WYCLIFFE BIBLE DICTIONARY

Charles F. Pfeiffer, Howard F. Vos, John Rea
EDITORS

HENDRICKSON
PUBLISHERS

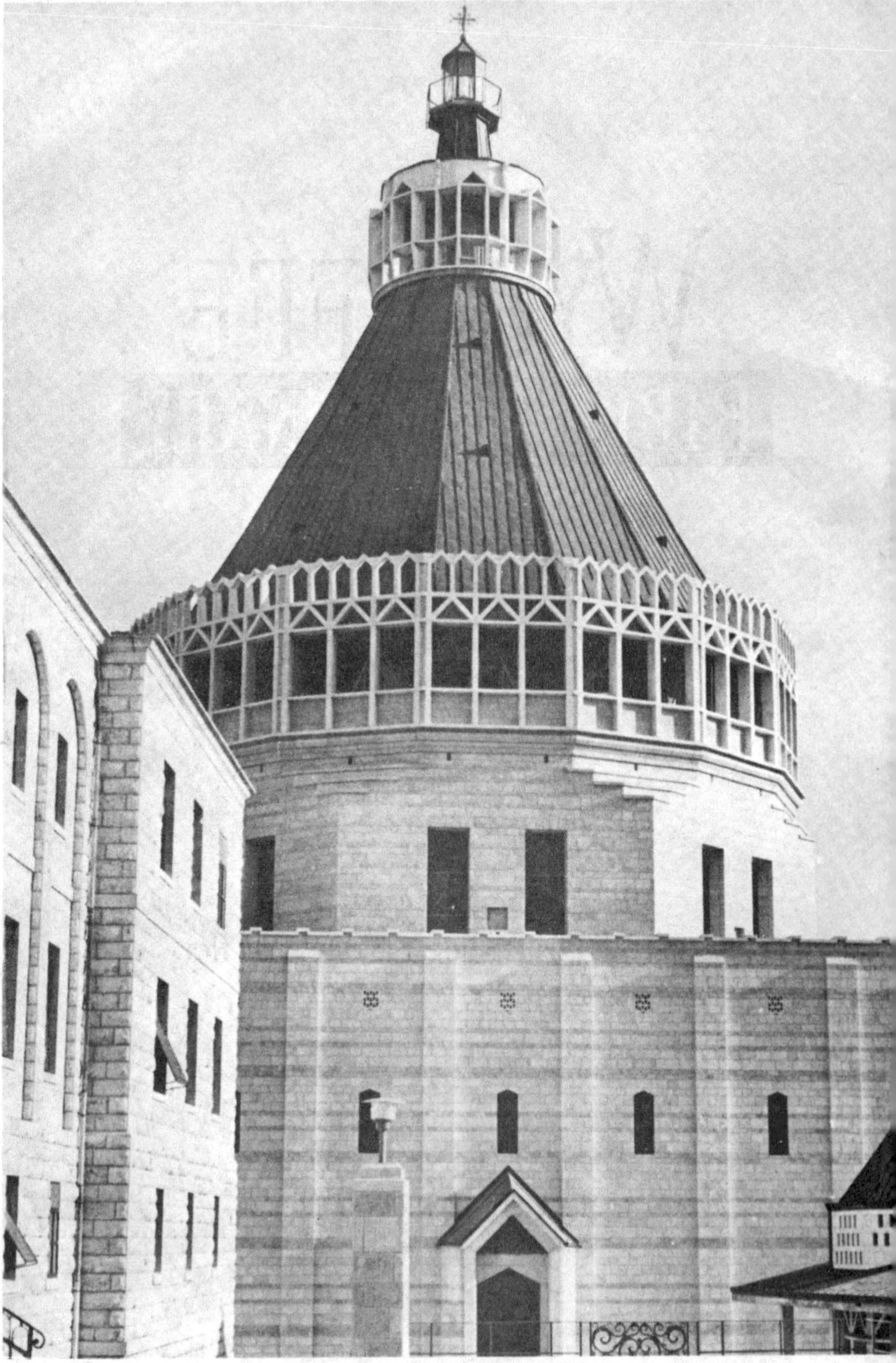

The New Church of the Annunciation, Nazareth. See Luke 1:25–38. HFV

WYCLIFFE BIBLE DICTIONARY

Wycliffe Bible Dictionary

Published by Hendrickson Publishers, Inc.
P.O. Box 3473
Peabody, Massachusetts 01961-3473

This book was first published in the United States by Moody Press in two volumes with the title *The Wycliffe Bible Encyclopedia,* copyright © 1975 by Moody Bible Institute of Chicago. The new one-volume Hendrickson Publishers, Inc. edition has been re-titled *Wycliffe Bible Dictionary* and is reprinted by permission.

Printed in the United States of America

ISBN 978-1-56563-787-0

Eighth Printing — September 2008

PREFACE

The two volumes of the *Wycliffe Bible Encyclopedia* are the product of the combined efforts of more than two hundred scholars in the several fields of biblical studies. While most of them are Americans, a number are citizens of other countries.

The project was begun in 1959 when the staff of Moody Press recognized the need to replace older Bible dictionaries and encyclopedias with a work that would be abreast of recent trends in theology and the newest discoveries in archaeology and linguistic research.

The committee established several basic guidelines for the WBE. First of all, its doctrinal articles must adhere to Christian orthodoxy, the fundamentals of the faith generally accepted by believers of conservative, evangelical persuasion. No article should contradict the belief that all Scripture is inspired of God and was verbally inerrant in its original manuscripts. In matters of eschatology the return of Christ is considered as occurring before His millennial reign on earth.

Second, the encyclopedia should be complete in the sense that every place and personal name in the Bible be listed and discussed, as well as all important doctrines and theological terms. Various articles on nonbiblical subjects have been included to provide historical and cultural background for the setting of the events in the Bible. This has been done because frequent references are made to such subjects as the Amarna letters, the Nuzu tablets, Hammurabi, Sumer, and the Moabite Stone. There terms are meaningless to the average reader of the Bible unless explained. Because the encyclopedia is limited to a discussion of subjects contributing directly to one's understanding of the Bible and Bible times, little attention has been given to matters of church history.

Third, the articles should be comprehensive enough to satisfy the informed layman, yet clear enough for the understanding of the average reader. For this reason Hebrew, Greek, and other foreign words have been transliterated.

Since the King James Version is still the most widely read Bible in evangelical churches, it has been followed for the spelling of proper names in the titles of the individual articles. Within the articles, however, the more accurate translations or transliterations found in the recent revisions are frequently used. Certain names and important words or terms which occur in newer versions but not in the KJV are discussed for the convenience of the reader. Names as spelled in newer versions are also listed, and are followed by a cross reference to the name as spelled in the KJV. For example, by the entry on Quirinius the notation is found: *See* Cyrenius. The latter is the spelling as given in the KJV. In referring to the personal name of God in the OT the editors have chosen the spelling *Yahweh* rather than *Jehovah*. The former spelling is now generally accepted by most OT scholars as more nearly approximating the correct pronunciation in ancient Israel.

The authors of all articles of 150 words or more in length are identified by their initials. Their position in the academic community is given in the List of Contributors. The reader is assured of having at his disposal an accurate, reliable, and up-to-date source of information for his study of God's Word. Differing viewpoints (within the boundaries of an evangelical position) are expressed, so that a rigid uniformity has not been imposed on the various articles.

Bibliographies attached to the longer articles are by no means exhaustive, but are added as a help to the reader by referring him to books and periodicals usually obtainable in the libraries of most Christian colleges in America. A special effort was made to refer to the more important articles in G. F. Bromiley's excellent translation of Kittel's famous work, the *Theological Dictionary of the New Testament*.

The usefulness of the encyclopedia has been greatly extended at the same time that duplication has been largely avoided by a system of cross references within and at the end of most articles. Another subject may be referred to either by the abbreviation *q.v.* (Latin *quod vide*, "which see") in parentheses following the mention of that word, or by the actual instruction "*See* . . ." naming that article.

In a number of areas it was deemed best to discuss the related individual items or units under a general topic instead of in separate articles. For example, all the animals, birds, fish, insects, and reptiles are discussed under Animals. Other examples are the long articles on Bible Manuscripts; Dress; Festivals; Food; Gods, False; Jewels; Minerals and Metals; Occupations; Plants; Versions, Ancient and Medieval; and Weights, Measures, and Coins. This arrangement enables the reader more easily to gain a comprehensive knowledge of a particular subject, if he so desires.

The original staff of editors was headed by Charles F. Pfeiffer. Associated with him were E. Leslie Carlson in Old Testament, Walter M. Dunnett in New Testament, R. Allan Killen in theology, and Howard F.

Vos for illustrations and archaeology. John Rea was later asked to fill the vacancy created by the death of Dr. Carlson. Subsequently, Dr. Rea was brought in as manuscript editor to expedite the editorial task through to completion. He was especially assisted by Dr. Vos, who as textbook editor of Moody Press, and later textbook consultant, read and evaluated the entire contents of the encyclopedia; and by James Mathisen, for several years assistant editor of Moody Press. Others who have rendered invaluable editorial assistance include Dwight P. Baker, Kenneth A. Domroese, Fred Dickason, Stanley N. Gundry, and Alan F. Johnson.

Special thanks are due to Miss Nettie Cox, who after her retirement from Moody Bible Institute as editor of promotional materials has served so ably and tirelessly as chief copy editor. Without her ability to organize the accumulating mass of manuscripts, her memory of details and sharp eye for errors, this project would have foundered. She was assisted by Mrs. Dorothy Martin during the many months of proofreading. Nor would the project have been completed without the constant supervision and practical involvement of Howard Fischer, production manager at Moody Press.

The authors and the editors acknowledge their indebtedness to the many fine Bible dictionaries and encyclopedias published in this century. Especially useful have been *Unger's Bible Dictionary* and *The New Bible Dictionary,* in all aspects; the *Pictorial Biblical Encyclopedia* (by G. Cornfeld), the *Seventh-Day Adventist Bible Dictionary* (by Siegfried H. Horn), *The Interpreter's Dictionary of the Bible* , and *The Biblical World* (by Charles F. Pfeiffer) in matters of archaeology, ancient history, and biblical customs; and *Baker's Dictionary of Theology* in doctrinal matters. *The Interpreter's Dictionary of the Bible* has served as the standard for the spelling and pronunciation of most of the names of persons, places, and events in the ancient history of the Near East. The table of abbreviations for periodicals, reference works, dictionaries, and versions reveals in fuller measure the wide scope of materials consulted by the contributors of the articles and by the editors. Color maps are inserted by special arrangement with C. S. Hammond and Company.

Numerous individuals and agencies have supplied illustrations for this work. A credit line appears with each picture but special recognition goes to those listed below who have all furnished a sufficiently large number of pictures to commend the use of abbreviations to designate them. Such abbreviations appear in parentheses in the following listing: British Museum, London (BM); Israel Information Service, New York (IIS); Lehnert and Landrock, Cairo (LL); Louvre Museum, Paris (LM); Moody Institute of Science (MIS); Metropolitan Museum of Art, New York (MM); Matson Photo Service, Los Angeles (MPS); Oriental Institute of the University of Chicago (ORINST); Dr. John Rea (JR); and Dr. Howard F. Vos (HFV).

LIST OF CONTRIBUTORS

Entries are made in order of authors' last names

W.A.A. ALCORN, Wallace A., Ph.D., Associate Professor of New Testament, Northwest Baptist Seminary, Tacoma, Wash.

G.A.A. ANDERSON, George A., Th.M., Professor of Bible, King College, Bristol, Tenn.

G.L.A. ARCHER, Gleason L., Jr., Professor of Old Testament, Trinity Evangelical Divinity School, Deerfield, Ill.

D.P.B. BAKER, Dwight P.

N.B.B. BAKER, Nelson B., Ph.D., Professor of English Bible Emeritus, Eastern Baptist Theological Seminary, Philadelphia, Penn.

D.B. BALY, Denis, Kenyon College, Gambier, Ohio.

D.C.B. BARAMKI, D.C., Ph.D., Curator of Museums, American University of Beirut, Lebanon.

L.B. BARBIERI, Louis, Th.D., Member of Faculty, Moody Bible Institute, Chicago, Ill.

G.W.Ba. BARKER, Glenn W., Th.D., Dean & Professor of Christian Origins, Fuller Theological Seminary, Pasadena, Calif.

K.L.B. BARKER, Kenneth L., Ph.D., Associate Professor of Semitics and Old Testament, Dallas Theological Seminary, Dallas, Tex.

D.M.B. BEEGLE, Dewey M., Ph.D., Professor of Old Testament, Wesley Theological Seminary, Washington, D.C.

R.H.B. BELTON, Robert H., Th.M. Member of Faculty Emeritus, Moody Bible Institute, Chicago, Ill.

T.H.B. BENDER, Thorwald W., Th.D., Professor of Philosophy of Religion and Theology, Eastern Baptist Theological Seminary, Philadelphia. Penn

T.M.B. BENNETT, T. Miles, Th.D., Professor of Old Testament, Southwestern Baptist Theological Seminary, Fort Worth, Tex.

S.H.B. BESS, S. Herbert, Ph.D., Professor of Old Testament and Hebrew, Grace Theological Seminary, Winona Lake, Ind.

E.M.B. BOHNETT, Earl M., M. Div., M.A., Dean of Education, Baptist Bible College, Denver, Col.

A.B. BOWLING, Andrew, Ph.D., Associate Professor, Biblical Studies and Philosophy, John Brown University, Siloam Springs, Ark.

J.L.B. BOYER, James L., Th.D., Professor of New Testament and Greek, Grace Theological Seminary, Winona Lake, Ind.

G.W. Br. BROMILEY, Geoffrey W., Ph.D., Professor of Church History and Historical Theology, Fuller Theological Seminary, Pasadena, Calif.

W.B. BROOMALL, Wick, M.A., Th.M., Atlanta School of Biblical Studies, Atlanta, Ga.

W.G.B. BROWN, W. Gordon, D.D., Dean Emeritus, Central Baptist Seminary, Toronto, Ontario, Canada.

S.G.B. BROWNE, S.G., Leprosy Research Unit, Uzuakoli, Eastern Nigeria

F.F.B. BRUCE, F.F., M.A., D.D., Rylands Professor of Biblical Criticism and Exegesis, University of Manchester, England.

S.F.B. BRYAN, Sigurd F., Th.D., Professor of Religion, Samford University, Birmingham, Ala.

D.W.B. BURDICK, Donald W., Th.D., Professor of New Testament, Conservative Baptist Theological Seminary, Denver, Col.

J.O.B. BUSWELL, J. Oliver, Jr., Ph.D., Dean Emeritus, Covenant Theological Seminary, St. Louis, Mo.

D.K.C. CAMPBELL, Donald K., Th.D., Dean, Dallas Theological Seminary, Dallas, Tex.

E.L.C. CARLSON, E. Leslie, Th.D., Professor Emeritus, Southwestern Baptist Theological Seminary, Fort Worth, Tex.

F.G.C. CARVER, Frank G., Jr., Ph.D., Professor of Biblical Theology and Greek, Pasadena College, Pasadena, Calif.

G.H.C. CLARK, Gordon H., Ph.D., Professor of Philosophy, Butler University, Indianapolis, Ind.

E.W.C. CLEVENGER, Eugene W., Th.D., Professor of Bible, Abilene Christian College, Abilene, Tex.

J.W.C. COBB, John W., Th.D., Professor Emeritus of Religion, University of Corpus Christi, Corpus Christi, Tex.

W.B.C. COBLE, William B., Th.D., Professor of New Testament Interpretation and Greek, Midwestern Baptist Theological Seminary, Kansas City, Mo.

S.M.C. CODER, S. Maxwell, Th.D., Dean of Education Emeritus, Moody Bible Institute, Chicago, Ill.

S.C. COHEN, Simon, D.D., formerly Hebrew Union College, Cincinnati, Ohio.

R.O.C. COLEMAN, Robert O., Th.D., Associate Professor of Biblical Backgrounds and Archaeology, Southwestern Baptist Theological Seminary, Fort Worth, Tex.

C.W.C. CROWN, C.W., M.D., Physician, Chicago, Ill.

T.B.C. CRUM, Terrelle B., M.A., Professor of Biblical Studies, Barrington College, Barrington, Rhode Island.

W.C. CULBERTSON, William, D.D., President Emeritus and Chancellor, Moody Bible Institute, Chicago, Ill.

R.D.C. CULVER, Robert D., Th.D., Professor of Systematic Theology, Trinity Evangelical Divinity School, Deerfield, Ill.

J.J.D. DAVIS, John J., Ph.D., Professor of Old Testament and Hebrew, Grace Theological Seminary, Winona Lake, Ind.

V.G.D. DAVISON, Vernon G., Ph.D., Professor of Religion and Greek, Samford University, Birmingham, Ala.

W.T.D. DAYTON, Wilber T., Th.D., President, Houghton College, Houghton, N.Y.

D.W.D. DEERE, D.W., Th.D., Professor Emeritus of Old Testament, Golden Gate Theological Seminary, Mill Valley, Calif.

R.B.D. DEMPSEY. Robert B.

C.E.D. DE VRIES, Carl E., Ph.D., Research Associate (Associate Professor), Oriental Institute, University of Chicago, Chicago, Ill.

C.F.D. DICKASON, C. Fred, Th.D., Member of Faculty, Moody Bible Institute, Chicago, Ill.

R.L.D. DOBSON, Robert L., Th.D., Professor of Bible, Howard Payne College, Brownwood, Tex.

H.L.D. DRUMWRIGHT, Huber L., Jr., Th.D., Dean and Professor of New Testament, Southwestern Baptist Theological Seminary, Fort Worth, Tex.

W.M.D. DUNNETT, Walter M., Ph.D., Member of Faculty, Moody Bible Institute, Chicago, Ill.

D.G.E. EADIE, Douglas G., Th.D., Ph.D., Professor of Religion, University of Redlands, Redlands, Calif.

R.E. EARLE, Ralph, Th.D., Professor of New Testament, Nazarene Theological Seminary, Kansas City, Mo.

L.R.E. ELLIOTT, L.R.

C.L.F. FEINBERG, Charles L., Ph.D., Dean, Talbot Theological Seminary, La Mirada, Calif.

P.F. FEINBERG, Paul, Ph.D., Assistant Professor of Philosophy of Religion, Trinity Evangelical Divinity School, Deerfield, Ill.

E.F. FERGUSON, Everett, Ph.D., Professor of Bible, Abilene Christian College, Abilene, Tex.

P.W.F. FERRIS, Paul W., Jr., M.Div., Graduate Student, Dropsie College, Philadelphia, Penn.

H.E.Fi. FINLEY, Harvey E., Ph.D., Professor of Old Testament, Nazarene Theological Seminary, Kansas City, Mo.

F.L.F. FISHER, Fred L., Th.D., Professor of New Testament Interpretation, Golden Gate Baptist Theological Seminary, Mill Valley, Calif.

H.D.F. FOOS, Harold D., Th.D., Member of Faculty, Moody Bible Institute, Chicago, Ill.

C.T.F. FRANCISCO, Clyde T., Th.D., Professor of Old Testament Interpretation, Southern Baptist Theological Seminary, Louisville, Ky.

H.E.Fr. FREEMAN, Hobart E., Th.D., Lecturer and Author, Graceland, Ind.

L. Ga. GALLMAN, Lee. Th.D., Professor of Religion, Samford University, Birmingham, Ala.

J.F.G. GATES, John F., S.T.D., Professor of Bible and Philosophy, St. Paul Bible College, Bible College, Minn.

N.L.G. GEISLER, Norman L., Ph.D., Professor of Philosophy of Religion, Trinity Evangelical Divinity School, Deerfield, Ill.

J.M.G. GERSTNER, John M., Ph.D., Professor of Church History, Pittsburgh Theological Seminary, Pittsburgh, Penn.

G.A.G. GETZ, Gene A., Ph.D., Associate Professor of Christian Education, Dallas Theological Seminary, Dallas, Tex.

R.G. GODDARD, Robert, Th.D., Member of Faculty, Moody Bible Institute, Chicago, Ill.

L.Go. GOLDBERG, Louis, Th.D., Member of Faculty, Moody Bible Institute, Chicago, Ill.

J.H.G. GREENLEE, J. Harold, Th.D., Missionary, OMS International

J.K.G. GRIDER, J. Kenneth, Ph.D., Professor of Theology, Nazarene Theological Seminary, Kansas City, Mo.

V.C.G. GROUNDS, Vernon C., Ph.D., President, Conservative Baptist Theological Seminary, Denver, Col.

S.G. GUNDRY, Stanley, S.T.D., Member of Faculty, Moody Bible Institute, Chicago, Ill.

G.H.G. HADDOCK, Gerald H., Ph.D., Associate Professor of Geology, Wheaton College, Wheaton, Ill.

E.F.Hai. HAIGHT, Elmer F., Th.D., Professor Emeritus of Religion, Louisiana College, Pineville, La.

P.S.H. HAIK, Paul S., Th.D., Member of Faculty, Moody Bible Institute, Chicago, Ill.

F.E.H. HAMILTON, Floyd E.

H.A.Han. HANKE, H.A., Th.D., Professor of Religion, Asbury College, Wilmore, Ky.

G.L.H. HARDING, G. Lankester, Daroun-Harissa, Lebanon.

L.O.H. HARRIS, Lindell O., Th.D., Chairman, Division of Religion, Hardin-Simmons University, Abilene, Tex.

R.L.H. HARRIS, R. Laird, Ph.D., Professor of Old Testament, Covenant Theological Seminary, St. Louis, Mo.

E.F.Har. HARRISON, Everett F., Ph.D., Senior Professor of New Testament, Fuller Theological Seminary, Pasadena, Calif.

G.W.H. HARRISON, G.W., Th.D., Professor of Old Testament and Hebrew, New Orleans Baptist Theological Seminary, New Orleans, La.

C.K.H. HARROP, Clayton K., Th.D., Professor of New Testament Interpretation, Golden Gate Baptist Theological Seminary, Mill Valley, Calif.

R.E.H. HAYDEN, Roy E., Ph.D., Professor of Biblical Literature, Oral Roberts University, Tulsa, Okla.

A.K.H. HELMBOLD, Andrew K., Ph.D., Professor of Humanities, Tidewater Community College, Portsmouth, Va.

E.W.H. HELSEL, E. Walter, Th.M., Professor of Religion, Seattle Pacific College, Seattle, Wash.

C.F.H.H. HENRY, Carl F.H., Ph.D., Professor at Large, Eastern Baptist Theological Seminary, Philadelphia, Penn.

D.E.H. HIEBERT, D. Edmond, Th.D., Professor of New Testament, Mennonite Brethren Biblical Seminary, Fresno, Calif.

H.W.H. HOEHNER, Harold W., Ph.D., Associate Professor of Bible Exposition, Dallas Theological Seminary, Dallas, Tex.

H.A.Hof. HOFFNER, Harry A., Jr., Ph.D., Associate Professor of Hittiology and Assyriology, Yale University, New Haven, Conn.

S.H.H. HORN, Siegfried H., Ph.D., Professor of Archaeology and History of Antiquity, Andrews University, Berrien Springs, Mich.

C.M.Ho. HORNE, Charles M., Th.D., Associate Professor of Theology, Graduate School of Theology, Wheaton College, Wheaton, Ill.

S.M.H. HORTON, Stanley M., Th.D., Professor of Bible, Hebrew, and Theology, Central Bible College, Springfield, Mo.

H.E.H. HOSCH, Harold E.

F.D.H. HOWARD, Fred D., Th.D., Professor of Religion, Wayland Baptist College, Plainview, Tex.

G.E.H. HOWARD, George E., M.A., Th.M., Ph.D., Associate Professor, Philosophy of Religion, University of Georgia, Athens, Ga.

F.R.H. HOWE, Frederic R., Th.D., Professor of Theology, Dallas Theological Seminary, Dallas, Tex.

H.A.Hoy. HOYT, Herman A., Th.D., President, Grace Theological Seminary, Winona Lake, Ind.

F.B.H. HUEY, F.B., Jr., Th.D., Associate Professor of Old Testament, Southwestern Baptist Theological Seminary, Fort Worth, Tex.

K.H. HUJER, Karel, D.Sc., Professor of

Astronomy and Physics, University of Tennessee at Chattanooga, Tenn.

C.J.H. HURST, Clyde J., Th.D., Professor of Bible and Philosophy, Hardin-Simmons University, Abilene, Tex.

C.M.Hy. HYATT, Cecil M., Th.D., Professor of Bible and Religion, California Baptist College, Riverside, Calif.

E.C.J. JAMES, Edgar C., Th.D., Member of Faculty, Moody Bible Institute, Chicago, Ill.

J.E.J. JENNINGS, James E., M.A., Assistant Professor of Archaeology, Wheaton College, Wheaton, Ill.

P.K.J. JEWETT, Paul K., Ph.D., Professor of Systematic Theology, Fuller Theological Seminary, Pasadena, Calif.

A.F.J. JOHNSON, Alan F., Th.D., Associate Professor of Bible and Apologetics, Wheaton College, Wheaton, Ill.

P.C.J. JOHNSON, Philip C. Th.D.,

R.L.J. JOHNSON, Robert L., M.A., Associate Professor of Bible, Abilene Christian College, Abilene, Tex.

E.S.K. KALLAND, Earl S., Th.D., Dean, Conservative Baptist Theological Seminary, Denver, Col.

J.L.K. KELSO, James L., Th.D., Professor Emeritus of Old Testament History and Biblical Archaeology, Pittsburgh Theological Seminary, Pittsburgh, Penn.

H.A.K. KENT, Homer A., Jr., Th.D., Vice President and Dean, Grace Theological Seminary, Winona Lake, Ind.

R.A.K. KILLEN, R. Allan, Th.D., Professor of Contemporary Theology, Reformed. Theological Seminary, Jackson, Miss.

W.H.K. KIMZEY, Willis H., Jr., Th.D., Professor of Religion, Union University, Jackson, Tenn.

M.A.K. KING, Marchant A., D.D., Professor Emeritus, Los Angeles Baptist College, Newhall, Calif.

M.E.K. KLINE, Meredith E., Ph.D., Professor of Old Testament, Gordon-Conwell Theological Seminary, Wenham, Mass.

F.H.K. KLOOSTER, Fred H., Th.D., Professor of Systematic Theology, Calvin Theological Seminary, Grand Rapids, Mich.

J.W.K. KLOTZ, John W., Ph.D., Professor of Natural Science, Concordia Senior College, Fort Wayne, Ind.

G.W.K. KNIGHT, George W., III, Th.D., Associate Professor of New Testament, Covenant Theological Seminary, St. Louis, Mo.

C.H.K. KRAELING, Carl H., Ph.D., Director Emeritus of Institute of Oriental Studies, University of Chicago, Chicago, Ill.

F.C.K. KUEHNER, Fred C., Th.D., Dean, Professor of Biblical Languages, The Theological Seminary of the Reformed Episcopal Church, Philadelphia, Penn.

W.L.L. LANE, William L., Th.D., Professor of New Testament and Judaic Studies, Gordon-Conwell Theological Seminary, Wenham, Mass.

H.C.L. LEUPOLD, H.C., D.D., Professor of Old Testament Theology, Evangelical Lutheran Seminary, Columbus, Ohio.

J.P.L. LEWIS, Jack P., Ph.D., Professor of Bible, Harding Graduate School of Religion, Memphis, Tenn.

N.R.L. LIGHTFOOT, Neil R., Ph.D., Professor of Bible, Abilene Christian College, Abilene, Tex.

R.P.L. LIGHTNER, Robert P., Th.D., Assistant Professor of Systematic Theology, Dallas Theological Seminary, Dallas, Tex.

F.D.L. LINDSEY, F. Duane, Th.D., Assistant Professor of Systematic Theology, Dallas Theological Seminary, Ft. Worth, Tex.

G.H.L. LIVINGSTON, G. Herbert, Ph.D., Professor of Old Testament, Asbury Theological Seminary, Wilmore, Ky.

G.C.L. LUCK, G. Coleman, Th.D., Member of Faculty, Moody Bible Institute, Chicago, Ill.

E.L.L. LUEKER, Erwin L.

L.A.L. LUFBURROW, Lawrence A.

J.C.M. MACAULAY, J.C., D.D., Dean, New York School of the Bible, New York City.

W.R.L.Mc. MC LATCHIE, Wm. R.L.

W.H.M. MARE, W. Harold, Ph.D., Professor of New Testament Language and Literature, Covenant Theological Seminary, St. Louis, Mo.

J.Ma. MATHISEN, James, M.A., Assistant Professor of Sociology, Aurora College, Aurora, Ill.

A.M. MERCER, Arthur, Th.D., Private Business, Dallas, Tex.

C.S.M. MEYER, Carl S., Ph.D., Graduate Professor of Historical Theology, Concordia Seminary, St. Louis, Mo.

J.R.M. MICHAELS, J. Ramsey, Th.D., Professor of New Testament and Early Christian Literature, Gordon-Conwell Theological Seminary, Wenham, Mass.

R.A.M. MITCHELL, Richard A., Institute for Mediterranean Studies, Berkeley, Calif.

H.M.M. MORRIS, Henry M., Ph.D., Institute for Creation Research, San Diego, Calif.

L.M. MORRIS, Leon, Ph.D., Principal, Ridley College, Melbourne, Australia.

R.M. MOUNCE, Robert, Ph.D., Professor of Religious Studies, Western Kentucky University, Bowling Green, Ky.

W.M. MUELLER, Walter, Th.M.

J.K.M. MUNRO, John Ker, Th.M., Director of Admissions, Columbia Bible College, Columbia, S.C.

J.M. MURRAY, John, Th.M., Professor of Systematic Theology Emeritus, Westminster Theological Seminary, Philadelphia, Penn.

W.E.N. NIX, William E., Ph.D., Director of Education, Beverly Hills Hospital, Dallas, Tex.

H.W.N. NORTON, H. Wilbert, Th.D., Dean of Graduate School of Theology, Wheaton College, Wheaton, Ill.

R.P. PACHE, Rene, J.D., President of Emmaus Bible School, Lausanne, Switzerland.

F.P. PACK, Frank, Professor of Bible, Abilene Christian College, Abilene, Tex.

J.B.P. PAYNE, J. Barton, Th.D., Professor of Old Testament Language and Literature, Covenant Theological Seminary, St. Louis, Mo.

A.T.P. PEARSON, A.T.

J.D.P. PENTECOST, J. Dwight, Th.D., Professor of Bible Exposition, Dallas Theological Seminary, Dallas, Tex.

G.W.P. PETERS, George W., Ph.D., Professor of World Missions, Dallas Theological Seminary, Dallas, Tex.

I.G.P. PETERSON, Irving G.

C.F.P. PFEIFFER, Charles F., Ph.D., Professor of Ancient Languages, Central Michigan University, Mt. Pleasant, Mich.

C.H.P. PINNOCK, Clark H., Ph.D., Professor of Systematic Theology, Regent College, Vancouver, British Columbia.

R.E. Po. POWELL, Ralph E., Th.D., Professor of Theology and Philosophy of Religion, North American Baptist Seminary, Sioux Falls, S.D.

R.E. Pr. PRICE, Ross E., Ph.D., D.D., District Superintendent, Rocky Mountain District, Church of the Nazarene, Billings, Mont.

W.T.P. PURKISER, W.T., Ph.D., Associate Professor of English Bible, Nazarene Theological Seminary, Kansas City, Mo.

A.F.R. RAINEY, Anson F., Institute for Holy Land Studies, Jerusalem, Israel.

R.G.R. RAYBURN, Robert G., Th.D., President, Covenant Theological Seminary, St. Louis, Mo.

J.R. REA, John, Th.D., Theological Lecturer and Editor

A.M.R. RENWICK, Alexander M., D.D., Professor Free Church College, Edinburgh, Scotland.

R.L.R. REYMOND, Robert L., Ph.D., Associate Professor of Systematic Theology, Covenant Theological Seminary, St. Louis, Mo.

J.A.R. REYNOLDS, J.A., Th.D., Professor of Religion, Mary Hardin-Baylor College, Belton, Tex.

R.C.R. RIDALL, R. Clyde, Th.D., Associate Professor of Theology and Biblical Literature, Olivet Nazarene College, Kankakee, Ill.

R.V.R. RITTER, R. Vernon, Th.D., Professor of Religious Studies, Westmont College, Santa Barbara, Calif.

D.M.R. ROARK, Dallas M., Ph.D., Professor of Philosophy, Kansas State College of Emporia, Emporia, Kan.

J.W.R. ROBERTS, J.W., Ph.D., Professor of Bible, Abilene Christian College, Abilene, Tex.

I.R. ROBERTSON, Irvine, Th.M., Member of Faculty, Moody Bible Institute, Chicago, Ill.

E.B.R. ROBINSON, Earl B.

D.R.R. ROSE, Delbert R., Ph.D., Professor of Biblical Theology, Asbury Theological Seminary, Wilmore, Ky.

C.C.R. RYRIE, Charles C., Ph.D., Dean of Doctoral Studies, Dallas Theological Seminary, Dallas, Tex.

A.C.S. SCHULTZ, Arnold C., Th.D., Lecturer in History, Roosevelt University, Chicago, Ill.

S.J.S. SCHULTZ, Samuel J., Ph.D., Professor of Bible and Theology, Wheaton College, Wheaton, Ill.

D.R.S. SIME, Donald R., Ph.D., Vice President, University Affairs, Pepperdine University, Malibu, Calif.

J.H.S. SKILTON, John H., Ph.D., Professor of New Testament, Westminster Theological Seminary, Philadelphia, Penn.

E.B.S. SMICK, Elmer B., Ph.D., Professor of Old Testament, Gordon-Conwell Theological Seminary, Wenham, Mass.

R.L.S SMITH, Ralph L., Th.D., Professor of Old Testament, Southwestern Baptist Theological Seminary, Fort Worth, Tex.

W.M.S. SMITH, Wilbur M., D.D., Professor Emeritus of English Bible, Trinity Evangelical Divinity School, Deerfield, Ill.

J.A.S. SPRINGER, J. Arthur, D.D., Member of Faculty Emeritus,

Moody Bible Institute, Chicago, Ill.

B.C.S. STARK, Bruce C., Th.D., Professor of Philosophy, Ashland College, Ashland, Ohio

F.R.S. STEELE, Francis R., Home Director, North Africa Mission

D.S. STEPHENS, Douglas, Th.D., Member of Faculty, Moody Bible Institute, Chicago, Ill.

H.G.S. STIGERS, Harold G.

N.J.S. STONE, Nathan J., Th.M., Member of Faculty Emeritus, Moody Bible Institute, Chicago, Ill.

R.S. STRICKLAND, Rowena, Th.D., Professor of Bible, Oklahoma Baptist University, Shawnee, Okla.

G.G.S. SWAIM, Gerald G.

M.C.T. TENNEY, Merrill C., Ph.D., Professor of Bible and Theology, Graduate School of Theology, Wheaton College, Wheaton, Ill.

J.D.T. THOMAS, J.D., Ph.D., Professor of Bible, Abilene Christian College, Abilene, Tex.

J.A.T. THOMPSON, John A., Cairo, U.A.R.

D.D.T. TIDWELL, D.D., Th.D., Professor in Christianity, Houston Baptist College, Houston, Tex.

G.H.T. TODD, G. Hall

W.B.T. TOLAR, William B., Th.D., Professor of Biblical Backgrounds, Southwestern Baptist Theological Seminary, Fort Worth, Tex.

S.D.T. TOUSSAINT, Stanley D., Th.D., Assistant Professor of Bible Exposition, Dallas Theological Seminary, Dallas, Tex.

A.E.T. TRAVIS, Arthur E., Th.D., Professor in Christianity, Houston Baptist College, Houston, Tex.

J.L.T. TRAVIS, James L., Th.D., Faculty (Bible), Blue Mountain College, Blue Mountain, Miss.

J.W.T. TRESCH, John W., Jr., Belmont College, Nashville, Tenn.

G.A.T. TURNER, George A., Ph.D., Professor of Biblical Literature, Asbury Theological Seminary, Wilmore, Ky.

R.V.U. UNMACK, Robert V., Th.D., Professor of New Testament, Central Baptist Theological Seminary, Kansas City, Kan.

C.V. VAN TIL, Cornelius, Ph.D., Professor of Apologetics Emeritus, Westminster Theological Seminary, Philadelphia, Penn.

E.J.V. VARDAMAN, E. Jerry, Th.D., Associate Professor of Biblical Archaeology, Southern Baptist Theological Seminary, Louisville, Ky.

H.F.V. VOS, Howard F., Th.D., Ph.D., Professor of History, The King's College, Briarcliff Manor, N.Y.

L.L.W. WALKER, Larry L., Ph.D., Associate Professor of Old Testament, Southwestern Baptist Theological Seminary, Fort Worth, Tex.

W.B.W. WALLIS, Wilber B., Ph.D., Professor of New Testament, Covenant Theological Seminary, St. Louis, Mo.

J.F.W. WALVOORD, John F., Th.D., President, Dallas Theological Seminary, Dallas, Tex.

B.M.W. WARREN, Bern M., Th.D., Professor of Biblical Studies, Western Evangelical Seminary, Portland, Ore.

J.W.W. WATTS, J. Wash, Th.D., Professor Emeritus of Old Testament and Hebrew, New Orleans Baptist Theological Seminary, New Orleans, La.

J.D.W.W. WATTS, John D.W., Th.D., Professor of Old Testament, Serampore College, India.

C.J.W. WENZEL, Charles J., B.D., Member of Faculty, Columbia Bible College, Columbia, S.C.

W.W.W. WESSEL, Walter W., Ph.D., Professor of New Testament, Bethel College, St. Paul, Minn.

J.C.W. WHITCOMB, John C., Th.D., Director of Postgraduate Studies, Grace Theological Seminary, Winona Lake, Ind.

J.T.W. WILLIS, John T., Ph.D., Associate Professor of Bible, Abilene Christian College, Abilene, Tex.

D.L.W. WISE, Donald L., M.A., Member of Faculty, Moody Bible Institute, Chicago, Ill.

D.J.W. WISEMAN, Donald J., O.B.E., M.A., Professor of Assyriology, University of London, London, England

A.W.W. WONDER, Alice W., Th.D., Professor of Religion, Texas Wesleyan College, Fort Worth, Tex.

G.E.W. WORRELL, George E., Director of Youth Evangelism, Texas Baptist Convention

E.M.Y. YAMAUCHI, Edwin M., Ph.D., Associate Professor of History, Miami University, Oxford, Ohio

K.M.Y. YATES, Kyle M., Jr., Th.D., Associate Professor of Old Testament and Archaeology, Golden Gate Baptist Theological Seminary, Mill Valley, Calif.

J.D.Y. YODER, James D., Th.D., Professor of English Bible and Biblical Languages, Evangelical Congregational School of Theology, Myerstown, Pa.

E.J.Y. YOUNG, Edward J., Ph.D., Professor of Old Testament, Westminster Theological Seminary, Philadelphia, Pa.

F.E.Y. YOUNG, Fred E., Ph.D., Dean, Professor of Old Testament, Central Baptist Theological Seminary, Kansas City, Kan.

R.F.Y. YOUNGBLOOD, Ronald F., Ph.D., Professor of Old Testament, Bethel Theological Seminary, St. Paul, Minn.

ABBREVIATIONS

Books of the Bible

Old Testament

Gen	II Chr	Dan
Ex	Ezr	Hos
Lev	Neh	Joel
Num	Est	Amos
Deut	Job	Ob
Josh	Ps	Jon
Jud	Prov	Mic
Ruth	Eccl	Nah
I Sam	Song	Hab
II Sam	Isa	Zeph
I Kgs	Jer	Hag
II Kgs	Lam	Zech
I Chr	Ezk	Mal

New Testament

Mt	Eph	Heb
Mk	Phil	Jas
Lk	Col	I Pet
Jn	I Thess	II Pet
Acts	II Thess	I Jn
Rom	I Tim	II Jn
I Cor	II Tim	III Jn
II Cor	Tit	Jude
Gal	Phm	Rev

Apocrypha and Pseudepigrapha

Bar (Baruch)
Bel (Bel and the Dragon)
Ecclus (Ecclesiasticus) or Sir (Wisdom of Jesus Son of Sirach)
I Esd (Esdras)
II Esd
I Macc (Maccabees)
II Macc
Tob (Tobit)
Wisd (Wisdom of Solomon)

Bible Translations, Reference Works, Periodicals, etc.

AASOR	*Annual of the American Schools of Oriental Research*
AB	Amplified Bible
AJA	*American Journal of Archaeology*
AJSL	*American Journal of Semitic Languages and Literatures*
ALUOS	*Annual of Leeds University Oriental Society*
ANEP	*The Ancient Near East in Pictures*, J. B. Pritchard
ANET	*Ancient Near Eastern Texts*, J. B. Pritchard
ANT	*Apocryphal New Testament*, M. R. James
AOTS	*Archaeology and Old Testament Study*, D. Winton Thomas
ARE	*Ancient Records of Egypt*, J. H. Breasted
Arndt	Arndt-Gingrich, *Greek-English Lexicon*
A-S	Abbott-Smith, *Manual Greek Lexicon of the New Testament*
ASAE	*Annales du service des antiquités de l'Egypte*
ASOR	American Schools of Oriental Research
ASV	American Standard Version (1901)
BA	*Biblical Archaeologist*
BASOR	*Bulletin of American Schools of Oriental Research*
BC	*The Beginnings of Christianity*, Foakes-Jackson and Lake
BDB	Brown, Driver, and Briggs, *Hebrew-English Lexicon of the Old Testament*
BDT	*Baker's Dictionary of Theology*
BETS	*Bulletin of the Evangelical Theological Society*
BJRL	*Bulletin of the John Rylands Library*
BS	*Bibliotheca Sacra*
BW	*Biblical World*, Charles F. Pfeiffer
CAH	*Cambridge Ancient History* (12 vols.)
CBQ	*Catholic Biblical Quarterly*
CHT	*Christianity Today*
CornPBE	G. Cornfeld, *Pictorial Biblical Encyclopedia*
D	Deuteronomist source
DeissBS	Deissmann, *Bible Studies*
DeissLAE	Deissmann, *Light from the Ancient East*
DOTT	*Documents from Old Testament Times*
DSS	Dead Sea Scrolls

E	Elohist source
EA	El-Amarna letters or tablets
EBC	*Everyman's Bible Commentary*
EBi	*Encyclopaedia Biblica*
EDNTW	*Expository Dictionary of New Testament Works,* W. E. Vine
EGT	*The Expositor's Greek Testament,* W. R. Nicoll
EQ	*Evangelical Quarterly*
ERV	English Revised Version (1881–85)
Euseb. Hist.	Eusebius, *History of the Christian Church*
EV	English Versions
ExpB	*The Expositor's Bible*
ExpGT	*The Expositor's Greek Testament*
ExpT	*The Expository Times*
FLAP	Jack Finegan, Light from the Ancient Past
GTT	*Geographical and Topographical Texts of the Old Testament,* J. Simons
HBD	*Harper's Bible Dictionary*
HDAC	*Hastings' Dictionary of the Apostolic Church*
HDB	*Hastings' Dictionary of the Bible*
HDCG	*Hastings' Dictionary of Christ and the Gospels*
HE	*The Ecclesiastical History of Eusebius*
HERE	*Hastings' Encyclopaedia of Religion and Ethics*
HGHL	*Historical Geography of the Holy Land,* G. A. Smith
HNTC	*Harper's New Testament Commentaries*
HR	Hatch and Redpath, *Concordance to the Septuagint*
HTR	*Harvard Theological Review*
HUCA	*Hebrew Union College Annual*
IB	*Interpreter's Bible*
ICC	*International Critical Commentary*
IDB	*Interpreter's Dictionary of the Bible*
IEJ	*Israel Exploration Journal*
ILN	*Illustrated London News*
Interp	*Interpretation*
IOT	*Introduction to the Old Testament,* R. K. Harrison
IQM	War Scroll from Qumran Cave 1
ISBE	*International Standard Bible Encyclopaedia*
J	Jehovah (Yahwist) source
JAOS	*Journal of the American Oriental Society*
JASA	*Journal of the American Scientific Affiliation*
JBL	*Journal of Biblical Literature*
JBR	*Journal of Bible and Religion*
JCS	*Journal of Cuneiform Studies*
JEA	*Journal of Egyptian Archaeology*
JerusB	Jerusalem Bible
JETS	*Journal of the Evangelical Theological Society*
JewEnc	*Jewish Encyclopaedia*
JFB	Jamieson, Fausset and Brown, *A Commentary on the Old and New Testaments*
JNES	*Journal of Near Eastern Studies*
Jos *Ant.*	Josephus, *Antiquities of the Jews*
Jos *Wars*	Josephus, *The Jewish Wars* .
JPS	Jewish Publication Society, *Version of the Old Testament*
JQR	Jewish Quarterly Review
JSS	*Journal of Semitic Studies*
JTS	*Journal of Theological Studies*
KB	Koehler and Baumgartner, *Lexicon in Veteris Testamenti Libros*
KD	C. F. Keil and Franz Delitzsch, *Commentary on the Old Testament*
Kittel	Rudolf Kittel, *Biblica Hebraica*
KJV	King James Version (1611)
LAE	see DeissLAE
LB	Living Bible
LSJ	Liddell, Scott, Jones, *Greek-English Lexicon*
LXX	Septuagint – Greek translation of the Old Testament
MM	Moulton and Milligan, *The Vocabulary of the Greek Testament*
MNT	*Moffatt's New Testament Commentary*
MSt	McClintock and Strong, *Cyclopaedia of Biblical, Theological and Ecclesiastical Literature*
MT	Masoretic Text
NASB	New American Standard Bible
NBC	*New Bible Commentary,* F. Davidson
NBD	*New Bible Dictionary,* J. D. Douglas
NEB	New English Bible
Nestle	Nestle (ed.), *Novum Testamentum Graece*
NIC(NT)	*New International Commentary (on the New Testament)*
NJPS, NJV	New Jewish Version of the Jewish Publication Society
NPOT	*New Perspectives on the Old Testament*
NT	New Testament
NTS	*New Testament Studies*
Onom.	*Onomasticon,* Eusebius

OT	Old Testament
P	Priestly source
PEQ	*Palestine Exploration Quarterly*
Phillips	J. B. Phillips, New Testament in Modern English
Ptol.	Ptolemy of Alexandria (Claudius Ptolemaeus)
PTR	*Princeton Theological Review*
RA	*Revue d'assyriologie et d'archéologie orientale*
RB	*Révue Biblique*
RSV	Revised Standard Version
RV	Revised Version
SBK	Strack and Billerbeck, *Kommentar zum Neuen Testament aus Talmud und Midrasch*
SCM	Student Christian Movement
SDABD	*Seventh-day Adventist Bible Dictionary*
SHERK	*New Schaff-Herzog Encyclopedia of Religious Knowledge*
SOTI	*A Survey of Old Testament Introduction,* Gleason L. Archer
SP	Samaritan Pentateuch
SPCK	Society for the Promoting of Christian Knowledge
Tac. Ann.	Tacitus *Annals*
TAOTS	D. Winton Thomas, *Archaeology and Old Testament Study*
Targ.	Targum
TBC	*Tyndale Bible Commentaries*
TDNT	*Theological Dictionary of the New Testament,* Kittel
TNTC	*Tyndale New Testament Commentaries*
TR	Textus Receptus (Received Text)
TWNT	*Theologisches Wörterbuch zum Neuen Testament,* Kittel
UBD	*Unger's Bible Dictionary*
VBW	*Views of the Biblical World,* Benj. Mazar
VT	*Vetus Testamentum, Martin Noth*
Vulg.	Vulgate Version
WBC	*Wycliffe Bible Commentary,* Pfeiffer and Harrison
WC	*Westminster Commentaries*
WH	Westcott-Hort, *Text of the Greek New Testament*
WHG	*Wycliffe Historical Geography of Bible Lands,* Pfeiffer and Vos
W Int D	*Webster's International Dictionary*
WTJ	*Westminster Theological Journal*
ZAW	*Zeitschrift für die alttestamentliche Wissenschaft*
ZPBD	*Zondervan Pictorial Bible Dictionary*
ZPBE	*Zondervan Pictorial Bible Encyclopedia*

General

A.D.	*anno domini* (in the year of our Lord)
Akkad.	Akkadian
Arab.	Arabic
Aram.	Aramaic
art.	article
B.C.	before Christ
c.	*circa* (about)
CA	critical apparatus
cen.	century
cf.	*confer* (compare)
chap(s).	chapter(s)
col.	column
com.	commentary
d.	died, or date of death
E	east
ed.	edited, edition, editor
e.g.	*exempli gratia* (for example)
Egyp.	Egyptian
Eng.	English
et al.	and others
f., ff.	following (verse or verses, page, pages, etc.)
fem.	feminine
fig.	figuratively
ft.	foot, feet
gal.	gallon(s)
Gr.	Greek
Heb.	Hebrew
ibid.	*ibidem* (in the same place)
id.	*idem* (the same)
i.e.	*id est* (that is)
illus.	illustration
intro.	introduction
L., Lat.	Latin
l.	line
lit.	literal, literally
loc. cit.	*loco citato* (in the place cited)
marg.	margin, marginal reading
mil.	millennium
MS(S)	manuscript(s)
N	north
n.d.	no date
NE	northeast
No.	number
NW	northwest
op. cit.	*opere citato* (in the work cited)
orig.	original
p., pp.	page, pages
par.	paragraph
pl.	plural
publ.	publication, published
q.	source
q.v.	*quod vide* (which see)
re	pertaining to, connected with, concerning
rev.	revised, revision
Rom.	Roman

S	south	trans.	translation
SE	southeast	viz.	*videlicet* (namely)
sec.	section	vol.	volume
sing.	singular	v., vv.	verse, verses
s.v.	*sub verbo* (under the word)	W	west
SW	southwest		

GUIDE TO PRONUNCIATION

ā as in late
ā̍ as in vacation
â as in care
ă as in add
a as in infant
ä as in father
ȧ as in ask
á as in testament
ē as in eve
ē̍ as in depend
ĕ as in pet
ĕ̍ as in silent
ë as in porter
ī as in like
ĭ as in till
ĭ̍ as in glory
î as in marine
ō as in oat
ō̍ as in obey
ô as in Lord
ŏ as in hot
ŏ̍ as in connect
o͞o as in moon
o͝o as in book, put
ū as in fuse
ū̍ as in unite
û as in turn
ŭ as in rub
ŭ̍ as in consensus

A

AARON (âr'ŭn). Aaron is known best as the head of the Heb. priesthood. He was a descendant of Levi, the son of Amram and his wife Jochebed (Ex 6:20). A younger brother of Miriam, he was three years old when his brother Moses was born (Ex 7:7). He had four sons by his wife Elisheba: Nadab, Abihu, Eleazar, and Ithamar. The first two died before the altar (Lev 10:1-2) and the succession went to Eleazar upon the death of his father (Num 20:26).

Aaron first appears in the biblical narrative as Moses' assistant and spokesman. In response to God's command, Aaron, who had remained in Egypt during the 40 years of Moses' absence, went forth to meet Moses at "the mount of God" and reintroduced him to the Heb. community in Egypt (Ex 4:27-31). Moses was to receive God's message directly and it was Aaron's task to relay this message to the people (Ex 4:16). Aaron also accompanied Moses when they appeared in Pharaoh's presence with the request that Israel be permitted to hold a feast in the wilderness (Ex 5:1). It was Aaron who did miracles in Pharaoh's presence as evidence that their authority came from God Almighty (Ex 7:10). Later, during the battle with the Amalekites, Aaron, assisted by Hur, held up the hands of Moses until Israel was victorious (Ex 17:8-12).

Aaron appeared at Mount Sinai as an elder who, as representative of his people, was allowed, with Moses, Aaron's two sons, and 70 elders, to approach the very presence of the Lord (Ex 24:1-11). After this, while Moses was to be alone with God in the mountain, Aaron was appointed by Moses to be the interim leader of the people (Ex 24:13-18). It was during this period of Aaron's greatest responsibility that he failed his trust most tragically. Less than 40 days after he had been face to face with the God of Israel, Aaron yielded to popular pressure and sanctioned the people's lapse into idolatry. When confronted by Moses, he attempted to evade responsibility for his role in the apostasy (Ex 32:21-24). Strangely, no mention is made of any punishment for Aaron.

Later, his weakness showed up in petty jealousy which led him to join with his sister Miriam in a complaint against Moses because of the latter's claim to be God's spokesman and because of his marriage to a Cushite woman (Num 12). Miriam was punished, but again Aaron was not disciplined, perhaps because of his priestly office. Aaron and Moses together later faced a rebellion which subsided when Aaron with his censor made intercession for the people (Num 16:47). The consequent budding of Aaron's rod served to vindicate Aaron and his priesthood before the entire nation (Num 17). He died in Mount Hor at the age of 123 (Num 20:28).

Aaron's chief significance was his establishment of the priesthood. His was the responsibility of appearing in God's presence, as representative of the nation, to intercede for them and to present their sacrifices. The priesthood, thus established, lasted until A.D. 70. Although not listed among the heroes of the faith (Heb 11), Aaron is named as the God-appointed high priest who helped prepare the people for the greater high priesthood of Christ (Heb 5:4).

G. A. T.

AARONITE (âr'ŭn-īt). A term descriptive of one whose descent was from Aaron, the founder of the priesthood and brother of Moses. In I Chr 12:27 the 3,700 fighting men under Jehoiada who joined David at Hebron are so designated (translated in RSV as "of the house of Aaron"). The same Heb. phrase is translated "for Aaron" (RSV) in connection with Zadok (I Chr 27:17), distinguishing descendants of Aaron from the other Levites (Josh 21:4, 10, 13).

AB (ăb). The Babylonian name of the fifth Heb. religious month (July-August) and the eleventh civil month. *See* Calendar.

ABADDON (*à*-băd'ŏn). This word occurs six times in the OT (RSV) as the name of a place (Job 26:6; Prov 15:11; 27:20; Job 28:22; Ps 88:11; Job 31:12). In the first three it is a synonym for Sheol, in the next for death, in the next for grave, and in the last it is possibly to be taken in a general sense for ruin. In the NT the word occurs once (Rev 9:11) as the name of the angel who reigns over the world of the dead (Gr. *Apollyon*), especially of punishment. *See* Apollyon; Dead, The.

ABAGTHA (*à*-băg'th*à*). Name of one of the seven eunuchs of Ahasuerus (Xerxes I) mentioned in Est 1:10 (one of several Persian characteristics of the book). Abagtha was sent by the king to accompany Queen Vashti to the royal feast, since he was a guard for the king's harem. *See* Eunuch.

ABANA (ăb'*à*-n*à*). The first of the two rivers of Damascus which Naaman (*q.v.*) preferred to Jordan (II Kgs 5:12); modern Nahr Barada. Both Abana and Barada may have been used at one time, the former partially preserved in the name of one of Barada's branches, Nahr Banias (HDB). The latter is taken from the mountain

The Abana River (modern Barada) as it flows through downtown Damascus. HFV

which is its source, Amana (Song 4:8), Amana of Assyrian writers (Montgomery, *Kings*, ICC, p. 377), modern Zebedani.

Rising in the Anti-Lebanon range 23 miles NW, it is doubled in volume by the torrential 'Ain Fijeh as it cascades down the mountain. Crossing the plain of Damascus it fans out into several branches, at last to be lost in a marshy lake to the E. The beauty and fertility of Damascus are primarily because of its clear, cool waters creating what Arabic writers have fondly called "the garden of Allah." If appearance were all, Naaman's partiality could hardly be avoided.

ABARIM (ăb'*ȧ*-rĭm). The promontories at the western edge of the plateau of Moab, overlooking the Jordan Valley and the Dead Sea. Viewed from the W in the valley below, they appear to be a mountain range rising to a height up to 4,000 feet above the Dead Sea. Here the Israelites camped briefly (Num 33:47-48). From Mount Nebo (Pisgah, *q.v.*) Moses saw Canaan (Num 27:12; Deut 32:49). Jeremiah (22:20, RSV) links Abarim with Lebanon and Bashan because of the hilly nature of its terrain.

ABBA (ăb'*ȧ*; Aramaic "father"). Especially a name by which God was addressed in prayer. In the NT it occurs three times, being accompanied by the Gr. equivalent (Mk 14:36; Rom 8:15; Gal 4:6). But this Aramaic term may lie behind numerous references to God as Father where only the Gr. is given in the NT.

See Adoption; God.

ABDA (ăb'd*ȧ*)

1. The father of Adoniram, an officer in charge of forced labor under Solomon (I Kgs 4:6).

2. The son of Shammua, a Levite of the family of Jeduthun, who resided in Jerusalem after the Exile (Neh 11:17). In I Chr 9:16 (RSV) he is called "Obadiah, the son of Shemaiah."

ABDEEL (ăb'dē-ĕl). Father of Shelemiah (Jer 36:26), who served Jehoiakim. Shelemiah was ordered by the king to help arrest the prophet Jeremiah and his scribe Baruch.

ABDI (ăb'dī)

1. A Levite, father of Kishi and grandfather of David's singer Ethan (I Chr 6:44).

2. A Levite, father of Kish who served at the beginning of Hezekiah's reign, considered by some to be the same as 1 above (II Chr 29:12).

3. One of the sons of Elam in Ezra's time who put away his foreign wife (Ezr 10:26).

ABDIEL (ăb'dī-ĕl). A son of Guni, father of Ahi, who was a Gadite living in Gilead or Bashan (I Chr 5:15-17).

ABDON (ăb'dŏn)

1. A Levitical city in Asher, assigned to the Gershonites (Josh 21:30; I Chr 6:74). It is probably modern Khirbet 'Abdeh, in the hills 12 miles NE of Acre. Possibly "Abdon" should also be read where RSV has "Ebron" and KJV "Hebron" in Josh 19:28 (Kittel, BH; BDB, p. 715).

2. A judge of Israel for eight years (Jud 12:13-15). He was son of Hillel of Pirathon, an Ephraimite hill-country town seven miles SW of Shechem; modern Far'atah. A special point is made of the family status symbols—70 ass colts ridden by his 70 sons and grandsons.

3. A courtier of Josiah, king of Judah, sent to inquire the meaning of the book of the law found in the temple (II Chr 34:20). He is also called Achbor (II Kgs 22:12, 14; probably also in Jer 26:22; 36:12).

4. A Benjamite of Gibeon, firstborn of Jehiel and Maacah, and brother of Saul's grandfather, Ner (I Chr 8:30; 9:35-36).

5. One of several Benjamites dwelling in Jerusalem (I Chr 8:23, 28).

ABEDNEGO (*ȧ*-bĕd'nē-gō). The Babylonian name given to Azariah, a companion of Daniel in exile (Dan 1:1-7). The name, meaning "servant of Nebo," was given him by his captors. Since Nebo was a chief god of Babylon, it is believed that scribes changed it to "nego" to avoid honoring a heathen deity.

Abednego was among the Heb. captives taken to Babylonia by Nebuchadnezzar in 605 B.C. (Dan 1:1). With his compatriots he refused to eat the "unclean" food while learning Chaldean culture in the king's court. After this he became one of the king's counselors or wise men (Dan 1:20) and was later promoted to an administrative position (Dan 2:49). His fame comes from his refusal to deny his God even under threat of death (Dan 3:12-18). After miraculously surviving the fiery furnace he was given a further promotion by the chastened tyrant. He is named in I Macc 2:59 and referred to in Heb 11:33-34.

ABEL (ā'bĕl)

1. The second son of Adam, who was a shepherd. His offering to God was from the "firstlings of his flock," an offering more acceptable than Cain's offering of grain and vegetables. Whether Abel's was preferred because it involved the shedding of life and hence was symbolic of life, or whether it was offered in a more sincere spirit, is not made explicit. In jealous rage Cain killed Abel and tried to evade responsibility. Abel became a type of the martyrs who suffer for their faith (Mt 23:35). He was honored by Jesus and appears in the catalog of heroes of the faith (Heb 11:4). While his offering was superior to that of Cain, it was inferior to that of Jesus Christ (Heb 12:24). Of Abel it may be said that he was the first shepherd, the first to offer animal sacrifices, the first righteous man (Mt 23:35; I Jn 3:12), and the first martyr. He was victim of the same kind of insane jealousy which took the life of Jesus.

2. Abel ("meadow") is a term compounded with several other place names; e.g., Abel-maim.

3. Apparently identical with Abel-beth-maachah *(q.v.)* in II Sam 20:18.

G. A. T.

ABEL-BETH-MAACHAH (ā'bĕl-bĕth-mā'*a*-k*ȧ*). Alternately Abel (II Sam 20:18); Abel-maim (II Chr 16:4); Beth-maachah (II Sam 20:14–15, RSV). *See* each.

A fortified city in the tribe of Naphtali, located W of Dan, about 12 miles N of Lake Huleh in the N of Israel. It overlooked the intersection of the important trade route running from the Mediterranean to Damascus with the one coming N from Hazor. It is the place where Sheba, son of Bichri, took refuge when his revolt against David failed (II Sam 20:13–18). It was among the Israelite towns captured by Ben-hadad of Damascus (I Kgs 15:20) and later by Tiglath-pileser (II Kgs 15:29). It corresponds to modern Tell Abil in Israel.

ABEL-MAIM (ā'bĕl-mā'ĭm). An alternate form of Abel-beth-maachah *(q.v.)* in II Chr 16:4.

Tell Abil, the site of Abel-Beth-Maachah. JR

ABEL-MEHOLAH (ā'bĕl-mē-hō'l*ȧ*). Probably a place E of Jordan, though the site is not exactly located, to which the Midianites fled from the valley of Jezreel when pursued by Gideon (Jud 7:22). It is best known as the home of the prophet Elisha (I Kgs 19:16, 19–21). In Solomon's administration it was a part of the district which lay on both sides of Jordan, centered in Bethshean (I Kgs 4:12).

ABEL-MIZRAIM (ā'bĕl-mĭz'rā-ĭm). Alternate place name of Atad, which lay E of the Jordan and N of the Dead Sea, at which the funeral procession of Jacob paused to mourn the patriarch before entering Canaan to bury him (Gen 50:11). Previously called the "threshing floor of Atad," it now became known as the "mourning of Egypt" because of the mighty men of Egypt who took part in the ceremony (Gen 50:7). There is a possible play on the words *'ābel,* "meadow," and *'ēbel,* "mourning." Apparently new inhabitants of the Negeb made the direct route to Hebron too dangerous.

ABEL-SHITTIM (ā'bĕl-shĭt'ĭm). A place earlier called Shittim *(q.v.)* on the plains of Moab at which Israel camped before crossing the Jordan to attack Jericho. During this encampment (Num 33:49), the Balaam episode (Num 22–24), the invasion of the camp by Midian idolatry (Num 25), and the war with Midian (Num 31) took place.

ABEZ (ā'bĕz). A name used for the town Ebez (see Josh 19:20, RSV), located in the territory of Issachar.

ABI (ā'bī). In II Kgs 18:2 Abi is cited as the name of the mother of Hezekiah, king of Judah. She is alternately called Abijah *(q.v.)* as in II Chr 29:1.

ABIA (*ȧ*-bī'*ȧ*)

1. Grandson of Solomon through Rehoboam, father of Asa (I Chr 3:10; Mt 1:7).

2. Descendant of Aaron, who was head of the eighth division of David's priestly order (I Chr 24:10, "Abijah"). Zacharias, father of John the Baptist, belonged to this division (Lk 1:5).

See Abijah.

ABIAH (*ȧ*-bī'*ȧ*). Variant form of Abijah *(q.v.)*.

1. The second son of Samuel who was appointed judge of Beer-sheba, whose conduct hastened Israel's demand for a king like other nations (I Sam 8:2–5; I Chr 6:28).

2. The wife of Hezron (I Chr 2:24).

3. One of the sons of Becher and grandson of Benjamin (I Chr 7:6, 8).

ABI-ALBON (ā'bī-ăl'bŏn). One of the 30 mighty men (II Sam 23:31) surrounding David, serving him as a bodyguard. Abi-albon is called Abiel *(q.v.)* in the parallel passage in I Chr 11:32.

ABIASAPH (*ȧ*-bī'*ȧ*-săf). Probably same as Ebiasaph. A Levite who is the last mentioned descendant of Levi through Korah (Ex 6:24). There exists a difference of opinion as to his identity with Ebiasaph, an ancestor of the great musician Heman of David's time (I Chr 6:23, 37; 9:19).

ABIATHAR (*ȧ*-bī'*ȧ*-thȧr). A priest of the old line of Eli. Apparently his father's name was Ahimelech (I Sam 22:20) and one of his sons had the same name (II Sam 8:17). (*See* Ahimelech.) When Saul slew the priests of the Lord at Nob, Abiathar escaped and fled to David, before whom he served and bore the ark of the Lord when occasion demanded. Frequently (at least eight times) Zadok and Abiathar are mentioned together (Zadok always first) as the high priests of David's time. In Absalom's rebellion, Abiathar remained true to David's cause. However, afterward in Adonijah's attempt to secure the throne, Abiathar cast in his lot with Adonijah and was therefore ultimately deposed by Solomon, and commanded to dwell in his home town Anathoth. Solomon spared him for having faithfully shared in David's afflictions. In the deposition of Abiathar, the doom foretold upon the house of Eli was fulfilled, as noted in I Kgs 2:27. If in II Sam 8:17 Zadok and Ahimelech are unexpectedly mentioned together, it may be that Abiathar had Ahimelech as his assistant because of his own old age.

When Jesus says in Mk 2:26 that David came to request the showbread when "Abiathar was priest," whereas I Sam 22:11 ff. says that Ahimelech filled that office, apparently the son Abiathar is named as the one who stood out more prominently.

H. C. L.

ABIB (a'bĭb)

1. Young ears of barley (Heb. of Ex 9:31; Lev 2:14), ripe but still soft, eaten either rubbed or roasted (KB).

2. This Canaanite name was applied to the month (March-April) in which the barley ripened. As "the beginning of months" (Ex 12:2) and "the first month" (Lev 23:5) of Israel's national life, Abib was a witness year by year to the Lord's part in the crisis experience of the Exodus events, ritually remembered in the Feast of Unleavened Bread (Ex 13:4; 23:15; 34:18) and the Passover (Deut 16:1) during this month.

Abib is equivalent to the Babylonian Nisan, by which name the month was called after the Captivity (Neh 2:1; Est 3:7). It is not clear whether Josephus' distinction between the ritual and civil years, beginning, respectively, in the spring (Nisan) and fall (Tishri), is of early or late origin (Jos *Ant.* i.3.3). *See* Calendar.

ABIDA, ABIDAH (*ȧ*-bī'd*ȧ*). A son of Midian and a grandson of Abraham and Keturah (I Chr 1:33). The name is spelled Abidah in Gen 25:4 (KJV).

ABIDAN (*ȧ*-bī'd*ȧ*n). The son of Gideoni (Num 1:11). As a prince of the tribe of Benjamin he represented that tribe at the census in the wilderness (Num 2:22), and was also present at the dedication of the tabernacle (Num 7:60, 65).

ABIEL (ā'bĭ-ĕl)

1. A Benjamite, probably the father of Ner, who was Saul's and Abner's grandfather (I Sam 9:1; 14:51).

2. An Arbathite, one of David's mighty men (I Chr 11:32), called in II Sam 23:31 Abi-albon. The name occurs also in Akkadian and in ancient S Arabic, meaning "El is my father."

ABIEZER (ăb'ĭ-ē'zẽr), **ABIEZERITES** (ăb'ĭ-ē'zẽ-rīts)

1. Founder of a family to which the judge Gideon belonged, called Jeezer or Iezer in Num 26:30 (see KJV and RSV). The term Abiezerites identifies the descendants of Abiezer (Jud 6:11, 24; 8:32).

2. A family descended from Manasseh to which land in Canaan was given (Josh 17:2; I Chr 7:18).

3. A member of David's 30 mighty men, a Benjamite (II Sam 23:27; I Chr 27:12).

ABIGAIL (ăb'ĭ-gāl)

1. The wife of Nabal of Maon, near Carmel, in the territory of the tribe of Judah. She was a woman "of good understanding and beautiful." When Nabal treated David churlishly and so irritated him that he would have taken vengeance on Nabal, Abigail, hearing of her husband's folly, prepared a substantial gift of food and took it to David and his men. With discreet words of reconciliation she checked David's anger and saved her husband's life. But about ten days later Nabal died, apparently of a stroke. David admitted that the woman had prevented him from committing grievous folly by seeking to take his own vengeance on his enemy (I Sam 25).

David felt free to woo the woman after this, having been deeply impressed by her practical discretion and levelheadedness. When David was constrained to flee to Gath, he took Abigail with him (I Sam 27:3). Abigail was but one of the six wives David had in those early days. In Hebron she bore him a son by the name of Chileab, his second son (II Sam 3:3). However in I Chr 3:1 this son is called Daniel.

2. The name of a sister of David, who became the mother of Amasa (I Chr 2:16 f.).

H. C. L.

ABIHAIL (ăb'ĭ-hāl)

1. A Levite, the father of Zuriel, who was chief of the family of Merari in Moses' day (Num 3:35).

2. The wife of Abishur, a Jerahmeelite of the tribe of Judah (I Chr 2:29).

3. The son of Huri of the tribe of Gad, head of a family in Bashan in the time of Jotham, king of Judah (I Chr 5:14).

4. One of the wives of Rehoboam, a descendant of Eliab, David's older brother. She was

not strictly a daughter of Eliab as the text states or she would have been far too old for Rehoboam (II Chr 11:18).

5. The father of Esther and uncle of Mordecai (Est 2:15; 9:29).

ABIHU (*ȧ-bī'hū*). The second son of Aaron (Ex 6:23), who was consecrated to the priesthood with his three brothers, Nadab, Eleazar, and Ithamar (Ex 28:1; Num 3:2; I Chr 24:1). With his older brother Nadab, Abihu went with the elders of Israel and with Moses and Aaron up the mountain of God (Ex 24:1, 9). When he and his brother Nadab offered "strange fire" on the altar, they were instantly killed (Lev 10:1-2). The prohibition against the use of intoxicants which follows this account (v.9) has led some commentators to assume that the brothers were drunk when they died. They were childless (Num 3:4; I Chr 24:2).

ABIHUD (*ȧ-bī'hŭd*). A Benjamite, the third son of Bela (I Chr 8:3).

ABIJAH (*ȧ-bī'jȧ*)

1. A son of Jeroboam I, king of Israel. When the boy was gravely ill, Jeroboam sent his wife in disguise to appeal to the prophet Ahijah. The prophet, warned by God, told her that for the sin and apostasy of Jeroboam God's judgment would sweep his descendants away, and as for Abijah, "when thy feet enter into the city the child shall die" (I Kgs 14:12). The child died as prophesied, saved from the wrath to come, "because in him there is found some good thing toward Jehovah" (I Kgs 14:13, ASV).

2. The son of Rehoboam and his successor on the throne of Judah (II Chr 12:16). He is also called Abia in I Chr 3:10 and Abijam in I Kgs 14:31; 15:1-8. His mother was Maachah (I Kgs 15:2) or Michaiah (II Chr 13:2), the granddaughter of Absalom. The chief episode of his brief reign of three years was the battle in which he decisively defeated Jeroboam of Israel. The remarkable thing about the battle was a speech by Abijah to the opposing army in which he proclaimed God's presence with Judah and rebuked the Israelites for their apostasy (II Chr 13). Nevertheless he walked in the sins of his fathers, imitating their debasing polygamy with 14 wives (I Kgs 15:3; II Chr 13:21).

3. A descendant of Aaron and a priest in the time of David. He was made head of the eighth of the 24 courses into which David divided the whole priesthood for service (I Chr 24:10).

4. The daughter of Zechariah and wife of King Ahaz (II Chr 29:1). Her name is given as Abi in II Kgs 18:2. She was the mother of King Hezekiah.

5. A priest, the father of Zichri (Neh 12:1-4, 17), who returned with Zerubbabel to rebuild the temple after the Exile. If it is the same one, at a great age he also sealed the covenant of Nehemiah, binding the people in rededication to God (Neh 10:7).

P. C. J.

ABIJAM (*ȧ-bī'jȧm*). A king of Judah, successor to his father Rehoboam (I Kgs 14:31–15:8). Abijam may be an alternate spelling since he is also referred to as Abijah (*q.v.* 2).

ABILENE (*ăb-ĭ-lē'nē*). A territory on the eastern slopes of the Anti-Lebanon Mountains, named after its capital, Abila, which was about 18 miles NW of Damascus on the SW bank of Wadi Barada, the ancient Abana River (II Kgs 5:12). It was the tetrarchy of Lysanias (Lk 3:1, only Bible reference). *See* Lysanias. A contemporary inscription at Abila confirms this. In A.D. 37 it was given by the emperor to Herod Agrippa I. From A.D. 44 to 53 the territory was administered by procurators. In the latter year it was confirmed by Emperor Claudius to Herod Agrippa II. Toward the end of the century it was once more made a part of the province of Syria. It is identified with the village called es-Suk, or Suq Wadi Barada, in a wild and scenic region of limestone cliffs and gorges.

ABIMAEL (*ȧ-bĭm'ā-ĕl*). One of the sons of Joktan, a descendant of Shem, supposed founder of a tribe among the Arabians (Gen 10:28; I Chr 1:22). Such names with a medial *m* are found both in S Arabic (*Abmi-'athtar*) and Akkadian (*Ili-ma-abi*).

ABIMELECH (*ȧ-bĭm'ĕ-lĕk*)

1. The earliest OT man to bear this name was the king of Gerar, an early Philistine inhabitant of Palestine, who should be distinguished from the later warlike Philistines who at the end of the 2nd mil. migrated from their homeland in Caphtor (probably Crete, *q.v.*) and settled along the southern coast. It is highly probable that these "sea people" arrived in Palestine in waves of migration throughout the 2nd mil., Abimelech's clan being among the early settlers. Gerar is believed to be located some few miles SE of Gaza.

Abraham told Abimelech the half-truth that Sarah was his sister (Gen 20:2-18). Abimelech, whose wife was barren, assumed Sarah was unmarried and espoused her to be his wife. He became cognizant of the whole truth through a dream by which he learned also that Abraham was a prophet of the Lord who could pray for him. After some chiding of Abraham, the good Philistine Abimelech not only returned Sarah untouched but also gave Abraham gifts of cattle, servants, and silver. Abraham's prayer for Abimelech was answered with fruitfulness of womb for his entire household. Later there was a slight rift between the two wealthy households over possession of a well (Gen 21:22-32). The swearing of a covenant brought peace and gave the Hebrews their name for the oasis at Beer-sheba ("the well of swearing"). *See also* Philistines.

2. Another king of Gerar in the time of Isaac was called Abimelech (Gen 26:1, 6-17). Isaac's experience was very similar to that of his father Abraham. He too went to Gerar be-

Probable ruins of the Temple of Baal Berith (Judg 9:46-49) at Shechem. HFV

cause of famine. Fearful of his life because of his wife's beauty, Isaac said that she was his sister. Abimelech learned the whole truth and rebuked Isaac. Isaac's success through agriculture and reopening the wells dug by his father made the people envious, so that Abimelech asked him to leave. Later, a covenant was made between Isaac and Abimelech, as had been done between Abraham and the first Abimelech (Gen 26:26-31).

3. In the title of Ps 34 Achish, the Philistine king of Gath in the time of David (I Sam 21:10), is called Abimelech. It is possible that Achish *(q.v.)* was his native name and that he was known among the Canaanites as Abimelech (cf. the Assyrian king Tiglath-pileser III who was also called Pul in parts of his realm). Or Abimelech may have been a popular title for kings among the Hebrews. It is a well-known fact that Egyptian titulary consisted of five names for each king.

4. The son of Gideon (Jud 8:30–9:54) bears the title Abimelech. Related through his mother to the people of Shechem who worshiped the god Baal-berith, Abimelech received money from the treasury of Baal-berith and with it procured wicked men to help him slay his 70 brothers. The people at Shechem quickly proclaimed him king. Jotham, the youngest, however, escaped and lived to speak a parable against his presumptuous brother. In this parable he likened Abimelech to a bramble bush lording it over all the trees, and prophesied that the men of Shechem and Abimelech would destroy each other. In three years the prophecy began to be fulfilled when the people of Shechem turned against Abimelech.

Another complication is introduced into the narrative with the appearance of Gaal, the son of Ebed, who gained the confidence of most of the men of Shechem. However Zabul, a ruler of Shechem, informed Abimelech of this situation, and Abimelech by means of an ambush drove Gaal and his people away.

But Abimelech still had to win the city of Shechem, which took some ingenious military tactics (Jud 9:43-45). Finally the city was taken and sown with salt, a measure designed to spoil the soil for years to come. As was usually the case, many of the lords of Shechem took refuge in their citadel in the temple of the god Berith. The bloody Abimelech set fire to the temple tower and burned them alive. In the process of taking Thebez, a nearby city, the people likewise took refuge in their strong tower, but Abimelech's purpose to burn it was frustrated by a woman who dropped a piece of millstone on his head breaking his skull, and thus ending his wicked career.

E. B. S.

ABINADAB (*ȧ*-bĭn'*ȧ*-dăb)

1. An older brother of David (I Sam 16:8; 17:13).

2. A son of Saul who died with him in the battle of Gilboa (I Sam 31:2; I Chr 8:33; 9:39; 10:2). He is also called Ishui in I Sam 14:49.

3. The best known personage who bore this name was the man of Kirjath-jearim in whose house the ark of God rested for 20 years and from whose house David, not without trouble, brought the ark up to Jerusalem (I Sam 7:1; II Sam 6:3-4; I Chr 13:7).

4. The "son of Abinadab" (I Kgs 4:11, KJV) is rendered "Ben-Abinadab" in ASV, RSV.

ABINOAM (*ȧ*-bĭn'ō-*ă*m). A native of Kadesh in Naphtali, father of Barak (Jud 4:6, 12; 5:1, 12). The name is found also in ancient S Arabic inscriptions.

ABIRAM (*ȧ*-bī'răm)

1. A Reubenite, son of Eliab, who with his brother Dathan joined On and Korah (a Levite) in organizing a jealous conspiracy against Moses and Aaron in the wilderness (Num 16:1,12,24-27; 26:9; Deut 11:6; Ps 106:17). He perished miserably (with Korah and Dathan) when the earth miraculously cleft asunder and "swallowed them up" (*c.* 1430 B.C.).

2. The firstborn son of Hiel the Bethelite (I Kgs 16:34), who died when his father foolishly relaid the foundation of Jericho (*c.* 870 B.C.). His tragic death fulfilled Joshua's remarkable prophecy (Josh 6:26). (*Perhaps* Hiel revived an ancient Canaanite custom and offered his firstborn son as a foundation sacrifice.)

ABISHAG (ăb'ĭ-shăg). According to I Kgs 1:4, this was an exceedingly beautiful unmarried young woman (Heb. *na'arâ b^e^tulâ*) who cared for King David in his old age. Though one of her duties, in the words of the king's servants, was to be "in thy bosom, that my lord the king may get heat" (I Kgs 1:2), there can be no inference that she became his wife (v. 4, RSV). Her purpose was only to make the aged man comfortable. "They covered him with clothes, but he gat no heat." After David's death Adonijah, an older half-brother of Solomon who was a rival contender for kingship, asked Solomon for Abishag's hand in marriage. Solomon interpreted this as a possible claim on the throne in the eyes of the people and forthwith had Adonijah put to death.

ABISHAI (*ȧ*-bĭsh'ā-ī). A grandson of Jesse and cousin of David, being the son of David's sister Zeruiah who bore three sons, Abishai, Joab, and Asahel (I Chr 2:15-16). Abishai appears to have been a capable though impetuous soldier completely devoted to David as the Lord's anointed. In I Sam 26:6-9 Abishai went with David by night into the camp of the sleeping Saul and was restrained from killing Saul with the latter's own spear. He joined his brother Joab in pursuing the hapless Abner, who was forced to kill their brother Asahel during a skirmish resulting from a belt-wrestling joust (II Sam 2:18-24).

There are numerous examples of Abishai's devotion to David and his character as a military hero. Facing Ammonites and Syrians before and behind, Joab divided his army giving his brother Abishai the less heroic warriors to fight Ammon while Joab fought the Syrians; both experienced victory (II Sam 10). It took an army and the forceful General Abishai to slay 18,000 Edomites in the valley of salt and put up garrisons in Edom (I Chr 18:12-13). He was wholly the soldier in his thinking; treason deserved death. When the Benjamite Shimei cursed the exiled David, Abishai wanted to slay him immediately. "Why should this dead dog curse my lord my king? let me go over, I pray thee, and take off his head." But David looked on this misfortune as of the Lord (II Sam 16:7-14). Later, in II Sam 19:21 when David forgave Shimei, once again it was Abishai who called for execution.

Abishai commanded one of the three regiments of David's army-in-exile which brought the Absalom rebellion to a swift conclusion. In the Sheba rebellion, Joab and Abishai took command from their ill-chosen cousin Amasa and pursued after the rebel to the frontier settlement Abel-beth-maachah, whence Sheba's head was thrown over the wall to them (II Sam 20). In David's later years Abishai delivered the king out of the hand of a Philistine giant, after which David no longer went out to battle (II Sam 21).

According to II Sam 23:15-18, Abishai seems to have been the leader of the three mighty men who risked their lives to bring David a drink from the well in Bethlehem. Here also we are told he slew 300 with his spear.

E. B. S.

ABISHALOM (*ȧ*-bĭsh'*ȧ*-lôm). This is the fuller form found in I Kgs 15:2; II Chr 11:20 of the more common name Absalom *(q.v.)*.

ABISHUA (*ȧ*-bĭsh'ū-*ȧ*)

1. A Benjamite, a son of Bela (I Chr 8:4).
2. A descendant of Aaron, he was the son of Phinehas, the priest, and ancestor of Ezra (I Chr 6:4, 50; Ezr 7:5).

ABISHUR (*ȧ*-bī'shûr). A man of Judah, the second son of Shammai, listed in the genealogy of Jerahmeel. He was the husband of Abihail (I Chr 2:28-29).

ABITAL (*ȧ*-bī'tăl). One of David's wives (fifth), the mother of Shephatiah, who was born in Hebron (II Sam 3:2, 4).

ABITUB (*ȧ*-bī'tŭb). A Benjamite born in Moab, a son of Shaharaim (I Chr 8:8-11).

ABIUD (*ȧ*-bī'ŭd). The Gr. form of Abihud *(q.v.)*, who was a descendant of Zerubbabel and the father of Eliakim, being mentioned in the NT as an ancestor of Jesus (Mt 1:13).

ABJECT. A plural noun in Ps 35:15 from Heb. *nēkeh* probably meaning "slanderers" or "railers." RSV has "cripples."

ABLUTION. This is an act of washing the body. In Scripture there are only a few doubtful references to washing for sanitary purposes. These references, the bathing of Pharaoh's daughter (Ex 2:5), of Bathsheba (II Sam 11:2), and of the harlots of Samaria (I Kgs 22:38, RSV), are each also capable of explanation as religious ablutions. Religious ritual washings were universal in the ancient Near East. "In the minds of the ancients there was a close connection between the notion of purity or cleanness and the notion of being consecrated to God" (R. deVaux, *Ancient Israel, Its Life and Institutions,* p. 460).

The evolutionary religious concept explains the entire OT system of clean and unclean and of ritual washings as arising, like the idea of holiness, from taboo, and makes of it all a base element in Heb. religion ("Unclean," HDB; cf. de Vaux, *op. cit.*, pp. 463, 464, where taboos

Ruins of a highly decorated ablution tank adjacent to the temple of Jupiter at Baalbek. It measures about sixty-five by twenty-five feet.
HFV

are said to be "remains of old superstitious rites"). Whatever forms and ideas may have been carried over from pre-Mosaic times, it is certain that ablutions were designed by God, "having as their object the cultivation of holiness and of the spiritual life. . . . The great obstacle to holiness is sin; while that death again, which is the consequence of sin, puts an end to man's life . . . permeates the entire man; nor does it merely desecrate the soul . . . but it also defiles the body . . . turns it into the very dust of death" (C. F. Keil, *Biblical Archaeology,* I, 378).

Keil's view is further that water as a principal cleansing medium of ordinary life was used to symbolize spiritual forgiveness of sin. This connection between defilement and death explains how the Levitical purifications ranked side by side with sacrifices and together formed the main features of worship in the Mosaic system. Thus the law was able all the better to fulfill the purpose for which it was designed, of awakening and keeping alive in man the consciousness of sin and guilt and of the need for cleansing of the inner nature (see Keil, *ibid.,* pp. 378–384).

The Levitical ablutions were of four kinds: (1) washing of the hands (Lev 15:11); (2) washing of hands and feet (Ex 30:19; 40:31); (3) bathing of the whole body (Num 19:19; Lev 22:4–6); (4) sprinkling with a special water ("water of separation," Num 19:9).

Baptism is a form of ritual ablution which arose among the Jews apparently in connection with initiation of proselytes. Authorities state that a stranger who desired to become a proselyte of the covenant of righteousness, i.e., in the fullest sense an Israelite, had to be circumcised and baptized, and then offer sacrifice. Baptism was by self-immersion in a pool (see HDB, I, 239; Edersheim, *Life and Times of Jesus the Messiah,* II, xii; Schürer, *History of the Jewish People,* II, ii, par. 31, p. 319). Baptism and other ablutions were prominent among the Essenes (Jos *War* ii. 8.5) as witnessed by the findings at Qumran (F. M. Cross, Jr., *The Ancient Library of Qumran,* pp. 49, 50, 70). John's and Jesus' use of baptism is well-known.

Except for the rites of baptism and feet washing (Jn 13), ritual ablution is as foreign to NT Christianity as the sacrifices of the Mosaic law. For the Christian, ceremonial defilement does not exist (Mk 7:6–23; Mt 15:3–20), hence no need for ritual washing. Jesus fulfilled this aspect of the law as well as the others. Baptism by whatever mode and feet washing whether viewed as a rite or only as a Gospel incident have no connection with ritual uncleanness, hence no connection with OT ritual or interpretation.

See Baptism; Bathe, Bathing; Foot Washing; Hands, Washing of; Unclean.

Bibliography. A. Oepke, "*Louō,* etc.," TDNT, IV, 295–307.

R. D. C.

ABNER (ăb'nẽr). A cousin of Saul and commander of Israel's army (I Sam 14:50–51; 17:55). He occupied the place of honor at feasts and was Saul's bodyguard during the desert campaign against David (I Sam 20:25; 26:5–15). After the death of Saul and Jonathan, Abner became leader of Israel and made Ishbosheth king, succeeding his father Saul (II Sam 2:8–10). When offended by Ishbosheth, Abner decided to support David as king over all Israel (II Sam 3:8–10). Incensed by David's acceptance of this allegiance, and embittered because Abner had killed his brother Asahel (in self-defense), Joab murdered Abner at the gate of Hebron (II Sam 3:27). His death was mourned by David and all Israel (II Sam 3:31–34; I Kgs 2:32).

ABOMINATION. There are a total of 12 Heb. and Gr. words translated "abomination" or "abominable." The biblical languages, like our own, have a variety of expressions, some close synonyms, others not, to express degrees and varieties of abhorrence.

The chief idea represented in the four Heb. nouns is revulsion at great wrong in religious matters. Since there is only one true living God, an invisible spiritual being without bodily parts, all forms of idolatry and all ceremonies and objects connected with idolatry are abhorrent to God. This attitude is shared by His people and His prophets. Heb. *tô'ēbâ* is the chief word in the OT used in this connection. The same abhorrence pertains to moral evil. Hence *tô'ēbâ* is used of that as well (Jer 7:7–10). The verb *tā'ab* from which *tô'ēbâ* is derived is less specialized in meaning, though translated similarly. It expresses displeasure of all sorts, from dislike of certain foods (Ps 107:18) to loathing for idols (Deut 7:26).

Heb. *sheqeṣ* seems to be a technical word for revulsion at the use of flesh of unclean animals for food or sacrifice (Lev 7:21; 11:10–13, 20, 23, 41, 42). The related *shiqûṣ* is chiefly a term of contempt for idols and idolatry, especially in the prophets (Isa 66:3; Jer 4:1; 32:34; Ezk 7:20). The verb *shāqaṣ,* translated "abomination" (Lev 11:11, 13), from which these two words are derived, likewise expresses the revulsion a Heb. was expected to have toward things morally or religiously wrong.

Disgust at petty dishonesty is expressed once as abomination (Mic 6:10, "abominable"), though the Heb. word used here ordinarily means to be angry.

The NT words rendered "abomination," "abominable," etc. (Mt 24:15; Lk 16:15; Tit 1:16; I Pet 4:3; Rev 21:8), are simply the OT Heb. ideas discussed above in Gr. garb.

See Sacrilege.

R. D. C.

ABOMINATION OF DESOLATION. This expression appears in Mt 24:15 and Mk 13:14. Matthew states that it is that "spoken of by Daniel the prophet." The Gr. phrase is quoted almost exactly from the LXX of Dan 9:27 (as well as Theodotion's Gr. translation which replaced the LXX in early Christian centuries). Similar expressions are found in Dan 8:13 ("transgression of desolation"), Dan 9:27 ("for the overspreading of abominations he shall make it desolate"), Dan 11:31 ("the abomination that maketh desolate"), of which, as stated, the LXX of Dan 9:27 is cited in the NT.

An act whereby a pagan idol is introduced into the precincts of the holy temple at Jerusalem is obviously intended by Jesus. Liberal interpreters of Daniel hold that the three passages in Daniel all refer to an act of Antiochus Epiphanes, pagan king of Syria, who desecrated the temple in 165 B.C. Thus Jesus was mistaken or else never really said what is attributed to Him in Mt 24:15 and Mk 13:14. Certain conservatives feel the prophecy was fulfilled in events of the 1st cen. A.D. associated with the destruction of Jerusalem. Others assert that Paul's expansion of the prophecy in II Thess 2 (as most agree it is) requires that there is some reference here to a final Antichrist who shall make his appearance at the end of the present age (G. R. Beasley-Murray, *Jesus and the Future* and *A Commentary on Mark 13*). *See* Abomination; Antichrist; Beast (Symbolic).

R. D. C.

ABRAHAM (ā'brȧ-hăm)

Authenticity and Date of His Background

Though archaeology has provided no direct contact with Abraham, abundant evidence has accumulated which, far from contradicting the biblical story, has led many critical scholars to accept the account as a genuine reflection of the period it claims to represent. This evidence is in the form of documentary sources which establish the cultural traditions reflected in the biblical account.

The Nuzu texts which present the common law of the Hurrians (biblical Horites, *q.v.*), who dominated parts of Mesopotamia *c.* 1500 B.C., have cast light on such traditions as Abraham's adoption of his servant Eliezer as heir (Gen 15:2–4). In Nuzu such slave adoptions were common practice by childless couples. For the eventual inheritance, the adopted male adult traded his caring for the adopting parents in their old age and his providing them proper burial ceremonies. But Nuzu provided that a natural son like Isaac, even if born after such adoption, always received primary inheritance rights.

Again, both Nuzu and Hammurabi's law-code tell how a childless wife was obliged to provide her husband a handmaid with hopes a son might be born. Abraham's reluctance to send Hagar off (Gen 21:11) reflects the protection by Hurrian law of the handmaid under those circumstances.

Another cultural tradition, which does not fit later (Mosaic) Heb. law and therefore must come from an earlier time, is Abraham's purchase of the field of Machpelah (Gen 23). Cappadocian texts reflect Hittite feudal laws which apparently made it necessary for Abraham to pay full price (23:9, NASB) to obtain legal title and to purchase the entire field from Ephron the Hittite, because with full ownership went the feudal obligation or services due the ruler of the land, according to Hittite law (BASOR, # 129, pp. 15–18). Abraham was accustomed to such business transactions and was able to weigh out to Ephron the 400 shekels of silver as "current money with the merchant." It was not coinage, but as the Heb. says, "silver which passes to the merchant," meaning unalloyed bars or rings of silver.

The Plains of Mamre. HFV

Although Abraham himself is not known from extrabiblical sources, the name is attested in its Babylonian form, Abamram (BASOR, # 83, p. 34), as are the names Nahor (cf. city of Nahor, Gen 24:10), Terah and Serug (Gen 11:22, 24) as towns mentioned in the Mari texts and other Assyrian documents (cf. John Bright, *A History of Israel*, p. 70).

One of the most interesting chapters in the story of Abraham is Gen 14 which deals with the battle of the four kings of the E against the local monarchs. Archaeologists consider this chapter to be most detailed in its authenticity. (*See* Amraphel; Arioch; Chedorlaomer; Tidal.) The geographical accuracy of Gen 14 is undisputed. Moreover, the rare technical term (*ḥanîkim*) used for Abraham's retainers (Gen 14:14) appears in the Egyptian Execration texts and in a letter from Taanach dated to the first half of the 2nd mil. B.C. The occurrence of this rare, early word lends tremendous authenticity to the text.

Abraham's travels from Mesopotamia and his wanderings in Palestine accord well with the general picture that archaeology has obtained for the early 2nd mil. This was a time when Palestine was receiving new nomadic groups and the central hill country where Abraham chose to live was sparsely populated, while the Jordan Valley, coastal regions, and other agricultural domains were dominated by the Canaanites and others. Abraham was probably part of this great movement of people usually identified as Amorites (Gen 15:16), which would explain Abraham's alliances with the Amorites Aner, Eshcol, and Mamre (Gen 14:13, 24), and the justification for Ezekiel accusing the erring nation of having an Amorite father (Ezk 16:3-5). Abraham spent some time in the Negeb and along the trade route from Kadesh-barnea to Shur (eastern border of Egypt). Not for centuries before or after the Middle Bronze I period (2100-1850 B.C.) were there known settlements in the Negeb. Ruins of way stations, dated to that time by pottery, dot the inland caravan route through the northern Sinai desert.

An exact date for Abraham cannot be pinpointed by means of archaeology, though most authorities settle on the early 2nd mil. By using the biblical figures and assuming no gaps, a date of *c*. 2000 B.C. for the birth of Abraham may be obtained. This fits well with archaeological data.

Objection has been raised regarding the occurrence of the term Philistine *(q.v.)* in Gen 21:32, 34. The warlike Philistines of David's day did not arrive in the coasts of Palestine until *c*. 1200 B.C. It has been pointed out by C. H. Gordon, however, that the Indo-European Sea people, such as the Minoans from Crete, had been migrating into Canaan all through the 2nd mil. The Canaanized Abimelech of Gerar was probably part of an earlier wave of peace-loving "Philistines," although the name Philistine itself may be anachronistic, coming from the hostile peoples of Saul's and David's time. *See* Chronology, OT; Patriarchal Age.

History and Significance of His Life

Abram began his life in Ur of the Chaldees in Mesopotamia. From there Terah, his father, moved the family to Haran. Both Ur and Haran were centers of moon worship. His father's name, Terah, possibly means "Ter is (the divine) brother." Ter is believed to be a dialectic variant for the moon-god and was especially popular in the district of Haran as is borne out by Assyrian records (J. Lewy, HUCA, 19, p. 425). But Abram was called away from this pagan background by the voice of God to go to a land divinely promised to his seed.

The Mosque of Hebron which covers a cave thought to be the Cave of Machpelah, burial site of Abraham and other members of the Patriarchal family. HFV

After arriving in Palestine Abram spent his days mainly near three centers in the S, Bethel, Hebron (Mamre), and Beer-sheba. He had apparently entered Canaan from the E, as Jacob did on his return from Padan-aram, crossing the Jordan near Succoth and stopping first to worship God outside Shechem (Gen 12:5-7). Near Bethel, however, Abram built his second altar (Gen 12:8; 13:3) and called on the name of the Lord Yahweh. After a brief sojourn in Egypt because of famine, Abram returned to the place of the altar near Bethel and effected a separation with his nephew Lot, who chose to dwell in the verdant plain of the Jordan where the Canaanite cities of Sodom and Gomorrah were situated. Then Abram journeyed S to the highland plain called Mamre (Hebron) at the southern end of the central mountain range. Here he built another altar to the Lord.

Following the recovery of Lot and his household from the hands of their Mesopotamian captors, Abram paid tithes to Melchizedek, king of Salem. Whether or not Salem was Jerusalem cannot be proved, but the text is clear that Melchizedek was a priest-king representing El Elyon—another appellation for Abraham's God. Gen 20-22 tells of Abraham's sojourn in the Negeb, especially around Beer-sheba. The biblical account states that Abraham both dug the well and named the place Beer-sheba ("the well of swearing") because of the covenant he made with Abimelech, the Philistine chieftain in that area.

God renewed His promise to Abram on several occasions (cf. Gen 13:14-18; 15; 17; 22:15-19). Emphasis is laid on Abram's faith in the promise of God concerning both a land and a seed despite his wife's continued barrenness and age. Abram's name, meaning "exalted father" or "my father is exalted," was changed to "Abraham" meaning "father of a multitude." God's covenant with him was sealed by the sign of circumcision, and eventually Isaac, a son of promise (Gal 4:28), was given to this one who ever after was to be known as "the father of all them that believe" (Rom 4:11). Indeed, Abraham believed God's promise of a son in his old age and "it was reckoned to him for righteousness" (Gen 15:4-6; Rom 4:1-4; Jas 2:22-23; Gal 3:6; 5:6). Before Isaac was given through Sarah's dead womb (Heb 11:11), her Egyptian handmaid Hagar bore Ishmael, through whom the Arabs of this day trace their origin to Abraham.

Isaac's name comes from the Heb. root *ṣāḥaq*, meaning "to laugh." Abraham's laughter (Gen 17:17) seems to have been an expression of joy or even amazement, while Sarah's laugh-

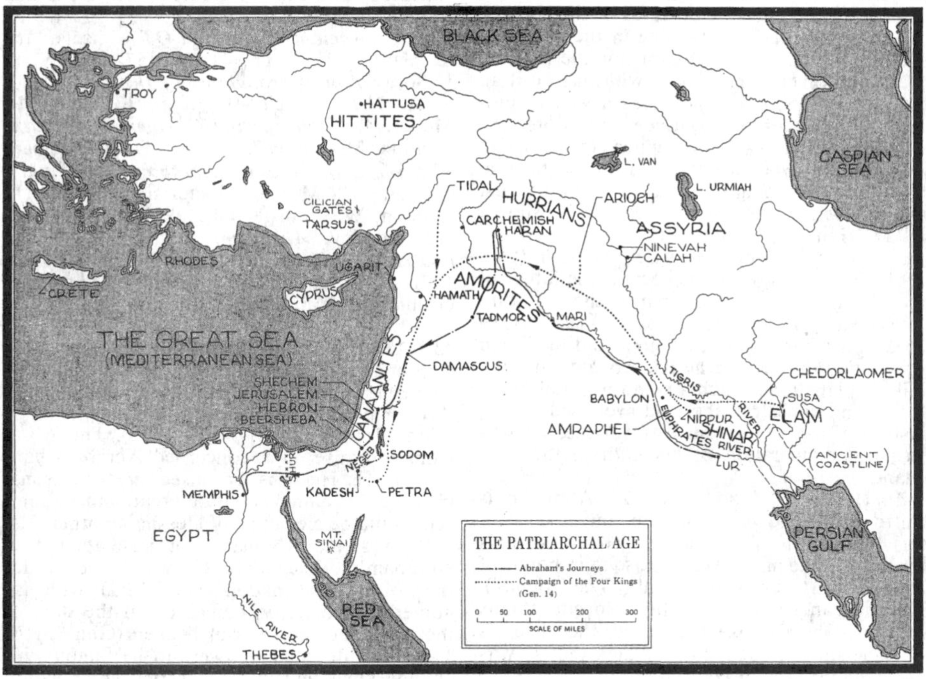

The Journeys of Abraham

ter (Gen 18:11-15) was an expression of disbelief which she shamefacedly disavowed. In due time Isaac became the focal point of all Abraham's hopes; this explains the importance of the episode of the offering of Isaac in Gen 22. The dilemma Abraham experienced was that God's promise could not be fulfilled if Isaac died and yet God was asking Abraham for Isaac. Heb 11:17-19 gives the divine commentary on this event, showing how Abraham's faith in God's faithfulness triumphed, "accounting that God was able to raise him [Isaac] up, even from the dead" (v. 19) if necessary, to fulfill His promise. *See* Abrahamic Promise.

Other episodes in the life of Abraham picture him not as a generic figure about whom legend has become encrusted (as certain critics have claimed) but in warm human tones. Most of the biblical account deals with him from his seventy-fifth year on (Gen 12:4). That Abraham was 100 and Sarah was 90 when Isaac was born, far from being late Midrash, is a key part of the original story, i.e., that Abraham worshiped the God who performs the impossible. It is true that the biblical account touches on a relatively small segment of his life, yet these comparatively few chapters (Gen 12-25) present a surprisingly well rounded picture of the patriarch. He was seminomadic but very different from the average bedouin of today, for Abraham was well-to-do in cattle, silver, and servants. He was a man of peace, but could use his retainers (Gen 14:14) for an occasional skirmish.

Abraham had face-to-face encounters with the Almighty, entertained angels (Gen 18:1-8), and received the word of God in dreams (Gen 15:12-17). Most importantly, he is called a prophet by God in Gen 20:7, where Abimelech, the king of Gerar, is warned that Abraham had the gift of intercession. He used this gift successfully in Abimelech's behalf (Gen 20:17-18) but was unsuccessful in his intercession for Sodom (Gen 18:23-30), undoubtedly because his estimate of that city was wrong. *See* Sodom; Bab edh-Dhra.

Twice Abraham seems to have been protecting his own skin by using the half-truth that Sarah was his sister while hiding the fact that she was also his wife (Gen 12:11-13; 20:5). Isaac did the same thing (Gen 26:6-11). *See* Abimelech. These episodes, however, when properly understood, show that Abraham and Isaac, although afraid, were not deliberately walking the borderline of moral turpitude. The patriarchs came from Haran, an area controlled by the Hurrians. Hence they were evidently both practicing a cherished Hurrian custom, which E. A. Speiser (The Anchor Bible, Genesis, pp. 91-94) calls the wife-sister relationship. Both Sarah and Rebekah were eligible for this privileged status according to Hurrian legal practice. The patriarchs hoped to use as a diplomatic device this special status of their wives, who enjoyed superior standing in their society. Neither the pharaoh of Egypt nor the ruler of Gerar, however, was familiar with this Hurrian custom, and had to be convinced it was a legitimate exercise of prerogatives and protection enjoyed by sister-wives of upper-class Hurrian society. Yet God intervened for Abraham in both cases, teaching him that the walk of trust and obedience was the new course he should follow (Gen 12:17; 20:3, 17f.).

Abraham had another wife, Keturah (Gen 25:1-4), through whom he became the father of the Midianites and others, but as the Scripture says, "He gave all that he had to Isaac" (Gen 25:6). Abraham died "in a good old age" and was buried in the cave he had bought from the Hittites. His taking such a step for burial of his family and himself in the land promised to him instead of back in his ancestral homeland was strong demonstration of his faith in the covenant.

In II Chr 20:7 and Jas 2:23 Abraham is called the friend of God. The universality of this title for the father of the Heb. nation is reflected in the name of the mosque in honor of Abraham at Hebron, Al-Khalil ("The Friend"). No one can be sure that this mosque stands over Abraham's burial cave in the field of Machpelah, but Gen 23:19 states that it was indeed in the area of Hebron.

E. B. S.

Abraham in the NT

The name of Abraham occurs 74 times in the NT, more than that of any other OT saint except Moses (79 times). God is the "God of Abraham" (Mt 22:32; Acts 7:32), and Abraham lives on in conscious fellowship with Him (Lk 16:22; *see* Abraham's Bosom). Abraham was the ancestor of Messiah (Mt 1:1) and the father of the Israelites according to the flesh (Mt 3:9; Jn 8:33; Acts 13:26). But he becomes the spiritual father of all who share in his faith by the Spirit (Rom 4:11-16; 9:7; Gal 3:16, 29; 4:22, 31). Abraham's faith led to his justification and thus typifies the kind of faith we must exercise (Rom 4:3-11). The demonstrations of his faith in his obeying God's call to leave Mesopotamia and in his offering of Isaac are mentioned as outstanding examples of faith in action (Heb 11:8-19; Jas 2:21).

J. R.

Bibliography. William F. Albright, *Archaeology, Historical Analogy, and Early Biblical Tradition,* Baton Rouge: Louisiana State Univ. Press, 1966, pp. 22-41. Jack Finegan, *In the Beginning,* New York: Harper, 1962, pp. 85-121. Nelson Glueck, *Rivers in the Desert,* New York: Farrar, Strauss & Cudahy, 1959, pp. 60-110. Angel Gonzalez, *Abraham, Father of Believers,* trans. by R. J. Olsen, New York: Herder & Herder, 1967. James L. Kelso, *Archaeology and Our OT Contemporaries,* Grand Rapids: Zondervan, 1966, pp. 13-27. K. A. Kitchen, *Ancient Orient and OT,* Chicago: Inter-Varsity, 1966, pp. 41-56, 153-156. W. S. LaSor, *Great Personalities of the OT,* Westwood, N.J.: Revell, 1959, pp. 13-30. F. B. Meyer, *Abraham: or the Obedience of Faith,* London: Morgan & Scott, n.d. D. J. Wiseman, *The Word of God for Abraham and Today,* G. Campbell Morgan Memorial Lecture #11, London: Westminster Chapel, 1959. C. Leonard Woolley, *Abraham: Recent Discoveries and Hebrew Origins,* London: Faber & Faber, 1936. Geerhardus Vos, *Biblical Theology,* Grand Rapids: Eerdmans, 1954, pp. 79-105.

ABRAHAMIC PROMISE. The promises given to Abraham embodied in the Abrahamic covenant first appear in Gen 12:1-3, followed by three important confirmations and applications (Gen 13:14-17; 15:1-7; 17:1-19). The Abrahamic promise, first, concerned Abraham himself *(q.v.).* He was promised great personal blessing, his name would be great, and he himself would be a channel of blessing to others.

Second, the Abrahamic promise related to Abraham's descendants. He was to be the father of a great nation (Gen 12:2) with innumerable posterity, compared to the dust of the earth and the stars of heaven (Gen 13:16; 15:5). His descendants were to be famous, including kings and more than one great nation (Gen 17:6). It is significant that all these promises have already been literally fulfilled.

Third, the promise of title to the land to which God had directed Abraham was made sure to Abraham's posterity as an "everlasting" possession (Gen 17:7-8). The extensive boundaries of their possession are given in great detail (Gen 15:18-21) and confirmed by a solemn covenant sealed with blood (Gen 15:8-17). The implication that the nation would continue forever in keeping with its title to the land was later confirmed in Jer 31:35-37. To these broad promises detailed predictions are added, such as the sojourn in Egypt (Gen 15:13-14) and emphasis on the fact that only a portion of Abraham's seed would inherit the full promise.

Fourth, through Abraham "all the families of the earth" would be blessed. This promise went beyond Abraham's physical lineage and concerned all nations. It was fulfilled in the coming of Jesus Christ and His provision for the sins of the whole world. Through Abraham's posterity, also, the Scriptures have been written through which God speaks to the entire world. The antagonism between Gentiles and Israel is anticipated in Gen 12:3 in the statement that God would bless those who bless Abraham's seed and curse those who curse it.

Scholars have differed as to whether the promises to Abraham should be considered literally or nonliterally. The nonliteral interpretation regards Abraham's seed as the divine community or body of believers throughout all ages and the promise of the land is spiritualized to represent the promise of heaven.

Abraham, however, understood the promise concerning his seed to be literal, and this was confirmed by God's refusal to recognize Abraham's servant or Ishmael (Gen 15:2-4; 17:15-22). The specific promise to Abraham's seed was first narrowed to Isaac, later to Jacob, and through Jacob channeled to the 12 patriarchs, the sons of Jacob. The promise of the land was also interpreted literally throughout the OT. Not only was the promise of the land confirmed to Isaac (Gen 26:1-5) and then to Jacob (Gen 28:13-15), but it was given to Moses (Deut 30:1-5) and Joshua (Josh 1:3-4). Israel was assured that, though scattered, ultimately they would be restored to their land never to be dispersed again (Amos 9:14-15).

The NT seems to justify the concept that there is a sense in which all believers are children of Abraham. Gal 3:6-9 states that "they which are of faith, the same are the children of Abraham." However, the particular aspect of the Abrahamic promise cited relates this, according to Gal 3:8, not to Israel but to that aspect of the covenant which originally belonged to the Gentiles, namely, "in thee shall all nations be blessed." The fact that the NT uses the expression "children of Abraham" to include those who are not physical descendants of Abraham but who, like Abraham, believed in God (Gal 3:9) does not cancel the promises to Israel as a nation or the promise of the land to them.

The Abrahamic promise will involve the restoration of Israel to the land, as promised Abraham in Gen 15:18-21 and numerous other OT prophecies (Isa 11:11-12; 12:1-3; 27:12-13; 43:1-7; 48:8-17; 66:20-22; Jer 16:14-16; 23:3-8; 30:10-11; 31:8, 31-37; Ezk 11:17-21; 20:33-38; 34:11-16; 39:25-29; Hos 1:10-11; Amos 9:11-15; Mic 4:4-7; Zeph 3:14-20; Zech 8:4-8). The Abrahamic promises are, therefore, foundational declarations of the purposes of God beginning with Abraham's day and finding their fulfillment throughout human history.

See Covenants.

J. F. W.

ABRAHAM'S BOSOM. This figurative phrase depicts the blessedness of the believer in paradise following death. Although used in rabbinic Judaism, the only scriptural occurrence of this expression is in Christ's parable of the rich man and Lazarus (Lk 16:19 ff.). At his death Lazarus the beggar is carried by angels to Abraham's bosom, while the rich man after his burial is tormented in Hades.

According to the OT, at death one goes to be with his fathers (Gen 15:15; 47:30; Deut 31:16; Jud 2:10). Since Abraham was the father of the Jews (Lk 3:8; Jn 8:39 f.), a concrete form of this expression was to go to father Abraham (IV Macc 13:17). A simple variation of this was to speak of the life hereafter in terms of Abraham's bosom.

In rabbinic Judaism the phrase had two distinguishable meanings, and interpreters are divided as to the precise meaning of the phrase in this parable. To lie or sit in Abraham's bosom may express figuratively the loving fellowship which exists between Abraham and his believing descendants in heaven in analogy to the paternal tenderness of a father for his son (Jn 1:18). Others think the figure focuses primarily on the heavenly banquet where, according to the Roman manner of feasting employed also by the Jews, Lazarus reclined at table with his head in the bosom of Abraham, his host (Jn 13:23; 21:20).

Perhaps both elements are applicable to the parable. Since Scripture generally depicts the joy of heaven in terms of a banquet feast (Mt 8:11; Lk 13:28-29; 14:16 ff.), it is natural to see this implied in the picture of the poor beggar who was fed by the crumbs from the rich man's table now enjoying the abundance of the heavenly banquet. But intimacy and fellowship are not excluded from the picture. The lonely outcast beggar is now enjoying the blessedness of heaven in the intimate company of the father of believers. And since Lazarus is in Abraham's bosom, it also appears that he has received the place of honor at the banquet.

Interpreters also differ as to whether Abraham's bosom depicts a place which is a division or compartment of Hades. In Jewish writings Sheol-Hades is often the place of the dead in general, including both righteous and unrighteous. In the pseudepigraphal Enoch chap. 22, there are even four divisions to Hades where the dead await the day of judgment. But here Abraham's bosom and Hades are distinct places. Jesus speaks of the rich man only in Hades, and there he sees Abraham "afar off" and is told that "a great gulf" is fixed between them so that transfer is impossible. Abraham and Lazarus are in bliss, while the rich man in Hades suffers torment and requests water to cool his tongue. These dreadful conditions appear as the inherent consequences of being in Hades.

The eschatological implications are clear, for the faith of Lazarus leads to the joy of everlasting life (Abraham's bosom), while the riches of the unbelieving rich man cannot protect him from the torment of hell (Hades).

The context offers no support for the view of some Roman Catholics that Abraham's bosom refers to the *limbus patrum,* a place where the OT believers enjoy peace while awaiting Christ's perfect redemption. In Egypt other motifs led to an interpretation of Abraham's bosom in which the element of cool water and refrigeration were emphasized.

For further bibliographical references see SBK, II (1924), 226-227; SBK, IV (1928), 1018-1019; TWNT, III (1938), 825-826.

See Abraham; Death; Paradise; Sheol.

F. H. K.

ABRAM (ā'brăm). The original name used for Abraham *(q.v.)* in Gen 11:27–17:5. The name occurs in Old Babylonian, Egyptian texts of the 19th cen. B.C., ancient S Arabic, and on a Ugaritic inscription. To these heathen the name probably meant "my (divine) father is exalted."

ABSALOM (ăb'sȧ-lŏm). David's third son, born to Maacah the daughter of Talmai, king of Geshur, at Hebron (II Sam 3:2-3; I Chr 3:1-2). The author of the book in which the Absalom narratives occur (II Sam 13–19) is primarily concerned with the Lord's righteous acts in the formative years of the Davidic dynasty. For the author, Solomon (and not the firstborn Amnon nor the third son Absalom nor the fourth Adonijah, etc.) was God's choice as David's successor. An appreciation of this emphasis helps to explain the selection of two events in Absalom's life (Amnon's murder, II Sam 13:1-38; and Absalom's conspiracy and rebellion, II Sam 13:39–19:8) in preference to others. The writer intends to show how the Lord punished David for adultery and murder, and yet kept His promise to perpetuate David's dynasty (announced by Nathan in II Sam 12:10-14; 7:12-16).

Nathan announced three ways in which God would punish David. (1) Bathsheba's child (a son, II Sam 11:27, and thus possible heir to the throne) would die (II Sam 12:14). Who would succeed David? Could it be Amnon? Prodded by Jonadab (his "friend," II Sam 13:3-7, a "court confidant"; cf. Hushai, David's "friend," II Sam 15:37; 16:16; I Chr 27:33), Amnon raped his half sister (Absalom's full sister) Tamar; and (David having failed to avenge this act) two years later Absalom had Amnon killed and then fled to his maternal grandfather. Could, then, David's successor be Absalom? Five years passed before David fully reinstated him. But now Absalom moved swiftly to gain the throne. Adopting pagan customs (which Talmai taught him?), he appeared publicly in a chariot escorted by a cortege of runners. He secured the sympathy of the ten northern tribes by posing as their advocate. Within four years (LXX; not 40 years–apparently due to mishearing, a Heb. copyist wrote *'arbā 'îm shānāh* for *'arbā' shānîm* in II Sam 15:7), under pretense of fulfilling a vow, Absalom went to Hebron and claimed the title "king" (II Sam 15:10); then seized Jerusalem for his capital. But his success ended when Joab had him murdered (defying David's explicit command) in the forest of Ephraim. Finally, could the successor to David be Adonijah? He attempted to seize the throne in David's old age, only to be denounced by the aged king's own appointment of Solomon (Bathsheba's son!) as his successor.

Traditional tomb of Absalom in the Kidron Valley, Jerusalem. HFV

(2) The sword would not depart from David's house (II Sam 12:10). Absalom had Amnon murdered for raping his sister; Joab had Absalom slain for conspiracy and rebellion; and Benaiah killed Adonijah for asking to marry Abishag (I Kgs 2:13-25).

(3) One of David's own house would conspire against him and go in publicly to his concubines (II Sam 12:11-12). Absalom stole the hearts of the men of Israel (II Sam 15:6), proclaimed himself king at Hebron, and seized Jerusalem without a battle. Following Ahithophel's advice, he went in to David's ten concubines publicly, thereby strengthening his claim to the throne and asserting his complete domination of David's empire (II Sam 16:20-23).

But despite the magnitude of David's sins and the period of uncertainty concerning the identity of his successor, God remained faithful to His promise that David's dynasty would be established forever in Israel. Solomon became king in his father's stead (I Kgs 1).

Bibliography. E. R. Dalglish, "Absalom," IDB, I, 22-23. H. W. Hertzberg, *I and II Samuel: A Commentary, Old Testament Library,* Philadelphia: Westminster, 1964. Eugene H. Maly, *The World of David and Solomon (Backgrounds to the Bible Series),* Englewood Cliffs, N.J.: Prentice-Hall, 1966. J. Weingreen, "The Rebellion of Absalom," VT, XIX (1969), 263-266.

J. T. W.

ABSTINENCE. This is a general term applicable to any object or action from which one refrains for a certain time and for some particular purpose, especially for the cultivation of the spiritual life. It is usually a voluntary self-discipline and may consist in an entire renunciation or a very slight partaking of some pleasure or necessity, as eating, drinking, etc. Sometimes it pertains to the total abstinence from something positively harmful or forbidden, as fornication, prohibited food, intoxicating alcoholic beverages, or debilitating drugs. Extreme abstinence may take the form of asceticism. It may be distinguished from temperance, which is a moderate use of food or drink, etc. Fasting is a specific form of abstinence, namely, from food. *See* Fasting.

In the OT the eating of blood was forbidden (Gen 9:4). Other instances of mandatory abstinence are recorded (Gen 32:32; Ex 22:31; Lev 3:17; 10:9; 11:4 ff.; Num 6:3; Deut 14:21), related to the dietary regulations of the Israelites in general and the priests and Nazarites in particular. These dietary restrictions were largely set aside in the NT (Acts 15:19-20, 28-29). Paul leaves the matter of abstinence from food up to the individual's conscience and the Spirit's guidance, and urges loving consideration for one another (Rom 14; I Cor 8). In matters involving morals, apostolic commands to abstain from evil are obligatory (I Thess 4:3; 5:22; I Pet 2:11).

While His life was the supreme example of self-denial, our Lord neither taught nor practiced asceticism, although His public ministry was preceded by 40 days of fasting in the wilderness. He condemned artificial piety and ostentation (Mt 6:16-18).

Abstinence, according to the Bible, is never good and valuable in itself, but is so only when it fosters a holy and useful life. It is a means, not an end in itself.

R. E. P.

ABYSS (lit., "no bottom"). This word appears only nine times in the NT. It is translated seven times as "the bottomless pit" (Rev 9:1, 2, 11; 11:7; 17:8; 20:1, 3). In two other occurrences the rendering is "the deep" (Lk 8:31; Rom 10:7).

The NT usage apparently grew out of its frequent usage in the Septuagint. Here it usually is the translation of *tehôm*, beginning at Gen 1:2. Primary reference in each case is simply to the depths of the ocean (e.g., Ps 77:16). Those interpreters who suppose the Hebrews adopted the pagan cosmology of the ancient Near East imagine all sorts of references to mythology in the word (see BDB, pp. 1062-1063). This much only needs to be conceded: that the language and outlook of the OT being phenomenal, i.e., employing the common language of appearance, the depths of the sea are cited poetically as the opposite of the vault of heaven above. Paul employs similar language, using the word abyss in Rom 10:6-7.

Taken, then, as the remote opposite of heaven, the abode of God, the word is employed as a name for the present abode of wicked spirits. This is the better understanding of Rom 10:7 (Jesus did not send demons to dwell in a lake, Lk 8:31), and of every other NT use save Rom 10:6-7 where the word simply designates the farthest possible position downward.

Study of the word in the LXX, classics and NT supplies no information for a geography of the nether world. *See* Bottomless Pit; Dead, The; Hell.

R. D. C.

ACACIA. *See* Plants.

ACCAD (ăk'ăd). Spelled Accad in English Bibles (KJV, ASV, RSV), it is in Heb. *'akkad* (Gen 10:10). The city of this name (in modern historical literature commonly spelled Akkad) was located in lower Mesopotamia not far S of present day Bagdad and a bit N of ancient Babylon. In certain early tablets the spelling is Agade. The exact site of Agade is not known.

Lower Mesopotamia (i.e., S and E of the neck formed by the near approach of the Tigris and Euphrates) in later OT times was called Babylonia, but as early as the Third Dynasty of Ur (Abram's city), located in the far S of the territory, the area was known as Sumer and Akkad (ANET, p. 159 *et al.;* FLAP, p. 10), indicating the early prominence of Akkad. During the Old Akkadian period (*c.* 2360-2180 B.C.) a certain Sargon founded a dynasty of Semitic-speaking kings at Akkad (Agade) who ruled all of lower Mesopotamia. Under Sargon I and Naram-Sin, his grandson, the realm was extended till the king of Agade could be styled "the mighty, god of Agade, king of the Four Quarters." His empire extended from Elam to Syria.

The strong impression left by this kingdom of Agade upon later generations is seen in the fact that more than a millennium and a half later Nabopolassar, Nebuchadnezzar and Nabonidus, kings of the Neo-Babylonian Empire, were sometimes called "the king of Akkad" (FLAP, pp. 220, 222, 227; Donald J. Wiseman, *Chronicles of the Chaldean Kings,* pp. 67-69). Furthermore, the chief Semitic language of the region and the cuneiform writing came to be known as Akkadian (of which Assyrian and Babylonian are dialects), referred to respectfully by Ashurbanipal, king of Assyria (668-633 B.C., the Asnapper of Ezr 4:10), as "the obscure Akkadian writing which is hard to master" (FLAP, p. 216).

R. D. C.

ACCEPT, ACCEPTABLE. These English words translate a variety of Heb. and Gr. words. In the OT "to accept" (from *rāṣâ*) means "to receive with pleasure and kindness" (Deut 33:11; Ps 119:108), becoming part of the sacrificial terminology that indicated the acceptability *(rāṣôn)* of an offering to God (Lev 22:20; 23:11; Isa 60:7).

Contrary to pagan belief, the biblical teaching is that one's sacrifices and prayers are acceptable to God only when the man's person is first of all acceptable to Him (Hos 8:13; Jer 6:20; Mal 1:9 f.; note the order in II Sam

Crusaders' Wall, Accho. IIS

24:23-25). Only moral uprightness (Prov 21:3; Job 42:7-9) and the sacrifices of a repentant, sincere heart (Ps 19:14; 40:6-8; 51:15-17) are recognized as truly acceptable with God. The Lord's acceptance of Abel's offering (Gen 4:4f.) was a witness that Abel's person had already been accepted. Through his offerings presented in faith "he received approval as righteous, God bearing witness by accepting his gifts" (Heb 11:4, RSV), whereas Cain was admonished that his offering would be accepted if he would do well (Gen 4:7).

An "acceptable time" (Ps 69:13; Isa 49:8; II Cor 6:2) or "acceptable year" (Isa 61:2) is a time of favor or grace *(rāṣôn),* hence the favorable season or opportune moment when God is still offering His salvation.

The basic Gr. word for "accepted," "acceptable" *(dektos)* means "welcomed," "appreciated," as in Lk 4:24. In the NT the grounds of divine acceptance are never ceremonial, but always spiritual (Rom 12:1; Phil 4:18; I Tim 2:3; I Pet 2:5). Our Lord does not accept the person (shows no partiality, lit., does not receive the face) of anyone (Lk 20:21; Gal 2:6); rather, the one who fears God and practices righteousness is acceptable to Him (Acts 10:35), demonstrating genuine repentance by appropriate works (Acts 26:20). None, however, can achieve perfect acceptability by his own works, for all have fallen short of the glory of God (Rom 3:9-23). Jesus Christ alone is fully accepted by the Father. ("This is my beloved Son, in whom I am well pleased," Mt 3:17.) In Him as the Beloved and through Him as the Mediator, men secure their standing and fundamental acceptance with God (Eph 1:6).

J. R.

ACCESS TO GOD. "1. The act of bringing to. 2. Access, approach . . . that friendly relation with God whereby we are acceptable to Him and have assurance that He is favorably disposed toward us" (Thayer).

The OT believer approached God through a priest, after offering sacrifices for his sins; the NT believer approaches Him directly because of and through Jesus Christ. The concept of access can be properly understood only by the OT revelation that God is King, and therefore to be approached through a worthy and qualified representative (Ps 47:7).

Christ reconciled both Jew and Gentile to God by the cross, broke down the middle wall of partition between Israel and the Gentiles, and removed the hostility between God and man (Eph 2:16), thus making possible access to God for both (Eph 2:18).

Access to the grace of God through saving faith—the ability to believe in Christ as our Saviour—also is dependent upon His having first made peace with God through the blood of His cross (Rom 5:2; Col 1:20).

Because of what Christ did and because He is ever at the throne of God as our Advocate, even when we have sinned (I Jn 2:1), we are encouraged to come to God with boldness (Eph 3:12; Heb 4:16).

R. A. K.

ACCHO (ăk'ō). A town on a promontory across the bay to the N from Haifa and Mount Carmel. Furnishing the best anchorage in the area, it long commanded the approach to the rich plains of Esdraelon and the coast road to the N. Though within the territory of Asher, it was not conquered by the Hebrews (Jud 1:31). During the Greek and Roman sway it was called Ptolemais after the first Egyptian king of that name. Paul visited it (Acts 21:7). The Crusaders, considering it the key to the Holy Land, won it at great cost. Now Haifa and Beirut have overshadowed it as centers of trade.

ACCOUNTABILITY. Not a biblical term but it expresses the biblical concept of man's responsibility to God. Man knows by what he learns through consciousness that he is answerable for his actions, and this is confirmed by his conscience and by the revelation of Scripture.

Christ says man is accountable for what he says, even for idle words (Mt 12:36), and for what he does, particularly for the way he uses the money, gifts, and talents which the Lord has bestowed (Mt 25:14-30; Lk 19:11-27). Paul speaks of the deeds done by the Christian while alive "in the body" (II Cor 5:10): of his responsibility to consider a weaker brother in his actions (Rom 14:10) even though all things are lawful for him (I Cor 6:12; 10:23); of his own responsibility to keep his body under and control his passions lest he become disapproved in the ministry—a castaway (I Cor 9:27). In Romans Paul also speaks of responsibility for obedience to civil rulers, and hence to laws of the state (Rom 13:1-7).

The Christian will not be judged with the unbeliever, since he is judged regarding possible rewards; there is no condemnation possible for him (Rom 8:1), only the exposure of what is proved to be dross (I Cor 3:12-15). His judgment occurs before the Millennium, as proved by the fact Christ promises rulership over cities to the good servants in the parable of the pounds (Lk 19:17, 19). It is clear this judgment of the believer's works must be complete before he reigns with Christ on the earth (Rev 5:10; 20:4-6). *See* Rewards.

R. A. K.

ACCURSED

1. Heb. *qᵉlālâ,* a form of curse used throughout the ancient Near East as a malediction expressing a wish that evil may overtake someone. In the ancient usage, curses frequently had the effect of protecting the terms of treaty contracts by being directed toward future violators of the agreement. As translated in Deut 21:23, "he that is hanged is accursed of God," it refers to the abject criminal who after he has been put to death is impaled on a tree or stake. Only the worst of cases was so punished and hence the person was considered accursed of God (cf. Josh 8:29; 10:26-27; II Sam 4:12; Gal 3:16). In Isa 65:20 a form of this word occurs denoting the longevity of life even on the accursed sinner in the future millennial age. RSV translates this word "accursed" in Ps 119:21.

2. Heb. *ḥerem,* a word meaning "devoted thing," used especially in the book of Joshua (cf. 6:17, 18; 7:1 ff.; 22:20) in connection with Canaanite cities and all their inhabitants. A thing which is accursed or banned is irrevocably withdrawn from common use. Consequently it was either set apart for the use of the Lord in the priestly service or utterly exterminated. It was common in ancient warfare to "devote," or put under the ban, the enemy and everything which belonged to him. So Mesha, king of Moab (*c.* 830 B.C.), relates how he "devoted to destruction" for the god of Ashtar-Chemosh the entire Israelite city of Nebo, "slaying all, seven thousand men, boys, women and girls and maid-servants" (ANET, p. 320). It was also practiced by the Assyrians (II Kgs 19:11). Whoever took the "devoted" thing for himself, as Achan did (Josh 7), became himself "banned" and was mercilessly destroyed with all persons and property attached to him. In later rabbinical use the practice became equivalent to excommunication.

3. RSV translates Heb. *zāʿam* as "accursed" in Mic 6:10 (KJV "abominable").

4. *NT use.* Each of the four occurrences of this word in the KJV are renderings of Gr. *anathēma* (cf. Rom 9:3; I Cor 12:3; Gal 1:8-9) which is the LXX word for section 2 above. In pagan usage it referred to a "votive offering." Paul desired that it might be possible for him to be "banned" from Christ in order, as it is commonly inferred, that his Jewish brethren might find Christ as their Lord (Rom 9:3).

On another occasion Paul remarks that no man speaking by the Spirit of God can say Jesus is "accursed" (I Cor. 12:3). Apparently some in the church (gnostics?) made certain esoteric statements that in fact degraded the high position of Jesus to that of one who deserved the death He died (Godet). Hence Paul states that all true manifestations of the Holy Spirit exalt Jesus as Lord.

Again, Paul relegates to "utter destruction" all those who do not love the Lord Jesus Christ (I Cor 16:22). He also states that the gospel he proclaimed was the only way of salvation, and those who pervert it are accursed or irremediably assigned to judgment because of the serious consequences of invalidating the grace of God in the preaching of Jesus Christ (Gal 1:8-9).

See Achan; Anathema; Curse; Devote; Oath.

A. F. J.

ACCUSED. Three important examples in the Bible of persons being accused are Daniel, Christ and Paul.

Daniel was accused of praying to his God when all were ordered to make supplications to Darius only (Dan 6:4-24). Daniel's three Heb. companions had previously been accused of disloyalty because they would not bow to the image of King Nebuchadnezzar (Dan 3:8-12).

Christ was accused of many things but of six in particular:

1. Desecrating the Jewish sabbath, because (a) His disciples gathered and ate some grain on the sabbath (Mt 12:1-8). He replied by citing two examples from the OT and giving three reasons for permitting His disciples to do this. David entered the house of God and took the sacred showbread for his famished soldiers (I Sam 21:6); and the priests on the sabbath day profaned the sabbath and were blameless (Num 28:9-10, 24). The reasons given are that Christ is greater than the temple, i.e., He has authority over it and what is holy (Mt 12:6); God is seeking mercy and compassion from His own above ritual sacrifice (v. 7); Christ, the Son of Man, is the one who has authority over the sabbath itself (v. 8). (b) Christ also healed on the sabbath. Jesus defended His action by pointing out that His accusers did good and saved life on the sabbath (Mt 12:11; Lk 6:9), and that man is worth much more than the sheep they would rescue (Mt 12:12). The sab-

bath was made for man anyway, and not man for the sabbath (Mk 2:27).

2. Fellowshiping with publicans and sinners, that is, with the common people and the unsaved (Mt 9:11; Lk 7:34). His defense was that He came not for the righteous but to bring sinners to repentance (Mt 9:13).

3. Forbidding men to pay tribute to Caesar (Lk 23:2). This accusation was untrue because He had paid tribute Himself (Mt 17:24-27), and declared that appropriate tribute should be given both to God and to Caesar (Mt 22:17-21; Mk 12:14-17).

4. Claiming to be God by forgiving sin, which of course He did (Lk 5:20-24).

5. Planning to destroy the temple and to rebuild it in three days, though He really spoke of His own body (Mt 26:61; Jn 2:19-21).

6. Claiming to be Christ the very Son of God (Mt 26:63), and to this He gave His assent (Mt 26:64).

Paul was falsely accused of the Jews as the instigator of sedition against the Roman government, and as being a profaner of the temple and a member of the Nazarenes (Acts 24:5-6).

The Christian realizes that he is being accused by Satan daily before the throne of God (Job 1:6-12; 2:1-8; Rev 12:9-10), but rejoices that Christ stands there also as his Advocate to plead His shed blood and to defend him (I Jn 2:1-2). Christians shall also suffer from false accusations by those around them, but are not to allow themselves to be found in a position in which they are rightfully accused of wrongdoing (I Pet 3:17; 4:12-19). Believers in Christ can overcome Satan, the accuser of the brethren, on the basis of the blood of the Lamb and the word of their testimony (Rev 12:11). *See* Accuser.

R. A. K.

South bank of the Hinnom Valley showing Potter's Field with burial caves. HFV

ACCUSER

1. A human accuser, plaintiff in any lawsuit (Gr. *katēgoros,* Jn 8:10; Acts 23:30, 35; 24:8; 25:18); an opponent in court or in general (Gr. *antidikos,* Mt 5:25, RSV; Lk 12:58; 18:3); "false accuser" (Gr. *diabolos,* II Tim 3:3; Tit 2:3).

2. Satan (the adversary, I Pet 5:8) is an accuser of the believers (Rev 12:10). He comes before the throne of God and points out all their weaknesses and faults and sins (Job 1:6 f.; 2:1-8). But the day will come, just before the time of the Great Tribulation, when he and his angels will be cast out of heaven into the earth (Rev 12:7-10). Meanwhile, in the face of Satanic accusations, Christ intercedes on behalf of believers at the right hand of God the Father. He pleads for them on the basis of His sacrificial death (Rom 8:34), so that no other being has any right to condemn the Christian. *See* Adversary; Devil.

ACELDAMA (*ȧ*-kĕl'd*ȧ*-m*ȧ*). This term for "field of blood" is found only in Acts 1:19. The piece of land, which was formerly known as the potter's field (cf. Jer 18:2; 19:1, 2; Mt 27:7), was purchased by the priests with the betrayal money which Judas returned (Mt 27:3-10). Their intention was to use the ground as a cemetery for strangers. Tradition locates the site S of Jerusalem, on the S side of the valley of Hinnom near its junction with the Kidron Valley. The name apparently has reference to the blood money used in its purchase (Mt 27:6-7) and to the gruesome death of Judas (Acts 1:18-19).

ACHAIA (ā-kā'y*ȧ*). In the NT Achaia refers to the southern portion of Greece, Macedonia being the northern portion (Acts 19:21; Rom 15:26; II Cor 1:1; I Thess 1:7, 8). By Claudius' direction, in A.D. 44 it was governed by a proconsul (e.g., Gallio in Acts 18:12, ASV), appointed by the Roman senate; the emperor governed his provinces through procurators. Its chief cities were Athens *(q.v.)* and Corinth *(q.v.)* the capital with its seaport Cenchrea, although Sparta to the S and Megara, Thebes, and Delphi to the N were famous from antiquity.

ACHAICUS (*ȧ*-kā'ĭ-k*ŭ*s). A companion of Stephanas and Fortunatus, who visited Paul at Ephesus and perhaps brought a letter from the church at Corinth (I Cor 7:1; 16:17).

ACHAN (ā'kăn). Variant of Achar in I Chr 2:7; also in certain LXX and Syriac MSS.

A man of Judah who secretly appropriated for himself some of the spoils of war at the fall of Jericho (Josh 7:1-26; 22:20). The Lord revealed to Joshua that Israel's defeat at Ai was caused by the presence of sin in the camp. When the sacred lot specified Achan as the offender, he confessed to coveting, stealing, and concealing in his tent fine clothing, silver, and gold, all of which was under the sacrificial ban, "devoted to the Lord for destruction" or "for the treasury" (Josh 6:17-19, RSV; cf. S. R. Driver on I Sam 15:33). Achan and his family were stoned to death, and their bodies and possessions were burned in the valley of Achor ("troubling") S of Jericho.

Theft would have carried only the penalty of restitution with double indemnity (Ex 22:4, 7) even in a peacetime situation. Achan violated the special sanctity of "devoted things" which were forever removed from common use. He had dared to put them among his "own stuff" (Josh 7:11).

The ancient concept of community solidarity everywhere underlies the story: (1) the covenant unity of Israel as a "devoted" (i.e., "sanctified") people (cf. Ex 13:11-15; 4:23) assured them of the Lord's protection; (2) Achan's offense associated him with the Canaanites who were "devoted to the Lord for destruction" (i.e., "accursed") and separated him from the protection of the covenant (Josh 6:17-18; 7:15); (3) Achan's offense became Israel's offense until they separated themselves from the "devoted things" whose end had to be destruction (Josh 6:18; 7:11-12); (4) all Achan's family and possessions had suffered the taint of the "devoted things" and shared his responsibility and destruction (Josh 7:24-25).

R. V. R.

ACHAR (ā'kär). This is a variant form of Achan *(q.v.)* found in I Chr 2:7.

ACHAZ (ā'kăz). In Mt 1:9 the KJV makes use of this name for Ahaz *(q.v.)*

ACHBOR (ăk'bôr)

1. The father of Baal-hanan, a king of Edom (Gen 36:38-39; I Chr 1:49).

2. An officer in the government of Josiah who was deputized to examine the book of the law (II Kgs 22:12, 14; Jer 26:22; 36:12). He is called Abdon in II Chr 34:20.

ACHIM (ā'kĭm). According to Mt 1:14, Achim was the fifth of the ancestors of Joseph the husband of Mary.

ACHISH (ā'kĭsh). King of Gath (home of Goliath and member of the Philistine pentarchy) to whom David twice resorted when a fugitive from Saul. Achish still ruled early in Solomon's reign (I Kgs 2:39, here, "son of Maachah"; cf. "son of Maoch," I Sam 27:2; consonantal similarity suggests identity).

David first fled to Achish alone (I Sam 21:10-15) offering himself for service in the palace (21:15). Recognized as the slayer of Goliath (cf. v. 11 with 18:7), in fear David feigned madness and escaped (22:1).

On his second flight to Achish, now accompanied by his 600 seasoned guerrillas, David was made welcome (I Sam 27:1-12). The Philistine king granted him and his men the border town of Ziklag. This association was hardly an

The mound of Gath, where Achish was king and where Goliath lived. HFV

unmixed blessing for either, since it contained for David self-contradictory elements: a sense of responsibility to Achish, whose feudatory vassal he had become (I Sam 28:1-2); a built-in loyalty to his own nation resulting in raiding Philistine allies instead of the Judean Negeb as claimed (I Sam 27:8-12); a deep sense of divine mission and personal restraint. David was spared fighting Israel in the battle on Gilboa by Philistine skepticism of David's loyalty (I Sam 29:1-11).

Achish has left his imprint on the sacred record: (1) he appears as Abimelech *(q.v.)* in the superscription of Ps 34; (2) David, appointed to the bodyguard of Achish (I Sam 28:2), maintained a Pelethite (Philistine) bodyguard when king (II Sam 8:18, *et al.*).

R. V. R.

ACHMETHA (ăk'mĕ-thȧ). A city reaching at least back to the days of Cyrus (about 550 B.C.). Here the decrees of Cyrus were found that authorized the Jews to rebuild the temple at Jerusalem (Ezr 6:2). The city is on high elevation (about 6,000 ft.) and thereby provided a good summer resort. Darius I may have used it for a part-time capital of Persia.

Achmetha is referred to many times in the Apocrypha but under the name of Ecbatana. Known today as Hamadan, this city of Iran has a population of about 50,000 and is located on the road from Baghdad to Teheran.

ACHOR (ā'kôr). A valley lying W of Jericho where Achan (Achar, I Chr 2:7) and his family were stoned to death (Josh 7:24, 26). It is also on the N boundary of Judah (Josh 15:7). A future millennial change is found in Isa 65:10; Hos 2:15.

ACHSA, ACHSAH (ăk'sȧ). The name of Caleb's daughter (I Chr 2:49). Caleb had been assigned the unconquered Kirjath-sepher. He promised his daughter to anyone who would capture it for him. Caleb's kinsman Othniel won the right to marry Achsah (Josh 15:16 ff.; Jud 1:12 ff.).

ACHSHAPH (ăk'shăf). A city in the land given originally to the tribe of Asher (Josh 19:25). It was a city-state under one of the kings allied against Joshua (Josh 11:1; 12:20). Though its exact location is disputed by authorities, all agree it was near the Mount Carmel ridge.

ACHZIB (ăk'zĭb)

1. A town in the Shephelah of Judah near Keilah and Mareshah (Josh 15:44; Mic 1:14). Micah makes a pun on its name, which means "deceitful" or "treacherous." Achzib seems to be mentioned in Lachish letter #8. Perhaps it is the same as Chezib (*q.v.;* Gen 38:5).

2. A Canaanite town assigned to Asher (Josh 19:29) on the Mediterranean coast eight miles N of Acre. It is doubtful whether the tribe of Asher ever occupied this city (Jud 1:31). Sennacherib claims to have overwhelmed the fortress city Akzibi (ANET, p. 287). In 1941–42 two large cemeteries with over 70 rock-cut tombs were excavated, from which were recovered quantities of Phoenician pottery, figurines, scarabs and jewelry. Recent excavations at the site have revealed a Hyksos-type fortification, plus six more levels of occupation dating from the 9th to the 4th cen. B.C. Many pieces of imported Gr. and Cypriot pottery testify to Achzib's commercial connections in the Israelite, Persian and Hellenistic periods.

J. R.

ACRE

1. An area, lit., "yoke" (I Sam 14:14, RSV; Isa 5:10), which likely means the amount of ground a yoke of oxen could plow in a day.

2. A Western name since the Crusades for the city of Accho *(q.v.),* which was given to Asher but never conquered (Jud 1:31). This city lies at the N end of a fine plain about eight miles long, with modern Haifa on the S end. It was called Ptolemais during the period of Hellenistic influence, and is the port where Paul landed on his way to Caesarea (Acts 21:7).

ACROPOLIS (*ă*-crŏp'ō-lĭs). The higher part of a city; especially a fortified eminence overlooking an ancient Gr. town. Among cities with an acropolis were Philippi, Athens, and Corinth, which Paul visited on his second missionary journey.

By far the most famous acropolis was that of Athens. On the plateau at its summit, magnificent structures were erected in classical times. Celebrated for their architectural excellence were the Parthenon, preeminent shrine of Athe-

The Acropolis at Corinth (which towers to a height of almost 1900 feet) with the temple of Apollo in the foreground. HFV

Entrance to the Acropolis at Athens today. HFV

na; the Erechtheum, another temple dedicated to Athena and Poseidon; the Propylaea; and the temple of Athena Nike. In the Parthenon was a statue of Athena, more than 40 feet in height, made by Phidias of gold and ivory. Between the Parthenon and the Erechtheum was the bronze statue of Athena Promachos, 30 feet high, also made by Phidias. The shining helmet and spear were visible far off at sea. On the summit of the acropolis and on its sides were additional temples, statues, and other structures. Here human artistic effort achieved some of its most notable triumphs, but the dedication to false religion pointed up the inability of the natural man to find the truth of God. The spiritual need of a city filled with idols deeply moved the apostle Paul (Acts 17:16-34).

J. H. S.

ACROSTIC. A literary device found in some of the poetry of the OT either to aid memory or to provide strophic divisions. The kind employed in the OT is alphabetic in character. The best example is Ps 119 in which the first word in each of the first eight verses begins with the first letter of the Heb. alphabet; the next eight verses begin with the second letter of the alphabet. In succession, eight verses are assigned to the rest of the 22 Heb. consonants, making a total of 176 verses. However, Ps 34 has only 22 verses, since the first word of each verse begins with a Heb. letter in alphabetic order. Ps 25, 37, 111, 112, and 145 are similar but are not quite so regular; some have one or more letters missing or transposed. Parts of Ps 9 and 10, which are one psalm in the LXX, are alphabetic.

In Prov 31, each verse of 10-21 begins with a Heb. letter in alphabetic order. Several alphabetic acrostics occur in Lamentations. Chaps. 1, 2 and 4 each contain an acrostic of 22 verses, with one verse to each Heb. letter, but not always in precise order. Chap. 3 has three verses for each letter of the alphabet. Nah 1:2-10 is thought by some to be partially alphabetic, but this is not clear in the Heb. text. Some have held that acrostic poems are late in date, but the position is not founded on fact.

G. H. L.

ACTS, THE BOOK OF. The Acts of the Apostles, the fifth book of the NT, is the second volume of the earliest history of Christianity, of which the first volume is the Gospel according to Luke. The essential unity of the two volumes is marked by the common address to Theophilus (Lk 1:1-4; Acts 1:1); by the allusion in Acts to a "former treatise . . . concerning all that Jesus began both to do and to teach" (ASV), which fits the content of the Gospel; by a common emphasis on the person and work of the Holy Spirit; by the

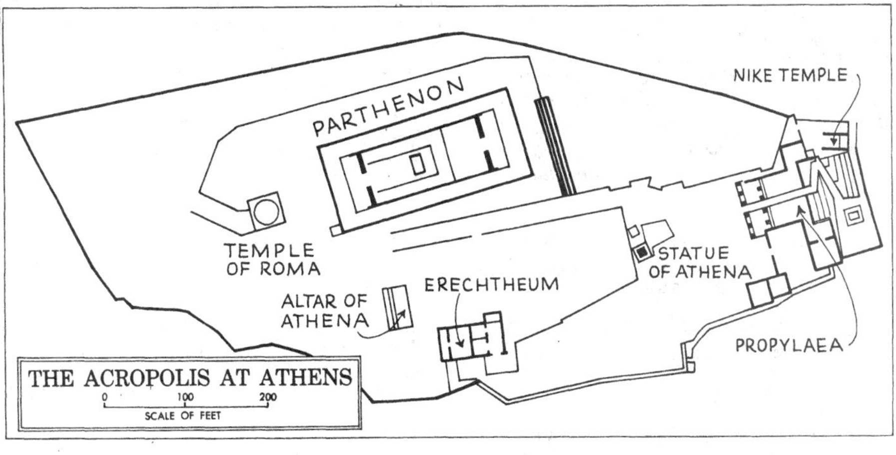

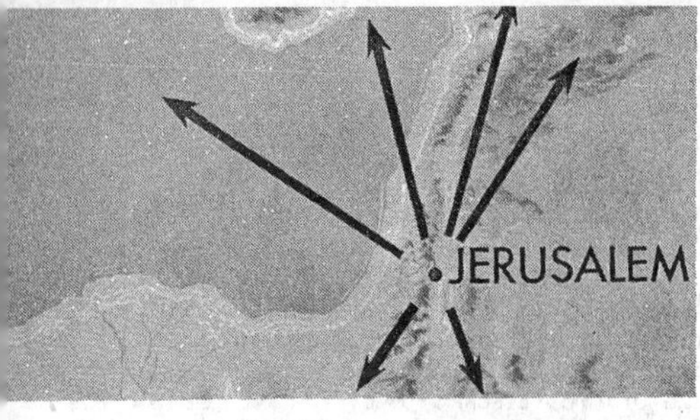

The Book of Acts tells how believers preached the Gospel in Jerusalem, Judea, Samaria, Syria and in much of the Eastern Mediterranean World (cf. Acts 1:8). MIS

close resemblance of the language of the two documents; and by the confirmation of tradition which uniformly ascribes the authorship to Luke, the friend and companion of Paul. The title was probably given to it when the Gospel was combined with Matthew, Mark, and John into a distinct group of narratives of the life of Jesus, leaving Acts to become the chronicle of a later period. The division took place at an early date, since the oldest extant list of canonical books treats it as a separate writing.

Content

Although it is called the Acts of the Apostles, or even Acts in some MSS, it does not narrate the deeds of all the earliest followers of Jesus. The record is selective, and is apparently motivated by a desire to trace the growth of the Gentile church from the day of Pentecost through the expansion to Antioch, and then through the Pauline mission to Rome. The organization is largely biographical, focusing on such personalities as Peter, Stephen, Philip, Barnabas, and Paul.

Acts is organized in three stages, based on the words of Jesus quoted in Acts 1:8: "But ye shall receive power, when the Holy Spirit is come upon you: and ye shall be my witnesses both in Jerusalem, and in all Judea and Samaria, and unto the uttermost part of the earth" (ASV). The first stage marks the Jewish foundation beginning in Jerusalem; the second stage of transition involves the development of new ideas and movements in the direction of the Gentile world; and the third stage covers the Gentile mission of Paul which carried him from Antioch across Asia Minor to Rome.

Outline

The Beginnings of the Christian Church

I. The Period of Inception: Jerusalem, 1:1–8:3
   - A. The Commission of Christ, 1:1-8
   - B. The Preparation for Pentecost, 1:9-26
   - C. The Founding of the Church at Jerusalem, 2:1–6:7
   - D. The Ministry of Stephen, 6:8–8:3

II. The Period of Transition: Antioch, 8:4–11:18
   - A. The Ministry of Philip (Samaria), 8:4-40
   - B. The Conversion of Paul, 9:1-31
   - C. The Ministry of Peter (Caesarea), 10:1–11:18

III. The Period of Expansion: Rome, 11:19–28:31
   - A. The Transfer to Antioch, 11:19–12:25
   - B. The First Missionary Tour, 13:1–14:28
   - C. The Council at Jerusalem, 15:1-35
   - D. The Second Missionary Tour, 15:36–18:22
   - E. The Third Missionary Tour, 18:23–21:14
   - F. The Arrest and Defense of Paul, 21:15–28:31

The first section of Acts introduces the theme by reference to the last words of Jesus before His ascension, in which He commanded the disciples to remain in Jerusalem for the coming of the Holy Spirit. At His descent on the day of Pentecost they were empowered to preach that Jesus had risen and that He was the true Messiah. Peter's sermon called for repentance and baptism on the part of believers. Three thousand converts were added to the band of disciples. Through a series of persecutions the church grew until it numbered at least 5,000, including converts from the Jewish priesthood.

The ministry of Stephen extended the church into foreign-speaking synagogues. His arrest and trial before the Sanhedrin marked a turning point in the life of the church. His statement that "the Most High dwelleth not in houses made with hands" (Acts 7:48) implied an outlook broader than that of Judaism, and the persecution accompanying his death compelled the Christians to scatter into other fields.

The period of transition marked advance into new territory and the commencement of a ministry among other peoples. Philip's preaching to the Samaritans and to the Ethiopian eunuch (8:5-40), Peter's entrance into the household of the Roman centurion Cornelius (10:1–11:18), and the startling conversion of the chief persecutor, Saul of Tarsus (9:1-30), broke down the barriers of prejudice and fear. Some of the refugees began a work among the Gentiles at Antioch, which became the basis for an empire-wide missionary movement.

The missionary campaign comprised three successive tours. The first, conducted by Paul and Barnabas, covered Cyprus and the southern part of the province of Galatia (Acts 13:1–14:28). The second by Paul, Silas, Timothy, and Luke, revisited the churches of S. Galatia, and penetrated the provinces of Macedonia and Achaia (15:36–18:22). The third included a three-year ministry in the province of Asia, centering in Ephesus, followed by a thorough inspection of the churches in Macedonia and Achaia (18:23–21:14). The council at Jerusalem settled the important question whether the Gentiles needed to keep the law in order to become Christians (15:1-35).

The arrest of Paul in Jerusalem, his imprisonment and hearings before Jewish and Roman officials, and his voyage to Rome conclude the narrative with his preaching in the imperial city (21:15–28:31). The story ends abruptly, perhaps because the author had finished the account as he knew it and had no more to say. He had, however, achieved his objective of tracing the progress of the gospel message from Jerusalem, the center of Judaism, to Rome, the metropolis of the Gentile world.

Authorship

Acts has been traditionally ascribed to Luke, a Gr. physician, who was a companion of Paul on his second and third journeys. His presence is indicated by the use of the pronoun "we," which occurs first in Acts 16:10-17, reappears in 20:5–21:17, and again in 27:1–28:16. The author joined Paul at Troas, went with him to Philippi, where he apparently remained until Paul returned on the third tour, and then accompanied him all the way to Rome. He did not share Paul's imprisonment in Jerusalem and Rome, but remained near him. Paul alluded to "Luke, the beloved physician" in his correspondence from prison (Col 4:14; Phm 24), and at a later date spoke of him again (II Tim 4:11).

Irenaeus, one of the early Church Fathers (*c.* A.D. 180), quotes Acts as the product of Luke, "the disciple and follower of the apostles" (*Against Heresies* I. xxiii.1). It is possible that Luke was the brother of Titus, another of Paul's companions, who is never mentioned in Acts, and that he is characterized by Paul in II Corinthians as "the brother whose praise in the gospel is spread through all the churches" (II Cor 8:18, ASV). The letter was written while Luke presumably was still in Philippi and when Titus was in Macedonia.

Internal evidence shows that the author was a highly literate Greek who had traveled widely and who was a keen observer. Hobart *(The Medical Language of St. Luke)* argued that Luke's language proved that he was a physician because of the medical terms he used. It may be that Hobart exaggerated the technical significance of Luke's vocabulary, but Luke seems to have had a greater interest in disease and in healing than other Christian writers. All indications that can be drawn from Acts support the traditional authorship.

Date

The *terminus a quo* of Acts is the close of Paul's first imprisonment, *c.* A.D. 61/62, for the book could not have been written earlier than the events which it describes. The Tübingen School of the 19th cen. assigned it to the middle of the 2nd cen., believing it to be an apologetic work written to gloss over differences in the church that occurred in the preceding era. Others have dated it late in the 1st cen. on the assumption that Luke used as a source the works of Josephus, which were not written before A.D. 90. Luke, however, may have had independent access to the same information that Josephus used. The general accuracy of his allusions to places, persons, and events, insofar as they can be corroborated by archaeology and history, indicates that Luke was a contemporary of what he described. Despite the author's keen interest in Paul, the absence of any reference to his epistles is scarcely explicable if Acts were written after their collection and publication. For these reasons a date before A.D. 65 seems most acceptable.

The Value of Acts

Acts is a document of primary historical value both for the history of the church and of the ancient world. Apart from Acts the gap between the Gospels and the epistles would be almost unbridgeable, for no explanation would be available for the transition from the ministry of Jesus to the doctrine and evangelism of the church. Almost all authentic extant knowledge concerning the apostolic leaders and the geographical extent of their mission is derived from this book. Acts does not afford a complete account, but it provides leading facts and general principles that aid historical interpretation.

The allusions to contemporary occurrences enable scholars to relate Christianity to the world of its day. The death of Herod Agrippa I (Acts 12:21-23); the proconsulship of Gallio (18:12-17); the administrations of Felix (23:24) and Festus (24:27), procurators of Judea; the technical names of officials in the districts of the Roman Empire, such as praetors and lictors at Philippi (16:35, ASV marg.); "rulers of the city" at Thessalonica (Gr. *politarchs,* 17:6), and Asiarchs at Ephesus (19:31, ASV); the linguistic differences that obtained in different sections of the empire (14:11; 21:37, 40); and the accurate geographical detail of the final voyage to Rome (Acts 27-28)) provide reliable information for modern historians, and show that the author was accurately informed.

The doctrinal and spiritual value of Acts is great. The primitive teaching of the church is outlined in the speeches which Acts preserves; and the emphasis upon the work of the Holy Spirit and upon the basis of the missionary enterprise constitutes a pattern for the experience and practice of succeeding generations.

Bibliography. E. M. Blaiklock, *The Acts of the Apostles (Tyndale Commentaries),* Grand Rapids: Eerdmans, 1959. F. F. Bruce, *Commentary on the Book of Acts (The New International Commentary),* Grand Rapids: Eerdmans, 1954. F. J. Foakes-Jackson and Kirsopp Lake, *The Beginnings of Christianity,* Part I: *The Acts of the Apostles,* 5 vols., London: Macmillan, 1920-35. Richard B. Rackham, *The Acts of the Apostles,* WC. A. T. Robertson, *Luke the Historian in the Light of Research,* New York: Scribner's, 1923.

M. C. T.

ADADAH (ăd′ȧdȧ). A town in the southern part of Judah, associated with Kinah and Dimonah (Josh 15:22).

ADAH (ā'dȧ)

1. One of the two wives of Lamech (Gen 4:19–23), the mother of two famous sons, Jabal and Jubal.

2. Esau had a Hittite wife by the name of Adah who was the mother of his son Eliphaz (Gen 36:2–16).

ADAIAH (ȧ-dā'yȧ)

1. A native of Boscath in Judah. He was the father of Jedidah, wife of Amon and mother of Josiah king of Judah (II Kgs 22:1).

2. A Levite of the family of Gershom, an ancestor of Asaph, a celebrated musician in the time of David (I Chr 6:41). Probably the same as Iddo (v. 21).

3. A son of Shimei or Shema of Benjamin, an important resident of Jerusalem before the Exile (I Chr 8:13, 21).

4. A priest and important family head who served in the temple after the return from Exile (I Chr 9:10–12; Neh 11:12).

5. The father of Maaseiah, one of the captains used by Jehoiada to guard the child Joash when he was proclaimed king (II Chr 23:1).

6. A son of Bani after the Exile who was condemned as one who had taken a foreign wife (Ezr 10:29).

7. The son of another Israelite named Bani, also listed with those who had put away their foreign wives (Ezr 10:39).

8. A man of Judah, father of Hazaiah, whose descendants were prominent men in Jerusalem after the return from Exile (Neh 11:5).

P. C. J.

ADALIA (ȧ-dā'lĭ-ȧ). One of the ten sons of Haman who was slain by the Jews at the order of Mordecai (Est 9:8).

ADAM (ăd'ȧm). The first man, from whom the entire human race descended. The NT presents Adam as the representative of humanity and relates the whole problem of sin to his original transgression.

As to the meaning of this name, etymology cannot offer any positive help. Three possibilities rival one another. The word may come from the similar word *'ădāmâ*, which means "the red soil"; or from the root *dāmâ*, which means "be like" (reference to *d^emût*, i.e., "likeness," Gen 1:26; 5:1); or from the Akkad. root *adâmu*, which means "to make or produce." Perhaps the last deserves the preference.

The Bible states that God created Adam (Gen 2:7), placed him in the garden of Eden (2:8–15), gave him the command regarding the tree of the knowledge of good and evil (2:16–17), and lastly put woman at his side as his mate in a separate act of creation (2:18–25). God blessed them, conferring prosperity on them by the power of His spoken word, and ordered them to multiply and to be masters of all living creatures on earth (1:28). When subjected to a temptation by the serpent, Adam succumbed, as his wife had before him. This marks the event commonly known as the Fall. Immediately after the Fall, the altered lot of our first parents became known through their actions and through the doom that God assigned to them. They were not cursed. In His great mercy, the Lord suffered them to continue to live for a while and provided them with their first garments. But He did expel them from the garden in which they had dwelt. They had children, in fact a number of them (cf. Gen 5:4). Adam himself died at the age of 930 years (Gen 5:5).

Adam was a historic personage, not merely a poetic figure or a mythical person. In the OT the word *'ādām* is used more than 500 times in the sense of mankind as well as in the sense of a proper name. Both uses appear in the Genesis record, but only from Gen 4:25 onward can it definitely be claimed that the specific person Adam is exclusively under consideration. Before that, he usually is thought of as the representative man, although the term Adam in Gen 3:17, 21 seems to occur without the definite article, suggesting that in these verses the name is meant and the specific person is in view. See also Gen 5:1, 3–5.

There are two accounts of Adam's creation: Gen 1:26–28 and 2:4–7, 20–23. The usual explanation of this fact by modern higher critics is that these two accounts trace back to two separate sources that the author used, and to reinforce this point, the near incompatibility of the two accounts is often stressed. But quite apart from sources, about which we must always speak with great caution, it appears that the account of Gen 1 is quite summary in fashion and agrees with the pattern of the work of the six creation days; whereas the record of Gen 2 is supplementary—in no sense contradictory to chap. 1—supplying certain details that are very essential to the understanding of what follows. This latter viewpoint is generally held by conservative biblical scholars.

In this dual record two factors are found in man: God made him of the dust of the earth (2:7) and breathed into his nostrils the breath of life. There was a lower and a higher strain in his being. Secondly, he was made in "the image of God" (1:26–27), a meaningful claim which is not defined by the writer in any way. The supplementary account (Gen 2) also gives the exact manner in which Eve was created; it tells of the location of the garden, and also of the two unusually significant trees. So also man's duties in this early state of existence were outlined: he was to till and keep the garden (2:15).

Divine grace manifested itself in that only one commandment was laid upon the man, that he was not to eat of the tree of the knowledge of good and evil. This command was violated with tragic consequences.

The almost startling fact about this narrative of Adam and the Fall is that there are very sparing references to it in the OT. A comparison of the original Heb. would show that there could be a reference to Adam in Deut 32:8; Job 31:33; Hos 6:7, ASV. It may be safe to assume that the basic character of the event of man's creation and Fall was generally accepted without further ado. The full theological evaluation of the Fall came later, in the writings of the apostles.

Almost equally strange is the fact that in the apocryphal books, the references to Adam and his basic importance are numerous.

The passages of the NT that refer to Adam are Mt 19:4-6; Rom 5:12-21; I Cor 15:22, 45; I Tim 2:13-14; Jude 14. In each of these, it can hardly be doubted that Adam is regarded as a historical figure. Rom 5 is particularly strong: two persons are contrasted—Adam and Christ—and the wide sweep of the consequences of their deeds. Of these two, the one is as much a historical figure as the other.

See Anthropology; Creation.

Bibliography. James O. Buswell, III, "Adam and Neolithic Man," *Eternity*, XVIII (1967), 29 ff., for various views of the date of Adam. J. Barton Payne, *The Theology of the Older Testament*, Grand Rapids: Zondervan, 1962, pp. 213-231, helpful both for content and further bibliography. Geerhardus Vos, *Biblical Theology*, Grand Rapids: Eerdmans, 1954, pp. 37-55.

H. C. L.

ADAMAH (ăd'*ȧ*-mȧ). A fortified city assigned to Naphtali (Josh 19:36).

ADAMANT. *See* Minerals.

ADAMI (ăd'*ȧ*-mī). The lone mention of this border town in Naphtali (Josh 19:33) has brought various suggestions from scholars. The translators of the KJV decided it was a separate town from Adami-Nekeb, while the ASV translators made the two one town. (*See* Nekeb.) Its identification is not certainly known. Perhaps it may be associated with the pass in the hills going to the Jordan River S of modern Tiberias, possibly with Khirbet Damiyeh, a large Bronze Age site five miles SW of Tiberias.

ADAR (ā'där)

1. Used in KJV as the name of a city in Judah (Josh 15:3), but perhaps it should have been spelled Addar *(q.v.)*.

2. Most likely this word came from Babylonia and was first used by the Jews there to indicate the twelfth month of their sacred calendar; therefore, it appears in Ezr 6:15; Est 3:7, 13; 8:12; 9:1, 15, 17, 19, 21. It was timed from the new moon in our February until the new moon in March. *See* Calendar.

ADBEEL (ăd'bĭ-ĕl). The third son of Ishmael and therefore the name of an Arabian tribe (Gen 25:13; I Chr 1:29). It was located in NW Arabia close to Kedar and Nebaioth.

ADDAN (ăd'*ȧ*n), **ADDON** (ăd'ŏn). Some of the people who returned to Jerusalem from Babylon with Zerubbabel were from Addan in Babylonia (Ezr 2:59). They were unable to establish their identity with Israel (Neh 7:61).

ADDAR (ăd'är)

1. A city on the border of Judah W of Kadesh-barnea (Josh 15:3, RSV), called by the double name Hazar-addar in Num 34:4.

2. The son of Bela and grandson of Benjamin (I Chr 8:3). Elsewhere called Ard (Gen 46:21).

ADDER. *See* Animals: Cobra IV.8.

ADDI (ăd'ī). The father of Melchi and the son of Cosam (Lk 3:28) in the Lucan genealogy of Jesus.

ADDON (ăd'ŏn). *See* Addan.

ADER (ā'dẽr). A distinguished man of Benjamin, son of Beriah, who lived at Aijalon (I Chr 8:15).

ADIEL (ā'dĭ-ĕl)

1. One of the noted warriors of the tribe of Simeon who helped to take certain cities from the original inhabitants (I Chr 4:36).

2. A priest, the son of Jahzerah, who was among the people returning from the Exile (I Chr 9:12).

3. The father of the treasurer Azmaveth in the days of King David (I Chr 27:25).

ADIN (ā'dĭn). The representative of a family in Exile some of whom returned to Jerusalem under Zerubbabel (Ezr 2:15), and some later perhaps under Ezra (Neh 7:20; 10:16).

ADINA (ăd'ī-nȧ). One of the mighty men under David, captain of 30 men, a member of the tribe of Reuben (I Chr 11:42).

ADINO (ăd'ī-nō). The reference in II Sam 23:8 may not be the name of a person, and perhaps should be related to I Chr 11:11. One of the shades of meaning of the word Adino in Heb. is "slender," which may suggest the spear used by these mighty warriors of David.

ADITHAIM (ăd-ī-thā'ĭm). A city in the Shephelah section of Judah (Josh 15:36).

ADJURE. To make or cause one to swear by some higher being or object, which put one under obligation to speak the truth. Two Heb. and two Gr. words carry the same general thought. The Heb. words *'alâ* and *shāba'* are used in connection with oaths (I Sam 14:24; Josh 6:26; I Kgs 22:16; II Chr 18:15). The Gr. words are *exorkizō* and *horkizō*, used where Jesus was put under oath (Mt 26:63), and where demons spoke to Him (Mk 5:7; see also Acts 19:13). *See* Oath.

ADLAI (ăd'lā). The father of Shaphat, a shepherd of David's royal flocks in the valleys (I Chr 27:29).

ADMAH (ăd'mȧ). One of the towns in the Dead Sea basin with Sodom and Gomorrah, conquered with them by the kings from the E, and then destroyed with them in divine judgment (Gen 10:19; 14:2, 8; Deut 29:23). The fate of Admah is presented as a warning against all Israel (Hos 11:8).

ADMATHA (ăd-mā'thȧ). The third in rank of the princes of Persia who sat with King Xerxes (Ahasuerus); these were counselors to the king (Est 1:14; cf. Ezr 7:14).

ADNA (ăd'nȧ)

1. One of the men from Pahath-moab who was condemned by Ezra because of his marriage to a foreigner (Ezr 10:30).

2. A priest who served during the high priesthood of Joiakim in the days of Nehemiah (Neh 12:15).

ADNAH (ăd'nȧ)

1. When it was learned that the Philistines refused to allow David and his force to join them against Saul, some of Saul's own men deserted him and joined David at Ziklag. One of these was a captain named Adnah (I Chr 12:20).

2. One of the captains under Jehoshaphat (II Chr 17:14).

ADONI-BEZEK (ȧ-dō'nī-bē'zĕk). A petty king of the Canaanite town of Bezek, he had unmercifully amputated the thumbs and great toes of 70 other "kings." (This incapacitated them for ancient warfare; they could neither handle weapons nor pursue an enemy.) When Bezek fell before the fierce warriors of Judah and Simeon, Adoni-bezek fled. However, he was captured alive and received the same cruel treatment which he had inflicted upon his royal captives. Incredible as it may seem, he recognized his punishment as an act of retributive justice (Jud 1:5-7). He died at Jerusalem.

ADONIJAH (ăd'ō-nī'jȧ)

1. The fourth son of David by Haggith (II Sam 3:4; I Chr 3:2). When David was at the brink of death, Adonijah desired to succeed David to the throne, for at that time he was the oldest living son. Gathering chariots, horsemen, and 50 men, Adonijah enlisted the aid of Joab, commander of the army, and Abiathar, the high priest. However, other generals, priests, Nathan the prophet, and David's bodyguard refused to follow him. They favored Solomon as the new king. While Adonijah called for a meeting of his supporters at En-rogel in the valley below Jerusalem, Bathsheba, Solomon's mother, and Nathan the prophet made an urgent plea to David that Solomon be crowned immediately. David quickly granted their petition and gave instructions for the coronation of Solomon at the spring of Gihon close by Jerusalem. Zadok the priest anointed Solomon king, and he was proclaimed king of Israel amid the wild acclaim of the people (I Kgs 1). In a few days, Adonijah rashly requested that Abishag, David's last attendant, be given him for a wife. In anger, Solomon sent Benaiah to kill Adonijah. The command was promptly carried out (I Kgs 2:13-25).

2. In Jehoshaphat's reform, another Adonijah, a Levite, assisted a group of princes and priests in teaching the people the law of God (II Chr 17:7-9).

3. Among those returning to Jerusalem from Exile was an Adonijah (also called Adonikam) who set his seal to the covenant made during Ezra's reform (Ezr 2:13; Neh 7:18; 10:16).

G. H. L.

ADONIKAM (ăd-ō-nī'kȧm)

1. The representative of a family that returned with Zerubbabel from Exile and that numbered 666 (Ezr 2:13), or including the representative, the family numbered 667 (Neh 7:18).

2. Part of the above family waited to come with Ezra. This group was composed of 60 males (Ezr 8:13).

ADONIRAM (ăd'ō-nī'răm). A public official in charge of forced labor during the reigns of David, Solomon, and Rehoboam (I Kgs 4:6; 5:14; 12:18). After the ten northern tribes revolted, Rehoboam foolishly sent Adoniram (perhaps to collect their taxes), but the insulted Israelites stoned him to death at Shechem (*c.* 922 B.C.). He is also known as Adoram (II Sam 20:24; I Kgs 12:18) and Hadoram (*q.v.;* II Chr 10:18). When the latter spelling occurs one should carefully distinguish this unpopular taskmaster from (a) Hadoram, a son of Joktan in the genealogy of Shem (Gen 10:27; I Chr 1:21), and (b) Hadoram, a son of Tou, king of Hamath (I Chr 18:10).

ADONI-ZEDEK (ȧ-dō'nī-zē'dĕk). An Amorite king of Jerusalem at the time of the Conquest (Josh 10). Impressed by the initial successes of Israel and by the military potential of their newly formed alliance with Gibeon (Josh 9), he took the initiative in forming a five city military alliance against Israel. By attacking the city of Gibeon he hoped to greatly weaken the Israelite position as well as punish the Gibeonites for their defection. Joshua made an overnight march, arriving in time to assist his ally. The miraculous intervention of God and the resultant decisive Israelite victory were celebrated in song in the Book of Jashar, a portion of which is quoted in Josh 10:12-13.

Adoni-zedek and his royal allies hid in a cave at Makkedah. After the destruction of all their armies they were taken out, humbled and slain, and, after sundown, entombed in the same cave.

ADOPTION. The word itself is used in the Bible only in a theological sense. In a civil or legal sense the practice of adoption was exemplified outside the cultural milieu of Israel in the adoption of Moses (Ex 2:10; Acts 7:21, RSV) and of Esther (Est 2:7, 15).

In patriarchal times the ancient Near East practiced something akin to adoption. The discovery of the Nuzu tablets has disclosed the custom whereby a childless couple adopted an adult son who would serve them in life and bury them at death. In return this adopted son would receive the inheritance, unless a son was later born to the couple, in which case the natural born son would then become chief heir (see ANET, pp. 219 f.). While no laws of adoption are found formulated in the OT, such a custom may well be reflected in the relationship of Abraham and Eliezer (Gen 15:2-4). Something close to legal adoption may also be seen in respect to Jacob's grandsons Manasseh and Ephraim (Gen 48:5), with a recognized adoption formula, "let my name be named on them," appearing in v. 16 (cf. Code of Hammurabi #185, ANET, p. 174). Possibly Laban placed Jacob in the status of an adopted son wherein Jacob had to perform service (Gen 29:15) and which gave Laban legal rights to Jacob's children (Gen 31:28, 43, 55). Other cases of adoption may be alluded to in I Kgs 11:20 and I Chr 2:34-35.

The details of these OT practices do not appear to have a direct bearing on the NT usage of the term. Paul is the only one to employ the Gr. word *huiothesia* and then he does so only five times (Rom 8:15, 23; 9:4; Gal 4:5; Eph 1:5). In Rom 9:4 he refers to the privileged position of the Jews as God's elected people, alluding to Ex 4:22 where the Lord calls Israel His son, His firstborn (cf. Deut 7:6-8; Isa 43:6; Jer 3:19; 31:9; Hos 11:1).

In the other passages, however, the apostle's usage reflects not the Hebraic but the Hellenistic world, emphasizing the freedom of a son in the household contrasted to the bondage of a slave.

Adoption was a very common part of the Graeco-Roman way of life. If there were no children in a family, the husband would adopt a son to whom he could give the inheritance. The person being adopted might have living parents but this would not prevent the adoption proceedings, because families were often willing to give up their children if they would thereby have a better chance in life. Once a child was adopted, the natural father had absolutely no more authority over him, and the adoptive father had complete control over his new son. A notable example of this practice in Roman history comes from the administration of the emperor Augustus. Realizing he had no responsible heir to his throne, he adopted an heir. When he outlived one heir, he adopted another, and finally settled on Tiberius, who succeeded him in A.D. 14.

Reflecting this understanding of adoption in the Hellenistic world, Paul employed the term to denote that legal act of God's grace by which believers become sons of God. Their relationship to God *as children* results from the new birth ("He gave the right to become children of God," Jn 1:12, NASB); whereas their adoption signifies that they as children have been placed in the position of *adult sons* (Gal 4:1-7). This is in contrast with the unique ("only begotten") sonship of Jesus Christ, who is Son of God by nature (Jn 1:14).

As in civil adoption, so in a spiritual sense, the following features may be noted: (1) Adoption is taking one for a son who was not so by nature and birth. (2) It is being adopted to an inheritance—in the spiritual sense, an inheritance which is incorruptible and undefiled (Rom 8:15-17; Gal 4:5-7). (3) It is the voluntary act of the adopter—spiritually the heavenly Father exercises His sovereign will in the matter (Eph 1:5)—mediated by Christ through the instrumentality of the Holy Spirit (Gal 4:4-6). (4) It means that the adopted bears the name of the adopter and can call him "Father" (Isa 56:5; 62:2; 65:15; Rev 2:17; Rom 8:15; I Jn 3:1). (5) It means that the adopted becomes the recipient of the compassion and care of his heavenly Father (Eph 1:3-6; cf. Lk 11:11-13), and is accepted into full family rights and privileges, received back as a son and not a servant in the case of the prodigal (Lk 15:19-24). (6) In the eschatological aspect the entire creation will benefit from the adopted one receiving the deliverance of his body from decay and death (Rom 8:23).

See Family; Inheritance.

Bibliography. Sherman E. Johnson, "Adoption," HDB rev., p. 11. C. F. D. Moule, "Adoption," IDB, I, 48 f. CornPBE, p. 319.

C. M. H.

ADORAIM (ăd′ō-rā′ĭm). A city in southern Judah rebuilt and fortified by Rehoboam (II Chr 11:9). It has been identified with Dura, five miles SW of Hebron.

ADORAM (*ȧ*-dō′răm). Alternate form of Adoniram *(q.v.)*.

ADORATION. This term does not occur in KJV, ASV, or RSV, although the idea is expressed in the OT *shāḥâ*, "worship," "bow oneself before"; and in the NT *proskuneō*, "worship," "kiss the hand," "do reverence to," "adore," and less frequently by *sebomai*, "revere," "adore," "be devout," and *latreuō*, "worship publicly," "minister," "serve," "render religious homage." *See* Worship.

ADORN. A word meaning "to polish" or "to arrange," it came to be used for dress, especially women's dress (I Tim 2:9; I Pet 3:3, 5; Rev 21:2). Figuratively, we are to adorn the doctrine of God (Tit 2:10).

ADRAMMELECH (*ȧ*-drăm'ĕ-lĕk)
1. One of the Syrian or Mesopotamian gods brought to Samaria when the kingdom of Israel fell (II Kgs 17:31), likely the deity Adad-milki ("Adad is king"). *See* Gods, False.
2. A son of Sennacherib. He and a brother assassinated their father and fled to Armenia (II Kgs 19:37; Isa 37:38).

ADRAMYTTIUM (ăd-r*ȧ*-mĭt'ĭ-*ŭ*m). Mentioned only once in the Scriptures (Acts 27:2) when Paul was placed on a ship from this seaport in Mysia of the Roman province of Asia.

ADRIA (ā'drĭ-*ȧ*). Paul and the party with him being taken to Rome drifted in Adria for 14 days (Acts 27:27). The northern part of the body of water between Italy and Dalmatia was from Etruscan times called the Adriatic Sea, but according to Livy, Strabo, Ptolemy and Josephus, the sea as far S as the island of Crete was designated as Adriatic. Thus when Luke wrote in the 1st cen. A.D. about the voyage, he used the current designation and called the waters "Adria" in which they were drifting.

ADRIEL (ā'drĭ-ĕl). King Saul had promised his daughter Merab to David, but instead he gave her in marriage to Adriel (I Sam 18:17-19). Later Saul gave his daughter Michal to David in marriage. Perhaps some scribal corruption accounts for Michal being recorded as the mother of five boys that David allowed the Gibeonites to hang in payment for Saul's offense to them. Their mother was Merab the wife of Adriel (II Sam 21:8). The RSV has corrected this on the authority of two Heb. MSS and the LXX.

ADULLAM (*ȧ*-dŭl'*ȧ*m), **ADULLAMITES** (*ȧ*-mīts). A city in the Shephelah of Judah, usually listed with some other cities that can more easily be identified (Josh 12:15; 15:35; II Chr 11:7; Neh 11:30; Mic 1:15). Near the city were several caves in which David and his men stayed for a while (I Sam 22:1; II Sam 23:13; I Chr 11:15). The Adullamites were citizens of Adullam.

ADULTERY. Sexual intercourse of a married person with other than the marriage partner. Adultery was generally condoned in pagan cultures, particularly on the part of the male, who though married was not charged with adultery unless he cohabited with another man's wife or a betrothed maiden.

Adultery is strictly forbidden in both the OT (the seventh commandment, Ex 20:14; Deut 5:18; punishable under the law with death by stoning, Lev 20:10; Deut 22:22 ff.) and the NT (Rom 13:9; Gal 5:19; Jas 2:11). Jesus extended guilt for adultery, as He did in the case of other commandments, to the purpose or will to commit it as well as to the act itself (Mt 5:28).

Adultery is technically distinguished from fornication, which is intercourse between unmarried persons. However, the Gr. *porneia,* uniformly translated "fornication" in the KJV, properly includes all lewdness and sexual irregularity (cf. MM; and Vine, EDNTW). For this reason, many churches regard Mt 5:32 and 19:9 as allowing divorce with remarriage in cases where the prior marriage was broken by reason of adultery. Others refuse to acknowledge any valid basis for remarriage after divorce, and view all such as resulting in adultery in the sight of God. However, it must not be concluded because this exception is absent from the Synoptic parallels and from Paul's analogy in Rom 7:2-3 or his treatment in I Cor 7:10-11 that it therefore is not authentic. Exactly the reverse may be the case. It may have been so universally recognized as not to require restatement each time divorce and remarriage were mentioned.

The attitude of Jesus toward the woman taken in adultery as recorded in Jn 8:1-11 has been questioned on the grounds that this passage is lacking in the best ancient MSS, and where it does occur, the readings vary widely. However, "it is unquestionable that it forms part of the authentic tradition of the church" (A. J. MacLeod, "John," NBC). Christ did not condone sin in the woman, nor did He condemn her to death by stoning as her accusers suggested. "The truth in Him rebuked the lie in the scribes and Pharisees. The purity in Him condemned the lust in her" (C. J. Wright, *Mission and Message of Jesus,* p. 795), and He bade her go and sin no more.

A consistent biblical use of the term adultery (Heb. *nā'aph;* Gr. *moicheia*) is metaphorical, to represent the idolatry or backsliding of the nation and people espoused to God. Examples of this are Jer 3:8-9; Ezk 23:27, 43; Hos 2:2-13; Mt 12:39; Jas 4:4. Such use is based on the analogy of the relationship between God and His people as resembling the relationship of husband and wife, a common feature of both OT (Jer 2:2; 3:14; 13:27; Hos 8:9) and NT (Jn 3:29; Rev 19:8-9; 21:2, 9). Marriage as involving both a legal covenant and a bond of love is a fitting symbol of the relationship between Christ and His Church (Eph 5:25-27).

Polygamy as a legalized relationship between the male and subordinate wives and concubines was permitted in OT times, but forbidden in the NT (e.g., I Tim 3:2, 12). It did not involve the sin of adultery.

In spite of strict biblical injunctions, adultery became widespread at different times, being particularly offensive as part of the Canaanite worship of the Baals, involving "sacred" prostitution. Indications of common moral laxity are found in such references as Job 24:15; 31:9; Prov 2:16-19; 7:5-22; Jer 23:10-14. The case of David was particularly notorious, giving occasion for the enemies of God to blaspheme (II Sam 11:2-5; 12:14). That general laxity prevailed in NT times is clearly seen in Mk 8:38; Lk 18:11; I Cor 6:9; Gal 5:19; Heb 13:4, and in more than 50 references in the NT to the concept of fornication *(porneia, porneuō, pornē, pornos). See* Fornication.

Bibliography. F. Hauck, "*Moicheuō,* etc.," TDNT, IV, 729–735.

W. T. P.

ADUMMIM (*ȧ*-dŭm'ĭm). The pass through red marl hills with the modern Arabic name of Tal'at ed-Damm ("ascent of blood") is thought to be the ancient Adummim. The Scriptures indicate it is on the general line between Jericho and Jerusalem (Josh 15:7; 18:17). It may be the setting for Jesus' story of the good Samaritan (Lk 10:30).

ADVENT, SECOND. *See* Christ, Coming of.

ADVERSARY. In 32 of its 57 KJV occurrences, "adversary" is the translation of *ṣar* (or related forms) meaning "foe." It refers primarily to enemies of Israel (Ex 23:22; Jer 50:7; cf. Est 7:6; Ps 69:19), but also to a rival wife (I Sam 1:6) or sinful Judeans (Isa 1:24). Adversaries execute God's wrath (Ps 89:42; Amos 3:11; cf. Lam 2:4), but will be overcome (Ps 81:13–14; Jer 30:16; cf. Isa 59:18; Nah 1:2). Heb. *śāṭān* (*see* Satan) may describe a human adversary (I Sam 29:4; II Sam 19:22), or even the angel of the Lord (Num 22:22).

Of NT words rendered "adversary," *antikeimenos* means simply "opposer" (Lk 13:17; 21:15; I Cor 16:9; Phil 1:28; I Tim 5:14; cf. Arndt); but *antidikos* signifies opponents in a lawsuit (Mt 5:25; Lk 12:58; cf. Job 31:35; Isa 50:8), as well as more generally the devil (Lk 18:3; I Pet 5:8).

See also Devil.

ADVOCATE. Arndt defines the Gr. word *paraklētos* for "advocate" as "one who appears in another's behalf; mediator, intercessor, helper" (p. 623). *See* Paraclete.

John says that one only deceives himself when he says he has no sin (I Jn 1:8), while he makes God a liar when he says he has never sinned (v. 10). At the same time, if anyone commits sin he does have an "advocate with the Father, Jesus Christ the righteous" (I Jn 2:1). To understand what John means, one must realize he also has an adversary who constantly stands to accuse him before God, even Satan (cf. Zech 3:1–7; Job 1:6–12; 2:1–7; Rev 12:10). In Christ's work as Advocate He pleads His own substitutionary atonement for the believer's sins and defends him against the attacks of Satan before God.

AENEAS (ē-nē'*ȧ*s). The name of a paralytic "sick of the palsy" and bedridden for eight years whom Peter healed, saying, "Jesus Christ maketh thee whole" (Acts 9:32–35). The healing resulted in a great spiritual awakening at both Lydda and Sharon. It illustrates very well the purpose of NT miracles as an attestation by God to the ministry of the early church, and identifies the disciples' work with that of Christ. *See* Healing, Divine; Miracles.

AENON (ē'nŏn). John baptized here because there was much water. In Jn 3:23 it is said to be near Salim. Though the exact site is unknown, it is located by Eusebius (*Onomasticon* 40:1–4) W of the Jordan, eight miles S of Scythopolis or Beth-shan.

AEON. This represents a Gr. word which is used in the NT of an age (cf. the present age, this age, the coming age, that age, Mt 12:32; Mk 10:30; Lk 18:30; 20:35; Gal 1:4, RSV). It is also used of worlds and universe (Heb 1:2). It is employed especially in certain phrases to express the ideas of forever and forever and ever (Jn 6:51, 58; Gal 1:5). For an introduction to recent discussion of its force as applied to eternity, see James Barr, *Biblical Words for Time*. Barr contends that Cullmann's vocabulary study has failed to prove that there is lexical foundation for his view that no qualitative distinction can be drawn between the NT conceptions of time and eternity, and claims that eternity is merely time in its entirety or time without end or limit. *See* Eternity; Time.

J. H. S.

A lively controversy exists over the use of the word in such a passage as Mt 24:3 (cf. Mt 13:39–40; Lk 18:30; I Cor 10:11; Heb 9:26) where the disciples said to our Lord, "Tell us, when shall these things be? and what shall be the sign of thy coming, and of the end of the world [age or aeon]?" Young, in his concordance, sees it as being used here in the sense of age, and classifies it along with many other NT uses which, though translated "world" in the KJV, express time and can be, therefore, better translated "age" or "dispensation."

Actually the decision as to which translation is correct is dictated in such places not so much by exegetical details as by the fact one is either amillennial or premillennial. The premillennialist has no difficulties with the literal translation "age," but the amillennialist feels he must eliminate such a meaning for such verses as this and Mt 13:39, "the harvest is the end of the aeon" (cf. II Cor 4:4; Gal 1:4), lest it support the literal idea of the thousand year reign of Christ on the earth. The primary meaning "age" should be given preference over the secondary one "world" except where it does not fit (e.g., Heb 11:3; cf. I Cor 2:6; II Cor 4:4), or the context demands the meaning "world" (Heb 1:2).

At the same time it should be realized that the Heb. concept of time and of dispensations in time was applied in a much wider sense than our term age; everything was related to particular periods or points of time. *See* Dispensation.

Bibliography. James Barr, *Biblical Words for Time,* Naperville: Allenson, 1962. Oscar Cullmann, *Christ and Time,* London: S. C. M. Press, 1951.

R. A. K.

AFFLICTION. The unsaved suffers afflictions because of his sins (Ps 107:10, 39); the Christian, because of the curse of sin and death upon the world, because of Satan (Job 1:6-12; 2:1-7), and because the fallen world hates righteousness and the light (Jn 15:18; 3:20). Moses chose to "suffer evil [literal] together with the children of God, rather than to enjoy the pleasures of sin for a season" (Heb 11:25).

Yet this does not explain fully the afflictions which come upon the believer. Seen in a deeper dimension, they are all part of Rom 8:28—"all things work good to them that love God"—in the sense God sends afflictions for the Christian's good. Paul, who knew the greatest of trials, calls the believer's afflictions "light" compared with the glory which follows when he goes to be with the Lord (II Cor 4:17).

According to our Lord, the time of greatest affliction, the Great Tribulation, will occur just prior to His second coming (Mt 24:21, 29-30; cf. Rev 7:14; Rev 6-19), and He says except those days be shortened, no one will be left on the earth (Mt 24:22).

The term "the afflictions of Christ," used by Paul in Col 1:24, does not refer to any lack in the sufferings of Christ which is completed by believers. The Roman Catholics teach that it is possible to help fill out these sufferings and add to the work of Christ, just as it is possible to do works of merit which are added to His works. Paul is here referring to the sufferings borne by Christ's Body, the Church, and speaks in this way because of the close spiritual union between the Lord and His own. The Lord refers to this union in Jn 17:21 as He prays, "That they all may be one; as thou, Father, art in me, and I in thee, that they also may be one in us."

See Agony; Suffering.

R. A. K.

AGABUS (ăg'*a*-bŭs). A prophet from Jerusalem (Acts 11:27-30) who predicted a widespread famine in the inhabited world (the Roman Empire). This occurred in the days of Claudius (A.D. 41-54), relief being sent probably between the years 45-46 by the Antioch church in Syria to the Jerusalem Christians. Presumably, the same Agabus is intended in Acts 21:10, 11, where his prediction made in A.D. 59 to the church at Caesarea was dramatically presented by his binding himself with Paul's girdle, warning Paul of impending imprisonment if he insisted on going up to Jerusalem.

That Agabus may have been a native of Antioch rests on the very slender evidence of a few MSS which read "one of us" instead of "one of them" in Acts 11:28.

AGAG (ā'găg). The king of the Amalekites, who was captured and his life spared by Saul, although the prophet Samuel had commanded that all Amalekites be put to death. When Samuel went out to meet Saul after the king had returned from the victory, the bleating of the sheep belied his claim of perfect obedience. He tried to blame the people for sparing Agag and the cattle, but Samuel would not accept the excuse. Saul then confessed his sin, but it was too late, for Samuel predicted the loss of his kingdom. Samuel demonstrated the need of full obedience by personally slaying Agag in the presence of the people (I Sam 15:8-33). Earlier, an Agag had been mentioned in the prophecy of Balaam, who declared that Israel's king would be higher than Agag (Num 24:7).

AGAGITE (ā'g*a*-gīt). Haman (*q.v.*), who was the first officer in command under Ahasuerus (Xerxes I), was an Agagite (Est 3:1, 10; 8:3, 5; 9:24). Josephus (*Ant.* xi.6.5) associated this name with Amalek. It was Agag the king of the Amalekites whom Saul brought back to Israel and thus aroused the anger of Samuel (I Sam 15:8, 33). If this association is correct, one can understand Mordecai's disrespect for Haman.

An Akkadian inscription of Sargon II mentions Agag as a district in Media.

AGAPE (ā-gă'pā). The agape (Gr. for "love") was the common meal or love feast of the early church. Besides satisfying hunger and distributing to the poor, it was a means for expressing unity and brotherly love. *See* Love Feast.

Though mentioned specifically only in Jude 12 and II Pet 2:13 (in some MSS), the custom was known in the NT (Acts 2:42, 46; 20:11; I Cor 10:16; 11:24) and in post-canonical literature (Didache, Ignatius, Tertullian, Chrysostom, Augustine, *et al.*). Jewish feasts and Gentile guilds furnished precedent for such an expression of fellowship.

At first, after the pattern of the Lord's Supper, the meal seems to have been associated with the Eucharist. Later, the sacerdotal emphasis tended to separate the two and to associate the latter with fasting. Never having been entirely universal or essential to Christian practice, faced with abuses from within, and coming under suspicion of the heathen who imagined an evil motive, the meal fell more and more into disuse by the 4th cen. However, it is still preserved by some religious bodies (Mennonites, Dunkards, and some German Baptists).

W. T. D.

AGAR (ā'gär). The Gr. version of the Heb. Hagar (*q.v.*). It is used allegorically by Paul in Gal 4:24-25.

AGATE. A precious stone. *See* Jewels; Minerals.

AGE. *See* Eternity; Time.

AGEE (ā'gē). The father of Shammah, one of

David's mighty men. He is called a Hararite (II Sam 23:11).

AGONY. This word (Gr. *agōnia*) is found but once in the NT (Lk 22:44). It describes the climax of the mysterious conflict and unspeakable suffering of our Lord in the garden. Coming from *agōn,* "contest," and *agō,* "to drive or lead," as in a chariot race, it has the root idea of the struggle and pain of the most severe athletic contest or conflict. From Demosthenes on, it has been used of severe mental struggles and emotions.

The agony of soul wrought pain upon the body of Jesus until "his sweat became as it were great drops of blood falling down upon the ground" (Lk 22:44, ASV). Blood mixing with the ordinary watery perspiration is medically termed diapedesis. It results from agitation of the nervous system, turning the blood out of its natural course and forcing the red particles into the skin excretories (Fausset, *Bible Encyclopedia*). Other cases are on record, such as Charles IX of France on his death bed and a Florentine youth unjustly condemned to death by Sixtus V.

The anguish of Christ seems to have reached an unbearable level even before the bloody sweat, for an angel came and strengthened Him (Lk 22:43). It was then that He was able to pray the more earnestly and to sweat blood.

The meaning of the agony is in the thrice repeated cry, "If it be possible, let this cup pass from me" (Mt 26:36-46; Mk 14:32-42; Lk 22:39-46). It was not the pains of physical death from which Jesus shrank. It was the prospect of becoming the bearer of sin. There was an instinctive, agonizing shrinking of His whole being from the horror of bearing the sin of the whole world and the withdrawal of the light of God's face. None but the perfect Christ could compass the weight of all man's guilt, anguish, sorrow, and pain as He consented to be bruised and crushed by our iniquities. The NT reserves the word agony for this one supreme redemptive contest. *See* Affliction; Suffering.

W. T. D.

AGORA (ăg'ŏ-rȧ). The gathering place was the public open space in town, city, or country where the people congregated. From its use for display and exchange of goods, it was called the marketplace or bazaar. It was often at or near the gate of the city, as the bazaar of Old Jerusa-

The Church of All Nations at the foot of the Mount of Olives covers the traditional rock of agony. To the left of the church is the Garden of Gethsemane. HFV

The Agora at Athens with the reconstructed Stoa of Affalos in the background. HFV

lem just inside the Damascus Gate. But business fanned out into adjoining areas, which came to be known as the street of the bakers or of the coppersmiths.

Marketing was only one of the activities. Children assembled for song, dance, and play (Mt 11:16, 17; Lk 7:32); the idle awaited employment or sought the latest gossip (Mt 20:1-16); those who wanted to attract attention came where people assembled (Mt 23:3-7; Mk 12:38; Lk 11:43; 20:46); the sick sought treatment (Mk 6:56); preliminary hearings for trials were held here where rulers could be found (Acts 16:19); and the public gathering served as a sounding board of free speech for religious, philosophical, and political discussion (Acts 17:17). The agora of Athens was the scene of peripatetic (sauntering) schools of philosophy.

W. T. D.

AGRAPHA (ăg'rȧ-fȧ). Commonly used to refer to alleged sayings of Christ not written in the Gospels (or in the NT; as, e.g., a few of His sayings which appear in Acts and the epistles).

A number of alleged sayings of Jesus are found in non-canonical sources. First, a few are preserved in later MSS of the NT; e.g., the one in Codex Beza after Lk 6:4 (in the footnotes of Nestle). Also some of the early Church Fathers added a number of sayings of Jesus, like that of Justin: "In whatsoever things I shall take you, in these I shall judge you" (Dial. with Trypho 47). These are, however, very few, unimportant, and are probably only fanciful citations.

In 1897 and 1903 Grenfell and Hunt found three papyri in Egypt that occasioned much interest. These included about 14 "sayings" of Jesus, half of which equal sayings in the Gospels. The non-canonical sayings are out of character; therefore surely not genuine. One of the more famous ends, for example, in pantheism: "Raise the stone and thou shalt find me; cleave the wood and there I am." The source of these sayings is unknown, but it has been argued that they came from a 2nd cen. collection of sayings of Jesus (ISBE art. *Logia*). This conclusion is now largely confirmed, though some reconstruction of damaged portions has been shown to be fallacious.

In 1946 there was discovered in Egypt at Chenoboskion *(q.v.)* an amazing cache of documents. Scme of these are in Coptic and include Gnostic works and apocryphal materials composed in Gr. in the 2nd cen. Related finds are the Bodmer papyri, including important early copies of books of the Gr. NT. The Gnostic works include a Gospel of Thomas (not the previously known Gospel of the Infancy allegedly by Thomas), which is a collection of 114 sayings of Jesus. These include the sayings discovered earlier by Grenfell and Hunt. Some of the others parallel our Gospels; some do not. Again, the non-canonical sayings are usually widely out of character and have little chance of being genuine. A work entitled The Gospel of Truth is a discussion of Gnostic views but gives no sayings of Christ. Another work is entitled The Gospel of Philip. All three are dated by F. L. Filson (BA, XXIV, 1961, pp. 8-18) and others as in the 2nd cen. They are Gnostic and help greatly in studying that movement. But there is no clear indication that any of these sayings are genuine. They add nothing clear, sure, or of value to our Gospels.

See Gnosticism.

R. L. H.

AGRICULTURE. The production of crops from the soil and the raising of livestock. The word "agriculture" is not used in the Bible, but the idea is conveyed by the term "husbandry" (Heb. *'ădāmâ,* II Chr 26:10; Gr. *geōrgion,* I Cor 3:9). The term "husbandman" is frequently used; e.g., Gen 9:20; Jer 31:24; 51:23; Mt 21:33-41; Jn 15:1; Jas 5:7.

Agriculture in the Bible. The importance of agriculture in the Bible is indicated by numerous references to the farmer and the shepherd. The many agrarian laws in the OT reflect the fact that throughout the whole period of Israel's national history the principal occupation was agriculture.

It is mentioned in connection with the earliest activities of the human race. Cain is said to have cultivated the ground (Gen 4:2). God was regarded as the founder of husbandry (Isa 28:26). No other area of Israelite life has supplied so many figures of speech to enrich the thought and language of the Bible as agriculture. The blessings of the messianic future are described in terms of fertile fields, fruit trees, and vineyards (Amos 9:14; Zech 8:12), while the disappointment of a crop failure was symbolical of sorrow or judgment (Isa 16:10). The language of Jesus illustrates the importance of figures related to the agricultural life of Palestine (Lk 6:43-44). Good examples are seen in the parable of the fig tree (Mt 24:32), the parable of the laborers in the vineyard (Mt 20:1-16), the parable of the sower (Mk 4:1-20).

The calendar and methods of the husbandman. The land was thought of as being the property of the Lord (Lev 25:23), and the husbandman enjoyed the privilege of its use. *See* Land and Property. The crops depended on the seasons, which in turn were determined by God. In many ways the religious calendar of the Israelites reflected the agricultural life of the people. The so-called Gezer Calendar (*see* Calendar), in seven lines of doggerel, provides a summary of the agricultural activities in the period of the beginning of the divided monarchy. The months are mnemonically arranged according to the main agricultural activities of the year. The three major festivals (Feast of Unleavened Bread, Feast of Weeks or Pentecost, and Feast of Tabernacles, Ex 23:14-17; Deut 16:16), which the Israelite was under obligation to attend in Jerusalem, were basically agricultural in character. They were related to the seasons and the products of the soil, and were observed at the beginning and at the end of the grain harvest, and the final ingathering of all the crops of the year.

The agricultural year began with the advent of the early rains, which had the effect of softening the ground baked hard by the heat of the summer sun. The early or former rains began during the latter half of October. Delay of these rains, or scanty rains in the spring or the "latter rain," would endanger the crop.

The major supply of water for agriculture was from the rains and dew (Gen 27:28, 39; I Kgs 17:1; Hag 1:10), but underground water sources were sometimes utilized. Some irrigation was developed by the use of Jordan River water, and by channels from cisterns hewn out of rock (Ps 1; Deut 8:7; Ezk 17:8). Israel's greater dependence on the rains is contrasted with Egypt's total dependence on irrigation (*q.v.*) in Deut 11:10-12. The dependence of Israel upon the Lord for His gift of rain is indicated in many references (Deut 11:14; Jer 3:3; 5:24; Joel 2:23; Zech 10:1). The farmer's major enemy was drought; but locusts, plant mildew, hot sirocco winds and pillaging in war also might take a heavy toll.

The principle of crop rotation is suggested in the regulation that a field *(q.v.)* should lie fallow for one year in every seven (Ex 23:10). Plowing was done usually with a simple plow drawn by oxen or cows, and reaping with a sickle of

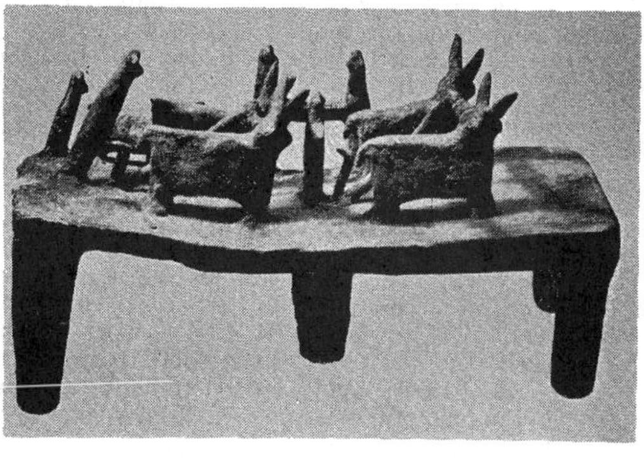

A terracotta model of a plowing scene, third millennium B.C. Cyprus Museum

Israelis harvesting olives. IIS

wood and flint, or of iron (Deut 16:9; 23:25; Jud 14:18; I Kgs 19:19; Job 1:14; Amos 6:12). Threshing *(q.v.)* and winnowing were done on a hard threshing floor. Oxen trod out the grain and sometimes a threshing sledge was used (Isa 28:27*a*; 41:15). Flails or sticks were sufficient to beat out the smaller harvests (Isa 28:27*b*; Jud 6:11, RSV). In winnowing the threshed grain, the workers tossed it by means of a pitchfork, shovel, or "fan" *(q.v.)* into the air to permit the breeze to blow away the fine chaff (Mt 3:12; Ps 1:4). The heavier kernels fell at their feet. To remove bits of straw the grain was sifted (cf. Lk 22:31). The cut straw and stubble could be used as fuel, or was left in the field and burned (Lk 3:17; Isa 47:14; Mal 4:1).

The ass and the mule also served as draft animals. The farmer used his goad also to break the clods. The ground was leveled with an implement resembling a stone boat, or with a roller (Job 39:10; Isa 28:24–25; Hos 10:11). The seed was sown by hand. Spelt, barley, and wheat were frequently placed in the furrow, and in the time of the Mishna the seed was plowed in.

The products of agriculture. The general diet of Israel is reflected in such references as I Sam 25:18 and Num 11:5, and together they indicate the variety of foods which could be grown in ancient times. Three products dominated the market in Palestine—wheat, wine, and olive oil (Ps 104:15; Joel 2:19); these were also the chief exports. Thus the four most important branches of agriculture were the growing of grain, vineyards, olives and the raising of flocks. *See* Vine; Wine; Plants; Shepherd; Animals.

Of the grains, wheat was the most valuable product (I Kgs 5:11). It was sown in late October or early November when the rains had started, and was harvested during the end of May or the beginning of June. Barley was more common and was used for bread (Jud 7:13; II Kgs 4:42). It was also used for fodder (I Kgs 4:28), which perhaps indicates that it was considered an inferior grade of food. Barley was sown the same time as wheat but could be grown on poorer soil and was harvested about a month earlier (Ruth 2:23). Spelt was also cultivated (Ex 9:32). The Heb. word is translated "rie" in the KJV. Spelt was sown around the edges of the barley and wheat fields (Isa 28:25). It apparently was an inferior species of wheat. Flax was another important crop (Josh 2:6; Isa 19:9; Hos 2:5, 9). Rope and linen cloth were made from flax.

The fig was a significant delicacy. It was, together with the date, an important source of sugar. The sycamore fig, which was an inferior type, was treated in a special way to improve its quality. In Amos 7:14, the prophet says that he was "a dresser [or pincher] of sycomore trees." The fig was used for medicinal purposes as appears from Isa 38:21. The date palm tree was widely used and was grown especially in the Jordan Valley (Deut 34:3; Jud 1:16). Dates were made into cakes, as were figs, and there was also date honey and date syrup.

Legume-producing plants were lentils and beans, which were sometimes used for the making of bread (II Sam 17:28; Ezk 4:9). Melons and cucumbers constituted part of the diet and were particularly refreshing in such a hot cli-

A threshing scene near Jerash, Jordan. HFV

mate. As is the case today, the poor might live for months on bread and melons or cucumbers alone. Leeks, garlic, and onions were used for seasoning. Cummin and coriander are mentioned (Isa 28:25; Ex 16:31). The NT adds anise, mint, rue, and mustard (Mt 13:31; 23:23; Lk 11:42). *See* Food; Harvest.

Bibliography. ANEP, figs. #84-102. Denis Baly, *The Geography of the Bible,* New York: Harper, 1957, especially pp. 97-108. A. C. Bouquet, *Everyday Life in NT Times,* New York: Scribner's, 1954, pp. 74-94. CornPBE, pp. 17-30, 238-243. E. W. Heaton, *Everyday Life in OT Times,* New York: Scribner's, 1956, pp. 97-112. Madeleine S. and J. Lane Miller, *Encyclopedia of Bible Life,* New York: Harper, 1944, pp. 1-24. William M. Thomson, *The Land and the Book,* Grand Rapids: Baker, 1954. Lucian Turkowski, "Peasant Agriculture in the Judean Hills," PEQ, CI (1969), 21-33, 101-112. G. Ernest Wright, *Biblical Archaeology,* rev. ed., Philadelphia: Westminster, 1962, pp. 183-187.

A. C. S.

A plowing scene from a tomb of a noble at Thebes, Egypt. Gaddis, Luxor

AGRIPPA I, HEROD (hĕr'ŏd *ȧ*-grĭp'*ȧ*). He is called Herod the King in Acts 12:1. He was a son of Aristobulus and Bernice, and grandson of Herod the Great and Mariamne. The royal Asmonean line, though nearly extinguished by the murderous jealousy of Herod the Great, was preserved in Agrippa. In him the kingdom of Herod came again to glory.

Agrippa was born about 10 B.C. and moved to Rome at the age of six. He was brought up with Drusus, son of Tiberius; with Antonia, wife of Drusus; and with Claudius. Though but a private citizen, he was far-seeing and cultivated every opportunity of advancement. His brilliant prospects made available a supply of money for luxury and extravagance. But after Drusus died suddenly in A.D. 23, the emperor declined to receive the high-spirited young man. His companions forsook him. Deeply in debt, he fled from Rome to a fortress in Malatha in Idumea.

His wife, Cypros, through his sister Herodias, wife of Herod Antipas, obtained a position for him as a market overseer at Tiberias with aedile rank and a small annuity (Jos *Ant.* xviii.6.2). Having quarreled with his brother-in-law, who made him feel his dependent position, he fled to Flaccus, proconsul of Syria. Convicted of a bribe, he fled again, and, as he was about to sail for Italy, was arrested for a sum of money owed to the Roman treasury. He escaped to Alexandria, where his wife procured a loan for him. Thence he sailed to Puteoli and was favorably received by the aged Tiberius. Back in Rome, he made fast friends with Caius Caligula, heir presumptive to the Roman throne. One day he expressed the wish that Caius might soon succeed to the throne. Reported to the emperor, he was cast in prison.

When Caligula succeeded Tiberius (A.D. 37), he freed Agrippa, gave him the tetrarchy of Philip and the territory of Lysanias II with the title of king, exchanged the iron chain with which he had been bound for a gold one of the same weight, and induced the Senate to invest him with the rank of praetor. Herod Antipas and his wife, being jealous of the distinctions conferred, sailed to Rome to supplant him in the emperor's favor. Agrippa anticipated the action by countercharges against Antipas of treasonous correspondence with the Parthians. When the charges were not answered, Antipas was exiled, and the tetrarchies of Galilee and Perea were added to Agrippa in A.D. 39. Then when Caligula was assassinated and the imperial crown was offered to the weak and indifferent Claudius, it was Agrippa who led him to accept the honor. In A.D. 40 Claudius added Judea and Samaria to Agrippa and confirmed the grant of the tetrarchy of Lysanias. He then possessed the entire kingdom of Herod the Great. In addition, he begged from Claudius the kingdom of Chalcis for his brother (who was then called Herod of Chalcis) and obtained consular rank for himself.

His reign over the total domain was for only three years, but it was considered a happy one for the Jews. He was the most affable and popular ruler of the Herodian family. He showed such tact and respect for the feelings of his countrymen that the Talmud and other Jewish literature praise him as a pious and beloved devotee of their religion.

The first act by which Agrippa celebrated his return to Palestine was one of piety. The golden chain which Caligula had bestowed on him, he hung up within the limits of the temple, over the treasury, as a memorial. At the same time, he presented a thankoffering, "because he would not neglect any precept of the law," and bore the expenses of a large number of Nazarites that they might discharge the obligation of their vows (*Ant.* 19.6.1).

Agrippa won the gratitude and good wishes of the Jews by persuading Caligula to desist from his attempt to have his own statue placed in the temple in Jerusalem. This was done with real hazard to his own security and fortunes. Two other attempted favors to the Jews were less successful. In order to strengthen the fortifications of Jerusalem, the capital, he began to build on the N of the city a powerful new wall which, according to Josephus, would have made the city impregnable. But at the instigation of Marsus, governor of Syria, Claudius issued an injunction against its continuance. Of still more importance was Agrippa's conference of princes at Tiberias. Five Roman vassal kings answered the invitation. Again the governor of Syria was suspicious of their designs. He appeared at Tiberias and ordered the other guests to return home without delay.

Agrippa I liked to live in Jerusalem and was strictly careful of the laws of the Jews while there, letting no day pass without its appointed sacrifice. The Talmud relates how as a simple Israelite, he with his own hand presented the firstfruits in the temple (Mishna, *Bikkurim,* iii. 4). When he betrothed his daughter Drusilla to King Antiochus of Commagene, he made him promise first to be circumcised. By such displays of piety he gave abundant satisfaction to the people and befriended the Pharisees. At the Feast of Tabernacles in A.D. 41, he read Deut 17:15, according to the old custom, and burst forth in tears at the words, "Thou mayest not set a stranger over thee, which is not thy brother." The people cried out, "Be not grieved, Agrippa! Thou art our brother!" His strong desire to please the Jews seems to be the reason for his persecution of the Christians (Acts 12:1-3), whom the Jews hated.

It is too much to believe that Agrippa was a Pharisee by conviction. His piety was only in the Holy Land. Elsewhere, he was a liberal patron of Gr. culture. In Berytus he cultivated pagan magnificence, building a beautiful theater, an amphitheater, baths, and piazzas. Games and sports of all kinds were celebrated, including gladiatorial combats in which, on one occasion, 1,400 men were killed. While coins stamped in Jerusalem had no offensive images, those minted outside bore likenesses of Agrippa or the emperor. He was more affable and sly than Herod the Great, but was moved more by a desire for peace than by piety.

In A.D. 44 he celebrated games at Caesarea to honor the emperor and to make vows for his safety. A number of principal persons in the province attended. The second day he appeared in the theater in a garment interwoven with silver. At the close of his address to the people they saluted him as a god. He did not rebuke them. A sharp pain seized him and he died five days later, in his fifty-fourth year. The NT calls it an act of God (Acts 12:23). With him the Herodian power had virtually run its course. He left three daughters (Bernice, Mariamne, and Drusilla) and a son of 17 (Agrippa), to whom the Romans were not yet ready to entrust the government.

See Herod. For bibliography *see* Herod.

W. T. D.

AGRIPPA II, HEROD. The only son of Agrippa I and Cypros, he was the last of the royal Herodian line. Marcus Julius Agrippa, as he was named, received a royal education at Rome in the palace of the emperor. Being only 17 when his father died in A.D. 44, he was considered too young to rule over the difficult kingdom of the Jews. Claudius sent Cuspius Fadus as procurator and thus restored the land of the Jews to a Roman province. In the meantime, the youth was useful to his countrymen at Rome through his influence at the court.

When his uncle, Herod of Chalcis, died (A.D. 48), Claudius conferred on Agrippa the little province of Chalcis with the oversight of the temple and the right to appoint the high priest. This latter right he exercised from time to time down to A.D. 66, but his impulsive appointments offended the Jews. Agrippa continued to reside in Rome, for the most part at least, until A.D. 53, when Claudius, in exchange for Chalcis, bestowed on him the larger tetrarchies which had formerly been held by Lysanias and Herod Philip. Later, Nero added important parts of Galilee and Perea, including Tiberias, Tarichea, and the lands belonging to them. The title of king was permitted.

Agrippa's private life was blighted by scandal. His sister Bernice, widow of Herod of Chalcis, moved to his house in A.D. 48 and soon had the weak man in her control. Their incestuous relationship was commonly discussed in Rome as well as among the Jews. To stop the report, Bernice married Polemon of Cilicia, but soon returned to her brother and apparently resumed the old relations.

The public policy of his reign reflected complete dependence upon Rome. He provided auxiliary troops in the Parthian campaign of A.D. 54. When the new procurator Festus arrived in Palestine, he and Bernice hastened with great pomp to offer him a welcome (Acts 25:13, 23). His coins, almost without exception, bore the names and images of the reigning emperor (Nero, Vespasian, Titus, and Domitian). He seems to have been more of a visitor at Jerusalem than a resident. His gestures toward Jewish law were less extravagant than his father's and proved less convincing to the people.

However, Agrippa did seek to keep on good terms with Judaism. His brothers-in-law, Azizus of Emesa and Polemon of Cilicia, were required to be circumcised. Questions of law were put by the king directly or indirectly to Rabbi Elieser. Even Bernice took a vow in Jerusalem, shaving her head and going barefoot. But the general, undisguised mood was one of indifference. Rather than please the Jews by quick condemnation of Paul, as his father would likely have done, he indulged his curiosity with a hearing (Acts 26:1). Then admitting the force of Paul's argument, he straightway dismissed it (Acts 26:28). His interest was in external matters. He imported wood from Lebanon to support the temple when its foundations began to sink, allowed the psalm-singing Levites to wear the linen garments of the priests, and paved Jerusalem with marble. But he had no reputation for personal piety.

When in A.D. 66 the revolution broke out, Agrippa earnestly warned the nation against revolt. When the peace party was defeated, Agrippa stood unflinchingly loyal to Rome, even though much of his territory joined the rebellion. He entertained the Roman general Vespasian magnificently in Caesarea Philippi, fought on the Roman side, was wounded at the siege of Gamala, became a companion of Titus (to whom the war had been entrusted), and almost certainly joined in the festive celebration at Caesarea Philippi to rejoice over the destruction of the Jews in the war. His loyalty to Rome was rewarded by additions to his territory. But he and Bernice resided in Rome, where he died in the reign of Trajan in A.D. 100 without heir. His kingdom was undoubtedly incorporated in the province of Syria.

See Herod.

W. T. D.

AGUR (ā'gûr). The writer of Prov 30.

AH. An emotional term usually expressing hesitance or complaint (Jer 1:6; 4:10; 14:13; 32:17; Ezk 4:14; 9:8; 11:13; 20:49).

AHAB (ā'hăb)

1. A false prophet, son of Kolaiah. He was deported to Babylon and denounced by Jeremiah (Jer 29:21).

2. The seventh king of Israel, son and successor of Omri. In the book of Kings he appears as both a politically strong and a spiritually weak king. On the secular side, he was able to win the respect of both friend and foe. On the religious side, his syncretistic practices spelled the doom of the house of Omri. His reign is listed as 22 years (I Kgs 16:29), which Thiele gives as 874 to 853 B.C. (*The Mysterious Numbers of the Hebrew Kings,* p. 61).

His political marriage with Jezebel resulted in mixed blessing and curse. The attendant alliance with Ethbaal, king of the Tyrians and father of Jezebel, brought increased trade, wealth, and a growing merchant class to Israel. However, Jezebel brought with her a form of Baalism which clashed head on with the worship of the Lord. With fanatical zeal, she pushed forward the cult associated with Baal-Melcarth and Asherah, gradually engulfing Ahab by her ruthless vigor. Later Ahab introduced this form of Baalism into Judah by giving his daughter Athaliah in marriage to Jehoram, son of Jehoshaphat.

Ruins of Ahab's palace, Samaria. HFV

Neither Ahab nor Jezebel was able to stand unopposed. Elijah, the Tishbite, appeared repeatedly as an accusing conscience. He was the champion of the common man as he confronted Ahab in the vineyard of Naboth. He was the champion of the worship of God in the victory on Mount Carmel.

While the Elijah stories present Ahab as weak and dominated by Jezebel, other aspects of his reign demonstrate his stronger points. His building operations were extensive and outstanding. At Samaria, he continued the construction begun by his father Omri. Excavations at Samaria have illustrated how strong were the walls which later were to withstand three years of seige. Carved ivories from Samaria are illustrative of the furnishings which went into his "house of ivory" at Jezreel. It was during his reign and possibly on his orders that Jericho was rebuilt by Hiel of Bethel. Other cities were rebuilt and fortified during this period.

Ahab's reign was a time of constant international conflict. He is shown fighting against the Syrian kingdom of Damascus (I Kgs 20), fighting with them against the Assyrians in the battle of Qarqar (records of Shalmanezer III), and finally aligned with Judah against Ben-hadad of Syria at Ramoth-gilead (I Kgs 22). In this battle to win back Ramoth-gilead from the Syrians, Ahab was struck down by an arrow shot at random. The king died, and his kingdom declined rapidly after his death, Moab and other subject areas rebelling and winning independence from Israel (II Kgs 1:1).

K. M. Y.

AHARAH (*ȧ*-hâr'*ȧ*). A son of Benjamin (I Chr 8:1). The list of the sons of Benjamin given in Gen 46:21 does not include Aharah, but Ehi may be the same. In Num 26:38 the third son of Benjamin is called Ahiram.

Ahasuerus (Xerxes) here stands behind his enthroned father (Darius); from the treasury at Persepolis, the Persian capital. ORINST

AHARHEL (*ȧ*-här'hĕl). Perhaps a descendant of Caleb. It is certain he was of the tribe of Judah and son of Harum (I Chr 4:8).

AHASAI (*ȧ*-hā'sī). A priest among those who returned from Exile (Neh 11:13). This name is spelled Ahzai in RSV. He is also called Jahzerah (I Chr 9:12).

AHASBAI (*ȧ*-hăs'bī). A Maachathite, the father of Eliphelet, one of the mighty men of David known as the "thirty" (II Sam 23:34). In the parallel passage (I Chr 11:35*b*–36*a*), his name seems to be Ur.

AHASUERUS (*ȧ*-hăzh'ōō-ĕr'*ŭ*s). Better known by his Gr. name Xerxes (486–465 B.C.), he was the son of Darius I and father of Artaxerxes I. Scripture indicates that he ruled a vast empire from India to Ethiopia (Est 1:1; cf. Herodotus 7:9), deposed Vashti as queen in 483 B.C., and chose Esther in 478 B.C. Four years later he gave permission to Haman to destroy the Jewish nation; but the plot was thwarted by the providence of God (473 B.C.). This great deliverance is celebrated at the Feast of Purim (Est 9:28). *See* Esther; Esther, Book of.

Ahasuerus (Xerxes) is depicted in the book of Esther as a fickle and vain monarch, and this seems to be confirmed by other historical sources. Because of a rebellion in Babylon, he had the city partially destroyed (482 B.C.). Two years later his great fleet was defeated at Salamis and Samos, and his army was routed at Plataea when he tried to conquer the Greeks.

The taking of a new wife in his seventh year (Est 2:16) fits Herodotus' description of the new interest he manifested in his harem after the disastrous Gr. campaign (9:108). Various court intrigues plus work on the new palace at Persepolis occupied his remaining years until he was assassinated in his bedchamber, August, 465 B.C.

Ezr 4:6 was formerly applied to Cambyses (530–522 B.C.), but it is definitely a reference to Xerxes, constituting part of a parenthetical summary of opposition to the rebuilding of Jerusalem and its walls (Ezr 4:6–23). Although he is not named, Xerxes was probably the fourth Persian king after Cyrus mentioned in Dan 11:2 (following Cambyses, Pseudo-Smerdis, and Darius I): "the fourth shall be far richer than they all: and when he is waxed strong through his riches, he shall stir up all against the realm of Greece" (ASV).

The Ahasuerus of Dan 9:1, father of Darius the Mede, is not otherwise known to history.

J. C. W.

AHAVA (*ȧ*-hā'v*ȧ*). A Babylonian town along a small river or canal of the same name on whose banks Ezra assembled the Jews who were to return to Jerusalem with him (Ezr 8:15, 21, 31).

AHAZ (ā'hăz). The twelfth ruler of Judah, son of Jotham. He was 20 years of age when he ascended the throne, and he reigned for 16 years (732–716 B.C.; see II Kgs 16:2; II Chr 28:1). Ahaz was given to idolatry, following the practices of the northern kingdom. He even went so far as to sacrifice a son to pagan gods.

Politically, Ahaz was at odds with Pekah, king of Israel, and with Rezin, king of Syria. They decided to attack Jerusalem and set a puppet, "the son of Tabeel" (Isa 7:6), on the throne of Judah, but they were unsuccessful. However, the Edomites took advantage of Judah's plight by capturing Elath on the Gulf of Aqaba (II Kgs 16:5–6).

The prophet Isaiah lived in Jerusalem at the time and sought to encourage Ahaz by giving him the virgin birth prophecy as a sign of God's delivering power (Isa 7:3-17), but Ahaz refused to accept the challenge to believe God. Instead, he sent messengers, with some of the temple treasure, to enlist the aid of Assyria's Tiglath-pileser III, who promptly destroyed Damascus (*c.* 732 B.C.). Ahaz went to Damascus where Tiglath-pileser gave him specifications for a new altar for the temple court (II Kgs 16:7-10).

The Chronicles give a more vivid account of Ahaz's wickedness and the devastation of Judah by Syria and Israel. Pekah is said to have slain 120,000 soldiers and taken captive 200,000 of the inhabitants of Judah. However, the prophet Obed warned Pekah to be merciful or else suffer divine punishment. In response to this message, the Israelites properly clothed the captives and returned them to Judah (II Chr 28:5-15). The Chronicler notes that the Philistines also had taken several cities from Ahaz at this time, and that after the Assyrians had helped Ahaz by destroying Syria and Israel, they turned on him, exacting tribute. Ahaz spent his last days as a helpless puppet of Assyria (II Chr 28:16-27).

G. H. L.

AHAZIAH (ā'h*ȧ*-zī'*ȧ*)

1. Ahaziah followed Ahab, his father, to the throne of Israel in 853 B.C. and reigned two years. He joined Jehoshaphat, king of Judah, in building a merchant fleet, but it displeased God and the fleet was destroyed (I Kgs 22:40, 48-53; II Chr 20:35-37). Ahaziah accidently fell out a second story window and was severely hurt. He sent messengers to Ekron to inquire of Baalzebub whether he would recover, but Elijah, at God's bidding, stopped the messengers and sent them back with word that Ahaziah would die. In anger, Ahaziah sent 50 soldiers twice to bring Elijah to him, but fire from heaven struck each company dead. The captain of a third company of 50 soldiers begged Elijah for mercy; so at God's command Elijah went to Ahaziah and warned him personally of his coming death. Within a short time, Ahaziah died (II Kgs 1). His brother Jehoram became the next king.

2. There was also a king of Judah by the name of Ahaziah who reigned but a short time in 841 B.C. He was a nephew of Ahaziah of the northern kingdom of Israel and a grandson of Ahab, for his mother was Athaliah, Ahab's daughter. His father was Jehoram, son of Jehoshaphat. Ahaziah was 22 years old when he ascended the throne and soon joined with Joram, king of Israel, in an expedition against Syria. The battle was lost, Joram was wounded, and Jehu, one of his generals, rose in revolt. He killed Joram and Jezebel and wounded Ahaziah, who later died at Megiddo but was buried in Jerusalem (II Kgs 8:28–9:37). The account in II Chr 22:7-9 emphasizes the guilt of Ahaziah and condemns his alliance with Joram (Jehoram) by stating that it was because of their close friendship that Jehu killed him. Ahaziah was also called Jehoahaz (*q.v.;* II Chr 21:17; 25:23).

G. H. L.

AHBAN (ä'băn). One of the sons of Abishur by Abihail in the genealogy of Jerahmeel, a man of Judah (I Chr 2:29).

AHER (ā'hẽr). A Benjamite (I Chr 7:12). Identified in the ASV marg. as the Ahiram of Num 26:38.

AHI (ā'hī)

1. Chief of the Gadites in Gilead in Bashan (I Chr 5:15).

2. A son of Shamer (I Chr 7:34).

AHIAH (*ȧ*-hī'*ȧ*). Three OT characters are so identified in KJV, though elsewhere (and throughout ASV) this same name appears as Ahijah (*q.v.*).

1. A warrior (I Chr 8:7; possibly the same as the earlier Ahoah, 8:4), who, with Naaman, was led by Gera to take captive two sons of Ehud.

2. A great-grandson of Eli, through Phinehas and Ahitub (brother of Ichabod), and high priest during Saul's early reign (I Sam 14:3). He brought the ark to Gibeah at the battle of Michmash (14:18) and later encouraged Saul to seek God (14:36). Ahiah was succeeded by his younger brother Ahimelech (I Sam 22:9), unless these two are to be equated (KD, *Samuel,* pp. 136-7).

3. A son of Shisha (I Kgs 4:3) who, with his brother Elihoreph, served Solomon as "scribe" (secretary of state, or finance, II Kgs 22:3-9; Isa 22:15; 36:3; *see* Scribe), as his father (*q.v.*) had under David (II Sam 8:17; 20:25; I Chr 18:16).

J. B. P.

AHIAM (*ȧ*-hī'*ȧ*m). One of David's mighty men of the company of "thirty," a son of Sacar (I Chr 11:35) or Sharar (II Sam 23:33).

AHIAN (*ȧ*-hī'*ȧ*n). Of the family of Shemidah, of Manasseh's tribe (I Chr 7:19).

AHIEZER (ā'hī-ē'zẽr)

1. A representative of the Danites who assisted Moses in the census. The son of Ammishaddai (Num 1:12; 2:25), he was also captain of the rear guard for the march (Num 10:25).

2. From Gibeath, he came to David's aid at Ziklag. He was a leader of the Benjamite bowmen (I Chr 12:3).

AHIHUD (*ȧ*-hī'hŭd)

1. An Asherite leader, son of Shelomi (Num 34:27). He was appointed to divide the W Jordan territory among the ten tribes in that area.

2. A head of the house of Benjamin (I Chr 8:7), a son of either Heglam (RSV) or Gera

(KJV). The Heb. phrase "he removed them" (KJV), may be rendered as the name "Heglam," thus changing the father from Gera to Heglam.

AHIJAH (*ȧ*-hī'*jȧ*). In KJV this name sometimes appears as Ahiah (*q.v.*).

1. An Ephraimite from Shiloh, a prophet of God, who, meeting Jeroboam returning from exile in Egypt, tore his own new garment into twelve pieces and gave ten pieces to Jeroboam, indicating God's intention to make him king over the ten tribes of the northern kingdom (I Kgs 11:29-39). Much later, when he had become king, at the serious illness of his son, Jeroboam sent his disguised wife to now blind Ahijah to inquire whether the child would recover. By revelation, Ahijah knew the disguised queen and predicted the child's death (I Kgs 14:1-18). He wrote of Solomon's "acts" (II Chr 9:29).

2. The father of Baasha, king of Israel (I Kgs 15:27, 33).

3. A son of Jerahmeel, and descendant of Judah through Pharez and Hezron (I Chr 2:25).

4. A Pelonite, one of David's mighty men (I Chr 11:36). *See also* Paltite.

5. A Levite set over the treasures of the house of God in David's reign (I Chr 26:20). LXX translates the Heb. as "the Levites, their brethren."

6. A chief of the people in Nehemiah's day, among those who sealed a covenant to walk uprightly before God (Neh 10:26; cf. 10:14). The name is translated Ahiah in RSV.

H. G. S.

AHIKAM (*ȧ*-hī'kăm). The son of Shaphan the scribe, he was a companion of Shaphan and Hilkiah the priest when Shaphan read to King Josiah a copy of the law found in the course of repairing the temple. He was sent with Hilkiah, Achbor, Shaphan and Asahiah to inquire of Huldah the prophetess concerning the future of Judah relative to the curses read out of the law (II Kgs 22:8-14). Through the protection of Ahikam, Jeremiah was saved from death at the hands of false prophets (Jer 26:24). Ahikam was the father of Gedaliah, governor of Judah under the Babylonians (II Kgs 25:22).

AHILUD (*ȧ*-hī'lŭd). Father of the recorder Jehoshaphat under rule of David (II Sam 8:16; I Kgs 4:3; I Chr 18:15) and, probably, the father of Solomon's district officer Baana (I Kgs 4:12).

AHIMAAZ (*ȧ*-hĭm'ā-ăz)

1. The father of Ahinoam, wife of Saul first king of Israel (I Sam 14:50).

2. One of two sons of Zadok who was high priest in David's time when Absalom raised rebellion against David (II Sam 15:27; I Chr 6:8, 53). With Jonathan, son of Abiathar a priest, Ahimaaz was to carry information to David concerning Absalom's plans and movements from Zadok and Abiathar in Jerusalem (II Sam 15:35-36). News of Absalom's plan to trap David in some corner was transmitted to them in En-rogel by a woman. They were seen by one who informed Absalom, but after concealment by a woman in Bahurim safely took the news to David (II Sam 17:15-21). At the death of Absalom in the Wood of Ephraim (*q.v.*), when Ahimaaz requested permission to bear the news to David, Joab refused it, but Ahimaaz persisted and finally was given permission. He gave David incomplete news, however; but Cushi soon made known the fact of Absalom's death (II Sam 18:19-32).

3. An officer of Solomon in the tribe of Naphtali responsible for provisions for Solomon's table for the seventh month. His wife was Solomon's daughter Basmath (I Kgs 4:7, 15).

H. G. S.

AHIMAN (*ȧ*-hī'măn)

1. A son of Anak, and probably founder of a family of Anakim (Num 13:22), he was one of the giants (*see* Anak) driven from Hebron by Caleb (Josh 15:14; Jud 1:10).

2. A Levite who served as porter for the house of God (I Chr 9:17).

AHIMELECH (*ȧ*-hĭm'ē-lĕk)

1. A son of Ahitub, a priest at Nob (I Sam 22:9), from whom David, pretending to be on King Saul's business, received showbread for food and the sword of Goliath when he fled from Saul (I Sam 21:1-9). (Mk 2:26 places this event in the time of Abiathar [*q.v.*], son of Ahimelech.) Ahimelech's aid to David was reported to Saul by Doeg the Edomite, who had observed them. Saul interpreted it as treachery on the part of all the priests. On the basis of this unsubstantiated report Saul ordered Doeg to slay Ahimelech and 84 other priests. Doeg also put the sword to the town of Nob, from which Abiathar alone escaped to bear the news to David (I Sam 22:6-20).

2. Son of Abiathar and grandson of Ahimelech. He was a priest with Zadok, son of Ahitub, in David's reign (II Sam 8:17; I Chr 24:3, 6, 31).

3. A Hittite and follower in David's band when Saul pursued him (I Sam 26:6).

H. G. S.

AHIMOTH (*ȧ*-hī'mŏth). A Levite, son of Elkanah and brother of Amasai (I Chr 6:25).

AHINADAB (*ȧ*-hĭn'*ȧ*-dăb). A purveyor in Mahanaim for Solomon, he was the son of Iddo (I Kgs 4:14).

AHINOAM (*ȧ*-hĭn'ō-ăm)

1. The daughter of Ahimaaz and wife of Saul (I Sam 14:50).

2. One of David's wives, a woman of Jezreel (I Sam 25:43). Captured by the Amalekites, she was rescued by David (I Sam 30:5), and lived

with him in Hebron while he was king of Judah (II Sam 2:2). She was mother of David's eldest son, Amnon (II Sam 3:2).

AHIO (*ȧ*-hī'ō)

1. The son of Abinadab, who with his brother Uzzah was entrusted with the ark when David made his first attempt to take it to Jerusalem (II Sam 6:3-4).

2. Considered the proper name of a Benjamite, son of Elpaal (I Chr 8:14-16).

3. Son of Jehiel, brother of Kish; a Benjamite (I Chr 8:30-31; 9:35-37).

AHIRA (*ȧ*-hī'r*ȧ*). A prince of the tribe of Naphtali and son of Enan. He helped Moses with the census during the wilderness wanderings (Num 1:15; 2:29; 7:78; 10:27).

AHIRAM (*ȧ*-hī'răm). The third son of Benjamin; the head of the family called Ahiramites (Num 26:38). Also referred to as Aharah (I Chr 8:1).

AHISAMACH (*ȧ*-hĭs'*ȧ*-măk). From the tribe of Dan, father of Aholiab, he was one of the craftsmen of the tabernacle and its equipment (Ex 31:6; 35:34; 38:23).

AHISHAHAR (*ȧ*-hĭsh'*ȧ*-här). A descendant of Benjamin through Bilhan and Jediael (I Chr 7:10).

AHISHAR (*ȧ*-hī'shär). The household overseer for Solomon (I Kgs 4:6).

AHITHOPHEL (*ȧ*-hĭth'ō-fĕl). A resident of Giloh, a town in SW Judah (II Sam 15:12; Josh 15:51). One of David's counselors (II Sam 15:12), he was the father of Eliam, one of David's mighty men (II Sam 23:34). Though a discerning and skillful counselor (II Sam 16:23), he was morally unstable, ready to betray David by giving counsel as to how to destroy him (II Sam 17:1-4). When Absalom accepted instead the adverse counsel of delay of Hushai, who was there purposely to defeat Ahithophel's counsel (II Sam 15:34), Ahithophel understood the result to mean the end of the rebellion, and anticipating his punishment when David would return, he went home and hanged himself (II Sam 15:31-34; 16:15; 17:23).

AHITUB (*ȧ*-hī'tŭb)

1. A priest in the line of Ithamar, son of Aaron. He was grandson of Eli the priest at Shiloh, son of Phinehas, and father of Ahimelech the priest (I Sam 14:3).

2. A priest in the line of Eleazar, son of Aaron (I Chr 6:3-7), son of Amariah the priest, and father of Zadok, priest in David's time (I Chr 6:8). He was an ancestor of Ezra (Ezr 7:1-2).

3. A priest, also in the line of Eleazar, son of Aaron, son of a second Amariah and father of a second Zadok (I Chr 6:3-11).

AHLAB (ä'lăb). A town in the territory of Asher from which the Canaanites were not driven out (Jud 1:31). Probably a textual corruption of Mahalab (Josh 19:29, RSV), a town on the coast between Tyre and Achzib, mentioned by Sennacherib as Mahalliba.

AHLAI (ä'lī)

1. The daughter of Sheshan (I Chr 2:31, 34).

2. The father of Zabad (I Chr 11:41).

AHOAH (*ȧ*-hō'*ȧ*). Son of Bela of the family of Benjamin (I Chr 8:4).

AHOHITE (*ȧ*-hō'hīt). A descendant of Ahoah (II Sam 23:9, RSV; I Chr 11:12,29). Apparently used to designate a hero of David's time.

AHOLAH (*ȧ*-hō'l*ȧ*). A symbolic name (hinting at Israel's schismatic tent-shrine) used in Ezk 23 for the kingdom of Samaria. The unfaithfulness of Israel and Judah was symbolically portrayed in the persons of Aholah and Aholibah (Oholah and Oholibah in RSV), who became harlots while married to the Lord. Aholah's activities were painted in lurid detail in order to show the heinousness of Israel's sin against a background of the unchangeable character of God (Ezk 23:49). Israel's unfaithfulness, begun in Egypt, included political involvement with Assyria and syncretistic worship (Ezk 23:5-10). In poetic justice these very paramours became ministers of divine judgment (Ezk 23:9-10). Samaria was defeated and carried captive by Assyria in 722 B.C.

AHOLIAB (*ȧ*-hō'lī-ăb). A craftsman of the tribe of Dan, son of Ahisamach, appointed by Moses to assist Bezaleel in the construction of the tabernacle and its furnishings (Ex 31:6). He was filled with the Spirit of God for his construction task and teaching ministry (Ex 35:34-35). *See* Bezaleel.

AHOLIBAH. *See* Aholah.

AHOLIBAMAH (*ȧ*-hŏl-ĭ-bā'm*ȧ*)

1. The wife of Esau, granddaughter of Zibeon the Horite (Gen 36:20, 25; cf. v. 2). In Gen 36:2 Zibeon is called a Hivite, evidently a textual corruption, since in v. 20 he is clearly a Horite (Kittel), i.e., the name applied to the early occupants of Seir (Gen 14:6), whose personal names were Semitic in contradistinction from the Horites of central Palestine who were non-Semitic Hurrians, called Hivites in Heb. (Gen 34:2) (E. A. Speiser, AASOR, XIII [1931-32], 26-31). Aholibamah's name is not found in the other lists of Esau's wives (Gen 26:34; 28:8-9).

2. Chief of an Edomite clan (Gen 36:41; I Chr 1:52).

AHUMAI (*ȧ*-hū'mī). Head of a family of Judah, the son of Jahath (I Chr 4:2).

AHUZAM (*ȧ*-hŭz'*ȧ*m). In the genealogy of Judah, he is mentioned as a son of Ashur (I Chr 4:5-6).

AHUZZATH (*ȧ*-hŭz'ăth). The adviser and friend of Abimelech, king of Gerar. He went with Abimelech to Beer-sheba to make a covenant with Isaac (Gen 26:26-31).

AI (ā'ī). A city of the Canaanites situated E of Bethel. Its name means "ruin." After Joshua had conquered Jericho, he sent men to spy out Ai. On the advice of the spies, Joshua sent 3,000 soldiers against Ai, but they suffered defeat. In distress, Joshua prayed for guidance. God answered that someone had sinned by stealing some of the devoted spoil of Jericho. Achan of Judah was singled out as the culprit and, with his family, was promptly stoned to death. Joshua then sent out 30,000 soldiers and by clever strategy captured and destroyed Ai (Josh 7-8).

Evidently a new town was built nearby, for Isaiah speaks of an Aiath through which the Assyrians marched on their way S to Jerusalem (Isa 10:28). Among those who returned from Exile were 223 from Bethel and Ai (Ezr 2:28; see Neh 7:32 where the number is 123). Nehemiah also speaks of an Aija near Bethel (Neh 11:31). Jeremiah mentions an Ai, but it was E of the Jordan in Ammonite territory (Jer 49:3).

The identification of Ai with any known site near Bethel has been a difficult problem for archaeologists. In 1933-35 Judith Marquet-Krause partially excavated a mound known as et-Tell two miles SE of Bethel, but found that though the site had been founded about 3000 B.C., it had been destroyed no later than 2000 B.C. It was occupied again after 1200 B.C., for about a century. This would mean that no city existed on this mound at Joshua's time.

Some scholars then suggested that the story of the destruction of Ai was actually that of the fall of Bethel (*q.v.*), since excavations at the village of Beitin (Bethel?) have revealed that that city was reduced to ruins by the invading Israelites (see reference to Bethel in Jud 1:22-26). On the other hand, legitimately it could be argued that ancient Ai was located elsewhere near Bethel, or that the remains of the city destroyed by Joshua had been washed or blown away, or that its ruins lay under the present village of Deir Dibwan immediately SE of et-Tell (R. K. Harrison, *Introduction to the Old Testament,* Eerdmans, 1969, pp. 121f., 177, 327ff.; John Rea, WBC, pp. 213f. at Josh 7).

G. H. L.

Et-Tell, supposed site of Ai. JR

Attempting to solve the problem of Ai, Joseph A. Callaway began in 1964 a new series of excavations at et-Tell. Four seasons of digging confirmed that the site was not occupied between 2500 and 1200 B.C. Furthermore, his investigations within Deir Dibwan and at several nearby ruins, including Khirbet Haiyan that might possibly have been Ai, revealed nothing earlier than the Herodian period. Callaway believes the large (25 acre) Early Bronze Age city commanded the trade route into the hill country from Jericho from *c.* 2900 to 2500 B.C. and may have become a center of Egyptian influence before it was burned and left a stark ruin. The Iron I Age Israelite village on et-Tell covered less than three acres and was unfortified (BA, XXVIII [1965], 26-30; JBL, LXXXVII [1968], 312-320). David Livingston has suggested a new possibility for the location of Bethel (*q.v.*) at Bireh, and that Ai may then identify with the small unnamed ruins a mile and a half SE of Bireh ("Location of Biblical Bethel and Ai Reconsidered," WTJ, XXXIII [Nov., 1970], 43).

J. R.

AIAH (ā'y*ȧ*)

1. Son of Zibeon, brother of Anah, a Horite (Gen 36:24 [Ajah]; I Chr 1:40).

2. The father of Saul's concubine Rizpah (II Sam 3:7; 21:8, 10, 11).

AIATH. *See* Ai.

AIJA. *See* Ai.

AIJALON. *See* Ajalon.

AIJELETH SHAHAR (ā'jĕ-lĕth shā'här), **AIJELETH HASH-SHAHAR** (ā'jĕ-lĕth hăsh-shā'här). Perhaps the name of a tune used by the chief musician for Ps 22. The tune name probably means "hind of the dawn." *See* Music.

AIN (ä'ēn)

1. The name of the sixteenth letter of the Heb. alphabet. *See* Alphabet.

2. In OT times, several towns bore this name, meaning "well," which was also compounded with place names in NT times. In an account of the boundaries of Israel's inheritance (Num 34:1-12; cf. Ezk 47:15-23), Ain is said to lie within the eastern boundary near Riblah and N of the Sea of Galilee.

Another Ain is designated as a city in the Negeb within Judah's portion (Josh 15:32) but also belonging to the tribe of Simeon, whose heritage was within Judah (Josh 19:7; I Chr 4:32). A parallel account in I Chr 6:59 calls this place Ashan. This city was occupied by Aaronic priests and was located near Hebron (Josh 21:16).

In the post-Exilic period, Ain appears to be identified with En-rimmon (Neh 11:29), although these places are distinctly separated in the references above. Tradition has held that Ain Karem, a village four miles W of Jerusalem, was the birthplace of John the Baptist. A spring, Ain Feshkha, on the W shore of the Dead Sea, was important in the life of the Qumran community.

G. H. L.

AIN FESHKHA (ä'ēn fĕsh'kȧ). A slightly mineral spring on the NW shores of the Dead Sea, emerging at the foot of the Judean hills which here are close to the sea. It lies about two miles S of Khirbet Qumran, at the southern extremity of the narrow plain which represents the end of the Jordan Valley. Immediately S of the spring the cliff descends steeply into the sea and blocks further progress except on foot.

A group of buildings at the spring belonging to the Essene settlement of Qumran was discovered in 1956 and excavated in 1958. These are contemporary with the main settlement, *c.* early 1st cen. B.C. to A.D. 69. The connection is clearly attested by identical pottery and coins found at the two sites. The installations can be divided into three groups of which the central, a rectangular building with inner courtyard surrounded by rooms, would seem to be partly living quarters, while the southern part was connected with agricultural affairs, and the northern, as suggested by the excavator Père de Vaux, was concerned with the tanning of hides and skins. The practice of a modest form of agriculture would certainly have been possible, for there are several smaller, slightly mineral springs there and the remains of long walls which appear to be ancient field boundaries. The soil is, however, rather salty, setting a limit to the type of vegetation which could be grown.

The suggestion that the northern group of buildings was concerned with tanning is based on the peculiar layout of cisterns, channels and shallow basins which constitute this group, and is difficult to explain in terms of ordinary everyday usage. Analyses of deposits from basins and channels do not contradict the suggestion, and experts in the trade consider the installation perfectly suitable for such a purpose; but nothing can be proved definitely. The community, however, was a self-contained one, and it is probable that they produced somewhere on the premises the skins necessary for writing material, etc., and this is certainly the most likely place for such work.

See Archaeology; Dead Sea Scrolls.

G. L. H.

The Valley of Ajalon where the sun stood still.
HFV

AIR. Used in the language of the supernatural as the lowest of the three divisions: the atmosphere or air, the sky, and the highest or third heaven (II Cor 12:2, 4). The air is the dwelling place of Satan, "the prince of the power of the air" (Eph 2:2), and of his demonic hosts (cf. Eph 6:12).

AJAH. *See* Aiah.

AJALON (ăj'ȧ-lŏn). Variant of Aijalon.

1. A valley town on the Philistine border in the Shephelah (Josh 10:12; II Chr 28:18). It is mentioned in the Amarna letters and the list of Shishak's conquests in Palestine. Ajalon is identified with modern Yalo, 13 miles NW of Jerusalem, guarding the lower end of the pass of Beth-horon. It was a Levitical city of Dan for the Kohathites (Josh 21:20, 24; I Chr 6:69). Later it was included in Benjamin (I Chr 8:13). Fortified by Rehoboam (II Chr 11:10), it was then captured by the Philistines (II Chr 28:18).

2. A village in the tribe of Zebulun, site unknown, where Elon was buried (Jud 12:12).

AKAN (ā'kăn). A Horite (Gen 36:27). *See* Jaakan.

AKELDAMA. *See* Aceldama.

AKHENATON (ä'kĕ-nä'tŏn). Succeeded his father, Amenhotep III, as ruler of Egypt *c.* 1370 B.C. He inspired the Amarna revolution (*see* Amarna, Tell el-), which displaced the older gods by the Aton, or sun disk. He deified the light of the sun, devising a new symbol for the new god: the sun disk with diverging rays radiating downward, each ending in a human hand. Some of these hands held the *ankh,* "life" symbol. There is evidence that this "solar monotheism" had its roots in the time of

Akhenaton, Nefertiti, and a daughter worship the sun disk with rays ending in human hands.
LL

A statue of Akhenaton in the Cairo Museum.
LL

Amenhotep III, and perhaps as far back as Thothmes IV.

Since Akhenaton sought to exterminate the old gods, he chiseled from the inscriptions the plural "gods" and every occurrence of the word "Amon." However, attempts to eliminate the old cults never penetrated to the masses. The priests of Amon in Thebes, the capital, stirred up trouble. As a result, Akhenaton was compelled to choose a new location for the capital near the site of modern Tell el-Amarna. Here, 300 miles N of Thebes, he built Akhetaton, "Horizon of the Aton," and occupied it in the sixth year of his reign. Aton worship was made the official state religion. The king changed his own name from Amenhotep IV, "he in whom Amon is content," to Akhenaton (variously spelled Ikhnaton), "he who is beneficial to Aton."

He married his sister, Nefertiti, a zealous devotee of Aton worship. Due to his preoccupation with the religious, literary, and artistic reforms, the great empire erected by Thothmes III crumbled. The Hittites absorbed the vassal states in Syria. Nomads overran Palestine. (Some see in this the early period of the judges following Joshua's conquest. Others believe that certain archaeological evidence would favor a later date for that event.) The Egyptian fortifications and center at Gaza were destroyed. The priests and army began to conspire against Akhenaton. He married his daughter Merit-Aton to his brother Smenkhare, and made him co-regent. Shortly after Akhenaton died, *c.* 1357–1353, he was succeeded by Tut-ankh-Amon, Nefertiti's half brother, and Enekhes-en-Amon, who returned the capital to Thebes.

A. K. H.

AKKUB (ăk′ŭb)

1. The son of Elioenai, descendant of David (I Chr 3:24).

2. A Levite who was head of a family of gatekeepers in the post-Exilic temple (Ezr 2:42; Neh 7:45; 11:19; 12:25; I Esd 5:28).

3. The name of a Nethinim family of temple servants (Ezr 2:45; I Esd 5:30).

4. An expounder of the law; a Levite (Neh 8:7; I Esd 9:48).

AKRABBIM (*ȧ*-krăb'ĭm). The name (meaning "scorpions") of the ascent of a mountain pass on the southern border of Canaan on the route up from the Arabah through the Negeb highlands to Beer-sheba (Num 34:4; Josh 15:3, RSV; Jud 1:36). *See* Hazazon-tamar.

ALABASTER. *See* Minerals.

ALAMETH (ăl'*ȧ*-mĕth). A Benjamite, the son of Becher and the grandson of Benjamin (I Chr 7:8). In RSV the name is spelled Alemeth (*q.v.*).

ALAMMELECH (*ȧ*-lăm'ē-lĕk). A town located in Asher. The exact site is unknown but probably it was on the border of Zebulun in the southern region of the plain of Acco (Josh 19:26).

ALAMOTH (ăl'*ȧ*-mŏth). A term in music, likely referring to the falsetto or maiden soprano voice, or to a musical instrument used for accompaniment (I Chr 15:20). *See* Music.

ALARM. A sound of battle, usually used in relation to blowing the trumpet for announcing war or victory (Num 10:5–6; Jer 4:19; 49:2; Zeph 1:16).

ALEMETH (ăl'ē-mĕth)

1. A descendant of King Saul. His father was either Jarah (I Chr 9:42) or Jehoaddah (I Chr 8:36).
2. Known also as Almon, a city of Benjamin (I Chr 6:60; Josh 21:18).

ALEPH (ä'lĕf). The first letter of both the Phoenician and Heb. alphabets. It is a consonant having no counterpart in the English alphabet. From aleph the Gr. *alpha,* a vowel, is derived. It is used to begin the first word of each verse in the first section of Ps 119, called the acrostic psalm. *See* Alphabet.

ALEXANDER (ăl'ĭg-zăn'dẽr). A fairly common NT name.

1. Alexander, son of Simon of Cyrene who was compelled to carry the cross for Jesus (Mk 15:21). Because of this allusion to Alexander as one known to the Christian community, it has been assumed that he and his brother became Christians.
2. An Alexander in the Sanhedrin (Acts 4:6) before whom Peter and John were brought for trial. Nothing further is known of him.
3. A leader of the Jews in Ephesus at the time of the riot against the Christians (Acts 19:33). Prompted by his fellow Jews because of his prominence, he attempted to quiet the uproar, fearing, perhaps, that the heathen would not distinguish between Jew and Christian in their fanaticism.
4. Alexander the coppersmith (II Tim 4:14), an enemy and antagonist of Paul who "did me much harm." If this warning to Timothy implies that he lived in Ephesus, this Alexander may be the same as 3, thus a fellow craftsman of the silversmiths. However, the reference may mean an opposing witness to Paul at his Roman trial. In this case, further identification would be very difficult.
5. Another Alexander in Ephesus (I Tim 1:20) is mentioned as one who had made shipwreck of his faith and had been sternly disciplined by Paul. Since the name was so common, it would be precarious to identify this fallen Christian with either 3 or 4.

P. C. J.

ALEXANDRIA (ăl'ĭg-zăn'drĭ-*ȧ*). An important Gr. city founded by Alexander the Great in 332 B.C. and built around a small Egyptian town called Rakote, dating back to 1300 B.C. It is located near the point where the western branch of the Nile empties into the Mediterranean. With two spacious harbors, it became a famous commercial center, exporting Egyptian grain to Rome and serving as a focal point for trade with India, Arabia, and parts of Africa.

Alexander never saw the completed city, but his body was brought there from Perdiccas for interment. His Egyptian territories were taken over by his general Ptolemy, who left Memphis and made Alexandria his capital and founded the dynasty which continued until the death of Cleopatra (30 B.C.). Alexandria reached its height under the first three Ptolemies: Ptolemy I (Soter), 323–285 B.C.; Ptolemy II (Philadelphus), 285–247 B.C.; and Euergetes, 247–222 B.C.

A "museum" was established and became a center of learning and culture. Like a modern university, the museum had research professors and included lecture halls, laboratories, observatories, parks, zoos, and a library approaching 700,000 volumes. Jewish legend says the Septuagint translation of the OT was made especially for the museum.

Other famous structures included the Pharos lighthouse, towering nearly 450 feet high over the harbor; the Temple of Serapis, which was

Alexandrian waterfront and skyline. Egyptian State Tourist Administration

designed for the worship of the god which combined the Osiris cult with the Apis (bull) cult; the royal tombs, and the palace in the Rakote sector. Here the apocryphal book of Wisdom was written, and the famous Philo tried to reconcile Gr. philosophy and Heb. religion in the 1st Christian cen. *See* Philo.

Famous men of Alexandria included the mathematicians Euclid, Eratosthenes and Hipparchus, and the astronomers Aristarchus and Claudius Ptolemy, who respectively viewed the universe as heliocentric and geocentric.

By the 1st Christian cen. Alexandria was the second city of the Roman Empire, with a population of at least 600,000. It was the home of Apollos (Acts 18:24), and from its port sailed two of the grain ships used by the centurion to transport Paul to Rome (Acts 27:6; 28:11). It had a large Jewish community because Alexander had treated the Jews kindly, and some Jews from Alexandria returning to Jerusalem had formed a synagogue (Acts 6:9). There was a tradition, according to Eusebius, that John Mark founded the church at Alexandria, but this lacks support.

Following in the footsteps of Philo's allegorical method of interpreting the Scriptures, early converts to Christianity from Judaism turned to Gnostic (*see* Gnosticism) forms of thinking and formed a school at Alexandria under the direction of Basilides. Clement of Alexandria (*c.* A.D. 150–*c.* 220) and his foremost pupil Origen (*c.* 185–*c.* 254) directed a Christian catechetical school that was more orthodox and more closely attached to the church at large, although it, too, preferred allegorical or "spiritual" interpretation. The Epistle to the Hebrews *(q.v.),* because of its use of terminology beloved at Alexandria and its frequent reference to the OT, has been associated with an Alexandrian background, perhaps even with Apollos.

A. K. H.

ALEXANDRIAN (ăl′ĭg-zăn′drĭ-*ȧn*). A native of the Egyptian city of Alexandria (*q.v.*), which numbered more than 600,000 inhabitants in the first Christian century. The Alexandrians were quite cosmopolitan, as their location and previous history would prescribe. Most of the inhabitants of the city were either Egyptians (in the sector of Rakote), Greeks (in Brucheum), Romans, or Jews (in the eastern sector). The latter, comprising about one-fourth of the population, had equal rights with Greeks until Caligula took them away. The great museum, with its eminent scholars, had given the city two centuries of cultural and literary pre-eminence. As a result of the siege of Alexandria by Julius Caesar, when much of the library in the museum was burned, this importance had about disappeared by the end of Cleopatra's reign, only to be replaced 200 years later by another period of greatness when Alexandria led the world in philosophy and theology.

A. K. H.

ALGUM, ALMUG. *See* Plants.

ALIAH (*ȧ*-lī′ă). A duke of Edom, descended from Esau (I Chr 1:51). The name is also spelled Alvah (*q.v.*).

ALIAN (*ȧ*-lī′ăn). A son of Shobal in Edom (I Chr 1:40). The name is also spelled Alvan *(q.v.).*

ALIEN. A foreigner (*q.v.*), one who is denied the privileges of a specific group to which he is not considered to be a member; sometimes the sense of the word stranger (KJV).

ALLEGORY. A "prolonged metaphor" (longer and more detailed) in which objects or events are understood as symbolic or typical of meanings in another realm of discourse. An allegory is distinguished from a parable in that an allegory makes each detail representative of truth or meaning, whereas a parable stresses one central truth. A hard and fast line is difficult to draw, since many parables lend themselves to allegorizing. The allegory differs from the fable in that it is more true to life and fact than is the fable, in which animals or objects may speak or act in human ways (cf. Jotham's fable of the trees choosing a king, Jud 9:7–15).

The word occurs but once in the KJV (Gal 4:24, *allēgoroumena,* "being allegorized") in connection with the application of the history of Sarah and Hagar to the covenant of grace in contrast with the covenant of law. The Gr. word is derived from *allos,* "other," and *agoreuō,* "to speak in a place of assembly"; and came to mean speaking not in the primary sense of the words but in such a way that the stated facts illustrate principles.

Other biblical allegories occur in Ps 80:8–19; Isa 5:1–7, and in the allegory of the sower and the seed, Lk 8:4–15. The door of the fold and the Good Shepherd of Jn 10:1–16, 26–29 are properly regarded as allegories. It must be noted, however, that the meaning of *parabolē,* "parable, a placing beside" (derived from *paraballō,* "to throw or lay beside, to compare") may in fact include what is meant by allegory. RSV translates Heb. *māshāl* (KJV, "parable") with "allegory" in Ezk 17:2; 24:3. Outside the Bible, Bunyan's *Pilgrim's Progress* is the best-known example of a religious allegory.

The allegorical interpretation of the OT became prominent in Alexandria with Philo, and was taken over by such Christian Fathers as Justin, Clement, and Origen. Origen distinguished three levels of truth in Scripture: the literal or "fleshly," the moral, and the spiritual. These were said to correspond to man's body, soul, and spirit. Jerome introduced the use of allegory into Roman Christianity, but it was largely rejected by the reformers. Unrestrained allegorizing is subject to the obvious abuses of excessive subjectivity and imagination.

It must be recognized, however, that the NT

itself views parts of OT history allegorically; e.g., the Church is the new Israel, delivered from bondage to sin in a new Passover, receiving a new covenant in Christ's blood, subject to a new law given from a new mount, and led into a second rest by a new Joshua. Paul so speaks in I Cor 10:1-12 (cf. also Heb 3–4). *See* Parable; Type.

W. T. P.

ALLELUIA. This word occurs only in Rev 19:1, 3, 4, 6, KJV (ASV and RSV spell the expression hallelujah). It is a transliteration of the Gr. *allēlouia,* which in turn is a transliteration of the Heb. *hal^{e}lûyāh,* a liturgical expression which means "praise the Lord." In the LXX, the Gr. word occurs as the title of Ps 104–106, 110–118, 134–135, 145–150. It is found within the LXX text only in Ps 150:6. The word has come directly into the English language without change as a religious expression. Within the psalms to which it is attached there is an emphasis on the power and wisdom of God as these are witnessed to in His deeds.

ALLIANCE. Although this word does not occur in the KJV or ASV, it does appear four times in the RSV. Its basic idea is conveyed by the Heb. noun *b^{e}rît,* meaning "league," "confederacy," "covenant"; the verbs *ḥātan,* meaning "affinity," "join in marriage"; and *nûaḥ,* meaning "to be at rest," "to be confederate"; and the noun *qesher,* which usually has the negative meaning "conspiracy," "treason."

The earliest alliance described in Scripture was between Abraham and the Amorites Mamre, Eshcol, and Aner. They joined forces long enough to rescue Lot from his captors (Gen 14:13-24). Abraham entered a more lasting alliance with Abimelech at Beer-sheba (Gen 21:22-32), as did Isaac later (Gen 26:26-31).

No prohibition or stigma was placed against these early alliances; but the Mosaic law later repeatedly placed a ban against foreign alliances, particularly with Canaanites. The prohibition against joining the Canaanites was based chiefly upon religious grounds. The newly formed nation was as yet too weak to withstand the enticements of Canaan's sex worship, so God through Moses sought to isolate Israel. The pagan altars, temples, and images were torn down lest the young people become ensnared by Baalism (Ex 23:32-33; 34:12-13). To protect the Israelites further from this corruption, intermarriage was prohibited, lest in the intimacy of marriage the pagan idolator corrupt the Israelite (Deut 7:2-4). After the Conquest, when Israel became entangled with waywardness, the reason for God's judgment upon them was traced back to Israel's violation of this ban (Jud 2:2).

Besides the alliance which the Gibeonites by trickery concluded with Joshua, there were no official ties with other nations until the time of Solomon. David had friendly relationships, based on personal covenants, with the kings of Moab, Ammon, Gath, and Hamath; but it seems that Solomon was the first to establish an international league with a foreign nation. This was done with Hiram of Tyre in connection with building the temple and operating fleets in the Red Sea and in the Indian Ocean (I Kgs 5:1-18; 9:26-28). The full implications of this league did not come to light until the marriage of Ahab with Jezebel, a daughter of a king of Tyre. Baalism immediately took over the religious life of Israel but was vigorously opposed by Elijah, Elisha, and Jehu. Judah felt some evil results of this marriage when Jezebel's daughter, Athaliah, became queen of Judah.

In the triangular quarrels of Judah, Israel, and Syria, several leagues were forged. At one time, Asa of Judah purchased the aid of Ben-hadad of Syria against Baasha of Israel (I Kgs 15:18-19; II Chr 16:3). Later, Ahab of Israel gained the help of Jehoshaphat of Judah against Syria (I Kgs 22; II Chr 18:1). After Ahab's death, Ahaziah of Israel sought to join Jehoshaphat in building a merchant fleet, but God was displeased and the fleet was destroyed (II Chr 20:35-37). In Isaiah's time, Rezin of Syria and Pekah of Israel joined against Judah, but Ahaz of Judah purchased the help of Assyria, which quickly destroyed Syria, reduced Israel to the status of a satellite, and finally made Ahaz its puppet (II Kgs 16:5-8). The last tragic alliance was between Zedekiah and Egypt, which act brought Babylon against Judah and utterly destroyed Jerusalem (Jer 37:1-8; Ezk 17:15-17). *See* Covenant.

G. H. L.

ALLON (ăl'ŏn)

1. A Simeonite prince, a descendant of Shemaiah (I Chr 4:37).

2. In Josh 19:33 it is better translated (see ASV, RSV) as a common noun meaning "oak." The word "plain" in Jud 4:11 should also be rendered "oak" as in ASV and RSV.

ALLON-BACHUTH (ăl'ŏn-băk'ŭth). Rebekah's nurse Deborah was buried under this tree (its name meaning "oak of weeping"), near Bethel (Gen 35:8). It also may have been the site of the palm tree of the prophetess Deborah located between Ramah and Bethel (Jud 4:5).

ALLOTMENT. The terms "allotment," "inheritance" (*q.v.*) and "portion" (*q.v.*) are used of land and, by extension, of one's position in life.

Josh 13–19 describes the allotment assigned to each of the Israelite tribes in Canaan following the conquest. Reuben, Gad, and half the tribe of Manasseh had settled E of the Jordan, but the remaining nine and a half tribes were assigned land in the area W of the Jordan and the Dead Sea (cf. Num 32; 33:54; 34:13). Since the Promised Land belonged to the Lord, He had the right to assign it as He chose. Eleazar, the priest at Shiloh, and Joshua, Moses' successor, in cooperation with the tribal leaders (Josh

14:1-2; 19:51), determined the will of God and revealed to the people their tribal inheritance. The means of determining the allotment is not specified. It may have been by the use of Urim and Thummim, two stones in the breastplate or pouch on the ephod of the high priest (Ex 28:28-30).

The land of Canaan is described as the "lot of the righteous" (Ps 125:3). The tribe of Levi had no territorial allotment, but Levitical cities were established among the tribes (Josh 21).

C. F. P.

ALMIGHTY. Used 48 times in the OT, of which 31 are in the book of Job, to translate Heb. *shaddai*. *See* God, Names and Titles of; El.

ALMODAD (ăl-mō'dăd). A people who lived in southern Arabia descended from the first son of Joktan (Gen 10:26; I Chr 1:20).

ALMON (ăl'mŏn). A Benjamite city in which the priests lived (Josh 21:18). It is also called Alemeth (I Chr 6:60).

ALMON-DIBLATHAIM (ăl'mŏn-dĭb'lȧ-thā'ĭm). A stopping place in the journeyings of Israel after Dibon-gad and before the mountains of Abarim (Num 33:46-47). Probably the same as Beth-diblathaim (*q.v.*; Jer 48:22).

ALMOND. *See* Plants.

ALMS, ALMSDEEDS. These words occur in the NT only, as the translation of the Gr. *eleēmosynē*, derived from *eleos*, "mercy"; *eleeō*, "to show mercy"; and *eleēmōn*, "merciful." The Gr. word means "pity, mercy, kindness," as well as the kind act or benefaction itself, in which the effect is taken for the cause. Essentially, alms is relief to the poor in the modern sense of charity. ("Charity" in the KJV is a translation of *agapē*, "love," and is a much broader term, as e.g., I Cor 13:3.) "Alms" and "almsdeeds" are now archaic as English words.

The OT uses *ṣedeq* or *ṣᵉdāqâ*, "righteousness," "justice," in a number of instances to mean the duty of caring for the poor (e.g., Deut 24:13; Ps 24:5; Prov 10:2; 11:4; Mic 6:5), and this term is translated *eleēmosunē* in the LXX of Deut 25:15 and Dan 4:27. The propriety of this usage is seen in view of the constant OT concern for widows. the fatherless, strangers, and the poor—a complete contrast with ancient Gr. and Rom. attitudes. To do what the law so clearly required was *ṣᵉdāqâ*, "righteousness."

The law of Moses was very definite on the care of the poor. In the Book of the Covenant (Ex 20–23), the poor were protected against usury and the taking of garments in pledge for loans (Ex 22:25-27; cf. Lev 25:35-36), and were provided for in the sabbatical year (Ex 23:11). In the Holiness Code (Lev 17–22) provision was made that gleanings be left in the field for the poor (Lev 19:9-10; cf. Ruth 2) and that wages be paid promptly (Lev 19:13). Later provisions in Leviticus protected the property of the poor from permanent alienation (25:25-30). Deuteronomy is replete with directions for a second tithe for the poor (14:28-29); generosity in providing for their needs (15:7, 11); provision for them at the stated festivals (16:11-14); and permission to satisfy hunger in vineyard and field (23:24-25). See also Deut 24:13, 19-22; 26:12-13.

Job in his "oath of purgation" cites his generosity to the poor (Job 29:12-16). Special blessing was promised those who assisted the oppressed (Neh 8:10; Prov 19:17). The prophets declare the care of the poor to be God's will (Isa 58:4-7; Ezk 18:7; Dan 4:27; Amos 2:6-7).

In the NT the same concern is seen. Jesus gives directions for almsgiving as characteristic of the religious spirit (Mt 6:1-4). Luke particularly stresses the Lord's sympathy for the poor and outcast (Lk 3:11; 6:30; 12:33). The early church viewed almsgiving as an evidence of Christian love (Acts 9:36; 10:2, 4; Rom 12:13; Eph 4:28; I Tim 6:18; Heb 13:16; I Jn 3:17-19). The NT gives particular attention to the motive in giving in relation to ability (Mk 12:42-44; II Cor 8:12; Acts 11:29).

W. T. P.

ALMUG TREE. *See* Plants: Algum.

ALOES. *See* Plants.

ALOTH (ā'lŏth). Used only in I Kgs 4:16. *See* Bealoth.

ALPHA AND OMEGA (ăl'fȧ, ō-mĕg'ȧ). The first and last letters of the Gr. alphabet, used in Rev 1:8; 21:6 as a title of God, and in Rev 22:13 of Christ. In the latter reference the added phrases give the meaning of the expression: "the beginning and the end, the first and the last." Additional parallel phrases indicating the same basic concept appear subjoined to the expression, such as, "the Lord, which is, and which was, and which is to come, the Almighty" (Rev 1:8). Thus is signified the sovereignty of Christ, as of God in Isa 44:6; 48:12.

As the Alpha, He alone is in possession of the knowledge of the origin of the earth and man; and having absolute authority over them, He alone has the power to make all things new (Rev 21:5-6). As the Omega, the last, He is in possession of the future and alone can "tell us what is yet to be" (Isa 44:7, RSV). He can banish death and Hades (Rev 20:14), punish the wicked eternally (Rev 21:8), and determine the final reward for all men (Rev 22:12; Jn 5:22).

The importance of this term being applied to Christ (Rev 22:13) cannot be overlooked. In other terms the NT concurs with John's designation by asserting the primacy of Christ in and over all creation (Col 1:15-18; Heb 1:1-3; Mt

28:18), His absolute power over life and resurrection (Jn 5:21, 25-26, 28-29), and His sovereignty in the final judgment (Jn 5:22, 27). Rev 1:17-18 asserts that the firstness and lastness of Christ are supremely validated by His resurrection from the dead.

W. M. D. and A. F. J.

ALPHABET. An alphabet is a series of letters which represent significant phonetic values arranged in a socially accepted order. The word alphabet is a combination of the names of the first two letters of the Gr. alphabet, *alpha* and *beta*.

Alphabetic writing was preceded by other methods of written communication. Pictures etched in ancient caves conveyed meaning, although the words they were intended to represent cannot be read. By 3000 B.C. two systems of writing, both based on pictorial characters, developed in the Near East. The Egyptian system of picture writing, or hieroglyphs, so called because of their association with the priesthood, contained both syllabic and alphabetic elements. Pictures could represent sounds, corresponding in some instances to individual letters of later alphabets. The Egyptians, however, never dropped the nonalphabetic elements from their writing system, so that they cannot be credited with actually producing an alphabet.

The Sumerians, who were dominant in the Tigris-Euphrates valley during the last half of the 4th and the 3rd mil. before Christ, used a system of wedge-shaped characters impressed in clay or cut into stone. Originally a system of picture writing, the cuneiform characters, as the wedges are now called, developed into a system of syllables and word signs in which the earlier pictorial element lost its significance. The cuneiform system of writing was adopted by the successors to the Sumerians—Assyrians, Babylonians, Hittites, and other peoples of the Fertile Crescent. *See* Writing.

Discoveries at Serabit el-Khadem in the Sinai Peninsula show that slaves of the Egyptians who worked the turquoise mines used alphabetic writing in the early 15th cen. B.C. A dagger with an alphabetic inscription dating to the 16th cen. B.C. has been discovered at Tell ed-Duweir (biblical Lachish), and comparable material has been excavated at Gezer, Shechem, Megiddo, and Beth-shemesh.

In 1929 documents in an alphabetic cuneiform script were discovered at Ras Shamra (*q.v.*), ancient Ugarit, in northern Syria. The Canaanite cuneiform alphabet seems to have been invented by someone who knew both the alphabetic principle and the cuneiform system of writing. By combining both ideas he invented an alphabet which would be suitable for writing on clay tablets. Hundreds of texts were found at Ras Shamra, dating from the 15th and the 14th cen. B.C. Other texts using the same alphabet were subsequently discovered at Beth-shemesh and in the vicinity of Mount Tabor. In 1949, Professor C. F. A. Schaeffer found at

The Ahiram Sarcophagus, from Gebal, with an alphabetic inscription from the eleventh century B.C. National Museum, Beirut

Ras Shamra a tablet of the 14th cen. B.C. listing the 30 letters of the Canaanite cuneiform alphabet in their alphabetic order. The arrangement of the letters is similar to that used for the Phoenician or NW Semitic alphabet, with which the Sinai script is related.

The Old Hebrew (palaeo-Hebrew) script is the form of Heb. writing which is similar to that used by the Phoenicians. A royal inscription of King Shaphat-baal of Gebal (Byblos) in this alphabet dates back to 1600 B.C. The sarcophagus of a Phoenician king named Ahiram contains an inscription which tells how the son of Ahiram made the coffin for his father "as an abode forever." Ahiram, whose name is similar to the biblical Hiram of Tyre, probably reigned in the late 11th cen. B.C.

The oldest extant Heb. writing, the Gezer Calendar, dated around the 10th cen. B.C., is written in this Old Hebrew-Phoenician type script, as is the Moabite Stone (*c.* 840 B.C.), which gives the Moabite version of the revolt mentioned in II Kgs 1:1; 3:4-5.

A variant of the Old Hebrew-Phoenician method of writing was used by the Arameans, whose alphabet used "square letters" in contrast to the more angular shape of the NW Semitic alphabet. About 200 B.C. the Hebrews, influenced by the Aramaic language which was commonly spoken by post-Exilic Jews, adopted the square form of the letters. With few exceptions, this is the form of the alphabet used in the Dead Sea Scrolls, dated from the 2nd cen. B.C. to the 1st cen. after Christ. The square letters are used in printed Heb. Bibles and in other printed literature in Heb.

According to Gr. tradition, the alphabet was brought to Boeotia in central Greece by a Phoenician prince of Tyre named Cadmus. Since *kedem* is the Semitic word for east, the tradition with the name Cadmus derived from the root *K-d-m* seems to reflect the fact that Greece received her alphabet from the east, i.e., Phoenicia. The Semitic origin of the Gr. alphabet is further illustrated by the names of

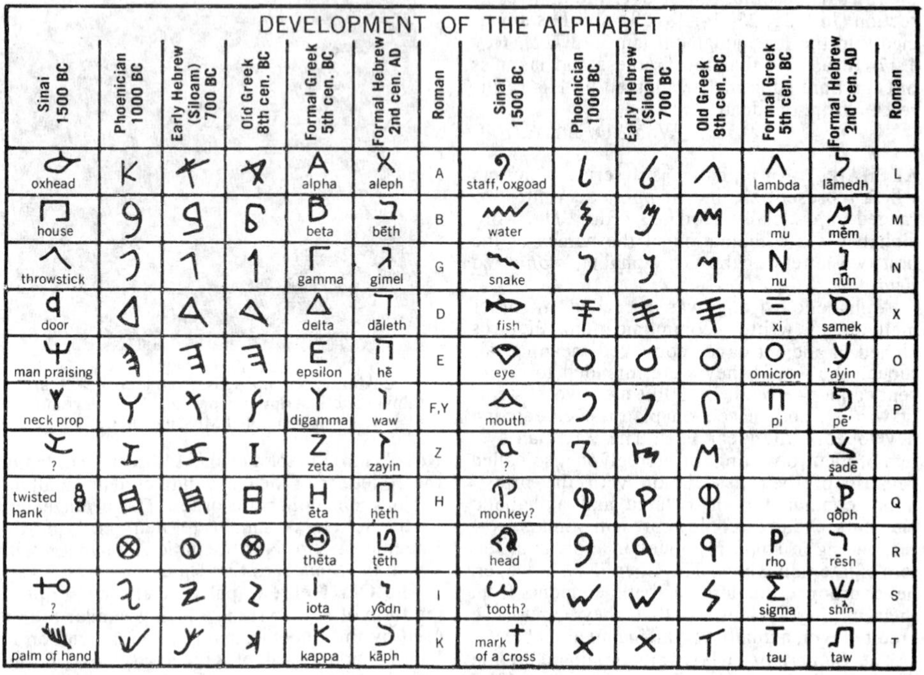
DEVELOPMENT OF THE ALPHABET
Sinai 1500 BC
Phoenician 1000 BC
Early Hebrew (Siloam) 700 BC
Old Greek 8th cen. BC
Formal Greek 5th cen. BC
Formal Hebrew 2nd cen. AD
Roman
oxhead
alpha
aleph
A
house
beta
bēth
B
throwstick
gamma
gimel
G
door
delta
dāleth
D
man praising
epsilon
hē
E
neck prop
digamma
waw
F,Y
?
zeta
zayin
Z
twisted hank
ēta
hēth
H
thēta
ṭēth
?
iota
yōdn
I
palm of hand
kappa
kāph
K
staff, oxgoad
lambda
lāmedh
L
water
mu
mēm
M
snake
nu
nūn
N
fish
xi
samek
X
eye
omicron
'ayin
O
mouth
pi
pē'
P
?
ṣadē
monkey?
qōph
Q
head
rho
rēsh
R
tooth?
sigma
shin
S
mark of a cross
tau
taw
T

Chart showing development of alphabet. JR

the letters. Gr. *alpha, beta, gamma* are clearly parallel to Semitic *aleph, beth, gimmel.* The words mean nothing in Gr. except the letters they name, whereas in Heb. they reflect early picture writing when they represented, respectively, an ox, a house, and a camel. It is thought that the Greeks learned of the alphabet through trade with the Phoenicians. After it proved useful for commercial purposes, it was adopted for literary use. By 700 B.C. even painters of pottery jars had learned the art of writing.

While cuneiform writing continued in use to the 1st cen. B.C., the simplicity of alphabetic writing caused it ultimately to displace other systems. Cuneiform and hieroglyphic writing were used by learned and priestly classes, but all normal persons could readily learn to communicate through alphabetic writing. All the biblical writers seem to have used alphabetic writing—Hebrew, Aramaic, or Greek. By the time of the judges, a young man whom Gideon met by chance could write down the names of the chief men of his city (Jud 8:14, RSV). *See* Languages; Writing.

Bibliography. W. F. Albright, "The Early Alphabetic Inscriptions from Sinai and Their Decipherment," BASOR #110 (1948), pp. 6–22; *The Proto-Sinaitic Inscriptions and Their Decipherment,* Harvard Theological Studies #22, Cambridge, Mass.: Harvard Univ. Press, 1968. Frank M. Cross, Jr., "The Evolution of the Proto-Canaanite Alphabet," BASOR #134 (1954), pp. 15–24. David Diringer, *The Alphabet,* New York: Philosophical Library, 1948. Ignace J. Gelb, *A Study of Writing,* Chicago: Univ. of Chicago Press, 1952.

C. F. P.

ALPHAEUS (ăl-fē'ŭs). One of many Gr. names in common use by Jews in 1st cen. Palestine.

1. The father of Levi the tax collector (Mk 2:14).

2. The father of James, one of the disciples of Jesus (Mk 3:18). The identification with either Cleophas (Jn 19:25) or Cleopas (Lk 24:18) seems unlikely. On these problems *see further* under Cleophas, Cleopas, James, Levi, Matthew.

ALTAR. In the Heb. OT, the usual word for altar is *mizbēaḥ,* "place of sacrifice," which is derived from the verb *zābaḥ,* "to slaughter," "to sacrifice." In Ezr 7:17 there occurs the Aramaic *madbaḥ,* formed from the same word. Such Aramaic words may be expected after the return from the Captivity. Two other terms for altar seem to be derived from the Akkad. language. In Ezk 43:15–16 the expressions *har'ēl,* "mountain of God"(?) and *'ărî'ēl* (of uncertain meaning) are translated "altar" in KJV, and "altar hearth" in ASV.

Patriarchal Altars

As far as is recorded, Noah is the first person in the OT to have built an altar. Upon it he offered as a burnt offering one animal from each kind of clean animal and bird which had been preserved in the ark. Abraham built an altar at Shechem, one near Bethel (Gen 12:6–8), and one at "Mamre, which is in Hebron" (Gen 13:18). Later, he built one on Mount Moriah where God provided a substitute sacrifice for Isaac (Gen 22:9–13). According to the record, Isaac built only one altar, that at Beer-sheba (Gen 26:23–25), whereas Jacob erected one at Shechem (Gen 33:18, 20) and one at Bethel (Gen 35:1–7). No description is given of the size, shape, or construction of any of these altars.

Mosaic Altars

Apart from the altars of the tabernacle, Moses is said to have reared an altar after the battle with the Amalekites (Ex 17:15), and also after the revelation of the covenant law on Sinai (Ex 24:4–5). Beside this altar 12 pillars, one for each tribe, were erected, and upon the altar burnt offerings were placed. The Pentateuch also mentions two other occasions when altars were built apart from the tabernacle. Balaam, a non-Israelite, built seven altars at each of three different places, and upon each altar sacrificed a bullock and a ram (Num 23:1, 14, 29). Moses instructed the elders of Israel to erect an altar of unhewn stones on Mount Ebal. Upon this altar they were to sacrifice peace offerings, and on large plastered stones near the altar they were to inscribe the words of the law (Deut 27:4–8). Joshua carried out this injunction faithfully several years later (Josh 8:30–32).

Though only the construction of the altar on Mount Ebal is described in these passages, the Pentateuch contains several sets of instructions concerning the building of altars. After Moses came down from Mount Sinai, he told the people that altars could be constructed either of earth or of unhewn stones. Steps could not be used with either type, lest the nakedness of the priest be exposed (Ex 20:24–26). The altar on Mount Ebal was of this kind and, presumably, also those built by the tribes of Reuben, Gad and the half tribe of Manasseh (Josh 22:10, 34), by Gideon (Jud 6:26–27), Samuel (I Sam 7:17), Saul (I Sam 14:35), David (II Sam 24:18, 25), and Elijah (I Kgs 18:30).

Tabernacle and Temple Altars

Moses received word from the Lord that the tabernacle should have two altars: the brazen altar of burnt offering, which was located in the courtyard, and the altar of incense in the holy place.

The brazen altar, built by Bezaleel (Ex 27:1–8; 31:2–5; 38:1–7), was made of acacia wood and was covered with bronze. It was seven and one-half feet square, four and one-half feet high, and had horns on its upper four corners. Within, it was equipped with a grating of bronze which had four bronze rings, one at each corner. The altar could be transported by means of two wooden poles overlaid with bronze, which were slipped through rings on the sides of the altar.

Canaanite altar at Megiddo, dating to about 2700 B.C. HFV

The brazen altar was placed just inside the main entrance of the courtyard and was in direct line with the door of the tabernacle. Upon it were sacrificed the animal and cereal offerings of Israel (Ex 40:6, 29). When the altar was consecrated, a sin offering was made for its atonement each day for seven days. It was also anointed with oil. After its consecration, the altar was holy, and whatever touched it was regarded as holy (Ex 29:36–37, 44; 30:28; 40:10; Lev 8:11; Num 7:10–88).

The brazen altar of burnt offering was also a place for refuge for the innocent man accused of murder (Ex 21:12–14; I Kgs 1:50; 2:28). He could plead for mercy by holding on to the horns of the altar.

The brazen altar which Solomon designed for the temple was larger than that in the tabernacle. It measured 20 cubits (30 feet) square and 10 cubits (15 feet) high (II Chr 4:1). It was repaired by Asa (II Chr 15:8), but was replaced by Ahaz, who constructed a new altar after an Assyrian model (II Kgs 16:14–17). Hezekiah ordered the altar to be restored and cleansed for service (II Chr 29:18–24). Manasseh at first ignored the brazen altar, but in later life restored it to its proper function (II Chr 33:16).

Evidently the brazen altar was destroyed by the Babylonians after the fall of Jerusalem (II Kgs 25:14). Before the second temple was built, the returned exiles rebuilt the altar in the courtyard and reestablished its proper service (Ezr 3:1–6).

While in captivity, Ezekiel envisioned a great altar in a future temple, and recorded its size and shape in some detail. There were to be three stages. The base would be 24 feet square, the second stage 21 feet square, and the final stage 18 feet square. The total height would be about 16 feet. Steps would ascend to the altar on its E side (Ezk 43:13-27). Some speculate that rather than a vision of a future temple this is a description of the altar built by Ahaz which was still standing in the temple court at the time Ezekiel was taken away as a captive.

Limestone altar of incense, Megiddo. Palestine Archaeological Museum, Jerusalem

The golden altar, or altar of incense, was much smaller than the brazen altar. It was covered with gold, and was placed in the holy place of the tabernacle before the curtain of the holy of holies. The frame of the altar of incense was made of acacia wood measuring one and one-half feet square by three feet high. Its upper four corners had horns or projections and its sides had rings. Through the rings were slipped wooden poles covered with gold for carrying the altar. On it the high priest offered incense morning and evening. Once a year the high priest made atonement by placing blood upon its horns (Ex 30:1-10; 40:5, 26-27). After the sons of Korah had rebelliously offered incense contrary to the law and were punished by death, their bronze censers were fashioned into a cover for the golden altar as a memorial (Num 16:36-40).

Solomon made an altar of cedar, overlaid it with gold, and placed it in the holy place of the temple (I Kgs 6:20, 22; 7:48). However, David is said to have given his son the specifications for the temple and its furniture, including the altar of incense (I Chr 28:18). This altar is not mentioned again in the OT. Presumably, it also was destroyed when Jerusalem was captured by the Babylonians. Although the OT has left no record to this effect, it is likely the second temple was equipped with an altar of incense, since the NT speaks of such an altar in Herod's temple that followed it.

Nonbiblical Jewish Literature

References to the altars of the temple appear in Jewish literature of the intertestamental period. In the Letter of Aristeas (100 B.C.), the author makes the observation that water was piped to the base of the brazen altar from underground cisterns in order that the blood of the animal sacrifices might be washed away (*The Apocrypha and Pseudepigrapha of the Old Testament,* ed. by R. H. Charles, Oxford: Clarendon Press, II, 83-122). Antiochus, the Gr. ruler of Syria and Palestine (175-163 B.C.), carried away the golden altar and other valuables from the temple, and erected a sacrilege, an image of Jupiter, by the altar of burnt offering (I Macc 1:21, 54). After defeating the Greeks, Judas the Maccabee tore apart the altar of burnt offering and built a new one of unhewn stones (I Macc 4:44-49; *ibid.,* I, 59-124).

Both altars of the tabernacle are described by Josephus (*Ant.* iii. 6.8). His description of the altar of incense differs from the scriptural record only in one detail. Josephus noted that at the top of the golden altar there was a golden grate edged with a golden crown to which the rings were attached. In another place, Josephus (*Wars* v. 5.5-6) observed that in the temple of his day (1st cen. A.D.) 13 kinds of incense were offered on the golden altar in order to honor God as the possessor of all things. Also, he noted that the altar of burnt sacrifice was 75 feet square at the base and 23 feet high. A gradual incline approached it from the E. In the Mishnah (treatise "Middoth" III, trans. by H. Danby, pp. 593-595) mention is made that the measurements in Ezk 43:13-27 are from the center to the outer edge, so each figure should be doubled, i.e., the base should be 48 feet square instead of 24, etc. Further, the men who returned from the Exile added a six foot extension to the S and to the W sides of the base. The inclined ramp is located on the S side of the altar and is said to be 24 feet wide and 48 feet long.

Altars Found by Archaeologists

In Palestine, archaeologists have identified many objects as altars. The use of altars of burnt offering and of incense was widespread among the pagan non-Israelite people in ancient Palestine and in neighboring countries. From a small Early Bronze Age shrine built against the inner side of the city wall at Ai, archaeologists have brought to light an altar of plastered stones.

At Megiddo the remains of three temples from *c.* 1900 B.C. were unearthed. Against the back wall of each was a raised mud-brick platform serving as an altar table not only for offerings but also for images of the gods. In the temple courtyard in obvious relation to these buildings was found a round mound of stones and rubble which was used for burnt offerings. It is six and a half feet high and 29 feet in diameter, with six steps on one side. The period of 1475–1225 B.C. at Lachish yielded three successive temples, each with benches and mud-brick altars. The latest of these was approached by means of three steps at one side and measured about 29 inches square and three feet high. An irregular mound with steps was found in a Late Bronze temple courtyard at Bethshan. At Hazor about 1300 B.C., an altar was hewn from a huge block of limestone, about 40 inches square and 90 inches long and weighing around five tons. It had a place for burnt offerings and a basin for either blood or liquids. Clay stands from many locations have been thought to have been incense burners.

From the 10th cen. B.C. have come relatively small cut stone altars, some with horns on their upper corners. Most are from Megiddo, Tell Beit Mirsim, and Shechem. These have been regarded as altars of incense. In II Chr 34:4, 7; Ezk 6:4, 6 and other passages the Heb. word *ḥammanîm,* translated "images," is found. This is now known to refer to small stone incense altars with four feet, of the 6th to the 5th cen. One such altar inscribed in Aramaic, beginning with the word "incense offering," came to light at Lachish.

Significance and Abuse of Hebrew Altars

The altars built for the tabernacle and for the temple, then, were not completely different from those of Israel's neighbors, but their function in worship was brought in line with the covenant concept of the relationship between God and Israel. The altar of burnt offering was the place where sacrifices for atonement and communion were to be offered. The golden altar was where God's majesty was honored by means of burning incense.

Actually, the sanctuary altars were not always employed in the worship of Israel's true God. Frequently, idolatry polluted the spiritual life of the Israelites, and the sacrifices offered on the altars became a snare to them (Amos 3:14; 5:21–22; Isa 1:11–13; 27:9). When Jeroboam formed the rebellious ten tribes into a nation, he built altars and sacrificed to the calves which he had made (I Kgs 12:32). This act was condemned by a prophet of God (I Kgs 13:3–5). Ahab set up an altar to Baal in Samaria, an act which angered God (I Kgs 16:32; cf. Hos 8:11; Jer 17:2). Josiah was commended because he destroyed pagan religious tools

A small altar in the theater at Salamis, Cyprus. Sacrifices were commonly made before dramas were performed. HFV

which were used at the temple altars, and also destroyed unlawful altars which were located outside Jerusalem (II Kgs 23:4–20).

In the New Testament

The Gr. word for altar most frequently appearing in the NT is *thysiastērion.* Referring to the altar of burnt offering in the temple, it occurs in Mt 5:23–24; 23:18–20, 35; Lk 11:51; Rom 11:3; I Cor 9:13; 10:18; Heb 7:13; Rev 11:1. But in a few places altar has a spiritual sense (Heb 13:10; Rev 6:9). In reference to the golden altar of incense, this Gr. term appears in Lk 1:11 and a very similar word in Heb 9:4 to designate the altar in the earthly temple built by Herod. But elsewhere the golden altar is symbolic of intercessory prayer (Rev 8:3–5) or of judgment (Rev 9:13; cf. Rev 14:18; 16:7). In order to explain the seeming contradiction in Heb 9:4, which states that the golden altar of incense stood in the holy of holies, it has been suggested that on the Day of Atonement the high priest brought this altar inside the veil for that part of the ceremony involving the burning of incense before the ark (Lev 16:13).

Another Gr. word for altar, *bōmos,* is used in Acts 17:23 for a pagan altar in Athens. An altar of this type has been unearthed in Ephesus.

Bibliography. W. F. Albright, *Archaeology and the Religion of Israel,* Baltimore: Johns Hopkins Press, 1946. G. Cornfeld, *Adam to Daniel,* New York: Macmillan, 1961. W. Harold Mare, "The Greek Altar in the NT and Intertestamental Periods," *Grace Journal,* X(1969), 26–35. Roland de Vaux, *Ancient Israel,* New York: McGraw-Hill, 1961. G. E. Wright, *Biblical Archaeology,* Philadelphia: Westminster, 1957.

G. H. L.

AL TASCHITH (ăl-tăs'kĭth; Heb. "do not destroy"). More correctly Al-tashheth (RSV). A title annotation found in Ps 57, 58, 59, 75. Its significance is uncertain, but it may have been the name of a Heb. tune to which these psalms were sung. Or, as in the case of other musical terms in the psalm titles, it may be a subscript belonging to the previous psalm. Psalms 56, 57, 58, and especially 74, seem to voice the pleas of David and Asaph for God not to destroy them nor allow the righteous to be destroyed by their enemies.

ALUSH (ā'lŭsh). One of the encampments of the Hebrews as they fled Egypt under the leadership of Moses, between Dophkah and Rephidim. Mentioned only in Num 33:13-14.

ALVAH (ăl'vȧ). A chief of Edom descended from Esau, referred to in Gen 36:40 and again in I Chr 1:51, where the same name is spelled Aliah.

ALVAN (ăl'vȧn). The eldest son of Shobal, a clan chief in the land of Edom (Gen 36:23). The name is spelled Alian in I Chr 1:40. It is probably a Hurrian (Horite) name.

AMAD (ā'măd). A city of Canaan assigned to the tribe of Asher in the division of the land after the Conquest (Josh 19:26).

AMAL (ā'măl). A son of Helem listed among the descendants of Asher in I Chr 7:35.

AMALEK (ăm'ȧ-lĕk), **AMALEKITES** (ȧ-măl'ĕ-kīts)

1. A grandson of Esau and son of Eliphas by Timna, his concubine. Amalek became a chieftain in Edom and gave his name to a seminomadic group roaming the wilderness S of Canaan (Gen 36:12, 16).

2. A people called Amalek or Amalekites against whom the Israelites often fought from the days of Moses to the reign of David. The mention in Gen 14:7 of "all the country of the Amalekites" through which Chedorlaomer campaigned does not prove that Amalekites already existed in Abraham's time, but simply designates the territory as it was known to the author of Genesis and his readers.

The main territory of the Amalekites seems to have been the Negeb desert (Num 13:29) between Beer-sheba and Sinai. The extent of their wanderings is summed up in I Sam 15:7 as "from Havilah as far as Shur, which is east of Egypt" (RSV)—from NW Arabia to the eastern border of Egypt along the line of the modern Suez Canal.

Migrating in search of suitable oases in what may have been a drought year, the Amalekites attacked Israel at Rephidim near Mount Sinai (Ex 17:8), for which ultimate destruction was decreed for them (v. 14; Deut 25:17-19). They were declared the objects of perpetual warfare (Ex 17:16), and continued to be numbered among the enemies of Israel (Ps 83:7). After rebelling against the Lord, the Israelites sought to enter Canaan from the S, but were disastrously defeated by the Amalekites and Canaanites in the hills of the Negeb N of Kadesh-barnea (Num 14:43, 45). Balaam described Amalek as "the first of the nations" (Num 24:20), either because of their antiquity in that region (I Sam 27:8) or because they were the first to attack the fledgling nation of Israel (Ex 17:8).

The Amalekites joined with neighbors twice in oppressing Israel during the period of the judges. They helped Eglon, king of Moab, to capture Jericho (Jud 3:13; for "the city of palm trees"—Jericho see Deut 34:3). As camel-riding bedouin they accompanied the Midianites in their harvesttime raids throughout Israel in the time of Gideon (Jud 6:3), but Gideon defeated them in the valley of Jezreel (6:33; 7:12-22). At one time there had been a settlement of Amalekites on a hill in the land of Ephraim (Jud 12:15; cf. 5:14).

King Saul carried out a systematic military campaign against the Amalekites (I Sam 14:48; 15:1-8). He selfishly refused to slaughter their healthy cattle and to execute their king Agag (15:9-33). Evidently he also failed to exterminate all of them, for they continued to raid the settled communities in S Judah during the later reign of Saul (I Sam 30:1-2). David made a reprisal raid to recover the wives and children taken from Ziklag (30:3-20). It was he who effectively crushed Amalek (I Sam 27:8-9; II Sam 8:11-12), so that they are heard of no more until the last remnant was wiped out by 500 Simeonites in Mount Seir in the reign of Hezekiah (I Chr 4:43).

H. G. S.

AMAM (ā'măm). One of the villages near Beer-sheba assigned to the tribe of Judah in the division of the land. Mentioned only in Josh 15:26.

AMANA (ȧ-mā'nȧ). A peak in the Anti-Lebanon range (Song 4:8), probably S of the Amana (Abana) River valley. It is called Umânum and Ammana in Akkad. inscriptions. Sargon II obtained alabaster there.

AMARIAH (ăm-ȧ-rī'ȧ)

1. A descendant of Aaron through Phinehas, the son of Meraioth, and father of Ahitub (*q.v.*; I Chr 6:3,4,7,52); an ancestor of Ezra (Ezr 7:3).

2. A second priest, son of Azariah who was high priest in the time of Solomon (I Chr 6:9-11).

3. A descendant of Levi through Kohath, the father of Hebron, of whom he was the second son (I Chr 6:1,2; 23:19; 24:23).

4. A third priest, declared high priest by Jehoshaphat in Jerusalem in his reforms in Judah after the death of Ahab (II Chr 19:1, 8-11). He was probably the Amariah who was the son of Azariah (I Chr 6:11).

5. A Levite under Kore, the son of Imnah the Levite, appointed by Hezekiah to distribute among the Levites the freewill offerings of the people, as well as the oblations and the most

holy things (II Chr 31:14–15). He officiated in one of the cities of the priests.

6. A descendant of Bani (called Binnui in Neh 7:15) whose descendants returned with Zerubbabel from Babylon. In the time of Ezra he had taken a "strange" (non-Israelite) wife (Ezr 10:42; Neh 12:2, 13), from whom Ezra took an oath that he would put away his foreign wife (Ezr 10:19).

7. A priest in the time of Nehemiah who sealed a covenant with him and others (Neh 10:1–8) to serve the Lord (9:38). He was probably the same one who married a strange wife (cf. Neh 12:1–7 with 10:1–8).

8. A descendant of Judah through Perez (Neh 11:4), some of whose descendants dwelt in Jerusalem after the Exile.

9. A descendant of Hezekiah, king of Judah, and ancestor of Zephaniah the prophet who prophesied in the days of Josiah, king of Judah (Zeph 1:1).

H. G. S.

AMARNA LETTERS (*ȧ*-mär'n*ȧ*). The group of official letters found in 1887, with subsequent discoveries, at Tell el-Amarna in Egypt (*see* Amarna, Tell el-) now comprises about 375 clay tablets. They were written mostly in Babylonian cuneiform to the pharaohs Amenhotep III and Akhenaton (*q.v.*). This correspondence, covering the period roughly from 1400 to 1360 B.C., came from (1) rulers of the four nations comparatively equal in strength to Egypt: Assyria, the Hittites, Mitanni, and Kassite kings in Babylon; (2) vassal princes in Canaan and Syria under Egyptian control; and (3) various Egyptian officials in those lands. It is evident that Akkadian was the diplomatic language of the entire Near East at this time, even between the Egyptian overlord and his Asiatic vassals. This great influence of Babylonian culture on Canaan is confirmed by the discovery in 1946 at Megiddo of a fragment (*c.* 1400 B.C.) of the Gilgamesh Epic (Babylonian flood account). The Amarna letters, therefore, possess extraordinary importance for reconstructing the culture and history of the Near East in the early 14th cen. B.C. More than 200 of the Amarna tablets are in the Berlin Museum, over 80 are in the British Museum, and the rest are in museums in Cairo, Oxford, Paris, and Brussels.

Among the vassal princes heard from are those of Byblos or Gebal, Sidon, Tyre, Hazor, Akko, Megiddo, Gezer, Ashkelon, Lachish, Shechem, and Jerusalem. But never mentioned in these letters are the towns of Jericho, Ai, Bethel, Gibeon, and Hebron, taken or destroyed by Joshua. The vassals in Canaan complain to the pharaoh of hostility between their own city and neighboring towns, and call for help to meet the raids of small bands of Habiru or 'Apiru (*see* Hebrew People). These cannot be exclusively identified, however, with the invading Israelite army under Joshua, for Habiru are mentioned in various documents all during the 2nd mil. B.C. and throughout the Near East as mercenary troops or vagrants. Nevertheless it is possible to see a picture of conditions in Palestine that prevailed early in the period of the judges when the Israelites were no longer operating as a united force.

In the Amarna period there were only four main city-states left in southern Palestine, whereas in Josh 10 nine cities having a king are mentioned. The Israelites had initially conquered and even recaptured some of these cities (e.g., Hebron and Debir), but in other cases, such as Jerusalem, they were unable to take the stronghold, or the Canaanites reoccu-

Amarna letters from King Labaia and Arzawa to Akhenaton in the Cairo Museum. LL

pied and held the city (e.g., Lachish) after the Israelite army returned to Gilgal. Disunity prevailed in the Amarna age, quite unlike the league of Amorite kings (Josh 10) or the Canaanite confederacy (Josh 11) that unitedly opposed Joshua. In certain specific instances the term Habiru in the Amarna letters may refer to Israelites. If so, the fact that according to tablets from 'Abdu-Heba of Jerusalem (ANET, pp. 487 ff.) Lab'ayu the prince of Shechem was in league with the Habiru may explain why Joshua did not find it necessary to attack and capture that city when the Israelites held the covenant ceremony at nearby Mount Ebal (Josh 8:30–35).

Bibliography. W. F. Albright, "The Amarna Letters," ANET, pp. 483–89. Gleason L. Archer, Jr., SOTI, pp. 164, 253–59, 265. F. F. Bruce, "Tell el-Amarna," TAOTS, pp. 3–20. Edward F. Campbell, Jr., "The Amarna Letters and the Amarna Period," BA, XXIII (1960), 2–22; *The Chronology of the Amarna Letters,* Baltimore: Johns Hopkins Univ. Press, 1964. CornPBE, pp. 40 ff. J. A. Knudtzon, *Die El-Amarna Tafeln,* Leipzig, 1907–15. George E. Mendenhall, "The Hebrew Conquest of Palestine," BA, XXV(1962), 66–87. Samuel A. B. Mercer, *The Tell el-Amarna Tablets,* New York: Macmillan, 1939. Charles F. Pfeiffer, *Tell el-Amarna and the Bible,* Grand Rapids: Baker, 1963.

J. R.

AMARNA, TELL EL- (tĕl-ĕl-*à*-mär'n*à*). The modern name of ruins and tombs on the E bank of the Nile, *c.* 190 miles S of Cairo. Tell el-Amarna is the site of ancient Akhetaton, "Horizon of Aton," built *c.* 1370 B.C. by Pharaoh Amenhotep IV, who changed his name to Akhenaton (*q.v.*) and instituted the so-called Amarna revolt. This revolution, possibly stemming from the cosmopolitanism of the empire of Thutmose III, involved religious, artistic, and literary changes. In religion, there was a new universalism, tending toward monotheism. Aton, the sun disk, was worshiped by the pharaoh and his family as the creator of all men, the benevolent father caring for all his creatures. Those in the court worshiped Akhenaton, the reputed son of this solar deity. Initiating this new worship brought so much opposition in Thebes, the royal residence and center of the worship of Amon-Re, that the young pharaoh moved the capital down stream to this new site. After his death the weakling pharaoh Tutankhamon was forced to return the capital to Thebes.

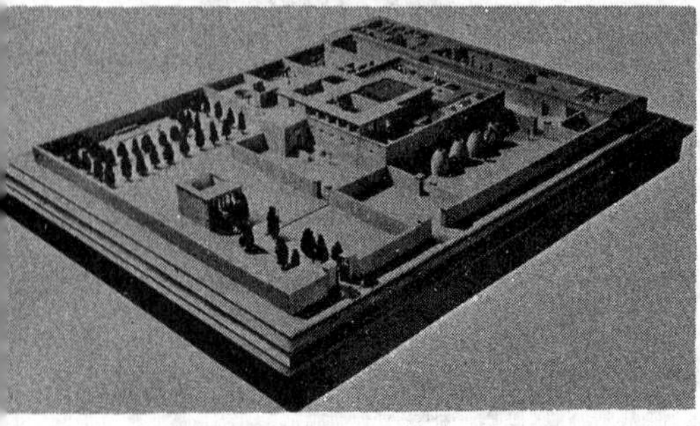

A model of a house and estate at Amarna, *c.* 1375–1330 B.C. ORINST

Excavations of the unimposing ruins of Tell el-Amarna, which stretches about five miles along the Nile but is only about 1,100 yards in width, indicate that the city was built in haste. The site had lain unnoticed and unidentified until 1887. In that year a local woman, while digging in the ruins for waste to use as fertilizer in her garden, happened on the royal archives of Akhetaton. These are known as the Amarna letters (*q.v.*) or tablets. Beginning in 1891 W. M. Flinders Petrie uncovered much of the palace. Later expeditions traced the plan of the city and explored about 25 tombs cut into the side of the hills to the E where Akhenaton's nobles were buried.

A hymn to Aton (ANET, pp. 369 ff.), with many parallels to Ps 104, was discovered at Amarna in the tomb of Eye, a courtier of Akhenaton. Direct dependence of Ps 104 on this hymn is doubtful, however, since contemporary Egyptian literature abounds in similar expressions, and the monotheism of the psalm goes far beyond the monolatry of the Aton worship.

Along with the Aton worship, Akhenaton fostered *ma'at,* "truth," in art and social life. Animals were depicted as if caught in action by a high-speed camera. Scenes of the royal family are presented in an informal, natural manner which differs from the earlier stylized art forms. The natural and familiar scenes, however, were so overdone that Akhenaton's own sickly figure, with pot belly, became the norm for all Egyptian portraits in that period.

A. K. H.

AMASA (*à*-mā'sà)

1. Nephew of David, son of his sister Abigail and Jether an Ishmeelite (I Chr 2:13–17); cousin of Joab, son of Zeruiah, Abigail's sister (II Sam 17:25). After Absalom's revolt failed, David forgave Amasa and made him captain of his forces in place of Joab (II Sam 19:13). On the fall of Absalom, Sheba sought to keep the revolt alive (II Sam 20:1–2). David instructed Amasa to assemble the army to pursue Sheba, but he delayed too long (II Sam 20:4–5). David then sent Abishai, cousin of Amasa and brother of Joab (II Sam 20:6; I Chr 2:16), who was among the troops. At Gibeon the forces of Amasa and Abishai met (II Sam 20:7–8). Feigning to kiss him, Joab seized Amasa by his beard and slew him with his sword (II Sam 20:9–10).

2. An Ephraimite who helped deliver the Judeans taken captive by Pekah (II Chr 28:12).

AMASAI (*a*-mā'sī)

1. A Levite of the family of Kohath. He was the father of Mahath, the ancestor of Samuel (I Chr 6:25, 35).

2. One of the chief captains of David. With a group of men from Judah and Benjamin he deserted Saul and joined David at Ziklag. By some he is supposed to be the same as David's nephew Amasa (*q.v.*), the son of Abigail (I Chr 12:18).

3. A priest in the time of David who blew a trumpet before the ark as it was brought up from the house of Obed-edom to Jerusalem (I Chr 15:24).

4. A priest in the days of Hezekiah. His son Mahath took an active part in the great revival and cleansing of the temple under Hezekiah (II Chr 29:12, 15).

AMASHAI (*a*-măsh'ī). Son of Azareel among the priests chosen by lot to live in Jerusalem at the time of Nehemiah (Neh 11:13).

AMASIAH (ăm'*a*-sī'*a*). Son of Zichri; a commander from Judah in Jehoshaphat's army who had volunteered for the Lord's service (II Chr 17:16).

AMAW (ā'mô). The name of the homeland of the prophet Balaam (Num 22:5, RSV), translating Heb. *'ammô*, "his people" (KJV). W. F. Albright (BASOR #118 [1950], 14-20) recognized this term to be the name of the country called *'Amau* on the inscribed statue of Idrimi excavated by Leonard Woolley at Alalakh, which may be dated variously *c.* 1450 B.C. (Albright) or 1375 (Woolley, Sidney Smith). Amaw, which lay between Aleppo and the Euphrates River, was ruled at that time by the king of Alalakh (near Antioch-on-the-Orontes). Amaw was also mentioned by an Egyptian officer of Amenhotep II. These references to Amaw from *c.* 1400 B.C. tend to confirm an early date for Moses, the Exodus, and Balaam. After *c.* 1370 B.C. that area was under Hittite control and was known to biblical writers as "the land of the Hittites" (cf. Josh 1:4; Jud 1:26). *See* Pethor; Balaam.

AMAZIAH (ăm'*a*-zī'*a*)

1. The ninth ruler of Judah, a son of Joash and Jehoaddan (Jehoaddin in II Kgs 14:2, RSV). Twenty-five years of age when he ascended the throne, he reigned for 29 years. There is disagreement on the dates of his reign. E. R. Thiele has placed the beginning of Amaziah's reign at 796 B.C. with a co-regency with his son Uzziah from 790 to 767 B.C. (*The Mysterious Numbers of the Hebrew Kings,* pp. 71-72). But W. F. Albright has proposed the dates 800-786 B.C. without a co-regency (*From the Stone Age to Christianity,* pp. 404 ff.). Because his father had been assassinated by servants in the royal household, Amaziah first had to ferret out and kill these murderers before his throne was secure (II Kgs 12:19-21; 14:6; II Chr 24:25-27; 25:3-4).

Though accounted as a good king, Amaziah was warlike in temperament. He soon organized a large army of 300,000, plus 100,000 hired from Israel. However, on the advice of a man of God, he discharged the soldiers from Israel, making them so angry that they killed 3,000 Judahites. Amaziah attacked and subdued the Edomites, but preserved their idols for his personal use, for which a prophet condemned him (II Chr 25:5-16). Amaziah challenged Jehoash, king of Israel, to battle. The battle was fought at Beth-shemesh, and Amaziah was defeated and captured. Jehoash broke down the N wall of Jerusalem and robbed the temple of its treasure (II Kgs 14:8-14; II Chr 25:17-24). Judah apparently became a vassal of Israel throughout the remainder of Amaziah's reign. Amaziah was assassinated at Lachish by rebels who pursued him from Jerusalem. He was buried in Jerusalem (II Kgs 14:19, 20; II Chr 25:27, 28).

2. A Simeonite, father of the prince Joshah (I Chr 4:34, 38).

3. A Levite, an ancestor of Ethan, a singer in the services of David's tabernacle (I Chr 6:45).

4. A priest during the reign of Jeroboam II, known because he commanded Amos to cease prophesying at Bethel (Amos 7:10-17).

G. H. L.

AMBASSADOR. In the KJV the following three Heb. words are translated "ambassador"; *mal'āk,* meaning "messenger" (II Chr 35:21; Isa 30:4; 33:7; Ezk 17:15); *m^e^lîṣ,* meaning "intercessor" or "interpreter" (II Chr 32:31); and *ṣîr,* meaning "ambassador" (Josh 9:4; Prov 13:17; Isa 18:2; Jer 49:14; Ob 1). The general OT use of the term was to designate a temporary messenger sent on a special mission representing a king or a government (*see* Herald).

In the NT the Gr. word *presbeia,* "embassage," is used in Lk 14:32 of a group of ambassadors sent with a request for a peaceful settlement of difficulties (cf. Lk 19:14 where *presbeia* is translated "message"). Paul employed the verb *presbeuō* (II Cor 5:20; Eph 6:20) in a figurative sense describing his ministry as a representative of Christ. The Gr. papyri show that both these words were commonly used in the Hellenistic world in the official relationships of cities and rulers (MM). Deiss LAE, p. 374, indicates that *presbeuō* and *presbeutēs* were the terms used to designate the emperor's legate. Thus, Paul claimed for himself the lofty dignity of representing heaven's King, Jesus Christ, and as Christ's ambassador he brought the message of reconciliation to a world at enmity with God. In Eph 6:20 the apostle appears as an ambassador in prison because of the message which he proclaimed.

D. W. B.

AMBER. *See* Minerals.

AMBUSH. A military tactic involving the placing of armed men in a hidden or unexpected location for a surprise attack. Used effectively by Joshua against Ai (Josh 8), by the men of Shechem and Abimelech (Jud 9:25, 35), in the battle against Gibeah (Jud 20), and by King Jeroboam (II Chr 13:13). Paul's life also was threatened by an ambush (Acts 23:16, 21; 25:3). Because of the deceit involved, ambush is sometimes used in a derogatory sense (Jer 9:8; Ps 17:12; Ps 64:4; Prov 1:11, 18, RSV).

AMEN (ā'mĕn'). This was the customary Jewish assent to commands (I Kgs 1:36) and prayers (Neh 5:13; 8:6), and is rendered in LXX by the optative of wish (*genoitō*), "So be it." Jesus used it before statements to certify what followed (Mt 5:18, "verily"). Christians employed it after prayers to signify the listener's approval (I Cor 14:16). The noun is used as a title for Jesus (Rev 3:14); cf. "God of (the) Amen" (Isa 65:16, Heb.). The Heb. *'āmēn,* "firmness," is derived from the verb root *'āman,* "to believe." In Gen 15:6 Abram believed in the Lord and said "Amen" to God's promise (see Meredith G. Kline, "Abram's Amen," WTJ, XXXI [1968], 1-11).

AMETHYST. *See* Jewel.

AMI (ā'mī). The head of a family included among the descendants of Solomon's servants who returned from Exile to Judah under the leadership of Zerubbabel (Ezr 2:57). He is also called Amon (Neh 7:59).

AMIABLE. An older English word meaning "lovely," and used to describe God's dwelling place in Ps 84:1 (KJV).

AMINADAB (*ȧ*-mĭn'*ȧ*-dăb). This name appears in the genealogies of Jesus (Mt 1:4 and Lk 3:33) in KJV only. It has been changed to Amminadab in RSV. *See* Amminadab.

AMITTAI (*ȧ*-mĭt'ī). The father of the prophet Jonah (II Kgs 14:25; Jon 1:1).

AMMAH (ăm'*ȧ*). A hill facing Giah on the way to the wilderness of (i.e., E of) Gibeon, which marked the end of Joab's pursuit of Abner (II Sam 2:24). The hill probably was at the crest of the wilderness descent into the Jordan Valley.

AMMI (ăm'ī). Heb. word meaning "my people," given by Hosea as the new name of the third child of his adulterous wife Gomer (Hos 2:1). The original name, Lo-ammi ("not my people," Hos 1:9), symbolized the sad rejection of God's covenant by His wayward people Israel. Ammi conveyed the hope of restoration (Hos 2:21-23) and is applied to the new Israel by NT writers (Rom 9:25; I Pet 2:10).

AMMIEL (ăm'ĭ-ĕl)

1. A man of the tribe of Dan. One of the 12 spies sent out by Moses to look over Canaan. He was with the majority who brought an unfavorable report and died under God's judgment (Num 13:12).

2. A Manassite of Lodebar in Gilead. He was the father of Machir who protected Mephibosheth, the lame son of Jonathan, and also received David fleeing from Absalom (II Sam 9:4-5; 17:27).

3. The father of David's wife Bathsheba (I Chr 3:5). In II Sam 11:3, by transposition of the second and third consonants, he is called Eliam.

4. A Levite, doorkeeper in the temple. One of the sons of Obed-edom (I Chr 26:5).

AMMIHUD (*ȧ*-mī'hŭd)

1. The father of Elishama, who was chief of the tribe of Ephraim in the days of Moses (Num 1:10).

2. The father of Shemuel who was appointed from the tribe of Simeon as a divider of the Promised Land (Num 34:20).

3. The father of Pedahel, prince of the tribe of Naphtali, a divider of the land (Num 34:28).

4. The father of Talmai, king of Geshur and father-in-law of David. Absalom fled to his grandfather's court after slaying his brother Amnon (II Sam 13:37).

5. A descendant of Perez of the tribe of Judah. His son Uthai was among the first to return to Jerusalem after the Exile (I Chr 9:4).

AMMINADAB (*ȧ*-mĭn'*ȧ*-dăb)

1. The father of Nahshon, prince of the tribe of Judah in the days of Moses (Num 1:7; 2:3; 7:12, 17; 10:14). He was the father also of Elisheba, the wife of Aaron (Ex 6:23). Amminadab was the ancestor of Boaz and David and is listed in the genealogy of Jesus Christ (Ruth 4:19-20; I Chr 2:10; Mt 1:4; Lk 3:33; spelled Aminadab in NT).

2. Named in I Chr 6:22 as the son of Kohath and father of Korah. In I Chr 6:2, 18 and in Ex 6:18, 29 he is called Izhar (*q.v.*).

3. One of the chief Levites of the family of Kohath in the time of David. He was one of those privileged to carry the ark of the Lord from the house of Obed-edom to Jerusalem (I Chr 15:10).

4. The name occurs on two ancient Ammonite seals and in an inscription of Ashurbanipal, where it is the name of the king of Ammon (ANET, p. 294).

AMMINADIB (*ȧ*-mĭn'*ȧ*-dĭb). Occurs only in Song 6:12, KJV where it is taken to be the name of a charioteer otherwise unknown. RSV regards it not as a proper name but emends it to read "in a chariot beside my prince." The text of this verse is generally regarded as having been corrupted in transmission, as it does not clearly make sense as it stands in the existing Heb. texts.

AMMISHADDAI (ăm'ĭ-shăd'ī). The father of Ahiezer of the tribe of Dan at the time of the Exodus (Num 1:12). This Heb. name was borne by an Egyptian official in the late 14th cen. B.C.

AMMIZABAD (*ȧ*-mĭz'*ȧ*-băd). The son of David's military leader Benaiah (I Chr 27:6).

AMMON (ăm'ŏn). The son of Lot by his younger daughter (Gen 19:38). His descendants are called Ammonites (*q.v.*), and sometimes Ammon (Ps 83:7). Ammon is also used as a place name in Neh 13:23.

AMMONITES (ăm'ŏ-nīts). A people descended from a son of Lot by his younger daughter, who gave birth to Benammi in a cave near Zoar, now called Zi'ara. They dispossessed the Zamzummims and dwelt in their place (Deut 2:20–21). Their country lay between the Arnon and Jabbok Rivers to the NE of Moab, protected by a strong border on its N side (Num 22:24). Rabbah (*q.v.*) or Rabbath (modern 'Ammān) was its chief city (Deut 3:11). In 1961 a fragment of a royal Ammonite monument from the 9th cen. B.C. was discovered in the ruins of the ancient citadel at Amman, written in Aramaic script (BASOR #193 [Feb., 1969], pp. 2–19).

No Ammonite could enter the nation of Israel even to the tenth generation (Deut 23:3). The Israelites were not to meddle with nor distress them on the way to Canaan (Deut 2:19).

The Ammonites joined with the Amalekites and Eglon the king of Moab to smite Israel in the time of the judges and to occupy Jericho, "the city of palm trees" (Jud 3:13). Israel later worshiped the Ammonite gods, was subjugated by these enemies for 18 years, and was finally delivered by Jephthah (Jud 10:6–11:33). Nahash, king of the Ammonites, threatened Jabesh-gilead, but was routed by Saul (I Sam 11:1–11; 12:12). David was a friend of Nahash or of his son with the same name (II Sam 10:2), but Nahash's son insulted David's messengers of peace and David thereupon sent Joab and Abishai to punish the people (II Sam 10:1–11:1). When David fled from Absalom, Shobi, son of Nahash and brother of Hanun, brought supplies to David at Mahanaim (II Sam 17:27–28). Zelek, one of David's mighty men, was an Ammonite (II Sam 23:37). Solomon loved Ammonite women among other foreign women, and worshiped Milcom, the god of the Ammonites, building a high place for his worship (I Kgs 11:1, 5, 7, 33). This god was the chief deity of their religion. Naamah, the mother of Rehoboam, was an Ammonite (I Kgs 14:21, 31).

When the Ammonites joined with the Moabites and Edomites to attack Jehoshaphat, God sent confusion among them so that they destroyed each other (II Chr 20:1–23). Zabad, son of the Ammonitess Shimeath, with Jehozabad, son of the Moabitess Shimrith, conspired against Joash, king of Judah, and slew him (II Chr 24:26; II Kgs 12:21). Uzziah received tribute from the Ammonites among others whom he subjected (II Chr 26:8). Jotham, son of Uzziah, again subjected them to tribute (II Chr 27:5). In his reforms Josiah defiled the high place which Solomon had built in Jerusalem for Milcom, the god of the Ammonites (II Kgs 23:13). The Lord sent the Ammonites against Jehoiakim and Judah because of the sins of Manasseh (II Kgs 24:1–4).

A street scene in Amman, Jordan, site of Rabbath-Ammon, capital of the Ammonites. Richard E. Ward

The practices of the Ammonites still infected Israel in the days of Ezra (Ezr 9:1). Tobiah, an Ammonite, obstructed the rebuilding of both the temple and city of Jerusalem (Neh 2:10, 19; 4:3, 7). The Ammonites were threatened with destruction (Amos 1:13–15; Zeph 2:8–11), punished (Jer 9:26), and were to become obedient to God's people (Isa 11:14).

Archaeological evidence indicates that the Ammonite civilization flourished from 1200 to 600 B.C. The W approaches to the capital at Rabbah were protected by a strong line of border fortresses. The fortress towers could be circular, square or rectangular. Ammonite tombs in the vicinity of Amman reveal a prosperous material culture during the Iron II period (900–600 B.C.), made possible by controlling the lucrative caravan trade across the desert from Arabia. Yet the Ammonites seem to have retained an essentially nomadic type of social structure as late as the 7th cen. B.C. (George M. Landes, "The Material Civilization of the Ammonites," BA, XXIV [1961], 65–86).

H. G. S.

AMNON (ăm'nŏn)

1. Oldest son of David, born at Hebron (II Sam 3:2; I Chr 3:1). He raped his half sister Tamar, and in retaliation was murdered by order of Absalom, her full brother (II Sam 13).

2. One of the sons of Shimon of the tribe of Judah (I Chr 4:20).

AMOK (ā'mŏk). One of the leading priests who returned to Judah with Zerubbabel after the Exile (Neh 12:7, 20).

AMON (ăm'ŏn)

1. Governor of the city of Samaria under Ahab, keeper of the prophet Micaiah, while Ahab with Jehoshaphat fought Syria (I Kgs 22:2, 10, 26; II Chr 18:25).

2. King of Judah, son of Manasseh, who succeeded his father at age 22 and reigned two years (II Kgs 21:19–21). He was distinguished by his evil deeds. Worshiping idols (v. 21), he thus forsook God (v. 22). Unlike his father Manasseh, Amon did not repent of his wickedness, exceeding his father in his evil deeds (II Chr 33:23). He was murdered in his palace by his servants (II Kgs 21:23), and the people made his son Josiah king in his stead (v. 24). Amon is numbered among the ancestors of Christ (Mt 1:10).

3. A descendant from among the servants of Solomon (Neh 7:57, 59).

4. The name of an Egyptian divinity in the name of the Egyptian city No-Amon (called "No," Jer 46:25); also called Thebes, the capital of upper Egypt. Amon replaced the sun-god Ra as head of the Egyptian pantheon. Under his ensign, the Hyksos were expelled from Egypt. *See* Gods, False.

H. G. S.

AMORITES (ăm'ŏ-rīts). The Amorites of the OT derived their name from a Semitic word (Akkad. *Amurru*) which means "westerner." The Amorites in Palestine were a part of a movement of western Semitic nomads *c.* 2100–1900 B.C. who appeared in all parts of the Fertile Crescent. They are included in the Genesis table of nations as a people of Canaan (Gen 10:16), reflecting the mid-2nd mil. B.C. viewpoint of that passage. The Beni-Hasan tomb paintings of Egypt (*c.* 1900 B.C.) depict 37 bearded Amorites bringing their wares into Egypt on donkeys. Kathleen Kenyon believes the single burials of the Early Bronze-Middle Bronze period (2100–1900 B.C.) at Jericho may be those of invading Amorite seminomads. Oldenburg contends that the Amorites introduced the worship of Baal-Hadad in the region of Canaan, which eventually displaced the worship of the god El.

In southern Babylonia the Larsa Dynasty (*c.* 1950 B.C.) was founded by Amorites. In the following century the Amorites took over such important centers as Babylon and Eshnunna. Mari on the mid-Euphrates had an Amorite king during the days of Hammurabi (*c.* 1750 B.C.) whose own dynasty had been founded by an Amorite. The Amorites formed the basis of the Assyrian stock who settled on the Tigris between the Zab tributaries. It has been conjectured that Abraham's family was among the

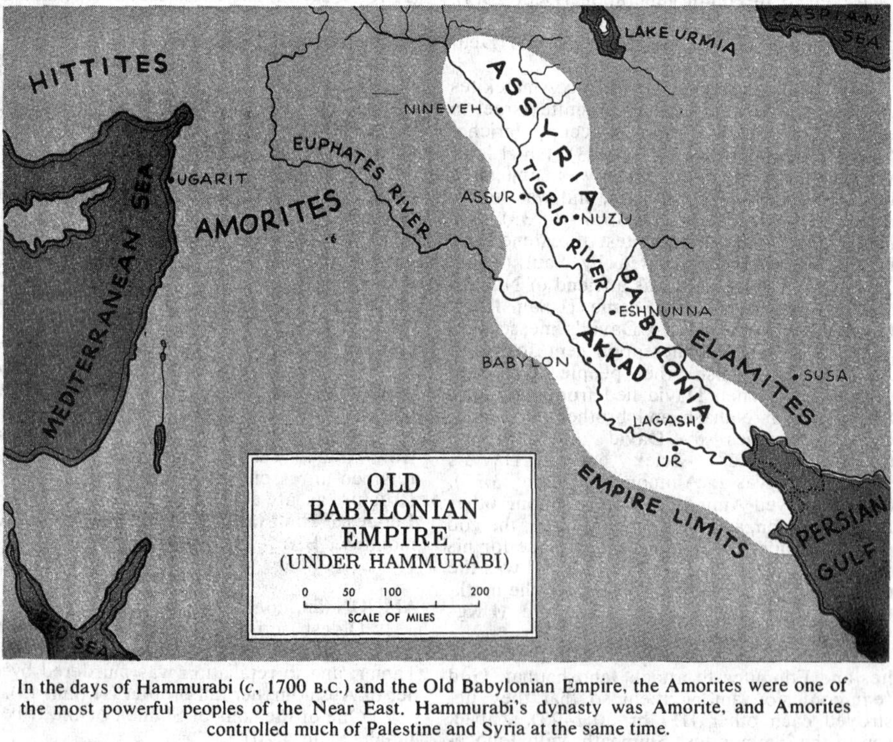

In the days of Hammurabi (*c.* 1700 B.C.) and the Old Babylonian Empire, the Amorites were one of the most powerful peoples of the Near East. Hammurabi's dynasty was Amorite, and Amorites controlled much of Palestine and Syria at the same time.

Amorite invaders of Canaan. Ezk 16:3 tends to support this by saying of Judah, "Thy father was an Amorite, and thy mother a Hittite."

The Amorites, who spoke a NW Semitic dialect, settled in various regions of Palestine, notably N of the Arnon but especially N of the Jabbok River. It was here that the Israelites under Moses encountered them and their king Sihon, who, like the Moabites and Edomites, refused to let Israel pass. The Hebrews celebrated their victory over the Amorites in the ballad song of Num 21:27-30. Moses also conquered the land of Og, king of Bashan, who is designated an Amorite in Deut 4:47.

According to Gen 14:13 some of the Amorites who settled in the Hebron area were allies of Abraham. Some of these Amorites dwelt on the W bank of the Dead Sea at En-gedi (Hazezon-tamar, Gen 14:7). They were subdued by the four kings from Mesopotamia (Gen 14). Shechem who fell in love with Dinah (Gen 34) was an Amorite. Jacob alludes to this episode in Gen 48:22 (Heb. text) when he bequeathed the town of Shechem to Joseph. Joseph's bones were eventually buried near this old Amorite-Hebrew stronghold (Josh 24:32).

After Joshua's invasion of Canaan, a league of five Amorite kings headed by Adonizedek of Jerusalem opposed the Israelite army near Gibeon (Josh 10). During the time of the judges the descendants of the Amorites in the S of Judah were still in the land. Their pressure forced the Danites to move N, while another pocket of Amorites who lived near the valley of Aijalon was put to forced labor by the Ephraimites (Jud 1:34-36). Solomon eventually put to slave labor all the remnants of non-Israelites left in the land, including the Amorites (I Kgs 9:20-21) who had tricked Joshua into an alliance (Josh 9).

Sometimes the OT seems to use the term Amorite as representative of all the Canaanite tribes in Palestine (cf. Gen 15:16). Perhaps this reflects the fact that their dialect was practically undistinguishable from their 3rd mil. predecessors in Palestine commonly called Canaanites. The Amarna letters use the term Amurru of the entire region of Syria-Palestine, revealing how numerous the Amorites became in Canaan. On the other hand, there are passages which make a distinction between the Amorite and the Canaanite and other groups, especially when the people whom the Lord would drive out were listed (cf. Ex 34:11). Also the Amorite had a common preference for the hill country along with the Hittite and the Jebusite (Hurrian), while the Canaanite dwelt by the sea (Num 13:29).

Later in history the autonomous Canaanite seafarers were called Phoenicians by the Greeks, while the Amorites were assimilated and disappeared as a distinct people in Palestine. Because of their degraded religious practices, this assimilation was stoutly resisted by the spiritual leaders of Israel from Joshua (Josh 24:15) down to Ezra (Ezr 9:1-3).

Bibliography. Giorgio Buccellati, *The Amorites of the Ur III Period,* Naples: Institute Orientals di Napoli, 1966. Kathleen M. Kenyon, *Amorites and Canaanites,* London: Oxford Univ. Press, 1966. Ulf Oldenburg, *The Conflict Between El and Baal in Canaanite Religion,* Leiden: E. J. Brill, 1969, pp. 151-163.

E. B. S.

AMOS (ā'mŏs). An 8th cen. prophet, Amos (Heb. *'āmôs,* "burden bearer") was unique in his bold ministry to the kingdom of Israel in that he was a native of Judah. He did not have his training in the religious schools or prophetic guilds of his day. To the contrary, he denied any previous connection with the formal religious community (Amos 7:14-15). He placed himself in the midst of the world in which he lived, a shepherd (1:1) and a dresser of sycomore fig trees (7:14). His familiarity with rural life is reflected in his selection of language: lion, bear, and serpent (5:19); locusts and grass of the land (7:1); and basket of summer fruit (8:1). He made his living in the wilderness or dry pastureland near Tekoa (cf. II Chr 11:6; Jer 6:1), a village situated about ten miles S of Jerusalem and 12 miles W of the Dead Sea.

Three statements in Amos 1:1 indicate the time Amos lived: (1) Uzziah was king of Judah; (2) Jeroboam was king of Israel; (3) it was two years before the earthquake. Critical study seems to place the convergence of these three near 760 B.C.

Amos was a prophet, a speaker for God, but not of his own choosing (cf. Paul, Jeremiah and Isaiah); it was rather at the command of God (7:15). His comprehension of the spiritual scene of his day has led many to classify him as the beginning of a new order of prophets. His ministry led him to Bethel, the center of religious apostasy in the northern kingdom (I Kgs 12:26-33). The last years before the fall of Israel were characterized by great material prosperity. Still enjoying the luxury of military victory during the reign of Jeroboam II, Israel allowed temporal security to replace her trust in the living God.

Amos' denunciation of Israel (Amos 2:6-16) can serve as an outline for a study of the social, moral, and religious condition of the people. Socially, two distinct classes had developed, the poor and the rich. The rich were seeking greater riches by any means (2:6-7). Moral evils were rampant. Drunkenness and sexual license were at an abominable level (2:7-8). Religious perversion was at a gross high. For the most part idolatry was common (2:8). The faithful were scorned, chastised and mocked (2:12). The depth to which the people had fallen is characterized in their seeming indifference to their position as a delivered and cared-for nation (2:9-11). Repentance and obedience were imperatives, the only escape from imminent judgment.

Amos or the compiler (cf. superscription and third person portions of the narrative) arranged this material into three major divisions. Likely the book contains only a portion of Amos' words spoken at Bethel. If the book had an editor other than Amos himself, possibly he was also from Judah and was a companion of the prophet on his trek northward, for the nature of the text indicates early recording of the prophet's message.

Chaps. 1 and 2 are viewed as one division, including a preface (1:1-2) in which Amos' theme is announced that the wrath of the Lord is imminent, and a setting forth of judgments against Israel and her neighbors. A second division is comprised by chaps. 3-6. These are in turn subdivided, each section introduced by "Hear this word" (3:1; 4:1; 5:1). The final division, chaps. 7-9, contains a series of five visions (7:1-3; 7:4-6; 7:7-9; 8:1-14; 9:1-10) interrupted by an historical account of his visit to Bethel (7:10-17). Perhaps at that time he proclaimed the warning messages of chaps. 1–6. His preaching seems to have been inspired by the words accompanying the fourth vision found in 7:4-6 (cf. 2:6-7). An epilogue (9:11-15) foretelling the restoration of the Davidic kingdom closes the work.

The key verses of the book may be 3:2–that judgment is determined according to privileges, so that God's chosen covenant people above all others will not escape–and 4:12, a summons to covenant renewal.

The book may be outlined in this way:

The Lion of Amphipolis stands guard at the ancient site as it did in Paul's day. HFV

I. Judgments Against Near Eastern Nations, Chaps. 1–2
   1. Prophecies against heathen neighbors, 1:3–2:3
   2. Wrath upon the two covenant nations, 2:4-16
II. Proclamations Against Israel, Chaps. 3–6
   1. The fact of Israel's guilt, 3:1-15
   2. The depravity of Israel, 4:1-13
   3. Coming punishment for Israel's sin, 5:1-17
   4. The inescapable captivity, 5:18-27
   5. The peril of complacency, 6:1-14
III. Five Visions Concerning Israel, 7:1–9:10
   1. Devouring locusts, 7:1-3
   2. Flaming fire, 7:4-6
   3. Plumbline; opposition of the priest of Bethel, 7:7-17
   4. Basket of ripe fruit, 8:1-14
   5. Judgment of the Lord on Bethel's apostate altar, 9:1-10
IV. Promise of Restoration, 9:11-15

Amos' theological motifs can be summarized briefly as the holy character of the sovereign God, the requirement by God of social justice, the moral and religious infidelity of the covenant people shown in utter disregard for the law of Moses, the reality of judgment, salvation through repentance, and the ultimate restoration and realization of God's purposes.

See Israel, Kingdom of; Prophet.

Bibliography. W. Brueggemann, "Amos IV: 4-13 and Israel's Covenant Worship," VT, XV (1965), 1-15. B. B. Copass, *Amos,* Nashville: Broadman, 1939. Richard S. Cripps, *A Critical and Exegetical Commentary on the Book of Amos,* London: SPCK, 1929. William R. Harper, *Amos and Hosea,* ICC, 1905. R. L. Honeycutt, *Amos and His Message,* Nashville: Broadman, 1963. A. S. Kapelrud, *Central Ideas in Amos,* Oslo: Aschehoug, 1956. H. G. R. Mitchell, *Amos, an Essay in Exegesis,* New York: Houghton Mifflin, 1900. Norman H. Snaith, *Amos, Parts I and II,* London: Epworth Press, 1945-6; *Amos, Hosea and Micah,* London: Epworth, 1956. John D. W. Watts, *Vision and Prophecy in Amos,* Grand Rapids: Eerdmans, 1958.

R. O. C.

AMOZ (ā'mŏz). The father of the prophet Isaiah (Isa 1:1; II Kgs 19:2, *et al.*). A Palestinian seal bearing the inscription "Amoz the Scribe" may have belonged to Isaiah's father since Amoz is a rare name. This may indicate Isaiah was from a family prominent in government.

AMPHIPOLIS (ăm-fĭp'ō-lĭs). Mentioned once in the NT (Acts 17:1). This city was visited by Paul on his second missionary journey. It was called Amphipolis ("surrounded city") because the site on which it was located was enclosed on three sides by the Strymon River which curved around it, the E side being open. According to Thucydides (*Peloponnesian War,* iv. 103 ff.), a wall protected this E side, and it was strengthened and enlarged at various times. Thucydides was intimately familiar with Amphipolis, since he tried unsuccessfully to relieve it in time of seige (*c.* 422 B.C.). His failure resulted in his 20-year exile from his country. He mentions that the town was valuable for "the timber that it afforded for ship building."

Jackson and Lake (*Beginnings of Christianity, Acts,* IV, 202) point out that Paul's journey between Philippi and Thessalonica along the Egnatian Way was 100 Roman miles and seems to have been divided into these three stages: Philippi to Amphipolis (33 Roman miles); Amphipolis to Apollonia (30 Roman miles); Apollonia to Thessalonica (37 Roman miles). This suggests to them that Paul used horses to make this part of his journey.

The coins of Amphipolis during Paul's time frequently depict Artemis Tauropolis riding on a bull, indicating the close contact the area had with Asia, being located only three miles from the Mediterranean. No archaeological work has been carried on as yet at Amphipolis (which reaches back to the 1st cen. A.D.), though a Byzantine-period Christian complex has been discovered.

E. J. V.

AMPLIAS (ăm'plĭ-*ă*s). A common name, frequently given to slaves. It is a shortened form of Ampliatus. Paul greets Amplias in Rome by calling him "my beloved in the Lord" (Rom 16:8). An early Christian tomb in the cemetery of Domitilla in Rome bears the inscription "Ampliat."

AMRAM (ăm'răm)

1. Grandson of Levi, son of Kohath, and the father of Moses and Aaron (Ex 6:18, 20; Num 26:59).

2. A son of Bani, who had married a foreign wife and was required by Ezra to put her away (Ezr 10:34).

AMRAMITES (ăm'r*ȧ*-mīts). The descendants of Amram who formed a branch of the priestly family of Kohathites (Num 3:27; I Chr 26:23).

AMRAPHEL (ăm'r*ȧ*-fĕl). The king of Shinar, who joined with other kings in a battle in the valley of Siddim during the days of Abram (Gen 14). *See* Abraham. Because of some similarity of the names in Heb., attempts formerly were made to identify him with Hammurabi, the famous king of Babylon. The first and last Heb. letters of Amraphel, however, cannot be equated with the Akkad. *ḫ* and lack of an *l*, respectively, in the name Hammurabi. It more likely would be the Amorite name *Amur-pi-el* or *Amuru-âpil(i)*.

W. F. Albright believes the name "Amraphel" may be associated with Emudbal, the name of an important Amorite tribe which gave its name to a region between Elam and Babylonia at least by 1800 B.C., according to the Mari tablets (BASOR # 163, pp. 49 f.; *Yahweh and the Gods of Canaan,* Garden City: Doubleday, 1968, pp. 68 f.

See Chedorlaomer.

AMULET. Amulets are decorative or magical objects worn on the person or installed in the home. They are usually made of semiprecious stone, such as carnelian or soft stone covered with glaze. As objects of magic they are intended to protect against evil spirits and assure the welfare of the wearer and his family. Amulets are usually pierced and worn around the neck.

Styles of amulets discovered in Palestine were often borrowed from Egypt where scarabs were common. The scarab was shaped like a beetle, usually made of stone, with a religious design or name on its under flat surface. Horus eyes served as symbols of the magic activity of the goddess Isis in restoring life to her husband Osiris.

Images of gods or teraphim (*q.v.*) were also common amulets (Gen 35:4). Palestinian excavations have yielded many Astarte figurines—images of the fertility goddess with exaggerated sexual features designed to insure fertility. Isaiah denounced the women of Israel for their pride and their ostentatious display of a variety of jewelry including crescent-shaped ornaments and amulets, which may have been more for decorative than magical use (Isa 3:18-21, NASB; cf. Jud 8:21, 26). *See* Magic.

C. F. P.

AMZI (ăm'zī)

1. Son of Bani of the tribe of Levi (I Chr 6:46).

2. A priest, the son of Zechariah (Neh 11:12).

ANAB (ā'năb). A town in the hill country of Judah conquered by Joshua (Josh 11:21) and allotted to the tribe of Judah (Josh 15:50). The site is now called Khirbet 'Anab, 13 miles SW of Hebron. The city was repeatedly mentioned in Egyptian texts of the Nineteenth Dynasty as Qrt-'nb, corresponding to the Heb. Kiriath-anab ("city of Anab").

ANAH (ā'n*ȧ*). Son of Zibeon and father of Aholibamah, the wife of Esau (Gen 36:2, 24). In I Chr 1:38-41 Anah is identified as a brother of Zibeon. This may be a different person, or the name may be loosely used to refer to a family group.

ANAHARATH (*ȧ*-nā'*ȧ*-răth). A town allotted to the tribe of Issachar in the conquest of Canaan (Josh 19:19), now en-Na'urah, five miles NE of Jezreel. Also mentioned in the list of towns captured by Thutmose III about 1479 B.C.

ANAIAH (*ȧ*-nā'y*ȧ*). One of the post-Exilic leaders who stood at Ezra's right hand when he read the book of the law (Neh 8:4), and who assisted Nehemiah in sealing the covenant (Neh 10:22).

ANAKIMS (ANAKIM, ANAK) (ăn'ȧ-kĭm). A tribe inhabiting the land of Palestine especially in the S near Hebron in pre-Israelite times. The term probably developed from the ascriptive title "people of the neck" or "necklace" (from Heb. *'ănāq*, "necklace," cf. Prov 1:9; Song 4:9) to a proper name for the tribe. Apparently all these tribal groups were destroyed by Joshua except the coastal settlements at Gaza, Gath, and Ashdod (Josh 11:21-22).

Twice the Bible refers to "the city of Arba the father of Anak" (Josh 15:13; 21:11), which could indicate either that a prominent man or ancestor of the Anakim was called Arba, or that we should understand the expression as a proper name of the city, i.e., "Kiriath-arba" or Hebron (cf. Gen 23:2), in which case the city was the ancestral home of the Anakim.

In the Execration texts of Egypt now in the Berlin Museum, dated *c.* 1900 B.C., there is an incantation directed toward certain enemy cities and territories among which are Palestinian areas and which names specific rulers of an area called "Iy-'aneq," who could well be the Anakim of biblical materials (ANET, p. 328). These pottery fragments represent the ritual cursing of Pharaoh's enemies by breaking jars upon which the names were inscribed.

The biblical materials indicate that very large stature (perhaps exaggerated by their neighbors) was attributed to the Anakim which tended to produce fear among their enemies (cf. Num 13:22, 28, 33; Deut 2:10-11, 21; 9:2). *See* Dolmens; Giant. In Num 13:33, RSV, they are mentioned as descendants of the "Nephilim," who are elsewhere described as being the pre-Flood sons of the union between the sons of God and the daughters of men (Gen 6:4). The Anakim were also known as Rephaim (*q.v.;* Deut 2:11, RSV).

E. C. B. Maclaurin believes that the term Anak may have been a Philistine title of rank, and that the Anakim were hereditary rulers of the Philistines who early came to Palestine from the Mycenaean world ("Anak/'Anax," VT, XV [1965], 468-474). A cuneiform tablet from Asshur mentions Anaku as a place in the Aegean area. R. de Vaux suggests the Anakim made up a corps of mercenary troops for one of the Canaanite principalities (*Ancient Israel,* p. 219).

A. F. J.

ANALOGY. The relation of similarity or likeness between two objects of thought, used as a basis for inferring other resemblances less obvious. The word is derived from the Gr. *ana,* "according to"; and *logos,* in this use, "proportion" or "ratio." The Gr. word occurs twice in the NT: Rom 12:6, translated "proportion," from which comes the phrase "analogy of faith"; and Heb 12:3 in the verb form, translated "consider," pointing out the resemblance between the sufferings of Christ and those of His followers.

Analogies are widely used in the Bible in the effort to convey truth about God and spiritual things to minds limited by the human and material. Thus, God is our heavenly Father (Deut 32:6; Ps 68:5; Isa 63:16; Mt 6:9; 23:9; Rom 8:15-16), we are joint heirs with Christ (Rom 8:17; Gal 4:7), and many more too numerous to list. All parables involve an element of analogy.

The anthropomorphisms of the Bible (i.e., attributing to God human form, feelings, and actions) must be considered as analogies; e.g., God is spoken of as having hands (Ex 7:17), eyes (II Chr 16:9), ears (Isa 5:9), mouth (Isa 1:20); and being able to walk (Gen 3:8), sleep (Ps 44:23), see (Gen 6:12), hear (Ex 16:12), write (Ex 31:18), breathe (Job 4:9), smell (Gen 8:21), and many others. *See* Anthropomorphism.

The strength and value of analogical reasoning depends on the degree to which the objects compared are essentially similar. Incidental resemblances are never safe bases for analogy. Analogy in theology is inescapable, but must be used with caution.

W. T. P.

ANAMIM (ăn'ȧ-mĭm). An Egyptian group (Anamin in RSV) referred to only in Gen 10:13 and I Chr 1:11.

ANAMMELECH. *See* Gods, False.

ANAN (ā'nȧn). One of the post-Exilic leaders who assisted Nehemiah in sealing the covenant with God (Neh 10:26).

ANANI (ȧ-nā'nī). The seventh son of Elioenai of the tribe of Judah (I Chr 3:24).

ANANIAH (ăn'ȧ-nī'ȧ)

1. The father of Maaseiah and grandfather of Azariah (Neh 3:23), the grandson assisting in the rebuilding of a section of the wall of Jerusalem.

2. A town in the territory of Benjamin (Neh 11:32) which was inhabited by Jews after the Exile. It is possibly to be identified with Bethany ("house of Ananiah"), which is two miles E of Jerusalem, probably taking its name from the members of the family of Ananiah who settled there.

ANANIAS (ăn'ȧ-nī'ȧs)

1. Ananias and Sapphira *(q.v.),* husband and wife, of Acts 5:1-11. In sharp contrast to the unselfishness of other church members, they pretended to give to the Jerusalem church the total sale price of their property while they actually retained part for themselves. Peter rebuked Ananias, who was immediately struck down in death by divine judgment. A few hours later Sappnira was likewise judged for the same effort to deceive. It is important to notice that Peter predicted rather than decreed these judgments which were God's act. The severity of

ANIM (ā'nĭm). A town allotted to the tribe of Judah after the conquest under Joshua (Josh 15:50). Identified with Khirbet Ghuwein et-Taḥta, 11 miles S of Hebron.

ANIMALS OF THE BIBLE. The biblical approach to animal classification is quite different from that used by the scientific community today. Thus, in Gen 1:20–30; 2:19–20 organisms are classified as great sea monsters, aquatic creatures, winged birds (1:21), cattle (domesticated animals), creeping things, and beasts of the earth, i.e., wild beasts (1:24). A similar scheme of the classification of fauna is found in Lev 11. Essentially the approach of the Bible to classification is an ecological one, i.e., the Bible classifies organisms on the basis of the habitat which they occupy, and lumps together, for example, all aquatic organisms regardless of their anatomical structure.

The modern system of classification is based on structure—anatomy and morphology—and consequently biologists place into one category the whale, the lion, and the bat because of anatomical similarities even though they occupy three different habitats. The Bible, on the other hand, would classify together the shark, the fish, and the mollusk even though their internal and external structures are different.

Any system of classification is arbitrary. There is no right way, nor can any series of categories that show some system be regarded as wrong. Most scientists today find a system of classification based on anatomy and morphology to be the most useful one; however, there are some men today who believe it would be profitable to pay more attention to ecology and other branches of biology in classifying organisms.

Classification by Anatomy and Morphology

I. Porifera
  Sponge

II. Coelenterates
  Red Coral

III. Annelida
  1. Leech
  2. Worm

IV. Arthropoda
  A. Arachnids
    1. Scorpion
    2. Spider

  B. Insects
    1. Ant
    2. Bee
    3. Beetle
    4. Crimson Scale
    5. Flea
    6. Fly
    7. Gnat
    8. Locust
    9. Louse
    10. Moth
    11. Wasp

V. Mollusca
  1. Mollusk, Purple
  2. Oyster, Pearl

VI. Chordates
  A. Fish
  B. Amphibians
    Frog
  C. Reptiles
    1. Cobra
    2. Crocodile
    3. Gecko
    4. Leviathan
    5. Lizard
    6. Lizard, Dabb
    7. Serpent
    8. Viper

  D. Birds
    1. Buzzard
    2. Cormorant
    3. Crane
    4. Cuckoo
    5. Dove, Turtledove
    6. Eagle
    7. Fowl, Domestic
    8. Goatsucker
    9. Goose
    10. Hawk, Sparrow
    11. Heron
    12. Hoopoe
    13. Ibis
    14. Kestrel
    15. Kite
    16. Lammergeier
    17. Ostrich
    18. Owl, Barn
    19. Owl, Little
    20. Owl, Long-eared or Great
    21. Owl, Scops
    22. Partridge
    23. Peacock
    24. Pelican
    25. Pigeon, Rock
    26. Quail
    27. Raven
    28. Sea Gull
    29. Sparrow
    30. Stork
    31. Swallow
    32. Swan
    33. Swift
    34. Vulture, Black
    35. Vulture, Egyptian
    36. Vulture, Griffon

  E. Mammals
    1. Antelope
    2. Ape
    3. Ass
    4. Bat
    5. Bear
    6. Boar, Wild

7. Camel
8. Cattle
9. Coney
10. Deer
11. Dog
12. Dugong
13. Elephant
14. Fox
15. Gazelle
16. Goat
17. Hare
18. Hedgehog
19. Hippopotamus
20. Horse
21. Hyena
22. Ibex
23. Jackal
24. Leopard
25. Lion
26. Mole Rat
27. Monkey
28. Mouse
29. Mule
30. Onager
31. Ox, Wild
32. Pig
33. Porcupine
34. Sheep
35. Sheep, Mountain
36. Vole
37. Weasel
38. Whale
39. Wolf

Classification by Biblical System

I. Cattle
1. Ass or Donkey
2. Beeves; see Cattle, I.6
3. Bull, Bullock; see Cattle, I.6
4. Calf; see Cattle, I.6
5. Camel
6. Cattle
7. Dog
8. Dromedary; see Camel, I.5
9. Goat
10. Greyhound; see Fowl, Domestic, III.14
11. Horse
12. Mule
13. Ox; see Cattle, I.6
14. Pig
15. Sheep
16. Swine; see Pig, I.14

II. Beasts of the Field
1. Antelope
2. Ape
3. Ass, Wild; see Onager, II.29
4. Badger; see Dugong, V.3
5. Bear
6. Behemoth; see Hippopotamus, II.20
7. Boar
8. Chamois; see Sheep, Mountain, II.36
9. Coney or Rock Badger

10. Deer, Hart or Stag, Hind or Doe, Roe, Roebuck
11. Dragon
12. Elephant
13. Ferret; see Gecko, IV. 16
14. Fox
15. Gazelle
16. Hare
17. Hart; see Deer, II.10
18. Hedgehog
19. Hind; see Deer, II.10
20. Hippopotamus
21. Hyena
22. Ibex or Wild Goat
23. Jackal
24. Leopard
25. Lion
26. Mole; see Mole Rat, IV.25
27. Monkey; see Peacock, III.40
28. Mouse; see IV.27
29. Onager or Half Ass
30. Ox, Wild, or Unicorn
31. Porcupine
32. Pygarg; see Antelope, II.1
33. Roe; see Gazelle, II.15
34. Roebuck; see Deer, II.10
35. Satyr
36. Sheep, Mountain
37. Unicorn; see Ox, Wild, II.30
38. Weasel; see IV.36
39. Wild Ass; see Onager, II.29
40. Wild Ox; see II.30
41. Wolf

III. Flying Creatures
1. Bat
2. Bee
3. Bittern; see Hedgehog, II.18; Heron, III.21
4. Buzzard
5. Cock; see Fowl, Domestic, III.14
6. Cormorant
7. Crane
8. Cuckoo or Cuckow
9. Dove or Turtledove
10. Eagle; see Vulture, Griffon, III.54
11. Eagle, Gier; see Vulture, Egyptian, III.53
12. Falcon; see Kestrel, III.25
13. Fly
14. Fowl, Domestic
15. Glede; see Kite, III.26
16. Gnat
17. Goatsucker or Nighthawk
18. Goose
19. Hawk, Sparrow
20. Hen; see Fowl, III.14
21. Heron or Bittern
22. Hoopoe
23. Hornet; see Wasp, III.55
24. Ibis
25. Kestrel or Falcon
26. Kite or Glede
27. Lammergeier
28. Lapwing; see Hoopoe, III.22
29. Locust

30. Moth; see IV.26
31. Nighthawk; see Goatsucker, III.17
32. Osprey; see Vulture, Black, III.52
33. Ossifrage; see Lammergeier, III.27
34. Ostrich
35. Owl, Barn or White
36. Owl, Little
37. Owl, Long-eared or Great
38. Owl, Scops
39. Partridge
40. Peacock
41. Pelican
42. Pigeon or Dove
43. Quail
44. Raven
45. Seamew or Sea Gull; see Cuckoo, III.8
46. Sparrow
47. Sparrow Hawk; see Hawk, Sparrow, III.19
48. Stork
49. Swallow
50. Swan
51. Swift
52. Vulture, Black, or Osprey
53. Vulture, Egyptian
54. Vulture, Griffon, or Eagle
55. Wasp or Hornet

IV. Creeping, Swarming Things
1. Adder; see Cobra, IV.8; Serpent, IV.30; Viper, IV.34
2. Ant, Harvester
3. Asp; see Cobra, IV.8
4. Beetle
5. Cankerworm; see Locust, III.29
6. Caterpillar; see Locust, III.29
7. Chameleon; see Lizard, IV.21
8. Cobra
9. Cockatrice; see Serpent, IV.30
10. Cricket; see Beetle, IV.4
11. Crimson Scale Insect
12. Dragon; see II.11
13. Flea
14. Fly; see III.13
15. Frog
16. Gecko
17. Gnat; see III.16
18. Grasshopper; see Locust, III.29
19. Hornet; see III.55
20. Horseleach; see Leech, V.6
21. Lizard
22. Lizard, Dabb
23. Locust; see III.29
24. Louse
25. Mole Rat
26. Moth
27. Mouse
28. Palmerworm; see Locust, III.29
29. Scorpion
30. Serpent, Snake
31. Spider
32. Tortoise; see Lizard, Dabb, IV.22
33. Turtle; see Dove, III.9
34. Viper
35. Vole
36. Weasel
37. Worm

V. Aquatic Organisms
1. Coral
2. Crocodile
3. Dugong or Sea Cow
4. Fish
5. Frog; see IV.15
6. Leech
7. Leviathan, Sea Monster
8. Mollusk, Purple
9. Onycha
10. Oyster, Pearl
11. Sea Monster (Lam 4:3); see Jackal, II.23
12. Sponge
13. Whale

Following the biblical system of classification we find mention of:

I. Cattle

Cattle are domesticated animals which include:

1. **Ass** or **Donkey,** *Equus asinus.* The ass is of purely African origin. Three wild races are known: a NW African race which is extinct; a NE African race which, if not extinct, is close to extinction; and a Somalian race which survives to the present but did not play an important part in domestication. The second of these, the Nubian ass, was believed to have been domesticated in the Nile Valley in early historic times. (For Old Kingdom tomb reliefs see VBW, I, 109; II, 184.) Bones of this form have been found in Palestine at Tell ed-Duweir and date from between 3000 and 2500 B.C.

The first mention of the ass in the Bible includes male and female asses among the animals which Abram acquired in Egypt (Gen

A Palestinian Ass. HFV

Oxen and an ass hitched together for threshing near Jerash, Jordan. HFV

12:16). The ass was primarily a beast of burden (Gen 42:26; I Sam 16:20; 25:18); it was driven but never bridled. W. F. Albright has emphasized the widespread use of asses for trade by the 20th cen. B.C. In caravans of 300 up to 1,000, each carrying loads of 150–200 pounds, the donkey needed fodder and water en route. Hence way stations with cisterns filled from dammed-up wadis were built in the Negeb and along the Sinai road to Egypt in Abraham's time (*Archaeology, Historical Analogy, and Early Biblical Tradition,* Baton Rouge: Louisiana State Univ. Press, 1966, pp. 28–40).

From the time of the Middle Kingdom on, the ass was used for riding in Egypt, but only the Jews and Nubians rode asses regularly. The ass was also used for threshing grain and for pulling the plow. In Arab countries today peasants plow with an ass and a cow or a camel hitched together (VBW, I, 279). The law, however, forbade plowing with an ass and an ox hitched together (Deut 22:10).

The ass was rather highly regarded by the Jews. It was considered an economic asset. An individual had to have an ass for minimum existence (Job 24:3), and the individual's wealth was counted by the number of asses which he possessed (Gen 12:16; 24:35; Job 1:3). The ass was an acceptable gift (Gen 32:13–15). The ass shared the rest of the sabbath (Deut 5:14). Numbers records the report of Balaam's ass which spoke (Num 22:22–35). People of influence rode asses (Jud 10:4; 12:14; I Sam 25:20); and the ass became a symbol of the Messiah's peaceable coming (Zech 9:9; Mt 21:1–7).

Elsewhere the ass was almost universally despised. Apparently its stolid temperament annoyed man. It has been considered inferior to the horse and the mule, and it has been generally regarded as the beast of the poor. Its patience has been likened to that of a slave. Yet the milk of asses was supposed to have medicinal properties and was highly regarded. The ass was often used to turn the large millstone of Roman times (cf. Mt 18:6, NASB marg.). Its dietary requirements are very simple: it can live on stubble, thistles, straw and a very small amount of grain.

See also Onager, II.29.

2. **Beeves.** *See* Cattle, I.6.

3. **Bull, Bullock.** *See* Cattle, I.6.

4. **Calf.** *See* Cattle, I.6.

5. **Camel,** *Camelus dromedarius* L. The camel is unintelligent, ill-natured and quarrelsome; it is a slow breeder. Yet it is a blessing to tribes living on the border of deserts because it is especially adapted to this habitat. Its feet padded with a thick elastic mass of fibrous tissue are adapted to walking on desert soils. It can go without water for a long period of time, and it can subsist on vegetation which grows on saline soils (photo, VBW, II, 85).

The camel is used primarily for transportation of merchandise, household equipment, and persons. It can carry a load weighing 600 pounds or more. A camel can be hitched to a plow where lands are temporarily arable. Because they are smelly and cannot be kept penned, camels are not used in cities.

There are two varieties within the one-humped species, the slow burden-bearing camel (Gen 37:25) and the fast dromedary (I Sam 30:17). Because Babylon is seen being attacked by Elam and Media, Isa 21:7 may refer to the Bactrian camel, *C. bactrianus.* This camel has two humps and longer hair but is not as fast as the swift dromedary.

Abraham had camels in Egypt (Gen 12:16), and Job at first had 3,000 camels (Job 1:3) and then 6,000 (42:12). While large scale camel nomadism does not seem to have begun until toward the end of the 2nd mil. B.C. (Jud 6:5), Sumerian texts from the Old Babylonian period list camels and indicate their domestication. Also camel bones and figurines have been found at various Near Eastern sites well before 1200 B.C. (K. A. Kitchen, *Ancient Orient and OT,* 1966, pp. 79 f.).

A camel at market day in Beer-sheba. HFV

Camels were used for swift travel (Gen 24:31). A riding camel can cover from 60 to 75 miles in a day as opposed to a normal day's journey of 20 miles. They were also used as mounts in time of war (Jud 6:5). Camels were used as burden bearers, especially of spices (Gen 37:25). Their wool was important (Mt 3:4); a rough cloak of camel's hair is still worn by Bedouin today. A camel's hair garment was also a sign of the prophetic office (Zech 13:4). Camels were eaten by the Arabs, who also drank their milk (Gen 32:15). However, the camel was forbidden to the Jews as food (Lev 11:4; Deut 14:7).

6. **Cattle,** *Bos primigenius.* The term "cattle" (Heb. *b^ehēmâ* or *miqneh*) is frequently used to refer to all domestic animals or livestock (Gen 1:24; 2:20; 7:23; 47:6, 16, 17; Ex 9:3–7; Num 3:41, 45). Occasionally it is used to refer to all large domestic animals (Num 31:9; 32:26), though sometimes the English word in KJV refers only to sheep and goats (Gen 30:32, 39–43; 31:8, 10; Isa 7:25; 43:23); in such cases it renders either Heb. *śeh* or *ṣō'n*. *See* Herd.

Usually, however, the English word refers to what we commonly speak of today as domestic cattle of the bovine species. Domestication is believed to have begun before 4000 B.C. (For reliefs, paintings, and models of cattle from Egyptian tombs see VBW, I, 59, 104, 117.) Cattle require considerable attention from the community and a reasonably high degree of community organization.

Some authors believe that milk rather than meat was the foremost consideration in the domestication of cattle and that in early civilization meat supplies came chiefly from wild game. Cattle also supplied strong hides that supplanted wood in the manufacture of shields. Their dung was a source of fuel when wood was scarce (Ezk 4:15). They were also used as beasts of burden and for traction, though oxen were more commonly used in this way. Still it is believed that the development of wheel transportation was associated more closely with cattle than with any other animal.

Bulls are referred to in Gen 32:15, so that cattle breeding was widely practiced by patriarchal times. Successful breeding by a bull is referred to in Job 21:10. Inlaid friezes found at Tell el-Obeid near Ur, dating to the middle of the 3rd mil. B.C. show bulls and a dairy scene with the milking of cows (ANEP, #98, 99). Strict laws in Mesopotamia and Israel penalized the owner of a bull that gored a man or other cattle (Ex 21:28–36). Bulls are sometimes employed figuratively as pictures of strength or violence (Deut 33:17; Ps 22:12; 68:30; Isa 10:13).

Bulls were widely used for sacrifices (for Egyptian tomb painting see VBW, I, 181). For this purpose they had to be at least eight days old (Lev 22:27). They might be used as a general sacrifice (Lev 22:23; Num 23:1) or for special sacrifices (Jud 6:25; I Sam 1:24). They were also used in particular sacrifices such as the consecration of priests (Ex 29:1), the dedication of the altar (Num 7), purification of Levites (Num 8), sin offerings (Lev 16), the day of the new moon (Num 28:11), the Passover (Num 28:19), the Feast of Weeks (Num 28:27), the Feast of Trumpets or of the new year (Num 29:1–2), the Day of Atonement (Num 29:7–8), and the Feast of Booths (Num 29:12–38). The latter feast exacted the largest number of bulls for burnt offerings of all the annual feasts, with a total of 71 being slaughtered during the course of eight days.

Calves are referred to as "sons of the herd" in Gen 18:8–9; I Sam 6:7; 14:32. The calf or heifer (*'ēgel*) was a symbol of peacefulness (Isa 11:6). It also was used figuratively to refer to Gentile peoples (Ps 68:30). A calf's head decorated the back of Solomon's throne (I Kgs 10:19, RSV). Calves were sometimes fattened in the stall (Amos 6:4; Mal 4:2; Lk 15:23) or kept around the house (I Sam 28:24). They supplied veal (Gen 18:7), which was considered a delicacy for the wealthy (Amos 6:4); yet calves also supplied meat for all Saul's army at the great slaughter of the Philistines (I Sam 14:32).

Cattle were subject to the law of firstlings (Ex 13:12). Cattle were a mark of wealth (Gen 13:2) and were considered proper booty of war (Josh 8:2).

Aaron made the golden calf as a rival for the

Farmers leading well-fattened cattle. Wall relief from the tomb of Ptah-hotep, Saqqara, Egypt. LL

Sacrificing a bull (lower register). Tomb of Menna, Thebes. Gaddis, Luxor

ark of the covenant (Ex 32; Deut 9:16, 21). Even if the image was intended only to be the pedestal for the invisible Yahweh (cf. Egyptian and Syrian deities standing on a lion or a bull, ANEP, #470–474, 486, 500, 501, 522, 531, 534, 537), it was especially offensive because the calf was a symbol of fertility related to Egyptian and Canaanite cultic practices. Two calves were made by Jeroboam I for his shrines at Bethel and Dan (I Kgs 12:28–33); denunciations of calf worship were directed at these (Hos 8:5–6; 13:2).

The ox is the adult castrated male of *Bos primigenius*. Oxen were used as draught animals (Num 7:3; Deut 22:10; 25:4). They usually fed on grass (Num 22:4; Ps 106:20), but they also ate straw (Isa 11:7) and salted fodder (Isa 30:24, NASB). They could be kept in a stable (Lk 13:15). Oxen could not be offered as sacrifices because they had been castrated (Lev 22:24). In passages (e.g., Ex 20:24; I Sam 6:13) which seem to say that oxen were sacrificed to God, it must be noted that the Heb. words *bāqār* and *shôr* can also mean "cattle" and "bull," respectively. Oxen could be used as food but they were not a common article of diet. Possession of an ox and an ass was regarded as the bare minimum for existence in an agricultural economy (Job 24:3; cf. Ex 20:17). *See also* Ox, Wild, II.30.

7. **Dog,** *Canis familiaris*. The dog is believed to have been the earliest of all domesticated animals. It is thought to have been valuable as a scavenger and to have been associated with man in hunting. The modern dog is thought to have come from the Indian wolf, *C. lupus pallipes*.

The dog is generally looked down on in the Bible (Prov 26:11; II Pet 2:22), and biblical writers seem to show no familiarity with the warm personal human-dog relationship which we know. The dog is pictured as a scavenger haunting streets and dumps (Ex 22:31; I Kgs 22:38; Mt 15:26; Lk 16:21). Isa 66:3 seems to point to a non-Yahvistic cult which sacrificed dogs.

Dogs were often used in hunting, according to paintings in Egyptian tombs, and there is reference to dogs herding sheep in Job 30:1. In general, however, "dog" was a term of contempt (I Sam 17:43) or of excessive humility (II Sam 9:8; 16:9; II Kgs 8:13). The "price of a dog" (Deut 23:18) meant the earnings of a male cultic prostitute. Dogs are also used to refer to lascivious and wicked persons (Isa 56:10–11; Mt 7:6; Phil 3:2; Rev 22:15).

8. **Dromedary.** *See* Camel, I.5.

9. **Goat,** *Capra hircus mambrica*. The goat is probably the earliest ruminant to be domesticated. Its wild ancestor seems to have been the bezoar goat, *C. aegagrus* Erxleben. The Mesolithic Natufians are believed to have tamed wild goats in Palestine by *c.* 9000 B.C. The goat of Bible times was probably the Syrian or Mamber variety (photo, VBW, I, 183).

Sheep are more important where cattle can be kept for milk, but where pasture is scarce and thorny scrub dominates over grass, and where cattle are difficult to keep because of lack of good food and water, goats become important. Not only are they able to live under conditions that do not suit sheep, but they also produce large quantities of milk. The goat does not supply fat as does the sheep, and since its hair is coarse the wool is rather scarce.

A herd of goats, Jerash, Jordan. HFV

Goats have voracious appetites and they were responsible for much of the damage done to the land in Palestine, breaking down terraces, destroying forests, and bringing about soil erosion by eating off all cover.

In Palestine the goat has hollow backward curving horns and is of lighter build than the sheep. It is commonly black and was the principle source of milk (Prov 27:27). Its flesh served as meat (Lev 7:23; Deut 14:4), and its hair was the raw material used for weaving tent cloth and for various domestic purposes (Ex 26:7; 36:14; I Sam 19:13, 16). The skin was tanned as leather, and a whole hide was turned into a skin bottle by sewing shut the leg and neck apertures (Gen 21:14; Josh 9:4).

The goat was a recognized form of wealth. It was subject to the law of firstlings (Num 18:15), and had to be eight days old before it could be offered as a sacrifice. A year-old male goat was one of the animals offered at the Passover (Num 28:22), and two goats were offered on the Day of Atonement (Lev 16:7 ff.; *see* Azazel). It was also used for many other specific sacrifices.

The goat is used in a figurative and symbolical sense in Song 4:1 and 6:5 for the bride's black hair; in Mt 25:30–46 for the wicked; and in Isa 14:9; Ezk 34:17; Dan 8:5–8; Zech 10:3 for various human leaders. *See also* Satyr, II.35.

10. **Greyhound.** *See* Fowl, Domestic, III.14.

11. **Horse,** *Equus caballus orientalis.* Two races of wild horses have survived into modern times: Przewalski's horse, which roamed about Mongolia until modern firearms put an end to most of them after World War I and the Russian Revolution; and the tarpan, a horse of southern Russia which became extinct in the Ukraine in 1851. The domesticated horse seems to be derived from the tarpan. The original site of domestication is believed to be Turkestan (see Hilzheimer, "The Evolution of the Domestic Horse," *Antiquity,* IX [1935], 133–139).

The horse apparently was domesticated, according to skeletal remains, at Sialk on the Iranian plateau by the 5th mil. B.C. and perhaps at Beer-sheba in the next millennium. It was known in Sumer during the Ur III Dynasty, mentioned in the Cappadocian (19th cen. B.C.) and Mari (18th cen.) tablets, and shown on 19th–18th cen. B.C. Anatolian seals with four horses drawing a solid-wheeled chariot (BASOR # 77, p. 31; # 163, p. 43). A horse skeleton was found at the Middle Kingdom Egyptian fortress of Buhen in the Sudan. The Hyksos conquerors achieved success largely by horse and chariot warfare.

The horse was introduced only very gradually into Israel, however. Joshua was commanded to hough or hamstring the horses of the Canaanites (Josh 11:6, 9), and David hamstrung most of the horses captured from Zobah, though he kept enough for a hundred chariots (II Sam 8:4). Solomon greatly increased the number of horses in the Jewish kingdom and maintained large stables at various cities (I Kgs 10:26) such as Megiddo, Hazor, and Gezer (I Kgs 9:15), major regional defense centers. Ahab's horses are mentioned in I Kgs 18:5, and records of Shalmaneser III state that Ahab furnished 2,000 chariots in the coalition against Assyria. Ruins of stables excavated at Megiddo date to his reign and reveal stalls and mangers for 450 horses.

In early Israel the horse was opposed as a symbol of pagan luxury and dependence on physical power for defense (Deut 17:16; I Sam 8:11; Ps 20:7; Isa 31:1). In addition, horses may have been used in heathen religious processions (II Kgs 23:11). Horse trading is mentioned already in Gen 47:17, and was carried on by Solomon between Egypt and Syro-Hittite principalities (I Kgs 10:28–29, RSV).

Most biblical references to horses refer to their use in war, but horses were also used in transportation. Riding seems to have been much less popular than the use of chariots, and cavalry units were not introduced until the 12th cen. B.C., by the Medes and Cimmerians. Joseph rode in Pharaoh's second horse-drawn chariot (Gen 41:43) and Absalom made a display by riding a horse-drawn chariot (II Sam 15:1). Naaman traveled by horse and chariot (II Kgs 5:9). Later, horses were so common in Jerusalem that the royal palace had a special horse gate (II Chr 23:15), and a gate of the city itself was known as the horse gate (Neh 3:28; Jer 31:40). *See* Jerusalem: Gates. Mordecai rode the royal horse as a sign of honor (Est 6:8–11). *See* Horseman.

Horses were also used by the wealthy for hunting (ANEP, #183, 184, 190); the only biblical reference to such hunting (Job 39:18) connects them with pursuing the ostrich. Horses were forbidden as food though they may have been eaten in Samaria during the siege (II Kgs 7:13). There seems to have been little use of horses in connection with agriculture or in the bearing or pulling of burdens. Isa 28:28 may refer to the use of horses in threshing grain, though this is uncertain. Horses are often spoken of figuratively (Ps 32:9; Song 1:9; Jer 5:8;

Horses were used by the wealthy for hunting. Here King Ashurbanipal of Assyria hunts lions. From his palace at Nineveh. BM

12:5; etc.) and in contexts of judgment (Hab 3:8; Zech 1:8; 6:1-8; Rev 6:2-8; 9:17; 19:11 ff.).

12. **Mule.** This is a hybrid, ordinarily sterile, the offspring of a male ass and a mare. Gen 36:24 reports that mule breeding was developed by the Edomites and Horites, though this may be a mistranslation; RSV uses the words "hot springs" rather than "mules." Because cross breeding was forbidden in the law (Lev 19:19), the Israelites procured mules from the Gentiles. They may have been obtained from the Phoenicians, since Tyre imported horses and mules (Ezk 27:14). They did not appear in Israel until David's reign (II Sam 13:29), possibly because of the rarity of horses among the Hebrews. Mules were used chiefly by members of the royal palace and by nobles. King David rode on a mule, and Solomon rode to his anointing upon King David's mule (I Kgs 1:33). Absalom met his death riding on a mule (II Sam 18:9). Mules were less common than horses, camels, and asses in the post-Exilic community (Ezr 2:66).

13. **Ox.** *See* Cattle, I.6.

14. **Pig,** *Sus scropha.* The pig is the most prolific and abundant supplier of meat and fat for the kitchen. Pigs cannot be driven; they are of value only to a settled farmer.

Wild pigs were found in Palestine, as well as in many other countries today. Ps 80:13 refers to the destructiveness of the wild boar which attacks growing crops. *See* Boar, II.7.

The pig symbolizes filth and ugliness. It eats fecal material, vermin, rodents, carrion, and the like (II Pet 2:22). Prov 11:22 refers to the incongruity of a golden ring in the nose of an animal showing these characteristics. There is a similar reference in our Saviour's statement in Mt 7:6 about casting pearls before swine. The prodigal's degeneration is shown by his being forced to feed pigs and eat their food in his poverty (Lk 15:15-16). The Gadarene demons took refuge in the herd of swine feeding on the bluff, overlooking the Sea of Galilee (Mt 8:28-32).

According to Lev 11:7 and Deut 14:8 the eating of the flesh of pigs was forbidden to the Jews. Pre-Semitic inhabitants of Palestine killed and ate pigs freely. In intertestamental times Antiochus used the pig as a test of loyalty to the Jewish faith by requiring its consumption (II Macc 6:18). Pig blood was also sprinkled on the temple altar to desecrate it (I Macc 1:47).

Pigs were frequently used in worship among heathen people (Isa 65:4; 66:3, 17), and this may account for their being forbidden to the Jews as food. Evidence in Palestine shows that

A shepherd anointing his sheep (cf. Ps 23:5). @ MPS

swine were sacrificed long before Hellenistic times. Pig bones were found in the grotto below the rock-cut place of sacrifice at Gezer. A similar underground chamber with vessels containing piglet bones at Tirzah dates to the Middle Bronze Age; and at Ai were unearthed alabaster fragments of a statuette of a pig ready to be sacrificed. Among the Greeks the agrarian rites of the swine god Adonis were popular. Swine were sacrificed to Aphrodite, and in Greece and Asia Minor to Venus. In addition, pigs were sacrificed in connection with oaths and treaties; in the *Iliad* Agamemnon sacrificed a boar to Zeus and Helius.

It is possible that the eating of pork was forbidden because the pig carries many worm parasites such as the trichina; yet this is true of other meat animals. Some people are allergic to pork in hot weather, and this has also been suggested as the reason for the Jewish taboo. The same taboo exists among the Moslems and existed in certain social strata in Egypt.

15. **Sheep,** *Ovis orientalis.* Next to the goat the sheep is believed to be the earliest ruminant tamed by man. It may have been domesticated as early as the 6th mil. B.C. with the aid of the dog, before agriculture itself was fully developed. However, the Bible reports that Abel kept sheep (Gen 4:2). The first sheep to be domesticated was probably the argali *(Ovis ammon),* a variety of the urial *(Ovis vignei)* which is a mountainous species still existing in Turkestan and Mongolia. Five breeds had reached Mesopotamia by 2000 B.C.; these were all of urial stock. *See also* Sheep, Mountain, II.36.

There are more than 500 references to sheep in Scripture, including mention of rams and lambs. Sheep represented the chief wealth and total livelihood of pastoral peoples, providing food to eat, milk to drink, wool for making of cloth and covering for tents. Its skin and bones were also used. In addition, the sheep was a medium of exchange and a source of sacrifices. The number of sheep raised in ancient times was prodigious. Mesha, king of Moab, paid a tribute (annually?) of 100,000 lambs and the wool of 100,000 rams (II Kgs 3:4). Reuben, etc., took 250,000 sheep from the Hagrites (I Chr 5:21). Thutmose III carried off 20,500 sheep from Megiddo (ANET, p. 237).

Good grades of wool suitable for garments developed on the sheep in climates with relatively cold winters; flax was grown to make linen in milder climates. Wool has finer quality as a fabric than does flax.

Sheepshearing (VBW, II, 150) was often a time for festival (II Sam 13:23). The sheep known in Israel (photo in VBW, I, 182; II, 81) was the broadtailed sheep *(O. orientalis vignei* or *O. laticaudata)* of which the tail weighs from 10 to 15 pounds and has always been considered a delicacy. Thus the Lord asked for this choice part as a sacrifice (Ex 29:22-25, RSV).

The ram represented great strength and fittingly symbolized Medo-Persia in Daniel's vision (Dan 8:3). For Persian ram's head made of gold, see VBW, IV, 207.

Because of the very nature of the sheep—gentle and submissive (Isa 53:7; Jer 11:19, RSV), defenseless (Mic 5:8; Mt 10:16), and in constant need of guidance and care (Num 27:17; Mt 9:36)— the Bible often draws an analogy between sheep and the believer. *See* Shepherd; Flock.

16. **Swine.** *See* Pig, I.14.

II. Beasts of the Field

A number of general references to wild animals may be found in the OT (Lev 26:22; II Kgs 14:9; Job 39:15; Ps 50:11; 80:13; Hos 13:8).

1. **Antelope,** *Oryx leucoryx.* These animals are very graceful and carry their heads considerably above the level of the back. They live in arid plains and deserts but are also found on rocky hillsides and in thick bush forests. Both sexes have long, permanent, hollow horns (not antlers) which go straight back. They are alert, wary, and keen sighted and form herds of from two to a dozen. When injured or brought to bay, the antelope attacks with his head lowered so that the sharp horns can point forward; in this way he can defend himself even against a lion.

Antelope feed on grasses and shrubs; they go to streams and waterholes to drink. When water is scarce they will eat melons and succulent bulbs.

The antelope was ceremonially clean. While exact identification of the Heb. terms is difficult, probably the *tᵉʾô* is the antelope (Deut 14:5; Isa 51:20, both RSV). The *dîshōn* (Deut 14:5) is translated "pygarg" in KJV following the LXX. It is a white-rumped antelope, perhaps the *Addax nasomaculatus* of N Africa and Arabia; RSV has "ibex."

A female antelope in the Biblical Zoo in Jerusalem. HFV

2. **Ape.** This term as it is used in Scripture (Heb. *qôph*) may well refer to monkeys and baboons rather than to true apes. Baboons were well known in Egypt where the god Thoth was often represented by a baboon. The common baboon is *Papio hamadryas*.

The term *qôph* is probably not a Heb. word. It may be derived from the Sanskrit *kapi* and from the Gr. word *kepos* which means long-tailed monkey. The LXX renders it "the tailless ape." If Ophir is India as some believe, or Somaliland on the African coast as others believe, or some place on the Persian Gulf as still others believe, the animals which Solomon received were in all probability a mixed lot (I Kgs 10:22; II Chr 9:21). Quite likely they were tailed primates, not true apes, like those the Egyptians brought back from Punt (tomb painting, VBW, II, 224).

3. **Ass, Wild.** *See* Onager, II.29.

4. **Badger.** *See* Dugong, V.3; *also* Coney or Rock Badger, II.9.

5. **Bear,** *Ursus arctos syriacus*. The bear is a large, heavy, big-headed mammal with short powerful limbs and a short tail. The eyes and ears are small. Bears have a plantigrade walk: they walk on both sole and heel as a man does.

Bears are usually peaceful and inoffensive, but if they think they must defend themselves (Lam 3:10), their young (II Sam 17:8; Prov 17:12; Hos 13:8), their food supply (Prov 28:15), or their own territory (II Kgs 2:24; Amos 5:19), they are formidable and dangerous adversaries (see Egyptian relief, VBW, II, 255). David was the champion bear killer of the Bible (I Sam 17:34–37).

The senses of sight and hearing of the bear are not too good, but their sense of smell is excellent. Bears are omnivorous: they subsist largely on a diet of vegetables, fruits, insects, and fish. The Palestinian bear is a Syrian version of the brown bear. In biblical times it seems to have roamed over all parts of Israel.

6. **Behemoth.** *See* Hippopotamus, II.20.

7. **Boar,** *Sus scropha*. Wild boars do not attack unless molested, but they are dangerous when aroused. They travel in bands of from six to 50 and are most active in the evening and early morning hours. The body is covered with stiff bristles and usually some finer fur, but the body covering is often quite scant. They have four continually growing tusks, two in each jaw. Boar hunts were common in Mesopotamia.

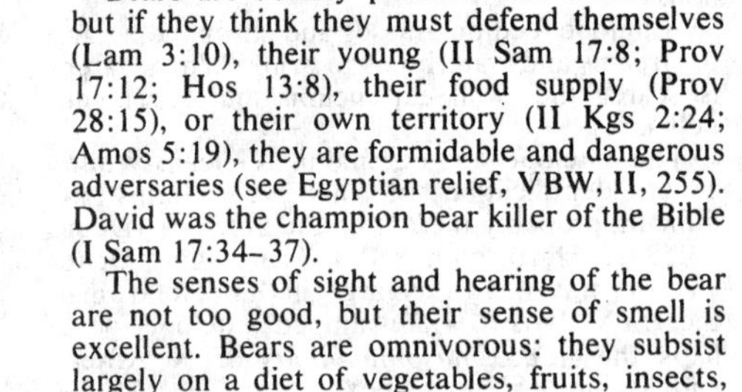

Catching deer in a net, palace of Ashurbanipal, Nineveh. BM

Wild pigs are mainly vegetarian, feeding on roots, nuts, grains, and plant stems. They may damage gardens and farms (Ps 80:13). *See also* Pig, I.14.

8. **Chamois.** *See* Sheep, Mountain, II.36.

9. **Coney** or **Rock Badger,** *Procavia capensis*. The coney is a small ungulate, the only species of the group found outside Africa. It looks like a rabbit, but its ears are quite inconspicuous. It does not burrow as rabbits do, but lives in rocky regions (Ps 104:18; Prov 30:26). It has black whiskers that may be as long as seven inches.

The coney is not a ruminant, but the constant motion of its jaws may suggest that it chews its cud. While for this reason it was probably included with other cud-chewing animals, it did not have cloven hoofs; thus God forbade it as food to the Jews (Lev 11:5; Deut 14:7).

The coney lives in small colonies of from six to 50 animals. It is mainly diurnal, but also comes out on warm moonlit nights. The animal is exclusively a vegetarian. Its flesh is eaten by some natives.

10. **Deer, Hart** or **Stag, Hind** or **Doe, Roe, Roebuck.** Deer are ruminants and were considered clean animals (Deut 12:15, 22; 14:5). Only the males have antlers. Deer antlers grow annually and are solid; this distinguishes the deer from the antelope and gazelle.

Three species of deer are known from Palestine: the red deer, *Cervus elaphus;* the Persian fallow deer, *Dama mesopotamica;* and the roe deer, *Capreolus capreolus*. The red deer (probably the Heb. *'ayyāl*, "hart" or "stag"; fem. *'ayyālâ*, "hind") stands about four feet high at the shoulder. It is gregarious, each group remaining in a definite territory. They graze and browse (Lam 1:6) during the morning and late afternoon. The sexes remain in separate herds. It was celebrated for its leaping (Isa 35:6) and sure footedness in the mountains (Ps 18:33; Song 2:8–9, 17; 8:14; Hab 3:19). Its thirst was evident when pursued (Ps 42:1). (For Assyrian relief of stag attacked by lion see ANEP, #355.)

The Persian fallow deer (I Kgs 4:23, KJV) may now be extinct. The antlers were flattened and palmated (VBW, II, 96). This deer traveled in small groups, feeding mainly on grass in the morning and evening.

The roe deer (Heb. *yaḥmûr*, Deut 14:5; I Kgs 4:23, RSV) is a small graceful animal, dark reddish brown in summer and yellowish gray in winter. Its antlers are about one foot long and have three points. This deer prefers sparsely wooded valleys and the lower slopes of mountains, grazing in open grasslands. These usually associate in family groups of the doe and her offspring. They are shy, yet very curious. The roe deer barks like a dog when disturbed. They are excellent swimmers with all senses well developed.

The hind or doe usually has a single offspring (Job 39:1; Ps 29:9; Jer 14:5), though twins occur with some degree of regularity. (For photo of fawn, see VBW, IV, 143.) The fawn is able to stand on its legs within a few hours of its birth. The hind illustrated grace and charm (Gen 49:21; Prov 5:19).

11. **Dragon.** The KJV translates the plural Heb. word *tannîm* as "dragons" when it clearly refers to desert animals (e.g., Ps 44:19; Isa 13:22; Jer 9:11; Mic 1:8; Mal 1:3), most likely meaning the jackal (*see* II.23). The similar word *tannîn* is singular with a plural form *tannînîm,* also rendered "dragon" or "dragons" in KJV and often in RSV. It refers to serpents in Ex 7:9, 10, 12; Deut 32:33, and perhaps in Ps 91:13; to the crocodile in Ezk 29:3; 32:2; to primordial sea monsters and possibly dinosaurs in Gen 1:21; Job 7:12; Ps 148:7; Jer 51:34; and perhaps in Ps 74:13; Isa 27:1; 51:9 to creatures familiar to the ancient reader from his general knowledge of Canaanite and Babylonian mythology. *See* Leviathan and Whale, V.7, 13.

The mythology of Babylonia describes such monsters or dragons in primordial conflict with Marduk (ANEP, #523); they represented the principle of evil (Tiamat and her troupe of dragons and demons, ANET, pp. 62–67). In Babylon, dragons constructed in relief with glazed bricks decorated the Ishtar Gate (ANEP, #761). Horned serpents appear frequently in Mesopotamian art (ANEP, #454, 511, 519, 520, 537).

In the book of Revelation the dragon is primarily a symbol of Satan, the archenemy of God and His people (12:3–17; 13:2, 4, 11; 16:13; 20:2).

12. **Elephant,** *Elephas africanus* and *E. indicus.* While there are no references in Scripture to the elephant itself, there are a number of references to ivory (I Kgs 10:18, 22; 22:39; Ps 45:8; Song 5:14; 7:4; Ezk 27:6, 15; Amos 3:15; 6:4). The elephant's tusk is the source of ivory, which is carved into ornaments and jewelry and used in making various pieces of furniture. *See* Ivory. At least four Assyrian kings reported hunting elephants and capturing them.

There are two species of elephants: the African and the Indian. The Indian elephant once roamed wild in N Syria and was hunted near Carchemish by Pharaoh Thutmose III (ANET, p. 240). Tiglath-pileser III as late as 735 B.C. received elephant hides and ivory as tribute (ANET, p. 283; cf. ANEP, #353). Elephant tusks have been found in the Jordan Valley.

The Indian elephant lends itself readily to domestication. In addition to its use as a beast of burden, it was used in battle in the ancient world. The Seleucid leader Lysias employed 32 elephants against the Jews in the Maccabean war (I Macc 6:30).

The African elephant is larger than the Indian elephant and untameable. The elephant is

אחזו לנו שעלים
שעלים קטנים מחבלים כרמים
TAKE US THE FOXES THE LITTLE FOXES
THAT SPOIL THE VINES
A fox in the Biblical Zoo, Jerusalem.IIS

the largest land mammal, weighing about three tons. The tusks may weigh up to 200 pounds.

13. **Ferret.** *See* Gecko, IV.16.

14. **Fox,** *Vulpes vulpes palaestinae.* The fox is a small dog-like carnivore with a bushy tail half its body length. It is smaller than a wolf and is normally a nocturnal solitary animal. The fox is omnivorous: it eats small animals, insects and fruit (Song 2:15). The fox is intelligent and has considerable endurance. It can run at speeds up to 30 mph. It has a keen sense of sight, smell, and hearing, and at times seems almost to have a sense of humor.

Usually the fox excavates its own burrow. It is known for its slyness, but the Hebrews also thought of the fox as insignificant (Neh 4:3; Lk 13:32). Some OT references, such as Ps 63:10 and Lam 5:18, are to jackals, for only the latter hunt in packs and tend to act as scavengers. Tristram found two varieties of fox in Palestine in the 19th cen. Feliks reports three varieties of fox in Israel today. How many of these existed in biblical times is not known.

15. **Gazelle,** *Gazella dorcas* and *G. arabica.* The gazelle (Heb. *ṣebî,* KJV "roe," "roebuck"; Gr. *dorkas*) is a small, dainty, graceful antelope with recurved horns. Two varieties exist in Palestine, the dorcas gazelle, which is pale fawn in color and 21 or 22 inches tall; and the Arabian gazelle, which is dark smoky fawn color and 24 or 25 inches tall. Both sexes have hollow horns.

Gazelles formed an important part of the diet of the early inhabitants of Jericho. The dorcas gazelle may have been domesticated and kept in the same way as goats. Apparently gazelles were kept as domestic animals in the Old Kingdom of Egypt. It could not be used for Jewish sacrifice, but could be eaten as food (Deut 12:15, 22; 14:5; 15:22, RSV).

In biblical times the gazelle was probably the game animal most hunted by the Jews (Prov 6:5; Isa 13:14). Pharaoh Tutankhamon hunted gazelles and ostriches with bow and dogs (ANEP, #190). The gazelle is said to have graced Solomon's table (I Kgs 4:23, RSV). It was not easy to catch because of its great speed (II Sam 2:18; I Chr 12:8; Prov 6:5, all RSV). It is also referred to in Song 2:7; 4:5; 7:3 (all RSV).

Herds are still found in the Negeb. Herds usually consist of from five to ten animals, but larger herds assemble in the varieties that migrate in the fall to lower elevations and new feeding grounds. The Bedouin hunt gazelles with falcons and dogs. The falcon annoys the gazelle and injures it so that dogs can overtake it.

16. **Hare,** *Lepus europaeus judaeus, L. capensis,* and *L. arabicus.* The hare is found in both open country, preferably near or on cultivated land, and in woods, usually deciduous. It is an herbivorous rodent and is different from the rabbit; no rabbits are found in Palestine.

A man sacrificing a gazelle, palace of Sargon II, Khorsabad, Assyria. LM

While not a true ruminant according to modern classification in that it does not have a four-chambered stomach, the hare does rechew its food. There is a process of partial regurgitation of material that is too hard for little cells in the stomach to absorb initially; thus the hare actually chews food previously swallowed (E. P. Schulze, "The Ruminating Hare," *Bible-Science Newsletter,* VIII [Jan. 15, 1970], 6).

Hares have very long ears and large hind feet; their feet are well furred (Egyptian relief, VBW, I, 186). Hares do not dig or occupy burrows; in this way they differ from true rabbits which do. Hares are mainly nocturnal and spend their inactive hours hiding in vegetation. They eat grasses and herbaceous matter, also twigs and the young bark of woody plants.

The hare was ceremonially unclean (Lev 11:6; Deut 14:7) apparently because while it appeared to chew its cud it did not have cloven hoofs. The consumption of hares is forbidden also among the Arabs, Chinese and Lapps.

The hare was widely hunted by other peoples in ancient and modern times (Assyrian relief, ANEP, #185). Yet its great speed, its prolific breeding, its timidity and its caution save it from extermination by its many enemies.

17. **Hart.** *See* Deer, II.10.

18. **Hedgehog,** *Erinaceus* sp. L. The hedgehog is an insectivore; the porcupine (*q.v.,* II.31), often confused with the hedgehog, is larger and is a rodent. This animal is characterized by a slow rolling walk, but it can run rapidly. It is a good swimmer and is generally active at night. Its spines are used to cushion itself as well as for protection.

The hedgehog roots in the fallen leaves of hedges and thickets, feeding on seeds and grubs, beetles, snails, snakes, lizards, young birds, mice, and carrion. It rolls into a ball for defense, covering its vulnerable belly.

Bodenheimer reports three species in Palestine. The Egyptian regarded the hedgehog as a bad omen. It is used in Scripture as a symbol of an inhabited area that has become desolate (Isa 14:23; 34:11; Zeph 2:14, all NASB; KJV, "bittern").

19. **Hind.** *See* Deer, II.10.

20. **Hippopotamus,** *Hippopotamus amphibius.* The hippopotamus is a large, thick-skinned amphibious ungulate with a large head, a bulky hairless body, and short legs. At the present time it is found only in the rivers of Africa, but there is considerable fossil evidence of hippopotami in Palestine, and they may have existed in the swamps of northern Galilee and the Jordan Valley. They are frequently found in the art and literature of pharaonic Egypt (VBW, IV, 132). Many have thought that this may be the animal principally in mind in Job 40:15–24 called behemoth. The Egyptian *pehemu* means "ox of the water."

21. **Hyena,** *Hyaena hyaena.* The hyena is a stockily built carnivore with coarse hair and an erect mane of long hairs along the neck and

ANIMALS OF THE BIBLE

back. Hyenas live in holes in banks or among rocks. They are mainly nocturnal but are not ordinarily noisy or aggressive. Their cry, however, is a disagreeable, unearthly sound. Usually they feed on carrion; they have jaws so powerful that they can crush bones. When the carrion supply is inadequate, they will kill sheep, goats, and small animals. If threatened, they growl and erect their mane, but they rarely fight.

Hyenas are known as scavengers; in Africa they eat the domestic refuse in the villages. The striped hyena is said to be the second most common predator in Palestine; here it prefers rocky districts and even rock tombs. It may exhume human bodies.

The hyena is not mentioned in KJV but appears as Zibeon in Gen 36:2, 14, 20, etc., as a personal name and in Gen 14:2, 8; Deut 29:23; I Sam 13:18 as a place name, Zeboim, which seems to indicate hyenas were common in the area. RSV translates *'î* as "hyena" in Isa 13:22; 34:14; Jer 50:39. The hyena is mentioned in Sir 13:18.

A statue in green schist of Thueris, Egyptian hippopotamus goddess in the Cairo Museum. LL

22. **Ibex** or **Wild Goat,** *Capra ibex nubiana.* The ibex (Heb. *yā'ēl,* "wild goat," KJV) is a species of wild goat which still lives in small numbers in the cliffs close to the Dead Sea (I Sam 24:2). Its slender legs and sharp cloven hoofs enable it to cling to narrow rock ledges, to jump between them, and to climb steep cliffs. Usually the ibex is found in rugged mountain country, rocky crags and meadows, just below the snow line (Ps 104:18). In Job 39:1 they are called *ya'ălê-sāla',* "goats of the crag or rock"; in RSV, "mountain goats."

These animals frequently gather in herds of from five to 20. They graze and browse, being active in the afternoon and sometimes feeding throughout the night.

The large horn of the ibex was at one period made into the shofar, which was blown in the second temple to announce the new year and the jubilee year.

23. **Jackal,** *Canis aureus.* The jackal (Heb. *tan,* often "dragon" in KJV) is smaller than the true wolf, and its tail is shorter (for photo see VBW, III, 258). It is similar to the fox (*q.v.,* II.14) but with shorter ears and longer legs. Its tail is drooping or erect compared with the long and horizontal tail of the fox. These animals usually prowl at night, singly, in pairs, or in packs through open savannah country. They eat small mammals, poultry, fruit, vegetables, and carrion. They spend their days in thickets and in clumps of vegetation. Often they obtain scraps from the kill of the larger carnivores. They are fast runners; their running speed is about 33 mph.

The cry of the jackal is an unnerving wailing howl (Mic 1:8, RSV; cf. Job 30:28–29). Scripture references in the RSV and NASB are chiefly to jackals prowling around ruined cities and wilderness areas. References include Neh 2:13; Ps 44:19; Isa 13:22; 34:13; 35:7; Jer 9:11; 14:6; 49:33; 51:37; Lam 4:3; 5:18; Mal 1:3.

24. **Leopard,** *Panthera pardus tulliana.* The leopard has the widest range across the earth of any of the large cats. In rocky areas it lives in caves, but in forested regions it lives in thick vegetation. Many lived in the vicinity of Mount Hermon in OT times (Song 4:8). It is a wary and cunning animal, formidable and ferocious (Jer 5:6; Hos 13:7; cf. Isa 11:6). It has survived in Palestine into the 20th cen. A.D.

The leopard is swift on the ground (Hab 1:8) and agile in trees. When it cannot consume all its prey, it caches the remainder in a tree. Its color is yellowish bespeckled with black spots (Jer 13:23; photo and tomb painting, VBW, III, 109). Daniel and John saw leopards in their visions as symbols of world powers (Dan 7:6; Rev 13:2).

25. **Lion,** *Panthera leo persica.* The lion is a large tawny colored carnivore which preys chiefly on hoofed mammals and charges by a series of leaps and bounds. Within the historic period, the lion ranged in Europe and Palestine. The Palestinian animal was the Asiatic or Per-

ANIMALS OF THE BIBLE

King Ashurnasirpal of Assyria hunting lions from his chariot. BM

sian lion. The males are heavily maned. The mane stops at the shoulders but covers much of the belly. It cannot climb and is mainly nocturnal, returning to its lair or thicket by day (Jer 4:7; 25:38; Nah 2:11–12).

Lions were common in biblical times in all parts of Palestine. The Heb. language has at least seven words for lion and young lion, and the beast is referred to over 130 times in the Bible. It gradually declined and became extinct shortly after A.D. 1300. The lion was present in Mesopotamia until the end of the 19th cen. Lion hunting was the sport of kings in Assyria (ANEP, #184) and Egypt (ANET, p. 243).

The roaring of the lion comes only on a full stomach, i.e., after it has consumed its prey (Ps 22:13; Ezk 22:25; Amos 3:4). The lion is a bold (II Sam 17:10; Prov 28:1), destructive animal (Ps 7:2; Jer 2:30; Hos 5:14; Mic 5:8), the enemy of the flock (Amos 3:12), whose roaring inspires fear in domestic animals (Amos 3:8; see VBW, III, 174–235; I Pet 5:8). Like all great cats, lions sometimes become maneaters (I Kgs 13:24–28; 20:36; II Kgs 17:25–26; Ps 57:4; Dan 6:7–27). They prefer open country, savannas, and plains.

Lions played an important part in the political (I Kgs 10:19–20) and religious symbolism of the Near East (see many references in ANEP). In Assyria and Babylonia the lion was regarded as a royal beast (Dan 7:4). A large basalt stela from the mid-2nd mil. B.C. was found at Beth-shan depicting a dog and a lion fighting (ANEP, #228). The lion was the mightiest of beasts to the Jew and illustrated a king's regal bearing (Prov 30:29–31). Thus it symbolized rulership (Gen 49:9; Num 24:9) and even became a title of Christ (Rev 5:5). The lion remains a favorite zoo animal among oriental-style rulers; the emperor of Ethiopia still exhibits the royal lions.

26. **Mole.** *See* Mole Rat, IV.25.
27. **Monkey.** *See* Peacock, III.40.
28. **Mouse.** *See* Mouse, IV.27.

Diorite statue of the Egyptian lion goddess Sekhmet. MM

29. **Onager** or **Half Ass,** *Equus hemionus hemihippus.* The onager or Syrian wild ass (Heb. *pereʼ*) is intermediate between the true horse and the true ass. Its ears are longer than those of a horse but shorter than those of the ass. It is also known as the kulan, the kiang, and the djiggetai. For Assyrian bas reliefs see VBW, III, 98; IV, 128; ANEP, #186. The front hoofs are narrow, there are chestnuts on the forelegs only, and the tail is short haired for a long distance from its root so that it appears to be tufted.

The Sumerians were able to domesticate the onager, but the horse superseded it. In Ur it was used to draw chariots, for a number were buried with their vehicles in a royal grave *c.* 2500 B.C. Later it was a favorite quarry of the Babylonian and Assyrian kings.

The onager seems to have been very common in the steppe lands near Israel where it is described as a freedom-loving desert animal (Job 24:5; 39:5-8; Ps 104:11; Isa 32:14; Jer 2:24; Hos 8:9). Ishmael was to be a wild ass of a man (Gen 16:12, RSV), one who could not adjust to communal life. Drought seems to have been responsible for the decimation of the onager in biblical times (Jer 14:6). Nebuchadnezzar dwelt among the wild beasts including the onager (Aram. *ʽărād,* Dan 5:21).

30. **Ox, Wild** or **Unicorn,** *Bos primigenius.* This animal (Heb. *rᵉʼēm,* Akkad. *rīmu,* described in Job 39:9-12; for Assyrian relief see VBW, IV, 129) is clearly the wild ox, a large, fierce, fleet, intractable animal. It has a long lean rump with a straight back and a long narrow head. The two horns (Deut 33:17, RSV; "unicorns" should be singular in KJV) are straight and as long as the head. These were its outstanding characteristics (Num 23:22; 24:8; Ps 22:21).

It is also known in Europe as the aurochs. In Germany it is known as *Auer;* in Latin it was *urus.* It existed in the wild state until the 17th cen. A.D. when it became extinct, though Bodenheimer reports rumors of individual specimens surviving in the mountain valleys of Kurdistan. Hunting of this animal was the preferred sport of Assyrian kings. Tiglath-pileser I hunted it in the Lebanon Mountains *c.* 1100 B.C. (cf. Ps 29:6).

At one time *rᵉʼēm* was thought to be the oryx or antelope; the Arabs call the oryx *riʼm.* The translators of the LXX called *rᵉʼēm* "monokeros" (unicorn) on the basis of relief representations of the aurochs in strict profile which they found on Babylonian mosaics and Egyptian drawings. Because it was in strict profile, only one horn was seen, hence "unicorn." The Vulgate translated *rᵉʼēm* "unicornus" and Luther followed with the phrase "Einhorn." There is no question today that the *rᵉʼēm* is the wild ox and that the author of Job was referring to this and not to a mythological animal (see also ANEP, #183; VBW, I, 228).

Kings often symbolized their dominion by wearing a helmet with two wild ox horns (VBW, IV, 57; cf. Ps 92:10 with 132:17-18).

31. **Porcupine,** *Hystrix* sp. The porcupine is a true rodent as opposed to the insectivore hedgehog, and lives in forested areas, rocky hills, ravines and valleys. It has long quills, which when raised give the appearance of a crest. This animal is almost entirely nocturnal. It burrows by day into a natural cavity or crevice. The old world porcupine rarely climbs trees as the new world porcupine does. Porcupines eat fruit, bark, roots and other succulent vegetation. They may also eat carrion. While its flesh is edible, it was not classed among the clean animals for the Israelite. A porcupine may weigh as much as 60 pounds.

Heb. *qippôd* in Isa 34:11 is translated "porcupine" in ASV and RSV, but "bittern" in KJV; KJV also has "bittern" for this word in Isa 14:23; Zeph 2:14, where RSV has "hedgehog."

32. **Pygarg.** *See* Antelope, II.1.

33. **Roe.** *See* Gazelle, II.15.

34. **Roebuck.** *See* Deer, II.10.

35. **Satyr.** The satyrs (Heb. *śāʽîr*) of Isa 13:21; 34:14 (KJV, RSV, JerusB) were evidently hairy creatures (from Heb. *śēʽār,* "hair") and almost certainly wild goats, since Heb. *śāʽîr* is also the word for "he-goat." RSV also translates this Heb. word as "satyrs" in Lev 17:7 and II Chr 11:15, where KJV has "devils." At the latter reference WBC (p. 400) suggests that instead of mythological satyrs or hairy demons, "as claimed by 'liberal' criticism," the *sᵉʽîrîm* were simply goat idols, used in conjunction with the golden calves which Jeroboam I of Israel had set up.

36. **Sheep, Mountain,** *Ovis orientalis.* The European chamois *(Rupicapra)* is not found in Bible lands. Thus in Deut 14:5, for Heb. *zemer* the KJV "chamois" may refer to one of several varieties of wild sheep known in the Mediterranean area. The above species occurs wild in Armenia and Persia. For *zemer* Tristram suggested the *Ovis tragelaphus,* a sheep about three feet high with long curved horns, familiar to the Bedouin.

37. **Unicorn.** *See* Ox, Wild, II.30.

38. **Weasel.** *See* IV.36.

39. **Wild Ass.** *See* Onager, II.29.

40. **Wild Ox.** *See* II.30.

41. **Wolf,** *Canis lupus.* The wolf travels in bands of up to 30 animals that arise from a family group (for photo see VBW, III, 280). They hunt singly or in relays, usually at night (Jer 5:6). Wolves have acute hearing and sight, but rely chiefly on scent and usually catch their prey in a swift and open chase. The wolf is known for its boldness, fierceness, and voracity (Gen 49:27; Hab 1:8). It commonly kills more than it can eat or take away. Its usual food is small mammals, such as mice, fish, crabs, and carrion. In Egypt, Rome, and Greece the wolf was considered sacred.

Wolves are intelligent, social creatures, faithful to their own kind; they mate for life. Wolves were well known in Palestine. Except for Isa 11:6; 65:25; Jn 10:12, the scriptural references to wolves are all figurative, usually the symbol of enemies and wicked men (e.g., Ezk 22:27; Zeph 3:3; Acts 20:29).

III. Flying Creatures

1. **Bat.** Bats are flying mammals; they have hair and provide milk for their young. They orient themselves by echo location and take shelter in caves, crevices, tree cavities, buildings, and also in exposed places on trees. In colder areas they hibernate or migrate. The normal resting position for a bat is hanging head downward. Because they fly with their legs as well as with their wings, they may properly be said to swim through the air.

Most bats are insectivorous. These bats are relatively small in size and obtain insects in flight. Many insectivorous bats also eat some fruit. In addition, there are fruit-eating bats which feed exclusively on fruit and some green vegetation. These usually live and feed in groups. They are tropical because they can live only where fruit is constantly ripening, although some have been observed in Palestine. Fruit-eating bats may be large with a wing spread of almost five feet. A third group are flower-feeding bats which eat pollen and nectar. They are small with long pointed heads and long tongues. They are found only in the tropics and semitropical regions.

Vampire bats are known only from the New World. There are only three species; these eat blood by making a small incision and lapping it up. Carnivorous bats are of all sizes; these prey on birds, lizards, and frogs. Fish-eating bats catch fish at or near the water surface.

Tristram reports eight varieties of bats in Palestine in the 19th cen. One of these, the little brown bat, *Myotis* sp., is worldwide in its distribution. It is insectivorous and probably actually has the widest natural distribution of any terrestrial mammal except man. Little brown bats are mostly cave dwellers. The females form maternity colonies which may number in the tens of thousands.

Two species of mouse-tailed bats, *Rhinopoma* sp., are found in Palestine. The tail is nearly as long as the head and body combined. These are often colonial. They roost in caves, rock clefts, wells, pyramids, palaces, houses, and they are insectivorous.

The slit-faced or hollow-faced bats also are found in Palestine. These, too, are insectivorous and roost in groups of from six to 20.

The bat is unclean (Lev 11:19; Deut 14:18), and is a symbol of desolation (Isa 2:20–21).

2. **Bee,** *Apis mellifica.* There are many references to bees in the Bible. The land of Israel was described as a land flowing with milk and honey. Honey and dates were the only major sources of sugar available to ancient man. It is believed that the honeybee was not domesticated until the Hellenistic period in Palestine so that earlier references are to wild honeybees. Passages such as Jud 14:8 refer to honey; other passages such as Deut 1:44; Ps 118:12; and Isa 7:18 allude to the irritable, vindictive nature of the bee and the painful stings which it inflicts.

In getting honey every attempt was made by the ancients to protect the colony in order to preserve this source of sugar. In Egypt the bee was considered sacred. The Philistines and the Hittites practiced beekeeping in their cities. A bee swarm was as valuable as a sheep, though the price of honey itself was low. Honey was sometimes eaten with the honeycomb (Song 5:1).

3. **Bittern.** *See* Hedgehog, II.18; Heron, III.21.

4. **Buzzard,** *Buteo buteo*. This bird was ritually unclean (Heb. *'ayyâ,* Lev 11:14; Deut 14:13, both JerusB), as were all predatory and carrion-feeding birds. It resembles the kite (KJV in above verses), though its tail is straight and not cleft. It is said to have wonderfully sharp eyesight (Job 28:7*b*) and will trail its prey for hours.

5. **Cock.** *See* Fowl, Domestic, III.14.

6. **Cormorant,** *Phalacrocorax carbo carbo*. The Heb. word *shālāk* implies a bird that hurls itself or dives upon its prey (Lev 11:17; Deut 14:17). The common cormorant is a large black goose-like bird which feeds on fish. It is known from the Mediterranean coast, from the Jordan River, and from the Sea of Galilee. The cormorant is repeatedly depicted in Egypt and in Palestine.

7. **Crane,** *Grus grus*. Cranes are tall wading birds resembling the stork and the heron but with shorter talons. Its plumage has a silvery gloss, and the feathers of the tail are wavy. It feeds on plants, insects, and worms. Large flocks of cranes flying in a wedge-shaped formation pass over Palestine annually on their way to Africa from the northern countries of Europe and again on their return flight. Jer 8:7 refers to the crane's migratory habits. Their general call is best described as a bellowing, but during flight they are said to emit a chattering sound; this latter seems to be what is referred to in Isa 38:14.

8. **Cuckoo** or **Cuckow,** *Cuculus canorus canorus*. The term used in Lev 11:16 and Deut 14:15 (KJV) may refer either to the common cuckoo or to the great spotted cuckoo, *Clamator glandarius*. The cuckoo is a small, drab brown bird. It is best known because of its parasitic habits. It acts as a brood parasite, laying its eggs in the nest of another species after pushing out one of the eggs of the host species. The young cuckoo hatches before the host species and evicts the young host species. The foster parents raise it as their own.

The cuckoo is an insect eater, yet in Scripture it is considered unclean, implying that either it is a predator or a carrion eater. For that reason some believe that the term actually refers to the sea gull (RSV, JerusB) or sea-mew (ASV) and not to the cuckoo. Gulls, terns, and petrels are all common on the seashore and lakes of Palestine.

9. **Dove** or **Turtledove,** *Streptopelia turtur.* The plumage of the dove or turtledove (Heb. *tôr;* Akkad. *tūrtu;* Gr. *trugōn*) is of many hues—red, blue, and violet. It migrates to Israel in the spring (Jer 8:7) and awakens the groves with its call (Song 2:12, RSV). It is smaller than the pigeon but is more beautiful. It cares for its young much as does the pigeon by regurgitating food. The psalmist employed the word metaphorically as a term of affection, "the soul of thy dove" (Ps 74:19). It was a clean bird that could be used for sacrifice (Gen 15:9; Lev 1:14; 5:7; 12:6; Num 6:10; Lk 2:24). *See also* Pigeon, III.42. (See Heinrich Greeven, *"Peristera,"* TDNT, VI, 63–72.)

10. **Eagle.** *See* Vulture, Griffon, III.54.

11. **Eagle, Gier.** *See* Vulture, Egyptian, III.53.

12. **Falcon.** *See* Kestrel, III.25.

13. **Fly,** *Musca* sp. Flies (Heb. *zᵉbûb)* are important causes of epidemics and food spoilage. The reference in Eccl 10:1 seems to be *Musca domestica* which ruins the ointment. The fly symbolizing Egypt in Isa 7:18 seems to refer to *Tabanus arenivagus* which attacks both man and animal. The swarms of insects in the fourth plague (Ex 8:21–31) may refer to the house fly, to the bluebottle fly *(Calliphora erythrocephala),* the dog fly, the Barghas midge, or the Tabanid fly *(Stomoxys calcitrans).*

The maggots of Job 25:6 and Isa 14:11, and the worms of Ex 16:24; Job 7:5; 17:14 are probably fly larvae. *See* Worm, IV.37. The domestic fly is very common in all parts of Israel, chiefly in dung heaps and garbage. The female lays her eggs out of which a white maggot emerges which feeds on refuse. After a few days the maggot develops into a cocoon out of which the adult insect emerges. In the summer this whole cycle lasts just about twelve days so that a fly can breed about twenty generations a year. Philistine inhabitants of the city of Ekron worshiped a god named Baal-zebul, "Baal the Prince," who was dubbed Baal-zebub, "Lord of flies," by God-fearing Israelites in a mocking pun (II Kgs 1:2).

14. **Fowl, Domestic,** *Gallus gallus domesticus.* Domesticated poultry are probably derived from the red jungle fowl of India. They seem to have been known already in OT times (Prov 30:31, RSV; not the "greyhound," KJV). A seal of Jaazaniah (cf. II Kgs 25:23) dating *c.* 600 B.C. bears the figure of a fighting cock; it was found at Tell en-Nasbeh, the site of ancient Mizpah.

Poultry were considered a symbol of fertility. The Jews carried a cock and a hen in front of bridal couples. The cock is still used as a timekeeper and an alarm clock in eastern countries (cf. Mt 26:34). *See* Cockcrowing. The motherly concern of the hen was familiar to Jesus' hearers (Mt 23:37). The reference in Neh 5:18 to fowls or poultry for Nehemiah's table is probably to wild game.

15. **Glede.** *See* Kite, III.26.

16. **Gnat,** *Culex, Anopheles,* etc. The references in Ex 8:20–28; Ps 78:45; 105:31 to "swarms of flies" (KJV, RSV) may be to the mosquito, to the harvester gnat, to the Barghas of the Arabs, or to the sandfly. These references seem to fit a swarm of these insects that plagued the inhabitants and pestered them in their daily life not unlike the lice which occurred in the preceding plague. Gnats frequently had to be strained out of wine to which they were drawn while it fermented (Mt 23:24).

17. **Goatsucker** or **Nighthawk,** *Caprimulgus* sp. There are several species of these birds found in Palestine, similar to the American whippoorwill (Lev 11:16*b;* Deut 14:15*b*). The goatsuckers were thought by the ancients to milk goats. They resemble owls with a flat head, large eyes and soft plumage which results in a noiseless flight. They are insectivorous, catching their prey on the wing. They migrate from Africa to Europe each year.

18. **Goose,** *Anser anser.* Geese are long-necked, web-footed water birds. They are easily domesticated. They were known to the Greeks, and domestic geese are mentioned in the Odyssey. They may have been domesticated already in Egypt in the Old Kingdom and certainly were domesticated by New Kingdom times. They were used for food and for sacrifice.

Geese were similarly used for food and sacrifice in ancient Mesopotamia. The breeding of geese was widespread in Canaan in biblical times; ivory carvings of the 13th or 12th cen. B.C. showing geese found at Megiddo attest to this fact (VBW, II, 210). Geese graced the table of King Solomon, according to I Kgs 4:23, where they are referred to as "fatted fowl."

Snaring ducks and geese. Wall relief in tomb of Ka-Gemni, Saqqara, Egypt. LL

The Egyptian god Horus represented as a hawk. LL

19. **Hawk, Sparrow,** *Accipiter nisus.* The Heb. *nēṣ* was ceremonially unclean (Lev 11:16; Deut 14:15) and probably is the sparrow hawk. It is not a permanent resident in Palestine, but stops off as it migrates from N to S. This southward migration is mentioned in the book of Job (39:26).

The sparrow hawk (photo, VBW, I, 188) is slightly larger than the kestrel with short feathers and a long tail. The tail acts as a rudder and helps the bird change its course very swiftly in flight, so that it can maneuver in the air when it chases small warblers and other birds. It does not seize its prey on the ground as does the kestrel, but hunts small birds in flight and attacks them. The Egyptians embalmed sparrow hawks as well as kestrels; all hawks were highly regarded by them. The god Horus was depicted with the head of a hawk or falcon. The sparrow hawk's back is grayish brown and its belly white with black and brown bars.

20. **Hen.** *See* Fowl, Domestic, III.14.

21. **Heron** or **Bittern,** *Ardea* sp. The heron is a wading bird with a long thin neck and long legs (photo, VBW, I, 188). There are at least seven varieties reported by Tristram in Palestine. According to Deut 14:18 and Lev 11:19, the heron was ceremonially unclean. Driver believes these references are to the cormorant, but most scholars believe they refer to one of the herons.

The characteristic mark of these birds is a comb-like growth on the inner side of the third toe. The white heron attains a length of over three feet, while the dwarf heron is only about 22 inches long. All herons feed on fish, small reptiles, and insects. They are a nuisance in artificial fish ponds.

22. **Hoopoe,** *Upupa epops.* The hoopoe (Lev 11:19; Deut 14:18, both RSV; "lapwing," KJV) is one of the most beautiful birds of Israel with colored plumage, a lovely crown-shaped crest on its head, and a long slender curved bill. In the fall it migrates to the S. It is listed as unclean, possibly because it searches for grubs and small insects in repulsive places such as dunghills.

23. **Hornet.** *See* Wasp, III.55.

24. **Ibis,** *Threskiornis aethiopica aethiopica.* The ibis (Lev 11:17, RSV following the LXX; "great owl," KJV) is a wading bird unknown in Palestine in the 19th and 20th cen. A.D., but possibly known there in biblical times. It was well known in ancient Egypt where it was sacred to Thoth. The ibis was classed as unclean; it eats mollusks and crustaceans. At one time it was very common in Egypt, but it has largely vanished today with the disappearance of the swamps along the Nile. The RSV does not consistently translate *yanshûp* as "ibis"; in Deut 14:16 and Isa 34:11, RSV follows the other versions by rendering it "great owl" or "owl."

On right, herons; on left ducks, geese, and pigeons. Wall relief from tomb of Ptah-hotep, Saqqara, Egypt. LL

the vicinity of the incubated eggs are intended to serve as food for the young.

The stupidity of the ostrich appears when it is hunted and cornered because it fails to take the evasive action which might save it. In open country, however, it is very wary and runs at great speed to escape. In contrast to the partridge, it will run away from its eggs and chicks when pursued. Its speed is proverbial: Tristram reports the maximum stride from 22 to 28 feet and a speed of 26 mph. To bag an ostrich was considered the feat of a hero (ANEP, #190, 706).

35. **Owl, Barn** or **White,** *Tyto alba*. Tristram reported that in 19th cen. A.D. Palestine there were eight varieties of owls, of which five were quite plentiful. It is difficult, however, to identify a particular variety with a certain Heb. word in the OT. Thus the following four owls can be only approximate identifications.

The barn owl (Heb. *tinshemeth*) is ritually unclean (Lev 11:18*a*; Deut 14:16*c*). It may get its Heb. name from the snoring sound that it makes when breathing. It has a frightening voice and somewhat sinister features so that at times it has been considered to be demonic; yet it is a useful bird that devours rodents that ravage the fields and damage houses. It sleeps during the day and is active at night. Its sense of hearing and sight are well developed. Its color is light brownish-yellow with a white mask around the eyes and cheeks. The whole leg is covered with feathers that protect it against the bites of its struggling victims. It has a large head and wide pop eyes; for this reason it is sometimes called the monkey-faced owl.

The KJV follows the Vulgate in translating *tinshemeth* as "swan," while the RSV renders it "water hen" after the LXX.

An ostrich in the Biblical Zoo. Jerusalem. HFV

36. **Owl, Little,** *Athene noctua lilith*. Like all other owls, this is ritually unclean (Heb. *kôs*, Lev 11:17*a*; Deut 14:16*a*). It is the smallest of all nocturnal birds of prey (photo, VBW, I, 188). Chiefly insectivorous, at times it feeds also on tiny birds. It is the most common owl in Palestine, dwelling among ruins (Ps 102:6*b*, RSV), tombstones, rocks, and in thickets. Its voice sounds like that of a dying person. On occasion it may be observed perching on a rock with its large eyes gazing off into the distance. It was this pose that the ancient Greeks considered a sign of wisdom. They considered it sacred to the goddess Athena.

The famous "owl" of Athens, standard currency of the Eastern Mediterranean during the Athenian Empire period (fifth cen. B.C.). G. L. Archer & W. S. LaSor

37. **Owl, Long-eared** or **Great,** *Asio otus*. This bird is mentioned in the Bible among the birds of desolation that will inhabit the devastated Edom (Isa 34:11). It gets its Heb. name *yanshûph* ("hisser," from *nāshap*, "to blow, hiss") because of the snoring or panting sound which it makes when breathing. For this reason G. R. Driver thinks it is the screech owl. It feeds on rodents, rats, and mice, devouring them skin and all and expelling the undigested waste through its mouth. It hibernates in Israel among ruins and in groves.

The great owl stands nearly two feet tall. The color is mouse gray with gray-brown spots and black stripes. As its name indicates, it has tufted "ears." Like other predatory birds, it was considered ritually unclean (Lev 11:17; Deut 14:16). For another possible translation of *yanshûph* see "Ibis."

38. **Owl, Scops,** *Otus scops*. The scops owl has two horn-shaped crests of hair-like feathers on its head, perches in an inclined posture, and hops and dances like a goat. During the hatching period the male's hooting sounds like a moan. It feeds chiefly on insects and mice. During an invasion by mice or locusts these owls appear in large flocks and help destroy the pest.

Biblical references may be either Isa 13:21 (NASB, Heb. *'ōaḥ*, KJV "doleful creatures") or Isa 34:15 (Heb. *qippôz*, KJV "great owl"). Others think the *qippôz* is a variety of snake (NASB, JerusB).

39. **Partridge,** *Alectoris graeca werae, A. graeca cypriotes,* and *Ammoperdix heyi heyi.* The partridge referred to in I Sam 26:20 is probably the sand partridge *(Ammoperdix)* found near the Dead Sea; in Jer 17:11, the chukar *(Alectoris).* They are the most common game birds in Palestine. The main hunting season seems to have been in July. It is caught by continuously chasing it (cf. I Sam 26:20), by snares, or by a hunter hiding in a deer blind. The bird finds refuge among the bushes with which its brownish-green feathers blend. It is a prolific breeder, otherwise it probably would have become extinct. The young are able to run about seeking food and shelter almost immediately after hatching. The explanation of the partridge's gathering a brood which she did not hatch (Jer 17:11, RSV) seems to lie in the fact that the hen partridge lays two batches of eggs, one for herself and one for the cock to incubate.

40. **Peacock,** *Pavo cristatus.* The peacock is a native of India where it is a shy, fast runner. Occasionally the peacocks fly in small flocks. Because it is not native to Palestine, the Heb. word *tukkîyîm* in I Kgs 10:22 and II Chr 9:21 is thought by some to be a reference to old world monkeys brought from E Africa, or to guinea hens from the Upper Nile. Since *tukî* is mentioned along with ivory, most likely from the African elephant, the *qōph* (*see* Ape, II.2), the monkey is the most probable identification

A pelican in the Biblical Zoo, Jerusalem. HFV

(see IDB, II, 252*a*). The Heb. term is similar to an Egyptian word for monkey in inscriptions regarding expeditions to Punt (Somaliland). Large and small monkeys were among the tribute received by the Assyrian king Ashurnasirpal II (ANET, p. 276).

41. **Pelican,** *Pelecanus onocrotalus.* Pelicans were known to the ancient Egyptians and Assyrians. Many scholars doubt that the Heb. *qā'at,* an unclean bird (Lev 11:18; Deut 14:17) that inhabited the wilderness (Ps 102:6) and ruins (Isa 34:11; Zeph 2:14, KJV "cormorant"), refers to the pelican and believe the *qā'at* is one of the owls or vultures. But the roseate pelican, with white plumage and large yellow pouch under its lower bill, does frequent rivers, lakes, and marshes of Palestine. After flying out to sea as far as 20 miles to swoop down upon fish near the surface, the pelican often retires inland to a deserted spot to digest its enormous meal. Thus the pelican may well be the lonely bird of the psalmist (102:6).

42. **Pigeon** or **Dove,** *Columba livia.* The dove (Heb. *yônâ;* Gr. *peristera*) or young pigeon (Heb. *ben yônâ*) mentioned in the Bible seems to be the wild rock pigeon from which our domestic pigeon is descended; the term is a loose one applying to any small species of pigeon. Some were colored silvery gray with greenish-gold irridescent plumage on the wings (Ps 68:13; for photos, see VBW, I, 184; III, 88).

The pigeon or dove was apparently one of the first birds to be domesticated, since Noah released a dove toward the end of the Flood (Gen 8:8-12). One variety still lives in a semiwild state on the roofs of Jerusalem. It roves over the fields, feeds on weeds, and returns at dusk to its home (Isa 60:8). The dove was offered as a sacrifice by the poor and the Nazarite (Lev 5:7; Num 6:10). It was widely used for food. Its throaty moaning is referred to in Isa 38:14; 59:11; Ezk 7:16; Nah 2:7. Its powers of flight were well known (Ps 55:6). Solomon comments on the beauty of its eyes (Song 1:15; 4:1; 5:12). He also calls attention to its gentleness and loyalty to its mate (Song 2:14; 5:2; 6:9). The dove often built its nest in the rocks and cliffs (Song 2:14; Jer 48:28). Usually the dove was regarded as a symbol of innocence (Mt 10:16); yet in Hos 7:11 the dove is said to be senseless and foolish. In II Kgs 6:25 there is a reference to the sale of dove dung *(q.v.),* presumably used for food because of famine conditions during the siege of Samaria. *See also* Dove, III.9.

43. **Quail,** *Coturnix coturnix.* These are short-winged, sandy-colored gallinaceous (poultry-like) birds, the smallest of the subfamily *Phasianinae* which includes pheasants and partridges. Quail of the Mediterranean region winter in the Sudan and migrate northward in vast flocks in the spring. Their flight at night with the wind is exhausting, so that when they alight they are easily caught with nets and even with bare hands (for painting, see VBW, I, 149).

Tristram says that quail are considered the most delicate eating of all game.

Enormous flocks of quail twice served as food for the Israelites in the wilderness of Sinai when they were driven down in the desert miraculously by the winds (Ex 16:13; Num 11:31; Ps 105:40). In the second case they must have been flying along the Gulf of Aqaba and were blown off course by an east wind (Ps 78:26–28). They are preserved by drying in the sun (Num 11:32).

44. **Raven,** *Corvus corax.* The raven is a large (three pound, 26 inch long) passerine (sparrow-like) bird related to the rooks, jackdaws, magpies, and jays. Its most conspicuous feature is its glossy-black, irridescent plumage (Song 5:11; for photo, SEE VBW, I, 189). Other members of the *Corvidae* are less soberly colored. It is found almost everywhere in the world except in the South Pacific.

Noah sent out a raven first from the ark (Gen 8:7); it must have fed on floating victims of the Flood. The raven is essentially a scavenger and thus was ceremonially unclean (Lev 11:15; Deut 14:14); but it will attack defenseless young animals (Prov 30:17). Aristophanes in his *Birds* similarly reports that crows peck out the eyes of their prey. It will even attack lambs, small mammals, birds, and reptiles. Ravens find food for themselves and their young quite readily, without help from man (Job 38:41; Ps 147:9; Lk 12:24). They pair for life. They prefer desolate uninhabited areas as their home territory (I Kgs 17:4, 6; Isa 34:11). Apparently the Heb. *'ōrēb,* "raven," refers to the entire family of *Corvidae.* Tristram reports eight species of the family in Palestine: three ravens, two jackdaws, one crow, one rook, and one chough.

45. **Seamew** or **Sea Gull.** *See* Cuckoo, III.8.

46. **Sparrow,** *Passer domesticus.* The sparrow referred to in Ps 84:3; 102:7 (KJV); Prov 26:2 (RSV); Mt 10:29, 31; Lk 12:6–7 is a passerine bird of the finch family and is generally considered to be of little worth. The Heb. word *ṣippôr* is the general term for "bird" and especially would refer to small birds, such as sparrows, finches, thrushes, blackbirds, and starlings. The common or house sparrow was known in ancient Greece and Egypt. There it had the reputation of invading fields in big swarms and picking seeds from them.

47. **Sparrow Hawk.** *See* Hawk, Sparrow, III.19.

48. **Stork,** *Ciconia alba.* The stork is a long-legged, wading white bird with glossy black wings, which eats aquatic organisms, garbage, small mammals, birds, and reptiles. It is related to the heron and is ceremonially unclean (Lev 11:19; Deut 14:18). Flocks of storks pass through Israel during the September migration on their way to central and southern Africa, and likewise in the spring on their return flight to their home in northern Palestine, Syria, and the whole of Europe. Their faithful tending of the young is proverbial, as is also their habit of returning annually to the same nesting place.

Jeremiah mentions the uncanny instinctive knowledge the stork has of the time of his migration (Jer 8:7; for photo, see VBW, III, 103). Ps 104:17 refers to its nesting in a treetop when a suitable building is not at hand. Tristram reported the black stork, *C. nigra,* as well as the white stork in 19th cen. Palestine. The black stork is common around the Dead Sea valley and nests in trees; hence it may be the species referred to in Ps 104:17.

The stork has large powerful wings, the flapping of which produces a strong rushing sound referred to in Zech 5:9. It has very long legs and connecting membranes between the toes to prevent it from sinking in the mud. The red bill is sharp and long, serving to seize and lift the prey out of water. In Europe the stork nests on rooftops and lives in the same place year after year.

49. **Swallow,** *Hirundo rustica.* The swallow is a small, nearly black, fork-tailed passerine bird with long, tapered wings, noted for its graceful flight. It resembles the swift in shape and life habits, but it has a shorter tail. The Heb. *d^erôr* (Ps 84:3; Prov 26:2) is quite certainly the sparrow; but in Isa 38:14; Jer 8:7 the *sîs* should rather be translated as the swift (*q.v.*).

50. **Swan,** *Cygnus* sp. Two species of swans are found in the Middle East as passing migrants, *C. olor, C. musicus.* Swans are the best musicians known among the birds and were considered sacred to Apollo. They sound like flutes and harps. Swans will fight only if attacked. They are often attacked by eagles. The scriptural references in Lev 11:18*a* and Deut 14:16*c* (both KJV) may not be to the true swan, but the Heb. term *tinshemet* may be the water hen (RSV) or the barn owl (*q.v.,* III.35).

51. **Swift,** *Apus* sp. Swifts (Heb. *sîs*) arrive in Palestine in late winter (Jer 8:7), and immense flocks fill the cities with their cries. They usually arrive sometime between February 20 and 25. The swift, like the swallow, has long, bent wings and a cleft tail which enables it to attain great speed as it skims the ground and sweeps through the air. It is a useful bird devouring a great many harmful insects which it catches in its mouth in flight. The swift makes its nest in the rooftops, in nooks and crannies of the walls in Palestinian cities. To build its nest it uses straw and feathers which are cemented together with saliva from its mouth. Other swifts live in caves and clefts of rocks. The plaintive cry of the swift is referred to in Isa 38:14.

52. **Vulture, Black,** or **Osprey,** *Aegypius monachus.* The black vulture is ceremonially unclean ("osprey," Lev 11:13; Deut 14:12, KJV, RSV). Its Heb. name *('oznîyā)* may be derived from a root meaning "powerful." Its body length is a little over a yard with a wing spread of over three yards. The feathers are black, and the head and the upper part of the neck are bald like those of other carrion eaters. It nests in

the Jordan Valley and seems to have been rather abundant in biblical times, but today it is quite rare. It has a cere, a small waxlike membrane at the base of the beak, of livid flesh color. It feeds on carcasses and on carrion (e.g., II Sam 21:10; see VBW, II, 195). Some observers report that it drives goats and sheep over precipices and then it devours them.

53. **Vulture, Egyptian,** *Neophron percnopterus.* This vulture, too, is ceremonially unclean (*rāḥām*, "gier eagle," KJV; "carrion vulture," RSV; in Lev 11:18; Deut 14:17). It is also known as Pharaoh's hen and has a plumage that is basically white with a naked head and a yellow neck. Its feet are pink. The Egyptian vulture breaks bones left by other vultures. Its flight is slow and easy and its voice a croak. It is the smallest of all the carrion-eating birds found in Palestine.

An eagle or vulture in the Biblical Zoo, Jerusalem. HFV

54. **Vulture, Griffon,** or **Eagle,** *Gyps fulvus.* Until a generation ago the griffon vulture, the "eagle" of the OT (Heb. *nesher,* Lev 11:13; Deut 14:12; VBW, I, 188) was one of the most common birds in Palestine, but today it is on the verge of extinction. Many have been killed by eating poisonous bait meant for foxes and jackals. In addition, its reproduction is limited; the female lays only one or two eggs a year. It nests in crags and on clifftops (Job 39:27-28; Jer 49:16; Obad 4), and gives special care to the fledglings for seven weeks (Deut 32:11; VBW, I, 292). It often basks on rocks at midday and can fly swiftly (Deut 28:49; Job 9:26) or can hover with easy movements. It can soar until it almost disappears in the sky (Prov 23:5; 30:19; Isa 40:31). Its call is a growling note.

The vulture was considered a symbol of sovereignty and domination in the ancient Near East. Thus Ezekiel compared the kings of Egypt and Babylon to mighty vultures (Ezk 17:3, 7). The Egyptian goddesses Nekhbet and Mut were represented as vultures (VBW, III, 171).

Like other carrion eaters (Prov 30:17), its neck is bald or very thinly covered with white down (Mic 1:16). This baldness seems to prevent the clumping of the feathers through the clotting of the blood as it plunges its head into the viscera of the carrion. The griffon vulture is the largest bird of Palestine, about four feet in length and measuring ten feet between wing tips. Its beak is extremely strong but its toes are short, fitted with blunt talons. The middle toe is equal in length to the others, unlike that of other birds of prey which use it to seize their victims. Keen-sighted, it hovers at great height watching for dying or dead animals. It plummets swiftly upon the corpse (Job 39:29-30; Hab 1:8).

In some passages the true eagle must be meant. Ezekiel saw in vision four living creatures, each with four faces, one of which was like an eagle's (Ezk 1:10), and John saw similar beings, one like a flying eagle (Rev 4:7). Palestine has two varieties, the more common imperial eagle, *Aquila heliaca heliaca,* and the golden eagle, *Aquila chrysaëtos.* The latter can fly three or four miles in ten minutes, and may have evoked the comparison in II Sam 1:23; Jer 4:3; Lam 4:19.

Other biblical references include Ex 19:4; Ps 103:5; Jer 49:22; Hos 8:11; Mt 24:28; Rev 12:14.

55. **Wasp** or **Hornet,** *Vespa orientalis.* The hornet, a large stinging wasp, is mentioned three times in the Bible (Ex 23:28; Deut 7:20; Josh 24:12). The common species in Palestine, a yellow and red-brown insect, is larger and more dangerous than an ordinary wasp. Its sting paralyzes its victim before it sucks out the vital fluids. The hornet is an important enemy of the honey bee; it lies in ambush for honeybee workers and then invades and destroys the hive.

The hornet is a social insect with the division of labor among queen, workers, and drones. It builds a comb with characteristic hexagonal cells of a paper-like substance. In addition to feeding on honey it feeds on fruit and gnaws at the bark of trees using this in building its comb.

The biblical references may be figurative for the panic and terror that the invading Israelites would instill in Canaanite hearts (cf. Deut 11:25); or the hornet may symbolize actual military power. John Garstang (*Joshua-Judges,* New York: Richard R. Smith, 1931, p. 259) believed the hornet represented the armies of Egypt because the wasp was one of the emblems of the pharaohs (VBW, I, 158).

IV. Creeping, Swarming Things (Chiefly insects, amphibians, and reptiles)

1. **Adder.** *See* Cobra, IV.8; Serpent, IV.30; Viper, IV.34.

2. **Ant, Harvester,** *Messor* sp. Ants are exceedingly abundant all over Palestine; 31 kinds are now known in that land. Ants only rarely enter houses made of stone or mud brick; thus a long, ancient omen listed the dire consequences to a house or its owner if one of many varieties of ants would be seen in it (Bodenheimer, *Animal and Man in Bible Lands,* pp. 97 f.).

Ant nests are ordinarily underground in Palestine to protect the ants against excessive heat. They frequently have special chambers which serve as nurseries, granaries, or fungus gardens.

Particularly interesting are the references in Prov 6:6–8 and 30:25 to ants which store up grain in the summer. At one time critics doubted the activity of these harvester ants. It was even suggested that these references resulted from faulty observation: that Solomon had seen the white larval cases and had mistaken these for grains of wheat. We now know that several species of this genus build granaries, flat chambers connected by galleries and irregularly scattered over an area averaging two yards in diameter and about a foot deep in the soil. They collect seeds from the ground or pluck them from plants, remove the envelopes, and discard the chaff and the empty capsules on kitchen middens outside the nest. During the winter an average-sized nest may contain a half pint of seeds. The ants first bite off the head or radicle, the softest part of the kernel, which prevents germination in the seeds, or they may spread them out in the sun to dry; some seeds germinate in spite of this. The individual granaries may be five inches in diameter and a half inch high. Some nests may be 25 to 40 feet in diameter and six to seven feet deep with several entrances.

3. **Asp.** *See* Cobra, IV.8.

4. **Beetle,** *Coleoptera.* Beetles are insects with chewing mouth parts and two pairs of wings, the fore pair of wings being hard and sheath-like and the hind pair being membranous and folded under the fore pair. Some beetles are carnivorous, others chiefly herbivorous. Some are aquatic, some produce a secretion which blisters the skin, some damage fabrics, some damage crops, and some feed on other insects which are harmful to man.

The beetle is referred to in Lev 11:22 (Heb. *ḥargōl*), where it is mentioned as edible. The reference here may well be to the cricket (RSV), one of the orthoptera (related to grasshoppers and locusts), rather than to the beetle. In ancient Egypt the beetle or sacred scarabaeus, the *kheper,* was a symbol of the sun-god Ra, and the scarab seal and amulet became extremely popular.

5. **Cankerworm.** *See* Locust, III.29.

6. **Caterpillar.** *See* Locust, III.29.

7. **Chameleon.** *See* Lizard, IV.21.

8. **Cobra, Egyptian,** *Naja haje.* References to the adder or asp (Heb. *pethen,* Job 20:14–16; Deut 32:33; Ps 58:4–6; 91:13; Isa 11:8) seem to be to the Egyptian cobra. It is one of the most poisonous snakes, attaining a length of about 80 inches. It is common in Egypt, but at the present time it has become extinct in Palestine. Cobras extend a hood when disturbed by expanding ribs on the sides of the neck and head. Their fangs are permanently erect, not movable as in the vipers. The poison attacks the nervous system of the victim causing muscular paralysis; that of the viper attacks chiefly the circulatory system. The Egyptian cobra is related to the Indian cobra which is frequently charmed. Ps 58:6 may be a reference to the practice of snake charmers in extracting the fangs of cobras. The "fiery serpents" (Num 21:6; Deut 8:15) perhaps were cobras, "fiery" (Heb. *sārāph*) referring to the burning fever caused by their venom. The winged or flying serpents (*sārāph*) of Isa 14:29; 30:6 may refer to the extended hood or to the lightning-like strike.

9. **Cockatrice.** *See* Serpent, IV.30.

10. **Cricket.** *See* Beetle, IV.4.

11. **Crimson Scale Insect,** *Kermes* sp. The scriptural references to "scarlet" (KJV) or crimson (Heb. *tôla'at shānî,* lit., "scarlet worm"; e.g., Ex 25:4; 26:1; 39:1 ff.; Lev 14:4–6; 14:51 f.; Num 19:6; Prov 31:21; Song 4:3; Isa 1:18; Jer 4:30) refer to a dye derived from the larvae or the eggs on the bodies of female kermes or cochineal scale insects. The Arabs called the insect *qirmiz,* from which our word "crimson" is derived. The LXX translated the color as *kokkinos,* normally rendered "scarlet" in English, from the Gr. *kokkos,* so named because the female insect looks like a berry. The females actually secrete and remain under waxy scales on plant tissue. These attach themselves to the kermes oak, Q. *coccifera coccifera,* a native of the Near East and the Mediterranean area (illus., VBW, I, 190).

The dye industry and trade in the paste made from these insects undoubtedly flourished among the Phoenicians, although "scarlet" thread was used in patriarchal times (Gen 38:28, 30), and the merchant Ili-ittiya of Nuzu promised to deliver by caravan to the palace "rouge extracted from worms," along with other products. It takes 70,000 insects to make a pound of dye which today sells for about three dollars a pound and is used in cosmetics, rouge, food coloring, beverages, and medicine. Today the insects live on the prickly pear and other cacti. The rich red color is actually extracted from the eggs of the female. By applying pressure on the part of the body containing the eggs the red substance oozes out. *See* Color: Crimson.

12. **Dragon.** *See* II.11.

13. **Flea,** *Pulex irritans.* There are many species of fleas in Palestine besides the common flea. They are wingless parasites that have

sharp jaws and suck out blood from the bodies of humans and animals. The body is wedge shaped, enabling the flea to burrow into the folds of the skin and hide there. The female lays her eggs in dust heaps which accumulate in the corners of rooms, and the eggs hatch into small white larva which pupate in a cocoon. Soon adult fleas appear which immediately attach themselves to the body of their host. The female requires blood for the development of her eggs.

The most dangerous fleas are those of the rat which transmit the organism responsible for bubonic plague.

The references in I Sam 24:14 and 26:20 seem to be to a very small and despicable creature.

14. **Fly.** *See* III.13.

15. **Frog,** *Rana* sp. The frog is mentioned as the second of the ten plagues inflicted on the Egyptians (Ex 8:2–14; Ps 78:45; 105:30). Frogs are amphibians, living part of their lives in the water and part on land. The female lays her eggs in the water; after about a week the eggs hatch into tadpoles. Gradually through metamorphosis the tail is lost and limbs are acquired. Frogs must maintain a moist skin since they must take in oxygen through the skin as well as through their lungs; thus they must always remain close to water. They feed on insects and worms. Frogs are found throughout Israel. They inhabit chiefly lowlands where their croaking is heard in the spring and on summer evenings.

The frog would be expected to fall in the category of the creeping or swarming creatures which in general were termed ceremonially unclean (Lev 11:29-31). However, since the frog was not specifically listed, the rabbis did not consider it one of the animals that defiled through contact. Maimonides said, "Only those animals mentioned in the law are defiling, but not the serpent, the frog, and the tortoise." Instead, the Jews classified the toad as unclean, believing it to be the *ṣāb,* the last creature of Lev 11:29 (*see* Lizard, Dabb, IV.22).

In Rev 16:13 certain foul spirits are said to look like frogs. The ancient Egyptians made the frog a symbol of life and origin, and an emblem of Heqet, the patron-goddess of birth. She is depicted with a frog's head, giving life to the newborn. Thus the deity was discredited when the power of Yahweh afflicted Egypt with the very animal that was her symbol (cf. Ex 12:12).

16. **Gecko,** *Hemidactylus turcicus.* The gecko is a reptile listed in Lev 11:30, RSV (KJV, "ferret"), as a ritually unclean creeping creature similar to the lizard. The reference in Prov 30:28 is to the insectivorous Turkish gecko which climbs walls and enters through the windows with the help of hand-shaped limbs. There are seven species of geckos in the Holy Land; all of them are insectivorous.

17. **Gnat.** *See* III.16.

18. **Grasshopper.** *See* Locust, III.29.

19. **Hornet.** *See* III.55.

20. **Horseleach.** *See* Leech, V.6.

21. **Lizard,** *Lacerta* sp. Lizards are listed as ceremonially unclean (Lev 11:29–31); in addition, their carcasses defile through contact (11:32–36). There are ten types of lizards, including the land crocodile and the chameleon, in Palestine which vary in color and size (see photos of chameleon and green lizard, VBW, I, 189). Lizards are reptiles: their skin is covered with scales. The lizard is a useful creature because it captures harmful insects and worms. Like other reptiles it lays eggs with shells softer than those of the birds and with no clear division between the yolk and the white. Both extreme heat and cold inactivate them, since they are variable-temperature organisms.

22. **Lizard, Dabb,** *Uromastix aegyptius.* In Lev 11:29 (RSV) the Heb. *ṣāb* is described as ceremonially unclean. KJV translates this "tortoise" but the reference seems to be to a lizard. It attains a length of about 24 inches and is found chiefly in the Negeb. The Dabb lizard is herbivorous, an unusual trait since most lizards are insectivorous. It has a hard rough skin. The

A lizard in the Biblical Zoo, Jerusalem. IIS

body is green with brown spots. It has a short, rounded head and a powerful tail encircled with a row of strong spines which it uses as a weapon of defense.

23. **Locust.** *See* III.29.

24. **Louse,** *Anoplura*. Lice (Heb. *kēn, kinnām*) were one of the ten plagues inflicted upon the Egyptians (Ex 8:16–19; Ps 105:31). The identification of these with lice is in dispute, though Feliks believes they were lice. Others suggest that the term refers to the gnat, the mosquito, or some other insect. The reference, they suggest, may be to the harvester gnat, the Barghas of the Arabs, a small midge which enters the eyes, ears, and nose of field workers during harvest (RSV above and Isa 51:6); to the Anopheles mosquito which transmits malaria (JerusB), or to the sandfly which carries dengue fever. Some identify the flies of the next plague with gnats (*see* Gnat, III.16) which seems likely, so that these may well have been true lice.

Lice were such a pest in biblical times that Egyptian priests and others shaved their heads. The Talmud distinguishes between the head louse and the body louse. Lice suck blood and are nuisances in this way. In addition they carry a number of diseases.

25. **Mole Rat,** *Spalax ehrenbergi ehrenbergi Nhrg*. The mole rat is neither a mole nor a rat, but rather a rodent from six to nine inches long which burrows in any area where the soil is suitable for digging. It is heavy-bodied, short-legged, and powerful, with projecting incisors and small claws. It has no tail and is mole-like in appearance, but neither true moles nor shrews have ever been found in Palestine. The mole rat builds breeding mounds in the wet winter season, which resemble those of pocket gophers, and less complex resting mounds in the summer. Both have rather complex tunnel systems. The mole rat feeds on roots, bulbs, tubers, and various other subterranean plant parts and does extensive damage to agriculture. Its body is adapted to underground life; it has no ears and only rudimentary eyes. The Libyans believe that touching a mole rat will result in blindness. Scriptural references are Isa 2:20 (Heb. *ḥăparpārâ,* from *ḥāpar,* "to dig") and probably Lev 11:29 (JerusB; "weasel," KJV and RSV; Heb. *ḥōled*).

26. **Moth,** *Tineola* sp. The clothes moth lays its eggs on wools or furs and the larvae feed on these. The destructive qualities of this insect are referred to in Job 13:28; Ps 39:11; Isa 50:9; Hos 5:12; Sir 42:13; Mt 6:19–20; Lk 12:33; and Jas 5:2. Isa 51:8, "worm," refers specifically to the larvae of the clothes moth. In all cases it is the larvae which does the damage; the adult is quite harmless and feeds mainly on the nectar of flowers. It is easily crushed (Job 4:19, JerusB). The moth is used as a symbol of disintegration, decay, and weakening. There are hundreds of species of moths other than the clothes moth in the Holy Land; they are harmful to leaves, flowers, fruits, trees, and seeds. As with the clothes moth, it is the larva which damages.

27. **Mouse,** *Mus musculus praetextus*. The mouse (Heb. *'akbār*) was pronounced unclean because being short-legged it was considered to be one of the creeping creatures (Lev 11:29). Both commensals, which inhabit dwellings, and wild forms of mice are known. The commensal forms tend to have longer tails and to be darker in color. The wild forms are active chiefly at night. Mice are good climbers and even good swimmers. Wild mice eat many kinds of vegetables, such as seeds, fleshy roots, leaves, and stems. At times they store food.

The word *'akbār* (Lev 11:29; I Sam 6:4–5; Isa 66:17) is probably a general term for various rats and mice. Tristram reports 23 varieties of mouselike rodents in 19th cen. Palestine. Mice and rats cause food spoilage, damage to household articles, and transport the host fleas of typhus, spotted fever, and bubonic plague bacteria. The latter may have caused the tumors or swellings among the Philistines (I Sam 6:5); but *see* Vole, IV.35. Isa 66:17 refers to a pre-Exilic Canaanite cultic practice in which mice were eaten; in this case the rodent may have been the hamster. For image of mouse found in Middle Bronze Age obelisk temple at Byblos, see VBW, II, 119.

28. **Palmerworm.** *See* Locust, III.29.

29. **Scorpion,** *Buthus quinquestriatus*. There are a dozen species of scorpions found in Palestine, but 90 percent are yellow scorpions. These are arthropods, three to five inches long (for photo, see VBW, III, 160), belonging to the same group (arachnids) as the spiders, slow nocturnal invertebrates which rest beneath stones by day and prey on insects and other arachnids. It carries at the end of its tail a poisonous sting which is fatal to its prey and extremely painful to man (Rev 9:3, 5, 10; cf. I Kgs 12:11, 14) and often dangerous (Lk 11:12). Scorpions symbolized Ezekiel's evil countrymen (Ezk 2:6) and the demonic forces of Satan (Lk 10:19). The scorpion is mentioned as frequenting the Sinai desert (Deut 8:15).

30. **Serpent, Snake,** Suborder *Ophidia*. Nine Heb. words and four Gr. words are found in Scripture referring to snakes or to various species of them. Heb. *naḥash* (31 times) and Gr. *ophis* (14 times) are the generic terms, always translated "serpent." The Heb. word is an onomatopoeic imitation of its hissing or of the sound this reptile produces as it scrapes its scales along the ground (cf. Jer 46:22). Many types of snakes lay eggs (Isa 59:5), although some retain the eggs in the body until ready to hatch.

The asp is probably the cobra (*q.v.*, IV.8), while the adder belongs to the viper class (*q.v.*, IV.34). The cockatrice of the KJV (Isa 11:8; 14:29; 59:5; Jer 8:17) was a fabulous serpent in English literature, supposedly hatched from a cock's egg, and thus has been replaced by "adder" in RSV.

Serpents were associated with worship in the Canaanite religion, and symbolized evil deities among many other peoples. Stelas have been unearthed at several sites in Palestine and Syria which depict a god or worshiper with a snake winding around the legs or body (W. F. Albright, *Archaeology of Palestine,* Penguin Books, 1960, p. 97, fig. 20; see also references to "serpent" in ANEP). Because the Israelites were burning incense in pagan worship of the bronze serpent of Moses (cf. Num 21:8-9), King Hezekiah destroyed it in his religious reform (II Kgs 18:4). *See* Brazen Serpent.

See also Cobra, IV.8; Viper, IV.34.

31. **Spider.** There are between 600 and 700 different species of spiders in Palestine. These are different from insects in that they, like scorpions, have four pairs of legs instead of the three pairs which characterize insects. All are equipped with poison glands, the effectiveness of which varies. A few can kill insects only, but others can kill even birds and mice. Most spiders are web builders. In Job 8:14 and Isa 59:5, 6 the web is referred to as a symbol of frailty and insecurity. Prov 30:28 seems to refer not to the spider but to the gecko (*q.v.,* IV.16).

32. **Tortoise.** *See* Lizard, Dabb, IV.22.

33. **Turtle.** *See* Dove, III.9.

34. **Viper,** *Cerastes* sp., *Echis colorata* and *Vipera palaestina.* For photos of the second and third species, see VBW, III, 87. There are several species of true vipers (*Viperidae*) in SW Asia, all poisonous with curved fangs that spring down when ready to strike; they are difficult to identify exactly. Pit vipers *(Crotalidae),* with facial or sensory pits such as the rattlesnake and copperhead, inhabit only the Americas. Heb. *'eph'eh* is the word translated "viper" in most English versions (Job 20:16; Isa 30:6; 59:5), but its exact identity is uncertain. The extremely venomous horned viper *Cerastes Hasselquistii* which is found in Palestine may attack horses (Heb. *sh^e^pîpōn,* Gen 49:17). It is 12 to 18 inches long and lies in ambush, sometimes burrowing in the sands so that only the two eyes and the hornlike protrusions on its head are visible. These two "horns" may be employed as bait for small birds which frequent caravan routes looking for refuse. The "adder" (KJV) or "viper" (RSV) of Ps 140:3 (Heb. *'akshûb*) may be a very similar species of horned viper *(Cerastes cornutus).*

The reference in Acts 28:3 (Gr. *echidna;* also Mt 3:7; 12:34; 23:33) is probably to *Vipera aspis,* which is smaller than the common viper and is found in southern Europe. It is pugnacious and lies flat glaring at its opponent. Each time it inhales and exhales it hisses. This viper strikes very rapidly.

35. **Vole,** *Microtus guentheri.* The reference in I Sam 6:5 (Heb. *'akbār*) is probably to a vole, very likely the Levant vole, *Microtus guentheri.* They have short tails; this distinguishes them from the mice. Voles prefer moderately moist meadow lands and swampy areas, where they have clearly defined surface runways. Some dig short round burrows and live among the rock crannies. The vole is strictly vegetarian, having substantial food requirements; within 24 hours most voles consume nearly their own weight in seeds, roots, bark, and leaves. The Levant vole not only ravishes agriculture but may also spread disease.

The vole is cyclic; e.g., in the western U.S. at peak periods, they may number up to 12,000 per acre. Others believe the *'akbār* is a mouse (*q.v.,* IV.27) or rat which carries the bacteria of bubonic plague and of a type of typhoid fever transmitted to human beings by fleas. Some believe the emerods or tumors of I Sam 5:9-12 refer to bubonic plague attacking the abdominal parts of the body.

36. **Weasel,** *Mustela* sp. Weasels are small carnivorous mammals mentioned in Lev 11:29 (KJV, RSV, based on the LXX and Vulgate); they are listed among the creeping things that swarm and that were ceremonially unclean. They are characterized by long slender bodies and short legs. They have well-developed anal scent glands. Weasels are solitary animals and tend to be nocturnal. They hunt by scent.

It is possible that the animal (Heb. *ḥōled*) referred to in Leviticus is not the weasel but the mole rat (*q.v.,* IV.25).

37. **Worm.** In most cases references to worms are to maggots (Heb. *rimmâ;* feeding on spoiled manna, Ex 16:24; on corpses, Job 21:26; 24:20; Isa 14:11; on open wounds, Job 7:5) or to the larvae of insects (Heb. *sās,* Isa 51:8). In Deut 28:39; Jon 4:7 the vine weevil *(Cochylis ambiguella)* is probably referred to; it destroys vines by boring into their stems.

In some cases men are humiliated by being likened to worms (Job 25:6; Ps 22:6; Mic 7:17) which may be *Lumbricus terrestris,* a segmented worm which lives in burrows consuming soil and leaf mold.

The Gr. *skōlēx* (Mk 9:48) refers to the worm or maggot that eats dead flesh. In Acts 12:23 the related adjective *skōlēko-brōtos,* "eaten by worms," describes the fatal abdominal worm disease of King Herod Agrippa.

V. Aquatic Organisms

1. **Coral,** *Corallium rubrum.* Corals represent the calcareous skeletons of marine organisms of a low order. The famous red coral of the Mediterranean and Red Sea is widely used for jewelry. While alive it is green in color and shrublike in appearance, looking very much like a plant growing in the water, since the animals are sessile or immobile. As soon as the coral is removed from the water it grows hard and red in color. The red coral is fished with nets or cut off with sharp iron tools. It is also used both externally and internally as a medicine. Two words in Heb. may refer to coral, *rā'môt* (Job 28:18; Ezk 27:16) and *p^e^nînîm* (Job 28:18; Prov 8:11; 20:15; 31:10; Lam 4:7); but the latter almost certainly are pearls (*q.v.,* V. 10).

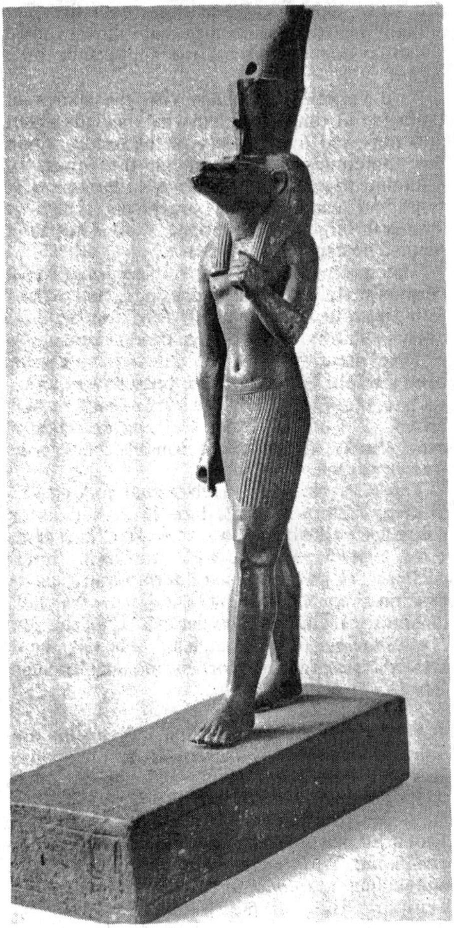

Sobek the Egyptian crocodile god in bronze. LM

2. **Crocodile,** *Crocodilus vulgaris*. The crocodile is the largest of all existing reptiles, attaining a length of 25 feet (photo, VBW, IV, 133). Until the beginning of the 20th cen. it was found in marshes and small coastal rivers of western Palestine. It was considered sacred by the Egyptians (for Sixth Dynasty relief see VBW, III, 187). The description of the leviathan (Heb. *lôtan*) in Job 41 is almost certainly based on that of the crocodile, although in other passages leviathan was a mythical creature used symbolically of the forces of evil (*see* Leviathan, V. 7). The pharaoh is probably symbolized by a crocodile, the "dragon" of Ezk 29:3, and Nebuchadnezzar likewise (Jer 51:34).

3. **Dugong** or **Sea Cow,** *Dugong dugong*. The dugong (Heb. *taḥash*) is an herbivorous aquatic mammal, similar to the manatee of Atlantic tropical coastal waters, about 11 feet long and weighing up to 650 pounds. It occasionally swims along the shores of the Red Sea to sleep or feed its young in one of the caves. It has a large, thick skin which the Bedouin made into footwear (cf. Ezk 16:10). This may be the animal referred to as badgers (KJV) or goats (RSV) in Ex 25:5; 26:14; 35:7, 23, the skin of which was used for the covering of the tent of testimony. The dugong was also caught for its blubber and oil and now is almost extinct. In view of the human-like breasts of the female, dugongs are probably the sirens and mermaids of mythology.

4. **Fish,** *Pisces*. Fish are frequently mentioned in the Bible without ever giving specific names which enable us to identify a particular species. Since time immemorial fish have constituted one of the staple foods of mankind, and they still serve as the chief source of protein throughout the world. For photos of catfish and edible fish from the Sea of Galilee, see VBW, I, 187.

The trade in fish was highly developed in biblical times. One of the gates of Jerusalem was called the Fish Gate (Neh 3:3; Zeph 1:10). In Egypt fish were speared and netted; hook-and-line fishing was also practiced. Lev 11:10-12 permitted the Jews to eat the bony fish or pisces which have fins and scales, but forbade the eating of cartilaginous fish such as the shark, the eel and the catfish which have no scales. *See* Occupations: Fishing; Fins.

5. **Frog.** *See* IV.15.

6. **Leech,** *Haemopis* or *Aulostoma gulo*. These are wormlike blood-sucking animals which are referred to in Prov 30:15. It is likely that the reference here is to the horseleech, though it may be to the ordinary medicinal leech, *Hirudo medicinalis*. This latter is abundant in springs and ponds from the Negeb to Galilee. It adheres to the body of human beings and animals which submerge themselves in water, injects an anticoagulant, and sucks their blood.

At one time leeches were widely employed in medicine to draw blood when it was thought that disease was caused by bad blood.

7. **Leviathan, Sea Monster.** This term (Heb. *liwyāthān*), which occurs in Job 3:8; 40:38 (MT); Ps 74:14; 104:26; Isa 27:1, may refer to larger marine animals, such as the large jellyfish, whales (*see* V. 13), sharks, or to large reptiles, such as the crocodile (*see* V. 2). In addition, this may well include some forms now extinct, such as the ichthyosaurs and the plesiosaurs, extinct marine reptiles similar to the dinosaurs. The scriptural term may also recollect some of the dinosaurs which spent part of their lives half-submerged in shallow streams, lakes, and oceans. *See also* Dragon, II.11.

8. **Mollusk, Purple,** *Murex trunculus* and *M. brandaris*. In the ancient world purple dyes of all shades ranging from red to purple were highly valued. These were obtained from a mollusk or sea snail which inhabited the waters off Crete and Phoenicia (photo, VBW, V, 177). The secretion is produced by the hypobranchial

gland of the mollusk, and the shade is regulated by using different species, altering the ratio, adding ingredients such as kermes (*see* Scarlet Scale Insect, IV.11), or varying air and light exposure time in the process of producing the dye. Tyrian purple was obtained by a double dyeing. Deposits of *Murex brandaris* and *M. trunculus* shells have been found in dyeing beds along the Mediterranean.

The Hebrews had to import purple goods (Ezk 27:16). Purple was a sign of distinction, royalty, and wealth. Lydia was a "seller of purple" or of cloth so dyed (Acts 16:14). Other Scripture references include Ex 25:4; 28:5-6, 15; Num 15:38; II Chr 2:7; Est 8:15; Prov 31:22; Song 3:10; Ezk 27:7; Dan 5:7. *See also* Purple.

9. **Onycha.** An ingredient of the sacred perfume (Ex 30:34), probably an aromatic oil obtained by roasting the closing valve muscle of certain marine mollusks or the Red Sea snail.

10. **Oyster, Pearl,** *Pinctada margaritifera.* While the word "pearl" does not occur in the OT of the KJV, it is found in the RSV, JerusB, and others, for Heb. *p^enînîm* (Job 28:18; Prov 8:11; 20:15; 31:10; Lam 4:7; KJV "rubies"). The pearl is a highly valued gemlike deposit, chiefly calcium carbonate, formed around a grain of sand in the shells of oysters or certain other mollusks. Pearls of fine quality are obtained from oysters in the Persian Gulf, off Ceylon, and in the Red Sea. In the latter area the pinna oyster occasionally yields translucent pink pearls, which may explain the comparison with ruddy bodies in Lam 4:7 (see *Unger's Bible Dict.,* 1957, p. 742).

In the NT the Gr. *margaritēs* unquestionably means "pearl." Pearls were in great demand for jewelry then as now (Mt 13:45-46; I Tim 2:9; Rev 17:4; 18:12, 16). Likening spiritual wisdom and other blessings to pearls, Jesus warned against casting them before swine (Mt 7:6). Each of the gates of the New Jerusalem is described as consisting of a single pearl (Rev 21:21).

11. **Sea Monster** (Lam 4:3, KJV). *See* Jackal, II.23.

12. **Sponge,** *Euspongia* sp. The sponge is the skeleton of a simple marine animal, *Euspongia officianalis.* It is a porous body composed of tubules and cells, lined with amoeboid substance. The vital action of these protozoa keeps up a steady action of water through the channels. Sponge fishing was well known in the Mediterranean area in ancient times. It was practiced particularly along the Anatolian and Syrian coasts. The references in Mt 27:48 and Mk 15:36 are to the use of sponges in absorbing liquids. Sponges were harvested by divers; their work was considered "hard and woeful."

13. **Whale,** *Balaenoptera physalus, Physeter catodon.* This is the largest of all living creatures, including those that have become extinct. Whales are air-breathing mammals. Their young are born alive and nourished with milk. They are generally devoid of hair except for a few stray whiskers. When they spout they are actually breathing; moisture from their exhaled breath condenses, giving the appearance of a spout.

Two varieties of whales visit the shores of Palestine at times. The fin whale weighs about 200 tons and lives mainly in the arctic region but sometimes passes through the Straits of Gibraltar to reach the eastern Mediterranean. It feeds on small marine organisms which it strains through its whale bone; it does not have teeth. The esophagus is narrow.

The sperm whale, about 60 feet long, has a curiously shaped head which looks like a battering ram and has teeth. It feeds on big fish, even on sharks. It has a large throat opening.

The "great fish" of Jon 2:1 need not have been a whale but could have been a large shark such as the Rhineodon, the whale-shark, which grows 70 feet and lacks the terrible teeth of other sharks. In any event, Jonah's deliverance was miraculous.

The KJV translates Heb. *tannîn* as "whale" in Gen 1:21; Job 7:12; Ezk 32:2. The latter reference probably is to a crocodile. The Heb. word, elsewhere in the KJV translated "dragon" (*q.v.,* II.11), is a general term for any sea or river monster. In Mt 12:40 the Gr. for "whale" is *kētos,* evidently following the LXX in Jon 2:1, *kētei megalō,* "great fish." The Gr. word also is a general term for sea monster or huge fish.

Bibliography. Emmanuel Anati, *Palestine Before the Hebrews,* New York: Knopf, 1963. Michael Avi-Yonah and Abraham Malamat, eds., *Views of the Biblical World,* 5 vols., Jerusalem: International Publishing Co., 1960. Raoul Blanchard and M. DuBuit, *The Promised Land,* New York: Hawthorn, 1966. F. S. Bodenheimer, *Animal and Man in Bible Lands,* Leiden: Brill, 1960; "Fauna," IDB, II, 246-256. George S. Cansdale, *All the Animals of the Bible Lands,* Grand Rapids: Zondervan, 1970. Robert A. M. Conley, "Locusts: Teeth of the Wind," *National Geographic,* CXXXVI (1969), 202-226. George R. Driver, "Birds in the Old Testament," PEQ, LXXXVI (1955), 5-20; LXXXVII (1955), 129-140. Jehuda Feliks, *The Animal World of the Bible,* Tel-Aviv: Sinai, 1962. Joseph P. Free, "Abraham's Camels," JNES, III (1944), 187-193. Frederick R. and George F. Howe, "Moses and the Eagle: An Analysis of Deut. 32:11," JASA, XX (1968), 22-24. George F. Howe, "The Raven Speaks," JASA, XXI (1969), 22-25; "Job and the Ostrich," JASA, XX (1968), 107-110. Willy Ley, *The Lungfish, the Dodo, and the Unicorn,* New York: Viking, 1948. Alice Parmelee, *All the Birds of the Bible,* New York: Harper, 1959. James B. Pritchard, ed., *The Ancient Near East in Pictures,* Princeton: Princeton Univ. Press, 1954. William M. Thomson, *The Land and the Book,* Hartford: Scranton, 1910. H. B. Tristram, *The Survey of Western Palestine: The Fauna and Flora of Palestine,*

London: Palestine Exploration Fund, 1884. Ernest P. Walker, et al., *Mammals of the World,* Baltimore: Johns Hopkins, 1964. Robert S. Wallace, "Birds of the Bible," Atlanta, Georgia, 1939, unpublished sermon quoted in George J. Wallace, *An Introduction to Ornithology,* New York: Macmillan, 1955. Lulu Rumsey Wiley, *Bible Animals,* New York: Vantage, 1957. Frederick E. Zeuner, *A History of Domesticated Animals,* New York: Harper and Row, 1963.

J. W. K.

ANIMATION. Animation means "making animate" or "alive," "quickening." Two main examples are found in Scripture. (1) The creation of man. "The Lord God formed man of the dust of the ground, and breathed into his nostrils the breath of life; and man became a living soul" (Gen 2:7). (2) The vision of the valley of dry bones, when, as the prophet prophesied to the wind, these came together and lived, signifying the regeneration of the nation Israel at the second coming of Christ (Ezk 37; cf. Rom 11:26–29; Zech 12–14).

Animation is to be distinguished from resurrection, which has to do with the body, in that it signifies the giving of life itself to the lifeless. In the first example, Adam was made a living soul; and in the second example, new life, which comes with the soul's regeneration, will be given to the Jews who are alive at the second coming of our Lord.

The term is sometimes used theologically to denote that quality of Holy Scripture which through the Holy Spirit produces spiritual life in receptive lives. Thus, "The word of God is living and active . . ." (Heb 4:12, ASV); and "being born again . . . by the word of God, which liveth and abideth for ever" (I Pet 1:23). This quality is one of many features which distinguishes the canonical Scripture from other mere human writings.

R. A. K. and A. F. J.

ANIMISM (ăn′ĭ-mĭz′m). This is the view that such things as trees, rocks, mountains, etc., are possessed of separate spirits which can either help and bless, or hinder and curse man. Such spirits are to be placated by certain acts and offerings. Animism differs from pantheism, which sees one spirit or god as present and identified with all things, in that it attributes separate spirits to each object. It agrees, however, in seeing the divine as present in the material.

Many evolutionary anthropologists place animism as the fourth of seven upward evolutionary steps in the progressive development of religion: dynamism, manaism, fetishism, animism, totemism, polytheism, and monotheism. The whole theory of such an evolutionary development is to be rejected for three reasons. (1) It is impossible to prove such a development ever occurred. (2) Even the lower forms of primitive religion have myths concerning a "high god" or a "sky god" who is a perfect, holy being and never does anyone any harm. Such a study of the mythology and folklore of any pagan tribe reveals the fact that a primal revelation of God is to be found in their mythology, even though it has disappeared from their direct historical knowledge. (3) The Bible teaches that at the very beginning God created man in His own image and after His own likeness, and that He talked with man and taught him about Himself. This particular primal revelation is, of course, found only in the Bible, but it fits and explains, as no other view can, the presence of the myths of the "high god" and the "sky god" in paganism.

R. A. K.

ANISE. *See* Plants.

ANKLET. An ornament worn around the ankle like a bracelet on the wrist. As found in tombs and numerous excavations, usually anklets were made of bronze. When used in pairs or with ankle chains, they would make a tinkling sound as one walked. Denounced by Isaiah as frivolous (Isa 3:18, RSV). *See* Dress.

ANNA (ăn′*a*). This is the Gr. form of Hannah, meaning "grace." *See* Hannah.

Anna the aged prophetess who was present at the dedication of the infant Jesus was the daughter of Phanuel, a descendant of Asher (Lk 2:36–38). Her age has been variously reckoned from 84 to 105 years. She had been married for seven years, following which she had been a widow, either for 84 years or until her eighty-fourth year. That she actually had living quarters in the temple is unthinkable, for no one lived there permanently. Luke's account suggests that Anna was one of the godly remnant looking expectantly for Israel's Messiah.

ANNAS (ăn′*a*s). The Jewish high priest appointed about A.D. 6 by Quirinius, governor of Syria. While Annas was deposed in A.D. 15, his prestige and control of the temple still continued in that five of his sons and his son-in-law Caiaphas became high priests after him. Luke was indicating the real state of affairs when he deliberately wrote, "Annas and Caiaphas being high priest" (singular, Lk 3:2, Gr.). Thus Annas took a leading part at the time of the crucifixion of Jesus (Jn 18:13, 24) and at the trial of Peter and John (Acts 4:6).

ANOINT. In the Scriptures, the practice of anointing with oil, either with or without perfume, had both a secular and a religious significance. In the Heb., two words were used: *sûk* (which occurs only nine times) and the more common word *māshaḥ,* from which comes the noun *māshîaḥ,* known in English as Messiah, "the Anointed One." The Gr. words are: *aleiphō,* which is comparable to *sûk;* and *chriō,* from which comes the title Christ, the counterpart of Messiah.

The Heb. *sûk* designated an everyday practice of rubbing the body with olive oil after bathing, or pouring oil on the head of a guest (Deut 28:40; Ruth 3:3; Est 2:12). However, it was prohibited during mourning (II Sam 12:20; 14:2; Isa 61:3; Dan 10:3). In Ex 30:31-32, where the term is translated "pour," it is specifically stated that the sacred oil was not to be used for common purposes.

In only one place in referring to persons does the term *māshaḥ* seem to indicate a nonreligious act of anointing the body (Amos 6:6). The basic meaning of *māshaḥ* is "to smear." It appears in Jer 22:14 in the sense of painting a royal chamber. Mention is made in II Sam 1:21 (RSV) and Isa 21:5 of anointing shields, which may mean no more than applying oil as a preservative.

In classical and in NT Gr. *aleiphō* is the preferred term for the secular practice of anointing the body after bathing or to show honor to a guest (Lk 7:38, 46; Jn 11:2; 12:3). It can, however, designate the act of anointing the sick (Mk 6:13; Jas 5:14) and the dead (Mk 16:1). In Jn 9:6 *epichriō,* "to rub on," is used of the mud with which Jesus anointed the eyes of the man born blind, and Rev 3:18 employs *egchriō,* "to rub in," for anointing the eyes with salve. The spiritual application was derived from the use of olive oil in physical healing. The Gr. *myrizō,* "to anoint with aromatics," is found in Jesus' statement that Mary had anointed His body beforehand for burying (Mk 14:8).

For a religiously oriented act of anointing, the Heb. OT prefers verbal and nominal forms of *māshaḥ*. The first such instance was Jacob's deed of anointing the stone at Bethel after his vision (Gen 31:13). Priests and high priests were anointed (Ex 28:41; 29:7, 36). Kings were anointed (I Sam 9:16; 16:3, 12-13; II Sam 2:4). Prophets were sometimes anointed (I Kgs 19:16). The tabernacle, its furniture, and its vessels were anointed (Ex 30:26-28). The anointing separated the thing or person unto God for special service, thus becoming sacred and untouchable (I Sam 24:6; 26:9). Frequently, the anointing was regarded as an act of God, because He commanded it to be done (cf. I Sam 9:16 with 10:1), and was associated with the outpouring of the Spirit of the Lord (I Sam 10:9; 16:13; Isa 61:1).

In the OT, the concept of anointing is associated with the future Messiah (Ps 45:7; 89:20; Isa 61:1; Dan 9:24). The Gr. word *chriō* carries these concepts into the NT, where God is always involved. In references to OT priests, kings, and prophets, it has the same function as *māshaḥ*. In Lk 4:18, Jesus applied the anointing mentioned in Isa 61:1 to Himself. Peter related the anointing of Jesus with the Holy Spirit (Acts 10:38), and Paul connects the anointing with the seal of the Spirit and proof of the Christian's relationship to Christ (II Cor 1:21-22). Thus the NT writers understood anointing metaphorically, that it is an enduement of spiritual power and understanding (I Jn 2:20, 27). In the OT it is associated with the kingly office (I Sam 10:1-9; 16:13), but in the NT it is associated with Christ and with Christian witnesses within a context of proclaiming the gospel.

G. H. L.

ANSWER. *Noun.* Chiefly from Heb. *dābār,* "word," and *ma'ănâ,* "answer," in OT; and *apokrisis,* "answer," and *apologia,* "defense," in Gr. NT. In the OT, the idea is that expressed by the English "answer" (II Sam 24:13; Job 32:3; Prov 15:1)—"a soft answer turneth away wrath." In the NT, *apokrisis* appears four times in the sense of giving an answer to a question; *apologia* appears eight times conveying the idea of making a defense—although II Cor 7:11 is best translated "clear yourselves" (ASV), and I Pet 3:15 "answer" in the sense of explaining or defending one's faith.

Verb. In the OT chiefly from Heb. *'ānâ,* "to answer," and *'āmar,* "to say"; in the NT from Gr. *apokrinomai,* "to answer," which occurs almost 200 times. The principal uses are: (1) reply to a question (I Sam 4:20; Mt 11:4; Lk 3:11); (2) reply to a request or command (Mt 4:4; 12:39); (3) response to a situation that demands a reply, although no question has been asked (Mt 17:4; Jn 2:18; I Sam 9:17); (4) rebuttal (Job 9:14; Mt 3:15; 27:12); (5) continuation of a discourse (Mt 11:25; Mk 10:24).

J. McR.

ANT. *See* Animals, IV.2.

ANTEDILUVIANS. In contrast to evolutionary concepts of human origins, the Scriptures clearly assert that the very earliest men were possessed of all the necessary talents for high cultural achievement. Cain, the son of Adam, built a city, and his immediate descendants lived in tents, domesticated cattle, invented musical instruments ("the harp and pipe"), and forged "every cutting instrument of brass and iron" (Gen 4:17-22, ASV). Noah had sufficient tools and skills for building a gigantic ark according to divine specifications (Gen 6:14-16). Great length of life and a unity of language doubtless contributed to a rapid development of the arts and sciences.

Parallel to the growth of civilization was the ripening of spiritual depravity. Cain, the first man born of woman, set the pattern for the age by murdering his own brother and complaining that God's punishment was unfair (Gen 4:1-15; I Jn 3:12). To be sure, some outstanding men of God lived during this period, such as Abel, Enoch, Lamech, and Noah; but the race as a whole sank to abysmal depths of sin (Gen 6:5-12; Mt 24:38; Jude 14-15). It is possible to interpret Gen 6:1-4 in terms of a race of wicked men of giant stature (Heb. *nᵉphīlîm;* cf. Num 13:33) born of men who had permitted themselves to be totally possessed by demons ("sons of God," Job 1:6). Because of such widespread acts of depravity, God's long-suffering came to an end (Gen 6:3; I Pet 3:20). With the exception of Noah's family, "the world that then was, being overflowed with water, perished" (II Pet 3:6), and another chapter of human history began.

See Anthropology; Ark, Noah's; Creation; Flood.

J. C. W.

ANTELOPE. *See* Animals, II.1.

ANTHROPOLOGY. The science or the knowledge of man, where he came from, what he is, and what are his future potentialities and destiny. The term anthropology can be used to define the entirely secular scientific study of these details when such theories as (1) organic evolution and theistic evolution, entirely apart from or versus fiat (i.e., by order) creation, are considered as explanations of man's origin; (2) pure behaviorism and operationalism, either apart from or versus the biblical view of the image of God in man and its effacement by sin, are examined to explain man's present condition; and (3) pure naturalism, with its extinction of individual personal existence at death, is adopted either apart from or versus the biblical supernaturalistic view of the immortal soul, which teaches that the soul is destined to an endless future existence after death.

Generally, as taught in colleges or universities, anthropology is presented according to theories which entirely disregard revealed biblical anthropology. When biblical anthropology is considered, secular theories can throw some light on the principles revealed in Scripture. This is more by contrast, however, than by common agreement, as is seen in the following study of the Bible's revelation concerning man.

The origin of man. God created man (male and female) by an act of fiat creation (Gen 1:27). The Bible allows no room for any theory of either organic or theistic evolution so far as the creation of man is concerned. Adam was created first, and immediately started to name the animals God had already created as God brought them before him. He looked for the fellowship of an I-thou relationship, similar to that which he already enjoyed with God from the beginning, but could not find it among the lower form of creation (Gen 2:20). Then, and only then, did God create Eve as his helpmeet (2:21-22).

Modern anthropologists usually ignore the biblical explanation altogether. To keep abreast of biological research the Christian may wish to allow much more room for development of phyla (those groups, larger than species, now considered the basic separate classes of beings created by God, from which species and kinds developed). However, he cannot accept the biblical record and go further in any theory of man's origin than to see him as a separate phylum, created from the beginning as a fully developed, self-conscious moral being. There are the clear statements of Genesis (chaps. 1-3) and the NT teaching that sin entered the world by one man, Adam, and passed upon all mankind through him as the federal head of the human race (Rom 5:12 ff.), as well as Christ's statement that God made man male and female at the beginning (Mt 19:4; Mk 10:6). These are evidences for man's creation as man, apart from any evolutionary development from protoplasm up to rational being.

A straightforward, literal acceptance of man's direct creation as a fully developed individual (rather than as the result of a long evolutionary process, even though that process is theistic evolution) is required by the following considerations: (1) The Genesis account clearly states such to be the case. (2) Jesus Christ declares the same to be true (Mt 19:3 ff.). (3) Paul in Rom 5:12-21 (as he holds that Adam is the first man) and in I Cor 15:45-47 expresses the same view. (4) The doctrine of the federal headship of Christ rests upon the federal headship of Adam, so that we read, "As in Adam all die, even so in Christ shall all be made alive" (I Cor 15:22). If Adam was not a real person, how can the Scripture compare him with Christ? The comparison is faulty and fails except they both are true representatives. (5) The reason that no fallen angel can be redeemed, while fallen men can be redeemed, is that angels are not members of a race, and therefore Christ could not die as their representative and be their Saviour. Never is Satan called the representative of even the fallen angels. Each one who rebelled did so as individually as each one who went on to eternal righteousness, both by individual decision.

The Shorter Catechism states that God created man "for His own glory," and declares that man's chief end is to enjoy God and glorify Him forever. God did not need man! Already in the Trinity He enjoyed an I-Thou relationship and the blessings of personal communion, as well as a social relationship in that any two persons of the Trinity could join to minister to the third. Why then did He create? To show forth His person with all its glories and bring glory and honor to His own name. This was to be demonstrated not only by those who worship Him with the homage due the Creator by the creature, but also by those who love Him for His sovereign grace and love manifested to them in their redemption through Christ. The angels could never be an illustration of the latter. *See* Creation.

The antiquity of man. Few if any scholars now feel that Ussher's chronology gives a satisfactory answer (creation in 4004 B.C.). It is quite commonly accepted by evangelicals that many of the names mentioned in OT genealogical tables stand for leading genealogical names, and that the lists cover much longer periods of time (and often cover hundreds of years) than at first thought. By the carbon 14 method (*see* Carbon 14 Dating) and the potassium-argon method anthropologists have tried to push the age of man back many millennia and even over a million years. Some conservative scholars are now speaking of a possible 100,000 years. Further knowledge with regard to radioactive factors and changes in cosmic radiation above the earth, however, may well cause the figures to be revised back much closer to a possible 25,000 to 10,000 years, or even less. For ethnic divisions of mankind *see* Nations.

The nature of man. Man is the highest of God's creatures, aside from the angels (Ps 8:5–8; Heb 2:6–9). He was the consummation of God's creation and given dominion over the earth and a charge to subdue it (Gen 1:26–27). For men's salvation alone did God send His only begotten Son to redeem them by the cross.

Man is bipartite in nature. He is composed of both body and soul or spirit. The angels are simply unipartite and pure spirit. The trichotomist position that man is tripartite—spirit, soul, and body—is based primarily on I Thess 5:23, "I pray God your whole spirit and soul and body be preserved blameless . . . ," and on Heb 4:12, "piercing even to the dividing asunder of soul and spirit." In the light of other Scripture, these seeming distinctions between soul and spirit can best be explained as differences of function or different aspects of the personality of the immaterial part of man. *See* Inner Man.

Certain important consequences follow: (1) Men are all members of a race, the human race. (2) Men as bipartite creatures will never be entirely complete without some physical "tabernacle" to house the soul. Hence, resurrection becomes a very important fact for man (cf. II Cor 5:1 ff.). (3) Being a combination of body and soul, man is subject to problems which arise from sin. The soul is subject to what are called psychosomatic problems (where difficulties in the mind cause sickness in the body), and somatic-psychic problems (where a sickness of the body becomes such an obsession of the mind that it becomes the cause of mental illness). (4) Since man was ordained to have a body, he must, except in the case of the creation of Adam and Eve, come into existence by physical generation and be a member of the human race.

So far as his spirit or soul is concerned, man was made by God according to His own image, after His own likeness (Gen 1:26–28). In what does this image consist? (1) Man, like God, is a person; both he and God have the characteristics of personality: intellect, will, emotion, self-conciousness, and a moral nature. Animals, in contrast, while they may show something of the first three, lack self-consciousness and a moral nature. (2) Man enjoys in a finite degree the communicable attributes of God: wisdom, power, holiness, goodness, love, justice, and truth. Yet he is entirely distinguishable from God in that he does not possess God's infinity, eternity, and unchangeableness, nor His omniscience, omnipotence, and omnipresence.

The fall affected God's image in man. Roman Catholics maintain that image and likeness are distinct qualities and that man lost only the latter. The "likeness" (Lat. *similitude*) of God was a *donum superadditum,* an additional supernatural gift extended to man at creation, by means of which he was to be able to control the degenerating effects of the physical body. This man lost when he fell but regains in salvation.

Protestants claim that the image of God was not entirely lost by man when he fell, but was only defaced. (Barth is an exception at this point, first, in that he sees the image in the fact God made man male and female and, second, that he insists the creation-image was entirely lost by his fall, yet retained by Christ and restored to man in redemption, and that these two facts exist simultaneously for every man whether he accepts them or not.) Man is still man but has become totally depraved by sin. Beginning with regeneration, the image, which is of course perfect in Christ, is gradually restored as the believer is renewed in knowledge (Col 3:10), righteousness, and true holiness (Eph 4:24). *See* Image of God.

God's original goal for man. This can only be understood properly when compared with that of the angels. It coincided with their goal to the extent that both angels and mankind started out in a state of innocency, and that both were given the opportunity to attain to a state of confirmation in righteousness. It differed in the manner in which this was to be accomplished. The holy angels so kept God's law and obeyed His will that they were individually confirmed; those that sinned defied His law and were eternally lost. Adam and Eve, on the other hand, were warned of the consequences (negative results) if they would not love God but disobey through eating of the forbidden fruit, and thereby sin and fall. Thus, God made an agreement, which, for the sake of simplicity and because of its particular character, has been called by the Reformed theologians the covenant of works. If man had kept this agreement, or covenant, he would have been confirmed in righteousness and would have gone on to eternal blessedness, just as the holy angels did (positive results).

But how do we come to this conclusion since it is not stated in the Bible? God, who is unchangeable, must deal with all His moral creatures in the same manner, whether they are angels or men. Does He not say, "I am the Lord, I change not" (Mal 3:6)? The development and confirmation of a holy, righteous character became a fact in the existence of the holy angels; the same, therefore, must have been a possibility for God's other personal creatures, men.

The redemption of man. But all mankind fell in Adam. The guilt and taint of Adam's sin were inherited and the lack of original righteousness was accompanied by the corruption of each man's entire nature. Therefore if man was to be saved from eternal separation from God and hell, an adequate plan of salvation was demanded. This provision of salvation is called in the NT the gospel or good news. Though regarded by worldly philosophers as foolishness (I Cor 1:18), and proving to be a stumbling block to the self-righteous who would save themselves by their own good works (v. 23), this gospel is God's almighty power to salvation and contains God's highest wisdom (v. 24). It corresponds completely to the needs of sinful, rebellious, fallen man.

By a study of the life of Christ, plus the revelation found in Ps 40:6–8, we are able to understand to some extent the plan of redemption developed in eternity past: (1) Christ was to lay aside His glory and become a man, taking upon Himself a physical body and a complete human nature (Ps 40:6–8; Heb 10:5–9; Phil 2:5–8). (2) He was to keep God's law as a man, the God-man, perfectly (Gal 4:4; cf. Mt 3:15; Heb 2:10). That He did so is proved by the fact that He led a sinless life (Jn 8:46; Heb 5:8–9; 9:14; I Pet 2:22). (3) He was to offer Himself as a substitutionary sacrifice in our place (Isa 53:10–11; Heb 10:5–9; I Pet 2:24) and die under the penalty of our sins. (4) The result or reward would be the salvation (Jn 1:29; 3:16) of all who repented of their sins and believed, and this salvation would cover believers of all ages (Rom 3:25–26).

In that Christ was made of a woman and made under the law, and kept that law perfectly in His life, He fulfilled in our stead the covenant of works which had been given to Adam. In that He died under the condemnation pronounced for breaking that covenant, He bore its penalty.

The present results for us of Christ's active and passive obedience, outlined above, are: (1) justification of believers before God, who sees us in Christ as having judicially fulfilled the law and borne its penalties; (2) deliverance from the penalty and power of sin; (3) the presence of the Holy Spirit in the believer. He can now dwell in us fully, since sin in us, our fallen nature, is a judged and condemned thing (Rom 8:3); and He can keep the law of God through us (8:4).

The future results of Christ's obedience are: (1) the complete removal of the fallen nature at the believer's physical death or at the second coming of Christ, whichever occurs first; (2) the reception of a resurrection body like that of Christ's (Rom 8:23; Phil 3:21; *see* Resurrection of the Body); (3) enjoyment of all the bliss and glory of eternal life in the presence of God.

Man's eternal future. In matters of eschatology and the prophecies concerning the future, wide variances of opinion appear. While the facts of a visible return of Christ and the future resurrection are accepted by all evangelicals, there is not agreement about the events which will occur afterward. Three main views are held: (1) Amillennialism – There will be no literal, physical rule of Christ on the earth. The OT prophecies predicting a glorious kingdom encompassing the earth (*see* Kingdom of God) and Rev 20:4 ff. are to be taken spiritually rather than literally. The OT references speak of the effect of the gospel in the Church Age; Rev 20, of the condition of those who have died in Christ. After Christ's second coming will occur the one final resurrection and great judgment. (2) Postmillennialism – The church, by its preaching prior to Christ's second coming, will usher in the Millennium on earth, a period of peace of approximately 1,000 years. (Some say we are in the Millennium now.) (3) Premillennialism – After Christ's second coming, He will establish a thousand years of peace in which the gospel will continue to be preached on earth. Satan will be bound for all this period, but will be loosed again at its close. Then those who have refused the gospel in spite of Christ's presence on the earth will rise against the Church. At that time Christ will destroy His enemies, and the final judgment of the wicked will take place. *See* Eschatology.

This last view does particular honor to the unfathomable grace of God in that it teaches that God's patience and mercy extend far beyond anything the other views can admit. (Acceptance of the premillennial position is based on many additional arguments from Scripture, however.) At the same time, it stresses even more clearly the total sinfulness of sin. There might be some seeming rational excuse for rejecting Christ and the gospel today, but what excuse can there be during the visible, personal reign of Christ on the earth when men have demonstrated before their very eyes the wonderful blessings of salvation in the lives of the resurrected saints who shall reign with their Saviour? Those in the first resurrection, namely, the righteous dead, and those believers who are alive on the earth at the rapture, will all have resurrection bodies like Christ's resurrection body and be freed of their fallen nature.

All who are saved now receive the earnest or down payment of their complete salvation in the form of the Holy Spirit (Eph 1:14; II Cor 1:22; 5:5). Other future installments of salvation for all believers are the removal of the fallen nature at death or when Christ comes, depending on which comes first, and then a resurrection body at Christ's second coming.

Bibliography. Herman Bavinck, *Our Reasonable Faith,* Grand Rapids: Eerdmans, 1956, pp. 184–220. Wayne Frair and P. William Davis, *The Case for Creation,* Chicago: Moody Press, 1967. R. Laird Harris, *Man: God's Eternal Creation,* Chicago: Moody Press, 1971. Charles Hodge, *Systematic Theology,* Grand Rapids: Eerdmans, 1952, II, 1–306. John W. Klotz, *Genes, Genesis and Evolution,* St. Louis: Concordia, 1955. J. Gresham Machen, *The Christian View of Man,* Grand Rapids: Eerdmans, 1937. Russell L. Mixter, *Evolution and Christian Thought Today,* Grand Rapids: Eerdmans, 1959. James M. Murk, "Anthropology," *Christianity and the World of*

Thought, ed. by Hudson T. Armerding, Chicago: Moody, 1968, pp. 185-211. Erich Sauer, *The King of the Earth* (The Nobility of Man According to the Bible and Science), Grand Rapids: Eerdmans, 1962. A. E. Wilder-Smith, *Man's Origin, Man's Destiny*, Wheaton: Shaw, 1968. P. A. Zimmerman, ed., *Darwin, Evolution and Creation*, St. Louis: Concordia, 1959.

R. A. K.

ANTHROPOMORPHISM AND ANTHROPOPATHISM. By anthropomorphism is generally meant the ascription of human form to God, and by anthropopathism, the ascription of human feelings, passions, emotions and suffering to God. Theologians in general agree that both anthropomorphic and anthropopathic terms in the Bible are ascribed to God in a metaphorical sense. Only the sect of the Audians (in the 4th and 5th cen.) held to a strictly literal interpretation of such words. Christians differ greatly as to the real nature of this phenomenon.

In ascribing various attributes to God the Bible represents Him as:

Having human organs—eyes and eyelids (Ps 11:4; 34:15; Hab 1:13), fingers (Ps 8:3), feet (Ex 24:9-11; Isa 66:1), nose (Ex 15:8; II Sam 22:9), ears (Ps 17:6; 31:2), hands (Ps 95:4; 139:5), and even hair (Dan 7:9).

Having human emotions. Scripture speaks of God as having joy (Isa 65:19; Zeph 3:17), grief (Jud 10:16; Heb 3:10, 17), anger (Deut 1:37; Jer 7:18-20), hatred (Ps 5:5-6; Prov 6:16), wrath (Ex 32:10; Ps 2:5, 12; Rev 15:7), love (Jer 31:3; Jn 3:16; I Jn 4:16).

Executing human actions. The Scripture describes God as knowing (Ex 3:7; Lk 16:15), thinking (Ex 32:14; Ps 40:17), remembering (Gen 9:16; Jer 31:34), speaking (Gen 2:16; Ex 7:8), hearing (Ps 6:8-9; Acts 7:34), repenting (regretting, feeling sorry, Gen 6:6; Ex 32:14), and resting (Gen 2:2; Ex 20:11).

Having human relations. The Lord is called a shepherd (Ps 23:1; cf. Jn 10:11), a judge (Gen 18:25; Isa 33:22), a farmer (Jn 15:1), a bridegroom (Mk 2:19-20), a husband (Isa 54:5; Jer 31:32), a builder (Ps 127:1; Heb 11:10), a doctor (Ex 15:26; Ps 103:3; 147:3). Further He is likened to a lion (Rev 5:5), a lamb (Rev 5:6, 12), an eagle (Deut 32:11-12), a hen (Mt 23:37), the sun (Mal 4:2), a star (Rev 22:16), a rock (Ps 18:2), a tower (Ps 61:3; Prov 18:10), and a shield (Ps 28:7; 84:11).

Though the Bible speaks of God in such terms, they are only figures of speech which convey deeper truths. God is spirit and therefore beyond any human description. For example, since He is omniscient, all expressions of His knowing, thinking, and remembering really show that He is intensely and constantly interested in the world and man; since He is omnipotent, the expression of His forming the heavens with His fingers reveals that He was infinitely precise and personal in creation and forming all things, including man.

Two approaches are helpful in considering the anthropomorphic descriptions given in the Bible. The first is based upon a study of the particular nature of our knowledge of God. What is the nature of these descriptions? It can be any one of three: (1) Univocal. The anthropomorphic expression means literally exactly what it says. This theologians in general reject. (2) Equivocal. A statement does not mean what is says and therefore can communicate no certain meaning or knowledge. Some Reformed theologians have come very close to taking this viewpoint when they have overstressed the inability of human words to communicate truth from God and any revelation concerning Him in particular. (3) Analogical. A statement is to be taken as a comparison based either upon comparatives that are absolutely different (Aquinas) or comparisons which do have a univocal element in them. It is the univocal element in an analogy which enables it to communicate knowledge. For example, "Like as a father pitieth his children, so the Lord pitieth them that fear him" (Ps 103:13). The univocal element in this is the concept of a father and his mercy toward his own child. We know what fathers are and how they pity their errant children, and to this extent we can understand God's compassion for those who reverence Him. Further, since man is made in the image and likeness of God, man's organs, actions, feelings, emotions and relations can all become legitimate means for the description of God.

Specific data given in the Scripture can offer a sound approach to the question of anthropomorphism. For example, such a categorical statement as that given by Christ to the woman at the well, "God is a Spirit: and they that worship him must worship him in spirit and in truth" (Jn 4:24). Again, there are some descriptions of God given both in the OT and the NT. The closest to a visual one may be that given in Ex 24:9-11: "There was under his feet as it were a paved work of a sapphire stone, and as it were the body of heaven in his clearness." The two "as it weres" clearly indicate that the description is figurative. Though Moses saw God in Ex 33:18-23 he saw only His "after parts," or as R. Laird Harris translates this along with J. O. Buswell, His "after effects," namely, evidences of His glory and power (*A Systematic Theology*, J. O. Buswell, p. 31). Warnings against making images and likenesses of God point to the supernatural non-corporeal nature of God. Moses wrote, "Ye heard the voice [sound] of the words, but saw no similitude; only ye heard a voice" (Deut 4:12), and warned against all images and likenesses (Deut 5:6-9, 22-28).

How are the anthropomorphic terms used of God to be understood? Though they are clearly figurative in nature, they communicate such real knowledge of God as that He is active, attentive even to the smallest details of man's life, sympathetic with all his weaknesses, patient, kind, and loving. *See* Analogy.

Certain problems arise with anthropopathisms. How can God who is immutable (Ps 102:26-27; Mal 3:6; Heb 13:8; Jas 1:17) be said to change His mind and to repent (Jon 3:10; Ex 32:14; I Sam 15:35), particularly when Scripture says He cannot repent (Num 23:19; I Sam 15:29)? Looked at from man's standpoint, God appears to change His mind—remember He does have feelings and emotions—but looked at from the fact of His omniscience, He knows what is to come to pass and has already ordained that it be so.

Divergent views are held about anthropomorphisms and anthropopathisms. Karl Barth, for example, sees them as a part of the *welthaftigkeit,* the "worldliness" that adheres to Scripture because man cannot express the "absolute otherness" of God. Only in the ineffable event of a personal experience of revelation does man come to know God. The difficulty with this view is that it actually makes any real knowledge of God impossible, that is, any knowledge that can be communicated from man to man. If Barth is right, then the anthropomorphisms in the Bible are really the perversions of revelation caused by man's forcing timeless eternal truth into time-space categories.

In paganism man himself has built up concepts of God made in the image and likeness of fallen man (Rom 1:23). Feuerbach rejected the Bible's explanation at this point and said that in Christianity man had simply projected an image of himself and turned and worshiped this image, and that this is the explanation of the origin of Christianity (*The Essence of Christianity*). But in Rom 1:18 ff. Paul by revelation explains how man once knew God, yet did not want to retain Him in his knowledge and therefore made images of himself, of fourfooted beasts and creeping things, and turned and worshiped these instead of God.

Anthropomorphism plays a very necessary part in revelation. It shows that God is really a person with intellect, will and emotions, a moral nature and self-consciousness, giving proofs of all these marks of personality. In recent years the "God is Dead" theologians have claimed that the transcendent God of the Scripture is either dead or died at Calvary (T. J. J. Altizer, cf. Wm. Hamilton); or that the concept given in the Bible of God is outdated, is no longer tenable and needs to be changed (Paul Tillich. Bishop Robinson); or that the term God is empty and meaningless and illogical (Paul Van Buren), and in at least one if not all of these senses dead. The anthropomorphisms and anthropopathisms of the Bible offer a needed answer to such views, in that they prove the image of God and the image of man are sufficiently alike that man can have a knowledge of God and know Him personally.

Bibliography. Herman Bavinck, *The Doctrine of God,* Grand Rapids: Eerdmans, 1951, pp. 83-98. J. O. Buswell, *A Systematic Theology,* Grand Rapids: Zondervan, 1962, 1, 29-36. Charles Hodge, *Systematic Theology,* Grand Rapids: Eerdmans, 1952, I, 335-345. A. H. Strong, *Systematic Theology,* Philadelphia: Judson Press, 1953, pp. 250 f.

R. A. K.

ANTICHRIST. *Names and references.* The term "Antichrist" appears only in I Jn 2:18, 22; 4:3; II Jn 7. If one holds that the Scriptures present a growing unity on this doctrine, and that an eschatological person, the final Antichrist to be indwelt by Satan (Rev 13), is yet to be manifest, he must relate a large number of biblical names and references to him. These begin with the "seed" of the serpent (Gen 3:15) and end with "the beast" (Rev 20:10). Most important are the "little horn" on the fourth beast of Dan 7:7 ff.; "the prince that shall come" (Dan 9:26); "one who makes desolate" (Dan 9:27, RSV); the willful king of Dan 11:36-39; "man of sin" and "son of perdition" as well as "the lawless one" (II Thess 2:3, 8, ASV); and "the beast" (Rev 11:7; 13:2 ff.). Jesus referred to Antichrist as one setting up an idol in God's temple in the days just before His second advent (Mt 24:15; *see* Abomination of Desloation).

Meaning. Antichrist means one who is against Christ or who is a substitute for Him. John saw his "spirit" or doctrine (Docetism?) in the world in the 1st cen. (I Jn 4:3). The OT doctrine of Belial (the Heb. *b^elîya'al* occurs 27 times in OT; once in NT, II Cor 6:15; cf. Beelzebub, Lk 11:15-19) probably refers to the same concept. *See* Belial.

Interpretations. Emphasizing one aspect or another of Scripture teaching, several types of interpretation have appeared in Christian circles.

1. "Principle of evil" view. Advocates propose that Antichrist is a personification of some evil principle, power(s), or idea(s) of the world, always until the end of time in opposition to the kingdom of God. I and II John seem to portray Antichrist in this way, and surely this must be part of the truth. At various times this principle has been identified with current movements (e.g., Communism, Fascism).

2. "Institution of evil" view. This is an appropriate name for the idea that the Roman Empire or the Papacy or the Muslim religion, etc., is the Antichrist. This approach is common among preterist and historicist interpreters of Revelation.

3. "Person of evil" view [not personification] is still another. Some contemporary man who seems particularly dangerous to Christianity in the opinion of the interpreter has frequently been held to be the man of sin of II Thess 2 or the Beast of Revelation and Daniel. In the early Middle Ages Muhammad was the favorite candidate. Later the popes would find various offending emperors or heretics likely holders for the label while conversely these men or their followers put the label on the current pope. In Reformation times, depending on whose side the interpreter was, the pope or

Martin Luther would be charged with the unwelcome name. Napoleon, Kaiser Wilhelm II, Mussolini, etc., have been proposed.

4. "Popular fallacy" view. Liberal (modernist) writers usually hold that Antichrist in the NT only reflects ancient pagan myths still believed by the early Christians, or Jewish notions carried over into Christianity by the first Christians. Such interpreters read II Thessalonians and Revelation not as God's Word but only as a source of early Christian opinion.

5. Among evangelicals, far more common is what may be called the "organic" view. This is the opinion that good and evil have parallel development and reach ultimate consummation in a personal Christ and in a personal Antichrist, and that these meet in final conflict at the second advent of Chirst. Postmillennialists (e.g., A. H. Strong, *Systematic Theology,* p. 1008), amillennialists (e.g., C. F. Keil, *Commentary on Daniel* at 9:26 - 27), and premillennialists (e.g., Alva J. McClain, *The Greatness of the Kingdom,* pp. 452 - 453) agree in this.

The doctrine. Though Daniel and Revelation have more material on this subject, the most detailed systematic treatment is in II Thess 2. Examination yields information that a consummately evil person called "the man of sin," "son of perdition," and "lawless one" (ASV) shall some day "be revealed." This revelation is to take place before (presumably shortly before) "the day of the Lord." With revelation of the man of sin will come a general apostasy from true religion, or "falling away." He will oppose God, exalt himself, demand divine honors, and in a general way be consummate godlessness and Antichrist. His coming will be the fruition of evil forces ("the mystery of lawlessness") now operating (II Thess 2:7). His success shall come, temporarily, by Satanic power and divine permissive providence (vv. 9 - 12), but ultimately he shall be slain by Christ's own manifestation at His coming (v. 8). (See also Rev 13:1 ff.; Dan 7:8 ff.; 11:36 ff.) Jesus speaks of him as one who comes in his "own name" (Jn 5:43).

See Beast (symbolic); Man of Sin; Devil.

Bibliography. W. Bousset, *The Antichrist Legend,* 1896. James Oliver Buswell, *A Systematic Theology of the Christian Religion,* Grand Rapids: Zondervan, 1962, II, 371 - 383, 390 - 396, 465 - 481.

R. D. C.

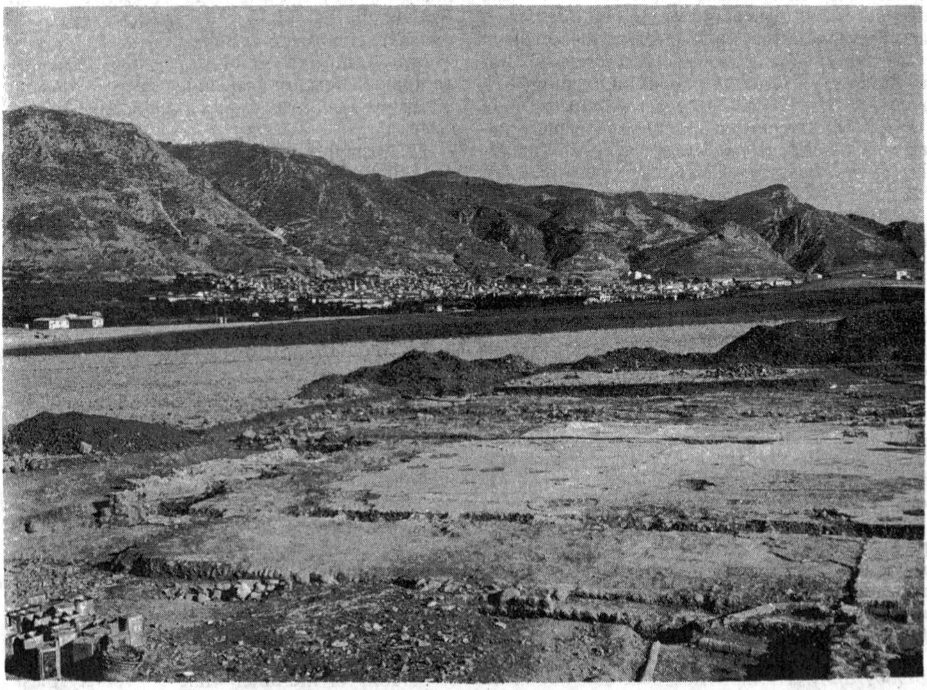

Excavations at Antioch of Syria. Princeton University

ANTIOCH (ăn'tĭ-ŏk). Sixteen Antiochs were established by Seleucus Nicator, founder of the Seleucid Empire in 312 (or 306) B.C. in honor of his father, Antiochus. Only two of these are mentioned in the NT: one in Syria, the other in Pisidia.

1. Antioch in Syria, the capital, was one of five Antiochs in Syria alone. Founded in 301 B.C., it became the greatest of all the Antiochs. In the 1st cen. it was the third largest city of the Roman Empire, with a population frequently estimated to have been 500,000. It was called "the Beautiful and the Golden," the "Queen of the East" from its location and magnificent buildings.

Located some 15 miles from the Mediterranean harbor of Seleucia, it lay on the N bank of the Orontes River in a broad and fertile valley at the foot of the snow-crested peaks of Mount Silpius. Crowding caravans from N, S, and E converged upon its marketplaces, while boats from the Mediterranean waited in port to unload their burdens and be refilled again. Retired government officials spent their fortunes there, surfeiting themselves with its exotic delicacies, gambling their gold coins on the chariot races, and relaxing daily in its great public baths. From its founding it was cosmopolitan. Jews enjoyed the same privileges given to Greek traders.

The city was divided into four quarters from 175 B.C. onward, separated by one long colonnade and a second shorter one intersecting it obliquely. Temples, theaters, baths, and Roman streets, when destroyed by earthquakes (as in A.D. 37) or by wars (several revolts in 1st cen.) were promptly rebuilt by the vigorous citizens. Today its population numbers barely 42,000.

Syrian Antioch is very important in the early history of the Christian church. Nicholas, one of the original deacons, was a proselyte of Antioch (Acts 6:5). During the persecutions following Stephen's stoning, many Jerusalem Christians fled to Antioch where they preached to Greek-speaking Jews (Hellenists) and to Greeks (Hellenes). (Gr. MSS are divided and we can argue for either word as original in Acts 11:20, but the context clearly implies both Hellenists and Hellenes were found in the congregation.)

Barnabas greatly strengthened the ties of fellowship between the Antiochian congregation and the mother church at Jerusalem (Acts 11:22 - 30), secured Paul's services for them as a teacher (Acts 11:25 - 26), and in company with Paul carried their relief money to Jerusalem (Acts 11:27 - 30). The disciples were given the name "Christians" first in Antioch (Acts 11:26). Paul was sent out from the Antioch church on his three great missions to Cyprus, Asia Minor, and Greece (Acts 13:1 ff.; 15:36 ff.; 18:23 ff.). The first great church council at Jerusalem was occasioned by the question whether it was necessary to circumcise Gentile converts, and it is fair to say the broader view of Antioch prevailed over the narrower view of Judea (Acts 15; cf. Gal 2:4 - 14).

In the ancient church, Antioch was famous for Ignatius, the bishop and martyr (*c.*A.D. 110) whose letters we still read; and for its school and great teachers, Chrysostom (*c.* 390) and Theodore of Mopsuestia (*c.* 390) who urged a literal and historical interpretation of the Bible over against the allegorizing tendencies of Clement and Origen of Alexandria in Egypt. *See* Archaeology.

The chalice of Antioch (found near Syrian Antioch in 1916), sometimes claimed to be the Holy Grail used by Jesus and His apostles at the first communion, is a plain silver cup set in a filigree holder bearing figures thought to represent Jesus and several apostles. It is now believed to date from the 4th or 5th cen. A.D.

See Archaeology.

Bibliography. Glanville Downey, *Antioch in the Age of Theodosius the Great,* Norman: Univ. of Oklahoma Press, 1962; *A History of Antioch in Syria,* Princeton: Univ. Press, 1961. Bruce M. Metzger, "Antioch-on-the-Orontes," BA, XI (1948), 69 - 88. Richard Stilwell (ed.), *Antioch-on-the-Orontes,* Princeton: Univ. Press, 1938.

2. Antioch near Pisidia, a city of Phrygia in southern Asia Minor. It was called Pisidian Antioch to distinguish it from the many other cities of the same name founded by Seleucus Nicator in honor of his father, probably soon after 301 B.C. It was a garrison point commanding the great Roman road connecting Ephesus with the Cilician Gates, a mountain pass just above Tarsus. After 25 B.C. Rome made it a city of Galatia, then elevated it to colony status shortly before 6 B.C. Roman roads henceforward connected it with the other colonies (e.g., Lystra) founded in the district.

On his first mission Paul planted a church in Pisidian Antioch (Acts 13:13 - 52) and its witness was heard throughout the "region" (Acts 13:49); only in Ephesus and Thessalonica were there comparable results. Jews were present in great numbers from 200 B.C. onward and no doubt their proselyting efforts had prepared many Gentile hearts for the gospel. By reaching "the Jew first" (Rom 1:16), Paul could furnish leadership to the infant church which knew the OT Scriptures and the synagogue service upon which Christian worship was based. (Note in Acts 13:43 ff. emphasis on Jews and proselytes.) Noble women among the Gentiles were drawn in great numbers from paganism to Judaism, according to Juvenal VI:543 and Jos *Wars* II.20.2, and likewise they readily embraced the Christian faith (Acts 13:50). Paul's sermon is given at length in Acts 13.

The "South Galatian" theory (*see* Galatia) claims Pisidian Antioch belonged to the region of Phrygia (a geographical term used by Greeks) and Galatia (a political term used by

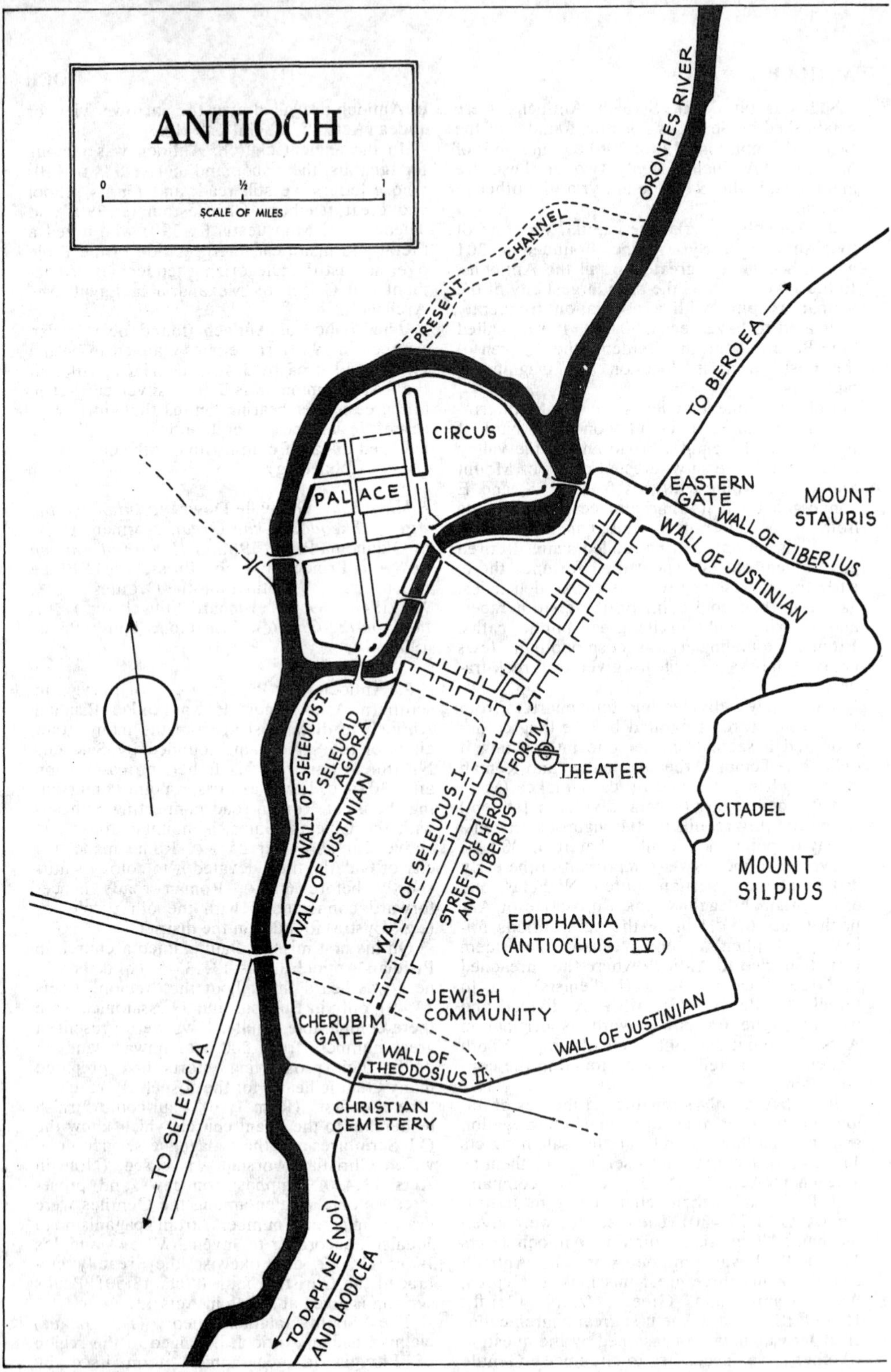

A Map of Antioch of Syria in New Testament Times.

the Roman government) according to Acts 16:6 and 18:23. Along with Iconium, Lystra, and Derbe, Antioch is one of the "Galatian" churches to which Paul wrote his letter.

On the less probable "North Galatian" theory, Pisidian Antioch lay too far S in Phrygia to be one of the churches to which Paul wrote; they were rather at Tavium. Ancyra and Pessinus, cities not mentioned in Acts or the NT except as Acts 16:6 and 18:23 refer to Phrygian (geographical) and Galatian (geographical northern part of the political province) territory.

Bibliography. David Magie, *Roman Rule in Asia Minor,* Princeton: Univ. Press, 1950, I, 457-463. David M. Robinson, "A Preliminary Report on the Excavations at Pisidian Antioch and at Sizma," AJA, XXVIII (Oct., 1924), 435-444.

T. B. C.

ANTIPAS (ăn'tĭ-păs). A contraction of Antipater.

1. While this was the name of the father of Herod the Great (Jos *Ant*. xiv. 1.3-4), it was best known as the name of one of the several sons of Herod the Great. He was the son of Herod and Malthace, and the brother of Archelaus (Mt 2:22) and Philip, known as Herod the tetrarch (Lk 3:1, 19) and notorious for his marriage to Herodias, Philip's wife.

After John the Baptist had appeared before him and had been beheaded for accusing Herod of adultery (Mk 6:17-29), Jesus was sent to him by Pilate to be examined (Lk 23:7-11). He was known for his evil deeds (Lk 3:19) and was called "that fox" by Jesus (Lk 13:31-32), an expression probably referring to his slyness. *See also* Aretas; Herod.

2. An early Christian martyr mentioned in Rev 2:13 as "my faithful martyr" resident at Pergamum (*q.v.*).

W. M. D.

ANTIPATRIS (ăn-tĭp'ȧ-trĭs). This city is mentioned only once in the NT (Acts 23:31). Paul and the 470 Roman soldiers guarding him stopped there when he was being transferred by night from Jerusalem to Caesarea. The site overlooks the plain of Sharon, *c*. 30 miles NW of Jerusalem and 28 miles S of Caesarea. The town was elaborately beautiful in the time of Herod (*c*. 9 B.C.) and renamed after Herod's father, Antipater; it was originally known as Kaphar Saba (see Jos *Ant*. xiii, 15.1; xvi.5.2).

Unquestionably a town stood there many centuries before the time of Jesus. Antipatris most likely was located at Ras el-'Ain ("head of the spring"), which spring is the most copious in all of Palestine and forms the main constant source for the Aujeh River (i.e., the Yarkon). Today most of this water is drained off by pipeline to the Negev.

Pre-Christian pottery (Hellenistic, Iron and Bronze Ages) was found here in 1946, corroborating the view that this site was OT Aphek (*see* Aphek 3). Josephus said it was located near the tower of Aphek (*Wars* ii.19.1), and in the Hellenistic period it was probably called *Pēgai* ("springs"; it is referred to in a document from the time of Ptolemy Philadelphus, cf. *Pap, d. Soc. Ital.* IV, 406). There are impressive remains (a large fortress and caravansary, etc.) from the Arabic-Crusader period there today. It invites excavation, which has not been carried on to any real degree as yet. In the Talmudic period it was on the border between northern Judea and Galilee (cf. *Gittin* VII.7; *Yoma* 69*a*). From the 4th cen. on it was one of the main stations for pilgrims.

Bibliography. Conder and Kitchener, *Survey of Western Palestine, Memoirs* II, 134, 258 ff. Emil Schürer, *History of the Jewish People in the Time of Jesus Christ,* New York: Scribner's, 1891, II, 1, 130-131.

E. J. V.

ANTITYPE. "Something that corresponds to or is foreshadowed in a type or symbol" (Webster). Christ is the messianic reality which fulfills many particular pre-messianic figures in the OT. For example, as the Lamb of God He is the antitype and fulfillment of the Passover lamb (I Cor 5:7). Christian baptism symbolizes the salvation which is in Christ and is the antitype (Gr. *antitypon*) of the salvation which was offered in Noah's ark (I Pet 3:21, NASB). In Heb 9:24 the term is used in a slightly different manner as the sections of the OT tabernacle are called the antitypes of God's heavenly tabernacle in the sense that the Mosaic tabernacle was the fulfillment or subsequent earthly reality of the eternal heavenly tabernacle, its pattern (cf. Heb 8:2, 5). *See* Types.

Reconstruction of the Castle of Antonia. Sisters of Zion, Jerusalem

ANTONIA (ăn-tō'nĭ-ȧ). A fortress rebuilt by Herod the Great NW of the temple, not named in the Bible but referred to in connection with Paul's arrest in Jerusalem. In the time of Nehemiah it was a citadel related to the temple (Neh

2:8; 7:2, RSV). Later this site was occupied by a castle of the Asmonean high priest-kings (Jos *Ant.* xv.11.4; xviii.4.3; *Wars* i.21.1). When Herod ordered the temple to be rebuilt (*c.* 22 or 19 B.C.), this structure at the NW corner of the temple area was also remodeled as a palatial guard tower and royal residence, and renamed in honor of Mark Antony, the friend and patron of Herod. It stood on a cliff of the Tyropeon Valley nearly 75 feet high, and had four massive towers, each 75 - 100 feet tall, at its four corners. Its courtyard was paved with great stone slabs three feet square and a foot thick.

For the NT student the primary importance of Antonia rests in the fact that Paul was imprisoned in the barracks (Gr. *parembolē*, "castle," KJV) until he was transferred to Caesarea (Acts 21:37; 22:24; 23:10, 16, 32). The high priest's garments were also stored here and released by the Romans only during the time of the Jewish festivals.

H. P. Vincent has argued that Antonia is to be identified with the pretorium with its pavement (Jn 18:28; 19:13) and that Jesus was tried here before Pilate. Strong reasons weigh against Vincent's view. The pretorium more likely referred to Herod's palace in Jerusalem. *See* Pretorium.

Bibliography. Soeur Marie Aline de Sion, *La forteresse Antonia à Jérusalem et la question du Prétoire,* Paris: Galbalda, 1956. P. Benoit, "Pretorie, Lithostrotos," *Revue Biblique,* LIX (1952), 531 - 550. Millar Burrows, "The Fortress Antonia and the Praetorium," BA, I (1938), 17 - 19. Superior Godeleine, *Le Lithostrotos d'apres des Fouilles Recentes,* Jerusalem: "Notre-Dame de Sion," 1932. Soeur Marie Ita of Sion, "The Antonia Fortress," PEQ, C (1968), 139 - 143. E. Schürer, *A History of the Jewish People in the Time of Jesus Christ,* 5 vols., 1896, see references to Josephus, Tacitus, etc. H. P. Vincent, "Le Lithostrotos Evangelique," *Revue Biblique,* LIX (1952), 513 - 530.

E. J. V.

ANTOTHIJAH (ăn'tō-thī-*jȧ*). A descendant of Benjamin. In RSV the spelling is Anthothijah (I Chr 8:24).

ANTOTHITE (ăn'tō-thīt). A short form of Anethothite (*q.v.*), a dweller in Anathoth.

ANUB (ā'nŭb). The son of Coz of the tribe of Judah (I Chr 4:8).

ANVIL. A heavy piece of metal used by smiths to receive hammer taps or blows when shaping metal implements or objects. Referred to only in Isa 41:7.

APE. *See* Animals, II.2.

APELLES (*ȧ*-pĕl'ēz). A Christian in Rome whom Paul greeted and designated as one "approved in Christ" (Rom 16:10). It was a frequently used name among Greeks and Jews according to inscriptional evidence.

APHARSACHITES (*ȧ*-făr'sȧ-kīts), **APHARSATHCHITES** (*ȧ*-făr'săth-kīts). A name used to transliterate an Aramaic or Persian term, understood in KJV as referring to the name of a people resettled in Samaria by Asnapper (Ashurbanipal), the Assyrian king. Found in Ezr 4:9; 5:6; 6:6, KJV. RSV translates the word as "governors" following the example of I Esd 6:7.

APHARSITES (*ȧ*-făr'sīts). Found only in Ezr 4:9, KJV, referring to a tribe resettled in Samaria by the Assyrian king Asnapper (Ashurbanipal). RSV translates the word as "Persians." Herzfeld believes it refers to neo-Babylonian officials (IB, III, 601).

APHEK (ā'fĕk)

1. A city by this name (Aphik in Jud 1:31), perhaps to be identified with Tell el-Kurdaneh six miles SE of Acco, was within Asher's territory (Josh 19:30) but was not conquered at first by the Israelites.

2. The Syrians fled to a city named Aphek in Bashan (E of the Sea of Galilee) after being defeated by Ahab (I Kgs 20:26 - 30).

3. An ancient Canaanite city which lay within the territory of Ephraim in the plain of Sharon. It was located at Ras el-'Ain, a copious spring that forms the headwaters of the Yarkon River. The presence here of Middle Bronze, Late Bronze, and Iron I Age potsherds agrees with the mention of Aphek in the Egyptian Execration texts and as the first town captured by Amenhotep II on his second Asiatic campaign (*c.* 1440 B.C.). Aphek appears again in an Aramaic letter of a Palestinian prince, Adon, to Pharaoh Hophra *c.* 600 B.C. (BASOR, # 111 [Oct., 1948], 24 - 27). Its king was slain by Joshua (Josh 12:18), but later the Philistines defeated the sons of Eli near the place and captured the ark (I Sam 4:1 - 11). The Philistines used Aphek as a staging area for their forces before attacking Saul in Jezreel. At the time, David and his men were a part of the Philistine forces, but were dismissed before the battle began because some Philistine generals did not trust David (I Sam 29).

In Roman times, the city of Antipatris (*q.v.*) was built near the ancient ruins of Aphek by Herod the Great and named after his father. After his arrest in Jerusalem, Paul was brought by night to this place while on his way to Caesarea (Acts 23:31).

G. H. L.

APHEKAH (*ȧ*-fē'k*ȧ*). A town in the southern hill country of Judah allotted to that tribe after Joshua's conquest (Josh 15:53).

APHIAH (*ȧ*-fī'*ȧ*). A Benjamite ancestor of King Saul (I Sam 9:1).

APHIK (ā'fĭk). *See* Aphek.

APHRAH (ăf'rȧ). *See* Beth-le-aphrah.

APHSES (ăf'sēz). A descendant of Aaron appointed by lot to priestly duties under King David (I Chr 24:15, KJV). Appears as Happizzez in RSV.

APOCALYPSE. From the Gr. word *apokalypsis,* an uncovering or unveiling, a disclosure of truth, a manifestation or return to view, the English word has come to mean a certain type of prophetic literature featuring end-time judgments of this world and visions of the next world. In addition to the canonical apocalypses in the books of Ezekiel, Daniel, and Zechariah in the OT and of John in the NT (*see* Revelation, Book of), there were numerous fanciful Jewish and early Christian apocalypses included among the Apocrypha (*q.v.*).

APOCRYPHA (ȧ-pŏk'rĭ-fȧ). Commonly used to designate a collection of edifying books not included in the canon of Scripture.

Terminology

Apocrypha as a Gr. adjective, neuter plural, meaning "hidden things," is to be found in Dan 2:22 (Theodotian); Sir 14:21; 39:3, 7; 42:19; 43:32; 48:25; and in the NT in three passages (Mk 4:22; Lk 8:17; Col 2:3). In early usage it was about equivalent to *esoterikos*—writings intended for the inner circle and capable of being understood by no others—"kept for the wise among people" (cf. IV Ezr 14). But with Augustine (*De civ. dei* xv.23), a second idea of obscurity of origin or authorship is suggested. Since the time of Jerome it has designated noncanonical books, and since the time of the Reformation a definite collection of such books. Carlstadt defined "Apocrypha" as writings excluded from the canon whether or not the true authors of the books were known.

Attitudes Toward OT Apocrypha

The OT Apocrypha is comprised of 14 or 15 books which are usually found in MSS of the LXX or the Vulgate, but which are not included in the Heb. canon. The Prayer of Manasseh and II Esdras are exceptions. The latter appears in no Gr. MSS and the Prayer of Manasseh is not in all of them. In contrast, the books of the Pseudepigrapha with few exceptions are never found in biblical MSS.

No exact record has survived giving the process and basis by which the apocryphal books were excluded from the canon. The exclusion for Pharisaic Jews had already taken place by the time of Josephus (cf. *Apion i.* 8), who states that the canonical books are 22 in number and that they date between the time of Moses and Artaxerxes. The apocryphal books, commonly dated from the 2nd cen. B.C. to the 1st cen. A.D., were too late to qualify. Some of the books have historical mistakes and represent questionable ethics and theology.

The earliest list of OT canon (Melito of Sardis; cf. Eusebius H. E. iv. 26.14) does not include the Apocrypha. No book of the Apocrypha is directly quoted in the NT; but the books are frequently cited by early Christian writers. In the Eastern and Western churches the books came to form an integral part of the canon and were scattered throughout the OT, generally placed near the books with which they have affinity.

OT Apocrypha deals in the main with persons, events, and themes closely related to OT and post-OT figures. Though composed by Jewish writers, likely in Hebrew and Aramaic, and though communities like the Dead Sea group possessed an undefined number of outside books, the Apocrypha has largely been preserved by Christians. However, despite Akiba's threat that he who reads the outside books has no part in the world to come, there were medieval Jewish translations of some of the books.

The Apocrypha has exercised considerable influence upon art and upon English literature through the centuries. Common proverbs and familiar names have been derived from these books. Most early English Bibles (Wycliffe, Coverdale, and Geneva) contained these books as an appendix, but as early as 1629 they were omitted from some editions of the KJV. The major translating committees have translated the Apocrypha as a separate volume; but since 1827 Bibles published by the British and American Bible Societies have omitted these books.

Four attitudes have crystallized toward the Apocrypha since the time of the Reformation. The Council of Trent (1546) affirmed the canonicity of these books as found in the Vulgate edition and anathematized him who denied their place. This declaration was further confirmed by the Vatican Council of 1870. In Catholic writers the books are often called "Deutero-canonical" with no distinction of authority to be implied from the term. Catholics tend to use the term Apocrypha to designate the group of books the Protestants call Pseudepigrapha.

A second attitude is to be found in Protestant writers. When Luther issued his German Bible, he put six books in an appendix at the end of the OT with an introduction: "Aprocrypha: these books are not held equal to the sacred Scriptures and yet are useful and good for reading." The sixth article of the Church of England states: "And the other books the church doth read for example of life and instruction of manners, but yet doth it not apply them to establish any doctrines." On special holy days sections of Tobit, Wisdom, and Sirach are read by the Episcopal Church in America.

The third attitude is seen developing with the rise of the Puritans who rejected the books as of no religious value: "Not to be otherwise approved or made use of than any other human writing." The term Apocrypha came to have a derogatory sense meaning unauthentic.

A fourth attitude, widely held today, shifts

the point of emphasis from that of the canonical status of the books to that of their historical value for supplying information on the times between the OT and NT period. They are invaluable for supplying information on the historical and religious conditions out of which they arose. The messianic idea, the doctrines of wisdom, law, sin, good works, demonology, angels, and eschatology are all dealt with.

Contents of OT Apocrypha

I Esdras is a narrative survey of events, parallel to the narrative of Ezra and Nehemiah, surrounding Zerubbabel and the return of Ezra and his work. The most charming part is the story of the three guardsmen who debate over the strongest thing in the world and conclude that it is Truth.

II Esdras is an apocalypse in which the writer has Ezra raise questions seeking to justify the ways of God in permitting calamities to befall Zion.

Tobit is a novel purporting to depict the life of the Jew in captivity. Its purpose is to teach moral lessons. Prayer and almsgiving are praised. The duty of burying the dead and of marrying within Judaism is set forth.

Judith is a patriotic short story extolling the deeds of a Jewish widow who delivered her people even as Esther brought deliverance.

The Additions to Esther are six supplementary passages added to complete the canonical story. They must be read in their proper place in the story as they stand in the LXX, rather than as a collection at its end as in the RSV, in order to be intelligible. They add a religious note to an otherwise secular book.

The Wisdom of Solomon consists of Wisdom-type literature in which idolatry is mocked and wisdom is praised. The fates of the righteous and the wicked are contrasted.

Ecclesiasticus is a miscellaneous collection of wise sayings dealing with all areas of life. Proverbs is the nearest canonical parallel. The book culminates in the "Praise of the Fathers" which surveys the merits of the OT worthies.

Baruch is a lament over the fall of Jerusalem which confesses the guilt of Israel and promises a restoration in prophetic fashion.

The Letter of Jeremiah is a satire on the follies of idolatry.

The Prayer of Azariah is an addition to Daniel which purports to express sentiments of the three Hebrews when in the fiery furnace.

Susanna is a detective story designed to extol the wisdom of Daniel, who demonstrates the innocence of the falsely accused woman.

Bel and the Dragon also extols the wisdom of Daniel and satirizes idolatry.

The Prayer of Manasseh purports to express the penitence of the OT's most wicked king. The theme is suggested by II Chr 33:12.

I Maccabees is a narrative of events leading up to and covering the Maccabean revolt. The book is a historical source of considerable merit.

II Maccabees covers the same material as the first part of I Maccabees, but adds religious sentiments and attempts to demonstrate that the miraculous played a significant part in the victory. *See* Maccabees.

NT Apocrypha

The Aprocryphal NT is a body of literature of undefined limits. It differs from the OT Apocrypha in that it is seldom found in biblical MSS. In general, infancy and passion Gospels, acts, epistles, and apocalypses are the categories treated. It is unlikely that they preserve any authentic deeds or sayings of their heroes. Rather, they are amplifications of themes suggested by the canonical books. The writers attempted to supply information on periods where biblical material is wanting, such as the hidden years of Jesus' life or details about what the man might have seen who was caught up into the third heaven (II Cor 12:2). The miraculous element is usually heightened.

The books tend to make propaganda for views which the writer thought were significant. Early heretics used these means to spread their views. In 1947 the known material of this sort was considerably enlarged by the discovery of a Gnostic library in Egypt containing portions of 13 codices in Coptic. Back of these are thought to lie Gr. materials that may be dated in the 2nd cen. A.D. *See* Chenoboskion; Gnosticism.

Considerable misimpression has been fostered about the Apocrypha by such titles as "The Lost Books of the Bible," for it has by no means been established that these books were ever a part of the Bible. Some NT apocryphal writings were already known to early Church Fathers. On the other hand, composition of this type of material has continued on down to modern times. The materials of the earlier period are most satisfactorily presented in the edition of M.R. James, while modern examples are evaluated by E. J. Goodspeed.

Bibliography. L. H. Brockington, *A Critical Introduction to the Apocrypha,* London: Duckworth, 1961. E. J. Goodspeed, *Modern Apocrypha,* Boston: Beacon Press, 1956. Robert M. Grant, *Gnosticism,* New York: Harper, 1961. M. R. James, *The Apocryphal New Testament,* Oxford: Clarendon, 1924. Bruce M. Metzger, *An Introduction to the Apocrypha,* New York: Oxford, 1957. B. F. Westcott, *The Bible in the Church,* London: Macmillan, 1905.

J. P. L.

APOLLONIA (ăp'ŏl-lō'nĭ-*ȧ*). Apollonia of Mygonia in Macedonia was one of the dozen or so towns of this name in the ancient world. (For list of other places named Apollonia, see A. H. M. Jones, *Cities of the Eastern Roman Provinces,* p. 560; see also B. V. Head, *Historia Numorum,* pp. 895 ff.). There were three Macedonian towns of this name. The one referred to in Acts 17:1 was situated S of Lake Bolbe.

According to Strabo, Cassander took the people from Apollonia, as well as other surrounding cities, and settled them in Thessalonica when he built that town for his wife (daughter of Philip of Macedonia) and named it after her (Strabo, *Geography*, Fragments of Book VII, Loeb ed. III, 343).

The apostle Paul passed through Apollonia on his second missionary journey as he traveled the Egnatian Way from Philippi to Thessalonica, a distance of *c.* 85 miles. It was *c.* 34 miles from Philippi to Amphipolis, 21 from Amphipolis to Apollonia, and 30 from Apollonia to Thessalonica. The whole district of Macedonia was much more fertile and prosperous than the region around Athens. The economic importance of this area is not generally recognized, but is quite obvious to the modern traveler. Adequate rainfall accounts for the lush aspect of this region. Apollonia (modern Pollina) is still settled by a small handful of people. See also W. M. Leake, *Travels in Northern Greece*, iii.458.

E. J. V.

APOLLOS (*ȧ*-pŏl'*ŏs*). The name is a shortened form of Apollonius. He is described in Acts 18:24–28 as an Alexandrian Jew, an eloquent man, and one "mighty in the scriptures." He had been "instructed" (lit., "catechized," cf. Lk 1:4) in "the way of the Lord"; that is, he knew of the teachings of the followers of Jesus (cf. Acts 9:2, "the Way"). His teaching, done with fervency, concerned "the baptism of John" (cf. Lk 7:29).

His preaching in Ephesus, listened to by Priscilla and Aquila, was not incorrect; rather, it was incomplete. They explained to him "the way of God" more accurately; that is, the rest of the message was made known to him, particularly concerning the ascension of Christ and the advent of the Holy Spirit. That these elements seemed to be lacking in his initial preaching is implied by Acts 19:1–3.

Other NT passages giving information about Apollos are I Cor 1:12; 3:4–6, 22; 4:6; 16:12 and Tit 3:13. We learn there that he had been associated with Paul, and that he had become one of four "party favorites" in the church at Corinth (along with Cephas, Paul, and Christ). Paul referred to him as a "fellow worker" and as "our brother," although making it clear that he himself had "laid the foundation."

Apparently Apollos' eloquence had made an impression on the Corinthians, and Paul took pains to emphasize that he (Paul) "did not come with superiority of speech or of wisdom" (I Cor 2:1, NASB), and that their faith "should not rest on the wisdom of men, but on the power of God" (v. 5).

Apollos seems to have become aware of the problem of tensions in the Corinthian church, and although Paul encouraged him to revisit them, he declined to go at that time (I Cor 16:12). Tit 3:13 appears to indicate that he was with Titus in Crete at a later date.

W. M. D.

APOLLYON (*ȧ*-pŏl'yŭn). A Gr. word meaning "destroyer," translating the Heb. *'ăbaddôn* (the lower or nether world, "perdition"), used of the angel of the bottomless pit (Rev 9:11). In Prov 15:11 (RSV) Sheol and Abaddon are linked together as the location and the state of the dead. Bunyan, in his *Pilgrim's Progress*, equated Apollyon with Satan.

APOLOGETICS. The term is derived from the Gr. verb *apologeomai*, meaning "to give an answer back," "reply," "defend one's position," and the Gr. noun *apologia*. In its narrowest sense it means the defense of the faith of the individual Christian. In a broader sense it is the answer of the Christian to attacks upon himself, his doctrine and faith, and all the revelation given in the Scriptures. In its fullest sense apologetics is the defense and justification of the Christian faith and of the revelation given in the Holy Scriptures against the attack of doubters and unbelievers, plus the development of a positive evangelical presentation of the facts given in the Bible, the reasonableness of God's revelation to man in Scripture, and its ample sufficiency alone to meet the complete spiritual needs of man. Apologetics is then not only a negative and defensive but also a positive and offensive exercise. It is not only to be used in defense of the gospel but also in its propagation.

The study of apologetics. This can be divided into three periods as found in three eras of church history.

1. *New Testament apologetics.* The Gr. verb *apologeomai* is used to express the idea of self-justification or self-excuse (Rom 2:15; II Cor 12:19) and also the noun *apologia* (II Cor 7:11); but particularly in the sense of replying to attacks on one's faith and convictions, and offering a defense. Acts 7 is often called Stephen's apology as he replied before the Jewish Sanhedrin to the accusations of false witnesses (Acts 6:11–15).

Paul speaks of being set for "the defense of the gospel" (Phil 1:7, 17). He made two "apologies" for his position: the first before Festus (Acts 24:10; 25:8; cf. v. 16), and the second before Agrippa (Acts 26:2). When he appealed for the privilege to do the same before Caesar (Acts 25:8–16), his request was finally granted. Each of these apologies contains both a negative defensive and a positive evangelistic element. For example, Paul used his defense as an introduction to the gospel in such an effective manner that Felix trembled (Acts 24:25), while Agrippa cried, "Almost thou persuadest me to be a Christian" (Acts 26:28). Even if the other interpretation of the latter verse, "Would you so easily persuade me to be a Christian?" is adopted, the positive evangel in Paul's apology still clearly appears by the effect produced in Agrippa.

2. *Apologetics in the early and medieval church.* Justin Martyr wrote his *Dialogue with*

Trypho (*c.* A.D. 150). Origen answered many antichristian arguments in his *Kata Kelsou* (*Contra Celsus*) (*c.* 235), and Athanasius published his *Contra Gentes* (*c.* 315). But the most important apology of all was Augustine's *City of God* (A.D. 426).

Until the church became recognized by Constantine the Great, it found itself accused of cannibalism and sexual promiscuity because of having to meet in secrecy in such places as the catacombs. In contrast, after it was imperially recognized, it had to face charges of worldliness. It was to explain the latter that Augustine wrote and took as his thesis the City of God in contrast to the city of the world.

In the Middle Ages apologetics struggled with the questions of faith—with regard to facts such as the Trinity and the incarnation, knowable only by faith—versus reason, and the facts of science and of the material world which are amenable to reason. Aquinas made a partial synthesis which has become the official position of Romanism: by reason man can argue to the existence of God and even know God, and yet the Trinity and the incarnation are inaccessible to reason, given by revelation, and received by faith alone.

3. *Modern apologetics*. For the purpose of study and helpful analysis it proves valuable to consider both Roman Catholic and Protestant apologetics.

(a) Roman Catholic apologetics is characterized by the fact it attributes both the origin and (infallible) interpretation of the Scriptures to the church; and by the fact that it teaches that rational theology is possible and exists as well as revealed theology: by the use of the human reason man can come to a knowledge of the person and existence of God and even to salvation. The reason why man fails to come to the truth by rational theology is not his fallen condition, but rather the indolence of those mentally equipped to achieve by this means and the rational inability of the rest. Because of this laziness on the part of some and inability of the rest, God has chosen in His grace to give revelation.

The Roman Catholic church has developed a very thorough apologetic of its own. Starting in 1908, the pope appointed continuous commissions to investigate thoroughly and issue reports on the Deutero-Isaiah problem, the J.E.D.P. theory, form-Geschichte, etc. Able church writers have produced such effective books on apologetics as *The Faith of Our Fathers* by Cardinal James Gibbons, a defense of the Roman Catholic church; and *Katholieke Geloofsverdediging* by Cardinal Brocardus Meijer, a very thorough, able work on apologetics in general, in Dutch. As a result of Rome's scholarly commissions and of such a complete work in apologetics as that by Meijer, the Roman Catholics are presenting a convincing defense of their faith which is winning many from the modernist fold where no such defense is given for a Christian faith.

(b) Protestant apologetics. There is a strong element of apologetics present in Calvin's *Institutes* where it is presented in combination with theology. The most famous and effective works in apologetics proper, however, before our times, are Joseph Butler's *Analogy of Religion* (1736) and A. B. Bruce's *Apologetics or Christianity Defensively Stated* (1892). The latter has been the standard orthodox work in English for many years. Its place has been taken lately largely by the writings of Edward John Carnell: *An Introduction to Christian Apologetics* and *A Philosophy of the Christian Religion,* and of Bernard Ramm: *Protestant Christian Evidences, Types of Apologetic Systems,* and *The Christian View of Science and Scripture.*

While Carnell and Ramm have led the evangelical cause in apologetics with admirable work in many areas of the field, both have had difficulties in places, particularly with regard to the absolute infallibility of the Bible in the original writing, and others have had to come to their rescue at this point.

The value and place of apologetics. Considering its length, the OT contains relatively little use of apologetics. In Job 32–37, however, is a corrective by Elihu to the false or inadequate views of Job and his three friends regarding God and theodicy. The Lord Himself replies to Job to convince of His sovereignty and Job's inability (Job 38–41). A number of the psalms appeal to God's activity, in providential care (e.g., Ps 104, 107) and history (Ps 105, 106), to evoke praise and trust and to show the folly of idolatry (Ps 115). Especially Isaiah among the prophets proclaimed God's apology against the pagan deities, challenging the idol-worshiping Gentiles to prove the reality and power of their gods by the test of prophecy and fulfillment (Isa 41:21–29; 43:8–13; 44:6–20; 45:18–25; 46:1–11; 48:1–6).

The NT gives apologetics a much more important place. The early Church Fathers were constantly called upon to defend their faith against heathen philosophers, agnostics, and heretics.

In apologetics we are called upon to show the reasonableness and rationality of the Christian faith and of its revelation as given in the Bible. This is accomplished by such means as a comparison of science with Scripture, a consideration of archaeology and biblical facts and history, an appeal to the fulfillment of predictive prophecies, a study of the proofs of inspiration and infallibility of the Bible, and an application of reason to the question of the existence and nature of God.

The Protestant apologists do not teach that a complete natural theology is possible merely by the application of man's reason in the formulation of five or more theistic proofs (proofs of the necessary and actual existence of God). Rather, as far as the human reason can go—and that includes the formulation of the theistic arguments, namely, the cosmological (existence of world), ontological (existence of an idea of God), the teleological (existence and manifestation of design and purpose in the world and man) and the moral arguments (existence of a moral nature in man)—it is only reasonable to conclude that a rational, purposeful, moral Person exists and is the cause of both the universe and man. The Bible states by revelation that such is the case, and in Rom 1:18 ff. we learn that God holds man responsible to come to the conclusion that God exists.

Therefore the Protestant apologist neither fully rests his case upon reason—as the Roman Catholic with his natural theology, nor does he completely reject the place of reason—as some of the extreme orthodox Protestants (e.g., Abraham Kuyper in his *Principles of Sacred Theology* and Cornelius Van Til in his *The Defense of the Faith,* who emphasize the helplessness of the human mind in sin and the necessity of the renewing power of the Holy Spirit). Instead, recognizing the frailty of human reason since the Fall of man, he gives it a corroboratory function subsidiary to revelation. In other words, the laws of logic, the facts of life and of the cosmos, and the propositional revelations found in the Bible are all to be given their proper place in the attainment of final truth and the formulation of our apologetic system.

Apologetic methods. It becomes most important to develop a thorough and satisfactory apologetic method. This is all the more necessary since the Christian must defend himself against not only the passing theories of science but also the errors of worldly philosophy. No successful defense is possible until one is able not only to see the error or errors against which he contends, but also to understand their philosophical foundations.

Therefore our cause is greatly strengthened when we insist upon the fact that we have a Christian philosophy of existence, namely, an explanation for *(a)* the origin of reality, consisting of the world and men; *(b)* reality itself, as consisting of objects (*res extensa*), and ideas or thoughts (*res cogitata*)—the two of which we clearly define and distinguish; *(c)* the destiny of the world and man. All philosophers are called upon to give their own explanation of these three things.

A workable and thorough defense of the Christian viewpoint on any opinion sought, therefore, includes the following: (1) a fair and thorough description of an opponent's view; (2) a presentation of the value of that view to one who holds it; (3) a consideration of its philosophical basis and a clear presentation of its fallacies, both on logical and philosophical grounds; (4) an examination of the view in light of the confessions and creeds of the church; (5) an examination to see what theological advantages it may offer and what theological problems it may raise; (6) a presentation of the scriptural view of the matter in discussion and proof of its reasonableness, and a clear description of how the biblical view escapes the philosophical and the theological problems raised by an erroneous view.

Besides the main works in apologetics already mentioned, there have been many very valuable books on specific aspects of the faith, such as the virgin birth, the resurrection, miracles, the infallibility of the Scriptures, etc. These can be found readily in the extensive bibliographies attached to books by Carnell and Ramm mentioned above.

The aim of apologetics. This includes: (1) making contact with those who hold an erroneous or dangerous view, or who attack the Christian revelation and faith; (2) finding an area in which the problem can be discussed impartially, and proving the weakness of the view in question first in some neutral area common to all, such as philosophy or logic; (3) showing the theological problems raised; (4) expounding the church's convictions in its confessions and creeds and exegeting what the Scripture teaches, while showing the reasonableness thereof. The common ground sought for conversation with the adversary does not have to entail any compromise, such as attempted by some recent apologetics, nor does it force Scripture upon the doubter or the agnostic. By considering every aspect of a problem before taking up the Scripture itself, it opens the mind of an opponent to consider God's own position and answer.

Bibliography. A. B. Bruce, *Apologetics,* Edinburgh: T. & T. Clark, 1892. E. J. Carnell, *An Introduction to Christian Apologetics,* Grand Rapids: Eerdmans, 1952; *A Philosophy of the Christian Religion,* Grand Rapids: Eerdmans, 1952. Robert Flint, *Agnosticism,* New York: Scribner's, 1903; *Anti-Theistic Theories,* Edinburgh: Blackwood, 1879. Brocardus Meijer, *Katholieke Geloofsverdediging,* Roermond: Romen & Zonen, 1946. Bernard Ramm, *Protestant Christian Evidences,* Chicago: Moody Press, 1953; *Types of Apologetic Systems,* Wheaton, Ill.: Van Kampen Press, 1953; *The Christian View of Science and Scripture,* Grand Rapids: Eerdmans, 1954.

R. A. K.

APOSTASY (Gr. *apostasia,* "a falling away or defection from the faith").

While the Gr. word is used only twice in the NT (Acts 21:21; II Thess 2:3), it is found in the LXX several times, as in Josh 22:22, to express rebellion of the people from God, and in II Chr 29:19 of the casting away of the holy temple vessels.

Apostasy is possible only for nominal Christians. In the case of real believers, the Scripture declares that God either brings them back through suffering and chastisement (I Cor 11:29-30; I Cor 5:5) or removes them through death (I Cor 11:30). In the case of apostates, though He may allow them to remain, He withdraws from them all possibility of repentance and salvation (Heb 6:1-6; 10:26-31).

Apostasy is to be distinguished from ignorance or a lack of knowledge, as well as from heresy, which is mistaken knowledge (II Tim 2:25-26). Men can be saved from ignorance but not from apostasy. It is characterized by a deliberate rejection of Christ's deity (I Jn 2:22-23; Jude 4) and His atoning death (Phil 3:18; II Pet 2:1; Heb 10:29). *See* Backsliding.

R. A. K.

APOSTLE. The Gr. *apostolos* comes from the verb *apostellein,* "to send away," "send forth." Noun and verb are used by the LXX to translate Heb. *shālaḥ* and its derivatives. These Heb. and Gr. words are occasionally used for messengers with emphasis on the sender, so that the agent becomes an extension of the personality and influence of the master (Gen 45:4-8; I Kgs 14:6). K. H. Rengstorf, T. W. Manson, and others have attempted to trace the NT word to the Jewish *shalîaḥ* (used of a representative whose functions cannot be transferred; representative of religious authority, either of an individual or group; God's agent). *Apostolos,* used for "messenger" or "agent," is also found in classical Gr. (Herodotus i.21; v. 38; cf. Euripides, *Iphigeneia in Aulis,* 688).

In the NT the word "apostle" is used with both a broad and a narrow meaning. All apostleship focuses on Jesus, who is *the Apostle* (Heb 3:1-6) sent by God to be the Saviour of the world (I Jn 4:14). Although John does not use the noun, he frequently uses the verb and describes functions of Jesus as the Apostle of God. He was sent by God (Jn 7:28-29; 8:42) to speak the words of God (3:34), to do God's works (5:36; 6:29) and will (6:38), to reveal God (5:37-47), to give eternal life (17:2-3). All subsequent apostleship centers in God through Jesus Christ (Jn 17:18-26; 20:21-23) and mediates Christ in word and person (Mt 10:40; Lk 10:16).

Matthew and Mark use "apostle" only once for the Twelve who were sent on a missionary journey (Mt 10:2; Mk 6:30). Here the word designates a function rather than status. During

The Sea of Galilee near the place where some of the apostles must have been called to be "fishers of men." CCR

Jesus' ministry, the Twelve were not primarily messengers but select men who were initiated into the coming kingdom and therefore regarded it their duty to call Israel to repentance and ultimately judge it (Mt 19:28-30).

Luke frequently and almost exclusively calls the Twelve "apostles" (Lk 6:13; 9:10; 17:5; 22:14; 24:10; Acts 1:26; 2:43; 4:35, 37; 5:2, 12, 18; 8:1. Exceptions: Lk 11:49; Acts 14:4, 14). The apostles were eyewitnesses of the earthly activity of Jesus and hence testified that Jesus was the risen Lord (Lk 24:45-48; I Jn 1:1-3). The prerequisites for apostolic replacement in this unique function are given in Acts 1:21-22. Luke's list of the apostles (Lk 6:14-16; Acts 1:13) corresponds to the list of the Twelve given in Mt 10:2-4 and Mk 3:16-19. Matthew lists the disciples in pairs, supposedly as sent out by Jesus. Thaddaeus (Matthew and Mark) was identical with Judas the son of James (Luke). Peter, James, and John formed an inner circle within the Twelve and were present at the transfiguration (Mt 17:1-9; Mk 9:2-10; Lk 9:28-36) and in Gethsemane (Mt 26:36-46; Mk 14:32-42; Lk 22:39-46). The Twelve were selected to be the companions of Jesus and proclaim the gospel (Mk 3:14). During Jesus' ministry, the Twelve served as His representatives, a function shared by others (Lk 10:1).

Apparently the position of the apostles was not permanently fixed before the resurrection (Mt 19:28-30; Lk 22:28-34; cf. Jn 21:15-18). The risen Christ made this select group of witnesses of His ministry and resurrection permanent apostles and witnesses that Jesus is the Lord, commissioned them as missionaries, instructed them to teach and baptize (Mt 28:18-20; Mk 16:15-18; Lk 24:46-48), and completed the process with the sending of the Holy Spirit on Pentecost (Lk 24:49; Acts 1:1-8; 2:1-13). In the earliest period, the 12 apostles were the only teachers and leaders of the church, and other offices were derived from them (Acts 6:1-6; 15:4). Apostleship did not imply permanent leadership. Though Peter initiated missions to Jews (Acts 2) and Gentiles (Acts 10:1–11:18), James replaced him as leader among Jews, and Paul among Gentiles.

Paul uses "apostle" in a broad sense for a messenger or agent (II Cor 8:23; Phil 2:25; possibly Rom 16:7). This broader usage made it possible to speak of false apostles (Rev 2:2). Usually, however, Paul uses the word for a group of witnesses who had seen the risen Lord and had received a specific call to an apostleship. This group was larger than the Twelve (Acts 15:5-6). Included in it were James the Lord's brother (Acts 15:13; Gal 1:19), Paul (Rom 1:1; I Cor 1:1; 9:1-2; 15:8-10; Gal 2:7-8), probably Barnabas (I Cor 9:1-6; Gal 2:9; cf. Acts 14:4, 14), and possibly others (Rom 16:7). The risen Lord, however, whom Paul witnessed is identical with the historical Jesus witnessed by the Twelve. Hence Paul's proclamation must be identical with that of the Twelve (I Cor 15:11; Gal 1:18; 2:7-10; cf. Acts 15).

John emphasizes the work of the Spirit who witnesses through the words of the apostles (Jn 15:26-27). Through the preaching of the gospel, Jesus the risen Lord is contemporary to the hearers, and places them on the same footing with the eyewitnesses (cf. I Cor 3:21-23).

The members of the church are priests, kings, servants of God, and saints who use their gifts for the edification of the whole church (I Cor 12:1-11; I Pet 2:9; Rev 1:6; 5:8, 10; 7:3) and, like the apostles, mediate Christ (Mt 25:40, 45; Mk 9:37; Lk 9:48) and will reign with Him (Rev 3:21).

The apostles, however, through the witness of their word, will always be the norm and foundation on which Christ builds His church (Eph 2:20; Rev 18:20; 21:14). Apostles are the first of Christ's gifts to the church (Eph 4:11) and of God's appointed ministers in the church (I Cor 12:28-29).

For details on the Twelve, see under name of each, including Matthias.

Bibliography. Oscar Cullmann, "The Tradition," *The Early Church,* ed. by A. J. B. Higgins, Philadelphia: Westminster, 1956. J. N. Geldenhuys, *Supreme Authority,* Grand Rapids: Eerdmans, 1953. E. J. Goodspeed, *The Twelve,* Philadelphia: Winston, 1957. Arnold Ehrhardt, *The Apostolic Succession,* London: Lutterworth, 1953. J. B. Lightfoot, *Saint Paul's Epistle to the Galatians,* rev. ed., London: Macmillan, 1890, and subsequent reprints, pp. 92-101. T. W. Manson, *The Church's Ministry,* Philadelphia: Westminster, 1948. K. H. Rengstorf, "*Apostellō-apostolos,*" TDNT, I, 398-447.

E. L. L.

APOSTOLIC, APOSTOLICAL. Pertaining to or descending from the apostles. The term is used to designate men who were companions of the apostles and those Church Fathers who were contemporary with the apostles. A supposed apostolic source was claimed by use of the titles Apostolic Constitutions and Apostolic Canons for writings of the 4th cen.

In an ecclesiastical sense, apostolic succession refers to the assumed uninterrupted line of Christian ministry descendant from the apostles. The assembled bishops of the Councils of Orleans (A.D. 511) and Macon (A.D. 581) were described as apostolic. In time the popes restricted the term to themselves as spiritual descendants of Peter, and the Council of Rheims (A.D. 1049) declared the pope to be the sole apostolic primate. The Roman Catholic church has since employed the term in various connections; e.g., apostolical decree.

APOSTOLIC AGE. The time from Pentecost (*c.* A.D. 30) to the death of the apostle John (*c.* A.D. 100) during which the apostles were exerting influence among the churches. The era readily divides itself into the pre-Pauline (*c.* A.D. 30-40), Pauline (*c.* A.D. 40-67), and post-Pauline (*c.* A.D. 67-100) periods. During the first period Christianity was largely confined to Jerusalem and the Jewish people. There was no attempt to make a definite break with Judaism as yet. Church life was marked by simplicity, purity, and power. In the Pauline period a transition occurred from a Jewish to a Gentile-Jewish church with a corresponding empire-wide expansion. Numerous problems began to take shape, such as the Judaistic perversion in Galatia, irregularities in Corinth, and the Colossian heresy. The chief figure of the post-Pauline period was the apostle John, whose death brought the Apostolic Age to its close. By that time Christianity had been firmly planted in all the lands from Jerusalem to Rome.

D. W. B.

APOSTOLIC COUNCIL. The designation sometimes used of the Jerusalem assemblage of apostles and elders (*c.* A.D. 49-50) recorded in Acts 15. As a result of the reception into the churches of uncircumcised Gentiles (Acts 11:19-21, RSV; 13:46-48; 14:27), the ultra-Judaistic party began to press strenuously for the adoption of the Jewish law in addition to faith in Christ as a condition of Gentile salvation. The ensuing controversy led to a council in Jerusalem (Acts 15:1-2), which apparently developed along the following lines: an open meeting of the church (15:4-5), a session of the church leaders (15:6-11), and a resumption of the general church meeting (15:12-29). After testimony from Paul, Barnabas, and Peter concerning the evident fact that God had saved uncircumcised Gentiles, the council agreed on a twofold decision: (1) Gentiles were not to be required to submit to the law of Moses (15:19), and (2) Gentiles were to be asked to abstain from practices which would hinder social relations between Jewish and Gentile believers (15:20, 28-29). Historically and theologically, this was an epoch-making decision. As a result, Christianity was to be not merely a Jewish phenomenon but a universal faith. Furthermore, it became the accepted view of the church that salvation is by faith alone.

D. W. B.

APOTHECARY. *See* Occupations.

APPAIM (ăp'ĭ-*ă*m). A descendant of Hezron of the tribe of Judah (I Chr 2:30-31).

APPAREL. *See* Dress.

APPEAL. A judicial term referring to the request of an inferior to his superior for either mercy or justice. The Shunammite woman appealed to the king of Israel for her land (II Kgs 8:3). Job appealed to God for mercy (Job 9:15). Paul appealed to Caesar for justice (Acts

25:11). Used also in RSV in an informal sense in NT epistles as a request for godly Christian behavior (e.g., Rom 12:1; I Cor 1:10; Heb 13:22). *See* Exhortation.

APPEARANCES OF CHRIST. The Gospels record five appearances of Jesus on the day of His resurrection. The first was to Mary Magdalene (Jn 20:11 - 18). The second was to "Mary Magdalene and the other Mary" as they were returning from the empty tomb (Mt 28:1 - 10). It is obvious that these might be taken as the same incident. But Mark adds a third person to the group (Mk 16:1) and seems to suggest that the first appearance was to Mary Magdalene alone (Mk 16:9, if genuine). The third appearance was to the two disciples on the way to Emmaus (Lk 24:13 - 32). The fourth was to Simon Peter (Lk 24:34; I Cor 15:5). The fifth was to the disciples, with Thomas absent (Lk 24:36 - 43; Jn 20:19 - 25).

In the following 40 days Jesus appeared: (1) to the eleven disciples (Jn 20:26 - 31); (2) to the seven disciples beside the Lake of Galilee (Jn 21:1 - 14); (3) to "above five hundred brethren" (Mt 28:16 - 20; I Cor 15:6); (4) to James (I Cor 15:7); (5) at the ascension (Lk 24:44 - 51; Acts 1:3 - 11).

The purpose of these appearances was to convince the disciples of the bodily resurrection of Jesus, and therefore the validity of His saving work in His life and on the cross as the true Messiah. They also fulfilled Scripture and taught the disciples things they could not grasp beforehand.

For OT appearances of the pre-incarnate Son of God *see* Theophany.

R. E. and E. B. R.

APPEARING. *See* Christ, Coming of; Millennium.

APPHIA (ăf'ĭ-*ȧ*). A Christian woman in Colossae, one of the addressees of the book of Philemon, probably the wife of Philemon (*q.v.*). Apphia was a common female name in western Asia Minor, as inscriptions show.

The Appian Way. HFV

APPII FORUM. Used in Acts 28:15; Forum of Appius in RSV. It is still called Foro Appio. This commercial station is one of the two places ("Three Taverns," nine to ten miles N, is the other) mentioned in Paul's itinerary between Puteoli and Rome. Inscriptions have been found here. One of Emperor Nerva states explicitly: ". . . at the Forum of Appius." In the same vicinity a milestone was discovered which indicated that Appii Forum was located 43 Roman miles (*c.* 40 English miles) from Rome.

The place itself was named after the censor, Appius Claudius Caecus, who also initiated (*c.* 312 B.C.) the famous Appian Way as well as the aqueduct named in his honor. Pliny (III.v.9) mentions Appii Forum among the towns of Latium. Strabo (v.233) says that a mule-operated canal cut through the Pontine marshes and ran parallel to the road, which was especially used by travelers at night: ". . . embarking in the evening, and landing in the morning to travel the rest of their journey by road." Horace (*Satires* I.v.3 - 6) interestingly describes the activity of its boatmen and travelers. The marshes nearby (largely drained in the time of Mussolini) then added to the tedium of its life since mosquitoes and other insects were spawned there in great numbers. Horace complains that the waters about the town were bad, its rooms were crowded and expensive, and travelers could not sleep because of the noise of frogs and the sting of mosquitoes. It is easy to understand how much Paul needed encouragement when Christian brethren from Rome met him here!

E. J. V.

APPLE. *See* Plants.

APPROVE. The Gr. verb *dokimazō* and its derivatives are used particularly of testing and purifying metals, and hence metaphorically of the testing of the Christian in such passages as I Pet 1:7: "That the proof [*dokimon*] of your faith, being more precious than gold which is perishable, even though tested [*dokimazomenou*] by fire . . ." (NASB). Four main uses of "approval" are:

1. Self-examination of the Christian to prove himself as to his faith (II Cor 13:5), his own works (Gal 6:4), and particularly before attending communion (I Cor 11:28).

2. Examination of others, such as when Israel tested God (Heb 3:9); deacons are tested for office in the church (I Tim 3:10); and the spirit in others is tested to see if they are orthodox and have the Holy Spirit or the spirit of Antichrist (I Jn 4:1).

3. Self-preparation for God's approval. Paul urges young Timothy in II Tim 2:15, "Study [*spoudason*, lit., "hasten"] to show thyself approved [*dokimon*] unto God, a workman that

needeth not to be ashamed, rightly dividing the word of truth." The idea of preparation through study is so apparent in this verse that the translators chose to bring out this aspect rather than Paul's stress upon the need of speed in the preparation of oneself for the Lord's service.

4. God's testing of His servants through trials and tribulations before He is ready to open new and greater doors of service. James speaks of this in his epistle, urging one to "count it all joy when ye fall into divers temptations . . . for when he is tried, he shall receive the crown of life . . . " (Jas 1:2, 12). Just as examinations precede entry to high school, university, etc., so trials precede promotions in the life of the believer in God's economy.

At the same time, the Christian is constantly in danger of losing God's approval and blessing upon his ministry because of allowing his fallen nature to have its own sinful way. Therefore even Paul as a mature missionary writes: "I keep under my body, and bring it into subjection: lest by any means, when I have preached to others, I myself should be a castaway" (*adokimos*, "become disapproved," I Cor 9:27).

R. A. K.

APRICOT. *See* Plants.

APRON. *See* Dress.

AQABAH, GULF OF (ä'kȧ-bä). An arm of the Red Sea reaching N, located E of the Sinai peninsula and W of Midian in Arabia. Geologically it is part of the Arabah and Jordan rift which continues the fault northward. Elath (*q.v.*), a seaport, is located at its northern end. *See also* Ezion-geber.

AQUILA (ăk'wĭ-lȧ). A Jew from Pontus in N Asia Minor, resident in Rome, where he and his wife Priscilla (*q.v.*) became Christians. The edict of the emperor Claudius (*c.* A.D. 49) expelling Jews from Rome, forced this couple to migrate to Corinth, where they set up a branch of their tentmaking or leather-working business, and met Paul, who joined them because that was his trade too (Acts 18:1–3). When Paul left Corinth in A.D. 52, they accompanied him as far as Ephesus, where they settled for some years. Early in their residence there, they gave hospitality to the Alexandrian Jew Apollos (*q.v.*) and repaired deficiencies in his knowledge of Christianity (Acts 18:18–26). By A.D. 57 they were probably back in Rome, according to Rom 16:3. Claudius' expulsion edict doubtless lapsed for practical purposes with his death in A.D. 54. According to II Tim 4:19, they seem to have located in Ephesus again. The picture of such tradespeople moving from place to place, probably leaving branches of their business here and there in charge of a manager, is quite true to conditions of life under the Roman Empire. Wherever they lived, Aquila and Priscilla provided the local church with accommodation in their home (Rom 16:5; I Cor 16:19). On one occasion, possibly in Ephesus, they risked their lives for Paul (Rom 16:4).

F. F. B.

AR (är). A Moabite city located near the Arnon gorge E of the Salt Sea (Num 21:15, 28). When Isa 15:1 was written it had been destroyed. Its exact site has not yet been determined.

ARA (âr'ȧ). A descendant of Asher (I Chr 7:38).

ARAB (âr'ăb)

1. A city, identified with Khirbet er-Rabiyeh, seven miles SW of Hebron, allotted to the tribe of Judah after the conquest by Joshua (Josh 15:52).

2. A bedouin inhabitant of the Arabian peninsula, neighbors of the Hebrews to the S and E of Palestine. The word originally meant "waste" or "desloation." That they were tent-dwellers in the wilderness is indicated in Isa 13:20 and Jer 3:2.

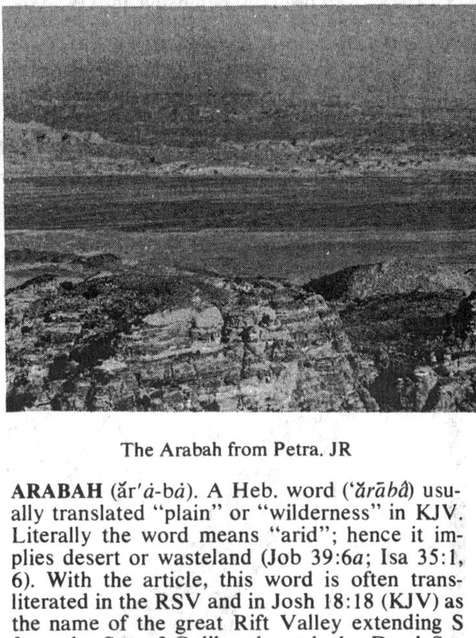

The Arabah from Petra. JR

ARABAH (ăr'ȧ-bȧ). A Heb. word (*'ărābâ*) usually translated "plain" or "wilderness" in KJV. Literally the word means "arid"; hence it implies desert or wasteland (Job 39:6*a*; Isa 35:1, 6). With the article, this word is often transliterated in the RSV and in Josh 18:18 (KJV) as the name of the great Rift Valley extending S from the Sea of Galilee through the Dead Sea and continuing to the Gulf of Aqabah. Sometimes this name is connected with the northern part of this valley, called el-Ghôr by the Arabs (Deut 1:7; 3:17; Josh 11:2, 16) and sometimes with the portion S of the Dead Sea, which the Arabs call Wadi el-'Arabah (Deut 1:1; 2:8). This depression reaches the lowest point on the earth's surface at the Dead Sea (1,275 feet below sea level at the surface of the sea; in addition, the Dead Sea is 1,300 feet deep at its lowest point). It divides eastern from western Palestine, geographically and historically.

Archaeological remains confirm indications in the patriarchal narratives that this valley was more thickly populated in the Bronze Age than later. In ancient times, especially during Solomon's reign, copper and iron were mined and smelted in the southern Arabah, notably at Punon (modern Feinan), Mene'iyeh, Khirbet en-Nahas, and Mrashrash. Such deposits were known or foretold in Moses' day (Deut 8:9).

The plains (*'arābôth*) of Moab (Num 22:1; 26:3; etc.) are the Moabite portions of the Arabah. Likewise the plains of Jericho (Josh 4:13; 5:10; II Kgs 25:5; Jer 39:5) refer to the Arabah near that city.

The Sea of the Arabah (Deut 3:17; 4:49; Josh 3:16; 12:3; II Kgs 14:25, RSV) is the Dead Sea. The Brook of the Arabah (Amos 6:14, RSV) is a stream flowing into the Arabah and marking the southern boundary of Jeroboam II's kingdom, perhaps the valley of Zered (Wadi el-Hesa. Num 21:12; Deut 2:13). *See* Dead Sea; Jordan; Palestine II.B.3. f.

J. A. T.

ARABIA (*à*-rā'bĭ-*à*). A peninsula in SW Asia, bounded on the W by the Red Sea, on the S by the Indian Ocean, on the E by the Persian Gulf, and on the N by modern Jordan, Syria, and Iraq. Its area is almost one million square miles, about one-third the size of continental U.S.A. Classical geographers divided it into three parts: Arabia Petrea, including Sinai, Edom, Moab, and eastern Transjordan, named after the area's greatest city, Petra; Arabia Deserta, the Syrian and central deserts; and Arabia Felix, the "happy," fertile southern area.

In S Arabia kingdoms arose which owed their prosperity largely to trade and spices: the Sabean kingdom, or Seba (Ps 72:10; Isa 43:3; 45:14), organized at least as early as the 10th cen. B.C.; the Minaean kingdom of Ma'în *c.* 400 B.C.; the kingdom of Qataban in the 4th cen. B.C.; and the two Himyarite kingdoms from the 1st cen. B.C. to the 6th cen. A.D. Much of Arabia is desert, except for some fertile areas in the mountainous section of the S coast, which precipitates rainfall. Oases, including biblical Dedan, Tema, and Dumah, line the caravan routes along which perfumes of S Arabia and products of Africa and India were carried to Palestine and thence to Mediterranean countries.

Biblical references to Arabia sometimes include both the N and S portions (II Chr 9:14), but sometimes indicate only the NW portion, Arabia Petrea (Gal 1:17; 4:25). The many places in Arabia mentioned in the Bible show

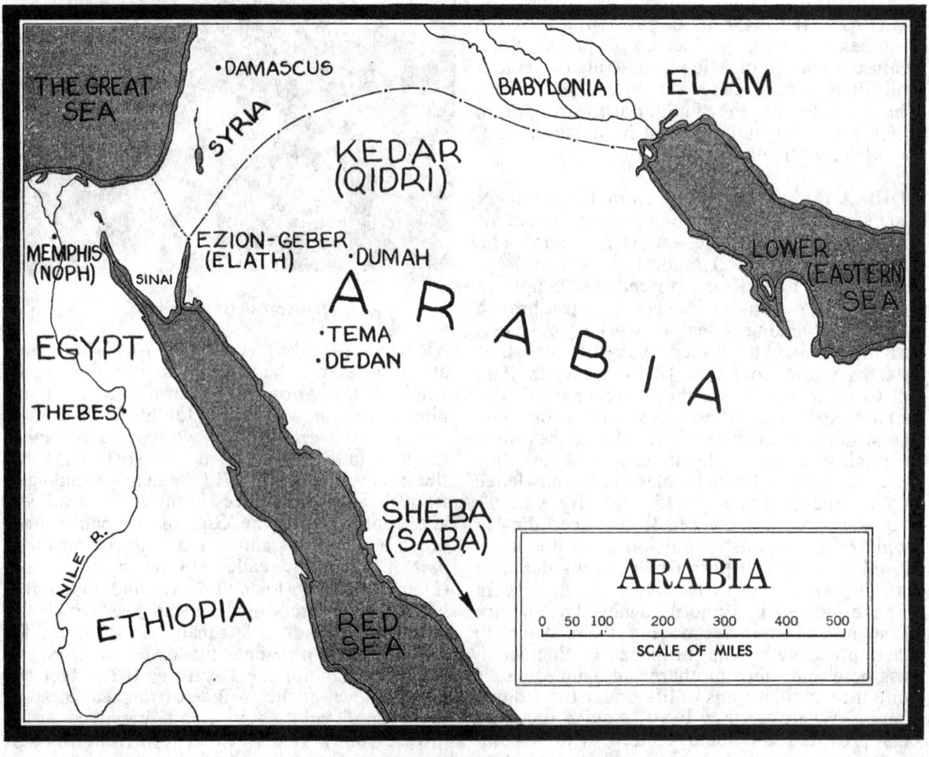

an early and detailed knowledge of this country and include Buz, Dedan, Dumah, Ephah, Havilah, Hazarmaveth, Hazor (Jer 49:28), Massa, Mesha, Midian, Parvaim, Raamah, Sabtah, Seba, Sephar, Sheba (called "the south" in Mt 12:42), "the hill country of the east" (Gen 10:30, RSV). Some important biblical events took place in the NW portion of Arabia, notably the giving of the law at Sinai and the wandering in the wilderness.

Products of Arabia mentioned in the Bible include frankincense and perfumes (I Kgs 10:2, 10), gold (I Kgs 10:2, 10, 15), precious stones (Ezk 27:22), onycha (Ex 30:34), coral and pearls (Job 28:18, RSV), camels (Gen 37:25), sheep and goats (Ezk 27:21), asses (Num 31:28), horses (Job 39:19-25), dates (Ex 15:27). Since A.D. 1932 oil has been marketed from the world's largest known petroleum deposits.

Wild animals connected with Arabia in the Bible are lion (Job 38:39-40, no longer found in Arabia), mountain goat (Job 39:1-4), wild ass (Job 39:5-8), wild ox or unicorn (Job 39:9-12, now extinct), jackal and hyena (Isa 34:13-14, RSV), gazelle (Isa 13:14, RSV), poisonous serpents (Num 21:6), and flying, i.e., springing, serpents (Isa 14:29). The following birds are associated with Arabia: raven (Job 38:41), ostrich (Job 39:13-18, last seen in Arabia in A.D. 1941), hawk (Job 39:26), eagle (Job 39:27-30), quail (Num 11:31), owl and kite (Isa 34:15, RSV).

See Arabians.

J. A. T.

ARABIANS (*ȧ*-rā'bĭ-*ȧ*ns). The Heb. *'ărab* literally denotes "arid," the dry steppe land. The Arabah (*'arabâ*), the dry Dead Sea valley, comes from the same word root. Hence the *'ar^{e}bîm* were the wanderers in the desert wilderness, or nomads (II Chr 17:11; 21:16; 22:1; 26:7). In Assyrian cuneiform records they are called *Arubu* and *Aribi,* a term used for the nomads of Media as well as for those of Arabia. Even the Koran uses *a'rab* (plural of *'arab*) for the Bedouin, as contrasted with the settled people.

As for the inhabitants of Arabia, some of the sons of Joktan (Gen 10:25-30), of Cush (Gen 10:7), of Keturah (Gen 25:1-4), and of Ishmael (Gen 25:13-16) can be identified with places and tribes in Arabia. Other Arab tribes mentioned in the OT include the Amalekites, Hagarites, Kedarites, Kenites, Meunim (identified by LXX with Minaeans), and perhaps (though some of these may be Canaanites) the Gezrites, Kadmonites, and Kenizzites. Another name for Arabians is "children of the east" (*b^{e}nê qedem,* Jud 6:3). *See* Arabia.

Historical events involving Arabians in the OT include the Midianite raids on Palestine in the time of Gideon (Jud 6-8), the first recorded large-scale use of camels; and the Queen of Sheba's visit to Solomon (I Kgs 10:1-10), reflecting the wealth and commerce of S Arabia. Arabians paid tribute to Jehoshaphat (II Chr 17:11), raided Jerusalem in the reign of Jehoram (II Chr 21:16-17; 22:1), and were defeated by Uzziah (II Chr 26:7). The conquest of N Arabian tribes by the Assyrians is referred to in Isa 21:13-17 and by the Babylonians in Jer 25:23-24; 49:28-30. By the 5th cen. B.C. Arabs pushed the Edomites out of Mount Seir (Ob 7). Nehemiah was opposed by Geshem the Arabian (Neh 2:19), who is known from inscriptions as king of Kedar, a tribe who then dominated the N Arabians.

In the Apocrypha, "Arab" (e.g., I Macc 11:16-17) usually refers to the Nabataeans (I Macc 5:25), who made Petra their capital and controlled the trade routes around Palestine. They were sometimes allied with the Maccabees (I Macc 9:35) and sometimes with the Syrians (I Macc 5:39; 12:31). *See* Nabataeans.

Arabians were among the Jews and proselytes who heard the gospel in Jerusalem at Pentecost (Acts 2:11). They may have come from the Nabataean kingdom in Transjordan, or perhaps from farther S. The governor of Damascus, representing the Nabataean king Aretas IV (9 B.C.—A.D. 40), set guards to catch Paul, who nevertheless escaped (II Cor 11:32-33).

In culture, Arabians are Semites (Gen 10:25-30), as indicated by their languages. N Arabians lived in the wilderness (Jer 3:2) in tents (Isa 13:20) made of black goats' hair (Song 1:5). They were camel riders (Gen 37:25). Arabian caravans brought spices, gold, and precious stones from S Arabia, and sheep and goats of N Arabia to Palestine and Syria (I Kgs 10:2; Ezk 27:20-22), and Arab merchants also transferred products of Africa and India (I Kgs 10:22). Jer 9:26; 25:23; 49:32 (RSV) mention the Arab custom of cropping the hair, which is referred to by Herodotus (iii.8) and is depicted in Assyrian bas reliefs of Arabs fighting from their camels.

Arabia was known for its wise men (I Kgs 4:30), among whom were Agur (Prov 30:1) and Lemuel (Prov 31:1), two kings of Massa, a tribe of Ishmael (Gen 25:14). The wisdom book of Job reflects its background in NW Arabia. The advanced culture of the ancient S Arabians is illustrated by the great temple of Ilumquh, the moon-god at Ma'rib, the Sabaean capital; large dams and canals for irrigation; sculpture in stone; casting in bronze; goldsmith's work; and by many religious and historical inscriptions.

The general Arabian term for god was *il* (cf. Heb. *'el*) or *ilah* (cf. Heb. *'elōah*), but the ancient Arabians revered many gods, including a moon-god; a sun-goddess, Shamash; and their son, the morning star, 'Athtar. The Koran mentions several pagan gods: al-Lat, al-'Uzza, and al-Manat (Qur'an 53:19, 20), Wadd, Suwa', Yaghuth Ya'uq, and Nasr (71:23). Arabians feared demons called jinn (Qur'an, 72).

Like the Israelites, the Arabians practiced circumcision, pilgrimage, and sacrifice, including a sin offering. Among their religious functionaries were priest-diviners and seers.

Bibliography. R. L. Bowen and F. P. Albright, *Archaeological Discoveries in South Arabia,* Vol. II, Baltimore: Johns Hopkins Univ. Press, 1958. CornPBE, pp. 116-120. Butrus Abd al-Malik and John A. Thompson, "Arabia," BW, pp. 45-50. P. K. Hitti, *History of the Arabs,* 6th ed., London: Macmillan, 1956. J. A. Montgomery, *Arabia and the Bible,* Philadelphia: Univ. of Pennsylvania Press, 1934. G. Ryckmans, *Les religions arabes préislamiques,* 2nd ed., Louvain: Publications Universitaires, 1951. J. Starcky, "The Nabataeans: A Historical Sketch," BA, XVIII (1955), 84-106. G. W. Van Beek, "Recovering the Ancient Civilization of Arabia," BA, XV (1952), 2-18; "Frankincense and Myrrh," BA, XXIII (1960), 70-95. Brian Doe, *Southern Arabia,* New York: McGraw-Hill, 1971.

J. A. T.

ARAD (âr'ăd)

1. A son of Beriah, a Benjamite (I Chr 8:15).
2. A Canaanite city in the Negeb whose king fought against the Israelites when they were on their way to Mount Hor (Num 21:1, 33:40, RSV). In the KJV of these verses "king Arad" should read "king of Arad." Joshua later vanquished its king (Josh 12:14). Arad is mentioned again in Jud 1:16 as a city on the border of the wilderness of Judah where the Kenites settled.

The site has generally been identified with Tell 'Arâd, about 17 miles S of Hebron, but the excavations carried out there under the direction of Y. Aharoni and R. Amiran since 1962 have shown that Tell 'Arâd was inhabited only during two periods: from *c.* 3200 to *c.* 2900 B.C. and from the 10th cen. B.C. to the Byzantine period. Hence this site was uninhabited during the period of the wilderness wandering of Israel and at the time of Joshua's conquest, and the Arad of Moses' and Joshua's time must have been somewhere else. The excavators have therefore come to the conclusion that Tell 'Arâd represents another Arad which, although not mentioned in the Bible, appears in the victory inscription of Pharaoh Shishak, while the Canaanite Arad of the Bible existed at Tell Malḥata, *c.* eight miles SW of Tell 'Arâd, where Middle and Late Bronze Age Canaanite remains have been found (IEJ, XII [1962], 144-145; Yohanan Aharoni and Ruth Amiran, "Arad: a Biblical City in Southern Palestine," *Archaeology,* XVII [1964], 43-53). B. Mazar argues on the basis of Jud 1:16-17 that the entire region of the eastern Negeb was called Negeb Arad, so that there was no *town* of Arad during the 2nd mil. B.C. ("The Sanctuary of Arad and the Family of Hobab the Kenite," JNES, XXIV [1965], 297-303).

S. H. H.

During Solomon's reign a strong square fortress with casemate walls *c.* 165 feet on a side and a typical Solomonic city gate was erected on Tell'Arâd to guard the kingdom's SE border with Edom. After this fortress was destroyed, probably by Pharaoh Shishak, another with a solid wall 13 feet thick and a second smaller wall on the lower slope was built in the 9th cen. A water tunnel below the latter wall enabled water carriers using donkeys to fill large plastered cisterns beneath the citadel buildings. Over 200 ostraca were found during five seasons of excavations, over half of them written in Heb. from the time of the monarchy. Seventeen are addressed to Eliashib, evidently the commander of the fortress in the time of Nebuchadnezzar. One of these mentions the "house of Yahweh" and was apparently sent from Jerusalem. Another orders men to be sent from Arad to Ramath-negeb against a threatening Edomite attack (Y. Aharoni, "Three Hebrew Ostraca from Arad," BASOR # 197 [1970], pp. 16-42).

The most surprising discovery at Tell 'Arâd was an Israelite temple within the citadel rebuilt several times and in use from the 10th to the 7th cen. B.C. It evidently functioned as a royal border sanctuary until King Josiah's reform (II Kgs 23:5, 8) along with other such probable temples at Gilgal, Beer-sheba, and Geba (Amos 5:5; 8:14; II Kgs 23:8), just as the northern kingdom had border temples at Dan and Bethel. Its E-W axis was the same as that of the tabernacle and Solomon's temple, and in a courtyard until the time of Hezekiah's reign (cf. his reform, II Kgs 18:4) there was an altar for burnt offerings built of many stones exactly five cubits square and three cubits high, as in the tabernacle (Ex 27:1). Heb. ostraca found in these levels contain names of priestly families known from the OT (Y. Aharoni, "Arad: Its Inscriptions and Temple," BA, XXXI [1968], 1-32).

J. R.

ARAH (âr'*a*). A man of the tribe of Asher (I Chr 7:39). His numerous descendants returned from the Exile with Zerubbabel (Ezr 2:5; Neh 6:18; 7:10).

ARAM (âr'*a*m), **ARAMEANS** (ăr'*a*-mē'*a*nz). Aram was the name of at least three men in the Bible:

1. The fifth son of Shem (Gen 10:22-23). From this lineage came several Semitic groups.
2. Son of Kemuel, nephew of Abraham (Gen 22:20-21). This kin group settled about Haran, whereas Abraham moved to Canaan. Hence Aram came to designate a land area and a language called Aramaic.
3. The third son of Shamer of the tribe of Asher (I Chr 7:34).

As the name of a people called the Arameans, the term occurs about 65 times in the books of Samuel, Kings, and Chronicles. Following the LXX (*Syria*), the KJV calls these people Syrians (Amos 1:5; 9:7; Isa 7:2, 4, 5, 8; 9:12; 17:3; Jer 35:11; Ezk 16:57; 27:16).

As a reference to the land of the Arameans, the translation "Syria" appears in KJV in

II Sam 15:8; Hos 12:12, but in Num 23:7 KJV has Aram. Of the people and the land together, or of the gods of that country, "Syria" occurs in Jud 10:6; Isa 7:8 and more than 40 times in Kings and Chronicles.

Aram is most likely a non-Semitic appellation. In geographical terms Aram seemed to refer to that land area which was bounded by the Tigris River, the Arabian Desert, the Taurus Mountains, and the land of Phoenicia. Assyrian inscriptions usually limit Aram to the plains E of the Euphrates River.

Sometimes Aram is connected with other names, which seem to designate limited land areas. Aram of Damascus (II Sam 8:6, RSV) would refer to territory immediately about Damascus. Aram-maacah (I Chr 19:6, RSV), Beth-rehob and Zobah populated by Syrians or Arameans (II Sam 10:6) all designate small provinces E of the Jordan and NE of Galilee. The KJV uses Syria instead of Aram in each of the above instances.

Late in the 3rd mil. B.C., nomadic Arameans pushed westward out of the NE section of the Arabian Desert and were deflected to the NW by the Amorite settlements on the Euphrates River. They settled around Haran, sometimes called Aram-Naharaim (KJV has Mesopotamia in Gen 24:10; Deut 23:4; Jud 3:8). See also Padan-aram (*q.v.*) in Gen 25:20; 28:2, 6, 7; 31:18; 33:18, and Padan in Gen 48:7. From Aram came Rebekah (Gen 24) and to it Jacob fled (Gen 28).

The Arameans are first mentioned in Akkad. texts, perhaps *c.* 2250 B.C., but certainly in some around 2000 B.C. From the Amorite city of Mari have come texts which refer to the Arameans as early as the 18th cen. B.C. Tablets from Ugarit (14th – 13th cen. B.C.) also mention Aram, as well as the Amarna letters.

By the 12th cen. B.C., Aram was strong enough to make itself felt in international affairs. By the 9th cen. B.C. it had become an effective buffer state between Assyria and Palestine. Damascus, a fruitful oasis on the plain E of the Anti-Lebanon range, was made the capital of Aram (Syria).

David conquered Syria and controlled it during his reign (II Sam 8:5-6; I Chr 18:5-6). After the breakup of the kingdom during the reign of Rehoboam, the Syrians became independent, with the dynasty of Hezion in power.

During the kingdom period, Israel, Judah, and Syria were a quarrelsome triad. At one time Judah and Syria teamed up against Israel (I Kgs 15:18-20). At another time Israel and Syria joined forces against Judah (II Kgs 16:5); and according to Assyrian inscriptions, Israel under Jehu united with Ben-hadad (*q.v.*) of Syria and others to stop the westward march of the Assyrian Shalmanezer III at Qarqar in 853 B.C. Finally, Ahaz of Judah joined with Assyria against Israel and Syria (II Kgs 16:7-18). As a result, Tiglath-pileser III destroyed Damascus in 732 B.C., and the power of Aram (Syria) was broken forever. Many of its people were carried into captivity by the Assyrians. *See* Aramaic; Syria; Damascus.

Bibliography. R. A. Bowman, "Arameans, Aramaic, and the Bible," JNES, VII (1948), 65-90. CornPBE, pp. 121-126. A. Malamat, "The Kingdom of David and Solomon in Its Contact with Aram Naharaim," BA, XXI (1958), 96-102. Benjamin Mazar, "The Aramean Empire and Its Relations with Israel," BA, XXV (1962), 98-120. Roger T. O'Callaghan, *Aram Naharaim,* Rome: Pontifical Biblical Institute, 1948. Merrill F. Unger, *Israel and the Arameans of Damascus,* London: James Clarke, 1957.

G. H. L.

ARAMAIC (ăr'*ȧ*-mā'ĭk). A general term for some Semitic dialects related to Hebrew. Besides isolated words in the OT, Aramaic is found in Ezr 4:8–6:18; 7:12-26; Dan 2:4*b*–7:28; Jer 10:11. Some Aramaic expressions occur in the NT. The originals of some of the apocryphal and pseudepigraphal books were written in Aramaic. The translations of the OT into Aramaic are called Targums. Inscriptions in an Aramaic alphabet on stone from Syria are dated as early as the 10th and 9th cen. B.C.

In their rise to power, the Assyrians developed Aramaic into the common language of their empire, for rulers and merchants. Inscriptions of this official Aramaic occur on weights, seals, pottery, and on cuneiform tablets as summaries of their content. At Sinjirli, a statue of Bar Rekub shows a scribe as though writing Aramaic letters. There is reference to Aramaic as a diplomatic medium in II Kgs 18:13-37. A bronze bowl with Aramaic letters has been found in Greece, and inscriptions have been found in Egypt dating from the Assyrian period.

Both the neo-Babylonian (605-538 B.C.) and Persian (538-330 B.C.) empires utilized Aramaic in their correspondence, of which abundant samples have been found. The Borchardt collection has 13 letters in Aramaic written on leather. These came from Egypt and were official Persian correspondence. Aramaic written on papyri has been found in Egypt, the most famous coming from Elephantine and dating from the 5th cen. B.C. *See* Elephantine Papyri.

During the Exile the Jews adopted Aramaic as their tongue and borrowed the Aramaic script for their Scriptures. In Jesus' day Galilean Aramaic was common. Among the Christians who went to the upper Euphrates Valley the language soon became known as Syriac, written with a different script.

G. H. L.

ARARAT (ăr'*ȧ*-răt). A high plateau on the far E border of modern Turkey, N of biblical Haran and SE of the Black Sea. The Tigris and Euphrates Rivers are formed by the confluence of streams which spring up in this region. Gen 8:4 records that Noah's ark rested "upon the mountains of Ararat" after the Flood. This does not necessarily mean that the ark stood upon one of the two peaks which rise from the plateau. These peaks, Great Ararat, which rises some 17,000 feet above sea level, and Little Ararat, which is nearly 13,000 feet high, have been given the name of the region of which they are a part, just as Sinai may be either the mountain on which the commandments were given or the desert or peninsula surrounding this summit. In II Kgs 19:37 and Isa 37:38, the "land of Ararat" is translated "land of Armenia" in the KJV. In Jer 51:27, the "kingdom of Ararat" (Urartu of Akkad. inscriptions, e.g., ANET, pp. 305, 316) is one of the kingdoms summoned to destroy Babylon. *See* Armenia.

Since World War II several expeditions have explored in this region looking for Noah's ark. Their efforts have frequently been hampered by Soviet suspicion that continued activity near the Russian border involved spying. A large wooden structure has been found encased in ice on Mount Ararat. Wood samples taken from the site have been tested by the carbon 14 method of dating, but interpretations of the results conflict. In any case, these materials do not seem to date early enough to have anything to do with Noah. Much further investigation of the area will evidently be required.

G. A. A.

ARAUNAH (*á*-rô'n*á*). A Jebusite, an inhabitant of Jebus ("which is Jerusalem," Jud 19:10; I Chr 11:4). The non-Semitic form of his name may stem either from the Hittite title *arawanis* meaning "noble," or from the Hurrian title *iwirne* meaning "chief, ruler, lord." In II Sam 24:16 his name is preceded by the definite article in Heb. and explained in v. 23 as *hammelek,* "the king." In either case it would tend to confirm the foreign ancestry of some of Jerusalem's aboriginal inhabitants (Ezk 16:3).

Araunah (also called Ornan, I Chr 21:15) owned a threshing floor on Mount Moriah which he sold to King David as a place for an alter to Yahweh. God had smitten Israel three days with a plague and 70,000 died because of King David's sin in numbering the people (II Sam 24:10–15; I Chr 21:1, 8–14). According to God's instructions, the prophet Gad told the king to build an altar on the threshing floor. Araunah would have given the land and oxen for sacrifice, but David felt he must pay fully (50 silver shekels in II Sam 24; 600 gold shekels in I Chr 21, the higher figure probably for the whole area). Heaven answered by sending fire to consume David's offerings (I Chr 21:26) and Yahweh stopped the plague. David determined this as the place for the temple, and it was here that Solomon later built the temple (II Chr 3:1).

W. G. B.

ARBA (är'b*á*). A leader of the Anakim and founder of the city of Hebron (Josh 14:15), whose original name, Kiriath-arba, means the "city of Arba" (also Josh 15:13; 21:11).

ARBATHITE (är'b*á*-thīt). Abialbon, one of David's mighty men, was so designated (II Sam 23:31; cf. I Chr 11:32). The word indicates an inhabitant of Beth-arabah.

The Dome of the Rock on the site of the threshing floor of Araunah. HFV

ARBITE (ăr'bīt). A dweller in the town of Arab (Josh 15:52). Paarai, one of David's warriors, is so designated (II Sam 23:35).

ARCH. The English word "arch" occurs 15 times in the KJV and only in the plural (Ezk 40:16-36). It is the translation of two similar forms of the Heb. word *'ēlām,* which is related to Heb. *'ûlām,* "porch," "vestibule." The words thus mean generally "porch," differing slightly in emphasis. They designate an entry room or pillared hall or covering of some sort in front of a building or gate. The three main gates to the outer court of Ezekiel's temple are described as each having a vestibule at its inner end (Ezk 40:7-26), while each of the three gates leading to the inner courtyard have a vestibule at its outer end (Ezk 40:27-37).

The earliest known true arch in Palestine occurs at Lachish in a 5th cen. B.C. Persian residence. The arch and vault became common in the great buildings of Herod the Great's reign. The arch as a weight-carrying device was developed in Mesopotamia and then borrowed by other countries. This architectural feature was highly perfected and widely utilized by Roman engineers of the empire period. Greeks and Egyptians generally employed the post-and-lintel type of construction, though the corbeled arch was used by the early Aegean builders (e.g., in the Mycenaean "beehive" tombs).

See Architecture; Porch.

H. G. S.

ARCHAEOLOGY

Nature and Purpose of Biblical Archaeology

The word "archaeology" comes from two Gr. words, *archaios* and *logos,* which mean literally "a study of ancient things." But the term has been much more refined than that and usually applies to a study of excavated materials belonging to a former era. Bible archaeology may be defined as an examination of ancient things which have been lost and found again, as those recovered objects relate to the study of Scripture and the portrayal of life in Bible times.

While archaeology is defined variously in the popular mind, it is basically a science. Knowledge in the field is acquired by systematic observation or study, and facts discovered are evaluated and classified into an organized body of information. Moreover, archaeology is a composite science because it seeks assistance from many other sciences, such as chemistry, anthropology, and zoology.

Of course, some subjects of archaeological investigation (such as obelisks and temples of Egypt and the Parthenon at Athens) have never been "lost" at all, but perhaps a knowledge of their original form and purpose and the meaning of inscriptions on them have been lost.

Corbeled arch at Mycenae. HFV

Functions of Biblical Archaeology

Archaeology performs the very useful service of helping us to understand the Bible. It reveals what life was like in biblical times, what obscure passages of Scripture really mean, and how the historical narratives and context of the Bible are to be understood.

Archaeological study also helps to confirm the accuracy of the biblical text and its contents. It has shown the falsity of some higher critical theories of biblical interpretation. It has helped to establish the accuracy of the Gr. and Heb. originals and to show that the biblical text has been transmitted with a remarkable degree of accuracy. And it has confirmed the accuracy of many passages of Scripture, e.g., statements concerning numerous kings and the whole patriarchal narrative.

One should not be dogmatic in his statements concerning confirmation, however. Archaeology has also created numerous problems for the Bible student. For instance, recovered Babylonian and Sumerian accounts of the creation and the Flood having striking parallels to the OT and questions of origin plague the Bible scholar. One is also troubled by the problem of interpreting the relationship between the Ras Shamra texts and the Mosaic code. But one can confidently believe that answers to the problems will be forthcoming. To date there has not been an instance of archaeology conclusively demonstrating the Bible to be in error

Why Ancient Cities and Civilizations Disappeared

It may be argued that ancient civilizations and cities disappeared because of the judgment of God. Scripture is full of such indications. But there are simple naturalistic explanations that can also be briefly noted. Cities were usually built on easily defensible sites possessing a good water supply and located near important trade routes.

Such sites were at a premium in the ancient Near East. So if some catastrophe brought about the destruction of a town, the tendency was to rebuild on the same location. A town might be largely destroyed by earthquake or invasion. Famine or pestilence might depopulate a city or territory. In the latter instance, the inhabitants might conclude that the gods had leveled a curse on them and they might fear to return. Uninhabited sites would quickly fall into ruins. And when former inhabitants returned or when new settlers came into the area, they usually simply smoothed out the rubble and built a new city. Thus mounds or tells rose up with many superimposed layers of habitation. Sometimes the water supply dried up, rivers changed their courses, trade arteries were rerouted or political fortunes changed—resulting in the permanent abandonment of a site.

Excavating a Mound

The biblical archaeologist may undertake excavation of a mound for many reasons. If the mound he attacks is known to cover a biblical site, he probably seeks to uncover the layer or layers of occupation having relevance for the biblical narrative. He may be looking for a city which is known to have existed but has not yet been identified. Perhaps he seeks to resolve doubts concerning proposed identification of a site. Possibly he is searching for information concerning Bible characters or events that will help to illuminate the Scripture narrative.

Once the excavator has chosen a site to dig and has made proper arrangements to do so (including permits, finances, equipment and staff), he is ready to begin operations. A careful surface exploration is usually carried out first to learn all that can be ascertained from pottery or other artifacts on the surface, to discover whether a configuration of ground houses the remains of a building, or to figure out something of the history of the mound. Then a contour map of the mound is drawn and a sector or sectors chosen where digging is to be carried on during a season of excavation. These sectors are then usually subdivided into one meter squares to facilitate labeling of finds.

The usual method of excavation today is stratigraphic. That is, each successive layer or stratum of occupation is carefully uncovered until bedrock is reached. All objects are photographed where found, and then carefully lifted from location and labeled and recorded. The pieces of a broken jar are put in a basket and later glued together. Since stratigraphic excavation is so expensive, time-consuming, and destructive, the tendency is to clear only part of

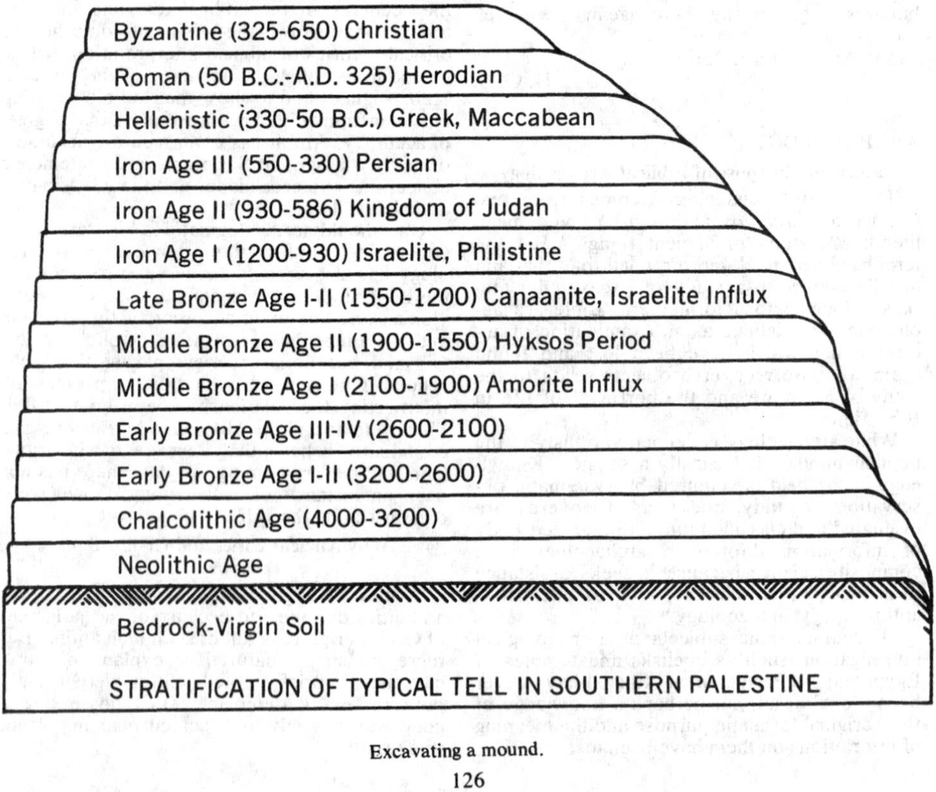

Excavating a mound.

ARCHAEOLOGY

a layer. In that way a fairly clear picture of the history of the mound may be drawn and there will be something left for future excavators to evaluate if they desire to do so.

Archaeology and the Text of the Bible

While most people think of huge monuments and museum pieces and exploits of kings when biblical archaeology is referred to, they have become increasingly aware that inscriptions and manuscripts also have an important contribution to make to biblical study. Although most archaeological work used to center on biblical history, today it is increasingly concerned with the text of the Bible.

Intensive study of the more than 3,000 NT Gr. MSS dating from the 2nd cen. A.D. and following has shown that the NT text has been remarkably preserved in transmission from the 3rd cen. to the present. Not one doctrine has been perverted, and Westcott and Hort concluded that only about one word in a thousand of the Gr. original has serious question upon it.

It is one thing to demonstrate that the NT text has been remarkably preserved from the 2nd cen. to the present; it is quite another to show that the Gospels, for instance, did not gradually evolve into their present form during the early centuries of the Christian era or that Christ was not gradually deified by Christian legend. At the turn of the 20th cen. a new science was born that would help to show that neither the Gospels nor the Christian view of Christ evolved into their present form. B. P. Grenfell and A. S. Hunt excavated in the Fayum district of Egypt (1896 - 1906), finding large quantities of papyri and launching the science of papyrology.

The papyri, written on a kind of paper made from the papyrus reed of Egypt (*see* Papyrus), include a wide variety of topics presented in several languages. The number of fragmentary papyrus MSS containing portions of the NT now stands at 77. These fragments help to confirm the general text found in the longer vellum MSS dating to the 4th and following centuries, and to bridge more of the gap between the later MSS and the originals.

Phenomenal has been the impact of papyrology upon biblical study. Many of the papyri date to the first three centuries after Christ. Thus it is possible to establish the development in the grammar of that period, and on the basis of the argument from historical grammar, to date the composition of NT books to the 1st cen. A.D. In fact, one fragment of the Gospel of John found in Egypt can be dated on the basis of paleography *c.* A.D. 125. Allowing time for the book to get into circulation, a date toward the end of the 1st cen. must be assigned to the fourth Gospel—and that is what Christian tradition has always assigned to it. No one doubts that the other three Gospels date to a period somewhat earlier than John. If the NT books were written during the 1st cen., they were written close to the events they record and there was no time for an evolutionary development to occur.

But the contributions of the mass of papyri of all types do not stop here. They have shown that NT Gr. is not some form of language invented by NT writers, as formerly thought. Instead it was generally the language of the people of the first centuries of the Christian era. Fewer than 50 words in the NT were coined by the apostles. Moreover, the papyri have shown that NT grammar was good grammar, judged by 1st cen. standards rather than those of the classical period. Furthermore, the non-biblical Gr. papyri have helped to clear up the meaning of uncertainly understood NT words and to throw new light on others fairly well understood.

The story of OT textual criticism can hardly be told here. Suffice it to say that OT MSS are not as close to their originals in time as those of the NT, but they were copied with greater care and have fewer variations.

Until recently, the oldest-known Heb. MS of any length did not date earlier than the first part of the 10th cen. after Christ, and the oldest complete Heb. Bible dates about a century later. Then, in the spring of 1948, the religious and academic worlds were rocked with the announcement that an ancient Isaiah manuscript had been found in a cave near the NW corner of the Dead Sea. Since that time a total of 11 caves in that area have disgorged their treasures of scrolls or fragments. Tens of thousands of leather fragments and some of papyrus have been recovered. While most of the materials are non-biblical, fragments representing over a hundred MSS bear Scripture portions. So far, all OT books except Esther are represented in the finds. As might be expected, fragments of OT books quoted most in the NT (Deuteronomy, Isaiah, Psalms) are most numerous there also. The longest and most nearly intact biblical scrolls include two of Isaiah, one of Psalms and one of Leviticus.

The significance of the Dead Sea Scrolls is tremendous. They have pushed the history of the OT text back 1,000 years (after much controversy the date has been assigned to the first centuries B.C. and A.D.). They have provided an abundance of critical material for research on the OT comparable to what has been available to NT scholars for many years. Third, the Dead Sea Scrolls have provided a more adequate context for the NT, demonstrating, for instance, the essential Jewish background of the Gospel of John —rather than a Gr. background as scholars have frequently asserted. Fourth, they help to establish the accuracy of the OT text. The Septuagint (Gr. OT) has been shown by studies in the scrolls to be more nearly accurate than often thought. And it has been demonstrated that there were other families of texts besides the Masoretic (traditional), which has served as the text of Heb. Bibles for so long. Yet, when all of the evidence is in, perhaps it will be demonstrated that the true text of the

OT is 95 percent or more what has been in the Masoretic Text all along. In this connection, it is interesting to note that one of the Isaiah MSS tallies almost exactly with the Masoretic Text. Fifth, the scrolls provide new material to help establish the meaning of Heb. words. *See* Dead Sea Scrolls.

The Dead Sea Scrolls are not the only important textual discovery of this century bearing on OT textual study. The Ras Shamra texts of the 15th and 14th cen. B.C. (see below under excavations) unearthed in 1929 ff. have done much to put Heb. religious practices into their proper context and to shed light on the meaning of certain Heb. words. The Mari and Nuzu texts (see below) have also played their part in illuminating the OT text. *See* Bible Manuscripts.

The Temple of Zeus at Athens. HFV

Excavations of Biblical Sites

No two writers will agree on a selection of excavated biblical sites for comment in a short survey such as this. Since hundreds of cities have now received archaeological attention, the choice becomes increasingly difficult. Some have been chosen because of their importance in ancient times, some because they figure prominently in the Bible narratve, and others because they illuminate the biblical narrative.

1. *Antioch of Syria*. Excavations were carried on at this early headquarters of Christianity (1932–39) by Princeton University, with the cooperation of the Baltimore Museum of Art, the Worcester Art Museum, and the National Museum of France, under the general direction of Richard Stillwell. The main features of the city were recovered, and the near equivalent was accomplished for the suburb of Daphne and the port of Seleucia. The acropolis of the city was discovered on Mount Stauris; the location of the two principal intersecting colonnaded streets was plotted; and the circus, probably erected originally in the 1st cen. A.D., was found and excavated. Villas, aqueducts, and baths in abundance were found at Antioch and her suburbs. Several churches were uncovered, but none date to the 1st cen. Probably most amazing of all the finds at Antioch were the well executed mosaics, dating from the 1st to the 6th cen. after Christ. *See* Antioch.

2. *Athens*. Archaeological work at Athens began after the Greek Archaeological Society was founded in 1837. Since then French, German, American, British, Austrian, Italian, and Swedish schools have been established there, in that order. Excavations of structures or areas familiar to Paul during his ministry at Athens include the Gr. and Rom. marketplaces, the acropolis and the structures of the S slope of the acropolis, and the great temple of Zeus. The most prodigious single undertaking involved clearance of 16 acres of the Gr. agora by the American School of Classical Studies since 1931, largely financed by John D. Rockefeller, Jr. Gr. archaeologists excavated the acropolis down to bedrock 1884–1891, and the 367- by-315-foot Roman market between 1890 and 1931. The Greek Archaeological Society (1886–1901) and the German School (1922–23) worked on the temple of Zeus which measured 286 by 62 feet. *See* Athens.

3. *Babylon*. Knowledge of ancient Babylon comes from the excavations of Robert Koldewey, who excavated there for the German Oriental Society, 1899–1914. Since he found the earliest strata of occupation to be under seepage water, nearly everything uncovered dated to the time of Nebuchadnezzar, except for one

Reconstruction of Babylon (after Unger). ORINST

spot where a few houses of the Hammurabi period were reached. Despite the general destruction of the city, the excavators were able to gain an accurate picture of the layout of the city, to outline its major buildings, procession street, and the famous Ishtar Gate. One of the major structures was the great brick ziggurat or staged tower some 295 feet high and composed of seven successively smaller stages or stories, on the topmost level of which stood a temple. *See* Babylon.

The Temple of Apollo at Corinth. HFV

4. *Caesarea*. Built by Herod the Great and dedicated about 10 B.C., Caesarea (*c.* 25 miles S of Haifa) was the Rom. capital of Palestine in subsequent decades. Here Paul was imprisoned for two years and here Origen and Eusebius lived and ministered. The Crusaders occupied the site for almost two centuries, and it has lain in ruins ever since the Muslims destroyed it in the 13th cen. The massive crusader walls and some adjacent areas were excavated by the Israelis in 1960. In the same year the Link Expedition conducted extensive underwater exploration around the harbor of this first good artificial port the Hebrews built on the Mediterranean. The circular breakwater which enclosed the harbor was charted and numerous pieces of pottery and other artifacts were found, the most important of which was a coin interpreted as picturing the ancient harbor and waterfront. In 1961 Italian archaeologists discovered a stone inscription in the theater bearing the name of Pontius Pilate. *See* Caesarea.

5. *Corinth*. Corinth was the great commercial center of Greece where Paul ministered for 18 months. In 1896 the American School of Classical Studies began excavation here under the general direction of R. B. Richardson and has continued intermittently ever since, working on the city proper, the acropolis, and the

Remains of the Roman Period at Caesarea. IIS

nearby sanctuary of Poseidon where the Isthmian games were held. Of special interest to the Bible student is the excavation of the great agora, or commercial and political center of the city, measuring 600 feet E and W, and 300 N and S. In the center of the agora still stands the bema or judgment seat at which Paul appeared before Gallio. *See* Corinth.

6. *Ephesus*. John T. Wood launched archaeological work at Ephesus in 1863 when he began his search for the great temple of Diana. This he finally located in 1869, and then spent five more years excavating the structure. At the same time he cleared the immense theater (Acts 19:31) on the W slope of Mount Pion. In 1897 Austrian excavators began to work on the city proper and have, with interruptions, continued there to the present. They have uncovered the street that led to the harbor and a great street that ran through the city, as well as numerous structures along both sides of the thoroughfare. The great 360-foot square Hellenistic agora is very largely excavated, and shops of silversmiths have been found there. *See* Ephesus.

Shops adjoining the Hellenistic Agora at Ephesus. HFV

Entrance to the water supply system, Hazor. HFV

7. *Ezion-geber.* Ezion-geber (Tell el-Kheleifeh) is known in the OT as the headquarters of Solomon's fleet (I Kgs 9:26) and was built by him at the N end of the Gulf of Aqabah. Nelson Glueck's excavation of the site in 1938 revealed that it was also an important copper smelting center where partially roasted ore from the Arabah to the N was prepared for shipment. Glueck also found that there were five main periods of occupation beginning with Solomon. What were thought to be blast furnaces or foundries of the Solomonic town were considered to be the finest yet discovered in the ancient world.

This feature of the excavations, however, has recently been challenged by Beno Rothenberg who has shown the improbability of the structures being used as smelting furnaces, and suggests that they were rather warehouses for goods being shipped along the trade routes which intersected at Ezion-geber (PEQ, 94 [1962], pp. 5 - 61). *See* Ezion-geber.

8. *Hazor.* Prominent in the leadership of opposition to Joshua in northern Palestine (Josh 11), Hazor was one of the largest cities of Canaan. It was located nine miles N of the Sea of Galilee and consisted of a high bottle-shaped mound some 2,000 feet long and 25 acres in extent and a lower rectangular plateau about 2,300 feet wide and 3,300 feet long. John Garstang excavated here briefly in 1928, but a more detailed excavation was made by a Hebrew University expedition under the direction of Yigael Yadin, 1955 - 58 and 1968 - 69. The last city in the rectangular enclosure had an estimated population of 40,000 and presumably was destroyed by Joshua or by Barak. Solomon and Ahab were probably responsible for building towns on the upper mound during the 10th and 9th cen. B.C. *See* Hazor.

9. *Jerash.* Jerash (perhaps the NT Gerasa) was one of the Decapolis, a chain of ten Hellenistic cities located in the Palestinian region. Many followed Jesus from the Decapolis (Mt 4:25; Mk 5:20; 7:31). Serious excavation began

A view across the ancient site of Jerash from one of the theaters. MIS

ARCHAEOLOGY

there in 1920 under the supervisio[illegible]-estine Department of Antiquities, and since 1948 the government of Jordan has continued the work. The magnificent city which has been laid bare provides a good example of the Graeco-Roman influence of Decapolis in the midst of Jewish religious exclusivism. While many of the remains date to the 2nd cen. A.D., a theater and temples to Zeus, Artemis, and Tiberius are among the structures dating to Jesus' day. *See* Gerasa.

10. *Jericho.* Excavations at OT Jericho were first carried on by Ernst Sellin and Carl Watzinger for the German Oriental Society, 1907-9. The archaeologists demonstrated that the town had covered only some six to eight acres, small enough for the Israelites to have marched around in 15 minutes. The British archaeologist John Garstang worked at the site 1929-36 and identified the double walls of City D as belonging to the city of Joshua's day. He claimed that they fell outward around 1400 B.C. Kathleen Kenyon, reopening the Jericho excavations 1952-58 for the British School of Archaeology in Jerusalem, concluded that the walls Garstang dated to Joshua's time actually dated to the period 3000-2000 B.C. She believed Joshua captured Jericho 1350-25 B.C. Excavations at nearby NT Jericho were conducted by James Kelso in 1950 and James Pritchard in 1951. They found remains of the Herodian palace and other structures of this winter capital of the Herods. *See* Jericho.

11. *Jerusalem.* The beginnings of archaeological work in Jerusalem date to the establishment of the Palestine Exploration Fund in 1865 and the work of Charles Warren in 1867 ff. From 1894 to 1897 F. J. Bliss and his architect A. C. Dickie did important archaeological and architectural work in the old Heb. capital. Captain Parker in 1909-11 cleared the entire system of tunnels related to the Gihon spring. E. L. Sukenik undertook excavation of the line of the N wall between 1925 and 1940.

In addition to these few examples, many other archaeological efforts have been undertaken in Jerusalem, but it will of course be impossible to carry on any large scale expeditions there because the ancient city is largely covered by modern habitation. Since nearly all these expeditions were conducted before proper stratigraphical records were understood, the British School of Archaeology in Jerusalem and the Ecole Biblique undertook in 1961 to survey the old city. In 1962 and succeeding years they were joined by the Royal Ontario Museum. Fère R. de Vaux, A. D. Tushingham, and Kathleen M. Kenyon were codirectors. A significant step has been made in clearing up problems related to the E wall and the area of the old Jebusite city. New evidence was also found to suggest that the site of the Church of the Holy Sepulcher was outside the wall of Jerusalem at the time of the crucifixion. Israeli soundings in 1969 found that the Herodian bridge across the Tyropeon Valley to the W side

Excavations adjacent to the Western Wall of the Temple in Jerusalem. HFV

of the temple area was as wide as a four-lane highway. *See* Jerusalem.

12. *Megiddo.* Among the fortress cities constructed by Solomon (I Kgs 9:15), Megiddo (Tell el-Mutesellim, located S of the plain of Esdraelon) was excavated by the Oriental Institute of the University of Chicago (1925-39) under the leadership of Clarence Fisher, P. L. O. Guy, and Gordon Loud. Stratum IV has been identified as the Solomonic level. There two stable compounds were found, capable of holding about 450 horses and a large number of chariots. Although Yigael Yadin of the Hebrew University in more recent excavations at the site feels that these stables date to Ahab's day, it seems probable that Solomon built them and that they were remodeled by Ahab. *See* Megiddo.

13. *Nineveh.* Excavations at Nineveh were begun by A. H. Layard in 1847 and continued during the last century by Hormuzd Rassam and George Smith for the British Museum and Victor Place for the French. Later, British Museum expeditions there were led by L. W. King and R. C. Thompson in 1903-5, and M. E. L. Mallowan in 1931-32. Ancient Nineveh is represented by 7½ miles of ramparts surrounding two great mounds—Kouyunjik and Nebi Yunus. Most of the archaeological work has centered on the former, where Layard uncovered the palace of Sennacherib, and he and others worked on the palace of Ashurbanipal with its great library. The palace of Esarhaddon was discovered in the mound of Nebi Yunus. Nineveh is as yet only partially excavated. *See* Nineveh.

14. *Pergamum* (Pergamos). Since 1868, when Carl Humann began to excavate at Pergamum, German archaeologists have been working at the site, which consists of an older hill city and a lower city of Roman imperial times. The hill city has now been largely excavated. There the great altar of Zeus was uncovered, identified by some as Satan's throne

The Altar of Zeus, Pergamum. HFV

(Rev 2:13), as well as two agoras, the gymnasium, several temples, the world-famous library, and palaces and a theater. The lower city, which was just being built in the apostle John's day, is largely covered by the modern city; but archaeological work was attempted there just prior to World War II. Near the lower town was the world-famous health center dedicated to Asklepius, god of healing, which is still receiving archaeological attention. *See* Pergamum.

15. *Philippi.* The first city in Europe to hear the Christian gospel was Philippi, and the church there was dear to the heart of the apostle Paul. While some excavation has been conducted at Philippi since World War II, the main work was done at the site by the French School at Athens, 1914–38. The 300-by-150-foot rectangular forum has been completely uncovered. Though rebuilt in the 2nd cen., it had essentially the same plan in Paul's day. The French also worked on the acropolis and uncovered the theater and Byzantine churches. *See* Philippi.

16. *Rome.* While archaeological work in Rome has been extensive, only a fraction of it has any relation to Scripture. Excavations on the Palatine Hill began about 1725 and have continued intermittently to the present. Part of the palace of Tiberius (reigning emperor when Christ was crucified) has been uncovered, but most of the construction on the hill was built by Domitian (who exiled John to the Isle of Patmos). Since 1907 work has been in progress on the recovery of Nero's Golden House on the Oppian Hill. First archaeological work at the Forum (political, social and economic center of the city and probable place where Paul appeared before Caesar) was done in 1788, and it has been carried on periodically to the present. A considerable amount of attention has also been devoted to the Circus Maximus, a great entertainment center in Paul's day, located between the slopes of the Aventine and Palatine. Excavation under the Vatican began in 1940 and has continued since World War II. Opinions of archaeologists vary on whether Peter's tomb was located there and whether it has been found. *See* Rome.

17. *Samaria.* Excavations at Samaria, capital of the northern kingdom, began with a Harvard expedition under the leadership of George A. Reisner, 1908–10. J. W. Crowfoot led a second expedition, 1931–33, in which Harvard cooperated with four other institutions. The British School of Archaeology in Jerusalem and others excavated at the site in 1935. Excavations at Samaria uncovered the palace begun by Omri and Ahab and added to by later kings, the city walls, cisterns for water storage during long sieges, large amounts of ivory, and ostraca. The latter, about 70 in number, were inscribed pieces of pottery dating to the early 8th cen. B.C., and tell something of the handwriting, religious and economic conditions of the time. Remains of construction by Herod the Great also came to light. *See* Samaria.

18. *Shechem.* Shechem (Tell Balatah) figures often in the OT narrative. It was, e.g., the town near which Abraham built his first altar, and served as the first capital of the kingdom of Israel under Jeroboam. I. E. Sellin and others connected with the German Oriental Society excavated at Shechem between 1913 and 1934. G. Ernest Wright, now at Harvard, began a new series of excavations at the site in 1956 under the auspices of Drew University, McCormick Theological Seminary, and the American Schools of Oriental Research. Various institutions have cooperated in the almost annual expeditions of recent years. Shechem probably reached its height between 2000 and 1500 B.C. A discovery of particular interest to the Bible student is an extensive Late Bronze Age temple which may have been the house of Baal-berith of Jud 9:4. *See* Shechem.

19. *Susa* (Shushan). Winter capital of the Persian Empire, Susa appears in the OT under the name Shushan (Neh 1:1; Est 1:2; Dan 8:2). The royal palace there was begun by Darius I

A griffon in bas relief from the palace at Susa, fifth to fourth century B.C. LM

ARCHAEOLOGY

(522 - 486 B.C.) and enlarged and beautified by later kings. Darius tells of bringing materials for it from Egypt, Lebanon, and India. French excavators have conducted the work at Susa. M. A. Dieulafoy pioneered there in 1884 - 86 and Jacques de Morgan and others directed excavations at the site 1897 - 1912. The three fragments of the Code of Hammurabi were discovered at Susa in 1901 - 2. Especial attention was devoted to the palace, which included three courts of varying size surrounded by large halls and apartments. The walls of sun-dried brick were covered with whitewash on the inside but were decorated with panels of beautifully colored glazed bricks probably during the reign of Artaxerxes II (404 - 359), well after the days of Esther and Nehemiah. Motifs of these panels included winged bulls, winged griffins, and spearmen of the guard. *See* Shushan.

20. *Ur.* In 1854 J. E. Taylor identified Tell Mukayyan in S Iraq as Ur and excavated there briefly. R. Campbell Thompson and H. R. Hall led two expeditions there in 1918 under the auspices of the British Museum. But the main work at the site was done by a joint expedition of the University Museum of Philadelphia and the British Museum in a protracted excavation headed by Sir Leonard Woolley (1922 - 34). Woolley found that Sumerian civilization flourished at Ur at a very high level as early as 2500 B.C. But the city was at its height 2070 - 1960 B.C., during which time Abraham may have left it, depending on how one figures the OT chronology. At that time its population numbered in the tens of thousands, and its people engaged in extensive commercial and industrial activity, enjoyed substantial educational opportunities, and built such great public structures as the brick ziggurat or stage-tower of Nanna (200 feet long by 150 feet wide and 70 feet high). *See* Ur.

Excavations of Sites Important for Biblical Study

1. *Ain Feshkha* and *Qumran.* The spring Ain Feshkha is located some 10 miles S of Jericho, and it is in this region just W of the Dead Sea that the caves are located which contained the Dead Sea Scrolls. To date at least 11 caves in the region have yielded scrolls and scroll fragments since the original discovery in 1947. Immediately N of Ain Feshkha was Khirbet Qumran, excavated in 1953 - 56 and discovered to have been the center of an ascetic sect akin to the Essenes and a place where many of the DSS were produced. The scrolls include portions of all OT books except Esther. A complete Isaiah MS, a second fairly complete Isaiah scroll, an almost complete scroll of Leviticus, and an almost complete copy of about 40 psalms are the longest and most important biblical MSS among the discoveries. The DSS provide important new information on the historical background of Scripture and important new materials for textual criticism. *See* Ain Feshkha; Dead Sea Scrolls.

The ziggurat at Ur. BM

2. *Boghazköy.* Mentioned many times in more than a dozen books of the OT, the Hittites were an important people of Asia Minor hardly known until Hugo Winckler led a German Oriental Society excavation at Boghazköy (the Hittite capital 90 miles E of Ankara) in 1906 ff. A find of special importance was the royal archives, consisting of about 10,000 cuneiform tablets. Temples, walls, and other construction have come to light in subsequent seasons of excavation. German excavators have again been working at this great 300-acre site regularly since World War II. *See* Hittites.

3. *Mari.* Mari (Tell Hariri) is located on the Euphrates almost due E of Byblos. André Parrot of the Louvre led annual excavations at the site 1933 - 38 and 1951 - 56. Most dramatic of the finds were the royal palace and the royal archives of the early 2nd mil. B.C. The palace boasted more than 250 rooms, courts, and corridors and covered more than six acres. More important to biblical study, however, were the royal archives, containing upward of 20,000 clay tablets. These consist of royal correspondence from many kingdoms of western Asia and a large number of business documents. These tablets have helped to modify our knowledge of the chronology of the 2nd mil. B.C. and have told much about the Amorites and thus about the patriarchal period. The names Peleg, Serug, and Nahor (Gen 11:16, 22, 24, 27) appear as names of towns in the Mari tablets. *See* Mari.

4. *Nippur.* Nippur, some 50 miles SE of Babylon, was an important Sumerian site. The first excavations there were conducted by the University Museum of Philadelphia, 1889 - 1900, under the leadership of J. P. Peters and others. Since Nippur was a religious and commercial center dedicated to the great earth-god Enlil, the city's principal building was the temple of Enlil. Near the temple was found the temple library comprising some 20,000 tablets of the 3rd and early 2nd mil. B.C. Among the religious texts important for biblical study were the Sumerian flood account and Sumerian King List, which mentions long-lived

patriarchs. Among the business houses of the mound thousands of tablets were found, dating from the 3rd mil. to the 5th cen. B.C. Since World War II many seasons of excavation have been conducted at the site by the Oriental Institute of the University of Chicago and the University Museum of Philadelphia with notable success. Several large temples have been investigated, foundation deposits discovered and additional tablets excavated. *See* Nippur.

5. *Nuzu.* Excavations at this NE Iraq site were conducted 1925–31 by the American Schools of Oriental Research under the direction of Edward Chiera. Harvard, the University Museum of Philadelphia, and other institutions cooperated in the operation. Of particular significance was the discovery of about 1,500 clay tablets in Nuzian private homes, dating to about 1500 B.C. and revealing striking parallels to the patriarchal narrative. Moreover, it should be pointed out that the Nuzians were Hurrians, related to the long-lost Horites of the OT. *See* Nuzu; Horites.

6. *Persepolis.* Persepolis was one of the great capitals of Persia and became the main capital under Darius I. Xerxes (probable husband of Esther) and Artaxerxes I (to whom Nehemiah ministered) continued construction there. The Oriental Institute of the University of Chicago excavated at Persepolis 1931–39 under the direction of Ernst Herzfeld and Erich Schmidt. The chief buildings were erected on a large rectangular terrace and included the palace of Darius, a building which probably served as his reception hall, and an audience hall begun by Darius I and completed by Xerxes (195 feet square). It was covered by a wooden roof supported by 72 stone columns. Also on the terrace stood a third large reception hall with 100 columns started by Xerxes and finished by Artaxerxes I, the harem of Darius, and the royal treasury. *See* Persia.

7. *Ras Shamra.* Ras Shamra (ancient Ugarit) was located on the Syrian coast opposite Cyprus. Excavated from 1929 until World War II and since 1950 by C. F. A. Schaeffer, the site has provided hundreds of texts dating from the 15th and 14th cen. B.C. These Canaanite documents are very significant for understanding the Heb. language, and reveal as well the nature of Canaanite religious practices at the time of the Heb. Conquest. *See* Ras Shamra.

A relief from the palace area at Persepolis. ORINST

Bibliography. William F. Albright, *The Archaeology of Palestine,* rev. ed., Harmondsworth, Middlesex: Penguin, 1960. George A. Barton, *Archaeology and the Bible,* 7th ed., Philadelphia: American Sunday School Union, 1937. George E. Bean, *Aegean Turkey,* London: Ernest Benn, 1966. Millar Burrows, *What Mean These Stones?* New Haven: American Schools of Oriental Research, 1941. Jack Finegan, FLAP. Joseph P. Free, *Archaeology and Bible History,* 2nd ed., Wheaton: Scripture Press, 1956. David N. Freedman and Jonas C. Greenfield (eds.), *New Directions in Biblical Archaeology,* Garden City: Doubleday, 1969. Nelson Glueck, *Rivers in the Desert,* Philadelphia: Jewish Publication Society, 1959. Kathleen Kenyon, *Archaeology in the Holy Land,* 2nd ed., New York: Praeger, 1965. William S. LaSor, *Amazing Dead Sea Scrolls,* 2nd ed., Chicago: Moody, 1959. Paul MacKendrick, *The Greek Stones Speak,* New York: St. Martin's Press, 1962. Charles F. Pfeiffer, ed., BW. Ira M. Price, O. R. Sellers, and E. L. Carlson, *The Monuments and the Old Testament,* Philadelphia: Judson, 1958. James B. Pritchard, ed., ANET, ANEP. D. Winton Thomas, ed., AOTS. John Arthur Thompson, *The Bible and Archaeology,* Grand Rapids: Eerdmans, 1962. Merrill F. Unger, *Archaeology and the Old Testament,* Grand Rapids: Zondervan, 1954. Donald J. Wiseman, *Illustrations from Biblical Archaeology,* Grand Rapids: Eerdmans, 1958. G. Ernest Wright, *Biblical Archaeology,* rev. ed., Philadelphia: Westminster, 1962.

H. F. V.

ARCHANGEL. That there are ranks among both the good and evil angels is clear in Eph 3:10 and 6:12. The evil angels are led by Satan and the elect angels by the archangel Michael (Rev 12:7).

The word "archangel" occurs only twice in the Bible (I Thess 4:16; Jude 9) and there is only one angel so designated–Michael ("who is like God"). In the OT he appears as the guardian angel of Israel (Dan 10:21; 12:1) and he has great authority (Dan 10:13). His power and authority will be used in behalf of the Israelites particularly during the time of Jacob's trouble.

Rabbinical traditions concerning Michael are many. He is called "great high priest in heaven" and "great prince and conqueror." In the Book of Enoch he is called one of the archangels (implying others).

In the NT the voice of the archangel will be heard at the return of the Lord for His people (I Thess 4:16). Michael is seen in the apocalyptic vision of John as leading the angelic armies of heaven against Satan and his host of evil angels (Rev 12:7). As a result of this conflict Satan is cast out of heaven. The reference in Jude 9 poses problems for some in connection with its being quoted from the Assumption of Moses. However, if one believes that its inclusion in the inspired text guarantees the accuracy of the facts reported (but only those facts which are included and not the entire account in the Assumption), then we learn that the archangel (1) had something to do with the burial of Moses; (2) had no prerogative in himself to pronounce judgment on Satan; and (3) is dependent on the greater power of God.

See also Angel; Michael.

C. C. R.

ARCHELAUS (är'kē-lā'ŭs). Son of Herod the Great by the Samaritan woman Malthace; governor over Idumea, Judea, and Samaria (4 B.C.–A.D. 6). On the death of his father, Archelaus at first appeared to be conciliatory to the Jews, but in a short time his true nature was revealed by the slaying of 3,000 persons during an uprising at the Passover season. As a result, when he went to Rome to obtain Caesar's confirmation of his rulership, the Jews also sent a delegation to protest his appointment (Jos *Ant.* xvii.11.1 f.). Some are of the opinion that Christ referred to this event in Lk 19:12–27. His brother Antipas also appeared before Augustus to contest their father's will, desiring to obtain the kingdom for himself. Finally, however, Archelaus was appointed ethnarch of Idumea, Judea, and Samaria, with the promise that he was to become king if he proved to be worthy (Jos *Ant.* xvii.11.4).

His rule, like his father's, was marked by numerous building projects. By many unwise and cruel acts he brought the hatred of the people upon himself. His domestic relationships were particularly offensive to the Jews. After being married to Mariamne for some time, he fell so deeply in love with Glaphyra, the widow of his half-brother Alexander, that he divorced his first wife and married Glaphyra (Jos *Wars* ii.7.4). He was also guilty of replacing the high priests at will. His treatment of his subjects is described by Josephus as barbarous and tyrannical (*Ant.* xvii.13.2; *Wars* ii.7.3). The only mention of him in the NT occurs in Mt 2:22, where Joseph is said to have settled in Galilee because he feared Archelaus. After ruling for more than nine years, Archelaus was recalled to Rome following accusations made by both Jews and Samaritans. On his arrival, he was deposed and banished to Vienna in Gaul (Jos *Ant.* xvii.13.2).

D. W. B.

ARCHERS. Men armed with bows and arrows. For many centuries archers, on foot, riding in chariots, or mounted, formed the backbone of the armies of the ancient Near East. In the OT the archer stands for military activity, and bows and arrows for military equipment generally (Gen 49:23–24; Ps 127:4–5; Hos 1:5; R. de Vaux, *Ancient Israel,* pp. 243–244). When Job wished to say God was making war against him, he said he had been made a target for God's archers (Job 16:12–13). Saul, Uriah, and Josiah were shot by archers (I Sam 31:3; II Sam 11:24; II Chr 35:23).

Archers from the guard of king Ashurbanipal at Nineveh, seventh century B.C. LM

Bows were usually of wood. To string a bow with its ox gut string, one end was secured with the foot while being bent, hence the archer was one who "treads a bow" (I Chr 8:40; Jer 51:3). Arrows were tipped with bone, stone, bronze, or iron and were called "sons of his quiver" (Lam 3:13, ASV marg.) or "son of the bow" (Job 41:28, ASV marg.).

See Bow and Arrow.

ARCHEVITES (är'kē-vīts). A group of people deported to Samaria by the Assyrian king Asnappar or Ashurbanipal (Ezr 4:9). They are identified with the Babylonian city of Erech of Gen 10:10 (IB, III, 601) and translated in RSV as "the men of Erech." *See* Erech.

ARCHI (är'kī). *See* Archite.

ARCHIPPUS (är-kĭp'ŭs). Mentioned twice in the NT (Col 4:17; Phm 2). In Colossians, Archippus is urged to take heed to his ministry. Paul is here perhaps commending Archippus for past service and encouraging him for future tasks, with no thought of a rebuke. In Philemon, Paul greets Archippus after Philemon and Apphia in a manner suggesting he may have been their son, and calls him a "fellow soldier," likely because Archippus had shared with Paul in some experience of service or suffering for the sake of Christ (cf. Phil 2:25).

Lightfoot has argued that Paul in Colossians is reproving Archippus for being remiss in the service of Christ. Believing that Archippus served the church at Laodicea, Lightfoot thinks of Archippus as being lukewarm like the whole church at Laodicea later became (cf. Rev 3:14 ff.). John Knox, however, has argued that Archippus was the main addressee of the so-called Epistle to Philemon and thus likely the pastor of the church at Colosse, not Laodicea; and that the service *(diakonia)* which Archippus was urged to perform was, as the owner of Onesimus, to release him so that he might do the work of an evangelist. This is not an obvious interpretation, however, of "the ministry which thou hast received in the Lord" (Col 4:17). *See* Philemon, Epistle to.

Bibliography. Henry Cowan, "Archippus," HDAC, I, 89. John Knox, *Philemon Among the Letters of Paul,* rev. ed., New York: Abingdon, 1959. J. B. Lightfoot, *Colossians,* 3rd ed., London: Macmillan, 1879, pp. 72 ff. For the occurrence of this name in Egyptian papyri and inscriptions from Asia Minor, see Arndt.

E. J. V.

ARCHITE (är'kīt). An inhabitant of a town or clan along the border of Ephraim and Benjamin between Luz and Ataroth (Josh 16:2, RSV). Hushai, David's loyal counselor, was an Archite (II Sam 15:32; 16:16; 17:5, 14).

ARCHITECTURE. The art of building, herein limited to Palestine from 2000 B.C. to A.D. 100.

In the Old Testament

The usual city of several thousand people was perched atop a hill or city mound five to ten acres in extent, and was protected by a strong wall with one or two gates. With no proper street planning before the Hellenistic age, the city contained only an unimpressive assortment of houses crammed together, reached by winding unpaved alleys. Many people, mainly the peasants engaged in agriculture, lived in surrounding unwalled villages (Deut 3:5) or in huts and tents outside the fortified city, seeking refuge within it only in time of attack. Most essential to the location was an adequate fresh water supply. Thus many towns (e.g., Jerusalem, Gibeon, Megiddo, Lachish, Gezer, Zarethan) had elaborate stepped tunnels to reach the spring or well when besieged. Around 1300 B.C. plastered cisterns and catchbasins came into use to collect rainwater, supplementing the town well. On the whole, building styles were simple and practical, for Israel was always the cultural borrower and never the innovator.

A diagram of the northern gate at Megiddo. HFV

Fortifications. For centuries after the Hyksos period the Canaanites and even the Israelites made use of any remaining features of the Middle Bronze Age defenses. These consisted of stone or brick walls perhaps 25 to 30 feet high at the top of an artificial slope (or glacis) of battered earth with a ditch at the bottom to protect the walls from enemy battering rams. Egyptian sculptured reliefs depict bearded Canaanite defenders standing on crenellated battlements. Early in the Israelite monarchy casemate walls were constructed, consisting of two parallel walls connected by a series of cross walls. The "rooms" thus formed could be filled with earth in times of siege to strengthen the wall against battering machines (cf. Ezk 26:9). Later in the monarchy, single walls 20 feet or more thick were built with alternating recesses and salients to expose attackers.

The gate was the key to the city's defense since it was the most vulnerable point. While Jerusalem had a number of gates, most Israelite cities had only two, one for chariots and, on the opposite side of town, a smaller one for donkeys and pedestrians only. The road leading up to the main gate was planned so that attackers carrying shields with their left hands would have the wall and its defenders on their right flank. The gate was part of a strong tower or had bastions on each side (II Chr 26:9). Usually in the gateway the road ran between two sets of massive stone piers (pilasters) or projecting jambs—sometimes three as at Shechem—with guard chambers between (II Sam 18:24). Stairs gave access to the tower roof where a sentinel stood watch (II Kgs 9:17). The double doors of the gate (Isa 45:1; Neh 6:1) consisted ordinarily of two wooden sections, sometimes overlaid with bronze plating (Isa 45:2) and held shut with one or more horizontal bars of wood, bronze (I Kgs 4:13), or iron (Ps 107:16), passing into openings in the gateposts (Jud 16:3). At Megiddo, as in the present Damascus Gate of Jerusalem, the axis of the gate turned 90 degrees between the two sets of portals to prevent a straight shot through the gate by enemy archers. Solomon's architect planned identical gates with four pairs of pilasters for Hazor, Megiddo, and Gezer (cf. I Kgs 9:15).

Public buildings. In Canaanite cities the local king of the city-state and a few of his nobles built two-story houses with ceilings supported by stone pillars. Solomon rebuilt certain cities as centers for his administrative districts (I Kgs 4:7–19). As at Megiddo, these probably contained near the gate a "palace" with many rooms to house the city garrison as well as the provincial governor and his retinue, and stables for the horses of the royal chariotry (I Kgs 9:19). Storehouses held the jars of grain, wine, and olive oil collected as taxes, as at Dothan, Shechem, and Gezer. A large stone-lined silo pit was constructed at Megiddo during the reign of Jeroboam II to store the grain harvested from the fertile plain of Esdraelon. The fortified building at Ezion-geber, formerly dubbed a copper smelter, is now interpreted as having been a storehouse granary.

Except at these store-cities and the royal citadels at Samaria, Jerusalem, and Ramat Rahel, Israelite Palestine gives little evidence of monumental architecture of the styles current in Egypt and Phoenicia. But King Solomon did hire carpenters and masons from Tyre and Gebal to prepare the cedar timber and stones for his temple (I Kgs 5:6, 18). Quite clearly Phoenician masons were also employed at Megiddo, and by King Omri and King Ahab at Samaria later on. At these sites parts of walls remain consisting of closely jointed and smoothed limestone blocks laid in a pattern of alternating headers and stretchers. The oldest known masonry of this type was uncovered at Ugarit.

Solomon's courtyard was built with a foundation of three rows of hewn stones topped by a row of cedar beams (I Kgs 6:36; 7:12), a common architectural feature in the ancient Near East to withstand earthquake shocks. Probably above the timber joists bonding the stones together were laid further courses of stones or of bricks, as at Ezion-geber and Samaria. The citadel enclosed by two walls on the summit of Samaria was approached from the E through a gate with a monumental forecourt ornamented by pilasters with "proto-Ionic" capitals. These have been found also at Megiddo and Ramat Rahel near Jerusalem, at the latter site decorating the facade of a palace in the royal citadel built probably by King Jehoiakim (cf. Jer 22:13 ff.). An Egyptian-style monolithic tomb of the period of the Jewish monarchy can be seen at Silwan across the Kidron Valley from old Jerusalem. Perhaps the sepulcher of the pro-Egyptian steward Shebna (Isa 22:16) or even of King Hezekiah (II Chr 32:33) followed this architectural style.

See Temple for special features of these buildings.

Private houses. The house of the better-class Israelite consisted of several rooms facing a courtyard, which was used for all household tasks (II Sam 17:18), the largest room for the family, another for the cattle, and a third for a general storeroom ("closet," Mt 6:6). These rooms were small, 12 to 15 feet square or less. As at Gezer, house walls generally consisted of common field stones with wide, irregular joints filled with mud and stone chips. Each family built its own house, expert masons being employed only on royal residences, temples, or city walls. The average man plastered the inside walls with mud; the wealthy could afford to panel their walls with cypress or cedar wood ("cieled," Hag 1:4, KJV). In all periods the floors were made of hard-packed clay or plaster polished with rubbing stones.

A casemate wall of ancient Hebrew construction at Ramat Rahel, near Jerusalem. HFV

Roofs were flat, supported by wooden beams laid from wall to wall. Smaller rafters (Song 1:17) crossed these, then brushwood or reeds, above which was a layer of earth several inches thick coated with heavy plaster, rolled after a rain to keep the roof watertight. The roof was reached by an outside staircase from the courtyard and was made safe by a parapet required by the Mosaic law (Deut 22:8). Such a roof, sometimes shaded by awnings, had many uses (Josh 2:6; I Sam 9:25; Isa 15:3; Acts 10:9). Some built roof chambers (I Kgs 17:19; II Kgs 4:10, RSV), in effect making theirs a two-story house. Only a palace, however, would have an ornamental or latticed window balustrade such as the one from which Jezebel looked out (II Kgs 9:30–33), in accordance with a favorite artistic theme of the ancient Near East showing a lady standing at the state window. Stone-lined sewers have been discovered in many Canaanite and Israelite towns.

Paneled effect of Herodian masonry on the Western Wall of the Temple. HFV

In the New Testament

One lasting result of the Hellenization of the Mediterranean world was the founding or rebuilding of some 350 Hellenistic cities, more than 30 of them in Palestine. These 30, among them the cities of the Decapolis *(q.v.)*, were concentrated mainly in Transjordan and along the coast. They stood out architecturally because of their systematized town planning with principal streets and rectangular blocks, monumental arches, theaters, public baths, gymnasiums, temples, and above all the typically Gr. *agora* (forum or marketplace). Gerasa in Gilead with its spectacular ruins is the chief example of one of these cities. The Nabateans incorporated many of these architectural features in their rock-cut city of Petra. Predominantly Jewish towns, however, had refused to Hellenize, even though prominent Jewish families took on western ways, as seen in the mausoleum of the Tobiads in Transjordan and the Maccabean-age tombs in the Kidron Valley. The average Jewish houses remained small and crowded together, with flat roofs and the rooms opening on a courtyard separated from the street by a wall with its gate-door (Acts 12:13), all purely utilitarian in architectural style.

It was the great building program of Herod the Great (30–4 B.C.) that most deeply affected the architecture of Judea. He erected a remarkable chain of castles with aqueducts, great cisterns, and dungeons. Remains of these can still be seen at Masada and Herodium near Bethlehem. His supreme achievements were the complete renovation of the second temple in Jerusalem, and the transformation of Caesarea and Samaria (which he renamed Sebaste) into major cities. His masonry is recognizable everywhere by squared blocks of faultless jointing with drafted borders producing a paneled effect. He introduced cut-stone vaulting, making possible the harbor at Caesarea, the vast substructures of the Jerusalem temple area, and great viaducts that spanned the Tyropean valley (Wilson's and Robinson's Arches). His attempts, however, to ingratiate himself with the Jewish populace by this program only earned him their undying hatred. By and large, they bitterly opposed his temples built in other cities as tributes to the Greek and Roman gods, and they refused to appreciate the blending of prevailing Hellenistic forms in structure and ornament with their native Oriental motifs. *See* Arch.

See articles on the various cities mentioned herein.

Bibliography. "Ancient Cities"; "Cities, Canaanite, Israelite, Hellenistic," *Pictorial Biblical Encyclopedia,* ed. by Gaalyahu Cornfeld, New York: Macmillan, 1964. J. W. Crowfoot, Kathleen M. Kenyon, E. L. Sukenik, *The Buildings at Samaria,* London: Palestine Exploration Fund, 1942. R. W. Hamilton, "Architecture," IDB. G. Ernest Wright, *Biblical Archaeology,* rev. ed., Philadelphia: Westminster, 1962.

J. R.

ARCTURUS (ärk-tū̄r'*ŭ*s). A large bright star or constellation referred to in Job 9:9; 38:32, KJV. RSV translates the Heb. word as the "Bear." The precise modern equivalent is not known, although either the constellation of Ursa Major, the Great Bear, or of Aldebaran is a possible reference. *See* Astronomy.

ARD (ärd), **ARDITE** (är'dīt). One of the descendants of Benjamin who founded a clan in Egypt (Gen 46:21; Num 26:40).

Ard is alternately Addar (*q.v.;* I Chr 8:3).

ARDON (är'dŏn). One of the sons of Caleb of the tribe of Judah (I Chr 2:18).

ARELI (*ȧ*-rē'lī), **ARELITES** (*ȧ*-rē'līts). A son of Gad who went to Egypt with the house of Jacob (Gen 46:16). The Arelites were descendants of Areli (Num 26:17).

AREOPAGITE (ăr'ē-ŏp'*ȧ*-gīt). A member of the Areopagus council. One such member is named in Scripture, Dionysius (*q.v.;* Acts 17:34). *See also* Areopagus.

AREOPAGUS (ăr'ē-ŏp'*ȧ*-g*ŭ*s). Philosophers of Athens brought Paul to the Areopagus to hear an explanation of his teachings. Areopagus (Acts 17:19) is the equivalent of Mars Hill (Acts 17:22), for Mars was the Roman name for the god of war and Ares the Gr. name. Actually Areopagus could signify a 377-foot hill in Athens NW of the acropolis, or the name of the venerable council which traditionally had met on the hill. By Paul's day the council did sometimes meet in the agora, but the Gr. of Acts 17:19 probably should be translated "up to" and seems to signify that this meeting took place on the hill. Acts 17:19 probably refers to the hill and Acts 17:22 to the council ("in the midst of Mars hill" is an impossible rendering of the Gr.).

While the Areopagus had once held a place of supreme importance in the political and religious affairs of the state, during the 5th cen. B.C. it lost its political power and became largely a criminal court. In Roman times it was charged mainly with religious and educational affairs. Sir William Ramsay believed that the Areopagus had power to appoint or invite lecturers at Athens and that for that reason Paul was brought before the council. *See* Athens; Dionysius the Areopagite.

H. F. V.

The Areopagus. HFV

ARETAS (ăr'ĕ-tȧs). Mentioned only in II Cor 11:32 in the NT. The name was used by the kings of Nabatean Arabia whose capital was Petra. This was Aretas IV (9 B.C.–A.D. 40), whose daughter was married to Herod Antipas (*q.v.*) until the latter divorced her to marry Herodias. As a result of Herod's act, along with border disputes between the two (cf. Jos. *Ant.* xviii.5.1), Aretas declared war in A.D. 36, a war which resulted in the destruction of Herod's army.

Probably about this same time the incident recorded in II Cor 11:32 took place. Exactly what Aretas' jurisdiction in Damascus was is not clear, for the province of Syria was officially under Roman jurisdiction. Some scholars think that the governor or ethnarch at Damascus under Aretas was ruler only of the Nabatean citizens resident in the vicinity of the city. Others suppose that the Roman emperor Caligula (A.D. 37–41) may have handed over the control of Damascus to Aretas as a friendly gesture.

See Damascus; Ethnarch.

W. M. D.

ARGOB (är'gŏb)

1. The southern part of Bashan in northern Transjordan, extending on the S to the Yarmuk River and on the W to Geshur and Maachah (Deut 3:4–5, 13–14). It included the 60 fortified cities which comprised the northern portion of the kingdom of Og. It should be distinguished from northern Gilead, S of the Yarmuk where the "unwalled towns" of Deut 3:5*b* (i.e., the *ḥavvôth* Jair, Deut 3:14*b*; Jud 10:4) were located (I Kgs 4:13). This distinction, however, is not clear in Josh 13:30. Rabbinic Targums identified Argob with Trachonitis (modern el-Leja), but this is generally rejected in favor of the more fertile area to the W (Driver, *Deuteronomy,* pp. 48–50). Moses assigned this area to the half tribe of Manasseh (Deut 3:13–14). In Solomon's fiscal administrative organization Argob was the northern half of the district assigned to the son of Geber, one of Solomon's 12 administrative officials responsible for the supply of food for the court (I Kgs 4:13).

2. An Israelite noble associated with Pekah (II Kgs 15:25). However, Argob and Arieh possibly should be omitted from v. 25 and added to v. 29 as place names, as in RSV (cf. also KB; BDB; Kittel marg.; Smith, *An American Translation;* James A. Montgomery, ICC, *The Books of Kings*).

R. V. R.

ARIDAI (âr'ĭ-dī). One of the ten sons of Haman slain by the Jews in the story of Queen Esther (Est 9:9).

ARIDATHA (ăr'ĭ-dā'thȧ). A son of Haman killed in Susa by Jewish loyalists (Est 9:8). This was probably a Persian name of uncertain meaning.

ARIEH (ȧr'ī-ȧ). Along with Argob, Arieh was involved in the conspiracy of Pekah and the murder of King Pekahiah (II Kgs 15:25, KJV and RSV marg.).

ARIEL (âr'ĭ-ĕl)

1. The hearth of the altar of burnt offering in Ezekiel's temple (Ezk 43:15–16). *See* Hearth.

2. A leader whom Ezra sent to Casiphia, presumably a Babylonian Levitical settlement, to seek ministers for the temple (Ezr 8:16–17).

3. A symbolic name for Jerusalem (Isa 29:1–2, 7). Its usage favors the root meaning "hearth of God" rather than the similar root for "lion." Jerusalem under divine judgment, despite its holy associations, will be as a great bloody altar with the slain everywhere around it.

4. Its occurrence in the Heb. text of II Sam 23:20 (ASV) and I Chr 11:22 (ASV) is enigmatic, but may suggest the strength of the two slain (KJV). Preferably, by introducing "sons of," the Septuagint makes it the name of a Moabite whose two sons were slain by Benaiah (RSV).

ARIMATHAEA (ăr'ĭ-mȧ-thē'ȧ). A town mentioned only in the Gospels as the home of Joseph who requested the body of Jesus from Pilate and buried it in his own new tomb (Mt 27:57; Mk 15:43; Lk 23:51; Jn 19:38). Luke's reference, which states it was a city of the

Jews, would identify it with the territory of Haramantha (Rathamin) mentioned in I Macc 11:34 as being added to the northern border of Judea by the Syrian king Demetrius II Nicator (145 B.C.) from possessions then belonging to Samaria. Eusebius' *Onomasticon* apparently calls it "Remphthis" (Rantis) and locates it as part of the city territory of Diospolis. While sometimes also called Ramah, it should not be confused with Ramah (Ramleh or er-Ram) in Benjamin, six miles N of Jerusalem. However, Arimathaea is identified by some as Ramathaim-zophim ("the two Ramahs" or "twin heights") in the land of Ephraim where Samuel was born (I Sam 1:1, 19). The exact location still remains uncertain although many place it about 20 miles E of Tel-Aviv and Joppa. *See* Ramah.

A. F. J.

ARIOCH (âr'ĭ-ŏk)

1. King of Ellasar, one of the Mesopotamian coalition, who campaigned successfully against the rebellious cities of the Arabah (Gen 14:1, 9), capturing Lot who was in turn rescued by Abram. He is not clearly identifiable from extrabiblical sources. Most recent attempts, through the Mari tablets, to equate with Arriwuk, son of Zimrilim of Mari, would demand a 17th cen. B.C. date, seemingly too late for Abraham (cf. Gerhard von Rad, *Genesis,* p. 171; Martin Noth, VT, I, 136–140; W. F. Albright, "Archaeology of Palestine," *Old Testament and Modern Study,* p. 7; H. H. Rowley, *From Joseph to Joshua,* pp. 63–66). The similarity to Arriwuk does show that Arioch was an authentic Hurrian name during the 2nd mil. B.C. in N Mesopotamia.

See Abraham; Ellasar.

2. Nebuchadnezzar's captain of the guard, commissioned to slay the wise men for their inability to tell Nebuchadnezzar his dream (Dan 2:14–15, 24–25). His commission was never executed. He informed Daniel, who through divine revelation succeeded where the other wise men had failed.

R. V. R.

ARISAI (âr'ĭ-sī). A son of Haman slain in the revenge of the Jews under Queen Esther (Est 9:9).

ARISTARCHUS (ăr'ĭs-tär'kŭs). A Macedonian from Thessalonica (Acts 19:29; 27:2), probably of Jewish ancestry (Col 4:10–11), who accompanied Paul on his third missionary journey. At Ephesus he was dragged into the theater in the silversmiths' riot (Acts 19:29). From there he journeyed with Paul through Macedonia to Greece (Acts 20:2), and with others sailed directly to Troas where they awaited arrival of Paul who followed by way of Philippi (Acts 20:3–6). Aristarchus sailed with Paul to Rome for trial (Acts 27:2), and evidently shared his imprisonment (Col 4:10). Paul's alternating references to him and Epaphras as "fellow prisoner" and "fellow worker" in the closing greetings may suggest that this was a voluntary sharing in which these faithful friends took turns (cf. Phm 23–24). According to tradition he was martyred under Nero.

ARISTOBULUS (ăr'ĭs-tŏb'ū-lŭs). Paul sent greetings to "them which are of Aristobulus' household" (Rom 16:10). Lightfoot's well-known view is that this man was a brother of Herod Agrippa I and that these people were his slaves, now the property of the emperor. Bruce suggests that the next verse, "Salute Herodion my kinsman" (Rom 16:11), is thus very fitting. Possibly Herodion was a member of the household of Aristobulus.

ARK, NOAH'S. Noah's ark was a colossal barge which God commanded Noah to build for the purpose of keeping alive members of his family and two of every kind of land animal through a universal flood (*see* Flood) which would come upon the earth in 120 years (Gen 6:3, 14–21). The ark (Heb. *tēbâ,* from the Egyptian *db't,* meaning "chest," "box," or "coffin," and found elsewhere only in Ex 2:3, 5) was not a ship with sloping sides, rudder, and mast, but rather a bargelike repository intended only to float and to withstand the impact of waves. Shaped thus, its carrying capacity was one-third greater than a ship of similar length and width, and it would have been almost impossible to capsize.

The ark was constructed of gopher wood (cypress?) and was protected by an inner and outer coating of pitch or bitumen (Heb. *kōper*). The three decks were divided into rooms (Heb. *qinnîm,* "nests"). Around the entire vessel just below the roof was an opening for light; and in one side was a door (Gen 6:14–16). See Alexander Heidel, *The Gilgamesh Epic and Old Testament Parallels,* pp. 233–35; and Bernard Ramm, *The Christian View of Science and Scripture,* pp. 229–31.

The ark was 300 cubits long, 50 wide, and 30 high (Gen 6:15). Assuming that the basic Heb. cubit was 17.5 inches (cf. R. B. Y. Scott, "Weights and Measures of the Bible," BA, May, 1959, pp. 22–27), the ark was 437.5 feet long, 72.92 feet wide, and 43.75 feet high. Since it had three decks, its total deck area was about 95,000 square feet. The total volume of the ark would have been 1,396,000 cubic feet, giving it a gross tonnage of about 13,960 tons, which is well within the category of large metal ocean-going vessels today. As early as 1609–21, Peter Janson of Holland built a large model of the ark and demonstrated the efficiency of its design and proportions. Not until the last half of the 19th cen. was a ship built with dimensions exceeding that of the ark.

Noah and his sons probably hired many men to assist them in the construction of the ark. By the very nature of the case, the project must have gained worldwide attention, and the universal rejection of Noah's faithful warnings during this final testing period of 120 years was the basis upon which Noah "condemned the world" (Heb 11:7). Noah's ark-building faith stood out in startling contrast to the unbelief of the human race "when the long-suffering of God waited in the days of Noah, while the ark was a preparing, wherein few, that is, eight souls, were saved through water" (I Pet 3:20, ASV).

For well over a century, scholars have debated whether the ark was sufficiently large to carry two of every kind of air-breathing animal in the world, plus an additional five of each "clean" kind. It must be recognized, in the first place, that two or more similar "species" of modern taxonomy may be included within one Genesis "kind." But more important, the vast majority of the nearly one million species of today are marine creatures which could have survived outside the ark. A leading systematic taxonimist, Ernst Mayr, lists 17,600 species of mammals, birds, reptiles, and amphibians. So we may assume that there were probably not more than 35,000 individual vertebrate animals in the ark, the average size being that of a sheep. Since a standard two-decked railroad stock car (with an effective capacity of 2,670 cubic feet) can carry about 240 sheep, only 146 stock cars would be needed to carry 35,000 animals of this average size. But the ark had a carrying capacity equivalent to that of 522 stock cars; so it is obvious that it was entirely adequate for its God-intended purpose (see John C. Whitcomb, Jr., and Henry M. Morris, *The Genesis Flood*, pp. 65-70).

When fully laden with its cargo (Gen 6:21), the ark sank into the water 15 cubits, or one-half its height. This seems to be the implication of Gen 7:20 ("fifteen cubits upward did the waters prevail"), for if the Flood had not covered the mountains by at least 15 cubits, the ark could not have floated over them. On the same day that the waters began to assuage (exactly 150 days after the Flood began), the ark rested on the highest peak of the mountains of Ararat (Gen 8:4); but an additional 221 days elapsed before Noah was permitted to disembark (8:14-16).

Concerning the subsequent history of the ark, Scripture is silent. In spite of rumors to the contrary, it is doubtful that its remains will ever be discovered. Sufficient for the Christian is the testimony of God's Word that such a structure once existed and that for more than a year it served as the only refuge for the human race and air-breathing animals in the judgment of a universal deluge. *See* Ararat.

Bibliography. Alexander Heidel, *The Gilgamesh Epic and Old Testament Parallels,* 2nd ed., Chicago: Univ. of Chicago Press, 1949. John C. Whitcomb, Jr., and Henry M. Morris, *The Genesis Flood: The Biblical Record and Its Scientific Implications,* Philadelphia: Presbyterian and Reformed, 1961.

J. C. W.

The traditional spot where Moses was rescued from the Nile. HFV

ARK OF BULRUSHES. When the mother of Moses could no longer hide the baby Moses, she placed him in an ark made of rushes or papyrus reeds caulked with pitch (Ex 2:3), to avoid killing the child in accord with Pharaoh's cruel decree (Ex 1:22). Bulrushes *(q.v.)* of this type were plentiful on the shores of the Nile River. There is no support that Moses' mother used papyrus reeds for the small basket because she was following an ancient belief that such rushes were effective in warding off crocodile attacks.

ARK OF THE COVENANT. This was a chest made of acacia wood, about four feet long, two and a half feet wide, and two and a half feet high. It was overlaid with gold inside and out (Ex 25:11) and had a ring of gold at each corner or foot through which poles were passed to carry it. The lid of the ark, the *kappōreth* or "mercy seat" (Ex 25:17), was made of pure gold. At each end of the mercy seat was a cherubim made of hammered gold.

The ark *('ārôn)* is referred to some 200 times in the OT under 22 different designations. It is called the ark (Ex 25:14), the ark of Jehovah (I Sam 4:6, ASV), the ark of God (Elohim, I Sam 4:18), the ark of the covenant (Josh 3:6), the ark of the testimony (Ex 25:22). This various terminology for the ark may reflect a difference in date and authorship of the various sources, but this is not necessarily so.

The ark seems to have served various functions during its history. It was built by Moses (Deut 10:5), or actually by Bezaleel (Ex 31:2, 6-7; 37:1-9), at Sinai. According to Num 10:33-36 it served as a guide to Israel in the wilderness, and Num 14:44 adds that when the rebels at Kadesh-barnea went out to possess the Promised Land, neither Moses nor the ark went with them. In these passages the ark serves as a symbol of the presence of God. The ark is spoken of as the throne of God (I Sam 4:4; II Sam 6:2; cf. Jer 3:16).

The idea of the ark as a war palladium is a

very common one in the OT. The ark was very prominent in the story of the capture of Jericho (Josh 6-7), and in the struggle with the Philistines when the ark was captured (I Sam 4:11), at which time it is said that "the glory is departed from Israel" (I Sam 4:21). Even in defeat God did not abandon His throne on the ark but wrought havoc among the Philistine captors. The power of the ark can be seen in the curses it brought upon the Philistines (I Sam 5) and upon Uzzah (II Sam 6:7). G. Henton Davies has argued that the ark may be mentioned a number of times in the Psalms under the term *'ōz*, "strength" (cf. "The Ark in the Psalms," *Promise and Fulfillment*, F. F. Bruce, ed.; also cf. Ps 132:8; 78:59-61; 105:4).

One other function of the ark was to serve as the container of the tablets of the law or covenant. This concept is reflected in the name "the ark of the testimony" (Ex 25:16; Num 4:5; Josh 4:16).

When the ark was returned from the Philistines, it came to Beth-shemesh *(q.v.)* and then was removed to the house of Abinadab in Kirjath-jearim where it stayed for approximately 20 years (I Sam 7:2). Although the ark was now in Israel, it was probably, in effect, still under the control of the Philistines. This fact would explain why Saul had nothing to do with the ark and why "all the house of Israel lamented after the Lord" (I Sam 7:2).

When David came to the throne he set out to make Jerusalem the political and religious capital of all Israel. In doing so he brought the ark to Jerusalem and made it the center of worship (II Sam 6; Ps 132). Solomon built his temple to house the ark (I Kgs 6:19; 8:1-9). From this time on the historical books seldom mention the ark (cf. II Chr 35:3). It is very probable, however, that it was used in some of the great religious festivals in Jerusalem during the monarchy. At least four psalms (24, 68, 118, 132) reflect a cultic procession around Jerusalem probably during one of the major festivals, at which time the ark may have been carried in front by the priests (cf. Ps 68:24-25; 118:26-27; 24:7-10; 132:8-9).

The final fate of the ark is a mystery. A reference to it in Jer 3:16 seems to suggest that it would be destroyed or captured (by the Babylonians in 586 B.C.). The prophet was saying that in the latter days the ark (as the throne of God) would not be missed, or come to mind, or be made again, because Jerusalem shall be called the throne of God. There is an apocryphal tradition found in II Esd 10:22; II Macc 2:4-5 which claims that Jeremiah hid the ark along with the tent and the altar of incense in a cave on Mount Nebo before Jerusalem was destroyed. George Adam Smith says, "This was a most unlikely thing for him to do" (*Jerusalem*, Vol. 2, footnote 4, p. 256).

The ark was the visible symbol of the presence of God. It had served a real need in the early days of Israel's history. But when the danger arose that it might become a fetish in Israel, God allowed it to be captured and destroyed.

See Tabernacle.

Bibliography. Frank M. Cross, Jr., "The Priestly Tabernacle," *The Biblical Archaeologist Reader*, ed. by G. Ernest Wright and David Noel Freedman, Anchor Books, Vol. I, Garden City: Doubleday, 1961. G. Henton Davies, "The Ark of the Covenant," IDB, I, 222-226. Roland de Vaux, *Ancient Israel*, trans. by John McHugh, New York: McGraw-Hill, 1961, pp. 297-301. Walther Eichrodt, *Theology of the Old Testament*, trans. by J. A. Baker, Philadelphia: Westminster, I (1961), 107-112. Gerhard von Rad, "The Tent and the Ark," *The Problem of the Hexateuch and Other Essays*, trans. by E. W. Trueman Dicken, Edinburgh: Oliver & Boyd, 1966, pp. 103-130. Marten H. Woudstra, *The Ark of the Covenant*, Philadelphia: Presbyterian and Reformed, 1965.

R. L. S.

The Plain of Armageddon or Jezreel. IIS

ARKITES (är'kīts). A tribe descended from Canaan (Gen 10:17; I Chr 1:15). The present site, Tell 'Arqah, is located in Syria along the coast N of Tripoli. The city is mentioned in several Egyptian records from the 19th to the 14th cen. B.C., as well as by Tiglath-pileser III of Assyria (ANET, p. 283).

ARM. As a noun it is used mostly in a poetic sense in the Bible to symbolize strength or power. The "outstretched arm of God" refers to His providential care (Ex 6:6; Deut 4:34; 9:29; Ps 89:10; Isa 51:9; *et al.*). The breaking of an arm means the loss of power or health (Job 31:22; Ps 10:15; Jer 48:25; *et al.*). Although frequent in the OT, it appears but three times in the NT and in each case in imitation of OT usage of the arm of the Lord (Lk 1:51; Jn 12:38; Acts 13:17).

ARMAGEDDON (är-mȧ-gĕd'ŭn). A Heb. name used only in Rev 16:16 for the gathering place for the "battle of that great day of God Almighty" associated with Christ's second coming (Rev 16:14-15). It is usually interpreted as Mount (Heb. *har*) Megiddo. The pass of Megiddo leads through the Carmel range and has been the scene of many famous battles.

It is possible that the Revelation uses Megiddo as a type of bloody conflict as it uses Sodom as a type of sinful Jerusalem (Rev 11:8). Since the eschatological battle (Zech 14:2 and elsewhere) is at Jerusalem, some have identified Armageddon with Jerusalem. But the verse may merely mean that Megiddo *(q.v.)* will be the bivouac area for the great conflict. It is important to note that Rev 16:13-16 only announces the battle. The actual conquest of the three evil powers by Christ in His coming is given in the succeeding section, Rev 19:11–20:3, which describes in detail the battle of the great day of God Almighty.

R. L. H.

ARMENIA (är-mē'nĭ-ȧ). The KJV translation of Ararat *(q.v.),* following the LXX in II Kgs 19:37; Isa 37:38. A later name for Ararat, it first occurs as Armina in the inscriptions of Darius I at Behistun. The Assyrians had used Urartu.

Armenia centered about Lake Van and the Araxes Valley. Traditionally, Mount Ararat has been located in the mountains of Armenia. The Araxes Valley linked the Iranian plateau with the plateau of Asia Minor, and served as the sanctuary for oppressed people from the S.

The Urartian kingdom flourished in the 9th and 8th cen. B.C. It was very rich in mineral resources, with fertile plains along its deep river valleys. After Assyria regained her might under Tiglath-pileser III, the Assyrian kings frequently pillaged Urartu and took thousands of captives. See T. Özgüc, "Urartu and Altintepe," *Archaeology,* XXII (1969), 256-263.

The Medes conquered Urartu early in the 6th cen. B.C. A people with an Indo-European language moved into the plateau and blended with the natives. These newcomers seem to have belonged to the Thraco-Phrygians of Asia Minor.

The Seleucids took over from Persia, but Armenia revolted in 190 B.C. Artaxias founded Armenia, which was strongest under Tigranes I (96-55 B.C.). He was defeated, however, by the Romans in 69 B.C. and surrendered to Pompey (66 B.C.), giving up Syria which he had ruled for over 14 years. In A.D. 303 Tiridates III was converted to Christianity, which became the state religion.

G. H. L.

ARMINIANISM. Arminianism is that form of Protestant theology which bears at least some resemblance to the teachings of James Arminius (1560-1609). In its authentic form it refers especially to the doctrine that predestination is conditioned upon man's free response to grace—as taught by Arminius, the Remonstrants, John Wesley, and conservative evangelicals of this century, such as the late H. Orton Wiley (see his three-volume *Christian Theology,* 1940-46). In its unauthentic form, it has come to be associated with Socinian, Unitarian, Universalist, Latitudinarian, and other liberal theologies, which carried to extremes certain germinal persuasions of Arminius, especially his tolerance and his emphasis upon human freedom. Lambertus Jacobus van Holl, referring to these unauthentic developments, speaks of "the increasing involvement of Arminianism in liberal theology" ("From Arminius to Arminianism in Dutch Theology," *Man's Faith and Freedom,* p. 27).

Antecedents of Arminianism

Arminius did not originate what is called Arminianism, but was simply its ablest exponent. Just before he became associated with such teachings as conditional predestination, a whole array of scholars were either tending in that direction or teaching that doctrine.

Well known is the fact that the erudite Erasmus taught human freedom, as opposed to Luther's Augustinian view, although Erasmus was humanistic and therefore quite unlike the later Arminius.

Melanchthon seems to have gravitated in the direction of conditional predestination (see Caspar Brandt, *The Life of James Arminius,* pp. 32-34).

Anabaptists, later better known as Mennonites, taught that the provision for salvation is universal and that men cast the deciding vote on whether they will be damned or redeemed.

While Zwingli and Calvin taught unconditional predestination, their view was by no means held universally even in their own Switzerland. At Zurich, the distinguished Bullinger questioned for a time Calvin's teaching; and Jerome Bolsec of Geneva opposed the view, as did Charles Perrot of Geneva.

In Holland, a few decades before the Synod of Dort (1618-19), most ministers tended to conditional predestination. Theodore Beza, Calvin's son-in-law and successor at the Geneva Academy where so many ministers were trained for the Reformed churches, came to expect that many of the students from the Low Countries would be conditionalists—although he himself was a supralapsarian, i.e., one who believed that the decree to elect some individuals and to damn others was made prior to Adam's creation and fall.

At the newly founded university at Leyden in Holland, most of the teachers were "Arminian" during the six years Arminius studied there (1775-1781). Nor had the Belgic Confession and the Heidelberg Catechism, the two main creeds for the Reformed churches prior to the Canons of Dort, taught unconditional predestination—unless it was by implication. Arminius was quite sure that they had not clearly taught that doctrine.

In England, in 1595, William Barrett was denied the B.D. degree at Cambridge because he rejected the Calvinistic views of Cambridge's William Perkins. At about this time, theologian Peter Baro was deposed from his position at Cambridge for the same reason (see Carl Bangs, "Arminius and the Reformation," *Church History,* June, 1961, p. 7).

But of all these, Arminius was distinctly the ablest. "Of all the actors in that movement [the recoil from Calvinism], so fertile of mighty actors, no one played a more conspicuous, important, and trying part than Arminius" (John Guthrie, "Translator's Preface," *The Life of James Arminius,* by Caspar Brandt, p. XIV).

Arminius' Teachings

Arminius' "Declaration of Sentiments" (see *The Writings of James Arminius,* I, 193), delivered by him before the governmental authorities at The Hague in 1608, spells out his own views and gives 20 arguments against the supralapsarianism of Leyden University's Francis Gomarus. Arminius' arguments condensed say that the doctrine is unsound because it makes God the author of sin.

It is in this treatise, too, that Arminius presents his distinctive doctrine of the divine decrees. Whereas the supralapsarians taught that the decree to save and to damn certain individuals preceded the decree to create them, Arminius taught that the first decree was to send Christ to redeem sinful men; the second was to receive into favor those who repent and believe; the third was to help all men to do this repenting and believing (prevenient grace); and the fourth was to save and damn individuals according to God's foreknowledge of the way in which they would freely respond to His offer of grace.

Important to an understanding of Arminius' teachings, too, is his view of human freedom. He was not a Pelagian in this regard, although he was so accused even in his own lifetime. Unlike the ancient Pelagius, he believed in a racial fall caused by Adam's sin; and while he believed that "the power of willing" was retained in men after the Fall, he believed that it is not possible for fallen men, unaided by prevenient grace, to exercise that capacity of freedom toward any good thing. Of fallen, natural man, Arminius wrote: "In this state, the free will of man toward the true good is not only wounded, maimed, infirm, bent, and weakened; but it is also imprisoned, destroyed, and lost. And its powers are not only debilitated and useless unless they be assisted by grace, but it has no powers whatever except such as are excited by divine grace. For Christ has said, 'Without me ye can do nothing' " (*The Writings of Arminius,* ed. by Nichols, I, 526).

He also wrote: "The mind, in this state, is dark, destitute of the saving knowledge of God, and, according to the apostle, incapable of those things which belong to the Spirit of God. For 'the animal man has no perception of the things of the Spirit of God' (I Cor 2:14)" *(ibid.).* Hear him also say: "Exactly correspondent to this darkness of the mind, and perverseness of the heart, is the utter weakness of all the powers to perform that which is truly good, and to omit the perpetration of that which is evil" (*ibid.,* p. 527). In support, he quotes Christ: "A corrupt tree cannot bring forth good fruit" (Mt 7:18), and "how can ye, being evil, speak good things?" (Mt 12:34). Among other supports, he also mentions Jn 6:44: "No man can come to me, except the Father draw him." After quoting Jn 8:36, that only those are free "whom the Son hath made free," he says: "It follows, that our will is not free from the first fall; that is, it is not free to good, unless it be made free by the Son through his Spirit" (*ibid.,* p. 528).

It has often been supposed that Arminius held the doctrine of entire sanctification, or Christian perfection (see this error in *Man's Faith and Freedom,* pp. 66–79). But Arminius did not teach this doctrine. It is true that at times he seemed to suggest the Wesleyan teaching. Of sanctification he says that it is for believers only, that it is an act, that it is received by faith (*Works,* II, 120). He even says that it is "the purification from sin" (*ibid.,* p. 121). Yet he withdrew such suggestions of a Wesleyan understanding right within such passages, saying, e.g., "This sanctification is not completed in a single moment; but sin . . . is weakened more and more . . ." (*ibid.*). He also wrote, "Who can deny, when the Scriptures affirm, that there are in us the remains of sin and of the old man as long as we survive in this mortal life" (II, p. 263).

Arminius tried to make theology really biblical. He felt that Stoic philosophy instead of the Bible was the basis of Augustine's doctrine of unconditional predestination; for the Stoics taught that there is a law of necessity written into the very nature of existence, to which law both God and men are subject. Arminius felt also that the creeds often become more authoritative than Scripture, and he believed that both the Belgic Confession and the Heidelberg Catechism should be interpreted, and perhaps corrected, by the Bible.

Arminius was also irenic. He was a peace-loving man who called not for rigid uniformity of belief but for tolerance. It is ironic that during his last years and just after his death the people of Holland took sides so heatedly on the matter of predestination that some wondered if the issue might give rise to a civil war.

Arminius followed practical interests instead of the merely speculative. He wrote, "For the theology which belongs to this world is practical . . . . Theoretical theology belongs to the other world . . . . For this reason, we must clothe the object of our theology in such a manner as may enable it to incline us to worship God, and fully to persuade and win us over to that practice" (*Writings,* I, 60).

For centuries it was generally thought that Arminius had earlier been a supralapsarian Calvinist, and that he had switched to the espousal of conditional predestination. Supposedly this change took place after he had been asked to support supralapsarianism against the type of conditional predestination which the Dutch humanist Richard Coornhert was advocating, and against the sublapsarianism of certain ministers of the town of Delft—sublapsarianism being the view that God's decree to save or damn certain individuals was made after the free sin and fall of Adam. Peter Bertius had stated that Arminius changed from supralapsarianism to conditional predestination. Bertius made this claim in a funeral oration at the time of Arminius' death, and the statement seems to have influenced those who have written about Arminius ever since.

While the matter has not been resolved, Carl Bangs, the principal authority on Arminius of the present time, has made an interesting case for the theory that Arminius was a conditionalist right through the years, and did not earlier espouse supralapsarianism (see Carl O. Bangs, *Arminius and Reformed Theology,* Univ. of Chicago Library, 1958). Bangs mentions the fact that the only primary evidence contrariwise is the statement of Bertius, but that Bertius had not been so close to Arminius as some have supposed. Bangs also says that Beza expected his Dutch students to be conditionalists, and thus did not clash with Arminius, but instead recommended him highly on the completion of his studies. As to why Arminius was asked to support supralapsarianism, Bangs points out that, (1) another person, Martin Lydius, had first been asked, who in turn asked Arminius; and that (2) perhaps the request for Arminius to do this was designed to drive him out into the open with his conditionalism. One factor which this does not explain, however, is why Arminius should have accepted such an assignment, if indeed he was already an opponent of supralapsarianism.

Arminianism in Holland

In 1610, the year after Arminius' death, 42 ministers and two educators met at The Hague and drew up and signed a statement which in general concurred with what Arminius had taught. Written by John Uytenbogaert, Arminius' close friend from student days at Geneva onward, it came to be called the *Remonstrance,* and its signers, the Remonstrants. This document, addressed to the government of Holland, enumerated five doctrines held by Uytenbogaert and his associates, and was designed to gain official permission for the promulgation of those doctrines in Holland's Reformed churches.

The *Remonstrance* discusses certain problems and also outlines five doctrinal differences between Calvinism and what was soon called Arminianism. In the first part of the document, the Remonstrants treated the place of confessions in the church, and stated that they are helpful, but that they may be changed at any time, and that only the Holy Scriptures are authoritative.

An interesting statement in the first part of the document, also, is its view that secular authorities have the right to enter into theological disputes in order to preserve peace and prevent schisms. The Remonstrants probably figured that secular authorities would be more tolerant and more objective as arbiters of theological disputes than ecclesiastical authorities would be. Aside from the matter of whether this would give the state the right to dominate the church, it was a stance on the part of the Remonstrants which, if followed in the upcoming years in Holland, might well have guaranteed for Arminianism an official status. As it turned out, an ecclesiastical "court" was later called (1618–19) which outlawed Arminianism.

The second part of the *Remonstrance* rejects the five articles of Calvinism and sets forth the five opposing positions of the Remonstrants. The first of the five, summarized, is what might be called conditional predestination: that God purposes to save those who repent and believe, and to damn those who do not.

The second main point of the Remonstrant position is that Christ died "for all men and for every man," and not simply for a segment of the race who had been previously destined for salvation (see Philip Schaff, *The Creeds of Christendom,* III, 545 ff.).

The third point has to do with what can be called prevenient grace—God's purpose to help sinful men to turn to God.

The fourth point is that this grace may be resisted, and is not, as the Calvinists were saying, irresistibly received.

The fifth and last point is that, having become "incorporated into Christ by true faith," Christ "keeps them from falling" only if they continue to believe. But while the Remonstrants are cautious on the matter, they imply that if a saved person does not continue to cooperate with Christ he will become "devoid of (saving) grace."

When the *Remonstrance* was published, the Calvinist party issued a Counter-Remonstrance in which they answered it.

Arminianism Outlawed in Holland

Holland was now divided. In 1610 and 1612 conferences were held to help heal the dispute, but were not successful. In 1614 the government forbade pulpit discussion of the disputed doctrines. Then in 1617 Prince Maurice, who wanted the dispute decided in favor of Calvinism, called for a national synod to meet at Dort the following year. According to the Memoirs of Simon Episcopius, this prince was enlisted by the Calvinists on their side of the controversy against the great statesman van Olden Barnevelt. Maurice was jealous and afraid of him, and saw in the religious dispute an opportunity to unite the provinces under his control.

It was decided to make the meeting at Dort a national synod for the United Netherlands, composed of six delegates from each of the seven provinces. These delegates were to be chosen by provincial synods; and because of certain maneuverings, even from the provinces of Holland and Utrecht, where the Arminians were in the majority, almost all the delegates were Calvinists. Indeed, in all there were only three Arminians among the 42 official delegates; and in addition to the official ones, 33 foreign delegates were invited as guests, all of them Calvinists. Besides all this, the three Arminian members were prevented by the rules from defending Arminianism, and they quit the sessions before taking the "Calvinistic" oath as delegates. While Arminian spokesmen were permitted on a few occasions to answer the charges made against them, there was no open debate on the merits of the two theologies.

This synod condemned Arminianism as heresy, and forbade its propagation in the Low Countries – in the seven states, that is, of the 17 states which comprised the entire Low Countries, the seven being officially called the United Netherlands, or the Dutch Republic. The synod's sessions concluded in May, 1619, having begun in November, 1618. In July, 1619, the synod's *Sentence* was approved by the government, and the Arminian leaders were ordered banished or imprisoned. It was illegal to hold Remonstrant meetings, or to support or harbor any of their ministers. Spies were hired to report the leaders if any of them returned to their families for visits. Some 18,000 became martyrs, slaughtered by hired mercenaries of the contra-Remonstrant party.

In spite of all these deterrents to their faith, the Remonstrants often met together; and survived, even if they did not flourish. In 1619 they set up an organization called the Remonstrant Reformed Brotherhood, led by John Uytenbogaert, Simon Episcopius (a pupil of Arminius), and one Grevinchovius. When Prince Maurice died in 1623, the ban against the Remonstrants was lifted. They organized the Remonstrant Reformed Church Community, which still exists as the Remonstrant Brotherhood. In 1634 they started a theological college at Amsterdam with Episcopius as its head and as its first professor of theology. The college still exists as a part of the University of Leyden (see G. O. McCulloh, ed., *Man's Faith and Freedom,* 1962, pp. 5–7).

Outside of Holland

Arminius and Arminians in general have made frequent mention of the fact that both the Greek and the Latin Fathers prior to Augustine (354–430) had been conditionalists. Already it has been mentioned that the Mennonites, who flourished in Germany, were Arminians.

The Moravians, who moved to Count Zinzendorf's large estates at Herrnhut in Germany and who went forth from there as missionaries to many world areas, were Arminian. Their belief that anyone may be saved, thrust them into extensive and committed missionary work at a time when not many Christians were similarly motivated. It was through their work in America and England that their Peter Böhler met John Wesley in London and helped him to experience the strangely warmed heart.

In England, there were some conditional predestinationists prior to Arminius' espousal of that doctrine with disputations and publications. Peter Baro, at Cambridge, has already been mentioned. His successor (1608), John Playfere, lectured and published on free will and redemption as possible for all men. So did Archbishop Laud early in the 17th cen., although he went to Pelagian extremes, denying original sin (see John Fletcher, *Works,* II, 276, 277).

The Quakers, mystical and not doctrinal in their interests, and therefore "Arminians without Arminius," nonetheless taught basically what Arminius did – that anyone may be saved.

John Goodwin taught Arminianism in England in the middle of the 17th cen., and directly influenced Wesley in that direction (see William Strickland's Ph.D. dissertation on Goodwin, Vanderbilt University, 1967). Jeremy Taylor and William Law also taught Arminianism and likewise helped to mold the founder of Methodism.

Many English divines prior to the time of John Wesley (1703–1791) taught an aberrant Arminianism. Pelagian, Socinian, Arian, Universalist, and Latitudinarian impurities were introduced into the Arminian opposition to Calvinism. This is why John Wesley wrote, "To say, 'This man is an Arminian,' has the same effect on many hearers as to say, 'This is a mad dog.' It puts them into a fright at once . . ." ("The Question, 'What Is an Arminian?' Answered," *The Works of John Wesley,* X, 358). Yet when Wesley started a periodical in 1778, he was brave enough to call it *The Arminian Magazine*.

Actually, in England, and in Wales as well, there were and are two wings of the Arminian movement. Geoffrey Nuttall, in a paper presented in 1960 in Holland at the four hundredth anniversary of Arminius' birth, says: "Self-confessed Arminianism in England is to be found, in the main, in one or the other of two contrasting movements. One of these two movements leads into Arianism, Socinianism, and Unitarianism, and eventually decreases in numbers and influence. The other remains Trinitarian and evangelical, and increases" ("The Influence of Arminianism in England," *Man's Faith and Freedom,* ed. by G. O. McCulloh, 1962, p. 50). Nuttall actually traces the "unauthentic" wing in the records of local congregations in Wales and England, and supports by first-hand historical study his statement that the unauthentic wing tends to decrease in numbers.

It would not take such a study to prove that the other wing, Wesleyan Arminianism, "Arminianism on fire," has tended to increase in numbers and influence. So effective, in fact, is the influence of Wesleyan Arminianism that university students in England, a few years ago, found themselves writing an examination on the topic "Since Wesley We Are All Arminians."

Methodism is the movement through which Arminianism was most widely disseminated in America. With the word that anyone may be saved, Methodist circuit riders, lay and ordained, spread the doctrine of conditional predestination as America's frontier moved westward. Thus Methodism became the largest Protestant denomination in the United States, being overtaken by the Southern Baptists only in the 1950's.

Besides being promulgated in America by Methodism, authentic Arminianism has been taught in this country by the United Brethren, the Salvation Army, many Wesleyan denominations including the Church of the Nazarene, and by numerous other groups.

The Present Situation

Arminianism and Calvinism are not now so far apart as they were, say, during the first half of the 20th cen.

On the Arminian side, even within its Wesleyan strain, i.e., "Arminianism on fire," Pelagian tendencies had developed. John Miley, who taught at Methodism's Drew Theological Seminary during the latter years of the 19th cen., opposed the representative theory of original sin's "transmission," which theory both Arminius and Wesley had espoused, and taught a so-called genetic mode view: that original sin is received from one's parents (see his *Systematic Theology,* II, 506). In addition, Miley taught that no racial guilt resulted from Adam's sin, whereas Arminius and Wesley had taught that guilt as well as depravity accrued to the race, but that the guilt was removed by Christ's atonement as a "free gift" (Rom 5:16-17) for the entire race (cf. Robert E. Chiles, *Theological Transition in American Methodism 1790-1935,* 1965).

Besides Miley, who was studied widely by Wesleyans, Olin Alfred Curtis, his successor at Drew, also tended in a Pelagian direction, away from an emphasis upon grace and toward an overemphasis upon free will. His major work, *The Christian Faith* (1905; reprinted by Kregel in 1956), was probably the most widely used theology textbook in Wesleyan-Arminian circles prior to the publication of H. Orton Wiley's three-volume *Christian Theology* (1940-46). Curtis is Kantian in that volume when he says, "Deeds are moral . . . only when they express a man's own conception of duty . . ." (p. 61). So Kantian is Curtis that he cannot let God's grace come through unconditionally to infants who die. He has them accepting Christ for themselves in the intermediate state. Says he, "In the intermediate state all these children come to full personal experience just as surely as our children do in this life" (p. 404). For Curtis, man is so free that "any motive in the conscious range can be selected . . ." (p. 44).

Also Pelagian in tendency were Boston University's E. S. Brightman and A. C. Knudson. Brightman's *A Philosophy of Religion* (1940) shows this, as well as others of his works. Knudson defined freedom as the power of "contrary choice" (*The Principles of Christian Ethics,* p. 82). He could say that, apart from grace, men can choose contrariwise, because, for him, the Fall is "legendary" (p. 94).

Such men as Miley and Curtis, Brightman and Knudson were mentors to many Wesleyan-Arminians and influenced them in a Pelagian direction.

What Arminius taught on freedom has been shown. John Wesley was in basic agreement with Arminius on freedom. Like Arminius, he taught that man casts the deciding vote whether he will be saved or damned. But for Wesley, as for the earlier "freedomist," man does not, cannot, of himself, cast an assenting vote. Speaking of John Fletcher and himself, Wesley says that they "absolutely deny natural free will" (see Burtner and Chiles' *Compend of Wesley's Theology,* pp. 132-133). Wesley continues, "We both steadily assert that the will of fallen man is by nature free only to evil" *(ibid.).*

Believing that to deny original sin is to be a heathen, Wesley held a view of the racial fall which is a bit extreme. He taught that all men are " 'conceived in sin,' that hence there is in every man a 'carnal mind,' which is enmity against God; which is not, cannot be, 'subject to' His 'law'; and which so infects the whole soul that 'there dwelleth in' him, 'in his flesh,' in his natural state, 'no good thing'; but 'every imagination of the thoughts of his heart is evil,' only evil, and that 'continually' " (*Standard Sermons,* II, 223). Wesley even figures that every descendant of Adam is ". . . dead to God, wholly dead in sin; entirely void of life of God; void of the image of God" (*Works,* ed. by Emory, 401).

If man is not "void" of the image of God, the image is at least utterly defaced. This is why Arminian-Wesleyans agree with Wesley that "salvation begins with what is termed (and very properly) preventing grace; including the first wish to please God, the first dawn of light concerning his will, the first slight transient conviction of having sinned against him" (*ibid.,* VI, 509).

Within the past decade or two, within "Arminianism on fire," Pelagian tendencies have waned and authentic Wesleyan-Arminianism has exerted itself. This is in part because of the widespread use of the late H. Orton Wiley's *Christian Theology,* which is admittedly more idealistic in places than Arminius and Wesley were (e.g., I, 255-319), but which nonetheless is basically Arminian in the authentic sense. It is in part because of a revival of first-hand study of Arminius and Wesley. The waning of purely philosophical interests and the resurgence of biblical engagement have figured most importantly in this return to the persuasions of Arminius and Wesley. For proof of such a return, see *The Word and the Doctrine*, a composite volume issued in 1965 by the National Holiness Association, containing 37 papers given at a 1964 national conference on Wesleyan-Arminian theological distinctives.

At the same time, Calvinism is tending to become less Calvinistic. Not many prominent Calvinists at present espouse the supralapsarianism of Theodore Beza and Francis Gomarus of Arminius' time, nor even the sublapsarianism of the Synod of Dort. Nor do such scholars, by and large, teach the unconditional predestination contained in the Westminster Confession. Those of the Christian Reformed Church (Calvin Seminary) still do, along with distinguished scholars at Westminster Theological Seminary. But several Calvinist scholars connected in recent years with Fuller Theological Seminary, for example, write quite as evangelical Arminians might. *Christianity Today,* by far the most widely disseminated and influential evangelical magazine for ministers in our time, is not at all rigidly Calvinistic. Many such persons now teach that anyone may be saved; but in general they do still teach the unconditional security of believers—eternal security. Yet it is an interesting fact that Robert Shank, in his *Life in the Son,* 1960, a Baptist, has tended to undermine even the doctrine of eternal security.

It may be that in the future there will be still more of a convergence of the Arminian and Calvinistic theologies, as the vain philosophies of men wane in their influence and as evangelicals are taught more and more by Holy Scripture.

Bibliography. James Arminius, *The Writings of James Arminius,* trans. by James Nichols and W. R. Bagnall, Grand Rapids: Baker, I–III, 1956. Carl Bangs, *Arminius and Reformed Theology,* Ph.D. dissertation, Dept. of Photoduplication, Univ. of Chicago Library, 1958; "James Arminius and the Remonstrants," unpublished B.D. thesis, Nazarene Theological Seminary, 1949. E. S. Brightman, *A Philosophy of Religion,* New York: Prentice-Hall, 1940. Edward John Carnell, *The Kingdom of Love and the Pride of Life,* Grand Rapids: Eerdmans, 1961. Robert E. Chiles, *Theological Transition in American Methodism 1790–1935,* New York: Abingdon, 1965. George L. Curtiss, *Arminianism in History,* New York: Hunt and Eaton, 1894. Simon Episcopius, *Memoirs of Simon Episcopius,* ed. by Calder Frederick, London: Simpkin and Marshall, 1835. J. Kenneth Geiger, ed., *The Word and the Doctrine,* Kansas City: Beacon Hill Press, 1965. John Guthrie, *The Life of James Arminius,* Nashville: Stevenson and F. A. Owen, 1857. A. C. Knudson, *The Principles of Christian Ethics,* New York: Abingdon-Cokesbury, 1943. Gerald O. McCulloh, ed., *Man's Faith and Freedom,* New York: Abingdon, 1962. O. Glenn McKinley, *Where Two Creeds Meet,* Kansas City: Beacon Hill Press, 1959. John Miley, *Systematic Theology,* New York: Eaton and Mains, 1894. Robert Shank, *Life in the Son: A Study in the Doctrine of Perseverance,* Springfield, Mo.: Westcott Publishers, 1960. Wm. Fairfield Warren, *In the Footsteps of Arminius,* New York: Phillips and Hunt, 1888. H. Orton Wiley, *Christian Theology,* Kansas City: Beacon Hill Press, 1940–46. Mildred Bangs Wynkoop, *Foundations of Wesleyan-Arminian Theology,* Kansas City: Beacon Hill Press, 1967.

J. K. G.

Armlets and bracelets adorn this mythical figure at the Assyrian palace of Nimrud. LM

ARMLET. A ring or band usually of metal worn on the upper arm, as distinguished from a bracelet, worn on the wrist. It was an ornament or status symbol and could be worn by either men or women (Ex 35:22). Armlets were counted as spoils of war (Num 31:50). King Saul wore one (II Sam 1:10), but later Isaiah condemned them as frivolous (Isa 3:19).

ARMONI (är-mō'nī). A son of King Saul and his concubine Rizpah. David delivered him along with others of Saul's family to the Gibeonites to be hanged, to avenge Saul's slaughter of the Gibeonites (II Sam 21:8–9).

ARMOR, ARMS. Various kinds of weapons are mentioned frequently in the Bible, both literally and figuratively (as illustrative of spiritual warfare). Yet little detailed description is given of the many different weapons. However, it is known that the weapons of the nations of the Near East were essentially the same, with certain modifications and variations. Representations in sculpture of the weapons of the Assyrians, Chaldeans, Egyptians and Hittites on their ancient monuments greatly assist us in knowing more definitely what the battle pieces of the Hebrews were like.

Offensive Weapons

The rod or staff was the simplest implement, which might have been weighted on one end with a stone or copper mace-head like a club. It could be quite a threatening weapon, whether used in self-defense or in attack of an enemy (Prov 25:18, "maul," KJV; "war club," RSV). It was either carried in the hand or attached to the wrist by a loop. *See* Rod; Staff.

The sling was another simple instrument among the most ancient devices of warfare (Job 41:28), used commonly by shepherds to drive off animals attempting to attack or molest their flocks or to turn straying sheep. *See* Sling. The sling was usually made from a strip of leather, although sometimes it was woven into a belt from rushes, hair, or animal sinews, which widened to about two inches in the middle and formed a hollow in which a smooth object was placed. After being swung several times around the head with great force, one of the strings of the sling was released to discharge the missile. Both smooth stones and pellets of lead were used, carried in a bag or piled at the feet of the soldier. They could be hurled as far as six hundred feet!

Slingers formed a part of the regular army and at times certain nations employed large numbers of slingers in their armies as part of the light infantry, together with the archers. It will be remembered that this was the weapon used by David to kill the giant Goliath (I Sam 17:40–50). The chosen 700 left-handed Benjamites were noted for their skill and accuracy with the sling (Jud 20:16).

The bow and arrow constituted a very important weapon of war, as well as for hunting, and is thought to have been the principal weapon of offense. Evidence indicates its early use among the Hebrews (Gen 21:20; 27:3; 48:22). Use was not limited to common soldiers, but captains high in rank and even kings' sons employed the bow and arrow and were skilled in its use (II Kgs 9:24; I Sam 18:4). The tribe of Benjamin seems to have been particularly expert in archery (I Chr 8:40; 12:2; II Chr 14:8; 17:17). *See* Bow and Arrow; Archer.

Bows were made of flexible seasoned wood, copper, or bronze, and ranged greatly in size and style. The string was made from bindweed, natural cord, hide, or the intestines of animals. The bow was strung by hand, usually bending it with the foot since it required much strength. Arrows, constructed from reed or light wood, were tipped with sharp stone, bronze, and iron, and were often poisoned and provided with barbs. They were about 30 inches long and winged with three rows of feathers. In times of siege they were dipped in pitch, wound with flax or hemp, and ignited to start fires. The quiver in which arrows were kept was carried on the soldier's back, at his side, or fastened to a chariot. Archers on foot and mounted comprised a formidable element of the fighting forces.

A Persian panel showing spearmen of the guard from the palace at Susa. LM

The spear, javelin, or lance had a wooden shaft of varying lengths and weight with a metal point or head made from brass or iron, usually with a double edge. Infantry spears were shorter (about the height of a man) than those of the cavalry. Javelins were generally lighter and shorter than spears. When not in use these weapons were carried across the soldiers' backs (I Sam 17:6, RSV). They were employed by the heavy-armed troops and were used both for thrusting and throwing. Stuck in the ground in front of a tent, a spear indicated the quarters of a king (cf. I Sam 26:7). It was the heavier spear, *ḥănît,* Saul's favorite weapon, that he hurled at David (I Sam 18:11; 19:10) and later at Jonathan (I Sam 20:33), and not a javelin as KJV translates. There also existed a lighter missile called a dart, but little is known about it.

The sword or dagger (Heb. *ḥereb*) is the most frequently mentioned weapon in the Bible, being used both for offense and defense. The blade was constructed of iron or bronze and varied greatly in length, weight, and style, usually being two-edged. It normally hung on the left side from a girdle, housed in a sheath. Often the hilt was highly ornamented, especially those

An Assyrian archer draws his bow. From the palace of Ashurbanipal, seventh century B.C. LM

Two Assyrian servants armed with swords, from the palace at Khorsabad, eighth century B.C. LM

of kings. Swords were used to hit, cut, and thrust. Short swords or daggers sometimes had three sides and were carried under the belt or the clothing (Jud 3:16, 21). In the hands of a skilled soldier the sword was a deadly and much-feared weapon.

Battle-axes and maces were among the most primitive weapons. They were used for cleaving, as clubs, and as throwing missiles. Wooden maces were bound with bronze, had metal hand guards, and were probably studded with iron spikes. Used by the heavy infantry in hand-to-hand fighting, they were also issued to charioteers. Battle-axes were two or more feet long with variously shaped metal blades (often curved or circular), wielded by infantrymen to batter down enemy gates and towers (Ezk 26:9). *See* Axe.

Chariots were not used by the Israelites until the time of Solomon, who built 4,000 stalls for his horses and chariots (I Kgs 4:26). They were boxlike vehicles closed in front and open in the rear, likely made of wood and overlaid with iron or bronze, resting on an axle which connected the two wheels. Usually three persons stood in the chariot, the driver, the warrior, and the shield bearer. *See* Chariot.

Siege weapons, such as the battering ram, engine *(q.v.),* and catapult, were used for breaching walls and throwing stones, arrows, darts *(q.v.),* and other objects (up to 300 pounds weight; some missiles could be hurled more than a quarter of a mile). Some rams required as many as 200 men to move; others were hung in movable towers and were threatening instruments of war. The Hyksos built sloping ramparts to defend their cities against battering rams as early as 1600 B.C.

Defensive Armor

The shield or buckler was the oldest and most common weapon of defense. The Israelites had chiefly two varieties. A large shield *(ṣinnâ)* used by the heavy-armed infantry, covered the whole body, and was either oval or rectangular in shape (Ps 5:12; II Chr 11:12; 25:5). Sometimes a special shield bearer was employed. A small light shield *(māgēn),* used by archers and for hand-to-hand fighting, was round (II Chr 17:17). Shields were made of wood or wicker overlaid with leather, although sometimes bronze and copper were used. They were rubbed with oil to preserve them and to make them shine in the sun (II Sam 1:21; Isa 21:5). Ornamental shields were plated or made with gold. When not being used in actual combat, the shield was strapped over the shoulder and kept in a cover (Isa 22:6).

Helmets were made of differing materials and in various shapes by the ancient nations. Originally they were more like skullcaps and worn only by prominent persons, but later it became common for ordinary soldiers to wear them for protection. Materials from which they were made included wood, linen, felt, rushes, leather, and brass. Sometimes helmets were furnished with flaps and covered with metal scales to protect the ears, neck, and shoulders. *See* Helmet.

The coat of mail, habergeon, cuirass, or breastplate was also used at first only by prominent men. At a later period when the soldiers were provided with such body armor, theirs were made of leather, linen or felt, whereas the leaders' were made of bronze. Often it protected the back as well as the breast; sometimes it had leather flaps which hung from the waist-

King Ashurnasirpal II of Assyria in his chariot. BM

line. Certain styles had small iron plates fitting closely over each other and sewn on a leather jacket. The "nails" used in its construction were likely the pins which were used to fasten the metal scales. Smaller plates or scales and narrower rows were used where greater flexibility was needed, as at the throat and neck. Some coats of mail covered the thigh nearly to the knee, being bound with a girdle at the waist to prevent its pressing too heavily on the shoulders. More often a second piece was employed to cover the body below the waist, like a short skirt detached from the girdle. Wire netting was also used to cover the top part of the body. Kings and principal chariot warriors wore long coats of mail reaching to the ankles or to the knees. *See* Cuirass; Corselet; Habergeon.

The girdle, from which the sword usually hung, was of leather studded with nails or metal plates. With light armor it was sometimes broad and placed around the hips. It was known also to have been worn from the shoulder like a scarf.

Greaves, armor to protect the leg between the knee and the ankle, were widely used among the ancients, but apparently not commonly among the Israelites. Made of brass or leather, they were tied with thongs around the leg and above the ankle. Military boots are mentioned in Isa 9:5 (RSV), likely a leather half-boot studded with heavy nails.

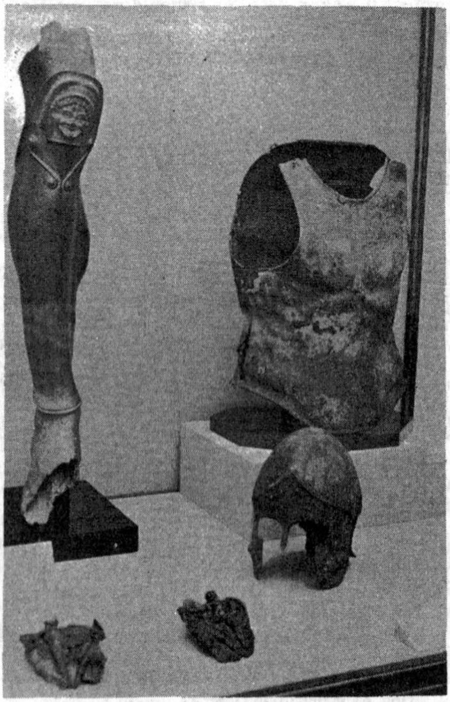

Greek armor of the fifth century B.C. BM

Spiritual Armor

In the well-known passage in Eph 6:10–17 the Christian is exhorted to put on the whole armor of God (*panoplia tou theou;* 6:11, 13). The word *panoplia,* "full armor" (NASB), is a fusion of two Gr. words, *pan* ("all") and *hopla* ("weapons"), and refers to the full combat equipment of a soldier: It is used figuratively to indicate the complete provision of spiritual virtues with which God endows His child for the war against evil (see also Rom 13:12; II Cor 6:7; 10:4–6). Every believer is inextricably engaged in the warfare that rages in the spirit realm between Christ with His angels and Satan with his demonic forces of wickedness.

The apostle Paul symbolizes vital elements of Christian character for one's defense against the accusations of the devil (cf. Rev 12:10) by various pieces of the Graeco-Roman armor of his day. Truth in the sense of personal honesty, sincerity, and dependability must be girded on the loins, the biblical seat of one's emotions (cf. Isa 11:5). The breastplate of practical uprightness in daily life protects the heart, the biblical seat of one's personality, conscience, and will (cf. Isa 59:17). The sandals are equated to preparedness in, or a skillful working knowledge of how to apply, the promises of the gospel of peace, so that one need not be anxious but have firm footing on the slippery ground of external circumstances. The large (four-by-two-feet) rectangular shield (*thyreos*), which could interlock with those of the soldiers on either side to form a solid wall, suggests one's faith acting together with that of fellow believers to present a united front against insidious, devilish attacks. The helmet of salvation perhaps symbolizes assurance of salvation, so necessary to protect one's mind from doubts and fears. The only offensive weapon listed by Paul is the sword of the Spirit, here described as the Word (*rhēma*) of God, i.e., every spoken command or prophetic utterance coming from God through one of His servants (Lk 1:37 [ASV], 38; 5:5; Mt 4:4; Heb 1:3; cf. Hos 6:5; Mt 10:19 f.; I Cor 12:8–10).

Bibliography. CornPBE, pp. 126–136. A. Oepke and K. G. Kuhn, "*Hoplon,* etc.," TDNT, V, 292–315. Yigael Yadin, *The Art of Warfare in Biblical Lands,* 2 vols., New York: McGraw-Hill, 1963.

R. E. Po.

ARMOR BEARER. A companion to an important warrior in the period of the Conquest and monarchy who was responsible for carrying a shield and perhaps weapons to assist in battle. Stories of Abimelech, Jonathan, and Saul all involve their armor bearers (Jud 9:54; I Sam 14 and I Sam 31). Joab, David's general, had ten armor bearers (II Sam 18:15).

ARMORY. Refers to military equipment kept in a storehouse (II Kgs 20:13) or to the place where such collections were kept (Neh 3:19).

Used poetically of God's power against the Chaldeans (Jer 50:25). In Song 4:4 the Heb. word *talpîyôth* ("armoury," KJV) perhaps refers to the courses of stone in the tower of David, likened to the rows or layers of the beloved's necklace.

ARMY. The Israelites were not intended by God to be a warlike people with a large standing army. Because of their strategic location at the crossroads of three continents, however, they found it necessary to make adequate preparations for their defense against hostile attacks. In the OT two Heb. words often signify "army": *ḥayil,* literally meaning "strength, force" (cf. armed forces), and *ṣābā',* "host, army." God is frequently called Yahweh of hosts, and the name is transliterated as Lord of Sabaoth in Rom 9:29 and Jas 5:4.

The first recorded use of armed forces in the history of the Jews is that of Abraham's conflict with the king of Elam and his confederates (Gen 14), in which Abraham displayed heroic military leadership with a band of 318 retainers.

Military organization of the Jews began with the Exodus from Egypt. It was not so much, especially at first, that they were armed for warfare as that they were arranged by tribes and divisions as a body of troops for the march through the wilderness. After Sinai they were divided into divisions or army corps; certain gradations of military rank existed. Except for the Levites, men of 20 years of age and older who were fit to go to war were assigned a post in the army (Num 1:3, 47-50; 31:14). Certain individuals were exempt from military service: those who were newly married, those who had built a new house or planted a vineyard, the fearful and fainthearted (Deut 20:5-8). As footmen in the desert their weapons were the simple arms for attack and defense. It is evident that their journeyings in the wilderness prepared them for the discipline and tactics of a military company.

Under the brilliant leadership of Joshua and following the conquest of Canaan, there was further development of military organization, strategy, and equipment. United action of the armed forces was jeopardized, however, by tribal jealousies and rivalries which threatened the national solidarity. Individual tribes generally defended their own territory and people; only great emergencies united the armies of the various tribes in common action. There was no regular, permanent army at this time. When emergencies arose, God raised up a leader who summoned the men of Israel to war against their enemies, and when the exigency passed the forces were disbanded. Armies thus drafted were divided into companies of thousands, hundreds, fifties, and still further into families under appointed officers. Provisions for the army were the responsibility of each tribe (Jud 20:10), were supplied by rich landowners (I Sam 25), or from the natural resources of the land. The soldiers' pay generally consisted only of supplies, plus a portion of the spoil.

Wooden models of a contingent of Egyptian soldiers found in a tomb dating to about 2000 B.C. LL

It was not until the monarchy that Israel had a professional or standing army. (Comparatively little progress had been made in military affairs from the time the Jews had entered Palestine.) Saul and David had bands of select warriors, the nuclei of which served as the kings' bodyguards. David developed a national militia of 12 regiments, each of which was called up for duty for one month in the year under their appointed officers. Over the entire army there was a commander-in-chief or "captain of the host" (I Sam 14:50; II Sam 24:2), a role only rarely assumed by the king himself after Saul's reign.

Samuel had warned the leaders of Israel that a professional soldiery would be needed under a monarchy (I Sam 8:10-12). But the severe oppression of the mighty Philistines necessitated systematic military preparations on the part of King Saul to withstand invasions and to free the people from their heavy yoke of bondage, as well as to achieve a national unity in Israel. General Joab of David's army, though rough and unscrupulous, was well known for his military genius. His tactical brilliance revolutionized Israel's warfare, particularly his skill in the art of siege warfare which he taught David's soldiers.

Although peace generally prevailed during Solomon's reign, there was no diminution of the armed forces. Many cities resembled fortresses and required strong garrisons for their defense. Disregarding the divine prohibition of horses (Deut 17:16; I Kgs 10:26-29), Solomon added vast numbers of horses and chariots to the army's equipment, and later lancers and mounted archers were also added. Palestine's hilly interior was not suited for the use of chariots, but as the foreign relations of Israel extended in the direction of Syria and Egypt in later times, it was thought advantageous and militarily necessary to employ chariots against enemy forces, especially in the flat plains regions. But this proved to be an expensive and often impractical addition to Israel's army. The oppressive cost and the forced military service and labor created intense dissatisfaction, eventually contributing to the disruption of the kingdom. Foreign troops, such as the Cherethites and Pelethites, mainly of Philistine origin, were sometimes hired as mercenaries.

Extraordinarily large numbers are sometimes given for the military statistics (e.g., I Sam 11:8; II Chr 26:12–13). It is thought that some of these are not necessarily to be understood in a strictly literal numerical sense, but may have been figurative or territorial terms. Or the numbers may not have been transmitted correctly in the recopying of MSS. Another possibility is that the Heb. *'eleph* translated "thousand" can also mean in various contexts "clan" or "clan leader, chieftain." In some passages such men are further designated as mighty men of valor (e.g., II Chr 14:8; 17:13–18). *See* Number.

Little is known about the order of battle and the exact arrangement of troops in the field, but it seems that the heavy-armed troops (spearmen) came first, followed by slingers and archers, supported by horses and chariots. Division into three bodies is frequently mentioned, the heavy-armed troops and two divisions of light-armed soldiers. Various purposes were served by this arrangement: the provision of a center and two wings for combat; various strategic combinations of the divisions according to special needs; relays for the night watches. Maneuvers varied according to the strategy of the enemy forces or the lay of the land.

Fighting was generally limited to the dry season. Operations were suspended when the rainy autumn weather came and resumed again in the spring. Sentries were appointed to keep a vigilant guard of the camp at night. When the army went forth into battle a detachment remained to protect the camp and to serve, if necessary, as a reserve or to provide an escape for the chief.

In the NT, the Roman army is most frequently mentioned, especially the Roman legions (varying from 3,000 to 6,000 soldiers), which were commanded by chief captains or tribunes. Legions were divided into bands or cohorts, which were subdivided into maniples, which in turn were divided into centuries (originally comprised of 100 men) under the command of centurions. Special groups, independent cohorts of volunteers, are mentioned in Scripture, such as the Augustan and the Italian bands (Acts 10:1; 27:1); also there was the praetorian guard (Phil 1:13, RSV).

See Armor; Host; Legion; War.

Bibliography. Yigael Yadin, *The Art of Warfare in Biblical Lands,* 2 vols., New York: McGraw-Hill, 1963.

R. E. Po.

ARNAN (är'năn). A remote descendant in the royal family of David through Zerubbabel (I Chr 3:21).

The Arnon River. JR

ARNON (är'nŏn). A perennial stream of Transjordan flowing 30 miles through a deep gorge into the Dead Sea slightly N of its mid-point; modern Wadi el-Mojib. At the time of the Conquest it separated Moab from the Amorite kingdoms to the N. It was from this vicinity that Israel issued its challenge to Sihon, king of Heshbon (Num 21:13–14, 21–24, 28), and moved northward to conquer the whole of Gilead and Bashan (Deut 2:24, 36; 4:48; Josh 12:1–2). Upon assignment of tribal allotments, the Arnon became the southern boundary of the territory of Reuben (Deut 3:12, 16; Josh 13:15–16). Balak, king of Moab, met Balaam here to solicit his favor and to seek his curse on Israel (Num 22:36).

The territory N of Arnon had previously been controlled by Moab so that the portion opposite Jericho was still called the "plains [fields] of Moab" (Num 22:1; 26:3; 36:13; *et al.*), but Sihon had driven the Moabites over Arnon (Num 21:26, 28). The Moabites under Eglon attempted its recovery in the period of the judges (Jud 3:12–30), as also in the late 9th cen. when Mesha claimed victory over Israel in his votive stela (Moabite Stone), building a highway and numerous forts along the N of the Arnon (line 26; cf. Nelson Glueck, *The Other Side of the Jordan,* pp. 138–139). An elegy over the ultimate fall of Moab witnesses indirectly to the temporary successes Moab had enjoyed (Isa 15:4; Jer 48:20).

R. V. R.

AROD (âr'ŏd), **ARODI** (ăr'ō-dī). A son of Gad (Gen 46:16) and founder of the clan. The Arodites were descendants of Arod (Num 26:17).

AROER (*à*-rō'ēr)

1. A city strategically located on the N bank of the Arnon gorge; modern Arair, three miles SE of Dhiban. It was the southernmost city of the Amorite king Sihon (Deut 2:36; 4:48; Josh 12:2), hence also Reuben's southernmost city (Josh 13:16). This was David's starting point in

Transjordan for his census (II Sam 24:5). Aroer appears also in the Heb. of Jer 48:6, but the text is uncertain (RSV: "like a wild ass"). Aroer was lost to Hazael (II Kgs 10:33). Mesha records rebuilding it (Moabite Stone, line 26). Jeremiah represents Aroer as Moabite at that time (Jer 48:18-19). Hotham, the "Aroerite" in a Reubenite context, suggests this Aroer (I Chr 11:44; cf. v. 42).

2. A town in the territory of Gad "opposite" (RSV: "east of") Rabbah (modern Amman), capital of the Ammonites (Num 32:34; Josh 13:25); exact location uncertain. LXX of Isa 17:2 is to be preferred to the Heb., reading "her cities" (RSV) instead of "Aroer."

3. A town of southern Judah to whom David gave a part of the spoil retrieved from the Amalekite raiders of Ziklag (I Sam 30:28); modern Ararah, 12 miles SE of Beersheba. "Adadah" of Josh 15:22 should probably also be so read.

R. V. R.

ARPAD (är'păd). Twice spelled Arphad (Isa 36:19; 37:13). A N Syrian city-state, spelled *'Arpad* in Heb., *'rpd* in an Aram. inscription, and *Arpadda* in Akkad. records. The site of Arpad, now *Erfâd,* lies 30 miles N of Aleppo. The Assyrians under Adad-nirari III despoiled the city first in 806 B.C., and again under Ashur-dan III in 754 B.C. Tiglath-pileser III after another conquest of the city in 740 B.C. made its territory into an Assyrian province. Twenty years later Arpad rebelled and received its punishment by Sargon II. In the OT it is most often mentioned in connection with its destruction by the Assyrians (II Kgs 18:34; 19:13; Isa 10:9; 36:19; 37:13; Jer 49:23).

ARPHAD (är'făd). *See* Arpad.

ARPHAXAD (är-făk'săd). Listed in Gen 10:22, 24 as a son of Shem, born two years after the Flood (Gen 11:10) and living to the age of 438 years (Gen 11:13). The name may refer not only to an individual but to a tribe of people descended from Shem. The name Arrapachitis (Ptol. vi. 1-2), a region between lakes Van and Urmiah in Armenia, perhaps stems from his name.

ARROW. *See* Armor; Bow and Arrow.

ARTAXERXES (är'tă-zûrk'sēz). The fifth monarch after Cyrus the Great to rule over the Persian Empire. To distinguish him from two later kings of the same name, he was known as Artaxerxes I (Longimanus). He reigned from 464 to 423 B.C., twice as long as his father Xerxes (Est 1:1). *See* Ahasuerus.

Not a dynamic ruler, Artaxerxes had suffered humiliations at the hands of the Greeks and by revolts in Egypt and Syria. Enjoying life in his palace cities, he entrusted military campaigns to his generals and the rule of the provinces to relatives and friends. Thus he was only too glad to stabilize matters in Palestine by heeding the requests of first one faction and then another.

In 458 B.C., he gave Ezra permission to return to Jerusalem to revive and strengthen the temple services (Ezr 7). A few years later the Jews must have begun to repair the city walls too, for about 446 B.C. Artaxerxes allowed Rehum and Shimshai to halt the project (Ezr 4:7-23). Not only did they stop this work, but also broke down the walls and burned the gates (Neh 1:3). This led the cupbearer of Artaxerxes, a Jew named Nehemiah, to ask permission to rebuild the city walls, which favor was graciously granted in 445 B.C. (Neh 2:1-8). In 443 B.C., Nehemiah obtained permission from Artaxerxes to return again to Jerusalem to carry out reforms (Neh 13:6).

J. C. W.

ARTEMAS (är'tĕ-mĭs). A companion of Paul whose name is linked with Tychicus in a proposed mission to Crete to relieve Titus (Tit 3:12). The name is generally considered to be Gr. (*contra.* Jerome), possibly a shortened form of Artemidorus, a familiar name in Asia Minor, or the masculine form of Artemis. According to tradition, he was one of the 70 disciples of Lk 10:1.

ARTEMIS. *See* Gods, False.

ARTILLERY. The KJV translation of the word rendered "weapons" in I Sam 20:40, RSV. From the context ("Jonathan gave his weapons to the lad") and from the modern meaning of the word "artillery," it is clear that the RSV is a more accurate translation. *See* Armor.

ARTS. *See* Occupations.

ARUBOTH (ȧ-ro͞o'bōth). The town of Ben-hesed, one of Solomon's officers (I Kgs 4:10). It may be identified with the modern Arab town of 'Arrabeh, two miles SW of Dothan in Manasseh.

ARUMAH (ȧ-ro͞o'mȧ). A town near Shechem where Abimelech resided (Jud 9:31, 41).

ARVAD (är'văd), **ARVADITE** (är'vȧ-dīt). A port city of northern Phoenicia, located on the island of Ruad, which lies *c.* two miles off the mainland and *c.* 30 miles N of Tripolis. The city is mentioned first in the Amarna letters (14th cen. B.C.) as Arwada, in Assyrian records as Armada, Aruda, Aruadi, etc., in classical writings as Aradus, and in Hebrew as *'Arwād.*

The Arvadites are listed in Gen 10:18 and I Chr 1:16 as descendants of Canaan, while Ezekiel mentions the mariners and soldiers of Arvad as having served the city of Tyre in its defense (Ezk 27:8, 11). The city repeatedly fought against the Assyrians, and at other periods was tributary to Assyria. Nebuchadnezzar II mentions its king as one of his vassals.

ARZA (är′zȧ). The steward of King Elah of Israel at whose house in Tirzah the king was drunk when he was assassinated by Zimri (I Kgs 16:9).

ASA (ā′sȧ). The third king of Judah, son and successor of Abijah. His 41-year reign began with a ten-year period of peace, during which a program of religious reform was started. His aim was to rid the land of heathen idols and worship. His zeal for God was shown by the dethroning of Maachah, his grandmother, the acting queen mother, for erecting an image of Asherah, the Canaanite goddess of fertility (I Kgs 15:12–13; II Chr 15:16). (For the problem of Asa's mother and grandmother having the same name, *see* Maachah.) Also during this period Asa built fortified cities and fielded an army (II Chr 14:1–8).

It was probably in the 11th year of his reign that a great army invaded Judah from the S, led by Zerah, the Ethiopian. Asa put his trust in the Lord and attacked the invaders. God gave the victory (II Chr 14:9–15). *See* Zerah.

Following this victory, Asa heeded the advice of Azariah, the prophet, and completed the reformation begun earlier. The people were called together and induced to renew their covenant with God (II Chr 15:1–15).

During the 16th year of his reign (the 36th year of the divided kingdom), the border war with Israel was continued. Baasha, king of Israel, invaded the territory of Benjamin and fortified the city of Ramah. His purposes were (1) to recover the territory lost to Abijah, Asa's father, and (2) to control the area N of Jerusalem. Asa took what was left of the temple treasures and sent them to Ben-hadad, king of Syria, asking him to break his pact with Baasha and attack Israel. Ben-hadad complied, forcing Baasha to withdraw from Ramah. Asa conscripted labor and used the materials gathered at Ramah to fortify the cities of Geba and Mizpah (I Kgs 15:16–22; II Chr 16:1–6).

Hanani, the seer, condemned Asa for his alliance with Syria instead of reliance upon the Lord. Asa became enraged, casting Hanani into prison (II Chr 16:7–10).

During his 39th year as king, Asa became diseased in his feet and failed once more to seek help from God, calling on the physicians instead (I Kgs 15:23; II Chr 16:12). Asa died in the 41st year of his reign and was buried with royal honors in the city of David (I Kgs 15:24; II Chr 16:13–14).

R. O. C.

ASAHEL (ăs′ȧ-hĕl)

1. A brother of Joab (David's army commander) and one of the three sons of Zeruiah (David's sister). Asahel was an officer in David's army (II Sam 23:24; I Chr 11:26). He was known for his fleetness ("as swift of foot as a wild gazelle") in his pursuit of Abner following the battle of Gibeon. This event ended in his own death by impalement upon Abner's spear (II Sam 2:18–23). The whole incident issued in the treacherous murder of Abner at Hebron and David's lament for Abner's politically untimely death (II Sam 3:26–39).

2. A Levite named Asahel was commissioned by King Jehoshaphat as an itinerant instructor of the law and sent through "all the cities of Judah" teaching (II Chr 17:8).

3. Another Levite bearing this name was placed under Cononiah by Hezekiah with the group charged with overseeing "the contributions, the tithes and the dedicated things" (II Chr 31:12–13).

4. The father of the Jonathan who, in the time of Ezra, opposed the appointment of a commission to study Jewish intermarriage of the period (Ezr 10:15, ASV).

R. O. C.

ASAHIAH. *See* Asaiah.

ASAIAH (ȧ-zā′yȧ)

1. "King's servant" to Josiah, member of a delegation he sent to Huldah the prophetess to inquire the meaning of the words of the book of the law found in the renovation of the temple (II Chr 34:20). Incorrectly written "Asahiah" in II Kgs 22:12, 14, KJV.

2. Princely descendant of Simeon who in the time of Hezekiah dispossessed the Mennim near Gedor (Gerar?) (I Chr 4:34–41).

3. A Levite, chief of the 250 descendants of Merari assembled by David to assist in bringing up the ark from the house of Obed-edom to Jerusalem (I Chr 15:6, 11). Probably the same as in I Chr 6:30.

4. A "Shilonite" (i.e., descendant of Shelah, son of Judah, Num 26:20) dwelling in Jerusalem after his return from captivity (I Chr 9:5, RSV). Possibly the same as Maaseiah in Neh 11:5 (RSV) since the list is otherwise similar.

ASAPH (ā′săf)

1. Asaph the son of Berachiah, a Levite, is the most prominent of this name in the Bible. An outstanding musician in the days of David, he was appointed along with another Levite, Heman, as minister of music in the center of worship in Jerusalem (I Chr 6:39; 15:17, 19; 16:5, 7, 37; 25:1–2, 6–9). Eleven of the psalms (73–83) are attributed to Asaph by the traditional editorial notes. The descendants of Asaph for hundreds of years retained this office of musicians before the Lord, and the term "sons of Asaph" became almost equivalent to chorister or musician (Ezr 2:41; 3:10; Neh 7:44; 11:17, 22; 12:35–36). *See* Psalms, Book of.

2. The father of Joah, the court chronicler or recorder in the days of Hezekiah (II Kgs 18:18, 37; II Chr 29:13; Isa 36:3, 22).

3. The ancestor of some of the Levites who returned from the Exile (I Chr 9:15). This may be the same as 1.

4. A Levite of the family of Korah whose descendants were appointed gatekeepers of the

Lord's house by David (I Chr 26:1; called Ebiasaph in 9:19).

5. An officer of the king of Persia who may have been a Jew; he was "keeper of the king's forest" (Neh 2:8).

A Heb. seal bearing the name Asaph was found at Megiddo.

P. C. J.

ASAREEL (*ȧ*-sâr'ĭ-ĕl). One of the four sons of Jehaleleel of the tribe of Judah (I Chr 4:16).

ASARELAH (ăs'*ȧ*-rē'l*ȧ*). A son of Asaph who was selected by David for the service of prophesying (I Chr 25:2). Also called Jesharelah (v. 14).

ASCENSION OF CHRIST. The bodily transfer of our Lord from the earthly to the heavenly sphere of existence. The primary account of this event appears in Acts 1:9-11; the secondary references in Mk 16:19 and Lk 24:51 are rendered questionable by inferior textual evidence. However, the ascension is assumed as the foundation for numerous statements in the NT (e.g., Col 3:1; Rom 8:34; Heb 8:1). In fact, there is hardly a NT writer who does not give testimony, direct or indirect, to the truth of the ascension.

According to Luke, the event took place 40 days after the resurrection (Acts 1:3) near Bethany (Lk 24:50) on the Mount of Olives (Acts 1:12). The text explains that He was taken up into a cloud (Acts 1:9). Whether the cloud was that of the Shekinah glory or a natural cloud of vapor, the record does not make clear. The ascension was anticipated in the OT in Ps 68:18; 110:1, and Christ spoke of it prophetically in Jn 6:62; 20:17.

Objection has been raised concerning the ascension by those who approach the record from a purely naturalistic viewpoint. They assert that such violation of the law of gravity is unthinkable. However, for those who accept the possibility of supernatural intervention in the world, the ascension is no problem. Given an omnipotent God, both resurrection and ascension are easily conceivable.

Others view the ascension as being merely a symbolical representation of Christ's entrance into divine glory. This is an attempt to retain the spiritual value of the ascension account without sacrificing the concept of the natural world as a closed system not susceptible to supernatural intrusion.

The significance of the ascension is manifold. (1) For Christ Himself it meant exaltation to a position of glory as victorious Lord, the Head of the Church (Eph 1:20-23; Phil 2:9). (2) It also made possible the coming of the Holy Spirit to indwell the believer as Divine Helper (Jn 16:7; Acts 2:33) and to convict the world of sin, righteousness, and judgment (Jn 16:8-11). (3) The ascension signifies the identification of the Christian with Christ; he is seated with Him positionally in the heavenlies (Eph 2:6; Col

Chapel of the Ascension atop the Mount of Olives. HFV

3:1-3). (4) The ascension initiated Christ's high priestly advocacy before the Father in the believer's behalf, a truth which is given major treatment in the Epistle to the Hebrews (4:14-16; 6:20; 7:25; 8:1; 9:24). (5) For the future, the fact that Christ ascended means that He will return to the earth in the same manner in which He left (Acts 1:11).

D. W. B.

ASENATH (ăs'ē-năth). Daughter of Potipherah, Egyptian priest of On, who was given to Joseph for his wife by Pharaoh. She was the mother of Ephraim and Manasseh (Gen 41:45, 50). In Heb. her name is a transliteration of the Egyptian name 'Iws-Nît ("she belongs to [the goddess] Neith").

ASER (ā'sẽr). The Gr. form of the Heb. Asher found only in the NT (KJV) in Lk 2:36 and Rev 7:6. Asher *(q.v.)* was a son of Jacob by Zilpah, and the tribe descended from him.

ASH A tree. *See* Plants.

ASHAN (ā'sh*ă*n). A village allotted to Judah after the Conquest (Josh 15:42), reassigned to Simeon (Josh 19:7; I Chr 4:32), and finally given to the sons of Aaron (I Chr 6:59). It has been identified with Khirbet 'Asan, four miles NW of Beer-sheba. The Chor-ashan (Borashan, ASV, "cistern of Ashan") of I Sam 30:30 is the same town.

ASHBEA (ăsh'bē-*ȧ*). The town in the tribe of Judah noted for its linen workers (I Chr 4:21). RSV renders it Beth-ashbea.

ASHBEL (ăsh'bĕl), **ASHBELITES** (ăsh'bĕ-līts). One of the sons of Benjamin (Gen 46:21) and ancestor of the Ashbelites (Num 26:38; I Chr 8:1). Apparently Ashbel was also called Jediael (I Chr 7:6).

ASHCHENAZ (ăsh'kĕ-năz). Another form of Ashkenaz *(q.v.)*. Ashchenaz is used in I Chr 1:6 and Jer 51:27.

ASHDOD (ăsh'dŏd). Probably the capital of the five Philistine cities. Located three miles inland and 18 miles NE of Gaza, it controlled a junction on the coastal trade route. Tablets discovered at Ugarit indicate that Ashdod was one of three Palestinian cities that traded with the northern Canaanite capital in Syria during the 14th and 13th cen. B.C.; the other two were Acco and Ashkelon. Ashdod was allotted to the tribe of Judah (Josh 15:46 f.), but its Anakim inhabitants enabled the city to resist Joshua's army (Josh 11:22; 13:1-3).

When the Philistines captured the ark of the covenant, they placed it in the temple of Dagon there. On each of two nights the image fell, and finally broke. A plague of tumors also descended upon the city. In panic, the Ashdodites gave the ark to Gath and then to Ekron, which returned it to the Israelites (I Sam 5-6). Ashdod was not captured by Judah until the reign of Uzziah (II Chr 26:6).

The Assyrians took the city in the 8th cen., calling it Asdudu. A revolt occurred while Ahimiti was governor, and the city was destroyed by Sargon II in 711 B.C. (ANET, pp. 284-287; cf. Amos 1:8; Isa 20:1). During the next century Ashdod was weak (see Jer 25:20; Zeph 2:4; Zech 9:6).

In Nehemiah's day the city joined with others to oppose the rebuilding of Jerusalem's walls. Nehemiah protested that half the children of Jews who had wives from Ashdod did not speak Hebrew (Neh 4:7-8; 13:23-24). Idolatry in Ashdod, by Hellenistic times called Azotus, provoked the Maccabees to attack it (I Macc 5:68; 10:84). In the NT, the city is referred to in Acts 8:40. It had been restored by Herod and Gabinius and was presented to Salome, Herod's sister, by Augustus Caesar.

Ashdod is now known as Esdud. The ruins consist of an acropolis of 17 acres and a lower city spreading over at least 90 acres. Excavations beginning in 1962 have revealed 20 levels of human settlement, from Early Bronze Age II to the end of the Byzantine period. Throughout the Late Bronze Age (1550-1200 B.C.), Ashdod was a large walled city. A cylinder seal of the Middle Babylonian style belongs to the period, and many pottery imports show commercial relations with Cyprus and the Mycenaean cultural area of Greece. The last Late Bronze Age city was totally destroyed, leaving a thick level of ash after 1250 B.C., but the conqueror is still unknown.

Five strata belong to the era of the Philistines *(q.v.)*. The ruins reveal that they reached the peak of their power in the first half of the 11th cen., i.e., before Saul became king. Their city wall, built of sun-dried bricks, was 20 feet wide. The earliest Philistine stratum yielded pottery resembling in decoration a style found in Cyprus from the period after 1230 B.C. This suggests Ashdod was settled by an early wave of Sea-Peoples coming via Cyprus. Three seals have been found engraved with signs resembling the Cypro-Minoan script in use in the E Mediterranean sphere *c.* 1300-1150 B.C. A potters' quarter was unearthed in the lower city area dating to the 8th cen. B.C. Its destruction may be attributed to Uzziah. Fragments of a basalt stela bearing cuneiform characters of a type found in Sargon's capital attest to the Assyrian domination by that king.

Bibliography. Moshe Dothan, "Ashdod: a City of the Philistine Pentapolis," *Archaeological Discoveries in the Holy Land,* New York: Thomas Crowell Co., 1967, pp. 129-137; "Ashdod of the Philistines," *New Directions in Biblical Archaeology,* ed. by D. N. Freedman and J. C. Greenfield, Garden City: Doubleday, 1969, pp. 15-24; "Tel Ashdod, 1969," IEJ, XIX (1969), 243 ff.

G. H. L.

ASHDOTHITES (ăsh'dŏth-īts). Found in Josh 13:3, it is a less acceptable form of Ashdodites, resulting from anglicizing the name. *See* Ashdod.

ASHER (ăsh'ĕr). *Personal history*. Asher was the eighth son of Jacob and the second by Zilpah, Leah's maid (Gen 30:12-13; 35:26). Jacob's blessing on Asher is found in Gen 49:20. He had four sons and a daughter (Gen 46:17; I Chr 7:30).

The tribe. Descendants from Asher at the time of the Exodus numbered 41,500 adult males (Num 1:41). At the second census the number was 53,400 (Num 26:47). On the march this tribe was placed with Dan on the N of the tabernacle along with Naphtali. It was allotted territory in the N, which formed the northern boundary of Palestine. This extended southward to S of Carmel, about 60 miles in extent. On the E were the territories of Zebulun and Naphtali; on the W was the Mediterranean (Josh 19:24-31).

This territory brought the tribe into contact with the Phoenicians, who were famous for their extensive commerce. But Asher failed to drive the Canaanites out of their cities (Jud 1:31-32). The method of taking possession of their allotted land seems to have been by peaceful penetration rather than by outright conquest. They gave their energies to the cultivation of the olive; thus the mention in Deut 33:24 that they would dip their feet in oil.

Egyptian records from the reigns of Seti I (1319–1304 B.C.) and Rameses II (1304–1234 B.C.) speak of the hinterland of Phoenicia as *'I-ś-r* or *Asaru,* which seems to indicate that the tribe of Asher had already settled in this area. Here is clear evidence for the earlier date of the Exodus and Conquest. *See* Exodus, The.

The tribe did not distinguish itself during all of Israel's history. It was not adventurous or enterprising (Jud 5:17). In David's time it was not even mentioned in the list of chief rulers (I Chr 27:16 ff.). In Hezekiah's godly reign it responded to his call for observance of the Passover (II Chr 30:11). Anna, the prophetess, was a member of this tribe (Lk 2:36).

C. L. F.

ASHERAH. *See* Gods, False.

ASHES

1. A special word, *deshen,* really "fatness," denotes the burnt wood of the altar soaked with fat (I Kgs 13:3, 5), which was in pots (Ex 27:3), or on the E side of the tabernacle altar (Lev 1:16), or deposited outside the camp (Lev 4:12; cf. Jer 31:40).

2. Another word, *pîaḥ,* used twice, is really "soot." Moses tossed skyward before Pharaoh two handfuls from a kiln to bring sores on man and beast (Ex 9:8, 10).

3. The common word *'ēper* is the same as "dust," loose and crumbled. These ashes may be useless remains of complete destruction, as when God turned Tyre "to ashes upon the earth" (Ezk 28:18; cf. Mal 4:3; II Pet 2:6; Lam 3:16). To express dire distress, whether of mourning or repentance, the impassioned Oriental often used ashes. They might be on the head, as of dishonored Tamar crying aloud (II Sam 13:19); in the garment of sackcloth, as of Mordecai bewailing the decree to annihilate the Jews (Est 4:1; cf. v. 3); sat on to show deepest repentance, as the king of Nineveh (Jon 3:6; cf. Isa 58:5; Mt 11:21 parallel to Lk 10:13); mixed with dust (Job 42:6); or used more fervently to seek the Lord (Dan 9:3).

Ashes, then, symbolized deepest humility, as when Abraham pled for Sodom (Gen 18:27); or even humiliation, as when Job had "become like dust and ashes" (Job 30:19). They might symbolize futility, as of idolatry (Isa 44:20) or paltry proverbs (Job 13:12). Ceremonially, the ashes of the red heifer were used in "the water for impurity" (Num 19:9; Heb 9:13).

What a wonderful promise of the evangelical prophet that the Lord would grant mourners a diadem instead of ashes (*pe'ēr* instead of *'ēper,* Isa 61:3)! *See* Beauty.

W. G. B.

ASHIMA. *See* Gods, False.

ASHKELON (ăsh'kĕ-lŏn). This city on the Mediterranean coast, about 30 miles S of Tel-Aviv, was among five principal cities of the Philistines (Gaza, Ashdod, Gath and Ekron being the other four, Josh 13:3). Each city was controlled by a "lord." Together, the cities posed the most serious threat to the independence of Israel during the period of the judges.

The Goddess of Victory standing on the globe supported by Atlas in the antiquities park, Ashkelon. HFV

From Ashkelon, the Philistines sent back with the ark one of the golden tumors (I Sam 6:17). With Gaza, Ashdod, and Ekron, the city was bitterly denounced by Amos (Amos 1:7 f.). It is mentioned also by David (II Sam 1:20) and the prophets (Jer 25:20; Zeph 2:4, 7; Zech 9:5). Worship of Dagon by the inhabitants of Ashkelon is indicated in the Tell el-Amarna tablets *c.* 1380–1350 B.C.

Ashkelon was captured by Jonathan, brother of Judas the Maccabee (I Macc 10:86; 11:60). Though the Herodian family was connected with Idumaea, there is evidence that Herod the Great was born at Ashkelon (Eusebius, *Eccles. Hist.* 1.7.11 and Justin *Dialogue, c.* 52). Herod built baths and costly fountains there (Jos *Wars* i.21.11). Ruins from the time of his reign were uncovered in excavations in the 1920's, in addition to evidence of occupation from the Philistine period and as early as 1800 B.C.

R. L. J.

ASHKENAZ (ăsh'kĕ-năz). The eldest son of Gomer and great-grandson of Noah through Japheth (Gen 10:3; I Chr 1:6, ASV). Also the name of a tribe mentioned in Jer 51:27 (ASV), coming from eastern Armenia, associated with Ararat and Minni, who as barbarians were instruments of God's wrath against Babylon. The identification with Assyrian *Aš-gu-za-a,* the Scythians of the 7th cen. B.C., is reasonably certain, because cuneiform documents of Esarhaddon mention them as allies of the Mannai (Minni) in their revolt against Assyria. Medieval Jews wrongly connected the term with Germany, so that German Jews are called Ashkenazim.

ASHNAH (ăsh'nȧ). Two villages in the Shephelah or foothills of Judah are given this name (Josh 15:33, 43). Their exact location has not been determined. The first is thought to be 'Aslin, located on the edge of the coastal plain W of Jerusalem. The second has been identified by some with Idhna between Hebron and Lachish, about 30 miles SW of Jerusalem.

ASHPENAZ (ăsh'pē-năz). Master of the eunuchs in the court of Nebuchadnezzar, king of Babylon (Dan 1:3). The meaning of the name is unknown. It is perhaps of Persian origin, and has been found on an incantation text at Nippur.

Ashpenaz held a position which was common in Oriental courts. One in this position could attain great influence with the ruler and was sometimes treated by him as a confidential servant. His office placed him in control of the other eunuchs employed in the palace, and consequently put the royal harem in his charge. He was also entrusted with the training of youths for the service of the king. This latter responsibility does not necessarily imply, however, that Daniel and his three friends were made eunuchs. Yet see Isaiah's prediction in Isaiah 39:7.

ASHRIEL (ăsh'rĭ-ĕl). Found only in I Chr 7:14. The name is more properly spelled Asriel *(q.v.).*

ASHTAROTH (ăsh'tȧ-rŏth)

1. The plural form of Ashtoreth, a Canaanite goddess (Jud 2:13; 10:6; I Sam 7:3-4; 12:10; 31:10). *See* Gods, False.

2. One of two chief cities, along with Edrei *(q.v.),* of Og, king of Bashan (Deut 1:4; Josh 9:10; 12:4; 13:12, 31; I Chr 6:71; cf. Gen 14:5), located at Tell Ashtarah about 20 miles E of the Sea of Galilee. This area is traditionally in the region of Uz, homeland of Job (HDB, rev. ed., p. 63). The name may be an abbreviated form of the place name Ashteroth-karnaim *(q.v.),* either the name of the Canaanite goddess Ashtoreth compounded with Karnaim ("two horns") meaning "Ashtoreth of the two horns," or it may designate one of the twin cities along the King's Highway which alternated as the capital of Bashan. It is known as *Aštarti* in the Amarna tablets.

ASHTEROTH-KARNAIM (ăsh'tĕ-rŏth-kär-nā'ĭm). A city in Bashan occupied by the Rephaim, prehistoric inhabitants of Canaan (Gen 14:5), and apparently dedicated to the worship of the primary female deity of the Canaanites, the goddess of fertility. By Hellenistic times Atargatis, the Syrian goddess, may have been worshiped there (II Macc 12:26) rather than Ashteroth. Ashteroth was often represented in art wearing a two-horned headdress like the Egyptian cow-goddess Hathor.

A more probable meaning of the name according to Eusebius' *Onomasticon,* however, is "Ashteroth near Karnaim," in which case it may be identified with the town Ashtaroth *(q.v.),* capital of King Og (Deut 1:4), at modern Tell Ashtarah, 21 miles E of the Sea of Galilee. Under Aramaean and Assyrian rule a town called Karnaim (Carnaim) by the Jews (Amos 6:13, RSV; I Macc 5:26, 43 f.) eclipsed Ashtaroth in size and became the regional capital. It may be identified with the site of *Sheikh Sa'ad,* three miles NE of Tell Ashtarah.

H. L. D.

ASHTORETH. *See* Gods, False.

ASHUR (ăsh'ŭr). A great-grandson of Judah, born posthumously to Hezron by his wife Abiah (I Chr 2:24). The name is more correctly spelled Ashhur in RSV (Heb. *'ashḥûr*). He became the founder of Tekoa through the seven children that were borne by his two wives, Helah and Naarah (I Chr 4:5). The LXX makes him a son of Caleb by Ephrathah.

ASHURBANIPAL (ăsh'ŭr-băn'ĭ-pȧl). The last of the great kings of Assyria (668-626 B.C.). The Assyrian Empire was supreme by this time, but this supremacy had to be maintained by the constant strong arm of the military to keep down revolts. Though not without military ability, Ashurbanipal appears to have had more

A fragment of the Babylonian creation epic from Ashurbanipal's palace. BM

interest in cultural pursuits than conquest. Under his father, Esarhaddon, Assyrian suzerainty spread into Egypt, and Ashurbanipal inherited an uprising by Tirhakah the Nubian (Ethiopian, cf. II Kgs 19:9). The revolt was crushed and Memphis taken, but Ashurbanipal restored the Delta princes to their positions. The man who was to become Pharaoh-necho (II Kgs 23:29) was carried to Assyria, later released and was set up as ruler in Sais. A final attempt to restore Nubian power by Tirhakah's nephew, Tanutamon (Tandamane), in 663 B.C., brought the Assyrian army all the way S to Thebes. The sacking of this famous city by Ashurbanipal left a lasting impression, as can be seen from Nahum's reference to it (Nah 3:8, RSV). Ashurbanipal himself considered this triumph a noble accomplishment.

Almost immediately a native Egyptian ruler, Psamtik I (663–609 B.C.), started another rebellion and this time with the aid of Lydian mercenaries he overcame rival princes and succeeded in driving Assyrian forces out of Egypt. Ashurbanipal's apparent indifference to this loss may have been for two reasons. First, Assyria was overextended in Egypt; and secondly, Ashurbanipal preferred peaceful enterprises. A less aggressive policy is evidenced also by the swift conclusion of the inherited seige of Tyre, accomplished probably by offering Ba'alu, its king, easier terms of surrender. On the other hand, the presence of the Cimmerians, hordes of wild nomads in the N, may have made many a prince happy to wear the protective mantle of Assyrian might. Gyges of Lydia (in western Asia Minor) felt it wise to flatter Ashurbanipal by acknowledging the latter's supremacy, though he was beyond the Assyrian sphere of power. But at almost the same time Gyges encouraged Psamtik's liberating of Egypt with Lydian mercenaries. Left alone to face an overwhelming enemy, Gyges' capital city Sardis fell into the hands of the Cimmerians in 652 B.C.

In 652 Ashurbanipal also became absorbed with the rebellion of his own brother Shamash-shum-ukin, who ruled over the Babylonian province. It was perhaps the preoccupation of Ashurbanipal together with the Egyptian success which encouraged this general movement toward rebellion. Elam had been reduced to a dependent state and new princes appointed in 663 B.C., the very year of Psamtik's success. The southern Chaldeans had a long history of opposing Assyrian domination of Babylonia. An unwise administration of Babylonia, in which Shamash-shum-ukin was king but all local governors were responsible to Ashurbanipal, and constant pressures from anti-Assyrian elements like the Chaldeans, finally led Shamash-shum-ukin secretly to ally himself with Elam, the Chaldeans, the Arameans, the Aribi, Egypt and others. The result was the most difficult struggle the Assyrian army had faced for decades. It was the first time the Assyrians were met by warriors trained in their

ASHU

Ashurbanipal in his war chariot. LM

own school. The struggle continued from 651 to 648 B.C. Internal strife weakened the Elamites, which gave Ashurbanipal opportunity to cut off the city of Babylon and to starve it into submission. Shamash-shum-ukin died in the flames of his own palace. Ashurbanipal did not sack the city but devoted himself to a year of personal rule and restoration, after which another puppet king, Kandalanu, was set up.

Ashurbanipal was not as generous with the Elamites who stubbornly championed the rebellious activities of the Chaldean leader Nabu-bel-shumati. This action provoked Ashurbanipal's last campaign against Elam when he virtually exterminated the Elamite nation, leaving the capital Susa uninhabitable. Elamite history thus came to an end and a void existed in this region until the coming of the Persians.

From 669 to 639 B.C., when the sources for his reign came to an abrupt end, Ashurbanipal was a successful ruler, as Assyrian rulers go. In the last years of his reign, however, ill-health and internal dissensions plagued the king. He died in 626 B.C. and Ashur-etil-ilani, his chosen son, had to fight a usurper to take the throne. This marked the beginning of the end of the Assyrian Empire.

Ashurbanipal was a scholar and archaeologist, or at least an antiquarian. As a trained scribe he took avid interest in literary and cultural matters. He had scribes collecting and copying into late cuneiform writing thousands of documents which became the basis for his famous library in Nineveh. The discovery of this library by Layard and Rassam in the

gave birth to the serious study of
AS ges written on clay and stone in
m
ay of his predecessors, Ashurbanipal
at builder. He embellished his archi-
ith the usual reliefs. The quality of this
unequalled in Assyria and, in the depic-
animals, ranks with the best relief work
world. Assyrian culture had reached its
but was destined to be short-lived.

It appears that the Asnapper of Ezr 4:10 is Ashurbanipal, for among the people this Asnapper brought to Samaria were Susanchites and Elamites (Ezr 4:9), which agrees well with the final destruction of Elam described above.

Ashurbanipal ruled approximately during the period paralleled by the reigns of Manasseh, Amon, and Josiah, kings of Judah. The Israelites had already fallen to the Assyrian Sargon II (721 B.C.). The prophetic ministries of Isaiah, Micah, Nahum, and possibly Zephaniah were also contemporary with his reign.

E. B. S.

Ashurnasirpal II at a banquet. BM

ASHURITES (ăsh'ŭ-rīts). A tribe in northern Israel, located between Gilead and Jezreel, part of the realm of Ishbosheth (II Sam 2:9). Many follow the Targum emendation, reading this name as the men of Asher (cf. Jud 1:32). It could hardly be the Asshurim of Gen 25:3, for these were a tribe in northern Arabia.

ASHURNASIRPAL II (ăsh'ĕr-năs'ĭr-păl). After nearly two centuries of decline, the Assyrian army began again the work of conquest in the reign of Tukulti-Ninurta, the father of Ashurnasirpal II (884–859 B.C.). To the latter fell the task of completing the conquest and organizing the realm. Though with typical Assyrian cruelty, this work was done efficiently and with considerable forethought. His greatest expansion was to the W where he marched to the Mediterranean coast, assimilating many new provinces and placing numerous Aramean princes under heavy tribute. In his annals he frequently boasts of the ferocity with which he put down many a revolt, crucifying thousands and flaying alive captured rulers. His, however, was a time of comparative peace for Assyria, and he sometimes avoided battle, especially in strong and distant places such as Damascus.

Ashurnasirpal was interested in building and art. He moved the capital from Nineveh to Calah (Gen 10:11) and rebuilt this city with the help of captured Aramean artisans. He invited 69,574 persons to a great feast when he dedicated the new capital in 879 B.C. (cf. the 120,000 persons of Nineveh in Jonah's times, Jon 4:11). But the Assyrians themselves were artists of no little talent as is evidenced by the great inscribed reliefs of Ashurnasirpal and the man-headed lion colossus discovered in his palace at Nimrud (Calah). The lone example of Assyrian sculpture in the round is itself a statue of this notable Assyrian monarch (ANEP, #439). *See* Assyria; Calah.

E. B. S.

ASHVATH (ăsh'văth). A great-grandson of Asher, the last of the three sons of Japhlet of the family of Heber (I Chr 7:33).

ASIA (ā'shȧ). In the NT, Asia generally refers to the Roman province created *c.* 129 B.C. after Attalus III had earlier (133 B.C.) willed his kingdom of Pergamos to Rome. Asia included the countries of Mysia, Lydia, Caria, and most of Phrygia, plus several islands and coastal cities. At first Pergamos was the capital, but the seat of government was later moved to Ephesus. Asia was governed by a procurator or a proconsul appointed by the Senate. The annual assembly of representatives from all districts was presided over by the Asiarch *(q.v.)*. The city of Smyrna also vied with Ephesus for chief honors.

Jews from Asia were present in Jerusalem on the day of Pentecost (Acts 2:9). On his second journey, Paul was prevented from preaching in Asia (Acts 16:6); but on the third journey his ministry was extensive, and all Asia "heard the word" (Acts 19:10). Rev 1:11 lists the "seven churches of Asia" as Ephesus, Smyrna, Pergamum, Thyatira, Sardis, Philadelphia, and Laodicea.

R. L. J.

ASIA, CHURCHES OF. *See* under their respective names. *See* Asia.

ASIARCHS (ā'shĭ-ärk). These were officials and possibly "high priests of the temples of Asia" (Ramsay and Lightfoot), though some authorities challenge this designation. There were chief men of equal rank in other provinces (cf. Syriarch, Pamphyliarch, etc.). They must have been men of means, as they incurred considerable expense while presiding over the public games held in celebration of religious rites in honor of the gods and the emperor. It is believed that they formed a type of council which managed the business of the *Commune Asiae*. They offered friendly advice to Paul at Ephesus (Acts 19:31, ASV). The office was one of power and prestige in view of the control exercised over the priesthood and of religion in general.

ASIEL (ăs'ĭ-ĕl). Great-grandfather of Jehu, a Simeonite "prince" mentioned in I Chr 4:35.

ASKELON. *See* Ashkelon.

An inscription from Izmir bearing the title Asiarch in the fourth line. HFV

The province of Asia occupied the western third of Asia Minor.

ASNAH (ăs'nȧ). The head of a family of Nethinim who returned from the Exile with Zerubbabel (Ezr 2:50).

ASNAPPER (ăs-năp'ẽr). This spelling is used in Ezr 4:10. RSV uses Osnappar. *See* Ashurbanipal.

ASP. *See* Animals: Cobra, IV.8.

ASPATHA (ăs-pā'thȧ). The third son of Haman, put to death by the Jews (Est 9:7).

ASPHALT. *See* Minerals: Bitumen.

ASRIEL (ăs'rĭ-ĕl), **ASRIELITE** (ăs'rĭ-ĕ-līt). A Gileadite family descended from Manasseh through Machir (Josh 17:2; Num 26:31). The spelling of the name as Ashriel in I Chr 7:14 is probably a scribal error.

ASS. *See* Animals, I.1. For Wild Ass, *see* Animals: Onager, II.29.

ASSEMBLY. From several Heb. words, especially *qāhāl* (tribal gathering-council, Gen 49:6), which came to signify the community of Israel in whole or in part. From Gr. *ekklēsia*, originally it meant any public assembly of citizens summoned by a herald. In a Gr. city, the *ekklēsia* was the whole assembly of free-born citizens. Though sometimes translated "assembly" (Acts 19:32), *ekklēsia* in the NT chiefly means church *(q.v.)*. The original word is from *ek-kaleō* ("call out"), but various meanings are associated; e.g., "the meeting" (convened) assembly, community or society of Christ's disciples, association, *et al.;* also *synagōgē*, a "coming together," as in Jas 2:2. *See* Synagogue; Congregation; Church.

ASSHUR (ăsh'ŭr), **ASSUR** (ăs'ŭr)

1. A son of Shem (Gen 10:22; I Chr 1:17), from whom the Assyrians were descended. The name appears in Gen 10:11 (KJV) as if it were the name of a person, but the verse should be rendered as in the RSV: "From that land he [Nimrod, vv. 8–10] went into Assyria, and built Nineveh."

2. The land of Assyria (Ezr 4:2; Ezk 27:23; 32:22; Hos 14:3). The Assyrian city named Asshur is not mentioned in the Bible. *See* Assyria. The chief god of the Assyrian pantheon bears this name.

3. An Arabian tribe (Num 24:22, 24; Ps 83:8), also known as the Asshurim *(q.v.;* Gen 25:3) and perhaps the Ashurites of II Sam 2:8–9.

ASSHURIM (ăsh'ŭr-ĭm). Found only in Gen 25:3. A son of Dedan, or his descendants, traced back to Abraham and Keturah.

ASSIR (ăs'ẽr)

1. A son of Korah of the Kohathite branch of the tribe of Levi (Ex 6:24; I Chr 6:22)

2. A son of Ebiasaph, descendant of 1 above (I Chr 6:23, 37).

3. A son of Jeconiah (Jehoiachin) (I Chr 3:17), the king of Judah who was carried captive to Babylon by Nebuchadnezzar in 597 B.C. (II Kgs 24:8–15). The fact that a son of that name is mentioned nowhere else, and that the line of descent was carried through Salathiel (Mt 1:12; Lk 3:27, RSV, Shealtiel) has led to the conjecture that the supposed name should be translated as a common noun, "the captive" (I Chr 3:17, RSV). If this translation is correct, the article in the Heb. text must have been dropped in textual transmission.

ASSOS (ăs'ŏs). Referred to once in the NT (Acts 20:13–14) in connection with the final stages of Paul's third missionary journey. On leaving Troas, the companions of Paul traveled by ship around Cape Lectum, sailed between the island of Lesbos and the mainland, and took Paul on board at Assos (a distance of 35 miles by sea). Paul took the shorter land route between Troas and Assos (21 miles in a straight line, but somewhat farther as the road ran). There must have been some practical reason for this plan, but the author of Acts does not make it clear. Perhaps contrary winds indicated that Paul would have much more time at Assos if he journeyed by land rather than by sea.

Assos was on the site of the present village of Behramkoi. It was founded by Aeolians of Lesbos (Mytilene) *c.* 900 B.C. The acropolis, which was located on a steep volcanic cone *c.* 770 feet above sea level, overlooked the Gulf of Adramyttium, half a mile away. A temple of Athena crowned the top. Assos has excellent architectural remains and city walls which date from the Hellenistic and Roman periods. Its 4th cen. B.C. fortifications are some of the best preserved of their kind. Strabo (XIII.1.58) indicated they were two miles around and 65 feet high.

Assos was famous as the home of Cleanthes, who succeeded Zeno as leader of the Stoic school (3rd cen. B.C.). Aristotle also lived there three years. It was noted for various products in the ancient world. It seems to have been a center for animal breeding, for we hear incidentally that Eumenes II bought some famous white boars there (see Rostovtzeff, *Social and Economic History of the Hellenistic World,* Oxford: Clarendon Press, 1941, I, p. 563). Assos also was a center for the finest white limestone *(lapis Assius),* used for the manufacture of sarcophagi (see Pliny, *Natural History,* II.95; Augustine, *City of God,* XVIII.5). In the Hellenistic period Assos was renamed temporarily Apollonia (Pliny, *Natural History,* V.123). It was well known for the fine wheat which grew in the area and was exported to Rome in Paul's day (cf. Acts 27:2).

A bronze plaque from Assos dating from the time of Caligula (A.D. 37) has been discovered which mentions that the people of Assos welcomed the reign of this emperor (who had visited Assos with his father Germanicus, in A.D. 18) and pledged their loyalty to him (see for convenience a photo of this bronze tablet in *The Good News: The New Testament with Over 500 Illustrations and Maps,* New York: American Bible Society, n.d., p. G18). For drawing and translation of original text of this plaque to Caligula, see Clarke, Bacon, Koldewey in bibliography below, p. 66). Interestingly, in this tablet the people take an oath to be faithful by swearing to "... Zeus Soter and the Deity Caesar Augustus [i.e., Octavian], and the pure Virgin [i.e., Athena Polias], whom our fathers worshipped ...."

Bibliography. J. T. Clarke, *Report on the Excavations at Assos,* 1881, Boston: A. Williams and Co., 1882. The inscriptions of Assos were published separately by J. R. S. Sterrett, *Papers of the American School of Classical Study at Athens,* Vol. I, Boston: Damrell and Upham, 1885, pp. 1-90. J. T. Clarke, *Report on the Investigations at Assos,* 1882, 1883, Part 1, New York: Macmillan, 1898. See especially the combined volume, J. T. Clarke, Francis H. Bacon, Robert Koldewey, *Investigations at Assos,* 1881-1882-1883, Cambridge, Mass.: Archaeological Institute of America, 1902 (yet as the Epilogue by Bacon on p. 315 notes, this book was not finally released until 1921 due to high printing costs).

E. J. V.

ASSUR. *See* Asshur.

ASSURANCE. The realization by redeemed people that they are truly saved. Eternal security is the work of God which guarantees salvation forever, while assurance is the realization of this fact by the individual. The Gr. word usually translated "assurance" is *plērophoria* (Rom 4:21; Col 2:2; I Thess 1:5; Heb 6:11; 10:22).

The ground for assurance is threefold. First, there is the objective revelation from God that those who believe in Jesus are truly redeemed (Rom 3:25; I Jn 5:13). Second, there is the certainty of the committal of faith which results in God's keeping His promise to save (Rev 3:20). Third, there are the subjective experiences of the realities of the Christian faith. The experiences of being led by the Spirit, answers to prayer, love for the brethren are such that nurture assurance in the believer's life (Rom 8:14; I Jn 3:21-22; 2:10).

ASSYRIA (*ȧ-sĭr'ĭ-ȧ*). Assyria is a triangular-shaped section of land E of the middle Tigris between 35° and 37° N latitude, bounded in antiquity on the N by the mountains of Armenia and Kurdistan, on the E by the Median range, on the S by the Upper Zab River, and on the W by the Tigris River. The later Assyrian Empire at its height was bounded on the W by the Mediterranean and the Libyan Desert, on the E by the Persian Gulf and what later became Persia, on the N by the old Hittite Empire in Asia Minor and the Caucasus, and on the S by the Arabian Desert.

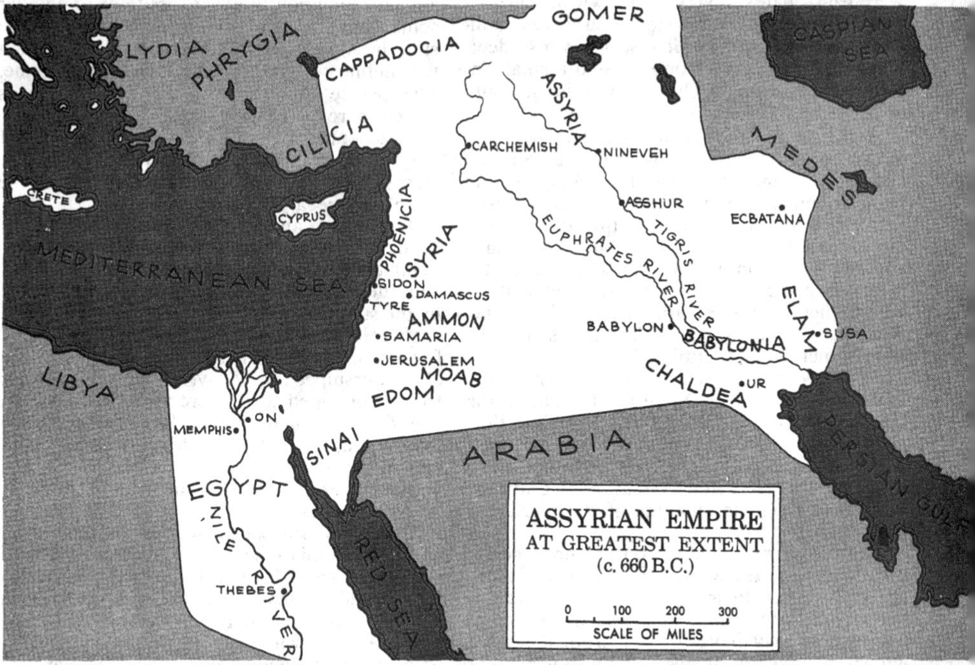

ASSYRIAN EMPIRE
AT GREATEST EXTENT
(c. 660 B.C.)

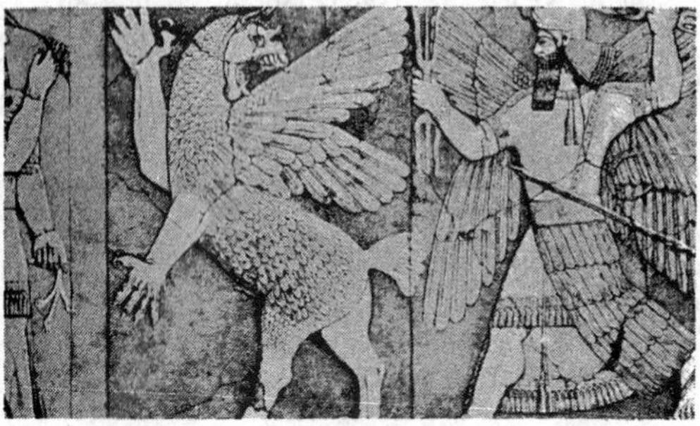

Assyrian relief showing fight between gods and a monster. ORINST

Since Assyria proper was a highland limestone plateau, it had a more invigorating climate than that of Babylonia. It was cold and wet in the winter, but rather warm during the summer months. The major river in the country was the Tigris (biblical Hiddekel, cf. Gen. 2:14), which originated in the mountains of Armenia about 25 miles from the source of the Euphrates. It flowed swiftly (Hiddekel means "the arrow-swift river") through the hills of Assyria and joined the Euphrates before emptying into the Persian Gulf. Other important rivers were the two Zab Rivers and the Khoser River, on which was situated Assyria's best known city, Nineveh. For the most part, the land was hilly, with well-watered plains along the Tigris River. The hills were covered with oak, plane and pine trees, while the main products of the country were fruits, dates, olives, wine, wheat and barley. Larger wild beasts included bears, panthers, wolves, lynxes, foxes, marmots, deer, lions, and wild boar. Domesticated animals included goats, camels, sheep, oxen, horses, and dogs.

Assyria was undoubtedly founded by Babylonian colonists. "From that land he [Nimrod and his descendants] went into Assyria, and built Nineveh, Rehoboth-Ir, Calah, and Resen between Nineveh and Calah; that is the great city" (Gen 10:11-12, RSV). Some Sumerians apparently lived in Asshur, the early capital, for a temple dedicated to Ishtar was found there with Sumerian architectural designs. The Assyrian people were Semitic with strains of Hurrian, Sumerian, and Hittite.

An early literary reference to Assyria was found in a tablet from Nuzu written during the Old Akkad. period (*c.* 2350 B.C.). Nuzu (Yorgan Tepe) lay E of Asshur, the capital, near Kirkuk in modern Iraq. It was here that much evidence was also found that related to the social and religious customs of the patriarchs (*see* Nuzu).

The Assyrians of historic times were a fierce, war-loving (cf. Isa 33:19) people, much more aggressive than their neighboring Semitic cohorts of Babylonia. This spirit of competitiveness may have derived from the more temperate climate or the circumstances that faced Assyria. The most important cities of Assyria were Calah (*q.v.*), Nineveh (*q.v.*), Asshur (*q.v.*), Arbela and Khorsabad (*see* Sargon).

The language of the Assyrians differed only dialectally from that of the Babylonians. Under the influence of the Babylonians, the Assyrians wrote in cuneiform script on clay tablets. These tablets were usually pillow-shaped, about two by one and a quarter inches, or large flat pieces 16 by 10 inches. Sometimes a barrel-type clay prism was used to record important materials. The contents of the tablets varied from royal and private letters, lists of taxes, bills of sale and receipts, to mythological, astrological and incantation texts. In the Assyrian vocabulary, there were a number of Sumerian loan words. This necessitated grammars and vocabulary lists.

In the cultural program of Ashurbanipal (*q.v.*), agents were employed to ransack the libraries of Babylonia and to send their contents to Nineveh, where royal scribes copied and edited the ancient texts. Later came commentaries on these texts, and there were prepared even some interlinear translations of the texts to help students understand the ancient language of the Sumerians. Many thousands of these tablets were discovered by excavators in the royal library of Nineveh. So much literature and of such a varied nature has been found that a separate department on Assyriology has been created in leading institutions in both America and Europe.

Often a tyrant at home, the king was general of the army in the field and rarely missed an annual expedition to exact tribute or to plunder some country. The whole organization of the state in Assyria was built around the king and was military in nature. The king was supreme. The palace dominated, and the temple was merely a royal chapel attached to the palace. This accounts for the preponderant size of the king's palace in comparison to the temples of Assyria. In Babylonia, a theocratic state, the temples were larger than the palace.

The culture and religion of Assyria were essentially Babylonian except for the predominance of the national god, Asshur. Asshur was the incarnation of war, represented in art by the sun disc, topped by an archer shooting a shaft. He was always honored as the divine founder of the nation. Babylonian deities were also worshiped in Assyria. Two important triads worshiped there were Anu, Bel, and Ea, and Shamash (sun deity), Sin, and Ramman (storm-god). Sometimes Ishtar replaced Ramman in the second triad.

Since there was an abundance of stone in Assyria, the natives did not build with brick as in Babylonia. Instead of painted or tiled walls as in Babylonia, they faced the palaces with sculptured slabs. However, the quality of sculpture lagged behind that of relief, and thus the statuary was quite inferior to that of Babylonia. Soft alabaster was used to decorate the halls with sculptures in low relief, while fine marbles, hard limestone, and basalt were worked into stone vessels, pillars, altars, etc. The winged lion and the human-headed bulls at the entrance to buildings were famous forms of Assyria (cf. Dan 7:4). The British Museum and the Louvre afford excellent opportunities to see the Assyrian wall reliefs. There are war scenes, triumphal processions, pictures of private life, etc., depicted on the walls that were removed from Assyria by British and French excavators during the 19th cen.

The early history of Assyria was permeated with Babylonian influence. Although there is evidence of Assyrian merchant colonies in Asia Minor shortly after the fall of the Ur III Dynasty (*c.* 2000 B.C.) in the thousands of clay business documents (Cappadocian tablets) found at Kanesh (Kultepe), the early authority in Assyria was Babylonian and Amorite. Even when Assyria asserted her independence under Shamshi-Adad I (1813–1781 B.C.), there continued from 1800 to 1380 B.C. to be exerted strong pressures by the Hittites from Asia Minor, by the Hurrians from the N, and in particular by the Egyptians under the influence of Thutmose III, the Napoleon of Egypt.

Knowledge of Assyrian history has come largely through the efforts of excavators. To launch archaeological investigations, Layard dug at Calah and Nineveh 1845–51 and Botta at Khorsabad 1843–45. Rawlinson and others continued activities during the 19th cen. The British School of Archaeology in Iraq has done thorough excavation from 1949 to 1963 at Nimrod (Calah, *q.v.*). From these excavations has come a mine of inscriptions. As these inscriptions were translated and interpreted, the history of Assyria began to unfold. Because of the widespread influence of Assyria, evidences important for Assyrian history have been located in non-Assyrian sites. A stele of Sargon was found in Cyprus; a stele of Esarhaddon at Zinjirli on the borders of Cilicia; a letter from Ashur-uballit, king of Assyria, to Amenhotep IV, king of Egypt, at Tell el-Amarna in Egypt; and statues of Assyrian kings at Dog River near Beirut. The biblical record is very helpful for the later period, but the classical histories of Greece and Rome add little to the accurate knowledge of ancient Assyria.

While the Babylonians dated their years with names, the Assyrians devised a modification of the year name by a system known as the eponym canon. They named each year after a particular official who was selected by lot to govern that year. Lists of these officials, in their order of succession, are fairly complete from 911 to 668 B.C. In these lists, the ruling official sometimes added a chronological statement, and thus a sketchy history of the past could be ascertained.

One of the early rulers, Tiglath-pileser I (1114–1076 B.C.), left a rather full account of a lengthy reign and a series of conquests. He claimed to have conquered 42 countries with their princes. He was distinguished by his restoration of cities and the acclimatizing of all sorts of useful trees and plants.

Shalmaneser III (858–824 B.C.) also had a long and effective rule. His record relates 33 campaigns. He strengthened his conquests by placing governors over the conquered districts. During his reign, Assyria began to loom large on the horizon of Israel. The Kurkh stele tells of contact between Shalmaneser and Israel at the battle of Qarqar (853 B.C.). Here Shalmaneser met the combined forces of Damascus, Hamath, Bedouin Arab nomadic forces, and King Ahab of Israel. According to the Assyrian record, Ahab provided 2,000 (or 200) chariots and 10,000 foot soldiers. The battle was not decisive, as Shalmaneser had to fight the same foes in 849 B.C., and again in 846 B.C. In 842 B.C., he defeated Hazael of Damascus, and according to his famous Black Obelisk (now in the British Museum) he claimed tribute from Tyre, Sidon, and Jehu, king of Israel. Jehu's tribute is interesting: it included silver, golden cups and buckets, a golden bowl, a golden vase with pointed bottom, tin, a scepter, and *puruḫati*-fruits (ANET, p. 281; DOTT, pp. 48 f.).

Tiglath-pileser III (745–726 B.C.) was one of Assyria's most celebrated warriors. He took the title of the 12th cen. Assyrian hero, causing many scholars to see in the careful destruction of his predecessor's records and his scanty remarks about his origin, the rise of a commoner to kingship. He was tremendously successful in his concerted drive to revive the Assyrian Empire. He secured the boundaries to the N, E, and S, and then moved W to claim for Assyria a port on the Mediterranean. His drive was not

Bas relief showing Ashurnasirpal II of Assyria being anointed by a magical figure. BM

A human-headed winged bull from the palace of Sargon II of Assyria, weighing thirty to forty tons.
LM

just to annex land, but to gain control of the caravan routes that plied the coastal regions and thus to pour the wealth of the world into the coffers of Assyria. Tiglath-pileser III is the Pul of II Kgs 15:19-20, according to I Chr 5:26 (Anchor Bible). After defeating the Chaldean king who had made himself king of Babylon, Tiglath-pileser III was crowned king of Babylon in 728 B.C. He took there the name of Pulu. Previously, in 732, he had defeated Syria and annexed it along with the northern part of Israel to the Assyrian Empire (II Kgs 15:29).

Sargon II (722-705 B.C.) seems to have been a son of Tiglath-pileser III. He tried to reproduce the reign of the great Sargon of Akkad. In 722 B.C. he was present at the fall of Samaria and deported more than 27,000 Israelites to cities in Assyria and Media (cf. II Kgs 18:9-11). He replaced the deportees with natives from Syria and Babylonia. These intermarried with the Israelites left in Samaria and were called by the Hebrews the Samaritans.

Sennacherib ("Sin [the moon-god] has increased the brothers"), 705-681 B.C., followed Sargon II. He claimed ancestry from Gilgamesh, the semidivine Babylonian hero. He conducted many campaigns, one of which was at Kish against Merodach-baladan, the Chaldean, who sent an embassy to visit King Hezekiah of Judah (Isa 39:1-2). Sennacherib took from him the city of Babylon in 703 B.C. and spoiled it, deporting over 208,000 people as captives. In 701 B.C., Sennacherib appeared on the Mediterranean coast, accepted tribute from Phoenicia, isolated Tyre and took, according to his records, 46 cities of Judah, deported 200,150 people, and shut up Hezekiah "like a bird in a cage" in Jerusalem (ANET, p. 288). Where he deported all these people is not known. Apparently he took much of his spoil to the capital city of Nineveh. Some say his records really meant that he claimed an oath of allegiance from that number. Others conjecture that he displaced them to Babylon from where he had taken approximately the same number. This is an interesting conjecture; but according to Assyrian records, he destroyed the city of Babylon for its insurrection.

One of the great puzzles concerning Sennacherib is the account of his great loss of soldiery in an attack on Jerusalem. One suggestion has been made that there were really two campaigns, and that the loss of 185,000 soldiers occurred in the second investiture. Esarhaddon's annals suggest that there was a second campaign. The biblical narrative says that Tirhakah, king of Ethiopia, was on the scene of battle. This would make this battle *c.* 691 B.C. (*see* Sennacherib). The Assyrian king died *c.* 681 B.C. and was succeeded by his son, Esarhaddon, whom he had apparently appointed regent of Babylonia. Even before Sennacherib's death, Esarhaddon began to restore the city of Babylon.

Ashurbanipal (*q.v.*) succeeded Esarhaddon and ruled 668-633 B.C. He was noted for his cultural interests and for the famous Nineveh library whose cuneiform treasures have unlocked the door to many secrets of Assyriology.

About 612-609 B.C., the Assyrian Empire gave way to the Neo-Babylonian Empire led by Nabopolassar and his son Nebuchadnezzar II. After the fall of Nineveh in 612 B.C. to the Babylonians and Medes, Haran and Carchemish soon surrendered, and the lion of Assyria gave way to the eagle of Babylon.

Bibliography. Georges Contenau, *Everyday Life in Babylon and Assyria,* New York: St. Martin's Press, 1954. CornPBE, pp. 136-146. C. J. Gadd, *The Fall of Nineveh,* London: Oxford Univ. Press, 1923; *The Stones of Assyria,* London: Chatts and Windus, 1936. M. E. L. Mallowan, *Twenty-five Years of Mesopotamian Discovery,* London: British School of Archaeology in Iraq, 1956. A. T. Olmstead, *History of Assyria,* 1923, Chicago: Univ. of Chicago Press, 1960 (reprint). A. Leo Oppenheim, "Assyria and Babylonia," IDB, I, 262-304; *Ancient Mesopotamia: Portrait of a Dead Civilization,* Chicago: Univ. of Chicago Press, 1964. Andre Parrot, *Nineveh and the Old Testament,* London: SCM Press, 1955. H. W. F. Saggs, *The Greatness That Was Babylon,* New York: Hawthorn Books, 1962.

F. E. Y.

ASTAROTH (ăs'tȧ-rŏth). The KJV spelling of the town Ashtaroth (*q.v.*) in Deut 1:4. *See also* Gods, False: Ashtoreth.

ASTARTE. *See* Gods, False: Ashtoreth.

ASTONISHMENT. The translation of five Heb. words and one Gr. word. Most important in the OT is *shammâ* ("astonishment" or "desolation," as in Jer 8:21), along with *shāmēm, shimmāmôn, timmāhôn* ("astonishment" or "consternation," as in Deut 28:28) and *tar'ēlâ* ("astonishment," "reeling," or "staggering," as in Ps 60:3). The lone word in the NT is *ekstasis* ("astonishment," "amazement" or "trance," as in Mk 5:42). There are in addition a number of related verbal forms, particularly in the NT, where *ekplēssomai* (Mk 1:22), *existēmi* (Lk 2:47), *thambeomai* (Mk 10:24) and *periechō* (Lk 5:9) occur.

In the OT, *shammâ* is used 14 times, ten being in Jeremiah, and is closely associated with such words as "desolation," "hissing," and "curse." Most of the references apply to a disobedient Israel and dismay over the fate that would consequently befall the nation. Moses prophesied that if Israel would not hearken to the voice of the Lord her God, she would be scattered among the nations of earth, and she would become "an astonishment, a proverb, and a byword" among these nations (Deut 28:37).

Jeremiah, living at the time of the Babylonian destruction of the nation, described its impending fate. Eight of his references (8:21; 25:9, 11, 18; 29:18; 42:18; 44:12, 22) apply to the state of the Jews under judgment. The same word is then applied to their captor Babylon. She, in turn, would become "an astonishment" among the nations of the earth (Jer 51:37, 41) at the hand of the Lord.

Thus the word was usually related to the dread of judgment, and often included the idea of the unexpected or the awesome. Sinful man stood in the presence of a holy and righteous God.

The NT word *ekstasis* (in this sense) occurs only in Mk 5:42 where it is combined with *existēmi:* "And they were astonished with a great astonishment." Here the context includes the response to one of Jesus' miracles (raising the daughter of Jairus from the dead), where those present were "beside themselves" (NEB).

People were astonished *(ekplēssomai)* at Jesus' teaching (Mt 7:28), for it was full of fresh vigor and came with great authority. Even as a lad in the temple, He caused astonishment *(existēmi)* at His insight (Lk 2:47). His parents, too, were amazed *(ekplēssō,* Lk 2:48). The reports of His resurrection also caused the disciples to be astonished (Lk 24:22). In fact, the chief human reaction to the manifestations of deity in Jesus Christ, as emphasized throughout the Gospel of Mark, is that of fear, amazement, astonishment, and the like. The short ending of that Gospel closes with the note of awe in the hearts of the women disciples who had seen the empty tomb (Mk 16:8).

In Acts the same kind of response to divine intervention is described. For instance, the Jews were astonished when God imparted the Holy Spirit to Gentiles (Acts 10:45). The disciples were astonished that Peter had been released (miraculously) from prison (12:16). Sergius Paulus, the Roman proconsul of Cyprus, was astonished when he saw and heard the power of God through Paul (13:12), and he became a believer.

There is only one occurrence of any of the Gr. terms cited above later than Acts. In II Cor 5:13 *existēmi* is translated "beside ourselves," in the sense of being ecstatic and considered insane. Evidently the word "astonishment" (and its related terms) is primarily tied to a description of the wonderful, supernatural works of God through our Lord (in the Gospels) and His designated apostles (in Acts).

See Fear; Holiness.

Bibliography. Georg Bertram, "*Thambos,* etc.," TDNT, III, 4-7; "*Thaume,* etc.," TDNT, III, 27-42.

W. M. D.

ASTROLOGY. *See* Astronomy; Magic.

ASTRONOMY. The science of the stars, the most ancient of all human intellectual preoccupations. Its beginnings are lost in the dawn of prehistory of man's civilization. Since the age of mythology, astronomy has occupied a leading role among all the sciences and arts. By the very nature of the object of its study—heavenly appearances—it was closely associated with man's religious life and observances.

Its original name was astrology, generally described as the mother of astronomy. By the 18th cen. A.D. this designation was abandoned because of the exclusive astrological drift into horoscopic prognostication of man's future based on the 12 zodiacal signs. This practice, a remnant of the age of mythology, became unacceptable to the scientific and rational discipline of the science of astronomy. Yet even rational astronomy continued to be the source of religious inspiration, with Newton himself and later Eddington as outstanding examples.

With the rise of the French school of materialistic philosophy at the turn of the 19th cen. and the formation of Laplacian determinism in the evolution of the physical world, astronomy also became the source of agnostic and atheistic tendencies. This concurred with the emergence of a new astronomy in which the universe was thought to consist only of matter and energy. The new science became cosmical physics or astrophysics. But simple faith continued to be sustained by the overwhelming wonders of the universe. "The heavens declare the glory of God." However, triumphant victories in such intellectual fields as spectrum analysis, which in the nature of light of radiant stars established the universality of matter, kept undermining the ancient faith. Consequently, there then emerged that school of philosophy which advocates the primacy of matter in the universe, a universe with nothing supernatural in its character. The result of this trend is dialectic materialism.

If classical, descriptive astronomy was concerned in the position of celestial objects, in the orbits of planets, comets and multiple stars, astrophysics today investigates the nature, origin, and behavior of matter and energy that constitutes all the stars in the universe. Astrophysics, therefore, becomes closely related to atomic or nuclear physics. For this very reason, astrophysics encourages the student of creation to consider such speculations on the origin of matter and of the universe that continue to follow the trend of mechanistic determinism and the picture of a universe without God. Some authoritative doctrinaires holding this school of thought go even so far as to advocate that all wisdom is now attainable. They boast of the triumphs of experimental science, which maintains that the universe consists only of matter without any supernatural character, and that all the laws of the universe and the higher forms of life, including consciousness, are mere results of more complex and arbitrary oscillations of some ultimate particles of the universe, such as electrons, protons, or neutrons.

They further maintain that the entire universe is knowable, which means that it is only a question of time when man will learn everything so far unknown.

However, the contemporary revolution in physics, known as quantum physics, reveals entirely new and unpredictable regions of an unknown universe which indicates an inevitable end of the transient Laplacian illusion. New phases of quantum physics, combined with unforeseen aspects of the Einsteinian universe, reveal that the objective character of physical phenomena is undescribable in imaginative terms. On the borderline of the perceptible, comprehensible, and conceivable, the explorer once again encounters a certain transphenomenal realm. This realm is irrevocably forever inaccessible both to man's perception and his imagination; it can neither be perceived nor imagined. In other words, after the most ingenious language of modern mathematical astrophysics and the seemingly genial cosmogony of most advanced intellects, man once again returns to the simple biblical statement: "In the beginning, God created the universe."

In biblical times the science of astronomy was in its infancy. The Egyptians observed that the heliacal rising of the Dog Star Sirius—which they identified with their god Soth—at times coincided with the annual rising of the water of the Nile. Such readings were made for practical agrarian purposes, not for theoretical studies. Around 700 B.C. systematic reports of the movements of heavenly bodies were given to the Assyrian kings, especially data pertaining to eclipses. But such information largely aided the court diviners, and no mathematical computations were made.

Much earlier texts from the time of Hammurabi record observations of the planet Venus. Various German scholars, such as O. Neugebauer, T. G. Pinches, A. J. Sachs, and J. N. Strassmaier, have studied the mathematical and astronomical texts of ancient Mesopotamia and have concluded that early Babylonian astronomy was very crude. Yet as early as the time of Job, or of the writing of his book, the major constellations were noted and designated by specific names (Job 9:9; 38:31 ff.; cf. Isa 13:10; Amos 5:8).

It was not until the Hellenistic era that texts reveal any consistent mathematical theory of lunar and planetary motion. In this period the concept of the 12 signs of the zodiac and the accompanying horoscopes seem to have been developed. The terms "height" and "depth" (Rom 8:39) were used by astrologers for the celestial spaces above and below the horizon, to speak of the rising and setting of the stars which supposedly control the fate of men (Merrill C. Tenney, *New Testament Times,* p. 123).

In Greece it was during the Classical Age that astronomy first began to develop as a true science. Thales (d. 546 B.C.) declared the theory of the earth's roundness and predicted the year of a solar eclipse. The mathematician Anaximander (611–547 B.C.) taught that the earth revolves about its own axis and that the light of the moon is reflected sunlight. Pythagoras and his school (530–400 B.C.) held that the sun is the center of the planetary system, and also believed that the earth rotates on its axis.

The Israelites do not appear to have devoted much attention to astronomy, perhaps because astrology (*see* Magic) and worship of the heavenly bodies were forbidden by the law (Deut 4:19; 18:10–11; see also II Kgs 17:16; Jer 19:13; Ezk 8:16). Such worship was practically universal among the neighboring nations (Isa 47:13; Jer 27:9; Dan 2; Amos 5:26).

In I Cor 15:41 the apostle Paul refers to the differing degrees of brightness or glory between sun, moon, and stars in order to illustrate the possibility of variations among those who will receive glorified resurrection bodies. These will be celestial *(epourania)* bodies (I Cor 15:40, 48–49), of another or different *(hetera)* kind from the terrestrial (*epigeia,* I Cor 15:40; II Cor 5:1) or natural human bodies we now have (I Cor 15:44–46). Angels at present are considered as celestial or heavenly beings (*epouranion,* Phil 2:10; cf. Lk 9:26).

See Star; Magi; Magic; Arcturus; Orion; Pleiades; Moon; Sun; Calendar.

Bibliography. CornPBE, pp. 146–150. M. J. Dresden, "Science," IDB, IV, 236–244. O. Neugebauer, *The Exact Sciences in Antiquity,* 2nd ed., Providence, R.I.: Brown Univ. Press, 1957. Merrill C. Tenney, *New Testament Times,* Grand Rapids: Eerdmans, 1965.

K. H. and J. R.

ASUPPIM (*ȧ*-sŭp'ĭm). The KJV in I Chr 26:15, 17 transliterates this as a proper noun. Literally, it means "gatherings," "stores." The RSV translates here as the temple "storehouse," and in Neh 12:25 as "the storehouses of the gates."

ASYLUM. The custom of flight to sacred places to secure at least the temporary protection of a deity was known to ancient man in all areas of the earth. The ancient Greeks and Romans found asylum at the altars, temples, and holy shrines. Even the statues of Roman emperors afforded such, and the Roman legions in their campaigns used the standard with the eagle to provide asylum.

The two chief places among the Hebrews were their altars and the cities of refuge. Ex 21:14 provided that a person be taken from the altar to be executed. I Kgs 1:50; 2:28 indicate that the altar of the house of God was so used. Laws preventing abuse of such a place of refuge for criminals deserving of death appear in Lev 4:2 ff.; 5:15–18; Num 15:27–31. The cities of refuge (*q.v.,* Num 35:6; Josh 20:7–9) served as asylums complementary to the law of the avenger of blood (*see* Blood, Avenger of). Here one could flee and be shielded from the avenger until his trial. Here also the inadvertent slayer found refuge. (Cf. also II Sam 14:4–11.)

Among Christians, the church altar (later the building and grounds) served as such. But many abuses necessitated definite reforms. Modern law affords asylum to the accused until he is convicted.

R. E. Pr.

ASYNCRITUS (*ȧ*-sĭng'krĭ-tŭs). A believer greeted by Paul in Rom 16:14. The name, meaning "incomparable," appears among the freedmen of Augustus.

ATAD (ā'tăd). A threshing floor in Transjordan (Gen 50:10). *See* Abel-Mizraim.

ATARAH (ăt'*ȧ*-r*ȧ*). The second wife of Jerahmeel and mother of Onam (I Chr 2:26).

ATAROTH (ăt'*ȧ*-rŏth)

1. A town E of the Jordan given to the tribe of Reuben but evidently fortified by Gad; modern Khirbet 'Attārûs, about eight miles NW of Dibon (modern Dhiban) (Num 32:3, 34). On the Moabite Stone *(q.v.)* Mesha said the Gadites had "always" dwelt there (ANET, p. 320).

2. A town on the S border of Ephraim toward the W (Josh 16:2), perhaps the same as Ataroth-addar (Josh 16:5), probably Khirbet 'Attāra near Tell en-Nasbeh.

3. A border town of Ephraim (Josh 16:7), perhaps the prominent mound of Tell el-Mazar, according to Nelson Glueck, which guards the route up the Wadi Fari'a from the Jordan valley toward Shechem and overlooks the ford across the Jordan at Adamah leading to the Jabbok valley.

4. A town in Judah near Bethlehem; referred to as "Ataroth, the house of Joab" (I Chr 2:54).

ATER (ā'tẽr)

1. The ancestral head of one of the large families of returning exiles (Ezr 2:16; Neh 7:45).

2. The chief of a family of returning exiles who with Nehemiah sealed the covenant (Neh 10:17).

ATHACH (ā'thăk). A city in S Judah, probably near Ziklag, to which David sent gifts from the booty taken from the defeated Amalekites (I Sam 30:30).

ATHAIAH (*ȧ*-thā'y*ȧ*). A man of Judah, son of Uzziah. He was a post-Exilic inhabitant of Jerusalem (Neh 11:4).

ATHALIAH (ăth'*ȧ*-lī'*ȧ*). Her father, Ahab, was seventh king of the northern kingdom of Israel; her mother, Jezebel, Ahab's Phoenician wife. Her husband was Jehoram, fifth king of Judah, who, evidently under his wife's influence, murdered his six brothers and restored Baal worship which his father Jehoshaphat had suppressed. The marriage seems to have been prompted by a political desire to bring Judah under the control of Israel. Apparently even the nonaccession year system of Israel was adopted by Judah at this time. After Jehoram's death in 841 B.C., the Arabs killed all his sons except Ahaziah, who became king under Athaliah's guidance. Athaliah saw to it that her son promoted Baalism and fully cooperated with Joram, king of Israel. But Ahaziah was killed along with Joram that same year by Jehu, one of Joram's generals, when a joint expedition against the Syrians failed.

Taking advantage of the fact that none of Ahaziah's sons were old enough to ascend to the throne, Athaliah seized power and proceeded to exterminate the royal household of Judah. However, the infant Joash was saved by Ahaziah's sister Jehosheba. Unknown to Athaliah, Joash was hidden in the temple for six years by Jehosheba and her husband Jehoida, the priest (II Kgs 11:1–3; II Chr 22:10–12). Athaliah promoted a reign of terror against all her opponents and installed Baalism as the religion of Judah. She made the high priest Mattan her personal priest in Baal worship.

At an opportune time, Jehoida publicly proclaimed Joash the new king of Judah in the temple court with the support of the temple guard. When Athaliah heard the celebration which followed the coronation ceremony, she ran into the temple area crying, "Treason! Treason!" but no one rose to aid her. So she was seized and slain near the horse gate of the palace (II Kgs 11:12–20; II Chr 23:11–15). Her reign was 841–835 B.C.

G. H. L.

ATHEISM. The biblical adjective *atheos* occurs only once in the NT (Eph 2:12). It is translated "without God," and signifies an idolatrous religious state, not a state of atheism as the word is now commonly understood. There is no biblical noun for "atheism" or "atheist," but the idea is described in such passages as "The fool hath said in his heart, There is no God" (Ps 14:1; 53:1).

The American Association for the Advancement of Atheism was incorporated in New York state in 1925; and in 1929 the League of Militant Atheists was organized "to carry out the communist aim of destroying the religious foundations of the old society." (Very brief bibliographical references to these two atheistic movements are found in the *Twentieth Century Encyclopedia of Religious Knowledge*, I, 91 f.). One can find no information about these dogmatic atheistic movements in current editions of such general reference works as the *Encyclopaedia Britannica* nor even the compendious *World Almanac*.

The history of atheism, ancient (Lucretius) and postmedieval, is well set forth in Robert Flint's *Anti-Theistic Theories*. Albert Camus gives a history of European atheism in his book, *The Rebel*.

Dogmatic atheism today is far from being dead, but it generally prefers to wear other names, such as naturalism. In *Naturalism and the Human Spirit,* H. T. Costello gives as a thesis of the naturalists, "There is no supernatural." He continues, "The naturalist now looks up to the great white throne, where once sat great Jove himself, and exclaims, 'Thank God, that illusion is gone' " (pp. 295 f.).

Ludwig A. Feuerbach (1804–1872) is correctly classed as a materialistic atheist. He taught that *"Mann ist was er isst"* ("Man is what he eats") (see Wilhelm Windelband's *History of Philosophy,* p. 641). Yet a current article on "Atheism" (*Encyclopaedia Britannica, II,* 600) suggests that one is not an atheist if, as Feuerbach claims (*Essence of Christianity,* Eliot tr., p. 21), though denying the existence of God, he accepts the value of the attributes "love, wisdom, justice."

The atheism about which Christians are chiefly concerned is not so much the dogmatic denial that in some form "God is," as the denial that in Christ He is the "rewarder of them that diligently seek him" (Heb 11:6).

J. O. B., Jr.

ATHENIAN (*ȧ*-thē′nē-*ȧ*n). A dweller of the ancient city of Athens (Acts 17:21).

ATHENS (ăth′ĕnz)

Geography. Athens was the political, cultural, and economic center of Attica in eastern Greece. The Athenian city-state was coextensive with the roughly triangular 1000-square mile peninsula of Attica (about equal to Rhode Island). Located about four miles from the Aegean, Athens was served during her most important period by her seaport at the Piraeus. The driest region of Greece with

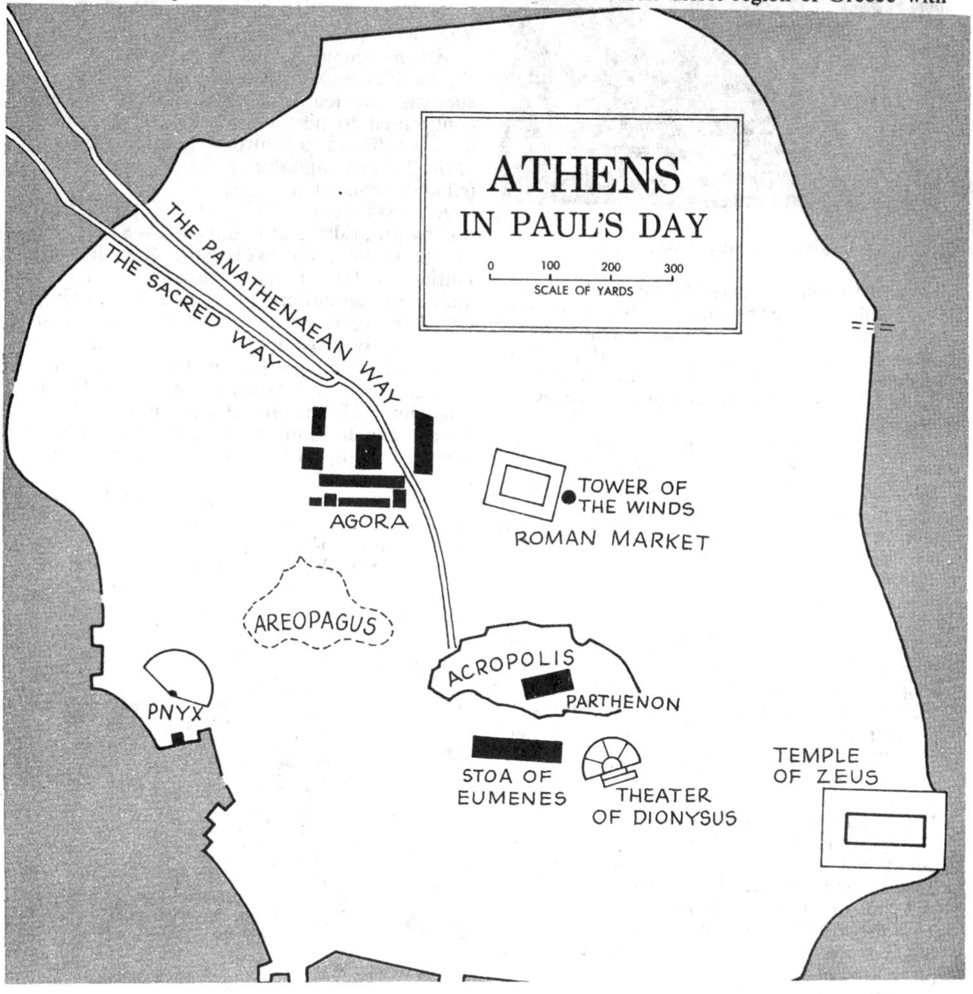

The Tower of the Winds. HFV

an annual rainfall of only 16 inches, Attica had a soil only about one-quarter arable. Resources in ancient times included excellent clay beds for pottery manufacture, the famous marble of Pentelicus, and the lead and silver mines of Laurium in the S of the peninsula (exhausted by the Christian era).

History. Although Athens was an important center in Greece during the Mycenaean era (*c*. 1400–1150/1100 B.C.), the city lost much of her early power and prestige during the subsequent Dorian invasion and Dark Ages. For centuries it remained a backward little country town with little interest in trade. During the 7th cen. the power of the monarchy was broken and an aristocracy established in its place.

Discontent resulting from agrarian problems opened the way for Solon to make sweeping economic, political, and social changes early in the 6th cen. He wiped out slavery for debt, strengthened the power of the assembly, and encouraged foreign artisans to settle at Athens. Development of the Athenian olive oil and pottery-making industries date to this time. The Pisistratid family ruled as tyrants or dictators during the latter half of the 6th cen., bringing about land reforms and encouraging the industrial and commercial development of the state and urbanizing Athens.

In the struggle that followed the expulsion of the tyranny from Athens, Cleisthenes rose to power and in 508 was given authority to reform the government. He became the real founder of the Athenian democracy and was responsible for creation of the famous Council of 500.

Athens was heavily involved in the Graeco-Persian wars. She supported the revolt of Miletus against Persia in 499 and defeated the Persians at Marathon in 490. In 480 Persians occupied Athens but the population was evacuated. The next year Athens led in the great naval victory over Persia at Salamis. In 478 Athens organized the Delian League as a defense against Persia but later turned it into an Athenian Empire.

Income from the empire made possible the golden age of Athens in the days when Pericles held the reins of government (461–431). The full democracy was developed in those days and extensive beautification of the Acropolis (*q.v.)* engaged in to make Athens a fit center of the empire and a fit home for her patron goddess Athena.

Rivalry with Sparta led to the Peloponnesian War (431–404), which resulted in destruction of Athens' empire, fortifications, and fleet. During the 4th cen. Athens built a small empire, but she was defeated by Alexander the Great and contributed to his invasion of Persia. Macedonia continued to control Athens during much of the 3rd cen., and during the 2nd cen. Athens fell under control of Rome.

Athens suffered terribly during the occupation by Mithridates of Pontus in 88–87 B.C. and the subsequent revenge of the Roman Sulla. During the 1st cen. A.D. Athens was primarily known for her cultural prowess and her university. The empire and the silver mines were gone and great rival centers of the E Mediterranean competed effectively for her trade. Despoiling of the city's art treasures came with Nero's rebuilding of Rome after the fire of A.D. 64. But Roman emperors of the 1st and 2nd cen. contributed heavily to building and other needs of Athens.

Biblical connections. Paul stopped briefly in Athens on his second missionary journey to wait out the storm of opposition raised against him at Thessalonica. Apparently he did not have a plan for evangelization of the city. He ministered in the Athenian synagogue and

Acropolis at Athens in classical times. After D'ooge

agora (Acts 17:17). At the latter he would have seen such important structures as the council chamber, the mint, the stoa of Attalus, and the temple of Hephaestus on an adjoining hill.

Epicurean *(q.v.)* and Stoic *(q.v.)* philosophers brought him before the Areopagus *(q.v.)*, which probably met on the 377-foot hill S of the agora *(q.v.)*. There he delivered his famous speech, in which he referred to "temples made with hands" (Acts 17:24), no doubt alluding to the famous temples of the Acropolis to the E of Areopagus. There the Parthenon, Erechtheum and temple of Athena Nike still stood intact. Farther E stood the great temple of Zeus. His reference to an inscription "TO THE UNKNOWN GOD" is supported by the 2nd cen. Gr. writer Pausanias, who saw altars at Athens to "gods called unknown." The American School of Classical Studies has excavated the agora and worked in other areas of Athens. *See* Archaeology.

H. F. V.

ATHLAI (ăth'lī). An Israelite who in the days of Ezra was one of those compelled to put away his foreign wife (Ezr 10:28).

ATONEMENT. The word "atonement" is an Anglo-Saxon term which has the force of "at-one-ment," a "making at one." It speaks of a process of bringing those who are enemies into harmony and unity, and thus it means reconciliation.

In the NT, the Gr. *katallagē,* "reconciliation," is once translated "atonement" in KJV (Rom 5:11); it describes the work or action of God in Jesus Christ by which the sinner is reconciled to God. This reconciliation, however, is not merely any reconciliation. It takes place in a definite setting of OT teaching and practice, so that the English Bible not unjustly uses the term "to make atonement" for the Heb. verb *kippēr,* which signifies appeasement or propitiation *(q.v.)*.

Under the Mosaic law atonement for sin was achieved by the death of a sacrificial victim. The shedding of its blood was the evidence of its death. "For the life of the body is in the blood; and I have appointed it for you to make atonement upon the altar in behalf of your lives; for it is the blood that makes atonement by reason of the life [of the victim]" (Lev 17:11, orig. trans.).

Biblical atonement has a definite form, this specific reconciliation being effected by the death of Jesus Christ in His incarnation, life, death, resurrection and ascension. Thus this particular atonement is to be understood in terms of its specific background and reality, rather than in terms of the general concept. *See* Reconciliation.

The biblical concept. In both the OT and the NT the need of reconciliation is posed by the gracious, wise, and omnipotent resolve of God to satisfy His holiness and justice and yet fulfill His purpose even for sinful, guilty, alienated, and impotent man. Man in his sin is obviously unfit for fellowship and an eternal destiny with God. Yet man is neither able to absolve his guilt nor to free himself from transgression. The OT sacrifices were certainly not designed as a means of human self-atonement. They pointed to the atonement offered by Christ. For the fulfillment of the divine purpose in man, there is need of a substitutionary sacrifice as the basis of forgiveness, liberation, and restitution.

On a human reckoning, this might not seem to present any problem. God might simply abandon man on the one side, or declare and make him righteous on the other, in an arbitrary acceptance in spite of sin. As self-revealed in Holy Scripture, however, God is holy and loving as well as righteous, and therefore He was not willing that man should perish. But being righteous, He neither would nor could condone man's guilt or receive him in his sin. Reconciliation as accomplished by God is thus His self-consistent action for the divine restoration of fellowship between Himself, an absolutely holy God, and fallen, sinful man.

The problem of reconciliation was that of saving man in an act of perfect righteousness and judging him in an act of love. It should be emphasized, however, that this was no problem with God. He was not as it were brought to a stand and forced to seek a solution. He was not confronted by an inner tension in His own being which demanded integration. It may seem to us that the love and the righteousness of God pulled different ways, so that the first reconciliation had to take place within God Himself; but this is a false conception. We perceive the problem only as we see it in the light of the answer, and it was a problem only in terms of human understanding.

How could there be an action in which justice was done both to the righteousness of God on the one side and His love on the other, when it was a matter of saving guilty and impotent men? In His eternal wisdom and power, in the inner consistency of His own being, God had in Himself from the very first the answer to this question. Worked out historically in the action recorded in Scripture, this answer lay in the person and work of Jesus Christ, the incarnate Son, in whom all the demands of righteousness were met, both actively in His life as He kept the law perfectly in our stead, and passively in His death as He died under the penalty of the broken law. Thus the purpose of absolute justice and love was accomplished, man being freed from the guilt and power of sin and restored to eternal fellowship with God.

Four aspects of Jesus Christ and His work are here considered.

1. He was both God and man, so that He could act for both parties and yet also in one cause. While the incarnation was not itself the atonement, it was its indispensable basis. God now dealt with mankind only in the one Man who is Himself both God and man, so that

already there was in this new work an indissoluble relationship.

2. He fulfilled the law of God and attained righteousness, overcoming temptation and manifesting consistent obedience even to the death of the cross. He thus merited to the full the divine good pleasure, but in such a manner that there was in Him no rift between the divine love and the divine righteousness.

3. In fulfillment of His obedience, He bore the righteous judgment of sin as the one for the many. Thus sin was not condoned, yet it was judged in an act which was itself the crown of obedience and therefore acceptable to the Father. Judged in the innocent Saviour, sinful man can be accepted in Him even in judgment. The act of judgment was thus both an act of grace and salvation.

4. He was raised the third day from the dead, so that the sinner judged in Him is also victoriously renewed through Him. In virtue of the new life in Christ, the sinner is thus freed from the power as well as the guilt and penalty of sin, and can live the new life of fellowship to which he is restored.

Scriptural formulations. To describe the tremendous and inexhaustible reality of this great work of reconciliation, the Bible uses many forms of expression. It was an act of redemption in which the price paid by another, and finally by God Himself, was the precious blood of Christ (cf. Mk 10:45; Gal 3:13; Eph 1:7; I Pet 1:18–19). It was an act of conquest, in which the powers of evil, i.e., sin, death, the devil and hell, were overthrown (cf. Rom 8:37; Col 2:15). It was an act of sacrificial propitiation, in which the pleasing self-offering of the Innocent was accepted representatively for the guilty (cf. Rom 3:25; 5:12–21; Heb 2:17). It was an act of penal judgment, in which the divine wrath was suffered by the Just for the unjust (Isa 53:10–11); and therefore in one act God was just and yet also the justifier of those who trust in Jesus Christ (Rom 3:26 ff.).

In all these statements there is an element of metaphor. They are drawn from familiar social, military, cultic and forensic situations. Yet this does not mean that the metaphors do not represent facts. They are not to be evaluated simply as the efforts of the writers to express God's work in familiar concepts and categories. They cannot be dismissed as relative expressions which may be replaced by new and better ones as insight into the work of God increases. As the divine order lies behind human life in general, so there is a reality of divine and eternal content behind these descriptions of the divine work of reconciliation, even though some of the details in the divine wisdom may remain a mystery. Man is in fact enslaved, and God liberated him at a price. There is in fact a conflict, and Jesus Christ on the cross triumphed in and by the defeat of Satan and the powers of evil. Separation between the holy God and sinful man is a reality, but it was bridged by the offering of Christ which was well-pleasing to God. There is a holy, wise, just, good law and God is righteous. Transgression and guilt exist and therefore bring judgment. But judgment was executed as the penalty fell on the righteous One in place of the guilty. These are solid and enduring realities which cannot be ignored in any attempted restatement.

The history of the doctrine. In the patristic age the discussion of the doctrine of atonement was largely dominated by the concepts of redemption and victory, though other motifs were also present. Irenaeus stressed the full identification of Christ with man as the second Adam, and His freeing of man from the devil by the ransom of death. Later writers, like Athanasius and Gregory of Nyssa, brought out the great importance of the incarnation in this regard, either in the principle of God's identification with man, or by the stratagem whereby the devil was lured by the bait of humanity and caught on the hook of divinity (cf. also Augustine and John of Damascus). The latter idea introduced a certain incongruity, as does also the discussion whether the ransom was paid to God or to the devil (Origen). Perhaps an even greater danger lurked in the approximation to a cosmic or metaphysical reconciliation by the simple equation of God and man irrespective of the cross. Nevertheless, the period shows a fine grasp of reconciliation not only as victory but also as intellectual and physical as well as spiritual liberation, and for the most part, the crucifixion was seen to be the critical point in the whole downward and upward movement of Christ the Reconciler.

The medieval period gave fresh prominence to the legal aspect which Augustine appreciated. A particularly fine statement is made in the famous *Cur Deus homo?* of Anselm, where the greatness of sin, the significance of divine holiness, the demand for satisfaction, and therefore the absolute necessity of the incarnation and crucifixion, are all convincingly declared. If Anselm also added less satisfactory elements, e.g., the idea of an equivalent payment and the transfer of a merited but superfluous reward, he certainly held the essentials of a true biblical concept. Bernard of Clairvaux preferred the more common patristic understanding, and Thomas Aquinas attempted a large-scale synthesis in his usual mode. Abelard sounded a new but defective note with his suggestion that the death of Christ was a demonstration of love which brought reconciliation by changing the sinner; and Scotus and Occam introduced the element of arbitrariness with their argument that it was only because of the inscrutable divine will that the death of Christ was an acceptable basis of forgiveness.

The Reformation fathers followed for the most part the Anselmic line, though with significant modifications. True, Luther loved to speak in terms of victory and liberation, but he also spoke plainly of Christ bearing the actual punishment of sin (as distinct from offering an equivalent satisfaction). Melanchthon developed this thought of penal suffering in his *Loci communes,* and Calvin gave it forceful formulation in the definition: "Christ took upon Himself and suffered the punishment which by the righteous judgment of God impended over all sinners, and by this expiation the Father has been satisfied and His wrath appeased" (*Institutes,* II, 16, 2). For all the legal emphasis, Calvin's understanding was perhaps that one which stresses the primary scriptural aspect. Christ is the High Priest who reconciled us by His self-oblation and who still ministers on our behalf in His heavenly intercession.

In the post-Reformation age, Grotius tried to see in Christ an example given on a governmental basis to deter man from sin and yet satisfy the principles of good government. Moberly attempted to preserve the thought of a vicarious offering, but primarily in terms of penitence rather than punishment. Many recent writers, e.g., Rashdall, Storrs, Hanson, and to some degree Dodd, show great hostility to the full biblical Reformation understanding. Yet few are prepared to make it entirely subjective, that is, to make it rest on the response of the sinner aside from the satisfaction of God's holiness. In the most diverse circles there may be seen an insistence on the objectivity and even the penal nature of the work of Christ. B. B. Warfield, James Denney, J. K. Mozley, E. A. Knox, and Leon Morris may be quoted in this regard. But so, too, may L. Hodgson and Vincent Taylor to some degree, though in more guarded terms. The exegetes are almost unanimous that this is the witness of Scripture itself, as admitted by candid opponents like Rashdall and Storrs, who explained their position by claiming a better insight than the apostles. Emil Brunner and especially Karl Barth, with his thoroughgoing outworking of substitution, have added some scriptural and historic facets again, but have fallen into Schliermacher's error of a realistic view of true atonement which logically negates the need of personal faith in Christ.

Three points may be briefly made in conclusion. First, the reality of reconciliation is so vast that no single simple statement of one aspect can claim to be adequate. The Bible itself presents different aspects in order the better to encompass the whole. From this it follows, secondly, that we are not confronted by sharp alternatives in which the choice of one necessarily excludes all others. The various presentations all bring out elements of the truth of reconciliation comprehensively. Thirdly, however, this does not mean that we are in a sphere of relativity where each view of the Church Fathers is as good as another, and therefore we may pick and choose either arbitrarily or at random. There is an absolute reality of atonement which can be expressed fully only by accepting all of the biblical aspects or formulations. Proper weight must thus be attached to each of these if there is to be comprehension of what God Himself has really done for the redemption of His elect.

See also Christ, Passion of; Forgiveness; Salvation; Reconciliation.

Bibliography. Karl Barth, *Church Dogmatics,* IV, 1, 2, 3, trans. by G. T. Thomson, Edinburgh: T. & T. Clark, 1936. John Calvin, *Institutes of the Christian Religion,* 8th Am. ed., Grand Rapids: Eerdmans, 1949, I, 506–512, 551–585. Thomas J. Crawford, *The Doctrine of the Holy Scripture Respecting the Atonement,* 4th ed., Grand Rapids: Baker, 1954. Robert H. Culpepper, *Interpreting the Atonement,* Grand Rapids: Eerdmans, 1966. James Denney, *The Christian Doctrine of Reconciliation,* New York: Doran, 1918; *The Atonement and the Modern Mind,* London: Hodder & Stoughton, 1903. Vernon C. Grounds, "Atonement," BDT, pp. 71–78. J. Hermann and F. Büchsel, "*Hilaskomai,* etc.," TDNT, III, 300–323. David Hill, *Greek Words and Hebrew Meanings,* Cambridge: Univ. Press, 1967, chap. on *hilaskesthai.* Thomas H. Hughes, *The Atonement, Modern Theories of the Doctrine,* London: Allen & Unwin, 1949. R. B. Kuiper, *For Whom Did Christ Die?* Grand Rapids: Eerdmans, 1959. Leon Morris, *The Apostolic Preaching of the Cross,* Grand Rapids: Eerdmans, 1956, pp. 114–117, 142–156, 161–223, 277–280. John K. Mozley, *The Doctrine of the Atonement,* London: Duckworth, 1947. J. Barton Payne, *The Theology of the Older Testament,* Grand Rapids: Zondervan, 1962, pp. 246–257, 378 ff.

G. W. Br.

ATONEMENT, DAY OF. *See* Festivals.

ATROTH (ăt′rŏth). The KJV translation of a town of Gad listed in Num 32:35, near Jogbehah. The name should be combined with Shophan, giving the compound name Atroth-shophan, as in RSV. The town was probably near the larger Ataroth (Num 32:3, 34), from which its name was derived, and acting as its outpost. A site, Rujm 'Atarus, on a lofty hill a mile and a half NE of Ataroth (Khirbet 'Attarus), may be its location.

ATTAI (ăt′ī)

1. A half Egyptian, father of Nathan; mentioned in genealogy of Jerahmeel of the tribe of Judah (I Chr 2:35–36).

2. A Gadite, one of David's mighty men who joined him at Ziklag (I Chr 12:11).

3. Son of Rehoboam and younger brother of Abijah, king of Judah (II Chr 11:20).

ATTALIA (ăt′*a*-lī′*a*). A city on the coast of Pamphylia, visited by Paul on his first missionary journey (Acts 14:25). It was founded *c.* 165–150 B.C. (see A. H. M. Jones, *Cities of the Eastern Roman Provinces,* p. 130) by Attalus II Philadelphus (159–138 B.C.) of Pergamum to be an outlet to Egypt and Syria (Strabo XIV. 667). Strabo placed Attalia to the W of the Catarrhactes River; Ptolemy on the other hand

Augustus Caesar. HFV

placed it to the E (v. 5.2). Perhaps the river changed its course. It was punished by the Roman consul P. Servilius Isauricus (*c.* 77 B.C.) for aiding Zenicetes in his piracy (see Jones, p. 105) by being added to the Roman province thereafter.

Coins were struck from the time of the founding of the city and its name is spelled thereon as *Attaleōn* ("belonging to Attalia"). When Paul was there, the main type of coin showed Claudius on the obverse, and on the reverse Athena dressed in a crested Corinthian helmet (cf. G. F. Hill, *B. M. C., Catalogue of Greek Coins; Lycia, Pamphylia, Pisidia* [London: 1897], Plate XXIII, 8). It should be remembered that the people of Attalia claimed kinship with the Athenians. Attalia struck coins as late as Cornelius Valerianus (d. A.D. 255).

The situation of this port city, rising as it does by tiers from its harbor, is still picturesque and is partly responsible for its continued existence and commercial activity. Ruins there are traceable to the Roman and Hellenistic periods. It is called Antalya today.

Bibliography. A. H. M. Jones, *Cities of the Eastern Roman Provinces,* Oxford: Clarendon, 1937, pp. 105, 130–131, 133–134, 145, 557. Karl Lanckorońoski-Brzezie, *Städte Pamphyliens und Pisidiens,* Wien: F. Tempsky, 1890, pp. 7–32, 153–163. David Magie, *Roman Rule in Asia Minor,* Princeton: Univ. Press, 1950, I, 28, 261 f., 285, 288, 291, 620, 691; II, 1133, n. 4, 1169, n. 20, 1365, 1615 f. W. M. Ramsay, *Historical Geography of Asia Minor,* London: John Murray, 1890, p. 420. An inscription published in the *Bulletin de correspondence hellenique* (1883, p. 260) proves that in the late 3rd cen. Attalia became a Roman colony. It reads: "... the glorious colo[ny] Attalia ..." For other inscriptions from Attalia see Robert, *Revue des Etudes Greques,* LXI (1948), 198 f.

E. J. V.

ATTIRE. *See* Dress.

ATTITUDES. *See* Mind and Attitudes.

AUGUSTUS (*ȧ*-gŭs′tŭs). The first of the Roman emperors (27 B.C.–A.D. 14) and the successor of the noted Julius Caesar. His reign was especially marked by two things: a time of peace (the *Pax Augusta*) and his great building programs ("I found Rome built of sun-dried bricks; I leave her clothed in marble"). He gave impetus to the restoration of religion.

In the NT, his name is indelibly inscribed together with the story of the birth of Jesus (Lk 2:1–20). It seems not accidental, either, that the angel's words on that occasion included "peace among men."

His full name was Gaius Julius Caesar Octavianus, and the title Augustus was bestowed upon him by the Senate in 27 B.C., making him the commander-in-chief of the armies. The title implied divinity, but he did not claim such for himself.

Although he was Julius Caesar's adopted heir, Augustus had to fight to inherit Caesar's legacy. First he and Mark Antony had to defeat forces responsible for Caesar's assassination led by Brutus and Cassius. The battle took place near Philippi in 42 B.C. Later he was forced to war against Antony and Cleopatra, defeating them at Actium in western Greece in 31 B.C. Augustus brought an end to the Roman Republic and introduced the empire period. By careful organization of the provinces, he consolidated the empire, leaving a conquered area

Tomb of Augustus, Rome. HFV

of more than three million square miles at his death. He was succeeded by his adopted heir Tiberius.

See also Caesar.

Bibliography. William James Durant, *Caesar and Christ, The Story of Civilization*, New York: Simon and Schuster, III (1935), Chap. XI. Herbert Jennings Rose, *Ancient Roman Religion*, London: Hutchinson's Univ. Library (1948), Chap. IV. Suetonius, *The Twelve Caesars*, trans. by Robert Graves, Harmondsworth: Penguin, 1957.

W. M. D.

AUL. A thin, sharp instrument mentioned in the Bible only in connection with the piercing of the ear of a Heb. slave who out of love willingly took a vow of perpetual slavery (Ex 21:6; Deut 15:17). Many specimens of auls made of bone, wood, flint, or metal have been unearthed in the Near East from earliest periods onward.

AUTHORITY

Terms. The Gr. *exousia* is the chief word translated as "authority" in the NT. Originally it signified the power and freedom of choice (e.g., I Cor 7:37, NEB). Ancient wills expressed the "right" of the testator to dispose of his property as he wished. In the NT *exousia* is used in the sense of one's rights. Paul spoke of his rights as an apostle (I Cor 9:1–14). Those who wash their robes have the right to the tree of life (Rev 22:14), even as Christ gives the right to become children of God to those who receive Him (Jn 1:12).

Then *exousia* came to mean the rightful power to act or possess or control, as in the case of the sale proceeds of the property of Ananias and Sapphira (Acts 5:4). Whereas *dynamis* primarily denotes physical power or ability, *exousia* usually signifies the warrant or power that is in some sense lawful (e.g., Acts 9:14; 26:10, 12). The uniform teaching of the Bible is that the only rightful power in the created universe is that of the Creator. Absolute authority belongs to God alone, all other authority being subordinate and derivative.

While the English word is not used of God in the OT, the concept of His authority appears in passages speaking of His sovereign and everlasting rule (Ps 66:7; 89:9; 103:19; Isa 40:10; Dan 4:17, 34–35) and His universal kingship (Ps 47; 93; 95:3–5; etc.). He is recognized as the Judge of all the earth (Gen 18:25) who has the last word in all the affairs of men. In OT times God exercised authority over and governed His people through the agency of the elders and also the priests, judges, and kings whom He raised up or appointed (Jud 2:16; II Sam 7:8). They were enabled to govern by God-given wisdom (Prov 8:15–16). See "Government, Authority and Kingship," CornPBE, pp. 354–369. Especially the prophets were His servants to proclaim His messages (Jer 1:7–10) and write down His authoritative instruction (*tôrâ*). They were bound to no earthly superior and so spoke with His divine authority to people, priest, and king alike.

The ultimate authority of God. The Bible plainly states that the true source and seat of authority is in God. Paul writes that there is no authority except from God (Rom 13:1), and Jesus argues that God alone need be feared, because He alone has authority to cast into hell (Lk 12:5). God's authority over mankind consists in His unchallengeable right and power to deal with men as He pleases, just as the potter has *exousia* over the lump of clay (Rom 9:21). Man is not to attempt to unravel the mystery of future times and epochs which God the Father has fixed by His own authority (Acts 1:7).

Jesus Christ's authority is both original and derived. As the Son of God, His authority is original because He is Himself God, the Co-creator and sharer in all the Father's works (Jn 5:19–21). He had within Himself the power or authority to lay down His life and to take it up again, although the charge or directive to do so He had received from His Father (Jn 10:18). He did not have to pray to God for help or hesitate to assume complete authority in the presence of storms or disease or demon-possession. He took it upon Himself to forgive sins, the prerogative of God alone (Mk 2:5–10). He dared to go beyond the precepts of the law of Moses, which was accepted as of divine origin (Mt 5:22, 28, 34); thus He taught as one having authority in Himself (Mt 7:29).

Because the Word of God is fully inspired by the Spirit of God, it has supreme authority for men (*see* Inspiration). The prophets spoke the word of the Lord—"thus saith the Lord"; and the apostles were Christ's commissioned witnesses and representatives (Mt 10:40; Jn 14:26; 15:26–27; 20:21; Acts 1:8; 26:16–18). They were given His authority to build up the Church (Mt 16:18–19; II Cor 10:8; 13:10). God bore witness with them by signs and miracles and gifts of the Holy Spirit (Heb 2:3–4). Their message was received "not as the word of men, but for what it really is, the word of God, which also performs its work in you who believe" (I Thess 2:13, NASB). *See* Apostle.

Even Jesus Christ as man accepted and submitted to the authority of the OT. During His temptation He quoted Scripture to Himself in the presence of Satan as the reason why He should not follow the devil (Mt 4:1–10). In His controversies He appealed over and over again to the Scriptures as the final authority to answer His critics (e.g., Jn 10:33–36; Mt 22:23–46). He clearly demonstrated that the proper school of authority is not the individual's reason or conscience (rationalism) or religious tradition (Mk 7:1–13) but the Word of God, the Bible.

The documents of the NT were early recognized as Scripture (cf. I Tim 5:18 with Lk 10:7; II Pet 3:15–16) and considered profitable and thus authoritative (II Tim 3:16). It is through the Bible, then, that God the Son now speaks and exercises divine authority.

The authority delegated to men. As man and Messiah, Christ's authority is not only original but also delegated to Him by His Father (Jn 17:2). He implies as much when He counters the question of the Jewish leaders who asked, "By what authority are You doing these things, and who gave You this authority?" (Mt 21:23-27, NASB). He praises the centurion for recognizing that He too is under authority (Mt 8:8-10). He plainly states that the Father gave Him authority to pass judgment, gave it to Him because He is Son of man—the *human* Messiah (Jn 5:27). This is clearly reminiscent of the vision of Daniel in which one like a Son of Man stood before the Ancient of Days and received everlasting sovereignty and glory and kingship (Dan 7:13-14; *see* Son of Man). His great commission to His disciples has finality because all authority has been given to Him in heaven and on earth (Mt 28:18).

Men have authority only as God commits it to them (Jn 19:11). This is true both within the church and in the realm of civil government where secular (Roman) officials are called "authorities," ministers of God to punish evildoers (Rom 13:1-7). Christians are to honor and submit themselves to these kings and governors (I Pet 2:13-17; Tit 3:1; cf. Mt 22:21), unless it requires a direct disobedience to God (Acts 4:19; 5:29).

Within the God-ordained family unit the man is "head," has authority over the woman (Eph 5:23) and over his children (I Tim 3:4, 12). Thus the wife should not teach or exercise authority over her husband (I Tim 2:12) but be subject to him (Eph 5:22; I Pet 3:1-6). The husband should exercise leadership of the home as his duty in all humility, gentleness and love, recognizing that Christ as his Head has granted authority to him (I Cor 11:3). In turn, he should fully respect his wife's sphere of responsibility and show appreciation for her competence in handling the details of housekeeping. Children are to obey their parents in harmony with the fifth commandment (Eph 6:1-3; Col 3:20).

Christ delegated His authority not only to the apostles who had, properly speaking, no successors in the matter of producing inspired Scriptures, but also to every disciple. He gave power and authority over all demons and to heal diseases both to the twelve (Lk 9:1) and to the seventy (Lk 10:1, 9, 17, 19). Miraculous signs, the credentials of the ambassador of Christ, accompanied those who believed in the apostles (Mk 16:16-20).

Such power is granted to the believer because by God's grace he is seated or enthroned with Christ in the heavenly places, in the spirit realm or sphere of all spiritual activity (Eph 1:19-20; 2:6). Every Christian, therefore, occupies potentially the throne of Christ. In the spiritual warfare with Satanic forces the believer should exercise his delegated authority and in faith compel the powers of evil to obey in the name of Jesus (Eph 6:12; Acts 3:16; 4:30; 16:18). He is to bring every thought captive to the obedience of Christ (II Cor 10:4-5). He can reckon on the power of the Holy Spirit (Rom 15:13, 19) and the protection of the blood of Christ (Rev 12:11), symbolic of Christ's victory at Calvary over the Satanic principalities and powers (Col 2:14-15).

The authority usurped by Satan. The exercise of power by the devil and his demonic spirits and their domain are often termed *exousia* (Lk 4:6; 22:53; Acts 26:18; Eph 2:2; Col 1:13). While Satan has usurped his power from God, it nevertheless has been handed over to him (Lk 4:6). Thus he holds it only by God's permission and as God's unwilling agent (Rev 2:10).

Angelic beings are sometimes called "powers" or "authorities" (*exousiai,* Eph 3:10; Col 1:16), and these include the evil spirits (Eph 6:12; Col 2:15). But in every case their authority is only secondary, for Christ has been raised "far above all rule and authority and power and dominion, and every name that is named, not only in this age, but also in the one to come" (Eph 1:21, NASB). The great claim of the NT is that the whole world of supernatural beings and their authority are entirely subordinate to God.

Bibliography. Werner Foerster, "*Exousia,* etc.," TDNT, II, 562-575. J. Norval Geldenhuys, *Supreme Authority,* Grand Rapids: Eerdmans, 1953; "Authority and the Bible," *Revelation and the Bible,* ed. by Carl F. H. Henry, Grand Rapids: Baker, 1958, pp. 371-386. J. I. Packer, "Authority," NBD, pp. 111-113. Bernard Ramm, *The Pattern of Religious Authority,* Grand Rapids: Eerdmans, 1957. T. Rees, "Authority," ISBE, I, 333-340. Benjamin B. Warfield, *The Inspiration and Authority of the Bible,* Philadelphia: Presbyterian and Reformed, 1948.

J. R.

AUTHORIZED VERSION. The King James Version (KJV) of A.D. 1611. *See* Bible, English Versions.

AVA (ăv'ȧ). A city from which colonists were sent to Samaria to replace the Israelites removed by the conquest of the Assyrians in 722 B.C. (II Kgs 17:24). The Avites made idols which were called Nibhaz and Tartak (II Kgs 17:31), perhaps deliberate Jewish corruptions of the names of Syrian deities. Ava may be identified with Ivah (II Kgs 18:34), probably modern Tell Kefr 'Aya on the Orontes River. *See* Ivah.

AVEN (ā'vĕn)

1. Aven is the name applied by Ezekiel (Ezk 30:17) to the famous Egyptian worship center of On (Gen 41:45), also called Heliopolis. As he prophesied of the desolation to be visited by God upon Egypt, this world renowned city for the worship of Ra the sun-god

is described by the prophet as Aven—"nothingness."

2. The same scorn of idolatrous places of worship is found in Hos 10:8 where the sites of Israel's apostasy are described as the "high places of Aven, the sin of Israel."

3. Amos 1:5 speaks of the "plain [or valley] of Aven" in connection with God's judgment of Syria. If this reference is to Baalbek, the center of Baal worship in Syria, the false gods are again scorned as "vanity."

AVENGER OF BLOOD. *See* Blood, Avenger of.

AVIM (ăv'ĭm), **AVITES** (ăv'īts)

1. An aboriginal Canaanite people who lived in the area around Gaza. At the time of the Philistine invasions, all except a small remnant were destroyed (Deut 2:23; Josh 13:3). *See also* Hazerim.

2. A city S of Bethel in Benjamin (Josh 18:23).

3. Inhabitants of Ava (*q.v.;* II Kgs 17:24) in Syria, mentioned in II Kgs 17:31 as an idolatrous people transported to Samaria.

AVITH (ā'vĭth). The city or home of Hadad, son of Bedad, fourth king of Edom, who ruled before there were any kings in Israel (Gen 36:35; I Chr 1:46).

AWL. *See* Aul.

AXE. Axes were among the commonest tools of Palestine (Isa 10:15). With other such tools they required hard toil (II Sam 12:31; I Chr 20:3, both RSV).

As to material, earliest cutting tools were of bone, flint, or stone, later bronze, and beginning about 1200 B.C., iron. (The "axe head" in II Kgs 6:5 is really "iron," as in v.6.) The Philistines tried to prevent Israel from using this superior metal when they overflowed the lowlands of Palestine at the beginning of the Iron Age; at least I Sam 13:19-22 is so interpreted (G. Ernest Wright, *Biblical Archaeology,* rev. ed., Philadelphia: Westminster Press, 1962, pp. 91-94).

The butt of the axe head might be perforated to receive a thong by which to fasten it to the wooden helve or handle. The accidental murder anticipated in Deut 19:5 and the loss of the borrowed axe in II Kgs 6:5-6 suggest that the head often worked loose.

The shape of the axe varied, so that the seven different Heb. words which the KJV renders "axe" could be translated axe, pick-axe or adze (with cutting edge at right angle to the handle), billhook, chisel, pick—all of them cutting tools, mostly for wood, sometimes for stone (in Palestine especially limestone).

Abimelech and his men cut brush with axes to set fire to the tower of Shechem (Jud 9:47-49). Attackers of cities cut down trees (Jer 46:22) for siegeworks, for which no fruit trees might be taken (Deut 20:19-20). An axe might be used as a blade for shaping the wooden core of an idol, to be overlaid with precious metals (Jer 10:3-4). The enemies of Israel hacked down the wooden decorations of the temple with axes (Ps 74:4-7). Pick-axes or adzes were employed to cut stones for altars (but Israel's altars were to be of natural stones only, Ex 20:25), or for the temple of Solomon, whose stones, some of tremendous size, were all prefabricated (I Kgs 6:7; 7:9-11).

The axe occurs in the NT only in the words of John the Baptist (Mt 3:10; Lk 3:9), who illustrated threatened judgment by an axe laid at the roots of a fruit tree, ready to cut it down if the tree were useless.

W. G. B.

AX HEAD. *See* Axe; Armor.

AZAL (ā'zȧl). Found only in Zech 14:5 (KJV). It is conjectured that this is the name of a site near Jerusalem. Two places are suggested: Beth-ezel (Mic 1:11), or the name of a place that ceased to exist and is suggested in the name of Wady Yasul, a tributary of the Kidron. The Heb. meaning is "side or slope."

AZALIAH (ăz-*ȧ*-lī'*ȧ*). A son of Meshullam and father of Shaphan, the scribe under Josiah (II Kgs 22:3; II Chr 34:8).

AZANIAH (ăz-*ȧ*-nī'*ȧ*). A Levite, son of Jeshua, who signed the covenant after the Exile (Neh 10:9).

AZARAEL (ăz'*ȧ*-rā'ēl), **AZAREEL** (ăz'*ȧ*-rēl)

1. One of the family of Korah who defected from Saul to David at Ziklag (I Chr 12:6). He is listed with the warriors of Benjamin, especially skilled in using the sling with either right or left hand.

2. A Levite, son of Heman, who was appointed by David to minister in music in the sanctuary (I Chr 25:18). He is called Uzziel in I Chr 25:4.

3. A prince of the tribe of Dan who was appointed by David to be chief captain over his tribe at the time of the numbering of the people (I Chr 27:22).

4. An Israelite of the family of Bani after the return from Exile. He had taken a foreign wife and thus came under the judgment of Ezra (Ezr 10:41).

5. A priest in the days of Nehemiah (Neh 11:13; 12:36). He was the father of Amashsai, a "mighty man of valor," residing in Jerusalem. He is probably the man mentioned as a member of the band of trumpeters at the dedication of the wall.

P. C. J.

AZARIAH (ăz-*ȧ*-rī'*ȧ*). This was a common name in Heb., especially among the families of the priestly line of Eleazar, whose name means "whom Yahweh has helped." It is closely related to the name Ezra, which means simply "help." The Scriptures mention the following persons as having borne this name:

1. The son of Ahimaaz (I Chr 6:9) who, according to I Kgs 4:2, seems to have succeeded his grandfather Zadok in the high priesthood under Solomon. Since his father died before Zadok, the notation in I Chr 6:10 undoubtedly applies to him rather than his own grandson.

2. A son of Nathan who served as captain of Solomon's tax collectors (I Kgs 4:5).

3. The tenth king of Judah whom Isaiah refers to as Uzziah (*q.v.;* II Kgs 14:21; 15:1, 6, 7, 8, 17, 23, 27; I Chr 3:12. See also II Kgs 15:13; II Chr 26:1; Isa 1:1; 6:1).

4. A son of Ethan of the tribe of Judah (I Chr 2:8).

5. The son of Jehu with Egyptian descent through the daughter of Sheshan (I Chr 2:38–39).

6. The son of Johanan, who served as high priest during the reigns of Abijah and Asa (I Chr 6:10).

7. The son of Hilkiah and the father of Seraiah (I Chr 6:13–14).

8. The son of Zephaniah the Kohathite, ancestor of the prophet Samuel (I Chr 6:36; see also I Chr 6:24).

9. A prophet during the reign of Asa whose father's name was Oded (II Chr 15:1–8).

10. and 11. Two of the sons of Jehoshaphat, king of Judah (II Chr 21:2).

12. King of Judah (II Chr 22:6; also called Ahaziah in v. 1).

13. A son of Jehoram, and a captain in Judah. He helped overthrow Athaliah and enthrone Joash (II Chr 23:1).

14. The high priest who withstood King Uzziah when he took to himself priestly prerogatives (II Chr 26:17–20). A contemporary of Isaiah.

15. The son of Johanan and a captain of Ephraim during the reign of Ahaz (II Chr 28:12). He returned the captives and the spoil that were taken in the invasion of Judah by Pekah.

16. A Kohathite who was father of Joel in the reign of King Hezekiah (II Chr 29:12).

17. A Merarite who was the son of Jehalelel in the time of Hezekiah (II Chr 29:12).

18. A chief priest during the reign of Hezekiah who cooperated with the king in the cleansing of the temple (II Chr 31:10, 13).

19. A bitter enemy of Jeremiah (Jer 43:2 ff.).

20. The companion of Daniel whose name was changed to Abed-nego, a royal captive in Babylon (Dan 1:6, 7, 11, 19).

21. The son of Maaseiah, who helped repair the walls of Jerusalem (Neh 3:23–24).

22. A Levite who assisted Ezra in expounding the law (Neh 8:7). Possibly the same as 21.

23. One of the priests who sealed the covenant with Nehemiah, and who probably is to be identified with the one who assisted with the dedication of the city wall (Neh 10:2; 12:33). Possibly the same as 21.

R. E. Pr.

AZAZ (ā'zăz). A Reubenite, the son of Shema and father of Bela (I Chr 5:8).

AZAZEL (*à*-zā'zĕl). This word means "scapegoat," "removal," or "far removed" (Lev 16:8, 10, 22, 26). A footnote in the Berkeley Version says: "The name Azazel is derived from Azalzeh ('dismissed one') thus properly thought of as the scapegoat." Gesenius in his Heb. lexicon declares: "I have no doubt that it should be rendered *averter*." He suggests a more correct form to be *'azalzêl* meaning "to remove," "to separate." It may be considered as an intensified form of the Semitic root *'azal,* found in Arabic. Thus the term seems to stand (in its untranslated form in recent versions) as a symbol of the transfer of guilt and the complete removal of sin.

The Gr. term used by the LXX translators signifies "a sending away, or a getting rid of." Jerome seems to have considered the term to be a compound of *'ēz* and *'āzal,* "goat" and "to depart," for his Latin term is *Caper emissarius* in the Vulgate Version. Brown, Driver, and Briggs (*Hebrew Lexicon,* p. 736) remind us that "in the ritual of the Day of Atonement" it indicates "entire removal of sin and guilt from sacred places into the desert on the back of a goat; symbolic of entire forgiveness." Oehler, in his *Theology of the Old Testament,* thinks it has reference to "an evil spiritual power" (p. 350) or to "a wicked demon" (p. 159).

The name appears in the pseudepigraphical book of Enoch where Azazel designates the angel of cutlery, weapons, and metallurgy (8:1); a teacher of unrighteousness (9:6); who is bound and cast into darkness in the desert pit or abyss (10:4); to whom there is no peace, but severe sentence of bonds (13:1); and is later named among the fallen angels (69:2).

Among the Arabs, the name refers to an evil demon. Those who regard it as a demon of the wilderness appeal to such passages as Ps 106:37; Deut 32:17; Lev 17:7; II Chr 11:15; Isa 13:21; 34:14; Mt 12:43 ff.; Lk 11:24 ff.; Rev 18:2.

The Epistle of Barnabas (7:6–11; mid. 2nd cen. A.D.) definitely considers this scapegoat to be a type of Christ our Sinbearer (cf. Isa 53:4–6). And so it has been treated frequently in later Christian thought.

Others suggest that the term has special reference to the place of banishment, or that it may specify a curse offering to the author of demoniacal sin (cf. Gal 3:13).

Radical liberals view it as simply a relic of some ancient magical pagan rite which was incorporated into Judaism. The Caffers of South Africa have a ceremony in which a goat is taken into the presence of a sick man, where the sins of the kraal are confessed over it and a few drops of blood from the sick are allowed to fall on the head of the goat, which is then turned out into an uninhabited part of the veldt. Thus the animal becomes a vehicle for the expulsion of evil, which evil, being transferred to the animal, is lost in the desert.

Evangelical Christians see here a type of the removal of sin and guilt achieved in the person of our Saviour, and for that reason, they are loath to think of the "scapegoat" as an offering for the placating of a demon.

See Festivals: Day of Atonement.

R. E. Pr.

AZAZIAH (ăz-*à*-zī'*à*)

1. A Levitical musician appointed to play the harp when the ark was brought to Jerusalem from Obed-edom (I Chr 15:21).

2. The father of Joshea, prince of Ephraim, in the reign of David (I Chr 27:20).

3. A Levite overseer of the tithes under Hezekiah (II Chr 31:13).

AZBUK (ăz'bŭk). The father of a certain Nehemiah (not the governor of the same name) who took part in rebuilding the wall of Jerusalem after the Exile (Neh 3:16).

AZEKAH (*à*-zē'k*à*). A city located on a high hill NE of Lachish and SW of Jerusalem. Her king joined the enemies of Israel in Joshua's day and suffered defeat at the hands of the Hebrews (Josh 10:10–11). Near this city the Philistines encamped when David killed Goliath (I Sam 17:1). During the divided monarchy Rehoboam fortified Azekah (II Chr 11:9) and it remained an important fort when Nebuchadnezzar attacked Jerusalem in 588 B.C. On that occasion it was one of the last remaining strongholds of Judah (Jer 34:7). One of the Lachish letters (No. IV), written at that time by an officer in charge of an outpost near Azekah, mentions that he could not see fire signals from Azekah (ANET, p. 322). It is not certain whether this implies Azekah had already fallen to the Babylonians. The city again figured in Heb. history after the return from Babylonian captivity (Neh 11:30).

It is identified with Tell Zakariyeh in the Shephelah or foothills region of Judah (Josh 15:35), guarding the lower end of the valley of Elah (Wadi es-Sant), *c.* 16 miles W of Bethlehem. F. J. Bliss and R. A. S. Macalister in 1898–99 uncovered an inner citadel fortified with eight large towers, perhaps built during Rehoboam's reign.

H. F. V.

Mound of Azekah. HFV

AZEL (ā'zĕl). A Benjamite, a descendant of Jonathan (I Chr 8:37).

AZEM (ā'zĕm). A town in the Negeb district of Judah later assigned to Simeon (Josh 15:29; 19:3). It is spelled Ezem in I Chr 4:29. Since it is mentioned near Arad in the list of towns pillaged by Pharaoh Shishak, it may be identified with Umm el-'Azam, 12 miles SE of Beer-sheba.

AZGAD (ăz'găd). The head of a family, of whom 1,222 male members returned to Palestine with Zerubbabel (Ezr 2:12; Neh 7:17 [2,322]), and again 110 male members returned with Ezra (Ezr 8:12). Azgad set his seal to Ezra's covenant (Neh 10:1, 15). The name occurs in the Aramaic papyri from the ruins of the Jewish colony at Elephantine in Egypt.

AZIEL (ā'zĭ-ĕl). A shortened form of Jaaziel (*q.v.;* I Chr 15:18). A Levitical singer who played the psaltery (I Chr 15:20).

AZIZA (*à*-zī'z*à*). One of the sons of Zattu who obeyed Ezra and put away his foreign wife (Ezr 10:27).

AZMAVETH (ăz-m*à*'vĕth)

1. A member of David's elite corps of 30 valiant men (II Sam 23:31; I Chr 11:33). He was a native of the town of Bahurim in Benjamin, just E of Jerusalem. He was probably the father of the two young Benjamites who deserted Saul to join David at Ziklag (I Chr 12:3).

2. The son of Jehoaddah, a descendant of Jonathan through Mephibosheth (Meribbaal) (I Chr 8:36; 9:42).

3. The son of Adiel and an important officer over the king's treasury in the time of David (I Chr 27:25).

4. A village, also called Beth-Azmaveth (*q.v.),* on the border of Judah and Benjamin, five miles NE of Jeruslaem; modern Hizmeh. The village might well preserve the name of the mighty man of David's day (i.e., see 1 above). From this town came 42 exiles who returned in the days of Zerubbabel (Ezr 2:24; Neh 7:28; 12:29).

AZMON (ăz'môn). A place on the southern border of Judah; location uncertain (Num 34:4–5; Josh 15:4).

AZNOTH-TABOR (ăz'nŏth-tā'bŏr). A place at the SW corner of the border of Naphtali, evidently on the lower slopes of Mount Tabor (Josh 19:34). *See* Tabor, Mount.

AZOR (ā'zŏr). One of the post-Exilic ancestors of Jesus (Mt 1:13–14).

AZOTUS (*ȧ*-zō'tŭs). The LXX and NT form (Acts 8:40) of Ashdod *(q.v.)*.

AZRIEL (ăz'rĭ-ĕl)

1. One of the heads of the half tribe of Manasseh E of the Jordan (I Chr 5:24).

2. The father of Jerimoth who was a chief of Naphtali (I Chr 27:19).

3. The father of Seraiah who was commanded by King Jehoiakim to arrest Baruch and Jeremiah (Jer 36:26).

AZRIKAM (ăz'rĭ-kăm)

1. One of the sons of Neariah, a descendant of Zerubbabel in the family of David, in the period after the return from Exile (I Chr 3:23).

2. One of the six sons of Azel, a Benjamite descendant of Saul and Jonathan, probably after the Exile (I Chr 8:38; 9:44).

3. A Levite of the family of Merari, one of whose descendants is listed as a dweller in Jerusalem in Nehemiah's time (I Chr 9:14; Neh 11:15).

4. The most prominent Azrikam was "commander of the palace" under Ahaz (II Chr 28:7, RSV). He was slain by Zichri of Ephraim during the attack of Pekah and Rezin on Judah.

AZUBAH (*ȧ*-zū'b*ȧ*)

1. A wife of Caleb and mother of three sons (I Chr 2:18–19).

2. A daughter of Shilhi and the mother of King Jehoshaphat (I Kgs 22:42; II Chr 20:31).

AZUR (ā'zŭr)

1. The father of Hananiah, the false prophet from Gibeon (Jer 28:1).

2. The father of Jaazaniah, one of those who gave wicked counsel to the city of Jerusalem (Ezk 11:1).

3. One of the chief Israelites who signed the covenant in the days of Nehemiah (Neh 10:17, Azzur).

AZZAH (ăz'*ȧ*). The KJV translation of Heb. *'azzâ* in Deut 2:23; I Kgs 4:24; Jer 25:20. The Gr. form, Gaza, is more commonly used. *See* Gaza.

AZZAN (ăz'*ȧ*n). The father of Paltiel, a prince of the tribe of Issachar who was one of the commissioners selected to divide the land among the tribes (Num 34:26).

AZZUR (ăz'ŭr). Found only in Neh 10:17. *See* Azur.

B

BAAL, BAALIM. *See* Gods, False.

BAALAH (bā'*ȧ*-lă)

1. A border city of northern Judah, better known as Kirjath-jearim or Kirjath-baal (*q.v.*), five miles W of Jerusalem on the road descending to the coast (Josh 15:9 – 10, 60), where the ark remained after its return from Philistia (I Chr 13:6).

2. A ridge, probably the hill of Mughar, some 20 miles farther W, arising out of the Philistine plain between Ekron and Jabneel (Josh 15:11).

3. A city of Simeon in southern Judah (Josh 15:29), modern Tulul el-Medhbah, identifiable with Balah (Josh 19:3) and Bilhah (I Chr 4:29), which see.

BAALATH (bā'*ȧ*-lăth). A town fortified by Solomon (I Kgs 9:18; II Chr 8:6). It was in the original territory of Dan (Josh 19:44), probably near Gezer.

BAALATH-BEER (bā'*ȧ*-lăth bē'ēr). A border city of the tribe of Simeon, apparently also known as Ramah (*q.v.*) of the Negeb (Josh 19:8; I Sam 30:27). The shrine of a Canaanite goddess was located here and was simply referred to as Baal (I Chr 4:33). An early 6th cen. B.C. Heb. ostracon from Arad mentions Ramath-negeb and illuminates the area of the S boundary of the kingdom of Judah (BASOR # 197 [1970], pp. 16 – 28).

BAALBEK (bāl'bĕk). A site of magnificent ruins, about 40 miles NW of Damascus in the Beqa', the wide plain between the Lebanon and Anti-Lebanon. Some scholars have identified it with the Aven of Amos 1:5 (RSV). It seems to have been a center for the worship of Baal or Hadad before it became known as Heliopolis, "City of the Sun," in the Seleucid period. Under Augustus the city became a Roman colony and its cult was much favored. The first three centuries of the Christian era witnessed its greatest prosperity. Magnificent temples were erected to the god Bacchus and to the triad Jupiter (identified with Baal, at that time recognized as the sun-god), Mercury, and Venus. The great Jupiter temple was commenced by

Antoninus Pius (A.D. 138 - 161) and completed under Caracalla (211 - 217), whose mother was a Syrian lady.

When the Arabs conquered Baalbek in 634 the great temple was converted into a citadel. Two severe destructions were carried out by the Mongols, first by Hulagu in 1260 and later by Tamerlane in 1401. It again suffered greatly from an earthquake in 1759. Since 1900 excavations and restoration work of the ruins have intermittently been carried out, first by a German expedition and recently by the Lebanese government.

S. H. H.

BAAL-BERITH. *See* Gods, False.

BAALE OF JUDAH (bā'ă-lē of Jū'dȧ). A town of Judah (II Sam 6:2), the same city as Baalah or Kirjath-jearim (*q.v.*; I Chr 13:6).

BAAL-GAD (bāl-găd'). Located in the valley of Lebanon, near Mount Hermon, marking the northern boundary of Joshua's conquests (Josh 11:17; 12:7; 13:5). May have been where Gad, the god of fortune, was worshiped. Site unknown.

BAAL-HAMON (bāl-hā'mōn). Solomon had an extremely successful vineyard here (Song 8:11). Site is unknown.

BAAL-HANAN (bāl-hā'năn)

1. A king in Edom, son of Achbor (Gen 36:38; I Chr 1:49).

2. A man appointed by David as caretaker of the olive and sycamore trees in the Shephelah (I Chr 27:28).

BAAL-HAZOR (bāl-hā'zôr). A height NE of Bethel where Absalom apparently had a farm and invited the other sons of David to a festival. Ammon was slain by the servants according to Absalom's plans (II Sam 13:23-29).

BAAL-HERMON (bāl-hûr'mōn). A height near Mount Hermon on the N border of Manasseh, E of the Jordan. It was not captured by the Israelite conquest (Jud 3:3; I Chr 5:23).

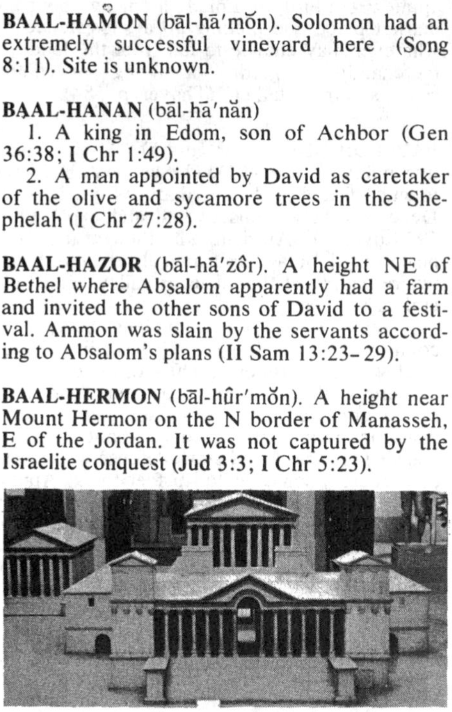

Reconstruction of the temple complex at Baalbek in the National Museum, Beirut. Entrance through the massive propylea leads up to the temple of Jupiter. The temple of Bacchus stands on the left. HFV

The temple of Bacchus at Baalbek. HFV

BAALI (bā'ȧ-lī). The Heb. word *ba'al* means "owner," "husband," "master" (KB), and the suffix *ī* adds the personal possessive "my." The term "Baal" had come to be applied to a Semitic deity (particularly the storm-god Hadad) and to local fertility deities, "owners" of the cities. There was also another word for husband (*'īsh*) which, in contrast, had its cultural association in the primitive marriage relationship (Gen 2:22-24). In Hos 2:16 there is a play on these two words (cf. KJV and RSV) with respect to the Lord. The prophet pointed to a time of regeneration and covenant renewal when the Lord's steadfast love would have triumphed over Israel's unfaithfulness, and she would call Him "my Husband" (*'ishī*). The names of the Baals no longer in her heart, they will no longer be on her lips (Hos 2:17-23).

BAALIM. *See* Gods, False: Baal.

BAALIS (bā'ȧ-lĭs). An Ammonite king who sent Ishmael to murder Gedaliah shortly after Nebuchadnezzar's capture of Jerusalem (Jer 40:14).

BAAL-MEON (bāl-mē'ŏn). An Amorite city of N Moab, assigned to the Reubenites and rebuilt by them. Also known as Beth-baal-meon (*q.v.*; Josh 13:17; Ezk 25:9). It is mentioned on the Moabite Stone (line 9) as held by Mesha, king of Moab, *c.* 830 B.C., and later taken by the Israelites (Ostracon 27 from Samaria); but by Ezekiel's time it was back in the hands of Moab (Ezk 25:9).

BAAL-PEOR. *See* Gods, False.

BAAL-PERAZIM (bāl-pē-rā'zĭm). A place near the valley of Rephaim where David won a victory over the Philistines shortly after he became king of Israel (II Sam 5:18-20; I Chr 14:9-11; Isa 28:21). *See* Perazim, Mount of.

BAAL-SHALISHA (bāl-shăl'ĭ-shȧ). A fertile valley where early crops were raised. It was from here that a man brought 20 loaves of barley and fresh ears of grain to Elisha and the school of the prophets at Gilgal (II Kgs 4:42). Some scholars identify the site with Shalisha mentioned in I Sam 9:4, SW of Shechem.

BAAL-TAMER (bāl-tā'mȧr). A place near Gibeah in Benjamin where the Israelite army took its last stand and successfully attacked the city (Jud 20:33). The site has not been positively identified.

BAAL-ZEBUB. *See* Gods, False.

BAAL-ZEPHON (bāl-zē'fŏn). One of the three sites mentioned near the Red Sea in connection with the Israelites' crossing (Ex 14:2, 9). The exact location is unknown, but the divinity for whom the place was named is mentioned in Ugaritic, Egyptian and Phoenician literature as a sea- and storm-god. *See* Exodus, The.

BAANA (bā'*ȧ*-n*ȧ*)

1. The son of Ahilud, an overseer for Solomon in the S district of the plain of Jezreel from Megiddo to the Jordan (I Kgs 4:12).

2. The father of Zadok, who helped in rebuilding the walls of Jerusalem in the time of Nehemiah (Neh 3:4).

See also Baanah 3.

BAANAH (bā'*ȧ*-n*ȧ*)

1. Son of Rimmon, of the tribe of Benjamin. He and his brother Rechab were captains in Ishbosheth's army. They traitorously slew Ishbosheth while he was sleeping at noon in his house. Taking his head, they fled to Hebron and presented it to David. Enraged by their act, David ordered them slain. With hands and feet cut off, their bodies were hung by the pool in Hebron (II Sam 4:2-12).

2. The father of Heleb, one of David's 30 heroes (II Sam 23:29; I Chr 11:30).

3. A son of Hushai, overseer of one of the 12 districts of Solomon in Asher and Bealoth (I Kgs 4:16). His name should be translated Baana, as in RSV.

4. One who returned from Babylon with Zerubbabel, and signed Ezra's covenant (Ezr 2:2; 7:7; 10:27).

BAARA (bā'*ȧ*-r*ȧ*). A wife of Shaharaim (I Chr 8:8).

BAASEIAH (bā'*ȧ*-sē'y*ȧ*). An ancestor of Asaph, the musician, and a Levite of the family of Kohathites (I Chr 6:33, 40). Perhaps the name should be Maaseiah (*q.v.*).

BAASHA (bā'*ȧ*-sh*ȧ*). A son of Ahijah of the tribe of Issachar. He became third king of Israel by destroying Nadab, son of Jeroboam I, at Gibbethon (I Kgs 15:27). He thoroughly exterminated all members of Jeroboam's family, thus fulfilling prophecy (I Kgs 14:6-16). After establishing his capital at Tirzah, he made war against Asa, king of Judah. Baasha entered the territory of Benjamin and began to build a fortress at Ramah, about five miles N of Jerusalem. Since the E-W trade route crossed the highlands just N of Ramah, this move threatened to set up an economic blockade against Jerusalem. He withdrew because Asa persuaded Ben-hadad of Syria to attack Baasha from the N. The prophet Jehu predicted judgment because of Baasha's wicked ways. Baasha reigned for 24 years and was buried at Tirzah. The destruction of Baasha's dynasty by Zimri (I Kgs 16:9-12) became a symbol of divine judgment (I Kgs 21:22; II Kgs 9:9). His story is found in I Kgs 15:16-22, 27-34; 16:1-7; II Chr 16:1-6.

G. H. L.

BABBLER. The English word refers to one who talks incoherently or foolishly. The term is supposed to have been formed from the childish ba ba (cf. Eccl 10:11). The Gr. word *spermologos* was applied contemptuously to Paul by some Athenian philosophers (Acts 17:18). The word means literally a seed picker, and was applied to a bird, or a man "lounging about the market place and picking up a subsistence by whatever may chance to fall from the loads of merchandise . . . getting a living by flattery . . . an empty talker" (Thayer, p. 584).

BAB EDH-DHRA (băb'ĕd-drä). A site about five miles E of the Dead Sea, just E of the tongue of land (el-Lisan) that juts out into the Dead Sea. It was discovered and explored in 1924 by W. F. Albright, who thought it to be a place of pilgrimage and annual religious feasts where people of the adjacent valley came several days a year.

Several excavation campaigns have been conducted at the site since 1965, directed by Paul W. Lapp. Before 3000 B.C. people began to camp at the site and buried their dead there in underground chambers radiating outward from the tomb shafts they dug. About 2800 B.C. massive mudbrick and stone defense walls were constructed, some up to 40 feet thick. Apparently this was a fortified town, occupied down to the 23rd cen. B.C. Its inhabitants continued the use of shaft tombs but mainly constructed single-room mudbrick charnel houses which were found filled with human bones and pots as well as some copper weapons. The destroyers of this Early Bronze Age town, and their descendants, camped in the vicinity until *c.* 2000 B.C. and continued to use the site as their cemetery also, employing cairn burials consisting of a shallow pit in which was placed a single skeleton together with some jars. All in all, an estimated 20,000 tombs with some three million pots made up the cemetery of Bab edh-Dhra.

If this was the burial ground and religious center or "high place" for Sodom (*q.v.*) and the other cities of the nearby plain, as Albright suggested, it would be expected that a sudden destruction of those cities would cause discontinuance of the use of their cemetery, as did in fact occur about 2000 B.C. Two similar walled hilltop sites for pagan worship have been found in the Negeb, all dating around 2000 B.C.

J. R.

The ziggurat at Babylon, cast in the Oriental Institute Museum. ORINST

BABEL, TOWER OF (bā'bĕl). This expression does not occur in the OT, but is used to describe the tower built by the early inhabitants in the plain of Shinar. The word "tower" is *migdol* (Canaanite, "watch tower"). Basically, the people built the tower to fortify their city against God in their refusal to spread out and repopulate the earth after the Flood (Gen 11:4).

The Mesopotamian temple towers, called in Assyro-Babylonian *ziggurratu* ("pinnacle, mountain top"), are often thought to help in understanding the form of the Tower of Babel. The oldest extant ziggurat, however, at ancient Uruk (biblical Erech, Gen 10:10, modern Warka), dates back only a little before 3000 B.C. These temple towers were rectangular, built in stages, accessible by stairs from the court to the top of the second story, and from there to the top by outside staircases.

The foundation consisted of stamped down clay, buttressed with layers of brick and bitumen. In Babylonia there was no stone locally available in the alluvial plain near the rivers, but an abundance of clay. Thus many elaborate buildings were constructed entirely of sun-dried or kiln-baked clay bricks. Bitumen (slime, pitch, tar) was also available and was used for mortar. Normally in a ziggurat there were three stages, but some reached seven stages. The chapel atop the tower held the image of the deity in whose honor the ziggurat was built. The temple tower at Borsippa had seven different colors, one for each stage.

There are two suggestions for the location of the biblical Tower of Babel. (1) Most writers follow the tradition handed down by Jews and Arabs identifying it with the temple of Nabu in Borsippa (Birs Nimrud), *c.* ten miles S of Babylon. Birs Nimrud is explained as a corruption of Birj Nimroud—Tower of Nimrod (cf. Gen 10:9). (2) Others locate it in Babylon. There was in Babylon an ancient ziggurat which was begun in the second millennium B.C. Called Etemenanki ("the house of the foundation of heaven and earth"), it stood a short distance to the N of Esagila, the temple of Marduk. It was like a step pyramid, 300 feet square at the base and about 300 feet high above the foundation. Nebuchadnezzar called it the Tower of Babylon.

The writer of Genesis sees this tower as the symbol of human pride and ambition, and says that it was destined to fall even before it was finished. No one knows where it was or is. One Jewish tradition claimed that fire fell from heaven and split it to its foundation. Another tradition maintained that the wind blew it down. The biblical writer used the story to account for the origin of various languages in the human race. Man's pride and disobedience led to confusion and dispersion, as did Adam and Eve's sin. *See* Tongues, Confusion of.

Bibliography. Hugo Gressmann, *The Tower of Babel,* New York: Univ. Publishers, 1960. Alfred Jeremias, *The Old Testament in the Light of the Ancient East,* New York: Putnam's, 1911. André Parrot, *The Tower of Babel,* trans. by E. Hudson, New York: Philosophical Library, 1955. Merrill F. Unger, "Semites and Babel Builders," *Archaeology and the Old Testament,* Grand Rapids: Zondervan, 1954

F. E. Y.

BABYLON (băb'ĭ-lŏn). An ancient city-state situated on both banks of the river Euphrates in the land of Shinar (later called Chaldea), *c.* 40–50 miles S of modern Baghdad and 300 miles N of the Persian Gulf. Its name was derived from the Akkad. *babilu*—"gate of god." It eventually became the capital city of the Babylonian Empire, and the name was used in the OT to designate both the city and the country.

The beginnings of the city are obscure, except for the biblical passage that ascribes the founding of Babylon to the descendants of Cush and the followers of Nimrod (Gen 10:8-10). According to Gr. tradition, Belus (Babylonian Bel or Merodach) was the founder. Archaeological excavations have revealed the presence of a Sumerian culture in and around Babylon that antedates the Akkadian-Semitic civilization.

Description. Many ancient writers have given accounts of the size, splendor, and significance of Babylon. Although there is some disagreement among them concerning the actual size of the city, all are agreed on its magnitude and its influence. Since stone was scarce in the area, and the quality of wood (mainly palm trees) was inferior, the city was constructed largely of brick made from the clay deposits

Reconstruction of Babylon, showing the Procession Street, the Ishtar Gate, and in the right background the Hanging Gardens and the ziggurat. ORINST

nearby (cf. Gen 11:3, ASV marg.—"brick for stone, and bitumen for mortar"). Herodotus, the Gr. historian who visited Babylon after the conquest of Cyrus while it still preserved much of its original splendor, related that the city was a great square 56 miles in circuit. He also referred to the huge moat that surrounded the double walls of the city. These walls were very high and quite wide (cf. Jer 51:58). Atop the walls were chambers facing each other, with space between the rows for a four-horse chariot to turn around. One hundred gates, 25 on each side, all with bronze-plated doors, pierced the city walls (cf. Isa 45:2). The streets of the city were laid out in an orderly fashion as symmetrical as a modern American housing development. Houses three and four stories high lined the well-planned streets. The two halves of the city were joined by a bridge consisting of stone piers covered with movable platforms of wood. Royal palaces, heavily guarded, were at either end of the bridge, and a tunnel beneath the river connected the palaces.

Another famous structure in the city was the temple of Belus, described by Herodotus as occupying one of the squares into which the city was divided. This temple was greatly enlarged and beautified by Nebuchadnezzar. Berossus, the Babylonian historian in the days of Alexander, wrote his history of Babylonia from the inscriptions taken from the temple walls. The temple tower or ziggurat was devoted to astronomical purposes, for which the Babylonians were famous. The first recorded eclipse of the sun was observed with accuracy in Babylon in 721 B.C.

The palace of Nebuchadnezzar also adorned the city of Babylon, as did the Hanging Gardens, said to have been built by Nebuchadnezzar to gratify his wife Amytis, who retained strong sentiment for the hills and groves in her native Media. These gardens were called one of the seven wonders of the ancient world.

The famed Processional Avenue led from the Ishtar Gate to the Ishtar (comparable to Ashtoreth in the OT) temple and to the Esagila temple. Both sides of the street were lined with life-size lions and dragons in relief on enameled brick.

Rulers. The first famous ruler of Babylon was the Amorite Hammurabi (*c.* 1728-1686 B.C.), sixth king of the strong First Dynasty of Babylon. Especially known for the law code which bears his name, he also extended the boundaries of his empire to Mari in the N. A Hittite raid ended this dynasty shortly after 1600 B.C. Kassites from the NE overran the country for several centuries, ruling from Dur Kurigalzu (modern 'Aqarquf), a few miles W of Baghdad. From the time Tukulti-Ninurta I (1235-1198 B.C.) captured Babylon, it was periodically under the sway of the Assyrians, until the death of Ashurbanipal late in the 7th cen. B.C. In 626 B.C. Nabopolassar declared himself king of the city, and under his son Nebuchadnezzar II (605-562 B.C.) Babylon reached her most glorious heights. Merodach or Marduk, patron deity of the city, became, with the gradual rise of Babylon to supremacy in the area, the head deity of the Babylonian pantheon, and is called in the OT Bel. He is pictured symbolically on monuments as a fiery dragon.

Babylon and the Bible. Mentioned along with Babylonia more than 200 times in the Bible, Babylon played a significant role in the life of the Hebrews. Abraham brought with him in his pilgrimage from this area, the language, culture, and faith that left certain influences upon the stream of Heb. life. Babylonia, along with Assyria, constantly affected the development of the Heb. nation, and Babylonia served as a second Egypt in influencing Heb. life and thought through the enforced Babylonian Exile that followed the fall of Jerusalem and the collapse of the Judean state. Merodach-baladan, ruler of Babylon in the 8th cen. B.C., carried on correspondence with Hezekiah, king of Judah (II Kgs 20:12-19; Isa 39:1-8); and Daniel and his three Heb. companions were the captives of the Babylonians in the capital city (Dan 1–5).

Isa 13–14; 21:1-10; and Jer 50–51 spoke of the coming fall of Babylon. They pictured it as an earth-shaking event in the magnitude of its impact upon civilized nations. It would become a desolated, ruinous heap. According to ancient Mesopotamian records, Sennacherib first invested the city and flooded it by means of canals to wreak vengeance on the city for its insurrection. Cyrus the Great, Darius Hystaspes, Xerxes (who punished rebellions in the city by destroying palaces, temples, and walls *c.* 480 B.C.), and finally Alexander the Great made conquest of the city. Alexander planned to restore the city and make it the capital of his empire, but failed because of his untimely death. Then in 312 B.C., Seleucus Nicator founded and fortified Seleucia on the Tigris, some distance from Babylon, and transferred the seat of the empire to that city. From that time, Babylon rapidly declined and never regained the status of a city. At the beginning of the Christian era only a small group of astronomers and mathematicians were living in Babylon. Many of the cities in the vicinity, such as Hilla, used the sun-dried and kiln-baked bricks of the once great city to build new walls, houses, and dams, even as prophesied (Isa 13:19-22; Jer 50:23-26; 51:24-26). Babylon thus lives only in the building of new cities.

In the NT, therefore, the references in Rev 14:8; 16:19; 17:18 to Babylon probably refer to the city of Rome. Tertullian, Jerome, and Augustine so viewed these references. A less likely theory is that the reference to Babylon in I Pet 5:13 referred to a place in Egypt now located in Old Cairo.

Excavations. The major archaeological undertaking at Babylon was led by Robert Koldewey, who excavated there for the German Oriental Society, 1899-1914. Since the earliest strata of occupation at the site now lie under water, nearly everything found is dated to the

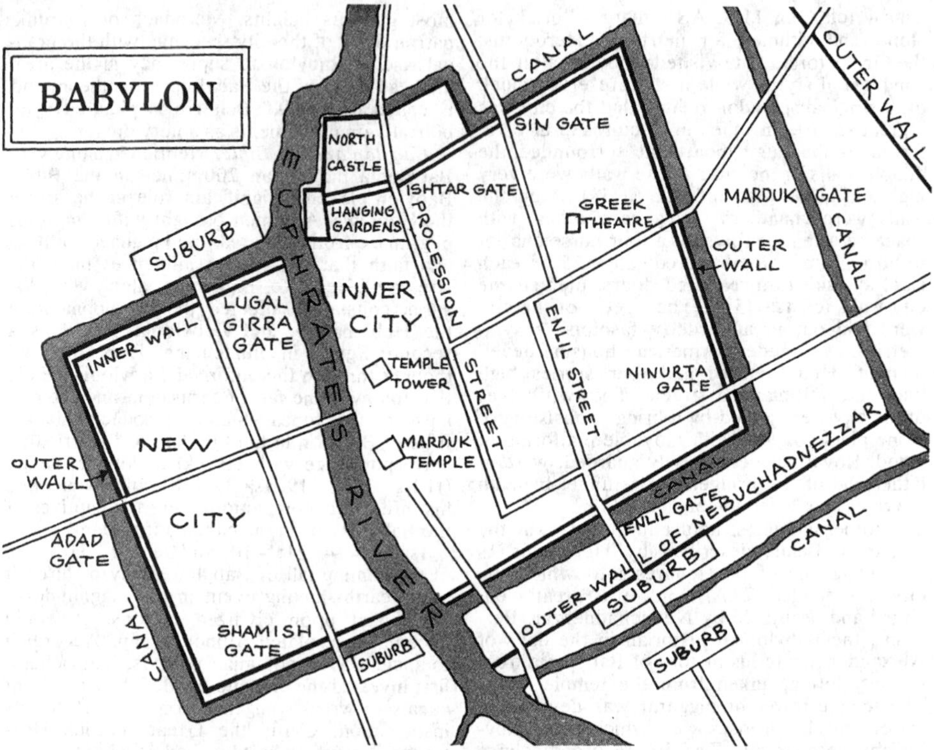

time of Nebuchadnezzar. Although the whole city had been badly ruined, it was possible for the expedition to recapture an accurate picture of the layout of the city and to outline its major buildings. *See* Archaeology.

Bibliography. Albert Champdor, *Babylon,* trans. by Elsa Coult, New York: Putnam, 1959. Edward König, *The Bible and Babylon,* trans. by W. T. Pilter, London: The Religious Tract Society, 1905. Gerald A. Larue, *Babylon and the Bible,* Grand Rapids: Baker, 1969. G. F. Owen, *Archaeology and the Bible,* Westwood, N.J.: Revell, 1961. André Parrot, *Babylon and the Old Testament,* London: SCM, 1958. H. W. F. Saggs, *The Greatness That Was Babylon,* New York: Hawthorne, 1962; "Babylon," TAOTS, pp. 39–56.

F. E. Y.

BABYLON, MYSTERY. A term used in Scripture (Rev 17:5, 7; cf. 18:2, 10) to typify paganism in an all-inclusive sense, as it is seen by God. In certain passages of the OT the concept of Babylon emerges into an archetypal figure for the proud, God-defying forces of this world (Isa 13–14; 21:1–10; 47; Jer 50–51). In the NT it is even more clearly a type of pan-deism formed from a synthesis of Christianity and paganism; this is indicated symbolically in the description of the woman riding on the Beast (Rev 17:1 ff.). The designation "mystery" does not mean that it refers to something unrevealed, but rather something revealed from heaven to all who will listen and read, though it can be understood only by the believer in Christ and with the aid of the Holy Spirit.

The Jerusalem Bible translates the term "mystery" (Rev 17:5) as, "On her forehead was written a name, a cryptic name," indicating that "Babylon" is meant symbolically. In John's day Rome (city, empire, civilization, emperor worship) was the contemporary embodiment of Babylon. Rome was built on seven hills (Rev 17:9), and "blasphemous names" (Rev 17:3) or divine titles were given to Roman emperors. Roman harlots customarily displayed their names on their brows (Rev 17:5).

But Babylon is more than the Rome of history. It prefigures the apostate ecclesiastical system of the end time (Rev 17; 19:2) as well as the political power of the Antichrist (Rev 14:8; 16:19; 18:10–24). It is a demonic kingdom, the habitation of demons and the haunt of every unclean spirit (Rev 18:2). This Babylon is clearly considered to be the successor of the pagan kingdom denounced in the OT prophetic books, for echoes from the taunt songs of the prophets concerning Babylon are heard in Rev 17–18 (Rev 17:1, 15 with Jer 51:13; Rev 17:2, 4; 18:3, 9 with Jer 51:7; Rev 18:2 with Isa

21:9; 13:21–22; Rev 18:5 with Jer 51:9; Rev 18:7 with Isa 47:7–8; Rev 18:8 with Isa 47:9; Rev 18:21 with Jer 51:63–64).

R. A. K. and J. R.

BABYLONIA (băb-ĭ-lō'nĭ-*ă*)

The Land and Its People

Babylonia is located in the alluvial plain between the Euphrates and Tigris Rivers at the eastern end of the Fertile Crescent in western Asia. Scarcely 40 miles wide, it comprises about 8,000 square miles and is approximately the size of New Jersey. The city of Babylon (*q.v.*) was its capital, and the land of Babylonia was called "land of Shinar" (Gen 10:10; 11:2; Isa 11:11) and the "land of the Chaldeans" (Jer 24:5; 25:12; Ezk 12:13). It is bounded on the N by Assyria, on the E by the plains at the foot of the Zagros Mountains, on the S by the Persian Gulf, and on the W by the Arabian Desert from which it is separated only by a narrow strip. The deposits of silt, carried by the Tigris and Euphrates Rivers in their course toward the Persian Gulf, extend the land area approximately 72 feet a year, or one and one-half miles each century. Some scholars believe that the rate of deposit was much greater in antiquity.

The climate is extremely warm in summer. The rainy season continues from November through February, but total rainfall during those months is less than ten inches. The fertility of the soil was fantastic. Two harvests each year and 50- to 100-fold reaping of grain sown was not unknown in antiquity. Irrigation canals, well arranged and properly attended, added to the productivity of the soil, which was enriched annually by the new topsoil silt brought into the valleys by the yearly inundations of the Euphrates and the Tigris. Ancient authors called Babylonia the bread basket of the world and the cradle of civilization—the site of the Garden of Eden. However, long neglect of cultivation has rendered much of Babylonia an arid waste. Only the visible embankments and trenches attest the presence and courses of those ancient irrigation canals so vital to the teeming masses that once filled the Babylonian plain. Recent estimate of the population of this area is given as 7 million, but with a potential of 50 million should the full use of the waters of the Euphrates and the Tigris be utilized.

Wheat was the main harvest, while sesame was also grown. Date palms were introduced from Arabia, providing for the inhabitants wine, vinegar, honey, sugar, flour for baking, matting for wicker work, wood for construction, and even food for fattening oxen and sheep. Man could live almost exclusively from the fruit of the date palm. Reeds that grew along the river canals were used in construction of boats and for fencing around the fields.

The canal systems virtually joined the Euphrates to the Tigris and became in themselves means of transportation as well as the sources for irrigation. One was called the royal canal and joined the two rivers, with water sufficiently deep and wide to convey large boats. Tradition makes it the canal built by the biblical Nimrod, while critical scholarship accredits it to a Babylonian king. Ps 137:1–2 speaks of the rivers (canals) of Babylon. Lions, panthers, jackals, foxes, wild boar and wild oxen roamed the marshlands, while cattle, sheep, goats, donkeys, and dogs served the needs of man in domesticated service. The elephant, the wild ass, and the camel were also known.

Since stone was extremely scarce in the alluvial plain, and the date palm was of inferior quality for construction purposes, most of the cities in Babylonia were constructed on mounds with the use of sun-dried or kiln-baked bricks made from the abundant clay found everywhere. The bricks varied considerably in size, and many of them were stamped with the name of the king for whose use they were made, which lends considerable assistance in deciding the chronology and history of the many structures. The kiln-baked bricks were used to finish the outer layers of public buildings and in important foundation structures, for their resistance to weather made them more durable than that of the sun-dried bricks. Stones were imported when necessary for special monuments or other building needs.

In the early period, the country was divided between the Akkadians in the N and the Sumerians in the S. Babylon, Borsippa, Kish, Kutha, Sippar, and Agade (founded by Sargon I) were Akkadian cities; Ur (the home of the patriarch Abraham), Eridu, Nippur, Lagash, Umma, Larsa, and Erech were Sumerian cities. Some of these cities go back to 4000 B.C. or even earlier.

The Sumerians spoke an agglutinative language (like Turkish) which belongs to an unclassified group of languages called for convenience, Turanian. They developed a cuneiform script from an earlier pictographic writing form. The language spoken by the Babylonians belongs to the N group of Semitic languages and is related to Phoenician, Aramaic, and Heb. It was called cuneiform from the Latin *cuneus*—"wedge," which was the form the signs took from the stylus used to form the symbols. The script ran from right to left with no spaces between the words. Writing was usually done on clay tablets, virtually indestructible when baked. Thus extensive records of Mesopotamia have been preserved and large collections have been uncovered by excavators. The Akkadians, upon defeating the Sumerians, borrowed their form of writing, modified it, and made it the basis of all cuneiform writing which continued in existence until a century before the Christian era.

The origin of the Sumerian peoples is uncertain. Some scholars have seen in the root *smr* the basic root *sm* (shem) with a phonetic complement "r" and maintain that they are the descendants of Shem and are really a Semitic people. From the monuments they have left, it appears that their facial features resemble Asiatics, and from the trees and animals portrayed on their cylinder seals, it has been conjectured that they came from the mountains to the N and E. Their work with metals and inlaid jewelry has never been excelled. *See* Sumer.

Historical Developments

At first, the cities of Babylonia were independent kingdoms—city-states. But finally dynastic centers began to arise to protect the area from invaders and to organize the indispensable irrigation systems. About 2500 B.C. Ur established a hegemony over most of Sumer. Sargon I of Agade, *c.* 2350 B.C., created in the true sense a Semitic empire when he defeated all the Sumerian cities and founded the city of Agade (Accad) as the first capital of the Semitic Empire. Their dynasty continued until about 2200 B.C.

Among the early conquerors of Babylonia were the Gutians and the Amorites. Hammurabi (18th cen. B.C.), an Amorite, led Babylon in a victorious campaign against neighboring cities and made of it the capital of a political empire. His administration was excellent, great public works were instituted, law and order prevailed, and his fame became immortal in his codifying of the laws known as the code of Hammurabi. It was a law code that protected the interests of the noble and furthered the interests of the upper classes. Many comparative studies of the Heb. and Hammurabi codes have been made. While there do appear to be many similarities, the differences are greater. Heb. law was unique in its elevated monotheism, its rejection of administration of justice according to one's social class, and its concept of moral law. *See* Hammurabi.

After the Hammurabi dynasty came to an end in the 16th cen., Babylonia did not figure significantly in world history until the Chaldean Empire of Nebuchadnezzar (6th cen. B.C.) became the terror of western Asia. *See* Babylon; Chaldea; Chaldeans; Nebuchadnezzar.

Babylonian Religion

With the rise to supremacy of the city of Babylon, Marduk, the patron deity of the city, became the head deity of the Babylonian pantheon. A new year festival called the "akitu" festival was held annually in his honor, wherein a mock battle between the king and the dragon of the deep was reenacted to commemorate Marduk's primeval victory over chaos. The purpose of the festival was to usher in the new year with a ritual form so as to ensure peace, prosperity, and happiness throughout the entire year.

Other deities worshiped by the Babylonians were Anu, god of heaven; Enlil, god of wind and earth; Ea, god of the underworld—who together formed a triad of deities. Another important triad was Sin, the moon-god of Ur and Haran, the early haunts of the family of Abra-

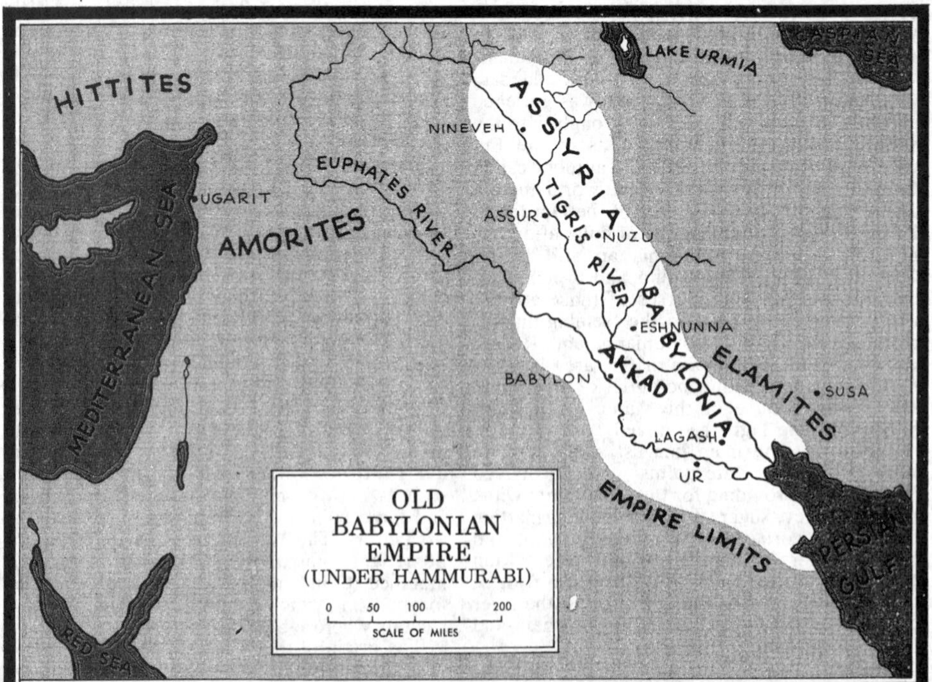

ham; Shamash, the sun deity; and Ishtar, goddess of love and war, the counterpart to Astarte of the Phoenicians, Ashtoreth of the Bible, and Aphrodite of the Greeks. Other significant deities were Nabu, the god of writing, and Nergal (brother of Marduk), the god of war and famine. *See* Gods, False.

The gods of Babylonia were, in their origin, personifications of the various forces of nature. Babylonian religion was thus a worship of nature in all its parts, paying homage to both friendly and hostile superhuman beings, often depicted in the human, animal, or human-animal form. No deity was all-powerful—not even the heads of the various triads of deities. Each deity had a province wherein he or she ruled. In fact, each large city had its own deity to whom the inhabitants of that city gave homage. The deities were created out of the existing materials of the world and were subject to the natural order. Some deities died as did man. The rising gods were the Babylonian expressions of man's longing for transcending the pattern of the natural order. Beneath the deities was the world of demons, endowed with various qualities and characteristics, but of limited influence.

The deities were worshiped in various temples, many times on temple towers. The temple towers (ziggurats) consisted of lofty structures rising in huge stages one above the other, composed for the most part of solid brick and ascended by a staircase on the outside. Several of these temple towers were three or four stories high with extremely wide bases. At the top of the structure was a shrine in which stood an image of the deity to whom the tower temple was dedicated. Some of the ziggurats were constructed so that the angles were oriented toward the points of the compass. These temple towers dominated the surrounding houses and were more imposing than the royal palaces.

To each temple was attached a trained and highly organized priesthood devoted to the worship of its god and to the preserving of the ritual and body of traditions. The priests were remunerated with the regular offerings and the revenue from endowed temple lands. The role of priesthood in Babylonia was higher than that exercised in Assyria. Babylonia was a theocratic society, governed by the priestly order, which sanctioned a kingship that was subordinate to the religious order, but powerful enough to carry out the law that regulated Babylonian society.

Several great pieces of literature have come from Babylonia. Besides the law code of Hammurabi are the Creation and Flood stories found at Nippur and elsewhere and the Descent of Ishtar into Hades.

Babylonian influence in Heb. affairs was at its highest peak during the period of the Exile. Several Heb. families of the Captivity were involved in business transactions in the area of Nippur as stated in tablets found there, and the

Marduk, chief god of Babylon, became the head of the Babylonian pantheon as the city extended its power over the whole area of Babylonia.

coinage of Babylon influenced the monetary system of the Hebrews. It is quite likely that the synagogue movement developed among the Hebrews in the Babylonian Exile, and the spirit of Judaism, born in this period, was carried by Ezra the scribe from Babylonia to Jerusalem.

During the early Christian centuries, the Babylonian Talmud was created in the Heb. schools in and about Nehardea, Pumbeditha, and Sura. These schools eventually died out, and the center of Judaism shifted to Palestine and Europe.

Bibliography. Georges Contenau, *Everyday Life in Babylonia and Assyria,* trans. by K. R. and A. R. Maxwell-Hyslop, London: E. Arnold, 1954. G. S. Goodspeed, *A History of the Babylonians and Assyrians,* New York: Scribner's, 1906. Samuel N. Kramer, *History Begins at Sumer,* New York: Doubleday, 1959. A. Leo Oppenheim, *Ancient Mesopotamia,* Chicago: Univ. of Chicago Press, 1964. H. W. F. Saggs, *The Greatness That Was Babylon,* New York: Hawthorne, 1962.

F. E. Y.

BABYLONISH GARMENT. (Heb. "mantle of Shinar") Shinar was the name by which the Israelites knew Babylonia. The garment stolen by Achan (Josh 7) cannot be described exactly but probably was very fine embroidered cloth, woven entirely of gold thread.

BACA (bā'kȧ). If the valley of Baca (Ps 84:6) was ever an identifiable place, its location is now unknown but may have taken its name from the presence of balsam trees (cf. II Sam 5:23 - 24, RSV). The word, however, is from a root meaning "to weep" (BDB and KB *s.v.*). It is probably preferable here to consider it a common noun rather than a place name and translate as "valley of tears" (Arthur Weiser, *The Psalms,* pp. 565, 567; *et al.*). Men who find their strength in the God to whose sanctuary they make pilgrimage, men "in whose heart are the highways to Zion" (Ps 84:5, RSV), discover hidden springs and enjoy refreshing rains even in the place of desolation (cf. Ps 23:4; Hos 2:15). The eyes which can see the springs through the tears can also see Zion's God (Ps 84:7).

BACKBITE. The Heb. word so translated means "to wander about as a slanderer" (Ps 15:3). Another Heb. word is used in similar manner to describe evil speaking (Prov 25:23).

BACKSLIDING. A term used in the OT by God of Israel, particularly in Jeremiah, where the nation is spoken of as backsliding children (Jer 3:22), a backsliding daughter (Jer 31:22), and in Hosea where He calls Israel a backsliding heifer (Hos 4:16). Children who get into evil and a daughter who chooses a life of sin are familiar examples to people of all ages, and a backsliding heifer is a particularly expressive term to any farmer to portray stubbornness.

In the OT, backsliding speaks of a return or turn back to the old life of sin and the worship of false gods; in this day, a return to a former life of sin and spiritual idolatry, that is, to materialism and the worship of things rather than God. As used today in modern religious parlance, the term refers to the spiritual state of individual Christians.

The view that the backslider who though once saved has become lost again, fails to see that the Christian's *standing* must be distinguished from his *state*. Positionally, that is. as far as his standing is concerned, he is in Christ and eternally justified. He is safe against anything or anyone taking away his eternal life, since both Christ and the Father hold him in their hands (Jn 10:28 - 29). And yet the Christian's *state* is subject to change, since he is still imperfect and able either to progress or regress. The Christian's *standing* is spoken of in Col 2:10 - 13 as a perfection equal to Christ's; his *state* (I Cor 3:1 - 4; Rom 7), as one in danger of a constant degeneration into carnality. Backsliding invokes chastening from God (Heb 12:6; I Cor 11:32), and results in the loss of rewards (II Cor 5:10; I Cor 3:15), loss of fellowship (I Jn 1:7), removal from a place of usefulness (I Cor 5:5; 11:30), and sometimes even calls for removal from this life by death (I Cor 11:30). *See* Apostasy.

R.A.K.

BADGER. *See* Animals: Dugong, V. 3.

BAGS. Bags in OT times were of bark, cloth, and skin, and of varied size. They were often purses (Isa 46:6; Prov 1:14; 7:20) and, since money was uncoined metal, might be of considerable size (II Kgs 5:23; Gen 42:35). The figurative use in I Sam 25:29 (translated "bundle"), suggests sealing (cf. Hos 13:12, "bound up"; Job 14:17); but in Hag 1:6 such a sealed money bag was worthless if it had holes, and figuratively illustrated a man's life when God was neglected. A bag was often used for weights of stone (Prov 16:11); the deceitful man had two kinds in his bag (Deut 25:13; Mic 6:11). The shepherd's bag appears in both the OT and NT (I Sam 17:40, 49; Mt 10:10; Lk 10:4, RSV).

In the NT the bag functioned as a purse for coins (Lk 12:33; 22:35). Judas' "bag" (KJV), however, was actually a small case or "money box" (Jn 12:6; 13:29, RSV) (Arndt, *s.v. glōssokomon).*

BAHARUMITE (bȧ-hä'rū-mīt). An inhabitant (I Chr 11:33) of Bahurim (*q.v.*); also called a Barhumite (II Sam 23:31).

BAHURIM (bȧ-hū'rĭm). Modern Ras et-Temim, a highway village E of Olivet, where Phaltiel and Michal parted as she was being returned to David (II Sam 3:15 - 16). Here Shimei cursed David (II Sam 16:5; 19:16; I Kgs 2:8), and Jonathan and Ahimaaz hid in the well of a man in Bahurim (II Sam 17:18).

BAIL. *See* Surety.

BAJITH (bā'jĭth). A Moabite place name found only in Isa 15:2. Some suggest that the Heb. *bayit* may be an altered reading for *bat* ("daughter"), which would then be rendered: "The daughter of Dibon has gone up to the high places to weep" (RSV). Such a rendering is grammatically weak because the verb is masculine in Heb. RSV marg. reads: "The house and Dibon are gone up to the high places to weep," which may be the proper rendering. *See* NASB.

BAKBAKKAR (băk-băk'ẽr). A Levite of the sons of Asaph and resident of Jersulaem (I Chr 9:15).

BAKBUK (băk'bŭk). Family head of post-Exilic temple servants, one of the Nethinim (Ezr 2:51; Neh 7:53).

BAKBUKIAH (băk'bȧ-kī'ȧ)

1. A high official of the Levites in Jerusalem immediately after the Exile (Neh 11:17).

2. A gatekeeper of the temple in Nehemiah's time (Neh 12:25) related to or the same as 1.

BAKE. *See* Food: Cook, Cooking.

BAKEMEATS. *See* Food.

BAKER. *See* Occupations.

BALAAM (bā'lăm). A prophet whose sin and failure made him an example to warn later ages (Num 22–24). Having defeated the Amorite kings Sihon and Og, and thus acquiring all the land from the Arnon to Mount Hermon, the Israelites settled in the plains of Moab to prepare for the invasion of Canaan. Though they had already passed by Moab in peace, the sight of this victorious host on his borders alarmed Balak, king of Moab. After consulting with his Midianite allies, he sent an embassy to Pethor in Amaw, part of Mesopotamia, to call the renowned prophet Balaam to their aid. If the identification of Pethor (*q.v.*) with Tell Ahmar near Carchemish should prove correct, it would locate the home of Balaam near Haran, once the home of Abraham. This suggests the possible source of Balaam's knowledge of God. *See* Amaw.

The embassy from Balak offered rewards of wealth, honor, and power if Balaam would come to curse Israel, but God's will was very clear. "Thou shalt not go with them; thou shalt not curse the people: for they are blessed" (Num 22:12). Refusing the first delegation, the covetous prophet succumbed to the tempting offer of a second embassy and obtained permission from God to depart for Moab. On the journey, an angel of the Lord, unseen by Balaam but manifest to the ass he rode, barred the way. The poor beast three times sought to avoid the apparition and brought the angry prophet to the point of beating him, when Balaam's eyes were opened and he was made aware of the Lord's opposition. In fear, he offered to return home, but he was ordered to continue on to Moab where he would speak "only the word that I shall speak unto thee" (Num 22:35).

Balak received the prophet with great expectation and led him to a Baal sanctuary high above the plain where he could look upon Israel. After the appropriate sacrifices, Balaam opened his mouth to speak, but the words that came forth were the words of the Lord; not in cursing but in blessing. A second and third high place only brought forth more blessings, until the frustrated and enraged king commanded the unhappy prophet to begone.

Before he departed, Balaam proclaimed one more word from the Lord. This famous prophecy told of a star, the symbol of a great king, who would arise in Israel in the far off future days. The sign of a star in connection with the promised King-Messiah is found only here in the OT. It is significant that the wise men who followed that star to Bethlehem came from the east, possibly the same area from which Balaam himself had come.

The defeated and humiliated prophet departed for home, but not to stay. Determined still to gain the promised reward, Balaam conceived a plan whereby God Himself would destroy Israel. Let Balak send the young people of Moab to mingle with the Israelites and draw them away from God to the degrading worship of Baal. The plan was highly successful (Num 25), but the results were not as Balaam had planned. God's judgment came quickly upon His people, and the sinners were thoroughly cleansed from the congregation. Then the Lord commanded Moses to smite Moab for their wily attack (Num 25:16-18). In the ensuing battle, the prophet Balaam was slain, falling in defeat with those who had sought his aid (Num 31:8).

The NT warns against the "error" (Jude 11) and the "way" of Balaam (II Pet 2:15). Balaam is a type of all those who, knowing God, yet turn their backs upon Him to grasp at the temporal goods of an evil world. Rev 2:14 speaks of the wicked "doctrine of Balaam," the teaching that would lead God's people to indulge in the sins of the flesh as though God were indifferent. *See* Divination; Prophecy.

P.C.J.

BALAC (bā'lăk). The same as Balak (*q.v.*). Balac is found only in Rev 2:14.

BALADAN (băl'ȧ-dăn). The father of Merodach-baladan, king of Babylon (II Kgs 20:12, RSV; Isa 39:1).

BALAH (bā'lȧ). A town of Simeon in the Negeb, perhaps SE of Beer-sheba (Josh 19:3). It may be the same as Bilhab (*q.v.*) in I Chr 4:29 and Baalah (*q.v.*) in Josh 15:29.

BALAK (bā'lăk). A king of Moab who was frightened by Israel's conquest of the kingdoms of Sihon and Og and in desperation hired Balaam (*q.v.*), from Pethor on the Euphrates, to curse Israel. The Lord would not permit Balaam to curse but rather bless. However, Balak succeeded in a roundabout way by following Balaam's advice and seducing the men of Israel to idolatry, thus bringing God's judgment upon themselves (Num 22–25; 31:8, 16; Josh 24:9; Jud 11:25; Mic 6:5; Rev 2:14).

BALANCES. Three words are used to picture balances: *qāneh,* "cane, beam of the scales" (Isa 46:6 only); *peles,* "indicator, level beam of the scales" (Isa 40:12; Prov 16:11 only); and *mō'zᵉnayim,* "a pair of pans, balances" (16 times). The only NT reference is *zugos,* "yoke or beam of the balance" (Rev 6:5). Down to the Persian period, money consisted of lumps or rings of gold or silver and was weighed (e.g., Gen 23:16; Jer 32:10).

"Balance" is used mostly in connection with the divine demand for business honesty (Lev 19:36; Ezk 45:10). A just balance is God's work (Prov 16:11)! But "balances of deception are the Lord's abomination" (Prov 11:1), for that is oppression (Hos 12:7). Here "diverse weights" (Heb. "a stone and a stone," Prov 20:10, 23), "a bag of stones of deception," and

Weighing of the heart of the scribe Ani in the afterlife by the gods Anubis and Thoth. Egyptian scales are clearly shown. BM

"balances of wickedness" (Mic 6:11) to falsify (Amos 8:5), imply a heavier weight to buy with and a lighter one to sell with. *See also* Weights, Measures, and Coins.

The balance might also represent heavy calamity (Job 6:2-3), or simply moral integrity (Job 31:6) or the lack of it (Dan 5:27; Ps 62:9).

W. G. B.

BALDNESS. Mentioned infrequently in the OT and not at all in the NT, natural baldness was probably uncommon in biblical times. Semites or Asiatics are usually depicted in ancient Near Eastern art with long hair and beards. Baldness was considered a defect which detracted from one's beauty (Isa 3:24), for gray and white hair were looked upon as a crown of glory (Prov 16:31; 20:29). *See* Hair. It was the duty of the priest to distinguish between natural baldness and that caused by leprosy (Lev 13:40-44).

The address to Elisha, "Go up, thou bald head" (II Kgs 2:23), may be an allusion to a tonsure worn by prophets and thus a mockery of his office, for Elisha was not yet an old man.

Baldness artificially produced was a mark of mourning in the ancient Near East in later times (Isa 15:2; 22:12; Jer 16:6; Ezk 7:18; Amos 8:10; Mic 1:16), although it had been forbidden to the Israelites on the ground of their being a holy people (Deut 14:1-2). It is thought that the pagan Canaanites shaved off hair to provide their dead with that life-giving stuff (cf. Samson's hair) which would enable the dead to live on in the realm of death. Arabs today often lay hair on the grave of the dead. A female prisoner-of-war whom her captor desired to marry was first to be allowed to mourn her parents with the sign of shaving her head (Deut 21:10-13). The priests especially were not to follow heathen mourning rites and customs such as shaving the head and cutting off the corners of their beards; thus wearing tonsures was forbidden to them at any time (Lev 21:1-5, RSV; Ezk 44:20). Yet for the Nazarite, who was to let his hair grow long, shaving the head marked the conclusion of his vow (Num 6:9, 18).

J. R.

BALM. *See* Plants.

BAMAH (bā'mȧ). The word is retained in its Heb. form only in Ezk 20:29. Doubtless the prophet's question is a contemptuous play on words regarding the people's worship at a heathen high place: "What [*mâ*] is the high place [*bāmâ*] whereunto ye go [a form of the verb *bô'*]?" *See* Bamoth.

BAMOTH (bā'mŏth). This name appears in KJV in Num 21:19-20 as a camping ground on the journey of Israel N of the Arnon canyon. The site may have been identical with Bamoth-baal (*q.v.*; Num 22:41, RSV; KJV, ASV, "the high places of Baal") where Balak took the prophet Balaam to observe Israel, a locality mentioned in Josh 13:17.

The name is plural form of *bāmâ,* "elevation," "a height," and appears in Heb. in this sense in Deut 32:13; II Sam 1:19, 25; Ps 18:33; Mic 3:12; Ezk 36:2; Hab 3:19. In a specialized sense the Heb. word means a sacred hill shrine with an altar or chapel (e.g., I Kgs 11:7; 12:32; 13:32; 14:23; Jer 7:31; etc.). *See* High Place.

BAMOTH-BAAL (bā'mŏth-bāl'). A place N of the Arnon River in Moab where Balak took Balaam that he might see Israel. There he sacrificed and sought to curse Israel (Num 22:41, RSV; 23:1 - 12). Later it was assigned to the tribe of Reuben (Josh 13:17). Apparently the same city is called Beth-bamoth in the Moabite inscription (ANET, p. 210).

BAND. A term used in describing army units, such as a cohort. *See* Army.

BANI (bā'nī)

1. A Gadite warrior, one of David's 30 mighty men (II Sam 23:36).
2. A chorister of the Levitical family of Merari in David's time (I Chr 6:31, 46).
3. The progenitor of a family of the tribe of Judah whose descendants are listed among those returning from the Exile (I Chr 9:4; Ezr 2:10; 10:29, 34).
4. A member of the family of Bani with the same name. He is listed among those condemned by Ezra for having a foreign wife (Ezr 10:38).
5. A Levite prominent in the reforms of Nehemiah (Neh 8:7; 9:4 - 5; 10:13 - 14). One of his sons, Rehum, was active in the building of the wall (Neh 3:17). He is one of the men who assisted Ezra at the great reading of the law, by causing the people to understand the meaning of that which was read, probably by "targumming," that is, translating into Aramaic. He took part also in the prayer of dedication of the wall and sealed the covenant. Another of Bani's sons was appointed overseer of the Levites (Neh 11:22). *See also* Binnui.

P. C. J.

BANISH. The Hebrews had no legal banishment prescribed by the Mosaic law as a punishment, as did the Greeks and Romans. But individuals cast out of the land by war (Isa 16:3-4), or self-exiled because of crime (II Sam 13:37-38; 14:13-14) or some other reason (e.g., David), were all "banished."

The Heb. formula for serious crimes not worthy of death was "to cut off" (Lev 17:4; Ex 12:15; Num 19:20). This has been taken to mean death, but more probably it was a form of excommunication (Ezr 7:26). The individual was barred from all communion, social and religious, within the fellowship of Israel. In later times, this took the form of exclusion from the temple or synagogue (Jn 9:21, 34-35).

BANK. The ancient world did not have banks in the modern sense of the institution. The word translated "bank" in the NT is the common word "table." It is used to refer to the ordinary dining table, and also for the tables of the money changers (Lk 19:23). These exchangers would take deposits of money on which they paid interest and use it either for trade or for lending at a higher rate of interest. That is Jesus' reference in Mt 25:27. Another aspect of the business was to exchange coins of one denomination for another, or foreign money for current coins, which was a highly lucrative business. From the Phoenicians, who seem to have invented the practice, the business of money changing had spread throughout the Roman Empire by NT times. *See* Occupations: Money Changers. In Moses' day, the simple pastoral economy of Israel did not call for such complicated financial transactions. Loans were made between friends in case of need, and taking interest was forbidden (Ex 22:25; Lev 25:37). For commercial loans in Solomon's time see note on Prov 6:1 in *Wycliffe Bible Commentary*. *See* Borrow; Occupations: Banker.

P. C. J.

BANNER. Two words are used in Heb. in the sense of a banner: *degel,* "something conspicuous," and *nēs,* "lifted up, exalted." The banners of Bible times were poles or standards with some identifying marking or figure, rather than the flags and pennants of our day. They were used as rallying points either in peace or war (Num 21:8-9), and served as identification for the various tribes and nations (Num 1:52; 10:14, 25; Ps 20:5). The ancient standard of Ur (from 2500 B.C.), a wooden panel inlaid with a mosaic of shell and lapis lazuli, shows the antiquity of standards. A 13th cen. B.C. silver-plated bronze cult standard, showing a goddess head with snakes, was found at Hazor. The banners of Rome with their eagles and other insignia are familiar ensigns (*q.v.*).

BANQUET. *See* Food.

BAPTISM (Gr. nouns *baptismos* and *baptisma*; Gr. verbs *baptizō* and *baptō*).

Three different views are held concerning the real meaning of baptism. The Baptists and others who baptize by immersion maintain that it signifies the believer's identification with the death, burial, and resurrection of Christ, and therefore insist it must be done by a complete immersion in the waters of baptism. Those who practice pouring maintain it signifies the outpouring of the Holy Spirit upon the believer and his infilling with the Spirit. The Reformed, Methodists, and Anglicans, who sprinkle, maintain baptism signifies the cleansing away of the believer's sins by the blood of Christ. They, and those who pour, baptize infants, while immersionists baptize only those who have reached sufficient maturity to themselves believe in Christ.

The reasons for these wide divergences stem, first, from the use of *baptō* and *baptizō* in classical Gr. For example, Charles Hodge, the great Presbyterian theologian, says the following: "*Baptō* means (1) to dip, (2) to dye by dipping, (3) to dye without regard to mode. . . . (4) It also means to gild . . . (5) to wet, moisten or wash, (6) to temper . . . (7) to imbue. . . . As to the classical use of *baptizō,* it means (1) to

Apparently the Standard of Ur, pictured here, served as a kind of flag or banner. BM

immerse or submerge . . . (2) to overflow or cover with water . . . (3) to wet thoroughly or moisten, (4) to pour upon or drench, (5) in any way to be overwhelmed or overpowered" (*Systematic Theology,* III, 527). However, this only introduces the arguments which ensue and which are summarized below. The actual question is, how are the words used in the OT and particularly in the NT? Second, the fact that several different things are spoken of as baptism, such as the outpouring of the Holy Spirit (Mt 3:11; Acts 1:5); identification with Christ's death, burial, and resurrection (Rom 6:3-5; cf. Mk 10:38; Lk 12:50; Col 2:12); and OT cleansings by sprinkling (Heb 9:10, 13, 19, 21).

The Case for Immersion

This rests upon the following arguments:

1. The general use of *baptō* and *baptizō* in secular and classical Gr. Both those who teach immersion and those who teach sprinkling accept the fact that it is largely used there to express to dip and to immerse. Thus the meaning to sprinkle appears to have been a secondary meaning in Gr.
2. A simple acceptance of the translation of *baptizō* in several places in the KJV and other English versions of the NT gives the impression immersion was the mode (Mt 3:6; Mk 1:5, 8-10; Acts 8:38).
3. A stress upon certain passages in the OT in which both of the Gr. words are used of immersion. For example, Naaman was told to dip (*baptizō*) seven times in the Jordan (II Kgs 5:10, 14); Nebuchadnezzar was wet (*baptō*) with the dew of heaven (Dan 4:33); and the priest was told to dip the tip of his finger in the blood (Lev 4:17; cf. Josh 3:15; I Sam 14:27; Ps 68:23).
4. The baptism of proselytes in the intertestamental period. The Dead Sea Scrolls throw some light upon this custom, though it is a question whether they prove very much. First, they reflect customs of such an extremely ascetic group as the Essenes and these cannot be regarded as being identical with the customs of orthodox Jews; and, second, the mode of cleansing they required of proselytes is not too clear.
5. Since the exhortations to be baptized by John the Baptist were directed to adults who repented of their sins, and by Christ and the disciples to those old enough to believe, it is argued that baptism is a sacrament or ordinance to be dispensed only to those who have first believed. Certain pertinent rational arguments are added to support the view, such as the futility of baptizing a baby who cannot know what is being done either to him or for him, in contrast to the meaningfulness of baptism when it is given to those who have already believed in Christ.
6. The difference between the OT and NT and between law and grace. In the OT the stress is upon "this do and thou shalt live," and in the NT, upon God's grace and man's faith. The emphasis upon obedience in the old dispensation stands in contrast to that of belief in the new. Circumcision and the covenant which accompanied it have been discontinued, and baptism and personal confession of faith have been introduced.
7. The NT teaching that believers are baptized into Christ's death, burial, and resurrection. This is taken to express the true significance of baptism. Only immersion can properly and fully express what burial with Christ in His death means (Rom 6:3-5).
8. Christ's particular teaching. He said of His coming death on the cross, "I have a baptism to be baptized with: and how am I straitened till it be accomplished!" (Lk 12:50); and He asked His disciples, "Can ye

BAPTISM

drink of the cup that I drink of? and be baptized with the baptism that I am baptized with?" (Mk 10:38).

Highpoints in the immersionist view. (1) The atoning death of Christ and His bodily resurrection are witnessed to, and thus the gospel is given in a most dramatic form. (2) Saving faith is stressed. (3) This method enables the participant to confess his faith publicly and even add a personal testimony, which enhances the sealing aspect of baptism as the sign or token of the new covenant on the one hand, and witnesses to salvation on the other. (4) A most important phase of the gospel is expressed. (5) This particular meaning for baptism has strong support from Christ and the Scripture.

The Case for Pouring

This rests upon the NT teaching concerning baptism and the Holy Spirit. When clean water is poured upon the participant, it signifies the outpouring of the Holy Spirit upon the believer. Certain arguments are presented to support this mode, such as:

1. John the Baptist's teaching. John, when baptizing those who had repented of their sins, said that he baptized only with water, but Christ would baptize with the Holy Ghost and fire (Mt 3:11).

2. Christ's teaching. Though Christ left all baptisms to His disciples (Jn 4:2), still they soon were baptizing more than John (Jn 4:1). After His resurrection and just before the ascension, Christ told the disciples to wait for the promise of the Father, and, taking up the teaching of John, He said, "For John truly baptized with water; but ye shall be baptized with the Holy Ghost not many days hence" (Acts 1:5). This appears, in contrast to Rom 6:3-5, to identify baptism with the infilling of the Holy Spirit. Some Reformed writers place much of their stress upon this passage (cf. Robert G. Rayburn). Of course Peter explained the actual outpouring of the Spirit at Pentecost as a fulfillment of Joel's prophecy (Acts 2:16-21; Joel 2:28-32) and preached that those who repented and were baptized should receive the Holy Spirit (Acts 2:38-39).

Highpoints of the pouring view. (1) It stresses the person and work of the Holy Spirit and the importance of the Spirit-filled life. (2) It emphasizes a particular truth in baptism stressed by both John the Baptist and Paul. (3) It has the support of Christ's own words and interpretation in Acts 1:5.

The Case for Sprinkling

This rests upon the following considerations:

1. Certain OT commands to sprinkle. Consideration is given to OT passages where sprinkling is enjoined for cleansing (Ex 24:6-8; Lev 14:7; Num 19:9, 17), and their classification in Heb 9:10 as divers baptisms (*diaphorois baptismois*). In the ensuing passage in Hebrews the sprinkling of the ashes of the red heifer on the unclean (Num 19:9, 17), the sprinkling of both the Book of the Covenant of the law and of the people by Moses (Ex 24:6-8) after the giving of the law, and cleansing of certain other sins are all given as examples of baptism.

2. The continuity between circumcision and baptism. This is taught in Col 2:11-12 where the two are used of circumcision and baptism in Christ, either interchangeably or as two parts of the same thing. Peter concluded his plea at the end of his sermon at Pentecost, when calling upon those present to repent and to be baptized that they might receive the Holy Ghost, with the declaration, "For the promise is unto you,

A baptism in the Jabbok River, Jordan. Courtesy Richard E. Ward

and to your children [*teknois*]" (Acts 2:38 - 39), making clear that the blessings of baptism extend to the whole family and to their descendants. Had he not included their children, the Jews who heard him would have objected that the gospel in the NT offered them less than the law in the OT.

3. Continuation of the covenant. At circumcision the children of OT believers came under a covenant relationship with God—they became children of the covenant. Unless baptism extends to children, this aspect of covenantal relationship for infants ceased with the coming of Christ. Since this was a very precious doctrine to the OT saint, and entitled him to special blessings from God, it would be amazing that it could have disappeared without mention or controversy in the NT, and adult baptism have taken its place to the exclusion of the believer's children, particularly since the dropping of circumcision itself brought such a strong reaction (cf. Acts 15:1 ff.; Gal 2:1 ff.). The conviction that the covenantal relationship for children continued, with the baptism of children taking the place of circumcision, is strengthened by the fact that there is not even a suggestion of any objection being raised that with the introduction of baptism a covenantal relation had been removed.

Baptismal pool in the sixth century church of St. John at Ephesus. HFV

4. The unity of the plan of salvation. If God commanded His OT saints to circumcise their children and to enter into a covenant with Him to rear them in the fear and nurture of the Lord, promising to be their God and the God of their children, and if He is unchangeable, why should He change His way of dealing with children in the NT age? A covenant sealed by circumcision was God's way of bringing salvation to the OT family, and unless otherwise revealed, a covenant sealed by baptism should be His way in this present age. God's unchangeability and the unity of the plan of salvation, by faith through sovereign grace, call for a continuation of His same plan for the salvation of children in the NT age.

5. John the Baptist's office and training. John was an OT Levite and a priest in his own right. His father was a priest who served in the course of Abia (Lk 1:5). John, as the forerunner of Christ and the liaison between OT and NT believers, had to follow exactly the instructions given to Moses in the Pentateuch for sacrifices and cleansings. However, the OT cleansings were by sprinkling, except in cases where the body of an individual had actually become infected with sores or contaminated by disease and in certain cases of bodily discharges (cf. Lev 15:1 ff.; 22:1–9; Num 5:2; cf. Lev 14:2 f.). That John's mode of baptism was a sign of cleansing is also clear from the fact that he connected it with repentance from sin on the participant's part, and purging or cleansing on God's part: "He shall baptize you with the Holy Ghost, and with fire . . . and . . . thoroughly purge his floor" (Mt 3:11- 12), and that the only dispute over his baptism was regarding purification (Jn 3:25) or cleansing.

Yet the question as to whether John the Baptist might have practiced the mode of baptism administered to proselytes, namely, immersion (G. F. Moore, *Judaism,* I, 334 f.), is admittedly impossible to answer dogmatically. First of all, the Jewish evidence from the Mishnah and the Talmud comes too late to be entirely conclusive (from A.D. 200 to 400). Then the earliest Christian evidence for the use of immersion comes from about A.D. 100. Even if the Jewish evidence proves that immersion was practiced for proselytes entering Judaism by John's time, this does not necessarily mean John adopted this practice. It is to be remembered that no Jew would readily submit to what was reserved as a proselyte baptism without real objections. Would John have used a mode which would appear certain to raise protests? Or did he simply follow the OT modes of ceremonial priestly cleansing? The latter conclusion appears certain to the Reformed people, particularly since no controversy arose concerning his mode. The only question discussed regarding John's baptism so far as the NT records go, was the broad doctrine of purification or cleansing itself (Jn 3:25).

If John by revelation introduced a new kind of cleansing, namely, by immersion rather than by sprinkling, then of course that should be adopted. However, at no point did he suggest he was bringing in some new method of cleansing. Nor did he ever have to explain or defend the mode he used.

6. Lack of any NT passages that conclusively prove immersion. The Reformed group maintains there is no passage on baptism in the NT which cannot be explained more naturally by sprinkling than by immersion, whether it be the baptism of John, that of the 3,000 at Pentecost, of the Philippian jailer at midnight, or the Ethiopian eunuch in the desert. Further, in no place does the Gr. require translation of a particular instance of baptism as by immersion. For example, as certain writers point out (E. B. Fairfield, *Letters on Baptism,* pp. 73-76; John Scott Johnson, *Baptism,* p. 30), to express "from" the Gr. is merely *ek* or *apo,* and to express "to" is *eis;* but to express "out of" it is unquestionably *ek,* once with the verb and once with the noun (Mk 5:8; 7:31; Lk 4:22), and to express "into" *eis* is unquestionably used, once with the verb and once with the noun (Jn 20:3-6). At His baptism Jesus was baptized by John *eis* the Jordan (Mk 1:10) and went up *apo* the water (Mt 3:16), but in neither case is the preposition repeated so as to prove absolutely that Christ either went fully under the water or came up from immersion in the water.

At the same time the Reformed group sees particular cases in the NT in which they feel immersion would seem to be impossible. How could Jews immerse couches before they took their meals, and how could Pharisees accuse Christ of not taking a bath by immersion before He ate when water was very scarce and kept in home cisterns (Mk 7:3-4)? How could 3,000 be baptized by immersion right in the city of Jerusalem, or a jailer at midnight (Acts 16:30-34)?

7. The stress upon the gospel in sprinkling. In sprinkling, the Reformed people signify that the blood of Jesus Christ alone can cleanse from sin. They maintain that they thus express the gospel in its most fundamental form. Someone may never understand the doctrine of identification with Christ in His death, burial, and resurrection, biblical and wonderful as that truth is, and yet he may go to heaven. But no one can go to heaven except he accept and believe that the blood of Jesus Christ cleanses from sin.

8. Family salvation retained. In the OT God ordered the parents to make a covenant to rear their children in His fear and nurture, and commanded circumcision as a seal of their faith. God is intensely interested in the salvation of children and does not entrust them to believers of either Testament without requiring a pledge, or covenant, binding the parents to teach and instruct the children and bring them up for God.

The Reformed feel that few understand what the baptism of a child really means. It is first of all a confession of the faith of the parents that only the blood of Jesus Christ can cleanse away their own sin, and that that same precious blood alone can take away the sin of their child. Second, it is an agreement and pledge to care for and train the child whom God has given, for God; to teach him the Scriptures and how to pray, and to endeavor to lead him to a saving faith in Jesus Christ. When parents do this, God promises to be the God of their children. Thus it becomes a covenant between the parents and God, and the child is the child of the covenant. But the covenant does not save. Salvation is possible only by God's sovereign grace; thus the salvation of the child is actually and finally of grace. When he comes to the age of accountability, he must himself accept and confess Christ as his own personal Saviour.

Highpoints of the sprinkling view. (1) This particular mode signifies and stresses the fact that only by the shedding of Christ's blood can one's sins be washed away. Therefore, like immersion, it gives the gospel in baptism, though in an even simpler and more fundamental form. (2) It maintains what is called the unity of the covenant of grace, or the continuity of the one plan of salvation in the OT and NT. (3) It supports the doctrine of the unchangeability of God. (4) Family salvation becomes a reality for believing parents of both Testaments. The importance of children, and of their nurture in the faith and their being won to Christ, is emphasized. (5) The acceptance of John the Baptist's mode of baptism by the Jews is explained.

Why Are There Three Modes of Baptism?

Is one mode in particular, and its peculiar significance, to be maintained so completely over the others as to deny that blessing can be found in the others too? This would be hard to sustain, since the Baptists and other immersionists appear to have won more to Christ than those who practice either of the other modes. The answer is to be found in the facts that: (1) Each mode of baptism teaches a separate, vital biblical truth. Immersion teaches identity with Christ's death, burial, and resurrection; pouring teaches the baptism or infilling of the believer with the Holy Spirit; and sprinkling teaches the washing away of sins by the blood of Christ. Therefore each, when properly understood and taught, brings great blessing. (2) They all are only phases or parts of what baptism in its entirety covers. Each mode is based upon what is called in the NT a baptism—and yet the Scripture categorically states there is only one baptism. Paul writes in Eph 4:4-6 that there is one Holy Spirit, one God and Father of us all, "one Lord, one faith, one baptism." This leads to the realization that all three modes or "baptisms" are only parts of a greater whole. But what is this whole?

In the Lord's Supper Christ's substitutionary death is commemorated until He comes again. It would be strange if baptism only repeated the same truth. The problem of the two sacraments or ordinances signifying the same thing is solved when we see that, while the Lord's Supper signifies Christ's death, baptism covers the application of the benefits of Christ's death to the believer by the Holy Spirit.

The first thing the Holy Spirit does is to apply the blood of Christ to cleanse away sin—signified by sprinkling; the next is to identify the believer with the death, burial, and resurrection of Christ—signified by immersion; and the last is to come and indwell God's purchased vessel—signified by pouring. Thus we are led to see that baptism signifies more than many scholars at first thought; that each of the three views is true as far as it stresses a phase of the total meaning of the sacrament or ordinance, and therefore is accompanied by blessings when properly understood and taught and used; that immersion has brought blessing to countless thousands, and still, sprinkling is blessed as it stresses an equally fundamental truth of the gospel. All inclination to ridicule and make light of each other's viewpoint vanishes when once the particular biblical truth others are trying to demonstrate and teach is understood. Baptists learn a new respect for Presbyterians and Presbyterians for Baptists, and those who omit the ordinances both of baptism and the Lord's Supper (Salvation Army and the Quakers) receive a new understanding of the different views and modes practiced by others.

Bibliography. Herbert S. Bird, "Professor Jewett on Baptism," WTJ, XXXI (1969), 145-161. J. Oliver Buswell, Jr., *Systematic Theology,* Grand Rapids: Eerdmans, Vol. II. Edmund B. Fairfield, *Letters on Baptism,* Philadelphia: Gordon Holdcrott, n.d. Charles Hodge, *Systematic Theology,* Grand Rapids: Eerdmans, III (1952), 526-611. Paul Jewett, "Baptism (Baptist View)," *Encyclopedia of Christianity,* ed. by E. H. Palmer, 1964, I, 517-526. Albrecht Oepke, "*Baptō,* etc.," TDNT, I, 529-546. A. H. Strong, *Systematic Theology,* Philadelphia: Judson, 1953, pp. 930-959.

R. A. K.

BAPTISM FOR THE DEAD. Paul speaks of this practice when presenting his arguments for the bodily resurrection in I Cor 15. He argues: (1) "If there be no resurrection of the dead, then is Christ not risen . . . then is our preaching vain . . . . But now is Christ risen" (vv.12-20). (2) If the dead do not rise, why are some baptized for (or above, *hyper*) the dead (v. 29)? (3) If He be not risen, why do we risk our lives hourly to preach a risen Lord (v. 30)?

Many explanations have been given of the expression "baptism for the dead." These may be divided into two classifications.

Early views: (1) Early Christian writers suggested a vicarious baptism undergone by believers for other believers who died unbaptized. Tertullian offers this explanation (de Resurr. 48; Adv. Marc. 5:10). Epiphanius speaks of such a custom among the Cerinthians but not among Christians (Haer. 28:6). H. A. W. Meyer (*Critical and Exegetical Handbook to the Epistles to the Corinthians,* pp. 364-368) accepts such a view. (2) Chrysostom considers that it means the believer is baptized for his dead body, in order to show he believes it will live as a resurrection body.

Modern views: (1) That some were being baptized on behalf of those who died unbaptized, whether believers or not. This view is held and practiced by Mormons today. (2) That some were encouraged to be baptized by the example of early Christian martyrs, this being a testimony to their faith in the resurrection of the body. (3) That all who are baptized are baptized "for the good of the dead," in the sense the resurrection cannot occur till a certain number are saved (Olshausen). (4) That erstwhile Gentile pagans who became Christians through the testimony of loved ones now departed were baptized for the sake of their dead, i.e., in order to be reunited with them at the resurrection (J. K. Howard, "Baptism for the dead: a Study of I Corinthians 15:29," E.Q., XXXVII [July, 1965], 137-141). (5) That many are baptized over the graves of the departed (G. J. Vossius; F. W. Grossheide, *Korte Verklaring,* I Corinthians, pp. 196-7).

Though the explanation offered by Vossius and Grossheide may not appear so convincing to Western minds, it has several points in its favor. It offers a view that may fit the person and the writings of Paul. He would not use an unscriptural vicarious baptism as an argument to true believers for the resurrection, and if he did, certainly not without any explanation. In Europe and Asia burial beneath the floor of a church is a common practice. Those being baptized in such churches would testify by their baptism that they believed their bodies, and those of the dead beneath them, would rise at the resurrection. In the 1st cen. A.D., however, Christians were not yet building their own churches, but baptized their converts in convenient pools or rivers.

R. A. K.

BAPTISM OF FIRE. In announcing the baptism of the Spirit, John the Baptist twice declared that Christ would also baptize with fire. Having said that, he immediately mentioned the judgment by which the Saviour ". . . will burn up the chaff with unquenchable fire" (Mt 3:11-12; Lk 3:16-17). The "baptism of fire" is therefore the terrible punishment by which sinners will be judged in the last day (cf. Mt 13:30, 41-51; 25:41, 46; see also in Mal 3:2-3 the appearance of Him who will be like "the refiner's fire"; *see* Occupations: Refiner).

In a similar passage, Christ declares that "every one shall be salted with fire" (Mk 9:49). This appears to be applied to believers as well as unbelievers, but with this tremendous difference: *the believer* recognizes that he is guilty and liable to judgment, but he believes that Jesus has been smitten in his place and judged by the fire of divine justice. If now such a man "shall not come into condemnation" (Jn 5:24), it is because in Christ the fire has already passed on him. Henceforth he is willing that the Spirit of holiness judge and burn in him all impurity, "for our God is a consuming fire" (Heb 12:28-29). On the other hand, *the unbeliever* will know all the severity of the "unquenchable fire," the "everlasting fire," and the "lake of fire and brimstone" (Mt 3:12; 25:41; Rev 20:10, 15). *See* Brimstone; Punishment.

R. P.

BAPTISM OF THE SPIRIT. After the repeated announcements of John the Baptist concerning the baptism of the Holy Spirit (Mt 3:11; Mk 1:8; Lk 3:16; Jn 1:33), Christ solemnly stressed the promise of the Spirit's coming (Acts 1:4-5). The two historical fulfillments mentioned in the NT occurred at Pentecost (Acts 2:1-4) and in the house of Cornelius (Acts 11:15-16). These two groups of believers were added to the church at the very moment they received the baptism of the Spirit. Paul confirms this by giving in I Cor 12:13 the clearest definition in the NT.

Effected by the divine Spirit, this baptism has as its result the placing of every believer "in Christ," making him a member of Christ's Body, and at the same time uniting him to all the other children of God. The tense of the verb "we were all baptized ..." (RSV) indicates that here it is a matter of the initial experience coinciding with the new birth. The man already regenerated need not therefore look again for the baptism of the Spirit, nor for a "new baptism" (that which does not exist), but rather for the fullness of the Spirit constantly renewed.

Baptism shows death and resurrection, the burial of the crucified sinner with Christ, and the birth of the regenerated man, born from above by the Holy Spirit (Jn 3:3). It marks the break with the past and the entrance by faith into the new sphere of life in Christ: "Buried with him in baptism, wherein also ye are risen with him through the faith of the operation of God... [you] hath he quickened together with him" (Col 2:12-13). We "were baptized into his death ... buried with him by baptism into death: that like as Christ was raised up from the dead ... even so we also should walk in newness of life" (Rom 6:3-4). "For as many of you as have been baptized into Christ have put on Christ" (Gal 3:27). These texts speak first of all of the baptism of the Spirit, which alone is capable of producing such a work in us: death and resurrection with Christ, new birth and the receiving of a superior nature which is the basis of a transformed life.

Water baptism shows by an external and visible means that which the baptism of the Spirit has produced in the spiritual realm. Since the believer dies and is resurrected with Christ, it is understandable that the church often practiced water baptism by the immersion of the convert (*see* Baptism). The old man, crucified with Christ, disappears under the water, and it is a new man which comes out of it, dead to sin and regenerated unto a new life (Rom 6:3-4; Col 2:12). Water baptism is, therefore, the affirmation and sign of that which the baptism of the Spirit has effected in the depth of the heart. The two are so bound together that Paul could state in reality that there is only *one baptism* (Eph 4:5). It is the baptism of the Spirit (death and resurrection with Christ) that saves a believer, and in water baptism he gives the answer of a good conscience toward God (I Pet 3:21).

Participation in this gracious operation of God is assured to all who become members of the Body of Christ by faith (Col 2:12; I Cor 12:13).

See Holy Spirit, Filling of; Unction.

R. P.

BAR

1. A piece of wood or metal (Heb. *b^e^rîaḥ*) used as a support, fastening or barrier (e.g., Ex 26:26-29; Neh 3:3; Jon 2:6).

2. A bolt or bar (Heb. *min'āl*, "to fasten"). The word is used only in Deut 33:25, RSV ("shoes" in KJV).

BAR-. A prefix, this is the Aramaic for the Heb. *ben* ("son"), e.g., Bar-jonah, "son of Jonah" (Mt 16:17). *Bar* is the original word translated "son" in Ps 2:12 and Prov 31:2.

BARABBAS (băr-ăb'*ȧ*s). All four Gospels (Mt 27:16; Mk 15:15; Lk 23:18; Jn 18:40) mention this man who was released by Pilate in preference to Jesus. A notorious prisoner arrested for robbery, sedition, and murder, he has become the source of many imaginative narratives describing what may have happened to him when the full realization broke upon his conscience that a "good man," God's Son, had been crucified in his place. The custom of releasing a prisoner at Passover is not mentioned outside the NT.

The reading of his name as Jesus Barabbas (Mt 27:16 f.) was known to Origen (*c.* A.D. 200), is found in the early Syriac version (*c.* A.D. 200), and a few cursive MSS (dating after A.D. 900), but it is not found in the oldest and best texts. Probably it originated as a scribal error due to the proximity of Jesus' name in Mt 27:17.

See Crime and Punishment; Pilate; Zealot.

T. B. C.

BARACHEL (băr'*ȧ*-kĕl). A descendant of Buz (Gen 22:21), Barachel was the father of Elihu, one of Job's friends (Job 32:2, 6).

BARACHIAH. *See* Berechiah.

BARACHIAS (băr'*ȧ*-kī'*ȧ*s). In Mt 23:35 he is called the father of Zacharias, who seems to have been the Zechariah referred to in II Chr 24:20-22, the son of Jehoiada the priest (*see* Zacharias for discussion of the problem of parentage).

Barachias is also spelled Berechiah (*q.v.*) in the OT.

BARAH. *See* Beth-barah.

BARAK (bâr'*ȧ*k). A military leader from the tribe of Naphtali who, under the direction and encouragement of the prophetess Deborah (*q.v.*), delivered the northern tribes of Israel from bondage imposed by Jabin, king of Hazor. Jabin (*q.v.*) had a seemingly invincible army with 900 chariots of iron, led by a mercenary Sisera, possibly an Egyptian or a Hittite. Deborah, a judge in Ephraim, called upon Barak as the chosen of the Lord to gather an army from Zebulun and Naphtali. The Israelites met on Mount Tabor, while Sisera, alarmed by the revolt, assembled his army on the plain of Esdraelon by the river Kishon. A violent thunderstorm caused the Kishon to overflow its banks, rendering the iron chariots useless in the swampy ground. Attacked by the Israelites, the Canaanites fled in panic. Sisera himself died at the hands of a woman, Jael, in whose tent he had sought refuge (Jud 4–5).

Barak is named among the great heroes of faith in Heb 11.

P. C. J.

BARBARIAN. This word is not found in the OT, though the LXX uses it; e.g., Ps 114:1. It is used five times in the NT. "Barbarian" may be a repeated syllable imitative of a foreigner, "bar bar." Similarly Egyptians called non-Egyptians *berber*. So it means speaking an unintelligible tongue in I Cor 14:11.

Plato divided his world into barbarians and Hellenes. The word may therefore mean non-Greek of both language and culture. Luke does not in any derogatory way call the Semitic Maltese barbarians, that is, non-Greeks, natives (RSV), in Acts 28:2, 4.

After the Persian War (493-479 B.C.) the Greeks came to use "barbarian" with the sense of rough and crude. So Rom 1:14 may mean that Paul is "debtor to those who speak Greek and to those who do not, and (so) to the cultured and to the uncultured." In Col 3:11 he defines "Greek and Jew" as "circumcision and uncircumcision," and puts Scythian right after barbarian, for Scythians were barbarians par excellence. *See* Foreigner.

W. G. B.

BARBER. *See* Hair; Occupations.

BAREFOOT. Two words are used in the Heb.: *yāḥēp*, "unshod" (II Sam 15:30; Isa 20:2-4); and perhaps *shôlāl* in Mic 1:8, "stripped," and in Job 12:17, 19, "spoiled."

BARHUMITE (bär-hū'mīt). A probable variant of Baharumite (cf. II Sam 23:31 with I Chr 11:33), denoting an inhabitant of Bahurim (*q.v.*).

BARIAH (bā-rī'*ȧ*). A descendant of David in the Zerubbabel line, son of Shemaiah (I Chr 3:22).

BAR-JESUS (bär-jē'sūs). Alternative name for the magician Elymas, who opposed Barnabas and Saul in Cyprus (Acts 13:6). *See* Elymas.

BAR-JONA (bär-jō'n*ȧ*). A surname of Simon Peter (Mt 16:17). *See* Bar-.

BARKOS (băr'kŏs). Ancestor of certain Nethinim (*q.v.*) who returned with Zerubbabel and were temple servants (Ezr 2:53; Neh 7:55).

BARLEY. *See* Plants.

BARNABAS (bär'n*ȧ*-b*ȧ*s). A Levite of Cyprus and member of the primitive church of Jerusalem. His personal name was Joseph; the patronymic Barnabas was given him by the apostles to indicate his character ("son of encouragement," Acts 4:36, RSV). He is first mentioned for his generosity in selling some land and handing over the price to the apostles for the relief of the poorer members of the church (Acts 4:36 f.). He next appears in Acts 9:27 as lending his good offices to Saul of Tarsus when Saul returned to Jerusalem in the third year after his conversion, and commending him to the apostles as a genuine believer. This suggests that he was previously acquainted with Saul.

When, some years later, news came to the apostles in Jerusalem of the large-scale Gentile evangelization being undertaken in Syrian Antioch by Christian Hellenists, refugees from the persecution which started in Judea after Stephen's death, they sent Barnabas to Antioch as their commissioner to investigate the situation and take such action as he judged appropriate. They could not have sent a more suitable man.

The nearer harbor area pictured here is where Barnabas and Paul landed at Salamis on Cyprus on the first missionary journey. HFV

Far from being shocked at the innovations that he found, Barnabas was delighted to see how the grace of God was at work in the conversion of pagans at Antioch, and he encouraged the evangelists and the young converts with all his might. After some time, he felt the need of a colleague in the supervision of this growing work, and brought Saul/Paul from Tarsus to help him.

After a year's collaboration in Antioch, Barnabas and Paul were released by the church there to undertake a more extensive ministry. They traversed Cyprus from E to W, and then crossed to Asia Minor, where they preached the gospel and planted churches in the cities of S Galatia. Barnabas' young cousin, John Mark of Jerusalem, accompanied them on this journey as far as the coast of Asia Minor, and then returned home.

The incident of Gal 2:11 ff. may be dated shortly after Barnabas and Paul returned to Antioch. Even Barnabas was disposed to follow the example of Peter and others and withdraw temporarily from table-fellowship with Gentile Christians to avoid offending visitors from Jerusalem.

On two occasions Barnabas and Paul visited Jerusalem as delegates from the church of Antioch. The first was when they brought a gift for the relief of the Jerusalem church in time of famine (Acts 11:30). It was probably during this visit that they had the interview with the Jerusalem leaders at which their apostleship to the Gentiles was recognized (Gal 2:1-10). The second was when they attended the Jerusalem council (Acts 15) to discuss and decide with the Jerusalem leaders the terms on which Gentile converts should be admitted to church fellowship.

Shortly after this, Barnabas and Paul parted company because they disagreed about taking Mark with them again. Barnabas took Mark and continued to evangelize Cyprus. But Paul always refers to him with affectionate esteem as a fellow missionary among the Gentiles (I Cor 9:6). From the fact that Paul requested John Mark to be sent to help him years later, "for he is profitable to me for the ministry" (II Tim 4:11), we can conclude that Barnabas did as much for Mark as he had earlier for Paul.

F. F. B.

BARREL. The word used in KJV refers to a large earthenware jar used for carrying water, storing grain, etc. (I Kgs 17:12, 14, 16; 18:33). The Heb. word *kad* is more properly translated "pitcher" (KJV) or "jar" (RSV) in Gen 24:14-20; Eccl 12:6; Jud 7:16-20. *See* Pottery.

BARREN. To the Hebrews, children were a blessing from the Lord (Ps 127:3-5), and childlessness was an affliction, a judgment of God (Ex 23:26; Deut 7:14; Lev 20:21). For a woman to be barren was the ultimate in sorrow and shame. She felt that she had failed in the prime reason for her existence, and she was looked upon as one whom God had smitten. Regardless of her position or other blessings, she was in sorrow until a child should be born (I Sam 1). It was a legal practice in Abraham's day to claim the child of one's husband by a handmaid as one's own to avoid the disgrace of sterility (Gen 16:1-2; 30:3-4). *See* Family; Marriage.

BARSABAS (bär′sȧ-băs)

1. Joseph, surnamed Justus, nominated with Matthias to succeed Judas Iscariot (Acts 1:23).

2. Judas, a prophet in the Jerusalem church, who with Silas accompanied Paul and Barnabas to deliver the decision of the Jerusalem council to Antioch. He later returned to Jerusalem and nothing more is known of him (Acts 15:22-33).

BARTHOLOMEW (bär-thŏl′ō̇-mū). The English and Gr. forms simply transliterate the Aramaic name meaning "son of Tolmai" or "Talmar," a name found in the Gr. OT in several forms and in Josephus. Bartholomew is named in all four lists of the 12 apostles (Mt 10:3; Mk 3:18; Lk 6:14; Acts 1:13) and always immediately after Philip. Study of the lists indicates pairing and grouping into four. This suggests Bartholomew and Philip were companions in the second group headed by Philip.

It is also conjectured that Nathanael (meaning "God's gift") is a surname of Bartholomew since the Synoptic Gospels pair Philip and Bartholomew, whereas John pairs Philip and Nathanael. In addition, the Synoptics never mention Nathanael, and John never mentions Bartholomew. Attempts to identify him with Matthew or Matthias, or John the son of Zebedee have proved vain. On the other hand, some scholars give up the attempt to identify Nathanael with one of the Twelve. If his identification with Nathanael is correct, however, then Philip brought Bartholomew (Nathanael), a native of Cana of Galilee (Jn 21:2), to acknowledge Jesus as the Messiah (Jn 1:45-46). The beautiful description of his encounter with Jesus is found in Jn 1:47-51. An Israelite indeed, without guile, Jesus disclosed Himself to him as God's Son, Israel's King, and then promised more and fuller divine insights through the days of discipleship to come.

Nothing further is known of Bartholomew from the NT. Traditions concerning him are very untrustworthy. They begin with Eusebius (A.D. 325), state several fields of preaching, and several forms of martyrdom. He is often made one of the 70 disciples (Lk 10:1).

See Nathanael.

T. B. C.

BARTIMAEUS (bär-tĭ-mē′ŭs). The name of a blind beggar whose eyes Jesus opened as He went on His last journey from Jericho to Jerusalem. Bartimaeus' healing as recorded in Mk 10:46-52 presents a remarkable profession of faith in the person of Christ—"thou son of David"—and His power—"Lord, that I might receive my sight" (vv. 47, 51).

A problem, however, has arisen since Lk 18:35-43 speaks of a blind man receiving his sight as Jesus "was come nigh unto" Jericho, while Mark says as He left Jericho. Further, Mt 20:29-34 speaks of two blind men, while Mark and Luke mention only one.These may well be three separate incidents. Yet they can be reconciled as one if the expression "was come nigh" (Lk 18:35) merely means Jesus was near, and the two writers Mark and Luke picked out the blind beggar who did the speaking and ignored a second with him.

R. A. K.

BARUCH (bâr'ŭk)

1. The son of Neriah and brother of Seraiah (King Zedekiah's chamberlain, Jer 51:59), said by Josephus (*Ant.* x.9.1) to have come from a very illustrious family (cf. Jer 51:59; Bar 1:1). He was Jeremiah's friend and private secretary (Jer 32:12; 36:4). *See* Jeremiah.

Upon being forbidden to prophesy in the temple area, Jeremiah dictated his oracles to Baruch, who then read them to the people. Baruch was arrested by King Jehoiakim, and the scroll (*q.v.*) containing Jeremiah's prophecies was cut to pieces with a knife and burned in the fire. Baruch and Jeremiah then were obliged to rewrite the oracles.

Along with Jeremiah, Baruch witnessed the destruction of Jerusalem by the Babylonians in 586 B.C. and thereafter went to live at Mizpah. But after the untimely death (murder) of Gedaliah, the newly appointed Babylonian governor of Judea, at the hands of the anti-Babylonian faction, Baruch was accused of unduly influencing Jeremiah (cf. Jos *Ant.* x.9.6) to dissuade the people from leaving Judea (Jer 43:3). Along with Jeremiah, he was forced to accompany those who fled into Egypt for fear of Babylonian reprisals (Jos *Ant.* x.9.6).

Tradition says he survived Jeremiah and went eventually to Babylon, where he lived for 12 years after the fall of Jerusalem, his death occurring in 574 B.C. But another tradition holds that he and Jeremiah died at the same time in Egypt.

A large number of spurious writings have been attributed to him, the most important of which are the apocryphal book of Baruch and the pseudepigraphical Apocalypse of Baruch.

2. The son of Zabbai (Zacchai, ASV marg.), who aided Nehemiah as he repaired the wall of Jerusalem (Neh 3:20).

3. One of the priests who sealed the covenant in Nehemiah's time (Neh 10:6); possibly the same as 2.

4. The son of Col-hozeh, descendant of Perez the son of Judah (Neh 11:5).

R. E. P.

BARZILLAI (bär-zĭl'ā-ī)

1. A wealthy octogenarian of Gilead, E and N of Jordan, who met David at Mahanaim (Gen 32:2) near the Jabbok River during the king's flight from Absalom, and gave provisions to David's men (II Sam 17:27-29). As he and David parted at the Jordan on the king's return, he refused the royal invitation to move to the palace and its delights, and asked rather to die at home, though at Barzillai's suggestion his son Chimham (*q.v.*) took his place (II Sam 19:31-40). David, dying, charged King Solomon to show loyalty to Barzillai's sons (I Kgs 2:7).

2. Barzillai's name continues as that of returning priests of Ezra's time, descended from one of "the daughters of Barzillai the Gileadite" (Ezr 2:61 parallel to Neh 7:63).

3. Another Barzillai, of Meholah, possibly also in Gilead, was paternal grandfather of five of the seven sons of Saul, whom the Gibeonites hanged (II Sam 21:8 f.).

W. G. B.

BASHAN (bā'shăn). Bashan, meaning "fertile plain," was the name of the area E of the Sea of Galilee and the Jordan River. It was bounded on the N by Mount Hermon and on the E by Jebel Druse, extending on the W to the slopes of the Sea of Galilee and the upper Jordan. Bashan extended S about six miles beyond the Yarmuk River. It was a tableland 1600-2300 feet high with excellent wheat fields, pastures for cattle (Mic 7:14; Jer 50:19), and the groves of oak trees which have now disappeared. Bashan includes 350 square miles of petrified lava fields from which the Gr. name Trachonitis (Lk 3:1) was given to the region.

Bashan was the kingdom of Og at the time of the Exodus. It boasted 60 cities (Num 21:33; Deut 29:7) including Karnaim his capital, Ashtaroth (Deut 1:4), Salcah, Kenath and Edrei where he was defeated. Later, Gr. cities of Hippos, Dion and Abila were in the region, which included the districts of Argob and Golan (Deut 3:4; 4:43). Bashan was assigned to the E half of the tribe of Manasseh.

Archaeologists claim that the area was continuously occupied from about the 32nd cen. B.C. Its fields of dolmens (*q.v.*) may date to that early period. Taken from the Amorite king Og at the time of the Conquest (Deut 3:1-3), Bashan subsequently became a battleground between Israel and the Arameans (II Kgs 10:32-33). The area may have been mentioned as *Ziri-bashani* in the Amarna letters. In later times it was identified with Hauran and Hellenistic-Roman Batanaea.

In the Bible, the prosperity of Bashan is frequently used as a symbol of arrogant pride. The cruel enemies that beset the righteous are "strong bulls of Bashan" (Ps 22:12). The pleasure-seeking women of Samaria are addressed as "cows of Bashan" (Amos 4:1). God's judgments will be on the haughty and proud who are like "the cedars of Lebanon" and "the oaks of Bashan" (Isa 2:13). The rich city of Tyre, soon to meet God's judgment, had oars for its ships made from the oaks of Bashan (Ezk 27:6).

In Moses' blessing on the tribes we read, "Dan is a lion's whelp: he shall leap from Bashan" (Deut 33:22). Lions lurked among the trees of Bashan, affording the imagery of Dan as a tribe that could be ferocious like a lion. *See* Palestine II.B.4.*a.*

C. F. P.

BASHEMATH (băsh'ĕ-măth)

1. Esau's wife, the daughter of Elon the Hittite (Gen 26:34), probably to be identified with, or considered a sister of, Adah who is listed as the wife of Esau (Gen 36:2).

2. Another wife of Esau, the daughter of Ishmael and sister of Nebajoth (Gen 36:3, 4, 10, 13, 17). She is also called Mahalath (Gen 28:9). As a daughter of Ishmael she would also be a descendant of Abraham. Esau married her because his parents were displeased with his other wives (Gen 28:8; 26:34-35).

3. A daughter of Solomon, the wife of Ahimaaz, a quartermaster in the service of King Solomon for the province of Naphtali (I Kgs 4:15). The name is here spelled Basmath.

BASIN, BASON. Several words are translated "basin" (or "bason") in KJV. Basins were usually metal.

1. The Heb. word *'aggān,* a large banqueting bowl or crater; used also for catching and sprinkling blood in sacrifice (Ex 24:6). A smaller size may also have existed ("cups," Isa 22:24).

2. Heb. *kepôr* ("bowl," RSV), somewhat smaller, used in the temple service; of gold and silver (I Chr 28:17; Ezr 1:10; 8:27).

3. Heb. *mizrāq,* a large banqueting bowl (Amos 6:6), similar to 1 above. When used in a sacrificial ritual, it was of bronze (Ex 27:3; Num 4:14; I Kgs 7:40, 45), silver (Num 7:13; II Kgs 12:13), or gold (I Kgs 7:50; II Kgs 25:15).

4. Heb. *sap,* a bowl of indeterminate size with both sacrificial (Ex 12:22; Jer 52:19) and secular uses (II Sam 17:28).

5. Heb. *niptēr,* a washbasin (Jn 13:5). Such a foot basin is also mentioned in Ps 60:8; 108:9 (*sîr raḥaṣ,* "washpot," KJV; "washbasin," RSV). Examples have been excavated at Samaria and Mizpah (Tell en-Nasbeh).

See Pottery.

R. V. R.

BASKET. Woven or plaited of reeds or straw, baskets had many uses; exact size and shape is not always clear. One type, often carried on the head, was used for both secular and sacrificial purposes (Gen 40:16-18; Ex 29:3, 23, 32; Lev 8:2, 26, 31; Num 6:15, 17, 19; Jud 6:19). A rough wicker basket was used for transporting the heads of the sons of Ahab (II Kgs 10:7), figs (Jer 24:1-2), and the burdens of the slave laborer (Ps 81:6, "pots"). A type used as a fruit basket in Amos 8:1-2 doubled as a cage for birds (Jer 5:27, *see* Cage). Another was used for produce (Deut 26:2-4; 28:5, 17).

The ark of bulrushes in which the baby Moses was placed by his mother (Ex 2:3, 5) was probably a small basketlike chest with a cover made of bulrushes or papyrus (*see* Ark of Bulrushes; Bulrush; Reeds).

By the use of different Gr. words Mark (8:19-20) differentiates the types of baskets used for collection of the fragments after the feeding of the 5,000 (Mt 14:20 and parallels) and the feeding of the 4,000 (Mt 15:37 and parallels). The latter kind was used to lower Paul over the wall (Acts 9:25, but cf. II Cor 11:33 where the word used is one for a large rope basket).

R. V. R.

BASMATH (băs'măth). *See* Bashemath 3.

BASTARD. An illegitimate child or, particularly in the OT, a child sprung from an incestuous union (BDB, *s.v.*), or from a marriage within the prohibited degrees of affinity (Lev 18:6-20; 20:10-21). In the Deuteronomic law, such offspring were to the tenth generation (Deut 23:2) excluded from the covenanted community, "a people holy to the Lord your God" (Deut 14:2; Ex 19:5-6). The Moabites and Ammonites as a result of their incestuous origin (Gen 19:30-38) suffered the same blemish and the same exclusion (Deut 23:3; cf. Driver, *Deuteronomy,* ICC, pp. 260 f.). That this applied only to the males of these peoples was generally recognized by rabbinic interpreters. Witness also the acceptability of Boaz's marriage to Ruth the Moabitess. David the king was a third generation descendant of this union (Ruth 4:17).

The same Heb. word translated "bastard" in Zech 9:6 is better rendered "mongrel people" (RSV), that is, the proud Philistine city of Ashdod would as a result of divine judgment suffer the humiliation of being inhabited by a mixed population.

The illegitimate child's second-rate position in the family (e.g., Jud 11:1-3) resulted in lack of parental attention, including the discipline that would normally be exercised toward those in whose future the parent was most concerned. This fact lies behind Heb 12:7-8 where God's discipline of His spiritual children is the mark of their having the full standing of sonship (cf. Prov 3:11-12; Arndt, *s.v.;* MM, *s.v.*).

R. V. R.

BAT. *See* Animals, III.1.

BATH. *See* Weights, Measures, and Coins.

BATHE, BATHING. There is no distinction in terminology between bathing and washing only part of the body. References to the former, apart from ritual ablutions, are very limited: Pharaoh's daughter (Ex 2:5); Bathsheba (II Sam 11:2, RSV); possibly Ruth (3:3). The bathing of Naaman (II Kgs 5:14) and the impotent man at Bethesda (Jn 5:2-7) had therapeutic aspects. The hot climate and dusty roads of Palestine made washing of hands, face, and feet a frequent necessity (Gen 19:2; 24:32; 43:31; II Sam 11:8). Guests were provided water to wash their feet (Gen 18:4; Jud 19:21; Lk 7:44). To do so for them was the responsibility of a servant (I Sam 25:41), hence the significance of Jesus' example in humility (Jn 13:1-10; cf. I Tim 5:10).

Most of the biblical references are related to ritual washings: of offerings (Ex 29:17; Lev 1:9, 13; 8:21; 9:14; *et al.*); of priests (Ex 30:20; Lev 8:6; Num 8:21); of clothing and/or bodies of those ceremonially unclean (Lev 14:9; 15:5-27 *passim;* Num 19:10; *et al.*).

To wash the hands on the occasion of possible or presumed guilt was an assertion of innocence (Deut 21:6-7; Mt 27:24).

It was only after contact with Hellenistic civilization that gymnasia and public baths found a place in Palestine (Jos *Ant.* xix.7.5; I Macc 1:14). The hot springs at Tiberias and Gadara were renowned for their therapeutic powers (Jos *Ant.* xvii.6.5; xviii.2.3).

See Ablution; Unclean.

R. V. R.

BATHSHEBA (bǎth-shē'bȧ). The daughter of Eliam (II Sam 11:3) and granddaughter of Ahithophel the Gilonite (II Sam 23:34), the trusted friend and counselor of David who later betrayed him. She was married to Uriah the Hittite, one of the many foreign mercenaries attracted to the court of David. In the absence of Uriah in the Ammonite war, David took Bathsheba as his paramour. The illicit love affair ended with the murder of Uriah and the death of the child born of the adulterous union (II Sam 11–12).

David and Bathsheba were then married legally and she became the mother of four sons: Solomon, Shimea, Shobab, and Nathan (I Chr 3:5; Bath-shua is an alternate spelling of Bathsheba). As Solomon's mother, Bathsheba is included in the genealogy of Christ (Mt 1:6).

It was at the insistence of Bathsheba, supported by the prophet Nathan and the priest Zadok, that Solomon was crowned king, preventing the plot of his brother Adonijah to seize the succession to the throne. Bathsheba last appears as the unwitting tool of Adonijah who, in asking for the hand of David's wife Abishag in marriage, laid a claim to the kingdom (I Kgs 1–2).

P. C. J.

BATH-SHUA (bǎth-shū'ȧ). An alternate form of Bathsheba (*q.v.*), mother of Solomon (cf. I Chr 3:5; II Sam 12:24).

BATTERING RAM. *See* Armor.

BATTLE. *See* Warfare.

BATTLE AXE. Used only in Jer 51:20. *See* Armor; Axe; Maul.

BATTLE BOW. *See* Armor.

BATTLEMENT. A row or course of stones with openings on top of walls or fortifications. From these openings stones, arrows, lances were hurled on attacking soldiers (Zeph 1:16; 3:6, RSV).

In Deut 22:8 a battlement or parapet was to enclose the open flat roof of a house, mainly to keep people from falling from it. The flat roof was used for recreation and entertaining guests, since there one could be cooled by the evening breeze.

BAVAI (bǎv'ī). Son of Henadad who aided in the rebuilding of the wall of Jerusalem (Neh 3:18); perhaps called Binnui in Neh 3:24.

BAY (COLOR). *See* Colors.

BAY (COVE)

1. The bay or cove at the NW corner of the Dead Sea (Josh 15:5; 18:19), formed by the delta of silt at the mouth of the Jordan River.

2. The shallow bay at the S end of the Dead Sea (Josh 15:2), S of el-Lisan, the "tongue" or delta-peninsula extending from the E shore of the sea. The waters of this bay may now cover the ruins of Sodom and Gomorrah.

BAY TREE. *See* Plants.

BAZLITH (bǎz'lǐth). The ancestor of a family group included among the Nethinim (*q.v.*), members of which returned from Babylonian Exile. The spelling is sometimes Bazluth and Bazloth; the correct rendering is difficult to determine (Ezr 2:52; Neh 7:54).

BAZLUTH (bǎz'lŭth). Another form of Bazlith (*q.v.*).

BDELLIUM. *See* Minerals: Bdellium; Plants: Bdellium.

BEALIAH (bē-ȧ-lī'ȧ). One of the Benjamites who joined David's outlaw band at Ziklag. He was one of the mighty men who could shoot arrows and sling stones with either the right or the left hand (I Chr 12:2, 5).

BEALOTH (bē'ȧ-lŏth)

1. A town in southern Judah (Josh 15:24), perhaps the same as Baalath-beer (Josh 19:8).

2. A town or locality in Solomon's ninth administrative district (Aloth, KJV) located in the old territory of Asher in the N (I Kgs 4:16, RSV).

BEAM. A word used to translate several Heb. and Gr. terms referring to large timbers in constructing floors and ceilings or roofs of buildings (I Kgs 6:9; 7:2-3; II Kgs 6:2, 5). The word also refers to the large bar on which the warp was wound in the loom, called "the weaver's beam" (Jud 16:14; I Sam 17:7; I Chr 11:23). In I Kgs 6:36; 7:12 reference is made to an architectural feature common in the Near East during the 2nd mil. B.C., the use of a framework of wooden beams to strengthen a wall on a stone foundation against the shock of earthquakes. The term was used by Jesus in a figurative sense in contrast to a mote (*q.v.*) or speck (Mt 7:3).

BEANS. *See* Plants.

BEAR. *See* Animals, II.5.

BEAR (CONSTELLATION). Translated "Arcturus" in Job 9:9; 38:32, but "Bear" in RSV. *See* Astronomy.

BEARD. *See* Hair.

BEAST. *See* Animals.

BEAST (SYMBOLIC). This expression is frequently used in Scripture in a figurative or symbolic sense. It may symbolize especially tyrannical monarchies. The four beasts in Dan 7:3, 17, 23 represent four kingdoms (Babylon, Medo-Persia, Greece, Rome). The fourth beast (Dan 7:7-8, 19-26) is said to have ten horns. Among these ten (symbolic of ten contemporary kings immediately before the coming of the Most High) arises an eleventh ("little horn") who destroys three and dominates the rest.

Christian interpreters generally unite in identifying this "little horn" with the beast "out of the sea" of Rev 13:1 ff. and 17:3 ff. who has "seven heads and ten horns." This is the same as the man of sin or son of perdition of II Thess 2:3-10 (*see* Man of Sin; Antichrist). Identification is based on similarity and doctrinal unity rather than specific scriptural statement.

Most of the features of the fourth beast of Dan 7 are incorporated into John's vision of "the beast," a final personal Antichrist. This beast forms an unholy trinity with a second beast "out of the earth" (Rev 13:11) and the "dragon" (Satan, Rev 13:2) in imitation of and opposition to the Holy Trinity. The first beast apparently even fakes a resurrection (13:3) and performs other false miracles (13:13 ff.). He persecutes the saints (13:7) and gains world power, but is destroyed by Christ at His coming (19:20). *See* Abomination of Desolation; Deceiver.

For a preterist view see H. B. Swete, *The Apocalypse of John. The Apocalypse* by Joseph Seiss provides an elaborate premillennial futurist interpretation. An excellent homiletical treatment is found in *The Apocalypse Today* by Thomas F. Torrance.

"Beast" in Rev 4 translates a Gr. word which should be rendered "living creature" (*q.v.*).

R. D. C.

BEATING. This was a common form of punishment throughout the East. Beating administered with a rod should be distinguished from scourging inflicted with a whip of several lashes, often reenforced with sharp pieces of metal or bone (II Macc 6:30; 7:1; Mt 10:17; Acts 22:25).

Israel's foremen were beaten by Egyptian taskmasters for failure to meet brick production quotas (Ex 5:14, 16). (Cf. Egyptian Eighteenth Dynasty tomb painting where taskmaster says to brickmakers, "The rod is in my hand; be not idle," Alleman and Flack, *Old Testament Commentary*, p. 214.) Such beatings as legal punishment in OT law were administered to the prisoner in a prone position and proportioned to the offense with a 40 stroke maximum. Jewish practice reduced it to "forty stripes save one" to avoid breaking the Deuteronomic law by miscalculation (II Cor 11:24). Beating of a child was essential as a disciplinary measure to save him from worse evil (Prov 23:13-14). An owner might beat his slave, short of immediate death, without penalty (Ex 21:20-21).

Paul and Silas were beaten before being thrown in prison at Philippi (Acts 16:22-23). On the ground that this was an infraction of his rights as a Roman citizen, Paul demanded and received a public apology (Acts 16:37-39); yet

The dungeon at the traditional site of the Palace of Caiaphas showing the place where prisoners were beaten. The prisoner's hands were tied at the two holes over the archway at the left. Courtesy St. Pierre en Gallincante

he was beaten on two other occasions (II Cor 11:25).

See Crime and Punishment; Punishment; Scourge.

R. V. R.

BEATITUDES. *See* Sermon on the Mount.

BEAUTY. The biblical concept of beauty blends two areas: the aesthetic that touches man's experiences of beauty and art, as well as the recognition of the moral, ethical and spiritual aspect of what is divinely and eternally good and righteous. The Bible does not purport to supply answers for a critique into the meaning and value of human experiences in beauty and art; the Gr. thinkers speculated philosophically concerning the aesthetic. As the divinely inspired writers speak of their encounters with the majesty, honor and glory of the one holy God in His being as well as in His work, one cannot help seeing something of the "beauty of holiness" of God and the work of His creation (though marred now) pronounced as "good." Out of this, in a practical way, the Bible recognizes beauty in every area of the human experience.

A number of terms express in a variety of meanings the many facets of beauty. In the OT there is *pā'ar,* "to beautify," "glorify." The nouns *tip'ārâ* and *tip'eret* are "beauty," "finery," "glory" (Isa 44:13; 52:11). The Heb. verb *yāpâ* means "be fair," "be beautiful" (Ezk 16:13), while the noun and adjective *yāpeh* carries the same meaning. The Heb. root *tā'ar* ("mark out," "delineate") emphasizes as a noun *tô'ar,* "fair of form," "handsome form" or "shapely figure" (Est 2:7). *Hādar* (root idea of "to swell") and its derived forms denote "beauty," "majesty," "honor," "splendor" (Ps 8:5; 29:4). *Nā'â* (or, *nāwâ*) emphasizes "to be comely," "beautiful" (Song 1:10). *Ṣābâ,* "to swell" (or, Arabic "to shine"), carries in its derivative *ṣᵉdî* the ideas of "beauty," "glory," "ornament" (Ezk 7:20). The same word is the Heb. for the beautiful, graceful gazelle (Song 8:14). The noun *hôd* indicates "glory," "majesty," "honor," "comeliness," "beauty" (Ps 45:3). *Ḥāmad,* "to desire," "to delight" in a good sense ("covet" in an evil sense), expresses the same idea in its derivatives (Ezk 23:6, 23; Hag 2:7). *Nā'ēm,* "to be delightful," indicates through its derivatives "pleasant," "agreeable," "lovely" (II Sam 1:23; Ps 16:11). Other words are, e.g., *tôb,* "handsome," "fair," "goodly," "pleasant," "pleasure"; and *ḥēn,* "grace" or "beauty" in several instances (Prov 1:9; 3:22; 17:8).

In the NT, there are *asteios,* "elegant," "fair," "comely"; *euprepeia,* "well-looking," "grace," "beauty"; *kalos,* "beautiful"; *timē,* "honor"; and *hōraios,* "prime" or "blooming," thus, "attractive."

Usages of the various terms from concordances indicate wide ranges of descriptions. *Women* are described as beautiful: Rachel was "fair of form" and "beautiful to behold" (Gen 29:17). Certain *men* are described as handsome: David had "beauty of eyes and good appearance" (I Sam 16:12); the ruler of Tyre was "perfect in beauty" which made him proud (Ezk 28:12, 17). Specific *body parts* are mentioned: Ezekiel had "a pleasant voice" (Ezk 33:32); the feet of the messenger of God's news are comely (Isa 52:7; Rom 10:15); the "fair" woman in the Song had beautiful eyes, hair, teeth, lips, etc., described with appropriate similes (Song 4:1 f.). *Garments* are considered as beautiful and attractive: the high priest's garments were for "honor and beauty" (Ex 28:2); Joseph was arrayed in fine linen of an important office (Gen 41:42); and the glorified saints are ornamented in white garments (Rev 3:4-5).

Countries, cities, Jerusalem, temple, etc., are all described as beautiful under various terms and figures; e.g., Zion (Ps 48:2 f.), the temple (Acts 3:2), the crown of Ephraim (Samaria, Isa 28:1-4), Tyre (Ezk 27:3), nature (Mt 6:29), etc. *Art work* of all kinds was the product of the wise-hearted (Ex 35–39), and the aesthetic in architectural designs was recognized and appreciated (I Kgs 6–7; Eccl 2:4-10). In *eschatological* expressions, the Jerusalem of the future is described as a city of brightness and beauty (Isa 62:1-4).

Moving into the *moral, ethical,* and *spiritual* aspects, a strong emphasis is noted: the face of an old man is to be honored (Lev 19:32); the woman who anointed Jesus before His passion did a beautiful work to be remembered as a memorial (Mt 26:10, 13); the sons who are wise in God's wisdom wear a crown of beauty (Prov 4:9); the right kind of speech is likened to the art work in apples of gold (Prov 25:11); the commandments of God (or, the Word of God) are to be regarded greater than the best art work (Ps 119:127); the Lord is to be worshiped in the "beauty of holiness" (Ps 96:9), etc. The *Messiah* in the days of His flesh had no comeliness (Isa 53:2), but "in that day" He will be "for beauty and honor" (Isa 4:2).

Therefore, the Bible has distinctive terms describing the God of majesty, who is arrayed in glory and beauty, and deals "in grace and loving-kindness." His activities are a delight to the heart and eye. Thus, within a theocentric context, in a unique presentation, there is seen the proper union of moral and spiritual beauty and the aesthetic. The lines of contact between the human and divine in the appreciation of beauty are, in the end, an emphasis upon the uniqueness of the God of the whole cosmos.

In Zech 11:7, 14 God as the divine shepherd of Israel is depicted as taking two staffs which He calls "Beauty" (*nō'am*) and "Bands" (*ḥōbelîm*), the first representing the Lord's gracious, pleasant covenant relationship with His people, and the second, the brotherly union (RSV) of Judah and Israel. The breaking in half of the staffs represented the annulment of the covenant and the dissolution of the bonds uniting the descendants of Jacob.

L. Go.

BEBAI (bē'bī). A chief of returning exiles from the Captivity (Ezr 2:11; 8:11; 10:28; Neh 7:16; 10:15).

BECHER (bē'kĕr)

1. Second son of Benjamin (Gen 46:21; I Chr 7:6, 8). The other available lists of the sons of Benjamin do not mention Becher (Num 26:38–41; I Chr 8:1–40). There may have been considerable confusion in textual transmission. On the other hand, the Benjamin genealogy in I Chr 8 probably contains lists of Benjamite families and their dwelling places at a particular period (Jacob M. Meyers, *I Chronicles,* Anchor Bible, XII, 59 f.), perhaps in the time of Ezra. Becher is thought to have been omitted in Num 26 because of the small number of his descendants in the early history of the tribe. By David's time the Becher clan could send 20,200 men to war (I Chr 7:2, 9). But after the Exile the clan had once again become insignificant.

2. A son of Ephraim, progenitor of the Bachrites (Num 26:35; Becherites, RSV). This son and clan are not included in the LXX. In I Chr 7:20 there is a "Bered" but no "Becher." BDB considers the former the correct form in Num 26:35 (cf. Gray, *Numbers,* ICC, p. 393). Evidence is inconclusive.

R. V. R.

BECHORATH (bĭ-kôr'ăth). One of Saul's ancestors of the tribe of Benjamin, the father of Zeror (I Sam 9:1).

Wooden bedstead covered with thick gold and mesh of linen cord, from the tomb of Tutankhamon. LL

BED. A number of terms are used, often interchangeably, which are rendered "bed" or the equivalents: "pallet," "couch," or "litter." The form depended on the economic status of the individual. The simplest was a place on the dirt floor where a person might recline with his only covering his outer garment (Ex 22:27; Deut 24:13), or a rug or blanket (Jud 4:18; Isa 28:20). Most common was a reed mat or pallet rolled out along the wall at floor level or on an elevated ledge that would serve as a seat during the day. Such a bed could be carried with ease (II Sam 17:28; Lk 5:25; Jn 5:5–8), and could also serve as a litter for transporting the sick (Mk 6:55). Larger homes had separate bedrooms (II Kgs 11:2) often on a second level (I Kgs 17:19); the balustraded rooftop was a common sleeping place.

That beds on legs were rather common would appear from Jesus' use of them as illustrations in teaching the masses (Mk 4:21;Lk 8:16). Among the wealthy they were very elaborate and highly ornamented. Amos charged the luxury-loving Israelites with sleeping on "beds of ivory" (i.e., ivory inlay, Amos 6:4). The harlot of Proverbs enticed to a couch "decked with coverings, colored spreads of Egyptian linen," and "perfumed with myrrh, aloes and cinnamon" (Prov 7:16–17, RSV). Ptolemy of Egypt sent ten beds with silver feet as a gift to Eleazar, high priest at Jerusalem (Jos *Ant.* xii.2). Sennacherib of Assyria listed beds with ivory inlay as a part of Hezekiah's tribute (ANET, p. 288). Xerxes' palace could boast beds of gold and silver (Est 1:6).

R. V. R.

BEDAD (bē'dăd). The father of Hadad, king of Edom (Gen 36:35; I Chr 1:46).

BEDAN (bē'dăn)

1. A judge mentioned only in I Sam 12:11. Bedan is probably a corruption of either Abdon or Barak, as found in LXX. In Jud 12:13–15 Abdon is recorded as one of the regular judges of Israel, while Barak and Deborah's exploits are told in Jud 4 and 5.

2. From the tribe of Manasseh, a son of Ulam (I Chr 7:17).

BEDCHAMBER. Two Heb. expressions are so translated.

1. The Heb. words *ḥădar mishkāb,* enclosure or room for lying down (Ex 8:3; II Sam 4:7; II Kgs 6:12; Eccl 10:20).

2. The Heb. words *ḥădar hammiṭṭôth,* rooms for (storing) beds (II Kgs 11:2; II Chr 22:11). *See* Chamber.

BEDEIAH (bē-dē'yȧ). A son of Bani who was compelled to give up his foreign wife in the time of Ezra (Ezr 10:35).

BEDSTEAD. *See* Bed.

BEE. *See* Animals, III.2.

BEELIADA (bē-ē-lī'ȧ-dȧ). A name meaning "Baal knows," given to a son of David born in Jerusalem (I Chr 14:7). According to II Sam 5:16 and I Chr 3:8 perhaps the name was altered to Eliada, "God knows."

BEELZEBUB (bē-ĕl'zē-bŭb). This name designates Satan as the "chief of the devils" (Lk

11:18). The perverted Pharisees accused Jesus of exorcising demons (Lk 11:15, 19), of having (Mk 3:22), or even being, this fallen prince (Mt 10:25; 12:24). Beelzebub (from II Kgs 1:2) is the Syriac and Latin Vulgate (hence KJV) rendering of the Gr. NT's *Beelzeboul* (cf. ASV marg.), probably meaning "lord of the height" (IDB, SBK, TWNT; cf. Eph 2:2, "prince . . . of the air"). Ugaritic myths thus speak of *z-b-l B-'-l*, "exalted Baal." No definite connection can be made between Baalzebub (II Kgs 1:2, "lord of flies") and the NT *Beelzeboul*. Alternative doubtful derivations include *Ba'al zebûl*, "lord of the dwelling" (cf. Mt 10:25; "they have called the *master of the house* Beelzebul"), or "lord of dung" (II Kgs 1:2; the Philistine deity Baalzebul [?] mocked as Baalzebub, "lord of flies"). *See* Baal-zebub under Gods, False; Devil.

J.B.P.

BEER (bē'ĕr)

1. A stopping place on the NE border of Moab as Israel approached Canaan (Num 21:16–18). Here the Lord provided water in a well dug by their princes and remembered in song. This may be the Beer-elim ("well of heroes") mentioned in a Moabite context in Isa 15:8, possibly in Wadi eth-Themed NE of Dibon.

2. The city to which Jotham fled after reciting the parable in which he denounced his brother Abimelech to the men of Shechem (Jud 9:21). Location is uncertain, possibly modern el-Bireh about eight miles N of Beth-shan (Beisan). This is not to be confused with the el-Bireh N of Jerusalem.

BEERA (bē'ê-rȧ). A descendant of the tribe of Asher, the eleventh son of Zophah (I Chr 7:37).

BEERAH (bē̇-ê'rȧ). A prince of the tribe of Reuben who was deported by Tiglath-pileser III in the 8th cen. B.C. (I Chr 5:6).

BEER-ELIM (bĭr-ē'lĭm). A village name meaning "well of Elim" in Moab (Isa 15:8); possibly the same as Beer (*q.v.*; Num 21:16) where the Israelites stopped during their wilderness journey.

BEERI (bē-ē'rī)

1. Name of a Hittite whose daughter Judith was one of Esau's wives (Gen 26:34).

2. Father of the prophet Hosea (Hos 1:1).

BEER-LAHAI-ROI (bĭr'lȧ-hī'roi). The Heb. *be'ēr laḥay ro'î* means "well of the Living One who sees me." This was a fountain of water in the wilderness, between Kadesh and Bered on the road to Shur (the eastern line of Egypt's border fortresses), where the Lord's watch care was revealed to Hagar. Also a place where Isaac dwelt for some time (Gen 25:11, RSV). The site is unknown, possibly about 50 miles SW of Beer-sheba.

Excavations of an underground Chalcolithic settlement at Beer-sheba. HFV

BEEROTH (bē̇-ē'rŏth). One of the cities of the Gibeonite alliance with whom Joshua made a treaty of peace (Josh 9:16–18). It was assigned to Benjamin (Josh 18:25) and was evidently near the Ephraimite border (II Sam 4:2–3, 5–9). It was the home of Ishbosheth's assassins. One of David's "mighty men," Naharai, armor bearer of Joab, was from Beeroth (II Sam 23:37; I Chr 11:39). Men of Beeroth are listed among the post-Exilic community (Ezr 2:25; Neh 7:29).

Exact location is disputed, several sites having strong advocates: (1) el-Bireh, one mile E of Ramallah; (2) Tell en-Nasbeh, one mile S of el-Bireh (Albright), but more likely to be Mizpah; (3) Nebi Samwil, about two miles SW of Tell en-Nasbeh.

BEEROTHITE (bē̇-ē'rō-thīt). A native or inhabitant of Beeroth (*q.v.*). These inhabitants succeeded in deceiving Israel and in making a covenant with them (Josh 9:3 ff.). *See also* Berothite.

BEER-SHEBA (bēr-shē'bȧ). A city in the territory of Simeon (Josh 19:1–2) and reckoned among "the uttermost cities of the tribe of the children of Judah" (Josh 15:21, 28). It marked the southern extent of the land (cf. Jud 20:1; I Sam 3:20; II Sam 3:10; 17:11). Its name may mean "well of seven" (Gen 21:30 f.), or "well of (the) oath" (Gen 26:31–33).

In this area Hagar wandered with Ishmael (Gen 21:14). Abimelech of Philistia and Abraham entered into a covenant here (Gen 21:27–32). Abraham planted a tamarisk tree at Beer-sheba (Gen 21:33), and returned to the town after the offering of Isaac on Moriah (Gen 22:19). Isaac returned here from his sojourn in the valley of Gerar (Gen 26:17, 23). Jacob fled from Beer-sheba to escape the wrath of Esau (Gen 27:41; 28:10). On his way to Egypt, Jacob offered sacrifices at Beer-sheba (Gen 46:1).

Joel and Abiah, sons of Samuel, judged in Beer-sheba (I Sam 8:2). Elijah stopped at

Beer-sheba on his way to the Mount of God (I Kgs 19:3). The mother of Joash, king of Judah, was from Beer-sheba (II Kgs 12:1; II Chr 24:1). During the divided monarchy the town had a sanctuary that was visited by pilgrims from the northern kingdom (Amos 5:5; 8:14; cf. II Kgs 23:8). The family of Shimei of the tribe of Simeon lived here (I Chr 4:28). Some of the children of Judah lived here after the Captivity (Neh 11:27, 30).

Beer-sheba's importance spiritually is attested by God's appearance here to Hagar (Gen 21:17), to Isaac (Gen 26:23-24), and to Jacob (Gen 46:1-2).

Twenty-eight miles SW of Hebron the 25-acre Tell es-Seba' lies *c.* two miles to the E of the modern city. Here Israeli archaeologists noticed ruins of a fortress of the kingdom of Judah, measuring approximately 465-by-265 feet, headquarters for controlling the Negeb trade routes (IEJ, XVII [1967], 9, 15). Four seasons of excavation, begun in 1969 and directed by Yohanan Aharoni, revealed Roman, Hellenistic and Israelite structures. The oldest city wall, over 13 feet thick, was built in the late 10th cen. B.C. The well-preserved 8th cen. wall from the reign of Uzziah or Hezekiah was of brick casemate construction atop a steep glacis reminiscent of Hyksos fortifications, testifying to the great pains taken in protecting the city. Inside the walls were two royal store houses, each *c.* 55 feet long, with a row of pillars for supporting the roof. Astarte figurines, a small incense burner, and a miniature horned altar suggest the spiritual condition of the inhabitants. The city reached its greatest extent in the 7th cen. B.C. It was similar in nature to the fortress at Arad (*q.v.*). Excavations at a site S of the present city by Jean Perrot uncovered dwellings of the Chalcolithic Age (4000-3100 B.C.), with stone and copper maceheads and fertility cult images.

Beer-sheba is a rapidly growing Israeli city (*c.* 70,000-75,000 in 1968) which serves as an administrative and distribution center for the Negev. The environs, particularly to the N and the W, are being developed agriculturally, thanks to irrigation largely from the Yarkon River project.

W. C.

BEESHTERAH (bē-ĕsh'tē-rȧ). A Levitical city given to Manasseh; also called Ashtaroth (*q.v.*; cf. Josh 21:27; I Chr 6:71). Beeshterah is an abbreviation or contraction for Beth-Ashtaroth, "the temple of Ashtoreth."

BEETLE. *See* Animals, IV.4.

BEEVES. *See* Animals: Cattle, I.6.

BEGGAR. The Gr. word *ptōchos* has reference to "crouching" or "cringing," hence to one who was "a beggar." According to MM, *Lexicon,* it always had a bad sense before biblical usage (in the Gospels).

In the NT, a "beggar" might wait for food scraps (Lk 16:21) or money (Acts 3:2 f.). The word was also associated with Jesus' disciples, who were not allowed to carry a "beggars' bag" but were dependent on people for their food (Mt 10:10, NASB marg.), and with the virtue of "poverty" (e.g., "Blessed are the poor in spirit," Mt 5:3).

BEGINNING. The word "beginning" appears in Gen 1:1 and Jn 1:1 in a specialized, absolute sense. In Gen 1:1 the beginning is not the first of the creative acts, but rather the act by which the whole of creation is initiated. The beginning is thus apart from that which begins, transcending time (cf. "the beginning of his way," Prov 8:22; cf. also Heb 1:10, quoting Ps 102:25). It is the immediate act of God, prior to time and transcending time. Creation is seen as dependent on the God who was in the beginning—before time.

Jn 1:1 states that the *logos,* "the Word" by which the eternal, invisible God is revealed to man, was with God (the Father) and was in essence Deity "in the beginning." The Father and the Son are thus presented as co-equal and co-eternal. Before time, before the beginning of the creative process by which the universe and mankind came into being, God was—without beginning or end—and the "Word" was present sharing in the divine essence and glory. John contrasts the position of the Word as "in the beginning" with God, yet in historical time entering the world and dwelling among us (Jn 1:1; 1:14).

The Lord Jesus Christ is called the Beginning (*archē*) by both Paul (Col 1:18) and John (Rev 3:14; 21:6; 22:13; cf. the Alpha and the Omega, Rev 1:8). The Gr. philosophers expressed the First Cause of all things by the same term, *archē.*

See Creation; Logos; Time.

Bibliography. Gerhard Delling, "*Archē,* etc.," TDNT, I, 479-484.

C. F. P.

BEGOTTEN. *See* Only Begotten.

BEGUILE. *See* Guile.

BEHEMOTH. *See* Animals: Hippopotamus, II.20.

BEKAH. *See* Weights, Measures, and Coins.

BEL. *See* Gods, False.

BELA, BELAH (bē'lȧ)

1. Another name for Zoar (*q.v.*), one of the five cities of the plain with Sodom and Gomorrah (Gen 14:2, 8).

2. A descendant of Esau who is listed as the first king of Edom (Gen 36:32-33; I Chr 1:43-44). From the name of his father, Beor, the same name as the father of Balaam, some

have thought he may have been a Chaldean rather than an Edomite.

3. The eldest son of Benjamin (Gen 46:21). From him were descended the Belaites, one of the main family groups of Benjamin in the time of Moses (Num 26:38, 40; I Chr 7:6–7; 8:1, 3).

4. The son of Azaz of the tribe of Reuben who dwelt in Gilead (I Chr 5:8).

BELAITE (bē'lā-īt). A descendant of Bela (Num 26:38).

BELIAL (bē'lĭ-ĕl). The literal meaning of the OT Heb. word *belîya'al* is "useless," "without worth." It is usually employed as a term descriptive of a person; e.g., "a son of Belial" or "a man of Belial." An approximate meaning is our colloquial expression "a good-for-nothing." But the contexts of most passages suggest definite forms of evil, not just the absence of good. The evil men of Gibeah who abused the Levite's concubine in Jud 19:22 f. are called "sons of Belial." When Hannah prayed for a son in the temple, moving her lips but making no sound, Eli the priest, concluding she was drunk, thought her to be "a daughter of Belial" (I Sam 1:16). In Prov 6:12 the term is equated with the Heb. *'āwen* which often means "iniquity." In Ps 41:8, "a thing of Belial" (Heb.) is an evil disease, while in II Sam 22:5 and Ps 18:4 "the floods of Belial" are equated with "the waves of death."

E. B. S.

BELIEVE. The verb form is related to faith, meaning "to have confidence in," "to trust," "to accept as true and reliable." In the NT it often has the force of "obey"; e.g., "believe the gospel" (Mk 1:15; I Thess 2:13) and "obey the gospel" (Rom 10:16; II Thess 1:8; I Pet 4:17; cf. Rom 1:5).

"Believe" is used to translate the Heb. *'āman,* "to build up or support," "to render firm or faithful," "to trust," "to stand still"; and the Gr. *pisteuō,* "to have faith or trust," "put trust in," "commit"; or more rarely *peithomai,* passive, "to assent, rely," "have confidence in," "be persuaded."

When used with God or Christ as its object, to believe means three things: (1) to assent to the truth of what He says or makes known; (2) to receive and trust Him personally; and (3) to commit oneself to Him in obedience. "Believe" is often used with the preposition "in" or "on"; e.g., "Believe on the Lord Jesus Christ, and thou shalt be saved" (Acts 16:31), to stress elements of trust and commitment. Believing must not be intellectualized and considered only in terms of assent to truth. Truth about God is necessary ("He that cometh to God must believe that he is, and that he is a rewarder of them that diligently seek him," Heb 11:6), but it is not sufficient ("Thou believest that there is one God; thou doest well: the devils also believe, and tremble," Jas 2:19, and are still demons!).

In the religious sense, believing depends upon divine revelation, and is always related to that revelation in the personal and written Word. Believing is thus the human response to the initiative God has taken in His redemptive acts, which are made known to men through the written and preached Word: "For whosoever shall call upon the name of the Lord shall be saved. How then shall they call on him in whom they have not believed? and how shall they believe in him of whom they have not heard? and how shall they hear without a preacher? and how shall they preach, except they be sent? . . . So then faith cometh by hearing, and hearing by the word of God" (Rom 10:13–15, 17). In the high priestly prayer Jesus said, "Neither pray I for these alone, but for them also which shall believe on me *through their word*" (Jn 17:20).

Since faith is response to grace, it involves no element of merit. We are not, strictly speaking, saved *by* faith; rather it is *through* faith: "By grace are ye saved through faith; and that not of yourselves: it is the gift of God: not of works, lest any man should boast" (Eph 2:8–9).

See also Faith.

W. T. P.

BELIEVERS. A term (from Gr. *pisteuō,* "to trust," "to rely upon") applied to Christian converts (Acts 5:14; I Tim 4:12). It is thought by B. B. Warfield that "believer" was the first name given to Christians ("The Biblical Doctrine of Faith," *Biblical Doctrines*). Certainly the great stress in the teachings of Christ is that men are to believe in Him (Jn 3:16, 38; 5:24; 10:26–30; cf. Rom 10:9–10; I Jn 5:1; Heb 11:6). The Philippian jailer asked what he must do to be saved and was told, "Believe on the Lord Jesus Christ, and thou shalt be saved, and thy house" (Acts 16:31). In Romans and Galatians Paul stresses that Abraham was justified by faith, that is, by believing God, and that this is the only way in which man can be saved (Rom 3:28; Gal 2:16, 21).

Believers are those who have exercised saving faith by taking Christ as their own personal Saviour on the authority of the Word of God, the Bible, and thus have obtained a position of sonship to God. They are spoken of as "in Christ" (Eph 1:3; I Cor 1:2; Rom 8:1). Their position in Christ is sealed in the Holy Spirit, in whom they are baptized unto the death, burial and resurrection of Christ (Eph 1:13; I Cor 12:13; Rom 6:3; Gal 3:27). This position is the basis of all the Christian's spiritual possessions. Because of his sonship, he is obligated to live in accordance with his position and with the character of his heavenly Father (Eph 4:1; Mt 5:48; Rom 6:11).

R. A. K.

BELL. Two different Heb. words are translated "bell."

1. Heb. *pa'ămôn,* lit., "striker." A bell of

gold which, alternating with pomegranates of blue, purple, and scarlet fabric, encircled the bottom of the high priest's blue linen robe (Ex 28:33 f.; 39:25 f.). Ben Sirach stated the purpose thus: "to send forth a sound as he went, to make a sound that might be heard in the temple, for a memorial to the children of his people" (Sir 45:9). That is, the sound of the bells reminded the worshiper of the effective mediatorial ministry of the priest in his behalf before God. Ex 28:35 (RSV) states: "Its sound shall be heard when he goes into the holy place before the Lord, and when he comes out, lest he die." The sound of the bells indicated to the worshiper that his mediatorial representative was properly robed to minister acceptably in his behalf in the Divine Presence. That these bells were a relic of a primitive fear of evil spirits that might otherwise assemble about the doors of the sanctuary can hardly be proved (cf. Driver, *Exodus, Cambridge Bible,* p. 308). Bells were not used as a call to worship before the Christian era.

2. Heb. *m*ᵉ*ṣillâ,* lit., "a tinkler." A bell was used as an ornament on the harness of horses (Zech 14:20). When inscribed "Holy to the Lord," they became symbols of the total integration of life within the all-pervasive divine holiness in the Messianic Age. Since a cognate of this Heb. word meant "cymbals" (I Chr 13:8; Ezr 3:10, *et al.*), some have supposed these bells to be more like bangles which made a tinkling sound from striking together when the horses moved. However, Assyrian excavations have illustrated the use of clapper type bells as ornaments on the harness of war horses.

R. V. R.

BELLOWS. Although the word *mappuaḥ,* "bellows," occurs only in Jer 6:29, there are allusions to the use of bellows in Isa 54:16 and Ezk 22:21. Since wood and charcoal burn easily and may be simply fanned, bellows were used in forges and furnaces for smelting and refining purposes. Pictures of bellows may be seen in the tomb of Senusert II (*c.* 1892 B.C.). They were made of two leather bags secured and fitted on a frame, from each of which a large reed pipe extended to carry the air to the fire. They were worked by the operator's foot pressing alternately upon the two skins till they were deflated, and then pulling up the skins by means of a string in each hand. Two pairs of bellows were used for one forge, one on either side.

BELLY. The words translated in Scripture as "belly" are from various roots signifying "soft," "hollow," "round," that describe the physical features of the abdominal region. The term is used quite generally to refer to the outer belly (Song 5:14), womb (Ps 22:10), stomach (Ps 17:14), and the lower abdomen in general.

The term is also widely used in a figurative sense. Because of its connection with food, it sometimes stands for carnal, worldly satisfactions (Phil 3:19). Because it designates the inner anatomy, it is used in Heb. thought as a figure of the inner self, of the intellectual and emotional life (Jn 7:38; Job 20:20).

BELOMANCY. A method of divination by arrows, a number of which were marked in certain ways, then mixed and drawn at random. References in the OT are in Hos 4:12 and Ezk 21:21. This practice was condemned by the prophet Hosea. *See* Magic.

BELOVED DISCIPLE. *See* John the Apostle.

BELSHAZZAR (bĕl-shăz'ár). The ruler in Babylon who was killed when the city was captured in October, 539 B.C. His name (Babylonian *Bel-shar-uṣur*) means "May Bel protect the king." The LXX and Theodotion in his Gr. version called him Baltasar. Although he is mentioned in Dan 5:2, 11, 13, 18 as having Nebuchadnezzar as his father, he was really the son of a later king called Nabonidus (Akkad. *Nabu-na'id*). Yet there is a likelihood that Belshazzar's mother was the daughter of Nebuchadnezzar (*q.v.*), making him the grandson of the great Chaldean king. At any rate, the use of "father" here can signify simply a predecessor, just as in ancient usage the term "son" often referred to a successor in the same office whether or not there was a blood relationship (e.g., "son" in the nomenclature "Jehu, son of Omri" in the Assyrian inscriptions, which must mean successor).

Critical scholarship had long questioned the statements in Dan 5 regarding the kingship of Belshazzar, for it is certain that Nabonidus remained alive until after the fall of Babylon in 539 B.C. Various clay tablets from Babylonia, however, have revealed that Belshazzar shared the throne as coregent or king with his father. From the site of Ur came a tablet with the text of two dreams for which the man involved studies the stars in regard to a favorable interpretation "for my lord Nabonidus, king of Babylon, as well as to a favorable interpretation for my lord Belshazzar, the crown prince" (ANET, p. 309, n. 5). Also there exist two legal documents dated to the twelfth and thirteenth years of Nabonidus that include oaths sworn by the life of Nabonidus, the king, and of Belshazzar, the crown prince, a unique type of oath in cuneiform literature.

A tablet in the series known as the Babylonian Chronicle states that Nabonidus (556/555–539 B.C.) stayed in Tema from the seventh through the eleventh years of his reign, while the crown prince, his officials, and his army were in Akkad (i.e., Babylonia), and that during those years the festival of the new year was omitted (ANET, p. 306). The so-called "Verse Account of Nabonidus" complains that the king, when his third year was about to begin, "entrusted the 'Camp' to his oldest son, the firstborn, the troops everywhere in the country he ordered under his command. He let everything go, entrusted the kingship to him and, himself, he started out for a long journey," invading Arabia, capturing Tema (*q.v.*), rebuilding the town, and making his residence there (ANET, p. 313). A Harran inscription gives ten years for the exile of Nabonidus. Just why he chose to live in Tema for so long a time is not known, but it may be conjectured that he needed to be near this important outpost to keep down the Arab tribes that threatened his commercially lucrative caravan route that passed through Tema, or that in favoring Sin, the chief god of Ur and of Harran, his home town, he found himself at odds with the hierarchy and formalized worship of Marduk, the city-god of Babylon.

Therefore Daniel is not unhistorical in portraying Belshazzar as the reigning king in Babylon. Nabonidus did eventually return to Babylonia, and was present in the land when Cyrus' army attacked. He had brought idol-gods from other cities to Babylon, perhaps for safekeeping, but was in Opis at the time. Nearby Sippar was seized without battle, and Nabonidus fled. After Cyrus took Babylon, Nabonidus returned there and was arrested, all according to the Nabonidus section of the Babylonian Chronicle (ANET, p. 306).

Other Babylonian inscriptions give details of Belshazzar's administration and of his gifts to sanctuaries in Babylon and to the temples in Erech and Sippar, up to the fourteenth year of his father's reign. The scriptural record, however, emphasizes his blasphemous feast during which he used the sacred vessels brought by Nebuchadnezzar to Babylon from the conquest of Jerusalem.

Bibliography. Raymond P. Dougherty, *Nabonidus and Belshazzar,* Yale Oriental Series, XV, New Haven: Yale Univ. Press, 1929. FLAP. ANET. H. H. Rowley, *Darius the Mede and the Four World Empires in the Book of Daniel,* Cardiff: Univ. of Wales Press, 1959. E. J. Young, *The Prophecy of Daniel,* Grand Rapids: Eerdmans, 1949.

F. E. Y. and J. R.

BELTESHAZZAR (bĕl-tē̆-shăz'ẽr). The name given by the prince of the Babylonian eunuchs to Daniel (Dan 1:7). *See* Daniel.

BEN

1. Ben is the Heb. word for son. Usually it referred to the male child. However, it was used also as a term of kindliness or endearment even when no blood relationship existed. In I Sam 3:6, 16, Eli calls Samuel his son. It was frequently used as a prefix in proper names; e.g., Ben-oni, "son of my sorrow" (Gen 35:18); Benjamin, "son of the right hand" (Gen 35:18); Ben-ammi, "son of my people" (Gen 19:38).

On occasion it was used descriptively when followed by a word indicating a characteristic. "Strong man" in I Sam 14:52 is literally, "son of strength." "Sons of Belial" (Jud 19:22) were worthless, base fellows or scoundrels.

The term may also designate membership in a guild or class, as one who had learned the trade from his father or by apprenticeship. The "sons of Mahol" (I Kgs 4:31) were members of a musical guild.

2. A Levite (I Chr 15:18), in KJV included in the second rank of Levites, but probably in error. The name is omitted in LXX, and does not occur in the similar list of v. 20.

R. B. D.

BENAIAH (bē̆-nā'yȧ)

1. A Levite, the son of Jehoiada of Kabzeel (II Sam 23:20) from southern Judah (Josh 15:21). Jehoiada was probably the leader of the priests who joined with the army at Hebron to place David on the throne of all Israel (I Chr 12:23, 27). Benaiah began his career as the commander of a division of 24,000 soldiers in the third month on a monthly basis during David's reign (I Chr 27:5). He was listed in the second rank among the heroes of David's great men (II Sam 23:20–23; I Chr 11:22–25). His feats of prowess included the killing of a lion that strayed into the Judean hills, the slaying of two lionlike (mighty) men of Moab, and the disarming and slaying of an Egyptian giant. He served as commander of David's chosen troops, the Cherethites and the Pelethites (II Sam 8:18). In the rebellion of Absalom (II Sam 15:18; 20:23), and in the attempt of Adonijah to seize the throne (I Kgs 1:8), Benaiah remained loyal to David. Along with Nathan and Zadok, Benaiah espoused the cause of Solomon and assisted in Solomon's coronation at Gihon, just outside Jerusalem (I Kgs 1:38–40). As chief of the bodyguard of the king, he executed Adonijah (I Kgs 2:25), Joab (I Kgs 2:34), and Shimei (I Kgs 2:46) on the orders of Solomon. During Solomon's reign, Benaiah replaced Joab as commander-in-chief of the army.

2. A Pirathonite, one of David's heroes of the second rank (II Sam 23:30; I Chr 11:31) who commanded the army in the eleventh month (I Chr 27:14).

3. A prince of the families of Simeon who was among those who took Gedor from the Amalekites for pastureland (I Chr 4:36, 39–41).

4. A Levite who played a musical instrument before the ark when David brought it to Jerusalem (I Chr 15:18, 20; 16:5).

5. One of the priests appointed to blow the trumpets before the ark when David brought it to Jerusalem (I Chr 15:24; 16:6).

6. A Levite, descendant of Asaph, the son of Jeiel and grandfather of Jahaziel (II Chr 20:14).

7. A Levite in the time of Hezekiah appointed to be one of the overseers of the temple offerings (II Chr 31:13).

8–11. Four men who put away their foreign wives in the days of Ezra and Nehemiah (Ezr 10:25, 30, 35, 43).

12. The father of Pelatiah, a prince in Israel (Ezk 11:1).

F. E. Y.

BEN-AMMI (bĕn-ăm'ī). Son of Lot's younger daughter, from whom sprang the Ammonite tribe (Gen 19:38). This son was born soon after the destruction of Sodom. The account of his birth, as well as that of Moab, was commonly regarded as an expression of Israel's intense hatred and contempt toward these two nations.

BENCH. In the prophet's lamentations over Tyre in Ezk 27:6, he says: "They have made thy benches of ivory inlaid in boxwood, from the isles of Kittim" (ASV). The word benches here evidently stands for the benches of the boat whose mast (v. 5) and oars (v. 6) have just been described in the vivid figures of speech in which the city itself is pictured as a merchant ship. Since the Heb. word *qeresh* in the plural denotes boards in the tabernacle (Ex 26:15–29) but here is used in the singular, the more recent versions and lexicons have suggested "deck" or "prow" as the meaning.

BENE-BERAK (bĕn'ē-bĕr'ăk). A city in the territory of Dan (Josh 19:45), represented by the modern village of Ibn Ibrak, about four miles SE of Jaffa.

BENEDICTION. The invocation of blessing, and the expression in prayer for happiness and well-being. Technically, benediction is the act of a minister in pronouncing blessing upon others in the name and in the stead of the divine Lord. Thus benediction may be distinguished from prayer for blessing in which a minister voices the desire of his own heart and of the people for God's blessing. In the narrower sense, the Aaronic benediction in the OT (Num 6:24–26) and the apostolic benediction in the NT (II Cor 13:14) are true benedictions. Eph 3:20–21; Heb 13:20–21; and Jude 24–25 are often used as benedictions in a broader sense of the term, but are more properly prayers for the blessing of the Lord upon the people.

Benediction is implied in the "blessing" of patriarchal times; e.g., Melchizedek (Gen 14:19–20; Heb 7:6), Isaac, and Jacob (Heb 11:20–21). The Aaronic benediction was pronounced by the priest with uplifted hands after the morning and evening sacrifices, the people responding with "amen" (cf. Lev 9:22; Lk 1:10, 21–22). Levites (II Chr 30:27) and kings (II Sam 6:18; I Kgs 8:55) in OT times also pronounced benedictions. Benediction is expressed as Jesus blessed the children (Mk 10:16), and His disciples (Lk 24:50).

Protestants reject the Roman Catholic view that the value of the benediction increases with the hierarchical rank of the functionary pronouncing it. Catholic dogma claims objective worth for the benediction by authorized officials. Protestants recognize the subjective and spiritual value of the benediction as received in faith by its subjects.

W. T. P.

BENE-JAAKAN (bĕn-ē-jā'ă-kăn). Described as "Beeroth of the children of Jaakan" (Deut 10:6), the place is called Bene-jaakan in the list of stations (Num 33:31–32). From Gen 36:27 (ASV marg.) and I Chr 1:42 the Bene-jaakan seem to be descendants of Seir, the Horite. The western border of Seir or Edom near Mount Hor is the probable situation of the wells of this clan.

BENE-KEDEM (bĕn-ē-kē'dĕm; "children of the East"). From references such as Gen 29:1; Job 1:3; Jud 6:3, 33, it seems that the term Bene-kedem refers to the peoples of the Arabian deserts, and primarily to the tribes of Ishmael and Keturah. Some of these seem to have spoken a dialect which was understood by the Israelites (Jud 7:11–15).

BENEVOLENCE, DUE. The KJV of I Cor 7:3 reads, "Let the husband render unto the wife due benevolence," but ASV and most other versions read simply "her due" (Gr. *opheilēn*), what she has the right to expect (Jerusalem Bible), what he owes her. It is a direction dealing with "the duty of cohabitation" (Alford).

BEN-HADAD (bĕn-hā'dăd). Contemporary with the rise of the state of Israel under David and Solomon, a dynasty of forceful kings built up the powerful rival kingdom of Syria N and E of Israel, with its capital at Damascus. Until both nations were finally swept away by Assyria, there was continual warfare between them.

1. Ben-hadad I, the son of Tabrimmon (I Kgs 15:18), was one of the strongest and most aggressive of the Syrian kings. About 890 B.C., opportunity was given him to advance greatly his kingdom and authority. Attacked by Baasha of Israel, who fortified Ramah just five miles N of Jerusalem, Asa, king of Judah, sent a great treasure to Ben-hadad, begging him to attack Israel in the N. Asa was saved, but Syria was placed in a position of great advantage, threatening both Heb. kingdoms (I Kgs 15).

In the days of Ahab of Israel, Ben-hadad invaded the country with a great host and besieged Samaria. Whether this was the same Ben-hadad has been questioned, but the inscribed stela of Ben-hadad found in northern Syria in 1940 seems to settle the fact that it was (W. F. Albright, "A Votive Stele Erected by Ben-hadad I of Damascus to the God Melcarth," BASOR #87 [1942], 23–29). The siege was broken and the Syrians driven out. A year later on the plains of Aphek Ahab again defeated the Syrian king (I Kgs 20). Instead of exercising the rights of victor, Ahab entered into an alliance with his defeated enemy. The strange action, unexplained in Scripture, is made clear from Assyrian records. The rising great empire of Assyria threatened both kingdoms, and the alliance was for mutual protection. The Monolith inscription of Shalmaneser III describes the decisive battle of Karkar in 853 B.C. when Assyria was halted, at least for a time, by a coalition, prominent among whom were Ahab and Ben-hadad.

Ben-hadad I seems to have been the Syrian king who was warring against Israel in II Kgs 6:8–7:16 (see 6:24), and not the ineffective Ben-hadad II, who did not begin to reign until *c.* 800 B.C. at the very end of Elisha's life. The king of Israel in Samaria at the time (6:9, 23, 26; 7:12) was probably the wicked Jehoram (*q.v.*). After a long reign Ben-hadad was assassinated in 841 B.C. by the hands of a trusted general, Hazael (II Kgs 8:7 - 15).

2. Ben-hadad II, a weak king, son of Hazael, is mentioned in the Aramaic inscription of Zakir, king of Hamath, under the name of Bar-hadad. He was defeated by Jehoash of Israel, as prophesied by both Amos (Amos 1:4) and Elisha (II Kgs 13), losing all the territory gained by his father.

P. C. J.

BEN-HAIL (bĕn-hāl'). One of the princes of Judah who was sent by Jehoshaphat to teach in the cities of Judah (II Chr 17:7).

BEN-HANAN (bĕn-hā'năn). A son of Shimon, registered with the tribe of Judah (I Chr 4:20).

BENINU (bē-nī'nū). A Levite who with Nehemiah and others sealed a covenant with the Lord (Neh 10:13).

BENJAMIN (bĕn'*jà*-mĭn)

1. A son of Bilhan, the head of a family of warriors (I Chr 7:10).

2. An Israelite, the son of Harim, who divorced his foreign wife after the Exile (Ezr 10:32). He assisted in the rebuilding of the walls of Jerusalem (Neh 3:23) and the Benjamin gate in the temple area (Neh 12:34), the scene of one of Jeremiah's imprisonments (Jer 20:2).

3. The youngest of the children of Jacob and the only one of the 13 born in Palestine. He was born somewhere between Bethel and Ephrath (Bethlehem), his mother Rachel dying in the act of giving birth. She called him Ben-oni ("son of my sorrow"). Jacob, fearing the consequences of such a name, renamed him Benjamin ("son of the right hand," or "son of the South," i.e., southerner, Gen 35:16-18). The Samaritan Codex gives his name as Benjamin, "son of days," i.e., "son of old age" (cf. Gen 44:20). Philo, the Testament of the Twelve Patriarchs, and Ibn Ezra preferred this reading.

After Joseph was sold to the Ishmaelites, Benjamin became the favorite of his father Jacob, as well as of his brothers. Since he is called a lad in Gen 44:20, 22, his sons and grandsons were most likely born after Jacob brought the entire clan to Egypt during the famine (Gen 46:21; see Leupold, *Genesis,* p. 1115). There is little besides the events in Gen 24-44 concerning Benjamin himself; later references concern the tribe of Benjamin.

Tribe of Benjamin. In the census list in Num 1:36-37, Benjamin is next to the smallest tribe with 35,400 members; and in the census list in Num 26:41, the tribe is in sixth position with 45,600 members. In the wilderness journeyings, Benjamin was on the W side of the tabernacle along with Ephraim and Manasseh (Num 2:18-24).

In the allotting of the land by Joshua and the elders, Benjamin drew the hill country S of Ephraim and N of Judah. It was in the form of a parallelogram, 26 miles long by 12 miles wide. The eastern boundary was the Jordan; the western one was Kirjath-jearim (the later western boundary included Ono and Lod). The northern boundary was Bethel, and the southern, the Valley of Hinnom. The boundary between Benjamin and Judah ran next to the city of the Jebusites (Jerusalem). Therefore the temple was built adjacent to the old tribal border. This may have played some part in Benjamin's choice to stand with Judah when the northern tribes seceded.

The territory of Benjamin was, for the most part, hilly. The names of Geba, Gibeah, Gibeon all suggest hills, and Ramah, Ramathaim and Mizpeh indicate heights. The other significant cities in Benjamin were Bethel, the site sacred to Jacob's theophany, and Kirjath-jearim, the place where the ark rested for 20 years. The land was open to attack from the Moabites on the E and from the Philistines on the W. The fortress cities in the land of Benjamin made life hard for the courageous Benjamites. They are characterized by the epithet "fierceness." They were the only tribe to have pursued archery to any purpose, and their skill with the bow (I Sam 20:20, 36; II Sam 1:22) and the sling (Jud 20:16) was celebrated.

The second deliverer in the period of the judges was the Benjamite Ehud (Jud 3:15). This tribe joined with Deborah and Barak in the struggle against Jabin and Sisera (Jud 5:14). It gave to Israel her first king, Saul, the gentleman farmer from Gibeah (I Sam 9:1-2). The tribe was nearly exterminated when it protected miscreants who attacked the concubine of the Levite sojourner at Gibeah (Jud 19–20). The tribe of Benjamin stayed with Judah in the drive to restore Israel to the dynasty of Solomon (I Kgs 12:21; II Chr 11:1). Rehoboam strengthened Judah by fortifying and garrisoning several cities in Benjamin and dispersing members of his own family throughout the tribe in order to secure his position.

The history of Benjamin finally merges with that of Judah. Men of Benjamin returned with the Judeans under Zerubbabel (Ezr 2; Neh 7) and took back their old towns (Neh 11:31 - 35).

Extrabiblical references. In 1933 the city of Mari on the middle Euphrates yielded a store of clay tablets that dated back to the 18th cen. B.C. Among these tablets were some that told of the Banu Yamina (sons of the South). The French excavator of Mari, A. Parrot, attempted to tie these references to those of Benjamin in the OT and concluded that the tribe of Benjamin was of Mesopotamian origin. However, in the same tablets were references to the "sons of the North." These designations may have been to distinguish two tribes in Mesopotamia rather than to refer to the Benjamites of the OT.

F. E. Y.

BENJAMIN GATE. *See* Jerusalem.

BENJAMITE (bĕn'jȧ-mīt). One belonging to the tribe of Benjamin (e.g., Jud 3:15; I Sam 9:1-2; II Sam 20:1; Phil 3:5). *See* Benjamin.

BENO (bē'nō). A descendant of Merari through Jaaziah (I Chr 24:26-27), if Beno is a proper name, as it seems in v. 27.

BEN-ONI (bĕn-ō'nī). The name, which means "son of my sorrow," that was given by the dying Rachel to her new-born son. But the name was changed by his father Jacob to Benjamin (Gen 35:18). *See* Benjamin.

BEN-ZOHETH (bĕn-zō'hĕth). A son of Ishi of the house of Judah (I Chr 4:20).

BEON (bē'ŏn). An old Amorite city on the frontiers of Moab, known fully as Beth-baal-meon (*q.v.*; Josh 13:17); more briefly Baal-meon (*q.v.*; Num 32:38) or Beth-meon (Jer 48:23), as well as Beon (Num 32:3). It was assigned to the Reubenites and rebuilt by them (Num 32:2-5). The city was held by Mesha, king of Moab, and was in the possession of the same people in the 6th cen. B.C. (Ezk 25:9; Jer 48:23). In Jerome's day it was still a considerable town, about nine and three-quarter miles from Heshbon. The ruins, now called Main, lie in the N Moabite territory, four miles SW of Medeba.

BEOR (bē'ôr)

1. The father of Bela, king of Edom (Gen 36:32).
2. The father of the seer Balaam (Num 22:5). He is called Bosor in II Pet 2:15.

BERA (bĕr'ȧ) King of Sodom (Gen 14:2), who in the battle of Siddim was subdued by Chedorlaomer.

BERACHAH (bĕr'ȧ-kä)

1. A Benjamite who joined David at Ziklag (I Chr 12:3).
2. A valley where an army invading Judah in the days of Jehoshaphat was destroyed (II Chr 20:26). The name still lingers as Bereikut, a ruin about four miles NW of Tekoa, six miles SW of Bethlehem, and a little E of the road from Bethlehem to Hebron.

BERACHIAH. *See* Berechiah.

A street scene in Berea. Courtesy E. W. Saunders

BERAIAH (bē-rā'yȧ). One of the sons of Shimhi, listed as a member of the tribe of Benjamin (I Chr 8:21).

BEREA (bē-rē'ȧ). A city of southern Macedonia in the district of Emathia (Ptolemy's *Geography,* iii.12). Strabo says distinctly that the "city Berea lies in the foothills of Mount Bermium" (Strabo *Fragments,* VII.26; see the Loeb edition, Vol. 3, 351). The region about Berea was watered by the river Haliacmon. A few miles to the SE this river left the Olympian range and flowed into the Thermaic Gulf. Berea was *c.* 50 miles SW of Thessalonica, the chief metropolis of Macedonia at this time; 30 miles S of Pella, the birthplace of Alexander the Great; and *c.* 20 miles W of the Thermaic Gulf. Leake (*Travels in Northern Greece,* III, 290 ff.) describes the town as beautifully situated and states that its modern name is Verria. In NT times it was evidently a prosperous city with a Jewish colony.

Paul and Silas found their way to Berea when pressure forced them out of Thessalonica (Acts 17:10). They had hoped to return to Thessalonica, but since this was not permitted (I Thess 2:18), they made their way to Athens, where Timothy later met them. Apparently Paul and Silas had a rather brief stay in Berea, but it cannot be exactly determined how many days they were there. Ramsay, however, conjectures that Paul and Silas stayed in Berea some months (*St. Paul the Traveller and the Roman Citizen,* p. 234). The Jews in Berea were more openminded than those in Thessalonica, listening eagerly to Paul's message and studying the Scriptures to see if what he said was really true (Acts 17:11).

Finally, Paul and Silas were forced to leave Berea due to rabble-rousers who stirred up the people against these apostles (Acts 17:13-14). Acts 20:4 mentions that Sopater, one of Paul's close friends and fellow travelers, was from Berea. According to the Apostolic Constitutions, VII, 46, Onesimus was the first bishop of the church of Berea.

E. J. V.

BERECHIAH (bĕr'ē-kī'*a*)

1. A descendant of Jehoiakim and Jehoiachin born in captivity. He was a brother or son of the leader of the return from Exile, Zerubbabel (I Chr 3:20).

2. A Levite of the family of Gershom, the father of the celebrated musician of Israel, Asaph. Berechiah was appointed as one of two "doorkeepers of the ark" when it was brought up from Obed-edom to Jerusalem (I Chr 6:39, RSV; 15:17, 23).

3. A Levite, son of Asa, who returned from the Exile to settle near Jerusalem (I Chr 9:16).

4. A prince of Ephraim in the time of Pekah. When Oded the prophet warned the Israelites against taking into bondage the host of captives they had secured in their war against Judah, Berechiah and three others led the way in persuading their brethren to restore the captives (II Chr 28:12).

5. The father of Meshullam, a family head who assisted in building the wall of Jerusalem in Nehemiah's day (Neh 3:4, 30; 6:18).

6. The son of Iddo and father of Zechariah the prophet (Zech 1:1, 7).

P. C. J.

BERED (bĕr'ĕd)

1. A place in the wilderness of Shur, to the W of Kadesh, and not far from Beer-lahai-roi (Gen 16:7, 14).

2. The son of Shuthelah of the house of Ephraim (I Chr 7:20), supposed by some to be the same as Becher (Num 26:35). *See* Becher 2.

BERI (bĕr'ī). An Asherite, son of Zophah, of the family of Heber (I Chr 7:36).

BERIAH (bē-rī'*a*)

1. The son of Asher and ancestor of the family of Beriites (*q.v.*; Gen 46:17; Num 26:44–45; I Chr 7:30–31).

2. One of the sons of Ephraim. He was born after some of his brothers had been slain by the Gathites, and was called Beriah "because it went evil with his house" (I Chr 7:23).

3. A Benjamite, the son of Elpaal, who with his brothers settled in the area of Aijalon (I Chr 8:13, 16).

4. A Levite of the family of Gershom in the time of David. Because they had few sons, he and his brother Jeush were counted as one house in the ordering of the Levitical courses (I Chr 23:10–11).

BERIITES (bē-rī'īts). The descendants of Beriah, a son of Asher, and father of Heber and Malchiel, and head of the family of the Beriites (Num 26:44).

BERITES (bĕr'īts). The descendants of Beri, a warrior of Asher (I Chr 7:36). They are mentioned only once in Scripture (II Sam 20:14) as followers of Sheba, whose abortive rebellion against David followed closely the defeat of Absalom (II Sam 20). They followed him to the city of Abel of Beth-maachah where he was killed. After the death of their leader, the Berites were permitted to depart in peace.

The RSV translates the word "Bichrites" (*see* Bichri) following the lead of both the LXX and Vulgate. Sheba was the son of Bichri of the tribe of Benjamin, and the RSV editors have conjectured that it was his own kinsmen who followed him, not the obscure northern Berites.

BERITH. *See* Gods, False: Baal-berith.

BERNICE (bĕr-nēs'). The name occurs three times in the NT designating the oldest daughter of Herod Agrippa I (Jos *Ant.* xviii.5.4). She was born in A.D.28 and was early married to Marcus, the son of Alexander (Jos *Ant.* xix.5.1). After his death, Bernice was given by Agrippa to his brother Herod, king of Chalcis. To this union two sons were born (Jos *Ant.* xviii.5.4). When Herod of Chalcis died in A.D. 48, she "lived a widow a long while" and was assumed to have been involved in incestuous relations with her brother Agrippa II (Jos *Ant.* xx.7.3) with whom she appears in the book of Acts (25:13, 23; 26:30). "She persuaded Polemo, who was king of Cilicia, to be circumcised and to marry her" (Jos *Ant.* xx.7.3), but soon left him and returned to her brother. Eventually she came into contact with the Roman rulers Vespasian and Titus, to both of whom she became a mistress (Tacitus, *Hist.* ii.81; Suetonius, *Titus,* 7). *See* Herod; Agrippa I; Agrippa II.

J. McR.

BERODACH-BALADAN. *See* Merodach-Baladan.

BEROTHAH (bē-rō'th*a*), **BEROTHAI** (bē-rō'thī). A town situated between Hamath and Damascus (Ezk 47:16). It is probably identical with Berothai, a city which was once subject to Hadadezer, king of Zobah, but was captured by David and yielded him large booty in brass (II Sam 8:8; in I Chr 18:8 called Chun, *q.v.*). Identified with Ain Berdai or Bereitan, S of Baalbek.

BEROTHITE (bē-rō'thīt). Probably a man of Beeroth (*q.v.*). The name is associated with Naharai, Joab's armor bearer (I Chr 11:39).

BERYL. *See* Jewels.

BESAI (bē'zī). One of the Nethinim (*q.v.*) and founder of a family who returned with Zerubbabel to Jerusalem (Ezr 2:49; Neh 7:52).

BESODEIAH (bĕz'ō-dē'y*a*). Father of Meshullam, who helped to repair the gate of Jerusalem (Neh 3:6).

BESOM (bē'zŏm). This word occurs only once in Scripture: "I will sweep it with the besom of destruction" (Isa 14:23). This refers to what was in store for Babylon. The Heb. word *maṭ'ăṭē'*, rendered "besom," is close of kin to the verb *ṭē'ṭē'tî*, rendered "I will sweep." In early English "besom" was synonymous with "broom," and is still so used in some parts of England.

BESOR (bē'zôr). A torrent bed or brook S of Ziklag mentioned in the account of David's pursuit of the Amalekites (I Sam 30:9-10, 21). Perhaps it is the present Wadi Ghazzeh, which rises near Beer-sheba and empties into the Mediterranean SW of Gaza.

BETAH (bē'tȧ). A city of Aram-zobah taken by David from the king of Zobah, called Tibhath in I Chr 18:8.

BETEN (bē'tĕn). A village of Asher (Josh 19:25) mentioned between Hali and Achshaph. Eusebius identified it with the village of Beth-beten, about seven and a half miles E of Acre.

BETH (bĕth; "house"). The second letter of the Heb. alphabet. *See* Alphabet. Originally it was a rude representation of a dwelling, whence it derives its name. In compound place names Beth means "place of," "abode of," "temple of," "house of." It came also to be used for the number "two." It became Gr. *beta* and Latin and English *b*.

BETHABARA (bĕth-ăb'ȧ-rȧ). A place beyond the Jordan at which John baptized (Jn 1:28). The name survives at the ford called Abarah, 12 miles S of the Sea of Galilee and NE of Bethshean. This is the only place where this name occurs in Palestine. The site is as near to Cana as any point on the Jordan, and within a day's journey. The principal Gr. MSS here read "Bethany" (*q.v.*). Others connect Bethabara with the Beth-barah (*q.v.*) of Jud 7:24.

BETH-ANATH (bĕth-ā'năth). An ancient fenced town in Naphtali (Josh 19:38) from which the Canaanites were not expelled (Jud 1:33). Today it is the modern village of Ainatha in the mountains of upper Galilee about 12 miles NW of Safed.

BETH-ANOTH (bĕth-ā'nŏth). A town in the mountains of Judah near Gedor (Josh 15:59). It is the present Beit 'Ainun, a mile and a half SE of Halhul.

BETHANY (bĕth'ă-nĭ)

1. The village of Bethany, the home of Lazarus, Mary, and Martha (Jn 11:1), was situated on the E side of the Mount of Olives about two miles E of Jerusalem (Jn 11:18). Jesus visited Bethany on occasion (Mt 21:17; 26:6; Mk 11:1, 11, 12; Jn 11:1; 12:1) and chose a spot near it to be the site of His ascension (Lk 24:50).

Bethany. HFV

2. "Bethany beyond the Jordan" was on the E side of the Jordan River where John baptized (Jn 1:28). There is some evidence that the site might have been called Bethabara ("house of the ford") as well as Bethany (FLAP, p. 301).

BETH-ARABAH (bĕth-ăr'ȧ-bȧ). One of the six cities in the wilderness of Judah on the NE boundary between Judah and Benjamin (Josh 15:6, 61; 18:22), called simply Arabah in Josh 18:18. It is situated near 'Ain-el-Gharba in the Wadi el-Kelt.

BETH-ARAM (bĕth-ā'rȧm). In Num 32:36 called Beth-haran (*q.v.*). A town in the E Jordan Valley in the territory of Gad and rebuilt by the Gadites (Josh 13:27). It is identified with Tell Iktanû on the S side of the Wadi er-Rameh (Wadi Hesban), about seven miles NE of the mouth of the Jordan. It is also known as Beth-aramphtha, where Herod had a palace. The place was called Livias by Herod Antipas in honor of the wife of Augustus. Here Herod possibly celebrated his birthday (Mt 14:6-12).

BETH-ARBEL (bĕth-är'bĕl). A place mentioned as having been plundered by Shalman (Hos 10:14). Some have identified Beth-arbel with Arbela of Galilee (Jos *Ant.* xii.11.1; xiv.15.4), modern Irbid in the hills W of the Sea of Galilee. However, it is more likely that Eusebius was correct in identifying it with Irbid in Gilead, which was called Arbel in his time (*Onomasticon* 14:18). This site was occupied from the Bronze Age until the Persian period. The city was probably conquered by Shalmaneser III during one of his campaigns in Syria and Bashan (841 and 838 B.C.).

BETH-AVEN (bĕth ā'vĕn). A town in the territory of Benjamin, near Ai, E of Beth-el (Josh 7:2), W of Michmash (I Sam 13:5; cf. 14:23), and on the border of a wilderness (Josh 18:12). This name, meaning "house of wickedness," was given in contempt to Beth-el by Hosea after it had become a seat of idolatry and corrupt worship (Hos 4:15; 5:8; 10:5).

BETH-AZMAVETH (bĕth-ăz′mȧ-vĕth). A village in the vicinity of Jerusalem, also called Azmaveth (*q.v.*), where 42 of its inhabitants returned from the Babylonian Captivity (Neh 7:28; Ezr 2:24). Some of the singers at the dedication of the restored walls resided on its field (Neh 12:29). Its site is perhaps Hizmeh, midway between Geba and Anathoth.

BETH-BAAL-MEON (bĕth′bāl-mē′ŏn). The town's full name (Josh 13:17), but also written Baal-meon (Num 32:38; I Chr 5:8; Ezk 25:9), Beth-meon (Jer 48:23), and Beon (*q.v.*; Num 32:3). The town was built by the children of Reuben along with Nebo, "their names being changed" (Num 32:38). As Beth-baal-meon it was given by Moses to the tribe of Reuben (Josh 13:15–17). King Mesha named it on the Moabite Stone as a city he fortified. It appears in Jer 48:23 as one of the cities of Moab. Eusebius' *Onomasticon* speaks of it as a large village near the hot springs, i.e., Callirrhoe, in Wadi Zerka Ma'in, nine miles from Heshbon.

BETH-BARAH (bĕth-bâr′ȧ). A place on the Jordan S of the valley of Jezreel. Some suppose it to be the same as Bethabarah (*q.v.*). Owing to its waters, it was a locality difficult for the Midianites to cross (Jud 7:24). This is probably S of Beth-shean in the region N of the mouth of the Wadi Farah.

BETH-BIREI (bĕth-bĭr′ī). A town belonging to Simeon in the Negeb (I Chr 4:31), called Beth-lebaoth (*q.v.*) in Josh 19:6 and Lebaoth (*q.v.*) in Josh 15:32. The site is not identified.

BETH-CAR (bĕth-kär′). A place, probably a height, to which the Philistines were pursued by the Israelites after the second and decisive battle of Ebenezer (I Sam 7:11). Ain Karim, four and a half miles W of Jerusalem, is a possible site.

BETH-DAGON (bĕth-dā′gŏn)

1. A city in the territory of Judah in the lowlands of the Shephelah (Josh 15:41). It is provisionally identified with Khirbet-Dajun.

2. A town on the border of Asher (Josh 19:27), apparently to the E of Carmel, and is probably Jelamet el-Atiqa, at the foot of Carmel.

Both places were doubtless once seats of Dagon worship.

BETH-DIBLATHAIM (bĕth-dĭb-lȧ-thā′ĭm). A town on the tableland of Moab once in possession of Israel and mentioned with Dibon and Nebo (Jer 48:22). It is probably the same as Almon-diblathaim (*q.v.*; Num 33:46 f.). Mesha claims to have fortified it along with Medeba and Baal-meon. It has been identified with the double ruin Deleilât esh-Sherqîyeh two and one-half miles NE of Khirbet Libb.

James Kelso excavating a Canaanite worship center at Bethel. HFV

BETHEL (bĕth′ĕl; "house of God")

1. A town in the southern part of Israel, evidently in the vicinity of Ziklag. Probably Bethel, Bethul and Bethuel (*q.v.*) are names by which it was known (Josh 19:4; I Sam 30:27; I Chr 4:30). Its site is not currently identified.

2. A town on the border between Benjamin and Ephraim, about ten miles N of Jerusalem and S of Shiloh (Jud 21:19), near Ai (Gen 12:8).

Originally called Luz (*q.v.*; Gen 28:19; Josh 18:13), it was visited by Abram early in his sojourn in the Promised Land (Gen 12:8). Later he stopped here on his return from Egypt and the Negeb (Gen 13:3). Jacob had his dream here while on his way to Padan-aram (Gen 28:19). Upon Jacob's return from Padan-aram, he built an altar here and called the place El-bethel (*q.v.*; Gen 35:6–7). Deborah, Rebekah's nurse, was buried here (Gen 35:8). The town was assigned by the drawing of lots to Benjamin (Josh 18:22). Afterward, the Ephraimites possessed it (I Chr 7:28). It was a place of worship (Jud 20:18; I Sam 10:3). Samuel judged Israel here as one of the places in his circuit (I Sam 7:16).

Jeroboam I made Bethel one of the two seats of worship for Israel, erecting here one of the golden calves (I Kgs 12:28–29; cf. Jer 48:13). A man of Judah came to Bethel to announce the birth of Josiah (I Kgs 13:2). An old prophet, who proved the undoing of this man of God, lived here (I Kgs 13:11). The contemporary prophets Hosea and Amos both spoke against Bethel (Hos 10:15; also known as Bethaven [*q.v.*], 5:8–9; 10:5, 8; Amos 3:14; 5:5). The king of Assyria established a priest in Bethel (II Kgs 17:27–28). Josiah (cf. I Kgs 13:2) destroyed the altar and high place of Bethel (II Kgs 23:15–16). People of Bethel returned here after the Captivity (Ezr 2:28; Neh 7:32).

Archaeological research was carried on at the supposed site of ancient Bethel (modern Beitîn) by W. F. Albright in 1934 and by James L. Kelso in 1954, in 1956–57, and in 1960. The modern town is built on a large section of the southern part of ancient Bethel, preventing excavation here. It has been ascertained that a street N of Beitîn is built over the N wall of the old city. Pottery from a house adjoining the N wall of the ancient town would indicate that this level was occupied by the Hyksos, *c*. 1700 B.C. No recognized ruins of the holy place erected by Jeroboam I have been discovered. His shrine may have been outside the city walls on the site of Abraham's or Jacob's altar.

In 1957 Kelso discovered an inscribed S Arabian clay stamp seal at Beitîn, almost identical to one found *c*. 1900 by T. Bent at Meshed in the Hadhramaut region of Arabia. The stamp was used to seal the bags or sacks used as containers in the incense trade between Israel and S Arabia *c*. the 9th cen. B.C. (BASOR #151, pp. 9–16; #163, pp. 15–18; #199, pp. 59–65).

There is no evidence of a break in occupation between the early 8th cen. and the 6th cen. (BASOR #56, p. 14). Bethel was destroyed late in the 6th cen. B.C. There are references to the town in Josephus (*Ant.* xiii.1.3; *Wars*, iv.9.9).

More recently David Livingston has argued that Bethel should be located at el-Bireh just E of modern Ramallah and two miles SW of Beitîn. It is dominated by the height Ras et-Tahuneh, where Jeroboam may have built his temple, and lies on the natural crossroads for the whole area ("Location of Biblical Bethel and Ai Reconsidered," WTJ, XXXIII [Nov., 1970], 20–44).

W. C.

BETHELITE (bĕth'ĕl-īt). The term was applied to a man named Hiel (*q.v.*) who was a native of Bethel and in the days of Ahab rebuilt the city of Jericho (I Kgs 16:34).

BETH-EMEK (bĕth-ē'mĕk). A town within the territory of Asher (Josh 19:27). It is probably modern Tell Mimas, about six and a half miles NE of Acre.

Stone cups for watering sheep at the Pool of Bethesda, illustrative of Psalm 23:5. HFV

BETHER (bē'thĕr). Found only in Song 2:17, translated in RSV by the adjective "rugged"; ASV, "craggy." Probably it refers either to a type of difficult terrain over which, however, a mountain deer could move swiftly and safely, or to the city of Bether which is presently identified with Khirbet el-Yehud, just above modern Bittir, about seven miles SW of Jerusalem.

BETHESDA (bē-thĕz'dȧ). The name of a pool with five porticoes mentioned only in Jn 5:2 where the afflicted came for healing when the waters were troubled. Here Jesus healed the man who had been unable to walk for 38 years. In 1888, N of the temple area in Jerusalem, K. Schick uncovered the outlines of a large double pool, i.e., twin rectangular pools lying N and S, with a rock partition 20 feet thick on which the fifth portico was constructed. The area of the pools measured *c*. 150-by-300 feet.

One of the best ancient MSS of the NT (Codex Sinaiticus), one other later Gr. MS and Eusebius have *Bēthzatha* (the name of the northern extension of Jerusalem according to Josephus – Arndt, p. 139) rather than *Bēthesda*. This name has been included in recent editions of Gr. texts (e.g., Nestle; Aland-Black). The copper scroll from Cave III near Qumran, however, lists 64 different hiding places for the temple treasures, with locations 57–60 in and around "Beth-Eshdatain." Since this Heb. form of the name has a dual ending, it fits in precisely with the archaeological discovery that Bethesda was, in fact, a double pool (Jerry Vardaman, "Bethesda, Pool of," BW, pp. 140 ff.; VBW, V, 142).

J. Mc R.

BETH-EZEL (bĕth-ē'zĕl). Probably a town in the Philistine plain (Mic 1:11). The reference may suggest that no help will be found in a neighbor town, for it has its own "mourning." It is probably Deir el-'Aṣal, two miles E of Tell Beir Mirsim.

BETH-GADER (bĕth-gā'der). An unidentified town in Judah, listed with Bethlehem and Kirjath-jearim. It is associated with Hareph, son of Hur and grandson of Caleb (I Chr 2:51). Hareph was "father" or founder of the city. *See* Geder; Gedor.

BETH-GAMUL (bĕth-gā'mŭl). Town of Moab in the tableland near the Arnon River, marked for divine judgment (Jer 48:23).

BETH-GILGAL (bĕth-gĭl'găl). Probably a town eight miles NE of Jerusalem mentioned by Nehemiah (Neh 12:29) as residence of a group of Levites belonging to the clans of singers.

BETH-HACCEREM (bĕth-hăk-kē'rĕm). A town in Judah, modern Khirbet Salih, near Ramat Rahel, two miles N of Bethlehem. Its name means "settlement of the vineyard." The list of hidden treasure on the Dead Sea Copper Scroll locates Beth-haccerem just before the tomb of Absalom which was in the Valley of the King (II Sam 18:18). A similar identification is made in the *Genesis Apocryphon,* another of the Qumran scrolls (BW, p. 142).

Because of its height, Jeremiah mentions Beth-haccerem as a signal point in a time of invasion (Jer 6:1). Predicting a terrible imminent invasion from the N, *c.* 625 B.C. (Jer 1:13 ff.; 4:6; 6:22; 10:22), Jeremiah calls on Tekoa ("blast"), 11 miles S of Jerusalem, to give a trumpet blast, and on "Vineyard Settlement," a third of the way there, to raise a fire signal on its hill.

Such signals are known in the Euphrates Valley from the Mari letters 11 centuries earlier. In the last days of Judah's kingdom, before Nebuchadnezzar destroyed it, signal telegraph was used by the Jewish army, according to correspondence of 589 B.C. found at Lachish, where the word for "signal" is the same as Jeremiah used (*maś'ēt,* "sign of fire," KJV, properly a "lifting up"; in Jud 20:38, 40 "flame," KJV, or "smoke signal," JerusB).

In post-Exilic times when the walls of Jerusalem were being rebuilt, men from the district of "Vineyard Settlement" repaired the Gate of Ash Heaps (Neh 3:14), just as other groups from N, E and S of the capital labored on other gates.

Bibliography. Yohanan Aharoni, "*Beth-haccherem,*" TAOTS, pp. 171 - 184.

W. G. B.

Bethlehem. HFV

BETH-HAGGAN (bĕth-hăg'ăn). Translated "the garden house" in II Kgs 9:27, but probably the name of a town seven miles S of Jezreel toward which Ahaziah fled. This is modern Jenin, also called En-gannim (*q.v.*).

BETH-HARAN (bĕth-hâr'ăn). A fortified town of Gad with folds for sheep (Num 32:36), identical with Beth-aram (*q.v.*).

BETH-HOGLA (bĕth-hŏg'lă). A town near the mouth of the Jordan River mentioned as marking the N border of Judah (Josh 15:6) and the S border of Benjamin (Josh 18:19), about five miles SE of Jericho ('Ain Ḥajlah).

BETH-HORON (bĕth-hôr'ŏn). The name of twin towns near the old shrine of the Canaanite god Horon, on the road from Jerusalem to the Mediterranean.

Joshua, after a surprise attack to defend the new ally Gibeon against the confederacy formed in alarm by five kings under Adonizedek of Jerusalem, chased the fleeing enemy through the pass of the two Beth-horons some four miles W (Josh 10). More destruction during the rout was done by "great stones from heaven" than by Israel's swords. Joshua even commanded the sun to "be silent." that is, "be motionless," or, as the story continues, it "stood in the middle of the sky." As Joshua stood on the height of the pass, the sun was on Gibeon to the E and the moon on the "Valley of Stags" to the W, which increased the slaughter. This crucial victory assured the conquest of southern Judah. *See* Sun.

Among the tribes the Beth-horons lay near the boundary between Ephraim (Josh 16:3, 5) and Benjamin (18:13-14). These two towns and surroundings were a possession for the Kohathite Levites (Josh 21:22). In the time of Saul parties of Philistine raiders spread from their central camp at Michmash toward Beth-horon (I Sam 13:18).

Solomon's fortifications through his kingdom included the two Beth-horons, upper and lower (I Kgs 9:17; II Chr 8:5). After overrunning the territory of Rehoboam, Egyptian Shishak listed Beth-horon among the 156 places taken, on the sculpture celebrating the victory. The captives appear to be Amorites with fair skin, light hair, blue eyes, and long heads. King Amaziah of

Judah spent 100 talents hiring mercenaries of Israel against Seir. But when he did not use them, they fell upon cities of Judah, including Beth-horon, for slaughter and booty (II Chr 25:13).

Here Judas Maccabaeus won his second victory over Syria (I Macc 3:16, 24). Here, too, in the Roman war against them the rebellious Jews cut in pieces a considerable army under Cestius Gallus in A.D. 66 (Jos *Wars*, ii.19.8–9).

W. G. B.

BETH-JESHIMOTH (bĕth-jĕsh'ĭ-mŏth), **BETH-JESIMOTH** (bĕth-jĕs'ĭ-mŏth). A town three miles E of the mouth of the Jordan River. Mentioned (Num 33:49) as the point from which the camp of Israel stretched five miles N to Abel-shittim; as S end of Jordan Valley (Josh 12:3); and in the allotment of Reuben (Josh 13:20). In an oracle against Moab, Ezekiel (25:9) mentions it as a frontier town of Moab. It is probably Tell el-'Azeimeh.

BETH-LE-APHRAH (bĕth-lē̆-ȧf'rȧ; "house of dust"). An unknown place name (Mic 1:10, RSV), probably same as Ophrah of Benjamin or of the Philistine plain. There is here a play on words, for Micah declares, "Roll thyself in the dust" as an act of mourning.

BETH-LEBAOTH (bĕth-lē̆-bā'ŏth). A town in the S of Judah, assigned to the Simeonites (Josh 19:6). It is the same as Lebaoth (*q.v.*) in Josh 15:32 and as Beth-birei (*q.v.*) in I Chr 4:31.

Church of the Nativity, Bethlehem. HFV

BETHLEHEM (bĕth'lē̆-hĕm; "house of bread"). A name used 40 times in the OT and eight times in the NT.

1. A place in Zebulun's territory seven miles NW of Nazareth (Josh 19:15). It is suggested by some that Ibzan, one of the judges, came from this Bethlehem in the N (Jud 12:8).

2. A village on a Judean hill about five miles

Interior of Church of the Nativity, Bethlehem. Courtesy Semerdjian, Jerusalem

S of Jerusalem, center of a fruitful area also called Ephrath or Ephratah ("cornland"; cf. Ruth 4:11; I Chr 2:5; 4:4). In this territory, though not right at Bethlehem (Zelzah, I Sam 10:2, near Ramah, Jer 31:15), Rachel died and Jacob buried her (Gen 35:16 – 20; 48:7).

In one of the Amarna letters (# 290), dating a little after 1400 B.C., the prince of Jerusalem tells that *Bit-Lahmi,* a town in his domain, has gone over to the side of the 'Apiru (ANET, p. 489). In the time of the judges Bethlehem was the home of a self-seeking Levite (Jud 17:7–9) and a run-away concubine (19:1–2, 18). From this city Ruth's in-laws fled to Moab in a time of famine (Ruth 1:1–2). In Bethlehem her great-grandson David was born (I Sam 17:12) and there Samuel anointed David king (I Sam 16:13). Three of his mighty men broke through the Philistine garrison to draw David a drink from the well near Bethlehem's gate (II Sam 23:13–17; I Chr 11:15–19). His relative Asahek was buried here (II Sam 2:32). Rehoboam fortified the town (II Chr 11:6). After the Exile some "sons of Bethlehem" returned (Ezr 2:21; Neh 7:26).

Prediction had been made that "great David's greater Son" would be born here (Mic 5:2), as the scribes of Herod's day knew (Mt 2:4–6), and their people had heard from the Scripture (Jn 7:42). Indeed, here Joseph and Mary came to be enrolled in the empire's census (Lk 2:4–5), and to the shepherds the angel said that the Saviour, Christ the Lord, was born "in the city of David" (Lk 2:11). Emperor Constantine's Christian mother Helena built the original church in A.D. 325 on the site of the traditional cave of the virgin and her Son.

See City of David.

W. G. B.

BETHLEHEMITE (bĕth'lē-hĕm-īt). An inhabitant or native of Bethlehem (*q.v.*), a town of Judah five miles S of Jerusalem. It identifies Jesse, father of David (I Sam 16:1, 18; 17:58), and Elhanan (II Sam 21:19) who slew a brother of the giant Goliath.

BETH-MAACHAH (bĕth-mā'*a*-k*a*). A city far to the N near source of the Jordan River. So named in II Sam 20:14–15, but also named Abel-beth-maacah (*q.v.*) in I Kgs 15:20 and II Kgs 15:29, as well as Abel (*q.v.*) in II Sam 20:14, 18. In II Samuel it is the city in which Joab besieged rebelling Sheba. In I Kings it is included among cities smitten by Ben-hadad of Damascus. In II Kings it is mentioned as a city in Naphtali captured by Tiglath-pileser, king of Assyria, about 732 B.C.

BETH-MARCABOTH (bĕth-mär'k*a*-bŏth). A city of Simeon in extreme S of Judah (Josh 19:5; I Chr 4:31). It is conjectured that this might be one of the stations Solomon built for his chariots and horsemen (I Kgs 9:19; 10:26).

BETH-MEON (bĕth-mē'ŏn). A city of Moab included by Jeremiah with others in the coming destruction of the nation (Jer 48:23). Same as Beth-baal-meon, Baal-meon and Beon (*q.v.*).

BETH-NIMRAH (bĕth-nĭm'r*a*). A city in Transjordan opposite Jericho originally assigned to Gad (Num 32:36; Josh 13:27), a fenced city with folds for sheep. It was also named Nimrah (*q.v.*; Num 32:3) and Nimrim (*q.v.*; Isa 15:6), and was included by the prophet among the cities of Moab whose ample springs would dry up and whose territory would produce no grass. The site has been identified with Tell el-Bleibil, six miles E of the Jordan in the Wadi Sha'ib.

BETH-PALET (bĕth-pā'lĕt). Listed by Joshua (15:27) among "the uttermost cities of . . . Judah" (v. 21), near the border of Edom S of Beer-sheba. In Neh 11:26 (here called Beth-phelet) it is mentioned as a village of Judah. The site is uncertain; Aharoni suggests Tell es-Saqati (*The Land of the Bible,* Westminster, 1967, p. 356). Tell el-Far'ah, 18 miles S of Gaza, with which Flinders Petrie identified the town, is now identified with Sharuhen. Beth-pelet (RSV spelling) must have been a settlement of the Pelethites (*q.v.*).

BETH-PAZZEZ (bĕth-păz'ĕz). A town in the land allotted to Issachar (Josh 19:21) in the N.

BETH-PEOR (bĕth-pē'ôr). A town *c.* ten miles E of Jordan at its mouth. When Moses delivered the messages of Deuteronomy, the Israelites were encamped in the valley "over against Beth-peor" (Deut 3:29; 4:46). Moses was buried in this valley by the Lord (Deut 34:6) but the exact spot was unknown to man. Beth-peor is included in the allotment of land made by Moses to the tribe of Reuben (Josh 13:20). It perhaps can be identified with Baal-peor (*q.v.*) and with Khirbet esh-Sheik Jāyil, six miles W of Heshbon at the edge of the Moabite plateau. *See also* Peor.

BETHPHAGE (bĕth'f*a*-jē). A town on the E slope or ridge of the Mount of Olives on or near the Jericho-Jerusalem road. Mentioned by Synoptic Gospels (Mt 21:1; Mk 11:1; Lk 19:29) in connection with Jesus' journey with His disciples from Bethany to Jerusalem on the day of the triumphal entry. Tentatively it has been located at the present Kefr et-Tur, NW of Bethany, on the summit of the Mount of Olives (Emil G. Kraeling, *Bible Atlas,* Chicago: Rand McNally, 1956, pp. 396–398). Here Jesus' disciples secured the young donkey for Him to ride.

BETH-PHELET. *See* Beth-palet.

BETH-RAPHA (bĕth-rā'f*a*). A name occurring in the genealogy of Judah (I Chr 4:12), possibly referring to a clan which dwelt in a place by the same name.

BETH-REHOB (bĕth-rē'hŏb). A town, probably identical with Rehob (*q.v.*; Num 13:21), in the N of Canaan, near which the Danites built Laish-Dan (Jud 18:28). It is probably the same as the Rehob (No. 87) in Pharaoh Thutmose III's list of captured towns. In II Sam 10:6, 8 Rehob designates a city-state and district occupied by the Aramaeans, who supplied soldiers to assist the Ammonites against David. The site, though uncertain, possibly lay in Coele-Syria between the Lebanon ranges N of Dan. (See M. F. Unger, *Israel and the Aramaeans of Damascus,* p. 42).

BETHSAIDA (bĕth-sā'ĭ-d*a*). This name is Aramaic for "house of hunting," in Bible instances, "of fishing"; so in English it could be called "fishtown." Two cities by this name are mentioned seven or eight times in all four Gospels.

1. Bethsaida-Julias, on the E bank of the upper Jordan about a mile N of the Lake of Galilee, was named by Herod Philip, tetrarch of Ituraea and Trachonitis (Lk 3:1), after the daughter of Caesar Augustus–Julia's Bethsaida (Jos *Ant.* xviii.2.1). It is probably to be identified with modern et-Tell. Near here, in "a desert place," i.e., a sparsely inhabited region, our Lord in a tremendous nature miracle fed the 5,000 on "an extensive plain" (Lk 9:10 ff.). In another retirement from Galilee E across the lake, on His way to the region of the same Philip's Caesarea near Mount Hermon, Jesus stopped at this Bethsaida to restore the sight of a blind man in two unique stages (Mk 8:22 ff.).

2. The home of Philip, Andrew and Peter (Jn 1:44) was NW of the lake in the fertile plain of Gennesaret (Mk 6:45, 53) near Capernaum (Jn 6:17) in the province of Galilee (Jn 12:21). Its name could refer to the fishing quarter of that important town on the lake, except that Jesus twice denounced Bethsaida separately from Capernaum for its blind unbelief (Mt

Mound of Bethshan, Roman theater in foreground. IIS

11:21, 23; Lk 10:13, 15). If there was another city of the same name on the W shore of the lake, probably all the biblical references refer to it rather than some to Bethsaida-Julias.

Some further confusion arises in connection with the reference to the pool of Bethesda in Jn 5:2. In certain ancient Gr. MSS (B, W, P66), "Bethsaida" is read instead in this passage. It is probably a corruption for either Bethesda (KJV) or Bethzatha (RSV).

W. G. B.

BETH-SHAN (bĕth'shăn), **BETH-SHEAN** (bĕth-shē'ăn). The first spelling occurs in I and II Samuel; the latter in Joshua, Judges, I Kings and I Chronicles.

Beth-shan was the most important fortress guarding any Jordan River crossing. It was located at the E end of the vale of Jezreel (modern Tell el-Husn), whose road carried the heavy traffic from Egypt and the Mediterranean coast to Damascus. Identification is confirmed by two Egyptian texts which mention the name. Although the site of Beth-shan was occupied as early as 4000 B.C., the city's major historical period occurred during Egyptian suzerainty when, for approximately three centuries during the Late Bronze Age, it served as a key fortress in that nation's Asian empire. The last Pharaoh to occupy it was Rameses III during whose reign the Philistines entered Palestine in force.

Joshua was unable to capture Beth-shan, for his troops were infantry only and unable to cope with the iron chariots of its defenders (Josh 17:16). In hopes that the larger tribe might later take the city, Joshua allotted Beth-shan to Manasseh in the distribution of the land, although geographically it was in the territory of Issachar (Josh 17:11); but Manasseh also failed (Jud 1:27). During the Amarna period men of Gath-carmel acted as a garrison for the Egyptians. Pharaoh Seti I *c.* 1310 B.C. placed two stelae in Beth-shan, one of which mentions that the Habiru were attacking a nearby town (ANET, pp. 253 ff.). An Egyptian father and son dedicated a stele to the Sumerian god Mekal in a temple found in Level IX (14th cen. B.C.). Many cult objects were found in this and the next four levels that show Beth-shan was a center of snake worship.

The Philistines later occupied the city, evidenced by anthropoid clay coffins showing the Philistine style headdress. Saul's last battle was fought at nearby Mount Gilboa. His armor was placed as a votive offering to Ashtaroth, the greatest of the Canaanite goddesses. Her temple (I Sam 31:10) is probably the northernmost of the two sanctuaries found by the excavators in Level V. Saul's body and those of his sons were displayed on the walls of Beth-shan, from which they were rescued at night by the valiant men of Jabesh-gilead as a token of respect for his earlier rescue of that city (I Sam 31:12). David added Beth-shan to his empire, and Solomon incorporated it into the new fiscal district whose capital was Megiddo. Shortly after Solomon's death, Pharaoh Shishak plundered Beth-shan, according to his inscription at Karnak.

The next historical reference to the city is in intertestamental times when the city is also called Scythopolis. In Maccabaean times, John Hyrcanus captured the city but spared its population of mixed Jews and Gentiles. Pompey made it a free city, and it remained such throughout Roman times.

As one of the Decapolis (*q.v.*), Beth-shan gained considerable prosperity. This fact is attested to by remains of the magnificent theater and other structures of the period. Major excavations at the site were conducted by the University of Pennsylvania 1921–23, 1925–28, 1930–33, revealing 24 strata of settlement back as far as the 4th mil. B.C.

Bibliography. G. M. Fitzgerald, "Beth-shean," TAOTS, pp. 185-196. Henry O. Thompson, "Tell el-Husn – Biblical Beth-shan," BA, XXX (1967), 109-135. J. A. Thompson, "Beth-shan," BW, pp. 143 ff.

J. L. K

BETH-SHEMESH (bĕth-shĕm'ĭsh). The name Beth-shemesh means "house of the sun (god)," reflecting the fact that the pre-Israelite Canaanites had shrines to many deities in the land of Canaan. Many of these names continued into Israelite times. At least four places named Beth-shemesh are mentioned in the OT:

1. A town in the valley of Sorek on the N border of Judah (Josh 15:10) 15 miles W of Jerusalem and 15 miles NE of Tell ed-Duweir (Lachish). Located in the Shephelah on the site of Tell er-Rumeileh, Beth-shemesh was a frontier post near the border between Judah and the Philistines. It was doubtless also called Ir-shemesh (*q.v.*; Josh 19:41), which was jointly allotted to the tribe of Dan. At the division of the land of Canaan, Beth-shemesh was assigned to the Levites (Josh 21:16) as one of 48 Levitical cities (Josh 21:41–42).

After the Philistine victory at Aphek (I Sam 4) the ark was taken to Ashdod, and then to Ekron, Philistine cities where God's judgment brought a plague on Israel's enemies (I Sam 5). The Philistines then sent the ark to Beth-shemesh (I Sam 6:10–7:2), where it remained until it was taken to Kirjath-jearim, in the hills W of Jerusalem. Beth-shemesh was in Solomon's second administrative district (I Kgs 4:9).

It was the scene of a battle between Jehoash of Israel and Amaziah of Judah in which Amaziah was defeated and taken prisoner (II Kgs 14:11–14; II Chr 25:20). As a border city it was frequently threatened by the Philistines (cf. II Chr 28:18).

Beth-shemesh was excavated by Duncan Mackenzie from 1911 to 1913 for the Palestine Exploration Fund, and by C. S. Fisher and Elihu Grant under the sponsorship of Haverford (Pa.) College from 1928 to 1931. Archaeological evidence indicates that the first settlement (Stratum VI) was during the Early Bronze Age, from the 23rd to the 21st cen. B.C. It apparently was taken and settled by the Hyksos (Stratum V) and later destroyed, perhaps by Amenhotep I of Egypt or his successor Thutmose I, *c.* 1525 B.C. Beth-shemesh flourished during the 15th to the 13th cen. B.C. as is evidenced by its houses, lime-plastered cisterns, granaries, and heavy fortifications (Stratum IV). A smelting furnace of this period used imported copper ore. Two interesting inscriptions were found in this level: an ostracon with proto-Sinaitic characters, and a 14th cen. tablet in the alphabetic cuneiform used at Ugarit. From the period of the judges (Stratum III) bronze work was discovered, with some iron weapons and jewelry of probable Philistine origin. Much of the pottery was also of Philistine design. Stratum III was destroyed by fire, probably in the wars between Israel and the Philistines in the time of Saul or David.

To the period of David (*c.* 1000 B.C., Stratum II*a*) belong granaries and a palace or citadel on an earth-filled platform, or Millo, such as was built in Jerusalem. Protection (presumably from the Philistines) was afforded by a casemate wall. Evidence of oil and wine production comes from grape and olive presses.

Occupation ended during the 10th cen., perhaps at the time of Shishak's invasion (925 B.C.). Rehoboam did not rebuild Beth-shemesh, but instead he strengthened Zorah on the hill above. Beth-shemesh was reoccupied during the 9th cen., but it was a poorer city (Stratum II*b*). During the time of Ahaz, the Philistines took the city (II Chr 28:18) but it was retaken, probably by Josiah. A jar handle seal bears the inscription, "Belonging to Eliakim, steward of Yaukin" (i.e., Jehoiachin, king of Judah, 597 B.C.). The armies of Nebuchadnezzar destroyed Beth-shemesh (Stratum II*c*) along with other cities of Judah (588–587 B.C.).

Following the return from captivity the Jews did not regain Beth-shemesh, which was possibly in Philistine territory (cf. the mention of Ashdodites in Neh 4:7). The site was not reoccupied until the Hellenistic period (Stratum I). The last archaeological remains are of a 4th or 5th cen. A.D. monastery.

Bibliography. J. A. Emerton, "Beth-shemesh," TAOTS, pp. 197–206. Elihu Grant, *Beth Shemesh,* Progress of the Haverford Archaeological Expedition, 1929; *Ain Shems Excavations,* I–III, Haverford, 1931–34. Elihu

Grant and G. E. Wright, *Ain Shems Excavations,* IV–V, Haverford, 1939.

2. A city in Issachar near the Jordan River (Josh 19:22). It may be el-'Abeidiyeh guarding a ford over the Jordan *c.* two miles S of the Sea of Galilee.

3. A Canaanite city in Naphtali (Josh 19:38) which Naphtali was not able to occupy (Jud 1:33). Possibly the same as 2, or the village of Haris, SSE of Tyre.

4. The Heb. rendering of On in Egypt. The temple of the sun-god Re was at On, which the Greeks called Heliopolis. The city of On is five miles NE of modern Cairo. Jeremiah prophesied that the Lord would break the images of Beth-shemesh and burn with fire the houses of the gods of Egypt (Jer 43:13).

C. F. P.

BETH-SHEMITE (bĕth-shēm'īt). An inhabitant of Beth-shemesh (*q.v.*) on the western edge of Judah, specifically, Joshua the Beth-shemite (I Sam 6:14, 18), in whose field the cart bearing the ark of the covenant came to rest.

BETH-SHITTAH (bĕth-shĭt'*à*). A town between the valley of Jezreel and the Jordan on the route followed by the Midianites in flight before Gideon (Jud 7:22).

BETH-TAPPUAH (bĕth-tăp'ū-*à*). A town in the mountains of Judah (Josh 15:53), probably the modern village of Taffuh, about three and a half miles NW of Hebron. Another town was known simply as Tappuah (*q.v.*).

BETHUEL (bē-thū'ĕl)

1. The youngest child of Nahor, Abraham's brother, and Milcah (Gen 22:20, 22). He became father-in-law to Isaac (Gen 22:23; 24:50). This close relationship stemmed from Abraham's desire that his only son by Sarah should not marry a Canaanite but an Aramaean (Gen 25:20) from "home" (Gen 24:3–4). Isaac's desire, in turn, for his son Jacob was like Abraham's for him, a wife from the same family (Gen 28:2).

2. The name Bethuel is attached to a town in the territory of Simeon (I Chr 4:30), spelled Bethul in Josh 19:4. *See* Bethel 1.

BETHUL (bĕth'ŭl). A city in Simeon (Josh 19:4), the same as Bethuel (*q.v.*).

BETH-ZUR (bĕth-zûr'). A fortified town in the hill country of Judah (Josh 15:58). It is identified with Khirbet et-Tubeiqah, four and a half miles N of Hebron, settled by Calebites (I Chr 2:45) and fortified by Rehoboam (II Chr 11:7).

Resettled after the Babylonian Exile in the time of Nehemiah (Neh 3:16), Beth-zur was the most important strong point on the border facing Idumea. Near here Judas Maccabaeus defeated a Syrian army in 165 B.C., and then fortified the city (I Macc 4:29, 61). Beth-zur was later starved into surrender by the Syrians (I Macc 6:31, 49–51). It was finally recovered *c.* 143 B.C. by Judas' brother Simon (I Macc 11:65 f.).

Excavations on the site by Albright and Sellers in 1931 and by Sellers in 1957 revealed huge defense walls of the Hyksos period and occupation during the 12th–11th cen., the 8th and 7th cen., and the Hellenistic age. They showed that *c.* 110 B.C. the town was abandoned, suggesting that after John Hyrcanus conquered Idumea, the Jewish garrison at Beth-zur was no longer needed there and was withdrawn.

S. C.

BETONIM (bĕt'ō-nĭm). A town in the territory of Gad, E of the Jordan, given by Moses (Josh 13:26). It is identified with Khirbet Batneh near es-Salt.

BETRAY. The underlying Gr. words mean "to deliver over." This is precisely what Judas did in betraying Christ (Mt 26:14–16, 47–50; Mk 14:10–11, 43–46; Lk 22:3–6, 47–48; Jn 18:3–5), which accounts for most occurrences of the word in the KJV. The hideousness of betrayal is made more poignant by the Lord's quotation from Ps 41:9: He "which did eat of my bread hath lifted up his heel against me." The circumstances of Judas' treachery and the awful results for himself have forever stamped him as a "devil" (Jn 6:70) and the "son of perdition" (Jn 17:12).

Judas' motivation for his act of treachery has been traced to ambition, covetousness, and jealousy. Baffled ambition turned him to treachery when he did not find in Christ the worldly advantages he desired. Covetousness and jealousy were manifest in his reaction to Jesus' anointing and the subsequent rebuke he received from the Lord when he hypocritically lamented the "waste" (Jn 12:1–8). Frank Morison in *Who Moved the Stone?* (pp. 30–39) shows how Judas was in a most favorable position for carrying out his resolve to betray Christ. *See* Judas.

W. B. W.

BETROTHAL. *See* Marriage.

BEULAH (bū'l*à*). A name prophetically applied to the land of Palestine after it should be repeopled by an Israel restored to God's favor after the Captivity (Isa 62:4). As Israel's name is changed from "forsaken," to "my delight is in her" (Hephzibah), so the once desolate land shall be called "married" (Beulah), for it will again be populated.

BEWITCH. This word, found in Acts 8:9, properly means "astonish" or "amaze," and is so translated in the ASV and RSV. The Gr. word *baskainō* in Gal 3:1 means "bewitch" or "deceive." Judaizers had charmed the Galatian Christians to a point where they had ceased to reason.

BEYOND JORDAN, BEYOND THE RIVER. The deep rift of the Jordan River divides Palestine E and W. The Heb. term "beyond the Jordan" is used numerous times of the land E (Deut 1:1; 3:8, RSV) and also a number of times of the land W of the Jordan (Deut 3:20, 25; 11:30). The phrase thus acquires a technical meaning something like "Jordania." In the KJV the same Heb. phrase is sometimes rendered "this side Jordan" (Deut 1:1; 3:8, etc.). While some have maintained that the term indicates the geographical proximity of the author, it is a reasonable supposition that the phrase had become a standard designation for the territory E of Jordan regardless of where the writer happened to be (SOTI, p. 244). In the instances where the term refers to the W area, it should be understood literally rather than as the technical term.

In the NT the Gr. term "beyond the Jordan" is translated numerous times as the territory E of the Jordan known as Perea (e.g., Mt 4:25) and only once as the region W of the Jordan (Mt 19:1)

The term "beyond the river" is the Persian designation for the land W of the Euphrates, and in the reign of Darius I included Palestine-Syria within its bounds (cf. Ezr 4:10-20; 5:3; Neh 2:7, 9; 3:7). This is the same Heb. expression for the KJV "on this side the river."

W. G. B. and A. F. J.

BEZAI (bē'zī)

1. One whose descendants, numbering 323, returned from Exile with Zerubbabel (Ezr 2:17; Neh 7:23).

2. The name of a chief or clan that, with Nehemiah, sealed the covenant with God (Neh 10:18).

BEZALEEL (bē-zăl'ē-ĕl)

1. The son of Uri, son of Hur, of the tribe of Judah. This gifted artist, endowed by the Spirit of God with knowledge and ability in all sorts of craftsmanship, was called by God to be the chief artisan in the construction of the tabernacle in the wilderness. With him was associated another gifted man, Aholiab (*q.v.*) of the tribe of Dan (Ex 31:1-6). These two not only had the responsibility of designing the various parts of the tabernacle, according to the divinely revealed plan, but of teaching other Israelites the skills necessary for the actual building (Ex 35:30-35). Bezaleel himself was not only chief artist but chief artisan, and as the ultimate authority he is said to have made all the various parts of the tabernacle (cf. Ex 37:1 ff.). Skills necessary for fabricating structures similar to the tabernacle, for working the precious metals and for cutting and mounting the jewels were practiced and highly valued during the 2nd mil. B.C. in Syria, Palestine and Egypt (R. K. Harrison, IOT, pp. 403 ff.). *See* Jewel; Occupations: Metalworker, Woodworker.

2. A priest of the family of Pahath-moab in the days of Ezra. One who had married a foreign wife (Ezr 10:30).

P. C. J.

BEZEK (bē'zĕk)

1. The residence of Adoni-bezek ("lord of Bezek") in Judah, near Gezer, inhabited by Canaanites and Perizzites, taken by Judah and Simeon (Jud 1:4-5). *See* Adoni-bezek.

2. The place where Saul marshaled his army before going to the relief of Jabesh-gilead, probably Khirbet Ibziq, in Ephraim, about 13 miles NNE of Shechem (I Sam 11:8).

BEZER (bē'zĕr)

1. A city of refuge designated by Moses and also Joshua in the territory of Reuben E of the mouth of Jordan in the tableland (Deut 4:43; Josh 20:8). It was assigned by lot as also a place of residence for the family of Merari of the tribe of Levi (Josh 21:36; I Chr 6:63, 78).

2. A son of Zophah of the family of Asher (I Chr 7:37).

BIBLE. That collection of books of the OT made by the Jews, and of the Gospels, Acts, epistles, and book of Revelation made by the early Christian church, which the church recognizes as the divinely inspired record of God's revelation of Himself and of His will for mankind.

Names. The Gr. *biblion,* sing.; *biblia,* pl., are diminutive of *biblos,* which means any kind of written document, though originally one written on papyrus (*biblos*). The English word "Bible" comes from the Latin *biblia,* a fem. sing., meaning "book." The singular in Latin witnesses that the 66 books—39 in the OT and 27 in the NT—reveal such a unity of thought and purpose that together they form one book.

The first usage in the early church of the term *ta biblia,* "the books," for the Bible in the above sense is reported to be found in II Clement XIV:2 (*c.* A.D. 150), "The books and the apostles declare that the church existed from the beginning." Daniel, however, had already spoken of the Scriptures, particularly the prophecies existent in his time, as "the books" (Heb. *sepārîm,* Dan 9:2). Several synonomous expressions referring to the OT are found in the NT, such as "the writings" or "the scriptures" (*hai graphai; ta grammata*). The briefest is simply "the scriptures" (Mt 21:42—called "this scripture" in Mk 12:10, the parallel passage; Mt 22:29; Lk 24:32; Jn 5:39); "the scripture" (Acts 8:32; Gal 3:22); "the holy scriptures" (Rom 1:2; II Tim 3:15, "the sacred writings," RSV); "the other scriptures" (II Pet 3:16).

Several other terms descriptive of the OT canon are found in the NT, such as "the law" (Mt 5:18; Lk 16:17; Jn 12:34); "Moses and the prophets" (Lk 16:29; 24:27); "the law and the prophets" (Mt 22:40; Lk 16:16); or possibly even more fully, "the law of Moses. . . the prophets. . . and . . . the psalms" (Lk 24:44).

Languages. The OT was written in Heb., except for a few passages in Aramaic found in Ezr 4:8–6:18; 7:12-26; Jer 10:11; Dan 2:4–7:28. The original Heb. text contained no vowels. These were added by the Jewish Masoretic scholars in the 6th cen. A.D. and later, following ancient traditional pronunciation.

The Heb. text was translated into Gr. between 250 and 150 B.C. This earliest version of the OT is called the Septuagint or the LXX (the "seventy," since it was purported to be the work of 70 translators). Using the Dead Sea Scrolls as a basis, R. Laird Harris dates the LXX at about 200 B.C. (*Inspiration and Canonicity of the Bible*, p. 99). In numerous cases the NT quotes from the LXX rather than from the Heb. text.

The discovery of Gr. papyrus fragments in the Egyptian desert written in Koine, that is, in the common or vernacular Gr. of NT times, has explained the main differences between the NT and classical Gr. The NT was written in the common (Koine) vernacular language of the 1st cen., even as Martin Luther used the common German of the times in his translation of the Bible. *See* Bible Versions.

Scope and dimensions. The Bible used by Protestants contains 66 books, 39 in the OT and 27 in the NT. The books accepted in the OT are the same as the books accepted by the Jews as canonical. They speak of 24 books in the OT because of the fact that they consider I and II Samuel, I and II Kings, I and II Chronicles, Ezra-Nehemiah, and the 12 Minor Prophets as each one book. Josephus (*Against Apion* i. 8) refers to the fact that there are only 22 books in the OT to correspond to the 22 letters in the Heb. alphabet, but he probably combines Ruth with Judges and Lamentations with Jeremiah in order to arrive at 22.

The Roman Catholic church includes in the OT as canonical most of the Apocrypha: Tobit, Judith, Wisdom, Ecclesiasticus (also called Sirach or Ben Sirach), Baruch, I and II Maccabees, and some additions to Esther and to Daniel. The Greek Orthodox church does likewise. The Church of England, in accord with the Lutheran church, follows Jerome in holding that the apocryphal books may be read "for example of life and instruction on manners; but yet doth not apply them to establish any doctrine" (Article VI). The Ethiopic Bible includes I Enoch and the Book of Jubilees. *See* Apocrypha.

The Jews divided the OT into three sections: (1) the Law, the five books of the Pentateuch written by Moses; (2) the Prophets, which was subdivided into the Former Prophets, and included Joshua, Judges, Samuel and Kings, and the Latter Prophets, which included Isaiah, Jeremiah, Ezekiel, and the book of the Twelve Prophets; (3) the Writings, which contained the rest of the OT: the Psalms, Proverbs, and Job; then the five Scrolls: Canticles, Ruth, Lamentations, Ecclesiastes, and Esther; and finally Daniel, Ezra-Nehemiah, and Chronicles.

The Jews used the above order in their text, but the LXX revised this to form a more chronological and logical order. The LXX order has been retained by the Christian church.

The books of the OT are divided by the Christian church into four sections: (1) Law, namely, the Pentateuch. (2) History, comprising Joshua, Judges, Ruth, I and II Samuel, I and II Kings, I and II Chronicles, Ezra, Nehemiah, and Esther. (3) Wisdom and poetry, namely, Job, Psalms, Proverbs, Ecclesiastes, Song of Solomon. (4) Prophecy, namely, Isaiah, Jeremiah, Lamentations, Ezekiel, Daniel, Hosea, Joel, Amos, Obadiah, Jonah, Micah, Nahum, Habakkuk, Zephaniah, Haggai, Zechariah, and Malachi. Isaiah, Jeremiah, Ezekiel, and Daniel are called the Major Prophets, the other 12, the Minor Prophets.

The NT is composed of 27 books which are usually divided into four parts also: (1) Gospels, namely, Matthew, Mark, Luke, and John. (2) History of the early church, namely, Acts. (3) Epistles. These are sometimes divided into (a) Church Epistles: Romans, I and II Corinthians, Galatians, Ephesians, Philippians, Colossians, I and II Thessalonians; (b) Pastoral Epistles: I and II Timothy, Titus, and a personal epistle to Philemon; (c) Catholic (or General) Epistles: Hebrews, James, I and II Peter, I, II, and III John, and Jude. (4) Prophecy: book of Revelation.

Text of Scripture. The Bible was written over a period of approximately 1,500 years. The five books of Moses can be dated *c*. 1400 B.C. and the last book of the NT, Revelation, *c*. A.D. 90. In spite of the fact that the original manuscripts are not now extant, and that only handwritten copies existed down to the invention of printing, still the condition of the text has been remarkably preserved. The Heb. OT has been substantially verified by the LXX, and by the Heb. biblical manuscripts of the Dead Sea Scrolls which date in places back to the same period as the LXX. The existence of around 4,500 manuscripts of the NT in Gr., dating from *c*. A.D. 125 up to the invention of printing, provide a wealth of attestation to the NT. Added to this evidence are the versions, such as the Old Latin and Syriac, going back to A.D. 150, and the Latin Vulgate translation made by Jerome (382-405).

Chapter and verse divisions. The books of the Bible originally had neither chapters nor verses. Jews of pre-Talmudic times divided the OT into sections of convenient length for reading in the synagogues. Verse division marks of the OT appeared somewhat later, but our modern system was devised by Rabbi Nathan in the 15th cen. and came into Christian usage through Paginius' Latin Bible of 1528. Probably it was Stephen Langton (d. 1228), archbishop of Canterbury and supporter of the Magna Charta, who worked out the present chapter divisions. The verse divisions of the NT appeared first in a Gr. NT published in 1551 by Robert Stephens, a Paris printer. In 1555 he

Thus far all Old Testament books except Esther have been represented in the Dead Sea Scrolls. Here scholars scrutinize scroll fragments. Palestine Archaeological Museum, Jerusalem

published an edition of the Latin Vulgate, which was the first Bible to have the present chapters and verses. The first English Bible with such divisions was the Geneva edition of 1560.

Message. The Bible, though written over a long period of time, and by writers who often did not know each other, reveals a marvelous unity of thought. The writers all agree in their views of a divine revelation concerning: (1) Man's condition and needs. They depict man's sinful, fallen condition; his inability to save himself; God's revealed will to save man through a substitutionary sacrifice, and the salvation of man through saving faith alone. (2) God's covenant with Israel. He covenanted with Israel through Abraham to give them both a Saviour and a kingdom. This covenant was expanded and developed in all the ensuing covenants, namely, the Sinaitic with Moses and Israel, and the Davidic. It was both expanded and replaced by the new covenant in the NT (Mt 26:28; Heb 8:6-13). The term OT actually refers to the old covenant, the Latin word "testament" having been adopted to translate the Heb. *b^erîth* and the Gr. *diathēkē* (Mt 26:28). (3) Types and antitypes. All the types given in feasts, ceremonies, and sacrifices in the OT are fulfilled in Christ and the Church in the NT. For example, the Feast of Passover typified Christ as our passover and sacrificial lamb (Jn 1:29; Mt 26:19; I Cor 5:7). *See* Antitype. (4) Prophecies. Many specific prophecies concerning the coming of Christ the Messiah and of His sacrificial death were fulfilled in His life and death. Others concerning His coming to rule in His kingdom are still future.

The Bible and criticism. Two forms of criticism have been applied to the Bible, lower and higher. Lower criticism concerns the establishment of the exact wording of the text of Scripture, and great progress and much reason for confidence have attended its scholarly application. The Dead Sea Scrolls have done much to confirm the reliability of the words of the OT in particular, and to clear up quotations by the NT writers from the Septuagint at the points in which it differs from the Masoretic Text.

Higher criticism, which can be used constructively to study the origin of the facts in the Bible and the authenticity of the authorship of the different books, has all too often been used in a destructive manner. Rejecting supernaturalism as a general principle, the critics have endeavored to prove that Moses did not write the Pentateuch; that Isaiah did not write all the book designated by his name; that the fourth Gospel was not written by John the apostle; and that the Synoptic Gospels are not the product of the three evangelists, Matthew, Luke, and a man called Mark who was guided by Peter, but are accounts based upon sources or documents which have been drastically edited and collated. Detailed studies by evangelical scholars have answered in a careful manner the attacks on the OT. Some of these are James

Orr, Oswald T. Allis, Edward J. Young and Gleason L. Archer. In refuting the attacks of the higher critics on the NT, the following men among others have given worthwhile and scholarly answers: R. Laird Harris, Donald Guthrie and Ned B. Stonehouse. See bibliography below.

See Bible, English Versions; Bible Interpretation; Bible Manuscripts; Canon of Scripture, the OT and the NT; Versions, Ancient and Medieval.

Bibliography. Oswald T. Allis, *The Five Books of Moses,* 1943; *God Spake by Moses,* 1951; *The Unity of Isaiah,* 1950, Philadelphia: Presbyterian and Reformed Pub. Co. Gleason L. Archer, *A Survey of Old Testament Introduction,* Chicago: Moody Press, 1964. William Henry Green, "The Canon," *General Introduction to the Old Testament,* New York: Scribner's, 1898. Donald Guthrie, *New Testament Introduction,* London: Tyndale Press, 3 vols., 1965. R. Laird Harris, *Inspiration and Canonicity of the Bible,* Grand Rapids: Zondervan, 1957. James Orr, *Problem of the Old Testament,* New York: Scribner's, 1906. Ned B. Stonehouse, *Origins of the Synoptic Gospels,* Grand Rapids: Eerdmans, 1963. Edward J. Young, *Introduction to the Old Testament,* Grand Rapids: Eerdmans, 1949.

R. A. K.

BIBLE DICTIONARIES. In the last 300 years there have been nearly 300 Bible dictionaries published in the English language—some small and some extending to many volumes, some carrying the names of many of the greatest biblical scholars of their respective generations, while some appear anonymously.

Augustine, as early as A.D. 367, expressed a wish that someone would produce a work on the names found in Scripture, "such as Eusebius has done in regard to the history of the past." But the church had to wait 12 centuries before any such volume appeared.

Early Dictionaries

The earliest work of this kind probably was done by John Marbeck (1550), followed by a Latin dictionary of the Bible by a German Lutheran, M. I. Flacius (1567). The beginnings of a dictionary of the Bible in English was a work by William Patten. This appeared in London in 1575 (200 pages), the title of which indicates its scope—*The Calendar of Scripture, wherein the Hebru, Chaldean, Arabian, Phenician, Syrian, Persian, Greek and Latin names of—Men, Weemen, Idols, Cities, etc., in the Holly Byble—is set and Turned into Our English Toung.*

The first really important Bible dictionary appearing in English was the one compiled by Thomas Wilson, *Complete Christian Dictionary,* first published in 1612, and appearing in four other editions within 35 years. The text extends to 948 unnumbered pages, concluding with a unique dictionary for the book of Revelation of 131 pages, and a dictionary of the Song of Solomon of 49 pages.

The greatest Bible dictionary appearing in Europe before the middle of the 19th cen. was by one of Europe's great Catholic scholars, Augustin Calmet (1672-1757), published in Paris in 1722. It was translated into English and published in London in 1732 in six folio volumes with the title *An Historical, Critical, Geographical, Chronological, and Etymological Dictionary of the Holy Bible.* This was the ideal of biblical encyclopedias from the time of its first appearance. It was published in revised form in four volumes, then in five volumes, and again in abbreviated editions, even being published in Boston in 1832 and in London in 1847, thus still being issued 125 years after its first appearance. The last volume contains an enormous bibliography of biblical literature extending to 600 columns. This was probably the only great Bible dictionary in English that was translated from a European language.

John Brown of Haddington (1722-1787) published *A Dictionary of the Holy Bible Containing Definitions of All Religious and Ecclesiastical Terms . . . and a Biographical Sketch of Writers in Theological Science,* in the middle of the 18th cen. A fifth edition of Brown's work appeared in 1839 embracing about 95,000 words. Early in the 19th cen. Charles Buck (1771-1815) published his *Theological Dictionary,* London, 1802, in two volumes. It has often been reprinted and revised, down to as late as 1850. It is a work of great erudition.

The earliest important Bible dictionary by an American was *The Dictionary of the Bible* by Howard Malcolm (1799-1879), London, 1828; third edition, Boston, 1830; and an enlarged edition, Boston, 1853. It sold 130,000 copies within 20 years.

A New Era for Bible Dictionaries

One might say that a new era for Bible dictionaries began with the appearance in 1845 of the *Cyclopedia of Biblical Literature* by John Kitto (1804-1854). His enlarged edition of 1862-67 extended to about 3,340,000 words. Here for the first time an edition of a Bible dictionary made use of a great number of contemporary biblical scholars, more than 40 of them, from Great Britain, Germany, and America. Some biblical subjects are treated with greater fullness than any other similar work; e.g., ten double-column pages are devoted to the subject of Adam, 45 pages are devoted to "Burial in Tombs," and there is a superb survey of biblical concordances, etc. An abridgment of the third edition appeared as late as 1894.

In this same decade (1849) there appeared an excellent one-volume work, *The Biblical Cyclopedia,* by John Eadie (1810-1876), which called for 17 editions within 40 years.

In 1860, the first volume of the *Dictionary of the Bible,* edited by Sir William Smith (1813-1893), was published. This proved to be the most influential Bible dictionary of the 19th cen. The complete three-volume work contains more than 3,100 pages. This dictionary saw innumerable editions, the most important of which was the American revision edited by Professor H. B. Hackett, to which an additional staff of 27 scholars contributed. With this work began the strong emphasis on articles relating to historical and geographical subjects, incorporating the constantly multiplying results of archaeological discovery. Smith's dictionary has appeared in many forms, revised, abbreviated, etc., and parts of it stolen for other later dictionaries.

In the same decade, Patrick Fairbairn (1805-1874) issued his *Imperial Bible Dictionary* (1865), which in the later edition of 1885 appeared in six quarto volumes. It is still a treasure house of biblical lore.

The well-known biblical commentator A. R. Fausset (1821-1910) published his *Englishman's Critical and Expository Bible Encyclopedia,* London, in 1878, a work of some 950,000 words, with excellent articles on prophetic subjects, and with unusually full treatment of such subjects as David, Christ, etc. This was republished by an American firm in 1949.

William Blackwood, an American clergyman, in 1873 published his *Potter's Complete Bible Encyclopedia* in two quarto volumes of 2,000 pages, certainly the most beautiful Bible dictionary that had been published up to that time, with more than 3,000 illustrations.

The most important one-volume Bible dictionary edited by an American was the *Dictionary of the Bible* by John D. Davis (1854-1926), first appearing in 1898; the fourth edition in 1924, which was reprinted in 1954. A revision by H. S. Gehman appearing in 1944 with the title *The Westminster Dictionary of the Bible* was more liberal than the original work by Davis.

In 1899 there began to appear in four large volumes the most liberal of all Bible dictionaries up to that time, *The Encyclopedia Biblica,* edited by T. K. Cheyne and J. S. Black, London, 1899-1903. A large number of articles in this encyclopedia were written by the German rationalist P. W. Schmiedel, who repudiated all biblical miracles including the resurrection. A noted review commented, "It is not a dictionary of the Bible: it is a dictionary of the historical criticism of the Bible."

Twentieth Century Dictionaries

In the first decade of the 20th cen. began to appear the remarkable series of dictionaries edited by James Hastings (1852-1922). *A Dictionary of the Bible* in five volumes was published in 1898-1904, followed by a single volume in 1909, really an improvement over the preceding work. A thoroughly revised edition edited by F. C. Grant and H. H. Rowley appeared in 1963, with 150 contributing editors. The latter is a beautiful piece of typography, with excellent colored maps, but lacking bibliographies.

In 1908 appeared the two-volume work *A Dictionary of Christ and the Gospels;* and in the next decade, 1916-1918, *The Dictionary of the Apostolic Church,* also in two volumes. These last two works are far more important for the Bible student today than the earlier five-volume work. Some of the best scholars in the Western world contributed to these volumes on NT subjects. The volumes relating to the Gospels include articles by B. B. Warfield; "Fact and Theory" by C. W. Hodge; an article on the Holy Spirit by James Denny; and an extended article on "The Character of Christ" by T. B. Kilpatrick.

A one-volume work, *A Standard Bible Dictionary,* edited by Nourse and Zenos, appeared in 1909, revised by M. W. Jacobus as *A New Standard Bible Dictionary,* New York, 1936, with 55 contributors, extending to nearly a million words.

The most helpful conservative Bible dictionary of this century, up to the time of its publication, was the *International Standard Bible Encyclopedia* (ISBE), edited by James Orr, Chicago, 1915, in five volumes of more than four million words. It includes articles by 200 contributors, with discussions of such subjects as Chronology, Astronomy, Jesus Christ, Inspiration, etc. It has proved a boon to students of the Scriptures for the last half century, and a revision is now being carefully prepared. One of the invaluable features of this work is the five exhaustive indexes extending to over 840 columns.

Necessarily passing by numerous Bible dictionaries, certainly the most important one-volume work published in the last half century is *The New Bible Dictionary* under the editorship of the staff of the Inter-Varsity Fellowship of London, a work of over 1,400 pages, appearing in 1962, produced by 140 contributors, with many illustrations and the most modern maps. Of great value are the rich articles on OT historical subjects by K. A. Kitchen and Donald J. Wiseman, together with the latter's carefully prepared tables setting forth the most important archaeological discoveries since early in the 19th cen., with full bibliographic references.

The largest Bible dictionary attempted since ISBE is *The Interpreter's Dictionary of the Bible* (1962), in four volumes, in modern format, the work of 253 biblical scholars and authorities on various related subjects. There are something over 1,000 illustrations, together with a series in color of the Westminster maps. Historical and archaeological subjects are considered with fullness and general satisfaction. In many places, however, the work is extremely liberal, with the denial of the Mosaic authorship of the Pentateuch, insisting that Daniel was a product of the 2nd cen. B.C., etc. The NT articles are far more conservative and satisfying than the OT.

Other important one-volume Bible dictionaries that have appeared since World War II include *Harper's Bible Dictionary* (1952) by Madeleine S. and J. Lane Miller; *Unger's Bible Dictionary* (1957) by Merrill F. Unger, a thorough revision of the *Bible Encyclopedia* (1900) by Charles R. Barnes; the *Seventh-Day Adventist Bible Dictionary* (1960) by Siegfried H. Horn; *The Zondervan Pictorial Bible Dictionary* (1963) edited by Merrill C. Tenney with more than 65 contributors; and the *Pictorial Biblical Encyclopedia* (1964) edited by Gaalyahu Cornfeld and assisted by over two dozen Israeli Bible scholars and archaeologists.

Word Studies

Mention should be made of some volumes that are devoted exclusively to the study of specific words found in the Scriptures. Among these, one of the most widely used was *The Bible Word Book, a Glossary of Archaic Words and Phrases in the Authorized Version of the Bible,* compiled by William Aldis Wright, first published in London in 1866, with a second revised edition in 1884. There is also *The Theological Word Book of the Bible* edited by Alan Richardson, London, 1950. Some of the articles here are quite extensive, as the one on the Spirit of 26 columns, with a good bibliography. Another very helpful work is by W. E. Vine, *An Expository Dictionary of New Testament Words,* published in London in 1940, in four volumes.

Some of the more important dictionaries of theology include one of extended significance, *The Dictionary of Doctrinal and Historical Theology* by J. H. Blunt, second edition 1872, a work of 800 double-column pages. Though very few probably consult it now, there are still great treasures in *The Cyclopedia of Biblical, Theological, and Ecclesiastical Literature* edited by John M'Clintock (1814 - 1870) and James Strong (1822 - 1894), New York, 1867 - 1881, two volumes, with two supplementary volumes. There is also the still valuable work *The New Schaff-Herzog Encyclopedia of Religious Knowledge,* published in 12 volumes, appearing in 1908. A work that contains a great mass of invaluable information but today almost wholly forgotten is *The Concise Dictionary of Religious Knowledge* edited by Samuel Macauley Jackson (1851 - 1912), first appearing in two volumes, 1889 and 1890, with a third edition in 1898.

Geoffrey W. Bromiley is performing a tremendous service to English readers by translating the voluminous German work *Theologisches Wörterbuch zum Neuen Testament* edited by Gerhard Kittel (1888 - 1948) and Gerhard Friedrich (1908-). The original work was begun in 1932.

An excellent recent volume is *Baker's Dictionary of Theology* edited by Everett F. Harrison, 1960. This is an invaluable work from a conservative standpoint, with articles by 140 contributors. The bibliographies are most commendable.

From time to time a number of denominations have issued separate ecclesiastical encyclopedias. The still very important work, *The Catholic Encyclopedia,* was published in New York from 1907 to 1914 in 16 volumes. *The Jewish Encyclopedia,* 12 volumes, appeared earlier, 1901 - 1906.

W. M. S.

BIBLE – ENGLISH VERSIONS. The Bible came to the British Isles in a Latin version. In the 1st cen. there were two versions of the OT, Heb. and Gr. But the early Christians found a Latin version necessary, both for the OT and the growing NT, especially because of their missionary work in N Africa where Latin was the dominant language. Before the end of the 2nd cen. some of the books of the Bible had been translated into Latin, for writers of the 3rd cen. show wide acquaintance with Latin versions.

These versions became so multiplied and varied that Pope Damasus assigned to Jerome the task of producing a standard Latin text, which was completed in A.D. 405. This came to be called the Vulgate, which was the standard text most widely used for more than a thousand years, and is still the official text of the Roman Catholic church. It could be that some of the Roman soldiers sent to Britain had copies of portions of the Bible in Latin, though of this we have no evidence.

For nearly 200 years following the departure of the last Roman troops from Britain, A.D. 410, almost nothing is known of the experiences of Christians in England. But monasteries were springing up throughout Ireland so that by A.D. 600 the study of sound literature held the uppermost place and was pursued with a thoroughness and intensity unknown elsewhere in Europe at that time. During this period the Book of Armagh was written, partly in Irish, partly in Latin, containing a non-Vulgate text of the NT. There is no trace of a vernacular Bible in the Celtic church.

Following the coming of Christianity to England in 597 through the mission of Augustine, the first archbishop of Canterbury, Bibles were sent to the early church at Canterbury by Pope Gregory (540 - 604), some of the volumes adorned with silver and jewels, all in the Latin tongue.

Early English Translations

The earliest translation of any part of the Bible into Anglo-Saxon was expressed in songs, initiated by the beautiful songs of Caedmon (d.680), of whom Bede says, he "sang first of the creation of the world and the beginning of mankind and of the story of Genesis . . . and of Christ's incarnation, and of His passion, and of His ascent into heaven; of the coming of the Holy Ghost and the teachings of the apostles." Many of these songs were carefully preserved and can be read today. About this time the famous Christian epic known as *The Christ* was composed, and also that exquisite gem of literary composition *The Dream of the Rood.*

The greatest scholar in Britain in the 8th cen., the Venerable Bede, confessed, "I gave all my attention to the study of the Scriptures." While Bede's writings were in Latin, he did undertake the translation of the Gospels into Anglo-Saxon, and on the day of his death (735) was dictating the concluding lines of the Gospel of John. None of these translations have come down to us.

The earliest written translation of the Gospels into Anglo-Saxon now existing dates from about the 10th cen. The elegantly written Lindisfarne Gospels were originally in Latin (*c.* 700), but *c.* 950 an interlinear translation in Anglo-Saxon was inserted. Alfric, the abbot of Eynsham, writing *c.* 990, acknowledged that the English at that time "had not the evangelical doctrines among their writings . . . those books excepted which King Alfred wisely turned from Latin into English." About 1000 there was a Wessex version of the Gospels.

For two centuries following the Norman invasion (1066) there was an almost total check upon the producing of vernacular literature in Britain, for the Normans introduced and constantly used the French language. By the 14th cen., however, the general use of the French language in England had practically ceased, and there began the production of genuine native literature accompanied by a revival of vernacular Bibles and portions of the Bible. Two English versions of the Psalter were produced at this time. The work by Richard Rolle (d. 1349), which attained great popularity, contained the Latin text of the Psalter, following verse by verse with an English translation and commentary.

Great Bible Translators

The first of the great Bible translators of Britain was *John Wycliffe* (1320 - 1384). Wycliffe's one great desire was to make the Scriptures available in the language of the people, even though a large part of the population of Britain at that time could not read. He also hoped that the availability of the Scriptures in the vernacular would bring about a reformation in the church, and for this reason he has since been called "the morning star of the Reformation." His NT translation was completed in 1380 and the OT in 1382, making this the first complete Bible in the English language. The Apocrypha (*q.v.*) was included, interspersed among the OT canonical books, but with a note in the preface to the OT that these were "without the authority of belief." At least 170 manuscript copies of this Bible, in one edition or another, have survived, and for 150 years it was the only complete English Bible in use. Its greatest shortcoming was that it was a translation from the Latin Vulgate and not from the original Heb. and Gr. Scriptures.

The next distinguished translator of the Bible was *William Tyndale* (1492 - 1536). Educated at Oxford, Tyndale was thoroughly acquainted with Heb. and Gr., and thus for the first time an English NT was produced translated directly from the Gr. Tyndale was in frequent fellowship with the great Gr. scholar Erasmus, and may have met Luther.

It was Tyndale who said to an opponent, "I defy the Pope and all his laws; if God spare my life, ere many years I will cause a boy that driveth the plow shall know more of the Scriptures than thou dost." Since the Wycliffe Bible had appeared, Gutenberg had invented printing with movable type, and had produced the great Mazarin Bible, the Latin Vulgate text, in 1456. Soon manuscript Bibles ceased to be written. Tyndale's NT, and later the OT, appeared in printed form, and thus with copies available for the common man, they were eagerly purchased by people throughout Britain.

The printing of Tyndale's Bible had to be carried on outside Britain, at Hamburg, Worms, and Cologne. Not for the first time but now with greatest intensity, the authorities vigorously attempted to suppress all these efforts of Tyndale and his group. King Henry VIII issued a proclamation in 1530 that read in part as follows: "His highnes hath therfore semblably

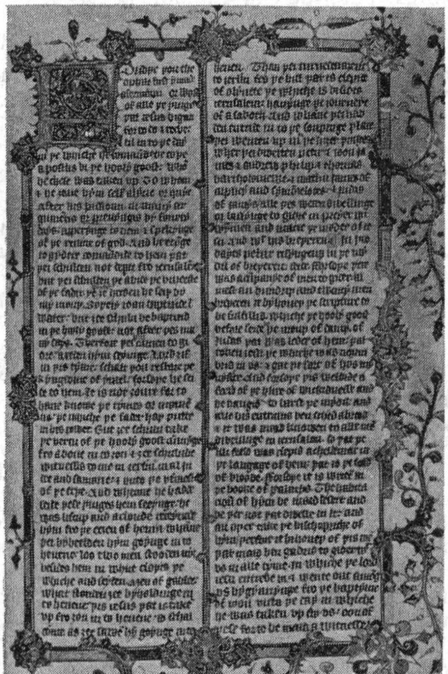

A page from the Wycliffe Bible. BM

BIBLE – ENGLISH VERSIONS

there vpon consulted with the sayd primates and vertuous, discrete, and well lerned personages in diuinite forsayde, and by them all it is thought, that it is not necessary, the sayde scripture to be in the englisshe tonge, and in the handes of the commen people: but that the distribution of the sayd scripture . . . dependeth onely vpon the discretion of the superiours, as they shall thynke it conuenyent. And that hauing respecte to the malignite of this present tyme, with the inclination of people to erronious opinions, the translation of the newe testament and the olde in to the vulgare tonge of englysshe, shulde rather be the occasion of contynuance or increace of errours amonge the sayd people, than any benefyte or commodite towarde the weale of their soules. And that it shall nowe be more conuenient that the same people haue the holy scripture expouned to them, by preachers in their sermons, accordynge as it hath ben of olde tyme accustomed before this tyme . . . that the same bokes and all other bokes of heresy, as well in the frenche tonge as in the duche tonge, be clerely extermynated and exiled out of this realme of Englande for euer."

Betrayed by a friend, Tyndale was martyred in Brussels in 1536. He himself never saw a completed English Bible as a result of his own labors. However, a complete translation by *Miles Coverdale* (1488–1569), later the bishop of Exeter, did appear based upon Tyndale's work. In contrast with the persecution of Tyndale and the attempt to suppress his version, Coverdale did his work under the patronage of Thomas Cromwell.

Miles Coverdale's English translation of the Bible was based on Latin versions, Tyndale's work, and Luther's and Zwingli's German translations. Appearing in 1535, this was the first Bible to be published (i.e., printed) in English, although not all of it based on the original Gr. and Heb. Here for the first time in English Bibles, the books of the OT were arranged in the order in which they are found in Bibles today. Interestingly, from Coverdale's Bible onward the Apocrypha (*q.v.*) has not been printed along with the canonical books of the OT but is placed in a separate appendix at the close of the OT.

A folio edition of the Scriptures appeared in 1537 affirming the translation to be by one *Thomas Matthew,* now recognized as John Rogers, an associate of Tyndale. This translation was "set forth with the King's most gracious license."

A later edition revised by Coverdale (1539) contained a preface by Archbishop Cranmer, and so became known as the *Cranmer Bible* (also called the *Great Bible* because of its size). This was the first authorized Bible and copies were placed in every church. Various editions underwent careful revision. In 1541 King Edward issued a proclamation for the English Bible to be set up in churches, and a part of this proclamation may be read again with profit:

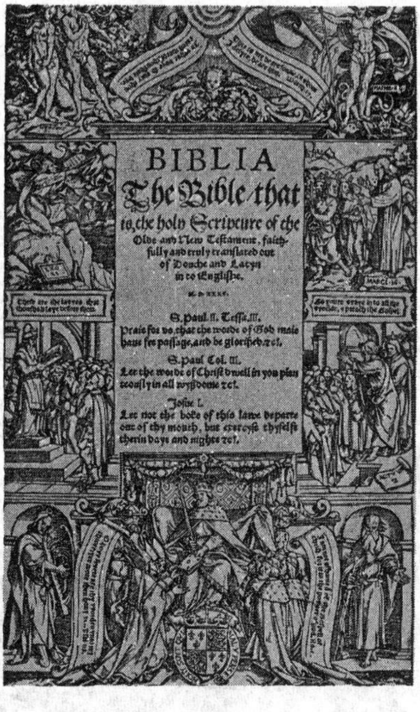

Title page of the Coverdale translation, the first printed English Bible. BM

"It was ordenyed and commaunded . . . that in al and synguler paryshe churches, there shuld be prouyded by a certen day nowe expyred, at the costes of the curates and paryshioners, Bybles conteynynge the olde and newe Testament, in the Englyshe tounge, to be fyxed and set vp openlye in euery of the sayd paryshe churches. The whiche Godlye commaundement and iniuntion was to the onlye intent that euery of the kynges maiesties louynge subiectes, myndynge to reade therin, myght by occasyon thereof, not only consyder and perceyue the great and ineffable omnipotent power, promyse, iustice, mercy and goodnes of Almyghtie God, but also to learne thereby to obserue Gods commaundementes, and to obeye theyr soueraygne Lorde and hyghe powers, and to exercyse Godlye charite, and to vse themselues, accordynge to theyr vocations: in a pure and syncere christen lyfe without murmure or grudgynges. . . . and not that any of them shulde reade the sayde Bybles, wyth lowde and hyghe voyces, in tyme of the celebracion of the holy Masse and other dyuyne seruyces vsed in the churche, nor that any hys lay subjectes redynge the same, shulde presume to take vpon them, any common dysputacyon, argumente or exposicyon of the mysteries therein conteyned, but that euery suche laye man shulde humbly, mekely and reuerentlye reade the same, for his owne instruction, edificacion and amendment of hys lyfe, accordynge to goddes holy worde therin mencioned."

Title page of the Bishops' Bible.

Other Early Bibles

During the reign of Queen Mary (1553–1558), no Bible was printed in England, and its use in the churches was forbidden. However, a group of scholars in Geneva, in 1560, produced an unauthorized English version called the *Geneva Bible*. This was the most accurate version up to that time. The NT was edited by William Whittingham, who was married to Calvin's sister. Calvin wrote an introductory epistle.

For the first time, marginal notations called attention to variations in the Gr. MSS. This was the first English version to use numbered verses as separate paragraphs. The verse divisions of Robert Estienne (or, Stephanus), originally employed in his Gr. NT in 1551, were also used. It was the first Bible to be printed in Roman type instead of the old block letters, the so-called Old English type.

This was the Bible used by Shakespeare, John Bunyan, Oliver Cromwell, so fervently studied by the Puritans and brought over on the *Mayflower*. Designated as "the People's Book," it held a preeminent place among English versions for 75 years.

From 1560 to 1644, 140 editions of the Geneva Bible or NT appeared. Certain Geneva Bibles printed in 1599 omitted the apocryphal books for the first time. The first Bible to be printed in Scotland was a Scottish edition of the Geneva Bible, in 1579.

The popularity of the Geneva Bible persuaded the Anglican authorities, after the accession of Queen Elizabeth to the throne in 1558, that they should produce a Bible which could bear the authority of the Church of England. Proposed by Archbishop Parker, he appointed a committee for such a work. Since the scholarship of these bishops was not equal to that of the group that had produced the Geneva Bible, they used the Great Bible as their basis, checking with the Gr. and Heb. text. The finished work was called the *Bishops' Bible*. Nineteen editions were printed from 1568 to 1606. It was endorsed by convocation in 1571. In the 1572 edition Parker published in parallel columns the Psalter of the Great Bible and the Psalter of the Bishops' Bible.

Until the rather free translation (NT, 1944; OT, 1949) by the late Msgr. Ronald A. Knox, the *Douay Bible* had been the only English Bible approved by the Roman Catholic church. The NT, translated from the Latin, was published under the leadership of Gregory Martin in 1582 by the English Catholic University, then located in exile at Rheims in northeastern France and it was thus known as the *Rheims New Testament*. The OT, for the most part a translation of the Latin Vulgate by Martin, was published in 1609–10 when the English University had returned to Douay in northwestern France and hence the name the Douay Bible.

The poorest part of this version is acknowledged to be the Psalter, which has been rightly characterized as "a translation of a translation of a translation." There is heavy emphasis in this version on ecclesiastical terms. "Repentance" is here translated "penance." Here are such unfamiliar words as "exinanited," "donanes," and "commersation." Instead of "shewbread," this version reads "proposition of loaves." "Deacon" is translated "minister" and "elder" is translated "priest." Eph 3:9 is made to read, "the dispensation of the sacrament." The Douay NT was extensively used by the King James revisers, but the OT was published too late for any such influence. An authority on this subject does not exaggerate in saying that today "the Douay Old Testament is a forgotten book." The apocryphal books appear interspersed throughout the OT in this version.

Translation of the King James Version

With all these various translations available, and with a growing knowledge in Britain of Heb. and Gr., the time was ripe for the greatest single undertaking in the area of translation in the history of English literature, the production of what came to be known as the Authorized Version, or the King James Version (KJV).

In the summer of 1603, King James I, on his way to London to receive the English crown, was presented with a petition of grievances by the clergy of Puritan convictions, which led him to call for a conference at Hampton Court, January 14–16, 1604. During this conference, Dr. John Reynolds, president of Corpus Christi College, Oxford, moved that a new translation of the Bible be undertaken. Though opposed by the majority, this motion was accepted by the king, and the undertaking was begun at once with 54 of the outstanding biblical scholars in Great Britain engaged in this task. They were divided into six groups, three to work on a translation of the OT, two on the NT, and one on the Apocrypha.

Dr. H. Wheeler Robinson has well summarized the qualifications of this group: "The Oxford group was headed by Dr. John Hardinge, regius professor of Hebrew, and included Dr. John Reynolds, the originator of the project, 'his memory and reading were near to a miracle'; Dr. Miles Smith, who 'had Hebrew at his fingers' ends'; Dr. Richard Brett, 'skilled and versed to a criticism in the Latin, Greek, Chaldee, Arabic and Ethiopic tongues'; Sir Henry Saville, editor of the works of Chrysostom; and Dr. John Harmer, professor of Greek, 'a most noted Latinist, Grecian and divine.'

"The Cambridge committee was at first presided over by Edward Lively, regius professor of Hebrew, who died in 1605 before the work was really begun, and included Dr. Lawrence Chaderton, 'familiar with the Greek and Hebrew tongues, and the numerous writings of the rabbis'; Thomas Harrison, 'noted for his exquisite skill in Hebrew and Greek idioms'; Dr. Robert Spalding, successor to Lively as professor of Hebrew; Andrew Downes, 'one composed of Greek and industry'; and John Bois, 'a precocious Greek and Hebrew scholar.'

"The Westminster group was headed by Lancelot Andrewes, dean of Westminster, afterward bishop of Chichester, of Ely, and finally of Winchester, 'who might have been interpreter general at Babel . . . the world wanted learning to know how learned he was'; and included the Hebraist Hadrian Saravia, and William Bedwell, the greatest living Arabic scholar."

In method, the separate panels were to consider the work of each other panel, and differences were to be resolved first by correspondence, and that failing, by the general meeting at the end, which was composed of two representatives from each of the three main centers of translation (Oxford, Cambridge, Westminster). The final session, which brought together and edited the whole work, lasted nine months. Though begun in 1607 the translation was not completed until 1610 and published in 1611.

In the famous preface to this version is a superb statement regarding the work and value of translation: "Translation it is that openeth the window, to let in the light; that breaketh the shell, that we may eat the kernel; that putteth aside the curtaine, that we may looke into the most Holy place; that remooueth the couer of the well, that we may come by the water, euen as *Iacob* rolled away the stone from the mouth of the well, by which meanes the flockes of *Laban* were watered. Indeede without translation into the vulgar tongue, the vnlearned are but like the children at *Iacobs* well (which was deepe) without a bucket or some thing to draw with: or as that person mentioned by *Esay*, to whom when a sealed booke was deliuered, with this motion, *Reade this, I pray thee,* hee was faine to make this answere, *I cannot, for it is sealed.*"

It was not long before the KJV crowded out all preceding translations as far as the public reading of the Scriptures was concerned. At last England was reading the same Bible at home which they also heard read from the pulpits of their churches. The distinguished English scholar of a generation ago, Dr. Albert S. Cook well said: "It thus became bound up with the life of the nation. Since it stilled all controversy over the best rendering, it gradually came to be accepted as so far absolute that in the minds of myriads there was no distinction between this version and the original texts, and they may almost be said to have believed in the literal inspiration of the very words which composed it."

The translators of the Revised Version nearly three centuries later declared: "We have had to study this great version carefully and minutely, line by line; and the longer we have been engaged upon it the more we have learned to admire its simplicity, its dignity, its power, its happy turns of expression, its general accuracy, and, we must not fail to add, the music of its cadences, and the felicities of its rhythm."

Even such a non-Christian as Thomas Huxley gladly acknowledged that the KJV "is written in the noblest and purest English, and abounds in exquisite beauties of pure literary form; and, finally, that it forbids the veriest hind who never left his village to be ignorant of the existence of other countries and other civilizations, and of a great past stretching back to the furthest limits of the oldest civilizations of the world."

English and American Standard Versions

While a number of versions appeared during the 17th and 18th cen., and particularly some important new translations from the Gr. NT, more than 250 years went by before there was any united effort to produce a new standard version. Much had happened in the world of biblical scholarship since 1611, e.g., the discovery of the great Sinaitic manuscript by Tischendorf (*see* Bible Manuscripts). On February 10, 1870, Bishop Wilberforce submitted the following resolution to the Upper House of Convocation of the Province of Canterbury: "That a committee of both Houses be appointed, with power to confer with any committee that may be appointed by the Convocation of the Northern Province, to report upon the desirableness of a revision of the Authorized Version of the New Testament, whether by marginal notes or otherwise, in all those passages where plain and clear errors, whether in the Hebrew or Greek text originally adopted by the translators, or in the translation made from the same, shall, on due investigation, be found to exist."

In May of the same year, a committee made some suggestions. Among them were: "1. That it is desirable that a revision of the Authorized Version of the Holy Scriptures be undertaken. 2. That the revision be so conducted as to comprise both marginal renderings and such emendations as it may be found necessary to insert in the text of the Authorized Version. 3. That in the above resolutions we do not contemplate any new translation of the Bible, or any alteration of the language, except when in the judgment of the most competent scholars such change is necessary."

Fifty-four of the best biblical scholars in Britain pledged themselves to cooperate in this undertaking. Two groups of 27 members each commenced work in June of that same year, the NT company meeting on 407 days within 11 years, and the OT company on 792 days in 15 years. The NT appeared on May 17, 1881, and the OT in 1885.

Among other virtues, the poetical passages throughout the Bible were printed as such. Many words that had become outdated and antique were modernized, and innumerable passages were more accurately translated. A great number of varied renderings were inserted in the margin, and the entire system of cross-references was completely revised. While verse numbers were retained, apart from the poetical passages the text was printed in paragraphs, and these paragraph divisions were most carefully determined.

The text of the English revision of the NT was sent ahead to New York and published in America May 20, 1881. Two Chicago daily newspapers received the text of Matthew through Romans in history's longest telegram (*c.* 118,000 words). Type for the remainder was set from copies arriving by fast train in the evening of May 21, so that they published the entire NT for their public May 22. Three million copies of this were sold in the United States and Great Britain in the first twelve months.

The verdict of Prof. F. F. Bruce exactly states what is the general opinion by the best authorities, that this version "is still the most useful edition of the Bible for the careful student who knows no language but English." But concerning the NT Charles H. Spurgeon once remarked, "It is strong in Greek, weak in English." This evaluation still stands and the fact observed has hindered this version and its American counterpart from being a "people's" version.

BIBLE – ENGLISH VERSIONS

The English committee invited American biblical scholars to participate with them in this undertaking, an invitation that was gladly accepted. But differences arose about certain methods of procedure and the American committee decided to publish its own revised version, though exchanging notes with the British revisers, and promising not to publish its complete work for 14 years after the English revision had appeared. It has been generally agreed that the American Standard Version (ASV), which was published in 1901, was in many ways superior to the English one. It is estimated that in the NT of these revised versions there are about 30,000 alterations from the KJV text or, as someone has estimated, about four and one-half alterations for each verse.

Revised Standard Version

In 1937 the International Council of Religious Education initiated work for a complete new revision, undertaken by 32 American biblical scholars. The Revised Standard Version (RSV) NT was published in 1946 and the entire Bible in 1952. While many passages in this text aroused fierce criticism, in some places there was actually a return to the earlier KJV. For example, II Tim 3:16, which had been badly mutilated in the ASV, was now made to read, "All scripture is inspired by God and profitable, etc."

The chairman of this work, Dean Luther Weigle of Yale, wrote of this new version at the time of its publication: "It was in effect a new translation, and for three reasons. The first is that no adequate revision can be made except upon the basis of a thorough study of the Greek text, and as careful procedure in putting its meaning into English, as would be required in the case of a new translation. The second is that the committee has used the new evidence concerning the Greek text and the new resources for understanding the vocabulary and grammar of the Greek New Testament which have been afforded by the remarkable discoveries of the past sixty years since the revisions of 1881 and 1901 were made. The third is that the present committee was not obliged, as the former committees were, to maintain the peculiar forms of Elizabethan English in which the King James Version is cast." In this text the use of the name "Jehovah" was dropped and the title "Lord" was substituted. While archaic forms of pronouns were discarded, quotation marks were not introduced.

W. M. S.

Translations into Modern Speech by Committees or Groups of Scholars

New English Bible (NEB). In 1946 the General Assembly of the Church of Scotland approached the Protestant churches of Great Britain suggesting a completely new translation of the Bible into contemporary English. The proposal met with approval, and a translation called the New English Bible was produced.

This version stems from an interdenominational joint committee of English Protestants under the direction of C. H. Dodd, commissioned to make a "completely new translation" of the Bible "rather than a revision of any earlier version." It was to be both a "faithful rendering of the best available Greek text into the current speech of our time and a rendering which should harvest the gains of recent biblical scholarship."

The NT appeared in March, 1961, and has been widely adopted by many British and American groups. Since a new Gr. text has been constructed for this project, it marks an innovation in committee translations where formerly standard critical editions of the Gr. text were used. However, in a number of cases, in our judgment, this new text follows questionable and slender manuscript evidence in the readings it adopts (e.g., Jn 13:10; 19:21; Mk 8:26; Phil 2:16). The OT was published in March, 1970.

Many attractive features and qualities, ranging from a pleasing format and style to clarity and forcefulness, have contributed to the NEB's present popularity. However, a number of general weaknesses can be cited. It falls prey to excessive interpretive paraphrases and free translations in many instances (e.g., Jn 16:8–11; Rom 5:15). For this reason, it is difficult to classify the NEB as either a literal translation with some paraphrase, or as a true paraphrase. Furthermore, there are no italics to indicate where words and phrases are added in English in order to complete the sense. Parentheses are used ambiguously for both the added words and parenthetical thought.

New American Standard Bible (NASB). A well-qualified group of evangelical American biblical scholars issued the NT of the New American Standard Bible in 1963, and the whole Bible in 1971. They stated as their purpose "to adhere to the original languages of the Holy Scriptures as closely as possible and at the same time to obtain a fluent and readable style according to current English usage." The basis for their work was the ASV of 1901.

In this revision helpful marginal notes and cross-references are found on the outer edge of the page; paragraphs are designated; quotation and punctuation marks follow modern practice. "Thou," "thy" and "thee" are changed to "you" except in the language of prayer when speaking to Deity. The number of the word "you" is designated "you^{s}" or "you^{pl}" when it cannot be determined from the context. Italics indicate words not present in the Gr. text but justified in the translation.

The translators indicate that, while giving attention to the latest available Gr. MSS, the attempt is made "to render the grammar and terminology of the ASV in contemporary English." Where the literalness of the ASV is not possible, a more current English expression is used, but the literal rendering is indicated in the margin.

This version is an accurate translation free from archaic expressions and suitable for careful Bible study and for Scripture memorization, which is not always the case with paraphrases or amplified versions.

Confraternity Version. The NT was first published in 1941 by the Episcopal Confraternity of Christian Doctrine. It is a revision of the Rheims-Challoner NT translated from the Latin Vulgate. The latest evidence for the Vulgate text is followed, but it is indicated that ". . . if the Latin disagrees from the Greek to such an extent to affect the meaning, attention is given in the footnotes" and the Greek is followed. The text is divided in paragraph style but with the verses numbered within the paragraphs.

There is a colloquialness in this translation that lends itself to a good understanding of the Scripture. Some of the footnotes, however, contain Roman Catholic dogma, as in I Tim 2:5 where this is said to mean "mediatorship as a man," or in Mt 1:25 which is said to mean that "Mary's perpetual virginity" is not impaired in the least.

In 1948 a new translation of Genesis appeared and therefore a start was made on a translation of the OT based on the Heb. rather than the Latin. The entire Bible was published in 1970 under the title New American Bible.

The translation has an easy reading style and follows the text quite closely, though in the introductions there are evidences of higher critical scholarship.

Revised Standard Version Roman Catholic Edition. The Catholic Bible Association of Great Britain has been responsible for this Roman Catholic edition. The statement in the foreword has been that the different religious branches – Protestant, Catholic and otherwise – can use just about the same Bible. However, this edition, while not changing the bulk of the NT RSV, does incorporate some 67 changes that reflect Roman Catholic dogma.

But in the OT, "it was not thought necessary to make any changes at all." The usual amount of footnotes is carried. Of course the apocryphal books are included along with the OT text. Thus the objections already indicated concerning the regular RSV apply to the Roman Catholic edition as well.

Berkeley Version in Modern English (1958). The NT portion is a private version by Gerrit Verkuyl, whose desire was to produce a translation less interpretive than Moffatt's, more American than Weymouth's and less tied to the KJV than the RSV. Working from the best Gr. MSS, Verkuyl did produce a version with clear idiomatic English. The archaic expressions with obscurities of speech are minimized. Yet there are a number of stiff expressions.

Much the same is true of the OT. Many scholars, each responsible for his own work, did the translation on portions assigned to them, but the whole Berkeley Version is essentially a series of private ventures with no formal committee revision procedure. Messianic prophecies with regard to Christ are carefully preserved.

The version carries chronological notations in the headings of many of the chapters, while the footnotes have moral and ethical suggestions along with the other explanatory remarks.

The Torah, the Five Books of Moses. Published in 1963, this is the first phase of a Jewish translation of the entire OT, of which the other books are still in process of translation. There is an English translation by Jewish scholars of the Heb. OT dating from 1917, largely modeled on the idiom of the ASV, but the present version is a new translation into modern English. The text reads smoothly and is free from expressions difficult to understand. In instances where the context demands extra words that are not in the Heb. text, paraphrase is used, but the additional words are bracketed. Where the text is controversial, there are variant readings in the footnotes, thus allowing some choice for the reader. It is noted that in Ex 3:14, the holy name for God is left untranslated. The reading is, "Thus shall you say to the Israelites, '*Ehyeh* sent me.' " Some questionable translations may be seen in Gen 2:17; 3:15; Num 24:17; Deut 6:4.

The translation is basically the work of one man, Harry M. Orlinsky, noted Jewish scholar, although two other scholars (H. L. Ginsberg and E. A. Speiser) and three rabbis acted as a reviewing committee. The three rabbis represented the three branches of American Judaism.

The Anchor Bible. It is known as an ecumenical venture and is under the editorial supervision of William F. Albright and David N. Freedman. The first volumes were published in 1964, Genesis and the Epistles of James, Peter and Jude. For each book of the Bible there is an accurate English translation conveying the meaning of the Heb. and Gr. texts and yet adapting the translation to modern American English. However, in many instances the translation follows the biblical text quite literally (e.g., Ps 1; Jn 1). There are some curious paraphrases (e.g., in Jn 3:1 where Nicodemus is "a member of the Jewish Sanhedrin").

With the translation there are explanatory notes and a commentary considering historical and critical matters. There is no ecclesiastical organization behind the project, which is international and interfaith since Catholic, Protestant, and Jewish scholars from many parts of the world contribute the individual volumes. Each Bible book is the work of one scholar who is an expert in that area of Bible study. It should be noted that most scholars hold the theologically liberal view.

Amplified Bible. This appeared in several stages, the NT in 1958 and culminating in the whole Bible in 1965. The complete edition has been extensively revised, especially in the OT. The translation is new and generally accurate in the revised edition. As its chief feature it amplifies different shades of meaning in the original Heb. and Gr. by multiplying English words. For example, whereas in Isa 7:14 the KJV reads, "Behold, a virgin shall conceive," the AB has, "Behold, the young woman *who* is unmarried *and* a virgin, shall conceive." Footnotes bring together a multitude of conservative comments on the text of every page.

While in some instances it is no doubt helpful to have more than one English word to translate the original, yet out of the several shades of meaning represented by the various word amplifications, only one – not all – of the meanings fit a given context. In other words, though a single English word seldom says all an author intended, a multiplication of words usually says more than he actually meant to convey. However, many find enrichment in the understanding of Scripture through the approach of the AB.

The Jerusalem Bible (1966). This Roman Catholic version produced in England is the English equivalent of the French *La Bible de Jerusalem* (1956) prepared by the Dominican Biblical School in Jerusalem under the general editorship of Père Roland de Vaux. The introductions and copious footnotes are a direct translation from the French, while the text was usually translated directly from the original languages and simultaneously compared with the French when questions of variant reading or interpretation arose. The desire of the English general editor Alexander Jones and his collaborators was to translate the Bible into "contemporary" English.

The divine name Yahweh is used throughout the OT. As one would expect, the books of the Apocrypha are distributed among the Historical Books, the Wisdom Books, and the Prophets instead of keeping them in a separate section. The poetic passages are printed as verse and the lines with fewer stresses in the Heb. are indented. The text is divided by bold-type section and paragraph headings to enable the reader to see at a glance what is the subject matter before him.

The introductions and the interpretive notes follow the trend among Roman Catholic scholars to accept a modified documentary theory of the Pentateuch, believing there are three streams of tradition in Genesis to Numbers; to hold to composite authorship for the book of Isaiah; and to date the writing of Daniel to *c.* 165 B.C. On the other hand, messianic prophecies are clearly noted and often explained in the footnotes (e.g., the passages in Isaiah regarding the "servant of Yahweh," at 42:1). The explanatory footnotes in the NT are in general theologically sound; with the book of Romans, e.g., they are nearly as long as the text of that book and provide excellent evangelical comments. Helpful supplements include an extensive chronological table for general and biblical history, and an index of the biblical themes in the footnotes.

The New World Translation. Published by the Watchtower Bible and Tract Society in 1953, this version indicates how a distinctive cult (Jehovah's Witnesses) can translate the Bible to suit its own purposes, often without the substantiation of any kind of good biblical exegesis. Of course where no theological bias is involved, the translation can be in fairly good idiom. Yet this cult denies the deity of Christ and the equality of the Son with the Father, and thus Jn 1:1 is translated ". . . and the word was *a* god."

Also, the word "Jehovah" is often substituted in the NT for the word "Lord," although "Jehovah" is not used when referring to the Lord Jesus Christ personally. Thus there is an inconsistency to support a particular bias.

Some Private Translations into Modern Speech

The New Testament in Modern Speech. This is perhaps the first modern speech version translated by an individual (1902). R. F. Weymouth first ascertained the sense of the Gr. text and then proceeded to express that sense in 20th cen. English. In other words, Weymouth was interested in how an inspired writer would have written had he lived in this age. The values of Gr. verbs, shades of meaning of words used and a keen appreciation of Gr. cases are all reflected in this translation. Note how I Jn 1:6 is translated: ". . . while we are living in darkness," or note the expression in Lk 15:1: "Now the tax-gatherers and the notorious sinners were everywhere in the habit of coming close to Him to listen to Him."

In general the earlier editions were doctrinally sound. Later editions, revised by Weymouth's successors, were somewhat influenced by liberal doctrine.

Twentieth Century New Testament. This British translation began in 1890 when a mother and pastor's wife, Mrs. Mary Higgs, together with Ernest Malan, an engineer, decided to produce a translation of the NT in everyday speech that young people could understand. They were joined gradually by more housewives, businessmen, and ministers until the committee had grown to 35 persons, including three recognized scholars. Their work was done with meticulous care and a thoroughly sound procedure; it was released in 1904 (Moody Press reprint, 1961). TCNT contains a minimum of paraphrase and interpretation and shows both accuracy and clarity.

The Bible by James Moffatt. The translation of the whole Bible by Moffatt was completed and published in 1926. He attempted to provide an entirely new version that would produce the same effect as the original text on those who read and heard it. Moffatt was a careful scholar, especially in the NT (1913). The version is free and quite vigorous. It does not sound like the familiar KJV (e.g., Gen 1:1, "This is the story of how the universe was formed"). Finer shades of meaning in the Gr. tenses are graphically brought out in the NT (cf. Lk 7:45; 8:23; Rom 8:13; I Jn 1:6).

In spite of these qualities, Moffatt's version has serious weaknesses. He affirmed that he found "freedom from the theory of verbal inspiration," and this view is reflected in his rendering of some of the great doctrinal passages of both OT and NT. In the Pentateuch, in accord with the documentary theory, he attempted to indicate the multiple authors by alternating Roman and italic type. He also rearranged the text as he thought best in some places (cf. Jn 13 – 16), and since he held to a diminished view of the deity of Christ, he reduced to a minimum the thrust of the great passages on that doctrine (e.g., Jn 1:1 – 5; Phil 2:5 – 8; Col 1:15 – 18; Heb 1:3). The virgin birth of Christ is placed in question by using a decidedly inferior text reading that refers to Joseph as "the father of Jesus" (Mt 1:16).

The New Testament in the Language of the People. This was translated and first published in 1937 by C. B. Williams, then professor of Greek at Union University, Jackson, Tenn., and reprinted by Moody Press in several editions. It is noted primarily for its accuracy in rendering the tenses, word pictures, and fine shades of grammatical meaning in the Gr. which are often passed over in other translations. While it lacks something in literary quality and smoothness, it rewards the careful reader of the NT by additional help from the Gr. in a modern-speech rendering.

This translation is not to be confused with the *New Testament in Plain English* by Charles Kingsley Williams, published in 1949 and reprinted by Eerdmans in 1963. The latter volume is an excellent basic English version with about a 2,000 word vocabulary suitable for children or foreigners learning English.

The New Testament in Modern English by J. B. Phillips (1958). This version is highly colloquial, a deliberate presentation of vivid and idiomatic language, using paraphrase very freely to bring out the meaning of difficult passages. It has become one of the most widely used translations of the NT in recent years.

With his *Four Prophets* (1963), Phillips began the translation of the OT using Amos, Hosea, Micah and Isa 1–35. These four prophetic passages were chosen because of their relevance today. Phillips admits that the OT cannot be translated so quickly and readily as the NT.

On the whole, the OT is a good and intelligible translation, although some objectionable features might be cited. In Isa 6:5 the prophet describes himself as a "foul-mouthed man," which can have an altogether different doctrinal meaning than the KJV of "a man of unclean lips." Hos 2:2 reads, "Tell her to wash the paint from her face," instead of "Let her put away her harlotries from before her presence," thus giving the passage a different connotation from what was intended. In general, however, many a difficult passage has been clarified, while paragraph headings are an aid to understanding.

The New Testament in the Language of Today by William F. Beck (1963). Prompted by the desire to put the NT in "the living language of today and tomorrow," Beck, aided by the most recent manuscripts and papyri discoveries, prepared a completely new translation, which was published by Concordia Publishing House. It has also been included in the *Four Translation New Testament* published in 1966 by Moody Press.

While lacking in forcefulness, NTLT is generally accurate, clear, and free from interpretation and paraphrases. It does a good job of following the Gr. text and at the same time attempts to render the words in their nearest single-word English equivalent. For example, "behold" in the KJV becomes "look" in the NTLT; "serpent" in KJV is simply "snake" in Beck's rendering; "blessed" in the beatitudes (Mt 5:3–12) of the KJV becomes "happy" in the NTLT.

The Letters of Paul by F. F. Bruce (1965). This is an avowed extended paraphrase by one of England's greatest evangelical NT scholars.

Bruce points out that in a paraphrase "the paraphrast includes much more of his own interpretation and exposition than a translator would deem proper." Therefore, the accuracy of such a rendering hinges largely on the scholarly ability of the translator. To guard against false conclusion from his paraphrase, Bruce has included on each facing page the ERV, which he deems the most accurate literal rendering.

Living Bible. Starting in 1962 with *Living Letters,* a paraphrase of the NT epistles, Kenneth N. Taylor published the *Living New Testament* (1967) and has now completed the series covering the entire Bible. His work immediately gained popularity so that by 1967 three million copies of Living Letters and Living Gospels had been printed. Also available is a parallel edition of the Living New Testament with the KJV. The earlier translations were carefully revised for the 1967 edition of the complete NT, and a general revision by a paraphrase revision committee is planned for every five years.

There is an undeniable freshness and clarity in Taylor's style that awakens interest. This results from the paraphrast's skill in using colloquial speech and free rendering of passages. Another reason for the clarity is interpretive selection. In practically every instance where the Heb. or Gr. texts are ambiguous, allowing alternatives, Taylor has adopted one view and rendered it clearly.

For example, the problem of what kind of faith James is talking about is decided by the additional interpretive word "real" faith (Jas 2:20); the problem of the sense of "she shall be *saved* in childbearing" (KJV) is interpreted in Living Letters as "He will save their souls" (I Tim 2:15); the meaning of "Can two walk together, except they be agreed?" is fixed by the interpretive paraphrase, "For how can we walk together with your sins between us?" (Amos 3:3). This leads to clarity, but it also fixes interpretation when equally sound alternate views are possible.

Much of Taylor's very free paraphrase is plainly commentary and should be so recognized. True paraphrase involves the modernized English equivalent of what is in the text itself, while the commentary introduces something which is not there in order to elucidate the meaning of what is there. In Jn 1:11, e.g., Taylor adds the whole sentence, "Only a few would welcome and receive Him." Besides being historically inaccurate, this statement is not in the Gr. text, but the reader is not informed of this.

The New Testament, An Expanded Translation by Kenneth S. Wuest, late professor of Greek at Moody Bible Institute (1961). Using "as many English words as are necessary to bring out the richness, force and clarity of the Gr. text," the translation is intended as "a companion to, or commentary on, the standard translations."

Wuest wished to stay clear of paraphrase and interpretation. The translation is commendable for attempting to reproduce the feeling of the Gr. text as a Gr. student would read it. For example, the KJV of Lk 15:20 reads, ". . . and fell on his neck and kissed him," while Wuest translates, ". . . he fell on his neck and tenderly kissed him again and again." Sometimes the expansion gets out of hand, as in Acts 17:18 where the one Gr. word *spermologos* (KJV, "babbler") is rendered, "This ignorant plagiarist, picking up scraps of information here and there, unrelated in his own thinking and passing them off as the result of his own mature thought."

Despite certain weaknesses of paraphrase and some questionable Gr. exegesis, this version is helpful as a commentary-type translation and a supplement in understanding certain idioms and shades of thought in the Gr. text.

Good News for Modern Man, the New Testament in Today's English Version (TEV). Published by American Bible Society, this translation has had an unexpected sales boom since its publication in 1966. Its author, Robert G. Bratcher, steers a healthy course between the inaccuracies of excessive paraphrase that have spoiled many recent translations and the obscurity of meaning in the more literal versions. This has the combined strengths of general accuracy with everyday language, conservative handling of the text, and general theological faithfulness to the intent of Scripture. Interesting line drawings on almost every page, outlines and cross-references of the general material, and a glossary of Bible terms at the back offer several added and helpful features.

The TEV, however, contains some weaknesses of various types. While interpretive paraphrase is at a minimum, the author unnecessarily biased the translation in a few places toward a particular interpretation of the text. In I Jn 5:6, "... he came with the water of his baptism and the blood of his death," Bratcher interpreted the words "water" as Christ's "baptism," and "blood" as His "death." The different "tongues" of I Cor 12 and 14, which may well be languages, are rendered as "strange sounds," which is not justified by the Gr. text and biases the interpretation toward ecstatic utterances.

Some criticism has been offered in the way the version translates certain passages referring to the "blood" of Christ by the "death" of Christ (cf. Eph 1:7; Col 1:20; Rom 3:25; 5:9; Acts 20:28; I Pet 1:19; Rev 1:6). While it would be easy to accuse the translator of theological motives in these cases, the fact that in numerous other places the word "blood" is retained (cf. Lk 22:20; Jn 6:53-56; I Cor 10:16; 11:27; Heb 9:22) seems to indicate he is not opposed to this concept but has been motivated out of concern for modern readers understanding that the "blood" was often used as a synonym for "death" in ancient days (cf. Mt 27:4, 25).

A. F. J. and L. Go.

Bibliography. Ward Allen, trans. and ed., *Translating for King James* (the notes of John Bois), Nashville: Vanderbilt Univ. Press, 1969. Dewey Beegle, *God's Word into English,* New York: Harper, 1960. F. F. Bruce, *The English Bible,* London: Oxford Univ. Press, 1961. Charles C. Butterworth, *The Literary Lineage of the King James Bible,* Philadelphia: Univ. of Pennsylvania Press, 1941. Herbert Dennett, *A Guide to Modern Versions of the New Testament,* Chicago: Moody, 1966. Stanley L. Greenslade, ed., *The Cambridge History of the Bible,* Cambridge: Cambridge Univ. Press, 1963 (a monumental work). Geddes MacGregor, *A Literary History of the Bible,* Nashville: Abingdon, 1968. Gustavus S. Paine, *The Learned Men,* New York: Crowell, 1959 (about those who produced the KJV). Alfred W. Pollard, *Records of the English Bible,* New York: Oxford, 1911. Hugh Pope, *English Versions of the Bible,* rev. and amplified by S. Bullough, St. Louis: Herder, 1952 (by a Roman Catholic scholar, with a full bibliography and extended lists of versions and translations). Ira Price, *The Ancestry of Our English Bible,* New York: Harper & Bros., 3rd rev. ed., 1956. H. Wheeler Robinson, ed., *The Bible in Its Ancient and English Versions,* London: Oxford Univ. Press, 1940, rev. ed., 1954. Philip Schaff, *A Companion to the Greek Testament and English Version,* 4th ed., New York: Harper & Bros., 1894. Luther A. Weigle, *The English New Testament from Tyndale to the Revised Standard Version,* New York: Abingdon-Cokesbury Press, 1949. B. F. Westcott, *A General View of the History of the English Bible,* 1868; 3rd ed. rev. by W. A. Wright, New York: Macmillan, 1927.

BIBLE INTERPRETATION. All communication must be properly interpreted by the hearer or reader. Witness Philip's question to the Ethiopian treasurer, "Do you understand what you are reading?" (Acts 8:30), indicating the need for interpretation.

The basic word hermeneutics (Gr. *hermēneia,* verb *hermēneuō*) means "to interpret," "to expound," "to explain," and further includes to translate from a foreign language into a familiar language (Jn 1:38, 42; 9:7). In the OT the English term occurs, e.g., in Prov 1:6 regarding the interpretation of a proverb.

Joseph was enabled to interpret (Heb. *pātar*) dreams in Egypt (Gen 40:12; 41:8-15), and Daniel was given the interpretation (Aram. *pᵉshar*) of several dreams (Dan 2; 4; 7:16) and the mysterious handwriting (Dan 5). The term *pesher* was used by the Qumran community for their interpretations of OT prophetical passages (*see* Dead Sea Scrolls).

In the NT the compound Gr. word *diërmēneuō* is used of Jesus expounding the OT prophecies regarding His suffering and glory (Lk 24:27) and of interpreting a message in an unknown tongue (I Cor 12:30; 14:5, 13, 27).

A distinction ought to be maintained between inspiration (*q.v.*) and interpretation. Inspiration relates to the nature of the Bible, its trustworthiness, because it is the word of God written (II Tim 3:16); interpretation relates to the meaning of the Bible. It is, therefore, quite possible for persons to agree on the former while having great difference of opinion regarding the latter. For example, two persons might agree that Gen 1 is a trustworthy record, yet disagree about the meaning of the word "day" in the passage.

During the early centuries of church history two basic schools of interpretation arose, one in Alexandria, Egypt, the other in Antioch, Syria. Only a summary of their principles can be included here, described by way of contrast. First, the Alexandrian school emphasized the allegorical approach (one thing stands for or teaches something else), while the Antiocheans insisted upon a more literal meaning, or the original sense of any passage.

Second, the Antiocheans laid more stress upon a study of any passage within its immediate and wider context, a practice not always followed by the Alexandrians.

Third, greater reliance upon the traditions of the church in interpreting Scriptures was found in Alexandria than in Antioch. For the latter, Scripture was its own interpreter.

Fourth, with regard to the inspiration of the Bible, the Alexandrian stressed the abnormal, or trancelike, state of the writer, while the Antiocheans emphasized his consciousness and the heightening of his perceptions by the work of the Holy Spirit. Thus the latter provided for a greater degree of individuality being preserved in the writing of Scripture.

The interpreter of the Bible is similar to a

workman with a task before him. He is an intelligent being, and he sees what needs to be done. What else is required? Two things: *spiritual insight* and *good tools*. The former is supplied by the ministry of the Holy Spirit in the life of the believer (Jn 14:26; I Cor 2:10-13; I Jn 2:27; cf. Eph 1:17); the latter we now discuss. Admittedly, some of these tools, or principles, will be more available to some than others.

1. Determine the meaning of the original language of any passage for the original readers. Ideally, this calls for a knowledge of Hebrew, Aramaic, and Greek. Practically, it means the interpreter needs to use the best translations of the Bible available to him. In this connection, he ought to learn something of the purpose for which the author wrote and the historical circumstances out of which the writing arose. The Scriptures are part of a larger historical and cultural context. In the OT, Israel was related, in one way or another, to the Egyptians, the Assyrians, the Babylonians, the Persians (to name a few); in the NT, the church emerged from a Jewish background and arose in the Greco-Roman world. The languages of the Bible reflect these various cultures; thus the interpreter must be knowledgeable of and sensitive to the use of words in their various settings.

For example, the word "save" (Gr. *sōzō*) was a common term of the 1st cen. world. The secular usage included saving from death, rescuing from physical danger, saving from disease or demon-possession, and preserving one's physical well-being (e.g., Mt 8:25; 14:30; Mk 3:4; 15:30-31; Jas 5:15). In addition to these, in the NT the word is used of saving from spiritual or eternal death (e.g., Lk 9:24; 19:10; Jn 3:17; 5:34; 10:9; Rom 5:9-10).

2. Interpret the words of any given verse or paragraph within its immediate context. The context is the ultimate determinant of word meanings. While the dictionary will provide various possibilities, the context will aid in narrowing the choice. For example, why translate the Gr. word *paraklētos* as "Comforter" in Jn 14:16 and as "Advocate" in I Jn 2:1? Or what is the difference between the word "law" in Rom 7:9 and in Rom 8:2? Furthermore, the context of the Bible as a whole must be included. The principle of "the analogy of Scripture" is a corrective to isolated interpretations and a guard against the danger of pet theories based upon limited data.

3. Discover the literary nature of the passage under study. Is it to be taken in the natural, normal sense of the language? Or is it figurative? Is it a narrative of events? Or is it discourse or didactic material, meant to teach a specific idea? This calls for some knowledge of customs within the culture involved, and of the idioms by which ideas are made clear.

Often there is no problem in deciding matters of this kind. For example, the parables of Jesus are regarded as illustrations of ideas, figurative language to clarify concepts. Idea: the kingdom of heaven. Illustration: a man who sowed good seed in his field (Mt 13:24-30). Not so simple is the meaning of the words "a great mountain burning with fire was cast into the sea" (Rev 8:8). Is it a description of a meteorite-like object falling into water? Or is it depicting the fall of some great ruler, rejected by God and cast down among men? Possibly more difficult yet is the interpretation of the phrase "a thousand years" (Rev 20:2-7). Does it mean an actual thousand years? Or a round number of years? Or a long period of time (regardless of specific length)? Or is it a symbol of completeness? The history of biblical interpretation shows that these questions are not always easily decided.

4. Interpret the Bible in terms of the principle of progressive revelation. Put simply, this means that God revealed things gradually, not all at one time. Partly, this was because of the stages in which the divine program was being fulfilled (cf. Heb 1:1-2); partly, because of man's state of unreadiness to receive and understand the message (cf. Jn 16:12).

On occasion, this principle involved adding to what had been given earlier. Jesus told His disciples, "I have yet many things to say unto you, but ye cannot bear them now" (Jn 16:12); the Holy Spirit would teach them when He came. In other instances, there was a fuller interpretation of previous teachings, e.g., "Ye have heard that it was said. . . but I say unto you" (Mt 5:21-22). Here our Lord explained the essential character of the commandments.

5. Interpret the language of the Bible regarding the natural world as that of appearance and popular rather than technical or scientific. Yet, at the same time, *popular* terminology is not synonymous with *errant* or *invalid*. The Bible does not theorize about nature; it simply states facts in a non-technical manner.

Illustrations of this form of language are found in expressions describing the sun rising (Eccl 1:5; Mt 5:45), or the earth having four corners (Isa 11:12), a form of speaking preserved in our speech until this day. Notice, too, the manner in which the various elements in the creation are described: a "firmament" (Gen 1:6-8); "grass," "herb," "fruit tree" (Gen 1:11); "living creature" and "fowl" (Gen 1:20). None of these are technical names. They are all common, popular terms, intelligible to the ordinary reader. Simply put, too, are observations of the water cycle of nature: the rivers flow from their sources into the sea; then by evaporation and condensation the waters return again to their sources (Eccl 1:7).

Another illustration of this same principle is found in the book of Ecclesiastes as a whole. The writer makes observations on various human experiences and natural conditions, then draws certain deductions therefrom. The book is essentially a commentary on life by nature, a continual round of activity, unsatisfying to the one caught in it. A final solution to the human dilemma occurs at the end of the book (12:13-14).

To return to the question of the identification and interpretation of various literary types, a knowledge of these is indispensable to the interpreter. A concise discussion has been written by J. Stafford Wright from which the following are adapted, with some added illustrations:

Literal fact. A statement of events as they occurred, to be interpreted in its simple sense (e.g., Jn 1:35-42).

Substantial or compressed fact. A statement compressing irrelevant details in the interest of a main impression (cf. Lk 24:44-53 with Acts 1:1-11, the latter indicating that there were 40 days between the resurrection and the ascension, a fact not given in the former passage).

Metaphor. A word or group of words indicating a resemblance between two ordinarily different things (e.g., Gen 2:7 which describes God's creative activity under the figure of a potter; cf. Rom 9:20-21).

Parable. A story based on an ordinary life situation, used to convey the meaning of an idea or concept. Commonly used in the teaching of Jesus, this literary device could drive home a point effectively. See the examples in Lk 10:30-35 (where one point is basic, answering the question, "Who is my neighbor?") and Mt 13:24-30, 36-43 (where Jesus explains both the one point and the many details).

The recent key works on this figure are by C. H. Dodd, *The Parables of the Kingdom* New York: Scribner's, 1936; J. Jeremias, *The Parables of Jesus* (trans. by S. H. Hooke), London: SCM Press, 1954; A. M. Hunter, *Interpreting the Parables,* Philadelphia: Westminster, 1960; and in a number of his other books on the Gospels. Among the older, standard books mention should be made of R. C. Trench, *Notes on the Parables of Our Lord,* 14th ed. rev., London: Macmillan, 1882; A. B. Bruce, *The Parabolic Teaching of Christ,* New York: A. C. Armstrong & Son, 1894; and G. Campbell Morgan, *The Parables and Metaphors of Our Lord,* New York: Revell, 1943. The last three tend to be more conservative in their attitude toward the Bible, while the first three have indicated many new insights into the problems related to interpreting the parables. *See* Parable; Parables of Jesus.

Symbol. An object or person which has no importance in itself but rather in what it portrays. Many of these are found in the visionary apocalyptic writings (e.g., Dan 7:2-3,17; Rev 1:12, 16, 20), as well as in the prophets' teaching techniques (e.g., Ezk 37:15-28). *See* Symbol(ism).

Type. An object or person having significance of its own, yet is used to represent something or someone else. While often abused by interpreters, the type holds a large place in Scripture. The original plan of the tabernacle (Acts 7:44; Heb 8:5), the first Adam (Rom 5:14), and the experiences of the Israelites in the wilderness (I Cor 10:6, 11) are all called types (Gr. *typos*) of something greater. Probably the NT use of certain OT figures is the proper starting point for interpretation of others. *See* Type.

Allegory. The use of a story, which may or not be factual, to depict a certain truth. Jotham's tale (sometimes called a "fable") in Jud 9:7-15 is one clear example; the story in the Song of Solomon may be another; while Paul's use of Hagar and Sarah (Gal 4:21-31) seems to be a third. *See* Allegory.

Myth. While the use of this word is always in an unfavorable sense in the NT (I Tim 1:4; 4:7; II Tim 4:4; Tit 1:14; II Pet 1:16), probably resulting from the apostles' response to Gnostic excesses, the term basically means an account, whether or not true in itself, used to teach a truth about human experience.

For the OT, much formerly regarded by liberal critics as mythical (e.g., the patriarchal narratives in Genesis) has been shown by archaeological investigation to be a part of early Semitic culture (the Nuzu tablets and the Mari documents are important evidence here). A valuable monograph on the historical and theological backgrounds is G. E. Wright's *The Old Testament Against Its Environment*; see also W. F. Albright, *The Biblical Period*; and W. Keller, *The Bible as History*.

For the NT, the arguments of Rudolf Bultmann for the mythical nature of much of the Gospel narratives has been countered by recent arguments for the historicity of early Christianity (e.g., F. V. Filson, J. W. Montgomery, W. Pannenberg, N. Stonehouse, M. C. Tenney). Within the NT itself, see I Cor 15:1-4; I Jn 1:1-4; II Pet 1:15-18. Luke wrote of the factual nature of the events of the life of Christ, even His ascension into heaven (Acts 1:1-11). *See* Myth(ology).

Saga. A psychological and interpretative reaction of some person involved in an important event. Examples of this figure would be the song of Deborah (Jud 5) or the song of Moses and the Israelites after crossing the Red Sea (Ex 15). Saga fills a relatively minor role in biblical literature. In modern critical theories it is often suggested as the source of various other OT and NT types of literature, thus casting doubt on their authenticity.

The interpreter of the Bible, therefore, needs genuine spiritual insight into that which he reads, and honest diligence in his pursuit of understanding. And what he understands ought to end in glory to God and to richness of life in Christ.

A final summary of the approach to study is as follows: (1) Read the text prayerfully, asking God for wisdom; (2) study the immediate and surrounding contexts; (3) give attention to other major related biblical passages; (4) investigate available theological, historical, archaeological, and psychological/sociological evidences which bear upon the problem involved; (5) choose the resulting interpretation which seems most in harmony with clear evidence (including the whole of Scripture); (6) be willing to await further light rather than make a bad choice at the moment.

Bibliography. E. C. Blackman, *Biblical Interpretation,* Philadelphia: Westminster, 1959. F. J. Denbeaux, *Understanding the Bible,* Philadelphia: Westminster, 1958. A. M. Derham, *A Christian's Guide to Bible Study,* New York: Revell, 1963. F. C. Grant, *How to Read the Bible,* New York: Collier, 1961. A. M. Hunter, "The Interpreter and the Parables," *New Testament Issues,* R. Batey, ed., London: SCM, 1970. A. B. Michelsen, *Interpreting the Bible,* Grand Rapids: Eerdmans, 1963. B. Ramm, *Protestant Biblical Interpretation,* Boston: Wilde, 1956. Milton S. Terry, *Biblical Hermeneutics,* Grand Rapids: Zondervan, n.d. J. D. Wood, *The Interpretation of the Bible,* London: Duckworth, 1958. J. Stafford Wright, *Interpreting the Bible,* London: Inter-Varsity, 1955.

W. M. D.

BIBLE MANUSCRIPTS

The Old Testament

The original MSS of the OT (*autographa*) are not available, but the Heb. text is amply represented by both pre- and post-Christian MSS.

I. *The Number of Hebrew Old Testament Manuscripts*

The first collection of Heb. MSS made by Benjamin Kennicott (A.D. 1776–80), published by Oxford, listed 615 MSS of the OT. Later Giovanni de Rossi (1784–88) published a list of 731 MSS. The main MS discoveries in modern times are those of the Cairo Geniza (*c.* 1890f.) and the Dead Sea Scrolls (DSS) (1947f.). In the Cairo synagogue attic storeroom alone were discovered some 200,000 MSS and fragments (Paul E. Kahle, *Cairo Geniza,* p. 13; Ernst Würthwein, *The Text of the Old Testament,* p. 25); some 10,000 of these are biblical (Moshe Goshen Gottstein, "Biblical Manuscripts in the United States," *Textus* [1962], p. 35). According to J. T. Milik, fragments of about 600 MSS are known from the DSS, not all biblical. Gottstein estimates that the total number of OT Heb. MS fragments throughout the world runs into the tens of thousands (Gottstein, *op. cit.,* p. 31).

II. *Major Collections of Old Testament Manuscripts*

Of the 200,000 Cairo Geniza MS fragments, some 100,000 are housed at Cambridge. The largest organized collection of Heb. OT MSS in the world is the Second Firkowitch Collection in Leningrad. It contains 1,582 items of the Bible and Masora (see V. Nature of OT MSS, 3) on parchment, 725 on paper, plus 1,200 additional Heb. MS fragments (the Antonin Collection, Würthwein, *op. cit.,* p. 23). The British Museum catalog lists 161 Heb. OT MSS. The Bodleian Library catalog lists 146 OT MSS, each one containing a large number of fragments (Kahle, *op. cit.,* p. 5). Gottstein (*op. cit.,* p. 30) estimates that in the United States alone there are tens of thousands of Semitic MS fragments, about 5 percent of which are biblical (500 plus MSS).

III. *Description of Major Old Testament Hebrew Manuscripts*

The most significant Heb. OT MSS date from between the 3rd cen. B.C. and the 14th cen. A.D. (For terms and names pertaining to the Masoretes see V. Nature of OT MSS, 3.)

1. Dead Sea Scrolls. The most remarkable MSS are those of the DSS (*q.v.*) which date from the 3rd cen. B.C. to the 1st cen. A.D. They include one complete OT book (Isaiah) and thousands of fragments which together represent every OT book except Esther.

2. Nash Papyrus. Besides these unusual finds, which are about a thousand years older than most of the earliest OT Heb. MSS, there is extant one damaged copy of the Shema (from Ex 20:2 f.; Deut 5:6 f. and 6:4 f.). It is dated between the 2nd cen. B.C. (William F. Albright, "A Biblical Fragment from the Maccabean Age: The Nash Papyrus," JBL, LVI [1937], 145–176), and the 1st cen. A.D. (Kahle).

3. Oriental 4445 (Or 4445). This British Museum MS is dated by Ginsburg between A.D. 820 and 850 (*Introduction,* pp. 249 f., 269 f.), the Masora notes being added a century later. But Kahle (*op. cit.,* p. 118) argues that both consonantal Heb. texts and pointing (the added vowel points or marks) are from the time of Moses ben Asher (10th cen.). Since the Heb. alphabet consists only of consonants, Heb. writing normally shows only these letters, with a few of the letters being used in varying degrees to represent some of the vocalic sounds. This MS contains Gen 39:20–Deut 1:33.

4. Codex Cairensis. A codex is a manuscript in book form with pages. According to a colophon or inscription at the end of the book, this Cairo Codex was written and vowel-pointed in A.D. 895 by Moses ben Asher in Tiberias in Palestine (Würthwein, *op. cit.,* p. 25). It contains the Former Prophets (Joshua, Judges, I and II Samuel, I and II Kings) and the Latter Prophets (Isaiah, Jeremiah, Ezekiel, and the Twelve). It is symbolized *C* in Kittel's *Biblia Hebraica* (BH).

5. Aleppo Codex of the whole OT. It was written by Shelomo ben Baya'a (Kenyon, *Our Bible and the Ancient Manuscripts,* p. 84), but according to a colophon it was pointed (i.e., the vowel marks were added) by Moses ben Asher *c.* A.D. 930. It is a model codex, and although it was not permitted to be copied for a long time and was even reported to have been destroyed (Würthwein, *op. cit.,* p. 25), it was smuggled from Syria to Israel. It has now been photographed and will be the basis of the new Heb. Bible to be published by the Hebrew University (Gottstein, *op. cit.,* p. 13). It is a sound authority for the Ben Asher text.

6. Codex Leningradensis (B 19 A). According to a colophon or note at the end, it was copied in Old Cairo by Samuel ben Jacob in A.D. 1008 from a MS (now lost) written by Aaron ben Moses ben Asher *c.* A.D. 1000 (Kahle, *op. cit.*, p. 110), whereas Ginsburg held it was copied from the Aleppo Codex (pp. 243 f.). It represents the oldest dated MS of the complete Heb. Bible that is known (Kahle, *op. cit.*, p. 132). Kittel adopted it as the basis for his BH from the 3rd ed. on, where it is re; e-sented under the symbol *L.*

7. Babylonian Codex of the Latter Prophets (MS Heb. B 3). This is sometimes called the Leningrad Codex of the Prophets (Kenyon, *op. cit.*, p. 85) or the [St.] Petersburg Codex (Würthwein, *op. cit.*, p. 26). It contains Isaiah, Jeremiah, Ezekiel, and the Twelve. It is dated A.D. 916, but its chief significance lies in the fact that through it, punctuation added by the Babylonian school of Masoretes was rediscovered. It is symbolized as V (ar)^{p} in BH.

8. Reuchlin Codex of the Prophets, dated A.D. 1105, now at Karlsruhe. Like the British Museum MS *Ad.* 21161 (*c.* A.D. 1150), it contains a recension of Ben Naphtali, a Tiberian Masorete. These have been of great value in establishing the fidelity of the Ben Asher text (Kenyon, *op. cit.*, p. 36).

9. Cairo Geniza MSS. Of the about 10,000 biblical MSS and fragments from the Geniza (storehouse for old MSS) of the Cairo synagogue now scattered throughout the world, Kahle identified over 120 examples copied by the Babylonian group of Masoretes. In the Firkowitch Collection are found 14 Heb. OT MSS dating between A.D. 929 and 1121. He contends also that the 1,200 MSS and fragments of the Antonin Collection come from the Cairo Geniza (Kahle, *op. cit.*, p. 7). Kahle provided a list of 70 of these MSS in the prolegomena to BH, 7th ed.

There are other Geniza MSS scattered over the world. Some of the better ones in the United States are in the Enelow Memorial Collection housed at the Jewish Theological Seminary, New York (cf. Gottstein, *op. cit.*, p. 44 f.).

10. Erfurt Codices (E 1, 2, 3) are listed in the University Library in Tübingen as MS Orient. 1210/11, 1212, 1213. Their peculiarity is that they represent more or less (more in E 3) the text and Masora of the Ben Naphtali tradition. E 1 is a 14th cen. MS containing the Heb. OT. E 2 is also of the Heb. OT, probably from the 13th cen. E 3 is the oldest, being dated by Kahle and others before A.D. 1100 (cf. Würthwein, *op. cit.*, p. 26).

11. Some lost codices. There are a number of significant but now lost codices whose peculiar readings are preserved and referred to in BH. Codex Severi (Sev.) is a medieval list of 32 variants of the Pentateuch (cf. CA to Gen 18:21; 24:7; Num 4:3), supposedly based on a MS brought to Rome in A.D. 70 which Emperor Severus (A.D. 222–235) later gave to a synagogue he had built. Codex Hillel (Hill.) was

Samaritan high priest and Samaritan Pentateuch. HFV

supposedly written *c.* A.D. 600 by Rabbi Hillel ben Moses ben Hillel. It is said to have been accurate and was used to revise other MSS. Readings from this MS are cited by medieval Masoretes and are used in the critical apparatus (CA) of BH in Gen 6:3; 19:6; Ex 25:19; Lev 26:9 (cf. Würthwein, *op. cit.*, p. 27). A critical apparatus lists the variant readings to the text which the editor considers are significant for translators or necessary for establishing the text.

12. Samaritan Pentateuch. The separation of the Samaritans from the Jews was an important event in the history of the post-Exilic period of the OT. It probably occurred during the 5th or 4th cen. B.C., and was the culmination of a long process. At the time of this schism one would suspect that the Samaritans took with them the Scriptures as they then existed, with the result that there came into being a second Heb. recension or revised text of the Pentateuch. This Samaritan Pentateuch (SP) is not a version in the strict sense of the word, but rather a MS portion of the Heb. text itself. It contains the five books of Moses, and is written in a Paleo-Heb. script quite similar to that found on the Moabite Stone, Siloam inscription, Lachish

letters, and in particular some of the older biblical MSS from Qumran. Because the Samaritan script is a derivative of the Paleo-Heb. script which was revived in the Maccabean era of nationalistic archaizing, and because of the full orthography of the SP, Frank M. Cross, Jr., believes that the SP branched off from the pre- or proto-Masoretic text in the 2nd cen. B.C. (*The Ancient Library of Qumran,* Garden City: Doubleday, 1958, pp. 127 f.).

The Samaritans were the descendants of those members of the ten northern tribes who were not deported by the Assyrian kings in their conquest of the kingdom of Israel. After the capital city of Samaria fell to Sargon II in 722 B.C., this ruler claims to have led away 27,290 of its inhabitants (ANET, pp. 284 f.). He brought in Gentile colonists from other parts of his empire, who eventually intermarried with the remaining Israelites. The Samaritan Sanballat (*q.v.*) opposed the relief measures of Nehemiah because Zerubbabel earlier had refused to let the Samaritans help rebuild the temple in Jerusalem. The rift between the Jews and the Samaritans widened, so apparent in the Gospels describing the time of Christ. Alexander the Great gave them permission to build their own temple on Mount Gerizim (later destroyed by John Hyrcanus in 128 B.C.), and they made their own recension of the Heb. books of Moses with modifications to provide scriptural authority for worshiping on that mountain. *See* Samaritans.

A form of the SP text seems to have been known to such early Church Fathers as Eusebius of Caesarea and Jerome. It did not become available to scholars in the West, however, until 1616 when Pietro della Valle discovered a MS of the SP in Damascus. A great wave of excitement arose among biblical scholars. The text was published in an early portion of the Paris Polyglot (1632) and later in the text of the London Polyglot (1657). It was quickly regarded as being superior to the MT; but it became relegated to relative obscurity after Wilhelm Gesenius in 1815 adjudged it to be practically worthless for textual criticism. In more recent times the value of the SP has been reasserted by A. Geiger, Paul E. Kahle, Frederic Kenyon, *et al.*

So far as is known, no MS of the SP is older than the 11th cen. A.D. Although the Samaritan community esteems one roll, which it claims was written by Abisha, the great-grandson of Moses, in the thirteenth year after the conquest of Canaan, their authority is so spurious that the claim may safely be dismissed. The oldest codex of the SP bears a note about its sale in A.D. 1149 – 50, but the MS itself is much older. One MS was copied in 1204, while another dated 1211 – 12 is now in the John Rylands Library at Manchester, and still another, dated *c.* 1232, is in the New York Public Library.

The standard printed edition of the SP is in five volumes by A. von Gall, *Der hebräische Pentateuch der Samaritaner* (1914–18). It provides an eclectic text based on 80 late medieval MSS and fragments. Although Gall's text is in Heb. characters, the Samaritans wrote in an alphabet quite different from the square Heb. Nevertheless, their script, like the Heb., descended from old Paleo-Heb. characters.

In all there are about 6,000 deviations of the SP from the MT, many of them being merely orthographic and trivial. In about 1,900 instances the Samaritan text agrees with the LXX against the MT. It must be argued, however, that some of the deviations from the MT are alterations introduced by the Samaritans in the interests of preserving their own cultus as well as the N Israelitic dialectal peculiarities, while the MT perpetuates any Judean dialectal features.

In the early Christian era the SP was translated into the Aram. dialect of the Samaritans, known as the Samaritan Targum. It was also translated into Gr., called the *Samaritikon,* from which about 50 citations are preserved in the notes on Origen's *Hexapla.* After the 11th cen. several translations of the SP were made into Arabic (cf. Paul E. Kahle, *The Cairo Geniza,* 2nd ed., pp. 51–57). [This section on the SP is by W.E.N.–Ed.]

IV. *Printed Hebrew Bibles*

(See Kenyon, *op. cit.,* pp. 86–88; Gottstein, *op. cit.,* pp. 8–10; Würthwein, *op. cit.,* pp. 27–30.)

1. Bologna ed. of the Psalms (A.D. 1477).
2. Soncino ed. of the complete OT with vowel pointing (A.D. 1488). There were also editions in Naples (1491–93) and Brescia (1494).
3. Complutensian Polyglot Bible by Cardinal Ximenes at Alcala, Spain (1514–17) in Heb., Gr., Aram. Targum, and Latin. A polyglot is a multiple-columned edition containing the original language and various other translations for means of comparison.
4. Antwerp Polyglot (1569–72).
5. Paris Polyglot (1629–45) ten vols.
6. London Polyglot (1654–57) six folio vols.
7. First Rabbinic Bible (1516–17). Produced by Felix Pratensis and published by Daniel Bomberg. It was a considerable critical achievement (in four vols.) and served as the basis of the Second Rabbinic Bible.
8. Second Rabbinic Bible (1524–25) by Jacob ben Chayyim and published by Daniel Bomberg in four vols. It was based on late MSS which provide the basis of the *textus receptus* (TR), a text presumed to be identical to that of the original MSS. Until 1929 it was found in Kittel's 1st and 2nd eds. of BH (where it is called Bombergiana or B).
9. J. H. Michaelis ed. (M[1]) (A.D. 1720). A Protestant pietist of Halle who followed in the main the text of Jablonski's 1699 ed. Its critical apparatus (CA) contains the most important readings of the Erfurt MSS.
10. Kennicott ed. (1776–1780) used 615 MSS (mostly late) and 52 printed eds. The text follows the ed. of van der Hooght (1705).

11. Meir Halevi Letteris (1852) two vol. Heb. Bible based to a marked extent on MS Erfurt 3, readings of which are found in Michaelis (1720). He may have used MS or folio 121 of Marburg (Gottstein, *op. cit.*, p. 8).

12. De Rossi (1784–88) produced not an ed. but a collection of variants from 1,475 MSS and eds. The collection is greater than Kennicott's but most variants are not substantial.

13. S. Baer (B) (1869–95) with the collaboration of Franz Delitzsch endeavored to produce a correct form of the Masoretic text using old MSS and eds., but their methods of "correcting" the text are questionable, according to Kahle and Würthwein. They followed the text of Wolf Heidenheim (1757–1832).

14. Ginsburg ed. (1894) used earlier and better MSS.

15. C. D. Ginsburg (G) produced for the British Foreign Bible Society (1926) a new ed. of Ginsburg's earlier work (1894) with variants of 70 MSS and 19 printed eds. (mostly 13th cen.) including Or 4445 which Ginsburg dated A.D. 820–50.

16. *Biblia Hebraica* (1929) 1st and 2nd eds. based on Bomberg (1524–25), containing variants from 10th and 11th cen. *Codicis Jemensis* (*V*[ar]J) edited by R. Hoerning (1889).

17. *Biblia Hebraica* (1939) 3rd ed. based on codex Leningradensis (L) or BI9A (from A.D. 1008) with the small Masora of Ben Asher in the margin.

18. *Biblia Hebraica* (1951) 7th ed. includes DSS Isaiah and Habakkuk variants for the first time.

V. *Nature of Old Testament Manuscripts*

Although the official text of the OT was transmitted with great care, it was inevitable that certain copyist errors would creep into the texts over the hundreds of years of transmission into thousands of MSS.

1. Types of MS errors. There are several kinds of copyist errors which produce textual variants (cf. Archer, SOTI, pp. 48–50): (*a*) Haplography is the writing of a word, letter, or syllable only once when it should have been written more than once. (*b*) Dittography is writing twice what should have been written only once. (*c*) Metathesis is reversing the proper position of letters or words. (*d*) Fusion is the combining of two separate words into one. (*e*) Fission is the dividing of a single word into two words. (*f*) Homophony is the substitution of one word for another which is pronounced like it (e.g., "two" for "to"). (*g*) Misreading of similarly shaped letters. (*h*) Homoeoteleuton is the omission of an intervening passage because the scribe's eye skipped from one line to a similar ending on another line further down the page. (*i*) Accidental omissions where no repetition is involved (as "Saul was . . . year(s) old," I Sam 13:1, RSV). (*j*) Misreading vowel letters for consonants.

2. Rules for textual criticism. Scholars have developed certain criteria for determining which reading is the correct or original one. Seven may be suggested (cf. Archer, *op. cit.*, pp. 51–53): (*a*) The older reading is to be preferred since it is closer to the original. (*b*) The more difficult reading is to be preferred because scribes were more apt to smooth out difficult readings. (*c*) The shorter reading is to be preferred because copyists were more apt to insert new material than omit part of the sacred text. (*d*) The reading which best explains the other variants is to be preferred. (*e*) The reading with the widest geographical support is to be preferred since such MSS or versions are less likely to have influenced each other. (*f*) The reading which is most like the author's usual style is to be preferred. (*g*) The reading which does not reflect a doctrinal bias is to be preferred. (Cf. Würthwein, *op. cit.*, pp. 80–81, for further textual principles.)

3. History of the OT text. The Sopherim (from Heb. meaning "scribes") were the Jewish scholars and custodians of the OT text between the 5th and the 3rd cen. B.C. whose responsibility it was to standardize and preserve the OT text. They were followed by the Zugoth ("pairs" of textual scholars) in the 2nd and 1st cen. B.C. The third group were Tannaim ("repeaters" or "teachers") who extended to A.D. 200. Their work can be found in the *Midrash* ("textual interpretation"), *Tosefta* ("addition"), and *Talmud* ("instruction") which latter is divided into *Mishnah* ("repetitions") and *Gemara* ("the matter to be learned"). The Talmud gradually was written between A.D. 100 and 500.

Between A.D. 500 and 950 the Masoretes added the vowel pointings and pronunciation marks to the consonantal Heb. text received from the Sopherim, on the basis of the *māsôrâ* ("tradition") which had been handed down to them. The Masoretes were scribes who codified and wrote down the oral criticisms and remarks on the Heb. text. There were two major schools or centers of Masoretic activity, each largely independent of the other, the Babylonian and the Palestinian. The most famous Masoretes were the Jewish scholars living in Tiberias in Galilee, Moses ben Asher (with his son Aaron) and Ben Naphtali, in the late 9th and 10th cen. A.D. The Ben Asher text is the standard text for the Heb. Bible today as best represented by Codex Leningradensis (B 19A) and the Aleppo Codex.

4. Families of OT texts. Despite the minor variations within the Masoretic Heb. text (MT), it represents one broad textual family, even if all the MSS cannot be traced to a single archetype (as Kahle has argued that they cannot be).

The other two basic families of similar variants are the LXX and the Samaritan Pentateuch (SP). Thanks to the discovery of the DSS there are now Heb. MS representatives of all three text types: (*a*) The Proto-Masoretic text type is represented by findings of MSS of Isaiah, Ezekiel, the Twelve, and most MSS of

One of the most important of the Dead Sea Scrolls is the complete manuscript of Isaiah (1QIs^{a}), dating prior to 100 B.C. Courtesy *Biblical Archaeologist*

the law from Cave IV of Qumran. (*b*) The Proto-Septuagint text type, which often varies in its use of numbers from the MT, is represented by MSS of Samuel (4Q Sam^{a,b}), Exodus (4Q Ex^{a}), and Jeremiah (4Q Jer^{a}) which is one-eighth shorter in the LXX. (*c*) The Proto-Samaritan text type is also represented by the DSS Paleo-Heb. MS of Exodus (4Q Ex^{b}) (cf. Patrick W. Skehan, "Exodus in the Samaritan Recension from Qumran," JBL, LXXIV [1955], 182-187), and one of Numbers (4Q Num^{b} in "square" script).

5. Quality of the OT text. What does a comparison of the OT textual variants among the three textual families reveal about the state of the OT text? The SP contains *c*. 6,000 variants from the MT, but most of these are a matter of orthography (spelling, etc.). Some 1,900 of the variants agree with the LXX (e.g., in the ages given for the patriarchs in Gen 5, 10). Some of the SP variants are sectarian, such as the command to build the temple on Mount Gerizim, not at Jerusalem (e.g., after Ex 20:17). It should be noted, however, that most MSS of SP are late (13th - 14th cen.) (see von Gall, *Der hebräische Pentateuch der Samaritaner,* 1914-18) and none is before the 10th cen. (Kenyon, *op. cit.,* p. 93). Many of the LXX variants from the MT are a matter of numbers, as "75 souls" (LXX) rather than "70 souls" (MT) in Ex 1:5. The LXX is now supported by fragments from the DSS (cf. Millar Burrows, *The Dead Sea Scrolls,* New York: Viking Press, 1955, and *More Light on the Dead Sea Scrolls,* New York: Viking Press, 1958, chaps. 13-14).

With the discovery of the DSS, scholars have Heb. MSS one thousand years earlier than the great MT MSS which enable them to check on the fidelity of the Heb. text. The result of comparative studies reveals that there is a word-for-word identity in more than 95 percent of the cases and the 5 percent variation consists mostly of slips of the pen and spelling (Archer, *op. cit.,* p. 19). To be specific, the Isaiah scroll (1Q Isa) from Qumran led the RSV translators to make only 13 changes over the MT, eight of which were known from ancient versions and few of which are significant (cf. Burrows, *The DSS,* p. 320). More specifically, of the 166 Heb. words in Isa 53 only 17 Heb. letters in 1Q Is^{b} differ from the MT. Ten letters are a matter of spelling, four are stylistic changes, and the other three comprise the word for "light" (add in v.11) which does not affect the meaning greatly (Laird Harris, "How Reliable Is the Old Testament Text?" *Can I Trust My Bible?* Chicago: Moody, 1963, p. 124). Furthermore this word is also found in that verse in the LXX and IQ Is^{a}.

We may conclude then with Kenyon that "the Christian can take the whole Bible [see NT below] in his hand and say without fear or hesitation that he holds in it the true word of God, handed down without essential loss from generation to generation throughout the centuries" (*op. cit.,* p. 55).

The New Testament

The original MSS of the NT are not available but, like the OT, they are represented by an abundance of MS copies.

I. *The Number of Greek New Testament Manuscripts*

In 1964 there were known to be 4,969 Gr. MSS of the NT: 76 papyri, 250 uncials, 2,646 minuscules, and 1,997 lectionary MSS (Metzger, *The Text of the New Testament,* pp. 31-33). But it must be remembered that this total increases yearly as new MSS come to light. About 95 percent of these date from the 8th through the 13th cen. (Greenlee, *Introduction to New Testament Textual Criticism,* p. 62). This would mean that there are *c*. 250 MSS from the 2nd through the 7th cen.

Compared to other books from the ancient world, the total ages and numbers of NT MSS are remarkable. Some ancient works survive on a single MS, e.g., Velleius Paterculus' compendious history of Rome, which was lost in the 17th cen. Even the first six books of the *Annals* of Tacitus are known through one MS dating from the 9th cen. Homer's *Iliad* survives by 647 MSS. Compared with almost 5,000 NT MSS the evidence for most other ancient works is meager. Of course most of these MSS are only portions of the NT; about 50 of them are of the complete NT. The least well attested book of the NT, Revelation, is preserved by about 300 Gr. MSS, only ten of which are uncials (Metzger, *op. cit.,* p. 34).

II. *Nature and Date of New Testament Greek Manuscripts*

Textual critics today classify the Gr. text of all NT MSS, according to the similarity of the slight variations in wording, into four main types or families—Alexandrian, Caesarean, Western, and Byzantine (Greenlee, *op. cit.,* pp. 117 f.). This classification relates to the characteristics of the Gr. text contained in the MSS. But when considered in terms of appearance and date, the NT MSS are divided into three major groups, all in codex form with pages—papyri, uncials, minuscules:

A. Papyrus MSS. MSS from the 2nd and 3rd cen., so named because written on material made from the pith of the papyrus reed. Of the 76 papyrus MSS of the NT, the following are the earliest and most significant.

1. P 52 John Ryland Fragment (A.D. 117–138). It contains Jn 18:31–33, 37–38 and is the oldest known fragment of the NT. Because of its early date and where it was found (Egypt) it tends to confirm that the Gospel of John was a 1st cen. composition.

2. P 66, 72, 75 Bodmer Papyri (*c.* A.D. 200). P 66 contains most of John (mixed Alex. and West. text types). P 72 is the earliest known copy of Jude, I Peter and II Peter (similar to Alex. type). P 75 contains the earliest copies of Luke and John (Alex. type like B).

3. P 45, 46, 47 Chester Beatty Papyri (*c.* A.D. 250) together contain most of the NT. P 45 consists of 30 leaves from the Gospels and Acts (mostly Alex. and West. text type). P 46 has 86 leaves of Paul's epistles (mostly Alex. text type). P 47 contains ten leaves of the book of Revelation (Alex. text type).

B. Uncial (Majuscule) MSS. MSS from the 4th to the 9th cen., so named because the Gr. letters were formed or printed as large, separate letters called "uncials."

1. B, Codex Vaticanus (A.D.325–350). This is the oldest extant uncial MS, on vellum. It contains both OT (LXX) and NT, except Genesis (1–46), some of Kings (10–13), Psalms (106 - 138), and Heb 9 through Revelation. Mk 16:9 - 20 and Jn 7:53 – 8:11 are intentionally omitted from the text. It is a good example of the Alex. text type.

The Bodmer Papyrus showing John 1:1–14. Bodmer Library

The John Rylands Fragment of John 18: 31–33. John Rylands Library

2. Aleph (χ), Codex Sinaiticus (A.D. 340). Because of its antiquity, accuracy, and completeness (all of the NT and half of the OT), it is one of the most important of all Gr. biblical MSS. It too leaves out Mk 16:9–20 and Jn 7:53 – 8:11. It is generally Alex. text type with strains of West. readings.

3. C, Codex Ephraemi Rescriptus (*c.* 345). Most of the OT is missing and II Thessalonians and II John of NT plus parts of other books. It is a palimpsest ("rubbed out") rescriptus ("rewritten"), i.e., the codex in which the Gr. text of Scripture was originally copied was much later erased by Ephraem, who wrote his sermons on the pages. By chemical reactivation Tischendorf was able to decipher the almost invisible original writing. The text type is a compound of all major types, but it agrees frequently with the Byzantine.

4. A, Codex Alexandrinus (*c.* A.D. 425). Originally this vellum MS contained the entire Gr. Bible plus I and II Clement and the Psalms of Solomon. The NT now lacks Mt 1:1 – 25:6; Jn 6:50 – 8:52; and I Cor 4:13 – 12:6. The text

is written in two columns to the page. It is, as its name might suggest, of the Alex. text type.

5. D, Codex Bezae (*c.* A.D. 450 or 550). This is the oldest known bilingual (Gr. and Latin) MS of the NT. It contains the Gospels, Acts, and III Jn 11 - 15 with many small omissions (Latin only). It is representative of the West. text type but has a remarkable variation from the usual NT text type.

6. D², Codex Claromontanus (*c.* A.D. 550). It is also bilingual and contains much of the NT missing in D, with distinctly West. readings.

7. E, Codex Basiliensis (8th cen.) is a MS of the four Gospels with a Byzantine text type.

8. E², Codex Laudianus (6th or 7th cen.) is the earliest MS with Acts 8:37. The text is mixed but mostly Byzantine.

9. H³ (or Hᵖ), Codex Coislinianus (6th cen.) is an important codex of Paul's epistles with an Alex. text type.

10. I, Codex Washingtonianus II (5th or 6th cen.) has portions of all Paul's epistles and Hebrews except Romans, with a good Alex. text resembling Aleph and A.

11. L, Codex Regius (8th cen.) is a badly written copy of a good text type, often like B. It contains two endings for Mark, a shorter one (see RSV footnote of Mk 16:8) and the longer one (vv. 9-20 of KJV).

12. P², Codex Porphyrianus (9th cen.) has all the NT but the Gospels (with some omissions). One of the few uncials containing the book of Revelation. The text type is mixed.

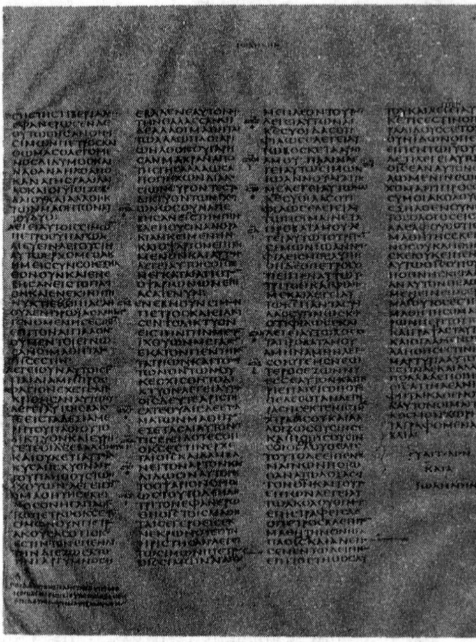

Codex Sinaiticus opened to John 21:1-25. BM

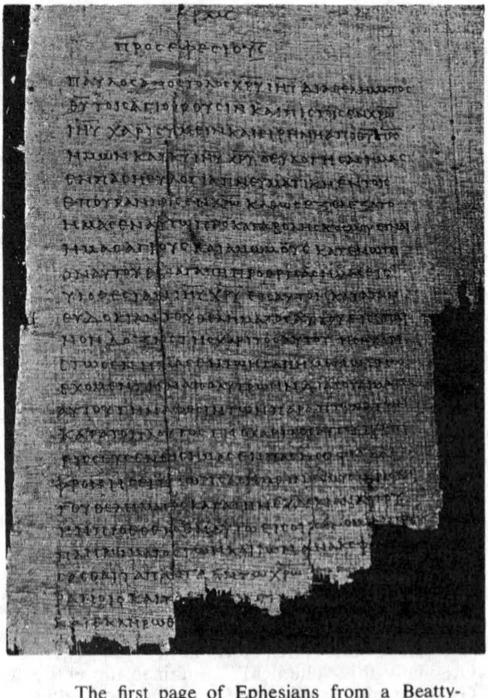

The first page of Ephesians from a Beatty-Michigan papyrus. University of Michigan Library

13. W, Codex Washingtonianus I (4th or 5th cen.). It contains the Gospels, portions of all Paul's epistles except Romans (with some omissions). Mark has a different insertion following the long ending (see Metzger, *op. cit.*, p. 54). The text is a mixture of types.

14. Theta (*θ*), Codex Koridethi (9th cen.) is a MS of the Gospels, mostly Byzantine except that Mark resembles the 3rd or 4th cen. text used by Origen and Eusebius, a Caesarean text type.

It should be noted that of the many uncial MSS of the NT the most important ones (Aleph, B, A, and C) were not available to the KJV translators prior to 1611. The only uncial available for the KJV was D and it was used only slightly.

C. Minuscule MSS. These NT MSS from the 9th to the 15th cen. are so named because the style of handwriting used was modified cursive (small letters which were sometimes connected and capable of being written rapidly) called "minuscule." Although the minuscule MSS are late, some of them have value as copies of good and earlier texts. Of these the following families may be mentioned.

1. The Alex. family represented by MS 33, "the Queen of the cursives," which contains

the whole NT except Revelation. It is mostly Alex. with traces of Byzantine text.

2. The Caesarean text type is represented by family 1 which includes MSS 1, 118, 131, and 209 (from 12th-14th cen.). Mark is similar to Theta (θ), a Caesarean text type.

3. An Italian subfamily of the Caesarean (11th - 15th cen.) is represented by family 13 including MSS 13, 69, 124, 230, 346, 543, 788, 826, 828, 983, 1689, and 1709 (the first four MSS were formerly thought to be Syrian text type). An interesting characteristic of family 13 MSS is that they contain the passage on the woman taken in adultery (Jn 7:53–8:11, KJV) after Lk 21:38.

Some other noteworthy MSS. MS 28 (11th cen.) is of the Gospels, having many noteworthy Caesarean readings in Mark. MS 61 (15th or 16th cen.) is of the whole NT and the first one containing 1 Jn 5:7, the single basis on which Erasmus reluctantly inserted this doubtful passage in his Gr. NT (A.D. 1516) and which eventually came into the KJV. MS 81 (A.D. 1044) of Acts is one of the most important minuscules, frequently agreeing with Alex. text type. MS 565 is very beautiful with gold letters on purple vellum. It has all four Gospels, closely akin to Theta (θ) in support of Caesarean text. MS 579 (13th cen.) of the Gospels is a good Alex. text of all but Matthew, often agreeing with Aleph, B, and L. MS 700 (11th or 12th cen.) has some 2,724 deviations from the received text, 270 of which are found in no other MSS (cf. Metzger, *op. cit.,* p. 64). MS 1739 (10th cen.) is an important copy of 4th cen. Alex. type with marginal notes from Origen, Eusebius, *et al.*

Space does not permit a listing and description of lectionaries, church service books containing selected Scripture readings usually from the Gospels and sometimes from Acts or the epistles. About 2,000 Gr. lectionaries are known, most of them dating from the 7th to the 12th cen.

III. *History and Editions of the Greek New Testament*

A. Period of composition (1st cen.). Most if not all the NT books were composed between A.D. 50 - 100. Some authors hold that Galatians and James were composed before this (see Merrill C. Tenney, *NT Survey,* Eerdmans, 1962, pp. 262 - 268).

B. Period of reduplication (2nd and 3rd cen.). During this period the books of the NT were usually copied rather carefully by professional scribes, but sometimes hastily and imperfectly, often because of persecution. For this reason there arose a multiplicity of early variants in the text. And even though the Christian scholars at Alexandria attempted an early criticism and editing of the Gr. text, the unnoticed textual errors which they inherited, plus the unintentional errors which they created by editing and revision, were transmitted in the MSS which they ordered to be written. Thus there came into being the basis of textual problems later scholars would have to face.

C. Period of standardization (4th-15th cen.). Beginning with Eusebius there was a new era of more careful and faithful copying of the NT text. But critical comparison and revision of the text were rare. Rather than criticism there was a process of standardization so that by the 8th cen. the older text types (Alex., Caesarean, West.) were standardized and replaced by the Byzantine. As a result, the mass of NT MSS produced between 8th and 15th cen. (95 percent of all NT MSS) are largely Byzantine in type.

D. Period of crystallization (16th and 17th cen.). With the invention of printing came some editorial revisions of the Gr. text, but basically it was a matter of crystallizing in printed form what was already abundant in MS forms (viz., the late Byzantine text). What previously had been standardized now became established.

1. The Complutensian Polyglot (A.D. 1514) of Cardinal Ximenes was the first to be printed, but it was not approved by the pope for publication until 1520. The MS basis has never been determined, though he claimed they were ancient MSS lent to him by the pope (cf. Metzger, *op. cit.,* p. 98).

2. The Erasmus Gr. NT (A.D. 1516) was the first to be published. In order to beat Cardinal Ximenes, Erasmus made a hurried ed. based on about a half dozen Gr. MSS (10th-12th cen.) only one of which was non-Byzantine (MS 1) but which he used least. In his 3rd ed. he included I Jn 5:7 (KJV) on the basis of MS 61. In his 4th and 5th eds. he omitted this verse and used better MSS, but the cheaper more popular 3rd ed. became the basis for the later "received text" or *textus receptus* (TR), the Gr. text presumed to underlie the KJV of 1611.

3. Robert Estienne (Latinized as Stephanus of Paris) issued four eds. of the Gr. NT (1546, 1549, 1550, 1551). The 3rd ed. was the first Gr. NT to have a critical apparatus (CA), using 14 codices including D and the Complutensian Polyglot. His 3rd ed. followed Erasmus' 4th and 5th eds. almost exactly. The text of Stephanus' 4th ed. (1551) is the same as in his 3rd ed., but for the first time the text was divided into numbered verses. It was the work of Stephanus that was considered the TR in Great Britain and America (Greenlee, *op. cit.,* pp. 70-71). The first English NT (Geneva, 1557) to incorporate both the modern chapter and verse divisions was based on his 4th ed.

4. Theodore Beza published four eds. of the Gr. NT (1565, 1582, 1588-89, 1598) plus five reprints. Despite the fact that Beza annotated his work with several Gr. MSS which he had collected, including D and D^2 as well as MSS collated by Henry Stephanus (son of Robert S.), the text he printed differed little from that of Stephanus (1551). Beza's NT succeeded in popularizing the TR, and the KJV translators made large use of his last two eds.

5. The Elzevir brothers (Bonaventure and

Abraham) published seven eds. of the Gr. NT between A.D. 1624 and 1678 (Greenlee, *op. cit.*, p. 71). Their purposes were more commercial than critical, and their 2nd ed. (1633) was so widely sold that it became the accepted Gr. text in continental Europe.

E. Period of criticism (18th to 20th cen.). With the Gr. NT widely available, scholarly interest in the best possible text increased and new MSS came to light. The goal has been to produce an edited critical text of the Gr. NT which, by critical comparison and evaluation of all the MS evidence, most closely would approximate what was in the autographs or original MSS.

1. Dr. John Fell issued a Gr. NT (1675) drawn from the Elzevir NT (1633) which claimed to use variants from 100 MSS and ancient versions including the Gothic and Bohairic versions for the first time.

2. John Mill published a Gr. NT in 1707 using the Stephanus text of 1550, but including a prolegomena and index using nearly 100 MSS and 32 printed eds. of the NT. Mill refers to 3,041 of the almost 8,000 verses of the NT, collecting some 30,000 variants.

3. Richard Bentley did not publish a NT but a prospectus (1720) for a work he never completed; this contained a specimen of Rev 22 which forsakes the TR more than 40 times.

4. Daniel Mace anonymously published *The New Testament in Greek and English* (1729), choosing from Mill's CA the variants that common sense told him were better than the TR; thus he often anticipated the readings of much later scholars.

5. Johann Albert Bengel published a Gr. NT (1734) which printed the text of the TR with preferred variants in the margin chosen on the textual principle that "the difficult is to be preferred to the easy reading." Bengel was also the first to classify MSS into two great groups: Asiatic and African.

6. Johann Jacob Wettstein published the TR (1751-52) with the preferred readings in the CA, arguing that "manuscripts must be evaluated by their weight not by their number." He was the first to designate uncials by capital Roman letters and minuscules by Arabic numbers—a system used to the present.

7. Johann Salomo Semler (1725-91) did not publish a Gr. NT, but he further developed Bengel's classification of MS families into three recensions: Alex., West., and Eastern.

8. William Bowyer, Jr., produced a critical ed. of the Gr. NT (1763) largely following Wettstein's judgment, bracketing familiar passages which lacked good textual support (as Mt 6:13; Jn 7:53–8:11; Acts 8:37; I Jn 5:7).

9. Johann Jacob Griesbach published three eds. of the Gr. NT (1774-1806), collated a large number of MSS, categorized the families as Alex., West., and Byzantine, and developed 15 canons of criticism of which the following is a sample: "The shorter reading . . . is to be preferred to the more verbose" (cf. Metzger, *op. cit.*, p. 120). Because of his influence, scholars began to abandon the TR.

10. Karl Lachmann published the first Gr. NT (1831) whose text rested wholly on critical principles. A second ed. followed (1842-50) in which he explained his principles and silenced some criticism.

11. Constantin von Tischendorf published eight eds. of the Gr. NT (1841-1872) plus 22 vols. of texts of NT MSS, the most important of which was Aleph, which he had discovered in the St. Catherine monastery at Mount Sinai. His 8th ed. of the Gr. NT (1869-72), based primarily on Aleph, differs in 3,572 places from his 7th ed. and it contains a comprehensive CA with all the variants known to his time.

12. Samuel P. Tregelles published his critical Gr. NT (1857-72) based on sound textual principles; he is responsible for leading England away from the TR.

13. In 1881-82 B. F. Westcott and F. J. A. Hort published *The New Testament in the Original Greek,* but it was used in advance by the translators of the ERV (1881). The work of Westcott and Hort (WH) was so extensive and prevailing that with it the TR was vanquished. On the basis of their study they formulated four families or similar groupings of MSS: Syrian (A and late minuscules), West. (D, D^2), Alex. (C, L), and Neutral (Aleph, B).

14. John W. Burgon (1813-88) and F. H. A. Scrivener led a futile battle against the WH text in favor of the TR.

15. Bernhard Weiss edited a Gr. NT (1894-1900), using intrinsic probability as a guide, concluding that B is the best and resulting in a text like WH.

16. Alexander Souter's Gr. NT (1910) reproduced that of Archdeacon Edwin Palmer, which lies behind the ERV (1881), but added a CA. In the 1947 ed. evidence of the Chester Beatty Papyri was added.

17. Von Soden's Gr. NT (1913) is based on principles different from WH and results in a text closer to the TR than any other modern critical text but generally confirms the WH text. He classes all MSS into K (Koine or Syrian), H (Hesychian of Egypt), and I (Jerusalem or Palestinian), all three recensions based on a lost archetype used by Origen and corrupted before him by Marcion and Tatian. Other scholars feel he gave too much value to K and that I is too heterogeneous (Metzger, *op. cit.*, pp. 142-143).

18. Present state of the NT text. Recently Canon Streeter has rejected WH "Neutral" and discovered a new family, the Caesarean, thus leading to a reclassifying of the families in order of preference: Alexandrian (including WH "Neutral"), Caesarean, Western, Byzantine (formerly "Syrian").

From 1898 until recently Erberhard Nestle's *Novum Testamentum Graece* has been the most widely used critical Gr. NT. It is based on a combination of WH, Tischendorf, and Weiss texts. It was slightly revised for the British and

Foreign Bible Society by G. D. Kilpatrick (1958). The United Bible Societies have published *The Greek New Testament* (1966), edited by Kurt Aland, Matthew Black, Bruce Metzger, and Allen Wikgren, which for the first time includes readings from 52 important lectionary MSS (9th–14th cen.).

IV. *Nature of New Testament Manuscripts*

1. John Mill had collected some 30,000 variants in NT MSS by A.D. 1707.

2. F. H. A. Scrivener counted nearly 150,000 variants by A.D. 1864. It is estimated that there are some 200,000 to date (Neil R. Lightfoot, *How We Got the Bible,* Grand Rapids: Baker, 1963, p. 53). On the surface this seems like an enormous number; but it is a very misleading figure, for the variants occur in only 10,000 different places in the NT (e.g., if one word is misspelled in 2,000 MSS it is counted as 2,000 variants). Furthermore, the vast number of variants do not affect the meaning of a passage (see Geisler and Nix, *General Introduction to the Bible,* pp. 360–367).

3. WH estimated that only one-eighth of all variants had any weight and only about one-sixteenth rise above "trivialities" and can be called "substantial variations." This would leave the text over 98 percent pure.

4. Ezra Abbot estimated that nineteen-twentieths (95 percent) of the variants were "various" rather than "rival" readings and nineteen-twentieths (95 percent) of the "rival" readings make little difference in the sense of the passage.

5. Philip Schaff calculated that of the 150,000 variants known in his day only 400 affected the sense, only 50 were of real significance, and not one of these affected any article of faith.

6. A. T. Robertson said that the real concern is about one-one thousandth of the text (i.e., the text is 99.9 percent pure of significant variants). When this is compared with Homer's *Iliad* where 5 percent of the text is in doubt, or the Mahabharata which has 10 percent corruption, it may be safely concluded that the Bible is the most accurately transmitted major work from the ancient world (cf. Metzger, *Chapters in the History of New Testament Textual Criticism,* pp. 144 f.).

Bibliography. Norman L. Geisler and William E. Nix, *A General Introduction to the Bible,* Chicago: Moody Press, 1968. Harold J. Greenlee, *Introduction to New Testament Textual Criticism,* Grand Rapids: Eerdmans, 1964. Paul E. Kahle, *Cairo Geniza,* 2nd ed., Oxford: Blackwell, 1959. Frederic Kenyon, *Our Bible and the Ancient Manuscripts,* 5th ed., rev. by A. W. Adams, New York: Harper, 1958. Bruce M. Metzger, *The Text of the New Testament,* New York: Oxford Univ. Press, 1964. Bleddyn J. Roberts, *The Old Testament Text and Versions,* Cardiff: Univ. of Wales Press, 1951. Bruce K. Waltke, "The Samaritan Pentateuch and the Text of the Old Testament," NPOT, pp. 212–239. Ernst Würthwein, *The Text of the Old Testament,* trans. by Peter R. Ackroyd, Oxford: Blackwell, 1957.

N. L. G.

BIBLIOMANCY. A form of divination by which the Bible is opened at random and the reader is guided by the first verse that meets the eye. The practice goes back to ancient times, when the Greeks and Romans in the same way consulted the works of Homer and Virgil. In the Middle Ages such things as the demands of duty and the discerning of the future were divined from the Bible. It is not to be doubted that instruction and comfort can come from chance readings of Scripture, but it is to be denied that God's Word should be so studied.

BICHRI (bĭk'rī). The father of Sheba, a Benjamite, who rebelled against David. Sheba is identified as the son of Bichri eight times in II Sam 20.

BIDKAR (bĭd'kär). A captain in the service of Jehu when he killed King Jehoram and earlier a fellow officer serving King Ahab (II Kgs 9:25).

BIER (bēr). Found only twice in KJV. King David followed the bier bearing the body of Abner (II Sam 3:31). Christ touched the bier of the only son of a widow in Nain (Lk 7:14). The word means "coffin" and refers to a simple open litter or flat wooden frame on which the dead body was borne from the house to the grave. *See* Burial.

BIGTHA (bĭg'thȧ). One of the seven eunuchs or chamberlains in charge of the harem of the Persian king Xerxes (Ahasuerus). He was commanded to bring Vashti to the king's banquet (Est 1:10–11).

BIGTHAN (bĭg'thăn), **BIGTHANA** (bĭg-thā'nȧ). One of two eunuchs or chamberlains of Xerxes (Ahasuerus) whose conspiracy against the king was known to Mordecai. Upon Mordecai's testimony through Queen Esther, the men were hanged (Est 2:21; 6:2). Bigthan was possibly identical with Bigtha (*q.v.*).

BIGVAI (bĭg'vī)

1. The head of a great family that returned in 536 B.C. with Zerubbabel to rebuild the temple (Ezr 2:2). The importance of the family can be judged by the fact that the "sons," probably including all retainers, are numbered 2,056 (Ezr 2:14). Two sons of Bigvai, Uthai and Zaccur, returned with Ezra in 458 B.C. in a company of 72 men (Ezr 8:14, RSV).

2. In Neh 10:16 there is a Bigvai listed with the princes of Israel who set their seal to the covenant made in 444 B.C. under Nehemiah. Unless he was very old this is unlikely to be the same as 1.

BILDAD (bĭl'dăd). Bildad, the Shuhite, was the second of Job's three friends (Job 2:11; 8:1;

18:1; 25:1; 42:9). The patronymic Shuhite has been taken to refer to Shuah, one of the sons of Abraham and Keturah (Gen 25:2). The Assyrian land of *Shûḫu* was S of Haran, near the middle Euphrates and may have been the land of Bildad.

Bildad attributes the sufferings of Job to his sins, as do the other friends. Bildad's argument is based upon the traditions of the wise and ancient words that had come down from past ages. His appeal to tradition is irrelevant to the situation and fails to convince Job. Although Bildad is solemn and gracious in manner, his second speech is a horrible description of the unrighteous man, as he assumes Job to be (Job 18).

BILEAM (bĭl'ē-ăm). A town of Manasseh W of Jordan assigned to the Levite family of Kohath (I Chr 6:70). *See* Ibleam.

BILGAH (bil'gȧ)

1. A descendant of Aaron, and in the time of David head of the 15th of the 24 divisions of the priests who officiated in the temple (I Chr 24:14).

2. A priest or priestly family who accompanied Zerubbabel on the return from Captivity (Neh 12:5, 18).

BILGAI (bĭl'gī). Found only in Neh 10:8. It is probably the same as Bilgah (*q.v.*), but named among those who sealed the covenant (Neh 10:1).

BILHAH (bĭl'hȧ)

1. A slave girl whom Laban gave to his daughter Rachel when she married Jacob (Gen 29:29), and whom Rachel gave to Jacob as a concubine (Gen 30:3-4). She became the mother of Dan and Naphtali by Jacob (Gen 30:5-8). After the death of Rachel she committed incest with Reuben (Gen 35:22).

2. Town in the territory of Simeon, S of Judah (I Chr 4:29), probably the same as Balah and Baalah (*q.v.*).

BILHAN (bĭl'hăn)

1. A Horite chief, son of Ezer, descendant of Seir (Gen 36:20, 27; I Chr 1:42).

2. A descendant of Benjamin, son of Jediael, father of seven sons who were heads of houses (I Chr 7:10).

BILL

1. Heb. *sēpher kerîtût,* "scroll," "document of cutting off"; LXX *biblion apostasion,* "a bill of divorcement" (cf. Deut 24:1, 3; Isa 50:1; Jer 3:8). According to the law of Moses, divorce transactions were to be formally certified by written documents. Archaeological discoveries have furnished modern students of the Bible with extensive evidence of these materials so that it is possible to study actual copies of such divorce contracts. Document 19 published in *Les Grottes de Murabba'at* (*Discoveries in the Judean Desert,* II, Oxford: Clarendon Press, 1961) tells of a certain "Mary and Joseph" who divorced each other. The document is prepared in duplicate, witnesses attested it, the woman was free to marry any other Jew. Each document was written twice, so that if the divorcing partner lost a copy of the bill, another original copy could be supplied! (See also V. A. Tcherikover and A. Fuks, *Corpus Papyrorum Judaicarum,* II, Cambridge, Mass.: Harvard Univ. Press, 1960, p. 10, No. 144 and the references there.) In the Hellenistic period, Jewish divorce contracts written outside Palestine used the legal forms customary in the same pagan contracts of time and place.

2. In the NT Gr. *biblion apostasion,* "a document of divorce" (Mk 10:4) follows the LXX expression. Jesus showed familiarity with the Mosaic provisions of divorce, but went beyond Moses as interpreted by certain rabbis of His day, in taking a position against the laxity with which divorce was granted.

Gr. *gramma,* "writing," "bond," "letter" (Lk 16:6). The papyri supply students with thousands of examples of receipts, I.O.U.'s, business contracts, accounts, etc. A. Deissmann raises the possibility that perhaps the "bill" of Lk 16:6 is to be explained by the practice of drawing up such a document in two copies, one "inner" (closed) and the other "outer" (open). He describes a receipt in which the outer text reads *30* drachmae, while the inner text reads *40* (Deiss LAE, p. 33, n. 3).

E. J. V.

BILSHAN (bĭl'shăn). One of 10 or 11 chief men or princes who returned to Jerusalem from Babylon with Zerubbabel (Ezr 2:2; Neh 7:7).

BIMHAL (bĭm'hăl). A son of Japhlet of the line of Asher, who was a son of Jacob (I Chr 7:33).

BINDING AND LOOSING. These words were common in rabbinical circles in both a legislative and a judicial sense. They were employed to mean: (1) to forbid or permit, (2) to condemn or acquit, and (3) to retain sins or to forgive.

Christ's conferral on Peter of the power to bind and loose (Mt 16:19) has been variously interpreted through the Christian centuries as referring to binding decisions concerning right and wrong, to the power to excommunicate or restore church members, and to the retention or forgiveness of sins. The Roman Catholic church insists that this power is legislative, judicial, and administrative, and that it was committed to Peter and his successors, the popes.

It should, however, be noted that the power was not only promised to Peter (Mt 16:19) but also to the other disciples (Mt 18:1, 18). Another significant factor is the tense of the verbs employed. The assertion that the earthly binding and loosing are accompanied by similar actions in heaven is expressed by the Gr. future perfect periphrastic construction, meaning that whatever is bound or loosed by the apostles shall have (already) been bound or loosed by God Himself. The apostles, therefore, are merely repeating or declaring what God has already done.

In view of the preceding context in Mt 16:19, it would appear that the power to bind and loose is related to that of the keys, which, in turn, were to be employed to open the doors for entrance into God's kingdom, misused by Jewish scribes (cf. Mt 23:13; Lk 11:52). Some, however, explain the passage eschatologically, as applying to the reign of the saints over the earth in the Millennium (A. J. McClain, *The Greatness of the Kingdom*, pp. 329 f.).

Parallelism with Jn 20:23 suggests that binding and loosing refer to forgiving or retaining sins, the factors which determine entrance into the kingdom. An instance of the exercise of such authority is afforded in Acts 10:43. Peter announced that acceptance of Christ and the gospel brings loosing from sin's penalty, and rejection leaves one bound for judgment. These terms may also include the power to excommunicate or reinstate (Mt 18:15-18), as well as the authority to prohibit or permit various actions such as those described in Acts 15:23-29 and I Cor 5. It should be clearly understood, however, that this latter power was given to the apostles, and there is no scriptural indication or example that it was to be transmitted to papal successors.

According to Mt 18:18 disciple-believers may bind the power of Satan and his demonic hosts or loose persons from his grip by declaring what Christ has already accomplished in destroying the works of the devil (cf. Heb 2:14-15; I Jn 3:8; Rev 12:11).

D. W. B.

BINEA (bĭn'ĭ-*ȧ*). A son of Moza, a descendant of King Saul through Jonathan (I Chr 8:37; 9:43).

BINNUI (bĭn'ū-ī). A name common at the time of Israel's return from Exile.

1. The father of a Levite named Noadiah (Ezr 8:33). The latter assisted in weighing the silver, gold, and vessels which Ezra brought from Babylon.

2. The son of Pahath-moab (Ezr 10:30). During the revival under Ezra, this lay Israelite agreed to put away his foreign wife (or wives).

3. The son of Bani who did the same (Ezr 10:38).

4. A Levite, the son of Henadad, who accompanied Zerubbabel to Jerusalem (Neh 12:1, 8). He helped repair the wall (Neh 3:24), and signed a covenant of loyalty to the Lord (Neh 10:9). He may also be the same as Bani (*q.v.*) who assisted in the great assemblies under the ministry of Ezra (Neh 8:7; 9:4-5).

5. The head of a large family who came to Jerusalem with Zerubbabel (Neh 7:15). He is to be identified with the Bani of Ezr 2:10, and probably with the Bani of Neh 10:14 or Bunni (Neh 10:15).

D. W. B.

BIRD. *See* Animals, III.

BIRSHA (bûr'sh*ȧ*). King of Gomorrah who joined in a league in an unsuccessful war against Chedorlaomer. The latter made Lot and his family captive (Gen 14:1-12).

BIRTHDAY. There are two biblical references to birthdays: (1) On Pharaoh's birthday he made a feast for his servants and granted amnesty to his chief butler whom he had previously imprisoned (Gen 40:20). (2) The birthday of Herod Antipas was celebrated with a banquet for his "courtiers and officers and the leading men of Galilee." Entertainment included the dancing of Salome, daughter of Herodias, who was rewarded with the head of John the Baptist on a platter (Mt 14:6; Mk 6:21-28, RSV).

The Gr. *genesia* originally was a celebration on the birthday of a deceased person (Arndt, *s.v.*), but came to have broader application, and in the papyri it was always a birthday feast (MM, *s.v.*). That it might also be a feast on the anniversary of the accession date of a ruler has never been demonstrated (cf. Edersheim, I. 672).

The birth of a son was an occasion for rejoicing (Ruth 4:14; Jn 16:21; Jos *Ant.* xii. 4.7), but Jeremiah, in great despondency, came to curse the day of his birth (Jer 20:14-15; cf. Job 3:3). According to Herodotus, the ancient Persians also celebrated a birthday with a feast (i.133). In Egypt such celebrations can be documented back to the 13th cen. B.C. apart from the biblical reference above.

R. V. R.

BIRTHRIGHT. *See* Firstborn.

BIRZAVITH (bûr-zā'vĭth)

1. Son of Malchiel, great-grandson of Asher (I Chr 7:31).

2. A town "fathered" or settled by Malchiel, a descendant of Asher. Because several Asherite clans seem to have settled in the hill country of Ephraim, it is possibly the present Khirbet Bir Zeit, four miles NW of Bethel (Beitin), where Judas Maccabeus pitched his last camp (Jos *Ant.* xii.11.1) (Aharoni, *The Land of the Bible*, p. 223).

BISHLAM (bĭsh'l*ȧ*m). A Persian official, possibly satrap, who complained to Artaxerxes against the Jews under Zerubbabel who were rebuilding the city (Ezr 4:7).

BISHOP. The word *episkopos* occurs five times in the NT: once of Christ (I Pet 2:25), and in four places of "bishops" or "overseers" in local churches (Acts 20:28; Phil 1:1; I Tim 3:2; Tit 1:7). The verb *episkopeō* occurs in Heb 12:15 ("watching") and (in some NT MSS) I Pet 5:2 ("exercising the oversight," ASV), while the noun *episkopē* in the sense of an "office of an overseer" appears in Acts 1:20 ("bishopric") and I Tim 3:1.

It is generally agreed that the term "bishop" in the NT is equivalent to "elder" (*presbyteros*), the latter occurring often in Acts as well as in I Tim 5:17, 19; Tit 1:5; Jas 5:14; I Pet 5:1, 5. *See* Elders. (The sense in II Jn 1 and III Jn 1 is not wholly clear, as is the case of the "four and twenty elders" in Revelation.)

Lightfoot (*Philippians*, pp. 96 f.) summarizes the NT evidences for the identity of the terms as follows: (1) In Phil 1:1, Paul salutes the "bishops and deacons," and it seems incredible that he would omit the second order (viz., elders) if it was distinct, as elders formed the staple of the ministry of a NT church; (2) in Acts 20:17, Paul summoned the "elders" of Ephesus to Miletus, yet addressed them as "bishops" (Acts 20:28, ASV); (3) Peter appealed to the "elders" to fulfill the office of bishops (I Pet 5:1-2); (4) Paul described the qualifications for the office of a "bishop" (I Tim 3:1-7) followed by a "deacon" (I Tim 3:8-13), yet in I Tim 5:17-19 he calls these ministers "elders"; (5) yet more plainly in Tit 1:5 the apostle speaks of "elders," then of a "bishop" (Tit 1:7).

Both the Gr. and Jewish backgrounds of "bishop" are illuminating, though not as conclusive NT usage. In its etymology, the word means an "overseer" or "one who watches." On the other hand, in usage it was varied. The one who "watched" or "protected" assumed an attitude of graciousness toward the one under his care. Further, the word came to denote an office of one kind or another, whether financial, administrative, or social, either secular or religious.

The Greeks thus described their gods: a being who gave particular attention to the one who worshiped him. And the god had a particular sphere of responsibility, protection, and judgment. When used of men, the idea of protective care is still essential to the activity of the individual. In Gr. life the word also designated an office. The *episkopos* could be an official of the state, an officer of a local society (as those who supervised the relief of the poor in a city), or those who supervised building projects and possibly controlled the money designated for the work.

Jewish usage was similar. In the LXX at Job 20:29, the Heb. word for "God" (*'ēl*) is rendered *episkopos* (*para tou episkopou*). Thus, the "Episkopos" is the One who judges the wicked, rendering to him his heritage. Men are so designated also, whether as officers (Num 31:14), overseers (or supervisors, II Chr 34:12,17) responsible for money for workmen, or, in a religious sense, as officers (or watchmen) in the temple (II Kgs 11:18). The Syrian king Antiochus IV appointed "inspectors" (or governors) over Israel (I Macc 1:51), men who were to enforce his policies.

Both the name and the office of "elder" are essentially Jewish (Lightfoot, *op. cit.*, p. 96; cf. Beyer, TDNT, II, 618). Particularly, the name is linked with the governing council of every Jewish synagogue, whether in Palestine or the Diaspora. Both in the OT (cf. Josh 20:4; Ruth 4:2; Ezr 10:14) and the NT (cf. Lk 7:3) the case is the same. And in the Jerusalem Sanhedrin "elders" formed a part of the group (cf. Mk 8:31; Lk 20:1; Acts 4:5). *See* Elder.

It seems hardly surprising, therefore, that these terms *episkopos* and *presbyteros* were employed for leaders in the NT church. They were terms at hand, and already connected with organizations current in Gr. and Jewish life. While certain changes were, of course, necessary in view of the nature of the Christian church and the prevailing circumstances, the familiar names were kept and used.

The NT usage of *episkopos* and *presbyteros* is important. That they both referred to the same individual in the NT has already been considered, but what was the function fulfilled by each? From an examination of Acts 20:17, 28 it would seem that the term "elder" designated the status of the men, i.e., they were the recognized leaders of the Ephesian church. On the other hand, "bishop" or "overseer" is used with particular reference to their ministry: to feed the church of God. In I Pet 2:25 the terms "shepherd" and "bishop" are linked together of Christ. Selwyn (*I Peter*, p. 182) regards the latter term as an interpretation of the former, rather than the introduction of a new idea, appealing to Acts 20:28 for support. Ezk 34:11-13 combines the same two terms, as does also I Pet 5:2.

In Phil 1:1, the term *episkopos* is joined with *diakonos* ("deacon"), the latter appearing here for the first time, but the function of neither is specified. It is only in the Pastoral Epistles that the description of this ministry is made clear (I Tim 3:1-7; 5:17 ff.; Tit 1:5-9). The following seems to characterize the teaching given there:

1. In I Tim 3:1, the word *episkopē* has reference to an office which a man may seek. Both in Acts 14:23 and Tit 1:5, the "elders" were appointed. The word used in Acts (*cheirotonēsantes*) occurs again in the NT only in II Cor 8:19 where one was "appointed by the churches" to travel with Paul. In Athenian life it referred to voting "by stretching out the hand." The term in Titus (*katastēsēs*) occurs also in Acts 6:3, where the apostles told the congregation to "look out" (*episkepsasthe*) from among them seven men whom they would "appoint" (*katastēsomen*), over the serving of tables.

2. The "bishop" in I Tim 3:1-7 must be a man possessed of high moral qualities (vv. 2-3), an apt teacher (v. 2), one in control of his own family (vv. 4-5), spiritually mature (v. 6), and held in high regard by unbelievers (v. 7). The necessary qualifications for "elders" in Tit 1:5-9 are similar. God's work calls for godly and gifted men.

3. In the NT, the number of these persons in

any particular place was plural. The use of the singular in I Tim 3:2 and Tit 1:7 refers to "the bishop as a type" rather than number. "There is no reference to monarchical episcopate" (Beyer, TDNT, II, 617).

In I Tim 5:17 ff., there may be indicated a bridge between the NT "presbyter" and the later development into the elevation of one above the others. Those elders who "rule well" were to be counted "worthy of double honor." That some would labor particularly "in the word and in teaching" seems to indicate already a division of responsibility. Does this possibly stand in contrast to the apostles' word in a much earlier day: "It is not fit that we should forsake the word of God, and serve tables" (Acts 6:2, ASV)?

The historical progression of the meaning of *episkopos* into "the episcopate" may be traced in the writings of the Church Fathers. It was not thus advanced in Clement of Rome (First Epistle to the Corinthians), but begins to appear in the *Didache*, in Ignatius (Epistles), where it is "your godly bishop and your presbyters"; then is well developed in Irenaeus (*Against Heresies*), and Cyprian (Epistles). Yet it is notable that even in the 2nd cen. and on into the Middle Ages, the 1st cen. equivalence of the terms was maintained (e.g., by Chrysostom, Jerome, Augustine, and others).

Bibliography. Hermann W. Beyer, "*Episkopos*, etc.," TDNT, II, 599–622. T. M. Lindsay, *The Church and the Ministry in the Early Centuries*, London: Hodder and Stoughton, 1910.

W. M. D.

BISHOPRIC (Gr. *episkopē*). The English word is found only in Acts 1:20 (KJV; "office" in RSV) and quoted by the apostle Peter from Ps 109:8. The reference is to Judas' position as an apostle. In I Tim 3:1 the same Gr. word is used of the office of bishop; in I Pet 2:12 the word is translated "visitation."

Bishopric in later times was the office of overseer or the district over which the bishop or elder was in charge. *See* Bishop; Elder.

BIT. A part of the bridle or halter inserted in the animal's mouth to which the reins were fastened to control the animal's movement (Ps 32:9; Jas 3:3). *See* Bridle.

BITHIAH (bĭ-thī'*á*). An Egyptian princess, a daughter of Pharaoh and wife of Mered of the tribe of Judah. The meaning of her name ("daughter of Yah[weh]") suggests that she became a believer in the Lord (I Chr 4:18).

BITHRON (bĭth'rŏn). Found only in II Sam 2:29. Bithron apparently is not a proper place name but designates the ravine or shortcut by which Abner and his men came up from the Jordan Valley to his capital at Mahanaim, S of the brook Jabbok. RSV translates the phrase, "the whole forenoon."

BITHYNIA (bĭ-thĭn'ĭ-*á*). A Roman province (after 74 B.C.) of NW Asia Minor situated near the Bosphorus and the Propontis (modern Sea of Marmara). It is mentioned only twice in the NT (Acts 16:7; I Pet 1:1). On his second missionary journey (*c*. A.D. 49–50) Paul was restrained from entering Bithynia by the "Spirit of Jesus" (RSV), and thus he proceeded on to Europe via Troas.

It is obvious that Christian work was started in Bithynia before A.D. 63 since I Peter is addressed to believers in this area by that time. It is possible that Christianity was planted in Bithynia long before Paul attempted to go there. Since Pontus was at that time connected with Bithynia (after 65–63 B.C.), Christianity could have been introduced there shortly after Pentecost (cf. Acts 2:9). At an early period Paul determined not to labor where other missionaries had already laid a foundation of believing Christians before him (Rom 15:20). In the NT period Bithynia was a senatorial province (after 27 B.C.) and its capital was at Nicomedeia. The propraetor Pliny the Younger was sent by Trajan to Bithynia as governor (*c*. A.D. 111–122). He reported (see Letter 96) that Christianity (which he calls a "superstition") was so strongly rooted in Bithynia at that time that it ". . . has spread not only in the cities, but in the villages and rural districts as well. . . ." The strength of the Christian movement then is also shown by the fact that prominent Roman citizens were included in the fellowship of Christians, and it is significant that many of the pagan temples in Bithynia were "almost deserted" according to Pliny.

Bibliography. J. Weiss, *Realencyclopädie für protest. Theol. und Kirche*, X, 553 ff. For a convenient source on Pliny and Trajan's reply, cf. Henry Bettenson, *Documents of the Christian Church*, London: Oxford Univ. Press, reprinted 1959, pp. 3–6. For convenient maps of Bithynia and Pontus in relation to other provinces see William M. Ramsay, *Historical Commentary on the Galatians*, London: Hodder and Stoughton, 1899, map facing p. 1. For coins see *B.M.C. Catalogue of Greek Coins: Pontus, Paphlagonia, Bithynia, Bosporus*, London: 1889.

E. J. V.

BITTER. In one form or another, the word is used 65 times, mostly in the OT. It may be of things concrete, as herbs (Ex 12:8; Num 9:11); or water, as at Marah, "bitter," i.e., brackish (Ex 15:23); or in the water trial for a woman's adultery (Num 5:16–28); of the stomach (Rev 10:9–10); and even of people (Hab 1:6).

The word may describe actions, whether with words (Ps 64:3), or weeping (e.g., Peter's, Mt 26:75 parallel to Lk 22:62), of cursing (Rom 3:14 from Ps 10:7), or crying out (Gen 27:34).

Again it may describe feeling of soul (Job 3:20), whether in resentment (Col 3:19; Heb 12:15) or total wickedness (Acts 8:23), or even evil destiny (Prov 5:4; Eccl 7:26).

BITTER HERBS. *See* Plants.

BITTERN. *See* Animals, III.3.

BITUMEN. *See* Minerals.

BIZJOTHJAH (bĭz-jōth'jȧ). A town in the S of Judah near Beer-sheba (Josh 15:28).

BIZTHA (bĭz'thȧ). One of seven eunuchs or chamberlains serving King Ahasuerus or Xerxes (Est 1:10).

BLACK. *See* Colors.

BLASPHEMY. The concept involved an intentional and defiant dishonoring of the nature, name, or work of God by word or action (II Kgs 19:3, 6, 22; cf. 18:22) Sometimes it was directed toward men or objects closely associated with God; e.g., Israel (Isa 52:5), the mountains of Israel (Ezk 35:12), the temple (I Macc 7:38). The idea was also expressed euphemistically by use of the root *bārak,* the usual term for "bless," the actual intent being obvious from the context (I Kgs 21:10, 13; Ps 10:3; Job 1:5, 11; 2:5, 9; cf. A. Murtonen, VT, IX [1959], 171).

Blasphemy is often stated as being against the name of the Lord (Lev 24:11, 16; Ps 74:10, 18; Isa 52:5). This terminology led the Jews to a superstitious regard for the name itself. Some of the Qumran MSS, e.g., although written in the later "square" script, have the divine name written in the older script, to avoid profaning it with the newer, common characters. Likewise, the Jews dared not pronounce it, so in reading they substituted "Adonai" for "Yahweh." As a reminder to the reader, they wrote the vowel signs of Adonai with the consonants of Yahweh, and in the LXX wrote *kurios,* the Gr. of Adonai, "Lord."

Blasphemy was a capital offense, execution among the Jews being traditionally by stoning (Lev 24:11-16; cf. Naboth's fate, notwithstanding the falsity of the charge, I Kgs 21:10, 13). In the case of Jesus, the charge of blasphemy was based on His having claimed divine prerogatives (Mt 9:3; 26:64-65; Mk 2:7; Jn 10:33, 36; 19:7), but since the capital punishment entailed was administered under Roman jurisdiction, execution was by crucifixion. Stephen was stoned for blasphemy (Acts 6:11; 7:56-58).

In the NT, following classical Gr. usage, *blasphēmeō* and its substantives are often related to men and an injury of reputation; i.e., "slander" (Rom 3:8; I Cor 4:13; 10:30; Tit 3:2; cf. Arndt, *s.v.*).

For blasphemy against the Holy Spirit, *see* Sin; Holy Spirit, Sin Against.

Bibliography. Hermann W. Beyer, *"Blasphēmeō,* etc.," TDNT, I, 621-625.

R. V. R.

BLASTING. This word refers to the effect upon grain or other plants caused by the hot E wind which blows upon Palestine from the Arabian Desert. The winds usually continue for two to three days at a time, and in the ripening time will cause severe damage. This blight is included among the divine curses upon a disobedient Israel (Deut 28:22-24; Amos 4:9; Hag 2:17). In Solomon's prayer (I Kgs 8:37; II Chr 6:28), blasting is included among the curses removed by a merciful God in response to the cry of His people. Occasionally the wind brought with it a cloud of locusts (II Chr 6:28).

BLASTUS (blăs'tŭs). Described in Acts 12:20 as "the king's chamberlain," he was appealed to by the populace of Tyre and Sidon in the face of the wrath of Herod Agrippa I. These cities were dependent upon the king for their food, even as they had been dependent upon Solomon in the days of Hiram (I Kgs 5:9-11; 9:11-13).

BLEMISH. The English word occurs often in KJV, mostly in Leviticus, Numbers and Ezekiel, representing three Heb. and two Gr. words. Of the Heb. words, *tāmîm* means "entire" or "complete," hence "without blemish." Heb. *m*ᵉ*'ûm, mûm* means "something stained," or "spot" or "blot." The third, *t*ᵉ*ballul* (used only in Lev 21:20) denotes a white spot in the eye causing obscure vision, probably a cataract (*see* Diseases). Blemish occurs only three times in the NT. Each time the Gr. word *mōmos* means "blot" or "flaw" (or, negatively, "without flaw").

To summarize: the sacrifices of the OT were to be "without blemish"; Christ was a sacrifice "without blemish" (I Pet 1:19); and the Church is to be one day "without blemish" (Eph 5:27).

BLESS, BLESSING. The act of one person blessing another can be considered under several headings.

1. God blessing man (Gen 1:28; 12:2; 22:17; 32:29; Ex 20:24; 23:25; Deut 1:11; 15:10; II Sam 6:11; Ps 28:9; 45:2; 107:38; Eph 1:3; Heb 6:14). God's blessing, since it is that of an omniscient, omnipotent, omnipresent God, is always fully effective, both in supplying man's needs in this life and eternal life in the world to come (Mt 6:33; Jn 10:27-30; Mt 25:34; Rev 22:14).

2. Man blessing God (Ps 63:4; 103:1-2; 104:1; 145:1-3) in which man recognizes and praises those great qualities which adhere to God's person, and expresses thanks and gratitude to Him and His name.

3. Men blessing each other in particular prayers, such as a father blessing his sons just before his expected death, which prayers were accompanied by a prophecy, as when Isaac blessed Jacob and Esau (Gen 27:26-40), when Jacob blessed his sons (Gen 49:1-27), when Moses blessed the children of Israel (Deut

33:1-29), and when Simeon blessed the holy family (Lk 2:34).

4. Priests in the OT blessing the Lord's people (Lev 9:22-23; Num 6:24-26; I Sam 2:20), and Christian leaders doing so in the NT (Col 1:9-14; Heb 13:20-21) in prayers and benedictions.

5. The blessing of food before it is eaten, as for example the cup at Jewish feasts, which was done by Christ as He instituted the new covenant in His blood (Mt 26:26-28). The church continued this custom in the Lord's Supper as indicated in I Cor 10:16: "The cup of blessing which we bless, is it not the communion of the blood of Christ?"

The description of the state of blessedness or happiness is often introduced by the distinctive words Heb. *'ash^{e}rê* (Ps 1:1; 2:12; 32:1-2; etc.) and Gr. *makarios* (Mt 5:3-11; 11:6; etc.), both of which denote one who is truly happy before the Lord.

Bibliography. Hermann W. Beyer, "*Eulogeō*, etc.," TDNT, II, 754-765.

R. A. K.

BLESSING, CUP OF. The apostle Paul in I Cor 10:16 states that participation in drinking the cup at the Lord's Supper brings a blessing, for in so doing we commemorate the Lord's death on the cross. *See* Lord's Supper.

BLESSINGS AND CURSINGS. *See* Covenant: Mosaic or Sinai Covenant.

BLIGHT. *See* Blasting (I Kgs 8:37; II Chr 6:28; Amos 4:9; Hag 2:17, RSV).

BLINDNESS. One of the many common physical ailments of biblical times. It was often inflicted upon prisoners of war by barbaric nations (Jud 16:21; II Kgs 25:7). On occasion it was a punishment of God for sin (Gen 19:11; Acts 13:11). The physically blind are frequently listed with the dumb (Mt 15:30) and the lame (Lk 14:21) who received healing from Jesus. It is not strange that the reign of the Messiah should be described by Isaiah as a time when "the eyes of the blind shall be opened" (Isa 35:5). *See* Diseases.

In a figurative sense the word is used of spiritual ignorance caused by unbelief (II Cor 4:4; Mt 15:14; 23:17), and of spiritual immaturity (II Pet 1:9). *See* Judicial Blindness.

BLOOD (Gr. *haima*). The red fluid circulating in the bodies of animals and men which signifies the "life" principle in the OT (Gen 9:4; Lev 17:11; Deut 12:23). Because "the life is in the blood" the OT forbade eating blood or bloody meat (Lev 3:17; Deut 12:16). Though all foods were made clean by Christ (Mk 7:18-19; Acts 10:13-15), this prohibition was applied to Gentile Christians in the apostolic decree of Acts 15 out of consideration for the consciences of their Jewish brethren (Acts 15:19-20).

Blood denotes the physical origin of human life (Jn 1:13; Acts 17:26). The expression "flesh and blood" speaks of man in his weakness, brief life, and limited knowledge (Mt 16:17; Gal 1:16; I Cor 15:44-50; Eph 6:12). It stands for human nature in Heb 2:14 where Christ shares fully our humanity, even to the giving of His life.

Shedding blood is violently taking the life of another, or murder (Acts 22:20; Rom 3:15). God condemns the shedding of the blood of the righteous and the innocent (Gen 9:6; Prov 6:17; Mt 23:35; 27:4; Rev 6:10). The term "blood" is sometimes used for the bloody death itself (Mt 23:30; 27:24; Lk 11:51). To have another man's blood on one's hands was to bear the guilt for the death of another (II Sam 1:16; I Kgs 2:37; Prov 28:17). Symbolically Pilate washed his hands to be free from the innocent blood of Jesus, while the mob shouted, "His blood be on us, and on our children" (Mt 27:24-25). Judas' betrayal of Jesus brought "a reward for a bloody deed" (Arndt, p. 22) and with this reward "the field of blood" was bought with blood money (Mt 27:6, 8).

Blood also played a significant role in the religious practices of the OT. It is worthwhile noting that blood was not a basic element of sacrifice and had no special function or meaning in the rituals of any of the other ancient Near Eastern or Mediterranean peoples (McCarthy, "The Symbolism of Blood and Sacrifice"). The sacrificial system of the law, based on the earlier animal sacrifices of the patriarchal period, called for the slaying of the victim on behalf of the sinner, and the sprinkling of its warm blood by the priest as proof of its death for atonement for sins (Lev 17:11-12). In the sacrifices death was required of the victim so that its life might be offered to God as the substitute for the repentant sinner. Sin was thus cleansed ("covered with blood") and guilt taken away (Heb 9:22).

This background forms the basis for the place of the blood of Christ in the NT. The shedding of His blood on the cross ended His earthly life, which He voluntarily gave to die in our place as the Lamb of God slain to redeem us (I Pet 1:18-20; Rev 5:6, 9, 12); and the sprinkling of that blood made atonement for the sins of all men (Rom 3:25). Following the pattern of the Jewish Day of Atonement (Lev 16), Christ is our atoning sacrifice (Heb 9:11-14; I Jn 2:2; Rev 1:5), and also our sin offering (I Pet 1:18-19; Rev 5:9). As Moses sealed the covenant between God and ancient Israel at Sinai with sprinkled blood (Ex 24:8; cf. Heb 9:19-21), so the new covenant of Jer 31:31-34 was sealed by Christ's blood (Heb 9:14-15; 10:14-19, 29; 13:20). In instituting the Lord's Supper, Jesus spoke of the cup as "the new covenant in my blood" (I Cor 11:25; Lk 22:20; cf. Mk 14:24).

Christ is also referred to as the great peace offering, reconciling Jew and Gentile (Eph 2:14-17) as well as all things through His blood (Rom 5:9-10; Col 1:20). The sinner is delivered from slavery to sin through the release (redemption) which Christ's blood has purchased (Eph 1:7; Col 1:14). Thus the Church is described as "purchased with his own blood" (Acts 20:28). By the blood of Christ Christians have been justified (Rom 5:9), loosed from sins (Rev 1:5), sanctified (Heb 13:12), and will be redeemed eternally (Rev 7:14 - 15). To "eat the flesh and drink the blood" of Christ is to receive all the gracious benefits which His death and life-giving blood can bring to the believer (Jn 6:53 - 56).

See Atonement; Sacrificial Offerings; Sacrifices.

Bibliography. Johannes Behm, "*Aima,* etc.," TDNT, I, 172-177. Dennis J. McCarthy, "*The Symbolism of Blood and Sacrifice,*" JBL, LXXXVIII (1969), 166-176. Leon Morris, *The Apostolic Preaching of the Cross,* Grand Rapids: Eerdmans, 1956, pp. 108-124 (Chap. III, "The Blood"); "Blood," BDT, pp. 99 f. A. M. Stibbs, *The Meaning of the Word 'Blood' in Scripture,* Monograph Series, London: Tyndale Press, 1947.

F. P.

BLOOD AND WATER. *See* Cross; Diseases: Sufferings and Death of Christ.

BLOOD, AVENGER OF. In the OT, if a man killed another, the man closest of kin to the dead was expected to kill the slayer and was called "the avenger of blood" (Heb. *gô'ēl haddām*).

This practice may perhaps be traced to Gen 9:5 f., where God lays down the rule for mankind after the Flood that he who sheds man's blood shall in turn have his blood shed by man. Antiquity finds this rule in force among many nations and tribes. In the course of time it is not surprising that this law of blood revenge came to include the accidental slayer along with the guilty murderer, and so the practice came to be the source of unwholesome feuding between individuals and tribes.

The need of curtailment of this practice was so strongly felt in Mosaic days that in the covenant law (Ex 20:22–23:33) a clear distinction was made between intentional murder and accidental slaying, and provisions were made for the safeguarding of the innocent (Ex 21:12-14).

This led to the establishment of cities of refuge (*q.v.*; Num 35:9-34; Josh 20:1-9), where the man who had accidentally slain another might take refuge from the avenger of blood and be safe until a fair trial had established either guilt or innocence. In the former case he would be handed over to the proper authorities, but in the second instance he could claim asylum in the city of refuge until the death of the incumbent high priest. Then the whole case was declared closed, evidently a legal custom comparable to the expiration of our statutory period of limitations.

Nothing directly messianic is involved in the term "avenger of blood."

Bibliography. Moshe Greenberg, "Avenger of Blood," IDB, I, 321.

H. C. L.

BLOOD, ISSUE OF. *See* Diseases.

BLOODY SWEAT. The expression comes from the statement in Lk 22:44, "his sweat was as it were great drops of blood." Only Luke, a physician (Col 4:14), tells of this unusual phenomenon in the agony of Christ in Gethsemane. Many insist that his statement was written in medical terminology (e.g., W. K. Hobart, *Medical Language of Luke,* p. 82) and that he was describing a physiological rarity–the emitting of blood through the transpiratory glands. Cases are on record of such phenomena caused by extreme grief or terror (cf. Henry Alford, *Greek Testament,* 7th ed., I, 648). It is further urged that the word "blood" would not have been used at all for mere comparison, for why should drops of sweat resemble blood any more than anything else? Luke could simply have said, "His sweat became great drops."

Others feel equally strongly that "Luke by the use of Gr. *hōsei* says plainly enough that he is using a simile, and is speaking neither of a change of the sweat into drops of blood nor of a mixture of sweat with blood" (Norval Geldenhuys, *Commentary on the Gospel of Luke,* p. 577). *See* Diseases: Sufferings and Death of Christ.

The exact nature of the visible signs of Jesus' agony may be irrelevant, because textual evidence suggests verses 43 and 44 may not have been in Luke's original manuscript.

J. McR.

BLOT. Two Heb. words and one Gr. word are used for "blot," "blotted," "blotteth," and "blotting." One Heb. word means basically "to rub" or "blot out." The other means a spot or blemish (*q.v.*). The Gr. word means to "erase" or "obliterate." Usually, the word is followed by "out."

Two things in particular are referred to in connection with being blotted out: names and sins. God threatens to blot out the name of Israel (Deut 9:14), and the name of the Israelite who breaks His covenant (Deut 29:20); but says He will not blot out of the book of life the name of the overcomer (Rev 3:5).

David prays for his own sins to be blotted out (Ps 51:1, 9); Jeremiah and Nehemiah for the sins of certain enemies not to be blotted out (Jer 18:23; Neh 4:5). Ps 109:14 is similar. The blotting out of sins has a very definite theological meaning, in the sense of forgiveness. God is the One who blots out Israel's sins for His own sake (Isa 43:25; 44:22), and Peter says sins will be blotted out upon repentance and conversion (Acts 3:19).

J. A. S.

BLUE. *See* Colors.

BOANERGES (bō'ă-nûr'jĕz; "sons of thunder"). A surname Jesus gave James and John, sons of Zebedee, when He ordained them apostles (Mk 3:17), referring to their fiery zeal (see Mk 9:38; Lk 9:54).

BOAR. *See* Animals, II.7.

BOAST. *See* Glory.

BOATS. The people of ancient Israel were not a seafaring people, a fact that is strikingly illustrated by the very scattered mention of ships or boats in Scripture. The Jordan River was not safely navigable and the Dead Sea had no value for fishermen or other voyagers. For ventures on the great seas the Israelites depended upon the Phoenicians and other nations to bring them goods from afar or transport them. Except for a "ferry" described in II Sam 19:18 to cross the Jordan, and the small lifeboat mentioned by Paul in Acts 27, the boats of Scripture, as distinguished from large ships (*q.v.*), almost entirely refer to the small fishing vessels that in Jesus' day swarmed on the Sea of Galilee.

These little boats were the tools of a great industry that in later times almost completely disappeared. William M. Thomson, in *The Land and the Book* (p. 401), which described 19th cen. A.D. Palestine, could find hardly a boat on Galilee where once they had been so numerous, because of the Arab's dislike for open water.

The fishing boats were small, scarcely larger than a good sized row boat. They carried one sail, but for the most part were propelled by rowing. They were large enough to carry Jesus and His disciples and even provided a place where Jesus might rest on the steerman's "cushion" (Mt 8:23 f.; Mk 4:38; Lk 8:22 f.; KJV misleadingly translates "ships"). Although these boats were very small, at times pirates used them on the Sea of Galilee to raid towns along the shore. Miniature naval battles were fought as the authorities sought to clear the waters of these pirates.

For the Christian these little boats will always have a special appeal. It was from them that Jesus preached, in them that He passed across the sea to His ministry. To such a boat He walked on the waves and from it He stilled the storm.

See Ships.

P. C. J.

BOAZ (bō'ăz)

1. A Bethlehemite of the tribe of Judah, great-grandfather of David (Ruth 2:4; I Chr 2:12). He was an honorable and wealthy landowner from Bethlehem (Ruth 2:1–3), a kinsman of Elimelech, Naomi's husband (1:1; 2:1). Ruth went to glean in the fields (cf. Deut 24:19) and happened to select the fields of Boaz (Ruth 2:3). Acting under Deut 25:5, the law of levirate marriage, Naomi instructed Ruth what to do in order to have Boaz perform the part of redeemer-kinsman (Ruth 3:1–11). However, a kinsman of nearer relation had first rights and obligations (3:12–13). When he had to decline the duty of near kinsman, Boaz announced he would do so and married Ruth (4:1–11). Their union was blessed by a son who was named Obed.

2. The left pillar of the two at the front of Solomon's temple (I Kgs 7:15–22). *See* Jachin.

BOCHERU (bō'kĕ-rōō). A son of Azel, a descendant of King Saul through Jonathan (I Chr 8:38).

BOCHIM (bō'kĭm). A place W of Jordan near Gilgal, probably so named (lit., "the weepers") because Israel wept there at the remonstrance of the angel of the Lord (Jud 2:1, 5).

BODY. In the KJV no less than 14 Heb. words are translated "body" in the OT. But most of these indicate a part of the body. Five of them literally mean "back." A common one, *beten,* means "belly" or "womb." Another refers to the "thigh." Still another describes the body as a "sheath." Another word means "bone" or "skeleton." Heb. *geshem* is most commonly translated "rain." But five times the identically appearing Aramaic word is rendered "body" in Dan 3–7. Another word means "carcass." Heb. *nephesh* is translated "body" four times, but its most common renderings are "soul" (428 times) and "life" (119 times). It means a living organism. The Hebrews did not have the concept of a physical body as we have it now. Nor did they seem to differentiate sharply between the body and the spirit, as we do. Perhaps *bāśār,* "flesh," comes the nearest to making this distinction.

A Roman merchantman of the first century.
Department of Classics, New York University

In the NT the common Gr. word for "body" is *sōma* (145 times). Here the difference between body and spirit is more evident. But *sōma* is used mostly in a figurative sense in the NT–for the whole man, for the body of sin, and for the Church.

Bibliography. E. Schweizer and F. Baumgärtel, "*Sōma*, etc.," TDNT, VII, 1024 - 1094.

R. E.

BODY OF CHRIST

1. A human body was prepared for the eternal Son of God that He might dwell among men (Heb 10:5). This He assumed in the incarnation (*q.v.*), when the Word became flesh (Jn 1:14; I Jn 4:2). To achieve our salvation it was essential that He take a real human body (Heb 2:14 - 16; 10:20); thus He is a perfect High Priest (Heb 2:17–3:1; 4:14–5:10) and a perfect substitute (Heb 9:12 - 14, 26 - 28; I Pet 2:24). The transformation of His own body in His resurrection is a prototype and guarantee of a similar resurrection body for each believer (Phil 3:21; I Cor 15).

2. The bread which was broken and appointed to be eaten at the Lord's Supper *(q.v.)*, over which Christ spoke the words, "This is my body" (Mt 26:26; etc.). The broken bread represented His body which was to be wounded and scourged for our healing (Isa 53:4-5; Mt 8:17; I Pet 2:24).

3. The beautiful figure of the human body with its component parts is used by Paul in I Cor 12 (cf. Rom 12:4-8; I Cor 10:17; Eph 1:22-23; 2:16; 4:15-16; 5:23; Col 1:18, 24; 2:19; 3:14-15; Heb 13:3) to describe the relationship and unity of all believers in the Church of Jesus Christ (cf. Gal 3:27). The Church is *metaphorically* the body of Christ in relation to His headship (Eph 1:22 f.). But the NT nowhere indicates that the Church is the continuation of the incarnation or is to be identified with Christ's incarnate body or is Christ Himself. All believers are indwelt by and baptized in the one Holy Spirit unto or with reference to this one body (I Cor 12:13). Each believer is given particular spiritual gifts with which to minister in the body (v. 11); each fulfills some very necessary function in regard to the other members of the body (vv. 14-31), which function is chosen by God according to His own wish and plan (vv. 11, 18). The full spiritual understanding of this figure to express the life and internal ministrations and order of the Church is the secret to a successful, efficiently operating church. *See* Church; Head of the Church; Spiritual Gifts.

Bibliography. Alan Cole, *The Body of Christ: A New Testament Image of the Church,* Philadelphia: Westminster, 1964.

R. A. K. and J. R.

BOHAN (bō'hăn). A descendant of Reuben after whom a stone was named which marked the NE boundary of Judah where it bordered on Benjamin (Josh 15:6; 18:17).

BOILS. *See* Diseases: Skin.

BOLDNESS. The concept of boldness is seldom expressed verbally in the OT. Prov 28:1 does state: "The righteous are bold as a lion," where the verb *baṭah* connotes their confidence based upon active trust in the Lord. In like manner courage in the OT is not thought of as an independent virtue but as an inner strength and determination inspired by God (Deut 31:7; Ps 27:14; 31:24).

In the NT, however, there are three different word roots that carry the idea of boldness. The verb *tolmaō* contains the element of daring, of action that rises above fear (Mk 12:34; 15:43; Acts 7:32; Rom 5:7; II Cor 11:21; Phil 1:14). The second, *tharrheō*, denotes confidence and hope in God (II Cor 5:6, 8; Heb 13:6), confidence in men (II Cor 7:16), and boldness in human relations (II Cor 10:1-2). It is the third word, *parrhēsia*, however, which strikingly characterizes the early Christians. It denotes speaking freely and boldly, and carries the old Athenian tradition of unhindered, democratic speech. The disciples followed the example of their Teacher, who spoke out openly (Jn 7:26) and plainly (Mk 8:32; Jn 11:14). The apostles on numerous occasions exercised great boldness of speech in the face of their opponents (Acts 4:13, 29; 9:27; 13:46; 14:3; 28:31). Such boldness is attributed to the filling of the Holy Spirit (Acts 4:31). Paul testifies of his own boldness to preach and teach the gospel to his converts (I Thess 2:2; II Cor 3:12; Phm 8). At times, however, he felt the need of prayer that he might continue to speak boldly for the Lord (Eph 6:19 f.).

This new outspoken courage marked Christian believers in every phase of their lives (Phil 1:20). Absolutely devoid of self-confidence, they were fully assured of the finished work of Christ in their behalf, of His continual power and presence with them, and of the mighty promises of God. Thus the Christian knows he can approach God directly with full confidence of an immediate audience (Heb 4:16; 10:19, 22). This provides strong assurance in prayer (I Jn 3:21 f.; 5:14 f.). Nor need the believer shrink from Christ at His second coming but he may have bold confidence before Him on the day of judgment if His love is perfected in him (I Jn 2:28; 4:17). It is by holding fast to his confidence in Christ (*parrhēsia,* Heb 3:6; Eph 3:12)–not throwing it away (Heb 10:35)–that the believer may enter the rest which God has provided for him by Jesus Christ, who has accomplished the necessary work of conquering the Christian's enemies (Heb 3:14; 4:3, 11).

Bibliography. Heinrich Schlier, "*Parrhēsia*, etc.," TDNT, V, 871 - 886.

J. R.

BOLSTER. In KJV the word is found only in I Sam 19:13, 16, where it designates the head of the bed where a "pillow of goat's hair" had been placed, and in I Sam 26:7, 11, 12, 16, where it indicates the place Saul's spear had been stuck in the ground at the side of his head.

BOLT. *See* Lock.

BOND. In the KJV, bond represents four Gr. and four Heb. words meaning "chain," "fetter," "slave," or, in a figurative sense, a moral or legal obligation.

In Acts 8:23, the "bond of iniquity" seems to mean the fetter that consists of unrighteousness. In Eph 4:3, "bond of peace" means the bond that consists of peace; that is, peace itself is the bond. In Col. 3:14, love is the bond which unites all the virtues in perfect unity. This word *syndesmos* also means "ligament" in an anatomical sense (Col 2:19, RSV).

In Col 2:14 (ASV and RSV) "bond" appears as the translation of *cheirographon* (KJV, "handwriting"). Here the figure refers to a written document. What was this bond? The just condemnation of the law against sin. Christ blots out, takes out of the way and nails to the cross, the cancelled bond. The reference to ordinances refers to the specific requirements of the law, or the specifications, in legal usage, of the general charge against us. When the law condemns, God and conscience bring to bear specifications of our transgressions. Paul became aware of the law when an awakened conscience specified transgression of the command, "Thou shalt not covet" (Rom 7).

W. B. W.

BONDAGE. *See* Service.

BONDMAID, BONDMAN, BONDSERVANT. *See* Service.

BONE. Four words are used for "bone" in the Bible.

1. The Heb. word *gerem* is used metaphorically of character or personality in Prov 17:22; 25:15.

2. Heb. *'eṣem* refers to bone or substance (Gen 2:23; Ex 13:19; II Sam 21:12); to the body or physical frame (Lam 4:8); to the substance of the sky, i.e., to "very" heaven (Ex 24:10, ASV); to the center of one's being or the seat of sensation (Job 20:11; Jer 20:9).

3. Heb. *qāneh* is used in Job 31:22 and translated "socket" in the RSV.

4. The Gr. word *osteon* is translated "bone" in Mt 23:27; Lk 24:39; Jn 19:36; and in some MSS of Eph 5:30 and Heb 11:22.

BONNET. *See* Dress: Dress of Priests.

BOOK. *Old Testament.* The Heb. word for "book" is usually *sēper,* which is probably a loan word from the Akkadian. It is suggested that in Akkad., the root signified a "task," then the document outlining the task, then the verb meaning "to send" a document. At all events, *sēper* means "book" or "letter." The derived verb signifies "count" or "relate." The participle *sōper* designates either a scribe or the officer who mustered troops.

The form of the book in OT times varied. The "letters" of II Kgs 20:12 were likely clay tablets as had been used in Mesopotamia since the invention of writing before 3200 B.C. In Palestine, the Hebrews usually used Egyptian papyrus, or possibly skins, for writing material. The Heb. alphabet was not adapted to writing on clay. The Heb. book, such as the Book of the Covenant (Ex 24:7), was doubtless a scroll such as is seen in Egyptian pictures. Such scrolls (*q.v.*) were well adapted for long literary pieces. Five scrolls would easily hold the five books of Moses. The later word for such a scroll is *m*ᵉ*gillâ* (Jer 36:28). The Dead Sea Scrolls (*q.v.*) now give us many examples of such rolls written on leather as early as 225 B.C. The whole book of Isaiah coming from 150 B.C. is in a fine state of preservation.

Shorter writings were sometimes folded up and tied or sealed. Examples of this format are found in the papyri of *c.* 500–400 B.C. from the Jewish colony of Elephantine in Egypt. *See* Elephantine Papyri.

Many books are mentioned in the OT, some known and some unknown. The book of the law of Moses is repeatedly mentioned. Joshua also wrote a section in the book of the law of God (Josh 24:26). Several of the prophets refer to their books. Daniel evidently had a collec-

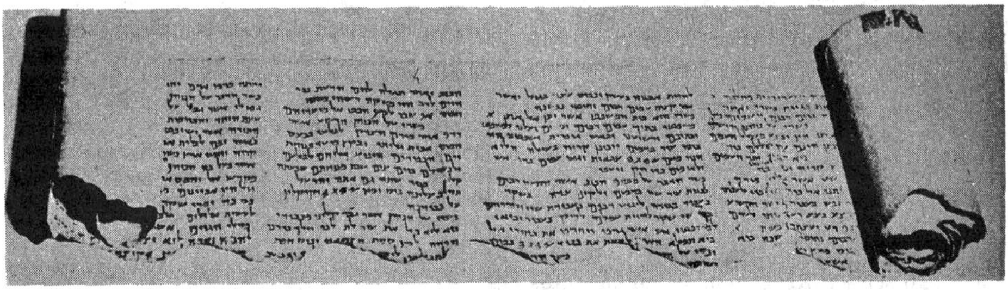

A Hebrew scroll book – the Habakkuk Commentary from the Dead Sea Scrolls. Y. Yadin and The Shrine of the Book.

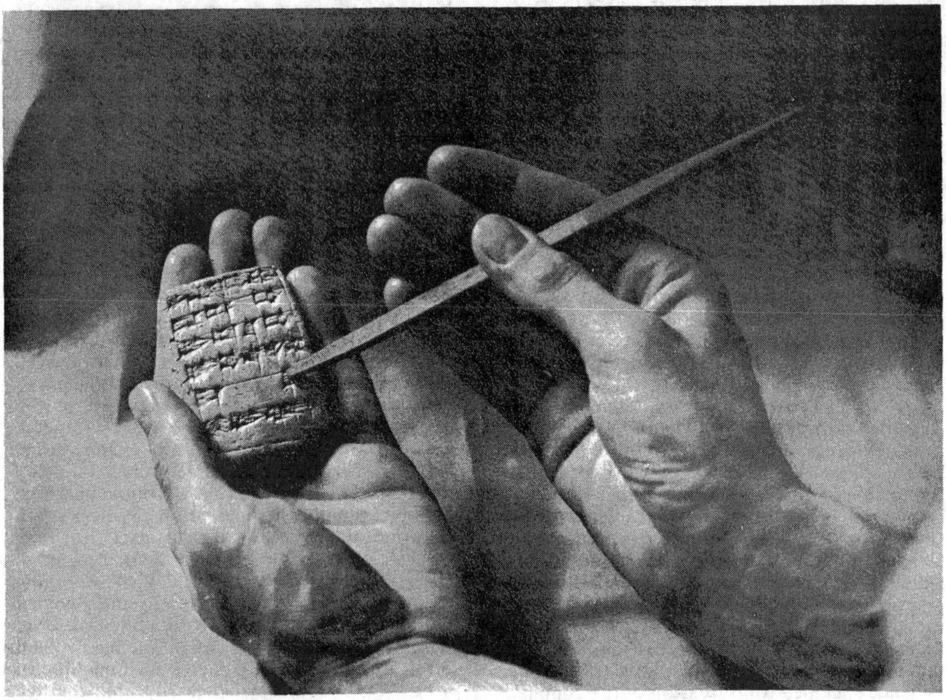

A Babylonian "book" written on a clay tablet. ORINST

tion of sacred books among which was Jeremiah (Dan 9:2; cf. BDB, p. 707).

Ancient kings kept court records in books (Est 6:1; Ezr 4:15). There were such chronicles of the kings of Israel and Judah (I Kgs 14:19, 29). Chronicles refers to the books of successive prophets as its sources (II Chr 9:29; 20:34; 32:32; etc.). Since we know its sources were Samuel-Kings, we may argue that these books were the very works of those prophets. An enigmatic reference is to the book Jasher (Josh 10:13; II Sam 1:18). Jasher means "the upright," and Israel was named Jeshurun (Deut 32:15; 33:26). Jasher just may have been an early chronicle of the history of the nation.

New Testament. The Gr. for "book" is *biblion* or *biblos* from which we get Bible, *the* Book. The Gr. word in turn seems to be derived from the name of the town Byblos, the Syrian port through which the Egyptian papyrus was imported into Palestine and Syria and transshiped to Greece.

The word "book" in the NT several times refers to OT writings, which were clearly scrolls (Lk 4:17). The shorter compositions of Paul and Peter are called "epistles." They would perhaps have been folded instead of rolled into scrolls. Revelation and John's Gospel are called "books" (Rev 22:18; Jn 20:30). Matthew's Gospel begins, "The book of the generation of Jesus Christ" which reminds us at once of Gen 5:1. Paul asks for his books in II Tim 4:13.

It is regularly supposed that the apostles wrote on scrolls except for the shorter letters. But the Rylands papyrus fragment of John's Gospel dating from *c.* A.D. 125 was written on pages like our books in the form called a codex. It is possible that some of the NT writings were originally in codex form. This would explain the very early collection of the Gospels into one unit of material and the Pauline epistles into another unit. The modern codex form of book probably helped in the spread of the NT as a unit, and, conversely, the wide use of the NT helped in the widespread adoption of the codex form of books. *See* Scroll; Writing.

R. L. H.

BOOK OF LIFE. *See* Life, Book of.

BOOK OF THE COVENANT. Moses read from "the book of the covenant" when reporting to the people the laws given to him by God on Mount Sinai (Ex 24:7). The expression probably refers to the collection of laws found in Ex 20:22–23:33.

BOOT. The word does not occur in KJV, but in the RSV the word is found in Isa 9:5, which is translated "battle" in KJV. The Heb. word involved, *s^e'ōn,* probably is derived from an Assyrian word meaning "shoe" or "sandal." *See* Sandal; Dress.

BOOTH. A hut made of wattled twigs or branches, common as temporary buildings for a person (Jon 4:5), for soldiers (II Sam 11:11; I Kgs 20:12), for harvesters (Lev 23:33 ff.). Job (27:18) used a watchman's booth as a symbol of impermanence. *See* Festivals: Feast of Tabernacles.

BOOTY. *See* Spoil.

BOOZ (bō'ŏz). The Gr. form of Boaz (Mt 1:5; Lk 3:32). *See* Boaz.

BORDER. In the OT the Heb. word is *g^{e}bûl,* meaning "border," "boundary line," "edge," "margin" (Num 34:6; Deut 3:16; Jud 11:18; Ezk 43:13). It can mean a bounded country or district included within borders (Gen 10:19). In the NT the Gr. word is *horion,* meaning "limit" or "border" and always in the plural (Mt 4:13; cf. 2:16; 8:34).

BORN AGAIN. To be born again is to experience the creative, life-giving work of the Holy Spirit. He regenerates (Jn 3:5) those who are dead in trespasses and sins, so that they are quickened or made alive spiritually (Eph 2:1, 5), and are changed from being the children of the devil (Jn 8:44; Eph 2:2–3) to becoming the children of God (Jn 1:12), His sons and daughters (Rom 8:16–17). When a person is born again he becomes a partaker of the divine nature of Christ (Gal 2:20; Eph 2:10; Col 1:27; I Pet 1:23; II Pet 1:4).

Interpretations of the expression "born of water and of the Spirit" (Jn 3:5) have been various. (For details see commentaries.) Both in John's Gospel (see 1:33; 7:37–39) and in the OT (see Ezk 36:25–27; Isa 44:3) the two elements are joined. In Nicodemus' own day, the ministry of John the Baptist, which emphasized both cleansing through repentance and the coming of the Spirit, would have been illustrative. The water was the sign; the work of cleansing by the Spirit was the thing signified. Both are important, and joined together they complement the ideas of repentance and faith (Acts 20:21) which bring salvation.

Need for the new birth. God warned Adam and Eve that the day they rebelled against Him by disobeying His command they would die (Gen 2:17). They died spiritually when they ate of the forbidden fruit (Rom 5:12), with the result that no matter how moral, upright, and law-abiding any of their descendants may be, each man in his heart is totally depraved and sinful. He has a fallen nature, being blind to sin and unable to save himself (Jn 3:6; Ps 51:5; I Cor 2:14; Rom 8:7–8), and needs cleansing from his sins and personal salvation (Ps 51:7; Mt 26:28; Jn 13:8; Tit 3:5; Heb 1:3; 10:14).

Christ explained to Nicodemus, who was a member of the Jewish Sanhedrin and a leading theologian of his day, that he must be born again (or "from above," as some translate *anōthen* in Jn 3:3, 7). For "that which is born of the flesh is flesh"—by our parents we experience a physical birth and enter into the world as human beings, and "that which is born of the Spirit is spirit"—by the Holy Spirit we receive spiritual birth and become children of God.

The tests of the new birth. One reason men have sometimes ignored the doctrine of the new birth is that they have overlooked the fact it is set forth not only in John 3 but also in I John. In John's epistle he goes into the matter of the new birth more fully, giving the marks or proofs whereby a man may know whether he has been born again. (1) Such a one does not practice sin (I Jn 3:9; 5:18). (2) He has true Christian love toward others (4:7, 20; cf. 3:14–15), particularly toward other Christians (5:1). (3) He loves God and keeps His commandments (5:2–3). (4) He overcomes the world, that is, lives a victorious Christian life (5:4–5). When these proofs are missing, either the person is only a nominal Christian and not really saved, or he is a Christian who is living a defeated, disobedient life. *See* New Birth; Regeneration.

Bibliography. F. Büchsel and K. H. Rengstorf, "*Gennaō,* etc.," TDNT, I, 665–675. Herman A. Hoyt, *The New Birth,* Findlay, Ohio: Dunham Pub. Co., 1961.

R. A. K. and W. M. D.

BORROW, BORROWING. In its usual sense in Scripture, borrowing means just what it does in our own times. The root meanings of the Heb. words "to be joined (to another)" (Deut 28:12; Ps 37:21; Neh 5:4) and "interweave" (Deut 15:6) suggest the close relationship that obtains between borrower and lender. We lend not only our goods but ourselves, and we not only borrow another's possessions but become a part of his life. For borrowing as a commercial transaction, *see* Bank; Loan.

Chief interest in the term comes as a result of the unfortunate KJV translation in Ex 3:22; 11:2; 12:35, where the word "ask" was translated "borrow." Modern versions have translated correctly according to the context. The word so translated in these verses is the usual Heb. word "to ask." In some cases, as here, it bears the implication "to demand."

The use of the word "borrow" has given rise to a serious ethical question. It is assumed that the Lord was commanding the Israelites to deceive their neighbors into thinking that they intended only to borrow their valuables for a few days, but then they departed forever from the land with these goods thus fraudulently obtained. Actually the Israelites were told to demand from their masters that which would represent the wages of the many years of slavery when they labored without pay. God said, "Ye shall not go out empty" (Ex 3:21). They were to "despoil" the Egyptians (Ex 3:22; 12:36) as surely as though they had been a great army, conquering and despoiling its foe. Thus God's victory over Egypt would be clearly marked. It is obvious, then, that in these passages there is no moral problem of a God who counsels fraud and deceit. Any attempts to justify Israel's "borrowing" have been unnecessary. In two other passages (Ex 22:14; II Kgs 4:3) the verb "ask" seems to be translated properly by "borrow."

P. C. J.

BOSCATH. *See* Bozkath.

BOSOM

1. Bosom refers to the human breast both literally and figuratively in Scripture. One holds a child or clasps a loved one to one's bosom (Num 11:12; Ruth 4:16; I Kgs 3:20). The bosom is also the place of affection and love, the inner self (Deut 13:6; Ps 89:50; Prov 6:27). It describes the place of special intimacy (Jn 1:18). The term "Abraham's bosom" *(q.v.)* refers to heaven, where the "Father of the faithful" receives His children to final peace and rest (Lk 16:22).

2. A use of the term "bosom" peculiar to the East is also found. The long flowing garments, bound at the waist by a girdle, provide a convenient carrying place, like a bag, in the fold of material over the breast. Thus the word often refers to this pocket where bread, grain, even lambs were carried (Ex 4:6-7; Prov 17:23; Isa 40:11).

BOSOR (bō'sôr). Gr. form of Beor, father of Balaam (II Pet 2:15). *See* Beor.

BOTCH. *See* Diseases: Skin.

BOTTLES. The most widely used bottles in the East, even today, are made of leather. Usually the skin of a kid or goat, though even a cow, camel, or buffalo, was used. The animal's head and feet were cut off, and it was then skinned. The hide was usually tanned and smoked, the openings were sewn up and sometimes sealed with pitch, and the "bottle" was ready for use. It was a highly portable vessel. Carried on the back, filled with water or milk, it was one of the most essential articles of any household. It was even used as a churn; when filled with milk it was shaken until it formed an oily butter.

By use the skins became stretched and dry and in time would split. This is the point of Jesus' parable of new wine in old wine skins (Mt 9:17). The new wine would ferment and expand; the old skin, having no stretch left, would split and lose the wine.

Earthenware bottles and jars were also used, but these were fragile and easily broken. For costly perfumes there were tiny flasks of glass, gold, or silver. *See* Cruse.

P. C. J.

A goatskin "bottle." JR

BOTTOMLESS PIT. The expression occurs only in Rev 9:1-2, where at the sound of the fifth angel the pit was opened by one possessing the key and beings came forth resembling locusts but having faces like men (Rev 9:7). Their physical make-up equipped them for their mission, "to hurt men five months" (Rev 9:10).

The word abyss *(abyssos)*, however, stands alone frequently, and in both Scripture and early religious literature indicates the opposite extreme of heaven (cf. Testament of Levi 3:9 where the plural is used of a third category or realm of things, along with the heavens and the earth, that are shaken by the presence of God. In I Clement 28:3 the plural is used in the same categorization in a quotation from Ps 139:7-8). Paul makes a similar categorization in Phil 2:10 and speaks of "things under the earth" *(katachthonios)*. This third realm called the abyss was also called Hades (Gr. in LXX of Ps 139:8) and considered to be the abode of the dead (Rom 10:7; Acts 2:31) and of demons (Lk 8:31). The devil himself is kept in the abyss according to John's revelation (Rev 20:3). Some feel that the word thus means "the depths of hell" (Arndt, p. 55), but this cannot be clearly established. *See* Abyss; Hades; Hell.

J. Mc.R.

BOW, BOWING. An act of obeisance. Many Heb. and Gr. words signify the act of bending one's knees and bowing down in humility before a superior. The custom symbolized (1) servitude (Gen 27:29); (2) homage, respect, or reverence, e.g., when Abraham bowed before the three angels (Gen 18:2), Lot before the two angels (Gen 19:1), Ruth before Boaz (Ruth 2:10), Bathsheba before David (I Kgs 1:16); (3) worship (Ex 20:5; Ps 72:9; Mic 6:6; Ps 99:9, "worship," lit., "bow down"); (4) mourning and sorrow (Ps 38:6; 44:25).

In many cases the suppliant bowed so completely that hands and face were on the ground, i.e., he prostrated himself (Gen 48:12; Num

22:31; I Kgs 1:31; Lk 24:5). The custom of bowing seven times, as Jacob did before Esau (Gen 33:3), is verified by the frequently used statement in the Amarna letters that the writers "fall seven times and seven times" at the feet of Pharaoh (ANET, pp. 483-490). The Roman soldiers showed their contempt for Christ by mockingly bowing before Him as the king of the Jews (Mt 27:29; Mk 15:19).

See Worship.

A. F. J.

BOW AND ARROW. Used as an instrument in hunting and warfare from very earliest days in biblical lands. In the Bible references, the bow (Heb. *qeshet)* dates back to the patriarchal period where it appears to have been used both as a weapon by the nomad (cf. Gen 21:20) and for hunting (Gen 27:3). Later references indicate it became part of the warriors' equipment (Isa 13:18). The Philistines seemed to excel in the art of archery which led David to require special training to be given to the Israelites (II Sam 1:18). Seen in the hand of the symbolical white-horseman of the apocalypse (Rev 6:2), it may indicate warfare and conquest or, as others interpret, a bloodless victory (no arrows).

The earliest bows were constructed of wood often plaited with leather or bark for added strength (Job 20:24; Ps 18:34, RSV). The Hyksos introduced the compound bow, which contained laminations of bone, horn or ivory to increase its elasticity and shooting power. Some bows were even laminated with bronze strips for the same purpose. Such bows were expensive and were carried usually by princes and leaders. For example, in the campaign of the Egyptian pharaoh Thutmose III at Megiddo (*c.* 1480 B.C.), only 502 bows were taken while over 900 chariots and 2,000 horses were captured (ANET, p. 237). Larger battle bows (Zech 9:10; 10:4) were strung by placing the foot on one end of the bow and bending down the upper end to notch the string. Apparently from this procedure archers were known as "bow treaders." Strings were made of ox gut.

Arrows were made of reed or light wood notched at one end for the string and tipped at the other with flint, bone, or bronze. Tips were often barbed or dipped in poison (Job 6:4).

Arrows are once associated in the Bible with the occult divination (Ezk 21:21) practiced by the Babylonians, and were used in magical or symbolic rites (II Kgs 13:15-19). The bow and/or arrow sometimes symbolizes divine judgment (Ps 7:13; 38:2; 64:7), violence (Ps 11:2; 57:4), or military might (Gen 49:24; I Sam 2:4; Hos 1:5). *See* Archers; Armor, Arms; Hunt; War, Warfare.

A. F. J.

BOW IN THE CLOUDS. The regular Heb. word *qeshet* for "bow" is used in Gen 9:13, 14, 16 for the rainbow, which symbolized God's covenant with mankind that He would never again

An Assyrian warrior, palace of Sargon II of Assyria at Khorsabad. LM

flood the earth with water as in the days of Noah. Whether this phenomenon appeared for the first time in nature at this point, as C. F. Keil concludes in commenting on Gen 9:8-17 (KD, *Pentateuch,* I, 154), or gained a new significance as a "sign" to the inhabitants of the earth, is not clear.

Both Ezekiel (1:28) and John (Rev 4:3; 10:1) see the rainbow associated with the throne of God's judgment, probably signifying the grace and mercy of God in the midst of judgment.

BOWELS. The KJV rendering of several Heb. words and the consistent rendering of the Gr. *splagchna.* In addition to its literal meaning (II Sam 20:10; Acts 1:18), the word is also used to refer to the reproductive capacity of man (II Sam 7:12; Isa 48:19), and the center of his emotions (Song 5:4), equivalent to the heart in Western literature. The ASV renders the Gr. *splagchna* in various ways to indicate emotion: (1) tender mercy (Lk 1:78; Phil 1:8; 2:1); (2) affections (II Cor 6:12; 7:15); (3) heart of compassion (Col 3:12); (4) heart (Phm 7, 12, 20); and (5) compassion (I Jn 3:17).

The bowels were probably felt to be the center of emotion because of the reaction of the stomach to excitement. Though "heart" is a more poetic word than "bowels," it is no more accurately used, because emotion originates in the mind.

BOWL. A shallow, hollow-shaped vessel, such as a basin or cup. *See* Dish. The word bowl is used to translate a variety of Heb. words. Bowls were made of earthenware, metal, or wood. *See* Pottery.

Gideon wrung water from fleece into a bowl (Jud 6:38). Bowls like cups in the shape of almonds decorated the lampstand in the tabernacle (Ex 37:17-20). Larger gold and silver bowls were used for the ritual service in the temple (I Chr 28:17). Dissolute revelers in Israel would drink wine from costly bowls (Amos 6:6). "Bowl" is used instead of "vial" in the revised versions of Revelation (e.g., Rev 16:1 ff.).

BOWMAN. *See* Armor; Bow and Arrow.

BOWSHOT. A way of indicating the distance (only in Gen 21:16) between an archer and his target, about 50 yards.

BOX. A small case, cruet, or flask with cover for keeping oil or ointment, such as Elisha used in anointing Jehu (II Kgs 9:1, 3); alabaster jar *(alabastron)* of the NT (Mt 26:7; Mk 14:3; Lk 7:37).

BOX TREE. *See* Plants.

BOY. Two Heb. words are used: *yeled,* "one born" (Joel 3:3; Zech 8:5), and *na'ar,* "youth" (Gen 25:27), used of young Esau and Jacob. The latter word covers the age range from an infant (I Sam 4:21) to a warrior such as Absalom (II Sam 18:5, 12), with a stress on youthfulness.

BOZEZ (bō'zĕz). Name of the northern of two cliffs which stand on each side of the valley of Michmash (I Sam 14:4). *See* Geba; Michmash.

BOZKATH (bŏz'kăth). A town in the lowlands of Judah between Lachish and Eglon (Josh 15:39), the birthplace of the mother of King Josiah (II Kgs 22:1).

BOZRAH (bŏz'rȧ)

1. A very ancient city, a capital of Edom, about 18 miles SE of the Dead Sea (Gen 36:33; I Chr 1:44; Isa 34:6; 63:1; Jer 49:13, 22; Amos 1:12), identified with the village of Buseirah on a virtually impregnable spur of a ridge, guarded on three sides by deep wadis.

2. Mentioned in Jer 48:24 as a city of Moab, possibly the Reubenite city of refuge known as Bezer *(q.v.)*.

BRACELET. Used to translate five Heb. words which describe an ornament worn by both men and women. King Saul wore a bracelet on his arm (II Sam 1:10) and the Israelites gave bracelets as an offering to the Lord (Ex 35:22). Bracelets were used as a sign of wealth (Gen 24:22). Isaiah prophesied the removal of such finery as a future punishment by the Lord for the proudness of women (Isa 3:19).

Bracelets were made of bronze, iron, glass, ivory, silver, and gold and are found in many shapes and designs, some inlaid with many precious stones. They are found in abundance throughout the lands of biblical times.

See Dress; Jewels, Jewelry.

BRAMBLE. *See* Plants.

BRANCH. This term translates 18 Heb. and four Gr. words. These include six distinct connotations:

1. The natural meaning is evident when it is said, "the fowls of the heaven . . . sing among the branches" (Ps 104:12), or that the fig tree's budding branches are a sign of approaching summer (Mt 24:32). *See* Plants.

2. The three arms on each side of the central shaft of the golden candlestick or lampstand are termed branches (Ex 25:31-36; 37:17-22).

3. The making of booths of tree branches under which to dwell during the Feast of Tabernacles gives a ceremonial connotation (Lev 23:40 ff.; Neh 8:14 f.).

4. Branches may be part of a figure representing some important person, as Job (Job 29:19); the chief butler (Gen 40:9 f.); Joseph (Gen 49:22); Nebuchadnezzar (Dan 4:12, RSV).

5. "Branch" depicts God's blessings on faithful Israel, as well as His chastisement for their disobedience. Israel under chastisement: "The Lord will cut off from Israel . . . branch and rush in one day" (Isa 9:14); Israel the "green olive tree . . . the branches of it are broken" (Jer 11:16); and many others. Like judgment is visited on heathen nations and rulers because of their sins: Moab (Isa 16:6-8); Egypt (Ezk 31:2-14); Nebuchadnezzar (Dan 4:13-14). Paul also uses the metaphor of natural branches broken off the olive tree to describe the result of Israel rejecting Jesus (Rom 11:19-21). Jesus employs a similar figure to warn fruitless disciples (Jn 15:6). Israel under blessing: "But you, O mountains of Israel, shall shoot forth your branches, and yield your fruit to my people Israel; for they will soon come home" (Ezk 36:8, RSV; also Ezk 19:10 f.; Ps 80:8-11).

6. The culmination of all OT branch symbolism is found in those foregleams of the coming Messiah (Heb. *ṣemaḥ,* "sprout," Isa 4:2; Jer 23:5; 33:15; Zech 3:8; 6:12; Heb. *neṣer,* "green shoot," Isa 11:1 f.). Isa 4:2 ("In that day shall the branch of the Lord be beautiful and glorious") does not give the branch definite personality as does Isa 11:1 f., but the results of His presence (4:3-6) are so similar as to leave little doubt that both passages refer to the

coming Branch. The remaining passages are clearly personal and messianic.

After His resurrection Jesus became the Vine and His disciples the branches (Jn 15:1-8).

L. R. E.

BRAND. Three Heb. words are used in connection with this expression: (1) *'ûd,* "a bent stick," used to stir the fire (Amos 4:11; Zech 3:2); also "firebrand" (Isa 7:4; *see* Firebrand); (2) *lappîd,* a waving torch similar to a lightning flash (Jud 15:4-5); (3) *ziqqîm,* "sparks, embers, or firebrands" (Prov 26:18; Isa 50:11).

BRASS. *See* Minerals and Metals: Bronze.

BRAY. Two Heb. words are translated "bray."

1. In Job 6:5 *nāhaq* is used to refer to the harsh cry of the ass; and in Job 30:7, figuratively, to the senseless talk of mockers.

2. In Prov 27:22 *kātash* is used to refer to the severe but futile chastisement of a fool, which is likened to being crushed or pounded small in a mortar.

BRAZEN. Used of articles made of brass. *See* Metals.

BRAZEN SEA. *See* Tabernacle: Laver.

BRAZEN SERPENT. During the period of the wilderness wanderings, Israel murmured against the Lord. As a disciplinary measure, God sent "fiery serpents" among them (Num 21:5-9). Probably these were cobras, whose bite produced a burning fever. When the stricken people imploringly turned to Moses, he at the command of God made a brass (copper) serpent, no doubt a replica of the viper with the stinging, deadly bite which had already bitten them. One should not consider this as sympathetic magic, for it probably served as a symbolic reminder of the divine displeasure. Centuries later it became a rallying point for idolatrous worship in Israel which caused the godly Hezekiah to destroy it (II Kgs 18:4). Christ refers to it figuratively as a type of His own approaching death on the cross (Jn 3:14), as being "made sin for us" (II Cor 5:21) and as bearing our judgment.

See Animals, IV.8, 30.

J. F. G.

BRAZIER. A pan, usually metal, for holding live coals, placed for heating on the floor in the middle of the room. In Jer 36:22-23 (KJV, "hearth") it refers to the heating device in King Jehoiakim's winter palace on which he burned Jeremiah's scroll as he cut it to pieces with a knife. *See* Hearth.

BREAD. *See* Food.

BREAD OF FACES, BREAD OF PRESENCE. The Heb. term referring to the showbread in the tabernacle or temple. Twelve loaves were kept on the table in the holy place at all times, being exchanged for fresh loaves every week (Ex 25:30). *See* Showbread.

The significance of the "bread of faces" is seen perhaps best in its literal meaning, "bread of the presence" (Num 4:7, RSV). Not only was the never-ceasing presence of God thus symbolized, but also the fact that God's presence was to be considered as more vital than bread.

BREAKER, THE. A messianic title found only in Mic 2:13. The KJV translation of Heb. *happōrēṣ* (RSV, "He who opens the breach"), it is used of the Lord as the deliverer of regathered Israel pictured as a flock in an enclosure and besieged by its enemies. In an earlier time God had broken through *(pāraṣ)* David's enemies the Philistines like a bursting *(pereṣ)* flood, so that King David had named that place Baal-perazim—"the Lord of breaking through" (II Sam 5:20, RSV marg.). A literal rendering of Mic 2:13 follows: "The Breach-maker will go up before them; they will break through and pass through the gate and will go out by it; yes, their King will pass on before them, even Yahweh at their head." Christ is also the Breaker figuratively for the individual believer as "He breaks the power of cancelled sin and sets the prisoner free." (Cf. Lev 26:13; Isa 61:1; Ezk 34:27.)

J. R.

BREAKFAST. *See* Food: Meals.

BREAST. The common Heb. word, translated variously in the KJV as "breast" (Gen 49:25), "teats" (Isa 32:12), and once by the Old English "paps" (Ezk 23:21), always refers to the female breast. In the NT, the Gr. word *stēthos* translated "breast" refers always to the male chest (e.g., Lk 18:13; Jn 13:25; Rev 15:6). The Gr. *mastos* is apparently synonymous, but is rendered "pap" in the NT (Lk 11:27; 23:29) and refers to the female breast, except in Rev 1:13 where it is used of Christ. *See also* Bosom.

BREASTPLATE. *See* Armor; Dress (of High Priest); Priest, High.

BREECHES. *See* Dress: Dress of Priests.

BRETHREN. *See* Brother.

BRIBE, BRIBERY. The Heb. word *shōḥad* means a gift; but in a corrupt sense, a bribe. Heb. law condemned the giving or receiving of gifts or bribes in order to pervert justice (Ex 23:8). References are made to its use to corrupt judges and rulers (Job 15:34; I Sam 8:3; Ps 26:10; Isa 33:15; Ezk 22:12). In this sense *kōper* is used in I Sam 12:3 and Amos 5:12. This Heb. word is used of the atonement money or ransom, and in the latter passage implies a payment for a man that was murdered so that the rich murderer might go free.

BRICK. The earliest bricks of which there is written record were in the city and tower of Babel (Gen 11:3). The ruins of Mesopotamian houses reveal the use of beaten clay and bricks in their foundations as early as approximately 4000 B.C. (Joseph Free, *Archaeology and Bible History*, pp. 37-38). Ancient Babylonia, Egypt, Assyria, and even Palestine found them a cheap and convenient building material, especially where stone was scarce or hard to use. The exact extent of their use is hard to trace because unburned bricks, after the houses and walls fall, gradually form a heap of earth not distinguishable from the surrounding soil.

In Egypt the bricks were invariably crude or unburned. When kiln-burned bricks are found, they are known to be of Roman time. Crude bricks were made of a black loamy earth or mud which was thoroughly "slipped" or mixed and formed in a bottomless box, which came off to let the brick bake in the sun. It often became so hard that a blow of a hammer would be required to break it. To render it more cohesive, chopped straw or stubble was added (Ex 5:7-18). (See *ibid.*, pp. 91-92, for confirmation of the cohesive action of straw and even of water in which straw has soaked.) When feed was in short supply, the straw was consumed by the beasts. This greatly added to the difficulty of the brickmakers, who had to collect stubble, or labor under severe handicap. Modern excavations at Pithom (Ex 1:11) show that most of the bricks of the store city were made of mud and straw baked in the sun (probably the work of the Heb. slaves). In some of the upper courses rushes had been substituted for straw, and still other bricks had no fibrous material.

Egyptian bricks were generally about 16 x 8 x 6 inches. For walls they were laid flat. For arches they were laid edgeways. They were frequently stamped on one side with hieroglyphics of the name of the pharaoh or of some edifice belonging to the pharaoh. The bricks that have survived from early Egypt appear to have been made under government monopoly. The rulers gave the distasteful and unhealthful task to captive Asiatic foreigners, among whom were the Israelites. In the tomb of the grand vizier Rekh-mi-Re at Thebes is a much-publicized picture of some light colored bondsmen (possibly Hebrews) employed in bringing water, digging clay, kneading it, pressing it into molds, carrying the bricks and piling them up for use. The picture is complete with whips and goads and the superintending officer.

In Palestine and Syria the same methods were often used. Where building stone was scarce, houses were made of sun-baked brick. When the bricks were laid, the house was plastered inside and out with the same material and whitewashed or painted with gray or yellow earth. The outer coating had to be renewed from year to year. Isa 9:10 refers to the superiority of hewn stone over brick.

Brick-making along the Nile. Wet clay is poured into a wooden frame, which is then lifted and used to repeat the process. HFV

Ancient Babylon used kiln-baked bricks which were frequently held together by hot bitumen (Gen 11:3). These bricks were generally about 12 x 12 x 3½ inches. They were often stamped with cuneiform characters. Many thousands bore the name of Nebuchadnezzar. Vitrified bricks of different colors were common. Assyrians used sun-baked bricks more freely for buildings, though they also used kiln bricks for flooring or paving of courts or palaces. Painted, glazed, and even gilded bricks have also been found at Nineveh and other Assyrian cities.

See Architecture; Building.

W. T. D.

BRICKMAKER. *See* Occupations.

BRIDAL GIFT. *See* Marriage.

BRIDE, BRIDEGROOM. The bride is a translation of Heb. *kallâh* and Gr. *nymphē,* referring to a betrothed or recently wedded woman (Isa 61:10; 62:5; Jer 7:34; Jn 3:29). The same Heb. word is translated "spouse" in Song 4:8–5:1. The most important usage is with reference to the Church as the Bride of Christ (Rev 21:2, 9; 22:17; also II Cor 11:2; Eph 5:25 ff.). The Gr. word *gynē,* "wife," is also closely related, as in Mt 1:20.

The bridegroom is the counterpart of the bride. The Gr. *nymphios* is the "bridegroom" (Jn 3:29; Rev 18:23). The Heb. word *ḥātān* means "bridegroom," "husband," or "son-in-law" according to the context. Christ used the term of Himself in the parable of the ten virgins (Mt 25:6). The "friend of the bridegroom" was one who arranged the details of the marriage and had a prominent place in the wedding festivities (Jn 3:29).

See Bride of Christ; Marriage.

Bibliography. J. Jeremias, "*Nymphē,* etc.," TDNT, IV, 1099–1106. T. C. Mitchell, "The Meaning of the Noun *HTN* in the OT," VT, XIX (1969), 92–112.

W. M. D.

BRIDE OF CHRIST. One of the seven figures used to set forth the relationship of the Church to Christ: the branches and the Vine (Jn 15:1–11), the sheep and the Shepherd (Jn 10:1–30), the stones and the Chief Cornerstone (I Pet 2:4–8), the priests and the High Priest (Heb 2:17; 4:14; 7:26; I Pet 2:9), the new creation and the Last Adam (I Cor 15:45–50), the members and the Head of the Body (I Cor 12; Eph 4:4–16), the bride and the Bridegroom (Rev 19:7–9; cf. Eph 5:21–32). *See* Bride, Bridegroom.

The Church, composed of those who have been saved by grace through faith, forms the Bride of Christ. Those already with the Lord, together with those still alive at the rapture, will at that event receive resurrection bodies (I Thess 4:14–17; I Cor 15:51 f.). As members

The clay brick wall of the hall of justice at Ur.
Carl DeVries

of the Church they will celebrate the marriage supper of the Lamb with Christ (Rev 19:7–9) close to the time of His return to put down His enemies (Rev 19:11–21). Our Lord Himself foretold the occurrence of this marriage in the parable of the ten virgins in which He stressed the fact that the day and the hour of His coming for His own is unknown (Mt 24:36; 25:1–13), and the consequent need to be ready at all times with oil in our lamps—perhaps a figure of salvation in the sense that the Christian is the temple of the Holy Spirit (I Cor 6:19). *See* Marriage of the Lamb; Head of the Church.

At present, then, the marriage of the Church to Christ has not been consummated. She is to be living as a virgin betrothed to her future husband (II Cor 11:2), belonging to Christ under marriage contract (i.e., the covenant of redemption). He has sought His bride in love and is even now sanctifying her that she might be without spot or blemish when He will present the Church to Himself in splendor (Eph 5:23–27, RSV). This present time of purification of the Church is reminiscent of the twelve months of beautifying through which Esther and the other maidens went, before being brought in to the king (Est 2:12). The Bride of Christ joins in the last prayer of the Bible as she waits for Him to return for her: "And the Spirit and the bride say [to Jesus], Come! . . . Amen. Even so, come, Lord Jesus" (Rev 22:17, 20).

In connection with the theme of the bride and the Bridegroom, NT teaching speaks of wedding guests (Mt 22:1–14), "sons of the bridechamber" (Mk 2:19 f., ASV), and even a best man or friend of the Bridegroom, viz., John the Baptist (Jn 3:27–30). OT imagery includes bridal attendants along with the king's daughter or bride in the beautiful poetic prophecy of the coming messianic wedding (Ps 45:13–15). The interpretation as to the identity of these guests and attendants is not theologically certain.

Ultimately the Bride will reign with her Husband over the new earth, as the joint metaphor of the holy city, the new Jerusalem, "coming down from God out of heaven, prepared as a bride adorned for her husband" (Rev 21:2, 9–10), seems to indicate.

R. A. K. and J. R.

BRIDECHAMBER. *See* Marriage.

BRIDLE. The several words in Heb. and Gr. for "bridle" are used rather loosely in the Bible to refer to either bit *(q.v.),* bridle, rein *(q.v.),* or halter, whatever may have been used to guide or check an animal. Usually it was no more than a leather strap with a loop over the upper lip. Sometimes a ring was placed in the nose or lip and the animal was led about. A basket of rope network was also in use as a sort of muzzle.

The references in Scripture are largely figurative. The nations, and particularly Israel, are spoken of as though they were refractory animals who must be trained and curbed, or punished (II Kgs 19:28; Isa 30:28; 37:29; Ezk 29:4). That these expressions are not entirely figurative is seen by some of the Assyrian monuments in which captives of war are actually led on a strap with a ring through the lip.

God's law is also referred to as that which controls and guides (Ps 32:8–9). The point of Ps 39:1 is somewhat dimmed by the KJV translation "bridle." The psalmist actually says, "I will muzzle my mouth."

P. C. J.

BRIER. *See* Plants.

BRIMSTONE. *See* Minerals.

BRONZE. *See* Minerals and Metals.

BROOCH. Used in plural by RSV (KJV, "bracelets") for a class of gold jewelry brought as offerings by men and women of Israel (Ex 35:22). Keil and Delitzsch suggest "clasp or ring." It could be "buckle or brooch." *See* Bracelet.

BROOK. In the OT "brook" derives its meaning from the following Heb. words: (1) *naḥal,* which describes a valley with a stream or a river in it (Num 21:12), or the stream alone (Deut 9:21); (2) *'āphîq,* which refers to the actual bed of the stream (Joel 1:20, RSV); (3) *yeʾōr,* which almost always refers to a large river such as the Nile, the canal-arms of the Nile, or the Tigris; but in Isa 19:6–8 it is translated "brook" in referring to the channels of the Nile in the delta; (4) *mîkāl,* which is found only in II Sam 17:20 and is of uncertain meaning.

In the NT the Gr. word for the brook Kidron in Jn 18:1, *cheimarrhos,* describes a stream which flows in the winter.

BROOM. *See* Plants.

BROTHER. This term is used extensively in Scripture to express a wide variety of relationships. The natural use has reference to a blood relationship, whether immediate or remote: (1) sons of the same parents or parent (Gen 43:29; Gal 1:19); (2) near relatives (Gen 29:15); (3) fellow tribesmen (Num 16:10); (4) kindred tribes (Jud 20:23); (5) fellow countrymen (Ex 2:11); (6) cognate nations (Ob 10); (7) fellow human beings (Gen 9:5).

The figurative use expresses a relationship of affinity or similarity which is not necessarily based on a physical connection: (1) likeness (Job 30:29; Prov 18:9); (2) similarity in rank or office (Ezr 3:2); (3) friendship (II Sam 1:26); (4) relationship of allies (Amos 1:9).

The most distinctive NT usage of the term "brother" is that which expresses a spiritual relationship. It is a common designation for a Christian (Acts 9:17; I Cor 5:11; Phm 16), and is suggestive of the family nature of the Christian community (Gal 6:10) in which God is Father (Phil 1:2; I Jn 5:1) and all believers are brothers. This relationship is not merely figurative but is based on a spiritual birth which makes its recipients fellow possessors of a new life (II Pet 1:4). The Christian community is called a brotherhood (I Pet 2:17) and as such is to be marked by love (I Jn 5:1). Its members are to cultivate brotherly love (Gr. *philadelphia*) toward each other (II Pet 1:7). The fact that they are brothers should significantly affect their conduct. They are to share with the needy brother (I Jn 3:17–18); they are to show hospitality to one another (III Jn 5–6); they are not to take each other to court (I Cor 6:1–8); they are not to place a stumbling block before a weaker brother (I Cor 8:9–13); they are to admonish those who sin (II Thess 3:15).

Background for this distinctive NT use of the term is obviously to be found in its OT employment to refer to a fellow Israelite. However, it may well be that the custom of the Pharisees of calling themselves *ḥăbērîm,* "companions" or "brethren," has a bearing upon the Christian usage. It may also be significant that the members of the Qumran community referred to one another as brothers.

D. W. B.

BROTHERLY KINDNESS. Translated thus twice in II Pet 1:7 from the Gr. *philadelphia;* more literally, "love of the brethren" (I Pet 1:22, ASV marg.), or as the same noun is elsewhere rendered, "brotherly love" (Rom 12:10; I Thess 4:9; Heb 13:1). The biblical connotation of *philadelphia* is not that of love simply for one's blood brothers, as in all previous pagan writings, but for the broader brotherhood of true believers (cf. Arndt). Those who have been adopted into divine sonship through faith in Christ (Jn 1:12) become necessarily brothers in their relation to each other (Mt 23:8; Rom 8:17; Eph 4:15–16; cf. "neighbor" in OT, Lev 19:17). Brotherly kindness thus forms an indispensable (I Jn 4:20) element in the Christian's growth in sanctification (II Pet 1:7) and exhibits itself in harmoniousness (Acts 2:46; Rom 12:16), sincerity (I Pet 1:22), affection and esteem for fellow disciples (Rom 12:10; cf. Gal 6:10; Lev 19:34 for others also), zealously maintained (Heb 13:1; I Pet 1:22). Pagans witnessing this unique selflessness could only exclaim, "Behold how they love one another!" (Tertullian, *Apologeticus,* cf. Jn 13:35). *See* Love; Charity; Brother.

J. B. P.

BROTHERLY LOVE. *See* Brotherly Kindness.

BROTHERS OF OUR LORD. The NT contains a number of references to the brothers of Christ (Mt 12:46 ff. and parallels; Jn 2:12; 7:3, 5, 10; Acts 1:14; I Cor 9:5; Gal 1:19). Their names, as listed in Mt 13:55, were James, Joses, Simon, and Judas.

Since the days of the early church, the relationship of these individuals to Jesus has been under discussion. Some have held that they were stepbrothers, sons of Joseph by a former marriage. This theory, which was advanced by such men as Origen, Eusebius, and Epiphanius, is based on the conjecture that Joseph was considerably older than Mary. A similar view postulates that the brothers were sons of Joseph by a levirate marriage with the widow of Cleophas, his brother. Neither of these theories has sufficient basis to warrant serious consideration.

Of much wider acceptance is the view, which is officially held by the Roman Catholic church, that the brothers were in reality cousins of Jesus. James, the Lord's brother, is identified with James the son of Alphaeus (Lk 6:15) and with James the less (Mk 15:40), and is thus considered to be one of the 12 apostles (Gal 1:19). Judas and Simon (Mt 13:55) are also taken to be apostles (Lk 6:15–16). Mary, the wife of Cleophas, is said to be a sister of the mother of Jesus (Jn 19:25), and Cleophas is identified with Alphaeus (cf. also Mk 6:3; 15:40). It is asserted, therefore, that these brothers were sons of Mary, the sister of Christ's mother, and thus cousins of Christ.

This view, however, is open to several serious objections: (1) It is not possible to identify Christ's unbelieving brethren (Jn 7:5) with the apostles. (2) Scripture clearly distinguishes the brothers of the Lord from the apostles (Jn 2:12; Acts 1:13–14). (3) It is unthinkable that sisters would have the same name. Jn 19:25 probably refers to four women rather than three. (4) There is no sound basis for identifying Alphaeus with Cleophas. (5) This view is in reality based on the Roman Catholic dogma of the perpetual virginity of Mary.

The most natural interpretation of the passage involved considers the brothers to be half brothers of Jesus, born of Mary subsequent to the birth of Christ. It is significant that they are repeatedly associated with Jesus' mother (Mt 13:55–56; Jn 2:12; Acts 1:14). Furthermore, Luke, writing a number of years later, calls Jesus Mary's firstborn son (Lk 2:7), which indicates that other sons followed. In addition, Matthew's statement that Joseph "knew her not till she had brought forth her firstborn son" (Mt 1:25) argues against perpetual virginity. The NT contains nothing which demands anything other than the natural interpretation of the term brother. In fact, history indicates that it was the development of the Roman Catholic Marian doctrine which made necessary the deviations from the natural view.

D. W. B.

BROTHER'S WIFE. A brother's wife is to be respected and her person not violated (Lev 18:16; 20:21). *See* Levirate Marriage.

BROWN. *See* Colours.

BRUISED. This word appears a number of times in the Bible as a translation for several different words. It is used principally of grain that has been crushed (Lev 2:14, 16; II Sam 17:19) and of reeds that have been broken (II Kgs 18:21). But the latter use always has a deep religious significance. (1) Egypt is the reed that is to be crushed (II Kgs 18:21); (2) weak disciples are bruised reeds for whom God cares (Isa 42:3; Mt 12:20); (3) Satan would bruise the heel of Christ, i.e., cause suffering and death; but Christ would bruise the head of Satan, i.e., destroy his power (Gen 3:15); (4) through the bruising of Christ (i.e., crucifixion) salvation from sin has been made possible (Isa 53:5, 10; Lk 4:18); (5) God will bruise Satan ultimately (i.e., triumph) (Rom 16:20).

BRUISES. *See* Diseases.

BRUTISH. One who is irrational and unreasonable. RSV usually translates the word "stupid" (Ps 49:10; 73:22; 92:6; Jer 10:8, 14, 21; 51:17), and therefore unteachable. Such are also crude, uncultivated, thoughtlessly ignorant. Brutish counsel (Isa 19:11) is foolish and unreasonable. In self-criticism Agur regarded himself as brutish (Prov 30:2), indicating his lack of knowledge.

BUCK. *See* Animals, II.10.

BUCKET. Found only in Isa 40:15 and Num 24:7. The bucket was a skin with two wooden crosspieces at the top attached to a rope, for drawing water.

Leather bucket used at a well. JR

BUCKLE. *See* Brooch.

BUCKLER. *See* Armor.

BUFFET. The Gr. word *kolaphizō,* "to strike with the fist," "to beat," signifies rude maltreatment, whether in derision (Mt 26:67; Mk 14:65), affliction (I Cor 4:11), opposition (II Cor 12:7), or punishment (I Pet 2:20).

BUILDERS. *See* Occupations.

BUILDING. Buildings included homes, temples, city walls and other fortifications. *See* Architecture. Mud bricks dried in the sun (*see* Bricks) were used for the ordinary home, or stone if available. Roof timbers would be covered with clay or thatch.

Solomon's and Herod's temples were made with costly materials by trained artisans of their times. The disciples shared the great pride of the Jews in their magnificent temple (Mk 13:1).

Foundations were often laid on the leveled ruins of previous towns and villages destroyed by invaders or fire.

"Building" is used figuratively also. It may refer to a family line, as in God's promise to build David a house (II Sam 7:27); or to the building which is God's church (I Cor 3:9); or to the building of Christian character (Jude 20).

See Occupations.

BUKKI (bŭk'ī)

1. Son of Jogli and representative Danite chief who assisted in the division of the land (Num 34:22).

2. Fourth in descent from Aaron through Eleazar (I Chr 6:5, 51), and ancestor of Ezra (Ezr 7:4).

BUKKIAH (bŭ-kī'*a*). A Levite, a son of Heman, leader of the sixth company of 12 musicians who served in the temple worship (I Chr 25:4, 13).

BUL (bo͞ol). Name of the eighth month of the pre-Exilic Jewish year (I Kgs 6:38), corresponding to October-November. The name appropriately means rain or shower, for this is the beginning of the rainy season. *See* Calendar.

BULL. *See* Animals, I.3.

BULLOCK. *See* Animals, I.3.

BULRUSH. *See* Plants.

BULWARK. Translation of five Heb. words: (1) *ḥēl* (Isa 26:1) and (2) *ḥêlâ* (Ps 48:13), meaning "strong objects," ramparts or citadel; (3) *māṣôd* (Eccl 9:14) and (4) *māṣôr* (Deut 20:20), meaning a fortress or siegeworks used against a city; (5) *pinnâ* (II Chr 26:15), corner tower(s) of a fortification. *See* Fort; Citadel.

Mummy-shaped coffin of wood of King Tutankhamon of Egypt. LL

BUNAH (bū'n*a*). The son of Jerahmeel of the line of Judah (I Chr 2:25).

BUNCH. Only one word is properly translated "bunch," *'ăguddâ,* "a bunch of hyssop" (Ex 12:22). "Bunch" in II Sam 16:1 and I Chr 12:40 (Heb. *ṣimmûq*) means a cluster or bunch of raisins. In Isa 30:6 *dabbeshet* means a "camel's hump," as in RSV.

BUNDLE. A pouch which could be closed and used especially for items of value (e.g., money, Gen 42:35; Prov 7:20) and designed to be kept near the person for safekeeping. The essential concepts are those of safety and value. In Hag 1:6, since the bag has holes, it is the life without God, soon empty of all value, even material. The supreme and intimate preciousness of the lover (Song 1:13) is expressed by the bundle of costly perfume pressed close to the breasts. Abigail tells David he is "bound in the bundle of the living" (I Sam 25:29, RSV), literally, "with the Lord thy God." God had seen value in David and had become his intimate associate and guarantor of his safety (cf. the variant concepts of being enrolled in the "book of the living," Ps 69:28, RSV; Ex 32:32–33; Dan 12:1).

BUNNI (bŭn'ī). Apparently the name of three Levites:

1. A Levite who helped Ezra teach the people (Neh 9:4).
2. An ancestor of Shemaiah (Neh 11:15).
3. A leader or family that, with Nehemiah, sealed the covenant (Neh 10:15).

BURDEN

1. The Heb. word *maśśā'* literally comes from the root *nāśā,* which means "to lift up" any load carried by beast (Ex 23:5) or man (Num 4:15). Figuratively, as a responsibility of a leader, people may be a burden (Num 11:11); a man may be a burden to himself (Job 7:20); the psalmist speaks (38:4) of iniquities as a burden. Possibly taxes are referred to as a burden in Hos 8:10.

The word *maśśā'* is frequently used of the message and utterance of a prophet (Isa 13:1; 15:1; etc.) against the nations, and translated "oracle" in RSV. It is used also of the words of Agur and Lemuel in Prov 30:1; 31:1, translated "oracle." The term *mas'ēt,* of the same derivation, is used of foolish oracles (Lam 2:14) by false prophets.

2. Other words, e.g., *sēbel* (Neh 4:17) and *sōbel* (Isa 9:4) are derived from *sābal,* "to bear a load," translated "burden." In Exodus (1:11; 2:11; 5:4-5; 6:6-7), *sᵉbālâ* is used and refers to the total hardship placed upon the Hebrews by the Egyptians.

E. F. Hai.

BURIAL. The manner of disposing of dead bodies in biblical times varied from country to country. In Egypt the outstanding burial practice for nobles and royalty was the unique method of embalming (*see* Embalm). The internal organs were removed from the body cavity and replaced by linen cloth and a resinous gum. The body was then wrapped in yards of linen bandages from the toes to the head. If the deceased was a king or high official, the body was enclosed in a case of plaster-like substance which was painted with the face of the dead person and otherwise engraved with various markings. The mummy was then encased in several coffins. Such was, no doubt, the method used in embalming Joseph (Gen 50:26), though Jacob's preservation would probably have been less elaborate (Gen 50:2-3). In the case of pagan Egyptians, the body was buried with helpful items for the future life and often with portions from the Book of the Dead. Kings were buried in elaborately prepared tombs, some of which were housed in pyramids as late as the Twelfth Dynasty in the time of the patriarchs.

Excavated Babylonian tombs also indicate that great care was taken to prepare the body for burial and for the future life. Personal items to be used in the next life were placed with the body, as in the royal tombs of Ur *(q.v.)*. The greater the dignity of the deceased, the larger the tomb and the more extensive were the provisions for the hereafter. Poorer people were buried in simpler graves accompanied by food and personal effects. For Canaanite tombs at Jericho with well-preserved furniture and dried food, *see* Tomb.

Heb. burials, like those in other countries with warm climate, usually took place on the day of death (Deut 21:23; Acts 5:5-10). The seeming haste, a sanitary measure occasioned by the heat, was also necessitated by the ceremonial laws of the clean and unclean which warned against the touching of a dead body (Num 19:11-14). If the family was prosperous enough to own property, a cave was used (Gen 49:29-31), or a tomb was hewn out of rock in which were carved a number of shelves or niches for the various members of the family (II Kgs 21:18, 26; 23:30). In NT times such a tomb would often be closed with a circular rolling stone set in an inclined groove (Mk 16:3-4). The rocky hills around Jerusalem, as well as those in other places, contained many

Sarcophagus of Ramses III of Egypt. LM

Phoenician sarcophagus from Byblos, late second millennium B.C. HFV

rock-hewn tombs (Lk 23:53; Jn 19:41; Mk 5:3).

Poorer people buried their dead in graves dug in the earth and covered them with stones. Such a cemetery was found near the monastery at Qumran by the Dead Sea with 1,200 graves placed in rows. The Early Bronze Age cemetery at Bab edh-Dhra contained thousands of graves. Only leading men were allowed to be buried within the city walls (I Kgs 2:10). A graveyard for paupers was located outside the S wall of Jerusalem (Mt 27:7-8; Acts 1:19).

The Hebrews neither embalmed nor cremated their dead except in rare instances (Gen 50:2-3, 26; I Sam 31:11-13). It was customary to wash the body (Acts 9:37), apply spices and ointment (Lk 23:56; Jn 19:39-40), and wrap it in strips of linen cloth (Jn 19:40). The face was tied separately with a napkin and the hands with linen cloths (Jn 11:44). The body was carried to the burial place on a bier or litter (Lk 7:12, 14). The use of professional mourners was quite common where finances permitted (Mk 5:38).

The denial of proper burial to a man or to toss his body into a common pit of corpses indicated the greatest disgrace heaped upon the reputation of the deceased (Isa 14:18-20; Jer 22:18-19). Burning the body was a punishment fit for a criminal (Lev 20:14; 21:9; Josh 7:25). The Mishna forbade cremation as idolatry ('Abodah Zarah I.3).

Christian burial in NT times was viewed in the light of the resurrection hope. Death was referred to as sleep (I Thess 4:13) and the grave as a place of rest (Gr. *koimētērion* from *koimaō*, "I sleep," the source of the English word "cemetery"). The body, as the temple of the Holy Spirit (I Cor 6:19) and as the subject of resurrection (I Cor 6:13-14), was viewed with respect. Pagan excessiveness in mourning was discouraged (I Thess 4:13). Burial was also used symbolically to depict the believer's positional identification with Christ in death to sin (Rom 6:4-5). Many also view this passage as referring to burial in the waters of baptism.

Sarcophagus of the Greek period at Tyre. HFV

A graveyard for paupers located just east of the Kidron Valley (center) in Jerusalem. Pictured are some of the caves in which burials took place. HFV

A Chalcolithic practice of placing the bones of a decomposed corpse in an ossuary (a terra-cotta or stone box two to three feet long) was revived about the 3rd cen. B.C. In a tomb dating *c.* A.D. 50, between Jerusalem and Bethlehem, E. L. Sukenik in 1945 found eleven ossuaries on which charcoal inscriptions had been made. These included the sign of the cross, possible laments to Jesus, and the name Simeon Barsaba. The latter name is not known elsewhere except in Acts 1:23; 15:22. Here may be "the earliest evidence for the presence in Jerusalem of the first Christian community" (André Parrot, *Golgotha and the Church of the Holy Sepulchre,* p. 119). In another cemetery on the Mount of Olives were discovered in 1954 a number of ossuaries with NT names, such as Jairus, Salome, Martha, Mary, Simon son of Jonas, one with a carefully drawn cross, and another with the three letters I, X, B standing undoubtedly for *Iēsous, Xristos, Basileus* (i.e., Jesus Christ King). The Christian catacombs in Rome contain many inscriptions expressing the faith of the early church (see FLAP, pp. 451-491).

See Bier; Cross; Dead, The; Embalm; Funeral; Grave; Mourning; Tomb.

Bibliography. Eric M. Meyers, "Secondary Burials in Palestine," BA, XXXIII (1970), 1-29. Roland de Vaux, *Ancient Israel,* New York: McGraw-Hill, 1961, pp. 56-61.

D. W. B. and J. R.

BURNING. Burning, the act of consuming combustible material by fire, is used in Scripture in both a literal and a figurative sense. Sacrifices were burned on the altar of burnt offering, signifying total consecration to God (Lev 6:9). Lamps burned continually, with pure olive oil as the fuel (Lev 24:2; Rev 4:5). Incense was continually burning on an altar in the holy place of the tabernacle and, later, the temple (I Kgs 9:25). The burning of spices near the body of King Asa was performed as a royal funeral rite (II Chr 16:14; cf. 21:19; Jer 34:5). The bush from which God called Moses (Ex 3:2; *see* Burning Bush) and the mountain from which the law was given, are both described as burning (Deut 5:23). A burning coal from the altar was applied to the lips of Isaiah (Isa 6:6-7, NASB).

Punishment by fire was practiced in Babylonia (Jer 29:22). Shadrach, Meshach and Abed-nego were cast alive into a burning, fiery furnace (Dan 3:6, 11, 15-26). In ancient Israel, however, burning as a punishment was used only in cases of aggrieved prostitution and incest (Gen 38:24; Lev 20:14; 21:9). Some scholars suggest that stoning preceded burning in these instances. It is known that the corpses of criminals executed by stoning were sometimes burned with fire, as in the case of Achan and his family (Josh 7:25). Divine punishment by fire sometimes fell directly from God (Lev 10:2, 6).

Figuratively the word "burning" is used to describe the anger of the Lord (Josh 7:26; Ps 69:24, RSV); everlasting punishment (Isa 33:12, 14; Rev 19:20; 21:8); physical pain (Job 30:30); idolatrous or sexual lust (Isa 57:5, RSV; I Cor 7:9); and fervent, flattering lips (Prov 26:23). In the context of worship, burning indicates purification (Isa 6:6-7; I Pet 1:7) and total devotion to God (Lk 24:32; Jn 5:35). In human relationships, a burn or burning speaks of the sense of pain and suffering, either physical (Lev 13:24-25) or emotional (II Cor 11:29).

See Fire.

C. F. P.

BURNING BUSH. The flaming bush by which God attracted Moses' attention and revealed Himself at the time of Moses' call to become Israel's deliverer (Ex 3:2-4). The Heb. word for "bush," *seneh,* is found only in this passage and Deut 33:16. It was probably an unidentified thorn bush of the acacia family. *See* Plants: Bush.

The blazing flame which did not consume the bush and with no human agent to kindle it illustrated to Moses the self-sufficiency and unapproachable holiness of God; it was not a symbol of the afflictions of Israel in Egypt, as many commentators have suggested. The JerusB brings out the proper sense of Ex 3:2: "There the angel of Yahweh appeared to him in the shape of a flame of fire, coming from the middle of a bush." Thus the flame as a symbol of deity (cf. Gen 3:24; 15:17; Ex 13:21; 19:18) and the audible voice of God declaring the holiness of the place enabled Moses to recognize that God was dwelling in the bush, as he later recalled (Deut 33:16). That he used the term "the angel of the Lord" (KJV) in v. 2 in narrating this incident is no contradiction, because this expression often signifies a special manifestation of Yahweh, a theophany or appearance of the pre-incarnate Son of God. *See* Moses.

J. R.

BURNT OFFERING. *See* Sacrificial Offerings.

BUSH. *See* Plants.

BUSHEL. *See* Weights, Measures and Coins.

BUSYBODY. Three different Gr. words are used, all meaning the same thing: (1) *periergos,* meaning "to be overly officious," "to be a busybody" (I Tim 5:13); (2) *periergazomai,* meaning "to make oneself always too busy," "to be a busybody" (II Thess 3:11); (3) *allotriepiskopos,* meaning "a meddler in other men's matters" (KJV, ASV), "mischief maker" (RSV). The use of *episkopos* suggests that Peter was referring to an "overseer" or "bishop" (I Pet 4:15).

BUTCHER. *See* Occupations.

BUTLER. *See* Occupations.

BUTTER. *See* Food.

BUZ (bŭz)

1. The name of a region (Jer 25:23) probably somewhere in N Arabia, possibly the Bazu of the Assyrian inscriptions. *See* Buzite.

2. The second son of Nahor and Milcah, and nephew of Abraham (Gen 22:21).

3. A descendant of the tribe of Gad (I Chr 5:14).

BUZI (bū'zī). The father of the prophet Ezekiel (Ezk 1:3), and consequently a member of the priestly house of Zadok.

BUZITE (bū'zīt). One belonging to the Arabian tribe of Buz. Elihu, one of the friends of Job (Job 32:2), is called a Buzite, and may have belonged to a tribe of that name, against which judgments were denounced by Jeremiah (Jer 25:23).

BUZZARD. *See* Animals, III.4.

BYBLOS. *See* Gebal.

BYWAYS. Used in Jud 5:6 to mean a back road or path that a traveler sometimes took.

C

CAB. *See* Weights, Measures and Coins.

CABBON (kăb'ŏn). An unidentified place in the Shephelah or foothills of Judah near Eglon (Josh 15:40). It is possibly the same as Machbenah (I Chr 2:49).

CABUL (kā'bŭl)

1. A village in the borderland between Asher and Zebulun, about ten miles NE of Mount Carmel, in the Galilean hills (Josh 19:27).

2. A region embracing 20 villages given to Hiram of Tyre by King Solomon (I Kgs 9:10 - 13). Hiram was displeased with the gift, calling it "Cabul," by some taken to mean worthless or good-for-nothing, but by others taken to mean a borderland region, perhaps unproductive, and as an inland area of small value to a sea power. According to II Chr 8:2, Solomon fortified this region and colonized it with Israelites, suggesting that he regained possession of it.

CAESAR (sē'zẽr). The term was the surname of the Julian family, as in the name Caius Julius Caesar. In the NT it is applied to four Roman emperors: (1) Caesar Augustus (Lk 2:1); (2) Tiberius Caesar (Lk 3:1); (3) Claudius Caesar (Acts 11:28; 17:7, where he is called only Caesar; Acts 18:2, where he is called Claudius); Nero (Acts 25:10-12; 26:32; Phil 4:22). *See* each name.

The expression "the things that are Caesar's" (Lk 20:25) came to be used in opposition to "the things that are God's," that is, the earthly realm versus the heavenly realm. Thus a principle was introduced to guide the disciple of our Lord in the extent of his responsibilities to the world and to God (cf. Acts 4:19 f.; 5:29).

Crusader Walls and Moat at Caesarea. HFV

CAESAREA (sĕs'ȧ-rē'ȧ). Two cities in the NT are so named.

1. Caesarea was the capital of Judea under the Roman procurators (e.g., Pilate). It had been rebuilt and renamed from Strato's Tower to Caesarea Sebaste (in honor of Augustus) by Herod the Great. Located on the coast about 30 miles N of Jaffa (old Joppa) and about 65 miles NW of Jerusalem, it was a magnificent city containing many palaces and lavish public buildings, and a seaport, in this latter respect being adulated by Josephus. It was here that King Herod Agrippa I, in Luke's account, "was eaten of worms, and gave up the ghost" (Acts 12:19*b*-23).

A city of mixed population, leading to frequent Jewish-Gentile friction, it is connected in Acts with various evangelistic efforts. Here lived Philip the evangelist (one of the seven deacons, Acts 6:5), together with his four daughters who prophesied (Acts 21:8-9). Peter, while residing at Joppa, was called to preach to "a certain man in Caesarea," the Roman centurion Cornelius, a God-fearer (Acts 10:1-2, 24; 11:11-12). Paul saluted the church at Caesarea on his return from his missionary journey (Acts 18:22); then later he was held prisoner here for two years under Felix and Festus (Acts 23:23–26:32). He "reasoned" with Felix and often the procurator "communed with him" (Acts 24:25-26). And before Festus and Herod Agrippa II Paul expressed his fervent desire for their conversion (Acts 26:29).

An Italian expedition excavating the site in 1959-61 discovered a stone inscription from the city theater bearing the word "Tiberieum" (dedicated to the emperor Tiberius), and on the next two lines, "[Pon]tius Pilatus . . . Military Procurator." This is the first reference to Pilate (cf. Lk 3:1) on an inscription (BW, p. 156).

In 1962 excavators found in a synagogue at Caesarea part of a list of the 24 priestly courses and the cities in which the priests lived, including a reference to the 18th course as coming from the city of Nazareth (BW). *See also* Archaeology.

2. Caesarea Philippi was N of the Sea of Galilee on the SW slope of Mount Hermon. It was renamed by Herod Philip (the tetrarch), son of Herod the Great and Cleopatra of Jerusalem, in honor of Tiberius Caesar (Jos *Ant.* xviii.2.1). This Gr. city (earlier called Paneas after the god Pan) is notable in the NT as the scene of Peter's great confession (Mt 16:13 ff.; Mk 8:27), and probably the transfiguration of Christ (Mt 17:1-8). The name "Philippi" distinguished it from the Caesarea on the sea. In NT times the city was an important center for

Remains of the Temple of Augustus at Caesarea. HFV

Greco-Roman civilization and culture. Josephus indicates that its population was largely pagan (*Life,* xiii). Some suggest the city was the OT Baal-gad (Josh 11:17; 12:7; 13:5). *See* Baal-gad.

Ewing (HDB), in a descriptive passage, says that "no spot in Palestine can compare with this in romantic beauty." Its abundant vegetation, the beauty of Mount Hermon to the NE, its crag towering up to 8,000 feet above the valley, and the waters which comprise the fountainhead of the Jordan River, all combine to a magnificent scenery. The modern village of Banyas stands among the ruins of the once splendid city.

W. M. D. and A. F. J.

CAGE. In Jer 5:27 the Heb. word means the wicker basket in which the fowler placed the captured birds. Such baskets, filled to capacity with living birds, were probably a familiar scene in the markets of ancient cities. *See* Basket.

CAIAPHAS (kā'ȧ-făs). Joseph Caiaphas was high priest *c.* A.D. 18–36. He was son-in-law and successor of Annas. Appointed by the Roman procurator Valerius Gratus (Pilate's immediate predecessor), he was deposed by Vitellius, "president of Syria" (Jos *Ant.* xviii.2.2; 4.3).

The earliest mention of him is in Lk 3:2: "Annas and Caiaphas being the high priests." This odd expression evidently reflects the fact that whereas the latter legally held the position of high priest, Annas continued to wield the power of that office. *See* Annas.

The next notice is in Jn 11:49–53, where Caiaphas advised that Jesus' life should be sacrificed to save the nation. He feared that the Prophet from Nazareth would precipitate a political revolution, which might result in the whole nation being destroyed by Rome. The evangelist comments (Jn 11:51) that Caiaphas spoke better than he knew. As high priest he uttered a prophecy that Jesus would die on behalf of the Jews and all mankind. Reference is made to this again in Jn 18:13–14.

Steps leading to St. Peter's in Gallicantu, presumably the site of Caiaphas' palace. Jesus may have walked on these Roman steps. HFV

The Jewish leaders followed the advice of Caiaphas and from that very day "took counsel together" to put Jesus to death (Jn 11:53). Mathew (26:3–5) describes a meeting of the Sanhedrin – "the chief priests, and the scribes, and the elders of the people" – at the palace of "the high priest, who was called Caiaphas," two days before the Passover of the Passion. Here the leaders of the nation conspired to take Jesus "by subtilty" and kill Him. They did not wish to arrest Him during the feast, for fear of an uprising of the people. But Judas Iscariot's offer to betray Him secretly caused them to change their minds.

After a preliminary hearing before Annas, Christ was sent to Caiaphas (Jn 18:24) – perhaps just from one apartment to another in the same palace. Here the Sanhedrin had gathered (Mt 26:57). The true character of the high priest is shown in this Jewish trial of Jesus. The Sanhedrin "sought false witness against Jesus, to put him to death" (Mt 26:59). When Christ refused to reply to these false accusations, Caiaphas put Him under oath to tell whether He was the Messiah. When He answered in the affirmative and applied to Himself the language of Dan 7:13, the high priest "rent his clothes" and declared that Jesus had uttered blasphemy (Mt 26:65). The Sanhedrin gave judgment that He was guilty of death, and delivered Him to the Roman governor for execution. The last mention of Caiaphas is in Acts 4:6.

R. E.

CAIN (kān)

1. The older brother of Abel, Cain is pictured in Genesis as the first child to be born of the first parents, Adam and Eve. The name is explained as meaning "gotten" (from Heb. *qānâ,* Gen 4:1), but the exact form *qayin* can also mean "spear" or "smith." He was a "tiller of the ground" (v.2).

Cain brought an offering to the Lord "of the fruit of the ground," while Abel offered "of the firstlings of his flock" (vv. 3-4). God accepted Abel's offering, but not Cain's. Three reasons for God's rejection of Cain's offering have been suggested. The first is that Abel offered the best he had, while Cain did not. But there is no clear indication of that in the account. The second is that Cain brought a bloodless offering, and thus offended Deity by posing as righteous and not in need of any sacrifice for sin. This theory has strong theological appeal. It assumes previous divine instruction as to what type of offering must be brought for making atonement for sin. There is indication that such a revelation had been given by the use of the verb form in Gen 4:3 that can mean customary action.

Without ruling out the possible validity of these two theories, we must note that a third one seems to have also a firm scriptural support. This holds that Cain's attitude was wrong. Heb 11:4 says it was "by faith" that Abel offered a "more excellent sacrifice" than did Cain.

Cain was reproved by the Lord for his jealous anger. Instead of repenting, he killed his brother, and was cursed away from home for his sin (Gen 4:6-12). He moved to Nod, where he built a city and raised a family. He must have married a daughter or granddaughter of Adam and Eve.

In the NT Cain is mentioned in Heb 11:4; I Jn 3:12; Jude 11.

2. A town in the southern part of Judah (Josh 15:57).

R. E.

CAINAN (kā'nán)

1. Son of Enos and great-grandson of Adam, mentioned in Gen 5:9-14 and Lk 3:37.

2. Son of Arphaxad, mentioned in Lk 3:36, which seems to follow Gen 10:24; 11:12-13 of the LXX (and also I Chr 1:18 of the Alexandrine text of the LXX).

CAKE. *See* Food.

CALAH (kă'lȧ). This Assyrian city, now called Nimrud after its founder Nimrod (Gen 10:11-12), was already ancient when the Assyrian king Ashur-nasir-pal II (884-859 B.C.) chose it for his capital. It lay at the confluence of the Great Zab and Tigris Rivers *c.* 20 miles S of Nineveh.

Here the pioneer archaeologist Sir Austen Henry Layard began his excavations in Assyria, digging this site 1845-51. Rassam and Loftus followed him, 1852-55. The British School of Archaeology in Iraq resumed work at Calah, with a series of campaigns directed by

Ivory panels from Calah showing Egyptian influence. BM

The Black Obelisk of Shalmaneser III; in the second panel Jehu of Israel pays tribute to the Assyrian king. ORINST

M. E. L. Mallowan and David Oates 1949–61.

The main citadel was built by Shalmaneser I *c*. 1250 B.C. In the first years of his reign Ashur-nasir-pal II constructed in Calah (Heb. *Kālaḥ*, Akkad. *Kalḫu*) a new canal partly underground from the Upper Zab River to the city wall. He added a palace of brick faced with stone, decorated with characteristic Assyrian reliefs of religious ceremonies, hunting and battle scenes. Its doors were guarded by two colossal winged man-headed lions. This monarch was also responsible for the temple of Ninurta, in which were found an unusually excellent lion in high relief and two poorly preserved statues of Nabu with inscriptions by the city governor Bel-tarṣi-ilsuna. These mention Adad-nirari III (811–782 B.C.) and his queen mother Sammu-ramat (Semiramis of Gr. legend).

This latter king was so proud of his control of Babylonia that he built in Calah a replica of the temple of Ezida at Borsippa. Across the walled city from the acropolis Shalmanezer III erected *c*. 840 B.C. a tremendous fortified palace and arsenal, 18 acres in extent. The greater walled city with its armories and gates covered nearly 900 acres, and had a population of perhaps 60,000.

From Calah Tiglath-pileser III (744–727 B.C.) and Sargon II (721–705 B.C.) marched via Nineveh across the N Syrian plains to attack Palestine. After the latter conquered Samaria, he stored much booty in Calah, and a list of Jewish names written in Aramaic seems to suggest that captives from the northern kingdom were removed to Calah. Late in his reign Sargon built a new royal city at Khorsabad, and Sennacherib removed the capital to Nineveh; but Calah remained the military headquarters of the empire until it was burned in 612 B.C. by the Medes and Babylonians.

Other notable finds from Calah are the famous Black Obelisk showing the Israelite king Jehu (or his ambassador) paying tribute to Shalmanezer III; the rare statue in the round of Ashur-nasir-pal II; glazed tile and many objects of ivory and bronze showing Egyptian motifs and Phoenician craftsmanship; the great treaty

A royal servant from the palace at Calah, ninth century B.C. LM

tablet of Esarhaddon of 672 B.C. made with various Iranian princes; and the Banquet Stele, discovered in 1951, which describes the feast of dedication in 879 B.C. for the newly rebuilt capital to which Ashur-nasir-pal II invited 69,574 guests. They came from all parts of the kingdom and spent ten days consuming 2,200 oxen, 16,000 sheep, 10,000 skins of wine, and 10,000 barrels of beer. Cf. the number of sacrificial animals offered at the dedication of Solomon's temple – 22,000 oxen and 120,000 sheep, for seven days (I Kgs 8:62–66).

See Assyria.

Bibliography. M. E. L. Mallowan, *Nimrud and Its Remains,* 2 vols., London: Collins, 1966.

E. B. S.

CALAMUS. *See* Plants.

CALCOL (kăl'kŏl). Variant of Chalcol (I Kgs 4:31).

A Judahite (I Chr 2:6), one of several brothers, "sons of Mahol," each of whom was celebrated for wisdom. In I Kgs 4:31 they are compared in wisdom with Solomon. Since the word *māḥôl* is elsewhere found as a musical term (Ps 149:3; 150:4), "sons of Mahol" may mean members of an orchestral guild, with exceptional wisdom or skill in the composition of hymns. The name Kalkol appears in a 13th cen. B.C. Egyptian inscription found at Megiddo, as the name of a great Canaanite musician at Ashkelon.

CALDRON. An earthenware vessel for cooking, of undefined size and characteristics. In I Sam 2:14 the vessel was for use in the sanctuary; in Mic 3:3 the vessel was for domestic use. The Heb. word *sîr* is translated caldron in Jer 1:13 (ASV); 52:18 (KJV); Ezk 11:3, 7, 11. It was distinctly a large pot, employed both for domestic use and in the sanctuary.

CALEB (kā'lĕb)

1. Caleb, the son of Jephunneh of the tribe of Judah, was one of the 12 spies sent in from Kadesh-barnea to explore the land of Palestine (Num 13:6). While ten of the spies brought back an adverse report, discouraging the people from attempting the conquest of the Promised Land because of the great cities and the fearsome inhabitants, "the sons of Anak" (Num 13:33), Caleb and Joshua pleaded with Israel to go forward, trusting in the Lord (Num 13:30; 14:6–9). Although Israel failed to enter the land at that time because of unbelief, the Lord promised Caleb and Joshua that they would have a part in the occupation of the country because of their faith and loyalty (Num 14:24, 30). Caleb stands as a great monument of faith because he "wholly followed the Lord" (Num 32:12; Deut 1:36).

At the end of the 40 years of wandering under God's judgment, Caleb with Joshua entered the Promised Land and was a part of the great conquest. After the decisive victories of Joshua had subjugated the land as a whole, it became the responsibility of each tribe to occupy the territory that had been assigned to it by lot. Although he was now an aged man, Caleb set an example to the nation by the faith and vigor with which he claimed his possessions. Caleb asked for the city of Kiriath-arba in the hill country to the S. This was the city of Arba, "the greatest man among the Anakim," those giants who had so frightened the spies many years earlier (Josh 14:6–15, RSV). It is as though Caleb wished to show the people of Israel that their fathers could have entered the land 40 years before had they only believed.

As an inducement to the young men of his tribe, Caleb offered his daughter Achsah in marriage to the young man who would take the city of Kirjath-sepher (Josh 15:16; Jud 1:12). It was his own nephew Othniel, inspired by the reward and his own faith, who led the assault that took the city, and with it won the hand of Achsah (Josh 15:17 ff.; Jud 1:13 ff.). Othniel became the first of the judges of Israel in the years that followed (Jud 3:9).

There is no discrepancy between this account of the conquest of Caleb and the statement that Joshua "wiped out the Anakim" (RSV) and "took the whole land" (Josh 11:21, 23). It is clear in the book of Joshua that the organized resistance to Israel was broken by the two great victories at Gibeon and Hazor (Josh 10–11). After that it was only a question of the individual tribes moving into the assigned territories and taking over the cities one by one. As in modern warfare, the commander-in-chief is accredited with the whole operation. In great measure the tribes failed fully to possess the land because of their lack of faith and courage in wholly following the Lord (Jud 1:27 ff.). Here, as at Kadesh-barnea, the valiant Caleb set an example of what it means to follow God.

There is some question as to the exact ancestry of Caleb. The genealogy in I Chr 2:18 mentions Caleb as the son of Hezron. On the other hand, Jephunneh the Kenezite is called Caleb's father in Num 32:12. The Kenezites, descendants of Kenaz, seem to be one of the Edomite tribes roaming the deserts of Sinai (Gen 36:15). It was into one of these tribes, the Kenites, that Moses had married (Jud 1:16; 4:11). The migration of Israel northward attracted some of these people, and they joined themselves in faith to the Lord and to His people. Caleb's family was attached to the tribe of Judah, and Caleb quickly gained a place of leadership. Although the chief of the tribe was Nahshon, son of Amminadab (Num 2:3), it was Caleb who represented the tribe as a spy and later as one of those who divided the land into tribal areas (Josh 21:12). It is said that Caleb was given his portion "among the children of Judah" (Josh 15:13), implying that he was not actually a member of that tribe. Centuries later, in the days of Saul and David, the Calebites were still a distinct family in Judah and their part of the country seems to have been a separate enclave in the tribe (I Sam 25:3; 30:14).

2. The son of Hezron (I Chr 2:18-19) and grandson of Judah (I Chr 2:3-5). He was the great-grandfather of Bezaleel (Ex 31:2; I Chr 2:20), chief artisan of the tabernacle. He is called Chelubai in I Chr 2:9. Possibly he is the same as 1.

3. The son of Hur (I Chr 2:50) and grandson of 2 according to the Heb. The LXX and Vulgate connect this Caleb with the preceding verses (cf. I Chr 2:42-50 with I Chr 2:18-19), which would make him the same as 1.

P. C. J.

CALEB-EPHRATAH (kā'lĕb-ĕf'rȧ-thȧ). On the basis of I Chr 2:24, this is thought to be a place in the vicinity of Bethlehem where Caleb, the son of Hezron, an ancestor of David, died. This place is not mentioned elsewhere in the Bible, and the LXX of the passage reads: "And after the death of Hezron, Caleb went in to Ephratha, the wife of Hezron his father; and she bore him Ashur the father of Tekoa." It is possible that Ephratah was a second wife of Caleb's father Hezron whom Caleb took to establish his claim to the inheritance (cf. II Sam 16:22).

The Gezer Calendar. ORINST

CALENDAR. Palestine was a land without political unity until the time of the Heb. united monarchy. Among peoples who lived under city-state rule centered around an important temple, the tendency was to develop separate menologies or ecclesiastical calendars. In the ancient Near East the best documented calendars of this type were those of the Sumerians. One determines the provenience of a Sumerian business document by the month name appearing in the date formula. Not until the strong central government of Hammurabi did the Babylonian month names begin to take the place of local menologies.

The evidence from Palestine bears witness to a similar system of local rather than national menologies.

First, there is a noticeable silence of any official month names used continuously by the Jews before they took the Babylonian names during the Babylonian Exile.

Secondly, it is important to note that three of the month names which were used in pre-Exilic Israel are Phoenician names. These are Ziv (*ziw*), Ethanim (*'ētānîm*) and Bul (*bûl*), which are mentioned only in I Kgs 6 and 8 in connection with building and dedicating the temple. The month Abib (*'ābîb*, Ex 13:4; 23:15; 34:18; Deut 16:1) usually associated with the above names is not attested in Phoenician sources.

Thirdly, *yeraḥ* is primitive Semitic and in Heb. is the older poetic word for "month." In Phoenician, Ugaritic and the Gezer Calendar, *yeraḥ* is regularly employed. The more common prosaic Heb. idiom in the Bible is *ḥōdesh*. The contrast between these two words is striking in I Kgs 6:38, "in the month (*yeraḥ*) Bul, which is the eighth month" (*ḥōdesh*).

In this light it is significant that in every usage of *'ābîb* the term *ḥōdesh* is employed. This, along with the fact that *'ābîb* is not attested in Phoenician sources, gives reason for assuming it belonged to another calendar.

The fourth piece of evidence comes from the meaning of *'ābîb*. In Ex 9:31 Pharaoh's barley was ruined by the hail because *haśś^{e}'ōrâ 'ābîb*, "the barley was freshly ripened." In Ex 13:4 the phrase *b^{e}ḥōdesh hā'ābîb* clearly means "in the month of the freshly ripened barley." Therefore *'ābîb* is an agricultural common noun incorporated in the month name of an early agricultural menology in use among the Hebrews.

The evidence for a fifth menology is the Gezer Calendar written by a schoolboy on a limestone tablet dating from the late 10th cen. B.C. It is still another completely distinct local calendar based on agricultural seasons.

Both *yeraḥ* and *ḥōdesh* are words associated with lunation, the time elapsing between two successive new moons, averaging 29 days, 12 hours, 44 minutes and 2.8 seconds. Although *ḥōdesh* (from *ḥādāsh*, "new") originated from observation of the moon's renewal, the word was by no means limited to this exact connotation. This is seen in Gen 29:14, where Jacob dwelt with Laban *ḥōdesh yāmîm*, "a month of days."

Egypt developed a solar calendar having 30-day months irrespective of the renewing of the moon, but here again the 30-day period must have originated from lunation since 30 days is an approximate lunation and could refer

HEBREW MONTHS, FESTIVALS, AND SEASONS

Lunar Month	Preexilic Hebrew Name	Postexilic Babylonian Name	Modern Equivalent	Festivals	Agricultural Season
1	Abib (Ex 13:4; 23:15; 34:18; Deut 16:1)	Nisan (Neh 2:1; Est 3:7)	Mar.-Apr.	1st: New Moon 10th: Passover lamb selected (Ex 12:3) 14th: Passover lamb killed (Ex 12:6-7; Lev 23:5) 15th-21st: Unleavened Bread (Lev 23:6-8) 16th: Wave sheaf offered (Lev 23:10-14)	Latter (spring) rains Green figs and leaf buds Barley harvest begins Flax harvest
2	Ziv (1 Kgs 6:1,37)	Iyyar	Apr.-May	1st: New Moon 14th: Later Passover for those unclean in 1st month (Num 9:10-11)	Dry season begins
3		Sivan (Est 8:9)	May-June	1st: New Moon 6th: Feast of Weeks (Feast of Wheat Harvest, Pentecost), loaves of wheat flour offered on 50th day from 16th of Nisan (Ex 23:16; Lev 23:19-21)	Wheat harvest Early or first-ripe figs
4		Tammuz	June-July	1st: New Moon	Vine-tending
5		Ab	July-Aug.	1st: New Moon	First-ripe grapes Olives in lowlands
6		Elul (Neh 6:15)	Aug.-Sept.	1st: New Moon	Olive and grape harvest Dates and summer figs
7	Ethanim (1 Kgs 8:2)	Tishri	Sept.-Oct.	1st: Blowing of Trumpets (Rosh Hashanah, New Year, Lev 23:24). Beginning of civil year 10th: Day of Atonement (Yom Kippur; Lev 16; 23:27-32) 15th-21st: Feast of Ingathering (Ex 23:16) or Tabernacles (Succoth, Booths, Lev 23: 34-43) 22nd: Holy convocation (Lev 23:36; Num 29:35)	Olive harvest completed Vintage Early (autumn) rains begin Plowing begins
8	Bul (1 Kgs 6:38)	Marcheshvan	Oct.-Nov.	1st: New Moon	Barley and wheat sown
9		Kislev (Neh 1:1; Zech 7:1)	Nov.-Dec.	1st: New Moon 25th: Dedication (1 Macc 4:52-59; Jn 10:22)	Planting continued
10		Tebeth (Est 2:16)	Dec.-Jan.	1st: New Moon	Winter rains, occasional snow in hill country
11		Shebat (Zech 1:7)	Jan.-Feb.	1st: New Moon	Almonds blossom
12		Adar (Ezr 6:15; Est 3:7)	Feb.-Mar.	1st: New Moon 14th-15th: Purim (Est 9:17-28)	Citrus fruit harvest; hoeing flax
(13)		Adar Sheni	c. 7 times in 19 years		

to nothing else, and the hieroglyph for "month" is the crescent.

There is no evidence in the Bible of any such uniform solar month; indeed, the new moon festivals are quite important and called for special sacrifices, the blowing of trumpets, and feasts (Num 28:11–15; Ezr 3:5; Neh 10:33; II Chr 2:4; 8:13; I Sam 20:18–34).

Since lunation and agricultural seasons are two phenomena early employed by the Hebrews for time reckoning, when they are used together as is clear from these calendars, one concludes that intercalation was necessary. Otherwise the agricultural festivals, which were based on annual solar seasons though expressed in terms of lunar months, could not have kept on representing the proper agricultural event. The Sumerian lunar calendars were also tied to the seasons, hence they also intercalated according to need. For example, a second month of *še-kin-kud* is frequently attested in order to keep the season of harvest approximately in place in the calendar.

The Hebrews in rustic simplicity achieved a solar year by making the months agree with agricultural seasons and intercalating when necessary. The Egyptians, though pioneers in the sophisticated non-lunar months which we have inherited through the Romans, made a small error; small, though big enough to send the "seasons" on a 1,460 year cycle around the true solar year, commonly called the Sothic Cycle because the year was measured by the first appearance of the star Sothos on the horizon at exact sunrise. They neglected the one-quarter of a day which we make up with our leap year.

The Hebrews outgrew their simple agricultural calendars as they too became more sophisticated. When Solomon built the temple, he employed Phoenician technicians. Just as Phoenicians supplied materials and served as craftsmen, it is reasonable to believe that Phoenicians also kept the records of building progress. The Phoenician month names Ziv, Ethanim, and Bul were used by Phoenician scribes, and are found in the OT only in connection with the building and dedicating of Solomon's temple. That these months are defined by the Heb. numbered months suggests that sometime during the monarchy, for administrative reasons, this system of numbered months was employed. It was quite likely instituted all at once by the central authority of the crown.

The numbered system was evoked by the administrative needs of the monarchy when, for example, tax collection and conscription brought about the need for a uniform calendar throughout the realm. Tax administration might become an acute problem if each community had its own menology. The Egyptians had for a long time numbered the months from one to four within each of the three seasons. The Heb. monarchy merely improved on this by straight 1 to 12 numbering. Such may not have originally affected the common people who would continue their provincial ways, but crown officials would be forced to go by the national reckoning. In the book of Jeremiah only the numbered system is used.

After the Exile the Jews, like other subject peoples in the world empires of Assyria, Babylonia, and Persia, were gradually forced into using the Babylonian names. This change was effected by a strong central government that cut across national lines. Although a Persian government official, Nehemiah seems to have preferred the Babylonian names. Ezra, the scribe and priest, in all but one instance uses the Judean numbered designation. The book of Esther uses both, giving dual references. Likewise the Elephantine papyri use dual references giving both the Babylonian and Egyptian month names; for in Egypt of Persian times the old numbered system was given up in favor of festival names. Gradually later Judaism adopted the Babylonian names to the exclusion of other systems.

The Jews at various times in the OT employed at least five different calendars:

1. The *'ābîb* calendar, a local agricultural menology, this being the only month name we have from it. The new year began in the spring, the system followed for the festivals outlined in the Levitical law.

2. The Gezer Calendar, which is the only extant example of another local menology. It began with the two months of olive harvest, our early autumn. This inscription is on a small tablet of soft limestone discovered during Macalister's excavation of Gezer in 1908. W. F. Albright believes it was written *c.* 925 B.C. in verse in good biblical Hebrew:

> *His two months are (olive) harvest,*
> *His two months are planting (grain),*
> *His two months are late planting;*
> *His month is hoeing up of flax,*
> *His month is harvest of barley,*
> *His month is harvest and feasting;*
> *His two months are vine-tending,*
> *His month is summer fruit*

(ANET, p. 320; see also DOTT, pp. 201 ff.).

3. A Phoenician calendar with months named *Ziv*, *'Ētānîm*, and *Bûl*, all attested in Phoenician sources and used in the Bible only where Phoenician personnel were concerned.

4. The numbered system which came about through practical demands under the monarchy. We know that Gezer was incorporated into Solomon's realm upon the capture of Gezer by Solomon's Pharaonic father-in-law. The multiplicity of such local calendars doubtless precipitated the numbered system. Solomon's civil year apparently began in the autumn with the Feast of Trumpets (Lev 23:24 f.). The dedication of his temple (I Kgs 8:2) was postponed for eleven months (cf.6:38), apparently in order to make it a part of the autumnal new year festival (Rosh Hashana).

5. The Babylonian month names, which were forced on the entire Near East as a con-

sequence of the ancient world empires. Their new year was in the spring.

During the intertestamental period pious Jews developed a perfectly regular calendar in order to insure the proper observance of their holy days. As learned from the Book of Jubilee (written between 135 and 105 B.C.) the year consisted of 364 days divided into four series of three months each, the first and second months always having 30 days and the third 31 days. The first day of the first month was always Wednesday, so that the eve of the Passover was on Tuesday every year. This was the calendar observed by the Qumran community for dating their religious festivals (see Finegan, *Light from the Ancient Past,* pp. 580–587). Some scholars have suggested Jesus and His disciples were following this system in eating the Passover meal in advance of the date officially observed in Jerusalem (Finegan, pp. 596 f.).

See Era; Festivals; Time.

Bibliography. F. F. Bruce, "Calendar," NBD, pp. 176–179. CornPBE, pp. 176 ff. S. J. DeVries, "Calendar," IDB, I, 483–488. Jack Finegan, *Light from the Ancient Past,* 2nd ed., Princeton: Princeton Univ. Press, 1959, pp. 552–598. J. van Goudoever, *Biblical Calendars,* 2nd ed. rev., Leiden: E. J. Brill, 1961.

E. B. S.

An Apis bull. LM

CALF. *See* Animals, I.6.

CALF, GOLDEN

1. While Moses was absent in Mount Sinai, Aaron made an image of a bull calf which he announced as the god who brought Israel out of Egypt (Ex 32:1–20). The worship and play conducted before this image so angered Moses upon his return that he broke the tablets of stone containing the law of God and made the people ingest the image, reduced to fine powder, with their drinking water. This idolatry may have been patterned after Egyptian and Semite bull-cults in the Egyptian Delta with their symbolism of strength and fertility.

2. In order to hold the loyalty of the people after their revolt from Rehoboam by cutting them off from the temple at Jerusalem, Jeroboam set up rival centers of worship in Bethel and Dan and installed a golden (bull) calf in both places (I Kgs 12:28–32). Whether Jeroboam intended to displace the worship of God or merely to give some visible aid to His worship, these calves did become objects of worship (Hos 10:5–6; 13:2).

It should be noted that some peoples of this part of the world thought of their gods as invisibly seated or standing on the back of an animal that would be reproduced in wood or metal at a cultic center. Possibly Jeroboam had this in mind when setting up the calves in Israel.

J. K. M.

CALKER. *See* Occupations.

CALL, CALLED, CALLING. Although "call" has many ordinary usages in the Scriptures, its chief importance is as a specifically theological term. The verb form *(kaleō),* when used technically, refers to God's (rarely Christ's) call to men to participate in the blessings of redemption. The benefits may be described as God's call unto His glory (I Pet 5:10; II Pet 1:3); to eternal life (I Tim 6:12); unto fellowship with His Son (I Cor 1:9); and from darkness unto His marvelous light (I Pet 2:9).

The call is dependent upon God's divine purpose (Rom 8:30; 9:11), established through the free grace of God (Gal 1:6, 15), and reaches men through the proclamation of the gospel (II Thess 2:14), so becoming man's one hope (Eph 4:4). The calling is directed not only to man's salvation but to his behavior. Thus Christians are called not to uncleanness but to sanctification (I Thess 4:7); to patience in suffering (I Pet 2:21); to freedom (Gal 5:13); and to life in peace (I Cor 7:15).

The noun form "calling" *(klēsis)* appears in the NT in a technical sense exclusively. The invitation is to enter the kingdom of God, to receive it as a gift and possession. Included in the invitation is a decided emphasis on the sovereign initiative of God. "For the gracious gifts of God and his calling are irrevocable" (Rom 11:29, NEB). "Think what sort of people you are, whom God has called . . . God has chosen what the world counts folly . . . so there is no place for human pride" (I Cor 1:26-28, NEB; cf. Eph 4:4). But this divine call requires a human response as well. "All the more then, my friends, exert yourselves to clinch God's choice and calling of you" (II Pet 1:10, NEB; cf. also II Thess 1:11).

The call may be spoken of as a call from heaven (Heb 3:1) and as a call to the heavenly life (Phil 3:14). It is also a holy calling (II Tim 1:9), which is not open to human understanding but requires spiritual discernment (Eph 1:18).

The verbal adjective "called" *(klētos)* is used in two ways. In the majority of cases it has in view the call to salvation (so Rom 1:6-7; I Cor 1:24; Jude 1; Rev 17:14); but a new dimension appears in Rom 1:1 and I Cor 1:1 where calling becomes effectual in terms of an office—"called to be an apostle."

It is Matthew's parable about the wedding feast ("many are called [*klētos*], but few are chosen" [*eklektoi*], Mt 22:14) that provides the text with the greatest difficulty. Contrary to the practice in other instances (see especially Rev 17:14; but also Rom 8:28 f.), the elect here are distinguished from those who are called. In spite of K. L. Schmidt's warning that we do not know the Aramaic wording behind the text (TWNT, III, 496), the context clearly supports the distinction. The dialectic tension of which the verse speaks cannot be located in the fact that in some instances many are called and in other instances only few are called, as Schmidt maintains. It is rather that many are invited but few are accepted. What the text asserts is that God as the inviter has the sole prerogative to qualify those who may attend. The purpose of the utterance is not to give comfort to the chosen few. In the parable the call to the many has been extended and refused. Those who are gathered are men originally passed by. But even they are not exempt from judgment. Each must have his wedding garment to be accepted (chosen).

The parable is a warning. It reiterates what is taught elsewhere in Matthew (cf. Mt 5:20) and particularly in the immediate context. In the parable of the vineyard just preceding, the conclusion is that he "will rent out the vineyard to other vinegrowers, who will pay him the proceeds at the *proper* seasons . . . . Therefore I say to you, the kingdom of God will be taken away from you, and be given to a nation producing the fruit of it" (Mt 21:41, 43, NASB).

In Mt 23:3 the theme is continued in Jesus' condemnation of the Pharisees who preached but did not practice righteousness. Merit consists not in being one of the few, but in possessing a righteousness acceptable to God. *See* Chosen; Election; Vocation.

Bibliography. Alan Richardson, *A Theological Word Book of the Bible,* New York: Macmillan, 1960, pp. 39 f. J. L. Schmidt, "*Kaleō,* etc.," TDNT, III, 487-501. K. Stendahl, "The Called and the Chosen," *The Root of the Vine,* New York: Philosophical Library, 1953, pp. 63-80.

G. W. Ba.

CALNEH (kăl'nĕ), **CALNO** (kăl'nō). The name of a city or village in NW Syria referred to in Amos 6:2 and Isa 10:9. Although today Calneh is often equated with Assyrian *Kunalū'a (Kinalū'a),* the present site of which is believed by some to be a large tell one mile E of Ḥarîm, the best identification still remains that of I. J. Gelb (cf. *American Journal of Semitic Languages and Literatures* 51 [1935], pp. 189-191) who equates Assyrian *Kullāni* (Calneh) with modern Kullan Köy, about ten miles SE of Arpad. Canneh *(q.v.),* though located in the same general area (cf. Ezk 27:23), was perhaps a different site.

Heb. *kalnēh* in Gen 10:10 should doubtless be revocalized to read *kullānâ,* "all of them" (cf. RSV), as in Gen 42:36 (cf. also Prov 31:29), since no Calneh is known in Babylonia (cf. W. F. Albright in JNES, III [1944], 254 f., R. Youngblood in *Bethel Seminary Quarterly,* XI [1962], 8 f.). LXX *pántes,* "all," translating the Heb. consonants *k-l-n-h* in Amos 6:2, further demonstrates such a revocalization to be not without foundation.

R. Y.

CALNO (kăl'nō). A city which had fallen to the Assyrians, cited as an example to Israel of the futility of offering resistance to them (Isa 10:9). This is probably the Kulnia associated with Arpad and Hadadezer in the Assyrian "tribute list." It is also called Calneh (*q.v.*) and mentioned with Hamath in Amos 6:2. It may be modern Kullan Köy, 20 miles NW of Aleppo.

CALVARY (kăl'vȧ-rĭ). The word occurs in only one place in the Bible (Lk 23:33). It comes from the Vulgate, which in all four Gospels (Mt 27:33; Mk 15:22; Lk 23:33; Jn 19:17) translates the Gr. word *kranion* ("a skull") by *calvaria,* the Latin word for skull. Strangely, the KJV translators gave the correct English equivalent, "a skull," in three of the Gospels. For some unknown reason they varied this in the

Gordon's Calvary. Garden Tomb Assn.

The Church of the Holy Sepulchre covers the traditional site of Calvary. G. Semerdjian

case of Luke, adopting a Latinism. Thus by literary accident the term appeared in what became the most widely used English version. Though based on this one odd occurrence, the term "Calvary" has taken on such rich devotional and theological associations that its value guarantees it a permanent place in the Christian vocabulary.

The location of Calvary is uncertain. The traditional site, fixed in the 4th cen. by Helena, the mother of Emperor Constantine, is in the Church of the Holy Sepulchre. But this is inside the present N wall of Jerusalem (where the N wall was in Jesus' day is not yet established by archaeologists) and it is implied that Christ died outside the wall (Heb 13:12). For this reason some have preferred "Gordon's Calvary," a skull-shaped rock some 250 yards NE of the Damascus Gate.

See Cross; Golgotha.

R. E.

CALVINISM. This is the name of that system of theological thought which was brought to its most complete expression by the great Swiss reformer John Calvin (1509–64). It is also called Reformed doctrine. Its emphases include predestination and the sovereignty of God. It must not be forgotten that Calvinism holds, besides its distinctives, to those doctrines common to all historic Christianity, such as the full truthfulness of Scripture, the Trinity, the deity of Christ, His supernatural miracles, bodily resurrection, etc. Without these basic and fundamental doctrines a theology cannot properly be called Calvinistic or Reformed.

Although Calvin gave the Reformed doctrine its most thorough formulation, the theology had long been held. Calvin would have been the first to have denied its novelty. He found it in the Church Fathers and, of course, in the Bible. This theology and its main opposing view, now called Arminianism *(q.v.),* were much discussed through the Middle Ages in the Latin church. Augustine was a prominent protagonist of the position later held by Calvin. Indeed, Calvinism is often called Augustinianism. In the Council of Trent in 1545, the Roman Catholic church, partly in reaction to the reformers, officially espoused the Arminian view.

Martin Luther's view on the sovereignty of God was very similar to Calvin's. His tract on *The Bondage of the Will* speaks strongly of total depravity. Later, Lutheran thought on these matters inclined more toward Melancthon's Arminian views. In post-Reformation days a reaction set in and in Holland Jacob Arminius (1560–1609) advocated a greater emphasis on free will. His five theses were condemned by the Synod of Dort (1618) which formulated the famous five points of Calvinism remembered by the acronym TULIP: total depravity, unconditional election, limited atonement (now often called definite atonement), irresistible grace, and perseverance of the saints (or as now sometimes put, the perseverance of God in the saints).

Prominent Calvinistic creeds are the Westminster Confession, the Heidelberg Catechism, the Belgic Confession, and the Scotch Confession of 1560. The Arminian position has been adopted especially in Methodism; the Calvinistic, in Presbyterian, Reformed, the older Episcopal, and many of the older Baptist churches.

It must be remembered that Calvinism does not deny free will. It declares that God's sovereignty extends to all things and persons, but that His sovereign control in some inscrutable way does not deny man's free moral agency and responsibility. Note also that the problem of sovereignty and freedom was not originated by Calvinism or even by Christianity. Plato struggled with the problem and concluded with belief in a creator limited by his refractory materials. Muslim theologians also face the problem and adopt the position of fatalism. Calvinism does not claim to solve the problem, but only to put it in the Scripture focus and leave it there, not going beyond what is written.

R. L. H.

CAMEL. *See* Animals, I.5.

CAMEL'S HAIR. In Mt 3:4 and Mk 1:6 the outer garment of John the Baptist is said to have been of camel's hair. It is rather long and woolly in texture, and when woven makes a coarse, durable textile which both ancient and modern Bedouins have found suitable for clothing or tent coverings. Toward the spring when the camel is shedding, the hair of the neck, back and hump is either clipped or pulled in handfuls or licks. It is then woven on hand looms and made into camel's hair cloth. Elijah's mantle of "haircloth" (II Kgs 1:8, RSV) and the "hairy mantle" mentioned in Zechariah (13:4, RSV) may be OT references to this textile.

CAMON (kā'mŏn). Camon is found in KJV, but in other versions is spelled Kamon. It was where Jair, the Gileadite judge, was buried (Jud 10:5), probably in Gilead.

CAMP

1. The most common Heb. word for camp is *maḥăneh,* which probably comes from a root meaning "to bend or curve." Hence it is thought that the Heb. camp in the seminomadic period was usually in a circle with the tents surrounding the cattle and sheep, and wagons surrounding the women and children in times of travel, for protection from attack. The same Heb. word is used of a caravan of travelers (Gen 32:7–8, "company"); of a band of angels (Gen 32:2); of all the tribes of Israel encamped around the tabernacle (Num 2:17); of the camp of the armies of Israel (Josh 6:11; I Sam 4:3, 5); of the funeral "company" of Jacob (Gen

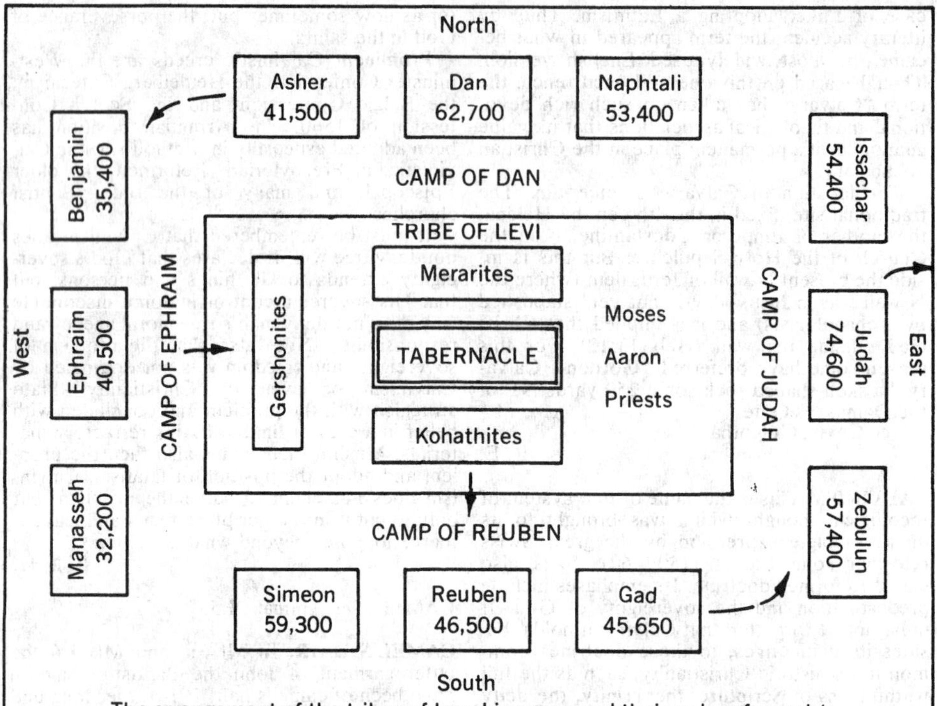

The arrangement of the tribes of Israel in camp and their order of march/ (based on Num 2,3 with arrows indicating order in line of march)

50:9). The temple is even called "the camp of the Levites" in I Chr 9:18 (RSV).

2. Once (II Kgs 6:8) the Heb. *taḥănōt*, "camp," "encampment," occurs. The form of the word is related to 1 above.

3. The Gr. word for camp, *parembolē*, refers to the barracks of the Roman army in Acts 21:34 (RSV). In Heb 13:11, 13 the sin offering is mentioned as being burnt outside the camp of Israel. A figurative reference to the militant saints is made in Rev 20:9.

R. L. S.

CAMPHIRE. *See* Plants.

CANA (kā'nȧ). A Galilean village mentioned only in the fourth Gospel as the site of Jesus' first miracle (Jn 2:1, 11), as the place where He spoke the word to heal a nobleman's son lying sick in Capernaum (Jn 4:46), and as the home of Nathanael (Jn 21:2).

The location of Cana in Galilee (so called to distinguish it from a Cana in Coelesyria) has long been an open question in Gospel geography. Various identifications are:

1. Khirbet Kana, overlooking the Battof Valley (also called Plain of Zebulun or Plain of Netophah) nine miles N of Nazareth. This site was reidentified by Robinson (*Biblical Researches . . .*, III, 204–207). Dalman also argues for this site (*Sacred Sites . . .*, pp. 101–106). Etymologically, historically, archaeologically, and geographically, a strong case can be made for this locale as the true site of Cana. Archaeologists in 1963 discovered pottery of the Iron II, Hellenistic, Herodian, Late Roman, Arabic, and Crusader periods. This is important since Tiglath-pileser III mentions his capture of a town in Galilee named Qana (see ANET, p. 283). The Iron II sherds of Khirbet Kana strengthen its case as being the true Cana. Surface coins of the 1st cen. A.D. have been found here according to reports (cf. Kraeling, *Bible Atlas*, pp. 372–373), and the name ("reeds") is naturally accounted for by the fact that reeds once grew bountifully in the marshy Battof Valley (called the Asochis Valley in the NT period; cf. Jos *Life*, 41). This Cana was inhabited as late as the time of Quaresimus (17th cen.).

2. Others (De Saulcy, Vilnay?, Pilter, Farrar) favor Kefr Kenna. There is little tangible evidence to support this view, which was never popular before the Franciscans settled there in the 16th cen. "Tradition" located the site at Kenna to make it more convenient for travelers, since it was on the main road between Nazareth and Tiberias. But Eusebius says that Cana was in the area of the tribe of Asher, near Sidon (cf. *Onomasticon*, ed. Klostermann, pp.

116-117). Besides, other pilgrims speak of Sepphoris as being located between Nazareth and Cana, which would be out of the question for Kenna.

3. Ain Kana, S of er-Rene, has also been so identified, but this location has never been widely accepted.

Cana must have remained a strictly Jewish community throughout the Roman period, since the priestly family of Eliashib was settled here after the destruction of the temple in A.D. 70. The stone jars, used by the Jews for purifying (cf. Jn 2:6), are explained by several examples of such jars which still are to be found at 3rd cen. synagogues in Galilee (see photos), or certain pedestal urns, made of soft limestone, which date from the Herodian period and have been found at various places in Palestine (cf. *Gallery Book, Palestine Archaeological Museum; Persian, Hellenistic, Roman, Byzantine Periods,* p. 35, freestanding 1092; and for a photograph [of one found at Ain Feskha], cf. Roland deVaux, *L'Archelogie et Les Manuscrits de la Mer Morte,* London: 1961, p. xxxiv). The Talmud speaks of lustral vases which contained the water and the ashes of a red heifer located at the entrance of the court of Israel in the temple enclosure (cf. Parah, iii.3).

Bibliography. See books referred to above. M. Avi-Yonah, *Views of the Biblical World,* Jerusalem: International Publishing Co., 1961, V, 138. Ch. Clermont-Ganneau, "La mosique de Kefr Kenna," *Recueil d'Arch. Or.,* Paris: Leroux, 1901, pp. 345-360, 372-373. W. H. Dixon, "Itineraries of Our Lord," PEQ (1878), pp. 67-73. Samuel Klein, *Beitrage zur Geographie und Geschichte Galiläas,* Leipzig: Rudolf Haupt, 1909, pp. 56 ff. Clemen Kopp, *Das Kana des Evangeliums,* 1940. E. W. G. Masterman, "Cana of Galilee," PEQ (1914), pp. 179 ff. W. T. Pilter, "Where is Cana of Galilee?" PEQ (1883), pp. 143-148. W. M. Thomson, *The Land and the Book,* Hartford: Scranton, II, 303-306. Zeller, "Kefr Kenna," PEQ I (1869-70), 71-73.

E. J. V.

CANAAN (kā'nǎn), **CANAANITE** (kā'nǎ-nīt). A personal name applied to the youngest son of Ham (Gen 9:18); a tribal name for peoples supposedly descended from him; and a geographical name describing the territory occupied by those descendants.

As a tribal name, Gen 10:15-19 lists eleven subdivisions, Ex 13:5 lists five, Ex 23:23 lists six, Deut 7:1 lists seven, and Gen 15:19-21 lists ten. Omission in the other lists of the last five names of the Gen 10 list may result from their unimportance. The additions to the Gen 15 list may be primarily of tribes in the Negeb and the Sinai peninsula.

As a geographical term, Canaan at one time was the name of the land along the Mediterranean from modern Syria to S of Gaza. However, throughout most of OT times it referred

Remains of the Canaanite city of Hazor destroyed by Joshua. Yigael Yadin

to all the territory W of the Jordan. Taking its name from the chief tribal group inhabiting it, the land was called *Keᵉna'an,* according to both Gen 10 and native Canaanite-Phoenician tradition as transmitted by Sanchuniathon and preserved by Philo of Byblos.

The Canaanites can be traced back before 3000 B.C. to the founding or rebuilding with strong walls of such cities as Jericho, Beth Shean, Beth Yerah and Megiddo. About 2200/2100 B.C. a wave of Amorite *(q.v.)* invasions into Syria and Canaan greatly influenced Canaanite civilization. The Early Bronze Age cities of the Canaanites fell before the nomadic chieftains, who often camped on the ruined sites and buried their dead in tombs nearby, as at Jericho. As these Amorites amalgamated with the Canaanites, towns again began to multiply in Palestine *c.* 1900 B.C., revealing a change from nomadic to urban civilization. This is documented by comparing the 20th cen. Egyptian Execration texts now in Berlin with the similar 19th cen. texts in Brussels. The earlier series lists several headmen with Amorite names for several localities, suggesting seminomadic conditions. In the latter set of texts the following are some of the Canaanite towns listed, naming only one ruler for each: Jerusalem, Shechem, Accho, Achshaph, Tyre, Hazor, Aphek, Ashtaroth, Pella, Shutu (Sheth, Num 24:17), and Byblos (BASOR #83, pp. 33 f.).

Beginning *c.* 1750 B.C. the Canaanites broke with Egyptian and other cultural influences and began to develop their own culture and art. Known at this time as the Hyksos, they established many commercial contacts with the Aegean world. From 1800 until 1500 B.C. there was a great movement of Hurrians (biblical Horites) and some Indo-Iranians (including Hittites) into Syria and Palestine, so that the Canaanites of the Late Bronze Age became a very mixed race.

Linguistic evidence shows the presence or influence of Canaanites in the Sinai peninsula about 1500 B.C. Their culture reached its peak

Roman columns frame the Crusader castle, below which stand the Canaanite walls of Gebal (Byblos).

at Ras Shamra (Ugarit) about 1500 B.C. After 1400 B.C. the Canaanites in Canaan were being disrupted by the Israelite and Aramaean invasions as documented by the Amarna tablets. *See* Joshua, Book of. In the 12th cen. the Sea Peoples (including the Philistines) from the Aegean Sea region took possession of the Canaanite seacoast from Gaza to S of Joppa and destroyed Ugarit and Tyre. Shortly afterward Aramaeans took over most of the northern territory of the Canaanites, establishing the kingdom of Damascus (Syria), which became so troublesome to later Israelite and Judean kings. As a result of these invasions, the Canaanite territory shrank to one-tenth of its original extent. This led to a new Canaanite capital being established at Tyre as the center of a colonizing empire. Byblos and Sidon became leading cities in this era.

From these outposts, traders and colonizers set forth in the 9th cen. to found colonies on Sardinia, with settlements on Cyprus antedating them, and those at Carthage not much later. These traders even colonized Spain (ancient Tartessus or Tarshish, *q.v.*). However, historians make a division in Canaanite history and culture at *c.* 1100-1000 B.C., calling the period subsequent to that date "Phoenician" *(q.v.)*. This term probably is derived from Gr. *phoinos,* "purple" *(q.v.),* referring to a famous and expensive dye made by the Phoenicians from the murex shellfish. With the defeat of Tyre by Nebuchadnezzar in 572 B.C. the Canaanites/Phoenicians ceased to be of importance in biblical history.

Linguistically, the Canaanites spoke and wrote a language very closely related to, if not the antecedent of, classical biblical Heb. The earliest evidence for a Canaanite dialect is found in the inscriptions of the Sinai turquoise mines at Serabit el-Khadem, dating to *c.* 1500 B.C. The decipherers say these inscriptions are adaptations of Egyptian hieroglyphics by the acrophonic principle to a Canaanite dialect. These adapted figures were later stylized into the Canaanite script of *c.* 1000 B.C., the almost identical Phoenician script of the 8th cen. (as known at Karatepe). Probably most of the OT was written in a similar script. Although they were in contact with four other styles of writing—Egyptian hieroglyphs, Byblian syllabic writing, Akkadian syllabic cuneiform, and Ugaritic alphabetic cuneiform—the Canaanites rejected them in developing their own alphabetic script. From the Phoenicians, *c.* 800 B.C., the Greeks borrowed the alphabet which is used by most modern Western languages. *See* Writing.

The literary character of the Canaanite civilization is attested by a whole library of religious literature found in the house of the chief priest between two temples at the site of ancient Ugarit. Beginning in 1929, an extensive literature in a dialect closely related to early Heb. was recovered in the Ras Shamra Ugaritic tablets. The mythological texts, Ba'al and Anath, Dan'el and Aqhat, and Keret (cf. ANET, pp. 129 ff. for H. L. Ginsburg's translations; also translated in T. H. Gaster's *Thespis*), not only show the religious myths and ideas of Canaanite culture, but also are verbally and stylistically quite similar to early Heb. poetry, especially the song of Miriam (Ex 15), the song of Deborah (Jud 5), the blessing of Moses (Deut 33), and Ps 29 and 68. The Heb. poets borrowed much of their style and vocabulary from the Canaanites without, however, taking over their religious ideas. Through the Bible, the Canaanites have passed on some of their literary forms to the world.

Canaanite religion left its impress upon the OT in two ways: (1) certain mythological themes (e.g., Leviathan) were borrowed by the Hebrews for illustrative purposes and some practices and cult objects (e.g., incense altars) adapted to the worship of God; (2) the reaction of the Heb. prophets against the false theology and impure, idolatrous worship. The former category includes some architectural features of the Solomonic temple and some of its furnishings. The latter classification includes the Heb. rebellion against Canaanite polytheism, its sensuality, worship of idols, and practices such as human sacrifice, sacred prostitution, eunuch priests, and serpent worship.

The pantheon of the Canaanites, according to the Ugaritic literature, was headed by El, the creator god, whose wife was Asherah. Their son (or grandson), Ba'al, was the god of fertility, the "activator" of all life, and the real power to be worshiped. His wife was Anath, the goddess of love and war. Other gods were Dagon, the grain god; Resheph, god of plagues; Shulman, god of healing; Koshar, the inventor god; and Mot, the god of death (*see* Gods, False). The OT presents a slightly different picture of the pantheon, with Ashtoreth (Ishtar) being the wife of Ba'al. Such variations from region to region are common in the ancient Near East. *See* R'as Shamra.

Canaanite cultic practices centered around elaborate rites of sacrifice of cattle, rams, ewes, lambs, wild animals, birds, doves. There is some evidence that they offered up the front shoulder as did the Hebrews. Altars were erected at high places; in connection there were sacred groves, trees, or carved wooden images of Asherah (*see* Gods, False; Heb. *'ăshērâ,* cf. Jud 6:25, RSV). Canaanite temples had a "holy of holies" with an idol enshrined, an altar of incense before its entrance, libation bowls and small lamps. Divination, snake worship and sacred prostitution were practiced. The latter was supposed to make the lands, domesticated animals, and human beings fertile and productive.

Evidence of the widespread influence of Canaanite religion can be seen in the mention of Ba'al-zephon in Egypt (Ex 14:2). This probably refers to a site where Ba'al of Saphon, "the lord of the North," was worshiped.

In material culture, from the middle to the end of the 2nd mil. B.C. the Canaanites were quite advanced as evidenced by their walled cities, buildings, pottery, ivory inlays and other artifacts.

Bibliography. William F. Albright, *The Archaeology of Palestine,* 2nd ed., Harmondsworth: Penguin Books, 1960; *Archaeology and the Religion of Israel,* 2nd ed., Baltimore: Johns Hopkins Univ. Press, 1956; *From the Stone Age to Christianity,* 2nd ed., Baltimore: Johns Hopkins Univ. Press, 1957; "The Role of the Canaanites in the History of Civilization," appendix to *The Bible and the Ancient Near East,* G. Ernest Wright, ed., New York: Doubleday, 1961; *Yahweh and the Gods of Canaan,* Garden City: Doubleday, 1968. CornPBE, pp. 179–196, 210–211. J. Gray, *The Legacy of Canaan* (supplement to VT, V), Leiden: Brill, 1957. Kathleen Kenyon, *Archaeology in the Holy Land,* London: Ernest Benn, 1960. George Ernest Wright, *Biblical Archaeology,* Philadelphia: Westminster 1957.

A. K. H.

CANAANITE, SIMON THE. *See* Simon; Zealot.

CANAL. The word "canals" occurs in several places in the ASV marg. (Ex 7:19; 8:5; Isa 19:6; Nah 3:8). In the account of the plagues (Ex 7:19), names are used descriptively to designate the different waters of Egypt: *neh̄ārôt,* "flowing streams," for the main branches or channels of the river Nile in the Delta, and *ye'ōrîm* for other streams, which by contrast must mean, as it should according to its use by the Egyptians, "the sluggish streams," i.e., "canals." It is so rendered by the revisers. It refers to the network of connecting waterways and irrigation canals from the Nile.

CANDACE (kăn'dȧ-ṣē). Queen of ancient Ethiopia or Cush, who is mentioned in Acts 8:27. Her kingdom, which is not to be confused with modern Ethiopia or Abyssinia, was the area known as Meroë in S Nubia or the modern Sudan (*see* Cush 3 and Ethiopia).

The writings of Strabo, Dio Cassius, and Pliny, and the inscriptions of pyramid tombs indicate that Candace was a common title (not name) used by a number of reigning queen-mothers between *c.* 300 B.C. and A.D. 300. The occasion for the reference in Acts was the conversion, under Philip, of the treasurer of one of these queens, a eunuch who may well have been a proselyte to Judaism returning from a Jewish feast. *See* Ethiopian Eunuch. John A. Wilson believes the queen referred to was Amanitēre, whose title appears in a cartouche as *Kntky,* "Candace." She ruled from A.D. 25 to 41 (JNES, XVIII [1959], 287).

D. W. B.

CANDLE. This word is found nine times in the OT as the rendering of *nēr,* and in the NT for *luchnos.* In all these references in the ASV the more exact rendering "lamp" is used. The candle, in our sense of the term, was unknown in antiquity. *See* Lamp; Pottery.

CANDLESTICK, GOLDEN. *See* Tabernacle.

CANE. *See* Plants.

CANKER. *See* Diseases.

CANKERWORM. *See* Animals: Locust, III.29.

CANNEH (kăn'ĕ). Mentioned only in Ezk 27:23. Located in Syria, it was connected with Haran and Eden as one of the places with which Tyre had commercial relations. The site is unknown. It is possibly the same as Calneh (*q.v.*).

CANON OF SCRIPTURE – OLD TESTAMENT. By "canon" is meant that list of OT books which is regarded as inspired and which can be accepted as the rule of Christian faith and conduct. In English Protestant Bibles there are 39 books in the OT canon. How and when were these books accepted as canonical and why were these accepted and no others?

The study of the OT canon is made somewhat difficult by the fact that the process of canonization took place in a distant time and there are practically no extrabiblical materials from those days to provide details of the process. Some points and general principles can be learned from the books themselves, but for some matters meager information must suffice. Of great assistance has been the discovery of the Dead Sea Scrolls. These copies of biblical and non-biblical books push back available information to the first and second pre-Christian centuries. They have greatly helped to confirm many points previously held by orthodox students of this subject.

Christ and the Canon

Fortunately, we are not left entirely to speculation or to the evaluation of meager information concerning the OT canon. Specific instruction concerning the books and how they are to be received comes from the teaching of the Lord Jesus Christ Himself. For the Christian, this is the highest authority. And it must be remembered that the teaching of Christ and the apostles is not only authoritative, but also is the best witness for the situation among the Jews in the 1st cen.

The witness of Christ and the NT is clear and explicit. Christ accepted the present 39 OT books and no others as being the Word of God, entirely true and authoritative for His people. Inasmuch as this conclusion is widely accepted, it is only necessary to summarize the evidence.

In the Gospel of Matthew alone, Christ in His teaching specifically quotes from or refers to the OT some 31 times, referring to it as authoritative Scripture, the Word of God, etc. Many other instances occur in the remaining Gospels. In the whole NT, the OT is specifically quoted more than 250 times, according to lists of quotations in Nestle. There are many more allusions of equal significance. The OT is quoted for its ethical teaching, and for its spiri-

CANON OF SCRIPTURE – OLD TESTAMENT

tual revelations as well as for its historical facts. Jesus appeals to the OT account of the creation of Adam and Eve, to Noah's flood, to Jonah's experience in the fish. He refers to the necessity of Scripture being fulfilled (Mt 26:54; Lk 24:44). He says that it was written by the Holy Spirit (Mk 12:36) and that even a tittle of it shall never fail (Lk 16:17). Much more could be added, but these passages are sufficient to show that Christ and the apostles utterly believed in and trusted the OT. Even in Mt 5, where Jesus sets His own word against what had been "said by them of old time," He is not contradicting the OT, but the scribal traditions. Note Mt 5:43 where He expresses agreement with the OT part of the quotation, but contradicts the scribal addition to it. For further discussion, see R. Laird Harris' *Inspiration and Canonicity of the Bible,* pp. 48–56.

All parts of the OT are given equal reverence. The three most frequently quoted books are Deuteronomy in the Pentateuch, Isaiah among the prophetic books, and the poetical book of Psalms. All the books are quoted or alluded to except Ruth, Ezra, Esther, Ecclesiastes, Song of Solomon, Lamentations, Obadiah and Nahum. These eight are all short books and doubtless were not referred to for lack of occasion. Moreover, the Jews included Obadiah and Nahum in one book with the other Minor Prophets, and these the NT often appeals to. They likewise often united Ezra with Nehemiah, which is probably alluded to. Ruth also was united into one book with Judges, as 1st cen. evidence shows. Thus only four small books of the OT are without specific NT witness.

At the same time, no other books are quoted as authoritative. Not one of the seven apocryphal books accepted in Roman Catholic circles is quoted in the NT. Three times Paul quotes from Gr. authors (Acts 17:28; I Cor 15:33; Tit 1:12). The last reference speaks of the Cretan author as a prophet, but all three quotations are obviously given for illustrative purposes and their sources are not regarded as authoritative. Likewise, in Jude 14 there is a quotation from the book of Enoch, where Enoch is said to have prophesied condemnation of sinners. Here too it seems justified to say that Enoch is quoted for purposes of illustration and confirmation. The text of Enoch is uncertain, as it exists only in a translation of a translation, except for portions found in the Dead Sea caves. It was not accepted by the Jews as authoritative, nor does it ever appear in any Christian list or enumeration of canonical books. It can therefore be presumed that Jude quoted it for its inherent value and not as authoritative. It is thus clear from the quotations that Christ and the NT used the 39 books of the OT and no other as canonical.

This witness from quotations is fully supported by the references of Christ and the apostles to the OT as a whole. Once Christ spoke of the OT as the "law of Moses . . . the prophets and . . . the psalms" (Lk 24:44). In the context it is plain that this was a name for the "scriptures" or "all the scriptures" (Lk 24:45, 27). More often, Christ used the designation "the law and the prophets" or "Moses and the prophets" (Mt 5:17; 7:12; 11:13; 22:40; Lk 16:16, 29, 31; 24:27), which is used also by the apostles (Jn 1:45; Acts 13:15; 24:14; 26:22; 28:23; Rom 3:21).

There is no doubt as to what books were included by these designations. Josephus was a Jewish historian who was a contemporary of the apostles. In a well-known passage (*Against Apion* i.8) he states that the Jews held sacred only 22 books – 5 of the Law of Moses, 13 of Prophets, and 4 of "hymns to God and precepts for the conduct of human life." These 22 books are quite obviously the present 39. The difference arises because the 12 Minor Prophets were written on one scroll and called one book; I and II Samuel, I and II Kings, I and II Chronicles were each counted as one book; so also were Ezra and Nehemiah, Judges and Ruth, Jeremiah and Lamentations.

Various authors in the centuries after Josephus also counted the books as 22 (or 24 with Lamentations and Ruth counted separately). Thus Melito (A.D. 170) gives a list including exactly the present canon except for Esther. Origen (A.D. 250) counted 22 books, Tertullian (A.D. 200) counted 24. Jerome (A.D. 400) says that the Jews accepted 22 books, counted by some as 24. Augustine (*c.* 400) is the only ancient authority for including the extra apocryphal books, but even he declares the apocryphal books not fully authoritative (see evidence given in detail in William Henry Green, *General Introduction to the OT, the Canon,* pp. 160–175). It is therefore clear that "Moses and the prophets" on the lips of Jesus meant just the present 39 OT books and none other. On the authority of Christ one can be confident that the present canon of the OT is the correct one.

The Dead Sea Scrolls and the Canon

It is of some importance, however, to inquire further and learn how this canon arose. Obviously, Christ only approved a canon that was already recognized. Discovery of the Dead Sea Scrolls has opened up the whole picture of the intertestamentary times in a way not heretofore thought possible. Indeed, the contribution of the Dead Sea Scrolls to study of the OT canon may prove to be one of their major values. Evidence from the scrolls is of two kinds. First, they witness to the existence and widespread use of the OT books at an early date. Second, they show the attitude of Jews of those times toward the Scriptures.

As is well known, the scrolls contain copies of every book of the OT except Esther, which has not yet been identified. The dates range from the 3rd cen. B.C. to the 1st cen. after Christ, with the majority, apparently, falling in the 1st cen. B.C. Copies are in various states of

 CANON OF SCRIPTURE – OLD TESTAMENT

preservation, from the first scroll of Isaiah, readable and practically complete through the entire book, to the fragments of Chronicles, which are only about six lines long and badly eaten by ancient bookworms. Some books, notably Deuteronomy, Psalms, Isaiah, and the Minor Prophets, are found in several copies. Important finds from the 3rd cen. include fragments of Exodus, Samuel and Jeremiah. Other portions of special value include a copy of Ecclesiastes from 150 B.C. and portions of Daniel from *c.* 110 B.C. For details, see J. T. Milik, *Ten Years of Discovery in the Wilderness of Judea,* pp. 20–43. *See also* Dead Sea Scrolls.

It can thus be said that all OT books (except possibly Esther) were known, loved, and used by the Essenes. But this alone does not prove that these books were regarded as canonical. For this, it is necessary to turn to the second type of evidence, quotations of these books in the non-biblical writings of the Essenes.

The chief non-biblical writings quoting Scripture extensively are the Manual of Discipline, the Thanksgiving Hymns, the Damascus Document (previously known but now authenticated by portions found in the caves), and the Rule for the Final War. Further information comes from commentaries on sacred texts and on testimonial booklets stringing together messianic passages.

The Manual of Discipline insists that the law of Moses is inviolate and a man shall be excommunicated if he "transgress a single word of the law of Moses" (viii, 22; translation of Theodor H. Gaster, *The Dead Sea Scriptures,* Doubleday Anchor Books, 1956, p. 57). Both Exodus and Isaiah are quoted as Scripture.

The attitude of the Damascus Document is similar, but its witness more extensive. It also speaks largely of the law of Moses and explicitly quotes every book of the Pentateuch as Scripture. It does the same for the prophets:

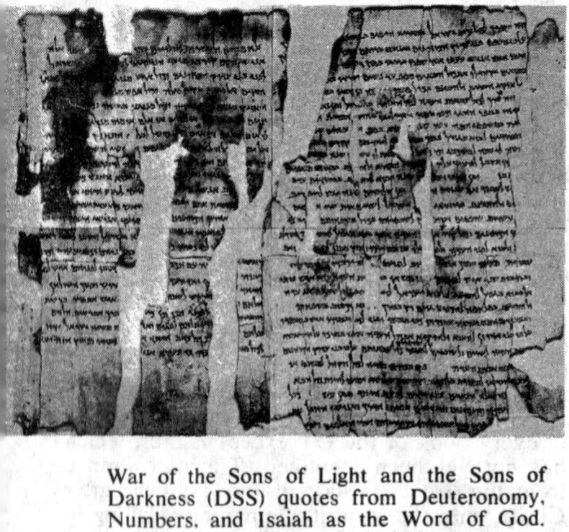

War of the Sons of Light and the Sons of Darkness (DSS) quotes from Deuteronomy, Numbers, and Isaiah as the Word of God. Palestine Archaeological Museum

Isaiah, Ezekiel, Hosea, Amos, Micah, Nahum, Zechariah, and Malachi. Even the book of Proverbs is specifically quoted as Scripture. Many other biblical books are alluded to. Some non-canonical books might perhaps be used by the author, but there is only one clear allusion or reference to such a book. It says that certain matters "are spelled out with equal exactness in the Book of the Divisions of the Times into their Jubilees and Weeks" (xvi, 4; Gaster, *op. cit.,* p. 85). This is obviously the Book of Jubilees written, probably, early in the 2nd cen. B.C.

The Thanksgiving Hymns give a picture of the devotional life of the Dead Sea community. They have no formal citations of Scripture, but the comment of Gaster is: "It is true that they are, in the main, mosaics of biblical quotations" (*op. cit.,* p. 112). According to Gaster's notes, all OT books are utilized except Joshua, Ruth, Chronicles, Nehemiah, Esther, Song of Solomon, Joel, and Haggai. The authors were steeped in the present OT books, though in this type of devotional literature specific quotations are not to be expected. There is little if any dependence on non-canonical books.

The piece often called the War of the Sons of Light and the Sons of Darkness adds little to the above. It quotes from Deuteronomy, Numbers, and Isaiah as the Word of God.

In addition to this evidence, several commentaries exist on portions of Scripture. Non-canonical scriptures were not thus used, giving further witness on the limits of the Dead Sea canon. So far, commentaries have been identified on portions of Genesis, Isaiah, Habakkuk, Hosea, Micah, Nahum, and Psalms.

Also some documents have been found which string together Scripture passages, especially verses bearing on messianic prediction. Such documents use verses from Numbers, Deuteronomy, Joshua, Isaiah, Ezekiel, Amos, and Psalms. Daniel is reported to be thus used, although all the passages are not yet published. A non-canonical book, provisionally called Psalms of Joshua, seems to be quoted in one of the testimonia (not yet published in full), but the piece may be quoted because of the verses from the canonical Joshua cited therein (J. M. Allegro, "Further Messianic References in Qumran Literature," JBL, LXXV [1956], 185 f.).

To summarize, the extant Dead Sea sectarian writings quote or refer to as Scripture the five books of Moses and Joshua, I and II Samuel, Psalms, Proverbs, Isaiah, Ezekiel, Daniel, Hosea, Amos, Micah, Nahum, Habakkuk, Zechariah, and Malachi. This is a total of 20 books out of the present 39. It is to be noted that books of all sections of the OT are treated as equally inspired. Furthermore, many of the remaining books are utilized in the Thanksgiving Hymns as explained above. For instance, Job does not appear among the books just listed, but it was repeatedly used in the Thanksgiving Psalms, as is also the case with Jeremiah. If

CANON OF SCRIPTURE – OLD TESTAMENT

the usage in the Thanksgiving Hymns is added to the positive evidence of canonicity, all 39 OT books are covered except Ruth, Chronicles, Nehemiah, Esther, Song of Solomon, Joel, and Haggai. But the last two were united with the other Minor Prophets in the term "the twelve prophets" (Sir 49:10, before 180 B.C.), and Ruth was by the Jews attached to Judges, and Nehemiah to Ezra. Thus actually all but Chronicles, Esther, and Song of Solomon are covered. The evidence for canonical acceptance may not be watertight and conclusive for all, but it is positive for most of the books, and satisfactory for all but these three.

Divisions of the Canon

The earliest witness to the Jewish classification of the OT is the prologue to the apocryphal book of Ecclesiasticus (Wisdom of Jesus the Son of Sirach), which speaks three times of "the law and the prophets and the other books of our fathers" in slightly varying phraseology. It has been argued that the third division was not yet definite, because it is referred to three times in different words.

The next time this threefold division is used is in Lk 24:44 where Jesus speaks of the "law of Moses and . . . the prophets . . . and the psalms." The next instance is Josephus (*Against Apion* i.8), referred to above, where for the first time the contents of the three divisions are given as 5 books of Law, 13 books of Prophets, and 4 books of "hymns to God and precepts for the conduct of human life." Philo of Alexandria, a contemporary of Christ, also says of the sect of the Therepeutae that they had "laws, and oracles uttered by prophets, and hymns and the others by which knowledge and piety are increased and perfected" (*de vita contemplativa,* § 3). This sounds much like Josephus' division and seems to be usually passed over by those who suppose the Egyptian canon was different from that in Palestine. This threefold division does not occur in the Mishna of *c.* A.D. 200. It apparently does not appear again until about A.D. 400 in the Talmud (Baba Bathra, 14*b*–15*a*) and the writings of Jerome. The Talmud names 5 books in the Law, 8 in the Prophets, and 11 in the Writings – 24 in all.

Many conclusions have been drawn from the threefold division of the canon as found in the present Heb. Bible and the Talmud and these four ancient witnesses. But there are two things to observe about it. First, it is by no means sure that the threefold division of today – substantially that of the Talmud – goes back much before A.D. 400. The only previous witness as to the details of the grouping of the books is Josephus who groups them as 5 of Law, 13 of Prophets, and 4 of hymns and precepts. For some strange reason, authors have paid little attention to this witness of Josephus, but his testimony is clear and weighty. Indeed, Philo's terminology seems to support it.

The second observation concerning this threefold division is that parallel to it there was another, the twofold division. This is clearly seen in the NT witness as outlined earlier. Fourteen times the NT speaks of Moses and the Prophets or uses similar terms. It is out of the question to say that the NT authors did not yet recognize the third division books as canonical. All the major books of the third division of the Talmud are quoted in the NT and quoted as authoritative. It is clear, rather, that there was a twofold classification of the whole OT parallel with the threefold. Later Christian authors use this terminology also (Ignatius, *Epistle to Smyrnaeans,* chap. 5; *Epistle to Diognetus* [*c.* A.D. 130], chap. 10; Irenaeus, *Against Heresies,* i.3.6).

But the new evidence of the Dead Sea Scrolls is that this terminology is pre-Christian and Palestinian. It existed at an early date side by side with references to a threefold classification.

Such a reference has long been known in II Macc 15:9 where Judas comforted his army out of "the law and the prophets." The assumption has sometimes been made that this only referred to the first two divisions of the Heb. Bible (5 books of Law and 8 of Prophets), the third division not yet having been canonized. This was pure assumption. To begin with, the first two divisions of Josephus' day would have 5 books of Law and 13 of Prophets. Besides, who can now think that the Psalms were not canonized by the days of II Maccabees?

The Dead Sea Scrolls clarify the matter, for side by side with clear acceptance of practically all the books of the OT canon they evidence usage of the twofold division, so common in the NT.

Thus the Manual of Discipline exacts a pledge of all initiates to do what is good "in accordance with what He has commanded through Moses and through His servants the prophets" (i.2–3; Gaster, *op. cit.,* p. 39). This clearly refers to the entire sacred corpus and is as early as the reference in the prologue of Ecclesiasticus. Another probable reference speaks of the "study of the law which God commanded through Moses to the end that, as occasion arises, all things may be done in accordance with what is revealed therein and with what the prophets also have revealed through God's Holy Spirit" (Manual of Discipline, viii.15–16; Gaster, *op. cit.,* p. 56). The Prophets, notice, are not a lesser revelation than is the Law and they are quoted repeatedly in the Dead Sea literature as the word spoken by God.

In the Damascus or Zadokite Document twice again such terminology is used. In interpreting Amos 5:26–27 the writer(s) used a slightly variant text; Gaster translates the portion as follows: "I will exile *Sikkuth* your king and *Kiyyun* your image, the star of your God . . . beyond Damascus." The comment is made that "the expression 'Sikkuth your king' refers to the books of the law" and that "the expression 'Kiyyun your image' refers to the

 CANON OF SCRIPTURE – OLD TESTAMENT

books of the prophets" (*Zadokite Document,* vii.15-18; Gaster, *op. cit.,* p. 70). Another instance is translated by Gaster as follows: "The commandments of God which he had given through Moses and through his holy anointed priest Aaron" (v.21-vi.1; Gaster, *op. cit.,* p. 67). But the words "priest Aaron" are not in the original. It is better to translate more strictly: "The commandments . . . through Moses and through his holy anointed ones." This is suggested by Chaim Rabin (*The Zadokite Documents,* 1954, p. 20). He remarks (p. 8n.) that "anointed ones" is equivalent to "prophets."

Thus the Dead Sea Scrolls show that substantially the present OT was held by the community as of divine authority and these books were subsumed under the names "the law and the prophets," or "Moses and the prophets."

Although it has been argued that the original designation of the OT was twofold, and that later a threefold classification was used (R. L. Harris, *Inspiration and Canonicity of the Bible,* p. 147 f.). further reflection suggests that the varying usage may be due to sectarian differences. It is not impossible that the Jerusalem Jews of official Pharisaic and Sadducean opinion divided the canon into three parts and that the Essene sect divided it into only two parts. In that case it would explain the NT terminology which here as often would tend to reflect Essenic usage.

The Critical View

There is no justification whatever for the view held by destructive critics in general, which makes the threefold division a basis for a theory of three stages in the development of the canon. This view alleges that the Pentateuch was canonized first about 400 B.C. After that, the Prophets (Joshua, Judges, Samuel, Kings, Isaiah, Jeremiah, Ezekiel, and the 12 Minor Prophets) were accepted about 200 B.C. Last of all, the 11 other books called the Writings (Heb. *Kethuvim;* Gr. *Hagiographa*) were canonized at the Council of Jamnia about A.D.90.

Evidences for this view are not impressive. There is no proof of any canonizing of the Pentateuch at 400 B.C. There are no contemporary non-biblical documents bearing on the question. As far as evidence goes, the Pentateuch could have been canonized much earlier. But critical thought will not allow this because, it is held, the Pentateuch was not completed until about 400. There are biblical verses to the contrary, as is noted subsequently, but these are explained away.

The Prophets were canonized somewhat later, the theory holds. If the Prophets had been accepted at 400, they would have been included in the Law. But they were not, so they must have been canonized at a later time. It is known that the 12 Minor Prophets were canonized by about 180 B.C. when Ecclesiasticus mentions them as a unit (49:10). So likely this canon was closed shortly before that date. The clinching argument is that Daniel is not among the Prophets. Clearly Daniel belongs among the Prophets. Chronicles also belongs among the Prophets as truly as does Kings. But Chronicles was written around 200 B.C. and Daniel about 168 B.C. (they say) – just too late to get into the canon of the Prophets. This suggests that 200 B.C. was the closing date. The Psalms also were not fully collected until after 168 B.C. as there are some Maccabean psalms allegedly after that time.

The Writings are therefore a miscellaneous collection which were accepted at various times from 200 B.C. to A.D. 90. At this date there supposedly was a council held in Jamnia in Palestine at which the Jews, now dispersed and seeking guidelines for faith, discussed the canonicity of several books, notably Ruth, Esther, Proverbs, Ecclesiastes, Song of Solomon, and Ezekiel. Objections were at last overcome and the canon forever closed.

This is a neat theory almost universally held by destructive criticism. Orthodox students following William Henry Green (*op. cit.,* p. 81) have usually countered by alleging that the three divisions answer to three types of authorship, rather than to three periods of time. The Law was by Moses, the next eight books were by prophets, the Writings were by men who had the gift of prophecy but not the prophetical office. One may ask, however, how we know that Judges was written by a prophet and Daniel was not! And can we say that David the king had not the office of a prophet (cf. Acts 2:29 f.), whereas Joshua the captain did?

Other questions must embarrass the views of criticism. Dead Sea discoveries have moved F. M. Cross now to claim that Chronicles was written *c.* 400 B.C. (F. M. Cross, *The Ancient Library of Qumran,* p. 141). Fragments of Ecclesiastes dated at 150 B.C. have convinced most that it was written by 250 B.C. at least. Why then were these not included in the canon of the Prophets? As mentioned above, the book of Proverbs was quoted as Scripture in the Zadokite Documents which were written close to 200 B.C. When we add the considerable regard shown for Proverbs by Ecclesiasticus at 180 B.C., we wonder why Proverbs did not make it into the canon of the Prophets, which was supposedly closed only very shortly before. Now with the Dead Sea copies available, practically no one speaks of Maccabean psalms any more!

Also, the so-called Council of Jamnia is a very shadowy thing. There is no contemporary information on it. Moreover, the books there questioned were questioned not for admittance into the canon, but as to their continued acceptance. This is clear, because Ezekiel was also questioned and it was admittedly among the Prophets since 200 B.C.! The questioning of Proverbs means nothing, because, as already seen, the Dead Sea Scrolls accepted it as Scripture long before. So did the NT. Any discussion of rabbis at Jamnia proves absolutely nothing about the close of the canon. It only shows that questions of canonicity keep popping up!

But the main fact opposed to the critical view (and also the view of Green *et al.*) is that the threefold canon of the Talmud is simply not the exclusive and original division. Why explain the absence of Daniel from the Prophets when the oldest definite witness, Josephus, makes it quite explicit that this book was among the Prophets! Why explain the presence of Daniel among the Writings when the Dead Sea Scrolls and the NT show that many Jews in that time used no such classification at all!

Some branches of Jewry indeed had a threefold division. But the contents of those three divisions were subject to change without notice. Josephus (and probably Philo) had only four books among the Writings. The Talmud had 11. Origen counted 22 books and thus did not have Ruth and Lamentations among the Writings. Tertullian, counting 24, would have placed them there if, indeed, he used the threefold scheme.

It has been suggested that this shifting of books from one division to another was for liturgical reasons. The Law and Prophets were divided at an unknown date into weekly synagogue lessons. Some of the other small books were read entire at annual feasts. Such practices may have caused these differences in the Jewish divisions of their Scriptures, but this is only theorizing. The facts, however, are sure. The threefold division cannot be made the basis of a three-stage canonization.

The Old Testament Witness to Its Canon

It may yet be asked if the OT itself gives an indication as to when and why these 39 books were accepted. For the period before the Dead Sea Scrolls there is no non-biblical information, but the OT books themselves speak with considerable clarity, though not in detail.

That the OT in general accepted the law of Moses as canonical is clear. Moses commanded that it be read at the Feast of Tabernacles every seventh year (Deut 31:9–11). Nehemiah records that he did this (Neh 8:1–18), and further says that the people lived in booths fulfilling the law of Moses. This law is given in Lev 23:40 ff.

Joshua recognized the law of Moses as the law of God (Josh 1:7, 8; 23:6). But Joshua added a writing to the law of God (Josh 24:26) and 600 years later the book of Joshua is quoted as the word of the Lord (I Kgs 16:34).

Deut 18:15–22 predicts a succession of prophets culminating in the great Prophet and demands credence for the Lord's prophets. Certain tests are given that the people may know a true prophet—fulfilled prophecy, miracle, agreement with God's previous word.

It should be noted that the OT historical books follow in connected sequence. The death of Joshua is recorded in Jud 2:7–9 and these verses form the conclusion of Joshua. Judges and Ruth go together, and Ruth ends with a genealogy going up to the time of David. Samuel-Kings carry the story to the Captivity. The parallel history in Chronicles ends with two verses which are repeated in Ezr 1:1–2.

As is well known, Chronicles used the books of Samuel-Kings as its sources. What is not so well known is that Chronicles in a series of verses declares that its sources (Samuel-Kings) were written by a succession of prophets from Samuel to Jeremiah (see I Chr 29:29; II Chr 9:29; 12:15; 13:22; 20:34; 26:22; 32:32; 33:19; 35:25). Many of these prophets are known to us. They rebuked kings, preached reform, comforted God's people, and some have left books in their own names. The people were taught to heed their spoken words. Their writings were equally authoritative. Note the reception Jeremiah's writings had with the faithless king and the faithful remnant (Jer 36:4–32). Jeremiah's writings were to be accepted at once as the word of the Lord. Jer 36:4–6 says they were to be accepted because of prophetic authorship.

Likewise, II Kgs 14:6 refers to King Amaziah who about 825 B.C. heeded Deuteronomy as the word of the Lord by Moses. Jer 26:18–19 quotes a verse from the prophet Micah as the pronouncement of the Lord. Dan 9:2 says that Daniel had read in "the books" (Heb. "the article") a prophecy of the word of the Lord to Jeremiah.

The fact is that the OT is permeated with the idea of canonicity. Many prophets claimed to speak the word of the Lord, and their books repeat the claim. False prophets were exposed, but tests revealed the true prophet. In not a few places the prophets quote each other as canonical. In many more places the books refer to each other, as Hos 10:9 refers to Jud 20; Hos 11:8 to Deut 29:23; Prov 9:10 to Job 28:28.

Evidence is obviously not complete for all the OT books. But evidence is clear for the principles of their acceptance. Those written by prophets were accepted, and kings and priests were also sometimes prophets. Any man to whom God revealed His word was a prophet. Thus David and Solomon were prophets as truly as Joshua and Daniel. There are, of course, some books whose authorship is now not known. These were, however, classified by the Jews and by Christ as among the Prophets, and in the absence of the slightest evidence to the contrary, they may be thus accepted. God gave the Jews no test of an inspired book or list of canonical books. But He did give them very obvious and practical tests of a prophet, and it is clear that they accepted the writings of these prophets equally with their spoken words.

Some have held other tests of canonicity than prophetic authorship. The authority of the OT congregation has been suggested, but that certainly would not have helped in Jeremiah's

CANON OF SCRIPTURE – NEW TESTAMENT

day! Nonetheless, acceptance by the believing congregation or church universal is a significant point. Providential leading has been mentioned, and this doubtless operated insofar as God used providential means in preserving the writings of these prophets. But there is no hint in the OT that the messages oral or written of other than prophets should be revered. Likewise, there is no hint in the OT of Green's distinction between the gift of prophecy and the office of a prophet. Only one prophet in the whole OT was ever ordained to his office as far as is known – Elisha, and he wrote no book.

More common today is the idea that canonicity is determined by the inner testimony of the Holy Spirit. There is truth in this concept, but it is not always accurately expressed. The reformers emphasized this testimony, but not for questions of canonicity of particular books. The Spirit testifies rather to our being saved through being led to repentance and faith by the sacred doctrine, and thus testifies to the writings which contain that teaching. As Abraham Kuyper well puts it, the Spirit testifies to the *centrum* (*Principles of Sacred Theology,* pp. 560 ff.). From these central truths we can work out to other truths. From the fact of our salvation through Christ, we can conclude to His authority and the inspiration of the Scriptures that He recommends. But we cannot merely by reading a short passage such as the 25 verses of Jude know beyond a doubt that this is Scripture. At least Luther could not so identify James! And the question of the verses in Mk 16:9–20, which is a section almost as long as Obadiah, cannot be decided by an inner voice.

By and large the testimony of the Holy Spirit confirms the canonization of the 39 OT books. The apocryphal books have many good points and have been accepted as Scripture by many Christian people. But they will not stand *all* the tests or indeed any one of them – prophetic authorship, approval of Christ, acceptance by the church universal, or the testimony of the Holy Spirit. The 39 canonical books will pass them all.

See Hagiographa.

Bibliography. Archibald Alexander, *Evidences of the Authenticity, Inspiration, and Canonical Authority of the Holy Scriptures,* Philadelphia: Presbyterian Board of Publication, 1836. F. F. Bruce, *Second Thoughts on the Dead Sea Scrolls,* 2nd ed., Grand Rapids: Eerdmans, 1961. F. Buhl, *Canon and Text of the OT,* Edinburgh: T. & T. Clark, 1892. F. M. Cross, *The Ancient Library of Qumran,* Garden City, N.Y.: Doubleday, 1958. T. H. Gaster, *The Dead Sea Scriptures,* New York: Doubleday Anchor, 1956. Samuel R. L. Gaussen, *Theopneustia: The Inspiration of the Holy Scriptures,* reprint, Chicago: Moody, 1949. W. H. Green, *General Introduction to the OT, the Canon,* New York: Scribner's, 1899, xvii. R. Laird Harris, *Inspiration and Canonicity of the Bible,* Grand Rapids: Zondervan, 1957; "Was the Law and the Prophets Two-thirds of the OT Canon?" BETS, IX (1966), 163–171. Meredith G. Kline, "Canon and Covenant," WTJ, XXXII (1969), 49–67. W. S. LaSor, *Amazing Dead Sea Scrolls,* Chicago: Moody, 1956. J. T. Milik, *Ten Years of Discovery in the Wilderness of Judea,* London: SCM, 1959. E. J. Young, *Introduction to the OT,* Grand Rapids: Eerdmans, 1949.

R. L. H.

CANON OF SCRIPTURE – NEW TESTAMENT. What books belong in the NT? This is a question not often asked because there is such a complete agreement on the subject. All branches of Christendom explicitly state that they receive the 27 books of our NT as properly belonging to the sacred collection – the canon. There is considerable material to support this universal judgment of the church. It is true that because of the ravages of time, some of the evidence is lacking which was available in the early centuries of this era. On the other hand, some new material has been recently discovered. The evidence must therefore be scrutinized with care. This evidence comes largely from the writings of the early Church Fathers and from the works also of heretics of those days. Some evidence can be gleaned from the pages of the NT itself.

For this article the general conclusions of conservative NT scholarship with regard to the origin of the individual books are assumed. If one held the old liberal view that John's Gospel is a late 2nd cen. production, then of course its apostolic authorship would be ruled out. Happily, that view has been adequately disproved and our study may be based upon the conclusion that John, and the other Gospels, too, are from the 1st cen., even from the middle decades for the Synoptics. The point is that general introduction, which considers the canon, must base itself in part on special introduction, which considers in detail the date and authorship of the individual books. For these details, reference may be made to articles on the books themselves.

There is considerable evidence available for study of the early use and acceptance of the NT books. The first witness comes from the days when John, the last surviving apostle, was still alive. Clement of Rome wrote an extensive epistle at about A.D. 95. The epistles of Ignatius and of Polycarp come from only a few years later. These men had probably all talked with one or more of the apostles. They knew some of the NT authors firsthand. They had surely seen some of the original writings.

The next stage of the investigation concerns the second generation of Christians – those who wrote at about A.D. 140. These had talked with those who had known the apostles. More extensive writings have survived from this period. The names of Justin Martyr and Papias stand out. By this time also, there were some who had departed from the faith. We must reckon

CANON OF SCRIPTURE – NEW TESTAMENT

with Marcion and also with the heresy of Gnosticism. New information is available on Gnosticism. Former students sometimes felt that Christianity was heavily influenced by this heresy. It appears now that the Gnostic philosophy – which claimed a secret and esoteric knowledge – was a later and somewhat weird attempt to unite Christian doctrine with Gr. philosophy. Of especial interest now is the recently discovered work called "The Gospel of Truth" written, evidently, by the Gnostic Valentinus at about this time.

A third stage of study is at about A.D. 170 when evidence becomes abundant for almost all parts of the NT. From this period there are the extensive writings of Irenaeus and the nearly complete listing of NT books called the Muratorian Canon. Of course, there is also much other minor material bearing on the subject. Even this age – 70 years after the death of the last apostle – is not so far removed from the earliest times. Irenaeus was a pupil of Polycarp who in turn had been a disciple of the apostle John. So the extensive information given by Irenaeus is of great value even though not from the earliest time.

There is no great need to trace the subject through the giants of the later ages – Tertullian and Clement of Alexandria, and Cyprian of about A.D. 200; then Eusebius, the church historian, and Athanasius, the defender of orthodoxy, in A.D. 325. These men in some cases round out the picture, but their witness is hardly necessary. The NT canon was fixed to all intents and purposes before their time. This can be said in spite of the fact that the first listing of NT books exactly agreeing with our Bibles was in Athanasius' Festal Letter of A.D. 367. The point is, that although no list before this exactly agrees with our own (there actually are very few earlier lists in any case), there still is a great deal of evidence from which the canon of the earlier periods may be constructed.

Furthermore, absolute unanimity on the canon at an earlier time does not preclude someone's reopening the discussion at a later date. It is well known that Luther questioned somewhat the canonicity of James. Yet James had been accepted by the whole church for well over a thousand years. Likewise, in an earlier day there was a group of heretics called the *Alogi* (those who were opposed to the Logos doctrine of Jn 1:1). These people in the 3rd cen. denied the canonicity of all the Johannine writings. Yet before this all the Johannine writings had been fully accepted as canonical. The lesson is that every witness is not to be accepted at face value. There are offshoots and backslidings which need not seriously trouble us. As van Unnik reminds us, "The way that led to the formation of the canon was, however, a zig-zag road" (H. C. Puech, G. Quispel and W. C. van Unnik, *The Jung Codex,* p. 125). Van Unnik holds that the canon was substantially settled earlier, despite these controversies of the 3rd cen. regarding certain books.

For these reasons it is possible to omit detailed study of the later centuries and concentrate on the history of the acceptance of the NT books in three stages. First may be chosen the period of about A.D. 170 when data becomes really abundant. Working backward to about A.D. 140, we find there is a broad witness in several authors. Finally we shall study the period from A.D. 95 to 120 in the writings of those who were themselves contemporary with and companions of the apostles. We shall finish this survey of history by an investigation of the claims and witness of the NT itself.

The Period of A.D. 170

The writings of Irenaeus which remain fill 263 large pages in *The Ante-Nicene Fathers* (A. Roberts and J. Donaldson, ed., Vol. 1). Irenaeus was an important figure in France in the early days. He was born in Asia Minor about A.D. 130 and was a friend of Polycarp in his youth. He became a bishop of the church in Lyons, Gaul, and was in close touch with the church at Rome, opposing it more than once. He wrote his great work *Against Heresies* after the intense persecution of A.D. 177, and finally gave his life with many of his flock in the awful times of Severus (A.D.202). His witness is of great value because of its extent and also because he was in a position to know the facts of the origin and acceptance of the NT books.

In Irenaeus we perceive a kindred spirit. His trust in Christ was deep, and his regard for the NT is clear. In one passage he presents an early form of the Apostles' Creed (*ibid.,* p. 330). In another place he likens the inspiration of God by the Holy Spirit to a man playing music on a lyre (*ibid.,* p. 276). He says, "I am entirely convinced that no Scripture contradicts another" (*ibid.,* p. 230), thus evidencing belief in its inerrancy. He evidently regarded the NT as a unit, for he calls it "the evangelists and apostles," paralleling it with the term "the law and the prophets" for the OT (*ibid.,* p. 320).

The extent of the canon for Irenaeus is rather plain. He quotes extensively from the NT, summarizes the teaching of all the Gospels, tells how they were written, and then goes on to summarize from the apostolic epistles arguments against the Gnostic heresies of his day. Irenaeus refers by name (i.e., citing the author) to 18 NT books, and seven more are quoted. Only the tiny books of Philemon and Jude pass unnoticed, and this is surely because he lacked occasion to use them.

Irenaeus' references are interesting. He declares that there are necessarily four Gospels as there are four winds of heaven, four faces on the cherubim, etc. (*ibid.,* p. 230). He insists that Paul was truly an apostle (*ibid.,* p. 439) and quotes by name most of his epistles in Book V of his work. In the second Pfaffian fragment preserved from a lost work, he quotes Hebrews as Pauline (*ibid.,* p. 574). He cites Revelation as written by John the apostle "no very long time since, but almost in our day, towards the end of Domitian's reign" (i.e., about A.D. 95, *ibid.*, p. 559 f.). In fact, Irenaeus quotes practically the whole NT, referring to it as Scripture, apostolic, verbally inspired, and absolutely true. No other book written in the Christian era is quoted as Scripture. Indeed, the spurious Gospel of Thomas and the Gnostic Gospel of Truth are indignantly rejected (*ibid.*, pp. 345 and 429), as "agreeing in nothing with the Gospels of the apostles." Irenaeus bases everything on "the scriptural proof furnished by those apostles who did also write the Gospel," and adds, "The apostles, likewise, being disciples of the truth are above all falsehood" (*ibid.*, p. 417).

Supplementing the testimony of Irenaeus is the Muratorian Canon. This interesting list of NT books is known from a Medieval fragment and was composed about A.D. 170. The history of the fragment is not known, and it is tantalizingly brief. The first lines are missing, but it begins by mentioning "the third Gospel," Luke, and therefore it witnesses to Matthew and Mark as well. All the other NT books are listed with brief comments, except Hebrews, James, I and II Peter. Inasmuch as Hebrews, James and I Peter are well attested before this and II Peter also is used by Irenaeus, Westcott concludes that the fragment was copied from a MS with a break in it (B. F. Westcott, *A General Survey of the History of the Canon of the New Testament,* 6th ed., p. 219). The fragment mentions two epistles of John, which are taken by Westcott to be II and III John. It also quotes from I John. Thus the fragment agrees with Irenaeus and complements his witness. The two together give our NT exactly.

The Muratorian Canon (printed in *Ante-Nicene Fathers,* V, 603 f.) rejects the Shepherd of Hermas as not from the apostles. It mentions the Apocalypse of Peter as received by some but not by others, and names some spurious epistles of Paul. It is a discerning witness both in what it accepts and what it rejects. Other witnesses from this period tell the same story with individual variations.

Two translations of the NT were made around this time. The Eastern Church made the Syriac version called the Peshitta. Little is known of its origin, and early MSS do not remain. It apparently lacked II and III John, II Peter, Jude, and Revelation. There were no extra books. The Old Latin Version, used largely in Carthage, was made before A.D. 200. It apparently lacked II Peter, James, and Hebrews, though the evidence on Hebrews is unsure. Again, there were no added books. Putting these two versions together, we may say that the church agreed on our NT books and none other, except that some doubts were expressed on the shorter epistles and Revelation. Actually, we have abundant evidence for Revelation at an early time. The Eastern Church was clearly in error in excessively narrowing its list.

CANON OF SCRIPTURE – NEW TESTAMENT

The Days of Justin Martyr – A.D. 140

Justin is the earliest Christian author whose writings have been preserved in considerable extent. His two *Apologies* and the *Dialogue With Trypho* cover 110 large pages of material. His date is not certain, but he seems to have been born in Neapolis (modern Nablus near ancient Shechem) and to have been martyred in A.D. 148 (Westcott, *op. cit.*, p. 99 n); others say 165 (*Ante-Nicene Fathers,* Vol. 1, 159 f.). He was a philosopher in his early days and carried over his philosophic bent into his writings. They show a boldness and a Christian humility which are still impressive. We also have fragments and shorter pieces from several of his contemporaries which add to the evidence for his age.

Justin refers to a number of the NT books by name and clearly uses others. According to Westcott, he uses all the Gospels, Romans, I and II Corinthians, Colossians, II Thessalonians, Hebrews and Revelation (Westcott, *op. cit.*, pp. 114 f., 167 ff.). His treatment of the Gospels is interesting. Writing as he did for non-Christians, he used the unique phrase "Memoirs of the Apostles," adding that they "are called Gospels" *(Ante-Nicene Fathers,* p. 185). He describes a Christian Sunday worship service as consisting of reading of the "Memoirs of the apostles, or the writings of the prophets," with a sermon, prayer, communion service, and collection (*ibid.*, p. 186)!

Justin's doctrine of Scripture is clearly that of full belief: "I am entirely convinced that no Scripture contradicts another." He adds that if a contradiction be imagined, "I shall admit rather that I do not understand what is recorded" (*ibid.*, p. 230). It is true that in this passage he was discussing the OT, but his reverence for the Memoirs is so clear that the statement can fairly be applied to the rest of the NT that he used.

Justin gives valuable information on the authorship of the Gospels. He says, "The apostles, in the Memoirs composed by them, which are called Gospels" have delivered to us the Lord's Supper. But he also quotes an item found only in Luke and says it is recorded "in the Memoirs which I say were drawn up by His apostles and those who followed them" (*ibid.*, p. 251).

Also he refers to an incident recorded only in Mark saying, "When it is said that He changed the name of one of the apostles to Peter; and when it is written in the Memoirs of him that this so happened, as well as that He changed the names of other two brothers . . . this was an announcement of the fact that it was He by whom Jacob was called Israel" (*ibid.*, p. 252). Westcott has noted that "him" in this quotation can only refer to Peter, and thus the Gospel of Mark is designated as the Memoirs of Peter (*op. cit.*, p. 114). Justin was doubtless aware that Mark wrote the second Gospel, but he was also aware of the witness of Papias and others

CANON OF SCRIPTURE – NEW TESTAMENT

that Mark wrote it down as Peter gave it. This could put Mark in a position similar to Tertius who wrote down Romans for Paul (Rom 16:22) or Silas whom Peter used on another occasion (I Pet 5:12). In this sense the Gospels are referred to by Justin indiscriminately as the work of "apostles" or as the work of "apostles and those who followed them." Note also the expression of Justin quoted above: "It is written in the Memoirs of him [Peter]." This formula of citation is one regularly used for the quotation of Scripture. It is clear that Justin had our Gospels, called them Gospels, and used them as Scripture. As already mentioned, he also uses seven other NT books. He refers to these more or less informally, but on one occasion quotes Revelation by name, ascribing it to the apostle John (*Ante-Nicene Fathers,* Vol. 1, 240).

Several other shorter witnesses for Justin's day have long been known. Basilides, the Gnostic heretic, and the Epistle of Barnabas add very little to Justin's testimony, but it is interesting that Basilides quotes I Corinthians and Romans as Scripture. The Epistle to Diognetus, probably somewhat earlier than Justin, includes allusions to Acts, Galatians, Ephesians, Philippians, I Timothy, Titus, and I Peter in addition to some of those quoted by Justin. Diognetus has one of the early references to the Bible as a unit: "The fear of the law is chanted, and the grace of the prophets is known, and the faith of the Gospels is established, and the tradition of the apostles is preserved, and the grace of the church exulted" (*ibid.,* p. 29). It is clear that the central books of the NT were received on a par with the OT at this time.

Papias is another witness, somewhat earlier than Justin. His works included a five-volume exposition of the oracles of the Lord, but unfortunately all have perished except a few quotations in other books. He is noted for his statement that Mark wrote down Peter's preaching and Matthew wrote his Gospel originally in Aramaic. Papias also mentions I John and "the Epistle of Peter" by name (*ibid.,* p. 155).

Until quite recently, only these half dozen witnesses remained from the mid-2nd cen. Now, however, the sands of Egypt have yielded new treasures. At Chenoboskion (*q.v.*), a little N of Thebes, peasants in 1945 found a cache of Gnostic writings (known as the Nag Hammadi Gnostic Texts, see BW, pp. 402–410). There were 13 books containing about 49 works. One of these books, the Jung Codex, was eventually spirited out of Egypt and is being published.

One of the interesting writings of the Jung Codex is the Gospel of Truth, written by the heretic Valentinus about A.D. 140. Irenaeus had attacked this work in his book *Against Heresies* (III.11.9), but no copies of it had survived. Now it is available (Kenneth Grobel, *The Gospel of Truth).* It is not an attempted fifth Gospel, but an exposition of what Valentinus thought to be the true gospel, i.e., Gnosticism. But in his writing Valentinus quotes from or alludes to many NT books. Tertullian at A.D. 200 had written that Valentinus, though a heretic, had used all the NT. This one writing of Valentinus supports Tertullian's estimate.

In the study, *The Gospel of Truth and the New Testament,* van Unnik parallels the wording of Valentinus with many passages of the Gr. NT and concludes, "It is clear that the writer of the Gospel of Truth was acquainted with the Gospels, the Pauline epistles, Hebrews and Revelation, while there are traces of Acts, I John and I Peter" (*The Jung Codex,* by H. C. Puech, G. Quispel, and W. C. van Unnik, 1955, p. 122). This covers all the NT except small books totaling 11 chapters! He adds, "Round about 140–50 a collection of writings was known at Rome and accepted as authoritative which was virtually identical with our New Testament" (*ibid.,* p. 124). It will be remembered that Diognetus already put this collection on a par with the OT Scripture. The testimony of Valentinus is a welcome voice confirming the previously known witnesses and adding important details.

The Earliest Age – A.D. 95-120

Now take a further step backward to A.D. 95–120. This period overlapped the times of the apostle John. It includes three well-known witnesses, Clement of Rome, Ignatius, and Polycarp, all three of whom had known the apostles and two of whom sealed their faith in blood.

Clement wrote to the Corinthians at about A.D. 95. He quotes from I Corinthians by name and clearly uses Matthew, John, Romans, Ephesians, Hebrews, James, and possibly I Timothy and Titus (cf. Westcott, *op. cit.,* pp. 25 f., 48). Some of the quotations from Mathew have parallels in Mark and Luke, so it is not impossible that these Gospels are included in Clement's testimony.

Ignatius was a bishop in Antioch around the end of the 1st cen. The *Martyrdom of Ignatius (Ante-Nicene Fathers,* Vol. 1, 129) places his arrest in the reign of Trajan, but there is some uncertainty whether he was martyred in 107 or 116. In any case, his witness is valuable and significant. He wrote epistles to seven different churches as he was being carried to Rome for martyrdom. In these letters he quotes Ephesians by name. In his letter to the Philadelphians he seems to refer to NT writings as a corpus: "I flee to the Gospel as the flesh of Jesus and to the apostles as to the presbytery of the church. And let us also love the prophets" (*ibid.,* p. 82). We may compare the similar wording of Justin given above.

Again, he refers to some whom "neither have the prophets persuaded nor the law of Moses, nor the Gospel even to this day" (*ibid.,* p. 88). Another such reference is that we should "give heed to the prophets, and above all, to the Gospel" (*ibid.,* p. 89). He quotes verbatim from

Matthew, I and II Corinthians, and Ephesians, and clearly uses the phraseology of Luke, John, Romans, Galatians, Philippians, I Thessalonians, and I Timothy. Gregory remarks, "The Gospels of Matthew and John appear to have been either his favorites or the ones better known to him. He knew the epistles of Paul well" (C. R. Gregory, *Canon and Text of the New Testament,* p. 71). Ignatius and Clement together witness to the bulk of the present NT.

Shortly after Ignatius' martyrdom, Polycarp wrote a letter to the Philippians which has fortunately been preserved. Polycarp was instructed by the apostles, according to Irenaeus, and was in turn Irenaeus' teacher. He therefore directly links Irenaeus to the Apostolic Age. Polycarp was martyred in his old age about A.D. 155. But the best date for this epistle is shortly after Ignatius' death, therefore either 108 or 118 (cf. Westcott, *op. cit.,* p. 38). It is an early and precious monument of Christian antiquity.

Polycarp quoted the NT copiously. In the *Ante-Nicene Fathers* quotation marks are used to set off excerpts from Matthew, Luke, Acts, Romans, I Corinthians, Galatians, Ephesians, I and II Thessalonians, I and II Timothy, I Peter, and I John. Other books are clearly alluded to. Westcott claims the use of II Corinthians, Philippians, and possibly Ephesians and II Peter in addition (*ibid.,* p. 49). In Chap. XII Polycarp quotes Eph 4:26 as Scripture and in his previous chapter, he quotes I Corinthians and Philippians by name.

Putting together these three great men who began their Christian life in apostolic times, we see that they used the bulk of the NT. They refer by name to I Corinthians, Ephesians, and Philippians, and speak of the NT books as a united whole and as Scripture. The only NT books not witnessed to in these very early writings are Mark, Colossians, Philemon, II and III John, Jude, and Revelation.

Even these omissions are not unexplainable. Matthew and Mark are so very parallel that it is likely that quotations from Mark are concealed under the material from Matthew. Colossians was fully recognized in the next age, and was probably omitted in these early writings for lack of an occasion to quote it. The absence of Philemon, II and III John, and Jude from the list is not surprising either, as they are each but a chapter long and would have less chance of being quoted. With regard to Revelation, we should remember that it was probably written only about 20 years before the last of these men wrote. But Polycarp's pupil Irenaeus gives very explicit testimony concerning the date and authorship of Revelation. Indeed, Irenaeus uses all these books except Philemon and III John. We need not question them because of the silence of the very earliest witnesses.

The New Testament Testimony to Itself

Having traced the reception of the NT books back to the very edge of the apostolic times, we have found that there is evidence that practically all of them were accepted by the men who had learned from the apostles themselves. What was the beginning of this practice? What principle did the early church follow in selecting these books?

Two points should be emphasized to begin with. First, the apostles did not unthinkingly write miscellaneous letters and histories which were piously gathered only in a later age. Rather, the apostles wrote their works consciously and commanded the faithful to receive them.

Secondly, the early church did not pick and choose 27 books out of a mass of good literature, even apostolic literature. No early author refers to a lost writing of the apostles or clearly quotes from such, as far as we can tell. There may have been lost letters of Paul, but none were consciously rejected by the early church. Actually, it may be questioned if any were ever lost. Col 4:16 may well refer to the epistle to the Ephesians which may have been a general letter ("Ephesians" is not in some texts of Eph 1:1), and I Cor 5:9 may be an epistolary aorist referring to the letter Paul was then writing. Contrary to some statements, the spurious books of Barnabas, Apocalypse of Peter, Shepherd of Hermas, etc., may have fooled a few people, but they were never accepted in any serious fashion.

As to Paul's conscious intention in writing, there is clear witness in his next to earliest epistle, "If any man obey not our word by this epistle . . . have no company with him" (II Thess 3:14). In his first epistle he claims that his preaching is not the "word of men," but "the word of God" (I Thess 2:13). In his great epistle of I Corinthians he speaks similarly (I Cor 2:13), and further he insists that "the things that I write unto you are the commandments of the Lord" (14:37). This is not contradicted, as some think, by his statements in I Cor 7:10, 12, etc., where he distinguishes his word from the Lord's. There he is only concerned to quote the words of Jesus on earth. It should be noted that Paul – and Luke – often refers thus to Jesus as "the Lord" before His crucifixion (cf. Mt 26:75 with Lk 22:61). Paul quotes the spoken words of Jesus where possible, but adds his own where the direct command of Jesus was lacking.

There is a reason why Paul could make these claims. He was an apostle. He makes much of this office (I Cor 15:8–9; 9:1; II Cor 11:5; 12:11–12). So do the early authors Clement, Ignatius, etc. They never confuse themselves with the apostolic circle. Similarly, John makes the claim of inspiration in Rev 1:1–3 and 22:18–19.

Christ had chosen the apostles for a purpose. He had promised them the Spirit in a special way. Jn 14:26 promises that He will quicken their memory concerning the words of Jesus. Jn 16:13 promises them that the Spirit will show them future things. The apostles are counted

 CANON OF SCRIPTURE – NEW TESTAMENT

equal to the OT prophets by all the early authors. It is no wonder that their works were promptly equated to the OT Scripture.

This was already done in the NT itself. Three times one author calls the work of another inspired. The best known is II Pet 3:15-16 which refers to the epistles of Paul as Scripture. I Tim 5:18 quotes Lk 10:7 as Scripture. And Jude 17-18 quotes II Pet 3:3 as part of the words spoken by the apostles. These witnesses are not inconsequential. But they are directly in line with the witness of the post-apostolic fathers.

The above study of the early Church Fathers, plus other passages on the subject that could be cited, shows that the early church received as authoritative all the books written by apostles. This is stated categorically by Stonehouse: "It is clear that apostolicity was the organizing principle of the NT of the Old Catholic Church," i.e., the church of about 170 (Ned B. Stonehouse, *The Apocalypse in the Ancient Church,* pp. 4-5).

Warfield in his valuable studies on this subject admits that "apostolic authorship was, indeed, early confounded with canonicity" (B. B. Warfield, *Revelation and Inspiration,* p. 455). Warfield's own view is that those books were canonized which the apostles either wrote or declared that the church should accept. This view is quite safe, for the early witnesses show that the NT books were all by apostles except possibly Mark, Luke, Acts, Hebrews, James, and Jude. These books were used as early as the others, however (though the witness for Jude is not clear in the earliest time), and it is surely clear that they were accepted in the age of the apostles.

But there is more. The same witnesses who tell that Mark wrote his Gospel also tell that he wrote down Peter's preaching. The Gospels of Mark and Luke are called works of apostles by Justin Martyr. Tertullian later presents the same view (*Ante-Nicene Fathers,* Vol. 3, 252). Apparently these books were written under the superintendence of the apostles and thus were certified by them.

Much has been made of Hebrews as if it were not written by Paul. But we should note that no voice before A.D. 200 said it was non-Pauline. It was used by Clement at A.D. 95. The newly found Gospel of Truth by Valentinus makes definite use of it. In Egypt the claim of its Pauline authorship can be traced back through Clement of Alexandria to Pantaenus of about 140. And in Rome, Irenaeus not only uses Hebrews extensively, but in the second Pfaffian fragment refers to it as Pauline (see details in R. L. Harris, *Inspiration and Canonicity of the Bible,* p. 264). There has always been the problem that the language of Hebrews seems somewhat different from that of Paul's other epistles, but the thought and argument is quite Pauline. The truth may be that the book is by Paul, but was written for him by another helper (but not by Luke).

As to James and Jude, these were written by brothers (Jude 1) and we apparently have a twofold choice. There was a pair of brothers, James and Jude, in the apostolic company (Lk 6:16). There seems to have been another pair who were half brothers of Jesus – though this has been denied (Mt 13:55). The problems are complicated, but it would seem possible for men in this station to whom Christ had especially appeared after His resurrection (I Cor 15:7) to be counted as apostles extraordinary, if indeed these passages do not refer, after all, to the one pair of brothers, the sons of Alphaeus, the apostles.

In conclusion, it should be reemphasized that the early church did not falter in establishing its rule of faith, nor was there a welter of conflicting opinion with many different books now accepted, now rejected. In the later times of the 3rd cen. when the living witnesses had passed away, there was actually more debate and uncertainty than in the age immediately following the apostles. At first all the Gospels were fully accepted, and were not questioned in the 2nd cen. except by the heretic Marcion who denied the authority of all the apostles except Paul. Moreover, most of the Pauline epistles, including Hebrews, were used and several were quoted by name by the early writers who had known the apostles. We may lack as full evidence as we would wish for some of the smaller epistles, because the works of Papias and others have perished; but we should always remember that though we lack full evidence, Irenaeus, Justin, and such men had abundant evidence in their possession. As Tertullian challenged, if one questions these things, he may go to the churches where the original writings of the apostles were preserved (*Ante-Nicene Fathers,* Vol. 3, 260). These early men had the facts. We have most of them too. But as to some of the lesser supported epistles where our evidence is meager, we can safely rest in the testimony of such valiants for truth of the early days.

See Epistles, General; Inspiration.

Bibliography. A. H. Charteris, *The New Testament Scriptures,* New York: Carter, 1882. C. R. Gregory, *The Canon and Text of the New Testament,* New York: Scribner's, 1907. R. Laird Harris, *Inspiration and Canonicity of the Bible,* Grand Rapids: Zondervan, 1957. Everett F. Harrison, *Introduction to the New Testament,* Grand Rapids: Eerdmans, 1964. H. Puech, G. Quispel and W. C. van Unnik, *The Jung Codex,* ed. by F. L. Cross, New York: Morehouse-Gorham, 1955. Herman Ridderbos, "The Canon of the New Testament," *Revelation and the Bible,* ed. by C. F. H. Henry, Philadelphia: Presbyterian and Reformed, 1958. A. Roberts and J. Donaldson, ed., *The Ante-Nicene Fathers,* 9 vols., Buffalo: Christian Literature Publishing Co., 1886. H. C. Thiessen, *Introduction to the New Testament,* Grand Rapids: Eerdmans, 1954. Theodor

Zahn, *Introduction to the New Testament,* Grand Rapids: Kregel, 1953.

R. L. H.

CANTICLES. *See* Solomon, Song of.

CAPER, CAPERBERRY. *See* Plants.

CAPERNAUM (kȧ-pûr'nā-ŭm). After His rejection at Nazareth, Jesus determined to make Capernaum, on the Sea of Galilee, His headquarters. Matthew called it "his own city" (9:1). Here occurred some of the most significant events of His ministry. Nearby, the Master called as disciples the fishermen Simon, Andrew, James, and John (Mk 1:16–21, 29), and the tax collector Levi (Mt 9:1–9; cf. Mk 2:13–14). In the town He healed the centurion's servant (Mt 8:5 f.; Lk 7:1 f.), Peter's mother-in-law (Mt 8:14–15; Mk 1:30; Lk 4:38–39), the paralytic (Mt 9:1 f.; Mk 2:1 f.; Lk 5:18), and a demon-possessed man. Here also occurred the dispute over greatness (Mk 9:33–37), the discourse of Jn 6 (see v. 59), and other events in the life of Christ.

The location of Capernaum has been problematical, but the town is now almost certainly identified with Tell Hum on the NW shore of the Sea of Galilee about two and a half miles SW of where the Jordan enters the sea. Capernaum is a Gr. corruption of the Heb. *Kefar-Nahum,* "village of Nahum," so-called because the prophet's tomb used to be shown there. Tell ("mound of") (Na) Hum is linguistically equatable with Capernaum.

It is to be remembered that Jesus pronounced a curse on Capernaum for her unbelief (Mt 11:23). The town degenerated in the 6th cen., and became uninhabited. The Franciscans bought the site in 1894 and cleared the ruins of an ancient synagogue there. This limestone structure had an interior of about 70 by 50 feet. Oriented S toward Jerusalem, it was joined on the E by a colonnaded court. Along the E and W sides of the lower floor of the prayer hall were stone benches for worshipers. An upper floor was probably used by women. The synagogue was decorated with figures of palm trees, vines, eagles, lions, centaurs, and boys carrying garlands. Although the structure probably dates to the 3rd cen. A.D., it very likely stood on the site of an earlier synagogue—perhaps in the same place and following the same plan as the

The Capernaum Synagogue. IIS

one built by the Roman centurion (Lk 7:5) and the one in which Jesus taught. Excavations are presently being conducted in an area between the synagogue and the shore of the Sea of Galilee. Remains of an early Christian church have come to light there.

H. F. V.

CAPH. The eleventh letter of the Heb. alphabet. *See* Alphabet. This letter is used in the KJV as the heading of the eleventh section of Ps 119, where each verse begins with this letter.

CAPHTOR (kăf'tôr), **CAPHTORIM** (kăf'tô-rĭm). According to the Bible, Caphtor is the place of origin of the Philistines (Amos 9:7; Jer 47:4; cf. Gen 10:14; Deut 2:23). The name appears first as Kaptara in an Akkadian text which locates it "beyond the Upper Sea" (*c.* 2200 B.C.), available in a later MS copy. Other references are found in tablets from Mari and Ugarit. By the term *keftiu* Egyptian texts of *c.* 2200 to 1200 B.C. identify this with Crete *(q.v.)*, an island kingdom with which Egypt had commercial relations. Some scholars think it more likely that the term was used by the 13th cen. to designate the Aegean islands. The Philistines are called Cherethites (*q.v.*) in Zeph 2:5 and Ezk 25:16, and the LXX translates this "Cretans." The theory that Caphtor is to be identified as Crete rests, therefore, upon the LXX and the Egyptian texts. *See* Philistines.

A recently published tablet from Mari, dated *c.* 1780–1760 B.C., mentions a Caphtorite merchant stationed at Ugarit to whom a shipment of tin was sent (IEJ, XXI [1971], 31–38).

G. A. T.

CAPPADOCIA (kăp'*ȧ*-dō'sh*ȧ*). An inland province of Asia Minor, bounded on the E by the Euphrates River, on the N by Pontus, on the W by Lycaonia, and on the S by the Taurus Mountains. It was a wild, barren, mountainous country, with the highest peak (Arqâeus) reaching 13,100 feet. The earliest references to Cappadocia are from the time of Hammurabi, when it was part of the Babylonian Empire. It was occupied by Hittite civilization from 2000 B.C. In later years, it was a satrapy of Persia, and was made a Roman province in A.D. 17. Visitors from Cappadocia were in Jerusalem at Pentecost (Acts 2:9), and Peter addresses one of his epistles to scattered Christians in this province (I Pet 1:1). Caesarea in Cappadocia was an early center of Christianity, and Basil was its most famous son. It remained a part of the Eastern Empire until captured by the Seljuk Turks in the 11th cen.

C. K. H.

CAPTAIN. This term occurs some 214 times in the canonical Scriptures (KJV), of which 182 occurrences are in the OT. The word is the KJV translation of 14 different Heb. and four Gr. terms. It means an officer or leader either civilian or military.

1. By far the most frequent term in the OT is *śar* where it means "the captain of the guard"

Decorations of the Capernaum Synagogue. HFV

(Gen 37:36), the "captain of the host" (II Sam 10:16), or chariot officer (I Kgs 22:31). Among the men in the Bible thus designated were Joseph's master Potiphar, Abner (II Sam 2:8), Phicol (Gen 21:22), and captains of thousands, hundreds, fifties and tens in the army of Israel (Num 31:48; Deut 1:15).

2. Heb. *nāśî'* or "exalted one," was applied exclusively to the tribal leaders in the book of Numbers.

3. "Governor" is the meaning of *peḥâ*, usually a reference to officers in foreign armies; e.g., Dan 6:7, "the princes, the counselors, and the captains" (see RSV).

4. Heb. *rab* (25 occurrences) designated the leader of the occupying troops of the Babylonians (Jer 39:9).

5. Heb. *shālîsh* is translated "captain" 13 times and refers to subordinate officers in Israel's army (II Kgs 10:25).

6–14. Heb. *rō'sh*, the word which is translated "captain" in ten instances, means "head." The other eight Heb. synonyms occur from one to six times each and are rendered in the RSV as "prince," a charismatic leader (I Sam 9:16), "sentry" (Jer 37:13), "marshal" (Jer 51:27), and "chief" (Josh 10:24). It is remarkable that such a variety of terms existed for which there seems to have been no technical precision in meaning.

15. The NT term normally used in the Roman army to designate the officer over the centurions was the *chiliarchos*, "chief captain," meaning the ruler of a thousand (Acts 21:31).

16. Gr. *stratēgos* in the term "captain of the temple" refers to the chief of police among the Jewish leaders. Such an officer was in charge of the men who went to arrest the apostles (Acts 4:1; 5:24, 26).

17. The *stratopedarchēs* occurs once (Acts 28:16) and means "chief of the camp."

18. Gr. *archēgos* means "pioneer" (RSV), "leader," or "founder," and is applied to Jesus in Heb 2:10.

G. A. T.

CAPTIVITY. The term "captivity" in the Bible can refer to the captivity of Israel or to that of other nations (Amos 1:5). From very ancient times victorious armies followed the practice of taking from their captives those they desired for slaves and wives (Deut 21:10 ff.). Such removal from their land nearly always meant the destruction of national existence and a feeling of severance from the care and protection of their local or national god; indeed, it implied the defeat of that deity (cf. Isa 52:2-5; Jer 50:29). Beginning with the Assyrians, a new technique for dealing with captive peoples was used, that of deportation. Great numbers of people were captured in war and deported and settled in another part of the empire. This practice was continued by the Babylonians, but was reversed by the Persians in 536 B.C.

There was hardly a time in Israel's history when all her people were at home in Palestine. In fact, Israel's history began in Egyptian bondage, and though that bondage is not referred to as a captivity, the people were slaves nonetheless and were not free to leave. There are three main oppressions of the people of Israel on foreign soil mentioned in the Bible: in Egypt, in Assyria, and in Babylon (cf. Isa 52:3-6).

Limited captivities for some Israelites probably began as early as the reigns of Rehoboam and Jeroboam I (*c.* 926 B.C.), when Shishak, pharaoh of Egypt, invaded Palestine (I Kgs 14:25-28). Tiglath-pileser III of Assyria (745-727 B.C.) captured the cities of Naphtali (II Kgs 15:29) and carried the inhabitants of the tribes of Naphtali, Reuben, Gad and E Manasseh (I Chr 5:26) captive to Assyria (*c.* 733 B.C.). In 722/21 B.C. the city of Samaria fell to Sargon II of Assyria and the captives were taken to Halah (cf. Ob 20, RSV) on the Habor, the river of Gozan, and to the cities of the Medes (II Kgs 17:6; 18:11). Sargon's inscription indicates that 27,290 Israelites were deported. By following heathen deities they had brought upon themselves the covenant curse pronounced by Yahweh their God for such disobedience (Deut 28:25, 32, 36, 41; II Kgs 17:7-23).

With the fall of the northern kingdom to Assyria, the fate of the covenant people lay with Judah. Again certain individuals or small groups were carried away captive until Jerusalem herself was destroyed in 586 B.C. and many of the people were deported to Babylon by Nebuchadnezzar. Three of Judah's last five kings were carried into captivity: Jehoahaz to Egypt, Jehoiachin and Zedekiah to Babylon. Daniel, Hananiah, Mishael, and Azariah were also carried away to Babylon. Jeremiah and Baruch were carried to Egypt against their wishes by some of their own countrymen. There were Jewish settlements already in Egypt when Jeremiah arrived. Such groups had come either as mercenaries or as refugees from Assyrian and Babylonian oppression.

Those taken as captives to Babylonia must have had times of bitterness. They were humili-

Prisoners of war represented on a relief in the palace of Ashurbanipal, Nineveh. LM

ated by the memory of the destruction of their beloved Jerusalem. If faithful to their God, they were subjected to the scorn and taunts of their captors (Ps 137). Yet life for the majority of the Israelites born in captivity does not seem to have been too hard. When the opportunity came for the Jews to return to Palestine in 536 B.C., only a small percentage came back. It has been estimated that at the time of Christ a million Jews were living in Egypt, a million more were living in Asia Minor and Syria, another million were living in Babylon, one hundred thousand were living in Italy and Sicily, and another hundred thousand were living in N Africa.

The Babylonian exile or captivity of Israel produced some remarkable prophetic personages, such as Ezekiel and Daniel. It was a period of great literary activity. It gave birth to the synagogue. It was at the very heart of the biblical understanding of divine judgment and revelation.

See Israel; Dispersion; Chronology, OT; Restoration and Persian Period.

R. L. S.

CARBON 14 DATING. This is a method of dating ancient objects made from organic substances, all of which contain carbon, by measuring the amount of radioactive carbon remaining after years of disintegration. The method was elaborated by Willard Libby of the University of Chicago and has been widely applied. It has proved useful and reliable in many instances, but problems and inconsistencies also have been observed. Its usefulness is admittedly limited to the last 50,000 years.

The method is based on the fact that there are two kinds (or isotopes) of carbon atoms—the normal kind called carbon 12 (atomic weight 12) and a heavy type with two extra neutrons in the nucleus called carbon 14. The latter kind is unstable and decomposes by radioactive decay into nitrogen. In the upper atmosphere cosmic rays strike atoms of nitrogen, which has seven neutrons and seven protons in its nucleus, and transform them into carbon 14, which has eight neutrons and six protons. This mingles with the normal carbon 12, which is in the atmosphere in the form of carbon dioxide and constitutes about one part in a trillion of the carbon in the air.

The carbon in the air is taken in by growing plants, and by photosynthesis is joined to water and becomes cellulose, starch, sugars, etc. These plants are then eaten by the animals, and thus all living things have the same proportion of carbon 14 and carbon 12 that the atmosphere does—about one part in a trillion. Even sea water has dissolved carbon dioxide, and the carbonates of seashells show approximately this same proportion.

However, when a living organism dies, it ceases to take in any more carbon from the atmosphere directly or indirectly. The radioactive carbon 14 in the dead organism slowly throws off energy and changes into nitrogen. The result is that after a sufficiently long time the object will have no carbon 14 left, but only the stable carbon 12. By measuring the amount of carbon 14 remaining in a sample, the age of the sample can thus be calculated. Experiments have determined that if a gram of pure carbon 14 is left for 5,570 years, one-half of it will have turned into nitrogen. If this is left another 5,570 years, another half will have changed and only one-fourth gram of carbon 14 will remain. After a third 5,570 year period, only one-eighth gram of carbon 14 will remain, and so on. This figure of 5,570 years is called the half-life.

In analyzing a sample of old organic material we must determine how much carbon 14 was there originally. This is done by assuming that the proportion of carbon 14 to carbon 12 in living things many years ago was the same as it has been recently, i.e., one to one trillion. Thus if we have a sample of old carbon weighing one trillion grams it would have had in it originally one gram of carbon 14 and all the rest carbon 12. If now we measure this sample and find only one-fourth gram of carbon 14, we conclude that the sample has lain dead for two half-lives, or 11,140 years. One gram of carbon taken from a living organism gives rise to approximately 15 disintegrations per minute from the carbon 14 it contains; a gram of carbon from a sample dead 5,570 years yields about 7.5 disintegrations per minute.

The method of analysis is relatively simple. A specimen of organic matter containing carbon is collected. It is carefully separated from any modern roots or mold, etc. Then it is burned and the carbon dioxide collected. This carbon dioxide is purified and the carbon from it is redeposited in a container. The container is placed in a space heavily shielded from stray radiation and the carbon 14 present is measured with a Geiger counter or similar device which counts the rate of breaking down of carbon 14. From these data the amount of carbon 14 can be calculated, and from the amount of carbon 12 present the original amount of carbon 14 can be calculated. The difference is a measure of the time taken for the carbon 14 decomposition.

There are certain assumptions and limitations in the method of which we should be aware. First, it is held that the rate of carbon 14 decay never changes. Experiments with pressure and temperature variation do not vary it. However, it is not so clear that stray radiation might not have some effect—probably slight in most cases.

A second assumption is that the proportion of carbon 14 to carbon 12 in the air has always been constant. This involves two other assumptions. First, that cosmic rays have always been the same. Actually we can observe minor variations in them but do not directly know the past situation. Their intensity in space may have been invariable, but their intensity in the stratosphere may indeed have changed. Secondly, it is assumed the amount of carbon 12 in the air has always been the same. But this is a questionable assumption. Coal-burning factories in recent years have increased the carbon 12 in the air. Volcanic activity could have changed it, as could other unknown circumstances. The extent of such variation would presumably not have been great, unless there were a revolution of climate or of the earth's circumstances. It could be theorized that if there were a great change of climate at the time of Noah's flood, dates determined from objects prior to the deluge would possibly be inexact.

One obvious limitation of the method is that it must be used on carbon. It therefore cannot date dry fossil bones, as these are largely calcium phosphate. If fresh bones were burned over a camp fire and the fat and marrow turned to charcoal, the charcoal could be dated, however. Wooden beams in Egyptian tombs have been dated satisfactorily. Charcoal from camp sites is another good subject.

A last limitation that comes to mind is that this method cannot date very old material. After about 50,000 years the carbon 14 remaining becomes so scarce that measurement is not practical. Therefore this method cannot date directly the bones of fossil men nor can it substantiate the claims of ages of 100,000 years, 300,000 years, etc., for them. These ages are still reckoned by the older geological methods, usually by comparison with glacial deposits.

The dates have proved acceptable with some exceptions back to 3000 B.C. when history begins in Egypt. The lowest levels of Jericho have been dated to 7000 B.C. by a series of self-consistent readings. The most glaring inconsistencies have been the datings of Jarmo in Iraq, which was clearly inhabited only a short time but whose datings vary from about 3300 B.C. to 9275 B.C. Something here is badly wrong. With this in mind, there is a tendency not to trust too implicitly an individual age determination, but to get a series of consistent dates, if possible.

On the positive side, carbon 14 of spruce logs in Wisconsin and of some glacial remains in Europe has, in the minds of most, brought down the age of the last glacier from 25,000 years ago to about 11,000 years. Since the interval after the last glacier is used to calculate the ages of the other glaciers, their dates should be correspondingly reduced, though this is usually not yet done. A notable exception is Albright (*Archaeology of Palestine,* pp. 51-61), who formulates a much lower chronology based on radiocarbon dating.

Another striking use of the method is to date the entombment of the Siberian mammoths at about 11,000 years ago. Albright suggested a correlation of the last glacier and what he speaks of as "traditions of the Great Flood" at about 9000 B.C. (*From the Stone Age to Christianity,* 2nd ed., p. 9). Much work remains to be done, but certainly something of major proportions happened at a time given as about 9000 B.C. by carbon 14 dating.

Bibliography. L. J. Briggs and K. F. Weaver, "How Old Is It?" *National Geographic Magazine,* CXIII (1958), 234-255. W. F. Libby, *Radiocarbon Dating,* 2nd ed., Chicago: Univ. of Chicago, 1955. E. A. Olson, "Radiocarbon Dating," JASA, XI (1959), 2-11.

R. L. H.

CARBUNCLE. *See* Jewels.

CARCAS (kär′kăs). One of seven chamberlains ordered to summon Queen Vashti before King Ahasuerus (Est 1:10).

CARCASE. The spelling is now carcass. It refers to the dead body of a beast (Jud 14:8), or sometimes in a contemptuous way to the dead body of a human being (Josh 8:29). The use of the word as applied to a living body is not found in either the OT or NT.

A Syro-Hittite bas relief from Carchemish. Hittite Museum, Ankara

CARCHEMISH (kär′kĕ-mĭsh). Also spelled Charchemish in II Chr 35:20 (cf. Jer 46:2).

A city on the upper Euphrates mentioned in ancient records from the beginning of the 2nd mil. B.C. as *Karkamis* in Babylonian documents, as *Kargamish* and *Gargamish* in Assyrian inscriptions, as *Krkmsh* in Egyptian records, and as *Karkemish* in Hebrew. It was an important administrative center in the Hittite Empire;

several Syrian city-states (such as Ugarit) were, as vassals of the Hittite king, subject to Carchemish, according to royal Hittite archives found at Ras Shamra. After the end of the Hittite Empire (*c.* 1200 B.C.), Carchemish retained its Hittite culture and became an independent and important Hittite city-state. It paid tribute to Ashurnasirpal II of Assyria (884-859 B.C.) and to Shalmaneser III (859-824 B.C.), but was also often at war with Assyria. In 717 B.C. the city was destroyed and its population deported by Sargon II (722-705 B.C.). However, it rose again to importance, and after the fall of Nineveh in 612 B.C. was occupied by the Egyptians under Pharaoh Necho (see II Chr 35:20), who made it the center of his control over Syria for a few years. In 605 B.C. he was defeated there by Nebuchadnezzar II, according to the Babylonian Chronicle and Jer 46:2.

The site of ancient Carchemish, now called Jerablus, lies 63 miles NE of Aleppo, on the W bank of the Euphrates. It was excavated for the British Museum 1876-79 and 1912-14. In the first season of excavations in 1878 a large number of Syro-Hittite sculptures and Hittite hieroglyphic inscriptions came to light. Excavators of the second expedition discovered a fortified citadel at the summit of the mound, below which lay the city which was protected by a wall pierced with monumental gateways set between flanking towers. The lower part of the walls of these towers was covered with Hittite sculptures and inscriptions. Remains of a temple and a palace were also found, but they were not sufficiently investigated.

The main feature of the city was an irregular piazza or town square at the foot of the citadel approached from the S section of the city by a processional gateway. A monumental stairway led from this piazza up to the citadel on the N.

Bibliography. William Hallo, "Carchemish," BW, pp. 165-169. D. G. Hogarth, C. L. Woolley and T. E. Lawrence, *Carchemish,* London: British Museum, 1914, 1921, and 1952.

S. H. H. and D. C. B.

CARE, CARES. A number of Heb. and Gr. words are translated by the English word "care." In the OT the following terms are each so rendered once: *deʼāgâ,* meaning anxious care (Ezk 4:16); *ḥărādâ,* referring to a fearful anxiety (II Kgs 4:13); and *dābār,* meaning word or matter (in I Sam 10:2 a matter for concern). In Phil 4:10 the infinitive *phronein,* which is translated substantivally, refers to the act of thinking of someone. In II Cor 7:12; 8:16, *spoudē* is used in the sense of earnest concern. The NT term most commonly rendered by the noun "care" is *merimna* (Mt 13:22; Lk 21:34; II Cor 11:28; I Pet 5:7), which depicts anxiety as a destructive attitude or state of distraction.

CAREAH (kȧ-rē'ȧ). Father of the captains Johanan and Jonathan, who came to Gedaliah, the Babylonian governor of Judah (II Kgs 25:23). In other Scriptures the name is spelled Kareah (*q.v.*).

Mount Carmel with Haifa at its foot. IIS

CARMEL (kär'mĕl)

1. A mountain promontory 556 feet high situated between the plain of Esdraelon and the Mediterranean Sea (Jer 46:18). It was so called because of its thickly wooded aspect, which was even more striking in ancient times than it is today (Isa 33:9; Amos 1:2; 9:3; Mic 7:14). From a single peak, however, the name passed to the range of hills associated with it, thus designating the mountainous ridge more than 20 miles in length, from three to eight miles in breadth to the W and NW of Esdraelon, 1,742 feet above sea level at its summit.

Because of exposure to the sea winds, Carmel is well watered. Ancient sanctuaries to the weather deities were built on its heights; thus it was a fitting site for the contest between Elijah and the prophets of the Canaanite storm-god Baal (I Kgs 18). The Egyptians called Carmel a sacred cape, and in the Amarna letters from Canaanite princes it was known as Ginti-Kirmil. Carmel, meaning "garden" or "orchard," is famed in literary composition for its natural beauty (Song 7:5; Isa 35:2; Nah 1:4).

From 1929 to 1934 Garrod and McCown, under the auspices of the British School of Archaeology and the American School of Prehistoric Research, excavated caves on the lower western slopes of Mount Carmel known as Wadi el Mugharah, "valley of the caves." Specimens include evidence of a flint industry from early Paleolithic to Mesolithic times, as well as human bones of both Neanderthal man and Homo Sapiens. Animal bones in the caves have also thrown light on climatic changes in Palestine during the Stone Age (BW, p. 397).

2. A city of Judah, in the uplands near Hebron, named with Maon and Ziph (Josh 15:55). It was the scene of incidents in the lives of Saul and David. Saul set up a memorial stone there

Carmel Caves. HFV

(I Sam 15:12). It was the home of Nabal, the churlish and drunken flock-master, whose widow Abigail David married (I Sam 25); and also of Hezrai, one of David's mighty men (II Sam 23:35; I Chr 11:37). It is represented by the modern el-Kermel, about ten miles to the SE of Hebron. There are considerable ruins from Crusader days.

V. G. D.

CARMELITE (kär'mĕ-līt). A native of the Judean Carmel. Among those thus named were Nabal, the husband of Abigail (I Sam 30:5, etc.), and Hezrai, one of David's mighty men (II Sam 23:35).

CARMI (kär'mī), **CARMITES** (kär'mīts)

1. A son of Reuben, and founder of a tribal family (Gen 46:9; Ex 6:14; Num 26:6).

2. A Judahite (I Chr 2:7), son of Zabdi, according to Josh 7:1, and father of Achan, who is given the name of "Achar" in I Chr 2:7. The Carmi of I Chr 4:1 is probably a scribal variant of Caleb *(q.v.)*.

The Carmites were a family of Judah whose head was Carmi.

CARNAL. This word occurs only in the NT, although "carnally" is found three times in the OT (KJV). "Carnal" appears in the NT 11 times, "carnally" once. "Carnal" means "pertaining to the flesh." The noun *sarx* basically means the flesh of an animal or person, or the meat of an animal. However, in the NT, "carnal" has sometimes to do with literal flesh, and sometimes with the old Adamic fallen human nature to be found in all men alike. For the literal use, see Rom 15:27; I Cor 9:11; II Cor 10:4; Heb 7:16; 9:10; for the metaphorical, Rom 7:14; 8:7; I Cor 3:1, 3, 4 where reference is to the old nature, or "old man."

Paul admits to being carnal, that is, still having a fallen nature. He says the carnal mind is enmity against God, and brands the Corinthian Christians as carnal, which he defines as behaving like natural, unregenerated men. When he says "to be carnally minded is death" (Rom 8:6), he is talking of those who have only a fallen nature and have not the new nature, those who are unsaved.

See Anthropology; Flesh.

J. A. S.

CARNELIAN. *See* Jewels.

CAROB. *See* Plants.

CARPENTER. *See* Occupations: Carpenter, Craftsman.

CARPUS (kär'pŭs). Mentioned only in II Tim 4:13 as a man of Troas with whom Paul left his cloak. Such a reference seems to indicate a degree of friendship, or possibly that Paul had stayed in his home. The word *phelonēs* (alternate spelling of *phainolēs*) was used of a coarse outer garment worn to protect one against the elements while traveling. Had Paul just "forgotten" his cloak? Or possibly, due to warm weather, had he temporarily left it behind?

CARSHENA (kär-shē'nȧ). The first named among the "seven princes of Persia and Media" under King Ahasuerus (Est 1:14).

CART. The Heb. term *'ăgālâ* is translated both "cart" and "wagon" *(q.v.)*. In I Sam 6:7–14 the Philistines made a new cart to transport the ark of God back to Israel. Such Philistine carts with two solid wheels are depicted in a relief of Rameses III at Medinet Habu, *c.* 1170 B.C. In II Sam 6:3 and I Chr 13:7 a cart was used by Uzzah and Ahio to bring the ark to Jerusalem from the house of Abinadab. Isa 28:27–28 refers to a cart wheel used as a threshing instrument, and Amos 2:13 may refer to the same thing in the words "a cart . . . full of sheaves."

In Ps 46:9 the Heb. term *'ăgālâ* is translated "chariot" in the KJV, and probably refers to supply wagons used for military purposes.

CARVING. *See* Occupations.

CASEMENT. *See* Lattice.

CASIPHIA (kȧ-sĭf'ĭ-ȧ). An unidentified place in N Babylonia near the river Ahava, on the route from Babylonia to Jerusalem, to which Ezra sent for "ministers for the house of our God" (Ezr 8:17).

CASLUHIM (kăs'lŭ-hĭm). The name of an unidentified people mentioned in Gen 10:14 and I Chr 1:12 as descended from Mizraim (Egypt).

CASSIA. *See* Plants.

CASTANET. *See* Music.

CASTAWAY (Gr. *adokimos,* "not approved, rejected, disqualified").

While this Gr. term occurs a number of times in the NT, the only passage where the KJV translates it "castaway" is I Cor 9:27. Etymologically it is related to the verb *dokimazein,* which means to test or to approve as a result of testing. *Adokimos,* then, describes a person or an object which has been tested and disapproved. These words were used of such things as metals, coins, and horses.

In I Cor 9:27, however, the context demands an athletic setting, perhaps drawn from the Isthmian games held near Corinth. The picture is that of a contending athlete who is disqualified because of an infraction of the rules. In saying that he had preached (Gr. *kēryssein*) to others, Paul seems to be drawing upon the imagery of the herald (Gr. *kēryx*) who announced the rules of the game. The apostle was engaged in the contest of Christian life and service. In fact, he had proclaimed to others the standards for that life. It would have been most tragic if the very one who had announced the rules should, through submission to his carnal nature, violate those rules and be disqualified from further participation and thus from the reward. In so speaking, Paul is not referring to the loss of salvation, but to the forfeiture of reward for service. The crown (Gr. *stephanos*) of I Cor 9:25 was the wreath of pine or olive leaves placed on the head of the victorious athlete, a figure commonly used in the NT to picture the believer's reward. *See* Crowns.

D. W. B.

CASTING. *See* Occupations: Metal, Workers in.

CASTLE. Ordinarily a fortified place, building, or citadel *(q.v.).* Several words are translated "castle" in the KJV; only two in the RSV. It is used in the sense of encampment in Gen 25:16; Num 31:10; I Chr 6:54 (KJV). "Castle" (RSV is better than "palace" in Neh 7:2. The castle referred to in Acts 21:34 was the Roman fortress of Antonia attached to the temple area. The RSV and NASB "barracks" does not sufficiently indicate its strength as a fortress.

CASTOR AND POLLUX. *See* Gods, False.

CASTRATION. The act of emasculating by removing the testicles. Castrated animals were not acceptable as sacrificial offerings (Lev 22:24, RSV). This operation performed on a human resulted in his being known as a eunuch *(q.v.).* The Mosaic law excluded such a man from the congregation *(q.v.)* of the Lord (Deut 23:1, RSV), but God promised through Isaiah to relax this prohibition (56:3-7), which was fulfilled under the new covenant (see Acts 8:27, 38).

CATAPULT. An ancient military machine used for discharging darts, stones, or other objects. The motive power was obtained by a strong lever working on an axis, which was tightly strained with twisted ropes and suddenly released. Although this machine is not mentioned specifically in the Bible, it was in common usage by the Assyrians and other peoples during the 1st mil. B.C. It may be referred to under the term "engines" in II Chr 26:15, invented to shoot arrows and great stones. *See* Engines; Armor.

CATERPILLAR. *See* Animals: Locust, III.29.

CATHOLIC EPISTLES. A traditional designation for the last seven epistles in the NT. *See* Epistles, General.

The term "catholic" is derived from Gr. *katholikos,* "general," "worldwide," "universal." With the exception of II and III John, each of which is written to an individual person or church, these epistles were addressed to a wider audience than one local church or individual. Later, the word "catholic" was applied to epistles which were universally accepted by the church and were orthodox in doctrine; thus the term became synonymous with "genuine" or "canonical."

CATTLE. *See* Animals, I.6.

CAUL

1. A word applying to a membrane fastened to the liver and mentioned along with fat and kidneys which Aaron's sons were to burn on the altar (Lev 3:4-5). One explanation is that it refers to the fatty mass which covers the liver *(q.v.).* Another is that it denotes the "liver-net, or stomach-net, which commences at the division between the right and left lobes of the liver" (KD on Lev 3:4).

2. In Hos 13:8 "the caul of their heart" may be understood to mean "the enclosure of the heart, i.e., their ribs or their breast" (IB).

3. In Isa 3:18 the word "cauls" refers to a kind of headdress.

CAUSEWAY. This word occurs in I Chr 26:16, 18, and refers to a series or flight of steps leading up into the temple.

CAVALRY. *See* Army; War.

CAVE. The soft limestone hills of Palestine are marked by innumerable artificial and natural caves. During prehistoric times many of the caves were used for human shelter, as shown by the artifacts discovered in them. Later, Lot and his daughters occupied a cave (Gen 19:30), as did David (I Sam 22:1), and Elijah (I Kgs 19:9). Human occupation of caves continued all through the biblical period. Jewish sectarians apparently lived in some caves and stored precious manuscripts in others near Qumran by the Dead Sea. The inn at Bethlehem at the time of the birth of Jesus was built over a cave which was used as a stable. Even today many caves in Judea are used as places of shelter for man and beast.

Caves were used in conducting heathen ritualistic practices (Isa 65:4, Berkeley), as at Gezer. There are many references in the Bible to

Numerous caves dot the cliffs at Qumran. HFV

caves used as places of refuge (Josh 10:16; Jud 6:2; I Sam 13:6; 22:1; II Sam 23:13; Heb 11:38). Caves were natural burial places and were used as tombs in every period of human history. Abraham purchased the cave of Machpelah for use as a tomb for Sarah (Gen 23:19). This cave became the sepulcher of Abraham, Isaac, Rebekah, Leah, and Jacob (Gen 25:9; 49:30–31; 50:13). In the NT the tomb of Lazarus was a cave (Jn 11:38). Caves were also used as prisons (Jer 37:16–17; 38:6), and as cisterns. *See also* Den; Pit.

A. C. S.

CEDAR. *See* Plants.

CEDRON. *See* Kidron.

CELESTIAL BODIES. *See* Astronomy.

CELIBACY. Remaining in an unmarried state for conscientious, religious, or moral reasons. The term is often confined to men, but applies equally to women, such as the vestal virgins of heathenism and the nuns of Roman Catholicism.

As a phenomenon, celibacy is not confined to Roman Catholicism. The Buddhist priests and many of their laity practice the strictest and most exacting rules of celibacy, as do many heathen witch doctors.

The practice is justified among Roman Catholics, first, upon the basis of Christ's words in Mt 19:4–12: "There be eunuchs, which have made themselves eunuchs for the kingdom of heaven's sake" (v. 12); and, second, upon Paul's insistence that the unmarried state is preferable (I Cor 7:8, 40). Christ's statement certainly does not command celibacy—only some can bear it. Rather, He commended marriage as ordained of God from the beginning (Mt 19:3 ff.). Paul saw celibacy as expedient for him and certain others in his day. He thought the Lord's coming was too near, the time too short to become involved in marriage (I Cor 7:29). Celibacy leaves men free of the cares of marriage. Yet it can be dangerous, and must then not be attempted (v. 36 f.). Paul spoke of himself as being as free to have a wife of his own as Peter and the brothers of Christ (I Cor 9:5). Paul's position was that celibacy, in his opinion, was the best for him (I Cor 7:6, 40).

The Roman Catholic view of physical nature actually lies behind this practice of celibacy. Having adopted the heathen view that the material, the body in particular, is inherently evil, as it is expressed in neo-Plotinian philosophy, this church seeks holiness for its priests and nuns through a life of absolute poverty, chastity, and obedience led in monasteries and nunneries. The pagan practices of a similar nature also have contributed to a certain syncretistic adoption of heathen customs in the matter. Celibacy often leads to great evil and gross sin, since it places impossible burdens upon both men and women, as has often been proved by the testimony of those who have left Romanism.

Paul thoroughly condemns those who forbid to marry (I Tim 4:3; cf. Col 2:16–23) when he says this will be a mark of apostates in the latter days. The mention of the 144,000 as virgins in the Great Tribulation of Rev 14:1, 4 may bear out Paul's conviction that in times of great persecution it can be expedient that the Lord's servants be unmarried.

R. A. K.

CELLAR. In I Chr 27:27–28 the word means merely storehouses or rooms where wine and oil were stored. In Lk 11:33 (ASV) the Gr. word means literally "a hidden place," i.e., anything similar to a vault, crypt, or cellar.

CENCHREA (sĕn'krē-*a*). This seaport of Corinth was about nine miles from the metropolis, on the E side of the isthmus. Paul embarked from Cenchrea at the close of his first visit to Corinth (Acts 18:18). It was the site of a church by the time of the writing of Romans, where mention is made of Phoebe, a servant (deaconess) of that church (Rom 16:1).

Area of the old port of Cenchrea. JR

CENSER. The Heb. *maḥtâ,* commonly translated "censer," is a general word meaning any sort of firepan. It is used not only for true censers, i.e., vessels in which coals of fire were placed to burn incense (Lev 10:1; 16:12; Num 16:6 ff.), but of ordinary firepans used to carry away the ashes of the altar (Ex 27:3) and of snuffdishes, the trays used to catch the debris of the lamps when they were trimmed (Ex 25:38; 37:23).

Another Heb. word, *miqtereth,* means literally "a vessel to burn incense" (II Chr 26:19; Ezk 8:11). This specialized utensil may have been a decorated rod ending in a small hand-shaped bowl as found in Egypt. In the NT the KJV translation "golden censer" of Gr. *thumiatērion* in Heb 9:4 probably refers to the golden altar of incense in the holy place of the tabernacle rather than a censer (cf. RSV). *See* Altar; Incense.

The censers were ordinarily made of copper or bronze, but in some cases they were of gold (I Kgs 7:50; II Chr 4:22; Rev 8:3, 5). Since they were a part of the tabernacle or temple, they were treated as sacred objects (Num 4:14), and even in the hands of rebels they were holy, having been dedicated to God (Num 16:36-40).

Scripture contains no description of size or shape of the censers. They were probably either shallow pans or bowls when used as true censers, or flat, shovel-like utensils when used as ash pans. The censers of Korah and his company could be flattened out and used to plate the altar of burnt offering (Num 16:39). According to Jewish tradition they were of various sizes and had long or short handles (Mishnah Yoma iv.4). *See* Firepan.

A similar utensil was the small ladle or spoon *(kaph),* literally a "hand" or "palm" (Ex 25:29; 37:16; Num 4:7; I Kgs 7:50; II Kgs 25:14). Stone or marble incense spoons have been found at Tell Beit Mirsim (ANEP, #592), at Megiddo (BA, IV [1941], 30), and at Hazor (BA, XX [1957], 40 and fig. 7). On some of these a hand is carved with the fingers grasping the "cup" of the ladle. A hollow tube opens into the cup, perhaps to enable one to blow on the incense to speed its burning. The Twelfth Dynasty tomb of Amenemhet depicts a priest carrying a long white (ivory?) handle ending in a cupped "hand" supporting a bowl in which incense is burning (*Illustrated Family Encyclopedia of the Living Bible,* II, 75).

P. C. J.

CENSUS. The biblical concept of enrollment, numbering, or census is found in the Heb. *pāqad,* "to visit," "examine," "review," "muster," "number"; also *sāpar* and *mānâ*; the Septuagint *arithmos,* "number," "amount," "sum," "unit of troops"; the NT *apographē,* "list," "inventory," "taxing" (KJV), "census," "registration" (cf. *kēnsos,* "tribute money," "poll tax," Latin *census*); and the Latin *descriptio,* "a marking out," "transcript," "copy."

An instance of numbering is found in Ex 38:26, soon after the Exodus, while Israel first encamped at Sinai. It was to raise necessary funds to build the tabernacle. Another census occurred one year later (Num 1:2-3; cf. Jos *Ant.* iii.12.4), to ascertain the people's military strength. A later census revealed the number of males 20 years and upward (Num 26:1-2). *See* Number. In the reign of David a census revealed his military potential (I Chr 21:1-6; cf. differing totals in II Sam 24:1, 9; Jos *Ant.* vii.13.1). Solomon completed David's census and included the foreigners and aliens (I Chr 22:2; II Chr 2:17-18). During the centuries that followed, numerous instances of the recorded military strength of both Israel and Judah appear (see I Kgs 12:21; II Chr 13:3, 17; 14:8-9; 17:14-19; 25:5-6; 26:11-15, etc.). Such information was essential for taxation.

Each country had its system of taxation and census taking. Fluctuating property values caused differing evaluations. In Athens, for example, an assessment was held every year, or every third or fifth year (Aristotle, *Polit.* v.7.6). Before and after the days of the Republic, it was customary for the Romans to have "enrollments by households," where persons and property would be taxed by families. The censors would query each family head regarding the name, age, financial and legal status of each member of his household (cf. Cic. *Laws* iii.3; Livy xliii.14).

In NT times, rather complete records were kept by Emperor Augustus because of his thorough reorganization of the Roman Empire. Papyri finds from Egypt reveal that at this time a census was taken every 14 years (cf. P. Oxy. 255 in Milligan, *Greek Papyri,* pp. 44-47), and such general procedures would affect Palestine. Mention is made of three enrollments taken during the rule of Augustus (Sue. *Aug.* xxvii; cf. Tac. *Ann.* i.11). The second of these is generally understood to have been around 8-4 B.C. Most biblical scholars identify the taxing of Lk 2:1-2 with this particular census and thus show reason for the journey of Joseph and Mary to Bethlehem. Josephus (*Ant.* xviii.1.1), however, mentions a taxing while Quirinius ruled Syria, which the latter administered after Archaelaus, the son of Herod the Great, was deposed from office in A.D. 6. How long or often Quirinius remained in office is a matter of dispute. This census mentioned by Josephus is associated with the one which caused Judas the Galilean to revolt (Acts 5:37). For a complete discussion of this intricate problem, *see* Chronology of the NT; Cyrenius; Taxing.

Bibliography. F. F. Bruce, "Census," NBD, p. 203. CornPBE, pp. 196-199. G. E. Mendenhall, "The Census Lists of Numbers 1 and 26," JBL, LXXVII (1958). George Milligan, *Selections from the Greek Papyri,* Cambridge: Univ. Press, 1927. Alfred Plummer, "Quirinius," HDB, IV. William M. Ramsay, *The Bearing of Recent Discovery on the Trust-*

worthiness of the New Testament, London: Hodder and Stoughton, 1915. Ramsay, *Was Christ Born at Bethlehem?* London: Hodder and Stoughton, 1898. J. A. Sanders, "Census," IDB, I, 547.

R. V. U.

CENTURION. An officer in the Roman army (Acts 21:32; 22:26; 23:23) in command of a century (100 foot soldiers, more or less). The number of centurions in a legion was 60 and in a cohort (KJV, "band") was ten.

In the NT, four centurions are mentioned, all in a favorable light: Cornelius, stationed at Caesarea, through whom it was made evident that Gentile believers also received the Holy Spirit (Acts 10); Julius, who treated Paul kindly on his trip to Rome (Acts 27:1, 3, 43); the centurion of Capernaum who sought aid for his servant (Mt 8:5–13); and the centurion who announced his faith at the cross (Mt 27:54).

CEPHAS (sē'făs; Gr. *kēphas,* from Aram. *kēpa',* "rock or stone").

A name given by Jesus to the apostle Simon (Jn 1:42; I Cor 1:12; 3:22; 9:5; 15:5; Gal 2:9). Peter is the Gr. equivalent of Cephas. *See* Peter; Simon; Simeon.

CHAFF. *See* Plants.

CHAIN. The term "chain" is used in two different senses. Chains were used, as were ropes, for binding prisoners (Jer 39:7; 52:11; Nah 3:10; Acts 12:6; 21:33; 28:20). More frequently we read of ornamental chains and necklaces strung with precious stones, particularly pearls (Jud 8:26; Ezk 16:11). Such chains were made of precious metals and often served as a sign of rank. Both Joseph and Daniel were given such chains or necklaces (Gen 41:42; Dan 5:29). Ornamental necklaces are also mentioned in Prov 1:9 and Song 1:10; 4:9. Ornamental chains formed part of the decoration of the Jerusalem temple (I Kgs 6:21; 7:17; II Chr 3:5–16). *See* Jewels, Jewelry; Fetters.

CHALCEDONY. *See* Jewels.

CHALCOL. The same as Calcol (*q.v.*).

CHALDEA (kăl-dē'*á*). From at least the 10th cen. B.C. southern Babylonia bordering the Persian Gulf was called by the Assyrians *Kaldu*-land (Babylonian *kashdu;* Heb. *kaśdîm*). In 626 B.C. a dynasty from this area ruled in Babylon and subsequently the name was used by foreigners (Jer 50:10; Dan 3:8; Ezk 11:24) as a synonym for the whole of Babylonia. *See* Babylonia; Chaldeans.

CHALDEANS (kăl-dē'*á*ns). The Gr. name *Chaldaioi* (Heb. *kaśdîm)* designated a group of Semitic tribes living in the "sea-lands" of southern Babylonia. It is first found in texts of *c.* 1000 B.C. but is probably a much older name. It is likely that seminomads of the Kaldu occupied the deserts of N Arabia (Job 1:17) and settled in the Persian Gulf area late in the 3rd mil. B.C. Thus the city of Ur in their territory continued to be called "of the Chaldees" (Gen 11:28; Acts 7:4), perhaps to distinguish it from a city (Ura') of the same name in northern Mesopotamia.

During the 2nd mil. Babylon was ruled by chiefs from these "sea-lands" for brief periods. From the reign of Adad-nirari III (*c.* 810 B.C.) the Chaldean tribes paid homage to the Assyrian conquerors of N Babylonia. Then in 734 Ukin-zēr, head of the Chaldean tribe of Bit-Amukkani, seized the throne of Babylon for a few months before he was defeated at Sapia. Two other tribal leaders, Balasu of Bit-Dakkuri and Marduk-apla-iddina (the biblical Merodach-baladan) of Bit-Yakin, paid their dues, and their lands were spared.

The latter took the initiative at a time of Assyrian weakness to regain the throne for the Chaldeans in 721–710 B.C. His embassy to Hezekiah of Judah seeking support for his opposition to Assyria, despite Isaiah's warning of the dangers of such action to Judah (Isa 23:13) and his prophecy of the coming defeat of the Chaldeans (Isa 43:14), could be dated to the time of Merodach-baladan's defeat by Sargon II in 710 B.C. or by Sennacherib after the Chaldeans had once more seized the throne in Babylon in 703/2 B.C. Isaiah referred to Babylon itself by the poetic phrase "daughter of the Chaldeans" (Isa 47:1) and correctly used Chaldean as a synonym for Babylonia at this time (Isa 13:19; 47:1; 48:14).

In 626 B.C. Nabopolassar, another native Chaldean, was enthroned in Babylon by popular acclaim. He soon won the whole country as far N as the Middle Euphrates and, with the Medes, sacked Nineveh in 612. He was succeeded by his son Nebuchadrezzar II (605–581 B.C.), who defeated the Egyptians at Carchemish in 605 and made all the kings of Palestine, including Jehoiakim of Judah, his vassals. Jeremiah makes frequent reference to the Chaldeans at this time since the Babylonian army marched annually to Palestine in the first 12 years of Nebuchadrezzar's reign (Jer 21:4, *et al.*).

In 601 B.C. the Babylonian army was defeated by the Egyptians, and Jehoiakim, who had been a vassal for three years, now broke with Babylon. Retribution followed in late 598 and early 597 when, according to the Chaldean (or Babylonian) Chronicle (626–594 B.C.), which is an objective and accurate source for the history of this period, "Nebuchadrezzar marched to the city of Judah, capturing it and its king. He put a king of his own choice on the throne. He took much spoil and sent it back to Babylon." This capture of Jerusalem and Jehoiachin on March 16, 597 B.C., at the beginning of the great Exile, as at the sack of Jerusalem ten years later, was the work of Chaldean army units (II Kgs 24).

The Chaldean or Neo-Babylonian Empire at its height.

Later rulers of the Chaldean dynasty included Evil-Merodach (Awel-Marduk), Nabonidus, and his co-regent Belshazzar, whom Daniel calls "king of the Chaldeans" (Dan 5:30). Darius the Mede ruled "the kingdom of the Chaldeans" after the fall of Babylon to Cyrus in October, 539 B.C. (Dan 9:1). *See* Babylon. Daniel used "Chaldean" to describe the whole of Babylonia and its inhabitants (Dan 3:8). Ezekiel extended the use to those neighboring countries under its jurisdiction (Ezk 23:23).

The language of the Chaldeans (Dan 1:4) was only a dialect of Aramaic; thus "Chaldee" as at one time applied to the non-Hebrew sections of Daniel and Ezra is technically incorrect.

While others used Chaldean to describe all the people, the Babylonians themselves later reserved the name for priests who specialized in astronomy and mathematics (the science of which originated in Babylonia) or used these sciences for astrology, horoscopes, or other omen practices. This special use of Chaldean to denote a "wise man" (attested by Herodotus) appears to have been developed in the 6th cen. B.C. (Dan 2:10; 5:11).

Bibliography. A. Leo Oppenheim, *Ancient Mesopotamia: Portrait of a Dead Civilization,* Chicago: Univ. of Chicago Press, 1964. D. J. Wiseman, *Chronicles of Chaldean Kings (626–556 B.C.),* London: British Museum, 1956.

D. J. W.

CHALDEE. *See* Aramaic; Chaldeans.

CHALK. *See* Minerals and Metals.

CHAMBER. Equivalent to a room, especially a private one (Gen 43:30; Jud 16:9). The word "room" is preferred in present-day English. Chamber is used of the rooms in the temple, whether in Solomon's temple (I Chr 9:26, 33) or the post-Exilic temple (Ezr 8:29), or especially in the temple of Ezekiel's vision (Ezk 40:17, *et al.*).

Sometimes the chamber was a room on the upper level of a house, either the second story or on the roof (II Sam 18:33). The Lord cautioned the disciples against any rumor that He would be in a secret chamber at the time of His final return (Mt 24:26).

CHAMBERING. A sexual sin mentioned as one of the works of darkness in Rom 13:12–13 (Gr. pl. *koitais,* "debauchery," "illicit intercourse"). The sing. form *koitē* occurs in Lk 11:7 as "bed," and in Heb 13:4 as the marriage "bed." In Rom 9:10, Rebekah "conceived" (*koitēn*) by Isaac. Thus the original passage condemns the prostitution of a natural (and divinely ordained) relationship.

CHAMBERLAIN. *See* Occupations: Chamberlain.

CHAMELEON. *See* Animals: Lizard, IV.21.

CHAMOIS. *See* Animals: Sheep, Mountain, II.36.

CHAMPION. In I Sam 17:51 *gibbōr,* rendered "champion," means "hero," "mighty man." In I Sam 17:4, 23, "champion" is a good translation of the Heb. word meaning "man of the middle places," i.e., the man who stands between two armies to decide the case of one against the other.

CHANAAN. *See* Canaan.

CHANCE. To the Hebrews Yahweh was a God of law and order, and therefore there is very little room for "chance" in their theology. In most instances where the idea is used it is the thinking of someone other than a Hebrew. In the Gr. translation of the OT (LXX), the word *tychē* is found twice, once in Gen 30:11 where Leah said, "With *fortune*" (ASV marg.; KJV, "a troop cometh"); and in Isa 65:11 (lit.), "preparing for the demon a table, and filling up for *chance* a mixed drink." In view here is the heathen god of chance, called Fortuna by the Romans. The idea of chance is found in the statement of the Philistines, that if their effort to determine the cause of their calamities turned out a certain way, they would call them a chance, that is, bad luck (I Sam 6:9). There are other instances where the same word is used: "chanceth him by night" (Deut 23:10); "her chance was to light on the portion of the field" (Ruth 2:3); "something hath befallen him" (I Sam 20:26); "one event happeneth to them all" (Eccl 2:14-15).

There is also the Heb. word *qārā'*: "If a bird's nest chance to be before thee in the way" (Deut 22:6); again, "and there happened to be there a base fellow" (II Sam 20:1, ASV). *Pega'* is the Heb. word used in Eccl 9:11: "Time and chance happeneth to them all," and I Kgs 5:4, "neither adversary nor *evil occurrent* [misfortune, RSV]."

V. G. D.

CHANCELLOR. The title of Rehum (Ezr 4:8, 9, 17) meaning literally "lord of judgment." The term designates a Babylonian office, viz., that of the "master or lord of official intelligence," or "postmaster" (Sayce).

CHANGE OF RAIMENT. This expression occurs in three different passages in the OT (Gen 45:22; Jud 14:12, 13, 19; II Kgs 5:5, 22-23). The peoples of the ancient Near East were fond of brightly colored and ornamented garments and changed into such at weddings and other festive occasions. Kings and men of rank kept a large wardrobe of these (cf. II Kgs 10:22), partly for their own use (Prov 31:21; Job 27:16; Lk 15:22), partly to give away as presents (Est 6:6-11; and see above). Included in long lists of gifts exchanged between the pharaoh in the Amarna age and various kings in Babylonia, Syria and Palestine are many types of clothing, with up to 41 garments of a certain kind (e.g., EA #14, 22, 25, 29, 31*a*, 34). Another Heb. word, *maḥălāṣôt* (KJV, "changeable suits of apparel," Isa 3:22; "change of raiment," Zech 3:4) is better translated "festal robes" as in NASB. *See* Dress.

J. R.

CHANNEL. In the KJV two words are translated "channel."

1. Heb. *'apîq* refers to the streambed or riverbed (Isa 8:7; cf. Joel 3:18, RSV), or to deep ravines in the ocean floor (II Sam 22:16; Ps 18:15; cf. Ezk 35:8; 36:4, 6, RSV).

2. Heb. *shibboleth* refers to the flowing stream of the Euphrates River (Isa 27:12). The Heb. term appears as a test of dialect in Jud 12:6, where it refers to the channel or stream of the Jordan.

See Canal.

CHAOS. The Gr. term from which this word is transliterated *(chaos)* does not occur in the Bible. In ancient mythologies it carried the idea of confusion and is commonly used to describe the condition of the earth at the time the Spirit of God moved upon the face of the waters (Gen 1:2-4). In this passage the concept of chaos would then be a synonym for the word "void" (Heb. *bōhû,* Gen 1:2) in the expression "waste and void."

The idea of Gen 1:2, however, is not best understood by the English "confusion." Rather, the original Gr. meaning of *chaos* as void or desolate should be understood. The Heb. word (*bōhû*) never occurs in the OT except with the corresponding word, as in Gen 1:2, "waste" (Heb. *tōhû*), which is used in Isa 45:18 to mean "uninhabited" and both terms appear in Jer 4:23 referring to Jerusalem after the Babylonian invasion in the 6th cen. B.C. Jeremiah says, by way of further explanation, "I beheld, and, lo, there was no man" (Jer 4:25).

J. McR.

CHAPEL. An expression in Amos 7:13 (KJV), elsewhere translated "sanctuary." Here it is indicative of the dependence of this national shrine at Bethel on the court of King Jeroboam II of Israel.

CHAPITER. Chapiter is the rendering of three Heb. words used in Kings, Chronicles, and Exodus to designate the topmost part of a pillar.

The capitals of the two pillars of Solomon's temple were called *kōteret,* "crown" (I Kgs 7:16 ff.). *See* Jachin and Boaz. They had bowls (pommels, II Chr 4:12-13), apparently to hold oil for a continuing flame. The exact style of the pillars is unknown. The Heb. *ṣepet,* "capital," in II Chr 3:15 is a synonym. *See* Architecture.

The tops (*rô'sh,* "head or top") of the pillars of the door of the tabernacle tent were gold leafed (Ex 36:38). The tops of the pillars of the fence (*rô'sh*) were silver plated (Ex 38:17, 19, 28). This treatment caused the parts to glisten in the sunlight.

CHARASHIM (kär'ȧ-shĭm, "craftsmen"). The expression "valley of Charashim" is found in I Chr 4:14 (KJV). In ASV and RSV Ge-harashim is used. This valley in Judah was where a certain Joab founded a community of metal craftsmen, inhabited after the Exile by the tribe of Benjamin (Neh 11:35, see also ASV marg.). It may be identified with Sarafand el-Kharab, about five miles SW by W of Lydda (Lod) in a dale that slopes into the valley of the Nahr Rubin, or with the broad valley between Lod and Ono on the main road between Joppa and Jerusalem.

CHARCHEMISH. *See* Carchemish.

CHARCOAL. *See* Coals; Minerals and Metals.

CHARGER. Two Heb. words and one Gr. word denote this utensil.

1. The Heb. word *q^e'ārâ,* originally meaning "hollowness" but later signifying "plate" or "dish," indicates one of the gifts the tribal chiefs presented at the tabernacle dedication (Num 7:13, *et al.*).

2. The Aramaic word *'ăgarṭāl* (etymologically uncertain) is used of the "vessels" or "basins" given to the returning Jewish exiles by Cyrus (Ezr 1:9).

3. The Gr. word *pinax,* "board" or "plank," came to denote anything flat as "tablet, disc, dish, platter." Such a flat, narrow-rimmed charger, usually one to three feet in diameter (HDCG), was used to bring John the Baptist's head to Salome when her dancing pleased Herod Antipas (Mt 14:8, 11; Mk 6:25, 28). "Charger," an English word, is better translated "platter."

CHARIOT. The common Heb. words for chariot, *rekeb* and *merkāb,* probably come from a root meaning "to mount and ride." Heavy-wheeled vehicles drawn by asses are attested in Mesopotamia as early as the end of the 4th mil. and throughout the 3rd mil., as seen at Ur, Kish, and Tell Aqrab. The lighter spoke-wheeled, horse-drawn war chariot is depicted on Cappadocian cylinder seals in the time of Hammurabi (*c.* 1750 B.C.). It was the use of the speedy horse-drawn chariot that enabled the Hyksos to overrun Syria and Palestine and to conquer and control Egypt from about 1730 to 1580 B.C.

The first reference in the OT is to Joseph's chariot (Gen 41:43), probably patterned after the solid-wheeled chariots drawn by four horses shown on 19th–18th cen. B.C. seals from Anatolia. Other references to Egyptian chariots are in Gen 46:29; 50:9; Ex 14–15; Josh 24:6; II Kgs 18:24.

State chariot of King Tutankhamon of Egypt. LL

When the Israelites came into Canaan, they found inhabitants in the plains whom they could not drive out because of their chariots of iron (Josh 11:4-9; Jud 1:19; 4:13). Joshua burned the chariots and hamstrung the horses that he captured in the battle against Jabin, possibly because they would have been of little use to people living in the hill country (see also the commandment of the Lord in Deut 17:16). *See* Armor.

Although David hamstrung some horses he captured, in one battle he saved enough horses for 100 chariots (II Sam 8:4). It was Solomon who built the chariot cities of Hazor and Megiddo to protect the northern frontier, Beth-horon, Gezer, and Baalath overlooking the Philistine plains, and Tamar in the Arabah to guard against the Edomites (I Kgs 9:15 - 19). Solomon had 1,400 chariots and 12,000 horsemen (I Kgs 10:26). He was also a middleman in the trade of horses from Cilicia (Kue) and chariots from Egypt (I Kgs 10:28 - 29, RSV).

The stele of Shalmaneser III mentions Ahab's 2,000 chariots which he furnished for the battle of Qarqar. The stables for 450 horses excavated at Megiddo are now dated to his reign.

Chariots continued to be used on a much smaller scale in Israel until NT times. The most familiar reference to a chariot in the NT is that which the Ethiopian eunuch was riding when Philip preached the good news of Jesus to him (Acts 8:27–28).

R. L. S.

CHARITY. Used 27 times in the KJV, including eight times in I Cor 13 for *agapē,* to signify human love for another person, often in the sense of benevolence. It is not used for the Gr. *charis,* which indicates grace, favor, goodwill. The Gr. *agapē* goes far deeper than the modern concept of charity, welfare, and generosity.

The use of "charity" in I Cor 13 (KJV) does not refer to almsgiving, since v. 3 uses it in the broad sense of love to all. The KJV translates the Gr. *agapē* as "charity" 27 times and as "love" 82 times, both mostly in Paul's writings. The difference must be determined by the context.

Charity shows man's love to man predicated on God's love to man. The word comes from the Latin *caritas,* which influenced Wycliffe and the Roman Catholic translators. Tyndale and most modern translators prefer to translate the Gr. *agapē* as "love," which avoids the narrower modern implication of generosity to needy people or worthy causes, and conveys the idea of man's loving attitude and action to his fellowman as a result of divine grace (Mt 22:37–40; Rom 13:8; I Cor 13). *See* Brotherly Kindness; Love.

E. B. R.

CHARM, CHARMER, CHARMING. *See* Magic.

CHARRAN. *See* Haran.

CHASE. *See* Hunting.

CHASTE, CHASTITY. Used to indicate inward, personal purity which shrinks from contamination or pollution, consequently free from defilement generally (I Pet 3:2), and from carnality and sexual sins (II Cor 11:2, "pure," RSV; Tit 2:5). *See* Purity.

CHASTEN. *See* Chastisement.

CHASTISEMENT. This is the KJV translation for the Heb. word *mûsār* and the Gr. word *paideia.* RSV prefers to use "discipline," which more closely represents the basic meaning of the original words. The primary significance is that of education, correction, guidance. The idea of punishment may be involved in the word, but unless the context indicates otherwise, punishment is to be viewed as corrective, as a part of the training process.

The basic idea involved in the biblical use is that God deals with His people as a father deals with his children. He disciplines and trains His people (primarily the nation Israel in the OT and the individual believer in the NT) to produce in them the qualities that conform to His own desire for them. The basic passage in the NT is Heb 12:6–8 where the writer states that chastisement (discipline) is a sign of sonship; the absence of it is a sign of illegitimacy.

Chastisement from God is to be viewed as an act of love and mercy. The believer, rather than rebelling against God's discipline, should recognize it as an act of fatherly love on God's part and correct his ways. Christian fathers are admonished by Paul to emulate God in bringing up their children in the discipline *(paideia)* and admonition of the Lord (Eph 6:4).

See Punishment.

F. L. F.

CHEBAR (kē'bär). A river in the land of the Chaldeans, on the banks of which some of the Jewish exiles, including the prophet Ezekiel, were settled. It was there that Ezekiel (*q.v.*) saw some of his visions (Ezk 1:1, 3; 3:15, 23; 10:15, 20). It has been identified as a navigable canal called *naru Kabari,* "great river," in Akkadian cuneiform tablets, just E of the ancient site of Nippur adjoining one of the great ship canals of Babylonia.

CHECKER WORK. Network or latticework used as ornamentation on the top of the pillars of Jachin and Boaz before the porch of the temple (I Kgs 7:17, 21). *See* Jachin and Boaz.

In Ex 28:4, 39 a different Heb. word is translated by RSV as a "coat of checker work" or "broidered coat," referring to the checked design used in making the high priest's tunic.

Checker work also refers to a net (Job 18:8) and a lattice (II Kgs 1:2). *See* Lattice.

CHEDORLAOMER (kĕd'ŏr-lā-ō'mẽr). A king of Elam who led a coalition of Mesopotamian and northern Syrian kings to put down a rebellion of five vassal kings in the Vale of Siddim, the Salt Sea (Dead Sea) area (Gen 14:1–5). The latter may have stopped tribute payment of bitumen, copper or salt, natural resources highly prized in Mesopotamia. After the defeat of Sodom and Gomorrah and capture of Lot by Chedorlaomer and his allies, Abram pursued them to Hobah, N of Damascus (Gen 14:15), and rescued Lot (Gen 14:17). *See* Abraham; Ellasar.

Although the places and peoples named and linguistic archaisms establish the antiquity of Gen 14, it is not possible to suggest an historical identification of Chedorlaomer free of problems. The proposal by W. F. Albright (BASOR #88 [1942], p. 34) that he may be Kutir-nahhunti I of Elam (*c.* 1625 B.C.) has chronological difficulties (see now BASOR # 163, pp. 49 f.). The name Chedorlaomer is a genuine Elamite construction, *Kutir* (or *Kudur)–lagamar,* and means "servant of the (goddess) Lagamar"; however, it cannot be equated with any known Elamite ruler.

Since Abraham lived *c.* 2000 B.C., the most likely time in Mesopotamian history when such a campaign could have taken place would be after the collapse of Sumerian rule during the Ur III Dynasty (2113–1991) and before the powerful control of Babylonia under Hammurabi (1792–1750 B.C.). Elamites, Amorites (*see* Amraphel) and Hurrians (*see* Arioch) are known to have been active in Mesopotamia during the Isin and Larsa dynasties (1991–1786 B.C.).

H. E. Fi.

CHEEK. The freshness and roundness of the cheek was a sign of youthful beauty (Song 1:10; 5:13). To be smitten on the cheek was regarded as a deadly insult (Job 16:10; Mic 5:1; Mt 5:39). Even a slave preferred a blow to a buffet on the cheek. "Thou dost smite all my enemies on the cheek" (Ps 3:7, RSV) is symbolic of their utter destruction.

CHEESE. *See* Food.

CHELAL (kē'lă). One of the eight sons of Pahath-moab who were forced by Ezra to give up their foreign wives after their return from Captivity (Ezr 10:30).

CHELLUH (kĕl'*ú*). One of the sons of Bani, mentioned in a group having foreign wives who were forced by Ezra to give them up after their return from Captivity (Ezr 10:35).

CHELUB (kē'lŭb). May be a variant of Caleb.

1. A descendant of Judah, a brother of Shuah and father of Mehir (I Chr 4:11).

2. Father of Ezri, one of David's officers and evidently his chief gardener (I Chr 27:26).

CHELUBAI (kê-lū'bī). A form of Caleb (I Chr 2:9, 18). He is mentioned here as the brother of Jerahmeel and Ram, and son of Hezron. Caleb (or Chelubai) is listed also as the son of Jephunneh the Kenezite (Num 32:12) and as the brother of Kenaz, Othniel's father (Josh 15:17). He was one of the men sent by Moses to spy out the land of Canaan (Num 13:6, 30), and was the conqueror of Hebron (Josh 14:13). *See also* Caleb.

CHEMARIM (kĕm'*á*-rîm). A word of Aramaic origin meaning "priest." The RSV translates this plural form as "idolatrous priests." The KJV transliterates the term "chemarims" in Zeph 1:4, but as "idolatrous priests" in II Kgs 23:5 and "priests" in Hos 10:5. All three passages show these priests involved in false worship. The Peshitto, however, uses the term favorably in connection with the Levitical priests and Jesus (Isa 61:6; Heb 2:17; 3:1; 4:14-15). The root idea is still uncertain. The word occurs in ancient Phoenician, Palmyrene, and Nabataean texts and in the Amarna letters as *kamiru*. Jews at the fortress of Elephantine near Aswan used the word when speaking of the Egyptian priest of the god Khnum.

CHEMOSH. *See* Gods, False.

CHENAANAH (kĕ-nā'*á*-n*á*)

1. The father of Zedekiah, the false prophet who incited Ahab against Micah (I Kgs 22:11, 24; II Chr 18:10, 23).

2. One of the seven sons of Bilhan, son of Jediael of the tribe of Benjamin, a mighty warrior at the time of David (I Chr 7:10).

CHENANI (kĕ-nā'nī). One of eight Levites mentioned as singing some religious song at Ezra's public reading of the law (Neh 9:4). The names represent either Levitical houses or individuals chosen to lead the worship of the people.

CHENANIAH (kĕn-*á*-nī'*á*)

1. A leader of the Levites over "the songs," or the "lifting up" of the ark of the covenant as it was brought by David's command from the house of Obed-edom to Jerusalem (I Chr 15:22, 27).

2. An Izharite, who with his sons was appointed "to outside duties for Israel, as officers and judges" (I Chr 26:29, RSV). This probably refers to duties outside the temple.

CHENOBOSKION (chĕn-ō-bŏs'kê-ŏn). The ancient Gr. name of a village (Coptic *Shênêsit*) in upper Egypt where a large collection of Gnostic books was discovered. Now called Qasr es-Sayyad, Chenoboskion lies near the town of Nag Hammadi, some 30 miles NW of Luxor. Here, sometime in 1945, natives accidentally discovered 13 well-preserved Coptic codices on papyrus with leather covers. One of them found its way to the Jung Institute at Zürich, Switzerland, while the other 12 codices came eventually to the Coptic Museum in Cairo. These volumes contain 49 treatises, of which some are duplications, but 44 of them are different. The majority of these works had been lost for many centuries and were known only by name or through quotations given in the writings of Church Fathers who refuted them. Most of these works are written in the Sahidic dialect of Coptic, but several appear in the Subakhmimic dialect. These manuscripts were written in the 3rd and 4th cen. A.D., but they are all translations of Gr. works of greater antiquity, which originally were composed in the 2d cen. A.D.

The Chenoboskion papyri contain Gnostic works of a great variety: discussions and treatises, dialogues, prayers, gospels, epistles, and apocalypses. From early church writings it is known that some of these works were attributed to the Gnostic Valentinus (middle of the 2nd cen. A.D.), and others to the Gnostic sects of the Sethians, Archontics and Barbelognostics. Up to the present time only a few of the Chenoboskion have been published in full, but even these few provide some idea of the literature of these sects. Among the most important of the published works belong the following three so-called gospels: (1) the Gospel of Thomas, a collection of 114 sayings of Jesus, of which some were already known from Gr. papyrus fragments found at Oxyrhynchus in Egypt; (2) the Gospel of Philip, also a collection of sayings, which is characterized by a strong dualism and which stresses the four elements of water, earth, wind, and air that correspond to faith, hope, love, and knowledge: and (3) the Gospel of Truth, which is a conglomeration of different phases of Gnostic philosophy, but has no semblance of what ordinarily is considered a gospel.

See Agrapha; Canon of Scripture–NT; Gnosticism.

Bibliography. J. Doresse, *The Secret Books of the Egyptian Gnostics,* New York: Viking Press, 1960. F. V. Filson, BA, XXIV (1961), 7-18. V. R. Gold, BA, XV (1952), 70-88. Andrew K. Helmbold, *The Nag Hammadi*

Gnostic Texts and the Bible, Grand Rapids: Baker, 1967. W. C. van Unnik, *Newly Discovered Gnostic Writings,* Naperville, Ill.: Allenson, 1960.

S. H. H.

CHEPHAR-HAAMMONAI (kē'fȧr-hā-ăm'ō-nī). A settlement meaning "village of the Ammonite" in the territory of Benjamin (Josh 18:24), so called perhaps because Ammonites lived there. Some identify it with Kefr'ana, a site of ruins about two miles NE of Bethel.

CHEPHIRAH (kĕ-fī'rȧ). A Hivite city in Benjamin's territory (Josh 18:26) which followed Gibeon's lead in making peace with Israel (Josh 9:17). It was resettled after the return from Babylonian exile (Ezr 2:25; Neh 7:29). The present-day site is Khirbet Kefireh SW of el-Jib (Gibeon).

CHERAN (kĕr'ȧn). The fourth son of Dishon, a Hurrian clan chief, listed in the genealogical tables of Seir. Evidently the founder of a Hurrian subclan in Edom (Gen 36:26; I Chr 1:41).

CHERETHITES (kĕr'ĕ-thīts)

1. A body of people in the Negeb or southern Palestine (I Sam 30:14), neighbors to the SE of the Philistines (cf. Ezk 25:16; Zeph 2:5). Ezekiel predicts judgment on them because of the Philistine revenge against Judah, indicating the close association of the two. The name (Heb. *kerētî*) probably echoes the word Crete *(q.v.),* ancient Caphtor *(q.v.).* They would thus be Cretans, relatives of the Philistines. The Carites were probably the same peoples (II Sam 20:23, variant reading in the *Kethibh;* II Kgs 11:4, 19, RSV, not "captains" as in KJV).

2. Mercenaries along with the Pelethites forming David's bodyguard, led by Benaiah son of Jehoiada (II Sam 8:18; 20:23; I Chr 18:17), probably recruited from the Cherethites during the time he fled from Saul. They stood by David when Absalom rebelled (II Sam 15:18), and proved their loyalty once again by being present at Solomon's coronation (I Kgs 1:38, 44). Foreign mercenaries have no family or local loyalties and tend to be well disciplined, as Cyrus H. Gordon points out, who equates these Cherethites with Cretans (*The World of the Old Testament,* pp. 171 f.). *See* Philistines.

H. G. S.

CHERITH (kĕr'ĭth). A brook where Elijah was told to hide from Ahab and was miraculously fed by ravens (I Kgs 17:2-7). The expression "facing" or "before" Jordan seems to favor a site in Gilead E of Jordan rather than the Wadi Qelt, the traditional site W of Jordan near Jericho.

CHERUB

1. Cherub (kĕr'ŭb) was an Israelite who returned from Captivity but was of a group who "could not prove their fathers' houses or their descent, whether they belonged to Israel" (Ezr 2:59; Neh 7:61, RSV). It could possibly be an unknown Babylonian place name instead of a person.

2. Cherub (chĕr'ŭb; pl., cherubim) is a celestial being of the angelic order belonging to the spiritual realm. The Semitic peoples pictured the cherubim as winged lions and bulls, having human faces, guarding temples and palaces. The biblical representations stress the human likeness but also indicate the animal characteristics. They guarded the way to the tree of life (Gen 3:24); a representation was fastened to the mercy seat of the ark (Ex 25:18 ff.) in the holy of holies (II Chr 3:7-14). They evidently have to do with the holiness of God violated by sin. Ezekiel identified them as the "living creatures" (*q.v.*) which he saw by the river Chebar (Ezk 1:5 f.; 10:20). Many identify the living creatures of the book of Revelation (4:6 f., RSV) with the cherubim. The number of wings varies. *See* Angel.

L. O. H.

CHESALON (kĕs'ȧ-lŏn). A city on the northern boundary of Judah, bordering Dan (Josh 15:10). Usually identified with modern Kesla, about nine miles W of Jerusalem on a mountain ridge to the S of Wadi el-Humar.

CHESED (kē'sĕd). The fourth son of Nahor (Abraham's brother) and Milcah (Gen 22:22). Probably the ancestor of an Aramean tribe referred to as the Casdim or Chaldeans.

The Monastery of Elijah by the traditional Brook Cherith. G. Semerdjian

CHESIL (kē'sĭl). A town in the extreme S of Judah named with Eltolad and Hormah (Josh 15:30). The name is not mentioned again. Chesil evidently corresponds with Bethul (Josh 19:4), Bethuel (I Chr 4:30), and Bethel (I Sam 30:27). *See* Bethel.

CHEST. Two Heb. words mean "chest," referring to an object rectangular in shape and usually made of wood.

1. Heb. *'ārôn* is uniformly used for the ark of the covenant except in two instances: (1) The bones of Joseph were placed in a "coffin" which was carried to Palestine (Gen 50:26). (2) King Joash and Jehoiada the priest had a chest placed in the temple beside the altar to receive free-will offerings for the repair of the temple (II Kgs 12:9; II Chr 24:8-11).

2. Heb. *g^enāzîm* is used in its plural form in connection with things collected or hidden, as treasures (Est 3:9), and chests for keeping valuables, treasure chests (Ezk 27:24).

CHESTNUT. *See* Plants.

CHESULLOTH (kė-sŭl'ŏth). A town in Issachar on the border of Zebulun (Josh 19:18). It seems to be the same as Chisloth-tabor (*q.v.;* Josh 19:12). It is identified with the modern Iksal on the northern edge of Esdraelon, about three miles SE of Nazareth.

CHETH. The eighth letter of the Heb. alphabet. *See* Alphabet. This letter is used in KJV as the heading of the eighth section of Ps 119, where each verse begins with this letter.

CHEZIB (kĕ'zĭb). The place where Judah's third son, Shelah, was born (Gen 38:5). It is probably to be identified with Achzib *(q.v.),* a town in western Judah, mentioned along with Mareshah and Keilah as belonging to Judah (Josh 15:44). From its grouping it seems to be the same also as Chozeba (I Chr 4:22).

CHICKEN. *See* Animals: Fowl, Domestic, III.14.

CHIDON (kī'dŏn). The name of the threshing floor where Uzzah was struck dead for touching the ark when the oxen stumbled (I Chr 13:9-10). However, the parallel passage in II Sam 6:6 has the threshing floor of Nachon *(q.v.).* The reference may indicate the owner of the threshing floor. There is no certain knowledge concerning either name.

CHIEF. The translation of a large group of Heb. words in the OT, usually designating the leader of a family, clan, or tribe, or in connection with certain official terms and titles. The ASV and RSV use "chief" where the KJV uses "duke" in referring to clan and tribal leadership (Gen 36:15; Ex 15:15; I Chr 1:51). Certain official terms are used, such as "chief butler" (Gen 40:9), "chief of the captains" (I Chr 11:11), "chief of the fathers of Israel" (II Chr 19:8), "chief of the nations" (Amos 6:1), and "chief priest" (II Chr 19:11). The NT uses such terms as "chief of the demons" (Lk 11:15), "chief Pharisee" (Lk 14:1), "chief of the Jews" (Acts 28:17), "chief city" (Acts 16:12), and "chief captain" (Gr. *chiliarchos,* RSV, "tribune," NASB, "commander," Acts 21:31, etc.). *See* Captain; Tribune.

CHIEF OF THE THREE. The official title of Adino the Ezrite, or Eznite (II Sam 23:8). The ASV reads: "These are the names of the mighty men whom David had: Josheb-basshebeth a Tahchemonite, chief of the captains; the same was Adino the Eznite, against eight hundred slain at one time." The obscure Heb. of this verse has led the RSV to omit the phrase "the same was Adino the Eznite," substituting the phrase "he wielded his spear." The phrase "chief among the captains" (KJV) is then translated as "chief of the three" in RSV.

CHIEF PRIEST. *See* Priests.

CHIEFS OF ASIA. *See* Asiarchs.

CHILD SACRIFICE. *See* Sacrifice, Human.

CHILDBEARING. One evidence that creation lies under God's curse is the travail which ordinarily accompanies the birth of a child (Gen 3:16). Often, indeed, the Bible alludes to the pangs of parturition as pain at its most painful (Ps 48:6; Isa 13:8; 21:3; 26:17; Jer 4:31; 6:24; 13:21; 22:23; 50:43). Yet from a biblical perspective childbearing is not just a burden; it is, paradoxically, a woman's highest privilege and greatest joy (Ps 113:9; Isa 54:1; Jn 16:21). Sterility, on the contrary, is a supreme affliction (Gen 11:30; I Sam 1:1–2:5; II Sam 6:23; Lk 1:7).

Under the Mosaic law childbearing rendered a woman ceremonially unclean; 50 days for a daughter, 40 days for a son. At the end of that time a sacrifice for purification was presented (Lev 12; Lk 2:22-24). The older practice of the "churching" of women, a public thanksgiving for the safe deliverance of child and mother, no doubt developed from this OT purification ordinance. This observance, in Protestant churches at any rate, has been largely abandoned.

Paul's statement concerning childbirth in I Tim 2:15 has called forth a number of diversified views, ranging from ordinary childbirth to an allusion to the incarnation (cf. Dean Henry Alford, *The Greek New Testament).*

V. C. G.

CHILDHOOD OF CHRIST. Knowledge of the childhood of Christ depends upon three sources: historical, cultural, and indirect evidence.

1. *Recorded facts.* These are the recorded incidents surrounding the birth and early babyhood of Christ, followed by complete silence

until His twelfth year when He went with Joseph and Mary to the temple to attend the Feast of the Passover at Jerusalem. The main events at His birth include the time and place (Mt 2:1 ff.; Lk 2:1 ff.), and the annunciation to the shepherds and their visit to the manger to worship the Christ Child (Lk 2:8–20). On the eighth day He was circumcised, and at that time He received His name (Lk 2:21). At His presentation in the temple on the fortieth day, Mary offered a pair of turtledoves or two young pigeons, as was appropriate for the poor (Lev 12:8; Lk 2:22–24).

This last ceremony was marked by Simeon's prophecy that Jesus was God's means of salvation for both Jew and Gentile, though His coming would be rejected by many in Israel (Lk 2:25–35). This prophecy was corroborated by Anna, an aged woman serving God day and night in the temple with fasting and prayer, who foretold that Jesus was the one sent for the redemption of Jerusalem (Lk 2:36–38).

It was probably after the circumcision and dedication that the wise men inquired in Jerusalem and then visited Mary and Joseph and the Babe in Bethlehem, since the flight to Egypt followed that visit so shortly (Mt 2:1–14). After the death of Herod, Joseph and Mary and the Child returned to Palestine and lived quietly in Nazareth (Mt 2:19–23). We may well surmise that Joseph and Mary told Jesus the amazing events and the prophecies attending His birth, and that these details greatly enriched His childhood.

In Lk 2:42–50, the boy Jesus, at 12 years of age, showed great insight into His peculiar relationship to God. His question addressed to Joseph and Mary, "Did you not know that I had to be in My Father's house?" ("in the things of My Father?" NASB and marg.) shows a consciousness that God, not Joseph, was His true Father. These first quoted words of Jesus, referring to His sonship, were the mark of His awareness of His mission on earth.

2. *Culture and customs.* A study of Jewish customs and culture, particularly as they are recorded in the OT and were revealed to Israel as the will of God, adds much to our knowledge of the childhood of Christ. The feasts and religious observances filled much of the life of the Israelite (*see* Worship). The Feast of the Passover was celebrated in every family, followed by the Feasts of Unleavened Bread, First Fruits, Pentecost, Trumpets, Day of Atonement, and Feast of Tabernacles. Some of these feasts lasted a week. Although the main celebrations occurred at Jerusalem, nevertheless observances of a lesser nature must have been held in the local synagogues.

The Jewish home had Scripture on its doorposts, the constant daily teaching and discussion of the Bible (Deut 7:6–9; 11:18–20), and memorization of the Heb. Scriptures, in addition to the weekly sabbath services in the synagogue. We know that Christ learned to read (Lk 4:17) and write (Jn 8:6–8). Like every Jewish boy, He was taught a trade, and by carpentry probably supported Himself, His mother Mary, and the family after Joseph's death, until He was baptized and led by the Holy Spirit into His public ministry (Mt 3:13–17; Lk 4:1, 14). Justin Martyr speaks of His making "plows and yokes" (*Dial.* 88).

3. *Inferences from Christ's own references to childhood.* Jesus must have been intensely interested in nature because of His references to foxes, birds (Mt 6:26; 8:20; 13:32; Lk 9:58; 12:6), hen and chickens (Mt 23:37), flowers (Mt 6:28–30), and the weather (Mt 16:2–3; Lk 12:56). He must have entered into and played the games which other children played (Mt 11:16–17).

In all, Jesus enjoyed a very normal and healthy childhood. His parents were humble, honest, hard working, and devout. His mother in particular was an example of patience and love (Lk 2:19, 51); Joseph a man of integrity, yet compassionate (Mt 1:19–25) and of real faith. Christ's childhood experiences undoubtedly were those of a boy who spent much time in the out-of-doors, coupled with a thorough training in a trade. Through it all He developed both mentally and physically. His teaching proved the former and His physical endurance the latter. Besides this, He matured spiritually in His fellowship with God, and socially in His relationships with His fellowmen (Lk 2:40, 52).

The so-called infancy gospels, the Protevangelium of James and the Gospel of Thomas, are apocryphal writings of the 2nd cen. A.D. They contain purely legendary incidents such as miracles wrought by Jesus as a small boy. In later centuries other writings copied and enlarged on these imaginative stories.

R. A. K.

CHILDREN. Parenthood, as the Bible sees it, is an incontestable proof of God's favor. The pious Israelite, therefore, responded to the birth of his child with gratitude and joy (Ps 127; 128:3), and his wife shared these emotions (Ps 113:9). Indeed, the larger their family, the greater was the thankfulness of a heaven-blessed couple. In the context of a rather simple agricultural economy, this reaction was entirely understandable. Hence the problem of planned parenthood never appeared on the horizon in ancient Palestine. Hence, too, voluntary childlessness was viewed as reprehensible.

The birth of a boy, however, was far more welcome than that of a girl. To the Jews the pagan practice of destroying female infants was anathema, yet only mild enthusiasm greeted a daughter's arrival.

Hebrew mothers, one may assume, prided themselves on delivering their own children with ease (Ex 1:19), although on occasion they had the help of midwives (Gen 35:17; 38:28; Ex 1:15–19). Immediately after parturition infants were bathed; then they were rubbed with salt to harden their skin; after that they were wrapped in swaddling bands (Ezk 16:4; Lk

2:7). Suckling was the rule rather than the exception (I Sam 1:21-23; Isa 49:15; cf. Ex 2:7; II Kgs 11:2). The weaning of a child at two or three years of age was the occasion for both feast and sacrifice (Gen 21:8).

When only eight days old, males were circumcised, a rite which Yahweh explicitly commanded in Gen 17:10. Circumcision was not primarily an act of purification; essentially it was an act of incorporation, the sign that a boy had become a member of the covenant community (Lev 12:3). A parallel ceremony for girls evolved to mark their official entrance into God's people.

Names were customarily bestowed at the same time (Lk 2:21). Since in Semitic culture a spiritual significance, a kind of numinous influence, was attached to names, the father had the privilege of choosing what his child would be called; no doubt in practice the choice was a matter of mutual agreement between husband and wife (Lk 1:57-63).

The firstborn male in a family occupied a unique position; his status as future head of the family was indicated by a special designation, *bᵉkôr,* the Heb. term Mary must have applied to her own Son (Lk 2:7). In remembrance of the Exodus judgment upon Egypt, the firstborn belonged to the Lord. Within a month after his birth, however, following official presentation in the temple, he was ransomed by an offering (Ex 13:12-16; Num 8:17; Lk 2:22-23).

For the first few years of life both boys and girls were in the care of their mothers. The girls, of course, remained under maternal supervision, helping in the home, carrying water, learning to spin, or perhaps tending sheep, and gleaning in the fields. Boys, as they grew, were supervised by their fathers, serving as apprentices in the paternal occupation.

Education, too, was the father's responsibility. This was chiefly religious and moral in nature (Ex 13:8; Deut 4:9-10; 6:4-7; 7:9; Josh 4:4-8), a thorough indoctrination in history, Torah, and ritualism. Something of the tenderness of a child's upbringing in Israel may be glimpsed in passages such as Isa 66:12; Hos 11:3; cf. Mk 9:36-37. Something of the severity which likewise prevailed, a severity which sprang from the absolute authority of the parents, may be seen in passages like Ex 21:15-17 and Deut 21:18-21. And something of the play in which children engaged may be gathered from passages like Zech 8:5 and Mt 11:16-17.

Formal schools seem to have appeared about a century before our Lord was born. Extensions of the synagogue, they enrolled a child at five and subjected him to a program of rote memorization which centered in the Torah. By 13 this training ended, as a boy legally came of age, entered into the court of men, and assumed the duties of reciting the Shema, fasting regularly, and making pilgrimages. Some rabbis argued that girls should not be educated, but they seem to have acquired a rather thorough knowledge of Scripture; e.g., Mary's repeated allusions to the OT in her Magnificat (Lk 1:46-55).

The duties of parents *(q.v.)* with respect to their children are set forth in, e.g., Prov 22:6; Eph 6:4; Col 3:21; I Tim 5:8; Tit 2:4. The duties of children, on the other hand, are stated in, e.g., Ex 20:12; Eph 6:1-3; and Col 3:20.

In the Bible, references to childhood are sometimes used psychologically to denote a stage of ignorance and immaturity (Lk 7:32; I Cor 13:11; Eph 4:14; Heb 5:13); sometimes they are used ethically to denote a state of innocence, simplicity and trust (Mt 7:9-11; 18:1-5; 19:13-15; I Cor 14:20); and sometimes they are used spiritually to denote a faith-established relationship to God (Mt 5:9; Jn 1:12; Rom 8:14-17).

See Family; Education.

Bibliography. Henri Daniel-Rops, *Daily Life in the Time of Jesus,* New York: Hawthorn, 1962, pp. 118-133. Edith Deen, *Family Living in the Bible,* New York: Harper, 1963, pp. 86-93. Albrecht Oepke, "*Pais,* etc.," TDNT, V, 636-654.

V. C. G.

CHILDREN OF GOD. With a few exceptions, this phrase is equivalent to sons of God. In the OT it denotes chiefly a relationship to God by covenant, not by physical descent as is found in other Semitic or pagan religions. Man was *created* in the image of God, not begotten, and Israel's sonship was dependent upon grace not nature. Moreover, not all men are addressed as children of God. Israel collectively can be spoken of as God's son (Ex 4:22), or the nation generally may be called the children of God (Deut 14:1); but only the actual or messianic King can be called the Son of God (Ps 2:7).

In the NT, sonship is indissolubly linked with the sonship of Christ (Rom 8:17; Jn 1:12). Because He is Son (Mt 2:15; 3:17), He also leads many other sons to glory (Heb 2:10).

In Pauline parlance men become children of God by adoption (Rom 8:15, 23; Gal 4:5; Eph 1:5). This is made possible by coming to God the Father through Christ (Gal 3:26). Sonship is attested to by the Spirit (Rom 8:14, 16). Although on earth it is imperfect and incomplete, in the resurrection at the return of Christ it will be made perfect (Rom 8:21, 23, 29; I Jn 3:1).

In the language of John and Peter, sonship is described in terms of rebirth (Jn 1:12-13; I Jn 3:9; 4:7; 5:1, 4; I Pet 1:23). Some have held that in the NT the children of God *(tekna)* and the sons of God *(huioi)* should be differentiated, the former term being more appropriate for the birth metaphor and the latter to adoption. Such a distinction should be advanced with great caution. It is true that John uses *tekna* for Christians and reserves *huios* for Christ. Paul, however, seems to use *huioi* and *tekna* interchangeably when referring to Christians.

G. W. Ba.

CHILDREN OF ISRAEL. *See* Israel.

CHILEAB (kĭl'ĭ-ăb). The second son of David, born to him at Hebron by Abigail, the widow of Nabal the Carmelite (II Sam 3:3). He is called Daniel in a corresponding account (I Chr 3:1).

CHILION (kĭl'ĭ-*ŭ*n). One of the two sons of Elimelech and Naomi, who migrated from Bethlehem to Moab. Chilion married the Moabitess Orpah, and died childless in Moab (Ruth 1:2, 5; 4:9).

CHILMAD (kĭl'măd). A city or district mentioned along with Asshur, Haran, Canneh, and Eden as having supplied merchandise to Tyre (Ezk 27:23). Chilmad may possibly be identified with Charmon (Charmande), a town in Babylonia near the Euphrates.

CHIMHAM (kĭm'hăm). One of the sons of Barzillai the Gileadite (Jos *Ant.* vii.11.4), who remained loyal to David while the latter was in exile at Mahanaim (II Sam 19:37–40). David urged Barzillai *(q.v.)* to return to Jerusalem with him and receive royal favors, but he declined because of his age and asked that David confer the favors upon Chimham (II Sam 19:31–40). Chimham seems to have received a pension and some land near Bethlehem, known four centuries later as the "habitation of Chimham" (I Kgs 2:7; Jer 41:17).

CHIMNEY. The word more properly means "lattice" or "window." The word "chimney" is found only in Hos 13:3. RSV translates the passage: ". . . like smoke from a window." The houses had no chimneys.

CHINNERETH (kĭn'*ĕ*-rĕth), **CHINNEROTH** (kĭn'*ĕ*-rŏth)

1. An early name, probably Canaanite, for the Sea of Galilee (Num 34:11; Deut 3:17; Josh 11:2; 12:3; 13:27), perhaps because the lake is lyre or harp shaped (from Heb. *kinnôr,* "lyre"). *See* Galilee, Sea of.

2. A fortified city of Naphtali (Josh 19:35). It was included as *knnrt* in a list of towns conquered by Thutmose III of Egypt (*c.* 1475 B.C.). Its site is Tell el-'Oreimeh, on the lake shore two and a half miles SW of Capernaum.

3. The area around the city of Chinneroth (Josh 11:2), usually identified with the plain of Gennesaret (Mt 14:34), and thus a district of Naphtali W of the Sea of Galilee, conquered by Ben-hadad of Syria (I Kgs 15:20), spelled Cinneroth in KJV. The Gr. name *Gennēsaret* was more correctly *Gennēsar,* according to I Macc 11:67, Josephus, the Talmud, Gr. MS D, and several ancient versions of Mt and Mk. The derivation of the Gr. name is not certain.

L. O. H.

CHIOS (kī'ŏs). A rocky and mountainous island in the E central region of the Aegean Sea, about five miles from the mainland of Asia Minor, W of Smyrna. It was famous for its wines, figs, and aromatic resins. Paul's ship anchored for the night off Chios as he returned to Jerusalem at the end of his third missionary journey (Acts 20:15). Along with other places, it claimed to be the birth place of Homer. Its chief city and port, also called Chios, was a free city belonging to the Roman province of Asia in Paul's time. Today Chios (Khios) is a town of 22,000.

CHISEL. A carpenter's tool used in the making of a wooden idol (Isa 44:13, JerusB). The Heb. term *maqṣu'ôth* is probably better translated "chisels" instead of "planes" (KJV, RSV, etc.). In Isaiah's time the more primitive chisel and adz still were used in place of the plane.

CHISLEU (kĭs'lū). The third civil or ninth ecclesiastical month of the Jewish year corresponding to November-December (Neh 1:1; Zech 7:1). The derivation seems to be from the Akkad. word *kislīmu*. *See* Calendar.

CHISLON (kĭs'lŏn). The father of Elidad, who as one of the leaders of Benjamin was selected to help divide the portion of Canaan W of the Jordan among the nine and one-half tribes (Num 34:21).

CHISLOTH-TABOR (kĭs'lŏth-tā'bôr). A town in Galilee bordering the territories of Issachar and Zebulun. It seems to be the same as Chesulloth (*q.v.;* Josh 19:18). It is identified with the modern Iksal, a village about four miles W of Mount Tabor near Nazareth.

CHITTIM (kĭt'ĭm). The Heb. word is used in both a broad and narrow sense. In its narrower sense it meant the island of Cyprus (Isa 23:1, 12; Jer 2:10; Ezk 27:6). Josephus refers to Cyprus as follows: "Cethimus possessed the island Cethima; it is now called Cyprus: and from that it is that all islands, and the greatest part of the sea-coasts, are named Cethim [equals Kittim] by the Hebrews" (*Ant.* i.6.1). The city of Citius, or Cition, on Cyprus seems to have given its name to the island. In Num 24:24; Dan 11:30 Chittim evidently refers to Rome. The earliest reference (Gen 10:4) makes this term apply to the descendants of Javan, indicating the Greek-Latin races of the Mediterranean area including Cyprus.

CHIUN. *See* Gods, False: Kaiwan.

CHLOE (klō'ē). A woman, evidently a Christian, whose household servants or slaves informed Paul, who was working in Ephesus at the time, of partisan divisions and moral disorders in the church at Corinth (I Cor 1:11). It is not known whether she lived in Corinth or Ephesus. However, she was well-known to Paul and the Corinthian church.

CHOENIX. *See* Weights, Measures, and Coins.

CHORASHAN (kôr-ā'shăn). Found only in I Sam 30:30 (KJV). RSV refers to the city as Borashan. It is probably the same as Ashan. Located in the Shephelah, it was originally assigned to Simeon, but in David's administration it became a Levitical city of Judah (Josh 15:42; 19:7; I Chr 4:32; 6:59). *See* Ashan.

CHORAZIN (kō-rā'zĭn). A small town in the hills, about two miles N of Tell Hum (Capernaum) and thus as far inland from the Sea of Galilee. Identified with Kerazeh, the town exhibits extensive ruins from the 3rd to 4th cen. A.D., including a synagogue of black basalt stones richly decorated with sculptures of animals and representations of grape gathering and grape pressing. Jesus performed many great works there without winning disciples, and upbraided the townsfolk for their unbelief (Mt 11:20–22; Lk 10:13).

CHOSEN. The Heb. and Gr. words translated "chosen," based on the verbs *bāḥar* and *eklegomai,* involve a comparison of two or more objects or persons. The choice suggests a certain privilege, position, or purpose. Human choices on the basis of character or skill are evident in Scripture, such as choosing wives (Gen 6:2), captains and soldiers (Ex 15:4; 17:9; Jud 20:15–16), and Yahweh as one's God (Josh 24:15, 22). The church in Jerusalem chose seven deacons on the basis of their spirituality and wisdom (Acts 6:3, 5); and the church chose men who had already risked their lives for Christ to accompany Paul and Barnabas to Antioch with the decision of the Jerusalem council (Acts 15:22, 26).

God also chooses, but His choice depends upon grace rather than merit. Israel was not chosen to be His special people because of its numbers (Deut 7:6–7; 10:15; Neh 9:7–8; Isa 43:20; 44:1–2; Acts 13:17); nor is the Christian believer selected because of his natural talents (I Cor 1:26–31) but for God's glory and to manifest His love. He chose David to be king over Israel not on the basis of his outward appearance (I Sam 16:7, 12). The Servant of Yahweh (Isa 42:1) would have no stately form or majesty but would be despised and rejected by men (Isa 53:2–3). As individual believers we were "chosen before the foundation of the world" (Eph 1:4; cf. Rom 8:29).

Can any of the chosen of God fail? What about Israel, for example? In Rom 11 Paul discusses at length their being rejected for a time and their final redemption, concluding his revelation with the words, "So all Israel shall be saved . . . for the gifts and calling of God are without repentance" (Rom 11:26, 29). Similarly, those whom God has foreknown as His own He will carry safely through every step of salvation to their final glorification (Rom 8:29–30). *See* Election.

Certain difficult questions arise concerning God's election or choice. How can man be called free if only those who are chosen are saved? In other words, where do God's sovereignty and grace and man's freedom meet in salvation? Briefly, man's freedom since the Fall is essentially a freedom to do evil. Without God's grace he may desire but cannot actually choose the good. At the same time God does not ignore the freedom of man but includes it in His sovereign grace when He does save a man.

The Chorazin Synagogue. HFV

Again, how can God be righteous and choose some while rejecting others? The answer to this is that God does not have to save any; and therefore those who are saved are actually the subjects of His unmerited favor, while those He passes by are victims of their own rebellion and sin.

See Call; Election.

R. A. K.

CHOSEN PEOPLE. In the OT the term *bāḥar* expresses "choose," and first occurs in connection with Israel in Deut 7:6, where they are commanded to destroy all pagan cult objects in Canaan because "thou art a holy people unto Jehovah thy God: Jehovah thy God hath chosen thee" (ASV). This was no matter of nationalistic pride, for God's choice was based upon His gracious love and His promise to Abraham, rather than upon the numbers or merit of the nation (v. 7). Hence, they were a people saved only by grace and unconditionally committed to God's will and cause (Ps 105:6; 135:4). God's choice was later reaffirmed by His delivering Israel from Babylonian captivity (Isa 14:1) to fulfill a missionary role to the world as His servant (Isa 41:8; 44:1–2), especially in the person of the coming Christ, God's Chosen One *par excellence* (Isa 42:1). Other occurrences of the chosen people concept are in I Kgs 3:8 and Ezk 20:5. Important references in the NT are I Cor 1:26–28; Eph 1:4; Jas 2:5; and especially I Pet 2:9–10. *See* Election.

G. L. A.

CHOZEBA (kō-zē'bȧ). A city in Judah whose men were descendants of Shelah (I Chr 4:22). It is to be identified with Chezib (Gen 38:5) and Achzib (Josh 15:44). *See* Chezib; Achzib.

CHRIST. *See* Jesus Christ.

CHRIST, APPEARANCES OF. *See* Appearances of Christ.

CHRIST, ASCENSION OF. *See* Ascension of Christ.

CHRIST, COMING OF. The first and second comings of Christ as the Messiah are foretold in many OT prophecies. He was to come the first time as the suffering Messiah and to die as an atoning sacrifice (Isa 7:14; 52:13–53:12; Ps 16; cf. Acts 2:22-31; Ps 22:1-21; 31; 40:5-8; 41:9; 69:8-9, 21). He is to come the second time as the reigning, ruling Messiah, whose kingdom is to be a literal reign on the earth (Isa 9:6-7; 11:1 ff.; 66:15 ff.; Zech 12:10; 13:6; 14:1 ff.). The book of Revelation says the reign will be for one thousand years (Rev 20:4-6).

On the details of His first coming all Christians agree. On those of His second coming there is a wide divergence of opinion. The postmillennialist says the church will inaugurate a period of perfect peace, a millennium, and then Christ will come. The amillennialist says there is no literal earthly millennium; for them the passages which speak of a physical rule of the Messiah on the earth are not to be taken literally. The premillennialist says since the prophecies of His first coming were fulfilled literally, even though the Jewish leaders rejected their literal interpretation and would not receive Christ, the prophecies of His second coming are to be accepted as literal.

Four Gr. words are used for Christ's second coming: (1) *erchomai,* "to come" (Mt 24:3; 25:27; Lk 12:45; 18:5; 19:23); (2) *epiphaneia,* "appearing," "presence," which occurs six times, one in II Thess 2:8 and five times in the pastoral epistles (I Tim 6:14; II Tim 1:10; 4:1, 8; Tit 2:13); (3) *apokalypsis (apocalyptō),* "revelation" (apocalypse) or "unveiling" (Lk 17:30; I Pet 1:13); (4) *parousia,* which means "presence" and is used more frequently. It expresses the arrival and subsequent visit of a king or emperor (Mt 24:3, 27; I Cor 15:23; I Thess 2:19; 3:13; 4:15; II Thess 2:1, 8-9; Jas 5:7-8; II Pet 1:16; 3:4, 12; I Jn 2:28). See Albrecht Oepke, "*Parousia,* etc.," TDNT, V, 858-871.

Christ's second coming includes two phases: His coming in the air for His own at the rapture (Jn 14:3; I Cor 15:51-53; I Thess 4:13-18; Rev 16:15), and His coming to rule over the nations of the world (Zech 14:1 ff.; Rev 20:4-6).

The time of the rapture is a question to which three answers are given. It may be immediately preceding the Great Tribulation—the pre-Tribulation rapture view; in the middle of the Tribulation—the mid-Tribulation rapture view; or after the main part of the Great Tribulation but before the seven vials of wrath—the post-Tribulation rapture view.

The important thing, and that on which all premillennialists agree, is that the Scriptures of the OT and NT both teach Christ will rule in His millennial kingdom upon the earth. They base their conclusion upon a grammatical-historical interpretation of both fulfilled and unfulfilled prophecy in OT and NT. *See* Eschatology; Rapture.

R. A. K.

CHRIST, CRUCIFIXION OF. *See* Cross.

CHRIST, DEATH OF. *See* Atonement; Christ, Passion of; Cross.

CHRIST, DEITY OF. Jesus Christ is the Son of God and very God of very God. He is of the same substance with the Father and the Holy Spirit, and equal in power and glory (*see* Godhead). Everything, therefore, that can be said of the Father and of the Holy Spirit can be said of the Son. He is the Creator (Jn 1:1-3; Col 1:16; Heb 1:2), even as the Father (Gen 1:1; Rev 4:11) and the Holy Spirit (Gen 1:2) created. He is the Upholder and Sustainer of all things (Col 1:17; Heb 1:3), even as are the Father (Gen 8:21-22) and the Holy Spirit (Job 27:3; 33:4). He is the Redeemer (Rev 5:9; Rom 3:24; Titus 2:14), even as the Father (Isa 63:16).

Biblical proofs of the deity of Christ. The deity of Christ is proved by certain express statements in Scripture (Immanuel, or "God with us," in Isa 7:14 and Mt 1:23; Jn 1:1; Jn 1:18, RSV marg.; Rom 9:5; Tit 2:13, RSV; Heb 1:8). He claimed to be able to forgive sins (Mk 2:5, 10-11; Lk 7:48), which is the prerogative of God alone and was so recognized (Mk 2:7; Lk 5:21). He healed the sick (Mt 4:23-24; 8:14-17; 9:18-35; Lk 5:17-26; 7:18-23), and raised the dead (Lk 7:11-15; 8:41-42, 49-55; Jn 11:38-44; cf. 5:25-29). He controlled nature by stilling the waves (Mt 8:23-27). He acted creatively in multiplying the loaves and fishes (Mt 14:19-21; 15:32-38). He claimed to be God (Jn 10:33) and to be pre-existent with God (Jn 8:58; 17:5). He is equal with the Father (Jn 14:9; Phil 2:5-8) and one in essence with the Father (Jn 10:30). He alone of all men is worthy to be worshiped, an act prohibited toward mere created beings and reserved for God only (Jn 9:38; Phil 2:9-11; Rev 5:11-14; 19:10; 22:8 f.; Acts 10:25 f.).

Philosophical and theological proofs. If we are to have a God who is infinite in His person and in His relationships, this God must be triune in nature. *See* Trinity; Theism. Any view—such as the Muslim faith, Judaism, Jehovah's Witnesses—which states that there is only one person in the Godhead proves inadequate. Such a view presents a God who for the first time would have known a true subject-object relationship (the I-It relationship), would have had a real person relationship (the I-Thou relationship), or would have experienced an actual social relationship (the We-You), only after He had created both the world and man. This is the fatal defect in all Unitarian views. In that man knows and enjoys

CHRIST, HUMANITY OF

all these relationships, he would be greater in these respects than a non-triune God would have been before He created the world and man. Thus the eternal sonship and deity of Christ is philosophically tenable and necessary.

The deity of Jesus Christ is of the greatest importance for our salvation. Only an infinite person could offer an infinite sacrifice sufficient to satisfy God's divine justice and to atone for the sins of all who would believe. While sin started with a single act of disobedience, such as a forest fire starts with a single spark, it spread to all mankind; and its atonement—after sin had enveloped all of nature and of mankind—required not merely the act of a man but of the Almighty in His own omnipotent Son. *See* Incarnation.

R. A. K.

Nicene creed. In the 2nd and 3rd cen. A.D. widely divergent views of the relation of Jesus to God were expressed in the writings of various Christian leaders. Justin Martyr held that the Logos incarnated in Jesus Christ was a second God. Irenaeus emphasized the unity of God, or monotheism, while Paul of Samosata stressed the humanity of Jesus, saying He was a sinless man from birth. Sabellius believed the Father was born as Jesus Christ and suffered as the Son, the Father, Son, and Holy Spirit being three modes or aspects of God. Tertullian declared that God is one substance but three persons or parties in the divine administrative activity, and that Jesus was both God and man, one person but two substances or natures. Origen was basically orthodox but taught that while the Son was coeternal with the Father, yet Christ as the image of God is dependent upon the Father and subordinate to Him.

Early in the 4th cen. Arius, a presbyter in the Alexandrian church, maintained that the Son had a beginning and is not a part of God. The Father had created the Son in order that He might create the world. Such a controversy developed in the eastern part of the Roman Empire that Emperor Constantine summoned a council of the entire church that met at Nicaea in Asia Minor in A.D. 325. It was the first ecumenical council, with more than 300 bishops in attendance. The young Athanasius, a deacon of Alexandria, championed the orthodox position. The creed adopted by this council states that the Son is of the same substance (*homoousios*) with the Father. It reads as follows:

"We believe in one God, the Father Almighty, maker of all things visible and invisible, and in one Lord, Jesus Christ, the Son of God, the only-begotten of the Father, that is, of the substance (*ousias*) of the Father, God from God, light from light, true God from true God, begotten, not made, of one substance (*homoousion*) with the Father, through whom all things were made, those things that are in heaven and those things that are on earth, who for us men and for our salvation came down and was made flesh, suffered, rose again on the third day, ascended into the heavens, and will come to judge the living and the dead" (K. S. Latourette, *A History of Christianity,* New York: Harper, 1953, p. 155).

While Arius was banished and his position anathematized, in the decades that followed his disciples tried to override the council's decision. Athanasius for a time was given so little support by others that historians speak of *Athanasius contra mundum,* "Athanasius against the world." He died in 373. Three outstanding bishops from Cappadocia, Gregory of Nazianzus, Basil of Caesarea, and Gregory of Nyssa, took up the contest and argued that there is only one *ousia* (substance, essence) in which Father, Son, and Holy Spirit share, but that there are three *hypostases* (translatable into Latin by *personae,* persons). A second ecumenical council met at Constantinople in 381 to make a final end of the Arian controversy. The orthodox doctrine established at Nicaea was reaffirmed and the Nicene creed modified and enlarged to its present form.

J. R.

Bibliography. G. C. Berkouwer, *The Person of Christ,* Grand Rapids: Eerdmans, 1954, pp. 155-192. Loraine Boettner, *Studies in Theology,* Eerdmans, 1947, pp. 140-182. H. P. Liddon, *The Divinity of Our Lord and Saviour Jesus Christ* (Bampton Lectures, 1866), 15th ed., London: Longmans, Green & Co., 1891. Wilbur M. Smith, *The Supernaturalness of Christ,* Boston: Wilde, 1940.

CHRIST, HUMANITY OF. The Scripture bears witness in numerous ways to the humanity of Jesus Christ. He was "the son of Abraham" (Mt 1:1), "made of the seed of David according

During His earthly life, Christ spent many hours by the Sea of Galilee. IIS

to the flesh" (Rom 1:3), conceived of Mary the virgin (Lk 1:31), "made of a woman" (Gal 4:4), born of Mary (Mt 1:25; 2:11; Lk 2:7), "made flesh" (Jn 1:14; cf. Rom 1:3; I Tim 3:16). He was an infant (Mt 2:11, 14, 20, 21; Lk 2:7, 16), He "increased in wisdom and stature" (Lk 2:52), wrought as a carpenter (Mk 6:3), hungered (Mt 4:2; Mk 11:12), thirsted (Jn 4:7; 19:28), experienced the emotions of joy and sorrow (Lk 10:21; Jn 12:27), was crucified, and rose again from the dead. He is expressly called man (Jn 1:30; Acts 17:31; Rom 5:15; I Cor 15:21, 47; I Tim 2:5; Heb 2:6–9). Four characterizations sum up the doctrine of Christ's humanity.

1. The *reality* must be emphasized in opposition to any view which either asserts or implies mere appearance or semblance. It was this heresy John was called upon to combat, and he says it was of Antichrist (I Jn 4:1–3). There are more subtle ways, however, in which the reality of Christ's humanity may be compromised. Human nature is finite and there are, therefore, the limitations inseparable from Jesus' manhood. The meaning of many of His words and actions in the days of His flesh are missed if one does not take account of His speaking and acting in terms of His human nature, and thus with the limitations incident to it. Conspicuous in this respect is Mt 24:36 which, so far from being a difficulty, is a clear index to the limited knowledge belonging to His human consciousness and His dependence upon revelation for all that came within its compass.

2. The *integrity* of Christ's humanity means that all the attributes essential to manhood were His. He was body and spirit. He had human understanding, feeling, and will, and these must not be submerged in the attributes of Deity which were also His. The jealousy with which the church must maintain this integrity appears in what was central in His mission. In human nature He suffered and died. It would impinge upon the reality of the atonement to impair to any extent the completeness with which He acted in terms of human nature.

3. The *sinlessness* of Jesus distinguishes His human nature from that of all others. Limitations are not to be equated with sinful infirmities nor with fallibility. From conception He was the holy thing begotten (Lk 1:35); born of a virgin. He was holy, harmless, undefiled, and separate from sinners (Heb 7:26), and no one could convict Him of sin (Jn 8:46). Though tempted in all points like as we are, yet it was the qualification "without sin" that imparted to His ability to sympathize its matchless grace and virtue (Heb 4:15).

4. The *continuance* of His humanity is indispensable to the discharge of His heavenly ministry. In death, body and spirit were separated, the body laid in the tomb and the spirit dismissed to the Father. But body and spirit were reunited in the resurrection. In the integrity of human nature physically and psychically constituted He ascended to heaven, and continues His mediatorial ministry until at His advent He will return in this same human nature to judge the world and consummate the kingdom of God.

See Incarnation.

J. M.

CHRIST, HUMILIATION OF. The title "Christ" means "anointed"; it refers to that office which was undertaken in pursuance of God's saving and redeeming purpose. It is more proper, therefore, to speak first of all in terms of the humiliation of the Son of God. The latter title bespeaks His eternal and divine identity, and only against the background of such dignity may His humiliation be understood.

It would have been humiliation for the eternal Son of God to have come into this world and become man under the most ideal earthly conditions, a humiliation merely because of the disparity between God and man. It was not, however, into an ideal world that the Son of God came, but into this world of sin, and misery, and death. All the circumstances of His coming were conditioned by these facts. Not only so, He came to deal with sin, misery, and death; He took these upon Himself as the Sin-bearer to make an end of sin and abolish death for His people. The cross of Christ was self-humiliation to the lowest depths conceivable. Because of the dignity of His person as the one "in the form of God" and "on an equality with God" (Phil 2:6), and the damnation He took upon Himself as Sin-bearer, there is no parallel to this humiliation; it is inimitable and unrepeatable.

The humiliation began with the begetting in the womb by the Holy Spirit and conception by the virgin. The entrance into and development in the womb of one who was herself sinful, as all other members of the race, are indicative of the condescension. Jesus did not partake of Mary's sin but He did of her substance. The conditions under which Jesus was born at Bethlehem are expressive of the humiliation through which this Person must fulfill the design of His coming. The humble station in life at Nazareth, baptism of John at Jordan, temptation in the wilderness, weariness with toil, hunger and thirst, sufferings and persecutions, mockeries and insults in arraignment before the high priest and Pilate, the agony of Gethsemane—all exemplify the humiliation that converged upon and reached its climax in Calvary.

The humiliation did not end with the cross. His spirit went to paradise but His body was laid in the tomb. The Son of God was in the grave as respects His body and He remained under the power of death for a season. Only with the resurrection was humiliation ended. The resurrection was the first phase of that exaltation whereby is bestowed upon Him the highest exaltation conceivable (Phil 2:9).

See Kenosis.

J. M.

CHRIST, OBEDIENCE OF. *See* Obedience of Christ.

CHRIST, PASSION OF. The expression "passion of Christ" has its origin in the translation of the aorist infinitive of the verb *pascho* in Acts 1:3, where Luke speaks of the fact that Christ "showed himself alive after his passion by many infallible proofs." The verb here translated as a noun means "to suffer," and is used frequently to refer to the sufferings and death of Christ (Mt 16:21; 17:12), and specifically to the death of Christ in Lk 22:15; 24:26. The expression should not be confused with the "passions of men" referring to human emotion (Acts 14:15; Jas 5:17). Used of Christ, it embodies the thought of His sufferings and death on the cross.

The Garden Tomb, where many believe Christ was buried. HFV

The Prophetic Fulfillment

The sacrificial death of Christ was anticipated in the OT in the sacrificial system, and it was also the frequent subject of OT prediction (Ps 22; 69; Isa 53; Zech 12:10; 13:7; cf. Rev 1:7). Christ predicted His own sufferings and death constantly throughout His life ministry and especially toward its end (Mt 16:21; 17:22-23; 20:17-19; 26:12, 28, 31; Mk 9:31; 14:8, 24, 27; Lk 9:22, 44-45; 18:31-34; 22:20; Jn 2:19-21; 10:17-18; 12:7). It was anticipated in the announcement of John the Baptist (Jn 1:29) when Christ was introduced as "the Lamb of God, which taketh away the sin of the world," and especially in the Gospel of John in a number of classic passages (3:14-16; 6:51; 10:11; 11:49-52; 12:24; 15:13).

The crucifixion, a torturous death prescribed by Roman law for those who were not Roman citizens, together with the burial of Christ, is described in all four Gospels (Mt 27:31-56; Mk 15:20-41; Lk 23:26-49; Jn 19:16-37). The order of events in the Gospels includes the attempt of Jesus to carry the cross to the place of crucifixion. When He was unable to do this, Simon of Cyrene was compelled to carry the cross (Mt 27:32; Mk 15:21; Lk 23:26). John alone does not mention Simon. The place of crucifixion, described as Golgotha, is interpreted as "the place of a skull" (Mt 27:33; Mk 15:22; Jn 19:17). Luke alone calls it Calvary (Lk 23:33).

The order of events which followed the act of crucifixion is: (1) Christ's refusal of the drugged vinegar (Mt 27:34; Mk 15:23); (2) Christ's crucifixion along with two thieves (Mt 27:35-38; Mk 15:24-28; Lk 23:33-38; Jn 19:18-24); (3) His first statement on the cross, "Father, forgive them" (Lk 23:34); (4) the soldiers casting lots for His garment, in fulfillment of prophecy (Ps 22:18; Mt 27:35; Mk 15:24; Lk 23:34; Jn 19:23-24); (5) the mocking of the Jews (Mt 27:39-44; Mk 15:29-32; Lk 23:35-37); (6) the mocking of the two thieves, though later one believed (Mt 27:44; Mk 15:32; Lk 23:39-43); (7) the second statement of Christ, "Today shalt thou be with me in paradise" (Lk 23:43); (8) the third statement of Christ, "Woman, behold thy son" (Jn 19:26-27); (9) the three hours of darkness (Mt 27:45; Mk 15:33; Lk 23:44); (10) the fourth statement of Christ, "My God, my God, why hast thou forsaken me?" (Mt 27:46-47; Mk 15:34-35); (11) the fifth statement of Christ, "I thirst" (Jn 19:28); (12) the sixth statement of Christ, "It is finished" (Jn 19:30); (13) the seventh and final statement of Christ, "Father, into thy hands I commend my spirit" (Lk 23:46); (14) Christ dismissed His spirit (Mt 27:50; Mk 15:37; Lk 23:46; Jn 19:30). *See* Cross.

Immediately after His death, the veil of the temple was rent from top to bottom and graves were opened. Later, soldiers broke the legs of the two thieves, but finding Christ dead they pierced His side in fulfillment of Scripture (Jn 19:31-37; cf. Zech 12:10; Rev 1:7). The body of Christ was claimed by Joseph of Arimathea, who with Nicodemus prepared His body for burial and laid it in a new sepulcher in a garden. Christ's burial was followed by His resurrection on the first day of the week.

The Theological Significance of the Death of Christ

The central significance of the death of Christ is contained in three great words—redemption, propitiation, and reconciliation. According to Rom 3:24, believers in Christ are "justified freely by his grace through the redemption that is in Christ Jesus." The thought of redemption is that of deliverance by the payment of a price. The imagery involves both the redemption by purchase and the setting free of the object of redemption. Christ in His death also constituted a propitiation or satisfaction of the righteousness of God (Isa 53:11), as explained by the apostle Paul in Rom 3:25-26. Likewise, in His sacrifice "God was in Christ, reconciling the world unto himself, not imputing their trespasses unto them" (II Cor 5:19). Through the death of Christ, the sinner is transformed both in position and in nature, given eternal life, and thereby reconciled to God and His holy standards. *See* Propitiation; Reconciliation; Redemption.

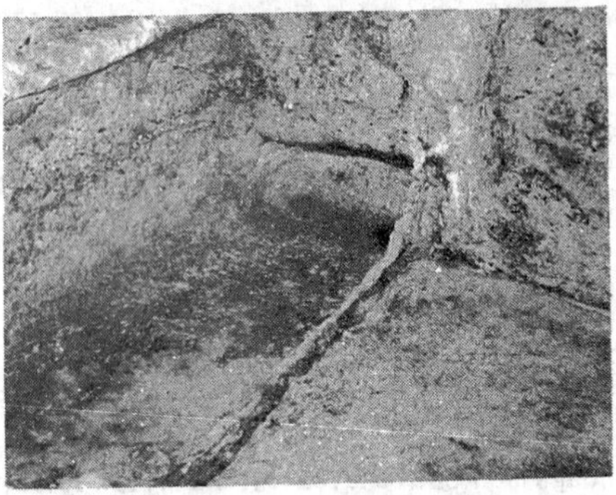

The crypt in the Garden Tomb where Christ is believed to have been buried. Photo Leon, Jerusalem

Different Theories of the Atonement

In the history of the church, various theories of the atonement have been advanced. Historic orthodoxy has supported the concept of a *substitutional atonement,* also described as vicarious or penal. This regards the death of Christ as primarily directed toward God and the satisfaction of His holy character and righteous demands in relation to sinners (cf. Jn 1:29; II Cor 5:21; Gal 3:13; Heb 9:20; I Pet 2:24). Substitutionary atonement is indicated by the use of prepositions *peri, hyper,* and *anti,* used in relating the sacrifice of Christ to the sinner. The view of A. H. Strong, called "ethical atonement," and that of Louis Berkhof are variations of this point of view.

A number of alternative viewpoints have been advanced. Early Church Fathers, such as Origen, Augustine, and others, held to the *ransom theory,* that the death of Christ was a penalty paid to Satan in the form of a ransom, a view largely abandoned today. The *recapitulation theory,* supported by Irenaeus, viewed the death of Christ as a phase of Christ's reenactment of all phases of human life, including being made sin, without excluding the idea of the satisfaction of divine justice.

The *commercial theory,* advanced by Anselm in the 11th cen., regards the atonement as essentially commercial or one of the satisfactions of God in the sense that it satisfies the honor of God. While not necessarily contradicting the substitutionary view, it falls short of being penal. The *moral influence theory,* introduced by Abelard in opposition to Anselm, is based on the premise that God did not require the death of Christ as an expiation of sin but only to demonstrate His love and fellowship in suffering. This view is followed by modern neoorthodox and liberal scholars in its modern form as the *example theory,* that Christ died as merely an example.

Various combinations of these theories have been offered, such as that of Thomas Aquinas, usually considered the norm for Roman Catholic theology, which accepts substitutionary atonement with some qualification. Aquinas held that God was under no necessity to offer atonement. Another view, that of Duns Scotus, denies the necessity of the atonement as far as the nature of God is concerned, and makes it an arbitrary choice on the part of God that He accepts the sacrifice of Christ as sufficient apart from whether it is or not.

Schleiermacher and Ritschl offered a *mystical experience theory,* a variation of the moral influence theory, that the death of Christ in a mystical way influences the sinner for good. The *governmental theory* of Grotius is another compromise between the example theory and orthodox substitutionary atonement, in which the death of Christ proceeds from the government of God rather than the character of God. The *vicarious confession theory* is based on the idea that God could forgive if man could adequately repent and confess his sins. Because he could not, Christ did it in his place.

The Scriptures support the substitutionary concept that Christ actually died in the sinner's place and that this provided a righteous ground for God to forgive and to save (Isa 53:11; Rom 3:25–26; I Pet 2:24). The death of Christ is therefore essential not only to human faith and salvation but to the divine program of redemption, and constitutes a fundamental of Christian doctrine.

See Kenosis; Atonement.

Bibliography. Lewis Sperry Chafer, *Systematic Theology,* Dallas: Dallas Seminary Press, 1948, III, 35–164. James Denney, *The Death of Christ,* ed. by R. V. C. Tasker, London: Inter-Varsity, 1952. Leon Lamb Morris, *The Apostolic Preaching of the Cross,* Grand Rapids: Eerdmans, 1955. Andrew Murray, *The Power of the Blood of Jesus and The Blood of the Cross,* London: Marshall, Morgan & Scott, 1951.

J. F. W.

CHRIST, RESURRECTION OF. *See* Appearances of Christ; Resurrection of Christ.

CHRIST, SECOND COMING OF. *See* Christ, Coming of.

CHRIST, SINLESSNESS OF. This expression refers to Christ's perfect freedom from sin not only in its outward aspect of acts of sin but also in its inward aspect of an inclination to sin.

Scriptural statements. The perfect sinlessness of Christ is foretold in the OT under the figure of the holiness and righteousness of the coming Messiah (Ps 45:7; 89:19; Isa 11:5; 32:1; 49:7; 53:9; 59:17; Jer 23:5; Zech 9:9). In the NT it is declared in many passages (Mk 1:24; Lk 1:35; 4:34; 23:40–41; Jn 1:29; 8:46; 10:36; 16:10; Acts 3:14; 4:27, 30; 13:28; Rom 8:3; II Cor 5:21; Heb 4:15; 7:26–27; 9:14; I Jn

3:5; I Pet 1:19, 23; 3:18; I Jn 2:29; 3:5; Jas 5:6; Rev 3:7).

Christ's sinlessness is typified in the OT by the perfection required of the sacrifices (Ex 12:5; Deut 15:21; cf. Jn 1:29; I Pet 1:19). It was declared in the NT by the testimony of the demons (Mk 1:24; Lk 4:34); by Pilate's wife as she pleaded, "Have thou nothing to do with that just man" (Mt 27:19); by Pilate as he said, "I . . . have found no fault in this man" (Lk 23:14); by Judas as he cried, "I have betrayed the innocent blood" (Mt 27:4); by the centurion as he said, "Truly this was the Son of God" (Mt 27:54; cf. Lk 23:47). It is evidenced by the fact that while others admitted they were sinners, Christ maintained Himself to be sinless (Jn 8:46); while others had sins to confess, Christ confessed no sins; while others must be born again, He never spoke of the need for Himself. He was not, as we, dead in trespasses and sins (Eph 2:1), but rather He was the resurrection and the life (Jn 11:25).

Theological aspects of Christ's sinlessness. Man finds himself guilty of three kinds of sin: (1) original sin, that is, the sin of Adam which is imputed to every man (Rom 5:12 ff.); (2) a sinful fallen nature which leads man to want to sin (Rom 7:17 ff.); (3) individual acts of sin. It is because man under the federal headship of Adam is fallen in Adam, that the NT says, "By one man sin entered into the world . . . for that all have sinned" (aorist, Rom 5:12), and "in Adam all die" (I Cor 15:22).

But Christ did not enter the world under the federal headship of Adam. He introduced a new headship, His own (I Cor 15:20-22, 45-49). In order to do this it was necessary that He not follow in Adam's line, but be born of a virgin. This the angel made clear to Mary as he said, "The Holy Ghost shall come upon thee . . . therefore also that holy thing which shall be born of thee shall be called the Son of God" (Lk 1:35). A better translation, supported by the margin in Nestle and by Westcott and Hort, is, "therefore also that which is born shall be holy, the Son of God." This reading answers Mary's question, "How can this be, seeing I know not a man?" (The Son of God can be born of Mary and be holy because this will occur by the power of the Holy Spirit.) This is the attestation of the angel Gabriel to Christ's incarnation in innate holiness.

Some problems. Certain passages have raised problems. Why did Christ say to the rich young ruler in Mark, "Why callest thou me good? There is none good but one, that is, God" (Mk 10:18; cf. Lk 18:19)? And why did He ask a different question in Matthew, "Why do you ask me about what is good? One there is who is good" (Mt 19:17, RSV)? The answer is possibly the fact that Christ asked two separate questions. He was leading the young man on, stepwise, from the question, "Why do you ask Me about what is right?" (Matthew), to, "Why callest thou Me good?" (Mark and Luke), in an endeavor to evoke saving faith and the answer, "Because You are God!" Thus seen, there is no hint given here by Christ that He is not God, but rather a pair of persuasive questions are so presented as to lead the young ruler toward making the conclusion that Jesus is God.

Concerning Christ's baptism, was not John's baptism one of repentance for the remission of sins? Yes, but Christ identified Himself with those He came to save. "He was made of a woman, made under the law," and, therefore, He must keep the law in its entirety. He was circumcised the eighth day (Lk 2:21), presented in the temple after the days of purification were over (Lk 2:22-24), and baptized in order "to fulfill all righteousness" (Mt 3:13-17; Lk 3:21-22).

Does the statement in Heb 5:7-8 regarding Christ learning obedience imply a stage in which Christ was not obedient? Christ learned obedience in connection with His suffering. He had come to do God's will (Heb 10:7-9), but this entailed terrible suffering and the agony of the sinless Son of God becoming sin, a sin bearer, for sinful man (II Cor 5:21). In this is seen the contrast between Adam's disobedience and Christ's obedience (Rom 5:19). *See* Temptation of Christ for the nature of Christ's sinlessness.

R. A. K.

CHRIST, TRANSFIGURATION OF. *See* Transfiguration of Christ.

CHRISTIAN. One who belongs or is devoted to Christ. This is one of several NT terms applied to followers of Christ. It is formed from Christ (Messiah) and the *-ianos* ending, which is from the Latin and is used only with proper names (cf. Herodians in Mk 3:6). The word occurs only three times in the NT: Acts 11:26; 26:28; I Pet 4:16. It was used first in Antioch, *c.* A.D. 43, and seems to have been given to the disciples by outsiders. (For a contrary opinion see Elias J. Bickerman, "The Name of Christians," *Harvard Theological Review,* XLII [1949], pp. 109-124.) The name most likely was used by Gentiles, since the Jews were still looking for the Messiah. The occasion was probably the large number of Gentiles who for the first time had become followers of Christ.

Several scholars feel that the name was given by enemies of the Christians. In favor of this view it is argued that the NT uses of the term have a note of hostility, and that the term *chrēstianos* was often applied to Christians. The word *chrēstianos* means "kindly" and was most likely used in derision. While it is true that in the NT "Christian" is used in relation to the outside world, it does not necessarily carry the implication of hostility in any of its three occurrences. Also, the word *chrēstianos* may have been a confusion of the word *christianos* and not the origin of it. If so, the term *christianos* most likely was used in a general way by outsiders to designate the followers of Christ, and not just by their enemies. Several considerations show the appropriateness of the term to designate the followers of Christ: the prophecy of a new name (Isa 65:15); references by Jesus (Mk 9:41; Lk 6:22); the apostles spoke in the name of Jesus (Acts 5:40); and believers were baptized in the name of Jesus (Acts 2:38).

D. R. S.

CHRISTIANITY. The religion founded by Jesus Christ. Following His ascension, the apostles in the power of the Holy Spirit preached in His name. They taught that He was God's Son, the Messiah; they gathered a community of believers; and they exhorted all to a holy life.

There is both a continuity and a discontinuity of Christianity with the religion of the OT. The life and teachings of Jesus, upon which Christianity is founded, are the culmination and fulfillment of the OT; and at the same time they represent the incarnation of the Spirit of God in a way radically different from anything which preceded. Although believing in the deity of Christ and the reality of the Holy Spirit in human affairs, Christianity has a strong monotheistic emphasis.

There has been great latitude in the historical development of Christianity. It is possible, however, to say that in the main the followers of Christ have stressed the historic and factual nature of the biblical revelation, and have attempted to follow it as the guide to faith and practice. Counting all adherents to Christianity there are at the present time about one billion Christians, the largest of all the world religions.

D. R. S.

CHRISTMAS. Tourists taking the Christmas pilgrimage to Jerusalem and Bethlehem are apt to be surprised at finding it celebrated there on three different days. Roman Catholics and most Protestants observe December 25. The Eastern Orthodox church holds to January 6, while the Armenian church observes January 19.

There is no evidence for the observance of December 25 before *c.* A.D. 300. Hippolytus, in his commentary on Daniel, is supposed to have been the first to compute the date. He believed that from the conception to the crucifixion of Jesus was exactly thirty-three years, and that both these events took place on March 25. That would make the birth, nine months later, fall on December 25. The weakness of these premises is obvious. In the 3rd cen. some favored April 18 or 19 for the birth of Christ, others March 28. A. H. Newman says: "The earliest record of the recognition of December 25 as a church festival is in the Philocalian Calendar (copied 354, but representing Roman practice in 336)" (SHERK, III, 47).

One objection often raised against observing Christmas is the claim that it is simply the old heathen festival of the sun Christianized. But it may have been intended to link this with the birth of the Sun of Righteousness (HDCG, I, 261).

R. E.

CHRISTS, FALSE. Those who claim to be the Messiah but are not. Jesus warned His disciples during the Passion week against such, saying that many would come in His name claiming to be the Messiah, and would deceive many. These pretenders were not to be believed (Mt 24:4, 11, 23-25; Mk 13:21-23; Lk 21:8). *See* Antichrist.

CHRONICLES, BOOKS OF. In the Heb. Bible Chronicles is called *dibrê hay-yāmîm,* "the words (affairs) of the days," meaning "the annals" (cf. I Chr 27:24). Other annals (now lost) are referred to in Kings (e.g., I Kgs 14:19, 29); but they cannot be our present I and II Chronicles, which were written a full century after I and II Kings. Jerome (A.D. 400) first entitled these books "Chronicles." Written as one book, they were divided into I and II Chronicles in the LXX (*c.* 180 B.C.). In the Heb. Bible, Chronicles closes the OT canon. Christ (Lk 11:51) therefore spoke of all the martyrs from Abel in the first book (Gen 4) to Zechariah in the last (II Chr 24).

Authorship

Chronicles does not explicitly state when or by whom it was written. The last recorded event is the decree of Cyrus in 538 B.C., releasing the Jews from their Babylonian captivity (II Chr 36:22). The book's genealogies extend to Pelatiah and Jesaiah (*c.* 500 B.C., I Chr 3:21), two grandsons of Zerubbabel, the leader of the returning exiles. The style and subject matter of Chronicles closely parallel Ezra, which carries on the history of the Jews from Cyrus down to 457 B.C. Both emphasize lists and genealogies, priestly activities, and reverence for the law of Moses. The last verses of II Chronicles (36:22-23), moreover, reappear as the opening verses of Ezra (1:1-3). Scholars, such as Albright (JBL, 40 [1921], 104-124), therefore, confirm the ancient Heb. tradition that Ezra may have written both Chronicles and Ezra. His total history would then have been finished *c.* 450 B.C.

Authorship by the "scribe" (Ezr 7:6) may explain Chronicles' repeated acknowledgment of written sources. These include prophetic records by Samuel (I Chr 29:29), Isaiah (II Chr 32:32), and a number of others (II Chr 9:29; 12:15; 20:34; 33:19), but especially "the book of the kings of Judah and Israel" (II Chr 16:11; 25:26; etc.). This last source cannot be our book of Kings, for verses such as I Chr 9:1 and II Chr 27:7 refer to it for further details on matters about which I and II Kings are silent. It must have been an extensive court record from which both Kings and Chronicles drew before it perished.

Contents

Chronicles seems to have been written as a part of Ezra's crusade to revitalize post-Exilic Judah in devotion to the law of Moses (Ezr 7:10). Starting in 458 B.C., Ezra campaigned to restore temple worship (Ezr 7:19-23, 27; 8:33-34), to save the Jews from mixed marriages with pagan neighbors (Ezr 9-10), and to rebuild Jerusalem and its walls (Ezr 4:8-16; 9:9). Chronicles, accordingly, consists of these four parts:

I. Genealogies, Adam to 500 B.C., I Chr 1-9
To establish family descent (cf. Ezr 2:59)
II. The Kingdom of David, I Chr 10-29
The ideal theocratic state
III. The Glory of Solomon, II Chr 1-9
Stressing the temple and its worship
IV. The History of the Southern Kingdom, II Chr 10-36
Especially, religious reforms and military victories of Judah's more pious kings

While paralleling the events of Samuel and Kings, the priestly annals of Chronicles lend greater emphasis to the building of the temple (I Chr 22, etc.), the holy ark, the Mosaic sacrifices, Levites, and the singers (I Chr 13; 15-16). At the same time they omit certain moralistic, personal acts of the kings (II Sam 9; I Kgs 3:16-28) and biographies of the prophets (I Kgs 17:1-22:40; II Kgs 1:1-8:15). This agrees with the placement of Chronicles in the third (non-prophetic) part of the Heb. canon; contrast the location of the prophetically authored and more homiletically minded books of Samuel and Kings in the second (prophetic) division. Finally, the Chronicler seems deliberately to pass over the deteriorating reign of Saul (I Sam 8-30, except his death, 31), David's disputed accession and later shame (II Sam 1-4, 11-21), Solomon's failures (I Kgs 11), and the whole deviant history of the northern kingdom of Israel. The disenchanted, struggling Jews of 450 B.C. were painfully aware of the results of sin; what they needed was the encouragement and inspiration of their former, God-given victories (such as II Chr 13-14, 20, 25).

Authenticity

These very emphases, however, have caused the majority of modern critics to reject Chronicles as mere Levitical propaganda, dreams of "what ought to have happened" (IB, III, 341), with numerous conflicting revisions as late as 250 B.C. (e.g., Robert H. Pfeiffer, Adam C. Welch, and W. A. L. Elmslie). The book's high numbers (e.g., one million invading Ethiopians, II Chr 14:9) have been particularly ridiculed, despite the clarifications of believing scholars (see Edward J. Young, *An Introduction to the Old Testament,* pp. 420-421). But once a liberal writer denies the Mosaic origin of the Pentateuch and of OT religion, as all do, then an open-minded evaluation of Chronicles becomes impossible. Chronicles' repeated validations of the laws of the Pentateuch leave him no alternative but to reject its historicity. Yet excavations at Ras Shamra, the Canaanitish city of Ugarit of Moses' own day, have confirmed the authenticity of just such religious practices (J. W. Jack, *The Ras Shamra Tablets: Their Bearing on the Old Testament,* pp. 29 ff.). Albright further observes that archaeological discoveries have established the historicity of many of the statements that were formerly found in Chronicles alone (BASOR # 100 [1945], 18). Though Chronicles does indeed emphasize the brighter side of Israel's history, it is not unmindful of the defeats (cf. I Chr 29:22 on the undisputed second anointing of Solomon, and II Chr 17:3 on the more creditable first ways of David). Both the prophetic woes of Kings and the priestly hopes of Chronicles are true, and both are necessary. While the moralizing sermons of Kings are indispensable, it is the sacrificial redemption of Chronicles that constitutes the distinctiveness of NT Christianity.

Bibliography. William F. Albright, "The Date and Personality of the Chronicler," JBL, XL (1921), 104-124. Willis J. Beecher, "Chronicles," ISBE, I, 629-635. Edward L. Curtis and A. A. Madsen, ICC. H. L. Ellison, "I and II Chronicles," *The New Bible Commentary,* ed. by Francis Davidson, Grand Rapids: Eerdmans, 1953, pp. 339-364. W. A. L. Elmslie, *The Books of Chronicles (Cambridge Bible for Schools and Colleges),* Cambridge: Univ. Press, 1916; "The First and Second Books of Chronicles," IB, III, 339-548. J. K. F. Keil and F. J. Delitzsch, KD. J. Barton Payne, "Chronicles," *Wycliffe Bible Commentary,* Chicago: Moody, 1962. A. M. Renwick, "I and II Chronicles," *The Biblical Expositor,* ed. by Carl F. H. Henry, Philadelphia: Holman, I (1960), 351-377. Israel W. Slotki, *Chronicles (Soncino Books of the Bible),* Bournemouth, England: Soncino, 1952.

J. B. P.

CHRONOLOGY OF THE OLD TESTAMENT. Biblical chronology in general and OT chronology specifically present many intricate and in some cases insoluble problems. For some periods of biblical history no detailed chronological sources are available, and even where such information is provided, the data often seems to be contradictory or incomprehensible. It is for these reasons that many differing chronological schemes have been worked out by scholars, and that absolute unanimity has still not been reached in the field, though an intensive study of the biblical and extrabiblical data has led to a great measure of agreement for the later periods of OT history.

Many editions of the KJV contain in the

CHRONOLOGY OF THE OT

margins OT dates which are the result of computations made by Archbishop James Ussher, first published in his *Annales* (1650–58). According to his scheme of reckoning, the creation of the world took place in 4004 B.C., exactly 4,000 years before Christ's birth. Since Ussher's dates were computed at a time when chronological data of the nations surrounding Israel was not yet available or only incorrectly understood, it is not surprising to find that his dates can no longer be considered a valid system of chronology. Three centuries of increasing knowledge in the field of ancient history have thoroughly outmoded them.

From the Creation to the Deluge

The only biblical data for this period is contained in the genealogical list of Gen 5 to which Gen 7:11 must be added. This list contains the age of one representative patriarch of each of ten successive generations. By adding up the ages which each patriarch had reached at the time his first son was born, a total figure of 1,656 years is obtained, according to the figures of the Masoretic Hebrew Text. These 1,656 years represent the time from the creation of Adam to the Flood in the six hundredth year of Noah's life.

However, the Samaritan Pentateuch, the LXX, and the statements of the Jewish historian Josephus vary greatly with regard to these figures, as Table I shows. In the LXX six of the ten patriarchs are given ages at the time of the birth of their sons that are 100 years higher than in the Masoretic Text. This lengthening of ages has the result that the period between the creation and the Flood according to the LXX is 2,242 years long. On the other hand, the figures of the Samaritan version are shorter in several instances, with the result that the period from the creation to the Flood is only 1,307 years long. According to Josephus, who follows closely but not completely the figures of the LXX, this period has a length of 2,256 years. These great divergences between the ancient sources make it understandably difficult to establish a convincing case for acceptance of one set of figures and rejection of the others.

Furthermore, it should be pointed out that commentators differ in their understanding of these genealogical lists. Some take them to indicate a direct succession of one generation after the other, from father to son, while others assume that a number of links have dropped out and that only some representative patriarchs are listed. A third group of interpreters considers the names given as dynasties of peoples. The two last-mentioned groups of interpreters therefore deny that the figures given in Gen 5 provide a basis for an estimate of the length of the period which lay between the creation and the Deluge.

In this connection it must be stated that the ancient methods of composing biblical genealogical lists are unknown to us. A comparison of such lists shows that hardly two parallel lists ever completely agree with each other. That the knowledge of the methods employed was already forgotten in the time of the apostles, with the result that the study of genealogies presented great difficulties and caused differences of opinion, can be concluded from the admonition of the apostle Paul to avoid disputations concerning "endless genealogies" (I Tim 1:4).

TABLE I

GENEALOGY OF THE PATRIARCHS FROM CREATION TO THE FLOOD

	Hebrew		*Samaritan*		*LXX*		*Josephus*	
	Age at Son's Birth	Age at Death	Age at Son's Birth	Age at Death	Age at Son's Birth	Age at Death	Age at Son's Birth	Age at Death
Adam	130	930	130	930	230	930	230	930
Seth	105	912	105	912	205	912	205	912
Enos	90	905	90	905	190	905	190	905
Cainan	70	910	70	910	170	910	170	910
Mahalaleel	65	895	65	895	165	895	165	895
Jared	162	962	62	847	162	962	162	962
Enoch	65	365	65	365	165	365	165	365
Methuselah	187	969	67	720	167*	969	187	969
Lamech	182	777	53	653	188	753	182	777
Noah	500	950	500	950	500	950	500	950
Noah's age at Flood	600		600		600		600	

*Later editions of the LXX give Methuselah's age at the birth of Lamech as 187 years, in an attempt to avoid the obvious difficulty of having Methuselah live 14 years after the Flood.

Secular records are entirely lacking for this period, and those given in the later Sumerian King Lists are legendary data. According to some lists ten kings, according to others eight kings, reigned over the country before the Deluge, to whom are given reigns averaging more than 20,000 years each.

It must therefore be concluded that neither the biblical records nor secular documents can give a final and definite answer to the question how long man has been on earth.

From the Deluge to Abraham

The biblical sources for the chronology of this period and problems connected with them are similar to those of the preceding era. Again nothing is available but genealogical lists (Gen 11:10–26), and they differ widely among the Masoretic Text, the LXX, the Samaritan Pentateuch, and Josephus, as Table II shows.

An additional uncertainty lies in the fact that the age of Terah at the time of Abraham is not clearly given. Gen 11:26 seems to imply that Terah was 70 years old when Abraham was born, but a comparison of Gen 11:32; 12:4; Acts 7:4 indicates that Abraham was probably born when his father had reached the age of 130 years. Taking this latter figure, the data of the Masoretic Text lead to a total of 352 years from the Flood to the birth of Abraham, the data of the Samaritan Pentateuch to 942 years, and of the LXX to 1,232 years. Both the Samaritan and the Gr. texts give to several patriarchs a higher age at the birth of their firstborn son than the Masoretic Text does. Furthermore, the LXX adds Cainan, with 130 years, to the list by putting him between Arphaxad and Salah. This additional name is also found in Lk 3:35–36, where the same genealogical list is preserved. This fact provides powerful support to the views of those who see in the genealogical lists of Gen 5 and 11 no absolutely complete records, but only selections or excerpts of longer lists of generations.

Exact chronologies of early Egypt and Mesopotamia, two countries from which early historical records are available, have not yet been established, but all available evidence indicates that history based on written records began in both countries about 3000 B.C. Hence, the Deluge, which preceded the establishment of historical Egypt and of Sumer, must have occurred at an earlier time.

From Abraham to the Exodus

For this period not only genealogical information is available but also some chronological data, although they also pose problems. A key statement for this period claims that the total length of Israel's sojourn at the time of the Exodus was 430 years (Ex 12:40). However, the Samaritan Pentateuch and the LXX include in this number not only the years spent in Egypt but also the years of the patriarchs' sojourning in Canaan, and the apostle Paul accepts this reasoning, as is seen from Gal 3:16–17. Paul here clearly shows that he considered the 430 years as beginning at the time when the promises were made to Abraham (Gen 12:1–4) and terminating with the giving of the law at Sinai.

If this interpretation is correct, the actual

TABLE II

GENEALOGY OF THE PATRIARCHS FROM THE FLOOD TO ABRAHAM

	Hebrew		*Samaritan*		*LXX*		*Josephus*
	Age at Son's Birth	Remaining Years	Age at Son's Birth	Remaining Years	Age at Son's Birth	Remaining Years	Age at Son's Birth
Shem (age 2 years after the Flood)	100	500	100	500	100	500	(omits)
Arphaxad	35	403	135	303	135	430*	135
Cainan					130	330	
Salah	30	403	130	303	130	330	130
Eber	34	430	134	270	134	370*	134
Peleg	30	209	130	109	130	209	130
Reu	32	207	132	107	132	207	130
Serug	30	200	130	100	130	200	132
Nahor	29	119	79	69	179*	129*	120
Terah	70	135	70	75	70	135	
Terah (at Abram's birth)	130	75	70	75	130	75	70

*Ancient texts of the LXX disagree on these figures. The figures here given are from the oldest LXX texts known.

time spent by the Israelites in Egypt from the time Jacob entered Egypt until the Exodus could have been only 215 years, because the migration of Jacob's family to Egypt took place 215 years after Abraham came to Canaan, as can be seen from the following data. Abraham was 75 years old at the time he entered Canaan and received God's promises (Gen 12:4). Abraham was 100 years old when Isaac was born (Gen 21:5), hence 25 years after Abraham's entry into Canaan. Isaac was 60 at the time of Jacob's birth (Gen 25:26), and Jacob was 130 at the time of his migration to Egypt (Gen 47:9, 28). Adding up the 25, 60, and 130 years makes 215 years from the beginning of the sojourn in Canaan to the beginning of the sojourn in Egypt, and if the 215 years are part of the total period of 430 years, the time spent by the Israelites in Egypt was another 215 years.

No other chronological statements are preserved for this period, and the genealogical data covering Israel's stay in Egypt are of doubtful value. Some of the people who lived at the time of the Exodus, such as Moses, Aaron, and Miriam, seem to be removed from Jacob by only four generations (Num 3:17–19; 26:57–59; etc.), while others, such as Joshua, are said to be removed from Jacob by 11 generations (I Chr 7:20–27). Hence, the genealogical lists cannot decide the question whether the Israelites spent the long period of 430 years or the shorter period of 215 years in Egypt. [Actually the LXX and Samaritan reading of Ex 12:40 merely state that "the children of Israel"—not including Abraham and Isaac—sojourned in Canaan and in Egypt 430 years. A few more than 30 years passed from Jacob's return from Padan-aram until he and his sons migrated to Egypt.—Ed.]

The date of the Exodus is disputed. Many scholars place the Exodus in the 13th cen. B.C. during the reign of the Nineteenth Dynasty kings, while others favor an Exodus date in the 15th cen. during the reign of the powerful kings of the Eighteenth Dynasty. The crucial text to determine the date of the Exodus is I Kgs 6:1, according to which Solomon began to build the temple in the fourth year of his reign, which coincided with the 480th year after the Exodus. The dates of Solomon's reign are fairly well established (see sections under United and Divided Kingdoms), and his fourth regnal year was the year 967/6 B.C. The month Zif, in which the work began, was a spring month, hence the building activity began in the spring of 966 B.C. Since this was the 480th year after the Exodus, that event must have taken place in 1445 B.C. *See* Exodus, The.

The invasion of Canaan took place 40 years after the Exodus (Num 33:38; Deut 1:3; Josh 5:6), hence after 1405 B.C. when the Hebrews began to make their inroads into Canaan in the Amarna period. The final destruction of the reused Hyksos-built city wall of Jericho possibly may be attributed to this invasion, as well as the fact that Jericho's cemetery shows that no burials took place after *c.* 1375 B.C. Also the destruction of a gateway in Area K at Hazor and of Debir's city C_1 may be attributed to the Israelite campaigns under Joshua (Josh 6:20–21; 10:39; 11:13). The destruction of Hazor and Debir in the 13th cen. B.C., of which the ruins also contain clear evidence, must therefore have occurred in the period of the judges. Recent discoveries at various sites in Transjordania have revealed that in some spots a sedentary population occupied eastern Palestine, contrary to earlier claims that it had been unoccupied from the 18th to the 13th cen. B.C. These evidences and others not mentioned here make it therefore plausible to believe that the Exodus took place in the 15th cen. B.C.

Using the year 1445 B.C. as the end of the period which begins with Abraham and terminates with the Exodus, the migration of Abraham to Canaan took place in 1875 B.C., his birth in 1950 B.C., and the migration of Jacob's family to Egypt in 1660 B.C.—during the Hyksos period. Joseph's position as vizier of Egypt can better be visualized under the foreign Hyksos rulers than in any other period of Egypt's history. The fact that horses and chariots are also first mentioned in the Bible in connection with the Joseph stories (Gen 41:43; 47:17) agrees with the historical fact that the Hyksos introduced horses and chariots into Egypt for the first time.

The Period of the Judges

A definite chronology for the period of the judges cannot be established for the following reasons: (1) no information is available with regard to the length of time that elapsed from the beginning of the conquest under Joshua (40 years after the Exodus) until the oppression of Chushan-rishathaim started, some time after Joshua's death; (2) the length of Samuel's judgeship is unknown; and (3) the total of all figures given in the book of Judges for the periods of oppression and of rest under the rule of judges considerably exceeds the total number of years available for this period. Therefore it must be concluded that some of the periods of oppression and rest overlapped.

Archaeological evidence has shown that Shechem and its great temple of Baal were destroyed *c.* 1150 B.C., which helps to date the approximate reign of Abimelech, since he was the king responsible for Shechem's destruction (Jud 9:46–49). Furthermore, the excavations of Shiloh revealed that that city was destroyed *c.* 1100 B.C., thus providing an approximate date for Eli's death, which occurred after the battle of Aphek and the capture of the ark (I Sam 4:11, 18), for it must be assumed that Shiloh was at that time destroyed by the victorious Philistines (Jer 7:12, 14; 26:6, 9).

The period of the judges began with the oppression of Chushan-rishathaim, the result of an apostasy of the Israelites. This apostasy had set in some time after the death of Joshua and the elders, during whose time Israel had served the

TABLE III

TENTATIVE CHRONOLOGY OF PERIOD OF THE JUDGES	B.C.
Invasion of Canaan	c.1405
Israel under Joshua and the elders (Jud 2:7)	c.1405 - c.1364
Othniel's liberation from Chushan-rishathaim's eight-year oppression (Jud 3:8)	c.1356
Rest of 40 years (Jud 3:11)	c.1356-c.1316
Ehud's liberation from 18-year Moabite oppression (Jud 3:14-15)	c.1298
80 years' rest of southern and eastern tribes (Jud 3:30)	c.1298-c.1218
Deborah and Barak's liberation after Jabin's 20 years of oppression in the N (Jud 4:3)	c.1258
Rest of 40 years in the N (Jud 5:31)	c.1258-c.1218
Gideon's liberation from seven-year Midianite oppression (Jud 6:1 ff.)	c.1211
Gideon's rule of 40 years (Jud 8:28)	c.1211-c.1171
Abimelech's kingship over Shechem (Jud 9:22)	c.1171-c.1168
Tola, Jair (Jud 10:1-3)	c.1168-c.1123
Jephthah's liberation from 18-year Ammonite oppression (Jud 10:8 – 11:33)	c.1105
Jephthah, Ibzan, Elon and Abdon (Jud 12:7-9, 11, 13-14)	c.1105-c.1074
Philistine oppression of 40 years (Jud 13:1)	c.1119-c.1079
Samson's exploits (Jud 14:1 – 15:20; 16:31)	c.1101-c.1081
Ark taken, Eli's death (I Sam 4:18)	c.1099
Battle of Ebenezer, Philistines defeated (I Sam 7:2-12)	c.1079
Samuel as judge (I Sam 7:15-17)	c.1079-c.1050

Lord (Jud 2:7-11; 3:7-8)—perhaps some 30 to 40 years after the conquest (*c.* 1370 B.C.). It ended *c.* 1050 B.C. when Saul was elected king (see next section). Hence, the whole period of the judges, from Othniel to Samuel, lasted approximately 320 years. Table III gives dates for the various periods of oppression, of political rest, and of the years of reign of the several judges. All dates are only approximate and are based on 1445 B.C. as the year of the Exodus, as well as on the statement of the judge Jephthah that in his time the conquest lay 300 years in the past (Jud 11:26). If the Exodus took place 200 years later, i.e., in the 13th cen. B.C., as many scholars believe, the period of the judges would have been only *c.* 120 years in length and all dates presented in Table III would have to be revised accordingly.

The United Kingdom

The OT provides no information with regard to the length of Saul's reign, but Paul in one of his sermons gives the length as "40 years" (Acts 13:21). Since he makes no point of exact chronology, it is entirely possible that the term "40 years," like that of the "450 years" in the preceding verse, was meant as a round number.

David's 40-year reign, however, may be regarded as established, since the number 40 is the sum of seven years of reign in Hebron and of 33 years in Jerusalem (II Sam 5:4-5; I Kgs 2:11; I Chr 29:27). One event is dated in his fortieth year (I Chr 26:31).

Solomon also reigned 40 years (I Kgs 11:42), which again may be a round number. His reign began before his father's death (I Kgs 1:32-48), but no information is given concerning the length of this coregency. However, the context of the story and the expressions used in I Chr 23:1 give the impression that Solomon's coronation took place shortly before David's death. Hence, we should not count on a great overlap of the reigns of the two kings. Solomon's death, which marked the division of the kingdom, occurred in 931 B.C. (see next section). This date can be considered to be fairly accurate, while the other dates given here for the reign of Saul, David, and Solomon are only approximate, since they depend on the accuracy of the number 40 for the length of reign of each of the three kings involved, and the assumption that Solomon came to the throne in the year of David's death.

Saul	*c.* 1050 - *c.* 1011 B.C.
David	*c.* 1011 - *c.* 971 B.C.
Solomon	*c.* 971 - *c.* 931 B.C.

In the section on Abraham to the Exodus reference was made to the beginning of the building of the temple by Solomon in the spring of 966 B.C., which according to I Kgs 6:1 marked 480 years after the Exodus. The correctness of this date hinges on the accuracy of the length of Solomon's reign. While the year of his death (931 B.C.) is fairly well established, the beginning of his reign in 971 B.C. is based on I Kgs 11:42, which mentions 40 years as the length of Solomon's reign. If Solomon came to the throne in 971 B.C., his first year began with the following New Year's Day in the autumn of 970 B.C., and his fourth year was 967/66 B.C. (autumn to autumn). Since the month Zif, during which the actual building activity started, was a spring month, we have to conclude that the beginning of the building of the temple must be dated in the spring of 966 B.C.

The Divided Kingdoms – Israel and Judah

For this period precise chronological data are available, giving for each king the length of reign, and also many synchronisms by dating the beginning of a king's reign in the regnal year of the monarch who at that time reigned in the rival kingdom. The mention of Assyrian kings in the records dealing with the history of the divided kingdoms also provides chronological evidence, as does the mention of kings of Israel or of Judah in Assyrian records. Furthermore, several synchronisms between kings of Judah and of Babylon are given in the OT, which serve as helps to establish an accurate chronology for the last period of the kingdom of Judah.

A study of all available evidence leads to certain conclusions with regard to the chronological methods employed by ancient scribes who produced the source material which forms

TABLE IV

CHRONOLOGY OF THE KINGS OF ISRAEL AND JUDAH

Israel	B.C.	*Judah*	B.C.
Jeroboam I	931–910	Rehoboam	931–913
		Abijam	913–911
Nadab	910–909	Asa	911–869
Baasha	909–886		
Elah	886–885		
Zimri	885		
Omri	885–874		
(Tibni	885–880)		
Ahab	874–853	Jehoshaphat	872–848*
Ahaziah	853–852	Jehoram	854–841*
Joram	852–841	Ahaziah	841
Jehu	841–814	Athaliah	841–835
Jehoahaz	814–798	Joash	835–796
Jehoash	798–782	Amaziah	796–767
Jeroboam II	793–753*	Azariah (Uzziah)	791–739*
Zachariah	753–752		
Shallum	752		
Menahem	752–742	Jotham	750–731*
Pekahiah	742–740		
Pekah	752–732*	Ahaz	735–715*
Hoshea	732–722	Hezekiah	729–686*
		Manasseh	696–641*
		Amon	641–639
		Josiah	639–608
		Jehoahaz	608
		Jehoiakim	608–598
		Jehoiachin	598–597
		Zedekiah	597–586

The dates follow Edwin R. Thiele, except with regard to King Hezekiah.

*The Hebrew reigns thus marked (*) are reckoned as overlapping; that is, the earlier years of one reign coincide with the closing years of the preceding reign, representing coregencies. The one exception is Pekah, whose years seem to have been reckoned from 752 B.C., ten years before he took over actual control of the kingdom by murdering Menahem's son Pekahiah.

the basis for a reconstruction of the history of the Heb. kings. The regnal years of all kings always coincided with the existing calendar years, and were not anniversary years as are the regnal years of modern rulers. However, the official years of kings in the ancient Near East were reckoned according to at least two different methods, and both methods were employed in the OT with regard to the kings of Israel and Judah. One method of reckoning was to count the year in which a king came to the throne as his "accession year" and then begin his "year one" with the following New Year's Day. According to the other method, a king began to count the year of his accession as "year one," and began "year two" at the following New Year's Day. In the latter case the calendar year in which a king came to the throne was officially counted twice, i.e., as the last year of the dead king, and as the first year of the incoming king. A study of all available evidence shows that the kings of Israel applied the non-accession-year system from Jeroboam I to Jehoahaz, but the accession-year system from Jehoash to the end of the kingdom, while the kings of Judah employed the accession-year system throughout their history, except for a short period from Jehoram to Joash, when, under the influence of the northern kingdom, the non-accession-year system was followed.

The chronology of this period is further complicated by two facts: (1) The kingdom of Israel used a calendar year that began in the spring with the month later called Nisan as its initial month, while the kingdom of Judah employed a calendar year that began in the autumn, with the month later called Tishri as its first month. (2) The scribes of both countries recorded synchronisms and other data of their own kings as well as that of the rival country according to the system employed in their own land.

Several kings associated their sons with them on the throne and thus created coregencies. Only one such coregency is expressly mentioned in the biblical record, that between Azariah (Uzziah) and Jotham (II Kgs 15:5), while other coregencies can be recognized either by double synchronisms such as those given for Jehoram (II Kgs 1:17; 3:1) and Hoshea of Israel (II Kgs 15:30; 17:1), or by a careful study of all available data. In Israel, King Pekah evidently counted a large portion of his regnal years simultaneously with those of his two rivals, Menahem and Pekahiah.

Because of the contact between the Heb. kings and the rulers of the Assyrian and Babylonian empires, whose chronologies from the 10th cen. B.C. are well established, a fairly accurate chronology in terms of B.C. dating can be obtained. The first of these contacts is the battle of Qarqar in the sixth year of Shalmaneser III, in which, according to the Assyrian records, King Ahab of Israel took part. The second contact is King Jehu's payment of tribute to the same Assyrian king in his eighteenth year. The Assyrian chronology of this period is firmly established by means of the Assyrian eponym lists through their mentioning of a solar eclipse that took place on June 15, 763 B.C. *See* Eclipse. Combined with the biblical synchronisms and regnal years of the Israelite kings involved, the information given by Shalmaneser III thus enables us to date with reasonable certainty Ahab's death in 853/52 B.C. and the accession of Jehu in 841/40 B.C. A further result of this information is the fixation of the chronology of the kings of Israel and Judah before the reign of Ahab and after that of Jehu. The computations based on this evidence lead to 931 B.C. as the year of the accession of Jeroboam I of Israel and of Rehoboam of Judah in the year of Solomon's death. This date has been used in the sections from Abraham to the close of the judges as the basis for the computation of chronological dates of the earlier biblical periods.

Also, the reign of some of the last kings of Judah can be dated fairly accurately through synchronisms with Nebuchadnezzar II of Babylon, such as those given in Jer 25:1-3 and in II Kgs 24:12, 17; 25:1-2, 8-9, since Nebuchadnezzar's regnal years are well established by an astronomical tablet of his thirty-seventh year, by many dated economic records, and by the Babylonian Chronicle.

Table IV presents the results of the most recent studies of all data as applied to the chronology of the kings of Israel and Judah. The dates presented follow for the most part the studies of E. R. Thiele (see bibliography), and deviate from them only with regard to the period of King Hezekiah. (The writer believes he has a more satisfactory solution of the chronological problems than has Thiele.)

Exile and Post-Exilic Period

The OT contains records of three successive captures of Jerusalem by Nebuchadnezzar II, each accompanied by the carrying away of captives. The first capture took place in the third year of King Jehoiakim (Dan 1:1-3), in 605 B.C. The second capture occurred March 16, 597 B.C., when young Jehoiachin surrendered to Nebuchadnezzar (according to the Babylonian Chronicle and II Kgs 24:12), while the third and final fall of Jerusalem took place in the eleventh year of King Zedekiah (II Kgs 25:2), in 586 B.C.

Babylon fell to Cyrus of Persia on October 12, 539 B.C. The same king allowed the Jews to return to their homeland, issuing a decree to this effect in his first year (II Chr 36:22; Ezr 1:1). Cyrus' first regnal year, according to Persian reckoning, lasted from the spring of 538 B.C. to the spring of 537 B.C., but according to Jewish reckoning from the autumn of 538 B.C. to the autumn of 537 B.C. Neh 1:1 and 2:1 provide evidence that the Jews in post-Exilic times reckoned the years of Persian kings according to their own calendar year, which began in Tishri, and not according to the Persian calendar year, which began in Nisan. The Aramaic papyri from Elephantine have furnished evidence that the same custom was employed by the Egyptian Jews in the 5th cen. B.C. (see bibliography under Horn and Wood). Hence, it can be concluded that Cyrus' decree was issued in 537 B.C., and that the return of the Jews took place during the following year, which was the seventieth year after the first captivity had begun, thus fulfilling the prophecy of Jeremiah concerning the length of the Exile (Jer 25:12; 29:10).

After the return of the Jews under Cyrus, the work of rebuilding the temple was commenced at once, but due to various difficulties it soon came to a halt. However, in the second year of Darius I (520/19 B.C.) the building activity was resumed, chiefly as the result of appeals made by the prophets Haggai and Zechariah (Ezr 4:24; 5:1-2; Hag 1:1-15; 2:1-9). The building was completed on Adar 3 of the sixth year of Darius (Ezr 6:15), which was March 12, 515 B.C.

The last events recorded in the OT took place under Artaxerxes I (465-423 B.C.). Ezra was sent to Jerusalem as plenipotentiary in Artaxerxes' seventh year (Ezr 7:7-9). If the reckoning of Ezr 7 follows that of Nehemiah, as there is every reason to believe it does since Ezra and Nehemiah were originally one book, Artaxerxes' seventh year was reckoned from the autumn of 458 B.C. to the autumn of 457 B.C. Accordingly, Ezra began his journey in the spring of 457 B.C. and arrived in Jerusalem in the summer of the same year.

After Nehemiah, a Jewish royal courtier, heard of the sad state of affairs at Jerusalem in the month Chislev of the twentieth year of Artaxerxes (Neh 1:1), he obtained an appointment as governor of Judah in Nisan of the same twentieth year (Neh 2:1-8). That was in April, 444 B.C. The last date mentioned in the OT is the thirty-second year of Artaxerxes (433/32 B.C.), when Nehemiah's first term as governor of Judah came to an end (Neh 13:6).

Bibliography. W. F. Albright, "The Chronology of the Divided Monarchy of Israel," BASOR #100 (Dec., 1945), 16-22. Joachim Begrich, *Die Chronologie der Könige von Israel und Juda,* Tübingen: J. C. B. Mohr, 1929. S. H. Horn and L. H. Wood, "The Fifth Century Jewish Calendar at Elephantine," JNES, XIII (1954), 1-20; "The Chronology of King Hezekiah's Reign," *Andrews University Seminary Studies,* II (1964). P. van der Meer, *The Ancient Chronology of Western Asia and Egypt,* 2nd ed., Leiden: E. J. Brill, 1955. R. A. Parker and W. H. Dubberstein, *Babylonian Chronology 626 B.C.-A.D. 75,* Providence: Brown Univ. Press, 1956. L. Pirot and V. Coucke, "Chronologie biblique," *Supplément au Dictionnaire de la Bible,* ed. by L. Pirot, A. Robert and H. Cazelles, Paris: Letouzey et Ane, I (1928), cols. 1244- 1279. Edwin R. Thiele, *The Mysterious Numbers of the Hebrew Kings,* 2nd ed., Chicago: Univ. of Chicago, 1955; "The Question of Coregencies Among the Hebrew Kings," *A Stubborn Faith,* ed. by Ed. C. Hobbs, Dallas: Southern Methodist Univ. Press, 1956, pp. 39-52; "Synchronisms of the Hebrew Kings," *Andrews University Seminary Studies,* I (1963), 121-138; II (1964). D. J. Wiseman, *Chronicles of the Chaldean Kings (626-556 B.C.) in the British Museum,* London: British Museum, 1956.

S. H. H.

CHRONOLOGY OF THE NEW TESTAMENT. The NT contains chronology in the sense that it records its story accurately and in orderly sequence. But it does not give a carefully dated chronicle. Hence attempt is made to take its historical data, compare it with information from other available sources, and to arrive if possible at specific dates for its major events.

Dates in the Life of Christ

His birth. The scriptural facts which are involved in the date of the birth of Christ are these:

1. Herod was king of Judea (Mt 2:1). The birth of Christ took place while Herod was still living, not long before his death (Mt 2:20, 22), yet possibly as much as two years before (Mt 2:7, 16). The Jewish historian Josephus identifies the year of this Herod's death as 4 B.C. He even tells the time of year, just before Passover, and records an eclipse of the moon which preceded his last illness. This eclipse has been dated astronomically as March 12, 4 B.C. So the spring of 4 B.C. was the date of Herod's death and the latest possible date for Jesus' birth. In light of Herod's concern for the precise time of the appearance of the star and his order to kill all the children of Bethlehem "from two years old and under, according to the time which he had diligently inquired of the wise men" (Mt 2:16), it seems probable that the birth took place at least one, perhaps two years earlier, therefore 6 or 5 B.C. It is clear, then, that the monk Dionysius Exiguus, who *c.* A.D. 525 introduced the present method of dating forward and backward "from the year of the incarnation of our Lord Jesus Christ," made an error in his calculations. On the basis of the data at his command, he fixed the birth of Christ as the year 754 of the Roman era instead of 750 or earlier.

2. The enrollment under Quirinius (Lk 2:2, RSV). What is known of this Roman official from outside the Bible is in harmony with what the Scripture here says of him, but it does not fix the date of this enrollment. *See* Census; Cyrenius.

3. Jesus' age at His baptism (Lk 3:23). "And Jesus himself began to be about thirty years of age" at the time of His baptism. Assuming that this means His age was close to 30, it ought to be possible to reckon back to the birth date of Jesus. The date of the beginning of John's min-

istry is carefully given by Luke (see below) and, as is shown later, was probably in A.D. 26. If the baptism of Jesus took place shortly after, which is the impression gained from reading the account, then subtracting "about thirty years" brings us to "about" 5 B.C. as the date of His birth. Obviously this is a very inexact reckoning, but it coincides with the date figured from the death of Herod.

4. The star of Bethlehem. Attempt has been made to fix the date of the nativity by identifying the star seen by the wise men as a natural phenomenon. Astronomers have pointed out that unusual conjunctions of planets did occur in 7 or 6 B.C. In China there is recorded a comet or nova which occurred in March, 5 B.C., and in April, 4 B.C. However, several arguments weigh against such an identification. The conjunction of planets was never close enough to be called "a star," and the date is too early, unless it is assumed that the wise men saw it long before they arrived in Jerusalem. Most important, however, is Matthew's statement that the star "stood over where the young child was." This would be impossible for any natural star; it demands a supernatural phenomenon, and renders the natural explanation unwarranted. Perhaps the unusual natural occurrence might have served to awaken interest on the part of the wise men, but it cannot help to date the birth of Christ.

5. What about December 25? Here it must be admitted freely that the date is only traditional, and relatively late tradition at that (4th cen. A.D.). Even the late tradition is divided between Dec. 25 and Jan. 6 (still observed by the Eastern church as celebrating both the birth and baptism of Christ). Both dates were previously observed as pagan celebrations, and were probably taken over in an attempt to replace the pagan ceremonies with Christian ones. The Scripture itself gives no clue. The winter season does not fit well with the gospel story. It is unlikely that shepherds would be in the fields with their flocks in midwinter.

The beginning of His public ministry.

1. The fifteenth year of Tiberius (Lk 3:1-2). Luke here gives a detailed date-reference for the beginning of the preaching of John. The baptism of Jesus followed soon after. This fifteenth year of Tiberius may be figured variously, depending on whether his years are counted from the time he succeeded Augustus, Aug. 19 or Sept. 17, A.D. 14, or from the time he was named joint ruler of the eastern provinces as coregent with Augustus, A.D. 12. Luke, as a provincial, may have chosen the latter method. To complicate the reckoning further, it is uncertain whether his regnal years were figured according to the accession year system or the non-accession year system. Thus the possible dates for "the fifteenth year of the reign of Tiberius Caesar" (Lk 3:1) are four: A.D. 26, 27, 28, or 29. Of these, the first is most probable.

2. The forty-sixth year of the temple (Jn 2:20). This reference to the temple cannot mean that in the past it had taken 46 years to complete it, for the building was still going on and was not completed until almost 40 years later. The statement is usually taken to mean that the temple had been begun just 46 years before that time: "It has taken forty-six years to build this temple" (RSV). Josephus says it was begun in the eighteenth year of Herod, or 19 B.C. The forty-sixth year, then, at Passover, would be the spring of A.D. 27. If Jesus' baptism occurred the preceding fall, A.D. 26, this coincides with and confirms the date arrived at above for the fifteenth year of Tiberius.

The length of His public ministry.

1. In the Synoptic Gospels. These Gospels give no information on which the length of the Lord's public ministry can be determined. It is often claimed that they reflect a ministry of only one year. But this certainly is overstating the case, for even in these Gospels there are indications of at least two other spring seasons besides the Passover at which He was crucified (Mt 12:1; Mk 2:23, "ripe grain"; Mt 14:19; Mk 6:39, "green grass").

2. The Passovers named in John's Gospel. John carefully lists a number of the annual Jewish festivals and relates them to the Lord's public ministry. This list includes at least three Passovers (Jn 2:13; 6:4; 12:1), necessitating a public ministry of more than two years. Taking the unnamed feast of Jn 5:1 to mean another Passover – and there are many arguments for so understanding it – this would add another year. Since the baptism and the beginning of Christ's ministry in Galilee preceded that first Passover by perhaps six months, the total period of the public ministry would be about three and one-half years.

The date of the crucifixion.

1. From previous findings. If, as indicated above, Christ's public ministry began in A.D. 26 and lasted through four Passovers, then the death of Christ occurred at the Passover season in the year A.D. 30. This is the most satisfying and fruitful method of figuring. All other methods presented here only confirm the results thus obtained, or are of such a nature that they may be made to fit whatever result has been previously obtained by this method.

2. Pontius Pilate. The governorship of Pilate, according to Josephus, was from A.D. 26 to 36. At the trial of Jesus it appears that Pilate already had had trouble with the Jews, the Galileans, and Herod; therefore it must not have been at the very beginning of his term in office. A Passover earlier than A.D. 28 would hardly fit.

3. Annas the high priest. The high priesthood of Annas offers another point of contact. Josephus states he was deposed about the time of Herod Philip's death, or about A.D. 34. This then becomes the latest possible date of the crucifixion.

4. Astronomical calculations. Elaborate attempts have been made to fix the year by calcu-

lating in what year the Passover fell on Friday. Assuming that the crucifixion was on Friday, and that the last supper was the Passover meal, it should be possible to arrive at an exact date. But this method of reckoning is beset by many difficulties. *(a)* While the almost universal tradition has placed the crucifixion on Friday, there have been and still are some scholars who dispute that interpretation, putting it instead on Thursday, or Wednesday. *(b)* Again, there is disagreement on the nature of that last supper, whether it was an ordinary meal or the Paschal meal. *(c)* There is disagreement whether the first day of the feast was Nisan 14 or 15. Of course anyone may choose his own from these alternatives and proceed to figure an exact date. Actually the many who have attempted to do so have come up with widely divergent results. However, the chief and fatal objection to this method is *(d)* the uncertainty as to how the Jews determined their calendar. If they calculated the first day of the month astronomically, the method ought to work. If they did it by actual observance of the appearance of the new moon, which is much more likely, then certainty is impossible. The unknown factors involved, therefore, would seem to make this method all but useless in ascertaining the date of the crucifixion.

Dates in Early Church History

Points of contact. Several references in the historical narratives of the book of Acts mention contact with persons or events in extrabiblical history. Only a listing of these and a brief summary of the information contributed by them are here given. For fuller treatment consult the bibliography.

1. Aretas, king of the Nabataeans (Acts 9:23-25; II Cor 11:32). There is no extrabiblical evidence that Damascus was under a Nabataean governor appointed by Aretas, but if it was, it must have been after A.D. 34, for there is clear evidence that the Romans governed the city before that date. But if this reference is to an ethnarch over only the Nabataean segment of the Damascus population, this could be true even when the Romans governed the city, and therefore nothing can be fixed as to date.

2. Death of Herod Agrippa I (Acts 12:21-23). Josephus and almost all other sources agree that Herod's death came in A.D. 44. An attempt to fix the time of year by identifying the occasion of Herod's display and oration seems unconvincing. From Acts 12:1-4, 19 it would appear that it followed Passover.

3. The famine under Claudius (Acts 11:28-30). Secular history confirms that widespread famine, or dearth, marked the reign of Claudius, but does not single out any date. Josephus tells of "the great famine in Judea" and the generous help of Queen Adiabene, but unfortunately his dating is not clear; either in the governorship of Fadus (A.D. 44-46) or of Alexander (A.D. 46-48), probably not earlier than 46.

4. Sergius Paulus, proconsul in Cyprus (Acts 13:7-12). Inscriptions have attested both the name and the title of this Roman official in Cyprus, but have not fixed the date.

5. The edict of Claudius (Acts 18:2). Again, extrabiblical sources mention Claudius' edict of expulsion of the Jews from Rome. The fifth century historian Orosius gives the date as the ninth year of Claudius, or about A.D. 49.

6. The proconsulship of Gallio in Achaia (Acts 18:12). Here there is strong possibility that the precise date may be fixed by extrabiblical sources. An inscription from Delphi mentions Gallio with the official title used in Acts, and is dated in the first half of the year A.D. 52. Since Roman proconsuls usually arrived at their posts and entered office in the early summer, this date may represent either the end or the beginning of his term. The incident in Acts seems to have taken place shortly after the arrival of Gallio; therefore Paul's 18 months in Corinth coincide fully or in part with the year between the summers of A.D. 51 and 52.

7. The procuratorship of Felix (Acts 23-24). Felix became procurator of Judea in A.D. 52. There is some evidence that he had held a subordinate position under his predecessor, so that Paul's statement that he had been "many years a judge" (Acts 24:10) does not demand a date later than A.D. 55 or 56. Also, Drusilla (Acts 24:24) could not have been his wife before A.D. 54 (she had been given in marriage to another in A.D. 53). So Paul's first appearance before Felix might have been as early as A.D. 55 or 56, but not before A.D. 54.

8. Festus succeeds Felix (Acts 24:27). This very crucial time-reference, unfortunately, cannot be dated with certainty. There is abundance of information from Josephus and other sources, but it has been understood in widely different ways. For full discussion, see the works listed in the bibliography and E. M. B. Green, "Festus," NBD, p. 421. The most that can be concluded is that Festus (*q.v.*) replaced Felix between A.D. 57 and 60, perhaps earlier in that period than later.

9. The days of unleavened bread (Acts 20:6-7). Attempt has been made to reason backward from Monday when Paul left Troas to Thursday as the day of the week when the Passover occurred that year; then to identify the year by astronomical calculation; result, A.D. 57. For reasons indicated above (see date of the crucifixion) this line of reasoning is unconvincing.

10. The single prefect (Acts 28:16). According to Conybeare and Howson, after the death of Burrus (A.D. 62), Rufus and Trogellinus were made joint prefects. Since at Paul's arrival in Rome a single prefect is mentioned, it could not have been after A.D. 61.

An illustration. In spite of these many contacts with extrabiblical history and many more references to periods of time within the Acts and the epistles, there is still only a relative chronology. The precise date for even a single event is not fixed, yet the order of events and their relative position have been carefully checked and confirmed. An illustration may help. The various events described in the book of Acts may be likened to the links of a chain. Certain of these links, which represent the points of contact described, are fastened so that they can come and go only within certain definite limits. It is readily seen that such a chain would be quite flexible, and could be stretched or compressed into many different patterns according as one might pull one link to its latest extremity and push another to its earliest limit. But with all its flexibility, the links would still remain in the same order and the same relative position with respect to one another and to the outside facts to which they were linked. To carry the illustration one step further, if the size of the various links is narrowed down by reasonable deductions from the events themselves, the chain will become more and more fixed. To this we turn next.

Additional data from the NT. Besides these direct points of contact with secular history, there are many indications within the book of Acts and the epistles which help to date with some confidence the intervening events.

1. The council at Jerusalem (Acts 15). Two lines of approach are open. It is possible to reason forward from the famine in Claudius' time, which, as seen above, must not be earlier than A.D. 46. Acts 13:1 suggests that Paul and Barnabas must have spent some time in Antioch before they started out on the first missionary journey, and Acts 14:28 indicates a considerable period after their return before the calling of the council at Jerusalem. The first journey itself must have taken at least a year and a half (Turner's estimate; Ramsay makes it two years and three or four months). If the whole interval then be estimated at a minimum of three years, A.D. 49 would be the earliest probable date for the council. Or reasoning back from the year 52 (or 51) for Paul's trial before Gallio (the interval includes the entire second journey and the 18 months in Corinth), any date later than 49 for the council seems improbable.

2. Paul's visits to Jerusalem. The book of Acts lists five visits of Paul to Jerusalem, while in his epistle to the Galatians Paul mentions two and gives some important chronological data in relation to them. There seems little doubt that the first visit of Gal 1:17–18 refers to the first visit of Acts 9:26. This is dated three years after his conversion. But there is sharp difference of opinion regarding the visit mentioned in Gal 2:1. The older traditional view identified it with Acts 15 and the council at Jerusalem. Others argue that it should rather be identified with the famine relief visit of Acts 11:27–30; 12:25. Paul says this visit came "fourteen years after" (Gal 2:1). If Paul made this trip to attend the Jerusalem council A.D. 49, then beginning with that date and taking the inclusive way of figuring, the conversion of Paul would be in A.D. 35. Taking the 14 years as being in addition to the three, his conversion would be in A.D. 32. If this visit is identified instead with the famine relief visit in A.D. 46, the conversion of Paul would be in A.D. 32. Of course the 14+3 manner of reckoning would be impossible in this case.

3. The date of Paul's martyrdom. It may be inferred from several factors that Paul was not martyred at the end of his two years imprisonment of Acts 28. The way Acts mentions the "two whole years" (v. 30) gives the impression that the period had come to an end. Paul's letter to the Philippians, usually thought to have been written during that Roman imprisonment, reflects Paul's own expectation that he would be released. The Pastoral Epistles seem best explained on the theory that Paul was released and carried on a continuing ministry for some time, and then again was imprisoned in Rome. This reconstruction of the last years of Paul's life is strongly confirmed by early Christian tradition.

The only evidence for the date of Paul's death is found in this early tradition, and it is quite clear and definite. It associates the martyrdom of both Peter and Paul with the persecution of Nero which followed the great fire of A.D. 64.

One of the arguments which has been strongly urged for a later date than A.D. 64 is the supposed difficulty in fitting a release from the first imprisonment, a more or less extended further missionary career, a rearrest and second imprisonment, into the period between Paul's first imprisonment in Rome, and the year 64. This difficulty was especially prominent in the older traditional system of dating which accepted a late date for the procuratorship of Festus. If Paul appeared before Festus as late as A.D. 60, he would have arrived in Rome in 61, and the two years of this imprisonment would be 61–63. No time is left for these later travels before 64. But if Paul's meeting before Festus were in 57 or 58, as seen above is possible and probable, then his first Roman imprisonment would have ended in 60 or 61 and plenty of time is left before A.D. 64.

A Resultant Table of Approximate Dates

Birth of Christ	6 or 5 B.C.
Death of Herod	March, 4 B.C.
Beginning of John's ministry	A.D. 26
Baptism of Jesus	A.D. 26
Duration of Christ's public ministry	3½ years
Crucifixion and resurrection	Passover, A.D. 30
Conversion of Paul	32
Martyrdom of James, death of Herod Agrippa I	44
Famine relief visit of Paul and Barnabas to Jerusalem	46

First missionary journey of Paul	47–48
Jerusalem council	49
Second missionary journey of Paul	49–52
Eighteen months in Corinth	Summer, 50-Spring, 52
Third missionary journey of Paul	52–56
Three months in Corinth	Winter, 55/56
Arrest in Jerusalem	Spring, 56
Caesarean imprisonment of Paul	56–58
Voyage to Rome, shipwreck	Late fall and winter, 58
First Roman imprisonment of Paul	59–61
Release and final travels of Paul	61–63
Second Roman imprisonment, martyrdom	64/65

Bibliography. James L. Boyer, *New Testament Chronological Chart,* studygraph chart, Chicago: Moody Press. Jack Finegan, *Handbook of Biblical Chronology,* Princeton: Univ. Press, 1964. F. R. M. Hitchcock, "Dates," HDCG I, 408–417. W. M. Ramsay, *St. Paul the Traveller and the Roman Citizen,* Grand Rapids: Baker, 1951. Merrill C. Tenney, *New Testament Times,* Grand Rapids: Eerdmans, 1965, pp. 134–138, 158 f., 164–178, 203, 206 ff., 216, 242–246, 275 ff., 294 ff. C. H. Turner, "Chronology of New Testament," HDB I (1903), 403–425.

J. L. B.

CHRYSOLYTE. *See* Jewels.

CHRYSOPRASUS. *See* Jewels.

CHUB (kŭb). A place or nation in alliance with Egypt and mentioned along with Ethiopia, Libya and Lydia (Ezk 30:5). The ASV transliterates a corrected Heb. reading by "Cub," while the RSV translates the corrected reading as "Libya" (*q.v.*).

CHUN (kŭn). One of the cities of Hadarezer, king of Syria, plundered by David for its brass and copper for use in building the temple (I Chr 18:8). The city is called "Cun" in ASV and RSV. The parallel passage in II Sam 8:8 has "Berothai" (*q.v.*).

CHURCH

Origin of the Term

The English word "church" is derived from the Gr. adjective *kyrikon (kyriakon)* which means "belonging to the Lord." The substantival form can be rendered simply as "the Lord's house" and is used to designate a Christian place of worship.

In the NT, however, "church" translates the Gr. *ekklēsia* which never refers to a place of worship but has in view an assembly of people. In the overwhelming majority of cases, *ekklēsia* indicates a local company of believers.

The circumstances under which *ekklēsia* became the accepted term for Christian congregations remain uncertain. The word does appear in the NT in the utterance of Jesus recorded in Mt 16:18 and 18:17. However, unless Jesus spoke Gr. on these two occasions, a possibility which remains much in doubt, *ekklēsia* in this text more likely reflects the terminology of Matthew and the early church. Moreover, there is no way to determine what Heb. or Aram. word Jesus may have used, for *ekklēsia* could be used to translate at least three different Semitic words.

Neither is it probable that *ekklēsia* owes its origin to the first believers in Jerusalem. In Acts there is a variety of what appear to be self-designations of the members of this community, such as "the brethren," "the disciples," "followers of the way," or "saints"; but there is no evidence that they called themselves "the church."

More than likely it was among the Gr. speaking Jewish Christians and their Gentile adherents that the name was first introduced and that in the context of their own cultural tradition. In the Gr. world *ekklēsia* commonly referred to an assembly. It was also used technically to refer to the regularly scheduled assemblies of the citizens of a Gr. city. Acts 19:39 provides an example of this usage when the town clerk of Ephesus remonstrates with the people that they should refer any action against Paul's companions to the lawfully constituted *ekklēsia*.

It is also possible that Jewish Christians in the Hellenistic world introduced the term *ekklēsia* because it was one of the two primary expressions used in the LXX to designate the people of God. Nearly 100 times *ekklēsia* renders the Heb. word *qahal,* meaning "assembly." The other main word used to translate *qahal* was *synagōgē,* but this term had already been appropriated by the Gr.-speaking Jewish community to designate their gathering places. *See* Assembly.

By whatever means the word *ekklēsia* drew the attention of Christians, its swift rise to general usage and its predominance over other competing terms cannot be accepted as accidental. Two factors appear responsible. First in importance is the awareness on the part of Christians of the parallel development which they sustained to the people of God in the OT. The OT "assembly" was established when God summoned Israel at Mount Sinai (Deut 5:22; 9:10; 10:4; 18:16) and by His own word and act the covenant community was created. From this time forth the Israelites became the *qahal (ekklēsia)* of God, "actively engaged in God's purposes of revelation and salvation, caught up in the mighty events whereby God intervenes redemptively in history and involved in the forward thrust of the covenant toward final and universal fulfillment" (T. F. Torrance, "The Israel of God," *Interpretation,* X, 306).

Correspondingly, the NT *qahal* or *ekklēsia* was duly summoned of God by His own divine Word, the Eternal Logos. It too had been ordered into existence as a "covenant" community, and receiving the new covenant in Jesus' blood was "caught up" in God's great redemptive program. Thus believers, by the use of this name, bore witness that they stood in direct succession to Israel as inheritors of the hope of Israel. The use by Christians of other expressions that had traditionally referred to Israel would support this contention. Early Christians are spoken of in the NT as "the elect," "Abraham's seed," "the twelve tribes," "strangers of the dispersion," and the "Israel of God."

The coming into existence of the church was recognized by Christians as a fulfillment in part of the covenant made with Abraham and Moses. With the Israelites God had covenanted that He would establish a people for His own possession who should receive His promises. They would be His "own possession," "a kingdom of priests," "a holy nation," the bearer of His light to the nations (Ex 19:5-6).

In I Peter it is precisely in these terms that the community of the NT is addressed. They are "elect according to the foreknowledge of God the Father, through sanctification of the Spirit, unto obedience and sprinkling of the blood of Jesus Christ . . . begotten . . . again unto a lively hope by the resurrection of Jesus Christ from the dead, to an inheritance incorruptible, and undefiled, and that fadeth not away" (1:2-4). They are "precious, . . . living stones . . . built up a spiritual house, an holy priesthood, to offer up spiritual sacrifices" (2:4-5). They have become "an elect race, a royal priesthood, a holy nation, a people for God's own possession, that [they] may show forth the excellence of him who called [them] out of darkness into his marvelous light" (2:9, ASV).

The second factor in the eventual choice of the term *ekklēsia* by the Christian community is related to the Jewish rejection of Messiah. A new people of God had been established. Appropriate to this people was the selection of a term from the LXX which historically referred to the people of God, a name familiar by its usage and associations, sacred because of its appearance in the divine Book, and unappropriated by the Jewish opponents.

G. W. Ba.

What could be more natural than the selection of *ekklēsia*, a term neutral enough that it could be adapted to the many fresh understandings which belonged to the new hope?

Origin of the Church

Much difference of opinion exists concerning the date of the origin of the church. Did it begin at Pentecost, or was it merely constituted in its NT form at that time?

Those who believe it started at Pentecost point out that Christ's statement in Mt 16:18, "I will build my church," is in the future tense and alludes to a time at least subsequent to this utterance. Further, they argue that one be-

St. Peter's Church at Antioch of Syria. A Crusader facing encloses a cave believed to have been used by Christians for worship purposes in the early days of the Church. HFV

comes a member of the church by the baptism in the Holy Spirit, which act joins him to or identifies him with the mystical body of Christ (I Cor 12:13 ff.). The baptism in the Holy Spirit was future in the Gospels (Mt 3:11; Mk 1:8; Lk 3:16; Jn 1:33) and in Acts 1:5. It is past in Acts 11:15-16. Where else could one logically begin the baptism than at Pentecost? If the beginning of the baptism in the Holy Spirit, by which one becomes a member of the church, occurs at Pentecost, then the church must begin there.

Moreover, they refer to Paul's teaching in Eph 3:2-11 and stress that he speaks of "the mystery . . . which in other ages was not made known unto the sons of men, as it is now revealed unto his holy apostles and prophets by the Spirit" (vv. 3-5).

Others reply that this passage clearly does not deny the prior existence of the church but only says that its extension was not made known to them as it was to the apostles. In other words, while the OT certainly gave indications that the Gentiles would receive the gospel when the Messiah came (Isa 9:2; 11:10; 42:6; 49:6; 60:3; 66:12; Amos 9:12), it did not make clear the abolishment of the division or middle wall of partition between Jew and Gentile (Eph 2:14; 3:9).

To this they add that the unity of the covenant of grace—that salvation has at all times and under all dispensations been offered on the basis of God's grace through believing faith—and the teaching of Rom 4 concerning justification by faith, before the law in Abraham's case, under it in David's case, and in the NT times, call for the existence of the church in the OT and its continuity into the NT.

R. A. K.

Nature of the Church

The true church is one, as indicated by the singular use of the term in Ephesians and several other passages when referring to all believers (I Cor 15:9; Gal 1:13; Col 1:18, 24; I Tim

3:15). Yet there were many local groups known as "the church" in that locality. W. C. Robinson explains the paradox: "Wherever the church meets she exists as a whole, she is the church in that place. The particular congregation represents the universal church, and through participation in the redemption of Christ mystically comprehends the whole, of which it is the local manifestation" (BDT, p. 124).

The significant feature of each local church and the universal church is its relationship to God and to Jesus Christ: "the churches of God in Christ Jesus" (I Thess 2:14, NASB). The church is God's because He has established it by the supernatural acts of coming to earth in the person of the Son via the virgin birth, purchasing a people by the substitutionary sacrifice of His Son, raising Him from the dead to provide eternal life, and sending forth the Holy Spirit to fill and equip His saints.

At least eight NT figures represent the relation of Christ to His church: (1) the Shepherd and the sheep (Jn 10:1-30; Acts 20:28; Heb 13:20); (2) the Vine and the branches (Jn 15:1-17); (3) the Cornerstone or Foundation and the stones of a holy temple (Eph 2:20-22; I Cor 3:9-17; I Pet 2:4-8); (4) the High Priest and the kingdom of priests (Heb 5:1-10; 6:13-8:6; I Pet 2:5, 9; Rev 1:6); (5) the Head and the many membered body (Eph 1:22-23; 4:4, 12, 15; 5:23, 30; I Cor 12:12-27; Col 1:18; 2:19); (6) the Bridegroom and the bride (Jn 3:29; II Cor 11:2; Eph 5:25-33; Rev 19:7-8); (7) the Firstborn or Firstfruits among many brethren (Rom 8:29; I Cor 15:20, 23; Rev 1:5); (8) Master and slaves (Eph 6:5-9; Col 3:22-4:1; I Cor 7:22-23; Rom 6:18, 22; Phil 1:1). These and other descriptions reveal that the life of the church, her holiness, and her unity are in Christ (Col 3:3-4; I Cor 1:30; Gal 3:28; Jn 17:21-23).

Ministry and Mission of the Church

As a body, a living organism, the church was to grow to mature manhood, "to the measure of the stature which belongs to the fulness of Christ" (Eph 4:13, NASB; cf. vv. 14-16). To aid in this development Christ gave gifts to His church in the form of men to fulfill various tasks. Some were apostles, and others were prophets, evangelists, and pastor-teachers, to equip the saints for the work of ministering (Eph 4:11-12). Since every member of the church was baptized in the Spirit, every member had one or more spiritual gifts to edify the others in the community of believers (I Cor 12:4-13; Rom 12:3-8; *see* Gifts, Spiritual). Each was to serve according to his calling and ability (I Pet 4:10-11).

The church was also to grow in the sense of expansion. Every believer was to be a witness of Christ through the empowering of the Holy Spirit (Acts 1:8), taking the gospel to every creature and making disciples of all the nations (Mk 16:15; Mt 28:19; *see* Commission, Great).

While every believer enjoyed an equal position under Christ the Head, the church was organized in order to insure its practical, orderly functioning here on earth. In one sense the apostles and prophets were its foundation (Eph 2:20), the authorized representatives of Jesus Christ to complete the revelation of His Word to His people. In this primary sense of apostleship there could be no succession of apostles subsequent to those who had witnessed the ministry and resurrection of Jesus (Acts 1:21-22; *see* Apostle). In order to preside over and give direction in the local churches, the apostles instituted the offices of deacon (Acts 6:1-6) and elder (Acts 14:23; 20:17-38; Phil 1:1; I Tim 3:1-7; Tit 1:5-9; I Pet 5:1-4; Jas 5:14).

In whatever capacity each believer served, it is significant to note that he was chosen and then guided and energized by the Spirit. In a manner not specified, the Holy Spirit revealed that Barnabas and Paul were to be sent out as missionaries (Acts 13:1-3). Similarly the elders at Ephesus were made leaders of the community by the Spirit (Acts 20:28). Prophetic utterance accompanied the charismatic gift bestowed on Timothy at his ordination (I Tim 4:14). Paul and Silas were directed by the Spirit to Troas (Acts 16:6-8).

Thus the chief ministry of the church was to minister to her Lord (Acts 13:2*a*), to worship Him as priests by the indwelling Spirit (Phil 3:3) and to carry out His will on earth by performing His works through the power of His Spirit (Jn 14:12, 16-17). The aura of the supernatural characterized the church at every turn.

J. R.

Bibliography. James Barr, *The Semantics of Biblical Language,* London: Oxford Univ. Press, 1961, p. 119. J. Oliver Buswell, Jr., *Systematic Theology,* Grand Rapids: Zondervan, 1963, I, 418-429; II, 216-280. J. Y. Campbell, "The Origin and Meaning of the Christian Use of the Word *Ecclesia*," JTS, XLIX (1948), 130. Edmund P. Clowney, "Toward a Biblical Doctrine of the Church," WTJ, XXXI (Nov., 1968), 22-81. Charles Hodge, *Systematic Theology,* Grand Rapids: Eerdmans, 1952, III, 546 ff. P. H. Menoud, "Church, Life and Organization of," IDB, I, 617-626. Paul S. Minear, "Church, Idea of," IDB, I, 607-617. Leon Morris, "Church Government," BDT, pp. 126 f. William Childs Robinson, "Church," BDT, pp. 123-126; "The Nature of the Church," *Christian Faith and Modern Theology,* ed. Carl F. H. Henry, New York: Channel Press, 1964, pp. 389-399. K. L. Schmidt, "*Ekklēsia*," TDNT, III, 501-536. T. F. Torrance, "The Israel of God," *Interpretation,* X (1956), 305.

CHURL. The word occurs only in Isa 32:5, 7. It probably means "avaricious" or "fraudulent." The RSV translates the term as "knave." The term "miserly" also fits the context very well.

CHURLISH. The term means "severe," "hard," or "rough." Nabal, whose widow Abigail later married David, was described as "churlish and ill-behaved" (RSV), "evil in his doings" (I Sam 25:3).

CHUSHAN-RISHATHAIM (kū'shăn-rĭsh-*ȧ*-thā'ĭm). A king of Mesopotamia (Aram-Naharaim) who oppressed Israel for eight years not long after the time of Joshua. He was defeated by Othniel, the first of the judges (Jud 3:7-11). The identity of the king is a mystery. Even his name is actually an epithet, "doubly wicked Chushan," probably applied by his Israelite subjects. The most likely identification is with an obscure Hittite conqueror from Qusana-Ruma, a district in northern Syria. He had overcome the Mitanni (Mesopotamia; *see* Horites) in Aram and then turned S against Israel (cf. Unger, *Israel and the Aramaeans of Damascus*, pp. 40 f.).

Because Cushan is used as a parallel to Midian in Hab 3:7, some have conjectured that the king was from this country and overcame only Judah, from whence the deliverer Othniel came.

CHUZA (kū'z*ȧ*). Steward of Herod Antipas, probably managing his property. He was the husband of Joanna, a Galilean woman who, having been cured of a disease or possession of an evil spirit, followed and supported Jesus (Lk 8:2-3; 24:10).

CIEL, CIELD, CIELING. *See* Architecture: Private Houses.

CILICIA (sĭ-lĭsh'*ȧ*). Geographically Cilicia referred to the area of SE Asia Minor between Pamphylia on the W, the Amanus Mountains on the E, Lycaonia and Cappadocia on the N, and the Mediterranean on the S. It had a coastline of about 430 miles, extending from the E boundary of Pamphylia to the S end of the Gulf of Issus. It was roughly co-extensive with the modern Turkish Vilayet of Adana. Politically (in Paul's day at least) Cilicia designated the Roman province first organized in 102 B.C. to deal with the pirate menace. It encompassed the E part of the geographical area. When Luke spoke of the "sea of Cilicia" (Acts 27:5), he probably had in mind the Mediterranean opposite the entire geographical region. Since Paul used Roman political terminology, he must have applied Cilicia to the Roman province only (Acts 21:39; 22:3; 23:34).

Cilicia was commonly divided into two territories almost as dissimilar in their physical characteristics as they could be. The W part, Cilicia Tracheia ("Rugged Cilicia"), was a tangled mass of mountains of the Taurus range descending abruptly to the sea, with a narrow tract of land along the coast and little or no plain country. The mountains of Tracheia were valuable only for their timber (chiefly cedar),

The Cilician Gates, strategic pass through the Taurus Mountains about thirty miles north of Tarsus. Robert McKay

and this rugged terrain succeeded effectively in cutting off the inhabitants from much peaceful contact with the rest of the world. In 67 B.C. Pompey wiped out the pirates who had their hideouts in the impassable hills.

The E part of Cilicia was known as Cilicia Pedias ("Lowland Cilicia"). This region had much in its favor from a geographical standpoint. Its land was fertile and grew cereals of all kinds, and its flax made possible a thriving linen industry. Timber from the nearby mountains moved through Cilician ports. Goats living on the slopes of the Taurus, where snow lies until May, grew magnificent coats used in the famous tentmaking industry of the area. It will be remembered that Paul followed this trade (Acts 18:3). Pedias was located on one of the great trade arteries of the ancient world. Trade routes from the Euphrates and Syria met about 50 miles E of Tarsus (*q.v.*), chief city of the province and Paul's birthplace, and entered the city as a single road. It then proceeded through the Cilician gates, a pass through the Taurus Mountains 30 miles to the N, and led across south central Asia Minor to Ephesus. Paul, accompanied by Silas, undoubtedly took this route to Derbe on his second missionary journey (Acts 15:41; 16:1).

Around 38 B.C. Cilicia Pedias was transferred to the province of Syria. It seems to have been administered by the Roman governor of Syria until A.D. 72, when Vespasian recombined both regions of Cilicia into a single province. Therefore Paul and Luke, both writing before A.D. 72, are strictly correct in speaking of Syria and Cilicia together (Gal 1:21; Acts 15:23, 41).

Jews had settled in Tarsus and other Cilician cities after the conquests of Alexander the Great. A certain synagogue in Jerusalem was frequented by Jews who returned from Cilicia and other lands of the Dispersion (Acts 6:9); one of them may have been Saul of Tarsus.

In OT times the region of Cilicia Pedias was known to the Hittites as Kizzuwatna. Its Mycenean Greek settlers apparently called it Khilakku, mentioned in late Assyrian records (ANET, pp. 284, 297). The Syrians named the area Qu'e, according to annals of Shalmaneser III and Tiglath-pileser III (ANET, pp. 277, 282 f.) and the Old Aramaic inscription of Zakir, king of Hamath and Luʿash, from the early 8th cen. B.C. (DOTT, pp. 242–246). The name Kue appears in modern versions of the Bible as a land from which Solomon imported horses (I Kgs 10:28; II Chr 1:16, RSV, NASB). Cilicia was famous for raising great numbers of horses.

Bibliography. W. F. Albright, "Cilicia and Babylonia under the Chaldean Kings," BASOR, # 120 (1950), pp. 22–25. J. D. Bing, "Tarsus: A Forgotten Colony of Lindos," JNES, XXX (1971), 99–109. M. J. Mellink, "Cilicia," IDB, I, 626–628. H. F. Vos, "Asia Minor," WHG, pp. 336–344.

H. F. V.

CINNAMON. *See* Plants.

CINNEROTH. *See* Chinnereth 3.

CIRCLE. The word has reference to the vault of the heavens (Isa 40:22). The same word is also translated "circuit" (*q.v.;* Job 22:14). Yahweh is represented by Isaiah as sitting upon the circle of the earth and by Job as walking upon the vault of heaven as it arched over the earth.

CIRCUIT. Used to represent several Heb. words in various meanings.

1. Heb. *sābab,* "to revolve"; a regular tour of inspection (I Sam 7:16). Eccl 1:6 mentions the circuit of the winds.

2. Heb. *teqûpâ,* "revolution"; the sun's orbit (Ps 19:6); the completion of a year (Ex 34:22).

3. Heb. *ḥûg,* "circle"; the vault of the heavens (Job 22:14).

CIRCUMCISION (Heb. *mûlâ,* Gr. *peritomē*). Circumcision is literally the surgical removal of the prepuce or foreskin of the male sexual organ. Similar operations on women are known but are infrequent and religiously meaningless. Circumcision is practiced by many peoples, especially in tropical and subtropical regions. Their number is variously estimated to include one-seventh to one-fifth of the earth's population.

In Egypt (Jer 9:25–26; Josh 5:4–9) and among Semitic peoples generally, circumcision seems to have been practiced in antiquity. A relief in the Sixth Dynasty tomb of Ti (*c.* 2300 B.C.) at Saqqarah in Egypt depicts the operation of circumcision on 13-year-old youths. Exceptions in the Near East were the Babylonians, Assyrians, and Philistines. Apparently among many the practice was given up in later times, or only employed loosely. Under the Roman Caesars in Egypt, only sons of priests were circumcised. Josephus (*Ant.* xiii.9.1) reports that John Hyrcanus had to force the Edomites to be circumcised.

The original significance of this practice is uncertain. Various possibilities include hygiene in preventing infection; facilitating intercourse; initiation into manhood; sacrifice similar to that for the firstborn; or as a protective measure against demons. All of these may have had significance somewhere, and all are in some sense reflected in the OT.

Apparently circumcision was first given religious significance in the OT where it is prescribed as the required external sign or seal (Gen 17:11; Acts 7:8; Rom 4:11) that one belonged to the covenant people of the Lord. Of course, this applied only to the male members of the people. Circumcision was a fitting sign for the chosen people of God because spiritual purity and holiness were to characterize their walk. Since the corruption of sin often manifests itself with peculiar force in the sexual life, God required His people to symbolize the sanctifying of their lives by the purifying of the organ by which life is reproduced.

Curiously, this prescription occurs chiefly in narrative passages of Scripture (Gen 17:10–14; 34:15–17; Josh 5:2–7). In the actual legal sections it is required only in Lev 12:3. It appears again in the narrative related to Passover (Ex 12:44, 48). Nowhere are there instructions as to how it is to be carried out. Apparently stone (flint) knives were used by the child's father (Ex 4:24–26; Josh 5:3). Gen 17:12; 21:4; Lev 12:3 set the time as the eighth day after birth. It was vitally important that Moses, God's newly appointed leader of His covenant people, carry out the rite of circumcision on his own son(s), lest God slay Moses for disobedience (Ex 4:24–26; cf. Gen 17:14). Some think Moses himself may not yet have been circumcised (Jerusalem Bible, p. 83, note *e*. See also H. Kosmala, "The 'Bloody Husband,'" VT, XII [1962], 14–28).

Circumcision gained in importance during the Exile as a sign to distinguish Jews from Babylonians, but its earlier significance is stressed in the repeated scorn poured on the

Philistines as "uncircumcised" (Jud 14:3; 15:18; I Sam 14:6; 17:26, 36; 18:25; 31:4; II Sam 1:20; 3:14; etc.).

The OT also uses the term in an applied or symbolic sense. In Deut 30:6 the Lord promises to "circumcise thine heart" (cf. also Deut 10:16; Lev 26:41; Jer 4:4; 6:10; Ezk 44:7, 9). Circumcision of the heart or ear evidently was understood to mean overcoming spiritual hindrances to obedience. (Cf. reference to Moses as of "uncircumcised lips," Ex 6:30.)

Post-biblical Judaism under the influence of Pharisaic emphasis on individual piety through keeping the law laid great stress on circumcision. This only made the position of the Jews more difficult in the Graeco-Roman world and provided occasion for taunts and even persecution under Hadrian. The pressure led some to attempt a second operation to disguise or remove the sign of circumcision. Orthodox Jews reacted by placing even greater value on it as Israel's highest honor and badge (Midrash Rabbah on Numbers, 12:10; Midrash Tehilloth, 40; etc.). They even ascribed circumcision to Adam, Seth, Noah, and Melchizedek. It is therefore strange that neither the Mishna nor any other official document of the times has a section on circumcision. It is possible to follow the exact prescription for the rite in Talmudic times. The Babylonian Talmud states that the Jews accepted the ceremony with joyfulness (*Shabbath* 130*a*).

Islam took over circumcision from the Jews. It is not demanded by nor even mentioned in the Koran, but is practiced by tradition which traces Arab ancestry to Abraham through Ishmael (Gen 17:20). The normal age for circumcision is 13, since Ishmael was circumcised at that age (Gen 17:25). In Islam circumcision is clearly a puberty rite in which the boy is led to the scene in girl's clothes. They also occasionally have parallel rites for girls. But circumcision in Islam never has had the importance that it does for Jews.

In the NT circumcision was first recognized as a proper prescription of the law (cf. the accounts of Jesus, Lk 2:21; John the Baptist, Lk 1:59–60; Paul, Phil 3:4–5. See also Jn 7:22). But in Antioch the Christians first denied its necessity for church membership (Acts 15). This decision was later supported in the so-called Jerusalem council (Acts 15:6ff.). Evidently the argument continued, however, as seen in the writings of Paul (especially Romans and Gal 5:2, 6; 6:15; Col 3:11). It was linked with the larger question of the necessity for the Christian to fulfill the whole law.

The positive meaning of circumcision in the NT lay not in fulfilling the law but as the sign of God's chosen people in the previous history of revelation (Acts 10:45; 11:2; Rom 3:1–2; 4:12; 15:8; Gal 2:7–9, 12; Eph 2:11; Col 4:11; Tit 1:10). Circumcision is a part of God's order which contained the promise of the Messiah. True circumcision was a seal of faith (Rom 4:9–11). Faith was essential. True circumcision "not done with human hands" consists in laying aside the "body of flesh" in the Christ-circumcision, i.e., being buried with Him in baptism and raised with Him (Col 2:11–12). Whoever serves God in spirit and boasts only of Christ is truly circumcised (Rom 2:28–29; Phil 3:3).

The OT stresses spiritual as well as fleshly circumcision. The NT values only the former while giving it deeper meaning in relating it to Christ's crucifixion and resurrection.

See Concision.

Bibliography. L. H. Gray, L. Spence, G. Foucart, D.S. Margoliouth, G.A. Barton, "Circumcision," *Encyclopaedia of Religion and Ethics*, III (1910), 659–680. Rudolf Meyer, *"Peritemnō*, etc.," TDNT, VI, 72–84.

J.D.W.W.

CIS (sĭs). The Gr. form of Kish (*q.v.*), the father of King Saul (Acts 13:21).

Cistern and altar at the high place, Petra.

CISTERN. The Heb. word *bôr* means "pit, dungeon, sepulchre."

Usually cisterns were tanks hewn from the porous limestone rock, or pits artificially constructed, of varying dimensions with sides and bottom sealed by lime plaster, invented about 1200 B.C. Most of the cisterns were roughly bottle shaped with one or more openings at the top through which water was drawn in containers. In a land where rainfall is small, it is exceedingly important that the water supply, collected during the rainy season (November–April), be carefully preserved. Water was essential for domestic use, irrigation, and ceremonial cleansings. Excavations reveal that it was not uncommon for cisterns to have steps leading to the bottom, chiefly to assist in the cleaning operations or in ceremonial cleansing.

In ancient times, cistern users would often close the opening with flat stones or boards, over which sand was spread, to prevent its use by unlawful hands. A cracked rock, a split wall, or an insufficiently sealed tank, resulting in a broken cistern was looked upon as a great calamity (Jer 2:13). The reference to a wheel broken at the cistern (Eccl 12:6) not only symbolizes the ending of life but suggests the way water was pulled up for use.

Cisterns have been used as dungeons. Examples of this are seen in the experiences of Joseph (Gen 37:22-24) and Jeremiah (Jer 38:6-13). It also was customary to make men responsible for their cisterns, for if a man's animal should fall into a neighbor's unclosed cistern, the cistern owner was required to pay for the loss (Ex 21:33-34; cf. Jos *Ant.* iv.8.37). By persuasive speech, the Rabshakeh, the crafty Assyrian commander, tried to lure the people of Judah to surrender Jerusalem by offering every man "his own fig tree and his own cistern" (II Kgs 18:31). The remains of ancient cisterns are still to be seen.

R. V. U.

The citadel of Aleppo, Syria. JR

CITADEL. This term means a stronghold or fortress. Several Heb. terms are used to describe the various aspects and elements of fortification. The Heb. word *'armôn* suggests a stronghold of a city, a palace, castle, or citadel (I Kgs 16:18; II Kgs 15:25). The most famous stronghold in the OT was the citadel of Jerusalem which David conquered, and thus conquered the city (II Sam 5:7-9; I Chr 11:5, 7). The term usually comprehends many buildings. This word and other Heb. words are translated variously, such as tower (Ps 122:7, RSV), fenced city or fortress (Isa 17:3), siegeworks (II Kgs 25:1, RSV), high fortifications (Isa 25:12, RSV), stronghold (Jud 6:26, RSV), palace (Isa 32:14), and fortress of the temple (Neh 2:8, RSV). *See* Fort; Bulwark.

CITIES OF REFUGE. Among the 48 cities given to the Levites throughout Israel, six were by the command of God to be appointed as cities of refuge, or asylum, "for the manslayer" (Num 35:6-7). Moses himself selected three of these on the E side of the Jordan River: Bezer in Reuben, Ramoth-gilead in Gad, and Golan in Manasseh (Deut 4:41-43). Later under Joshua the other three were named, being in the main part of the land W of Jordan: Kedesh in Naphtali, Shechem in Ephraim, and Hebron in Judah (Josh 20:7). These were conveniently located in northern, central, and southern areas of the land. Roads were to be built and kept open to these important cities (Deut 19:3).

An ancient practice, said to exist even now in the Near East, was for the closest relative of a slain man to act as "avenger of blood" (Num 35:12, 19; Deut 19:12). This custom was permitted to continue under the Mosaic law, but with certain restrictions. If one had killed another unintentionally ("unawares," Num 35:15), he could flee immediately to one of these cities of refuge and there find sanctuary. The deliberate murderer who had killed intentionally was not allowed to claim this privilege (Num 35:16 ff.). The one to whom it properly belonged, however, was safe from the avenger as long as he stayed inside his city of refuge. When the high priest died, he was free to leave the city and dwell safely at home again (Num 35:25-28). *See* Blood, Avenger of.

That the cities of refuge were a type of Christ is hinted in Heb 6:18. "The apostle alludes to this when speaking of those who fled for refuge to lay hold upon the hope set before them" (Fairbairn, *Imperial Standard Bible Encyclopaedia,* IV, 161). To Christ we flee for refuge, and in Him we are safe from the divine Avenger of blood (Rom 5:9; 8:1, 31, 34). The greatest sin of this age—the murder of Jesus Christ—is classified by God as a sin of ignorance (Acts 3:17; I Cor 2:7-8). Unsaved men little realize the "exceeding sinfulness of sin." Sanctuary is open to all who will flee for refuge to Christ (Jn 6:37). The saved ones will never again leave this "city of refuge" because their High Priest will never die (Heb 7:25).

G. C. L.

CITIES OF THE PLAIN. The Heb. word *kikkār,* for "plain," refers to the "basin" of the Jordan. These cities included Sodom, Gomorrah, Admah, Zeboiim, and Bela (Zoar), located in the Valley of Siddim or Salt Sea (Gen 14:8). By far the most famous (or infamous) of these cities were Sodom and Gomorrah (*q.v.*), which according to Gen 19 were completely destroyed by fire. The wickedness of these cities, along with the resulting judgment, is often referred to in the Scriptures (Deut 29:23; Isa 1:9; 3:9; Jer 50:40; Ezk 16:46; Mt 10:15; Rom 9:29) as a precedent to be avoided.

Opinion differs among scholars as to whether these cities were located at the northern or southern end of the Dead Sea. According to tradition and the judgment of most scholars, the probable site was at the southern end of the Salt Sea. The abundance of salt and bitumen in this area lends credence to this theory. Reports that the remains of the cities have been seen from the air have not been substantiated. It is not improbable that the cities are underneath the shallow water at the southern quarter of the sea.

The cities are first glimpsed in biblical history in Gen 13:10 where the apparent proximity to the "well watered" Jordan Valley might seem to argue for a location to the N. Because of the fertility of the valley compared to that of the hill country of Canaan, Lot chose it as his residence.

The cities were really city-states, each with its own "king" (Gen 14:2). After a war with Mesopotamian kings, these cities became vassal states of Chedorlaomer, king of Elam, for a period of 12 years. In the thirteenth year they rebelled and found themselves at war again with Chedorlaomer and his three allies (Gen 14:9). They were defeated and Lot's family and others were captured and taken away. Abraham attacked the victorious allies, defeated them, and recovered both the captives and the goods (Gen 14:13-16).

The destruction of two of these cities, Sodom and Gomorrah, is detailed in Gen 18—19. The destruction, as a result of a fire from heaven, consumed four of the cities, the inhabitants of the valley, and "what grew on the ground" (Gen 19:25). The small town of Zoar apparently was located at some distance from Sodom and Gomorrah. Lot and his daughters lodged here temporarily after leaving Sodom and before they fled to the hills behind the city (Gen 19:20-30). In Wisd 10:6 these cities are called the Pentapolis (Five Cities).

G. A. T.

CITIZENSHIP. *Hebrew citizenship*. Among the Jews in OT times the stress was on the membership of the Israelite in a religious organization, rather than on his relationship to the city or the state (Eph 2:12, "commonwealth of Israel"). Non-Israelites had the protection of the same law as the Israelites, but were not allowed to insult the Israelites in any way concerning their religious beliefs. The good citizen was the good member of the Jewish theocracy. The advantage of the Jew over the Gentile was spiritual and not judicial.

Roman citizenship. This made persons equal in judicial rights to the inhabitants of Rome. It was granted by emperors to provinces and cities, or to individuals because of special services rendered to the emperor or the state, and was even obtainable by purchase at times (Acts 22:28). It entitled the holder to exemption from such shameful punishments as scourging or crucifixion, and also gave the right of appeal to Caesar in certain cases.

Paul's citizenship. Either Paul's father or an ancestor had obtained Roman citizenship and Paul had it by birth. He sometimes used his Roman privileges (Acts 16:37-39; 22:25-29; 23:27; 25:10-12; 26:32).

Christian citizenship. All believers are citizens of a heavenly commonwealth and ought therefore to live in accordance with such a position (Phil 1:27; 3:20; cf. Acts 23:1). As citizens of the kingdom of God (Heb 11:16; 12:22 f.; 13:14; I Pet 2:9-11), they shall reign with Christ in His millennial kingdom and then enter the new heavens and the new earth (Rev 5:10; 20:4-6; 21—22). *See* New Heavens and New Earth; Millennium; Eternal State and Death.

R. A. K.

CITRON. *See* Plants.

CITY. As in modern times so also in the ancient world, the line of demarcation between "city" and "town/village" was nebulous. There seems to have been no distinction in the several Heb. words for city: *'îr, qiryâ* and *qāret*. Heb. *sha'ar* ("gate") frequently stands by *synecdoche* for "city," especially in Deuteronomy. A rule-of-thumb classification characterized the city as walled, the village or town as unwalled (Lev 25:29-31; Deut 3:5). All such distinctions, however, were more convenient than scientific, since Bethsaida, e.g., is called a city in Mt 11:20-21; Lk 9:10; Jn 1:44, but a town in Mk 8:22-23. In ancient Israel, it was typical for a city (the "mother," cf. II Sam 20:19, RSV) to be surrounded by a cluster of villages (the "daughters," cf. Num 21:25, Heb.), the former exercising a certain hegemony over the latter in a characteristic city-state relationship (cf., e.g., Josh 15:32).

Such city-states (cf. Latin *cīvitās*) with all the refinements of civilization sprang up originally in Mesopotamia during the Proto-Literate period (*c*. 3500 B.C.), in turn stimulating a similar development in Egypt and the Indus Valley slightly later. Hazor (Josh 11:1-5, 10) was the largest city in Palestine in the second millennium B.C. with a population of perhaps 50,000. During the Amarna period (*c*. 1375 B.C.), there were four main city-states (Gezer, Jerusalem, Lachish, and probably Hebron) in southern Palestine, whereas in the time of Joshua's conquest the number was nine (including in addition Debir, Eglon, Jarmuth, Libnah, and Makkedah; cf. Josh 10).

The earliest cities in the hill country of Palestine usually occupied a limestone knoll near a spring. Successive periods of habitation and destruction would result in the formation of mounds or "tells" (cf. Josh 11:13, Heb.), many of which modern excavators have laid bare. The more important of such cities would be enclosed by massive, buttressed walls (Num 13:28; Deut 1:28; 9:1) with towers at the corners and flanking the gates (II Chr 26:9), fortified as a last means of defense by a citadel (*q.v.*) or a "strong tower within the city" (Jud 9:51), and interlaced by a network of streets

A reconstruction of Megiddo in the days of Solomon and Ahab. ORINST

which were often narrow, crooked, and dirty (Isa 10:6). Occasionally certain cities were set aside for specialized functions and became, e.g., chariot cities (II Chr 1:14), store cities (I Kgs 9:19), or merchant cities (Ezk 17:4).

During the Hellenistic period, many of the old cities were rebuilt, but new ones were also established by Gr. conquerors and colonists. These newer cities (Gr. *polis*) were plotted according to the city plan devised by Hippodamus of Miletus, consisting of streets intersecting at right angles with a centrally located marketplace. The same pattern was followed by city builders during the early Roman period (cf. Mt 6:5). Somewhat later the Roman city came to be characterized by an avenue of columns leading from a triple gate through the center of the city and crossed by one or more secondary streets. *See* Acropolis.

Spiritually speaking, the Bible recognizes that while the city is the repository of cultural life (Gen 4:17, 21-22), it also tends to become the receptacle of evil propensities (Gen 4:19, 23-24; 19:1-38) which concentrate themselves in the capital city (Mic 1:5). Eventually all earthly cities will thus have to be destroyed (Mic 5:11, 14) in anticipation of the final establishment of the heavenly and "holy city, new Jerusalem" (Rev 21:2). *See* Babylon; Jerusalem, New.

Bibliography. "Ancient Cities (of Palestine)," CornPBE, pp. 44-107, 210-221.

R. Y.

CITY, FENCED. The Heb. expressions *'îr b^e-ṣûrâ, 'îr (ham)mibṣār,* and *'îr m^{e}ṣûrâ* are all translated "fenced city" in KJV and refer to cities surrounded by walls or fortifications as opposed to unwalled villages. Such a rendering is found in I Sam 6:18; II Sam 20:6; Jer 5:17; Ezk 36:35; Dan 11:15; Hos 8:14; Zeph 1:16, and more than once each in Numbers, Deuteronomy, Joshua, II Kings, and II Chronicles. Heb. *'îr māṣôr* is similarly so rendered in II Chr 8:5. "Defenced city" renders *'îr b^{e}ṣûrâ* three times in Isaiah and *'îr (ham)mibṣār* four times in Jeremiah, while *qiryâ b^{e}ṣûrâ* is so translated in Isa 25:2.

In all the above references, ASV and RSV translate "fenced" and "defenced" uniformly as "fortified."

See further Fence; Fort; Gate; Tower; Wall.

CITY, HOLY. For Christians and Jews, there is but one "holy city"–Jerusalem (Neh 11:1, 18; Isa 48:2; 52:1; Mt 4:5; 27:53; Rev 11:2; 21:2). For Muslims, Jerusalem is the third holiest city next to Mecca and Medina, and Palestinian Arabs call it El Kuds, "the holy (place, city)." Most major religions of the world have their "holy cities," including Eleusis in Greece, Thebes in Egypt, Benares in India, and Kyoto in Japan. In the Bible, rivals for this distinction included Shechem (Gen 12:6-7, RSV; cf. Josh 8:30-35), Gilgal (Josh 4:20; I Sam 11:14–12:25), Mizpah (I Sam 10:17-25), and Bethel (I Kgs 12:26-33). For Christians, not even Nazareth or Bethlehem rank with Jerusalem in emotional appeal. *See* Jerusalem; Jerusalem, New.

CITY, LEVITICAL. *See* Levitical Cities.

CITY OF DAVID

1. This name is applied to the most ancient section of Jerusalem, the SE hill of Jerusalem also called Mount Zion. The Jebusite fortress which stood here was conquered by David, who then moved his capital from Hebron and built a new palace and citadel (II Sam 5:7, 9; I Chr 11:5, 7). He made his new royal city the center of Israel's religious life by bringing to it the ark of the covenant from the house of Obed-edom (II Sam 6:10-16). King Solomon brought up the ark out of the city of David to the temple on Mount Moriah to the N (I Kgs 8:1; II Chr 3:1; 5:2).

Hezekiah, in constructing the Siloam tunnel, brought the waters of Gihon down to the W side of the city of David (II Chr 32:30). Manasseh rebuilt and considerably heightened the outer wall of the citadel of David; his repairs encircled the Ophel (*q.v.*) as far as the Fish Gate in the Tyropean valley (II Chr 33:14, JerusB). David, Solomon, and many other kings of Judah were buried within David's original city. *See* Jerusalem.

2. The town of Bethlehem in Judea, the home of David, is called the city of David (Lk 2:11). *See* Bethlehem 2.

L. O. H.

CITY OF DESTRUCTION. *See* Irhaheres.

CITY OF GOD

1. A term used to describe Jerusalem (Ps 46:4; 48:1, 8). It was the city which God chose to be His habitation among the tribes of Israel (Deut 12:5). *See* Jerusalem.

2. This term is used also to describe heaven, or the New Jerusalem (Heb 11:10; 12:22; Rev 3:12;21;22). *See* Jerusalem, New.

CITY OF PALM TREES. *See* Jericho.

CITY OF SALT. *See* Salt, City of.

The Jerusalem David conquered is now barren (foreground) and lies south of the later Temple area. HFV

CITY, TREASURE. The Israelites built two such cities, Pithom and Raamses, for Pharaoh (Ex 1:11). The produce of the land was stored in the cities. Certain cities were set aside by Solomon for stores of food, chariots, and horsemen (I Kgs 9:19). Benhadad conquered the store cities of Naphtali (II Chr 16:4). Jehoshaphat built store cities in Judah (II Chr 17:2). *See* Pithom; Raamses.

CLASPS. This word means "a bend," especially a hook made to fit in an eye for fastening. The KJV translates the term as "taches" (an English word of French origin) or as "hooks," while the ASV and RSV translate the term as "clasps" (Ex 26:11; 35:11; 36:13; 39:33). The clasps were fastenings of gold (Ex 26:6; 36:13) or bronze (Ex 26:11; 36:18) by which the linen curtains and the goat skin hangings of the tabernacle were held together.

CLAUDA (klô'dȧ). A small island about 23 miles from the SW shore of Crete. Spelled Cauda in ASV and RSV, it is now called Gaudos or Gozzo. On Paul's journey to Rome his ship sailed under the lee of Clauda after a storm prevented its reaching a safe harbor at Crete (Acts 27:16).

CLAUDIA (klô'dĭ-ȧ). A Christian woman at Rome who sent her greetings to Timothy (II Tim 4:21). This is all that Scripture tells of her. Legend has made her the mother of Linus, mentioned in the same verse (*Apostolical Constitutions* vii, 21), and identified by Irenaeus and Eusebius as a bishop of Rome.

So great a modern scholar as Alford (*Greek Testament,* III, 104-105) has given considerable attention to the hypothesis that Claudia may have been a British maiden, converted to Christianity and later married to Pudens (mentioned before Linus in II Tim 4:21). This conjecture, based on an inscription found in England, is admittedly rather fanciful and very doubtful.

CLAUDIUS (klô'dĭ-ŭs). The fourth Roman emperor, who reigned A.D. 41–54. He was a nephew of Tiberius Caesar (A.D. 14–37), under whose rule Jesus' ministry was carried on. Between these two emperors came the short rule of Caligula, who greatly antagonized the Jews by his cruel policies toward them. Claudius revived the more generous attitude of Augustus and Tiberius, the first two Roman emperors, who had been conciliatory toward the Jews.

The Emperor Claudius. BM

At the beginning of his reign Claudius issued an edict in favor of the Jews of Alexandria, who had been undergoing persecution. Josephus reports part of it as reading thus: "I will, therefore, that the nation of the Jews be not deprived of their rights and privileges on account of the madness of Caius; but that these rights and privileges, which they formerly enjoyed, be preserved to them, and that they may continue in their own customs" (*Ant.* xix. 5.2). Josephus further relates that Claudius sent an edict throughout the world in which he wrote: "Upon the petition of king Agrippa and king Herod, who are persons very dear to me, that I would grant the same rights and privileges should be preserved to the Jews which are in all the Roman empire, which I have granted to those of Alexandria, I very willingly comply therewith" (*Ant.* xix. 5.3). "Agrippa" was Herod Agrippa I, grandson of Herod the Great. Claudius gave him the territory ruled by his grandfather, with the title of king.

Claudius is mentioned by name only twice in the NT. In Acts 11:28 a famine is recorded as occurring in his reign. Historical records indicate that famines were frequent and severe in this period (Suetonius, *Claudius* 18). In fact, the emperor's life is said to have been threatened on this account (Tacitus, *Annals* xii. 43). The situation was partly due to the carelessness of his predecessor.

Aquila and Priscilla are said to have been compelled to leave Rome when Claudius made a decree expelling all Jews from that city (Acts 18:2). The correctness of this reference is confirmed by Suetonius (*Claudius* 25).

The unfortunate emperor was murdered by his wife Agrippina in A.D. 54.

R. E.

CLAW (lit., "hoof"). The mark of a "clean" animal was: "Every animal that parts the hoof and has the hoof cloven in two, and chews the cud, among the animals, you may eat" (Deut 14:6, RSV). The KJV describes the worthless shepherd as tearing off even the "claws" of the sheep, while the RSV uses the term "hoofs" (Zech 11:16).

CLAY. *See* Minerals.

CLEAN, CLEANNESS. The translation of several Heb. and Gr. words having the idea of physical cleanness, and then of moral purity. The term is used in the physical, ceremonial, ethical, figurative, and spiritual senses, with the uses frequently overlapping. The chief usage is the ceremonial, applied to persons, places, or things (Lk 5:14; Heb 9:13, 22; II Chr 23:19; Isa 52:11). The idea of cleanness is also applied to animals and birds (Gen 7:2; Deut 14:11). *See* Food: Meat.

The importance of "cleanness" for Israel is that the nation should reflect in her national life the qualities which she ascribes to Yahweh. The spiritual ideal of cleanness is reflected in the OT mainly in Job, Psalms, and the Prophets. "Cleanness" is necessary to fellowship with Yahweh (cf. Ps 15). The greater emphasis concerning spiritual cleanness is found in the NT (Jn 13:11; Acts 18:6; I Jn 1:7, 9). *See* Chaste; Purity; Sanctification.

Bibliography. R. Meyer and F. Hauck, "*Katharos,* etc.," TDNT, III, 413–431.

CLEFT

1. A space or opening, usually narrow, made by cleavage, as the "clefts of the rocks" (Ex 33:22; Isa 2:21; Amos 6:11; Mic 1:4).

2. The split in the hoof of an animal (Deut 14:6; cf. Lev 11:3).

CLEMENT (klĕm'ĕnt). A fellow worker with Paul at Philippi and saluted by Paul in his letter to the Philippian church as one whose name was in the book of life (Phil 4:3). Attempts to identify him with Clement of Rome fail largely because Clement of Rome lived at the end of the 1st cen., and Paul's friend was evidently a mature person at the time of Paul's letter, *c*. A.D. 63.

CLEOPAS (klē'ō-păs). One of the two disciples to whom Jesus revealed Himself in the breaking of bread at Emmaus on the afternoon of His resurrection (Lk 24:18). Some would identify this Cleopas with Cleophas (KJV) or Clopas (RSV) in Jn 19:25, the husband of one of the Marys who stood at the cross. Others would go further and identify both of these with Alphaeus (Mt 10:3; Mk 3:18; Lk 6:15; Acts 1:13), the father of James the apostle (the second by that name). While Clopas and Alphaeus may well come from the same Heb. root (Alford, *Greek Testament,* I, 101), it does not appear that these men should be identified with Cleopas.

CLEOPHAS (klē'ō-făs). A close relative of a woman named Mary who stood by the cross (Jn 19:25). The Gr. text does not indicate whether his relationship was that of husband, son, or father, although it would be most probable that he was her husband. The following attempts at further identification have been made:

1. Cleophas (Gr. *klōpas;* RSV, Clopas) has been identified with Cleopas (Gr. *kleopas,* Lk 24:18), which is doubtful since the latter is a thoroughly Gr. name while the former seems to be of Semitic origin.

2. Cleophas has also been identified with Alphaeus (Mt 10:3), on the assumption that both names are transliterations of the Aramaic *ḥalpay*. That this view is based on a number of arbitrary assumptions weakens its possibility.

3. Cleophas has been thought to be the brother of Joseph, as Hegesippus suggested, but there is no biblical indication of such a relationship.

In view of the lack of evidence, it would seem best to view Cleophas, Cleopas, and Alphaeus as different individuals.

D. W. B.

CLERK. *See* Town Clerk.

CLOAK, CLOKE. The outer garment. *See* Dress.

CLOSET. In Heb. *ḥuppâ,* KJV, "closet," means a canopy, as in Isa 4:5, RSV; the verb form means "to cover." Originally it evidently referred to the tent set apart for the bride. Later it signified the bride's chamber (Joel 2:16). In the NT the Gr. term *tameion* (Mt 6:6; Lk 12:3, 24) refers to a store chamber or inner chamber. The NT stresses the ideas of privacy, even secrecy, and storage, as suggested in the terms store chamber, upper chamber, secret chamber, inner room, and private room.

CLOTH, CLOTHES, CLOTHING. *See* Dress.

CLOTHES, RENDING OF. *See* Rend.

CLOUD. The word is used many times. Basically, it refers to the literal clouds in the sky, as in Gen 9:13, 14, 16; Lk 12:54. However, it is frequently used figuratively as in Ezk 8:11; Heb 12:1. The word is also used in another sense to indicate the presence of God to guide His people (Ex 13:21, 22; 40:34-38), or to protect them (Ex 14:19).

Literal. Unlike Lower Egypt, Palestine enjoys considerable rainfall, but it is limited almost entirely to the winter—from October 15 to May 1. During the summer—May 1 to October 15—there is practically no rain and few clouds. Hence, "the winter is past, the rain is over and gone" (Song 2:11).

Figurative. The dissipation of a thick cloud is used to represent the blotting out of Israel's sins (Isa 44:22). A cloud veiled the glory of the Lord from Moses' sight, and the people's, when the law was given (Ex 19:9; 24:15-18), and at other times also (Ex 16:10; 34:5). The Lord promised to appear in a cloud upon the mercy seat in the most holy place on the Day of Atonement (Lev 16:2). A cloud representing the glory of God appeared when the tabernacle was originally set up (Ex 40:34-35), and when the ark was brought into the first temple (I Kgs 8:10-11). Clouds are often spoken of in connection with the unapproachableness of God, as in Job 22:14; Ps 18:11, 12; 97:2.

At the transfiguration, a cloud overshadowed the three disciples and the voice of God spoke from it acknowledging Jesus as His beloved Son (Mt 17:5; Mk 9:7; Lk 9:34-35). Jesus said He would come again "in a cloud with power and great glory" (Lk 21:27; see also Mt 24:30; Mk 13:26; Rev 1:7). Paul speaks of believers being caught up in the clouds (or, in clouds) when Christ comes for His own (I Thess 4:17). Thus clouds, being in the sky, seem to be used repeatedly in Scripture to remind us of God: His glory and His guidance, His distance and His presence.

J. A. S.

CLOUD, PILLAR OF. *See* Pillar of Cloud and Fire.

CLOUT. A patch or piece of cloth, a rag, a portion of cloth applied to mend a tear. The Gibeonites in deceiving Joshua came with "old shoes and clouted" (Josh 9:5). Rags and torn bits of cloth were used to prevent the ropes from cutting Jeremiah's flesh when he was being pulled up from the dungeon (Jer 38:11-12).

CLUB. An offensive weapon, probably the most primitive of all weapons. Several words may be translated "club."

1. Heb. *tôtāḥ,* "bludgeon" or "club" (Job 41:29). The LXX translated it as "hammer," "mallet"; the KJV has "dart."

2. Heb. *mappēṣ,* "war club" (Prov 25:18; Jer 51:20). The KJV has "maul" and "battle axe"; the RSV has "war club" and "hammer."

3. Gr. *xulon,* something made of wood such as a "cudgel," "stick," "staff" (Mt 26:47, 55; Mk 14:43, 48; Lk 22:52). The KJV has "staves," while the RSV has "clubs." These were carried by the crowd in arresting Jesus in Gethsemane.

CNIDUS (nī'dŭs). A Gr. city of Caria on the coast of SW Asia Minor. It was located at the tip of a long narrow peninsula jutting out into the sea for 90 miles. Its location placed it between the islands of Rhodes and Coos (Cos). Paul sailed by Cnidus on his journey to Rome (Acts 27:7). The ruins of Cnidus are the only objects of interest on the peninsula today.

COALS. This translates five different Heb. words in the OT and two different Gr. words in the NT. Although no mineral coal has been found in Palestine, wood was used to make a fire of coals such as is described in Jn 18:18; 21:9. The coal was actually charcoal made by subjecting wood to a smothering process, and was used then as in recent times for heat (Isa 47:14) as well as cooking (Isa 44:19; Jn 21:9), and by the blacksmith (Isa 44:12). The Gr. *anthrax* (Rom 12:20) refers to charcoal when Paul says (quoting Prov 25:22) that one may heap coals of fire upon someone's head by returning good for evil. *See* Minerals and Metals.

COAST. This word is translated variously as "border," "boundary," "coast," "territory," or "region" in the RSV (Num 34:11; Josh 1:4; Jud 1:18; Acts 27:2). Where the KJV has "coast," the RSV usually has "border" or "boundary." The seacoast itself is seldom mentioned (Acts 27:2; Lk 6:17). *See* Border.

COAT. *See* Dress.

COAT OF MAIL. *See* Armor.

COBRA. *See* Animals, IV.8.

COCK. *See* Animals, III.14.

COCKATRICE. *See* Animals: Serpent, IV.30.

COCKCROWING. All four Gospels give Jesus' prophecy that Peter would deny Him three times: Mark, "before the cock crows twice" (14:30); the others merely, before the cock crows (Mt 26:34; Lk 22:34; Jn 13:38). Mark therefore refers to a "second" cockcrowing (14:68, 72), the others do not (Mt 26:74–75; Lk 22:60–61; Jn 18:27). Numerous explanations for this difference are offered. Possibly Mark's two cockcrowings give the more precise and detailed account—consistent either with the priority of Mark or with Peter himself as Mark's source of information—while the other evangelists generalize into the one cockcrowing which was later and more commonly heard.

COCKLE. *See* Plants.

COFFER. A small chest or box which the Philistines placed upon the cart with the ark (I Sam 6:8, 11, 15). In this they placed the golden mice and emerods when they returned the ark to the Hebrews.

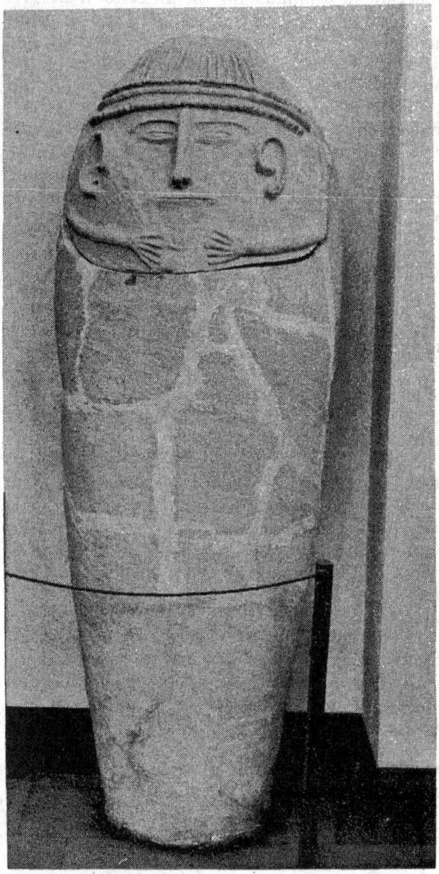

A pottery coffin from Bethshean. Palestine Archaeological Museum

COFFIN. Coffins were seldom used by the Hebrews, who buried their dead wrapped in cloths or sheets. The only exception in the Bible is the case of Joseph, who died as a nobleman in Egypt (Gen 50:26). His embalmed body was likely placed in a wooden Egyptian coffin or mummy case. For this unusual instance the Heb. word *'ārôn* was employed; it is rendered "chest" in II Kgs 12:9–10 and very frequently "ark." Numerous coffins from the Middle Kingdom period of Egypt (*c.* 2050–1750 B.C.) are displayed in our museums. These are often shaped in human form and elaborately decorated inside and out. Joseph's remains were carried, presumably in his coffin, by the Israelites into Canaan for final burial (Josh 24:32). *See* Burial; Tomb.

COHORT. The tenth part of a legion, usually about 600 men. The KJV has "band," while ASV marg. has "cohort" (Mt 27:27; Mk 15:16; Acts 10:1; 21:31; 27:1). It may also be used of a small detail (Jn 18:3, 12, ASV marg.). A cohort was stationed in Jerusalem in the tower of Antonia adjacent to the temple (Jos *Wars* v.5.8). *See* Army; Legion.

COIN. *See* Weights, Measures, and Coins.

COL-HOZEH (kŏl-hō'zē). A man of Judah whose father was Hazaiah (Neh 11:5). His son Shallum rebuilt the Fountain Gate in the time of Nehemiah (Neh 3:15).

COLLAR

1. The opening of a robe or shirt through which the head is inserted (Job 30:18; cf. Ex 28:32; Ps 133:2, RSV). *See* Dress.
2. A decorative ornament hung around the necks of Midianite camels (Jud 8:26).
3. A pendant or necklace (Prov 1:9; Song 4:9).
4. A pillory or instrument of torture into which a person's head was placed (Jer 29:26, RSV; Ps 105:18, RSV).

COLLECTION. The word collection is found in two passages in the KJV (II Chr 24:6, 9; I Cor 16:1). However, in the OT the original is more properly rendered "tax." In the NT the word *logeia* is used (found only here) which refers to a voluntary gathering of money for charitable purposes. The use of this word in the sense of "collection" is abundantly confirmed by the papyri. It is closely related to the usage of *koinōnia* ("contribution") in Rom 15:26. The collection made among the Gentile churches for the poor saints at Jerusalem by Paul and delivered at the peril of his life (Acts 21:17-36; 24:17) was a visible sign of the inward and essential unity of apostolic Christianity. *See* Alms.

COLLEGE. The residence of the prophetess Huldah (II Kgs 22:14; II Chr 34:22). The Heb. term evidently means a district or suburb of the city. The KJV has "college" while the RSV has "second quarter." The same term is translated as "second" in Zeph 1:10 where the reference is to a quarter of the city.

COLLOPS. The only reference to this term is in Job 15:27. The KJV reads "maketh collops of fat on his flanks," while the RSV reads "gathered fat upon his loins."

COLONY. A group of self-governing Roman citizens settled in foreign communities. Roman colonies were established primarily for three purposes: (1) to serve as strategic outposts; (2) to resettle poor citizens and thus take them off the relief rolls; (3) to provide land for veterans. In addition, sometimes a community would be granted colonial status by Rome to honor its inhabitants and to strengthen its ties with the imperial government.

The word "colony" occurs only once in the NT (Acts 16:12). Philippi was a Roman colony originally settled by the veterans of the battle fought between the forces of Antony and Octavian (later Emperor Augustus) and Brutus and Cassius in 42 B.C. Subsequently Octavian settled other colonists there.

COLOR, COLORS. *See* Colours.

COLOSSE (kŏ-lŏs'ē). A city located on both sides of the Lycus River in Phrygia, about 12 miles from Laodicea in SW Asia Minor. The histories of Colosse, Laodicea, and Hierapolis were closely associated. The great trade route from Ephesus to Tarsus and Syria went through Colosse and made it a prosperous city by the time of Xerxes (Herodotus vii.30). The city had owed its wealth chiefly to its red or violet woolens, called *colossinus*. But it was already declining in importance by Paul's day because of competition especially from Laodicea (*q.v.*), and no letter was sent there by John when he wrote the churches in Asia (Rev 1-3).

The Christian church in Colosse may have been founded by Epaphras (Col 1:2; 4:12). Paul had not visited Colosse previous to his epistle to them (Col 2:1). The church seems to have met in the home of Philemon, a prominent layman (Phm 2).

COLOSSIANS, BOOK OF. The Epistle to the Colossians is almost universally regarded as a genuine writing of the apostle Paul. Three times the writer calls himself Paul (Col 1:1; 1:23; 4:18). The great concepts of the person and work of Christ, death and resurrection with Christ, harmonious domestic relationships, and the new man in Christ are unmistakably Pauline. Repeatedly the genuineness of Ephesians is argued because of its similarity to Colossians, assumed without question to be Pauline. Furthermore, "the external attestation to Colossians is all that can be desired" (H. C. Thiessen, *Introduction to the New Testament,* p. 229).

One of four writings usually called the Prison Epistles, Colossians is a companion epistle to Philemon, both of which were apparently written about the same time (perhaps A.D. 60-61) and carried to their destination by Paul's co-worker Tychicus (Col 4:7-9), who was to take the slave Onesimus back to Philemon. Because of these associations, it is argued that Philemon lived at Colosse and was a leading member of that church, which may have met in his house (Phm 2). As far as we know, Paul never personally ministered in Colosse; however, the assumption that his co-laborers evangelized there while he was at Ephesus (Acts 19:1-10) is valid. At least, he felt a personal responsibility for this church.

Purpose for Writing

The immediate occasion of writing to the Colossians was the projected mission of Tychicus, coupled with a report brought to Paul from Colosse by Epaphras (1:7-9; 4:12). Apparently this report informed Paul of insidious errors, both doctrinal and practical, that had crept into the church. Often called the Colossian heresy, these errors combined Judaistic elements with ascetic and Gnostic teachings akin to those features which later developed into a full-blown Gnostic system. Designating it as an example of man-made religion, R. H. Lightfoot summarizes the features of this heresy as: rationalism, heresy of intellect (Col 2:8); ceremonialism, heresy of religious instinct (Col 2:16, 20-22); mysticism, heresy of spiritual consciousness (Col 2:18); and asceticism, heresy of the moral will (Col 2:23) (*St. Paul's Epistles to the Colossians and to Philemon,* pp. 71-111).

The basic purpose of Colossians is to combat these heresies, which Paul meets "not by indignant controversy, for as yet they were only undeveloped; not by personal authority, for these Christians were not his converts; but by the noblest of all forms of controversy, which is the pure presentation of counter truths" (F. W. Farrar, *Messages of the Books,* p. 312). Hence, a key idea for the entire epistle is in 2:9-10 and 1:19-20. The complete Christ, giver of a complete salvation, when personally experienced, is the complete answer to error, both theological and practical.

Plan of the Epistle

The emphasis in Col 1:12-20 is on Christ in whom dwells all the fullness of the Godhead bodily. As to His person, He is the image—the likeness, representation, manifestation—of the invisible God. In reference to creation, He is its Sovereign, Creator, Sustainer, and to it He gives essential meaning. First to be resurrected from the dead, He is the beginning, the Head of the Body, the Church. The work of Christ is here described as reconciliation, both cosmic and personal, made possible by the peace He secured by His death.

In Col 2:11—3:4, Paul then shows how that "in Him ye are made full." This vital experience in Christ is described negatively as being buried with Christ and is symbolized by spiritual circumcision and baptism. Positively, being in Christ is to be made alive with Him. The means of realizing this experience is faith in the workings of God. God raised Christ from the dead after our Lord had defeated all spiritual enemies and cancelled the indictment of sin by assuming in full the demands of its penalty (2:11-15). This work, then, constitutes the basis of personal salvation. Practical consequences follow. Negatively, they are a rescue from the error and a repudiation of the error with all its features. This is involved in dying to the old way and manner of living (2:16-23). Positively, vital experience in Christ will mean a new kind of living—seek heaven, think heaven—and a new hope (3:1-4).

What follows in Col 3:5—4:6 are detailed practical expressions of new life in Christ. New character must come—put to death the old nature, seeing that the new nature has been put on (3:5-14); new life principles must be adopted—peace ruling in the heart, the Word dwelling there, and grace inspiring the heart's song (3:15-17); new conduct must show in domestic relationships, in evangelism among the worldly (3:18—4:6).

Outline

The Christian in Christ—
Antidote to Error

I. The Gospel at Work Among the Colossians, 1:1-14
II. The Person and Work of Christ, 1:15-23
  A. Christ as seen in all His relationships is pre-eminent, vv. 15-20
  B. Christ's work is described as reconciliation, vv. 21-23
III. Paul's Ministry of the Mystery of Christ, 1:24—2:5: His spirit, authority, message, method, strength, goal
IV. The Personal Experience of Christ, 2:6—3:4
  A. Man-made religion—the enemy of faith
  B. The complete Christ and complete experience in Him is the answer to all error
  C. Vital Christian experience
    1. Described negatively: buried with Christ
    2. Described positively: raised with Christ
    3. Means of realization: faith in the working of God
    4. Grounds or basis: the working of God
  D. The practical consequences of experience in Christ, negative and positive
V. Life in Christ Expressed in Personal Character and Relationships, 3:5—4:6
VI. Paul's Personal Interests and Salutations, 4:7-18

Bibliography. John Eadie, *Commentary on the Epistle of Paul to the Colossians,* Grand Rapids: Zondervan, reprint. R. C. H. Lenski, *The Interpretation of St. Paul's Epistle to the Colossians,* Columbus: Lutheran Book Concern, 1937. J. B. Lightfoot, *St. Paul's Epistle to the Colossians,* Grand Rapids: Zondervan, reprint. Alexander Maclaren, "The Epistle of Paul to the Colossians," ExpB. H. C. G. Moule, *The Epistle of Paul the Apostle to the Colossians,* Cambridge: Univ. Press, 1894. W. R. Nicholson, *Oneness with Christ,* Grand Rapids: Kregel, 1951. A. T. Robertson, *Paul and the In-*

tellectuals, rev. by Archie Robinson, Nashville: Broadman, 1959. James S. Stewart, *A Man in Christ,* New York: Harper, 1935.

E. W. H.

COLOURS

1. "Under colour" in Acts 27:30 (KJV) means simply "on the pretense of" (NASB).

2. The abstract word for color does not actually occur in the OT or NT. In each case where the translators have so employed our English word, the word in the original has a different basic meaning.

In most OT occurrences the Heb. word means simply "appearance" (cf. Lev 13:55; Num 11:7; Ezk 1:4, 7, etc.; Dan 10:6). The coats of many colors of Joseph (Gen 37:3) and Tamar (II Sam 13:18-19) were most probably ankle-length coats with long sleeves which, as the Tamar reference illustrates, were worn by the upper classes. The ordinary coat reached only to the knees and had no armholes. Several Heb. words with meanings like "variegated," "many colored" also occur (cf. Ezk 16:16; 17:3; I Chr 29:2; Prov 7:16, RSV).

All NT references are not separate Gr. words but extensions of the basic color mentioned.

3. Color as a specific light phenomenon in both OT and NT. When one seeks to identify the various names of colored objects in the Bible he is perplexed at the paucity of words used and the difficulty of matching the terms with standard colored objects which we know. This does not necessarily mean that the Oriental lacked a sense of appreciation for color, but rather that he failed to analyze and define color effects. The biblical indefiniteness should be understood as part of the general cultural heritage of the ancient Near East and not a particular defect of the Hebrews.

In the ancient use of colors on pottery, glazed bricks, glassware, tomb walls, sarcophagi, wood, and fabrics there does not seem to be the elaborate blending of colors which characterizes modern coloring, but rather the striking effects produced by highlighting the basic colors. It may be noted in this connection that often the main distinction in reference to the color of an object is not in its specific hue, but rather its classification as somber or brilliant, lightish or darkish. This concern for color value or brilliance is apparently a phenomenon noticed in other ancient literature such as Homer and Old English poetry (R. W. Corney, "Colors," IDB, I, 657).

The following is an attempt to identify the main specific colors mentioned in the OT and NT:

Bay, or red. Probably better understood as a reference to the strength or vigor of the horses referred to in Zech 6:3, 7 and not to the color (so RSV, "steeds," v. 7; cf. JerusB).

Black. The English word translates at least eight different Heb. words indicating shades of darkness from dark brown to gray to blackish. Black is used to describe the color of hair (Lev 13:31, 37; Song 5:11), skin (Job 30:30; Song 1:5-6, where the reference is not necessarily racial but "sunburned" or dark brown), human face (Lam 4:8), horses (Zech 6:2, 6), flocks (Gen 30:32 ff., RSV), heavens (I Kgs 18:45, as a sign of rain), brooks because of ice (Job 6:16). The Gr. word for black in the NT is used of hair (Mt 5:36), one of the four horses of the Apocalypse (Rev 6:5), and the darkened sun (Rev 6:12). In Heb 12:18 a different Gr. word signifies blackness or darkness of Mount Sinai when the law was given, and the same word literally describes the "blackness of darkness" (II Pet 2:17; Jude 13, NASB marg.; RSV has "nether gloom of darkness").

Blue. Probably a purple-blue obtained from Mediterranean mollusks or shellfish and, although considered inferior to the royal purple dye, was a very popular color used in the tabernacle fringes, veil and priestly vestments (Ex 25:4; 26:1; Num 4:6-7, 9; 15:38) and in Solomon's temple (II Chr 2:7, 14; 3:14). This color appears also in Ahasuerus' palace and his royal robes (Est 1:6; 8:15). Qumran (Essene) priests wore an embroidered purple and blue girdle at the occasion of battle (1QM 7:10; cf. Ex 39:28-29). The word blue does not occur in the KJV or RSV of the NT.

Brown. The KJV form of the same word for black (*q.v.*) in the sense of "sunburnt" or "swarthy" in Gen 30:32-33, 35, 40.

Crimson. A red color of varying shades derived from the eggs of female kermes or cochineal insects. After the eggs were removed from under the outer shell of the female insect, they were carefully rolled into a large ball from which the dye was then extracted. This color is applied to materials used in Solomon's temple (II Chr 2:7, 14; 3:14); metaphorically to the blood redness of Israel's sins of shedding innocent blood (Isa 1:18), and apparently to the face paint of a harlot (Jer 4:30). *See* Scarlet; Animals: Crimson Scale Insect, IV.11.

Gray. Applied to the color of the hair of the aging (Gen 42:38; 44:29, 31; Deut 32:25; I Sam 12:2; Job 15:10; Ps 71:18; Prov 20:29; Isa 46:4; Hos 7:9). The same word is rendered "hoar" or "hoary" in other passages (cf. I Kgs 2:6, 9; Isa 46:4; etc.).

Green. Several Heb. words are so translated. In each case the usual reference is to the color of vegetation, and along with red and white forms one of the definite color words in the OT (cf. Gen 1:30; 9:3; Ex 10:15; Job 39:8; Ps 37:2). Sometimes the color is a yellow-green such as "green gold" (Ps 68:13, RSV) or the greenish color of leprous spots (Lev 13:49; 14:37). In the NT the references are all to green grass or trees (Mk 6:39; Rev 8:7; 9:4). A metaphorical usage occurs in Lk 23:31 where Jesus apparently likens the future distress to come upon the rebelling Jewish people to the rapid burning of a "dry" tree, contrasting it to the undeserved distress He was encountering in

His scourging and crucifixion which He alluded to as the burning of a "green" tree.

Grisled ("dappled" in RSV). The term denotes literally, "spotted with hail" and is used of the "mottled," "spotted" or perhaps "dappled gray" color of certain apocalyptic horses (Zech 6:3, 6) and goats (Gen 31:10, 12).

Purple. Probably this color was considered the most valued of the ancient dyes. Its various red-purple hues were derived from Mediterranean mollusks or shellfish of the Gastropoda class. Phoenicians (from Gr. *phoinos,* "red-purple") have been cited in ancient documents as the discoverers of this dye color (cf. Ezk 27:7). The name Canaan ("land of the purple") was apparently derived from the dye. According to Pliny, the most valuable shade was that of congealed blood. Garments dyed in the color were used in the tabernacle (Ex 26:1, 31) and in the priestly attire (Ex 28:4-6; 39:1, 28-29; cf. 1QM 7.11, where along with blue, white, and scarlet clothing the Qumran priests attired themselves for battle). Royal garments customarily contained the purple dyed fabrics (cf. Midianite kings, Jud 8:26; Solomonic chariot seat, Song 3:10; Babylonian and Persian kings' apparel, Dan 5:7, RSV; Est 1:6), as well as those of wealth (Prov 31:22; Jer 10:9; Ezk 27:7, 16). Apparently the earlier Roman kings did not wear purple (cf. I Macc 8:14).

In the NT Lydia of Thyatira (Acts 16:14) was a dealer in the costly purple dye. The rich man was clothed in purple in the story Jesus told about the beggar Lazarus (Lk 16:19). The symbolical significance of purple denoting royalty figures in the robes of mockery in Jesus' trial (Mk 15:17, 20; Jn 19:2, 5), and the whore mentioned in Revelation (cf. 17:4; 18:12, 16). *See* Purple; Animals: Purple Mollusk, V.8.

Red. While this color may be a dye artificially obtained from insects, vegetables, and minerals (Ex 25:5; 26:14; etc.), the most frequent use in the Bible is to designate the natural color of certain objects. For example, red is used of the color of skin (Esau's, Gen 25:25; David's, "ruddy," I Sam 16:12; 17:42); the color of the eyes after wine has been drunk (Gen 49:12; Prov 23:29); of pottage (Gen 25:30); of the sacrificial purification heifer (Num 19:2, 5-6, 8-10); of spots of suspected leprosy (Lev 13:19); of war shields (Nah 2:3). In Isa 63:1-2, a word-play exists between the word Edom ("red," v. 1) and red in "red [Heb. *'ādōm*] like him that treadeth in the winefat" (v. 2). The latter statement refers to the Messiah's blood-spattered clothing resulting from His work of judgment (v. 3). A different Heb. word *(hāmar)* occurs in Ps 75:8 translated "red" but the meaning is probably "foaming" (RSV) or "fermented."

In the NT the Gr. word *pyrros* and cognates are used of the color of the sky as "fiery red" (Mt 16:2-3); one of the four horses in the Apocalypse (Rev 6:4); and the color of the satanic dragon (Rev 12:3).

Scarlet. A dye color indistinguishable in the Bible from crimson (*q.v.*) and derived in the same manner from the bodies of certain female insects and used for fabrics and yarn (Gen 38:28, 30; Josh 2:18, 21; II Sam 1:24; Nah 2:3; Prov 31:21); lips (Song 4:3); figuratively for sins (Isa 1:18). Scarlet was also part of the Qumran priests' attire (1QM 7.11). In the NT scarlet is used to designate the color of wool (Heb 9:19); the robe put upon Jesus by the Roman soldiers in mockery (Mt 27:28); and together with purple comprises the clothing worn by the symbolic woman in Revelation (17:4) which may signify her magnificence. The businessmen of the world mourn over the loss of their market for scarlet when the woman is destroyed (Rev 18:12). *See* Animals: Crimson Scale Insect, IV.11.

Sorrel. Found in Zech 1:8, RSV, as one of the colors of the apocalyptic horses. The Heb. word is related to the Assyrian and Arabic word for "red blood" or "redness." It may refer to having a ruddy tinge over white (BDB).

Vermilion. A bright red pigment made in modern times from mercuric oxide, but probably from an iron oxide in ancient times that was known as red ocher. It was a brilliant color and apparently connected with costly painting of rooms and pottery. Jeremiah accused King Jehoiakim of building himself a house painted with vermilion while he neglected justice and practiced oppression (Jer 22:14). It is connected with the figures of Babylonian men painted on the walls by which the adulterous Judah was seduced to intercourse (Ezk 23:14). These figures were war scenes, depicting the triumphal processions of the Babylonian rulers with which the Assyrian palaces were adorned (cf. Keil, *Ezekiel,* KD). Heathen idols are described as being painted with this red ocher in the apocryphal book of the Wisdom of Solomon (13:14) and the Greeks used the color for painting pottery (Pliny, *Nat. Hist.,* XXXV.152).

Violet. Found in the RSV of Jer 10:9 (KJV, blue). The Heb. word is everywhere else rendered "blue."

White. While there are several Heb. words which are rendered white, the most common is *lābān,* which can be detected in the word "Lebanon" that probably was so named because of Mount Lebanon's snow-tipped peaks. It is generally the natural color of various objects, such as teeth (Gen 49:12), snow (Isa 1:18), hair (Mt 5:36), horses (Zech 1:8; 6:3), tree branches (Joel 1:7), bleached garments (Eccl 9:8; Dan 7:9). In the NT "whitewashed" (Mt 23:27; Acts 23:3; KJV, "whited") is used metaphorically much like our use of a deliberate attempt to portray outwardly something as good but which in reality is bad. White garments clothed the transfigured Christ (Mt 17:2), angels (Mt 28:3; Jn 20:12; Acts 1:10), and various clothed personages in the book of Revelation (3:4; 4:4; 7:9; 19:8, 14).

Yellow. A word describing the color of gold

in Ps 68:13, but elsewhere a greenish-yellow, and hence translated greenish in Lev 13:49; 14:37. In Lev 13:30, 32, 36 a different Heb. word describes the color of the hair in a person afflicted with leprosy in the region of the head or beard.

Color symbolism. It is very difficult to assign specific symbolic significance to the colors found in the Bible because of the general lack of emphasis on distinctive hues in the majority of cases, and because only a few colors in a few places are given any definite meaning in the text. Furthermore, there is no principle that demands that once a color is mentioned in a certain symbolic sense it always retains that same sense uniformly through the biblical periods. The contemporary cultural significance of colors appears to have influenced the biblical writers more than a uniform scriptural fixity. The following colors seem to be identified in some contexts with the stated associations.

Black: mourning (cf. Jer 4:28; 8:21; 14:2; Isa 50:3; Job 30:30), treachery (Job 6:15-16), perhaps hopelessness (Mic 3:6, RSV; Jude 13).

Blue: bonds of wisdom compared to a cord of blue in the apocalyptic book of Ecclesiasticus (6:30); associated with kings, therefore figurative of royalty.

Crimson: sin is so described (Isa 1:18).

Green: occasionally used to refer to places of idolatrous practices (cf. Deut 12:2; I Kgs 14:23) which were luxuriant with trees. Since the color is usually associated with luxuriance and abundance of vegetation, it easily suggests that which is flourishing and healthy (cf. Job 15:32; Ps 23:2; 37:35; Jer 11:16).

Purple: usually associated with kings and the wealthy, hence the color of royalty, honor, status.

Scarlet: associated with sins (Isa 1:18); some suggest it as the color of sacrifice or blood-shedding.

White: symbolic of purity, holiness, righteousness (Dan 11:35; 12:10; Isa 1:18).

Most of the other symbolic designations that are made can offer no more than educated guesses. Even regarding the rich tabernacle colorings, some suggest that they all imply nothing more than that the presence of the King of kings is there, as opposed to others who find a symbolic significance in each of the colors used.

A. F. J.

COLT. *See* Animals, I.1.

COMB. The honeycomb (e.g., I Sam 14:27; Prov 24:13; Lk 24:42). *See* Animals: Bee, III.2; Food: Honey.

COMFORT. The OT terms *nāḥam*, "to sigh with," and *sāʿad*, "to support and refresh," imply an expression of sympathy, giving of encouragement. The NT terms express the idea of strengthening, encouragement, speaking with consolation. The most common, *parakaleō*, means "to call to one's side" particularly to help. Men comfort one another (Gen 37:35; Job 6:10; Phil 2:19), and God is the divine source of comfort (Ps 119:76; Isa 49:13; II Cor 1:4). The actual experience of comfort in the fellowship of the church is the work of the Holy Spirit, appropriately termed "the Comforter" (Jn 14:16, 26; 15:26; 16:7). *See* Paraclete. Comfort is one of the three main results of prophesying (I Cor 14:3). KJV often translates the original terms with "consolation" (*q.v.*). *See* Exhortation.

Bibliography. Gustav Stählin, "*Paramytheomai*, etc.," TDNT, V, 816-823.

COMFORTER, THE. *See* Holy Spirit.

COMING OF CHRIST. *See* Christ, Coming of.

COMMANDMENTS, TEN. *See* Ten Commandments.

COMMERCE. While this word is not used in KJV, it includes in its scope the terms "merchant," "merchandise," "trade" and "traffic." *See* Occupations: Merchant.

Palestine was situated on or near the chief commercial highways of the ancient world, being traversed by roads connecting Babylonia and Egypt and the Far East with the Mediterranean area. *See* Travel and Communication. International trade early benefited those who lived in Canaan. Abraham, for example, was rich in cattle, silver and gold (Gen 13:2). W. F. Albright suggests that Abraham may have been involved in the profitable caravan trade, leading donkey caravans back and forth across the Negeb and the Sinai desert between Palestine and Egypt (*Yahweh and the Gods of Canaan,* 1968, pp. 58-73).

The patriarch had come from one of the great commercial centers of the ancient world, Ur, the capital of Sumer. The Sumerian cities traded far and wide. Tablets from the Ur III dynasty (2070-1960 B.C.) deal with the exchange of slaves and houses, the borrowing of commodities, and the loaning of grain, dates and silver at interest. Even before that, Gudea, king of Lagash, tells of obtaining gold from Anatolia and Egypt, silver from the Taurus Mountains, cedar from Lebanon, copper from the Zagros ranges, diorite from Ethiopia, and timber from Dilmun, which may refer to Bahrain or the Indus Valley civilization (S. N. Kramer, "Sumer," IDB, IV, 457). From *c.* 1950 to 1750 B.C. the Assyrians traded extensively with Asia Minor where they established as many as nine merchant colonies. Over 3,000 tablets from Kanesh (Kültepe) reveal that Assyrian traders lived under the protection of native princes while they bartered their goods in exchange for the gold and silver which was so plentiful in E Anatolia.

The earliest biblical account of bargaining and selling is Abraham's transaction with Ephron the Hittite (Gen 23:3-20). The use of the word "merchant" (v. 16) implies that the standard of the silver weighed out was fixed by usage among the merchants of that period. Reparations or compensation could be made for intangible damages by means of such money (Gen 20:16). Gold and silver in the form of bars or rings, as well as manufactured vessels and jewelry, were in use among the settled inhabitants of the area, although the metals were probably imported. Eliezer gave jewels of silver and earrings and bracelets of gold to Rebekah (Gen 24:22, 53). The *qesitah* was a specific form of money in the early 2nd mil. B.C., probably an ingot of precious metal (Heb., Gen 33:19; Job 42:11). The book of Job mentions iron, bronze, lead, crystal, jewels, the art of weaving, merchants, gold from Ophir, sapphire (lapis lazuli) whose only ancient source was Afghanistan, topaz from Ethiopia, all indicating an advanced state of commerce during the patriarchal period. The inhabitants of Arabia, living between India and Egypt, seem to have had a monopoly of trade between these countries, as well as with spices grown in S Arabia.

Egypt was prominent among the trading nations, along with the Ishmaelites or Midianites. It was a caravan of the latter, carrying spices, balm and myrrh, that took Joseph to Egypt (Gen 37:25; 39:1). Slaves were obviously also a part of their merchandise. Grain was exported from Egypt and paid for by silver (Gen 41:57; 42:3, 25, 35). The colored cloth used in the tabernacle was probably made and dyed in Egypt (Ex 25:4, 5). Evidences of widespread trade with Babylonia and Syria, known from the Amarna tablets, are seen in Num 31:50; Josh 7:21; Jud 5:30; 8:24.

After their settlement in Canaan, the Israelites became involved in commerce. At first, they had a natural self-sufficient economy. Each household grew its food and made all the tools and clothing needed. Other necessary articles or metals were supplied by wandering blacksmiths such as the Kenites (*q.v.;* Jud 1:16; 4:11)—the name means "smith"—and merchants. The latter were mostly Canaanites or Phoenicians. The word "Canaanite" became a synonym for "merchant," "trader" or "trafficker" (Job 41:6; Prov 31:24; Isa 23:8; Hos 12:7; Zech 14:21, RSV).

Previous to the Exile, Israel was not usually noted for commerce; trade was not the occupation of many of its people. The law made little regulation of such. Rather, just and righteous dealings were emphasized in general (Lev 19:35-36; Deut 25:13-16; 28:12). This absence of any manufacturing code is in itself a witness to the early date of the laws of the Pentateuch. The tribes near the sea and near Phoenician territory may have had some maritime trade (Gen 49:13; Deut 33:18; Jud 5:17).

During the reign of Solomon, however, Israel developed extensive external trade. A number of the wise sayings in Proverbs pertain to business matters, such as warnings regarding surety (Prov 6:1; 11:15; 17:18; 20:16; 22:26). The virtuous wife is commended for her small-scale commercial endeavors (Prov 31:13-18, 24). Solomon levied tariffs on merchantmen (I Kgs 10:15). He apparently exploited the copper deposits in the Arabah and was also a large exporter of wheat and oil, which was paid to Hiram of Tyre for timber and the use of skilled workmen (I Kgs 5:6 ff.). Sidon and Tyre with the nearby mountains furnished the best and most durable timber for shipbuilding. Their craftsmen built ships and made other products for export. The Phoenicians led by Tyre were esteemed as the great commercial nation and famed for knowledge of navigation (Ezk 27).

Solomon also acted as middleman in the profitable trading of horses and chariots between Kue (Cilicia) and Egypt, and his royal merchants as agents sold many to the Hittite and Aramean principalities (I Kgs 10:28-29, RSV). Every three years from Ezion-geber (*q.v.*) he sent ships to Ophir for gold, silver, ivory, apes and peacocks. He had built for him a fleet of cargo ships designed like those the Phoenicians were sailing to their mining colonies at Tarshish in Spain (I Kgs 10:22). He also fostered the spice trade with Arabia (I Kgs 10:15). His example apparently could not be followed on any large scale by his successors, although Jehoshaphat vainly tried to revive trade to Ophir (I Kgs 22:48). Jonah had to embark on a ship with Gentile sailors for Tarshish, showing that his countrymen were not active in maritime affairs at that time.

After the division of the kingdom, Israel traded with Phoenicia and Syria, while Judah dealt with Egypt, its southern neighbor, olive oil being its chief export (Hos 12:1). Ahab of Israel gained the right to establish trading markets or bazaars (KJV, "streets") in Damascus of Syria (I Kgs 20:34). The treasuries of the kings must have been accumulated partly at least by trade. Isaiah (3:18-24) speaks of the luxuries of feminine apparel not native to Israel. Tribute was often paid in kind, as sheep

Model of a ship used by Queen Hatshepsut of Egypt in trading expeditions about 1500 B.C.
Art Gallery and Museum, Glasgow

and wool from Moab (II Kgs 3:4). Hezekiah paid Sennacherib with silver and gold stripped from the house of the Lord (II Kgs 18:15 - 16).

During this period certain towns seem to have specialized in certain trades, such as the dyeing industry evidenced by the many stone vats in the excavations of Tell Beit Mirsim. Gibeon enjoyed a prosperous business in making and selling wine. *See* Occupations.

It is probable that the commercial genius of the Jews began to appear during the Exile. They acquired both wealth and positions of importance in Babylonia (Neh 1:11; 5:17). Many of those who stayed there became clients or agents of big commercial firms, such as the business house of the Murashu sons in Nippur, according to tablets written in the reign of Artaxerxes I (ANET, pp. 221 f.). After the return from the Exile, the Jewish community in Judah was poor and there was little business except at Jerusalem. Ezra (3:7) mentions oil exported to Tyre and cedar imports. Tyre sent fish to Palestine (Neh 13:16). Nehemiah's exhortation to the people to stop profaning the sabbath indicates that buying and selling were carried on.

Domestic trade in Israel included the shipping of salt from the Dead Sea, cattle and wool from the pastures E of the Jordan, and grain from the plain of Esdraelon. These were sent to various markets. Zephaniah implies one at Jerusalem (1:11).

The town markets were chiefly open spaces near the gates to which the producer brought his goods for direct sale to the consumer (II Kgs 7:1; Neh 13:15-16; Zeph 1:10). Later, traders intruded into the temple where the outer courts were utilized (Zech 14:21; Mt 21:12; Jn 2:14).

During the Hellenistic period, Jews did business with colonies in Alexandria, Antioch of Syria, Asia Minor, Greece, and even in Rome. Greek mercenary troops, craftsmen and merchants had been active along the E Mediterranean coast for centuries (Edwin Yamauchi, *Greece and Babylon,* pp. 26-93). Herod built the port of Caesarea, as Simon Maccabeus had built Joppa, to care for the maritime trade.

In Maccabean times it had become customary for villagers to carry products to town once a month. Later, market days were traditionally twice a week, on Monday and Thursday. Special services were held in synagogues on these days.

While its position was extremely unfavorable for trade, Jerusalem was the commercial center of the entire country in the time of Christ. Woolen garments were produced there and sold in the markets of the city. Tanners obtained skins from the temple sacrifices. Olives were processed in and around Jerusalem in such presses as Gethsemane, and the oil was probably the only export of the city. Spices were made into ointments and sold in its markets (Mk 16:1; Lk 23:56; Jn 19:39). The craftsmen were organized in guilds and grouped their small shops, open to the street or bazaar, in separate sections or quarters. The building trade flourished in Jesus' day, and stone was easily quarried in the vicinity. As Joachim Jeremias concludes, it was the religious significance of the Holy City which made its trades flourish and the enormous revenues of the temple which enabled Jerusalem to import its necessary food (*Jerusalem in the Time of Jesus,* p. 28; see his chapters on industries and commerce, pp. 3 - 57).

Bibliography. G. A. Barrois, "Trade and Commerce," IDB, IV, 677-683. "Trade," CornPBE, pp. 687-691. Walter Duckat, *Beggar to King,* Garden City: Doubleday, 1968, Appendix I: "Commerce and Trade," pp. 287-298. Donald Harden, *The Phoenicians,* London: Thames & Hudson, 1962, pp. 157-179. Joachim Jeremias, *Jerusalem in the Time of Jesus,* Philadelphia: Fortress Press, 1969. J. L. Kelso and E. M. Blaiklock, "Trade and Commerce," NBD, pp. 1287-1290. W. F. Leemans, "Old Babylonian Letters and Economic History," *Journal of the Economic and Social History of the Orient,* XI (1968), 171-226. Nimet Özgüc, "Assyrian Trade Colonies in Anatolia," *Archaeology,* XXII (1969), 250-255. H. W. F. Saggs, *The Greatness That Was Babylon,* New York: New American Library, a Mentor Book, 1962, pp. 262-287. Edwin Yamauchi, *Greece and Babylon,* Grand Rapids: Baker, 1967.

I. R.

COMMISSION, GREAT. The post-resurrection command of Jesus Christ to His disciples as recorded in Mt 28:19-20; Mk 16:15-18; Lk 24:46-49; Jn 20:21-23; and Acts 1:4-5, 8.

Its integrity. The authenticity and genuineness of the Great Commission passages, especially as found in Matthew and Mark, have been assailed by representatives of rationalism and higher criticism, the former on theological grounds and the latter on manuscript evidence. Evangelical scholarship, however, has defended both the genuineness as well as the authenticity of the passages and held its line well on the basis of internal and external evidences.

Its interpretation. The interpretation of the Great Commission passages has differed greatly through the centuries and has caused considerable discussion. Debate has revolved around numerous questions: Were these words spoken to the disciples as apostles of Jesus Christ? Did they constitute a part of the unique assignment to the apostolic office? Or were they addressed to the apostles as representatives of the church of Jesus Christ and thus are a part of the church's commission unto the end of the age? Again, what is the interrelationship between baptizing and teaching? Is the latter a coordinate with or a subordinate to the former since the conjunctive "and" is missing between vv. 19 and 20 of Mt 28? Or is teaching associated with baptizing and not merely subsequent to it? And how are baptizing and teaching related to making disciples? What is the real meaning of baptizing "into" the name? Why is the word "name" used in the singular when it is followed by an enumeration of the three persons of the Godhead?

Evangelical scholarship has sought to answer these questions very much in keeping with the presentation which follows, believing that the commission is addressed to the church and must be obeyed to the end of the age, and that it must be interpreted in the light of total revelation.

Few commentators deal exhaustively with the Great Commission passages. Recently two exegetical studies of note have appeared. The first is by Karl Barth, the second by Robert D. Culver. Neither man attempts to investigate the full scope of the Great Commission; both limit their studies to the Gospel of Matthew passage. Thus these are only partial considerations of the Great Commission.

Its relationship to Christianity. The Great Commission is not an isolated command arbitrarily imposed upon Christianity. It is a logical summation and natural outflow of the character of God as He is revealed in the Scriptures (Ezk 33:11; I Tim 2:4; II Pet 3:9); of the missionary purpose and thrust of God as unfolded in the OT (e.g., Isa 49:6; 56:3–8; Jon 3:10; 4:2, 11), and historically incarnated in the calling of Israel (Gen 12:1–3; Ex 19:5–6; Isa 42:6–7, 19); of the life, theology and saving work of Christ as disclosed in the Gospels (Mt 9:35–11:1; Lk 19:10; Jn 10:16); of the nature and work of the Holy Spirit as predicted by our Lord and manifested on and after Pentecost (Acts 2:17; 13:2, 4; 16:6–10); and of the nature and design of the church of Jesus Christ as made known in Acts (2:9–11, 21, 39; 13:46–49; 15:7–18) and the epistles (Rom 10:18; Eph 2:11–22; 3:8–11; Col 1:6, 23). Christ prophetically declared that His gospel will be preached throughout the whole world as a testimony to all nations before the end comes (Mt 24:14). The fulfillment of this is previewed in the heavenly scene described in Rev 7:9–10. The commission is thus firmly anchored in the total body of revelation, both OT and NT. It forms an organic unit and an integral part within that revelation, and receives its true meaning and force only if seen in this larger relationship.

The Great Commission does not make Christianity a missionary religion. The latter is such because of its source, nature, and total design. The apostles became missionaries not because of a commission but because Christianity is what it is and because of the indwelling Holy Spirit who is a Spirit of missions. Christ Himself speaks of the mission of the Holy Spirit as a witnessing mission (Jn 15:26; 16:8–15). Thus, if the particular words of the Great Commission had never been spoken, or if having been spoken they had not been recorded or preserved, the missionary thrust and responsibility of the church would not be in the least affected. The thrust of missions prospers wherever Christianity is truly known, thoroughly believed and genuinely experienced.

Its value. Nevertheless, it is of immense value that the Great Commission was spoken by our Lord and recorded by the Holy Spirit through the Gospel writers. While it does not create new duties for Christianity, this final order of Jesus Christ sharply focuses the missionary thrust and responsibility beyond reasonable doubting and disputing. Again, its singularity as the principal command of the Lord in His resurrection ministry marks it off as unique among His words and makes it more than just one commission among many commands to the disciples. Its restatement by every one of the Gospel writers witnesses to its living tradition in the early church, and the book of Acts demonstrates its dynamic in the original movement of Christianity.

Its composite nature. The Great Commission is a composite command. Its record in all four Gospels and in Acts is unique among the words of Christ and points up its significance in the mind of each writer, its richness and fullness of content, and the unity and design of each of the Gospels. They all culminate in the Great Commission and point in a common direction. Christianity is centrifugal in nature and thrust.

The fact that each of the four evangelists gives the Great Commission in one form or another needs to be noted. No one gives it in its completeness. While each of the evangelists presents it from his own point of view and with his own emphasis, together they supplement each other, making a complete whole as the following outline shows:

Matthew – the authority, the all-inclusive goal and the time-extension of the work
Mark – the method and geographical scope of the work
Luke – the message and the universality of the work
John – the spiritual equipment and the spiritual nature of the work

Only as we see the whole outline as presented in the four Gospels do we see the total Great Commission.

Its scope and pattern. An analysis of the Great Commission reveals two imperatives in the original Gr. that give direction to the commission. These are found in Matthew and Mark in the words "make disciples" and "preach the gospel." Thus the Great Commission is like an ellipse with its twofold foci. While in former years of the modern missionary movement beginning with William Carey the emphasis was upon the Markan focus – "preach the gospel" – and evangelism was the all-out thrust of missions, the emphasis today is upon Matthew's focus – "make disciples" – and church planting has come to the foreground. The Bible would emphasize both and keep them in proper balance. The two imperatives are supplemented by the participles "going" (Mk 16:15; Mt

28:19), "baptizing" (Mt 28:19; cf. Mk 16:16), "teaching" (Mt 28:20).

There are no imperative verbs relative to witnessing or preaching in Luke, John or Acts. However, there is a scriptural ("thus it is written," Lk 24:46) and a spiritual ("receive ye the Holy Spirit," Jn 20:22) force back of these words so that a command to witness is not necessary; indeed, it would seem out of place. The dynamic of the Word and the Spirit take the place of the imperative.

A study, then, of the composite Great Commission as recorded in the four Gospels produces the following facts. The all-inclusive *goal* is to *"make disciples"* of all nations. In order to accomplish this purpose:

1. Christians must engage in an intensive and extensive heralding of the gospel among the nations of the world, communicating meaningfully the gospel of God as recorded in the Scriptures.
2. Christians must lead people into an experience of the grace of God made available through the death and resurrection of Jesus Christ and offering forgiveness of sin in His name to all who will believe the gospel.
3. Christians must separate people from their old sinful relationships (without deculturizing them) and build them into the new congregation of God through the practice of baptism.
4. Christians must indoctrinate them in the precepts of the Master and thus by the renewing of their minds mold them into true Christian discipleship.

Such is the pattern of our ministry according to the Great Commission. None of the essentials may be omitted or neglected. Neither does time exhaust the dynamics nor the validity of the commission. Christ's commands bind every Christian to the task until the end of the age. *See* Evangelists; Witness.

Bibliography. Karl Barth, *The Theology of the Christian Mission,* ed. by Gerald Andersen, New York: McGraw-Hill. Robert D. Culver, "What Is the Church's Commission? Some Exegetical Issues in Matthew 28:16-20," ***Bulletin*** *of Evangelical Theological Society,* X (1967), 115-126. Joachim Jeremias, *Jesus' Promise to the Nations,* trans. S. H. Hooke, Naperville, Ill.: Allenson, 1958, includes an excellent bibliography. George E. Mendenhall, "Missions," IDB, III, 404 ff. John R. W. Stott, "The Great Commission," ChT, XII (1968), 723-725, 778-782, 826-829. John M. L. Young, "Theology of Missions, Covenant-centered," CT, XIII (1968), 162-165.

G. W. P.

COMMUNION. *See* Lord's Supper.

COMMUNION OF SAINTS. Gr. *koinōnia,* translatable as "communion" or "fellowship," designates a common sharing or participation in something. It (and its cognate forms) describes the fellowship of true believers with their Lord and with one another. The essential teachings regarding this truth may be set forth thus:

Communion arises out of the new birth (Jn 3:1-12), and is therefore restricted to those who are "in Christ" (II Cor 5:17). Their common spiritual paternity makes them one common brotherhood (Heb 2:11-13).

Thus communion represents the spiritual unity that binds believers to Jesus Christ and to each other (Jn 15:1-10; 17:21, 23; Eph 4:3-16). This unity transcends natural bounds (Gal 3:28; Col 3:11), although it does not thereby abolish providential differences between believers (I Cor 7:20-24; Eph 6:5-9).

This communion finds its visible outlet in the mutual sharing of material blessings (Rom 12:13; 15:26-27; II Cor 8:4; 9:9-14; Gal 6:6; Phil 4:14-16). In the apostolic community at Pentecost this sharing took the form of a community of goods, although it is not evident that this innovation became a precedent for subsequent times (but cf. I Tim 6:18; Heb 13:16).

On a higher level, communion provides for the free use of spiritual gifts, even though these gifts are not equally bestowed upon all believers (Mt 25:15; I Cor 12:1-31). Within the Christian community places of leadership are just as important as places of submission (Phil 2:29; I Thess 5:12-13; II Thess 3:14; Heb 13:7, 17).

Restricted to the regenerated, the communion of saints necessarily excludes all other relationships incompatible with it. The child of God can no longer participate on the spiritual level in the plans and programs of unregenerate humanity (Ps 1:1-2; 26:4-5; I Cor 5:9-11; II Cor 6:14-18; Eph 5:7, 11; I Tim 5:22).

This communion may be interrupted or hindered either by sin (I Cor 5:1-7; I Jn 1:6-10), or by error in conduct (II Thess 3:6-15), or in doctrine (I Jn 2:19; II Jn 9-11). It is therefore very necessary for the believer to safeguard his life scrupulously (I Cor 6:1-20).

In the present life the communion of saints finds its highest realization in the fellowship with the Triune God (I Cor 1:9; II Cor 13:14; Phil 2:1; I Jn 1:3). In Christ's sufferings (Phil 3:10; I Pet 4:13) the believer finds a fellowship that is visibly portrayed in the Lord's Supper (I Cor 10:16, 20-21; 11:20-34).

This blessed communion reaches its consummation in the eternal fellowship of believers with the Triune God and with one another (Ps 73:23-26; Mt 8:11; Heb 12:22-24). This communion constitutes a paramount blessing of the glory of heaven (Rev 5:9-14; 7:9-17). *See* Fellowship.

W. B.

COMMUNITY OF GOODS. With a large segment of the world's population under the political and economic control of communism and with an increasingly widespread discussion of communist theory everywhere in the world, the question often arises whether the Bible recommends or even enjoins communal ownership of goods.

It is true that Jesus commanded a rich young ruler to sell his goods and give to the poor (Lk 18:18–30), but the reason for the command was to test the extent of his faith, not to enforce a social or economic leveling. It should be remembered that on another occasion when the disciples argued that Mary's anointing of the Master was a waste and that the money might better be given to the poor, Jesus remarked, "Ye have the poor always with you; but me ye have not always" (Mt 26:11).

As far as the early church and Scripture regarding it are concerned, there is only one locale where communal ownership of goods was practiced and only two passages referring to it. In Jerusalem, after the descent of the Holy Spirit on Pentecost, the brethren of the new fellowship of Christians enjoyed a remarkable unity, extending to holding all things in common. Those who had wealth pooled it, and all drew from the common treasury as they had need (Acts 2:44–45).

After an outbreak of persecution, the Holy Spirit again moved upon the believers in Jerusalem. Again it is said that they held all things in common; no one was in need. Barnabas was singled out as a well-to-do person who sold property and contributed to the common treasury. In this context appears the account of the death of Ananias and Sapphira. They sold property too, but were more concerned with a reputation for philanthropy than for honesty. They kept back part of the proceeds though they said they gave all as they presented their gift to the common treasury. God would not condone sin in the nascent Christian church any more than in the early days of Heb. national occupation of Canaan (when He judged Achan, Josh 7), and He struck down both Ananias and Sapphira. Power was linked to purity in the launching of the Christian church (Acts 4:32–5:11).

What conclusions may be drawn, then, concerning the biblical approach to communism? In the first place, the Bible certainly does not support Marxist Communism with its anti-God philosophy and its concept of class warfare. Numerous passages (e.g., Eph 6:5–9; Col 3:22–4:1) admonish good relations between workers and employers. Second, communal ownership of property among believers seems to have been restricted to Jerusalem. Whether in Antioch of Syria, Philippi or Thessalonica, believers practiced private ownership of property, and there is no indication they were encouraged to pool their resources. They were, however, urged to give to various collections for the poor saints in Jerusalem. Moreover, there is no proof that communal ownership of property continued indefinitely in Jerusalem. Furthermore, apparently communal ownership of property was optional in Jerusalem. In his judgment, Peter focused on Ananias' dishonesty. He made it clear that Ananias did not have to sell his property, and once he did, he did not have to give the proceeds to the common treasury. His sin was in claiming to have given all, when he held back a part (Acts 5:3–4).

There seems to have been a special, temporary need for a communal ownership of property in Jerusalem. Many Jews of the Dispersion, in Jerusalem for the Jewish feast of Pentecost, were converted and lingered on, enjoying spiritual blessing. There was little means of support for them. Probably many of them would have been cut off by their families socially and economically if they had returned home. Likewise, many Palestinian Jews were cut off from their society after conversion and no longer had a means of livelihood. Moreover, at best Jerusalem Jews in NT times had a difficult economic position. The economic pinch on believers there was great indeed. A communal treasury seemed necessary for the time being, as did numerous collections by Paul for the "poor saints in Jerusalem."

If believers today wish to live in an arrangement where Christians have communal ownership of goods, they should feel free to do so; but the Scripture does not oblige them to live in this fashion. And they should not sit in judgment on other believers who prefer to enjoy the private ownership of property. All should remember that they are merely stewards of all God has given them and that they are enjoined to exercise a faithful stewardship of possessions entrusted to them. *See* Fellowship; Steward.

H. F. V.

COMPASS. Various Heb. words are used. The noun forms suggest a circle or sphere (Prov 8:27; Job 26:10); a compass, circuit, or margin (Ex 27:5; 38:4); compass or instrument for describing a circle (Isa 44:13); what is round about (I Kgs 7:35). The verb forms frequently mean to surround, go round about (Gen 2:11; Deut 2:1; Jer 31:22; Ps 18:4; Isa 50:11); to be or go round about (Josh 15:10; 18:14; 19:14); to encircle (I Sam 23:26; Lk 21:20); to set around (II Kgs 6:14); and other variations.

COMPASSION. *See* Mercy.

COMPEL. The English word carries the ideas both of force and persuasion. Several words convey various aspects of these ideas. (1) It may mean "to urge or constrain" (I Sam 28:23); (2) "to force" (II Chr 21:11), "to press" (Est 1:8), "impress" for service (Mt 5:41; 27:32), "to constrain" by force or entreaty (Lk 14:23).

CONANIAH (kŏn-*ȧ*-nī′*ȧ*). A chief of the Levites in the reign of King Josiah (II Chr 35:9).

CONCISION (Gr. *katatomē*, "to cut down or cut off," "mutilate").

Used by Paul once in Phil 3:2 where he

contemptuously speaks of physical circumcision, considered by the Judaizers to be necessary for salvation, as a type of mutilation in comparison with the true spiritual circumcision of those who worship God in the Spirit. He suggests that those who were unsettling the Galatians should mutilate (Gr. *peritomē*) themselves (Gal 5:12). This passage may refer to emasculation, such as found in the Cybele-Attis cult. In Col 2:10-11 Paul speaks of a circumcision "made without hands" in Christ, and equates it with baptism into Christ's death (cf. Rom 6:3-5). True circumcision then is that phase of baptism in which the Holy Spirit identifies the believer with all Christ has done for his justification. *See* Baptism; Circumcision.

CONCUBINE. Though lawfully united to a man in marriage, the concubine was a secondary type of wife and inferior to a full wife. Concubinage was a natural part of a polygamous society. The custom was recognized and regulated in the code of Hammurabi (13th cen. B.C.), and also in the laws of Moses (Ex 21:7-11; Deut 21:10-14). Concubines were usually taken from among Heb. or foreign slaves or from foreign captives. They enjoyed no particular rights in family affairs and could be sent away with a mere present and their children excluded from an inheritance (e.g., the sons of Hagar and Keturah, Gen 25:1-6). Though their children were regarded as legitimate, they were treated as secondary when it came to inheritances.

In patriarchal times following Mesopotamian customs concubines particularly served to continue the line of a family when the real wife was barren (Gen 16:3). Levirate marriage, on the other hand, supplied this need when the husband died without descendants. Then his brother was to take the widow to wife (Deut 25:5-10; cf. Mt 22:23 ff.).

Some men who had concubines in the OT were Nahor (Gen 22:24), Abraham (Gen 25:6), Jacob (Gen 35:22), Eliphaz (Gen 36:12), Gideon (Jud 8:31), Saul (II Sam 3:7), David (II Sam 5:13; 15:16; 16:21), and Solomon (I Kgs 11:3). The problems and dangers of the practice are shown in the OT, particularly in Solomon's case where his many wives and concubines caused him to permit pagan worship and thus to sin (I Kgs 11:1-8).

The later prophets encouraged monogamy (Mal 2:14 ff.). Prov 31 urges this as the ideal. In His teaching on marriage (Mt 19:3-9) Christ implied that polygamy was among the things permitted by Moses only because of the hardness of men's hearts (Mt 19:8), thus showing that it is excluded for all Christians. The teaching of the epistles is clear that any leader of a church must be the husband of only one woman (I Tim 3:2, 12; Tit 1:6), and that every believer should love his wife (singular) as himself (Eph 5:33). *See* Family; Marriage.

R. A. K.

CONCUPISCENCE (kŏn-kū′pĭ-sĕns). A term used theologically to express the evil desires and lusts which beset fallen man (Rom 7:8; Col 3:5; I Thess 4:5).

There exists a great difference of opinion among Roman Catholics over the true nature of this word, and between Catholics in general and Protestants. Augustine confined it to sexual lusts; others extended it to all inordinate desires, hence the lack of agreement. Aquinas saw it as sin, but in general Roman Catholics do not regard concupiscence itself as sin. The Council of Trent spoke in negative terms and straddled the issue. It was thought of as something that gives cause to sin. Man was created with it, and the *donum superadditum*, the added gift of original righteousness, held it in control until man fell. It is counteracted in baptism and by *gratia infusa*, infused grace, at regeneration. It is clear that it is something for which man cannot be held responsible when looked upon in this way.

The biblical Reformed view sees concupiscence as the lust which leads to sin, developed when man rebelled against God and fell. It is sinful in itself, and reveals the corruption of man's whole nature and sin in him. Not only acts of the will are sinful, but willful thoughts (Gen 6:5; Mt 5:28). Paul speaks of it in Rom 7 as that which caused him to sin. It can be conquered only through recognizing that the fallen nature in us is judged (Rom 8:3); then walking by the Spirit and letting Him keep the law of God in us (Rom 8:4), which is the Spirit-filled life. *See* Covetousness; Lust.

R. A. K.

CONDEMNATION (CONDEMN). An unfavorable decision or sentence rendered by either human or divine agency. In the OT, the verb "condemn" in almost every instance translates the Heb. word *rāsha'*, meaning "condemn as guilty," and is used in civil relations (Deut 25:1; Ps 94:21; Job 34:17) and in ethical and religious relations (Job 9:20; 10:2; Ps 37:33; Prov 12:2; Isa 50:9; 54:17).

In the NT, occasionally the English words "condemn" and "condemnation" are used to translate the shorter Gr. words for "judge" and "judgment" (*q.v.*). The context makes it clear whether it is simply a decision rendered or an unfavorable sentence imposed by God or man (cf. Jn 3:17, 19; 5:24; Lk 23:40; Jas 5:12).

The more frequent Gr. word is *katakrinō* and is to be distinguished from the previously mentioned words in that it refers either to the sentence or to the punishment following the sentence (MM, p. 328) rather than to the simple act of deciding in judgment. Only the context can determine the precise nature of the sentence. For example, in Mk 10:33 and Mt 20:18 the condemnation or sentence is to physical death; in II Cor 7:3 Paul refers to a condemnation or reprimand of behavior before others. In some places the reference is to God's condemnation and seems to refer to God's sentence of permanent judgment upon the sinner and all that that implies (Mt 12:41-42; I Cor 11:32; II Cor 3:9; II Pet 2:6).

In Rom 5:16, 18 Paul refers to the divine condemnation of the whole human race in Adam. While some make a distinction here between the sentence and its legal punishment or execution (e.g., Deissmann, *Bible Studies,* pp. 264 ff.), others perhaps rightly point out that in divine condemnation in distinction to human, the sentence and its execution—the beginning at least—can never be separated (TWNT, p. 951). For those who are "in Christ Jesus" there is no longer either the divine sentence or the legal punishment for sin resting upon them (Rom 8:1). The difficult expression of Paul that "God condemned sin in the flesh" (Rom 8:3) seems to assert that God both judged and executed punishment for man's sin upon Jesus who became flesh (incarnate).

A further word *(katadikazō)* is used in basically the same sense as *katakrinō* for the rich landlords punishing the poor innocent laborers (Jas 5:6); for the words untruthfully spoken and held as evidence to sentence those who reject Christ (Mt 12:37); for the act of holding persons personally guilty rather than acquitting them (Lk 6:37); and for the Pharisees' pronouncement upon the disciples of their guilt for threshing and eating grain on the sabbath day (Mt 12:7).

A somewhat different word *(kataginōskō)* is used in I Jn 3:20-21 concerning our heart condemning us. The word means to "scorn" and is used of self-judgment, perhaps in the idea of "guilt feeling," and admits either to the sense that God is behind the guilt feeling showing us that something is wrong, or that God's knowledge is greater than our own feeling of guilt and we should persuade our hearts to His point of view (cf. Rom 14:22; Gal 2:11).

A. F. J.

CONDUIT. Expressed in Heb. by *te'ālâ,* "channel," "trench"; in Gr. by *hydragōgos,* "water carrier," "irrigation channel"; and in Latin by *aquaeductus,* "conduit," "aqueduct."

Usually a conduit was an open trench running along the surface of the ground; but there were also underground piped channels. Remains of numerous conduits may be seen in the Near East; for example, at Caesarea, Qumran, and Jerusalem. Clay pipes fitted into stone blocks can be seen at Laodicea. Such a conduit brought water from the neighboring hills. Biblical references are to the water works of Jerusalem in Isaiah's time (II Kgs 18:17; 20:20; Isa 7:3; 36:2; cf. Sir 24:30; 48:17; FLAP, pp. 190 f.).

Roman aqueduct at Caesarea. HFV

CONEY. *See* Animals, II.9.

CONFECTION. A perfume made by the temple apothecary (Ex 30:35). The KJV translates the same term as "ointment" while the ASV has "confection," referring to a mixture of medicines or perfumes made by the sons of the priests (I Chr 9:30).

CONFECTIONARY. This term is found only once in the KJV of the OT. I Sam 8:13 reads: "He will take your daughters to be confectionaries" ("perfumers," ASV). They seemed to have formed part of a perfumers' guild (Neh 3:8; II Chr 16:14).

CONFECTIONER. *See* Occupations: Perfumer.

CONFESSION. The word means to make an open avowal, usually with undertones of a change of position. Nearly all the biblical passages can be classified under two heads: a confession of sin, or a confession of faith. Confession of sin is made to God (Ps 32:3-6; I Jn 1:9), to the one who has been wronged (Lk 17:4), to a spiritual adviser (II Sam 12:13), or to the congregation of believers (I Cor 5:3 ff.; cf. II Cor 2:6 f.). Confession of faith is to be made openly before men (Mt 10:32; Rom 10:9; I Tim 6:12-13; Heb 3:1; 4:14; 10:23). In the end, all men will be forced to confess the lordship of Christ (Phil 2:11). *See* Forgiveness.

Bibliography. Otto Michel, "*Homologeō,* etc.," TDNT, V, 199-220. John R. W. Stott, *Confess Your Sins: The Way of Reconciliation,* Philadelphia: Westminster Press, 1964.

CONFIDENCE. *See* Boldness.

CONFUSION OF TONGUES. *See* Babel; Tongues, Confusion of.

CONGREGATION. The Heb. words *qāhāl* ("assembly") and *'ēdâ* ("congregation") are the most frequently used terms to designate a gathering of Israel for religious or political purposes (BDB). It has been supposed, on the basis of Ex 12:6 and Num 14:5, that the "assembly" constituted only a part of the "congregation";

Water channel atop the Roman aqueduct at Caesarea. HFV

but this distinction, in the light of Lev 4:13 and Num 16:3 (ASV and RSV), cannot be pressed too far. Prov 5:14 uses the two terms as synonyms.

The only valid distinction between these terms seems to be in the fact that *qāhāl* represents Israel as the ideal people of God, whereas *'ēdâ* designates the nation as a political entity here upon earth. This latent meaning of *qāhāl* in certain messianic passages in the Psalms (22:22, 25; 35:18; 40:9-10; 89:5; 107:32; 149:1) puts this term in the forefront as the spiritual prototype of the Christian *ekklēsia* ("church"). Justification for this word parallelism may be seen in the quotation of Ps 22:22 in Heb 2:12, where *qāhāl* is translated by *ekklēsia*. However, *'ēdâ* also has its spiritual implications (Ps 1:5; 74:2).

It should be noted that ASV translates *qāhāl* as "assembly" in all places except in Genesis (28:3; 35:11; 48:4), Jeremiah (31:8; 44:15; 50:9), and Ezekiel (16:40; 17:17; 23:24, 46-47; 26:7; 27:27, 34; 32:3, 22-23; 38:4, 7, 13, 15). "Assembly" is, however, used in Jer 26:17; and strangely, "congregation" is found in II Chr 31:18. "Company" is used in the passages noted as exceptions. On the other hand, ASV translates *'ēdâ* as "congregation" in all places except where, designedly, it uses "swarm" (Jud 14:8), "multitude" (Ps 68:30) and "company" (Num 16:5 f., 11, 16, 40; 27:3; Job 15:34; 16:7; Ps 22:16; 86:14; 106:17-18).

Membership in the congregation of Israel was on the basis of circumcision (Gen 17:1-14). However, "strangers" could become members by submitting to this same rite (Ex 12:48 f.). They thus assumed the same rights and responsibilities as native-born Israelites (Ex 12:19; Num 9:14; 15:15 f., 29). Membership could be lost ("cut off") by rebellion against God's laws (Gen 17:14; Ex 12:15, 19; 31:14; Lev 17:10, 14; Num 9:13; Ezr 10:8). Some were automatically excluded because of physical deformity or ancestral sins (Deut 23:1-8; Neh 13:1-3; Lam 1:10).

The congregation was called together by trumpets (Num 10:2-8). Such purposes as the following justified the calling of the congregation: to receive new legislation (Lev 8:1-4); to perform religious ceremonies (Ex 12:47; II Chr 30:1-13); to hear important messages (Josh 23:2; 24:1; Ezr 8:15 f.); to act on moral issues (Jud 20:1; Ezr 10:1-19); to ratify a covenant (II Chr 15:9-15); to crown a king (I Sam 10:17-25; II Sam 5:1-3; I Kgs 12:20). Often, however, the nation was represented by elders and/or chiefs (Ex 3:16; 4:29 f.; 12:21; 17:5; 24:1, 9-11; 34:31 f.; Num 31:13). Their decisions were accepted as final (Josh 9:15, 18; 22:30-34; Ezr 10:14, 16).

The congregation of Israel during and after the conquest of Canaan met at such places as Shiloh (Josh 18:1; 22:12), Shechem (Josh 24:1, 25), and Mizpeh (Jud 10:17; 11:11; 20:1; I Sam 10:17). The congregation met at Hebron to crown David king (II Sam 5:1-3), but afterward Jerusalem became the focal point of national gatherings (I Chr 13:2; 15:29; II Chr 23:2 f.; 30:1-13, 25-26). The Jews continued to make Jerusalem their national center after returning from exile in Babylon (Ezr 10:1, 9).

In two passages in the NT (Heb 10:25; Jas 2:2), the Christian gathering is called a synagogue (*synagogē*). Once Israel is called an *ekklēsia* (Acts 7:38). But *ekklēsia*, "a called out group," eventually became the specific term for the Christian church as the divide between the church and Judaism grew wider and wider. Although some features of the church, e.g., rule by elders (Acts 15:2, 23), undoubtedly came from the Heb. "congregation," the church was a new society, a separate community. It was made up of men of various nations and classes who by salvation were transformed into "one body in Christ": they were no longer Jews or Gentiles, slaves or freemen (Gal 3:28-29; Col 3:11, 15). Their new citizenship was in heaven (Phil 3:20, NASB).

The members of this new congregation were commanded to keep themselves "unstained by the world" (Jas 1:27, NASB), because friendship with the world (Jas 4:4) crowds out love for God (I Jn 2:15-17). They could expect persecution from the world. While they did not belong to the world, their Leader had not chosen to remove them from the world (Jn 17:14-15) and had given them a responsibility to win as many from the world as possible (*see*

Commission, Great). Thus the Christian church as a whole has not isolated itself from the rest of human society. *See* Assembly; Church; Synagogue.

Bibliography. John W. Flight, "Man and Society," IDB, III, 250 ff. Marvin H. Pope, "Congregation, Assembly," IDB, I, 669 f. J. A. Selbie, "Congregation," HDB, I, 466-467.

W. B.

CONGREGATION, MOUNT OF THE. This phrase is found in Isa 14:13, which places the mountain in the sides or recesses of the N. It does not refer to Zion, for Zion was neither in the northern part of the earth nor was it located to the N of Jerusalem. In his predictive taunt song Isaiah depicts the kings of the nations speaking to the king of Babylon (cf. v. 4) in terms of the thinking of his people, who did not have the throne of their god in the midst of them as did the Israelites. The Babylonians placed the abode of their god on the summit of the northern mountains which were lost in the clouds. The high boast of the Babylonian king of self-deification, inspired by Satan (Lucifer), doomed him to be cast down to the lowest depths. Various terms in Isa 14:12-14, RSV, such as "Day Star," "son of Dawn," "the Most High," and "the mount of assembly" of the gods, are common also in Canaanite mythology as known from the Ras Shamra (*q.v.*) texts. The Canaanites located this mountain at Jebel 'Aqra, N of Ugarit. *See* Lucifer.

W. B.

CONGREGATION, TABERNACLE OF. *See* Tabernacle.

CONIAH (kō-nī'ȧ). This king of Judah is called Coniah in Jer 22:24, 28; 37:1, but he was known also as Jeconiah and Jehoiachin *(q.v.)*.

CONONIAH (kŏn-ō-nī'ȧ). A Levite, appointed with his brother Shimei by Hezekiah the king and Azariah the ruler of the house of God, to oversee the oblations, tithes and dedicated things (II Chr 31:12-13).

CONQUEST. *See* Exodus, The; Joshua; Joshua, Book of.

CONSCIENCE. Conscience is that faculty of a person that tells him he ought to do that which he believes to be right and that he ought not to do that which he believes to be wrong. It is not that by which one distinguishes right and wrong, since that is learned from teaching or environment, but that which prods one to do right and to refrain from wrong. The apostle Paul once did wrong, yet in a "good conscience" (Acts 23:1), which means that he was misinformed as to right conduct, but he still did that which he at that time believed right.

Conscience is an innate characteristic, found universally in men, that becomes active when one reaches the age of accountability. It is the "sense of moral awareness" or of *oughtness* in man, called the "categorical imperative" by Kant. The word is from the same root meaning as the words for consciousness and conscientiousness, but in its common NT usage means moral awareness. The conscience serves: (1) to accuse or excuse us (Rom 2:14-15), (2) to punish us when violated, and (3) to give us a sense of divine approval as well as self-approval when we do right. This is true since the very existence of the conscience calls for the existence of a Moral Governor of the universe, to whom we must all some day give account. *See* Law.

Bibliography. Christian Maurer, "*Synoida, Syneidēsis,*" TDNT, VII, 898-919. Roy B. Zuck, "The Doctrine of the Conscience," BS, CXXVI (1969), 329-340.

J. D. T.

CONSECRATION. This is primarily an OT word in the KJV and is used to translate a number of Heb. verbs and their derivative nouns (*ḥāram,* "to devote"; *qādash,* "to set apart"; *mālē',* "to fill the hand"; and *nāzar,* "to separate"). The common idea of these Heb. words brought out in KJV seems to be that of setting something or someone apart to the peculiar service of the Lord: priests (Ex 28:1-3; 30:30), things (Josh 6:19), feast days (Ezr 3:5), sacrifices (Lev 7:37), gain (Mic 4:13). The word is also used to describe the procedure by which one who has been defiled may regain admittance to the Lord (Num 6:7-12).

In the NT, the KJV uses the word to translate two Gr. words. Heb 10:20 declares that Jesus has consecrated (*enkainizō,* "renewed") a new and living way to God. Heb 7:28 shows that Jesus is eternally consecrated (*teleioō,* "perfected") as our great High Priest.

RSV prefers to use this word to translate *hagiazō,* usually translated in KJV by "sanctify" or "sanctification." The root idea is still that of separating from secular (worldly) use to divine service. There are a few instances of things being separated to God (cf. Mt 23:17, 19), but primarily the idea is that of separating people to God. The emphasis shifts from the exceptional individual to the whole body of Christians. The act of consecration takes place primarily at the time of conversion. The actor is always God; the object is man (cf. Heb 2:11). However, the idea of separation to and equipment for service is found in the case of Jesus (Jn 17:19) who is said to have consecrated Himself, and of the apostles (Jn 17:17) whom God so consecrated. A few passages seem to involve the growth or development of the Christian in holy living (cf. I Thess 5:23).

Of particular interest is the fact that the adjective for this verb *(hagios)* is one of the most common designations for the believer, usually translated "saint." The idea in the word is that every believer is a saint, a consecrated one, one who is separated from the world and belongs to God. Being a saint is our vocation, and becoming saintly is our goal in life. The modern practice of applying the word only to great Christians, especially of a previous age, is completely unbiblical. The biblical usage justifies us in saying that every true believer is a saint; he has been consecrated by God to Himself through Jesus Christ. *See* Saint; Dedicate.

F. L. F.

CONSOLATION. *See* Comfort; Holy Spirit.

CONSTELLATIONS. *See* Astronomy; Star.

CONSUMPTION

1. Heb. *shaḥepheth,* "wasting away." A punishment which would follow disobedience to God and His laws (Lev 26:16; Deut 28:22). Other diseases and punishments are also listed.

2. Heb. *kālâ,* "destruction," "completion," or "full end." The KJV uses the term "consumption," but the ASV and RSV use the terms "destruction" (Isa 10:23; 28:22), "full end" and "decreed end" (Dan 9:27).

3. In Isa 10:22, "consumption" ("full end," RSV) is the rendering of a different Heb. term from the above references.

CONTENTION. Several Heb. and Gr. words are used to suggest contention, strife, and wrangling. The contention may be physical, oral, or spiritual. It may describe a man's nature (Jer 15:10; Hab 1:3). Pride may bring contention (Prov 13:10). Christians are admonished to avoid contentious wrangling (I Cor 1:11; Tit 3:9). The sharp dispute between Barnabas and Paul (Acts 15:39) may refer more to a state of irritation and inner incitement than to an outward expression of contention.

CONTENTMENT. "The acceptance of 'things as they are' as the wise and loving providence of a God who knows what is good for us, who so loves us as always to seek our good" (IDB).

Moses was content to dwell with Jethro (Ex 2:21). The brothers of Joseph were pleased to listen to Judah in selling Joseph (Gen 37:27). Jesus urges contentment (Mt 6:19–34) with regard to desires for material things. John the Baptist urged the Roman soldiers to be content with their wages (Lk 3:14). Paul reminds Timothy that godliness with contentment is great gain (I Tim 6:6–8). The secret of contentment lies in the Christian's fellowship and union with God (Phil 4:11–13; 3:8–9).

CONTRACT. *See* Covenant.

CONTRITION. Found only in the OT in KJV (cf. Ps 34:18; Isa 57:15; Ps 51:17; Isa 66:2). The literal meaning of the word is to be bruised or broken. Biblical usage is limited to a description of the worshiper who approaches God with a "crushed" spirit over his sins. The implication is always that God will receive and forgive one who comes to Him in such a spirit. A NT parallel is found in II Cor 7:10 where "godly sorrow" for sin is looked upon as a precondition of true repentance. Possibly parallel in thought is the beatitude, "Blessed are they that mourn: for they shall be comforted" (Mt 5:4).

CONVERSATION. The KJV translation of Heb. *derek,* "way (of life)" in Ps 37:14; 50:23, and of Gr. *anastrophē, politeuma,* and *tropos* (once, Heb 13:5). This 17th cen. meaning of conversation always connoted ethical and moral conduct, behavior, or life-style in contrast with the modern meaning of the term as social intercourse and friendly talk.

The Gr. words translated "conversation" in Phil 1:27 (*politeuō*) and 3:20 (*politeuma*) refer to discharging one's obligations as a citizen in his civil life and to "citizenship," respectively.

The KJV uniformly rendered the 13 occurrences of the noun *anastrophē* by "conversation," whereas the modern English versions have employed a variety of terms to render the word; e.g., "manner of life," "behavior," "conduct." In Paul's epistles KJV has "ye have heard of my conversation" (Gal 1:13); "put off concerning the former conversation" (Eph 4:22); and "be thou an example . . . in conversation" (I Tim 4:12). Paul used the verb *anastrephō* in II Cor 1:12, "we have had our conversation in the world"; in Eph 2:3, "we all had our conversation in times past"; and in I Tim 3:15, where KJV does have "how thou oughtest to behave thyself in the house of God."

Peter employed the noun frequently in exhorting his readers to demonstrate holy, honorable, chaste conduct in keeping with a holy life (I Pet 1:15; 2:12; 3:2, 16; II Pet 3:11). By her godly behavior the Christian wife may without nagging win her husband who is disobedient to the word of God (I Pet 3:1). James used the noun in 3:13 to teach that individual deeds of the man with godly wisdom must stem from consistent good behavior. Heb 13:7 speaks of the model behavior of Christian leaders, "whose faith follow, considering the end of their conversation."

Placed in a contemporary setting, the dynamic Christian life is relevant. By his words and deeds the Christian communicates meaningfully the truth of God which he has believed and received into his own life. Honesty and love are the normal experiences of Christian living (Heb 13:18), in contrast with the deceitful, vain and filthy life-style of the non-Christian (I Pet 1:18; II Pet 2:7, 18). *See* Example; Liberty.

H. W. N.

CONVERSION. This means literally to turn, and is used to translate the Heb. word *shûb,* and the Gr. word *strephō* and its derivatives, especially *epistrephō.* The words are sometimes used in the Bible in a literal sense of turning physically to or from something (cf. Mt 9:22; Acts 9:40). The meaning which is primary and spiritual denotes a spiritual revolution. It is used in the bad sense of being converted from the right to the wrong in two passages (Gal 4:9; II Pet 2:21). However, the good meaning of turning from the undesirable to the desirable is the usual one. In this sense, it is used both of unbelievers and Christians.

When used of unbelievers, it denotes the change of heart or mind (related to repentance and faith) which enables one to receive the grace of God in salvation (cf. Acts 3:19). Though conversion is thought of as an act of man in contrast to justification and regeneration which are solely acts of God, the implication is always present that thoroughgoing conversion can only be accomplished by the help of the Holy Spirit. Conversion implies a complete repudiation of sin and a trustful surrender to Christ as Lord. *See* Repentance.

When used of believers, it denotes a return to a proper relationship with God which may have been broken by moral failure (cf. Peter, Lk 22:32) or by departure from true doctrine (cf. Jas 5:19–20).

The spiritual use of this word is illustrative of the fact that the Christian vocabulary, at first, was primarily figurative. The necessity of expressing spiritual concepts without an established vocabulary drove the apostles to adopt many common words and convert them to their own uses.

Bibliography. Georg Bertram, "*Strephō*, etc.," TDNT, VII, 714–729.

F. L. F.

CONVICTION. Used only in the NT and primarily with the meaning of bringing one to a realization of his own guilt or attempting to do so. The Gr. word *elegchō* is variously translated in the KJV by "convict," "convince," "reprove," "rebuke," and "tell one's fault." The various means by which conviction is brought about are: the reproof of a wronged brother (Mt 18:15); the message of the preacher (cf. Lk 3:19; I Tim 5:20; II Tim 4:2; Tit 1:9, 13; 2:15); the Holy Spirit dwelling in the congregation (Jn 16:8); coming to the light (Jn 3:20; Eph 5:13); the law (Jas 2:9); the Lord (Heb 12:5; Rev 3:19); the church (Eph 5:11; I Cor 14:24); and the coming of the Lord (Jude 14–15).

Faith is said to be the means by which men come to a conviction of the truth of creation (Heb 11:3). The Jews were challenged to convict Jesus of any sin (Jn 8:46); perhaps the judicial idea of convicting by evidence in court is approximated in this passage. In general, conviction is thought of in the NT as a necessary precondition to repentance and conversion.

F. L. F.

CONVOCATION. A religious gathering on a sabbath or certain sacred days. Usually "holy" precedes the word (Lev 23:2–4, 7–8, 21, 24, 27, 35–37; Num 28:18). It is a technical phrase in priestly regulations. The same Heb. words appear elsewhere (Ex 12:16: Isa 1:13; 4:5) meaning a "solemn assembly." A summoned assembly held under particularly holy circumstances for the observance of sacred rites and occasions, such a convocation was part of the great festivals in Israel. They were called sabbaths and were regarded as rest days. Such assemblies belonged to the picture of eschatalogical hope (Isa 4:5). The same Heb. word (without the qualifying "holy") is once used in the sense of "reading aloud" from the Torah (Neh 8:8). Jews came to use the term as a synonym for Scripture.

COOK, COOKING. *See* Food; Occupations: Cooks.

COOS (kō'ŏs). An island off the coast of Asia Minor near the province of Caria, 111 square miles in area. It was at the entrance to the Thermaic Gulf. The island is famous as a fertile place and as an emporium for various products and for banking. Coos (or Cos) lay on the main shipping route between Greece and the E. Josephus states that Herod the Great provided for perpetual annual revenues for the people of Coos to maintain the office of Gymnasiarch (see *Wars* i.21.11). An important inscription has been found on the island which mentions Herod Antipas, tetrarch of Galilee. This inscription can be translated: "To Herod [the] Tetrarch, son of Herod the Great, Philo, son of Aglaos [by adoption?], but by physical nature son of Nikon, his host [lit., 'guest friend'] and friend of Herod the Tetrarch [has erected this monument]."

Just when Herod Antipas made a journey to Coos is not certain, but it was probably in connection with a stop he also made on the island of Delos some time during A.D. 6–10. Around the year A.D. 6, Archelaus, his brother, who had been ethnarch of Judea, was removed and likely Herod Antipas made a trip to Rome at that time to protect his own interest, which might have been threatened, since he gave a donation about this time to the temple of Apollo on the island of Delos. It is highly probable that at this same time he also gave new benefits which his father Herod the Great had earlier provided (see above reference in Josephus). The inscription, therefore, is likely to be dated at that time.

Coos is mentioned in the NT in Acts 21:1 in connection with Paul's final journey to Jerusalem. It was natural that the famous island of Coos should be mentioned in connection with Paul's journey. It was a well-known and historic isle (it is mentioned as early as Homer) and as such was a well-known landmark. Coos was the site of the first school of scientific medicine.

Here the great Hippocrates, father of medicine, practiced early in the 4th cen. B.C.

One of the best short descriptions of Coos is by W. M. Ramsay in HDB. The island is referred to in Strabo, *Geography,* p. 657 ff.

E. J. V.

COPING. An obscure architectural term used in connection with the building of the temple by Solomon (I Kgs 7:9). It reads: "All these were made of costly stones, hewn according to measure . . . from the foundation to the coping" (RSV). It evidently refers to the highest or covering course in the wall. *See* Architecture.

COPPER. *See* Minerals and Metals.

COPPERSMITH. *See* Occupations.

COPY. *See* Type.

COR. *See* Weights, Measures, and Coins.

CORAL. *See* Animals, V.1; Jewels.

CORBAN (kôr'băn). A sacred gift, money or service dedicated to God to be used for a religious purpose (Lev 1:2; 2:1; 3:1; Num 7:12-17; Mk 7:11). The Pharisees, who were zealots for the temple, held that when a person said to his father or mother concerning his possessions, "That wherewith thou mightest have been profited by me is Corban" (Mk 7:11, ASV), the possessions were consecrated to God and he was released from using any of them to benefit his parent. Jesus condemned this practice as a casuistic use of religion to avoid the obligation of the commandment to honor father and mother by aiding them in their needs. Josephus (*Wars* ii.9.4) shows that Corban money could not be diverted for secular use even if for public welfare. *See* Vows.

Bibliography. K. H. Rengstorf, *"Korban,"* TDNT, III, 860-866.

CORD. Used to translate the Heb. words *ḥebel, ḥûṭ, yeter, mêtār, 'ăbōt,* and the Gr. *schoinion,* the most frequent being *ḥebel.* The meaning includes not only cord or rope but also string, thread, twine, measuring line, bowstring, etc. The materials used depended on what was available for the strength required. They included flax, goat's hair, camel's hair, date tree fibers, reeds, rushes. Strong cords were made of camel's hide, still used by the Bedouin for drawing water.

The following are some of the uses of this word in the OT: (1) To lower men over walls and Jeremiah into a dungeon (Josh 2:15; Jer 38:6, 11-13). (2) To drag stones so as to destroy a city, or to draw a cart (II Sam 17:13; Isa 5:18). (3) As the tacklings of ships (Isa 33:23). (4) To bind expensive clothing or hangings of a palace (Ezk 27:24; Est 1:6). (5) As a measuring line (Amos 7:17; Mic 2:5). (6) As an easily broken thread (Jud 16:12). (7) As a scarlet thread, or literally, "the cord of this thread of scarlet" (Josh 2:18). (8) As a threefold cord (Eccl 4:12). (9) As a bowstring (Job 30:11). (10) To hold up a tent, or as the cords of the tabernacle (Ex 35:18; 39:40; Num 3:26, 37; 4:26, 32; Isa 54:2; Jer 10:20). (11) As a twisted cord used as a fetter (Jud 15:13-14; Ps 118:27). (12) As twisted cords or golden chains on the high priest's breastplate (Ex 28:14, 22; 39:15).

The harbor at Coos. E.W. Saunders

Cord in the NT is made of rushes and used only once, where Jesus made a whip (Jn 2:15). However, the same Gr. word is used for the ropes that hold a ship's boat in place (Acts 27:32).

Figurative uses of cord include the following: (1) Of one who is bound with his sins (Prov 5:22). (2) The cords of wickedness (Isa 5:18) or affliction (Job 36:8). (3) The cord of life (Eccl 12:6). (4) The cords of a father training his child to walk, which is figurative for a guiding principle (Hos 11:4). (5) A figure of authority or restraint (Ps 2:3; 129:4).

E. C. J.

CORE (kō'rē). A Gr. or variant form in Jude 11 of Korah (*q.v.*). Korah was a cousin of Moses and Aaron (Ex 6:21), who led in a rebellion against their leadership (Num 16:1-49).

CORIANDER. *See* Plants.

CORINTH (kŏr'ĭnth). A very ancient city; the earliest settlers came in the 5th or 6th mil. B.C. But Corinth of the classical period was really established with the Dorian invasion. About 1000 B.C. these Gr. people settled at the foot of the acropolis of Corinth. Occupying a place of safety, they also controlled the main overland trade route between the Peloponnesus and central Greece, as well as the Isthmian route. Coming early to a height of prosperity, the city colonized Syracuse on Sicily and the island of Corcyra and achieved a peak of prosperity through commercial and industrial development. Corinthian pottery and bronzes were exported widely over the Mediterranean. About the middle of the 5th cen. the city's fortunes declined as a result of the effective competition of Athenian industrial production. During the classical period Corinth controlled about 248 square miles of territory, approximately one-fourth the size of Rhode Island.

It is not possible to tell the history of Corinth in detail. Suffice it to say that she clashed with Rome during the 2nd cen. B.C., was finally destroyed by the Romans in 146 B.C., and lay virtually uninhabited until Julius Caesar refounded it in 44 B.C. The growth of Corinth was rapid, and by the time of Paul or soon thereafter it became the largest and most flourishing center in S Greece. It served as capital of the Roman province of Achaia, with a population estimated variously from 100,000 to several hundred thousand.

The later history of Corinth has no special value to the NT student. The city suffered various catastrophes until in 1858 when obliterated by an earthquake it moved to a new site on the Corinthian gulf; hence excavators of the American School of Classical Studies were able to discover what the place was like in NT times.

In Paul's day the city lay about one and a half miles S of the Corinthian gulf on the N side of its acropolis at an altitude of *c.* 400 feet. The Acrocorinthus or acropolis hill towered *c.* 1,500 feet over the city to an altitude of 1,886 feet. The city and its acropolis were enclosed by a wall over six miles in circumference. Outside the walls in the surrounding plain stretched grain fields, olive groves, vineyards, and other agricultural holdings of the city.

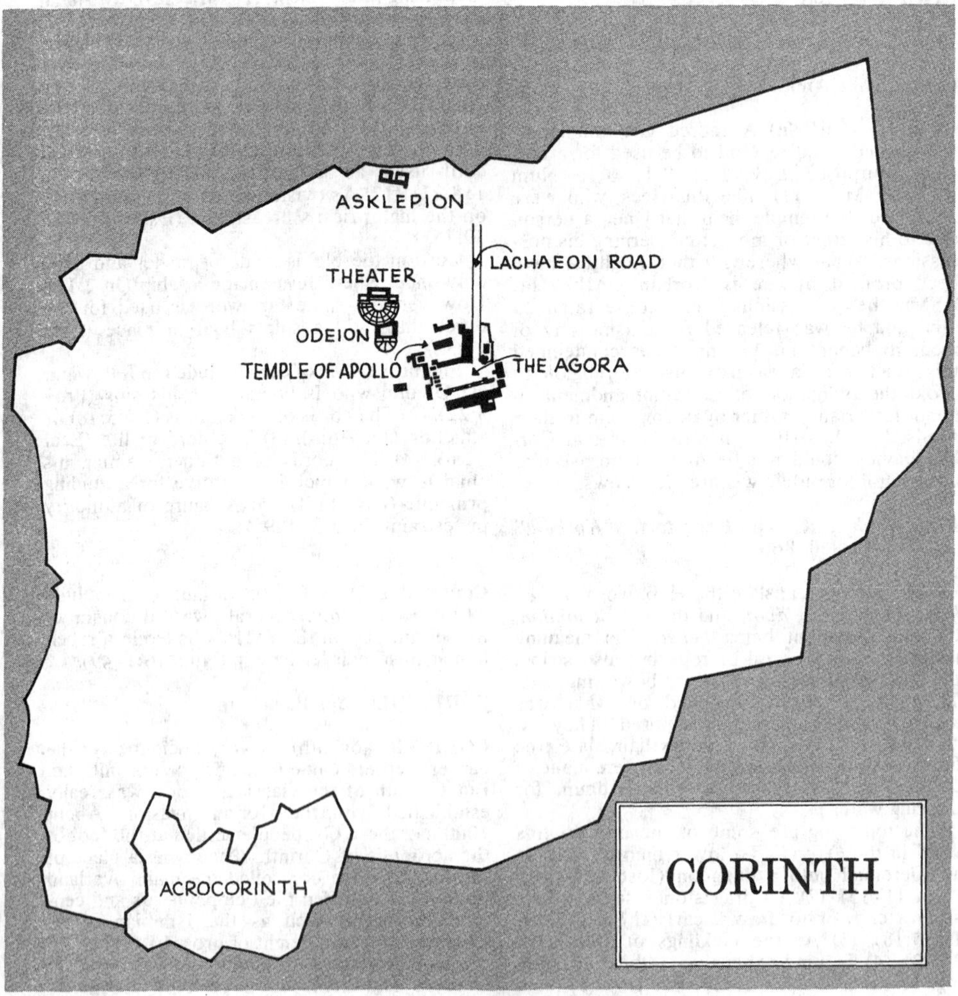

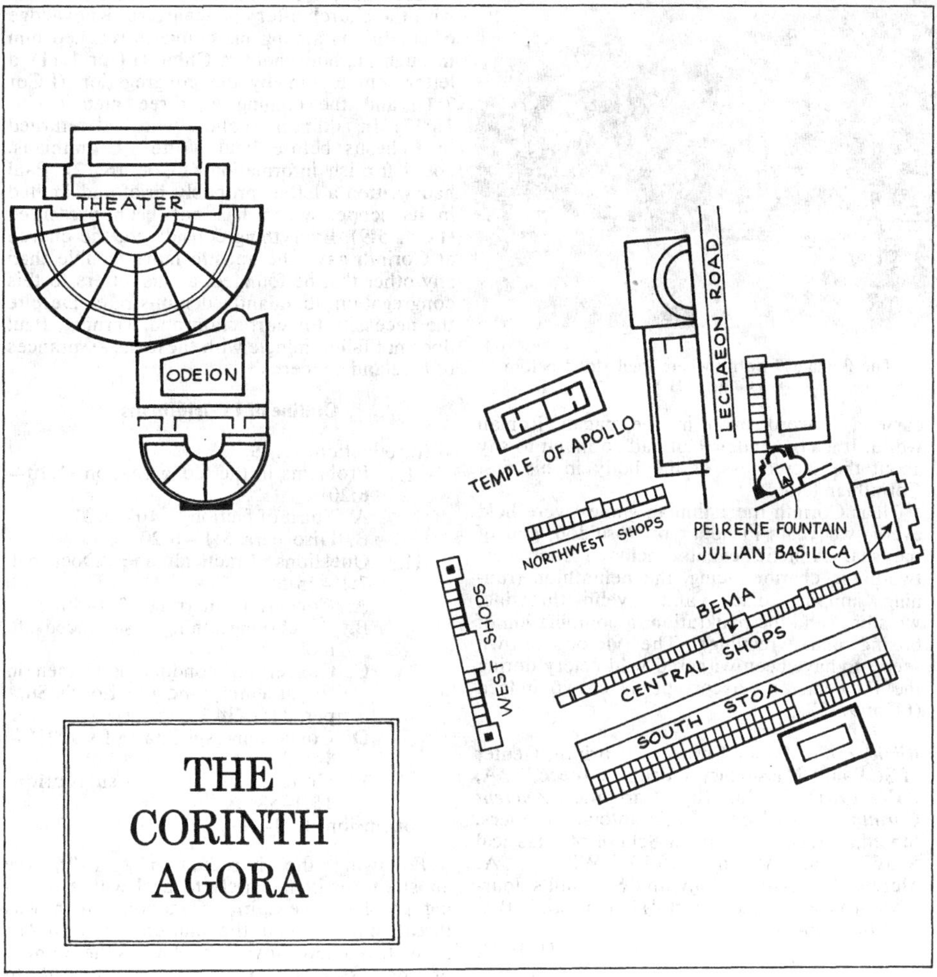

In the N central part of town stood the Agora, nerve center of the metropolis. The Agora was almost 700 feet E and W and about 300 feet N and S. Following the natural configuration of the land, the S section was about 13 feet higher than the N part. At the dividing line of the two levels was a row of low buildings flanking a rostrum or bema, which served as a speaker's stand for public addresses and a judgment seat (*q.v.*) for magistrates. Here Paul appeared before Gallio (*q.v.*), governor of Achaia, as a result of Jewish accusations to the effect that he had broken the law (Acts 18:12-13). Along the S side of the Agora stood a stoa or colonnaded shopping center about 500 feet long. Here and on the NW side near the temple of Apollo were shops for meat and wine merchants, probably the "shambles" or market which Paul referred to in I Cor 10:25 (KJV). An inscription was found near the theater stating that Erastus (*q.v.*; probably mentioned in Rom 16:23) the aedile (city treasurer) had laid the pavement at his own expense.

As to nonphysical aspects of Corinth, it should be noted that much of the population was mobile (sailors, businessmen, government officials, *et al.*) and was therefore cut off from the inhibitions of a settled society. To make matters worse, religious prostitution was commonly practiced in connection with the temples of the city. For instance, according to Strabo, 1,000 priestesses or slave girls of the Temple of Aphrodite on the acropolis were employed in religious prostitution. An inscription reveals they had their own seats in the theater NW of the Agora. From the social mobility and the evils of religious practices there arose a general corruption of society. "Corinthian morals" be-

The Bema at Corinth where Paul stood before Gallio. HFV

came a byword even in the pagan Roman world. It is no wonder Paul had so much to say about the sacredness of the body in his first Corinthian letter.

Near Corinth the Isthmian games were held every two years in honor of Poseidon, god of the sea. Athletic events included footraces, two-horse chariot racing, the pentathlon (running, jumping, discus and javelin throwing, wrestling) and the pankration (a combination of boxing and wrestling). The victor's crown seems to have been withered wild celery during the 1st cen. A.D., a corruptible crown indeed (I Cor 9:25).

Bibliography. Oscar Broneer, "Corinth, Center of St. Paul's Missionary Work in Greece," BA, XIV (1951), 78-96. Rhys Carpenter, *Ancient Corinth,* rev. by Robert L. Scranton and others, 6th ed., Athens: American School of Classical Studies at Athens, 1960. William A. McDonald, "Archaeology and St. Paul's Journeys in Greek Lands, Part III: Corinth," BA, V (1942), 36-48.

H. F. V.

CORINTHIANS, I AND II. These letters belong to the second group of Paul's writings, usually designated as soteriological because of their concern for the message of salvation. The others in the same group are Galatians and Romans.

In the course of his European mission Paul came to Corinth from Athens and began his labors in the synagogue. Doubtless Priscilla and Aquila assisted. Later, Silas and Timothy helped in the work (II Cor 1:19). After Paul's departure at the end of a ministry of 18 months, Apollos came and carried on for a time (Acts 18:24, 27-28; I Cor 3:5). The church seems to have been composed mainly of Gentiles, for the testimony in the synagogue was soon terminated by the opposition of the Jews (Acts 18:6-7). This conclusion is supported in several respects by the first epistle (e.g., I Cor 12:2).

CORINTHIANS, I AND II

According to his custom, Paul made contact with the church after his departure. Knowledge of conditions among his converts reached him through the household of Chloe (I Cor 1:11), a letter sent to him by the congregation (I Cor 7:1), and the coming of three men (I Cor 16:17). In addition Apollos, who had returned to Ephesus before Paul wrote I Corinthians, could furnish information (I Cor 16:12). Paul had written a letter, probably brief and limited in its scope, which has not been preserved (I Cor 5:9). Everything considered, the church at Corinth gave the apostle more trouble than any other that he founded, as his letters to this congregation abundantly demonstrate. Despite the necessity for correction and warning, Paul does not fail to mingle with these his assurances of love and concern.

Outline of I Corinthians

Introduction, 1:1-9
- I. Problems in the Congregation, 1:10–6:20
  - A. Spirit of faction, 1:10–4:21
  - B. Disorders, 5:1–6:20
- II. Questions Practical and Doctrinal, 7:1–15:58
  - A. Concerning marriage, 7:1-40
  - B. Concerning things sacrificed to idols, 8:1–11:1
  - C. Concerning conduct of women in the assembly and the Lord's Supper, 11:2-34
  - D. Concerning spiritual gifts, 12:1–14:40
  - E. Concerning the resurrection, 15:1-58

Conclusion, 16:1-24

Following the introduction (1:1-9), the apostle turns immediately to deal with a pressing problem, the spirit of faction which was threatening to rend the church (1:10–4:21). Some had a fierce loyalty to Paul as the founder of the assembly, others were attached to Apollos, and still others to Cephas (Peter), even though, as far as is known, he had not visited the place. A fourth segment, disgusted with their fellows, turned against all human leadership (1:12). Paul shows that only Christ merits their devotion. He died for them. They were baptized in His name. The ministry has a place, but only in the sense of workers who labor together under God (3:9). All the ministry belongs to the church as a whole, not to a section of it (3:21-22). Christianity is not a philosophy with various schools of thought led by teachers who have their own coteries of disciples.

The next problem to be faced was a grievous case of immorality (5:1-13). In being lax about discipline and even being puffed up over this situation, the church must share in the guilt. Blame attaches to the believers also for taking their grievances against one another to pagan magistrates for settlement (6:1-8). Reverting to the problem of morality along broader lines than in chap. 5, the apostle teaches the sanctity of the body (6:9-20).

Marriage and related matters claim attention (7:1-40); then the question of eating food which has been offered to idols (8:1–11:1). It was hard for these young Christians to break the hold of their former environment. They needed help, too, regarding the conduct of women in the assembly and the proper observance of the Lord's Supper (11:2-34).

The Corinthians, being Greeks, loved self-expression, so they treasured the gift of tongues. Paul treats the whole question of spiritual gifts, not forbidding tongues but calling for greater interest in the gift of prophecy, and for supreme concern for love, which is greater than all the gifts (12:1–14:40).

The letter comes to a climax with its teaching on resurrection (15:1-58). Gr. philosophy was not hospitable to a doctrine of bodily resurrection. But if Christ was so raised (and the Corinthians had accepted this, 15:3-11), the resurrection of believers is guaranteed thereby.

The closing chapter deals with plans and personalities (16:1-24).

This letter was written about A.D. 55 or 56. The identity of the bearer is not certainly known.

Outline of II Corinthians

I. Gratitude for God's Consolation, 1:1–2:13; 7:5-16
II. The Glory and Suffering of the Christian Ministry, 2:14–7:4
III. Christian Giving, 8:1–9:15
IV. Paul's Ministry Contrasted with That of False Apostles, 10:1–13:14

Opposition to Paul, which had been fostered to some extent by the factions (I Cor 4:18-21) and which centered in his apostleship and authority (I Cor 9:1-3), was fanned by the arrival in Corinth of men who claimed to belong to the Christian fellowship and to be of apostolic rank (II Cor 11:13). One of the believers, apparently taken in by their propaganda, turned against Paul and encouraged others to do so (II Cor 2:5 ff.; 7:12). It seems that the apostle felt it necessary to leave his work at Ephesus temporarily to make a hurried trip to Corinth to settle the unrest (II Cor 2:1; 12:14; 13:1-2). Even this face-to-face encounter was not successful. On his return to Ephesus Paul penned a letter filled with anguish and tears (II Cor 2:4; 7:8), sending it by the hands of Titus. Anxiety over the outcome compounded his troubled situation at Ephesus, where he faced the danger of death (II Cor 1:8 ff.). Leaving the city, he passed through Troas (II Cor 2:12-13) and finally met Titus in Macedonia and learned with relief of the improvement of conditions at Corinth (7:5 ff.).

This news led to the writing of II Corinthians, wherein the apostle defends and expounds his ministry (2:14–7:4). He had some unfinished business with the church, including the raising of a fund for the poor saints at Jerusalem (cf. I Cor 16:1-4). To this he now gives attention (chaps. 8-9).

The unwholesome influence of his opponents, the false "apostles," still lingered to some extent, so Paul levels an attack on them (chaps. 10-13). He challenges them to match his record of service tinged with suffering for Christ's sake (11:22-29). Nothing in Paul's writings is so critical as these chapters. He complains that his friends have allowed themselves to be browbeaten by these interlopers (11:19-20), and by failing to stand up for him themselves have forced him to make his own defense against these attacks (12:11).

Some students have seen in these final chapters of the book the letter to which Paul makes reference as written following his trip from Ephesus. The great difficulty in accepting this judgment is that the character of the two portions is quite different. There is nothing to suggest tears of anguish and sorrow in this broadside with which the second letter closes, yet such was the nature of the communication which Paul wrote in that crisis.

It appears that II Corinthians, written only a few months after the first epistle, was sent by the hand of Titus (8:6).

Bibliography. James Denney, *The Second Epistle to the Corinthians,* ExpB, New York: Armstrong, 1900. Frederic Godet, *Commentary on St. Paul's First Epistle to the Corinthians,* 2 vols., Edinburgh: T. & T. Clark, 1889. F. W. Grosheide, *Commentary on the First Epistle to the Corinthians,* NICNT, Grand Rapids: Eerdmans, 1953. Charles Hodge, *An Exposition of the First Epistle to the Corinthians,* 1857, Grand Rapids: Eerdmans, 1950 (reprint); *An Exposition of the Second Epistle . . . ,* 1859, Eerdmans, 1950 (reprint). P. E. Hughes, *Paul's Second Epistle to the Corinthians,* NICNT, Grand Rapids: Eerdmans, 1962. G. Campbell Morgan, *The Corinthian Letters of Paul,* New York: Revell, n.d. Leon Morris, *The First Epistle of Paul to the Corinthians,* TNTC, Grand Rapids: Eerdmans, 1958. Alfred Plummer, *A Critical and Exegetical Commentary on the Second Epistle of St. Paul to the Corinthians,* ICC, New York: Scribner's, 1915. Archibald Robertson and Alfred Plummer, *A Critical . . . Commentary on the First Epistle . . . Corinthians,* ICC, 2nd ed., Scribner's, 1911. A. T. Robertson, *The Glory of the Ministry,* New York: Revell, 1911. R. V. G. Tasker, *The Second Epistle of Paul to the Corinthians,* TNTC, Grand Rapids: Eerdmans, 1958. A. F. Walls, "Corinthians, Epistles to the," NBD, pp. 252-257.

E. F. Har.

CORMORANT. *See* Animals, III.6.

CORN. A term found in Bibles published in England (KJV, NEB, etc.). It is the translation of several Heb. and Gr. words for cereal grains such as wheat and barley (e.g., Gen 27:28; 41:35; 42:1; Deut 16:9; Mt 12:1). Modern American versions usually have "grain" where KJV has "corn." The term must not be mistaken for Indian maize, a cereal native only to the Western Hemisphere.

See also Food.

CORNELIUS (kôr-nēl'yŭs). This man is of particular significance in two ways: he is the first recorded Gentile convert to Christianity; and the story of his conversion is told twice. Apart from the threefold repetition of Saul's epochal conversion, this is unique in Acts. The conversion of Cornelius is related in Acts 10. Peter, when reproached at Jerusalem for eating with uncircumcised Gentiles, retold the incident as his best defense (Acts 11:1-18). At the famous council of Jerusalem (A.D. 48) he alluded to this significant event as proof that God designed to save the Gentiles by grace apart from the Mosaic law (Acts 15:7-11).

Cornelius is identified as a centurion (*q.v.*) of the Italian cohort stationed in Caesarea (Acts 10:1). Since Publius Cornelius Sulla in 82 B.C. had freed 10,000 slaves and given them the family name Cornelius, this was a common name in the Roman Empire at this time, and also an honorable one.

The centurion is described as "a devout man, and one that feared God with all his house, who gave much alms to the people, and prayed to God always" (Acts 10:2, ASV). There has been considerable dispute as to exactly what this means. Was he a full proselyte to Judaism? Most scholars are agreed that he was not. He has commonly been labeled a "proselyte of the gate." But Kirsopp Lake maintains that there was no such category. Gentile worshipers in Jewish synagogues were proselytes only if they were circumcised and observed all the regulations of the Mosaic law ("Proselytes and God-Fearers," *Beginnings of Christianity*, V, 74-96). Cornelius was not a proselyte but a God-fearer. The Gr. word for "devout" means "pious, godly." It seems clear that Cornelius had accepted monotheism, and worshiped the true God in the synagogue. It appears equally clear that he had not heard the definite Christian gospel preached before this. In a vision he was instructed to send for Peter who would tell him how to be saved (Acts 11:12-14). Peter preached salvation through the name of Jesus (Acts 10:43). Cornelius and his company accepted the message of Christ and the Holy Spirit was poured out on them (Acts 10:44).

R. E.

CORNER GATE. A gate at the NW corner of Jerusalem. Located 400 cubits from the Ephraim Gate (II Kgs 14:13; II Chr 25:23), its defenses were torn down by Jehoash, king of Israel. Uzziah later built a tower there (II Chr 26:9). Jeremiah prophesied that Jerusalem would be rebuilt "from the tower of Hananel to the Corner Gate" (Jer 31:38, RSV).

See Jerusalem.

CORNERSTONE. Either a stone tying two walls of a building together (Isa 28:16), or the keystone capping and completing the building (Ps 118:22). Figuratively, Christ's passion and resurrection are the "cornerstone" or fulfillment of the OT (Mk 12:10 f.; Acts 4:11; I Pet 2:4-7; Rom 9:33; 10:11). The Church is represented as a building erected on the foundation of the prophets and apostles, Christ Jesus being the cornerstone (Eph 2:20). Daughters are referred to as cornerstones, to be regarded as of great worth (Ps 144:12).

The significance of the keystone in an arch is often ascribed to a cornerstone. In modern architecture its value is slight, frequently only as the stone giving the date of the building. For churches and sacred edifices a special dedicatory service is generally held for the laying of the cornerstone. Sometimes documents are deposited in it, symbolizing that the past is the foundation for the future. *See* Headstone.

CORNET. *See* Music.

CORRECTION. This word is used for reform, amendment, restoration, discipline. Correction is a function of a father with his children (Prov 23:13; 29:17; Jer 2:30; Heb 12:9) and of God with His people (Job 5:17; Prov 3:12; Heb 12:7, 9). Both Heb. and Gr. terms imply a twofold meaning: to instruct, guide, reason with; and to punish, chastise, reprove. The whole process of child rearing is in view in correction, as suggested by the most common Gr. term *paideuō*, "to train up a child," involving both positive guidance and negative discipline in the case of wrongdoing. That the Word of God is profitable for correction (II Tim 3:16) refers to its value for improvement of life and character in the believer. The Gr. term here means "restoration to an upright state." *See* Chastisement.

CORRUPTION. This word translates various nouns from the Heb. root *shāḥat* (OT) and Gr. root *phtheirō* (NT), "to ruin," "destroy." Corruption may be physical: blemished animals (Lev 22:25); disfigured faces (Dan 10:8); desecrated shrine, whose high place is therefore called "mount of corruption" (*q.v.*; II Kgs 23:13); perishable bodies (I Cor 15:42, 50; Acts 13:36; cf. Isa 38:17, pit of *belî*, "nothingness," bodily annihilation); or creation under the curse (Rom 8:21). The very important passage in Ps 16:10 predicts Christ's resurrection (Acts 2:27, 31; 13:34-35, 37) from decomposition (Job 17:14, worm-eaten; cf. Ps 49:9; Jon 2:6). The RSV renders Ps 16:10 as if the reference is to David's deliverance from approaching the "pit" of death (from another Heb. root, *shûăḥ*, "sink down," hence "pit trap," Ezk 19:4, 8; cf. *The Biblical Expositor,* II, 58-60). Corruption also denotes moral depravity (II Pet 1:4; 2:19) and final spiritual judgment (Gal 6:8; II Pet 2:12*b,* Arndt, p. 865). *See* Death; Immortality; Pit; Sheol.

CORRUPTION, MOUNT OF. A hill E of and near to Jerusalem where Solomon had built places for the worship of Ashtoreth, Chemosh, and Milcom (I Kgs 11:7, RSV). Josiah destroyed them (II Kgs 23:13). The site evidently referred to the southern height of the Mount of Olives. Later, Christian tradition referred to it as the "Mount of Offense." It was also called the "Mount of the Ointment," a term used for the Mount of Olives (*q.v.*).

CORSELET. Defensive armor for the body. It evidently refers to the protective covering for the chest, abdomen, and back. It is referred to as "breastplate," "habergeon," and "coat of mail." Armor of this nature was worn by Nehemiah's workers (Neh 4:16), by the soldiers of King Uzziah (II Chr 26:14), by Goliath (I Sam 17:5), and by Ahab (I Kgs 22:34, "harness," KJV). Paul uses this term figuratively (Eph 6:14). *See* Armor.

COSAM (kō'săm). An ancestor of Jesus, the son of Elmodam and the father of Addi, in the fifth generation before Zerubbabel (Lk 3:28).

COSMETICS. Materials used for beautification. Ointments, perfumes, eye paint, and possibly henna were widely used by Egyptian and Hebrew women in biblical times (Prov 27:9; Rev 18:13). Jezebel painted her eyes (II Kgs 9:30, RSV), and beauty applications were valued by many (Jer 4:30). Ivory combs, hairpins, alabaster flasks and palettes for ointment, bronze mirrors, and rouge pots have been found in many excavations. The hot, dry climate made the use of lotions for the skin essential, and perfumes counteracted body odors. The offering of ointments for guests was a part of the hospitality pattern of NT times (Lk 7:37 f.).

COSMOS. *See* World.

COTTAGE. This word appears in the KJV in Isa 1:8 (Heb. *sukkâ,* "hut"); Isa 24:20 (Heb. *m^e^lûnâ;* "hut" in RSV); Zeph 2:6 (Heb. *kārōth,* "hewn out place"; translated "Crete" in LXX, and "meadows" in RSV).

The word "cottage" has changed considerably in meaning from its original significance. It is related to the word "cote," a stall for animals (cf. Milton, *Comus,* 344). "Might we but hear the folded flocks, penned in their wattled cotes." Chaucer used the term to signify a humble dwelling: "A poore widow somedeal stoopen in age, was whilom dwelling in a narrow cottage" (*Canterbury Tales:* "Nun's Priest's Tale," 1:2).

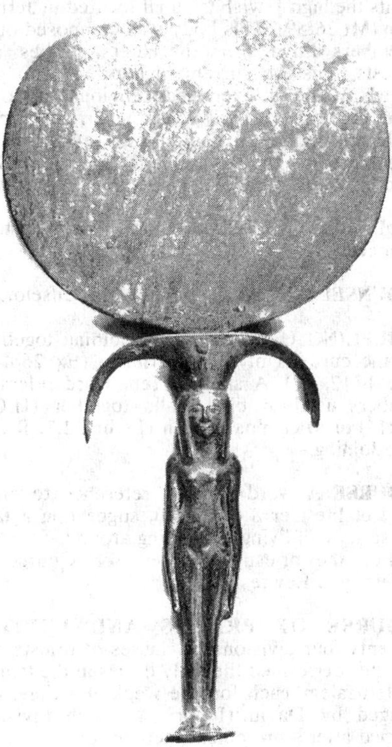

A bronze mirror of the Egyptian Empire period. LM

The term as found in the OT always preserves this connotation of a lowly kind of structure, and not the neutral significance of the word as employed in contemporary usage. In Isa 1:8 it refers to a temporary frame which would be covered with foliage to protect a worker from the sun while he guarded the vineyard during the time the grapes ripened. The other Heb. words translated "hut" or "cottage" also suggest a flimsy type of construction.

E. J. V.

COTTON. *See* Plants.

COUCH. *See* Bed.

COULTER. Plowshare, a sharp metal point attached to plowbeam (from Heb. "to cut in or dig"). The Philistines sharpened these tools for the Israelites before iron became plentiful in Palestine (I Sam 13:20-21). *See* Plow.

COUNCIL. This is the KJV translation for three biblical words: (1) Heb. *rigmâ,* "crowd," "assembly" (Ps 68:27); (2) Gr. *symboulion,* "a joint council" (Mt 12:14; Acts 25:12); (3) Gr. *synedrion,* often transliterated "sanhedrin." Except for Mt 10:17 and Mk 13:9, where it refers to lesser courts, the latter form always represents the high Jewish tribunal located in Jerusalem (Mt 26:59). This body was composed of 70 members drawn from the elders, scribes, and priests, plus the current high priest who presided. While it exercised religious authority over all Jews, its civil power was restricted to Palestine and concerned only those matters not preempted by the Roman authorities. *See* Sanhedrin; Apostolic Council.

COUNCIL OF JERUSALEM. *See* Apostolic Council.

COUNSELOR. *See* Occupations: Counselor.

COUPLING. Used to indicate joining together, as the curtains of the tabernacle (Ex 26:4-5; 36:11-12, 17). A similar Heb. word refers to timbers used to bind walls together (II Chr 34:11) or to clamps of iron (I Chr 22:3, RSV). *See* Joining.

COURSE. A word used in reference to one's way of life (Jer 8:6; 23:10), suggesting a fast, loose style of living or running around.

For the priestly courses *see* Course of Priests and Levites.

COURSE OF PRIESTS AND LEVITES. Twenty-four divisions or classes of priests and Levites performed the daily duties in the temple at Jerusalem, each for one week at a time. Arranged by David (I Chr 24), each division, named after a prominent member of the family, was subject to its president. Zacharias, John the Baptist's father, belonged to the eighth division, that of Abia (Lk 1:5).

In 1962 while excavating a synagogue at Caesarea archaeologists discovered fragments of a marble inscription that originally named the 24 priestly courses and the city where each moved after the destruction of the temple in A.D. 70. Nazareth is listed as the city of the 18th course, the town's earliest mention outside the NT (IEJ, XII, 137 ff.).

COURT. An area without a roof enclosed by buildings or walls. The tabernacle had an outer court enclosed by curtains (Ex 27:9 ff.). Solomon's temple had an inner court for the priests marked off by stone walls (I Kgs 6:36), and another outer court. *See* Tabernacle; Temple.

Ancient houses were often protected from direct entrance from the street by a forecourt enclosed by a wall; in other houses the living quarters would be built around a central court. The RSV has "court of the high priest" instead of "palace" (KJV, Jn 18:15). Rev 11:2 speaks of a huge court outside the temple proper in John's vision. *See* House; Architecture.

COURTS, JUDICIAL. *See* Law, Administration of.

COUSIN. There is no word for cousin in the OT, but "kinsman" or "relative" was used to denote that relationship. Marriage between cousins was common (Gen 24:15; 28:2; 29:10, 19; 36:3).

COVENANT. In Heb. "covenant" is designated *berît*, and *berît kārat* signifies "to make (lit., 'cut') a covenant." In Gr. the term is *diathēkē* (which can mean both "pact" and "last will and testament"), and the verb *diatithēmi* (cf. Acts 3:25; Heb 8:10; 9:16; 10:16).

A covenant is an agreement between two or more persons in which the following four factors or elements are present: parties, conditions, results, security.

The biblical covenants are important as the key to two great facets of truth: *Soteriology*—God's plan through Jesus Christ to redeem His elect is unfolded in an ever-widening and deepening manner in the successive covenants. *Prophecy*—the Abrahamic, Palestinian, Davidic, and new covenants open up the whole panorama concerning Christ's first and second advents, and His thousand year millennial reign on the earth. Most of the great covenants reveal facts concerning both the suffering, sacrificial Messiah, and the ruling, reigning Messiah. The manner in which these two lines of prophecy are to be interpreted finally determines one's eschatology, whether it is to be amillennial, postmillennial, or premillennial. The question must be faced as to whether the method to be applied to both lines of prophecy is the same or different. Upon this must depend the decision on the millennial question and the interpretation of much contained in each of the covenants. *See* Millennium.

Parties. These may be: (1) Individual men, such as Abraham and Abimelech (Gen 21:27) or Jacob and Laban (Gen 31:44-46), when each man subjected himself to certain conditions and offered a proof to secure the covenant made. (2) Nations, as when Nahash the Ammonite tried to force a covenant upon Jabesh-gilead in I Sam 11:1 ff., or the Israelites were foolishly led to make a covenant with the Gibeonites (Josh 9:6-16). (3) God and man were the parties of the great kingdom-messianic covenants, such as the Abrahamic covenant (Gen 12:1-7; 15; 17:1-14; 22:15-18), the Palestinian covenant (Deut 29-30), and the Davidic covenant (II Sam 7:4-16; Ps 89:3-4, 26-37; 132:11-18). (4) God the Father and Jesus Christ were the chief originating parties of the covenant of redemption (Ps 40:6-8; Heb 10:5-14), Christ being the Mediator of this covenant, while God and individual men (Heb 7:9 ff.) and God and Israel (Jer 31:37) were its efficacious partners. The Father and the Son were the chief parties of the covenant of grace. God the Father covenanted with Christ to save by grace those who believe in the Son and His substitutionary death. This covenant became the foundation of Rom 4 and Heb 11, the two *loci classici* or main passages concerning justification by faith in the NT. Individuals in the OT entered into this covenant through their saving faith in and acceptance of the type of Christ in the OT, and in the NT by the same faith with acceptance of the antitype, even Jesus Christ Himself.

Conditions. In every covenant certain conditions are stated. This applies both to those covenants which are unilateral, namely, announced by God to man and promulgated as certain to come to pass, and to this extent unconditional; and also to those which are bilateral, namely, to those covenants which are entirely conditional upon the acceptance and fulfillment thereof by both parties. All human covenants are bilateral and conditional. Covenants between God and man can be mainly unilateral, e.g., the Abrahamic covenant, Davidic covenant, new covenant; or bilateral, e.g., the Mosaic covenant. Still there is confusion if we do not see that even the essentially unilateral covenants have a bilateral aspect insofar as their application has regard to individual men. This can be seen in the fact that, as Paul writes in Rom 9, though the covenants belong to Israel, "they are not all Israel, which are of Israel . . . the children of the promise are counted for the seed" (Rom 9:6, 8). They apply to the elect.

Further, we see that the seal or sign or token of one's having accepted the covenant relationship by an act of individual faith is a step of obedience, even in the Abrahamic covenant, the sign of which was circumcision (cf. Gen 17:10-11 where the sign was stated as a part of the individual application of the covenant, "This is my covenant . . . every man child among you shall be circumcised"). Any attempt to separate the unilateral element of the Abrahamic covenant from its individual application becomes artificial, and the acknowledgment therefore of both factors—unilateral and bilateral—in such a covenant becomes necessary. In like manner water baptism is the sign or seal of one's membership in the new covenant community. Examination shows that the unilateral elements in a covenant are prophetic, and thereby immutable; and the bilateral elements are soteriological, and therefore conditional to the extent they are dependent upon personal acceptation by faith, with motivation coming through God's sovereign grace.

Results. These can either be promises of blessing when the covenant is kept, or warnings of punishment when the covenant is broken, or both. For example, in the Abrahamic covenant there was promise of a seed (who according to Gal 3:16 was Christ; cf. Gen 12:1-3; 13:16; 22:18), of a land, of fame, and of a great posterity. These facts were prophetic and certain. At the same time there was a conditional aspect, for each believing participant had to be circumcised as a seal of his faith, even as in the case of Abraham (Gen 17:9-17; Rom 4:11). Those who refused to be circumcised broke the covenant (Gen 17:14). This rite pointed to Christ "in whom we [Christians] are circumcised . . . by the circumcision of Christ" (Col 2:11). All this is conditional to the extent it is based upon saving faith.

Security. The security given to guarantee the fulfillment of a covenant was usually an oath. For men, it was an oath of such solemn character that it partook of the nature of a will or testament. The idea is that just as a testator cannot change his will when dead, so neither can a covenanter change his covenant. One way in which this was signified was by the slaying of an animal, dividing it into two parts, and then the passing of both parties between the halves (Gen 15:9 ff.). Christ sealed the new covenant with His death (Heb 9:15-17), having instituted the Lord's Supper to commemorate that death (Mt 26:28; Mk 14:25; I Cor 11:25-26). Again, sometimes a gift was made (Gen 21:30), or a sign set up, such as a cairn or heap of stones (Gen 31:52).

Since God can swear by nothing greater than Himself, He confirmed His covenants either by swearing by Himself (Deut 29:12; Heb 6:13-14), as when confirming His covenant with Abraham, or by swearing by His providential control of the world, as when He announced the new covenant in Jer 31:35; 33:20.

Kinds of Covenants

Two main kinds of covenants in the Bible need to be considered, those specifically designated as covenants, and those implied but not so designated. For the sake of distinction they can perhaps best be called biblical and theological covenants.

Specific Biblical Covenants

1. *Noahic covenant.* This is the first clearly mentioned covenant in the Scriptures. It was promised to Noah in Gen 6:18 and is recorded in Gen 8:20-9:17. This covenant was chiefly unilateral in that God was the initiator and maker, not requiring a promise of acceptance and compliance on the part of Noah as the Israelites vowed at the foot of Mount Sinai (see Ex 19:8).

The *parties* to this covenant were God and the earth (Gen 9:13) or Noah and all his descendants (Gen 9:9, 16, 17). Hence it was universal in its scope. Nevertheless it had *conditions,* namely, that mankind would be fruitful, multiply, and fill the earth (9:1, 7), and that they must not eat flesh with the life, i.e., the blood, still in it (9:4). In this sense the covenant was conditional, for God brought judgment upon mankind at the Tower of Babel in the form of confusion of language in order to force them to scatter and populate the earth when they were deliberately defying the purpose and command of God (Gen 11:4-9). The *results* were the promise of God never again to destroy the earth by deluge (Gen 8:21; 9:11, 15), with the concomitant promise of the regularity of seasons (Gen 8:22). The *security* that God would keep this covenant as long as earth shall last is found in its sign or token, the rainbow (9:12-17).

2. *Abrahamic covenant*. This is generally considered to be a unilateral covenant in the sense that it was announced by God in the first place without any attached conditions. A bilateral element does appear, however, in Gen 17:1: "I am the Almighty God; walk before me, and be thou perfect," and in the last repetition and confirmation of the covenant to Abraham in Gen 22:16 ff., when God says, "By myself have I sworn . . . because thou hast done this thing, and hast not withheld thy son, thine only son: that in blessing I will bless thee . . . because thou hast obeyed my voice."

The *parties* to this covenant were God and Abraham. The *condition*, as revealed above by God to Abraham after he had shown his willingness to obey God's command to offer up Isaac, was faithful obedience (cf. Heb 11:17-19). The *results* were the promises of God to make Abraham's posterity into a great nation (Gen 12:2); to increase his seed as the sands of the sea (Gen 22:17); to bless those who should bless the Jewish people and curse those that should curse them (Gen 12:3); and to give to Abraham's seed, that is, to Israel, Palestine and the territory from the River of Egypt to the Euphrates. Finally, and most important of all, the whole world was to be blessed through his seed, which was Christ (Gal 3:16), and Christ in turn was to have rulership over all His enemies (Gen 22:17-18). The *security* for this great covenant was God's oath by Himself and His great name (Gen 22:16; Heb 6:13-18), as well as the shedding of the blood of sacrifices (Gen 15:9, 10, 17).

3. *Mosaic or Sinai covenant*. In this covenant there is the appearance of a new factor, that of a particular form. The Abrahamic covenant was very simple and direct. The Mosaic, while still direct, was much more complex. It employed the contemporary form of suzerain-vassal covenants then in vogue in the ancient Near East in which the great lord or suzerain dictated an agreement to his vassals or servants. A recent study of Hittite treaties or covenants of the mid-2nd mil. B.C. has revealed that a parallel form existed between these and God's covenant with Israel. Each had six elements.

(1) A preamble: "I am the Lord thy God" (Ex 20:2*a*). This identified the author of the covenant and corresponded to such an introduction as, "These are the words of the son of Mursilis, the great king, and king of the Hatti land, the valiant, the favorite son of the storm-god, etc. . . ." (ANET, p. 203).

(2) A historical prologue: "which have brought thee out of the land of Egypt, out of the house of bondage" (Ex 20:2). In Deuteronomy, which is the second giving of the covenant and of the law, the historical prologue is greatly expanded in order to cover how God led Israel through the wilderness right to the threshold of the Promised Land (Deut 1:6–4:49). Moses is repeating and expanding the covenant given at Sinai to bring it up to date and to prepare Israel for entry into the Promised Land. In the Hittite covenants the suzerain reminded the vassal ruler of the benefits he had enjoyed hitherto as a vassal of his kingdom, as a basis for the vassal's gratitude and future obedience.

(3) The exclusive stipulations or obligations of the covenant: "Thou shalt have no other gods before me. Thou shalt not make unto thee any graven image . . . thou shalt not bow down . . " (Ex 20:3-5). One typical Hittite covenant reads: "But you Duppi-Tessub remain loyal to the king of the Hatti land. . . . Do not turn your eyes to anyone else" (ANET, p. 204). In its first form in Ex 20 the covenant opens with the Ten Commandments and continues on through Ex 31. In Deuteronomy it opens with the law in chap. 5 and continues on through chap. 26.

(4) Sanctions, namely, blessings and curses which accompanied the keeping or breaking of the covenant. In its first promulgation in Exodus, the Mosaic covenant contains those specifically attached to the Ten Commandments, e.g., "visiting the iniquity . . . and showing mercy" (Ex 20:5-6); and, "Honor thy father and thy mother; that thy days may be long . . ." (Ex 20:12). In addition, further sanctions and warnings are given with the promise of guidance and protection by the Lord's presence (Ex 23:20-33; for other blessings and curses see Lev 26). But in Deuteronomy there are two chapters of blessings and curses to be read publicly and expounded at the covenant renewal ceremony (27-28), followed by the so-called Palestinian covenant (29-30). Blessings and curses were also written into the ancient treaties of western Asia.

The biblical confirmation or surety for keeping a covenant was either an oath or the death of the one who made the covenant. "The terms oath and covenant often are used as synonyms in the OT, as are the terms oath and treaty in extrabiblical texts"—so Gene M. Tucker concludes ("Covenant Forms and Contract Forms," VT, XV [1965], p. 497). In essence, an OT covenant was an oath, a sworn agreement. God confirmed the Mosaic covenant by an oath, called in Deut 29:12 ff. "his oath, which the Lord thy God maketh with thee" (cf. Deut 32:40; Ezk 16:8; Neh 10:29). The parties making a covenant were to become as if dead so that they could no more change their minds and revoke it than can the dead (Gen 15:8-18; Heb 9:16-17). Thus the blood of sacrificed animal substitutes was sprinkled at the covenant ratification ceremony to represent the "death" of the parties to the covenant (Ex 24:3-8). In the current Hittite treaties of Moses' time an oath on the part of the suzerain was not a feature; rather they stressed the oath of loyalty on the part of the vassal.

(5) Witnesses. The Hittite treaties called a long list of deities to witness the document. In the Sinai and other biblical covenants pagan

gods were obviously excluded. Instead, memorial stones could be a witness (Ex 24:4; cf. Josh 24:27); heaven and earth were called upon as witnesses (Deut 30:19; 31:28; 32:1; cf. 4:26); the scroll of the law was deposited by the side of the ark to be a witness (Deut 31:26); and Moses' song itself would remind the people of their covenant vows (Deut 31:30–32:47). In the covenant renewal service at the end of Joshua's life the people themselves acted as the witnesses (Josh 24:22).

(6) The perpetuation of the covenant. This was seen in the care for the safekeeping of the treaty documents by depositing them before or under the idol of a heathen god of the nation which was party to the treaty, in contrast to the tablets of the Mosaic covenant being placed within the ark of the covenant in Israel (Ex 25:16, 21; 40:20; Deut 10:2); and in the periodic reading in public and instruction to children both of the Hittite covenants and the Mosaic covenant. The law was recorded on plastered stones and read aloud at the ceremony when the blessings and the curses were pronounced by half of Israel on Mount Ebal and half on Mount Gerizim after they entered the land (Deut 27:9 ff.; Josh 8:30-35). The whole law was reread publicly every seven years at the Feast of Tabernacles (Deut 31:9-13).

Several important conclusions have been reached as a result of the comparison of the Mosaic covenant with ancient suzerainty treaties of that day: (*a*) God spoke to Israel in a form which was suitable for His purpose but which also was familiar to the people of that day. Some of the finer details of the form even prove that the Mosaic covenant must be placed before 1200 B.C., because Aramaic and Assyrian treaties of the 1st mil. B.C. lack several of the distinctive elements common to the Hittite and the Sinai covenants (see Meredith G. Kline, *The Treaty of the Great King*, p. 42 f.). (*b*) The particular Hittite covenantal form of Deuteronomy leads us to see that the stress is more upon its covenantal meaning than its legal meaning. (*c*) Study shows the two tablets of the law were not two stones with four commandments on the first and six on the second, but two stone copies of the same treaty or covenant, one for God—kept in the ark—and one for Israel. The same was true of all Hittite and Assyrian treaties: two copies were made, one for the suzerain king and one for the vassal king.

Certain important differences must not, however, be overlooked. The Mosaic covenant as made by God was based upon love and grace rather than mere power. Further, it had as its goal the salvation of God's elect rather than their mere submission and obedience.

Returning to the spiritual significance of this covenant, we might conclude that the conditional element outshadows the unconditional. Does it teach "this do, and thou shalt live" (cf. Lk 10:28) in the sense that eternal life for the OT believer depended on keeping God's law? If so, works were of meritorious value up until the cross! Or does God mean that we are to live in the light of this law? Christ in the Sermon on the Mount taught the latter view when He exegeted several commandments and said, "Be ye therefore perfect, even as your Father which is in heaven is perfect" (Mt 5:48). He applied the law for the purpose of the continuing sanctification of the believer and not for his justification. In Lev 18:5 the same application of the law is made: "Keep my statutes . . . which if a man do, he shall live in them" (that is, in their sphere). When we see that this covenant opens with grace: "I am the Lord thy God, which brought thee out of the land of Egypt; out of the house of bondage" (Ex 20:2), and we add to this a consideration of the facts given above, we are led to see it as full of grace. The Mosaic covenant then becomes both a schoolmaster to bring us to Christ, with all its types which point to Him, and a standard to guide the deportment of both the OT believer and the Christian.

4. *Palestinian covenant* (Deut 29-30). Though a part of the renewal of the Mosaic covenant, this covenant is considered separately by some. The *parties* are God and Israel. The *conditions* are that God will bless Israel if she remains faithful to Him, and He will curse her if she turns from Him, as expressed in the blessings and the curses promulgated from Mount Gerizim and Mount Ebal (Deut 27:9 ff.). The *results,* after all the blessings and the curses have been experienced by Israel in the course of her history, are that, if and when she repents, God will regather her from the utmost parts of the earth, reestablish her in Israel and bless her. The *security* for the covenant is found in the ordinances of heaven and of earth (Deut 30:19).

This covenant has a unilateral aspect—promises and rewards for keeping the covenant, and curses as the consequence of breaking it. The assurance was given that national repentance of Israel will most surely occur (Deut 30:1-10). Yet there is also a bilateral aspect—Israel must repent. This repentance will come to pass because of God's sovereign grace in the lives of individual Jews when Christ returns (Zech 12:10-14; 13:6; cf. Isa 66:19-20). God's ordinances take into consideration both what man will do in his freedom, and what God plans to do in His sovereign grace. Both these elements appear in the Palestinian covenant.

5. *Davidic covenant* (II Sam 7:4-16; Ps 89:3-4, 26-37; 132:11-18; cf. Isa 42:1, 6; 49:8; 55:3-4). This was basically a unilateral covenant in which God promised David first a secure reign for his son and successor Solomon, and then a kingship that should continue forever in the Messiah. Isaiah speaks of the Messiah Himself as both this covenant and its fulfillment (Isa 42:1, 6; 49:8). Yet it had a bilateral element, in that for the individual king it contained conditional elements (II Sam 7:14-15).

6. *New covenant.* Like the Sinaitic covenant, with Moses as the mediator between God and His chosen people (Acts 7:38; Gal 3:19), so the new covenant was also established between God and a redeemed people, with Christ the Son of God acting as mediator (I Tim 2:5; Heb 8:6; 9:15; 12:24). In contrast, however, the new covenant is far superior to the old or Mosaic covenant, for it is based on better promises and a better sacrifice (Heb 8:6; 9:23). It speaks of a time when God will write His will within the minds and hearts of His people in such a manner that men will no more need to teach one another His will, and when He will forgive the sin of His people Israel (Jer 31:31-37). The writer of Hebrews uses the OT revelation of this covenant to prove that Christ is both the Redeemer and the Mediator for man's sins (Heb 9:7-9; 10:5-16). Christ referred to this covenant as He announced at the institution of the Lord's Supper, "This is my blood of the new testament [covenant]" (Mk 14:24).

Is there any conditional element in this covenant? Yes, to the extent the believer takes Christ as his Saviour and testifies to his faith that Christ's blood was shed for the remission of his sins, and thus individually becomes partaker of the new covenant. Yet there is an unconditional, unilateral, prophetic aspect to this covenant in that it also speaks of a time when all Israel, all the Jews, will know its blessings. Certainly this Gosepl Age cannot yet claim that no man needs to teach his neighbor or brother God's law. This part of the covenant can be applied only to the Millennial Age. *See* Covenant, New.

Theological Covenants

These covenants are thus named because they are discovered by applying the definition of covenant to an agreement recorded in Scripture. Where such facts as contracting parties, conditions, results, and security are present, there is a covenant. Such covenants, which some theologians consider to be woven into the warp and woof of the Scriptures, are the covenant of works, the covenant of grace, and the covenant of redemption. These are usually discussed in the writings of Reformed theologians who follow the covenant theology of Johannes Cocceius (1603-1669).

To those who object to the classification of God's agreement between Himself and Adam before the Fall as a covenant of works, and His agreement with men for their salvation after the Fall as a covenant of grace, the following may be said: (1) God's agreement with David in II Sam 7 is not designated a covenant there, but it is named a covenant in Ps 89:3, 28. (2) It is only possible to develop a true systematic theology by the application of inductively developed definitions. This is what is done in establishing the theological covenants. (3) We are faced with the necessity of laboriously repeating the agreement God announced to Adam when He created him, and its conditions and results, or classifying the same. When we call it a covenant we are simply using a definitive term rather than unnecessarily repeating data.

1. *Covenant of works.* The *parties* were God and Adam before the Fall. The *conditions,* positive: love God and obey Him and love others; negative: do not disobey God or rebel against Him; do not eat of the tree of the knowledge of good and evil. How can we determine the positive result when it is not stated? Quite simply. God is holy and unchangeable; therefore the way in which He dealt with the earliest order of rational beings, the angels, is the way in which He must deal with all the rest of His creatures. Those angels who loved and obeyed Him became the holy angels—they were confirmed in righteousness; those who rebelled became the fallen angels. The tree of the knowledge of good and evil in Eden was the test for man. Not to eat of it represented obedience and love; to eat, disobedience and distrust. The *results* revealed in this covenant were life for obedience and love, as for the holy angels; and death for disobedience and rebellion, as for the fallen angels. God's word, because He is the truth, was the *security.*

2. *Covenant of grace.* The *parties* are God and man through the Lord Jesus Christ, or, perhaps better, God and Jesus Christ and men as they become united with Christ by faith in Him. This concept of a covenant of grace between the Father and the Son in which salvation is offered to sinners may be found in Eph 1:3-6, where it is written that God chose us in Christ before the foundation of the world. See also II Tim 1:9; Tit 1:2; Jn 3:17; 17:4-10, 21-24. The *condition* again is saving faith, expressed in the OT by such acts of faith as that of Abel (Heb 11:4), Abraham and David (Rom 4:3, 6-8), and by acceptance of Jesus Christ as revealed in the NT. The *results* are eternal life for the believer and eternal condemnation for the unbeliever.

3. *Covenant of redemption.* Whether there is an additional covenant of redemption to the covenant of grace is debated by the covenant theologians. Charles Hodge was the leader of those in the United States who make a distinction and see two separate covenants. J. O. Buswell, Jr., argues strongly that they are one and the same (*Systematic Theology,* II, 122 ff.).

The covenant of redemption may be defined as a unilateral agreement between the Father and the Son, which contains a second covenant between God and His people. This covenant appears clearly in two places: in Ps 40:6-8, where the Son is talking to the Father and speaks of the sacrifice God desires from Him; and in a passage which quotes these verses, Heb 10:5-16, where we are told God takes away the first covenant, namely, the Mosaic, to establish the second: "By the which will we are sanctified through the offering of the body of Jesus Christ once for all" (v. 10). We are then told (Heb 10:15-17) that the Holy Spirit endorsed this truth when He foretold the new covenant in Jer 31:33-34. The insight of Archibald McCaig is particularly helpful at this point: "The 'New Covenant' here spoken of is practically equivalent to the Covenant of Grace established between God and His redeemed people, that again resting upon the eternal Covenant of Redemption made between the Father and the Son, which, though not so expressly designated, is not obscurely indicated by many passages of Scripture" ("Covenant, The New," ISBE, II, 731).

It is of value to distinguish the covenant of redemption from the new covenant, since the covenant of redemption becomes a most important test in the detection of a Unitarian view, such as found in the teachings of Karl Barth. If there is no ontological Trinity of three Persons in the Godhead, there can be no covenant of redemption between the Father and the Son. Since Barth teaches merely three modes of revelation of one single Person, he must reject this covenant. His Unitarianism excludes a covenant or direct communication in word or prayer between the Persons of the Godhead.

Interrelationship of the Covenants

This connection between the various covenants can be likened to a series of stairsteps—each is added to and based on the ones preceding it. The interrelationship may be illustrated by the fact that the Davidic and the new covenants are both contained in and are extensions of the Abrahamic covenant. Abraham was promised a kingdom and a land, and these were given in further detail in the Davidic covenant. He was also given the gospel, for "the scripture . . . preached the gospel beforehand to Abraham" (Gal 3:8, RSV), and this was delineated much further and in greater detail in the new covenant.

Again, the covenant of works, though broken by Adam and though its consequences came upon all mankind, was taken up by Christ, as He was "made of a woman, made under the law, to redeem them that were under the law" (Gal 4:4-5), and kept perfectly by Him for us and in our stead. Further, on the cross He bore the penalty of the broken law for us. We in turn are saved by the covenant of grace, which depends upon Christ having ended for us the covenant of works; first by fulfilling its demands, and second by bearing its penalties against sin (Rom 10:4).

Bibliography. Karl Barth, *Church Dogmatics,* Edinburgh: T. & T. Clark, 1936. Louis Berkhof, *Systematic Theology,* Grand Rapids: Eerdmans, 1949. J. Oliver Buswell, Jr., *A Systematic Theology of the Christian Faith,* Grand Rapids: Eerdmans, 1962. K. A. Kitchen, *Ancient Orient and Old Testament,* Chicago: Inter-Varsity, 1966, pp. 90-102. Meredith G. Kline, *The Treaty of the Great King,* Grand Rapids: Eerdmans, 1963; *By Oath Consigned,* Grand Rapids: Eerdmans, 1968; "Canon and Covenant," WTJ, XXXII (1969), 49-67; "The Correlation of the Concepts of Canon and Covenant," NPOT, pp. 265-279. George E. Mendenhall, *Law and Covenant in Israel and the Ancient Near East,* Pittsburgh: Biblical Colloquium, 1955. John J. Mitchell, "Abram's Understanding of the Lord's Covenant," WTJ, XXXII (1969), 24-48. J. Barton Payne, *The Theology of the Older Testament,* Grand Rapids: Zondervan, 1962; "The B'rith of Yahweh," NPOT, pp. 240-264. Gottfried Quell and Johannes Behm, "*Diathēkē,*" TDNT, II, 106-134. Gene M. Tucker, "Covenant Forms and Contract Forms," VT, XV (1965), 487-503. Donald J. Wiseman, "The Vassal-Treaties of Esarhaddon," *Iraq,* XX (1958), 1-28. John M. L. Young, "Theology of Missions, Covenant Centered," ChT, XIII (Nov. 22, 1968), 162-165. *See also* Covenant, New.

R. A. K. and J. R.

COVENANT, ARK OF. *See* Ark of the Covenant.

COVENANT, BOOK OF THE. *See* Book of the Covenant.

COVENANT, NEW. This is God's arrangement by which He established a new relationship of responsibility between Himself and His people (Jer 31:31-34). The phrase the new covenant also is a synonym for the NT, and thus refers to the 27 books of the NT or the New Covenant. But in this article the phrase is considered only in connection with that covenantal relationship between God and His people which is designated as a new covenant.

The designation of the covenant. When first mentioned, this covenant was called "new" (Jer 31:31), for it was set in contrast with Israel's primary or older covenant, namely, the covenant of the Mosaic law. This same contrast is also made in Heb 8:6-13.

The provisions of the covenant.

1. The new covenant provides an unconditional, grace relationship between God and "the house of Israel and the house of Judah." The frequency of the use of the phrase "I will" in Jer 31:31-34 is striking.
2. It provides regeneration in the impartation of a renewed mind and heart (Ezk 36:26).
3. It provides for restoration to the favor and blessing of God (Hos 2:19-20).
4. It includes forgiveness of sin (Jer 31:34*b*).
5. The indwelling ministry of the Holy Spirit is one of its provisions (Jer 31:33; cf. Ezk 36:27). This also includes the teaching ministry of the Spirit.
6. It provides for the exaltation of Israel as head of the nations (Jer 31:38-40; cf. Deut 28:13).

The foundation of the covenant. The foundation of all the covenant blessings is the blood of Christ. In the upper room the night before His death, the Lord stated that the cup symbolized "the blood of the new covenant" (Mt 26:28), and that this blood shed would be the foundation for all the blessings of that covenant. The disciples would have thought of no other covenant than the one prophesied by Jeremiah.

The people of the covenant. There is no question that the OT revelation of the new covenant links it with the nation Israel. This is specifically stated in the words of establishment (Jer 31:31). This fact is reaffirmed in Isa 59:20-21; 61:8-9; Jer 32:37-40; 50:4-5; Ezk 16:60-63; 34:25-26; 37:21-28. It is also a logical deduction from the fact that the contrasting Mosaic covenant was made with Israel, and from the fact that in its establishment, the perpetuity of the nation Israel and her restoration to the land is vitally linked with it (Jer 31:35-40). The NT adds the truth that believers in Christ have a better covenant (Heb 8:6) and that they are ministers of the new covenant (II Cor 3:6).

Amillennialists understand the NT teaching to indicate that only the Church is now fulfilling the promises of the new covenant and that there will be no other fulfillment. Premillennialists disallow an exclusive fulfillment by the Church and teach either that the covenant is still only for Israel, and will be fulfilled by her in the millennium; or that the Church has some relationship to the covenant but that this does not replace the future millennial fulfillment by Israel.

The amillennial interpretation is based on its consistent insistence that the Church during this age is fulfilling all of Israel's promises, which would quite naturally include the promises of the new covenant. The premillennial interpretation is built on the sharp distinction made in the system between Israel and the Church. (Cf. O.T. Allis, *Prophecy and the Church,* pp. 154 ff., and C. C. Ryrie, *The Basis of the Premillennial Faith,* pp. 105 - 125.)

The fulfillment of the covenant. Whatever relationship the Church may have to the new covenant, it seems clear from the NT that it will be fulfilled in its original provisions to Israel at the second coming of Christ (Rom 11:26-27). There is no question that the covenant to be fulfilled at that time is the new covenant, for the reference to taking away sin is a promise contained in the new covenant. The question is only, who is "Israel," who will be saved then, and who will enjoy the benefits of the new covenant? Premillennialists and even some amillennialists (Charles Hodge, *Epistle to the Romans,* pp. 584-5) say that this is a reference to the Jewish people, but other amillennialists insist that it is the Church and that fulfillment is now, not at the second coming of Christ (Allis, *op. cit.,* p. 156). This appears inconsistent with the principle of plain interpretation, since the nation of Israel is so clearly mentioned.

Premillennialists are faced with the question of the relation, if any, of the believer today to the new covenant. Some have said that there is no relationship (J.N. Darby, *Synopsis of the Books of the Bible,* V, 286). Others follow the view of the notes of the Scofield Reference Bible (p. 1297), which applies the one new covenant to both Israel in the future and the Church in the present. A few others see two new covenants—one for Israel and one for the Church (L. S. Chafer, *Systematic Theology,* IV, 325). Note that all agree on a future fulfillment by Israel in the millennium.

Concerning the Church's relation to the covenant, it seems best understood in the light of the progress of revelation. OT revelation of the new covenant concerned Israel alone. The believer today is saved by the blood of the new covenant shed on the cross. All spiritual blessings are his because of this, and many of his blessings are the same as those promised to Israel under the OT revelation of the new covenant. However, the Christian believer is not promised blessings connected with the restoration to the Promised Land, and he is not made a member of the commonwealth of Israel. He is a minister of the new covenant, for there is no other basis than the blood of that covenant for the salvation of any today. Nevertheless, in addition to revealing these facts about the Church and the new covenant, the NT also reveals that the blessings promised to Israel will be experienced by her at the second coming of Christ (Rom 11:26 - 27).

See Church; Covenant; Kingdom.

Bibliography. O. T. Allis, *Prophecy and the Church,* Philadelphia: Presbyterian and Reformed, 1945. Alva J. McClain, *The Greatness of the Kingdom,* Grand Rapids: Zondervan, 1959, pp. 157-160. Leon Morris, "Covenant," *The Apostolic Preaching of the Cross,* Grand Rapids: Eerdmans, 1955, pp. 60 – 107. Charles C. Ryrie, *The Basis of the Premillennial Faith,* New York: Loizeaux Bros., 1953; "Covenant Theology," *Dispensationalism Today,* Chicago: Moody Press, 1965, pp. 177-191. Wilber B. Wallis, "Irony in Jeremiah's Prophecy of a New Covenant," JETS, XII (1969), 107-110. *See also* under Covenant.

C. C. R.

COVENANT OF SALT. Agreements or compacts between individuals were usually ratified by eating together (Gen 31:44, 54; Ex 24:7-11). Seasoning the food to be eaten with salt signified the permanence and inviolability of the treaty or covenant being made or remembered (II Chr 13:5; Ezr 4:14, RSV). When the covenant was made with God, the food was first sacrificed to Him (Lev 2:13; Num 18:19; Ezk 43:24). Nomads of the Middle East still eat "bread and salt" together as the sign and seal of a brotherhood covenant.

COVERING THE HEAD. In I Cor 11:2-16 Paul commanded women to have their heads covered while at public worship. In the plan of God, man has headship over the woman. It was unseemly, then, in a gathering where both men and women were present in the house of God, that women should be without a token of this subjection. Women should not therefore object to wearing a veil, for this simply answered to the long hair covering which they already had. Women who refused to wear a veil manifested a spirit of independence, which was unbecoming and which would find its logical expression in cutting the hair so as to look like a man (vv. 5-6). This condition was considered by Paul contrary to nature (vv. 14-15). In no church at that time was it the custom to permit the women to be without a veil (v. 16). Actually, in the final analysis, the covering of the head represented the subjection of the woman to the man.

F. C. K.

COVERLET. Found in II Kgs 8:15, RSV. A mat or coarse cloth used to smother Ben-hadad.

COVERT FOR THE SABBATH. *See* Sabbath, Covert for the.

COVETOUSNESS. The tenth commandment forbids covetousness of all sorts when it speaks of a neighbor's house, wife, servant, cattle, draft animal, and of any of his possessions (Ex 20:17). The NT declares covetousness to be a form of idolatry (Col 3:5) or worship of goods and possessions, and condemns it along with other cardinal sins (Mk 7:22; Lk 12:15; Rom 1:29; Eph 5:3; Col 3:5; I Thess 2:5; II Pet 2:3).

It was covetousness which Christ saw in the rich young ruler when the Lord quoted him five of the six commandments of the second table of the law, and then challenged him with the tenth by enjoining him to sell all he had and give the proceeds to the poor (Lk 18:20-22). Barnabas, in contrast, probably fearing covetousness and knowing of the rich young ruler, sold all he had and gave it to the church (Acts 4:36-37).

Paul cites covetousness as a key illustration of sinfulness, saying that "sin, finding occasion, wrought in me all manner of coveting" (Rom 7:8, ASV). In I Tim 6:10 we read, "The love of money is the root of all evil." The Gr. says "a root." This love stems from covetousness and can become the source of all kinds of evil (e.g., Ananias and Sapphira, Acts 5:1-11; cf. Ahab and Naboth's vineyard, I Kgs 21:1-19).

Some forms of covetousness are even more subtle, such as gambling, lotteries, bingo, etc., in which the player or participant often fails to analyze his own motive and detect covetousness. It is essentially covetousness which causes one to want to keep up with others when he knows that doing so extends him beyond his means and causes him to purchase what he really does not need.

Bibliography. Gerhard Delling, *"Pleonektēs,* etc.," TDNT, VI, 266-274.

R. A. K.

COW. *See* Animals, I.6.

COZ (kŏz). The father of Anub and Zobebah. Coz is found only in I Chr 4:8. It is also spelled Koz (*q.v.*).

COZBI (kŏs'bĭ). A Midianite princess slain by Phinehas, thus averting a plague (Num 25:6-15). In Akkadian *kuzbu* means "voluptuousness."

CRACKLING. The noise of burning thorns or stubble sometimes used as firewood, which flashes up and burns out quickly, leaving nothing but ashes (Eccl 7:6).

CRACKNELS. Used only in I Kgs 14:3. *See* Food.

CRAFT, CRAFTSMAN. *See* Occupations.

CRAFTINESS, CRAFTY. These terms are used for cunning or guile. Crafty refers to one who is sly and tricky in getting his own way (Job 5:12-13; 15:5; I Cor 3:19), or who is even unscrupulous or deceitful (Lk 20:23; II Cor 4:2; Eph 4:14). Paul caustically quotes the Corinthians' opinion of him in II Cor 12:16 in order to refute their insinuation.

CRANE. *See* Animals, III.7.

CREATION. The work of God in bringing all things into existence. The definitive passage is Gen 1:1, upon which must rest all biblical theology. God the Creator is a personal trinity, omnipotent, omnipresent, and omniscient. God alone is eternal, and is both immanent and transcendent with respect to His creation.

True creation must be *ex nihilo* (from nothing). The idea that the present universe has been developed out of prior materials, though commonly held in other religions and philosophies, has no basis in either Scripture or physical science. The translation of Gen 1:1 which treats it as a dependent clause (i.e., "When God began to create the heavens and the earth, the earth was without form and void") is inadmissible. This opening verse is rather an absolute statement asserting the initial creation of the heavens and the earth out of nothing. Neither is it a mere title nor summary of that which follows; rather, it is the first statement in the narrative of the order of the events of creation.

Since Gen 1:1 is the only verse in the chapter which mentions the creation of the heavens, it must be comprehended within the scope of the summary statement of Gen 2:1, which asserts the completion of the creation of both the heavens and the earth.

Complete creation. It is of paramount importance to recognize that Scripture teaches a *finished* creation. This fact is emphasized by the repeated statements to this effect in Gen 2:1-3, and by the institution of the sabbath as a memorial of God's finished work (see also Ex 20:11; 31:17; Ps 33:6, 9; Neh 9:6; Heb 4:4, 10; II Pet 3:5). Thus creation is no longer taking place, except in occasional acts of a miraculous nature. The normal, uniform processes of nature by which God now is providentially upholding all things (Heb 1:3; II Pet 3:7) are thus not processes of creation at all. Scientific study of present processes can therefore lead to no understanding whatever of the events of the creation period, since these events were brought about by divine creative processes which we are not now able to investigate.

A fragment of the Babylonian Creation epic from the palace of King Ashurbanipal of Assyria. BM

This teaching of Scripture is supported scientifically by the law of conservation of mass and energy, the first law of thermodynamics, which is the most basic and best-proved law of all science. Neither energy nor mass (except in mass-energy interchanges) is now being either created or destroyed. The universal reservoir of energy (which really includes everything in the physical universe) must therefore date from a primeval period of creation, just as the Bible declares.

Apparent age. If creation was not brought about by means of present processes, then the *only* way by which we can know anything of the events, manner, order, or date of creation is for God to reveal these things. This is exactly what He has done in the creation record in Gen 1 and 2, as well as in many other passages of Scripture. There is therefore no valid reason to doubt in any way the exact accuracy of the events recorded in these passages. These great events occupied a six-day period. Each act was complete and each was adjudged by God to be "good." The total creation He called "very good" (Gen 1:31). Necessarily, these created entities must, at the instant of their creation, have had an "appearance of age." This is most obvious in the case of Adam and Eve, who were created as mature individuals, but it must also have been true in the case of all other objects, both animate and inanimate. The entire universe was established as a functioning whole from the instant of creation. In fact, it is philosophically as well as scripturally impossible even to conceive of a substance truly created without some appearance of age. This does not in any wise involve God in deception, as some claim, since He has clearly revealed this to be the case in His Word.

Evolution. It may therefore be categorically asserted that processes of evolution, whether theistic or atheistic, cannot account for the constitution of the universe and its inhabitants. Evolution by definition involves a general increase in order and organization, from simple to complex and from lower to higher. In its usually presented scientific framework, it involves great ages of slow changes, guided upward by the process of natural selection. This is purportedly explained by the principle of uniformity of operation of present processes—a principle explicitly contradicted by the creation account.

Furthermore, the Scriptures indicate that because of the entrance of sin there now exists a universal curse on the earth (Gen 3:17-19; Rom 8:19-22), manifested in a universal tendency toward decay and death. Thus, although change is everywhere evident in the world, this change is not evolutionary but rather deteriorative. This teaching of Scripture is verified scientifically by the second law of thermodynamics, which states that there is in every system—whether physical or biological—an innate tendency toward decrease of order and complexity. At the most, therefore, evolution can only be a local and temporary phenomenon, and cannot possibly have the status of a universal law such as the laws of conservation and deterioration. Thus it is impossible to attribute the creation to any form of evolution.

Summary. Creation, according to Scripture, was accomplished as a series of divine acts, bringing material entities into existence out of nothing. These were highly organized and completely functioning from the beginning, and thus were formed with an appearance of age. The creation was completed and finished during a special period in the past, following which God "rested" and is no longer creating, except in isolated instances of supernatural intervention. Present physical and biological processes are providential rather than creative, and so can give no information whatever concerning the creation period. This information can come only by divine revelation, which is given in the Bible.

Thus there remains no reason why we cannot or should not accept the creation record of Genesis as a historical, literal, factual account of the specific events which took place during that period. *See* Adam; Genesis.

Bibliography. J. O. Buswell, Jr., *A Systematic Theology of the Christian Religion,* Grand Rapids: Zondervan, 1962, pp. 135-137. J. O. Buswell, III, "Adam and Neolithic Man," *Eternity,* XVIII (1967), 29-30, 39, 48-50. Alexander Heidel, *The Babylonian Genesis,* Chicago: Univ. of Chicago Press, 1951, pp. 89-92. W. G. Lambert and A. R. Millard, *Atra-Ḫasīs: the Babylonian Story of the Flood,* New York: Oxford Univ. Press, 1969. James M. Murk, "Evidence for a Late Pleistocene Creation of Man," JASA, XVII (1965), 37-49. Robert C. Neville, *God, the Creator,* Chicago: Univ. of Chicago Press, 1968 (a philosophical defense of the theory of divine creation). J. Barton Payne, *The Theology of the Old Testament,* Grand Rapids: Zondervan, 1962, p. 133. A. E. Wilder Smith, *Man's Origin, Man's Destiny,* Wheaton: Shaw, 1968. John C. Whitcomb and Henry M. Morris, *The Genesis Flood,* Nutley, N.J.: Presbyterian and Reformed Pub. Co., 1961, pp. 223-227, 232-234, 344-346. Edward J. Young, "The Relation of the First Verse of Genesis 1 to Verses 2 and 3," WTJ, May, 1959, pp. 134-145. R. Laird Harris, *Man—God's Eternal Creation,* Chicago: Moody, 1971, pp. 25-71.

H. M. M.

CREATURE(S). In Heb. a creature, *nepesh,* is any living being (Gen 1:21, 24; 2:19), even as God breathed "the breath of life" into man and he became a living "soul" (*nepesh,* Gen 2:7). The English word is also used to refer to all created animate beings both human and animal in the total creation (Gen 2:19; Rom 8:19-22), but elsewhere is applied specifically to animals or water creatures (Gen 1:20-21, 24; 9:10, 12, 15-16; Lev 11:46).

In the NT the word so translated (Gr. *ktisis*) means either (1) an individual thing or being created, "created thing" or "creature" (Rom 8:39; Heb 4:13); (2) the sum total of everything created, "creation" (Mk 13:19; II Pet 3:4).

Paul describes a redeemed man as a "new creature" (II Cor 5:17; Gal 6:15). Since the word is Gr. *ktisis,* Paul means that a redeemed man is a "new creation."

See Living Creatures.

CREATURES, LIVING. *See* Living Creatures; Cherubim.

CREDITOR. *See* Debt; Loan.

CREEK. Found only in Acts 27:39 ("bay" in RSV) as a translation of the Gr. *kolpos* meaning "bay," "gulf" of the sea (Arndt, p. 443). Paul was shipwrecked on the shore of the bay of the island of Melita (*q.v.*) or Malta. The traditional gulf is located on the NE tip of the island and is known today as St. Paul's Bay.

CREEPING THING. *See* Animals, IV.

CRESCENS (krĕs'ĕnz). Crescens was the assistant of Paul mentioned in II Tim 4:10. He went to Galatia, but there is no indication of the reason. No trustworthy tradition exists concerning him, though tradition has suggested that he was one of the 70 sent out by Jesus, and that he founded the church in Vienna.

CRESCENTS. Used in Jud 28:21, 26, RSV. It is translated ornaments in KJV. *See* Amulets.

CRETANS. *See* Crete.

CRETE (krēt). The fourth largest island in the Mediterranean (Sicily, Sardinia, and Cyprus being larger). Located 60 miles S of Cape Malea in the Peloponnesus and 110 miles W of Cape Krio in Asia Minor, Crete became a seed bed and distributing center for the cultures of the Near East from the 4th to the 1st mil. B.C.

Comprising an area of 3,200 square miles, Crete is of elongated form—160 miles from E to W and 6 to 35 miles from N to S. In the center of the southern coast is Cape Lithinos, the southernmost point of the island. Immediately to the E of that is the small bay of Kali Limenes or Fair Havens, where the ship carrying Paul took refuge (Acts 27:8). A little less than 25 miles SW of Cape Lithinos lay the rocky, treeless isle of Clauda (Cauda, RSV; modern Gavdo), which Paul's ship passed as it began to fight the storm which eventually blew it to Malta (Acts 27:16).

During the 2nd mil. B.C. Crete was the center of the famous Minoan civilization (CornPBE, pp. 13-17). Caphtor (*q.v.*), home of the Philis-

A reconstructed entrance to the palace at Knossos, Crete. Mimosa

A large storage jar (*c.* 4–5 feet high) from the palace at Knossos (1500–1400 B.C.) in the British Museum. BM

tines (Jer 47:4; Amos 9:7), is commonly identified with Crete. *See also* Cherethites. Rome conquered the island 68/67 B.C. and made it a separate province. Paul may have evangelized it on a fourth missionary journey. At any rate, he sent Titus to organize the church there (Tit 1:5). He quoted one of the Cretan philosophers, Epimenides (*c.* 600 B.C.) who said of his countrymen, "Cretans are always liars, evil beasts, lazy gluttons" (Tit 1:12, NASB), a line in the same poem which Paul also quoted in Acts 17:28.

H. F. V.

CRIB. A feeding trough for animals (Prov 14:4; Isa 1:3; Job 39:9). Government stables at Megiddo during the era of the kings had mangers hollowed out of stone blocks. *See* Manger.

CRICKET. *See* Animals: Beetle, IV.4.

CRIME AND PUNISHMENT. A crime is an act or omission that violates the law forbidding such an act. Punishment (*q.v.*) imposes a penalty on the one responsible for the crime. Crime in the secular sense is regarded as an offense against society, and punishment ensues in the name of society. However, in biblical administration of justice, punishment ranges widely in extent and refinement, from prosecution by injured individuals as in the time of the patriarchs (Gen 38:24), to a well defined prosecution by society through a recognized body of judges and courts as in the NT. In all this development, there is a religious basis.

The body of the law in the OT provides the fundamental biblical base for the definition of crime and punishment. Extrabiblical Jewish traditional materials in the intertestamental period give amplification and modification of these bases which are reflected in the NT. The presence of Roman penal law is also seen in the NT. The body of law in the OT should also be seen against the wider background of ancient Middle Eastern law, in agreement with it in many facets but also divergent from it because of a distinctive theocratic tie with Israel's special revelation.

An OT Theology of Crime and Punishment

The OT view of crime. Since Israel was a theocracy, criminal law in the OT differs from the Middle Eastern legal procedures of other ancient peoples. Crimes are regarded as an offense against Yahweh, and thus, crime is sin. The theocracy had a body of divinely given law and was held responsible for its practice. If there was any laxity in disciplining individual offenders, God held the whole community responsible and He would bring judgment on the community (Lev 26:3–45; Deut 28). These passages indicate that idolatry, immorality and murder were crimes involving the whole community in its common share of guilt and therefore punishment involved itself in public action.

Thus, laws existed in the theocratic relationship between the nation and Yahweh pertaining to the community's responsibility as well as to the individual's moral choices. There was also overlap in the two considerations that posed some real problems in legal procedure of determining guilt and punishment; e.g., in the slaying by the "avenger of blood" of one involved in an accidental homicide when the latter left the city of refuge before the appointed time. While the action would be wrong, the avenger would not be charged, since "blood-guilt" consideration was a serious community responsibility.

The most often used words describing crimes come from the root verbs *ḥāṭā'* ("miss the mark," usually rendered "sin"), *pāsha'* ("revolt," or "refuse subjection to rightful authority," usually rendered "transgress"), and *'āwâ* ("bent," or "crooked," usually rendered "do iniquity"). The words are rendered differently in various situations; thus the contexts need to be examined to see if the criminal acted against God or man.

A number of terms are used to describe those committing offenses and crimes. There is the "wicked" or "guilty" one (Deut 25:2) and the "offender" (I Kgs 1:21). An offender guilty of a capital crime was "guilty of death" (Num 35:31) and the offense could be described as "worthy of death" (Deut 19:6). Another penalty was to be "cut off" (Lev 7:20), and seems to imply the death penalty (cf. Lev 18:8, 29; 20:11). Later development of the law in *Mishnah Makkoth* 3:1, 2 implies that "cut off" standing by itself suggested another penalty, e.g., scourging, etc. Other terms for crimes speak of "breach of faith against the Lord" (Lev 6:2, RSV), wrongdoing as "punishment" (I Sam 28:10), and to commit "folly" (Josh 7:15). A more complete list of crimes and their punishments is given later.

The OT view of punishment. "The judgment is God's" (Deut 1:17) and the punishment of evildoers is an expression of divine justice. A person who was punished for a misdeed was reckoned to have appeared in judgment before the Lord (Deut 19:17). The penal laws were meant to be obeyed, with dire consequences of punishment for disobedience, because observing the law was doing "that which is right in the eyes of the Lord thy God" (Deut 13:18). Other expressions in the administration of justice need to be recognized; e.g., "If the thief is not found, the owner of the house shall come near to God . . ." (Ex 22:8, RSV; KJV has "judges" for "God"). "God" is understood here as the judge himself called Elohim and who was the representative of God.

Source Materials

The Pentateuch. In the establishment of the theocracy, one sees a stricture of exercise in function by taking from the head of a family the power of life and death exercised in the time of the patriarchs (Gen 38:24; Ex 21:20). Blood revenge was still retained but restricted under theocratic controls. At Sinai and Abel-shittim God gave the theocratic nation a revelation of detailed legislation, codified in the Mosaic writings.

The historical development of criminal law seems to involve four major codes: (1) the Decalogue (Ex 20:2-17); (2) elaboration in the judicial and ritualistic specifications of "the book of the testament" (Ex 20:22–23:33) which united the nation in its religious and political life; (3) the priestly codes (comprising primarily Leviticus and Num 5; 6; 9:1-14; 10:1-10; 15; 18; 19); (4) the Deuteronomy codes.

However, Moses received all this material during the period of the wilderness experience, beginning with the Decalogue on Mount Sinai in 1447 B.C. and ending with the Deuteronomy materials given on the plains of Moab in 1407 B.C., just before Israel entered Canaan. One can discern development in the details of a law, e.g., the law of accidental homicide, from the book of the testament to Deuteronomy as additional material was added (Ex 21:13; Num 35:9-15, 22-28; Deut 19:1-10). Also, depending on particular needs, a given judicial aspect was emphasized in one area more than in another, or it was mentioned in one code and not discussed in another. For example, the Exodus materials treat in detail concerning injuries to person and property, but deal with only one aspect of immorality concerning seduction; Deuteronomy treats the matter of crimes upon women, wedded or single, but does not mention seduction. This does not mean, however, that offenses involving chastity were not known during the Sinai encampment.

In general, the body of the Mosaic law emphasizes that God is the Lawgiver and the One who validates the law; that accidental death and murder must be treated differently; that there is no death penalty in a crime pertaining to a property right; that punishment in cases of the principle of *lex talionis* excludes the practice of one human dying for another; and that no class distinction is observed in ascertaining punishment. The body of the law is also distinct in its comprehension and application from that of other law codes of Middle Eastern peoples in the 2nd mil. B.C. (see below).

Upper part of the Code of Hammurabi, showing Hammurabi receiving his laws from the sun god. LM

Middle Eastern law. A knowledge of other law codes of Middle Eastern countries contemporary with the patriarchs and Moses is necessary in order to provide proper background and contrast. Pertinent to this period are the laws of Eshnunna of the 19th cen. B.C., the Hammurabi code of the 18th cen. B.C., the Middle Assyrian

CRIME AND PUNISHMENT

laws of the 15th-13th cen. B.C., and the Hittite laws ranging from the 19th-13th cen. B.C.

In treating the well-known Hammurabi's *lex talionis,* appearing earlier than the book of the testament, some scholars have questioned the divine origin of Moses' laws. It is granted that there were legal patterns present as a part of a common Middle Eastern culture and heritage familiar to all peoples of the region. However, there were important points of contrast between the Pentateuchal codes and the Hammurabi code and other codes of the ancient Middle East. Thus, it was God who sanctioned the Mosaic materials throughout, while Hammurabi's code existed in no such form (except for one initial reference to its supposed receipt from the sun-god). Moses' law had one standard of justice for all, while Hammurabi's material presented an elaborate class distinction. The Pentateuchal insisted on sexual purity, with divorce permitted only for one specific cause (Deut 24:1), but Hammurabi's code recognized temple prostitutes as one social class and divorce was common. Moses' laws had a unique regard for social consciousness that reached even to an enemy (Deut 23:7); it forbade replacement of the slain by another person and sacrificing life to protect property.

What has been indicated for the Hammurabi code applies to a greater or lesser extent to the other codes. The primary thrust of the penal law was economic, and a secular legal system represented the state and the king as the ones who gave and validated the codes, in contrast to the Mosaic law.

Further development in the OT. Extra-biblical material from Palestine covering the period from the judges to the end of the OT monarchy is almost lacking as contrasted with a wealth of material in criminal cases, court documents, etc., in Mesopotamia. In 1960 an ostracon from the time of Josiah was found in Israel near Yavneh-Yam. It is the plea of a conscripted agricultural worker to the local governor that his overseer had wrongly impounded his garment for not delivering a full quota of grain (S. Talmon, "The New Hebrew Letter from the Seventh Century B.C. in Historical Perspective," BASOR #176 [Dec., 1964, pp. 29-38). The few biblical references in the non-legal literature to criminal situations in the period just indicated are brief and treat only some unusual circumstances.

When there are references to points of law in the Prophets and Writings, there is sometimes an agreement with the criminal code and sometimes a deviation from it. In most instances deviations resulted from the people's syncretization of Canaanite practices, which had a thoroughly adverse effect upon public morals and led to an increase in criminal actions. The prophets denounced this synthesis and championed greater adherence to the revealed materials. But the greatest amount of biblical material dealing with ethics, which in turn would aid in the control of criminal situations, was in the Proverbs of Solomon. This book should be regarded as second to the Pentateuchal codes in explaining and amplifying the precepts in the laws. Prevention of crime is stressed in Proverbs concerning the sanctity of life, regard for private property, and the use of sex as God had prescribed.

Non-legal biblical literature gives some application of the law concerning crimes involving the state and the king. Saul abused the criminal code in slaughtering the priests of Nob contrary to the concept of vicarious punishment (I Sam 22:19), while in another place he condemned the trafficking in spiritism (I Sam 28:9). David was involved in criminal action in the Bathsheba affair. Also he indicated a knowledge of the penal codes in Nathan's story of the confiscation of the poor man's lamb (II Sam 12:1-6). One full account of a legal procedure, although an abuse, is the case of Naboth and the false charge of cursing God and the king (I Kgs 21:10, 13). During his reign, Jehoshaphat saw that Judah had need for the application of a good judicial system (II Chr 19:4-11). A trial for treason appears in Jer 26; prosecution and defense argued alternately for Jeremiah, who was charged with "worthy of death." Jeremiah was cleared, but Uriah, another prophet, suffered a miscarriage of justice. The period of the monarchy closed with a wide gap between an actual legal practice and the demands of the Mosaic law.

Jewish traditional materials. The post-Exilic period began to see, under Ezra, a restoration of the ordinances of the law in the life experiences of a resettled people. There was no official monarchy, but Ezra and those who succeeded him fenced the legal system with further restrictions to guard against the deviations from the commandments.

The end of the intertestamental period and the 1st cen. A.D. saw the production and further development of a body of literature and materials concerning views on the biblical law. The *ḥîṣônîm* literature (that outside the canon)—the Apocrypha (e.g., Tobit and Judith) and the Pseudepigrapha (e.g., Jubilees)—is a valuable witness. Main line Judaism had its legal sources in appropriate materials of the Tannaim (lawyer rabbis of the 1st cen. B.C. to *c.* A.D. 200). This material appeared in written form by A.D. 200 in the Mishnah (first part of the Talmud). Included with the Mishnah are the Tannaitic commentaries on the legal materials in the Pentateuchal books, e.g., the *Mekilta* on Exodus, the *Sifra* on Leviticus, and the *Sifre* on Numbers and Deuteronomy. This literature is still used as source materials for judicial rendering on points of Jewish law in connection with biblical materials. The writings of Philo (*On the Special Laws*) and Josephus (*Ant.* iv.8) are also pertinent.

Crime and Punishment in the OT

Crimes concerning society as a whole. These were crimes that affected the whole nation. One of these was to *defy the law.* It was a gross crime to act with impudence and defiance toward the priest and the judge as these officials sought to minister. The penalty in this case was death in order to put away evil from Israel (Deut 17:12). This was to serve as a warning to the rest of the people that they should not act in defiance of the law either.

Another crime of this nature involved *perverting and obstructing justice.* False reports were not to be received, and one was not to join with the wicked to be an unrighteous witness. One was not to join in a false cause to twist judgment, especially when the poor were involved inasmuch as the latter could not defend themselves (Ex 23:1-2, 6-7). There was to be impartiality; equal justice was to prevail for both poor and wealthy (Lev 19:15). Here was a unique contrast with other Middle Eastern codes that had respect for all kinds of classes and many times favored the wealthy over the poor.

Bribery as a crime against society was forbidden; bribes were regarded as blinding the ones receiving them (Ex 23:8).

Closely associated with bribery was *perjury,* which was strictly forbidden (Deut 5:20). The penalty for perjury consisted in punishing the false witness to the extent that he had thought to do to his victim (Deut 19:16-20).

Crimes against individuals. Within the biblical context, individual life has dignity and grace associated with it and any harm to that life is of a serious nature. Accordingly, a number of areas whereby harm could come to the individual life was spelled out.

At the head of the list of crimes which could result in bodily harm was *murder.* The Decalogue indicated that one was not to murder (Ex 20:13). Murder was regarded as marring the image of God (Gen 9:6). The unrequited blood of the murdered one was considered as polluting the land (Num 35:33). Some of the cases of premeditated murder were spelled out: coming presumptuously in guile upon a neighbor to kill him (Ex 21:14); smiting a person with various instruments in enmity or with hatred so that death ensues (Num 35:16-21). Striking a father or mother was considered murder (Ex 21:15, RSV). It was regarded as murder when death was caused from an induced miscarriage (Ex 21:22-23). It was considered murder to sacrifice a child to a foreign god (Lev 20:2-3). The penalty in all these instances was death. In cases of murder, the offender was not allowed to ransom his life (Num 35:31-33). There is no parallel in this matter between the biblical codes and other Middle Eastern codes, e.g., Assyrian, Hittite and the Hammurabi codes. The biblical text emphasizes the sanctity of human life.

Different degrees of guilt were recognized when human life was taken. When the killing was without premeditation, the offense was called manslaughter. When there was accidental death, the offending party was to flee to a city of refuge (Ex 21:13; Num 35:15). An appropriate penalty would then be established by the judges (Num 35:22-28). Death as a result of self-defense seems to have been recognized and the one who killed was blameless (Ex 22:2).

The cursing of one's parents was considered heinous and was regarded as having his blood upon him (Lev 20:9), a form of murder. The case of a rebellious son who would not listen to his parents, and who had established a pattern of perversity in spite of continued correction and chastening, was considered the same as a murderer; this action carried the death penalty (Deut 21:18-21).

Also considered crimes against individuals were *rape* and *seduction* (see next section dealing with crimes of a sexual nature).

Assaults of various categories were also treated in the code. In the case of a fight between two individuals, and one was harmed but did not die, the offending party had to pay for any damages as well as lost wages (Ex 21:18-19). When a master struck his servant so that he died, then the servant would be avenged; but if the servant continued to live, the master would not be punished (Ex 21:20-21). One sees here an unparalleled law in the Middle East for its interest in the slave as a human being rather than as chattel. However, if the master struck the servant so that he lost either an eye or a tooth, the servant was to be freed (Ex 21:26-27). When a man caused a pregnant woman to miscarry but the woman did not die as a result, then the offender had to pay damages as assessed by the wronged husband and the judges (Ex 21:22). In the case of an assault by an animal, the animal was to be put to death (Ex 21:28-32; see section below under penalties for murder).

A householder could slay a burglar breaking into his house at night, but was forbidden to do this in the daytime (Ex 22:2-3). The assumption was that the burglar at night would not hesitate to kill, and thus the case of law at this point. The Hammurabi code did not make this distinction since theft alone was sufficient to justify killing the offender. Other Middle Eastern laws did make the distinction of night and daytime robbery as the biblical law does.

Crimes of an ethical nature were also considered an affront against individuals. There was to be no *lying* one to another (Lev 19:11*b*). In the same category, *slander* and *talebearing* were expressly forbidden (Ex 23:1; Lev 19:16).

Honest weights and measures were to be used in dealing with each other and any *falsifying* was also considered an injustice against God. The penalty inferred here was that dwelling in the land could be jeopardized (Deut 25:13-16).

Stealing and selling a man was an extreme ethical violation and a disgrace to human dignity. This practice carried the death penalty (Ex 21:16; Deut 24:7).

Specific crimes of a sexual nature. Strict regulatory procedures were spelled out in the area of morality with measures of penalty which might sound harsh from the modern point of view. However, moral deviations were regarded as serious, especially since the basic structure of society was involved, the family unit. While similar in a number of ways, distinction in one aspect from other Middle Eastern codes is that biblical law regarded the marriage bond as divinely sanctioned.

In the case of *rape,* the penalty for the man who committed this crime was death (Deut 22:25 - 26). Concerning *seduction,* when a man enticed a maid who was not engaged into sexual intercourse, then the maiden was to be married to this individual. However, if the maiden's father refused this action, then the offender had to pay money for the dowry of the misused maiden (Ex 22:16 - 17).

Adultery was considered a crime and was forbidden (Ex 20:14). A number of instances of adultery were spelled out in the law. When there was coition between a married woman and a man not her husband, and they were caught, then both suffered the penalty of death (Deut 22:22). The same would apply if an engaged woman in a populated area had illicit relations with a man not her fiancé: both suffered the penalty of death (Deut 22:23-24). However, if an engaged woman in a sparsely settled area entered into illicit relations, only the man was put to death inasmuch as the woman could always claim she had protested but no one heard her cries (Deut 22:25-27).

In still another case, if a virgin not engaged had been forced by a man into sexual intercourse, then the man had to pay 50 shekels of silver and she had to be his wife; the man had no right to put her away as long as he lived (Deut 22:28-29). In a further curious situation, if a man was suspicious of his wife's actions, he could appeal to the "law of jealousies," the instruction for cases of jealousy (Num 5:29-30). In an oath before the priest, the suspected woman would drink water mixed with the dust from the tabernacle floor and rest her case before the Lord. If she was guilty, she would become ill, and thus her guilt would be established (Num 5:12-31). A man and another man's bondmaid caught in immorality were to be scourged but not put to death, since the slave was not a freewoman. In this case the man could obtain forgiveness through the proper sacrifice (Lev 19:20-22).

Sexual relations with those near of kin were expressly forbidden. The list of persons considered close of kin included the immediate family, the immediate in-laws, step-mother or step-father, aunts, uncles, nieces, nephews, or double marriages involving a mother and daughter, or two sisters (Lev 18:6-18). The penalty in these cases of *incest* was death (Lev 20:11, 12, 14, 20, 21).

Sodomy (Lev 18:22) was punished by the death of both parties (Lev 20:13). In the case of bestiality (Lev 18:23), both the offending person and beast were put to death (Lev 20:15-16).

Indecent assault by a woman upon a man when defending himself resulted in a penalty in kind for the woman (Deut 25:11-12).

The case of *willful relations* with a woman during her menstrual period called for the death penalty (Lev 15:24; 18:19; 20:18).

Improper dress, where either sex wears the clothing that pertains to the opposite sex, is described as an abomination to the Lord; however, no penalty is prescribed by the law (Deut 22:5).

In the matter of *prostitution,* the law prohibited sacred or cult prostitutes of both sexes among the Israelites (Deut 23:17). While parents were forbidden to sell their daughters to be common harlots (Lev 19:29), it was recognized that such harlotry could not be strictly controlled (Deut 23:18).

Crimes of a religious nature. Because of the seriousness of these crimes, primarily against God, the penalties called for the death sentence.

Apostasy involved an individual's attempting to lead members of his family or close friends astray to worship gods other than Israel's true God (Deut 13:6-11). Or apostasy occurred in a case of proved subversion where whole communities were led astray to serve pagan deities (Deut 13:12-16). In addition there was the concept of *ḥerem,* pertaining to an object banned from common use or "devoted to destruction." This related to anything associated with paganism, the idols and their decorations (Deut 7:25), the people involved in sacrifices to them (Ex 22:20), or as indicated, subverted communities. One connected with *ḥerem* became *ḥerem,* and thus one who appropriated to himself objects regarded as *ḥerem* became *ḥerem,* accursed or under the ban (Josh 7:11-26).

Blasphemy of the name of the Lord, Israel's God, by either an apostate Israelite or a foreigner, was considered a heinous crime (Ex 20:7; Lev 24:16).

False prophets and *dreamers* prophesying in the name of foreign gods were not to have any audience. Even in cases where these individuals predicted short range prophecies that came to pass, they were not to receive attention for this demonstration. Their predictions were permitted by God to prove the Israelite in his loyalty to Him (Deut 13:1-5).

Sabbath desecration was another crime with serious consequences, for no labor was to be done on the day set aside particularly for worship (Num 15:32-36).

Men or women *possessing familiar spirits* (or

understood as being demon possessed) were not to be tolerated but must be executed (Lev 20:27). Neither was *sorcery* permitted (Ex 22:18).

Crimes concerning property. Personal property was held to be inviolate and each one was to respect the possessions of others. This high regard prompted a number of situations which were treated to demonstrate this respect. In all these cases specific restitution had to be made (see below, concerning punishment for crimes).

The eighth commandment definitely stated that no one was to steal, and therefore *theft* was condemned (Ex 20:15). Specific cases of theft are mentioned, e.g., stealing cattle or sheep (Ex 22:1, 7), and taking more of the neighbor's vineyard or grain fields than could be eaten at the moment (Deut 23:24-25).

Burglary as a specific case of theft was recognized, in which a thief would break into someone's property to steal for personal gain (Ex 22:1-4). *Arson* was a crime against property and considered loss where buildings containing stored grain as well as fields of grain were set on fire (Ex 22:6).

Killing someone else's beast of burden was forbidden (Lev 24:18, 21). If a hole or a pit was not covered and someone's beast fell into the pit or hole so that the animal was injured or killed, then the negligent party had caused a loss of property (Ex 21:33-34). Care was taken for property in the case of an animal injuring or killing a neighbor's animal. The live animal was to be sold and the money divided, or if a negligent owner did not properly guard an unruly animal, then payment was based on beast for beast (Ex 21:35-36).

Removing landmarks or changing boundary lines between neighbors was condemned (Deut 19:14).

It was regarded as *trespassing* when a man turned his beasts of burden loose in his neighbor's fields to cause loss or destruction (Ex 22:5).

Penalties for crimes. The criminal code recognized degrees of crimes and therefore recommended degrees of penalty. Some of these sentences seem inhumane from today's point of view, but it must be recognized that certain of these crimes, if allowed to go unchecked, had serious national consequences. Schooling a nation in its legal system would lead the people to recognize the holy position of their theocracy in which God Himself was regarded as the Ruler.

The rule of the *lex talionis* limited punishment to strict retaliation in order to prevent excessive revenge. In the case of murder, it was a life for a life, or capital punishment as we know it today (Gen 9:6). Note that this applied even before the Mosaic covenant. But the Mosaic law did also specify the eye for eye, the tooth for tooth, hand for hand as well as the life for life (Ex 21:24-25; Num 35:33). However, apart from murder, the emphasis too many times was on the negative outlook in the interpretation. The sacred Scripture emphasized positively the equity in the punishment. For example, if there was an eye injury, the life of the offending party could not be taken; or if there were an arson case, the offender was not to be maimed or killed. There was to be strict and equal justice, which seems to be the intent of the law.

In the case of murder, no ransom or fine was allowed. Neither was there any sacrifice specified in the sacrificial system for murder; e.g., David could only put himself at the mercy of God when confronted with his sins of adultery and murder (II Sam 12:13). The penalty for murder was the death of the murderer.

In only one instance was there an exception (Ex 21:28-32). This was the case where a negligent owner, after being warned of his rampaging ox, did nothing to restrain it and someone died as a result. In this case, both ox and owner were to be put to death. However, he could ransom himself with the consent and at a sum determined by the kin of the victim. Under the Hammurabi code, in cases of negligence where children died as a result of an unruly ox, etc., the child of the offender was put to death. Ex 21:31 and Deut 24:16 repudiate this practice in Mesopotamian law and emphasize a more humane outlook.

An extreme punishment of *burning* was reserved for those involved in unusual immorality cases; e.g., a man involved with both his wife and her mother, or in the case of a priest's daughter engaged in harlotry (Lev 20:14; 21:9). But even before the law was given, the penalty recognized by the patriarchs for a woman given over to the fertility cult rites of priestess-prostitute (*qedēshā*) was burning (Gen 38:24).

Mutilation was meted out to the woman attempting to help her husband engaged in a fight with another person. She was to lose her hand for indecent assault upon her husband's assailant (Deut 25:11-12). There are few other specific corporal penalties in biblical law. The Middle Eastern laws contain many mutilation specifications based on retaliation that involved ears, eyes, noses, lips, whole faces, etc. Unusual modes of execution, e.g., dismemberment as indicated in Hittite laws or being thrown to the beasts (Dan 6:12), were not a part of Israel's penal code.

Cutting off from the people was another general type of penalty, but the specific kind of punishment many times was not described. It could mean death, banishment, or loss of inheritance because there would be no children to carry on the family line. The context in a few cases indicates what is meant as to the kind of punishment.

Some examples deserving cutting off were: eating blood along with the flesh in violation of the sacredness of the blood (Lev 17:14), being engaged in the many moral deviations practiced by the pagans (Lev 18:29; 20:17-18), sacrificing children as burnt offerings to pagan deities (Lev 20:3), being engaged as accomplices to the ones offering their children (Lev

20:4), becoming involved with those having familiar spirits (Lev 20:6), disregarding the Passover (and thereby disregarding the whole religious system under the law, Num 9:13), continuing willful disregard of the Word of God (Num 15:30–31), and an obvious contemptuous disregard for the ceremonial purity under the law (Num 19:13, 20). *See* Cutting Off.

Hanging was used in certain instances where the crime was worthy of death; after death, the body was hanged or impaled on a stake and bore a special curse of God (Deut 21:22–23). The only specification was that the body was not allowed to remain on the tree overnight but was to be buried on the same day of the execution so that the land would not be defiled.

Stoning was the judgment for those proved to be apostates (Deut 17:5), for those who blasphemed the name of Israel's God (Lev 24:16), for those who sacrificed their children as burnt offerings to pagan idols (Lev 20:2), and for those who had familiar spirits or were wizards (Lev 20:27). In addition, stoning was the judgment for continually stubborn and rebellious sons (Deut 21:19–20), for a bride who could not disprove a charge of immorality (Deut 22:21), and for one who desecrated the sabbath day (Num 15:32–36). In the punishment of stoning, the witnesses to the crime had the privilege of throwing the first stones (Deut 17:7).

In cases where the judges meted out *scourging* and *beating* as a penalty for the wrongdoer in a controversy, any amount up to the limit of 40 stripes was the judgment. The limit of 40 was specific or else there would be no justice and the offender's dignity would be utterly degraded (Deut 25:2–3).

Banishment was a punishment meted out in the post-Exilic period for those who would disobey some of the laws of God or the land (Ezr 7:26). At that time *confiscations of property and excommunication* from the congregation were the penalty for those who refused to part with their non-Israelite marriage partners (Ezr 10:8).

Imprisonment mentioned in the Mosaic covenant lasted only a short time, until it could be ascertained from the Lord what penalty was to be applied to the offender; e.g., in the cases of sabbath desecration and blasphemy (Num 15:34; Lev 24:12). At a later point in Israel's history, imprisonment and the stocks were a part of the penal system of the government, since some of God's prophets were put in prison; e.g., Micaiah (II Chr 18:25–26), Jeremiah (Jer 20:2; 29:26).

Search warrants and sanctions were permitted in the case of a man who kept some of his neighbor's goods for a time and then couldn't return them when called for, indicating they had been stolen (Ex 22:8).

Restitution was an important part of the criminal code of the law. If a beast of burden harmed another, the repayment was animal for animal (Lev 24:18). Theft, denial of things found, burglary, things entrusted for safekeeping and falsely declared to be stolen, etc., were all the bases for restitution, and replacement was to be made plus 20 percent extra. Lev 6:1–7 and Num 5:5–8 deal with voluntary return of property. In all Middle Eastern law, in comparison, there were legal specifications of capital punishment for theft. In one exception in the Hammurabi code there were instructions for punishment in damages amounting to 10 and 30 times the amount stolen. However, this was almost tantamount to a death penalty, for if restitution could not be made, the thief suffered death. Continuing, restitution in kind was to be made for stolen or borrowed property; e.g., animals stolen which had been delivered for safekeeping, and animals or goods that were destroyed when the owner was not there to witness it (Ex 22:12, 14, 15).

In other cases of *compensation* and/or *damages*, an offending party in a fight had to pay lost wages and medical expenses for the injured party (Ex 19:21). A fine of 30 shekels of silver was assessed along with the loss of the ox, in case the ox gored a servant (Ex 19:32); the theft of an ox for food or profit required five oxen for payment, while four sheep were payment for the theft of one sheep (Ex 22:1). A burglar was to make full restitution for his theft, or if he had no money for payment, he was to be sold into servanthood (Ex 22:3). A burglar found with the stolen animal in hand was to repay double (Ex 22:4). A man who fed his animals in his neighbor's fields was to make repayment in kind out of the best of his own fields or vineyards (Ex 22:5), and an arsonist was to make full payment for crops or property destroyed (Ex 22:6).

Punishment was to be meted out for the offender's crimes only; no penalties were to be paid by the defendant's parents or children (Deut 24:16). Punishment was to be handled by the judges or elders and no one was to avenge himself when wronged (except in the case of the avenger of blood for premeditated murder, Lev 19:18; Deut 25:2).

Crime and Punishment in the NT

Jewish law. It should be recognized that the NT is not some kind of body of law. Many situations and instructions in the NT touch on points of the legal code; what is displayed is the Jewish and Roman practice of law (or lack of it) in that period. Legal situations are difficult to determine; the NT authors did not write comprehensive legal briefs and give majority and minority opinions. There are differences of opinion on points of law at crucial passages even in the trial of Jesus as well as in the lengthy trials of Paul in spite of the space devoted to the accounts. There are numerous sources in Jewish and Roman law, however, that give general background for NT materials concerning offenses and punishments.

Beginning with 37 B.C., Judea was governed

by Herod the Idumean in the name of Rome, and starting in the year A.D. 6, Roman procurators. In spite of the occupation, there was leeway in Jewish internal autonomy by the high priesthood and Sadducean hierarchy in matters involving Jewish law and custom. Religious jurisdiction also seems to have been granted by the Romans to Jewish communities in the Diaspora whereby Jewish religious matters could be handled by competent leadership under supervision by the Jerusalem high priesthood.

Jus gladii, or capital punishment, was largely under the jurisdiction of the Romans, taken from Jewish authority during Pilate's governorship (*Shabbath* 15*a*), although there were instances of capital trials and executions without known Roman interference. Tannaitic records indicate executions by burning in a strictly religious question (*Mishnah Sanh.* 7:1, 2). The NT records Peter's trial with the possibility of execution (Acts 5:27–33) and the power of the high priest to execute (Acts 26:10). Any foreigner, including Romans, could be slain if they trespassed into the well-defined temple area; the warning against entry on pain of death was plainly displayed in Greek (Jos *Ant.* xv. 11.5). Making the capital charge of blasphemy under the Mosaic code, the Sanhedrin voted for the death penalty when they felt that Jesus wrongfully testified He was the Messiah and equal with God (Mt 26:63–66). On this occasion, the Roman authority was involved as well in the death penalty since Pilate eventually concurred in the decision. However, *Mishnah Sanh.* 7:5 does not cover in the matter of blasphemy all that was involved in the trial of Jesus.

The Mishnah prescribes stripes as corporal punishment in the tractate *Makkoth.* Offenses against the codes carried certain penalties. When penalties were not specifically mentioned, 40 stripes were prescribed, although 39 stripes or less were applied also to show leniency or care for the culprit. The penalty of flogging served as a frequent deterrent to wrongdoing and was applied quite often (Mt 10:17; Acts 5:40). Religious authorities also used the penalty of excommunication from the synagogues as a means for enforcing conformity to the codes and traditions (Lk 6:22; Jn 9:22).

Roman law. It was within the jurisdiction of the Roman governors and procurators to handle all situations involving peace and order. Josephus gives illustrations of Roman pronouncements for sedition in the cases of Theudas and Judas the Galilean (Acts 5:36–37; *Ant.* xx.5.1). A similar illustration is provided concerning the execution of John the Baptist by Herod Antipas (*Ant.* xviii.5.2). Pilate's charge and basis for execution of Jesus seemed to be treason from the inscription, "King of the Jews." There were some who regarded the disciples of Jesus as rebels against Rome (Acts 5:34–39), while Paul was picked up by the authorities as a leader of sedition (Acts 21:38). Both Romans and Jews could arrest and examine, but it was the prerogative of the Romans only to execute.

Roman execution of capital punishment was by crucifixion when slaves and other lower class people were involved, although beheading was also used on occasion (*Mishnah Sanh.* 7:3; Mt 14:10). Lifetime consignment to work in the mines, called *vincula* or "bonds" (word usage, Acts 23:29), was practically a punishment of living death. Scourging was used often, either as a punitive measure or to derive needed information for judicial proceedings (*Ant.* xv.8.4; Acts 22:24). Detention in jail was common, pending the court proceedings or execution (Acts 24:26–27), and sometimes the stocks were used to restrict further the prisoner's freedom (Acts 16:23–24).

A law enacted during the reign of Augustus prohibited scourging or imprisonment for a Roman citizen. Paul, having been born in the free city of Tarsus, was a Roman citizen, and appealed to this advantage on a number of occasions (Acts 16:37; 22:25–29). However, there were times when Paul was not able to prevent scourging (II Cor 11:25) or perhaps refused to claim this privilege (II Cor 11:24).

Roman citizens in the provinces, when tried for capital charges, had the right to a trial before a council comprised of the governor of the province and other leaders of the province (in the case of Paul, Acts 25:12, 23). However, the Roman citizen in this situation could also refuse this procedure and seek judicial audience with the emperor in Rome. As to Paul's case, a number of undesirable as well as technical factors induced him finally to appeal directly to the Roman emperor (Acts 25:11–12; 26:31–32).

Bibliography. H. J. Cadbury, "Roman Law and the Trial of Paul," *The Beginnings of Christianity,* V, New York: Macmillan, 1933. H. Danby, trans., *The Mishnah,* New York: Oxford Univ. Press, 1933. D. Daube, *Studies in Biblical Law,* n.p., 1937. G. R. Driver and J. C. Miles, *The Assyrian Laws,* New York: Oxford Univ. Press, 1935; *The Babylonian Laws,* I and II, Oxford: Clarendon Press, 1952 and 1955. E. W. Edersheim, *The Laws and Polity of the Jews,* London: Religious Tract Society, n.d. H. E. Goldin, *Hebrew Criminal Law and Procedure,* New York: Twayne, 1952. M. Greenberg, "The Biblical Conception of Asylum," *Journal of Biblical Literature,* LXXVIII, Philadelphia: Society of Biblical Literature, 1959. A. Gulak, "Law, Jewish," *Encyclopedia of the Social Sciences,* IX, New York: Macmillan, 1937. F. Josephus, *Antiquities of the Jews, Loeb Classical Library,* Cambridge: Putnam, 1930. J. Z. Lauterbach, trans., *Mekilta,* London: Routledge, 1949. P. L. Maier, *Pontius Pilate,* New York: Doubleday, 1968. G. F. Oehler, *Theology of the Old Testament,* Grand Rapids: Zondervan, n.d. J. B. Payne, *Theology of the Older Testament,* Grand Rapids: Zondervan, 1962. Philo, *On the Special Laws, Loeb Classical Library,* Cambridge: Harvard Univ.

Press, 1937–38. J. B. Pritchard, ed., ANET, Princeton: Univ. Press, 1955. H. W. Saggs, *The Greatness That Was Babylon,* New York: Hawthorne, 1962. A. N. Sherwin-White, *Roman Society and Roman Law in the New Testament,* Oxford: Clarendon Press, 1963. J. M. P. Smith, *The Origin and History of Hebrew Law,* Chicago: Univ. of Chicago, 1931.

L. Go.

CRIMSON. *See* Colours; Animals, IV.11.

CRISPING PINS. Once thought to refer to metal objects used for curling hair. RSV translates the Heb. *ḥărîṭîm* as "handbags" in Isa 3:22, here probably highly ornamented bags carried by women. The expression is defined in KB as a bag (originally made of bark) or purse. Naaman gave two talents of silver to Gehazi in two such bags (II Kgs 5:23). *See* Bags.

CRISPUS (krĭs'pŭs). The ruler of the synagogue *(archisynagōgos)* in Corinth who "believed on the Lord with all his house" (Acts 18:8). He was one whom Paul baptized, along with Gaius and the household of Stephanas (I Cor 1:14, 16). Tradition records that he became bishop of Aegina (Apostolic Constitutions, VII, 46).

See Synagogue.

CROCODILE. *See* Animals, V.2.

CROCUS. *See* Plants.

CROOKBACKED. *See* Diseases.

CROP. Craw or pouch which serves as a receptacle for food in the neck of birds or fowl, discarded before the sacrifice (Lev 1:16).

CROSS. An upright post with horizontal beam fastened across it near the top of which convicted persons were executed in the Roman world.

Forms. (1) *Crux simplex,* the simple cross, namely, a single post or upright stake; (2) *crux commissa* or *crux humilus,* St. Anthony's, in the shape of a *tau* or "T"; (3) *crux decussata,* St. Andrew's, in the form of an "X"; (4) *crux immissa,* the Latin cross; (5) St. George's, formed with two pieces of equal length; (6) triple cross, three crosses in a row, used by priests and church dignitaries from the 5th cen. on.

It is generally accepted that Christ was crucified on a *crux immissa,* or Latin cross, since the Scripture declares that the inscription, "This is Jesus the King of the Jews," was set over His head (Mt 27:37; cf. Mk 15:26: Lk 23:38; Jn 19:19). Neither the St. Andrew's cross nor the St. Anthony's would seem to have permitted this to be done. Early Christian tradition affirms that it was on a Latin cross that Jesus died (Irenaeus, *Against Heresies,* ii.24.4; Justin, *Trypho,* 91).

The *tau* cross consisted of the upright *stipes* or stake permanently planted in the execution field. Its top was tapered to a point. The *patibulum,* a wooden crossbar weighing some 125 pounds with a hollow cup whittled from its center, fitted over the tip of the *stipes.* Some authorities are convinced this was the cross preferred by Roman executioners and that the title plaque could be fastened to a stick and nailed to the *patibulum* above the criminal's head.

The sign of the cross may have been used by early Jewish Christians of Jerusalem before the city's destruction in A.D. 70. Ossuaries (rectangular stone chests for human bones) were found in 1945 in the suburb of Talpioth, one of which was marked on each of the four sides with a rough cross, like a plus sign. A similarly marked ossuary was included in an apparently Christian cemetery on the Mount of Olives (FLAP, pp. 331 ff.). At Herculaneum, destroyed in A.D. 79 by the eruption of Mount Vesuvius, a house was excavated which showed a Latin cross incised in the plastered wall above a small wooden cabinet taken to be a prayer stool or an altar (FLAP, pp. 363 f.).

Symbol or emblem. The cross is emblematic of a death died under the greatest guilt and the deepest curse. Thayer says of the cross that it was "the well-known instrument of most cruel and ignominious punishment, borrowed by the Greeks and Romans from the Phoenicians; to it were affixed among the Romans, down to the time of Constantine the Great, the guiltiest criminals, particularly the basest slaves, robbers, the authors and abettors of insurrections, and occasionally in the provinces, at the arbitrary pleasure of the governors, upright and peaceable men also, and even Roman citizens themselves" (J. H. Thayer, *A Greek-English Lexicon of the New Testament,* p. 586). For the Christian the cross therefore becomes the sign that Christ has borne the guilt and thus paid the penalty for his sins.

In the OT, death was by stoning (Deut 21:20–21), and then often the dead body was hung or impaled upon a tree or stake as a warning (Deut 21:22–23; Josh 10:26). This hanging of a body on a tree was regarded as a particular mark of accursedness (Deut 21:23), thus explaining Gal 3:13, "Christ hath redeemed us from the curse of the law, being made a curse for us: for it is written: Cursed is every one that hangeth on a tree." The cross *(stauros,* "stake") is often called the "tree" *(xylon)* in the NT (Acts 5:30; 10:39; I Pet 2:24), thus connecting it with the OT concept of the deepest humiliation and shame (Heb 12:2). Here may be seen the continuity of the one idea of shame and curse as it is expressed in two different cultures.

The one condemned to crucifixion was first scourged or flogged with a *flagrum,* a whip with several leather thongs the ends of which were tipped with lead balls or sheep bones. Then the near naked victim was forced to carry the heavy *patibulum,* or crossbar of his cross, to the place of his death. The intensity of Christ's sufferings even before His actual crucifixion is revealed by the fact that after a night of torture and scourgings He was too weak to carry His own cross. It was therefore placed upon Simon of Cyrene (Mt 27:32; Mk 15:21; Lk 23:26).

At Golgotha the soldiers would have flung Jesus to the ground and stretched His arms upon the crossbar for size. The executioner would take a square spike about a third of an inch thick at its head and drive it with a single blow between the carpal or wrist bones at the heel of the victim's hand (not through the palm). Usually it tore through the median nerve. Edward R. Bloomquist, M.D., explains that the tissue of the palm "cannot bear weight and the victim would drop to the ground within minutes after being elevated" (p. 48).

He further explains that the feet were nailed (through the second metatarsal space) in order to give the victim a cruel "step" to support himself so that he could breathe. Otherwise the sagging body hanging on its arms went into a tetanic spasm which prevented exhalation. The victim would then quickly suffocate from an inability to use his respiratory muscles. As the hours wore on the body became soaked with perspiration, thirst became intense, and pain and shock were tremendous. *See* Nail for 1968 discovery in a tomb near Jerusalem of an iron nail through the heel bones of a crucified victim.

Breaking the legs meant that the victim could no longer lift himself on the nail in order to breathe, and he soon died (Jn 19:32). Since Jesus was already dead, the soldiers merely administered their usual *coup de grace* by stabbing a lance along the right side of the sternum and into the heart ("A Doctor Looks at the Crucifixion," *Christian Herald* [March, 1964], 35, 46–48).

When one discovers what it meant to be hanged upon a tree in the OT dispensation, and to be crucified in Christ's day, he understands one of the reasons the cross was a stumbling block to the Jews (I Cor 1:23; Gal 5:11). Another reason was that it signified the utter impossibility of justification by works, even by keeping the perfect law of God (Rom 9:31–33). At the same time the preaching of the cross was foolishness—the thoughts of a moron—to the Greeks with their philosophies. Yet it frees the power of God to save men and reveals His infinite wisdom (I Cor 1:24). The more the believer understands of sin, its origin, nature and power, the fall of man and what devastation came thereby, the more he sees the wonder and sufficiency of Christ's substitutionary death upon the cross.

Figurative meanings of the cross.

1. Taking up one's cross. Christ says, "If any man will come after me, let him deny himself, and take up his cross [Luke adds, daily], and follow me" (Mt 16:24; Mk 8:34; Lk 9:23). Here it becomes clear from the analogy of carrying the *patibulum,* mentioned above, that Christ calls upon believers to be ready to sacrifice their selfish interests and daily to bear reproach, misunderstanding and shame in their service for Him, even as He did in His life and death (Mt 10:38; 16:24–26; Mk 8:34–38; Lk 9:23–26).

2. The preaching of the substitutionary atonement. This is the meaning attached to the cross in many places in Paul's epistles (I Cor 1:18; Gal 6:14; Phil 3:18; Col 1:20). It expresses the whole concept of Christ bearing our sins as our representative (II Cor 5:21; I Pet 2:24). Through the cross, Christ reconciled the sinner to God and made peace between Him and the sinner (Col 1:20), so that God is now propitious or well-disposed toward the sinner, and Paul could therefore write, "We pray . . . in Christ's stead, be ye reconciled" (II Cor 5:20; cf. Rom 5:10). See Leon Morris, *The Apostolic Preaching of the Cross,* 1955.

3. A symbol of the believer's union with Christ and sharing in a new divine life. In Christ's death the believer died in Him to sin and to the world-system (Rom 6:4 ff.; Gal 6:14), and now is to live like Paul, who writes, "I have been crucified with Christ; and it is no longer I who live, but Christ lives in me; and the life which I now live in the flesh I live by faith in the Son of God, who loved me, and delivered Himself up for me" (Gal 2:20, NASB).

See Burial; Christ, Passion of; Golgotha.

Bibliography. Johannes Schneider, "*Stauros,* etc.," TDNT, VII, 572–584.

R. A. K. and J. R.

CROWN. An ornamental circlet or head covering symbolic of royalty or of special status or achievement.

Origin. Crowns in the ancient Near East are the development of two common headdresses, the turban and the cloth or leather headband. The headband early gave rise to the metal diadem, such as the ornate golden wreaths with beads and gold pendants or rosettes of Queen Shubad of Ur, dating back to the 25th cen. B.C. (ANEP # 72). A copper headband belonging to an Amorite chieftain from *c.* 2000 B.C. was found in a Jericho tomb, and Flinders Petrie discovered a diadem of strip gold patterned with dots at ancient Gaza (Tell el-'Ajjul). Such crowns were sometimes set with precious stones (Zech 9:16). Among the Greeks and Romans the headband became the garland of leaves or flowers given to victorious athletes or to prominent citizens. In imitation of the Hellenistic practice some Jews prior to the time of Christ were crowning themselves with roses and olive wreaths during times of revelry and rejoicing (Wisd 2:8; Jth 15:13).

Ancient monarchs in the biblical world wore a great variety of caplike crowns or turbans (*q.v.*). The conical headdress of Assyrian kings consisted of a cloth wrapped repeatedly around the head and adorned with bands of colored embroidery or precious stones. The turban and diadem were sometimes combined into a composite crown (Ezk 21:26, NASB). The elaborate double crown of Upper and Lower Egypt incorporated the red crown of Lower Egypt (a fez-like cap with spiraled wire at front and tall projection at rear) and the white crown of Upper Egypt (tall, conical cap with a bulbous top). Whatever crown the pharaoh wore, the royal insignia of the *uraeus* or cobra always adorned the front to symbolize power and terror to his enemies.

Old Testament. The official headpiece of the high priest of the Israelites, and later of their kings (II Sam 1:10; II Kgs 11:12), is denoted by the Heb. term *nēzer,* which means "consecration" (cf. Lev 21:12, KJV with NASB). It describes the diadem or plate of gold, inscribed

Queen Shubad of Ur (c. 2500 B.C.) shown wearing her crown. BM

with the words "Holy to the Lord," and attached to the priest's turban with a blue cord (Ex 29:6; 39:30; Lev 8:9; cf. Ex 28:36–38; *see* Diadem). The *nēzer* signified not only the rank and authority of the wearer but also the sacred nature of his office. In the cases of both priest (Ex 29:6–7) and king (II Kgs 11:12) the coronation involved anointing with the holy oil (IDB, I, 746). The crown of David was the emblem of God-given kingship in Israel (Ps 21:3; 132:18). When the crown was removed and profaned in the dust, the visible kingdom came to an end (Ps 89:39; cf. Prov 27:24; Lam 5:16; Ezk 21:26).

Heb. *'ăṭārâ* is a more general word for crown, used for crowns and head ornaments of various sorts. It denotes the bejeweled gold crown taken by David from the king of Ammon at Rabbah (II Sam 12:30). It may be the queen's crown as well as of the king (Jer 13:18), Mordecai's gold crown (Est 8:15), or King Solomon's on his wedding day (Song 3:11). The latter may refer to a garland of flowers worn by both bride and bridegroom (Ezk 16:12), a custom still observed in some parts of the Orient. Zechariah was commanded to make an ornate crown of silver and gold circlets for the head of Joshua the high priest, probably a double crown to symbolize the future uniting of the priestly and regal offices in the one person, Messiah (Zech 6:11–14, NASB).

This word for crown was also used metaphorically in the poetic and prophetic books of honor and glory (Job 19:9; Prov 4:9) conferred in the form of a bountiful harvest (Ps 65:11) and of riches to the wise (Prov 14:24), in the form of a virtuous wife (12:4) and of grandchildren (17:6), and appearing as gray hair on the head of the righteous (16:31). God has crowned man, represented now by Jesus the Son of man, with glory and majesty (Ps 8:5; Heb 2:7, 9). The Lord crowns the believer "with lovingkindness and tender mercies" (Ps 103:4), and will Himself be the beautiful crown of His people instead of the proud crowns worn by the drunken nobility of Ephraim (Isa 28:1, 3, 5). Millennial Jerusalem will be a glorious crown, a kingly diadem in the Lord's hand (Isa 62:3, NEB).

Persian royalty wore the tiara or crown (Heb. *keter*) made in the form of a skull cap encircled by a battlemented gold diadem decorated with rosettes and representations of jewels (ANEP # 462; Est 1:11; 2:17; 6:8). Originally the term diadem meant a blue band trimmed with white around the tiara and signifying royalty among the Persians (Arndt, p. 181). Figuratively, the prudent make knowledge their crown (Heb. *yaktirû,* Prov 14:18).

Other Heb. words rendered "crown" are *zēr,* a border or molding of gold around the edge of the ark, table of showbread, and altar of incense (Ex 25:11, 24; 30:3); and *qodqōd,* the crown or top of the head (Gen 49:26; Job 2:7; etc.).

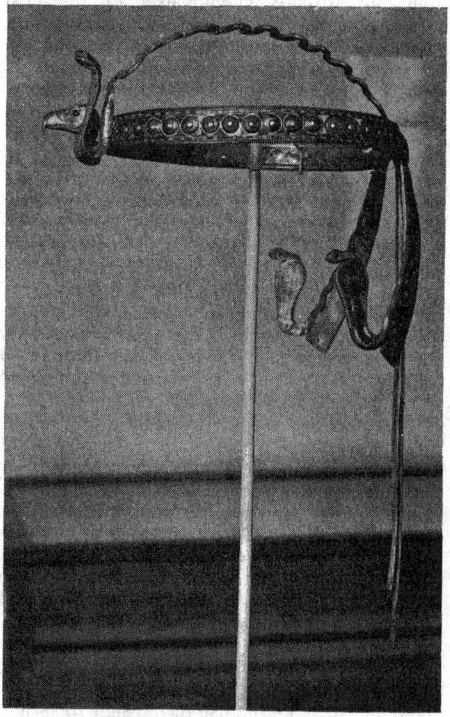

Crown of King Tutankhamon of Egypt. It is a gold band decorated with rosettes inlaid with carnelian. In front are the royal emblems of the vulture and cobra. LL

New Testament. Outside the book of Revelation the "crown" (*stephanos*) refers to a wreath, whether it be the literal crown of thorns mocking Jesus' claim to kingship (Jn 19:2, 5) or the garland of leaves symbolizing victory and reward. At the Isthmian games near Corinth winners were awarded a crown of celery leaves which would soon wither, suggesting the "corruptible crown" for which Paul says athletes in his day contended (I Cor 9:25; Oscar Broneer, "The Apostle Paul and the Isthmian Games," BA, XXV [1962], 16 f.). Instead, Christians seek the reward of an unfading crown of glory (I Pet 5:4), which has its basis in eternal life (Jas 1:12; Rev 2:10). Like the athlete, we must compete according to the rules (II Tim 2:5, NASB), for the crown may be taken from us (Rev 3:11). Paul states that it is the crown or reward for righteousness, awarded at the time of Christ's return to all those who have loved His appearing (II Tim 4:8). It is the hope of seeing Christ in His coming glory that causes believers to purify themselves (I Jn 2:28; 3:2–3). The apostle Paul also writes that his converts are his crown of rejoicing, his prize to be proud of (I Thess 2:19; Phil 4:1).

The golden *stephanos* in Revelation is worn by beings of high rank: the 24 elders (4:4, 10). the rider on the white horse (6:2), the demonic locust-like creatures (9:7), the woman Israel representing the people of God (12:1), and Christ waiting to come as judge (14:14). In 19:12, however, He wears the regal crown of many diadems (*diadēma*). Impersonating Christ and opposing God's sovereign rule, the devil and Antichrist will wear many diadems before their overthrow (Rev 12:3; 13:1).

See Diadem; Garland; Judgment; Rewards.

Bibliography. Walter Grundmann, "*Stephanos,* etc.," TDNT, VII, 615–636.

J. R.

CROWN OF THORNS. *See* Plants.

CRUCIBLE. The Heb. word means "to refine or melt." KJV uses the term "fining pot." It was a container, probably made of thick pottery, used for melting silver (Prov 17:3; 27:21, RSV). *See* Refine.

CRUCIFIXION. *See* Cross; Jesus Christ.

CRUSE. A small, elongated pottery decanter about four to six inches tall. Possibly a narrow-necked jar (Heb. "gurgler"), such as used by Jeroboam's wife to take a gift of honey to Ahijah the prophet (I Kgs 14:3; same word for "bottle" in Jeremiah's object lesson, Jer 19:1, 10); or a pan (open, shallow bowl) in which Elisha had put salt when he healed the water supply of Jericho (II Kgs 2:20); or a jug, flask, or canteen as a water bottle for Saul (I Sam 26:11, 12, 16) and Elijah (I Kgs 19:6), and an oil container for the widow of Zarephath (I Kgs 17:12, 14, 16). *See* Bottles; Pottery.

CRYSTAL. *See* Jewels.

CUBIT. *See* Weights, Measures, and Coins.

CUCKOO, CUCKOW. *See* Animals, III.8.

CUCUMBER. *See* Plants.

CUIRASS (kwē-răs'). A coat of mail made of interwoven heavy metal wire or links, or a breastplate (I Sam 17:5; Job 41:13, RSV; Neh 4:16, RSV; II Chr 26:14, RSV). *See* Armor; Breastplate; Coat of Mail.

CULTS. These are particular systems of religious worship with special reference to rites and ceremonies. The cult(us) is the focal point of a religion and eventually assumes forms and symbols which most clearly reveal the distinctive character of the religion. As the focus of religious life, the cult(us) becomes the point at which the sense of the sacred is most highly concentrated, and thus serves as an index to the innermost quality of religion. The term is also descriptive of minority religious groups holding beliefs regarded as unorthodox or spurious, and in this sense it was applied to early Christianity by the officials of the Roman state religion.

The religion of Israel was in constant conflict with, but eventually triumphed over, the base cults of her neighbors, such as the worship of Baal and Asherah with their many prophets and priests (I Kgs 18:19). The extremely degraded nature of these cults with temple prostitutes (*see* Harlot) and child sacrifices has been made startlingly clear by the Canaanite tablets found at Ras Shamra (*q.v.*) and Phoenician burials near Carthage.

The early Christian church doubtless inherited numerous forms and customs of worship from the Jewish synagogue; but it is very doubtful if pagan worship, such as that of the mystery religions, exercised an appreciable influence on early Christian worship. Research has rather conclusively shown that external and superficial resemblances do not necessarily prove dependence. In certain particular instances the most that seems probable is a similarity in terminology, a terminology to which Christianity gave a new content and meaning.

See Gods, False; Worship.

T. M. B.

CUMI (kū'mĭ). *See* Talitha Cumi.

CUMMIN. *See* Plants.

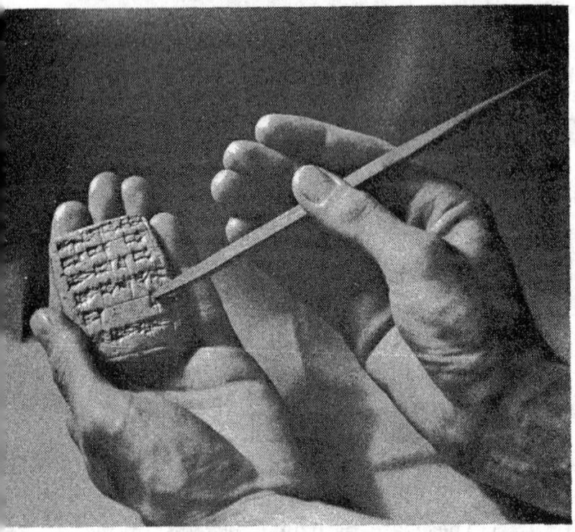

Babylonian clay tablet with stylus in correct position for writing Cuneiform. ORINST

CUNEIFORM. The name for the peculiar script developed in Mesopotamia around 3000 B.C. and used in modified form for many languages down to the 2nd cen. B.C. The name means, literally, "wedge-shaped" since the individual characters are composed of groups of wedge-shaped impressions made by a triangular stylus in soft clay. Though used for the most part on clay, this script was also used on stone, metal, and terra cotta. (Other quite independent scripts using wedge-shaped characters were devised much later. See Ugaritic and Persian below.)

Apparently developed in its original pictographic form in order to signify personal ownership of goods, and especially offerings deposited in temples, the early incised pictures were scratched on lumps of soft clay used to seal jars. In time, as they changed into linear symbols, the underlying pictographs became entirely unrecognizable. Later, the symbols were constructed of complex groups of wedge-shaped impressions of varying size. Gradually the number and size of the wedges diminished until by the 6th cen. B.C. a sign once composed of 20 or more wedges required only five.

That the Sumerians invented the script is attested by the fact that the original reading of the signs was in the Sumerian language. For example, the picture of a fish was read *ha*, Sumerian for "fish," and the picture of a human head was read *sag*, Sumerian for "head." Soon pictures of objects were used for abstract ideas associated with the object. For example, the picture of a foot (Sumerian *DU*) was also read as *gub*, "to stand," and *gin*, "to go." A further development was the use of the individual signs for words that sounded like the word for the original pictured object though completely unrelated to it. Note the use of the sign *BI* (a jug) for the pronominal element "its" which is also pronounced *bi* in Sumerian. Next the signs were used in their syllabic value alone with no reference to the pictured object at all but simply as part of a spelled-out word. For example, the sign *RA*, originally the picture of a net, was used for *-ra*, a suffixal dative element in Sumerian.

Concomitant with this development in the use of the script for the Sumerian language there was adaptation so that it could also be used to write Semitic Akkadian. This development followed much the same lines. In addition, Akkadian translations were substituted for the various Sumerian readings of the signs, and at the same time, the syllabifying process was accelerated. The five basic types of signs in Akkadian documents were: word signs, syllabic signs, determinatives (symbols indicating that the following word was a personal name, a geographic term, a kind of stone, plant, animal, utensil, etc.), phonetic complements (a syllable written after a word sign to indicate its pronunciation), and numerals.

Perhaps the cuneiform syllabic system seems unwieldy to us, but it was sufficiently flexible to become the basic script for many languages beyond the tongue of its inventors. It was used by scribes to write Elamite, Hurrian, Hittite, and Urartean. On the other hand, Egyptian hieroglyphs remained local and were never used for any other language. In fact, syllabic cuneiform scripts continued in use long after alphabets were invented.

Its flexibility may be demonstrated in another way. The documents written in this fashion include just about every conceivable type of literature; e.g., business letters, contracts, receipts, lists, personal letters, myths, hymns, poems, proverbs, historic annals, monumental inscriptions, mathematical texts, grammatical texts and vocabularies. Literally hundreds of thousands of business documents have been recovered. Data from such documents together with government records have permitted a remarkably detailed reconstruction of daily life and political events more than 3000 years ago, in some cases to a greater degree than can be done for many parts of Europe of only a few centuries ago.

But first cuneiform inscriptions had to be deciphered. This was a difficult task performed with brilliance and diligence, chiefly by Grotefend, Rawlinson and Hincks, by the mid-19th cen. They began with Persian royal inscriptions of Darius and his successors in an entirely different script from that developed by the Sumerians. The script appears similar, however, in that it is composed of signs made up of groups of wedges. But the similarity ends there. The Persian script consists of 36 alphabet-like characters plus some special word signs, word dividers and determinatives.

These royal inscriptions were noticed by travelers to the Orient in the 17th cen., after having been unknown for centuries. Comparison of the Persian royal names found in these inscriptions with the same names in Sassanian and Gr. records provided vital clues. The larger number of signs in the parallel Neo-Babylonian inscriptions indicated a more complex script. It was assumed to be alphabetic in character with many helping signs. The multitudes of clay tablets uncovered by Botta at Khorsabad in 1843 and by Layard at Nineveh in 1845 helped considerably, especially by providing ancient lists of signs with their readings compiled by Assyrian scribes long ago. In fact, without the hundreds of similar tablets found later at Nippur, probably very little of the Sumerian language would yet be known.

Another cuneiform script of independent development consisting of 36 alphabetic signs arose in Syria in the 15th cen. B.C. It records a Semitic language called Ugaritic which is closely related to Hebrew. The tablets were discovered at Ras Shamra by Claude F. A. Schaeffer in 1929 and were deciphered by Hans Bauer, Edoward Dhorme, and Charles Virolleaud among others. The texts are chiefly poems of myths, epics and legends.

Eventually, Canaanite alphabetic scripts, with later modifications by the Greeks and Romans, completely replaced the cuneiform scripts and they passed into oblivion until archaeologists resurrected them and recovered the information they contained.

See Writing; Ras Shamra.

Bibliography. Edward Chiera, *They Wrote on Clay,* Chicago: Univ. of Chicago Press, 1938. Johannes Friedrich, *Extinct Languages,* New York: Philosophical Library, 1957. Samuel Noah Kramer, *From the Tablets of Sumer,* Indian Hills, Colo.: Falcon's Wing Press, 1956.

F. R. S.

The Chalice of Antioch is apparently a very early communion cup (some would date it to the first century) and may have representations of the apostles on it. MM

CUP. Besides its literal use as a drinking vessel, bowl, goblet or laver (*see* Pottery), the term is also used in a figurative sense in the Scriptures. By metonymy it may refer to what it contains (Prov 23:31). It is also used with the genitive of the person who bestows the drink (I Cor 10:21). Symbolically it is used of life itself, an expression of destiny in both the good and evil sense.

The inheritance of the saints is the portion of their cup (Ps 16:5); the state of the wicked is theirs (Ps 11:6). There is the cup of sorrow (Mt 26:39; Mk 14:36; Lk 22:42; Jn 18:11) and the cup of consolation (Jer 16:7). It symbolizes an abundant share of blessings, prosperity, joy, even salvation (Ps 23:5; 116:13); or a share of afflictions (Ps 75:8; Isa 51:17). It may be the cup of God's wrath, punishment, vengeance (Isa 51:17, 22; Lam 4:21; Ps 11:6; 75:8), the cup of judgment (Ps 11:6; 73:10; 75:8; Isa 51:17, 22; Jer 25:15–28; Ezk 23:31–34). The wine of harlotry, with which Babylon intoxicated the nations, becomes the wine of God's wrath for them, i.e., the wine cup of His passionate wrath (Rev 14:8, 10; 16:19; 18:3; 19:15).

Gold cup from Vaphio, Greece (c. 1500 B.C.). Mimosa

For Christ Jesus it was the cup of violent death (Mt 20:22–23; Jn 18:11). The martyrdom of Christians is described as sharing in the cup of Christ (Martyrdom of Polycarp 14:2; cf. Mt 20:23; Mk 10:39). The cup which the Father gave His Son to drink makes the cup of the new covenant in His blood a cup of blessing (I Cor 10:16) for the forgiveness of sins.

The eucharistic cup is often made of precious metals, sometimes embellished with precious stones, although it is also made of less costly materials. The *calix ministerialis* was used in the Roman church until the high Middle Ages for communing the faithful *subutraque* (under both kinds, with bread and wine). The *calix offertorius* is used at the Roman Mass for the common participation by the officiant, but with bread alone. At baptism the *calix baptismalis,* which contained a mixture of milk and honey, was drunk.

In Bohemia the reform movement of the early 15th cen. demanded the giving of the cup to the laity, a concession granted by the Council of Constance, although this did not satisfy the calixists entirely. The European reformers of the 16th cen. denounced the withdrawal of the cup from the laity, for Christ commanded of this cup, "Drink ye all of it." In Protestant and Lutheran churches the sacrament is administered *subutraque,* under both kinds, as it is also in the Orthodox churches, both Eastern and Russian, and some of the Uniate churches. In many Protestant congregations individual communion cups are used; Anglican and many Lutheran churches use the "common cup" (one chalice from which all communicants drink in turn).

C. S. M.

CUPBEARER. *See* Occupations: Cupbearer.

CURE. *See* Diseases; Healing, Health.

CURIOUS ARTS. The translation "curious arts" ("magic arts," RSV) of a Gr. article (*ta*) and adjective (*perierga*) with this usage is found only in Acts 19:19. The adjective originally means excessively busy; then meddlesome, relative to the concerns of others; and finally, as regards the future, inquisitive to the extent of using magical or occult arts as a means of information and discovery.

Such arts were a specialty in Ephesus (Acts 19). Magicians and astrologers were present in large numbers and carried on a brisk trade in charms, books of divination, and rules for interpreting dreams. The so-called "Ephesian spells," or "Ephesian writings," were small strips of parchment on which were written letters or monograms. These strips were kept in small silk bags which were worn on the arm as charms or amulets (*q.v.*).

In the OT such arts played a much less important role in Israel than in other countries of the ancient Near East. In fact, the Mosaic law forbade many such practices (Deut 18:9–13). That they were known among the Israelites, however, is seen from references to them in the prophets (Jer 27:9; Mic 5:12; Mal 3:5) and in certain incidents (e.g., the witch of Endor, I Sam 28), as well as the fact that amulets are often found in archaeological excavations in Palestine.

See also Magic; Divination.

T. M. B.

CURSE. The several Heb. and Gr. words for curse denote the expression of a wish or prayer that evil might befall another. This idea found a wide variety of uses in Israel's life and was universally known among her neighbors. The terms of a contract or treaty were protected by curses or imprecations directed at any future violator of the agreement (see ANET, pp. 205 f.). Similar security measures are found in royal inscriptions where curses were pronounced upon any one who might alter or destroy the inscription (ANET, pp. 267 f.). Curses were also directed against murderers (Gen 4:11–12), as well as against enemies who in the future might harm one (II Sam 18:32) or who were presently harming one (Jer 12:3). Indeed, wherever protective and punitive measures were lacking or inadequate, curses were employed.

Cursing, when applied to God, is an anthropomorphic term expressing divine displeasure or vindictive justice (e.g., Gen 3:14–19; 5:29; 12:3). The natural antithesis of all such curses is blessing.

The efficacy of a curse depended basically upon divine approval and execution. In the Heb. mind, the spoken curse was considered to be the active agent for harm, clothed with the power of the soul which sent it forth. But only the individual who was a faithful servant of Jehovah had a source of true power; hence it was the living God who ultimately wielded the power of the curse or spell. Therefore, a curse (or a blessing) once soberly uttered might not be recalled or revoked (Gen 27:27–40; cf. I Sam 14:24–30, 43–45).

The Mosaic law forbade the cursing of father or mother (Ex 21:17) on penalty of death, the prince of the people (Ex 22:28), and one that was deaf (Lev 19:14). Blasphemy, or cursing God, was a capital offense (Lev 24:10-16). But curses pronounced against individuals by godly men (e.g., Gen 9:25; 49:7; Deut 27:14-26; II Sam 3:29; 39; Josh 9:23) were not the expressions of passion, impatience, or revenge; they were prophetic predictions or statements of the divine decree, and therefore not such as God condemned.

Cursing or imprecatory psalms are those in which the psalmist pronounced a curse on the enemies of Israel (Ps 83:9-17) or on his personal opponents or oppressors (Ps 69:21-28). To understand these prayers which are so foreign to the NT, one must remember that the revelation of the OT was preparatory to that of the NT, and was therefore incomplete. Furthermore, the curse in the ancient Near East, including Israel, was considered a legitimate means of defense. Also, the language of the Oriental was more impassioned and for the Israelite more concrete than ours.

In the NT the cursing of enemies or persecutors is forbidden by the example and word of Jesus (Lk 23:34; Mt 5:44). Paul, however, cursed those who did not love Christ (I Cor 16:22) or who preached a gospel different from his (Gal 1:8 f.). He was willing to become accursed himself, if by so doing his own people would more readily accept his Christ (Rom 9:3). The "curse of the law" is the sentence of condemnation which is pronounced on the transgressor (Gal 3:10), and from which Christ redeemed us by having been made a curse for us (Gal 3:13). *See* Accursed; Anathema; Devote; Dedicate; Oath.

Bibliography. Herbert C. Brichto, *The Problem of "Curse" in the Hebrew Bible,* JBL Monograph Series, XIII, 1963. Chr. Senft, "Curse," *A Companion to the Bible,* J. J. von Allmen, ed., New York: Oxford Univ. Press, 1958. N. H. Smith, "A Study of the Words 'Curse' and 'Righteousness,'" *The Bible Translator,* III (1952), 111-114.

T. M. B.

CURTAINS. Ten curtains covered the tabernacle of Moses and became synonymous for the tabernacle itself (*q.v.*). Hangings were also used for the door and for the gate of the court about the tabernacle (Ex 26:1-14, 31-37; 27:9-18). A veil or curtain separated the holy of holies from the holy place.

The veil was torn at the death of Jesus Christ from the top to the bottom (Mt 27:51; Mk 15:38; Lk 23:45), and so access was opened to the inner sanctum (cf. Heb 6:19). This was symbolic of the direct access to God secured by Christ, since He opened the way through the veil, that is, through His flesh (Heb 10:20). *See* Veil.

CUSH (kŭsh)

1. The son, possibly the eldest, of Ham and grandson of Noah (Gen 10:6-8). He was the father of several sons, or nations, including Nimrod.

2. A Benjamite enemy of David, according to the ancient title of Ps 7.

3. The people and land of Cush. The word is usually but not consistently translated Ethiopia in the KJV. The designation Ethiopia is misleading, for it did not refer to the modern state of Ethiopia or Abyssinia. The biblical Cush (Egyptian *Kôsh*) bordered Egypt on the S, the land of Nubia or modern Sudan. The dividing line seems to have been at the first cataract, at the city of Syene, modern Aswan (Ezk 29:10). Egyptian Dynasty XXIII was Cushite, and one of its kings is mentioned as the opponent of Sennacherib (II Kgs 19:9). *See* Ethiopia.

4. Another land, described as compassed by the river Gihon (Gen 2:13). Since this river flowed in the same area as the Tigris and the Euphrates (Gen 2:10-14), the land has been located in western Iran, home of the Kassites, a powerful people who ruled Babylonia in Moses' time.

P. C. J.

CUSHAN (ko͝o'shăn). A name formed from Cush, whose meaning is in doubt. It is used as a parallel to Midian (Hab 3:7) and may be an older, poetical name for this land or its inhabitants who were descended from Cush. Some have suggested that the name stands for Chushan-rishathaim (*q.v.*), a Mesopotamian king who oppressed Israel some eight years before he was defeated by Othniel (Jud 3:8-10). This is highly improbable, even though Josephus refers to this king as Chusan (*Ant.* v. 3.2).

CUSHAN-RISHATHAIM. *See* Chushan-rishathaim.

CUSHI (ko͝osh'ī)

1. Great-grandfather of Jehudi, a prince of Jeremiah's day (Jer 36:14).

2. The father of the prophet Zephaniah (Zeph 1:1).

3. In II Sam 18:21-32, the messenger sent by Joab to announce to David the success of the battle against Absalom as well as his death. Here the RSV renders the Heb. *the Cushi,* "the Cushite," i.e., the Ethiopian.

CUSHION. *See* Bed.

CUSTOM. The word refers in its widest legal sense to all rules of law not derived directly from specific acts of law-making bodies. In a more restricted sense it refers to a popular usage which under certain conditions may serve as a source of law.

In the OT it is one of a number of related words variously translated as "tax," "toll," "tribute," or "custom," depending on the version used (cf. Ezr 4:13, 20; 7:24). In the NT it is the rendering of the Gr. *telos*, usually meaning an indirect tax on goods, as opposed to a tax on property or person (Mt 17:25; Rom 13:7). *See* Taxes.

CUSTOM, RECEIPT OF. The place at which Matthew sat when Jesus called him (Mt 9:9; Mk 2:14; Lk 5:27). A revenue or tax office, which arose from the practice of the Roman government in selling to the highest bidder the privilege of collecting taxes within a certain province or city. The buyer paid a stipulated sum for the privilege and was free to collect more if he so desired.

Matthew's place of business was a toll booth or customs office (*telōnion*), perhaps near the wharves in Capernaum. He collected tariffs or duties levied on goods shipped across the Sea of Galilee from the territory of Philip to that of Herod Antipas, or on merchandise in transit on the road from Jerusalem to Tyre or Damascus. *See* Taxes.

CUTH (kūth), **CUTHAH** (kūth'ȧ). An ancient city in Babylonia, *c.* 15 miles NE of Babylon. In 1880 Hormuzd Rassam identified Tel-Ibrahim, a mound about 3,000 feet in circumference and about 280 feet high, as the site.

The only mention of Cuth or Cuthah in the OT is found in II Kgs 17:24, 30, where it is listed as a source of the mixed population of Samaria. When Sargon II, king of Assyria, deported people from the northern kingdom of Israel, he transplanted inhabitants from other areas to take their place. Among these the Cuthians were sufficiently prominent that the rabbinical Jews applied their name to the Samaritans generally, and words peculiar to the Samaritans were called Cuthian. Contract tablets, the great temple Ê-meš-lam (dedicated to Nergal, god of the underworld), the ruins of the city itself, and the exterior remains extending for miles around, all indicate a flourishing city with foundations going back to Sumerian times. There are marks of greatly enhanced development after the destruction of Babylon.

Reference is made in II Kgs 17:30 to the introduction of the pagan cult of Nergal into Samaria. The racial amalgamation and the religious apostasies brought to Samaria go far to account for the animosities of Judah toward the Samaritans during the restoration.

W. T. D.

CUTTING OFF. In the OT a penalty or form of punishment used primarily, though not exclusively, for various offenses against the ceremonial laws (e.g., Lev 17:3–4). The agent of the "cutting off" was either God (Lev 17:10) or the community (Lev 18:29). Older interpreters held the view that this method of punishment always involved the death penalty. This is hardly correct in spite of the implication of such a passage as Ex 31:14. Although the death penalty was at times associated with "cutting off," its more probable meaning was that of expulsion from the religious or civil community.

This type of punishment found in the early Israelitish community was doubtless the basis for the later "excommunication" among the Jews which resulted in exclusion from the synagogue, either temporarily or permanently depending on the nature of the offense committed. Evidence of a similar form of discipline has been found among the members of the Qumran community. Discipline in the early Christian communities was naturally patterned after that of the parent religion, and numerous similar practices are found in the NT (II Thess 3:14; I Cor 5:1-5, 13; I Tim 1:20).

See also Crime and Punishment; Excommunication.

T. M. B.

CUTTINGS IN THE FLESH. The biblical attitude gives no place in worship for cutting, gashing, or disfiguring the body in any way. (*See* Circumcision, an entirely different practice.) If not a belief in the sacredness of life, there was at least a profound respect for the body as God's creation, and therefore no place was given to mutilating or disfiguring it in the name of Yahweh. The common mourning practice of non-Israelites of scratching the arms, head, and face was prohibited by Moses (Lev 19:28; 21:5). In addition, the Mosaic law prohibited tattooing (Lev 19:28). Respect for a sound, whole body is emphasized in the bodily birth defects or injury sustained after birth which disqualified one of Aaron's family from the priesthood (Lev 21:18-24).

However, among the worshipers of Baal and Asherah it apparently was a common custom to cut and disfigure the body. This is illustrated by the frenzied action of the Baal priests during the contest between Elijah and Jezebel's priests on Mount Carmel (I Kgs 18:28). Adoni-bezek cut off the thumbs and great toes of his enemies (Jud 1:6-7); Philistines gouged out the eyes of Samson (Jud 16:21) and of the men of Jabesh-gilead (I Sam 11:2).

H. E. F.

CYMBAL. *See* Music.

CYPRESS. *See* Plants.

CYPRUS (sī′prŭs). The third largest island of the Mediterranean (after Sicily and Sardinia), it has an area of 3,572 square miles. Visible from both Asia Minor and Syria on a clear day, it is about 43 miles from the former and 60 miles from the latter. The surface is almost evenly divided between mountain and plain.

So extensive was Cyprus' export of copper in ancient times that the English word copper is derived from its Gr. name *kypros*, through the Latin *cuprum*. OT references to Kittim or Chittim (e.g., Gen 10:4; Num 24:24; Isa 23:1) are commonly identified with Cyprus (CornPBE, pp. 13-17). The Romans took the island in 58 B.C. and transferred the capital from Salamis (*q.v.*) on the E to Paphos on the W coast. Paul and Barnabas landed at Salamis on their first missionary journey (Acts 13:5) and ministered throughout the island, embarking at Paphos for Asia Minor after some success in missionary efforts (Acts 13:6-13). Later, Barnabas and John Mark preached on Cyprus (Acts 15:39).

H. F. V.

Bronze statuette of a horned god, twelfth century B.C. Enkomi, Cyprus. Cyprus Museum

CYRENE (sī-rē′nĭ), **CYRENIAN** (sī-rē′nĭ-*a*n). A city in N Africa midway between Carthage and Alexandria. Cyrene was founded as a Gr. colony in 630 B.C. In 331 B.C. it submitted to

Alexander, in 321 B.C. came under the Ptolemies, and passed to Rome in 96 B.C. Renowned as an intellectual center, at its zenith it had a population of 100,000. Ruins of beautiful buildings now mark the site. Cyrene and Cyrenians figure in Mt 27:32; Mk 15:21; Lk 23:26; Acts 2:10; 6:9; 11:20; 13:1.

CYRENIUS (sī-rē'nĕ-ŭs). The KJV form of Quirinius (ASV), taken from the Gr. *kyrēnios*. In Lk 2:2 he is called "governor of Syria," and was responsible for carrying out the census of Caesar Augustus.

Publius Sulpicius Quirinius was a Roman senator, later elected consul, and "of great dignity" (Jos *Ant.* xviii.1.1). He was sent to Syria by Augustus to carry out a taxation edict of the emperor. (To this point both Josephus and Luke [Acts 5:37] agree, for they both refer to an event *c.* A.D. 6, in the days of the rise of "Judas the Galilean.") At his death in A.D. 21, Tiberius requested the Senate that the occasion "be celebrated with a public funeral" (Tacitus, *Annals* iii.48).

The chronological problem arises in connection with the "first census" mentioned in Lk 2:2. Of this there is no other mention, and some have rejected Luke's history. Several factors, however, ought to be considered. First, it seems that Quirinius had been appointed by Augustus to serve as legatus of the emperor during the period 10–6 B.C. in the E, and may have held a governorship in Syria. Second, we know by the discovery of receipts and decrees among the papyri of Egypt that regular Roman enrollments were instituted on the basis of a 14-year cycle. Other inscriptions indicate Augustus first ordered the imperial census. The earliest known census papyrus document certainly dated is from A.D. 34; other similar papyri are regarded by some as belonging to A.D. 20 or even A.D. 6. Fourteen years earlier would thus fall in the period of about 8 B.C. Third, the example of an edict in Egypt in A.D. 104, issued by one Vibius Maximus, ordered all persons "to return to their domestic hearths" to be enrolled (Deiss LAE, p. 271). The similarity to Luke's language is clear. Finally, the fact that Luke calls this incident "the first census" taken by Quirinius in Syria may imply that Quirinius also supervised a second census, namely, the one of A.D. 6, mentioned in Acts 5:37. *See also* Census.

Bibliography. F. J. Foakes-Jackson and Kirsopp Lake, *The Beginnings of Christianity,* London: Macmillan, IV, 61 f. J. N. Geldenhuys, "Commentary on the Gospel of Luke," *New International Commentary on the New Testament,* Grand Rapids: Eerdmans, 1956, pp. 99–106. W. M. Ramsay, *Was Christ Born at Bethlehem?* New York: Putnam's Sons, 1898, pp. 227–248. Merrill C. Tenney, *New Testament Times,* Grand Rapids: Eerdmans, 1965, pp. 134–138.

W. M. D.

Tomb of Cyrus. ORINST

CYRUS (sī'rŭs). Son of the earlier Cambyses, of the royal race of the Achaemenians, and the founder of the Persian Empire. Isaiah prophesied of him as anointed of God to conquer kings and fortified places and to set the Jews free from captivity (Isa 44:28; 45:1–14). Under his liberal policies the Jews were permitted to return from the Exile (Ezr 1).

The history of Cyrus is complicated by early accretions of fable and romance. Even Herodotus, who lived within a century of the time of Cyrus, refers to these embellishments. Ctesias, a half century later, lived in the Persian court and drew from the Persian archives, but these were also affected. Xenophon's *Cyropaedeia* is thought to be more of a historical romance than accurate biography. The best sources are thought to be Herodotus, Persian and Babylonian chronicles, and inscriptions.

Cyrus was probably named for his grandfather, who had also been king of Anshan, capital city of Elam. The name Cyrus, being Elamite, is of doubtful meaning.

Herodotus (i.107 ff.) gives a stirring account of one version of Cyrus' origin. The wealthy Median king Astyages gave his daughter Mandane in marriage to Cambyses, a Persian ruler, to prevent any danger of her offspring being a rival to the Median throne. Persia was then a relatively poor and perhaps dependent land. It was also at a safe distance. Because of a dream, the Median king plotted to destroy the male offspring of this union. A shepherd, however, saved and reared Cyrus. As he became an extraordinary lad, he was discovered and returned to his parents and grandfather. Then he had access to the skills and resources of Median royalty and yet maintained the Persian hardy spirit. Friends and admirers in both countries paved the way for his sudden rise to power, as did the discontent of the people under the tyranny and injustice of the Median ruler.

Whether or not these events and relationships were all reported accurately, Cyrus first succeeded his father on the throne of the province of Anshan (559 B.C.), and then suddenly rose to the combined throne of Medo-Persia, aided by mass defection from the Median army. This was about 550 B.C., while Nabonidus reigned in Babylon. Cyrus took Ecbatana and carried its spoil to his own city.

Croesus, king of fabulous Lydia in Asia Minor, alarmed and covetous, made powerful Gr. alliances and crossed the Halys River to invade the dominions of the Medes and Persians. Cyrus overwhelmed him, conquered Lydia, and made Croesus a captive.

The great test was Babylon with its massive walls and its prestige of centuries of rule. It was particularly impregnable because of the vast area within the walls where food could be stored and even produced, because of its great wealth, and because of the Euphrates River which flowed through the city. Cyrus is said to have stationed a portion of his army at the place where the river entered the city and another where it left. The rest of the army deepened the canals in the Euphrates Valley and diverted the river temporarily. In October, 539 B.C., the army marched in by way of the riverbed under the leadership of Gobryas (Akkad. Ugbaru), who died a week later (ANET, p. 306).

The invasion seems to have been without battle. Dissatisfied with the reign of Nabonidus and Belshazzar, the people sued for peace and were granted it. They were governed by an official also named Gobryas (but Akkad. Gubaru; ANET, p. 306 does not clarify this distinction), whom Cyrus appointed vice-regent of the city. He is probably to be identified with Darius the Mede (Dan 5:31; 6; 9:1; see John C. Whitcomb, Jr., *Darius the Mede*).

With the throne of Babylon came the decision of the fate of the Heb. captives. In keeping with the generous policy of restoring people to their own lands and religion, Cyrus permitted the Jews to return from exile. Another reason may have been to create a buffer nation between Egypt and the Persian satraps.

The manner of Cyrus' death is uncertain. He crossed the Araxes to the N and attacked the Massagetae. His army was destroyed by the Scythians. It is thought that he lost his life in the battle. After a reign of 29 years, he was succeeded by his son Cambyses, in 530 B.C.

Cyrus is thought by most commentators to have been the subject of Daniel's vision of the ram with two horns, representing the Median and the Persian divisions of his empire (Dan 8:3-4, 20). *See* Babylon; Darius Hystaspes; Persia.

Bibliography. Ronald E. Manahan, "The Cyrus Notations of Deutero-Isaiah," *Grace Journal,* XI (Fall, 1970), 22-33. A. T. Olmstead, *The History of the Persian Empire,* Chicago: Univ. of Chicago Press, 1948, pp. 34-58.

W. T. D.

D

DABAREH (dăb'*à*-rĕ). A variant of Daberath (*q.v.*) found in Josh 21:28.

DABBASHETH (dăb'*à*-shĕth). A hill town (the name means "hump") of uncertain location on the border of Zebulun (Josh 19:11).

DABERATH (dăb'*à*-răth). Variant of Dabareh in Josh 21:28.

A Levitical town lying on the boundary line of Zebulun (Josh 19:12) and Issachar (Josh 21:28, RSV), probably modern Deburiyeh, at the foot of Mount Tabor. A strategic location, it may have been the site of the defeat of Sisera by Barak (Jud 4:14-22).

DAGGER. A short sword. Where the KJV translates the word "dagger," later versions translate it "sword" (Jud 3:16). Archaeologists arbitrarily distinguish swords from daggers by length, 40 centimeters (*c.* 16 inches) being the dividing point. Swords or daggers in biblical time were basically of two types: the straight and the bent (sickle). *See* Sword; Armor.

DAGON. *See* Gods, False.

DAILY. Pertaining to that which is done, occurs, or issues each day. Israelites counted their day from one sunset to the next (Ex 12:18; Lev 23:32). But the Israelites also understood by "day" the time during which the earth was lighted up in contrast to night (Gen 1:5; Dan 8:14).

For the expression "daily bread" in the Lord's Prayer, *see* Food: Bread.

DAILY OFFERING OR SACRIFICE. *See* Sacrifice.

DALAIAH (d*à*-lā'y*à*). Found only in I Chr 3:24 (KJV). This name is more correctly spelled Delaiah (*q.v.*).

DALE, THE KING'S. A valley in the immediate vicinity of Jerusalem, perhaps at the head of the Valley of Hinnom. It was the site where Abram after his victory over Chedorlaomer was met by the king of Sodom and by Melchizedek, king of

Damascus. HFV

Salem (Gen 14:17–18). It was the location of Absalom's memorial (II Sam 18:18). The latter reference calls it the King's Valley (RSV). According to Gen 14:17 it was in ancient times called the Valley of Shaveh.

DALETH (dä'lĭth). The fourth letter of the Heb. alphabet ("d" in English). *See* Alphabet. As such it is used in Ps 119 to designate the fourth part, each verse of which begins with this letter. The Heb. word *daleth* means "door," and this was the appearance of a daleth in its earliest pictographic form.

DALMANUTHA (dăl-mȧ-nū'thȧ). The place of landing by Jesus and His disciples after feeding the 4,000 (Mk 8:10). The location is unknown but thought to be on the W shore of the Sea of Galilee, somewhere S of the plain of Gennesaret. Probably the same as Magdala (Magadan, ASV) in Mt 15:39. Sometimes it is identified with the home of Mary Magdalene, but without evidence.

DALMATIA (dăl-mā'shĭ-ȧ). A name originally applied to the land of Dalmatae, a warlike Illyrian tribe. Later, the southern portion of the province of Illyricum was called by this name. Finally it was applied to the entire province lying on the E shore of the Adriatic. Paul records in II Tim 4:10 the departure of Titus to this province. It is unknown whether churches had been established there before his visit.

DALPHON (dăl'fŏn). The second of the ten sons of Haman who were put to death by the Jews after the triumph of Queen Esther (Est 9:6–13).

DAM. The ordinary word for female parent. Heb. law prohibited the destruction of the dam on her nest and the young birds at the same time (Deut 22:6–7). An animal was not to be taken for slaughter before it had been seven days with its mother (Ex 22:30; Lev 22:27).

DAMAGES. The usual translation of a Heb. term expressing any affliction, or loss of value, or permanent injury to persons or things (Ezr 4:22).

DAMARIS (dăm'ȧ-rĭs). A woman of Athens who, with Dionysius the Areopagite and certain others, was converted when Paul spoke on Mars Hill (Acts 17:34). The singling out of her name with that of Dionysius may indicate some personal or social distinction (cf. Acts 13:50; 17:12).

DAMASCENES (dăm'ȧ-sēns'). The inhabitants of Damascus (*q.v.*) under Aretas, the Arabian or Nabataean ruler, were called Damascenes (II Cor 11:32).

DAMASCUS (dȧ-măs'kŭs). Damascus (Gr. *damaskos,* Heb. *dammaśeq,* Aram. *darmeśeq,* I Chr 18:5; II Chr 28:5), the chief city of ancient Aram (Isa 7:8), has had a long history reaching back to prehistoric times. The *'Ăram Darmeseq* of I Chr 18:6 corresponds to modern Damascus. The city was known to the Egyptians as Apum according to the Saqqara Execration texts (19th cen. B.C.) and appears in both the records of Thutmose III (15th cen.) and the Amarna letters (14th cen.). The Assyrians knew it as *Dimashqi* and *Bīt-Haza'-ili* (House of Hazael). It is well watered by the clear rivers called Abana and Pharpar (II Kgs 5:12).

It is first mentioned in the OT in Gen 14:15 as the scene of Abraham's rescue of Lot. His servant Eliezer may have come from there (Gen 15:2; see William F. Albright, *Yahweh and the Gods of Canaan,* Garden City: Doubleday, 1968, pp. 65 f., n. 30). By the time of David, Damascus was an influential city-state and the focal point of various coalitions. When the town sent troops to help Hadadezer of Zobah against David, David captured the city and placed a garrison there (II Sam 8:5–6; I Chr 18:5).

In Solomon's day Rezon of Zobah captured Damascus and made it the capital of the city-state of Aram (Syria, I Kgs 11:24). His successors Hezion and Tabrimmon strengthened the city. Asa of Judah made an alliance with Ben-hadad, son of Tabrimmon, when Baasha of Israel attacked him (I Kgs 15:18–19). Either the same king or Ben-hadad II (Akkad. Adad-idri) restored to Ahab cities which had been taken from Israel, and gave Ahab concessions in Damascus, perhaps to secure Ahab's help in an anti-Assyrian coalition (I Kgs 20:34). At the great battle of Qarqar in 853 B.C., Ahab of Israel fought beside Ben-hadad and ten other kings against Assyria. Some time later Ahab was killed fighting the "king of Aram" (I Kgs 22:29–36).

The prophet Elijah was sent by God to anoint a certain Hazael as the future king of Aram (I Kgs 19:15). Later, Elisha, who had healed the general Naaman (II Kgs 5), went to

DAMASCUS

Damascus and the sick Ben-hadad sent Hazael to inquire whether he would recover. Hazael slew the old king and ruled in his place (II Kgs 8:15). In the years that followed Hazael invaded Israelite lands. When Joram of Israel opposed him he was wounded in battle (II Kgs 8:29).

For some years prior to 800 B.C. Damascus suffered from repeated Assyrian attacks. In 843 B.C. Shalmaneser III besieged Hazael in Damascus. He withstood the siege but suffered badly. When the Assyrians withdrew, Hazael attacked Israel again and occupied all of Transjordan (II Kgs 10:32 f.). He even reached the coastlands of Judah in the days of Joash of Judah (II Kgs 12:17; 835–796 B.C.). In 805–803 B.C. the Assyrians under Adadnirari III attacked Hazael, and again in 797 B.C. King Shalmaneser IV attacked Damascus. These repeated assaults so weakened the city that J(eh)oash of Israel was able to recover the towns Israel had lost to Hazael (II Kgs 13:25).

During the years that followed, Aramaean states were at war with one another while Assyria was occupied elsewhere. Then in 739 B.C. both Menahem of Israel and Rezin of Damascus became vassals of Tiglath-pileser of Assyria. They broke free for a time and sought to

East Gate, Damascus. HFV

"Street Called Straight," Damascus. HFV

form an anti-Assyrian coalition. When Judah refused to join, Pekah of Israel and Rezin of Damascus marched on Judah (II Kgs 16:5; II Chr 28:5–8). Ahaz appealed to Tiglath-pileser for help and the latter launched a series of attacks in 734–732 B.C. which ended in the death of Rezin, the fall of Damascus in 732 B.C., and in the loss of areas of Israelite territory (II Kgs 15:29; 16:9 f.). This result had been foretold by Amos (1:4 f.) and Isaiah (8:4; 17:1).

At that time Ahaz of Judah was summoned to Damascus to pay homage and was required to place a copy of a pagan altar which was there in the temple in Jerusalem (II Kgs 16:10–12; II Chr 28:23). Thereafter, Damascus was a town in the Assyrian province of Hamath and lost all political significance, although it was a center of trade (Ezk 27:18). It was regarded as the ideal border of Israel (Ezk 47:16 ff.; 48:1; Zech 9:1 f.). See Aram, Aramaeans.

Under the Seleucid rulers Damascus was only the second city of Syria. In 111 B.C. Antiochus IX made it the capital of Coele-Syria. The Nabataeans took it in 85 B.C. but lost it to Tigranes the Armenian king. Finally it became a Roman town from 64 B.C. to A.D. 33. It was later governed by an ethnarch of Aretas IV (9

B.C.–A.D. 40), the Nabataean king (II Cor 11:32). Paul visited synagogues here after his conversion (Acts 9:8–25), but had to escape over the wall of the city when troubles arose (Acts 9:25; II Cor 11:33). He returned later after a period in Arabia (Gal 1:17).

The present East Gate of the old city probably dates from Roman times. It consisted of three archways, but two of the three arches are now walled up. The street which goes W from this gate becomes one of the bazaars of the city and is still called "Straight Street"; it probably preserves the line of "the street called Straight" of Acts 9:11.

In the early part of the Christian era Damascus was secondary to Antioch. It fell to the Arabs finally in A.D. 634.

Bibliography. A. Dupont-Sommer, *Les Araméens,* Paris: A. Maisonneuve, 1949. A. Jepsen, "Israel und Damaskus," *Archiv für Orientforschung,* XIV (1942), 153–172. Merrill F. Unger, *Israel and the Aramaeans of Damascus,* Grand Rapids: Zondervan, 1957. WHG, pp. 219, 234–239, 255–257.

J. A. T.

DAMMIM (dăm'ĭm). *See* Ephes-dammim; Pas-dammim.

DAMNATION. The condition of being sentenced to eternal punishment is the idea underlying the KJV translation "damnation" of the three different Gr. words: *apōleia* in II Pet 2:1; *krima* in Mk 12:40; Rom 3:8, and elsewhere; and *krisis* in Mt 23:33; Jn 5:29. This meaning has come to be so fully identified with the word that damnation is almost universally associated with condemnation to future punishment. The root meaning of *krima* and *krisis* is simply "condemnation" or "judgment"; that of *apōleia* is "destruction." The idea of unending judgment is not in these words themselves, but is sometimes provided in the Scriptures by the modifying adjectives or prepositional phrases; e.g., Mt 23:33, RSV, "the judgment of hell [Gehenna]." In certain places, particularly I Cor 11:29, it is a mistake to imply eternal condemnation by translating *krima* as damnation, for the context indicates clearly that the apostle is speaking of penal judgment in this life which falls upon those who partake of communion in an unworthy or hypocritical manner. *See* Judgment.

R. G. R.

DAN (dăn), **DANITES** (dăn'īts). One of the sons of Jacob by Bilhah (Gen 30:5–6). He had an only son, Hushim (Gen 46:23) or Shuham (Num 26:42). His father Jacob's final prophetic benediction was figurative of Dan and his descendants. "Dan shall judge his people, as one of the tribes of Israel. Dan shall be a serpent in the way, an adder in the path, that biteth the horse's heels, so that his rider falleth backward" (Gen 49:16–17, ASV). This is generally interpreted to mean that Dan would deal with the foes of Israel on a par with the other tribes. Moses referred to Dan as a lion's whelp that leapeth forth from Bashan (Deut 33:22).

The tribe of Dan was assigned an area in the central part of Canaan, facing the Mediterranean Sea. It had a common border on the N with Ephraim, on the E with Benjamin, and on the S with Judah. Its territory contained the towns of Zorah, Aijalon, Ekron, Eltekeh, and the borders of Joppa (Josh 19:40–46; 21:5, 23–24; cf. Jud 5:17).

It is apparent that the Amorites restricted Dan's effort to possess the allotted area. Being pressed for extra living space the Danites sent spies to the extreme northern border of Palestine, near the southern slopes of Mount Hermon, to look for new territory. They found a desirable place in the vicinity of Laish and with an expedition of soldiers they seized the territory. Then they slew the inhabitants and rebuilt the city under the name of Dan (Josh 19:47; Jud 18).

The expression "from Dan to Beer-sheba" is sometimes used to denote the northern and southern boundaries of the inhabited area of the Promised Land (Jud 20:1; II Sam 3:10, etc.).

H. A. Han.

DAN, CAMP OF (Mahaneh-dan, ASV, RSV). A locality W of Kiriath-jearim in the SW part of Palestine. In the story of Samson (Jud 13:25), it is a stretch of territory where the tribe of Dan, the last of the Israelite groups to attempt to settle in Canaan, had temporary encampments, but were not able to establish any permanent settlements because of the Philistines. In the Micah story (Jud 18:11–12, RSV marg.), however, the name is given to the place where the warriors of Dan encamped on their march to the N. It is possible, therefore, that the same name was applied both to a place and a territorial area.

See Mahaneh-dan.

DAN, CITY OF. A town near the sources of the Jordan River, commonly identified with Tell el-Qadi because the Arabic name means "mound of the judge," which corresponds with Dan, "judge" (see AASOR, VI, 16). Proverbially, it was the northernmost point in Israel, as exemplified by the expression "from Dan to Beer-sheba" and its variations (Jud 20:1; I Chr 21:2, *et al.).*

The original name of the town was Laish or Leshem (Josh 19:47; Jud 18:7). Under this name (written *rwś* in Egyp.) it appears before Hazor in Thutmose III's list of conquered towns (No. 31), and is found in the second group of Egyptian Execration texts from *c.* 1825 B.C. A Mari tablet, dated *c.* 1780 - 1760

The site of ancient Dan. JR

B.C., lists a tin shipment sent from the Euphrates city to the ruler of Laish with the Hurrian name of Wari-taldu (A. Malamat, "Syro-Palestinian Destinations in a Mari Tin Inventory," IEJ, XXI [1971], 35 f.). The Danites captured it and renamed it after their tribe (Josh 19:47; Jud 18).

In pursuit of the Mesopotamian invaders, Abraham had trekked as far as Dan (Gen 14:14). Some have suggested that this was another place, known from II Sam 24:6 as Dan-jaan. However, it seems more likely that Dan-jaan is a textual corruption which should be corrected on the basis of I Kgs 15:20 to read "Dan and Ijon."

The town had been known for its political and cultural association with Sidon (Jud 18:7, 28). After its conquest by the Danites, Jonathan, the son of Gershom, and his descendants served as priests until "the captivity of the land" (Jud 18:30). Jeroboam I established the cult of his golden calf there (I Kgs 12:28–30), which continued to thrive even after the reform of Jehu (II Kgs 10:29; Amos 8:14). Ben-hadad conquered it along with other towns in the region at the urging of Asa, king of Judah, who needed a diversionary action to help him escape the pressure of his rival Baasha, king of Israel (I Kgs 15:20; II Chr 16:4). A bowl with an Aramaic inscription "belonging to the butchers (or cooks)" was found at Dan and points to the Aramaean occupation of Ben-hadad I (PEQ, C [1968], 42 ff.).

In 1966 the Israeli Department of Antiquities began to probe the 65-foot-high mound. It was settled during the Early Bronze Age, and its chief fortifications were built in Hyksos times. All occupation in later periods was on the mound itself, except for an Iron Age II monumental building on the slope of the rampart and attached to the city wall. A thick layer of ash indicated destruction of the Late Bronze Age city, confirming the account in Jud 18:27 of the capture and burning of Laish by the Danites (IEJ, XVI, 144 f.).

In the following three seasons the city gateway on the E side of the mound was excavated, the largest ever discovered in Palestine. Probably built during the reign of Jeroboam I, the gate had a processional way of paved stones leading from the approaches of the mound and up into the city. Near the entrance were a 15-foot-long bench against the outer wall of one of the gate towers and a canopy-like structure with columns topped by decorated capitals at its four corners. Here the king may have sat in state (cf. I Kgs 22:10) during visits to Dan, or it may have served as the base for a statue with cultic significance. Near the NW corner of the mound the remains of the high place installation of Jeroboam possibly have been uncovered. Fine masonry using headers and stretchers enclosed the structure. It and the pottery, including five seven-spouted oil lamps, are typical of the period of the Israelite monarchy (IEJ, XIX [1969], 121 ff., 239 ff.).

A. F. R.

DANCE. The English word, in one form or another, occurs 25 or 30 times, mostly in the OT, and translates several Heb. and two Gr. words. One Heb. word means "to whirl, writhe"; another, "to spring, skip about"; and still another, "to revolve, whirl about." Of the two Gr. words, the more common suggests a "regular motion"; the other, "singing" (Lk 15:25), the word from which we get our English word "chorus."

There are various types of dancing in the Bible, usually by women: that representing joy, that representing worship, and that which might be classified as amusement. Examples of dancing for joy would include that referred to in Jud 11:34, where Jephthah's daughter met him, after his great victory over the children of Ammon, "with timbrels and with dances." Also included would be the rejoicing of the women at the victory of David over Goliath, when they sang and danced with tabrets (I Sam 18:6; 21:11; 29:5).

Examples of dancing in connection with worship are found in Ex 15:20; 32:19; Jud 21:19–23; II Sam 6:14–16. In the first of these references Miriam and other women are celebrating "with timbrels and with dances" the safe crossing of the Red Sea by Israel. In the second, the people are dancing, naked, before the molten calf of gold Aaron had fashioned for them to worship. In the third, the daughters of Shiloh, where the tabernacle and ark were located, go out into the fields to dance. Presumably this was a religious dance. In the last instance, King David, having brought the ark up to Jerusalem and being deeply stirred over this event, leaps and dances "before the Lord." The Psalms, too, refer occasionally to dancing (30:11; 149:3; 150:4).

The only example in the Bible of dancing as an amusement seems to be that of the daughter of Herodias (Mt 14:6; Mk 6:22). This was a prelude to the murder of John the Baptist. The dance as we know it today, performed by pairs of persons of opposite sex, seems to be entirely unknown in the Bible.

Acrobatic dancers pictured in the tomb of Mereruka, Sakkara, Egypt. LL

There are two other references to dancing in the NT which deserve notice. One is our Lord's comment in Mt 11:17 and Lk 7:32 concerning the people's rejection of John the Baptist and of Himself. He compares this to the refusal of children in the marketplace to respond either to gay music or to mournful. He says, "We have piped unto you, and ye have not danced; we have mourned unto you, and ye have not lamented." This and Job 21:11 f. indicate it was rather commonplace for children, at least, to dance for joy in biblical times. Probably this has always been true. The other instance is of similar import. In Lk 15:25, the elder son hears music and dancing in the house after his younger brother's return—again an example of dancing for joy.

Dancing in the Bible, therefore, except in the case of Herodias' daughter, seems to have little relationship to the sensual, but is rather associated ordinarily with joy, either because of circumstances or because of gratitude for the Lord's blessing.

See Games.

J. A. S.

DANIEL (dan'yėl). Daniel, an OT hero, is the main character of the book of Daniel. Of royal or noble birth (Dan 1:3), Daniel was taken captive to Babylonia by Nebuchadnezzar in 605 B.C., with other Jewish youths of like ability and attainments (1:1-7), where he spent the remainder of his life and gained distinction as statesman and prophet.

Daniel was instructed in the learning and language of the Chaldeans (1:4). He and his friends Hananiah, Mishael, and Azariah were offered the lavish menu of the heathen court. Since the royal fare was against the law of Moses and would render him less efficient, Daniel "purposed in his heart that he would not defile himself with the portion of the king's meat, nor with the wine" (1:8). At their request Daniel and his friends were allowed to eat vegetables and drink water for ten days and were then in better health than the other trainees. The supervisors discerned that these Jewish youths possessed great skill and wisdom. At the end of their training period they were recognized by the king as superior to all the other wise men at the royal court.

By divine revelation Daniel told the king his forgotten dream and its interpretation which included the doom of Nebuchadnezzar's kingdom (Dan 2). The king worshiped Daniel, honored his God, rewarded him with costly gifts (2:46-47), and "made him ruler over the whole province of Babylon, and . . . over all the wise men of Babylon" (2:48). Later, Daniel interpreted another of Nebuchadnezzar's dreams, telling the king that for a time he would lose his throne but would be restored to it after he had become thoroughly humbled (Dan 4).

God revealed through Daniel certain aspects of the messianic kingdom having to do with the course of history and the eternal age. *See* Daniel, Book of.

For more than 20 years (561-539 B.C.) nothing is recorded of Daniel, and he seems to have lost his position and fallen out of public favor. Then at the feast of Belshazzar (*q.v.*), coregent with his father Nabonidus, the queen (probably Belshazzar's mother, daughter of Nebuchadnezzar) remembered Daniel, who when sent for interpreted the strange handwriting on the wall (Dan 5:10-28). In accordance with his interpretation, Babylon fell that night (539 B.C.) to Darius the Mede. Though secular history at present does not know of a Darius the Mede, he is identified by competent scholars with Gobryas, governor of Babylon under Cyrus (John C. Whitcomb, *Darius the Mede*). Darius recognized Daniel's ability, made him chief of a board of three presidents, and "thought to set him over the whole realm" (Dan 6:3).

In religion Daniel still manifested the same uncompromising faithfulness. He defied Darius' decree and prayed to God rather than to the

Babylon as Daniel would have known it. The ziggurat stands in the foreground and Procession Street runs up the center of the picture. ORINST

king. He was cast into the den of lions, but was miraculously delivered (Dan 6). Daniel never compromised his convictions nor wavered in his loyalty to God. He lived until the third year of Cyrus (536 B.C.) being perhaps 90 years of age and still active.

Ezekiel referred to Daniel as a man of high wisdom and piety (Ezk 28:3) and placed Daniel alongside such worthies as Noah and Job (Ezk 14:14, 20), men renowned for their righteousness. Jesus referred to Daniel at least once (Mt 24:15).

C. J. H.

DANIEL, BOOK OF

General Characteristics

The book of Daniel occupies a unique place in the OT. It sets forth marvelous predictions of the coming of the Messiah and the kingdom of God. In the English Bible it is among the major prophets after Ezekiel; in the Heb. Bible it is among the Writings, the third division of the Jewish canon. In the Heb. Bible, Hebrew in Dan 1:1–2:4*a* and 8:1–12:13 points up Israel's significant role in international developments; Aramaic in Dan 2:4*b*–7:28 indicates the order of succession, character, and destiny of heathen nations.

Outline

- I. History of Daniel, chaps. 1–6
  - A. Daniel's youth and education, chap. 1
  - B. Nebuchadnezzar's image-dream, chap. 2
  - C. Faithfulness of Daniel's companions, chap. 3
  - D. Nebuchadnezzar's tree-dream, chap. 4
  - E. Belshazzar's feast, chap. 5
  - F. Daniel in the den of lions, chap. 6
- II. Visions of Daniel, chaps. 7–12
  - A. Vision of the four beasts, chap. 7
  - B. Vision of the ram and the he-goat, chap. 8
  - C. Daniel's prayer; vision of the 70 weeks, chap. 9
  - D. Daniel's last vision, chaps. 10–12
    1. The angel appears to encourage Daniel and predict the future, chap. 10
    2. Persia and Greece; struggles between Ptolemies and Seleucids; oppression under Antiochus Epiphanes, chap. 11
    3. The Messianic Age and its consummation, chap. 12

Date and Authorship

From ancient times Jewish-Christian tradition has declared that Daniel wrote the book during the Exile in the 6th cen. B.C. That the men of the Great Synagogue wrote the book of Daniel during the time of Ezra and Nehemiah, according to the Talmud, means that they copied it. The book purports to be serious history and claims that Daniel gave forth the prophecies contained therein. Jesus refers to "the abomination of desolation, spoken of by Daniel the prophet" in Mt 24:15.

The traditional view as to date and authorship has been seriously questioned. Porphyry, a Platonic philosopher of the 3rd cen. after Christ, held that the book was written in the 2nd cen. B.C. Many modern scholars hold that a pious scribe used the figure of Daniel, an ancient sage, to encourage loyalty to God and maintain enthusiasm for the national cause during the Maccabean revolt of 167–164 B.C. against the Seleucid ruler Antiochus Epiphanes. In this view the book of Daniel consists of spurious stories of Daniel in the Babylonian courts during the Exilic period and of visions ascribed to Daniel which traversed Israel's history from this period to the writer's own time, concentrating on the years of persecution and their consummation in the inauguration of the kingdom of God.

Despite prevalent critical opinion against the 6th cen. dating of the book, a gradual trend is discernible toward earlier dating. The discovery of Belshazzar's (*q.v.*) name on Babylonian clay tablets, and the probable identification by Whitcomb of Darius the Mede (*q.v.*) with Gubaru (Gr. *Gobryas*) have gone far to vindicate the 6th cen. historical accuracy of the book. Alleged linguistic and exegetical problems have been more than adequately answered by conservative scholars (SOTI, pp. 368 ff.). Qumran fragments of the book of Daniel (150 B.C.) are also weighing heavily in pushing back the date of the authorship of the book toward the conservative date.

Interpretations

Three principal competing interpretations of the book of Daniel are noted.

1. The first view says the book was written to encourage the Jews to constancy under the persecutions of Antiochus Epiphanes. It deals with history no later than 164 B.C. The fourth kingdom of chaps. 2 and 7 is Greece with primary reference to Antiochus as the "little horn" of 7:8, parallel with 8:9. The anointed one cut off (9:26) probably refers to the murder of the high priest Onias III, *c.* 170 B.C. (II Macc 4:33–38). The one who desolates in 9:27 is Antiochus, and the desolating abomination refers to his desecration of the altar in Jerusalem in 167 B.C. in the midst of Daniel's seventieth week (chap. 9). Sacrifices ceased, but were reinstituted in 164 B.C., the end of the seventieth week. The promise in chap. 12 is that God will vindicate the faithful and raise the martyrs from the dead to enjoy the blessings of the everlasting kingdom.

2. The second interpretation understands that the death of Christ occurred in the midst of the seventieth week, at which time Jewish sacrifices ceased and a covenant prevailed for many. Consequent upon the cutting off of the Messiah, a desolator appears over the temple which, now having become an abomination, is

destroyed. The fourth kingdom of chaps. 2 and 7 is Rome; the ten horns are ten early Roman emperors; the "little horn" is Titus Vespasianus who destroyed Jerusalem in A.D. 70. The emphasis in this interpretation is upon the messiah who, in being cut off, brought in eternal righteousness and made reconciliation for iniquity.

3. The third interpretation holds that Daniel's seventieth week is still future. The present Church Age was hidden from the OT prophets, but may be accounted for as a "parenthesis." The prophecy that "an anointed one shall be cut off" (9:26, RSV) looks to the death of Christ at the end of the sixty-ninth week. Israel will receive forgiveness for not having recognized their Messiah when "the times of the Gentiles" end and the Son of Man appears a second time. The second half of the seventieth week is identical with the Great Tribulation of Mt 24:15-28. The fourth kingdom of Dan 2 and 7 is Rome. The "little horn" is the Antichrist, the great leader of the revived Roman Empire who will appear at the end of the age in the midst of the seventieth week. At the end of the seventieth week the millennial reign begins.

See Nebuchadnezzar.

Bibliography. G. L. Archer, "The Aramaic of the 'Genesis Apocryphon' Compared with the Aramaic of Daniel," NPOT, pp. 160-169. R. D. Culver, *Daniel and the Latter Days,* New York: Revell, 1954. A. C. Gaebelein, *The Prophet Daniel,* New York: "Our Hope," 1911. E. W. Heaton, *The Book of Daniel,* London: SCM, 1956. G. R. King, *Daniel,* Grand Rapids: Eerdmans, 1966. H. Leupold, *Exposition of Daniel,* Columbus: Wartburg Press, 1949. D. J. Wiseman, *et al., Notes on Some Problems in the Book of Daniel,* London: Tyndale Press, 1965. E. M. Yamauchi, "The Greek Words in Daniel in the Light of Greek Influence in the Near East," NPOT, pp. 170-200. E. J. Young, *The Prophecy of Daniel,* Grand Rapids: Eerdmans, 1953.

C. J. H.

DAN-JAAN. *See* Dan, City of.

DANNAH (dăn'ȧ). A town in the mountain of Judah SW of Hebron, perhaps associated with modern Idnah (Josh 15:49).

DARA (där'ȧ). Found in I Chr 2:6. The preferred spelling is Darda (*q.v.*).

DARDA (där'dȧ). One of four men, sons of Mahol ("members of the orchestral guild," IDB), noted for wisdom, excelled only by Solomon (I Kgs 4:31). In I Chr 2:6 he is mentioned as a son of Zerah, son of Judah, and is called Dara (*q.v.*).

DARIC. A gold Persian coin worth about five dollars, known to the Jews after their return from Babylon (Ezr 8:27, RSV). The name is presumably derived from "Darius," the Persian king (522-486 B.C.), and is rendered "dram" in KJV. It is the first coin mentioned in the Bible. The writer in I Chr 29:7 may have been converting a monetary value of David's period to the equivalent amount in darics of his own day. The references in Ezr 2:69 and Neh 7:70-72 (RSV) to gold darics during the reign of King Cyrus (550-530 B.C.) prior to Darius' time may be similarly explained. *See* Weights, Measures, and Coins.

DARIUS (I) HYSTASPES (dȧ-rī'ŭs hĭs-tăs'pēz). The name in Old Persian was *Darayavaush;* in Babylonian, *Da-ri-ya-muš;* in Gr., *Dareios.* He is also known as Darius the Great.

Darius was a descendant through his father Hystaspes of Ariaramnes, a descendant of Hakhmanish (Achaemenae) the ancestor of Cyrus, but not of the royal succession. Darius was born in 550 B.C. and ruled from 522 to 486 B.C.

In his Behistun inscription Darius claims eight kings as his ancestors, but he came to the throne only by pressing energetically the claim of the elder side of Hakhmanish. At Cambyses'

Darius I enthroned with his son Xerxes standing behind him; from the treasury at Persepolis. ORINST

Tomb of Darius, Naksh-i-Rustam. ORINST

death in 522 B.C., revolt flared up over the empire with contestants in Susiana, Babylon, Media, Sagartia and Margiana. By alliance with the heads of six leading families of Persia and starting with a surprise attack, Darius slew Gaumata, who pretended to be Bardiya (Gr. *Smerdis,* Cambyses' murdered brother), in 521 B.C., and by 519 B.C. had suppressed all rebellions.

Darius extended his empire to the Caucasus and by 513 B.C. marched beyond the Bosphorus and crossed the Danube. Complete Persian control over the area, however, was prevented by Scythian attacks. Though having added Macedonia to his realm, he failed to add Greece when his host was defeated at Marathon, 490 B.C. He recorded his exploits in a trilingual inscription high on the cliff near Behistun (Bisitun), along the main trade route between Ecbatana (Achmetha, Ezr 6:2) and Babylon.

Darius then proceeded to reorganize the empire, putting it under a bureaucracy centered in himself, removing many of the native officials installed by Cyrus. He fixed coinage and introduced the daric. In the interests of E-W trade, he caused a canal to be dug from the Nile to the Red Sea and sent ships through it, according to hieroglyphic inscriptions.

He is the Darius mentioned by Haggai the prophet. In his second year, he affirmed Cyrus' benevolent policy respecting the Jews against the oppressions of Tatnai, governor of Samaria (Ezr 4:5; 6:6). On the request of the Jews, he ordered a search of the records, and the decree to restore the Jerusalem temple was found at Ecbatana (modern Hamadan) which he reaffirmed. To it he added the command that money and cattle be furnished to the project, forbidding at the same time further interference with it. The temple was completed in his sixth year, 515 B.C. (Ezr 6:1–15).

See Cyrus; Persia; Haggai.

H. G. S.

DARIUS THE MEDE. The ruler of "the realm of the Chaldeans" (Dan 9:1) under Cyrus (Dan 6:28), immediately following the death of Belshazzar (Dan 5:30–31). He is best remembered for his decree which resulted in the prophet Daniel's being cast into a den of lions (6:7–28). He is not to be confused with the later Persian monarch, Darius I Hystaspes (521–486 B.C.), for he was of Median extraction ("of the seed of the Medes," Dan 9:1), and his father's name was Ahasuerus (the Heb. equivalent of Xerxes; cf. the name of the son of Darius I; cf. Est 1:1). Darius the Mede was born in the year 601/600 B.C., for at the fall of Babylon (Oct., 539 B.C.), he was sixty-two (Dan 5:31).

One of the cardinal doctrines of negative criticism has been that the book of Daniel was authored by an unknown writer of the Maccabean age (*c.* 165 B.C.), who mistakenly thought that an independent Median kingdom ruled by Darius the Mede followed the fall of Babylon and preceded the rise of Persia under Cyrus. But Darius the Mede is not depicted in the book as a universal monarch. In fact, his subordinate position is clearly implied in the statement that he "was made king over the realm of the Chaldeans" (Dan 9:1). Also, the facts that Belshazzar's kingdom was "given to the Medes and *Persians*" (5:28); that Darius the Mede *received* the kingdom (5:31, ASV, RSV, NASB, JerusB); and that Darius found himself helpless to alter the "law of the Medes and *Persians*" (6:15) render the critical view untenable.

The publication during the early decades of this century of additional cuneiform texts from this period has enabled Bible students to gain a much clearer understanding of the fall of Babylon in 539 B.C. It seems quite probable that Darius the Mede was none other than Gubaru, the governor under Cyrus who appointed subgovernors in Babylon immediately after its conquest ("Nabonidus Chronicle," ANET, p. 306; cf. Dan 6:1). This same Gubaru (not to be confused with Ugbaru, governor of Gutium, the general under Cyrus who conquered Babylon and died three weeks later, according to the

Nabonidus Chronicle) is frequently mentioned in cuneiform documents during the following 14 years as governor of Babylon and the Region-Beyond-the-River (i.e., the entire Fertile Crescent). Gubaru thus ruled over the vast and populous territories of Babylonia, Syria, Phoenicia, and Palestine, and his name was a final warning to criminals throughout this area (cf. John C. Whitcomb, *Darius the Mede,* Presbyterian and Reformed Pub. Co., 1963, pp. 10-24). The fact that he is called "king" in Dan 6 is not an inaccuracy, even though he was a subordinate of Cyrus. Similarly, Belshazzar was called "king," even though he was the second ruler of the kingdom under Nabonidus (Dan 5:29).

The book of Daniel gives more information concerning the personal background of Darius the Mede than of Belshazzar or even of Nebuchadnezzar. He is the only monarch in the book whose age, parentage, and nationality are recorded. Although he was a subordinate ruler like Belshazzar, it is evident that he ruled Babylonia with far greater zeal and efficiency than did his profligate predecessor.

J. C. W.

DARIUS THE PERSIAN. Mentioned once in the OT in Neh 12:22. He was either Nothus, Darius II (423-404 B.C.) or Codomannus, Darius III (336-331 B.C.). Darius II authorized the keeping of the Passover by the Jews at Elephantine in Egypt (ANET, p. 491). Darius III was the king whose empire Alexander the Great conquered. The evidence for the identification rests on the fact that the priests Johanan and Jaddua are mentioned in the same verse. A Johanan appears as the high priest at Jerusalem in an Elephantine papyrus dated 407 B.C. (ANET, p. 492), which would favor an identification with Darius II. On the other hand, a Jaddua is mentioned as the high priest who greeted Alexander (Jos *Ant.* xi.7.2 and 8.4-5), which has inclined many scholars to favor an identification with Darius III.

The recent discovery of 4th cen. B.C. Samaritan papyri, which indicates that there was a sequence of governors called Sanballat, provides a new solution. It can be assumed that Darius the Persian was Darius II, and that the Jaddua mentioned in Nehemiah was not the same individual mentioned in Josephus but a grandfather of the latter. See Frank M. Cross, "The Discovery of the Samaria Papyri," BA, XXVI (1963), 121; "Aspects of Samaritan and Jewish History in Late Persian and Hellenistic Times," HTR, LIX (1966), 203 ff.

E. M. Y.

DARKNESS. This is expressed by 11 Heb. words, the most common of which is *ḥōshek* and several forms of *'ōpel;* and in Gr. by *skotia, skotos,* "darkness," and *zophos,* "gloom" or "blackness."

Physical darkness. This is particularly mentioned on four occasions in the Bible.

1. At the time of creation when "darkness was upon the face of the deep" (Gen 1:2). This was dispelled when God created light and commenced the generative process which is recounted in Gen 1:1–2:6, and ended in the creation of man (2:7-25).

2. The darkness of three days' duration which constituted the ninth judgment upon Egypt, "even darkness which may be felt" (Ex 10:21-23).

3. The darkness at the crucifixion (Mt 27:45), which continued for three hours, from the sixth to the ninth hour, as God hid from the wicked world the agonies of His Son upon the cross. This darkness was one of the series of miracles which happened at that time: earthquake (v. 51), darkness (v. 45), rending of temple veil from top to bottom (v. 51), resurrection of bodies of some of the saints (vv. 52-53).

4. Darkness at Christ's second advent. This darkness is prophesied by Isaiah, Joel, Christ and John (Isa 13:9-10; Joel 2:31; 3:15; Mt 24:29; Rev 6:12). It will be different from the second and third, though it too will accompany and signify judgment. While the others appear to have been local in nature, this darkness will cover the whole earth since the sun and the moon and stars are to be darkened.

Spiritual darkness. Darkness is also used in a figurative sense to designate spiritual ignorance and blindness (Eccl 2:14; 5:17; Isa 9:2; 29:18; 42:7; Jn 1:5; 8:12; I Jn 2:11) in contrast to light (Jn 1:5, 9; Isa 49:6).

The day of calamity and of sorrow is called a day of darkness (Isa 8:22; Joel 2:2; I Jn 2:8). The despair of the lost is as darkness (Mt 4:16; 6:23).

Since darkness offers a cover for committing evil, the expression "the works of darkness" is sometimes used (Rom 13:12; Eph 5:11).

Darkness is also used to express the condition of the dead apart from the light of the gospel (Job 10:21-22; 18:18; Col 1:13; I Pet 2:9); of the fallen angels kept in chains (II Pet 2:4; Jude 6); and of the final condition of the lost (Mt 22:13; 25:30; Jude 13).

R. A. K.

DARKON (där'kŏn). An ancestor of Solomon's servant Jaala. The "children of Darkon" returned from Exile with Zerubbabel (Ezr 2:56; Neh 7:58).

DARLING. A translation in KJV of the Heb. *yāḥîd,* "only" or "only one" (Gen 22:2, 12, 16). In Ps 22:20 and 35:17 later versions render it "life" or "dear life." It is poetically transferred to the psalmist's own life "as the one unique and priceless possession which can never be replaced" (*Oxford Hebrew Lexicon*).

DART. A sharp-pointed weapon as an arrow or light spear used for thrusting. Joab used three darts (pointed rods) to kill Absalom (II Sam 18:14). Darts or arrows were mechanically hurled in the Maccabean period (I Macc 6:51). At times these darts may have been wrapped in inflammable materials and ignited (Eph 6:16; cf. Ps 120:4). *See* Armor.

DATHAN (dā'thăn). A descendant of Reuben who, with his brother Abiram and others, followed Korah, the Levite, in rebellion against the authority of Moses and Aaron in the wilderness. Dathan and Abiram with their families and goods were swallowed up by the earth (Num 16; Deut 11:6; Ps 106:17).

DAUGHTER (Heb. *bath,* "daughter," "child," "descendant").One cannot determine the exact meaning of the Heb. word *bath* until he carefully considers the context, any more than he can for the word *ben,* "son," of which *bath* is the feminine counterpart.

The Heb. word *bath* appears about 150 times in the OT in contexts that would suggest the ordinary biological relationship. There is nothing unusual about this meaning of the word. Collectively, the term may refer to all the women of a community (Gen 34:1; Lk 23:28). It served also as a familiar form of address expressing respect and even compassion (Mk 5:34). *See* Family.

There are, however, figurative uses of the word which are of great significance. Seventy or more times in the Psalms and Prophets the word is so used, especially in the works of Jeremiah, where it appears 41 times. Sometimes the word "daughter" means a city (e.g., Isa 1:8; 10:32, referring to Jerusalem as the daughter of Zion). At other times the reference is to the inhabitants of a city or a kingdom (Isa 47:1 ff.; Jer 6:26; 46:24). Certain characteristics are heightened when used in conjunction with the term daughter (feminine beauty, Jer 6:2; the cry of anguish, Jer 8:19 ff.; the spirit of disobedience, Jer 31:22; or punishment decreed, Jer 51:33). The word is also applied to small villages attached to the mother city in a city-state community (Num 21:25; 32:42, marg., ASV).

J. W. C.

DAUGHTER-IN-LAW. This is the wife of one's son and is the translation of a term used also for "bride." The daughter-in-law joined her husband's family and came under the authority of her father-in-law (Gen 11:31). Incestuous relations with a man's daughter-in-law were forbidden, and death was the penalty for both, if this law was violated (Lev 18:15; 20:12).

DAUGHTER OF ZION. *See* Zion, Daughter of.

DAVID (dā'vĭd). The second king of Israel, founder of the united monarchy (1000–962 B.C.).

Sources

The main source for the life and times of David is the material found in the books of I and II Samuel and I Kgs 1–2. These accounts, especially II Sam 9–20 (the court history of David), are a realistic presentation of David by a contemporary historian. I Chr 11–29 contains a parallel account to Samuel-Kings with some additions and omissions. It is fuller than the Samuel-Kings account in the details of the temple arrangement and of lists of royal officers, and presents David in a more idealistic way than does Samuel-Kings.

Numerous references to David are also found in other OT and NT books. Secondary sources to David are stories in the Talmud, Koran, and in the rabbinic and Christian traditions of David. These add to the luster if not to the light of Israel's most beloved figure after the patriarch Abraham.

Name and Family

The name David may mean "beloved" from the noun *dôd* (cf. Jedidiah, "the beloved of the Lord," II Sam 12:25, ASV marg.). Scholars thought a few decades ago that it might be a title such as "captain." The term *dawîdum,* "army officer," occurs a number of times in the Mari texts, and the word *dwdh* once on the Moabite Stone. This possible derivation of David's name, however, is now seriously doubted or discarded (K. A. Kitchen, *Ancient Orient and Old Testament,* pp. 84 f.).

David was born in Bethlehem of Judah, a city about six miles S of Jerusalem, mentioned in the Tel el Amarna letters. This was the home of Boaz and Ruth, and became best known as the birthplace of the son of David, the Messiah of Israel.

David was the youngest child of a family of ten children (I Sam 16:10–11; I Chr 2:13–16 lists only nine; perhaps one child died young). His brothers' names were Eliab (Elihu?), Abinadab, Shimma, Nethaneel, Raddai, and

David trying on Saul's armor, pictured on Byzantine silver dish, c. 625 A. D. MM

Ozem. His sisters' names were Abigail and Zeruiah. According to II Sam 17:25, these girls were daughters of Nahash. Apparently David's mother had the two daughters by a previous marriage. The name of David's mother is unknown. His father, Jesse, a well-to-do, respected elder in Bethlehem, claimed to be of the lineage of Boaz. David was a son of Jesse's old age (I Sam 17:12).

Early Life

The first mention of David occurs in the account of the visit of the prophet Samuel to Bethlehem to select a successor to King Saul. At the sacrifice to which Jesse was especially invited, Samuel began to interview his sons as possible candidates for the kingship. One by one Jesse presented his boys, but none seemed to meet the divine specifications which Samuel sought in the new leader-to-be. Finally, Samuel asked Jesse to present his youngest son; whereupon David was summoned from his chore of sheep tending and won the approval of the prophet as God's man for the nation.

Although David was anointed in the presence of his brethren (I Sam 16:13), the exact purpose of the anointing was not made known to all present. It is thought by many scholars that those at the feast interpreted the ritual act as Samuel's choice of David to succeed him in the prophetic office, as Elijah the prophet had anointed Elisha, the young man to succeed him.

I Sam 16:12 states that David was ruddy (*'admônî*, "red," also used of Esau, causing many to believe David to be redheaded), had beautiful eyes, and was handsome. Far more important to Samuel and to Israel was the assurance that "the Spirit of the Lord came mightily upon David from that day forward." He was the choice of the prophet and of God for the task which faced the nation. He was to become the people's choice at a later time.

David came to public attention in Israel through two important events, one related to music, the other to physical prowess. In the search for a skilled musician to soothe the melancholia of Saul, David was recommended by a member of the court for the position. I Sam 16:18 (RSV) lists among his qualifications "skilled in playing, a man of valor, a man of war, prudent in speech, and a man of good presence." In addition to good looks and excellent musical talent, he came from a good family background, could fight if called upon, knew how to ease difficult situations with the right word, and possessed the charm needed of one in public service. It seemed that David possessed all the requisites of a young man destined for greatness. Again it is noted that "the Lord is with him." David's versatility commanded the attention of Saul, and David quickly attained a dual role in the royal court, king's armor bearer and private musician to the king. Since Bethlehem was but a day's journey from Gibeah, the house of King Saul, it is believed that David returned often to his home to

The Valley of Elah, where the fight between David and Goliath took place. HFV

continue caring for his father's flocks (I Sam 17:15). His prestige grew in both Benjamin and Judah by leaps and bounds.

The other event in David's early life that commanded national attention was his victory over Goliath, the Philistine giant, in the battle that took place in the valley of Elah (I Sam 17). Chap. 17 may refer to events prior to Saul's hiring David to play in his court, parenthetically included by the author to explain David's qualifications (I Sam 16:18). David left his home in Bethlehem to carry food to his warrior brothers and to return word to Jesse on how the battle fared. When he arrived in the camp, he learned that Goliath had been challenging the Heb. army for 40 days to provide a Hebrew to engage him alone in a contest to determine the outcome of the war. It was customary in Gr. warfare for two warriors to fight a duel to determine the outcome of a battle, rather than for two armies to engage in locked combat. (Achilles and Hector finally settled the Trojan War by a duel.) Since the Philistines controlled the metal industry and were skilled warriors from their youth, the Heb. host was at a serious disadvantage. Their equipment and military tactics were inferior to the superbly trained Philistine giant. To volunteer to fight him was sheer suicide. Saul knew the odds of winning and offered high stakes to any one who would volunteer: freedom from taxation for his father's house, and the hand of Saul's daughter in marriage.

David offered to accept Goliath's challenge and Saul gave him the best military equipment the Heb. army could muster. David refused the armor as being unwieldy and chose his own weapons, the weapons of a shepherd, stone and sling. With this instrument he had protected the sheep of his father's flock; with it he would attempt to protect the people of his Father's flock. He accepted the offer of Goliath with an expression of his heroic faith in God to give victory to His people. Goliath was defeated by the shepherd boy, his head taken to the metropolis of Jerusalem as a trophy of war, and his armor placed in David's tent (some would interpret "tent" to mean the tent at Nob).

The victory of David over Goliath brought him more permanently into the court of Saul. There he met Michal, the daughter of Saul, who was to become his wife. Here he also met the charming prince Jonathan. The story of their friendship and loyalty to each other is a masterpiece in biblical literature. Their friendship was of one soul in two bodies. The bond which united Jonathan to David was neither mere admiration for his heroic courage and extraordinary skill in using the sling, nor mere sympathy with him in his fervent love of country and common hatred of the uncircumcised Philistines, but was mainly their common faith in the covenant love of God for Israel. This unity of spirit won Jonathan to David, and he made with him a covenant of friendship and exchanged gifts in token of that friendship (I Sam 18:1–4).

Fugitive from King Saul

David performed his task so well that his fame spread through all the land. He became the favorite son of the common people and of the court (I Sam 18:5). Hymns were composed by the singing women lauding his exploits beyond those of the king himself. This caused a breach to develop between Saul and David. Saul attempted on several occasions to assassinate him (I Sam 18:11; 19:10), encouraged his court to put him out of the way, sent him on dangerous missions, and even proposed a seemingly impossible feat with the pretext that he should so distinguish himself in fulfilling it that he could become the worthy son-in-law to the king (I Sam 18:20–29). No plan of Saul nor any member of his court was able to eliminate David, for "the Lord was with him."

Saul's fears of David were legitimate, for he saw quite clearly that David, rather than Jonathan, would succeed him in the kingship. Jonathan knew the reality of his father's fears, but was of a gracious spirit and saw in David the better man to succeed to the throne of Israel in those troubled days. Jonathan tried several times to heal the rift between Saul and David but failed, and David finally had to flee for his life. His wife Michal helped him to escape the net of King Saul by a ruse. She placed a teraphim (household god) in David's bed, enlarged the torso of the dummy with a goat hair quilt, and covered it with a garment. Then she reported to the men whom Saul had sent to arrest David that he was ill. Saul ordered his men to bring David in his bed to the court, and the ruse was revealed. Saul's inquiry of Michal was met with carefully worded untruth (I Sam 19:11–17). Even Saul's family seemed to turn from him in favor of youthful David.

David fled first to Samuel at Ramah (I Sam 19:18). Undoubtedly he sought the influence and protection that the great religious leader could provide. He also needed to be reassured that God had a future for him in the scheme of national affairs. Some have conjectured that David offered to follow Samuel and to give up the rocky road to the throne. Saul's repeated attempts to capture David in Ramah met with signal failure (I Sam 19:18–24). David's next stop was at the sanctuary in Nob to secure weapons and food for a flight to Philistine Gath (I Sam 21). His method of securing aid has been seriously questioned, for he lied to get bread and a sword.

David made a wise choice in fleeing to the land of the Philistines. He received his basic boot training in warfare from the very people whom he was to challenge later on for the right to full control of Palestine. His newly acquired military knowledge would better equip him to fight Israel's most dreaded foe.

While in flight from King Saul, David collected a motley army. The dispossessed, those in debt, and the discontents gathered around him, and from this strange mixture David formed a hard core of loyal adherents. Many were non-Hebrews. With them he began a series of movements in the Negeb area of Judah. His flight from Saul offered him numerous opportunities to woo the clans of Judah to his cause. Many were disillusioned in Saul's program and in his tribal preferences, and were slowly but surely becoming backers of the movement that saw in David the champion of Israel's cause. David made many fine gestures for the support of Judah's clans by his gifts and protective policies. The marriages to Abigail and Ahinoam (I Sam 25) strengthened the alliances with powerful clans in the hills of southern Judah.

David's patience with and respect for King Saul are admirable. He did nothing that would overthrow Saul's kingdom, but merely kept one step ahead of the pursuing king. His healthy and religious respect for the anointed of the Lord and at the same time a steady building of his own program so as to be prepared when God should call him to assume leadership were his paradoxical objectives. That time came in the death of Saul and Jonathan in the battle on Mount Gilboa. Most of Israel mourned the death of the tragic King Saul. David wept with the nation and composed an elegy in honor of Saul and Jonathan (II Sam 1:17–27).

King of Israel

King at Hebron. David became king of the tribe of Judah (II Sam 2:4) before he became king of all Israel. His capital was in Hebron about 30 miles S of Jerusalem, from where he governed the affairs of Judah for seven and one-half years. Among his most strategic moves to enlarge his domain were the gestures of friendship toward the men of Jabesh-gilead in Transjordan (II Sam 2:4–7), recalling of Michal his wife, and acts of courtesy toward key Benjamite leaders. Slowly but surely David was able to woo the cohorts of the kingdom of Saul into the solid backing he had developed in Judah. All Israel finally crowned him king of Israel. He was the first king of united Israel and the founder of a dynasty which remained in power about 425 years. Few dynasties in the world have equaled the records of the family of David. The NT reveals the eternal nature of the kingdom of God in the true son of David, the King of kings, Jesus Christ.

King at Jerusalem. David had many wives and concubines who bore to him many sons and daughters. The most famous of his sons were Absalom, Adonijah, Amnon, and Solomon. Tamar was his most famous daughter. Tragedy struck hard and often in the family of David. Intrigue and rivalry always follow the careers of sons born to fathers who marry many wives. Absalom slew Amnon for the rape of Tamar; David's nephew Joab slew Absalom for treason; Solomon banished Adonijah for political reasons. The tragedy of David's life was his family problems. He could weld a nation of headstrong tribes into a solid unit, but his sons created chaos under his very eyes.

David's first act as king of all Israel was to choose a site for the capital that would be acceptable both to the northern and the southern tribes. Jerusalem was to become that place. David built his palace on Mount Zion, the SE hill captured from the Jebusites (II Sam 5:6-9), and he erected a number of government buildings to house his offices. His own experience and the period of the judges proved that a people's army was not dependable; he therefore created a professional army. It was composed of many Cherethites and Pelethites under the leadership of Benaiah of Kabzeel, and the 600 men under Ittai of Gath, an old friend from David's fugitive period. David waged war successfully against the Philistines, against Edom, Moab, Ammon, and Aram or Syria (II Sam 5; 8; 10; 12).

David's two most significant contributions to the life of Israel were (1) the unification of the 12 tribes into a monarchy whose capital was in Jerusalem; and (2) the plans for the centralization of worship in Jerusalem in a temple. He did this by establishing the worship of the people of Israel according to the Mosaic law as seen in the ritual of the ark. By placing the ark, the symbol of the invisible God, in the center of the state, David centralized the religious worship in Jerusalem and prepared the way for the temple. Subsequent history accredits to him not only the physical materials of the temple but much of the music that would constitute the worship of the temple (cf. I Chr 6:31; 16:7, 41-42; 25:1).

The Jews of later days looked back to David as the ideal king, and pictured as a second David the ruler of the happy day for which they hoped.

Evaluation

David was not without fault. The affair with

David ruled in Hebron for seven years before becoming king of all Israel. HFV

Bathsheba and the murder of Uriah indicate his human weaknesses. He often showed disrespect for the men who had been his staunchest supporters (e.g., Joab, and the army of Israel in the rebellion of Absalom). However, he was true to commitments, intensely loyal to friends, and more amenable to prophetic guidance than was Saul. He has been called the sweet singer of Israel; the founder of a dynasty of kings; a prophet; one beloved of God, for his heart was inclined toward God, and he knew how to repent and ask for God's grace.

Bibliography. William F. Albright, *The Biblical Period from Abraham to Ezra,* New York: Harper Torchbooks, 1963, pp. 50-53. John Bright, "The Age of King David," *Union Seminary Review,* Vol. 53 (1942), 87-109; *A History of Israel,* Philadelphia: Westminster, 1959, pp. 171-190. David Cooper, *David,* Los Angeles: Biblical Research Society, 1943. William J. Deane, *David: His Life and Times,* New York: Revell, n.d. James L. Kelso, *Archaeology and Our Old Testament Contemporaries,* Grand Rapids: Zondervan, 1966, chap. 5. Rudolf Kittel, *Great Men and Movements in Israel,* New York: KTAV Publishing House, 1968, chap. 6. F. B. Meyer, *David,* London: Morgan and Scott, 1910. Alan Redpath, *The Making of a Man of God: Studies in the Life of David,* Westwood, N.J.: Revell, 1962. Samuel J. Schultz, *The Old Testament Speaks,* New York: Harper, 1960, pp. 124-141.

F. E. Y.

DAVID, CITY OF. *See* City of David.

DAWN. *See* Dayspring; Time, Divisions of.

DAY. *See* Time; Time, Divisions of.

DAY OF ATONEMENT. *See* Festivals.

DAY OF CHRIST, THE. A NT expression occurring (with its equivalents) in I Cor 1:8; 5:5; II Cor 1:14; Phil 1:6, 10; 2:16. It looks more to a moment of time than to a period of time, the moment being when believers meet the Lord. It is that climactic time when the Church's pilgrimage is finished and she is joined to her Lord. It is related to believers only, and is associated with blessing, not judgment as is the day of the Lord (*q.v.*).

DAY OF GOD, THE. Found only in II Pet 3:12: "Looking for and hasting unto the coming of the day of God, wherein the heavens being on fire shall be dissolved, and the elements shall melt with fervent heat." It is identified by some with "the day of the Lord" (*q.v.*) spoken of in Isa 2:12-21; 13:9 f. (cf. Jer 46:10; Ezk 30:3; Joel 1:15; 2:1, 11; 3:14; Amos 5:18; Ob 15; Zeph 1:7, 14; Zech 14:1). It starts with the events which immediately precede the second coming of Jesus Christ and continues through the Millennium on till the creation of the new heavens and the new earth. That its duration is at least a thousand years is implied by the statement in II Pet 3:8 that "one day is with the Lord as a thousand years, and a thousand years as one day." The term is considered by others, especially those who are amillennial in viewpoint, as referring only to the renovation of the heavens and the earth by fire preparatory to the creation of the new heavens and the new earth. *See* Eschatology; Day of the Lord.

R. A. K.

DAY OF JUDGMENT. *See* Judgment.

DAY OF THE LORD, THE. This expression (and various equivalents, such as "that day") is the subject of both OT and NT revelation. An early occurrence (Amos 5:18-20) shows that the phrase was already a popularly used one. It is a time of judgment on Israel (Amos 5:18-20), of punishment on the nations (Isa 13:6, 9; Ob 15), and of the actual coming of the Lord and salvation for those who repent (Joel 2:28-32). Its coming will be as a thief in the night and will be preceded by signs (I Thess 5:1-2; II Thess 2:2). Thus the day of the Lord includes the period of the Tribulation and the millennial kingdom (II Pet 3:10). *See* Day of God.

DAY'S JOURNEY. *See* Weights, Measures, and Coins.

DAYSMAN. A judge, mediator, or arbitrator. Where the KJV translates the word "daysman," the RSV uses "umpire." "Daysman" is derived from "man's day" (I Cor 4:3, ASV marg.) in the sense of a day set for a man's trial. Job 9:33 says: "Neither is there any daysman betwixt us, that might lay his hand upon us both." The arbiter in the E lays his hand on both parties to show his authority and his desire to render an unbiased verdict. A good illustration of the daysman or mediator is found in Jesus Christ (cf. I Tim 2:5).

DAYSPRING. A poetic way of speaking of the dawn or of the sunrise (Job 38:12; Lk 1:78). In the latter passage the term refers to Messiah, with possible reference to Mal 4:2, "the Sun of righteousness shall arise."

DAY STAR (Gr. *phōsphoros,* "light giving"). Signifies the planet Venus (Lat. Lucifer), that star that precedes or accompanies the rising of the sun, the morning star. In II Pet 1:19 (cf. Lk 1:78; Rev 2:28; 22:16) the term is applied to Christ. Isaiah compares the king of Babylon to Lucifer (*q.v.*), son of the morning (Isa 14:12, RSV). The brightest of the planets is pictured as scheming to rise higher than the stars. In the desert the morning star is so brilliant that it appears as though the sun were about to rise. Even so Lucifer pretends to be the Sun rising with healing in his rays (cf. Mal 4:2). *See* Gods, False; Lucifer.

DEACON. The verb form (*diakonein*) means "to serve"; particularly, "to wait at table" (cf. Arndt, p. 183). It connotes a very personal service, closely related to a service of love. To the Greek, service was scarcely dignified; rather, one's goal should be self-development instead of self-abasement. While the LXX does not use the word *diakonein* ("to serve"), Judaism held a different view of service. It is exemplified in the second commandment: "Thou shalt love thy neighbour as thyself" (Lev 19:18; cf. Mk 12:31). Our Lord so taught when He washed His disciples' feet and then said, "For I have given you an example, that ye should do as I have done to you" (Jn 13:15).

The general uses of "deacon" in the NT have been classified by H. W. Beyer ("*Diakoneō,* etc.," TDNT, II, 81-93) and are given in the following adapted form: (1) "the waiter at a meal" (Jn 2:5, 9); (2) "the servant of a master" (Mt 22:13; Jn 12:26); (3) "the servant of a spiritual power," either good (Col 1:23; II Cor 3:6; Rom 15:8) or evil (II Cor 11:14 f.; Gal 2:17); (4) "the servant of God" (II Cor 6:3 ff.) or Christ (II Cor 11:23), as in Paul's case, or as applied to his fellow workers (I Thess 3:1-3; I Tim 4:6; Col 1:7; 4:7); (5) "the [heathen as] servants of God" (Rom 13:1-4); (6) "a servant of the church" (Col 1:24-25; I Cor 3:5).

In Gr. writings, the noun related closely to the verb in sense. It described a waiter at table, a servant, a messenger, a steward, and was even used with reference to specific occupations, as baker or cook. The term appears infrequently in the LXX, and then only in the secular sense. It describes the servants of the king in Est 1:10; 2:2; 6:3, 5. In Prov 10:4 (LXX only) the fool is to be "servant" of the wise. Josephus, historian of the Jewish nation, characterized Elisha as the "disciple and servant" of Elijah.

When did the diaconate first appear in the early church? Was it in Acts 6:1-6? In the passage dealing with the choosing and appointment of the seven, the word "deacon" does not appear. And while the terms *diakonia* ("ministry" or "service") and *diakonein* ("to wait at table") do appear (Acts 6:1, 2, 4), they are used, it would seem, in a nontechnical sense, i.e., they refer to workers and not to office bearers. This is indicated by the expressions "the ministry of waiting tables" and "the ministry of the word" where the same term applies to both types of service.

Lightfoot (*Philippians*, pp. 188f.) regards the seven as the first deacons, for (1) their duties were similar to what since that time has characterized the "diaconate," viz., the care of widows and orphans and deeds of charity; (2) it was a newly created office, neither patterned after the Levitical ministry nor the synagogue minister (the Chazan); and (3) the teaching ministry, e.g., of Stephen and Philip, was incidental to the office, being brought about by the necessity of the circumstances.

Rackham (*Acts*, pp. 82-86) concludes that the "office" in Acts 6 was "unique; i.e., unique in the same sense as was the apostolate." The seven correspond to the 12 disciples, and the full list of their names shows this relation. In these two groups, then, are the ancestors of presbyters and deacons.

In Rom 16:1, Paul made reference to Phoebe as a *diakonon* ("deaconess," *q.v.*) of the church in Cenchrea. Was she an officeholder or does the word simply describe her service in the Christian community? It is impossible to say, even as is the case in the reference to the "women" in I Tim 3:11 (RSV). Were these women the wives of deacons or were they "deaconesses"?

With reference to one who holds a specific office in the church, the word *diakonos* ("deacon") occurs in only two passages in the NT: Phil 1:1 and I Tim 3:8, 12. Phil 1:1 contains Paul's greetings to the "bishops and deacons." While no activities are specified here, they are two existent and related offices, regarded as distinct from the body of saints in general.

In I Tim 3:1-13, the same relation may be observed: "the bishop" (vv. 1-7) and "the deacons" (vv. 8-13). The "deacons" must be men of disciplined character and moral repute (vv. 8-9); they must qualify for the office by being "proved worthy" (v. 10); and they must be in control of their own households (v. 12). The fact that in their ministries of charity and aid they were in close contact with people and material possessions, called for special qualities of character. They were not to be "double-tongued," nor were they to be "greedy of filthy lucre" (v.8).

Paul does not specify how the deacons were to be chosen, yet they were to be first "proved," and Timothy was certainly expected to be able to approve them. The historical development of the office of deacon is linked with that of bishop. *See* Bishop for the question of selection.

Elsewhere in the NT Paul uses the term minister to denote his fellow workers in the gospel ministry – of Timothy (I Thess 3:2), Tychicus (Col 4:7), and Epaphras (Col 1:7). Paul's own ministry (I Cor 3:5; II Cor 3:6; 6:4; 11:15) and the ministry of Christ (Rom 15:8) are also so designated. These latter references indicate that the term is in no way applied to inferior service.

W. M. D. and A. F. J.

DEACONESS. The English translation of the Gr. *diakonos*, which is used of a helper or of a deacon as an official of the church. In Rom 16:1 Phoebe is mentioned as a *diakonos* in the church at Cenchrea. This would not necessarily imply that this was an official office. It could have been only an occasional or temporary act of service, or an office in the church. No clear recognition of the office of deaconess is found in the Pastoral Epistles. In the KJV and ASV Rom 16:1 is rendered "servant." In the ASV marg. it is translated "deaconess."

It is probable that there were in the different churches groups of women engaged in visiting those of their own sex in the same way as the deacons performed their duties. The rules given in I Tim 3:11 and Tit 2:3-5 as to the conduct of women have been referred to the office of the deaconess. I Tim 5:9-10 have also been suggested as requirements for the office. It is not certain that these passages refer to that office, although there existed such an order later in church history. Pliny the Younger, writing as governor of Bithynia to the emperor Trajan in A.D. 112, indicated that by that time there were deaconesses among the Christians whom he assigned to torture in that province.

D. L. W.

DEAD, THE. The word "dead" as an adjective is many times applied to individuals in the Bible from Sarah to Sapphira. The usual words referring to the dead are *môt* in the OT and *nekros* in the NT. The OT also uses the word *nepesh* (usually translated "soul") for a dead body, but this happens because the word often refers just to an individual and therefore to the body of the individual. Also the word *r^epā'îm* is used, usually translated "shades" in the RSV. The etymological meaning "sunken," "powerless ones" is questionable. In the NT, forms of the verb *thnēskō*, "die" and similar words, are also used to designate the dead. None of these usages greatly elucidate the condition of those who have departed this life.

The OT Teaching

On this subject the OT is not very explicit. This is an interesting reticence in view of the wild speculations of the surrounding peoples. The OT verses bearing on the question come largely from Job, Psalms, Ecclesiastes, Isaiah, and Ezekiel, and are made more difficult by their poetic backgrounds. The subject is complicated also by the use of such words as Sheol (*q.v.*), which is of uncertain etymology and whose precise meaning is debatable. Critical studies on the subject, moreover, are often vitiated by a preconception which reverses the datings of some OT books and passages, and finds OT ideas of immortality and resurrection only in post-Exilic times under foreign influence.

But the Psalms are now accepted as largely pre-Exilic and Ps 16:8-11; 17:15; 49:14-15; 73:23-26 seem to speak clearly of resurrection and immortality. In Ps 16:8-11 David is said by Peter to be knowingly predicting Christ's resurrection (Acts 2:30-31). (See the writer's treatment of these verses in *The Biblical Expositor,* Vol.2, 59 f.) Ps 17:15 may also refer to future resurrection rather than to awaking after death in glory. It is significant that in the NT, resurrection is called an awaking (Jn 11:11), though this is somewhat figurative as is the reference to death as a sleep. Ps 49:14-15 and 73:19-26 may well refer to the present state of the dead. Ps 73:19, 24 and Isa 57:1-2 particularly seem to emphasize the distinction between the destiny of the righteous dead and of the wicked.

There are several specific verses in Job teaching immortality, but equally significant is the total argument of the book. Job sees the inequities of this life, yet holds fast to his trust in a righteous God. The only answer to this problem even today is in the concept of a future life of rewards and punishment. The classic passage is Job 19:25, "I know that my redeemer liveth." An extensive treatment of this passage and of the whole subject is found in a valuable but little known study on afterlife in the OT by A. Heidel, *The Gilgamesh Epic and OT Parallels* (2nd ed., Chicago: Univ. of Chicago Press, 1949, pp. 173-223). This verse in Job refers to resurrection rather than to the state of the dead today.

Isa 25:8 and 26:19 are clear and there is no necessity to place these passages later than the days of Isaiah himself. They speak of a resurrection of the dead as Israel's future hope. The former verse is quoted expressly with regard to the resurrection in I Cor 15:55. Dan 12:2 is also a landmark. It has been suggested that the verse may be read, "And the many that sleep in the dust of the earth shall awake," taking the *min* ("from") as explicative rather than as referring to a partial resurrection which does not seem to be in this context (cf. Heidel, *op. cit.,* p. 220f.). These passages do not reveal the present state of the dead, however, except that they forbid the doctrine of the extinction of the person inasmuch as there is a future hope. The instances of resurrection recorded in the OT reinforce this conclusion.

The translations of Enoch and Elijah and the bringing up of Samuel bear more on the state of the dead and emphasize also that Israel knew there was a life beyond for the people of God. Elijah was taken up body and soul to God in glory. The translation might well have suggested that the ascent of the soul of the godly was usual; the ascent of the body was obviously unique.

The raising of Samuel (I Sam 28:7-25) presents several problems, but in any case it argues that Samuel was in conscious existence after death. Some have argued that the appearance was that of an evil apparition and not the real Samuel (Heidel, *op. cit.,* p. 189 f.). Others hold that Samuel really appeared by a miracle of God—not by the conjurings of the necromancer, who apparently was quite surprised (cf. *Wycliffe Bible Commentary,* p. 292). That Samuel was brought *up* does not necessarily mean that his spirit was in the grave or in a subterranean netherworld. It may only be a figure of speech from the fact that Samuel had been let *down* into the grave (so Heidel).

This conclusion would doubtless be more widely accepted were it not that certain verses appear on the other side of the ledger. They are mainly: Ps 6:5; 30:9; 39:13; 88:11-12; 115:17; 143:3; Job 3:17; 10:21-22; Eccl 9:5,10; Isa 38:10-11. James Orr points out ("Eschatology of the OT," ISBE, II, 974) that these verses are not to be pressed too literally: "Part of it is the expression of a depressed or despairing . . . or temporarily skeptical . . . mood; all of it is relative." Thus, the skepticism of Eccl 3:19—4:3 is not the final answer of the book to the question of the chief end of man (Eccl 8:12-13; 12:13). It would seem that some at least of the descriptions in the above verses apply not to the state of the dead, but to the condition of the body in the grave. The grave is indeed a place of silence, of darkness, of the worm and corruption; a place where the body is soon forgotten and where the tongue ceases to give praise. "The death of the devout costs Yahweh dear" (Ps 116:15, Jerusalem Bible), because his service to the Lord of worship, sacrifice, and thanksgiving ceases on earth altogether. But these verses do not teach that this is the condition of the spirit after death. See R. L. Harris, "The Meaning of the Word Sheol," BETS, IV (1961), 129-135.

Other representations portray the dead kings of the earth rising from their thrones in Sheol to greet newly fallen potentates (Isa 14:9-20; Ezk 32:18-32). This also is highly figurative. Heidel argues (*op. cit.,* p. 198 f.) that the treatment in these verses is "almost exclusively of the grave and not of the spirit world." Sheol may be a poetic word for "grave" and this explains the statements about its being a place of darkness, silence, etc. But as to the abode of the spirit, the godly Israelite, trusting in the living God as he did, died in peace expecting to awake in God's likeness (Ps 17:15).

The NT Doctrine

The NT has more light on the state of the dead, but it only extends the OT teaching. It also clearly teaches a future resurrection. There are many such passages and the resurrection of Christ Himself is basic to the whole picture.

But there is also more light on the condition

of the dead today. Christians "sleep in Jesus" (I Thess 4:14). This seems clearly to be a euphemism arising from the appearance of the dead body, for the redeemed in glory are active (Rev 6:9 ff.) and are concerned with events on earth. The transfiguration scene shows Moses and Elijah speaking with Jesus of the coming crucifixion (Lk 9:30-31). The lost are also conscious, terribly so, and they too are concerned with the present world (Lk 16:19-31). Some have held that the record of Dives and Lazarus is a parable. It may be, though it differs essentially from other parables. But in any case, Jesus' parables were always true to life illustrations, and the conclusion is clear that the dead are either in bliss or in torment now.

This was the comfort that Christ gave to the dying thief (Lk 23:43; "paradise" is equated to heaven in II Cor 12:2, 4), and Paul declares that to depart and be with Christ is "far better" (Phil 1:23). To be absent from the body is, for the Christian, to be present with the Lord (II Cor 5:8). Stephen at death was given a glorious glimpse into this heavenly home (Acts 7:56) and so was the aged apostle on Patmos (Rev 4:1).

There is a view that before the cross there were two compartments in Sheol and that Christ entered Sheol and delivered the redeemed from there, taking them to heaven at His crucifixion. Aside from the strangeness of this view, it has poor exegetical foundation. Eph 4:9 is appealed to, but that verse may merely identify the ascended Christ with the Jesus who descended to the earth in His incarnation. Another passage often quoted is I Pet 3:19-20. This may only mean that Christ in the days before the Flood preached by the Holy Spirit to Noah's contemporaries who are now "in prison." Actually Christ told us, as has been noted, where He went at His death—to His Father and to paradise. The NT assures us that at our death we shall be there too with Christ until He comes again. See especially such expressions as are found in II Cor 5:8 and Phil 1:21-23. *See* Burial; Death; Embalm; Grave; Eschatology; Funeral; Hades; Heaven; Hell.

Bibliography. For treatment of the corpse and burial customs see Roland de Vaux, *Ancient Israel,* trans. by John McHugh, New York: McGraw-Hill, 1961, pp. 56-61. Aubrey R. Johnson, *The Vitality of the Individual in the Thought of Ancient Israel,* Cardiff: Univ. of Wales Press, 1949, pp. 11-14, 71-74, 89-94.

R. L. H.

DEAD, BAPTISM FOR THE. *See* Baptism for the Dead.

DEAD SEA. Called in the OT the Salt Sea (Gen 14:3; Num 34:12; etc.), the Sea of the Plain or Arabah (Deut 3:17; 4:49; etc.), the East Sea (Ezk 47:18; Joel 2:20; etc.). It lies in the great rift of the Jordan Valley resulting from a great convulsion which shook the surface of the earth in prehistoric ages. At that time the mountain ranges of Lebanon and Anti-Lebanon rose above the great plain which embraced the entire area of Lebanon, Syria, Palestine, and Transjordan, and a deep cavity was formed between them, stretching from the foothills of the Amanus Mountains, through Coele-Syria, the Jordan Valley, the Dead Sea, and the Red Sea, and extending as far S as the Nyasa Lake in central Africa.

The Dead Sea

The surface of the Dead Sea averages about 1,290 feet below sea level. Its deepest point, near the NE corner, is some 1,300 feet lower. The sea today is about 50 miles long and up to 10 miles wide. It is fed principally by the river Jordan, but a number of springs and streams on both sides add their quota to its waters. It has no outlet, but the rate of evaporation is so great that the inflow of waters is able only to keep the surface level approximately constant. Thus the salt and potash deposits (25 percent of the water) have become more concentrated than in any other sea or lake in the world. The specific gravity of the water is greater than that of human beings and it is impossible for any person to sink in the Dead Sea.

The shallow area S of the peninsula El-Lisan, where Sodom and Gomorrah almost certainly lay, has at times been dry land, as submerged tree stumps testify. Ruins of an Edomite fort on the SW shore have been inundated at least twice since 1000 B.C. Between the days of Abraham (Gen 14:3) and the time of Moses the Dead Sea must have risen to cover the area of Sodom and the other cities of the plain.

There is a bed of asphalt at the bottom of the sea, from which fairly large pieces break loose from time to time and float on the surface (cf. Gen 14:10). The Greeks and Romans called it the Sea of Asphalt because of this feature. However, by the 2nd cen. after Christ it had acquired its more usual name from the fact that no fish or other marine animal can live in its waters. *See* Palestine, II.B.3.*e*.

The area around the Dead Sea has been inhabited by man since the Neolithic period, and the rugged country on both sides has afforded a refuge and a protection on numerous occasions to persecuted persons and groups. David, fleeing before Saul, took shelter at one time at the spring known as the waters of Engedi (I Sam 23:29–24:1). During the first Jewish revolt the Jews made their headquarters at the strategic position of Masada above the Dead Sea, whither they were followed by the Roman general Silva. Similarly, Herod the Great had refortified a Maccabean stronghold at Machaerus above its eastern shore. At his death it passed to Herod Antipas, and it was there that he slew John the Baptist. Below Machaerus, there is a hot water spring which was called Callirrhoë in ancient times because of its medicinal properties.

A short distance N of the Dead Sea, at a site called Ghassul, lie the ruins of a village which goes back to the Chalcolithic Age. The site has been excavated in recent years and has produced evidence to show that it was occupied between 4000 and 3200 B.C. at a time when Jericho appears to have been abandoned.

In recent years, the remains of a communal settlement which belonged to the Essenes have been discovered at Qumran, above the western shore of the Dead Sea. In the nearby caves, scrolls have been discovered, ranging in date from the 2nd cen. B.C. to the 1st cen. after Christ. *See* Dead Sea Scrolls.

D. C. B.

DEAD SEA SCROLLS

The Initial Discovery

The recovery of the Dead Sea Scrolls has been called "the greatest manuscript discovery of modern times." What enhances the value of the discovery is the paucity of written records from biblical times from Palestine.

In retrospect scholars were able to point to records of similar discoveries in the Dead Sea area. Origen used some texts found in A.D. 217 in jars near Jericho. A Nestorian patriarch, Timothy I (726–819), inquired about MSS found in a cave near Jericho, including "more than two hundred psalms of David." Al-Qirqisani of the 10th cen. A.D. referred to a sect called "Magharians" because their books were found in a cave. But in modern times no comparable MS discoveries had been made.

At the end of 1946 (or at the beginning of 1947) three members of the Ta'amireh Bedouin accidentally came upon a cave near Wadi Qumran NW of the Dead Sea. They discovered three sheepskin scrolls in a covered jar and removed them. In May or June, 1947, the Bedouin returned and removed four more scrolls from the cave. At the end of the year E. Sukenik of the Hebrew University purchased three of the scrolls (the incomplete Isaiah Scroll, the War Scroll, and the Thanksgiving Hymns).

It was not until April 11, 1948, that news of the discovery was released to the public. A month later Jewish-Arab hostilities erupted into a full-scale war, making further investigation by Israelis in the Qumran area impossible.

Early in 1949 Metropolitan Samuel of the Syrian Orthodox Church, who had secured the other scrolls (the complete Isaiah Scroll, the Manual of Discipline, the Habakkuk Commentary, and the Genesis Apocryphon), brought them to the U.S. In 1954 these were bought for Israel by Y. Yadin, the son of Sukenik, for $250,000, after they had been advertised in the *Wall Street Journal.*

Dating of the Manuscripts

Some scholars were skeptical of the antiquity of the documents. S. Zeitlin still vigorously argues that they are medieval MSS. The evidences for the date of the finds are as follows:

1. *Paleography.* J. Trever, who was at the American School of Oriental Research in Jerusalem in 1948, examined the scrolls in February and surmised their antiquity from a comparison of the script with that of the Nash Papyrus, a small fragment of the OT from Egypt and dated to the 2nd cen. B.C. His initial impression was confirmed by an authority on the subject, W. F. Albright.

2. *Radio-carbon analysis.* An analysis of cloth associated with the MSS yielded a date of A.D. 33 plus or minus 200 years (later revised to 20 B.C.).

3. *Excavations at Khirbet Qumran.* Excavations at Khirbet Qumran, the ruins of the monastery of Qumran, a mile S of the initial find, proved that the main levels of the settlement were in Hellenistic and Roman times.

4. *Coins.* Several hundred coins found in the excavations date the limits of the main period of occupation from 135 B.C. to A.D. 68.

Later Discoveries at Qumran

When the Ta'amireh Bedouin realized the monetary value of the MSS, they began to search the Judean desert for other finds. In 1952 they discovered Cave II close to Cave I. In the same year archaeologists led by R. de Vaux explored from 200 to 300 caves. In all, 11 caves have yielded MSS in the Qumran area.

In 1952, a mile N of the initial discovery, Cave III yielded the Copper Scroll. The most important discovery of all was that of a library in Cave IV in a terrace near Khirbet Qumran. This cave alone yielded some 40,000 fragments of 400 different MSS, one-fourth of which were biblical. Also in 1952 Caves V and VI were discovered near Cave IV.

In 1955 Caves VII–X were found in the area of Khirbet Qumran. These yielded relatively few MSS. In 1956 Cave XI was discovered to the N near Cave III. Next in importance to Caves I and IV, Cave XI gave up seven extensive MSS.

Some of the caves at Qumran. HFV

Other Discoveries Near the Dead Sea

1. *Murabba'at*. In 1951 the Bedouin discovered texts in caves in Wadi Murabba'at 11 miles S of Qumran. In 1952 archaeologists under L. Harding and R. de Vaux excavated four caves here. These caves yielded biblical documents, and also important letters and contracts from the period of Bar Kochba's revolt against the Romans in A.D. 132-135. One MS is the oldest Heb. papyrus ever found, dated to the 7th cen. B.C.

From the earliest level of occupation (4th mil. B.C.) came objects of wood, leather, basketry, and parts of a fish net—the first objects of such perishable material found in Palestine. The spectacular finds from Murabba'at have not received the notice they deserve, because they have been overshadowed by the even more spectacular Qumran materials.

In 1955 the Bedouin brought forward a MS which they said came from Murabba'at. It was a magnificent Heb. scroll, dated to the 2nd cen. A.D., of the Minor Prophets, extending from the middle of Joel to the beginning of Zechariah. It belongs to the proto-Masoretic Text type.

2. *Khirbet Mird*. Bedouin in 1952 discovered some Byzantine and early Arabic MSS at Khirbet Mird, six miles WSW of Qumran. This was the place where a famous monastery was established in A.D. 492 by Mar Saba. Explorations were conducted by R. de Langhe in 1953. MSS in Arabic, Gr. and Palestinian Aram. from the 5th to the 8th cen. A.D. were found. A Gr. fragment of *Andromache*, a play of Euripides, dates from the 6th cen. A.D. and is a thousand years older than the oldest MS of the play on parchment.

3. *Nahal Hever*. Here, three and a half miles S of En-gedi, the Israelis in 1960 made the first MS discoveries on their territory. They found 15 letters either to or from Bar Kochba: nine in Aram., four in Heb. and two in Gr. In 1961 in the same cave the Israelis found 65 more papyri and parchment documents, including important legal contracts. One of the letters from Bar Kochba was written on wooden tablets—the first such discovery in Israel. Bits of a MS were found by the Israeli team that proved to belong to a fragmentary copy of a Gr. version of the Minor Prophets purchased from the Bedouin in 1952. Its text is in agreement with that used by Justin Martyr *c*. A.D. 150. From Nahal Tse'elim, a few miles to the S of Hever, the first preserved arrow shafts of wood were found.

4. *Wadi Daliyeh*. In 1962 word reached Jerusalem that the Ta'amireh Bedouin had found still another cave, this time nine miles N of Jericho and seven miles W of the Jordan (therefore not strictly a "Dead Sea" site). The cave, called Mugharet Abu Shinjeb, was explored in 1963 under the direction of P. Lapp. Some 40 Aramaic papyrus documents were secured, pre-

cisely dated from 375 to 335 B.C. Hitherto very few texts from this century had been recovered. The MSS were entombed in the cave with perhaps 200 Samaritans attempting to flee from Alexander the Great in 331 B.C.

5. *Masada.* In 1963-65 Israelis under Y. Yadin excavated Masada, near the W shore of the Dead Sea opposite the Lisan peninsula. The last Jewish stronghold against the Romans in the first Jewish war, it fell in A.D. 73. In addition to a few biblical fragments and 26 fragments (some quite sizable) of the Heb. text of Ben Sirah, a scroll identical with the text of the Songs of the Sabbath Sacrifice from Qumran was found. This is the first time that a "Qumran" MS has been found outside a cave and in a stratified context.

OT Manuscripts from Qumran

Prior to the discovery of the Qumran MSS the oldest extant Heb. OT MSS came from the 9th and 10th cen. A.D., with the exception of a fragment known as the Nash Papyrus (2nd cen. B.C.), quotations in the Aramaic Magic Bowls (6th cen. A.D.), and fragments of over 120 6th-9th cen. A.D. biblical MSS from the geniza (storeroom) of a Cairo synagogue. The Jews made a practice of destroying worn-out MSS to save them from impious hands.

1. *Number and description.* The greatest importance of the Dead Sea Scrolls lies in the recovery of biblical MSS a full millennium earlier than the medieval copies. Of the some 500 MSS recovered from Qumran, 175, or one-third, are biblical. As of 1965 the following numbers of copies of OT books had been found in the 11 caves of Qumran: Genesis 15, Exodus 15, Leviticus 8, Numbers 6, Deuteronomy 25, Joshua 2, Judges 3, Ruth 4, Samuel 4, Kings 4, Chronicles 1, Ezra-Nehemiah 1, Job 4, Psalms 27, Proverbs 2, Ecclesiastes 2, Song of Solomon 4, Isaiah 18, Jeremiah 4, Lamentations 4, Ezekiel 6, Daniel 8, and the Minor Prophets 8. Of the Heb. canon only Esther is not represented. The most popular books were Genesis, Exodus, Deuteronomy, Isaiah, and Psalms.

The oldest text is an archaic Exodus fragment from Cave IV dated to 250 B.C. The text had to be read with the aid of infrared and ultraviolet photography.

Most of the texts were written in the so-called Aramaic script. But ten MSS including the books of the Pentateuch and Job were written in an archaizing script known as Paleo-Hebrew. The divine name was sometimes written in this script in other MSS.

2. *Textual traditions*

Masoretic Recension. The traditional Heb. text of the OT preserved in the medieval MSS is called the Masoretic Text (MT) after the editorial work of Jewish scribes known as Masoretes. They labored from the 5th to the

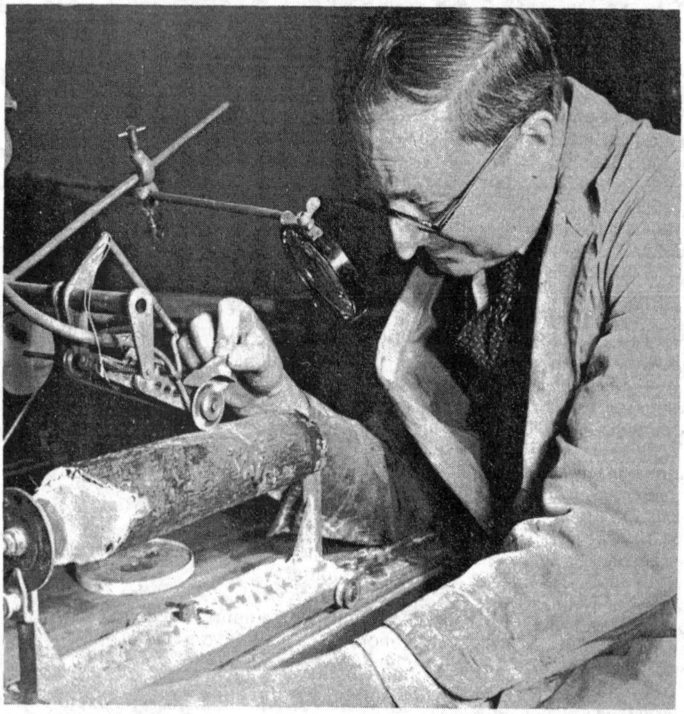

Professor H. Wright Baker of Manchester's College of Technology cutting the copper scroll from Cave Three. John M. Allegro

9th cen. A.D., introducing vowels into the consonantal text and adding notes in the margins.

Scholars were not sure how accurate the work of the Masoretes and their predecessors was. Some scholars dated the origin of the MT to the editorial activities of rabbis in the 2nd cen. A.D. Thanks to Qumran we now know that the MT goes back to an edition antedating the Christian era by several centuries, and that this recension was copied with amazing accuracy.

Most of the biblical MSS from Qumran belong to the proto-Masoretic tradition. This is especially true of the Pentateuch and the Latter Prophets. What effect the evidence of the complete Isaiah Scroll from Cave I (cited in the RSV as "one ancient MS") has made may be seen by comparing the RSV (1952) with the KJV in the following passages: Isa 3:24; 14:4, 30; 15:9; 21:8; 23:2; 33:8; 45:2, 8; 49:24; 51:19; 56:12; 60:19. Most of these 13 readings are not new, in that they have the support of some of the ancient versions. One may conclude therefore that in spite of the fact that the great Isaiah Scroll diverged considerably from the MT in spelling and grammar, it has not warranted any major changes in the substance of the text.

Septuagint Recension. The LXX, the Gr. translation of the OT begun *c.* 250 B.C., is next to the MT in importance for the reconstruction of the OT text. The majority of the 250 OT citations in the NT are from this version.

Where the LXX diverged from the MT, some scholars had assumed that the translators had taken liberties with their texts. Now it appears that many of these differences resulted from the fact that they were following a somewhat different Heb. text.

From Qumran have come Heb. texts that correspond to the LXX in the books of Exodus, Numbers, Deuteronomy, Job, Jeremiah and Samuel. The Jeremiah and Samuel MSS may help in obtaining a Heb. text superior to that of the MT.

Also found in Qumran were Gr. MSS of the LXX itself, of Exodus, Numbers and Leviticus. A text of Leviticus from Cave IV dated to 100 B.C. is now the oldest known LXX fragment. A Gr. MS of the Minor Prophets was recovered from the area of Wadi Khabra.

Other recensions. A Paleo-Heb. MS of Exodus from Cave IV is close to the Samaritan version. All known copies of the Samaritan version of the Pentateuch (SP) are written in a script derived from the Paleo-Heb. script used in some of the Qumran documents. The SP must now be dated to the 2nd cen. B.C. and not earlier as some had held. Since it exhibits expansive tendencies it is of little value in helping to obtain a better Heb. text.

There are also examples of Targums or Aramaic paraphrases of Leviticus and Job found at Qumran.

3. *Composition and canon.* The early dates of the biblical MSS from Qumran militate against extreme views of critics who place the

Qumran structures (airview). Palestine Archaeological Museum

composition of certain OT books in Maccabean times (2nd cen. B.C.).

Some critics dated the composition of Ecclesiastes to the 2nd or 1st cen. B.C. Yet Cave IV yielded a MS of Ecclesiastes dated to 175 - 150 B.C., which is certainly not the original text.

A 2nd cen. B.C. MS of the Psalms indicates that the collection of canonical Psalms was fixed before the Maccabean age. The 2nd to 1st cen. Hymns from Qumran are quite different from the canonical Psalms.

One MS of Daniel is dated to 120 B.C., bringing into question the alleged Maccabean date of its composition. A fragmentary Prayer of Nabonidus (*see* Nabonidus) shows that the Jews knew about the father of Belshazzar, though he is not mentioned by name in Daniel.

The biblical MSS from Qumran show affinities with a number of recensions. Those, however, from Murabba'at, including portions of the Pentateuch, Psalms, Isaiah and Minor Prophets, belong uniformly to the MT tradition. This lends credence to the Jewish tradition that the OT text was standardized at Jamnia in A.D. 95. Since all the texts from Masada (A.D. 73), including portions of Genesis, Leviticus, Deuteronomy, Psalms and Ezekiel, also belong to the MT tradition, standardization may have begun even earlier, at least in orthodox circles.

There is evidence that the sect at Qumran was more open than orthodox Jews in its concept of canonical books. They made use of a number of Apocryphal and Pseudepigraphical works, and probably considered the revelations embodied in their own sectarian writings as inspired. (Only commentaries that deal with canonical books have been found, it may be said.)

A Psalms Scroll from Cave XI, published in 1965, includes not only 36 canonical psalms but also eight other compositions. One of these is a prose piece ascribing to David the composition of 4,050 psalms. Another is a poem found in

Ben Sirah. One of the psalms is one known previously as Ps 151 of the LXX, Old Latin, and Syriac versions. Two others had been known from medieval Syriac texts.

Apocrypha and Pseudepigrapha

1. *Apocrypha*. The Apocryphal and Pseudepigraphical works, rejected by the Jews from the canon, were known to us previously only in translations. Qumran has now furnished the Heb. and Aram. originals of some of these works. Cave IV has yielded four Aram. and one Heb. MSS of Tobit. The composition of Tobit dated by scholars to the 2nd–1st cen. B.C. may now be pushed back to the 5th–4th cen.

A Heb. MS of Ben Sirah or Ecclesiasticus came from Cave II; a passage of chap. 51 was included in the Psalms Scroll from Cave XI. Fragments of the Heb. text of Sirah have also come from Masada. These are textually the same as the Heb. texts of Sirah recovered in the 1890's from the Cairo geniza, proving that the latter, though medieval MSS, were accurate copies of the text and not translations from Syriac as some had suggested.

A Gr. MS of the Letter of Jeremiah (Baruch 6 in the Vulg.) was found in Cave VII.

2. *Pseudepigrapha*. Fragments of ten MSS in Aram. of Enoch were found in Cave IV. Eleven MSS in Heb. of Jubilees were found in Caves I, II, and IV; fragments were also found at Masada. Three Aram. MSS of the Testament of Levi and one Heb. MS of the Testament of Judah were found. These MSS indicate that the date of composition for Jubilees and the Testaments must be pushed earlier than the end of the 2nd cen. B.C.

3. *The Genesis Apocryphon*. This scroll, called at first the Lamech Scroll, was one of the original seven documents from Cave I. It was not published until 1956, and then only in part. The MS is in Aram. and was copied at the beginning of the Christian era; its date of composition probably goes back to the early 1st cen. B.C. In style it resembles Jubilees or a Targum, commenting in a legendary vein on passages of Genesis. One passage, e.g., describes the beauty of Sarah in great detail.

Sectarian Documents

1. *The Damascus Document*. This composition, sometimes called the Zadokite Document, had been known from medieval MSS discovered in 1897 in the geniza (storehouse for old MSS) of a synagogue in Cairo. At least nine MSS of it have now been found at Qumran.

The Damascus Document gives important information about the history of the sect centered at Qumran. The reference to an exile to Damascus led some scholars to suggest an actual exodus to Syria after the earthquake of 31 B.C. struck Qumran. But since the oldest MS of the Damascus Document is dated back to 75–50 B.C., Damascus may be the prophetic name of Qumran itself.

2. *Manual of Discipline.* The manual was one of th seven scrolls from Cave I. Eleven more fragmentary MSS have been found in Caves IV and X. This gives detailed instructions concerning the entrance requirements of the sect.

3. *The Thanksgiving Hymns*. Another of the seven MSS from Cave I contained hymns. It is called *Hodayot* in Heb. and is also represented by five fragments from Cave IV. In all they include some 30 hymns, probably composed by a single individual, perhaps the Teacher of Righteousness.

4. *Commentaries*. Commentaries, called *Pesharim* in Heb., have been found on Ps 37, Isaiah, Hosea, Micah, Nahum, Habakkuk, Zephaniah. The Habakkuk Commentary, one of the original MSS from Cave I, gives important details about the persecution of the Teacher of Righteousness by the Wicked Priest. The Nahum Commentary makes clear reference to historic persons: to Antiochus (probably the IV, 175 - 163 B.C.) and to Demetrius (probably the III, who ruled 95–88 B.C.). The mention of the "Lion of Wrath" who crucified men is probably a reference to Alexander Jannaeus (103–76 B.C.).

5. *The War Scroll*. Another of the original scrolls from Cave I, the War Scroll describes in detail the tactics, equipment, and prayers that the Sons of Light will use in defeating the Sons of Darkness. The eschatological war, which will also be waged by angels, will last 40 years: six years with Edom, Moab, Ammon, etc.; 29 years with the kings of the N and the Kittim; and five years off for the sabbatical years. Some scholars have identified the Kittim with the Seleucids and others with the Romans.

6. *Miscellaneous documents*

a. Descriptions of the New Jerusalem have been found.

b. Mishmarot, MSS describing the courses of the priests adjusted to the solar calendar of the sect, have been found.

c. Testimonia, collections of OT texts related to the Messiah, may be similar to those used by NT writers, including as they did composite quotations.

d. A liturgical calendar makes reference to Queen Alexandra, Hyrcanus (I or II), and Aemilius.

e. An angelic liturgy contains "Songs of the Sabbath Sacrifice." A MS of this work was also found at Masada, indicating that sectarians of the Qumran type fought with the Zealots there in the last stand against the Romans in A.D. 73. (Some, e.g., C. Roth and G. R. Driver, have argued indeed that the sectarians were Zealots!)

f. A messianic horoscope and a cryptic document indicate that the sectarians were not opposed to the astrology of their day.

g. A *Florilegium* or anthology of midrashic comments on II Sam 7 and Ps 1–2.

h. An allegory called "The Wiles of the Wicked Woman," describing a group hostile to the sect.

i. In 1967 after the June War, Yigael Yadin announced the acquisition of a remarkable Qumran document which he has called "the Temple Scroll." The scroll, over 28 feet long, is now the longest known from Qumran. The style of its Heb. script dates it to the Herodian period. The text, which is yet to be published, deals with four subjects: (1) religious rules concerning ritual cleanness; (2) sacrifices and offerings; (3) statutes of the king and the army; (4) a detailed description of the temple. The scroll gives detailed prescriptions as to the building of the temple, perhaps to supply the description which David was said to have given to Solomon (I Chr 28:11). As the details of the projected temple do not accord with those of Herod's temple, this is further evidence that the sect had rejected the Jerusalem sanctuary. A unique feature of the new text is that the author seems to pass off the scroll as a divine decree from God. In quotations from the Pentateuch the third person singular of the text is regularly rendered as a first person singular.

The Copper Scroll

An unusual scroll of copper, eight feet long and 11 inches high, was found in Cave III in 1952. Because it had become very brittle it was not opened until 1955. The text, published in 1960 by J. Allegro, tells about the location in some 60 places of fabulous amounts of gold and silver. Allegro, who believes that it is a map of the temple treasures drawn up by Zealots fleeing from the Romans, made a survey of the identifiable sites in 1960—unfortunately without any results. The text in Mishnaic Heb. is the earliest extensive document in that dialect. Cross dates the writing of the Copper Scroll to c. A.D. 75. He and Milik regard the text as folkloristic.

Excavations at Khirbet Qumran

Khirbet Qumran, i.e., the ruins of the monastery at Qumran, is located a mile S of Cave I. The ruins have been known for some time. In 1851 F. de Saulcy had mistakenly identified the site as Gomorrah. It was not until several years after the discovery of the MSS in the caves that excavations were conducted from 1951–56 under G. L. Harding and R. de Vaux.

1. *Levels of occupation.* The earliest occupation dates to the 8th–7th cen. B.C., perhaps a fortress built by King Uzziah (II Chr 26:10). A circular cistern dates back to this period. The major settlement, that which can be associated with the MSS from the caves, began in the time of Hyrcanus I (134–104 B.C.). The site was abandoned after the earthquake of 31 B.C. and reoccupied around the time of Herod's death in 4 B.C. The site was then taken by the Romans in A.D. 68 and occupied by a small Roman garrison until A.D. 86. It was finally occupied by the Jewish rebels under Bar Kochba in A.D. 132–135.

2. *Buildings and objects.* Although no MSS as such were found in the ruins, pottery similar to that in which MSS were stored in Cave I was found. One potsherd was found on which a budding scribe had practiced the writing of the alphabet. Several hundred coins were found which helped to establish the dates of the occupation levels.

The main settlement covered an area 80 meters square. The most striking feature of Qumran is the number of cisterns and pools, some of which were used for the ritual immersions of the sect. The cisterns were supplied with water by an open aqueduct from the mountain to the W.

Low plaster tables (or benches) 17 feet long and 20 inches high were found together with inkwells. These came from a second-story room which many have called the *scriptorium,* the room used for the copying of the MSS. The largest room, 22 meters long and four and a half wide, served as the refectory for the sect's communal meals.

Some two miles to the S farm buildings were found at the spring of Ain Feshkha.

It has been estimated that some 200–400 persons lived at Qumran at one time. Most lived in huts or tents outside the buildings. A few lived in nearby caves, where signs of occupation have been found in 30 of them.

3. *The cemetery.* Toward the Dead Sea, separated from the Khirbet by a wall, was a sizable cemetery. The main cemetery contains about 1,100 burials, with about 100 burials in secondary cemeteries. In the main cemetery 31 graves were dug, and 13 in the other sections. The main cemetery gave up but one female skeleton and three children's skeletons (from the ages of six to ten). On the other hand, the secondary cemeteries yielded five female skeletons and one of a child, a much higher proportion. Those who identify the sectarians with the normally celibate Essenes may argue that the burial of females in the secondary sections may be an indication that they were not full-fledged members of the community or that their bodies may have been brought to Qumran from the towns where married Essenes lived. More recently, however, further excavations have uncovered more female skeletons in the main cemetery itself.

The Life of the Sect

Although the Manual of Discipline seems to address itself to a celibate community, the Rule of the Congregation and the Damascus Document speak of women and children. Some explain the difference by ascribing it to different stages in the community's history. What is clear is that the sect excluded anyone who was lame, blind, deaf, dumb, or was so aged that he tottered.

Those who wished to enter the sect had to undergo a probationary testing of two years. In the third year one would be admitted to provisional membership. Upon becoming a member, one would give up his material wealth to a common treasury.

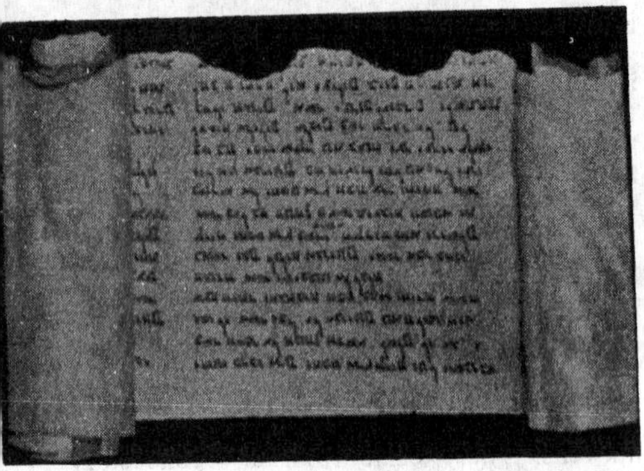

The Habakkuk Commentary. IIS

In addition to the manual work necessary to make the community self-sufficient, the members participated in the communal meals, ritual immersions, and above all in the study of Scriptures. In every group of ten, one man at least had to be studying or interpreting Scriptures at all times. The membership was divided into three shifts so that studies could be maintained throughout the night.

The sectarians were even stricter than the Pharisees in the maintenance of the sabbath. Discipline was severe. For falling asleep in the assembly one had to spend a month in isolation; likewise for foolish laughter; three months for indecent talk; six months for a deliberate lie; for slander against the community one was banished.

Beliefs of the Sect

1. *The angels and God.* Angels take a prominent role in the theology of Qumran. They fight along with the elect in the final war, and are more important than any messiah.

God is depicted as sovereign, predestinating men to either salvation or condemnation. The wicked, it seems, are not even allowed to repent.

2. *Sin and salvation.* Man is a frail creature, sunken in sin, "a spring of impurity, a furnace of iniquity." He can be saved only by the grace of God. The status of the elect is determined in part by his attitude to the Teacher of Righteousness. The sectarians explained Hab 2:4, which Paul cites as "The just shall live by faith," to mean faith in the Teacher. This does not, however, mean faith in an atoning Saviour but rather fidelity to the precepts of the Teacher. Salvation meant membership in the sect. One had a positive duty to hate outsiders.

3. *The Teacher of Righteousness.* This anonymous figure was not strictly speaking the founder of the sect, as he appeared some 20 years after the community had been groping "like the blind." He may possibly have been the author of the Thanksgiving Hymns, which give the greatest insight into the sect's views of sin and salvation. The Habakkuk Commentary, the Damascus Document, and the Commentary on Ps 37 provide but scanty information about the Teacher. He was a priest who was persecuted by the Wicked Priest, i.e., the corrupt high priest. Nowhere is it said that he was killed, let alone crucified as some have averred. Nor is there any justification in any of the scrolls for claiming the resurrection of the Teacher.

Scholars have tried to place the Teacher of Righteousness (TR) and the Wicked Priest (WP) in various historical contexts. (*a*) In the period 175–162 B.C. Rowley and Black would identify the TR with the Zadokite high priest Onias III and the WP with the Hellenizing Jason or his brother Menelaus. (*b*) In the period 162–152 B.C. Stauffer would identify the TR with the Hasidic Jose ben Joezer and the WP with Alcimus. (*c*) In the period 152–134 B.C. Milik, Cross, Sutcliffe, de Vaux, Vermes, Winter, J. Jeremias and Bruce would consider the TR some unknown person and the WP either Jonathan or his brother Simon. (*d*) In the period 134–76 B.C. Allegro and Brownlee would consider the TR some unknown person and the WP Alexander Jannaeus. The Hasmoneans from the time of Jannaeus' predecessor took over the high priesthood as well as the monarchy. (*e*) In the period 76–63 B.C. Dupont Sommer would consider Hyrcanus II as the WP. (*f*) At the time of the war with Rome in A.D. 66 Roth and Driver would identify the TR with the Zealot Menahem and the WP with Eleazar the son of Ananias the high priest. The most likely period seems to be 152–134 B.C. with Simon as WP.

4. *Messianic figures.* Many scholars see in the phrase "anointed ones of Aaron and Israel" a reference to two Messiahs, a priestly Messiah and a kingly Messiah, with the former having a role superior to the latter. This would correspond to the expectations reflected in the Testaments of the Twelve Patriarchs. Other scholars prefer to speak of one Messiah and a priestly companion. It is quite certain that the Teacher of Righteousness was not himself considered the Messiah. He may have fulfilled the role of the anticipated Prophet (Deut 18:18).

5. *Eschatology and afterlife.* The members of the sect believed that they were living in the last days before the coming of the Messiah(s) and the final battle with the wicked. The members believed in immortality for the elect. Certain passages in the Hymns may possibly reflect a belief in the resurrection of the dead. The wicked, however, were to be annihilated.

Identification of the Sect

The sect has been identified with many groups, ranging from the Hasidim, the Pharisees, the Zealots, on the one hand, to the Jewish-Christian Ebionites and medieval Karaites on the other hand. The most plausible identification is with the Essenes, a sect known from Josephus, Philo, and Pliny as an ascetic and generally celibate community living on the W shore of the Dead Sea.

Both the Qumran sectarians and the Essenes had a probationary period for initiates, ranked their members, held property in common, practiced immersion, partook of a common meal, refused the use of oil, held apart from the animal sacrifices of the temple, stressed God's predestination, and were intolerant of outsiders.

There are, to be sure, some discrepancies. The Essenes did not believe in the resurrection of the dead, whereas the sect may have held this belief. The Essenes rejected oaths, but the sect enjoined oaths on their initiates. These and other alleged differences are minor and can be explained. *See* Essenes.

Significance for NT Studies

1. *John the Baptist.* Since John was ascetic and celibate, lived in the Jordan Valley (thus near Qumran), and practiced baptism, some have suggested that he was reared at Qumran. But John's asceticism stemmed from the fact that he was a Nazarite. His baptism was a single rite and not the repeated washings of Qumran.

2. *Jesus.* Exaggerated comparisons between the Teacher of Righteousness and Jesus have been made, especially by A. Dupont-Sommer and J. Allegro. These views have been popularized by the journalist E. Wilson in a best seller. But in truth there are more contrasts than similarities.

Unlike the sect, Jesus did not withdraw from the world, did not reject the physically deformed, and did not hate outsiders. There is no evidence that the sect regarded the Teacher of Righteousness as pre-existent, as divine, as saving from sin by his death, as sinless, or as the Messiah of David who was also a priest after the order of Melchizedek.

3. *The Gospels.* Now that discovery has been made of actual documents in Heb. and Aram. from before the 2nd cen. A.D., the question of Heb. and Aram. originals of the Gospels may be reinvestigated.

The Gospel of John, considered to be very Hellenistic and dated by some scholars to the 2nd cen. A.D., is shown more clearly than ever to be a product of 1st cen. Palestine by virtue of its many parallels with the Qumran texts.

4. *Acts.* The communion of the church has been compared with the communal meals of the sect. The latter were not celebrated as sacraments, however; the elements did not represent anything. Both groups practiced a type of communism. This was voluntary in the book of Acts but required by the Qumran rules.

5. *Epistles.* Scholars sought to explain the use of the word "mystery" in Paul's epistles in terms of the Hellenistic mystery religions. This may now be explained more simply by the Semitic background of Qumran. Scholars have argued that the office of bishop in the Pastoral Epistles indicates a late date. The functions of the *m^ebaqqer* or "overseer" at Qumran were the same as those of the bishops in the Pastorals. This fact therefore invalidates the argument.

Of major importance for understanding the Epistle to the Hebrews is a document from Cave XI which deals with the enigmatic figure of Melchizedek. This new text describes Melchizedek as a heavenly deliverer similar to the archangel Michael. He is also portrayed as the "heavenly one" who will proclaim God's salvation. This may help to explain why the author of Hebrews stresses not only Christ's superiority to the Aaronic priesthood but also to the angels. Heb 7:3, which speaks of Melchizedek without parentage, is usually explained on the basis that his ancestors are not mentioned in Gen 14, but may be now interpreted in the light that Melchizedek was regarded as a suprahuman being.

The Six Day War and the Scrolls

Fortunately neither scroll materials at the Palestine Archaeological Museum in Jerusalem nor those in the museum in Amman were harmed or pilfered during the Six Day War. The Israeli government has taken the position that all archaeologists approved for activity on the W bank by the Jordanian government will have permission to continue their projects. Of course this applies to work on the scrolls. Scholars working in E and W Jerusalem before the war had no contact with each other, even by telephone. Now that is changed and research on the scrolls may be expected to benefit by interchange between the international teams.

Bibliography

GENERAL WORKS. John Allegro, *The Dead Sea Scrolls**, Baltimore: Penguin, 1965. F. F. Bruce, *Second Thoughts on the Dead Sea Scrolls*, London: Paternoster Press, 1956. Millar Burrows, *The Dead Sea Scrolls*, New York: Viking Press, 1955. Frank M. Cross, *The Ancient Library of Qumran**, Garden City, N.Y.: Doubleday, 1961. David N. Freedman and Jonas Greenfield, eds., *New Directions in Biblical Archaeology*, Garden City, N.Y.: Doubleday, 1969, William S. LaSor, *Amazing Dead Sea Scrolls and the Christian Faith**, Chicago: Moody Press, 1956. M. Mansoor, *The Dead Sea Scrolls*, Grand Rapids: Eerdmans, 1964. K. Schubert, *The Dead Sea Community*, New York: Harper, 1959.

STORY OF DISCOVERY. Athanasius Samuel, *Treasure of Qumran**, Philadelphia: Westminster, 1966. John Trever, *The Untold Story of Qumran*, Westwood, N.J.: Revell, 1965. Yigael Yadin, *The Message of the Scrolls**, New York: Grosset and Dunlap, 1962.

ARCHAEOLOGY OF QUMRAN. John Allegro,

*Paperback edition is available.

The People of the Dead Sea Scrolls in Text and Pictures, Garden City, N.Y.: Doubleday, 1958. R. de Vaux, *L'Archéologie et les Manuscrits de la Mer Morte,* London: Oxford Univ. Press, 1961.

TRANSLATIONS. A. DuPont-Sommer, *The Essene Writings from Qumran**, Cleveland: World Publ. Co., 1962. Theodor Gaster, *The Dead Sea Scriptures**, Garden City, N.Y.: Doubleday, 1964. G. Vermes, *The Dead Sea Scrolls in English**, Baltimore: Penguin, 1965.

DOCTRINES OF QUMRAN. F. F. Bruce, *Biblical Exegesis in the Qumran Texts,* Grand Rapids: Eerdmans, 1959. Helmer Ringgren, *The Faith of Qumran**, Philadelphia: Fortress Press, 1963.

QUMRAN AND THE BIBLE. M. Black, *The Scrolls and Christian Origins,* New York: Scribner's Sons, 1961. W. H. Brownlee, *The Meaning of the Qumran Scrolls for the Bible,* New York: Oxford Univ., 1964. Jean Danielou, *The Dead Sea Scrolls and Primitive Christianity**, New York: New American Library, 1962. R. Laird Harris, "The Dead Sea Scrolls and the Old Testament Text," NPOT, pp. 201-211. Lucetta Mowry, *The Dead Sea Scrolls and the Early Church**, Notre Dame, Ind.: Univ. of Notre Dame, 1966. Roland Murphy, *The Dead Sea Scrolls and the Bible**, Westminster, Md.: Newman Press, 1956. Jerome Murphy-O'Connor, ed., *Paul and Qumran,* Chicago: Priory Press, 1968. K. Stendahl, ed., *The Scrolls and the New Testament,* New York: Harper, 1957.

REFERENCE WORKS. Karl G. Kuhn, *Konkordanz zu den Qumrantexten,* Gottingen: Vandenhoeck and Ruprecht, 1960. A. M. Habermann, *Megilloth Midbar Yehuda,* Jerusalem: Machbaroth Lesifruth Publ. House, 1959. E. Lohse, *Die Texte aus Qumran,* Munich: Kösel-Verlag, 1964. [The last two works contain vocalized texts; Lohse also has a German translation facing the texts. For individual text editions with commentaries, see bibliographies below.]

BIBLIOGRAPHIES. C. Burchard, *Bibliographie zu den Handschriften vom Toten Meer,* Berlin: Töpelmann, 1957; 2nd vol., 1965. William S. LaSor, *Bibliography of the Dead Sea Scrolls,* Pasadena, Calif.: Fuller Theol. Seminary, 1958. Current bibliographies are being published in the journal *Revue de Qumran.* Cf. also James A. Sanders, "Palestine Manuscripts, 1947-1967," JBL, LXXXVI (1967), 431-440; J. Fitzmyer, "A Bibliographical Aid to the Study of the Qumran Cave IV Texts 158-186," CBQ, XXXI (1969), 59-71.

E. M. Y.

DEAF. Used in the Scriptures both in the physical sense and figuratively as expressing unwillingness to hear the divine message (Ps 58:4). It may also be used to signify incapacity to understand God's Word for want of spirituality (Ps 38:13).

*Paperback edition is available.

DEAL. *See* **Weights, Measures, and Coins.**

DEARTH. This word means scarcity or famine. The word originated from "dear"; that which is precious or dear is rare or scarce. The word is used in the KJV in Gen 41:54; II Kgs 4:38; II Chr 6:28; Neh 5:3; Jer 14:1; Acts 7:11; 11:28. In later translations "dearth" is replaced in most instances by such terms as "rare," "famine," "drought."

DEATH (Heb. *māwet;* Gr. *thanatos).* The cessation of natural or animal life; the state of having ceased to live; that separation, whether violent or otherwise, of the soul from the body whereby life as an organism is ended. So death has been variously defined as: "disunion of body and soul" – Tertullian; "departure of the mind from the body" – Cicero; "the suspension of personal union between the body and the soul, followed by the resolution of the body into its chemical elements, and the introduction of the soul into that separate state of existence which may be assigned to it by its Creator and Judge" – A. A. Hodge. Death may be thought of as that experience in which one's connection with the world of life is broken off or terminated. Theologically, it is the last event in the probationary history of the individual man.

Scientifically, death is a servant of the natural economy. Hence it is not a failure, but a sacrifice to secure a higher process of life, or at least to insure propagation of the species. Cf. Jesus' remark in Jn 12:24.

Scripturally, the idea of death is used or described: (1) In the sense of the process of dying (Gen 21:16). (2) Synonymously for poison (II Kgs 4:40). (3) To describe one in danger of perishing (Jud 5:18; cf. Paul's "in deaths oft," II Cor 11:23). (4) As a return to dust (Gen 3:19; Eccl 12:7). (5) As a removal of the breath of life (Ps 104:29). (6) As a departure or exodus from the body (Isa 38:12; II Cor 5:1; II Pet 1:13-15; cf. also II Cor 5:8-9). (7) As being unclothed of one's earthly garment (II Cor 5:3-4; II Pet 1:13-14). (8) As departure to a land of gloom and darkness (Job 10:21-22; 38:17). (9) As sleep (Ps 13:3; Jer 51:39; Jn 11:13 ff.; I Thess 4:15; Acts 7:60). (10) As loss of spiritual life (Rom 7:9-13; 8:6; Eph 2:1, 5; Col 2:13; Jude 12). (11) As an approaching ominous event that casts a deep, foreboding shadow (Heb. *ṣalmāwet,* "shadow of death," KJV; "deep darkness," RSV; Job 3:5; Ps 23:4; 44:19; 107:10, 14; Jer 2:6; Isa 9:2; Mt 4:16; Lk 1:79).

Death is personified (Job 28:22; I Cor 15:55; Rev 20:14) as a ruler, tyrant, or enemy (Job 18:13-14; Ps 55:15; I Cor 15:26; Rev 6:8); or as a hunter who lays snares for men (Ps 18:5; 116:3; Prov 13:14; 14:27).

Death appears constantly as the highest form of punishment that can be administered to transgressors (Gen 9:5-6; Ex 21:12; etc.). Capital punishment is therefore retributive and not merely reformatory. It served to purge out evil and to warn the nation (Deut 13:5-11). The final state of the unrepentant is called "the second death" (Rev 20:14; 21:8). But death in the scriptural sense never means annihilation of the person or extinction of being.

Death comes but once to each human organism (Heb 9:27), and while it is sure (Job 14:1-2), its advent is uncertain (Prov 27:1); but it is universal to mankind (Gen 3:19; Rom 5:12; I Cor 15:22). The grave is referred to as "the gates of death" (Job 38:17; Ps 9:13; 107:18), symbolizing the entrance to the abode of the dead and also the place from which death exercises its authority.

Man, in the case of his first parents, was placed only conditionally under the law of life. Eden yielded its rich fruitage to sustain his physical life. Deity walked and communicated with him to sustain his spiritual life, which was dependent upon communion with "the Father of his spirit."

Man's transgression of the will and commandment of God, involving as it did a breach of covenant, brought death as its penalty. Death is a consequence of sin (Rom 5:12; 6:23; Jas 1:15; Gen 2:17). Satan has instigated murders (Jn 8:44), and has used his power to inflict death as the means of gripping the human race in the bondage of fear (Heb 2:14). Therefore, Christ's redemptive work on behalf of mankind to deliver from both the penalty and the fear of death entailed His own death (I Cor 15:3; Rom 4:25; I Pet 3:18). By submitting to death He triumphed over it, abolished it, and brought to believers a blessed hope of life and immortality (II Tim 1:10). The sting of death has been removed (1 Cor 15:55-56), and the grave has been robbed of its victory for those who are "in Christ" (I Cor 15:22).

Hence, because of Christ's victory over death, it may even be desirable to the righteous person (Lk 2:28-30), for he will gain rest from his labors (Rev 14:13) and death introduces him into felicity (II Cor 5:8).

See Abraham's Bosom; Dead, The; Eternal State and Death; Christ, Passion of.

Bibliography. R. Bultmann, "*Thanatos,* etc.," TDNT, III, 7-25. H. F. Lovell Cocks, "Death," *Handbook of Christian Theology,* New York: Meridian Books, 1958, pp. 70-73. Olin A. Curtis, *The Christian Faith,* New York: Eaton & Mains, 1905, Chap. XX. A. B. Davidson, *Theology of the Old Testament,* New York: Scribner's, 1906, pp. 495-532. Franz Delitzsch, *A System of Biblical Psychology,* Edinburgh: T. & T. Clark, 1899, pp. 467-476. John Laidlaw, *Bible Doctrine of Man,* Edinburgh: T. & T. Clark, 1897, pp. 171-176. Alex. Macalister and Herman Bavinck, "Death," ISBE, II, 811-813. McClintock and Strong, *Cyclopedia of Biblical, Theological and Ecclesiastical Literature,* II, 712-715. G. F. Oehler, *Theology of the Old Testament,* Grand Rapids: Zondervan, reprint, pp. 166-174. Alan Richardson, "Death, etc.," *Theological Word Book of the Bible,* New York: Macmillan, 1951, pp. 60-61. H. Orton Wiley, *Christian Theology,* Kansas City, Mo.: Kingshighway Press, 1943, III, 212-215.

R. E. Pr.

DEBATE. The English word comes from the Latin *de,* "down"; *batuere,* "beat," and now means to discuss in an open, friendly manner. In early English it was true to its Latin origin and meant to quarrel or wrangle or contend for something. In the KJV it is used only in this latter sense of strife (Prov 25:9; Isa 27:8; 58:4; Rom 1:29; II Cor 12:20).

DEBIR (dē'bĭr). A name given to a king and to three cities in Canaan. The word may mean "innermost room of a shrine," then, "sacred city," and ultimately may have been substituted for an older name, just as Zion ("citadel") became synonymous with Jerusalem.

1. A king of Eglon according to the Heb. MT (Josh 10:3). He was one of the five kings in the Amorite coalition that attempted to halt Joshua's invasion.

2. A Canaanite royal city (Josh 10:38 f.; 12:13), inhabited by the Anakim (Josh 11:21). It is listed as Kirjath-sannah (*q.v.*) in the hill country of Judah (Josh 15:49), and was also formerly known as Kirjath-sepher (Josh 15:15; Jud 1:11). The city of Debir was later assigned to the Levites (Josh 21:15). Debir was initially conquered by Joshua (Josh 10:38-39), but had to be recaptured by Othniel, the son-in-law of Caleb (Josh 15:15-19; Jud 1:11-15).

It has been tentatively identified with Tell Beit Mirsim, 12 miles SW of Hebron. Excavations of that site (1926-1932) have shown that it was founded *c.* 2200 B.C., became a fortified Hyksos city, and that it later underwent several destructions, including those probably by the Israelites, by Shishak of Egypt, and by Nebuchadnezzar. During the 9th and 8th cen. B.C. Tell Beit Mirsim was a center of the textile dyeing industry, according to numerous vats found by the excavators under the leadership of M. G. Kyle and Albright (W. F. Albright, "Debir," TAOTS, pp. 207-220).

Two other sites proposed for Debir, which have upper and lower springs (Josh 15:19) and are higher in the hill country (Josh 15:48-49), are Khirbet Terrameh, five and one-half miles SW of Hebron, and Khirbet Rabūḍ, nine miles SSW of Hebron (GTT, p. 282). Investigation of the latter site since 1967 has revealed Late Bronze Age occupation.

3. A city in Gad (Josh 13:26), also called Lo-debar (*q.v.*), located in the eastern part of Gilead. It is mentioned in the story of David's flight from Absalom (II Sam 17:27), and was a bone of contention between Aram and Israel in the wars of Jeroboam II (Amos 6:13).

4. A place on the N boundary of Judah (Josh 15:7), near the valley of Achor. It perhaps is

Thoghret ed-Debr, seven and one-half miles NE of Jerusalem, on the Jerusalem-Jericho road.

S. C. and J. R.

DEBORAH (dĕb'ŏ-rȧ)

1. Rebekah's nurse, who accompanied Rebekah to Canaan (Gen 24:59). Her death at Bethel is recorded in Gen 35:8.

2. A prophetess who "judged" Israel in the 13th or 12th cen. She was one of those rare individuals who had a special charismatic gift of the Spirit of God (cf. Jud 6:34; 11:29; 14:6); as such she was recognized as a prophetess (Jud 4:4). She had her headquarters under "the palm tree of Deborah" between Ramah and Bethel (Jud 4:5), where the people or leaders of the various tribes came to have their disputes arbitrated and settled. Although she probably gained her reputation as an ordinary, non-military judge, she was best remembered by later generations as the one able to rally the scattered tribes of Israel to loyalty to Jehovah, and hence as their savior or deliverer from the oppression of Jabin, king of the Canaanites (cf. Jud 5). Her own contemporaries respected her as a "mother in Israel" (Jud 5:7).

The song of Deborah (Jud 5:2-31) celebrates the victory of Deborah and Barak over Sisera and is one of the oldest pieces of literature in the OT. Recent studies by W. F. Albright, Frank M. Cross, Jr., and others have demonstrated the archaic style and form of this poem by comparison with the ancient Canaanite tablets from Ugarit (*see* Ras Shamra). Thus this poem is very important not only for a contemporary description of the historical situation and theological perspective of the period of the judges, but for the form and style of the poetry and language of the period as well.

R. L. S.

DEBT, DEBTOR. In OT times the debtor was to be pitied. In fact, it was a mark of divine favor to be in the class of the lender (Deut 15:6; 28:12, 44). The penalty of nonpayment often was slavery (Lev 25:47; Isa 50:1; Amos 2:6; 8:6). The harshness of this custom is graphically portrayed in the case of the widow's two sons (II Kgs 4:1-7). Debtors joined the distressed and discontented who followed David (I Sam 22:2).

Debts often involved pledges and usury and these were burdensome. The verb *ḥābal,* "to take in pledge" (Deut 24:6, 17; Job 24:3, 9), denotes something binding and painful as well. Interest or usury, Heb. *neshek,* literally means "something bitten off" (note Hab 2:7, ASV marg.). The deprivations caused by interest-seeking creditors are to be seen in the hardship cases of Neh 5:1-11.

On the other hand, the oppressive severity of life for the Israelite debtor was meant to be mitigated by regulations of the Mosaic law. The seventh year was the year of release from all pecuniary obligations (Deut 15:1-2). On the taking of pledges, a creditor was not to take a widow's garment (Deut 24:17), nor a millstone (Deut 24:6). Clothes taken as security from the poor were to be returned before sundown (Ex 22:26-27). Also, it was not the creditor's prerogative to determine the nature of the pledge (Deut 24:10-12).

Usury, especially from the poor, was condemned (Ex 22:25; Lev 25:35-37; etc.). Usury is linked with unjust gain in Prov 28:8. The righteous lend (Ps 37:26), and a rich kinsman might redeem his brother (Lev 25:47-49). Under the predominantly agricultural economy of the Israelite culture in the OT period, loans were not commercial in purpose but charitable, granted to tide a poor farmer over a time of hardship. Hence the Pentateuchal laws did not regulate mercantile pursuits but directed one's attitude to his unfortunate neighbor. *See* Loan; Mortgage; Surety; Usury.

According to the NT, we are to "owe no man anything" (Rom 13:8) and to show kindness and generosity (Mt 5:42; 6:12; Lk 6:35). Debts were forgiven (Mt 18:23-35; Lk 7:41-42). On the other hand, the parable of the unjust steward gives evidence of a commercial credit system in the Graeco-Roman civilization (Lk 16:1-7), and the parables on the talents and pounds condemn the unfaithful for not making gain by usury through the facilities of a bank (Mt 25:27; Lk 19:23).

This subject has rich theological overtones. The sinner and the debtor are most certainly related. Note the use of the word for debtor, *opheiletēs,* in Lk 13:4 (cf. v.2), and the usages in Lk 11:4 and Mt 18:21, 24. Sin makes us all debtors to God, and brings on an enslavement from which there is no release except through divine redemption and forgiveness, which in turn is to be expressed through us toward others.

I. G. P.

DECALOGUE. *See* Ten Commandments.

DECAPOLIS (dĕ-kăp'ŏ-lĭs; Gr. *deka,* "ten," and *polis,* "city," meaning "the league of ten cities"). Pliny called the territory "Decapolita regio" (*Natural History,* V, 16). It began on the W side of the Jordan where the plain of Esdraelon opens out into the river valley, being a part of Galilee at one time; it stretched across the Jordan to the E, embracing the territory given to the tribe of Manasseh at the time of the division of the land (Num 32:33-42).

As indicated by the name, there were originally ten cities in the league. Most of them were built by the followers of Alexander the Great, and to some extent were rebuilt by the Romans in 65 B.C., who conferred upon these cities the privileges of their own coinage, courts, and army. Other towns were added to the league until a total of 18 were included. The original cities were Scythopolis (Beth-shan), Hippos,

The circular forum and main street of Jerash, one of the cities of the Decapolis. G. Trimboli

Gadara (extensive remains are visible and are now called Um Qeis), Pella (modern Khirbet Fahil), Philadelphia (Rabbah and modern Amman), Gerasa, Dion, Canatha (OT Kenath), Raphana, and Damascus which alone has continuously remained a city to this day. Scythopolis (modern Beisan) was the only city W of the Jordan. (It was excavated by University of Pennsylvania, 1921–33; cf. BW, pp. 143–5.)

The Gospels indicate a repeated contact with this territory by Jesus during His itinerations. Multitudes coming from Decapolis followed Him in the beginning of His ministry (Mt 4:25). The Gadarene demoniac bore witness to his healing in the region of Decapolis (Mk 5:20), where Jesus on more than one occasion traveled (Mk 7:31). *See* Beth-shan; Gadara; Gerasa.

H. L. D.

DECEIT, DECEIVER. Many Heb. and Gr. words appear in English Bibles as forms of the word "deceit." Basically it means a deliberate misrepresentation of the truth, especially in moral and spiritual matters, in order to mislead another person. The most frequently used Heb. root, *rāmâ,* and its derivatives, imply treachery and betrayal (e.g., I Sam 19:17; II Kgs 9:23). In the NT this concept is expressed chiefly by the Gr. *dolos,* "craftiness," "treachery" (Mk 7:22; Rom 1:29); by *apataō,* "to cheat," "seduce," "beguile" ("deceive you with vain words," Eph 5:6), and *apatē,* "seduction," "deceitfulness" (e.g., of riches, Mt 13:22; of evil, Heb 3:13); "deceitful lusts," Eph 4:22; and by *planaō,* "to go astray," "lead into error" (e.g., Mt 24:4–5,11,24).

While it is very possible to deceive oneself that he has no sin (I Jn 1:8; cf. I Cor 3:18), yet the source of all deceit and the arch-deceiver is the devil (*q.v.*), the one who deceives (Gr. *planōn*) the whole world (Rev 12:9; cf. 20:3,8,10). In the end time he will inspire a false prophet in league with the Beast (*q.v.*) to further his work of deception (Rev 13:14; 19:20; 20:10). The Antichrist himself, the man of lawlessness, will be energized by Satan to deceive many through signs and false wonders (II Thess 2:3–4, 8–10, NASB).

In the meantime many deceivers (*planoi*) have gone out into the world who refuse to acknowledge the truth about Jesus Christ (II Jn 7). John recognizes that these are antichrists, forerunners of the final Antichrist who is coming (II Jn 7; I Jn 2:18). Paul warns that there are false apostles, deceitful workers who masquerade as apostles of Christ (II Cor 11:13; cf. II Tim 3:13; Tit 1:10). He also states that in the latter times some will fall away from the faith because they pay attention to deceitful spirits and doctrines of demons (I Tim 4:1, NASB). While the Christian may be misunderstood and called a deceiver, even as were Paul (II Cor 6:8) and Jesus Himself (Mt 27:63), yet he will never resort to deceit or guile to extend the gospel (I Thess 2:3; II Cor 4:2).

See Guile.

Bibliography. Herbert Braun, "*Planaō,* etc.," TDNT, VI, 228–253.

J. R.

DECISION, VALLEY OF. The Heb. *'ēmeq heḥārûṣ* could be rendered "valley of judgment" or "valley of fate-decreed" (Joel 3:14). The

Heb. verb *ḥāraṣ* is used in Isa 10:22–23; 28:22 in the sense of destruction being decided or decreed for rebellious peoples. The valley of decision is identical with the valley of Jehoshaphat (*yᵉhôshāphāt,* "Yahweh hath judged," Joel 3:12). It is the place where someday God Himself shall judge all nations.

As early as the time of Eusebius of Caesarea (d. A.D. 340), this site was identified with the valley of the Kidron (E of Jerusalem). But this is pure conjecture. No valley of Palestine has ever borne this title. However,. when our Lord returns for judgment, the Mount of Olives shall be cleft in twain and a new valley will extend from E to W (Zech 14:4). *Perhaps* this is the enigmatic valley of decision.

DECREE, ROYAL. Royal decrees are public proclamations, usually in writing, issued by rulers to their subjects. Isaiah (10:1) condemns rulers who proclaim unjust laws. Such proclamations seem to have been inscribed on stone by command of the king.

Hezekiah issued a decree concerning the observance of the Passover after it had been neglected for some time (II Chr 30:5). Nebuchadnezzar issued various decrees, such as the death penalty for his wise men who were unable to declare his dream (Dan 2:9, 13, 15) and his order for all people to worship the image that he set up on the plains of Dura (Dan 3:10). Darius the Mede was tricked into establishing an injunction against anyone who prayed to any god or man besides himself (Dan 6:7–15, NASB).

The Persian king Cyrus issued a decree permitting the Jews to rebuild their temple (Ezr 5:13), a decree which was subsequently confirmed by Darius (Ezr 6:1–12). When the Persian king Ahasuerus divorced Vashti, this fact was made known through the kingdom by a decree (Est 1:19–22). He also let a decree be issued in his name to destroy all the Jews in his domain (Est 3:8–15; 4:3, 8). This was forestalled by a subsequent decree which Mordecai sent out in the name of the king that the Jews might defend themselves (Est 8:8–9:1).

A decree for a census issued by Caesar Augustus brought Mary and Joseph to Bethlehem prior to the birth of Jesus (Lk 2:1). At Thessalonica the enemies of Christ accused the apostle Paul of acting contrary to the decrees of Caesar (Claudius) in asserting that there was another king, namely, Jesus (Acts 17:1–7). This anticipated the persecutions of Christians until the time of Constantine, for Christians were considered disloyal citizens since they rejected the gods of the state, including the emperor who was worshiped as a god.

Ps 2:7 speaks of a royal decree from God Himself declaring that His Anointed (the Messiah, the Christ) is His Son. The Most High God announced His decree of humiliation to Nebuchadnezzar through the vision which Daniel interpreted (Dan 4:17, 24).

C. F. P.

DEDAN (dē'dan). The Dedanim (Isa 21:13) or Dedanites were an Arab people, descendants of Ham through Cush (Gen 10:7; I Chr 1:9), who intermarried with descendants of Abraham by Keturah (Gen 25:3; I Chr 1:32). That the name Dedan does not represent two separate peoples in these genealogies seems certain from the fact that in each case the brother of Dedan is named Sheba. They built the city of Dedan, 100 miles SW of Tema (*q.v.*), at a large oasis (el-'Ula, 175 miles NW of Medina, 350 miles SE of Petra) on the caravan route to S Arabia used by the Queen of Sheba. Thus they were known for their caravans and traders (Isa 21:13; Ezk 27:20; 38:13).

Dedan is mentioned in oracles against Edom (Jer 49:8; Ezk 25:13), indicating their close links with the Edomites and leading to the speculation that some Dedanites had settled in Edom. Dedan is mentioned in certain proto-Arabic Sabean and Minaean inscriptions, indicating its close contacts with these successive rulers of S Arabia (W. F. Albright, "Dedan," *Geshichte und Altes Testament,* Tübingen, 1953, pp. 1–12). *See* Arabia.

J. R.

DEDICATE, DEDICATION. To set apart or give to the deity or to a cause. Several Heb. terms are translated by this English concept, in verbal and substantive forms. The most frequent Heb. term, from the root word *qōdesh,* "apartness," "sacredness," "holiness," applies to men and to things set apart for divine service. Thus Ex 13:2, "Sanctify unto me all the firstborn." The things dedicated to God include treasure (Jud 17:3), spoils of war (I Chr 26:27), a field (Lev 27:18), and the temple (II Chr 7:5).

Of special usage is *ḥerem,* an antonym which denotes an object irrevocably devoted to one's God, or set apart for destruction. Any object or person that had been sacred to or associated with another deity must be "accursed," removed from any use by the layman (Deut 7:25–26; 20:17–18; Moabite Stone, line 17, ANET, p. 320). Usually this ban meant death or destruction, although certain objects captured in a holy war could be banned from common use and dedicated to sacred use in the sanctuary or by the priests (Num 18:14; Josh 6:19). *See* Curse. Achan disregarded the proscription imposed on Jericho and everything within it and was himself "devoted" (Josh 7:20–24; 8:26–27), while Rahab escaped a similar fate by aligning herself with God's covenant people (Josh 2:9–14).

See Consecration; Sanctification; Separation.

G. A. T.

DEDICATION, FEAST OF. *See* Festivals.

DEEP. The common Heb. root signifying "deep" or "low" is *'āmaq*. Another Heb. word, *tehôm,* refers to the ocean depths. While scholars have sought to derive this word from Akkad. *ti'amat,* the goddess of the salt water in the Babylonian creation epic (ANET, pp. 61-68), such borrowing cannot successfully be maintained, as Alexander Heidel has shown (*The Babylonian Genesis,* pp. 98-101).

The word *tehôm* is used: (1) of the primeval watery mass at creation (Gen 1:2; Ps 104:6; Prov 8:27); (2) of the sea (Ex 15:8; Isa 51:10; etc.); (3) of the subterranean reservoir of water (Gen 7:11; Deut 33:13); (4) in the figurative sense of profound: "Thy judgments are a great deep" (Ps 36:6; cf. 92:5); cf. " the deep things of God" (I Cor 2:10).

In the NT Gr. *abyssos,* "bottomless," refers literally to the depths of the Sea of Galilee (Lk 8:31, RSV) and figuratively to the underworld or abode of the dead (Rom 10:7, RSV) and of demons (Rev 9:1, 11; etc.). When used of water, *bathos* refers to the deep sea (Lk 5:4), and *buthos* is used only of ocean depths (II Cor 11:25). *See* Abyss; Hell.

R. L. D.

DEER. *See* Animals, II. 10.

DEFILE. In the OT this word is closely connected with the clean and the unclean (*see* Uncleanness) and the laws with regard thereto, as well as defilement of God's temple (Lev 15:31; 20:3; Num 19:13; Ps 79:1; Ezk 5:11), and the land (Jer 2:7; 3:9; 16:18). In the NT ceremonial defilement is shown to be only a type of moral defilement, and those who elevate the ceremonial above the moral are condemned by Christ (Mk 7:1-23). The extremes to which the Jews were going in cleansing cups, pots, tables and themselves were condemned by Christ. Not what enters the body defiles but what is said and done (v. 15). The keenness of the issue is revealed by the fact that the one known argument between John the Baptist and the Jews concerned purification (Jn 3:25). As a Levite and of the priestly order his baptism raised this question.

Peter had to learn by special revelation that nothing is actually unclean in itself (Acts 10:9-48). Paul advanced this teaching, though for expediency's sake he did once join in a Jewish purification ceremony. It is to be noticed, however, that this was the immediate cause of his Caesarean imprisonment (Acts 21:26 ff.).

R. A. K.

DEGREE. The Bible speaks of men of high degree (I Chr 17:17) and of low degree (Lk 1:52; Jas 1:9) with reference to their position in human society, whether they be exalted like David or of humble circumstances.

The deacons who serve well "purchase to themselves a good degree" (I Tim 3:13, KJV), i.e., they obtain for themselves a high standing or rank (Gr. *bathmos*) (NASB). Such a deacon gains a respected reputation in the church, and is also laying up treasures in heaven where he will have good standing at the judgment seat of Christ (H. A. Kent, Jr., *The Pastoral Epistles,* Chicago: Moody, 1958, p. 143).

For the "ten degrees" that the shadow of the sun turned backward for King Hezekiah (II Kgs 20:9-11; Isa 38:8) *see* Sun Dial. For a song of degrees (in titles of Ps 120-134) *see* Degrees, Song of.

DEGREES, SONG OF The KJV translation of the titles of Ps 120-134. The RSV and NASB call each "A Song of Ascents." The Heb. *ma'ălôt* literally means "goings up." The expression has been interpreted in different ways. Some see in it a reference to songs sung by pilgrims going up ("ascending") to Jerusalem (cf. Ps 122:4). Others suggest that it has specific reference to a supposed new year's festival with a ceremonial ascent to the temple, at which time these psalms were sung. The Mishnaic Tractate Middoth (ii.5) states that one of the 15 Psalms of Ascent was sung on each of the 15 steps leading from the women's court to the men's court of the second temple. The Levites sang these psalms, according to the Mishna, during the all-night ceremony of the first night of the Feast of Tabernacles.

Bibliography. J. Liebreich, "The Songs of Ascents and the Priestly Blessing," JBL, LXXIV (1955), 33-36.

C. F. P.

DEHAVITES (dē-hā'vīts). Mentioned among the groups for whom Rehum, the chancellor, wrote in Aramaic (Syrian) to Artaxerxes, the Persian king, filing a complaint against those who had recently returned from Babylonia to Jerusalem (Ezr 4:6-10). Along with the others they are identified as those who had been earlier transplanted by the great Asnapper (Ashurbanipal) from Babylonia and its neighboring regions to Samaria.

Formerly the Dehavites have been identified as a particular group like the Persians, Babylonians, etc. They were therefore thought to be the Daoi mentioned by Herodotus or the Dahae of Pliny and Virgil. This made them a tribe of the area to the E of the Caspian. The difficulty with this theory is that this region is far removed from Assyrian borders and, further, there is no mention of them in extant Assyrian documents. The more recent tendency is to follow a suggestion based on extrabiblical sources; that is, to read *dî-hû'* (or Targum *dîhû*) instead of *dehāwē',* meaning "that is" (cf. *hoi eisin* of Codex Vaticanus).

The resulting rendering is: "Susians, that is, the Elamites . . ." (cf. Ezr 4:9, RSV, "the men of Susa, that is, the Elamites . . .").

H. E. Fi.

DEKAR (dē'kär). The name of one of the 12 officers who provided food for King Solomon and his household (I Kgs 4:7, 9).

DELAIAH (dē-lā'yȧ)

1. A descendant of David through Zerubbabel; one of the seven sons of Elioenai (I Chr 3:24; KJV, Dalaiah).

2. A priest serving during David's reign who was leader of the 23rd course (I Chr 24:18-19).

3. A prince or officer, the son of Shemaiah, at the court of Jehoiakim. After hearing the words of prophecy from Jeremiah's scroll, he with Elnathan and Gemariah pleaded with the king not to burn the scroll (Jer 36:12, 25).

4. The ancestor of one of the post-Exilic families. Having lost the family genealogy, the sons "could not prove their fathers' houses or their descent" (Ezr 2:59-60, RSV; Neh 7:62).

5. The father of Shemaiah, a contemporary of Nehemiah. The builder rejected Shemaiah's counsel to flee and accused him of accepting hire from Tobiah and Sanballat (Neh 6:10-13).

R. O. C.

DELILAH (dĭ-lī'lȧ). A Philistine woman living in the valley of Sorek *c.* 1100 B.C., to whom Samson revealed the secret of his strength (Jud 16:4-22). The Wadi Sorek is the main pass leading W down from Jerusalem, through the Shephelah or foothills to the Maritime plain.

Although there were at least three women in Samson's life, it is Delilah who receives the greatest attention in Scripture. She succeeded where all others had failed in defeating Israel's champion. Samson "loved" this woman (Jud 16:4) and saw her frequently. Noting this, the leaders of the Philistines sought by bribery to accomplish what they had been unable to do by force. The bribe by which they persuaded her to deceive Samson was so large that it may imply that her loyalties were with Israel. However, her attachment to Samson may have been so strong that a large sum was required to betray her lover, even if he were an enemy of her nation. Each of the five Philistine rulers promised to pay her 1,100 pieces of silver (Jud 16:5). If shekels are meant, the total amount was nearly fourteen times the price paid by Abraham for a place to bury his wife (Gen 23:15).

Samson suspected that Delilah was interested in something other than romance and three times he misled her as to the source of his strength. On the third attempt, Samson apparently slept on her lap while she wove his hair into fabric on a loom. This time he left with loom and all. On her fourth attempt, Delilah accused him of lack of love day after day until he relented and told her the truth. The secret of his strength lay in his Nazarite vow which separated him unto God for special service, the symbol of this vow being the uncut hair. Delilah perceived now that his secret was laid bare, and with confidence summoned the Philistines, who came bringing the money. She again got him to sleep in her lap and then called an assistant to cut his hair. Delilah thus gained lasting infamy as the wily temptress who betrayed her lover for a large sum of money.

G. A. T.

DELIVERANCE. *See* Freedom; Liberation; Liberty.

DELUGE. *See* Flood.

DEMAS (dē'mȧs). Mentioned three times in the NT (Col 4:14; II Tim 4:10; Phm 24). This may be a shortened form of Demetrius (*q.v.*). He was a believer, and was evidently with Paul when he wrote Colossians and Philemon. Later, when writing II Timothy, Paul pens the dismal fact that Demas had forsaken him, "having loved this present world."

DEMETRIUS (dē-mē'trĭ-ŭs). At least five persons bore this name in biblical times.

1. Demetrius I, successor to Antiochus Epiphanes (162 B.C.), known for his intrigues, guile, and cruelty. In general he practiced repressive measures toward Jews in Palestine (I Macc 10:1-21).

2. Demetrius II, son of Demetrius I, who concluded a favorable treaty with Jonathan Maccabeus which he later violated. His generals were defeated at Hazor (I Macc 11:53 f.).

3. Demetrius III, ruler of Syria at the time of Alexander Jannaeus. During the latter's bitter quarrel with the Pharisees, he took their part, and thus extended his realm. Later, he was imprisoned and starved into submission by Philip Herod.

4. A Christian highly endorsed by John (III Jn 12).

5. The silversmith at Ephesus who accused Paul of endangering his trade and of imperiling the sanctity of the goddess Diana or Artemis (Acts 19:24 ff.). Because of this accusation, there ensued the riot in Ephesus which almost caused Paul and his companions to lose their lives. With the appearance of the town clerk, however, sanity was restored as he referred the rioters to their rights before the courts and their responsibilities as citizens (vv. 36-41).

J. F. G.

DEMONOLOGY. The study of the existence and activity of demons or evil spirits may be theologically classified under the doctrine of fallen angels. II Pet 2:4 and Jude 6-7 declare that some of the fallen angels are being kept in everlasting chains awaiting judgment. Some scholars consider this confinement merely a metaphor to express the fact that such beings are only specifically restrained by God as to their activities. Yet Christ's going in spirit during the time of His burial to proclaim His triumph to the imprisoned spirits that had been disobedient in Noah's day (I Pet 3:18-20,22*b*) points to an actual imprisonment of spirit-beings. By deduction one may infer that the demons which have been vexing mankind since the Flood are the remainder of the angels that followed Satan (Mt 25:41; Rev 12:7-9), for he is also called the prince of demons (Mt 12:24; cf. v. 26). Demons were considered to be evil angels in ancient Judaism.

Demons (devils, KJV) are unquestionably real, individual beings having personality and knowledge about God and humans (Jas 2:19; Acts 19:15). Their present domain is the spirit realm or supernatural sphere (Eph 6:12, Berkeley), but they desire to be embodied in living human or animal beings. Demons are able to invade or influence the minds of human teachers in order to suggest false doctrines (I Tim 4:1; I Jn 4:1-6; Jas 3:15). They actually commune with the souls of men in the case of mediums who yield to them. Demons will entice the rulers of the earth to assemble for the battle of Armageddon (Rev 16:14).

In the OT, evil or lying spirits possessed a certain freedom of action to tempt and thus test men, as revealed in the case of Job (Job 1-2). Yet they remained under God's ultimate control who uses or permits their activity to punish people for their sins (I Sam 16:14-16,23; 18:10; 19:9; I Kgs 22:21-23). Demons (*shēdîm*) were the reality behind the Canaanite gods or idols which many Israelites were tempted to worship (Deut 32:17; Ps 106:37; cf. I Cor 10:20-21; Rev 9:20). A specific form of such

Bronze figurine of the demon god Pazuzu, *c.* 800-600 B.C. ORINST

worship was the slaying of sacrifices for "devils" (KJV) or goat-idols (*śᵉʿîrîm,* Lev 17:7; II Chr 11:15). In translating *shēd* by Gr. *daimonion* in the LXX, the Alexandrian Jews gave clear evidence that they considered the gods to be more than mere objects of wood, stone or metal. In the LXX *daimonia* is also found in Ps 96:(95:)5 for "idols" and in Ps 91:(90:)6 for "destruction" with an apparent allusion to the noonday demon of heat known in ancient Greece as Pan or Artemis-Hecate. The LXX translators used *daimon* instead of naming the Canaanite god *Gad* in Isa 65:11 (KJV, "troop"; RSV, "fortune").

In the NT, demons are frequently said to take possession of men, and Christ therefore cast them out (e.g., Mt 4:24; 8:16; 9:33; 15:22). At times more than one demon may possess one person, as in the cases of the maniac of Gadara (Mk 5:1-17; Lk 8:30-33, 36) and of Mary Magdalene (Lk 8:2). Such demons often produce uncleanness, whether ritual, moral or spiritual (Lk 4:33-36; 6:18; 8:27-29; 9:42; 11:24-26).

The disciples were empowered and commissioned to heal all manner of diseases and to cast out demons (Mt 10:8; Lk 9:1; 10:17-20). They had grave difficulty, however, with certain demons and were told by Christ that these could be cast out only after prayer and fasting (Mk 9:14-29). The apostles effected deliverance for victims of demonic oppression by use of the name of Jesus (Acts 16:16-18; 19:12-17). The writings of the Ante-Nicene Fathers indicate that the church continued to exorcise demons well after the Apostolic Age. Even if Christ's promise in Mk 16:17, "And these signs shall follow them that believe; in my name shall they cast out devils" (part of the questioned ending of Mk 16:9-20), were not canonical, it would then be descriptive of conditions early in the 2nd cen. A.D.

Pastors and foreign missionaries testify to demon possession among many peoples of the world today, from primitive heathen tribes with animistic beliefs to highly educated persons in Europe and America. In numerous cases those who commit mass murders or suicide seem to have been impelled by wicked demons. It is urgent that Christian workers take seriously this doctrine and learn to exercise the authority of Christ to set free those who are demon oppressed or possessed. *See* Angels; Devil; Divination; Exorcism; Familiar Spirit; Madness; Principalities.

Bibliography. Paul Bechtel, "Witches in the Air"; Ray B. Buker, Sr., "Are Demons Real Today?" Derek Prince, "Release from Depression," *Christian Life,* XXIX (March, 1968). William H. Chisholm, *Vivid Experiences in Korea,* Chicago: Moody Press, 1938, pp. 42-46. Werner Foerster, "*Daimōn,* etc.," TDNT, II, 1-20. Kurt E. Koch, *Christian Counseling and Occultism,* transl. by Andrew Petter, Grand Rapids: Kregel, 1965. Russell J. Meade, *Victory Over Demonism Today,* Wheaton: Christian Life Publications, 1962. John L. Nevius, *Demon Possession and Allied Themes,* 5th ed., Revell, n.d. Charles R. Smith, "The New Testament Doctrine of Demons," *Grace Journal,* X, 26–42. Merrill F. Unger, *Biblical Demonology,* Wheaton: Van Kampen Press, 1953.

R. A. K. and J. R.

DEN. A number of Heb. and Gr. terms are translated "den," "cave," "pit," "cleft," "covert," or "booth." In the limestone mountains of Palestine are many dens or caves large and small. Even on the plains there are numerous pits or "lime sinks" which were sometimes used by the Arabs to store straw or grain. Perhaps into such was Joseph cast by his brothers (Gen 37:20). Jackals, wolves and other wild animals inhabited these dens or caves. Even people frequently made their homes in such (Jud 6:2), and here also robbers would hide (Jer 7:11). *See also* Cave; Pit.

DEN OF LIONS. The account of Daniel in the den of lions (Dan 6:7,12,16–24) rings true with the Persian background of this chapter. The Persian rulers, being Zoroastrians, held fire to be sacred, so that for them it would have been improper to execute by fire (cf. Dan 3). Kings of the 1st mil. B.C. frequently kept lions in captivity. Ashurnasirpal II (883–859 B.C.) bred them and kept large numbers of them at Calah.

The construction of such lions' dens is not known, but on the basis of the text, Edward J. Young (*The Prophecy of Daniel,* Grand Rapids: Eerdmans, 1949, pp. 136 f.) suggests it was an underground pit with a small opening in the top like a cistern. Possibly there was also one at the side through which the beasts were admitted and normally fed. It was very likely such a side entrance that was closed by the stone and sealed (Dan 6:17). The hole at the top was evidently too high for a man to escape without assistance (6:23).

J.R.

DENARIUS. *See* Weights, Measures, and Coins.

DENIAL OF CHRIST. *See* Deny; Peter.

DENY. The verb "deny" appears in three forms in the Gr. NT and in the LXX where it translates three different Heb. words. The three Gr. terms have been illuminated by papyri discoveries of the 1st and 2nd cen. A.D.

Gr. *arneomai* was used in the early Christian centuries to mean "disown" (MM, p. 78) and bears this meaning in such NT passages as Acts 3:14; Mt 10:33; II Tim 2:12–13; I Jn 2:22; I Tim 5:8; Tit 2:12 (cf. Arndt, p. 107). It also means simply to deny in the sense of saying no as in Mt 26:70; Acts 4:16; Heb 11:24. To deny oneself (Mt 16:24; Mk 8:34; Lk 9:23) means to set aside or renounce all personal ambition and self-interest in favor of the new claims of Christ upon one's life for unreserved commitment to Him and His gospel.

Gr. *aparneomai* was also used to mean "deny" in the sense of disown (MM, p. 53) as is seen especially in Peter's denials of Jesus in Mk 14:30–31, 72 and parallels, and in Mk 8:34 and parallels.

Gr. *antilegō* has been shown in the papyri to mean "contradict" in a passage where a man is told "not to agree now with his father, but to *oppose* him and make no contract" (MM, p. 48). This strong sense of "contradict" or "oppose" is found in Rom 10:21 (Isa 65:2), where God's judgment on Israel is that they were a disobedient and *opposing* people. Paul says the Jews opposed (*antilegō,* lit., "spoke against") his being set free at Caesarea (Acts 28:19). This word appears also in Tit 1:9; 2:9; Jn 19:12; Acts 13:45; and probably Lk 20:27. The church was everywhere "opposed" (Acts 28:22).

J. McR.

DEPRAVITY. *See* Fall of Man; Reprobate; Sin.

DEPUTY. The word occurs in the OT once (I Kgs 22:47) as the rendering of the verb *niṣṣāb,* to be appointed as a deputy or official; and twice (Est 8:9; 9:3, RSV) for *peḥâ,* a governor, subordinate to an official of higher rank. "Deputies" is also the RSV rendering of *segānîm* (Jer 51:28, KJV, "rulers").

In the NT, "deputy" (KJV) appears for Gr. *anthypatos,* "in lieu of one higher," uniformly rendered "proconsul" by RSV. Under the Roman system proconsuls were appointed by the senate to preside over the senatorial provinces as distinct from the imperial provinces which were administered by direct appointees of the emperor. The proconsuls mentioned in the NT were Sergius Paulus of Cyprus (Acts 13:7–8, 12) and Gallio of Achaia (Acts 18:12). See Acts 19:38 for the only other NT mention of proconsuls.

See Governor.

DERBE (dûr'bĭ). A town in Asia Minor in the SE corner of Lycaonia on the main road from Lystra to Laranda. On Paul's first missionary journey he came to Derbe after having been stoned at Lystra and made many disciples there (Acts 14:6, 20). Paul passed through Derbe on his second journey from Cilicia to Lystra (Acts 16:1) and likely visited there on his third journey. Gaius, one of Paul's disciples and companions, was from Derbe (Acts 20:4).

Since Sir William Ramsay identified Derbe with Gudelisin in 1890, that view has been generally accepted. But two inscriptions found in recent years have demonstrated rather conclusively that Kerti Hüyük is the correct site of ancient Derbe. Gudelisin is about 30 miles W of the modern Turkish town of Karaman (66 miles by road SE of Konya), and Kerti Hüyük is some 15 miles NW of Karaman.

Bibliography. M. Ballance, *Anatolian Studies*, VII (1957), 147-151. B. Van Elderen, "Derbe," BW, pp. 195 f.

H. F. V.

DESERT. Various Heb. words are translated "desert" or "wilderness" in the KJV of the OT. *Midbār*, the most common, is found approximately 280 times. It is usually translated "wilderness" (*q.v.*) but 12 times is rendered "desert." The word derives from a root meaning "to drive," i.e., drive herds to the fields (cf. HGHL, p. 656; Selbie, HDB, IV, 917). It should be remembered that shepherds must lead their sheep from one spot to another to provide sufficient fodder if the flocks are to survive on the sparse vegetation of the desert (cf. Lk 15:3-7).

The term Jeshimon (Heb. *yᵉshîmôn*) is more expressive but is found less frequently (14 times). Apparently it derives from a root meaning "to be desolate" (*yāsham*). The mountain of Pisgah overlooked this area of Jeshimon (Num 21:20) as did the height of Peor (Num 23:28). The region around Ziph (near Hebron?) is similarly designated (I Sam 23:19, 24; 26:1, 3). It is thus a vivid term for the expanse of desert known to the sacred writers, particularly the rugged terrain that encircled the Dead Sea.

Arabah, Heb. *'ărābâ* (Isa 35:1, 6; 40:3; Jer 2:6; 17:6; etc.), is a broad term that refers frequently to depressed plains, such as the one in which the Jordan River is located, as well as the low desert region to the S of the Dead Sea. Today this large valley is called the Arabah. KJV translates the Heb. term 42 times as "plain."

Another term, *ḥorbâ*, is translated "desert" in KJV in Ps 102:6; Isa 48:21; Ezk 13:4, but generally means a ruined city or area.

The Gr. term used in the LXX and the NT for desert is regularly *erēmos*, a deserted, abandoned, lonely place. In later pilgrim texts in Latin this term is transliterated as *heremus* or *eremus*.

A typical scene in the Wilderness of Judea. HFV

In Egypt the desert begins at the edge of the rich soil deposited over the centuries by the Nile flood. HFV

The Judean desert has often exercised significant influences upon the changing tide of Palestinian history. Much evidence of the importance of this region has come to light recently in the form of ancient documents from biblical times. The recovery of the Dead Sea Scrolls, because of the bone-dry atmosphere of certain areas in this vicinity, is one of the more dramatic contributions of the Judean desert in our day. Written materials have been found especially in the area of the Dead Sea (at the Wadi ed-Daliyeh, N of Jericho; Qumran; Khirbet Mird; Nahal Tse'elim; Nahal Hever; Masada; etc.) and in certain centers of the Negev as well (Nessana, etc.). Thus, the practical monopoly which the Egyptian desert had held in years past on such ancient writing materials no longer exists. *See* Dead Sea Scrolls.

Glueck's researches in the Negev have brought to light many forgotten facts about the desert areas between Beer-sheba and the Gulf of Aqabah (where Solomon, Uzziah, and Jotham had a large warehouse and shipping center at Ezion-Geber). He has surveyed the centers where teeming populations once thrived (especially under the Nabataeans), carefully utilizing as they did their natural resources. Also he and his assistants have helped modern biblical research to discover anew the sites and the routes which Abraham and the Israelites followed in their desert sojourns.

The desert being close at hand (vegetation completely disappears six miles E of Jerusalem as one journeys toward the Dead Sea), it afforded criminals (cf. Lk 10:30), political exiles (I Sam 22-26, David fleeing from Saul), as well as false messiahs (Mt 24:26; Acts 21:38; Jos *Wars*, ii.13.5; vii.11.1) a suitable base for their operations.

The desert also reminded the sacred poets of the marvelous creative powers of God, blossoming as it does when drenched by the seasonal rains (Isa 35:1). For this reason a word which is sometimes used for the desert is *tohu*, a term descriptive of the primeval chaos ("without form," Gen 1:2) which abounded before God brought order to His created world (see "waste," Deut 32:10; "wilderness," Job 12:24; Ps 107:40).

Herod the Great, realizing the strategic importance of the defense posts, maintained various desert fortresses, such as Masada, Machaerus E of the Dead Sea, and Herodium near Bethlehem. John the Baptist, being reared in the desert, drew illustrations from its life (vipers fleeing before a brush fire, etc.; cf. Mt 3:7).

Bibliography. Frank M. Cross, Jr., "A Footnote to Biblical History," BA, XIX (Feb., 1956), 12-17. Gustav Dalman, *Sacred Sites and Ways,* New York: Macmillan, 1935, IV, 81-98. B. Z. Eshel, *The Dead Sea Region,* Jerusalem: Kirjath Sepher, 1958. Nelson Glueck, *The Other Side of the Jordan,* New Haven: ASOR, 1940; *Rivers in the Desert,* New York: Farrar, Straus and Cudahy, 1959. Edward Robinson, *Biblical Researches in Palestine, Mt. Sinai and Arabia Petraea* (various entries, see esp. II, 218-222). Beno Rothenberg, *God's Wilderness: Discoveries in Sinai,* London: Thames & Hudson, 1961. George Adam Smith, HGHL, 26th ed., pp. 263-265, 269-273, 312-317.

E. J. V.

DESIRE. For the occurrence of this word translating Heb. *'ăbîyônâ* in Eccl 12:5 (KJV, RSV) *see* Plants: Caperberry.

DESIRE OF ALL NATIONS. This phrase, found in Hag 2:7 (KJV), has traditionally been interpreted as a prophecy of Christ. In this, Christian expositors were following rabbinical interpretation which applied it to the Messiah. Another ancient interpretation, found as early as the LXX, has come into favor in recent times. While the noun "desire" is singular, yet because the verb "come" is plural, the phrase is translated "the desired things" or "the treasures of all nations shall come in" (RSV). The context of the passage is certainly messianic, since the splendor of the post-Exilic temple was found not in its beauty but in the coming of Christ. Both interpretations are acceptable. The passage speaks either of the coming of Christ or of the tribute which all nations will render to Him. I Sam 9:20 illustrates how the term "desire of Israel" may refer to a royal person, and Dan 11:37 infers that "the desire of women" is a divine being.

P. C. J.

DESOLATION, ABOMINATION OF. *See* Abomination of Desolation.

DESTROYER. This term refers to the angel of death employed in the destruction of the firstborn in Egypt not found under the blood (Ex 12:23; Heb 11:28); also in connection with the punishment for David's sin in numbering the people (II Sam 24:15-16); in smiting the camp of the Assyrians (II Kgs 19:35); and in smiting Herod in Acts 12:23. *See also* Destruction.

DESTRUCTION. Of 33 terms used in the OT, the most common are Heb. *'ăbăddôn,* "destruction," "perishing"; *'êd,* "calamity," "distress"; *m*ᵉ*ḥittâ,* "dismay," "ruin"; *m*ᵉ*hûmâ,* "trouble," "destruction"; *sheber,* "breaking," "breach"; and of four in the NT, Gr. *apōleia,* "ruin," "loss"; *olethros,* "death," "destruction."

The word *'ăbăddôn* refers to a place of destruction, an abyss, and is very close in meaning to Sheol (Job 26:6; 28:22; 31:12; Ps 88:11; Prov 15:11). In the NT *apóleia* stresses the idea of utter loss (Mt 7:13; Rom 9:22; Phil 3:19; II Pet 2:1; 3:16) and can best be understood in the light of Christ's warning in Lk 9:25: "What is a man advantaged, if he gain the whole world, and lose [Gr. *apolesas*] himself, or be cast away?" Rev 9:11, ASV, speaks of "the angel of the abyss: his name in Hebrew is Abaddon, and in the Greek tongue he hath the name Apollyon" (i.e., the Destroyer). *See* Abaddon; Apollyon; Destroyer; Sheol.

DESTRUCTION, CITY OF. In Isa 19:18, by employing the phrase *'îr haheres,* "the City of Destruction" (NASB), the prophet seems to be making a deliberate punning allusion to *'îr haḥeres,* "the City of the Sun," a designation for the Egyptian city of On (*q.v.*), which the Greeks called Heliopolis. On the basis of certain MS evidence the RSV adopted the latter phrase, without however noting the emendation.

DEUEL (dū'ĕl). A Gadite, the father of Eliasaph, who was the leader of the tribe of Gad in the Exodus (Num 1:14; 7:42, 47; 10:20). The name probably comes from a Heb. term signifying "knowledge of God." In Num 2:14 the name is rendered Reuel, perhaps resulting from confusing the Heb. letters for "d" and "r." *See* Reuel.

DEUTERONOMY, BOOK OF. This is the last of the five books of the Pentateuch. Its name comes through the Latin Vulgate from the LXX title *deuteronomion,* "repetition of the law," based on a misunderstanding of the words "copy of this law" in Deut 17:18.

Ancient Jewish and Christian writers unanimously attribute this book to Moses. Jesus Christ and the various NT writers quote from it or allude to it nearly 100 times, often indicating that the citation came from Moses (e.g., Mk 12:19; Mt 19:8; Rom 10:19; I Cor 9:9). Modern critics deny that Moses wrote Deuteronomy, attributing the book in its present form to various writers and editors over a period of centuries.

The literary unity of this book of Moses is unmistakably evidenced by its remarkable structure. It exhibits in its total pattern and in numerous thematic emphases the legal form characteristic of ancient Hittite and Assyrian treaties; in particular, those of the vassal type. Moreover, in so far as there was an evolution in the documentary form of these treaties. Deuteronomy corresponds to the classic Near Eastern form attested in the time of Moses as over against that of the 1st mil. B.C. As sealed legal contracts these treaties were not subject to alteration.

The fact that Deuteronomy can be so identified confirms its own plain claims as to its Mosaic authorship and the occasion for which it was produced (see Deut 1:3; 31:9,22,24); and by the same token it belies the whole complex of modern higher critical theories concerning the origin of this book. Negative criticism since the days of Wellhausen regards Deuteronomy as the product of a prolonged process of expansion and alteration, completed, according to the majority opinion, in the 7th cen. B.C., though some date it in post-Exilic times and others trace it back to the pre-monarchic amphictyony.

The book may be outlined as follows:

I. Preamble: Covenant Mediator, 1:1-5
II. Historical Prologue: Covenant History, 1:6–4:49
III. Stipulations: Covenant Life, 5:1–26:19
IV. Sanctions: Covenant Ratification, 27:1–30:20
V. Succession Arrangements: Covenant Continuity, 31:1–34:12

Vassal treaties opened with the self-identification of the suzerain addressing himself to his servant. So the Deuteronomic preamble (1:1-5) identifies Moses as the speaker and mediator-representative of the heavenly King who was the true Lord of this covenant. The preamble also indicates the occasion to be the final assembly of Israel called by Moses just before his death. As was customary in the administration of covenants, the approaching death of the dynastic head (i.e., Moses) was the signal for a renewal of the covenant, requiring of the vassal (i.e., Israel) a recognition of the appointed dynastic successor (i.e., Joshua).

The purpose of the historical prologue was to cite benefits previously bestowed by the great King so that the vassal's allegiance might be motivated by a sense of gratitude. Beginning his rehearsal of the history of the Lord's relationship to Israel at the scene of the Sinaitic establishment of the covenant, Moses recalls God's faithful guardianship of Israel in spite of their fractiousness during the wilderness wanderings and the Transjordanian conquests, and he brings the account up to the present solemn ceremony with words of exhortation (1:6–4:49).

Stipulations dictated by the suzerain for the regulation of the vassal's life formed a third standard division in the treaties. Always the fundamental demand was for the vassal's perfect loyalty to the exclusion of allegiance to any other lord. Agreeably, the Deuteronomic laws open with the great commandment to love the Lord with all the heart, for He alone was Israel's God (5:1–11:32). The fact that suzerains, when renewing covenants, repeated their earlier demands with such modifications as might be necessary, explains the new version of the Decalogue (5:6 ff.). In the remainder of the legislation (chaps. 12-26), the primary principle was applied to specific areas of the Israelite theocracy in laws dealing with cultic-ceremonial consecration (12:1–16:17), judicial-governmental righteousness (16:18–21:23), the sanctity of the divine order (22:1–25:19), and the confession of God as Redeemer-King (26:1-19).

There follows the usual section presenting the treaty sanctions. It begins with directions for a concluding phase of the covenant renewal to be conducted by Joshua within Canaan (chap. 27). The curses and blessings of chaps. 28-30 provide a prophetic view of Israelite history, culminating in exile and restoration. They also constitute the divine threat and promise in terms of which Israel swore its oath of allegiance that day.

Gathered together in the final chapters (31-34) are elements relating to the continuation of the covenant; arrangements for Joshua's succession; the appointment of the covenant witnesses, namely, the treaty text deposited in the sanctuary, and the song of witness placed in Israel's mouth; Moses' testamentary blessings; and the record of Moses' death, the imminency of which was the occasion of the ceremony of which Deuteronomy is the documentary witness. *See* Covenant.

Bibliography. CornPBE, pp. 258-262, for recent theories of authorship. Kenneth A. Kitchen, "Ancient Orient, 'Deuteronism,' and the Old Testament," NPOT, pp. 1-24. Meredith G. Kline, *The Treaty of the Great King,* Grand Rapids: Eerdmans, 1963. Dennis J. McCarthy, *Treaty and Covenant,* Rome: Pontifical Biblical Inst., 1963. Gerhard von Rad, *Studies in Deuteronomy,* New York: Henry Regnery, 1953. Adam C. Welch, *The Code of Deuteronomy,* London: Oxford, 1924; *Deuteronomy: The Framework to the Code,* London: Oxford, 1932. Samuel J. Schultz, *Deuteronomy, The Gospel of Love,* Chicago: Moody Press, 1971.

M. G. K.

DEVIL (Gr. *diabolos,* "slanderer," "false accuser"). Identical with Satan, Adversary. He is once called *katēgor,* "accuser," in Rev 12:10, and is called Beelzebub (*q.v.*) in Mt 12:27.

The devil is a personal, superhuman, evil, created being, a fallen angel, without corporeal material form. He is represented in Scripture as the highest of all created archangels before his fall.

Though it is unpopular today to believe in

the personality of the devil, the Scripture teaches both his reality and his personality. The Bible credits Satan with the attributes, works, and names of a personal being. He is said "to deceive" the whole world (Rev 12:9), involving intellect; he goes forth with "great wrath" (Rev 12:12), exhibiting emotion; he "makes war" (Rev 12:17), thus doing the works of a person. Furthermore, he has various names which describe his character: "Satan," "Devil," "old serpent," "accuser" (Rev 12:9-10; 20:2).

Aside from Scripture the strongest argument for his being a real person is that denial of his personality would destroy our belief in the deity of Christ: ". . . if He [i.e., Christ] were not externally tempted to evil . . . if those evil suggestions to make stone into bread . . . did not come to Him from some living intelligence . . . external to Himself, then must they have come from *within;* and that being the case, He Himself needed a Saviour rather than *was one*" (F. C. Jennings, *Satan,* p. 5).

Satan is spoken of as "the adversary" in I Pet 5:8. He can and does transform himself into an angel of light (II Cor 11:14). At least some forms of sickness are caused by the devil, for Paul said his "thorn in the flesh" (II Cor 12:7) was "the messenger of Satan" (see also Lk 13:16; Job 2:7).

The devil assumed the form of a serpent to tempt Eve (Gen 3:1). He deceives and tempts men to sin (Eph 6:11; I Tim 3:7; Mt 4:1 ff.).

Satan was a created angel who apparently was included among the sons of God (Job 1:6). His original home was in heaven as the "anointed cherub that covereth" (Ezk 28:14, 16). The mention in Ezk 28:2 ff. of the prince of Tyre and the king of Tyre would seem to have reference to Satan, for he was said to have been in Eden (v. 13), and "thou wast perfect in thy ways from the day that thou wast created, till unrighteousness was found in thee" (v. 15, ASV). This would seem not to refer merely to the earthly prince of Tyre but to the devil who dwelt in him. Others do not see this as a reference to Satan.

The devil fell from his high estate by the sin of pride, and by seeking to usurp the throne of God. Jesus beheld Satan falling as lightning from heaven (Lk 10:18; cf. Isa 14:12-14). He is now called "the prince of the power of the air" (Eph 2:2), and "the prince of this world" (Jn 14:30). Some feel that before his power was broken by Christ's death and resurrection, Satan deceived the nations, but now, before the second coming of Christ, he is bound in respect to deceiving the nations, though not with respect to tempting people; and at the end of this age he will be loosed to deceive the nations once more (Rev 20:2, 7-8; cf. Mt 12:26-29). Others interpret Satan's binding to refer to the removal of his whole activity against God in the future Millennial Age and that today he is not only tempting people but also deceiving the nations by enticing them into complete independence of God (II Cor 4:4; 11:3).

Satan is the "father of lies," a "murderer," and the spiritual father, mentor, or master of evil men (Jn 8:44). But wicked as he is, he must still bow to the sovereignty of God (Job 1:10).

The devil is neither omniscient nor omnipresent, so apparently he depends on his followers, the wicked fallen angels (demons) who are subject to him, to be his agents in tempting men and indwelling those who are demon-possessed (Mk 1:23-27, 32-34; 3:11-12; etc.). He is called the "accuser of our brethren" (Rev 12:10; cf. Job 1).

He is already judged by God and awaits his doom at the final judgment (Rev 20:10; Mt 25:41). There is apparently no scriptural evidence for the common belief that the devil is now in hell presiding over the tortures of the damned. Peter declares in II Pet 2:4 that God cast down the sinning angels to Tartarus and committed them to pits of darkness to await the final judgment, but this is different from the lake of fire and brimstone (cf. II Pet 3:7).

See Accuser; Adversary; Antichrist; Belial; Deceiver; Demonology; Evil One; Lucifer; Satan.

Bibliography. Donald G. Barnhouse, *The Invisible War,* Grand Rapids: Zondervan, 1965. Lewis S. Chafer, *Satan,* Chicago: Moody, 1942. Werner Foerster and Gerhard von Rad, "*Diabolos,*" TDNT, II, 72-81. F. C. Jennings, *Satan: His Person, Work, Place and Destiny,* New York: A. C. Gaebelein, n.d. Merrill F. Unger, *Biblical Demonology,* 2nd ed., Wheaton, Ill.: Van Kampen Press, 1963, especially pp. 182-208.

F. E. H.

DEVILS. *See* Demonology.

DEVOTE, DEVOTED (Heb. *ḥērem*). This is a term connected with holiness, exclusion, separation, taboo, i.e., things placed under a ban and forbidden to common use. The *ḥarîm* was the area forbidden to all except the husband and eunuchs.

In the OT the "devoted thing" was that which was set apart to the Lord, and therefore belonged no longer to the owner, nor could it be used for sacrifice (Josh 6:18-19; 7:10-15; I Sam 15). Man was not to be offered in sacrifice, but certain persons and nations were doomed (devoted) by God, who alone has the prerogative of taking life as well as giving it. Sacrifice rests on a different ground, i.e., the voluntary offering of an innocent life of a creature without blemish, approved of God to represent the great Sacrifice. The pagan confounded the two ideas of the devoted thing under a ban (as criminals and captives), and the sacrifice of one's flock or herd as a voluntary offering in worship; but the Scripture writers keep them distinct. *See* Anathema; Curse.

R. L. D.

DEVOTED THING. *See* Anathema; Curse.

DEW. "Sprinkled moisture" is referred to indiscriminately as dew (i.e., condensation of water vapor on a cooled surface) and night mist (i.e., condensation of the air). Moisture and cold are necessary for the formation of dew. In moist areas, there is less dew because of the uniformity of the temperature night and day. Because of limited moisture in the atmosphere, there is little dew in the desert even though there is a marked change of temperature. Palestine, being located near the Mediterranean Sea, always had a large percentage of water vapor in the atmosphere. The clear skies contribute to rapid radiation of ground heat immediately following the sunset. This is turn cools the land, so that the moisture in the air condenses through contact with cool objects.

Since April through October is a dry season in Palestine, dew is imperative to revive vegetation. Dews are so heavy that the plants and trees are literally soaked with water. In Jud 6:38, the wetting of Gideon's fleece is indicative of the dew's heaviness. It is heaviest on the coast W of Beer-sheba, in the plain of Esdraelon, and at the sources of the Jordan beneath the slopes of Hermon (Ps 133:3). The dew descends mysteriously (Job 38:28); its origin is heavenly (Gen 27:28; Deut 33:28; Hag 1:10; Zech 8:12). It falls suddenly (II Sam 17:12), gently (Deut 32:2), and remains on the ground throughout the night (Job 29:19). Overexposure to dew is discomforting (Song 5:2; Dan 4:15, 23, 25, 33). It quickly evaporates in the morning (Job 7:9; Hos 6:4). Dew is normally expected during the hot summer harvest season (Isa 18:4; Hos 14:5; Mic 5:7). Its copiousness permits dry-farming.

Dew is a figure of speech for abundant fruitfulness (Gen 27:28; Deut 33:13); also it stands as a symbol of the "remnant of Jacob" blessing all people (Mic 5:7). Again dew serves as a figure of speech for an unaware thief (II Sam 17:12) and ephemeral religion (Hos 6:4; 13:3).

D. W. D.

DIADEM. Properly a diadem is not a crown but a band narrower than a crown; a circlet or ring for the head. The diadem originally was a strip of white cloth bound about the head, later of blue, and also ornamented with gold. The high priest's diadem (crown) was a gold plate tied to his turban by a blue cord and inscribed with the words "Holy to the Lord" (Ex 39:30, NASB). The Jerusalem Bible reads: "They also made the plate, the holy diadem, of pure gold, and engraved on it 'Consecrated to Yahweh,' as a man engraves a seal."

The bestowal of the diadem by God is a mark of His grace and favor, particularly the mark of Messiah (Isa 62:3). When Israel is to be restored to her millennial glory, God is said to be for her a diadem of beauty (Isa 28:5). Conversely, the withdrawal of the diadem indicates the debasing of the one wearing it, the removal of the favor of king or God (Ezk 21:26).

Job speaks of clothing himself with righteousness and justice as with a robe and a diadem (Job 29:14). In the NT the word diadem (Gr. *diadēma*) occurs only three times (Rev 12:3; 13:1; 19:12) as crown(s); it denotes a circlet. The last reference enumerates the crowns of the Son of God, denoting His sovereignty over all nations.

See Crown.

H. G. S.

DIAL, SUN. *See* Sun Dial.

DIAMOND. *See* Jewels.

DIANA (dī-ă'nȧ). This is the Latin name for the virgin goddess of hunting, also identified with the moon and Hecate, and patroness of childbirth. Her Gr. name was Artemis (meaning "prompt," "safe," or perhaps "pendant"). This twin sister of the sun-god Apollo, chaste goddess of nature and protectress of wild animals, especially of their young, was also regarded as the patroness of hunters. Armed with a bow and arrow and accompanied by a bounding stag, this goddess of the light by night (later of the moon) was a mighty huntress. To her the Spartans sacrificed a goat before each battle.

A statue of Diana excavated at Ephesus. HFV

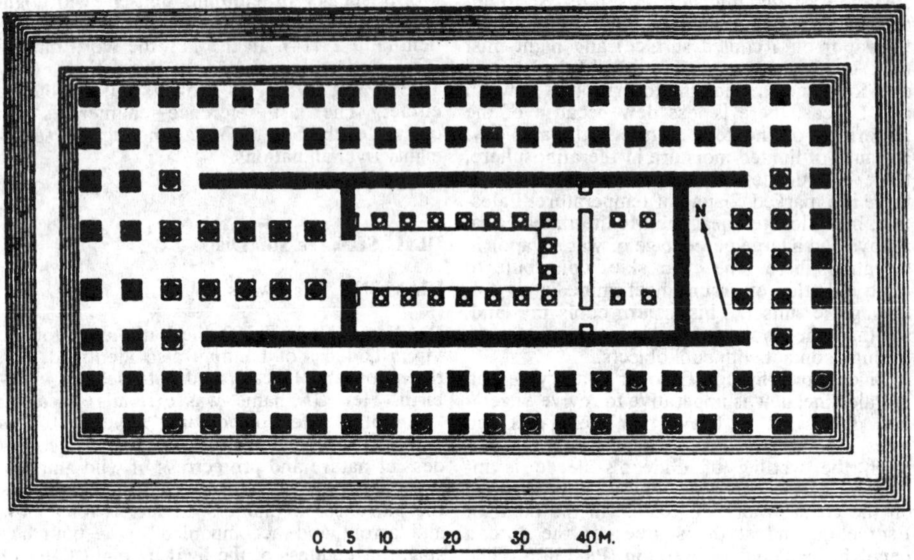

Plan of the Temple of Diana, Ephesus. From I. H. Grinnell, *Greek Temples*, Metropolitan Museum of Art

Young girls regarded her as the guardian of their maiden years. But in Asia Minor during Roman times she was identified with the Phrygian mother-goddess Cybele, a sensuous nature goddess, although images taken from the earlier yellow limestone temple at Ephesus picture her in less degrading light.

Diana of the Ephesians (Acts 19:24–37), as known from many statues of her image and as depicted on coins, had her thorax covered with three or four rows of pendant breasts, or possibly ostrich eggs, either of which were symbolic of fertility. The front of her garment was trimmed with sequences of lions, goats, and other sacrificial animals. Down the sides of her garment were alternate rows of nymphs, seashells, sphinxes, bees and roses. Her mural crown was decorated with signs of the Zodiac denoting the seasons, unlike the simple tiara symbolizing the crescent moon which was characteristic of the Gr. virgin huntress Artemis.

Originally the Artemis worshiped at Ephesus was not a Gr. divinity but was Asiatic. Ultimately the various goddesses of love in Syria and Asia Minor all owed their origin to the earlier Babylonian and Assyrian Ishtar through the link of the Phoenician Astarte. She impersonated the reproductive powers of man and animals and all other life. She assisted at childbirth. Associated thus with the various fertility cults she became the patroness of ceremonial prostitution, which was part of her worship at Ephesus.

The great temple of Diana at Ephesus, called the Artemision and considered as one of the seven wonders of the Hellenistic world, was the scene of an annual festival in her honor during the month of Artemisios (March–April). The religious ceremonies included athletic, dramatic and musical contests (*see* Games). Ephesus was proud of her position as "temple-keeper" of Diana (Acts 19:35), a boast which has been found on inscriptions excavated there. The temple treasury acted as a bank in which deposits were made by cities, kings and private persons (WHG, p. 362). Here the Ionians came with their wives and children, bringing costly offerings and presents to the priests. Her worship was characterized by sensuous orgies. Great throngs attended. Multitudes of female temple slaves or "priestesses" who came as virgins were here dedicated to service in the temple which may have included ritual or cultic prostitution.

The silversmiths of Ephesus carried on a lucrative business by the forging and sale of images of this goddess (Acts 19:23 ff.). Hence it was inevitable that Paul's message of Christianity should arouse their indignation because it jeopardized their trade. *See* Demetrius; Ephesus; Gods, False: Artemis; Goddess.

Bibliography. E. J. Banks, "Diana, Artemis," ISBE, II, 842 f. C. Cobern, *New Archaeological Discoveries,* New York: Funk & Wagnall, 1921, pp. 461–482. W. K. C. Guthrie, *The Greeks and Their Gods,* Boston: Beacon Press, 1951, pp. 99–106. Jane E. Harrison, *Prolegommena to the Study of Greek Religions,* Cambridge: Cambridge Univ. Press, 1922. C. H. Moore, *The Religious Thought of the Greeks, from Homer to the Triumph of Christianity,*

Cambridge: Harvard Univ. Press, 1916. M. P. Nilsson, *A History of Greek Religion,* Oxford: Clarendon Press, 1925. Cf. also the articles by M. M. Parvis and F. V. Filson on Ephesus in BA, VIII (1945), 61–73, 73–80.

R. E. Pr.

DIBLAIM (dĭb'lĭ-ăm). Gomer, Hosea's wife, was a "daughter of Diblaim" (Hos 1:3). The name comes from a Heb. term signifying "lump or double cakes of figs and raisins." Some have thought the name to be figurative, i.e., "Gomer the daughter of raisin cakes," meaning that she was wholly given up to her harlotry, since raisin cakes were used in certain fertility cult rites.

DIBLATH (dĭb'lăth). This word in Ezk 6:14 occurs as "Diblah" in ASV and "Riblah" in RSV. In the Heb. the "r" and "d" could easily have been interchanged. The correct term is likely Riblah (*q.v.*).

DIBON (dī'bŏn), **DIBON-GAD** (dī'bŏn-găd')

1. Dibon was one of the principal cities of Moab, and under Mesha it became the capital of the kingdom. The city stood on the site of modern Dhiban, a low mound which lies on the plateau of Moab a short distance W of the main highway between Amman and Kerak and about 10 miles N of the Arnon gorge (Josh 13:9).

Prior to the Israelite conquest of Transjordan under Moses' leadership, Dibon and all Moab N of the Arnon was overrun by Sihon, king of the Amorites (Num 21:30). One of the stations of Israel on the journey toward Canaan (Num 33:45), Dibon was taken from Sihon with his other possessions and assigned by Moses to Reuben (Josh 13:17). The city, however, was rebuilt by the stronger tribe of Gad and given the name Dibon-gad (Num 32:34). It was later taken over by King Mesha of Moab, who rebelled against Israel after the death of Ahab *c.* 853 B.C. (II Kgs 1:1: 3:4–5). According to the biblical account (II Kgs 3), Israel was initially victorious over Mesha; but Mesha later (*c.* 830 B.C.) set up a stele at Dibon (the famous Moabite Stone [*q.v.*] found there in 1868), boasting of his defeating Israel. He seems to have given the name of Qarhoh to the citadel of Dibon. Isaiah (15:2) and Jeremiah (48:18, 22) pronounced judgment upon Dibon in their prophecies against Moab.

From 1950 to 1956 the site of Dhiban was sounded and parts excavated by the American School of Oriental Research. The earliest levels of occupation belong to the Early Bronze Age. The most important discovery was the section of a city wall and huge gate towers with corner guard rooms, built of large blocks of masonry, each measuring on the average about 32 inches in length, 24 inches in width and over 18 inches in depth, and going back to the 10th through the 8th cen. B.C. This wall was rebuilt in all probability by King Mesha after the reign of Ahab in Israel. On the summit of the site was uncovered the foundation of a Moabite official building with walls averaging five feet in thickness and paved stone floors. Since the central room contained a fine incense stand and two adjacent rooms had fertility figurines, the building may have been a temple or a palace with a royal chapel. Inside the city walls a Nabataean structure of the 1st cen. B.C. was discovered, as well as the remains of a Roman bath of about the 3rd cen. A.D., and the foundations of a church of the Byzantine period. The site was last occupied by the Arabs of the early Umayyad period and appears to have been abandoned sometime during the 9th cen. A.D. See William H. Morton, "Dibon," BW, pp. 200f.

2. A village in Judah reinhabited by some of the Jews who returned from the Babylonian captivity (Neh 11:25), perhaps the same as Dimonah (Josh 15:22) in the Negeb.

D. C. B. and R. L. D.

DIBRI (dĭb'rī). A Danite, father of Shelomith and grandfather of the blasphemer who was executed by stoning (Lev 24:11).

DICTIONARIES, BIBLE. *See* Bible Dictionaries.

DIDRACHMA. *See* Weights, Measures, and Coins.

DIDYMUS (dĭd'ĭ-mŭs). A transliteration of the Gr. *didymos,* an alternative appellation for the apostle Thomas (Jn 11:16; 20:24; 21:2), probably used by Gr. speaking Christians. It appears in the papri as a proper name as well as a common noun meaning "twin." This is also the meaning of Aram. *te'ôma'* (Gr. *thōmas).* Instead of the name Didymus the RSV reads "the Twin." *See* Thomas.

DIET. The term applied to the daily allowance of food given by Evil-merodach, king of Babylon, to his royal captive Jehoiachin, king of Judah (Jer 52:34). The same Heb. word *'ărūḥâ* is translated "allowance" in II Kgs 25:30.

DIGNITIES. Persons higher in honor or glory (Gr. pl. of *doxa,* "glory"); probably angels as spiritual beings of preeminent dignity (II Pet 2:10; Jude 8). RSV translated the expression "the glorious ones."

DIKLAH (dĭk'lȧ). A descendant of Joktan (Gen 10:27; I Chr 1:21), and probably a tribe dwelling around an oasis (Diklah means "palm grove") in Arabia, perhaps at the S end of the Wadi Sirḥan *c.* 250 miles SE of the Dead Sea.

DILEAN (dĭl'ē-ȧn). A town of Judah in the Shephelah or foothills near Lachish (Josh 15:38). Identification not certain.

DILL. *See* Plants.

DIMNAH (dĭm'nȧ). A Levitical town in Zebulun

(Josh 21:35), probably a mistaken transcription for the name Rimmon, as given in I Chr 6:77. Rimmon (*q.v.*) may have been *c.* six miles NNE of Nazareth.

DIMON, WATERS OF (dī'mŏn). A stream E of the Dead Sea in the land of Moab (Isa 15:9), possibly the Arnon (Isa 16:2; Num 21:13, 26). The Vulg. and the famous Dead Sea Scroll (IQIsaa) read Dibon for Dimon. Jerome states that the two names were used interchangeably in his time. Some scholars think Isaiah purposely used the name Dimon to furnish a play on the sound of the Heb. word *dām,* "blood," in his line "the waters of Dimon shall be full of blood." RSV emends to Dibon.

DIMONAH (dĭ-mō'nȧ). A town in the Negeb of Judah, near Edom (Josh 15:22), not identified. It may be the same as the Dibon of Neh 11:25.

DINAH (dī'nȧ). The daughter of Jacob and his wife Leah (Gen 30:21). While going unescorted to visit with Canaanite girl friends she was raped by Shechem, son of Hamor the Hivite (Gen 34:2). Later the attacker wanted to take her in honorable marriage, and to this her brothers agreed, provided the Hivites would submit to circumcision. The stipulation was agreed upon and carried out; but despite the agreement, Dinah's two full brothers, Simeon and Levi, made a bloody attack upon the Hivite town and killed all the males, including Hamor and Shechem (Gen 34:1-29).

Jacob considered this treacherous act as unwarranted (Gen 34:30) and denounced it with horror just before he died (Gen 49:5-7). Because of this massacre the land fell to Jacob as the head of the tribe. At his death he bequeathed the land to Joseph (Gen 48:22).

DINAITES (dī'nȧ-īts). A name found in the KJV of Ezr 4:9, formerly understood as that of a people brought as colonists by Ashurbanipal (Asnapper) to Samaria. The word, however, is an official Aramaic title meaning "the judges" (so RSV, Jerusalem Bible, etc.), as the 5th cen. B.C. Elephantine papyri have shown.

DINE, DINNER. *See* Food: Banquet.

DINHABAH (dĭn'hȧ-bȧ). A city of Bela, king of Edom (Gen 36:32; I Chr 1:43). Location is uncertain.

DIONYSIUS THE AREOPAGITE (dī-ō-nĭsh'ŭs, ăr-ē-op'ȧ-gīt). An Athenian confessing Christ under Paul (Acts 17:34). As "the Areopagite" he was a prominent citizen, being one of the 12 judges forming the highest council. *See* Areopagus.

Tradition from another Dionysius, the bishop of Corinth in A.D. 171, through Eusebius and the Apostolic Constitutions, declares the Areopagite to be the first bishop of Athens, later suffering martyrdom under Domitian. Mistaken tradition also declares that he migrated to Rome, was sent to Paris, and is to be identified with the patron saint of France, Saint Denys (IDB). A considerable body of Neoplatonic literature bearing his name is forgery.

DIOTREPHES (dĭ-ŏt'rĕ-fēz). Mentioned only in III Jn 9-10, as one "who loves to be the first among them" (NASB), and who opposed the authority of the apostle John. Concerning those who did not agree with Diotrephes, it is said that he "cast them out of the church"—an early "excommunicator"!

DISCERNING OF SPIRITS. One of the gifts of the Spirit (I Cor 12:8-10; Eph 4:7-11). The discernment was as to whether or not one who prophesied, spoke in tongues, performed miracles, etc., was doing so by the Holy Spirit. The Gr. word *diakrisis* ("distinguishing," "discerning," "judging") is used only in two other places in the NT: in Heb 5:14, "to discern both good and evil," and Rom 14:1, "Now accept the one who is weak in faith, but not for the purpose of passing judgment on his opinion" (NASB). NT usage indicates that the meaning of I Cor 12:10 is an ability to judge as to whether one spoke or acted by the Holy Spirit or by a false spirit. *See* Gifts, Spiritual.

DISCIPLE. The Gr. word *mathētēs* for disciple used nearly 270 times in the Gospels and Acts denotes a pupil who submits to processes of learning under a teacher. The Gr. has entered the English language in the term mathematics, which means literally, "disposed to learn." In Attic prose, notably in Plato, it alludes to the students trained by a philosopher or rhetorician. The concept prevailed in the OT with "sons of the prophets," understudies of Samuel, Elijah, and Elisha, and later, Paul, "brought up at the feet of Gamaliel." In the NT, the term is used of the disciples of John the Baptist (Mt 9:14), the Pharisees (Mk 2:18), and Moses, indicating latter day adherents of his teachings (Jn 9:28).

In the epistles the term *mimētēs,* "follower," "imitator," occurs in exhortations to pattern one's life after God (Eph 5:1), the writer as an apostle (I Cor 4:16; 11:1; Phil 3:17; II Thess 3:7, 9), and other believers (Heb 6:12; 13:7). *See* Example.

In a broad sense, Jesus used "disciple" as descriptive of all His followers coming under the influence of His teaching, striving to conform to His principles. Luke refers to "the whole multitude of the disciples" (19:37). In Acts 6:2 he states that the Twelve summoned the multitude of the disciples. Jesus said, "If ye continue in my word, then are ye my disciples indeed" (Jn 8:31). Jesus' disciples then and ever are those who respond to His invitation, "Learn of me" (Mt 11:29).

In a restricted sense, disciple (also apostle) applies to the inner circle of the Twelve, called out of the greater company that they might be with Christ, hear Him expound the mysteries of the kingdom reserved for a select group, witness and later perform authenticating signs and wonders, and proclaim the gospel to the world.

The Twelve were as follows: Simon Peter, Andrew, James of Zebedee, John, Philip, Nathanael (also known as Bartholomew), Thomas, Matthew (called Levi), James of Alphaeus, Simon the Zealot or Canaanite, Judas the brother of James and sometimes called Thaddaeus, and Judas Iscariot.

Although lacking in higher education, as Hebrews they had a thorough grounding in the doctrines and history of their faith. Their obtuseness tried but never exhausted the patience of Jesus, who is no less forbearing with our limitations in His service. Their very dullness of comprehension constitutes an apologetic for the historical validity of what the Gospels relate concerning Jesus. Dr. A. B. Bruce said: "They were slow-minded persons, very honest but very unapt to take in new ideas. . . .We know that nothing but facts could make such men believe that which nowadays they get credit for inventing."

Bibliography. G. Kittel, "*Akolutheō*," TDNT, I, 210-216. K. H. Rengstorf, *"Manthanō,* etc.," TDNT, IV, 390-461.

G. H. T.

DISEASES. It is difficult to discuss the diseases mentioned in the Bible with any degree of certainty. One reason for this is that diseases are named according to symptoms and not pathological processes. Thus palsy (paralysis) could be caused by polio, trauma, hysteria, or a number of other diseases. It is not at all certain that the consumption of Lev 26:16 and Deut 28:22 was tuberculosis. Secondly, references to sickness are almost always incidental in the narrative. They are recorded more for their historical than for their medical significance. Finally, we are not sure which diseases existed in OT times (though autopsies on Egyptian mummies have shown evidence of tuberculosis, arteriosclerosis, arthritis, cancer, gallstones, bladder stones, schistosomiasis and smallpox). For an informative survey of medical knowledge and practice in ancient Mesopotamia and Egypt, see A. Dudley Dennison, "Medicine," BW, pp. 368-373.

The Israelites obviously had a working knowledge of anatomy. This is seen in their descriptions of the organs of sacrificed animals. The blood was correctly held to be the vital principle: "The life of the flesh is in the blood" (Lev 17:11). Emotional functions were sometimes assigned to certain organs. The heart, for example, was considered to be the center of the mind and will (Ezk 18:31). The expression "bowels of mercies" (Col 3:12) emphasizes the relationship between *psyche* ("soul") and *soma* ("body"), which has been corroborated in our day by psychosomatic research.

The Heb. words for disease and sickness come from the stems *ḥālâ* ("to be sick" or "weak") and *dawâ* ("to be ill"). These words are often modified by other descriptive phrases such as "sick and at the point of death." Heb. words for healing come from the stems *rāpā'* ("to heal," "stitch together," "repair"), and *ḥāyâ* ("revive," "restore to life"), and *'ārak* ("prolong").

The NT uses such Gr. expressions as *astheneia* ("weakness," "frailty"), *malakia* ("softness," "feebleness"), and *noseō* ("to be sick" or "ailing"). Gr. words for health and healing came from the stems *hygiainō* ("to be healthy" or "sound"), *therapeuō* ("to serve," "attend to," "heal," "cure," "restore to health"), and *iaomai* ("heal," "make whole").

Causes of Disease

Disease is but part of a broader concept—the suffering of man. In the Scriptures suffering is said to be one of the results of sin. God threatened to send disease on Israel if they disobeyed Him (Deut 28:15, 22, 27-28). Although disease was often considered as a direct punishment for disobedience (e.g., the sick man at the pool of Bethesda, Jn 5:14), it could also come from Satan, as it did in the case of Job (Job 2:7). Christ spoke of the crippled woman "whom Satan hath bound" (Lk 13:16). In addition, sickness could sometimes come for man's own good and for God's glory (e.g., Paul's "thorn in the flesh," *q.v.*, and II Cor 12:7-9).

The disciples, looking at disease only as punishment for sin, questioned Jesus about a man born blind. "Who sinned," they asked, "this man or his parents that he should be born blind?" (Jn 9:1-3). Jesus answered, "Neither hath this man sinned, nor his parents; but that the works of God should be made manifest in him."

It may not always be possible to distinguish whether an illness is the result of purely natural causes, an act of God, or the evil design of Satan. Perhaps all three may be active at the same time. Whatever the cause of a Christian's disease, however, he is promised that one day suffering will be removed, when God shall "wipe away every tear" and there will be pain no longer (Rev 21:4).

Physicians and Medicine

There are about a dozen references to physicians in the Bible. The Heb. root is *rāpā'* ("to heal"). Yahweh is referred to as "the Lord your healer" (Ex 15:26, RSV). The first reference to a physician is in Gen 50:2 (though it may be that these Egyptian physicians were only embalmers of the dead). Physicians in biblical times, as now, were called upon to heal sickness and relieve suffering (Job 13:4; Jer 8:22; II Chr 16:12).

Physicians were held in high regard by the Jews. The son of Sirach wrote about 190 B.C.: "Honor a physician according to the need of him with the honors due unto him, for verily the Lord hath created him; for from the most High cometh healing; and from the king he shall receive a gift. The skill of the physician shall lift up his head; and in the sight of great men he shall be admired" (Sir 38:1-3).

Physicians in NT times were trained in one of two ways. Most commonly a man served an apprenticeship with an established physician. He could also go to a type of medical school, usually associated with a pagan temple. The two schools we know most about were the medical schools at Pergamos and Alexandria.

The medicines used in biblical times were rudimentary and in most cases not very effective. Among those mentioned in the Bible were locally applied ointments (Isa 1:6), poultices (Isa 38:21), and balms (Jer 8:22; Gen 37:25). The leaves of certain trees were apparently used for herbs (Ezk 47:12). The mandrake, a member of the potato family, was superstitiously thought to promote fertility (Gen 30:14-16). The citizens of Laodicea are known to have had a medical school and to have prepared a powder or salve for weak eyes (Rev 3:18).

Wine was suggested as a stimulant (Prov 31:6), and was also used as an antiseptic. The good Samaritan bound up his patient's wounds "pouring on them oil and wine" (Lk 10:34). Paul recommended a little wine to relieve Timothy's gastric discomfort (I Tim 5:23). Sour wine mingled with gall and myrrh would have some sedative properties. It was offered to Christ, probably to ease His suffering (Mk 15:23).

Surgical treatment was usually minimal. The only operations mentioned in the Bible are circumcision, castration and the closing of wounds. But the code of Hammurabi regulated the charge of physicians for major operations and eye surgery in Babylonia, as well as for setting a broken bone and healing a sprained tendon (ANET, pp. 175 f.). The Edwin Smith papyrus from Egypt describes 48 surgical cases including such contingencies as accidental injuries and battle wounds.

Was the writer of the third Gospel and the Acts a physician? Internal evidence suggests that he was. He uses a large number of medical words found in Hippocrates, Galen and other medical writings, yet not found in the rest of the NT. He also notes medical particulars, such as the intensity of a fever, whether a disease was congenital or acquired, and which side of the body was affected (Lk 4:38; Acts 3:2; Lk 6:6). In writing about the woman with the issue of blood (Lk 8:43), he honestly states that she could not be healed by the physicians; but he is more polite to his profession than Mark who adds that she had "suffered many things of many physicians, and had spent all that she had, and was nothing bettered, but rather grew worse" (Mk 5:26). These factors tend to corroborate the other evidence that Luke "the beloved physician" (Col 4:14) was the author of the third Gospel and Acts.

Mosaic Health Laws

The law given by God to Moses contained remarkable rules pertaining to public health. Although the primary purpose of these regulations was to render a man ceremonially clean, hygienic cleanliness nonetheless was involved. What are the primary concerns of a public health officer today? Water and food contamination, sewage disposal, infectious diseases, health education—these are all dealt with in the Mosaic health laws.

It has been said that some of the health laws were too strict and perhaps unnecessary for public health, but it must be remembered that ancient man did not have our understanding of disease. To be overly strict for the sake of simplicity is better than to err in the other direction. We with our medical ability to distinguish between the dangerous and the harmless would not need to observe some of these same precautions, but this would not be true in their day. Again, it must be remembered that the initial reason for these ordinances was ceremonial purity.

The Mosaic health laws (Lev 11-15) include rules of circumcision, meat consumption, parturition, skin infections, contamination by secretions and excretions, disposal of the dead, personal cleanliness, and sexual relations.

Miracles of Healing

A number of healing miracles are recorded in the Bible. Other miracles, while not of healing but of judgment, are medical in nature. These include the plagues on Egypt (Ex 9:13-15; 12:12-13), the slaying of the Philistines before the ark (I Sam 5:6), the decimation of Sennacherib's army (II Kgs 19:35), Jeroboam's withered hand (I Kgs 13:1-6), and Gehazi's leprosy (II Kgs 5:27). Though God may have used natural disease processes, the supernatural is involved in their timing.

Miracles in the OT seem to center around the time of the Exodus and the ministry of Elijah and Elisha. Those recorded are more frequently miracles of nature, with less than a dozen involving healing (e.g., Abimelech, Gen 20:17; Miriam, Num 12:10-15; the brazen serpent, Num 21:5-9; the widow's son, I Kgs 17:17-24; the Shunammite's son, II Kgs 4:18-37; Naaman, II Kgs 5:1-14; Hezekiah, II Kgs 20:1-7).

On the other hand, the NT records a greater proportion of healing miracles. These were either performed by Christ or in His name. Of the 35 miracles of Christ recorded in the NT, 26 involve healings. In six of these instances demons were expelled. Careful details are given about many of these cases, especially by Luke the physician. Some of the people are even identified by name (Bartimaeus, Jairus' daughter, Mary, Lazarus; also Aeneas, Eutychus, and Publius' father in the Acts).

Some have tried to explain the healing miracles of Christ on a psychological basis. According to this theory the diseases cured were only functional or psychosomatic. It is true that people may have their diseases relieved by "faith" in men or things. But this type of cure is far removed from Christ's cure of such organic diseases as congenital blindness (Jn 9:1), advanced arthritis of the spine (Lk 13:11), metorrhagia or prolonged hemorrhaging (Lk 8:43), leprosy (Lk 5:12; 17:12), and even death (Lk 7:12; 8:49-55; Jn 11:1-44). Only by denying the reliability of the NT documents can all the healings of Christ be made psychological.

In addition to their predominantly organic nature, the healings of Christ were complete and instantaneous (with the exception of the man whose sight returned in two stages, Mk 8:22-25). Furthermore, they consisted of a number of different diseases which are difficult to treat even by today's medical techniques. Few if any were likely to recover spontaneously. And there is no evidence of any relapses occurring after Christ's healings. *See* Healing, Health.

Demon Possession

Demon possession is a phenomenon which seems to have occurred with more frequency at the time of Christ. Of the 26 persons healed by Christ, six are mentioned as having been demon possessed. Many other persons with no apparent physical maladies were set free from demonic oppression (Mt 8:16; Mk 1:34, 39; Lk 6:18). Little if any mention is made of demon possession in the OT. Christ and the NT seem to distinguish between ordinary illnesses and those accompanied by demon possession (Mt 10:8; Mk 1:34; Acts 5:16). Demon possession could be accompanied by physical symptoms (e.g., blindness, deafness and dumbness, Mt 12:22; Mk 9:25), neurological manifestations (e.g., epilepsy, Lk 9:39, 42), or mental symptoms (Lk 4:33; 8:27; Mk 7:25).

The diagnosis of demon possession, however, raises some difficult problems. What distinguished it from natural illness? How could a person recognize it as such? If there are any distinguishing features which typify the condition, they are suicidal tendencies and the demon's use of the person as a mouthpiece.

On the other hand, physical illness is often attributed in the Scriptures to Satan. Christ spoke of the arthritic woman as "this woman whom Satan hath bound" (Lk 13:16). Was she demon possessed? Jesus did not address any demon when He healed her. A. Rendle Short suggests a solution: "It is not that the scribes and Pharisees and common people diagnosed demon possession too often, but that their ideas were too crude, and they failed to recognize that there may have been a very much wider work of the devil" (*The Bible and Modern Medicine*, p. 121).

If this is true, then it may not be possible always to find specific signs to diagnose and distinguish demon possession from other diseases. *See* Demonology.

Skin Diseases

A number of skin lesions are mentioned in the OT. Some of these were to be imposed as afflictions on Israel for disobedience to the Lord (Deut 28:27). The *itch* is probably scabies, still known by that descriptive name. It is caused by an insect, *Acarus scabei*. *Scurvy* (RSV) is not what we know today as scurvy (caused by vitamin C deficiency) but rather a "scab" (KJV). The word comes from a root meaning "to scratch" or "be rough." This possibly covers a range of skin diseases including eczema and psoriasis. The *botch* (KJV) or *boil* (RSV) comes from a root meaning "to be inflamed" or "hot." Boils are common today though better controlled, thanks to modern antibiotics. Hezekiah's boil may have been a carbuncle or possibly anthrax (II Kgs 20:1, 7). Anthrax is contracted from cattle or the dried hides and hair of infected animals. Without treatment it may be fatal.

Leprosy is frequently mentioned in the Bible. Miriam, Naaman, and King Uzziah all contracted this disease. Instructions for its diagnosis are given in Lev 13; it apparently included more than what we today call leprosy (caused by the *Lepra bacillus* of Hansen). Unfortunately, the term leprosy has changed its meaning in the English language. Even in the Middle Ages the word was used to describe a number of different skin disorders such as ringworm. Harold M. Spinka states, "It is my opinion, that leprosy as well as the diseases mentioned in the differential diagnosis, e.g., chronic psoriasis vulgaris, syphilis, pemphigus and dermatitis herpetiformis, smallpox, fungus infections as well as the pyodermas were included under the general label of leprosy" ("Leprosy in Ancient Hebraic Times," JASA, XI [March, 1959], 17-22). That the leprosy of the OT is not identical with the leprosy of today is also demonstrated in the fact that there was a leprosy of houses and garments (Lev 13:47; 14:37)—probably some type of mold or fungus. *See* Leprosy.

Job's affliction has been the subject of much speculation. It is unlikely that he had ordinary boils, as they would not extend from head to foot and would not itch so severely (Job 2:7-8). The description may fit smallpox, which is of sudden onset, extensive, and may itch at one stage. However, a person with smallpox would probably be too ill to talk as Job did. Pellagra, psoriasis, eczema, dermatitis herpetiformis, and exfoliative dermatitis have all been suggested as possibilities. Dermatitis herpetiformis, a rare skin disease, would itch intensely, and would not severely affect Job's general health. Exfoliative dermatitis is generalized, chronic, miserable, very itchy and associated with boils from scratching.

Eye and Ear Diseases

Both congenital and acquired blindness are mentioned in the Bible. Infection with *tra-*

CURRENT CLINICAL DATA OF DISEASES CONSIDERED AS BIBLICAL LEPROSY*

Disease	*Degree of Contagion*	*Causative Agent*
Leprosy	++	Lepra bacillus of Hansen
Syphilis	++++	Treponema pallidum-bacteria
Smallpox	++++	Virus
Scabies	++++	Acarus scabei – a parasite
Favus	+++	Achorion Schoenleini-fungus
Tinea of scalp	++++	Microsporon audoini or lanosum fungus
Deep or systemic fungus infections	+++	e.g., Actinomysosis due to actinomyces bovis or Nocardia
Boils and furuncles	++	Staphlococcus and streptococcus-bacteria
Pemphigus	unknown	Unknown
Dermatitis herpetiformis	unknown	Unknown
Cancer of skin	unknown	Virus?

*Harold M. Spinka, M.D., "Leprosy in Ancient Hebraic Times." Paper presented at the 13th annual convention of the American Scientific Affiliation at Iowa State College; August, 1958. Reprinted from *Journal of American Scientific Affiliation,* March, 1959.

choma is still a common cause of acquired blindness in many parts of the world. This virus causes unsightly discharge and may have been Leah's problem (Gen 29:17). Perhaps her eyes were crossed (*strabismus*). Trachoma could have been Paul's thorn in the flesh (II Cor 12:7–10); his own words suggest some sort of eye trouble (cf. Gal 6:11 with 4:14–15; Acts 23:2–5). Smallpox can also cause an unattractive ulceration and scarring of the cornea, with loss of vision.

Cataracts were probably the cause of Isaac's and Eli's blindness in their old age. This is a progressive opacification of the lens of the eye. In Lev 21:20 the Heb. word for "blemish" (*q.v.*) suggests a spot causing confused sight, probably a cataract.

Ophthalmia neonatorum causes a severe conjunctivitis and blindness in newborn infants. It is usually a result of a gonorrheal infection in the mother. This probably accounted for much of the blindness present from infancy. There are also many types of congenital anomalies of the eye, which could result in total blindness from birth. *See* Blindness.

Deafness was also common in biblical times though its cause is difficult to determine.

Orthopedic Deformities

Orthopedic deformities would have been pathetic in a day when little could be done to correct them. The lame beggar whom Peter healed is such a case (Acts 3:2–8). Since he was lame from birth he may have had a congenital club foot, *spina bifida,* or cerebral palsy. The woman healed by Christ of an 18-year infirmity had a severe form of arthritis which bowed her forward (Lk 13:11–13). This sounds like rheumatoid arthritis, which affects women more than men.

Jacob's limp, acquired by his wrestling with the angel of God, may have been caused by a dislocated hip (Gen 32:25, 31–32). One can walk with a limp on an anterior dislocation. The acute pain and lameness may also indicate a ruptured intervertebral disc producing sciatic pain.

Neurological Diseases

Paralysis was evident in the Jewish population of Jesus' day. It was, no doubt, frequently caused by accidents as well as tuberculosis of the spine and polio. Paralysis is seldom mentioned in the OT.

The paraplegic healed by Christ (Lk 5:18) possibly had an injury or bony lesion of the spine, causing compression of the spinal cord. This would result in paralysis of the lower part of the body. The man healed at the pool of Bethesda (Jn 5:5–8) was only partially paralyzed. A birth injury, polio, multiple sclerosis, or a stroke could have caused this. The man with the withered hand was also partially paralyzed (Lk 6:6–10). His muscle atrophy could have resulted from inability to use his hand. He may have been a victim of injury, polio, or possibly amyotrophic lateral sclerosis, which affects the small muscles of the hand. The medically significant fact is that Christ healed him instantly and completely.

The centurion's servant (Lk 7:2; Mt 8:5) was also paralyzed. However, his condition was acute; he was close to death, and in great pain. This would suggest tetanus or an acute spinal cord compression from tumor, abscess or hemorrhage.

The Shunammite woman's son had a sudden onset of headache (II Kgs 4:18-20). He died within six hours of what may have been sunstroke, meningitis, subarachnoid hemorrhage, or more likely cerebral malaria.

Obstetrics

Sterility or barrenness was a problem affecting couples in biblical times as well as today. Sarah, Rachel, Manoah's wife, Hannah, the Shunammite woman, and Elisabeth all had this malady.

Deliveries in ancient Israel were usually performed with the mother on a birth stool (Ex 1:16) or sitting on the lap of another (Gen 30:3). [In the latter passage the practice referred to may be that of placing the new-born infant on the knees of the one who could give it legitimacy or the right to inheritance. – Ed.] After the baby's birth, the navel was cut, the baby washed in water, salt applied, and the baby wrapped in swaddling cloth (Ezk 16:4). Tamar was skillfully delivered of twins with one of them in a transverse presentation (Gen 38:27-30).

Mental Illness

There are only a few references to mental illness in the OT. David convincingly feigned madness (I Sam 21:12-15); Saul had recurrent depressions and showed paranoid symptoms (I Sam 16:14, 23; 18:8-11, 28-29; 19:9-10). Nebuchadnezzar had psychotic symptoms, living like an animal for seven years. R. K. Harrison classifies his illness as lycanthropy or boanthropy, a specific form of paranoia (IOT, pp. 1114-1117).

The writer of Prov 17:22 relates the emotions to the body, and thus anticipated psychosomatic medicine when he wrote, "A cheerful heart is a good medicine, but a downcast spirit dries up the bones" (RSV).

The relationship between mental illness and demon possession is uncertain and controversial. The "wild" man of Gadara (Mk 5:2-5) resembles what we would today classify as psychotic, although the other "demoniacs" healed by Christ had organic symptoms of physical illnesses.

Internal Diseases

High fever is a symptom rather than a disease. It could refer to malaria, typhoid, paratyphoid, smallpox, sunstroke, typhus, or a number of other diseases (Lev 26:16; Deut 28:22; Lk 4:38).

The *pestilence* sent by God upon the Philistines (I Sam 5:6, 9-12; 6:5) was probably bubonic plague. This disease was described by Hippocrates 400 years before Christ. It swept across Europe in the Middle Ages and has the characteristics of heavy mortality, sudden incidence, transmission by dead rodents, and the presence of enlarged inguinal glands (in the groin). It is interesting to note that the Philistines placed five golden images of the tumors and mice beside the ark. [Some have suggested that the "tumors" were hemorrhoids, following the KJV "emerods." – Ed.]

Another pestilence was used by God to destroy the army of Sennacherib (II Kgs 19:35). There are two diseases which could kill a large number of people within 24 hours – cholera and pneumonic plague. There would probably have been a few cases in the camp before the peak of the epidemic.

Giantism is caused by an endocrine disorder. Goliath is a familiar example and possibly had an anterior pituitary tumor. Og, king of Bashan, needed a bed about 13 feet long (Deut 3:11). A giant with 12 fingers and toes is described in II Sam 21:20.

Dropsy is caused by fluid in the tissues. It is symptomatic of certain diseases, the most common being heart failure. The man whom Christ healed with this condition may have been suffering with cancer, heart, liver or kidney disease (Lk 14:2).

Dysentery was the disease which caused the debilitating fever of Publius' father (Acts 28:8, NASB). In fulminating cases of bacillary dysentery there is evacuation of blood and mucous (hence the KJV "bloody flux"), and death may come quickly.

Medical science throws light on a number of *deaths* described in the Bible. King Asa died with a great disease of his feet (II Chr 16:12-14). His coffin was filled with perfumes. This suggests a gangrene of the feet which would have caused a foul odor. Gangrene (KJV "canker") was recognized as a decaying disease which eats away tissue in a part of the body, usually a limb (II Tim 2:17). It may be caused by injury or failure of the blood supply.

King Jehoram was stricken with an incurable disease which caused a prolapse of the rectum (II Chr 21:18-19). This may have been a severe amoebic dysentery or cancer of the rectum.

Nabal was probably a chronic alcoholic. Following an episode of acute alcoholism he apparently had a cerebrovascular incident (stroke). He was comatose for ten days and died without regaining consciousness (I Sam 25:36-38).

Ananias and Sapphira both died suddenly and without warning (Acts 5:1-10). They may have been struck with a coronary thrombosis.

Herod Agrippa was consumed by intestinal worms (Acts 12:23). He probably had an intestinal obstruction from parasitic round worms and may have died from a perforated bowel and its resulting peritonitis.

Sufferings and Death of Christ

Strong Christian tradition states that Jesus' sweat fell to the ground like great drops of blood as the result of His anguish in Gethsemane (Lk 22:44). This may have been the rare emitting of blood through the transpiratory glands. But verses 43 and 44 are doubted to have been written by Luke, according to the best MS evidence (*see* Bloody Sweat).

Over 100 years ago it was suggested by Stroud that Christ died of cardiac rupture (i.e., a broken heart). This has become a commonly held view, but it is quite unlikely. Cardiac rupture, apart from trauma, is rare and when it occurs affects those whose hearts are already seriously damaged. That Christ's heart was diseased is improbable in the light of His previous energetic activity and perfect physical condition to fulfill the sacrificial requirements (I Pet 1:19).

It has also been suggested that Christ died of asphyxia from impairment of respiration while on the cross. Prolonged upright positioning could also lead to venous pooling and to peripheral circulatory failure. The decrease in cardiac output and the resultant decrease in blood flow to the tissues would cause a lowered oxygen level in the brain.

Also compatible with both biblical history and medical probability is acute dilitation of the stomach. This is seen today as a rare and poorly understood post-operative complication. It may also follow a state of shock. The spear thrust would have released the accumulated watery fluid in the dilated stomach of our Lord. The blood probably came from the pierced heart and great vessels. Following this there would have been no question of death.

Whatever the immediate cause of His death, the importance of the crucifixion lies in the meaning of Christ's death. With Isaiah we can say, "He was wounded for our transgressions, he was bruised for our iniquities: the chastisement of our peace was upon him; and with his stripes we are healed" (Isa 53:5).

Bibliography. Charles J. Brim, M.D., "Job's Illness—Pellagra," *Archives of Dermatology and Syphilology,* XLV (Feb., 1942), 371-376. A. Dudley Dennison, "Medicine," BW, pp. 368-373. Roland K. Harrison, "Disease," IDB, I, 847-854; "Medicine," IDB, III, 331-334; *Introduction to the Old Testament,* Grand Rapids: Eerdmans, 1969, pp. 607-610 (on leprosy). Louis A. M. Krause, "Biblical Medical References," *Transactions of the New Jersey Obstetrical and Gynecological Society,* I (1956), 42-50. S. I. McMillen, *None of These Diseases,* Spire Book, Old Tappan, N.J.: Revell, 1967. "Medicine, Disease, Health," CornPBE, pp. 516-520. Albrecht Oepke, "*Iaomai,* etc.," TDNT, III, 194-215. A. Rendle Short, *The Bible and Modern Medicine,* Chicago: Moody Press, 1967. C. Raimer Smith, *A Physician Examines the Bible,* New York: Philosophical Library, 1950. Jacob Taub, M.D., F.C.A.P., "Endocrinology in the Bible," presented at the third World Assembly of the Israel Medical Assn., Jerusalem, August 16, 1955. J. V. Kinnier Wilson, "Gleanings from the Iraq Medical Journals," JNES, XXVII (1968), 243-247 (for a comparison of ancient and modern diseases). Nellie B. Woods, *The Healings of the Bible,* New York: Hawthorne Books, 1958.

C. W. C.

DISH

1. The "lordly dish" (Jud 5:25, KJV) represents the Heb. *sēpel 'addîrîm,* lit., "a bowl of nobles." Possibly in the time of the judges this was a handsome Cypriote milk bowl with "wishbone" handle. Or Jael's dish, her one prized possession, may have been a large bronze bowl, since Heb. *sēpel* is cognate to Ugaritic *spl,* a huge metal vessel (C. H. Gordon, *Ugaritic Manual,* 1955, p. 301), and to Akkad. *saplu,* a golden bowl or basin given by Jehu as tribute to Shalmanezer III (ANEP, #351-355). Gideon obtained enough dew to fill a bowl (*sēpel*) when he wrung his fleece (Jud 6:38). Among the Arabs today the word *sifl* denotes a large earthenware washbasin (Millar Burrows, *What Mean These Stones?* ASOR, 1941, p. 255). For the view that Jael's "dish" was a bulging skin milk churn see J. Kaplan, "Skin Bottles and Pottery Imitations," PEQ, July-Dec., 1965, pp. 144-149.

2. Heb. *sallahat* (II Kgs 21:13) is likely the popular ring-burnished bowl of Iron II Age. Since it had no handles to hang it up, it was turned over to dry.

3. Heb. *qeʿārâ* (Ex 25:29; 37:16; Num 4:7) was a gold dish or platter holding the bread of the Presence on the table in the tabernacle. The word is translated "charger" or "plate" (RSV) 14 times in Num 7.

4. In connection with the Last Supper, Gr. *trublion* refers to a large, deep dish or bowl, either of metal or perhaps of Roman style *sigillata* pottery, from which all could take food together (Mt 26:23; Mk 14:20). *See* Bowl; Pottery.

J. R.

DISHAN (dī'shăn). A Horite, the seventh and last son of Seir, who possessed mountains S of the Dead Sea. Dishan became a "duke" or "chief" (Heb. *'allûp*), i.e., "thousand"-leader (Gen 36:21, 30; I Chr 1:38). The name probably also designates a Horite clan.

Heb. *dîshān* has been compared with the Hurrian name Tai-sheni. *See* Horite. God enabled the descendants of Esau, i.e., Edom, to dispossess the Horites (Deut 2:12, 22).

DISHON (dī'shŏn). The name of two descendants of Seir, the Horite. The Heb. *dishôn* can mean "antelope," "mountain goat" (cf. Deut 14:5), but perhaps it is derived from the Hurrian name Tai-sheni.

1. Seir's fifth son, and head of one of the original Edomite tribes (Gen 36:21,30; I Chr 1:38).

2. Seir's grandson, the only son of Anah, and brother of Aholibamah, Esau's second wife (Gen 36:25; I Chr 1:41).

DISPENSATION. The Gr. word *oikonomia* means stewardship, management of a household, an economy or a dispensation. The greatest interest and importance centers around the last meaning.

While the term "dispensation" is used by all theologians to express God's method of dealing with men during different eras of biblical revelation before and since the Fall of man, great differences exist as to the correct meaning of the term. Dr. L. S. Chafer writes: "A dispensation is a specific, divine economy, a commitment from God to man of a responsibility to discharge that which God has appointed him" (*Systematic Theology,* VII, 122). The Scofield Bible states: "A dispensation is a period of time during which man is tested in respect to his obedience to some specific revelation of the will of God" (p. 5). Scofield also says, "Each of the dispensations may be regarded as a new test of the natural man and each ends in judgment" (*Rightly Dividing the Word of Truth,* p. 20).

Applying the above definitions, many dispensational theologians come to the conclusion that there are seven dispensations, namely: (1) Innocence—up to the Fall; (2) Conscience—from the Fall to Noah; (3) Human Government—from Noah to Abraham (Gen 8:20—9:27); (4) Promise—from Abraham to Moses (Gen 12:1—Ex 19:8); (5) Law—from Moses to Christ (Ex 20:1—31:18); (6) Grace—from the death of Christ until His second coming (Rom 3:24-26; cf. Eph 3:1-10); (7) Kingdom—the millennial reign of Christ on earth (Rev 20:4 ff.; cf. II Sam 7:8-17; Lk 1:31-33).

Reformed theologians in general reject both a dispensation of conscience and of human government, since conscience has been present always in man (Rom 2:15), and the command to subdue the earth was already given at creation (Gen 1:28). They teach from two to five dispensations: (1) two, namely, OT and NT (L. Berkhof); (2) three: OT, NT and kingdom (some premillennial Reformed theologians); (3) four: Adam to Abraham, Abraham to Moses, Moses to Christ, and the gospel dispensation (Charles Hodge); (4) five, namely, Hodge's four plus the millennial kingdom (some premillennial covenant theologians).

Reformed theologians in general are dissatisfied with Chafer and Scofield because they teach man has been under probation in each dispensation since the Fall, and that he could have met the specific test of any of the dispensational eras, and then the series would have ended. If so, the Reformed theologians reason, salvation was possible for man without the cross, and Christ therefore did not have to die. However, it must be realized that there are many who base their theology on a study of dispensations but reject the definition given by Scofield and Chafer. These groups may include the greater part of the evangelicals.

While the Reformed theologians differ in their opinions as to the number of the dispensations, they agree in asserting that only one plan of salvation has existed through all dispensations since the Fall of man. The divisions made—such as two by Berkhof and four by Hodge—are dependent on the detail into which each wants to carry his study of God's administration of salvation in the OT, rather than any disagreement in principle, and the question whether stress is placed upon dispensations or covenants or whether there is a balanced presentation of both.

It proves difficult to build a theology upon the biblical use of the Gr. word *oikonomia* since it is used in the sense of stewardship in nearly every case in the NT (Lk 16:2-4; I Cor 9:17; Eph 3:2; Col 1:25), except in Eph 1:10 where Paul speaks of God gathering all things into one "in the dispensation of the fullness of time." Nevertheless, great profit can come from a study of the increasing revelation of God's covenant of grace—namely, salvation by grace through faith—in the different eras or dispensations of OT and NT.

A study of the plan of salvation under each dispensation adds facets concerning soteriology which no fully developed system can afford to neglect.

See Covenant.

Bibliography. Louis Berkhof, *Systematic Theology,* Grand Rapids: Eerdmans, 1949, pp. 290-301. Lewis S. Chafer, *Systematic Theology,* Dallas: Dallas Sem. Press, 1948, IV, 16-21; VII, 121-123. Charles Hodge, *Systematic Theology,* Grand Rapids: Eerdmans, II (1952), 371-377. Charles C. Ryrie, *Dispensationalism Today,* Chicago: Moody Press, 1965.

R. A. K.

DISPERSION OF ISRAEL. From the time God gave Palestine to Abraham and his descendants as a permanent possession (Gen 13:14-17), the status of the nation Israel has been determined by its relation to that land. Those in the land were in the place of blessing. Those out of the land were "the captivity" (*gôlâ,* Ezr 1:11; 2:1), or the "dispersion" (*diaspora,* Jn 7:35). The former spoke of their relation to Palestine, and the latter of their relation to the peoples among whom they went. James (1:1, RSV) and Peter (I Pet 1:1, RSV) wrote to the converts among the Jews of the Dispersion.

The first absence of the nation from the land was predicted in Gen 15:13, where the Lord informed Abraham of the destiny of his descendants. A promise of restoration immediately followed (Gen 15:14). This prophecy was fulfilled in the Egyptian sojourn of the nation.

At the time of the return from the Egyptian bondage, God revealed to Moses, and through him to the nation, that dispersion would be His method of chastening them for disobedience and apostasy. This is clearly stated in Deut 28:15, 25; 30:1-4. Thus the nation was forewarned that unbelief and disobedience would be judged by expulsion from the land of promise. The prophets sent to both the northern and southern kingdoms warned of such an expulsion (Hos 9:3; Jer 8:3; Ezk 4:13) and stated clearly the cause for such a judgment (Jer 16:11-15), namely, that the nation had followed and served other gods and had forsaken the true God and refused to obey His law.

The northern kingdom (Israel) was carried into captivity by the king of Assyria, who relocated the deportees in Halah and in Habor by the river of Gozan and in the cities of the Medes (II Kgs 17:6). This deportation began in 722 B.C. when the Assyrians conquered Samaria. The indictment against Israel, listing the causes of the Exile, is given in II Kgs 17:7-20. In spite of the warnings by the prophets to the kingdom of Judah in the light of what happened to her N neighbor, the southern kingdom continued in unbelief and apostasy, and in 586 B.C. was carried captive to Babylon by Nebuchadnezzar (II Kgs 24:14; 25:6, 11). The reason for this dispersion is clearly stated to have been her rejection of the warning of the prophets and her continuance in idolatry (II Chr 36:13-16).

Other lesser deportations and relocations of Jews followed (*see* Elephantine papyri). Ptolemy I of Egypt (322-285 B.C.), at the time of his invasion of Palestine and capture of Jerusalem, transported many Jews to Alexandria, which subsequently became an important Jewish center. Antiochus of Syria (223 - 187 B.C.) transported about 2,000 families from Babylon, according to Josephus, and relocated them in Phrygia and Lydia (cf. the localities in I Pet 1:1). Pompey, after capturing Jerusalem in 63 B.C., carried many Jews to Rome to be sold as slaves. The latter, however, regained freedom and civil rights. After the destruction of Jerusalem in A.D. 70 by Titus, there was a further scattering.

In addition to these involuntary deportations, many Jews left Palestine voluntarily in pursuit of commercial interests. This took them to the important economic centers of the world, and most large cities had a Jewish settlement. Thus, it is not surprising to read in Acts 2:9-12 that Jews came to Jerusalem for the Feast of Pentecost from all over the known world. Although the deportees adjusted in language and culture to the society in which they settled, they maintained ties with Palestine and Judaism by pilgrimages to the three annual feasts, by the payment of the half-shekel temple tax as long as the temple stood, and by submission to the decrees of the Sanhedrin as long as it functioned.

During the 1st cen. of the Christian era it is estimated that a million Jews resided in Mesopotamia, another million in Antioch-on-the-Orontes and throughout present day Turkey, a million in Egypt centering around Alexandria, a hundred thousand each in Italy and N Africa, and two and one-half million in Palestine. Philo Judaeus (20 B.C.-A.D. 40) listed dozens of countries where Jews were scattered (*Legatio Ad Caium* 36).

While in dispersion the Jews settled down, frequently in comfortable surroundings (Jer 29:4-7), and made themselves an invaluable part of the business community. Circumstances were so pleasant in Babylon that, when permission was granted the Jews to return to Jerusalem to rebuild the temple, only a small remnant desired to undertake the rigors of the work. From the time of the Babylonian Captivity the number of Jews outside Palestine greatly outnumbered those in the land.

Another feature of the dispersion must not be overlooked. While the scattering was a judgment on Israel and Judah for unbelief and apostasy, yet it was meant for the blessing of the Gentiles. According to Ex 19:6 the nation was set apart by God to be a kingdom of priests, that is, they were to mediate between God and the Gentiles. They were to disseminate the revelation of the true God entrusted to them. The blessing of God on Abraham's seed was to be for all men (Gen 12:3). Yet the nation did not fulfill the responsibility entrusted to it. The law, which hedged Israel in from the Gentiles, was used to hide the truth God had revealed to Israel for the Gentiles. However, through the dispersion, the knowledge of God was brought, involuntarily, to the nations. A worldwide expectation of a Messiah-Redeemer was aroused as the dispersion brought a knowledge of God's promises to the Gentiles. Writers such as Tacitus, Suetonius, and Virgil anticipated a Blesser who would appear in Judea. Without doubt the Magi came to Judea to seek the King of the Jews because of the star and also knowledge gained from the dispersed nation (Mt 2:1-12).

The dispersion of Israel also had its effects on the preaching of the gospel in the NT era. The apostle Paul, in spreading the gospel through the Roman world, always began a ministry in a new city in the synagogue of the Jews, for he felt obligated "to the Jew first," to announce the fact that Israel's Messiah had come. The dispersed Jews were the first in any community to hear the gospel. Only after their rejection of his message did Paul turn to the Gentiles (as in Acts 18:6).

In Mt 12:31-37 Christ warned the nation of the dire results of following the leaders in their rejection of Him as Messiah, and concluded with a warning of judgment (Mt 12:41-45). He prophesied further dispersion for the nation by predicting the coming desolation of Jerusalem (Mt 23:37-39), which was fulfilled in A.D. 70, and promising that the city would be occupied by Gentiles until the second advent (Lk 21:24). In the Olivet Discourse Christ graphically prophesied a yet future overthrow of Jerusalem (Mt 24:15-21). This is only a reaffirmation of the prophecy of Zech 13:8-14:2, where the prophet foretold of an invasion during the Tribulation period in which Jerusalem would be destroyed and many of the inhabitants killed or scattered.

This eschatological dispersion is God's final chastisement of the nation before the Millennium. At the beginning of the Tribulation the head of the Roman Empire will make a covenant with the nation Israel, guaranteeing safety in the land of Palestine (Dan 9:27). The nation will occupy the land, trusting this political alliance to defend it. It will go even further and acknowledge that this ruler is its Messiah and God, and will worship him (Rev 13:11-18). God will cause the Gentile nations to come against Jerusalem to destroy it and to scatter the inhabitants, as He punished Israel previously in chastisement for its apostasy.

The predictions of dispersion contain also a promise of restoration to the land. It was in keeping with the promise of Deut 30:3-5 that the nation returned from the Babylonian dispersion. It is in fulfillment of such a promise as Deut 30:1-10 and that found in Amos 9:14-15 that Israel will be restored at the second advent of Christ and resettled in its land. Ultimately the answer to Israel's dispersion is its complete conversion (Isa 66:6-9; Jer 31:31-34) and restoration to Palestine under its Messiah (Isa 54:1-17; 60:1-6; 62:1-12) at the second coming of Christ.

Bibliography. Karl L. Schmidt, *"Diaspora,"* TDNT, II, 98-104. Merrill C. Tenney, *New Testament Times*, Grand Rapids: Eerdmans, 1965, pp. 88-91, 182 f. A. F. Walls, "Dispersion," NBD, pp. 318 ff.

J. D. P.

DISPERSION OF MANKIND. By means of confusing the speech of the people at Babel, God scattered mankind over the entire earth (Gen 11:5-9). Thus the posterity of Noah was divided (from Heb. *pālag,* Gen 10:25; Heb. *pārad,* 10:32) after the Flood. This dispersal occurred in the days of Peleg, probably within two or three centuries following the Noahic deluge (cf. Gen 10:25 with 11:10-19). Historically, the event must have occurred prior to the migration of peoples to the W Hemisphere, and to the founding of neolithic villages in the Middle East and of such early cities as Jericho in Palestine, Jarmo in Mesopotamia, and Catal Hüyük in Anatolia (all dated archaeologically before 6000 B.C.), for these sites furnish no evidence of disturbance by flood waters.

It is conceivable that much cultural knowledge was lost to mankind as a result of the confusion of languages, since one man could no longer communicate the knowledge of his particular skill to another. Thus many arts and crafts—agriculture, metallurgy, music (cf. Gen 4:20-22), perhaps even writing—died out, only to be rediscovered by laborious process much later after perhaps millennia of dark ages and primitive existence.

Gen 10 and 11 present a list of the principal descendants of Noah who might likely be known to the Israelites, including an account of the event which precipitated the division into many nations. The main criteria for classifying the subdivisions of mankind in this so-called Table of Nations were geographical ("in their lands"), linguistic ("after his tongue"), and political ("in their nations," Gen 10:5, 20,31). The basis was essentially ethno-geographic, however, because language can change completely as a result of conquest or migration.

Assuming Mosaic authorship for these chapters, one can more readily understand that the list of 70-odd ethnic groups mentioned in Gen 10 was compiled from the knowledge available to one educated in the courts of Egypt in the middle of the 2nd mil. B.C. Egypt had widespread diplomatic and trade contacts at that time with Libya, Cyprus, Cilicia, Crete, up and down the Red Sea, and with the Hittites in Anatolia and the Kassites in Babylonia. As a result of the conquests of Thutmose III she controlled Nubia and large areas of Canaan and Syria. This may help to explain why the Philistines are grouped under Mizraim (Egypt, Gen 10:13-14) and Canaan comes under Ham, although all evidence proves the Canaanites spoke a Semitic language from 2000 B.C. onward. The table definitely reflects a time before 1200 B.C., for Gaza is said to belong to the Canaanites (Gen 10:19), not to the Philistines. The brown, yellow, and red races are not mentioned, probably because these had no contact with Egypt nor with the Israelites in those days. *See* Gentiles; Nations.

Bibliography. Gleason L. Archer, SOTI, pp. 201-203. T. C. Mitchell, "Nations, Table of," NBD, pp. 865-869. E. A. Speiser, "Man, Ethnic Divisions of," IDB, III, 235-242. Merrill F. Unger, *Archaeology and the OT,* Zondervan, 1954, pp. 73-104.

J. R.

DISTAFF. In the process of spinning, the spindle-and-whorl (Heb. *pelek;* cf. Akkad. *pilakku*) which winds up the twisted fibers (Prov 31:19*b*). It is manipulated by back-and-forth action of the palms. The Heb. word also occurs in II Sam 3:29 as "staff" (KJV; "one who holds a spindle," RSV), condemning the male descendants of Joab to the feminine task of spinning. In Prov 31:19*a* the term "spindle" (RSV, "distaff") refers to the stick, or to the spinning bowl noted in Egyptian tomb models, either of which was used to hold the loose fibers. *See* Spin; Spindle.

DIVERS. In the KJV an archaic English word generally meaning either "several," "many" (e.g., Heb 1:1) or "diverse," "different in kind" (e.g., Deut 22:9), the rendering of several Heb. and Gr. words.

The Israelites, probably to avoid idolatrous practices of the Canaanites, were forbidden to bring together different kinds of materials, animals, or products, such as: (1) weaving garments of two kinds of material, particularly of wool and linen; (2) sowing a field with mixed seed; (3) yoking an ox and an ass together; (4) breeding together animals of different species, e.g., an ass and a horse to procure mules (Lev 19:19; Deut 22:9-11).

DIVINATION. The attempt to discern future events by such means as trances, visions, etc., or physical objects. These were varied: (1) rhabdomancy, the throwing of sticks or arrows into the air (Ezk 21:21; cf. Hos 4:12); (2) hepatoscopy, examination of the liver or other organs of an animal (Ezk 21:21); (3) teraphim, images used for divination (I Sam 15:23; Ezk 21:21; Zech 10:2); (4) necromancy, communication with the dead (Deut 18:11; I Sam 28:8; II Kgs 21:6) which was condemned in the law (Lev 19:31; 20:6) and the prophets (Isa 8:19-20); (5) astrology, reading the stars and coming to conclusions on the basis of their positions and relations to each other, which was pronounced vain in Isa 47:13 and Jer 10:2; (6) hydromancy, divination with water, done either by noting the reflections, or inducing a trance by this means. In order to confuse his brethren, Joseph had his servants suggest the goblet found in their sacks was for that purpose (Gen 44:5, 15); no approval of such a practice is implied. God sternly condemns all means of seeking hidden knowledge and knowledge of the future apart from His divine revelation.

To be distinguished from divination are the use of the lot, dreams, and signs. In the OT God used the casting of the lot for certain purposes, such as the allocation of territory for the ten tribes (Josh 18:10), the choice of the goat to be sacrificed on the Day of Atonement (Lev 16), the choice of a guilty person (Josh 7:14; Jon 1:7), the assignment of temple service (I Chr 24:5), and once in the NT for the choice of a successor to Judas' lost apostleship (Acts 1:15-26). It is significant that the use of the lot ceased with Pentecost. *See also* Urim and Thummim.

Dreams were a means used of God also for revelation, though it is significant that we read of no one specifically asking for guidance in that manner (e.g., Joseph's dreams, Gen 37:5-11; Nebuchadnezzar's dream, Dan 2; the dreams of Joseph, Mary's husband, Mt 1:20; 2:19).

In several instances OT believers asked God for a sign to guide them, such as when Gideon put out his fleece (Jud 6:37-40) and Jonathan took the particular reply of the enemy as his guidance from God (I Sam 14:8-10). In the use of the lot, it was commanded of God only for decisions which required more than human wisdom. In the case of dreams, it was God's way of giving a divine revelation only for the most extreme emergencies.

See Demonology; Enchantment; Familiar Spirit; Hepatoscopy; Liver; Magic; Necromancer; Teraphim; Witchcraft.

Bibliography. Yehezkel Kaufmann, *The Religion of Israel,* trans. by Moshe Greenberg, Chicago: Univ. of Chicago Press, 1960, pp. 42-53, 87-93.

R. A. K.

DIVINE HEALING. *See* Healing, Health.

DIVORCE. *In the OT.* In Deut 24:1-4 Moses permitted divorce of a husband from his wife if the husband found *'erwat dābār,* "some uncleanness" in her (lit., "a case of nakedness," or "nakedness of a thing"). The nature of such an accusation was so general that it led to two interpretations at the time of Christ: a narrower one taught by the school of Shammai, which confined it to unfaithfulness; and a broader view, taught by the school of Hillel, which extended it to include anything that might displease the husband. The requirement that a man give his wife a bill of divorcement gave the act a legal and official status, since it needed the aid of at least a Levite to execute it properly. The further rule forbidding him to take his wife back after she had married another showed the gravity of the act (Deut 24:4).

There were several circumstances, however, in which divorce was forbidden. When a man had openly and wrongfully accused his young bride of premarital unfaithfulness, he must pay damages to her father and thereafter "he may not put her away all his days" (Deut 22:19). Again, if a man had premarital relations with a maiden, he must first pay an indemnity to the father and then marry the girl. Because he had humbled her, he also was not allowed ever to divorce her thereafter (Deut 22:28-29; Ex 22:16-17).

In the case of adultery with either another married person or between a married and an unmarried person, the OT penalty was death (Lev 20:10; Deut 22:22). The same penalty applied even to a wife who had practiced fornication before marriage (Deut 22:21; cf. v. 23). Thus the possibility of divorce was replaced by the penalty of death in such cases. *See* Fornication.

One more example of divorce remains. The Israelites were commanded to put away unbelieving heathen wives by Ezra (Ezr 9–10) and Nehemiah (Neh 13:23 f.; cf. Mal 2:10-16), since these wives were leading them astray. The command in II Cor 6:14, 17 not to be unequally yoked with unbelievers deals with the same problem, but in both cases would apply only when the strange wife or husband was leading the believer into unbelief or heathenism. (See William R. Eichhorst, "Ezra's Ethics on Intermarriage and Divorce," *Grace Journal,* X [1969], 16-28.)

In the NT. The Pharisees approached Christ concerning the views of Shammai and Hillel and asked, "Is it lawful for a man to put away his wife for every cause?" (Mt 19:3 ff.). His answer throws light on Deut 24:1-4. Moses did not "command" that a bill of divorcement be given, as they maintained (v. 7). He merely suffered or permitted it because of the hardness of their hearts (v. 8). From the beginning, that is, from the first revelation of the nature and meaning of marriage in Gen 2:23-24, man was to have only one wife—"they shall be one flesh" and to have her permanently (Mt 19:6)—"cleave unto his wife" (Gen 2:24). The one exception permitting divorce, which Christ mentioned at this point, was fornication (v. 9; Mt 5:32).

In I Cor 7:10 Paul gives the further teaching of Christ concerning marriage and divorce as he writes, "Unto the married I command, yet not I, but the Lord. . . ." Paul is saying that he is writing what Christ taught. The wife is not to leave her husband because he is an unbeliever, for the unbelieving husband is sanctified by the wife (vv. 10, 14). To express it in theological terms, the covenantal family relationship made by a believer with God for himself and his children cares for the marriage. If the believing party leaves, he is not to marry again (v. 11) unless the unbeliever breaks the marriage vow by adultery or remarriage (cf. Mt 5:32; 19:9). However, if the unbeliever deserts his believing wife, then the believer seems to be considered free to remarry: "A brother or a sister is not under bondage in such cases" (I Cor 7:15). Some feel that homosexuality is also a reason for divorce since it is listed as an even greater sin than adultery, being "against nature" (Rom 1:26-27).

Two difficulties have arisen over Christ's teaching in the Gospels.

1. In Mark 10:11-12 and Luke 16:18 Christ makes no room whatever for divorce on any grounds; only in Matthew (5:32; 19:9) does He mention that divorce is allowed in case of fornication. Here we have to apply the principle that all the details must be gathered and scripture must be compared with scripture before we come to final conclusions. A complete inductive synthesis requires that all Christ taught on divorce, as recorded both in the Gospels and in I Cor 7:10 ff., be assembled before a final decision is made on Christ's teachings. To this must be added all else found on the subject in the NT in order to be sure of the NT doctrine of divorce.

How is Christ's view of divorce to be reconciled with the OT? How could Moses have been instructed of God to give such general permission? The condition of mankind at that time needs to be considered. These instructions were given to Moses because of the demoralized attitudes of man since the Fall. The ideal conditions which existed when God gave the original ordinance of marriage no longer existed. Moses was told to promulgate a civil law which would regulate divorce rather than a divine law, such as later revealed by Christ, which they could never keep in their unregenerate state. Such being the case, this civil law can well be a guide to man as he deals with unsaved persons and for civil laws even today, but it cannot be set up as the spiritual standard of the church. In the NT Christ removed the judgment of adultery and fornication from the realm of civil law, where they were punishable by physical death, and placed it fully under the judgment of the moral law and God Himself. Inasmuch as the moral law is a higher tribunal than the civil, He put it under an even severer judgment.

2. Christ did not mention adultery as a ground for divorce, but only fornication. Is it therefore not included? This can be explained first by the fact that the admission of the lesser sin of fornication implies the inclusion of the greater sin of adultery. Further, adultery was already considered in both Jewish and Roman law as a legitimate reason for divorce, and therefore would not require to be mentioned. To this must be added the fact that though fornication and adultery are separately mentioned in many cases (Mt 15:19; I Cor 6:9; Gal 5:19), fornication is often used alone to cover both (Acts 15:20; 21:25; Rom 1:29; Eph 5:3). The view generally held, therefore, is that by the use of the term fornication our Lord meant to cover the two. This is borne out further by the fact that the sinful conduct of Israel as Jehovah's wife is sometimes called adultery (Jer 3:8; Ezk 23:45) and sometimes fornication (Jer 3:2-3; Ezk 23:43). Again, in I Cor 7:2 fornication is used to cover either sin.

Summarizing the NT teaching, we find that divorce is permitted where there has been fornication or adultery, and in the case of willful desertion; but not because of some whim or even incompatibility. For such, only separation is permitted (cf. I Cor 7:10 ff.).

Some practical questions arise for the church. How is it to regard adultery and premarital relations? The latter is clearly the lesser sin. Paul was probably answering the question, "Is it good for a man to touch a woman?" in I Cor 7:1 ff., when he replied in the imperative mood, "Let every man have his own wife," or as Dr. J. O. Buswell, Jr., translates it, "Each man must have his own wife" (*Systematic Theology,* p. 386). The OT was very strict concerning fornication—the young people who had committed it must marry, yet it was lenient in comparison with adultery, when the offenders were to be stoned to death. The church should keep this in mind as it acts. *See* Incontinency.

What shall the church do about marrying divorced persons? Only the innocent party can be considered eligible for a church wedding. Some feel the same holds true for church membership. Others would urge a course of confession and discipline followed by restoration. Many churches refuse to give the divorced communicant membership, though with the open communion service not excluding him from the Lord's table. Churches with a closed communion tend to the former—discipline and restoration; those with an open one, to the latter.

See Bill; Family.

Bibliography. J. Oliver Buswell, Jr., *Systematic Theology,* Grand Rapids: Zondervan, 1963, I, 385–396. W. Fisher-Hunter, *The Divorce Problem,* Waynesboro: MacNeish Publishers, 1952. John Murray, *Divorce,* Committee on Christian Education, Orthodox Presbyterian Church, 1953; *Principles of Christian Conduct,* Grand Rapids: Eerdmans, 1957.

R. A. K.

DIZAHAB (dĭz'ȧ-hăb). One of several places listed in Deut 1:1 as defining the route the Israelites took between Paran or Horeb (Mount Sinai) and Moab in Transjordan where Moses was speaking. Since the name means "having gold," at one time gold may have been found there. Location is uncertain.

DOCTOR, DOCTOR OF THE LAW. *See* Occupations: Doctor, Lawyer.

DODAI (dō'dī). An Ahohite (I Chr 27:4). *See* Dodo 2.

DODANIM (dō'dȧ-nĭm). A family or race descended from Javan, the son of Japheth (Gen 10:4). If the Heb. spelling *dodānîm* is correct, this people may have been the ancient Danaoi (ANET, p. 262) or Dardani who were related to the Greeks and lived around Troy along the NW coast of Asia Minor. The LXX, however, reads *Rodioi,* and the MT of the parallel verse in I Chr 1:7 has Heb. *rôdānîm,* Rhodians or Greeks on the island of Rhodes (*q.v.*). The uncertainty is caused by the confusion of the very similar letters in Heb. of "r" and "d." Minoan, Mycenaean, and Dorian settlements have been identified on Rhodes from the OT period.

DODAVAH (dō'dä-vä). A man (RSV, Dodavahu) from Mareshah in Judah. His son Eliezer prophesied to King Jehoshaphat that for joining the wicked king Ahaziah of Israel in a maritime commercial venture, his fleet of ships would be wrecked (II Chr 20:37).

DODO (dō'dō). The name occurs in Akkad. as *Dudû*.

1. A descendant of Issachar, grandfather of the judge Tola (Jud 10:1).

2. An Ahohite, father of Eleazar, one of David's three mighty men or champions (II Sam 23:9; I Chr 11:12). He seems to be the same as the Dodai mentioned in I Chr 27:4 as commander of the division of David's royal troops for the second month.

3. A Bethlehemite, the father of Elhanan, one of David's 30 heroes (II Sam 23:24; I Chr 11:26).

DOE. *See* Animals, II.10.

DOEG (dō'ĕg). An Edomite who served King Saul. His name means "timid, anxious." He was "the chiefest of the herdmen that belonged to Saul" (I Sam 21:7). "As herds would form the main part of Saul's wealth, his chief herdsman would be a person of importance" (*Pulpit Commentary,* IV, 396).

When David, fleeing from Saul's insane wrath, received help from Ahimelech, the high priest at Nob, Doeg was present "detained before the Lord" (I Sam 21:7), perhaps in connection with some vow he had made. Later, he reported the incident to Saul (I Sam 22:9–10), who ordered the execution of all the priests. When Saul's bodyguard refused to obey this wicked command, the commission was transferred to Doeg, who fulfilled it with alacrity (v. 18), slaughtering 85 priests. (LXX increases this number to 305, while Josephus makes it 385.) It was a revolting crime and, though ordered by Saul, revealed also the bloodthirsty nature of Doeg. Evidently David, from previous experience with this Edomite, was not surprised when he received the sad report from Abiathar, son of Ahimelech, who alone escaped (I Sam 22:22). Allusion is made to Doeg and his part in this ugly affair in the title of Ps 52.

G. C. L.

DOG. *See* Animals, I.7.

DOLEFUL CREATURES. Animals or birds of uncertain identity (Isa 13:21). The Heb. *'ōḥîm* means howling creatures (RSV).

DOLMENS. Ancient hut-like structures with walls built of large vertical slabs of stone, usually with a single massive horizontal roof stone, weighing several hundred pounds each. They are found in many parts of the E Hemisphere, from W Europe through N Africa and Malta to S Russia and SW Asia. In Palestine there are several thousand individual dolmens located in dozens of sites that overlook the Jordan Valley from both sides.

While dolmens are usually interpreted as tombs, there is no real proof as yet that the builders constructed them for this purpose. Because no artifacts have thus far been discovered in or beside the empty dolmens, it is impossible to know who built them or when, according to James L. Swauger in "Dolmen Studies in Palestine," BA, XXIX (1966), 106–114. David Gilead, however, believes from all available evidence that the dolmens in Palestine were used in the 4th mil. B.C. for primary burials, and that after complete decomposition the skeletons were removed and reburied in communal burial caves ("Burial Customs and the Dolmen Problem," PEQ,C [1968], 16–26, 84; see also D. Webley, "A Note on the Dolmen Field at Tell el-Adeimeh and Teleilat Ghassul," PEQ,CI [June, 1969], 42 f.). It has been suggested that the huge stones were erected by some of the aborigines who roamed Palestine in pre-Abrahamic times. Large giant-like peoples known as the Anakim, the Emim, the Rephaim, and the Zamzummim are mentioned in Deut 2:10, 11, 20, 21; 3:11 (RSV). *See* Anakim; Giant; Rephaim.

After the six-day war in 1967 Israeli archaeologists investigated a vast field of thousands of dolmens of different sizes on the Golan Heights. The site is called Rujum Hiri, *c.* 15 miles E of the N end of the Sea of Galilee. Like Stonehenge in England, the megalithic structure consists of large, crude basalt stones in a series of concentric rings whose outer circle is over 500 feet in diameter. The circles are *c.* six feet high, and at the center is a stone pile 31 feet high. The purpose served by the structure is not known, and its date is not certain, although it is assumed to belong to the 4th or 3rd mil. B.C.

J. R.

DOLPHIN. *See* Animals: Dugong, V. 3.

DONKEY. *See* Animals, I.1.

DOOR. Referred to many times in the Bible. In KJV it translates seven Heb. and one Gr. word. Two Heb. terms are used frequently: *delet,* referring to the door itself, and *petaḥ,* a doorway or entrance. "Door" is used both literally and figuratively.

Literal usage (e.g., Gen 19:6, 9; II Kgs 9:10). Doors ordinarily were of wood, but sometimes were made of thick slabs of stone, both for houses and for tombs. Locks of wood, brass, or iron were used (Jud 3:24-25). In tents, doors were openings covered with flaps (Gen 18:1-2). *See* Gate; Hinge.

Figurative usage. Probably the most frequent use of door in a figurative sense is as a symbol of opportunity, especially for Christian witness and service (e.g., I Cor 16:9; II Cor 2:12; Col 4:3; Rev 3:8). Door is also used to represent the way by which a person enters into something. Christ Himself is the door by which one enters into salvation (Jn 10:9; cf. Acts 14:27; Hos 2:15). That which is near is said to be "at the door" (Mt 24:33; Jas 5:9; Rev 3:20; Gen 4:7).

See Joachim Jeremias, *"Thura,"* TDNT, III, 173-180.

G. C. L.

DOORKEEPER. Mentioned a number of times in both OT and NT. It sometimes signifies a gatekeeper, since both Heb. and Gr. words can refer to either door or gate. In important buildings, such as the temple, the position was evidently one of dignity and honor. In Ps 84:10 the translation "doorkeeper" is inaccurate. The allusion is to one who "stands at the threshold" (ASV marg.), such as the beggar of Acts 3:2. In the temple, there were a considerable number of Levites who served as doorkeepers (or porters, the same word in original; see I Chr 9:22). A few priests were also given this designation (II Kgs 25:18). Possibly the former served under the latter. These doorkeepers not only guarded the gates but also performed other services (II Chr 31:14). At the trial of Christ, the doorkeeper at the high priest's house was a girl (Jn 18:15-17). Sometimes private homes had doorkeepers (Mk 13:34).

See Porter.

G. C. L.

DOORPOST

1. Heb. *sap* (Ezk 41:16, KJV), better, "threshold" (*q.v.*).

2. Heb. *mashqôp* (Ex 12:7, KJV), "lintel" as in Ex 12:22, 23.

3. Heb. *meẓûzâ* (Ex 12:7, 22, 23; 21:6; Jud 16:3; etc.), usually rendered "doorpost" in RSV and as "side post," "door post," or "post" in KJV. Just as the Passover blood was commanded to be smeared on the doorposts and lintel of the Israelite house (Ex 12:7), so the words of the Shema (Deut 6:4, 5) were to be inscribed on the doorposts (Deut 6:9). It may be argued from a similar command in Deut 11:20 that this instruction was meant to be understood figuratively. But the ancient Egyptians inscribed their doorways with favorable omens in the names of their pagan deities, so it may be that the Israelites were told to replace that custom with one honoring their God. In early times, at any rate, Jewish homes had portions of the law either carved or inscribed upon the doorposts and fixed on the right-hand door jamb of every room in the house. Moslems today often paint sentences from the Koran over their front doors.

J. R.

DOPHKAH (dŏf'kȧ). A campsite of the Israelites between the Wilderness of Sin on the shore of the Red Sea and the oasis valley of Rephidim (Num 33:12-13). Identification is not certain, but suggestions are (1) the area of Serabit el-Khadim, an Egyptian copper and turquoise mining center, or (2) more likely in the Wadi Magharah leading to Wadi Feiran and Mount Sinai. *See* Sin, Wilderness of.

DOR (dôr). A Canaanite city on the Mediterranean coast between Caesarea and Mount Carmel, at the site of el-Burj by the harbor town of et-Tanturah. Excavations led by John Garstang in 1923-24 proved occupation had begun by the Late Bronze Age (1500-1200 B.C.). The king of Dor was a member of the confederacy of northern Canaanite kings headed by Jabin of Hazor, defeated by Joshua (Josh 11:2; 12:23). The city was assigned to Manasseh (Josh 17:11; I Chr 7:29), but was not taken over by Israelites (Jud 1:27) until the time of David and Solomon. Solomon made Dor the center of one of his administrative districts (I Kgs 4:11).

Meanwhile Dor had been occupied by the Tjekker who had invaded the coastal zone with the Philistines *c.* 1200 B.C. (ANET, p. 262), for the Egyptian emissary Wenamon found them living there *c.* 1100 B.C. (ANET, p. 26). The Assyrians claimed to have conquered Dor in the 8th cen. B.C. It fell into the hands of the Seleucids in the Maccabean struggle (I Macc 15:12-13,25). In 64 B.C. Dor was granted autonomy by Pompey. Josephus affirms that the Gentiles worshiped Apollo at Dor (Jos *Apion,* II. 10).

J. R.

DORCAS(dôr'kȧs). A Christian woman of Joppa whom Peter raised from death (Acts 9:36-42). *See* Tabitha.

DOTHAN (dō'thȧn). A picturesque site located a thousand yards E of the modern road from Samaria (Sebaste) to Jenin, said by Eusebius to be 12 miles N of Sebaste. The top of the tell is ten acres in area, dominating a broad fertile plain 1,000 feet above sea level. From the top an impressive view to the S and W is obtained of level fertile land under cultivation. A copious spring and large cisterns still supply water for the large flocks and herds in the area.

Dothan enters Bible history with the story of Joseph and his betrayal there, as he went to visit his brothers tending their flocks near the city (Gen 37). After the elder brothers had cast Joseph into a dry well or cistern, they decided to sell him to a caravan of spice merchants en route to Egypt. Then as now, the Dothan area has excellent pasturage, especially prized in dry seasons.

After this Dothan witnessed the invasion of Egyptians under Thutmose III (1504-1450 B.C.), who lists Dothan among the cities conquered (ANET, p. 242). Dothan is not mentioned in the Scriptures again until the Kingdom Period.

During the 9th cen. B.C., Elisha the prophet repeatedly warned the king of Israel of the movements of Syrian troops. The Syrian king suspected his own men of betraying his whereabouts, but was informed that Elisha knew the king's inner secrets and reported them to Israel's King Jehoram. Upon hearing this, Ben-hadad sent an army to capture the prophet. Dothan was surrounded during the night. The account says that in the morning, in answer to Elisha's prayer, the Syrian army was smitten by blindness, after which Elisha led them to Samaria where the king of Israel fed them and sent them home (II Kgs 6:8-23).

Dothan is mentioned several times in the fictional story of Judith (Jth 3:9; 4:6; 7:3, 18; 8:3). While the unknown author treats the geography of Palestine very loosely, he seems to place Dothan near the plain of Esdraelon and the range of hills known now as Mount Carmel and Mount Gilboa. His frequent mention of Dothan indicates it was a prominent town at the time of writing, *c.* 100 B.C.

Thus Dothan, located near the border between Manasseh and the plain of Megiddo, was near the caravan route and also near the scene of border conflicts. Even as late as 1967 its proximity to Jenin and the border between Jordan and Israel made Dothan a witness to armed conflict.

Dothan has been the scene of nine excavations, 1953-64, under the direction of Joseph P. Free with assistance of personnel from Wheaton College (Illinois). Approximately 20 levels of occupation have been identified. During the first season soundings 30 feet in depth at the crest of the S slope of the tell revealed 11 levels of occupation from the late Chalcolithic (3000 B.C.) to Iron I (1200-900 B.C.). An Early Bronze Age wall was exposed, 11 feet wide at the base, 9 feet wide at the top and 16 feet in height, vertical on the outside and sloping on the inside. A large stairway 13 feet wide with 18 steps was uncovered outside the city wall, presumably leading down to the springs and wells.

At the Middle Bronze level the skeleton of a two-year-old child was recovered, having been buried with a small jar and two juglets, all typical of the Middle Bronze Age. Since it had been placed in the foundation trench under the squared corner of a large wall, probably part of a rampart tower, this burial may well have been a child sacrifice incorporated in the wall during consecration (cf. Josh 6:26; I Kgs 16:34). The season produced nearly 400 artifacts, including flint blades, saddle querns, loom weights, bronze blades, a jar handle impressed by a Hyksos scarab, and a number of whole jars, pots, and bowls in stratification.

The second and third seasons concentrated on the top of the tell. Finds in the acropolis area included Hellenistic lamps and coins and Rhodian jar handles inscribed in Greek. Iron Age remains near the edge included a large Iron I crater or bowl with 14 handles, and an Assyrian "palace-ware" bowl from the Iron II level, mute evidence of 8th cen. B.C. Assyrian invasions.

The mound of Dothan. HFV

The 1955 expedition revealed a section of "Wall Street" of the Iron II city, averaging four feet in width and extending, as the 1956 expedition revealed, more than 100 feet; the house walls on either side were still standing seven feet high in places. A small pyxis jar of Late Bronze II or Iron I was located containing 15 pieces of metal objects, most of which were silver rings, bracelets and jewelry.

The 1956 season disclosed evidence of a thriving Iron Age city during the Kingdom Period of Israel's history. Evidence of destruction by fire was abundant. A piece of charred wood in an Iron Age level was later tested by radio carbon process and dated by Columbia University scientists as 885–725 B.C., contemporary with the prophet Elisha. An Arabic palace with 25 rooms arranged around a central courtyard, dated A.D. 1200–1400, was uncovered at the summit of the mound. Five adjacent depressions representing other courtyards suggest this building may have had as many as 150 rooms.

The expedition of 1958 began to uncover a large two storied building with flagstone or plastered floors, doorways made of well-cut stones and a room filled with 96 broken storage jars of uniform type that could be stacked. Remains of dozens more were found in other rooms. Some of the jars contained grain and some olive pits. At least two drains led from the building. Subsequent seasons showed a kitchen area with stone water basin for servants or guards. Several storage bins up to 14 feet in diameter held the wheat collected in the storage jars. The accumulated evidence indicates this was an administrative building first constructed during Solomon's reign and rebuilt *c.* 800 B.C. Nearby houses showed a later rebuilding during the divided monarchy and one final time after the Assyrian conquest of the land in 725–722 B.C. Assyrian pottery and jar burials suggest the conquerors occupied Dothan.

At the end of the 1959 season below the Early Bronze city wall on the W slope, a shaft was discovered leading down to the doorway of a large cave-tomb of the period of the judges. Its ceiling had collapsed on more than 3,200 pottery vessels, including at least three seven-lipped lamps, plus over 50 bronze objects such as daggers, spearheads, rings, bowls, and a lamp. The tomb had four distinct levels of burial from 1400 to 1100 B.C. It is the richest tomb yet found in Palestine.

Bibliography. Joseph P. Free, BASOR, Nos. 131, 135, 139, 143, 147, 152, 156, 160.

G. A. T.

DOUBLE. From the Gr. *diplous* (I Tim 5:17; Rev 18:6; Mt 23:15) and several Heb. words from the verb root *kāpal* (Ex 26:9; 28:16; 39:9) and *mishneh* (Gen 43:12, 15; Ex 16:5,22). The latter Heb. word also means a "copy" (Deut 17:18; Josh 8:32) and even indicates "second" in rank (Gen 41:43; II Chr 35:24) as well as "second" in age (I Sam 8:2; 17:13).

In the church, elders who rule well are worthy to be paid as well as praised (I Tim 5:17, "double honor"; the Gr. *timē*, "honor," means also "compensation"). A double-minded (Gr. *dipsukos*, "double-souled") man (Jas 1:7–8; 4:8; cf. Ps 119) is one who is divided in his thinking. One who is double-tongued is perhaps "not truthful" rather than merely repetitious (I Tim 3:8).

DOUBT. Doubt is that undecided state of mind in which one hesitates between two opposite conclusions. The doubter may have some degree of belief while he wavers in his opinions. Such was Peter, called by the Lord Jesus a man of little faith after he began to sink beneath the waves (Mt 14:31); also some who saw the risen Christ and yet doubted (Mt 28:17). In these passages the Gr. *distazō*, "to stand divided," is used. In such cases doubt may be provisional, waiting for more light (e.g., Acts 10:17–20).

Unless the honest doubter presses on to full faith, his doubt becomes sin, "for whatever does not proceed from faith is sin" (Rom 14:23, RSV). One must "ask in faith, with no doubting" (Jas 1:6, RSV). Such was Abraham (Rom 4:20), of whom it is said that he did not stagger, hesitate, doubt (*diakrinō*) through unbelief or lack of faith (*apistia*). Assured faith, with no doubts in his heart, enables one to claim the promises of God (Mt 21:21; Mk 11:23).

Other Gr. words rendered as "doubt" or one of its verb forms in the KJV have different emphases. The Gr. root *poreomai* connotes uncertainty (Jn 13:22; Acts 25:20) or perplexity rather than reasoned doubt (see RSV at Acts 2:12; 5:24; 10:17; Gal 4:20). In Jn 10:24 the people ask Jesus how long He will keep them in suspense (RSV). Gr. *meteōrizō* (Lk 12:29) suggests those having anxious minds, wavering between hope and fear.

J. R.

DOUGH. *See* Food: Bread, Flour.

DOVE, TURTLEDOVE. *See* Animals, III.9.

DOVE'S DUNG. "The fourth part of a cab" (1/4 cab equals *c.* 1/2 pint) of this substance was sold at an exorbitant price in Samaria during the siege (II Kgs 6:25). The Heb. words *ḥărê yônîm* are plain as translated, an example of the actual extremity of the siege. Josephus records that in their dire circumstances people were reduced to eating cattle dung during Titus' siege of Jerusalem (*Wars*, v. 13.7). Some commentators (e.g., WBC, p. 347) suggest the possible comparison with an Arabic herb named "sparrow's dung," but a parallel Heb. plant has not been found. *See* Plants.

DOWRY. When arrangements for a marriage were being made, several types of exchange of property might take place.

1. The suitor could be expected to give a

certain "gift" (Heb. *mōhar*) to the bride's parents and/or brothers (Gen 34:12; Ex 22:16; I Sam 18:25). This could entail much negotiation (Gen 34:8–12). Some see this as a possible survival of an early custom to purchase wives (Gen 24:53; 31:15; Ex 22:16–17; I Sam 18:25; Ruth 4:10; Hos 3:2). It is better explained as a compensation given to the bride's family, for she herself was neither bought nor sold. The amount given (or paid) varied according to the status and wealth of the bride, as for example with Jacob's service to Laban (Gen 29:18, 27). It might be replaced by deeds of valor (Josh 15:16; I Sam 18:25; Jud 1:12).

2. Gifts (Heb. *mattān*) were made by the bridegroom to the bride herself, as in the case of Isaac to Rebekah (Gen 24:22, 53; cf. Gen 34:12; Hos 2:19–20). In Akkadian the bridegroom's gift is *zubullû;* the cognate Aramaic form is *zebed,* used by Leah when she said, "God has endowed me with a good dowry" (Gen 30:20, RSV), and then called her sixth son Zebulun with the name based on the Akkadian spelling (E. A. Speiser, *Genesis, Anchor Bible,* p. 231).

3. A dowry was often given by the father of the bride to his daughter who was to be married, such as land to Achsah (Jud 1:15) and to Pharaoh's daughter (I Kgs 9:16), or a maidservant to Rebekah (Gen 24:61) and to Leah (Gen 29:24).

R. A. K.

DOXOLOGIES (Gr. *doxologia,* from *doxa,* "glory," and *logia,* "word"). Used in ecclesiastical Gr. to describe formulas expressing praise and glory to the Trinity. While the word itself does not occur in the Bible, expressions of praise often are found. In Jewish worship such expressions as "To Thee be glory forever" accompanied Heb. prayers. Similar formulas are found in the NT and characterized the worship of the early church (cf. I Cor 14:16). While exhibiting considerable variety in expression, they show a basic structure.

Westcott (*Epistle to the Hebrews,* pp. 466–467) lists 16 doxologies in the NT (Rom 11:36; 16:27; Gal 1:5; Eph 3:21; Phil 4:20; I Tim 1:17; 6:16; II Tim 4:18; Heb 13:21; I Pet 4:11; 5:11; II Pet 3:18; Jude 25; Rev 1:6; 5:13; 7:12). These he classified into three major groups: those ascribing glory to God alone; those ascribed to God either directly or through Christ (Rom 16:27; Jude 25); and those ascribed to Christ alone (II Tim 4:18; II Pet 3:18; Rev 1:6). Only three doxologies are found at the close of epistles (Rom 16:27; II Pet 3:18; Jude 25). Every doxology with one exception (II Pet 3:18, according to the best MSS) ends with the characteristic Amen. Some scholars include among the doxologies those expressions that begin with "blessed."

In later church history, Lk 2:14 with additions was called the "greater doxology" while the Gloria Patri (completely extrabiblical) was the "lesser doxology."

F. P.

DRAG. A large fishing net or seine, equipped with weights on the lower edge and floats on the upper, so that the net may be dragged along the bottom of a river or lake. Then the two ends are drawn together, enclosing any fish caught within the net. The Babylonian armies are described as fishermen who sacrifice to their dragnet (Heb. *mikmereth*), deifying the very weapons of their military successes (Hab 1:15–16). In Ezk 32:3 the more general word for net, *ḥērem,* is used in the specific sense of a dragnet (so RSV), used figuratively as God's means of catching pharaoh, the monster of the Nile. *See* Fishing; Net.

DRAGON. *See* Animals, II.11; V.7.

DRAGON WELL. Identified by many as the fountain En-rogel (*q.v.*) SE of the Jebusite and Davidic city of Jerusalem (Neh 2:13). Yet a spring much further up the Valley of Hinnom, or a well now dry in the Tyropean Valley, would better conform to the assumed location of the gates which Nehemiah mentions on his nocturnal inspection tour. RSV translates the verse Jackal's Well.

DRAM. *See* Weights, Measures, and Coins.

DRAUGHT. The Gr. *aphedrōn* in Mt 15:17; Mk 7:19 signifies a latrine or toilet. *See* Dung.

DRAUGHT HOUSE. Jehu, in contempt of Baal, ordered the temple of that heathen god to be demolished and the place turned into a public latrine to make the spot altogether unclean (II Kgs 10:27). Excavated latrines of this type consist of a simple building with a row of holes in stone slabs covering a drain through which water could be flushed, similar to many toilet facilities in Middle Eastern lands today.

DRAWER OF WATER. One of the lowest classes of servant (Deut 29:11). Yet such servitude was preferred to death by the Gibeonites, who in fear had submitted to the invading Israelites (Josh 9:21,23,27). Women (Gen 24:11) and young men (Ruth 2:9) drew water from the well as part of daily chores, but as a full-time occupation it was despised. Until recently men have made it their trade in the Middle East to peddle water carried in goatskins slung on their backs.

DREAM. A dream is a series of images or thoughts occurring during sleep. When these are unpleasant the cause is sometimes a physical disorder. Dreams can also be caused by powerful stimuli or suggestions and emotions which may be pleasant or unpleasant. These need not be of recent occurrence but can lie buried in the subconscious for a long period and, even though apparently forgotten by the individual, can make themselves felt in disturbing dreams. The psychologist and psychiatrist are always interested in their patient's dream life to find, if possible, a clue to the personality problems.

Dreaming and the prophetic office in the Bible seem to have been closely associated, although the dream coming to pass was not always to be regarded as of God and proof that He had spoken (see Deut 13:1-3,5). God did communicate His will through dreams on some occasions. He spoke to Abimelech and forbade his taking Sarah to be his wife (Gen 20:1-7). He spoke to Jacob at Bethel and confirmed the covenant promise (Gen 28:12-15). At Haran He appeared to Jacob and told him to return to his own land (Gen 31:10-13). When Joseph was in Egypt he interpreted Pharaoh's dream of the fat and lean cattle (Gen 41:1-9). Gideon overheard a Midianite soldier tell another man his dream of a barley cake tumbling into the camp of Midian and upsetting a tent. When Gideon heard their interpretation he worshiped God and returned to the camp of Israel to lead his people to great victory (Jud 7:9-15). Daniel interpreted two of Nebuchadnezzar's dreams, that of the great statue (Dan 2) and of the tree (Dan 4:1-28). Daniel had a dream of four great beasts (Dan 7:1-14) and a vision of the ram and the he-goat (Dan 8:1-14).

There are six references in the NT to dreams. Four of them came to Joseph the husband of Mary. The angel of the Lord appeared to him prior to the birth of Jesus and told him to take Mary to be his wife (Mt 1:20-21). After the birth of Jesus, the wise men were warned of God to return to their country another way (Mt 2:12). Joseph likewise was warned to flee into Egypt to escape the wrath of Herod (Mt 2:13), and upon Herod's death he was told to return to Israel, while in another dream he was directed to go to Galilee (Mt 2:19-22). Pilate's wife was disturbed in a dream concerning the innocency of Jesus (Mt 27:19).

It is debatable whether God communicates directly or indirectly by dreams in this day, although it is not to be thought impossible. There is one citation in Peter's explanation of Pentecost in which he said, "Your young men shall see visions, and your old men shall dream dreams" (Acts 2:17). These could refer to "types of extraordinary spiritual influence, and not as the precise forms in which the promise was to be fulfilled." God has given His written revelation and His Spirit to instruct and guide into all truth, so there is not much need for dreams today. In the epistles there is an absence of reference to them.

See also Vision.

Bibliography. Albrecht Oepke, "*Onar*," TDNT, V, 220-238. Richard L. Ruble, "The Doctrine of Dreams," BS, CXXV (1968), 360-364.

R. H. B.

Hittite clothing of the post-empire period (after 1200 B.C.) as seen on a bas relief from Marash. LM

DREGS

1. Dregs is the KJV translation of Heb. *shemārîm* in Ps 75:8; elsewhere "lees" of wine, as in Isa 25:6; Jer 48:11; Zeph 1:12. *See* Lees; Wine. As the wine was strained before drinking, so the psalmist uses the figure of the draught poured off from the top of God's cup of wrath to signify His restraint in judgment on the righteous, while the wicked shall drain the cup down to the dregs (cf. I Pet 4:17-18).

2. Heb. *qubba'at* means "goblet," "chalice" (Isa 51:17, 22). KJV renders, "Thou hast drunken the dregs of the cup of trembling, and wrung them out"; better, ". . . the chalice-cup of staggering and drained it" (51:17).

DRESS. The types, styles, and customs of the dress of Bible times have been preserved to a large extent by indications in the biblical record and by the archaeological findings of sculptures and tomb paintings in Babylonia and Egypt which depict Palestinians and Syrians. Of special importance are the Beni Hasan tomb paintings for the patriarchal era, the Megiddo ivories for the time of the judges, and the Black Obelisk of Shalmanezer III and Sennacherib's bas reliefs portraying the siege of Lachish for the kingdom period. To a lesser extent the costumes and dress customs of the orthodox Jews and simple people of modern Palestine help explain the ancient garments.

Materials of dress. The materials of attire depended on the means of the wearer, the civilization and culture, and the geographical loca-

Properly dressed members of the Roman Emperor Augustus' official family, as shown on his Altar of Peace in Rome. The Apostle Paul, a Roman citizen, probably would have worn the Roman toga, at least on occasion. HFV

tion. The first Scripture record of materials is in the statement that Adam and Eve "sewed fig leaves together, and made themselves aprons" (Gen 3:7). Animal skins were used early also (Gen 3:21), and sheepskins and goatskins were used widely (Heb 11:37). The sheepskin coat had sleeves and was worn over the tunic. Elijah's mantle may have been the skin of a sheep or other animal with the wool left on (I Kgs 19:19). Such rough garments were worn by prophets (Zech 13:4; Mt 7:15). Woven goats' hair was also known at an early period (Ex 26:7), and the sackcloth (*q.v.*) of mourners was of this material (cf. II Sam 3:31; Rev 6:12). The dress of John the Baptist was of camel's hair (Mt 3:4), which was a coarse woven cloth.

However, the favorite materials throughout Palestine were wool and linen (Lev 13:47–48, 52, 59). Sheepshearers were employed by Judah at an early time (Gen 38:12), and wool was a chief substance demanded as tribute (II Kgs 3:4). The prince of Megiddo wrote to the pharaoh that because of hostilities his men were not able to "pluck" the wool (EA #244, ANET, p. 485).

Linen (Heb. *bad;* Gr. *linon, sindōn*) was made from flax (I Chr 4:21; Prov 31:13; Mk 14:51; 15:46). It is interesting to note that angels appeared in linen (Dan 10:5; 12:6; Rev 15:6). The finest linen (Heb. *shēsh, bûṣ;* Gr. *byssos*) was manufactured chiefly in Egypt (Gen 41:42; Ezk 27:7). Herodotus mentioned four qualities, one so fine that each thread contained 360 fibers. The priestly vestments were made of this type of linen (Ex 28:6; etc.). *See* Linen.

The usual color of the Heb. dress was the natural white of the various materials or as bleached white by the fuller (*see* Occupations: Fuller). Such a color was appropriate not only for festive occasions but also as a symbol for purity (Eccl 9:8; Rev 3:4–5), since a spot or stain was readily detected (Isa 63:3; Rev 3:4). In Roman times the fuller also served as the cleaner of clothes.

Although it is not known when dyeing was introduced, scarlet thread was used at an early time (Gen 38:28), and purple was used as well (Acts 16:14; Rev 18:12). Purple was worn by Persian officers (Est 8:15), Midianite kings (Jud 8:26), and wealthy Tyrians (Ezk 27:7). Dyed robes were imported from other countries, particularly Phoenicia, and were worn only by the wealthy because of their expense.

Gold and silver thread were used for decoration. Figures too were added, much like the cherubim in the curtains of the tabernacle (Ex 36:8, 35). Such decorated robes were worn by royal personages (Ps 45:13; Acts 12:21) and the wealthy (Jud 5:30; Ps 45:14; Ezk 16:13). *See* Colors: Purple, Scarlet; Occupations: Dyer; Purple.

Articles of clothing. Because women's garments differed in detail not in kind, the usual articles of clothing were common to both men and women. The following articles were basic throughout Bible times. The most widely used term for clothing or garment in Heb. is *beged,* occurring some 200 times in the OT. In the NT Gr. *himation,* which has a specific meaning of robe or cloak, was also used in the general sense.

1. The loincloth or waistcloth (Heb. *'ēzôr;* KJV, "girdle") was a simple piece of cloth or leather worn by slaves and laborers about the hips like a kilt or apron and reaching from waist to above the knees (Isa 11:5; Jer 13:1-11). Elijah (II Kgs 1:8) and John the Baptist (Mt 3:4) wore leather waistcloths. Aprons were worn over the outer garment by workers in the Mediterranean world in Paul's day (Acts 19:12). A type of loincloth called an ephod was worn by those consecrated to God (I Sam 2:18; II Sam 6:14). *See* Girdle; Ephod 4.

2. The inner garment. The tunic or shirt (Heb. *k^etōnet;* Gr. *chitōn*) was the principal ordinary garment worn by men and women. It was worn next to the skin and was actually a long, rather tight-fitting shirt (inappropriately translated "coat" in KJV). The material used was leather, haircloth, wool, linen, or in modern times, usually cotton. It was probably made in two pieces and sewn together at the sides. The simplest kind was sleeveless, reaching only to the knees. A girdle or sash worn around the waist permitted its wearer to tuck the lower part of the tunic under it for freer movement (Jer 1:17; I Pet 1:13).

Another type worn by favored persons reached to the wrists and ankles. This was the kind probably worn by Joseph (Gen 37:3, 23), Tamar (II Sam 13:18), and the priests (Ex 28:4, 39). The garment Jacob gave to Joseph (Gen 37:3), though rendered "coat of many colours" in KJV, may well have been a sleeved tunic. This would also have been a mark of aristocracy, as the working classes usually wore a sleeveless shirt tunic.

The inner garment was worn by women as well as men (Song 5:3, RSV), although there was no doubt a difference in style and pattern. The tunic (*chitōn,* wrongly translated "coat" in KJV) is the garment mentioned in Lk 3:11; 6:29; 9:3 (and parallel passages) and Acts 9:39. The lower classes often wore only the tunic in warm weather. However, the higher classes would put on an outer garment when receiving callers or going outside, although they might wear just the tunic while at home. A particularly fine grade of undergarment was the *sādîn,* a fine white linen sheet to wrap around the body (Jud 14:12-13; Prov 31:24; Isa 3:23).

The term "naked" was often used of men clad only with their tunic. Thus it is said of Saul (I Sam 19:24) when he had taken off his upper garments; of Isaiah (Isa 20:2) after he had put off his sackcloth; of a warrior (Amos 2:16) when he had taken off his military cloak; and of Peter (Jn 21:7) without his fisher's coat.

3. The outer tunic or robe (Heb. *m^e'îl*). This was a looser and longer tunic, reaching to near the feet. It was open at the top so that it could be drawn over the head. It also had holes for the insertion of the arms. To cover a woman with one's "skirt" (*kānāp*) or corner of one's mantle or robe (I Sam 15:27; 24:4-5) symbolized protection and the right of marriage (Ruth 3:9). Uncovering the skirt of one's father meant lying carnally with one's mother or stepmother and was forbidden (Deut 22:30; 27:20).

Scripture indicates the use of tunic or robe by kings (I Sam 24:4), nobles (Job 1:20), prophets (I Sam 28:14), and sometimes youths (I Sam 2:19). However, these passages may refer to any robe worn over the inner garment. Nevertheless, when two tunics are mentioned as being worn at the same time (Lk 3:11), the second would be an outer tunic. Although travelers generally wore two tunics, disciples were forbidden to do so (Mt 10:10; Lk 9:3). The seamless tunic worn by our Lord (Jn 19:23, RSV) may have been of this outer type. Evidently this garment was optional, being worn by the higher classes or occasionally substituted for the outer garment.

4. The girdle. A loose tunic would hinder a person from walking freely, so a sash or belt was always worn when leaving home for any kind of journey (II Kgs 4:29; Acts 12:8). The "girdle" (Heb. *ḥăgôr, ḥăgôrâ*) normally was a long strip of cloth folded several times and wound around the waist over the tunic. The *ḥăgôr* could be simply a rope (Isa 3:24, RSV), but the waistband of a nobleman might be very elaborate, made of linen, embroidered with silk or gold and silver thread, and frequently studded with gold, precious stones, and pearls (e.g., "golden girdle," Rev 1:13; 15:6). It was generally a handbreadth in width. The girdles were fastened by a clasp or buckle of gold or silver. Fibula pins of bronze are regularly found

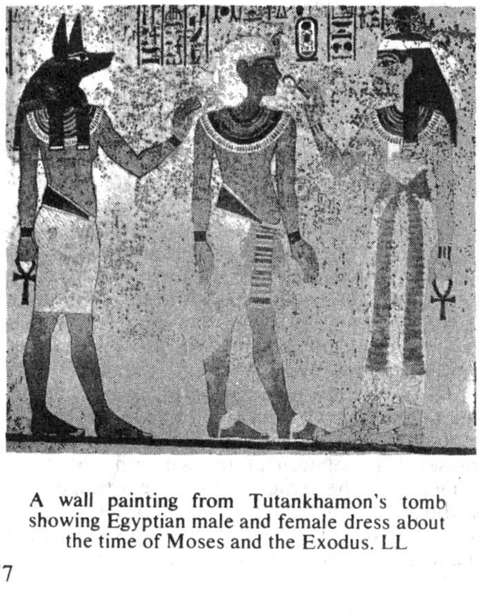

A wall painting from Tutankhamon's tomb showing Egyptian male and female dress about the time of Moses and the Exodus. LL

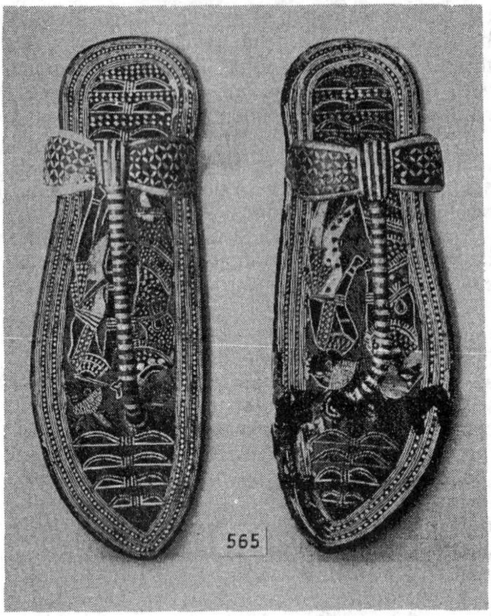

Sandals from the tomb of Pharaoh Tutankhamon. LL

in Palestinian excavations of Iron Age levels onward. The sash could also be tied in a knot so that the ends hung down in front.

The girdle was used to keep money (Mk 6:8, RSV). It also served as a belt to fasten a man's sword to his body (I Sam 25:13; II Sam 20:8). The girdle of women was generally looser than that of men and was worn about the hips, except when they were actively engaged (cf. Prov 31:17). *See* Girdle.

5. The outer garment or mantle (*śimlâ* or *śalmâ*). The ordinary outer garment was a large loose cloak which served the purpose of an overcoat. It was made of wool, goat's hair, cotton, or linen. It generally consisted of a large quadrangular piece of material, the size and texture varying with the demands of the wearer. It was worn over the shoulders in pleasant weather and wrapped like a heavy shawl around the body when necessary. When sleeping, the person would lie down on a rug or mattress and use his outer garment for a blanket. Thus the creditor was forbidden to keep the mantle of a borrower as a pledge overnight (Ex 22:26 f.; Deut 24:13). It was closely woven, warm, and in some cases waterproof.

This was the garment with which Elijah smote the waters of the Jordan, and it subsequently became Elisha's (II Kgs 2:8-13). Because of a violation of the sabbath, the Lord commanded the Israelites to make a fringe with a ribband or cord of blue on the borders of their mantles (Num 15:37-41). This was to remind them of the Lord and His commandments.

Because of its size, the outer garment could also be used to carry large burdens (Ex 12:34, RSV; II Kgs 4:39). Ruth even put six measures of barley into hers (Ruth 3:15, RSV). The *himation* of the NT ("cloak," "robe," Mt 5:40; 9:20; 24:18; Lk 6:29; 22:36; Jn 19:2; Acts 7:58; 22:20) was similar.

6. The headdress. Much of the time Israelites did not wear a head covering, except perhaps a headband of rope or cord (I Kgs 20:32). On occasions of war, a leather helmet was used. However, because of the direct rays of the sun, a turban (Heb. *ṣanîp*) was often worn by the better class of people. This was a piece of thick material wrapped several times around the head. It generally was made of linen or cotton and is mentioned by Job and Isaiah (Job 29:14, RSV; Isa 3:23, RSV). A single piece of cloth draped over the head and held in place with a cord or rope may have been used for protection by the Heb. peasant, just as the Bedouin wears the Arabic *kufiyeh* today.

7. The footgear. The shoes worn by the majority in Bible times were what we would call sandals (Heb. *na'al*; Gr. *sandalion*). The sole generally was made of leather, although felt, cloth, or wood were also used. It was bound to the foot by a leather thong (Gen 14:23; Mk 1:7). The sandals of women were sometimes made of animal skins. Women of rank had sandals elaborately embroidered with silk, silver, and gold. For some women, they were the richest articles of their attire. Sandals were universally worn throughout Palestine, even by the poor (Amos 2:6; 8:6). During mealtimes, the feet were uncovered (Lk 7:38; Jn 13:5-6); sandals were not worn indoors. They were used for military expeditions (Isa 5:27; Eph 6:15) and journeys (Ex 12:11; Josh 9:5, 13; Acts 12:8). The shoe could signify subjection or a transfer of property (Ps 60:8; 108:9; Ruth 4:7-8). *See* Sandal.

The dress of women. The dress of women was distinguished (Deut 22:5), not so much by kind, however, as by detail and quality of materials. They wore longer tunics and larger mantles than the men. The outer garment differed in elaboration, making it a distinctive robe. Isaiah mentions the "wimple" (KJV) or "cloak" (RSV), Heb. *miṭpaḥat* (3:22), a cape covering the head and neck. The skirt (*shûl*) means the lower flowing part of a garment. Figuratively, Jerusalem's "skirts" were lifted up to denote the shame of her illicit relationships (Jer 13:22, 26; Lam 1:9).

Women often wore veils, which were also distinctive. The veil (KJV, vail) was at first an article of ornamentation (Song 4:1, 3; 6:7, RSV), and both married and unmarried women appeared in public with their faces uncovered (Gen 12:14; 24:16; 29:10; I Sam 1:12). However, betrothed maidens did veil themselves in the presence of their future husbands, especially at the time of the wedding (Gen 24:65; 29:25). Tamar wore such a veil (*ṣā'îp*) to avoid recognition and to trick Judah by posing as a sacred prostitute (Gen 38:14, 19). The veil (*masweh*) which Moses would put on after being in the presence of God acted as a mask to conceal the departing of the radiance of his face (Ex 34:33-35; II Cor 3:13-16). Ruth's "vail" (*miṭpaḥat*) in which she carried home six measures of barley was a large shawl or cloak (Ruth 3:15). The Koran is responsible for much of the strictness in the use of the veil, for it forbade women to appear unveiled except in the presence of their nearest relatives (Koran 33:55, 59).

Some of the veils of modern Syrian, Arabian and Egyptian women are embroidered with colored silks and gold, and extend almost to the ground. The extravagant costumes of the women living in luxury in Jerusalem in Isaiah's day included many articles of jewelry as well as purses and perfume boxes (Isa 3:16-24, NASB). Since the woman's dress was distinct, the Mosaic law could forbid a man to wear woman's clothing and a woman to wear the garment of a man (Deut 22:5).

The dress of the priests. The priests and high priest were required to wear a distinctive dress when they were performing their priestly ministry. The *priests* were required to wear the following: (1) Drawers or short breeches (*mik-nesayim,* Ex 28:42), which reached from the loins to the thighs and were made of linen (Ex 39:28). (2) A long coat which had sleeves and was made of fine linen (Ex 39:27). (3) A girdle or sash (*'abnēt*) which was woven and variegated or embroidered with the same four colors used in the veil of the tabernacle and temple (Ex 39:29). (4) A cap or bonnet of linen. They were not allowed to have anything on their feet in the sanctuary (Ex 3:5; Josh 5:15).

The *high priest* was required to wear the following: (1) The breastplate, which was woven of blue, purple, scarlet, and fine linen yarn, embroidered with figures of gold. The 12 tribes of Israel were represented by 12 precious stones set in gold. It was securely fastened to the ephod and body by a series of cords and chains (Ex 28:13-28; 39:8-21). (2) The ephod was of the same material and fashion as the breastplate and was that upon which the breastplate was fastened (Ex 28:6-12; 39:2-7). *See* Ephod 2. (3) The robe of the ephod was blue, without seam, and worn under the ephod. The hem had blue, purple, and scarlet pomegranates alternating with bells of gold, which rang when the high priest went to minister (Ex 28:31-35; 39:22-26). (4) The girdle or sash was of the same material and fashion as the breastplate and ephod, and was used to hold the ephod firmly to the body (Ex 28:8). (5) The miter was a kind of turban which had a gold plate engraved, "Holy to Yahweh," and was fastened to the front of the miter with blue cord (Ex 28:36-38; 39:30-31).

The dress of the Pharisees. The Pharisees emphasized two articles of their religious garments which became distinctive to them. One of these, the phylactery (*q.v.*), was a small box of metal or a parchment band fastened by straps to the arm or forehead. It contained passages of Scripture referring to the Passover. The reason for wearing it is found in Ex 13:9, 16, where such objects, worn between the eyes, are called "frontlets" (*q.v.*). The other item was the blue fringes at the corners of the mantle (Num 15:37-38; Deut 22:12), which the Pharisees enlarged. Christ condemned them for their pride concerning these things without the appreciation of their true value, when He said that the Pharisees "make broad their phylacteries, and enlarge the borders of their garments" (Mt 23:5).

The dress of Jesus. In general, the clothes worn by Christ, as well as the disciples, were of

Bas relief of Shalmeneser III of Assyria showing King Jehu of Israel paying tribute to the Assyrian king and illustrating Hebrew and Assyrian dress of the ninth century B.C. ORINST

the simplest kind. It seems He wore a shirt or inner garment, since He removed His outer garments (pl., i.e., the tunic and mantle) before washing the feet of the disciples (Jn 13:4). His tunic was seamless (Jn 19:23, RSV) and therefore had short sleeves and fit closely at the neck. It would also indicate value and may have been given to Him by one of the women who ministered of their substance (Lk 8:3). Outside the tunic was a linen girdle or sash, wound several times around His waist. The mantle of woolen cloth was probably not white, for it became such during the transfiguration (Mk 9:3). It may have been blue or white with colored stripes and would have had the blue fringe or tassels at the corners. He wore leather sandals on His feet (Mt 3:11). He probably wore the customary white turban on His head, since no Jewish teacher of that day would appear with the head uncovered. This would have been wrapped around the head with the ends falling down over the neck. It probably fastened with a cord under the chin. Such a cloth, like a large handkerchief (KJV, "apron," *soudarion,* Lk 19:20, NASB; Acts 19:12), was used to cover the face of a corpse (Jn 11:44; 20:7). The disciples probably were dressed in similar fashion to Jesus.

The dress of foreign nations. The dress of foreign nations is occasionally referred to in Scripture. Included in the Babylonian garb worn by Daniel's three friends were the following articles (Dan 3:21, NASB): (1) the Aram. *sarbālîn* (KJV,"coats"), which were trousers or drawers and the distinctive feature of the Babylonian dress; (2) Aram. *peṭash* (KJV, "hosen"), which was a coat or inner tunic; (3) Aram. *karbelā'* (KJV, "hat"), the high pointed cap of the Cimmerians and Persians; and (4) Aram. *lebûsh* (KJV, "garment"), which was a general term for their other clothes.

Although the references to Gr. and Rom. dress are few, the traveling cloak referred to by Paul (II Tim 4:13) may have been a Rom. garment, the Lat. *paenula,* a circular cape used for protection against stormy weather.

The ornaments of dress. The Jewish men sometimes carried a staff or cane as an aid to travel through rough country or for purposes of protection. It was often ornamented at the top. Some men also wore a signet ring which served as the personal signature of its owner (Gen 38:18; Lk 15:22). This was generally worn on the right hand or suspended from the neck by a cord.

The women were more elaborate in their decoration and wore several types of ornaments. A favorite with them from the earliest times was the armlet or bracelet (Gen 24:22, 30, 47). Bracelets (*q.v.*) were sometimes worn even by men of rank (II Sam 1:10). These were made of ivory, precious metals, horn, cords, or chains. They could be worn on both arms, and some covered the forearm to the elbow.

The anklet (Isa 3:18) was generally so arranged that in walking a clanging or clapping sound was made which called attention to the wearer and enhanced her pride (v. 16). Sometimes small chains were fastened from one foot to the other in order to secure a more elegant step (Isa 3:20).

The necklace was another favorite ornament among the women. Men of rank and warriors of foreign nations also wore them. Persons of rank sometimes wore several. They were made of metal, stones, and pearls, and strung on a cord. Attached to them sometimes were other articles of finery, such as half-moons or crescents (Isa 3:18), smelling bottles (Isa 3:20, RSV), headbands with stellated studs (Isa 3:18), and serpent charms or amulets (Isa 3:20).

Earrings (*q.v.*) were universally worn by women (Ex 32:2; Ezk 16:12; Hos 2:13). They were made of bone, horn, or metal, and some that have been found have been rather large (as much as the width of four fingers in diameter). Some women would puncture the earlobe with as many openings as possible, and would then put a ring through each.

Nose rings were also a favorite and were used from the earliest times (Gen 24:22, 47, RSV). They were made of ivory or metal and often decorated with precious jewels. Isaiah lists these as well as other articles of ornamentation in rebuking the women of Jerusalem (Isa 3:18–26). *See* Jewelry.

Customs relating to dress. There are many significant customs associated with dress, and most arise from the particular type of wearing apparel. The outer garment or mantle had many secondary functions because of its size. It was used to carry a burden (Ruth 3:15) or as an impromptu saddle (Mt 21:7). It was used as a cover at night (Ex 22:27; Ruth 3:9). Because of its necessity, a creditor could not retain it after sunset (Ex 22:26; Deut 24:12–13).

Because the garments were loose and flowing, they were used in many symbolic ways. Rending them was a sign of grief (Gen 37:29, 34), fear (I Kgs 21:27), indignation (II Kgs 5:7; 11:14), and despair (Jud 11:35). Shaking the garments or shaking the dust off them was a token of renunciation (Acts 18:6). Spreading clothes before a person meant loyalty and joyous reception (II Kgs 9:13; Mt 21:8). If they were wrapped around the head, it was a sign of awe (I Kgs 19:13) or grief (II Sam 15:30). Casting them off meant excitement (Acts 22:23), and laying hold of them was a sign of supplication (I Sam 15:27; Isa 3:6).

Since the length of the outer garment made it inconvenient for active work, it was left in the house when working close by (Mt 24:18), thrown off when necessary (Jn 13:4; Acts 7:58), or girded up if traveling (I Kgs 18:46; II Kgs 4:29). Because the garments concealed the feet when sitting, a long, flowing robe was a sign of reverence (Isa 6:1). The greatest insult a Jew could receive was to shorten his garments (II Sam 10:4). Raising the skirt

A Syrian wears the typical pointed hat of his homeland as he presents tribute at the Persian palace at Persepolis. sixth century B.C. ORINST

of a woman implied her unchastity and was a great insult (Isa 47:2).

In many cases, the presentation of a robe was a sign of installation into office (Gen 41:42; Est 8:15; Isa 22:21), and taking the robe away was dismissal from office (II Macc 4:38). Presenting a robe worn by the giver was a token of great affection (I Sam 18:4). Being given the best robe was a mark of special honor (Lk 15:22). The number of such robes or vestments stored for the purpose of presents might be very large and formed a great part of the wealth of the individual (II Kgs 10:22). Sometimes such a wardrobe was superintended by a servant (II Chr 34:22). *See* Change of Raiment.

Bibliography. ANEP, figs. 1-66. E. P. Barrows, *Sacred Geography and Antiquities,* New York: American Tract Society, 1875. CornPBE, pp. 221-227. George B. Eager, "Dress," ISBE, II, 875-879. H. F. Lutz, *Textiles and Costume Among People of the Ancient Near East,* New York: Stechert, 1923. John M'Clintock and James Strong, "Attire," *Biblical, Theological and Ecclesiastical Cyclopaedia,* I, 529-534; "Dress," II, 886-892. Madeleine S. and J. Lane Miller, "Apparel," *Encyclopedia of Bible Life,* New York: Harper, 1944, pp. 48-64. James B. Pritchard, ed. consultant, *Everyday Life in Bible Times,* Washington: National Geographic Society, 1967. E. A. Speiser, *et al., Everyday Life in Ancient Times,* Washington: National Geographic Society, 1951.

E. C. J.

DRINK. Both water and sour milk were drunk by the Jews, but a sour wine often called vinegar was also used extensively by the common people (Ruth 2:14). People of wealth drank wine of a better vintage often mixed with water and spices.

The word is also used figuratively: "drink iniquity like water" (Job 15:16); "drink of the wrath of the Almighty" (Job 21:20); "drink of the river of thy pleasures" (Ps 36:8); "drink the wine of astonishment" (Ps 60:3); "tears to drink" (Ps 80:5); "drink the wine of violence" (Prov 4:17); "let him come unto me, and drink" (Jn 7:37), referring to the manner of receiving the Holy Spirit. *See also* Drink, Strong; Banquet; Food; Wine.

DRINK OFFERING. *See* Sacrificial Offering.

DRINK, STRONG. Alcoholic beverages in Bible times were made from pomegranates, grapes, barley, dates, and raisins. The term "strong drink" referred most likely to a strong barley beer, known from archaeological discoveries to have been very popular among the Egyptians and the Philistines. Strong drink (Heb. *shēkār;* Akkad. *šikaru*) refers to an intoxicating drink. In Palestine wine was almost always fermented grape juice.

Scripture is emphatic in its denunciation of strong drink. Aaron and his sons were not to drink wine nor strong drink when ministering in the tabernacle (Lev 10:9). This injunction applied also to their descendants. God through Isaiah pronounced woe upon those who drank all day (Isa 5:11) and upon those in authority who drank, for this impaired their judgment (Isa 5:22-23). The priests and prophets had "erred through strong drink" (Isa 28:7). Strong drink is the cause of poverty (Prov 21:17-20) and much sorrow and dissoluteness (Prov 23:29-35). Compare also Lk 1:15: "shall drink neither wine nor strong drink" *(sikera).*

In days of increasing alcoholism the rebuke of Prov 20:1 needs to be sounded abroad: "Wine is a scorner, strong drink a brawler, and whosoever gets drunk is unwise" (Berkeley). *See* Drunk, Drunkard; Drunkenness; Wine.

R. H. B.

DROMEDARY. *See* Animals: Camel, I.5.

DROPSY. *See* Diseases.

DROSS. *See* Mineral and Metals: Silver.

DROUGHT. This expression is connected with famine, one of the Lord's judgments in the OT. Water is usually at a premium in Palestine. Since rain was the chief source of water for both crops and human consumption, a prolonged drought spelled disaster for Palestine (cf. I Kgs 17:1; Jas 5:17). In addition to the partial failure of winter rains, the OT mentions frequent summer droughts (cf. Ps 32:4) caused by the blighting E wind (cf. Hos 13:15).

Religion and nature were tied together in the OT. The Lord taught His people that He is the controller of nature. Thus throughout Israel's history He used droughts and other calamities of nature to urge them to repent (cf. I Kgs 17:1; 18:17-18; Hag 1:6, 9-11; 2:16-17). Obedience and prosperity (cf. Ps 1:1-3; Prov 3:7-10; Isa 1:19), disobedience and want (cf. Lev 26:14-16) were biblical siamese twins. One of the aspects of the Messianic Age will be abundance of rain and fertility of nature (Joel 2:23 f.).

D. W. D.

DROWN. The Egyptian charioteers pursuing the escaping Israelites were drowned in the Red Sea (Ex 15:4; Heb 11:29). Drowning was never a Jewish method of capital punishment, nor was it a common practice in Galilee in Jesus' day; but it was known among Gentiles in the Graeco-Roman world (Mt 18:6). The Gr. *buthizō* is used figuratively in I Tim 6:9 of foolish desires that drown or plunge men into ruin.

DRUM. *See* Music.

DRUNK, DRUNKARD. Drunkenness is expressed in the Gr. NT by *methē* and the verbs *methuō* and *methuskō*. In the LXX *methuō* translates most often the Heb. *shākar,* which is used both literally (Gen 9:21) and figuratively (Jer 25:27) of intoxication. The many injunctions against drunkenness in the OT show that such was prevalent among the people of Israel (Deut 21:20; Lev 10:9; Prov 20:1; 23:20-21, 30-35; Joel 1:5; Nah 1:10; *et al.*). The geography and climate of Palestine are especially suited for growing the grapes from which wine is made. The abundance of wine is seen in the fact that it was traded commercially for incense and spices from Arabia (cf. BA, II [1939], 40). Intoxicants were also made from grain, as well as apples, dates, honey, and pomegranates.

Although there is no absolute prohibition of the use of wine in the NT (I Tim 5:23; Jn 2:7-9; Mt 11:19; Lk 7:34), it is clear that those who would live godly, especially those who take positions of leadership, will not be guilty of using it excessively (I Pet 4:3; I Tim 3:3, 8; Tit 1:7; 2:3). Drunkenness is not only contrasted to spirituality (Eph 5:18; Rom 13:13), but drunkards are to be excluded from the kingdom of God (Gal 5:21; I Cor 6:10; 5:11). *See* Wine; Drink, Strong.

J. McR.

DRUNKENNESS. Holy Scripture contains many cases of individual drunkenness, such as Noah (Gen 9:20-24), Lot (Gen 19:30-35), Nabal (I Sam 25:36), Uriah (II Sam 11:12-13), Amnon (II Sam 13:28), King Elah of Israel (I Kgs 16:8-10), and Ben-hadad of Syria (I Kgs 20:16). Drunkenness is implied in the account of Belshazzar's feast (Dan 5:1-4, 23). It must have been common in the times of the judges, for Eli quickly suspected Hannah of being drunken (I Sam 1:13-14; see also Prov 23:29-35; Isa 5:11, 22; 28:1, 3, 7-8).

Jesus warned His disciples against drunkenness, lest they be caught unprepared to meet Him at His return (Lk 21:34). Paul severely reprimanded the Corinthian Christians for drinking to excess at the Lord's Supper (I Cor 11:20-21), and admonished believers in Rome concerning drunkenness (Rom 13:13). He forthrightly taught that continuance in alcoholism barred one from the kingdom of God (I Cor 6:9-11; Gal 5:21). His command is absolute: "Do not get drunk with wine, for that is debauchery" (Eph 5:18, RSV). *See* Drink, Strong; Drunk, Drunkard.

J. R.

DRUSILLA (drū-sĭl'*ȧ*). The wife of Felix (*q.v.*), governor or procurator of Judea before whom Paul was brought at Caesarea (Acts 24:24). Born in A.D. 38, she was a Jewess, previously married to Azizus, king of Emesa, whom she left for Felix (Jos *Ant.* xx.7.1-2). As the youngest daughter of Herod Agrippa I, Drusilla belonged to the infamous family of the Herods. When Paul stood before Felix and Drusilla, the apostle spoke "concerning the faith in Christ Jesus," with the result that Felix was "terrified" as Paul "reasoned of righteousness, and self-control, and the judgment to come" (Acts 24:25, ASV). The effect on Drusilla is not recorded. *See* Herod.

DUGONG. *See* Animals, V.3.

DUKE. Around 1611 when the KJV was translated, "duke" was not a title but referred to a ruler or chieftain of a family or nation. Hence in Gen 36:15-43; Ex 15:15; I Chr 1:51-54 the KJV uses "duke" to translate Heb. *'allûph,* a tribal or clan leader of the Edomites or Horites. In Josh 13:21 (KJV) the Heb. plural of *nāsîk* is rendered "dukes," the ones anointed by Sihon, i.e., vassal princes to him.

DULCIMER. *See* Music.

DUMAH (dū'm*ȧ*)

1. A son of Ishmael and the presumed ancestor of a tribe in Arabia (Gen 25:14; I Chr 1:30), which gave its name to an oasis now called Dumat ej-Jendel, capital of the district known as the Jauf. Dumah lies about halfway between the Gulf of Aqabah and Kuwait on the Persian Gulf. It seems to be the same as the *Adumatu* conquered by Sennacherib (ANET, p. 691) and the *Adummu* overrun by Nabonidus of Babylonia on his campaign against Tema (ANET, p. 305). This may be the Dumah of Isa 21:11 (but see # 2), if during the 8th cen. B.C. the Edomites had extended their control over

200 miles eastward to include the oasis of el-Jauf.

2. Perhaps a symbolic name for Edom (Isa 21:11); the Heb. word means "silence." LXX has *Idoumaias,* i.e., Edom. But see # 1.

3. A town in the mountain district of Judah (Josh 15:52), probably the present ed-Dômeh, ten miles SW of Hebron. The name Rumah in II Kgs 23:36 perhaps is a misspelling for Dumah in Judah.

J. R.

DUMB. Dumbness in Scripture is attributable to several causes: (1) inability to speak by reason of a physical defect (Mt 15:30-31; cf. Ex 4:11); (2) an oppression by an evil spirit binding one's center of speech (Mt 9:32-33; 12:22; Mk 9:17, 25); (3) a psychological fear (Dan 10:15-19) or a feeling of guilt (Ps 39:9-11) or of inferiority in not knowing how to express oneself (Prov 31:8; cf. Ex 4:10-16); (4) a temporary judgment from God (Lk 1:20; Ezk 3:26).

DUNG. In KJV "dung" is used to render nine Heb. and two Gr. words. While these possess different shades of meaning, all are used to refer to excrement—waste matter discharged from the body—either of human beings or of animals. Dung is alluded to in several ways:

In connection with sacrifices. In the sin offering and the sacrifice of the red heifer, dung with other portions was to be burned "without the camp" (Ex 29:14; Num 19:5). Mal 2:3 refers to such dung being smeared on the faces of hypocritical offerers, signifying that God would allow them to be shamefully treated.

As fertilizer. The barren fig tree was to be "dunged" (Lk 13:8). Several times it was threatened that the bodies of the Jews or their enemies would be "as dung for the earth" (Ps 83:10; Jer 8:2).

As fuel. Ezekiel was to use it thus in connection with a prophetic sign (Ezk 4:12, 15). Cattle dung is still used as fuel in Mesopotamia and other lands. (On this use, see instructive notes in KD, *The Book of Job,* I, 377; KD, *The Prophecies of Ezekiel,* I, 82; Doughty, *Travels in Arabia Deserts.)*

As food in a last resort during famine (II Kgs 6:25). Documents outside Scripture also record such actions in times of extremity.

As a figure of worthlessness. In connection with divine judgments it is several times said that the bodies of various ones will be cast like dung on the earth (I Kgs 14:10; Zeph 1:17). Comparison is made here with the use of dung for fertilizer. In Phil 3:8 the apostle Paul considers fleshly honors as "but dung" ("refuse") compared with the privilege of knowing Christ.

The Dung Gate (Neh 2:13; 3:13-14; 12:31) was the one through which refuse was taken from the city of Jerusalem. *See* Jerusalem: Dung Gate.

G. C. L.

DUNG GATE. *See* Jerusalem: Gates and Towers 10.

DUNGEON. *See* Prison.

DUNGHILL. In KJV "dunghill" is the rendering of several different words meaning (1) a manure pit (Isa 25:10) or heap (Ezr 6:11; Lk 14:35); (2) an ash heap or garbage dump where the poor and beggars often stayed (I Sam 2:8; Ps 113:7; Lam 4:5).

DURA (dŭr'*ȧ*). The name of a plain in the province of Babylon where Nebuchadnezzar set up a golden image (Dan 3:1). Aram. *dûrā'* probably is derived from Akkad. *duru* meaning "wall," "circuit," perhaps referring to some of the outer fortifications of Babylon. The name survives in Nahr Dūra, a tributary which flows into the Euphrates *c.* five miles below Hilla. Nearby are some mounds or low hills called Tulūl Dūra.

DUST. Dust refers literally to small, powdery particles of earth, or is occasionally used as a synonym for the soil itself (Job 14:19; 38:38; Isa 25:12). From such humble material man's body was originally made by God (Gen 2:7), as well as the bodies of the other creatures (Eccl 3:20). To it the body eventually returns (Gen 3:19).

Dust is frequently used in the Bible as a figure of speech, and in a variety of ways. It sometimes speaks of a large number or great quantity (Gen 13:16; Ps 78:27; Zech 9:3). Conversely it is used to describe that which is very small (Deut 9:21; Ps 18:42; Isa 40:15). It speaks of a lowly position from which one is brought up (I Kgs 16:2) or a degraded position to which one is brought down (Ps 44:25).

To make something "like the dust" signifies complete destruction (II Kgs 13:7). Dust is frequently used as a synonym for the grave (Job 20:11; Dan 12:2). To speak of man as dust is to call attention to his frailty by an allusion to his humble origin (Gen 18:27; Ps 103:14). Dust is also a figurative expression for anything worthless (Zeph 1:17).

Most NT references have to do with Christ's command to His apostles to "shake off the dust of your feet" (Mt 10:14) when departing from a city which had rejected their divine message. "This symbolic act signifies that the feet of the heralds of the kingdom have actually been in the house or the town, and that they leave this their dust in witness to the fact that they were there but were forced to leave because they were unwelcome" (R. C. H. Lenski, *The Interpretation of St. Matthew's Gospel,* p. 396).

To throw dust at a person or in the air (II Sam 16:13; Acts 22:23) is said by some authorities to be a demand for justice (Conybeare and Howson, *The Life and Epistles of St. Paul,* p. 589). More likely, however, it was simply a gesture of contempt and hatred.

It was evidently quite common in Bible times to place dust on one's head as a sign of deep sorrow, grievous mourning, and complete humiliation (see e.g., Josh 7:6; Job 2:12; Lam 2:10; Rev 18:19). "The head, the noblest part of man, was thus placed beneath the dust of the ground from whence he was taken" (J. J. Lias in the *Pulpit Commentary,* Vol. 3, Part 2, p. 121).

G. C. L.

DUTY. Found six or eight times (excluding "due"). The duty of marriage is discussed in Ex 21:10; Deut 25:5, 7, in two different situations. Daily duty in connection with religious ritual is discussed in II Chr 8:14; Ezr 3:4. In Eccl 12:13, the word is supplied. The whole duty of man under the law was to fear God and keep His commandments. In Lk 17:10, Jesus says when we have done as commanded, we have merely done our duty. In Rom 15:27, Paul speaks of the duty of Gentiles to minister in material things to Jews who have ministered to them in spiritual things.

DWARF. The Heb. word *daq* is rendered "dwarf" in Lev 21:20, describing one who is physically disqualified from offering sacrifices. The term may indicate small size (perhaps caused by tuberculosis; *see* Diseases) or deformity resulting from withered limbs or some other malady. A dancing pigmy or dwarf was brought from central Africa as a gift to Pharaoh Pepy II of the Sixth Dynasty (*Everyday Life in Ancient Times,* National Geographic Soc., 1951, pp. 104 f.). The Egyptian god Bes was depicted as a grotesque dwarf figure (ANEP, # 663, 664).

DWELL. The translation of some 15 Heb. and Gr. words. Heb. *gûr* is often used of the stay of a foreigner, a transient, among the people (Lev 19:34).

Heb. *yāshab* conceives of one's dwelling as a sitting down, whether in a tent in the field or in a house in the town (Gen 13:12; Lev 18:3). Heb. *shākan* is used frequently of the Lord's dwelling among His people or in Jerusalem and means "to settle down and remain or dwell permanently." In the Gr. *katoikeō* (Acts 7:4) is similar to the Heb. *shākan.* Longer terms of stay are denoted by *menō,* "abide," "stay longer." *Oikeō* denotes "to have a house." *See* House; Tent.

The Gr. word for tent (tabernacle) is the root (*skēnē*) of a NT verb, *skēnoō,* describing the purpose of the life of Christ: like the tabernacle, He is the residence and manifestation of God's presence and glory among His people ("And the Word became flesh and tabernacled among us," Jn 1:14, NASB marg.). The Holy Spirit will abide (*menō*) in the Christian forever (Jn 14:17). The normal dwelling place or manner of life of the Christian is in the Father's love (I Jn 4:16).

H. G. S.

DWELLING. *See* Cave; Dwell; Habitation; House; Palace; Tabernacle; Tent.

DYERS. *See* Occupations.

DYSENTERY. *See* Diseases.

E

EAGLE. *See* Animals, III.53, 54.

EAR

1. The organ of hearing, our guarantee of God's ability to hear (Ps 94:9). Sometimes the external ear alone is meant, as in the piercing of a Heb. slave's earlobe for a sign of his choosing perpetual slavery (Ex 21:6; Deut 15:16 f.; Ps 40:6); also in the applying of blood on the right ear of the priest at his consecration (Ex 29:20), and of blood and oil at the leper's cleansing (Lev 14:14, 17). Figuratively, it speaks of an ability for spiritual understanding (Isa 50:4-5; contrast Isa 6:10; Jer 6:10).

2. Used of the fruiting spike of a cereal plant (Mk 4:28).

3. Archaic verb meaning to plow or till (I Sam 8:12; Isa 30:24).

Bibliography. Johannes Horst, "*Ous,* etc.," TDNT, V, 543-549. G. Kittel, "*Akouō,* etc.," TDNT, I, 216-225.

EARNEST (OF THE SPIRIT). "Earnest" is from the Gr. *arrabōn,* "surety," "pledge," a Semitic loan-word (cf. Heb. *'ērābôn,* Gen 38:17, 18, 20). It is a down payment given as a pledge or deposit that one will finally pay the full amount of the purchase price. The term "earnest money" is used today in the purchase of property.

The word is used three times in the NT (II Cor 1:22; 5:5; Eph 1:13-14). The last reference makes the biblical meaning clear: "In whom also after that ye believed, ye were sealed by that Holy Spirit of promise, which is the earnest of our inheritance until the redemption of the purchased possession unto the praise of his glory." The Holy Spirit was sent at Pentecost, just as money is given to guarantee a business transaction. His presence is a foretaste and pledge of what is finally to come. For the benefits to the believer in his completed salvation and total inheritance, *see* Salvation.

R. A. K.

EARRING. The Heb. word *nezem* signifies a ring and is used both of nose ring and earring. Its first use is in Gen 24:22 where the KJV has earring and the ASV has ring. From Gen 24:47 (ASV) it seems evident that nose ring is correct. Yet in Gen 35:4 earrings are definitely meant. Here the word is found in connection with Jacob's word to his household to discard the gods of the foreigner. They gave to him the foreign gods in their hand and the rings in their ears.

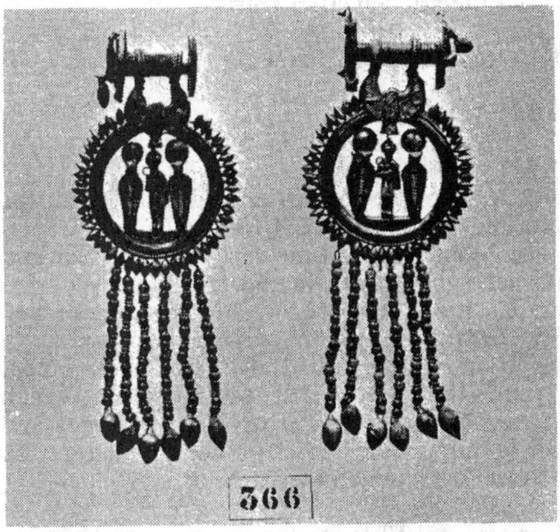

Gold earrings from the tomb of King Tutankhamon of Egypt. LL

From Ex 32:2-3 we learn that golden earrings were worn by Heb. women and both male and female children. Nothing is said of adult males wearing them. At this time they were fashioned into the golden calf. In Ex 35:22 either nose rings or earrings may be meant, but here the gold becomes an offering to the Lord for the construction of the tabernacle. Both men and women brought these rings, so if earrings were meant it shows that Heb. men did on occasion use them. However, Jud 8:24 indicates this was not the usual practice, for the men had earrings (or nose rings) because they were Ishmaelites.

The context of Prov 25:12 seems to favor earring instead of nose ring. Here it is used in a good sense of a thing of beauty. Thus the gold ring in itself was neither good nor bad, but could be used in idolatrous worship to make a golden calf, or given to the Lord, or worn as an object of beauty. In the NT the emphasis is that a Christian's adornment should not be outward but spiritual (I Tim 2:9-10; I Pet 3:3-4). *See* Dress.

A second word, *'āgîl,* translated earring in Num 31:50 and Ezk 16:12, emphasizes the idea of roundness.

The word *laḥash* means an amulet or charm. This word, translated in the KJV as "earring" in Isa 3:20, is "amulet" in ASV. The root means "to whisper" or "to conjure," and thus refers to charms of metal or jewels which were thought to have protective powers. Sometimes they were inscribed with magical formulas or were shaped like god-emblems, as among the Egyptians. *See* Amulet; Jewels.

C. J. W.

EARTH. This word has several meanings in the English Bible.

1. The distinctive name for our planet (Job 1:7).
2. The solid matter of the globe in contrast to the water and air (Gen 1:10).
3. The soil; the ground as a farmer would speak of it (II Kgs 5:17).
4. The inhabitants of the globe (Gen 11:1).
5. The world as lying in the evil one; thus "the things upon the earth" are sinful and the opposite of that which is heavenly and spiritual (Col 3:2, 5; cf. Phil 3:19).

The main Heb. words translated earth are (a) *'ădāmâ,* which signifies the reddish soil or ground (cf. Heb. *'ādōm,* "red"), from which man's body was made, and so he was named *'ādām,* "man" or "Adam" (Gen 2:7; 3:19); and (b) *'ereṣ,* which is not only translated "earth" but "land," thus denoting a country (Gen 21:21). Since this word may mean either the whole earth or just part of it, some passages may read "earth" in one translation and "land" in another (cf. Isa 10:23, KJV and ASV). *See* Land.

In the NT the usual Gr. word is *gē,* translated either "earth" with its various meanings or "land," especially the land of Judea (Mt 27:45). See Lk 23:44 for the parallel account and note how "earth" is used in the KJV and "land" in the ASV. Another word, *oikoumenē,* denotes especially the whole inhabited earth (Lk 21:26), and particularly the Roman Empire in NT times (Lk 2:1, "world"). *See* World; Creation.

C. J. W.

EARTHEN VESSEL, EARTHENWARE. *See* Pot; Potter under Occupations; Pottery.

EARTHQUAKE. A vibration of the earth caused sometimes by a cracking and shifting of rock beneath the surface. There are two major types, volcanic and tectonic. The Bible mentions a few; e.g., when (1) the law was given on Sinai (Ex 19:18; Heb 12:26); (2) the earth "swallowed . . . up" Korah, Dathan, and Abiram (Num 16:31-32); (3) Jonathan attacked the Philistine garrison at Gibeah (I Sam 14:15); (4) Elijah was on Horeb (I Kgs 19:11); (5) Uzziah was king of Judah (Amos 1:1; Zech 14:5); (6) Jesus died (Mt 27:51) and arose from the dead (Mt 28:2); (7) Paul and Silas were imprisoned at Philippi (Acts 16:26). Sometimes earthquakes are associated with divine judgment (Rev 6:12; 8:5; 11:13, 19). They will precede our Lord's second coming (Mt 24:7). The greatest earthquake of all time is yet future (Rev 16:18).

Natural theater on south side of Mount Ebal.
JR

EAST (Heb. *qedem,* lit., "front," or "before"; and *mizrāḥ,* "the place of dawning"; Gr. *anatolē,* "the rising" of the sun).

The Hebrews divided the world into four parts and described them as "corners of the earth" (Isa 11:12; Rev 7:1; 20:8), or as the "four winds" (Ezk 37:9). Like many Semitic peoples, the Hebrews looked to the East, "the place of dawning," as their basic direction. In describing the points of the compass, the "four corners," a person would face E, making that direction before, W to the rear, N to the left, and S to the right. *See* East, Children of the.

EAST, CHILDREN OF THE. The Heb. term *b^e^nê-qedem,* "sons of the east," was a general ancient designation of the peoples, mostly nomadic, living E of Palestine. They ranged as far N as Padan-aram where Laban (Gen 28:2; 29:1) and Balaam (Num 23:7) lived, and southward to Moab and Edom (Isa 11:14) and beyond (Ezk 25:4, 10) to Kedar among the Arab tribes (Jer 49:28). Many of these were descendants of Abraham by Keturah (Gen 25: 1-6). They invaded Israel along with the nomadic Midianites and Amalekites in the time of Gideon (Jud 6:3, 33; 7:12; 8:10-11).

The region of Qedem is mentioned in Ugaritic literature as well as in the Egyptian Tale of Sinuhe which reflects conditions in Palestine-Syria in the 20th cen. B.C. (ANET, p. 19). Job was "the greatest of all the men of the east" (Job 1:3). The men of the E had a special reputation for wisdom (I Kgs 4:30), which accords with the classification of the book of Job as Wisdom Literature.

J. R.

EAST GATE. *See* Jerusalem: Gates and Towers 14.

EAST SEA. The Dead Sea, on the eastern border of Canaan and Israel, is called the East Sea in Joel 2:20; Ezk 47:18; Zech 14:8 (RSV). *See* Dead Sea.

EAST WIND. *See* Wind.

EASTER. This word appears only once in the KJV (Acts 12:4). It is used there as a translation of the Gr. word *pascha,* which is translated correctly as "passover" in the 28 other places where it occurs in the NT. Revisions of the KJV consistently translate *pascha* as "passover" in all passages, including Acts 12:4 (cf. ASV, RSV, NEB). The English word "Easter" is thought to be derived from the name of a Teutonic goddess of spring, Eastre, and to have been adapted by Christians to its present usage about the 8th cen. after Christ.

EATING. *See* Food: Banquet.

EBAL (ē'bȧl)

1. An alternate form of Obal (*q.v.*; I Chr 1:22).

2. One of the sons of Shobal, son of Seir the Horite (Gen 36:20, 23; I Chr 1:40).

3. Mount Ebal, at the very center of Canaan, is the highest peak in the hill country of Samaria. Lying just N of Mount Gerizim and Shechem in the pass between, it rises to a height of 3,083 feet above sea level. Steep, barren, and rocky, Ebal was the site at which Joshua erected an altar of unhewn stones and wrote on plastered stones a copy of the law as Moses had commanded (Deut 11:29; 27:2 f.; Josh 8:30 ff.). The 12 tribes were divided upon Gerizim and Ebal for the blessings and curses, respectively, of the law.

EBED (ē'bĕd). Meaning "servant," Heb. *'ebed* is an element of many compound names. The following may be shortened from *'ebed-'ēl,* "servant of God," or *'ebed-yāh,* "servant of Yahweh":

1. The father of Gaal who headed the rebellion against Abimelech at Shechem (Jud 9:26-35).

2. The leader of the clan of Adin, who returned with Ezra from the Babylonian Captivity with 50 men (Ezr 8:6).

EBED-MELECH (ē'bĕd-mĕl'ĕk). This name meaning "servant of the king" may also have been a title equal to "king's minister." He was an Ethiopian (Cushite) eunuch at the court of King Zedekiah of Judah, perhaps in charge of the royal harem, an office which would give him private access to the king. He obtained Zedekiah's permission to rescue Jeremiah from the muddy bottom of an empty cistern (Jer 38:6-13). He was aided by three (one Heb. MS and LXX, v. 10) other men using ropes with old rags to pad the prophet's armpits. Later Jeremiah prophesied to Ebed-melech that for his kindness his life would be delivered in the approaching day of Jerusalem's destruction (Jer 39:15-18).

EBENEZER (ĕb'ĕ-nē'zĕr; "stone of help"). The name is mentioned three times in the Bible (I Sam 4:1; 5:1; 7:12). According to I Sam 7:12 it was the name given to a stone set up by

Samuel to commemorate the divine assistance given to Israel in battle, whereby they were victorious over the Philistines. Its position was carefully defined as a place between Mizpah and Shen, near Aphek. According to I Sam 4:1; 5:1, Israel 20 years previously had been soundly defeated there by the Philistines and the ark of God captured and taken to Ashdod. The writer used the name Ebenezer because the place was so known at the time of writing.

EBER (ē'bẽr)

1. Eber was a descendant of Shem (Gen 10:21, 24). He was the father of Peleg and Joktan, and the ancestor of various peoples called "all the children of Eber" (Gen 10:21; cf. Num 24:24), which phrase probably means the "Hebrews" in the broadest sense. Through Peleg, Eber became an ancestor of Abraham (Gen 11:16-26), and thus is in the messianic line (Lk 3:35). *See* Hebrew People.

2-5. Eber is also the name of a descendant of Gad (I Chr 5:13), two different descendants of Benjamin (I Chr 8:12, 22; cf. I Chr 8:17), and the name of a post-Exilic priest (Heb 12:20). *See* Heber.

EBIASAPH (ĕ-bī'ȧ-săf). An ancestor of Heman, a musician in David's time (I Chr 6:23, 37: 9:19). Probably the same as Abiasaph (*q.v.*).

EBONY. *See* Plants.

EBRONAH. Translated Abronah in RSV. A campsite of the Israelites near Ezion-geber (Num 33:34-35). Possibly it was at 'Ain ed-Defiyeh, a shallow water hole in the Arabah *c.* seven and one-half miles N of Ezion-geber.

ECCLESIASTES, BOOK OF. A treatise on a proper philosophy of life, and an outstanding example of OT Wisdom Literature.

Title

The title comes to us by way of the Vulg. from the LXX, where it means a member of the *ecclesia*. The Heb. form *qōheleth,* which scholars often transliterate, is a feminine participle used idiomatically of the one who convenes and addresses a public assembly or school, i.e., the officer of a *qahal,* the common word for assembly.

Author

Did the writer assemble proverbs (cf. I Kgs 4:32)? Sections of the book are such (e.g., 7:1-13; 10). Or was he an orator or debater? But the book seems meditation rather than argument. Most translate the word as "preacher" (so five times in 1:1, 2; 12:8-10 according to KJV, ASV, RSV, Berkeley).

Qoheleth is declared to be "son of David, king in Jerusalem" (1:1). Is he Solomon, or is he merely quoting a saying of Solomon's in v. 2 as the theme of his study? Scholars are divided as to Solomon's being the author. Yet in 1:12 we read: "I the Preacher was king over Israel in Jerusalem," i.e., up to the time of writing. The critical argument against Solomonic authorship is illogical, for the above statement is natural for one writing an autobiography. Beginning with chap. 3 Solomon uses proverbs which are based on his experience. He said, "I will be wise; but it was far from me" (7:23; contrast 1:16). It was a poor time compared to former days (7:10), for the government was corrupt near the end of his reign, and the subjects of the tyrannical king considered themselves oppressed (3:16; 4:1; 8:9; 10:5-7).

Was Qoheleth one or three? Some moderns say the preacher wrote in pessimism; he was augmented by a Wise Man with proverbs (e.g., 10:1-11:4), and he by a Pious One with more orthodox religious sentiments (e.g., 2:26). A final appendix (12:13 f.) commends the practice of the Jewish religion as man's whole duty. But could not one with keen mind both argue a case, adapt proverbs, and contend with doubts?

Qoheleth is never quoted in the NT, but Rom 8:20, speaking of creation subject to vanity, may have his theme as background; and our Lord's parable of the rich fool (Lk 12:16-21) is like the final sentence (Eccl 12:14).

While some scholars have suggested otherwise, the epilogue is by the preacher himself. He had wondered whether at death the spirit of man really does go upward to God (3:21), but now he is assured of a final judgment (12:14; cf. 11:9).

Time of Writing

The time of writing is held by some scholars to be the Persian period (which ended 333 B.C.) or even the succeeding Gr. period because of the occurrence of several words that seem to be Aramaic or Persian, but references to definite historical events seem quite indistinct. Solomon had more widely ranging international contacts than any after him (see Archer, SOTI, pp. 462-471).

Theme

The thought of these 12 chapters circles, rises and falls. At times it seems pessimistic, at times the cloud lifts. Though God is mentioned 20 times, 27 things vex the author with four main problems: life is unequal (2:12-26); the world is inscrutable (8:17); the future is uncertain (11:2, 6, 8 f.); death is dark (9:4-6, 10).

Yet there does appear to be a progression from an emphasis on vanity (Heb. *hebel,* "breath," "mist," anything transitory, frail, illusory, empty), mentioned 26 times in chaps. 1-6 and 12 times in chaps. 7-12, to an emphasis on wisdom, 11 times in chaps. 1-6 and 17 times in chaps. 7-12, and on being wise, 6 times in chaps. 1-6 and 15 times in chaps. 7-12.

The text, "How utterly futile, how utterly transitory, the whole thing is a puff of wind" (1:2; 12:8, orig. trans.), is true to realistic humanism. Life without God has no real meaning. Secularism can bring no lasting satisfaction. Faith, however, embraces the divine government. So in sum, "Banish moroseness from your heart; and remove evil from your flesh; for youth and the age of black hair are transient. Remember, then, your Creator in the days of your prime-of-life" (11:10–12:1, orig. trans.).

Outline

The Prologue, 1:1-11

Life, while not in itself evil, is a meaningless cycle, vain when lived apart from God and not used for His glory.

I. The Vanity of All Things, 1:12–6:12
   A. The failure of all humanistic attempts to give meaning to existence, 1:12–2:23
   B. The contrast of a life lived in observance of God's ordained order, 2:24–3:22
   C. The disappointments of earthly life, 4:1-16
   D. The futile efforts of the self-seeking life, 5:1-20
   E. The inadequacy of attainments esteemed by the world, 6:1-6
   F. Conclusion: Why argue with your Maker? 6:7-12

II. Words of Wisdom for Dwelling Amidst Vanity, 7:1–12:8
   A. General counsel about enduring values, 7:1-29
   B. Exhortation to obey the earthly king and fear the heavenly King even in wicked, perplexing times, 8:1-17
   C. How to cope with the fact of death, 9:1-12
   D. Wisdom better than folly, 9:13–10:20
   E. Exhortation to benevolence and cheerful industry in spite of possible trouble, 11:1-8
   F. Exhortation to youth to begin living for God while still young, before old age comes, 11:9–12:7
   G. Conclusion: Opening theme repeated that all is empty and transitory, 12:8

The Epilogue, 12:9-14

Summary: Fear God, and keep His commandments.

See Wisdom.

Bibliography. Gleason L. Archer, *A Survey of Old Testament Introduction,* Chicago: Moody, 1964, pp. 459-472; "The Linguistic Evidence for the Date of Ecclesiastes," JETS, XII (1969), 167-182. H. L. Ginsberg, "The Structure and Contents of the Book of Koheleth," *Supplements to VT,* III (1955), 138-149. Robert Gordis, *Koheleth—The Man and His World,* New York: Block Publ. Co., 1955. G. S. Hendry, "Ecclesiastes," NBC. Ernst W. Hengstenberg, *Commentary on Ecclesiastes,* trans. by D. W. Simon, Edinburgh: T. & T. Clark, 1876. Herbert C. Leupold, *Exposition of Ecclesiastes,* Columbus: Wartburg Press, 1952. J. Stafford Wright, "The Interpretation of Ecclesiastes," EQ, XVIII (1946), 18-34.

W. G. B. and J. R.

ECCLESIOLOGY (Gr. *ekklēsia,* "that which is called out," "the church"). The doctrine of the Church based upon an inductive study of the Scriptures. *See* Church. The most basic question involved is that of the origin of the Church. Two main views are held by orthodox theologians.

1. According to some theologians, the Church began with the NT. It was foretold by Christ at the time of Peter's confession (Mt 16:18). Following Christ's resurrection, He was exalted as "head over all things to the church, which is his body" (Eph 1:22-23). Pentecost was the day when the Church actually began, for by sending the Holy Spirit, God "baptized into one body" (I Cor 12:13) all believers, whether Jews or Gentiles.

This view is supported by the argument that the Church was a mystery, "not known unto the sons of men" but established and revealed by Christ (Eph 3:5). In it there is "neither Jew nor Greek, there is neither bond nor free, there is neither male nor female: for ye are all one in Christ Jesus" (Gal 3:28), the middle wall of partition having been taken away by His death (Eph 2:14-15). Those who were once separate, now through Christ "have access by one Spirit unto the Father" (Eph 2:18). This new relationship is based on our Lord's promise of the Spirit being "in" them (Jn 14:16-17).

2. According to the other view, that held by the Reformed theologians, the Church is composed of all the elect of all ages. There was a Church in the wilderness (Acts 7:38). Believers in the NT come to the "general assembly and church of the firstborn, which are written in heaven" (Heb 12:22-23). The mystery "that the Gentiles should be fellowheirs, and of the same body" with Jews (Eph 3:5, 9) was known by revelation to the OT believers (Isa 42:1-4; 60:3; Lk 3:6; Acts 13:47; 15:17), but not as fully "as it is now revealed . . . by the Spirit" (Eph 3:5). Since the promises to Abraham are to be shared by believers of all ages (Rom 4:13-16; Heb 11:39-40), the Reformed theologians see no possible distinction between the OT and the NT believers, either as to their basis of salvation in Christ and justification through faith (the unity of the covenant of grace), or their future destiny and rewards.

R. A. K.

ECLIPSE. The Bible contains no historical notice of an eclipse. The three-hour darkness beginning at noon during Christ's crucifixion cannot logically be attributed to an eclipse of the sun, because the moon is always full at the time of the Passover.

Eschatological descriptions of the "day of

the Lord," however, possibly foretell one or more eclipses in the future. Isaiah writes, "The sun will be dark at its rising and the moon will not shed its light" (13:10, RSV). Similarly, Joel says, "The sun and the moon shall be dark, and the stars shall withdraw their shining" (Joel 2:10; 3:15); "the sun shall be turned into darkness, and the moon into blood, before the great and the terrible day of the Lord come" (Joel 2:31; Acts 2:20). Amos even more clearly predicts a solar eclipse: "I will make the sun go down at noon, and darken the earth in broad daylight" (Amos 8:9, RSV). Other prophecies that may suggest such phenomena are Jer 4:23; Ezk 32:7-8; Zeph 1:15. Christ's Olivet discourse refers to these astronomical disturbances (Mt 24:29), and Rev 6:12 (RSV) repeats the thought, "And the sun became black as sackcloth, the full moon became like blood." At the sounding of the fourth trumpet there will be a partial restriction of solar, lunar, and stellar light (Rev 8:12).

James (1:17, RSV) may be implying the shadow of an eclipse by contrast when he writes, "... the Father of lights with whom there is no variation or shadow due to change" (i.e., in position of heavenly bodies, Arndt, pp. 97, 834). Job seems to have been aware of the phenomenon of the eclipse; in his cursing the day of his birth he exclaimed, "May murk and deep shadow claim it for their own, clouds hang over it, eclipse swoop down on it" (3:5, Jerus B).

The Bible is marked by the absence of belief in mythology, including astrology, such as the Babylonian myth of the eclipse of the moon, wherein the moon-god Sin is attacked by seven evil gods and must be rescued by the other great deities.

In ancient Assyria solar eclipses were observed and recorded, in one case as the chief event by which a year was distinguished in the lists of annual *limmu* officials. These records have been correlated with Assyrian king-lists giving the sequence and duration of reigns. In determining a chronological framework for a history of OT times the key is the note of that eclipse of the sun in the month *Simanu* in the *limmu*-ship of Bur-Sagale, the ninth year of King Ashur-dan III. By astronomical calculation this fell on June 15, 763 B.C., according to our calendrical system.

Other eclipses that would have been visible in Jerusalem occurred on Feb. 9, 784; June 5, 716; and Sept. 30, 610. Does Jeremiah allude to the latter in 15:9? Herodotus describes a battle that must have been fought about this date between Lydians and Medes when "day was suddenly turned into night" (*The Histories*, Penguin Classics, 1954, p. 42). In his canon or *Almagest* the Egyptian scholar Ptolemy (A.D. 70-161) recorded large amounts of astronomical data, including eight eclipses between 721 and 491 B.C. All his dates have been verified by modern astronomers. *See* Sun; Chronology, OT.

J. R.

ED (ĕd). A name appearing in Josh 22:34, transliterated from Heb. *'ēd*, "witness." The Heb. word has dropped out of the MT, but is obviously required by the context (see vv. 27, 28, 34*b*, where the word does appear). It is the name the two and one-half eastern tribes gave to an altar they built in the Jordan Valley, perhaps near the mouth of the Jabbok Valley. Their desire to have a monument to testify to the fact that they had a part in the Lord and in Israel was ill-founded, because God's method to preserve unity was to have *all* the tribes gather three times a year around the altar of sacrifice at *Shiloh* (Ex 23:17).

EDAR. *See* Eder 1.

EDEN (ē'dĕn; "plain" or "delight").

1. "And the Lord God planted a garden eastward in Eden" (Gen 2:8). Neither size nor boundaries of the garden are given. Adam, the first man, was put there to till and keep it. Eve was given to him as a helpmeet. Many fine trees were there: "The tree of life also in the midst of the garden, and the tree of knowledge of good and evil" (Gen 2:9). The man was told he could eat of the fruit of all the trees, "but of the tree of the knowledge of good and evil, thou shalt not eat of it: for in the day that thou eatest thereof thou shalt surely die" (Gen 2:17).

The term Eden gives the geographical location of the garden, an enclosed area. Eden (Heb. *'ēden*) is probably a common noun from the Sumerian *edin*, Akkad. *edinu* ("plain," "steppe land"), suitable for pasturage or cultivation, and characteristic of the Mesopotamian plain. "And a river went out of Eden to water the garden; and from thence it was parted, and became into four heads" (Gen 2:10). E. A. Speiser comments that the four separate heads, branches, or sources merged within Eden and went forth as one river *in* (locative use of Heb. *min*) Eden to water the garden (*Genesis*, The Anchor Bible, 1964, pp. 16-20). Two of these are well known: The Euphrates (*q.v.*), called in Scripture "the great river," and the Hiddekel, the old name for the river Tigris (*q.v.*). The other two, the Pison (*q.v.*) and Gihon (*q.v.*), which "compass" or meander through their respective lands, are not known. Some claim these are the four principal rivers of the ancient world, the latter two being the Indus and the Nile, respectively.

Many locations for Eden have been suggested, but the site cannot be determined because the surface of the earth after the Flood probably bears little resemblance to its antediluvian appearance. A likely site might be in the area of Babylon, where the Tigris and Euphrates come close together and the Diyala flows into the Tigris from the N and a large wadi drains into the plain from northern Arabia (Havilah?).

In the Sumerian texts the term *edin* was the pasturing ground of the Sumerian shepherds and seems to denote the grassy region between the plowed lands irrigated by canals from the

Tigris-Euphrates river system, specifically in the triangle between Nippur, Uruk (Erech), and Umma (Thorkild Jacobsen, "Mesopotamian Mound Survey," *Archaeology*, VII [1954], 54).

Sumerian literature contains the myth of the deities Enki and Ninhursag whose actions are centered around Dilmun, a fabled district near the head of the Persian or Arabian Gulf. The paradise-land of Dilmun is pure and clean and bright, with no death or sickness or old age, but lacking fresh water. Enki orders the sun-god to bring forth good water from the earth for Dilmun (cf. Gen 2:5-6). Later in the myth, a goddess is created for the healing of Enki's rib (*see* Eve). When Enki eats eight special plants, Ninhursag curses him, suggesting a parallel with the eating of the fruit of the tree of the knowledge of good and evil by Adam and Eve and the curse pronounced against them (see ANET, pp. 37-41; Samuel N. Kramer, *History Begins at Sumer*, pp. 144-149). While some scholars suggest that the Hebrews borrowed the concept of Eden from the Sumerians via the Babylonians or Canaanites, it is even more likely that both accounts refer to a real place and real events, the Sumerian version having become grossly distorted with mythological accretions over the centuries.

Paradise was apparently of short duration (cf. Gen 2:8 – 3:24). Following their sin, Adam and Eve were driven out of the garden, "lest he . . . take also of the tree of life . . . and live forever" (Gen 3:22). Their parting sight of that beautiful home was of a flaming sword guarding the way to the tree of life.

Strangely enough it was another sword, "the sword of the Spirit, which is the word of God" (Eph 6:17), that opened up to the sinner the fulfillment of the promise of a Redeemer first made in the Garden of Eden (cf. Gen 3:15). In the final chapter of the Bible the new paradise is seen. There the redeemed sinner can take of the tree of life and live forever (cf. Rev 22:14).

2. A locality in northern Mesopotamia (II Kgs 19:12; Isa 37:12; Ezk 27:23; Amos 1:5) mentioned as an embroidery market for Tyre; identified with Bit-adini in the Assyrian records, an Aramaean state between the Euphrates and the river Balikh. RSV has Beth-eden in Amos 1:5.

3. A son of Joah, a Gershonite Levite (II Chr 29:12; 31:15).

L. A. L. and J. R.

EDER (ē'dẽr), **EDAR** (ē'där), **ADER** (ā'dẽr)

1. A watchtower between Bethlehem and Hebron, where Jacob camped after Rachel's death and where Reuben had intercourse with Bilhah (Gen 35:21-22). KJV spells it Edar. Because of its proximity to Bethlehem where David was born, Micah (Mic 4:8) refers to it (*migdal 'ēder*, "O tower of the flock") and to Ophel ("the stronghold"), where David's citadel was built in Jerusalem, as symbols of the royal house of David.

2. A town in the Negeb of Judah (Josh 15:21), perhaps el-'Adar, five miles S of Gaza. The LXX, however, suggests that Arad (*q.v.*) is possibly the correct reading.

3. A Benjamite (I Chr 8:15, RSV), spelled Ader in KJV.

4. A Levite, descendant of Mushi, son of Merari (I Chr 23:23; 24:30).

EDIFICATION. The Gr. noun *oikodomē*, "edifice," "building up," "edifying," "edification," denotes the temple buildings in Mt 24:1; Mk 13:1-2, and appears metaphorically a dozen or more times in Paul's epistles. Believers as living stones (I Pet 2:5) are being built into the Church as a great "building" joined together and growing into a holy temple in union with the Lord Jesus Christ (Eph 2:21).

Each individual believer must be built up or edified for this ultimate purpose, strengthened and united with all other believers. The ascended Christ has given to His Church men with special ministries to equip the saints for this work of "building up" the body of Christ (Eph 4:12). This was the purpose of Paul's God-given authority, and his goal at all times (II Cor 10:8; 12:19; 13:10). Hence each Christian is to act unselfishly in order to edify his fellow believers in an attitude of love (Eph 4:15-16; Rom 14:19; 15:2; I Cor 8:1). His words should always be spoken to edify (Eph 4:29), especially in meetings of the local church (I Cor 14:26). Charismatic manifestations of the Spirit should always be controlled so that the hearers are edified. Prophesying best serves this purpose, although two or at the most three persons speaking in tongues, if followed by an interpretation in each case, may also edify the congregation (I Cor 14:3-13, 27-33).

Bibliography. Otto Michel, "*Oikodomeō*," TDNT, V, 136-144.

J. R.

EDOM (ē'dŏm). The term Edom means red. It has three possible origins: the red sandstone cliffs of the country (there is evidence that the country may have been called *'ĕdôm*, or "red," before Esau subjugated the Horites); Esau's red hair at birth; or the red pottage which Esau took in exchange for his inheritance (Gen 25:25-30).

Esau seems to have settled in a part of the Negeb S of Beer-sheba (Gen 28:9) which was called Seir at that time (Gen 32:3; 33:16; 36:8). This continued to be the homeland of the Edomites until after the time of Moses and Joshua, who came in contact with them just E of Kadesh-barnea (Num 20:14-21; 34:3; Deut 2:1-8) and S of Judah's tribal allotment (Josh 15:1, 21). *See* Esau.

The mountainous area which the Edomites (*q.v.*) invaded and made their headquarters from the 13th to the 6th cen. B.C. extends S from Moab, with the border at the river Zered, for about 70 miles to the Gulf of Aqabah. This territory consists of porphyry and colored sandstone mountains which contain the grandest rock scenery in the world. From these mountains of Transjordan the Edomites looked down upon a maze of cliffs, chasms, rocky shelves, and narrow valleys. This range E of the Arabah depression is actually the crested edge of a high, bleak plateau, covered by stones and spotted with patches of grain land and scattered woods. Its western cliff walls are steep and bare, black and red, rising from the pale yellow sands of the Arabah desert floor. So rugged is the terrain that the valley in which Petra is located can be reached by a deep gorge wide enough at times for only two horsemen to ride abreast. In addition to the wheat lands on the eastern plateau, the wider defiles provide some fertile fields and terraces for vineyards. Its 5,000 foot high promontories precipitate some of the moisture from the prevailing W winds that have passed over the Negeb, so that it is a comparatively well-watered land. Thus Mount Seir (*q.v.*) was a well-stocked fortress, with its copper and iron mines in the Arabah. Yet it was so high and lofty and locked in by precipice and jagged mountains that it was practically impregnable. It was this feature to which the prophet Obadiah referred in verses 3 and 4 when he wrote of Edom's dwelling in the clefts of the rock, setting his nest among the stars, and boasting, "Who shall bring me down to the ground?"

Living in this rich fortress-land, the Edomites enjoyed a civilization superior to that of the tribes of the surrounding deserts. Furthermore, they looked across to Palestine at their relatives the Israelites who were compelled because of their vulnerable borders to make alliances with surrounding nations in order to survive. The Edomites naturally absorbed something of the characteristics of their mountains. They were alone, aloof, unsympathetic and unmoved by the claims of pity and kinship. For this the Lord passed judgment on them: "For three transgressions of Edom, and for four, I will not revoke the punishment; because he pursued his brother with the sword, and cast off all pity, and his anger tore perpetually, and he kept his wrath for ever. So I will send a fire upon Teman, and it shall devour the strongholds of Bozrah" (Amos 1:11-12, RSV). This passage lists the two chief towns of Edom around 750 B.C., Bozrah (modern Buseireh), 20 miles SE of the Dead Sea, and Teman, identified by Nelson Glueck with a site strewn with Edomite potsherds known as Tawilan just E of the Petra valley.

Edom's self-sufficiency was enhanced by the position of the country located on several of the main trade routes of the ancient world. The masters of Mount Seir at times controlled the harbors of Aqabah, into which Solomon's ships had come with gold from Ophir. They swooped

Typical Edomite terrain. JR

down periodically upon the Arabian caravans and cut the roads to Gaza and Damascus. Mainly, however, the Edomites were traders, middlemen between Arabia and Phoenicia, thereby filling their caverns with both eastern and western wealth. This coveted position drew the envious fire of the Israelites—especially when the land of Edom was so cut off and so difficult to attack. Yet such kings of Judah as David, Amaziah, and Uzziah did invade Edom successfully and gained control of the oriental trade which flowed through the ports of Elath and Ezion-geber.

Bibliography. D. W. Deere, *The Twelve Speak,* New York: American Press, 1958, I, 45-50. Nelson Glueck, "Transjordan," TAOTS, pp. 433-445. G. A. Smith, *The Book of the Twelve Prophets,* New York: Harper, 1929, II, 177 ff.

D. W. D.

EDOMITES (ē'dŏ-mīts). The Edomites were a Semitic people descended from Esau (*q.v.*), who settled in the S of Palestine and Transjordan sometime during the 2nd mil. before Christ. Their kingdom was bounded on the N by the wilderness of Judea, the Dead Sea, and the river Zered (modern Wadi el-Hasa); on the E by the Syrian Desert; on the W by the Sinai Peninsula; and on the S by the Gulf of Aqabah. This territory, called Mount Seir (*q.v.*), was formerly occupied by the Horites (Gen 14:6), whom the Edomites dispossessed and settled in their place (Gen 36:8, 15-21). *See* Edom.

The Edomites are first mentioned outside the Bible in the Ugaritic tablets of Ras Shamra. In the Legend of King Keret, King Keret of Sidon is said to have advanced against the king of Edom, but the latter bought him off with some valuable presents and gave him his daughter Mesheb-Hory in marriage. Egyptian records from the late 13th cen. B.C. mention Bedouin tribesmen of Edom who were permitted to enter Egypt for food during a famine (ANET, p. 259).

The Edomites figure prominently in the Bible, often in the role of opponents to the Israelites. The first historical contact between the two took place when the Israelites were advancing on Palestine from the Sinai Peninsula. The Edomite territory lay along Moses' proposed route, so the Israelites sought permission to pass peacefully through their territory: "We will not pass through the fields, or through the vineyards, neither will we drink of the water of the wells; we will go by the king's highway, we will not turn to the right hand nor to the left, until we have passed the borders." The king of Edom refused this request even though an assurance was given to him by Moses that ". . . if I and my cattle drink of thy water, then I will pay for it" (Num 20:14–21).

The chief source of income of the Edomites came from trade and the fees collected for "protecting" the caravans carrying the incense from S Arabia to the Mediterranean coast. They also practiced agriculture, and cultivated wheat to a small extent; but rainfall is very scanty in that area. They grew vines and olives near those regions watered by natural springs. Another source of income came from copper mined in the Arabah. Their religion seems to have been polytheistic. Among the deities that can be traced from the names of their kings are Qos and Hadad.

The Edomites reached the height of their prosperity when the great empires of the past were weakened by the onset of the Aegean invasion and enjoyed an Indian summer between the 12th and the 10th cen. B.C. During the 13th cen. the Edomites had expanded their territory to include the mountains and forests of Transjordan. To protect their eastern border from raids from the desert dwellers, they erected a series of fortresses close enough to one another to communicate by fire signals. Nelson Glueck roaming over the sites of their ruined cities has collected a large number of potsherds from this period.

The Umm el Biyara or acropolis of Petra.

With the rise of David, the Edomites became vassals of the kingdom of Israel. It was probably David who destroyed fortresses of the Edomites on their western frontier W of the Arabah, as in the case of two 11th cen. B.C. forts near Jebel Usdum, the "Mount of Sodom." They remained in that state during the reign of his son Solomon (I Kgs 11:14–17), who built the port of Ezion-geber (modern Tell el-Kheleifeh near the present port of Aqabah), in the heart of Edomite territory (I Kgs 9:26). Solomon also opened up a number of mines and constructed a large smelting industry which has been studied by Jewish archaeologists in recent years.

On the death of Solomon and the division of the kingdom of Israel, the Edomites regained their independence. However, with the rise of the Assyrian Empire in the 9th cen. the Edomites began paying tribute to Assyria, and became involved in the numerous revolts against Assyrian rule that were instigated by Egypt. The lot of the Edomites was, however, a harder one than that of their neighbors, as they often found themselves paying tribute to Assyria on the one hand, and to the kingdom of Judah on the other.

A revolt against Judah appears to have taken place sometime during the 9th cen. B.C., but this was put down by Amaziah with great severity (II Kgs 14:7); Amaziah slew many Edomites by throwing them down from the high rock bastion within Petra (II Chr 25:12), now known as Umm el-Biyara. This action greatly weakened the Edomites and they ceased to play a great role in the history of the Near East. Nevertheless, the Edomites stood by rejoicing when Jerusalem was captured by Nebuchadnezzar (Ps 137:7), and the prophets denounced them for ill-treatment of their brother nation Judah (Jer 49:7–22; Ezk 25:12–14). Because of similar callousness on the part of Edom when Jerusalem was plundered in his day, Obadiah had forewarned the house of Esau that judgment would befall them should they ever gloat over Judah again (Ob 10–14).

It must have been soon after this event that the Nabataeans began to dislodge the Edomites from their country and occupied it in their stead. Already in 646 B.C. Ashurbanipal of Assyria had met the Nabataeans (*q.v.*) on his campaign against the Arabs near the land of Edom (ANET, pp. 297–300). It appears that with the reduction of their number and the loss of the greater part of their territory, the Edomites withdrew to S Palestine which later came to be called Idumea (*q.v.*). There appears to have been no relationship between the Nabataeans and the Edomites or Idumeans. Antipater and his son Herod the Great were both Idumean, and looked upon the Nabataeans as an alien people.

D. C. B.

EDREI (ĕd'rē-ī)

1. A city in the land of Bashan, modern Dera'a, about 30 miles E of the Jordan. Og, king of Bashan, came out of Edrei, which was built on a bluff overlooking the Yarmuk River and evidently on the S border of his kingdom, to intercept the invading Israelites. He lost the battle and his life, and all his territory was subjugated (Num 21:33–35; Deut 1:4; 3:1).

According to most biblical references, Og apparently used both Edrei and Ashtaroth (*q.v.*) as capitals (Josh 12:4; 13:12, 31). In one passage (Josh 9:10) it is simply stated that he lived in Ashtaroth. That this may be a textual problem is seen by examination of Deut 1:4 which, according to the Heb., could be rendered: "after he had defeated . . . Og, king of Bashan, who lived in Ashtaroth, in Edrei." However, the Gr. text (followed by RSV) is in harmony with the passages listed above. It reads: ". . . who lived in Ashtaroth *and* in Edrei." Ashtaroth was no doubt the main city, and Edrei was a secondary capital.

After the Israelite occupation of Bashan, Edrei was apparently destroyed (Deut 3:1–6) and does not receive further mention in the Bible. However, it was known in Roman sources by the name Adra or Adraene. Eusebius (*Onomasticon* 8:84) mentions it as a well-known city of Arabia, 24 miles from Bosora and six miles from Ashtaroth. Though the ancient tell has only received surface investigation, pottery fragments testify to occupation as ancient as the Early Bronze Age, with a large portion of sherds from the Early Iron Age. Probably in Hellenistic or Roman times a subterranean city with streets, shops, and cisterns was constructed in underlying caves in the basaltic rock (HGHL, p. 576; UBD, p. 287).

2. A town in the tribal inheritance of Naphtali, listed among its fortified towns (Josh 19:37). Several variations are known among the Gr. texts: *Ias(s)eir, Assapei, Edrain, Edraei, et al.* In the list it appears between Kedesh and En-hazor. Its general location may also be inferred from its place in Thutmose III's list of conquered towns (No. 91) where the name is written *'itr'* (ANET, p. 242). There it appears among the towns of northern Galilee such as Abel (-beth-maacah). A possible location for the ancient site is Tell Khureiba, S of Kedesh. However, recent researches have pointed to the tentative suggestion that Edrei be located near the modern Aitaroun.

A. F. R.

EDUCATION

Mesopotamian

Mesopotamian education involved the arduous process of learning cuneiform script. Students generally came from the upper classes of society. On rare occasions girls must have been educated as there is evidence of a few female scribes.

The early schools were probably associated with temples, but the famous school at Mari was located in the palace. Here were found rows of benches together with a collection of writing materials.

This school was called the *e-dubba,* "the house of tablets." The *ummia,* "headmaster," had under him specialized assistants, such as the *dubshar nishid,* "the scribe of counting"; the *dubshar kengira,* "the scribe of Sumerian," etc. Much of the actual supervision lay in the hands of an older student, the *shesh-gal,* "older brother."

Pupils learned various cuneiform signs by copying tablets prepared by the teacher, writing with a stylus on a moist clay tablet. Later they would copy excerpts of literary texts and study mathematics and the division of land. After the 2nd mil. B.C. when Sumerian was no longer a living language, scribes would have to memorize bilingual lists of Sumerian words and their Akkadian equivalents.

Students woke up early in the morning, fearful of being late, and took with them two rolls of bread for lunch. Discipline was severe. One lad in an essay recalls how he received seven canings from seven different staff members for poor writing, for talking without permission, etc. More severe punishment involved being locked up for two months.

Egyptian

Egyptian education prepared a scribal class of civil servants. Students from humble beginnings were able to succeed to eminent positions by virtue of their education. Moreover it meant, as teachers often reminded their pupils, a life free from taxes, poverty, and physical labor.

Schools were located in temple precincts, such as the Ramesseum. They were supervised by high officials of the departments for which students were training. The child went to school from about four or five to about 16 years of age.

He learned to copy accurately the pictographic hieroglyphs. His first efforts were made on ruled limestone flakes or potsherds. Only later would he advance to writing on papyrus, and at first on palimpsests, i.e., papyrus that had already been used and erased.

He had to learn the specialized vocabulary of his intended profession, including, for example, 96 names of Egyptian cities, 48 different baked meats. If he planned to work with the army, he had to learn the geography of Palestine, the organization of a military campaign, and the distribution of provisions. In the New Kingdom period the scribe also had to learn Semitic, Cretan, and other foreign names.

The boys' lessons lasted for half the day. When noon was announced the children left school "shouting for joy." Lunch consisted of three rolls of bread and a jug of beer.

The Egyptian word for education *sbꜣjt* comes from the root *sbꜣ*, "to chastise," "to punish." The teacher's motto was: "A youngster's ear is on his back; he only listens to the man who beats him." One student recalls how he was bound in the temple school for three months.

A painted limestone statue of a seated Egyptian scribe holding an open papyrus roll on his knees. LL

In spite of the rewards of a scribal career, there were delinquents. One teacher bemoaned a former pupil: "I am told, you are forsaking writing, and giving yourself up to pleasure. . . . You sit in the house and the girls encircle you. . . . A garland of flowers hangs about your neck, and you drum upon your belly."

Jewish

Jewish education was primarily religious, and until NT times was centered in the home. It was a father's duty to instruct his son about the religious traditions (Ex 12:26–27; Deut 4:9; 6:7).

It was essential that the child should learn to read the Scriptures. Happily the Heb. alphabet with its 22 letters was much easier than the hundreds of cuneiform or hieroglyphic characters of Israel's neighbors. In Isa 28:10, "precept upon precept" is literally, "*ṣ* after *ṣ*, and *q* after *q*," referring to the teaching of the alphabet. In Isa 10:19 we read, "And the rest of the trees of his forest shall be few, that a child may write them." The young man of Jud 8:14 "wrote down" (not as in the KJV, "described") the names of the elders of the city.

Formal schooling away from the home is not attested until the intertestamental era. Ben Sirach (*c.* 180 B.C.) speaks of a "house of learning" (Gr. *oikos paideias* for Heb. *bêth-midrash*). Under Jason (175–171 B.C.), the Hellenizing high priest, a gymnasium was established in Jerusalem (I Macc 1:14; II Macc 4:9; Jos *Ant.* xii.5.1). The gymnasium was the chief educational institution of Hellenism.

Simon ben Shetah (*c.* 75 B.C.) enacted a decree that children should go to school. The decisive development, however, came with the order of Joshua ben Gamala, high priest A.D. 63–65, that every town should have a school for children from the age of six.

According to a statement of Judah ben Tema (2nd cen. A.D.) in *Pirke Aboth* 5:21, the program of studies to be pursued was: (a) the Scriptures at the age of five; (b) the Mishnah—oral traditions—at ten; (c) the coming of age at 13; and (d) the Talmud—commentaries on the Mishnah—at 15. Young men were expected to marry at 18.

Girls were instructed at home, and were often betrothed at the age of 12 or 13. They did attend the synagogues, and some gained a good knowledge of the Scriptures (cf. the OT allusions in Mary's "Magnificat," Lk 1:46–55).

Most parents could not afford to allow their sons to have more than an elementary education. Some rabbis were contemptuous of those who had studied only the Scriptures, regarding them as ignorant *'am-hā'ārets,* "people of the earth" (cf. Jn 7:15; Acts 4:13). Those studying to become rabbis continued their education at the academy in Jerusalem, and were ordained at about 22.

Elementary classes met in the synagogues, with the *ḥazzan,* or attendant in charge of the scrolls, as the teacher. The teacher had to be a married man; no women were allowed to teach (cf. I Tim 2:12).

Children of various ages would sit on the floor before the teacher. The child would be taught to read the Scriptures aloud, beginning from Leviticus. He would proceed through most of the Scriptures, though some of the Hagiographa, e.g., the Song of Solomon, would not be taught to the immature student.

The stress was upon memory, and the method was repetition. One Mishnah teacher was said to have repeated the same lesson 400 times! Flogging was used with recalcitrant students. The Mishnah did not hold the teacher responsible if the student died from flogging. The Heb. word for education, *mûsār,* comes from the root *ysr,* "to chasten, to discipline."

The young boy's schooling began at daybreak and often continued until sundown. Some have questioned whether he took time

The "school" at Qumran.

out for a noon meal! School was shortened during the hot months of July and August to four hours. The day before the Sabbath was a half day, and there were holidays on religious festivals.

The academy at Jerusalem for prospective rabbis was distinguished by such teachers as Hillel and Shammai (1st cen. B.C.). Here Paul studied at the feet of Hillel's illustrious grandson, Gamaliel (Acts 22:3). Gamaliel was one of the few rabbis to permit students to study Gr. learning.

The rabbis, as a rule, did not receive recompense for their teaching, but supported themselves by working as millers, shoemakers, tailors, potters, etc. (cf. Acts 18:3). In fact, it was the duty of every father to teach his son a trade.

Greek

Gr. education or *paideia* (in the NT the word came to have the sense of "chastisement" in such passages as Heb 12:5, 7, 8, 11) was at first largely aristocratic and athletic. After about 450 B.C. the Sophists who taught rhetoric for pay revolutionized education. In the 4th cen. B.C. the great philosophic schools of Plato and Aristotle were established in two gymnasiums in the suburbs of Athens, the academy and the lyceum.

In the Hellenistic period the establishment of gymnasiums in every city founded by the Greeks in the Near East served as the primary means of preserving the Hellenic tradition and of assimilating non-Hellenes into Hellenic society.

Spartan education was a phenomenon by itself. Unlike the situation in other cities, education in Sparta was state sponsored. Girls received athletic training to make them robust mothers. At the age of seven boys were separated from their homes to live in barracks, to be subjected to a strict discipline intended to make them tough and obedient soldiers. Spartans were taught only the rudiments of reading and writing, and were considered uneducated by Athenians.

In Athens girls were taught the domestic arts at home. Boys went to school at seven. It was a truism that richer children went to school earlier and left later than poorer children.

Most families would have a *paidagōgos,* usually an elderly slave, who carried the boy's equipment, accompanied him to school, and quizzed him on his lessons. He was a combination of "nurse, footman, chaperon, and tutor" (cf. I Cor 4:15; Gal 3:24-25).

Gr. education equally stressed *gymnasia* (I Tim 4:8) for the body and "music"—a term which included literature—for the soul. The former instruction would be conducted in private *palaistras,* or "wrestling arenas," under *paidotribes,* literally, "boy-rubbers" from the practice of rubbing the body with oil and dust before the exercises. Running and hurling the javelin would be practiced in the public gymnasiums. The latter also contained halls where teachers, such as Socrates, would lecture.

Every young boy would be taught to sing and to play the lyre. He would learn the *stoichea,* i.e., the ABC's or rudiments (cf. Heb 5:12). His main text would be Homer, and secondarily, the dramatists and lyric poets.

The pupil went to school at daybreak, accompanied by his pedagogue who carried a lamp on dark winter mornings. Schools held from 60 to 120 students. The pupils sat on benches with their waxed writing tablets on their knees. The teacher sat on a chair on a platform. Pedagogues usually sat in the class also. From illustrations on pottery we see that the children brought their pet cats, dogs, and even leopards!

From the Mime of Herondas (3rd cen. B.C.) we can learn what happened to truant boys. A mother complains that her son would rather play knucklebones than go to school. He is not able to spell from dictation, and can read only with hesitation. When he is scolded he runs away to his grandmother. She therefore has the teacher whip her son until his hide is as mottled as a water snake.

When the boy reached the age of 18 and became of age, he was at last freed from the restrictive care of his pedagogue. From 18 to 20, Athenian youths, called *ephebes* during this period, underwent a compulsory, state-sponsored course of military and athletic training. In Hellenistic times the graduates of the ephebic training formed the upper class of Hellenized citizens. In Roman times the institution of ephebes at Athens formed the basis for the university there.

Roman

Even before Greece became a Roman province in 146 B.C. her cultural influence was felt at Rome. Cato the Elder (234-149 B.C.), who opposed Gr. learning, is said to have learned Gr. at the end of his life.

The Gymnasium at Salamis, Cyprus. The Palestra or wrestling area was located in the rectangle surrounded by the columns. HFV

The Romans copied the Greeks in using pedagogues for their children, often employing Gr. slaves. The great Cicero (106–43 B.C.) was as well-versed in Gr. as in Latin, having been educated at Rhodes (as were also Caesar and Antony) and at Athens. Quintilian (A.D. 40–118), the great authority on Roman education, held that Roman children should be taught Gr. before Latin. The satirist Martial (A.D. 40–104) and his colleague Juvenal complained that the women even made love in Gr.!

The pragmatic Roman outlook introduced some striking differences. Mathematics, geometry, and music were taught only insofar as they had practical applications. Rhetoric, not philosophy, was the subject that ranked supreme in higher studies. The Romans had little liking for the nudity of Gr. athletics. More to their taste were the horse races of the hippodrome and the gladiatorial games of the colosseum.

Girls attended the elementary schools with boys. Beyond that, some women were able to get such a knowledge of literature on their own that Juvenal complained: "How I hate them. Women who always go back to the pages of Palaemon's grammar, keeping all of the rules, and are pedants enough to be quoting verses I never heard."

Schools were sometimes held in a *pergula,* or "shed," in front of a house separated from the public by a thin partition. Students would sit on benches, while the teacher sat on a chair. For writing they began with waxed tablets; later they would use papyrus or even the parchment of a worthless manuscript. For arithmetic the pupil would use an abacus with *calculi,* pebbles.

The children attended the elementary school, which was called *ludus,* or "play," from the age of seven to ten or eleven. The elementary teacher was known as the *ludi magister*. Parents demanded much from him but paid him little, and at times only at the order of the courts. It was his task to teach the three R's. For the teaching of reading, texts with Aesop's fables were popular.

School began early—too early for Martial, who complained that the scoldings of the teacher kept him from getting his sleep. Hurrying off to school without breakfast, the lad would buy a little cake as he passed a baker's shop. Upon arriving he would say, "Good-morning, everybody. Let me have my place. Squeeze up a bit." After his morning's lesson he went home for a lunch of white bread, olives, dry figs, and nuts. He then returned to school, where the master upon examining his copy said, "You deserve to be whipped! All right, I'll let you off this time. . . ."

Discipline was a synonym for education. The phrase *manum subducere ferulae,* "to withdraw the hand from the rod," meant to leave school. Quintilian protested against the universal practice of flogging. He felt that praise, the spirit of competition, and even of play were better incentives than fear.

The boys would have the summer off from July to October and extensive holidays in December and in March. Every eighth day, which was a market day, was also a holiday. This was not enough for some, who pretended illness, rubbing their eyes with olive oil or taking cumin to make themselves pale in order to play hooky.

From the age of 12 to 15 or 16 when the young Roman became of age and donned his white *toga virilis,* he would attend the secondary or grammar school. This was called the *ludus litterarius,* and the teacher was called the *litteratus* or *grammaticus.* The main subjects were technical grammar and literature, primarily Homer and other Gr. texts. It was not until 25 B.C. that Latin texts, such as Virgil and Cicero, were also introduced.

Beyond grammar school until the age of 18 or 20, the young men received training in rhetoric. As Rome was transformed from a republic to an empire with the consequent restriction of political liberties, training in rhetoric became more and more artificial. Students were asked to declaim on either *suasoria,* which proposed some action, such as "Should Agamemnon sacrifice his daughter?" or on *controversia,* which dealt with some far-fetched case involving a conflict of laws.

Various figures of speech were taught. Paul uses about 30 different rhetorical figures in his writing. F. W. Farrar suggests that he may therefore have received some rudimentary training in rhetoric at Tarsus. On the other hand, the paucity of his classical allusions (Acts 17:28; I Cor 15:33; Tit 1:12) and the quality of his Gr. show that he did not receive very advanced classical training at that famed center of learning. He was probably sent to Jerusalem before he came of age at 13. Some scholars have argued that the word *anatethrammenos,* "brought up," in Acts 22:3, places Paul in Jerusalem at an even earlier age.

Whatever his training may have been, Paul forswears (I Cor 2:1) the use of the elaborate and pompous rhetorical language so commonly used by orators of his day to gain applause (e.g., Tertullus, Acts 24:1–8). Even Roman writers were disgusted. Petronius, a contemporary of Paul's, wrote: "No one would mind this claptrap if only it put our students on the road to real eloquence. . . . Action or language, it's all the same: great sticky honeyballs of phrases, every sentence looking as though it had been plopped and rolled in poppyseed and sesame."

See Children; Family; School; Schools. Hebrew; Teach.

Bibliography—General. W. Barclay, *Educational Ideals in the Ancient World,* London: Collins, 1959. Georg Bertram, "*Paideuō,* etc.," TDNT, V, 596–625. E. B. Castle, *Ancient Education and Today,* Baltimore: Penguin, 1964. H. I. Marrou, *A History of Education in Antiquity,* New York: New American Library, 1964. Karl H. Rengstorf, "*Didaskō,* etc.," TDNT, II, 135–165. W. A. Smith, *Ancient Education,* New York: Philosophical Library, 1955.

Mesopotamian. Cyril J. Gadd, *Teachers and Students in the Oldest Schools,* London: Univ. of London, 1956. Samuel N. Kramer, "Schooldays," *Journal of the American Oriental Society,* LXIX (1949), 199–215; *The Sumerians,* Chicago: Univ. of Chicago, 1963, Chap. 5.

Egyptian. Adolf Erman, *Life in Ancient Egypt,* New York: Macmillan, 1894, Chap. 14; *The Ancient Egyptians,* New York: Harper & Row, 1966, pp. 54–85, 189–242. T. Säve-Söderbergh, *Pharaohs and Mortals,* Indianapolis: Bobbs-Merrill, 1958, pp. 195–205.

Jewish. Nathan Drazin, *History of Jewish Education,* Baltimore: Johns Hopkins, 1940. Eliezer Ebner, *Elementary Education in Ancient Israel During the Tannaitic Period,* New York: Bloch, 1956. Nathan Morris, *The Jewish School,* London: Eyre & Spottiswoode, 1937. Fletcher H. Swift, *Education in Ancient Israel,* Chicago: Open Court, 1919.

Greek. F. A. G. Beck, *Greek Education, 450–350 B.C.,* London: Methuen, 1964. W. W. Capes, *University Life in Ancient Athens,* New York: Stechert, 1922. C. A. Forbes, *Greek Physical Education,* New York: Century, 1929. Kenneth J. Freeman, *Schools of Hellas,* London: Macmillan, 1922. E. Norman Gardiner, *Athletics of the Ancient World,* Oxford: Clarendon, 1955, Chap. 6. Moses Hadas, *Hellenistic Culture,* New York: Columbia Univ., 1959, Chap. 6. W. Jaeger, *Paideia,* 3 vols., Oxford: Blackwell, 1936–45. H. Michell, *Sparta,* Cambridge: Cambridge Univ., 1964, Chap. 6. Paul Monroe, ed., *Source Book of the History of Education for the Greek and Roman Period,* New York: Macmillan, 1910. W. W. Tarn, *Hellenistic Civilization,* London: Edward Arnold, 1959, Chap. 8. John W. H. Walden, *The Universities of Ancient Greece,* New York: Scribner's, 1912.

Roman. Jerome Carcopino, *Daily Life in Ancient Rome,* New Haven: Yale Univ., 1960, Chap. 5. Donald L. Clark, *Rhetoric in Graeco-Roman Education,* New York: Columbia Univ., 1957. George Clarke, *The Education of Children at Rome,* New York: Macmillan, 1896. A Gwynn, *Roman Education from Cicero to Quintilian,* Oxford: Clarendon Press, 1926. Jack Lindsay, *Daily Life in Roman Egypt,* London: Frederick Müller, 1963, Chap. 5.

E. M. Y.

EFFECTUAL CALLING *See* Call.

EGGS. *See* Food.

EGLAH (ĕg'lă). A wife of David and mother of Ithream, David's son who was born in Hebron (II Sam 3:5; I Chr 3:3). Some Jewish tradition has identified her with Michal, daughter of Saul.

EGLAIM. *See* En-eglaim.

EGLON (ĕg'lŏn)

1. The king of Moab, who was noted for his obesity. In league with the Ammonites and Amalekites, he subdued Israel as a divine punishment for their sins (Jud 3:12-14), occupying the city of palms, Jericho. Subject to him for 18 years, the Israelites paid tribute. After Ehud, the second deliverer in the book of Judges, had assassinated Eglon (Jud 3:15-25), Ehud roused and led the people of Israel to victory against Moab (vv. 26-30). *See* Ehud.

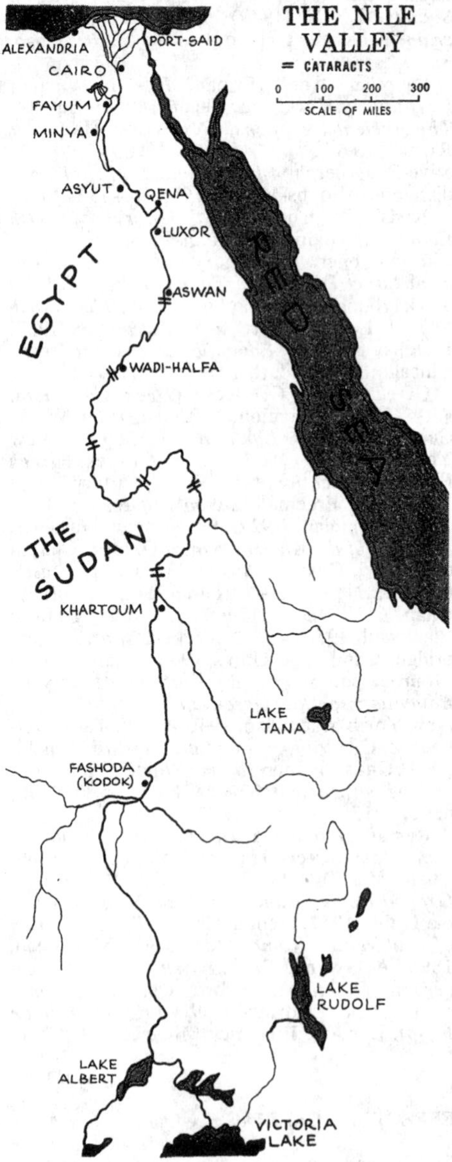

2. A Canaanite royal city which became part of the inheritance of Judah after the conquest of Palestine under Joshua (Josh 15:39). After the defeat of Ai and the peaceful capitulation of Gibeon, Debir, the king of Eglon, entered into a league with kings of four other cities to make war against Gibeon. This Amorite coalition was routed at the battle W of Gibeon by the Israelites (Josh 10:5-10). The five kings were captured and executed (10:22-26). Joshua then marched on the cities of the league, capturing and destroying them, including Eglon (10:34-35).

Eglon may be identified most likely with Tell el-Hesi, seven miles SW of Lachish. Excavating in 1890-93, Petrie followed by Bliss first applied the stratigraphic method at this site. A clay tablet, scarab seals, and a stamped jar handle prove the city was inhabited in Joshua's time.

R. B. D.

EGYPT (ē'jĭpt).

Name

The name Egypt is derived from the Gr. *aigyptos,* generally believed to be a corruption of the Egyptian *Ḥt-k3-ptḥ,* "the house of Ptah," a name given to the ancient city of Memphis, which was the oldest capital of united Egypt. The Heb. name for Egypt was *Miṣrayim,* a term whose form and meaning are uncertain. Often it is taken as a dual form and as such a reflection of the Egyptian "the Two Lands," a common Egyptian name for the country, based on its origin in the union of Upper and Lower Egypt. The Egyptians had a number of names for their land. A geographical designation, for example, made Egypt *Kemet,* "the Black Land," which contrasted the dark alluvial soil of the valley and the reddish hues of the surrounding desert.

Geography

Though at times in its ancient history the Egyptian Empire extended as far S as the Sixth Cataract of the Nile or included Palestine and Syria to the NE as far as the Euphrates River, Egypt proper was limited to NE Africa. Its N boundary was the Mediterranean Sea; to the E was the Red Sea; the S border was regarded as Aswan and the island of Elephantine; to the W, Egyptian territory reached into the Libyan Desert and took in the oases prominent in that area.

In reality the land of Egypt was even more restricted. Egypt was essentially an agricultural country and the arable and habitable land was

Truly "Egypt is the Nile." Beyond the alluvium laid down by the annual Nile flood stretches desert as far as the eye can see.
HFV

limited to the Nile Valley, a narrow strip of extremely fertile soil, varying from one to 12 miles in width. Since the distance from Cairo to Aswan is nearly 600 miles, it is apparent that the primary dimension of Egypt was length and that the dominant feature of Egyptian geography was the Nile.

It is practically impossible to exaggerate the importance of the Nile River to Egypt, for without its waters the whole country would be barren desert waste. The ancients were vitally aware of the role of the river; and in later times Hecateus, echoed by Herodotus, declared that Egypt was "the gift of the Nile" (*see* Nile). The river scoured out the valley, freighted down the alluvium, and annually watered the land by its life-giving flood. The country is almost rainless. Several inches of rain fall each year along the Mediterranean coast and Cairo has an occasional winter shower, but in Upper Egypt rain is a phenomenon. The annual inundation of the river, by saturating the ground, adding new soil, and bringing some organic material as fertilizer, has been the basis for the agriculture which has typified Egypt. Irrigation and water control were important, and even today the economy of the land centers on the river.

Just N of Cairo the Delta spreads out in characteristic shape, about 125 miles long and 115 miles wide. It was in the E part of this area, along the Wadi Tumilat, that the land of Goshen was located.

These features, the long tube of the river and the Delta, were the primary geographic basis for the division of the country into Upper and Lower Egypt (these terms based on altitude), though the latter consisted of the Delta plus a short part of the valley to the S. This division antedated the historic period and was never forgotten, for the name "the Two Lands" remained a popular name for Egypt and in many other traditional ways the bipartite origin of the country was remembered. For purposes of administration, the two areas were early divided into smaller parts, each with its distinctive name and emblem. In Gr. times these units were called nomes, with 20 of them in Lower Egypt and 22 in its S counterpart.

Geography contributed much to the course of the development of Egypt as a nation and as a center of culture. Though the dimensions of the land were a handicap to stable government and unified culture, the river was a good means of transportation and communication and served as a unifying and homogenizing factor. Over its long history Egypt lived in comparative security and stability, with opportunity to develop internally and to engage in the exchange of commodities and ideas with other lands.

By its unique setting the country was strikingly protected from periodic wholesale invasion. The valley was hemmed in by forbidding deserts of barren sand and jumbled rock cliffs. To the W lay the Libyan Desert and beyond that the vast Sahara; to the E was the Sinai Desert and farther S along the Red Sea the Nubian Desert. To the S the cataracts hindered foreign encroachment via the water route, and the addition of forts at strategic points made the S approach easily defended. The most vulnerable sections were the sides of the Delta, particularly near the sea. On the NW the Libyans sometimes posed a threat but generally were held in check by force of arms. The greatest danger lay in the NE, though Sinai formed a kind of buffer and the march along the desert coast was a tremendous feat for any army. In Middle Kingdom times this frontier was guarded by forts and checkpoints, for the kings were well aware of danger from this quarter. From this direction the infrequent invasions most characteristically came: Asiatics, Hyksos, Sea Peoples, Assyrians, Babylonians, Persians, Greeks.

Geography and climate were friendly to the Egyptians. Though the temperature range is quite great, it does not get down to freezing and the heat usually moderates at evening. Even the winds favored the land, for the prevailing N wind propelled sailboats on their upstream journey and provided refreshing coolness in houses oriented to receive the "sweet breezes of the north."

Its environment has made Egypt an outstanding area for the practice of archaeology. The presence of stone for building and art encouraged monumental architecture and statuary of both magnificent proportions and excellent finish. The absence of rain and frost preserved the monuments from these destructive elements, while the winds drifted in dry sand to cover them from sun and atmosphere, so that even fragile papyrus fragments and painted mud plaster are kept intact and fresh in appearance.

Religion

The study of Egyptian religion is exceedingly complex, for (1) the mass of source material is so great as to be unwieldy; (2) these materials vary greatly as to their nature, ranging from papyrus documents to the architecture and decoration of vast temple complexes; (3) the sources cover a tremendous span of time; (4) many of the records are very heterogeneous, for the scribes uncritically combined writings from different places and times.

The history of religion in Egypt has been given considerable attention. Some scholars have thought that there is evidence of a primitive monotheism in Egypt, though there was a great multiplicity of local gods, whose fortunes often varied with political history. With the union of the two lands, the king was identified with Horus, the falcon-god of Upper Egypt. Other divinities of importance included Ptah, the god of Memphis; Re, the sun-god of Heliopolis, who gained prominence at the time of the Fifth Dynasty; Amon-Re, the Theban god of empire; Osiris and Isis, later adopted by the mystery religions of Greece and Rome; Set, the enemy of Osiris and Horus; Hathor, the cow-goddess; Khnum, the god of Elephantine; Thoth, the god of writing and wisdom. Often the gods were grouped into triads or enneads.

Much has been written of the religious innovations of Amenhotep IV (Akhenaton), who attempted to advance the sun disc, Aton, as the sole or leading divinity. Once widely heralded as a kind of monotheism, the religion of Akhenaton has in recent times been more critically evaluated. Certainly the movement had political

Egyptian gods in bronze encrusted with gold and silver; Osiris left and Ptah right. LM

overtones; much of its content was not original and its practice was very limited. With the death of Akhenaton, Atonism soon disappeared and the priests of Amon regained their supremacy.

Egyptian religion had high ethical concepts, but much of the literature is concerned only with life after death and it is evident from the innovations of various periods that no final answers were found.

The religious life of Egypt made no contribution to the religion of the Bible, but it did affect the religious history of Israel, for the gods of Egypt were a source of serious apostasy (Ezk 20:5-9; 23:3, 8, 19-21, 27). The golden calf made at Mount Sinai and the later calf worship of Jeroboam I are concrete examples of this idolatry.

History

For some periods the chronology of Egypt is well established, but for others, such as the disturbed times called the "Intermediate Periods," considerably less is known. Egypt is fortunate, however, in the possession of fairly abundant materials for chronological study. From earlier historical times there is the Palermo Stone, which gives an abbreviated list of rulers and significant events down to the Fifth Dynasty. The Turin Papyrus extends the list of kings, but the document is incomplete and suffered irreparable damage during shipment to the Turin Museum. Other king lists are known from Sakkarah, Abydos, and Karnak. In addition, many historical references are dated in terms of the regnal year of the king. Records sometimes were cross-dated by the Sothic Cycle, a period of 1,460 years determined by the correspondence between the beginning of the yearly inundation and the heliacal rising of the Dog Star (Sothis, Sirius).

The cultures into which the predynastic period in Egypt is divided are named after "type-sites," at which a particular culture was first or most typically found by archaeologists. Consequently there are names such as Merimdian, Tasian, Badarian, Gerzean, etc. It is not possible to assign absolute dates to these cultures, though carbon 14 and similar tests may be used for approximate dating. Relative dates may be given on the basis of typology and for some of the periods the sequence is made certain by stratification, though excavated stratified sites are rare in Egypt. Sir Flinders Petrie, "the father of Egyptology," devised a system of sequence dating for Egyptian prehistory; this has been useful but now needs revision.

In the 3rd cen. B.C. an Egyptian priest-historian named Manetho divided the kings of Egypt into 30 dynasties, from the unification of the land until the conquest by Alexander the Great. Though little of his writing has come down to us, and that only as preserved by other writers, his system has been a convenience used by historians until the very

The step pyramid and its temple. HFV

present. The dynasties have been grouped into quite standard periods, which serve as useful labels in identification and discussion. Such an outline is presented here, with brief descriptions.

Protodynastic (Dynasties I-II; 3100-2700 B.C.). The traditional list of Manetho gives Menes as the first king of the Two Lands. Coming from Thinis in the S, he effected the union of Upper and Lower Egypt and set up his capital at "the White Wall," the city later known as Memphis. Some scholars believe that he is to be identified with Aha and/or Narmer. Large royal tombs of this period have been found at Sakkarah and Abydos.

Old Kingdom (OK, Dynasties III-VI; 2700-2200 B.C.). This period, the age of the great pyramid-builders, was one of the outstanding epochs of Egyptian history. Its architectural achievements are particularly famous; but equally noteworthy are its accomplishments in medicine, literature, and art. The proverbs of Ptahhotep, a vizier of Dynasty V, have been preserved and one of the best-known of the medical papyri, the Edwin Smith Surgical Papyrus, had its origins in the OK (*see* Diseases). The canons of Egyptian art were established, along with other cultural traditions which remained basically unchanged throughout Egyptian history.

The political dogma of this time pictured the king as an absolute ruler, aloof, austere, remote, unmoved by the vicissitudes of life and of time. The renowned statue of Khafre in the Cairo Museum conveys this impression of the king as a divinity incarnate but unapproachable, a most effective work of art.

Dynasty III saw the building of the step pyramid of Djoser at Sakkarah. Imhotep, the architect of this complex, was later regarded by the Greeks as identical with their god of medicine. Other pyramids were constructed during this period, but the largest of them still stand at Giza, the work of three kings of the Fourth Dynasty, Khufu, Khafre, and Menkaure, known to the Greek world as Cheops, Chephren, and Mycerinus.

Kings of the last two dynasties again had their pyramids at Sakkarah; from these tombs come the religious spells known as the Pyramid Texts. Fiscal difficulties, international problems, and related factors brought about the fall of the OK.

First Disintegration or First Intermediate Period (Dynasties VII–XI; 2200–2050 B.C.). This period was marked by political and social upheaval, confusion, and uncertainty. The breakdown of old values produced a pessimism reflected in the literature as men groped for meaning in life. Outstanding works include the Dialogue of a Man Weary of Life, the Song of Harper, and the writing of Ipuwer. Dynasties VII(?)-VIII had their capital at Memphis; IX–X, at Herakleopolis; XI, at Thebes.

Eventually the political situation stabilized when Mentuhotep II of Dynasty XI (*c.* 2060–2010 B.C.) crushed the rival king at Herakleopolis and another prosperous era eventuated with the *Middle Kingdom* (MK, Dynasty XI–XII; 2050–1786 B.C.). Many Egyptologists regard this as the greatest period of ancient Egypt. Art and architecture again flourished. This was the classical period of the Egyptian language and from the MK come the Story of the Eloquent Peasant, the adventures of the noble Sinuhe, and in religious literature the Coffin Texts. All the kings of Dynasty XII were named either Amenemhet or Senusert (Sesostris). The capital was located at It-towy near Lisht, not far from the Fayum.

This was an age of engineering projects, such as attempts to control the Nile waters and of imperialistic expansion. To the S, Nubia was occupied and protected by forts and to the NE there was increased activity in Sinai. During

The great pyramid. Herbert Lockyer, Jr.

Amenemhet III. LL

the dark times of disintegration the nobles had gained power, so that the early MK was a kind of feudal monarchy. About the middle of his reign Senusert III (1878–1843 B.C.) reduced the status of the provincial nobles and administered the entire country through the office of the vizier. How this was achieved is not revealed in the Egyptian records, but Joseph's purchase of the land for the pharaoh during the famine (Gen 47:20) supplies a possible explanation. The king was represented in statuary as a care-worn ruler, the concerned but efficient "shepherd" of the people. An increasing emphasis was placed on *ma'at,* "justice, right, the proper order of things."

The Second Intermediate Period (Dynasties XIII–XVII; 1786–1580 B.C.). Dynasties XIII–XIV were of minor importance; Dynasties XV–XVI were the Hyksos rulers, of whom later Egyptians spoke with contempt. The Hyksos, "rulers of foreign countries," became quite Egyptianized. Some scholars feel that they were able administrators and that Egyptian references to them were very biased. They introduced many elements into Egyptian culture including better weapons, which the native Egyptians adopted and used against them. Dynasty XVII, a local Theban house, initiated the fight to expel the Hyksos. The effort was successfully concluded by Ahmose, the first king of Dynasty XVIII. *See* Hyksos.

The New Kingdom or Empire (Dynasties XVIII–XX; 1580–1090 B.C.) was the high point of Egyptian territorial expansion, an age of conquest and material prosperity. The royal ideal now stressed the physical prowess of the divine king and made him the insuperable strong man and skilled athlete. Among the prominent rulers of this period the following may be singled out: (Dynasty XVIII) Hatshepsut, the woman-king, possibly the princess who found the infant Moses (Ex 2:5–10), is best known for her beautiful mortuary temple at Deir el-Bahri, with its fine reliefs showing her birth legend and a voyage to Punt. Thutmose III (1504–1450 B.C.) was the able military campaigner, whose 17 expeditions into Palestine-Syria really made the empire. According to the early date of the Exodus (*c.* 1445 B.C.), he would be the pharaoh of the oppression (Ex 2:15, 23; *see* Exodus, The); and his son Amenhotep II would then be the pharaoh of the Exodus (Ex 5–14). Amenhotep III, justly nicknamed "the Magnificent," noted for his luxurious living, and Amenhotep IV (Akhenaton), together were largely responsible for the temporary loss of the Asiatic empire through their rejection of pleas for help from that area (*see* Amarna Letters).

In Dynasty XIX, Seti I and Ramses II (1304–1234 B.C.) renewed Egyptian activity in the Asiatic provinces. According to the late date of the Exodus these two kings were the probable pharaohs of the oppression and the Exodus, respectively. The latter was famous also for his building achievements; his monuments and inscriptions mark him as a supreme egoist. His son Merenptah claimed to have destroyed Israel on a campaign to Palestine, the first extrabiblical mention of Israel.

Ramses III, the outstanding ruler of Dynasty XX, saved Egypt from an invasion of the Sea Peoples (including Philistines) and built his mortuary temple at Medinet Habu. The Empire Period was an age of cosmopolitanism, a characteristic which culminated in the collapse of the empire. Foreign influences sapped the strength of cultural features which were distinctively Egyptian; even the army became a mercenary force composed of foreigners.

The Post-Empire Period or Period of Decline (Dynasties XXI–XXX; 1090–331 B.C.) saw Egypt under foreign domination several times. In the Libyan Dynasty (XXII) Sheshonk (the biblical Shishak) successfully invaded Palestine (926 B.C.). Dynasty XXV was Kushite or Ethiopian, but these people were steeped in Egyptian tradition and were more Egyptian than the Egyptians of that time.

In spite of Assyrian invasions there was a resurgence of native energy in the *Saite Period* (Dynasty XXVI; 663–525 B.C.), but it was coupled with a backward look which generally hindered progress. Neco II (610–595 B.C.) tried unsuccessfully to dig a canal from the Nile to the Red Sea, but did send Phoenician ships which circumnavigated all of Africa.

A statue of Queen Hatshepsut from Deir el-Bahri. LL

In 525 B.C. Egypt came under Persian domination (Dynasties XXVII–XXX; 525–331 B.C.). In 331 Alexander the Great brought the native dynasties to an end; after his death (323 B.C.) Egypt was ruled by the Ptolemies until it became a province of Rome in 31 B.C.

Egypt and the Bible

Egypt appears in the Bible from Genesis to Revelation. The majority of the references are of an historic or prophetic nature and are found mostly in the OT. Egypt (Mizraim) is first mentioned in Gen 10:6, where the name appears in the Table of Nations as a son of Ham. It figures in the patriarchal narratives as a place of refuge for Abram at a time when famine swept through Palestine. Crop failure was rare in Egypt and its fertile soil produced both regularly and abundantly. It was natural for Egypt to play the role of breadbasket, and in Roman times large quantities of wheat were exported to Italy.

The presence of Asiatics in Egypt at about the time of Abram is illustrated by a frequently reproduced wall painting from the tomb of Khnumhotep II at Beni Hasan. Here some 37 Asiatics are shown bringing trade goods to Middle Egypt. Abraham's fears concerning his life and the seizure of Sarai for the king's harem were fulfilled in part. The varied literature from ancient Egypt provides no clear-cut parallels to this incident. Though the Tale of Two Brothers is sometimes cited in this respect, a reading of that story reveals that the circumstances were quite different. The wife of Bata wanted her husband killed so that she could be a member of Pharaoh's household.

The mention of camels in Egypt (Gen 12:16) early in the 2nd mil. B.C. is at present an unsolved problem, for there is no word for camel in hieroglyphic and the animal is not represented in the tomb scenes; further evidence is awaited. *See* Animals, I.5.

Since the Joseph narrative and the early part of Exodus are located in Egypt, the closest Egyptian-biblical relationships are found in these sections. Egyptian words and names, cultural practices, geographical features, and other aspects of Egyptian life appear in profusion. Some elements of Egyptian background include: Joseph's coat (Gen 37) of the style worn by Canaanite nobles bringing tribute to the pharaoh depicted in tomb paintings; the description of Potiphar as an Egyptian (Gen 39); the episode of the attempted seduction by Potiphar's wife, an account which has numerous parallels with the Tale of Two Brothers and its familiar sordid theme (Gen 39); the offices of royal butler and baker, the role of dreams in Egypt, the use of grapes (Gen 40); the raising of cattle, the relationship of cattle and the Nile, the production of grain (Gen 41); shaving (41:14); the destructive force of the east wind (41:27); the levying and collecting of taxes (41:34); the presentation of gold ornaments as an award for meritorious service (41:42); the use of chariots by royalty and nobility (41:42); the religious figure of the priest of On (Heliopolis) (41:45); divination (44:4–5); the location of the land of Goshen (Gen 45 ff.); embalming, mumification, and funerary ritual (Gen 50).

Ex 1 mentions the making of bricks, agricultural work, forced labor, and obstetrical methods. The description of the Nile in Ex 2 (babyhood of Moses) and Ex 7 (the first plague) is accurate and interesting. Moses' training in all the learning of the Egyptians (Acts 7:22) was not unusual, for children of W Semite nobles and officials were often sent to Egypt to be educated in court circles. The signs and the ten great plagues (*see* Plague) contain many evidences of a close acquaintance with Egypt, which testifies to the Mosaic authorship of the account. Familiarity with the excellence of Egyptian craftsmanship in gold and silver may be related to the Israelite demand for jewelry in Ex 11:2. The scene of the Egyptian chariotry pursuing the fleeing Israelites (14:9) reminds one of the battle reliefs in many Egyptian temples. The despairing attitude of the Israelites reflects their experience of slavehood and their deep respect for the Egyptian military (14:10). The bitter irony of their reproach of Moses, "Is it because there are no graves in Egypt" (14:11, RSV), has considerable force when one realizes that the desert edges of both sides of the Nile virtually constitute one vast extended cemetery from the Delta to Nubia.

Thutmose III. LL

Though the Israelites were successfully delivered from the land of Egypt, they did not soon escape its influence. Even while God was conferring with Moses on Mount Sinai the people on the plain below were worshiping a calf of gold (Ex 32), a form of the cattle worship of Egypt which was a recurring temptation to Israel. The pleasures of Egypt were also recalled; while enduring monotonous rations in the desert, the Israelites recollected the good food they had enjoyed in Egypt—fish, cucumbers, melons, leeks, onions, and garlic (Num 11:5–6).

Having reached Palestine, the Israelites were relatively free from Egyptian interference for some centuries. A few biblical scholars, however, have suggested a relationship between the oppressions and deliverances in the book of Judges and the periods of weakness and strength in Egypt. During this time the Egyptians were concerned mostly with the Great Road, the artery of commerce that lay in the maritime plain of Palestine (*see* Palestine II.B.1).

The decline of Egyptian power *c.* 1100 B.C. is evidenced in the account of the Egyptian representative Wen-Amon, who was treated with little respect on his venture to Phoenicia to obtain cedar wood (ANET, pp. 25–29). This weakness provided an opportunity for the rapid growth of the nation of Israel, particularly under David and Solomon. The first recorded contacts between Israelite and Egyptian rulers come in the time of Solomon, who married the daughter of the Egyptian king. The father-in-law captured and destroyed the city of Gezer and presented it to his daughter as a dowry (I Kgs 9:16). Solomon engaged in trade with Egypt (II Chr 1:16–17). His wisdom surpassed all the wisdom of Egypt (I Kgs 4:30).

Though Egypt had been a place of oppression for Israel, it was often considered a refuge. In Solomon's time it became a haven for political enemies of Solomon and a staging area from which they returned to plague him. Hadad, an Edomite who had fled to Egypt on the occasion of a foray by David into Edom, came back and became an active enemy of Solomon (I Kgs 11:14–20). Jeroboam the son of Nebat went to Egypt to escape Solomon's wrath. When he returned he became the first king of the northern tribes and "made Israel to sin" by his setting up of calf-idols at Bethel and Dan (I Kgs 12:26–33), another possible Egyptian influence on Israelite religion. With the division of the kingdom, Palestine was soon subjected to an Egyptian invasion. Sheshonk (biblical Shishak) sacked the temple of its treasures in the fifth year of Rehoboam (926 B.C.; I Kgs 14:25–26; II Chr 12:1–9).

Egypt continued to play a prominent part in Israelite political life and was overrated by those who saw in her a possible ally against the rising powers of Assyria and, later, Babylonia. Hoshea, the last king of Israel, in vain sent to So (the Delta city of Sais) to Pharaoh Tefnakhte (II Kgs 17:4). Isaiah and Jeremiah, as statesmen-prophets, saw the folly of this course and recognized Egypt under such a leader as Taharka (biblical Tirhakah, II Kgs 19:9) as only a "broken reed" (Isa 36:6; cf. II Kgs 18:21) on which one could not depend for support. Egypt was still much too strong for the military power of Judah, and when Neco II marched to aid the Assyrians in their last struggle against the Babylonians, Josiah, following his anti-Assyrian policy, made a foolhardy attempt against the Egyptians at Megiddo in 609 B.C. and lost his own life (II Kgs 23:29–30; II Chr 35:20–27). Ironically, the Babylonians won and later defeated Neco again at Carchemish in 605 B.C. Apries (biblical Hophra) is mentioned in a prophecy of Jeremiah (Jer 44:30).

Statue of Ramses II at Luxor Temple. HFV

After the capture of Jerusalem by Nebuchadnezzar and the murder of Gedaliah, the Palestinian remnant fled to Egypt in spite of the strong speech of Jeremiah against such a course (Jer 44). In Egypt they scattered to many places. Later records, such as the Aramaic papyri from Elephantine, indicate that even at Egypt's S border there was a group of Jews who had a temple and service and who kept in touch with Palestine. Also in the inter-testamental period the translation of the OT into Greek (the LXX) was accomplished in Egypt (3rd cen. B.C.).

In the NT the references to Egypt are concerned mostly with the OT record of God's dealings with Israel. Egypt was part of the current scene, however, for God directed Joseph to take Jesus and Mary to Egypt to save the Baby's life from the vengeful fury of Herod (Mt 2:13–15; cf. Hos 11:1). Among the foreign Jews who heard the languages and message of Pentecost were those of Egypt (Acts 2:10). Egypt was important in the history of the early church; documents from Egypt bear on both this history and the transmission of the text of the Scriptures.

The final biblical allusion to Egypt is in Rev 11:8, where Jerusalem is called "Sodom and Egypt." This allegorical usage makes Egypt a symbol of evil and of the perishing world-order. Typologists have overworked this aspect of Egypt, forgetting God's use of Egypt to preserve Israel in the time of Joseph (Gen 45:5–9) and His direction of Jacob to go to Egypt (Gen 46:3–4). The prophets uttered many severe predictions against Egypt, but the Lord also gave to Isaiah an oracle concerning Egypt which included the promise that Egypt would finally turn to the Lord and the gracious words of the Lord of hosts, "Blessed be Egypt my people" (see Isa 19:18–25).

C. E. D.

Bibliography. Butrus Abd al-Malik, "Egypt," BW, pp. 207-218. I. E. S. Edwards, *The Pyramids of Egypt,* Baltimore: Penguin, 1961. Ahmed Fakhry, *The Pyramids,* Chicago: Univ. of Chicago Press, 1961. Henri Frankfort, *Ancient Egyptian Religion,* New York: Harper, 1961. Alan Gardiner, *Egypt of the Pharaohs,* Oxford: Clarendon Press, 1961. William C. Hayes, *The Scepter of Egypt,* 2 vols., Cambridge: Harvard Univ. Press, 1953, 1959; "The Middle Kingdom in Egypt," Fasc. 3 (Chap. XX) for rev. ed. of *The Cambridge Ancient History,* Vol. I, Cambridge: Univ. Press, 1964 (and many other similar fascicles on Egypt). Kenneth A. Kitchen, "Egypt," NBD, pp. 337-353, with excellent bibliography. Martin Noth, "Thebes," TAOTS, pp. 21-35. Charles F. Pfeiffer and Howard F. Vos, "Egypt," WHG, pp. 47-93. George Steindorff and K. C. Seele, *When Egypt Ruled the East,* 2nd ed., Chicago: Univ. of Chicago, 1957. John A. Wilson, *The Burden of Egypt,* Chicago: Univ. of Chicago, 1951; "Egypt," IDB, II, 39-66.

EGYPT, RIVER OF. *See* River of Egypt.

EHI (ē'hī). A son of Benjamin (Gen 46:21). This is probably a contraction of the name Ahiram (*q.v.*) or a distortion in the text.

EHUD (ē'hŭd)

1. The son of Gera of the tribe of Benjamin, who was noted for being "a man lefthanded" (Jud 3:15). Ehud was raised up by God as the second deliverer among the judges. Through Ehud's leadership the 18 years of Moabite rule over Israel was ended. This was accomplished by a clever ruse. For the sake of gaining familiarity with Eglon, the king of Moab, and his palace, Ehud joined those who bore to Eglon the usual tribute from Israel. On the homeward trip. Ehud returned alone to Jericho from the sculptured stones ("quarries," Jud 3:19) at Gilgal. Not even Israel knew of his secret mission to Eglon (*q.v.*). He was able to gain a private audience with Eglon by indicating that he had secret information for the king, and was able to slay the Moabite king in his rooftop chamber with his concealed and specially crafted two-edged sword. Due to the ineptness of Eglon's servants, Ehud escaped without detection. The judge then marshaled the Israelites together in the hills of Ephraim and led them in battle against Moab. Ehud's battle strategy was based on the control of the fords of Jordan. Without the leadership of their king, Moab was defeated. In Jud 3:28 Ehud acknowledged the hand of God in this victory. The land then had relative peace for 80 years.

2. The name of a son of Bilhan, and great-grandson of Benjamin (I Chr 7:10), who was renowned as a mighty warrior.

R. B. D.

EKER (ē'kĕr). A post-Exilic descendant of Judah through Hezron and Jerahmeel (I Chr 2:27).

EKRON (ĕk'rŏn). The northernmost of the five main cities of Philistia (Josh 13:3). It was first assigned to Judah (Josh 15:11, 45-46); then to Dan (Josh 19:43) before that tribe moved N, after which it was temporarily taken by Judah (Jud 1:18). It was prominent in all stages of Israel's history, from the time the ark was taken there (I Sam 5:10) until the time of the prophet Zechariah (cf. Zech 9:5, 7). Sennacherib captured Ekron from a group of rebels who had turned its king, Padi, over to Hezekiah, evidently the leader in the opposition to the Assyrians (ANET, pp. 287 f.).

The site is now disputed. Edward Robinson, in the 19th cen., suggested that Ekron be identified with 'Akir, ten miles NE of Ashdod. Others identify it with Khirbet el-Muqenna', six miles SE of 'Akir (BW, p. 219). The latter site was probably the largest Iron Age city in Palestine, a walled town that covered 40 acres (J. Naveh, "Khirbat al-Muqanna'-Ekron," IEJ, VIII [1958], 87-100, 165-170).

EL (ĕl). The generic name for Deity shared by Hebrews (*'el*) and Canaanites, appearing in the cognate form *ilu* in Akkadian, *allah* in Arabic. It is seldom found in the OT except in poetical passages. When it does occur in prose narratives, it is usually in titles, such as El Roi (Gen 16:13, ASV marg.), El Shaddai (Gen 17:1), El Elyon (Gen 14:18); or in descriptive phrases, such as "God, the God of Israel" (Gen 33:20, RSV marg.), or "Yahweh, God of gods" (Josh 22:22, Heb.).

The original meaning of the word is uncertain. Some trace it to the idea "in front" or "first," since the word for "leading ram of the flock" is similar. Others derive it from the same root as the preposition "toward," in the sense of describing the object of all worship. Still others see its meaning in the verb " to tie," thus denoting the one who holds all things together.

Most scholars prefer to identify the essential idea as the one in the idiom "in the power of my hand," literally, "in the *'ēl* of my hand" (Gen 31:29; also Deut 28:32; Mic 2:1; Prov 3:27; cf. Neh 5:5). God is the all-powerful One, the Almighty (*q.v.*). The only suffix found on this word is the first common singular "my." In the later history of Israel, Elohim (*q.v.*) was usually preferred to El, but this earlier title was retained as a time-honored term of endearment. *See* God, Names of.

In the Ugaritic tablets, El is a proper name, the "high god" of the Canaanites. His position as king of the Canaanite pantheon was evidently usurped by the Amorite deity Ba'al-Hadad in the religious revolution that followed the coming of the Amorites from the Syrian desert plateau *c.* 2000 B.C. *See* God; God, Names and Titles of.

Bibliography. William F. Albright, *Yahweh and the Gods of Canaan,* Garden City: Doubleday, 1968, pp. 119-121, 124-128. Ulf Oldenburg,

The Conflict Between El and Baʿal in Canaanite Religion, Leiden: Brill, 1969.

C. T. F.

ELADAH (ĕl'ă-dȧ). A descendant of Ephraim (I Chr 7:20).

ELAH (ē'lȧ)

1. A prince of an Edomite clan (Gen 36:41; I Chr 1:52).

2. The father of Shimei, one of Solomon's administrative officers (I Kgs 4:18).

3. An Israelite king (*c.* 886–885 B.C.), son of Baasha (I Kgs 16:6, 8, 13–14). He was murdered by his successor Zimri.

4. Father of Hoshea, the last king of Israel (II Kgs 15:30; 17:1; 18:1, 9).

5. A family in the ancestry of Caleb (I Chr 4:15). Possibly this reference, as well as # 1 above, is to the place Elath (*q.v.*).

6. A family in the ancestry of Benjamin living in Jerusalem in post-Exilic times (I Chr 9:8).

ELAH, VALLEY OF (ē'lȧ). A valley which was the scene of the duel between David and Goliath (I Sam 17). Since the narrative indicates that the two armies confronted one another in strong positions on the heights, the valley is probably Wadi es-Sant, a steep-sided ravine W of Bethlehem, running from the heart of Judah to the Philistine plain.

ELAM (ē'lȧm) (PERSONS)

1. First son of Shem (Gen 10:22; I Chr 1:17); eponymous father of the Elamite people. *See* Elam (country), Elamites.

2. A chief man of the tribe of Benjamin who lived in Jerusalem (I Chr 8:24).

3. Son of Meshelemiah, a Korahite, one of the porters of the tabernacle in the time of David (I Chr 26:3).

4. The ancestral name of clans participating in the return from Exile (Ezr 2:7 and Neh 7:12; "the other Elam," Ezr 2:31 and Neh 7:34; Ezr 8:7; 10:2, 26).

5. A "chief of the people" (Neh 10:14). Possibly same as 4.

6. A priest and participant in the dedication of the wall of Jerusalem under Nehemiah (Neh 12:42).

ELAM (ē'lȧm) (COUNTRY), **ELAMITES** (ē'lȧ-mīts). Elam was located in SW Asia on a plain E of Babylonia and N of the Persian Gulf, watered by the Karun and Kerka Rivers. It corresponded approximately to Khuzistan in modern Iran.

Dating from the late 4th mil. B.C., the known history of the Elamites was one of constant strife and warfare with its more populous neighbors—Sumerians, Babylonians, Assyrians, and finally Persians, by whom the Elamites were ultimately absorbed. They seem, however, to have maintained rather consistently their independence in spite of repeated invasions attempting to gain control of the trade routes to the Iranian plateau.

The long history of this civilization is known through Mesopotamian documents and from inscriptions written by the Elamite kings in their own language. Most of the inscriptions were recovered at Susa, capital city of ancient Elam. In the early part of the 3rd mil. a proto-Elamite cuneiform existed alongside Sumerian cuneiform, but it died out as a result of the conquests of Sargon and the domination of his Akkadian Dynasty (*c.*2360–2180 B.C.). It was during this

Ruins at the ancient Elamite city of Susa as seen from the air. ORINST

period that the Elamite language produced the oldest known state treaty between Naram-Sin (Sargon's grandson) and the Avan Dynasty. Some proto-Elamite and Akkad. bilingual texts have come down to us from Puzur-Shushinak (2280 B.C.), a king of this Avan Dynasty. Later on, the Elamites used the Babylonian cuneiform signs for their language, as witnessed in that key to decipherment, the Behistun inscription written in Babylonian, Elamite, and Old Persian by the Persian king Darius I.

Many changes in Elamite culture took place during the Akkad. (Semitic) rule, for not only their peculiar form of writing but also their distinctive painted pottery disappeared, and the Sumero-Akkad. culture was adopted. Semites from Mesopotamia began to settle in this area in increasing numbers. Thus, while racially and linguistically the Elamites do not appear to have been of Semitic origin, it is probably on account of this Semitic influence that Elam is called a "son" of Shem in the Table of Nations (Gen 10:22; cf. I Chr 1:17).

Around 2000 B.C. the Elamites captured several cities in Babylonia, helping to bring to an end the supremacy of the Sumerian rulers of the Third Dynasty of Ur (2113–2006 B.C.) and sacking that city. It is in this period of Elamite strength that Chedorlaomer (*q.v.*; Gen 14:1–17) most likely rounded up confederates to march through Transjordan to collect tribute from the cities in the Dead Sea area. At the time of the Amorite First Dynasty of Babylon (*c.* 1894–1595 B.C.), whose sixth king was Hammurabi, several Elamite rulers are known, the first element of whose names was Kudur-. This fact tends to confirm that Chedorlaomer is an authentic Elamite royal name of that period.

Later, the Elamites periodically harassed Babylonia for several centuries (*c.* 1300–1120 B.C.). Shutruk-Nahhunte (*c.*1200 B.C.) returned from a successful raid against Babylon with the famous law code of Hammurabi as a trophy; it was rediscovered at Susa in 1901–2. Nebuchadnezzar I of Babylon reduced Elam once more, however, to the status of a Babylonian dependency, so that it is not heard of for some three centuries. After *c.* 740 B.C. the Elamites allied themselves with Babylonians as the almost constant enemy of the Assyrians, until Ashurbanipal nearly exterminated them (*c.* 645 B.C.). The void they left was filled in by Indo-European Persians, who made the ancient Elamite city of Susa into a Persian winter capital. It is called Shushan in the book of Esther; Neh 1:1; and Dan 8:2 (all KJV).

Isaiah had spoken of Elamite bowmen as captive mercenary troops in the Assyrian army that invaded Judah (Isa 22:6), and of Elamites in the army of Cyrus that would besiege Babylon (21:2). Jeremiah's prophecy against Elam (Jer 49:34–39) is puzzling unless it refers to the Persians who were overlords of the land formerly called Elam. Their return from captivity (v. 39) would then refer to the rise of the Persian Empire. Ezr 4:9 (RSV) names the "men of Susa, that is, the Elamites" as companions of Rehum and Shimshai, officials of the Persian government in Jerusalem, who opposed the rebuilding of post-Exilic Jerusalem. Elamites are also mentioned as present in Jerusalem on the day of Pentecost (Acts 2:9); these were Jews from the old region of Elam.

See Madai; Persia; Shushan.

T. M. B. and E. B. S.

ELASAH (ĕl-*á*/să)

1. Son of Shaphan and one of two messengers from Zedekiah to Nebuchadnezzar, who also delivered Jeremiah's message to the Judeans in Exile (Jer 29:3).

2. Son of Pashur and one of the post-Exilic priests who put away foreign wives (Ezr 10:22).

Elsewhere the name is rendered Eleasah (*q.v.*).

ELATH (ē'lăth). Alternately Eloth. Elath was located in biblical times at the head of the Gulf of Aqabah (*q.v.*). The name is still used by the state of Israel for a similarly located town whose Jordanian counterpart nearby is called Aqabah. The area is delightful in the winter months, living up to the resortlike connotation suggested in the Heb. meaning of the term (*'ēlat,* "palm grove"). The port facilities became very important for modern Israel when the United Arab Republic closed the Suez Canal to Israeli ships. The natural deepwater harbor at Elath allows the largest freighters and oil tankers to discharge or load at the docks. Cargo and oil can then be transshipped by highway and pipeline through the Negev to Haifa on the Mediterranean.

The origins of Elath are unknown, but it was probably an old Edomite center, as is indicated in Deut 2:8, where Moses and the children of Israel passed through the Edomite plain (the Arabah) that began at Elath and went N to Moab.

With David's conquest of the Edomites the area became important to the Israelites. Solomon made it the main port of the nation, though he also used the Phoenician ports on the Mediterranean coast. In I Kgs 10:22 (RSV) mention is made of Solomon's "ships of Tarshish," that is, a deep-sea fleet like those used by the Phoenicians who helped provide him with sailors and nautical knowledge (II Chr 8:17–18). Later, Jehoshaphat attempted to rebuild this fleet, but the attempt met with disaster (I Kgs 22:48).

According to II Kgs 14:22 Azariah (Uzziah) restored Elath, while II Kgs 16:6 relates that King Rezin of Syria drove the Jews out of Elath in the days of King Ahaz. Some (RSV and JerusB) would take the Heb. text of the latter passage to say that Edomites, not Syrians (*'dm* for *'rm*), actually occupied Elath, because of the northern attack on Judah by Resin and Pekah. According to II Chr 28:17, the Edomites were sharing in the spoils in those dark days, which was always the case when Judah was weak (II Kgs 8:20–22). *See* Ezion-geber.

E. B. S.

EL BERITH. *See* Gods, False: Baal Berith.

EL-BETHEL (ĕl-bĕth′ĕl; "God of Bethel"). The name given by Jacob to the scene of his vision of the ladder at Luz (cf. Gen 28:10-15) as he returned to Canaan (Gen 35:7). *See* Bethel.

ELDAAH (ĕl-dā′*ȧ*). The fifth son of Midian, the fourth son of Abraham by Keturah (Gen 25:2, 4; I Chr 1:32-33).

ELDAD (ĕl′dăd). One of the 70 elders summoned by Moses to help assume the responsibility of government. For some reason Eldad did not formally present himself at the tabernacle for ordination, but notwithstanding this, he too received the Spirit of the Lord and prophesied. Joshua expressed concern for Moses' honor because Eldad had not been formally ordained. Moses expressed a charitable view by acknowledging that the Spirit of God had been conferred, and expressed a wish that the Lord might put His Spirit upon all the people (Num 11:24-29).

ELDER. In the OT Heb. *zāqēn,* lit., "one who is bearded," designates a man of a certain official rank and position among his brethren. Among the Israelites there were two kinds of elders, the "elders of Israel" who were the heads of families or clans in the various tribes, and the "elders" of the towns built and settled after the Conquest.

Elders are mentioned in Mesopotamian texts from the 18th cen. B.C. onward as the representatives of the people, defending their rights but with no administrative functions. Many municipal duties were performed by the council of elders in the Hittite Empire. The elders of Gebal (Byblos) are mentioned in Ezk 27:9 and the assembly (of elders) of the prince of Byblos in the story of Wen-Amon (ANET, p. 29). The system of elders existed among other neighbors of Israel as well: Egypt (Gen 50:7; Ps 105:22, RSV), Moab and the Midianites (Num 22:4, 7), and the Gibeonites (Josh 9:11). The Heb. term is thus equivalent to the Homeric *gerontes,* the Spartan *presbys,* the Roman *senatus,* and the Arab *sheikh.*

The term *zāqēn* does not necessarily mean an old man, but does imply one of maturity and experience who has assumed leadership among his own kinsmen and in his town or tribe (cf. Num 11:16). Although the elders were not elected, during most of the periods from Moses to Ezra and on into the intertestamental era they were recognized as the highest authoritative body over the people. They acted as the religious representatives of the nation (Jer 19:1, RSV; Joel 1:14; 2:16) as well as handling many political matters and settling intertribal disputes (e.g., Phinehas and the ten tribal chiefs or elders, Josh 22:13-33). The town elders were a sort of municipal council whose duties included acting as judges in apprehending murderers (Deut 19:12), conducting inquests (Deut 21:2), and settling matrimonial disputes (Deut 22:15; 25:7).

The "elders of Israel," first heard of in Ex 3:16-18, were assembled by Moses to receive God's announcement of liberation from Egypt. The covenant was ratified at Mount Sinai in the presence of 70 of the elders of Israel (Ex 24:1, 9, 14; cf. 19:7), the "nobles" (KJV) or chief men of the nation (24:11). Later, 70 elders were specially anointed with the Spirit to aid Moses in governing the nation (Num 11:16-25). In cases when the whole community sinned, the elders of the congregation or community were to represent it in making atonement (Lev 4:13-15).

The authority of the elders was in principle greater than that of the king (cf. II Kgs 23:1). It was this group which demanded that Samuel appoint a king (I Sam 8:4-6), and they were parties to the royal covenant which established David as king (II Sam 5:3). In Babylon the elders were the focal point of the Jewish community in exile (Jer 29:1; Ezk 8:1; 14:1; 20:1-5), and after the return to Jerusalem they continued active (Ezr 5:5, 9; 6:7-8, 14; 10:8, 14).

Out of the Council of Elders (*gerousia*) of the Hellenistic period in Judah developed the Great Assembly (*Knesset*) of the Jews which in 142 B.C. granted great power to Simon the Maccabean leader (I Macc 14:28). The Great Sanhedrin with its 71 members, the supreme legislative body prior to A.D. 70, was the ultimate form of the institution of the "elders of Israel." *See* Sanhedrin. (See also "Government, Authority and Kingship," CornPBE, pp. 354-369.) For the office of elder in the NT churches *see* Bishop.

In his vision of heaven John saw 24 elders seated upon thrones surrounding the throne of God, clothed in white garments and wearing golden crowns (Rev 4:4). They fall down in worship and cast their crowns before God's throne (4:10; cf. 11:16; 19:4), and with their harps and bowls of incense, symbolizing the prayers of the saints, they sing a new song to the Lamb (5:8-10). As elders they represent God's people; their thrones and crowns symbolize a kingly role, while their acts of worship and the bowls of incense suggest a priestly function. Thus they seem to be the chief representatives of the redeemed as a kingdom of priests (Rev 1:6; cf. 20:6; I Pet 2:5, 9; Ex 19:6). Whether the number 24 suggests the 24 courses of the Jewish priesthood, or a combination of the 12 tribes of Israel (indicative of the OT saints) and the 12 apostles (the leaders of the NT saints), is debatable. For a detailed discussion of the identity of these elders see G. H. Lang, *The Revelation of Jesus Christ,* London: Paternoster Press, 1945, pp. 124-136.

Bibliography. W. Harold Mare, "Church Functionaries: the Witness in the Literature and Archaeology of the New Testament and Church Periods," JETS, XIII (1970), 229-239.

J. R.

ELEAD (ĕl'ĕ-ăd). A descendant of Ephraim, killed by the men of Gath while making a raid on their cattle (I Chr 7:21).

ELEALEH (ĕl-ē-ā'lē). A city of Transjordan in the area requested by the tribes of Reuben and Gad, rebuilt by Reuben (Num 32:3, 37); later a part of Moab (Isa 15:4; 16:9; Jer 48:34). Today it is identified as a mound called el-'Al.

ELEASAH (ĕl-ē-ā'sȧ). This name has the same Heb. form as Elasah (*q.v.*).

1. A descendant of Judah through Hezron and Jerahmeel (I Chr 2:33, 39-40).

2. A descendant of Saul (I Chr 8:33, 37; 9:43).

ELEAZAR (ĕl'ē-ā'zȧr). In addition to the following biblical references, the name appears also in a Jewish legal contract among the Dead Sea Scrolls.

1. The third son of Aaron and Elisheba (Ex 6:23; Num 3:2). He was consecrated to the priesthood with his father and brothers at Sinai (Ex 28:1, 4; Lev 8:2, 13). After God slew the older brothers when they presented unlawful fire (Lev 10:1-7), Eleazar and Ithamar continued to exercise priestly functions with Aaron (Num 3:1-4). Eleazar was placed over the Levites (Num 3:32) and assigned the care of the sanctuary and its vessels, etc. (Num 4:16; 16:37, 39; 19:3-4). He succeeded as high priest when his father Aaron died at Mount Hor (Num 20:25-28; Deut 10:6). Joshua was installed as Moses' successor before Eleazar the priest, who was to be Joshua's official counselor by making inquiry of the Lord (Num 27:18-22). He took part in the census at Shittim (Num 26:1, 63), and in the division of land to the eastern tribes (Num 32:2; 34:17) and later with Joshua to the western tribes (Josh 14:1; 17:4; 19:51; 21:1). He married a daughter of Putiel and she bore him Phinehas (Ex 6:25). Eleazar was buried near the home of his son, who succeeded him as high priest (Josh 24:33; Jud 20:28). Eleazar was the ancestor of the Zadokite priests, who in Solomon's time replaced Abiathar, a descendant of Ithamar, Eleazar's younger brother (I Chr 6:4-15; I Kgs 2:26-27, 35).

2. A Merarite Levite who died without sons. His daughters were married to kinsmen in order to keep the family inheritance within the tribe (I Chr 23:21-22; 24:28), in accordance with the regulation of Num 36:6-9.

3. The son of Abinadab, probably a Levite. He was consecrated to have charge of the ark while it was in his father's home in Kirjath-jearim after the Philistines had returned the ark (I Sam 7:1).

4. Son of Dodo; one of David's "three mighty men" (II Sam 23:9; I Chr 11:12).

5. A priest who assisted in the inventory of the temple treasure when it was brought back to Jerusalem by Ezra (Ezr 8:33).

6. A member of the clan of Parosh, listed among laymen in Israel who put away foreign wives during Ezra's reform (Ezr 10:25).

7. A priest who participated in the procession on the walls of Jerusalem during their dedication (Neh 12:42).

8. An ancestor of Joseph the husband of Mary (Mt 1:15).

J. R.

ELECT. "Chosen" or "selected." The main OT verb for this is *bāḥar*, a deliberated selecting of something or someone with attendant preference or pleasure. The NT verb *eklegomai* means to choose or select out of a larger group something or someone for oneself. The related adjectives *bāḥir* and *eklektos* are translated "elect" or "chosen" and are the result of an act of selection. The words are used of choices human (Gen 6:2; Deut 30:19; Lk 10:42; 14:7) and divine for salvation (Eph 1:4), and for service (Jn 15:16).

Various objects are termed "elect" or "chosen" by God: the nation Israel for special favor and purpose (Isa 44:1; 45:4); several individuals, such as Abraham (Neh 9:7), Aaron (Ps 105:26), David (I Sam 16:8 ff.); Jerusalem (II Chr 6:6); a remnant of Jews near the second coming of Christ (Mt 24:22; Isa 65:9); the Church, the body of Christ (I Pet 2:9; 5:13; Col 3:12; Tit 1:1); Christ Himself (Isa 42:1; I Pet 2:6); the "lady" (II Jn 1); and angels (I Tim 5:21). Elect men are chosen by God's grace (Rom 11:5) and love (Rom 8:33-39; 11:28; Eph 1:4-5) and according to His foreknowledge (I Pet 1:2); it is never on the basis of human merit (Rom 9:11; cf. II Tim 1:9). *See* Chosen; Election.

C. F. D.

ELECT LADY. A translation of the phrase *eklektē kyria* in II Jn 1. The meaning, long a puzzle to commentators, is probably to be found in one of two possible explanations: (1) a reference to an individual, named either "elect Kyria," Electa Kyria, or "the lady Electa"; or (2) a reference to a local Christian congregation under the symbol of a woman.

While the former meaning is possible, as the personal name Kyria was known in the ancient world, the contrast with III John makes it less likely. There John addressed his friend in the natural, normal way. On the other hand, the language of II John is indefinite and ambiguous.

More probably, then, John addressed a Christian congregation by use of the terms "the Lady chosen by God" (NEB). The idea of the election of the Church is common in the NT (see, e.g., Rom 8:33; Eph 1:4; Col 3:12; I Pet

1:1–2). Further, we find greetings being sent from "the church that is at Babylon, elected together with you" in I Pet 5:13. Furthermore, it was not uncommon to think of the community of God's people as a woman bearing children (Baruch 4:8–5:5; Gal 4:25; Rev 12).

Again, the alternating between the second person singular (II Jn 1–5) and the second person plural (vv. 6–12) and back again to the singular (v. 13) seems to favor the symbolic use of the phrase with reference to a church. Verse 13 could look in the same direction in the suggestion of sister churches greeting one another.

John's words in II Jn 5–6 are very similar to those in his first epistle (I Jn 2:3–10), a word given first by our Lord to His followers in Jn 13:34–35. Such words were given to the church generally, and seem less likely to have been written to one individual or family.

Bibliography. W. Foerster, TWNT (ExpT, Bromiley), III, 1095. B. F. Westcott, *The Epistles of St. John,* Grand Rapids: Eerdmans, 1950, pp. 223–224.

W. M. D.

ELECTION

Introduction

Election is the doctrine concerning God's divine choice of some individuals out of all mankind to become His own through regeneration and salvation. Election has to be related to but distinguished from God's decrees in general, predestination, foreordination and foreknowledge.

Election, the decrees of God, predestination and foreordination. The decrees of God encompass all that shall come to pass and include both foreordination and predestination. Predestination is confined in theological usage to God's decrees with regard to individual persons and their salvation, while foreordination covers all other events. They are the two parts of God's divine decrees in general.

Some Reformed scholars teach double predestination, that is, predestination to salvation for the elect and predestination to damnation for the lost (Augustine, Gottschalk, Calvin, Melanchthon and Luther, in their earlier period; L. Berkhof). Others teach the predestination of the elect and the passing by of the reprobate (C. Hodge, J. O. Buswell, H. C. Thiessen, L. S. Chafer). If God decrees to save one man and to damn another, then election and reprobation are two parts of the same. If predestination applies only to those whom God has chosen, then it describes that act in which God signs the projected life page or plan of the man whom He has chosen to save by divine grace. Foreordination, on the other hand, describes that act in which God signs the projected life page or plan of the man whom He has chosen to pass by and to leave to his own ways, which must inevitably lead to eternal loss.

Thus we see that for those who believe in double predestination, foreordination covers events but not individuals in any specific sense, while for those who believe in the predestination of the saved only, it applies to all God's decrees except those which have to do with the salvation of particular men.

Election and foreknowledge. Election is not simply foreknowledge, nor is it dependent upon foreknowledge. It includes God's foreknowledge as to what a man will do in his own freedom, but is dependent for its accomplishment upon God's sovereign grace. The Scriptures teach that God takes up what man will do in his freedom, and adds to this what He will do in His grace to save a man, to make effective His election of an individual.

Two controversies in particular have arisen within the church which have a bearing on election. First, that of Pelagianism versus Augustinianism. Pelagius argued for the ability of the natural man to accept Christ without sovereign grace, while Augustine maintained the doctrine of the total depravity of man and the need for sovereign grace. The Roman Catholic church chose a semi-Pelagian position, arguing that man has some ability but that this is insufficient without the help of seven kinds of steps of ascending grace. The Pelagian view leads to the conclusion that election, namely, God's choice of some, depends upon the foreknowledge of God; the Augustinian, that it depends on His good pleasure and grace. Arminius and the Arminians today argue like Pelagius, that election depends on God's foreknowledge.

Election and call. Two kinds of call are found in Scripture. A general call to all to repent and be saved (Isa 55:1; Mt 11:28), and an efficacious call (Jn 6:37, 44; Rom 8:29–30). The general call makes man cognizant of and responsible for what he ought to do; the efficacious call adds to this the sovereign enablement necessary to do it (Eph 2:8). It is the efficacious call which accompanies election. *See* Call.

We are now ready to consider the different phases of the biblical doctrine of election.

R. A. K.

The Vocabulary of Election

A wide variety of expressions is needed to describe the manifold aspects of election. Chiefly in the OT, *bāḥar* indicates a selection of one among other possible choices. It may describe a natural choice (Gen 6:2; Deut 23:16), a moral choice (Deut 30:19; Josh 24:15, 22; Ps 119:30, 173), or a divine choice (Deut 7:6; I Sam 10:24; Isa 41:8–9). The Heb. *bāḥar* and its cognate adjective *bāḥîr* are applied to such "chosen" objects as Abraham (Neh 9:7), Moses (Ps 106:23), Aaron (Ps 105:26), Israel (Ezk 20:5), David and Solomon (I Chr 28:4–6, 10), Jerusalem (II Chr 6:5 f.), the Messiah (Ps 89:3 f., 19; Isa 42:1), Zerubbabel (Hag 2:23), and the new Israel (Isa 43:20 f.; 65:9, 22). The verb *yāda',* "to know," is often used as an evident synonym of election (Gen 18:19; Ex 33:12, 17; II Sam 7:20; Ps 1:6; Jer 1:5; Amos 3:2; Nah 1:7).

The NT Gr. verb *eklegomai,* "to choose out for oneself," designates a discriminate choice after careful scrutiny (Lk 6:13; 10:42; 14:7; Acts 6:5). Of the 21 occurrences of this verb in the NT, God is the subject in seven places (Acts 13:17; 15:7; I Cor 1:27 twice, 28; Eph 1:4; Jas 2:5) and Christ is the subject in eight places (Mk 13:20; Lk 6:13; Jn 6:70; 13:18; 15:16, 19; Acts 1:2, 24). The adjective *eklektos,* "elect," is applied to Christ (Lk 23:35; I Pet 2:4, 6), to angels (I Tim 5:21), and frequently to believers. The noun *eklogē,* "election," is applied to Paul (Acts 9:15), to God's purpose (Rom 9:11), to Israel's believing remnant (Rom 11:5, 7, 28), and to Christians (I Thess 1:4; II Pet 1:10).

The truth of election is also involved in such words as "purpose," *prothesis* (Rom 8:28; 9:11; Eph 1:11; II Tim 1:9), "give" (Mt 20:14, 23; Jn 1:12; 3:27; 6:37, 65; 10:28 f.; 17:11; Heb 2:13), "know" (Jn 6:64; 10:14, 27; II Tim 2:19), "appoint" (I Thess 5:9; I Tim 2:7; I Pet 2:8), "prepare" (Mt 20:23; 25:34, 41), "determine" (Lk 22:22), "call" (Rom 8:28, 30; 9:11, 24-26; I Cor 1:2, 9; 7:20-22; Eph 4:1, 4; I Thess 2:12; 4:7; II Tim 1:9; I Pet 1:15; 2:9; 5:10; II Pet 1:3; Rev 17:14), and "calling" (Rom 11:29; I Cor 1:26; Eph 1:18; 4:1, 4; Phil 3:14; II Tim 1:9; Heb 3:1; II Pet 1:10).

The elect are certainly designated by such terms as these: "sheep" (Ps 100:3; Ezk 34:11-31; Mt 25:33; Jn 10:2-16, 26 f.), "flock" (Isa 40:11; Lk 12:32; I Pet 5:2), "one body" (I Cor 10:17; 12:12 f.; Eph 4:4), "the body of Christ" (I Cor 12:27; Eph 4:12), "seed" (Ps 22:23, 30; Isa 41:8; 45:25; 53:10; 61:9; 65:23; Rom 4:16; Gal 3:29; Heb 2:16), "people" (Hos 2:23; Acts 15:14; Rom 9:25 f.; 11:1 f.; II Cor 6:16; Tit 2:14; Heb 4:9; 8:10; I Pet 2:9 f.; Rev 21:3), "children," *teknia* (Jn 1:12, ASV; 11:52; Rom 8:16 f.; Gal 4:28), "sons," *hyioi* (Rom 8:14, 19; 9:26, ASV; II Cor 6:18; Gal 3:26, ASV; Heb 2:10; Rev 21:7), "brethren" (Mt 12:49; 25:40; Rom 8:29; Heb. 2:11 f., 17).

The Description of Election

Its selectivity. The doctrine of election excludes all theories of universal salvation. The following facts confirm this statement: (1) Selectivity is resident in the words designating election. For example, David "chose," *bāḥar,* five smooth stones for his sling (I Sam 17:40). It is perfectly evident, of course, that there were many more stones that David could have chosen. So likewise when God "chose" us in eternity (Eph 1:4), it is equally evident that He did not choose all. (2) Selectivity is confirmed by the "out of" passages dealing with this subject (Jn 15:19; 17:6; Acts 15:14; Gal 1:4; Col 1:13; I Pet 2:9; Rev 5:9; 7:9, 14; 14:3 f.). (3) Selectivity is manifested in the contrasting descriptions of the elect. They are the "sheep" (Jn 10:3-5, 11, 14-16); others are not (10:26). They are "written" in the Book of Life (Dan 12:1; Lk 10:20; Heb 12:23); others are excluded (Rev 13:8; 17:8). They respond to Christ (Jn 6:37, 39, 44, 65; 10:27 f.; Acts 13:48); others are unresponsive (Jn 8:43, 47; 10:26). (4) Selectivity is evidenced by the tragic descriptions of the lost. Such expressions as "not given" (Mt 13:11), "could not believe" (Jn 12:39), "perdition" (Jn 17:12; II Thess 2:3), "fitted unto destruction" (Rom 9:22), "were blinded" (Rom 11:7), "were appointed" (I Pet 2:8), "of old ordained" (Jude 4), "have not the seal of God" (Rev 9:4) point by way of contrast to the sovereign will of God in electing whom He chooses (Rom 9:14-24).

Its sovereignty. God's will is the sovereign cause of all His acts in eternity and in time. To His will are attributed His sovereignty (Eph 1:11), the creation (Rev 4:11), the course of history (Ps 115:3; 135:6; Dan 4:35; 6:27), the bestowal of blessings (Mt 11:25-27; 20:14-16), the Spirit's activity (Jn 3:8), regeneration (Jas 1:18), adoption (Eph 1:5), election (Rom 9:11, 18-24), and His good pleasure (Phil 2:13).

Thus, to be more specific, God's sovereignty in election is seen in His choosing (1) apart from the sinner's works (Rom 9:11; I Cor 1:26; Tit 3:4-7); (2) before the person's birth (Jer 1:5; Rom 9:11-13; Gal 1:15); (3) according to His sovereign purpose (Ex 33:19; Mt 11:25-27; Rom 11:33-36); (4) by sovereign discrimination (Rom 9:11-13, 19-23).

Its eternity. All of God's saving acts originate in eternity; therefore election must be eternal. (1) God's foreknowledge is eternal (Rom 8:29; I Pet 1:1-2); (2) God chose the elect in eternity (Eph 1:4; II Thess 2:13-14); (3) God promised the elect eternal life in eternity (Tit 1:1-2); (4) God inscribed the elect in His Book of Life in eternity (Rev 13:8; 17:8); (5) God chose the elect before their existence in this world (Jer 1:5; Gal 1:15; Eph 2:10; II Tim 1:9); (6) God gave the elect to Christ in eternity (Jn 17:2, 6, 24); (7) God prepared heaven, "eternal glory," for the elect (I Pet 5:10).

Its individuality. At this point we must recognize a distinction which is clearly indicated in the Scriptures. (1) The Bible speaks of a national election in the choice of Abraham and his posterity (Gen 12:1-2; Deut 4:37; 7:6-8; 10:15; Ps 105:6-15; Isa 41:8-9; Rom 9:4-5). But national election did not insure individual election (Mal 1:2-3; Rom 2:28-29; 9:27-33; 11:1-11; I Pet 2:8). (2) The Bible also speaks of an official election, that is, an election to some office or function. God sovereignly chose Moses (Ps 106:23), Aaron (Ps 105:26), the priests (Num 18:6 f.; Deut 18:5), Israel's kings (Deut 17:15; I Sam 10:24), the nations (Isa 45:1-7; Jer 27:5-7; Dan 2:37-40; 4:17, 25), the Messiah (Isa 42:1; I Pet 2:4, 6), and the apostles (Jn 15:16, 19) for their places in His plan. Sometimes, however, people were chosen to office, as illustrated in the lives of Saul (I Sam 13:14; 15:17-23) and of Judas (Jn 6:70; 13:2, 27; 17:12), who were not elected to salvation. (3) Apart from the limitations described above, the Bible never speaks of election as involving a race or group; election is always personal and individual. Those elected to salvation are described as individuals (Rom 16:13; Phil 4:2 f.); are referred to by personal pronouns (Rom 8:28-30; Eph 1:4); are distinguished from other individuals (Mt 24:22, 24, 31; Rom 9:21-29; I Cor 1:26-29); are declared to be from all groups of mankind (Rev 5:9 f.; 7:9).

Its certainty. God's plan of election is made definitely certain by the following factors: (1) God's purposes are definite and sure (Rom 11:29); no one can resist effectively His sovereign will (II Chr 20:6; Isa 45:9; Dan 4:35). God has eternally purposed the salvation of some (Rom 8:28-30). This purpose has been fulfilled (Rom 11:1-10) and is being fulfilled in the final completion of the entire number of the redeemed (Rom 11:11-36; Heb 11:39-40; 12:22-23). (2) The means ordained by God for the salvation of the elect are absolutely adequate. The Holy Spirit is sovereignly able to regenerate them (Jn 3:1-8). The gospel is God's power unto their salvation (Rom 1:16; I Cor 1:18, 24; 2:4; I Thess 2:13; Heb 4:12 f.; Jas 1:18; I Pet 1:3, 23). God convicts and brings them to salvation (Jn 16:8-11; Acts 16:14; Eph 2:1-10; Phil 2:13). Such persons come to Christ (Jn 6:37, 39; 17:2, 24) and are securely kept by God's power (Jn 10:27-29; I Pet 1:5; Jude 24). (3) The ultimate plan of God makes certain the salvation of those "ordained to eternal life" (Acts 13:48). God has prepared heaven for them (Jn 14:1-3); and He is now making equally certain that some will be there from all of earth's varied population (Rev 5:9; 7:9).

Its means. Those chosen to eternal life come to know Christ as their Saviour through the means ordained by God. They, like others, were in a state of spiritual deadness (Eph 2:1-3) before God worked faith in their hearts (Ps 110:3; Acts 11:18; 16:14; Eph 2:8) by the Spirit (I Cor 2:1-5; I Thess 1:4-5) and by His Word (I Thess 2:13; Heb 4:12; Jas 1:18). These God-given means are prerequisites of salvation (Rom 10:13-17). The gospel must be preached to all nations (Mt 24:14; 28:19; Acts 1:8); thus, by this means, the elect shall be gathered from all the earth (Mt 24:31; Rev 7:9). Through the ministry of God's elect others are brought into God's kingdom (Jn 17:20). Paul endured extreme suffering so that through his ministry the elect "may also obtain the salvation which is in Christ Jesus with eternal glory" (II Tim 2:10). The divine side stated in Acts 13:48 (those "ordained to eternal life believed") must not be divorced from the human side stated in Acts 14:21, ASV ("And when they had preached the gospel to that city, and had made many disciples," etc.). The mystery of election and human agency is the mystery of Deut 29:29.

Its assurance. It is absolutely certain, of course, that God knows those whom He has chosen (Num 16:5; Ps 37:18, 28; Nah 1:7). Christ likewise knows those chosen to eternal life (Mt 7:23; Jn 10:14, 27-30; 13:18; II Tim 2:19). God knows all things from eternity (Isa 41:26; 42:9; 45:21; Acts 15:18). The question arises, however, whether the elect can know their election and the election of others. The answer must be affirmative for these reasons: (1) God has revealed the election of certain ones. Ananias, for example, definitely knew that Paul was "an elect vessel" (Acts 9:15). Paul knew that Rufus was "chosen" (Rom 16:13; cf. II Jn 13). (2) Certain Christians evidently knew that they were among God's elect (I Thess 1:4; Jas 2:5; I Pet 1:1-2). They are even identified as such (Phil 4:3). (3) The elect are identical with the regenerate; therefore, since regeneration is knowable, election must also be knowable (Rom 8:15 f., 29-33; II Tim 1:12; I Jn 5:1-5, 13, 19-20). (4) God's Word declares the assurance of election to be one of the objectives of our Christian growth (Phil 2:12; II Pet 1:10). Christians can know that they belong to an elect people (I Pet 2:9-10).

Its results. Election is the positive side of predestination, and is thus the source of all good things planned for the redeemed. These good things are such as these: (1) Calling. Election always preceeds the historical call inviting the sinner to receive Christ (Rom 8:28-30; I Cor 1:26-29; II Thess 2:13 f.; II Tim 1:9; 2:10). This call becomes a living part of the Christian's experience of salvation (Rom 9:23 f.; I Cor 1:9, 24; I Thess 2:12; 5:24; II Thess 1:11; I Pet 1:15; 2:9; 3:9; 5:10). (2) Faith. Faith is God's gift (Eph 2:8) and the Spirit's fruit (Gal 5:22). The "vessels of mercy" are identical with those who believe (Rom 9:23-24, 33). Those "ordained to eternal life" believe (Acts 13:48). Those given to Christ by the Father believe in Christ (Jn 17:2, 6, 20). These "given ones" are "drawn" to Christ by a divine compulsion (Jn 6:37, 44, 47). (3) Justification. Faith is productive of the believer's justification (Rom 8:29-30, 33). Faith is described as the means of justification (Rom 3:22-30; 4:5, 20-24; 10:10; Gal 2:16; 3:11-14, 22); but the faith that justifies is "the faith of God's elect" (Tit 1:1). (4) Assurance. In addition to what is said above about assurance, it should be noted that a mutually reciprocal knowledge (*ginōskō*) exists between Christ and His sheep (Kn 10:14). Paul's "I know" is the human response to "the Lord knoweth them that are his" (II Tim 1:12; 2:19). (5) Perseverance. A necessary concomitant of election is perseverance. The elect are "kept by the power of God" (I Pet 1:1, 5). Those whom Christ knows as His sheep "shall never perish" (Jn 10:14, 27 f.). Those eternally called can never be separated "from the love of God" (Rom 8:30, 33, 35-39).

(6) Glorification. Here is the ultimate in the believer's election (Rom 8:30). God's elect will "obtain the salvation which is in Christ Jesus with eternal glory" (II Tim 2:10). This "eternal glory" follows earth's trials (I Pet 5:10). Those "redeemed from among men" are described as "without fault" (Rev 14:3-5; cf. Eph 5:27). Those who are "called, and chosen, and faithful" (Rev 17:14) are "clothed in fine linen, white and pure" (Rev 19:14, ASV).

Conclusions

It is quite evident that we should observe certain principles in teaching the doctrine of election. (1) We should go no further than God's Word takes us. There will always be mysteries about election that we can never fully explain or fathom. (2) Our duty is to preach the gospel in the power of the Holy Spirit to all (Mt 28:18-20; Acts 1:8; I Cor 2:1-5); God knows those who are His (II Tim 2:19). (3) Election should be a doctrine of hope and comfort to God's people—not a doctrine of horror and despair. Believers are encouraged to make their calling and election sure (II Pet 1:10).

These principles, held in proper balance, will enable us to avoid those extremes which are so often associated with this glorious truth.

See Chosen.

Bibliography. G. C. Berkouwer, *Divine Election*, Grand Rapids: Eerdmans, 1960. John Calvin, *Concerning the Eternal Predestination of God*, London: James Clarke, 1961. Hendley Dunelm, "Election," ISBE, III (1930), 925-927. John Gill, *The Cause of God and Truth*, London: W. H. Collingridge, 1855. G. E. Mendenhall, "Election," IDB, II, 76-82. G. Schrenk, "*Eklegomai*, etc.," TDNT, IV, 144-192. J. H. Thornwell, *Election and Reprobation*, Philadelphia: Presbyterian and Reformed, 1961. B. B. Warfield, "Predestination," HDB, IV (1902), 47-63. J. R. Willis, "Elect, Election," *Dictionary of Christ and the Gospels*, I (1906), 510-514.

W. B.

EL-ELOHE-ISRAEL (ĕl-ĕl'ō-hē-ĭz'rĭ-ĕl; "God is the God of Israel"). Jacob's altar at Shechem after he returned from Padan-aram (Gen 33:19-20). Here Abraham had erected an altar (Gen 12:7). The LXX renders Gen 33:20: "He built an altar and called upon the God of Israel."

ELEMENTS

1. The alphabet letters, thus symbolic of rudiments of a study or discipline, as in "the first principles [ASV, rudiments] of the oracles of God" (Heb 5:12).

2. Physical components of the world, which face destruction by fire (II Pet 3:10-12).

3. Spirits behind the physical components, which many Greeks personified as the ultimate principles of all existence and life and made objects of worship. These Paul attacked in Colossians, particularly in 2:8, 20; possibly also in Gal 4:3, 9—although probably he referred here to Jewish legalism as rudimentary or infantile religious thought.

See Rudiments.

ELEPH (ĕ'lĕph). A place in the vicinity of Jerusalem allotted to the tribe of Benjamin. In RSV it is called Ha-eleph (Josh 18:28). Its exact location is uncertain.

ELEPHANT. *See* Animals, II.12.

ELEPHANTINE PAPYRI. A highly significant group of papyrus documents was discovered between 1893 and 1908 on the island of Elephantine, opposite the city of Aswan at the First Cataract of the Nile. These letters and records, dated in the 5th cen. B.C., were written in Aramaic, the *lingua franca* of that era, very similar in style to the Aram. section of the book of Ezra. Some of the official documents were dated in both Egyptian and Jewish months, making them of great value to the ancient historian. The papyri consist of three sets of about a dozen documents each, two being family records and the third a community archive. Together they provide the earliest known documentation for the life of a Jewish community in the Diaspora (*see* Dispersion of Israel).

On the island of Elephantine during the Persian Empire a colony of Jewish mercenary soldiers was established to man the border fortress. The ancestors of these Jews may have been refugees from the Assyrian conquest of the northern kingdom of Israel in 722 B.C. Again, they may have been sent as troops to Egypt in the middle of the 7th cen. B.C. by Manasseh when he allied himself with the pharaoh in an attempt to throw off the Assyrian yoke. Or they may have arrived as refugees from Judah following their defeat at the hands of Nebuchadnezzar in 586 B.C. (Jer 42-43).

One of the documents is a copy of a letter written in 407 B.C. to the Persian governor of Judah (ANET, p. 492). The Jewish priests complained that priests of the Egyptian god Khnum had destroyed the Jewish temple at Elephantine, dedicated to Yahu (i.e., Yahweh). This letter names men in Palestine who are also mentioned in the book of Nehemiah: Sanballat, the governor of Samaria (Neh 4:1, etc.), and Johanan, the high priest (Neh 12:22-23).

The Jewish worship at Elephantine did not adhere rigorously to the Mosaic law. Deut 12:5-28 forbade offering sacrifices in any place other than at the central sanctuary where God's name would dwell. Also, other Semitic deities were worshiped, such as Ishum-bethel, Anath-bethel, Herem-bethel, and Anath-yahu. The latter may indicate a syncretizing tendency, perhaps especially on the part of the Jewish women, identifying Yahweh with the queen of heaven (cf. Jer 7:18; 44:17).

Bibliography. BW, pp. 220 f. DOTT, pp. 256–269. Bezalel Porter, *Archives from Elephantine: the Life of an Ancient Jewish Military Colony*, Berkeley: Univ. of California Press, 1968.

J. R.

ELHANAN (ĕl-hā'năn)

1. In I Chr 20:5 it is said that Elhanan, the son of Jair, slew Lahmi, the brother of Goliath the Gittite, but II Sam 21:19 (RSV) states that Elhanan, the son of Jaare-oregim, the Bethlehemite, slew Goliath the Gittite. The "oregim" is perhaps a scribal error based on "weaver" in the following line, thus making Jair and Jaare the same person. These two verses coupled with I Sam 17 present the problem of who killed Goliath.

Some scholars have contended, without good reason, that Elhanan was David's original name. Others have maintained that the text of I Chr 20:5 is preferred to a corrupt text in II Sam 21:19. (The Masoretic Heb. text of I and II Samuel has a number of textual corruptions.) Still others have concluded that Goliath was slain by Elhanan and his name attributed to the anonymous giant slain by David in the Valley of Elah.

2. A son of Dodo of Bethlehem, one of the 30 heroes in David's guard (II Sam 23:24; I Chr 11:26).

F. E. Y.

ELI (ē'lī). The last judge of Israel's Dark Ages. Eli's dramatic life story is recorded in I Sam 1–4, the book named after his successor. He was the priest of the "house of the Lord" at ancient Shiloh (I Sam 1:3, 7, 9) *c.* 20 miles N of Jerusalem, to whom the boy Samuel was brought to fulfill Hannah's vow (I Sam 1:1 – 2:11). The "house of the Lord" evidently was the tabernacle of Israel (cf. Josh 18:1; Jud 18:31), and the ark resided there (I Sam 3:3), suggesting that this sanctuary was the central shrine of the Israelites.

The biblical record is silent concerning Eli's ancestry; hence two traditions have arisen about his family tree: one, that he came from the Aaronic house of Ithamar (cf. Jos *Ant.* v. 11.5; I Chr 24:3); another, Eli came from the rival house of Eleazar (cf. II Esd 1:2–3; Ex 6:23, 25). By comparing I Kgs 2:27 with I Chr 24:3, one concludes that Phinehas, his son, and Eli himself were probably descendants of Aaron's youngest son, Ithamar. Abiathar's son Ahimelech is of the "sons of Ithamar" (cf. I Chr 24:3 with II Sam 8:17). No doubt Eli's family was of the ancient priesthood which ministered at Shiloh. Eli's descendants through Phinehas and his son Ahitub may have perpetuated the priesthood at Nob for a time (I Sam 14:3; 22:9 ff.).

Associated with Eli in this priesthood were his two incorrigible sons, Hophni and Phinehas (I Sam 1:3). The two sons conducted themselves so outrageously that they excited deep disgust among the people and rendered the service of the tabernacle odious in the people's eyes (I Sam 2:12–17, 22). Of this conduct Eli was aware, but contented himself with mild and ineffectual remonstrances (I Sam 2:23–24) when his position demanded severe and vigorous actions (I Sam 3:13). Because of their scandalous conduct and the laxity of parental discipline, a man of God pronounced doom upon them and their posterity (I Sam 2:27–36). This prophecy was confirmed by a revelation to the child Samuel which predicted the irremediable punishment of Eli's household (I Sam 3:11–14).

This announcement of judgment was partially fulfilled in the death of Hophni and Phinehas in the battle with the Philistines at Aphek (I Sam 4:11) and the ruthless murder of the priests in Nob by King Saul (cf. I Sam 22:9–20). But Abiathar slipped through the net and shared with Zadok the priesthood under King David (II Sam 15:24–29; 19:11). However, his removal by King Solomon restored the line of Eleazar in the person of Zadok, and was the final fulfillment of the ancient prophetic oracle (cf. I Kgs 2:26 f.).

The sunset of Eli's life was one of defeat, disappointment, and disaster. His end followed the sad news of the loss of the ark to the Philistines in the battle near Ebenezer. He fell over backward, broke his neck, and died *c.* 1000 B.C.: "He fell from off the seat backward by the side of the gate, and his neck brake, and he died; for he was an old man [ninety-eight years, v. 15] and heavy" (I Sam 4:18).

His prematurely born grandson was named Ichabod, i.e., "the glory of the Lord has departed" (I Sam 4:19–21). Eli brought to a climax the long, disastrous age of the judges and paved the way for the new age of the kings. Eli judged Israel 40 years and combined in his own person the offices of high priest and judge (I Sam 4:18). However, his record was marred and blighted by the shameful practices of his sensual sons and his dismal failure to remove them from their priestly service.

D. W. D.

ELIAB (ĕ-lī'ăb). The name occurs in Akkad. texts as *Ili-abi*.

1. A representative or "prince" of the tribe of Zebulun who assisted Moses in the census, etc. (Num 1:9; 2:7; 7:24, 29; 10:16).

2. A Reubenite, father of the rebels Dathan and Abiram (Num 16:1, 12; 26:8, 9).

3. An ancestor of Samuel descended from the Levite Kohath (I Chr 6:27), possibly the Eliel of verse 34 and the Elihu of I Sam 1:1.

4. The eldest son of Jesse and brother of David, tall and of regal appearance (I Sam 16:6–7; I Chr 2:13). He was in Saul's army and became furious when he heard young David inquiring about the reward for killing Goliath (I Sam 17:13–28). His daughter Abihail mar-

ried David's son Jerimoth, and their daughter Mahalath married Rehoboam (II Chr 11:18).

5. A Gadite warrior who joined the outlaw David at his wilderness stronghold (I Chr 12:8-9).

6. A Levite singer and harpist appointed to accompany the procession which brought the ark up to Jerusalem (I Chr 15:18, 20).

ELIADA, ELIADAH (ĕ-lī'*ȧ*-dȧ)

1. One of the sons born to David by a wife or concubine at Jerusalem (II Sam 5:16; I Chr 3:8). He is called Beeliada in I Chr 14:7.

2. Father of Rezon of Syria who was an implacable enemy of Israel during Solomon's reign (I Kgs 11:23; KJV, Eliadah).

3. A man of Benjamin, commander of 200,000 men in Jehoshaphat's army (II Chr 17:17).

ELIAH (ĕ-lī'*ȧ*). A variant form of Elijah (*q.v.*).

1. One of the "heads of the fathers" of Benjamin (I Chr 8:27-28).

2. A son of Elam, a priest, and one who had taken a foreign wife (Ezr 10:26).

ELIAHBA (ĕ-lī'*ȧ*-b*ȧ*). A Shaalbonite, one of David's special guard of 30 mighty men (II Sam 23:32; I Chr 11:33).

ELIAKIM (ē̆-lī'*ȧ*-kĭm). The name occurs on three scaraboid seals of the 6th cen. B.C. as "Belonging to Eliakim, attendant of Yaukin" (*l'lyqm n'r ywkn*). This Eliakim, not mentioned in the OT, was steward of Jehoiachin.

1. Son of Hilkiah; the royal chamberlain or official "over the household" of King Hezekiah, holding an office second only to the king. He represented Hezekiah during the interview with Sennacherib's officers (II Kgs 18:18, 26, 37). The king sent him on a delegation to Isaiah for advice (II Kgs 19:2-5). He must have been a highly capable and godly man, for Isaiah had prophesied that Eliakim would replace Shebna in office (Isa 22:20-24), and by the time of Sennacherib's invasion this had occurred.

2. A son of King Josiah. Pharaoh-nechoh placed him on the throne of Judah (II Kgs 23:34) and changed his name to Jehoiakim (*q.v.*).

3. A priest who took part in the dedication ceremony of the city wall (Neh 12:41).

4. The son of Abiud, descendant of David through Solomon and Zerubbabel (Mt 1:13).

5. The son of Melea, descendant of David through Nathan (Lk 3:30). These last two men occur in the genealogies of Jesus Christ.

J. R.

ELIAM (ē̆-lī'*ȧ*m). The name has been found on an ancient Heb. seal.

1. The father of Bath-sheba (II Sam 11:3); called Ammiel (*q.v.*) in I Chr 3:5, the two basic elements of the names, *'ēl* and *'am*, being interchanged. The name would mean "my God is a kinsman."

2. Son of Ahithophel and one of David's "mighty men" (II Sam 23:8, 13, 34); possibly the same as #1.

ELIAS (ĕ-lī'*ȧ*s). The NT form of Elijah (*q.v.*).

ELIASAPH (ĕ-lī'*ȧ*-săf)

1. A leader of the tribe of Gad, called the son of Deuel (Num 1:14; 10:20) or Reuel (Num 2:14). He presented Gad's offering at the tabernacle (Num 7:42-47).

2. Son of Lael, a chief of the Gershonites (Num 3:24).

ELIASHIB (ē̆-lī'*ȧ*-shĭb)

1. A priest, head of the eleventh of the 24 courses into which David divided the priesthood (I Chr 24:1, 12).

2. A post-Exilic Levite singer who had married a foreign wife (Ezr 10:24).

3. A layman, son of Zattu (Ezr 10:27).

4. Another layman, son of Bani (Ezr 10:36), in the same list as 2.

5. The high priest who was contemporary with Nehemiah; the son of Joiakim and grandson of Jeshua the priest in Zerubbabel's day (Neh 12:10). He directed the priests in rebuilding the Sheep Gate under Nehemiah (Neh 3:1), but later was guilty of allying with the hostile Tobiah and assigning him a room in the temple area over which Eliashib had charge (Neh 13:4-7). He even had a grandson who married a daughter of Sanballat, another opponent of Nehemiah (Neh 13:28).

6. A descendant of Zerubbabel (I Chr 3:24).

ELIATHAH (ĕ-lī'*ȧ*-th*ȧ*). A son of Heman, whose family (sons and brothers) was appointed by lot to be the twentieth division of musicians to serve in the temple (I Chr 25:4, 27).

ELIDAD (ĕ-lī'dăd). Son of Chislon of Benjamin. He was the tribe's representative in the group who worked under Joshua and Eleazar in apportioning the land W of Jordan among the tribes (Num 34:21).

ELIEL (ĕ-lī'ĕl)

1. A Kohathite Levite (I Chr 6:34), probably the same as the Eliab of I Chr 6:27 and the Elihu of I Sam 1:1.

2 and 3. Two mighty men or heroes in David's army (I Chr 11:46-47).

4. The seventh of the Gadite warriors who joined David at his wilderness stronghold and became officers (I Chr 12:11).

5. A Levite mentioned in connection with the removal of the ark from the house of Obed-edom (I Chr 15:9, 11).

6 and 7. Two Benjamite family heads (I Chr 8:20, 22).

8. A family chief of the Transjordanian half-tribe of Manasseh (I Chr 5:24).

9. A Levite overseer appointed by Hezekiah to assist in collecting tithes and offerings (II Chr 31:13).

ELIENAI (ĕl'ĭ-ē'nī). A head of a family in the tribe of Benjamin (I Chr 8:20).

ELIEZER (ĕl-ĭ-ē'zẽr). A name not to be confused with Eleazar.

1. Eliezer of Damascus (Gen 15:2), a servant and heir of Abram's house. The custom of childless couples adopting a son who would serve them as long as they lived, then at their death would inherit their property, has long been known from the Nuzi texts (cf. John Bright, *A History of Israel,* p. 71; C. H. Gordon, "Biblical Customs and the Nuzi Tablets," BA, III [1940], 1-12).

2. The second son of Moses and Zipporah, so named because of God's help in delivering Moses from the sword of Pharaoh (Ex 18:4; I Chr 23:15, 17; 26:25).

3. The grandson of Benjamin (I Chr 7:8).

4. One of seven priests who blew the trumpet before the ark when David moved it from the house of Obed-edom to Jerusalem (I Chr 15:24).

5. A ruler of Reuben in the time of David (I Chr 27:16).

6. A prophet who rebuked Jehoshaphat for joining with Ahaziah, king of Israel, in an expedition to Tarshish (II Chr 20:37).

7. The first of a group of 11 leading men of insight sent by Ezra to Iddo to seek out Levites to return to Jerusalem (Ezr 8:16 ff.).

8-10. Three men, a priest, a Levite, and a son of Harim, who in the time of Ezra had married foreign women (Ezr 10:18, 23, 31).

11. A person in the genealogy of Jesus as recorded by Luke (3:29).

R. L. S.

ELIHOENAI (ĕl'ĭ-hō-ē'nī). Variant of Elioenai (*q.v.*).

Head of a family of 200 males who returned to Jerusalem with Ezra (Ezr 8:4).

ELIHOREPH (ĕl'ĭ-hôr'ĕf). Son of Shisha who, with his brother Ahijah, served as scribe in Solomon's court (I Kgs 4:3).

ELIHU (ĕ-lī'hū)

1. The grandfather of Elkanah, Samuel's father (I Sam 1:1); called Eliel in I Chr 6:34 and Eliab in I Chr 6:27.

2. A Manassite captain who deserted King Saul to join David and his guerrillas on their way back to Ziklag (I Chr 12:20).

3. A Korahite gatekeeper among the able descendants of Obed-edom (I Chr 26:7).

4. One of David's brothers (I Chr 27:18); called Eliab in LXX and in I Sam 16:6; 17:13, 28; I Chr 2:13.

5. Job's young friend (Job 32:2-6; 34:1; 35:1; 36:1), the son of Barachel of the clan of Ram, a Buzite (Job 32:2), and thus a distant relative of Abraham (Gen 22:21). Jer 25:23 indicates that Buz was in Arabia. Related to the Hebrews (which may imply a deeper knowledge of their God), Elihu raises the discussion with Job to a higher theological level, showing that greater wisdom comes by inspiration than by human experience and tradition (Job 32:8-9), and urges Job to consider the wondrous works of God (37:14). *See* Job, Book of.

J. R.

Elijah and the widow's son. Stained glass, early sixteenth century Flemish. MM

ELIJAH (ē-lī'jȧ)

1. Elijah the prophet, whose name means "Yahweh is God," was active during the reigns of Ahab and Ahaziah in the northern kingdom (*c.* 875-850 B.C.). The account of his ministry begins in I Kgs 17 and concludes with the ascension of Elijah recorded in II Kgs 2. No genealogy, call to service, or background are given except the fact that he was identified as a Tishbite who resided in the land of Gilead E of the Jordan River.

Elijah was called to serve as a spokesman for God when the northern kingdom had expanded to its strongest position economically and politically since its secession from the Davidic rule in Jerusalem. Omri (885-874 B.C.), who introduced a policy of friendship with surrounding nations, sealed his alliance with Phoenicia by the marriage of his son Ahab to Jezebel, the daughter of Ethbaal, king of Tyre. Under the royal sponsorship of Ahab and Jezebel, the cult worship of the Tyrian Baal, Melqart, flourished in Israel. Ahab even erected a temple for Baal in the city of Samaria (I Kgs 16:32). Through his messages and miracles Elijah had the responsibility to remind the Israelites that they were God's people when the royal leadership was committed to Baal worship.

Elijah's first mission was to confront King Ahab with the announcement of an impending drought, reminding Israel's king that the Lord God of Israel, whom he had ignored, was in control of rain in the land where they lived (cf. Deut 11:10-12). Immediately Elijah secluded himself eastward toward the Jordan River. There he was sustained by water from the brook Cherith and by bread and meat miraculously supplied by the ravens. This "brook" (*naḥal*) is possibly the deep valley of the Yarmuk River in northern Gilead. When the water supply terminated because of the drought, Elijah was divinely instructed to go to Zarephath in Phoenicia where he would be sustained by a widow whose supply of flour and oil was miraculously extended until rainfall was restored to the land. Elijah's identity as a prophet or man of God was confirmed by the divine manifestation when the widow's son was restored to life.

In the third year of this drought Elijah was divinely bidden to contact Ahab and announce that God was about to send rain. During this time Ahab had made an intensive search for water to sustain his livestock, while Jezebel had killed many of the Lord's prophets. Some of the Lord's prophets, however, were secretly hidden and sustained by one of Ahab's officers named Obadiah. When the latter met Elijah, Obadiah was gravely concerned since Ahab's search for Elijah had intensified. Assured by Elijah that he would not disappear, Obadiah arranged for a meeting between Ahab and Elijah.

Although Ahab charged Elijah with being responsible for Israel's drought problem, the prophet boldly confronted Israel's king with his guilt in breaking the first commandment in worshiping Baal instead of God. In quick order Ahab complied with Elijah's instructions and arranged for a public meeting on Mount Carmel with the 450 prophets of Baal and 400 prophets of Asherah who were supported by Jezebel.

Mount Carmel and modern Haifa. Palphot, Hertseliya, Israel

On Mount Carmel the issues were clearly drawn by Elijah. Ahab's prophets were completely helpless to initiate any power of Baal to ignite the sacrifice they had prepared. Elijah in the meantime repaired the altar of the Lord and prepared his sacrifice. After he prayed to the Lord God of Abraham, Isaac, and Israel, Elijah's sacrifice was miraculously ignited before the public assembly of Israelites. The people responded to this demonstration of God's mighty act and confessed that Yahweh is God. Immediately Elijah ordered the execution of the cultic prophets and instructed Ahab to hurry back to Jezreel before the impending rain, even though the sky was clear. After Elijah's prayer the rain came in abundance. Elijah through divine enablement outran Ahab to the entrance of Jezreel, 18 or 20 miles to the E.

Threatened by Jezebel, the prophet Elijah escaped southward a day's journey past Beer-sheba. He was discouraged to the point of requesting death, but was divinely supplied with nourishment and then continued on to Mount Horeb. There he received a threefold commission: (1) anoint Hazael king over Syria; (2) anoint Jehu king of Israel; (3) anoint Elisha as his successor. On his return Elijah called Elisha to become his associate. The communication of the divine message to Hazael and Jehu was subsequently implemented by Elisha.

The boldest personal confrontation with King Ahab occurred when Elijah met the king in Naboth's vineyard. Jezebel had plotted the execution of Naboth, ignoring the right of land inheritance in ancient Israel (cf. R. de Vaux, *Ancient Israel,* trans. by John McHugh, McGraw-Hill, 1961, pp. 53 ff., 166 f.). Divine judgment upon the royal family was the verdict as Elijah delivered God's message. Since Ahab repented, the judgment was temporarily postponed.

Elijah outlived Ahab, who was killed in an Israelite-Syrian battle in 853 B.C. Elijah's prediction concerning Ahab was fulfilled when the dogs licked the king's blood.

After Ahaziah succeeded his father Ahab on the Israelite throne, he had a crippling fall. When Ahaziah sent servants to inquire of Baal the god of Ekron (mockingly called Baal-zebub, "Baal of flies," a pun on the real name Baal-zebul, "Baal the prince"), to ask if he would recover, Elijah was divinely commissioned to intercept the messengers. They were bidden to return to the king rebuking him for ignoring the God of Israel and warning him of impending death. After several attempts to arrest Elijah failed, the prophet was bidden to go with the third captain dispatched by the king. This time Elijah went to the king to deliver his message directly. Ahaziah did not recover but died as Elijah had predicted.

Near the end of Elijah's ministry, Elisha and some of the prophets associated with them sensed that their master was about to leave them. Elisha, however, bound himself by an oath that he would remain with Elijah. After a miraculous parting of the Jordan so the prophets could cross the river on dry ground, Elisha requested a double or firstborn's share of his master's spirit, thus desiring to be Elijah's principal spiritual heir (cf. Deut 21:17). The granting of this request was assured as Elisha saw Elijah ascend into heaven in a whirlwind.

Although Elijah's ministry was primarily in the northern kingdom, he did send a written communication to King Jehoram of Judah who succeeded his father Jehoshaphat. Jehoram was rebuked for ignoring the godly ways of Asa and Jehoshaphat, and following the idolatrous pattern of the kings of Israel (II Chr 21:12–15).

The miraculous element is very prominent in the ministry of Elijah. By this means he was confirmed as a spokesman for God in a time when the kings in Israel were to set the example of wholehearted commitment to God, but were instead devoted to idolatry.

In the OT there is another reference to Elijah in Mal 4:5 where he is mentioned as the forerunner of "the great and terrible day of Jehovah." One of the two witnesses of Rev 11:3–12 is possibly Elijah reappearing in fulfillment of this prophecy. The Jews expected him to return, as indicated in Ecclus 48:10, the Qumran Manual of Discipline (IX.11), and the Mishnaic literature.

Other NT references for further study are: Mt 11:14; 16:14; 17:1–13; 27:47–49; Mk 6:15; 8:28; 9:2–13; 15:35–36; Lk 1:17; 4:25–26; 9:8, 19, 28–36, 54; Rom 11:2–4; Jas 5:17–18.

Bibliography. CornPBE, pp. 273–276. Joachim Jeremias, "*Hēlias,*" TDNT, II, 928–941. James L. Kelso, "Elijah, the Abraham Lincoln of the Israelites," *Archaeology and Our Old Testament Contemporaries,* Grand Rapids: Zondervan, 1966, pp. 105–113. F. W. Krummacher, *Elijah the Tishbite,* trans. by John Cairns, London: T. Nelson & Sons, 1886. William S. LaSor, "Elijah: Rival Altars," *Great Personalities of the Old Testament,* Westwood, N.J.: Revell, 1959, pp. 126–135. F. B. Meyer, *Elijah, and the Secret of His Power,* London: Morgan & Scott, 1917. J. A. Montgomery and H. S. Gehman, *A Critical and Exegetical Commentary on the Books of Kings,* ICC, pp. 292–354. Leon J. Wood, *Elijah, Prophet of God,* Des Plaines, Ill.: Regular Baptist Press, 1968.

S. J. S.

2. A priest who had married a Gentile wife (Ezr 10:21).

3. A Benjamite chief (I Chr 8:27, RSV). *See* Eliah.

4. A layman who had married a foreign wife (Ezr 10:26, RSV). *See* Eliah.

ELIKA (ĕ-lī'kȧ). A Harodite, one of the 30 mighty men of David (II Sam 23:25). His name is not included in the parallel list of I Chr 11:26–47.

Brook Cherith (at bottom of ravine) and St. George's Monastery, marking traditional spot where ravens fed Elijah.

ELIM (ē'lĭm). Israel's second encampment in the wilderness of Shur after crossing the Red Sea (Ex 15:22–27; Num 33:8–10). It offered refreshment from 12 springs ("wells," KJV) and 70 palms, in contrast to the bitter waters of Marah in the previous camp. It is traditionally identified as Wadi Gharandel, the usual camping place for travelers from Egypt to Mount Sinai.

ELIMELECH (ĕ-lĭm'ĕ-lĕk). A man of considerable importance and holdings in Bethlehem-judah in the time of the judges; husband of Naomi and father of Mahlon and Chilion (Ruth 1:1 f.). By moving to Moab the family escaped Judah's famine. The sons' marriage to Moabites and the death of the three men led to the return of Naomi and one daughter-in-law, Ruth, to Bethlehem; Ruth's marriage to Boaz; and the birth to them of Obed, grandfather of King David, as related in the book of Ruth.

ELIOENAI (ĕl'ĭ-ō-ē'nī). A contracted form of Elihoenai (*q.v.*).

1. One of the sons of Neariah, a descendant of Zerubbabel, and the father of seven sons (I Chr 3:23–24).

2. One of the Simeonite chiefs, head of a numerous family (I Chr 4:36).

3. Son of Becher of the tribe of Benjamin and head of a father's house (I Chr 7:8).

4. The seventh son of Meshelemiah, a Korahite, a gatekeeper in the house of the Lord (I Chr 26:3; RSV has Eliehoenai).

5. A priest, one of the sons of Pashur, who put away his Gentile wife in the reform of Ezra (Ezr 10:22).

6. An Israelite, of the sons of Zattu, who put away his Gentile wife (Ezr 10:27).

7. A musician priest who took part in Nehemiah's dedication of the wall. Perhaps the same as 5 (Neh 12:41).

ELIPHAL (ĕ-lī'făl). Son of Ur (I Chr 11:35) and

Oasis in Wadi Gharandel, JR

one of David's 30 mighty men. Some identify him with Eliphelet (*q.v.*), the son of Ahasbai (II Sam 23:34).

ELIPHALET (ĕ-lĭf'*ȧ*-lĕt), **ELIPHELET** (ĕ-lĭf'*ĕ*-lĕt)

1. A son of David born in Jerusalem (I Chr 3:5-6; called Elpalet in I Chr 14:5).

2. The last of David's sons born in Jerusalem (II Sam 5:16, RSV; I Chr 3:8; 14:7, RSV).

3. A son of Ahasbai, one of David's mighty men (II Sam 23:34; cf. Eliphal [*q.v.*], I Chr 11:35).

4. A descendant of Jonathan (I Chr 8:33, 39).

5. A son of Adonikam who returned from Babylon with Ezra (Ezr 8:13).

6. A son of Hashum who divorced his Gentile wife after the Exile (Ezr 10:33).

ELIPHAZ (ĕl'*ĭ*-făz)

1. The eldest son of Esau who had a son named Teman (Gen 36:9-11), from whom the Edomite area took its name. Some have concluded that this was the Eliphaz (see 2) of Job's acquaintance.

2. The first and most prominent of the three friends of Job who came from great distances to comfort him when they heard of his affliction (Job 2:11). He is shown as a venerable sage of Teman in Edom, a place that was noted for its wisdom (Jer 49:7).

Doubtless the wisdom of Eliphaz was intended to be typical of the wisdom in the world of his time. This wisdom was a product of ages of thought, experience, and study. In his first speech (Job 4-5), he asserts that Job's condition is the natural effect of a cause, which cause he makes to include innate impurity and moral depravity. He promises restoration as a result of penitence. In his second speech (Job 15), Eliphaz is irritated by Job's words, which he feels hinder Job's devotion. He attributes them to iniquity and restates his depravity doctrine; he then goes into graphic detail concerning the fate of the wicked man. In his third speech (Job 22), he actually attempts to accuse Job of crimes and frauds committed when God was too far away to observe him.

His speeches are well-composed and wise but lacking in true human understanding and divine insight so as to be cold and of no avail. Their error was in an unyielding presupposition of Job's wickedness, an unsympathetic clinging to this theory resulting in the suppression of human friendship.

R. O. C.

ELIPHELEH (ĕ-lĭf'*ĕ*-lĕ). One of 14 special porters "of the second order" (I Chr 15:18) who, among others under David's leadership, were chosen from and by the Levites as instrumental accompanists in the ceremony of bringing the ark of the covenant to Jerusalem from the house of Obed-edom.

ELISABETH (ĕ-lĭz'*ȧ*-bĕth). The wife of the priest Zacharias (*q.v.*) and mother of John the Baptist (Lk 1:5-66). She was descended from Aaron and bore the name of his wife Elisheba (Heb. *'elîsheba'*, "my God has sworn," Ex 6:23). She and her husband, upright and blameless in their adherence to the law (Lk 1:6), could be included among those pious Jews who were eagerly awaiting the coming Messiah. The miraculous event (comparable to the births of Isaac and Samuel) of a son being born to this previously childless couple served both to confirm the announcement of the angel Gabriel to the virgin Mary (Lk 1:35-37), and to give the world a new prophet to prepare the way for the Messiah (1:76). When Mary her kinswoman (Gr. *sungenis,* 1:36) came to visit Elisabeth, the latter was filled with the Spirit and prophesied loudly, addressing Mary as the mother of her Lord (1:41-43). *See* John the Baptist; Mary.

J. R.

ELISEUS (ĕl'*ĭ*-sē'*ŭ*s). The form of the name Elisha used in the NT (Lk 4:27) and throughout the Douay Version. *See* Elisha.

ELISHA (ē-lī'sh*ȧ*). The attendant of Elijah (*q.v.*) and his successor as prophet in Israel. His Heb. name *'ĕlîshā'* means "God is salvation." Its Gr. form is *Elissaios,* as in Lk 4:27 (KJV, Eliseus).

Background. Elisha was the son of Shaphat from Abel-meholah (*q.v.*) in the Jordan Valley. The family must have had considerable means, for when Elijah came to extend him a call, Elisha was plowing with a yoke of oxen following eleven other teams. Although still quite young, Elisha responded eagerly and evidenced a godly upbringing by sacrificing his pair of oxen (I Kgs 19:16, 19-21).

Scope of ministry. His prophetic ministry covered the entire last half of the 9th cen. B.C. spanning the reigns of Jehoram, Jehu, Jehoahaz, and Jehoash of the northern kingdom. His influence extended from the widow in debt

(II Kgs 4:1) to the wealthy or prominent (4:8) and into the very palace of Israel itself (5:8; 6:9, 12, 21-22; 6:32–7:2; 8:4; 13:14-19). Furthermore, other kings (Jehoshaphat of Judah, II Kgs 3:11-19; Ben-hadad of Syria, 8:7-9) and high officials (Naaman of the Syrian army, 5:1, 9-19) sought his help. He changed the course of history by completing Elijah's commission (I Kgs 19:15-16) to anoint Hazael as king over Syria (cf. II Kgs 8:12-13) and Jehu as king over Israel (cf. II Kgs 9:1-10). Elisha's greatest contribution to the spiritual welfare of his country may well have been as principal of the schools of prophets at various centers, following in the tradition of Samuel (II Kgs 4:38-44; 6:1-7; cf. I Sam 19:20; *see* Sons of the Prophets).

Miracles. Elisha is best remembered, however, as a great miracle worker. No other person in sacred history is reported to have performed more signs and wonders, except Jesus Christ. A prophet like Moses (Deut 18:15), Elisha healed infected waters (II Kgs 2:19-22; cf. Ex 15:22-25) and produced water in the desert (II Kgs 3:9, 16-20; cf. Ex. 17:1-6). He paralleled the miracles of Elijah as he provided for the widow (II Kgs 4:1-7; cf. I Kgs 17:8-16) and restored the dead to life (II Kgs 4:18-37; cf. I Kgs 17:17-24). Anticipating the miracles of Christ, he healed the leper (II Kgs 5; cf. Mk 1:40-44; Lk 17:11-19) and multiplied the loaves (II Kgs 4:42-44; cf. Mt 14:16-21; 15:32-38). Again like our Lord, he was motivated by deep compassion as he responded to pleas for help by performing such feats as causing a borrowed axehead to float (II Kgs 6:5-7) and as he promised the Shunammite woman a son (4:11-17) and later advised her to flee the famine he predicted (8:1).

Character. In contrast to Elijah who tended to be an ascetic and to withdraw from the public eye, Elisha lived close to the people he served and enjoyed social life. He had a house in Samaria the capital city (II Kgs 6:32), but moved about the country constantly as Samuel had done. He frequently stopped to visit his friends at Shunem, even as Jesus stayed often with Mary and Martha. Elisha wept as he talked to Hazael, knowing full well the cruel suffering the latter would heap upon Israel (II Kgs 8:11-12). Yet he could pronounce judgment on the young fellows who ridiculed God's new prophet as a baldheaded leper (II Kgs 2:23-24; cf. Lev 13:40-46) and on the royal officer at Samaria for his mocking unbelief (II Kgs 7:1-2), just as severely as Elijah would have done and as Jesus called forth woe on the hypocritical Pharisees (Mt 23). Certainly Elijah's ministry was reproduced in John the Baptist (*q.v.*; Mt 17:10-13; *see also* Elijah); it is just as evident that the person and works of Elisha typify many aspects of our Lord's character and ministry.

Traditional fountain of Elisha at Jericho. JR

Introduction to his ministry. Elisha's first public service, as a chaplain to the armies of Israel and Judah in the time of King Jehoshaphat (II Kgs 3:11-19), may well have preceded the translation of Elijah (2:1-18). Elijah lived to write a letter of judgment to King Jehoram, Jehoshaphat's son (II Chr 21:12-15). On that campaign, then, Elisha was still the attendant of Elijah, the one "who has poured water on the hands of Elijah" (II Kgs 3:11). He had not yet been endued with the full power and spirit of his master. Perhaps this explains why he resorted to the practice of the day of calling for a minstrel to play before he could prophesy (3:15; cf. I Sam 10:5-6; I Chr 25:1).

At the time of Elijah's departure Elisha's request for a double portion recalls the law of inheritance of Deut 21:17. He was asking for the portion and rights of the firstborn son, in this case for the privilege of being the mighty prophet's chief successor. According to the Heb. text, *b^{e}rûḥăkā 'ēlāy,* he specified that the double portion might be in the form of (*b^{e}*) Elijah's spirit resting upon him (II Kgs 2:9). One should not infer, therefore, that Elisha was asking to be used twice as much or to be twice as powerful as his master.

Final ministry. When Elijah had gone up in the whirlwind, the younger prophet had acknowledged in his cry—"My father, my father, the chariotry of Israel and its horsemen!" (II Kgs 2:12)—that Elijah had been the real "army," the bulwark of spiritual defense for Israel in her time of apostasy. A half century later this same cry was directed by King Joash to Elisha (II Kgs 13:14). On his deathbed, the prophet was performing one last function, namely, to encourage the king to defend Israel against the Syrians (13:15-19). Such object lessons as having the king shoot an arrow and strike the ground repeatedly with his arrows, frequently accompanied prophetic oracles in the OT.

Even in his death the influence of Elisha continued. When a dead man was hastily buried in the same tomb during an enemy invasion, he was miraculously revived as his body touched the bones of Elisha (II Kgs 13:20-21).

J. R.

ELISHAH (ĕ-lī'shă)

1. Grandson of Japheth in the list of "heads of nations" in Gen 10:4 and I Chr 1:7. Josephus (*Ant.* i.6.1) identifies this name with the Aeolians.

2. A coastal region which sold blue and purple dye to Tyre (Ezk 27:7). Elishah is associated with Alashia, common to cuneiform records found in a number of places. Many call it a part of Cyprus other than Kittim (Ezk 27:6), possibly a non-Phoenician area. It has also been identified as Italy, northern Africa, Greece, and many other less prominent areas.

ELISHAMA (ē-lĭsh'ă-mă). The name occurs on ancient Heb. seals and in S Arabic inscriptions.

1. Son of Ammihud, leader of the tribe of Ephraim at the time of the Exodus (Num 1:10; 7:28). Joshua was his grandson (I Chr 7:26).

2. A son born to David in Jerusalem (II Sam 5:16; I Chr 3:8). The same name in I Chr 3:6 apparently stands for Elishua (*q.v.*; cf. II Sam 5:15–16; I Chr 14:5).

3. A prince and secretary to King Jehoiakim (Jer 36:12, 20–21), probably identical with the royal grandfather of Ishmael, who killed Gedaliah, the Babylonian-appointed governor of Judea (II Kgs 25:25; Jer 41:1).

4. A man of the line of Judah (I Chr 2:41).

5. A priest among a group of men appointed by King Jehoshaphat to teach the law in the cities of Judah (II Chr 17:7–9).

ELISHAPHAT (ē-lĭsh'ă-făt). One of five "captains of hundreds" who joined with Jehoiada the priest to seize the throne from Athaliah and establish Joash as king (II Chr 23:1).

ELISHEBA (ĕ-lĭsh'ĕ-bă). Daughter of Amminadab, a leader of the tribe of Judah. She was the wife of Aaron and mother of Aaron's sons Nadab, Abihu, Eleazar, and Ithamar (Ex 6:23). Thus she was the mother of the entire line of Aaronic priests. *See* Elisabeth.

ELISHUA (ĕl'ĭ-shū'ă). The sixth son born to David by a wife or concubine in Jerusalem (II Sam 5:15; I Chr 14:5). In I Chr 3:6 the name Elishama (*q.v.*) appears in his place in the list of David's sons.

ELIUD (ĕ-lī'ŭd). Listed in Matthew's genealogy of Jesus as the ancestor four generations before Joseph (Mt 1:15).

ELIZAPHAN (ĕl'ĭ-zā'făn), **ELZAPHAN** (ĕl-zā'făn)

1. A son of Uzziel who was a Kohathite Levite and a first cousin of Aaron (Ex 6:22; Lev 10:4; Num 3:30; in Exodus and Leviticus Elizaphan is contracted into Elzaphan). With his brother Mishael, he helped remove the bodies of Nadab and Abihu from the camp after they had offered "strange fire" on Yahweh's altar.

2. A son of Parnach who represented the tribe of Zebulun in the division of the land of Canaan under the supervision of Eleazar and Joshua (Num 34:25).

ELIZUR (ĕ-lī'zŭr). Chief of the tribe of Reuben who served as tribal military commander (Num 2:10; 10:18). He served under Moses and Aaron in the census of Israel taken in the second year of the Exodus travel (Num 1:5), and presented the tribe's offering at the tabernacle (Num 7:30–35).

ELKANAH (ĕl-kā'nă)

1. One of the sons of Korah who became the head of a clan (Ex 6:24; I Chr 6:23).

2. The father of Amasai and Ahimoth; son of Joel, descended from Korah through Ebiasaph (I Chr 6:25, 36).

3. The father of Zuph (Zophai) and Nahath, descended from No. 2 (I Chr 6:26, 35).

4. The son of Jeroham and father of Samuel (I Sam 1:1, 4, 8, 19, 21, 23; 2:11, 20; I Chr 6:27, 34). This man, descended from Elkanah Nos. 2 and 3, is described as an Ephraimite (Ephrathite) whose home was in Ramah in Ephraim (I Sam 2:11) and who, with his two wives, Hannah and Peninnah, made a religious pilgrimage to Shiloh each year to offer sacrifices (I Sam 1:3). Hannah was his favorite wife and this contributed, no doubt, to Peninnah's jealousy (I Sam 1:5–7).

5. One of the Levitical priests who dwelt in the hill country of Judea (I Chr 9:16).

6. A warrior from the tribe of Benjamin who deserted Saul's forces and joined David at Ziklag (I Chr 12:6).

7. A Levite in David's time charged with the responsibility for the custody of the ark (I Chr 15:23).

8. An official in the court of King Ahaz of Judah, who was said to have stood next to the king himself (II Chr 28:7).

The frequency of this name and the complexity of the genealogical lists have led some scholars to conclude that the term is used to denote the clan or family as well as individuals. Hence, in some cases one cannot be sure whether the individual or the clan is designated.

G. A. T.

ELKOSH (ĕl'kŏsh). The birthplace of the prophet Nahum (Nah 1:1). It is difficult to determine which city is meant; four suggestions have been made. (1) The 16th cen. Jewish writers identified Nahum as having been born of one of the ten northern tribes in exile in the town Al-Qush (Elkosh) N of Nineveh. (2) Capernaum in Galilee, the "village of Nahum." (3) Jerome's identification with Hilkesei (Elkoseh) in northern Galilee. (4) The more defendable position is the Elkosh in southern Judea near Beth-Gabre or the modern Beit-Jibrin between Jerusalem and Gaza.

ELKOSHITE. *See* Elkosh.

ELLASAR (ĕl'*á*-sär). The city or country ruled by Arioch (*q.v.*), an ally of Chedorlaomer (*q.v.*), who invaded Palestine in the time of Abraham (Gen 14:1, 9). Former identification of Ellasar with the S Babylonian city-state of Larsa must now be abandoned because the spellings of the two names cannot be equated. Also the cuneiform text bearing the name of the king of Larsa was formerly read as Eri-aku and thus seemingly was similar to Arioch; but now it is more correctly read as Warad-Sin. Recently scholars have suggested that Ellasar may be the town Ilanzura, between Carchemish and Harran in N Mesopotamia, mentioned in the Mari letters and in a Hittite text.

ELM. *See* Plants.

ELMODAM (ĕl-mō'd*á*m). Listed in Luke's genealogy (3:28) as Jesus' ancestor, the sixth generation before Zerubbabel and the twenty-fifth before Joseph.

ELNAAM (ĕl-nā'*á*m). According to the Heb. text of I Chr 11:46, he was the father of Jeribai and Joshaviah, two of 16 men added by the Chronicler to the list of David's guard, the "thirty," as found in II Sam 23:24–39 (cf. I Chr 11:41 ff.). The LXX says, "Eliel the Mahavite and Jeribai and Joshaviah, his son, and Elnaam and Ithmah the Moabite," making Elnaam himself one of the soldiers.

ELNATHAN (ĕl-nā'th*á*n)

1. A Jerusalemite, maternal grandfather of Jehoiachin (II Kgs 24:8). He was possibly also the son of Achbor, Jehoiakim's court officer (Jer 26:22), who also pled with Jehoiakim not to destroy Jeremiah's scroll (Jer 36:12–25).

2. Two "chief" men (Heb. text of Ezr 8:16) and one "teacher" summoned by Ezra to his camp on the river to Ahava. I Esd 8:44 lists one "chief" man.

ELOHIM (ĕl'ō-hĭm). A plural form of the Heb. noun *'ᵉlôah* describing Deity. Some erroneously regard it as the plural of El (*q.v.*), but it is not from the same root. It is usually translated "God," although sometimes it is a true plural and must be understood as "gods" (Ex 12:12; Gen 35:2, 4; Deut 29:18; 32:17). It is sometimes applied to men as God's representatives (Ex 21:6, RSV; 22:8–9, 28, RSV). The term may refer to angels (Ps 8:5, cf. RSV; 82:1), although these passages are debated.

Usually Elohim takes a singular verb. However, it seems occasionally to govern a plural form of the verb (Gen 20:13; 35:7; II Sam 7:23; Ps 58:11, Heb.). What is the significance of this apparent inconsistency? Some would regard it as evidence of the polytheistic origin of the term. In fact, other people of the same era used divine titles in a similar way. The Akkad. plural *ilanu* (gods) was applied to a single deity. Pharaoh was addressed as *ilania* ("my gods") by his Canaanite vassals in the Amarna letters. In the OT the plural Elohim is applied to Chemosh, the god of the Ammonites (Jud 11:24); Ashtoreth, the goddess of Sidon (I Kgs 11:5); and Baal-zebub of Ekron (II Kgs 1:2).

The significant fact, however, is not the origin of the word, for this cannot be definitely known. Rather, it is the way it is used of Israel's God in the OT. When used of Yahweh, it refers to the sole God of the world, who is addressed in the plural as the fullness of all Deity. We can be sure that no polytheistic elements are allowed to appear in Gen 1. Yet it is here that the plural is most obvious (Gen 1:26). Regardless of one's explanation of the reason for the plural emphasis here, he cannot ignore the plain meaning of the passage. In some sense God is plural; yet He is also singular (cf. the singular verbs in v. 27). Although the Christian doctrine of the Trinity is not taught in the chapter, it emerges from it.

See God; God, Names and Titles of.

C. T. F.

ELOI, ELOI, LAMA SABACHTHANI (ē-lō'ī, ē-lō'ī, lä'm*á* s*á*-băk' th*á*nī). The Heb. or Aram. words from Ps 22:1 spoken by Jesus in His fourth saying on the cross, quoted in Mk 15:34, and similarly in Mt 27:46, which has "Eli, Eli. . . ." Under the agony of crucifixion our Lord recited the opening words of a Davidic psalm depicting sufferings far more intense than David ever endured personally.

Jesus seems to have voiced the words not in Heb., but in His native Galilean Aramaic, *'ĕlohî, 'ĕlohî, lᵉmâ shebaqtanî,* "My God, My God, why hast Thou abandoned Me?" The word "eloi" is thought to be the Gr. transliteration of Aram. *'ĕlāhî,* as in Dan 6:22 (v. 23, Aram.), the sound possibly changed to *'ĕlohî* by provincial pronunciation. The commonly accepted text in Matthew has *ēli,* which transliterates the Heb. *'ēlî;* but it is a form also widely used in Aram.

The best Gr. MSS have *lema* in both the Mark and Matthew passages, which better represents Aram. *lᵉmâ* than Heb. *lāmâ,* in either case meaning "why."

"Sabachthani" appears to transliterate an Aram. word, for the original word in Ps 22 is Heb. *'ăzabtānî.* The Aram. verb *shᵉbaq,* "to leave, forsake, abandon," may be seen in Dan 4:23 and Ezr 6:7 ("let . . . alone"). The Targum of Ps 22 (the Targums were Aram. translations of the OT used in synagogues, still in oral form in the 1st cen. A.D.), has these words; thus it may have had a bearing on the form of Jesus' quotation.

Scholars, however, have reopened the debate whether Jesus would more naturally have used Heb. or Aram. The documents from Qumran and Wadi Murabba'at indicate that a form of Heb. influenced by Aram. may have been spoken quite generally in Palestine in the 1st cen. A.D., especially in religious contexts.

J. R.

ELON (ē'lŏn), **ELONITE** (ē'lŏ-nīt)
1. A Hittite, the father of Esau's wives Bashemath (Gen 26:34; 36:10) and Adah (Gen 36:2).
2. Second son of Zebulun, head of the family of Elonites (Gen 46:14; Num 26:26).
3. One of the judges, of the tribe of Zebulun, who served for ten years (Jud 12:11–12).
4. A town in the territory of Dan, the location of which is uncertain (Josh 19:43).

ELON-BETH-HANAN (ē'lŏn-bĕth-hā' năn). A Danite town which, with three others, provided one month's sustenance for Solomon's household (I Kgs 4:7–9). This may be the same as Elon 4 (*q.v.*).

ELOTH (ē'lŏth). An alternate form of Elath (*q.v.*).

ELPAAL (ĕl-pā'ăl). The head of a family of the tribe of Benjamin (I Chr 8:11–12, 18).

ELPALET (ĕl-pā'lĕt). A son of David born in Jerusalem (I Chr 14:5). He is called Eliphelet (*q.v.*) in I Chr 3:6; but is not included in the list of David's sons in II Sam 5.

EL-PARAN (ĕl-pâr'ăn). The southern extremity of the march of the kings with Chedorlaomer (Gen 14:6) before their swing northward through the city-states, which resulted in the capture of Lot and his rescue by Abraham. Many hold this to be another name for Elath (*q.v.*).

EL SHADDAI (ĕl-shăd'ī). *See* God; God, Names and Titles of.

ELTEKEH (ĕl'tĕ-kĕ). A city in the area of Ekron, Gibbethon, and Timnah, assigned to the tribe of Dan (Josh 19:44); then to the Kohathite Levites (Josh 21:23); and later taken by Philistines. Probably the place called Altaku by Sennacherib (*Hexagon Prism*), where he defeated an army of Egypt and her allies during his invasion of that section in 701 B.C., though the site is uncertain.

ELTEKON (ĕl'tĕ-kŏn). A city in the hill country of Judah (Josh 15:59), probably N of Hebron and W of Bethlehem. The site is uncertain, but some identify it as Khirbet ed-Deir.

ELTOLAD (ĕl-tō'lăd). A town of Judah near the border of Edom (Josh 15:30), given to the tribe of Simeon (Josh 19:4). It is probably the place called Tolad in I Chr 4:29. The site is unidentified.

ELUL (ē'lŭl). The sixth month in the Heb. sacred calendar and the last month of the civil calendar (Neh 6:15). It begins with the new moon of August and ends with the new moon of September. The Heb. name *'ĕlûl* seems to have been adopted during the Exile, as it does not appear in pre-Exilic writing. Early writings tended to refer to months by number. It was probably derived from the name of the Babylonian month of Elulu or Ululu. *See* Calendar.

ELUZAI (ĕ-lōō'zī). One of several warriors from the tribe of Benjamin, all noted for excellence with the bow and for ambidextrous use of the slingshot. They joined David's band at Ziklag (I Chr 12:5).

ELYMAS (ĕl'ī-măs). A Jewish magician at the proconsular court of Sergius Paulus in Cyprus who tried to dissuade Sergius from believing the message brought by Barnabas and Paul (Acts 13:6–11). For his opposition he was suddenly struck with temporary blindness. The name may be akin to Arabic *'alim,* "sage"; the Western text of Codex D reads *Hetoimas*.
See also Barjesus.

ELZABAD (ĕl-zā'băd)
1. One of several warriors from the tribe of Gad. Noted for use of the shield and spear, ferocity, and speed of foot, they joined David's band at Ziklag (I Chr 12:12).
2. One of six sons of Shemaiah, all Korahite gatekeepers (I Chr 26:7).

ELZAPHAN. *See* Elizaphan.

EMBALM. Processes of preparing the dead for burial varied considerably among Near Eastern countries during the biblical period. Embalming in antiquity differed somewhat in both tech-

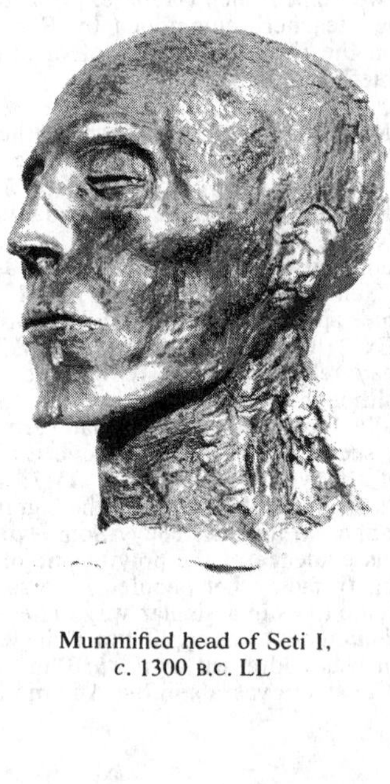

Mummified head of Seti I, *c.* 1300 B.C. LL

nique and purpose from the practice of today. The word originally indicated the treating of the body with spices or perfumes, as a preservant and deodorant, and as a mark of respect or honor. Climate, geography and religion affected the preservation of the dead. In Egypt in predynastic times the dead were interred in shallow graves dug in the edge of the desert; in the dry sand the bodies desiccated rapidly and were remarkably well preserved. With the development of the tomb, some of these advantages were lost.

Since the theological concepts of the Egyptians emphasized the survival of the body, the process of mummification was originated in which various organs of the body were removed. Herodotus later described methods of mummification in various price ranges (II, 85-88). The only mentions of the word "embalm" in the Bible are in connection with the bodies of Jacob (Gen 50:2-3) and of Joseph (v. 26). The Heb. verb *ḥānaṭ*, "embalm," means to spice, make spicy. This work was performed by the *rōpheʾîm*, "physicians," "repairers." Since spices such as natron, resins, and aromatics were used in mummification, the Egyptian context of Gen 50 indicates that the bodies of Jacob and Joseph were mummified. See Alfred Lucas, "Mummification," *Ancient Egyptian Materials and Industries*, 4th ed. rev. by J. H. Harris, London: St. Martin's Press, 1962, pp. 307-390.

The NT mentions the use of ointments in preparation for burial. The anointing of Jesus is described as burial preparation (Mt 26:12; Mk 14:8; Jn 12:7). In the burial of Jesus, Joseph of Arimathea and Nicodemus used "a mixture of myrrh and aloes, about an hundred pound weight" (Jn 19:39-40). The Galilean women also intended to anoint Jesus' body (Mk 16:1; Lk 23:55-24:1). The body was wrapped in linen cloth, with spices in the windings, according to Jewish custom (Jn 19:40; cf. Jn 11:44; Acts 5:6). Sometimes the corpse was merely washed and clothed to ready it for interment (Acts 9:37). Among the Jews no incisions were made in the corpse or organs removed, as in the mummification process.

See Burial; Dead, The; Funeral; Grave.

C. E. D.

EMBROIDERER. *See* Occupations.

EMEK-KEZIZ. *See* Keziz.

EMERALD. *See* Jewels.

EMERODS. *See* Diseases: Internal Diseases.

EMIM (ē'mĭm). These were giants inhabiting the land of Moab. They were once a tall and powerful people, comparable to the Anakim in stature (Deut 2:9-11). At the battle of the kings they were defeated by Chedorlaomer in the plain of Kiriathaim (Gen 14:5) during the time of Abraham. Apparently they belonged to the tribe of Rephaim although they are unknown outside the Bible. Their territory was later occupied by the Moabites. *See* Giant.

EMMANUEL (ĕ-măn'ū-ĕl). Gr. transliteration of the Heb. Immanuel, "God is with us." It is the form of the Heb. name in Mt 1:23 in which the evangelist quotes the words of Isaiah to King Ahaz (Isa 7:14), where the word is "Immanuel" in the prophetic announcement of the virgin birth of Christ.

See Edward E. Hindson, "Isaiah's Immanuel," *Grace Journal*, X (1969), 3-15.

EMMAUS (ĕ-mā'ŭs). A village mentioned only in Lk 24:13. One of the appearances of Jesus on resurrection Sunday was to two men walking from Jerusalem to Emmaus. The Lucan passage locates this village 60 stades from Jerusalem, or approximately six and three-quarter miles or 11 kilometers away. A variant reading, 160 stades, is found in a few uncial MSS, Si-

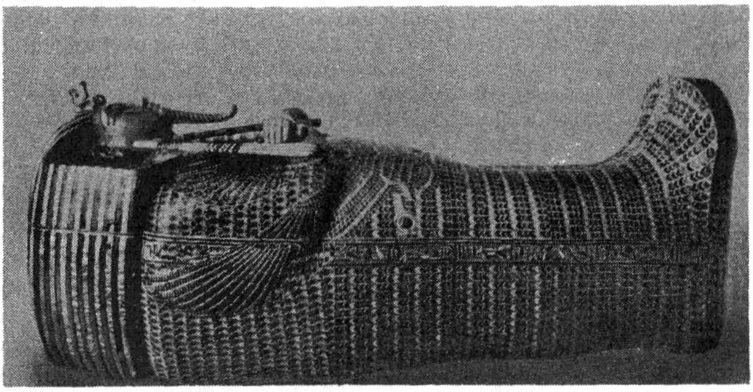

Mummy-shaped coffin of King Tutankhamon. LL

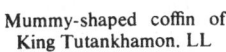

naiticus (4th cen.), N (6th cen.), K, Pi, and Theta (9th cen.), and a few minuscules and two versions; this distance is supported by Eusebius-Jerome, *Onomastikon*. The reading "60 stades" is found in P 75 (late 2nd or early 3rd cen.), B (4th cen.), A and C (5th cen.), and others. The evidence of P 75 (recently published Bodmer papyrus) and B (Codex Vaticanus) together establishes rather definitely the reading "60 stades."

Three identifications of Emmaus have been proposed: (1) The modern village of 'Amwâs (definitive publication: H. Vincent and F. M. Abel, *Emmaus: sa basilique et son histoire,* Paris: Librairie Ernest Lerous, 1932). However, this location would require the reading "160 stades," which is very doubtful in the light of the newer MS evidence. (2) A military colony of Vespasian, possibly present-day *Kaloniye,* called Ammaous by Josephus. The distance from Jerusalem is about 34 stades—rather difficult to correlate with the biblical record. (3) Present-day el-Kubêbe on the road to Joppa (definitive publication: P. B. Bagatti, *I Monumenti di Emmaus El-Qubeibeh e dei dintorni,* Jerusalem, Jordan: Franciscan Press, 1947). The remains here are definitely from the NT period, and the distance from Jerusalem agrees fairly well with the Lucan record, making this identification the preferred one.

B. Van E.

EMMOR (ĕm'ôr). The NT form of the Heb. name Hamor (*q.v.*) as transliterated into Gr. (Acts 7:16; cf. Josh 24:32).

EMPTIED. A word significant to the doctrine of Christ's incarnation (Phil 2:7, ASV, RSV, etc.). *See* Kenosis.

EN-. This prefix in Heb. stands for *'ayin* which primarily means "eye"; secondarily it means "fountain." Figuratively, it was anything which resembled the eye, a look or glance of the eye, an aspect or appearance of a thing. Thus, the usage for "spring" or "fountain" was derived. Many cities and places of Palestine and Syria were named from fountains in their vicinities, such as Engedi and En-gannim. Sometimes fountains themselves were so designated, as En-shemesh.

ENAM (ē'năm). A place in Judah adjacent to Adullam and Timnath in the Shephelah (Josh 15:34). It is conjectured that Enaim is another form of the same word (Gen 38:14, RSV). It was in the gate of Enaim or Enajim that Tamar sat before her interview with her father-in-law. The endings -im and -jim are interchangeable; thus the two names referred to the same place. In the KJV it is translated "an open place." The name means "double springs."

ENAN (ē'năn). A Naphtalite whose son Ahira was a prince at the time of the numbering of the children of Israel in the wilderness of Sinai (Num 1:15; 2:29; 7:83; 10:27). *See* Hazar-Enan.

ENCAMPMENT. *See* Camp.

ENCHANTER. *See* Magic.

ENCHANTMENT. In the KJV this is the translation of several Heb. words. It was used of the tricks of the Egyptian magicians (Ex 7:11, 22; 8:7), the auguries sought by Balaam (Num 24:1), the charming of a serpent (Eccl 10:11), and magical spells (Isa 47:9, 12).

Mosaic law forbad the practice of such enchantments (Deut 18:10; Lev 19:26; Isa 47:9). They constituted a peculiar temptation to Israel to apostatize.

See Magic; Divination.

END OF THE WORLD. *See* Eschatology.

ENDOR (ĕn'dôr). A town on the N side of the hill of Moreh, S of Mount Tabor which was assigned to the tribe of Manasseh, though it was located in the territory of Issachar (Josh 17:11). The ancient site was probably at Khirbet Safsafa about three-quarters of a mile NE of the former village of Indur which echoes the ancient name. Nearby are several ancient caves. Poetic tradition preserves the memory that Barak's victory took place in the vicinity of Endor (Ps 83:10). It was also the home of a witch consulted by King Saul (I Sam 28:7). *See* Familiar Spirit.

ENEAS. *See* Aeneas.

EN-EGLAIM (ĕn-ĕg'lĭ-ĭm). The name, found only in Ezk 47:10, refers to a site in conjunction with En-gedi between which places fishermen stand. Its exact location is in doubt; however, it is thought to have been on the W shore of the Dead Sea toward the mouth of the Jordan. Eglaim of Isa 15:8 is regarded as a different place since the initial letter is *alef* rather than *'ayin,* and the two letters are rarely if ever exchanged. The most probable location of En-eglaim is 'Ain Feshkha, one and a half miles S of Qumran.

ENEMY. One who hates another and seeks his hurt; a foe or adversary; also, a hostile nation or army.

A number of terms express in different ways the underlying idea of enemy. In the OT Heb. *'ōyēb* (possible original idea of breathing, blowing, puffing, an idea often applied to anger and hatred) is rendered "enemy" or "foe." Heb. *ṣār* (from *ṣārar,* "to press," "to compress" and thus to "oppress," or in this case, to treat one in a hostile manner) is translated as "adversary" and "foe" in addition to "enemy."

The noun *shōrēr* (specifically, a "defamer" or "slanderer," a Canaanism so used in the

Amarna letters according to M. Dahood, *Psalms II,* Anchor Bible, Garden City: Doubleday, 1968, pp. 25 f.) is also "enemy" in KJV and RSV.

Other words express the action of an enemy and are so indicated as such: *qûm,* "to rise up" against one; *śānē',* "to hate" and in its participle, therefore, a "hater" or "enemy"; *shûr,* "to lie in wait" against one. In the NT, Gr. *echthros* is rendered "enemy" or "foe."

In most instances, "enemy" in the OT describes the national enemies of Israel (Jud 3:1-3; etc.), but there are also references to personal enemies (Ex 23:4; I Sam 18:29; I Kgs 21:20; Mic 7:6; etc.); note particularly the Psalms (7:5; etc.). In the NT "enemy" for the most part indicates personal enemies (Mt 5:44; II Thess 3:15; etc.), but it also depicts foreign powers (Lk 1:71; 19:43).

Man becomes the enemy of God when he disobeys the divine commandments. He can incur God's wrath and jealous zeal in his disobedience (Deut 5:8-10; 7:10). The imprecatory psalms (*see* Psalms) express the psalmist's feelings as he regards God's enemies as his own; he then implores God to vindicate His own honor and righteousness by judging and punishing those who flout His commandments. Sinners are named by Paul the enemies of God (Rom 5:8, 10). The friend of the world is the enemy of God (Jas 4:4). Satan (*see* Devil; Satan) is the greatest enemy of all (Mt 13:39; Acts 13:10; cf. Jn 8:44). Death is regarded as the last enemy (I Cor 15:26) to come under the dominion of Christ.

The OT describes God as an enemy. He was the enemy to the enemies of Israel (Deut 28:7; II Chr 20:29). The prophets express their hatred for Israel's enemies and despisers of the Lord. This is not necessarily a sub-biblical ethic, for the inspired men were not merely expressing some personal diatribe against Israel's national enemies; their words and writings were the thoughts and sentiments of a holy God expressed against *His* enemies (Isa 14:25-27; Ezk 35:7; Obadiah; Nahum; etc.). Thus God was for Israel so as to deliver them out of Egypt (Ex 3:8), to guide them through the desert, and ultimately to give them the land of Canaan. Not only is this seen in the books of Moses, but the prophets continue this emphasis (Hos 11:1; Amos 2:9-10).

God also abandoned Israel to their enemies as a means of judgment on His people (Isa 10:5-6; Ezk 14:13-21; Lk 19:41-44), and therefore the prophets called God Israel's enemy (Lam 2:5). The prophets, though, recognized the positive aspect of the judgment, because if God did not judge Israel, they would have disappeared into the sea of nations. As difficult as it was, there was the dominance of the love of God in preserving a remnant of His people (Isa 54:7-8; Jer 30:14, 18; Dan 9:16, 24). In a peculiar emphasis also on the personal level, Job calls God his enemy (Job 13:24; 19:11).

On the other hand, there are many OT examples where God did good to the national enemies of Israel (e.g., to Nineveh in the book of Jonah). Jeremiah, for the well-being of his kinsmen, instructed the Judean captives to pray for their Babylonian masters (Jer 29:7). In many ways and through a number of circumstances Israel was to be a blessing to foreign nations even though these countries were enemies at times (Gen 12:3).

The OT instructed the individual Israelite to love his neighbor (Lev 19:18). While the Israelite was not told to love his enemy, yet he was *never* told not to love him; indeed, he was told to do his enemy good. Thus, Moses instructed his kinsmen to return any enemy's lost ox or ass and even help his enemy with his beast of burden (Ex 23:4-5). Saul said David was more righteous than himself since David repaid good for his enemy's evil (I Sam 24:17-19). Job stated in defense of his righteousness that he would be denying God if he rejoiced at the defeat of his enemy (Job 31:28-29). The wisdom writer in Prov 25:21-22 stresses the righteous man's duty: "If thine enemy be hungry, give him bread to eat; and if he be thirsty, give him water to drink: for thou shalt heap coals of fire upon his head."

The NT filled in the gap in the OT when Jesus stated that one should love and pray for his enemies (Mt 5:43-44). This love is demonstrated when we realize that God gave His Son on behalf of a world of enemies (Jn 3:16), and thus reconciled those hostile to Him (Col 1:20-22). Christ (Lk 23:34) and Stephen (Acts 7:60) are examples for us as they prayed for their persecutors. Paul emphasized the love of Christians for their enemies when he made the OT imperative (Prov 25:21-22) the NT ethic (Rom 12:14-21).

See Adversary; Sin; War; Wrath.

L. Go.

EN-GANNIM (ĕn-găn'ĭm)

1. A town in the Shephelah of Judah in the proximity of Zanoah, Tappuah and Enam (Josh 15:34).

2. Josh 19:21 and 21:29 mention a second such city in the tribe of Issachar. The Gershonite Levites were assigned this city with its suburbs as one of their possessions. It probably corresponds to the Ginea of Josephus (*Ant.* xx. 6.1) and may certainly be identified with the modern Jenin, a prosperous village on the southern edge of the plain of Esdraelon, with beautiful gardens, fruitful orchards and plentiful supplies of water from the local springs. Its location is approximately seven miles SW of Mount Gilboa on the main road from Esdraelon through Samaria to Jerusalem. Beth-haggan (II Kgs 9:27, RSV) is probably an alternate name for En-gannim.

EN-GEDI (ĕn-gĕd'ī). In ancient times an agricultural settlement watered by a copious spring ("spring of the goat-kid" or "spring of abundant waters") on the W shore of the Dead Sea (Ezk 47:10), about midway between the N and S ends in the general direction or vicinity of Hazazon-tamar (II Chr 20:2). It was included in the territory of Judah (Josh 15:62). In Solomon's time it was a fertile oasis in the midst of the desert where spice plants and vineyards were cultivated (Song 1:14). En-gedi was also famed in Jewish and Roman literature for its fine date palms.

Saul pursued David to this region, whereupon David and his men hid in a cave (I Sam 23:29; 24:1) while Saul slept nearby.

In the Middle Ages the terraced gardens and buildings were abandoned and became a deserted waste. Today travelers approach the area after a long trek through the desert inferno along the shores of the Dead Sea. The plain of En-gedi stretches 1,500 yards between two wadis or canyons descending to the Dead Sea. It is located in Israel, only a few miles S of the 1948–1967 Israel-Jordan border. After one climbs upward for a few hundred yards inland from the Dead Sea, the beautiful falls of En-gedi come into view. A crystal clear spring in the cliff above, 670 feet above the sea, cascades into a beautiful pool below. Most of the water runs into the Dead Sea, but in recent years members of an Israeli kibbutz (a communal settlement, mainly for immigrants) have utilized some of the water for irrigation purposes. The plain between the canyons is very productive and grows an abundance of vegetables and fruits, especially bananas.

Five seasons of excavations by Israeli archaeologists (1961–1965) in the En-gedi area have discovered a late Chalcolithic Age (*c.* 3300 B.C.) enclosure above the spring, probably a sacred place for the nomads and villagers of the Judean desert and its oases; a fortified mound (Tell el-Jurn) with five levels of occupation; an Israelite square watchtower by the spring; and two ritual pools from before A.D. 70 and a Roman bath (A.D. 70–135). The mound was first occupied from the reign of Josiah to the time of Nebuchadnezzar's control (*c.* 625–580 B.C.). The unusual pottery vessels suggest that this was an industrial center for the preparation of perfume from the balm cultivated nearby. En-gedi likely became a royal estate under King Josiah, with the perfumers organized in a guild. Later levels of Tell el-Jurn indicate En-gedi prospered in the Persian period (*c.*525–475 B.C.), under the Hasmonean kings John Hyrcanus and Alexander Jannaeus (135–76 B.C.), in the 1st cen. until destroyed by the Roman legion (A.D. 1–68), and during the Roman-Byzantine era (3rd–5th cen. A.D.).

Bibliography. B. Mazar, "Excavations at the Oasis of Engedi," *Archaeology,* XVI (1963), 99–107; "En-gedi," TAOTS, pp. 223–230. Mazar and I. Dunayevski, "Third Season," IEJ, XIV (1964), 121–130; "Fourth and Fifth Seasons," IEJ, XVII (1967), 133–143. Mazar, T. Dothan, and Dunayevski, "En-Gedi," *Excavations in 1961–1962,* Jerusalem: Dept. of Antiquities and Museums, 1966.

ENGINE. Translation of two words in Heb.: (1) *ḥishsh*^{e}*bōnôt* (II Chr 26:15), devices of war for hurling stones and arrows, i.e., catapults (*q.v.*); (2) *m*^{e}*ḥî q*^{e}*bōl* (Ezk 26:9), literally, "the smiting of an attacking engine," i.e., the blows of a battering ram (cf. RSV). *See* Armor.

ENGLISH VERSIONS, BIBLE. *See* Bible–English Versions.

EN-HADDAH (ĕn-hăd'ȧ). A village in the tribal territory of Issachar, near Remeth (Josh 19:21). It is perhaps modern el-Hadetheh, six miles E of Mount Tabor and six miles SW of the southern tip of the Sea of Galilee.

EN-HAKKORE (ĕn-hăk'ō-rē). Jud 15:19 mentions the experience of Samson after his exploit with the jawbone of an ass. His thirst was great and he called upon the Lord for water. Water was provided at Lehi and the name thereof was En-hakkore, "the spring of him that called." Its location is unknown.

EN-HAZOR (ĕn-hā'zôr). Josh 19:37 locates this village in the tribe of Naphtali adjacent to Kadesh, Edrei and Iron. Its site is unknown; however, some speculation exists relative to its identification with Khirbet Hazireh or Hazzur on the slopes about nine miles W of Kedesh.

EN-MISHPAT (ĕn-mĭsh'păt). Gen 14:7 identifies this place as Kadesh, probably Kadesh-barnea (*q.v.*). It is thought that there was a sanctuary there at which in ancient times a pagan priest gave oracles and decided disputes. The names Kadesh and Kedesh are connected with Canaanite cities that had heathen sanctuaries.

ENMITY. The Heb. *'êbâ* occurs five times in the OT (Gen 3:15; Num 35:21–22; Ezk 25:15; 35:5). The enmity in Gen 3:15 is between the serpent and Eve and between its seed and her seed, symbolic of the spiritual warfare between Satan and Christ and His followers. Individual hostility is in view in Num 35:21–22. The enmity in the Ezekiel passages is national.

The usage of the six occurrences of the Gr. *echthra* in the NT also reveals three kinds of enmity–hostility toward God (Rom 8:7; Jas 4:4), the enmity of individuals (Lk 23:12), and hostility between groups of people (Eph 2:14–16). The plural in Gal 5:20 (ASV) evidently refers to the various manifestations and forms of hostile feelings.

ENOCH (ē'nŭk)

1. The son of Cain (Gen 4:17) for whom a city was named.

2. The son of Jared (Gen 5:18) and the father of Methuselah (Gen 5:21; Lk 3:37). He is cited as a hero of faith (Heb 11:5).

It is said that "Enoch walked with God" (Gen 5:22), and as a reward for his holy walk he was translated to heaven without tasting death (Heb 11:5). Thus immortality or life after death was clearly taught in the early Genesis period. Jude 14–15 has excerpts from the Book of Enoch (1:9; 63:8; 93:3), which give a clear-cut sampling of the judgment which was preached by Enoch in this early period. While some may argue as to what source Jude actually used (written or oral tradition), it can be pointed out that inclusion of this quotation in a NT book canonizes his message and makes it Holy Writ. Some scholars believe that Jude was quoting from pseudepigraphical literature used by the false teachers in order to silence them with their own material.

The Book of Enoch was already in existence in the apostolic period. After being quoted in Jude and noticed by some of the Church Fathers, this book disappeared. No part of the Heb. original has come down to us, although there are fragments in Gr. and Ethiopic which scholars associate with this book. In caves near the Essene monastery by the Dead Sea were found parts of eight MSS. of I Enoch in Aramaic.

H. A. Han.

ENOS (ē'nŏs), **ENOSH** (ē'nŏsh). The son of Seth (Gen 4:26; 5:6) and the father of Cainan or Kenan (Gen 5:9–10; I Chr 1:1; Lk 3:37–38). The alternate spelling of Enos is Enosh. Little is known about him. His son Kenan was born when his father was 90 years of age and the length of Enos' life is recorded as 905 years. More significant is the statement that in his time men began to call on the name of Yahweh (Gen 4:26). The implication is that his birth is associated with the awakening of reverence or godly fear. The Genesis account presents Seth and Enos as successors of "righteous Abel." In contrast to Cain and his posterity, Seth and his descendants are portrayed as God-fearing and as custodians of the covenant relationship; this is the chief significance of Enos.

The Heb. term in the singular also occurs about 40 times as a common noun in the OT, chiefly in poetry, with the meaning parallel to that of *'ādām*, "man, mankind, human being."

G. A. T.

EN-RIMMON (ĕn-rĭm'ŏn). Some suggest that the name Rimmon refers to the Canaanite weather god. Neh 11:29 names En-rimmon as one of the places which the men of Judah reinhabited after their return from the Captivity. From the names of the surrounding cities, it is possible that this site is the same as that named in Zech 14:10; Josh 15:32; 19:7; I Chr 4:32. In the last three references the two names are listed separately; however, they are in close proximity to one another. En-rimmon has been identified with Khirbet Umm er-Ramāmîn, eight and a half miles NE of Beer-sheba.

Present-day well at Bir-Ayyub, lower left to right above; Hinnom Valley, Southwest Hill, City Wall. JR

EN-ROGEL (ĕn-rō'gĕl). Josh 15:7; 18:16 locate this site on the border of Benjamin and Judah. II Sam 17:17 sets forth En-rogel as the location where Jonathan and Ahimaaz stayed while awaiting the messages to be taken to David during the revolt of Absalom. I Kgs 1:9 records the event of Adonijah's abortive ascension to the throne of Israel as having taken place in this area.

Some question exists relative to the location of the site. Some identify it with Gihon, or the Virgin's Fount, Ain Sitti Miriam, and 'Ain Umm ed-deraj. Their arguments are set forth as follows: (1) It is the only real spring close to Jerusalem. (2) It fits more concisely with the boundary of Benjamin than any other. (3) The tradition of the death of James relates that he was thrown from the temple wall and clubbed to death in the valley of Kidron. (4) This spring is opposite a cliff face called Zaḥweileh, said to be the equivalent of "the stone of Zoheleth, which is by En-rogel" (I Kgs 1:9).

On the other hand, En-rogel has been identified with Bir-Ayyub for the following reasons: (1) It is a well some 125 feet deep which is fed by a spring at the bottom. (2) According to the account in I Kgs 1:9, Adonijah was at En-rogel feasting when in I Kgs 1:38 Solomon was acclaimed king at Gihon. Thus two different sites seem to be set forth. (3) Since it was not on the immediate route from Jerusalem to Jordan, it seems apparent that there would have been a better hiding place among the caves that were in its proximity in which Jonathan and Ahimaaz could secrete themselves. Thus, En-rogel is set forth as being in the precincts of Jerusalem, and somewhere in the southern extremity of the valley of Hinnom. This is the site that is called by the natives the "Well of Job" or Bir-Ayyub. The Arabic version of Josh 15:7 sets forth En-rogel as the "Spring of Job" or Ain Ayyub.

A description of this well is revealing. The gradual filling of the valley necessitated walling up the top of the old well or spring with large square stones, the lowest stage perhaps dating to Roman times. The water is pure and sweet, but not very cold. At certain times of the year the well overflows, giving the sense of "spring." Although some question exists concerning this site of En-rogel, it seems apparent that the location is Bir Ayyub. Some commentators have identified the dragon or jackal well of Neh 2:13 with Bir Ayyub, but probably wrongly.

C. M. H.

ENROLLMENT. *See* Census.

ENSAMPLE. *See* Example.

EN-SHEMESH (ĕn-shĕm'ĭsh; "fountain or spring of the sun"). Josh 15:7 and 18:17 locate En-Shemesh on the border between Judah and Benjamin, En-rogel and Adummim. It was E of Jerusalem about a mile beyond Bethany toward Jericho. It is identified with 'Ain el-Hôd, also called "the Well of the Apostles," on account of a tradition dating back to the 15th cen. which stated that the apostles drank from this well. It is the last spring on the road to Jericho. The rays of the sun are on it the whole day. Thus it is appropriately called the "Fountain of the Sun."

ENSIGN, STANDARD. An emblem or flag; a signal or warning sign.

1. Heb. *'ôt,* the "sign" or token "of their father's house" and thus of a tribal subdivision (Num 2:2). Ps 74:4 refers to the idolatrous emblems (see ANEP #469-573) or military ensigns which foes of God set up in the holy place.

2. Heb. *degel,* the military standard or banner of a fighting unit (Num 1:52; 2:2, 3, 10, etc.; 10:14, 18, 22, 25; Song 6:10). The word came to mean a division of an army in post-biblical literature. It was used this way in the Elephantine papyri and the Qumran scrolls, and the LXX translates *degel* by *tagma* or *taxis,* a body of soldiers (see Roland de Vaux, *Ancient Israel,* New York: McGraw-Hill, 1961, pp. 226 f.). The emblem was fastened to a wooden pole and was carried by a special standard-bearer as depicted in Sumerian and Egyptian art work (VBW, I, 202 f. on Num 2:2, 34).

Rabbinical tradition, continued in modern Jewish art, has perhaps partially preserved the figures portrayed on tribal standards of ancient Israel. The blessing of Jacob possibly provides a clue to the original emblems—Judah's, a lion (Gen 49:9); Zebulun's, a ship (Gen 49:13); etc. According to the Qumran apocalyptic scroll, "The War of the Sons of Light against the Sons of Darkness," inscriptions on the standards were to be changed with each new phase of the war. When the army of the righteous marched to battle their sign held high was to read: "The Community of God"; when fighting would begin it was to be changed to: "The War of God"; when their army returned to camp it was: "The Salvation of God."

The verb *dāgal* occurs in the victorious battle cry of trust in Ps 20:5, "In the name of our God we will set up our banners!" In Song 2:4 the beloved sings, "His banner over me was love." *See* Banner.

3. Heb. *nēs,* a standard or pole with an attached object. A bronze cult standard overlaid with silver found at Hazor bears the relief of a head of a goddess with two snakes on either side (VBW, I, 221 on Num 21:9). A bronze head covered over with gold, from a Late Bronze Age level at Beth-shan, probably adorned the top of a military standard (VBW, IV, 51 on Ps 115:4).

Moses placed a bronze serpent on a pole (*nēs*) as a signal for extending deliverance and healing (Num 21:8-9). In Num 26:10 the word translated "sign" indicates that Korah's death came as an act of judgment in order to convey a

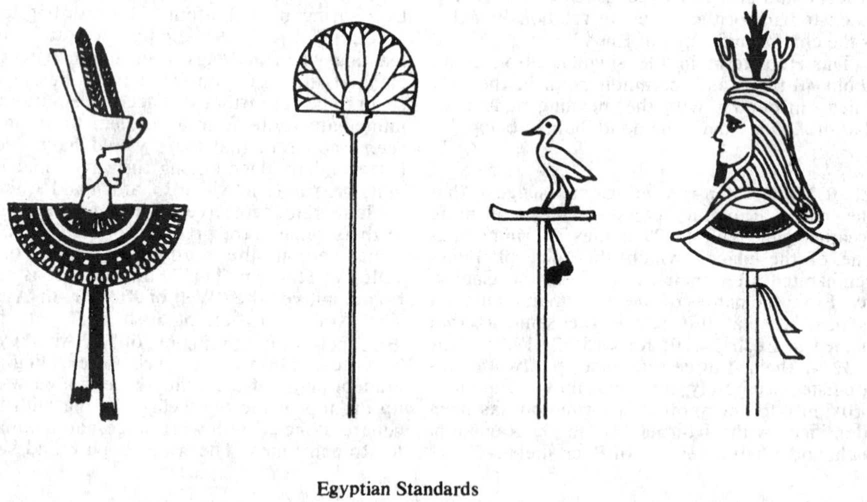

Egyptian Standards

warning. The simile of a signal standard alone on a bare hilltop depicts chastened Israel's lonely plight (Isa 30:17—"ensign," KJV and ASV; "signal," RSV). Assyrian officers would desert their ensign or standard in panic (Isa 31:9, RSV).

As an object raised aloft accompanied by the sounding of a trumpet, in certain prophetic declarations the *nēs* represents God's signal to summon enemy nations for Judah's judgment (Isa 5:26; Jer 4:6, 21) and for Babylon's downfall (Jer 50:2; 51:12, 27). God signals for all the world to watch the defeat of Cush or Ethiopia (Isa 18:3).

The *nēs* is a part of the prophetic imagery in predictions concerning the future regathering of Israel: "The root of Jesse shall stand as an ensign to the peoples" (Isa 11:10, RSV; and 11:12). It symbolizes that mood, movement, or condition which God will establish among the nations in order to effect the return of His people to their land (Isa 49:22—"standard," KJV; "ensign," ASV; "signal," RSV). It is the signal which will preface the heralding of the good news that salvation has come to the daughter of Zion (Isa 62:10).

Verbal forms of *nāsas,* considered to mean "lift up a standard," occur in Isa 10:18, "a standardbearer" (KJV); Isa 59:19, "the Spirit of the Lord shall lift up a standard against him" (KJV); Zech 9:16, "lifted up as an ensign upon his land" (KJV); and Ps 60:4, "Thou hast given a banner [*nēs*] to them that fear thee, that it *may be displayed* because of the truth."

H. E. Fi.

EN-TAPPUAH (ĕn-tăp'ū-*à*; "fountain of the apple or citron"). Located in Manasseh on the border of Ephraim (Josh 17:7). It is probably the same as or next to Tappuah (*q.v.*), located near the source of the river Kanah. Tappuah may be Sheikh Abu Zarad, nine miles SSW of Shechem, and the "spring of Tappuah" is probably to be identified with a spring about three miles N of Lebonah.

ENVY. Envy is an active principle of hostility aimed maliciously at the real or supposed superiority of another person. It originated in Satan's abortive attempt to usurp divine attributes (Isa 14:12-20). Eve imbibed this pernicious evil in yielding to Satan's insinuations (Gen 3:4-7). Envy prompted the first murder (Gen 4:5). Its ugly form appeared in Rachel (Gen 30:1), Joseph's brothers (Gen 37:11; cf. Acts 7:9), Saul (I Sam 18:8 f.), Israel (Ps 106:16). It even instigated the Jewish leaders to deliver Jesus to Pilate (Mt 27:18; Mk 15:10).

Gr. *phthonos,* which designates "envy" in all places except possibly Jas 4:5 (see ASV and NASB), characterizes human nature (Rom 1:29; Tit 3:3) and the "flesh" (Gal 5:19, 21). Its display among Christians is forbidden (Gal 5:26; I Tim 6:4; I Pet 2:1).

Gr. *zēlos* ("zeal"), while often righteously motivated (II Cor 7:7, 11; 9:2), can, when misdirected (Rom 10:2; Phil 3:6), easily become envy (Acts 13:45; 17:5; Rom 13:13; I Cor 3:3; II Cor 12:20; Jas 3:14, 16).

See Jealousy.

EPAENETUS (ē-pē'nē-tŭs). Paul's greeting to the Christians at Rome mentions Epaenetus as his beloved and as the first convert to Christ in Asia (Rom 16:5). The name was not uncommon; it is found in inscriptions both in Rome and Asia. In fact, one such inscription discovered in Rome makes reference to an Epaenetus as a native of Ephesus.

EPAPHRAS (ĕp'*à*-frăs). A "beloved fellow servant" and a "faithful minister of Christ," held in high esteem by Paul (Col 1:7-8; 4:12-13). In Phm 23 he is referred to as "my fellow prisoner in Christ Jesus." While the name is a contracted form of Epaphroditus, most do not connect him with the Philippian man of that name in Phil 2:25-30 (contra. Glover, *Paul of Tarsus*).

From Col 1:6-7 it appears that Colosse had received "the grace of God in truth" not from Paul himself but from Epaphras. On the basis of Col 4:13, he had been Paul's representative in evangelizing not only Colosse, but also Laodicea and Hierapolis. Later he shared Paul's imprisonment and sent greetings to Philemon.

EPAPHRODITUS (ē-păf'rō-dī'tŭs). One of two companions of Paul highly commended by him in Phil 2:25-30. The epithets are striking: "my brother and fellow worker and fellow soldier, and your messenger [*apostolon*] and minister to my need" (Phil 2:25, RSV). He had expended great energy both on behalf of the work of Christ and of Paul himself, even coming near death due to "hazarding his life" in aiding Paul (Phil 2:30), apparently in conveying to him the love-gift from Philippi (Phil 4:18).

EPHAH (ē'f*à*)

1. A branch of the Midianites (Gen 25:4; I Chr 1:33), living in NW Arabia, rich in camels and dromedaries (Isa 60:6). They are called Ḫaiapâ in Assyrian inscriptions of Tiglath-pileser III.

2. A woman of the family of Caleb (I Chr 2:46).

3. A son of Jahdai, family of Caleb, of Judah (I Chr 2:47).

4. *See* Weights, Measures, and Coins.

EPHAI (ē'fī). Jer 40:8 mentions Ephai the Netophathite as the father of some of the captains of the forces who were left behind in Judah at the carrying away of the captives to Babylon. These captains were identified with Gedaliah, the governor of the scattered, poverty-stricken Jews at Mizpah. Concurrent with Gedaliah's assassination, they were also put to death by Ishmael, the son of Nethaniah (Jer 41:3).

EPHER (ē'fĕr)

1. The second son of Midian and a descendant of Abraham through his marriage to Keturah (Gen 25:4).

2. The third son of Ezrah of the tribe of Judah (I Chr 4:17, RSV).

3. One of the five heads of their fathers' houses in the half tribe of Manasseh who dwelt between Bashan and Mount Hermon (I Chr 5:24). He was regarded as a famous and mighty man of valor.

EPHES-DAMMIM (ē'fĕs-dăm'ĭm). The site of a Philistine encampment preparatory to the Philistine attack on the Israelites (I Sam 17:1). It is located between Shochoh and Azekah. Goliath went forth from the camp to challenge Israel to send out one warrior to represent them. It has been suggested that the name ("border of blood") was derived from the frequent sanguinary encounters between the Israelites and the Philistines. Another conflict between these two nations is recorded in I Chr 11:13, where the abbreviated form, Pas-dammim, is used. The land, when freshly plowed, has a deep red color and this may account for the name. *See* Pas-dammim.

EPHESIANS. *See* Ephesus.

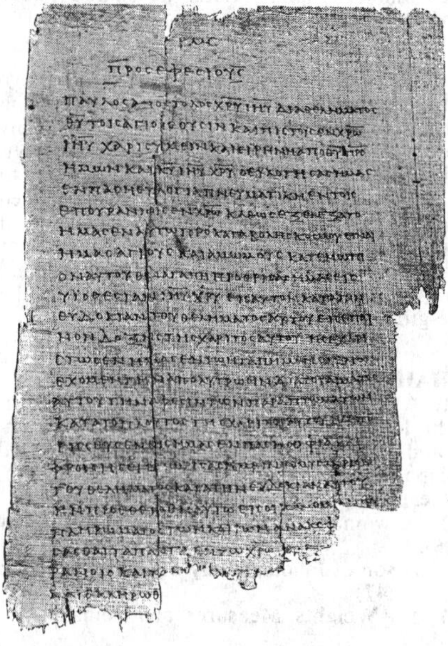

The first page of Ephesians from Beatty-Michigan papyrus. University of Michigan Library.

EPHESIANS, EPISTLE TO THE. The tenth book of the NT, classified along with Philippians, Colossians and Philemon as one of the Prison Epistles of Paul.

Authorship

Until the days of the 19th cen. higher criticism, Ephesians was universally held to be the work of Paul. Today, it is one of the four epistles which liberals in general deny as Pauline. (The others are I and II Timothy and Titus.) During the first three centuries it was ascribed to Paul by Marcion, Irenaeus, Clement of Alexandria, and Tertullian. Recent denial of Pauline authorship has, however, been based on internal evidence rather than external. Generally, four arguments are advanced in support of the critical position. (1) The vocabulary is said to contain 38 words not found elsewhere in the NT and 44 words not otherwise used by Paul. This argument fails to recognize the versatility of Paul and the influence of subject matter on vocabulary. (2) The style, it is noted, is smooth and deep-flowing, whereas Paul was a vigorous, rugged, controversial writer. Again, no room is left for Paul's versatility. Ephesians is, no doubt, an example of the apostle's style when he was not engaged in controversy, but, rather, in a more reflective type of writing. (3) Similarity to Colossians is taken to indicate that a later admirer of Paul used Colossians as his model in composing another letter in Paul's name. It is, however, much more natural to understand that Paul himself penned Ephesians shortly after Colossians, using with varying modification some of the terms and concepts employed in the letter to Colosse. (4) Doctrinal differences are interpreted as indicative of non-Pauline authorship. Careful analysis, however, reveals that the suggested differences are in no way inconsistent with Paul's teachings elsewhere. Allowance, again, must be made for the apostle's versatility. On the basis of the unanimous testimony of early church writers, and in light of the inconclusive nature of the critical arguments, it may be confidently asserted that Ephesians is the product of Paul's pen.

Recipients

Although the KJV contains the address, "to the saints which are at Ephesus," MS evidence and the general nature of the epistle have been taken to suggest that the letter was not confined to Ephesus alone. Two of the best MSS, the Vaticanus (*c.* A.D. 350) and the Sinaiticus (*c.* A.D. 375), as well as the Chester Beatty Papyrus P^{46} (*c.* A.D. 200), omit the words translated "at Ephesus." Furthermore, Basil the Great (A.D. 329–379) said that these words were not found in any ancient MSS. The impersonal nature of the epistle, and several passages which suggest that Paul was not personally acquainted with his readers (1:15; 3:2; 4:21), seem to call for a wider readership. There is, therefore, a reasonable possibility that Ephesians was originally a circular letter, perhaps sent to all the churches of the Roman province of Asia, of which the Ephesian church was the leading congregation. In time, because of the prominence of the latter church, the epistle may have come to be called by its name. The possibility that the letter was addressed to the church at Laodicea and is the so-called "lost" epistle to the Laodiceans ought to be carefully considered, particularly since there is considerable internal evidence to be found for its support.

An inscribed statue base along one of the main streets of Ephesus. HFV

Date and Place of Writing

The letter gives evidence of having been written during a prison experience (3:1; 4:1; 6:20). Although some, such as George S. Duncan in *St. Paul's Ephesian Ministry,* have argued for an Ephesian origin of the Prison Epistles, the traditional view of a Roman origin still commends itself to the majority of scholars. On this assumption, the epistle seems to have been written during Paul's first Roman imprisonment (cf. Acts 28:16-31), perhaps about A.D. 60-61. There is reason to believe that it was composed shortly after Colossians and sent along with that epistle and Philemon by the hand of Tychicus (Eph 6:21-22; Col 4:7-8).

Message of the Epistle

A key term in Ephesians is the word "mystery," the first occurrence of which is found in 1:9-10. Here Paul identifies the controlling theme of the epistle, namely, the design of God's overall plan. God purposes the ultimate union of all things in Christ, and the chief instrument which He is using during the present age to accomplish this goal is the Church. In this new community of redeemed people God has broken down the barrier between the Jew and the Gentile and united the two as one new man (2:14-15). This unification of two formerly opposing groups is but a token of the unity which is to be a reality among all who are members of the Body of Christ. In this new community of saints there are no legitimate barriers of nationality, race, color, or culture. The Church is one body in Jesus Christ, and as such it is, as Francis W. Beare asserts, the "harbinger of the ultimate unity of the whole creation" ("The Epistle to the Ephesians," IB, X, 606). From this first step in unification God will ultimately, according to His sovereign purpose, unite all things in Christ. This is the mystery of the grand design of God.

The unity of the Church is represented in Ephesians under three figures: the temple (2:19-22), the body (4:11-16), and the bride (5:21-33). Furthermore, in order that this unity may be more than theoretical, Paul insists that in its interpersonal relations the Church is to preserve "the unity of the Spirit in the bond of peace" (4:3).

Outline

I. Salutation, 1:1-2
II. Doxology, 1:3-14
    A. The choice of God the Father, 1:3-6
    B. The redemption wrought by Christ the Son, 1:7-12
    C. The sealing of God the Holy Spirit, 1:13-14
III. Thanksgiving and Prayer, 1:15-23
IV. Doctrinal Discussion, 2:1–3:21
    A. The redemption of Gentiles, 2:1-22
        1. Viewed personally, 2:1-10
        2. Viewed corporately, 2:11-22
    B. The ministry to Gentiles, 3:1-21
        1. Paul's commission, 3:1-13
        2. Paul's prayer, 3:14-21
V. Practical Discussion, 4:1–6:20
    A. Exhortation to unity, 4:1-16
    B. Exhortation to consistent living, 4:17–5:20
    C. Exhortations to various household groups, 5:21–6:9
        1. Wives and husbands, 5:21-33
        2. Children and parents, 6:1-4
        3. Slaves and masters, 6:5-9
    D. Exhortation to prepare for spiritual warfare, 6:10-20
VI. Conclusion, 6:21-24

Bibliography. F. F. Bruce, *The Epistle to the Ephesians,* Westwood, N.J.: Revell, 1961. Francis Foulkes, *The Epistle of Paul to the Ephesians,* TNTC. Charles Hodge, *A Commentary on the Epistle to the Ephesians,* Grand Rapids: Eerdmans, 1950. E. K. Simpson and F. F. Bruce, *Commentary on the Epistles to the Ephesians and the Colossians,* NICNT.

D. W. B

A view down one of the marble-paved streets of Ephesus, with the silted-in harbor visible in the distance between the first two columns on the right. HFV

EPHESUS (ĕf'ē-sŭs). The capital of the Roman province of Asia, located at the mouth of the Cayster River on the W coast of Asia Minor. Because of its fine harbor facilities and the roads which converged at that point, this city of more than 300,000 people became the most important commercial center of Roman Asia. It boasted numerous warehouses lining the banks of the river. Remains of an amphitheater can still be seen, measuring about 495 feet in diameter and capable of seating 25,000 people.

The origin of the city is hidden in legendary antiquity. However, about 1044 B.C. Gr. colonists under the leadership of Androclus drove out the previous inhabitants and established a Gr. city on the site. In 133 B.C. Ephesus, after a rather varied history, became a part of the Roman province of Asia.

The city was most widely known for its temple of Artemis (Diana, KJV), one of the seven wonders of the world. When the first temple was constructed is not known. The structure standing in Paul's day was begun about 350 B.C. It measured 340 by 100 feet, and its 100 columns stood more than 55 feet high. The goddess Artemis was originally an Anatolian fertility deity who had become partially Hellenized. In addition to its religious significance, the temple served both as a bank for the deposit and lending of money and as an asylum for fugitives. *See* Gods, False; Diana.

On his third missionary journey, Paul spent almost three years in Ephesus (Acts 19), no doubt because of its strategic position as a radiating center for the dissemination of the gospel. Timothy was later stationed there as an apostolic representative, giving assistance to local church leaders (I and II Timothy). Irenaeus and Eusebius indicate that the apostle John spent his last years in Ephesus, from which he wrote the five NT books ascribed to him.

See Archaeology.

Bibliography. E. M. Blaiklock, *Cities of the New Testament,* Westwood, N.J.: Revell, 1965, pp. 62–67. Floyd V. Filson, "Ephesus and the New Testament," BA, VIII (1945), 73–80. Merrill M. Parvis, "Archaeology and St. Paul's Journeys in Greek Lands," Part IV – Ephesus, BA, VIII (1945), 61–73. Howard F. Vos, WHG, pp. 357–365. Alfons Wotschitzky, "Ephesus: Past, Present and Future of an Ancient Metropolis," *Archaeology,* XIV (1961), 205–212.

D. W. B.

EPHLAL (ĕf'lăl). A descendant of Judah through Pharez, Hezron, and Jerahmeel (I Chr 2:37).

EPHOD

1. Father of Hanniel, a Manassite leader who helped direct the distribution of W Jordanian Canaan among the occupying tribes (Num 34:23).

2. A sleeveless shoulder vestment worn by the high priest over other garments (Ex 28:28–29; 35:27; 39:2–21; Lev 8:7). *See* Dress. In color it was gold, blue, purple and scarlet and was part of the ceremonial dress to which the oracle pouch containing the Urim and Thummim was attached.

In 19th cen. B.C. Assyrian texts from Cappadocia, the Semitic word *epādum* appears, and *'epādu* in Ugaritic materials (see G. R. Driver, *Canaanite Myths and Legends,* pp. 102 f.). W. F. Albright interprets the term as a wrap-around plaid robe, fastened at the shoulder and leaving one arm free. He believes the priestly ephod was similar to the Gr. *ependytēs,* a closely fitting outer garment which was often completely covered with gold, silver and other rich decoration (*Yahweh and the Gods of Canaan,* Garden City: Doubleday, 1968, pp. 200–203).

3. In I Sam 2:18 the boy Samuel and in II Sam 6:14 King David are described as being girded with a simple linen ephod, perhaps only a brief loincloth suitable for young children since Michal rebuked David for uncovering himself in public (II Sam 6:20). Thus it must have covered only the front of the body.

4. In several passages the meaning is obscure. The term ephod refers to an object used in obtaining oracles (I Sam 23:9–11; 30:7–8). In addition, in I Sam 14:18 the LXX reads: "Saul then said to Ahijah, 'Bring the ephod'; for it was he who carried the ephod in the presence of Israel" (JerusB), where "ephod" replaces the Heb. for "the ark of God" in the MT. I Sam 14:3 states that Ahijah was carrying (Heb. *nōśē'*, not "wearing") an ephod. In I Sam 2:28 Eli is reminded that the tribe of Levi was chosen, among other duties, "to carry the ephod" (JerusB; Heb. *lāśē'th,* from *nāśā'*). As Saul ordered Ahijah, so David on two occasions asked Abiathar to bring the ephod to him (I Sam 23:9; 30:7). Thus it was portable, yet large enough to hide Goliath's sword placed behind it (I Sam 21:9) in the sanctuary at Nob.

Gideon had made an ephod from the golden rings taken from the vanquished Midianites for his own city of Ophrah; it became the object of idolatrous worship for "all Israel" (Jud 8:26–27). Micah had such a cult object in his sanctuary (Jud 17:5; 18:14–20) along with teraphim and other images for the purpose of divination. Thus it may be concluded that this type of ephod was an oracular cultic instrument from which an answer could be obtained by means of inserting one's hand (I Sam 14:19). See Anthony Phillips, "David's Linen Ephod," VT, XIX (1969), 485–487.

R. O. C. and J. R.

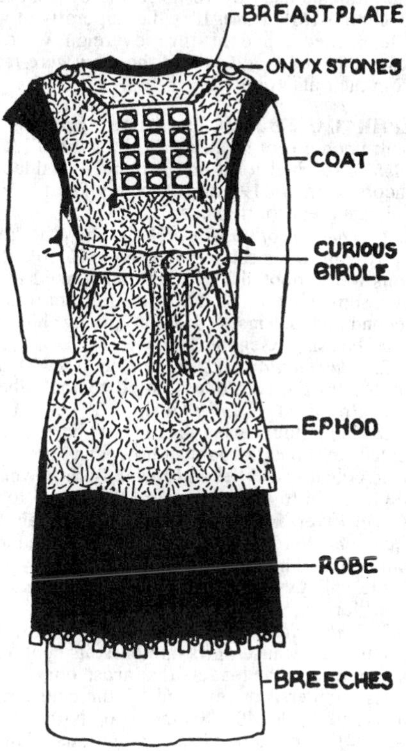

Priest in Ephod

The great theater mentioned in Acts 19, capable of holding twenty-five thousand. HFV

EPHPHATHA (ĕf'ȧ-thȧ). A transliteration of the Aramaic used by Jesus to the deaf-mute in Decapolis (Mk 7:34). It is the imperative form, "Be opened"; and at the sovereign word of Jesus the mouth and ears of the man were freed from their affliction.

EPHRAIM (ē'frā-ĭm). The name "Ephraim" is built upon a root meaning "to be fruitful" (Gen 41:52). Its dual form and prophecies added by Jacob (Gen 48:19) and Moses (Deut 33:17) indicate great fruitfulness.

1. *The son of Joseph.* The name was given by Joseph to his second son (Gen 46:20). Both sons were adopted by Jacob and ranked as his own sons (Gen 48:5). Though Ephraim was the second, Jacob insisted upon giving him the chief blessing (Gen 48:20).

2. *The territory.* Ephraim's name was also applied to the territory allotted to the tribe in the Promised Land (Josh 16; cf. I Chr 7:28-29). Boundaries have not been determined exactly. Roughly, however, they ran from Gilgal to Bethel and lower Beth-horon, W to Gezer, N to Lod, W toward the sea, N to tne Kanah River, E through Tappuah, Janobah, and Taanathshiloh to Ataroth, then S to Nasrath and Gilgal. This territory was hill country with fertile valleys and better rainfall than was enjoyed farther S.

3. *The tribe.* The tribe of Ephraim was prominent because of its numbers, its centers of influence, and the leaders that arose out of it.

Its numbers are revealed by the census lists in Num 1:33 (40,500) and in Num 26:37 (32,500). They fulfilled the predictions of Jacob and Moses.

Its centers at one time or another included: (1) Shechem, between Mount Ebal and Mount Gerizim, near the plot of ground willed by Jacob to Joseph and on which Joseph's bones were buried (Josh 24:32), near which the blessings and curses of the law were proclaimed from the lower slopes of the mountains (Josh 8:33-34); (2) Shiloh, where the ark was kept until the days of Eli (I Sam 1:3); (3) Bethel, the city on its southern border which became the more important of the two shrine centers established by Jeroboam I (I Kgs 12:26-33; Amos 7:10-13).

The Valley of Lebanon, north of Shiloh in the region of Mount Ephraim. JR

Its outstanding leaders included: (1) Joshua, the son of Nun, commander against the Amalekites at Rephidim (Ex 17:13), Moses' aid in the tent of meeting at Sinai (Ex 33:11), one of the 12 who spied out the Promised Land and one of the two who gave a good report (Num 14:6), successor of Moses as leader of all Israel, and who directed both the conquest and division of the land W of Jordan (Josh 14:1); (2) Samuel, the last of the judges, the seer to whom all Israel looked for the word of God, and the leader who prepared the way for the kingdom (I Sam 12:6-25); (3) Jeroboam, the son of Nebat, the first king over the ten tribes that rebelled against the house of David (I Kgs 12:19-20).

4. *The kingdom.* The name Ephraim was often used in the latter days for the northern kingdom (cf. II Chr 25:7; Hos 5:3; 6:10; 10:6; Isa 7:2; Jer 7:15). The calf worship set up by Jeroboam, the son of Nebat, led to moral corruption that ended in destruction and captivity, as prophesied by Amos, Hosea, Micah, and Isaiah. The prophets, however, predicted the restoration of a tiny remnant in the kingdom of the Messiah (Hos 14:8; Isa 11:13; Jer 31:7-9, 20; Ezk 37:16-23; 48:5; Zech 10:7).

J. W. W.

EPHRAIM, CITY OF. Jn 11:54 depicts Jesus leaving Judea and departing into the region near the wilderness to a town called Ephraim, because of the threat of violence by the priests after Lazarus' resurrection. The site may be modern et-Taiyibeh, situated on a conspicuous conical hill commanding a view over the valley of the Jordan and the Dead Sea. It is about five miles NE of Bethel and about 15 miles from Jerusalem. It has been identified with Ophrah (*q.v.*) of Josh 18:23 and I Sam 13:17, and also with Ephrain (Ephron, RSV), the city captured by Abijah from Jeroboam (II Chr 13:19). However, the Ephraim referred to in II Sam 13:23, to which Absalom invited all his family for the festivities relative to the sheepshearing, may be the same as the Mount Ephron of Josh 15:9; it is near Kirjath-jearim which is also called Baalah, corresponding to the Baal-hazor of II Sam 13:23.

C. M. H.

EPHRAIM GATE. *See* Jerusalem: Gates and Towers 6.

EPHRAIM, MOUNT OF. A comparison of Josh 17:15; 19:50; 20:7; 21:21; Jud 2:9; 3:27; I Sam 1:1 reveals the collective usage of the term; i.e., not any one single mount is set forth in every instance, but the reference is to the hill country or highlands which characterized the whole

The Shepherds' Fields with Bethlehem in the distance. HFV

territory of the tribe of Ephraim. This term applies to the greater part of the central ridge of Palestine on the W side of the Jordan, from N of Shechem S to Bethel.

EPHRAIM, WOOD OF. According to II Sam 18:6, the conflict between the forces of David and Absalom took place in this rugged tract which was overgrown with trees and shrubs. The context locates the area on the E of the Jordan River in the vicinity of Mahanaim. Since the territory of Ephraim lay W of the Jordan, the origin of the name of this thicket is unknown. Perhaps the name Wood of Ephraim resulted from the defeat of the Ephraimites at the hands of Jephthah and the Gileadites (Jud 12:1, 4–5); or the name may have been given at a later date, after the battle was over, as a reminder of Ephraim's folly. Another conjecture is that some Ephraimites were dissatisfied with their portion and made a colony in the area of Manasseh (Josh 17:14–18). The exact reason for this designation remains uncertain, however.

C. M. H.

EPHRAIMITE (ē'frā-mīt). In Josh 16:10; Jud 12:4, 5, 6, Ephraimite is used to denote anyone from the tribe of Ephraim (*q.v.*).

EPHRAIN (ē'frā-ĭn). One of the cities of Israel which Abijah took during his conflict with Jeroboam (II Chr 13:19; in RSV, Ephron, *q.v.*). It is conjectured that this is the same place referred to as Ephraim in the experience of Jesus recorded in Jn 11:54. *See* Ophrah; Ephraim, City of.

EPHRATAH (ĕf'rá-tá), or **EPHRATH** (ĕf'răth)

1. Ephrath is the ancient name of Bethlehem (Gen 35:16, 19; 48:7). Ruth 4:11 and Mic 5:2 seem to imply that Ephratah was a district in which Bethlehem was situated. Although the spelling differs they refer to the same area. Ps 132:6 mentions David's discovery of the ark after he heard of its being in Ephratah. The question is, what is meant by this use of the term? Does it mean the location in the area of Bethlehem, or can it mean some other? Some conjecture that it here means Kirjath-jearim, referred to as Ephratah. Since Kirjath-jearim was on the northern border of Judah, the term may also refer poetically to the tribal territories to the N of Judah. These are sometimes mentioned collectively by the name of their strongest tribe, Ephraim, whose nickname was Ephratah (meaning "fertility"; cf. Gen 49:22) as suggested by the usage of the term Ephrathite in I Sam 1:1; Jud 12:5 (Heb.); I Kgs 11:26.

2. The second wife of Caleb (I Chr 2:19, 50).

C. M. H.

EPHRATHITE (ĕf'rá-thīt). An inhabitant of Ephratah or Bethlehem (I Sam 17:12; Ruth 1:2). Elkanah, a Levite dwelling in the area of Ephraim, is called an Ephrathite (I Sam 1:1). Jeroboam is identified as an Ephrathite (I Kgs 11:26). The Ephraimites who sought to escape from Jephthah (Jud 12:5) were called Ephrathites (literal Heb.). *See* Ephratah.

EPHRON (ē'frŏn)

1. Son of Zohar, a headman among the sons of Heth who dwelt in an enclave at Mamre or

Hebron. He owned the cave of Machpelah (*q.v.*) which Abraham desired after Sarah's death for a family tomb (Gen 23:8-18). The elaborate purchase transaction between Abraham and Ephron, who required Abraham to buy also his land and its trees and thus pay all future dues on the property, parallels specific features and legal terms found in 2nd mil. B.C. Hittite laws and an Akkad. text from Ugarit (see K. A. Kitchen, *Ancient Orient and OT*, pp. 154 ff.). The price of 400 shekels of silver was exorbitant, for a hired laborer or craftsman earned only 1/30 shekel a day, or eight to 12 shekels a year (Code of Hammurabi, #273-277; ANET, p. 177). Yet in order to bury Sarah Abraham agreed to the price and terms without further argument. For the name Ephron cf. Apran in the Alalakh tablets. The "sons of Heth" may stem from proto-Hittites or Hattians migrating from Anatolia in the 3rd mil. B.C. *See* Hittites.

2. A mountain or hilly district between Nephtoah and Kirjath-jearim, on the border of Judah and Benjamin (Josh 15:9), probably in the forested region between Jerusalem and Beth-shemesh.

3. A town near Bethel which Abijah of Judah captured from Jeroboam I (II Chr 13:19, RSV, on the basis of the written MT, a Cairo Geniza fragment, LXX, and Vulg). The MT pointing or vocalization indicates *'eprayin*, KJV Ephrain (*q.v.*). It is probably the same as Ophrah (*q.v.*), a town of Benjamin (Josh 18:23), likely to be identified with the village of et-Taiyibeh, four and a half miles NE of Bethel.

J. R.

EPICUREANS (ĕp'ĭ-kū-rē'ănz). These were philosophers at Athens who confronted Paul along with the Stoics (*q.v.*; Acts 17:18). They followed the teachings of Epicurus (341-270 B.C.), an Athenian citizen though born on the island of Samos near Ephesus. Paul's familiarity with the philosophy is evident. Menander, writer and friend of Epicurus, is apparently quoted by Paul in I Cor 15:33 f. The Epicureans taught that the supreme good is pleasure or happiness (Gr. *hēdonē*); but it is the pleasure of the mind and the entire life, not the indulgence of momentary whims and instincts. Consequences of all actions should be considered before indulging in the activity. Epicurus was not a sensualist as is often charged. He denied providence, miracles, prophecy, and immortality, though modern writers claim he was not an atheist (cf. N. W. DeWitt, *Epicurus and His Philosophy*). Epicurus repudiated astrology and taught that religion was superstition; that to be happy one must be delivered from the fear of the gods. He developed an elaborate "atomic" theory. Lucretius (98-54 B.C.) was one of the best known interpreters of Epicureanism.

R. L. J.

EPILEPSY. *See* Diseases.

EPISTLE. In general usage the term epistle refers to written correspondence whether private or public. This broad use would include OT letters, although they are never specifically called epistles (II Sam 11:14-15; I Kgs 21:8-11; Ezr 4:11-22; Jer 29:1-29).

In the NT the Gr. *epistolē* occurs 24 times and is the designation of 21 of the NT writings. Of these, 13 are from the pen of Paul and seven or eight, depending on whether Hebrews is included or not, are traditionally classified as general or catholic epistles. The 13 letters of Paul are usually divided into four groups: eschatological (I and II Thessalonians), soteriological (Romans, I and II Corinthians, Galatians), prison (Ephesians, Philippians, Colossians, Philemon), and pastoral (I and II Timothy, Titus). The non-Pauline epistles have been called catholic because they were supposedly general in their destination. This, however, is not an accurate designation in the case of Hebrews and II and III John, which were sent to specific persons or groups.

In general, the NT epistles follow the standard form for an ancient letter as can be seen by study of the extensive papyrus correspondence which has been preserved. The usual epistolary order was: name of writer and recipients, greeting, prayer or wish for the readers' well-being, body of the letter, and closing greetings.

Some, following the lead of A. Deissmann, have made a distinction between letters and epistles. The former are said to be personal, non-literary pieces not intended for permanent use, whereas the latter are impersonal, literary pieces written for a more general readership and with the intention of permanency. Others have rightly insisted that this distinction is too sophisticated and oversimplified. Most of the NT epistles combine elements of both the letter and the epistle as distinguished by Deissmann. The NT correspondence was, for the most part, written in response to letters or personal word concerning problems or need which demanded authoritative treatment.

D. W. B.

EPISTLES, CATHOLIC. *See* Catholic Epistles; Epistles, General.

EPISTLES, GENERAL. Seven NT letters—James, I and II Peter, I, II, and III John, Jude—are so called because they do not contain specific addresses (notice the contrast with the Pauline epistles). The description "seven Catholic (*viz.*, indefinite and broadly addressed) epistles" was first given by the Church Father Eusebius (*Eccl. Hist.*, II, 23-25). However, even a cursory reading of the letters shows they are not all truly "general." I Peter was addressed to specific provinces in Asia Minor, III John was sent to one Gaius, and II John either to a local church or an individual.

Ready acceptance was not accorded these

letters in the early church. As late as the 4th cen. Eusebius stated that most of them were disputed, yet they were included in several important lists and manuscripts of the NT in the same century. Some of them, especially II Peter and James, have been contested in one way or another at various times until the present. (For details *see* Canon of Scripture, the NT.)

As far as major emphases are concerned, James and I Peter face the problem of suffering (see, e.g., Jas 1:2-4; 5:4-11; I Pet 1:6-7; 2:18-20; 3:14-17; 4:12-16). In fact, the words "suffer" or "suffering" appear at least 15 times in I Peter alone. The other letters reflect the rise of false teaching and how the early church opposed it (see II Pet 2:2-3; 3:1-7; I Jn 1:6-10; 2:22-23; 4:1-6; Jude 3-4).

See articles on the individual letters.

W. M. D.

EPISTLES, PASTORAL. *See* Pastoral Epistles.

EPISTLES, SPURIOUS. Among the apocryphal NT writings are a small number of epistles imitating those found in the NT canon but not ranking in importance with other types of apocryphal literature. The seven most important epistles are: the Epistle of the Apostles, Epistles of Christ and Abgarus, Epistle to the Laodiceans, Third Epistle to the Corinthians, Epistle of Lentulus, Epistles of Paul and Seneca, and the Apocryphal Epistle of Titus.

In the Epistle of the Apostles, 11 apostles (distinction is made between Peter and Cephas!) supposedly address "the churches of the east and west, of the north and south" and give a summary of the life and resurrection of Jesus. The work ends with an apocalypse from the risen Lord concerning the future.

The Epistles of Christ and Abgarus, found by Eusebius (*Ecclesiastical History,* I, 13), contains a letter addressed to Christ by Abgarus, king of Edessa, asking Him to come and heal the king and share his kingdom. Christ wrote and declined, but promised to send an apostle after His ascension. Thaddeus was sent, healed the king, and founded the Edessene church.

Both the Epistle to the Laodiceans and the Third Epistle to the Corinthians were suggested by references found in Paul's letters (Col 4:16; I Cor 5:9). Both had a rather wide circulation in the medieval period, though rejected by ancient scholars. The Laodicean epistle contains 20 verses copied from the genuine Pauline letters. This is not likely the same epistle mentioned in the Muratorian Fragment. The Apocryphal Epistle of Titus is a recent discovery.

The Epistle of Lentulus, written to the Roman Senate, gives a physical description of Jesus drawn from medieval paintings, although claiming to be from Lentulus, a Roman official in 1st cen. Judea.

The Epistles of Paul and Seneca are 14 short personal letters in which Paul and Seneca are represented as admiring each other, and Seneca extols Paul's inspiration.

F. P.

EPOCH. This is properly the starting point of an era or age, such as the first or second coming of Christ. However, the term is also used in a looser sense to signify an age or era which has been ushered in by a particular event and is characterized by that event. Thus we can speak of the epoch of the gospel, meaning the age of the dispensation of the gospel; and of the kingdom, signifying that of Christ's kingdom on the earth. *See* Time.

ER (ûr)

1. The firstborn son of Judah (Gen 38:7), whom the daughter of Shuah, a Canaanite, bore to him (vv. 3, 12; I Chr 2:3). Although Er was married to Tamar (Gen 38:6), he was childless, the Lord having slain him because of his wickedness (v. 7) in the land of Canaan (Gen 46:12; Num 26:19).

2. A descendant of Judah (I Chr 4:21), the namesake of his firstborn (cf. above).

3. The son of Jose and the father of Elmodam in the Lucan genealogy of Jesus (Lk 3:28-29).

ERA. An era is defined by Webster (2nd. ed. unabridged) as "a chronological order or system of notation computed from a given date as basis." There are no incontrovertible examples of such a concept in the OT, though some references border closely on it. The Exodus is used as the starting point for indicating the date of the building of Solomon's temple (I Kgs 6:1). The same very significant event is employed in connection with dating the death of Aaron (Num 33:38). It would seem natural for the Israelites to have continued to make the Exodus—which marked the beginning of the Heb. nation—the basis for their dating. Instead, they later followed the prevailing custom of the times in dating events by a certain year of a king's reign. This method was followed through the kingdom period, as both Kings and Chronicles testify.

Apparently the first era used by the Jews was the Seleucid era, which was widely observed in Syria. It dated from 312 B.C., when Seleucus Nicator took Babylon. The first distinctively Jewish era was that of the Maccabees, dating from Nov. 24, 166 B.C., the beginning of the Maccabean uprising against the Seleucids.

The Christian era supposedly dates from the birth of Christ. But that event took place at least as early as 4 B.C. Instead of B.C., Jewish writers use B.C.E.—before the common era (same as Christian era). The official Jewish era begins with the supposed date of creation, set at 3760 B.C. This has been used by the Jews since the 15th cen. A.D.

See Calendar.

R. E.

ERAN (ĭr'ăn), **ERANITES** (ĭr'*ȧ*-nīts). The son of Ephraim's oldest son, Shuthelah (Num 26:36). He was the father or head of the family called the Eranites.

Inscription found at Corinth mentioning Erastus. JR

ERASTUS (ĭ-răs'tŭs). A name used three times in the NT of a friend or friends of Paul. The Erastus of Rom 16:23 was a chamberlain or treasurer of the city of Corinth who sent his greetings to the Christians at Rome. He appears to be the same as mentioned much later in II Tim 4:20 as remaining in Corinth. It is hard to say if the Erastus sent by Paul from Ephesus into Macedonia is the same man (Acts 19:22). He is mentioned as one who specifically ministered to Paul, and may have followed him from Corinth to Ephesus in order to help him there. A Latin inscription carved into a stone paving block near the theater at Corinth states that for receiving the position of *aedile* (treasurer) Erastus laid this pavement at his own expense. Scholars generally agree that he is Erastus of Rom 16:23.

ERECH (ē'rĕk; Akkad. Uruk; Arab. Warka). The city of Nimrod in the land of Shinar (Gen 10:10). Situated on the Euphrates a little less than halfway between Babylon and the Persian Gulf, it was considered to be the home of Gilgamesh, the hero of the Mesopotamian flood story. Excavations of its extensive ruins have shown that it was occupied continuously for nearly 4,000 years, and has yielded the oldest known examples of writing, from *c.* 3300 B.C. (cf. BW, pp. 605-6).

Ezr 4:9-10 (see RSV) states that Asnapper (*q.v.*), the Assyrian Ashurbanipal, deported citizens (Archevites, *q.v.*) from Erech to Samaria.

ERI (ĭr'ī), **ERITES** (ĭr'īts). The fifth of the seven sons of Gad (Gen 46:16). Eri was the father or head of the family called the Erites (Num 26:16).

ESAIAS (ē-zā'yăs). NT (Gr.) form of Isaiah (*q.v.*).

ESARHADDON (ĕ'sȧr-hăd'ŏn). An Assyrian king, son and successor of Sennacherib (II Kgs 19:37; Isa 37:38); he reigned 681-669 B.C. Esarhaddon had to fight for his throne when his father was murdered. After his accession he began to rebuild Babylon, which his father had cruelly destroyed, as well as other cities and temples of Babylonia, probably because his mother was a Babylonian princess. His chief military efforts were directed toward subduing Egypt, which was continually stirring up rebellion in Palestine and Syria. His first expedition to Egypt in 675 B.C. met defeat, but on the second expedition his general occupied the whole Delta, conquered Memphis, and drove Pharaoh Taharqa (the biblical Tirhakah) up the Nile Valley. On his way to quell a revolt in Egypt in 669, Esarhaddon fell sick and died.

He was an extremely able ruler, waging successful wars against Syrian kings, the Cimmerians, and the Medes. To prevent trouble for his successor such as he had faced, he made his younger son Ashurbanipal crown prince, who then assumed an important share of the administrative duties. In 672 B.C. the high officials of Assyria had to take an oath to assure the succession of Ashurbanipal, who became king without any difficulty upon his father's death. In his inscriptions Esarhaddon claimed that Manasseh, king of Judah, paid tribute to him (ANET, p. 291). Since he ruled in Babylon as well as Assyria, the statement in II Chr 33:11 that Manasseh was carried captive to Babylon is not historically out of place. The Bible also speaks of Esarhaddon as one of the Assyrian kings who settled foreign colonists in Samaria (Ezr 4:2).

J. R.

Portal of the palace of Esarhaddon on Nebi Yunus at Nineveh. JR

ESAU (ē'sô). The son of Isaac and Rebekah, the elder twin brother of Jacob (Gen 25:24-26; 27:1, 32, 42; I Chr 1:34), is the traditional ancestor of the Edomites (cf. Gen 36; Mal 1:2-3).

The theory of the derivation of the word

"Esau" is connected with the hairy covering on his body at birth: "The first came forth red, all his body like a hairy mantle; so they named him Esau" (Gen 25:25, RSV; cf. also Gen 27:11).

These twins struggled (lit., "crushed one another") in the womb before birth (Gen 25:22). This was a prenatal foreshadowing of the relationship of Esau and Jacob in life as well as in their descendants (cf. Gen 25:23). This motif of the prenatal struggle of twins is also found in the traditions of other ancient peoples (IB, I, 665). At birth Jacob seized Esau's heel, indicating further the locked struggle of the future between these brothers and their posterities, the Israelites (the sons of Jacob) and the Edomites (the sons of Esau, cf. Deut 2:4).

Jacob revealed an eagerness from the first to gain advantage of his brother (cf. Hos 12:3). Esau was the firstborn, but Jacob would be his master. This prophecy is reiterated by other Jacob-Esau passages (Jer 49:8; Ob 6; Rom 9:10-13).

Jacob was the introvert and meditative type; but Esau was an extrovert and a man of the field who became a skillful hunter. He was the favorite of his father Isaac, while Jacob became the favorite of his mother Rebekah. Esau provided his father with his favorite meats from his hunting expeditions, but Esau's love for the chase became his downfall. One day as Esau returned, tired and hungry, Jacob was waiting for him with a steaming hot vessel of red pottage. As the aroma of this food hit Esau's nostrils he exclaimed, "Give me some of that red stuff," literally, "Pray let me swallow some of that red stuff—that red stuff there—for I am famished" (Gen 25:30). Since his lack of self-control was a weakness from birth, Esau must have this food and at once to satisfy his appetite! He paid a dear price in hastily agreeing to the demands of Jacob to surrender his birthright (Gen 25:30-34). Esau's sale of his birthright to Jacob is paralleled in the Nuzu tablets where one brother sells to another an inherited grove of fruit trees for only three sheep (Cyrus Gordon, BA, III [1940], 5).

The term birthright denotes the advantages and rights normally enjoyed by the eldest son. These included natural vigor of body and character (Gen 49:3; Deut 21:17), a position of honor at the head of the family (Gen 27:29), and a double share of the inheritance (Deut 21:15-17). When applied to tribes or nations, it conveys the idea of political and material superiority. This impulsive act stripped Esau of the headship of the people through which the redemptive purpose of God would flow. Also he forfeited the secular advantage of the firstborn son's share in the father's temporal goods.

With his birthright gone, Esau was still eligible to receive from Isaac the blessing of the oldest son if cunning, shrewd Rebekah had not risen to the occasion (Gen 27:1-10). Jacob accepted his mother's scheme, being assured by her that this was the appropriate and opportune thing to do (Gen 27:13). So with the bowl of savory food (lit., "that which is hunted") and his hairy mantle of disguise, he went to blind Isaac and requested the final blessing. Isaac's suspicions were aroused by the quick return and by Jacob's voice; but he was lulled by the hairy touch. Strengthened by the meal, Isaac's soul poured out all of its dynamic force in this one last prophetic act. The word "soul" (*nephesh*) here means the totality of one's power. The OT frequently alludes to the peculiar efficacy of the utterance of a dying man of God (Gen 48:10-20; 49:1-28; 50:24; Deut 33; Josh 23; II Sam 23:1-7; I Kgs 2:1-4; II Kgs 13:14-19). As a prophecy it approximated the divine word which carried within itself the power of its own fulfillment (cf. Isa 55:11; Jer 23:29).

Oral blessings or deathbed wills were recognized as valid in Nuzu as well as in patriarchal society (Gordon, *op. cit.*, p. 8). On the heel of the successful deception and the stolen covenant blessing, Esau returned from the field and served his father his favorite bowl of venison. As Isaac sadly related the theft, the loss suddenly dawned on Esau. He blamed Jacob altogether for his plight (Gen 27:34, 36), not recognizing that his earlier irreligious act of selling his birthright had become a fixed part of his character and he was unable to repent (Heb 12:16-17, RSV). So Esau received a blessing, but he was not to share in the fertile land of Palestine. "Behold, away from the fatness of the earth shall your dwelling be, and away from the dew of heaven on high" (Gen 27:39, RSV).

Esau at 40 years of age had married two Hittite wives which greatly distressed his parents. Isaac was gullible when Rebekah shrewdly used this parental heartbreak in her plan to send Jacob to Mesopotamia. Esau perceived that by marrying a non-Canaanite woman he would please his parents, so he married a relative of Ishmael (Gen 28:6, 9) in "the land of Seir." Since the land of Seir was a good environment for one who lived by the bow, Esau made it his permanent home.

Esau was living there when Jacob returned from Mesopotamia years later. As Jacob neared Palestine he dreaded to face his wronged brother and laid minute plans to allay Esau's anger. Also he earnestly petitioned God to soften Esau's attitude (Gen 32:3-21; 33:1-3). Esau, leading his 400 armed men, graciously embraced his guilty brother and received him without malice or recrimination (Gen 33:4-16). Although Esau cordially welcomed his brother, Jacob was dubious of Easu's complete forgiveness. With doubt in his mind, Jacob managed through deceit to travel a separate way toward Bethel, stopping long at Succoth and Shechem, while Esau returned to Seir (Gen 33:12-18).

In early life Esau lived shortsightedly as a youth of selfishness and impetuosity; but as a mature person he later exhibited generosity and forgiveness toward Jacob. Esau met his brother again about 20 years later at the death and burial of their father (Gen 35:29). Knowledge of Esau's latter years is nil.

If the old animosity was buried at the last meeting of the twin brothers, it was soon resurrected and handed down from generation to generation by their descendants. The history of their descendants is one of continuous fratricidal struggle. Israel's foes rose and fell like waves, but the Edomites were always their enemies. These two peoples scorned and hated each other with a relentlessness that finds no analogy between kindred and neighbor nations anywhere in history. From *c.* 1000 B.C. under King David to *c.* 120 B.C. under the Hasmoneans, Israel was at war with Edom. Between these two dates, prophet after prophet cried for vengeance upon Edom's heartless conduct. *See* Edom; Edomites; Idumaea.

Bibliography. Herbert Lockyer, *All the Men of the Bible,* Grand Rapids: Zondervan, 1958, pp. 113 f. A. Pieters, *Notes on Genesis,* London: Methuen & Co., 1913, pp. 245 ff., 255-263, 291-302, 312-321.

D. W. D.

ESCHATOLOGY. The term eschatology (Gr. *eschatos,* "last"; *logos,* "discourse"), meaning "the theology of last things," has been used since the 19th cen. to designate the division of systematic theology dealing with all that was prophetically future at the time it was written, i.e., prophecy now fulfilled, as well as unfulfilled prophecy. Important subjects of prophecy include predictions concerning Jesus Christ in both His first and second advents, Israel, the Gentiles, Satan, Christendom, the saints of all ages, the future Great Tribulation, the intermediate state, the resurrection of the dead, the millennial kingdom, the final judgments, and the eternal state. These themes may be classified as the divine revelation of the fourfold program of God for (1) Israel, (2) for the Gentiles, (3) for the Church, and (4) for Satan and the fallen angels.

Principles of interpretation. The concept of biblical prediction of future events depends upon the basic interpretive principles adopted. From the standpoint of historic orthodoxy, a detailed system of eschatology is impossible without assuming the authority and accuracy of the Scriptures. Radical liberalism has denied the possibility of the prediction of the future and has treated such Scripture as is seemingly prophetic as unauthoritative and merely expressing human hope or at best divine purpose already fulfilled. Moderate liberalism, represented by A. Schweitzer, recognizes that the NT taught the immediate end of the age, but holds that prophecy is not literally fulfilled and is only a vehicle to teach the general concept of future divine salvation and final judgment. Another deviation from historical orthodoxy is the view of C. H. Dodd who popularized "realized eschatology," the teaching that eschatology is principally divine purpose as fulfilled in the life of Christ rather than a detailed prediction of events. Karl Barth, the representative neo-orthodox scholar, considered prophecy as anticipating a consummation but as being incapable of giving clear particulars. These varieties of interpretation depend on the premise that the Scriptures are fallible records of the past and incapable of accurate predictions of the future.

Within orthodoxy which accepts the inerrancy of prophecy, two principal schools of thought exist that are distinguished by the extent to which they interpret prophecy literally. The oldest view interprets prophecy with the same degree of literalness as other Scripture. A later view uses a dual form of interpretation. Though following the literal and grammatical interpretation of Scripture as a whole, it interprets prophecy in a nonliteral way. The application of these two principles has led to a threefold division of orthodox eschatology. The oldest and most literal form of eschatology is the chiliastic or premillennial interpretation, which holds that Christ will reign on earth for 1,000 years after His second coming. The nonliteral type of interpretation of prophecy made popular by Augustine has led to the amillennial form of eschatology, which first became prominent with Origen in the 3rd cen. This view interprets the kingdom of God as a reign of Christ in the hearts of believers between the first and second advents, and hence denies an earthly millennial reign following the second advent.

Postmillennialism is a later derivative of amillennialism, often credited to Daniel Whitby (1638-1726), an English Unitarian. This theory, now held by only a few, interprets the millennial reign of Christ more literally than amillennialism and regards it as the last 1,000 years of the period between the first and second comings of Christ. Though often confused with amillennialism, it may be distinguished as more optimistic and to some extent more literal in its interpretation. The view gets its name from the teaching that Christ will return at the end of the earthly Millennium or utopia to judge all mankind. The most important interpretative question in eschatology, apart from belief in the authority of Scripture, is the use of the principle of literal interpretation. The most determinative doctrine is whether there will be a literal reign of Christ on earth after the second advent.

Prophecies concerning Jesus Christ. Messianic prophecy is the most important subject of the OT, as the fulfillment of it is the most prominent theme of the NT. Christ was to be born in fulfillment of the promise of a Saviour (Gen 3:15), of the line of Abraham (Gen 12:1-3), Judah (Gen 49:10), and David (II Sam 7:12-13); to be born in Bethlehem (Mic 5:2; Lk 2:4-7) of a virgin (Isa 7:14; Mt 1:23). Christ was to be a prophet (Deut 18:15), the divine Son of God (Isa 9:6-7), a priest (Ps 110:4), and a king (Zech 9:9). He was to die a shameful death on the cross for the sin of the whole world (Ps 22; Isa 53), only to be raised from the dead (Ps 16:10) and glorified (Dan 7:14). In His historic birth, life, death, and resurrection, many prophecies were fulfilled, and the promise was left to His disciples that He would return to establish His kingdom on earth (Mt 24:3, 27–31; 25:31–46; Acts 1:6–7, 10–11; Rev 1:7; 19:11–16). *See* Christ, Coming of; Jesus Christ.

Prophecies concerning Israel. First announced to Abram (Gen 12:1–3), God's program for Israel, the descendants of Jacob, predicted their continuance as a nation forever (Gen 17:7; Jer 30:11; 31:35–37), and their ultimate and permanent possession of the Promised Land (Gen 12:7; 13:14–15; 17:8). Israel was warned of several dispersions from the land and promised final regathering (Gen 15:13–14; Deut 28:63–67; 30:1–3; Jer 23:2–8; Ezk 39:25–28; Amos 9:14–15). The broad outline of their prophetic program is given in Dan 9:24–27. Premillenarians expect literal fulfillment of these prophecies; amillenarians find a nonliteral fulfillment in the church today.

Prophecies concerning Gentiles. The OT abounds in prophecies relating to Gentiles, beginning with the predictions concerning Noah and his posterity (Gen 9:25–27). Many later prophecies concern the nations surrounding Israel. Of major importance, however, is the revelation given through Daniel (Dan 2, 7, 8, 11) concerning four empires: Babylon, Medo-Persia, Greece, and Rome, covering the period called by Christ "the times of the Gentiles" (Lk 21:24), i.e., the period during which Jerusalem will be under Gentile domination beginning 605 B.C. and ending at the second coming of Christ. Many premillenarians believe the latter part of the fourth empire refers to a time yet future, just preceding the second advent.

Prophecies concerning the Church. The divine program for the present age, announced by Christ (Mt 16:18), is the outcalling of a body of saints composed of both Jews and Gentiles (Eph 2:11–16; 3:6) to form the Church (*q.v.*). Related to Christ in various figures such as the vine and the branches (Jn 15), the body (Eph 1:22–23), and the bride (II Cor 11:2; Eph 5:23–32), the Church will be completed at the rapture or catching up of the Church to heaven (Jn 14:3; I Cor 15:51–52; I Thess 4:13–17).

Pretribulationists consider the rapture will take place approximately seven years before the second advent proper (Dan 9:27); posttribulationists regard it as a phase of the second advent. The living members of the Church will be translated, i.e., given heavenly bodies at the rapture, when the dead in Christ will be raised (I Cor 15:51–52; I Thess 4:14-17). Rewards will be given to the Church after the rapture (I Cor 3:11–15; II Cor 5:10–11), and the Church will be with the Lord forever (I Thess 4:17). Amillenarians regard the rapture and resurrection as occurring at the second advent and as including all men, to be followed by the eternal state, in which the saved will be blessed and the unsaved will be punished. *See* Church; Rapture.

The intermediate state. Orthodox theologians hold that upon death all men go to the intermediate state, of torment for the unsaved and bliss for the saved, awaiting future resurrection and judgment (Lk 16:19–31; 23:39–43; II Cor 5:8; Phil 1:23; Rev 6:9–11; 7:9–17). *See* Dead, The; Death.

The millennial kingdom. According to the premillennial view, Christ will reign in person on earth for 1,000 years after His second advent. Satan will be bound and rendered inoperative (Rev 20:1–3). The period will be a golden age in which righteousness and peace will abound, war will be banned, and prosperity in the spiritual, economic, and political realms will be worldwide (Ps 72; Isa 2:2–4; 11:2–12; 65:17–66:24; Jer 23:2–8; 31:1–14, 31–34; 33:14–18; Amos 9:11–15). At the end of the Millennium, Satan will again be loosed, gain a large following, which will be destroyed by a judgment of fire from heaven (Rev 20:7–10). Amillenarians regard these prophecies as being fulfilled in the present age. *See* Kingdom of God; Millennium.

The final judgments. According to Scripture, all men will be judged (II Tim 4:1; Heb 9:27). Amillenarians regard this as a single event related to the second advent. Premillenarians view the final judgments as a series of events, beginning with the judgment of the righteous before the Millennium, and ending with the judgment of the wicked and Satan at the end of the Millennium (I Cor 3:11–16; II Cor 5:10; Rev 20:4–6, 9–15). The final destiny of the wicked is the lake of fire. *See* Gehenna; Hell.

The eternal state. Described in Rev 21–22, the locale of the eternal state is in a new heaven and a new earth in which is situated the New Jerusalem. The heavenly city is pictured as a place of great beauty, lavishly built of precious stones, the dwelling place of God as well as of the saints of all ages. *See* Eternal Life; Eternal State and Death; Heaven.

Taken as a whole, eschatology is the capstone of divine revelation, the grand culmination of the entire program of God for the ages and the principal reason for the creation of the material world. In it the eternal purposes of God for mankind will be realized with great blessing to all the saints.

Bibliography. Oswald T. Allis, *Prophecy and the Church,* Philadelphia: Presbyterian and Reformed, 1945 (amil.). Louis Berkhof, *The Kingdom of God,* Grand Rapids: Eerdmans, 1951 (amil.). Loraine Boettner, *The Millennium,* Philadelphia: Presbyterian and Reformed, 1958 (postmil.). John Bright, *The Kingdom of God,* Nashville: Abingdon, 1953 (neoorthodox). Herman A. Hoyt, *The End Times,* Chicago: Moody Press, 1969 (premil.). Alva J. McClain,

The fertile valley of Eshcol where the twelve spies picked grapes. HFV

The Greatness of the Kingdom, Chicago: Moody, 1959 (premil). René Pache, *The Future Life,* Chicago: Moody, 1962 (premil.); *The Return of Jesus Christ,* Chicago: Moody, 1955 (premil.). J. Barton Payne, *The Imminent Appearing of Christ,* Grand Rapids: Eerdmans, 1962 (posttrib.). Charles C. Ryrie, *The Basis of the Premillennial Faith,* New York: Loizeaux, 1953; *Dispensationalism Today,* Chicago: Moody, 1965. Wilbur M. Smith, *The Biblical Doctrine of Heaven,* Chicago: Moody, 1968. John F. Walvoord, *The Church in Prophecy,* Grand Rapids: Zondervan, 1964; *Israel in Prophecy,* Grand Rapids: Zondervan, 1962; *The Millennial Kingdom,* Findlay: Dunham, 1959; *The Nations in Prophecy,* Grand Rapids: Zondervan, 1967; *The Rapture Question,* Findlay: Dunham, 1957.

J. F. W.

ESDRAELON (ĕz-drā'lŏn). The Gr. name derived from Jezreel for the W portion of the valley of Jezreel (*q.v.*), including the valley of Megiddo (*q.v.*) or Armageddon (*q.v.*). *See* Palestine, II. B. 2. b.

ESEK (ē'sĕk). A flowing well dug under the direction of Isaac in the valley of Gerar near Rehoboth, over which the herdsmen of Gerar contended (Gen 26:20). Isaac gave it the name Esek because of the strife over it. The exact site is unknown.

ESHBAAL (ĕsh'bāl). The fourth son of Saul in the genealogical record of the tribe of Benjamin (I Chr 8:33; 9:39). In comparing this record with that found in II Sam 2:8, it appears that Eshbaal and Ishbosheth were the same person. Saul and three of his sons were killed in battle (I Sam 31:2). Only Eshbaal was left alive to assume the throne of his father. Because of later reluctance to pronounce the name "Baal," the uncomplimentary nickname Ishbosheth, "man of shame," was substituted. *See* Ishbosheth.

ESHBAN (ĕsh'băn). The second of four sons born to Dishon of the lineage of Seir the Horite, of the land of Edom (Gen 36:26; I Chr 1:41).

ESHCOL (ĕsh'kŏl)

1. A relative of Mamre and Aner, who formed an alliance with Abraham in Hebron, and joined his campaign in the rescue of Lot (cf. Gen 14:13–24).

2. A valley N of Hebron where the 12 spies sent out by Moses plucked huge clusters of grapes, symbolic of the fruitfulness of the land (cf. Num 13:23–24; 32:9; Deut 1:24). The vineyards in this wadi are still noted for their grapes.

ESHEAN (ĕsh'ĭ-*ȧ*n). A better spelling is Eshan (RSV). One of nine cities including Hebron in the hill country of Judah, grouped together in Joshua's division of the inheritance, according to Josh 15:52.

ESHEK (ē'shĕk). A Benjamite, brother of Azel, descended from Jonathan; he had three sons (I Chr 8:39).

ESHKALONITES (ĕsh'k*ȧ*-lŏ-nīts). In Josh 13:3 (KJV), the inhabitants of the Philistine city of Ashkelon (*q.v.*).

ESHTAOL (ĕsh'tā̆-ŏl), **ESHTAOLITES** (ĕsh't*ȧ*-līts). One of the 14 cities occupying the foothills or Shephelah of Judah (Josh 15:33). Josh 19:41 names Eshtaol and Zorah as part of the inheritance of Dan. The fact that both Judah and Dan had claims at Eshtaol may have been one of the contributing factors in the Danites' feeling crowded and their seeking for more space (Jud 18:2). Between Eshtaol and Zorah at Mahaneh-Dan the Spirit of God first stirred Samson to move against the Philistines (Jud 13:25, RSV). On the death of Samson (Jud 16:31), his brethren and kinsmen took his body and buried it between Zorah and Eshtaol in the burying place of his father.

Probably two or three centuries prior to Samson's day the Danites decided to expand (Jud 18:2). They sent five men of valor from Zorah and Eshtaol to spy out land in northern Canaan. Returning to Zorah and Eshtaol (Jud 18:8) they reported that the people lived securely and the land was large and good. In the light of their report, the people of Zorah and Eshtaol sent 600 men of war (Jud 18:11) to secure the land. Ancient Eshtaol may have been on the site of modern Eshua, about 13 miles W of Jerusalem.

C. M. H.

ESHTEMOA (ĕsh-tē̆-mō'*ȧ*), **ESHTEMOH** (ĕsh'tē̆-mō)

1. Son of Ishbah, Eshtemoa was a descendant of Caleb (I Chr 4:17).

2. A Maachathite, the son of Hodiah (I Chr 4:19).

3. The spelling Eshtemoh is found only in Josh 15:50. A city approximately eight miles S of Hebron, it is listed as one of a cluster of cities which occupied the hill country of Judah. Later, in distributing cities and their suburbs for occupation by the Levites (Josh 21:14), Eshtemoa was included. Thus, it became a Levitical city and a city of refuge in the territory of Judah. A family of Levites known as Kohathites became residents of Eshtemoa (I Chr 6:57). During his exile from Saul's court, David sent some of the spoil he had recaptured from the Amalekites to a number of towns in Judah including Eshtemoa (I Sam 30:28). The name of the present site is es-Semû'a.

C. M. H.

ESHTON (ĕsh'tŏn). A son of Mehir and the father of three sons, Beth-rapha, Paseah, and Tehinnah (I Chr 4:11-12), descendants of Judah.

ESLI (ĕs'lī). Esli is listed as the son of Nagge (Naggai, RSV) and the father of Naum (Nahum, RSV) in Jesus' genealogy, the eleventh generation before Jesus (Lk 3:25).

ESPOUSAL. Espousal, meaning "betrothal" or "engagement," was regarded almost as binding as marriage itself (Deut 20:7; 22:23, 25, 27-28; Hos 2:19-20; Lk 1:27; 2:5). This explains Joseph's concern over Mary and setting her aside (Mt 1:18-19). The betrothed man was sometimes called a husband (Deut 22:23; Mt 1:19) and the girl a wife (Gen 29:21; Deut 22:23-24; Mt 1:20). While the Bible does not legislate, except in Deut 22, about a broken betrothal, the code of Hammurabi did. It required that should the future husband break the engagement, the bride's father could keep the gift to the bride, and should the father of the bride renege, he would repay double the gift received. *See* Dowry. A man could declare his intentions and effect an engagement by spreading the skirt of his cloak over his beloved (Ruth 3:9; cf. Deut 22:30; 27:20; Ezk 16:8).

Figuratively, in the OT Israel is regarded as having been espoused or betrothed to Yahweh in the wilderness (Jer 2:2; cf. Ezk 16:8), but who through idolatry later became the adulterous wife of Yahweh (Hos 2:2, 16-23), now disowned but finally to be restored. In the NT the Church is called the espoused bride of Christ (II Cor 11:2; Eph 5:25-32; Rev 19:6-8).

R. A. K.

ESROM (ĕz'rŏm). This is the Gr. spelling of the OT name Hezron (*q.v.*). He is found in the genealogy of Jesus (Mt 1:3 and Lk 3:33).

ESSENCE, DIVINE. Our word "essential" comes from the word "essence." Both words are derived from the Latin *esse* which in English means "to be." The "essence" of a thing is that quality or characteristic which makes it to be what it is. For instance, the essence of a biped is that it has two feet, even as the essence of a quadruped requires an animal with four feet.

By divine essence is meant those characteristics God possesses which cause Him to be who He is. God is spirit, holiness, love, perfection. God possesses omniscience, omnipresence, and omnipotence. He does not depend for His existence on any other being; He is independent. He never changes in His character; He is immutable. He is not subject to the time process of the physical universe; He is eternal.

The revelation of the divine essence comes through God's actions. His revelation of Himself in Christ is the most authentic manifestation of His characteristics, attributes, and powers. "Divine essence" is but a generalized term for anything and everything that makes God to be uniquely Himself.

The word "essence" belongs to philosophy and theology rather than to the Scriptures. Theologians have argued as to whether man can really know the essence of God or only His attributes. Actually, to know God at all is to know Him through His actions. The actions of God reveal His character and powers. We can know God through what He has done and continues to do. God did not want us to know Him as an essence, a philosophical abstraction; but He revealed Himself, His divine essence, to us through Jesus Christ (Jn 14:9-11).

T. W. B.

ESSENES. For Judaism in the Roman period there were two alternatives to the issue of devout religious commitment: "party" life of the Pharisees and "sect" life of the Essenes. A party consists of people who join forces and efforts to make an impact upon society through reform. The purpose of the Pharisaic party was to restore sound life to Israel by being a good influence, and it accomplished its ends through careful organization, education and discipline. A sect, however, judges that society is beyond reform and sectarians withdraw in order to prepare for the judgment of God which must fall on a degenerate people. In the sectarian life of the Essenes, the cleavage between "the elect" and those outside the sect was emphasized by rites of initiation, acute discipline, and the claim that membership in the sect anticipates the messianic community.

Prior to the discovery and publication of the DSS material from Qumran, the Essenes had been known primarily through references made by Philo (*Quod omnis probus sit* xii-xiii (75-91), quoted by Eusebius (*Praeparatio Evangelium* viii. 12; *Hypothetica apud* Eusebius, *Praep. Evang.* viii.11) and Josephus (*Wars* ii. 8.2-3; *Ant.* xiii.5.9; xv.10.5; xviii.1.5). These authors agree that the Essenes kept aloof from normal society, living in communities which had a single treasury; that they practiced community of property and lived a diligent and frugal life under strict discipline. Both writers speak of the deep piety of the Essenes. Josephus describes their daily worship; their communal meal which was initiated and terminated with grace spoken by a priest; and the several stages of a three year probationary period, climaxed by stringent oaths which preceded the right of a candidate to touch the food of the community (*Wars* ii.8.5, 7). Little more was definitely known, however, for both Philo and Josephus expressed themselves in Hellenistic categories which invited a variety of conflicting interpretations.

The discovery of the remains of a sectarian library in 1947 near the NW shore of the Dead Sea and of the wilderness center at Khirbet Qumran from which they came, altered this situation. The majority of scholars involved with the study of the DSS believe the Essenes best fit the clues for the identity of the Qumran monks. Piecing together the archaeological and literary evidence which has accumulated, the Essenes emerge as a Jewish priestly sect which expressed itself in thoroughly Semitic categories, familiar from biblical and apocalyptic materials, whose history and organization, communal life and hopes, are now quite clear. Thus when Philo states that the Essenes reject all logical and natural philosophy except that which treats of God and creation, and that they are especially concerned with the ethical branch of philosophy, the Qumran texts clarify he is saying that the Essenes are interested only in biblical revelation and law.

The term "Essene" is probably a derivative from Aram. *'āsên, 'āsayyâ,* plural of *'āsê, 'āsyâ,* "healer"; or it may be the equivalent of Heb. *ḥasîdîm,* "pious ones." The *ḥasîdîm* are known from the Maccabean period and even before as those who were devoted to the law, and who chose death rather than violate their covenant with God (cf. I Macc 1:62 f.; 2:29–38, 42; 7:13–16; II Macc 14:6). From this group descended, apparently, both the Pharisees and the Essenes, each group developing along lines distinctive to itself, but claiming a common heritage. The name "Essene" was one given to the sect by outsiders, for it never occurs within the sectarian documents. The Qumran monks preferred to speak of themselves as "the Poor," "the Exiles," "the Sons of Light," or as "those who have entered into covenant," from which is derived the popular name for the group, "Covenanters."

The Essenes were a priestly movement. Although it is clear that both priests and laymen were to be found within the sect, priests dominated its councils and took precedence in its gatherings. The Manual of Discipline (1QS), by which the community was governed in the 1st cen. of this era, speaks often of "the priests and Levites" (e.g., 1QS i.18–24; ii.1–5, 11, 19–20),

Remains of the Qumran Community, Giovanni Trimboli

and more specifically of "the sons of Zadok the priests who keep the covenant" (1QS v.9; cf. ix.14; CD iii.21-iv.4). The Damascus Document (CD) speaks of "the sons of Zadok" as "the chosen of Israel, the men named with a name who shall stand at the end of the days" (CD iv.3-4). From this, and related evidence, it can be concluded that the Essenes were a priestly sect of the Zadokite line from which the high priests of Israel were to be anointed, but which was displaced by other lines in the priestly intrigues that preceded and accompanied the Maccabean revolt, *c.* 175-141 B.C.

The founder of the Essene movement is unknown by name, but is called in the documents "the Righteous Teacher," or perhaps "the Legitimate Teacher" (e.g., CD i.10-12). That he was a priest is now certain (4QpPs 37 ii.14-16; cf. 1QpHab ii.7-8), presumably of the legitimate but displaced Oniad-Zadokite line. Little is known of his life, but the texts indicate that he lived in a time of stress and was persecuted by a figure identified as "the Wicked Priest," who pursued him to his place of exile and violated the observance of the Day of Atonement among the Covenanters (1QpHab xi.4-16). The Righteous Teacher was primarily remembered by the Essenes as the man with revelatory insight, to whom God revealed the secrets of the prophets, and more specifically what would take place in the last generation (1QpHab viii.1-5; CD i.10-12).

The Damascus Document speaks of the Teacher having been "gathered in" (CD xx.1, 14), an expression used in the OT for natural death, but it remains uncertain how or when the Teacher died. The texts nowhere attach special significance to his death. The combined evidence of the texts and the coin sequence uncovered through excavation of the Essene center at Qumran suggests that it was toward the end of the troubled period, 175-141 B.C., that the Righteous Teacher led his faithful followers into exile where they could wait for God to vindicate them as His appointees to lead Israel in sacrifice and worship.

It was in 141 B.C. that the last of the Maccabean brothers, Simon of the priestly house of Hasmon, was confirmed as permanent ruling high priest by a nation grateful for the leadership the Hasmoneans had given to the successful revolt against Syria. The fact that the Hasmonean house was not of the legitimate Zadokite line was not considered a deterrent to this action. The decree confirming Simon in office expressly forbids any interference by laymen or priests, and prohibits the right of assembly without Simon's permission (I Macc 14:44-45). To the Essenes there was no course of redress but to wait for divine intervention. It is this series of events which best explains the character of the sect and reason for its founding by the Legitimate Teacher, whose activity is presented in the sectarian documents against a backdrop of apostasy on the part of Israel.

The men of the community are described as those who show fidelity to the Teacher (1QpHab viii.2-3), i.e., who have confidence in his teaching. The Manual of Discipline states that they retreated into the wilderness "to separate themselves from the abode of perverse men" (1QS viii.12-13), in keeping with the Levitical prescription for purity imposed upon priests.

The character of Essene communal life may be reconstructed from the texts as illumined by the results of several seasons of excavation at Qumran. The complex of buildings, which was clearly the center of a monastic community, contained a number of pools and cisterns, presumably where lustrations were practiced. The group ate at a common table according to prescriptions set forth in the Manual of Discipline (col. vi). They carried on an active literary work, copying biblical manuscripts and both familiar and previously unknown apocryphal and pseudepigraphic works. The discovery of long plastered benches thought to be writing desks, and inkwells, as well as practice ostraca for young scribes, indicates that the hundreds of manuscripts and fragments found in eleven of the nearby caves were placed there by members of the sect. Pottery found in the vicinity of the communal kilns is of the same type found in some of the caves containing the remains of the Essene library.

Essene occupation of the center is marked off by two major destructions. While the exact date for the founding of the center on the site of an old Israelitish fortress is uncertain, it was probably built during the reign of John Hyrcanus I (135-104 B.C.), to judge from the coin sequence. The first period of communal occupation was interrupted in Herodian times by the earthquake of 31 B.C., the ravages of which are still visible in the faulted steps leading into one of the cisterns. The center was abandoned and not resettled, to judge again by coins, until the early years of the ethnarch Archelaus (A.D. 6-14).

The wilderness sect lived out its remaining existence without interruption until the turbulent days of the First Revolt, when Vespasian's Tenth Legion destroyed the center in the summer of 68. The walls of this period are mined through, and in the ruins sealed with a layer of ash are iron arrowheads used by Roman legionnaires. Prior to the destruction the Essenes hid their library in nearby caves, with the result that the knowledge of the sect was not extinguished with the sect itself. While it would be erroneous to conceive of the Essenes as a sect restricted to the community in the desert at Qumran, the fact remains that we know of their life and practices only from this one center.

The Essenes clearly regarded themselves as the true Israel, constituting a remnant within apostate Israel. The promises to Israel they understood as being fulfilled in their own experience as a righteous congregation assuming a holy posture before God. Their writings reflect a strong election consciousness, and they eagerly anticipated "the day of vengeance" when God would vindicate His own elect (1QS i.11; ii.9; iv.12; v.12; ix.23). Essene perspective can be seen especially in their biblical commentaries, interpretations of portions of Scripture which are understood as coming into meaningful focus in the experiences of the community.

The fullest text which has been preserved is the Commentary on Habakkuk (1QpHab) containing 13 columns of fragmentary text. The interpretation of the first two chapters of Habakkuk, verse by verse, is controlled by the conviction that the prophecy has received its fulfillment in the life-situation of the community and its founder, the Righteous Teacher. This understanding was the work of the Teacher himself "to whom God has made known all the mysteries of the words of his servants the prophets" (1QpHab viii.1-5). It was he who made clear that the general time to which Habakkuk's prophecy looked forward was the extended period into which the Qumran Covenanters had entered.

Theirs was the last generation, and they keenly anticipated, to a degree higher than is elsewhere attested in the literature of the intertestamental period, the consummation. These expectations were made concrete in terms of "the coming of a Prophet and the Anointed Ones of Aaron and Israel" (1QS ix. 10-11), from whom deliverance and restoration to office would come. Here, and elsewhere (e.g., CD vi. 10; vii.21; xii.23; xiii.20; xiv.19; 1QSa ii.12-17), there is reference to an Anointed High Priest and an Anointed King who appear to be messianic figures. It is distinctive of Essene thought that the Anointed Priest takes precedence over the royal figure, a direct projection of the priestly character of the sect.

Although the Essenes are not mentioned in the NT, it is possible that some aspects of Jesus' teaching show alertness to Essene concepts. In Mt 5:43-44 Jesus refers to those who teach "You shall love your neighbor and hate your enemy." The command to hate one's enemy is not found in the OT or in the more familiar intertestamental literature, but it is found in the sectarian documents (1QS i.10; ii.21 f.; cf. x.19 f.). It is clear that Jesus' attitude toward many questions was contrary to the doctrine of the Essenes, and especially concerning the sabbath. While Jesus, as an argument for helping a man, could appeal to the common custom of assisting a sheep which had fallen into a pit on the sabbath (Mt 12:11 f.), the Essenes taught that neither an animal nor a man could be helped on the sabbath (CD xi.13-17). To the Essenes, devotion to the law meant the exaltation of biblical prescription over human life itself. *See* Dead Sea Scrolls.

Bibliography. Frank M. Cross, *The Ancient Library of Qumran and Modern Biblical Studies,* Garden City: Doubleday, 1958. A. Dupont-Sommer, *The Essene Writings from Qumran,* New York: Meridian, 1962 (the texts in translation). W. R. Farmer, "Essenes," IDB, II, 143-149. John L. McKenzie, "Qumran Scrolls," *Dictionary of the Bible,* Milwaukee: Bruce, 1965, pp. 710-716. Krister Stendahl, ed., *The Scrolls and the New Testament,* New York: Harper, 1957.

W. L. L.

ESTHER (ĕs'tẽr). A Jewish exile who lived in Persia during the reign of Ahasuerus (Xerxes, 486-465 B.C.). The name Esther was from Persian *stara,* "star," or from Ishtar, a Babylonian goddess. Her Heb. name was Hadassah, "myrtle." Esther was an orphan and was raised by her cousin Mordecai. Her beauty was the reason for her being numbered among the virgins brought to Ahasuerus for the selection of a queen to reign instead of Vashti. Esther was chosen and made queen and lived in the palace at Shushan (*q.v.*).

Esther is also noted for her bravery and her loyalty to her people. Risking her own life by having to reveal for the first time that she was Jewish, she made supplication to the king to sign a new decree to undo Haman's decree against the Jews.

Some accuse her of being heartless and vengeful in asking that the Jews might defend themselves and slay their attackers. However, careful study does not sustain these accusations. She exposed the evil plot of Haman and sought to save her people, but the royal decree obtained by her intercession was limited to self-defense (8:11). Notice that the Jews abstained from plunder (9:10, 16), and that no reprisals against women and children are mentioned. The only request that would reflect on Esther is for a second day of bloodshed and the display of the corpses of Haman's sons on the gallows (9:13). This may have been done to extend the right of self-defense to the Jews if necessary, and to prevent more bloodshed by showing that the leaders of the campaign against the Jews were dead, thus indicating the folly of further attacks.

R. B. D.

ESTHER, BOOK OF. In the Heb. Bible this book comes last in a group of five books bearing the title Megilloth, following Ruth, Song of Solomon, Ecclesiastes, and Lamentations.

Textual Considerations

Textual problems in this book are few. Esther is generally accepted as a unit. Only 9:20-32 and 10:1-3 are questioned. Eissfeldt considers 9:20 ff. as an addition explaining a change of date for Purim; but the fact that this passage does not change the date denies Eissfeldt's view. The summary nature of 9:20-32 accounts for any stylistic differences.

ESTHER, BOOK OF

Esther before Ahasuerus (Menescardi)). MM

Some dismiss 10:1-3 as annalistic and misplaced in an historical novel. However, its presence shows that the book of Esther is more than a novel. If 10:1-3 is obviously misplaced, no redactor would have included it in this fashion. Thus it may be concluded that the book of Esther in the Masoretic Text is in good textual condition and the work of one author.

Date

All evidence points to mid-5th cen. B.C. Est 10:2 indicates that it was written after the compilation of the annals of Ahasuerus (Xerxes, 486-465 B.C.). The author had an intimate acquaintance with the palace at Shushan (Susa), and this palace was burned within 30 years of the death of Ahasuerus (*q.v.*). Thus a date between 465 and the end of the reign of his successor, Artaxerxes I (464-424 B.C.), seems probable.

Author

The description of Mordecai in 10:3 precludes him as the author. The writer was probably an unknown Jew with personal knowledge of Shushan, the palace grounds and buildings, and Persian customs (see C. H. Gordon, *The World of the Old Testament,* Garden City: Doubleday. 1958, pp. 283 f., for the Iranian practice of *kitman* or dissimulation in Est 2:10; 8:17). He had access to Mordecai's writings, state annals, and royal decrees. Ezra or Nehemiah has been suggested as being the author, and the Heb. style compares closely with that of Ezra, Nehemiah, and Chronicles.

Outline of Contents

I. The Choice of a New Queen, Chaps. 1-2
  A. Vashti is deposed, 1:1-22
  B. Esther is made queen, 2:1-18
  C. Mordecai foils a plot against the king, 2:19-23
II. The Peril of the Jewish People, Chaps. 3-7
  A. Haman becomes furious at Mordecai, 3:1-5
  B. Haman plots to destroy the Jews, 3:6-15
  C. Mordecai persuades Esther to intervene, 4:1-17
  D. Esther invites the king and Haman to a banquet, 5:1-14
  E. The king makes Haman honor Mordecai publicly, 6:1-14
  F. Esther reveals Haman's plot to the king, 7:1-6
  G. Haman is hanged and Mordecai is promoted, 7:7-8:2
III. The Defense of the Jews, Chaps. 8-10
  A. A new edict is issued allowing the Jews to defend themselves, 8:3-17
  B. The Jews kill their enemies throughout the land, 9:1-16
  C. The Feast of Purim is inaugurated, 9:17-32
  D. Mordecai is advanced and is popular with his own race, 10:1-3

Historical Considerations

While Ahasuerus is commonly associated with Xerxes I (486-465 B.C.), in the LXX the name Ahasuerus was given throughout as Artaxerxes. The king in the book of Esther has therefore been identified by some scholars with Artaxerxes II (404-359 B.C.). The traditional identification seems correct for the following reasons:

Herodotus vii.8 relates that Xerxes called an assembly of princes in the third year of his reign to discuss a Grecian campaign. Est 1:3 refers to a princely gathering in that year. After the defeats of 480 and 479 B.C. Xerxes returned to Shushan several years later. Herodotus ix.108 states that he turned to private affairs. The book of Esther confirms this. Esther came to the harem in the sixth year (478 B.C.) and became queen (2:16) in the seventh (477 B.C.).

The book of Esther accurately describes the territory ruled by Ahasuerus (1:1, 3; 10:1). No other Persian ruler controlled the same domain.

Ahasuerus' character is correctly portrayed. He enjoyed the luxury and sensuality of court

A bull capital from one of the columns of the palace at Susa (biblical Shushan). LM

life and sometimes acted with brutality and cruelty. Thus Ahasuerus of the OT is characterized similarly to the Xerxes of Herodotus. Xerxes is known to have been capable of all attributed in the Bible to Ahasuerus. Although a law limited the Persian ruler to one wife, the palace ruins show that Darius and Xerxes had seraglios.

The author's accurate knowledge of the sections of the city and of details of the palace with its gorgeous furnishings (1:2, 5, 6; 2:11, 14; 3:15; 5:1; 6:4; 7:7-8) has been confirmed by French archaeologists. *See* Shushan.

A year's advance notice of the permission given to Haman by Xerxes to slaughter the Jews (Est 3:12-14) is historically understandable. It is in keeping with the value placed on lots among the Persians and with the psychological and military preparations necessary. If it be objected that so much notice would give the Jews opportunity to flee, it must be asked, where could they flee? There is no evidence of any mass migration of Jews during the 5th cen. B.C. to contradict Est 9:1-2 that they remained in their cities in the Persian Empire.

In recent years the historical accuracy of the story of Esther has been challenged on several counts. (1) Secular history knows nothing of a queen named Vashti or Esther in the reign of Xerxes, but rather his wife was Amestris, the daughter of a Persian general, according to Herodotus (vii.61). (2) Mordecai seems to be mentioned (Est 2:5-6) as having been carried away captive to Babylon (*c.* 597 B.C.) by Nebuchadnezzar. This would make him at least 122 years old when he was elevated to power in Xerxes' 12th year, while his young cousin Esther must have been at least 100 years younger. (3) The edict of Xerxes permitting the Jews to kill 75,000 of his subjects in one day (Est 9:16) seems improbable. These together with other problems of a more subjective nature form the main arguments against the historical accuracy.

In answer to these questions it may be noted that: (1) Herodotus omits many important people and events in his account. An outstanding example of this is his omission of Belshazzar (Dan 5), which recent archaeological discovery has verified. (2) The passage in Est 2:5-6 may be interpreted to mean that it was Mordecai's great-grandfather Kish who was taken captive by Nebuchadnezzar. A cuneiform inscription published by A. Ungnad in 1941 bears the name Marduk-ai-a (Mordecai), a Persian official and counselor in Susa during the reign of Xerxes. Late Babylonian inscriptions also reveal the frequent occurrence of the name Mordecai, indicating it was a common name of this period. *See* Mordecai. (3) The improbability of 75,000 Persians being slain in one day is not an impossibility. In the light of known Persian disregard for human life, especially when a member of the royal family was involved, and the thorough arming of the Jews throughout the province (Est 8:13; 9:5), "it is by no means incredible that the Jews could have encountered and overcome such a large number of foes" (SOTI, p. 405).

The vengeful slaughter of 75,000 has been condemned by some as immoral. It must be remembered, however, that Medo-Persian laws could not be repealed (cf. Dan 6:8, 12, 15, 17 with Est 1:19; 8:8). All Xerxes could do was to provide for the Jews' own self-defense. While the city of Susa rejoiced at the promotion of Mordecai, his rise could not abate *all* anti-Semitic feeling throughout the land (8:15-17). In an empire of 100 million, for perhaps three million Jews to kill 75,000 was not an excessive number. Government officials even helped the Jews (9:3). The latter also undoubtedly suffered some casualties, but the general OT custom of mentioning only the dead of the vanquished seems to be followed (see Keil, *The Books of Ezra, Nehemiah and Esther,* KD, pp. 307-310).

Lack of Mention of God

Acrostics notwithstanding, God is not mentioned in this book. In an atmosphere of hatred and opposition, it was not always expedient for the Jews to display their religion publicly. The Gentile populace resented the Jewish attitude toward idols, religion, foods, and mixed marriages. Thus without flaunting his religion, the author of this book conveys a spiritual emphasis.

Mordecai is shown to stand in the tradition of Shadrach, Meshach, and Abednego in refusing obeisance to Haman (Est 3:2 ff.). His refusal is understandable only on the basis of his strict adherence to the Decalogue. Fasting is a further indication of Jewish religious practice (4:16; 9:31). Est 9:31 speaks of the Jews' cry for help. Help from whom? Mordecai expresses his faith in God by telling Esther that if she fails, help will come from another source.

The outstanding religious motif is divine providence. The Jews learned under God's affliction what they would not learn under His forbearance. The author weaves the pattern of providence. Before Haman quarreled with Mordecai, Vashti's dismissal provided the occasion for Esther, a Jewess, to gain a position which enabled her to save her people. Mordecai had indebted himself to the king. Xerxes had a sleepless night at the right time and read in the right portion of the state records. All fits together. No Jew could have penned this without the intention of presenting the providence of God in the sparing of His people.

Bibliography. R. K. Harrison, *Introduction to the Old Testament,* Grand Rapids: Eerdmans, 1969, pp. 1085-1102. A. Macdonald, "Esther," NBC, pp. 380-386. L. B. Paton, "The Book of Esther," ICC, 1916. John C. Whitcomb, "Esther," WBC, pp. 447-457. J. Stafford Wright, "Esther, Book of," NBD, pp. 392 ff.; "The toricity of the Book of Esther," NPOT, pp. 37-47.

R. B. D.

ESTHER, FAST OF. *See* Festivals; Purim.

ETAM (ē'tăm)

1. One of five cities belonging to Simeon (I Chr 4:32). Two adjacent cities were Ain and Rimmon. Etam was located in the extreme southern part of Simeon, among the Negeb hills near Beer-sheba. Its exact site is unknown.

2. In II Chr 11:6 mention is made of a second site named Etam adjacent to Bethlehem and Tekoa, built by Rehoboam for defense in Judah. It was probably founded by a descendant of Hur of the tribe of Judah ("father of Etam," I Chr 4:3). The LXX includes Etam in a list of 11 towns in the hill country district of Bethlehem, not found in the Heb. MT in Josh 15:59-60. Josephus, in talking about the activity and splendor of Solomon, related: "There was a certain place, about fifty furlongs distant from Jerusalem, which is called Etham, very pleasant; it is in fine gardens, and abounding in rivulets of water; thither did he use to go out in the morning, sitting on high" (*Ant.* viii.7.3).

In the writings of the Talmud, 'Ain Etan is mentioned as being the most elevated place in Palestine, and from it ran an aqueduct to the temple. The site of Etan (Etam) is on an isolated hill a little to the E of 'Ain 'Atan, two miles SW of Bethlehem. According to Josephus (*Ant.* xviii.3.2), Pontius Pilate used temple funds to construct a 23 mile long aqueduct to Jerusalem, evidently from the three Hellenistic-Roman reservoirs now called Solomon's pools at Etam.

Pools of Solomon near Etam. JR

3. The rock of Etam (Jud 15:8, 11), where Samson stayed in a cave after smiting the Philistines, was also in Judah but lower in altitude ("he went down," v.8) in the Shephelah foothills. A cavern known as 'Araq Isma'in, two and one half miles SE of Zorah, suits the requirements of the story and affords an excellent view from its mouth high up on the N cliffs of the Wadi Isma'in.

C. M. H.

ETERNAL LIFE. A phrase appearing 30 times in the NT (KJV), of which 15 usages occur in the Gospel and epistles of John; and 43 times in the RSV, with 25 occurrences in the Johannine writings.

The word eternal (*aiōnios*) is derived from the word meaning "age," an indefinite period of time, hence, agelong, and consequently unending. Eternal life refers invariably to the life of God, or to the future state of the righteous (Mt 25:46). The Johannine writings define it in terms of knowing, making it synonymous with the experience of God (Jn 17:3). It cannot be earned by men, but is bestowed upon them as a gift in response to faith (Jn 3:15-16; I Jn 5:11; Rom 6:23), and becomes a perpetual source of power and refreshment (Jn 4:14). Eternal life is the vitality which God imparts to the human soul at the moment of personal conversion to Christ.

Eternal life is mediated through Christ (I Jn 5:11) and represents the totality of Christian experience in its vitality, in its duration, in its quality, and in its associations and content. It enables the believer to enter directly into the presence of God at death and enjoy the eternal bliss of heaven. Its opposite is eternal death, or severance from God (II Thess 1:9).

See Immortality; Life.

M. C. T.

ETERNAL SECURITY. *See* Assurance.

ETERNAL STATE AND DEATH

Death

Death is spoken of in three senses in the Bible.

1. *Spiritual death.* This is what occurred to Adam and Eve, and passed from them to the whole human race by imputation when they sinned and fell, even as God had warned (Gen 2:17; Rom 5:12). The continuance of man in a state of spiritual death is spoken of throughout the Bible (Rom 3:10-18; 5:12; I Cor 2:14; Eph 2:1, 5). This condition is abolished only by regeneration or what is called the new birth (Jn 3:3, 5 ff.; I Jn 5:1; cf. Eph 2:1, 5). *See* Born Again.

2. *Physical death.* This is the appointed portion of every man since the fall of Adam (Heb 9:27), except for those Christians who will be still alive at the rapture, at the second coming of Jesus Christ (I Cor 15:51-52; I Thess 4:14-17).

Some have endeavored to explain the prophecies of the return of Christ for His own, especially in I Thess 4:14-17, as Christ receiving the believer at death. This does violence, however, to the clear teaching of Scripture concerning Christ's returning visibly for His own as He promised (Jn 14:3, 6; Acts 1:11). Also it conflicts with those prophecies which foretell the snatching away and rapture of the Christian (Mt 24:36-41; I Cor 15:51-52; I Thess 4:14-17; cf. Christ's coming "as a thief" in Rev

16:15 with Mt 24:43; I Thess 5:2), and with the promise that the believer will not suffer God's terrible wrath against sin at the second coming (I Thess 5:9; II Thess 1:7-10; cf. Rev 3:10; chap. 16 and the vials of wrath).

3. *The second death.* This is the final, irreversible separation of the wicked from God and the righteous as they are cast into hell after the judgment of the Great White Throne (Rev 20:6, 14; 21:8; cf. 2:11).

Rev 20:6 states: "Blessed and holy is he that hath part in the first resurrection: on such the second death hath no power." According to this verse and v. 14, the second death comes after the thousand year reign of Christ on the earth (cf. Rev 5:10). *See* Dead, The; Death.

The Eternal State

Just when the believer will enter the eternal state is not certain. Some say immediately after the second coming of Christ. These teach that there will be one general judgment of all men at that time. Others say that Christ first establishes His visible kingdom on earth at His second coming and that the eternal state begins only after the Millennium. *See* New Heavens and New Earth; Millennium; Rapture. The premillennialist maintains that on the basis of an inductive study of the Scriptures the latter view, as explained in the articles referred to, best fits the teaching of the whole Bible.

1. *The nature of the eternal state.* This can be best understood by contrasting, first, the difference between the state of the believer today and in the Millennium; and then, the difference between the state of the saints who enter and enjoy the Millennium and of the saints in their eternal reign in the new heavens and the new earth.

The rulership of Christ and His kingdom, i.e., the kingdom of God, began in its hidden "mystery" form during the ministry of Christ on the earth (Mt 12:28; Lk 11:20; cf. parables of the kingdom in Mt 13). It has continued throughout the so-called Gospel Age. The kingdom will enter its second phase as Christ comes with His resurrected saints to rule in person over the whole earth at His second coming (Isa 66:15 ff.; Zech 14:5; Jude 14; Rev 20:4). At that time the resurrected saints will minister with Christ in resurrected bodies fashioned after the resurrected body of Christ (Phil 3:20-21; I Thess 4:14-17; Rev 20:4). They will have been freed from their fallen natures and the earth will have been freed from the curse (Isa 11:6-9; 65:25; Rom 8:18-23). Yet sin and death will continue for the people surviving on the earth at the beginning of the Millennium and for those who will be born during that time (Isa 65:20; Rev 20:7 f.). Peace will prevail, but will be maintained only by the strict rule of Christ, because man will still be sinful (Isa 65:20; Rev 2:27; 19:15; 20:7-10).

The final, eternal state begins with the creation of the new heavens and new earth (*q.v.*) "wherein dwelleth righteousness" (Rev 21:1; cf. II Pet 3:7-13). In it the wicked will be eternally separated from the righteous (Rev 21:27; 22:14-15), the former being finally consigned to the lake of fire and brimstone which is the second death (Rev 21:8).

The wicked will not be annihilated by the second death as judgment for their sins, any more than Christ was annihilated when He paid the penalty for our sins. The Beast and the False Prophet, cast into the lake of fire at Christ's return (Rev 19:20), do not suffer extinction of being, for they are still there in torment a thousand years later (Rev 20:10). The NT clearly teaches the endless duration of retribution (Mt 25:41, 46; II Thess 1:9; Jude 13; Rev 14:11; 19:3; 20:10). The nature of the punishment will include, in addition to whatever forms of physical suffering may continue, (1) exclusion from the immediate presence of God (II Thess 1:9) into outer darkness (Mt 25:30); (2) the gnawings of conscience and remorse (the undying worm, Mk 9:47-48; weeping and gnashing of teeth, Mt 25:30); and (3) probably the internal burning of the human spirit with no opportunity to express its sinful passions. *See* Gehenna; Hell.

2. *Blessings of the eternal state.* These include all the blessings enjoyed by the resurrected saints as they reign with Christ (see above), plus God's personal comfort as He wipes away all tears (Rev 21:4) and gives His own a specially prepared city, the New Jerusalem (Rev 21:9–22:5). In that city are the river of the water of life (Rev 22:1), the tree of life (Rev 22:2), and the very presence of God and His throne (Rev 22:3; cf. 21:22-23).

Certain questions arise concerning the final state of the believer. Will there not be sorrow over loved ones who died without Christ? Yes, but God will comfort us over such sorrows (Rev 21:4). Will there be time in heaven or will time cease? The meaning of the words "time shall be no more" in Rev 10:6 is not that time itself ceases but that the event being foretold is at hand. The idea that God is timeless or that eternity is static is not necessarily scriptural. Geerhardus Vos held that the eternal state will be progressive, opening up vista after vista, because hope, along with faith and love, will abide, and hope must have reference to a future even throughout eternity (Buswell, *Systematic Theology,* I, 46).

The philosopher Immanuel Kant saw God as timeless and spaceless, but only because he could not explain how the three infinites: God, time, and space, could all exist at one time. Kant therefore said that time and space are finite. However, this argument is fallacious since time and space are not created entities – as he supposed – but are merely relationships, for space between objects, and for time between events. It should be clear to all that more than one infinite can exist at one time. For example, God's infinite wisdom, power, holiness, etc., are not attributes of immensity and therefore do not conflict with infinite time and space. *See* Eternity; Time. Men are created beings, and thus are limited by time and space; but God is free from both time and space in the sense that His omnipresence overcomes the limiting effect of space, His omniscience that of time. *See* Eschatology; Eternity.

Bibliography. Rudolf Bultmann, "*Thanatos*, etc.," TDNT, III, 7–25. J. Oliver Buswell, Jr., *A Systematic Theology of the Christian Religion*, Grand Rapids: Zondervan, 1962, I, 29–54; II, 491–538. Harry Buis, *The Doctrine of Eternal Punishment*, Philadelphia: Presbyterian and Reformed, 1957. Herman A. Hoyt, *The End Times*, Chicago: Moody, 1969. C. S. Lewis, *The Great Divorce*, New York: Macmillan, 1946. S. D. F. Salmond, *The Christian Doctrine of Immortality*, 5th ed., Edinburgh: Clark, 1913. W. G. T. Shedd, *The Doctrine of Endless Punishment*, New York: Scribner, 1886. Henry B. Swete, *The Life of the World to Come*, New York: Macmillan, 1918.

R. A. K.

ETERNITY. In philosophic thought, both ancient and modern, eternity refers to something outside of or in contrast to time. In the biblical usage, however, the Heb. and Gr. terms for eternity always stand for time, either a specific era or a period of unknown and undivided quantity. The emphasis is on endlessness, indefinite duration.

The OT uses the Heb. word *'ôlām*; the NT employs the term *aiōn* (Herman Sasse, "*Aiōn*, etc.," TDNT, I, 197–209). These words may refer to exact periods as well as to undefined and incalculable duration. The eternity of God, for instance, means His continuous dominion over all time—past, present and future (Ps 10:16; 29:10; 90:1–2; 103:17–19; Isa 40:28; Jer 10:10–12). It must not be regarded as placing Him *outside* of time, as philosophy does. God effected our redemption at a specific moment in history. "When the fulness of the time came, God sent forth His Son" (Gal 4:4, NASB). Christ appeared to put away sins "at the climax of history" (Heb 9:26, NEB, lit., "at the consummation of the ages," His death viewed as the key event which completes or gives meaning to the ages), and He will appear a second time in history (Heb 9:28).

The Gr. NT frequently employs the plural *eis tous aiōnas*, "unto the ages," or *eis tous aiōnas tōn aiōnōn*, "unto the ages of the ages," to express the idea of eternity or forever (e.g., Rom 1:25; 9:5; 11:36; 16:27). The reference to God as the "King of ages" in I Tim 1:17 (RSV) really means the "eternal King."

See Aeon; Eternal State and Death; Time.

T. W. B.

ETHAM (ē'thăm). This proper name is given to both a place in Egypt and the wilderness on the E of the Red Sea. Ex 13:20 locates Etham between Succoth and the wilderness. Thus it must have been near the eastern end of the Wadi Tumilat and probably N of Lake Timsah. It was quite likely a border fortress, since the Heb. name *'ētām* is cognate to Arabic *othom*, "citadel," "stone fortification." Also *'ētām* may represent the Egyptian word *ḫtm* meaning "fortress." Nineteenth Dynasty papyrus letters mention fortresses in this area (ANET, p. 259).

Num 33:6–8 tells of the progress of Israel from Etham to Pi-hahiroth, whence they were led through the Red Sea. On the E side of it they went into the Sinai desert, which was known as the wilderness of Etham.

ETHAN (ē'thăn)

1. A son of Zerah, Judah's son by Tamar. He was the father of Azariah (I Chr 2:6, 8).

2. An Ezrahite of the tribe of Judah, known for his great wisdom (I Kgs 4:31) and mentioned in the title of Ps 89.

3. A Levite of the household of Merari (I Chr 6:44, 47; 15:17, 19) appointed as one of the temple singers by David. His name was apparently changed to Jeduthun after his appointment in the temple at Gibeon (I Chr 16:38–41).

4. A Levite of the household of Libni (I Chr 6:42–43; see also v. 20 and Num 26:58).

ETHANIM (ĕth'ă-nĭm; "perennial"). In I Kgs 8:2 the seventh month of the Jewish year is named Ethanim, which corresponds to Tishri of the later calendar. It was regarded as the month when only perennial streams were still flowing. It is mentioned in Phoenician inscriptions. At the time of the Exile, the name was replaced by the Babylonian name of Tishri. It corresponds to our September–October and is regarded as the beginning of the civil year for the Jews. *See* Calendar.

ETHBAAL (ĕth/baăl). The king of the Sidonians and the father of Jezebel, wife of King Ahab of Israel (I Kgs 16:31). Josephus further identifies him as the king of the Tyrians and Sidonians (*Ant.* viii.13.1). Menander the Ephesian referred to Ithobalus, the priest of Astarte, who reigned for 32 years as the king of Tyre after assassinating Pheles, the former king (Jos *Apion*, 1.18).

ETHER (ē'thẽr)

1. In the first division of the land a town was assigned to Judah by the name of Ether, together with Libnah and Ashan, in the foothills or Shephelah (Josh 15:42). This town may be located at Khirbet el-'Ater, four miles N of Lachish.

2. In the lot that was cast for Simeon (Josh 19:7), an Ether was assigned along with Ashan. While some geographers consider it identical with the Ether assigned to Judah, others identify it with Khirbet 'Attir, 15 miles NE of Beer-sheba.

ETHICS. *See* Example.

ETHIOPIA (ē-thĭ-ō'pĭ-*ȧ*), **ETHIOPIAN** (-*ȧn*). Cush (Heb. *kûsh,* borrowed from Egyptian *k3sh*) in most of its OT occurrences refers to the land variously known as Ethiopia, Nubia or the Sudan. It is located S of Egypt (therefore its frequent bracketing with Egypt; cf. Gen 10:6–8; I Chr 1:8–10; Ps 68:31; Isa 11:11; 20:3–5; 43:3; 45:14; Ezk 30:4, 9; Dan 11:43; Nah 3:9) and at times a part of the W Arabian peninsula (II Chr 21:16 and certain Assyrian inscriptions). The Al Amrān tribe of Arabia calls the region of Zebid in Yemen by the name Kūsh. Ezk 29:10; 30:6–9 (RSV) identifies its N border as Syene (modern 'Aswân, at the First Cataract of the Nile). Its S border was not clearly defined, but probably lay near Khartum at the junction of the Blue and the White Nile, a little upstream from the Sixth Cataract and a thousand miles S of Syene. Popular etymology defined the Gr. designation *Aithiopía* as the "Land of Scorched Faces" from *aíthein,* "to burn," and *ōps,* "countenance" (cf. Jer 13:23).

Nubia always attracted the attention of the Egyptian rulers because of its gold mines and the products of central Africa, such as ivory and ebony, which entered Egypt through Nubian traders (cf. Isa 45:14). The country was conquered by the strong kings of the Twelfth Egyptian Dynasty, lost during the Hyksos period, and reconquered by the Eighteenth Dynasty pharaohs. They penetrated as far S as the city of Napata at the Fourth Cataract and placed Kush under an Egyptian governor. The people of ancient Ethiopia—who were negroid, as appears from Egyptian art—adopted the Egyptian religion and culture so completely that the Egyptian way of life remained more conservative and lasted longer than in Egypt itself.

About 1000 B.C. Nubia regained its independence and established a kingdom with its capital at Napata. For an inscription telling of the nomination of an Ethiopian king of this period by the Egyptian god Amon-Re, see ANET, pp. 447 f. When Egypt became weak *c.* 750 B.C., the Nubians conquered Upper Egypt with its chief city of Thebes. About 725 Piankhi in a single campaign brought all the rest of Egypt under Nubian control except for a small portion in the Delta. Thus the Twenty-fifth Dynasty (715–663 B.C.) consisted of a series of Ethiopian rulers. The names of four of these have been preserved: Shabako, Shabataka. Taharka (the biblical Tirhakah, *q.v.*), and Tanutamun. These last two kings were driven back into Ethiopia by the Assyrian kings Esarhaddon and Ashurbanipal, who sacked Thebes in 663 B.C.

Nahum, who called Ethiopia the strength of Thebes (No-amon, 3:8–9), accurately reflects the Nubian control of that great city in Egypt. Toward the beginning of the Twenty-fifth Dynasty Isaiah delivered an oracle concerning the Cushites (chap. 18) and a prophecy (20:3–6) to warn Judah not to depend on Egypt and Ethiopia for help. Zephaniah (2:12) foretold Nubia's eventual doom, which was effected by the Persians (Est 1:1; ANET, p. 316). Meanwhile Ethiopian troops fought with Egypt in Jeremiah's day (46:9).

About 300 B.C. the royal residence of the Ethiopian rulers was transferred from Napata to Meroë at the Fifth Cataract. This kingdom, ruled by a succession of queens, each of whom carried the title Candace (*q.v.*; Acts 8:27), lasted until *c.* A.D. 355, and then gave way to the Abyssinian power of Aksum. During this period the population became predominantly Negro. The isolation of the Meroitic kingdom preserved its ancient Egyptian culture in stagnant form, as recent discoveries in the Nubian royal cemeteries at Meroë and Barkal indicate.

Other Ethiopians named in the OT are Zerah (*q.v.*, the leader of Egyptian mercenary forces, II Chr 14:9) and the slave Ebed-melech (Jer 38:7–12; 39:16). Joab sent a Cushite among his troops as one of his messengers to King David (II Sam 18:21–32, RSV). Ethiopian soldiers were frequently used as mercenaries in the Egyptian armies both before (II Chr 12:3) and after (Jer 46:9) their brief period of hegemony over Egypt. Persia later incorporated Ethiopia as the southwesternmost portion of its empire (Est 1:1; 8:9).

The hope expressed in Ps 68:31 that Ethiopia will stretch out her hands to God was realized in the conversion of the Ethiopian eunuch of Acts 8:26–39 who, according to tradition, became the first Christian evangelist to his people. *See* Ethiopian Eunuch.

Bibliography. Edward Ullendorff, *Ethiopia and the Bible,* New York: Oxford Univ. Press, 1968.

R. Y. and J. R.

ETHIOPIAN EUNUCH. Ethiopian tradition makes the man mentioned in Acts 8:26–40 the founder of Christianity in Ethiopia. Not identifiable from any reliable outside sources, he was possibly the state minister in charge of the treasury under Candace, queen of the Ethiopians. The designation "eunuch" is elsewhere translated "officer" or "chamberlain," and carries no special suggestion of mutilation. However, by usage the word had become synonymous with the Latin *castratus,* signifying one who had been emasculated. If physically a eunuch, the law of Deut 23:1 would have prohibited him from full communion in Judaism. He may have been a "proselyte of the gate." This is implied in his journey to Jerusalem to worship. *See* Candace; Ethiopia; Eunuch.

While traveling homeward, he was reading from the LXX, the Gr. translation of the OT. The place of his baptism, following his confession of faith in Christ, is believed to have been near Gaza.

I. R.

ETHIOPIAN WOMAN. The Cushite wife of Moses is so described in Num 12:1 (see RSV). Miriam and Aaron rebuked Moses for assuming authority beyond that which they possessed, and criticized his marriage to a person who was not of their national background, possibly lowering his prestige in the eyes of his contemporaries.

Two solutions are suggested for the problem of the Cushite woman. First, Zipporah, Moses' Midianitish wife (Ex 2:21), may have been called by this title. The name Cush has been applied to the territory stretching from Assyria on the E to Ethiopia on the W and S. The exploits of Nimrod, a descendant of Cush, in establishing Nineveh, are described in Gen 10:8-11. However, this term was never widely applied to this whole territory. Arabia may be recognized by the term Cush in I Chr 1:9, and by the related term Cushan in Hab 3:7. Thus, the term Ethiopian woman may reflect the fact that Zipporah came from a part of Arabia.

A second possible solution suggests that the term Ethiopian woman, as translated in KJV, applied to a second wife whom Moses married after the death of Zipporah. Neither event is stated in the Scriptures, however, and her background is not known. Josephus stated that Moses married a princess of Ethiopia after the battle of Saba (Meroë) and her delivering up of the city (*Ant.* ii.10.2). Another suggestion is that she may have been one of the mixed multitude who accompanied the children of Israel out of the land of Egypt (Num 11:4).

C. M. H.

ETHNAN (ĕth'năn). A son of Helah and member of the tribe of Judah (I Chr 4:7).

ETHNARCH (ĕth'närk). The Gr. term *ethnarchēs,* a governor of an ethnic group, occurs in II Cor 11:32, the "governor" of Damascus under the Nabataean king Aretas IV. "Ethnarch" was apparently a title of royalty granted to a dependent ruler, higher than "tetrarch" but lower than "king." Herod's son Archelaus was given the title of ethnarch of Judea (Jos *Ant.* xvii.11.4). After he was deposed in A.D. 6, "the government became an aristocracy, and the high priests were intrusted with a dominion over the nation" (*Ant.* xx.10). Thus Caiaphas had most of the powers of an ethnarch, and outranked the procurator Pilate in all matters not concerned with the safety of the state. That Caiaphas sent Jesus to Pilate for trial and sentencing suggests the nature of the crime attributed to our Lord. *See* Governor.

ETHNI (ĕth'nī). A Levite of the family of Gershom (I Chr 6:41). He was included in the genealogy of Asaph, one of the men set over the service of song in the house of the Lord after the ark had been restored by King David.

EUBULUS (ū-bū'lŭs). Paul listed Eubulus among the Christians who were active in the work at Rome by including a greeting to Timothy from him (II Tim 4:21). Since his was a Gr. name, it is assumed that he was a Gentile by birth. Nothing more is known about him.

EUCHARIST. *See* Lord's Supper.

EUNICE (ū-nĭs). The name, meaning "victorious," occurs but once in the Bible (II Tim 1:5). Eunice was Timothy's mother, and this gives her a measure of importance. She and her mother Lois are both described as women of genuine faith in the Lord, and they had apparently encouraged a similar faith in young Timothy. Eunice was a godly Jewess, married to a Greek. It is unlikely that she was a Christian believer before Paul's first visit to Derbe and Lystra, where she lived, but evidently she had taught Timothy the OT Scriptures thoroughly (II Tim 3:15), although he was not circumcised until Paul's second visit.

EUNUCH (ū'nŭk). The Heb. word translated "eunuch" (*sārîs*) also means "officer." Usually it indicates an officer for the women's quarters in a king's court. There were married eunuchs (Gen 39:1), but usually they were castrated (*q.v.*). Such men could be high officials as in the case of Potiphar or the Pharaoh's chief butler and baker (Gen 37:36; 40:1). Eunuchs (*sārîs*) served in the court of Ahab and Jezebel (I Kgs 22:9, ASV marg.), and the Persian king had one over his harem (Est 2:3, 14). The Heb. law excluded them from worship in the temple (Deut 23:1), but they were used by David in his court (I Chr 28:1, ASV marg.). Captives were often made eunuchs, although not always. Probably those used in the courts of Judah were foreigners. Isaiah advocated that those eunuchs who sought to keep the covenant should have their worship privileges restored (Isa 56:4 f.). Two Ethiopian eunuchs are mentioned specifically: Ebed-melech, who asked that Jeremiah be released from the well (Jer 38:7-13); and the pious man, an officer of Queen Candace, who was baptized after Philip explained the Scripture to him on the Gaza road (Acts 8:27-40). *See* Ethiopian Eunuch. To be "a eunuch for Christ's sake" probably meant to voluntarily give up marriage and family life to work for the kingdom (Mt 19:12).

A. W. W.

EUODIAS (ū-ō'dĭ-ăs). The KJV spelling, but it should properly be spelled Euodia (Phil 4:2, RSV). Euodia was a prominent woman in the church at Philippi who had a difference with another woman by the name of Syntyche. Paul exhorted them to settle their differences for the good of the church. What their difference was is not known. Some conjecture that it was a religious question rather than a personal quarrel. It is not known whether their positions in the church were official as deaconesses or if they were women in whose homes the church was accustomed to meet. However, the problem was so serious that it had been called to Paul's attention, and he sought even the intercession of a fellow worker in healing the breach of fellowship. An added incentive for this reconciliation was the memory of their former service with him in the work of the gospel.

C. M. H.

EUPHRATES (ū-frā'tēz). The largest river in western Asia. It has its source in central Armenia formed by the junction in Asia Minor of the Kara-su and Murad-su Rivers, from which it pursues a southeasterly course to the Persian Gulf. It is about 1,800 miles long. At Korna, about 100 miles from the gulf, it unites with the Tigris River. It is a very sluggish stream except in flood season and is not very deep until it combines with the Tigris, forming a delta which is composed of lakes and bays. The melting snow causes its rise about the middle of March, increasing gradually until June. The rise continues high for 30 to 40 days before it begins to fall. From the middle of September to the middle of October it is at its lowest.

The overflow of the Euphrates and the use of canals as in Egypt made possible bountiful crops that sustained a large population. Since the Mongolian and Mohammedan conquests, the land has been mostly unproductive, but now the Iraq government is restoring the canals and building dams.

Before its union with the Tigris it is navigable for only 1,200 miles by small boats. After its union, ocean-going vessels can go up as far as Basra. The Euphrates, with the Tigris, has carried silt to the Persian Gulf so that Ur, which some believe was just N of the gulf in Abraham's day, is now over 125 miles farther away.

Along or near its banks were such great cities in the historical past as Carchemish, Mari, Babylon, Ur, Erech, and Eridu. It is mentioned in the OT as "the river" (Deut 11:24), "the great river" (Gen 15:18; Deut 1:7; Josh 1:4), and twice in the NT (Rev 9:14; 16:12). It was the boundary of the Egyptian and Assyrian empires (II Kgs 24:7) and was prophesied to become the eastern boundary of the Heb. monarchy (Gen 15:18; cf. I Kgs 4:24).

E. L. C.

EUROCLYDON (û-rŏk'lĭ-dŏn). The term was commonly in use by sailors for an E or NE wind. It was a violent wind which frequently arose in the Cretan waters, swooping down from the mountains in strong gusts or squalls. The word is made up of two words, the Gr. *eyros,* meaning E wind, and a Latin word *aquilo,* meaning NE wind. Thus it seems to express a NE by E wind. It is still common that tempestuous winds from the E, S, and NE agitate the Mediterranean.

This was the tempestuous wind on the occasion of Paul's disastrous shipwreck (Acts 27:14). The ASV translates it Euraquilo.

An aerial view of the Euphrates. JR

EUTYCHUS (ū'tĭ-kŭs). The young disciple at Troas who sat in the open window of the third floor of a building where Paul was preaching. Falling asleep, Eutychus fell to the ground and was taken up dead. Paul extending himself upon the body restored him to life (Acts 20:5–12).

It has been disputed whether Eutychus was really dead or only in a swoon, and hence, whether a miracle was performed or not. Paul's words seem to indicate that the young man was not actually dead, but the words of Luke the physician are that he was "taken up dead." In Acts 14:19 Luke, referring to Paul's stoning, said the people, "supposing he had been dead," drew him out of the city. This is not the same phrase as in Acts 20:9 translated "taken up dead." The words in Acts 20:9 are too plain to justify modifying them to be read "taken up for dead," which the interpretation that he was not dead would require.

D. L. W.

EVANGELIST. One called to go about preaching the gospel, derived from the verb *euangelizō.* To evangelize is to bring good news to someone, specifically to announce information concerning Christian salvation (I Cor 15:1–4; *see* Gospel; Witness; Commission, Great).

The term is found three times in the NT. Evangelists are listed with apostles, prophets, pastors, and teachers as those called to share in building up the church (Eph 4:11 f.). Philip was called "the evangelist" (Acts 21:8). Although one of seven early chosen to relieve the apostles of the task of food distribution (Acts 6:5), he was especially noticed for his evangelistic activity. From Jerusalem he went to Samaria and preached with great success (Acts 8:4 ff.). From there he was sent to evangelize an officer of the Ethiopian court who was traveling home after visiting Jerusalem (Acts 8:26 ff.). He then preached the gospel from Azotus to Caesarea, where he had a home (Acts 8:40; 21:8).

Timothy, the young minister, was exhorted to do the work of an evangelist (II Tim 4:5) as an accompaniment of his pastoral oversight. It is clear that although apostles and others shared in the work of evangelizing, there were men whom God especially called for this task.

In later years the writers of the four Gospels were called evangelists because they recorded persuasively the foundations of the gospel of Christ.

N. B. B.

EVE (ēv; "life" or "life-giving"; exact meaning uncertain). Eve, the first woman, wife of Adam, and mother of Cain, Abel, Seth and other unnamed children, was made (lit., "built," Gen 2:22) by God from one of Adam's ribs. She was one with Adam yet subordinate to him and a helper for him (cf. I Tim 2:12; Gen 2:20).

The name Eve occurs only twice in the OT (Gen 3:20; 4:1), while the word "woman" is more commonly used. There is a biblical connection between the name Eve (from *ḥawwâ*, "to live") and her becoming the mother of the "living." Because Eve ate the forbidden fruit, she suffered certain judgments appropriate to her womanhood. (1) She and her seed were involved in the enmity between Satan and the redeemed. (2) Pain would accompany childbirth. (3) She would be subordinate to her husband.

In the Sumerian poem about the creation of deities at Dilmun (*see* Eden), the water-god Enki is dying from sickness in eight parts of his body. The goddess Ninhursag brings a cure for each member, including the rib, by giving birth to a special goddess. The one created for the healing of Enki's rib is called Nin-ti, "lady of the rib." But Sumerian *nin-ti* can also mean "the lady who makes live." Possibly this ancient literary play on words reflects in some way a common source with the Genesis account about Eve. (See Samuel N. Kramer, *History Begins at Sumer*, p. 146.) *See* Creation.

C. C. R.

EVEN, EVENING, EVENTIDE. *See* Time.

EVENING SACRIFICE. *See* Sacrifice.

EVERLASTING. *See* Eternity.

EVI (ē'vī). One of the five kings of Midian slain by the Israelites at the direction of Moses (Num 31:8). Josh 13:21 indicates that the land of Evi, along with that of the princes of Sihon and the other four chiefs of Midian, was given to the tribe of Reuben for an inheritance. It was on the E side of the Dead Sea.

EVIDENCE

1. The Heb. word *sēpher* means "writing," "letter," or "book." In Jer 32:10, 11, 12, 14, 16, 44 the prophet records the legal transaction involved in the purchase of a piece of property. Repeatedly he refers to the title deed or bill of sale which was drawn up, witnessed, and sealed in confirmation of the purchase of the field in Anathoth belonging to his uncle. Then he placed the documents in an earthen vessel for preservation against the time when property would again be bought and sold in the land of Judah.

2. The Gr. word *elegchos* is translated "evidence" in Heb 11:1. In this instance, the idea is conviction (RSV), a proof or the result of putting to the test and proving a thing, a sure persuasion in the heart. The RSV paraphrases the word "mouth" as "evidence" in the expression, "by the mouth of witnesses" (Mt 18:16; II Cor 13:1; Num 35:30; Deut 17:6; 19:15) and introduces the word "evidence" in I Tim 5:19.

C. M. H.

EVIL. Evil is the opposite of good (Gen 2:9, 17). As not good, it always proves harmful and causes loss and suffering.

Several kinds of evil can be differentiated: religious, moral, social, and natural. Religious or spiritual evil is the opposite of righteousness; it is sin (Ezk 20:43; 33:11–13; Mk 7:21–23). Such evil may be in the heart of man even without any act of transgression on his part (Gen 6:5; Mt 5:28). In Scripture words, thoughts, desires, conscience and heart may all be evil. The only antidote to such evil is the cleansing work of Christ.

Moral evil may depend on the customs of a culture, the specific taboos or prohibitions of a society or community. It may be punishable as a crime by civil authorities (Mt 27:23; Acts 23:9; Rom 13:4). It may be something that seems morally unfair, contrary to what one judges to be right (Eccl 2:18–21; 5:13–17; 6:1–2; 10:5–7, RSV). It may or may not be sin according to the Bible, since it may only be a *human* judgment of another's conduct.

Social evil can be seen in such problems as alcoholism, cheating in business, corruption in politics, inadequate opportunities for education, unemployment, poverty, racial discrimination, and war (Zech 7:9–10; 8:16–17). There are also varying degrees of moral and spiritual responsibility involved in these problems, both collectively and individually.

Natural evil or calamity concerns the havoc, loss and suffering caused by earthquakes, famine, fire, floods, disease. It is evil in this sense that God says He has created (Isa 45:7; Amos 3:6).

Not all evil is willed by man or is in his control. Evil in its larger meaning cannot be equated with sin (Eccl 12:1).

See Evil One; Iniquity; Sin (for bibliography); Wickedness.

T. W. B.

EVILDOER. In the Heb. the word is the participial form of a verb meaning "to break or to break into pieces." Hence an evildoer is one who breaks into pieces, destroys, makes evil whatever he does, acts wickedly, and afflicts others. Thus in Ps 26:5; 37:1, 9; Isa 1:4, and other passages, the writers are describing those who were offenders against God's law as well as those who were personal offenders against their fellowmen. *See* Malefactor.

EVIL-FAVOREDNESS. This term is found in Deut 17:1. It states the ritual unfitness of any animal that possessed a blemish of any kind. This included the lack of symmetry or a lean-fleshed condition of the animal as set forth in Deut 15:21. God required perfect animals in the sacrificial offerings. These two unwanted features, ill-favored and lean-fleshed, are combined in a description of the seven cows seen by Pharaoh in his dream (Gen 41:3; etc.).

EVIL-MERODACH (ē'vĭl–mĕr'ŏ-dăk). Akkadian *Amel-Marduk,* king of Babylon (562–560 B.C.), the son and successor of Nebuchadnezzar. Confirmation of his existence turned up during excavations at Susa (biblical Shushan). The Bible tells of Evil-merodach's releasing Jehoiachin, king of Judah, from prison after nearly 37 years and treating him kindly by having him at the king's table and granting him a permanent living allowance for the rest of his life (II Kgs 25:27–30; Jer 52:31–34). Ration tablets which mention Jehoiachin by name have been found in Babylon and support the accuracy of the biblical statement. According to the Babylonian historian Berossus, Evil-merodach's reign was "arbitrary and licentious," and he was the victim of a murderous plot by his brother-in-law Neriglissar (Nergal-sharezer, *q.v.*), who succeeded him (Jos *Against Apion,* i.20, Loeb ed.). Nabonidus passes over Evil-merodach in silence when he mentions as his predecessors and models Nebuchadnezzar and Neriglissar.

J. R.

EVIL ONE. One of the names given to Satan. The parables of the kingdom of God in Mt 13 mention two of Satan's ways to thwart the gospel. In the parable of the sower, "the wicked one" (ASV, "evil one") snatches away the word sown in the hearts of those who do not understand the gospel (v. 19). In the parable of the tares among the wheat, Satan places his own children alongside the children of God, where they will remain until the harvest at the end of the age (vv. 36–42).

The "evil one" as a personality is undoubtedly referred to by Jesus in the Lord's Prayer ("deliver us from the evil one," Mt 6:13, ASV), and in His high priestly prayer (". . . but that thou shouldst keep them from the evil one," Jn 17:15, ASV).

See Devil; Evil; Satan.

EVIL SPIRIT. *See* Demonology.

EWE. *See* Animals, I.15.

EXACTOR. This term is from a Heb. word meaning "to drive." In Isa 60:17 ("taskmasters," RSV) the word refers to officials who had oppressed the people. The same word is used in Ex 3:7 where it is translated "taskmasters" in KJV.

EXAMPLE. The KJV translation of the Gr. words *typos, hypogrammos, hypodeigma,* and *deigma*. The English term is used in illustrating different aspects of Christian conduct. The proper life style and value systems are thus demonstrated individually and collectively in the lives of Christ (Jn 13:15; I Pet 2:21), the prophets (Jas 5:10), Paul (Phil 3:17; II Thess 3:9), and the churches and their leaders (I Thess 1:7; I Tim 4:12; Tit 2:7; I Pet 5:3).

The negative example (*deigma,* "a thing shown, a specimen," Jude 7; *hypodeigma,* "figure, copy, example," II Pet 2:6) testifies to the severity of the judgment of God upon gross sexual immorality. The examples of disobedience (Heb 4:11) and idolatry and grumbling (I Cor 10:6–11) in the wilderness journeys of the Israelites serve as warnings to Christian believers. The remaining occurrences of the word "example" are positive references to exemplary living. These demonstrate the relevance of the centrality of Christ to one's ethical motivation, and the positive effects of godly living in enabling other men to comprehend the meaning of the Christian life.

The primary example for the Christian to follow is Christ Himself. He came to fulfill the law and the prophets (Mt 5:17), and thus He is the end of the law for righteousness to everyone who believes (Rom 10:4). Only in Christ can the requirement of the law—the divine standard for morality—be fulfilled in us (Rom 8:4). He taught with authority (*q.v.*) and gave a new and deeper interpretation to the Ten Commandments, the heart of the law (Mt 5:17–48; *see* Law of Moses) and "the core of the biblical ethic" (Murray, *Principles of Conduct,* p. 7).

Jesus' new commandment to His disciples is to love one another "even as I have loved you" (Jn 13:34). We know what love is and how to demonstrate love because God first loved us in Christ (I Jn 4:19). Paul's classic description of love in I Cor 13:4–7 is very likely based on the life of Christ. Jesus had taught, "Greater love hath no man than this, that a man lay down his life for his friends" (Jn 15:13), and then performed this supreme sacrifice Himself.

Christ promised to send the same Spirit that empowered Him to enable us to do His works (Jn 14:12; 16:7) and to bear the fruit of love (Gal 5:22). Thus the Spirit of Christ is the source of Christian morality, for He enlightens the conscience, one's ability to make moral judgments.

The Lord Jesus Christ is also our pattern of humility (Phil 2:5–8), of not pleasing oneself

(Rom 15:2-3), of meekness and gentleness (II Cor 10:1), and of liberality (II Cor 8:9). We are to imitate God (Eph 5:1) and be perfect like our heavenly Father in the sphere of moral character such as love and mercy (Mt 5:44-48; Lk 6:36). Christ is the model missionary for the Church to follow in carrying out its commission (*see* Commission, Great), for He said, "As my Father hath sent me, even so send I you" (Jn 20:21).

Jesus expected His disciples to identify with Him in His purpose and destiny after He cleansed them by His symbolic washing of their feet (Jn 13:1-17). The event occurred during the last night He was with them before His crucifixion. The foot washing example (*hypodeigma,* "copy") of Jesus provided an audio-visual demonstration to draw His disciples into the heart of His life view and motivation (13:15). Jesus told Peter that without this cleansing experience "thou hast no part with me" (13:8).

Long afterward, with the insights of a lifetime of Christian experience, Peter referred to Jesus' pattern for our lives: "For even hereunto were ye called: because Christ also suffered for us, leaving us an example [*hypogrammos*], that ye should follow his steps" (I Pet 2:21). The Gr. word indicates that the very life of Christ is the "writing copy" for His disciples, drawing them to intimate involvement with Him in His life of suffering and crossbearing. Peter seems to have in mind Jesus' repeated instruction on discipleship that requires complete self-denial (Mt 10:38-39; 16:24-26; Lk 14:26-33; 17:33; Jn 12:24-26).

Jesus presented His own model life as the basis of the Christian ethic. To follow Christ would demand denying oneself and taking the cross as the principle of living and the goal of all life (Mt 16:24). The exemplary Christian life was emphasized by Jesus when He said, "I always do the things that are pleasing to Him," the Father (Jn 8:29), and, "I do not seek My own will, but the will of Him who sent Me" (5:30), and, "I have come down from heaven, not to do My own will, but the will of Him who sent Me" (6:38, all NASB). This is the heart of the Christian ethic – the life that demonstrates the principle of the cross in all of Christian conduct and behavior.

It must be recognized, however, that Christ did nothing simply for the sake of example. The ideal of His perfect life will only condemn the sinner. The cross has power to lead men to holiness only as it first reveals the atonement made for their sins.

James (5:10) stresses the "example" (*hypodeigma*) of the OT prophets, who mediated the revelation of God through their preaching and teaching. The example of their sufferings is a testimony to patience for all Christians.

Meanwhile Paul illustrates by his own life the meaning of "example" for the Christians of his time. He declared his identity with Christ in terms of the cross in writing to the Galatians: "I have been crucified with Christ; and it is no longer I who live, but Christ lives in me" (2:20, NASB). Later he affirmed, "For to me, to live is Christ" (Phil 1:21).

Paul personalized the "example" by identifying himself with it in Phil 3:17, using the word *typos,* "mark of a blow, stamp, impress" (*see* Type). He urged the Philippians to observe those who walk according to the pattern they saw in him (3:17) and to practice these things themselves (4:9). His life-style and behavior stretched over a full generation of Christian witness and service. The Philippian Christians received his exhortation near the close of his confinement as a Roman prisoner. In one of his earliest epistles he had written to the believers in Thessalonica that he had worked to support himself "to offer ourselves as a model for you, that you might follow our example" (II Thess 3:9, NASB; cf. 3:7). Paul's conduct, therefore, demonstrated the validity of his message and the authority of the gospel in his life.

Such involvement in sacrificial living by faith in Christ enabled the two leading apostles to speak to both extremes of the generation gap of their times: Paul to Timothy, the NT representative of the youth generation, and Peter to the elders. Paul insisted that Timothy not allow any man to despise his youth; instead Timothy was commanded to be an example to the believers (I Tim 4:12). Peter, on the other hand, commanded the elders not to lord it over those allotted to their care, but to be "examples to the flock" (I Pet 5:3).

The Thessalonian Christians imitated the apostle Paul and the Lord, having received the word, the OT revelation as interpreted and fulfilled by Christ, "in much tribulation with the joy of the Holy Spirit." Consequently they became "an example to all the believers in Macedonia and in Achaia" (I Thess 1:6-7, NASB). The writer of Hebrews similarly describes the correlation of suffering and joy in the life of Christ, "who for the joy that was set before Him endured the cross" (Heb 12:2). The Thessalonians in their experience of suffering (I Thess 2:14; 3:3-4; II Thess 1:4-7) and joy seemed to fulfill Jesus' prayer for oneness with Christ in the Father and in the witness to God's love (Jn 17:21, 23).

Christian witness by example to other believers inevitably precedes the witness to non-believers on a broad scale. This was the case at Thessalonica (I Thess 1:7-8). Their witness to Christ was directly related to their behavior change. Their new conduct was clearly evident to the general population of Greece in that they had "turned to God from idols to serve the living and true God" (1:9).

The basis of such behavior change is established in the unique discipleship demonstrated by the same Thessalonian believers, who Paul said "became imitators of us and of the Lord" (I Thess 1:6, NASB). The key word to their discipleship is "imitators" (*mimētai*). Christian conduct, resulting in the change in behavior effected by conversion to faith in the living God, is based on imitating the Lord and His apostle Paul (cf. also I Cor 4:16; 11:1). The faith and patience of other believers and Christian leaders should also be imitated (Heb 6:12; 13:7).

In other words, Christian ethics has its foundations in the same principle of living as that of the Lord Jesus Christ. The commandments of God through His prophets and apostles and His Son, combined with the perfect example of Christ, provide the believer an absolute ethic rather than the ethical relativism of John A. T. Robinson's *Honest to God* (1963) and Joseph Fletcher's *Situation Ethics: The New Morality* (1966). The one all-inclusive principle of life is not intuitive love that relates to the need of another at the unique moment of personal encounter, but "whatever you do, do all to the glory of God" (I Cor 10:31), and to do it all in the name of the Lord Jesus (Col 3:17). The content of the Christian ethic is the will of God that must be done in love, "faith working through love" (Gal 5:6).

All of Christ's behavior was centered in His purpose to serve and to give His life a ransom (Mt 20:28). This was His pattern for His followers (20:25-27). Paul accepted it. So did the Thessalonian Christians. They had seen in Paul the example ("stamp") of Christ which gave meaning and understanding to them. They took this example for their own lives, including the affliction (*thlipsis,* "pressure, tribulation"). In such a context of Christian ethics, in the midst of suffering, imitating the life of Jesus and the conduct of Paul, those believers collectively and spontaneously shared a dynamically meaningful witness to Christ throughout Macedonia and Achaia.

The Christian example found first in Jesus and Paul issues in the kind of godly conduct that witnesses effectively through the combined body of the Church in any one area, strengthens the witness of Christian youth, and enables the behavior of the elders (pastors) to inspire a following in their flocks. The successful witness to Christ is centered on example.

See Conversation; Disciple; Grace; Justice; Law; Liberty; Love; Obedience.

Bibliography. Harvey Cox, ed., *The Situation Ethics Debate,* Philadelphia: Westminster, 1968. W. D. Davies, "Ethics in the New Testament," IDB, II, 167-176. J. Hempel, "Ethics in the OT," IDB, II, 153-161. John Murray, *Principles of Conduct,* Grand Rapids: Eerdmans, 1957. Sherwood E. Wirt, *The Social Conscience of the Evangelical,* New York: Harper & Row, 1968.

H. W. N.

EXCHANGER. *See* Occupations: Banker; Money Changer.

EXCOMMUNICATION. This is the judicial exclusion of unrepentant sinners from the rights and privileges of the communion of saints carried out by a local congregation. After admonition by one has failed, then by two or three, then by the congregation, the offender according to Mt 18:16-17 is to be as a "heathen man and a publican," or according to I Cor 5:13 is to be "put away from among yourselves," or according to I Tim 1:20 "delivered unto Satan." The ultimate purpose is to bring the offender to a realization of the seriousness of his offense and to lead him to repentance. It also removes offense from the church. *See also* Cutting Off.

Excommunication was used already in the time of the apostles. The primitive church continued the practice. The question of restoring the lapsed raised serious problems. Various councils dealt with the question about who was to be excommunicated, among them the Council of Elvira (*c.* A.D. 305), the Council of Cirta in Numidia (March, 305), and the Council of Ancyra (*c.* 314-319).

During the Middle Ages the "greater" and the "lesser" excommunication were in use; the distinction was abrogated in 1884. The Roman church regards excommunication as the prerogative of the pope, bishops, a few other dignitaries, and councils. In some cases a definite sentence of excommunication must be pronounced (*ferendae sententiae*); in about 50 others it is automatic (*latae sententiae*). Kings and princes were excommunicated, even for political reasons. The bull *Clerices laicos* (1296) declared that those levying taxes on the church without the consent of the pope or paying such taxes "*ipso facto* incur excommunication."

In the Reformation era the Anabaptists and related groups placed great emphasis on excommunication or the ban, declaring that a congregation in which public expulsion or orderly process of excommunication does not take place is not a true Christian congregation. A controversy arose among them regarding the "shunning" of banned persons. Calvin and his followers held that the exercise of church discipline was one of the marks of the church. He urged moderation of discipline and emphasized the corrective aspect of excommunication (*Institutes,* IV, 12, 10.11). The Westminster Confession (Chap. XXX), the Thirty-nine Articles (Article XXXIII), and the Apology of the Augsburg Confession (Article XI) affirm the obligation of the churches to employ excommunication. In established or state churches it is generally not used; even in voluntary churches in recent years it has largely fallen into disuse.

C. S. M.

EXECUTION. *See* Crime and Punishment.

EXECUTIONER. In Israel no office of executioner was necessary, for executions were in general performed publicly by the people (cf. Deut 17:5; 22:21, 24; Josh 7:25). The term "executioner" appears rarely in the English versions of the Bible. In the KJV it occurs only in Mk 6:27, where the Gr. *spekoulator* (lit., "spy, scout," but also "courier" and "executioner") is used of the soldier who beheaded John the Baptist. In the RSV "executioner" is found only in Ezk 9:1, where men were commissioned to slay people in Jerusalem. Military leaders and particularly the bodyguard of rulers often served as executioners; Benaiah, for example, fulfilled this function for Solomon (see I Kgs 2:25, 46).

EXERCISE, BODILY. Paul frequently referred to the athletic contests of his day to illustrate spiritual truth (see I Cor 9:24–27; I Tim 6:12; II Tim 2:5; 4:7). He was not opposed to bodily exercise (Gr. *gymnasia,* I Tim 4:8), but to the ascetic mortification of the body as practiced by the Essenes and other fanatical groups of his day.

EXHORTATION. Exhortation refers to language which is intended to incite and encourage. Many ideas are associated with the Gr. word *paraklēsis* in the NT. It is one of the gifts of the Spirit (Rom 12:8), but seems to be one aspect or purpose of prophesying (I Cor 14:3). It is used as hortatory instruction and consolation (Lk 3:18; Acts 11:23; 13:15; I Tim 4:13; Heb 12:5; 13:22); as entreaty meaning earnest supplication (II Cor 8:4); as consolation or solace (Lk 2:25); as comfort and consolation (Acts 15:31; Rom 15:4–5; II Cor 1:3, 5–7); as inspiring suitable motives (Rom 12:8; I Tim 6:2; Heb 3:13); as comfort in the sense of a cheering and supporting influence (Acts 9:31); and comfort as giving joy, gladness and rejoicing (II Cor 7:13). *See* Comfort; Prophesy.

EXILE. *See* Captivity.

EXISTENTIALISM

What is Existentialism?

It is a philosophy which finds its starting point in man with his hopes and fears, his surging ambitions and his devastating anxiety, guilt and pessimism.

A full-fledged philosophy covers three areas: (1) origin – the origin of the world, the universe, and man; (2) reality – the nature of reality and ability to understand and know it; (3) destiny – a view of the goal or destiny of the universe and man.

Some philosophical systems lack one or more of these. Materialism and pragmatism give no explanation of origin or of destiny, confining themselves to the phenomenon of existence. Existentialism forms a distinct system of philosophy because it is characterized by a starting point in man, not just in the universe as in materialism. It starts, however, not just with man as a phenomenon – for the psychology of behaviorism and the philosophy of pragmatism do this – but with either his inborn hopes and fears, or his inner problems with knowledge.

Negatively defined, existentialism is the opposite of essentialism. The essentialist begins with Being, The Absolute, The All or God; the existentialist begins with man and his inner struggles. Positively defined, existentialism is that explanation of reality and the origin and destiny of man and the universe which chooses to make as the starting point man and his problems regarding the attainment of knowledge, along with his hopes and fears, his surging ambitions, and his anxieties and guilt.

Kinds of Existentialists

Because they all start with man, there can be theistic, atheistic and agnostic existentialists.

Theistic existentialists. These believe in a God but start with man, his estrangement, guilt and anxiety, on the one hand, and his problems in regard to the knowledge of eternal truth and God, on the other. They can be subdivided into: (*a*) Protestant theistic existentialists – examples of whom are Karl Barth and Emil Brunner; (*b*) Roman Catholic theistic existentialists – Jacques Maritain and Gabriel Marcel; and (*c*) pantheistic existentialists – Paul Tillich and John A. T. Robinson.

Atheistic existentialists. Jean-Paul Sartre is an example. Nietzsche may possibly also be classed with Sartre, for he starts with man and concludes, "God is dead."

Agnostic existentialists. Martin Heidegger is an example. His position has been essentially one of indecision as to the existence of anything beyond man and the universe.

The History of Existentialism

Existentialism as a real philosophy began with Sören Kierkegaard (1813-1855). Existential elements appeared in many earlier philosophers but they were combined with other philosophic tendencies. Neither man nor man's problem with knowledge was made the full starting point.

Immanuel Kant (1724–1804) had raised the problem of knowledge before the time of Kierkegaard, and it formed a large part of the predicament in which the first full existentialist found himself. Kant argued that through his physical senses man receives a stream of impressions which, as they enter the mind, are stamped upon by the outer form of the mind, namely, space or place, and by the inner form, time. But time and space, Kant reasoned, cannot belong to the really real, the noumenon, because God is infinite and time and space are only finite. Man, then, who knows all that he does by learning in finite categories of time and space, does not know anything as God knows it, nor can he know God or His eternal truths. These are all timeless and spaceless.

Even by pure thought, that is, by "pure reason," man cannot know things as they are in God and as God knows them, because all of man's thoughts include time – it is the inner form of the mind. The net result of Kant's reasoning is that God Himself cannot communicate directly with man because man has no containers, no timeless-spaceless categories in which to receive timeless-spaceless eternal or really real truth.

Kierkegaard was faced with Kant's arguments about knowledge, on the one hand, and man's problems with sin, on the other. His guilt complex which led him to break his engagement with his sweetheart Regina, left him full of anxiety, despair and pessimism. Trying to express his agony of soul, he spoke of "sickness unto death." Attacks on the Bible and on the historicity of Jesus Christ shook his faith in the Bible.

Kierkegaard solved his problems over the paradoxes and absurdities which arose for him in the Bible, and his own guilt complex and need of redemption, by a synthesis of Kant's view of the problem of knowledge of God and his own existential hopes and fears. He claimed that God cannot speak directly to man because man has no thought forms in which to receive eternal, timeless-spaceless truth. Only indirect communication is possible. Even as Kierkegaard was trying to speak indirectly to his estranged fiancée in his books, and tell her why he had to break his engagement because of his own unconfessed sin of fornication, so God was speaking indirectly to us. According to Kierkegaard, man forces the eternal truth he receives from God into time-space categories. This is to be seen in the myths found in the Bible. Satan, the Fall, etc., are not historical figures and events but myths which contain some eternal truth. Some later existentialists, such as Barth, have preferred to call them sagas, saying myths are stories of things that never happened, while sagas tell of what happens over and over and is truth.

In his lifetime, no theologian or philosopher took Kierkegaard really seriously. Man was living in an age of reason and unbounded hope, and Sören's despair and pessimism found no place in the optimism of the age. However, near the end of World War I, as Karl Barth listened to the guns booming just beyond the border of peaceful Switzerland and wrestled with the bankruptcy of the social gospel and liberalism, they did find a sympathetic listener.

Barth wrote his *Romans* using all Kierkegaard's terms and concepts of indirect communication, contemporaneity, disjunction, myth, saga, etc. Soon he was a professor at Basel and had a group of theologians around him, which included Thorneyson and Brunner. However, Barth received such a reaction to his existential theology, as presented in his *Doctrine of the Word of God* in 1927, that he rewrote the whole book and published it as 1:1 of his *Church Dogmatics*. The Kierkegaardian terms were eliminated and he claimed that all the existentialism had been removed along with them; but the Kierkegaardian views still remained thoroughly ingrained in this new presentation of the doctrine of revelation.

God was described as *totaliter aliter,* totally other, and only indirect communication was possible. He lives in a timeless-spaceless "eternal now," but man can enjoy contemporaneity and the "eternal now" in the subjective experience of revelation. Revelation and salvation become synonymous; they are the same thing. Revelation occurs in the form of myth and/or saga, in spite of and through contradictions, etc. Christ as the Word becomes the real revelation, as man reads or hears the Bible.

Emil Brunner stoutly defended the possibility of general revelation. But he did not make the same effort to eliminate Kierkegaardian terms and hide Kierkegaardian concepts.

In its first theological form existentialism remained thoroughly theistic. It was called Crisis Theology (stressing the idea of God's judgment on man and sin) and neoorthodoxy (claiming that it was a return to a new form of orthodoxy in contrast to the old biblicism and fundamentalism).

It remained for a liberal, Paul Tillich, to make a synthesis between liberalism and neoorthodoxy. Tillich, like his liberal forefather in theology Schleiermacher and his forerunner in philosophy Hegel, was actually a pantheist.

Others who were either agnostics (Martin Heidegger) or atheists (Sartre) and who therefore admitted no revelation in the first place, had no real epistemological problems over it. They picked up the existential predicament of hope and fear, and of freedom and destiny, and developed existential philosophies of their own.

The Characteristics of Existentialism

The predicament of man. Man finds himself in a threefold predicament:

1. Estrangement. He is estranged from the world, his neighbor and himself. The theists add that he is estranged from God.

2. Anxiety. Kierkegaard said man must progress from anxiety to despair before he can make the leap of faith to salvation. Sartre has the hero of *The Flies* cry, "Human life begins on the far side of despair."

3. Detachment and extreme individualization. There is a singular lack of interest in the social and political. Karl Barth urged opposition to Hitler and the Nazis because they denied God, but he did not urge any stand against the communists, because this would mean entering the political and social realms. Extreme individual detachment is manifest in many of the atheistic and agnostic existentialists. Paul Tillich, because of his pantheism, was an exception and stressed involvement in his tensional dialectic between individualization-participation.

The possibilities of man. These are four in number.

1. Freedom. This characteristic of Renaissance humanism is particularly stressed by the atheistic and agnostic existentialists. In the theistic existentialists, and the neoorthodox in particular, freedom fades away, excluded by

God's sovereign grace. On the other hand, since Kierkegaard left the initiative of the leap to man, he allowed him freedom.

2. Autonomy. Man makes his own laws and sets up his own ethical system. The Ten Commandments are not propositional truth and revelation for Barth, but the place we receive our commission or our orders.

3. Decision. Greater importance is placed on making decisions than on the nature of the decisions made. Kierkegaard spoke of the leap of faith, the decision to believe what is contradiction, paradox, the absurd. A decision is important to the degree it is made without or contrary to evidence. Decision is good, according to Tillich, if made with the motive of love, even if it is a wrong one.

4. Intuitive knowledge. Man finds knowledge within himself. Plato had spoken of knowledge as recollection, but the existentialist sees it as something intuitive. Tillich, as a pantheist, sees it welling up from the depth of reason present in man, to appear in art and culture. The neoorthodox, since they deny propositional revelation and yet claim to experience revelation, are manifestly replacing biblical revelation with some form of self-knowledge.

The problems of man. Man's greatest problems are time and truth, and the effect of these on his existence.

1. Two kinds of time. Timeless-time or the "eternal now" is vertical and contemporaneous, while earthly time is linear and continuous.

2. Two kinds of truth. According to theistic existentialists truth partakes of the same dualism as time: eternal truth is timeless and spaceless; earthly truth is cumbered with the categories of finitude, time and space. Earthly truth is useful and of temporary importance but of no eternal significance. Heavenly truth is of eternal significance and all-important, but impossible to express in human terms.

3. Two existences. Man can simply continue to live like the mass of mankind in unauthentic existence, or he can transcend himself and enjoy authentic existence. Barth added still another existence as he spoke of every man existing in Christ as "the rejected" and "the elected one." This is man's "proper" existence.

Personal consequences.

1. Subjectivism. Man's knowledge of anything beyond what he can know through the senses depends entirely on what wells up within himself. There is no direct revelation from God in words and statements for the theistic existentialist (Barth, Brunner, etc.). Even the commands and teachings of Christ were later surrendered by Him and do not hold for us, according to Tillich.

2. Pessimism. Existentialism is essentially a philosophy of pessimism, originating in the frustration and disillusionment caused by the First World War. The atheist has no hope for the future. The theistic existentialist, with his tendency to extreme detachment and individualism, has no answer for man's social or political needs. The future offered after death is contentless since impossible of meaningful description.

The destiny of man.

1. Revelation. Only the theistic existentialist can offer any theory of a divine heavenly revelation of truth. His theory of indirect communication, coupled with the identification of revelation and salvation, expresses his view of man's goal on earth.

2. Reconciliation. This too is possible only for theistic existentialism. It is accomplished by a realistic theory of man's identification with what Christ has done and leads therefore to the restoration of all things, and universal salvation (Barth).

3. Self-transcendence. This is the term used by atheistic and agnostic existentialists, and by Tillich as a pantheist. Man can transcend himself and the mass to become free and enjoy authentic existence. It is the counterpart of salvation for the theistic existentialists.

4. Either oblivion or static history. There is no future since death is the end of all for the atheistic existentialist. Man merges back into Being or the Power of Being in which subject-object relationships are merged and identified in Tillich's pantheism.

The neoorthodox can offer little more than oblivion with their concept of an eternal contemporaneous now. Man's future in a timeless-spaceless eternity is indescribable beyond saying that past, present and future will all be one grand present, just as the events of history are all present in an endless set of volumes of history.

See God; Liberalism; Neoorthodoxy; Theology; Time.

Bibliography. H. J. Blackham, *Six Existentialist Thinkers,* New York: Harper, Torchbooks, 1959. Marjorie Grene, *Introduction to Existentialism,* Chicago: Univ. of Chicago Press, Phoenix Books, 1960. F. H. Heinemann, *Existentialism and the Modern Predicament,* New York: Harper, Torchbooks, 1958. Milton D. Hunnex, *Existentialism and Christian Belief,* Chicago: Moody, Christian Forum Books, 1969. Carl Michalson, *Christianity and the Existentialists,* New York: Scribners, 1956. J. C. Mihalich, *Existentialism and Thomism,* New York: Philosophical Library, 1960. David E. Roberts, *Existentialism and Religious Belief,* New York: Oxford Univ. Press, Galaxy Books, 1959. J. M. Spier, *Christianity and Existentialism,* Philadelphia: Presbyterian and Reformed Pub. Co., 1953.

R. A. K.

EXODUS, BOOK OF

The Name

The second book of the Torah (the law) was named *sh^emôth* by the Jews. They customarily entitled the books of their sacred Scriptures by one or more of the opening words, which for this book are *we'ēlleh shemôth,* "and these are the names. . . ." The English name is derived from its Latin name *Exodus,* in turn from the Gr. *exodos* of the LXX, meaning the "going out" or "departure" (occurring in the LXX at Ex 19:1; cf. Ps 104 [105]:38; 113 [114]:1; Heb. 11:22).

Theme and Contents

This is the great OT book setting forth redemption. Its purpose is to describe officially how Israel became the covenant nation of the Lord. While Heb. words translated "redeem" occur only in 6:6 and 15:13 (*gā'al*) and in 13:13-15 and 34:20 (*pādâ*), the concept of liberation from death, enslavement, and idolatry is found throughout. Repeatedly God declares Himself to be Yahweh, His name as the sovereign Deity making covenant with Israel (*see* God, Names of; Lord). He delivers them and brings them out of the land of Egypt; He takes them to Himself to be His people and to be their God; and He will bring them into the land promised to Abraham, Isaac, and Jacob (e.g., 6:6-8).

The continuity of God's redemptive plan is carefully, if briefly, shown in the introductory chapter. Connected as it is with Genesis by the Heb. conjunction "and," it bridges the gap from the time of Joseph in the patriarchal period to the birth of Moses during enslavement in Egypt. The next few chapters describe the birth, training, and call of this man whom God chose to be the human deliverer and covenant mediator for His people. In a series of confrontations Moses was unable to persuade the pharaoh to let the Israelite slaves leave Egypt. Even nine unusually severe plagues did not change his attitude but only hardened him further. The Lord's warning of a tenth plague killing the firstborn male in every house and flock in Egypt set the stage for the Passover ceremony to protect the Israelite homes, and for the consequent gathering of His people and their march to the Sinai border. Trapped at the Red Sea, they experienced God's mighty deliverance through the parted waters and sang a hymn of triumph in honor of Yahweh (14:1–15:21).

Moses led the nation through the desert until they camped in front of Mount Sinai (19:1-2). Along the way they saw the Lord work supernaturally several times to supply their need of water, food, and victory in battle. When the people agreed to keep the stipulations of the covenant which God as their theocratic ruler was about to make with them (19:8), they purified themselves and assembled at the foot of the mountain on the third day to participate in the covenant ceremony (19:9-19). Moses went up the mountain (19:20) to receive orally God's statement of His covenant with Israel (vv. 20-23). Then Moses returned (19:25) and repeated to the people the moral, social, and religious obligations of the covenant, which they unanimously accepted (24:3). He then wrote down all the words of the Lord and called it "the book of the covenant" (24:4*a,* 7), later receiving the moral code (the Ten Commandments) inscribed on two stone tablets by God Himself (24:12; 31:18). In the ceremony of covenant ratification the next day Yahweh's presence was represented by an altar and the 12 tribes by 12 pillars (24:4*b*-8). Then Moses as covenant mediator, the chief priests, and 70 elders representing the people ascended, saw the pavement of God's throne, and partook of the covenant meal (24:9-11).

Moses again climbed to the summit, this time for 40 days during which God revealed to him the plans for the tabernacle (*q.v.*), its furnishings and the priestly ministry in it, and the requirement to observe the sabbath as the sign of the covenant (chaps. 25–31). Meanwhile the people became impatient and demanded Aaron to make them an image of God (*see* Idolatry), thus breaking their covenant vow. Descending the mountain, Moses smashed the tablets of the law to symbolize this breach and had about 3,000 of the worst offenders executed (32:15-29). After Moses returned to the peak for another 40 days and interceded for the rest of the nation, God revealed Himself to His servant and promised to go Himself in the lead to Canaan (33:14) and drive out the heathen peoples (34:11). Fellowship was restored (34:31-33), and the people gladly responded with offerings to construct the tabernacle (35–39). When it was erected on the first day of the year, God sent His Shekinah glory to fill His earthly place of dwelling among His redeemed covenant people (40:34).

Outline

Preface: Link with Genesis, 1:1-7

I. God's Redemption of Enslaved Israel by Blood and Power from Egypt, 1:8–18:27
   - A. Background of the Egyptian bondage, 1:8-22
   - B. Preparation of the deliverer, 2:1–4:31
   - C. Contest with the oppressor, 5:1–11:10
   - D. Deliverance from Egypt, 12:1–15:21
     1. Redemption by sacrificial blood, 12:1–13:16
     2. Salvation by miraculous power, 13:17–14:31
     3. Song of triumph, 15:1-21
   - E. Training in the wilderness, 15:22–18:27
     1. Testing the redeemed, 15:22–17:16
     2. Governing the redeemed, 18:1-27

II. God's Relationship with Redeemed Israel by Covenant at Mount Sinai, 19:1–40:38
   - A. The covenant established with Israel, 19:1–24:18
     1. Preparations for receiving the covenant, 19:1-25

EXODUS, BOOK OF

2. Statement of the covenant, 20:1–23:19
3. Sanctions of the covenant, 23:20–33
4. Ratification of the covenant, 24:1–18

B. The worship of the covenant people, 25:1–40:38
1. Divine plan for tabernacle and priesthood, 25:1–31:18
2. Fellowship broken and restored, 32:1–34:35
3. Offerings for the tabernacle, 35:1–36:7
4. Its construction and erection, 36:8–40:38

Authorship and Date of Writing

The book of Exodus, as part of the Pentateuch, has been attributed by Jews to the hand of Moses ever since the time of Joshua (Josh 8:31-35; cf. "an altar of unhewn stones" with Ex 20:25). The Lord Jesus Christ quoted from the book of Exodus (3:6) and specifically called it "the book of Moses" (Mk 12:26; cf. Lk 20:37).

Internal evidences suggest that "the author must have been originally a resident of Egypt (not of Palestine), a contemporary eyewitness of the Exodus and wilderness wandering, and possessed of a very high degree of education, learning, and literary skill. No one else conforms to these qualifications as closely as Moses the son of Amram" (G. L. Archer, SOTI, p. 101).

The author of the Joseph narrative (Gen 37-50) and Exodus was well-acquainted with Egyptian names, titles, words, and customs. He correctly referred to the crop sequence for Lower Egypt (Ex 9:31-32). He spoke only of the shittim or acacia, the one known desert hardwood tree in the Sinai peninsula, as the source of lumber for the tabernacle (Ex 25:5, etc.); the acacia is not indigenous to Palestine except along the S shore of the Dead Sea. The "badger" skins used as the outer covering for the tabernacle (Ex 25:5; 26:14; etc.) were actually obtained from the dugong (Heb. *taḥash*), a sea mammal known in the Near East only in the waters of the Red Sea. He knew about the types of reeds in the marshes of the Nile delta (2:3) and that the desert sand begins abruptly at the edge of the cultivated fields (2:12). He seems to have been an eyewitness of the events and places mentioned in connection with the wilderness journey. For example, he listed for no apparent reason the exact number of springs (12) and of palm trees (70) at Elim (15:27). Moses was such an educated Israelite who had lived in Egypt (Acts 7:22) and who was thoroughly familiar with parts of the Sinai peninsula as well (see SOTI, pp. 101-109 for more details).

Furthermore, the book of Exodus states that Moses himself wrote down certain happenings and words soon after their occurrence. The "book" in which he recorded the battle with Amalek (17:14) was probably a leather scroll. It would be similar in function to the "annals" of Egypt and other ancient Near Eastern nations in which all the important events were recorded (cf. the daily records of the commanders of Thutmose III kept on "a roll of leather" in the temple of Amon, ANET, p. 237*a*). Moses personally transcribed all the words of the Lord contained in the Decalogue and the so-called covenant code (24:4). Later he was told by the Lord to write His additional directives when He renewed the covenant after the golden calf episode (34:27).

It is clearly stated that Moses put down in writing the complete words of the law when it

Thutmose III, Pharaoh of the Oppression according to the early date. LL

was renewed to Israel before his death, and that he delivered the record to the priests to place it beside the ark of the covenant (Deut 31:9, 24-26). He also wrote down the poem or song found in Deut 32 (Deut 31:19, 22). Thus there should be no question that Moses could write, that it was his habit to keep official records according to contemporary custom, and that he had his own source material which he could have used in writing the book of Exodus in its present form.

The date of writing, then, would be the date of Moses' life and the time of the Exodus (*see* Exodus, The: Date). Assuming he was the human author, he could have written the book during the 38 years of wandering in the desert around Kadesh-barnea after leaving Mount Sinai. Important confirmation of an early date for the book comes from a study of the ancient covenant or treaty forms used by sovereigns with their vassal nations in the middle of the 2nd mil. B.C. in the Near East. The pattern or format of God's covenant with Israel corresponds strikingly, e.g., with the suzerainty treaties of the Hittite emperors, suggesting that God employed the prevailing skeletal structure of covenant familiar to Moses from his education in the Egyptian court (*see* Covenant; G. L. Archer, "Old Testament History and Recent Archaeology from Moses to David," BS, CXXVII [1970], 103-106).

Another feature peculiarly reminiscent of the Egyptian New Kingdom (18th-19th Dynasties, 1570-1200 B.C.) is the structure of the tabernacle. Its linen curtains with figures of cherubim woven into the blue, purple, and scarlet tapestry work (Ex 26:1-6) were draped over a framework made of gilded shittim "boards" (KJV) or "frames" (RSV, 26:15-30). The closest known parallels in construction to this portable tent-sanctuary are the four rectangular gilded shrines, one within the other, over the sarcophagus of Pharaoh Tutankhamen (*c.* 1360-1352). These represented temples important in the life of the king. They were constructed of demountable wooden panels carefully joined together by means of mortice and tenon joints and sliding bolts, just as in the tabernacle, and assembled to fit neatly inside the royal burial chamber. A linen canopy or veil sprinkled with daisies of gilded bronze was over the second shrine (C. Desroches-Noblecourt, *Tutankhamen,* trans. by Claude, Garden City: Doubleday, 1965, pp. 49-54, 190-194). Since craftsmen trained or employed in Egypt, as Bezaleel may have been, could have known of this type of structure, it was not necessary at that period to spell out every detail in what to modern artisans is an enigmatic description (*see* Tabernacle; R. K. Harrison, IOT, pp. 403 ff.).

The members of the various schools of higher criticism have insisted that Exodus and the other books of the Pentateuch are composed of several independent documents and/or traditions compiled and edited many centuries after the time of Moses. The followers of the Graf-Wellhausen school divide Exodus into three main literary strata, the so-called J, E, and P sources. The post-Exilic Jerusalem priesthood supposedly interspersed background material and supplemented the older Jahwistic and Elohistic narratives with the account of the community's worship (Ex 25-31, 35-40). Wellhausen and other scholars held that the wilderness tabernacle was merely a late priestly idealization of the simple tent of meeting blended with the design and adornments of Solomon's temple. See a chart of the complicated division of the other chapters, verse by verse, into their documentary sources, reproduced in G. E. Wright, "Exodus, Book of," IDB, II, 193 f. Yet Wright recognizes that there are so many unknown factors in the transition of material that it is now considered difficult to be precise about such editorial work (*ibid,* p. 194).

Other scholars have propounded that there are additional documents that can be detected, a layman's source (Otto Eissfeldt) and a Kenite source giving Moses' history (Julius Morgenstern). Johannes Pedersen claims Ex 1-15 is the annual reliving of historical events, taking the form of a liturgical celebration of God's great victory, by the worshipers at the Passover festivals. Gerhard von Rad interprets the Sinai tradition (Ex 19-24) as a cultic legend. Martin Noth believes the book of Exodus is a combination of traditions: an oral Passover tradition of the deliverance from the plague and the miraculous rescue at the sea, with the story of Moses' birth, youth and call inserted into it; the recitation at certain central cultic festivals in Israel in which the making of the covenant was regularly re-enacted; narratives of the wanderings; and certain laws and creedal summaries inserted into the main Sinai narrative (*Exodus,* pp. 9-18). It is clear, therefore, that there is no consensus regarding authorship among the scholars who deny that Moses wrote the Pentateuch. *See* Canon of Scriptures, The OT; Genesis; Moses; Pentateuch.

The Hebrew Text

The Masoretic Text of Exodus is remarkably free from transcriptional errors (W. J. Martin, "Exodus, Book of," NBD, p. 405). A few affect the translation slightly. In 11:1 two Heb. words, *keshalleḥô kālâ,* "his sending away is final," may have been a scribe's marginal note that was later incorporated into the text (see JerusB and marg. note). In 23:3 an original *g* of the word *gādōl,* "a great man," may have been misread as *w,* forming *wedāl,* "and a poor man"; Lev 19:15 tends to corroborate this correction in that it has the same verbal construction, *lō' tehdar,* with *gādôl.* In Ex 34:19 apparently the Heb. definite article *h* became *t* in the uncertain form *tizzākār*; four ancient versions recognized this error and rendered the word "the male" (see RSV, NJV).

Many students of Exodus and Numbers have

questioned the magnitude of the numbers of the Israelites involved in the journeys. While it is probable that the transmission of numbers may have been more exposed to error than other words in the text, we cannot conclude that large figures are automatically suspect. There are problems in logistics of maintaining so many people and in tactics of getting a huge number of people to march quickly past a given point (e.g., the Red Sea) and through certain narrow valleys in the Sinai peninsula. Yet it is wiser to hold such difficulties in abeyance rather than to declare the text is corrupt. *See* Number; Numbers, Book of.

Bibliography. Gleason L. Archer, Jr., SOTI, pp. 209–226. Umberto Cassuto, *A Commentary on the Book of Exodus,* trans. by Israel Abrahams, Jerusalem: Magnes Press, 1967. G. A. Chadwick, "Exodus," ExpB. Samuel R. Driver, *Exodus (Cambridge Bible),* Cambridge: Univ. Press, 1911. Jack Finegan, *Let My People Go,* New York: Harper & Row, 1963. R. K. Harrison, IOT, pp. 566–588. Philip C. Johnson, "Exodus," WBC. H. R. Jones, "Exodus," NBC (rev. ed.). C. F. Keil and Franz Delitzsch, *Biblical Commentary on the OT, The Pentateuch,* Vols. I and II, Grand Rapids: Eerdmans (reprint), 1951. John Peter Lange, *Exodus,* trans. by Charles M. Mead, New York: Scribner, Armstrong, 1876. James Murphy, *Commentary on Exodus,* Edinburgh: T. & T. Clark, 1866. B. Davie Napier, *Exodus, The Layman's Bible Commentary,* Vol. 3, Richmond: John Knox Press, 1963. Martin Noth, *Exodus,* trans. by J. S. Bowden, London: SCM Press, 1962. J. Coert Rylaarsdam, "The Book of Exodus," IB, I, 831–1099.

J. R.

EXODUS, THE. The crucial event in Israel's history is the Exodus. It was the mighty deliverance performed by the Lord in bringing the entire people of Israel out from Egyptian slavery and into the Promised Land. This departure from Egypt and consequent migration toward Canaan under Moses' leadership was marked by many miracles. It resulted in the establishment of the Israelites as a nation in covenant agreement with God as their theocratic ruler. In its restricted sense the term covers the year of the ten plagues, the Passover, and the crossing of the Red Sea (Ex 7–15).

Historicity

No known Egyptian records refer to the Israelites in Egypt or to their departure. This complete lack of contemporary evidence has been used by some critics to argue against the Exodus as an historical event. But God's deliverance of Israel from bondage is referred to so often in the later books of the OT (see the numerous references to Egypt in a Bible concordance) that scholars now generally admit that a migration of some Israelites from Egypt did take place. Scholarly opinion varies widely, however, as to the date and whether the whole nation was involved in the Exodus or only some of the tribes of Israel.

Large movements of peoples from one land to another were not uncommon in antiquity. God reminds His people of His sovereign actions in the past by asking, "Did not I, who brought Israel out of the land of Egypt, bring the Philistines from Caphtor, and the Aramaeans from Kir?" (Amos 9:7, JerusB). In the late 15th cen. B.C. Hurrians of some 14 districts apparently left their homes within the Hittite kingdom and fled to the land of Isuwa in Hurrian country. They were later forced to return, however, by the powerful Hittite king Suppiluliumas, and a treaty was signed with the Hurrian king Mattiwaza (K. A. Kitchen, "Exodus," NBD, p. 402; see ANET, pp. 205 f. for part of the treaty).

Thus the account of the Exodus is unique in all of ancient literature in describing an entire people who were successfully delivered from an oppressive regime by the supernatural acts of their Deity.

The Biblical Account

Jacob and his sons had gone down to Egypt at the direction of God (Gen 46:1–7) to seek relief from the widespread famine in the Near East. Joseph, who had been installed as vizier (41:41–43), had them placed in the pasture-land of Goshen near Egypt's E border (46:31–34). The Israelites came to Egypt some 400 years before the Exodus (Ex 12:40). If the Exodus occurred *c.* 1445 B.C. (*see* section under "The Date"), then Jacob entered Egypt *c.* 1875 B.C. (or 1845 B.C., if the reading "in Canaan and in Egypt" of SP and LXX is adopted) during the illustrious 12th Dynasty, a time of strength and peace and unity throughout the whole country (Gen 41:43–48).

Sometime after Joseph's death *c.* 1800 (or 1770) B.C. a new king arose over Egypt, who refused to recognize the value of Joseph's ministry (Ex 1:8). Since the Israelites were more numerous than the new king and his own people (1:9), it is very likely that Ex 1:8–12 refers to the time of the Semitic Hyksos kings in Lower Egypt (*c.* 1730–1570 B.C.), not to later Egyptian kings. Antipathy between the Hyksos and the enslaved Israelites would explain why the latter did not choose to leave Egypt, or were not expelled, along with the foreign rulers.

The powerful 18th Dynasty pharaohs continued the harsh oppression for several more generations. In spite of this the Heb. slaves kept multiplying (Ex 1:7, 12, 20). At the time of Moses' birth measures were being applied to hinder this increase by throwing the newborn sons into the Nile. The infant Moses, however, was rescued by an Egyptian princess who adopted him. Thus he was educated in royal court circles (Acts 7:22), where he could learn about the contemporary peoples and their cultures.

The Israelites needed to be redeemed not only from economic servitude but also from spiritual bondage. They had turned in large measure to heathen deities during their four centuries of residence in Egypt (Lev 17:7; Josh 24:14; Ezk 20:5-9; 23:3, 19, 27). Thus at Sinai specific commandments were given to guard against their worshiping other gods (Ex 20:5-9; 23:13). Yet the urge for an idol of Egyptian style quickly produced the golden calf (Ex 32; Acts 7:39 ff.).

God heard the cry of His oppressed people and called Moses from his self-appointed exile. Having killed an Egyptian taskmaster, he had fled from the pharaoh and remained in the Sinai desert until after that ruler had died (Ex 2:23). Soon after Moses returned, God began to unleash the plagues on Egypt to force the new pharaoh to let His people go. These disasters to the life and economy of Egypt were also judgments on the gods of Egypt (Ex 12:12; *see* Gods, False). Although the plagues were supernatural in the exact timing and severity, they consisted in phenomena that were also natural to Egypt. The account is replete with authentic local coloring. Wherever the capital of Egypt was at the time, the pharaoh obviously was staying near the land of Goshen (Ex 5:6, 15-20). He must have been living in a secondary residence such as a temple guest house in a city (9:33) by the Nile (7:20-23; 8:3, 24), if not in the main royal palace.

The Lord gave Moses and Aaron very detailed instructions regarding the selection and killing of the yearling male lamb and the application of its blood on the doorway. This sacrifice was exceptionally important both for Israel's immediate survival and for redemptive typology (Ex 12:1-27, 43-49; 13:1-16). It was to be a passover or protective offering to the Lord (12:11, NJV), an offering to insure their protection when the Lord would go through the land of Egypt and strike dead the firstborn in every house.

The Israelites must have marched several days and nights after eating the lambs before reaching the shore of the Red Sea (*see* section under "The Route"). The mighty miracle of deliverance through the divided waters could not have been on the same night as the Passover, although the shedding of blood marked the time their freedom began (Ex 12:42, 51; 13:3, 4). It is remarkable that nowhere is it claimed that the people made any fight at all (Hebert, p. 14).

It must be stressed that the OT uniformly represents all the tribes of Israel as having taken part in the Exodus. All 12 sons of Jacob were with him in Egypt, along with their families which became the 12 tribes (Gen 46:5-27; Ex 1:1-5). They all surrounded him on his deathbed when he prophesied over them (Gen 49). Ex 12:41 plainly states that "all the hosts of the Lord went out from the land of Egypt." Moses erected 12 pillars at the foot of Mount Sinai to represent the tribes (Ex 24:4). All 12 names were to be engraved on the two shoulder stones of the ephod, and each of the 12 precious stones of the breastpiece was engraved with the name of a tribe (Ex 28:9-21; 39:6-14). Twelve loaves were to be placed on the table of showbread (Lev 24:5-6). The book of Numbers frequently mentions all 12 of the tribes of Israel. In Deuteronomy in referring to the spies Moses says, "I took twelve men of you, one man for every tribe" (1:23). All 12 tribes are named in connection with the command to pronounce the blessings and the curses between Mounts Ebal and Gerizim (Deut 27:12-13). The testimony of the book of Joshua is clear that all 12 tribes participated in the Jordan crossing (3:12; 4:2, 4, 9, 20-24).

Thus the OT teaches that the Exodus was a united movement from Egypt, all 12 tribes departing at once. And the entrance into Canaan was an invasion of the fighting men of all the tribes at the same time. Any evidence, therefore, concerning the history of one of the tribes during the latter half of the 2nd mil. B.C. is valid evidence for the history of the entire nation of Israel during that period.

This biblical data runs counter to the theories of many writers who follow the documentary hypothesis of the Pentateuch (*see* Exodus, Book of; Pentateuch). Most of them also subscribe to a late date for the Exodus. In order to handle certain extrabiblical evidence they have imagined either a twofold exodus and entry into Palestine in different centuries, or that some of the tribes of Israel never sojourned in Egypt at all. The interpretation of the Exodus event, then, is not merely a matter of chronology. It involves the origin of the religion of Israel, the historicity of the narratives, and the very inspiration of the Scriptures.

The Route

The exact route taken by the Israelites is difficult to determine. Nearly every place name mentioned in Ex 12-15 and the very meaning of the term "Red Sea" are in question. Therefore there are at least three main theories of the route of the Exodus. The higher critical attitude generally is that the account in Exodus appears to incorporate more than one geographical tradition, so that the present narrative is a reconstruction from several traditions without any certain knowledge of the places mentioned or of the actual route.

Those who believe the Heb. *yam sûph* refers to the Red Sea propose that the Israelites marched eventually S toward the head of the Gulf of Suez and crossed either the present gulf or the Bitter Lakes, connected at that time by a waterway with the Red Sea.

The proponents of a central crossing believe the Israelites proceeded E of Succoth to small Lake Timsah, the *yam sûph,* which should be

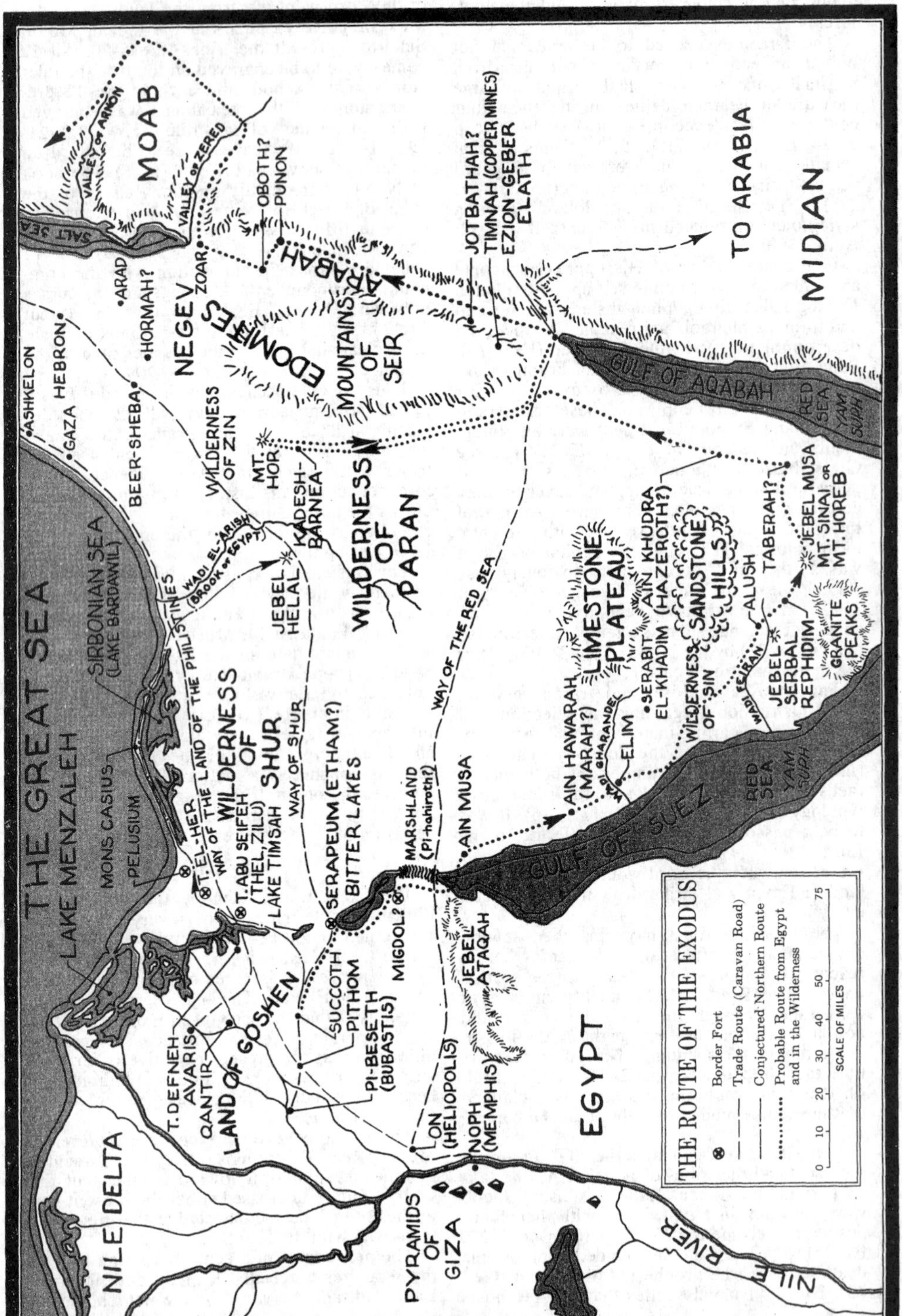
THE ROUTE OF THE EXODUS
Border Fort
Trade Route (Caravan Road)
Conjectured Northern Route
Probable Route from Egypt and in the Wilderness
SCALE OF MILES
0 10 20 30 40 50 75
THE GREAT SEA
LAKE MENZALEH
NILE DELTA
NILE RIVER
SIRBONIAN SEA (LAKE BARDAWIL)
MONS CASIUS
PELUSIUM
T. EL-HER
WAY OF THE LAND OF THE PHILISTINES
WADI EL-ARISH (BROOK OF EGYPT)
T. ABU SEIFEH (THEL, ZILU)
LAKE TIMSAH
WILDERNESS OF SHUR
WAY OF SHUR
T. DEFNEH
AVARIS
QANTIR
LAND OF GOSHEN
SUCCOTH
PITHOM
PI-BESETH (BUBASTIS)
SERAPEUM (ETHAM?)
BITTER LAKES
MIGDOL?
MARSHLAND (Pi-hahiroth?)
ON (HELIOPOLIS)
NOPH (MEMPHIS)
PYRAMIDS OF GIZA
JEBEL ATAQAH
EGYPT
AIN MUSA
WAY OF THE RED SEA
GULF OF SUEZ
RED SEA
YAM SUPH
AIN HAWARAH (MARAH?)
WADI GHARANDEL
ELIM
SERABIT EL-KHADIM
LIMESTONE PLATEAU
WILDERNESS OF SIN
SANDSTONE HILLS
AIN KHUDRA (HAZEROTH?)
ALUSH
WADI FEIRAN
JEBEL SERBAL
REPHIDIM
GRANITE PEAKS
TABERAH?
JEBEL MUSA
MT. SINAI OR MT. HOREB
JEBEL HELAL
KADESH-BARNEA
WILDERNESS OF PARAN
WILDERNESS OF ZIN
MT. HOR
ASHKELON
GAZA
HEBRON
BEER-SHEBA
HORMAH?
ARAD
NEGEV
ZOAR
SALT SEA
EDOMITES
MOUNTAINS OF SEIR
ARABAH
OBOTH?
PUNON
VALLEY OF ZERED
VALLEY OF ARNON
MOAB
JOTBATHAH?
TIMNAH (COPPER MINES)
EZION-GEBER
ELATH
GULF OF AQABAH
TO ARABIA
MIDIAN

translated as the "Reed Sea." The Jews then left Egypt by "the way of the wilderness" (Ex 13:18), which they equate with "the way of Shur" (Gen 16:7) going to Beer-sheba.

The theory of an extreme northern route supposes that after leaving Succoth the Israelites could not safely pass the Egyptian border fortresses, and thus turned NE to the Mediterranean in order to flank the wall of Egypt. They avoided the way of the Philistines (Ex 13:17) by traversing the sandy spit which divides the Sirbonian Sea lagoon (the Reed Sea for this view), now called Lake Bardawil, from the Mediterranean. Baal-zephon (Ex 14:2, 9) is supposedly a temple site to be equated with Mons Casius where Zeus was later worshiped on this narrow strip of land. But this conjecture is improbable, because the proximity of this route to the military road or way of the Philistines would have endangered Israel (Cassuto, p. 156). Also, an Israeli archaeological survey in 1967 found no Late Bronze Age potsherds at Mount Casius (IEJ, XVII [1967], 279 f.).

A strange variant of the southern theory has the Israelites cross near Suez and continue E to Ezion-geber, then S through the land of Midian in Arabia to volcanic mountains. This view supposedly explains the fire and smoke on Mount Sinai (Ex 19 the peaks of the S Sinai peninsula are not volcanic), Horeb being in Midian (Ex 2:15; 3:1), and the references to Seir, Paran, and Teman in Deut 33:2; Jud 5:4–5; Hab 3:3. For all these routes see Emil G. Kraeling, *Rand-McNally Bible Atlas,* Chicago: Rand McNally, 1956, Map V.

W. F. Albright and G. E. Wright have championed a northern view that claims that Baal-zephon is Tell Defneh (Tahpanhes, *q.v.*) and the Reed Sea is Lake Menzaleh. After crossing it the Israelites turned S to go to the traditional Mount Sinai in the S end of the peninsula. But the association of the god Baal-zephon with the port of Tahpanhes is based on a late Phoenician papyrus letter of the 6th cen. B.C.

The geographical data are as follows. The Israelites dwelt in the land of Goshen, also called "the land of Rameses" (Gen 47:11). As slaves they had built for the pharaoh the military depot or "store" cities of Pithom and Raamses (Ex 1:11). The Heb. name *gōshen* is the Gr. Gesem (Gen 45:10; 46:34–LXX), probably the Egyptian "Kesem of the East." Goshen almost certainly refers to the region E of the Nile delta, including the fertile 30 mile long Wadi Tumilat stretching from Bubastis on the E branch of the Nile to Ismailia near Lake Timsah.

Archaeologists have examined two sites in Wadi Tumilat. Tell el-Maskhuta, nine and a half miles W of Lake Timsah, was excavated by Naville in 1883; and Tell er-Retabeh, eight and a half miles farther W, was explored by Petrie. Hieroglyphic inscriptions at the former site probably identify it as Tjeku or a town in the Tjeku region, an area near the border of Egypt. Papyrus Anastasi VI mentions Tjeku as the place where famished Bedouin tribes of Edom were being sustained after being allowed to pass the fortress of Merneptah (ANET, p. 259). Another papyrus tells of the "enclosure-wall of Tjeku," evidently the line of fortresses guarding the desert border (*ibid.*). On philological grounds Tjeku may possibly be equated with Succoth (Ex 12:37; 13:20). This was the congregating point for the Israelites, their first encampment (Num 33:5) after leaving their slave dwellings. Heb. *sukkôth* literally means "booths," indicative of the temporary nature of their shelters on their journey.

Pithom (Pi-tum, Egyptian *Per-Atum,* "house of Atum") has been identified with Tell er-Retabeh by Sir Alan Gardiner. This is a small site, however, so that Uphill proposes Tell Hisn (Heliopolis, biblical On) in the NE suburbs of Cairo as Per-Atum (JNES, XXVII, 291–301). Thus the site of Pithom (Ex 1:11 only) remains uncertain.

Twenty-five miles NW of Tell el-Maskhuta and the area of Succoth lies Qantir. This is the probable site of Per-Rameses, the new capital city of Rameses II (see Uphill). Other scholars have equated Per-Rameses with Tanis (biblical Zoan, Ps 78:12, 43), the old Hyksos capital at San el-Hagar, 12–15 miles farther N. From the area of Rameses (Ex 12:37; Num 33:5) came many of the Israelites to begin the Exodus. The OT does not indicate, however, that this Rameses (or Raamses, Ex 1:11) was called Per-Rameses (which would be Pi-Rameses, after the pattern of Pi-tum=Per-Atum, Ex 1:11). The Heb. transcription omits the element *Pr* which always seems to precede the name of the city of Rameses in Egyptian inscriptions (Redford, VT, XIII, 409 f.). No 18th Dynasty inscriptions have been found at either Qantir or San el-Hagar, so that the biblical Rameses may have designated largely an agricultural area in Moses' time.

From Succoth the Israelites set out and encamped at Etham, at the edge of the wilderness (Ex 13:20). Because they were not led northward to take the shortest route to Canaan "lest . . . they see war" (Ex 13:17), Etham (probably=Egyptian *ḫ ṯ m,* "fort") cannot be one of the northern fortresses of the wall of Egypt. Rather a site to the E a day's journey (Num 33:6) would be expected. Ruins of such a fort are at Serapeum, half way between Lake Timsah and the Bitter Lakes, known later as "the fortress of Merneptah" (*see* above). It guarded the middle entrance route to Egypt known as "the way to Shur" (Gen 16:7).

Then the Lord ordered Israel "to turn back and encamp in front of Pi-ha-hiroth, between Migdol and the sea, in front of Baal-zephon . . . by the sea" (Ex 14:2, RSV). The sea must refer to the Red Sea where the miraculous deliverance took place (15:4, 22; Deut 11:4; Josh 2:10; 4:23; 24:6; Neh 9:9; Ps 106:7, 9, 22;

136:13-15), for as Ex 13:17-19 summarizes the entire journey, God did not lead them by the nearest way, the way to the land of the Philistines, but "led the people by a roundabout way of the wilderness—by the Red Sea" (orig. trans. of 13:18*a*).

The Heb. term *yam sûph,* "Red Sea" in KJV and RSV, has become an enigma. Many modern scholars translate it as "the Sea of Reeds" because in Ex 2:3, 5 and Isa 19:6 *sûph* is the word for a plant growing in abundance on the banks of the Nile, and because *sûph* seems equivalent to Egyptian *ṯwfi.* This etymological correspondence is not at all certain, however, and furthermore the Egyptian term *pr ṯwfi* is used only for a territory and never for a sea or a river (Simons, GTT, pp. 77 f.). If it were to mean "Sea of Reeds," then it probably does not refer to the known Red Sea, because no reeds grow anywhere along its shores.

When *yam sûph* occurs in an OT passage not referring to the Exodus miracle, it may designate the E arm of the Red Sea, the Gulf of Aqabah (I Kgs 9:26; Ex 23:31; Jud 11:16; Jer 49:21). The way of the Red Sea (Num 14:25; 21:4; Deut 1:40; 2:1) is best explained as the trade route across the Sinai Desert from Egypt to Arabia, connecting the two tips of the Red Sea at Suez (Clysma) and Ezion-geber (Elat), respectively. The LXX (and Acts 7:36; Heb 11:29) constantly rendered *yam sûph* by *hē eruthra thalassa,* the Red Sea as we know it today, except in I Kgs 9:26, where the adjective *eschatēs,* "last, farthest, end," supposes the reading *sôph.* Heb. *sôph* means "end" (Eccl 3:11; 7:2; 12:13; II Chr 20:16). Thus the term may originally have been *yam sôph,* "the Border Sea," that sea at the end of Egyptian territory (M. Copisarow, "The Ancient Egyptian, Greek and Hebrew Concept of the Red Sea," VT, XII [1962], 1-13; N. H. Snaith, "*Yam-Sôph*: the Sea of Reeds: the Red Sea," VT, XV [1965], 395-398).

According to Ex 10:19, "a mighty strong west wind" blew all the locusts from the entire country of Egypt into the *yam sûph.* The "west wind" is in Heb. literally a "sea wind," which in Palestine would be a W wind; here in Egypt it would be more a NW wind. Only the presently known Red Sea (not a marshy lake) is properly placed and large enough to cause the death of a huge locust horde. If the S route and the traditional Mount Sinai are accepted, *yam sûph* in Num 33:10-11 is easily explainable as the Gulf of Suez shoreline beyond the mouth of Wadi Gharandel in which the oasis of Elim is found, at the plain of el-Marḫah.

The three place names in Ex 14:2 cannot be identified with certainty under any theory. But in keeping with the most likely S theory, the probable route can be traced. After turning back from the frontier at Etham, the Israelites detoured on a SW course around the NW shore of the larger Bitter Lake. Then passing Jebel Jenefeh on the W they moved SE between Jebel Abu Hasan and "the sea," camping at Pi-hahiroth, which may mean "house of the marshes." Marshes exist around the S end of the Bitter Lakes, and on that height are ruins of a stone tower (Heb. *migdol,* Egyptian *mktl*), one of its three rooms being a shrine with hieroglyphic texts containing the names of Seti I and Rameses II.

While the possibility of identifying Baal-zephon with any of several sacred sites in the N is the crucial factor in the northern theories, the Canaanite deity Baal when introduced into Egypt was worshiped in many spots. C. Bourdon observed that an Egyptian papyrus giving an itinerary with the geographical names of the lakes lists four towers, one of which is the Tower of Baal-zephon (RB, LXI [1932], 370-392).

As early as the reign of Hatshepsut (1504-1483 B.C.), who sent ships via the Nile from Thebes to trade with Punt on the Somaliland coast, a channel must have connected the Bitter Lakes with the Gulf of Suez, and a canal in Wadi Tumilat joined the former with the E branch of the Nile near Bubastis. Therefore most scholars subscribing to the S route believe that the Bitter Lakes can rightfully be called part of the Red Sea, and propose that the Israelites crossed on a known ford at the narrow part of the lakes when the wind blew back all the water (a phenomenon observed by Napoleon, before the Suez Canal was dug).

On the other hand, the crossing path must have been very wide to enable all the Israelites to escape in one night. Also the waters returning to their normal state (Ex 14:27, NJV) were deep enough to cover all the chariot forces of Pharaoh. While the words of the song of Moses may be only figurative, they do speak of the depths of the sea, sinking to the bottom, the heart of the sea, and the mighty waters (Ex 15:5, 8, 10). Therefore a crossing through the present Red Sea S of the port of Suez or Clysma may best fit the data of the text. Here Israel would have been unable to escape by marching farther S along the W shore of the Red Sea, because the heights of Jebel Ataqah come right to the water. For the remainder of the route to Mount Sinai and Canaan, *see* Wilderness Wandering.

The Date

The key to the chronology of biblical events throughout the entire 2nd mil. B.C. is the date of the Exodus. There are two main views concerning this date: (1) the Israelites left Egypt during the 18th Dynasty *c.* 1450-1440 B.C., and (2) they did not depart until the 19th Dynasty during the 13th cen. The earlier date best accords with the 480 years between the Exodus and the beginning of Solomon's temple in the fourth year of his reign (*c.* 967 B.C.; I Kgs 6:1), the 300 years from the conquest of Transjordan to the time of Jephthah (Jud 11:26), and the length of the period of the judges. It claims Thutmose III (1504-1450 B.C.) to be the pharaoh of the oppression and Amenhotep II

(1450-1425) as the pharaoh of the Exodus. The chief arguments for the later date are the occurrence of the name of Rameses (or Raamses) in Ex 1:11 and 12:37, Glueck's surface explorations in Transjordan and the Negeb finding no important settlement ruins until after 1300 B.C., and destruction levels of a number of sites in W Palestine from 1250-1200 B.C.

Amenhotep II, Pharaoh of the Exodus according to the early date. HFV

The late date. The most reasonable explanation of this view is that the Exodus occurred early in the reign of Rameses II (1304-1237 B.C.), *c*. 1290 to 1280 B.C. Rameses' successor, Merneptah (1236-1223), claims on his victory stela about cities and peoples in Palestine to have laid Israel waste, along with his seed (ANET, p. 378). While "seed" may refer to offspring, more likely in keeping with Egyptian idiom the burning of growing crops is meant. Thus Israel seems already to have entered the Promised Land after the 40 years of nomadic wilderness wandering. But G. E. Wright and others insist that Israel must have been in Egypt at least during the early part of the reign of Rameses II in order to have worked on the construction of the city of Rameses (Wright, *Biblical Archaeology*, p. 60). They argue also that few if any building operations of Thutmose III are known to have taken place in the Nile delta, and that the 18th Dynasty capital was far upstream at Thebes.

The name Raamses in Ex 1:11 may not refer to the capital city Per-Rameses of Rameses II (*see* section under "The Route"). It may either be an anachronism, as it almost certainly is in Gen 47:11; or the name Rameses may go back to Hyksos times, even as the 19th Dynasty rulers traced their ancestry and tradition back to a Hyksos god or king named Seth, according to the "Stela of the Year 400" found at Tanis (ANET, pp. 252 f.).

The continuity of Ex 1–2 obviously implies that the beginning of the enslavement and the building of Pithom and Raamses took place before the birth of Moses. But Moses was 80 at the time of the Exodus (Ex 7:7). Thus, if the late date is correct, Moses would have been born *c*. 1370 in the 18th Dynasty (1570-1320). Therefore it is impossible both to hold that Rameses II was the pharaoh who ordered the Israelites to build the cities of Ex 1:11, and to believe Moses' age is correct.

The 18th Dynasty kings were very active in Lower Egypt. Thutmose III appointed two viziers over the country, one residing at Thebes and the other at Heliopolis near modern Cairo, where Thutmose erected two granite obelisks (now in New York and London). His son Amenhotep II is known to have left a monument to the god Amun-Re at Bubastis, at the W end of Wadi Tumilat. Here he also built a temple for the goddess Bastet. The armies of these two pharaohs must have used the facilities of this key city in the delta for their many Asiatic campaigns. A rock tablet at Tura shows that in Amenhotep's fourth year his overseer of works, Minmose, was still busy in the temples of the delta. Born at Memphis where he grew up (ANET, pp. 244 f.), Amenhotep took a keen interest in the affairs of Lower Egypt.

The late date proponents explain the 480 years of I Kgs 6:1 by suggesting this figure was an artificial date of secondary origin (Montgomery, *Kings*, ICC, p. 144). Supposedly it is based on a hypothetical 12 generations from Aaron to the priests of Solomon's day using the then accepted length of 40 years for a generation. But we know a generation is more closely 25 years long, giving a period of only 300 years from the Exodus to Solomon. While I Chr 6:3-8 and 50-53 list 11 priests from Aaron to Zadok (who anointed Solomon) inclusive, I Chr 6:33-37 has 18 generations from Heman in David's time to Korah in Moses' time. No accurate chronology, therefore, can be reckoned from the genealogies.

Nelson Glueck has charged that no Edomite or Moabite kings would have been encountered by Moses in the Negeb or Transjordan before they built their border fortresses in the 13th cen. B.C. (*The Other Side of the Jordan*, New Haven: ASOR, 1940, pp. 146 f.; *Rivers in the Desert*, New York: Farrar, Straus & Cudahy,

Huge fallen statue of Rameses II at Memphis, candidate for Pharaoh of Exodus according to the late date. HFV

1959, pp. 106, 109, 114 f.). He did not find one site or potsherd which could be ascribed to the Middle Bronze II or Late Bronze Ages (1900-1250 B.C.). His conclusions must now be modified, however.

A careful geographical study of the terms Edom (*q.v.*) and Mount Seir in Genesis to Judges reveals that Esau and his descendants lived in the Negeb W of the Arabah until after the time of Moses and Joshua. Not until the biblical records about Saul and David are the Edomites mentioned as residing in Transjordan (I Sam 14:47; II Sam 8:12-14, RSV; I Chr 18:11-13). Inscriptions from the reign of Thutmose III tell of his army warring in the Negeb (ANET, pp. 241, 243). Near ancient copper mines at Timnah (15 miles N of Elath, W side of Arabah) Beno Rothenberg excavated an Egyptian temple, dated by royal cartouches of Seti I (1318-1304 B.C.) and Rameses III (1198-1166). Much local pottery at the temple site and nearby smelting camps shows that tribes from Midian and the central Negeb hill country were employed in the Egyptian mining operations (PEQ, CI [1969], 57 ff.). The Canaanite king of Arad, who dwelt in the Negeb and fought against Israel (Num 21:1, RSV), evidently lived at Tell Malḥata (seven and a half miles SW of Tell Arad) which has a fine well and strong Canaanite fortifications including a solid brick glacis (IEJ, XIV [1964], 145 ff.).

Furthermore, the terms "king" of Edom (Num 20:14) and various "cities" of Edomite kings (Gen 36:32, 35, 39) need not prove that the Edomites were yet a sedentary people dwelling in fortified towns. The five kings of Midian (Num 31:8) in Moses' day and the two kings of Midian in Gideon's day (Jud 8:5, 12) were only nomadic chieftains. Kadesh-barnea had no permanent buildings and fortifications during Israel's wanderings, yet it is called "a city in the uttermost of thy [i.e., Edom's] border" (Num 20:16). It was only a tent city, like the "camps" (*maḥanîm*) of Num 13:19. It was God who forbade Israel to cross the territories of the Edomites and Moabites, not the superior strength of these peoples who prevented it (Deut 2:4-9).

Since World War II a number of tombs in the Amman-Mount Nebo region have yielded hundreds of Middle Bronze II and Late Bronze I (1800-1400) pottery vessels and scarabs. A Late Bronze Age temple with a large quantity of imported Cypriote and Mycenean pottery was discovered in 1955 at the airport of Amman (PEQ, XC [1958], 10-12; XCVIII [1966], 155-162; BA, XXXII [1969], 104-116). Beginning excavations at Heshbon in 1968 unearthed some Late Bronze sherds. Thus it seems that there was some sedentary occupation in Transjordan around 1400 B.C.

The late 13th cen. B.C. destruction levels of Beitin (Bethel?), Lachish, Tell el-Hesi (Eglon?), Tell Beit Mirsim (Debir?), and Hazor are attributed to the Israelite conquest of Josh 10-11 by such writers as G. E. Wright (*Biblical Archaeology*, pp. 81-85). While the poorer style of houses above the levels of burning at these sites may or may not prove Israelite occupation, it cannot prove it was Joshua's army which destroyed the cities at that time. The tribes continued to subdue their territories long after Joshua's death. He burned only Jericho, Ai, and Hazor (Josh 6:24; 8:19; 11:13). Hebron and Debir had to be recaptured (15:13-17), for Joshua did not settle or leave garrisons in the cities he took but led his entire army back to Gilgal (10:43). He did not conduct siege warfare but rather a series of lightning-like raids against key Canaanite cities with the purpose of destroying the morale and fighting ability of the inhabitants.

The early date. Positive support for this view comes from a comparison of Moses' exile with the long reigns of certain pharaohs, from settlement conditions in Goshen, the Dream Stela of Thutmose IV, the time of Balaam, the fall of Jericho around 1400 B.C., the history of Hazor, Egyptian mentions of Asher, and correspondences between the Amarna letters and the early period of the judges.

The combination of Thutmose III and Amenhotep II best fits the requirements of the pharaoh of the oppression and the pharaoh of the Exodus, respectively. Thutmose would be the ruler whose death is recorded in Ex 2:23, the same one from whom Moses fled in 2:15 (cf. 4:19). He reigned alone for 34 years (1483-1450 B.C.). The only other pharaohs of the 18th and 19th Dynasties whose reigns were long enough to include even most of Moses' exile and sojourn with Jethro were Amenhotep III (1417-1379), Horemheb (1348-1320), and Rameses II (1304-1237). But each of these three is disqualified because the king who followed could not be the pharaoh of the Exodus. The effeminate Amenhotep IV (Akhenaten, 1379–1362) built a new capital at Amarna, 200 miles up the Nile from Goshen, and rather neglected the delta region as well as the Canaanite princes appealing to him for help. Horemheb was the last king of the 18th Dynasty, and his successor, Rameses I, first 19th Dynasty king, ruled only a year and four months. Merneptah, son of Rameses II, shows in his stela that Israel was already in Canaan.

The plagues of the flies and the hail fell on all the land of Egypt but not on Goshen (Ex 8:22; 9:25–26). This suggests that while Goshen was on the edge of the land of Egypt, it was removed to some extent from the territory where the native Egyptians were residing. This would have been true during the 18th Dynasty whose kings left no traces in the easternmost delta. But during the 19th Dynasty, when the capital was probably at Qantir (*see* "The Route"), many of the principal building projects of Rameses II were in the Wadi Tumilat or Goshen region itself.

Thutmose IV (1425–1417 B.C.), the son and successor of Amenhotep II, set up a remarkable stela between the legs of the Sphinx at Gizeh. In a dream he was told that he would be given the kingdom (ANET, p. 449). If he had been the eldest son of his father, there would have been no purpose in a divine promise that he should someday become king. One may reasonably infer that the oldest son of Amenhotep must have predeceased his father, thus leaving the succession to his younger brother. This is in accord with the death of Pharaoh's firstborn son in the last plague (Ex 12:29).

In Num 22:5 we read that Balak "sent messengers to summon Balaam son of Beor, at Pethor on the River, in the land of the sons of Amaw" (JerusB). Pethor is the later Hittite city of Pitru, S of Carchemish on the Euphrates. The statue of Idri-mi from Alalakh, dated variously from 1450 to 1375 B.C., says he found sons of the land of 'Amau and sons of the land of Aleppo when he was in exile in Canaan (BASOR, # 118, p. 16). Only around 1400 B.C. was the land of 'Amau independent and not under the rule of either the Egyptians or the Hittites. From the time of Suppiluliumas (*c.* 1370 B.C.) Carchemish dominated the area, first within the Hittite imperial system and later as an independent city-state.

The first fortress city to fall before Joshua was Jericho. Miss Kathleen Kenyon has proved that Sir John Garstang misdated the parallel fortification walls that he attributed to Joshua's time. Nevertheless pottery evidence from the tell and from the tombs shows there was occupation of Tell es-Sultan in the Late Bronze I Age. Garstang's expeditions (1930–1936) discovered in 26 tombs containing pottery some 320 Late Bronze objects, including a series of royal Egyptian scarab seals ending with two of Amenhotep III (1417–1379 B.C.) but none of Akhenaten. Significantly, except in connection with the isolated Middle Building and two

The dream inscription of Thutmose IV shown on a stela between the paws of the Sphinx. LL

tombs which he attributes to the time of King Eglon (Jud 3:12–14), he found on the mound of Jericho next to no Mycenaen pottery. That began to enter Palestine *c.* 1400 B.C. Yet Pritchard at Tell es-Sa'idiyeh and Franken at Deir Allah 30 miles N in the Jordan Valley each found sizeable quantities of such ware. (See the penetrating analysis of the Jericho evidence in Wood, "Date of the Exodus," pp. 69–73).

On his northern campaign Joshua killed Jabin king of Hazor and set fire to the city (Josh 11:10–11). Later, Israelites under Deborah and Barak destroyed another king of Canaan that reigned in Hazor, also named Jabin (Jud 4:2, 23, 24). It is logical to associate the latest Canaanite level (1*a*) of the huge lower city with Jabin II. It was destroyed by fire in the second half of the 13th cen. B.C. and never reoccupied. In Area K of the lower city a gate (provisionally Late Bronze I of level 2) was destroyed in a violent conflagration. If it is correctly dated, this burning from around 1400 B.C. may have resulted from Joshua's action; there is no intervening evidence of destruction before the end of the Canaanite occupation.

The tribe of Asher settled in Galilee along the coast. An inscription of Seti I, dated *c.* 1310 B.C., lists a name in hieroglyphs *'i-ś-r* along with Megiddo and Kedesh (cf. Jud 4:6; J. Simons, *Handbook for the Study of Egyptian Topographical Lists Relating to Western Asia,* Leiden: E. J. Brill, 1937, p. 147, list XVII, 4). This may be the earliest extrabiblical reference to a specific Israelite tribe. It is mentioned again in Papyrus Anastasi I from the time of Rameses II (ANET, p. 477; Aharoni, *The Land of the Bible,* pp. 168, 171). Albright and K. A. Kitchen doubt that the Egyptian name is equivalent to Heb. *'āshēr,* but A. H. Gardiner believes that *'i-ś-r* may represent Asher (*Ancient Egyptian Onomastica,* I, 192 f.). In 1953 Aharoni found 19 small Iron Age settlements in upper Galilee which he believes were Israelite and began perhaps as early as 1300 B.C.

It is true that the small-scale forays of the Habiru and the inter-city fighting of the Amarna letters (*q.v.*) do not agree with the united invasion and disciplined campaigns of Joshua. The unrest in Canaan does harmonize with the early period of the judges, however, when the Israelites were turning to idols and "every man did that which was right in his own eyes" (Jud 17:6; 21:25). After Joshua died each tribe was responsible to conquer the Canaanites in its own possession, but in many cases the tribe was unsuccessful and co-existed with the heathen (Jud 1). The Habiru seem to have some connection with the Hebrews, however difficult that may be to define (*see* Hebrew People). It is significant that in Joshua's time there were nine city-states (cities with a king) in S Palestine, but Albright finds only four large ones *c.* 1375 B.C. according to a study of the Amarna tablets (BASOR, #87, pp. 37 f.). They are Gezer, Jerusalem, Lachish, and the city and land ruled by Shuwardata; the first two were never captured by Joshua, and Lachish may well have been reoccupied by Canaanites as were Hebron and Debir. It is noteworthy that Jericho, Ai, Bethel, and Gibeon are not mentioned in those letters.

A mediating position between the early and late date views is that of Miss Kenyon. On the basis of her excavations at Jericho she dates the fall of that city to the Israelites 1350–1325 B.C. (*Digging Up Jericho,* London: Ernest Benn, 1957, pp. 260–263). This would tend to support the LXX translation of I Kgs 6:1, which says Solomon began to build the temple in the 440th year of the exodus of the sons of Israel out of Egypt. If the LXX were correct, the Exodus would have occurred *c.* 1407 B.C. and the conquest of Jericho 40 years later, *c.* 1367, quite close to Miss Kenyon's 1350 B.C. There is no textual support for the LXX instead of the Heb. MT in I Kgs 6:1, however, and Miss Kenyon did not find enough remains of the late Bronze period at Jericho to discount Garstang's earlier discoveries.

In summary, the factual evidence can better be explained by the early date view; and to those who believe strongly in the inspiration of all Scripture the statements in I Kgs 6:1 (MT) and Jud 11:26 and supporting passages are conclusive for a date of the Exodus *c.* 1445 B.C.

Bibliography. Gleason L. Archer, SOTI, pp. 164 f., 210–223, 253–259 (early date). U. Cassuto, *Commentary on Exodus,* Jerusalem: Magnes Press, 1967 (S route, late date). Jack Finegan, *Let My People Go,* New York: Harper & Row, 1963 (S route, late date). L. H. Grollenberg, *Atlas of the Bible,* trans. and ed. by J. M. H. Reid and H. H. Rowley, London, 1956 (S route, late date). Gabriel Hebert, *When Israel Came Out of Egypt,* London: SCM Press, 1961 (late date, liberal but helpful to show theological importance). Siegfried H. Horn, "Exodus," SDABD, pp. 330–333 (S route, early date). K. A. Kitchen, *Ancient Orient and Old Testament,* Chicago: Inter-Varsity, 1966, pp. 57–78 (conservative, late date). John Rea, "The Time of the Oppression and the Exodus," BETS, III (1960), 58–69; "New Light on the Wilderness Journey and the Conquest," *Grace Journal,* II (Spring, 1961), 5–13. Donald B. Redford, "Exodus I.11," VT, XIII (1963), 401–418. Irwin W. Reist, "The Theological Significance of the Exodus," JETS, XII (1969), 222–232. H. H. Rowley, *From Joseph to Joshua,* London: British Academy, 1950 (late date). J. Simons, GTT, pp. 233–266 (S route). E. P. Uphill, "Pithom and Raamses: Their Location and Significance," JNES, XXVII (1968), 291–316; XXVIII (1969), 15–39. C. De Wit, *The Date and Route of the Exodus,* London: Tyndale Press, 1960 (S route, late date). Leon Wood, "Date of the Exodus," *New Perspectives on the Old Testament,* ed. by J. Barton Payne, Waco: Word Books, 1970, pp.

66–87 (early date). G. Ernest Wright, *Biblical Archaeology*, rev. ed., Philadelphia: Westminster, 1962, pp. 53–85 (S route, late date).

J. R.

EXORCISM. One who extracts an oath, an exorcist; from *exorkizō, orkizō,* "to extract an oath, to adjure." The verbal form *exorkizō* is used once in Mt 26:63 where the high priest says to Jesus, "I adjure thee by the living God, that thou tell us whether thou be the Christ," while *orkizō* is used three times in the same sense (I Thess 5:27; Mk 5:7; Acts 19:13). The noun is used once in Acts 19:13 of the vagabond Jews—"exorcists."

The exercise of exorcism consisted in the use of magical words and ceremonies for the purpose of expelling demons or evil spirits. It should be very clearly distinguished from the ministry of Christ in casting out evil spirits since He did so by His own power and authority. When His disciples cast them out in His name, they were depending upon this same power and authority (cf. Acts 3:6). The difference between the casting out of evil spirits and exorcism is made clear by two passages which complement each other, namely, Mt 12:22–30 and Acts 19:13 ff. In Christ's defense against the accusation of the Jews in Mt 12, that He cast out devils by Beelzebub, we find the Jews held the view that Christ was working in cooperation with the devil (v. 27). Jesus said that if such were the case, Satan's kingdom was divided against itself and could not stand (v. 26). He claimed that He had the ability to restrain and bind Satan and cast out evil spirits by the power of God, and that this proved the kingdom of God was come (vv. 28–29). To stop their criticism, He asked whether their children were casting out devils by Satan's power (v. 27).

Apparently Christ was referring to what they taught their own children about exorcism. Something of what this was can be learned from Josephus, the Apocrypha, and rabbinical writings. Josephus writes of the wisdom of Solomon in exorcism, attributing to him what were clearly heathen practices (*Ant.* viii.5). The apocryphal book of Tobit speaks of burning the liver of a fish in the ashes of incense to drive away a demon. Rabbinical writers go into long and obnoxious details of methods for exorcism. Yet in spite of this conglomeration of strange ideas, the Jews certainly would not be ready to admit they were casting out demons by Satan, and teaching their children to do the same. This fact Christ uses in His own self-defense.

In Acts 19:11 ff. some of the reprobate Jews, thinking that Paul was practicing mere exorcism in casting out spirits by the name of Jesus, decided to copy him. The answer of the evil spirit, "Jesus I know, and Paul I know; but who are ye?" (v. 15), shows the difference between the magical use of a name in exorcism and casting out demons by the power of God. The demon recognized the power of Jesus and the authority of Paul in Jesus' name, but not the magical exorcism in Jesus' name. Casting out evil spirits is different from exorcism.

See Demonology.

R. A. K.

EXPEDIENCY, EXPEDIENT. Expedient has two meanings: (1) the quality or principle of being adapted to ends which accomplish what is good; (2) the principle of doing what appears profitable or expedient under the particular circumstances apart from moral principles, often called pure expediency.

The wide scope of the word and its dual meaning causes much confusion. The second meaning is not found in the idea of expediency as used in Scripture. A distinction, therefore, needs to be made between the biblical use of the Gr. *sympherei,* the basic meaning of which is "what is profitable," and the idea of pure expediency. When Caiaphas says, "Consider that it is expedient for us, that one man should die for the people, and that the whole nation perish not" (Jn 11:50), and Christ, "It is expedient for you that I go away" (Jn 16:7), the idea of profit and the common good, rather than what suits the circumstances, is paramount. The Scriptures never teach us to make decisions apart from moral principles.

Again, when Paul says, "All things are lawful for me but all things are not expedient," while appearing at first glance to claim absolute Christian liberty, he still gives two reasons as the basis of decision: "I will not be brought under the power of anything"; "not all things edify" (I Cor 6:12; 10:23). Both are moral reasons and show that Paul's seeming amorality at this point is governed by good moral arguments, and his actions are determined by what will prove of permanent value, or real profit not only to himself but also to others.

Is pure expediency not present then in any sense in the NT? Yes, in the sense that eating things offered to idols or not eating them, and circumcision or uncircumcision are basically matters of Christian freedom. Still this is immediately tempered by the reaction of another man's conscience (Rom 14:13 ff.). In other words, while the Gr. word *sympherei* is not used to express pure expediency itself, there is an area of expediency revealed in Scripture. Since the ceremonial law has been done away with, there is nothing unclean in itself; since the antitype has come and fulfilled the law, circumcision has been fulfilled in Him (Col 2:11) and is revealed to be of the heart. Thus "expediency" in the NT is based upon what is profitable and morally good, first for others, whom we must not cause to stumble by doing what does not edify (I Cor 10:28); and second for ourselves, lest we become slaves to habit or "things," such as drink, etc. (I Cor 6:12).

See Flesh; Idols, Things Offered to.

R. A. K.

EXPERIENCE. Paul writes that "tribulation worketh patience; and patience, experience; and experience, hope" (Rom 5:3–4; cf. Jas 1:2–12), revealing a ladder of development which often occurs in the life of the Christian.

The proper relationship between revealed truth and experience must be carefully maintained, since revelation precedes Christian experience. We do not base our Christian ideas and decisions upon experience, but rather upon God's revelation, and experience corroborates the correctness of the decisions.

EXPIATE, EXPIATION. These terms are used in the RSV for Heb. *ḥaṭṭā't* (Num 8:7, "water of expiation") and *kāphar* (Num 35:33; Deut 32:43; I Sam 3:14; II Sam 21:3; Isa 27:9; 47:11), and for Gr. *hilastērion* (Rom 3:25), *hilaskomai* (Heb 2:17) and *hilasmos* (I Jn 2:2; 4:10).

The basic idea of expiation has to do with reparation for a wrong, the satisfaction of the demands of justice through paying a penalty. Propitiation carries in addition the idea of appeasing an offended person, of regaining the favor of a higher individual. Some feel that the idea of appeasing God, as one might appease an arbitrary tyrant, fails to do justice to the character of God as revealed in Christ. For this reason the term "expiation" is preferred as the translation for *hilastērion* by these recent scholars. But God is not seen as a temperamental, angry despot demanding his "pound of flesh." Rather we see Him in His holiness which cannot be undercut if He is to maintain His divine integrity. The demands of God's holiness are met in His love and mercy, His self-giving of Christ the only begotten Son as an expiation for our sins.

On the Day of Atonement in the history of Israel, the high priest entered the most holy place. First he sprinkled the blood of the sin offering upon the altar and then on the mercy seat "within the veil" where no one else dared enter (Lev 16:14). The writer of the Epistle to the Hebrews makes several references to Christ's ministry as our High Priest. After His death on Calvary, Christ entered the holy place of heaven once for all, not with the blood of bulls and goats, but with His own blood (Heb 9:11–14, 24–25; 10:10–14). Hebrews also tells us that the incarnation took place so that Jesus "might become a merciful and faithful high priest in the service of God, to make expiation for the sins of the people" (Heb 2:17, RSV).

Other NT writers also emphasize that through the sprinkling (shedding) of the blood of Christ reparation was made for our sins, a price was paid to remove the penalty from us (I Pet 1:18 f.). Forgiveness for sin could only be made by satisfying the holiness of God. God's reaction to sin cannot be anything else but judgment and condemnation, which Paul speaks of as the wrath of God (Rom 1:18 f.). The expiation made by Christ, His sin offering on our behalf, provided the objective ground for God's forgiveness of our sins; we are then justified if we receive Christ's priestly ministry as the Lamb of God by faith (Rom 3:25, RSV).

We may say then that Christ propitiated the holiness of God through becoming an expiation for our sins. The atonement does not mean the appeasing of an arbitrary potentate; it is the love of God coming to us in the self-giving of Christ. In this expiating ministry Jesus is described as our "advocate with the Father" (I Jn 2:1–2). "In this is love, not that we loved God but that he loved us and sent his Son to be the expiation for our sins" (I Jn 4:10, RSV).

See Atonement; Propitiation.

T. W. B.

Ancient peoples of the Near East feared the evil eye. In this mosaic from Antioch of Syria of early Christian date, all sorts of attacks are made on the evil eye. HFV

EYE. Eye denotes the physical organ of sight of man and beast and is used in many figurative applications. The eyes are affected by age, emotions, sleep, and death. They show emotional qualities, such as generosity (Prov 22:9), greed (Ps 10:8), arrogance (Isa 2:11; 5:15; II Kgs 19:22), envy (I Sam 18:9; Prov 28:22; Mk 7:22), evil desire (Isa 3:16; II Pet 2:14; I Jn 2:16). They are used of God in an anthropomorphic sense, showing His omniscience.

Painting around the eye was common for women in ancient Egypt and Babylonia, but among the Hebrews it is mentioned chiefly in connection with women of ill repute. The eyelids above and below the eyes were blackened with black powder of antimony or stibium. However, the translators of the KJV sometimes translated the word "eyes" by "face." Thus Jezebel actually painted her eyes (II Kgs 9:30, ASV). Jeremiah says, "Though thou enlargest thine eyes with paint" (Jer 4:30, ASV; cf. Ezk 23:40). *See* Eyes, Painting the.

The word "eyes" is used in a variety of other ways: (1) a fountain (*q.v.*), as the Heb. word is sometimes translated, probably stemming from the eye as a fountain of tears (cf. Jer 9:1); (2) color or gleam, since the eye sparkles like metal or jewels (Ezk 1:4; 8:2; 10:9); (3) face (Num 14:14); (4) visible surface of the earth (Ex 10:5, 15; Num 22:5); (5) forehead, as in "between thine eyes" (Ex 13:9); (6) presence, as in "before the eyes" (Heb. Gen 23:11); (7) individual opinion, as "in your eyes" (Gen 19:8); (8) favor or anger, as in "to set thine eyes upon" (Heb. Jer 39:12; Amos 9:8). The phrase "to keep as the apple [or pupil] of the eye" (Deut 32:10; Ps 17:8) means to preserve something with particular care.

E. C. J.

EYE, BLINDING OF. *See* Punishments.

EYES, COVERING OF THE. A difficult phrase used in Gen 20:16 of different interpretations. If the words refer to Abraham, the idea may be that Abraham when he professes to be Sarah's husband would act as a veil to those who may desire her. If the words refer to the money received by Abraham, the money may be as a veil to protect her from the wanton desires of others. More likely it refers to the money as a compensation or an "atoning gift . . . so that he may forget a wrong done (cf. Gen 32:21, and Job 9:24, 'he covereth the faces of the judges,' i.e., he bribes them)" (KD, I, 241).

EYES, PAINTING THE. The practice of painting the eyes is very ancient, being well attested in Egypt from even predynastic times. The material used was ground on a stone palette and often was kept in small jars of alabaster, tubes of wood, or similar containers. The early preference was for a green color (chrysocalla or malachite), but later black (galena) became more popular. A black form is known in modern times as *kohl,* a term derived from Arabic. Kohl was applied to the edges of the eyelids by either the fingers or special rodlike applicators. The resulting dark rim was thought to add contrasting brilliance to the eye. Though used primarily as a cosmetic, eye paint also appears in prescriptions for eye ailments.

In the Bible the use of eye paint always has evil associations. The Heb. verb *kāḥal,* "to paint (eyes)," occurs only in Ezk 23:40, in a description of the efforts of an adulteress to entice her victims. Eye paint (Heb. *pûk*) is mentioned twice in connection with makeup. Jezebel painted her eyes before she went to confront Jehu (II Kgs 9:30, RSV). Jer 4:30 (RSV) compares Judah and Jerusalem to a woman who enlarges her eyes with paint in an attempt to secure deliverance by seduction. Here the verb is *qāra',* basically "to tear," also "to make large or wide," graphically fitting the appearance of painted eyes. *See* Eye.

C. E. D.

EYESALVE. The medicine or powder referred to in Rev 3:18 was a compound of ingredients applied to the eyelids to strengthen the eyes. The medical school at Laodicea was famous for this preparation and its usage, according to Galen. The blindness of the Laodicean church was spiritual, however, and the intent of the command in Rev 3:18 was to urge those with inadequate spiritual discernment to seek a remedy for their condition.

EZAR (ē'zăr). This spelling of the name is used in place of Ezer (*q.v.*) in I Chr 1:38 for a son of Seir, the Horite, in the land of Edom (cf. Gen 36:21).

EZBAI (ĕz'bī). The name of one of David's mighty men, the father of Naarai (I Chr 11:37).

EZBON (ĕz'bŏn)

1. A son of Gad (Gen 46:16), also called Ozni (cf. Num 26:15–16).

2. One of the sons of Bela, thus a grandson of Benjamin (I Chr 7:7).

EZEKIAS (ĕz-ĕ-kī'ăs). The Gr. form of Hezekiah (*q.v.*), a king of Judah (Mt 1:9–10).

EZEKIEL (ē-zē'kyĕl). Ezekiel was one of the three writing prophets, along with Jeremiah and Daniel, at the time of the Babylonian Exile. While Jeremiah was ministering in Judah, and Daniel (deported in 605 B.C.) was serving at the court of Nebuchadnezzar (Dan 1:1–7), Ezekiel was preaching to the Jewish captives in Babylonia. He had been taken to Babylon with them and their king Jehoiachin (Ezk 1:2; 33:21) after the siege of Jerusalem in the eighth year of Nebuchadnezzar (597 B.C.; see II Kgs 24:10–16). The only other period of such fullness of prophetic testimony was the time of Isaiah, Hosea, Amos, and Micah in the latter half of the 8th cen. B.C. Ezekiel shows a closer relationship in concept and message to Jeremiah than to Daniel, who probably did not write down any of his prophecies until after the fall of Babylon in 539 B.C.

Ezekiel's name signifies "God strengthens." He was a priest (Ezk 1:3) of the family of Zadok. There is no evidence that Ezekiel had performed priestly functions in Jerusalem before he was exiled to Babylon, even though he seems to have been thoroughly familiar with the temple of Solomon and its cultus. Nothing is known of the personal history of Ezekiel beyond what is found in his book, and what is known of the times in which he lived. He is not mentioned in any other OT book, nor is he directly referred to in the NT, although much of the symbolism of the book of Revelation is clearly based on his visions.

Ezekiel is supposed to have been a young man at the time of the Exile, but it is claimed that his writings imply a more mature man. A number of his prophecies are carefully dated in the time of Jehoiachin's captivity. The date in Ezk 1:1 ("in the thirtieth year"), which has been the cause of much difference of opinion among the commentators, must refer to Ezekiel's own age of 30, the age when Levites entered their priestly duties (Num 4:23, 30, 39, 43). Thus he was born *c*. 627 B.C.

Ezekiel was married (Ezk 24:18) and lived probably in the village of Tel-abib near Nippur in Babylonia (3:15), in his own house (3:24; cf. Jer 29:1-7), to which the elders of Israel would come to consult with him (8:1; 14:1; 20:1). Most of the captives were settled along the river Chebar (1:3), now identified as a royal canal of Nebuchadnezzar, flowing from the vicinity of Babylon past Nippur to Erech (*see* Chebar). Fifth cen. B.C. clay tablets from Nippur tell of the Murashu Sons, merchants who did business with Jews during the Persian era, thus confirming the residence of Jews in this locale.

Ezekiel's wife died suddenly during his ministry, but the Lord expressly forbade him to mourn for her (24:16-18). The book is full of such personal experiences of the prophet (3:24-26; 4:4-8; 4:12; 5:1; 24:27). God intended the prophet to be a sign to Israel in the experiences of his life (24:24). He began his prophetic work in 592 B.C., in the fifth year of Jehoiachin's captivity when he was 30 years old (1:1-2). He prophesied for at least 22 years (29:17). Nothing is known concerning the end of his ministry.

At first Ezekiel's messages were not well received (14:1, 3; 18:19, 25), but with the passing of time his prophecies began to bear fruit, and finally the nation was cleansed of its idolatry. He began in a time of spiritual declension and uprooting. The prophet saw clearly that conditions among his people called for further judgment from the Lord, which did come in the third deportation from Judah in 586 B.C. When judgment had completed its work, then the need of the hour was consolation for the wounded nation.

Ezekiel has been spoken of as suffering from a mental disorder, even from a form of catalepsy, on the basis of such passages as 3:23–4:8 (H. Klostermann, *Theologische Studien und Kritiken,* 1877). Such a position arises from a failure to understand the nature of the visions and experiences of the prophet. His life and ministry were entirely under God's appointment.

He has been called "the father of Judaism" because of the influence he is said to have exercised on the later worship of Israel. A comparison may be drawn between the apostle John on the island of Patmos and Ezekiel at Chebar, both in a place of isolation and oppression by forces of the present evil world system.

C. L. F.

EZEKIEL, BOOK OF. This major prophetic work is named for the prophet whose divinely inspired messages and visions are recorded in it. It is the 12th book (of 24) in the Heb. Bible, the 26th book in the English OT.

Authorship and Date

Not until the 1920's did any scholars seriously challenge the genuineness and unity of the book of Ezekiel. J. Skinner wrote in 1898 (HDB, I, 817*a*): "Neither the unity nor the authenticity of Ezekiel has been questioned by more than a very small minority of scholars. Not only does it bear the stamp of a single mind in its phraseology, its imagery, and its mode of thought, but it is arranged on a plan so perspicuous and so comprehensive that the evidence of literary design in the composition becomes altogether irresistible." Nevertheless, critics have claimed several main difficulties in believing that the book is an authentic account of Ezekiel's ministry and that he wrote all the prophecies included in it.

First, Gustave Hölscher in 1924 claimed that all the pre-Exilic prophets of Israel and Judah proclaimed only doom and judgments against their respective nations, so that any passage promising a restoration and a golden age must necessarily have been added in the Persian period. Hölscher supported his criticism with a literary analysis based mainly on a contrast between the poetry and prose sections, and attributed to Ezekiel only 170 verses out of the total 1,273. But numerous writers, both ancient and modern, have composed beautiful poetry as well as prose. Furthermore, nearly all the OT prophets who warned of imminent divine punishment also predicted ultimate divine bestowal of grace upon a redeemed remnant of Israel.

Second, Robert H. Pfeiffer, following V. Herntrich, insisted that Ezekiel must actually have been living in Jerusalem when he delivered the prophetic messages of chaps. 4-24 (*Introduction to the OT,* Harper, 1948, pp. 535-543). His call to speak to a rebellious house (Ezk 2) and to be a watchman (Ezk 3) led him to return to Judah to address in person the Jews left in Jerusalem. He enacted symbolic prophecies for their benefit which they could not see if he were in Babylonia (e.g., 12:1-12); also he described conditions and events happening in his homeland, such as Pelatiah's sudden death (11:13) and Nebuchadnezzar's consulting omens at a crossroads as the Babylonian army approached Jerusalem (21:18-23).

Many modern scholars have adopted the view Pfeiffer has advocated because it would seem to be scientifically impossible for a man in Babylon to be ministering effectively to people hundreds of miles across the desert. But they discount the reality of visionary or spiritual transport (8:1-3; 11:24) and of direct revelation from God about immediate events in Jerusalem (e.g., 24:1-2). Furthermore, Ezekiel's words were relevant in Tel-abib, for in God's reckoning the 10,000 or more Jewish captives in Babylon (II Kgs 24:14) were as much His covenant people as those still in Judah. They were one in equally needing purification of heart and instruction concerning the reason for the destruction of their holy city. Moreover, as Jer 29 indicates, there was communication by ordinary travel between Palestine and Mesopotamia; thus the words and actions of Ezekiel could be reported to the Jerusalem community.

There are unconsciously designed bits of evidence that speak of a Babylonian locale for chaps. 1-24, such as a city map drawn on a clay tablet or brick (4:1-4)—a map of this kind has been found in the ruins of Nippur—and digging through a wall (12:1-7), possible of a mud-brick or adobe house common in Babylonia but not of the typical stone wall in the hill country of Judah. The many Babylonian words, idioms, and imagery also suggest that Ezekiel spoke and wrote in a proper Babylonian milieu (R. Tournay, "A propos des babylonismes d'Ezeckiel," RB, LXVIII [1961], 388-393). And as Carl G. Howie points out, Jews would have been very reluctant to admit that a genuine prophet was speaking outside the land, unless there were overwhelming evidence for such a conclusion (IDB, II, 206*a*; cf. Harry M. Orlinsky, "Where Did Ezekiel Receive the Call to Prophesy?" BASOR #122 [1951], 34-36). Therefore the interpretation of C. C. Torrey that the book was a pseudepigraph written in Palestine *c.* 230 B.C., a purely fictional account of events in the reign of Manasseh (*Pseudo-Ezekiel and the Original Prophecy,* 1930), may be dismissed.

Third, some scholars have argued that the presence of Aramaisms in the book must prove it was written in the post-Exilic period. But Aramaic had become the lingua franca of the Assyrian Empire from the latter half of the 8th cen. onward, and the Aramaic influence in Ezekiel is no more than one would expect for one writing in Mesopotamia in the 6th cen. B.C.

Others have rejected chaps. 38-39 and/or 40-48 as not belonging to Ezekiel because of their apocalyptic nature, this type of literature supposedly not having originated until the Hellenistic period. The same authors would date Daniel to the Maccabean period. Again one sees an antisupernatural bias at work, refusing to recognize the historical arguments in favor of the traditional 6th cen. B.C. date of these prophecies. The relative unimportance of Persia in Ezk 27:10 and 38:5 and its complete absence in chaps. 1-24 argue strongly for a time of writing before the rise of Cyrus *c.* 550 B.C. The gates of the future millennial temple (cf. 40:6-16) with three guardrooms on either side follow the pattern of excavated Solomonic gates at Megiddo, Gezer, and Hazor, whose plan was later discontinued, and was meaningful therefore only to one who had seen the temple of Solomon prior to its destruction in 586 B.C.

Purpose and Theme

The theme of Ezekiel is the glory and transcendence of the Lord. The Jews in exile must realize that their God has not been defeated by heathen powers but is justified in judging His own; that He is not limited to divine activity within the confines of Palestine but is present with them in far-off Babylon.

The vision of the throne-chariot of the Lord (Ezk 1) reveals the ability of God's governing power to go quickly anywhere on earth or above the earth—His omnipresence. He is enthroned above all creation—inanimate (represented by wind, cloud, and fire, 1:4) and animate (represented by the four cherubim; cf. Ezk 1:5-11 with 10:8; I Kgs 6:23-28)—symbolizing His omnipotence. Not only is He sovereign in His dealings with His chosen nation of Israel but also with the seven neighboring heathen nations that are exulting over her fall (Ezk 25-32). Them He will destroy for their pride and hatred of God's people (Babylon is not included, perhaps because that nation is the instrument of God's justice, cf. 29:17-20), but Israel He will purge and correct and restore as an act of His grace that will lead them to repentance (36:16-32). God's purpose is that both Israel and the nations "will know that I am the Lord"— a phrase that occurs some 30 times in 6:7—39:28.

The triumphant note of Ezekiel's prophecy is sounded in the last few words of the book: "the Lord is there." This will be the name, the very character, of the new, restored Jerusalem of the future millennial kingdom on earth. In a rebuilt literal temple, reminiscent of Solomon's, worship will be conducted with blood sacrifices, having sacramental but not propitiatory significance (Gleason Archer, SOTI, pp. 362 ff.). It will be a provisional economy pointing forward to the purely spiritual, eternal forms of worship without a temple promised in Rev 21:9—22:5.

Ezekiel was the first prophet to underscore the truth of individual responsibility (18:1-32; 33:1-20). Even though each may be a member of the covenant community, there is no such possession as inherited righteousness. Conversely, each may escape the judgment of his fathers by personally turning from his sins and observing God's ordinances.

Style and Literary Influence

Ezekiel uses more symbolism and allegory than any other OT prophet. His figures of speech are not dependent on heathen sources but have their foundation in the sanctuary of Israel and in the concepts of his predecessors, educated as he was under Levitical training. Nevertheless, he is unexcelled for the vividness of his poetic descriptions. Certainly he was a true mystic with an artistic imagination which the Spirit of God could employ to depict in human terms realities from the unseen spirit world (e.g., the king of Tyre evidently motivated by Satan, Ezk 28:11-19). None is so sensitive to the supernatural activity of the Spirit, and thus we turn to Ezekiel for much of the doctrine about the Holy Spirit in the OT.

Ezekiel shaped a type of prophecy known as the apocalyptic. It is characterized by the frequency of visions and emphasis on the future or eschatological period with its tremendous catastrophic movements and direct interventions from heaven. John was dependent on Ezekiel for many of the figures and concepts in the

Apocalypse (cf. Rev 1:15; 4:3, 6 with Ezk 1:22-28; Gog and Magog in Rev 20:8 with Ezk 38-39; the careful measuring and description of the city, etc., in Rev 11:1; 21:10-27 with Ezk 40-48; the river of life in Rev 22:1-2 with Ezk 47:1-12).

The significance of a good shepherd (Jn 10:1-30) is dependent on Ezk 34 as much as on Ps 23. The Lord Jesus seems to have turned to Ezekiel as well as to Dan 7:13-14 for the title He used most often of Himself, viz., the Son of Man. (For a thorough discussion of this term see Andrew W. Blackwood, Jr., *The Other Son of Man: Ezekiel/Jesus,* Baker, 1966, pp. 11-25.)

Contents

The book divides easily into two major parts separated by a collection of foreign oracles. The division is based on news of the siege and fall of Jerusalem (24:1-2; 33:21). Chaps. 1-24 in the main contain denunciations of the wickedness during the reign of Zedekiah, the last king of Judah, whereas chaps. 33-48 are occupied with promises to the future remnant of Israel.

A fourfold division of the book is also possible:

I. God's Commissioning of Ezekiel, Chaps. 1-3

II. Prophecies Concerning the Sins of Judah (dated 592-588 B.C., before the fall of Jerusalem), Chaps. 4-24

III. Prophecies Concerning the Punishment of Neighboring Nations (dated 587-585 B.C.; 29:17-21 dated 571 B.C.), Chaps. 25-32
  A. Against Ammon, Moab, Edom, Philistia, 25:1-17
  B. Against Tyre and Sidon, 26:1–28:26
  C. Against Egypt, 29:1–32:32

IV. Prophecies and Visions of Restored Israel in Their Land (dated 585-573 B.C., after the fall of Jerusalem), Chaps. 33-48
  A. Stages in the restoration and spiritual renewal of land and people, 33:1–39:29
  B. Visions of the future temple and worship in the glorious land, 40:1–48:35

Bibliography. G. A. Cooke, *The Book of Ezekiel,* ICC. H. L. Ellison, *Ezekiel: the Man and His Message,* Grand Rapids: Eerdmans, 1956. Carl G. Howie, *The Date and Composition of Ezekiel,* JBL Monograph Series, IV, 1950; "Ezekiel," IDB, II, 203-213. Anton T. Pearson, "Ezekiel," WBC, with bibliography of the older works. Samuel J. Schultz, *The OT Speaks,* New York: Harper, 1960, pp. 345-363. John B. Taylor, *Ezekiel: An Introduction and Commentary,* London: Tyndale Press, 1969. C. F. Whitley, *The Exilic Age,* Philadelphia: Westminster, 1957. Walter Zimmerli, "The Message of the Prophet Ezekiel," *Interp.,* XXIII (1969), 131-157.

J. R.

EZEL (ē′zĕl). There is wide difference of opinion as to the meaning of this word. Jonathan met David on their farewell parting (I Sam 20:19, 41 f.) by the stone Ezel (Heb. *hā'āzel*). The RSV, following the LXX, emends the passage to read, "beside yonder stone heap," and in v. 41 translates, "David rose from beside the stone heap." Regardless of the exact meaning, the field where David hid lay between Gibeah and Nob.

EZEM (ē′zĕm). *See* Azem.

EZER (ē′zĕr)

1. A son of Seir, the Horite, a native chief in Edom (Gen 36:21, 27, 30; I Chr 1:38, 42).
2. The father of Hushah, one of the descendants of Hur (I Chr 4:4).
3. A descendant of Ephraim who, with his brother Elead, was slain by the Gathites (I Chr 7:21).
4. The foremost of the Gadite warriors who joined David at Ziklag. They were famed for having boldly crossed the Jordan in the spring when it had overflowed its banks (I Chr 12:8-15).
5. A Levite, the son of Jeshua the ruler of Mizpah, who aided in building the wall of Jerusalem (Neh 3:19).
6. A priest who took part in the great dedication of the completed wall of Jerusalem in the days of Nehemiah (Neh 12:42).

EZION-GEBER (ē′zĭ-ŏn-gē′bẽr). In between the present-day cities of Elath and Aqabah in "no-man's land" lies the ancient site of the Solomonic fortified storehouse, which was built near the port anciently called Ezion-geber. It is identified with Elath (Eloth) in Deut 2:8; II Chr 8:17; I Kgs 9:26, and is also most probably to be identified with El-paran of Gen 14:6. *See* Elath. It is situated at the N end of the E arm of the Red Sea (*see* Aqabah, Gulf of). The Israelites encamped in this area when they left Sinai more than a year after departing from Egypt. From here they went on to Kadesh (Num 33:35-36).

Ezion-geber is not mentioned again in the OT until the time of Solomon. At this time (I Kgs 9:26-28; II Chr 8:17-18) Hiram (Huram), the king of Tyre, from whom Solomon had obtained both artisans and materials for building the temple, now sent him ships and sailors to ply the waters of the Red Sea from Ezion-geber. This commerce undoubtedly enriched both Solomon and Hiram and made good use of the products of copper mines located N of Ezion-geber along the Arabah, now known only from archaeological excavation. These "ships of Tarshish" (*q.v.*) took three years to make a round trip out of Ezion-geber to the foreign ports along the coasts of Africa, Arabia, and perhaps as far as India and Ceylon (I Kgs 10:22). Along with large quantities of gold (of Ophir) and silver, other articles of trade were ivory, spices, precious stones, wood (almug, I Kgs 10:11-12), apes, and peacocks. Solomon and his merchants became rich by shipping out of Ezion-geber copper, iron, olive oil, and possibly many products manufactured in Egypt, such as linen and chariots (I Kgs 10:28-29). Solomon had no great ports on the Mediterranean, but his alliance with the Phoenicians gave him access to their ports just as he gave Hiram of Tyre access to Ezion-geber. *See* Hiram; Navy.

Following Solomon, the activity of this port was a key to the prosperity of the land. Those kings of Judah who desired to show themselves powerful attempted to re-establish the fleet out of Ezion-geber. Jehoshaphat came nearest to success, but a storm or some other natural disaster destroyed the ships (I Kgs 22:48). A little known prophet, Eliezer of Mareshah, interpreted this disaster as punishment for Jehoshaphat's alliance with the wicked house of Ahab in the venture (II Chr 20:37). Throughout the rest of the history of the southern kingdom, whenever Judah was weak the Edomites took control of the Ezion-geber and Elath territory (cf. II Kgs 8:20-22; 14:22; 16:6; II Chr 28:17).

The port continued into Persian times as an important link between S Arabia, the coast of Africa, and the western world of the Mediterranean Sea. The excavations of Ezion-geber by Nelson Glueck prior to World War II (1938-40) amply prove this point. For example, Glueck discovered black Attic (Gr.) ware of the 5th cen. B.C., and two jars incised with S Arabian Minaean script in the 8th cen. B.C. level, which underline the prominence of Ezion-geber as a trade link (N. Glueck, BASOR #71 [1938], 15-16; #75 [1939], 19; #80 [1940], 3-10; #82 [1941], 3-16). Glueck's major find was Solomon's citadel with a large storehouse-granary for goods being shipped along the land and sea trade routes intersecting at Ezion-geber (BA, XXVIII [Sept., 1965], 70-87). A seal probably bearing the name of Jotham, the son of Uzziah, witnesses to the brief restoration of the port of Judah, according to II Kgs 14:22. *See* Archaeology; Commerce; Elath.

Bibliography. Y. Aharoni, "Forerunners of the Limes: Iron Age Fortresses in the Negev," IEJ, XVII (1967), 15-17. V. R. Gold, "Ezion-geber," BW, 233-237.

E. B. S.

EZNITE (ĕz'nīt). This word is used in a list of the mighty men of David, "Adino the Eznite" (II Sam 23:8). The meaning is uncertain. *See* Adino.

EZRA (ĕz'rȧ)

1. A priest who returned to Jerusalem with Zerubbabel (Neh 12:1, 13).

2. A priest in Nehemiah's time (Neh 12:33).

3. A priest-scribe, son of Seraiah (Ezr 7:1), who led a group of exiles back to Jerusalem. Best known from the book which bears his name, Ezra was designated in several ways: as priest (Ezr 10:10, 16; Neh 8:2), as scribe (Ezr 7:6; Neh 12:36), and as priest and scribe (Ezr 7:11-12, 21; Neh 8:9; 12:26). Although his work as scribe is well known, many fail to recognize the claim (Ezr 7:1-6) that his priestly lineage could be traced back through Zadok and Phinehas to Aaron. This placed him in the main stream of Jerusalem priesthood. His name is either a late form of *'ezrȧ*, "help," or an abbreviation of *'azaryahû*, "Yahweh helps."

Various sources of information are available for the reconstruction of Ezra's life and ministry. From the book of Ezra, the memoirs in the first person are of special importance (cf. most of Ezr 7:27–9:15). The Aramaic letters as well as the Heb. documents throughout the book give further background. The material in Neh 8-10 adds to the picture while also raising certain problems. There are also allusions to the work of Ezra in I and II Esdras of the Apocrypha.

His commission. In the seventh year of Artaxerxes (cf. below for problem of date), Ezra was commissioned by royal decree to go to Jerusalem for the purpose of evaluating the civil and religious conditions of the Judean community and instituting necessary corrective measures. He was given authority both in terms of money and goods for the temple and exemptions from taxation of the temple officials. Many have questioned the historicity of the sweeping authority given Ezra. Even though the powers are extensive, the king of Persia could well have needed the support of the provinces. He could gain gratitude without any risk to his empire by patronizing the needs of such neglected groups.

Ezra's commission also authorized him to gather a company of exiles who desired to return with him to Jerusalem. After mustering the group, fasting, and offering prayer, Ezra led them out on their journey. Reaching Jerusalem four months later, he presented his orders to the neighboring governors and turned over the temple vessels to the priestly officials. The community at Jerusalem was poor and backward compared with the culture of the Jewish group in Babylonia. It is difficult to estimate how much the arrival of Ezra meant to the struggling community at Jerusalem.

Date of his return. A superficial reading of the books of Ezra and Nehemiah leaves no doubt as to the chronological order of Ezra and Nehemiah. However, an unresolved controversy has raged since 1889 when Maurice Vernes made the suggestion that Nehemiah came first. (Cf. H. H. Rowley's essay, "Chronological Order of Ezra and Nehemiah," in *The Servant of the Lord and Other Essays on the Old Testament,* for a comprehensive listing of theories and scholars involved.) Rowley sums up the difficulty by saying: "It is therefore clear that bold claims, on the one side or the other, that the question is definitely settled are unjustified" (p. 135). Actually, no more than a balance of probability is justified at this point.

On the basis of the biblical text, Ezra appears to have arrived in 458 B.C., the seventh year of Artaxerxes I Longimanus (465-424 B.C.). According to many scholars, the king of Persia referred to should be Artaxerxes II Mnemon (404-358 B.C.). This would place Ezra's return in 398 B.C., long after Nehemiah's governorship. Three passages give the primary reasons for the later date: (1) Ezr 9:9 mentions the rebuilding of a wall, whereas the walls of Jerusalem were rebuilt by Nehemiah after his return in 444 B.C. (2) Ezr 10:1 suggests a greater population than Nehemiah found (cf. Neh 7:4). (3) Ezr 10:6 refers to Johanan (Jehohanan, RSV), as Ezra's contemporary, whereas Eliashib, the grandfather of a later high priest named Johanan, is the high priest in the time of Nehemiah (cf. Neh 3:1, 20; 12:22-23). It is known from the Elephantine papyri that a Johanan was high priest in 407 B.C. However, the arguments are not entirely conclusive, leaving the balance of probability in favor of the traditional order.

The long gap between the events in Ezra (458 B.C.) and the coming of Nehemiah (444 B.C.) also presents a problem. This has been explained as being occasioned by the alienation of the people toward Ezra over the compulsory divorces. However, Ezra may have returned to the Persian court and then have made a second visit to Jerusalem as a coadjutor to Nehemiah. Ezra's original commission may well have been a temporary appointment as in the case of Nehemiah. Surely the moral lapses which Nehemiah discovered would not have occurred if Ezra had been on the scene during the intervening years (458-444 B.C.). *See* Nehemiah.

His personality. Ezra was representative of those in Babylonia whose concern was for the nation's sacred heritage and writings. He was a diligent student of the law, a leading figure in the new order of scribes which had grown up during the Exile.

Much in Ezra reminds us of Nehemiah. They both demonstrated outstanding leadership qualities, unbounded energy, intense faith, and similar spiritual aims. However, Ezra's supreme work lay in his abilities as teacher, historian, critic, and linguist. While he was rigorous and narrow in matters of law, he was able to achieve lasting success. He gave determination and stubbornness to Judaism which made it able to resist the inroads of Hellenism. He was passionate and emotional but always exhibited strong faith in God. His asceticism was severe as he emphasized fasting and disciplined himself. Yet his interest in bringing back the temple vessels and treasures classifies him as a patron of sacred art.

His contribution. As a scribe, Ezra has always been remembered for his important editorial work on parts of the OT Scriptures. While much tradition has grown up around his name, he certainly was representative of those who helped in the collecting, arranging, and editing of the law.

As a religious leader, Ezra has a unique place in Jewish tradition, being often described as the true founder of Judaism, the second founder of the Jewish State, or the founder of the Great Synagogue. His work in renewing the spiritual power and vitality of Israel was indeed significant. Much of the work in adapting the pre-Exilic liturgical practices to post-Exilic Jewish worship can be credited to his spiritual leadership.

As a reformer, Ezra's name will always be linked with the enforced divorces with which he attempted to purify racial lines in order to preserve Israel's religious heritage. It is exceedingly difficult to justify the extreme measures employed as the homes of 17 priests, 6 Levites, 1 singer, 3 doorkeepers, and 86 laymen were torn asunder. However, it must be remembered that marriage in ancient times was viewed as a community matter.

Bibliography. John Bright, "The Date of Ezra's Mission to Jerusalem," *Yehezkel Kaufmann Jubilee Volume, Studies in Bible and Jewish Religion,* ed. by M. Haran, Jerusalem: Magnes Press, 1960, pp. 70-88. "Restoration and Persian Period; Ezra and Nehemiah," CornPBE, pp. 617-622. George Rawlinson, *Ezra and Nehemiah, Their Lives and Times,* London: Nisbet, 1891. H. H. Rowley, *The Servant of the Lord and Other Essays on the Old Testament,* London: Lutterworth, 1952. A. C. Welch, *Post-exilic Judaism,* Edinburgh: Blackwood, 1935. J. S. Wright, *The Date of Ezra's Coming to Jerusalem,* London: Tyndale, 1947.

K. M. Y.

EZRA, BOOK OF. The book which bears Ezra's name was originally combined with Nehemiah as a single volume. This was true in Heb. MSS until separated in a MS dated in A.D. 1448. However, the books were known as separate works to Origen and Jerome in certain Gr. MSS.

Outline

I. The First Return, 1:1–2:70
   A. Permission to return, 1:1-11
   B. Register of returnees, 2:1-70
II. The Rebuilding of the Temple, 3:1–6:22
   A. Altar and foundations of temple set up, 3:1-13
   B. Hindrances to the work, 4:1-5, 24
   C. Later opposition, 4:6-23
   D. Completion of the temple, 5:1–6:22

III. The Activity of Ezra, 7:1 – 10:44
 A. Commission to Erza, 7:1-28
 B. Coming of Ezra, 8:1-36
 C. Problem of mixed marriages, 9:1 – 10:44

Sources

The composite nature of the book is at once evident, especially so in the MT. The shift from first to third to first person pronouns and the alternating use of Heb. and Aram. are easily recognized. The book has combined the following:

1. Memoirs of Ezra (7:27 – 9:15). These were written in the first person. These may have been an abstract of the report which Ezra had to make to the Persian court.

2. Aramaic documents (4:7-16; 4:18-22; 5:7-17; 6:3-12; 7:12-26). These include letters, official and semiofficial documents.

3. Hebrew documents (1:2-4; 2:1-70; 8:1-14; 10:18-44). These undoubtedly came mainly from state archives.

Authorship

According to the Talmud (*Baba Bathra* 15*a*) and other evidences of Heb. tradition, Ezra wrote both the book bearing his name and the book of Nehemiah. However, it is almost universally held today that Chronicles, Ezra, and Nehemiah originally formed one work. Since the closing verses of II Chronicles also stand at the beginning of Ezra, the order has probably been reversed. The term the Chronicler is usually assigned to the author of the entire work. Although many scholars recognize Ezra as the Chronicler, others place the work of compiling these books toward the end of the 4th cen. (*c.* 330 B.C.). The great linguistic similarities, however, with 5th cen. Aram. papyri from the Jewish community at Elephantine, Egypt, argue for a date in Ezra's period. *See* Elephantine Papyri.

K. M. Y.

EZRAHITE (ĕz'rȧ-hīt). A descendant of Zerah of the tribe of Judah, as Ethan the Ezrahite (I Kgs 4:31; I Chr 2:16; Ps 89, title), whose wisdom was exceeded only by that of Solomon. Heman, his brother, is called the Ezrahite in the title of Ps 88. Or I Kgs 4:31 could mean that Ethan was an *'ezrāḥî*, a native, i.e., Israelite trained, as opposed to Heman, Chalcol, and Darda, members of a Canaanite orchestral guild ("sons of Mahol").

EZRI (ĕz'rī). A servant of David, the son of Chelub, placed over the tilling of the ground (I Chr 27:26).

F

FABLE. In the KJV and ASV NT, fable (which does not occur in the OT) is used to translate *mythos*. This Gr. word has also been translated "fiction" (Goodspeed), "myth" (NEB), "fairy tale" (Phillips, Tit 1:14), etc. At one time the word was almost synonymous with the Gr. *logos* and *rhēma*, "word" (cf. Trench, p. 337). Before NT times it had come to mean that which was fictitious as opposed to *logos* – the true expression or utterance (Jn 1:1). In the NT it carries this sense in all its occurrences (I Tim 1:4; 4:7; II Tim 4:4; Tit 1:14; II Pet 1:16). In these letters the word probably refers to fictitious stories concocted by Jewish teachers (Tit 1:14), based on the OT and devised to turn Christians away from the truth.

There are fables in the OT, though the term is not used to so designate them. Compare Jotham's fable of the trees choosing their king (Jud 9:7-21), and Jehoash's fable of the cedar of Lebanon and the thistle (II Kgs 14:8-10).

J. McR.

FACE. Used to denote the part of an object most exposed to view; hence, the face of the ground, water, sky, etc. In Scripture, it often denotes presence in the general sense; and when used of God, means His presence in a vivid sense. Adam and Eve hid from "the face of Jehovah," or from His presence. Because of the glory of God, Moses was told, "Thou canst not see my face: for there shall no man see me, and live" (Ex 33:20). Thus, no one in his present state of being can endure the full blaze of God's glory (I Cor 13:12; I Jn 3:2; Rev 22:4). However, when the brightness of His glory is veiled, man may behold such revelation (Gen 32:30; Jn 1:14). The "bread of the face" was the showbread, denoting God's presence. *See* Bread of Faces.

The word also implied favor, anger, justice, severity (Ps 44:3; 67:1; Dan 9:17; Gen 16:6, 8; Ex 2:15; Rev 6:16). "To hide the face" or "to fall on the face" expressed humility and reverence (Ex 3:6; Isa 6:2), and "the covering of the face" was a sign of mourning (II Sam 19:4). "To set one's face" denoted determination (Lk 9:51), and "to turn away one's face" expressed apathy or contempt (II Chr 29:6; Ezk 14:6).

Bibliography. Eduard Lohse, "*Prosōpon*, etc.," TDNT, VI, 768-780.

E. C. J.

FAIR. Several shades of meaning are found in the use of this word.

1. Heb. *ṭāhôr* means "to shine," "be bright"; hence, "clean," "pure," thus "fair." It is used of physical, moral, or ritual fairness (Prov 22:11, KJV "pureness"). Used physically it is opposed to filthy (Zech 3:3-5).

2. Heb. *ṭôb* means "to be bright," "cheer-

ful," "good," or "well." It also suggests beauty in the expression "fair young virgins" (Est 2:2).

3. Heb. *yāpeh* refers to "fairness as beautiful," such as a beautiful figure, beauty of aspect (Song 1:15-16; 4:1, 7; 6:10).

4. Heb. *leqaḥ*, "learning," is used of fair speech (KJV), captivating charms, learning or knowledge (Prov 7:21; cf. Rom 16:18).

5. Heb. *zāhāb* means "to shine or glitter" as gold, and suggests golden light as "fair weather" (Job 37:22, KJV); perhaps the aurora borealis is thus signified. In the NT "fair weather" translates the Gr. *eudia* (Mt 16:2).

FAIR HAVENS. A small bay on the S coast of Crete, about five miles E of Cape Lithinos. Paul's ship anchored there for a time while en route to Rome (Acts 27:8-12). The bay, which still retains its ancient name, is exposed on the E but protected on the SW by two small islands. Paul urged remaining there for the winter, but the ship's owner wanted to sail about 50 miles W of Phenice (Phoenix), a safer winter harbor. (Normally, ancient ships did not sail the Mediterranean during the stormy months of Nov. to Mar.) After leaving Fair Havens the vessel was driven from its course by a violent northeaster and ultimately was wrecked off Malta. *See* Melita.

FAIRS. Although "fairs" is one possible rendering of the Heb. word *ʿizzābôn*, it is translated in later versions by "wares," "merchandise." From Ezekiel's usage of the word it appears that it could mean either the place where trading was done or the objects involved in the trading (Ezk 27:12, 14, 16, 19, 27).

FAITH. Faith is a NT word. It occurs only twice in the OT of the KJV (Deut 32:20; Hab 2:4). The ASV translates the first reference (Heb. *'ēmûn*) "faithfulness." The ASV retains "faith" in the second text (giving "faithfulness" in the marg., Heb. *'ĕmûnā*), possibly because of the frequent quotation of the text in the NT, in which the idea is clearly that of faith in the active sense (cf. Rom 1:17; Gal 3:11; Heb 10:38). The equivalent OT word is "trust." The word "trust" and its related forms occur more than 150 times in the OT, the translation of a number of different Heb. words. The NT word *pistis* (see Arndt) is used both in the sense of faithfulness (Rom 3:3; Gal 5:22; Tit 2:10) and of trust (Mk 11:22; Mt 8:10; Lk 5:20; Rom 3:22, 28; etc.). *See* Faithfulness; Fidelity; Amen.

Faith is the basic virtue in the NT (I Cor 13:13; Heb 11:6; II Pet 1:5-7). Even so, there is no formal definition of faith in the Bible. Concerning the passage sometimes so presented (Heb 11:1), Dean F. W. Farrar observed: "The famous words with which this chapter opens are not so much a definition as a description. They are not a definition, for they do not, as St. Thomas Aquinas says, indicate the essence of faith. They tell us what faith does, rather than what it is—its issues, rather than its nature. 'Faith,' the writer says, 'is the basis of things hoped for, the demonstration of objects not seen.' This is what faith is in its results. It furnishes us with a foundation on which our hopes can securely rest, and with a conviction that those things exist which are not earthly or temporal, and which, therefore, we cannot see."

A proper definition of faith must take into consideration its complexity, for while the exercise of it may be said to be simplicity itself, it involves the whole personality. Knowledge is necessary (Rom 10:13-17). However, while intellectual grasp of the truth to be believed is not faith, it is part of it. Assent to the truth to be believed is necessary (Mt 9:28; Jas 2:19); however, assent may be no more than admitting the veracity of the thing to be believed, without carrying any committal with it. The element without which we do not have biblical faith, is the consent of the volition, or "the consent of the will to the assent of the understanding" (cf. Jn 8:30-31, ASV).

Saving faith, therefore, involves active personal trust, a commitment of oneself to the Lord Jesus Christ. But it is not the amount of faith that saves, it is the object of faith that saves. Great faith in the wrong object does not alter man's lost estate one iota. Little faith (so long as it is faith) in the right object must result in salvation. As an article of religion puts it: "We may thus rely on Christ, either tremblingly or confidingly; but in either case it is saving faith. If, though tremblingly, we rely on Him in His obedience for us unto death, instantly we come into union with Him, and are justified. If, however, we confidingly rely on Him, then have we the comfort of our justification. Simply by faith in Christ are we justified and saved" (Reformed Episcopal usage). In general biblical usage, to believe is to have such full-fledged faith in Christ, to entrust oneself to Him. The first term which the Christians used to describe themselves was "the believers" (Acts 2:44; 4:32; 5:14; etc.). *See* Believe; Believers.

It should be observed that there are most blessed and real results when an individual truly trusts the Lord Jesus Christ. There is not only a changed position before God (justification), but there is the beginning of the redemptive and sanctifying work of God. While the transformation of life is not the ground of salvation, it is the evidence of salvation. And without some such evidence (in greater or lesser degree), a question must be raised as to the genuineness of the faith of the individual. Within bounds, we agree with the dictum of Dr. C. I. Scofield: "Faith which does not impel to action, which does not result in a changed relation to God and Christ, which does not work transformingly in life, is not biblical faith." Unbelief everywhere in the Bible is equated with disobedience (cf. Jn 3:36, KJV with ASV), and is considered the most serious of sins (Heb 3:12-18).

The good works of a Christian are the result of and the evidence for the genuineness of his faith. It is an understanding of this fact which will solve the problem of some as to an alleged discrepancy between Paul and James. Paul certainly relates good works to faith (Eph 2:8-10). James surely is clear that he is speaking of justification before men (Jas 2:18—"show me," "show thee"; v. 22—"thou seest"; v. 24—"ye see"; v. 26), and that faith is proved by works (v. 22).

Faith is not only related to salvation from sin for the Christian, it is connected with God's providence and leading (Mk 11:22; Heb 11:6; Prov 3:5-6; Ps 37:3, ASV; Acts 27:25), with sanctification (Gal 3:1-3; Acts 26:18; II Cor 5:7; Gal 2:20, ASV; Col 2:6-7), with service (Rom 12:6; Gal 5:6; I Thess 1:3; II Thess 1:11; I Tim 6:12; Heb 11:33; Jas 2:22), and with prayer (Mt 21:22; Heb 11:6; Jas 1:5-8).

The relationship of repentance and faith is a frequently discussed theological question. In Paul's summation of his Ephesian ministry he spoke of "testifying both to the Jews, and also to the Greeks, repentance toward God, and faith toward our Lord Jesus Christ" (Acts 20:21; cf. 11:17-18; 26:18-20). It is probable that knowledge (*notitia*) and assent (*assensus*) precede repentance (a change of mind) as they precede trust (*fiducia*). Repentance, in this view, precedes trust. Thus faith is not genuine saving faith unless it involves repentance (*q.v.*).

Another theological question involving faith is that which is raised in any *ordo salutis* (order of salvation). One matter of concern is the relationship of regeneration and faith. The difference among evangelicals is represented by the Lutheran, the Arminian, and the Reformed conceptions. In the Lutheran view, calling, repentance, and regeneration are preparatory in the sinner's coming to Christ; since salvation is not imparted until the sinner exercises faith, it is necessary to maintain faith. The Reformed view regards regeneration, repentance, and faith as "blessings of the covenant of grace," not merely as preparatory or as conditions consummated by human initiative. In the Arminian concept, God grants grace to all men which enables them to believe and obey the gospel; a man is justified "on account of his faith."

Whatever view is held, it may be observed that there must be the response of faith for experiential salvation (Acts 8:37; 16:31; Eph 2:8). Indeed, such a concept is taught in the chapter on the new birth (Jn 3:14-16). Further, the Lord Himself spoke of the dead hearing His voice, and this reference must be to those spiritually dead (Jn 5:25-29; notice evident contrast in v. 29). However, there can be no question concerning either the sovereign choice of God (Acts 13:48; Rom 8:29, ASV; Eph 1:4-5), or the necessity of God's initiating the salvation of a man (Rom 3:10*b*-18; I Cor 2:14; Eph 2:8-9).

The expression "the faith" on occasion refers to "that which is believed, *body of faith* or *belief, doctrine*" (Arndt). The same lexicon says that "this objectivizing of the *pistis* concept is found as early as Paul." Even those scholars who acknowledge the usage of "the faith" in this sense, differ as to the references in which it appears. A suggested list follows: Lk 18:8; Acts 3:16; 6:7; 13:8; 14:22; 16:5; 24:24; I Cor 16:13; II Cor 13:5; Gal 1:23; 3:23-25; Eph 4:13; Phil 1:27; Col 1:23; 2:7; II Thess 3:2; I Tim 1:19; 3:9, 13; 4:1, 6; 5:8; 6:10, 21; II Tim 3:8; 4:7; Tit 1:13; Jas 2:1; Jude 3; Rev 14:12.

See Faith, The Christian; Faith, Rule of.

Bibliography. Rudolf Bultmann and Artur Weiser, "*Pisteuō*, etc.," TDNT, VI, 174-228. J. Oliver Buswell, Jr., *A Systematic Theology of the Christian Religion,* Grand Rapids: Zondervan, 1962, II, 175-186 (with good discussion of *pisteuō,* "to believe," in John's Gospel). Lewis Sperry Chafer, *Systematic Theology,* Dallas: Dallas Sem. Press, 1947-57, III, 372-378; VI, 293-294. Vernon C. Grounds, "The Nature of Faith," *Christian Faith and Modern Theology,* ed. by Carl F. H. Henry, New York: Channel Press, 1964, pp. 325-345 (including a discussion of Kierkegaard's understanding of faith and a full bibliography on the various aspects of faith). J. Gresham Machen, *What Is Faith?* Grand Rapids: Eerdmans, 1946 (the best volume on faith from an evangelical viewpoint). James I. Packer, "Faith," BDT, pp. 208-211. Benjamin B. Warfield, "Faith," HDB; *Biblical Doctrines,* New York: Oxford Univ. Press, 1929, Chap. 13; *Biblical and Theological Studies,* Philadelphia: Presbyterian and Reformed, 1952, pp. 375-444. See article on Theology for names and works of other recommended theologians.

W. C.

FAITH, THE CHRISTIAN. Christianity is that interpretation of existence which, as a thoroughgoing system of supernaturalism, stands in polar antithesis to atheistic naturalism. A radical monotheism, it is also the polar antithesis of polytheism. Teaching that God is self-subsisting, personal, living, ethical, dynamic, and sovereign, it is likewise the polar antithesis of pantheism and deism. Yet because it holds to the triunity of the Godhead, the Christian faith must be sharply differentiated from such species of monotheism as Judaism and Islam.

Structured upon the gracious activities of revelation and redemption, it postulates man's creation in the divine image; his apostasy, his guilt, his lostness; but his possibility of forgiveness through the miracles of incarnation, atonement, and resurrection—three history-splitting events which center in Jesus Christ. When the Mediator's person and work are appropriated by a sinner in trustful self-commitment, a new God-relationship is established. This experience is theologically formulated in the doctrines of regeneration, justification, and sanctification (*q.v.*). Christianity anticipates its Lord's second advent and His judgment of all mankind. Life, this faith holds, will continue eternally beyond death not in mere survival of disembodied souls but in a raising up of transformed bodies, with believers enjoying God's fellowship while unbelievers will endure unending punishment. And the dominant recurring theme of this cosmic drama is *sola gloria Deo* (to God be all the glory)!

V. C. G.

FAITH, RULE OF. Originally used to designate the summary of Christian doctrine taught to catechumens before baptism, the phrase, *regula fidei,* quickly became a technical term in theology; and as a synonym for the source and standard of belief, it likewise became the focus of significant controversy.

What is the norm of saving truth, the definitive criterion of dogma and practice, the canon of Christianity? Is it Scripture plus tradition, plus some ecclesiastical *magisterium* which functions as an authoritative interpreter? This has been the Roman Catholic and Greek Orthodox view, though Orthodoxy does not accept the papacy as the exclusive seat of interpretation, nor does it regard the pronouncements of any except the earlier church councils as binding. Is that criterion some mystical inner light? Disciples of Robert Barclay, the leading Quaker theologian, have so argued. Or is it a fusion of reason and conscience? With various modifications, liberalism has adopted that position. Or is it rather Scripture alone? This was the Reformation watchword, its *principium cognoscendi,* paralleling the material principle of justification by faith alone. Historic Protestantism contended—and still contends—that Scripture, Spirit interpreted, is the sole and sufficient norm of Christianity, rendering any extrabiblical supplement unnecessary.

Agreeing apologetically, Calvinists and Lutherans have divided on this issue polemically. Calvinists have taken rigorist ground, arguing that nothing is warranted unless Scripture expressly declares it. Lutherans have been less inflexible, accepting those practices which do not contradict Scripture. But all Reformed Christians concur with Chillingworth, "The Bible, the Bible alone, is the religion of Protestants."

Bibliography. Gabriel Moran, *Scripture and Tradition: A Survey of the Controversy,* New York: Herder & Herder, 1963. W. P. Patterson, *The Rule of Faith,* London: Hodder and Stoughton, 1912.

V. C. G.

FAITHFULNESS. God, as biblically revealed, is living and personal, hence the possessor of a certain character. Central to that character is faithfulness or utter dependability. Jas 1:17 brings out God's steadfastness, which is the antithesis of everything fickle and fluctuating. Very similar is II Tim 2:13 which declares that God's faithfulness is the corollary of His self-consistency. These NT passages highlight the same trait which is metaphorically expressed in those OT texts that call the Lord a Rock (Deut 32:4, 15, 18). In other words, God's character is the solid and unshakable foundation of reality. Hence His covenant is inviolable (Deut 7:9), His word more steadfast than the law-abiding framework of nature (Mt 7:24-27; 24:35; Lk 21:33). Because He is faithful, God's promises are infallibly reliable (Heb 10:23). God stands by His self-imposed commitments and carries through His self-initiated agreements. Forgiveness, therefore, is rooted in divine faithfulness (I Jn 1:9), as is His people's victory over life's hardest testings (I Cor 10:13; I Pet 4:19) and their perseverance as well (I Thess 5:24).

As the self-revelation of the divine character, Jesus Christ is fittingly designated the Faithful One (Rev 19:11), who with absolute fidelity discharges all the responsibilities of High Priest (Heb 2:17), Apostle (Heb 3:1-2), and Witness (Rev 1:5; 3:14).

This quality of the divine character finds its human reflection in men of faith (Hab 2:4). Like their divine Exemplar they manifest a steadfast trustworthiness in all their obligations (Mt 25:21; I Cor 4:2); they are tenaciously loyal even to the point of martyrdom (Rev 2:10). Responding to faith, the Holy Spirit produces in men this trait of faithfulness (Gal 5:22, RSV).

See Fidelity; God.

V. C. G.

FALCON. *See* Animals, III.25.

FALL OF MAN. *An historical event.* Scripture depicts the fall of Adam as a definite event taking place in human history. The account in Gen 3 is, therefore, not to be regarded as myth (so J. S. Whale: "Every man is his own Adam. Man's tragic apostasy from God is not something which happened once for all a long time ago. It is true in every moment of existence"). Nor is it to be taken as belonging to super-history (so Brunner: "The creation and the Fall both lie behind the historical visible reality"). Nor is it to be explained as an allegory, representing man's awakening to self-consciousness and personality (so Kant, Schiller, Hegel).

The NT takes the position that the fall of Adam is an historical event and an explanation of what happens today. Paul so closely links the respective headships of Adam and Christ that if Adam is looked upon as a myth, then Christ must be regarded as myth also (Rom 5:12 ff.; I Cor 15:21 ff.; see also I Tim 2:14). For Adam was the type of Him that was to come—"the last Adam" and "the second man" (I Cor 15:45, 47).

The details of the Fall are clear. Rather than confronting Adam, the tempter in the form of a serpent approached Eve. Not being the federal head of the race, and having received the command of God only indirectly, she would be less likely to assume a sense of responsibility. The course the tempter followed in Gen 3 lies behind every sin that is committed. First, there is the suggestion to doubt God's word ("Yea, hath God said....?"). Second, there is the prompting to disbelieve God's word ("Ye shall not surely die"). Third, there is the appeal to pride and self-sufficiency ("Ye shall be as God," ASV). Fourth, there is the actual disobedience to God's word (they "did eat").

The consequences of the transgression struck immediately. First, Adam and his wife became overwhelmed with a sense of guilt ("they knew that they were naked"). Second, they were aware of an estrangement between them and God ("they hid themselves"). Third, they received a sentence of curse ("sorrow," "sweat," "unto dust shalt thou return"). Finally, they were banished from the presence of God ("he drove out the man").

A "Temptation Seal" from Mesopotamia, showing a man and woman, a tree, and a snake. BM

The effects of the Fall. Though the Fall was indeed an historical event, it was not an isolated event. The consequences it brought upon mankind's first parents did not cease with their death. In their transgression they implicated their posterity and all creation (cf. Rom 8:18-25).

For their posterity the Fall introduced the *universality of sin* throughout the human race (Ps 143:2; Rom 3:1-12, 19-20, 23; Gal 3:22; I Jn 1:8, 10). As the *New England Primer* put it, "In Adam's fall, we sinned all." It is in the Fall of the human race in Adam that we are given the explanation why children are born sinners, why some die in infancy, and why all who survive, regardless of race, culture, and ancestry, commit voluntary transgressions.

The sin thus transmitted to the human race is called *original sin.* It is so named because (1) it is derived from the original root of mankind; (2) it is present in each individual from the time of his birth; (3) it is the inward root of all actual sins that defile the life of man.

As the result of original sin man is both a guilty and a polluted creature. In Rom 5:12-19 Paul stresses the solidarity of the human race, the federal headship of Adam over it, the unique significance of his first sin for all his posterity, and the guilt with its consequences under which all men now stand. The apostle reiterates the same truth in I Cor 15:22 ("In Adam all die"). If all die in Adam, it is because all sinned and are guilty in Adam. Every man is guilty, therefore, of having transgressed the expressed commandment of God and is, as a result, deserving of divine punishment.

Guilt, however, is but one result of original sin. The other is pollution. Man no longer possesses the original goodness with which he was created. In its place has come a perversity that controls his heart, mind, disposition, and will. This pollution of his entire nature is called *total depravity,* a term that needs to be guarded from misunderstanding. Total depravity does not suggest that every man is as bad as he can possibly become. Nor does it imply that he is incapable of thinking or doing any good whatsoever. Rather, we are to understand by the term that man is inherently corrupt in every part of his nature and is incapable of doing any spiritual good (that is, in relation to God). This total depravity is clearly taught in Scripture (Jn 5:42; Rom 7:18, 23; Eph 4:18; II Tim 3:2-4; Tit 1:15; Heb 3:12). *See* Depravity; Image of God.

But the effects of Adam's sin go beyond his descendants. Its consequences extend to the physical earth also. "Cursed is the ground for thy sake" (Gen 3:17; cf. Rom 8:20-22). As the image of God, the apex of creation, man was appointed God's vice-regent (Gen 1:26; Ps 8:4-8). When he, the crown of creation, fell, he brought catastrophe into everything over which he had dominion. This curse, which hangs like a pall over creation, will not be removed until Christ's second coming (Rom 8:18-23), at which time the effects of the Fall will finally be abolished, and a new heaven and a new earth, wherein righteousness dwells, will be established (II Pet 3:12-13). *See* Sin.

Development of the doctrine. Prior to the time of Augustine (5th cen.), not much can be found of formal exposition of the doctrine of the Fall of man in the writings of the Church Fathers. Augustine, in his controversy with Pelagius, stressed the fact that all men were seminally present in Adam and actually sinned in him. Pelagius, his opponent, denied such a connection between the sin of Adam and those of his posterity. Pelagianism taught that Adam's sin affected only himself, that every individual was born sinless, and was, therefore, inherently capable of living a sinless life. Only by way of setting a bad example did Adam's sin influence his descendants. The errors of Pelagianism have been perpetuated by the Socinians of the 16th and 17th cen. (forerunners of today's Unitarians), and by modern liberal theologians.

Roman Catholicism holds officially to a semi-Pelagian position, insisting that what man lost through the Fall was the gift of original righteousness. This gift was something extra added to man (*donum superadditum*) at the time of creation, and which, when lost, left man in his natural state. The Fall, therefore, constituted a negative evil (a loss of something added to man's nature) rather than a positive punishment. Thus, according to Roman Catholic theology, unregenerate man still possesses the ability to contribute works toward the attainment of his salvation.

Some of the reformers continued the Augustinian view that all men were seminally in Adam and thus shared in his transgression. Luther spoke of man's guilt because of the indwelling sin inherited from Adam. Calvin took the position that Adam was both the progenitor and the root of the human race; that therefore all his offspring are born with a corrupt nature; and that both the guilt of Adam's sin and their own inborn corruption are imputed to them as sin.

Later Reformed theologians laid greater emphasis on the federal or covenantal aspects of Adam's relationship to the race. According to them, Adam stood as the representative of the human race, and in his Fall mankind received both the guilt and the pollution of his sin. This view accords more with the parallel Paul sets up between Christ and those united to Him (Rom 5:12–19; I Cor 15:22, 45–49). In the case of Christ, it is representative headship that is indicated, a relationship that has its parallel in the one existing between Adam and his posterity.

In poetic terms Milton wrote one of the most profound statements concerning the nature of the Fall in the opening lines of his *Paradise Lost:*

"Of Man's first disobedience, and the fruit
Of that forbidden tree, whose mortal taste
Brought death into the world, and all our woe,
With loss of Eden. . . ."

Bibliography. H. Bavinck, "The Fall," ISBE, II, 1092 ff. L. Berkhof, *Reformed Dogmatics,* Grand Rapids: Eerdmans, 1941. Charles C. Hodge, *Systematic Theology,* Grand Rapids: Eerdmans, reprinted, 1952. J. Gresham Machen, *The Christian View of Man,* Grand Rapids: Eerdmans, 1937. J. Murray, *The Imputation of Adam's Sin,* Grand Rapids: Eerdmans, 1959. C. R. Smith, *The Bible Doctrine of Sin,* Naperville, Ill.: Alec R. Allenson, 1953.

F. C. K.

FALLOW DEER. *See* Animals, II.10.

FALLOW GROUND. The Heb. word *nîr* occurs twice in the OT (Jer 4:3; Hos 10:12), and is translated as "fallow ground" in the KJV. It signifies "tillable" or "untilled" ground.

The Heb. *nāṭash* has the thought of "fallow ground" in one instance (Ex 23:11). It means "to leave," "to let alone." The Israelites were required to allow the land to rest each seventh year.

FALLOW YEAR. *See* Sabbath.

FALSE CHRISTS. This term is found in Mt 24:24 and Mk 13:22. The idea is also expressed differently in Mt 24:5; Mk 13:6; Lk 21:8. Jesus said that many would come in His name claiming to be Christ. They would show signs and wonders, and thereby convince many that they were genuine. *See* Antichrist.

FALSE PROPHET, THE. The False Prophet (Rev 19:20; 20:10), also called the second Beast (Rev 13:11–18), is a religious leader who is associated with the first Beast, the political leader of the Tribulation period, as his subordinate. He appears in power in the middle of the Tribulation at which time the first Beast or Antichrist (*q.v.*) assumes worldwide political power (Rev 13:7) and he, religious power.

He is perhaps a Jew, since Rev 13:11 may indicate that he arises out of "the land," or Palestine. (In Gr. the word *gē* can mean either "earth" or "land.") He moves in the religious realm, for he appears as a lamb (Rev 13:11). He is energized by Satan, being given his power by the first Beast (Rev 13:12). He promotes the worship of the first Beast and forces the earth to worship him (Rev 13:12, RSV). His ministry and authority are authenticated by miracles and signs which he works by Satanic power (Rev 13:13–14). The unbelieving world is deceived by him and worships the first Beast as God (Rev 13:14–15). He holds the power of life and death to enforce the worship of the first Beast (Rev 13:15). His authority extends into the economic realm, and he uses this economic power to enforce his will (Rev 13:16–17). The believers of that day will be able to recognize him because of the sign given to identify him (Rev 13:18).

The False Prophet, together with Satan and the first Beast, form a triumvirate of evil, which is Satan's masterpiece of deception. The world will be dominated by them during the last half of the Tribulation period in the political, religious, and economic realms in imitation of God's worldwide rule over the earth in the Millennium by Jesus Christ, the Messiah.

J. D. P.

FAMILIAR SPIRIT. An expression occurring 16 times in the KJV, referring to a spirit of divination or to its medium or conjurer, translating Heb. *'ôb.* This term is related to similar words in Sumerian, Hittite, Akkadian, and Ugaritic, all probably coming from a common source. Originally it meant the ritual hole or pit dug in the ground to give underworld spirits access to the practitioner for a short time. Later the term was applied to the spirits which issued from the hole, and also to the necromancer himself/herself (Harry A. Hoffner, Jr., "Second Millennium Antecedents to the Hebrew *'ôb,*" JBL, LXXXVI [1967], 385–401). The practice of necromancy in the ancient Near East is reflected in the Gilgamesh epic: "Forthwith he opened a hole in the earth. The spirit of Enkidu, like a wind-puff, issued forth from the nether world" (ANET, p. 98); and in Isa 29:4 (RSV): "Your voice shall come from the ground like the voice of a ghost [*'ôb*], and your speech shall whisper out of the dust."

The term "familiar" is used to describe the alleged spirit of a deceased person because it was regarded by the Genevan revisers (1557-1560) as a servant (*famulus*) easily summoned by the one possessing it, or as belonging to the family (*familiaris*) and thus on intimate terms with the deceased person (Merrill F. Unger, *Biblical Demonology,* p. 144).

A parallel term in Heb., always occurring with *'ôb,* is *yiddeʻōnî,* from Heb. *yāda',* "to know," a "knowing" spirit, one with occult knowledge. The term is translated by "wizard" in KJV, RSV, etc., one who is made wise concerning the nether world by such a demon. The same medium might seek both types of demons: "one who consults a familiar spirit and a knowing-spirit" (Deut 18:11, lit.). Such a demon is well acquainted with the deceased human being and can imitate or impersonate him, deceiving the one desiring to communicate with the dead.

Other terms involved in necromancy are found in Deut 18:11, *dōrēsh el-hammēthîm* (lit., one who inquires of the dead; cf. Isa 8:19) and in Isa 19:3, *ha'ĕlîlîm* ("idols," or probably chthonic deities) and *ha'iṭṭîm* ("charmers"; better, "ghosts," from Akkad. *eṭimmu*), along with *hā'ōbôth* and *hayyiddeʻōnîm.*

The OT nowhere condemns necromancy on the ground that it is futile, but that it is rebellion against God on whom alone the Israelite believer was to depend (Lev 19:31; 20:6, 27; Deut 18:9-14), for the Lord had raised up prophetic spokesmen to reveal His will (Deut 18:15-22). Manasseh, as well as King Saul (I Chr 10:13), was guilty of trafficking with familiar and occult spirits (II Kgs 21:6; 23:4). In spite of these prohibitions many today find it fashionable to flock to spiritualist mediums for supposed messages from departed loved ones or for "proof" that there is no death or judgment to come.

The account of Saul when he sought counsel of the deceased Samuel through the medium of Endor (I Sam 28) exposes the fraudulency of spiritism. In the seance the witch, described as a *baʻălath-'ôb,* "mistress of a familiar spirit," expected to bring up the "control" spirit which would impersonate Samuel, but instead shrieked in fear at what happened. In this sole instance God sovereignly permitted the actual spirit of Samuel to speak in order to deliver a solemn rebuke to the apostate king. Normally the alleged spirit would speak somewhat favorably; in this unique case the inquirer (Saul) was condemned to die on the morrow, a warning for all time to come. *See* Demonology; Divination; Magic; Necromancy.

Bibliography. Raphael Gasson, *The Challenging Counterfeit,* Logos International, 1966.

J. R.

FAMILY

Terminology. Several words expressing the idea of family appear in the Bible. In the OT, Heb. *bayith* (lit., "house") may signify the family living in the house (e.g., I Chr 13:14) and often is translated "household" (e.g., Gen 18:19; Ex 1:1; Josh 7:18, *re* Achan who lived in a tent). More frequently found is Heb. *mishpaḥa* with the meaning of "kindred" (e.g. Gen 24:38-41), "family" or "clan," usually with a broader connotation than our English word "family" (e.g., Gen 10:31-32). The NT uses Gr. *oikia* ("house," "home," "household," e.g., Lk 19:9; Acts 10:2; 16:31; 18:8; I Cor 1:16) and *oikiakos* ("members of one's family group," Mt 10:25, 36).

Extent. The Jewish family or household included not only immediate members closely related by ties of blood or marriage, but also embraced slaves, hired servants, concubines, and even foreigners. Abraham circumcised every male of his household, from his son Ishmael to the slaves born in his house and those purchased from foreigners (Gen 17:23, 27). Note how extensive Jacob's family was considered to be, numbering all his children and grandchildren as 66, not counting his sons' wives (Gen 46:5-7, 26). Children were greatly desired amd were extremely important in the family economy, especially sons (Ps 127:3-5; 128:3; Ruth 4:11).

Status and role. The father exercised practically absolute authority in the OT family; hence the need to caution him not to provoke his children to wrath in the NT (Eph 6:4; Col 3:21). He symbolized tradition, the family ancestry, and its hope for the future. His duty was to lead the family in worship. When he did, his uprightness and devotion to God became an example to his descendants (e.g., Job 1:5); when he failed, he was bitterly denounced (Ps 78:8; Amos 2:6-7). The mother also had great influence behind the scenes, as in the case of Rebekah's advising Jacob (Gen 27:11-17). She comforted her children (Isa 49:15; 66:13) and was loved and respected by them. The eldest or firstborn son normally was prepared and trained for the future role of head of the family. Perhaps because of the extra duties and responsibilities as clan leader he was granted a double portion of the inheritance.

Biblical basis and principles of family living. God's initial pattern for marriage is recorded in Gen 2:18-25. As originally planned, it involved one man and one woman, physical union (Gen 1:28), and a new social unit (Gen 2:24). Upon these foundational principles the family was built, and throughout the OT the family was considered basic in God's dealings with men. Children were considered to be a gift and blessing from God (Gen 4:1; 33:5; Ps 113:9; 127:3; 68:6). Parents were responsible to train them (Deut 6:6-9; Prov 22:6), and fathers particularly were responsible to provide a consistent example in godly living. Failure in this respect would bring devastating results (Ex 20:4-5; Num 14:18), well illustrated in the apostasy of Israel (II Kgs 17:14; II Chr 33:22-25; Acts 7:51-53).

NT writers built upon the principles and ideals for family living which were established in the OT. Referring to the Genesis account, Jesus clarified and confirmed the concept of earthly permanency in the marriage relationship (Mt 19:3-6). Though the term "shall cleave" (Gen 2:24) strongly implies that this union was to be lifelong, Jesus left no doubt when He said, "What therefore God hath joined together, let not man put asunder" (Mt 19:6).

Paul elevated marriage to its highest level when he likened the husband to Christ and the wife to the Church (Eph 5:22-23). The husband, says the apostle, should "love . . . even as Christ also loved," and the wife is to submit herself to her husband as the Church is to submit to Christ (Eph 5:25, 22-24). The man, as a loving husband reflecting the unselfish and sacrificial attitudes of Christ Himself, should be the "head of the wife," giving her security and protection.

Jesus also elevated children to a prominent place in His divine plan when He taught not to offend them (Mt 18:6), not to despise them (18:10), and not to forbid them to come to Him (19:14). Paul reiterates an OT principle when he places the primary responsibility for child training upon the father's shoulders (Eph 6:4).

Both the OT and the NT provide a variety of practical instructions for successful marital and family relationships. The book of Proverbs especially is replete with these teachings. The child's effect on family morale (10:1; 15:20; 17:25; 23:24-25); the value of strict discipline (13:24; 19:18; 22:15; 23:13-14; 29:15, 17; cf. Heb 12:5-11); warnings against disobedience to parents (19:26; 20:20); and the aggravation of a nagging wife (19:13; 27:15)—these are some of the wise sayings regarding family problems.

The prosperous home is warned not to forget the Lord (Deut 6:10-12). Marriage to unbelievers is forbidden for God's people to prevent turning away to other gods (Deut 7:3-4; II Cor 6:14). I Cor 7 gives practical instructions regarding the problem of selfishness in marriage (vv. 1-5), tells what to do when one's mate is unsaved (vv. 12-16), and warns against the problem of divided loyalties (vv. 32-35). Jesus deals with the issue of divorce (Mt 19:3-11). and Paul gives instructions regarding remarriage (I Cor 7:39-40; Rom 7:1-3). Practical advice for wives and mothers may be found in Tit 2:3-5 and I Pet 3:1-6.

In addition to specific instructions, the Scriptures also give many significant illustrations which in turn provide principles for Christ-like family living. For example, Eli's sons and David's children are a potent reminder as to what happens when parents fail (I Sam 3:13; II Sam 12:10). Joseph is no doubt the supreme example in demonstrating family forgiveness (Gen 50:15-21).

Jesus illustrated proper parental attitudes toward the straying child with His parable of the prodigal son (Lk 15:11-24), but He also lays bare parental motives that are selfish (Mt 20:20-28).

There is no doubt that the teachings of the Bible elevate the family and its function to a level duplicated in no other literature or society. Though this divinely instituted social unit has failed in many instances to function at a proper level within the Christian community, God's holy pattern for family living is in no way invalidated.

Figurative use of the concept of family. In the new creation there is a new family relationship, with one Father, who is in heaven (Mt 23:9). A man may have to renounce his old family ties (Lk 14:26, 33) or may discover that his foes are those of his own household (Mt 10:35-36). Jesus Himself experienced this cleavage (Mk 6:4; Jn 7:5) and declared that His true brother and sister and mother are they that do the will of God (Mk 3:31-35).

The church becomes the family or household of God (Eph 2:19; I Tim 3:15; Heb 3:6; I Pet 4:17). Paul counts Timothy, Titus, and Philemon as his "children," and he exhorts Timothy to treat the members of the church at Ephesus as his own relatives (I Tim 5:1-2). He compares elders to fathers of a family (I Tim 3:5), and himself "begets" churches like a father (I Cor 4:15; cf. II Cor 6:13) or gives birth to them like a mother (Gal 4:19). As God's people, as His sons and daughters, we are to be separate and touch nothing unclean (II Cor 6:14-18).

See Adoption; Children; Divorce; Education; Home; House; Household; Husband; Father; Mother; Son; Daughter; Marriage; Inheritance; Parent; Women.

Bibliography. O. J. Baab, "Family," IDB, II, 238-241. "The Family," CornPBE, pp. 310-320. Larry Christenson, *The Christian Family,* Minneapolis: Bethany Fellowship, 1970. John W. Drakeford, *The Home: Laboratory of Life,* Nashville: Broadman Press, 1965. Alta Mae Erb, *Christian Education in the Home,* Scottsdale, Pa.: Herald Press, 1963. Oscar E. Feucht, *Helping Families Through the Church,* St. Louis: Concordia, 1957. Gene A. Getz, "The Christian Home," BS, CXXVI (1969), 16-21, 109-114. Ralph Heynen, *The Secret of Christian Family Living,* Grand Rapids: Baker, 1965. E. A. Judge, *The Social Pattern of the Christian Groups in the First Century,* London: Tyndale Press, 1960. G. Quell and G. Schrenk, "*Patēr*, etc.," TDNT, V, 945-1022.

G. A. G.

FAMINE. A general condition of extreme shortage of food. Bible history mentions numerous instances of famine during the days of Abraham (Gen 12:10), Isaac (Gen 26:1), Joseph (Gen 41:56-57), Elimelech and Naomi (Ruth 1:1), David (II Sam 21:1), Elijah (I Kgs 18:2; Lk 4:25), Elisha (II Kgs 6:25; 8:1), the final siege of Jerusalem (II Kgs 25:3).

During a famine in the "far country" the prodigal son was brought to his senses (Lk 15:14). One took place in the days of the Roman Emperor Claudius (Acts 11:28). In His Olivet discourse the Lord Jesus predicted famines during the tribulation period at the close of the age (Mt 24:7), and Revelation alludes to famine coming on Babylon the Great (Rev 18:8). One of the blessings promised to restored Israel is that there will be no more famines (Ezk 36:29-30).

There is reference to people paying high prices during famines for such unpalatable foods as asses' heads and doves' dung (II Kgs 6:25) and even turning to the most horrid kind of cannibalism (Deut 28:53-57; II Kgs 6:28-29).

Evidently in Bible days the natural causes most responsible for famine were drought (I Kgs 18:1, 2) and warfare in its various aspects (Ezk 6:11; II Kgs 25:2-3). However, it is many times pictured as a divine judgment on sin (II Sam 21:1; 24:13; I Kgs 8:37; II Kgs 8:1; Isa 51:19; Jer 14:12-18; Ezk 5:12). In this sense it is spoken of as one of God's "four sore judgments" (Ezk 14:21).

Yet promise is made that God will keep alive the godly in times of famine (Job 5:20, 22; Ps 33:19; 37:19), and best of all it is affirmed that famine, as well as other trials and tribulations, shall not separate us from the love of Christ (Rom 8:35-39). In a figurative sense "a famine . . . of hearing the words of the Lord" (Amos 8:11) is threatened to those who have despised and rejected the message of the Lord. This is the worst kind of famine of all.

G. C. L.

FAN. The noun forms are used twice in both the OT and NT (Isa 30:24; Jer 15:7; Mt 3:12; Lk 3:17). The meaning in all uses is simply "fan." Heb. *mizreh* is defined as a winnowing fan or fork, probably with six prongs, and Gr. *ptuon* is applied to the winnowing shovel used to toss grain into the wind. *See* Fork; Agriculture.

Forms of the verb *zārâ* are found four times translated as "fan" in the KJV (Isa 41:16; Jer 4:11; 15:7; 51:2), meaning "to winnow." The verb is used figuratively "to scatter" an enemy.

FANNERS. Used only once (Jer 51:2), and there the translation "fanners" is questionable. The ASV gives it the meaning of "strangers."

FARM, FARMERS. *See* Agriculture; Occupations: Farmer.

FARTHING. *See* Weights, Measures and Coins.

Ceremonial fan from the tomb of King Tutankhamon covered with gold. Around the edge of the head are holes into which ostrich feathers were fixed. LL

FAST, FASTING. Fasting in the Bible implies total abstinence (*q.v.*) from all food for a certain period. The length of time varied from daylight hours ("fasted that day until evening," Jud 20:26) up to 40 days, as in the cases of Moses, Elijah, and Jesus. People fasted either out of necessity during a food shortage (Acts 27:21, 33-36), because of loss of appetite resulting from deep emotions (as Hannah and Jonathan, I Sam 1:8, 18; 20:34), or for religious purposes.

The Heb. words are *ṣûm* (verb) and *ṣôm* (noun)—not found in the Pentateuch. The corresponding Gr. terms are *nēsteuō* and *nēsteia* from a root meaning "hunger." Other expressions used in the OT are "not eat bread" (I Sam 28:20; II Sam 12:17) and "to afflict one's soul." The latter is a phrase in the Mosaic law that may have included fasting (Lev 16:29, 31; 23:27, 32; *et al.*), and signifies to lower or humble oneself by self-denial as a proper expression of repentance.

The origin of the religious practice of fasting is lost in the dim past, but this discipline was widespread throughout ancient religions. In food-gathering (as opposed to food-growing) cultures fasting was often compulsory owing to the uncertainty of obtaining food. Possibly superstitious ignorance interpreted the scarcity of wild grains, fruits, and game as an expression of the divine will, and so men began to consider fasting as a religious duty. Thinking that the gods were jealous of the pleasures of mankind, men perhaps assumed that abstinence would propitiate their favor. On the other hand, the natural inclination to forego food during the grief of bereavement may have caused fasting to originate as a sign of mourning.

Fasting first appears in the OT as a voluntary act of individual piety. Moses twice fasted 40 days and nights in the presence of the Lord on Mount Sinai, taking neither food nor water (Deut 9:9, 18; Ex 34:28). While food may have been unavailable, abstention from water during these periods was probably voluntary, for there is a small well or spring in a cleft 100 feet below the summit of Jebel Musa. Yet Moses must have been supernaturally sustained, because the human body cannot endure lack of moisture for so long a time. Under ideal conditions a human has fasted from all food for 90 days and survived, according to Dr. Herbert M. Shelton who has supervised over 40,000 fasts (*Fasting Can Save Your Life,* Chicago: Natural Hygiene Press, 1964, p. 57). It is not specifically stated that Elijah (I Kgs 19:8) and Jesus (Mt 4:2) drank no water during their respective 40 day fasts. That they could continue to be active and not become weakened is the remarkable aspect in their cases (cf. Ps 109:24).

On long fasts hunger usually subsides by the end of the third day and does not return until the stored food reserves in the tissues of the body are used up ("and afterward he was hungry," Mt 4:2, RSV). This can take 40 days or longer; only then does starvation begin (Shelton, pp. 15, 23, 29–32). Before this stage fasting has many beneficial effects by permitting the body to secure physiological rest and be restored to health (*ibid.,* pp. 36–40, 48–52).

In most cases in the Bible fasting can be seen as a normal, voluntary result of the human state of mind. On his first prolonged stay on the mount Moses was too enraptured with the awesome presence of God, too absorbed with the divine revelations given him to want to eat. On his return he lay prostrate before God, heartbroken because of the rebellion of his people (Deut 9:18). The men of Jabesh-gilead and David mourned and fasted after bereavement (I Sam 31:11–13; II Sam 1:12; 3:35).

Fasting naturally seemed to reinforce the attitude of repentance and heartfelt confession, just as sackcloth and ashes did (I Sam 7:6; Ps 69:10–11; Jon 3:5, 8; Dan 9:3–5; Ezr 10:1, 6; Neh 9:1–2). After Elijah's rebuke, King Ahab thus repented of his crime toward Naboth (I Kgs 21:27–29). Perplexity, fear, and distress likewise evoked similar response (Jud 20:26; Est 4:3).

As an accompaniment of prayer, fasting often is something desirable to the godly man, not merely a matter of rigid self-discipline. During a fast one's mental and spiritual faculties seem more alert and sensitive to God's Spirit, and intercession seems easier, more effective. Thus David fasted while he prayed for his sick child (II Sam 12:16–23), and even for his sick enemies (Ps 35:13). Also Nehemiah fasted as he interceded for Israel (Neh 1:4–11).

The early Christians found fasting to be beneficial while seeking the will and direction of God (Acts 13:2–3; 14:23). During a three-week period of self-humbling and seeking to understand the future, Daniel ate no "pleasant bread," i.e., delicacies, nor meat nor wine (Dan 10:2–3). Such a non-total fast can be an effective aid to spiritual concentration and prayer. It may be advisable for those who must remain active or are too weak to endure a total fast.

God never seems to command His people to fast regularly, unless the "affliction of the soul" on the Day of Atonement includes fasting (Lev 16:29). The OT stresses rather the positive enjoyment of God and His blessings with gladness of heart (Ps 4:7; Prov 15:13; 17:22; Eccl 3:13; 9:7–9). God is not impressed with the act of fasting, especially when it does not signify turning from strife and oppression (Isa 58:3–5). Instead, fasting is acceptable only if it eventuates in acts of social justice and true charity, only if the motive for self-denial is one of love and desire to help the poor (vv. 6–11).

Nevertheless, in times of national emergency kings and spiritual leaders proclaimed special fast days to seek help from the Lord. When invasion from E of the Dead Sea was imminent King Jehoshaphat summoned all Judah to fast (II Chr 20:3). After the disasters of locust plague and drought Joel was ordered to have the priests sanctify a fast (Joel 1:14; 2:12, 15), although he insisted that the primary need was inward repentance, to rend their hearts and not their garments (2:13). Jeremiah took advantage of a fasting day to have the words of the Lord read to the people (Jer 36:6, 9). Ezra proclaimed a fast to pray for a safe journey to Jerusalem (Ezr 8:21, 23). Queen Esther begged Mordecai and the Jews to fast with her three days and nights before she approached King Ahasuerus (Est 4:16). Later, a national fast in preparation for the observance of Purim followed this pattern (Est 9:31).

Four annual fasts had arisen during the Babylonian exile, but they were observed, apparently, without divine authorization. Through His earlier prophets God had already expressed His mind concerning mere ceremonial worship. The emphasis upon positive wholesomeness in fellowship with God is clearly heard in His declaration that the four exilic fasts would become "joy and gladness and cheerful feasts" (Zech 8:19; cf. 7:3–10; Jer 14:12).

The value of the discipline of fasting is pointed out frequently in the Jewish intertestamental literature, although no specific mention of the religious fast may be found in the Qumran MSS published thus far. The Manual of Discipline states only that serious offenses could be punished by fining a community member part of his food ration (1Q S vi. 25). In the temple itself the godly Anna served the Lord with fastings and prayers (Lk 2:37). The Pharisees made much of fasting and regarded it as a meritorious work. It became the custom of the pious to fast on Mondays and Thursdays (Lk 18:12). If a man began to fast, his fast took priority over making sacrificial offerings and was regarded as more efficacious than almsgiving. *See* Festivals: Extrabiblical Jewish sacred seasons.

Jesus never required His disciples to fast. The term "and fasting" is not found in the best Gr. MSS at Mk 9:29 (nor in Acts 10:30; I Cor 7:5); Mt 17:21 is omitted entirely in the best texts. Yet while He denounced the hypocrisy of the Pharisees, He emphasized that fasting done in secret out of true devotion to God will be rewarded (Mt 6:16–18). He took it for granted that after His ascension His followers would feel the need to fast, even as John the Baptist's disciples did (Mk 2:18–20). Whether Paul's fastings were voluntary or resulting from lack of food (II Cor 6:5; 11:27) cannot be settled. The absence of any problem of fasting in Paul's letters suggests that it was not a prominent matter in the Gentile churches. According to the Didache (8.1), Christians by A.D. 100 could be exhorted to fast twice a week—on Tuesdays and Fridays, however! In the 2nd and 3rd cen. the pre-Easter and pre-baptismal fasts came to be widely practiced.

Bibliography. Johannes Behm, "*Nētis,* etc.," TDNT, IV, 924–935. Arthur Wallis, *God's Chosen Fast,* Fort Washington, Pa.: Christian Literature Crusade, 1968.

J. R.

FAT. The subcutaneous layer around the kidneys and other viscera which, like the blood, was forbidden by the Mosaic law to be used for food but rather was burned as an offering to God (mentioned several times in Lev 3, 4, 7, 8, 9). The offering had to be made on the very day the animal was killed so as to remove the temptation to eat that portion. The ancients considered fat and blood as the source of vitality and strength. Fat was the richest portion of the sacrificial animal. For this reason the fat was offered to the Lord as representative of the best part of each sacrifice.

FATHER. This term in the OT has a wide spectrum of meanings. These may be divided into literal and figurative uses.

Basically it refers to the male parent (Gen 2:24; 22:7; 48:1; etc.). One of the most basic and foremost ethical precepts of the OT and NT relates to the honor and obedience due to fathers. This esteem of parents was a characteristic of godliness even before the Decalogue was given. The father's authority over his family in the OT was absolute. He could sell his children into slavery (Ex 21:7) or have them put to death (Gen 22:2–10; cf. 21:9–14). The blessing or malediction of a father was of special significance and conferred benefit or injury (Gen 9:25–27; 27:27–40; 48;15–20; 49:1–28). The father also functioned as priest of the family before the formation of a formal priesthood (Gen 8:20; 22:13; Job, 1:5). *See* Family.

The term is employed in a literal sense to describe a forefather. Here the relationship may be more immediate as a grandfather (Gen 28:13; 31:42; 32:9) or great-grandfather (I Kgs 15:3; cf. 15:11, 24), or it may be more remote (Gen 15:15; II Kgs 15:38; 16:2; Ps 45:16).

A third literal meaning is found in its usage to refer to the ancestral progenitor of a nation or a people, as Shem (Gen 10:21), Abraham (Gen 17:4–5), Moab (Gen 19:37), etc.

It is in the figurative meanings that the more colorful concepts are found. The term describes one who is the author, maker, originator, or creator of something. God is said to be the Father of Israel because He formed the nation (Deut 32:6; Isa 63:16; 64:8; Jer 31:9). By implication He is the Father of nature (Job 38:28). Man can also be called father in the sense of originator, as in Gen 4:20–21 where it looks at men who brought into being a new mode of life.

Father also is used in a nonliteral sense as a term of endearment. In II Sam 7:14; I Chr 17:13; 22:10; Ps 68:5; 89:26 it is applied to God in His relationship with men. It implies His love will move Him to nourish and sustain. The word is also employed of man's association with another (Job 29:16; Isa 22:21). While endearment still is in view, the concept of sustenance comes to the fore here.

The term may describe one who is a teacher (I Sam 10:12). Quite often it refers to an adviser who possesses some authoritative position (Gen 45:8; Jud 17:10; 18:19; II Kgs 2:12; 6:21; 13:14).

Figuratively it becomes a term of respect (I Sam 24:11; II Kgs 5:13; cf. 8:9).

Finally, it is used in the OT to refer to some unstated but intimate association (Job 17:14).

As a term in the NT father (*patēr*) is also employed with literal and metaphorical meanings. Its basic concept, that of referring to the male parent (*q.v.*), is seen in Mt 2:22; Mk 5:40; Jn 4:53; etc. In the plural the word may look at both parents, the mother and father (Heb 11:23; cf. Eph 6:4; Col 3:21). As in the OT it is used of genealogical forefathers (Mt 3:9; Lk 1:73; Jn 8:39; Rom 9:10). In II Pet 3:4 it seems to have a technical sense in referring to the whole group of OT patriarchs.

Although the figurative meanings of the word are not as broad as in the OT, there are some that are essential for a proper understanding of the NT. It is employed once of a spiritual father, that is, of one who by his witness brought others to faith in Christ (I Cor 4:15). It is employed as a term of respect and honor (Mt 23:9; Acts 7:2; 22:1). In I Jn 2:13–14 it evidently portrays Christians who have matured in the faith. Figuratively it looks at one who is a prototype or archetype, one who originates a company of people with kindred spirit (Jn 8:38, 44; Rom 4:11–12, 16; cf. I Pet 3:6).

The word is also used of God as Creator and Father. *See* Father, God the; God.

Bibliography. Gottlob Schrenk and Gottfried Quell, "*Patēr,* etc.," TDNT, V, 945–1022.

S. D. T.

FATHER, GOD THE. In four senses God is Father: as Creator, as Father of Israel, as Father of Christ, and as Father of believers.

God is Father of mankind by creation (Acts 17:28–29; Lk 3:38; cf. Gen 1:27; Jas 3:9). The fatherhood of God in this sense is not a frequent subject in the Bible. Angels are called "the sons of God" (Job 1:6; 2:1; 38:7: cf. Gen 6:2) because they were created by God and/or because of their spiritual ties with God.

In the OT God is especially the Father of the nation Israel (Isa 63:16; 64:8; Hos 11:1). He sustains this relationship because the nation was created by Him (Deut 32:6; Mal 2:10). Israel as God's firstborn possesses a privileged position (Ex 4:22; Jer 31:9) and as such owns great promises (Jer 3:19). As a son Israel is to honor and serve God (Ex 4:23; Mal 1:6). Just as a natural father rears his children, so God desires to sustain Israel and make it great (Jer 3:19; cf. Ps 103:13; Prov 3:12).

In a very special sense God is the Father of Jesus Christ. Several concepts are revealed in this relationship. Especially the deity of Christ is evidenced (Jn 5:18). In Mt 3:17 messiahship is in view (cf. 17:5; Mk 9:7; Lk 9:35). The equality of the Son with the Father is seen in the Trinitarian name (Mt 28:19). The Lord Jesus is careful to maintain a strict distinction between God as His Father and God as the Father of believers (cf. Jn 20:17). Christ as God's Son is the revelation of the Father and the way of access to God (Mt 11:27; Jn 10:30; 14:6–7).

In seed form God is portrayed as the Father of individual saints in the OT (II Sam 7:14; Ps 103:13; Mal 3:17), but this concept finds maturation in the NT with the coming of Christ (cf. Mt 6:4, 6, 8, 9, 32). By creation God is the Father of all; by His grace He is the spiritual Father of believers. Sonship in the NT is portrayed in three aspects—regeneration (Jn 1:12–13; 3:6), adoption (Rom 8:15, 23; Gal 4:5; Eph 1:5), and transferal into the Son's kingdom (Col 1:13).

The Christian's close relationship with God is particularly seen in the formula, "Abba, Father," literally meaning, "Father, Father" (Mk 14:36; Rom 8:15; Gal 4:6). The first is an Aram. word which became colloquial in Heb. expressing the more intimate association of child and father. It is never used of God in the OT, and rabbinic literature rarely refers to God by this name and then only in a specific formula. However, Christ boldly said, "Abba." The second word is the regular Gr. word for father. The persistence of the formula in the NT may be due to the deep impression made on the disciples by the Lord's use of it. He evidently employed both the Aram. and the Gr.

See God; God, Names and Titles of.

S. D. T.

FATHER-IN-LAW. The Heb. husband's father (Heb. *ḥām,* Gen 38:13, 25; I Sam 4:19, 21) had authority over his son's wife (Gen 38:24), but was forbidden to marry her (Lev 18:15). Jacob lived for an extended period (Gen 31:41) with his wives' father, as did Moses (Heb. *ḥōtēn,* Ex 2:21; 3:1; 4:18; 18:1–27; etc.). Caiaphas cooperated with his father-in-law (Gr. *pentheros)* Annas (Jn 18:13). *See* Marriage.

FATHER'S BROTHER. Abraham was Lot's uncle and guardian (Gen 12:5). An uncle (Heb. *dôd)* could act as redeemer of property (Lev 25:49). In inheritance, paternal uncles followed brothers of the deceased (Num 27:10). Mattaniah (Zedekiah), Jehoiachin's uncle, succeeded him as king (II Kgs 24:17).

FATHER'S HOUSE. This usage in the OT is always of earthly significance, referring to the dwelling place of the family (Gen 24:23), or to the family itself (Gen 12:1), or to the tribe (Gen 24:40), or to the entire nation (Neh 1:6). *See* Family.

In the NT Jesus added two further ideas. He referred to the temple as His Father's house (Jn 2:16). In Jn 14:2 He speaks of the Christian's future home as "in my Father's house." *See also* Father; Heaven; Mansion.

FATHOM. *See* Weights, Measures, and Coins.

FATLING. In all the uses of this word reference is to a young calf that has been fed and is fat and firm. A calf was sometimes used as an offering. It was considered valuable property (Isa 11:6; Ezk 39:18), and was looked on as a table delicacy (Mt 22:4).

FATTED FOWL. This term, referring to fatted birds, is used only once in the OT (I Kgs 4:23 [Heb., 5:3]). The term translated the Heb. words *barbūrîm 'ăbûsîm.* The first of the two words stems from the root *bārar,* meaning "be pure" and thus white. Since ivory carvings from Megiddo show a row of barefooted peasants bringing fattened geese into town (VBW, II, 210), the "fatted fowl" for Solomon's table were likely white geese. *See* Animals, III.18.

FEAR. A term used both in the OT and NT in several very significant ways. The Scriptures speak of the following kinds of fear:

1. A holy fear (Heb. *yir'â*; Gr. *phobos*) which amounts to awe or respect for the majesty and holiness of God, a godly reverence (Gen 20:11; Ps 34:11; Acts 9:31; Rom 3:18). David speaks of this fear as clean and pure (Ps 19:9); Job and the psalmist, as the basis or beginning of all true wisdom (Job 28:28; Prov 1:7; Ps 111:10). This fear is God-given and enables man to respect God's authority, obey His commands, turn from evil (I Sam 12:14, 20–25; Ps 2:11; Prov 8:13; 16:6), and to pursue holiness (II Cor 7:1; Phil 2:12). Gentile converts to Judaism who believed in God were called God-fearers (Acts 10:2, 22; 13:26). *See* Worship.

2. A filial fear (Lev 19:3) which is based

upon the proper reverence of the child of God for his heavenly Father (Ps 33:18; 34:6–11; Prov 14:26–27; II Cor 6:17–7:1).

3. A fear for unforgiven sin which is caused by the work of the law written in the heart (Rom 2:15) and the knowledge of God's Word; e.g., Adam's fear when he sinned (Gen 3:10; cf. Prov 28:1); Felix as he heard Paul preach (Acts 24:25); that of men who reject the preaching of the gospel (Heb 10:27–31).

4. A fear, dread or terror (Heb. *paḥad*) of God's holiness on the part of the wicked at the Lord's coming (Ps 14:5; Isa 2:10, 19; Rev 11:11; 18:10, 15). Along with this we may consider a fear of His people that God places in other men's hearts to protect His own (Deut 11:25; II Chr 20:29–30).

5. A fear of man is also mentioned in Scripture. This may either be a proper respect for those in authority (Rom 13:7; I Pet 2:18), or a senseless dread (Num 14:9; Isa 8:12).

6. A fear for others and the danger in which they stand (I Cor 2:3; II Cor 11:3; 12:20–21).

7. A terror of the unknown (Lk 21:26) or of the uncanny (Job 4:14–16).

8. Cowardice or timidity (Gr. *deilia*), as in "a spirit of fear" (II Tim 1:7), and "let not your heart . . . be afraid" (Jn 14:27; cf. Mt 8:26; Mk 4:40; Rev 21:8).

Fear is sometimes falsely assumed to be the origin of religion, but fear alone in the sense of dread is not the positive force that draws men to God with an attitude of reverence, worship, and respect.

The Kierkegaardian concept of *Angst zum tode,* that anxiety which pursues man right through life until his death, falls under the third classification above, since it expresses the nagging anxiety which besets the unsaved. This fear, and the dread of appearing before a holy God, is eliminated—or ought to be—in the lives of believers (I Jn 4:18; cf. Rom 8:1, 33-34), though the fear of reverence and of respect for authority remains.

R. A. K.

FEAST. *See* Food: Banquet. For the various OT Jewish feasts *see* Festivals.

FEAST OF CHARITY. *See* Agape; Love Feast.

FEEBLE KNEES. The idea expressed in these words is found three times in the Bible (Job 4:4; Isa 35:3; Heb 12:12). In Job the Heb. word is *kāra'* and speaks of the bending of the knee through weakness. There is no indication of the cause, whether through disease or weariness. Isaiah uses *kāshal,* which means to totter in the ankles, but no cause is indicated. In the letter to the Hebrews *paralelumena* is the word; it indicates a sort of paralysis resulting from a cutting off of vital strength. In all uses the idea seems to be more figurative than literal, suggesting weariness and discouragement.

See Feebleminded.

FEEBLEMINDED. In I Thess 5:14 believers are instructed to "comfort the feebleminded," i.e., encourage those who are fainthearted or discouraged (Gr. *oligopsychos,* often in LXX). In the LXX the term covers a wide range of attitudes from being fearful (Isa 35:4), humbled or dejected (Isa 57:15), grieved or depressed in spirit (Isa 54:6; Ex 6:9), wounded or broken in spirit (Prov 18:14), to being short-tempered (Prov 14:29). Thus the word suggests one who is laboring under such trouble that his heart sinks within him, or who is grieving because of the death of loved ones.

See Feeble Knees.

FEET. *See* Foot.

FELIX, ANTONIUS (ăn-tō'nĭ-ŭs fē'lĭks). Procurator of Judea under Claudius and Nero (A.D. 52–60), and one before whom Paul was brought to trial in Caesarea (Acts 23:24–24:27). The descriptions by Tacitus (*Annals* xii. 54 and *Histories* v. 9) are classic: "He thought he could do any evil act with impunity," and "(He) exercised the power of a king in the spirit of a slave."

Felix listened to Paul's defense, postponed any decision pending more information from Lysias, the Roman commander in Jerusalem who had originally arrested Paul (Acts 21:33), often listened to and conversed with the apostle, but left him in prison, hoping for a bribe and also as a move pleasing to the Jews.

He had married Drusilla, a Jewess and a sister of Agrippa II, when she was about 16 years of age, after having persuaded her to leave her husband for him. Paul's reasoning with them (Acts 24:25) may be analagous to John the Baptist's accusing Herod Antipas and Herodias of an illicit relationship (Mk 6:18).

In A.D. 60, Felix was recalled by Nero and was replaced in office by Festus. *See* Festus.

W. M. D.

FELLOES. The English word means the rims of wheels supported by spokes. In I Kgs 7:33 these are parts of the wheels of the stands for the bronze basins or lavers in the court of Solomon's temple. The KJV so translated *ḥishshuqîm,* which more accurately means the spokes, whereas the KJV word "naves" immediately preceding it should be "rims" or "felloes" (see RSV, JerusB).

FELLOW. A term denoting, as in Gen 38:12, a friend, companion, associate, i.e., a fellow companion; or less personally, a fellow citizen or neighbor (Lev 19:18). The feminine in Heb., *re'ûth,* means fellow (woman) or neighbor (Ex 11:2). The name Ruth, meaning "friendship," is from the same root. The term "fellow" sometimes denotes contempt when used derisively, as "vain fellows" (II Sam 6:20). Other OT terms are *ḥābēr* (Ezk 37:16), and *'āmîth,* which is used prophetically of Christ in Zech 13:7. The NT synonyms are found in Mt 11:16;

20:13 (*hetairos*); Lk 5:7; Heb 1:9 (*metochos*). Cf. also fellow heir (Rom 8:17); fellow servant (Mt 18:28); fellow disciple (Jn 11:16).

FELLOWSHIP. Fellowship (Gr. *koinōnia*) means companionship or partnership and communion with others on the basis of something held in common. Christian fellowship can be considered under several headings.

Participants. The Christian's fellowship is first with God (I Jn 1:6), with Christ (I Cor 1:9), with the Holy Spirit (Phil 2:1; II Cor 13:14), with the Father and the Son (I Jn 1:3; Jn 14:6, 23, 26). It is second with fellow Christians (Jn 15:12; I Jn 1:3, 7).

Basis. The Christian's fellowship with men is, however, to be based, first, upon his clear confession that Christ is the promised Messiah and has truly assumed human flesh (I Jn 4:2–3; II Jn 7–11); and, second, upon his not living in open overt sins such as fornication, idolatry, covetousness, drunkenness (I Cor 5:11). Yet the Christian may company or mix with unsaved who have these sins, and will have to do so because he is a part of the world. That he is forbidden, however, to do so with Christians, shows the dangers of such overt sins not only to the Christian who lives in sin but also to others. Further, the Christian is forbidden to be unequally yoked together with unbelievers (II Cor 6:14–18). In the context Paul is speaking to those who have recently left heathenism. Still, the principle of separation from paganism is hard to distinguish from separation from those holding erroneous doctrines of Christ, particularly since the latter is forbidden by John (I Jn 4:2 f.; II Jn 7–11).

Means of fellowship. There are five specific kinds of fellowship or sharing enjoyed by the Christian.

1. Communion or fellowship together at the Lord's Supper (I Cor 10:16–21), in which the believer professes his faith in Christ's atoning blood and shows forth His death till He comes again (I Cor 11:23–26). Paul gives very careful instruction concerning this fellowship and warns us to examine ourselves before we take part in the Eucharist (I Cor 11:27–28).

2. Membership in the church. Our Lord established His NT Church, or body of called-out believers, on the public profession of Himself as Saviour (Mt 16:18). In Himself He established a vital unity, making of both Jew and Gentile one new "man" or "body" (Eph 2:14–16). He loved it as His own bride and gave Himself for it (Eph 5:25 f.). In the local churches or assemblies Christians are to be nurtured (Heb 10:24–25; cf. Mal 3:16) and to enjoy fellowship in the Word and prayer (Acts 2:42).

3. Giving, which is commanded (I Tim 6:18; Heb 13:16) and may consist in systematic giving on a regular basis (Rom 15:26; II Cor 8:4; 9:13), or it may occur in the gift of large sums or even all one owns at a particular time (Acts 4:36–37; 5:1–11). In cases where all is given, the gift is entirely at the discretion of the giver (Acts 5:4), though it may be necessary in certain cases because the particular individual is turning away from his besetting sin of covetousness (cf. the rich young ruler, Lk 18:18 f.).

4. Ministration to the saints, such as relief funds for other churches (Acts 11:29; Rom 15:25), help to Christians in need (Rom 12:13; II Cor 8:4) and perhaps other people as well (Heb 13:16), and sharing other people's burdens (Rom 15:1; Jas 5:16).

5. Fellowship in suffering. This refers to suffering as a member of Christ's body, partaking of "the fellowship of his sufferings" (Phil 3:10; cf. Col 1:24).

Is there not another fellowship, namely, that of the community of goods or Christian communism mentioned in Acts 4? The experiment of having all things in common was tried immediately after Pentecost. Since it is neither commended for future use nor condemned, and because it has never since been practiced by any except some of the smaller Christian groups, the general consensus is that it proved to be a failure, or was meant to be only a temporary expedient. *See* Community of Goods.

Limits of fellowship. The question as to how far the doctrine of Christian fellowship requires the church to go in the removal of denominational boundaries through merger and union has received increasing attention during the past 50 years. In 1923 all the Methodists, the Congregationalists and 55 percent of the Presbyterians united to form the United Church in Canada, and many other unions have occurred since in the U.S. Currently 25 million Protestants in the U.S. are working on a plan of church union. While undoubtedly many divisions within the body of Christ are unnecessary and harmful, the almost universal leveling of all distinctives in order to attain one great united church presents real questions and dangers.

Christ, it is true, prayed "that they may all be one . . . just as We are one" (Jn 17:21–22, NASB); nevertheless the basis upon which union is being fostered must be examined. Any unity founded upon the joining of those who truly believe Christ is the only begotten Son of God, who became incarnate, died on the cross to bear the sins of the believer, and rose in a resurrection body on the third day, with men or churches which do not believe these fundamentals of the faith, is unscriptural.

The move to bring about a reunion of Protestantism and Roman Catholicism also raises the problem of true biblical fellowship, though in another form. It is not the question as to who Christ is that separates Catholics and Protestants, but what Christ did. Did He offer the only sacrifice sufficient to save the sinner from his sin, or a sacrifice which was ineffectual without our good works? Is Christ the only mediator between God and man, or must we depend also on the intercessory work of Mary and the saints? Christ prayed for a unity of *fellowship,* not of *organization;* a unity in His new life and in the Spirit (II Cor 13:14) in which all the members of His one body are different (I Cor 12), not for a uniformity of structure. The eternal distinction and plurality of persons in the Trinity indicate that in making His comparison, Christ allows for diversity within the unity of His body (Jn 17:21-23). *See* Communion of Saints.

Bibliography. Friedrich Hanck, "*Koinos*, etc.," TDNT, III, 789-809.

R. A. K.

FEN. The Heb. word *biṣṣâ* is defined by BDB as a "swamp." The KJV translates the word in Job 8:11 as "mire" and in Job 40:21 as "fens." Thus a fen denotes a miry bog or marsh.

FENCE. Several Heb. words are used for fence.

1. The Heb. verb *gādar* designates "to surround with a wall," "to heap up stones for a wall" (Job 19:8; Lam 3:9). The nouns derived from the word mean either the wall itself or the area surrounded by it (Ps 62:3; "wall," Num 22:24; Prov 24:31; Isa 5:5).

2. Heb. *'āzaq* (Isa 5:2) really means "to dig and loosen with a mattock."

3. The verb *sākak* translated "fenced" in Job 10:11 (KJV) should be "knit together" as in RSV here and in Ps 139:13. *See* Hedge for passages containing the similar appearing root *sûk* or *śûk,* meaning "to hedge or fence up."

For fenced cities *see* City, Fenced.

FENCED CITY. *See* City, Fenced.

FERRET. KJV translation of *'ănāqa;* RSV has "gecko," a lizard. *See* Animals, IV.16, 21.

FESTIVALS. Observance of the sacred seasons and Jewish religious festivals constituted a significant aspect of the Heb. religion. These holy days and sacred seasons were decreed by God as His gifts to Israel. God purposed to preserve by them a remembrance of such sacred events as their divine election and deliverance (the Passover celebration), their sojourn in the wilderness (Feast of Tabernacles), their constant dependence upon Him for all temporal blessings and prosperity (Pentecost), their preservation in Persia (Feast of Purim), their need of cleansing and forgiveness (Day of Atonement). Many other spiritual lessons and blessings were also to be derived from the numerous festivals and holy days such as the sabbath, new moons, year of jubilee, and the like. Hence, the sacred seasons were based in large measure upon some significant historical event related to the national or religious life of Israel. Furthermore, like the temple and the Scriptures, the national religious festivals were important bonds of spiritual and national unity for the Heb. people.

Sabbatical Seasons

Weekly sabbath. In addition to the annual festivals, the celebration of the weekly sabbath (*shabbāt*) and the sabbatical feast days are also called "holy convocations" (*miqrā'ê qōdesh*) in Lev 23:2 ff. During the wilderness wanderings a holy convocation appears to have been a religious convocation of all males at the tabernacle. After Heb. settlement in Palestine, however, the universal command to appear at the sanctuary had reference only in regard to the three festival pilgrimages in which all males were to attend the feasts of Passover, Pentecost, and Tabernacles at Jerusalem (Ex 23:14-17; Deut 16:16). The holy convocation commanded for the weekly sabbath was to be *in all your dwellings,* that is, the sabbath was to be observed where the people lived.

1. Origin. The creation narrative in Genesis is concluded with an account of the hallowing of the seventh day by God, who rested from all His creative activity on that day. Although the term "sabbath" does not occur in this account, its verbal root (*shābat*) meaning "he rested or ceased" does occur (Gen 2:3). The Decalogue in Ex 20:8-11 assigns as the reason for requiring Israel to observe the sabbath the fact that God rested on this day after six days of creative work. Although there is no distinct mention of the observance of the sabbath in Genesis, some scholars hold that Moses apparently treats it as an institution with which they were already familiar as indicated by the words, "Remember the sabbath day, to keep it holy" (Ex 20:8); furthermore, a seven-day period is referred to in Gen 1:1-2:3; 7:4-10; 8:10-12; 29:27-28.

The first definite mention of the sabbath as a religious institution is found in Ex 16:21-30 in connection with the giving of manna. God commanded Israel in the wilderness that she was to observe the seventh day as a sabbath of rest from all labor by gathering a double portion of manna on the sixth day. That the day was already known to them, some believe, is evidenced by the Lord's rebuke to those who disobeyed: "How long refuse ye to keep my commandments and my laws?" (Ex 16:28). A short time later the observance was enjoined as the fourth commandment at Sinai (Ex 20:8-11).

Modern criticism assigns the origin of the sabbath to two different sources, which allegedly give conflicting reasons for its institution. Ex 20:11, it is argued, makes the sabbath a memorial of God's rest upon the completion of creation, whereas Deut 5:15 states that the sabbath is a memorial of the deliverance of Israel from Egypt. However, this view ignores the context of Deuteronomy. The sabbath was to be a perpetual covenant between God and Israel as His gift of refreshing rest; as such it served as a memorial of His rest from creative activity and was not specifically a memorial of the Exodus. The reference to the Exodus event in Deuteronomy is for the express purpose of reminding Israel that out of gratitude for their freedom and rest after a long period of servile labor, they ought also to allow rest for their servants who now were in a similar situation to their former condition in Egypt as slaves (cf. Ex

CHART OF JEWISH FESTIVALS

MONTHS	FESTIVALS	MONTHS	FESTIVALS
A'BIB (Heb. *'ābîb, green ears*), or NI'-SAN. Thirty days; first of *sacred,* seventh of *civil,* year. (March-April)	1. New moon (Num. 10:10; 28:11–15). 10. Selection of paschal lamb (Exod. 12:3). *Fast* for Miriam (Num. 20:1), and in memory of the scarcity of water (20:2). 14. Paschal lamb killed in evening (Exod. 12:6). Passover begins (Num. 28:16). 15. First day of unleavened bread (Num. 28:17). After sunset sheaf of barley brought to temple. 16. "First fruits," sheaf offered (Lev. 23:10, sq.). Beginning of harvest, fifty days to Pentecost (Lev. 23:15). 21. Close of Passover, end of unleavened bread (Lev. 23:6). 15 and 21. Holy convocations (23:7). 26. *Fast* for death of Joshua.	ETH'ANIM (Heb. *'ēthänîm, permanent*), or TIS'RI. Thirty days; seventh of *sacred,* first of *civil,* year. (Sept.-October)	1. New moon; *New Year;* Rosh Hashanah. *Feast* of Trumpets (Lev. 23:24; Num. 29:1, 2). 3. *Fast* for murder of Gedaliah (II Kings 25:25; Jer. 41:2); high priest set apart for day of atonement. 10. Day of atonement (Yom Kippur), "*the fast*" (Acts 27:9), i. e., the only one enjoined by the law (Lev. 16; 23:27–32); the first day of jubilee years. 15–21. *Feast* of Tabernacles, or Ingathering (Ex. 23:16; Lev. 23:34–43). 22. Holy convocation, palms borne, prayer for rain. (Lev. 23:36; Num. 29:35). 23. *Feast* for law being finished; dedication of Solomon's temple.
ZIV (Heb. *zîv, brightness*), or IYYAR. Twenty-nine days; second *sacred,* eighth of *civil* year. (April-May)	1. New moon (Num. 1:18). 10. *Fast* for death of Eli and capture of ark (I Sam. 4:11, sq.). 14. "Second" or "little" Passover, for those unable to celebrate in Abib; in memory of entering wilderness (Exod. 16:11). 28. *Feast* for death of Samuel (I Sam. 25:1).	BUL (Heb. *bûl*), or MARCHESH'-VAN. Twenty-nine days; eighth of *sacred,* second of *civil,* year. (October-Nov.)	1. New moon. 17. Prayers for rain. 19. *Fast* for faults committed during Feast of Tabernacles. 26. *Feast* in memory of recovery after the captivity of places occupied by the Cuthites.
SI'VAN (Heb. *sîvän*). Thirty days; third third of *sacred,* ninth of *civil,* year. (May-June)	1. New moon. 6. "*Feast* of Pentecost," or "*Feast* of Weeks," because it came seven weeks after Passover (Lev. 23:15–21). 22. *Fast* in memory of Jeroboam's forbidding subjects to carry first fruits to Jerusalem (I Kings 12:27). 27. *Fast,* Chanina being burned with books of law.	KISLEV (Heb. *kisleu*). Thirty days; ninth of *sacred,* third of *civil,* year. (Nov.-December)	1. New moon. 2. *Fast* (three days) if no rain falls. 6. *Feast* in memory of roll burned by Jehoiakim (Jer. 36:23). 14. *Fast,* absolute if no rain. 25. *Feast* of the dedication of the temple, or of Lights (eight days) in memory of restoration of temple by Judas Maccabaeus (cf. Jn. 10:22).
TAM'MUZ (Heb. *tămmŭz*). Twenty-nine days; fourth of *sacred,* tenth of *civil,* year. (June-July)	1. New moon. 14. *Feast* for abolition of a book of Sadducees and Bethusians, intended to subvert oral law and traditions. 17. *Fast* in memory of tables of law broken by Moses (Exod. 32:19); and taking of Jerusalem by Titus.	TE'BETH (Heb. *tĕbēth*). Twenty-nine days; tenth of *sacred,* fourth of *civil,* year. (December-Jan.)	1. New Moon. 8. *Fast* because the law was translated into Greek. 10. *Fast* on account of siege of Jerusalem by Nebuchadnezzar (II Kings 25:1).
AB (Heb. *'äb, fruitful*). Thirty days; fifth of *sacred,* eleventh of *civil,* year. (July-August)	1. New moon; *fast* for death of Aaron, commemorated by children of Jethuel, who furnished wood to temple after the captivity. 9. *Fast* in memory of God's declaration against murmurers entering Canaan (Num. 14:29–31). 18. *Fast,* because in the time of Ahaz the evening lamp went out. 21. *Feast* when wood was stored in temple. 24. *Feast* in memory of law providing for sons and daughters alike inheriting estate of parents.	SHE'BAT (Heb. *shᵉbät'*, or SE': BAT. Thirty days; eleventh of *sacred,* fifth of *civil,* year. (January-February)	1. New moon. 4 or 5. *Fast* in memory of death of elders, successors to Joshua. 15. Beginning of the year of *Trees* (*q. v.*). 23. *Fast* for war of the Ten Tribes against Benjamin (Judg. 20); also idol of Micah (18:11, sq.). 29. Memorial of death of Antiochus Epiphanes, enemy of Jews.
E'LUL (Heb. *'ĕlûl', good for nothing*). Twenty-nine days; sixth of *sacred,* twelfth of *civil,* year. (August-Sept.)	1. New moon. 7. *Feast* for dedication of Jerusalem's walls by Nehemiah. 17. *Fast,* death of spies bringing ill report (Num. 14:26). 21. *Feast,* wood offering. (Throughout the month the cornet is sounded to warn of approaching new civil year.)	ADAR (Heb. *'ădär, fire*). Twenty-nine days; twelfth of *sacred,* sixth of *civil,* year. (ADAR SHENI, *c.* 7 times in 19 years.) (February-March)	1. New moon. 7. *Fast* because of Moses' death (Deut.34:5). 8, 9. Trumpet sounded in thanksgiving for rain, and prayer for future rain. 13. *Fast* of Esther (Esth. 4:16). *Feast* in memory of Nicanor, enemy of the Jews (I Macc. 7:44). 14. The first *Purim,* or lesser *Feast* of Lots (Est.9:21). 15. The great *Feast of Purim.* 20. *Feast* for rain obtained in time of drought, in time of Alexander Janaeus. 23. *Feast* for dedication of Zerubbabel's temple (Ezra 6:16). 28. *Feast* to commemorate the repeal of decree of Grecian kings forbidding Jews to circumcise their children.

A chart of the festivals.

5:14–15). Thus both passages connect the sabbath with rest.

Some scholars have drawn parallels between the Babylonian *shabbatu* and the Heb. sabbath, but no such relationship is indicated from available evidence. Furthermore, Ezk 20:12, 20, indicates that the sabbaths were signs God gave to Israel to distinguish her from other nations.

2. Character and observance. The sabbath was to be observed by abstaining from all physical labor, whether done by man or beast. But the sabbath was not intended for selfish use in idleness; it was a divinely given opportunity, in freedom from one's secular labors, to strengthen and refresh the whole man, physically and spiritually. The sabbath had a benevolent design and was intended as a blessing, not a burden, to man (cf. Deut 5:14–15; Isa 58:13–14; Mk 2:27). Sabbath legislation is found in several OT passages; e.g., Ex 16:23 ff.; 20:8–11; 31:12–17; Lev 19:3, 30; Num 15:32–36; Deut 5:12–15. *See* Sabbath.

Monthly new moon. The first day of each month was designated as *rōʾsh ḥōdesh,* "the first or head of the month," or simply as *ḥōdesh,* "new moon" (Num 10:10; I Sam 20:5). Unlike the new moon of the seventh month, which was the first day of the civil new year and celebrated with a great festival, the regular monthly new moons were subordinate feast days celebrated with additional burnt offerings (Num 28:11–15), the blowing of trumpets (Num 10:10; Ps 81:3), family feasts (I Sam 20:5), spiritual edification (II Kgs 4:23), and family sacrifices (I Sam 20:6). As on all sabbatical feast days, all servile work ceased, except the necessary preparation of food (cf. Ex 12:16). The new moon and sabbath are closely related in several passages (e.g., Isa 1:13; Ezk 46:1; Hos 2:11; Amos 8:5).

The moon occupied an important place in the life of the Hebrews, since it was the guide to their calendar based upon the lunar month or period of the moon's circuit. Because of this, and the importance of the uniform celebration of the various periodic religious festivals by Jews everywhere, it was extremely important to determine the exact time of the appearance of the new moon. Thus the appearance of the smallest crescent signified the beginning of a new month and was announced with the blowing of the shofar or ram's horn.

Sabbatical year. The *shenat shabbātôn,* "year of rest" or sabbatical year, like the weekly sabbath, was designed by God with a benevolent purpose in view. Every seventh year debts were to be cancelled and the land was to lie fallow, the uncultivated increase to be left to the poor Israelite.

1. Observance. According to II Chr 36:21, observance of the sabbatical year had been neglected for about 500 years, the 70 year Captivity allowing the land to enjoy its neglected sabbaths, "for as long as it lay desolate it kept sabbath, to fulfill three-score and ten years" (ASV). After the Captivity, the people under Nehemiah bound themselves to the faithful observance of the seventh year, covenanting that "we would forego the seventh year, and the exaction of every debt" (Neh 10:31, ASV). Its observance continued during the intertestamental period (I Macc 6:48–53) and afterward (Jos *Ant.* xiv. 10.6).

2. Purpose. (*a*) A rest for the land (Lev 25:1–7). After the land had been sown and harvested for six successive years it was "to rest" or to remain fallow on the seventh year. This included the vineyards and olive yards also (Ex 23:10). This provision insured greater productivity for the soil by the periodic interruption of the incessant sowing, plowing, and reaping. (*b*) To enable the poor to eat (Ex 23:10–11). During this year, that which grew of itself in the fields, vineyards, and olive yards was not to be harvested, but left so "that the poor of thy people may eat: and what they leave the beast of the field shall eat." Lev 25:6–7 also includes the owner, his servants, the sojourner, cattle and beasts, as well as the poor of Ex 23:11, as those who were eligible to consume the natural produce of the sabbatical year. (*c*) Debts were to be cancelled (Deut 15:1–6). Each creditor was to cancel the debts of a brother Israelite at the end of every seven years, for it was called also "the year of release" (Deut 15:9; 31:10). This did not apply to a foreigner, from whom the debt could be collected (Deut 15:3). The release was so that absolute poverty and permanent indebtedness would not exist among the Israelites. In addition, they were not to disregard the needs of their poorer brethren by refusing to lend merely because the year of release was near (Deut 15:7–11). (*d*) In the sabbatical year the law was to be read for the instruction of the people at the Feast of Tabernacles (Deut 31:10–13). (*e*) Not simply on the sabbatical year, but also at the close of any six year period, those Israelites who because of poverty had made themselves bondservants to their brethren were to be released (Deut 15:12–18). In this case the year of release would be ascertained from the first year of indenture. The legislation respecting the sabbatical year was confined to the Israelites in the Holy Land and went into effect upon their arrival there (Lev 25:2).

Year of jubilee. Seven sabbatic cycles of years (i.e., 49) terminated in the year of jubilee (*shenat hayyôbēl*), lit., "the year of the ram's horn," the fiftieth year being designated thus from the custom of sounding the ram's horn (*yôbēl*) announcing its arrival (Lev 25:8–17). The fiftieth year is called "the year of liberty" (*derôr*) in Ezk 46:17 (cf. Jer 34:8, 15, 17) on the basis of Lev 25:10: "And ye shall hallow the fiftieth year, and proclaim liberty throughout the land . . . it shall be a jubilee unto you."

1. Nature of celebration. According to Lev 25:9, the year of jubilee was announced by the sounding of rams' horns throughout the land on the tenth day of the seventh month, which was also the great Day of Atonement. The year of jubilee was not, as some have thought, the forty-ninth year, and thus simply a seventh sabba-

Samaritan priests celebrating the Passover. Richard E. Ward

tical year, but was, as Lev 25:10 states, the fiftieth year, thus providing two successive sabbatic years in which the land would have rest. Certain regulations were issued to take effect during the year of jubilee. (*a*) Rest for the land (Lev 25:11–12). As in the preceding sabbatical year, the land was to remain uncultivated and the people were to eat of the natural increase. To compensate for this, God promised: "I will command my blessing upon you in the sixth year, and it shall bring forth fruit for three years" (Lev 25:21). In addition, other sources of provision were available, such as hunting, fishing, flocks, herds, bees, and the like. (*b*) Hereditary lands and property were to be restored to the original family without compensation, in the year of jubilee (Lev 25:23–34). In this manner all land and its improvements would eventually be restored to the original holders to whom God had given it, for He said, "The land shall not be sold in perpetuity; for the land is mine" (Lev 25:23, ASV). This regulation did not apply to a house within a walled city, which stood in no relation to a family's land inheritance (vv.29–30). (*c*) Freedom of bondservants was to be effected in the year of jubilee. Every Israelite who had because of poverty subjected himself to bondage was to be set free (Lev 25:29 ff.).

2. Purpose. There were several divine purposes in these regulations and provisions for the year of jubilee. (*a*) It was to contribute toward the abolishment of poverty by enabling the unfortunate and victims of circumstances to begin anew. (*b*) It would discourage excessive, permanent accumulations of wealth and property, and the consequent deprivation of an Israelite of his inheritance in the land. "Woe unto them that join house to house, that lay field to field" (Isa 5:8; cf. Mic 2:2). (*c*) It preserved families and tribes inasmuch as it returned freed bondservants to their own blood relations and families, and thus slavery, in any permanent sense, would not exist in Israel.

Special festival sabbaths. In addition to the weekly sabbath and the monthly new moon, there were seven annual feast days which were also classed as sabbaths. They were the first and last days of the Feast of Unleavened Bread (Lev 23:7–8), the Day of Pentecost (Lev 23:21), the Feast of Trumpets (Lev 23:24–25), the Day of Atonement (Lev 23:32), and the first and last days of the Feast of Tabernacles (Lev 23:34–36). There was one major distinction between these festival sabbaths and the weekly sabbath and Day of Atonement. On the latter, all work was strictly forbidden, whereas rest only from "servile" labor was required on the other sabbaths.

Pilgrimage Feasts

Feast of the Passover and Feast of Unleavened Bread. The Passover (*pesaḥ*) was the first of three annual pilgrimage festivals and was celebrated on the 14th of Nisan (post-Exilic name; formerly Abib, Ex 13:4, approximately our April), thereafter continuing as the Feast of Unleavened Bread from the 15th to the 21st. Nisan marked the beginning of the religious or sacred new year (Ex 12:2). The Heb. term *pesaḥ* is from a root meaning "to pass (or spring) over," and signifies the passing over (sparing) of the houses of Israel when the firstborn of Egypt were slain (Ex 12). The Passover itself refers only to the paschal supper on the evening of the 14th, whereas the following period, 15th to 21st, is called the Feast of Unleavened Bread (Ex 12; 13:1–10; Lev 23:5–8; Num 28:16–25; Deut 16:1–8).

1. Institution and celebration. The purpose for its institution was to commemorate the deliverance of Israel from Egyptian bondage and the sparing of Israel's firstborn when God smote the firstborn of Egypt. In observance of the first Passover, on the 10th of Nisan the head of each family set apart a lamb without blemish. On the evening of the 14th the lamb was slain and some of its blood sprinkled on the doorposts and lintel of the house in which they ate the Passover as a seal against the coming judgment upon Egypt. The lamb was then roasted whole and eaten with unleavened bread and bitter herbs. If the family was too small to consume a lamb, then a neighboring family could share it. Any portion remaining was to be burned the next morning. Each was to eat in haste with loins girded, shoes on the feet, and staff in hand.

2. Later observance. After the establishment of the priesthood and tabernacle, the celebration of the Passover differed in some particulars from the Egyptian Passover. These distinctions were: (*a*) the Passover lamb was to be slain at the sanctuary rather than at home (Deut 16:5–6); (*b*) the blood was sprinkled upon the altar instead of the doorposts; (*c*) besides the family sacrifice for the Passover meal, there were public and national sacrifices offered each of the seven days of the Feast of Unleavened Bread (Num 28:16–24); (*d*) the meaning of the Passover was recited at the feast each year (Ex 12:24–27); (*e*) the singing of the Hallel (Ps

113–118) during the meal was later instituted; (*f*) a second Passover on the 14th day of the second month was to be kept by those who were ceremonially unclean or away on a journey at the time of its regular celebration on the 14th of Nisan (Num 9:9–12).

The Passover was one of the three feasts in which all males were required to come to the sanctuary. They were not to appear empty-handed, but were to bring offerings as the Lord had prospered them (Ex 23:14–17; Deut 16:16–17). It was unlawful to eat leavened food after midday of the 14th, and all labor, with few exceptions, ceased. According to Josephus (*Wars* vi.9.3), each lamb was to serve ten to twenty persons, no ceremonially unclean men or women being admitted to the feast. After appropriate blessings a first cup of wine was served, followed by the eating of a portion of the bitter herbs. Before the lamb and unleavened bread were eaten, a second cup of wine was provided at which time the son, in compliance with Ex 12:26, asked the father the meaning and significance of the Passover feast. An account of the Egyptian bondage and deliverance was recited in reply. The first portion of the Hallel (Ps 113–114) was then sung and the paschal supper eaten, followed by third and fourth cups of wine and the second part of the Hallel (Ps 115–118).

3. Feast of Unleavened Bread. Both the Passover and the Feast of Unleavened Bread, which immediately followed, commemorated the Exodus, the former in remembrance of God's "passing over" the Israelites when He slew the firstborn of Egypt, and the latter, to keep alive the memory of their affliction and God's bringing them out in haste from Egypt ("bread of affliction," Deut 16:3). The first and last days of this feast were sabbaths in which no servile work could be done, except the necessary preparation of food. The Passover season marked the beginning of the grain harvest in Palestine. On the second day of Unleavened Bread (16th Nisan), a sheaf of the firstfruits of the barley harvest was presented as a wave offering (Lev 23:9–11). The ceremony came to be called "the omer ceremony" from the Heb. word for sheaf, *'ōmĕr*.

Feast of Pentecost. Pentecost, which is the Gr. word for "fiftieth," is called in Heb. *ḥag shābū'ōt*, i.e., "the feast of weeks" (Ex 34:22; Lev 23:15–22). It derived its name from the fact that it was celebrated seven weeks after the Passover on the fiftieth day (Lev 23:15–16; Deut 16:9–10). It is also called the "feast of harvest" (Ex 23:16) and the "day of firstfruits" (Num 28:26).

Pentecost was a one-day festival in which all males were to appear at the sanctuary, and a sabbath in which all servile labor was suspended. The central feature of the day was the offering of two loaves of bread for the people from the firstfruits of the wheat harvest (Lev 23:17). As the omer ceremony signified the harvest season had begun, the presentation of the two loaves indicated its close. It was a day of thanksgiving in which free-will offerings were made (Deut 16:10), rejoicing was expressed before the Lord, and special consideration shown the Levite, sojourner, orphan and widow (Deut 16:10–12). The festival day signified the dedication of the harvest to God as the provider of all blessings. *See* Firstfruits 3.

The OT does not specifically give any historical significance for the day, Pentecost being the only one of the three great agricultural feasts which does not commemorate some event in Jewish history. Later tradition, on the basis of Ex 19:1, taught that the giving of the law at Sinai was fifty days after the Exodus and Passover, and as a result *shābū'ōt* has also become known as the Torah festival. The book of Ruth, which describes the harvest season, is read at Pentecost. The significance of the day for the NT is set forth in Acts 2, when on the day of Pentecost the Church had its beginning. *See* Pentecost.

Feast of Tabernacles. The Feast of Tabernacles (*hag hassūkkôt*), the third of the pilgrimage feasts, was celebrated for seven days from the 15th to 21st day of Tishri, the seventh month (Oct). It was followed by an eighth day of holy convocation with appropriate sacrifices (Lev 23:33 ff.; Num 29:12-38; Deut 16:13–15). It was also called "the feast of ingathering" (Ex 23:16) for the autumn harvest of the fruits and olives, with the ingathering of the threshing floor and the wine press, which occurred at this time (Lev 23:39; Deut 16:13). It was the outstanding feast of rejoicing in the year, in which the Israelites, during the seven day period, lived in booths or huts made of boughs in commemoration of their wilderness wanderings when their fathers dwelt in temporary shelters. According to Neh 8:14–18, the booths were made of olive, myrtle, palm, and other branches, and were built upon roofs of houses, in courtyards, the court of the temple, and in the broad places of the city streets. Sacrifices were more numerous during this feast than at any other, consisting of the offering of 189 animals for the seven day period.

When the feast coincided with a sabbatical year, the law was read publicly to the entire congregation at the sanctuary (Deut 31:10–13). As Josephus and the Talmud indicate, new ceremonies were gradually added to the festival, chief of which was the *śimḥat bêt hashô'ēbâh*, "the festival of the drawing of water." In this ceremony a golden pitcher was filled from the pool of Siloam and returned to the priest at the temple amid the joyful shouts of the celebrants, after which the water was poured into a basin at the altar (cf. Jn 7:37–38). At night the streets and temple court were illuminated by innumerable torches carried by the singing, dancing pilgrims. The booths were dismantled on the last day, and the eighth day which followed was observed as a sabbath of holy convocation. The feast is mentioned by Zechariah as a joyous celebration in the Millennium (Zech 14:16).

Festivals and Holy Days of the Seventh Month

Feast of Trumpets. The new moon of the seventh month (1st of Tishri) constituted the beginning of the civil new year and was designated as *ro'sh hashshanâ*, "the first of the year," or *yôm terû'â*, "day of sounding" (the trumpet). Lev 23:23-25 and Num 29:1-6 are the only OT references to Rosh Hashanah, the regulations, prayers, and customs of which today fill volumes. The blowing of the shofar or ram's horn occupied a significant place on several other occasions, such as the monthly new moon and year of jubilee, but especially so at the beginning of the new year, hence its name—Feast of Trumpets. The Heb. calendar (*q.v.*) actually began with Nisan in the spring as the beginning of months (Ex 12:2); but since the end of the seventh month, Tishri, usually marked the beginning of the rainy season in Palestine when the year's work of plowing and planting began, Tishri was constituted the beginning of the economic and civil year. Business transactions, sabbatical years and jubilee years were all determined from the first of the seventh month. Later, Judaism associated many important events with Rosh Hashanah: the creation of the world; creation of Adam; the births of Abraham, Isaac, Jacob, and Samuel; the day of Joseph's release from prison, etc. (Ben M. Edidin, *Jewish Holidays and Festivals*, pp. 53-54).

The day was observed as a sabbatical feast day with special sacrifices, and looked forward to the solemn Day of Atonement ten days later. Rosh Hashanah (New Year's) and Yom Kippur (Day of Atonement) constitute what are called "high holy days" in Judaism. Rosh Hashanah has come to be considered as a day of judgment for one's deeds of the previous year. It is a day for retrospection, prayer, and repentance. On this day God judges all men for their deeds and decides who shall live or die, prosper or suffer adversity.

The Day of Atonement. The annual Day of Atonement (*yôm hakkippūrîm*) is set forth in Lev 16; 23:27-32 as the supreme act of national atonement for sin. It took place on the 10th day of the seventh month, Tishri, and fasting was commanded from the evening of the 9th until the evening of the 10th, in keeping with the unusual sanctity of the day. On this day an atonement was effected for the people, the priesthood, and for the sanctuary because it "dwelleth with them in the midst of their uncleannesses" (Lev 16:16, ASV).

1. The ritual. This was divided into two acts, one performed on behalf of the priesthood, and one on behalf of the nation Israel. The high priest, who had moved a week previous to this day from his own dwelling to the sanctuary, arose on the Day of Atonement, and having bathed and laid aside his regular high priestly attire, dressed himself in holy white linen garments, and brought forward a young bullock for a sin offering for himself and for his house. The other priests who on other occasions served in the sanctuary on this day took their place with the sinful congregation for whom atonement was to be made (Lev 16:17). The high priest slew the sin offering for himself and entered the holy of holies with a censer of incense, so that a cloud of incense might fill the room and cover the ark in order that he not die. Then he returned with the blood of the sin offering and sprinkled it upon the mercy seat on the east, and seven times before the mercy seat for the symbolic cleansing of the holy of holies, defiled by its presence among the sinful people. Having made atonement for himself, he returned to the court of the sanctuary.

The high priest next presented the two goats, which had been secured as the sin offering for the people, to the Lord at the door of the tabernacle and cast lots over them, one lot marked for Jehovah, and the other for Azazel (ASV). The goat upon which the lot had fallen for the Lord was slain, and the high priest repeated the ritual of sprinkling the blood as before. In addition, he cleansed the holy place by a sevenfold sprinkling, and lastly, cleansed the altar of burnt offering.

2. The goat for Azazel. In the second stage of the ceremony the live goat, the goat for Azazel, which had been left standing at the altar, was brought forward. The high priest, laying hands upon it, confessed over it all the sins of the people, after which it was sent into an uninhabited wilderness bearing the iniquity of the nation of Israel.

The precise significance of this part of the ceremony is determined by the meaning which is attached to the expression "for Azazel" (KJV, "for a scapegoat"). Basically, there are four interpretations: (*a*) Azazel was a *place* to which the second goat was sent. But such a place would have been left behind in the constant movement of Israel from Egypt to Palestine. (*b*) Azazel was a *person*, either Satan or an evil spirit. But the name Azazel occurs nowhere else in Scripture, which is unlikely if he were so important a person to divide the sin offering with God, which suggestion in itself has an offensive connotation. Moreover, demon worship is condemned in the same law in Lev 17:7-9. (*c*) Azazel was an *abstract noun* meaning "dismissal" or "complete removal." (*d*) More likely Azazel designates the goat itself. This view was held by Josephus, Symmachus, Aquila, Theodotion, Luther, Bonar, LXX, Vulg., KJV ("scapegoat"), and others. Hence the goat was called in the Heb. Azazel, meaning "the removing goat": "And Aaron shall cast lots upon the two goats; one lot for Jehovah, and the other lot for Azazel" (ASV), *for the removing goat*, i.e., for the remover of sins (Lev 16:8). Both goats were called an atonement and both were presented to the Lord. Therefore, both goats were looked upon as *one offering*. Since it was physically impossible to depict two ideas with one goat, two were needed as a single sin offering. The first goat by its death symbolized atonement for sins; the other, by confessing over it the sins of Israel and sending it away, symbolized their complete removal. Compare the analogy in Lev 14:4–7. *See* Azazel.

Feast of Tabernacles. The third and final sacred observance in the seventh month commanded by Scripture was the Feast of Tabernacles. Inasmuch as it was also one of the three pilgrimage feasts in which all males were to appear at the sanctuary, it is discussed under that category (see above).

Post-Exilic Festivals

Feast of Purim. This feast was instituted by Mordecai to commemorate the preservation of the Jews of Persia from destruction through the plot of Haman, as recorded in the book of Esther. The term Purim (*pûrîm*), which means "lots," was given to the festival because Haman had cast lots to ascertain which day he would carry out the decree to massacre the Jews. The festival was to last for two days, the 14th and 15th of Adar, with "feasting and gladness, and of sending of portions one to another, and gifts to the poor" (Est 9:20–22, ASV). The feast has always been popular with the Jews as Josephus (*Ant.* xi.6.13) attests, its celebration continuing down to the present time. Later generations began to observe only one day (14th). The preceding day (13th) is known as the Fast of Esther in commemoration of Esther's fast before seeking audience with the king on behalf of the Jews (Est 4:15–16). Services at the synagogue on Purim include the reading of the book of Esther. *See* Purim.

Feast of Dedication. The Feast of Dedication (*ḥanukkâ,* "dedication"), also called the Feast of Lights, is a significant, although extrabiblical, feast originating during the Maccabean period in commemoration of the purification of the temple and restoration of the altar by Judas Maccabeus in 164 B.C. (I Macc 4:36–61). The dedication of the altar was observed eight days from the 25th of Kislev (Dec.) and ordained to be observed yearly thereafter. According to II Macc 10:6–7, the feast was likened to the Feast of Tabernacles and celebrated by the carrying of boughs, palms, and branches, with the singing of psalms. Josephus called the feast "Lights" for he writes: "We celebrate this festival, and call it Lights. I suppose the reason was, because this liberty [i.e., restored political and religious freedom] beyond our hopes appeared to us" (*Ant.* xii.7.7). The use of lights during Ḥanukkah celebrations has always played a significant part, especially in the homes, synagogues, and streets of Palestine. The feast is mentioned in connection with Jesus' ministry in Jn 10:22 ff.

Subordinate extrabiblical Jewish sacred seasons. The seventh day of Sukkot (Tabernacles), the 21st of Tishri, came to be known as *hôshaʿnāʾ rabbāʾ,* "Great Hosanna" or "Great Help." The eighth day is now called *shᵉmînî ʿaseret,* "Eighth Day of Solemn Assembly," a holy convocation in which prayers for the homeland are offered. The following day (23rd Tishri) is *śimḥat tôrâ.* "Feast of the Law," a day of rejoicing and celebration marking the close of the yearly cycle of reading the Torah in the synagogues. The "Fifteenth Day of Shebat," or *Ḥamishâ ʿAsār Bishebāt,* marks the beginning of spring in Palestine and is celebrated by the planting of trees (cf. Lev 19:23; Deut 20:19). *Ḥag Bĕʿōmĕr* is celebrated on the 33rd day of the "omer" season (18th of Iyar) to commemorate the attempt by the Jews to regain their independence under Simon bar Kokheba (A.D. 132–135).

Fasts include, besides the Fast of Esther (*Taʿănît Esther*), *Asārâ Bᵉṭēbet,* "Tenth of Tebet," a fast in remembrance of the beginning of the siege of Jerusalem by Babylonia (II Kgs 25:1; Jer 39:1); *Shibʿâ ʿAsār Betammûz,* "Seventeenth of Tammuz," in token of the day the city was entered by the invaders (Jer 39:2; 52:6–7); *Tishâ Bĕʾāb,* "Ninth of Ab," to lament the day of the destruction of the city and temple (II Kgs 25:8–9; Jer 52:12–13); and the Fast of Gedaliah (third Tishri) to mourn the murder of Gedaliah in 586 B.C. *See* Fast.

Bibliography. Andrew A. Bonar, *A Commentary on the Book of Leviticus,* Grand Rapids: Zondervan, 1959. Ben M. Edidin, *Jewish Holidays and Festivals,* New York: Jordan Publ. Co., 1940. *Jewish Encyclopedia,* New York: Funk and Wagnalls, 1906. S. H. Kellogg, "The Book of Leviticus," ExpB. G. F. Oehler, "The Sacred Seasons,"' *Theology of the Old Testament,* Grand Rapids: Zondervan, n.d., pp. 323–352. J. Barton Payne, *The Theology of the Older Testament,* Grand Rapids: Zondervan, 1962, pp. 394–410, 524 f.

H. E. Fr.

FESTUS, PORCIUS (pôr'shŭs fēs'tŭs). The successor to Antonius Felix as procurator of Judea under Nero. According to E. Schurer, he was unable to undo the damage done by his predecessor, although he himself was disposed to rule well. Josephus (*Ant.* xx.8.9–11) presents Festus as a wise and just official, an agreeable contrast to Felix and to Albinus his successor.

The generally accepted date for his accession is A.D. 60, but many chronological problems are involved, and consequently the beginning of Festus' office has been placed as early as A.D. 55 and as late as A.D. 60. See bibliography below for representative viewpoints.

According to Acts 24:27, Paul had been in prison two years when Festus arrived in Caesarea. When the procurator, anxious to gain favor with the Jews, asked Paul if he would consent to being tried in Jerusalem (Acts 25:9), the apostle objected to what (in his mind) would have been a risky situation, and then made his classic reply: "I appeal unto Caesar" (Acts 25:11). Because Festus had no charge to send to Nero with the prisoner (Acts 25:25–27), he appealed to Herod Agrippa II to hear the case. *See* Agrippa II.

As he listened to Paul's impassioned witness, Festus retorted, "Paul, you are out of your mind!" (Acts 26:24, NASB). Apparently the apostle either sounded absurd to the procurator, or he had come "too close to home" in the matter of conviction of sin.

Bibliography. For A.D. 56: F. J. Foakes-Jackson and Kirsopp Lake, *The Beginnings of Christianity,* London: Macmillan, 1933, V, 464–474. For A.D. 58: C. H. Turner, "Chronology of the New Testament," HDB, I, 418 f., 424 f. For A.D. 59: William M. Ramsay, *Pauline and Other Studies in the History of Religion,* London: Hodder & Stoughton, n.d., p. 348. H. J. Cadbury, *The Book of Acts in History,* New York: Harper, 1955, pp. 9–10. For A.D. 60: Theodor Zahn, *Introduction to the New Testament,* Grand Rapids: Kregel, 1953, III, 469–478.

W. M. D.

FETTERS. Instruments used in securing feet and hands of prisoners. Fetters were made in pairs, usually of iron or brass. The word is always used in the plural. "He sent a man before them, even Joseph, who was sold for a servant: whose feet they hurt with fetters" (Ps 105:17–18). The word is sometimes used figuratively, as in Job 36:8–9: "And if they be bound in fetters, and be holden in cords of affliction; then he showeth them their work. . . ."

FEVER. *See* Diseases: Fever.

FIDELITY (Gr. *pistis,* "faithfulness," "trustworthiness"). The adjective *pistos* is usually translated "faithful." The word *pistis* is translated "fidelity" only once in the NT (Tit 2:10), although it is possible that in Gal 5:22 it should be so translated. In Rom 3:3, "the faithfulness of God" (RSV) is clearly "the fidelity of God."

A stone watchtower in a field near Samaria. HFV

There is a possibility that in Lk 18:8, "Shall he find faith on earth?" the meaning should be "fidelity." Two more passages, I Tim 6:11: "godliness, *faith,* love, patience," and II Tim 2:22: "follow righteousness, *faith,* charity," would make good sense if translated "fidelity." In all other NT uses of *pistis* the meaning would seem to be "faith" or "the faith" (*q.v.*).

When the word "fidelity" is used of God, as in Rom 3:3, the meaning is that God can be trusted not to change His character or disposition. He has the attribute of "fidelity." In Tit 2:10, "showing all good fidelity," slaves (servants) are enjoined to show the quality of faithfulness or fidelity. As Christians we are all to remain faithful to Christ, i.e., to have fidelity in our Christian life and faith, to manifest "the perseverance of the saints." In that way we will become "trustworthy." *See* Faith; Faithfulness.

F. E. H.

FIELD. The biblical term for "field" conveys the idea of an open area, while the term today may imply enclosure. The Heb. word *śādeh* (poetical form *śāday*) is the most common term for field in the OT. Frequently it is difficult to determine from the context the site and purpose of the territory (cf. Gen 2:5, 19; 4:8; Ex 1:14; 22:5; Deut 5:21, *et al.*). Sometimes the word is used to designate a large area ("country of Moab," RSV; or "field of Moab," KJV in Gen 36:35; parable of the tares in Mt 13:38, where "the field is the world"). The word is also used to designate a game resort (Gen 27:5), habitat of wild animals (Ps 80:13), a cultivated area (Ruth 2:2; Job 24:6; Ps 107:37), or a grazable pasture (Gen 34:5; Ex 9:21; Num 22:4). Jer 32:7 ff. records the details of the purchase of a field at Anathoth by Jeremiah during the siege of Jerusalem (588–586 B.C.).

Other Heb. words for a cultivated and non-cultivated field are: (1) *shedēmâ,* which is used only six times in the OT (cf. Deut 32:32; Isa 16:8); (2) *bar* (Aram.), used only in Dan 2:38; 4:12, 15, 21, 23, 25, 32; (3) *ḥûṣ,* sometimes translated "the outside" and frequently "abroad" (cf. Deut 23:13), but usually translated "field" as in Job 5:10; Prov 8:26, "in the open country"; (4) *ḥelqâ,* literally meaning "portion of ground," but usually translated "field" (II Sam 14:30); (5) *'ereṣ,* the common word for "earth" or "land"; (6) *yegēbîm,* which occurs only once in the OT and is usually translated "fields" in the various English versions (Jer 39:10). The Gr. words *agros, chōra* and *chōrion,* translated "field," may refer either to areas limited in size or to the open country (Mt 6:30; Lk 15:25; Jn 4:35; Acts 1:18).

The biblical "field" was generally not enclosed, but was indicated by stone markers (or landmarks) at the corners. Such stones could be easily removed (Deut 19:14; 27:17). Because of the lack of enclosure and of the usually unsettled conditions, a watchman was ordinarily employed, especially when the crops were nearing maturity (*see* Agriculture). Besides the danger of human intruders, there was sometimes danger of straying cattle or even cattle rustling (Ex 22:5), and of fire if a Samson (Jud 15:5) or an angry Absalom (II Sam 14:30) were about.

Fields were occasionally named after remarkable events, as Helkath-hazzurim, "the field of strong men" (II Sam 2:16), or after their use, as "the fuller's field" (II Kgs 18:17) or "potter's field" (Mt 27:7). *See* Fuller's Field; Potter's Field; Aceldama.

D. W. D.

FIG, FIG TREE. *See* Plants.

FIG LEAVES. *See* Dress: Materials.

FIGHT. *See* Warfare.

FILLET (fĭl'ĕt). The Heb. word *ḥûṭ* in Jer 52:21 is translated "fillet" in KJV; ASV translates it "line." Gesenius gives the meaning "a thread, line, rope or cord."

The word *ḥishshaq* is given the meaning "filletted" by KJV in Ex 38:28; ASV and RSV give it the meaning "made fillets." Gesenius gives the term "joinings," that is, the poles or rods used to join the top of the columns of the court of the tabernacle. In Ex 27:10–11, 17 these are prescribed to be made of silver.

FILTH, FILTHY. An alternate translation for Heb. *ṣô'â* which normally means "excrement" (Isa 4:4, a figure for sin), for Gr. *perikatharma* meaning "scrapings" or "refuse" (I Cor 4:13); or for *rhypos* (I Pet 3:21). Filthy can also be used in both literal (Isa 64:6; Ezk 36:25) and moral senses (Job 15:16; Ps 14:3; 53:3); or it may have the sense of "shameful" (Col 3:8).

FINE, FINES. *See* Crime and Punishment.

FINER. *See* Occupations: Refiner.

FINGER. This word is used literally of one of the five terminating members of the hand in relation to the OT priest and his ministry with the blood sacrifice (Lev 4:6; etc.); the rich man in Hades (Lk 16:24); Jesus' writing on the ground (Jn 8:6); doubting Thomas (Jn 20:25–27).

The term is also used figuratively or metaphorically to refer to the power or Spirit of God. Egyptian magicians said of the plagues, "This is the finger of God" (Ex 8:19). The tablets of stone were written by the finger of God (Ex 31:18; Deut 9:10). The heavens are the works of God's fingers (Ps 8:3). Jesus cast out demons with the "finger of God" (Lk 11:20).

FINING POT. A pot for refining metal, such as silver (Prov 17:3; 27:21). *See* Minerals and Metals; Silver; Occupations: Metal, Workers of.

FINISHER. This word (Gr. *teleiotes*) is used of Jesus in Heb 12:2. It is derived from *teleioō* which means "to carry through completely," hence, "to make perfect." Perhaps the idea intended in Heb 12:2 is that it is Jesus who as author or pioneer-leader of the faith-life "fulfilled the ideal of faith Himself, and so, both as a vicarious offering and an example, He is the object of our faith. . . . In this He is distinguished from all those examples of faith in chap. 11" (JFB), who were not to be made perfect (*teleiōthōsis*) apart from us (Heb 11:40).

FINS. Among the water creatures that were clean and could be eaten by the Israelites (Lev 11:9–12) were those that had fins and scales. The word "fin" is only used in denoting what may be eaten in the sea. The Heb. word is of uncertain origin. Fins are the membraneous structures on the body of fish used to propel or guide them in swimming. *See* Animals: Fish, V.4.

FIR. *See* Plants.

FIRE. Words for fire are used about 450 times in Scripture with both literal and figurative meanings. The literal uses include its employment for domestic purposes in cooking (Isa 30:14), lighting and for warmth (Jer 36:22; Mk 14:54; Jn 18:18; Acts 28:2); for melting, casting, working, and refining of metals (Zech 13:9; Mal 3:2); for burning refuse and contaminated articles (Lev 13:52, 57); as a means of destroying idolatrous objects (Deut 7:5; I Chr 14:12); as a destructive force in the form of lightning (Ps 29:7) and the burning of cities in time of war (Isa 1:7; Jer 34:2); as a severe means of punishment for grievous offenses (Rev 16:8–9); as the common means of making sacrifices to God. (The pagan custom of burning children in fire as a sacrifice was condemned.) *See* Fire Worship.

Figurative or symbolic uses include the representation of the divine presence, holiness, glory, guidance, and protection (Ezk 1:4, 13, 27; 8:2); God's jealousy (Ezk 36:5), wrath against and punishment of sin (Isa 10:16–17; Mk 9:48; Rev 18:8; 19:20; *see* Gehenna); evil (Isa 9:18), lust (Prov 6:27), and greed; war, trouble, suffering, and affliction (Job 5:7; Isa 29:6); purification and testing (I Pet 1:7; 4:12); the power of the word and truth of God (Jer 5:14; 23:29); prophetic inspiration (Jer 20:9); the zeal of saints (Ps 39:3; 119:139) and of angels (Ps 104:4; Heb 1:7); the Holy Spirit (Acts 2:3) and the glorified Christ (Rev 1:14); and eschatological judgment (Rev 20:9–15; 21:8).

The most important aspect of fire in the Bible is its use in worship and sacrifices to consume the burnt offerings and incense. The first explicit reference is Noah's offering to God (Gen 8:20–21). Later it was a central part of the continual sacrifices and constant worship of both the tabernacle and the temple in which the fire upon the altar was never permitted to die out (Lev 6:12–13). Fire upon the altar was miraculously sent from God (Lev 9:24; II Chr 7:1-3). Any fire started by man or obtained elsewhere than from the altar ("strange fire," Lev 10:1-2) was ritually unacceptable and incurred the divine wrath. Nadab and Abihu were punished with death by fire from God for using strange fire upon the altar (Lev 10).

The perpetual altar fire was to be replenished with wood every morning (Lev 6:12). Acceptance of the sacrifices was indicated by the fire of God suddenly consuming the offering. Fire from God signified the acceptance of certain special sacrifices (Jud 6:21; I Kgs 18:24, 38; I Chr 21:26)—Yahweh is "the God who answers by fire." Animals slain for sin offerings were consumed by fire outside the camp (Lev 4:12, 21; 6:30). Upon completing his vow, a Nazarite shaved his head and put the hair into the altar fire in which the peace offerings were being sacrificed (Num 6:18).

The law forbade any fire to be kindled on the sabbath day, even for cooking (Ex 35:3). Because of the dryness of the land during the hot season, the law provided that a restitution must be made by anyone kindling a fire which caused damage and loss to a field of grain (Ex 22:6).

Bibliography. Friedrich Lang, "*Pyr,* etc.," TDNT, VI, 928-952.

R. E. Po.

FIRE BAPTISM. *See* Baptism of Fire; Gods, False: Molech.

FIREBRAND. A burning stick taken out of a fire. Specifically, "firebrand" can designate a stick for stirring a fire, a fire missile, or a torch made from a stick with flammable material fastened on the end. It is used symbolically of a nation almost consumed but mercifully rescued from destruction, "a firebrand plucked out of the burning" (Amos 4:11; Zech 3:2). The kings of Israel and Syria are spoken of contemptuously as "these two smoldering stumps of firebrands" (Isa 7:4, RSV). Firebrands (or, embers, cf. Isa 50:11) are among the objects hurled by a madman (Prov 26:18). In a fit of anger Samson tied firebrands or torches to foxes' tails and set them loose in the fields of the Philistines (Jud 15:3-6).

FIREPAN. A firepan was a tray attached to a long handle used to carry live coals of fire, and probably ashes also. It is listed as one of the vessels for the altar of burnt offering (Ex 27:3; 38:3). The Heb. word *maḥtâ* is also translated 15 times in KJV as "censer" (Lev 10:1; 16:12; Num 4:14; 16:6; etc.), because the firepan had this function when used to hold live charcoal for the burning of incense. The same shaped utensil was used to hold the tweezers and for removing the burnt portions of the lamp wicks of the golden lampstand. In this case it was translated "snuffdishes" in KJV, "trays" in RSV (Ex 25:38; 37:23). The firepans were made of copper as a rule, but those used with the golden lampstand were of pure gold (Ex 25:38). *See* Censer.

FIRES. In Isa 24:15 the KJV translates the Heb. *'urîm* as "fires," but it is translated "east" in ASV and RSV. It is from the Heb. word translated "urim" in Urim and Thummim and denotes a glow as from fire—hence the idea of east as at sunrise. Where the KJV translates "burn with fire" (Ezk 39:9-10), the ASV and RSV use the words "make fires."

FIRE, STRANGE. *See* Fire.

FIRE WORSHIP. As a symbol of purity, or of the divine presence and power, or as one of the fundamental elements of nature, or as typifying the destructive forces of nature, fire has been worshiped by many peoples from the most ancient times. The idea of fire worship takes at least three directions in the Bible.

First, there is a definite relating of fire to God. This is evidenced by God's appearance to Abraham in ratifying His covenant (Gen 15:17), to Moses in the burning bush (Ex 3:2), and God's manifest presence in the pillar of fire over the camp of Israel (Ex 13:21). On Mount Sinai it is said that God descended in fire (Ex 19:18) and that the appearance of His glory was like devouring fire (Ex 24:17). Lev 9:24 states that fire came from the Lord and consumed the burnt offering. Lev 10:2 relates that fire from the Lord destroyed the two sons of Aaron. Because of the murmuring of the people against God, it is said that the fire of God burned among them (Num 11:1). These are only a few of the many instances where God is associated with fire in the OT.

In the NT John the Baptist promised that the Holy Spirit would baptize in fire (Mt 3:11, ASV). When the Holy Spirit came at Pentecost His presence is described as like cloven tongues of fire (Acts 2:3). Paul states that Christian service is to be tested by fire (I Cor 3:13). He says further that the Lord will return in flaming fire (II Thess 1:8). God specifically warns that His people must offer Him acceptable worship with reverence and awe, "for our God is a consuming fire" (Heb 12:29, quoting Deut 4:24).

Second, fire has to do with worship in a special way in the OT. The entire system of burnt offerings and, perhaps in a lesser way, the burnt incense, indicates that fire was instrumental in certain phases of worship. The offerings were consumed by fire and the aroma was wafted up to God symbolically. *See* Fire.

Third, the worship of fire as such did not enter into the Israelite concept and use of fire. However, there was a danger facing God's people because neighboring pagans perverted the use of fire in the worship of their deities. Outstanding were those who bowed to Molech, the god of the Ammonites. In Lev 18:21 and 20:1-5 Moses specifically forbids Molech worship, a part of which consisted in offering children by fire to him. The Israelites at times were enticed into this idolatry. Solomon went so far as to build a high place for Molech (I Kgs 11:7). Jeremiah reveals a practice of this worship (Jer 19:5; 32:35), and so does Ezekiel (20:31), although Josiah had seemingly purged the nation of this practice completely (II Kgs 23:10). *See* Gods, False: Molech. The article on fire worship in *Unger's Bible Dictionary* gives details of sacrifices to gods of fire in ancient Mexico and Peru.

A. E. T.

FIRKIN. *See* Weights, Measures, and Coins.

FIRMAMENT. The English term, derived from *firmamentum* in the Vulg., inadequately expresses the Heb. *rāqîa'*, which means "expanse" and describes the great vault or spread out expanse of sky surrounding the earth.

The firmament or atmosphere was created on the second day to separate the "waters from the waters" (Gen 1:6–7), i.e., the waters on the earth from the extensive water vapors (clouds) surrounding its surface. Into this expanse, which God called "heavens" (Gen 1:8), the sun, moon, and stars were set (Gen 1:14–18). The LXX renders the Heb. with *stereōma,* meaning a firm or fixed structure. In Col 2:5 this Gr. word, used metaphorically, is translated "stedfastness" (KJV) or "firmness" (RSV). However, it is the idea of expansiveness or extension rather than solidity that *rāqîa'* represents, a term derived from *rāqa'*, "to beat, stamp, or spread out."

Heb. cosmogony, contends the critical school, represented pre-scientific concepts allegedly visualizing the firmament as a rigid, solid dome (Job 37:18; Prov 8:28) supported on pillars (II Sam 22:8; Job 26:11), and containing fixed stars. The rains descended from the waters above the firmament through windows (Gen 1:7; 7:11; Mal 3:10). Such interpretation is hermeneutically unsound, confusing poetical metaphor and phenomenal language with literal prose. The obvious poetic metaphor, expressing the expansiveness of the firmament, is seen in Isa 40:22: God "stretcheth out the heavens as a curtain, and spreadeth them out as a tent" (cf. Isa 45:12). The OT describes the firmament as bright and transparent like crystal, sapphire, or glass (Ex 24:10; Ezk 1:22; Dan 12:3; Rev 4:6), revealing the handiwork of God (Ps 19:1), and signifying the seat of His power (Ps 150:1).

H. E. Fr.

FIRST BEGOTTEN. *See* Firstborn.

FIRSTBORN

Old Testament

The Heb. word *beḵôr* makes no distinction between the firstborn of human beings and that of animals (Ex 11:5; 12:29; 13:2). The sacrifice of the firstborn, as of the firstlings of flocks and firstfruits of the produce of the earth, was common in early times (Ex 23:16). Reference is made in II Kgs 3:27 to the sacrifice of the heir to the throne by Mesha, king of Moab, in an effort to save his people in time of war. The influence of surrounding paganism had its effect upon Israel. Scripture gives instances of the sacrifice of the firstborn by various kings of Israel (II Kgs 16:3; 17:17; 21:6). Jeremiah the prophet denied that such offering was by instruction from the Lord (Jer 7:31; 19:5). Other prophets also denounced the practice (Ezk 16:20–21; 23:37; Mic 6:7). It was contrary to that which was known of the character of God.

At the time of the first Passover, when the firstborn of Egypt were slain, Moses gave command that Israel was to "set apart unto the Lord all that openeth the matrix" (Ex 13:12–13). The male firstborn was considered holy to the Lord (Num 3:13, 40; 8:15–18). By destroying the firstborn sons of Egypt and sparing those of Israel, God acquired a special ownership over the latter. Since it was not feasible to select the firstborn of the entire nation and thus disturb the family organization, the Levites were substituted for them (Num 3:12–13). Previously the firstborn had been priest of the whole family. Now the exercise of the priesthood was transferred by this command of the Lord from the tribe of Reuben to that of Levi. The service at the sanctuary had to be carried out by the Levites, but all the firstborn after the Exodus were the peculiar property of the Lord, and had to be redeemed (Num 8:18). When the Levites were set apart by Moses, they numbered 22,000 (Num 3:39), though the firstborn of the 12 tribes of a month old and upward totaled 22,273 (Num 3:46). Therefore 22,000 were redeemed by the Levites, and 273 were redeemed by payment of 1,365 shekels, which was given to Aaron and his sons as compensation (Num 3:50–51). The rate was five shekels per person.

Distinction is to be noted between the firstborn of inheritance, and the firstborn of redemption.

Firstborn of inheritance pertains to the firstborn of the father by any of his wives, if he practiced polygamy (Deut 21:16 ff.; Gen 49:3–4). The firstborn of the father had authority over the family in place of the father (Reuben in Gen 37:21–30; 42:37), a double share of the inheritance (Deut 21:17), and the right to the priesthood. When Elisha asked Elijah for a double portion of his spirit (II Kgs 2:9), he was in effect asking for the portion of the firstborn, that he might be Elijah's chief and worthy successor.

It appears that the promises of God to the patriarchs were considered as attached to the line of the firstborn. Note the story of Jacob and Esau in Gen 25:30–34; 27:36. As the cases of Ishmael, Esau and Reuben show, it was possible for the father to deprive the firstborn of this right. Such action is noted as having been practiced in various parts of the Middle East in patriarchal times, as confirmed by a tablet found at Alalakh in Syria. Deut 21:15-17 forbade the arbitrary transfer of the right from the actual firstborn to the son of a favored wife. *See* Birthright; Inheritance. In succession to the throne, primogeniture was always considered, but was not always decisive (I Kgs 1:1, 5-39; I Chr 26:10; II Chr 11:22).

Firstborn of redemption relates to the firstborn of the mother, and applies to both man and beast (Ex 13:2). All firstborn Israelite males had to be redeemed, since they belonged in a peculiar way to the Lord (Num 3:12-13, 45-51). According to Talmudic tradition, the firstborn acted as officiating priests in the wilderness, until the erection of the tabernacle, when the office was given to the tribe of Levi. In the matter of redemption, there were distinctions.

1. The firstborn of a clean animal had to be brought into the sanctuary on the eighth day after birth (Ex 22:30). If without blemish, it was to be sacrificed, its blood sprinkled, fat burned, flesh eaten (cf. Deut 15:19 with Num 18:17). If the animal had a blemish, it lost its holy character, and the priest to whom it was given might eat it outside Jerusalem, as any common food (Deut 15:21-23). It could also be eaten by other persons. Deut 15:19 suggests that no work could be done with the firstling of bullocks, nor wool shorn from that of sheep. They could not be sold. They became holy at birth, dedication being unnecessary. They had to be sacrificed during the first year.

2. The firstborn of an unclean animal had to be redeemed when a month old according to the estimation of the priest, with the addition of one-fifth (Lev 27:27; Num 18:15). The firstborn of an ass was either ransomed by a sheep or a lamb, or its neck had to be broken (Ex 13:13; 34:20). In later times, the unclean animals could be redeemed with money, or the neck was broken and the body burned.

3. The firstborn son of a mother (not of the father), at the age of one month, had to be redeemed with five shekels (Ex 13:13; 22:29; Num 18:15 ff.; Neh 10:37). This was given to the priest either in money or in valuables "according to . . . estimation" (Num 18:16). The husband of several wives would have to redeem the firstborn of each. If the father failed to redeem, Jewish law required that the son had to redeem himself when he grew up. Tradition added that priests, Levites and Israelites whose wives were daughters of priests or Levites needed not to redeem their firstborn. Because of deliverance from the tenth plague, the firstborn were required to fast on the day preceding the Passover. If too young, the father fasted for him. If the father was a firstborn, some say that both mother and father fasted, he for himself, and she for her son.

Figurative usages. In Job 18:13 "the firstborn of death" refers to the disease which would eventuate in death. In Ex 4:22 and Jer 31:9 God likens His relationship to Israel to that of a father and his firstborn son. In Ps 89:27 the reference is narrowed to King David and his dynastic line, culminating in Jesus the Messiah.

Bibliography. I. Mendelsohn, "On the Preferential Status of the Eldest Son," BASOR 156 (Dec., 1959), pp. 38-39.

I. R.

New Testament

Firstborn is used literally in Lk 2:7 and Heb 11:28. The word designates Christ as the unique and eternal Son of God in Rom 8:29 and Heb 1:6 (ASV), holding first rank and complete authority over angels and all His brethren on earth. Twice the words "firstborn from the dead" point to the fact that Christ was the first to arise from the dead in immortal form (Col 1:18; Rev 1:5, ASV).

Erasmus suggested that in Col 1:15 the word should be accented on the penult so as to mean "original One who brought forth." If this suggestion is not acceptable, then "firstborn" here designates the One who has the *rights* of primogeniture, who has authority over all creation. Certainly it does not indicate that He ever began to exist.

Heb 12:23 literally refers to "the church of firstborn ones who are written in heaven." Every child of God, enrolled in "the book of life from the foundation of the world," being "a joint heir with Christ," an heir of "all things" unlimited, has in a real sense the position of a "firstborn" in God's household, privileged above all other men.

Bibliography. Wilhelm Michaelis, *"Prōtotokos,"* TDNT, VI, 871-881.

J. O. B., Jr.

FIRSTBORN, DESTRUCTION OF. *See* Plagues of Egypt.

FIRST DAY OF THE WEEK. *See* Lord's Day.

FIRSTFRUITS

1. *Individual offering of firstfruits*. The Mosaic law required the Israelites to bring to the house of the Lord "the first of the firstfruits of thy land" (Ex 23:19; 34:26). This was to include grain, wine, and oil, and was to be used for the support of the priests (Num 18:12; Deut 18:4). Instructions were given as to the manner in which the firstfruits were to be brought to the house of God and turned over to the priests, along with the ritual to be used at that time (Deut 26). However, the actual amount is nowhere stated in Scripture. "The Talmud fixed on the sixtieth as the least to be given of the produce, a thirtieth or fortieth as a liberal offering" (A. R. Fausset, *Bible Encyclopaedia*, p. 232). Evidently, in actual practice the firstfruits were brought in abundantly by the people during times of revival and reform (II Chr 31:5). It is significant that on at least one occasion when the priests of Israel were

apostate, an individual brought barley loaves of firstfruits to the prophet Elisha instead (II Kgs 4:42). After the Captivity, the returnees to Jerusalem covenanted to give the firstfruits faithfully, Nehemiah seeing that these were cared for and distributed to the priests in a systematic way (Neh 10:35–37; 12:44; 13:31). The book of Proverbs promises prosperity to those who honor the Lord with the firstfruits (Prov 3:9).

2. *The Feast of Firstfruits* (Lev 23:9–14). This was to be observed at the beginning of barley harvest, the first grain to come in. The first sheaf of the new crop, together with a sacrifice, was presented as a wave offering before the Lord on the day after the Passover sabbath. By this, acknowledgment was made that all came from God and belonged to Him, and none was to be used for food until this ceremony had been performed. The firstfruits were also a sample or specimen of the bounteous harvest of golden grain which would eventually follow because of God's providence.

3. *The Feast of Pentecost.* This is called by various names in the OT. Since it took place on the fiftieth day after the Feast of Firstfruits, it came to be known as Pentecost ("fiftieth") by the Jews (Acts 2:1; 20:16). As it thus occurred at the completion of wheat harvest, the firstfruits of the wheat were to be brought to the Lord at this time (Ex 34:22; cf. Ex 23:16; Num 28:26). This wheat was to be baked into two wave loaves in which leaven was to be used (Lev 23:17, 20). This is significant, as the ordinary meal offering was to contain no leaven (Lev 2:11). However, part of the unleavened offering was wholly offered to the Lord by burning it (Lev 2:9), while the loaves at Pentecost were presented to the Lord simply by waving them before Him, with no portion burned.

4. *Figurative use of firstfruits.* Both OT and NT warrant us in believing that the ceremonial presentation of the firstfruits had, beyond its obvious implications, a typical and symbolical significance. The chosen nation Israel is spoken of as God's "firstfruits," dedicated wholly to Him (Jer 2:3). A curse is pronounced on those who consume and destroy Israel, because they have infringed on that which belongs to the Lord.

Christ in His resurrection is "the firstfruits of them that slept" (I Cor 15:20, 23). The Feast of Firstfruits took place on the first day after the Passover sabbath. On this very day Christ rose from the dead (Mk 16:1–6). At Pentecost, 50 days later, the Holy Spirit came to mold the believers into one body, the Church (Acts 2:1; I Cor 12:13). The two loaves waved before the Lord at this feast may possibly represent Jewish and Gentile believers made one in Christ (Eph 2:14). This would explain the usage of leaven (speaking of corruption) in these loaves, as the believer, though saved, still has sin *in* him.

In another sense believers are spoken of as a "kind of firstfruits" (Jas 1:18). The Lord Jesus in His resurrection is *the* firstfruits. In Him we see a wonderful specimen of what God will eventually do for all believers. In each Christian God is seeking to perfect a holy life and character so that he will be a specimen or example of what God desires to do for all. Thus believers are a *kind* of firstfruits. The Holy Spirit, given now to all who believe on Christ, is also spoken of as a firstfruits (Rom 8:23), a wonderful sample, so to speak, of the full and complete blessings that lie ahead.

The present saved remnant in Israel is spoken of as "firstfruits" (Rom 11:16) and the 144,000 of the Tribulation period are likewise so designated (Rev 14:4). They are foretokens of a prophesied turning to the Messiah by the nation Israel. In similar manner, the first converts in any particular area are spoken of as "firstfruits" (Rom 16:5; I Cor 16:15).

In Ezekiel's glorious vision of the millennial temple and kingdom, it is indicated that the priests will once again be given the firstfruits (Ezk 44:30). Their portion of the land is spoken of as a "firstfruits" which they are not to "alienate" or allow to pass to others (Ezk 48:14).

See Festivals; Pentecost; Sacrificial Offerings.

G. C. L.

FISH. *See* Animals, V.4.

FISHER, FISHING. *See* Occupation: Fishing.

FISH GATE. *See* Jerusalem: Gates and Towers 4.

FISHHOOK. In the KJV this term is found only in Amos 4:2, which employs the two Heb. words *sîr dûgâ|*. The word *sîr*, "hook," means literally "thorn," and likely came to be used of a hook because of its resemblance to a thorn. It was an Assyrian practice, known from their palace sculptures, to lead away captives by hooks or rings in their noses or lips (ANEP #440, 447; cf. Isa 37:29; Ezk 29:4; 38:4, where *ḥāḥ* is the word for "hook"). Job 41:1 asks if you can draw out leviathan with a hook (*ḥakkâ*). This word came to be used to denote a fishhook because the hook fastens to the roof of the mouth or palate (*ḥēk*). It also is translated as "hook" in Isa 19:8 and Hab 1:15 in the RSV. Jesus instructed Peter to cast a hook (Gr. *agkistron*) into the sea to catch a fish (Mt 17:27). Bone fishhooks have been found in prehistoric settlements in Palestine, and iron fishhooks were excavated at Ezion-geber from the time of Solomon. *See* Hook; Occupation: Fishing.

A. E. T.

FISHPOOL. The Heb. word *b^{e}rēkâ* is translated "fishpool" in Song 7:4; but in II Sam 2:13; 4:12; Nah 2:8; Eccl 2:6 it is translated simply "pool." Versions other than KJV give the meaning in Song 7:4 as simply "pool." The word refers to an open pond of water.

FITCHES. *See* Plants.

FLAG
1. A standard. *See* Ensign.
2. A plant. *See* Plants.

FLAGON. In Isa 22:24 "flagons" (Heb. *neḇālîm*) refers to a clay storage jar (Lam 4:2) or a bag, usually made of dried whole skins of a goat or other similar animal, and was used for water, wine, milk, or other liquids.

It is generally thought that the Heb. word *'ăshîshâ* translated "flagon" in other OT passages in the KJV (II Sam 6:19; I Chr 16:3; Song 2:5; Hos 3:1) designates a "cake of raisins," made of pressed grapes and carried on a journey. It was counted as a delicacy and was an important item of food.

FLAKE. In Job 41:23 the statement is made that the "flakes" of the flesh of leviathan (*q.v.*) are joined in such a way that they cannot be moved. A better rendering may be "horny epidermic scales" (ISBE). The same Heb. word is translated "refuse" in Amos 8:6.

FLAME. *See* Fire

FLANK. This word is used only in the plural, as in Job 15:27. It refers to the section of the animal carcass near the kidneys called the loins. It is used five times in Leviticus and is translated "loins" in the ASV (Lev 3:4, 10, 15; 4:9; 7:4).

FLASK. The ASV marginal translation of Gr. *alabastron* (KJV "alabaster box") in Mt 26:7; Mk 14:3; Lk 7:37. RSV renders it "flask" in Lk 7:37. *See* Minerals: Alabaster; Pottery: Cruse; Vial.

FLAX. *See* Plants.

FLEA. *See* Animals, IV.13.

FLEECE. The Heb. word *gēz* is translated "fleece" (Deut 18:4; Job 31:20) and also "mown" grass (Ps 72:6; Amos 7:1). It speaks of that which is shorn. The similar form *gizzâ* is also translated "fleece" in Jud 6:37-40 where Gideon's experiences with the fleece are related. It seems that the word refers primarily to wool after it was shorn.

FLEET. *See* Swift.

FLESH. The Gr. NT term is *sarx* which has specific meanings of its own but also translates the Heb. term *bāsār*. The word occurs 143 times in the Gr. NT. The main biblical meanings of flesh may be classified as follows:

1. The soft substance of the animal organism which may be stripped off from the bones and is made up of muscles, blood, tissue, etc. (Lk 24:39; Jn 6:51; I Cor 15:39; Jas 5:3; Rev 17:16; 19:18, 21; Gen 2:21; Ex 12:8; Isa 31:3; Ezk 23:20).

2. The body. The whole material part of a living being, i.e., that which makes up its somatic existence (Gen 40:19; I Kgs 21:27; II Kgs 4:34; Eccl 12:12; Heb 5:7), and used with "blood" the whole phrase "flesh and blood" (*q.v.*), signifies the body (Heb 2:14).

3. The basis or result of natural generation and kinship or kindred (Gen 2:24; 37:27; Jn 3:6; cf. Rom 4:1; 9:3, 5, 8; I Cor 10:18; Gal 4:23, 29; Eph 2:11; Rom 11:14).

4. Corporeally conditioned living things, usually man but also animals (Gen 6:13; Num 16:22; Jer 12:12; 25:31; Isa 40:5-6; Joel 2:28; Mt 16:17; 24:22; Mk 10:8; Lk 3:6; Jn 1:14; I Cor 1:29; Gal 1:16; 2:16; Eph 6:12; I Pet 1:24).

5. The weak creaturely side of man's constitution in contrast with heart and soul with which it often occurs to designate the whole man. Thus it is used to indicate the external and secular as distinguished from the spiritual and religious (Gen 6:3; Ps 16:9; Isa 31:3; Mt 26:41; Mk 14:38; Rom 6:19).

6. In the ethical sense it has reference to the carnal nature, or that disposition in man which is prone to sin and is opposed to God (Gen 6:12; Rom 7:18; 8:6-8; I Cor 3:3; Gal 5:17, 19; Col 2:18; II Pet 2:10, 18; I Jn 2:16). This is the most important use for the Christian. The flesh, or fallen nature, lusts and wars against the Spirit as He works through the new nature, resulting in spiritual paralysis and defeat (Gal 5:17-24; Rom 7:14–8:1). This condition is overcome in the following manner: (*a*) Learning to distinguish the works of the flesh from those of the Holy Spirit (Gal 5:19-23: cf. I Cor 6:9-11; Rom 8:4-13). (*b*) Realizing by faith that the fallen nature is already under condemnation, even though it is not yet removed (Rom 8:3), and therefore the Holy Spirit can and does indwell the believer (Rom 8:9). (*c*) Surrendering and submitting ourselves to the leading guidance of the Holy Spirit (Rom 8:4-13; Gal 5:24-25; Eph 5:18 ff.), which is spoken of as "walking by the Spirit." *See* Carnal.

7. There are other terms in Scripture which indicate flesh in the sense of "butcher's meat," or that which is used for food.

In no case does the biblical idea imply the inherent evil of matter, nor is the body looked upon as a thing of shame.

To summarize: flesh, *physically,* indicates the body as possessing a soul, which the Spirit of God enables to exist in individual form; *ethically,* that whole life of the soul which is of a unit with the body, after the body has fallen a prey to the power of the senses and the principle of sin, i.e., the whole personality wrongly directed.

Bibliography. Ernest DeWitt Burton, "Galatians," ICC, appended note on *Sarx,* pp. 492-5. W. P. Dickson, *St. Paul's Use of the Terms Flesh and Spirit,* Glasgow: James Maclehose & Sons, 1883. K. Grayston, "Flesh, Fleshly, Carnal," *Theological Word Book of the Bible,* Alan

Richardson, ed., New York: Macmillan, 1950, pp. 83–84. W. G. Künnel, *Man in the New Testament,* trans. by J. J. Vincent, Philadelphia: Westminster, 1963. John Laidlaw, *The Bible Doctrine of Man,* Edinburgh: T. & T. Clark, 1879, pp. 74–86. J. A. Motyer, "Flesh, Fleshly," BDT, pp. 222–224. G. B. Stevens, *The Pauline Theology,* New York: Scribner's Sons, 1911, Chap. VI. H. Wheeler Robinson, *The Christian Doctrine of Man,* Edinburgh: T. & T. Clarke, 1913, especially chaps. I and II.

R. E. Pr. and R. A. K.

FLESH AND BLOOD. A term used several times in the NT (Mt 16:17; I Cor 15:50; Gal 1:16; Eph 6:12; Heb 2:14; cf. Jn 1:13) to express the idea of man, human beings, men. It is neutral in connotation, and while it does not imply any moral condition, it portrays man as he is, with his own resources, in contrast to God. The term "flesh," on the other hand, while it may be used in a similar neutral sense (Jn 1:14; 6:63; Acts 2:17; etc.), generally implies fallen sinful man and man's fallen nature in particular (Rom 7:18 ff.; 8:1 ff.; I Cor 5:5; Gal 5:17–24; Eph 2:3; Phil 3:3). *See* Flesh.

FLESH HOOK. The directions given Moses for the altar of burnt offerings included the "flesh hooks" (Ex 27:3), which were to be made of bronze in the tabernacle and gold in the temple (I Chr 28:17). I Sam 2:13 describes the flesh hooks as having three teeth and being used by the priest to take up his portion of the meat from the pots as it was boiling.

See Hook.

FLESH OFFERED TO IDOLS. *See* Idols, Things Offered to.

FLESH POT. These were pots which the Israelite slaves had used in Egypt in cooking meats (Ex 16:3). No details are given of the material or size. One of the uses of the *sîr,* a rather general term for "pot," was for boiling meats and vegetables (e.g., II Kgs 4:38–41; Jer 1:13; Ezk 11:3, 7, 11–"caldron"; 24:3-6; Mic 3:3). *See* Pottery.

FLINT. *See* Minerals.

FLOAT. A float was similar to a raft, formed of cedar logs tied together and floated to Joppa, as the word is used in I Kgs 5:9.

FLOCK (FIGURATIVE). This expression frequently was used of God's people. The prophets Isaiah, Jeremiah, Ezekiel, Micah and Zechariah all used flock in reference to Israel. For example, "He shall feed his flock like a shepherd" (Isa 40:11). Jeremiah accused false prophets of having scattered the flock of God (Jer 23:2). Ezekiel uses the word more than a dozen times in chap. 34 in a figurative sense of God's people. Jesus quoted Zech 13:7, using the term as applying to His disciples (Mt 26:31). He addressed His followers directly as "little flock" (Lk 12:32.) Paul admonished the Ephesian elders at Miletus to "take heed . . . to all the flock," and warned against the "wolves" who would ravage the flock (Acts 20:28–29). Jesus apparently used the expression "one flock" of the Church in Jn 10:16.

See Animals, I. 15; Shepherd.

FLOOD. The Noahic Flood, or Deluge, was the greatest single blow ever delivered by a holy God to this earth and its inhabitants. It was provoked by the universal apostasy and corruption of man, of whom it is written that "every imagination of the thoughts of his heart was only evil continually" (Gen 6:5). More space is devoted to a description of this universal aqueous catastrophe in the early chapters of Genesis than to the creation and the Fall. The technical term for "Flood" used in Gen 6–11 (and Ps 29:10) is *mabbûl,* which is translated by *kataklysmos* in the LXX, the same Gr. word being used in several of the NT references to the Flood (Mt 24:38–39; Lk 17:27; II Pet 2:5). The Flood is also referred to in Ps 104:6–9; Isa 54:9; Heb 11:7; I Pet 3:20; II Pet 3:3–7; and possibly Job 12:15.

The Chronological Order of Events

One hundred and twenty years before the Flood came, God began to warn men of their impending doom by instructing Noah to build a great ark (Gen 6:3, 14; I Pet 3:20). When the Flood began, only 40 days were required for the waters to reach their maximum depth, which was maintained for an additional 110 days (Gen 7.24). The ark settled on top of the highest peak in the mountains of Ararat and in 74 days the tops of the mountains were seen (Gen 8:5). Forty days later Noah sent out the raven, and then the dove three times at intervals of seven days. The covering of the ark was removed 29 days after this, and a final period of 57 days elapsed before the earth was sufficiently dry for disembarkation (Gen 8:14). Thus, the Flood lasted a total of 371 days (cf. E. F. Kevan, in *The New Bible Commentary,* p. 85).

The Geographical Extent of the Flood

A remarkable amount of biblical evidence is available for determining the geographical extent of the Flood. It is primarily to this evidence, rather than to the theories of modern scientists, that Christian students must pay heed in arriving at the correct answer to this highly controversial question. That the Bible clearly teaches a geographically universal flood in the days of Noah may be seen from the following considerations:

1. Gen 7:19–20 states that "all the high mountains that were under the whole heaven were covered" (ASV). Even if only one (instead of *all*) of the high mountains had been covered with water, the Flood would have covered the entire planet, for water must seek its own level.

2. Some of the most destructive floods in recorded history have come and gone within a matter of a few days, but the biblical deluge continued for over a year, seven months of this period being required for the waters to subside sufficiently for Noah to disembark from the ark in the mountains of Ararat.

3. Gen 7:11 states that "all the fountains of the great deep" (*t^{e}hôm rabbâ*) were "broken up" at the commencement of the Flood, and Gen 8:2 (cf. 7:24) indicates that these geologic upheavals continued for five months. Since "the great deep" refers to the oceanic depths in this context (cf. Gen 1:2), the Flood could not have been a merely local catastrophe.

4. Assuming that the cubit was 17.5 inches long, the ark's three decks had an area of 95,700 square feet, a volume of 1,396,000 cubit feet, and a gross tonnage (figured at 100 cubic feet of usable storage space per ton) of 13,960 tons (*see* Ark, Noah's). It seems fantastic that God would have commanded Noah to build such a gigantic vessel merely for the purpose of escaping a local flood.

5. Even more compelling is the consideration that if the Flood was to be local in extent, there would have been no need for an ark at all! Noah and his family, to say nothing of the animals, could have moved to some other region to escape a local flood. But the fact that he was commanded to provide refuge for representatives of *all* land animals in the world constitutes final proof that the Flood was geographically universal, for no one would care to defend the view that all land animals could have been destroyed by a local flood.

6. The local flood concept cannot be harmonized with the divinely inspired statements of the apostle in II Pet 3:3-7, for the one single event which he sets forth as having brought about a transformation, not of the earth only but also of the very *heavens,* is the Flood. It was the Flood that provided the transition from "the heavens from of old" to "the heavens that now are." It was the Flood to which Peter appealed as his final and incontrovertible answer to those who chose to remain in willful ignorance of the fact that God had at one time in the past demonstrated His holy wrath and indignation against sin by subjecting "all things" to an overwhelming, cosmic (*kosmos,* II Pet 3:6) catastrophe that was on a par with the final day of judgment, in which He will consume the earth with fire and will cause the very elements to dissolve with fervent heat. It would not be easy to excuse the apostle of gross inaccuracy when he depicts the Flood in such cosmic terms and in such a universal context, if the Flood had been only a local inundation after all.

7. The Bible teaches emphatically that *all men* outside the ark were destroyed by the Flood (Mt 24:37-39; Lk 17:26-27; I Pet 3:20; II Pet 2:5; and frequently throughout Gen 6-7). But it is impossible to assume that the human race was confined to the Mesopotamian valley (where a local flood would presumably have occurred) during the sixteen or more centuries that elapsed between Adam and the Flood, for at least three reasons: (*a*) the longevity and fecundity of the antediluvians would provide for a very rapid increase in population; (*b*) the prevalence of strife and violence would encourage wide distribution rather than confinement to a single locality; (*c*) evidence of human fossils in widely scattered parts of the world makes it difficult to assume that men did not migrate beyond the Near East before the time of the Flood. Therefore, it would have required a geographically universal flood to destroy a widely scattered human race (cf. John C. Whitcomb, Jr., and Henry M. Morris, *The Genesis Flood,* pp. 1-35).

It is a significant commentary on the clarity of the biblical testimony to the universality of the Flood that no known commentator, Jewish or Christian, ever suggested the local-flood view before A.D. 1655, and that even then the view found scarcely any supporters until after the rise of modern geology in the middle of the 19th cen. (cf. Don Cameron Allen, *The Legend of Noah,* Urbana, Ill.: Univ. of Illinois Press, 1949, pp. 66-112).

The Sources of the Flood Waters

In Gen 7:11 we are informed that on the very day the Flood began, "all the fountains of the great deep [were] broken up, and the windows of heaven were opened." From this we may assume, first, that vast suboceanic upheavals caused the seas to encroach upon the continental coasts and lowlands. Second, the entire antediluvian, invisible vapor canopy, which had been suspended in the upper atmosphere since the second day of creation (Gen 1:6-8), fell upon the earth. It is now known that if all the water in our present atmosphere were suddenly precipitated, it would only suffice to cover the earth to an average depth of less than two inches. Therefore, a continuous rainfall of 40 days and nights (nearly 1,000 hours) over most of the earth would have required a completely different mechanism for its production than is available today.

The fact that antediluvian climatology was indeed different from that which we know today is supported by biblical references to a vast canopy of water vapor suspended high in the antediluvian atmosphere ("waters above the firmament," Gen 1:7), to the absence of rainfall as we know it today (Gen 2:5), and to the appearance of rainbows for the first time after the Flood ("I do set my bow in the cloud, and it shall be for a token of a covenant between me and the earth," Gen 9:13). Such a vast expanse of water vapor would, of necessity, have created a greenhouse effect in the entire world, providing warm climates even in the polar regions. (The presence of vast coal deposits and of the frozen remains of tropical animals in polar regions clearly points to a sudden climatic change on a nearly global scale.)

Recently, scientists have discovered a region in the upper atmosphere, called the mesosphere (from about 25 to 50 miles high), where temperatures rise to above 50 degrees Fahrenheit (cf. Arthur Beiser, *Life Nature Library: The Earth,* p. 58). A vapor blanket of stupendous magnitude could be supported in this region. Since water vapor weighs only 0.622 times as much as dry air for the same conditions, it would not be significantly affected by the presence or absence of air or other gases in the region, the temperatures would remain high both day and night, and condensation nuclei such as salt particles (apart from which water vapor cannot condense) would not rise to that level (cf. Whitcomb and Morris, *The Genesis Flood,* pp. 255–58). When the hour of judgment finally came, God caused this upper ocean to collapse upon the earth in the form of torrential rains that continued without interruption for six weeks.

Geology and the Flood

A universal Flood which attained a mountain-covering depth within six weeks, maintained that level for 16 weeks, and subsided into newly formed ocean basins in 31 additional weeks, must, of absolute necessity, have accomplished a vast amount of geologic work in the crust of the earth.

1. In the first place, erosion and resedimentation must have taken place on a gigantic scale. The rapid rise of water level within 40 days would have created great sediment-carrying currents. The Scriptures specifically state that the waters were "going and returning continually" (Heb., Gen 8:3) when they began to assuage. Previous crustal balances, of whatever sort they were, must have been entirely upset by the great complex of hydrostatic and hydrodynamic forces unleashed in the floodwaters, resulting very likely in great earth movements. Associated with the volcanic upheavals and the great rains must also have been tremendous tidal effects, windstorms, and a great complexity of currents, crosscurrents, whirlpools, and other hydraulic phenomena. For decades and even centuries after the Flood itself ended, much more geologic work must have been accomplished as the masses of water settled into new basins and the earth adjusted itself to new physiographic and hydrologic balances.

2. Since the Flood destroyed "every living thing that was upon the face of the ground" (Gen 7:23), and in view of the great masses of sediment being moved back and forth and finally deposited by the floodwaters ("I will destroy them *with the earth,*" Gen 6:13), vast numbers of plants and animals must have been buried by the sediments, and under conditions eminently favorable to preservation and fossilization. This conclusion becomes inevitable when we realize that fossils are only rarely being formed in the earth today (cf. Wm. J. Miller, *An Introduction to Historical Geology,* 6th ed., New York: Van Nostrand, 1952, p. 12). Because the Flood was worldwide and comparatively recent (cf. below, "The Antiquity of the Flood"), most of the fossils that are now found in the earth's sedimentary rock beds must have been entombed there during the period of the Flood.

3. Finally, it may very fairly be inferred from the biblical record that it would now be impossible to discern geologically much of the earth's history prior to the Flood, at least on the assumption of continuity with present conditions. Whatever geologic deposits may have existed before the Flood, they must have been almost completely eroded, reworked, and redeposited during the Flood, perhaps several times. Such geologic time clocks as we may be able to use to date events subsequent to the Flood cannot therefore be legitimately used to extend chronologies before postdiluvian time. Even carbon-14 dating, which assumes basically unchanged atmospheric conditions indefinitely into the past, is valid only since the formation of a C-14 reservoir in the atmosphere following the collapse of the antediluvian vapor canopy. The basic premise of all such chronologies is uniformity; and, if the biblical record of the Flood be true, the premise of uniformity is, at that point at least, false. On the other hand, the relationship of the Flood to the earth's glaciers must be taken into consideration. Although many problems still remain, such as the exact chronology of the Pleistocene glacial period, the creation-catastrophe presupposition, based upon the inspired account of earth history in Genesis, has proved to be fruitful in approaching these problems.

The Antiquity of the Flood

Near Eastern cultures apparently have a rather continuous archaeological record (based on pottery chronology and occupation levels) back to at least the 5th or 6th mil. B.C.; and therefore it seems impossible to fit a universal flood into such an archaeological framework. Also the migration of man after the Flood to the Western Hemisphere, probably via the Bering Straits region, and the population expansion to the extremities of both North and South America, require a considerable amount of time. But there are several biblical evidences that point to rather long gaps in the genealogy of Gen 11, which would permit us to date the Flood long before Abraham.

(1) In the first place, the Scriptures give no total for the years between the Flood and Abraham, as they do for the time of Israel's sojourn in Egypt (Ex 12:40), even though totals are provided for the two numbers in the life of each antediluvian patriarch. (2) The genealogies of Gen 5 and 11 are symmetrical in form (ten patriarchs in each list, with the tenth in each case having three important sons named), suggesting the omission of other names, as in the parallel case of Mt 1. (3) If there were no gaps in the genealogy of Gen 11, *all* the postdiluvian patriarchs, including Noah, would still have

been living when Abram was 50 years old. *Three* of those who were born before "the earth was divided" at the judgment of Babel (Shem, Shelah, and Eber) would have actually outlived Abram. Eber, the father of Peleg, not only would have outlived Abram, but also would have lived two years after Jacob arrived in Mesopotamia to work for Laban. But Joshua said that Abram's fathers were idolaters, implying that Noah, Shem, and probably most of the others named in Gen 11 had long since died (Josh 24:2, 14, 15). (4) The biblical record implies that the judgment of Babel was a remote event in Abram's day, for he found ancient civilizations both in Canaan and Egypt. The strict chronology view, on the other hand, would date the Flood about 2460 B.C., several centuries after the building of the great pyramids of Egypt. (5) The term "begat" sometimes refers to ancestral relationships in the Bible. A careful comparison of Ex 6:20 with Num 3:17-19, 27-28 indicates that Amram was an ancestor of Moses and Aaron, separated from them by a span of 300 years. Similar wording in Gen 10:25, plus the fact that patriarchal life spans dropped suddenly between Eber and Peleg (Gen 11:16-19), suggests a large gap of generations between Eber and Peleg.

On the other hand, equally cogent arguments call for a date later than *c.* 7000 B.C. for the Flood: (1) The analogy of biblical chronology would be seriously strained if 5,000 years elapsed between the Flood and Abraham. Gaps of several centuries in OT genealogies are not unheard of, but gaps of thousands of years would be entirely out of proportion. (2) Because of the confinement of the human race to one region, it is highly improbable that Babel was judged more than a millennium after the Flood. But half of the postdiluvian patriarchs listed in Gen 11 lived in this pre-Babel period, leaving only Reu, Serug, and Nahor to link the judgment of Babel in the days of Peleg (cf. Gen 10:25) with the days of Terah. Thus, it is difficult to imagine how more than three or four thousand years could have elapsed between the judgment of Babel and the birth of Abram, or more than four or five thousand years from the Flood to Abram. (3) The remarkable similarities between the biblical and Babylonian Flood accounts preclude the possibility of a vast antiquity for the Flood, for the Babylonians could not have transmitted so many accurate details by oral tradition alone for more than a few thousand years (cf. Alexander Heidel, *The Gilgamesh Epic and Old Testament Parallels*). It may be concluded, then, that the judgment of the great Flood probably occurred from six to seven thousand years before Christ. *See* Chronology, Old Testament; Genesis.

Archaeological and Cuneiform Parallels

At the sites of several ancient Mesopotamian cities, notably Ur, Erech, Kish, Lagash, and Nineveh, levels of water-laid sediment of varying thickness have been discovered that can be dated to the 4th and 3rd mil. B.C. The archaeological contexts in each case indicate that the various destructions were local in character and do not all date from the same century. Hence these flood levels point to inundations of unusual severity caused by disastrous floodings of the Tigris and/or Euphrates Rivers, but not to a worldwide deluge of the proportions indicated in Genesis at the time of Noah.

Of more importance for a study of the biblical narrative are the various stories about the destruction of the world by a great flood which persist among many tribes on every continent and even on islands of the Pacific (Byron C. Nelson, *The Deluge Story in Stone,* pp. 165-190). The worldwide distribution of such flood stories cannot be accidental and should be considered as evidence for the historicity of the Genesis account.

Part of the Babylonian flood account from Ashurbanipal's palace. BM

Chief among extrabiblical narratives of a great flood is Tablet XI of the 12-tablet Gilgamesh epic written in Akkad. cuneiform. It was first discovered in 1872 by George Smith among the hoard of clay tablets brought back to the British Museum from the excavation of Ashurbanipal's palace at Nineveh. On his travels in search for immortal life, Gilgamesh met Utnapishtim, from whom he heard the story of the great catastrophe to mankind. The hero of the Deluge was called Ziusudra in the older Sumerian version written down by 2000 B.C. but circulating in Mesopotamia for many centuries before that. There are a number of close parallels between the experiences of Noah and Utnapishtim, as well as some obvious points of

The hero Gilgamesh in whose epic narrative the Babylonian flood account occurs. LM

divergence. Another Babylonian epic called the hero Atra-hasis.

In each case the hero was warned by deity of the impending flood; he built a boat in which he sheltered his family and animals; he sent out birds after the rain ceased; he sacrificed to deity after disembarking. But the polytheism of the Babylonian account stands in sharp contrast to the sober monotheism of Genesis 6-9. The gods of the Gilgamesh epic disagree with one another; they crouch like dogs and swarm like flies around Utnapishtim's sacrifice. The short duration of the flood—only seven days, and the proximity of Mount Nisir (in NW Persia, where Utnapishtim's craft came to rest) to Mesopotamia lead one to believe that details of a more recent local flood in the Tigris-Euphrates valley have been garbled with the oral tradition of the great Deluge of Noah's time. Certainly the many fanciful elements in the cuneiform accounts show that these are far less reliable than the Genesis narrative.

For a full translation of the Babylonian story see ANET, pp. 93-95, and for a translation of the Sumerian account, ANET, pp. 42-44.

Bibliography. Douglas A. Block, "Geology," *Christianity and the World of Thought,* Chicago: Moody Press, 1968, pp. 235-247. Alexander Heidel, *The Gilgamesh Epic and Old Testament Parallels,* Chicago: Univ. of Chicago, 1949. W. G. Lambert and A. R. Millard, *Atra-Ḫasīs: The Babylonian Story of the Flood,* New York: Oxford Univ. Press, 1969. Jack P. Lewis, *A Study of the Interpretation of Noah and the Flood in Jewish and Christian Literature,* Leiden: Brill, 1968. Byron C. Nelson, *The Deluge Story in Stone,* Minneapolis: Augsburg, 1931. André Parrot, *The Flood and Noah's Ark,* London: SCM, 1955. Donald W. Patten, *The Biblical Flood and the Ice Epoch,* Seattle: Pacific Meridian Publishing Co., 1966. A. M. Rehwinkel, *The Flood,* St. Louis: Concordia, 1951. Merrill F. Unger, *Archaeology and the Old Testament,* 3rd ed., Grand Rapids: Zondervan, 1956. J. R. van de Fliert, "Fundamentalism and the Fundamentals of Geology," JASA, XXI (1969), 69-81. John C. Whitcomb, Jr., and Henry M. Morris, *The Genesis Flood,* Philadelphia: Presbyterian and Reformed, 1961.

J. C. W.

FLOOR

1. The Heb. word *qarqa'* is used in referring to a floor of a building (Num 5:17). In the account of Solomon's building the temple, the word is used four times (I Kgs 6:15-16, 30). In I Kgs 6:5, 10 the noun *yāṣîa'* ("chambers," KJV) probably means stories or floors.

2. Heb. *gōren* signifies a threshing floor. It was a level place swept clean and used for treading out the wheat, often just outside the city gate (I Kgs 22:10, "in a void place"; see ASV marg.). Isaiah uses it in a figurative sense (Isa 21:10) of God's people who are trodden down as grain on a threshing floor. *See* Threshing Floor.

3. Gr. *halōn* designates a threshing floor in Mt 3:12 and Lk 3:17.

The threshing floor at Samaria.

FLOTES. *See* Float.

FLOUR. *See* Food.

FLOWERS. The Heb. word *peraḥ* is used figuratively in speaking of the blossom of the wicked going up like dust (Isa 5:24), of the blossom being over as symbolic of Ethiopia being ready for the pruning of judgment (Isa 18:5), and of the flower of Lebanon fading as a picture of judgment (Nah 1:4). Elsewhere this is the word for the blossoms on Aaron's rod that budded (Num 17:8), and it is used to speak of the flowerlike decorations on the branches of the golden lampstand (Ex 25:31-34; 37:17-20; Num 8:4; II Chr 4:21). The rim of the huge laver in Solomon's temple was shaped like the flower or calyx of a lily (I Kgs 7:26; II Chr 4:5, RSV, NEB).

Heb. *ṣîṣ* is used in comparing a man, his frailty, goodness, and works, to the fading flower (Ps 103:15). Heb. *ṣiṣâ* is used in a similar way of Ephraim's glorious beauty (Isa 28:4). The Gr. word *anthos* is found in the NT in a figurative sense in comparing man's life and glory to the frailty of a flower (Jas 1:10-11; I Pet 1:24).

Heb. *'ănāshîm* is translated in I Sam 2:33 (KJV, ASV) as the flower of age, denoting reaching the age of manhood (cf. our expression "in the bloom of life"). Similarly, Gr. *huperakmos* is used by Paul (I Cor 7:36) in speaking of a girl reaching womanhood, "the flower of her age."

The term *niddâ* is translated "flower" in KJV, but is given its more accurate meaning of "impurity" in ASV (Lev 15:24, 33).

See individual flowers under Plants.

A. E. T.

FLUTE. *See* Music.

FLUX, BLOODY. *See* Diseases.

FLY, FLIES. *See* Animals, III.13.

FOAL. *See* Animals: Ass, I.1.

FOAM. Three words are thus translated. Heb. *qeṣep* refers to foam as on water (Hos 10:7). The marginal reference in ASV gives "twigs" as a possible rendering. The word comes from *qāṣap*, which means "to break off or out," or "to be angry." Thus it could mean twigs broken off, or foam as the result of angry waves.

Foaming as froth at the mouth is indicated by Gr. *aphrizō* in Mk 9:18, 20 (cf. Lk 9:39). Jude's use of Gr. *epaphrizō* pertains to the foaming of waves on the sea (v. 13).

FODDER. The Heb. word *belîl* was used of a mixture of several kinds of grain as "wheat, barley, vetch and other seeds" (Gesenius), used in feeding livestock. The idea "mixed together" is indicated in the word. It is translated "fodder" in Job 6:5, "corn" in Job 24:6 and "provender" in Isa 30:24 in the KJV. *See* Provender.

FOLLOWER. *See* Disciples.

FOLLY. There is a variety of shades of meaning in the Heb. and Gr. words translated "folly." In general it expresses the unprofitable action or results of foolishness. Folly is the opposite of wisdom (*q.v.*).

1. Heb. *'iwwelet* is the word most often translated "folly," found frequently in Proverbs. It comes from the word meaning "to be a fool."

2. Heb. *kesel* is used twice (Ps 49:13; Eccl 7:25) and is related to the idea of confidence; hence, folly in the form of overconfidence. It is the folly that springs from inside a person.

3. Heb. *kislâ* is virtually the same word with a similar meaning as *kesel* (Ps 85:8).

4. Heb. *nebālâ* is folly signifying the weakness of decay from wickedness. This is the meaning of Nabal's name—emptiness or folly from inward wickedness (I Sam 25:25).

5. Heb. *sekel, siklût* suggest the folly that is due to thickheadedness (Eccl 2:3).

6. Heb. *tohŏlâ* denotes the folly that is sinful (Job 4:18).

7. Heb. *tiplâ* carries the idea of unsavory, without salt; hence, something silly because insipid. It is the folly of an idea or act when something is missing (Job 24:12; Jer 23:13).

8. Gr. *anoia* is the folly resulting from a lack of sense, without mind or understanding (II Tim 3:9), a madness expressing itself in rage (Lk 6:11).

9. Gr. *aphrosunē* (II Cor 11:1, 17, 21) is used by Paul to denote lightness or foolishness in speaking unwisely of himself in a way touching on self-glorying.

See Fool.

A. E. T.

FOOD. Man as originally created was a vegetarian. God appointed the fruits, nuts and grains of the garden of Eden for his food (Gen 1:29; 2:16). Immediately after the Flood, which had destroyed earth's vegetation, God permitted man to eat the flesh of animals (9:3), although he was forbidden to consume the blood (9:4). The prohibition concerning blood (*q.v.*) was repeated to the Israelites in the law of Moses (Lev 3:17; 7:26; 17:10; etc.). God also designated that only certain ritually clean animals were proper for their food (Lev 11; Deut 14; *see* Animals).

The food of the Israelites varied somewhat according to the period of their history and the area in which they were living. When they wandered as nomads in the wilderness, their diet was more limited than after they settled down in Palestine. Their meals generally were simple and largely vegetarian (Ruth 2:14; I Sam 17:17-18), but they served a variety of foods when they entertained guests. Prominent and wealthy persons naturally enjoyed richer foods as well as a larger quantity (Lk 16:19). The table of King Solomon was provided daily with luxurious fare—"thirty measures of fine flour and sixty measures of meal, ten fattened oxen, twenty free-grazing oxen, one hundred sheep, besides deer and gazelles, roebucks and fattened cuckoos" (I Kgs 4:22–23, JerusB).

Even after entering Palestine, food was often scarce because of droughts and the rocky soil and primitive methods of farming. *See* Famine. Food was therefore prized and used carefully, although the Jews did have their times of feasting. One of the factors which made Egypt and Babylonia prosperous was their abundant supply of food grown on well-irrigated and fertile soil.

The KJV often uses the terms "bread" and "meat" for food in general. There are, however, abundant references to specific foods which can be listed under various classes. Vegetables, fruits and grain comprised the chief foodstuffs of the Jews. An approximate idea of what these were may be obtained from a small limestone calendar found at Gezer from the 10th cen. B.C. *See* Calendar. It lists the chief crops and the months in which the farmer worked them.

The most important of the grains or cereals were wheat and barley. These were eaten raw, made into porridge, roasted or parched, or ground into flour or meal, and made into cakes or bread (leavened and unleavened). In times of famine bread was made from beans, lentils, millet and spelt. The pulse family included mainly lentils and coarse beans like our kidney bean. Other vegetables, most of which were eaten either raw or cooked, were squash, cucumbers, melons, leeks, onions, garlic, and various herbs (Num 11:5).

Fruit trees provided several varieties of food. Common were the olive, fig and vine, as suggested in Jotham's parable of the trees (Jud 9:8–15). Vines supplied grapes, a much prized food in the Orient, found in rich abundance in Palestine. Young grape leaves were used as a green vegetable; the older leaves were fed to sheep and goats. Grapes were eaten in their natural state, dried into raisins, and used to make wine. The date-palm tree is mentioned a number of times (Ex 15:27; Deut 34:3; Ps 92:12; Joel 1:12; Jn 12:13). Other fruits included pomegranates, various berries and nuts. The KJV "apple tree" was likely the apricot (Joel 1:12; Song 2:3; 8:5). Certain spices (cummin, dill, mint, mustard) and seasonings were grown or procured for cooking. Salt (*q.v.*) especially was considered to be a necessary ingredient.

Use of meat was generally limited to special occasions, such as weddings, family festivals (Mt 22:2–4), entertainment of guests (Gen 18:2, 7), and sacrificial meals (Lev 7:11–27). Food from "unclean" animals was forbidden by Jewish law: swine, camels, rabbits, etc. (Lev 11; Deut 14). "Clean" animals most often prepared for the table included goats (also kids), sheep (especially lambs), and young bulls or steers. Gazelles, harts and fowl, animals of the chase, were valued for food. Domesticated birds, together with their eggs (Lk 11:12), were a favorite by NT times.

Israeli olive harvest near Lydda. IIS

Milk from animals was a principal item of food, from which sour milk, curds, and cheese were obtained (Gen 18:8; II Sam 17:29). Honey was much enjoyed and relished, especially by children (Ps 19:10; Song 5:1).

Fish are not often mentioned in the OT, but in the NT, especially in the Gospels, they are frequently referred to as a common food, both fresh and cured. Edible insects, generally of the locust family (Lev 11:22), were regarded as delicacies when dried, roasted, boiled in water, or ground into a paste.

In the course of time and especially during the period of the kingdom, there came advances in the art of cooking and a taste for the delicacies enjoyed by the kings and nobles of neighboring peoples. After the Exile the Israelites imported many new varieties of food.

Specific items of food, methods of cooking, and types of meals are discussed in the following subtopics. For other foods not mentioned, *see* Agriculture; Animals; Drink; Drink, Strong; Plants.

R. E. Po.

Bakemeats. Any kind of bread, cakes, pastries, or baked goods prepared by bakers for the pharaoh (Gen 40:17). Honey was used as the sweetening ingredient (Ex 16:31).

Banquet. Banqueting was a popular social and religious function of biblical times. Ordinarily an entire feast was involved, but at times the word was used only of the drinking (Est 5:5–6). Interestingly, the several Gr. and Heb. terms most often used of banqueting literally mean "to drink," and one function of the Jewish prophet and Christian apostle was to speak against the constant reduction of festive occasions to drunken revelry (Amos 6:7; Rom 13:13; Gal 5:19–21; I Pet 4:3), particularly when these were religious in nature. *See* Drink, Strong.

Sacrifices were generally accompanied by a banquet involving the eating of at least part of the sacrificed meat (I Sam 9:13; II Sam 6:18–19). It is felt that the "love feast" of NT

Ancient olive press at Capernaum. Phalpot

times (Jude 12) may have developed from the sacrificial banquet or as fulfillment of the predicted messianic banquet (Isa 25:6). Like the prophet of the OT, Paul rebuked those who failed to distinguish (Gr. *diakrinō*) the Lord's Supper from mere banqueting (I Cor 11:20-34), even though the supper itself had been instituted during a Jewish festival (Mt 26:20-29). *See* Festivals.

In addition to religious celebrations, banquets were held on such occasions as sheep-shearing (II Sam 13:23), a marriage (Jud 14:10; Mt 22:2-4), the separation and reunion of friends (Gen 31:27; Lk 15:23-24), and the weaning of a son and heir (Gen 21:8). Banquets are mentioned at the birthdays of Pharaoh (Gen 40:20) and Herod (Mt 14:6), and there is evidence that mourners at a funeral took refreshments (Hos 9:4; II Sam 3:35).

Usually the banquet was held in the evening, and to begin too early was frowned upon as excessive (Isa 5:11). The cattle for the banquet were slaughtered in the early part of the day of the banquet (Mt 22:4). Some banquets lasted as much as seven days (Jud 14:12; Deut 16:13).

Invitations to the banquet were sent out by a servant (Mt 22:3), and in some cases, reminders were also later sent (Lk 14:17), but probably only in the case of larger banquets which required more extensive preparation. To spurn an invitation for insufficient reason was considered a great insult (Lk 14:18 ff.).

The normal posture at a feast before Amos' time was sitting (I Sam 16:11, Heb. "sit around"; I Sam 20:24 f.; I Kgs 10:5). During the monarchy the Syrian or Babylonian custom of reclining at meals was introduced among the nobility and wealthy (Amos 6:4; Ezk 23:41; Est 1:6). In the NT the phrase "to sit at meat" (*katakeimai,* lit., "to lie down," "recline") indicates that the banqueters lay on mats or couches around a central tray or low table (Mk 7:28). One supported himself on his left elbow, his right hand free for eating, his legs stretched out away from the table. Only this posture can explain how Mary could anoint Jesus' feet (Jn 12:3) or how the unnamed disciple could lean on Jesus' breast (Jn 13:23, 25).

In Graeco-Roman culture permanent benches were built U-shaped, called a triclinium, for nine to twelve or more persons. Each such setting had its place of honor (Lk 14:8-10, RSV). One assumes that in the case of large royal banquets where thousands were present (Dan 5:1) many tables with couches would have been used. Other terms also indicate that guests reclined during banquets (e.g., *anapiptō,* Lk 11:37; 17:7; Jn 13:12; *anaklinō,* Lk 7:36). Jesus spoke of the great joy and privilege of being in the kingdom of God in terms of "sitting down with Abraham, and Isaac, and Jacob" (Gr. *anaklinō,* Mt 8:11). This is taken by some to mean a great messianic banquet (Arndt, p. 55).

During the banquet, varying portions were given to guests by the host according to his desire (I Sam 1:5). Food at these banquets was also distributed to the poor (Neh 8:10) and to friends (Est 9:22). In addition to the meat and wine (often spiced, i.e., mixed, Prov 9:2, RSV), there were many kinds of food, the most choice of which was given to guests of special dignity (I Sam 9:24). *See* Drink; Drink, Strong; Wine.

Although at the three major feasts of the Jews it was the men who appeared before the Lord, women were not excluded from banquets (I Sam 1:9). The widow and the maid servant were to take part in the festivals (Deut 16:11). The practice of separating women at banquets was known among the Persians (Est 1:9).

Guests were received with a kiss as a matter of courtesy (Lk 7:45). The door was kept by a servant, and when the master was ready to

Dates almost ready for harvest. HFV

A banquet scene showing offering to Queen Makeri of Egypt. LM

begin the banquet, he shut the door himself to show that no more were to be permitted to enter (Lk 13:25). Thus the five foolish virgins were excluded from the marriage feast (Mt 25:10). Perfumes and scented oils were applied to the guests as anointing (Amos 6:6), and they also had their feet washed (Lk 7:36, 44). At weddings, garments were given to the guests for the occasion (Mt 22:11-12). It was considered an honor to be the recipient of a garment from a host (Rev 3:5).

In private banquets, the host presided over the festivities and cared for the details such as closing the door (Lk 13:25). When the banquets were larger and of mixed company, the custom was to choose a "ruler of the feast" (Gr. *architriklinos*) who would assume these duties (Jn 2:8). Guests were entertained by musical activities, dancing, and merrymaking in general (Jud 14:12; Isa 5:12; Amos 6:5; Mk 6:22; Lk 15:25). *See* Food: Meals.

J. McR.

Bread. The Heb. word *leḥem* is used 297 times in the OT and the Gr. *artos* 99 times in the NT. Bread was the most common and important food of the peasant. It was made from grain, with or without yeast, in different shapes. Generally it was used for the table, though often also in sacrifices. The word is sometimes used figuratively of physical necessity or of spiritual sustenance, or even of eternal life.

Bread might be made of barley, as in the Midianite's dream (Jud 7:13) or the 20 loaves brought to Elisha (II Kgs 4:42). At the feeding of the 5,000, John indicates that the boy's five loaves were of barley (Jn 6:9, 13).

Greeks frequently referred to white bread as "pure," i.e., white. Most loaves for the tabernacle were made of wheat (e.g., Ex 29:2). Emmer and oats were also raised in Palestine, though they are not mentioned in Scripture. Indian corn was unknown. ("Corn" in KJV is wheat or grain.) The dough was prepared simply by mixing the flour or meal with water and kneading the mixture. *See* Food: Dough; Flour.

"Little yeast ferments a big lump of dough" (a saying quoted in I Cor 5:6). The parable of the leaven had the woman baker "hide" a little yeast in three measures of flour (Mt 13:33). The rising took several hours. Kneading bowls are mentioned in Ex 8:3.

Unleavened bread was made at the time of the first Passover because Israel was hurried out of Egypt (Ex 12:39; cf. the witch of Endor hurrying to bake for Saul, I Sam 28:24, and Lot for his angelic visitors, Gen 19:3). In memory of Egypt the Jews ate this "bread of affliction" (Deut 16:3) for a week beginning with the Passover meal, but 51 weeks of the year they ate ordinary leavened bread. *See* Food: Leaven.

Fuel for baking was usually wood (Isa 44:14-15), but it might be dried grass inside a clay oven (Mt 6:30) with the loaves plastered on the outside and then turned (Hos 7:8). Fuel for baking might even be manure (Ezk 4:15). *See* Oven.

Professional bakers made bread in Jerusalem, for Jeremiah when in prison was given a loaf each day from "the bakers' street" (Jer 37:21). In the average home, however, bread was prepared by the wife (Gen 18:6) or a daughter (II Sam 13:8).

In size a loaf was one's thumb in thickness and as broad as a plate; thus loaves could be broken rather than cut. They usually were disk shaped, as indicated by the Heb. *kikkār* ("loaf," Jud 8:5; I Sam 10:3), but perhaps could be rings (Ex 29:23, Heb.), suspended around a pole to preserve them from mice, etc. So "breaking the staff or support of bread" meant famine (Lev 26:26; Ps 105:16; Isa 3:1; Ezk 4:16; 5:16; 14:13). *See* Food: Cake.

Bread kept too long became dry and crumbling (Josh 9:5, 12, JerusB). The Gilgamesh epic (XI, 225–229, ANET, p. 96) describes the various stages of bread mold.

Bread is a term used for food in general (II Sam 13:5–6, 10, RSV). To "eat bread" is to have a meal (e.g., Gen 3:19; 31:54; 37:25; 43:32; Prov 9:5; Eccl 9:7). Such food one should earn (II Thess 3:12). To "overflow with loaves" (Gr.) is to have plenty to eat (Lk 15:17). To go without a meal is not to eat bread (Mk 3:20). On a journey one usually took bread (Mk 6:8). Even animals and birds have their food or "bread" (Ps 147:9) and serpents their "meat" (*leḥem;* Isa 65:25).

A Jewish meal began with the father of the family taking a loaf, giving thanks, breaking and distributing it (cf. Christ in Mt 14:19; 26:26).

The uncommon Gr. adjective *epiousion,* translated "daily" in the only material petition of the Lord's prayer (Mt 6:11; Lk 11:3; *Didache* 8:2), may literally mean "for tomorrow"—the daily ration given out for the next day. The request may also be reminiscent of the provision of manna day by day to the Israelites.

Bread and clothing are essential for physical life (Deut 10:18), with water (Gen 21:14; I Kgs 18:4), or wine (Gen 14:18), and perhaps vegetables (Gen 25:34) or meat (I Kgs 17:6) or fruit (I Sam 30:12). It might be scant fare (I Kgs 22:27) or "bread of adversity and water of oppression" (Isa 30:20), or even "bread of pains," that is, bread earned by toil (Ps 127:2), the opposite of "bread of precious things," that is, delicacies (Dan 10:3; cf. Gen 49:20). But it is all important to remember that man does not live on bread or physical food alone, but in his total being on everything that proceeds from the mouth of the Lord (Deut 8:3; Mt 4:4).

Ceremonial use of bread was common. Much of it was unleavened (Ex 12:8, 18–20; 29:2; Lev 2:4), but leavened bread was used in a peace offering (Lev 7:13). The ceremonial loaf might be prepared from firstfruits and waved or swung in worship (Lev 23:17, 20).

What the KJV calls "shewbread"—continually (Num 4:7) supplied for a table in the tabernacle (Ex 25:23–30) and later in the temple (I Kgs 7:48), termed "holy bread" (I Sam 21:4), put there hot (I Sam 21:6), in rows (Ex 40:23; Neh 10:33, Heb.)—was by the Hebrews called "bread of (the) face," "presence bread," in the NT "loaves of the presentation" (Gr.; Mt 12:4; Heb 9:2). *See* Bread of Faces.

Manna was special "bread from heaven in abundance" (Ps 105:40; Neh 9:15), when God miraculously fed the multitudes of Israel 40 years in the wilderness (Ex 16:4, 15). It came with the dew (v. 14), six days a week (vv. 22, 25), and it could be cooked (v. 23). At times a complaining spirit loathed the light stuff (Num 21:5), though the apocryphal Book of Wisdom says this bread "provided every pleasure and suited every taste" (16:20)! *See* Food: Manna.

Metaphorical uses of bread in the OT are infrequent: the inhabitants of the land would be bread for Israel (Num 14:9), i.e., easily conquered. Bread and wine stand for the benefits of wisdom (Prov 9:5). But figurative uses play an important part in the NT. Leaven, ordinarily used in making bread, in the teaching of Jesus represented the teaching of the Pharisees and Sadducees (Mt 16:6, 11–12; parallel to Mk 8:15) and the hypocrisy or stage-play of the Pharisees (Lk 12:1). The parable of the leaven, like that of the mustard seed, illustrates the amazing growth of the kingdom, the mustard seed outward growth and the leaven inward. Leaven even here may represent evil, showing some kind of abnormal development. Paul in I Cor 5:6–8, employing rules for pre-Passover housecleaning, urged the corrupted church to "clean out the old leaven," which is "badness and wickedness." (Contrast Ignatius, d. A.D. 107, calling Christ the new leaven, Magnesians 10:2.)

Future bliss for the followers of Jesus was anticipated as eating bread at a banquet (Lk 14:15). In His discourse in Capernaum after the feeding of the 5,000, Jesus proclaimed Himself the bread of God that came from heaven (Jn 6:32–33 from Ex 16:4; Ps 78:24), and gives life to men (Jn 6:48, 51).

An ancient winepress in Jerusalem. HFV

In the supper which Jesus instituted, the broken bread represents His body smitten and broken for our healing (Mk 14:22 and the other Gospels; I Cor 10:16; 11:24; Isa 53:5; I Pet 2:24). For a believer to take of that bread is to show the most intimate communion with the Saviour. The one loaf also represents the many believers who form the mystical body of Christ (I Cor 10:17). *See* Lord's Supper.

Bibliography. T. Canaan, "Superstition and Folklore about Bread," BASOR #167 (Oct., 1962), 36–47.

W. G. B.

Butter. This is a milk product, translated "curds" in RSV, whether from camel, cow, goat, or sheep. With a cow and a couple of sheep one might live through hard times on butter and wild honey (Isa 7:15, 21, 22). Butter (Heb. *ḥem'â*) was made by pressing (sour) milk (Prov 30:33) so it would become curdled, like leben, yogurt, or cottage cheese. It was a staple article of diet, according to Abraham's menu (Gen 18:8), the lists of foodstuffs for Israel's land (Deut 32:13 f.), and the supplies taken to David in exile (II Sam 17:29). Sisera asked Jael for water and was given (sour) milk or curds, according to the use of synonyms in Heb. parallelism (Jud 5:25, RSV). Plenty of curds with olive oil made for a luxury diet (Job 20:17; 29:6). Parallel to oil, in Ps 55:21 it may be butter as we know it.

Cake. Several Heb. words translated "cake" in KJV describe the appearance of the loaf of bread (*q.v.*). Heb. *'ūgâ,* from a root meaning "to be round," signifies a round unsweetened cake or scone, a flat disk up to 18 inches in diameter. It was usually baked on hearthstones after raking away the coals (Gen 18:6; I Kgs 19:6). It needed to be turned to be properly done (Hos 7:8). Such cakes were never cut, always broken by hand. Manna could be crushed, boiled in a pot, and fashioned into round cakes (Num 11:8).

The *ṣelîl,* the barley cake which the dreaming Midianite saw rolling into his camp, must have been thicker. Heb. *ḥallâ,* from the root *ḥālal,* "to pierce, perforate," probably denotes ritual bread pierced with holes like the modern Passover cake (Ex 29:2, 23; Lev 2:4; *et al.*). The *rāqîq* was a thin, unleavened wafer (I Chr 23:29; Ex 29:2, 23; Lev 2:4; Num 6:15, 19) used in ceremonial offerings. Heb. *maṣṣôt,* translated "unleavened cakes" in Josh 5:11; Jud 6:19–21, is the usual term for unleavened bread (*see* Food: Leaven). The cakes (*kawwānîm*) of Jer 7:18; 44:19 (RSV) were marked with the features of the pagan goddess known as the Queen of Heaven, like a cookie pressed in a mold. Tamar made fancy cakes apparently in the shape of hearts, according to the Heb. *lᵉbibôt,* from *lēb,* "heart" (II Sam 13:6, 8, 10).

J. R.

Cheese. The coagulated curd of milk pressed into a solid mass (I Sam 17:18; II Sam 17:29; Job 10:10). The making of cheese was an important industry for the people of antiquity. Cheese was prepared by salting the strained curds, shaping them into disks, and drying them in the open air.

The term *ḥem'â* (Prov 30:33, "butter") refers to curdled milk. The term *ḥālāb* is used for ordinary milk, but in I Sam 17:18 *ḥărîṣê heḥālāb,* lit., "cuttings of milk," refers to a cheese made from sweet milk. The proper designation for cheese is *gebînâ* (Job 10:10).

Cooking. While most meals were not elaborate and the food was cooked simply compared to our standards, preparation took much time (Prov 31:15) because of the primitive hearths, ovens, cooking vessels (*see* Pottery), and utensils and lack of any prepared or packaged foods. Cooking was universally the task of the women of the household (Sarah, Gen 18:6; Martha, Lk 10:40).

Meat was either stewed or roasted. In the former case it was cut up into pieces (Ezk 24:3–5; Mic 3:3) and, perhaps with crushed wheat and vegetables, allowed to stew in a "pan, or kettle, or caldron, or pot" (I Sam 2:13–14). The broth could be served separately (Jud 6:19–20). Roasting was the oldest method of cooking meat. At first it was merely laid upon hot stones after removing the coals. Jesus cooked a fish for the disciples by placing it on the charcoal itself (Jn 21:9). Later, the meat was spitted and held over the flame or baked in a preheated pit, as the Samaritans do at their annual Passover feast (cf. Ex 12:8–9).

Vegetables were generally boiled (*see* Food: Pottage) and then mixed with olive oil, similar to our flavoring with butter. Grain was often parched (*q.v.*). Coarse wheat or barley meal was sometimes prepared as a porridge. But most often the grain was ground into flour, mixed with olive oil, and baked as bread (*see* Food: Bread; Cake).

J. R.

Corn. The KJV uses this term to translate several Heb. and Gr. words referring to various grains. Later American translations use the term "grain" or the word for one of the various types of grain. In modern English "corn" refers mainly to the Indian maize of America which was unknown in Eurasia before the 16th cen. *See* Parched Corn. The most common types of grain in Palestine were wheat, barley, millet, and spelt (emmer). *See* Grain.

Cracknels. A kind of hard bread or cake (*niqqudîm,* I Kgs 14:3). In Josh 9:5, 12 the Heb. word is used of the dry and "mouldy" or crumbled bread carried by the delegation from Gibeon.

Dough. A mixture (Heb. *bāṣēq*) of wheat or barley flour (or meal) with water or olive oil, kneaded in a wooden bowl or trough (Ex 12:34, 39; II Sam 13:8; Jer 7:18; Hos 7:4). Into the dough being kneaded, a bit of dough set aside

A baker's shop of the New Testament period at Pompeii. In the center stand four flour mills; ovens are located to the left. HFV

from the previous mixing would be worked, in order to make leavened bread. Heb. *'ărîsâ* seems to designate dough in its first stage of mixing (Num 15:20-21; Neh 10:37; Ezk 44:30), an offering of firstfruits from the mixing bowl as well as from the threshing floor.

Gr. *phyrama* translates these Heb. words for "dough" in the LXX and appears figuratively as "lump" in the sense of the whole loaf in the NT. In Rom 11:16 "the firstfruit" and "the root" stand for Abraham, through whom all the nation of Israel, referred to by "the lump" and "the branches," has been consecrated. In I Cor 5:6-7 "the lump" represents the entire congregation of Christian believers, whether unleavened (pure) or leavened by malice and evil. *See* Food: Bread; Leaven.

J. R.

Egg. Eggs of domesticated chickens did not become common food until after the 4th cen. B.C. Eggs of small wild birds were gathered for food (Isa 10:14), but when found in Israel, the hen or mother bird could not be taken also (Deut 22:6). The ostrich's habit of leaving eggs to be hatched in warm sand is mentioned in Job 39:13-14. Hatching out adders' (KJV, "cockatrice") eggs symbolized scheming evil (Isa 59:5). Jesus' reference in Lk 11:12 was doubtless to a hen's egg.

Fish. *See* Animals, V.4.

Flour. Three ideas are conveyed in the three Heb. words translated "flour" in the KJV. The Heb. word *bāṣēq* speaks of dough made by mixing flour with water and a bit of the previous day's batch of leavened dough (II Sam 13:8). Heb. *sōlet* refers to fine crushed flour and is used more frequently than either of the other two (Lev 2:1). Heb. *qemaḥ* was used of a coarser flour or meal. It is translated "meal" in I Sam 1:24; II Sam 17:28; Jud 6:19, ASV. The fine flour was made mainly from the inner kernels of wheat (Ex 29:2; Deut 32:14; Ps 81:16; 147:14), while barley, rye, and other grains were used for meal, the major difference being the texture since for the latter the entire kernel was used. Fine flour mingled with oil was used in unleavened bread (Ex 29:2) and in the meal offering (Ex 29:40). *See* Food: Bread.

After the grain was winnowed it was usually sifted (cf. Lk 22:31) and then ground into meal or flour between two millstones. Not until Hellenistic times did the rotary type of hand mill with two round stones become common. Throughout the OT the grinding was done by rubbing the upper, smaller stone back and forth over the grain placed on the larger stone. The sound of grinding early in the morning must have been common in the towns of Palestine before their destruction (Jer 25:10; Rev 18:22).

A. E. T.

Honey. Heb. *debash,* "honey," signified three sources of sweets: (1) grape or date honey, the Arabic *dibs,* a thick syrup made from dates or grape juice (Gen 43:11; I Kgs 14:3; II Kgs 18:32); (2) the honey of wild bees which was found dripping out of a honeycomb, perhaps in a hollow log, on the ground (I Sam 14:25 f.), in the skeleton of an animal (Jud 14:8-9), or in crevasses in the rocks (Deut 32:13; Ps 81:16; see also Mt 3:4; Mk 1:6); and (3) honey from domesticated bees (one of the products of "the field" collected as firstfruits during Hezekiah's revival, II Chr 31:5).

The term "honey" is used figuratively in the expression "a land flowing with milk and honey" (Ex 3:8, *et al.* 15 more times) to denote great fertility and abundance of food (PEQ, XCVIII [July-Dec. 1966], 166 f.). Canaan was indeed a source of much honey even before Moses' time. Thutmose III (1483-1450 B.C.)

brought back to Egypt hundreds of jars of honey from Syria-Palestine as tribute. Sinuhe sang the praises of that land *c.* 1950 B.C., exclaiming, "Plentiful was its honey, abundant its olives" (ANET, p. 19). At Ugarit the Canaanites lauded their country in the expression "The heavens rained oil; and the creeks ran with honey" (BA, XXVII [Dec., 1965], 121; cf. Job 20:17). Because of its sweetness honey is frequently employed in simile and metaphor in Heb. poetry (e.g., Ps 19:10; 119:103; Prov 16:24; Song 4:11; 5:1).

J. R.

Knead. Flour and water were placed in the kneading-trough in which a scrap of the previous baking had been left. The dough was worked by hand and allowed to stand until the scrap had leavened the lump (Gen 18:6; II Sam 13:8; Jer 7:18; Hos 7:4). The witch of Endor who hurriedly baked bread for King Saul did not have time for the fermenting, and thus baked unleavened bread (I Sam 28:24).

The kneading-trough was a shallow bowl usually made of wood or pottery. During the plague of frogs, even the kneading-troughs of the Egyptians were infested (Ex 8:3). The Israelites carried their kneading bowls as essential equipment when they left Egypt (Ex 12:34). The kneading-trough (KJV, "store") is among the objects of the Lord's blessing and cursing (Deut 28:5, 17).

Leaven. Bread was the staple commodity of food in biblical times, so much so that "our daily bread" was synonymous with one's whole diet. Except in times of unusual haste or unforseen circumstances (Ex 12:39), the bread was leavened. The leavening agent used to make the bread rise was a portion of a former mixture of leavened dough, preserved for the purpose, which was either dissolved in the water into which the flour was added in the kneading-trough, or "hid" in the flour itself which was kneaded into dough (Mt 13:33). *See* Food: Bread; Dough.

Unleavened bread (*maṣṣâ*) was used in the rituals of the Levitical law. There it seems to have had two special significances. 1. Unleavened bread was required in the Passover and the Feast of Unleavened Bread. It is also called "the bread of affliction" (Ex 12:34-39; 13:3; Deut 16:3-4). This kind of bread was required as a reminder that God had thrust the Israelites out of Egypt suddenly, without even sufficient time to allow their bread to rise. Hence they ate unleavened bread as they began their wilderness journey. Therefore, in both the Passover and the Feast of Unleavened Bread, designed as memorials of the deliverance from Egypt, unleavened bread was required. In these instances leaven does not seem to have an ethical significance. 2. Unleavened bread was required in the offerings made under the Levitical law (Lev 2:4; 6:16; 7:12). Leaven here does have an ethical connotation. It was excluded because the process of fermentation implied corruption. When used in an ethical sense, leaven speaks of evil or corruption.

Two exceptions to the general rule concerning the use of unleavened bread are to be noted. In the peace offering (Lev 7:13) and in the feast of the wave loaves (Pentecost) (Lev 23:17) leavened bread was to be offered. The explanation is to be found in the significance of these two events. The peace offering was a sweet-savor offering, revealing the Godward aspect of the death of Christ, in contrast to the nonsweet-savor offerings, which depicted the sinward aspect of Christ's sacrifice. In His death Christ reconciled the world to God (II Cor 5:19). He caused the warfare between man and God to cease, and established peace (Eph 2:14-18). Although "unleavened cakes mingled with oil" were offered (Lev 7:12) to show that Christ was separated from sin, leavened bread was also offered (Lev 7:13) as a symbol of the fact that Christ's reconciliation was for the sinful world.

In the feast of the wave loaves (Pentecost) it was also fitting to include leavened bread, for the two loaves symbolized the harvest that would be brought to God from among both Jew and Gentile by the work of Christ. That which was previously corrupt is after the cross offered to God as no longer corrupt but cleansed through the death of Christ.

In the figurative use of leaven in the NT, the ethical concept of the OT is retained. Christ used leaven as a figure of the false teaching of the Pharisees (Mt 16:6; Lk 12:1). This figure is explained in Mt 16:12, thus removing all doubt of its significance. Paul twice quoted a proverb using leaven in this ethical concept (I Cor 5:6; Gal 5:9), as the application of the proverb to the Corinthians shows (I Cor 5:7-8). This seems to be also the background of Peter's imagery in II Pet 1:4*b*. When Christ used leaven in the parable of the kingdom (Mt 13:33), while the ethical connotation may not be eliminated, the emphasis seems to be more on the effects of introducing leaven into meal: "all was leavened." In like manner, after the kingdom is introduced, it will ultimately encompass all. This is Christ's picture of the universality of His kingdom at His second advent.

J. D. P.

Manna. The word occurs first in KJV in Ex 16:15. Elsewhere in the OT all English versions uniformly render the Heb. word as "manna," which is merely an approximate transliteration; but in v. 15 ASV and RSV translate it as a question, "What is it?" Evidently, when the Israelites first saw it on the ground, they nicknamed it a "whatness," or colloquially a "whatdyacallit," which seems to be the literal meaning with reference to the mysterious quality of the divine bread.

Manna is said to have been small, round and white (Ex 16:14, 31). Left over night it ordinarily "bred worms, and became foul" (Ex 16:20, ASV). It melted in the hot sun. It was to be gathered daily, in the morning, an omer (about half a peck) per person. On the sixth day the people were to gather twice as much, to provide for the sabbath, when no manna was to be given. In this case it did not breed worms or become foul over the sabbath.

Manna tasted like "wafers made with honey" (Ex 16:31) or "butter cakes" (Num 11:8, NEB), and could be baked or boiled. Apparently it was like a seed in appearance and consistency, and like bdellium or gum resin in color. It was customarily ground before baking. After a time, many of the people came to dislike it violently (Num 21:5).

A pot of manna was gathered and kept as a memorial of this continuing miraculous provision by the Lord for the Israelites throughout the 40 years in the wilderness (Ex 16:32-35). Later, a golden pot of manna was placed in the ark in the tabernacle (Heb 9:4).

Manna is thought by many to be typical of Christ as the Bread of Life. The Lord's comments in Jn 6:31-35 seem to warrant this conclusion. "Hidden manna," which may refer to that in the ark, is promised in Rev 2:17 to the overcomer, implying the closest fellowship with the Lord in the coming kingdom.

See Food: Bread.

J. A. S.

Meal. This is the translation of two Heb. words, *sōlet* and *qemah*. The first refers to very fine flour or meal and is found in Gen 18:6; Ex 29:2; I Chr 9:29; Ezk 16:13, 19. The other word means flour or meal and is translated "meal" in the following passages: Gen 18:6; Num 5:15; I Kgs 4:22; 17:12, 14, 16; II Kgs 4:41; I Chr 12:40; Isa 47:2; Hos 8:7. The word "meal" occurs twice in the NT (Mt 13:33; Lk 13:21) where the Gr. word (*aleuron*) means fine flour or meal. The two most important grains among the Hebrews were wheat and barley (usually "corn" in KJV). When ground they were used for bread and for vegetable sacrifices ("meal offerings").

In Ruth 2:14 the Heb. word *'ōkel* ("meal") is used as a compound with the word for time (*'ēt*). The word denotes the portion of food eaten at any one time. In this passage the meaning is "mealtime" or "time of eating" (*see* Food: Meals).

Meals. Ordinary people in ancient Palestine ate only two regular meals a day—breakfast or lunch (our "brunch"), and supper or dinner (Ex 16:12; I Kgs 17:6). Heb. has no specific words to distinguish these meals, but in Gr. the former is *ariston* and the latter *deipnon* (see Lk 14:12, "luncheon or a dinner party," Phillips).

Aside from early snacks, the first proper meal came late in the morning, between 10:00 A.M. and noon (Ruth 2:14; cf. 2:7, 17). Peter became hungry about the sixth hour, i.e., noon (Acts 10:9-10). It was not a large meal. Boaz and his harvesters had only bread dipped in sour wine and parched grain (Ruth 2:14); Jesus provided bread and broiled fish (Jn 21:13). It was an hour for rest as much as for food.

The chief meal was eaten usually after sunset when it was too dark to work longer in the fields (Jud 19:16, 21). Unless a man had a slave (Lk 17:7-8), the women served the meal (Jn 12:2). If guests were invited, this meal became a feast or banquet (*see* Food: Banquet). Only men were seated at banquets (II Sam 13:23), although at ordinary meals women could eat with the men (Ruth 2:14). The communal practices of the Jerusalem church imply that after Pentecost male and female believers ate together daily (Acts 2:44, 46) as well as at the love feasts (I Cor 11:17-22, 33-34; Jude 12).

The Gospels reveal that "washing of hands" before meals was a religious requirement for Jews (Mk 7:1-5). At a banquet attendants brought bowls for washing the hands again after eating, since in biblical times no tableware was provided. Everyone ate out of the common bowl or platter with his fingers (Prov 26:15; Mk 14:20). Wine was usually not provided until the food had been served and eaten (Gen 27:25). At the Last Supper this order was followed as Jesus first broke the bread and then passed the cup.

Roman officials and wealthy persons often ate four meals a day, similar to our system with afternoon "tea" included. For a fuller description of Roman meals and cooking see A. C. Bouquet, *Everyday Life in New Testament Times,* Scribner's, 1954, pp. 70-73.

J. R.

Meat. This word was used in KJV for food in general, as it is in Scotland still. The "meat offering" (*minḥâ*, "oblation") of Lev 2, *et al.* is more properly a meal or cereal offering. The term signifying meat in the modern sense is "flesh" in KJV, as in Ex 12:8, 46 speaking of the meat of the Passover lamb (cf. also Ex 16:8, 12; 29:14, 31-34; I Kgs 17:6; Ps 50:13; *et al.*).

The Levitical laws of purity regulated which animals were considered ritually clean and suitable for offerings to God (Lev 11:2-23; Deut 14:4-20). Later in Judaism ritually pure food was designated *kōsher* (from Heb. *kāshar,* "to be right, proper," cf. Est 8:5). The distinction between clean and unclean animals dates from the earliest times (Gen 7:2; 8:20). Any domesticated beast permissible as a sacrifice to Yahweh was also deemed fit to eat by His covenant people. The criteria were whether the animal chews the cud and has a cloven hoof (Lev 11:3).

An underlying reason for excluding other animals, such as the pig, may be found in the danger of contracting such diseases as trichinosis, carried by swine. The principal reason, however, was no doubt a religious taboo against animals which the Canaanites and other pagans offered to their gods. Horses, swine, dogs, and mice (or rats) were connected with idolatrous rites often associated with the underworld (II Kgs 23:11; Isa 65:4; 66:3, 17). These and other beasts would be forbidden as food since animals were normally slaughtered only in connection with the offering of sacrifices. To eat their meat would make the Israelite "abominable" (Lev 11:43). For the prohibition con-

Peasant women bring offerings of a variety of food to Queen Ti as portrayed in her tomb at Sakkara, Egypt. LL

cerning stewing a kid in its mother's milk (Ex 23:19) *see* Food: Milk.

Many of the prohibited birds, insects, and reptiles (Lev 11:13–30) were worshiped in Egypt in the sense that as totems they represented Egyptian deities. No evidence exists that the game animals (Deut 14:5; 12:15; I Kgs 4:23) and birds not called unclean in the Mosaic code were ever totem gods in the ancient Near East. Egyptian Eighteenth Dynasty tomb paintings clearly show gazelle and quail as the object of the hunt (*see* Food: Venison). *See also* Clean.

The eating of any kind of blood, even of clean animals and birds, was absolutely forbidden on the grounds of the sacredness of life (Gen 9:4–6; Lev 17:10–14; Deut 12:16, 23–25; Acts 15:29). The life of the body was considered to flow in the blood, so that when the blood was shed, the very life itself was poured out. If not employed to make atonement (Lev 17:11), the drained blood was to be covered with dust.

Of the clean animals, a goat kid was the most frequently eaten, especially among the poor (hence the complaint of the prodigal's brother, Lk 15:29). But the favorite meal included a stall-fed calf (Prov 15:17) or choice sheep (Neh 5:18). Roast goose was a national dish in Egypt and may be the "fatted fowl" on Solomon's table (I Kgs 4:23). Chickens were known in Palestine by 600 B.C. (e.g., a seal showing a rooster found at Tell en-Nasbeh), but domestic poultry and eggs were uncommon before the Persian period.

J. R.

Mess. This nearly obsolete English word, now used only for meals in a military setting, occurs in KJV in Gen 43:34 and II Sam 11:8. Translating Heb. *maś'ēt,* the term means a portion of food or a gift "lifted" from the table of a ruler and given to an inferior as a largesse or token of friendship. The Heb. word occurs in this sense also in Est 2:18 ("gifts") and in Jer 40:5 ("reward," KJV; "present," RSV).

Milk. In biblical times people did not ordinarily drink fresh milk, probably because of lack of refrigeration. Milk was allowed to sour and then was made into curds (*see* Food: Butter) or cheese (*q.v.*). Goat's milk (Prov 27:27) was the most common, although sheep, cows, and even camels were also milked (Deut 32:14; I Cor 9:7). The importance of mother's milk for newborn infants is implied in Isaiah's figures (Isa 49:15; 66:11–12) and in Peter's simile regarding the necessity of spiritual nourishment from the Word of God (I Pet 2:2). For weaning from breast feeding (Isa 28:9), *see* Children.

The term "milk" was often used figuratively to denote abundance and fertility, both then (for the expression "milk and honey" *see* Food: Honey) and in the eschatological age (Isa 55:1; 60:16; Joel 3:18). In the NT "milk" represents the simplest form of the gospel, elementary Christian doctrine (I Cor 3:2; Heb 5:12–13). *See* Milk.

The prohibition of the Mosaic law against boiling or stewing a goat kid in its mother's milk (Ex 23:19; 34:26; Deut 14:21) evidently was given to combat a Canaanite sacrificial rite practiced to ensure the fertility of a field by sprinkling the resultant broth upon the earth.

Such a custom is mentioned in the Ugaritic poem, "Birth of the Gods" (G. R. Driver, *Canaanite Myths and Legends,* T. & T. Clark, 1956, p. 121).

J. R.

Parched Corn. This is roasted grain (Josh 5:11; Lev 23:14; Ruth 2:14; I Sam 17:17), probably wheat or barley (Ruth 2:14), not "corn" (*q.v.*). The threshed grain was roasted in a pan by keeping it in constant motion with a stirrer until the food was done. When prepared, such grain could be carried in quantity (I Sam 17:17) and used on a journey (Josh 5:11).

Pottage. Jacob made his famous pottage (Heb. *nāzîd*) by boiling red lentils (Gen 25:29–34). It was a common dish (Hag 2:12), a thick vegetable soup or stew, probably flavored with onions and occasionally bits of meat. Esau's sale of his birthright merely for a little pottage illustrates the cheap estimate he placed on his family rights. In Elisha's day one of the young prophets found a wild vine and cut up some of its gourds into the soup, inadvertently poisoning it (II Kgs 4:38–40).

Raisins. Raisins (Heb. *ṣimmûqîm*) were a favorite provision of persons on a journey (I Sam 25:18; 30:12; II Sam 16:1) because they were easily carried without spoilage (I Chr 12:40). Raisins were prepared by soaking bunches of grapes in oil and water, or in a solution of potash, and then spreading them in the sun to dry. Num 6:3 lists dried grapes as one of the prohibited foods for a Nazarite. The KJV "flagon," Heb. *'ăshîshâ,* more correctly is a raisin cake. *See* Flagon. These were considered delicacies suitable for feasts (II Sam 6:19; I Chr 16:3; Song 2:5). Cakes of raisins were used in pagan festivals (Hos 3:1) and no doubt as offerings to the fertility goddesses (cf. Jer 7:18; 44:19).

Savory Meat. Savory or tasty meat was requested by Isaac as he prepared to give his blessing to Esau (Gen 27:4, 7, 9, 14, 17, 31). The Heb. word means "delicacies" or "dainties" and was meat, particularly wild game, prepared in an appetizing way. Perhaps it was the deceiving of Isaac by Jacob that led the wise man to write the proverb that warns against desiring the "dainty meats" of the wicked (Prov 23:3, 6).

Venison. A KJV translation of two Heb. words (*ṣayid, ṣêdâ* from *ṣûd,* "to hunt") which technically referred to wild game of any kind (Gen 25:28; 27:3, 5, 7, 19 ff.). Venison came to mean usually deer, antelope, or gazelle meat. The Heb. term occurs also in Prov 12:27, in the KJV "hunting"; the Jerusalem Bible translates, "The idle man has no game to roast." BDB suggests, "The slothful man does not (even) flush his game." In Lev 17:13 Heb. *ṣayid* appears in the idiom "hunteth and catcheth," lit., "hunts a hunting of" or "hunts game whether animal or bird."

The same Heb. word was applied in a broader sense to any provisions of food (Job 38:41; Neh 13:15; Ps 132:15), especially to provisions for a trip (Gen 42:25; 45:21; Josh 1:11 ["victuals"[; 9:11, 14; etc.), perhaps because wild game was a frequent food of early nomads. *See* Food: Victuals.

Victuals. A common designation for food or provisions (cf. Gen 14:11; Lev 25:37; II Chr 11:11; Mt 14:15; *et al.*). This word is now seldom employed in the standard English language. KJV used it to translate such words as Heb. *'ōkel,* "food"; *leḥem,* "bread"; and *ṣêdâ,* "venison," "wild game," "provisions." *See* Food: Bread; Venison.

Bibliography. J. Behm, *"Esthiō,"* TDNT, II, 689–695. A. C. Bouquet, *Everyday Life in New Testament Times,* Scribner's, 1954, pp. 69–79. CornPBE, pp. 331–337. R. J. Forbes, *Studies in Ancient Technology,* III, Leiden: E. J. Brill, 1955, pp. 50–105; *op. cit.,* V, 1957, pp. 78–88, 97 f. E. W. Heaton, *Everyday Life in Old Testament Times,* Scribner's, 1956, pp. 81–115. K. A. Kitchen, "Food," NBD, pp. 429–433.

FOOL, FOOLISH. The term is used in Scripture with respect to moral and spiritual more than to mental or intellectual deficiencies. The "fool" is not one who does not think or reason, but who reasons selfishly and wrongly. In the OT the fool is the person who rejects the fear of the Lord, and thinks and acts independently as if he could ignore God's rule and blaspheme His name and mock at sin, all with impunity (Ps 14:1; 74:18, 22; Prov 14:8–9; etc.). In other passages the term has the more ordinary meaning, denoting one who is rash, loud-mouthed, or unreasonable.

The English word translates a number of Heb. and Gr. words. One word for "fool" in the Heb., *nābāl,* is also the name of an individual who personified folly, the man Nabal (I Sam 25:25). He was what he was not because of idiocy but because he was insensible to religious and ethical claims; even his own wife could not appeal to him (25:17). As such he might be termed spiritually senseless, as in Ps 14:1. Isa 32:6 gives a description of such a fool (see RSV): his mind plots iniquity, he practices ungodliness, utters error about the Lord, and neglects the hungry and thirsty. This type of person is actively irreligious and unkind. He is definitely a sinner (Gen 34:7; Josh 7:15; II Sam 13:12–13; Jud 19:23), practicing folly (*q.v.*).

Heb. *'ĕwîl* is found mostly in Proverbs and is described as one who despises advice and instruction (1:7; 10:8; 15:5), who lacks wisdom and good common sense (10:21; 11:29; 12:15; 24:7; Jer 4:22), and who is quick to talk back or act without thinking (10:14; 12:16; 14:17; 20:3, RSV; 29:9 RSV).

Heb. *kesîl* is used very frequently in both Proverbs and Ecclesiastes. This fool is characterized at length in Prov 26:1-12 and Eccl 7:4-9. The *kᵉsîl,* one who is dull and obstinate, hates knowledge (Prov 1:22; 23:9) and has no capacity to get wisdom (Prov 17:16); he is complacent and self-confident (Prov 1:32, RSV; 14:16; 28:26); he enjoys doing wrong (Prov 10:23; 13:19) and displaying his folly (Prov 13:16; 18:2); he shrugs off a rebuke (Prov 17:10); his speech is perverse (Prov 19:1), and he is prone to make many rash promises (Eccl 5:1-6).

Heb. *sākāl* occurs most often in Ecclesiastes; the term seems to stand for one who is willfully stubborn or thickheaded, who has eyes but does not see (Jer 4:22; 5:21; Eccl 10:3), as in the case of King Saul (I Sam 13:13; 26:21). Because this word is also applied to other kings in their transgression (David, II Sam 24:10; Asa, II Chr 16:9; Solomon [?], Eccl 2:12, 13, 19), perhaps *sākāl* can connote foolishness at an official level with consequent greater guilt. Derek Kidner includes the simple (*pᵉtî*) and the scorner (*lēṣ*) in the general category of fools (*The Proverbs,* Tyndale Press, 1964, pp. 39-42).

In the NT (using Gr. *anoētos,* "thoughtless") Christ rebukes the two on the Emmaus road and Paul rebukes the Galatians for lack of faith (Lk 24:25; Gal 3:1, 3). This term also describes the senselessness of the desires and lusts which drag men down into perdition (I Tim 6:9; Tit 3:3).

Gr. *asunetos* denotes someone without understanding (Mt 15:16; Mk 7:18) and is used to depict the hearts or minds of the God-denying heathen (Rom 1:21, 31).

As the rich fool (*aphrōn*) came to an untimely end because he failed to take into account the will of God, so Paul urges Christians not to be foolish but to understand what the will of the Lord is (Lk 12:20; Eph 5:15-17). This fool is heedless (Lk 11:40), without reason, ignorant (I Pet 2:15), and needs to be corrected (Rom 2:20). Paul uses this term of himself in sarcastically going along with the Corinthians' estimate of him (II Cor 11:16, 19; 12:6, 11).

In I Cor 1:18, 21, 25, 27; 2:14 *mōros* and its derivatives seem to connote man's attitude toward something unusual that has no intellectual explanation or that does not fit in with one's preconceived ideas. In turn, those who try to get by in the spiritual realm on their human reasoning are called foolish in God's sight (I Cor 1:20; 3:19; Mt 23:17). Thus the five foolish virgins were dependent on their own natural understanding (Mt 25:2, 3, 8; see Georg Bertram, "*Moros,* etc.," TDNT, IV, 832-847).

In Mt 5:22 the expression "thou fool" (*mōre*) may be the only pure Heb. (i.e., not Aramaic) word in the NT. Heb. *môreh* is an impious rebel against God, and is the expression which Moses used when he lost his temper at the chiding Israelites (Num 20:10). Its use would imply a murderous hatred.

I. G. P. and J. R.

FOOLISHNESS. *See* Folly; Fool.

FOOT. Great care was necessarily given the feet during Bible times because of the dusty roads, the absence of hose, and the open design of the sandals. Thus the host would wash the feet of a visitor, and this became synonymous with hospitality (I Tim 5:10). Such a menial task, done voluntarily, was a sign of complete humility, as exemplified by Christ (Jn 13:4-15).

The untying of the shoe latchets (*q.v.*) may refer to this same practice (Mk 1:7; Lk 3:16; Jn 1:27). Shoes were generally left outside one's house as well as the house of God. Moses was told to "put off thy shoes from off thy feet" (Ex 3:5; Acts 7:33), and Moslems still believe contact with the common ground brings defilement. The provision of shoes for Israel in the wilderness showed God's protection (Deut 8:4; 29:5). Nakedness of the feet in public was a sign of mourning (Ezk 24:17). Because of the delicacy of the Heb. language, the word was used for the private parts. Such phrases include "the hair of the feet," "the water of the feet," "to cover the feet," etc.

Other uses of the word are: (1) stability, "He set my feet upon a rock" (Ps 40:2); (2) the place of a learner, "to sit at the feet" (Deut 33:3; Lk 10:39; Acts 22:3); (3) affliction or calamity (Ps 35:15; 38:16; Jer 20:10); (4) take possession, to set one's feet (Deut 1:36; 11:24); (5) subordination, "to be under one's feet" (Ps 8:6; Heb 2:8; I Cor 15:27); (6) complete destruction, "treading under foot" (Isa 18:7; Lam 1:15). "To water with the foot" (Deut 11:10) may imply that channels of irrigation were turned with ease, as with the foot.

Bibliography. Konrad Weiss, "*Pous,* etc.," TDNT, VI, 624-631.

E. C. J.

FOOTMAN. Footman was used of a military infantryman (Num 11:21; I Sam 4:10; 15:4). An alternate Heb. word used stresses the activity of running and has the general idea of a runner or courier (I Sam 22:17). That the footman was often a runner is derived from the statement in Jer 12:5.

FOOTSTEPS. Two Heb. words are so translated.

1. Heb. *ʿāqēb,* literally, "the heel"; hence "heelprint," figuratively, "footstep" (Ps 77:19; 89:51; Song 1:8).

2. Heb. *paʿam,* "footfall," the tread of the foot on the ground; hence footstep (Ps 17:5). The idea is that of stepping or striding.

FOOTSTOOL. Heb. *kebesh,* translated "footstool," simply means that which is walked or stepped on, hence a stool, literally, "a stool of the foot" (Heb. *hădôm regel*). In the description of Solomon's throne it is said that "there were six steps to the throne, with a footstool of gold" (II Chr 9:18).

Footstool is used figuratively especially as the place of God's feet, and refers to the temple which David planned to build for Him, and to the earth (I Chr 28:2; Ps 132:7; Isa 66:1). It is also applied to God's enemies as His footstool (Ps 110:1).

Gr. *hypopodion* means "what is under the foot." James uses it once (Jas 2:3) as a place to sit. Just as in the OT, it is also used in a metaphorical sense in Mt 5:35; 22:44, and parallel passages; Acts 2:35; 7:49; Heb 1:13; 10:13. Here it carries the idea of the subjection of those who are under God's feet.

A. E. T.

FOOT WASHING. Foot washing was a common custom in Eastern lands. The effect of dusty or muddy roads upon feet shod with open sandals made it customary for water and a basin to be available at the entry of homes. A slave or the visitor himself performed the washing (Gen 18:4), although the host might do so as a mark of special favor (I Sam 25:41). It was discourteous to neglect the practice (Lk 7:44).

The washing of the disciples' feet by Jesus (Jn 13:1-17) had a deeper significance. His remark to Peter that "what I do thou knowest not now" showed that Jesus' intention went beyond the well-known custom. Many hold that Jesus was giving a lesson in humility by His example. Humility was certainly displayed by the washer. Yet Jesus said that if He did not perform this act, it would be Peter and not He that would be at fault. Thus He must have been teaching something about Peter's need, not His own virtues.

That spiritual cleansing was basic to Christ's purpose is seen in Jn 13:10-11, where lack of cleansing is specified of Judas. All except Judas were said to have been bathed (*leloumenos*—complete bath), but they still needed to have their feet washed (*nipsasthai*—partial washing). The complete bath referred to salvation as symbolized in baptism. The washing of the feet depicted the need that even believers have for cleansing from defilement which comes from contact with a sinful world.

That Jesus intended this act to be perpetuated by the church may be inferred from Jn 13:14-15. The practice of the Pedilavium may be seen in the early church from I Tim 5:10, and from such patristic notices as Tertullian (*De Corona,* Chap. 8), Athanasius (*Canon 66*), and Augustine (*Letter to Januarius*). The Synod of Toledo (A.D. 694) specified that the rite should be observed on Maundy Thursday. It is still practiced by some Protestant groups, including Brethren, Mennonites, Waldensians, Winebrennarians, and a few Baptists.

For Jewish religious ritual washings *see* Ablution.

H. A. K.

FORBEARANCE. This noun translates the Gr. *anochē* in its two occurrences in the NT. The word literally means "holding back," "stopping" (especially hostilities), and thus was frequently used for an armistice or truce. In Rom 2:4 the delay in a just God's inflicting wrath or punishment on the sinner is explained by the truth of His goodness (or "kindness," RSV), forbearance, and long-suffering ("patience," RSV). This delay is to give opportunity for, and to lead the sinner to, repentance. In Rom 3:25 it is stated that God has passed over sins during the former dispensation(s) in His divine forbearance until the perfect substitutionary sacrifice should be offered by His Son Jesus Christ. This concept of God's forbearance is also found in Neh 9:30.

The related verb *anechomai* is translated by "forbear" in Eph 4:2; Col 3:13, where Christians are commanded to forbear one another in love, to make allowances for one another, because love "covers a multitude of sins" (I Pet 4:8).

Other Gr. and Heb. verbs translated as "forbear" have the sense "to stop," "to cease," "to refrain from." *See* Long-suffering.

J. R.

FORCES. A military term meaning an army or military force, resources, powers, or fortress. Examples of use meaning a military force are found in Jer 40:7, 13; 41:11, 13, 16; as resources, in Isa 60:5, 11 (ASV, RSV, "wealth"); and as fortifications, in Dan 11:38 (ASV, RSV, "fortresses").

FORD. Without bridges, fords in Bible times necessarily were places of easy passage across a river. In some instances, at least, fords were places not only for men and animals to wade across, but also for wagons or carts to be driven across. Two in Transjordan were the ford of the Jabbok—Wadi Zerqa (Gen 32:22), and the ford of the Arnon—Wadi Mojib (Isa 16:2). Other references to fords in nearly every instance are to crossing places of the Jordan. They are mentioned in connection with Joshua's spies (Josh 2:7), Ehud's victory over the Moabites (Jud 3:28), the Shibboleth incident (Jud 12:5-6), and David's flight (II Sam 15:28; 17:16—"fords of the wilderness," ASV, RSV). None of these crossings can be identified with certainty today, but they must be located somewhere in the lower stretch of the Jordan as it approaches and empties into the Dead Sea. II Sam 19:18 should probably be translated, "And they crossed the ford to bring over . . ." (RSV).

"Fords of Babylonia" (Jer 51:31-32, RSV) apparently refer to crossing places of the Euphrates and its canals.

H. E. Fi.

FOREFRONT. The front part of a building, a place, or a battle. The KJV and ASV translate several Heb. terms as "forefront"; *pānîm,* "face" (II Kgs 16:14; Ezk 40:19; 47:1), but KJV renders Ezk 40:15 as "face" (ASV, "forefront"); *mûl pānîm,* "before or over against the face" (Ex 26:9; 28:37); *rō'sh,* "head" (II Chr

20:27); and *shēn,* "tooth" (I Sam 14:5; ASV, "front"). The RSV usually renders the first two expressions as "front," while it translates *rō'sh* literally and *shēn* as "crag."

FOREHEAD. This term is used frequently in its literal sense. Aaron and the high priests after him wore on their foreheads a gold plate (Ex 28:36, 38). The condition of the forehead aided the priest in determining leprosy (Lev 13:42-43; II Chr 26:20). David hit the forehead of Goliath with a stone (I Sam 17:49). Although cutting the body was forbidden (Lev 19:28), ownership markings were placed on the foreheads of slaves or devotees of a godhead. Such ownership by Yahweh is seen in Ezk 9:4, 6 where the word "mark" is the last letter of the Heb. alphabet (in early times made in the form of a cross). In the NT, the foreheads of the righteous (Rev 7:3; 9:4; 14:1; 22:4) and of the godless followers of Satan (Rev 13:16-17; 14:9; 17:5; 20:4) are marked. However, in Ezk 16:12, the jewel is a nose ring, not an ornament in the forehead as in the KJV.

Figuratively, forehead is used for obstinance (Ezk 3:7-9), and shame (Jer 3:3).

E. C. J.

FOREIGNER. Broadly, a Gentile or non-Israelite. The word included all aliens, wherever they resided. Foreigners could not partake of the Passover (Ex 12:43), enter the sanctuary (Ezk 44:9), be chosen king (Deut 17:15), or intermarry with Israelites (Ex 34:15-16). However, foreigners could be received into Judaism through circumcision (Gen 17:27).

A stranger (in ASV usually "sojourner") was one not having full citizenship but living in an Israelite home, in contrast with a foreigner staying in Israel temporarily. Although not an Israelite, the stranger had certain rights and duties. God admonished His people to be kind to him. "For ye know the heart of a stranger, seeing ye were strangers in the land of Egypt" (Ex 23:9). *See* Hospitality.

Many privileges and prohibitions were his, but not all the religious duties. He was free from circumcision, if he so chose. He could, on invitation, attend sacrificial feasts (Deut 16:11, 14). He was permitted to sacrifice to the Lord in the atonement for sins of the congregation unwittingly committed. He had the privilege of a sin offering, and the protection of a city of refuge. By circumcision, he was allowed to partake of the Passover (Ex 12:48). In early OT times, marriages with foreigners were frequently made, though not sanctioned. Later Ezra and Nehemiah vigorously tried to prohibit any foreign marriages (Ezr 10; Neh 13:23-31).

In the NT, among the Jewish people, foreigners and strangers were usually grouped together as Gentiles (*q.v.*). Strict Jews did not eat and drink with Gentiles (Acts 11:3). Due to conditions existing during and following the Exile, an attitude of hatred and scorn developed between Jew and Gentile, which continued through the Christian era. Following the finished work of Christ on the cross, another group, the Church, is referred to in addition to the Jews and Gentiles. Full membership in the Church is open to all who will accept Christ's sacrifice on the cross for sin. "Now therefore ye are no more strangers and foreigners, but fellow citizens with the saints, and of the household of God" (Eph 2:19). *See* Proselyte.

Bibliography. K. L. and M. A. Schmidt and Rudolf Meyer, "*Paroikos,* etc.," TDNT, V, 841-853. Gustav Stählin, "*Xenos,* etc.," TDNT, V, 1-36.

L. A. L.

FOREKNOWLEDGE. *See* Election.

FOREORDINATION. *See* Election.

FORERUNNER. The English word "forerunner" is an exact translation of the Gr. *prodromos.* Forerunner is the term used of one sent ahead, either as a spy to reconnoiter for those who are to follow, or as a herald to prepare the way for a coming king.

Although John the Baptist was in truth the forerunner of Jesus (see Mal 3:1: "I will send my messenger, and he shall prepare the way before me"; cf. Mt 3:3 with Isa 40:3), the term "forerunner" is never used of him in Scripture. In its only use in the NT the word is applied to the Lord Himself. In Heb 6:20 He is described as our "forerunner" who has entered into the presence of God, preparing the way for us who by His grace are to follow (cf. Jn 14:2; Heb 10:19-20).

FORESHIP. The front part of a ship, the bow or prow. The KJV renders Acts 27:30 "as though they would have cast anchors out of the foreship," but in v. 41 the same Gr. word is translated "and the forepart stuck fast" (ASV, "foreship"). The RSV uses "bow" in both instances.

FORESKIN. The fold of skin (prepuce) removed from the male organ in circumcision *(q.v.),* as "a token of the covenant" between God and the Hebrews (Gen 17:11). David presented Saul with 200 Philistine foreskins as proof of their slaughter and of his prowess (I Sam 18:27). In Hab 2:16 it refers to indecent exposure, although the LXX and Syriac versions and the Qumran Habakkuk Commentary have a similar word meaning "stagger." It is used figuratively of the obstinacy of carnal man ("foreskin of the heart," Deut 10:16; Jer 4:4).

FORESKINS, HILL OF. A place near Gilgal where the rite of circumcision, neglected during the wilderness wanderings, was performed on the males of Israel (Josh 5:3).

FOREST. *See* Plants.

FORGIVENESS. The doctrine of forgiveness,

prominent in both the OT and NT, refers to the state or the act of pardon, remission of sin, or restoration of a friendly relationship. Central to the OT doctrine is the concept of covering of sin from the sight of God represented by the Heb. word *kāpar* (Ps 78:38; cf. Deut 21:8; Jer 18:23). This is indicated in the various translations of the word such as "appease," "be merciful," "make reconciliation," and the most prominent use in the expression "make atonement," occurring 70 times in the KJV. In Lev 4:20 it is coupled with another prominent OT word for forgiveness with the meaning "to send away or let go." Accordingly, in Lev 4:20 it is stated: "The priest shall make an atonement [from *kāpar*] for them, and it shall be forgiven [from *sālaḥ*] them." A third Heb. verb, *nā'sā'*, occurs frequently with the idea of "lifting up" or "lifting away" sin (Gen 50:17; Ex 10:17).

From these passages it is clear that forgiveness depends upon just payment of the penalty for sin. The OT sacrifices provided this typically, and prophetically looked forward to the final sacrifice of Christ (cf. Acts 17:30; Rom 3:25). Forgiveness as a relationship between God and man depends upon the divine attributes of righteousness, love, and mercy, and is based upon the work of God in providing a suitable sacrifice. *See* Atonement.

The doctrine of forgiveness anticipated in the OT has its fullest revelation in the NT. Here three principal words are used in the original: (1) *aphiēmi* and *aphesis,* meaning "to send away," "remission" (Mt 6:12, 14-15; 9:2, 5-6; etc.); (2) *charizomai,* meaning "to be gracious" (Lk 7:43; Eph 4:32; Col 2:13; 3:13); and (3) *apoluō,* meaning "to loose away" (Lk 6:37). In the NT forgiveness is a part of the whole program of salvation provided for those who believe in Christ. In forgiveness the guilt of sin is pardoned and replaced by justification in which the sinner is declared righteous. Forgiveness is always included in the whole work of God for the sinner, is basically judicial, and provides pardon for the sinner. *See* Justification; Reconciliation.

Another major aspect of NT revelation concerns Christians who sin. Though judicially forgiven all sin, past, present, and future, when saved by faith (Jn 3:18; 5:24; Col 2:13; Rom 8:1), if sin enters the life of a Christian it affects his relationship to his heavenly Father. The forgiveness or restoration to fellowship which is necessary is accomplished by confession of sin (I Jn 1:9) and repentance (Lk 17:3-4; 24:47; Acts 5:31). The divine side is cared for by the efficacy of Christ's death and intercession (I Jn 2:1) in which Christ pleads for the sinner on the ground of His own sacrifice. *See* Confession; Repentance.

Two special cases related to forgiveness are cited in the NT: (1) the sin unto death, i.e., sin of such character that God takes His sinning child home to glory and cuts short any opportunity for further sin or testimony (I Jn 5:16; cf. I Cor 11:30-32); (2) the unpardonable sin, defined as attributing the miraculous power of Christ to Satan rather than to the Holy Spirit (Mt 12:22-32; Mk 3:22-30). Technically, the unpardonable sin is impossible today as Christ is not performing miracles in the same way. However, all sin becomes unpardonable if an individual passes from this life without availing himself of divine grace.

Forgiveness is also an obligation in the relationship between men, and believers are exhorted to forgive one another (Eph 4:32; cf. Mt 6:12, 14).

Bibliography. J. O. Buswell, Jr., *A Systematic Theology of the Christian Religion,* Grand Rapids: Zondervan, 1962, II, 74-77, 128-131. Hugh R. Mackintosh, *The Christian Experience of Foregiveness,* London: Nisbet, 1947. W. C. Morro, "Forgiveness," ISBE, II, 1132-1135. Leon Morris, "Forgiveness," NBD, 435 f. John Owen, *The Forgiveness of Sin,* New York: American Tract Society, n.d. Vincent Taylor, *Forgiveness and Reconciliation,* London: Macmillan, 1958.

J. F. W.

FORK. Literally, a three-pronged fork, an agricultural tool on the order of a pitchfork, used once in KJV in an obscure passage (I Sam 13:21). ASV translates *mizreh* as "fork" (Isa 30:24; KJV, "fan"), while RSV renders *mazlēg* (I Sam 2:13-14) and *mizlāgâ* (Ex 27:3; 38:3; Num 4:14; I Chr 28:17; II Chr 4:16) as "fork," a utensil of the tabernacle and temple.

The "fan" of Mt 3:12 and Lk 3:17 (Gr. *ptuon*) was a "winnowing fork" (RSV). *See* Fan.

FORM *See* Image of God.

FORNICATION. Used of illicit sexual intercourse in general (Mt 5:32; 19:9; Acts 15:20, 29; 21:25; Rom 1:29; I Cor 5:1). In a technical sense it is to be distinguished from adultery or social promiscuity after marriage (Gr. *moicheia;* Mt 15:19; Mk 7:21; Jn 8:3; Gal 5:19), and from rape, which is a crime of violence without the agreement of the other party. *See* Adultery; Divorce; Harlot.

Fornication and adultery are used figuratively in the Bible to express the disloyalty of Israel to God when idolatry is in view (Jer 2:20-37; Ezk 16; Hos 1-3). The terms are all too fitting, however, because the idolatrous fertility cult worship of the Canaanites as well as of the Greeks (*see* Corinth) often involved fornication with sacred prostitutes or priestesses. In Rev 17 the idolatry of the final apostate church, formed by a merging of many religions, is likened to an adulterous woman because of the utter worldliness of the church and her synthesis with paganism through a form of pan-deism.

Bibliography. F. Hauck and S. Schultz, "*Pornē,* etc.," TDNT, VI, 579-595.

R. A. K.

FORT, FORTIFICATION, FORTRESS. The most ancient fortified site thus far discovered is the Palestinian city of Jericho, which *c.* 7000 B.C. was surrounded by a massive stone fortification strengthened in at least one place by a large stone tower. Other cities of Palestine are known to have been strongly fortified from the early Bronze Age, which began *c.* 3300 B.C. and encompassed the inception of the city-state system in Palestine, to the Roman period. The earliest builders tended to occupy easily defensible sites, fortifying their cities with walls. Fortifications generally followed the irregular outlines of the hills and spurs on which the cities were built.

During the Middle Bronze Age (*c.* 2100–1550 B.C.), fortifications became more elaborate and powerful than at any other time in Palestinian history. In connection with the Hyksos movements of this period, a new type of fortification appeared in Egypt and in Syro-Palestine. As enclosures for horse-drawn chariotry, great rectangular camps up to half a mile long were constructed. These were surrounded by enormous sloping ramparts of packed earth *(terre pisée)*. The best example of such a camp in Palestine is at Hazor. Slightly later, similar ramparts, this time made of brick and stone and coated with hard-packed clay or with lime plaster, were used to strengthen city walls. They served to prevent erosion as well as to discourage invaders from attempting to scale the walls. In addition they probably served as an effective defense against the newly introduced battering ram. Other Middle Bronze Age innovations included new methods of constructing walls, gates, and towers in such a way as to force an enemy soldier, on entering the city, to expose his unshielded side. Such techniques greatly increased the difficulty of approaching and storming city gates.

Canaanite cities of the Late Bronze Age (*c.* 1500–1200 B.C.) were well fortified (cf. the description *'ārîm beṣûrôt*, "walled" or "fenced cities," used of them, e.g., in Num 13:28; Deut 1:28; 3:5; 9:1). At the beginning of Iron Age I (*c.* 1200–900 B.C.), however, the construction of fortifications in Palestine suddenly deteriorated. The feudal organization of the Canaanites had been able to make effective use of the corvée in building operations, while the loosely organized Israelite amphictyony was powerless to coerce its workmen. In addition, however, the introduction of bonded masonry made the previous massive construction techniques less necessary; and, indeed, Saul's castle at Gibeah (modern Tell el-Ful), though crudely built, demonstrates that Israelites were capable of erecting strong and relatively large buildings by the end of the period of the judges (last half of 11th cen.). It was a fortress built of massive polygonal masonry measuring *c.* 170 by 115 feet and surrounded by a double casemated wall (apparently with a tower at each of the four corners).

The casemate fortifications at Beth-shemesh

The King's Gate in the massive fortification walls at Boghazkoy, capital of the Hittite Empire. The gate is recessed in the wall and the walls are double, requiring a double gate. HFV

and Debir (modern Tell Beit Mirsim) can be confidently attributed to David. After capturing Jerusalem from the Jebusites, he proceeded to fortify it (David's Jerusalem is referred to as a "stronghold" in II Sam 5:9 [*meṣûdâ*] and I Chr 11:7 [*meṣād*]). Solomon, the great builder of united Israel, likewise shared in strengthening the fortified cities (cf. II Chr 8:5) of this period. Notable are the results of his labors still visible at Hazor, Gezer, and Megiddo. Defenses uncovered at Azekah (one of the "fortified cities" of Judah mentioned in Jer 34:7) and Mareshah have been attributed to Rehoboam (cf. the imposing list of "fortified cities" preserved in II Chr 11:5–10).

In the Transjordan region, many remains of Iron Age I fortifications have been discovered in recent years. Edomites and Moabites alike guarded their borders with fortresses (cf. the Moabite "strongholds" of Jer 48:18). The remains of the characteristic round tower forts of the Ammonites during the same period are often designated by the Arabic term *rujm el-malfûf* ("circular heap"). Transjordanian fortresses were commonly so situated that from each one those nearest on both sides were visible.

The best example of Iron Age II (*c.* 900–550 B.C.) fortifications in Palestine thus far excavated is the massive double wall of Tell en-Nasbeh (biblical Mizpah?) with its plastered revetment and well-preserved gate. The Judahite fortifications at this site witness to the ill will, not infrequently erupting into civil war, that obtained between Israel and Judah after Solomon's death. During this period Israel "built palaces" and Judah "multiplied fortified cities" (Hos 8:14, RSV).

Information regarding Iron Age III (*c.* 550–330 B.C.) fortifications is relatively scarce because of lack of physical remains, although Nehemiah restored the walls of Jerusalem during this period. Later strengthening of strategic Palestinian communities was stimulated by the Maccabean struggle for independence (cf., e.g., the remains of the Beth-zur fortress and those of the castle of Alexander Jannaeus on Qarn Sartabeh overlooking the Jordan Valley).

The arrival of the Romans in Palestine introduced changes in military architecture that sacrificed esthetic value for the sake of efficiency. The ruins of characteristically square Roman camps are observable throughout Palestine with many examples to be found in the Transjordan region. The most important of the massive fortifications of this period were constructed by Herod the Great, including particularly his fortress residence at Jerusalem and the Castle of Antonia (located at the NW corner of the temple area). He strengthened the defenses of Samaria (modern Sebaste) as well. His later namesake, Herod Agrippa I, is generally thought to be responsible for the so-called third wall of Jerusalem.

Since the nation of Israel was essentially and ideally a theocracy (cf. Ps 118:9, ASV), the OT emphasizes that true strength is found not in fortifications but in the Lord (Jer 5:17; Hos 8:14). Indeed, God is called a *mā'ôz* ("strength," "refuge") in II Sam 22:33; Prov 10:29; Isa 25:4; Jer 16:19; Joel 3:16; Nah 1:7; a *m^eṣûdâ* ("fortress," "stronghold") in II Sam 22:2; and a *miśgāb* ("high tower," "retreat") in 22:3. All three terms are also used of Him often in the Psalms. The character of Jeremiah resembled the unyielding nature of military defenses (Jer 1:18; 15:20), while Paul, in his well-known metaphor in II Cor 10:4, used the Gr. word *ochýrōma* ("stronghold") in reference to the vaunted arguments used by men to oppose the knowledge of God.

For descriptions of Assyrian, Babylonian, and Roman systems of fortifications *see* Babylon; Calah; Nineveh; Rome.

See also Bulwark; Citadel; City, Fenced; Gate; Tower; Wall.

Bibliography. Millar Burrows, *What Mean These Stones?* London: Thames and Hudson, 1957, pp. 97–104. Roland de Vaux, *Ancient Israel,* trans. by J. McHugh, New York: McGraw-Hill, 1961, pp. 229–236. Yigael Yadin, "Hyksos Fortifications and the Battering Ram," BASOR 137 (Feb., 1955), pp. 23–32; *The Art of Warfare in Biblical Lands,* 2 vols., New York: McGraw-Hill, 1963.

R. Y.

FORTUNATUS (fôr-tū-nā'tŭs). Mentioned but once (I Cor 16:17), Fortunatus is connected with two other men who, presumably, came from Corinth to Paul at Ephesus. The three are spoken of as having ministered to Paul in some way, and Paul uses this fact to administer a gentle rebuke to the Corinthian believers in general. He writes: "That which was lacking on your part they have supplied." Paul was evidently cheered by their coming.

FORUM. When mention is made of the forum, one usually thinks of the Imperial Forum at Rome. But every Roman city had a forum (roughly the equivalent of a Gr. agora), and some eastern cities (e.g., Athens) had a Roman agora or forum near the old Gr. agora. Moreover, near the Imperial Forum in Rome, Julius Caesar, Augustus, Nerva, Domitian, and Trajan built additional fora, as commercial and other needs demanded more space. The forum in every Roman city was the very hub of its life. *See* Agora; Market; Rome.

The Imperial Forum in Rome was bounded by the Palatine, Quirinal, Esquiline, and Capitoline hills. It was located where paths running down the valleys between the hills of Rome met. The Forum grew as Rome grew and was rebuilt from time to time. The area was drained by the Etruscans during the 6th cen. B.C. and became the political, religious, social, and economic center of Rome. As Rome grew, the more objectionable features of Roman business were removed from the Forum first. The

A reconstruction of the Castle of Antonia. Sisters of Zion, Jerusalem.

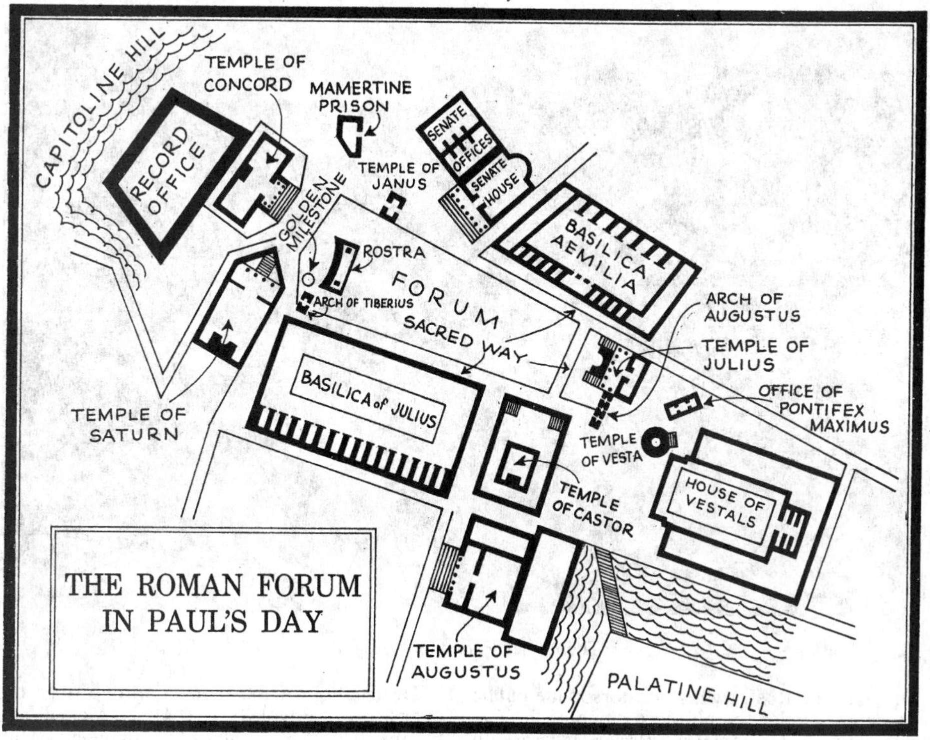

The Roman Forum in Paul's Day

smells of the fish market and the tumult of the vegetable market were removed about 300 B.C. In the early days there was no particular plan; the Forum was just a cluster of buildings. From about 200 B.C. to the time of Augustus a considerable amount of regularization took place. Augustus and Tiberius (about the time of Christ) gave the Forum its final ground plan but not its final buildings.

During these 200 years temples were rebuilt on a larger and more monumental scale and tended to take over the Gr. style. In addition, the Romans introduced the basilica, probably from Syria, with its large central hall and narrow side aisles. The Basilica Aemilia, the earliest in Rome, was built in the Forum *c.* 170 B.C. The Basilica Julia was started by Julius Caesar and finished by Augustus. The Romans used basilicas as law courts and business centers.

The Imperial Forum began to go out of regular use in the 5th and 6th cen. after Christ. During the medieval and early modern periods the area was used as a stone quarry. Stones found a use as building blocks as far away as Westminster Abbey in London.

As noted, the Forum was subjected to frequent reconstruction. Thus, effort is required to sort out the main buildings standing there when, for instance, the apostle Paul appeared before Nero. If he had entered the Forum on the Sacred Way from the E, he would have passed the large house of the vestal virgins, W of which was the Temple of Vesta. Vesta was the goddess of the hearth and was considered the patron of the fire that symbolized the perpetuity of the state. It was the responsibility of the priestesses to maintain this sacred fire and renew it annually on the first day of the year.

Just in front of the Temple of Vesta was the Regia or official residence of the head of the state religion. Next the apostle would have walked alongside the Temple of the Divine Julius (Caesar). When Paul came to the corner of the temple, the Sacred Way turned left, passed in front of the Temple of Julius and led straight to the steps of the Temple of Castor and Pollux. There the Sacred Way turned right again and passed the Basilica Julia, where Paul may have stood trial before Caesar (II Tim 4:16 f.).

As with municipal fora of Italy, so the Roman Forum was built up at one end. In Rome the W end dominated. Here on the Capitoline hill was a temple to Jupiter and at lower levels temples to Saturn and Concord. Before the lat-

The Roman Forum today. HFV

ter stood the Rostra where orators made public speeches. Under the northern slope of the Capitoline was the Mamertine Prison, where Paul was probably incarcerated (II Tim 1:16 f.; 2:9; 4:6). On the N side of the Forum stood the Senate chambers and the Basilica Aemilia.

H. F. V.

FORUM APPII. *See* Appii Forum.

FOUNDATION. Literally, the base or structure upon which a building or some object rests, as the foundation of the temple (II Chr 8:16), the base of the altar (Ex 29:12), the substratum of a mountain (Deut 32:22), a city (I Kgs 16:34) or its walls (Ezr 4:12). The Heb. *yāsad,* with its derivatives, and the Gr. *katabolē* are frequently used figuratively. Thus the term may refer to the security of the righteous described as "an everlasting foundation" (Prov 10:25), or to the frailty of man "whose foundation is in the dust" (Job 4:19). Temporally, it describes the beginning of the world; e.g., "the foundation of the world" (Mt 25:34; Eph 1:4); and poetically, the invisible foundational structure of the heavens (II Sam 22:8) and the earth (Ps 104:15).

Christ is designated in both Testaments as a "foundation" (Isa 28:16; I Cor 3:11). In the NT the term is used figuratively in reference to the first principles of the gospel (Heb 6:1-2); the teachings of the prophets and apostles (Eph 2:20); the eternal city (Heb 11:10; Rev 21:14); election (Eph 1:4; II Tim 2:19); the Christian life (I Cor 3); and is the subject of parables (Lk 6:48-49; 14:25 ff.).

Destruction of the foundation describes the overthrow of Egypt (Ezk 30:4), the wicked man by the figure of a house's foundation (Hab 3:13), and false prophets by the illustration of a wall (Ezk 13:14).

H. E. Fr.

FOUNDER. *See* Occupations: Goldsmith, Metal, Workers in, Refiner, Silversmith.

FOUNTAIN

1. A source of flowing water; a spring. This is to be distinguished from a well dug into the earth, or a cistern. One of the principal Heb. words translated "fountain" is *'ayin,* which also means "eye." In its compound form of *en (q.v.)* this word occurs in the names of many Palestinian cities, as En-rimmon (Neh 11:29); for Palestine, unlike Egypt, abounded in springs (Deut 8:7; 11:10). The Heb. *mabbûa'* has the idea of bubbling forth or gushing, as in Isa 35:7 where it is translated "springs."

2. A source of something other than literal water. The Heb. *māqôr* is often used this way. Thus is found the "fountain of life" (Ps 36:9), "of Israel" (Ps 68:26), "of her blood" (Lev 20:18). In Prov 16:22 and 18:4 it is translated "wellspring." The Gr. *pēgē* denotes both a spring of literal water (Jas 3:11-12) as well as the source of something else (Mk 5:29; Rev 21:6).

C. J. W.

FOUNTAIN GATE. *See* Jerusalem: Gates and Towers 11.

West end of the Roman Forum reconstructed.

FOWL. *See* Animals, III, 14.

FOWLER. In biblical times a fowler caught birds with snares. One kind of snare was a net *(reshet)* that pinned the bird to the ground (Hos 7:12). Another kind, called a gin, sprang up to cast a noose about a bird's neck (*môqēsh* in Amos 3:5*a*). Yet others, with doors or jaws which sprang shut when a bait was taken, have been found in Palestine and Egypt (*paḥ*, Ps 124:7; Amos 3:5*b*).

The action of a fowler in laying a snare has been used in the Bible in many different ways to illustrate the influence of evil persons and evil ways. In Jer 5:26 it is applied to wicked men that plot against others. In Jud 2:3 the worship of heathen gods is called a snare to Israel. In I Sam 18:21 Saul is said to have thought that the influence of his daughter Michal would be a snare for David. In II Sam 22:6 David spoke of the intention of his enemies as snares of death. In Prov 18:7 the lips of a fool are called "the snare of his soul." In I Tim 6:9 Paul said, "They that are minded to be rich fall into a temptation and a snare" (ASV).

See Snare.

J. W. W.

FOX *See* Animals, II.14.

FRANKINCENSE. *See* Incense; Plants: Frankincense.

FRAUD. *See* Crime and Punishment; Law.

FRAY. Literally, "to tremble, frighten, trouble," it is an archaic English word used in Deut 28:26; Jer 7:33; Zech 1:21. It is translated "frighten" in ASV and RSV in the first two references, and as "terrify" in the last.

FREEDOM. Freedom is exemption or release of one personality from domination by or obligation to another. The concept appears frequently in the Bible, especially in the passages dealing with the laws of slavery under the Mosaic regime, and also in the Pauline epistles, where the term is applied to individual spiritual life. When Abraham commissioned his servant to find a

The Peirene Fountain at Corinth. HFV

wife for Isaac, he required him to swear that he would not take Isaac back to the land from which Abraham had come, but that he would persuade the woman of his choice to come to Isaac. If the woman refused, the servant would be freed from his pledge (Gen 24:8, 41). To be free meant that the servant would not be expected to continue the search, but could consider his commission discharged.

Political freedom. Theory of government is not discussed at any length in the Bible. Autocratic rule prevailed in the time when it was written, but the germ of freedom can be found in the Christian revelation. In Paul's colloquy with the Roman colonel in charge of the garrison at Jerusalem, the latter said that he had bought his citizenship for a high price. Paul proudly affirmed that he was Roman born (Acts 22:28). Political freedom was usually inherited from one's ancestors, and was the privilege of the upper classes. It was an inalienable right unless some legal complications were involved.

Social freedom. Every member of the Jewish commonwealth was a free man except for captives of war who were made slaves, and for those who voluntarily sold themselves in order to pay a debt. Under the OT law a slave was usually freed upon completion of six years' service (Ex 21:2-6; Deut 15:12). When the slave had paid for his freedom by his labor, he was released to enter upon his own career.

Spiritual freedom. Freedom in the Bible is connected chiefly with the concept of liberation from sin. Jesus stated that every man who commits sin is the slave of sin, and that he can be freed only by the intervention of the Son of God who is able to break sin's yoke (Jn 8:32-36). The operation of the new life of the Spirit can deliver man from the depressing law of sin and death, and can engender the hope of ultimate liberation from the corruption that follows sin (Rom 8:2, 21). This freedom is not the product of legalism, but of faith (Gal 4:23-31).

Freedom, however, is not license, but is manifested in love (Gal 5:13). It is the voluntary operation of the will which motivates men to fulfill the purpose of God. To do right because it satisfies one's deepest desire is freedom.

The freedom of the human will is recognized by the Bible, though it is not discussed philosophically. It predicates the ability to choose one of two or more alternatives without external compulsion. God is also free; He may choose to do whatever He wishes (Dan 4:35). Because God is infinite personality and because man is finite, the freedom of man lies within the circle of the freedom of God. Man may at any moment decide to accept or to reject the alternative which that moment offers, but he cannot choose to avoid the consequences of his choice, nor can he refuse to respond to the alternative. To refuse to choose is in itself a choice. Furthermore, every choice modifies all subsequent choices. An act may be repudiated or counteracted, but it can never be recalled or undone. Man's freedom, then, is circumscribed by his previous acts in time, since the past affects the present. Because the present affects the future, apart from the intervention of God, man lives in an ever-narrowing circle of cause and effect, which must finally bind him completely.

Man has sinned, and the horizon of his freedom is consequently limited. He may choose whether or not he will commit some particular sin, but he cannot choose whether or not he will be a sinner. He can only acknowledge the fact, and accept the deliverance which God can provide. He may have the freedom to refuse it, but not to avoid the consequences of his refusal.

God enjoys perfect freedom because He is never under the necessity of acting contrary to His own nature. No external compulsion can have any effect on Him, because He created the universe and is sovereign over it. As the Absolute Good, He is superior to all obligation or coercion.

Because God is completely righteous, He is not limited by the restraint of evil. He is free to exercise His creative and redemptive powers as He sees fit at any time, and whatever He does must ultimately eventuate in good for all concerned. There can be no real conflict between the moral responsibility of man and the sovereign will of God, since the constitution of the universe, which embraces the option of moral choice, is established by divine decree. God has created the world with the possibility of freedom because it is an essential part of His nature. Although man's freedom is circumscribed by finiteness, it is no less genuine than that of God, who is infinite. Within the sphere allotted to man, he is free.

This freedom, however, has been seriously curtailed by sin. The evils that have been produced by the wrong choices of the past handicap the full exercise of free will, not because God has arbitrarily so ruled, but because in an ordered universe liberty can survive only within law. Liberty is not synonymous with chaos. In order to restrain evil, and to keep it from enslaving the world permanently, God must intervene by redemption. He retains the prerogative of final decision.

Both the freedom of man and the sovereignty of God are presented in scriptural revelation, often in the same or contiguous passages. Freedom is contingent upon abiding in the work of Christ, which involves an act of the will (Jn 8:31-32), but freedom is a gift of God, who alone possesses it fully (Jn 8:36).

See Example; Liberation; Liberty.

Bibliography. Heinrich Schlier, "*Eleutheros,* etc.," TDNT, II, 487-502.

M. C. T.

FREEDOM, YEARS OF. *See* Festivals; Jubilee.

FREEMAN. The KJV does not use "freeman" in the OT. The RSV, however, so translates the

Heb. word *ḥôrîm* ("free born, nobles" in Eccl 10:17, ASV marg.). In the NT *apeleutheros* (I Cor 7:22) refers to a freed slave, and in this particular reference, to one who has received spiritual freedom, while *eleutheros* (Gal 4:22-23, 30; Rev 6:15) concerns a free man as contrasted with a slave. *See* Freedom.

FREEWILL OFFERING. *See* Sacrificial Offering.

FRIEND, FRIENDSHIP. Two OT words, Heb. *rēaʻ* (and its derivatives), "friend," "neighbor," "companion"; and *'ōhēb* (participle of *'āhab,* "to love"), "lover," "beloved friend"; and two NT words, Gr. *hetairos,* "comrade," "neighbor," "friend"; and *philos,* "beloved friend," refer to comrades and close friends. Thus both the OT and the NT have words for a mere friend and one for a deeply affectionate friend.

The Bible speaks of two kinds of friendship: (1) between man and God in the case of Abraham (II Chr 20:7; Isa 41:8; Jas 2:23) and Moses (Ex 33:11); (2) between man and man, such as that between David and Hushai (II Sam 15:37; 16:16), between Elijah and Elisha (II Kgs 2), and between David and Jonathan, which is the most famous case of friendship in Scripture, a love that was "wonderful, passing the love of women" (I Sam 18:1; II Sam 1:26). There is one outstanding example between women, namely, that of Ruth with her mother-in-law Naomi (Ruth 1:16-18).

Solomon spoke many words of wisdom about friendship, such as: "A friend loveth at all times" (Prov 17:17); "Faithful are the wounds of a friend" (Prov 27:6); "There is a friend that sticketh closer than a brother" (Prov 18:24); and "Make no friendship with an angry man" (Prov 22:24).

The relationship experienced between Christ and the Twelve developed from that of teacher to disciple, through that of Lord to servant (Jn 13:13), into that of friend to friend (Jn 15:13-15). Judas, called "mine own familiar friend" (Ps 41:9), is the terrible example of an unfaithful friend (Mt 26:14-16).

R. A. K.

FRINGE. One of three symbols (the others were phylacteries and cylinders containing a parchment scroll attached to the door posts) that continually confronted the Jew, reminding him of the Lord's commandments. Four blue (white was permitted later) fringes of woven cords with tassels were to be attached to the four corners of the Jew's outer garment (Num 15:38-39; Deut 22:12). Jesus condemned the Pharisees (Mt 23:5) who, to be seen by men, made their fringes long.

FROG. *See* Animals, VI,15.

FRONTLETS. Israel was told that the great redemption wrought for them by God in Egypt and the word of God revealed to them by Moses was to be laid up in their hearts and souls. It was never to be forgotten but was to be ever before them, like "frontlets," i.e., a band or ribbon about the head and before the eyes (Ex 13:16; Deut 6:8; 11:18; JerusB, "circlet"). In later days this symbolic representation was taken literally by the Jews. Strips of parchment or papyrus were inscribed with passages from Scripture, placed in a small leather box and bound with thongs to the forehead (Mt 23:5). *See* Phylactery. By this literal, outward observation, the great spiritual need and obligation was neglected and God's Word lost its proper place in Israel's heart.

See Dress.

FROST. Frost is common in the higher areas of Palestine during the winter and may damage early crops and fruits (Ps 78:47; Heb. *ḥănāmāl*). Hoarfrost (Heb. *kᵉpôr*) is referred to in Ex 16:14; Job 38:29; Ps 147:16; Sir 43:19. It is the term for small ice needles which form during a cold, still night. The Heb. word *qeraḥ* in Jer 36:30 is translated "ice" in Job 37:10 by ASV and RSV, and "cold" in Gen 31:40 by RSV.

FROWARD. The translation in the KJV of several Heb. words signifying "contrary," "perverse," "subversive," etc. Heb. *hăphakpak* ("devious," Prov 21:8, JerusB) and *tahpukôt* ("mutinous," Deut 32:20, NEB; "perverse," "perverted," Prov 2:12, 14; 6:14; 8:13; 10:31-32; 16:28; 23:33, RSV) are derived from *hāphak,* "to turn, overturn," and emphasize an obstinate persistence in turning away from or overthrowing what is right or good. Heb. *'iqqēsh* ("twisted," Prov 2:15, JeruB; "crooked," Ps 18:26; Prov 17:20, RSV) and *'iqqᵉshût* ("crooked speech," Prov 4:24; 6:12, RSV) describe an evil man or thing as something crooked or twisted out of shape, not aligned with God's ways. Other words rendered "froward" also bring out the devious nature and stubborn depravity of fallen mankind.

FRUIT. The product of many plants and trees. Those most frequently mentioned in Scripture are grapes, figs, and olives, all of which are still grown in Palestine today. *See* individual entries under Plants.

Figurative. The term "fruit" is often used symbolically. Children are referred to as fruit (Ex 21:22; Ps 21:10) in such phrases as "the fruit of the womb" (Ps 127:3; Deut 7:13; Lk 1:42) and "the fruit of the body" (Ps 132:11; Mic 6:7). Praise is poetically described as "the fruit of the lips" (Isa 57:19; cf. Heb 13:15), and a man's words are called "the fruit of the mouth" (Prov 12:14; 18:20).

The term "fruit" is applied to the consequences of our actions and motives. "They shall eat the fruit of their doings" (Prov 1:31; Isa 3:10). "The fruit of wickedness" is the judgment incurred from wrong action (Jer 6:19; 21:14); and "the fruit of righteousness" is the good works that spring from the heart of a godly man (Phil 1:11). "The fruit of the Spirit" are the gracious habits and principles which the Holy Spirit produces in a Christian (Gal 5:22–23; Eph 5:9). Thus in this sense "fruit" may be said to be the total result that issues from any specific action or attitude. The fruit may be evil (Mt 3:10; 7:15–20; 12:33; Lk 6:43–46; Rom 7:5), but more often it is good (Ps 104:13; Mt 3:8; 21:43; Rom 7:4; Jas 3:17).

The disciples were urged to "bear fruit" (Mk 4:20; Col 1:10; Jn 15:4–8), and were criticized for being spiritually unfruitful (Mk 4:19; Tit 3:14; II Pet 1:8; cf. I Cor 14:14).

J. R.

FRYING PAN. A vessel in which the meal offering was cooked (Lev 2:7; 7:9), more properly a deep-fat pan or kettle. The pan used by Tamar (II Sam 13:9) was probably a frying pan.

FUEL. In the KJV, "fuel" stands for two Heb. words both meaning "food"; in these cases, food for fire (Ezk 15:4, 6; 21:32; Isa 9:5, 19). Fuel in biblical times was wood, charcoal (KJV, "coals" in Prov 26:21; also in Isa 44:12; 54:16 for the fire of the metalworker), perhaps chaff (Mt 3:12), and dry hay (Mt 6:30). For cooking, thorns might be used (Ps 58:9; Eccl 7:6), and in cities suffering from shortages during seige, animal and even human excrement was used (II Kgs 6:25; Ezk 4:12, 15).

FUGITIVE. A translation of five Heb. words with varying shades of meaning. The Heb. *bārîaḥ* means "one who flees or escapes" (Isa 15:5), as does *mibrāḥ* (Ezk 17:21); *nûa'* means "a roamer," "rover," "wanderer" (Gen 4:12, 14); *nōpēl,* "a deserter" (II Kgs 25:11), and likewise *pālît* (Jud 12:4). *See* Cities of Refuge.

FULFILL. *See* Prophecy, Fulfillment of.

FULLER. *See* Occupations.

FULLER'S FIELD. A well-known landmark of Hezekiah's day, just outside the city, near enough for the embassy of Sennacherib to be heard on the walls of Jerusalem. The uncertain site was near a conduit of the upper pool (II Kgs 18:17; Isa 36:2), probably near the Gihon spring in the Kidron Valley. Isaiah and his son met Ahaz here (Isa 7:3). The fuller's trade (*see* Occupation) required a water supply and ample area for drying the washed materials. *See* Field.

FULLER'S SOAP. *See* Occupations: Fuller.

FULNESS. The Gr. term *plērōma,* "fulness," that which has been filled, is used in Scripture in at least six ways.

1. *Time.* When the time had come and things were ready in God's plan: "When the fulness of the time was come, God sent forth his Son, made of a woman, made under the law" (Gal 4:4).

2. *History of the Gentiles.* The "fulness of the Gentiles," namely, the completion of God's plan to give the gospel specially to the Gentiles in the Church Age (Rom 11:25; cf. Lk 21:24).

3. *The deliverance of the kingdom by the Son to the Father.* This is called the "dispensation of the fulness of times" in Eph 1:10, in the sense that it covers the complete work of Christ in subduing all things to Himself. It closes with Christ delivering up the consummated kingdom of God to the Father (I Cor 15:24–28).

4. *Fulness of Israel.* This occurs with the regrafting of Israel into the true olive tree and the marvelous salvation of all that nation, at the second coming of Christ (Rom 11:12, 26–29; cf. Isa 66:8–9; Zech 12:10 ff.).

5. *Fulness of Christ.* The presence of the whole divine nature and of all the attributes of God in Jesus Christ (Jn 1:16; Col 1:19). "For in him dwelleth all the fulness of the Godhead bodily" (Col 2:9). So "Christ is, in a unique and complete sense, the incarnation of God Himself. Thus it is (Eph 4:10) that He fills all things" (C. F. D. Moule, "Pleroma," IDB, III, 827). In Eph 4:13 the "fulness of Christ" must mean that completeness, that maturity already realized in Christ Himself.

6. *Christ's sufficiency for us.* The complete sufficiency of Christ in His ministry of redemption and salvation so that believers are seen as "complete [*peplērōmenoi*] in him" (Col 2:10). The perfect tense of the Gr. passive participle indicates that positionally true Christians have already been made complete, with the result that they always shall be filled or completed in Christ. For "from His fulness we have, all of us, received – yes, grace in return for grace" (Jn 1:16, JerusB), i.e., "a grace answering to the grace (that is in Christ)." By experiencing the love of Christ we become filled with all the fulness of God (Eph 3:19).

Bibliography. Gerhard Delling, "*Plērēs,* etc.," TDNT, VI, 283–311.

R. A. K. and J. R.

FUNERAL. A funeral is the performance of cial rites for the dead, especially in the presence of the body and preceding burial or cremation. In Palestine in biblical times few burials were accompanied by elaborate services. Burial (*q.v.*) was performed as soon as possible after death, because of ceremonial defilement of the living and for practical considerations. Where the temperature was often high and no embalming was practiced, decomposition of the body occurred rapidly (*see* Embalm). It was customary to bury the body within a few hours after death. Consequently there was a lack of ceremony in burial. (See CornPBE, pp. 338–346.)

Though a number of burials are mentioned in

the Bible, the word "funeral" does not appear in the English versions. The account of Ananias and Sapphira illustrates the simplicity of burial and the shortness of the interval between death and interment. When Ananias died, the young men wrapped him, probably using the garments he wore, and carried him out and buried him (Acts 5:6). His wife was not even informed of what had happened. Some three hours later she came in, and within minutes she too died and shortly was buried beside her husband (Acts 5:10).

Often a procession escorted the corpse to its resting place. The funeral procession of Jacob was impressive for size, because Jacob was the father of the vizier of Egypt (cf. Gen 50:4–14, esp. vv. 7–9). A much more simple procession is mentioned in Lk 7:12, where the only son of a widow of Nain was being carried to his grave, accompanied by his mother and a large crowd from the town (cf. II Sam 3:31). Ordinarily a coffin was not used; the body was borne on a bier and placed directly into the tomb or grave (*see* Grave; Tomb). The funeral of Asa, king of Judah, was exceptional; he was laid on a bier filled with spices and a great fire was made in his honor (II Chr 16:14).

Funeral services in other parts of the ancient Near East were often quite elaborate, those of Egypt particularly so, because of the importance of funerary beliefs in Egyptian religion (see Montet, *Everyday Life in Egypt,* pp. 300–301).

See Dead, The; Mourning.

C. E. D.

FURLONG. *See* Weights, Measures, and Coins.

FURNACE. The English word "furnace" translates several Heb. and one Gr. word. Some of these refer to firepots used to bake bread or provide heat in dwelling houses; others to smelting furnaces in which metal is refined, or to kilns where bricks, pottery, etc., are hardened.

In a few passages the term is used literally; e.g., Dan 3 where three Heb. youths were thrown into a furnace used by the Babylonians for capital punishment, and Ex 9:8, 10 in which Moses was commanded to sprinkle "handfuls of ashes of the furnace" in connection with the sixth judgment on Egypt.

More often, however, the word is used as a figure of speech: (1) as a symbol of God Himself in His glory, holiness, and wrath (Gen 15:17; Ex 19:18; Isa 31:9); (2) as a symbol of intense suffering viewed as a refining process (Deut 4:20; I Kgs 8:51; Isa 48:10; Jer 11:4; Ezk 22:18, 20, 22); (3) as a simile to describe a fierce conflagration (Gen 19:28); (4) as a simile to depict the absolute purity of the Word of God (Ps 12:6); (5) as a graphic picture of the awfulness of the place of future punishment of wicked men (Mt 13:42, 50).

G. C. L.

FURNACES, TOWER OF. *See* Jerusalem: Gates and Towers 8.

FURNITURE. Cooking equipment and bed mats constituted the furniture of the very poor, the furnishings increasing with the wealth of the owners. Elisha's guest chamber was one of the better equipped rooms (II Kgs 4:10). The palaces contained costly and luxurious furniture (Est 1:6).

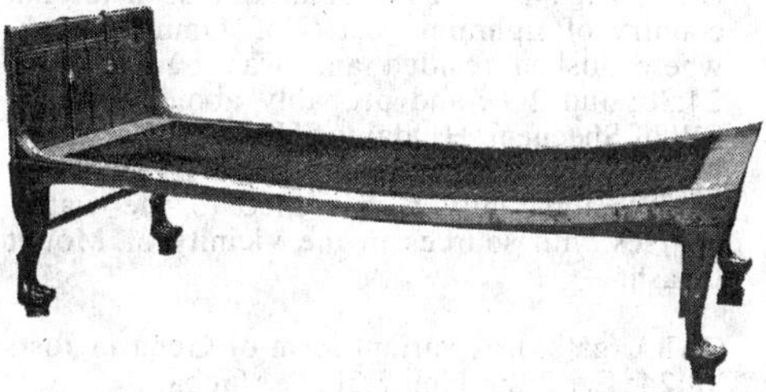

Wooden bedstead covered with thick sheet gold with mesh of string from tomb of Tutankhamon. LL

The term "furniture" (Heb. *kelî*) in the OT, with only one exception, refers to the brazen altar, laver, table of showbread, altar of incense, lampstand, and ark of the covenant of the tabernacle (*q.v.;* Ex 31:7–9; 35:14; 39:33). In Nah 2:9 the reference is to furniture in the palace of Nineveh. In Gen 31:34 "furniture" (*kar*) refers to the saddle of Rachel's camel.

FURROW. A shallow incision made by a plow (*q.v.*). Three different Heb. words are translated "furrow": (1) *telem,* "ridge, furrow" (Job 31:38; 39:10; Hos 10:4; 12:11); (2) *gedûd,* "cut, gash" (Ps 65:10); (3) *ma'ănāh* (Ps 129:3), figurative use of "furrow." ASV and RSV translate I Sam 14:14, "half a furrow's length."

Two other Heb. words are rendered "furrow" in the KJV: *'ônāh* (Hos 10:10), which is probably better understood as "transgressions" (see ASV) and "iniquity" (RSV); and *'ărûgāh* (Ezk 17:7, 10), "bed" in ASV and RSV.

FURY. Used particularly to express the burning anger and rage of man (Gen 27:44; II Sam 11:20; Est 1:12; 2:1); of the he-goat in Daniel's vision (Dan 8:6); and of God (Lev 26:28; Isa 42:25; 51:17 ff.; Jer 4:4; 10:25; Ezk 5:13; Zech 8:2). *See* Anger.

FUTURE LIFE *See* Life; Immortality.

G

GAAL (gā′*ăl*). Son of Ebed, evidently a Canaanite, and leader of a roving band of his relatives similar to the bands of Habiru mentioned frequently in the Amarna letters (*q.v.*). He organized a revolt of the Shechemites against Abimelech's rule, but was defeated outside the city as he and his rebels sallied forth to fight Abimelech and his approaching army. Zebul, the lieutenant-governor of Shechem, barred the gate to Gaal and his fleeing brethren as they sought refuge within the city walls (Jud 9:26–41).

GAASH (gā′ăsh). A hill or mountain in the hill country of Ephraim, just S of Timnath-serah, where Joshua resided and was buried (Josh 24:30; Jud 2:9), and probably about 20 miles SW of Shechem. Hiddai (or Hurai) was a native of "the brooks of Gaash" (II Sam 23:30; I Chr 11:32), apparently a reference to the water-courses with sources in the vicinity of Mount Gaash.

GABA (gā′*bȧ*). A variant form of Geba in Josh 18:24; Ezr 2:26; Neh 7:30. *See* Geba.

GABBAI (găb′ī; "tax collector," "exactor of tribute"). A prominent Benjamite among a tenth of the people selected to reside in Jerusalem after the Babylonian Captivity (Neh 11:8).

GABBATHA (găb′*ȧ*-th*ȧ*). An Aramaic term for what in Gr. was called *lithostrōtos*. The Gr. word means "paved with stones" and is translated in KJV and ASV "the Pavement" (*q.v.*). The Heb. word does not exactly correspond with the Gr. It points to the raised character of the place rather than its tesselated or mosaic nature. Jn 19:13 indicates it was the place from which Pilate gave formal sentence against Jesus. It was located adjacent to the praetorium or governor's residence in Jerusalem. If the praetorium (*q.v.*) can be identified as Herod's Tower of Antonia (*see* Antonia; Castle), then the ancient pavement in the basement of the Convent of Our Lady of Zion is very likely Gabbatha. The central area of this paved court measures about 2,500 square yards, with paving stones a yard square and a foot thick.

D. L. W.

GABRIEL (gā′brĭ-ĕl). An angel sent to Daniel in Babylon to explain to the prophet the vision of the ram and he-goat and to announce the prophecy of the 70 weeks (Dan 8:16–27; 9:21–27). After an interval of several centuries, Gabriel was sent to Jerusalem as the herald to Zacharias of the birth of John the Baptist (Lk 1:11–22) and to Nazareth as the messenger to Mary of the birth of the Messiah (Lk 1:26–38). In identifying himself to Zacharias, Gabriel described himself as one standing in the presence of God (Lk 1:19). In the Book of Enoch (a late Jewish apocalyptic work), Gabriel appears with Michael, Raphael, and Phanuel (Uriel) as one of the four highest angels (chaps. 9, 10, 40), or as one of the seven highest (chap. 20). In Moslem literature (Koran) he is represented as the agent through whom Mohammed obtained his "prophetic lore."

F. C. K.

GAD (găd)

1. Gad, son of Jacob; Gadites. The seventh son of Jacob by Zilpah, Leah's maid (Gen 30:9–10). At his birth Leah said, "A troop cometh: and she called his name Gad" (Gen 30:11). The reference to "troop" was prophetic of the high spirit and valor which characterized the descendants of Gad. This seems to be affirmed in the words of blessing by Moses in which it is stated that Gad "dwelleth as a lioness, and teareth the arm, yea, the crown of the head" (Deut 33:20 ff., ASV).

Qualities of valor are ascribed to the Gadites in these words: "Of the Gadites there separated themselves unto David into the hold to the wilderness men of might, and men of war fit for the battle, and could handle the shield and buckler, whose faces were like the faces of lions, and were as swift as the roes upon the mountains" (I Chr 12:8).

Gad had seven sons (Gen 46:16), and with the exception of Ezbon, each founded a family tribe (Num 26:15–18). Even though much is said about the descendants of Gad, little is actually recorded about the patriarch himself. At the beginning of the Exodus from Egypt to Canaan, the tribe of Gad numbered 45,650 "from twenty years old and upward, all that were able to go forth to war" (Num 1:24).

The territory assigned to the tribe was E of the Jordan, but it was mutually agreed with the other tribes that their warriors would cross over and help subdue the rest of the land before they would settle down (Num 32:20–32). The land of the Gadites included the southern part of

The "Pavement" excavated beneath the Convent of Our Lady of Zion. Sisters of Zion

Mount Gilead from the Jabbok River to Heshbon and from Rabbath-Ammon on the E to the Jordan River.

H. A. Han.

2. Gad, the seer. A prophet who advised David, while a fugitive, to leave Moab (I Sam 22:5). Later, he announced to David the Lord's choice of punishment for taking a census (II Sam 24:11-17; I Chr 21:9-17), and suggested the erection of an altar at "the threshing floor of Araunah" (II Sam 24:18-19; I Chr 21:18-19). He was one of the historians of David's reign (I Chr 29:29), and with Nathan encouraged David in forming the Levitical orchestra for "the house of the Lord" (II Chr 29:25). *See* Prophet.

3. Gad, a god of fortune. *See* Gods, False.

GADARA (găd'*à*-r*à*). Gadara (modern Umm Qeis) is located *c.* 1,200 feet above the Mediterranean Sea, yet *c.* 1,880 feet above the Sea of Tiberias, which it overlooks at a distance of six miles to the SE. It has a commanding view of the Jordan Valley and the Galilee area (on the hills behind, one can see all the way to Carmel), being situated on the W extremity of a mountain ridge between the valley of the Yarmuk to the N and the Wadi Arab to the S. Being surrounded on three sides by steep slopes, it was ideally situated to become a strong fortress. Its climate also is more bearable during the heat of summer than the Jordan Valley, or even the site of Amatha where famous warm springs were located three miles to the NE (the hottest spring being 115°).

A strategic road led from Tiberias to Damascus through Gadara, and another road branched off to go through Edrei all the way to the Persian Gulf. The aqueduct supplying the city with water came from Edrei, over 30 miles away. Important ruins similar to those at Gerasa (*q.v.*)–theaters, streets, buildings, inscriptions–are still visible, but practically no archaeological work has been attempted there.

Gadara served as an important Hellenistic fortress as early as *c.* 225 B.C., being taken by Antiochus the Great from Scopas, the general of Ptolemy Epiphanes. Later it was taken by Alexander Janneus (*c.* 100 B.C.), who forced its inhabitants to become Jewish proselytes. Pompey, being influenced by his freedman Demetrius, who was a Gadarene, rebuilt the city in 63 B.C. It was one of the original Decapolis (*q.v.*) cities and became the capital of Perea. Later (30 B.C.) Augustus gave the city to Herod the Great. After Herod's death (4 B.C.) it was transferred to the Roman province of Syria.

The character of the city was primarily Gr., but many Jews lived there and in the surrounding territory. At the beginning of the Jewish revolt its district was attacked by Jews, and as a means of revenge, Jewish citizens of the place were put to death or imprisoned. The citizens requested Vespasian to send a Roman garrison to defend the city against possible dangers, which was finally done. Several famous teachers came from Gadara, such as Philodemus (whose works were found on charred papyrus rolls at Herculaneum), Meleager, Menippus, Theodorus the orator (tutor of the emperor Tiberius), Oemaus, and Apsines.

In the NT, the district of the Gadarenes is mentioned as the place where the demoniac was cured with the consequent destruction of the herd of swine. There is a difficult textual problem connected with this incident (the best MSS being for Mt 8:28–"Gadarenes"; for Mk 5:1–"Gerasenes"; for Lk 8:26, 37–"Gerasenes" or "Gergesenes").

W. M. Thomson discovered a village on the lake shore named Khersa (Gerasa?) which is supposed by some to have been in the larger district of Gadara, which also is surmised to have reached to the Lake of Galilee. As A. T. Robertson notes (*Harmony of the Gospels*, New York: Harper, 1950, p. 71, n.): "... then the locality could be described as either in the country of the Gadarenes, or in the country of the Gerasenes" (cf. also VBW, V, 36). While there are steep banks for the lake at this point, no tombs are to be found there at the present. Many scholars (Schürer, p. 104; G. A. Smith, p. 631; Wroth, p. lxxxvii, who allows it) have noticed the fact that certain coins of Gadara show depictions of ships or triremes, and interpret this as evidence that the territory of Gadara reached the Sea of Tiberias. But Dalman (*Sacred Sites and Ways*, p. 178) takes a contrary view; a coin he found at Gadara reads that naval battles were arranged "*on the river.*" *See* Gerasa.

Bibliography. G. Dalman, *Sacred Sites and Ways*, New York: Macmillan, 1935, pp. 176-180. E. Schürer, *History of the Jewish People*, II. 1, pp. 100-104 (still indispensable). G. A. Smith, *Historical Geography of the Holy Land*, New York: Harper, 1931, see index. W. M. Thomson, *The Land and the Book*, Grand Rapids: Baker, 1954, pp. 375-378. C. Warren, "Gadara, Gadarenes." HDB, II, 79 f. W. Wroth, BMC, *Greek Coins of Galatia, Cappadocia, and Syria*, London: 1899, pp. lxxxvi ff., 304 ff.

E. J. V.

GADDI (găd'ī). One of the 12 spies sent by Moses to spy out Canaan. The son of Susi, he was the representative of Manasseh (Num 13:11).

GADDIEL (găd'ĭ-*ĕ*l). One of the 12 spies sent out by Moses to survey the land of Canaan. He was the son of Sodi and the representative of Zebulun (Num 13:10).

GADI (gā'dī). The father of Menahem, who became king of Israel after slaying Shallum (II Kgs 15:14, 17).

GAHAM (gā'hăm). One of the four sons of Nahor (*q.v.*) by his concubine Reumah (Gen 22:24).

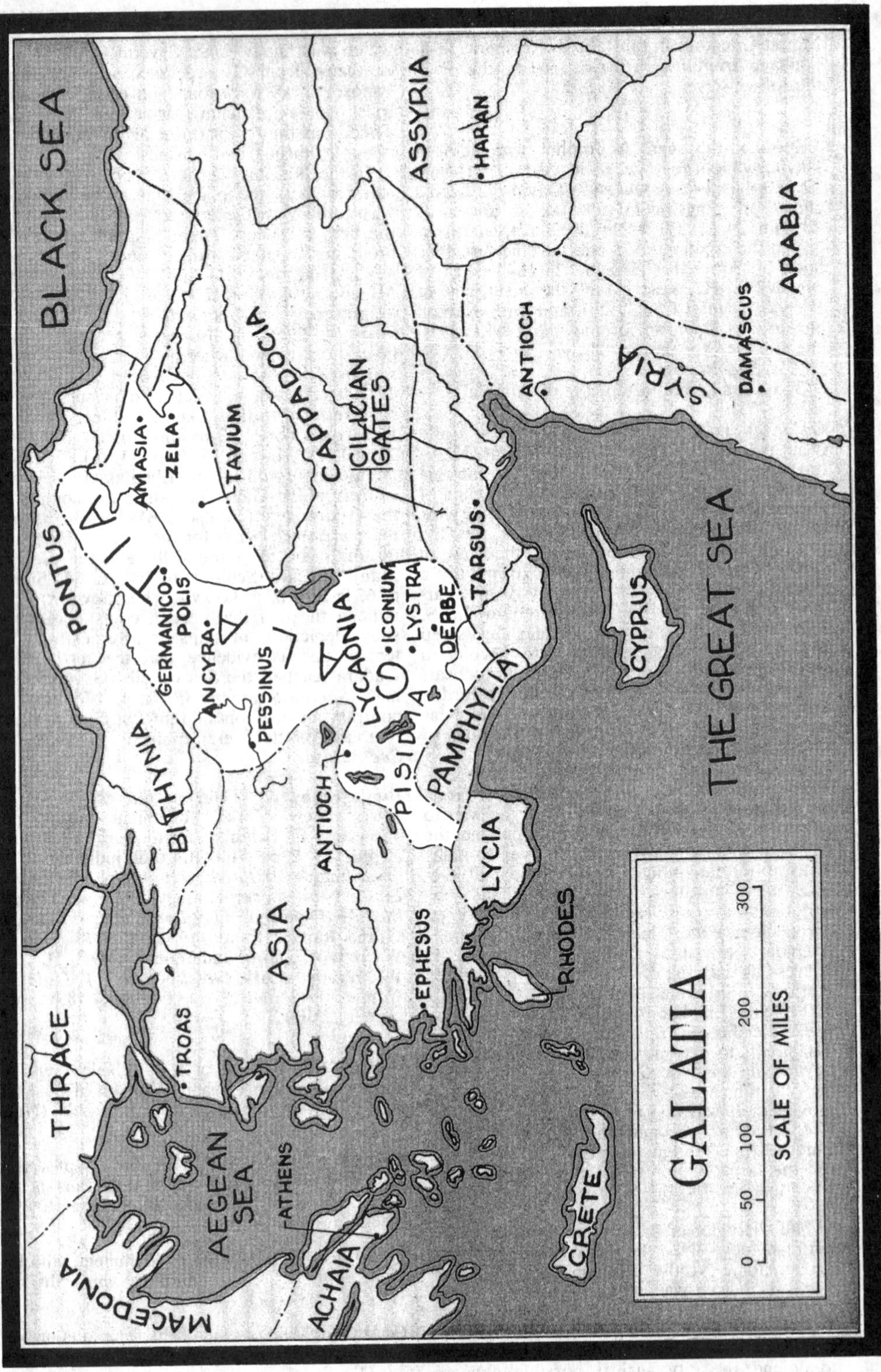
GALATIA
SCALE OF MILES
0
50
100
200
300
BLACK SEA
PONTUS
AMASIA
ZELA
TAVIUM
GERMANICO-POLIS
ANCYRA
PESSINUS
BITHYNIA
GALATIA
CAPPADOCIA
CILICIAN GATES
ASSYRIA
HARAN
ARABIA
ANTIOCH
DAMASCUS
SYRIA
TARSUS
DERBE
LYSTRA
ICONIUM
LYCAONIA
PISIDIA
ANTIOCH
PAMPHYLIA
LYCIA
CYPRUS
THE GREAT SEA
RHODES
EPHESUS
ASIA
TROAS
THRACE
AEGEAN SEA
MACEDONIA
ATHENS
ACHAIA
CRETE

GAHAR (gā'här). One of the chief Nethinim whose descendants were among those returning from the Babylonian Captivity with Zerubbabel (Ezr 2:47; Neh 7:49). *See* Nethinim.

GAIUS (gā'yŭs). This common Roman name occurs five times in the NT. How many different persons are referred to is uncertain, but probably four.

1. A Macedonian Christian who accompanied Paul on some of his journeys and was one of two men seized at the riot in Ephesus (Acts 19:29).

2. A Christian of Derbe in Lycaonia who was with Paul on his return from Macedonia, probably on his way to Jerusalem (Acts 20:4).

3. Paul's host at Corinth in whose house the Christians were accustomed to assemble (Rom 16:23). He is doubtless the same man mentioned in I Cor 1:14 as one of the few converts Paul had baptized at Corinth.

4. A Christian leader to whom III Jn is addressed (III Jn 1). John was evidently sure of this man's spiritual health, for he hoped his physical health and prosperity might be as good. Since this epistle was written late (*c.* A.D. 90), it seems likely that this is a different Gaius from any of the others.

J. A. S.

GALAL (gā'lăl). The name of two Levites whose descendants were among the returning exiles from Babylon. One was a descendant of Asaph (I Chr 9:15), and the other a son of Jeduthun, whose descendants "dwelt in the villages of the Netophathites" (I Chr 9:16; Neh 11:17).

GALATIA (gȧ-lā'shȧ). In the time of the NT the term Galatia was used in two senses, ethnic and provincial. Thus there are now two theories about the location of the churches addressed in Paul's epistle to the Galatians.

1. Ethnic Galatia. This term refers to that northern region of the large inner plateau of what we term Asia Minor. It draws its name from the Gauls or Celts who first invaded Italy *c.* 390 B.C. and later crossed the Bosporus and overran Asia Minor *c.* 278–277 B.C. They were defeated by Attalus I, king of Pergamum, *c.* 239, and as a result were confined to NE Asia Minor. Their vigorous and aristocratic spirit contributed to their separation from and rule over the more numerous tribes of the Phrygians and Cappadocians. The geographer Strabo indicates that the Galatians were grouped in three tribes with four governing units or tetrarchies to a tribe. They enriched themselves at the expense of their neighbors by plunder and extortion, sometimes also serving as mercenaries in local conflicts. They eventually settled, with their chief cities as Tavium, Ancyra (modern Ankara), and Pessinus. Their territory was bounded on the N by Bithynia and Paphlagonia, on the E by Pontus, on the S by Cappadocia and Lycaonia, and on the W by Phrygia. In 189 B.C. they were thoroughly defeated and plundered by the Roman army under Maulius Vulso, but were granted independence in 166 B.C. A Galatian leader, Deiotarus, sided with the Romans against Mithradates VI of Pontus (121–63 B.C.) in his continuing attempts to control all Asia Minor. After defeating Mithradates, Pompey confirmed Deiotarus in his ancestral kingdom and even added to his domains (63 B.C.).

2. The Roman province of Galatia. After the death of Amyntas, its last king, Augustus made Galatia a Roman province in 25 B.C., with Ancyra as capital. Its territory included, besides the old ethnic region, parts of Pontus, Phrygia, Lycaonia, Pisidia, Paphlagonia and Isauria. Included in provincial Galatia were the cities which the apostle Paul evangelized on his first missionary trip, i.e., Antioch, Iconium, Lystra, and Derbe (Acts 13–14). Lystra and Antioch were made Roman colonies, and all these cities attracted large numbers of Greeks, Romans, and Jews because of their geographical and economic importance. The Celtic tongue continued in private use in the N, but Latin became the official language, with Gr. permitted for business purposes.

3. The location of "the churches of Galatia." When Paul addressed his epistle to the Galatians, to what people did he refer? To those in the old northern and ethnic region, or to those in the southern region also included in the newer Roman province? The N Galatian theory holds that Paul addressed churches first contacted on his second missionary journey. After he had visited the southern territory he traveled through "the region of Phrygia and Galatia" (Acts 16:6). Advocates of this view say he entered old Galatia, visiting Pessinus and possibly Ancyra and Tavium before going on to Troas. They hold a second trip to the same territory is mentioned in Acts 18:23 where it says that he "went through the region of Galatia, and Phrygia, in order, establishing all the disciples" (ASV). This is the older of the two views, held by early Church Fathers and by more recent scholars such as Alford, Ellicott, Findlay, Godet, Lightfoot, and Moffatt.

The S Galatian theory holds that Paul wrote to the churches in the southern part of the Roman province which he contacted on his first missionary journey, i.e., Antioch, Iconium, Lystra, Derbe. These churches he revisited on his second journey (Acts 16:1–5) and possibly on the third (Acts 18:23). The main advocate of this view was Sir William Ramsay who did extensive archaeological research in Asia Minor. Most modern commentators, except for those in Germany, hold this view. Among them are Zahn, Burton, Duncan, Tenney, Bruce, and Hendricksen.

For an objective presentation of both N and S views see Everett F. Harrison, *Introduction to the New Testament,* pp. 257–59, and Donald Guthrie, *The Pauline Epistles, New Testament Introduction,* pp. 72–79.

While there is much to be said for either view and perhaps the issue cannot be settled with great certainty, the S Galatian view seems more probable for several reasons.

a. Paul's general habit of using official Roman terms, though not conclusive in itself, when coupled with the historical record in Acts and with the evidence of the epistle, strongly supports the view that Paul addressed the churches of the S as mentioned in Acts 13-14, and 16:1-5. Note I Cor 16:1 where Paul uses "Galatia" in context with other Roman provinces as Macedonia (16:5), Achaia (16:15), and Asia (16:19). Other references to Galatia are found in II Tim 4:10 and I Pet 1:1.

b. The lack of any definite evidence that Paul ever founded churches in N Galatia, in contrast to the easy connection to the southern cities whose extended historical background is supplied by Acts, is presumably in line with Luke's recognized purpose to supply background for Paul's epistles. Acts 16:6-8 and 18:23 are supports adduced for the N Galatian view. Acts 16:6-8 reads: "And they went through the region of Phrygia and Galatia, having been forbidden of the Holy Spirit to speak the word in Asia; and when they were come over against Mysia, they assayed to go into Bithynia; and the Spirit of Jesus suffered them not; and passing by Mysia they came down to Troas" (ASV). This passage indicates that after visiting the cities of S Galatia (16:1-5), Paul, being forbidden by the Spirit to go W into the province of Asia, headed N through a region ethnically Phrygian and Galatian (probably along the border of old Galatia). When he reached a point S of Bithynia and E of Mysia, he was directed by the Spirit to go W to Troas instead of N into Bithynia or E into old ethnic Galatia. There is no reference to extensive evangelism or founding of churches and no definite support here for the N Galatian theory.

In Acts 18:23 the order of the words is reversed and the reference is most likely to two adjacent regions. Paul departed from Syrian Antioch "and went through the region of Galatia, and Phrygia, in order, establishing all the disciples" (ASV). Burton prefers the explanation of the route that takes Paul to Tarsus and through the Cilician gates, through the extreme western part of old Galatia, and then through Phrygia, the eastern part of Asia. This would be consistent with Luke's ethnic use of the adjective "Galatian" in Acts 16:6 (NASB). Note there is no reference to cities or churches in any part of Galatia, either northern or southern. Luke gives no evidence of trying to furnish background to Paul's establishing churches at all. Thus there is no evidence in either passage cited of Paul's founding churches in the N.

c. A third reason for favoring the S Galatian view is that it better satisfies the exegetical considerations of the epistle. First, the southern portion of Galatia would more likely be familiar with the Jewish religion as Paul assumes. Second, the Judaizing teachers opposing Paul would have easier, quicker, and more likely access to the S. Third, the form of Paul's reasoning is more understandable if we assume that the decrees of Acts 15 had been delivered to the southern churches, as in Acts 16:1-5, and that the error presented to the Galatians was not that of Acts 15 (Gal 2:1-10) concerning justification by faith, but was directed primarily to Christians living by Mosaic law (as in Gal 2:11-21). Of course the doctrine of justification was logically affected, but the peculiar form of argument in Gal 3-4 does not hit it directly as does Romans.

Bibliography. E. D. Burton, *A Critical and Exegetical Commentary on the Epistle to the Galatians,* ICC. D. Guthrie, *The Pauline Epistles, New Testament Introduction,* London: Tyndale Press, 1961. Everett F. Harrison, *Introduction to the New Testament,* Grand Rapids: Eerdmans, 1964. M. J. Mcllinck, "Galatia," IDB, II, 336 ff. W. M. Ramsay, *A Historical Commentary on St. Paul's Epistle to the Galatians,* New York: Putnam's,1900; *St. Paul the Traveller and Roman Citizen,* London: Hodder and Stoughton, 1898. Howard F. Vos, WHG, pp. 332-337, 347-356, 383 ff.

C. F. D.

GALATIANS, EPISTLE TO THE

Significance

This short and fiery work of Paul is significant for several reasons. Interpretationally, there is a great contribution to the understanding of the gospel and ts practical implications. Historically, it saved Christianity from becoming a sect of Judaism in Paul's day, and later it fanned the fires of the Reformation. Doctrinally, it argues that since justification is by faith alone, so faith is the only proper sphere of Christian living. The new life is not legalism or license but liberty disciplined by grace and directed by the Spirit of God in love. It remains with exceeding relevance the protest against legalistic contamination of the gospel of grace and the proclamation of Christian liberty.

Authorship and Canonicity

Internal (within the book) and external (outside the book) evidence are both so decidedly in favor of the apostle Paul's authorship that it could not reasonably be doubted. Even destructive critics have recognized Galatians in the "normative group" of Paul (with Romans and I and II Corinthians). The writer calls himself Paul (1:1; 5:2). The book is so characteristic of Paul in vocabulary, style and content, so naturally developed in argument and personal allusions, so reflective of the heart and mind of the great apostle, that no one could have forged such a masterpiece. There is no suggestion of any worth from ancient times that anyone but Paul wrote it, or that it should not be in the canon of Scripture. It is found in the earliest lists of canonical books, in the earliest versions, and in references by Church Fathers and heretics. Galatians records God's words poured through the mold of Paul.

Date and Place of Writing

These cannot be fixed with certainty. Advocates of the N Galatian theory usually place it after Paul's second missionary journey, ranging from A.D. 52 in Ephesus to A.D. 57/58 from Macedonia or Achaia. S Galatian theorists vary from A.D. 48/49 at Syrian Antioch to the same later date and places as above. *See* Galatia. More exact dating depends on the interpretation of the Jerusalem visits mentioned in Gal 1-2. Exponents of the earliest date cannot allow that Gal 2:1-10 refers to the council of Acts 15 since these verses present a different emphasis and the decrees of the Jerusalem council are not cited as support by Paul; hence Galatians antedates the council (A.D. 48/49). The later dating by either theory identifies Gal 2:1-10 with Acts 15.

We may hold that Gal 2:1-10 refers to Acts 15 for several reasons. Lightfoot (*St. Paul's Epistle to the Galatians,* pp. 123-24) notes the determining similarities of geography, time, persons, subject of dispute, nature of the conference and result. Occurrence of two such similar incidents within a few years is so unlikely as to present great difficulty for any solution other than their identity. Those who hold this is not Acts 15 but Acts 11:30; 12:25 generally fail to see that Paul in Gal 1:13-24 does not intend to account for all his visits to Jerusalem, but only those which involved contact with the Twelve. There is no such contact in Acts 11; the Twelve may have fled from Herod (cf. Acts 12:1).

But if Paul wrote after Acts 15, why did he not appeal to the decision of the Jerusalem council to solve the Galatian problem? The answer is that he had done so in person (Acts 16:4); so later in his epistle he marveled at their deserting Christ (Gal 1:6). To refer to the Jerusalem decree would not now solve their problem, for it was a different one, like that of Peter (2:11-21); and both were logically the next step from the issue at the council. The issue had advanced to sanctification by faith and the relation of Christian living to Mosaic law. In Gal 2:1-10 Paul refers to a private aspect of the Jerusalem council; not primarily in support of his doctrine (independently received), but in support of his independence. Hence the different emphasis.

We may hold that Galatians was written on the third missionary journey from Ephesus, A.D. 52/53, or from Corinth or Macedonia, A.D. 54/55.

Recipients

Addressed to "the churches of Galatia," this is the only Pauline epistle written to a group of churches. They were all established by Paul (Gal 1:8, 11; 4:13-14, 19-20). If we hold the S theory and date the book after the Jerusalem council, Paul had delivered to them the council's decrees and they had prospered (Acts 16:4-5). The nucleus of the churches was Jewish, though they were composed mostly of Gentiles. To such a mixed group, a Judaizing compromise between Judaism and Christianity found many a point of contact. The question of Christian living according to Mosaic law and the breeding of two levels of righteousness (faith and faith plus law) might naturally arise and appeal to such a group. There appears no real evidence of the bold, assertive, proud character of northern Gauls; but the tone of Galatians and the type of problem that Paul dealt with in his letter would more naturally be expected of the subservient, susceptible S Galatians who were now seeking advancement under Rome. Such would well receive their new and inclusive title "Galatians."

Occasion and Purpose of Writing

Though some envision a dual problem of legalism and libertinism, the weight of the letter is directed against Judaistic and legalistic opponents. Jews outwardly espousing belief in Christ, to avoid persecution sought to promote the Mosaic law as a standard of Christian living. In doing this, they undercut the authority of Paul. They appealed to the Jerusalem apostles, to Abraham, and to the Mosaic law to picture Paul as a renegade apostle who, after he had received the gospel from the Twelve, stripped it of law to make it appeal to Gentiles; and by doing so, he offered a gospel with only half-standing before God. They insisted that a believer must also become a "son of Abraham" by being circumcised and keeping the law. Only this could he obtain full standing and inherit the fullest blessing of God in the Abrahamic covenant.

There is no evidence that the Judaizers outrightly denied justification by faith. They probably taught that faith in Christ was only the initial step into God's favor, and that the highest favor belonged to those who lived under the law. The Galatians had probably received the decrees of the Acts 15 council on justification by faith apart from law, and could not be confused by a frontal attack on that which Paul had delivered to them (Acts 16:1-5; Gal 1:9; 4:16). But this flank attack in the area of sanctification had "bewitched" the "unreflecting Galatians" (3:1), an address which immediately follows the story of Peter's similar error (2:11-21).

As a result, the Galatians were keeping Jewish seasons (4:9-10). They were hindered now in Christian living (5:7), in danger of becoming in bondage to law (4:21; 5:1) and losing fellowship with Christ (5:2, 4). There were seeds of division among them (5:15; 6:1). Of these things Paul was probably informed by a Galatian delegation.

GALATIANS, EPISTLE TO THE

Paul's purpose, then, is not to prove primarily that justification is by faith. His argument assumes this is true; and building upon the fact that justification has granted them perfect standing with God and full inheritance with Abraham, he seeks to establish that sanctification is in faith, apart from adherence to any part of Mosaic law (2:19; 5:18). This is the contention of the whole letter as seen in the key exhortation (5:1), the key question (3:3), and the significantly placed illustration of Peter's similar problem (2:11-21). Paul regards this error as a dangerous heresy, for the introduction of legalistic works anywhere into a grace system shatters grace and converts it into a system of works contrary to the gospel (1:6-9).

Paul must first reestablish his apostolic authority; then clarify that justification by faith has already granted them all the position they can gain; and finally exhort and instruct in regard to living by grace in faith.

Outline

Most analysts recognize three major divisions of thought with a salutation and a conclusion. Galatians may be outlined as follows:

- I. Salutation and Denunciation, 1:1-10
  - A. Salutation, 1:1-5
  - B. Denunciation, 1:6-10
- II. Personal: Authentication of the Apostle of Freedom, 1:11–2:21
  - A. Proposition: Paul's message is independent of men and directly from God, 1:11-12
  - B. Proof: History of Paul's independence from the 12 apostles, 1:13–2:21
    - 1. Independence verified: his authority separate from the apostles, 1:13-24
    - 2. Independence vindicated: his authority exercised with the apostles, 2:1-21
      - *a.* Recognition at the council of Jerusalem, 2:1-10
      - *b.* Refutation of Peter at Antioch, 2:11-21
- III. Doctrinal: Justification of the Doctrine of Freedom, 3:1–4:31
  - A. Principle argued: Righteousness and inheritance come by faith alone, not by law in any form, 3:1–4:7
    - 1. Personal experience, 3:1-5
    - 2. Progenitor Abraham, 3:6-9
    - 3. Pronouncement of law, 3:10-14
    - 4. Precedence of promise, 3:15-18
    - 5. Purpose of law, 3:19-22
    - 6. Position of superiority in faith, 3:23–4:7
  - B. Personal appeal, 4:8-20
    - 1. Circumstance of appeal, 4:8-11
    - 2. Content of appeal, 4:12-16
    - 3. Cause of appeal, 4:17-20
  - C. Pertinent allegory, 4:21-31
    - 1. Historical situation, 4:21-23
    - 2. Allegorical illustration, 4:24-27
    - 3. Personal application, 4:28-31
- IV. Practical: Expression of the Life of Freedom, 5:1–6:10
  - A. Life of liberty from the system of legalism, 5:1-12
    - 1. Command and injunction, 5:1
    - 2. Crucial issue, 5:2-12
  - B. Life of love in the Spirit of God, 5:13–6:10
    - 1. Exclusion of the life of love: license and lust, 5:13-15
    - 2. Empowerment of the life of love: the Spirit's control, 5:16-24
    - 3. Expression of the life of love: the Spirit's direction, 5:25–6:10
- V. Apostolic Conclusion, 6:11-18
  - A. Final Warning, 6:11-16
  - B. Final appeal, 6:17
  - C. Final benediction, 6:18

Analysis of Contents

After a pointed salutation emphasizing his apostolic authority, Paul denounces the heresy and warns those who would follow it of its seriousness.

The first major division (1:11–2:21) is an extended defense of his genuine and independent apostleship, which is intrinsically a defense of his gospel. His ministry and message are completely independent of men and directly from the risen Christ.

Paul supports this proposition with two major lines of proof (see outline). The proof is essentially a history of Paul's independence from the 12 apostles and their headquarters in Jerusalem. His independence is verified (1:13-24) by a review of his limited contact with them. He was an apostle before he met the others. After God had commissioned him, he did not confer with anyone concerning the content of his gospel but exercised an independent ministry. His independence is vindicated (2:1-21) on two occasions when he did come in contact with other apostles. In the first, at Jerusalem, the apostles, whose gospel the Judaizers claimed to teach, recognized Paul's message and authority. In the second, Paul had to rebuke openly the leading apostle to the Jews. And Peter accepted the rebuke. In both cases the apostles submitted to Paul on the issue of grace versus law. We take it that Peter's problem was essentially the Galatians' problem—to live by faith or by law.

In 3:1–4:31 Paul enlarges upon the argument he used with Peter. He first establishes what justification by faith has done, that he might move on to sanctification by faith. The principle argued is that justification by faith has given the believer a perfect standing before God, superior to and unimprovable by anything supposedly gained by living under law. Paul supports this with six lines of evidence (see outline). The Galatians must recognize that their salvation and early Christian experience were based on faith and not law. How foolish they were to begin in faith and then to seek to complete their position and practice by strict law-keeping.

The first doctrinal argument declares that just as Abraham was declared righteous and made an inheritor of the promises of God by faith, so those who trust Christ are declared righteous and made heirs. Paul then shows that the law can only curse sinners and cannot make righteous. In fact, Christ redeemed us from law that we might inherit the promises. The promise to Abraham, by which we also are blessed in Christ, takes precedence over law in time and nature. The law was given to reveal sin as transgression and to restrict the sinner to faith. Since the cross, we are no longer under law as a rule of life, but are full-fledged sons of God and so "sons of Abraham" and "heirs of promise." There is now no distinction between persons racially, socially, or sexually. Note that these blessings come upon all nations through the universal aspect of the Abrahamic covenant (Gal 3:8) and do not fulfill or abrogate the personal and national aspects of the covenant (Gen 12:1–3) regarding the nation and land of Israel. Paul's main argument ends at 4:7.

A very warm personal appeal is followed by a story from the law that illustrates the principle that the law begets slavery and cannot provide inheritance; whereas the promise taken by faith begets freedom and secures inheritance.

The fourth section calls for the practice of a life of freedom for which Christ saved us. It is a life of liberty from legalism in any system or form, a life free from license and domination by the sin nature within, and a life in faith expressed through love which is produced by the indwelling Spirit. The Spirit replaces the law as the Christian's sphere and guide of life. He will not lead contrary to the abiding moral demands of the law, but will produce the spiritual life, reflective of Christ, which the law could never produce. The Spirit is the power and the director of the new life of freedom that honors Christ and serves men.

The last section contains a warning that contrasts the Judaizers' devotion to the flesh with Paul's devotion to the cross; a final appeal not to follow the errorists; and a benediction asking for grace that they might follow Christ.

Bibliography. G. W. Barker, W. L. Lane and J. R. Michaels, *The New Testament Speaks,* New York: Harper & Row, 1969, pp. 185–191. Conybeare and Howson, *The Life and Epistles of St. Paul,* London: Longmans, Green and Co., 1901. C. J. Ellicott, *Commentary on St. Paul's Epistle to the Galatians,* Andover: Warren F. Draper, 1896. Charles R. Erdman, *The Epistle of Paul to the Galatians,* Philadelphia: Westminster, 1930. G. G. Findlay, *The Epistle to the Galatians,* ExpB. Everett F. Harrison, "Galatians," WBC, pp. 1283–1299. William Hendricksen, *New Testament Commentary, Exposition of Galatians,* Grand Rapids: Baker, 1968. C. F. Hogg and W. E. Vine, *The Epistle of Paul the Apostle to the Galatians,* London: Pickering and Inglis, 1922. J. B. Lightfoot, *St. Paul's Epistle to the Galatians,* London: Macmillan and Co., 1896. H. N. Ridderbos, *The Epistle of Paul to the Churches of Galatia,* Grand Rapids: Eerdmans, 1953. J. H. Ropes, *The Singular Problem of the Epistle to the Galatians,* Cambridge: Harvard Univ. Press, 1929.

C. F. D.

GALBANUM. *See* Plants.

GALEED (găl'ē-ĕd). Jacob gave this Heb. name (which means "the heap of witness") to the heap of stones commemorating the covenant between him and Laban, his father-in-law. The latter called it Jegar-sahadutha, the Aramaic equivalent of the Heb. Galeed. The site was in Gilead where Laban overtook Jacob before he reached the Jabbok. The event was observed with sacrifices, a covenant meal, and a final parting in peace (Gen 31:47–48).

GALILEAN (găl-ĭ-lē'ăn). Either a native or inhabitant of Galilee (Mt 26:69; Mk 14:70; Lk 13:1; Acts 1:11). Jesus (Mt 26:69) and Peter (Mk 14:70) were called Galileans, and the 12 apostles were all Galileans except Judas Iscariot.

Galileans were rather common people who were generous, impulsive, pious, nationalistic, and often more Hellenistic than the Judeans were. Although Galilee and Judea were only 60 miles apart, the people differed from each other in many respects. One difference was speech in which the pronunciation and accent of Galilean Aramaic identified Peter to the maid (Mt 26:73; Mk 14:70).

Galileans had different customs and simpler religious practices than the Judeans, so that the term Galilean was a reproach used by the Pharisees. People outside Galilee had a poor opinion of Galileans and believed therefore that a prophet could not come from Galilee (cf. Jn 1:46; 7:41, 52). Thus the term Galilean signified both geographical location and cultural type.

E. B. R.

GALILEE (găl'ĭ-lē). The northernmost section of three in Palestine W of the Jordan River. Northern Galilee is mountainous (up to 4,000 feet above sea level) extending S from the Leontes River (Nahr el-Litani), which terminates the Lebanons, *c.* 30 miles to Wadi esh-Shaghur that flows toward Acco (Ptolemais). Southern or lower Galilee is more level and thus more suitable for living and farming, bounded as it is on the S by the fertile Plain of Esdraelon. Roads across Galilee from all directions brought commerce from Egypt, Arabia, and Syria. Fruit and olive orchards thrived on the hills, and grain and grass in the valleys.

The Canaanites continued to dominate Galilee for a long time after Joshua's invasion (Jud 1:30–33; cf. 4:2). In Solomon's time Galilee had a mixed population so that he felt he could give 20 of its cities to Hiram of Tyre without great loss to Israel (I Kgs 9:11). After the Assyrian conquests *c.* 732 B.C. (II Kgs 15:29), Galilee once again became predominantly Gentile. Thus Isaiah called it "Galilee of the nations" (Isa 9:1; cf. Mt 4:15).

After Herod joined it to his kingdom, Galilee attracted a great many Jews. Josephus claimed it had 240 cities and villages (*Life,* 45) and could field an army of 100,000 men to fight against the Romans (*Wars,* ii.20.6).

In Jesus' time Galilee was part of the tetrarchy of Herod Antipas (4 B.C.–A.D. 30). Its chief cities were Capernaum, Nazareth, and Tiberias the capital. Jesus' apostles were from here, and His ministry was mostly at the N and W end of the Sea of Galilee, using Capernaum as His center. Both Jews and Gentiles still made up the population, with the northern section more Gentile than the southern and having more contact with Gr. and Rom. culture.

E. B. R.

The western shore of the Sea of Galilee as seen from the air. IIS

GALILEE, SEA OF. Named Galilee in Mt 4:18, it was also called Sea of Chinnereth (Num 34:11), Lake of Gennesaret (Lk 5:1), and Sea of Tiberias (Jn 6:1).

Lying nearly 700 feet below sea level 60 miles N of Jerusalem in the province of Galilee, the Sea of Galilee is a fresh water lake fed by the Jordan River, bringing down the snows of Mount Hermon and the Lebanons with the rains of the hills to form a lake nearly 13 miles long, eight miles at its greatest width, and from 80 to an estimated 700 feet deep.

The mild climate of the Plain of Gennesaret on the NW shore produced a year-round supply of vegetables, fruit, and grain. Elsewhere steep cliffs and mountains enclose the lake rising on the E as high as 2,700 feet to the fertile Hauran plateau. Cool winds rush down these slopes and stir up frequent sudden and violent storms on the warm surface of the lake (Lk 8:22 ff.).

A fishing industry thrived there on the abundant supply of fish with 22 known species (Mk 1:20).

In spite of the steep shoreline, nine cities of 15,000 or more population bordered the lake. Most prominent were Bethsaida-Julias, Tiberias, and Capernaum.

Bethsaida-Julias (*q.v.*) on the NE shore was built by Tetrarch Philip, son of Herod the Great, and named Julias in honor of Emperor Augustus' daughter. The feeding of the 5,000 (Mt 14:13 ff.) occurred near here.

Tiberias (*q.v.*) on the W shore was built by Herod Antipas (*c.* A.D. 25) and named for Tiberius Caesar. Its warm mineral springs made it a health resort. Hellenistic manners and morals thrived there so that most Jews, including Jesus, avoided it.

Capernaum (*q.v.*), only six miles N of Tiberias, was the home of Peter and Andrew. Here Jesus had His headquarters, called it His own city (Mt 9:1), performed many miracles, and called Matthew from the tax collector's booth. But still the city did not repent and so faced ruin (Mt 11:23–24).

On and around the Sea of Galilee Jesus performed 18 of His 33 recorded miracles, gave many teachings, and called His disciples.

See Tiberias, Sea of.

E. B. R.

GALL

1. A plant with bitter or poisonous fruit (*see* Plants: Gall).

2. A bodily organ or its secretion. The Heb. word *m^e^rōrâ* denotes the gall bladder in Job 20:25 (cf. NEB) and the bile, a bitter yellowish liquid secreted by the liver and stored in the gall bladder, in Job 16:13; 20:14. It is used figuratively in Job 13:26, translated "bitter things."

GALLERY. An architectural term used in the KJV and ASV to translate *'attîq,* a Heb. word of uncertain meaning. It is used in describing Ezekiel's temple in Ezk 41:16, "the galleries round about on their three stories" (RSV, "all three had windows with recessed frames"), and in Ezk 42:3, 5. It is a loan word from Akkad. *etēqu,* "to pass," and may therefore have the sense of a balcony passage or walkway. A variant Heb. form of *'attîq* is found in Ezk 41:15 (RSV, "walls").

The obscure Heb. word *rahaṭ* rendered "galleries" in KJV is translated "tresses" by ASV and RSV (Song 7:5).

GALLEY. *See* Ship.

GALLIM (găl'ĭm). A town in Benjamin apparently near Laish ("Laishah," ASV, RSV) and Anathoth, and so N of Jerusalem (Isa 10:30). Perhaps it is Khirbet Ka'kûl, three-quarters of a mile W of Anathoth. It was the home of Phalti ("Palti," ASV, RSV), the second husband of Michal (I Sam 25:44).

GALLIO (găl'ĭ-ō). The Roman proconsul of Achaia in Greece when Paul labored in Corinth on his second missionary journey (Acts 18:12-17). He was the son of M. Annaeus Seneca and was born in Cordoba, Spain, *c.* 3 B.C. His two younger brothers were Seneca, the philosopher and tutor of Nero, and Marcus Annaeus Mela, the geographer and father of the poet Lucan. Nero forced all three brothers to commit suicide *c.* A.D. 66.

He assumed the name L. Junius Gallio Annaeus when he was adopted by his wealthy friend Lucius Junius Gallio and introduced to a political career. Besides holding the consulship once in Achaia, where the climate made him ill according to a letter of Seneca, Gallio became a senator of Rome.

An inscription found *c.* 1905 at Delphi (45 miles NW of Corinth) reveals that Gallio was proconsul of Achaia after the 26th acclamation of Claudius as *imperator*. Jack Finegan argues convincingly that Gallio's arrival in Corinth, therefore, must be dated *c.* July 1, A.D. 51, placing Paul's coming there early in the year 50 (FLAP, 2nd ed., pp. 362 f.).

Gallio proved himself an impartial judge and a worthy Roman official when Paul was brought before him, because he refused to become involved in matters of religion. He paid no attention to the ensuing anti-Jewish demonstration.

J. R.

GALLOWS. A pole with a projecting arm for the hanging up of a dead body (Est 5:14; 6:4; 7:9-10; 8:7; 9:13-14, 25; cf. Gen 40:19, 22; 41:13). In the book of Esther it may mean to impale a body on a stake. The victim was usually dead before the body was placed on the gibbet. *See* Crime and Punishment; Cross.

GAMALIEL (gȧ-ma'lĭ-ĕl)

1. Gamaliel I ("the elder") was the son of Simon and the grandson of the famous Rabbi Hillel. He occupied an important position in the Jewish council and was held in respect (Acts 5:34-40). He was the first to bear the title "rabban" (our master) instead of the more common "rabbi" (my master). On occasion he was counselor to the Herods in legal-religious matters (Pesahim 88*b*). His importance is seen in the statement: "When Rabban Gamaliel the Elder died, the glory of the Law ceased and purity and abstinence died" (*Soṭah* 9.15).

Characteristic of the school of Hillel, Gamaliel was liberal in his outlook, showing moderate views toward the laws of the sabbath, marriage, and divorce (Rosh ha-Shanah 2:5; Yebamoth 16.7; Gittin 4.2, 3). In Acts 5:34-39 he is said to have counseled moderation in the treatment of the apostles. This can be interpreted as an example of his temperament. Another interpretation is that he spoke in irony against Sadducean skepticism toward the providence of God (James Moffatt, "Gamaliel," *Expositor,* 8th series, 5 [1913], p. 96). If this latter is true, the passage reflects the conflict between the Pharisaic tradition of Hillel and the Sadducean tradition of Shammai.

Ruins of ancient Corinth where Gallio was proconsul.

Gamaliel's mention of Theudas in Acts 5:36 raises a problem in regard to chronology. Josephus mentions a rebel named Theudas who was killed *c.* A.D. 44 during the procuratorship of Fadus (*Ant.* 20.5.1 ff.). Gamaliel, speaking before this event, places Theudas prior to the enrollment which took place in A.D. 6. Swain has suggested that the speech should be placed in Acts 12 just before the death of Herod (Joseph W. Swain, "Gamaliel's Speech and Caligula's Statue," *Harvard Theological Review,* 37 [1944], p. 342). This solves little, however, since Theudas was put to death, according to Josephus, after the death of Herod. It is possible that Josephus refers to another Theudas. Also, the reliability of Josephus may be doubted, since his various accounts of the Jewish wars do not always correspond.

The statement in Acts 22:3 that Paul was brought up at the feet of Gamaliel raises another problem. If Paul was taught by the moderate Gamaliel, why did he show such radical hatred toward the church? Why did he not mention Gamaliel in his letters? And why was he so completely different in his attitude toward the law? Some suggest that *para tous podas gamaliel pepaideumenos* should be translated by the general phrase, "brought under the influence of Gamaliel" (G. Corrie Clanville, "Gamaliel," ExpT, 39 [1918], pp. 39 f.). Others say that Paul did not study in Jerusalem, and that it is Luke's theological bias that places him there (M. S. Enslin, "Paul and Gamaliel," *Journal of Religion,* 7 [1927], pp. 360-375). In some ways, however, Paul reflects the Pharisaic tradition of his teacher. For example, he calls Isaiah Torah (I Cor 14:21), an expression fitting for a student of Gamaliel, for the Pharisees considered all Scripture as Torah. Another piece of evidence that Paul studied under Gamaliel is the passages in the Talmud referring to a student of Gamaliel called "that pupil." This designation is possibly a reference to Paul (Joseph Klausner, *From Jesus to Paul,* pp.

310 f.). Why Paul did not mention his famous teacher in his letters is a moot question. His conversion experience and new orientation may have been important factors.

2. The prince of the tribe of Manasseh (Num 7:54, 59; 10:23). He was appointed assistant to Moses in numbering the people at Sinai (Num 1:10; 2:20).

G. E. H.

GAMES. The Hebrews seem not to have been interested in athletics as a sport. There are no references to any purely athletic contests in the OT such as abound in Greco-Roman literature. Even the reference in Ps 19:5, ". . . rejoiceth as a strong man to run a race," is not necessarily speaking of a contest. The Semitic peoples rather found recreation and expressed their humor and lighthearted attitude in song and dance (cf. Job 21:11-12). *See* Dance; Music.

Samson employed a guessing contest to entertain wedding guests (Jud 14:12). *See* Riddle. The grim contest with swords between picked soldiers from Abner's and Joab's troops cannot be classed as a game (II Sam 2:12-17). In the end time, the streets of Jerusalem will be full of boys and girls playing children's games (Zech 8:5) such as tug-of-war, known in Egypt (ANEP #216, 217).

Wrestling (*q.v.*) was a sport common in the ancient Near East as clay figurines and tomb paintings attest. Beautifully wrought game boards, some being inlaid with ivory, shell, gold, and blue paste, have been found at Ur, Meggido, and other towns in Palestine, and in Egyptian tombs (ANEP #212-215; R. F. Schnell, "Games, Old Testament," IDB, II, 352 f.). Clay dolls, toys, and models of furniture have survived the ravages of time to indicate that the life of a child was not overly dull.

Gaming board from Ur. *c.* 2500 B.C. BM

Games were of tremendous importance, however, in the Gr. and Rom. world. The Greeks are remembered for their public games, the names of them lingering even in a modern context: Olympian, Isthmian, Nemean, Pythian. The Olympian games were the chief national festival of the Greeks, being given in honor of Zeus at Olympia every four years, and were chiefly gymnastic, though equestrian and musical contests were added. The Isthmian games were held at Corinth in a grove sacred to Poseidon, in the second and fourth years of each Olympiad. The Nemean games were held in the valley of Nemea, given in honor of Zeus at the end of each first and third years of an Olympiad, and consisted of gymnastic, equestrian, and musical contests, as did each of the others. The Pythian were next to the Olympian in importance, taking place in the third year of each Olympiad below Delphi. The prize for the winners was only a wreath of leaves, such as olive or laurel, but great honor was shown them by their fellow citizens.

Starting lanes for runners in the Pythian Games at the stadium of Delphi, Greece. HFV

GAMES

Among the Romans the number of the games increased until at the end of the Republic there were seven sets of games which occupied a total of 65 days. By the middle of the 2nd Christian cen., a total of 135 days out of the year was given over to these games, and by A.D. 354 the games claimed 175 days out of the year.

The major Roman games were the Ludi Romani, the oldest of the games, celebrated in honor of Jupiter; the Ludi Plebes which included dramatic entertainments; the Ludi Cereales, given in honor of the goddess Ceres; the Ludi Apollinares in honor of Apollo; the Ludi Megalenses in honor of the Great Mother; the Ludi Florales. The Ludi Circenses and the Ludi Augustales were celebrated during the period of the empire in memory of Augustus Caesar. These games were intimately connected with religious worship, being dedicated to the gods and goddesses. They were frequently under the direction of the priests, who superintended the games because they served the god in each instance.

For games that the government dedicated to the gods, the expense was met out of the public treasury. Eventually, the demands on the Roman public were so extravagant that the emperors found it necessary to underwrite a considerable part of the expense of public games out of the imperial purse. Not only Rome but other major cities and towns such as Ephesus found a considerable financial drain attached to the games that were celebrated locally, of which those at Rome would be more or less representative.

In addition to the public games that involved the entire population, many private games were given by individuals or organizations on occasions of special significance, such as births, marriages, and even funerals. Whereas admission to the public games was always free, private games many times charged admission and were frequently used by societies for fund raising. Sometimes these private games were donated by the wealthy to the public for the express purpose of gaining the good will of the populace. The cost of both the public and private games rose to staggering proportions by NT times.

Athletic games were especially favored by the Greeks but less favored by the Romans. The Romans favored those contests that involved danger and bloodshed. There were races, wrestling matches, throwing the discus and the javelin, and, of course, boxing. Among the Romans the chariot races in the circus were far more popular than the athletic races. The great race course in Rome, the Circus Maximus, could possibly accommodate 250,000 spectators. During the course of the race, the crowd went wild, and not infrequently there were riots. Large sums of money exchanged hands as the people bet on the outcome of the races; and the successful charioteer was able to amass a fortune.

A Roman game cut into the pavement of the Agora at Philippi. HFV

The gladiatorial shows, which attained such popularity among the Romans, were the most objectionable of all the games to the Christians. Such combats came to be a part of every important public occasion. Julius Caesar at one festival presented more than 300 pairs of gladiators in combat, while Trajan, rejoicing over his victory in Dacia, matched together 10,000 gladiators. The majority of the gladiators were prisoners of war or slaves, although occasionally criminals were condemned to fight in the arena. In Spain, Africa, Gaul, and the East there was a craze similar to that in Rome for the gladiatorial combats. They were, however, never very popular in Greece, except at Corinth, which was a Roman colony in NT times.

The Roman games were usually held in a stadium or a large circus arena. Some were of a temporary nature; others were permanent, the remains of which can be seen in the ruins of ancient civilization to this very day. The circular arena, or amphitheater, was designed for the combats of gladiators and wild beasts, and was first used in Italy. Eventually, every large town had its amphitheater. The most famous in Rome itself, known as the Colosseum, was begun by Vespasian, consecrated by Titus (A.D. 80), and finished by Domitian. It was 158 feet high and accommodated some 50,000 spectators. In this arena large groups were engaged in mock battle, fights between wild animals were staged and, occasionally, the arena was flooded so that small ships were able to conduct naval battles before the very eyes of the crowd.

The ancients also had various social games that attained wide popularity. The Greeks and Romans both had ball games. There were also among these people games of chance that employed dice. There was a game very similar to chess that was played on a board divided into spaces, the movements on the board being made with stones. A widely popular game was called "Odd and Even" (in Gr. *artiasmos* and in Lat. *ludere par impar*) in which coins, stones, or nuts were held in the hand; the opponent

The second century B.C. stadium at Rhodes, rebuilt by Italians before World War II. HFV

was to guess whether the number was odd or even.

The leaders of the early Christian churches condemned the forms of amusement that associated themselves with pagan religion and which controverted the Christian ethic. In the Treatises attributed to Cyprian, the games and amusements of his day were denounced because it was felt that participation in them involved idolatry. Tatian, Tertullian, and Clement denounced the games and similar amusements because of idolatry, immodesty, and brutality. It was, in fact, the opposition of Christianity that brought them to an end.

The references in Paul's epistles which liken the Christian life to the course of the athlete are many. He speaks of the self-discipline that is necessary if one is to win, and the necessity of abiding by the rules (I Cor 9:24 ff.). He speaks of life and one's ministry as a course to run (Acts 13:25; 20:24; Phil 3:14; II Tim 2:5; 4:7), and of running in vain (Gal 2:2) or running well (Gal 5:7). The author of Hebrews even likens the Lord Jesus to a runner who has covered the course before us (Heb. 12:1 f.). Even today these references to the contests of strength and endurance arouse us to run "with patience the race that is set before us."

Bibliography. A. C. Bouquet, *Everyday Life in New Testament Times,* New York: Scribner's, 1953, pp. 180–190. Jerome Carcopino, *Daily Life in Ancient Rome,* New Haven: Yale Univ. Press, 1940. Henri Daniel-Rops, *Daily Life in the Time of Jesus,* New York: Hawthorne, 1962. E. Norman Gardiner, *Greek Athletic Sports and Festivals,* London: Macmillan, 1910. E. W. Heaton, *Everyday Life in Old Testament Times,* New York: Scribner's, 1956, pp. 75 f., 80, 91–94. Harold Mattingly, *Roman Imperial Civilization,* New York: Doubleday, 1959. Madeleine S. and J. Lane Miller, *Encyclopedia of Bible Life,* New York: Harper, 1944, pp. 391 f.

H. L. D. and P. C. J.

GAMMADIM (găm'*ā*-dĭm). An obscure term found only in Ezk 27:11. It is translated "valorous men" by ASV, but the context seems to imply a proper name. Suggestions have been made to identify it with the city of Kumidi of the Tell el-Amarna letters, somewhere near Arvad in northern Phoenicia.

GAMUL (gā'mŭl). A chief of the Levites, who was chosen as head of the 22nd course of the priests when David organized them into 24 divisions (I Chr 24:17).

GANGRENE. *See* Diseases: Internal Diseases.

GAP. A break as through a wall, a tear, usually translated "breach," but as "gap" in Ezk 13:5; 22:30 (RSV, "breach").

GARDEN. *See* Plants: Garden.

GARDEN HOUSE. Mentioned in II Kgs 9:27, "when Ahaziah . . . fled by the way of the garden house." Since he fled in his chariot, pursued by Jehu, the "garden house" must have been some distance from the winter palace in Jezreel and may possibly be identified with En-gannim (*q.v.*: Josh 19:21), about "seven miles S of Jezreel at the foot of the ridge of Carmel" (IB, III, 235), modern Jenin.

GARDEN OF EDEN. *See* Eden.

GARDENER. *See* Occupations.

GAREB (gâ'rĕb)

1. One of David's mighty men who was numbered among the 30 (II Sam 23:38; I Chr 11:40), an Ithrite (*q.v.*), a member of a Kirjath-jearim family (cf. I Chr 2:53).

2. The name of a hill of uncertain site near Jerusalem to which the city would expand, according to a prophecy of Jeremiah (Jer 31:39). It is literally, "Hill of the Leper."

GARLAND. Found only in KJV in Acts 14:13, where the priests of Jupiter (Gr. Zeus) "brought oxen and garlands" to worship Paul and Barnabas as deities. Whether the garlands (Gr. *stemma,* "wreath") were for the apostles or oxen is not clear.

The ASV and RSV translate the Heb. *pe'ēr* ("headdress," "turban," "chaplet") as "garland" in Isa 61:3 ("beauty," KJV) and also v. 10 ("ornaments," KJV).

GARLIC. *See* Plants.

GARMENT. *See* Dress.

GARMITE (gär'mīt). An appellation of uncertain meaning used of Keilah, a descendant of Caleb of the tribe of Judah (I Chr 4:19).

GARNER. An archaic English word for a granary, barn, or storehouse. It is used in Joel 1:17

(Heb. *'ôṣār,* "storehouses," RSV), but it is elsewhere rendered "store," "storehouse," "treasure," "treasury." The Heb. term *mezew* (*māzû* or *mezāw*) is translated "garners" in Ps 144:13. The Gr. *apothēkē* is translated "garner" in KJV in Mt 3:12; Lk 3:17 (RSV, "granary") but elsewhere as "barn." *See* Storehouse.

GARNET. *See* Jewels.

GARRISON. A manned and provisioned military post or fortress. In the OT "garrison" is the translation of two Heb. words, both derived from the root *nṣb.* (1) Heb. *maṣṣāb* (I Sam 13:23; 14:1, 4, 6, 11, 15; II Sam 23:14) and a variant *maṣṣābâ* (I Sam 14:12). A similar form *maṣṣēbâ* is correctly rendered "pillars" by ASV and RSV in Ezk 26:11 where KJV has "garrisons." (2) Heb. *neṣîb* (I Chr 11:16; and most likely II Sam 8:6, 14; I Chr 18:13; II Chr 17:2). This word must be translated "officer" (KJV, RSV), governor, deputy or the like in I Kgs 4:19; II Chr 8:10, but "pillar" in the account of the punishment of Lot's wife (Gen 19:26). How to render the word in I Sam 10:5; 13:3-4 is a question among translators. Did Jonathan smite a Philistine garrison (KJV, ASV, RSV), official (IB, II, 931 f., 946), or pillar (Jerusalem Bible)?

In II Cor 11:32 the KJV renders the Gr. *phrourein* by "keep with a garrison," where RSV and NASB have simply "guard."

D. D. T.

GASHMU (găsh'mū). A variant form of Geshem (*q.v.*) found only in Neh 6:6. This Arab was an associate of Sanballat and Tobiah in their opposition to Nehemiah.

GATAM (gā'tăm). An Edomite chief or duke, the son of Eliphaz and grandson of Esau (Gen 36:11, 16; I Chr 1:36).

GATE. The rendering of five Heb. and three Gr. words. It is used of cities (Deut 3:5, *deleth,* "door"; I Kgs 17:10, *pethaḥ,* "opening"; Gen 23:10, *sha'ar,* "gate"); of the tabernacle (I Chr 9:19, *saph,* "threshold"); of the king (Dan 2:49, *tera',* "gate"); of the temple (Acts 3:2, *thyra,* "door"); of hell (Mt 16:18; *pylē,* "gate") and cities (Lk 7:12; Acts 9:24); and of houses and cities (Lk 16:20; Acts 12:13-14; Rev 21:12-25, *pylōn,* "gate"). See J. Jeremias, "*Pylē, Pylōn,*" TDNT, VI, 921-928.

City gates were made of wood (Neh 2:8; cf. 1:3; 2:13) and of bronze (KJV, brass; they were probably bound with heavy copper bands or sheathed in copper plates, as the gates of the Assyrian town of Balawat. ANEP #356-365). Some gates had towers as defensive elements (II Chr 26:9), and some were built of a series of gates hung on piers jutting out from a side wall, the outer gate sometimes protected by towers. *See* Tower. This was the Solomonic-type gateway with four pairs of evenly spaced piers found at Gezer, Hazor, and Megiddo (ANEP #721; BA, XXI [1958], 29-30, 46; XXIII [1960], 62-68; XXX [1967], 39 f.; XIII [1950], 42 ff.). Bars secured the gates when closed (Deut 3:5), some being made of bronze (I Kgs 4:13). The doors were formed to pivot at the jambs in stone sockets which, in Babylonia and Assyria in the more important buildings, sometimes had dedicatory inscriptions giving the name of the king and the god to whom the building was dedicated.

Many of the houses unearthed in Tell Beit Mirsim of the period 900-600 B.C. did not have door sockets. In the period 2200-1600 B.C. the large stone sockets give evidence of heavy doors for the houses. The conclusion to be drawn is that in the earlier period, times were unsettled and strong doors were needed, there being no country-wide police force. In the later period, since doors were frequently missing, betokening only a hanging in the doorway, the conclusion is that times were much more settled and that David and his successors had set up a national police force to protect the people (cf. I Sam 25:7-9). Lot's door (Gen 19:1-10) was mob-proof, fitting the early period and not the later period. *See* Door.

Hadrian's Gate provided entrance to the east end of Athens in the second century A.D. HFV

The gateway in Palestinian and Babylonian cities became a place of public hearings, legal transactions, and business (I Kgs 22:10; Deut 21:19 ff.; 22:13-21; Gen 23:10, 18; Ruth 4:1 ff.; II Sam 15:2 ff.; 19:8; II Kgs 7:1). Gates in larger cities were named, sometimes in accordance with the type of market conducted

The Golden Gate
In the wall of Jerusalem as seen from the Garden of Gethsemane. It was blocked up by the Turks in 1530 and is connected by some with the prophecy of Ezek. 44:1-3. Some would identify it with the Gate Beautiful. HFV

near it (e.g., Sheep Gate, Fish Gate, Old Gate, Neh 3:1, 3; 12:39). *See* Jerusalem: Gates. Gen 34:24 speaks of those going out at the city gate, and the context of the story would denote able-bodied males. The story of Ruth 4 would indicate them to be responsible men, and therefore Gen 34:24 and Ruth 4 would, by this phrase, denote the adult citizenry of the city. At Tell en-Nasbeh (biblical Mizpah) stone benches lining the walls forming the gate provided seats for the people conducting business there (ANEP #716, 717). Sometimes rooms for the gate garrison were provided above it (II Sam 18:24, 33).

In Heb 13:12 Jesus is said to have "suffered without the gate," i.e., outside the city. In this instance "gate" would signify the city of Jerusalem, fulfilling the OT type (Lev 4:12, 21; "camp" would be equal to "city"). Christ died to purify the "city" (household of faith) of God.

The term gate denotes the forces of hell in Mt 16:18; i.e., the devil and his armies of fallen angels and demons. It is the same idiom as in Gen 34:24. These shall not prevent God's Church from fulfilling God's will, nor can they overthrow it (II Tim 2:19).

H. G. S.

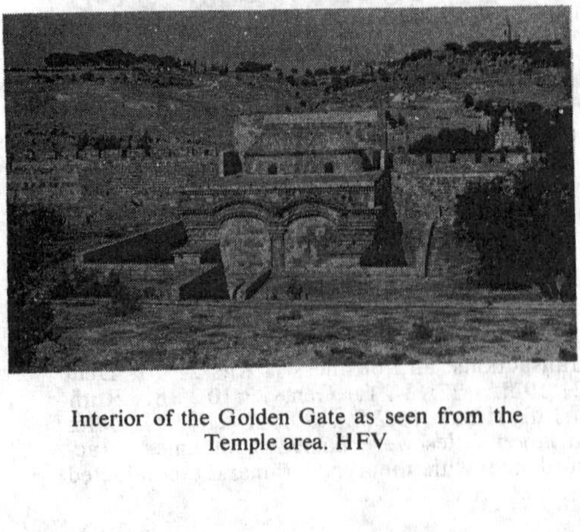

Interior of the Golden Gate as seen from the Temple area. HFV

GATE, BEAUTIFUL. The temple of Herod, which was the sanctuary in Jerusalem in the days of Jesus and the early church, was set in the midst of a huge courtyard, called the court of the Gentiles. Separating the outer court from the temple proper was a great wall, which in time of need made of the temple an actual fortress. This wall was pierced by nine gates by which Jews might enter to worship. According to the Mishnah, eight of the gates were 20 cubits high and 10 cubits wide. The great eastern gate, the principal entrance to the temple, was 50 cubits high and 40 cubits wide. This is undoubtedly that which the NT calls the Beautiful Gate (Acts 3:10). It was called the Gate of Nicanor in honor of its donor, and was also called the Corinthian Gate because its doors were made of Corinthian bronze. It was at this gate that the lame man sat who was healed by the power of the Lord through Peter (Acts 3:1-10). Against the background of this magnificent gate, Peter's words, "Silver and gold have I none" bear added significance.

P. C. J.

GATH (găth). A place name widely used in the Levant, meaning "wine press." Administrative documents from Ugarit list 29 different towns with a name of which the first element is *gt* (Gath) followed by a second element, e.g., *gt'ttrt*, "the wine press of Ashtaroth"; *gt gl'd*, "the wine press of Gilead." Therefore, it is not surprising to find several places with the name Gath in Palestine, since viticulture was a major industry in antiquity just as it is today.

There are numerous references to the Palestinian Gaths in both biblical and secular sources. Sometimes an additional element was added to the name to distinguish it from other Gaths, but in numerous instances the name Gath stands alone, and it is difficult for the interpreter to decide just which Gath is meant. The biblical Gaths which have such an additional designation are discussed under separate headings (*see* Gath-hepher; Gath of the Philistines; and Gath-rimmon). The locative ending *-ayim* may be added to produce the form Gittaim (*q.v.*). This town sometimes is referred to simply as Gath. The name Moresheth-gath contains this term as a second element, though it too may possibly be called simply Gath (II Chr 11:8; *see* Moresheth-gath).

At least four, or perhaps five, other Gaths in Palestine are known from sources outside the Bible. One of these is called *Gittipadalla* in the Amarna tablets (EA 250:12) and is written *ḏdpṯr* in Shishak's list (No. 34). From its position in the latter text, between Borim (No. 33; Khirbet Burin) and Yahem (No. 35; Khirbet Yamma) it is evident that this Gath-padilla should be identified with the village of Jatt on the northern coastal plain S of Mount Carmel. The same place is listed as *knṯ* in the list of Thutmose III (No. 70) in close association with other places known to be located in the northern Sharon, e.g., Soccho (No. 67; *swk,* Khirbet Shuweikat ar-Ras) and Yehem (No. 68).

The *Gintikirmil,* Gath-carmel, of the Amarna tablets (EA 288:26, 289:18) probably refers to the same town as Gath of the Philistines, now identified as Tell es-Safi (Y. Aharoni, "Rubute and Ginti-Kirmil," VT, XIX [1969], 137–145).

Another Galilean Gath is indicated by No. 44 of Thutmose III's list, written *kntišn,* listed after Ibleam (No. 43; Khirbet Bal'ama), which appears in an Amarna tablet (EA 319:5) as *Ginti-ashna.*

The fourth "Gath" in Thutmose's inscription, *kntit* (No. 93), probably represents the plural form *Gattoth.* Because of its position in the list alongside other towns in N Galilee, Aharoni has associated it with Gath Asher, written *qṯisr* in two topographical lists of Ramses II. He suggests that this Gath be identified with Jatt, a village in the ancient tribal territory of Asher (Yohanan Aharoni, *The Settlement of the Israelite Tribes in Upper Galilee,* Jerusalem: Magnes Press, 1957, p. 65 [Heb.]).

A. F. R.

GATH-HEPHER (găth-hē'fĕr). A town on the boundary of Zebulun (Josh 19:13, RSV), listed after Daberath (Dabburiya) and Japhia (Yafa) and before Eth-kazin (location unknown). It is known as the birthplace of the prophet Jonah, the son of Amittai (II Kgs 14:25). Jerome, in his commentary on the book of Jonah, states that Gath-hepher was situated two miles from Sepphoris (Saffuriya) on the road to Tiberias, and that the local inhabitants in his day pointed out the tomb of the prophet to interested passersby. This is evidently a reference to the village of Meshhed, which to this day displays a tomb of Nebi Yunas, an honor which it shares with several other places in Palestine, not to mention its famous rival at Nineveh. This village was only settled from the Roman period and later; but there was an Iron Age town on the nearby tell called Khirbet ez-Zurra', just SW of Meshhed.

A. F. R.

The Mound of Gath. HFV

GATH OF THE PHILISTINES. Home of one of the five Philistine lords (Josh 13:3, RSV). It was known as the home of giants (Josh 11:22), Goliath in particular (I Sam 17:4; II Sam 21:19–20; I Chr 20:4–8). Achish (*q.v.*) ruled there as king with apparent hegemony over all of the Philistine region (I Sam 21:10–15; 27:1–12; 28:1–2; 29:1–11). Y. Aharoni (VT, XIX [1969], 141–144) believes that Gath-carmel of two Amarna letters from 'Abdu-Heba of Jerusalem (#288, 289: ANET, pp. 488 f.) is identical with the later Philistine Gath.

According to one passage (I Chr 18:1) David conquered Gath; but the parallel text has another reading (II Sam 8:1). A Philistine king still reigned there in Solomon's day (I Kgs 2:39). The town fortified by Rehoboam was probably Moresheth-gath (*q.v.*), which is on a more logical line with the other towns in that list (II Chr 11:8). Hazael captured Gath on a foray into Palestine (II Kgs 12:17); Uzziah neutralized its power when he expanded Judah's own influence (II Chr 26:6); and Sargon II's annals mention a Gimti in the land of Ashdod (*q.v.*). After this, the only reference to Gath is in a proverbial expression (Mic 1:10; cf. II Sam 1:20).

Excavations have shown that no Philistine settlement existed at either Tell Sheikh el-Areini (five miles NW of Lachish) or Tell en-Najila (eight miles SW of Lachish). For these two sites see BW, pp. 571–574. Scholars have recently returned (Aharoni, *op. cit.,* p. 144) to the older suggestion ("Gath," ISBE, II, 1177) that Gath was located at Tell es-Safi (21 miles due W of Bethlehem, ten miles N of Lachish) which would place Gath close to Ekron (Tell Muqanna) and which suits the LXX account of I Sam 17:52 (see RSV). Tell es-Safi is at the W end of the Valley of Elah in which David killed Goliath. The site on its narrow spur of the Shephelah foothills juts out like a bastion, with very steep slopes on the N and W.

In 1900 Bliss and Macalister made soundings at the site and discovered pottery that corroborates the biblical data regarding its occupation. They noted a city wall of the Judean kingdom period and a Canaanite shrine enclosing an earlier high place with a series of standing stones (*Excavations in Palestine, 1898–1900,* pp. 28–43). But Moslem cemeteries on the mount have prevented large-scale excavations.

See Gath; Philistines.

A. F. R.

GATH-RIMMON (găth-rĭm'ŭn). The name of one or two towns in ancient Israel.

1. It appears in the list of Danite cities (Josh 19:45) in association with Jehud, Bene-berak, and Me-jarkon, the "waters of Yarkon." However, the city itself was to be a Levitical city (Josh 21:24; I Chr 6:69). It perhaps became an administrative center during the time of the united monarchy, since the area had remained unconquered by the Danites (Jud 1:34–35). Only during the expansion under David did Israel finally gain control over this region (cf. II Sam 8:1; I Chr 18:1).

The city called *knt* (No. 63), which is listed on Thutmose III's topographical list alongside Joppa (No. 62), Lod (No. 64), Ono (No. 65), and Aphek (No. 66), may be identical with Gath-rimmon because of the similarity of locale (for locations of the other towns mentioned above, cf. the respective articles). The city's apparent importance as a store city of the Levites under David's administration has led recent investigators to abandon the older identification of Gath-rimmon with the small, though prominent, Tell Abu Zeitūn in favor of Tell Jerisheh ("Napoleon's Hill"), a large site near the junction of Wady Musrara with the Yarkon River. Excavations there revealed that the site was an important town during the Late Bronze Age and continued to exist until sometime near the end of the 10th cen. B.C.

2. A Gath-rimmon appears with Taanach as one of the cities of Manasseh in Cis-jordan which was assigned to the Kohathite families of the Levites (Josh 21:25). The validity of this reference is disputed because of a textual difficulty. The parallel passage in I Chr 6:70 gives two entirely different towns in place of Taanach and Gath-rimmon, viz., Aner and Bileam (*q.v.*). This reading is supported by the LXX of Josh 21:25 which has *Iebatha* (a possible conflation of *Iebla*[*m*] and *Baithsa* or *Baithsan* which appear as variants in other LXX MSS in place of *Iebatha*). Whatever the solution to this knotty textual problem, the existence of a Gath-rimmon close to Taanach receives additional support from an Amarna tablet, which refers to a Gimti-rimmunima (EA 250:46) in association with Shunem. The northern Gath-rimmon can perhaps be identified with Rummana (169–214) in the vicinity of Taanach.

Bibliography. Benjamin Mazar, "The Cities of the Territory of Dan," IEJ, X (1960), 65–77; "The Excavations at Tell Qasile," IEJ, I (1950), 63, n. 6. E. L. Sukenik, "Excavations in Palestine, 1933–1934: Tell el Jerishe," *Quarterly of the Department of Antiquities, Palestine*, IV (1934), 208–209.

A. F. R.

GAULANITIS (gôl'ȧ-nī'tĭs). The area E of Galilee and bounded by the Yarmuk on the S, Hermon on the N, the Jordan on the W, and the desert on the E. It is not mentioned by this name in the Bible, but is derived from Golan (*q.v.*), one of the six cities of refuge assigned to the Gershonites (Josh 21:27; I Chr 6:71).

GAY. Translated as "gay" with reference to clothing in Jas 2:3, but rendered "fine clothing" by ASV and RSV.

GAZA (gā'zȧ). An important seaport town on the S coast of Palestine. The modern name Ghazzeh preserves the original first consonant (cf. Heb. *'azzâ*, Deut 2:23). During the Late Bronze Age it was the main Egyptian administrative center in their province of Canaan, of which it marked the southernmost extremity (Gen 10:19; cf. Acts 8:26). The original inhabitants were Avim, later replaced by Caphtorims (Deut 2:23; cf. Josh 10:41). Judah was supposed to inherit it (Josh 15:47) but failed to conquer it (Josh 13:2–3; Jud 3:3; Jud 1:18, LXX). Hence it became an important Philistine center (Josh 13:3; Jud 16; I Sam 6:17; *et al.*). The Assyrians conquered it several times in their struggle to control Palestine. King Hezekiah subdued Gaza (II Kgs 18:8), but Sennacherib later gave some Judean towns to its king. Pharaoh Neco took over the city on his northward march in 609 B.C. (Jer 47:1).

The town maintained its importance in Persian, Hellenistic, and Roman times. Alexander spent five months besieging it. Jonathan, Simon, and Alexander Jannaeus all fought with it, and the latter finally devastated the town in 93 B.C., so that certain writers referred to it as *erēmos*, "desert(ed)." Pompey placed the region of Gaza under the jurisdiction of the Roman province of Syria (62 B.C.). The Roman general Gabinius rebuilt Gaza in 57 B.C. on a new site by the sea, a little S of the old city. Thus in telling that Philip heeded the divine messenger to take the old road that descends from Jerusalem to Gaza, Luke correctly commented. "This city is deserted" (Acts 8:26, NASB marg.).

A. F. R.

GAZATHITES (gā'zȧ-thīts). The designation applied to the inhabitants of Gaza in Josh 13:3 ("those of Gaza," RSV) and rendered Gazites (*q.v.*) in Jud 16:2.

GAZELLE. *See* Animals, II.15.

GAZER (gā'zẽr). A variant form of Gezer (*q.v.*) in the KJV rendering of II Sam 5:25 and I Chr 14:16.

GAZEZ (gā'zĕz). A son and a grandson of Caleb bore this name (I Chr 2:46). The first Gazez was Caleb's son by his concubine Ephah, while the grandson was the son of Haran, another son of Caleb by Ephah.

GAZITES (gāz'īts). The inhabitants of Gaza (*q.v.*), the southernmost of the five principal Philistine cities.

GAZZAM (găz'ăm). The founder of a family of the Nethinim (*q.v.*), whose descendants were among the first exiles returning from Babylon (Ezr 2:48; Neh 7:51).

GEBA (gē'bȧ). Spelled Gaba in Josh 18:24; Ezr 2:26; Neh 7:30, KJV.

A city in the inheritance of Benjamin (Josh 18:24), today Jeba', an Arab village six miles NNE of Jerusalem between er-Ram (Ramah) and Mukhmas (Michmash). It occupies the hill (Heb. *geba'* means "hill," "height") on the S side of the gorge of the Wadi Suweinit, opposite Michmash (*q.v.*) on the N rim (I Sam 14:5, RSV). Geba is one of the four Benjamite cities in which dwelt priestly families (Josh 21:17; I Chr 6:60). Some of the inhabitants traced their lineage back to Ehud (I Chr 8:6), apparently to be identified with the judge of that name (Jud 3:15 ff.). The "meadows of Gibeah" (Jud 20:33, KJV) is understood by the Peshitta, LXX, and Vulg. as "west of Geba."

Geba is doubtless the site featured in the account of Jonathan's daring attack on the Philistines, because in I Sam 13:16 and 14:5 the Heb. MT has *geba'*, "Geba," not "Gibeah" (KJV). Most scholars believe that in I Sam 14:2, 16 *gib'â*, "Gibeah," is a scribal error for *geba'*, because one cannot view Michmash from Gibeah (Tell el-Ful), but it can easily be watched from Geba across the deep valley. Earlier the Philistines had established a garrison at Geba (I Sam 13:3), also known as Gibeath-elohim ("the hill of God," I Sam 10:5, KJV) because of its high place.

During the Judean kingdom, King Asa dismantled the walls of Ramah to fortify Mizpah and Geba on the two main roads to Jerusalem from the N (I Kgs 15:22; II Chr 16:6). Geba is also mentioned as a station of the Assyrian advance against Jerusalem (Isa 10:29). With the first returnees from the Exile came 621 descendants of citizens of Geba and Ramah (Ezr 2:26; Neh 7:30). The town belonged to the post-Exilic province of Judah (Neh 11:31); in its territory dwelt many of the temple singers (Neh 12:28 f.).

Benjamin Mazar ("Geba," EBi, II, cols. 411–412 [Heb.]) argues that there must have been another Geba, a city on the northern border of Judah, probably Khirbet et-Tell overlooking Wadi Jib. King Josiah defiled all the high places from "Geba to Beer-sheba" (II Kgs 23:8). In the same chapter it is clear that Bethel was also within the bounds of Judah during Josiah's time (II Kgs 23:4, 16), and Bethel is N of the Jeba' discussed above. A similar expression is "from Geba to Rimmon south of Jerusalem" (Zech 14:10), which seems to support the view that this Geba is the northernmost point in the Judean kingdom. It is also significant to note that in Roman times the boundary between Judea and Samaria was along the line *Jeshanah*–Geba–Chanot–Barkai (cf. also II Chr 13:19).

Eusebius (Onomasticon 74:2) refers to a Geba which was five miles N of Gofna on the way from Jerusalem to Shechem. The identification with et-Tel is supported by the fact that remains from Israelite through the Byzantine periods have been found there.

However, as Y. Aharoni points out (*The Land of the Bible*, 1967, pp. 350 f.), there is no need to assume that this Geba was directly on the border. In the time of Josiah Geba, like Beer-sheba, was an administrative center near the border, where cultic sanctuaries had been located prior to Josiah's reform.

A. F. R.

Phoenician Fortifications, Gebal. HFV

GEBAL (gē'bȧl)

1. An ancient Phoenician seaport, 25 miles N of Beirut, known by the Greeks as Byblos; modern Jebeil. Gebal is one of the most ancient sites yet excavated in the Near East, yielding human bone remains enclosed in large earthen pots dating back to Neolithic times (4000–3000 B.C.). By about 3100 B.C. Byblos was a center

Ancient harbor of Gebal. ORINST

of Egyptian influence, and vessels, known as Byblos travelers, plied the Mediterranean between Phoenicia and Egypt (BW, p. 154).

One of the most important finds uncovered at Gebal is the Ahiram sarcophagus (*c.* 1000 B.C.), discovered in 1923, containing an inscription written in early Phoenician alphabetic characters. The Gebalites were skilled craftsmen (I Kgs 5:18, RSV) and furnished the caulkers for the ships of Tyre (Ezk 27:9). Because they saw there imported Egyptian papyrus reeds made into scrolls, the Greeks named the city Byblos, meaning "papyrus." Byblos also means "book," and our word Bible is derived from the same word. See N. Jidejian, *Byblos Through the Ages,* Leiden: Brill, 1968.

2. An area between the Dead Sea and Petra referred to in Ps 83:7 as allied with the enemies of Israel. It is modern Gibal.

For illustration of Ahiram Sarcophagus, *see* Alphabet.

D. D. T. and A. F. J.

GEBER (gē'bĕr). The son of Uri and one of the 12 commissary officers of Solomon whose duty was to provide food and supplies for the king's household. He had charge of the 12th district consisting of Gilead (I Kgs 4:19).

Another of the commissary officers was Ben-Geber ("son of Geber," I Kgs 4:13), who was over the 6th district, consisting of 60 cities of Gilead and Bashan.

GEBIM (gē'bĭm). A city of unknown location in Benjamin between Anathoth and Nob, whose inhabitants are portrayed by Isaiah as fleeing before the approach of the Assyrian army (Isa 10:31).

GECKO. *See* Animals, IV. 16.

GEDALIAH (gĕd-*á*-lī'*á*)

1. Governor of Judah, appointed by Nebuchadnezzar after the destruction of Jerusalem *c.* 586 B.C. (II Kgs 25:22–26; Jer 40:6–41:18). Gedaliah was a member of a prominent and powerful family. His grandfather was Shaphan, probably the one who served as state secretary under King Josiah and reported the discovery of the book of the law to the king (II Kgs 22:10). Shaphan's son, Gedaliah's father, Ahikam, became Jeremiah's protector after the famous temple sermon (Jer 26:24).

Gedaliah set up his government at Mizpah, which was five or six miles N of Jerusalem; either at the modern site of Tell en-Nashbeh or Nebi Samwil. The length of Gedaliah's governorship is not known. Suggestions have ranged from two months to five years. Ishmael, a leader of a fanatic nationalist band and a member of the exiled royal family, murdered Gedaliah while he was a guest in the official residence in Mizpah (Jer 41:2).

A seal impression on clay once attached to a papyrus scroll and bearing the words, "To Gedaliah who is over the house," was found at Lachish. This seal would suggest that Gedaliah was probably the last prime minister of Judah, or administrator of the palace, since such a seal was borne by the chief official of the land next to the king (cf. G. E. Wright, *Biblical Archaeology,* p. 178).

2. A son of Jeduthun, an instrumentalist leader of the temple choir (I Chr 25:3, 9).

3. Grandson of Hezekiah and grandfather of the prophet Zephaniah (Zeph 1:1).

4. Son of Pashur, one of the princes of Jerusalem who advocated putting Jeremiah to death (Jer 38:1–6).

5. One of the priests who put away his foreign wife (Ezr 10:18).

R. L. S.

GEDEON (gĕd'ĭ-ŏn). Gr. form of Gideon (*q.v.*).

GEDER (gē'dĕr), **GEDERITE** (gē'dĕr-īt). An unidentified city of southern Palestine, whose king was captured by Joshua (Josh 12:13). It is probably the same as Beth-gader (*q.v.*). Baal-hanan, who had charge of David's olives and sycamores "that were in the low plains" (Shephelah), was a Gederite, a native of Geder (I Chr 28:28).

GEDERAH (gĕ-dĕr'*á*). A town in the Shephelah of Judah (Josh 15:36). I Chr 4:23 reads, "These were the potters and inhabitants of Netaim and Gederah; they dwelt there with the king for his work" (RSV). Gederah may possibly be identified with modern Jedireh, about 10 miles SE of Lud (Lod).

Some identify Gederah with a city of Benjamin from which came Jozabad, one of David's mighty men. It may be the same as a Jedirah near Gibeon or a Jedireh about three miles SW of Gezer.

GEDERATHITE (gĕd'ē-r*á*-thīt). An inhabitant of Gederah. This term is applied in I Chr 12:4 to Jozabad, one of David's mighty men, and in I Chr 4:23 in referring to the potters and inhabitants of Netaim and Gederah (ASV, RSV).

GEDEROTH (gĕ-dĕr'ōth). A city in the Shephelah of Judah, named with Beth-dagon, Naamah, and Makkedah in Josh 15:41. It is mentioned along with Beth-shemesh and Aijalon as taken by the Philistines during the reign of Ahaz (II Chr 28:18). It has been identified with Kedron, a place fortified by Cendebeus who was defeated here by John, son of Simon Maccabeus (I Macc 15:39; 16:9).

GEDEROTHAIM (gĕ-dĕr′ō-thā′ĭm). A village in the Shephelah of Judah near Zorah-azekah (Josh 15:36). Joshua's account lists it as the fifteenth city in an enumeration which suggests "fourteen cities with their villages." Accordingly, some scholars feel that the term "and Gederothaim" should read "and her sheep folds," or "and her places of enclosure." Thus this statement would refer to the preceding cities and leave the total at 14 as the verse suggests.

GEDOR (gē′dŏr)

1. One of the sons of Jehiel, a Benjamite, the "father" or founder of Gibeon (I Chr 8:31; 9:37).

2. A city in the hill country of Judah, assigned by Joshua to Judah at the division of the land (Josh 15:58). Men from Gedor came to David at Ziklag (I Chr 12:7). I Chr 4:4 states that Penuel was a "father" of Gedor, and I Chr 4:18 that Jered was likewise a "father" of Gedor. Since in this section other men are obviously listed as "fathers" or Israelite rebuilders of former Canaanite towns—Socho and Zanoah (I Chr 4:18) are towns in Josh 15:35-35—we may conclude that Penuel and Jered were the founding fathers of Israelite Gedor.

3. A city or valley where some of the Simeonites settled (I Chr 4:39). The location is unknown. The LXX has "Gerar" for Gedor in this verse.

GEHAZI (gē-hā′zī). The servant or youth (Heb. *na'ar*) of Elisha. He is referred to by name on three occasions (II Kgs 4:12 ff.; 5:20; 8:4) and may be the unnamed servant in II Kgs 4:43 and 6:15.

It was Gehazi who suggested to Elisha that the Shunammite's hospitality should be rewarded with the promise of a son, and later carried Elisha's staff and laid it on the dead child's face in a vain effort to restore the child's life (II Kgs 4:8-37).

Gehazi's greed is seen in his deceitful request from Naaman of a talent of silver and two festal robes in the name of his master Elisha, who had previously declined to accept a reward from Naaman (II Kgs 5:20-23). As a consequence of this sin, Elisha pronounced a curse upon Gehazi and his descendants to the effect that the leprosy of Naaman would cleave to them forever (II Kgs 5:27). Leprosy is a general term in the OT used for many types of skin diseases. Evidently this type which Naaman and Gehazi had contracted did not require isolation (cf. II Kgs 8:1 ff.; Lev 13:12-13). *See* Diseases: Leprosy.

The last picture of Gehazi in the OT is that of his relating to King Jehoram "the great things that Elisha hath done," especially the raising of the Shunammite's son (II Kgs 8:4-6). *See* Elisha; Naaman.

R. L. S.

GEHENNA (gē-hĕn′*a*). The Gr. form of the Heb. *gē-hinnom,* "valley of Hinnom" (Josh 15:8; 18:16); also called Topheth (II Kgs 23:10). The form *Gaienna* occurs in the LXX in Josh 18:16*b*. The word is used as the metaphorical name of the place of torment of the wicked after the final judgment. The valley was the place of the idolatrous worship of Molech, the fire god ("Ahaz . . . burnt incense in the valley of the son of Hinnom, and burnt his children in the fire," II Chr 28:3; cf. II Chr 33:6; Jer 7:31; 32:35; Lev 18:21). For this reason it was polluted by Josiah (II Kgs 23:10) to become a place of refuse and abomination.

The idea of a place of eternal spiritual punishment by fire is frequent in the OT (cf. Deut 32:22, "A fire is kindled in mine anger, and burneth unto the lowest Sheol," ASV. See also Lev 10:2; Isa 30:27, 30, 33; 33:14; 66:24; Dan 7:10; Ps 18:8; 50:3; 97:3). This concept combined with Jeremiah's prophecy of evil against the valley (Jer 19:2-10) developed a belief in a place of spiritual punishment to which the dread name Gehenna was given. Gaster (IDB) suggests that the application of the place name follows the analogy of using such Palestinian places as Armageddon (Rev 16:16; Zech 12:11), Jerusalem (Gal 4:26; Rev 21:2), or Sodom (Rev 11:8) for spiritual concepts.

It can be seen from Jewish literature that the idea was prevalent (Enoch 10:12-14: "[Sinners] will be led to the abyss of fire in torture and in prison they will be locked up for all eternity." Cf. also Enoch 18:11-16; 27:1-3; Judith 16:17; II Esd 7:36; Sir 7:17; Sibylline Oracles 1, 10:3; IQM 2:8; Talmud, Aboth 1:6; Assumption of Moses 10:10). Some Jewish writers thought the chosen people would be exempt and that the duration would be limited. Philo, however, taught that wicked Jews would be punished also, and that eternally (De Praem. et Poen. 921). The spiritual nature of Gehenna is further indicated by the fact that it was placed in the third heaven (Ascension of Isaiah 4:14; II Enoch 40:12; 41:2).

But the doctrine is most explicitly affirmed in Jesus' teaching. Jesus spoke of Gehenna as a place of future punishment. He spoke of "being cast into Gehenna" (Gr.; see RSV marg. in Mt 5:29; 18:8-9; Mk 9:45, 47; Lk 12:5); "the Gehenna of fire" (Mt 5:22); "destroy both body and soul in Gehenna" (Mt 10:28); "the condemnation of Gehenna" (Mt 23:33); "make him a son of Gehenna," i.e., one worthy of its punishment (Mt 23:15). It is used elsewhere in the NT only in Jas 3:6, "the tongue is set on fire of Gehenna." The NT clearly teaches that the punishment of Gehenna is eternal (Mk 9:47-48; Mt 25:46; Rev 14:11).

The book of the Revelation gives to Gehenna the name "the lake of fire" (19:20; 20:10, 14, 15; 21:8). Furthermore, since the Revelation equates the lake of fire with the "second death" (20:14), this apparently is also a synonym for describing Gehenna. In further confirmation of the identity of these terms in the Revelation with Gehenna, it may be noted that unbelieving men are therein consigned (20:15; 21:8), as well as Satan himself (20:10). It is also the eternal place of condemnation (20:10*b*).

See Dead; Eschatology; Eternal State; Hades; Hell; Hinnom; Punishment; Sheol; Tophet.

Bibliography. Joachin Jeremias, "*Geenna*," TDNT, I, 657 f.

J. W. R.

GELILOTH (gĕ-lī'lŏth). A technical Heb. term for administrative districts, as of the Philistines (Josh 13:2), translated "borders" or "regions." The Geliloth of Josh 18:17 lay on the boundary between Judah and Benjamin. It seems improbable to identify Geliloth with the Gilgal in the Jordan Valley, but it seems to be identical with the Gilgal of Josh 15:7. No positive identification is possible, but some point along the road from Jericho to Jerusalem, such as Tal'at ed-Damm, a hill near the so-called Good Samaritan Inn, may be intended. Josh 18:17, in speaking of the allotment to the tribe of Benjamin, reads: "Then it bends in a northerly direction going on to En-shemesh, and thence goes to Geliloth, which is opposite the ascent of Adummim" (RSV).

GEMALLI (gĕ-măl'ī). Father of the spy Ammiel from the tribe of Dan, sent out by Moses to spy out the land of Canaan (Num 13:12).

GEMARIAH (gĕm-*à*-rī'*à*)

1. The son of Shaphan and a scribe or priest who occupied a chamber in the New Gate of the temple during the reign of Jehoiakim (Jer 36:10). Gemariah was from an illustrious family. His father, Shaphan, was the secretary or a prominent minister in Josiah's time to whom Hilkiah first brought the book of the law when it was found in the temple (II Kgs 22:8). Gemariah's brother was Ahikam, who saved Jeremiah's life after his temple sermon (Jer 26:24). And Gemariah's nephew, Gedaliah, became governor of Judah after the fall of Jerusalem (Jer 39:14). Gemariah witnessed Jehoiakim's destruction of the first scroll of the book of Jeremiah. Together with Elnathan and Delaiah, he urged the king not to burn the scroll, but the king would not listen to them (Jer 36:25).

2. The son of Hilkiah, sent by King Zedekiah as an ambassador to Nebuchadnezzar, and the bearer of Jeremiah's letter to the Jewish captives in Babylon (Jer 29:3).

GENEALOGY

Definition

The Heb. word for genealogy, *yaḥaś*, occurs only once as a noun in the OT in the phrase "book of the genealogy" (Neh 7:5, ASV) where it is introducing a list of exiles returning to Jerusalem from Babylon. The verb *yāḥaś*, "to register," is always in the causative (*hithpael*) form and could be translated "to cause one's name to be recorded (enrolled) in genealogical tables" (I and II Chr, Ezr and Neh). In the NT the Gr. *genealogia*, "genealogy," occurs in I Tim 1:4 and Tit 3:9.

The idea is also conveyed in the OT by the Heb. word *tôl^edôth*, "generations" (*see* Generation), or the phrase "book of the generations" (Gen 5:1), and in the NT by Gr. *biblos geneseōs*, "book of the generation" (Mt 1:1). Thus the term "genealogy" can be defined as a list of names indicating ancestors or descendants of an individual or individuals, or it can mean the registration of the names of people for some reason.

Genealogical Lists

The principal lists are as follows:

1. Adam to Noah (Gen 5; I Chr 1:1-4). This gives the line of Seth, with ten names in each passage. In Genesis they are listed with a formula of *A* lived *x* years and begat *B*, and *A* lived after he begat *B y* years and begat sons and daughters, and all the days of *A* were *z* years, and he died. There are many variations for the *x* and *y* between the MT, SP, and the LXX, while the variations of the *z* in the various accounts are smaller.

2. The descendants of Cain (Gen 4:17-22). One notable feature of this earliest list in the Bible is that the occupation is mentioned for some of those listed.

3. The descendants of Noah (Gen 10; I Chr 1:4-23). This is the Table of Nations (*see* Nations).

4. The line from Shem to Abraham (Gen 11:10-26; I Chr 1:24-27). This list is similar to Gen 5 except the MT and the LXX do not give the total years that each man lived (conversely, the SP follows the formula of Gen 5 exactly).

5. The descendants of Terah (Gen 11:27-31).

6. The descendants of Nahor, Abraham's brother (Gen 22:20-24).

7. The descendants of Lot, son of Haran, Abraham's other brother (Gen 19:36-38).

8. The descendants of Abraham (Gen 25:1-4; I Chr 1:28-33).

9. The descendants of Ishmael (Gen 25:12-17; I Chr 1:29-31).

10. The descendants of Isaac (I Chr 1:34).

11. The descendants of Esau (Gen 36; I Chr 1:35-54).

12. The descendants of Jacob/Israel (Gen 46:8-27; I Chr 2-8).

a. Descendants of Jacob by Leah (Gen 46:8-15).

(1) Reuben (Gen 46:9; Ex 6:14; Num 26:5-11; I Chr 5:1-10).

(2) Simeon (Gen 46:10; Ex 6:15; Num 26:12-14; I Chr 4:24-38).

(3) Levi (Gen 46:11; Ex 6:16-26). The genealogy of Levi is important and extensive in the post-Captivity books. The reason for this is to demonstrate the continuance of the Levitical priesthood, both before, during, and after the Exile. The Levitical priesthood can be traced from the post-Exilic books in the following way: (*a*) Pre-Exilic, before David (I Chr 6:16-30); at the time of David (I Chr 6:31-48; 15:5-24); Jehoshaphat (II Chr 17:8); Hezekiah (II Chr 29:12-14; 31:12-17); Josiah (II Chr 34:8-13; 35:8-9). (*b*) Post-Exilic (Ezr 2:40-42; Neh 10:2-13; 12:1-24). (*c*) Aaronic high priesthood lineage (I Chr 6:1-15; Neh 12:26; Ezr 5:2; Hag 1:1, 12, 14; 2:2, 4).

(4) Judah (Gen 46:12; Num 26:19-22; I Chr 2:3–4:22). As with the Aaronic line, the line of Judah is important, for out of this line the Messiah was to come (Gen 49:9-10) and more particularly, He was to come out of David's line (II Sam 7:12-16; Ps 89:3-4, 28-30, 32-37). For the Davidic line in particular see I Chr 3:10-20; Ezr 3:2, 8; 5:2; Neh 12:1; Hag 1:1, 12, 14; 2:2, 23; Mt 1:6-16; Lk 3:23-31.

(5) Issachar (Gen 46:13; Num 26:23-25; I Chr 7:1-5).

(6) Zebulun (Gen 46:14; Num 26:26-27).

b. Descendants of Jacob by Bilhah (Gen 46:23-25).

(7) Dan (Gen 46:23; Num 26:42-43).

(8) Naphtali (Gen 46:24; Num 26:48-50).

c. Descendants of Jacob by Zilpah (Gen 46:16-18).

(9) Gad (Gen 46:16; Num 26:15-18; I Chr 5:11-17).

(10) Asher (Gen 46:17; Num 26:44-47; I Chr 7:30-40).

d. Descendants of Jacob by Rachel (Gen 46:19-22).

(11) Joseph (Gen 46:19-20; Num 26:28-37). However, two tribes came out of Joseph (cf. Gen 48:5, 8-20), namely, Manasseh (Num 26:29-34; I Chr 7:14-19) and Ephraim (Num 26:35-37; I Chr 7:20-27).

(12) Benjamin (Gen 46:19, 21; Num 26:38-41; I Chr 7:6-12; 8:1-40). King Saul was of Benjamin (I Chr 8:29-38; 9:35-44).

13. Genealogies of post-Exilic times. Those who returned with Zerubbabel (Ezr 2:2-61; Neh 7:7-64), and with Ezra (Ezr 7:1-7). Also there are several lists given in the post-Exilic books, two of which list both their names and their tribe (cf. I Chr 9:3-9; Neh 11:4-36). Post-Exilic genealogies are very important for establishing and preserving the homogeneity of the race. It was to show the continuance of the nation through a period of national disruption.

14. Genealogies of Christ (Mt 1:1-17; Lk 3:23-38). Both of these genealogies fit within the purpose of each of the books. Matthew demonstrates that Jesus is Israel's Messiah and King; thus he traces Jesus' lineage back through Solomon and David to show His kingly right to the throne, and ultimately back to Abraham with whom God made an eternal covenant concerning Abraham and his seed. In showing that Jesus is the Son of Man, Luke traces Christ's line back to Adam, the father of mankind.

One can see that genealogical lists can be either of descending or ascending order. For example, one observes this in Aaron's genealogy which is given in the descending order (i.e., *A* begat *B*) in I Chr 6:3-14, and in the ascending (i.e., *A*, the son of *B*) in Ezr 7:1-5. The same phenomenon occurs in Christ's genealogy (cf. Mt 1:2-16; Lk 3:23-38 respectively).

Purposes of Genealogies

First, they show the history of Israel. The earlier genealogies show Israel's kinship with and distinction from her neighbors. Adam is father of all mankind, but later on nations develop. Israel was, of course, the main interest to the biblical writers since it was for the benefit of that nation that the Abrahamic and Mosaic covenants were made.

Second, they are given to show the ancestry and preservation of the different tribes in Israel.

Third, the genealogies are for the preservation and the purity of Israel's Aaronic priesthood and the Davidic line which ultimately led to Christ, the long-awaited Messiah as seen in the Gospels. These genealogies not only were for the preservation of the line but also they were used to demonstrate the legitimacy of an individual in his office.

Fourth, the post-Exilic genealogies serve to demonstrate the homogeneity of Israel as a nation after their captivities. Thus, in conclusion, it can be seen that these genealogies were essentially the skeleton on which the history of Israel rested.

Genealogies and Chronology

Right at the outset it is very evident that there are genealogical gaps, at least in some of the genealogies. For example, although in the lineage only three generations are listed between Jacob and Moses (Ex 6:16-20; Num 3:17-19; etc.), there are in the lineage of Joshua eleven generations listed between Jacob and Joshua (I Chr 2:2; 7:20-29). Many more examples could be given (see Kitchen, pp. 54 f.).

The real crux of the relationship between genealogy and chronology comes in the genealogies of Gen 5 and 11. To say that other genealogies have gaps does not prove that these do, although Lk 2:36 includes the name Cainan as the son of Arphaxad, found in the LXX of Gen 11:12-13 but not in the Heb. MT. These are the only genealogies which give the age of the father at the birth of the son who serves as the next link in the genealogy. It may be that there are genealogical gaps in Gen 5, but since the age is given of the father who gives birth to the child, it is quite another matter to say one can have chronological gaps. Thus there may be gaps in the genealogy but not in chronology.

To have genealogical gaps in Gen 11 is even more difficult, for it is unlikely that many would have been grandfathers or great-grandfathers in their late 20's or early 30's as would be the case for those listed in this chapter! To be sure, as Green has indicated, these genealogies may show the longevity of life early in the earth's history, but this does not preclude that they cannot be chronologically accurate. In conclusion, it must be stated that this is a rather complex problem which is further aggravated by the fact of great differences in the figures given in the SP and the LXX. *See* Chronology, OT.

Bibliography. R. A. Bowman, "Genealogy," IDB, II, 362–365. Philip W. Crannell, "Genealogy," ISBE, II, 1183–1196. E. L. Curtis, "Genealogy," HDB, II, 121–137. William Henry Green, "Primeval Chronology," BS, XLVII (April, 1890), 285–303. Marshall D. Johnson, *The Purpose of Biblical Genealogies*, Cambridge: Cambridge Univ. Press, 1969. K. A. Kitchen, *Ancient Orient and Old Testament*, Chicago: Inter-Varsity, 1966, pp. 53–56. Abraham Malamat, "King Lists of the Old Babylonian Period and Biblical Genealogies," JAOS, LXXXVIII (1968), 170. T. C. Mitchell, "Genealogy," NBD, 456 ff. John C. Whitcomb and Henry M. Morris, *The Genesis Flood*, Nutley, N.J.: Presbyterian and Reformed, 1961, Appendix II, 474-489.

H. W. H.

GENEALOGY OF JESUS CHRIST. *See* Chronology, New Testament; Jesus Christ; Genealogy.

GENERATION.

1. The Heb. word *dôr* occurs *c.* 130 times in the OT and has the idea of a circle or cycle to be completed. Hence, it means the cycle of a man's life. It could have the idea of a man's life span, as in Gen 15:16. Abraham's descendants were to return to Canaan "in the fourth generation" after being afflicted 400 years in a land that was not theirs (15:13). Here *dôr* seems to be equivalent to Akkad. *dâru,* a lifetime, as seen in an inscription of Shamshi-Adad I of Assyria (see Kitchen, p. 54, n. 99).

Generally, however, it has the idea of a cycle beginning with a man's birth and ending with the birth of his son. It may speak of the generations of the past (Isa 51:8–9), of the future (Ps 49:11; Ex 31:16), of the past and future (Ps 102:24), of the present (Gen 6:9), or of the men of that generation (Ex 1:6). Besides the normal meaning, it also is used of a class of men both in a good sense (Ps 14:5; 24:6) and in a bad sense (Deut 32:5, 20). The Aram. cognate is used only four times with the general meaning of "generation" (Dan 4:3, 34).

2. The term *tôl^edôth* is used *c.* 40 times in the OT. The word is always in the plural and hence it has the meaning "offsprings" or "generations," being formed from *yālad* which means "to beget," "to bear." This word is more concerned with the descendants of a man, and consequently it is the term that is used in the genealogical history of a man or family (cf. its repeated usage in Num 1:20–40). It occurs frequently in Genesis, and on this basis the book may be divided into 11 sections, each being styled with the words "the generations of . . ." (2:4; 5:1; 6:9; 10:1; 11:10; 11:27; 25:12; 25:19; 36:1; 36:9; 37:2). Whether the term *tôl^edôth* introduces what is to follow (E. J. Young) or concludes what has preceded like a colophon on a cuneiform tablet (R. K. Harrison) is a technical point still being debated.

3. The Gr. word *genea* occurs around 40 times in the NT, and it is the common term in the LXX as a translation of *dôr*. It has the concept of the sum total of those born at the same time—contemporaries (Mt 11:16; 12:41), a period of time (Acts 15:21, NASB; Eph 3:5, NASB; Col 1:26), or a kind of people (Lk 16:8).

4. The Gr. *genesis* occurs five times in the NT (Mt 1:1, 18; Lk 1:14; Jas 1:23; 3:6, see NASB marg.) and is used chiefly in the LXX as a translation of *tôl^edôth*. It has the basic meaning of "origin," "birth," or "existence." Our name for the book of Genesis is from the Gr. title Genesis, which has the added meaning of "origin" or "generation." The whole book was thought of as the "Book of Generations" from this phrase as found in the LXX in 2:4*a* and 5:1.

5. Gr. *gennema* is used only four times in the NT (Mt 3:7; 12:34; 23:33; Lk 3:7). It has the basic meaning of "offspring" and in each case it is used in the phrase "generation of vipers," or "offspring of vipers."

6. Although *genos* occurs *c.* 20 times in the NT it is translated "generation" in the KJV only in I Pet 2:9. Basically the term connotes the meaning of "race," and it is so translated in the ASV, RSV and NASB.

In conclusion, the term "generation" has the basic meaning of a span of time, usually from a man's birth to the birth of his son. This span of time varies within the Scriptures, for according to Job 42:16 it was reckoned 30 to 40 years; in Deut 1:35; 2:14; etc., it was the 40 year period of the wilderness wanderings; and in Gen 15:13, 16 it was a period of approximately 100 years. The length of generations varies at different periods of history.

Bibliography. P. R. Ackroyd, "The Meaning of the Hebrew Dôr Considered," JSS, XIII (1968), 3-10. W. F. Albright, "Abram the Hebrew: A New Archaeological Interpretation," BASOR #163 (Oct., 1961), 50–51. R. K. Harrison, *Introduction to the Old Testament,* Grand Rapids: Eerdmans, 1969, pp. 543–551. K. A. Kitchen, *Ancient Orient and Old Testament,* Chicago: Inter-Varsity, 1966, pp. 53 f. F. J. Neuberg, "An Unrecognized Meaning of Hebrew Dôr," JNES, IX (1950), 215–217. E. J. Young, *An Introduction to the Old Testament,* Grand Rapids: Eerdmans, 1949, pp. 52–66.

H. W. H.

GENESIS (jĕn'ĕ-sĭs). The first book of the Bible and the first book of Moses is named from the Gr. title given to it in consequence of its subject matter. The name means "beginnings," or the name could refer to the genealogies which are so prominent in the early chapters (cf. Gen 2:4 and 5:1 with Mt 1:1). In Heb. the book was named after its first word, *b^e^rē'shît,* according to the usual Heb. practice. The word means "in the beginning."

Genesis is part of a larger work, the five books of Moses called the Pentateuch (*q.v.*). There is a uniform plan discernible in the Pentateuch. The early history goes down to the end of Genesis. Exodus carries on the history of Israel to the encampment at Sinai and the consecration of the tabernacle. Leviticus gives the laws, many of which were promulgated at Sinai. Numbers begins with the preparations for the first attempt to invade Canaan and carries the history to the end of the wilderness wanderings. Deuteronomy in large measure repeats the laws and histories of Sinai and the wilderness period in sermonic form, as the basis for the nation's renewal of its covenant vows. Genesis, then, seems to be part of the larger work, Scroll I of the Pentateuch. It is the only source for the pre-Exodus period; Deuteronomy does not rehearse this material. I Chronicles quotes extensively from the genealogies of Genesis, and other OT passages refer to it rather often. But Genesis is unique in its content.

Date and Authorship

The historic view. The time-honored view of the date and authorship of Genesis can be briefly stated. With one voice the Jews and the Christian church acknowledged the Mosaic authorship of the book until the rise of higher criticism in the 19th cen. It can hardly be doubted that this is the position witnessed in Neh 8–9. The book from which the Levites read is called the "book of the law of Moses" (Neh 8:1). But in Nehemiah's prayer (Neh 9) the history of Israel is summarized, beginning with creation and the call of Abram, continuing with the Exodus, Sinai, the rebellion at Kadesh-barnea, a quotation from Ex 34:6 (Neh 9:17), the wilderness experiences, the Transjordan conquest and, briefly, the later history of Israel. In short, the subject material of the whole Pentateuch beginning with Genesis is given. This witness gains somewhat from the tendency of recent scholars to agree with and ascribe the historic late 5th cen. dates to Ezra-Nehemiah and the books of Chronicles (F. L. Cross, *The Ancient Library of Qumran* [1961], p. 189; John Bright, *History of Israel* [1959], p. 383).

That Moses wrote the law is taught repeatedly in the OT (cf. Josh 1:7–9; 23:6; I Kgs

Abraham's well near Hebron as later incorporated into the temple of Hadrian. HFV

2:3; 8:53, 56; Ezr 7:6; etc.). In references to Israel's history, the events of Genesis are quoted in the same sequence with Exodus, Leviticus, Numbers, and Deuteronomy. In addition to the sequence in Neh 9, the historical Ps 105 is another case in point. Also the allusions in Hosea to the ancient history of the nation refer with equal facility to Genesis (Hos 12:3–4, 12), to Exodus (Hos 12:13; 13:4), to Leviticus (Hos 12:9), to Numbers (Hos 9:10), to Deuteronomy (ref. to Zeboim, Hos 11:8), and to later books. Genesis was clearly part of Israel's early sacred history.

In the NT Christ began at "Moses and all the prophets" expounding the messianic prophecies in "all the scriptures" (Lk 24:27). It is clear that Jesus considered the first book of the Bible Mosaic. Indeed, one of His names for the OT is "Moses and the prophets" (Lk 16:29, 31; cf. Jn 5:46–47; Mt 5:17; Lk 24:44). The apostles also used the terminology (Acts 26:22; 28:23). At the same time, Christ referred to many items in the Genesis record as part of the inspired Scriptures (Mt 19:4–6; 24:38; Lk 17:32; Jn 7:22). It is clear that Christ and the apostles held to the Mosaic authorship of Genesis. The Jewish historian Josephus expressly stated the same view in about A.D. 90 (*Against Apion* 1.8). No ancient authority of value brings this view into question.

As to the date of Genesis, the conservative position settles on the period of the wilderness wandering, about 1440–1400 B.C., because of the Mosaic authorship. The traditional date of the Exodus is calculated from the reference in I Kgs 6:1 as 480 years before Solomon began his temple. There is room for some slight elasticity here. The LXX text has 440 years. The date of Solomon's temple is about 960 B.C. With these figures the data in Jud 11:26 agree. An alternative dating of about 1250 B.C. is urged by some on the basis of certain archaeological data, but there seems to be no compelling reason to depart from the date most agreeable to the biblical text. *See* Exodus, Date of.

Critical views. With the rise of the rationalistic movement in Germany around A.D. 1800, the Mosaic authorship of all the Pentateuch was questioned. These views may be traced in any standard OT introduction (see Gleason L. Archer, *Survey of OT Introduction*, 1974, pp. 66–219).

The critical view has passed through several stages. First Genesis was divided into two documents on the basis of the different divine names Elohim and Jehovah (the Heb. consonants of which are YHWH). At first it was thought that these were two old documents woven together by Moses himself. Soon, however, the analysis was extended to the rest of the Pentateuch where the same phenomenon appears, and then the compiler was said to have lived long after Moses. The Mosaic authorship of the whole Pentateuch was thus denied.

It was noticed, however, that the general style of parts of the Elohim document differed from the Jehovah document, whereas other parts more or less resembled it. So the Elohim document was divided into an E_1 and E_2. The book of Deuteronomy was also isolated as containing much work of another source. There were thus four documents, E_1, E_2, J, and D. Some critics using similar criteria—that every alleged difference in style betokened a different author—divided up the Pentateuch into many fragments.

It remained for Wellhausen in about 1875 to set the patterns of thought for many years. He argued that these four documents, which he called J, E, D, P, could be dated by comparing their legal and historical references to the known history and legal picture of ancient Israel. If a document refers only to late legislation, the document is surely late.

One trouble with Wellhausen's theory was that in those days scholars were woefully ignorant of the history of the ancient Near East, let alone of the history of Israel, and Wellhausen all too often was left to reconstruct an artificial history. He did this quite confidently using the Hegelian philosophy of evolutionary progress, which was the last word in Wellhausen's day (1875). It is not remarkable, therefore, that when Wellhausen was done, he was able to show a beautiful progression in thought and culture from rude beginnings in Israel's history to its flowering expression in the 8th cen. prophets. It was a noble expression of Victorian ideology.

Two things have combined to overthrow Wellhausen's imposing edifice. First, the Hegelian philosophy of the evolutionary progress of history has largely given way to a more pessimistic existentialism since World War II. Secondly, the study of archaeology took great strides forward with the discovery of many additional clay tablets since the First World War and with the scientific unearthing of Palestinian cities. Whereas ancient history once began with Greece and Rome, and Herodotus was called the "father of history," now high school textbooks go back to 3000 B.C. for the start of written history, and there is much still earlier material in stratified sequence.

The notable thing, however, is that this wealth of ancient history fits beautifully with the biblical record. For example, the remains of people of Sumer who lived in lower Mesopotamia were discovered. The Bible called it the land of Shinar, which Heb. word is a good representation of "Sumer" (Gen 10:10; 11:2; 14:1). The Hurrian people were rediscovered with their customs and language. The Bible called them Horites. The ancient city of Uruk (biblical Erech) was uncovered and the oldest written tablets (from *c.* 3300 B.C.) were found there. The exploits of the great king Sargon of Accad of *c.* 2350 B.C. were discovered. Accad has not yet been identified, but Accad, Erech and Babel are all mentioned in Gen 10:10.

Ancient kings, ancient peoples, ancient cities, ancient cultures and ancient languages have been resurrected from centuries of oblivion. But the Bible all along preserved the kings,

The Patriarchs lived in tents and their "expanded families" must have created tent villages similar to those still to be seen in Palestine. HFV

cities and peoples in the right sequences and connections, and reflected the ancient cultures in the most natural ways. For a writing made up from a hodgepodge of sources by a later editor having very limited knowledge, this would be well-nigh a miracle. Archaeology has proved at least the substantial historicity of the biblical records. And nowhere has this work been more welcome than in the book of Genesis which, after all, concerns history of the distant past. Archaeological light is thrown on almost all parts of the book of Genesis. Further details are given under the discussion of the book's content.

In the early portions of Genesis the Flood story was divided by Wellhausen into two documents J and P, the first source written *c.* 850 B.C., the second *c.* 450 B.C. Since then the Babylonian flood story has been discovered. It dates from long before the time of Moses. The relation between this story and the Bible is uncertain. Possibly both depended on ancient records and reports of the Flood itself. But at least both the J document and the later P document have interesting parallels with the early Babylonian flood story. A natural conclusion is that the documentary division is artificial and Wellhausen's datings are quite arbitrary.

Especially the patriarchal narratives of Genesis have been supported by tablets from the town of Nuzu and elsewhere which give the legal and family customs of Hurrian settlers in Semitic (Amorite and Aramaic) lands. These customs evidently were known by the patriarchs from their residence in Haran and Ur, and the close similarity of the patriarchal practices to the Nuzu laws is striking. Standard OT introductions give details. One example will suffice. The birthright inheritance involving the double portion of a principal heir in Nuzu normally went to the oldest son. But it could be sold, and there is a case of the sale of a birthright for three sheep. Also it could be transferred by the father, and a case on record upholds the father's oral pronouncement in such a case (cf. Gen 48:17-20).

Notice that no such provisions or practices are found in Israel's later laws or history. The one passage in the Mosaic legislation dealing with birthrights forbids changing the natural order (Deut 21:15-17). Only in the patriarchal families are such customs witnessed. How would a late Israelite author like "J" at 850 B.C. or "P" at 450 B.C. know how to distinguish so accurately the ancient Mesopotamian background and customs of the patriarchs from the Mosaic legislation current in Israel?

Many such examples have driven recent OT scholars to accept the historicity even in detail of the patriarchal narratives. It is most difficult to combine this conclusion with Wellhausen's dictum of the late date of the alleged documents determined by comparing their background situations.

More recent critical study argues that the Pentateuch (and other historical books) were put together at a late date from early oral tradi-

The problem of water supply looms large in the patriarchal narrative. Here is the traditional well of Abraham at Beer-sheba. HFV

tions which were very faithfully preserved and transmitted. But opinions differ as to whether these oral traditions were all written down together after the Exile or were the background of J, E, D, and P, the usual Wellhausian documents which were combined after the Exile. In either case, the theory seems very unnatural. Writing was exceedingly common in all Mesopotamia and Egypt long before the patriarchal period. Why should it be thought that Israel alone of the nations had no written literature? This conclusion is especially odd when it is remembered that it was probably in Syria-Palestine that the alphabet was invented—the most convenient tool known for written expression!

It is true that ancient documents from Palestine have been almost completely lost except for the later Dead Sea Scrolls. But the explanation is not that they had no literature. It is simply that their literature has perished. If they had used cuneiform signs and had written on clay, the material would have lasted. But evidently they wrote on papyrus and skins. These items last well in the dry climate of Egypt, but in the rainy climate of Palestine they soon perish. It may indeed be true that the ancient Heb. people memorized much, and loved to recite their epics and religious literature. But that they did not also have the written word is pure theory. The archaeological support for the Genesis histories and laws is an impressive argument in favor of the witness of both the OT and the NT that Genesis and the rest of the Pentateuch is old, authoritative, and Mosaic.

Outline of Genesis

I. Pre-Abrahamic History, Chaps. 1-11
   A. Creation and Fall, 1-3
   B. Cain and his descendants, 4
   C. Antediluvian genealogy, 5
   D. The Flood, 6-9
   E. Postdiluvian nations and genealogy, 10-11

II. History of Abraham, Chaps. 12-25
   A. Call and settlement in Palestine, 12-13

B. Battle with the four kings, 14
C. Abrahamic covenant confirmed, 15–17
D. Sodom and Gomorrah, 18–19
E. Abraham and Abimelech, 20
F. The birth and offering of Isaac, 21–22
G. Death of Sarah, 23
H. Isaac's marriage and Abraham's death, 24–25

III. Isaac and His Sons, Chaps. 26–36
A. Isaac's history, 26
B. Jacob and the birthright, 27
C. Jacob at Haran, 28–31
D. Jacob again in Palestine, 32–35
E. The descendants of Esau, 36

IV. Joseph's History, Chaps. 37–50
A. Joseph's youth and dreams, 37
B. Judah's shame, 38
C. Joseph's slavery, 39–40
D. Joseph's exaltation, 41
E. Joseph and his brethren, 42–48
F. Jacob's prophetic poem, 49
G. Death of Jacob and of Joseph, 50

Content of the Book

Plan. It has often been pointed out that the author of Genesis wrote on a unified plan. In almost every case he tells the story of Israel proceeding from the general to the particular. He first tells of the entire world, or the entire race, or all the descendants of a man; then he concentrates on the specific, on a garden which he presents in detail, or the segment of the race important in the history, or the descendants of a man who carries on the line with which he is concerned.

Thus the first chapter deals with creation as a whole. Chaps. 2 and 3 give the picture of Adam, the fountainhead of the history. Chap. 4 gives the history and genealogy of Cain, who is not heard of again. Chap. 5, however, gives the genealogy of Seth which connects with Noah. After the Flood, the colonization of the whole Near East is given first in chap. 10; then comes the genealogy leading to Abraham. In the patriarchal histories, Ishmael is treated before Isaac; the descendants of Esau, before Jacob. Obviously Genesis as we have it is the work of one master mind, an author of competence using his materials skillfully and under the inspiration of the Spirit.

Creation narratives. Volumes have been written on the first chapter of Genesis. Two items are of special interest: first, the relation to Babylonian cosmogonies; and second, the relation to modern science.

As to the relation to Babylonian creation myths, the matter is discussed extensively in A. Heidel, *The Babylonian Genesis* (1951). The Babylonian story starts with warfare among the gods. The second generation of gods rebel against the first. Marduk is victorious. He vanquishes the goddess Tiamat and splits her dead body into halves making the heaven and earth. He creates man from the blood of her ally Kingu. There is no clear relation between the biblical account and the Babylonian stories.

As to scientific problems, the Genesis account gives few details. There is much truth in the statement that the Bible is not a book of science but of religion. Nevertheless, Genesis is clear that God made the worlds and is the Lord of nature as well as of spirits. Therefore where the Bible touches on science, it must be held to be correct when fairly and accurately interpreted. The Bible in Gen 1 and elsewhere declares that God created the worlds out of nothing. Matter is not eternal. With this view the current theories of science have no quarrel. One major claim is that all matter originated in a vast nuclear explosion some ten billion years ago. Science cannot say what caused the explosion. Genesis says, "In the beginning God. . . ."

The apparent great antiquity of the universe has been a problem. A theory of recent days has been that Gen 1:1 speaks of the distant creation of matter; v. 2 tells of a catastrophe which overtook creation at a fairly recent date; the following verses tell of quite recent events on the earth.

Another theory has been that the creative days of Genesis are not to be viewed as actual days in which events took place but as days on which God revealed certain items to Moses. They were "revelatory days." This view and variations of it do not seem to do justice to the meaning of the biblical text.

Another view, popularized by J. Whitcomb and H. Morris in *The Genesis Flood* (1961), suggests that the universe is not actually old. It appears to be old because God created it "fully grown" with the appearance of age. This view has some attractive features but has some philosophical problems too. Would God have created sedimentary rocks with fossils already in them? The view is usually associated with the idea that the Flood caused many fossils which are therefore of recent origin. It is a question if this view can be scientifically sustained.

A fourth view, held widely for many years, is that the days of Gen 1 were not 24 hour days but were periods of greater or longer extent. They began before the sun was established to mark the days, and the seventh day of God's rest from creation is still continuing, it would seem. This view is in general accord with scientific thought of today. Those who hold it argue that Gen 1:14 refers to the clearing away of dense clouds so that the sun and moon which were previously established became visible. The writer favors this view, but it should be remembered that scientific estimates of the age of the earth may well be wrong. Many present estimates depend upon astronomical and radiation theories which are of recent origin and which are not always self-consistent. There is room for reserve and further study of all these theories.

Gen 2:4–25 tells of the specific and separate creation of our first parents. The garden of

Eden was located in the Mesopotamian southland where the four rivers are located. (Ethiopia, Gen 2:13, is more properly Cush, the territory E of the Tigris.) Gen 2:5 probably refers not to the whole earth, but to paradise alone which was watered by irrigation from underground sources. (Heb. *'ēd,* "mist," from Akkad. *edû* seems to mean an underground flow.) Nothing in this section refers to anything in the earth outside of Eden. As to the alleged evolutionary origin of all species from one original germ and the evolutionary origin of man as well, cf. Carl F. H. Henry, "Theology and Evolution" in *Evolution and Christian Thought Today,* ed. R. Mixter (1959). *See* Creation.

The genealogical data. Four main genealogies are found in the early chapters: that of Cain (chap. 4), the antediluvians and postdiluvians (chaps. 5 and 11), and the Table of Nations (chap. 10). The contrast is plainest between chaps. 10 and 11. The so-called Table of Nations is not a genealogy at all. It is an outline of the result by Moses' time of the colonizing of the Near East after the Flood. In the movement of tribes and nations, some genealogical relations are involved; but in the peopling of Canaan, for instance (10:15-18), Canaan is said to "beget" peoples not individuals. Heth was apparently Indo-European, the Jebusite was probably Hurrian. The Amorite was of course Semitic but is found among the "sons" of Ham. One of the "sons" of Ham was Mizraim. This was the ancient name for Egypt and is a noun of dual formation referring to the union of upper and lower Egypt about 3000 B.C.

That there are omissions in the genealogies found in chaps 5 and 10 is a view widely held. Numerous other genealogies show such gaps. Thus four generations are reckoned from Levi to Moses (Ex 6:16-20), but the Levites in the generation of Moses and Aaron numbered 22,000 men (Num 3:39). Also, if the genealogy in Gen 11 is complete, Shem and his son Arphaxad actually outlived Abraham! This is not the picture one gets from the Abrahamic narratives. Recognition of these and other points has convinced most that Ussher's dates for creation (4004 B.C.) and the Flood (2350 B.C.) must be pushed back by an undetermined number of years.

The Flood narrative. The Bible plainly says that there was a flood, worldwide in its extent, sent by God to eradicate sinful mankind. The Mesopotamian peoples had a flood tradition, as did many other cultures. The Babylonian story has been studied and compared with the Bible by A. Heidel in *The Gilgamesh Epic* (1949). It is reasonable to conclude that similarities are found because both accounts reflect the actual occurrence.

Scientific evidence for the Flood is lacking, but so is evidence against it. Calculation of the size of the ark has often been made, and it has been shown to have the requisite capacity for all the animals (A. M. Rehwinkel, *The Flood,* St. Louis: Concordia Pub. House [1951], pp. 68 ff.). It may be that the Flood was not so simple a phenomenon as has been imagined. It could possibly have been a heavy deluge of rain, plus movements in the earth's crust making the ocean levels rise, plus heavy and long-continued snow in the higher altitudes and northern latitudes. It seems clear that there was a great change of climate about 10,000 years ago. The widely publicized Siberian mammoths apparently lived in a climate with buttercups (found in their mouths) and abundant grass. They were instantaneously frozen, some still on their feet, and have stayed frozen ever since so that their meat is preserved! *See* Flood.

Abraham's life. Abraham was undoubtedly not the only God-fearing man of that time. God surely had spoken to many individuals, such as Enoch before the Flood and Melchizedek afterward. But with Abraham, God determined to do a new thing—to gather His people into one place and by intensive revelation of His word and grace to prepare a large cohesive group of people for the advent of Christ and the blessing of the nations. It may be noted that Palestine was a land bridge, and the caravans of three continents crossed its boundaries. The Jews in Palestine and by their Messiah were truly to be a light to the nations (Isa 42:6; 49:6; 51:4).

God chose Abraham, instructed him in sacrifice, and gave him the covenant sign of circumcision. Circumcision was practiced in Egypt and elsewhere at the age of puberty, but as far as is known the infant circumcision of the Jews was unique in antiquity. It was a sign of both race and grace (Gen 17:14; Deut 30:6; Rom 2:29). Later the Abrahamic clan became welded into a nation by Moses. But the bases of the faith of Israel were clear in Abraham. Indeed, the ritual of sacrifice was as old as Adam. Abraham, believing in one true, living God, had a spiritual and ethical monotheism. He recognized human sin, offered sacrifices for cleansing, hoped in the Redeemer to come and in eternal heavenly fellowship with God (Gen 22:8, 18; John 8:56; Heb 11:10). The cultural background of Abraham is now brilliantly illuminated from Ur, Mari, Nuzu, and other discoveries. *See* Abraham; Patriarchal Age.

Isaac and Jacob. Isaac's life is little known, as he was overshadowed by his more famous father and son. Isaac, however, was a peaceful man who turned the other cheek to Abimelech (Gen 26:17-31). He too received the messianic promise (26:4). *See* Isaac.

Jacob has perhaps been dealt with harshly. He (really his mother) schemed for the birthright. But it should be remembered that it had been promised by God to the younger twin (25:23), and Jacob apparently desired the birthright for spiritual rather than monetary reasons. Jacob at Bethel consecrated himself to the Lord (28:20-22). Jacob and his wives ascribed the birth of their children to God's answer to prayer (Gen 30). Even Jacob's increase of his sheep, though due in part to his industry, partly to his superstition about prenatal influence and in part perhaps to some observation of principles of heredity, is nonetheless ascribed in the last analysis to God's providence (31:9, 42). Jacob's prayer at Peniel was based on God's promises as well as obedience to God's commands (32:9–12). In the wrestling with the angel Jacob asked for God's blessing rather than for material advantage (32:25–30). In dealing with Esau he ascribed all his advancement to God (33:11). *See* Jacob.

Joseph in Egypt. The story of Joseph has been a perennial favorite. Its real message is not merely the story of rags to riches, but how God in fine details of providence accomplished His perfect will. Joseph's future was foretold by God. Apparently Joseph believed it, though the rest of the family were irritated at his dreams.

When young men leave home for trade or war they often either grow tall or fall badly. Joseph grew tall. When no one was watching but God, Joseph lived for God even though he suffered because of his integrity. But in prison he still believed and maintained his character, and at last God blessed him and used him like few other individuals.

Joseph apparently became the grand vizier of Egypt under one of the foreign Asiatic Hyksos kings. The Hyksos period was *c.* 1750–1570 B.C., though various dynasties reigned in this period. Some have held that Joseph's ascendancy happened before the Hyksos (Exodus at 1440 B.C., I Kgs 6:1; bondage of 430 years, Ex 12:40, making Joseph's date 1870 B.C.). This view is argued by Gleason Archer (*op. cit.,* pp. 205–208) following John Rea ("Time of the Oppression and the Exodus," BETS, III [1960], 58–59).

An alternative view supported by the LXX is that the period of 430 years includes both the patriarchal residence in Canaan (215 years) and the Egyptian bondage (1655–1440 B.C.). Thus Joseph's governorship began during the Hyksos dynasty. The Hyksos introduced chariots into Egypt (cf. Gen 41:43). They changed land tenure so that all land was owned by the crown except temple lands. Thereafter the crown exacted a 20 percent tax (cf. Gen 47:20-26). However, the details are obscure partly because little is known of the Hyksos. The date of the Exodus itself is under debate, although the biblical evidence as given above seems clear (cf. I Kgs 6:1; Jud 11:26).

Joseph's sterling character was finally shown not in adversity but in prosperity, where he wisely and carefully tested his brethren, then freely forgave *and forgot.* Thus by his magnanimity he laid the basis for the expansion of Israel into the nation that God had predicted. No other man was more aware of God's overruling providence. *See* Joseph.

Genesis closes with the great messianic prophecy of Jacob (Gen 49:10, treated by the writer in an appendix in J. O. Buswell's *Systematic Theology of the Christian Religion* [1963]. II, 544). The touching story is briefly told of Jacob's death and burial in the cave of Machpelah, and Joseph's directions for his own embalming and eventual burial in the land of Canaan when God should have fulfilled His promises to Israel.

Bibliography. Gleason L. Archer, *A Survey of Old Testament Introduction,* Chicago: Moody Press, 1964. John Bright, *A History of Israel,* Philadelphia: Westminster Press, 1959. U. Cassuto, *Commentary on Genesis,* 2 vols., Jerusalem: Magnes Press, 1964. Jack Finegan, *Light from the Ancient Past,* 2nd ed., Princeton: Univ. Press, 1959. Cyrus H. Gordon, *The World of the Old Testament,* New York: Doubleday, 1958. Alexander Heidel, *The Babylonian Genesis,* 2nd ed., Chicago: Univ. of Chicago Press, 1951; *The Gilgamesh Epic and Old Testament Parallels,* 2nd ed., Chicago: Univ. of Chicago Press, 1949. Walter C. Kaiser, "The Literary Form of Genesis 1–11," NPOT, pp. 48–65. Ernest F. Kevan, "Genesis," NBC, 1953. Derek Kidner, *Genesis,* London: Tyndale Press, 1967. K. A. Kitchen, *Ancient Orient and the Old Testament,* Chicago: Inter-Varsity Press, 1966. H. C. Leupold, *Exposition of Genesis,* Columbus: Wartburg Press, 1942. E. A. Speiser, *Genesis* (Anchor Bible), Garden City, N.Y.: Doubleday, 1964. W. H. Griffith Thomas, *Genesis—A Devotional Commentary,* Grand Rapids: Eerdmans, 1946. J. A. Thompson, *The Bible and Archaeology,* Grand Rapids: Eerdmans, 1962. G. Van Groningen, "Interpretation of Genesis," JETS, XIII (1970), 199–218. John C. Whitcomb and Henry M. Morris, *The Genesis Flood,* Philadelphia: Presbyterian and Reformed Pub. Co., 1962. K. M. Yates, "Genesis," WBC, 1962; consult for further bibliography. Edward J. Young, *Genesis 3,* London: Banner of Truth Trust, 1966.

R. L. H.

GENNESARET (gĕ-nĕs'á-rĕt). The Gr. form of the Heb. name Chinnereth (*q.v.*) for the Sea of Galilee, found in the LXX and Mt 14:34; Mk 6:53; Lk 5:1. *See* Galilee, Sea of; Palestine, II. B. 3. *c.*

GENTILES. The plural of the word "nation" (Heb. *gôy*; Gr. *ethnos*) has sometimes been translated "nations," sometimes "Gentiles," sometimes "heathen." "Gentiles" has applied to all nations other than the Jewish without reflecting antipathy necessarily. "Heathen" has reflected a strong antipathy (II Kgs 16:3; Ezr 6:21; Ps 9:5, 15, 19).

In its early use, the word "Gentiles" or "nations" (*gôyim*) was applied without distinction to divisions among the descendants of Shem, Ham, and Japheth (Gen 10:5, 20, 31). The background for distinctions appeared in spiritual ideals for Israel held up by the Lord Himself. The promise concerning Abraham's seed (Gen 12:3) was interpreted by the first covenant at Sinai as making true believers in Israel an elect nation, chosen as a kingdom of priests to teach other nations about Yahweh (Ex 19:4–6). These ideals gave warrant for the description of

Israelites who "keep justice" and "do righteousness" as "thy nation," i.e., Yahweh's nation (Ps 106:5), while other nations are called "the nations," i.e., Gentiles (Isa 60:3; Acts 13:47). *See* Foreigners; Nations.

Perversion of the ideal relations led to emphasis upon the fact that "the nations" were identified with idolatry and basely corrupt (Lev 18:24). In turn Israelites often forgot to be priests of Yahweh. The forgetful Israelites considered Gentiles merely as "heathen" (Ps 9:5; 10:16).

The bitterness on both sides is marked for removal by missions. Hate is contrary to the heart of God (Jon 4:10–11). The Gentile nations are also to become the heritage of Messiah (Ps 2:8; Isa 42:1, 6; 49:6). Israelites and Gentiles are to be accepted as co-leaders in the messianic kingdom (Isa 66:12, 19–23). Followers of Jesus, Jews or Gentiles, are commanded to make disciples of all peoples (Mt 28:19–20). Paul described the redemption of Christ and faith in His work as resulting in the breaking down of "the middle wall of partition" between Jew and Gentile (Eph 2:14). This has reference to the partition wall which fenced out Gentiles from the inner courts of the Herodian temple. *See* Middle Wall of Partition; Commission, Great; Dispersion of Mankind; Nations.

J. W. W.

GENTILES, COURT OF THE. *See* Temple.

GENTLENESS. This term in English indicates moderation in action, refinement in mannerisms and disposition, and the absence of that which is precipitate and rough. The Heb. term is *'ānâ*, with the basic meaning "to bend low," "to condescend." Cf. God's clemency toward mankind (Ps 18:35). Four terms are used for gentleness in the NT:

1. Gr. *chrēstotēs* (Tit 3:4; Rom 2:4; II Cor 6:6; Eph 2:7; Gal 5:22; Col 3:12), with the general meaning of "benignity," "sweetness," "potential goodness," "moral goodness and integrity." Josephus ascribes it to the nature of Isaac. Old mellow wine was referred to as *chrēstos*. The pagans seemed to confuse *chrēstos* with the name of Christ, *Christos*, which could not be considered a total mistake in the light of Christ's nature. He Himself speaks of His yoke (Mt 11:30) as being *chrēstos*, i.e., one which does not chafe or irk or gall, but is smooth and even. Hence, the term suggests that gracious nature which mellows that which otherwise would have been harsh and austere.

2. Gr. *prautēs*, "gentleness," "mildness," "meekness," "forbearance" (I Cor 4:21; II Cor 10:1; Gal 5:23). The term seems also to specify courtesy, considerateness, and a humble, unassuming spirit (II Tim 2:25).

3. Gr. *ēpios*, "affable," "kindness toward someone" (I Thess 2:7; II Tim 2:24).

4. Gr. *epieikeia*, which would indicate that which is equitable, fair, mild, gentle, seemly, or a sweet reasonableness (Phil 4:5; I Tim 3:3; Tit 3:2). It is the opposite of contention and self-seeking, and is defined by Aristotle as "equity, or fairness of mind." Little wonder, then, that Paul specifies this as one of the qualities of a church official.

There is yet another similar term (*philanthrōpia*) which, while not translated "gentleness," carries the basic concept of "courtesy," "kindness," or "love to one's fellowman" (Acts 27:3; 28:2; Tit 3:4).

R. E. Pr.

GENUBATH (gē-nū'băth). Son of Hadad, the fugitive Edomite prince (I Kgs 11:19–20), who was brought up in Egypt with sons of Pharaoh. David's conquering of Edom necessitated the flight (I Kgs 11:15–20). Genubath's mother was a sister of Tahpenes, queen of the Pharaoh of Egypt.

GERA (gē'ra)

1. The son of Bela and grandson of Benjamin. In Genesis he is called the son of Benjamin and listed with those who went down to Egypt (Gen 46:21; I Chr 8:3, 5).

2. A Benjamite, the father of Ehud the judge (Jud 3:15).

3. A Benjamite of Bahurim, the father of Shimei who cursed David (II Sam 16:5; 19:16, 18; I Kgs 2:8).

4. The son of Ehud, a Benjamite, who was removed (KJV) or exiled (RSV) with his brothers to Manahath (I Chr 8:7).

GERAH. *See* Weights, Measures, and Coins.

GERAR (gē'rär). A city located in the southern extremity of Canaanite settlement. During the patriarchal period its inhabitants were known as Philistines (Gen 20:1 f.; 26:1, 6, 17, 20, 26). Some scholars suggest that Geder in Josh 12:13 may be a case of scribal confusion between *r* and *d* and should be read Gerar. This would associate the town with Hormah (*q.v.*) and Arad (*q.v.*). In I Chr 4:39–41 the LXX reads Gerara, while the MT has Gedor. The Simeonites occupied this area in Hezekiah's time. Asa defeated Zerah at Marisha and pursued his troops as far as Gerar (II Chr 14:13–14). Here the MT has Gerar, while the LXX has Gedor.

Eusebius (*Onomasticon*, 60. 7 ff.) described Gerar as being 25 miles from Eleutheropolis, which fits the location of Tell Abu Hureira (16 miles NW of Beer-sheba on the N side of the Wadi esh-Sheri'ah). Recent surveys have found ceramics on that site which show occupation during the Chalcolithic and in the Middle Bronze I and II plus the Iron Age periods. It is a huge tell of 40 acres with an upper citadel, possibly surrounded by a Hyksos glacis. Gerar is not mentioned in any existing Egyptian records or the Amarna letters.

A. F. R.

GERASA (gĕr'ȧ-sȧ). One of a league of ten semi-independent cities (the Decapolis of Mt 4:25; Mk 5:20; 7:31). Gerasa (Jerash) is pleasantly situated in an open, fertile valley E of the Jordan, i.e., in the OT land of Gilead. Its spectacular archaeological remains are now readily accessible via the northward extension of the Dead Sea highway. The site was occupied in the Bronze Age and a city must have existed there under a Semitic name in the Iron Age, but it is not mentioned in the OT. The extant remains are those of the Gr. city, founded probably by Antiochus IV (175–163 B.C.) under the name Antioch on the Chrysorrhoas, a N tributary of the Jabbok. It was greatly expanded and monumentalized in the Roman and Byzantine periods. It had a territory and presumably a constitution of its own. Macedonian citizens are mentioned in inscriptions. Alexander Jannaeus (107–76 B.C.) incorporated it in the Jewish state, therefore its Jewish inhabitants. It was restored by Pompey (63 B.C.) to such independence as it and the other cities of the league enjoyed thereafter under the Roman governors of Syria and Arabia.

Mark (5:1), followed by Luke (8:26, 37), associates with the "land of the Gerasenes" Jesus' healing of a demoniac, the story implying that the city territory extended to the shore of the Lake of Galilee. This association seems to have been doubted by Matthew who, according to the preferred reading, substituted "land of the Gadarenes" (Mt 8:28). Scribes copying Gospel MSS adapted Matthew, Mark and Luke to each other. The Caesarean text, influenced by Origen, substituted "land of the Gergesenes," to complicate the attestation further. Borders of city territories are only rarely known and those of Gerasa are unknown. The fact that Gadara and its territory lie between Gerasa and the Lake of Galilee explains Matthew's reading, but Gadara too is S of the Yarmuk River. The only corresponding free city E of the lake is Hippos. The location of Origen's Gergesa is unknown. *See* Gadara.

Main street, Jerash. HFV

Its colonnaded streets laid out in accordance with Roman city planning, Gerasa provides the best example of progressive urban development in Palestine in Roman times. Its monumental structures include a triumphal arch, hippodrome, temples of Zeus, of Artemis and of the Arabian god, a nymphaeum, two baths and two theaters. In Byzantine times the temple of the Arabian god was replaced by the Christian cathedral church, the fountain in its atrium being the site of the annual reenactment of the Cana miracle according to Epiphanius (*Panarion,* Her. 51:30, 1–2). It and ten other churches, one a rebuilt synagogue, have been excavated. Excavations (1927–1934) were conducted at the site by Yale University and the British and American Schools of Jerusalem. Further clearances by the Jordan Department of Antiquities are in process. See C. H. Kraeling, *Gerasa, City of the Decapolis,* ASOR, 1938. *See* Archaeology.

C. H. K.

GERASENE (gĕr'ȧ-sēn). A term derived from Gerasa, meaning an inhabitant of Gerasa (*q.v.*) or the nearby region. Two towns bear this name. The Roman Gerasa (Jerash) is too far distant from the Sea of Galilee. This term describes a district on the eastern shore of the Sea of Galilee where Jesus healed the demoniac (Mt 8:28; Mk 5:1; Lk 8:26, 37).

GERGESA. *See* Gadara.

GERGESENE (gûr'gĕ-sēn). To be identified with Gerasene. The terms "country of the Gerasenes" and "country of the Gadarenes" (Mk 5:1; Lk 8:26, 37, see KJV and RSV) are to be preferred to "country of the Gergesenes." *See* Gerasene.

GERIZIM (gĕr'ĭ-zĭm). A mountain 2,849 feet high in central Palestine S of the valley in which the city of Shechem was located. It is sometimes called the mount of blessing because Moses directed that the blessings were to be read from Gerizim while the curses were to be read from Mount Ebal on the opposite side of the valley (Deut 11:29; 27:12 f.; Josh 8:33).

A ledge part way up the mountain is popularly called Jotham's pulpit, from which he supposedly shouted his famous tree fable to the people below (Jud 9:7 ff.). The acoustic properties of the area make it possible for a voice to carry for great distances from certain spots on the mountain.

The Samaritans built a temple on top of Mount Gerizim, probably during the 4th cen. B.C. The Jewish Hasmonean king John Hyrcanus destroyed this temple in 128 B.C. However, the Samaritans still worshiped on Mount Gerizim in Jesus' day (Jn 4:20 f.), and continue to worship there now. The Samaritan synagogue is located in Nablus at the foot of Mount Gerizim.

Many traditions grew up around Gerizim. The Samaritans believe that there can still be seen the site of altars built by Adam, Seth, Noah, and Abraham. The last of these altars is said to have been erected for the sacrifice of Isaac.

Robert J. Bull of Drew University excavated at Tell er-Râs on the N slope of Mount Gerizim in 1964, unearthing the remains of a Roman temple in honor of Zeus erected by the emperor Hadrian (A.D. 117–138), and foundations of a Hellenistic structure which may have been the Samaritan temple destroyed by Hyrcanus (BASOR #180 [1965], pp. 37–41; AJA, LXXI [1967], 387–393).

In 1968 Robert Boling re-excavated a late Middle Bronze Age structure at Tananir, located on the lower N slope of Gerizim, *c.* 350 yards S of ancient Shechem. It was first discovered by G. Welter in 1931. The remains of four building phases (*c.* 1650–1540 B.C.) suggest a temple with rooms grouped around the central courtyard with a round stone pedestal for a sacred pillar. It is suggested Jotham may have stood on its ruins when he addressed the men of Shechem. A similar temple half the size was discovered at the Amman airport in 1955, also outside a city. One may assume these shrines served groups of tribes in covenant with one another (BA, XXXII [1969], 81–116).

R. L. S. and J. R.

Mount Gerizim. HFV

GERSHOM (gûr'shŏm)

1. The firstborn son of Moses and Zipporah who was born in Midian (cf. Ex 2:22; 18:3; I Chr 23:13–16).

2. Same as Gershon, the eldest son of Levi (cf. Gen 46:11; Josh 21:6; I Chr 6:1, 16–17, 22, 43; 23:6–7). His descendants are termed Gershonites (*q.v.*) or the "sons of Gershom" (cf. I Chr 6:62, 71; 15:7).

3. A descendant of Phinehas, who was a priest and the grandson of Aaron. He was one of the "heads of houses" who returned with Ezra from Babylonia (cf. Ezr 8:2).

4. The father of Jonathan, who served as priest to the idolatrous worship practiced by the Danites in the times of the judges (Jud 18:30). An alternate textual tradition reads: "Gershom, son of Levi," thus equating him with the son of Moses (see 1). The substitution of "Manasseh" for "Moses" is explained in the Talmud by asserting that Jonathan did the work of Manasseh, and was therefore counted in his family. Descendants of Gershom were separated from the priestly line of Aaron in a post-Exilic genealogy (I Chr 23:13–16), and Shebuel is named as "chief officer in charge of the treasuries" (I Chr 23:16; 26:24, RSV).

D. W. D.

GERSHON (gûr'shŏn). *See* Gershom 2.

GERSHONITES (gûr'shŏ-nīts). The descendants of Gershon or Gershom (I Chr 6:17, 62, 71), one of the three sons of Levi; thus one of the three clans or main divisions of the Levites. Three apparent attitudes as to the order of importance of these three divisions may be noted in the OT.

1. Gershon, Kohath, and Merari are named in that order in Gen 46:11; Ex 6:16; Num 3:17; 26:57; I Chr 6:1, 16; 23:6, probably because Gershon was Levi's oldest son. Gershonites are mentioned first in a census notation (Num 26:57), in the genealogy of I Chr 6:16–30, and in the list of servants for the temple assembled by David (I Chr 23:7–11).

2. The Gershonites appear second after the Kohathites in Num 4:34–49 and Josh 21:6, 27–33, probably since the latter became dominant because the family of Aaron belonged to their clan. The Joshua passage shows that the cities assigned to the Gershonites were far removed from the city (Jerusalem) of the eventual temple.

3. They are mentioned third in the Chronicles account of David's bringing the ark to Jerusalem (I Chr 15:4–7) and third in II Chr 29:12. No Gershonites are mentioned in I Chr 24; II Chr 20:19 and 34:12.

J. R.

GESHAM (gĕsh'ăm). In I Chr 2:47 Gesham is listed as a descendant of Judah through Caleb. The KJV has "Gesham," but ASV has "Geshan."

GESHEM (gĕsh'ĕm). An Arabian who was one of the chief opponents of Nehemiah's plan to rebuild the wall of Jerusalem in 445 B.C. (cf. Neh 2:19; 6:1-2). He is almost certainly the Gashmu in Neh 6:6. In these verses he is simply referred to as "the Arabian," but the probability is that he was the ruler (king) of the whole province of Arabia.

Geshem is mentioned in at least two inscriptions. A Lihyanite inscription was found at al-'Ula (biblical Dedan) in northwestern Arabia (cf. R. A. Bowman, IB, III, 681-682). An Aramaic inscription was on a silver bowl found at Tell el-Maskhutah (biblical Succoth) near the Suez Canal in Egypt. The inscription reads, "Qainu son of Geshem, king of Kedar." The bowl is now in the Brooklyn Museum. G. Ernest Wright says, "The evidence is accumulating that the territory ruled by his [Geshem's] dynasty was quite extensive, including southern Judah in which Lachish was a chief center, the ancient area of Edom, northern Arabia, Sinai, and some portion of the Nile Delta" (*Biblical Archaeology,* rev. ed., p. 207). He probably built the fine villa or palace and the so-called "solar temple" belonging to the Persian period found in the NE part of the ruined mound of Lachish.

R. L. S.

GESHUR (gĕsh'er). A small Aramean kingdom or city-state located in what is now Jaulan (NT period Gaulanitis), in the NW sector of Bashan. It is mentioned several times in the story of Absalom (II Sam 3:3; 13:37; 14:23, 32; 15:8), as Maacah, the daughter of Talmai, its king, was the mother of Absalom, and Absalom fled to that country after killing Amnon. The kingdom was apparently later absorbed into the larger Aramean kingdom of Damascus.

GESHURI (gĕsh'ŭ-rī), **GESHURITES** (gĕsh'ŭ-rīts). The inhabitants of Geshur, an Aramean tribe on the W border of Bashan (Deut 3:14; Josh 12:5; 13:11). The Geshurites were not expelled by the half tribe of Manasseh to whom the land had been allotted (Josh 13:13). Talmai, a ruler of Geshur, gave his daughter Maacah to David in marriage (II Sam 3:3). The Geshurites and Aram seized the cities of Jair in the land of Gilead (I Chr 2:23). The land of the Geshurites is listed as land yet to be possessed (Josh 13:2). This may suggest another group of Geshurites in the Negeb.

GETHER (gē'thĕr). One of the sons of Aram (Gen 10:23), probably a grandson of Shem (I Chr 1:17). Evidently an Aramean town and kingdom. The clan of which Gether was the founder has not been identified.

GETHSEMANE (gĕth-sĕm'á-nē). From an Aramaic word probably meaning "oil press." It is mentioned in Mt 26:36 and Mk 14:32 as an "enclosed piece of ground" (ASV marg.) to which Jesus returned with His disciples. Lk

In the foreground is the Church of all Nations with the Roman Catholic Garden of Gethsemane to the left. Farther up the Mount of Olives is the Russian Orthodox Garden of Gethsemane. HFV

22:39-41 identifies it only as a "place" (*topos*) on the Mount of Olives. It is called "a garden" located E of the brook Kidron in Jn 18:1. It was a rather extensive area because the main body of disciples sat there while Peter, James, and John went farther up the hill with Jesus. Jesus went still farther in this large olive grove to be alone to pray, leaving the three between Him and the other eight.

There are four rival claimants for the authentic site: the Franciscan (Roman Catholic) garden nearest the highway with gnarled olive trees up to 900 years old and the Basilica of the Agony (the Church of All Nations) housing a traditional Rock of the Agony; the one near the Tomb of the Virgin to the N; the Greek Orthodox to the E; and the large Russian Orthodox orchard farther up the hill adjacent to the Church of Mary Magdalene, the latter being the most "restful."

G. A. T.

GEUEL (gū'ĕl). The son of Machi, a member of the tribe of Gad. He was sent out by Moses as one of the 12 spies to search out the land of Canaan (Num 13:15).

GEZER (gē'zĕr). A city at the border of the Philistine plain and the northern Shephelah (Judean foothills). It overlooked miles of fertile fields and controlled the juncture of the arterial highway from Egypt to Syria and the main road from the Mediterranean coast up the valley of Aijalon to the interior of the hill country and Jerusalem. The mound of its ancient ruins is now called Tell Jezer.

During the Middle and Late Bronze Ages Gezer must have been an important city-state, as the strength of its fortifications and various records would indicate. It appears on lists of cities conquered by the Eighteenth Dynasty pharaohs Thutmose III and Thutmose IV. The Amarna tablets reveal that the rulers of Gezer, Milkilu followed by two men who were possibly his sons, were intermittently rebellious and loyal to Egypt (J. F. Ross, "Gezer in the Tell el-Amarna Tablets," BA, XXX [1967], 62-70). In his famous stele Merneptah boasts that he has seized Gezer, apparently one of the keys in pacifying Canaan (ANET, p. 378).

At the time of the Israelite conquest of Canaan, the king of Gezer was named Horam. He rushed to the aid of Lachish but was defeated in the field by Joshua (Josh 10:33), and is therefore listed among the conquered rulers (Josh 12:12). The city, however, remained in Canaanite hands (Jud 1:29) until Israel became strong enough to put the inhabitants to forced labor (Josh 16:10). It was intended for a Levitical city in the inheritance of Ephraim (Josh 21:21; I Chr 6:67; cf. Josh 16:3; I Chr 7:28). During David's wars Gezer was a strategic point on the Philistine border (II Sam 5:25; I Chr 14:16; 20:4, although II Sam 21:18 reads "Gob"). KJV uses the alternate spelling "Gazer" in II Sam 5:25 and I Chr 14:16.

Gezer was one of Solomon's major fortified centers after Pharaoh (probably Siamun of the Twenty-first Dynasty) had conquered it and given it as dowry to his daughter, Solomon's wife (I Kgs 9:15-19). Recent discoveries have shown that a Solomonic gate and casemate fortification wall at Gezer were almost identical to those at Megiddo and Hazor, the other two major forts in this passage (Yigael Yadin, "Solomon's City Wall and Gate at Gezer," IEJ, VIII [1958], 80-86). From the period of Solomon comes the Gezer calendar, a small limestone tablet inscribed in Heb. that poetically describes the agricultural activities of the 12 months of the year (*see* Calendar). On a temple in Egypt Pharaoh Shishak lists Gezer as one of his conquests on his campaign to Palestine (I Kgs 14:25; II Chr 12:2-4).

The Assyrian Tiglath-pileser III conquered Philistia in 734 B.C. and depicted the siege of *Gazru* (Gezer) on a relief in his palace at Nimrud (Calah). Two 7th cen. B.C. tablets written in Akkad. and found by Macalister at Gezer confirm Assyrian occupation of the city. In 142 B.C. Simon the Maccabee captured Gezer from the Seleucids, and later installed his son John Hyrcanus as commander of the army with headquarters at Gezer (I Macc 9:52; 13:43-53). Persian and Hellenistic remains on the mound and in tombs attest occupation at this time. See H. Darrell Lance, "Gezer in the Land and in History," BA, XXX [1967], 34-47.

Major excavations have been conducted at Gezer by R. A. S. Macalister, 1902-09 (for resumé see Fred E. Young, "Gezer," BW, pp. 254-7); and more recently by the Hebrew Union College beginning in 1964 (Wm. G. Dever, "Excavations at Gezer," BA, XXX [1967], 47-62; "The Water Systems at Hazor and Gezer," BA, XXXII [1969], 71-78; "Further Excavations at Gezer, 1967-71," BA, XXXIV [1971], 93-132).

A. F. R. and J. R.

GEZRITE (gĕz'rīt). According to the LXX and the *qerē'* reading of the Heb. text, this is the correct name of a desert tribe which lived in the region S of Israel, in the same general area as the Amalekites and the Geshurites (I Sam 27:8). It was against these three tribes that David and his men made their raids during his stay at Ziklag. Some texts of the LXX do not contain this word at all; others have variants such as *gezraion* or *gesraion*. The written Heb. text was *girzî*, while the traditional reading was *gizrî*. For this reason some English versions will be found to have Girzites in this passage.

It has been suggested that the inhabitants of Gezer are meant in this reference, but David could not possibly have made raids so far N without his Philistine overlord knowing it.

GHOST. The word occurs about 20 times in the KJV in the archaic expression "gave up the ghost." As the translation of several different

Heb. and Gr. words, the thought is that one has breathed out his last breath and expired. The literal Heb. expression in Jer 15:9 is "she has breathed out her life (or soul)," similar to Job 11:20, "a breathing out of life." At His crucifixion, it is recorded that the Lord Jesus "yielded up [Gr. *aphēken*] His spirit" (Mt 27:50, NASB), "breathed His last" (*exepneusen,* Mk 15:37, 39, NASB), or "gave up [*paredōken*] His spirit" (Jn 19:30, NASB). The ASV and RSV render Gr. *phantasma* as "ghost" in the terrified cry of the disciples upon seeing Jesus walking on the water, "It is a ghost!" (Mt 14:26; Mk 6:49, NASB). *See* Holy Spirit.

GIAH (gī'*à*). An unidentified place on the route followed by Abner in his flight, pursued by Joab (II Sam 2:24). LXX renders the Heb. *gîah* as Gr. *gai,* corresponding to the Heb. *gay',* meaning "valley."

GIANT. An abnormally tall and strong man of ancient times. "Giant" is a translation of several Heb. words.

1. Heb. *gibbôr* (Job 16:14) indicates simply a man great in deeds or in stature.

2. Heb. *rᵉpha'îm* (*see* Rephaim), a race evidently including numerous giants who were among the original inhabitants of Canaan, Edom, Moab, and Ammon. Chedorlaomer in Abraham's time defeated them (Gen 14:5; cf. 15:20). Israel defeated Og (*q.v.*), king of Bashan, one of this race (Deut 3:11; Josh 12:4; 13:12). His bed (or sarcophagus) is said to have been nine cubits long and four cubits wide. Other names of these people are the Anakim (*q.v.*; Deut 2:21), Emim (Gen 14:5; Deut 2:11), and Zamzummin (Deut 2:20). When Israel occupied Canaan, the remnant of these giants took refuge with the Philistines (Josh 11:22). Goliath (*q.v.*) of Gath was a descendant of one of these bands of giants. Others are mentioned by name in II Sam 21:16-22; I Chr 20:4-8. The region near Jerusalem formerly occupied by these giants or Rephaim was for some time referred to as the Valley of the Giants (Josh 15:8; 18:16) or the Valley of Rephaim (II Sam 5:18, 22). In the Ugaritic tablets Dan'el was called the man of Rapha or the Rapha-man (ANET, pp. 149-155). The Rephaim were frequently mentioned in administration tablets of Ugarit as an ethnic group. Many believe they erected the dolmens (*q.v.*) in Palestine.

3. Heb. *nᵉphilîm* is used in only two places (Gen 6:4; Num 13:33). The latter passage identifies the Nephilim (*q.v.*) with the sons of Anak, who in Deut 2:10-11 are connected with the Emim and in Deut 2:20 with the Zamzummim.

Identification of the Nephilim with the Rephaim, as in the foregoing references, does not fit so easily in Gen 6:4. One view of this passage holds that the "sons of God" were fallen angels which united physically with the "daughters of men" to produce a race of giants on earth. An opposing view holds that the relationship referred to here is simply the mingling of the godly line stemming from Seth with the ungodly line of Cain, the offspring of such unions being bold men, daring pioneers, individuals who flouted the laws of God and of society, as the latter part of the verse suggests: "these were the mighty men [*haggibbōrîm*] that were of old, the men of renown" (RSV).

The interpretation in Gen 6:4 hinges on the meaning given to Nephilim. Perhaps derived from *nāphal,* "to fall," the connotation may be "the fallen ones," referring to their fallen, wicked nature. Another meaning could be "the ones who fall" upon others, referring to their violent, tyrannical nature.

Extrabiblical evidence might lend support to the mixed angelic-human view, such as the Babylonian mythology with its Gilgamesh, a Sumerian demigod hero, and the whole Greek and Roman pantheon with its system of demigods and heroes, such as the rebellious Titans, born of the union between gods and mortals. Scriptures commonly cited in favor of this view include Job 1:6; 2:1; 38:7 (where "sons of God" are angelic beings), and Jude 6 with II Pet 2:4. But the latter passage implies that the fall and consignment to judgment of the angels was antediluvial, while Gen 6:4 states that however the "giants" were produced they reappeared after the Flood. Furthermore, Mt 22:30 states that angels are non-sexual.

Meredith J. Kline has suggested that the "sons of God" or "sons of the gods" of Gen 6:2 were antediluvian kings, following pagan terminology for divine kingship. They were noted for tyranny, city-building, and harems (cf. Gen 4:17, 19, 23). In taking as many wives as they wanted they were defying the pattern of monogamy which God had ordained (Gen 2:24), although as kings they acted as guardians of the general ordinances of God for human conduct (WTJ, XXIV [May, 1962], 187-204).

J. K. M. and J. R.

GIBBAR (gĭb'är). In Ezr 2:20 the "children of Gibbar" are mentioned among those who returned with Zerubbabel from Exile. However, the passage in Neh 7:25 has "children of Gibeon." It is possible that Gibbar is a corruption of "Gibeon."

GIBBET. *See* Gallows; Crime and Punishment.

GIBBETHON (gĭb'ĕ-thŏn). A town in west central Palestine in the territory of Dan listed with Eltekeh and Baalath (Josh 19:44). It was assigned to the Kohathite Levites (Josh 21:23). In early days of the northern kingdom Gibbethon belonged to the Philistines. Nadab was slain by Baasha while besieging it (I Kgs 15:27). Omri was besieging it when he was made king to succeed Zimri. It may possibly be identified with Kibbiah, which lies about 16 miles SE of Joppa.

GIBEA (gĭb'ē-*à*). A grandson of Caleb of the tribe of Judah (I Chr 2:49), whose father was

Sheva and whose mother was Maacah, Caleb's concubine (I Chr 2:48).

However, some think that the term is geographical rather than genealogical and refers more to a town in the hill country S of Hebron than to an individual (Josh 15:57). The term Gibea is probably a variation of the more common Gibeah (*q.v.*).

GIBEAH (gĭb'ē-*ȧ*). This is a Heb. word meaning a "hill," especially one used for heathen worship. It is in contrast to the stronger word *har*, "mountain."

1. As a place name its primary reference is to Gibeah of Benjamin, best known as Saul's home town (I Sam 10:26) and later his capital for Israel (I Sam 11:4; 23:19). The earliest reference to the city is in the listing of the cities of Benjamin (Josh 18:28) where the spelling is Gibeath.

Although the shameful story of the Levite's concubine appears at the close of the book of Judges (chaps. 19–20), the episode itself (cf. Hos 9:9; 10:9) took place only shortly after Joshua's conquest when Phinehas, the son of Eleazar, was still high priest (Jud 20:28) and the ark was at Bethel (Jud 20:18). (After this episode the ark was moved to Shiloh.) Tragedy again struck the city when seven of Saul's descendants were hanged because of that king's killing of the Gibeonites (II Sam 21:1–14). Here too is the story of the faithful Rizpah.

Gibeah contributed one of the "thirty" champions of David's army—Ittai, son of Ribai (II Sam 23:29); and at Ziklag two other warriors of Gibeah came to David's aid (I Chr 12:1–3).

Isa 10:29 predicts the city as falling before the Assyrians. Hosea also hears the war trumpet here (Hos 5:8). Gibeah the city also gave its name to the county seat (I Sam 14:2; 22:6).

Tell el-Fûl, three miles N of the Damascus Gate of Jerusalem, covers the ruins of the biblical city. W. F. Albright conducted brief campaigns here in 1922–23 and 1933. Further excavations were made in 1964 to check his findings (BA, XXVIII, 2–10). The small village which Albright found built directly on bedrock was doubtless the one described in Jud 19–20. The site lay dormant for a century or two until the Philistines fortified the mound. Saul or Jonathan captured the town (I Sam 13–14), and Saul erected his palace-fortress, following the Philistine plan. It was a large building, at least 169 by 114 feet with four corner towers.

When David moved the capital to Jerusalem, Gibeah declined and it was not rebuilt until about the 8th cen. B.C. The new city was short-lived, apparently being destroyed by Pekah and Rezin in their attack on Jerusalem about 735 B.C. It was rebuilt in the 7th cen., only to be destroyed in Nebuchadnezzar's conquest of Jerusalem. Later, there was a Hellenistic occupation and also one after the Roman conquest of Palestine, 63 B.C. The city was finally destroyed by Titus the day before he laid

The Mound of Gibeah with an unfinished palace of King Hussein of Jordan on top. HFV

siege to Jerusalem in A.D. 70. King Hussein of Jordan began to construct a palace on top of the mound just before the Six Day War in 1967.

2. A minor town on the plateau SE of Hebron in the tribe of Judah (Josh 15:57).

Bibliography. W. F. Albright, "Excavations and Results of Tell el-Fûl (Gibeah of Saul)," AASOR, IV (1924), 1–89; "A New Campaign of Excavation at Gibeah of Saul," BASOR #52 (1933), pp. 6–12. Paul W. Lapp, "Tell el-Fûl," BA, XXVIII (1965), 2–10. Lawrence A. Sinclair, "An Archaeological Study of Gibeah (Tell el-Fûl)," BA, XXVII (1964), 52–64; AASOR, XXXIV–XXXV (1960), 1–52.

J. L. K.

GIBEATH (gĭb'ē-ăth). A town of Benjamin (Josh 18:28), usually identified with Gibeah, Saul's capital (*see* Gibeah 2). The name means "hill" and is sometimes the first element in compound place names. The hill of Phinehas (Heb. *Gibe 'ath-Phînehas*) was the burial place of Eleazar, the son of Aaron, in Mount Ephraim (Josh 24:33); its location is unknown. Other translations of Gibeath in English versions are the hill of Moreh (*q.v.*), Jud 7:1; the hill of Hachilah (*q.v.*), I Sam 23:19; the hill of Ammah (*q.v.*), II Sam 2:24; the hill of Gareb (*q.v.*), Jer 31:39.

RSV in I Sam 10:5 transliterates the name of a city where a Philistine garrison was stationed as Gibeath-elohim, in most other versions rendered "the hill of God." Since I Sam 13:3 states that the garrison was in Geba (*q.v.*), this town apparently was also known as Gibeath-elohim because of its high place and its group of prophets.

GIBEATHITE (gĭb'ē-*ȧ*-thīt). An inhabitant of the city of Gibeah, a city of the tribe of Benjamin located between Jerusalem and Ramah (Jud 19:11–15). Some of David's mighty men were "of Gibea" (II Sam 23:29; I Chr 11:31; 12:3).

The Mound of Gibeon. HFV

GIBEON, GIBEONITES (gĭb'ĭ-ŏn, gĭb'ĭ-ŏ-nīts; "hill, hill-dwellers"). A city and people in the territory of Benjamin, now identified with the village of el-Jib. In the Bible the name occurs 45 times, the city being alluded to on 15 different occasions in biblical history. Gibeon (el-Jib) is located on a hill about 2,600 feet above sea level, and near the intersection of three roads leading to Joppa via the valley of Ajalon. It lies about six miles NW of Jerusalem and four miles SSW of Ramallah, near the old Jerusalem airport.

The identification of Gibeon with el-Jib was first suggested by Franz von Troilo in A.D. 1666, followed by Richard Pococke in 1738. Edward Robinson in 1838 noted the correspondence between the biblical name and the modern Arabic name and substantiated these earlier suggestions. This identification was challenged by Albrecht Alt who believed that biblical Gibeon and Tell en-Nasbeh are identical. Excavations at Tell en-Nasbeh dispelled this hypothesis, and the excavations at el-Jib under James B. Pritchard (1956-62) confirmed the earlier identification. The identification was made certain by the discovery of 61 inscribed jar handles, on 31 of which the name Gibeon had been incised in paleo-Hebrew. Few biblical sites have a more certain identification.

Gibeon's past, as reconstructed on the basis of excavations, can be traced to three millennia before Christ. Inhabitants of Gibeon in the Early Bronze Age (3100–2100 B.C.) built on bedrock as attested by the discovery of a room of this period containing 14 storage jars with distinctive Early Bronze handles. They were contemporary with similar jar finds in the Early Bronze remains at Tell en-Nasbeh, Jericho, and Ai. A burial cave which contained much pottery of this period was discovered in the hill on the E slope of the city.

During the Middle Bronze I period (2100–1900 B.C.) tent-dwelling seminomads dug shaft tombs, 55 of which have been cleared by the archaeologists halfway down the W slope of the hill. Each consisted of a cylindrical shaft *c.* four feet in diameter and from three to 13 feet in depth, which led down to a small opening into the burial chamber proper, measuring *c.* nine by six feet. In the chamber in 26 of these tombs were found four-spouted lamps, funerary jars, bronze javelins and daggers, or other artifacts characteristic of the Middle Bronze I period.

In the Middle Bronze II or Hyksos period the second actual city was built on the hill. A room belonging to this period, discovered on the NW edge of the site, contained 16 large MB II storage jars. The pottery of this period (1900–1550 B.C.) was far superior to that of Middle Bronze I in both design and texture. Artifacts in the 29 tombs of this period included bronze knives, toggle pins, scarabs, bone inlay and beads in addition to fine pottery. Multiple burials in one tomb was standard procedure of the period. This level of occupation came to an end at the close of the Hyksos period when the city evidently was destroyed by fire.

Evidence of the Late Bronze Age (1550–1200 B.C.) was found in seven tombs, revealing trade with Egypt and Cyprus. Among the finds were scarabs of Thutmose III (1504–1450 B.C.) and Amenhotep II (1450–1425). Cypriot imports included the distinctive long-necked jug (*bilbil*) of perfumed oil; pottery of domestic design and craftsmanship was inferior in technique to the imported wares. During this period the city entered into the mutual defense treaty with Joshua and the elders of Israel, thus avoiding the fate which befell their contemporaries among the Amorites (Josh 9).

Gibeon was the leading member of a group of four Hivite cities at the time of Joshua's conquest, the other three being Chephirah, Beeroth and Kirjath-jearim (Josh 9:17). These Hivite (or Horite) towns entered by deceit into a mutual assistance pact with Joshua and the elders of Israel, rather than remaining loyal to the Amorites of the area. As a result a coalition of five Amorite kings attacked Gibeon, but were defeated by Joshua's forces which had come from Gilgal in response to Gibeon's call for assistance as provided by the treaty (Josh 10:1–14). The episode indicates the binding obligations of an alliance made in the name of the Lord even when enacted without divine sanction (Josh 9:18). For comments concerning the sun and moon standing still, *see* Sun.

Gibeon was among the cities included in the territory of Benjamin (Josh 18:25) and was allotted to the descendants of Aaron (Josh 21:17). The Hivites inhabiting these cities were spared the fate of the other Canaanites but were made second-class citizens, assigned to be "hewers of wood and drawers of water" (Josh 9:27).

Iron Age I (1200–900 B.C.) was apparently the "golden age" of Gibeon. Archaeological discoveries which date from this period include two city walls. The older and outer wall was about five feet in thickness and more than a half mile in circumference, enclosing the 16 acre site. An inner wall constructed in the 10th cen. B.C. was much stronger, averaging 13 feet in thickness.

The city now appears in the biblical record as the scene of a joust between soldiers representing Abner and those of David, with David's men victorious (II Sam 2:12-17). Gibeon marked the last time the Philistines were a menace to Israel. After they made a raid up the valley, David's men fell upon them and "smote the Philistine army from Gibeon to Gezer" (I Chr 14:16, RSV).

Later, in David's reign during the rebellion of Sheba, Joab murdered Amasa "at the great stone which is in Gibeon" (II Sam 20:8).

Gibeon seems to have been the religious center of Solomon's realm during the early days of his reign. Here was located the tabernacle, the altar of burnt offering, a priesthood, daily sacrifices, and the "great high place" (I Chr 16:37-40; 21:29). It was here that Solomon participated in the first public dedicatory service of his reign and received a vision from God (I Kgs 3:4-5; cf. 9:2). The national religious center shifted from Gilgal (Josh 5:10) to the Shechem area (Josh 8:30-35) to Shiloh (I Sam 1:3) to Gibeon (I Chr 16:39) to Jerusalem.

Since no trace of Solomon's cultic installation has been discovered at el-Jib, Pritchard and others think it may have been located on Nebi Samwil, a conspicuous hill one mile S of el-Jib. Residents of Gibeon at this time included "Jehiel the father of Gibeon" (I Chr 8:29; 9:35). During the invasion by Pharaoh Shishak early in Rehoboam's reign (II Chr 12:2-9), Gibeon was among the many cities of Judah and Israel plundered according to Shishak's records in Egypt.

Inside stairway to the pool of Gibeon. James Pritchard

During the 6th cen. Gibeon again appears briefly in OT history as the hometown of the false prophet Hananiah, a contemporary of Jeremiah (Jer 28:1). During the Exile, in 582 B.C., Ishmael had murdered Gedaliah and his household at Mizpah and was returning with captives to the Ammonites. He was met by forces loyal to Johanan "at the great pool which is in Gibeon." A battle ensued in which the captives were released and their captor escaped by fleeing with eight companions to the sanctuary of the Ammonites in Transjordan (Jer 41:1-16).

In the memoirs of Nehemiah the Gibeonites are listed among those who helped build the walls of Jerusalem (Neh 3:7). The inhabitants of Gibeon had apparently been God-fearing people from the days of Joshua (cf. II Sam 21:4-6).

Josephus reports that in A.D. 66 the Roman governor Cestius camped at Gibeon as he traveled to and from Jerusalem via Beth Horon, to Joppa and the coast (*Wars* ii.19.1, 7).

Archaeologically speaking, Gibeon's most interesting era was during the kingdom period (Iron I and II, 1200-580 B.C.). The "great pool" of David's time may be the same as the enormous pit uncovered by Pritchard's expeditions of 1956 and 1957. This pit, dug perhaps in the early Iron Age, measures about 37 feet from rim to rim and has a depth of 35 feet, with a spiral stairway consisting of 40 steps and balustrade formed of the bedrock remaining when the pool was cut. Additional steps lead down through a rock tunnel to a large water chamber or cistern 82 feet below the surface. The largest of the eight springs near the city was reached by an enormous tunnel cut down through the rock with 93 steps leading from inside the city wall to the spring on the NE edge of the tell. In its walls were niches to hold lamps to provide light for the "drawers of water" (cf. Josh 9:27). Nearby were discovered more than 60 bell-shaped cellars cut out of the rock, capable of serving as cool storage places for wine kept in large jars and aged before being exported. Jar handles inscribed with the name GB'N (*Gibeon*) indicate a large distributing point in wine manufacture, and help to identify the site with certainty. The entire installation, including numerous winepresses and fermenting basins, the cellars, sherds of many jars, and more than 40 clay stoppers to fit into the mouths of the jars, could produce and store at least 30,000 gallons of wine. This winery was in use during the three centuries preceding the Exile, indicating that Gibeon was a thriving city engaged in industry and in trade with its neighbors.

Bibliography. James B. Pritchard, "The Water System at Gibeon," BA, XIX (1956), 66-75;

"Industry and Trade at Biblical Gibeon," BA, XXIII (1960), 23-29; "A Bronze Age Necropolis at Gibeon," BA, XXIV (1961), 19-24; "More Inscribed Jar Handles from El-Jib," BASOR #160 (1960), 2-6; *The Water System of Gibeon,* Philadelphia: Univ. of Penn. Museum, 1961; *Gibeon, Where the Sun Stood Still,* Princeton: Princeton Univ. Press, 1962; *The Bronze Age Cemetery at Gibeon,* Philadelphia: Univ. of Penn. Museum, 1963. W. L. Reed, "Gibeon," TAOTS, pp. 231-243.

G. A. T.

GIBLITES (gĭb'līts). Inhabitants of Gebal (*q.v.*).

GIDDALTI (gĭ-dăl'tī). A son of Heman (I Chr 25:4, 29), who was one of David's musicians, designated by David to prophesy with music in the sanctuary. The name is included in a list which seems to be a liturgical prayer in its origin.

GIDDEL (gĭd'ĕl)

1. The name of the head of a family of temple servants called Nethinim (Ezr 2:47; Neh 7:49).

2. Ancestor of one of the families of "Solomon's servants" among the returned exiles (Ezr 2:56; Neh 7:58; cf. I Kgs 9:21).

GIDEON (gĭd'ē-ŏn). A charismatic hero of Israel, son of Joash of the clan of Abiezer, of the tribe of Manasseh (Jud 6:11-8:35). He resided at Ophrah, E of the hill of Moreh between Beth-shean and Mount Tabor, a town in Issachar (cf. Josh 17:11). Like so many Israelites during the cycles of apostasy in the period of the judges, Gideon's father had turned to Baal worship. Few bothered to attend the feasts of the Lord at Shiloh, the one unifying factor that God had ordained to maintain a national sense of interdependency in Israel. Thus *c.* 1200 B.C. the Hebrews were easy prey for marauding Bedouin bands. Coming on camels from the deserts up Wadi Sirhan E of Amman, for seven consecutive years the Midianites invaded to steal livestock and plunder the ripening harvests. Likewise Amalekites, probably coming from the Negeb, raided as far as Gaza. Meanwhile the impoverished Jews, hiding in mountains and caves, began to cry to the Lord for deliverance.

During this oppression the angel of the Lord appeared to Gideon, probably then about 30 years old (cf. Jud 8:20). In order to keep his wheat hidden from the Midianites, he was beating it out in a winepress instead of treading it with animals on a threshingfloor, normally near the town gate. The divine messenger commissioned him to smite the Midianites, and manifested his true identity by having fire consume the food Gideon had prepared for him. That night the Lord tested Gideon's obedience by commanding him to destroy his father's altar of Baal and cut down the Asherah totem pole, and then to build a carefully constructed altar to Yahweh (Jud 6:11-27).

Gideon's other name, Jerubbaal (*q.v.*), is introduced in the account when his father shields him from the angry townspeople for his action by saying that Baal if a god should be able to contend for himself. Jerubbaal may have been the name given at birth to Gideon, "baal" meaning "lord" and signifying a title given to Yahweh, with the sense "May the Lord contend for me"; for it appears as his real name in Jud 7:1; 8:29, 35 and throughout chap. 9 as the father of Abimelech. ("Gideon," meaning "hewer," may have been a nickname or honorific title given him as a result of this incident.) Thus a new, popular explanation of his original name Jerubbaal arose: "Let Baal contend against him" (Jud 6:28-32). Later, when the name Baal was abhorred, this name was changed to Jerubbesheth ("Let the shameful one contend," II Sam 11:21).

The next time the Midianites and their allies swept into Israel, the Spirit of the Lord endued Gideon with power for a campaign of deliverance. He gathered an army from the tribes of Manasseh, Asher, Zebulun, and Naphtali. A novice in warfare himself, before going to battle he sought divine guidance and strengthening for his faith. God answered by signs of miraculous dew, first on the fleece, and the next night on the ground around it (Jud 6:35-40).

Because the highly mobile Midianites with their camels were encamped in the valley of Jezreel, Gideon and his men took position on Mount Gilboa above the spring of Harod (*'Ain Jalud;* cf. I Sam 29:1). At God's command in order to prevent pride, Gideon twice reduced his army, from an original 32,000 to 10,000 by sending home the cowards (cf. Deut 20:8), and then to a mere 300 by weeding out the careless. The faithful warriors, alert for ambushes, stood upright and kept one hand on their weapon while they dipped the other hand in the water and lapped from it, always ready for action (Jud 7:1-8).

God was revealing to Gideon step by step the only military tactics suitable for footsoldiers to defeat the vast camel-riding army of 135,000 (cf. 8:10). As A. Malamat shows, a small, closely knit, highly disciplined force—led by one thoroughly familiar with the terrain and knowing the morale of the enemy—could best stage a successful night assault ("The War of Gideon and Midian—A Military Approach," PEQ, LXXXV [1953], 61-65). Capitalizing on Bedouin fear of the dark, Gideon sprang the attack around midnight just after the Midianite watch was changed, the weakest moment in the sentry system. The element of surprise was augmented by every Israelite suddenly blowing a ram's-horn trumpet, breaking the jar which had concealed his smouldering torch (thus allowing it to burst into flame), and shouting the now-famous war cry, "A sword for the Lord and for Gideon" (7:20, RSV). Showing superb strategy, Gideon sent runners to have the Ephraimites cut off the enemy retreat at the fords of the Jordan (7:9-24). They captured two Midianite princes and brought the heads to

Gideon. He humbly and diplomatically allayed the bitterness of the men of Ephraim who reproached him for not summoning their help sooner (7:25–8:3).

Gideon continued the pursuit across the Jordan, capturing two more Midianite rulers. Because he had been refused assistance by the men of Succoth and Penuel, on his return he destroyed both places. He then executed Zebah and Zalmunna himself under the duty of blood revenge (cf. Num 35:19), because they had not spared his brothers living near Mount Tabor (Jud 8:4–21). The victory was so complete, so astounding, so wholly of God that "the day of Midian" seems to have become a proverbial expression for divine deliverance (Isa 9:4; cf. 10:26; Ps 83:11).

Gideon affords a splendid illustration of how God can use the least among men (Jud 6:15) when that one is fully yielded to His will and able to believe Him for miracles (6:13). Like Timothy, Gideon tended to be fearful (cf. 6:11, 22–23, 27; 7:10). But implicit reliance upon God and empowering by the Spirit made him a "mighty man of valour" (6:12), an outstanding example of one who "through faith subdued kingdoms" (Heb 11:32–33).

Gideon resisted the temptation of proffered hereditary kingship—his finest hour. But unwisely he made an ephod from the Midianite spoils given him (Jud 8:22–27). The ephod was probably a magnificent robe made of the gold and purple taken from his enemies. It proved a snare, however, to him and his house because he thus invaded the prerogative of the Aaronic priesthood, even though he perhaps meant only to use it in his office of civil magistrate (cf. I Chr 15:27). It also ensnared all Israel because they made it an object of worship. Like David, Gideon succumbed to the flesh in multiplying wives and concubines, with consequent tragedy among his offspring.

J. R.

GIDEONI (gĭd'ĭ-ō'nī). The father of Abidan, who was a leader of Benjamin in the wilderness (Num 1:11; 2:22; 7:60, 65; 10:24). Mentioned only in connection with his son.

GIDOM (gī'dŏm). The limit of the pursuit of Benjamin by the other tribes (Jud 20:45). It is a site in Benjamin near the rock Rimmon in the wilderness E of Gibeah. It may not be a proper name but may be used as an infinitive "till they cut them off." It is not mentioned elsewhere.

GIER EAGLE. *See* Animals, III.54.

GIFT. Several words with the basic meaning of "gratuity" come from the Heb. root *nāthan* meaning "to give." They were used of dowry (Gen 24:53; 34:12); a portion of inheritance (Gen 25:6; II Chr 21:3); a religious sacrificial offering (Num 18:11); an incentive to obtain favor from another (Prov 18:16; 21:14); and a bribe (Prov 15:27; Eccl 7:7).

Pecuniary assistance (Est 2:18) and a present given in token of respect (II Sam 19:42) are derived from the Heb. root *nāsā'* which means "to raise." It is translated "collection" in the KJV of II Chr 24:6, 9 and "tax" in the ASV. In II Sam 11:8 it is translated "mess" of food.

Heb. *minḥâ* is used of an oblation (II Sam 8:2, 6; I Chr 18:2, 6); *shōḥad* always means a bribe, a gift for the purpose of escaping punishment (Ex 23:8; Deut 10:17).

The Gr. words in the NT are related to the verb *didōmi: dosis* can be used with an active sense of "a giving" (Phil 4:15), or a passive sense of the "thing given" (Jas 1:17); *dōron* is used specifically of a "present" (Mt 2:11), yet not necessarily always gratuitous; *dōrea* denotes a gift which is also a gratuity (Rom 3:24, RSV).

God's supreme gift to mankind is His Son (II Cor 9:15; Jn 3:16). The Holy Spirit is the promised gift of the Father, sent by the Son, and to be received with active faith by Christian believers (Jn 14:16, 26; 15:26; 16:7; Acts 1:4–5; 2:33, 38–39; Gal 3:14). Through the Spirit are manifested spiritual gifts (I Cor 12:1–11). *See* Gifts, Spiritual.

Bibliography. Friedrich Büchsel, "*Didōmi,* etc.," TDNT, II, 166–173.

D. L. W.

GIFT OF TONGUES. *See* Tongues, Gift of.

GIFTS, SPIRITUAL. Three Gr. terms are involved in the apostle Paul's discussion of spiritual gifts in I Cor 12–14: *ta pneumatika* (I Cor 12:1; 14:1; see also Rom 1:11), "spiritual gifts, powers or manifestations"; *ta pneumata* (I Cor 14:12), "spirits" or manifestations of the Spirit; and *ta charismata* (I Cor 12:4, 9, 28, 30, 31; see also Rom 1:11; 12:6; I Cor 1:7; I Tim 4:14; II Tim 1:6; I Pet 4:10), "grace-gifts."

A spiritual or charismatic gift is a supernatural capacity or power bestowed upon a Christian believer by the Holy Spirit to enable him to exercise his function as a member of the Body of Christ (I Cor 12:4–27). These gifts are not to be considered natural abilities, but supernatural manifestations of the Spirit Himself (v. 7). They are not to be confused with spiritual graces or fruits of the Spirit—facets of Christ's character which every believer is to cultivate (Gal 5:22–23). They are not identical with spiritual offices—positions in the church whether for spiritual or temporal oversight of its affairs (elders, deacons, I Tim 3:1–13) or for public ministries (apostles, prophets, evangelists, pastor-teachers, Eph 4:11). Only certain believers are appointed to these spiritual offices (I Cor 12:28*a,* 29*a*)—Christ's gifts (*domata*) to His Church (Eph 4:8)—in view of specific charismatic endowments already evidenced in their lives.

In I Cor 12–14 Paul sets forth the unity, the diversity, the distribution, the order, the motivation, the permanence, the relative value, and the proper use of spiritual gifts. As to their unity, they are all given, administered and energized or inspired by the same Triune God

(12:4-6, 11). The one purpose of the Holy Spirit in so empowering Christians is always to glorify Christ (12:3), for the profit or common good of all (12:7).

As to their diversities or distinctions, they are called "gifts" (*charismata*) from the Spirit (12:4), "administrations," ministries or acts of service from the Lord (12:5), and "operations" or activities from God the Father (12:6). The apostle then names nine gifts: a word of wisdom, a word of knowledge, faith (not saving faith but exceptional faith to do the works of Christ, Jn 14:12), charismatic gifts of healings, workings of miracles or miraculous accomplishments, prophecy or prophetic utterances, discerning of spirits, speaking publicly in various kinds of tongues, and interpretation of tongues (12:8-10). Other charismatic gifts are mentioned in 12:28-30 (helps, administrations) and in Rom 12:6-8, so that no one list is exhaustive.

Various classifications of the gifts can be made, but perhaps that of I Pet 4:10-11 is the most satisfactory. Peter describes two main categories—gifts of utterance so that the possessor of the gift speaks forth as it were words spoken by God Himself, and gifts for practical service on a supernatural level. Paul makes a similar twofold classification when he states that the Corinthian believers were enriched with all utterance and all knowledge, not lacking in any charismatic gift (I Cor 1:5-7; cf. II Cor 8:7).

As to the distribution of the gifts, Paul says that they are given to "every man," i.e., to every believer (I Cor 12:7; see also I Pet 4:10). The Spirit is sovereign in granting these gifts, "distributing to each one individually just as He wills" (I Cor 12:11, NASB). It is possible for one individual to manifest more than one gift and to have more than one ministry. Paul, for example, was richly equipped, having the power to speak in tongues, to prophesy and to perform miracles, and was first a teacher (Acts 11:25-26; 13:1) and then an apostle (Acts 14:4, 14). Ordinarily, as in the church at Corinth, the gifts are widely distributed among the saints (I Cor 1:5-7; 12:29-30).

As to the order of the gifts, Paul teaches that some gifts are greater in their usefulness than others (I Cor 12:28, 31; 14:1-25). Yet none are to be ruled out or despised (I Cor 14:39; I Thess 5:20). The Corinthians were inclined to magnify the gift of tongues as most desirable, perhaps in keeping with the Gr. love of speech. But Paul puts it at the end of his lists (I Cor 12:8-10, 28-30).

As to the proper motive in desiring the gifts and the right motivation in using the gifts. Paul makes it very clear that love for others is the only true basis: "And moreover I am going to show you a way beyond comparison" (I Cor 12:31*b*, orig. trans.), a way *par excellence* (*kath' hyperbolēn*). Unless the gifts of tongues, prophesying, knowledge or helps are rooted in love, they are worthless (I Cor 13:1-3).

As to the permanence of the gifts, there is much difference of opinion. Obviously, the office of apostleship in the primary sense has been withdrawn. There is no proof in Scripture for apostolic succession from the Christ-appointed leaders of the church. In a secondary sense, however, many missionaries have done the work of apostles with extraordinary gifts and blessing from God. Again, the gift of prophecy in its primary sense of speaking forth and writing down the inspired, infallible Word of God has been sovereignly withdrawn; but believers may still speak forth a message impressed by God when they are under an anointing or prompting of the Spirit. Paul teaches that whereas love will never fail nor cease, the charismatic gifts will stop "when that which is perfect is come" (I Cor 13:10). Some have taught that by *to teleion,* "that which is perfect," Paul means the completed canon of holy Scripture; however, consideration of v. 12, which says that then we shall see face to face and know fully even as now we are fully known, seems to indicate that Paul is looking forward to the perfect state of things to be ushered in by the return of Christ from heaven (J. H. Thayer, *A Greek-English Lexicon of the New Testament,* p. 618).

A study of church history reveals that many of the charismatic gifts continued to be manifested long after the apostles were all dead (Adolf Harnack, *The Mission and Expansion of Christianity,* Harper Torchbooks, 1962, pp. 129-146, 199-205), and that on new mission fields and in times of spiritual revival the Lord still confirms His Word through the operation of supernatural gifts of the Spirit. Certainly the gifts of teaching, exhorting, sharing and ruling (Rom 12:6-8) or of helps and of governments (I Cor 12:28) are continuing functions, for the church will always need believers with such abilities.

As to the relative value of prophesying and speaking in tongues, Paul points out the limitations and the value of the latter gift to the individual for his own spiritual upbuilding and in his private praying and worshiping (I Cor 14:2, 4*a*, 14-18, 28*b*) as well as to the congregation for edifying when accompanied by the gift of interpretation (14:5, 13, 26-28). The one who prophesies, however, more directly and clearly helps the congregation by speaking a message of edification, exhortation or comfort (14:3). A third function of the gift of tongues is to act as a sign. This is evident when a language unknown to the one speaking it is recognized by a "foreigner" or unbeliever in the meeting (14:22; Mk 16:17, 20), as on the Day of Pentecost (Acts 2:4-12).

As to the proper use of spiritual gifts, Paul carefully instructs the Corinthian church in the orderly display of the gifts of utterance in their fellowship meetings. Only one is to speak at a time, and he is to permit the others to test his message, in order to prevent confusion and that all might be edified (I Cor 14:26-40). To correct abuse he does not prohibit the practice of the gifts, but ends by saying, "Let all things be done decently and in order" (v. 40).

Bibliography. Arnold Bittlinger, *Gifts and Graces,* trans. by H. Klassen, London: Hodder & Stoughton, 1967, a commentary on I Cor 12–14. Donald Gee, *Spiritual Gifts in the Work of the Ministry Today,* Springfield, Mo.: Gospel Publ. House, 1963. James G. S. S. Thomson, "Spiritual Gifts," BDT, pp. 497–500.

F. C. K.

Entrance to Virgin's Fount. JR

GIHON (gī'hŏn)

1. Gihon (from *gîaḥ,* "to gush forth") was the name given to one of the four rivers emerging from Eden "which flows around the whole land of Cush" (Gen 2:13, RSV), apparently meaning the area E of Mesopotamia (or possibly the Nile, which would extend Eden as far as the entire Fertile Crescent).

2. The Nile in Jer 2:18 is translated in the LXX as *Gēōn* (Gihon), perhaps influenced by Gen 2:13.

3. A spring which is Jerusalem's only known natural source of water and lies in the Kidron valley, E of Ophel, directly S of the present temple area. This never-failing spring accounts for the fact that Jerusalem has been occupied continuously for some eight millennia. As its name implies, it gushes forth an extra amount of water from its natural cave once or twice a day as the dry season ends, four or five times daily after a rainy winter.

Solomon was crowned at Gihon after his brother Adonijah made a futile attempt to claim the kingship at En-rogel (Job's Well), a few hundred yards down the valley (I Kgs 1:33). As the Assyrian armies of Sennacherib approached, Hezekiah took measures to deny this water to the invaders (II Chr 32:3–4) and assure its availability to the defenders by cutting a tunnel through the hill so that it emerged on the W side inside the city wall in what is now called the Pool of Siloam (II Chr 32:30; cf. II Kgs 20:20). This winding tunnel, 1,777 feet in length, averaging six feet in height by three feet in width, is the most famous of several rock-cut tunnels designed to assure access to the water.

An older conduit on a slightly lower level, led down the W bank of the Kidron. It began as a tunnel leading S from Gihon's cave until it emerged and became a surface channel. Schick traced it in 1901 to the S end of the hill of Ophel, where it presumably led to a pool older than the Pool of Siloam (cf. the "old pool" of Isa 22:11). A vertical shaft, discovered by Warren, appears to have been used by the Jebusites in pre-historic times (*see* Gutter with reference to II Sam 5:8). A higher level aqueduct or rock-cut channel was discovered by Schick in 1866 and may have been used for irrigation of the king's gardens (cf. II Kgs 25:4), probably the "waters of Shiloah that go softly" mentioned in Isa 8:6. At present Gihon, now known as "the Virgin's Fountain," is in a cave 30 steps below the ground level and is still visited by the local women in quest of water. *See* Siloam; Jerusalem; Hezekiah.

G. A. T.

GILALAI (gĭ-lā'lī). A Levitical musician who took part in the dedication of the wall of Jerusalem rebuilt under the leadership of Nehemiah (Neh 12:36).

GILBOA (gĭl-bō'*a*). Usually identified with a range of hills today called Jebel Fuqû'ah with an average elevation of 1,600 feet at the SE end of the plain of Jezreel (Esdraelon). It forms a watershed between the river Kishon and the Jordan as its eight-mile length curves SE, then S to merge with the central uplands of Samaria. Between Gilboa and the hill of Moreh to the N is the valley leading from Jezreel down to Beth-shan. Near its northern cliffs is the well of Harod where Gideon encamped (Jud 7:1). Gilboa's chief fame comes from the death of Saul and his sons on its NW slopes (I Sam 28:4; 31:1–8; II Sam 1:21).

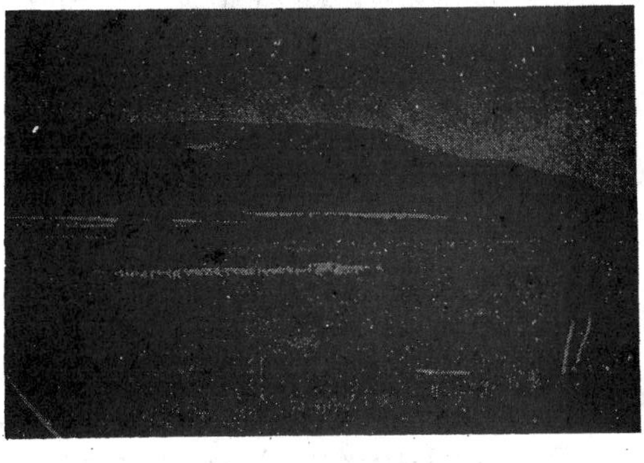

Mount Gilboa. JR

Another theory places Gilboa in the mountains of Samaria 15 miles or so E of Joppa near the Aphek of I Sam 29:1 (*see* Aphek 1), usually located at Ras el-'Ain (H. Bar-Deroma, " 'Ye Mountains of Gilboa,' " PEQ, CII [1970], 116-136).

GILEAD (gĭl'ē-ȧd)

1. The founder of the tribal family by that name (Num 26:29-30; Josh 17:1).

2. The father of Jephthah (Jud 11:1).

3. A Gadite (I Chr 5:14).

4. A mountainous region E of the Jordan River with an average height of 3,000 feet above sea level. It is bounded on the N by Bashan, on the E by the Arabian Desert, and on the S by Moab and Ammon (Deut 3:12-17). It is also known as Mount Gilead (but it is difficult to identify it with any particular mountain), the "land of Gilead" (Josh 22:15, 32) and "Gilead" (Ps 60:7; Gen 37:25).

The Jabbok River divides this area into two parts (Josh 12:2). Because it receives a rainfall of from 28 to 32 inches a year, N Gilead has many perennial streams descending to the Jordan. Much of it is still thickly wooded as it was in Absalom's day (II Sam 18:6-9). Gad received the south-central part of Gilead and Manasseh the northern. Reuben occupied the extreme southern part extending into Moab. The last interview between Laban and Jacob took place in Mount Gilead (Gen 31:21). The region of S Gilead is well suited for cattle raising and was eagerly applied for by the Reubenites and the Gadites (Num 32:1-5). Moses rebuked them for their willingness to settle down on the E side of Jordan before Canaan was finally conquered for the rest of the tribes (Num 32:6-15), but he reluctantly agreed to let them settle here. For recent discussion and bibliography see Nelson Glueck, "Transjordan," TAOTS, pp. 428-453.

5. A city in the region of Gilead (Hos 6:8).

The King's Highway and the mountains of Gilead. HFV

6. A mountain on the edge of the Valley of Jezreel (Jud 7:3) where Gideon ordered a reduction in number of the men who were to fight the Midianites. Another interpretation of the command, "Let him return and depart early from mount Gilead," translates the Heb. preposition *min*, "from," in its occasional sense of "toward," as in Gen 2:8; 12:8; 13:11. Mount Gilead then would be the same region as 4.

H. A. Han.

GILEADITES (gĭl'ē-ȧ-dīts). When the Heb. tribes arrived in the region E of the Jordan, Manasseh, Gad, and Reuben elected to take possession of that territory because they found it suitable for their flocks. Manasseh occupied the N, Gad the central, and Reuben the southern sector as far as the Arnon River. The exact borders between the three tribes cannot be defined with certainty because many of the cities named in the biblical record have not been identified.

One reference identifies the Gileadites with the descendants of Manasseh (Num 26:29). Jair and Jephthah are also identified as Gileadites (Jud 10:3; 11:1). Generally speaking, it is assumed that the Gileadites were the peoples occupying the greater Gilead region.

GILGAL (gĭl'găl)

1. Gilgal was Israel's first campsite after crossing the Jordan and main headquarters during the campaigns of conquest (Josh 4:19; 9:6; 10:6, 43; 14:6). Stones taken from the bed of the Jordan were set up in a memorial cairn. The name Gilgal, however, which means "circle," evidently belonged to the site already, for Moses seems to have known it (Deut 11:30). Perhaps to mark a burial site, as at Mycenae, the Canaanites had previously installed sculptured standing stones in a circle near Gilgal (Jud 3:19, RSV); the Israelites by establishing a memorial to Yahweh there, effectively counteracted the former idolatrous cult practices at the site. Nevertheless, Gilgal did not have an Israelite shrine until the 8th cen. B.C.; then, as at Bethel, unspiritual worship drew condemnation from Amos (4:4; 5:5) and Hosea (4:15; 9:15; 12:11). Both Gilgal and Bethel had been centers for the young prophets in training with Elijah and Elisha (II Kgs 2:1-2; 4:38), with an important road connecting the two towns.

Since Gilgal can be derived from the Heb. verb *gālal*, "to roll," the same was used by God through Joshua to serve as a reminder to Israel that He had rolled away the reproach or disgrace of all idolatrous Egyptian worship and lusting for Egyptian products still resident in their hearts by their submitting to circumcision there. Thus they were formally reinstated into covenant relationship with Yahweh and ceremonially fit to partake of the Passover festival (Josh 5:9-11). Later, Gilgal was the site of King Saul's coronation, his retreat and impetuous sacrifice, and his rejection as king (I Sam 11:15; 13:4, 7, 12; 15:12, 26, 33).

Gilgal is probably located just N of Khirbet el-Mefjir, about one and a quarter miles NE of OT Jericho (cf. Josh 4:19). James Muilenberg (BASOR #140 [1955] pp. 11-27) combines the testimony of the OT passages, Josephus' figure of ten stadia from Jericho, and his own small sounding in 1954 which unearthed pottery of the period 1200-600 B.C. to make this a convincing identification.

2. A place of the same name mentioned after Dor in a list of conquered kings (Josh 12:23), perhaps Jiljulieh bordering the plain of Sharon W of Shechem. In this verse, however, the LXX has Galilee instead of Gilgal.

3. A place on the border of Judah, "opposite the ascent of Adummim" (Josh 15:7, RSV); possibly the same as 1.

4. Many geographers seek to place the Gilgal of II Kgs 2:1 and 4:38, and perhaps of Deut 11:30, in the hill country of Ephraim, perhaps at Jiljulieh, eight miles NW of Bethel.

J. R.

GILOH (gī'lō). A city in the southern hills of Judah mentioned along with Jattir, Socoh, Debir, and Eshtemoh (Josh 15:48-51). It is called "Gilo" in II Sam 23:34 (RSV). Ahithophel came from here (II Sam 15:12). It is usually identified with Khirbet Jala, five miles NW of Hebron.

GILONITE (gī'lŏn-īt). An inhabitant of Giloh. Ahithophel is called a Gilonite (II Sam 23:34). The expression reads, "Eliam the son of Ahithophel of Gilo" (RSV).

GIMEL (gĭm'ĕl). The third letter of the Heb. alphabet, used in Ps 119 to designate the third section, each verse of which begins with this letter. *See* Alphabet.

GIMZO (gĭm'zō). A town in Judah bordering Philistia, captured by the Philistines in the days of Ahaz (II Chr 28:18). It is the modern Jimzu, a small village about three miles SE of Lydda.

GIN. Two words are translated "gin" in the KJV: *paḥ* in Job 18:9 and Isa 8:14; and *môqēsh* in Ps 140:5; 141:9; Amos 3:5. Both words are usually translated "snare." *Paḥ* is the snare and *môqēsh* is possibly the bait for the snare. It seems to have been a noose of hair or wire for snaring wild birds alive, horsehair for snaring small birds, and wire for snaring larger ones. *See* Snare; Trap.

GINATH (gī'năth). The father of Tibni, who was unsuccessful in his claim to the throne of Israel against Omri (I Kgs 16:21-22).

GINNETHO (gĭn'ĕ-thō). This term and Ginnethoi are evidently the same as Ginnethon (*q.v.*).

GINNETHON (gĭn'ē-thŏn). Variant of Ginnetho and Ginnethoi (Neh 12:4).

The head of a family of priests in the period of Joiakim (Neh 12:16). This name is also mentioned as being that of a priest who witnessed the covenant renewal under Ezra (Neh 10:6).

GIRDLE. There are several kinds of girdles, each used as an article of clothing. Heb. *'abnēṭ* was the special priestly linen sash (Ex 28:4, 39; 39:29; Lev 16:4; Isa 22:21); the *'ēzôr* was the common kilt or loincloth (II Kgs 1:8; Job 12:18; Isa 5:27; 11:5; Jer 13:1-11); the *ḥăgôr* or *ḥăgôrâ* was a soldier's belt (II Sam 20:8; I Kgs 2:5); and Gr. *zōnē* was a sash, belt, or loincloth. *See* Dress.

The word girdle is also used in a figurative sense. The girdle was a symbol of power, strength, and activity (Job 12:18, 21, ASV; 30:11; Isa 11:5; 22:21; 45:5; I Kgs 20:11), probably because it contained purses and weapons, or covered a man's vital and reproductive organs. Thus to gird (or girdle) up the loins denotes preparation for battle or any other activity (I Kgs 18:46; II Kgs 4:29; Lk 12:35; I Pet 1:13). *See* Armor.

To loose the girdle and give it to another was a token of great confidence and affection (I Sam 18:4). Girdles of sackcloth were worn in times of mourning to show humiliation and sorrow (Isa 3:24; 22:12). The "cleaving of the girdle to a man's loins" (Jer 13:11) illustrates the close adherence of the people of God to Him in loyalty. Righteousness and faithfulness are called the girdle or kilt of the Messiah (Isa 11:5). Because the *'ēzôr* was worn next to the skin, in figure it signifies that these are inseparable elements in His character.

E. C. J.

GIRGASHITES (gûr'gȧ-shīts). A Canaanite tribe (Gen 10:16; 15:21; Deut 7:1; Josh 3:10; 24:11; Neh 9:8; I Chr 1:14). In Heb. this term is always singular. These people were dispossessed by the Hebrews, with no sure indication of locality or to what branch of the Canaanites they belonged. The term is used in connection with the fifth son of Canaan (Gen 10:16).

The Girgashites evidently inhabited land to the W of Jordan (Josh 24:11). Some have identified the Girgashites with the Qirkishites of an Assyrian tablet. More likely the similarity is to the frequent personal names *Grgshy, Grgsh,* and *Grgshm* in the vowelless Punic texts from Carthage, and to the name *Grgsh* on a tablet from Ugarit. These occurrences would tend to confirm the Genesis record that the Girgashites were closely related to the Canaanites, later known as Phoenicians, who in turn founded Carthage.

GIRL. This term appears twice in the OT (Joel 3:3; Zech 8:5), in both instances in association with boys. The term may mean child, female, lass, or even damsel, as in Gen 34:4.

GISPA (gĭs'pȧ). An overseer of the Nethinim

(Neh 11:21). A comparison with Ezr 2:43 suggests that the term may be identified with Hasupha. This word may be a corruption of Hasupha, a family of temple servants among the returned exiles. *See* Hasupha.

GITTAH-HEPHER (gĭt'ȧ-hē'fẽr). *See* Gath-Hepher.

GITTAIM (gĭt'ā-ĭm). This is the name Gath with a common locative ending, *-ayim*, which is identical in form to the Heb. dual inflection. In II Sam 4:3 it is mentioned incidentally that the Beerothites (*q.v.*) had fled to Gittaim but that their town of origin, Beeroth, was reckoned to the tribe of Benjamin. In the post-Exilic period the Benjamites were also in possession of Gittaim (Neh 11:33). That the towns which follow Gittaim in this list, e.g., Hadid, Neballat, Lod, and Ono, are situated on the coastal plain inland from Joppa (for the location of each of these towns see their respective entries) is no coincidence. Eusebius (*Onomasticon* 72:2–3) located Gittaim between Antipatris and Yabneh. The town to which he referred is the Gitta of the Madebah map, which is placed between Beth Dagon and Lod (*q.v.*).

From the written texts it is clear that this town existed throughout the Israelite period, during the post-Exilic Age, and even into the Roman-Byzantine age. The Jewish community in Ramleh during the Middle Ages preserved the tradition that Gittaim was identical with their town. Ramleh was founded in the 8th cen. after Christ by Caliph Suleiman Ibn Abd el-Malik of the Umayyads. This combination of facts points to the identification of Gittaim with Ras Abu Hamid, a tell covering over 40 acres to the SE of the present town. Recent surface investigations of the site have shown that a large fortified town existed there from the Early Iron Age through the Early Arab period.

It is not impossible that some of the references to Gath (*q.v.*) are actually concerned with Gittaim. This was the suggestion of Mazar ("Gath and Gittaim," IEJ, IV [1954], 227–235; "The Cities of the Territory of Dan," IEJ, X [1960], 65–77), which was highly pertinent so long as Gath of the Philistines was thought to be in the southern part of the Philistine plain. However, with the tentative identification of that Gath with a more northerly locale (Tell es-Safi), the assumed confusion with Gittaim is no longer necessary. Nevertheless, it still deserves consideration, especially in regard to Hazael's campaign (II Kgs 12:17–18).

A. F. R.

GITTITE (gĭt'īt). An inhabitant of Gath. Gittites are mentioned along with the inhabitants of other Philistine cities (Josh 13:3). Some were found in Judah serving as a bodyguard to David with Ittai as their commander (II Sam 15:18 ff.; 18:2). Obed-edom, who cared for the ark for a time, was a Gittite (II Sam 6:10 f.; I Chr 13:13). Goliath and other giant Philistine warriors were Gittites.

GITTITH (gĭt'ĭth). A term found in the titles of Ps 8, 81, 84. It is a feminine adjective derived from Gath but with an uncertain meaning. It may denote a musical instrument manufactured at Gath. If this is right, the titles would mean "on the lyre which was brought from Gath." Some regard the term as denoting a melody or march popular in Gath, or "The March of the Gittite Guards." The LXX renders "concerning the vintage." It may indicate a vintage song, since the Heb. *gat* means "winepress."

GIZONITE (gī'zō-nīt). A designation which occurs in I Chr 11:34, "the sons of Hashem the Gizonite." Gizon is nowhere else mentioned in the OT.

GLAD TIDINGS. Good news; used in KJV in Lk 1:19; 8:1; Acts 13:32; Rom 10:15. *See* Gospel.

Hand mirrors might be made of bronze or silver. Here is a silver mirror with an obsidian handle from Egypt. LL

GLASS. Glass was manufactured as early as the Old Kingdom of Egypt (2850–2200 B.C.). Much of the sand of Egypt has a high content of calcium carbonate suitable for making glass. Because the technique of glassblowing was not developed until the 1st cen. B.C. by the Phoenicians, all glass objects in OT times were cast or made by welding sticks of glass around a core. By the time of Moses Egyptian craftsmen showed the greatest skill in beautiful colored beads, amulets and small vials for perfumes and unguents. Glass is mentioned only once in the OT (Job 28:17, RSV), Heb. *zᵉkûkît,* KJV "crystal," along with gold; this would indicate its rarity and high price in the ancient world.

By NT times the Romans were developing transparent glass. In his visions of heaven John saw a city of pure gold, like clear glass (Rev 21:18) and its street also of pure gold, "like transparent glass" (v. 21). He compared other surfaces to a "sea of glass" (Rev 4:6; 15:2). But the people still preferred bottles and other objects to be made of colored glass. The color was obtained by the addition of metal oxides. Even clear Roman glass objects have become iridescent because of the oxidation of mineral traces.

The "glass" in Ex 38:8; Isa 3:23; I Cor 13:12; Jas 1:23 refers to the highly polished bronze hand mirrors in vogue both in Egypt and in the Roman world. When Elihu said, "Hast thou with him spread out the sky, which is strong, and as a molten looking glass?" (Job 37:18), he had in mind the bronze mirror as a simile of the brazen summer sky.

See Minerals and Metals: Glass.

J. R.

GLASS WORKER. *See* Occupations.

GLEAN. To gather or to pick up what was left in the fields after reaping. It applied not only to grain but also to grapes and olives. Pentateuchal laws prohibited an owner from gleaning his own fields, so that the poor, the fatherless, the widow, and the stranger might have food (cf. Lev 19:9 ff.; 23:22; Deut 24:19-21; Ruth 2).

GLEDE. *See* Animals: Kite, III.26.

GLORIFY. With reference to the persons of the Godhead, glorify means to exalt, make glorious, and honor God in the human life of the believer by following those guides prescribed in the Bible. The Christian is to glorify God in his body (I Cor 6:20), that is, to set forth or manifest God's glory through a holy, godly, and completely yielded life. Primarily glorification came to Jesus Christ through His resurrection (Jn 12:16). The believer as sharing in this glorified resurrected life is to manifest Christlikeness and the fruit of the Holy Spirit (Mt 5:16; Gal 5:22). The Holy Spirit provides the source of power for this action (II Cor 3:17-18; Rom 8:13). *See* Glory.

GLORY. A major biblical concept, the word "glory" is the translation in KJV of a variety of Heb. and Gr. words, the most common being *kābôd* in the OT and *doxa* in the NT. Developing from the Heb. concept of "weight, heaviness, worthiness," the term "glory" in a doctrinal sense is used of God in Ps 19:1 and 63:2, speaking of the heaviness, awesomeness, or intrinsic worth of God's being.

Central to the OT usage of the term is the idea of the "glory of Yahweh" (Isa 6:3). In this sense, glory is linked to revelation, and consists of the manifestation of God's nature. The specific issue in Isa 6 is the revelation of holiness, and the majestic holiness and glory of God are closely related. At times in the OT this manifestation approximates an overpowering physical appearance of glory, splendor, or brilliance (Lev 9:23; Ex 33:18 ff.). This is theologically represented by the terms "presence," or "Shekinah glory."

In the NT the glory of the Lord is seen in connection with Jesus Christ in a variety of ways. The birth narrative in the Lucan account shows that the first advent of Messiah was marked by the appearance of the glory of the Lord (Lk 2:9, 14, 32). This glory, the fullness or sum of all the perfections of the Godhead, was veiled during the earthly incarnate ministry of Christ, except for a brief glimpse at the transfiguration (Lk 9:28 ff.), and at crucial points in Christ's ministry (Jn 2:11; 11:40). Heb 1:3 delineates Jesus Christ as the effulgence or radiation of the glory of God.

By sovereign grace, the NT believer is seen as sharing to some extent in this glory now (Rom 8:30; II Cor 4:6). In the resurrected state the believer will be conformed to the glorified Saviour to a far greater extent than now realized, and will share in the eschatological glory of Christ (I Pet 5:4; Rev 21:23). He will be free of the fallen nature and have a resurrection body.

Bibliography. R. Bultmann, "*Kauchaomai,* etc.," TDNT, III, 645-654. Gerhard Kittel, "*Doxa,*" TDNT, II, 233-255. Bernard Ramm, *Them He Glorified,* Grand Rapids: Eerdmans, 1963.

F. R. H.

GLUTTON. Essentially a voluptuary or a debauchee. In both OT and NT it is connected with drunkenness (Deut 21:20; Prov 23:21). Because our Lord was friendly to and went to the homes of publicans and sinners, He was accused of being a glutton and winebibber (Mt 11:19; Lk 7:34).

GNASH. To bite with the teeth or to grind the teeth in such a fashion as to show anguish, rage, or remorse. The OT uses the term in Job 16:9; Ps 35:16; 37:12; 112:10; Lam 2:16. Jesus speaks of the "gnashing of teeth" in Mt 8:12; 22:13; 24:51; 25:30. See also Mk 9:18; Acts 7:54.

GNAT. *See* Animals, III.16.

GNOSTICISM (nŏs'tĭ-sĭz-ĕm). A name applied to (1) a broad religious movement, basically dualistic and syncretistic, which spread throughout the ancient Near East immediately before and after the time of Christ; and (2) the religious systems exemplified by the "Great Gnostics" which flourished from the 2nd to the 4th cen. A.D. Gnosticism is used here in this latter sense.

Origins. While many have attempted to trace

Gnosticism to Iranian, Greek or Egyptian sources, it is now commonly accepted that the movement arose in a Judeo-Christian milieu. This is not a denial of probable pre-Christian elements in Gnosticism. However, the peculiar synthesis of ideas that gave birth to the "Great Gnostics" seems to have occurred in the late 1st cen. or early 2nd cen. A.D. It is evident that the movement began in a Heb.-Christian environment, probably in Syro-Palestine, because of the large number of Semitic names, idioms, and ideas appearing in early Gnostic works, such as the Apocryphon of John, the Gospel of Thomas, the Gospel of Philip; and the presence of distinctly Christian ideas, such as the sacraments, Christ the Redeemer, and the appeal to NT Scriptures.

Beliefs and practices. The more prominent of the "Great Gnostic" sects taught a system of doctrines which included (in variant forms) the following basic ideas: (1) a transcendent, ineffable Deity who is pure spirit; (2) a basic dualism between spirit and matter which necessitated the Pleroma (the chain of emanated beings linking the Great God with matter) to account for the origin of the universe; (3) a split within the Pleroma which resulted in the creation of material things and man by a Demiurge, the God of the OT; (4) a spark of the divine implanted in man at his creation; (5) the redemption and release of this divine spark by means of illumination, resulting in self-awareness (sometimes called "awaking from sleep" or "arousing from drunkenness"); (6) a Christ who redeems by being the Revelator or Illuminator rather than the suffering Saviour; and (7) salvation by knowledge, essentially self-knowledge.

Little is known about the ritual or cultic practices of the Gnostics. The Gospel of Philip seems to indicate that its readers practiced five sacraments: baptism, sealing, eucharist, chrism (anointing with olive oil), and bridal chamber. All these, except the final one, are found in orthodox Christianity. The practices of the Gnostics ranged from extreme asceticism to extreme libertinism, both extremes based upon the belief that the body was essentially evil.

Sects. The main bodies of Gnostics were the Valentinians (founded by Valentinus at Rome, *c.* A.D. 140), the Sethites (worshipers of Seth), the Ophites or Naasenes (who worshiped the serpent), the Barbelo-Gnostics (who stressed the role of Barbelo—the lower Sophia in Valentinianism), and the Marcionites (followers of Marcion, *c.* A.D. 145). Lesser groups included the Simonians (presumably followers of Simon of Samaria, Acts 8), the Carpocratians, the Paulicians, the Phibionites, and the Peratae. The latter named groups are not well represented in the surviving Gnostic literature.

Other groups closely related to the Gnostics include the Cerinthians and the Encratites of the 2nd cen. A.D., the Hermetics, and the Docetists. Lineal descent from the Gnostic movement can probably be ascribed to the Mandeans, a group still surviving in Iraq. Either through the Mandeans or directly, the Manicheans (who flourished 3rd to 5th cen. A.D.) borrowed certain Gnostic doctrines. The Manicheans left medieval manifestations in the Cathari (Albigenses) and the Bogomils.

Literature. Prior to 1955 the Gnostics were known mainly through (1) the descriptions of their beliefs and practices in the works of the Church Fathers, chiefly Irenaeus, Hippolytus and Epiphanius; and (2) the surviving Gnostic literature in Codex Brucianus (two Books of Jeu and an untitled work), and in Codex Askewianus (*Pistis Sophia*). In that year the publication of Codex Berolinensis 8502 made accessible the Gospel of Mary, the Apocryphon of John, and the Wisdom of Jesus Christ.

In the meantime, the Nag Hammadi Gnostic texts had been discovered in 1945, and with their publication (beginning in 1956) a wealth of Gnostic documents afforded the scholar first-hand insight into Gnostic doctrine and cult (*see* Chenoboskion). Today documents such as the Gospel of Truth, the Epistle of Rheginos, the Epistle of James, the Apocryphon of John, the Gospel of Thomas, the Gospel of Philip, and the Hypostasis of the Archons are available in English. Summaries of several other treatises have been published, and English translations of all 51 texts are projected. *See* Agrapha.

Biblical relationships. The Gnostic literature demonstrates the existence in the 2nd cen. of a NT canon almost identical with the formal canons adopted by the councils of Laodicea, Carthage, and Hippo. It also sheds light on textual variations and the history of textual transmission. The supreme importance of the literature is probably in the field of NT interpretation.

Some scholars have attempted to show that certain NT books are indebted to Gnosticism (John's Gospel) or are reactions against it (Colossians, Luke–Acts, Corinthians, Ephesians, Pastoral Epistles [*q.v.*], Johannine epistles). However, some of these scholars seem to be using the word "gnosticism" in the general meaning rather than referring to the central, unbiblical distinctives of the Great Gnostic sects. *See* Heresy.

Bibliography. Francis Crowfoot Burkitt, *Church and Gnosis,* Cambridge: Cambridge Univ. Press, 1932. Robert M. Grant, *Gnosticism, A Sourcebook of Heretical Writings,* New York: Harper, 1961; *Gnosticism and Early Christianity,* 2nd ed., New York: Harper & Row, 1966. Andrew K. Helmbold, *The Nag Hammadi Gnostic Texts and the Bible,* Grand Rapids: Baker, 1967. Hans Jonas, *The Gnostic Religion,* 2nd ed., Boston: Beacon Press, 1963. G. van Groningen, *First Century Gnosticism, Its Origin and Motifs,* Leiden: Brill, 1967. Robert McLachlan Wilson, *The Gnostic Problem,* London: Mowbrays, 1958.

A. K. H.

GOAD. A pointed stick used for driving animals. It could be used in combat (cf. Shamgar, Jud 3:31, who slew 600 Philistines). When a goad was tipped with iron the metal point had to be sharpened (I Sam 13:21). Eccl 12:11 indicates that words may serve figuratively as goads.

GOAT. *See* Animals, I.9.

GOAT'S HAIR, GOATSKIN. *See* Dress; Tabernacle.

GOATSUCKER. A nighthawk. *See* Animals, III.17.

GOAT, WILD. *See* Animals: Ibex, II.22.

GOATH (gō'ăth). A locality near Jerusalem, apparently near the SW corner of the city, listed after the hill of Gareb in Jer 31:39. In this passage the prophet describes the restored Holy City by proceeding around it in a counterclockwise direction. Goath thus may have been at the junction of the Kidron, Tyropoean, and Hinnom valleys.

GOB (gŏb). The exact location is unknown but at this place David's soldiers fought two battles with the Philistines (II Sam 21:18–19). The parallel passage in I Chr 20:4 lists Gezer as the locale of the contests. Gob, which is mentioned in the Amarna letters as Gubbu, may have been near the better-known Gezer. *See* Gezer.

GOBLET. A basin or curved bowl-shaped vessel. In Song 7:2 the beloved's navel or pelvis is compared to a goblet. The same Heb. term, *'aggān*, occurs in Ex 24:6 as "basins" and in Isa 22:24 as "cups."

GOD. The Bible stresses that man as a creature was especially made for knowledge of his Creator, who reveals Himself to man in nature, in conscience, and, moreover, in particular historical events. This divine disclosure, climaxed in Jesus Christ as God's self-revelation in flesh, is authoritatively narrated and interpreted by the Scriptures. The God of biblical theology is therefore decisively known from scriptural data, that is, from the prophetic-apostolic disclosure, centering in Jesus Christ as the incarnate revelation of Deity. By contrast, expositions by speculative philosophers aim to sketch the nature of God from His works alone, whether nature or man, or from the general movements of history.

The self-revealed God introduces Himself by name. Despite the fall of the human race into sin, He does not retire from the scene of history, but challenges speculative interpreters who introduce Deity simply by their own schematic views (e.g., Plato's Idea of the Good, Aristotle's Prime Mover, Hegel's Absolute, Tillich's Ground of Being). The biblical terms and names of God—generic, proper, and personal—supply, in fact, a dramatic introduction to the Creator, Preserver, Redeemer and Judge of life.

1. *The generic term: Elohim.* Genesis immediately refers the creation of the universe and man to *Elohim* (a generic term for deity, whose equivalent is *theos* in Greek, *Deus* in Latin, God in English). This plural noun (*'ĕlôah, 'ĕlōhîm*) in pagan usage signified plurality of gods, whereas the OT specifically excludes polytheism. (*a*) In prose, the plural form *elohim* commonly was used for deity (monotheistic or polytheistic), the rare singular form *eloah* being specially reserved for poetry (cf. Job, where *eloah* occurs more often than in all the rest of the OT). (*b*) Except when used of pagan gods (e.g., Gen 31:30; Ex 12:12), the plural *elohim* is uniformly used in the OT but with a singular adjective to exclude polytheistic misunderstanding. The intention or content, therefore, is more important than etymology or derivation for determining meaning. (*c*) The Genesis creation narrative refers the origin of the universe, and particularly man, to *Elohim,* whose creative activity distinguishes Him from the pagan myths of multiple competitive deities. (*d*) Although intimations of the doctrine of the Trinity sometimes have been traced to the plural form *Elohim,* the term more likely is a Heb. idiom that suggests plurality of majesty or plenitude of power in view of God's creation and governance of man and the world. When in the OT *elohim* carries the idea of plurality of persons, the reference is to pagan polytheism rather than to personal distinctions within a single deity. Without other hints in the OT, and without the explicit NT teaching, Trinitarianism could hardly be inferred from the term *elohim* itself. (*e*) Through its OT associations *elohim* does not remain simply a generic term for deity, but becomes a proper name also.

The title *Adonai,* from *'ādôn,* "master," "lord," "sovereign," is an attributive designation in view of the divine sovereignty. The word passed finally into use as a generic term for God. The corresponding NT term is *Kurios,* "Lord."

2. *Proper names: El Elyon, El Shaddai, Yahweh.* The remarkable turn in biblical theology is that the living God is progressively known through actual historical events in which He discloses Himself and His purposes. The generic terms for Deity thereby gain more specific content, become proper names, and these successively give way to later designations that reflect more fully the progressively revealed nature of God.

The word *El,* the most common term for Deity in the Semitic languages (but not the usual OT term), is often coupled with a noun or adjective (cf. *'el 'elyôn,* "God Most High," or *'el shaddai,* "God Almighty"). Thus it became a proper name for God.

El Shaddai became the characteristic patriarchal name for Deity in consequence of the divine covenant with Abraham. Whereas *Elohim* especially depicts God in the role of Creator, Maker and Preserver of man and the world, *El Shaddai* looks further to the divine constraint of natural processes for the purposes of His grace. The birth of Isaac the promised son, in the absence of any natural prospect, illuminates God as omnipotently materializing His gracious purpose in a finite and fallen creation. In the LXX and the NT, *El Shaddai* is translated *pantokratōr,* "Almighty," "Omnipotent One" (cf. II Cor 6:18; Rev 1:8; 4:8).

In the progress of the Heb. religious drama, earlier names for God fade into the background in view of the developing self-disclosure of God. Yet the name *El Shaddai* does not wholly replace *Elohim,* since the Hebrews retain all designations of Deity, sometimes interchangeably, often as circumstances may suggest one or another. The literary use of divine names, therefore, supplies no infallible clue to the literary development and authorship of the sacred writings.

The name par excellence for the God of Israel is *Yahweh,* found 6,823 times in the OT. Through Israel's deliverance from bondage in Egypt, adoption as a nation, and guidance to the Promised Land, the Redeemer-God is especially known by this name. The self-revealing God discloses Himself redemptively in a special way (I AM WHO I AM," Ex 3:14). *See* I Am.

The living God, who had earlier manifested Himself to the patriarchs in the capacity of *El Shaddai* (Ex 6:2 f.), was not wholly unknown to them as *Yahweh,* this name being found frequently in Genesis in the mouth of God, and even in Jacob's blessing (which no redactor would have altered!); from Abram onward, the name of *Yahweh* periodically enters the sacred record. But with the rescue of Israel and establishment of the theocracy, *Yahweh* becomes the distinctive OT name for the living God, who not only conforms fallen nature to grace, but shapes a new order of grace in the midst of this natural course of things. Hence the name *Jehovah* (an artificial English reconstruction of the Heb. YHWH, originally pronounced Yahweh or Yahveh) particularly emphasizes God's redemptive activity. Through superstition, the Hebrews came to avoid pronouncing the tetragrammaton (four-letter name) YHWH and substituted *Adonai.* In recent centuries, *Jehovah* has often served as the equivalent of *Yahweh* in English literature, hymnody, and Bible translations (e.g., the ASV). The Jerusalem Bible has adopted *Yahweh.*

Superimposing a framework of naturalistic development upon the Bible, higher critics have contended that the multiple names for God, especially *Elohim* and *Yahweh,* reflect divergent literary sources. This assumption was long a cornerstone of the now discredited JEDP hypothesis which resolved the Pentateuch (*q.v.*) into conflicting original sources. The attempt to explain the compounded name *Yahweh-Elohim* by documentary conflation has proved untenable, and JEDP are more and more acknowledged as artificially projected sources (on the precise content of which the critical scholars themselves have disagreed). *See* God, Names and Titles of; Lord.

3. *Personal terms: Father, Son, Spirit.* In the OT, God was revealed as Creator of all things, Lord of history, Judge of men and nations, and Redeemer of a chosen people. The NT lifts the revelation of God to even higher dimensions. Over against pagan superstition and speculation about the supernatural, the OT declared God to be transcendent to nature and man. Expressly forbidden were graven images which would not only localize Deity in time and space but also materialize Deity by denying the spirituality (invisibility and immateriality) of God. The NT revelation, presupposing that God is Spirit (Jn 4:24), adds the dramatic emphasis that the invisible God has become uniquely incarnate in Jesus Christ (Jn 1:14, 18).

The revelation of God in Christ discloses that God is a social being. In the one God there exists a society of divine persons; furthermore, this God seeks to restore doomed sinners to personal fellowship even at the cost of sacrificial death. The disclosure of "the name of Jesus," of eternal fatherhood and eternal sonship in the very being of God, moves on to the unveiling of God as triune by the revelation of "the name of the Father, and of the Son, and of the Holy Spirit" (Mt 28:19). The distinctive Christian affirmation about God is the doctrine of the Trinity. In a series of mighty redemptive acts the inner secret of God's being is made known. The God of Sinai, the outraged Creator ranged against transgressors of His law, is also the God of Golgotha, is "God with us," attested both by the gift of the incarnate Christ and by the gift of the indwelling Spirit by whom the Father draws near. *See* Godhead; Sonship of Christ; Trinity.

[The NT emphasizes the fatherhood of God. Jesus' most common designation for God was "Father." In Christian theology this term is reserved primarily for the first person of the Trinity. But the designation Father is sometimes used when referring to the one supreme God (I Pet 1:17; Isa 9:6, where "everlasting Father" connotes Messiah's true deity). The conception of God as Father is present in the OT, where it describes both a creative and a redemptive or covenant relationship. Malachi's contemporaries ask, "Have we not all one father? Hath not one God created us?" (Mal 2:10). Isaiah parallels the ideas of father and potter in calling upon God as Creator (64:8). In a unique sense God is the Father of Jesus Christ by eternal generation, expressive of an essential and timeless relationship.

More commonly in the OT the fatherhood of God expressed His covenant relationship with His people Israel. In His love He chose Israel and redeemed her from Egypt so that collectively the nation was considered the child or son of God (Isa 63:16; Ex 4:22; Hos 11:1). In this adoptive relationship Israel was to call God "my Father". (Jer 3:19) and was expected to honor Him as Father (Mal 1:6). Because the majority refused to show filial love expressed in obedience, the Lord was especially like a father to the God-fearing among the nation (Ps 103:13).

In the NT God's redemption reaches the individual first of all at the spiritual level. Salvation is viewed from two aspects, that of one's standing in Christ and that of the regenerating work of the Holy Spirit in him. Through identification with Christ by faith the believer is adopted into the family of God with all the privileges of an heir to call God "Abba! Father!" (Rom 8:15-17). *See* Abba. Under the other aspect he is regarded as born anew into the kingdom of God, partaker of the divine nature, and loved by the Father (Jn 3:3-7; II Pet 1:4; I Jn 3:1-2). Nowhere does Christ assume that this relationship exists between God and unbelievers. He never teaches that a redeeming fatherhood of God includes all men, but pointedly says to the censorious Jews, "Ye are of your father the devil" (Jn 8:44). *See* Father, God the.—J.R.]

4. *The attributive names or divine perfections.* While the personal names apply to the respective centers of consciousness in the one God, the attributes or virtues qualify the Godhead as a whole.

Theologians customarily have distinguished between the incommunicable attributes (self-existence, eternity, immutability, infinity, omniscience, omnipresence, omnipotence, unity) that emphasize His transcendence and are ascribable to God alone, and the communicable attributes that express the immanence of God and are shared in some degree by His creatures.

Through the influence of Kant and Schleiermacher, much Protestant theology in the recent past has been anti-metaphysical in temperament. Its preoccupation has been with God-in-relation to man (hence the communicable attributes) to the neglect of God-in-Himself. Protestant orthodoxy has repudiated this modernist "experiential centering" of theology which substitutes a "relational" for a "metaphysical" exposition of the nature of God. Instead of demeaning theology to an inference or induction from religious experience (as Protestant liberalism did), or trying to expound the divine attributes on a speculative rational basis (so medieval scholasticism), Protestant orthodoxy derives the content of its doctrine of God primarily from the Bible as an objectively communicated propositional revelation. The recent modern disbelief in propositional divine revelation has meant the loss also of objective knowledge of God. Karl Barth, in his later writings, sought to escape such neoorthodox subjectivity. But Barth halted short of affirming the objective inspiration of Scripture, and appealed vulnerably to an internal miracle of divine grace whereby the believer knows God truly.

The communicable attributes may be classified as spiritual (spirituality), mental (wisdom, veracity), moral (goodness, love, holiness, righteousness) and volitional (will, power to act). Theologians have had to contend with numerous temptations in expositing these perfections. Some have regarded these qualities as merely verbal distinctions with no objective basis in the nature of God (the pantheistic philosopher Spinoza reduced the attributes of Deity simply to thought and extension). Others have regarded every distinct biblical term as sufficient basis for attributing a different perfection to the divine nature.

By subordinating the righteousness or holiness of God to the love of God, Protestant liberalism nullified divine wrath. When righteousness is reduced to a form of benevolence, the resulting revision of the character of God leads logically to repudiating the doctrines of propitiatory atonement and of hell, and invites eschatological speculations about universal salvation or ultimate reconciliation for the lost. Neoorthodox theology claims to reaffirm the reality of the wrath of God. But it continues, even in a more complex manner, to submerge divine righteousness in divine love. Historic Protestant theology affirms that a basis exists in the nature of God to discriminate between righteousness and love as two distinct divine attributes which complement rather than exclude one another.

See Election; Godhead; Holiness, Holy; Incarnation; Sovereignty of God; Will of God.

C. F. H. H.

Bibliography. Robert Anderson, *The Silence of God,* Grand Rapids: Kregel, 1952. J. Oliver Buswell, Jr., *A Systematic Theology of the Christian Religion,* Grand Rapids: Zondervan, 1962, I, 29-182. Stephen Charnock, *Discourses upon the Existence and Attributes of God,* London: Henry Bohn, 1849. Gordon H. Clark, "God," BDT, pp. 238-248. R. A. Finlayson, "God," NBD, pp. 474-477. Charles Hodge, *Systematic Theology,* New York: Scribner, 1873, I, 191-441. H. Kleinknecht, G. Quell, E. Stauffer and K. G. Kuhn, "*Theos,* etc.," TDNT, III, 65-123. Robert C. Neville, *God, the Creator,* Chicago: Univ. of Chicago Press, 1968 (a philosophic defense of the transcendence and immanence of God). James Orr, *The Christian View of God and the World,* New York: Scribner, 1907, pp. 73-115. J. Barton Payne, *The Theology of the Older Testament,* Grand Rapids: Zondervan, 1962, pp. 120-176, and an annotated bibliography. J. B. Phillips, *Your God Is Too Small,* New York: Macmillan, 1961. Norman H. Snaith, *The Distinctive Ideas of the Old Testament,* London: Epworth Press, 1944. Augustus H. Strong, *Systematic Theology,* 11th ed., Philadelphia: Judson Press, 1947, pp. 52-110, 243-443. Geer-

GOD IS DEAD THEOLOGY

hardus Vos, *Biblical Theology,* Grand Rapids: Eerdmans, 1948.

GOD IS DEAD THEOLOGY. This viewpoint was presented in the 1960's by a new school of theology, calling the movement radical theology. It sprang up in the wake of the theologies of Paul Tillich and Rudolf Bultmann. The movement was composed of a number of theologians who vary considerably in their viewpoints but were united by the common theme "God is dead." They are generally known as the "God is Dead" theologians. They vary widely as to the meaning of this slogan, and were held together as much by other common factors as by their main tenet.

Different Views of the "Death of God"

1. *There never was a God* and now the very idea has died. This was the view of such an atheist as Nietzsche as he spoke of the "death of God," and his Madman cried, "Do we not hear anything yet of the noise of the grave diggers who are burying God? Do we not smell anything yet of God's decomposition? Gods too decompose. God is dead" (*The Madman).*

This atheistic view was presented in another form later by Feuerbach in his *Essence of Christianity* in 1841 as he spoke of religion, and the Christian religion in particular, as merely a projection of the human spirit. Albert Camus, in his famous book *The Rebel,* outlined the entire history of atheism as a movement.

2. *God has actually died.* T. J. J. Altizer, associate professor of Bible and Religion at Emory University, Atlanta, Georgia, wrote in *Radical Theology and the Death of God:* "We must realize that the death of God is an historical event, that God has died in our cosmos, in our history, in our *existenz*" (p. 11).

In a subsequent book, *The Gospel of Christian Atheism,* Altizer explained in detail his theory of how God has died over and over again, to appear each time in another "epiphany" or appearance. The incarnation of Jesus Christ and His crucifixion are to be seen as a Hegelian triadic dialectic in which the God of the OT epiphany, a changeless, immobile quiescent God (as the thesis), has negated Himself to become incarnate or flesh as Jesus Christ (as the antithesis), and then Jesus has negated Himself to become spirit, while God the Father has again negated Himself to become flesh. God the Father, now flesh, united with Jesus, now spirit, in the thesis to form "the Great Humanity Divine" or "the final coming together of God and man" (p. 107).

This triadic dialectic is the process of the death of God. And yet the death of God occurs again and again as a continuous process so that "we can say that God dies in some sense wherever he is present or actual in the world, for God actualizes himself by negating his original or given expressions" (p. 105). Altizer says of his position that "it is an atheistic view but with a difference" (*Radical Theology,* p. x).

3. *The old concept of God is dead.* The old biblical concept of a personal God is out of date and must be discarded, say these radical theologians. Modern man with his scientific viewpoint cannot accept the view of a "God out there." Paul Tillich spoke of the need perhaps to forget the name of God for a generation (*The Shaking of the Foundations,* p. 57) so that we may establish a new view of God as "the God above God" (*The Courage to Be,* pp. 182, 186) who is present as the Power of Being in everything while still being absent. Bishop John A. T. Robinson also speaks along the same lines in his *Honest to God* (p. 7). God is not a person or an object out there, but the Power of Being in everything that is.

4. *The very word "God" is logically meaningless.* The linguistic analyst argues that the term "God" corresponds to no reality which can be tested and proved in an empirical manner, and is therefore entirely contentless. Paul Van Buren reasoned in this manner in his book *The Secular Meaning of the Gospel.* We can talk meaningfully of Jesus Christ, because He was an historical person and there is at least empirical evidence for His existence, but not of "this literally nonsensical entity called 'God' " (p. 84). "Today we cannot even understand the Nietzschian cry 'God is dead,' for if it were so, how could we know? No, the problem now is that the *word* 'God' is dead" (p. 103).

5. *Various other views.* For some, God is merely in eclipse (cf. Martin Buber); for others, the God whom we have thought of as a problem solver is now the God who deals with man as no longer a child but mature (cf. Bonhoeffer's idea of the "coming of age" of humanity). Again, for such a man as William Hamilton, God is now silent, hidden, absent, so we must speak of the death of God, but that time will doubtless pass.

Uniting Characteristics

1. *Revolutionary activism.* The radical theologians see revolutionary action as called for in our day.

2. *Optimism versus pessimism.* The movement is a distinctly American reaction to the pessimism and the subjectivism of European existentialism. Its optimism is undoubtedly partly a result of the economic prosperity being experienced in both Europe and the United States today.

3. *Social action.* The great stress is upon social action in general in distinction to either individual or corporate spiritual renewal. The social, economic, and political aspects of life crowd out all the moral and spiritual.

4. *The slogan "God is dead."* While this is explained in all the diverse ways mentioned, still the slogan does indicate for many that the God of the OT has ceased to exist. God can be known only as He becomes united with universal humanity, that is, in Jesus as universal humanity.

5. *Universal humanity.* According to these

theologians, God has been done away with, but Jesus Christ has become united with fallen humanity. He can be touched in every human hand and seen in every human face.

6. *Secularized Christianity.* Man has become entirely secularized. Bonhoeffer spoke of man "coming of age" and reaching maturity. Man is now self-sufficient and has no need for God. Harvey Cox in *The Secular City* stresses the wholly secularized society of our day and proposes a secular gospel to meet man's needs. Bonhoeffer spoke of a "religionless Christianity" and how man must be spoken to in wholly secular terms; Cox spells this out for our day. The Christian is to work alongside the man of the world in his political, economic, and social endeavors. He should not come to his fellowman to help him with revealed principles or rules, but he should come simply as man with man to work out bit by bit the answers which prove successful because they are found to function.

7. *Situation ethics.* Most of the radical theologians are in distinct rebellion against the revealed ethical standards and moral laws presented in the Bible. They claim all ethical decisions can vary according to the particular circumstances in which a man finds himself as he applies the one principle of love. Premarital relations, adultery, lying and stealing, all may be right under certain circumstances (cf. Joseph Fletcher, *Situation Ethics*).

8. *The failure of the church.* According to their view, the church has failed and is failing, particularly today, to reach the masses of mankind. Its view of God is outdated in a modern scientific world. The church must mix with the world and enter into its social, economic, and political problems with a new secular gospel. The secular must replace the soul-winning gospel.

Historical Background

The God is Dead movement can be traced from early humanism through William Blake the poet, on to Nietzsche, and through Feuerbach, and on to the present. The Christian humanism of Erasmus has blossomed forth in the movement's confidence that man is quite well able to do without God because he can find absolute and radical freedom from all moral laws in a Christ who has become united with fallen humanity. Nietzsche could not bear to have a God who saw into his sinful heart, and therefore wrote, "He had to die; he looked with eyes which saw everything. . . .His pity knew no modesty: he crept into my dirtiest corners . . . on such a witness I would have revenge . . . the God that beheld everything and also man had to die!" With his Madman, Nietzsche put God to death in a literary manner. He finally broke down mentally under the strain, however. and died insane. Altizer leans heavily on Nietzsche for his argument that God has died, and others of the movement also quote him.

After Karl Barth failed to find any way to get propositional revelation from God with his Kierkegaardian theory of revelation (*see* Neoorthodoxy), and Bultmann emptied the teachings of Scripture completely with his demythologization, the radical theologians have turned to Nietzsche with his cry, "God is dead," and given the expression their own particular meanings. Bonhoeffer has given them certain inspirations with his suggestion of a "religionless Christianity" and a wholly secular presentation of the gospel, but since he continued to believe in the existence of God the Father and in confessional Christianity until the time of his death, their view that God is dead is not attributable to him.

The most important men in the American movement are Thomas J. J. Altizer, William Hamilton, Paul Van Buren, and Harvey Cox.

Analysis and Evaluation

The God is Dead theologians with their radical theology and revolutionary activism are challenging the true evangelical church to consider the Christian's responsibility toward the secular needs of man in the areas of economics, politics, and man's social needs. God charged man with the task of subduing and ruling the world (Gen 1:28), and this task has never been revoked. This is God's world, and therefore it is the Christian's world, even if Satan has usurped God's place in the hearts of fallen man. Therefore it is the Christian's duty to do all he can to subdue the world economically, socially, and politically. This was the concept of Abraham Kuyper and it has been worked out in detail by the Free University which he was instrumental in founding. The reformed view is that the Christian has as his duty the task of applying the revealed principles of justice, democracy, and morality found in the Bible to the world's needs. In contrast, these radical theologians think that they can change the world while at the same time denying the divinely revealed principles.

The evangelical Christian finds the God is Dead theology wanting for the following reasons:

1. The movement is essentially a rebellion against God-given law and morals. Man has always wanted absolute radical freedom, and these men are ready to destroy God in their own way, even as Nietzsche did in his way in order to gain such freedom.

2. These men maintain that we live in a scientific age and that modern man must base all his life on the scientific method. In science man finds physical laws by experimentation. If he breaks the physical law, then the law destroys him immediately. There are, however, also moral laws. If he breaks them, they in turn can destroy him; however, they do not necessarily react immediately. They may punish him in his old age or in his children's children. This tempts him to think that such laws may not

exist. The difference between the physical laws and the moral laws is that the former can be discovered by fallen man through functionalism, but the latter only through revelation! The reason functionalism fails at this point is that man, as fallen, cannot think correctly in moral matters. His total depravity incapacitates him and even prejudices him against revealed moral law.

3. All the arguments presented for the death of God are based finally upon a refusal to accept Jesus Christ at His own self-evaluation. He spoke of God as His Father, as being a person, and as hearing and answering both His prayers and those who are His children. He maintained that He was the Son of God, and indicated that He forgave sins because He was God. Any attempt, therefore, to take Christ only in part is a denial of who and what He is.

4. The God is Dead theologians are not Christians at all. They are merely humanists.

Bibliography. T. J. J. Altizer, *The Gospel of Christian Atheism,* Philadelphia: Westminster, 1966. Altizer and William Hamilton, *Radical Theology and the Death of God,* New York: Bobbs-Merrill, 1966. Harvey Cox, *The Secular City,* New York: Macmillan, 8th ed., 1966. Joseph Fletcher, *Situation Ethics,* Philadelphia: Westminster, 1966. Kenneth Hamilton, *God Is Dead,* Grand Rapids: Eerdmans, 1966. K. Hamilton, *Revolt Against Heaven,* Grand Rapids: Eerdmans, 1965. William Hamilton, *The New Essence of Christianity,* New York: Association Press, 1961. Gabriel Vahanian, *The Death of God,* New York: George Braziller, 1957. Paul M. Van Buren, *The Secular Meaning of the Gospel,* New York: Macmillan, 1963.

R. A. K.

GOD, NAMES AND TITLES OF. Five OT Heb. terms are of basic importance in discussing the various simple and compound names and titles of God. In the OT, just as in Canaanite religious literature, synonymous divine names often occur for the same deity as well as appellations used in parallelism in poetry. No inferences of polytheism can be drawn from such usage. For the significance in biblical times of the concept of "name," *see* Name(s).

1. *El*. The Heb. word *'ēl,* which has cognate forms in other Semitic languages, signifies "the strong one," a mighty being or leader, a god in the widest sense, whether true or false. Like *theos,* Deus and God, it is the generic term for Deity. The plural form *'ēlîm* in most contexts is to be translated "gods." These gods may be mere idols of wood, metal or stone (Isa 44:10, 15, 17; 46:6). *El* was the name of the "high god" or head of the Canaanite pantheon. Among the Israelites, *El* was often used of their God in describing Him and as an element in compound names (e.g., *El Shaddai,* "Immanuel"). *See* El.

2. *Elohim*. This plural form of the similar word *'ĕlōah* (found 42 times in Job) is used of gods and goddesses of the surrounding nations, but chiefly to signify the true God of Israel in the sense of the one supreme Deity (Gen 1:1, etc.; 3:5; Deut 4:35, 39; Jer 10:10). As the ordinary Heb. word for God, it corresponds to the common noun "god" in English, and is therefore applicable to the concept of deity in contrast to man and created beings. The plural form with reference to one particular deity is not unique to the Heb. OT, but the very frequent usage in Heb. was almost certainly encouraged by the Israelites' belief that their God was the only true God, and therefore that the sum and total of deity was inherent in Him. *See* Elohim; God.

3. *Elyon, El Elyon. Elyon,* the "Most High," is found alone as a designation for God in Num 24:16; Deut 32:8; II Sam 22:14; Ps 9:2, plus 11 times; Isa 14:14; Lam 3:35, 38. In the LXX and NT this title appears as Gr. *hupsistos* (e.g., Lk 1:32; Acts 7:48). The term *'El 'Elyôn,* the "most high God," is particularly significant as used by Melchizedek (Gen 14:18–20). The term refers to divine beings in the sacred literature of the Canaanites found at Ras Shamra (*q.v.*). *See* Most High.

4. *Yahweh*. This is the most significant name of God found in the OT in that it is the personal proper name Israel had for their God. For this reason in post-Exilic times it began to be considered so holy that it was never pronounced. Instead, usually the term *Adonai* was substituted. In the 6th–7th cen. A.D. the Jewish Masoretic scholars combined the vowels of *Adonai* with the consonants YHWH to remind the synagogue reader to pronounce the name as *Adonai*. But those consonants and vowels spell the name Jehovah, a form first attested about A.D. 1220. Jehovah is the spelling often used in the ASV, following its few occurrences in the KJV, to translate *Yahweh*. The substitution of the vowels can only be understood when we realize that the original Heb. Scriptures contained no written vowels. The Heb. words consisted of consonants alone, the vowels being provided by the requirement of the context, or by memory.

Yahweh was doubtless the approximate pronunciation of the tetragrammaton, the four-letter word YHWH, since transliterations into Gr. in early Christian literature have been found in the form of *iaoué* (Clement of Alexander) and *iabé* (Theodoret) pronounced "iave." The name is a variant connected with the verb *hāyâ,* "to be," from an earlier form, *hāwâ*

Strictly speaking, this is the only personal name of God belonging to Him alone. When Moses asked God what was the significance of His name, He replied, "I AM THAT I AM: and he said, Thus shalt thou say unto the children of Israel, I AM hath sent me unto you" (Ex 3:14). Thus God revealed to Moses what was the very inner meaning of His name as *Yahweh*. God followed with the declaration, "Thus shalt thou say unto the children of Israel, Yahweh

GOD, NAMES AND TITLES OF

the God of your fathers, the God of Abraham, the God of Isaac, and the God of Jacob, hath sent me unto you: this is my name for ever" (Ex 3:15). His very name was His promise to His covenant people that "He is" with them (cf. 3:12) to be their God and to supply every need. He had not explained the import of His name Yahweh to the patriarchs (cf. Ex 6:2-3).

There is strong reason to believe that Jesus picked up the thought inherent in the divine name when He said, "Before Abraham was, I am" (Jn 8:58). This identification of Himself with the declaration of God in Ex 3:14 would then have been so startling as to explain why the Jews took up stones immediately to stone Him (Jn 8:58-59). *See* I Am.

5. *Adonai.* An honorific title used both as an intensive plural of rank meaning "Master," "Sovereign," or "Lord," and as an appellative meaning "my Lord." Its alternate form occurs in Ps 110:1 which reads, "The Lord [*Yahweh*] said unto my Lord [*'ădōnî*]." Mt 22:41-45 shows how Christ identified this title with Himself. The Gr. equivalent is *Kyrios,* "Lord," representing both *Yahweh* and *Adonai* in the OT LXX. In the NT it is applied to Christ equally with the Father and the Spirit.

6. *Composite names for God.* There are in the OT special characterizations of God, both expressing and confessing such truths as:

a. God's power—*'Ēl Shaddai,* "Almighty God," probably meaning originally the "god of the mountain(s)" (Gen 17:1). The term Shaddai occurs alone 31 times in Job as an appellation for God.

b. God's eternity—*'Ēl 'Ôlām,* "the everlasting God" (Gen 21:33) and *'Attîq Yômîn,* "Ancient of Days," the One who judges and rules over the empires of the world (Dan 7:9, 13, 22).

c. God's special relationship to Israel. Accepting Israel as his new name (cf. Gen 32:28), Jacob confessed *'El-'elōhê-Israel,* "El (is) the God of Israel," when he bought a piece of land and erected an altar at Shechem (Gen 33:18-20, JerusB). Likewise Joshua in establishing the covenant at Mount Ebal (Josh 8:30), Deborah after her victory (Jud 5:3), and the prophets and psalmists (Isa 17:6; Ps 59:5; Zeph 2:9) acknowledged Yahweh to be the "God of Israel." "The Holy One of Israel" was a favorite title (*qᵉdôsh Yiśrā'ēl*) with Isaiah, who used it 29 times. He also spoke of God as the "mighty One of Israel" (Isa 1:24) and the "mighty One of Jacob" (Isa 49:26; 60:16), following Gen 49:24. See also the "Strength of Israel" (I Sam 15:29).

d. God's provision for the believer's needs. Abraham named the hill where he was about to offer Isaac *Jehovah-jireh.* He thus confessed that God had provided the needed sacrifice in the ram caught in the thicket which could substitute as a burnt offering instead of his son (Gen 22:13-14). *Yahweh Rōph'ekā,* "I am the Lord, your healer" (Ex 15:26, RSV), was God's promise to all who would diligently obey Him.

e. God's leadership—*Jehovah-nissi,* "The Lord is my banner," the name Moses gave to an altar he built to commemorate the defeat of the Amalekites (Ex 17:15). *Yahweh Rō'î,* the best loved name or description of all, is the familiar "The Lord is my shepherd" (Ps 23:1), with its many applications to leadership, provision, and protection.

f. God's peace—*Yahweh-shalom,* "The Lord is (my) peace," exclaimed Gideon after being visited by the angel of the Lord as he erected an altar in Ophrah and knew the peace of God in his heart (Jud 6:24).

g. The Messiah's most precious name, *Yahweh-tsidkenu,* "The Lord our righteousness" (Jer 23:6; cf. 33:16); the name and attribute by which the Messiah, Jesus Christ, was especially to be known (I Cor 1:30; II Cor 5:21; Phil 3:9; II Pet 1:1; I Jn 2:1).

h. The name of the New Jerusalem, *Yahweh-shammah,* "Jehovah is there," a prophecy in Ezk 48:35, which will be fulfilled in the New Jerusalem of Rev 21:22; 22:3.

i. God's heavenly title, *Yahweh Sabaoth,* "the Lord of hosts." This divine title, first found in I Sam 1:3, was used by David as he went to meet Goliath: "You come to me with a sword and with a spear and with a javelin; but I come to you in the name of the Lord of hosts, the God of the armies of Israel, whom you have defied" (I Sam 17:45, RSV). As the Lord of hosts He is mighty in battle (Ps 24:8, 10). The prophets often used the term. It is found in Jeremiah 88 times in the KJV either as "the Lord of hosts" or as "the Lord God of hosts," where it implies that the "hosts" are angelic forces of heaven constantly ready to do God's command (cf. Ps 89:5-8; 148:2; Mt 26:53). The expression "the Lord of Sabaoth" occurs untranslated in Rom 9:29 and Jas 5:4. *See* Host of Heaven.

7. *Other appellations.*

a. Rock (Heb. *sûr,* e.g., Deut 32:4, 15, 18, 31; I Sam 2:2; II Sam 22:3, 32, 47; 23:3; Ps 92:15; Heb. *sela',* e.g., Ps 18:2; 31:3; 42:9).

b. Father (e.g., Isa 63:16; 64:8; Mal 1:6; Mt 5:16, 45, 48; 6:9; etc.). *See* Father, God the; Abba.

c. King (Ps 10:16; 24:7-10; 44:4; 47:7; cf. I Sam 12:12). In the ancient Semitic world it was common practice to address one's deity as "King." Isaiah saw the Lord seated upon a throne and exclaimed, "Mine eyes have seen the King, the Lord of hosts" (Isa 6:1, 5).

d. Judge (e.g., Gen 18:25; Jud 11:27; Ps 50; 75:7; Acts 10:42; II Tim 4:8; Heb 12:23). This title referred to one of the functions of a king as ruler (Isa 33:22).

e. Shepherd. This title was frequently assumed by ancient monarchs to signify their benevolent rule of their people (e.g., Hammurabi in the prologue of his code). God is called the Shepherd of Israel (Ps 80:1), and is likened to one in Isa 40:11; Ezk 34:11-16. Thus it became an important title of the Lord Jesus Christ as the great Shepherd of the sheep (Heb 13:20; cf. I Pet 2:25; 5:4).

f. The First and the Last. Isaiah employs this expression to describe the eternal rule of Yahweh over the entire course of history from beginning to end (Isa 44:6; 48:12; cf. 41:4; 43:10; 45:21; 46:9-10). The risen, glorified Christ assumes the title as He speaks to John on the island of Patmos (Rev 1:11, 17; 2:8; 22:13).

g. Gr. *despotēs,* "lord," "master," "owner," denoted absolute ownership and uncontrolled power over slaves. It is used as a title for God in Lk 2:29; Acts 4:24; Rev 6:10, and for Christ in II Pet 2:1 and Jude 4. *See* God.

Bibliography. William F. Albright, *Yahweh and the Gods of Canaan,* Garden City: Doubleday, 1968. B. W. Anderson, "God, Names of," IDB, II, 407-417. Ada R. Habershon, *The New Testament Names and Titles of the Lord of Glory,* London: Nisbet, 1910. Andrew Jukes, *The Names of God in Holy Scripture,* London: Longmans, 1888. C. J. Labuschagne, *The Incomparability of Yahweh in the Old Testament,* Leiden: E. J. Brill, 1966. G. T. Manley, "God, Names of," NBD, pp. 477-480. Herbert F. Stevenson, *Titles of the Triune God,* Westwood, N.J.: Revell, 1956. Nathan J. Stone, *Names of God in the Old Testament,* Chicago, Moody, 1944. H. W. Webb-Peploe, *The Titles of Jehovah,* London: Nisbet, 1901.

R. A. K.

The goddess Demeter at Izmir. HFV

GODDESS. A term used only twice in the Bible: the Heb. *'ĕlōhîm* used of Ashtoreth, goddess of the Sidonians, in I Kgs 11:5, 33; Gr. *thea* of the goddess Diana in Acts 19:27, 35, 37.

Ashtoreth was the Heb. name of the Canaanite goddess Astarte. It is cognate with the Babylonian Ishtar, the goddess of sensuousness, maternity and fertility. The worship of Ashtoreth included most licentious practices. Israel commenced serving Baal and Ashtoreth in the times of the judges (Jud 2:13; 10:6). Solomon succumbed to her voluptuous worship and built high places for her and other heathen gods (I Kgs 11:5, 7-8, 33; II Kgs 23:13), in spite of God's earlier warnings (I Sam 7:3; 12:10).

Diana *(q.v.),* known among the Greeks as Artemis and the Romans as Diana, represented the same power over fruitfulness and birth which was worshiped as Ashtoreth in Palestine. She was regarded as mother goddess of the earth with her chief place of worship at the temple in Ephesus, where she was served by eunuchs and vestal virgins. The ritual of the temple consisted in sacrifices and ceremonial prostitution.

These two, Ashtoreth and Diana, who are essentially the same mother-goddess of Asia, are examples of the female images man has set up of himself—of his self-projections—mentioned in Rom 1:21-23 and worshiped, while the pagan gods are male examples. They personify man's unbridled passions and lusts and are deities made in man's fallen image and after his own likeness.

See Gods, False.

R. A. K.

GODHEAD. The word "godhead," compounded of "god" and "hood," later changed to "head," means that which is qualitatively of the nature of Deity. It refers not to any one person in the Trinity but rather the whole. The Shorter Catechism uses the term as it asks, "How many persons are there in the Godhead?" Three Gr. words are translated by this term in the KJV.

1. *Theion* is used once in Acts 17:29 by Paul as he speaks to the learned Greeks on Mars Hill about the unknown God whom they ignorantly worshiped, and contrasts His "Deity" (RSV) or "Divine Nature" (NASB) to the images of gold, silver and stone formed by the art and imagination of man.

2. *Theiotēs* in Rom 1:20 is a term particularly of quality and stresses the nature of God as divine. As man looks at creation he should come to two conclusions: the existence of a God who is powerful enough to cause it all to exist, and His "Diety" (RSV) or "Divine Nature" (NASB). By the use of *theiotēs* God's invisible qualities or attributes are indicated (see NASB, TEV).

3. *Theotēs* occurs in Col 2:9 and stresses the divine essence rather than attributes. "In him dwelleth all the fulness of the Godhead bodily." In Christ only, since He alone of the

Trinity became incarnate, does absolute and perfect Deity, all the divine essence, dwell in One who has a body.

The term Godhead stresses monotheism and the unity of the three persons of the Trinity, and guards against a polytheistic view of God. The OT categorically states, "The Lord our God is one Lord" (Deut 6:4). In the NT Christ declares, "I and my Father are one" (Jn 10:30). The doctrine of the Godhead develops this monotheistic concept further.

The doctrine of three persons in the one Godhead supplies certain very important philosophical needs. If God were a unitary person rather than a trinity of persons, the world and man would add basic new dimensions to Him. He would know added relationships when they came into being. To this extent a unitarian concept of God fails in that the God proposed by all Unitarians—be they Jewish, Muslim or Christian—needs the world and man to be fully developed. The world adds an "I-It" relationship; man adds an "I-Thou" and a "We-You" or social relationship. The Christian Trinity in contrast possesses all of these. The Son and the Spirit are objects to the Father, and each to the other. The Father and the Son have always enjoyed the "I-Thou" relationship, the personal encounter. Any two of the Trinity can minister to the third, and thus God forever knows the "We-You" or social relationship.

See God; I Am; Trinity.

R. A. K.

GODLINESS. Normally, "godliness" in the KJV is a translation of the Gr. *eusebeia.* Godliness broadly means practical Christian piety. It finds its basis in a proper knowledge of God (I Jn 5:18), its outworking in a yielded life to God through Jesus Christ (Rom 12:1), and its final goal as the development of the consciousness of God, and of such similar traits as righteousness, faith, love, patience, and meekness (I Tim 6:11; II Pet 1:6). The concept is developed extensively in the Pastoral Epistles, and is crystallized in the words, "but godliness with contentment is great gain" (I Tim 6:6; cf. I Tim 2:2, 10; 3:16; 4:7-8; 6:3, 5, 11; II Tim 3:5, 12; Tit 1:1; 2:12).

GODS, FALSE

Introduction

The most common Heb. words for "gods" are *'ēlîm* and *'ĕlōhîm,* denoting men of might and rank, angels, gods, and (*'ĕlōhîm* only) the Supreme Being. Whether or not both words are traceable to a single root is debatable. The former is probably from the root *'wl,* "to be in front of, precede." Some think the latter may come from a root *'lh,* "to be in awe of." The Gr. word *theoi,* used in the NT and the LXX to render *'ēlîm, 'ĕlōhîm,* may be connected with a root "to supplicate, to implore."

The meaning of the term must be determined by its actual usage. The ancient Near Eastern concept of "gods" varied somewhat from mod-

A Syrian deity standing on the back of a lion.
LM

ern ideas of "gods" as supernatural beings who were immortal. This was also true of the concepts of the pagan nations with whom Israel came in contact. For example, some gods, such as Baal and Tammuz, could and did die.

To the Hebrews, the "gods" of the nations about them were simply the powers in whom their neighbors and contemporaries believed. Those powers were the activators of the forces of nature: sun, moon, storm, flood, disease, etc. Each event had its activator. Hence there could be a multitude of gods according to pagan and primitive conceptions. Since there was no concept of an organized cosmos, there was no idea of a solitary Supreme Being, although each religion had its own chief, or father-god. Some gods were assumed to be local (I Kgs 20:28; II Kgs 17:26 f.) and limited in power. Other gods were conceived of as unlimited by geography, so certain prominent gods were worshiped across political and cultural lines (e.g., Ashtoreth, Baal, Hadad).

The biblical viewpoint regarding heathen deities affirms their subjective existence (Jer 2:28) in the mind and life of the devotee, but denies their objective reality (Jer 2:11). Of course, where deity and its image or idol were fused into one, the idol was an objective reality which the biblical writers acknowledge, while denying the objective existence of the deity represented by it.

In studying the gods of the Bible, a distinction must be made between the deities proper, and the idols or cult objects by which they were represented or worshiped. Sometimes the two were fused into one, while at other times the deity was kept distinct from his cult object. Baalim, asherim (sacred trees, groves), calves, the brazen serpent, and the teraphim (household idols) were all objects of worship. It is doubtful that there was a deity behind either of the latter two. The Baalim were representations of the local Baals, possibly in the form of bulls or calves. Sometimes the word is used of the deities without any reference to a cultic representation. The same is true of the asherim.

The golden calves of Jeroboam (I Kgs 12:28-30) have been thought by some to have been pedestals for Yahweh to ride on, replacing the ark as Yahweh's place of meeting His people. However, in keeping with the widespread use of the bull as a cultic symbol, it seems more likely that the calves were intended to be a fusion of deity and image, the deity being perhaps a fusion of Yahweh and the local Baal. Aaron's golden calf (Ex 32) may have been a fusion of Yahweh with the Egyptian god Apis, worshiped under the representation of a bull. Calf worship was denounced by Hosea (8:5-6; 10:5; 13:2).

A distinction must also be made between gods and demons. Frequently, when a nation conquered another nation, it demoted its gods to the status of demons and myths. Traces of this can be seen in the OT in such vague figures as satyrs (Lev 17:7; II Chr 11:15, both RSV, NEB), Lilith (Isa 34:14, JerusB), and Resheph (see below). Eventually the demoted pagan deity survived only in a language in mere hints of his former existence, such as in poetic symbolism (cf. Albright, *Yahweh and the Gods of Canaan,* pp. 183-193). This is evident in English in such expressions as "love-struck," i.e., "smitten by the arrows of Cupid." In this category can be put some of the OT references to Leviathan, the primeval serpent, the dragon, Rahab, and the Sea.

National Pantheons

Frequently the OT speaks of the gods of the various nations surrounding Israel in general terms. Here one encounters practically all the nations with whom Israel had contacts. Commonly the word "pantheon" is used in listing and discussing the gods of any ethnic or political group. However, this is a misleading anachronism. The Semitic idiom is "the assembly of the gods." This conclave is to be envisioned as an assemblage for concerted decision or action (as, e.g., U.S. Senate may meet without all senators being present) rather than a formal, methodical catalog of the deities worshiped by a particular people. With this distinction in mind, one can note the following pantheons mentioned in the Bible.

1. The gods of the Ammonites (Jud 10:6). The chief god was Moloch/Molech or Milcom.

2. The gods of the Amorites (Josh 24:2, 15; Jud 6:10; I Kgs 21:26; II Kgs 21:11). Since little Amorite literature has come down to us, secondary sources and inferences must be depended on for knowledge of this pantheon. Evidently it was somewhat like the later and succeeding Canaanite pantheon. The temple of Ishtar at Mari and the temple of Dagon at Babylon were probably Amorite shrines. Dagon/Dagan, Hadad, and Anath seem to have been Amorite deities forced upon the Canaanites by the invading Amorites from the middle Euphrates region, as inferred from the discoveries at Ras Shamra (Oldenburg, *The Conflict Between El and Ba'al,* pp. 146-163).

3. The gods of the Assyrians (Nah 1:14) come into purview in the OT in the 9th to the 7th cen. B.C. Chief god of this pantheon was Asshur, replacing the Sumerian Ea. The Assyrian pantheon was somewhat like that of Babylonia. In both localities Semitic deities replaced the older Sumerian gods, in some cases absorbing their functions and titles.

Stone tablet recording the refoundation of the temple of the sun god at Sippar, Babylonia, ninth century B.C. BM

4. The gods of the Babylonians (Isa 21:9; Ezr 1:7) were important to Israel in the closing centuries of the kingdom and during the Exile. There were more than 700 deities listed in Babylonia. The Semitic conquerors of the Sumerians accepted the native gods and added their own. This situation was further complicated by the fact that each city-state had its own pantheon.

At Lagash, in early times, Anu, the god of heaven, was worshiped along with Antu his wife. At Eridu the chief god was Enlil, god of earth, who was later succeeded by Marduk.

The Assyrian god Ashur. ORINST

Enlil's wife was Damkina, and his son was Marduk. These figures (except Marduk) were all Sumerian. Other gods of the Babylonians included Sin (Sumerian Nanna), the moon-god; Shamash, the sun-god and son of Sin; Ningal, the wife of Sin; Ishtar (Sumerian Innina), the fertility goddess, and her husband Tammuz; Allatu (Sumerian Ereshkigal), the goddess of the underworld; Namtar, herald of the god of death; Irra, the plague god; Kingsu, the goddess of Chaos; Apsu, the god of the underworld ocean; Nabu, the patron saint of science and learning; and Nusku, the god of fire. *See* Babylonia.

5. The gods of the Canaanites (*q.v.*) are mentioned along with those of other inhabitants of Canaan in connection with the Heb. conquest of the land. Other tribes mentioned in Ex 23:23; 34:11-17; Jud 3:5 f. and other passages include the Amorites, the Hittites, the Perizzites, the Hivites and the Jebusites. Except for the Hittites, and possibly the Hivites (Horites? i.e., Hurrians; cf. Gr. Gen 34:2; Josh 9:7), the other tribes were closely allied to the Canaanites and probably worshiped the same deities. The same was true of the Syrians mentioned in Jud 10:6, but there probably was some change in that pantheon in later times (see 11 below). The Canaanite pantheon is best known from the mythological texts of Ras Shamra, although other information comes from Philo of Byblos and biblical sources, as well as shorter literary texts in Aramaic and Phoenician.

The chief god and creator was El. His son (sometimes called his grandson) Baal (see below) was the storm and vegetation god. He was called "the one who prevails," "the exalted one, lord of the earth." In mythology, Baal is enthroned on a lofty mountain in the N. During Ahab's reign he became the chief god of Israel. Asherah was the wife of El and mother of 70 gods. In the Ras Shamra texts the goddess Anath is the sister and usually the wife of Baal, but in the OT Ashtoreth (i.e., Asherah) is usually his wife. At Tyre, home of Jezebel, Asherah is Baal's wife (cf. RSV; I Kgs 15:13; 18:19; II Kgs 21:7; 23:4). Other prominent Canaanite gods were Dagon, Moloch, Resheph and Rimmon (see below), and Mot (death).

6. The gods of Egypt are mentioned in the Heb. early premonarchic history and again in the 7th to the 6th cen. B.C. (Ex 12:12; Josh 24:14; Jer 43:12-13; 46:25). Since the gods of Egypt were constantly changing, fusing and syncretizing, depending in part upon the political fortunes of the nome or city at which a particular deity was paramount, it is difficult to give a brief survey of Egypt's "pantheon." However, the chief god was known by different names at different times and places. At Heliopolis he was known as Aten-Re-Khepri; at Elephantine as Khnum-Re; at Thebes as Amon-Re (see below); and at Amarna (*q.v.*) as Aton-Re. Re, the sun-god was thus fused with the local god of the nome. Triads of chief gods are noted at various times: Ptah, Sekhmet, Nefer Tem; Amon-Re, Mut, and Khonsu; Osiris, Isis, and Horus. These are all father-mother-son triads.

According to the Pyramid texts, the Book of the Dead, and other early Egyptian literature, there were over 1,200 deities known to the Egyptians. Chief of these deities were the following: Apis, the bull of Memphis (Ex 32; I Kgs 12:25-33 may refer to his worship); Hapi, the Nile god; Hathor, the goddess of love and beauty; Ma'at, the god of right and order;

The goddess Sekhmet. LM

The temple of Bacchus, god of wine, at Baalbek. HFV

Sothis, the dog star; Sihor, the god of the underworld; Shu, the god of the air; Thoth, the scribal god.

7. The gods of the Edomites are sometimes mentioned as the gods of Seir (II Chr 25:14; cf. v. 20).

8. The gods of the Hittites, although not referred to by name in the OT, are alluded to in Ex 23:23-24; 34:11-15; Jud 3:5-6. The chief Hittite god, Teshub, was a storm-god roughly equivalent to Baal. Possibly, therefore, the Hittites worshiped Canaanite deities as a result of their contact with the Canaanites, although Hittite proper names indicate that Indo-European deities were worshiped at least for a brief time (cf. William F. Albright, *Archaeology of Palestine,* p. 183).

9. The gods of the Moabites are mentioned in Num 25:1-2; Jud 10:6; Ruth 1:15; Jer 48:35. Their chief god was Chemosh, who is also called Athtar. In Babylonia in the 2nd mil. B.C., he was equated with Nergal, the god of the underworld.

10. The gods of the Philistines included Dagon, worshiped at Gaza and Ashdod (Jud 16:23; I Sam 5:1-7; I Macc 10:83); Ashtoreth, worshiped at Ashkelon (Herodotus i.105); and Baalzebub, worshiped at Ekron (II Kgs 1:2, 6, 16).

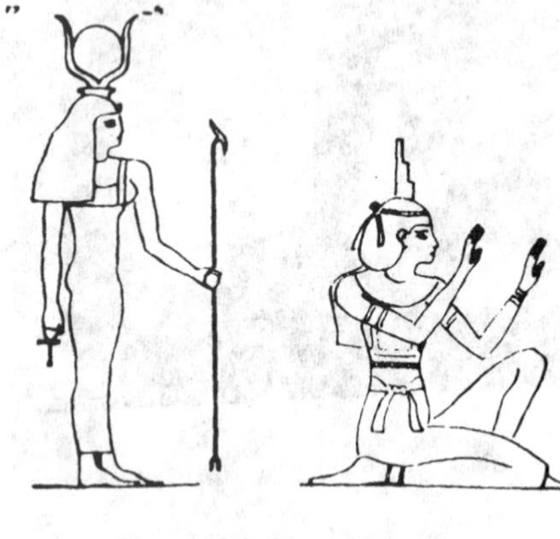

Picture of Hathor and Isis as is.

11. The gods of the Syrians (II Kgs 17:31; 18:34; II Chr 28:23; Isa 36:19) are probably variants of the older Canaanite pantheon. Theophoric names such as Ben-hadad and Tabrimmon bear witness to the worship of Baal under the guise of the Amorite Hadad, also known as Rimmon.

12. The Gr. and Rom. pantheons are not mentioned except in a general way (Acts 17:16, 18) in the NT.

The worship of astral deities is mentioned in Deut 4:19; II Kgs 23:5; Jer 19:13; Amos 5:26; Acts 7:43. An indirect reference to such entities may be found in Neh 9:6; Ps 148:1-4. A number of these astral deities are treated separately below.

The OT constantly condemns the worship of foreign deities (Deut 6:14) and pronounces judgment upon idolatry (Ex 20:3-5; 32:35; Num 25:1-9; Deut 5:7-9). Behind the awful judgment of Joel 1:4-20 was Israel's lapse into idolatry (cf. Joel 2:12 f.). The captivity is depicted as being brought on by the worship of other gods (II Kgs 22:17).

Individual Gods

Adrammelech (ȧ-drăm'ĕ-lĕk)–A deity worshiped by the people of Sepharvaim who were settled in Samaria by the Assyrians after 722 B.C. (II Kgs 17:31). Since "d" and "r" look alike in ancient Heb. script, the name may be a confusion of a NW Mesopotamian god Adad-Milki ("Adad is my king"). There is no evidence of a god named Adar. Cf. Anammelech below.

Amon (ăm'ŏn)–The chief deity of Thebes (Jer 46:25, RSV, NASB). He was represented by a ram with upward curving horns. When Thebes dominated Egypt following the fall of the Old Kingdom, Amon became the most important god and was called Amon-Re. His great temple at Karnak with its famous hypostyle hall has the highest columns in the world (70 feet). He became the national god par excellence, except for a brief time during the reform of Akhenaton (*q.v.*).

Anammelecn (ȧ-năm'ĕ-lĕk)–A deity worshiped by the people of Sepharvaim (probably Sabraim, located between Hamath and Damascus, II Kgs 17:31), who were settled in Samaria by the Assyrians after 722 B.C. The name probably means "Anu is king." There was a temple dedicated to Anu and Adad at Assur about this time. The worship of the Sepharvites, presumably including that of Anammelech, involved the sacrifice of children as burnt offerings.

Anath (ā'năth)–The name of a popular but savage Canaanite goddess of fertility who played a key role as the sister and consort of Baal in the important corpus of 15th cen. B.C. Semitic literature from Ras Shamra, known as the Ugaritic tablets. The Bible makes no direct

GODS, FALSE

The god Amon. MM

reference to her as a goddess, but rather to her sister goddess of fertility Astarte (Ashtoreth, I Kgs 11:5, 33). The two goddesses were at least partly fused in Canaanite thinking since Astarte and Anath were both worshiped as the spouse of Baal (cf. Jud 10:6; I Sam 7:4); this may be the reason for biblical silence on Anath.

Artemis (är'tĕ-mĭs)—In classical mythology, the sister of Apollo, daughter of Leto and Zeus, equated with the Roman Diana, the moon-goddess who was a huntress and protector of womanhood. However, Artemis of Acts 19:23–40 (NASB) has little in common with her classical namesake. She was really a Lydian mother-goddess, worshiped at the mouth of the Cayster River long before the Greeks came to Ephesus. At Ephesus, Artemis was the goddess of fertility. Her temple retinue included eunuch priests, attendants, and hierodules. Her image (Acts 19:35) probably was a meteorite. The silver shrines (Acts 19:24), as well as models of clay and marble, may have been replicas of the primitive sanctuary. The temple of Paul's day was one of the seven wonders of the world.

The worship of the Ephesian Artemis extended into Greece, Gaul, Rome, and Syria. The Nabateans of the 1st cen. A.D. worshiped the deity Atargatis, who is equated with Artemis. In NT times there was a temple of Artemis at Gerasa. *See* Diana; Goddess.

Asherah (*ȧ*-shē̆r'*ȧ*)—A deity whose name is frequently mistranslated in KJV following the LXX "groves." In a Sumerian inscription to Hammurabi she is called "the bride of Anu (heaven)." She was the chief goddess of Tyre, *c.* 1500 B.C. In the Ugaritic pantheon she is called *"Athiratu-yammi"* ("She who walks on the sea"). She was the consort or wife of El, and the mother of 70 gods, including Baal. Animal sacrifices were offered to her. She also bore the title "Holiness" as attested by an Egyptian nude figure of her bearing that inscription.

In Babylonian records Ashratum was known as a deity. In the Tell el-Amarna tablets her name occurs in the proper name "Abdi-Ashirta." The name is also found in S Arabia, indicating the widespread prevalence of her worship.

This goddess is not to be confused with Astarte, known in the OT in its plural form as Ashtaroth or Ashtoreth (*see* Ashtoreth below). In the OT her worship is associated with that of Baal (RSV: Jud 3:7; I Kgs 18:19; II Kgs 23:4).

The goddess Artemis or Diana in the Ephesus Museum. HFV

A column base from the temple of Artemis or Diana at Ephesus sculptured with life-size figures. BM

Gideon had to destroy his father's altar to Baal and the accompanying Asherah in order to qualify as a leader of Israel (Jud 6:25–30, RSV). Her worship during the Heb. kingdom is attested by the image made by Asa's mother (I Kgs 15:13, RSV) and the image set up by Manasseh in the temple (II Kgs 21:7, RSV). Josiah attempted to stamp out her worship (II Kgs 23:4–7, RSV).

Some OT passages indicate a coalescence of the deity with the cult object used in her worship (RSV: Ex 34:13; Jud 6:25–30; II Kgs 18:4), a phenomenon common in many religions. As a cult object, an *'ăshērâ* (pl. *'ăshērîm, 'ăshērôth)* (*see* Plants: Grove) could be made and destroyed by men (II Kgs 17:16; 23:6, 15, RSV); was made of wood (Ex 34:13; II Kgs 23:6–7, RSV); could be burned (Deut 12:3, RSV); stood upright (Isa 27:9, RSV); and was used in the worship of Asherah. Some scholars, on the basis of Deut 16:21 (RSV) and other evidence think it was a living tree. Most scholars, however, think it was an image of Asherah, perhaps a stylized tree of life, otherwise the silence of the prophets concerning it would be strange. But they do denounce idolatry, which would include the *'ăshērîm*.

Ashima (ȧ-shī'mȧ)—A deity worshiped by colonists from Hamath settled in Samaria by the Assyrians after 722 B.C. (II Kgs 17:30; Amos 8:14, RSV). There may be some connection with the deity mentioned in the Elephantine Papyri called Ashembethel.

Astarte—*See* Ashtoreth (following paragraph).

Ashtoreth (ăsh'tō̆-rēth; pl. ăsh'tȧ-rōth)—A deity variously known as Ishtar, Astarte, Venus, sometimes called the "queen of heaven." She was the goddess of the evening star or planet Venus, but may have been androgynous originally and thus also god of the morning star, likewise Venus (cf. S Arabic *'aṭtar,* "god of the morning star"). She was principally the goddess of sex and war. God's people altered her name from Astarte to Ashtoreth, vocalized with the vowels of the Heb. word *bōsheth,* "shame," as was Molech. Her association with Baal in the OT (Jud 2:13; 10:6; I Sam 7:4; 12:10) may indicate that she can be equated with Asherah in Palestine. Astarte grew in importance in Phoenicia and Palestine, while the cruel goddess of war Anath, sister and consort of Baal, occupies the place of prominence in the Ugaritic texts (Albright, *Yahweh and the Gods of Canaan,* pp. 128–135).

In the OT Ashtoreth is mentioned as being worshiped among the Hebrews during the days of the judges (Jud 2:13; 10:6); at Beth-shan where Saul's armor was placed in her temple (I Sam 31:10; I Chr 10:10); by the Zidonians (I Kgs 11:5, 33; II Kgs 23:13). Jezebel's father was an Astarte priest. Philo of Byblos says she was worshiped at Byblos and Tyre. The town name Ashteroth Karnaim (Gen 14:5) suggests a shrine for her worship existed E of the Jordan. Her fame spread to Egypt as evidenced by Astarte figurines and the translation of the poem "Astarte and the Sea Dragon." In Moab (Moabite inscription, ANET, p. 320) the name of her male equivalent Ashtar is compounded with Chemosh.

Baal (bā'ȧl, bāl; lit., "master, owner, husband")—The most important god of the Canaanite pantheon (*see* Canaan). From the 3rd mil. to *c.* 1500 B.C. the title is applied to the Amorite god of winter rain and storm, Hadad (see below). Hence, in the Canaanite pantheon he became the god of fertility with the bull as his symbol.

The widespread prevalence of his cult is attested by his name appearing in Babylonian, Aramaic, Phoenician, Punic, Ugaritic and Egyptian sources. During the Ramesside period he was equated with Seth. His titles were Zabûl, "exalted, lord of earth"; Ba'al Shamen, "lord of heaven" (in Phoenician, but not in the earlier Ugaritic); *Rōkēb 'ărufôt,* "rider on the clouds." The Egyptian place name Baal Saphon (lit., Baal of the N, Baal of Mount Casius) indicates his cult was known in Egypt. The OT refers to the many local Baal images as the Baalim, the plural form of Baal.

In the Ras Shamra texts he is the son of El (or, once, the son of Dagon). He overcomes the primeval waters. However he is slain by Mot and revived by Anath (fused with Athirat/Astarte). He also may have been identified with the Tyrian Melcarth, "lord of the city."

In the OT his worship became a serious rival to that of Yahweh. He was worshiped in the high places of Moab (Num 22:41). There were altars to him in the days of the judges (Jud 2:13; 6:28–32). Perhaps his worship reached its height in the days of Ahab and Jezebel (I Kgs 16:32; 18:17–40), although there were later revivals (II Kgs 3:2 f.; 10:18–28; 18:4, 22; 21:3; II Chr 21:6; 22:3). His worship was suppressed by Jehoiada (II Kgs 11:18) and Josiah (II Kgs 23:4–5).

GODS, FALSE

The worship of Baal was accompanied with lascivious rites (I Kgs 14:24; II Kgs 23:7). Kissing his image is attested (I Kgs 19:18; Hos 13:2). Child sacrifice by fire was part of his cult (Jer 19:5).

The worship of Baal was associated with Ashtoreth (see above; Jud 2:13). He is also associated with the goddess Asherah (see above; I Kgs 18:19; II Kgs 23:4, both RSV), and his altars frequently had asherahs nearby (RSV: Jud 6:30; I Kgs 16:32-33). It seems likely that during the Heb. monarchy Ashtoreth and Asherah had fused into one figure. Ahaz made images for the Baalim (II Chr 28:2); these may have been brazen bulls or calves. The worship of Baal was denounced by the prophets (Jer 19:4-5; Hos 2:17).

In addition to the direct influence of the Baal cult on the Hebrews, much of the Canaanite imagery applied to him is sublimated and applied to Yahweh in the OT. Yahweh is the "rider on the clouds" or heavens (cf. Deut 33:26; Ps 68:4; 104:3). Like Marduk in the conflict with Tiamat, the Canaanite Baal was the conqueror of the upsurging waters. This conflict, sometimes with a monster called Rahab or Leviathan, is re-echoed throughout the OT where Yahweh is depicted as the victor over all His foes. The motif of Yahweh's kingship and annual worship at the new year (Zech 14:16-19) has been traced by some to the idea of Baal's revivification, at the close of the combat, by the coming of the seasonal rains.

Baal of Thunder from Ras Shamra, Syria. LM

Baal-berith (bāl-bĕ-rîth'), "lord of the covenant"—An Amorite god with a shrine at Shechem (Jud 9:1-6). He is associated with the local Baals (Jud 8:33), so perhaps may be a local manifestation of the great fertility god of Canaan. Perhaps he was the same deity as El-berith (Jud 9:46, RSV), and is to be equated with the Semitic god of the underworld Hauron/Horon, whose name appears in Canaanite personal and place names.

Baal-peor (bāl pē'ôr), "the lord of Mount Peor"—A Moabite and Midianite god (Num 25:1-5; Deut 4:3; Ps 106:28; Hos 9:10).

Baal-zebub (bāl zē'būb)—The god of the Philistine city of Ekron (II Kgs 1:2, 6, 16). Opinion varies as to the meaning of this name. It was formerly thought to come from the Heb. root *zbb,* "to fly," hence as in the LXX, "lord of the flies." Most scholars now believe that the name of the god was Baal-zebul, "lord, prince" or "Baal the prince." In the Ugaritic texts Baal is described repeatedly as *zbl b'l 'arṣ,* "prince, lord of earth." The present form is explained as a mocking distortion, just as *bōsheth,* "shame," is often substituted for ba'al in personal names. The name of Jezebel, whose father's name was Ethbaal, contains the element *zbl* as an equivalent for *ba'al.* It is not surprising that her son Ahaziah preferred Baal-zebul to Yahweh. On the other hand, golden images of flies found in the excavations of Philistine sites may indicate that there truly was a god known as Baal-zebub, worshiped to appease the bothersome flies, or who gave oracles by the flight or buzzing of a fly (T. H. Gaster, "Baalzebub," IDB, I, 332).

Beelzebul (bē-ĕl'zē-būl)—A NT name applied to Satan (RSV, NASB: Mt 10:25; 12:24, 27; Mk 3:22; Lk 11:15, 18-19). KJV, following the Vulg., renders it Beelzebub (*q.v.*), probably a throwback, erroneously, to the Philistine god of Ekron, Baal-zebub, as found in the Heb. MT.

Bel (bēl)—The name of the Babylonian national sun-god Marduk. As Marduk, the son of Ea, he assumed the role of the Sumerian En-lil as conqueror of the chaotic waters. He was credited with conceiving the idea for the creation of man (ANET, p. 68), *contra* Canaanite El as the creator. In the OT Bel is associated with Nebo (Isa 46:1) and with Marduk (Jer 50:2). Other references to him are found in Jer 51:44, the apocryphal Bel and the Dragon (3:22), and Herodotus (i. 181).

Berith (Jud 9:46)—*See* Baal-berith.

Castor and Pollux (kăs-tŏr, pŏl'ŭks)—Astral deities, "the Twin Brothers," were children of Zeus and Leda (wife of the king of Sparta). They were the patron gods of sailors; the ship on which Paul sailed from Malta to Puteoli bore their insignia (Acts 28:11). Poseidon gave them power over winds and waves. Their temple at Rome stood next to the Basilica Julia in the Forum.

Chemosh (kē'mōsh)—The name or title of the god of the Moabites (Num 21:29; Jer 48:46). According to II Kgs 3:27 and the Mesha in-

GODS, FALSE

scription (ANET, p. 320) he was worshiped with child sacrifices. A sanctuary was built for him by Solomon (I Kgs 11:7), which was destroyed by Josiah (II Kgs 23:13-14). In the Mesha inscription he was equated with Ashtar (*see* Ashtoreth above). In addressing the king of the Ammonites Jephthah speaks of Chemosh as "thy god" (Jud 11:24), whereas the Ammonite deity was called Milcom/Molech (see below). But Molech may simply be a title of Chemosh, a god worshiped in common by the two related peoples. Jephthah's reference to Chemosh implying he admitted the god's existence was probably an *ad hominem* argument in appealing to the Ammonite king.

Chiun–*See* Kaiwan.

A bronze lion from the temple of Dagon in Mari (Iraq), second millennium B.C. LM

Dagon (dā'gŏn)–A name presumed to be related to Heb. *dāgān*, "grain," hence a vegetation deity. This is supported by a Ugaritic reference to Baal as "son of Dagon," perhaps viewing Baal as the dying and reviving vegetation deity. The idea of Dagon as a fish-god is not traceable earlier than Jerome, but is probably due to false etymology from Heb. *dāg*, "a fish."

Dagon is attested as a Babylonian deity. The name is found in theophoric names *c.* 2200 B.C. among the Amorites of Mesopotamia. There was a temple with two votive stelae commemorating sacrifices to Dagon found beside it, and older than that of Baal, at Ras Shamra, *c.* 2000 B.C. Philo of Byblos says Dagon was associated with El, the senior Phoenician god. First El and then Dagon may have been worshiped at that temple.

A theophoric place name (Josh 15:41; 19:27) indicates his worship in Canaan before the Philistine invasions. However, in the OT he is most famous as the god of the Philistines (Jud 16:23-24), who had an image of him at Ashdod (I Sam 5:2-4). He also was worshiped at Beth-shan (I Chr 10:10). The Ashdod temple was the locale where the Philistines put the Israelite ark. It was still in use in the Hasmonean period and was destroyed by Jonathan, the brother of Judas Maccabaeus, 147 B.C. (I Macc 10:83-84; 11:4).

Day Star (KJV, Lucifer), Heb. *hêlēl*, "bright one" (Isa 14:12)–He was evidently a deity who wanted to rise higher than all stars, but was obliged to come down to earth. This is illuminated by the Ugaritic story of Ashtar (Venus star) who was proposed as the occupant of Baal's throne when it was vacant during the dry season. However, Ashtar was too small to fill the throne so had to descend (ANET, p. 140).

The traditional exegesis of Isa 14:12 has equated Day Star (Lucifer) with Satan. This is based on the belief that Lk 10:18 refers to Isa 14:15. Some modern exegetes see the Day Star merely as a title for the king of Babylon.

Diana (Acts 19:24)–*See* Diana; *also* Artemis above.

El-berith (Jud 9:46, RSV), "god of the covenant"–*See* Baal-berith above.

Gad (găd)–A god of fortune (see Isa 65:11, KJV, RSV, JerusB). This name for a deity is found in Phoenician, Assyrian, and Aramaic. The LXX translates it *daimon*. ASV, RSV, NEB and NASB translate the name instead of transliterating it, but by capitalization show the translators believed it to be a deity or a hypostatization. In an Aramaic-Greek bilingual text from Palmyra, he is identified with *Tyche*, "fortune." Evidently his cult was popular in the Hauran region.

Hadad (hā'dăd), "thunderer"–A Semitic god known variously as Adad, Addu, Haddu, Had. He is equated with Rimmon and Teshub (Hittite storm-god). Haddu/Hadad was originally the proper name of Baal. In Babylonian and Assyrian art he is represented as a bull. His name is found on the Panamua inscription from Zinjirli where there was also a statue dedicated to Hadad. His worship persisted down to Hellenistic times. At Tannur in Transjordan there was a Nabatean temple to Hadad who assumed the role of Zeus (or vice versa).

The name Hadad may lie behind the KJV "Hadar" of Gen 25:15; 36:39. It was the divine element in names given to kings and princes of Edom in Gen 36:35-39; I Kgs 11:14-21; I Chr 1:46-51. He was worshiped at Damascus (II Kgs 5:18). Cf. above under heading "Baal."

Hadadrimmon (hā'dăd-rĭm'ŏn)–A deity worshiped with ritual mourning at Megiddo (Zech 12:11). Perhaps this is to be compared with Anath weeping for Baal her brother in Ugaritic text I AB (Cyrus H. Gordon, *Ugaritic Manual*, text 49; ANET, p. 139). Cf. preceding paragraph and Rimmon below. *See also* Hadadrimmon.

Hermes (hėr'mēz)–A Gr. deity mentioned in Acts 14:12 (RSV) which reflects his character as the god of eloquence and the divine herald. He was the son of Zeus, and half-brother of Apollo. As a master thief and trickster and god of good luck (whether honestly or dishonestly achieved) he was the patron saint of traders and thieves. In astral religion he was identified with Mercury. In Hellenistic times he was equated with the Egyptian scribal god Thoth. His epithet, "Hermes Trismegistus" ("thrice great"), indicates something of the importance he attained in the Hermetic religion of post-NT times.

Jupiter (jōō'pĭ-tẽr)—Sky god of the Latins, identified with Zeus in Hellenistic times. He is mentioned in Acts 14:12–13 and II Macc 6:2. *See* Zeus below.

Head of the god Hadad, from Carchemish, Syria. LM

Kaiwan (kī'wăn); KJV, Chiun (Amos 5:26)—He is probably identical with Remphan (KJV), Rompha (NASB) of Acts 7:43, and was probably an astral deity. In Babylonian the name *kayawânu* is given to Saturn; it is translated by *Raiphan* in the LXX of Amos. *See* Remphan below.

Lilith (lĭl'ĭth)—The "night hag" (RSV) or "screech owl" (KJV) of Isa 34:14. In Akkad. *lilītu* is a night demon who tempts men in their sleep. She was later associated in Semitic thought with the child-stealing witch. In Isaiah her companions are unclean birds and devouring animals.

Marduk (mär'dūk)—The state god of Babylon and foremost son of Ea. In the time of Hammurabi he was acknowledged as the chief deity with the functions of the Sumerian En-lil. In the new year festival ritual he was victorious over chaotic waters, thus re-enacting creation (cf. ANET, pp. 66 f.). Some recent scholars see these motifs influencing the OT in such concepts as enthronement and divine kingship. In Neo-Babylonian times Marduk is equated with Bel (cf. parallelism of Jer 50:2). The name is Hebraized as Merodach (II Kgs 25:27; Isa 39:1; Jer 52:31).

Meni (mĕ-nī')—A god of destiny and good luck mentioned in Isa 65:11 (JerusB). The word is translated in KJV as "that number," RSV and NASB as "Destiny," and NEB as "Fate." Perhaps the name is derived from the Egyptian god Menu. He is possibly an astral deity, one of the Pleiades. However, a god Manat is known in pre-Islamic Arabic culture (Koran, Sura 53:20). During the Assyrian Empire he was equated with Asshur, the chief god. There is probably no connection with the Phrygian god Men of Hellenistic times, who had his principal temple at Antioch of Galatia and was a god of healing and prosperous agriculture.

Mercurus (mẽ-kyŭ'ĭ-ŭs), **Mercury** (mẽr'cū-rĭ), Acts 14:12—*See* Hermes above.

Merodach—*See* Marduk above.

Milcom—*See* Molech, Moloch.

Molech (mō'lĕk), **Moloch** (mō'lŏk)—An Ammonite deity worshiped with human sacrifice (II Kgs 23:10; Jer 32:35). The first vocalization is based on Heb. *bōsheth,* "shame." There is evidence for a god Muluk in Mari *c.* 1700 B.C. Jud 11:24 may indicate the identity of Molech with Chemosh (see above), Molech/Moloch being a title. The name of Chemosh was compounded with Ashtar on the Moabite Stone. Since Ashtar equals the planet Venus, the evening star, and the latter appears as Shalim, "dusk," at Ras Shamra, Moloch could be an old Canaanite deity in another guise (cf. Jer 32:35).

This deity is called Milcom (same Heb. root) in I Kgs 11:7, Heb.; 11:33; II Kgs 23:13; Jer 49:1, 3 (RSV, following LXX; KJV translates "king," from same Heb. consonants). This is reversed in Amos 5:26 where RSV translates "king," while KJV reads "Moloch." Stephen quotes this passage in Acts 7:42–43, where "Molech" is strangely retained in RSV. Solomon built a sanctuary for Molech (I Kgs 11:7, 33) which was desecrated by Josiah (II Kgs 23:13). His worship was reproved by Zephaniah (1:5) in words which indicate he was an astral deity.

The forbidden practice of human sacrifice (Lev 18:21; 20:2–5) seems to have been widespread in Israel (II Kgs 16:3; 17:17; Ps 106:38; Jer 19:4–5, and many other passages). A recent attempt by Eissfeldt (followed by Albright, *Yahweh and the Gods of Canaan,* pp. 235–242) to remove Moloch from the list of deities to whom human sacrifice was offered does not seem to be satisfactory. On the basis of Punic inscriptions where *mlk* means a sacrifice made to confirm a vow, he said the OT "pass through the fire to Moloch" means "as a votive offering." However, while this would help explain the association of Baal and Moloch in Jer 32:35, yet Lev 20:5 (where harlotry certainly refers to idolatrous worship, not to an offering) and II Kgs 17:31 (where "to" Adrammelech and Anammelech certainly cannot mean "as") show that Moloch and other gods with names ending in the compound ______-melech must be understood as deities to whom sacrifices were offered.

Nebo (nē'bō)—Probably a transliteration of Akkad. *nabû,* "to announce." This Babylonian deity was regarded as the son of Marduk. Originally a water deity, he was later associated with writing and speech. His image was carried in the new year's procession. The cult of Nebo was popular in the Neo-Babylonian period (625–539 B.C.) where his name is the theophoric element in three of the six kings' names, e.g., Nebuchadnezzar. He had a special temple at Borsippa.

Nergal (nẽr'găl), probably from Sumerian *Ne-uru-gal,* "lord of the great city"—A Mesopotamian deity (II Kgs 17:30) worshiped by the Cuthites settled in Samaria after 722 B.C. by the Assyrians. Originally he was a god of fire and heat of the sun; then of hunting and disaster; finally the lord of the underworld. He was the consort of Ereshkigal, the mistress of hell. He was called "lord of weapons," which may be connected with the Heb. "Reshepho of the bow" (Ps 76:4[3]). As god of the underworld city he may have been equated with Mot of Ras Shamra. The Tyrian deity Melcarth (lit., "king of the city") was also an underworld god.

Nibhaz (nĭb'hăz)—A deity worshiped by Syrian colonists settled in Samaria after 722 B.C. by the Assyrians (II Kgs 17:31). There is to date no archaeological evidence for such a deity; so it has been suggested that the name is a corruption of Heb. *mizbēaḥ,* "altar," as also the temple was deified in the divine name "Bethel" at Elephantine two centuries later. The rabbis thought the name came from Heb. *nbḥ,* "to bark," but this is probably wrong.

Nisroch (nĭz'rŏk)—A deity worshiped by Sennacherib (II Kgs 19:37; Isa 37:38), who was killed in his temple. Several variant spellings of the name in the LXX all begin with *spiritus asper.* Since the name is unknown in Mesopotamian sources, it may be a corruption of the Assyrian Nusku. Nusku was a fire god, the son of the moon-god Sin and Nergal. His cult is attested at this period.

Queen of Heaven—[A pagan goddess to whom Israel, especially the women, offered sacrifice and worship in the last days of Judah (Jer 7:18). After the fall of Jerusalem and the disobedient departure of many of the Jews to Egypt, with a wicked perversion of reason, they insisted that it was while they worshiped the queen of heaven that things went well with them, and that only when Jeremiah had persuaded them to return to Yahweh had their troubles begun (Jer 44:17 ff.).

The false goddess is the Assyrian Ishtar or Astarte, the equivalent of the Ugaritic Ashirat. She was a mother-goddess and a symbol of fertility. Worship of the queen of heaven was to insure the fertility of field, flock and family (cf. Jer 44:17, "then had we plenty of victuals, and were well, and saw no evil"). In the 5th cen. B.C. the Jewish colony in Egypt on the island of Elephantine (Yeb) included in their strange syncretistic worship a goddess called Anath-bethel, who may be that same queen of heaven.—P. C. J.]

Pollux—*See* Castor and Pollux above.

Remphan (KJV, Vulg.), **Rephan** (RSV) (rĕm'făn, rē'făn)—An astral deity worshiped by the Israelites in the wilderness (Acts 7:43). The name is derived from the LXX Raiphan (Amos 5:26) where it is a corruption of Kaiwan (see above).

Resheph (rē'shĕf)—A Canaanite deity noted in offering lists and theophoric names from Ugarit, Egypt (Papyrus Harris, *c.* 13th cen.) and 8th cen. B.C. Syrian Aram. inscriptions. He is reportedly found sculptured in Egypt, holding the *ankh* ("life") sign. Conversely, in the Keret epic he is the god of plague and mass destruction. Many OT passages translate the name as a common noun, "pestilence," "thunderbolt,"

The god Reshef.

"flame," etc., where there is a covert allusion to this god. In the theophany of Hab 3:5, "and plague followed close behind" (RSV), some scholars consider it possible that the proper noun is meant. In Cyprian inscriptions (George A. Cooke, *Northwest Semitic Inscriptions,* pp. 55, 57), Resheph is equated with Apollo, who (*Iliad* i.51, 52) also caused plagues. As an underworld god, perhaps Resheph was identified with Nergal, Hauron and Melcarth.

Rimmon (rĭm'ŏn)—The name was originally thought to come from Heb. *rimmôn,* "a pomegranate," but now is clearly seen to be from Akkad. *ramānu,* "to roar," hence, "the thunderer." The chief god of Damascus, he was worshiped by Naaman and the king of Syria (II Kgs 5:18). He was the god of rain and storm. He was known among the Assyrians as Ramanu, a title of Hadad (see above), and identical with the Syrian Baal (see above). His name occurs in the Syrian name Tabrimmon, father of Ben-hadad (I Kgs 15:18).

Saccuth (săk'ŭth), **Siccuth** (sĭk'ŭth)—The latter spelling (ERV), based on the Heb. MT, is probably a variant (by Heb. *paronomasia* using vowels of *shiqquṣ,* "abominable thing") of Mesopotamian Sakkut (Amos 5:26, RSV). The LXX took it to be some form of Heb. *sukkāh,* "tabernacle." The KJV follows the LXX here, as do the KJV and RSV in Stephen's citation of Amos (Acts 7:43). In Mesopotamia, Sakkut has the same ideogram as Ninib, so it was an astral deity.

Succoth-benoth (sŭk'ŏth-bē'nŏth)—A deity worshiped by the colonists from Babylonia settled in Samaria after 722 B.C. by the Assyrians (II Kgs 17:30). The name in Heb. lit. means "booths of girls," but this must be a corruption. Assyriologists Rawlinson and Schroeder supposed the deity to be Ṣarpanitu, the consort of Marduk, who was popularly called *Zir-banîtu,* "seed creating." Franz Delitzsch thought the name might be the Heb. equivalent of *sakkut binîti,* "supreme judge," i.e., Marduk. The name may have some relation to Sakkuth (properly vocalized) of Amos 5:26 who is the same as Akkad. Ninib.

Tammuz (tăm'ŭz)—[A Mesopotamian deity after whom the fourth Jewish-Babylonian month (June–July) was named. The name occurs when the prophet Ezekiel finds some women in Jerusalem weeping for the god Tammuz (8:14). Tammuz was famous as a husband of Ishtar (*see* Ashtoreth above). His Sumerian prototype Dumuzi was a king of Erech in the early 3rd mil. B.C. who was deified as the consort of the city's protectress Inanna or Innin (corresponding to the Akkad. Ishtar). Gilgamesh accused her of betraying Tammuz, her lover, in the famous epic (ANET, p. 84). In Hellenistic times Tammuz was equated with Adonis, and Ishtar with Aphrodite/Venus. Swine, often associated with underworld cults, were his sacrificial animals.

It has long been supposed that the purpose of Inanna's (or Ishtar's) mythical descent to the underworld (ANET, pp. 52–57) was to resurrect her lover. Hence he was identified by Sir James Frazer in 1906, along with Adonis, Attis and Osiris, as an example of the dying and rising god. Although he was a shepherd and not a vegetation deity, Tammuz was represented as a fertility god who, like the vegetation, died in the heat of summer (at which time there was cultic wailing for him) and arose in the spring.

Thanks to the work of the sumerologist Samuel Kramer, we now have clear evidence that Dumuzi (Tammuz) was not thought to rise from the dead at all. In a newly translated poem, "The Death of Dumuzi," Inanna, in fact, has her husband dragged down to the netherworld as her substitute for not having properly mourned her absence. Henceforth all the identifications of Tammuz with Adonis and with other resurrected gods will have to be abandoned (e.g., A. Moortgat, *Tammuz*), and likewise those attempts to interpret the Bible on the basis of such an identification (e.g., Alfred Jeremias on the Joseph story, and Theophile Meek on the Song of Solomon [*q.v.*]). There is evidence of a *hieros gamos* or "sacred marriage" rite to insure the fertility of the land (not to be confused with the New Year *Akitu* rite in Babylon) between King Iddin-Dagan (*c.* 1900 B.C.), who was addressed as Dumuzi, and Inanna, who was probably represented by a hierodule. Sumerian love songs were also used in the Dumuzi-Inanna cult.—E. M. Y.]

Tartak (tär'tăk)—A deity worshiped by Arvites who were settled in Samaria after 722 B.C. by the Assyrians (II Kgs 17:31). The name may be a corruption of Atargatis, a goddess worshiped in Syria by the Aramaeans of Mesopotamia whose worship persisted down into Hellenistic times. Atargatis, in turn, may be a composite figure of Athirat (Ashtoreth of the OT) and Anath of the Ras Shamra pantheon.

Zeus (zūs)—The head of the Gr. Olympian pantheon mentioned in Acts 14:12 (RSV). His statue at Olympia was one of the seven wonders of the ancient world. His temple at Athens was the largest in Greece. His worship was still widespread in NT times, with representations in art found at Tarsus and temples at Gerasa, Tannur, and Salamis. In the Latin pantheon his equivalent was Jupiter. The fused figure of Zeus-Jupiter is in view in the NT reference. Oxen and sheep were sacrificed to him.

Bibliography. William F. Albright, *Archaeology and the Religion of Israel,* 3rd ed., Baltimore: Johns Hopkins Press, 1953; *Yahweh and the Gods of Canaan,* Garden City: Doubleday, 1968. Lloyd R. Bailey, "Israelite Êl Šadday and Amorite Bêl Šadê, JBL, LXXXVII (1968), 434–438. G. Cornfeld (ed.), "Canaan, Gods and Idols, Cult," CornPBE, pp. 179–191. G. R. Driver, *Canaanite Myths and Legends,* Edinburgh: T. & T. Clark, 1956. Henri Frankfort, *Ancient Egyptian Religion,* New York: Columbia Univ. Press, 1948. O. R. Gurney, "Tammuz Reconsidered," JSS, VII (1962),

Head of Zeus, Ephesus Museum. HFV

147–159. Arvid S. Kapelrud, *Baal in the Ras Shamra Texts,* Copenhagen: G. E. C. Gad, 1952; *The Violent Goddess: Anat in the Ras Shamra Texts,* Oslo: Scandinavian Univ. Books, 1969. Samuel N. Kramer (ed.), *Mythologies of the Ancient World,* Garden City: Doubleday Anchor Books, 1961; *Sumerian Mythology,* rev. ed., New York: Harper Torchbooks, 1961; *The Sacred Marriage Rite,* Bloomington: Indiana Univ. Press, 1969. Ulf Oldenburg, *The Conflict Between El and Baal in Canaanite Religion,* Leiden: Brill, 1969. Jean Ouellette, "More on 'Êl Šadday and Bêl Šadê," JBL, LXXXVIII (1969), 470 f. Raphael Patai, "The Goddess Asherah," JNES, XXIV (1965), 37–56. Edwin M. Yamauchi, "Tammuz and the Bible," JBL, LXXXIV (1965), 283–290; "Additional Notes on Tammuz," JSS, XI (1966), 10–15. For bibliography of Gr. religion and deities *see under* Diana.

A. K. H.

GOG (gŏg)

1. A Reubenite, son of Shemaiah (I Chr 5:4).

2. The prince of Meshech and Tubal (the Mushku and Tabali of the Assyrian inscriptions, Ezk 38:3). "Land of Magog" of Ezk 38:2 and "Magog" of Ezk 39:6 are probably incorrect since the former is not paralleled in 38:3 and the latter stands alone among several references to Gog. In Gen 10:2 Magog was the second son of Japheth, here the place being substituted for the personal name Gog. Placed between Gomer (Assyrian: *Gimirrai;* D. D. Luckenbill, *Ancient Records of Assyria and Babylonia,* II, 298, 352) and the Cimmerians, the land of Gog appears to be located in northern Armenia, W of the Caspian Sea. *See* Gomer.

Gog as a mighty commander of many peoples is to come from the N against Israel "brought forth out of the nations," dwelling "safely all of them" (Ezk 38:8) in unwalled villages, where Gog attacks them (vv. 11–12). He comes with great numbers (v.16), reminiscent of the Scythians (Ashkenaz, Gen 10:3) who invaded Asia Minor *c.* 630 B.C. The Lord will judge Gog with mighty plagues and will destroy him by the elements (Ezk 38:22–23). His forces will be buried in numberless graves (Ezk 39:5–16).

Rev 20:8–15 places the invasion of this people in the future; thus, Gog cannot be fulfilled in Gyges, king of Lydia in Asia Minor (d. 662 B.C.). Since the last recall of Israel from exile is that one just before the Millennium, and since Satan is loosed after that age for one last assault against God, some scholars believe that this invasion out of the N comes after the Millennium. The hordes would be the unconverted millennial descendants of the dwellers of the area N of eastern Turkey. Others hold that there will be one invasion from present-day Russia led by Gog before Christ returns (Ezk 38–39), and another led by Satan, similar to Gog's, after Christ's 1000-year reign (Rev 20:7–9).

See Hamon-Gog; Magog.

H. G. S.

GOLAN (gō'lăn). A city in Bashan of the Transjordanian half-tribe of Manasseh. Moses set it aside to be one of the three cities of refuge E of the Jordan (Deut 4:43; Josh 20:8), and it was one of the 48 Levitical cities (Josh 21:27; I Chr 6:71). It is probably to be identified with the modern Saḥem el-Jolan, *c.* 17 miles E of the Sea of Galilee. It later gave its name to the division of Bashan called Gaulanitis (*q.v.*), a flat and fertile tableland that was widely populated in Maccabean and Herodian times (Jos *Ant.* xiii.15. 3–4; xvii.8.1; xviii.4.6; *Wars* iii.3.5). It is called Jolan by the Arabs today.

GOLD. *See* Minerals and Metals: Gold; Ophir.

GOLDEN CITY. Isa 14, the taunt-song against Babylon, speaks (v.4) of the end of the golden city (Heb. *madhēbâ*). The translators, not finding the root in Heb., took it as Aramaic *dhb,* "gold," and therefore the derivation as "golden one," or "exactress of gold" (marg.). But now the Dead Sea Scroll 1Q Is[a] helps us see that the LXX, Syriac and possibly the Targum must have read *marhēbâ.* Heb. *d* and *r,* much alike, are often confused. This root means "storm against," "act arrogantly." The line is therefore better translated with its preceding parallel thought in the poetic couplet, "how the oppressor has ceased, how his arrogance has ceased!"

GOLDSMITH. *See* Occupations: Goldsmith

GOLGOTHA (gŏl'gŏ-thȧ). This is a Gr. word, derived from the Aramaic *gulgaltā'*, which means "a skull." Three times the place of the crucifixion is called the "place of a skull" (Mt 27:33; Mk 15:22; Jn 19:17). But what does this signify? Jerome said it was a place of public execution, where skulls lay around. In the past century the view has become popular that it means a skull-shaped hill. Gordon's Calvary, with its skull-shaped rock, holds sentimental attachment for many Protestants. The older tradition identifies Golgotha with the Church of the Holy Sepulchre, inside the walls. Both sites are uncertain. *See* Calvary.

Golgotha. HFV

GOLIATH (gŏ-lī'ăth). Goliath was either a descendant of the Rephaim (*q.v.*), a tall aboriginal people living in the Transjordan area of Ammon, of whom a scattered remnant took refuge with the Philistines after their dispersion by the Ammonites (Deut 2:20-21), or of the Anakim (*q.v.;* cf. Num 13:33; Josh 11:22), noted for their tall stature. The LXX (I Sam 17:4) and Josephus (*Ant.* vi. 9.1) say he was four cubits and a span, i.e., six feet nine inches tall, while the Heb. text states that he was six cubits and a span, or nine feet nine inches tall. Recovered skeletons of equal height from archaeological excavations at Gezer and other sites bear out the unusually tall stature of individuals in ancient Palestine at roughly the same period. *See* Giant.

Rabbinic literature records many legends about Goliath. According to these, his mother was Orpah (cf. Ruth 1:14), who walked 40 paces with Naomi and Ruth, and then returned to a profligate life in Moab. Goliath was born of her illegitimately. He boasted of having slain Eli's two sons (I Sam 4:11), and that he had stolen the ark of Israel (I Sam 4:17). The 40 days of his challenge to the Israelite army (I Sam 17:4-10) compared to the 40 paces of his mother Orpah, and it was done at the time of the reciting of the Shema!

The Vulgate calls him *vir spurius,* a bastard. The LXX refers to him as "the middleman" (I Sam 17:23); the Heb. text calls him "the man of the intervals" (I Sam 17:4, 23), i.e., the man who goes out as the champion in the space between two opposing armies. The cognate term in a prose text found at Ugarit signifies a middleman or intermediary (BASOR #150, p. 38).

The place where Goliath met his death was in the valley of Elah (I Sam 17:2), between Shochoh and Azekah, in the land of the tribe of Judah. The Israelites under King Saul were encamped on the N slope of the valley of Elah, and the Philistines were entrenched on the opposite slope. A narrow valley through which flowed a brook separated the two armies. Goliath the Philistine champion was attired in a bronze helmet and coat of mail, and carried both a spear and a sword. Bronze scales for coats of mail dating to the 15th cen. B.C. were uncovered at Nuzu. Records of such coats of mail and drawings of them were found in the inscriptions of the pharaohs engraved on temple walls of Karnak at Luxor, Egypt. The bronze "target" (KJV) or "javelin" (RSV), Heb. *kîdôn,* may have been a curved scimitar, since the *kîdôn* is so described in the Dead Sea War Scroll. A shield bearer preceded Goliath into the fray. The custom of two warriors engaging in a duel to settle a battle is well represented in the Homeric epics of Greece and in an Egyptian text that dates from the 20th cen. B.C. In the latter. Sinuhe shot his Retenu challenger with an arrow from a distance; then he finished off his fallen foe with the Retenu's own battle-axe and shouted the cry of victory over his back ("The Story of Sinuhe," ANET, p. 20, lines 109-145).

The religious significance of the contest is seen in the powerlessness of the Philistine gods to carry out Goliath's curse on David and in the battle cry of David, "I come against you in the name of Yahweh Sabaoth, the God of the armies of Israel that you have dared to insult" (I Sam 17:43, 45, JerusB). Also there is the fact that David placed the sword of Goliath, perhaps as an offering, in the sanctuary of Yahweh at Nob (I Sam 21:9). Ps 144 and Ps 151 (LXX and DSS) seem to be in tribute of David's victory.

An alleged contradicton seems to occur in II Sam 21:19 (ASV, RSV, etc.) which reports that "Elhanan the son of Jaare-oregim, the Bethlehemite, slew Goliath the Gittite, the shaft of whose spear was like a weaver's beam," while I Sam 17:50-51 (cf. 19:5; 21:9; 22:10, 13) asserts that David did so. Moreover, I Chr 20:5, clearly parallel to II Sam 21:19, states that "Elhanan the son of Jairi slew Lahmi the brother of Goliath the Gittite, the shaft of whose spear was like a weaver's beam" (RSV). It can be demonstrated in the Heb. that in the course of transmission of the text some copyists' errors have evidently been made in II Sam 21:19. While there are possible slight alternatives in seeking to harmonize the Heb. of

II Sam 21:19 and I Chr 20:5, it is clear that (*a*) David slew Goliath, and (*b*) Elhanan slew the brother of Goliath. For full discussion of the problem and possible emendation see S. R. Driver, *Notes on the Hebrew Text of the Books of Samuel,* Oxford, 1913; E. J. Young, *Introduction to the Old Testament,* Eerdmans, 1949, pp. 181f.; Archer, SOTI, p. 274.

F. E. Y. and J. R.

GOMER (gō'mẽr)

1. The eldest son of Japheth, and the father of Ashkenaz, Riphath, and Togarmah (Gen 10:2-3; I Chr 1:5-6). Gomer represents the people termed Gimirra by the Assyrians and Cimmerians by the Greeks. Indo-European nomads, in the 8th cen. B.C. they invaded the Near East from northern Europe via the Caucasus under pressure of the Scythians (*q.v.*). The Cimmerians attacked Urartu (Ararat) and Tabal N of Assyria, but were driven westward into Cappadocia by Sargon II. They went on to destroy the Phrygian kingdom (*see* Meshech) *c.* 695 B.C. and ransacked Lydia (*see* Sardis) before Esarhaddon and Ashurbanipal of Assyria defeated them. Alyattes of Lydia (605-560 B.C.) finally expelled them from Asia Minor. Their contemporary, Ezekiel, prophesied of a people called Gomer, evidently from the former territory of the Cimmerians, as joining the ranks of Gog (*q.v.*) in the end time (Ezk 38:6).

2. Daughter of Diblaim, the unfaithful wife of Hosea the prophet (Hos 1:3), and mother of Jezreel, Lo-ruhamah, and Lo-ammi (the second and third children may have been illegitimate). Her marital infidelity provided the stage for Hosea's dramatic parable of Israel's unfaithfulness to God. *See* Hosea.

J. R.

GOMORRAH (gŏ-mŏr'*ȧ*). Direct information on this city is very scant and can be arrived at mainly through its association with the cities which "were joined together in the vale of Siddim" near the Dead Sea. They are listed as Sodom, Gomorrah, Admah, Zeboiim, and Zoar (Gen 14:2-3). The twin cities of Sodom and Gomorrah were most intimately associated as cities of gross sin (Gen 18:20; Mt 10:15). Condemnation of Sodom is shared by the city of Gomorrah (Gen 18:20; II Pet 2:6; Jude 7).

It is generally assumed that these cities were located on the sloping plains between the hills of Judea and the shore of the Dead Sea, somewhere at the southern end. Archaeological probings have been made in this area, but no conclusive evidence has been found to identify Sodom or Gomorrah positively.

At the present time the southern end of the Dead Sea is very shallow. A broad delta or tongue of sand and stones, known in Arabic as el-Lisan, has been washed into this area from the E shore so that the water between the tip of el-Lisan and the W shore is only about three miles wide and not much deeper than the height of a man.

Jebel Usdum, a mountain of almost pure salt, is located on the SW shore of the Dead Sea. W. F. Albright and Melvin G. Kyle in 1924 made a thorough exploration of the southern shoreline of the Dead Sea S of el-Lisan. Their conclusion was that Sodom and Gomorrah must have been on the western side of the narrow plain, since Zoar (*q.v.;* Gen 19:20-23, 30), in an easterly direction toward the hills of Moab, seems to have been a safe place of refuge. This puts the doomed cities in a small plain, now covered by the Dead Sea, in front of the eastern side of Mount Usdum (see Melvin G. Kyle, *Explorations in Sodom,* 1928, pp. 130-138). *See* Sodom; Dead Sea.

H. A. Han.

GOOD. Good is that which is worthy of approbation because of its inherent moral value and because of its beneficial external effect. The Scriptures use the term in both of these moral and amoral senses. In the amoral sense, gold is spoken of as good (Gen 2:12), as well as cattle (Gen 41:26), trees (Mt 7:17), treasures (Lk 6:45), ground (Lk 8:8), etc. If salt has lost its savor it is "good for nothing" or of no practical value (Mt 5:13; Lk 14:34).

But the Bible speaks particularly of good in the moral sense; its teachings about this can be classified in the following manner.

God is the standard of all that is good. When the Scriptures describe what is good they do not apply some categorical imperative or moral standard to God, but present God Himself as the standard. The psalmist writes, "For the Lord is good; his mercy is everlasting; and his truth endureth to all generations" (Ps 100:5). This is neither an abstract quality in God nor a secular ideal of man, because all He plans, does, creates, commands and approves is good. In fact, no one is good without qualification but God (Mk 10:18). He is the norm, judge and decider of what is good, and man and things are good to the extent that they conform to Him and to His will.

God's works are good. They reveal His attributes of wisdom and power (Ps 104:24-32; Rom 1:19-20) and display His glory (Ps 19). Step by step as He formed creation He examined it to prove that it was good (Gen 1:4, 10, 12, 18, 21, 25), and when He finished it, "God saw everything" including man, "and, behold, it was very good" (v.31). There is no Barthian "*Das Nichtige*" or Manichean dualism, nor are there Roman Catholic degrees of being, in God's creation. Sin was originated by the creature and not the Creator. Sin (*q.v.*) did not come into existence because God could not do good without causing evil, but because the creature in his freedom of will caused it to exist.

God's gifts are good, because they express His beneficence, love, and mercy, and are for the good of the creature. James writes that every good and perfect gift comes from God (Jas 1:17). In His providence He does good to all men, both the just and the unjust (Mt 5:45; Lk 6:35; Acts 14:17), while as a perfect heavenly Father He gives good gifts in particular to His children (Mt 7:11).

In the OT God's goodness to His covenant people is foretold in the many promises of millennial blessings, which include the possession of the entire promised land (Deut 30:1-10; Isa 11:11-12; 66:19-20; Joel 3:1-20), a thousand years of peace (Isa 9:7; Rev 20:1-6); prosperity and plenty (Joel 3:17-20; Amos 9:13-15).

For the Christian, "all things work together for good to them that love God" (Rom 8:28), including chastening (Heb 12:10), temptations (Jas 1:2-12), trials (Ps 119:67, 71) and persecutions (II Cor 4:17). They drive him to God and to seek His blessing and the presence and power of the Holy Spirit.

God's commands are good. As God's law is a reflection of His holy character, so His commands are a revelation of His moral perfection and perfect will. The ideal moral standard of the Bible is to be like God the Father (Mt 5:48), as this has been revealed in the Scriptures and in the life and teachings of Jesus Christ. Christ came not to destroy the law of God but to fulfill it for our justification, and commended it as the guide for the walk of faith and obedience (Mt 5:17-19, 48).

Obedience to God's commands is good. Obedience pleases Him, is the basis of blessing and answered prayer (I Jn 3:22; 5:2-3), and blossoms forth into the performance of those good works for which the Christian has been saved (Mt 5:16; Eph 2:10; Col 1:10; II Cor 9:8).

In what sense can any works be called good? When they are in accordance with God's revealed standard and will (II Tim 3:16-17). When they stem from the right motive, namely, love to others and gratitude to God (II Cor 5:14; I Thess 1:3; Heb 6:10). When they are performed with the right aim, that is, for the extension of a knowledge of God and His glory (Mt 5:16; I Cor 10:31; cf. 6:20; I Pet 2:12).

The law of God is revealed to man in two ways: in positive form—love God and love your neighbor, which is the basis of the law (Rom 13:8-10); and in negative form—(except for the fourth and fifth commandments) as summarized in the Ten Commandments. God is love, and His holiness and love go hand in hand. Man too must combine love with righteousness in a Spirit-filled walk if his acts are to be truly good (Rom 8:3-4; Gal 5:22-23). Thus good works are works of love, such as Mary's anointing of Jesus Christ which is called by Him a good work (Mk 14:3-6; cf. Mt 5:13-16; Rom 12:9-21; 13:8-10).

In our understanding of good works, it is necessary to distinguish the three main uses of the law of God found in Scripture: (1) For justification. All men are born sinners and are therefore lost and need salvation. But they cannot save themselves since they cannot keep the holy law of God. One infraction breaks all the law (Jas 2:10). Christ, in contrast, came into the world sinless, kept the law of God perfectly, and then died under the penalty of the broken law—both for our justification. Therefore the Bible never presents to fallen man the keeping of the law as a means of self-justification, but says, "By the deeds of the law there shall no flesh be justified in his sight: for by the law is the knowledge of sin" (Rom 3:20). (2) For condemnation. The law of God convicts us of our sins and makes us guilty before God (Gal 3:24; cf. Lk 10:25-37; 18:20-22). (3) For sanctification. After we are converted, God's law becomes the standard for the Christian life as seen in the teachings of both Christ and Paul (Mt 5:17-48; Rom 13:8-10). It is only in the third sense that the Christian is spoken of as keeping the law of God, and then only by the indwelling power of the Holy Spirit.

See Example; Goodness; Law; Law of Moses; Sermon on the Mount.

R. A. K.

GOODLY TREES. *See* Plants.

GOODMAN. An archaic English word meaning the head of a family or master of a household. In 1611 the word meant "husband," as it still does in Scotland; hence in Prov 7:19 according to the context it is an accurate rendering of Heb. *hā'îsh,* "the man," RSV "my husband." In the NT Gr. *oikodespotēs* is translated "goodman" in KJV in Mt 20:11; 24:43; Mk 14:14; Lk 12:39; 22:11; and seven other times as "householder" or "master of the house." That he is the owner and not merely the chief steward is clear from a comparison of Mt 21:33 with verses 37-38 where his son is called the heir.

GOODNESS. In both the OT and the NT two elements appear in particular: a goodness which rests upon mercy (*ḥesed, chrēstotēs*) and one that rests upon God's moral goodness (*tôb, agathōsunē*). Thus, in some places God's kindness comes to the fore: "The earth is full of the goodness [loving-kindness, ASV] of the Lord" (Ps 33:5; cf. Ps 52:1; 107:8); "Despisest thou the riches of his goodness [kindness] . . . not knowing that the goodness of God leadeth thee to repentance?" (Rom 2:4). In others, God's perfection and goodness come forth (Num 10:32; Ps 16:2; 23:6; Gal 5:22; II Thess 1:11).

One of the fruits of the Spirit is goodness (*agathōsunē*), in the sense of Christian holiness and righteousness (Gal 5:22). This is in keeping with the goal of the Christian life, which is to be like our heavenly Father, both in character and action, even as Christ taught in the Sermon on the Mount (Mt 5:48).

See Good; Kindness.

R. A. K.

GOOSE. *See* Animals, III.18.

GOPHER WOOD. *See* Plants.

GOSHEN (gō′sh*e*n)

1. Goshen was the territory in Egypt in which Jacob and his family were granted royal permission to settle. It is called either "the land of Goshen" or simply "Goshen," and is related to "the land of Rameses" (Gen 47:11) and the store cities of Ex 1:11.

Goshen was located in the easternmost section of the Delta, NE of Heliopolis (biblical On, Gen 41:45). It is associated with the Wadi Tumeilat, a very fertile area which joins the Nile at Bubastis (Pibeseth, *q.v.*) with Lake Timsah at modern Isma'iliya, N of the Bitter Lakes. *See* Succoth.

The LXX relates Goshen (Gesem) to the Egyptian nome of "Arabia" (the twentieth nome of Lower Egypt, on the E border of the Delta, according to Ptolemy the geographer), preserving a tradition of the Hellenistic Jews of Egypt (cf. Gen 45:10; 46:34).

Joseph selected Goshen as the residence for his relatives, so that they would be near him and probably because the district was best suited for their pastoral livelihood (Gen 45:10; cf. 47:4; for a later parallel, see Breasted, *Ancient Records of Egypt,* III, §§ 636–638, and ANET, p. 259). When Jacob arrived in Goshen, Joseph went to meet him there (Gen 46:28–29; the LXX adds "at Heroonpolis"). Joseph told Pharaoh of the arrival of his family in Goshen (Gen 47:1) and presented five of his brothers to the king, who suggested that Joseph settle his relatives in "the best of the land" (v. 6), in Goshen, in accordance with their request (v. 4). Here the Israelites prospered and multiplied (v. 27). From here a large funeral procession went to Canaan to bury Jacob (Gen 50:7–9). At the time of the Exodus, Goshen was protected from the plagues of "swarms" (Ex 8:22) and of hail (Ex 9:26), which affected all the rest of Egypt. *See* Exodus, The; Plagues.

2. A district called Goshen was situated in the southern part of Judah, between the hill country and the Negeb (Josh 10:41; 11:16).

Plowing in the land of Goshen. MPS

3. There was a town by this name in the southern hill country of Judah (Josh 15:51); its location is uncertain. Aharoni (*The Land of the Bible,* p. 184) suggests that it is Tell el-Khuweilifeh, a site which others have identified as Ziklag (*q.v.*).

C. E. D.

GOSPEL. A word used only in the NT to denote the message of Christ. The Gr. *euangelion,* meaning "good tidings," became a technical term for the essential message of salvation. It is modified by various descriptive phrases, such as, "the gospel of God" (Mk 1:14, ASV; Rom 15:16), "the gospel of Jesus Christ" (Mk 1:1; I Cor 9:12), "the gospel of his Son" (Rom 1:9), "the gospel of the kingdom" (Mt 4:23; 9:35; 24:14), "the gospel of the grace of God" (Acts 20:24), "the gospel of the glory of Christ" (II Cor 4:4, ASV), "the gospel of peace" (Eph 6:15), "an eternal gospel" (Rev 14:6, RSV). Although distinctive aspects of the message are indicated by the various modifiers, the gospel is essentially one. Paul speaks of "another gospel" which is not an equivalent, for the gospel of God is His revelation, not the result of discovery (Gal 1:6–11).

The content of the gospel is clearly defined in the NT. It is the accepted message of the Christian church, for it was received by all believers, defended by their reason, and was a vital part of their experience. It was historical in its content, biblical in its meaning, and transforming in its effect. "Christ died for our sins according to the scriptures . . . he was buried . . . he hath been raised on the third day according to the scriptures . . . he appeared to Cephas . . ." are Paul's descriptive words (I Cor 15:1–6, ASV).

The gospel was not a loose accretion of early legends about Jesus, but was a well-organized set of teachings about His life and its significance, preached by the leaders of the early church in the first generation after His death. Although it was not reduced to a catechetical formulation, it was sufficiently uniform to be reflected in the writings of Matthew, Mark, and Luke, now called the Synoptic Gospels. A different form of the same preaching appeared in the Gospel of John. Because of the unique quality and content of the message, the writings embodying it were called the "Gospels." It is probable, however, that this technical use of the term does not appear in the narrative passages of the NT. Invariably when it is used it refers to the content rather than to the vehicle; the application of "Gospel" to the written work is later than the 1st cen.

The central truth of the gospel is that God has provided a way of salvation for men through the gift of His Son to the world. He suffered as a sacrifice for sin, overcame death, and now offers a share in His triumph to all who will accept it. The gospel is good news because it is a gift of God, not something that must be earned by penance or by self-improvement (Jn 3:16; Rom 5:8-11; II Cor 5:14-19; Tit 2:11-14). The gospel presents Christ as the mediator between God and men, who has been ordained by God to bring an erring humanity back to Himself.

See Evangelist; Glad Tidings; Law of Moses.

Bibliography. Gerhard Friedrich, *"Euaggelizomai,* etc.," TDNT, II, 707-737.

M. C. T.

GOSPELS, THE FOUR. The first four books of the NT canon, Matthew, Mark, Luke, and John, are called Gospels because they are the written record of the early preaching of the good news concerning Christ. They constitute a distinctive type of literature. They are not wholly biography, for they do not attempt to narrate all the facts of Jesus' career; nor are they only history; nor are they sermons, though they include preaching and discourses; nor are they simply news reports. All of these elements appear in them, combined in a new form of organization which appears only in Christian writings. These writings were intended to express the basic message of the early Christian preachers which was written to instruct believers in the certainties of their faith.

The first three, because of their close resemblance to each other in content and in viewpoint, are called the Synoptic Gospels. Although they differ in many respects, they follow the same general order of events, and deal largely with the ministry of Jesus in Galilee. John, the fourth Gospel, contains a different selection of events, narrates chiefly the work of Jesus in Judea, and interprets His life more from a theological standpoint than do the others.

From the very earliest period of the Christian church the Gospels have been acknowledged as valid records of the life of Jesus. The first writer to mention them by name was Papias of Hierapolis, who lived in the first third of the 2nd cen. According to the record given in the *Historia Ecclesiae* of Eusebius (iii.39), A.D. 350, Papias reported that "Matthew composed his history in the Hebrew dialect . . .," and that "Mark, being the interpreter of Peter, whatsoever he recorded he wrote with great accuracy, but not however in the order in which it was spoken or done by our Lord. . . ." Justin Martyr, *c.* A.D. 150, mentioned "the memoirs of the apostles, which are called Gospels," "composed by the apostles and those that followed them" (I *Apology* 66-67; *Dialogue with Trypho,* 10, 100, 103). Tatian, a Gnostic writer of the middle of the 2nd cen., combined the four Gospels into one harmony. They must, therefore, have been known and accepted as authority not later than the opening of the 2nd cen. Other works of the early 2nd cen., such as the Didache, the Epistles of Ignatius, and the Epistle of Barnabas, contain allusions which can be traced to Gospel sources, chiefly to Matthew's account. The recent discovery of the Gospel According to Thomas, containing very early specimens of the sayings of Jesus, simply confirms the previous existence of basic Gospel writings.

The Origin of the Gospels

The Christian church did not begin its evangelism by the distribution of literature but by public preaching. The witness of the apostles centered on the death and resurrection of Jesus (Acts 4:10), who, Paul said, "was delivered up for our trespasses, and was raised for our justification" (Rom 4:25, ASV). Wherever the early disciples went, they proclaimed the coming of Jesus as the promised Messiah of the OT, and told the story of His life and works. The climactic events of His passion constituted the initial message preached in any given locality. Paul reminded the Corinthians that "first of all" he had declared to them that "Christ died for our sins according to the scriptures; and that he was buried; and that he hath been raised on the third day according to the scriptures; and that he appeared . . . " (I Cor 15:3-5, ASV). Undoubtedly, however, the apostles did not confine themselves to these few facts, for their hearers would have desired more information about Jesus. The significant events of His life must have been narrated in order, making an account corresponding generally to the content of the existing Gospels.

Because of the numerous witnesses and the wide variety of discourses, parables, and episodes attributed to Jesus, there must have been many versions of the gospel story. The main facts, however, were fairly well fixed, and consequently the gospel tradition, as this oral preaching can be called, tended to become uniform in content.

From the beginning the new disciples were instructed formally in the "teaching of the apostles" (Acts 2:42), which must have contained the history and interpretation of Jesus' life, death, and resurrection. Without such teaching the Christian church would have lost its distinctive message. While the oral preaching may not have become stereotyped, constant repetition and the use of the material in the instruction of believers probably gave it a relatively settled form. Luke alludes to such procedure when writing to his friend Theophilus: ". . . that thou mightest know the certainty concerning the things wherein thou wast *instructed,*" Gr. *catechized* (Lk 1:4, ASV). The Gr. word implies the impartation of knowledge by word of mouth, and may mean formal teaching. Theophilus had already been orally informed of the general content of the gospel; Luke put the material into writing to confirm the facts that he already knew.

Since new believers constantly needed instruction, and since the original witnesses were gradually becoming unavailable either because of dispersion or death, a more permanent record became necessary. The transition from preaching to literature has not been preserved by any single account, and must be derived by inference from the hints that survive in the existing Gospels and in other early writings. Various theories have been propounded to explain the origin of the Gospels, particularly of the Synoptics, which present the peculiar problem of close verbal resemblances in some parts, and of widely differing content in others. The existence of these similarities and differences gave rise to the "Synoptic problem." Why, if these three Gospels were independently composed, do they resemble each other so closely? If they are not independent, why do they differ? *See also* Gospels, Synoptic.

Oral tradition. The apostles of Jesus who had associated closely with Him during the years of His ministry would have a vast fund of reminiscences from which to draw the outline of His life and the illustrations of His teachings. Since it would be impossible to recount in one message all that He did and said, the facts would have to be sorted so that only the most significant would be used. As they preached, they tended to repeat the essential events and teachings, such as the Sermon on the Mount, or the account of the passion, and to omit the smaller events which seemed of lesser importance. This constant repetition crystallized the message so that it became uniform with occasional variations. In writing, each author repeated the main narrative, endeavoring to reproduce it in accordance with the needs of his audience and with his divinely given purpose. The general facts and their significance would thus be the same for all; the organization and the illustrations would differ. Resemblances in the Gospels thus repeat facts common to all the preaching of the message by the church; differences are the result of varying selection of episodes and discourses fitted to the author's purpose.

The interdependence theories. Explanation of the resemblances and differences in the Synoptics by reproduction of various parts of the oral tradition, some identical and some different, did not satisfy the scholars of the late 18th cen. They and their successors pointed out that the resemblances were too close to be explained by purely verbal transmission. They argued that the Gospels must be dependent on each other. All possible permutations of order were suggested, but none could prove a conclusive case. Interdependence has been generally abandoned as an explanation of the Synoptic problem.

The documentary theories. A more recent theory proposes that the Synoptics were built on two primary sources, the Gospel of Mark and a hypothetical collection of Jesus' sayings and parables called "Q," from the German *Quelle* meaning "source." The theory owes its origin to the observation that almost the entire content of Mark is embedded in Luke and Matthew, and that while Mark and Matthew may agree against Luke, or Luke and Mark against Matthew, Matthew and Luke never agree against Mark. "Q" has been presumably reconstructed from the common discourse material existing in Matthew and Luke which does not occur in Mark. According to this "two-document" theory, Mark incorporated the main facts of the life of Jesus as they were currently preached and taught in the church. "Q" was composed of sayings and deeds of Jesus which had been noted for proclamation, but it was not an organized narrative. B. H. Streeter (*The Four Gospels,* 1936) extended the hypothesis to include two other "sources," "M" for Matthew's peculiar material, and "L" for Luke's specific contribution.

A plausible defense for the general documentary hypothesis can be offered on the ground that almost all the Markan narrative is incorporated into Matthew and Luke, and that collections similar to "Q" are known to have existed. Papyrus fragments of the sayings of Jesus have been discovered in the rubbish heaps of Egypt (see B. P. Grenfell and A. S. Hunt, *The Logia of Jesus,* and R. M. Grant, *The Secret Sayings of Jesus,* New York: Doubleday, 1960).

Such a theory, however, raises grave doubts concerning the independence and accuracy of Matthew and Luke. If the writers of these documents incorporated Mark wholesale, or with such modifications and additions as they saw fit, have they produced works which can be classed with his for authority and importance? Furthermore, no trace of "Q" has ever been found. Its existence is purely conjectural, founded on the assumption that Matthew and Luke must have had a single source for their common non-Markan material. The construction of the theory is wholly subjective, and there is disagreement among its proponents concerning what portions of the Gospel text may or may not belong to "Q." E. F. Scott, who accepts the documentary hypothesis, admits that "Q" does not represent a single document but a series of collections of Jesus' sayings that may have existed in many copies or editions (E. F. Scott, *Literature of the New Testament,* p. 41).

While it is possible that the writers of the Gospels may have used written sources, there is no reason why they could not have depended largely on firsthand knowledge or upon direct oral information for the bulk of their material; and there is little convincing evidence for the support of theories that place the time of production of the Gospels late in the 1st cen. or early in the 2nd. The writers themselves could have supplied most of the material credited to "sources." Streeter's theory does not necessitate two additional sources; he has simply assigned letters to the authors themselves.

Formgeschichte. The theory of *Formgeschichte,* a German word meaning "Form history" (English title, Form Criticism) was proposed by Martin Dibelius in 1919, who attempted to penetrate behind the "sources" to the oral tradition. He suggested that the material from which the Gospels were constructed originally circulated as short independent accounts which could be classified by their literary form for which he proposed a series of labels: the Passion Story concerning the end of Jesus' life; Paradigms, or stories of Jesus' works that were used as illustrations of His message; Tales, miraculous events which were narrated for the pleasure that they afforded the hearer; Legends, or stories of the lives of holy men, cited as examples; Sayings, epigrammatic utterances of Jesus which were used in exhortations. From the miscellaneous array of quotations and anecdotes, according to this theory, the first sermons were composed and later edited into the Gospels.

While it is not impossible that separate sayings and acts of Jesus may have been quoted and recorded in the Gospels, it is dubious whether so complicated a process really took place. Each of the Gospels bears marks of purposeful organization rather than of being the accidental accumulation of floating tradition.

The most definite evidence available concerning the origin of the Synoptic Gospels may be gleaned from the introduction to Luke. The writer acknowledges at the outset that others had attempted to produce narratives of the life of Jesus (1:1), but either he regarded them as unreliable, or else they were not available to his addressee. His statement, "It seemed good to me also . . . to write unto thee in order" (1:3), shows that he assumed an equal right with the others to create a life of Jesus, and that he possessed information which was superior in quality. The substance of his account would not be novel; it concerned "those matters which have been fulfilled [fully established] among us" (1:1, ASV). Luke took for granted that they were accepted by the church as a whole, and affirmed that they had been transmitted to him by men "who from the beginning were eyewitnesses, and ministers of the word" (1:2). The word "minister" is identical with the one used in Acts 13:5 to describe John Mark who was the attendant of Barnabas and Paul in their early ministry. Since Luke was not with them at that time, he may have obtained from Mark part of the information in his Gospel—a fact which might explain to some extent the identity of wording. In any case, Luke was careful to use authoritative informants. Furthermore, he was a contemporary of the general course of events (1:3), alert and conscientious both in the acquisition and in the transmission of information. Although the other two writers of the Synoptic Gospels do not explain their procedure with similar definiteness, the general order and content of their narratives bespeak equal accuracy.

The closing words of the fourth Gospel shed some additional light on this problem of composition. The writer states that "many other signs therefore did Jesus in the presence of the disciples, which are not written in this book: but these are written, that ye may believe . . ." (Jn 20:30-31, ASV). John was selective, taking from the store of facts about Jesus' life and teaching only such items as would serve his purpose. His Gospel has a specific objective, and he used only the materials that enabled him to attain his goal. Since the Gospels were not intended to be exhaustive, they should not be expected to provide a complete account of all that Jesus said and did, nor should they be regarded as inaccurate because they differ among themselves.

Perhaps the best explanation of the process of writing is that each of the four authors endeavored to present the central message about Jesus to his own constituency, and consequently used and arranged the materials independently. On the other hand, the message had been so often repeated that much of it was already fixed in form, so that it would be expressed in identical phraseology by anybody who used it. Furthermore, it is not impossible that the three authors, Matthew, Mark, and Luke, may have met each other at one time or another in their careers, and exchanged notes. The possibility of personal contact is at least as valid as that of documentary dependence.

The Gospel of Matthew

The Gospel of Matthew is the earliest known and the most widely used of the Gospels. As previously noted, Eusebius, a church historian of the 4th cen. after Christ, quoted Papias who said that "Matthew composed his history in the Hebrew dialect, and everyone translated it as he was able" (Eusebius, *Historia Ecclesiae*, iii.39). Since Eusebius did not quote all that Papias said, the meaning is uncertain. By "Hebrew" Papias could have meant Aramaic, the then current speech of Jewish Palestine. He does imply that Matthew contributed some definite information concerning Jesus which antedated the Gentile expansion of the church, and which consequently must have been known before A.D. 50. The Gospel quotations or allusions in the Didache (A.D. 125), the Epistle of Barnabas (A.D. 150), Ignatius' Epistle to the Smyrneans (A.D. 118), and Justin Martyr's *Dialogue with Trypho*, xlix (*c.* A.D. 140), accord more closely with Matthew than with any other Synoptic. The Gospel must have been in circulation by the end of the 1st cen., and probably considerably earlier.

Of the traditional author little is known. Matthew (Levi, as the Gospels call him) was a tax collector, stationed near Capernaum (Mt 9:9-10). He entertained Jesus at a dinner in his home, and abandoned his profession to become a disciple. There is no other mention of him except in the general list of the apostles (Mk 2:14; Lk 6:15; Acts 1:13). He must have been literate, for he would be compelled to keep accounts when he served the government. *See* Matthew.

The date of the Gospel is unknown, but its silence concerning the destruction of Jerusalem, its interest in Jewish prophecy, and its awareness of Jewish sentiment (Mt 28:15) point to an origin not much later than A.D. 50. Since the present Gospel exists only in Greek, it may be that its wide use among the Gentile Christians began with the dispersion from Antioch, and that it was first circulated extensively there between A.D. 50 and 65. Irenaeus (*c.* A.D. 180) stated that "Matthew also issued a written Gospel among the Hebrews in their own dialect" (*Against Heresies* iii, 1.1), confirming Papias' statement. Perhaps Matthew's Gospel was the first to incorporate in one account the teachings of Jesus which Matthew had transcribed, and the acts of Jesus which formed the core of apostolic preaching, as proclaimed by Peter and later digested by Mark. It may have been the earliest written account used in the transition from the Aramaic church of Jerusalem to the Gr. church of the Gentile mission.

The theme of the Gospel is the messiahship of Jesus, a topic prominent in primitive apostolic preaching. The opening genealogy makes Jesus heir of the promises given to Abraham and David. Six times in the first four chapters (Mt 1:22-23; 2:5-6, 15, 17-18; 3:3; 4:14) the events in His life are connected with the fulfillment of prophecy. The Sermon on the Mount emphasizes Jesus' relation to the law (5:17-20). He claimed to be a greater prophet than Jonah, and a greater king than Solomon (12:41-42). He accepted and commended Peter's confession that He was the Messiah (16:13-20), and He confirmed the claim on oath before the high priest (26:63-64).

Matthew's treatment of the gospel is predominantly topical. Rather than chronicling Jesus' activities by short episodes, as Mark does, he prefers to use large blocks of text, each of which is devoted to some one aspect of Christ's life and teaching. The first four chapters are concerned chiefly with the relation of the OT to the advent of the Messiah. The Sermon on the Mount (chaps. 5–7) is a sample of Jesus' preaching which states His essential ethical principles, and summarizes the main content of His teaching. Another block of text from 8:1 to 11:1 comprises a list of miracles of various types all illustrative of Jesus' power over nature, disease, and death. Chap. 13 contains eight parables of the kingdom, portraying both its inward and outward aspects. The conflict of Jesus with His opponents occupies chaps. 19-25, including the famous Olivet Discourse (24-25). The rest of the Gospel is devoted to the narrative of the passion.

The structure follows generally the chronological pattern of the other Synoptics. In biographical sequence it does not differ from them greatly, though it contains some material that they lack. The two largest sections of the book are marked by the phrase "from that time" (4:17; 16:21), which introduces first the beginning of Jesus' popular public ministry, and second, the decline which led to the cross. Matthew combines this rise and decline of Jesus' career with His messianic manifestation.

Several features of Matthew's Gospel are not duplicated in the others. The dream of Joseph (1:20-24), the visit of the Magi (2:1-12), the withdrawal into Egypt (2:13-15), the slaughter of the infants at Bethlehem (2:16), the dream of Pilate's wife (27:19), the suicide of Judas (27:3-10), the resuscitation of dead saints at the crucifixion (27:52), the bribing of the guard (28:12-15), and the baptismal commission (28:19-20) appear nowhere else. Ten parables are given only by Matthew: the tares (13:24-30, 36-43), the hidden treasure (13:44), the pearl (13:45-46), the dragnet (13:47-50), the unmerciful servant (18:23-35), the laborers in the vineyard (20:1-16), the two sons (21:28-32), the marriage of the king's son (22:1-13), the ten virgins (25:1-13), and the talents (25:14-30).

This Gospel stresses discourses and teaching. Seven important addresses are recorded: the preaching of John (3:1-12), the Sermon on the Mount (5:1–7:29), the commission of the disciples (10:1-42), the parables of the kingdom (13:1-52), the meaning of forgiveness (18:1-35), denunciation and prediction of the end (23:1–25:46), and the Great Commission (28:18-20). The emphasis is much more on teaching than on action or character development.

This Gospel is the only one in which the Church is mentioned (16:18; 18:17). The inclusion of Jesus' references to the Church indicates that the author was interested in the rise and growth of the institution. Perhaps he had in mind the development of the church at Antioch.

See Matthew, Gospel of.

The Gospel of Mark

Beginning with Papias, the early writers of the church unanimously ascribe the second Gospel to John Mark, a young companion of the apostolic band. The current tradition of the 2nd cen. was well summarized by Irenaeus (*c.* A.D. 180): "After their [Peter's and Paul's] departure, Mark, the disciple and interpreter of Peter, did also hand down to us in writing what had been preached by Peter" (*Against Heresies* iii. 1.1). This statement is repeated in substance by Origen of Alexandria (*c.* A.D. 250), Tertullian of Carthage (*c.* A.D. 200), and Jerome (*c.* A.D. 400), the translator of the Latin Vulgate. Neither on external nor on internal grounds is there any good reason for challenging the traditional authorship. The direct and artless narrative of Mark accords well with the known character of Peter, and with the type of preaching that was employed in the Apostolic Age.

According to the records of the NT, John Mark was the son of a woman named Mary who owned a home in Jerusalem, and was sufficiently affluent to have servants (Acts 12:12-13). It is possible that the "upper room" of the last supper was in her house, and that the pre-Pentecostal prayer meeting was held there. John Mark must have been acquainted with all the apostles, and must have been familiar with their preaching. It is probable that he may have seen Jesus during the last week of His life, if not before. He was a cousin of Barnabas, who took him to Antioch to work in the church with himself and Paul (Acts 12:25). He accompanied Barnabas and Paul on their first missionary journey (13:5), but left them at Perga (13:13). Paul refused to take him on the second missionary tour (15:36-39), but Mark continued in service with Barnabas. Evidently he succeeded, for in Paul's later epistles Mark is commended as a Christian worker (Col 4:10; II Tim 4:11). *See* Mark.

Mark was qualified to write a narrative of Jesus' life because he was personally acquainted with the apostolic band, because he had participated in the evangelistic ministry of the church, and because he may himself have been an eyewitness of the last scenes of Jesus' career. Two references in the Gospel seemingly point to Mark. One alludes to a young man who was in the garden of Gethsemane when Jesus was captured, and who narrowly escaped from the clutches of the arresting party (Mk 14:51-52). The episode does not occur in the other accounts, and is irrelevant to the main teaching of the passage. It takes on meaning only if it is an experience of the writer, who speaks from firsthand knowledge. Perhaps Mark, curious about the fate of Jesus, went to the garden to investigate, and was almost involved in the capture. He may have been the only witness to the prayer which the Lord offered on that occasion. The other reference relates to Simon, the Cyrenian, who carried Jesus' cross. Mark informs the reader that Simon was the father of Alexander and Rufus (15:21). There would have been no reason for this statement had the author not expected the two men to be known to his readers. Evidently he was a contemporary of the generation that immediately followed that of Jesus. While this allusion does not definitely identify him as Mark, it places him in the period and circle to which Mark belonged.

The place of writing is uncertain, but the general tradition connects the publication of Mark's Gospel with Rome. Mark's clear, terse, and concrete style would appeal to the practical Roman mind, for it stresses action rather than teaching. There are more Latinisms here in the Gr. text than in the other Gospels, such as the words "census" for "tribute" (12:14); "speculator" for "executioner" (6:27, KJV); *phragelloun* for Latin *flagellare,* "to scourge" (15:15); and *centurio* for "centurion" (15:39), where Matthew and Luke employ a Gr. equivalent. If Mark were not writing for a Roman audience, he may have been influenced by a Roman environment. Possibly he composed the substance of the Gospel in Palestine and finished it in Rome. It may have been written as a summary of the apostolic preaching to the Gentiles, to provide a résumé of Christian truth for the early converts.

The content of the Gospel is brief but inclusive. It contains a minimum of discourse material and a maximum of action, compressed into a series of episodes like candid camera pictures. Each presents Jesus in some one pose or action, and calls for a personal reaction on the part of the reader. In many instances the reaction of the public to Jesus is a part of the narrative.

The last 12 verses of the Gospel are lacking in the oldest MSS of the NT, Codex Vaticanus and Codex Sinaiticus, both of the 4th cen. Numerous other copies either omit them, or mark them with an asterisk to indicate that they are not contained in all the sources known to the scribe, and several of the early Church Fathers never quote them. In the existing MS tradition there are three different endings: the longer ending familiar to most readers, and two shorter ones which are obviously attempts to fill a gap. It is possible that Mark intended to conclude his Gospel at 16:8, as R. H. Lightfoot argues (*Locality and Doctrine in the Gospels,* pp. 1-23), but the ending is so abrupt that early damage to the original manuscript seems more probable. The longer ending, which is printed in most English translations, may date back to the 2nd cen., and represents a very early summary of the postresurrection events, whether it is Markan or not.

Mark's Gospel has certain definite characteristics. It emphasizes action rather than teaching. Very few discourses or parables of Jesus are reported, but Mark narrates more miracles than any of the other Gospel writers in proportion to length. He uses the historic present tense 151 times to make the story vivid. His language is terse but pictorial: "He saw the heavens *rent asunder*" (1:10, ASV); "The herd [of swine] *rushed* down the steep into the sea" (5:13, ASV); "They *laughed him to scorn*" (5:40); "They had a *few small fishes* " (8:7). The italicized words are phrases which illustrate the concise and vigorous quality of the Markan writing. The narrative moves rapidly, and is more concerned with changing the scenes than with continuity of reasoning. Nevertheless, this Gospel conveys a definite picture of Jesus, and from the variety of His acts it composes a unified portrait of a supernatural Person who can forgive sins, legislate human ethics, feed hungry crowds, heal the sick, and debate successfully with the sharpest intellects of His nation.

Mark specializes in portraying Jesus by the popular reactions which He evoked. He notes repeatedly that the crowds or disciples were "amazed" (1:27), resentful of His claims (2:7), querulous about His behavior (2:16), fearful of His power (4:41), "astonished" at His teaching (10:26; 11:18), awed by His wisdom (12:34). There are 23 such expressions of feeling that reflect the impressions that Jesus made on those who met Him. Mark does not attempt a general evaluation of Jesus; he simply records the popular reactions, and lets the reader form his own judgments.

The purpose of this Gospel seems to be evangelistic. It contains less teaching than Matthew and is less apologetic than Luke. The style is that of a street preacher, who attempts to hold the interest of his audience by lively anecdotes, pointed sentences, and pungent applications of truth. Mark makes his reader feel that he has witnessed the scenes described in the Gospel, and evokes from him the response that Jesus Himself would have created.

See Mark, Gospel of.

The Gospel of Luke

More information concerning the composition of the third Gospel is available than concerning the origin of Matthew and Mark, for the author has supplied a brief introduction (Lk 1:1-4) that explains his method and purpose in writing. This preface is a key to the book, which enables the reader to understand the motives which directed the writing of the Gospel and the circumstances under which it was produced. A comparison of this introduction with that of the book of Acts shows that the two documents were written by the same man, for both are addressed to Theophilus, and the introduction to Acts (1:1-5) speaks of a "former treatise" containing the life and works of Jesus. Since the vocabulary and style of the two works resemble each other closely, there can be no reasonable doubt that they had a common author.

This author was undoubtedly Luke, a companion of Paul, who is mentioned in the epistles as "the beloved physician" (Col 4:14). His birthplace is unknown, though it may have been Antioch of Syria, with which he seemed to be familiar. He joined Paul's company at Troas, on the second journey (Acts 16:10), and traveled with him to Philippi, where he probably remained as pastor of the church until Paul returned on the third journey (Acts 20:6 ff.). Throughout the rest of Paul's itinerary Luke was a constant associate, except that he seems to have been at liberty during Paul's imprisonment at Caesarea, for he is not mentioned in the account. He rejoined Paul on the voyage to Rome (Acts 27:1-2 ff.) and stayed with him for the rest of his life (II Tim 4:11).

See Luke.

Early tradition unanimously credits this work to Luke. Justin Martyr (A.D. 140) definitely quoted Luke 23:46, and ascribed his quotation to "the memoirs" (*Dialogue with Trypho* cv). The Muratorian Fragment (A.D. 170) attributed the third Gospel to Luke. Tatian (A.D. 140-150) included it in his *Diatessaron*. Marcion, the Gnostic (A.D. 140), accepted Luke as the only Gospel in his canon, though he altered its text considerably. Irenaeus (A.D. 170) quoted it extensively and acknowledged Luke explicitly as the author (*Against Heresies* iii.1.1).

The traditional view is supported by the internal evidence, for Luke is the only one of Paul's companions who could have written the book of Acts and, consequently, this Gospel. The language of both books shows a physician's interest in the sick and diseased, and some of his vocabulary is that which a doctor would be more likely to employ than a layman. Mark (1:30), in describing the illness of Peter's mother-in-law, says that she was sick with fever, but Luke (4:38) says that she was afflicted with "a great fever." Mark (1:40) speaks of a leper; Luke (5:12) says that he was "full of leprosy." Mark (3:1), in describing a cripple, says that he had a withered hand; Luke (6:6) observes that his *right* hand was affected. Mark (5:25-26) says that the woman with the issue of blood was not helped by the physicians but rather grew worse; Luke (8:43-44) implies that she was an incurable case.

Cadbury has objected that the language of Luke is not the technical jargon of a physician because there was none in the days of the NT (*The Style and Literary Method of Luke,* in *Harvard Theological Studies,* VI, 39 ff.). Cadbury may be right that the Gr. physicians did not have a separate medical terminology in the 1st cen., but his argument does not change the fact that Luke's vocabulary exhibits a physician's interests and viewpoint.

Furthermore, the writer seems to have had access to some informants that would have been available only to one who moved both in official circles and among the earliest associates of Jesus and the apostles. The first two chapters contain facts that could have been derived only from the family of Jesus. The author knew some of the apostles; among the women he mentions Mary Magdalene, and Joanna, the wife of Chuza, Herod's steward, who would have known Herod's court; and it is possible that he became acquainted with some of the persons mentioned in this Gospel, such as Zacchaeus, the publican of Jericho (19:2), and Cleopas, one of the two who traveled to Emmaus on the resurrection day (24:13, 18). Some of these witnesses, because of their convictions, had become active workers in the church, "ministers of the word" (1:2). Both by their experience and by their position they would be adequate sources for reliable information. Luke claims that he had been a contemporary of these men ("having traced the course of all things . . .,"ASV) for a considerable length of time, and that he was therefore qualified to write authoritatively concerning their testimony.

Luke's introduction implies that numerous accounts of the life of Jesus were already in circulation when he composed his Gospel (1:1). Whether he stated this fact solely to justify his right to produce another, or whether he was dissatisfied with the scope and accuracy of those already written is not perfectly clear. In any case, some attempts to write the facts concerning Jesus had already been made, so that the church was not devoid of literature. This Gospel presupposes a demand for such works, and the use of documents to propagate the faith.

The content of Luke's Gospel, according to

his own testimony, consists of "those matters which have been fulfilled among us" (1:1, ASV). The margin of the ASV reads "fully established," and the expression means "the facts generally accepted as settled." Luke was not attempting to introduce a novel teaching, but was transcribing the general story of Jesus' life as it had been confirmed by his own research or by the testimony of reliable witnesses. These matters were not novelties to his reader, for he had been "instructed" in them. The word instructed means literally, "to be informed by word of mouth," and may connote a regular course of instruction or catechizing. Evidently Luke did not confine himself to repeating church teaching, but he professed to convey the substance of the common oral instruction strengthened by information that he had acquired, and motivated by the consciousness that he possessed the authority of truth.

Luke did not specify whether by "order" he meant chronological sequence, logical continuity, or homiletical procedure. In general, his narrative followed the same order as those of Mark and Matthew, with some insertions. Perhaps he combined the biographical or homiletical sequence of the current preaching with his own didactic purpose, for he organized Luke and Acts around the ministry of the Holy Spirit in the life of Christ and of the early church. The governing purpose of this Gospel was to produce certainty in the thinking of its readers. The author could not have achieved this end had he built his narrative upon fiction or upon legend.

Although the date of production cannot be fixed exactly, it is most probable that the Gospel was written not later than A.D. 62. As the first half of the two-volume work of Luke-Acts, it must have been written before Acts. The latter was probably completed while Paul was still alive, quite likely at the end of his first Roman imprisonment. If the writer knew more concerning Paul's fate than the book of Acts records, it is unlikely that he would have ended his narrative without disclosing the facts. Probably he wrote no more because there was no more to tell. Paul's two years in Rome must have ended about A.D. 62. In that case the collection of material for the Gospel and its composition probably preceded that time. Luke would have had ample opportunity to interview the witnesses of Jesus' life and to visit the scenes of His ministry during Paul's two-year imprisonment in Caesarea. Even so radical a critic as Harnack argued that the Gospel of Luke cannot be much later than A.D. 80 (see Adolf Harnack, *Luke the Physician,* p. 163). It may be that it represents in some measure the gospel which Paul and other members of the Gentile mission preached.

The place of publication is not clear. Although the Gospel may have been composed during the first part of Paul's imprisonment, it may have been sent privately to Theophilus. After the completion of Acts, both may have been given to the Gentile Gr. churches. Both were probably published before the destruction of Jerusalem, for there is no reference to that event within their pages.

The destination is plainly marked in the introduction. The Gospel was dedicated to the "most excellent Theophilus" (Lk 1:3). "Most excellent" was an epithet usually reserved for royalty and nobility (Acts 23:26; 24:3; 26:25). Theophilus was almost certainly a man of high position and culture, probably a government official, who had become a friend of Luke and who was a new Christian. Perhaps the instruction which he had received in the church conflicted with the rumors concerning Jesus that had been familiar to him as a government officer, and he was desirous of ascertaining the truth of the matter. Luke wrote to him as a personal friend that he might dispel his doubts and lead him into an intelligent faith.

Luke's Gospel is the most literary of the four. Its introduction accords closely with the classical literary form for books. The ancestry, birth, youth, and introduction of Jesus to His public ministry are described with more detail than in other Gospels. In the section of the Gospel which is peculiarly Lucan (9:51–18:14), there are numerous parables and anecdotes which are unique, and which disclose the discernment and arrangement of a literary artist. The parables of the lost sheep, the lost coin, and the two sons in Lk 15 are short stories of high quality. Allowing for the fact that they were originally spoken by Jesus, their transcription shows the hand of a facile craftsman who knew how to write effectively.

Luke presents Christ as the Saviour of men, who is interested in the poor and downtrodden, and who has come to bring them deliverance.

Because of his desire to make the message of Christ convincing to Theophilus, Luke stresses the historical aspect of the gospel. He explains fully the environment from which Jesus came, gives His genealogy by natural descent rather than by tracing the royal line as Matthew does, and places the entire narrative in a chronological setting that relates it to the contemporary current of world affairs (Lk 2:1-2; 3:1-2). Though his approach is less didactic than Matthew's, he includes a large amount of Jesus' teaching so that His thought is adequately represented. Luke deals more with personalities than the other Synoptic writers, both in the contacts of Jesus with individuals, and in the literary characters of His parables. The connection of the Gospel with Acts reveals his historical perspective, for he was considering Jesus' life not as a unit by itself, but as the first part of the ministry which was continued through the leaders of the church who finally took the gospel from Jerusalem, the center of the Jewish world, to Rome, the center of the Gentile world. He saw in Christianity the manifestation of God's world plan, not simply the origin of a sect.

Tradition says that Luke was an artist who painted a picture of the Virgin Mary. Assuredly he was an artist in words. He alone of the Gospel writers preserves the four songs: the *Magnificat* (1:46-55), the *Benedictus* of Zacharias (1:68-79), the *Gloria in Excelsis* of the angels at Christ's birth (2:14), and the *Nunc Dimittis* of Simeon (2:29-32). His vocabulary is varied and colorful. His reproduction of the parables of Jesus, particularly those in the section peculiar to him (9:51 – 18:14), reveals literary skill of highest quality.

The Gospel is universal in its appeal. It presents Jesus as the Son of Man, who belongs to all humanity and who sympathizes with everybody. Luke alone relates the parable of the Good Samaritan, which shows that a neighbor is not determined by race or by culture, but by love. Women and children obtain greater recognition in his Gospel than in any other. He magnifies Jesus' ministry among the poor and oppressed. The *Magnificat* (1:53) says:

"The hungry he hath filled with good things;
And the rich he hath sent empty away."

Jesus' first words in the synagogue at Nazareth were a quotation from Isa 61:1: "The Spirit of the Lord is upon me, because he anointed me to preach good tidings to the poor . . ." (Lk 4:18, ASV). In the parables of the rich fool (12:16-21), the great supper (14:15-24), and the rich man and Lazarus (16:19-31), Luke has reflected Jesus' concern for the plight of the poor.

Luke stresses particularly two theological themes. Prayer is one of his most prominent topics. He notes Jesus' prayer at His baptism (3:21), at His withdrawal into the desert (5:16), before the choice of the twelve disciples (6:12), before the prediction of His death (9:18), before teaching His disciples (11:1), special intercession for Simon Peter (22:32), the prayer in Gethsemane (22:41), and on the cross (23:34, 46). A second theme is the Holy Spirit, who is mentioned more times than in Matthew and Mark combined. Luke indicates that all of Jesus' life was lived by the Spirit. The Spirit created His body (1:35); He was baptized with the Spirit (3:22), tried by the Spirit (4:1), commissioned by the Spirit for His life work (4:14, 18), encouraged by the Spirit in His work (10:21), and He enjoined His disciples to await the Spirit before they undertook their labors (24:49). Both of these themes are carried forward by Acts, which shows that they represent the author's interest as well as being historical facts.

The doctrinal content is not so pronounced as that of Matthew or John, but is sufficient to reveal the undercurrent of Christian theology. Luke presents Christ as the Son of God, whose sonship is attested by angels (1:35), by demons (4:41), and by God Himself (9:35). The concept of salvation is stated in Jesus' own words: "The Son of man came to seek and to save that which was lost" (19:10, ASV). In the concluding chapter Luke stresses the truth that Jesus is the predicted Messiah of the OT Scriptures, who "should suffer, and rise again from the dead the third day; and that repentance and remission of sins should be preached in his name unto all the nations . . ." (24:46-47, ASV). The climax of his teaching fulfills his avowed purpose to impart spiritual certainty to his reader.

See Luke, Gospel of.

The Gospel of John

The fourth Gospel differs strongly from the Synoptics in content and organization. So radical is the difference that some scholars have challenged its authenticity, saying that the Synoptic and Johannine accounts of the life of Christ cannot both be true. The Gospel of John contains no parables, few of the epigrammatic sayings of Jesus which are so common in the Synoptics, only seven miracles, five of which the Synoptics do not record, and a number of long argumentative discourses related to the person of Jesus that the Synoptics do not duplicate. The Gospel of John is organized more like a sermon than a biography, and deals with the life of Jesus as an incentive to faith rather than an attempt to summarize historical occurrences. By the critics of the 19th cen., from Bretschneider (1820) on, to more recent writers like James Moffatt (*Introduction to the Literature of the New Testament,* pp. 566-619) and Pierson Parker ("John the Son of Zebedee and the Fourth Gospel," JBL, LXXXI [1962], 35–43), the Johannine authorship has been widely denied.

The tradition that John the son of Zebedee was the writer is early, and is supported by considerable evidence. The Rylands Fragment, a small scrap of papyrus bearing on its two sides a few words from John, dates from the first quarter of the 2nd cen., and demonstrates that the Gospel was copied probably by A.D. 125. There are allusions in the Epistle to Barnabas (A.D. 125), the Epistles of Ignatius (A.D. 110), and Justin Martyr (A.D. 140) that seem traceable to this Gospel. Heracleon, a Gnostic who belonged to a school of thought flourishing between A.D. 140 and 180, wrote a commentary on the fourth Gospel. Tatian (A.D. 140) used it in his *Diatessaron,* so that there can be no doubt of its existence before the middle of the 2nd cen. From the time of Irenaeus (A.D. 170-180) the patristic testimony is almost unanimous that the fourth Gospel was the authentic product of John the beloved disciple.

The Gospel itself bears marks of its authorship. The writer was familiar with Jewish customs and traditions, and knew the OT. He was familiar with locations in Palestine, and had lived in Jerusalem and its environs. He professed to have seen Jesus, for he remarked that "we beheld his glory . . ." (1:14), and to have been present at the crucifixion (19:35). He noted the hour at which Jesus sat by the well of Sychar (4:6), the number and size of the waterpots at the wedding of Cana (2:6), the grass at the place of the feeding of the 5,000 (6:10), the numerous details concerning the death and burial of Jesus (chaps. 18-19). The final chapter of the book identifies him with the unnamed "beloved disciple" who was Peter's companion on the fishing expedition after the resurrection (21:7) and also in the investigation of the tomb (20:2). He must have been an intimate associate of Jesus, for he reclined next to Him at the last supper. Of Jesus' disciples who are mentioned by name, Peter, Andrew, Philip, or Nathanael cannot fill the requirement since they are mentioned in the third person. James and John, the sons of Zebedee, were present at the occasions mentioned above, but James could not have been the author since he was martyred at an early date, probably about A.D. 44 (Acts 12:2). By the simple process of elimination John the son of Zebedee is the one remaining possibility for authorship.

The objections that he was "unlearned" (Acts 4:13), that he was a Galilean rather than a Judean, and that his known character does not accord with the temperament of the author as deduced from the writing are not valid. Greek was spoken in Galilee, and although John may not have been primarily a literary man, he could have learned to express himself in the simple but good Greek of the fourth Gospel. If the book were written toward the close of his life, he would have had ample opportunity to improve both his language and his theological knowledge. The language of the fourth Gospel shows that its author possessed an ardent temperament which had been disciplined by contact with the world, and that he wrote from a perspective of many years in the ministry of Christ. The explanation of the words of Jesus concerning his longevity (Jn 21:22-23) implies that he must have survived to old age, or the explanation would not have been necessary for the author to include.

The great differences between the content of this Gospel and that of the Synoptics can be largely explained by assuming that the author was acquainted with the Synoptic tradition, the account of Jesus' life currently preached and incorporated in Matthew, Mark, and Luke, and that he was consciously attempting to add a supplement to it, while integrating with it simultaneously a new estimate of Jesus' life. A few chronological difficulties, such as the placing of the cleansing of the temple early in Jesus' ministry (2:13-22) and the sequence of the last hours of Jesus' life, have not yet been perfectly resolved. The Gospel is, however, authentic history, and should not be dismissed as mere theologizing.

Comparatively little is known concerning John, son of Zebedee. His father was a prosperous Galilean fisherman, who owned boats, and had hired servants (Mk 1:19-20). His mother was Salome, who may have been the older sister of Mary, Jesus' mother (Mt 27:56; Mk 15:40; Jn 19:25). John was a partner in the fishing business with his brother James, and with Peter and Andrew (Lk 5:10). All four men were probably among the early disciples of John the Baptist; perhaps John was the second member of the pair who first followed Jesus (Jn 1:35-37). If he were, he witnessed the wedding at Cana (2:2), and later quit the fishing trade to follow Jesus.

In the later ministry he participated in the general preaching of the Twelve (Mt 10:1-2). Both he and his brother were so aggressive that they were called "sons of thunder" (Mk 3:17), but Jesus' reproof disciplined their hasty tempers (Lk 9:49-55). John took the responsibility for Jesus' mother at the crucifixion (Jn 19:26-27), and was one of the first to realize the meaning of the resurrection (20:8). Both by his intimate knowledge of Christ and by his long spiritual experience he was well qualified to write an interpretative Gospel. *See* John.

The date of the fourth Gospel has been placed at various intervals from A.D. 40 to 140. Goodenough and Albright both argue, for different reasons, that John may have been written as early as A.D. 40 (Erwin R. Goodenough, "John a Primitive Gospel," JBL, LXIV [1945], 145-182; W. F. Albright, "Recent Discoveries in Palestine and the Gospel of John" in Davies and Daube, ed., *The Background of the New Testament and Its Eschatology*, pp. 153-171). A fair median date would be A.D. 85, at a time when the general gospel tradition had crystallized, and when doctrinal interpretation and controversy called for an authoritative presentation of the meaning of Jesus' career.

The place of production is unknown. Numerous hypotheses have been suggested: Palestine, Alexandria, and others. Irenaeus states (*Against Heresies* iii.1.1) that John published this Gospel during his residence at Ephesus in Asia. It was probably written for a church which had grown to maturity, and which was confronting the opposition of pagan philosophy. The explanation of Jewish phrases and customs (1:38; 2:6, 13; 4:9; 9:22; 18:28; etc.) indicates that it was intended for a Gentile audience. Quite probably the Gospel and the epistles were directed to the Gr. church of Asia.

The fourth Gospel is carefully organized, with definite literary and chronological divisions. Although the writer followed the sequence of Jesus' ministry by the successive Passovers, he paid less attention to biographical detail than to the interpretation of personality. His avowed aim was to create faith in Jesus as the Messiah, and to lead his readers into a new life as they believed. To this end his illustrative material and the progress of his argument are directed. The theme is eternal life, the life of God manifested among men, and it is developed in orderly fashion by presenting selected episodes from the life of Jesus that illustrate its meaning.

The prologue of the Gospel introduces the person of Christ as the Eternal Word, the expression of the Father, who became flesh in order to manifest eternal life to men. The plot of the Gospel is stated at the outset in the words, "The light shineth in the darkness; and the darkness apprehended [overcame, marg.] it not" (1:5, ASV). The manifestation of the life, like light, encountered the darkness, and a conflict immediately ensued. The history of this spiritual conflict is the scheme of interpretation for the life of Jesus. Two alternatives are presented: belief, which means receiving the light (1:11-12), and unbelief, which means rejecting the light (1:10-11). In the episodes that follow through the narrative, belief and unbelief, with their symptoms and consequences, are graphically illustrated.

The basis for belief consists of seven selected miracles or "signs" of Jesus: (1) turning the water into wine (2:1-11); (2) the healing of the nobleman's son (4:46-54); (3) the cure of the impotent man (5:1-9); (4) the feeding of the 5,000 (6:1-14); (5) the walking on the water (6:16-21); (6) the healing of the man born blind (9:1-41); (7) the raising of Lazarus (11:1-44). Each of these signs represents the sovereign power of Christ in some particular area of human need, and cumulatively they show His competence to cope with the forces that depress and degrade human life. Each miracle was a response to the faith of the principals involved, and at least five of them were performed to educate the disciples. John said specifically that these signs were selected for the purpose of promoting belief that Jesus is the Messiah (20:30-31).

The person of Christ is more important in this Gospel than His actions. His claims are stated in seven major uses of the phrase "I am." He said, "I am" the bread of life (6:35), the light of the world (8:12; 9:5), the door of the sheepfold (10:7), the good shepherd (10:11, 14), the resurrection and the life (11:25), the way, the truth, and the life (14:6), the true vine (15:1). Each of these equates Him figuratively with a common object which indicates one of His functions. As the bread, He is the sustenance of men; as the light, He is the guide of men; as the door, He provides access to security; as the shepherd, He assures protection; as the resurrection and the life, He achieves victory over death; as the way, the truth, and the life, He imparts certainty; as the true vine, He provides the vitality for fruitage.

More personal interviews are recounted in John than in any of the other Gospels. Some are short, like the conversation with the nobleman; some are long, like the trial before Pilate. Almost all of them illustrate Jesus' endeavor to evoke belief in Himself from the person with whom He was conversing.

The Johannine vocabulary is so distinctive that excerpts from this Gospel are easily identifiable. "Word," "life," "flesh," "hour," "sign," "lifted up," "works," "love" (two different Gr. verbs), "send," "beginning," "know" (two different Gr. verbs), "glory," "glorify," "abide," "perish," "Comforter," "the Father" contain concepts that are exclusively Johannine and that create a new representation of truth.

The Gospel emphasizes the deity of Jesus Christ, both in the claims of the Gospel itself, and in the confessions from the mouths of its characters. The prologue calls Him the Word of God (1:1-2); John the Baptist declared Him to be the Son of God (1:34); He descended from heaven (3:13); He was sent by God (3:34); the Samaritans called Him the Saviour of the world (4:42); He claimed equal honor with the Father (5:23), and professed to possess the same kind of life (5:26); the officers sent to arrest Him returned empty-handed, saying, "Never man [in contrast to God] so spake" (7:46, ASV). His statements, "Before Abraham was born, I am" (8:58, ASV) and "I and the Father are one" (10:30, ASV), were understood by His enemies to be claims to deity. At the same time, His humanity is stressed. He "became flesh" (1:14); He was tired (4:6), exasperated (4:48), harsh (8:44), sympathetic (11:33), agitated (12:27), affectionate (13:1), unselfish (18:8), loyal to family ties (19:26). John portrays the perfections of God manifested in the perfect humanity of Christ.

The characters are numerous and diverse. Among the disciples the writer characterizes by a few quick strokes of his pen the impulsive Peter, the quiet Andrew, Philip the materialist, Nathanael the student, Thomas the skeptic, Judas Iscariot the selfish, and "the beloved disciple" the confidant of Jesus. Among those whom Jesus encountered in His ministry were Nicodemus the learned teacher of Israel, the sharp but untaught Samaritan woman, the desperate nobleman of Cana, the supercilious and unbelieving brethren, the devoted Mary of Bethany, the indifferent Pilate, and the loyal Joseph of Arimathea. These and many others of lesser importance constitute the galaxy of men and women whose faith or unbelief reflected Jesus' influence upon them.

The language of John is simple, direct, and at times repetitious because of the constantly recurring technical terms which he uses. The structure of the Greek shows that the author had a good command of vocabulary and grammar, but that he possibly thought in Aramaic. The prologue has the form of Heb. poetry, somewhat resembling the Psalms in structure. The frequent use of "and" as a connective, the occasional use of Aramaic names such as Cephas (1:42), and the reiteration of propositions in slightly different wording (5:26-27) may indicate Semitic origin, though there is no proof that the Gospel was originally written in Aramaic.

The selection concerning the woman taken in adultery (7:53–8:11) is not found in the oldest MSS. Some include it, but indicate that it is not generally regarded as authentic, and one group of MSS locates it after Luke 21:38. Several Old Latin versions, three of the Old Syriac, the Coptic, Gothic, and the oldest Armenian version also omit it; nor is it contained in the recently discovered Bodmer Papyrus of the early 3rd cen. None of the earlier Church Fathers quote it, though it was recognized from the 5th cen. onward. A. T. Robertson said: "It is clear that it is not a genuine part of the Gospel of John" (*An Introduction to the Textual Criticism of the New Testament,* p. 210). It may, nevertheless, be a genuine episode in the life of Jesus, which was included in this text because it fitted the setting of the narrative. Its introduction shows that it was formerly part of a larger narrative, and it seems strange that this short anecdote should survive the loss of its context if it were not accepted as truth.

See John, Gospel of.

Each of the quartet of Gospels is needed for a rounded picture of Christ. Matthew depicts Him as the Messiah who fulfills OT prophecy and completes the redemptive purpose of God. Mark presents Him as the man of authority, who can overcome sickness, sin, and death, and who is Lord of all. Luke portrays Him as the perfect humanitarian, concerned with every aspect of human affairs. John declares that He is Deity, truly man and truly God. However much they may differ in approach and detail, they agree on the identity of the person of Christ, and they bear united testimony to His supernatural character.

Bibliography. F. F. Bruce, *Are the New Testament Documents Reliable?* London: Inter-Varsity, 1943. Austin Marsden Farrer, "On Dispensing with Q," *Studies in the Gospels,* ed. by D. E. Nineham, Oxford: Basil Blackwell, 1955, pp. 55–88. Edgar J. Goodspeed, *Matthew, Apostle and Evangelist,* Philadelphia: Winston, 1959. R. M. Grant and D. N. Friedman, *The Secret Sayings of Jesus, with an English Translation of the Gospel of Thomas* by William R. Schoedel, Garden City, N.Y.: Doubleday, 1960. Adolph Harnack, *The Sayings of Jesus,* trans. by J. R. Wilkinson, London: Williams and Norgate, 1908; contains Harnack's reconstruction of "Q." David Martin McIntyre, *Some Notes on the Gospels,* ed. by F. F. Bruce, London: Inter-Varsity, 1943. Edwin B. Redlich, *Form Criticism: Its Value and Limitations,* New York: Scribner's, 1939. A. T. Robertson, *Studies in Mark's Gospel,* New York: Macmillan, 1919; *Luke the Historian in the Light of Research,* New York: Scribner's, 1923. W. Graham Scroggie, *A Guide to the Gospels,* London: Pickering and Inglis, 1948. Vincent Henry Stanton, *The Gospels as Historical Documents,* Parts I, II, III, Cambridge: Univ. Press, 1923–1930. Burnett Hillman Streeter, *The Four Gospels,* 4th impression rev., London: Macmillan, 1936, pp. xxiv, 624. Theodor Zahn, *Introduction to the New Testament,* ed. by M. W. Jacobus, Grand Rapids: Kregel, 1953; see II, 307–617 and III, 1–354.

M. C. T.

GOSPELS, SYNOPTIC. As the term synoptic suggests (from *syn,* "together with," and *opsis,* "a sight, a view," thus "a seeing together"), Matthew, Mark, and Luke provide a presentation of Jesus and His ministry that has much in common. These features set them apart from the Gospel according to John, in which most of the material is peculiar to itself. In the Synoptics the public ministry of Jesus is prefaced by the preparatory work of John the Baptist and the baptism and temptation of our Lord. The ministry itself is pictured as occurring mainly in Galilee, consisting of Jesus' activities of teaching and healing, usually in terms of great throngs of people, as He moved here and there in the company of His disciples. The climax comes in the journey to Jerusalem and the events of the passion and resurrection.

The Synoptic Problem

When these three Gospels are considered apart from John and in relation to one another, certain agreements and differences come to light which in turn raise questions as to the origin of these writings. Did they emerge independently of one another, or did they make use of one another to some extent? If they made use of one another, this may help to explain the agreements, but by the same token the differences will be the more puzzling.

The measure of agreement between the Synoptics is actually quite surprising in view of the fact that Jesus was engaged for a period of approximately three years in an almost continuous ministry by word and deed. The amount of material available must have been tremendous. However hyperbolic Jn 21:25 may be in its affirmation that the world itself could not contain the books that should be written if all the deeds of Jesus were recorded, the clear intent is to give the impression that the reports in our Gospels are quite fragmentary. All we have is a selection.

The Synoptic problem, so-called, has to do with the mutual relations in the accounts. How can the similarities and also the differences in these three Gospels be explained? Before any kind of answer can be attempted, it is necessary to examine the phenomena of the Synoptics more closely.

The Data

First of all, as to the agreements among the Synoptics, one should consider *content* or subject matter. Westcott's analysis, though only approximate, is sufficiently precise for our purpose. Mark is found to have 93 percent of his material in common with Matthew and/or Luke; only 7 percent is peculiar to this Gospel. Matthew has 58 percent in common with other Synoptics and 42 percent that does not appear in the other two. Luke has 41 percent in common with the other two and 59 percent peculiar to this Gospel. To state the coincidences differently, roughly two-thirds of Mark is found in both Matthew and Luke, and almost one-third more in either Matthew or Luke. Mark has only thirty to forty verses that fail to appear in one or the other of the two remaining Synoptics.

As to *order* or sequence of the material, Mark's arrangement is usually shared both by Matthew and Luke. Where this is not the case, one or the other agrees with Mark. Matthew and Luke do not unite against Mark. When the Markan order is shared by the others, it is generally shared from the beginning to the end of a narrative.

With regard to *language and style,* one who is in position to study a Gr. synopsis where the accounts are placed side by side can better appreciate the situation, but an English harmony will provide considerable information. A good passage to test, one which contains the triple tradition (Matthew, Mark, Luke), is the account of the healing of the paralytic (Mt 9:1-8; Mk 2:1-12; Lk 5:17-26). While there is some variation, especially in the opening and closing statements, the main part of the narrative shows remarkable agreement in the vocabulary employed by all three writers. What is most striking of all is the preservation of a broken construction in the report of the actual performance of the miracle: "'But that you may know that the Son of man has authority on earth to forgive sins'—he says to the paralytic—'I say to you, rise, take up your pallet and go home'" (Mk 2:10-11, RSV, and parallels).

With respect to *differences,* it should be observed that as far as content is concerned, Mark has little to report of the *didachē* or teaching of Jesus, whereas Matthew and Luke contain many parables and considerable discourse material that is not parabolic. Lk 9:51–18:14 has much that appears only in this Gospel. Various details of the crucifixion and resurrection appearances turn up in a single record only. Matthew's account of the Sermon on the Mount is much more extensive than Luke's. The order of events in the temptation of Jesus varies between Matthew and Luke. Jesus' visit to the synagogue at Nazareth is put earlier in the Lucan narrative than in the other two. Many more examples could be given, including the use of synonymous terms rather than identical words in parallel accounts.

Explanation

While various attempts have been made to explain the relationship between them, no solution for the phenomena of the Synoptic Gospels has yet won universal acceptance.

1. *Oral tradition.* B. F. Westcott and Arthur Wright have suggested that oral tradition was the decisive influence, since several decades passed before our Gospels began to be written. During that time presumably the core of the material became somewhat fixed from telling and retelling. This could account for the agreements in the Synoptics, which were written to preserve this oral tradition. The differences could then be attributed to the special interests of the individual writers as well as to the particular needs of the people for whom they wrote.

This view, however, is not without difficulties. It is hard to see how the tradition could have been sufficiently safeguarded from alteration as it spread into the widely separated regions from which the written Gospels arose. Further, it is hard to understand how Mark, depending on this common tradition along with Matthew and Luke, could have utilized so little of our Lord's teaching. Furthermore, one would expect greater uniformity in the reports of what Jesus said in instituting the supper of His new covenant. It should be granted, however, that oral tradition must have played an important role, if not an exclusive one, in the preservation of the Gospel material, and even in the choice of written materials by each writer.

2. *Direct literary dependence.* The many agreements in content, in sequence, and in construction (language and style) are best explained in terms of some sort of literary dependence (recall especially Mk 2:10-11 and parallels). There can be little doubt that Mark is the source for the material in Matthew and Luke that agrees with it. Here the habitual following of the Markan order by the other evangelists is especially impressive. The conclusion of Markan priority is buttressed by the fact that Matthew and Luke contain alterations of Markan material at times in the interest of grammatical smoothness. In other words, Mark's record appears to be the more primitive. It is worth noting, too, that where the three Gospels have the same material, Mark's narratives are usually longer and more graphic. Matthew and Luke may have contracted Mark in such cases in order to allow room for material not derived from Mark. Ancient authors had to exercise care lest their book, which was in the form of a scroll, would become too unwieldy for convenient use.

There were people such as Augustine in the early centuries of the church who thought that Mark abbreviated Matthew. If this were the case, it is difficult to conceive how Mark could have omitted so much of the teaching of Jesus, such as that which is contained in the Sermon on the Mount. So this opinion has not been able to maintain itself.

3. *Two-document hypothesis.* It is clear, however, that Matthew and Luke could not have depended on Mark for everything, since they contain much discourse material that is absent from Mark. There is a strong possibility that they depended on a source, whether oral or written, that specialized in the sayings of Jesus. Modern scholars often refer to such a source by the designation "Q" derived from the first letter of the German word for source (*Quelle*). It is granted that the objective existence of such a source cannot be demonstrated historically, but it is felt that the data of Matthew and Luke

point to the necessity for such a source. Possible support for this theory may be found in the statement of Papias, quoted by Eusebius, that "Matthew collected the oracles (*logia*) in the Hebrew language, and each interpreted them as best he could." There is no clear evidence, however, that Matthew drew on Luke or vice versa. They seem to have written independently of each other.

Conclusion

If Mark and Q were sources for Matthew and Luke, most of the material in the latter two Gospels is accounted for, but not all. Judging from their nativity and passion narratives, as well as some other features, they each must have had access to information that was not a part of the central tradition of the early church. Some of it may have been gained by personal investigation. From Luke's prologue (1:1–4) it is evident that he had available to him the oral testimony of eye-witnesses plus the accounts of those who had written before he undertook his Gospel. The prologue informs us that he did some investigating of his own. So the possible sources for Gospel materials must have been many and varied. Apparently there was no prejudice against the use of sources, and this is quite natural, since much of the historical material in the OT was written up with the aid of earlier records (cf. Kings, Chronicles).

It would be a mistake, however, to look on the human authors of the Gospels as mere editors. Each one had a molding influence, under God, on the materials used, so that it is possible to detect a definite individuality impressed on each Gospel.

The search for the human factors that entered into the composition of the Gospels can go only so far. Beyond the sphere of this kind of investigation lies the mysterious and powerful inspiration or influence of the Holy Spirit upon the writers, leading them to the selection and use of their material. This is what gives their work authority for the church.

See Gospels, The Four.

E. F. Har.

Bibliography. Everett F. Harrison, *Introduction to the New Testament,* Grand Rapids: Eerdmans, 1964, pp. 136–145. Ned B. Stonehouse, *Origins of the Synoptic Gospels,* Grand Rapids: Eerdmans, 1963. B. H. Streeter, *The Four Gospels,* London: Macmillan, 1930. Merrill C. Tenney, *The Genius of the Gospels,* Grand Rapids: Eerdmans, 1951.

GOURD. *See* Plants.

GOUT. *See* Diseases.

GOVERNMENT OF GOD. *See* Theocracy; Israel; Israel, Kingdom of; King.

GOVERNMENT OF ISRAEL. *See* Israel; Israel, Kingdom of.

GOVERNOR. The English term is used broadly by the KJV in the OT for a variety of specialized Heb. words which designate some type of delegated official (e.g., Gen 42:6; 45:26; Jud 5:9; II Chr 1:2; 28:7; Jer 20:1; Zech 9:7). Heb. *peḥâ* (Akkadian *paḫatu*) was a general term that came to be used for governor during the Assyrian through the Persian periods (I Kgs 10:15; Ezr 5:3; 8:36; Neh 2:7; 5:15; Est 3:12). The *peḥâ* often exercised control by military power and is thus called a "captain" (e.g., II Kgs 18:24; Jer 51:23, 28, 57). This word has been found on several stamped jar handles from the post-Exilic level of Ramat Raḫel (IEJ, IX, 273 f.), proving that it was used as the title of the governor of the province of Judah during the Persian administration (Neh 5:14; 12:26; Hag 1:1; Mal 1:8). The Tirshatha (*q.v.*) was the honorific title for the governor of a province (Ezr 2:63; Neh 7:65; etc.).

In the NT, "governor" occurs most frequently for *hēgemōn,* "one who goes before," which denotes the emperor-appointed administrators in the provinces (Mt 10:18; I Pet 2:14) and especially the procurators in Judea (e.g., Pilate, Mt 27:2; cf. Acts 23:24; 26:30). *See* Pilate.

"Governor" is also used in II Cor 11:32 for the Gr. *ethnarchēs* (NASB, "ethnarch") of Damascus; in Gal 4:2 rendering *oikonomos* (RSV, "trustee"); in Jn 2:8–9 for *architriklinos* (RSV, "steward of the feast"); and in Jas 3:4 for the participial form, *euthynontos* (RSV, "pilot"). *See* Deputy; Ethnarch; Steward.

F. G. C. and J. R.

GOZAN (gō'zăn). A region along the Habor River near the Euphrates where the Israelites deported from Samaria were settled (II Kgs 17:6; 18:11). It is frequently mentioned in Assyrian records as Guzani. Assyria had already conquered it in 808 B.C. (cf. II Kgs 19:12). Oppenheim identified it with Tel Halaf on that river. Excavations have revealed documents of the 7th cen. B.C. with such Israelite names as Hoshea and Ishmael.

See Habor.

GRACE. The concept of grace is many-sided and subject to development in the Scriptures. In the OT *ḥēn,* "favor," is the unmerited favor of a superior to an inferior. In the case of God and man, *ḥēn* is demonstrated usually in temporal though occasionally in spiritual blessings, and in deliverance in both physical and spiritual senses (Jer 31:2; Ex 33:19). *Ḥesed,* "loving-kindness," is the firm loving-kindness expressed between related people and particularly in the covenants into which God entered with His people and which His *ḥesed* firmly guaranteed (II Sam 7:15; Ex 20:6).

In Gr. literature *charis* had the following meanings: (1) It was used of that which causes attractiveness, such as grace of appearance or speech. (2) It was used of a favorable regard felt toward a person. (3) It was used of a favor. (4) It was used to mean gratitude. (5) It was used adverbially in phrases such as "for the sake of a thing," *charin tinos*.

But it was not until the coming of Christ that grace took on its fullest meaning. His self-sacrifice is grace itself (II Cor 8:9). This grace is absolutely free (Rom 6:14; 5:15-18; Eph 1:7; 2:8-9). When it is received by the believer, it governs his spiritual life by compounding favor upon favor. It equips, strengthens, and controls all phases of his life (II Cor 8:6-7; Col 4:6; II Thess 2:16; II Tim 2:1). Consequently, the Christian gives thanks (*charis*) to God for the riches of grace in His unspeakable gift (II Cor 9:15).

The apostle Paul was the principal human instrument to convey the full meaning of grace in Christ. The NT offers grace to all, in contrast to the OT which generally restricted the offer of grace to God's elect people Israel. Grace in its fullest definition is God's unmerited favor in the gift of His Son, who offers salvation to all and who gives to those who receive Him as their personal Saviour added grace for this life and hope for the future.

Sovereign grace is not an arbitrary display of God's grace. In order to receive it man must believe. In order to enjoy it the believer must be obedient. Grace provides acceptance (Rom 3:24), enablement (Col 1:29), a new position (I Pet 2:5, 9), and an inheritance (Eph 1:3, 14). At least three motives are indicated in the NT as to why God acts in grace, especially in salvation. He does it to express His love (Eph 2:4; Jn 3:16), to be able to display His grace in the ages to come (Eph 2:7), and that redeemed man will produce good works (Eph 2:10). Sovereign grace is always purposeful, for the life under grace is a life of good works.

Bibliography. Leo G. Cox, "Prevenient Grace—a Wesleyan View," JETS, XII (1969), 143-150. Charles C. Ryrie, *The Grace of God*, Chicago: Moody Press, 1970.

C. C. R.

GRACE AT MEALS. Among the Jews, it was apparently customary at meals to give thanks over the bread, representing all the food, and over the wine, representing all the drink. This, says Edersheim, was because Psalm 24:1 states, "The earth is the Lord's, and the fulness thereof." Christians carried this custom over into their practice. It is suggested in the NT. Jesus gave thanks before distributing food to the 5,000 (Mt 14:19) and the 4,000 (Mt 15:36), before partaking of the Lord's Supper (Lk 22:19), and before eating with the two disciples at Emmaus (Lk 24:30). Cf. Acts 27:33-35; Rom 14:6; I Cor 10:30; I Tim 4:3-5.

GRAFF, GRAFT. This is a horticultural process by which the branches from a cultivated tree may be inserted and grafting take place. In Rom 11:17 ff. the apostle Paul employs this practice in reverse: the wild branches, the Gentiles, are pictured as grafted in to the good stock of the parent tree, the Israelites. This deliberate inversion heightens the picturesque figure of speech conveying the eternal truth of the rejection of national Israel and composition of true Israel—all believers. However, Paul warns that the new branch could be cut away if it proved faithless.

GRAIN. *See* Plants.

GRANARY. *See* Storehouse.

GRAPES. *See* Plants.

GRASS. *See* Plants.

GRASSHOPPER. *See* Animals: Locust, III.29.

GRATE. A bronze grating (RSV) or lattice for the altar of burnt offering before the tabernacle (Ex 27:4; 35:16; 38:4-5, 30; 39:39). The grating probably surrounded the lower half of the altar as a skirt, fastened to the ledge halfway up the altar and extending down to the ground, perhaps to prevent the priests from stepping in the sacrificial blood poured out at the base of the altar (Lev 4:7). Each corner of the grating had a bronze ring; through these went two bronze-covered poles to carry the entire altar (D. W. Gooding, "Tabernacle," NBD, p. 1233; fig. 176). *See* Altar; Tabernacle.

Herodian family tomb, Jerusalem (illustrates a "rolling stone" that would seal a tomb). HFV

Tombs carved from the mountainside at Petra. MIS

GRAVE. The words translated "grave" in KJV are the Heb. words *'î*, "ruin" (once); *qeber* and *q^ebûrâ*, "tomb" (about 40 times); *sh^e'ôl* (31 times); *shaḥat*, "destruction" (once); and the Gr. words *hadēs* (once); *mnēma* (once) and *mnēmion*, "tomb" (eight times). These words are also translated in other ways. *Qeber* and *q^ebûrâ* many times are rendered "sepulcher" or "burying place" as are *mnēma* and *mnēmion*. The translation "tomb" also is used. Heb. *sh^e'ôl* is also translated "hell" (31 times) and "pit" (three times) in the KJV. The RSV usually transliterates both *sh^e'ôl* and *hadēs*.

The burial customs of the Israelites are fairly clear from archaeology and biblical references. The OT speaks of burials both in house gardens (II Kgs 21:18) and in tomb complexes (Gen 23:20; I Kgs 14:31). Graves of the poor often were undoubtedly only shallow trenches, as in the large cemetery at Qumran. In other cases a cairn of stones was erected over the burial, as for Achan (Josh 7:26), enemy kings (Josh 8:29; 10:27), and Absalom (II Sam 18:17). Doubtless burial customs varied somewhat through the centuries.

The Hebrews apparently did not use coffins—none are found in native tombs—but buried their dead on a bier or low couch (II Sam 3:31; II Chr 16:14; Ezk 32:25; Lk 7:14), following a Canaanite custom as found in Middle Bronze Age tombs at Jericho.

Perhaps the most extensive burial chamber of Heb. times was found by Dr. Joseph P. Free at Dothan (BASOR, Dec. 1960, pp. 10–13; there is later unpublished material). Many bodies were found in the one tomb. The skeletons of those buried earlier were pushed to the sides to make room for the most recent burial. A notable feature was the many lamps found. Was the tomb left with a lamp burning or were the lamps used in funerary rites? Miss K. Kenyon found niches for lamps cut in the walls of tombs of an earlier date at Jericho (Kathleen Kenyon, *Archaeology in the Holy Land*, p. 139). Notice the mention of a burning at a burial in II Chr 16:14; 21:19. This was probably not a cremation, which was exceptional among the Hebrews.

In NT times tomb complexes were dug, as witnessed by the references to the tomb of Joseph of Arimathea. The Herodian family tomb in Jerusalem, Israel, is an undoubted example. The rolling stone that closed the low doorway is still intact. The so-called tombs of the Sanhedrin NW of modern Jerusalem, with their many chambers and niches for bodies, also may be dated prior to A.D. 70.

The poor were doubtless buried more simply.

The tomb of Clytemnestra at Mycenae, Greece, one of the so-called "beehive tombs."
Mimosa

From NT times come many ossuaries which perhaps reflect poorer burials. These are small stone boxes containing the bones of the dead which were collected after decomposition. They did not contain ashes; the Roman custom of cremation was apparently rejected. Some of these ossuaries are famous. NT names such as Miriam and Bar Jonah have been noted, but it is difficult to tell if these are Christian burials or Jewish (cf. G. E. Wright, *Biblical Archaeology*, p. 242). The famous Uzziah inscription refers to such a regathering of the bones of King Uzziah (*q.v.*).

The word *qeber* usually means simply "sepulcher." Occasionally it has a figurative use, e.g., Ps 5:9. In Isa 14:19 and Ezk 32:22, 25-26 the word is used in the dramatic scene of the kings of the earth who lie in their graves but stir themselves up to meet the kings of Babylon and Egypt as they also come to the grave. In these contexts *sheʾôl* is also used.

The word *sheʾôl* brings many problems. It is now usually defined as the place of departed spirits. This does not entirely fit the 31 places translated "grave" in KJV. Neither does it do justice to the statements that *sheʾôl* is a place of darkness, silence, and forgetfulness (Job 17:13; Ps 31:17; 88:3, 12). Some have concluded from such verses that the soul sleeps in *sheʾôl*. However, the problem is solved if these verses refer to the sleep of the body in the grave (*see* Dead). A. Heidel argues extensively that *sheʾôl* sometimes refers to the realm of the dead, sometimes to the grave (A. Heidel, *The Gilgamesh Epic and OT Parallels*, pp. 173 ff.). It may be argued that *sheʾôl* is a poetic word for "grave." It is used in poetic parallelism with *māwet*, "death," and *qeber*, "sepulcher" (R. L. Harris, "The Meaning of the Word Sheol," BETS, IV [1961], 129-135).

Of details of actual burial customs of the Hebrews, there is little evidence. Ananias and Sapphira were buried very promptly, as is still done among the Jews. G. E. Wright some time ago expressed doubt that food was left with the dead, though vessels clearly were (BA, VIII [1945], 17). Miss Kenyon found food in Jericho tombs, but this was of pre-Israelite date (*op. cit.*, p. 191). The Bible shows no cult of the dead in orthodox Heb. religion.

See Burial; Dead, The; Embalm; Funeral; Mourning; Sheol; Tomb.

R. L. H.

The false door from the Tomb of Nakht at Amarna, Egypt. Gaddis

GRAVE CLOTHES. The expression translates Gr. *keiriai* in Jn 11:44, the bandages or strips of cloth wrapped around a corpse to bind the arms and legs in a Jewish burial. After the body was washed (Acts 9:37)—but not further embalmed—it was generally wrapped first in a "clean linen shroud" (Mt 27:59, RSV).

GRAVEN IMAGE. An image (Heb. *pesel*) carved or sculpted from stone, wood, or metal, mentioned in the OT along with the molten image cast in a mold (e.g., Deut 27:15; Jud 17:3-4; II Chr 34:3). Since the Canaanites used these as idols—as archaeological discoveries in Palestine and Syria have verified—they were forbidden to the Israelites (Ex 20:4; Lev 26:1; etc.). *See* Idol.

GRAVER, GRAVING. *See* Occupations: Carving. Engraver.

GRAY, GREY. *See* Colors; Hair.

GREAT COMMISSION. *See* Commission, Great.

GREAT OWL. *See* Animals, III.37.

GREAT SEA. The large body of water known to us as the Mediterranean Sea (Num 34:6; Josh 1:4; 9:1; 15:12, 47; Ezk 47:10; etc.). It is also called the "uttermost sea" or the "hinder sea," i.e., the western sea (Deut 11:24; 34:2; Joel 2:20; Zech 14:8), the "sea of the Philistines" (Ex 23:31), the "sea of Joppa" (Ezr 3:7), or simply "the sea" (Num 13:29; Ezk 26:5, 16-18; 27:3; etc.; Jon 1:4; etc.; Acts 10:6, 32; 27:30; etc.). About 2,300 miles long, it was the chief sea known to the Israelites. According to some commentators, the expression may also be used figuratively in Dan 7:26 of the ocean or the masses of humanity. *See* Sea.

Violent winds from the NE made shipping unsafe during the winter months from October through February or March (Acts 27:14–28:11). Sandbars and rocky reefs were constant hazards, because the captains hesitated to leave the sight of land. Modern diving expeditions have found the wrecks of many an ancient ship with its cargo of wine jars or copper ingots or marble columns intended for the cities of Greece and Rome.

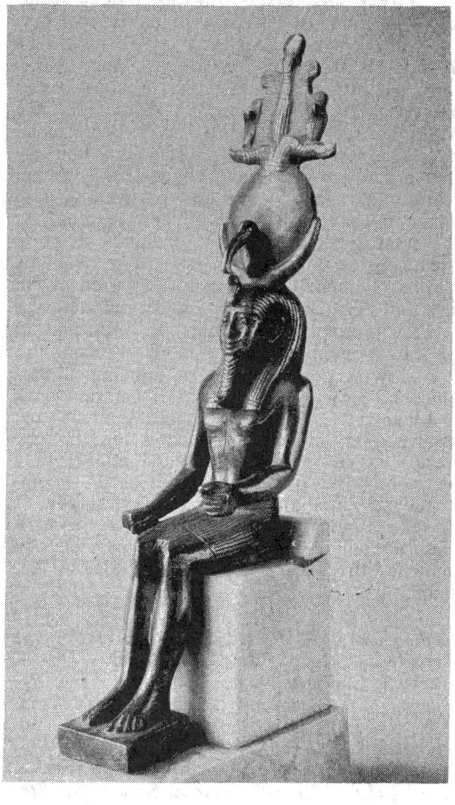

The Egyptian god Osiris cast in bronze. LM

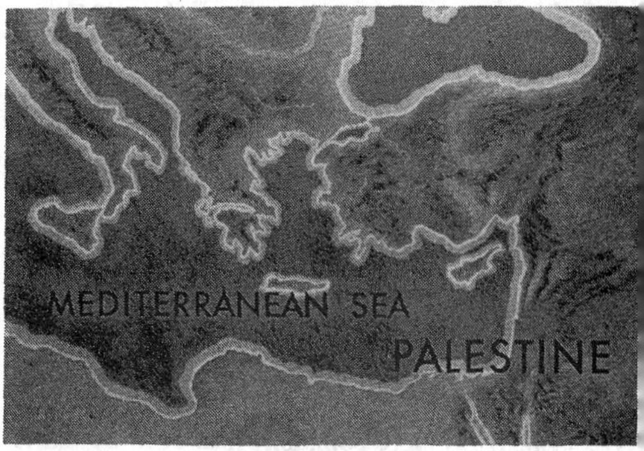

The "Great Sea." MIS

From 3000 B.C. onward the Egyptians carried cedar timber in their ships hugging the Mediterranean coast from Byblos (*see* Gebal) in Lebanon to the Nile delta. Minoan traders from Crete and later the Mycenaean Greeks dominated the Mediterranean during the 2nd mil. B.C. Throughout the 1st mil. B.C. the Phoenicians from Tyre and Sidon plied its waters and colonized its shores. With no natural harbors, the Hebrews never became a seafaring people; consequently they depended on Phoenician ships and sailors for maritime commerce and travel. Solomon employed the skills of Hiram's mariners (I Kgs 9:26-28; 10:11, 22). Jonah took passage on a Phoenician ship sailing from Joppa to Tarshish in Spain.

By NT times the Mediterranean had become virtually a Roman lake (*mare nostrum*) to connect Rome with many parts of her vast empire and to transport grain and other products to the capital from the provinces. A harbor was built at Acco in the Hellenistic period and renamed Ptolemais (Acts 21:7), and Herod the Great had constructed artificial harbor installations at Caesarea (*q.v.*). Thus Palestine came into direct communication with the western world, and since then has been at the crossroads of three continents.

J. R.

GREAVES. *See* Armor.

GRECIANS (grē'shănz)

1. Used in the OT once (Joel 3:6, KJV) for "the sons of Javanim," Javan being the Heb. word for Ionia or Greece.

The contacts of Jews with Greeks in OT times were limited but became considerable in the period between the Testaments. By the beginning of the Christian era the three centers of Jewish population outside of Palestine were Babylonia, Syria, and Egypt, the latter two areas being also centers of Hellenism. Large numbers of Jews were also located in Asia Minor and Rome. The contact of Jews with Gr. culture found creative literary expression at Alexandria, where the translation of the OT into Gr. was begun in the 3rd cen. B.C. and where Philo in the 1st Christian cen. expounded the OT in terms of Gr. philosophy. Even Palestinian Jews came under the Hellenizing influence.

2. In the NT "Grecians" (Gr. *Hellēnistai*) are mentioned in Acts 6:1; 9:29; and in some MSS at 11:20, and *Hellēnes* in the rest of Acts (14:1; 16:1, 3; 17:4, 12; etc.). This distinction is maintained by the translation of *Hellēnistai* as "Grecians" and *Hellēnes* as "Greeks."

"Grecians" (Gr. *Hellēnistai*) is a relatively rare word. It has not been found in Gr. or in Hellenistic Jewish literature. The verb form *hellēnizē* is more common. It is used by Christian writers to mean "to speak Greek," "to speak good Greek" (the classical meanings), or "to practice paganism," "to be pagan." Etymologically the verb has no special reference to language, and on the analogy of similar word formations should mean one who practices Gr. ways (whether a Gr. or a foreigner). It is this meaning which lies behind the usage for "pagan."

The following identifications of the "Grecians" in Acts (6:1; 9:29; 11:20) have been proposed.

a. The usual explanation is that they were Gr.-speaking Jews who were contrasted with the Aram.-speaking Palestinian Jews (*Ioudaioi*). This interpretation goes back to Chrysostom's homilies on Acts. There is difficulty in the contrast with "Hebrews" in Acts 6:1. "Hebrews" is not commonly used in a linguistic sense, and Paul, a Gr.-speaking Jew, called himself a Hebrew (Phil 3:5; II Cor 11:22).

b. A variation on the above takes "Grecians" and "Hebrews" in Acts 6:1 as meaning respectively, Jews who spoke *only* Greek, and Jews who *also* knew a Semitic language, without denying that both words in other contexts had wider connotations. This distinction between the two groups may have been reflected in the language used in their worship services and in the form of the Scriptures they read publicly. Such differences could account for the possibility of tensions, and at the same time avoid the problem that many Palestinian Jews would have spoken Gr. by preference so that a language distinction would not have been absolute between Palestinian and Diaspora Jews.

c. "Grecians" were Gr.-speaking Jews of the Diaspora living in Palestine, as opposed to the *Hellēnes* of the fourth Gospel who were Gr.-speaking Jews living beyond Palestine. It seems natural to connect the seven deacons whose names are all Gr., with the "Grecians" of Acts 6:1, and then to see a connection with the synagogues of the residents of Cyrene, Alexandria, Cilicia, and Asia (Acts 6:9) with whom Stephen was in dispute (see Acts 21:8, 16 for an association of Philip with Cypriot Jews). The same circle comes to mind as the antagonists of Saul, a native of Cilicia. Converts native to these regions opened up the Gentile mission at Antioch (Acts 11:19 f.; cf. 13:1).

d. The most radical interpretation is that "Grecians" are no different from "Greeks" (Gentiles). This view destroys the whole structure of Acts.

e. That Jewish proselytes are meant is unlikely, for it is more natural to distinguish Nicolas (Acts 6:5) as the only proselyte in the group than to consider all seven as proselytes and distinguish him only as from Antioch. His presence shows that those of pure Gr. culture were included among the "Grecians."

f. It has been argued that the "Grecians" were a religious party in Judaism opposed to the temple and its sacrificial cultus who were so named by their opponents. "Grecians" does appear only in the first half of Acts, which reflects Palestinian tradition.

g. The word may have its literal meaning of "act like a Greek," and so may describe both Jews (native or Diaspora) who did not conform to Palestinian customs and traditions (but were doctrinally orthodox) as well as Gentile pagans (at Antioch).

h. The word may be left as a general word for "Greek speakers," with the context deciding what kind—Jewish Christians in Acts 6:1, Jews of the synagogues in Acts 9:29, Gentiles in Acts 11:20.

In support of this last and broadest view, namely, "Greek speakers," in Acts 11:20 the MS evidence may slightly favor "Grecians" over the variant "Greeks." It seems unlikely that a scribe would have changed a common word into a rarer word and particularly one which introduces a more difficult reading. At the same time, the context demands that the preaching be done to non-Jews. The demands can be reconciled in "Grecian" as used in the sense of "Greek speakers," these imitating the Greeks in language, customs, or both, and so refer to the general population of Antioch.

Following the same line of thinking, if Stephen and his associates in Acts 6 can be identified with the Grecian party, then the first thrust of missionary activity in the early church came from this group and, as argued above, they were composed of those who spoke Gr. whether Jewish Christians, Jews of the synagogue, or Greeks. Philip began the mission to Samaria, and unnamed Jews from the Dispersion launched the work among the Gentiles at Antioch.

Bibliography. F. F. Bruce, *The Acts of the Apostles*, Grand Rapids: Eerdmans, 1952. Henry J. Cadbury, "The Hellenists," *The Beginnings of Christianity*, London: Macmillan, Vol. V, 1933. CornPBE, "Hellenism," pp. 379–388. C. F. D. Moule, "Once More, Who Were the Hellenists?" *Expository Times*, LXX (Jan., 1959), 100–102. Marcel Simon, *St. Stephen and the Hellenists in the Primitive Church*, New York: Longmans, Green, 1958. B. B. Warfield, "The Readings *Hellenas* and

Hellenistas, Acts xi.20," JBL, III (Dec., 1883), 113–127. Hans Windisch, "*Hellēn,* etc.," TDNT, II, 504–516.

E. F. and R. A. K.

GREECE. The reputation of Greece as a classical land has long been established. Its distinction as a Bible land is not so well fixed. Yet Greece provides the geographical stage for much of the NT drama. Here Paul preached at the prayer meeting site at Philippi and first brought the gospel to Europe, later becoming involved in the midnight scene at the local jail. Here he made his dramatic bid for acceptance before the Areopagus court on Mars Hill in Athens. Here he ministered at Corinth for 18 months. Numerous other Gr. towns figure in the NT account.

While Greece represents a national entity to the contemporary observer, it was never a whole sovereign state until winning its full independence from Turkey in 1829, and did not reach its present territorial limits until 1947. In ancient times Hellas (Greece) was that area inhabited by Gr. peoples, including the Gr. peninsula, islands of the Aegean and for many centuries the Asia Minor coast. Macedonia was not really a part of the Gr. world until the 4th cen. B.C., when Philip II and his son Alexander the Great made a conscious effort to bring Gr. culture to their kingdom. In most ancient times Greece was a collection of kingdoms and city-states; Alexander never really united it. Under the Romans it became two provinces, Macedonia and Achaia. With the decline of Rome in the W, Greece remained within the Byzantine Empire and with the fall of Byzantium passed on into the Ottoman Empire, of which it was a part until the last century.

Geography. If one includes in Greece the Gr. peninsula stretching S from Thessaly and Epirus and the Aegean islands, which is what Greece was in most of classical times, he is dealing with an area of about 30,000 square miles. This approximates the state of Maine. Like Maine, Greece is very mountainous; in fact, mountains cover about 70 percent of the land surface. No other country of the Mediterranean area presents a more tumbled surface than Greece. Although the placement of mountains in Greece is chaotic, there is a degree of symmetry. The Magnesian range extends S from Olympus in E Greece; the Pindus range lies between Thessaly and Epirus in central Greece; and the Epirus range stretches along the W coast. These are crossed by other ridges, dividing the country into a vast checkerboard of tiny valleys, few of which are more than a dozen miles long and more than half as wide. With communications so hampered, a provincialism developed in Greece such as has probably existed in no other historically important area of the world.

The coast of Greece is so deeply indented that she has the longest coastline in proportion to enclosed area of all important historical regions. The many indentations afforded numerous harbors. So the Greeks, unable to wrest a living from their rocky farms, became a seafaring people. It is easy, however, to overemphasize the place of the sea in Gr. economic life. The mountains sometimes cut off access to the sea and often were too barren to provide good ship timber. And during much of the year the sea was too stormy for sailing. Moreover, overseas trade was not vital in the early days when most of the communities of Greece were self-sufficient. It is important to observe that the best ports of Greece and many of her valleys lay on the E coast. Therefore her E areas received civilizing influences from the Orient first.

The Lion Gate at Mycenae. HFV

History. The earliest high development of civilization in the Gr. world occurred not on the mainland but on the island of Crete. There Minoan civilization began *c.* 3000 B.C. A combination of oriental and native elements, Minoan culture was palace-centered and reached its greatest prosperity 1600–1400 B.C. Often called "educators of Hellas," the Minoans left an indelible stamp on mainland developments. There, sometime after *c.* 2000 B.C., a wave of Indo-European peoples moved in from the N and established themselves. Ultimately they gained sufficient power to bring the Minoans of Crete under their control (*c.* 1500 B.C.). The greatest days of these Mycenaen peoples lasted 1400–1200 B.C. During this time they ranged far and wide over the Mediterranean, marketing their wares and in the latter part of the period tangled with Troy.

About 1200 B.C. another wave of Indo-European peoples moved in from the N and destroyed the Mycenaean kingdoms. The years *c.* 1100–800 are often known as the Greek Middle Age; at that time the old order

GREECE
MACEDONIA
PELLA
VARDAR R.
STRYMON R.
NESTRUS R.
EGNATIAN WAY
AMPHIPOLIS
NEAPOLIS
PHILIPPI
THESSALONICA
APOLLONIA
CHALCIDICE
THASOS
SAMOTHRACE
IMBROS
TROAS
HALIACMON R.
PYDNA
MT. OLYMPUS
BEROEA
EPIRUS
THESSALY
PHARSALUS
THERMOPYLAE
EUBOEA
AETOLIA
PHOCIS
CHAERONEA
DELPHI
BOEOTIA
THEBES
PLATAEA
MARATHON
ACHAEA
ATTICA
ELEUSIS
MEGARA
CORINTH
ATHENS
ELIS
MYCENAE
TIRYNS
OLYMPIA
CYCLADES
MESSENIA
SPARTA
LACONIA
0
50
100
SCALE OF MILES
CRETE
KNOSSOS

was dying out and a new order of small city-states was rising. Homer wrote his great epics around 850 B.C. The period 800–500 is frequently dubbed the Formative Age because at this time the typical political, economic, religious, and social institutions of the city-states of the Classical Age gradually appeared on the scene. At this time too Gr. peoples migrated all over the Mediterranean area—to Italy, France, Spain, Egypt, and elsewhere. To this deposit of Gr. peoples and culture Alexander and his successors would add. And Romans would imbibe a very large portion of the Gr. cultural heritage. As a result Greek was the language of communication of the entire Mediterranean world by the time of Christ, facilitating the spread of a gospel preached and written in Gr. And by that time the OT had been translated into Gr. (the Septuagint [LXX]) and was being studied in the some 150 synagogues of the Roman world, thus making preparation for the coming of the gospel.

In 512 B.C. Greece faced a new crisis when the Persians crossed the Hellespont and invaded Thrace. During subsequent years dramatic battles were fought at such places as Marathon, Thermopylae, Salamis, and Plataea, with the result that the Persians broke off attempts to subjugate the Greeks. Now the Greeks were free to experiment with their unique institutions in the small city-states of the Classical Age. Such experimentation would have been impossible if the superpower to the E had elected to make further efforts to bring the Hellenes to heel.

During the 5th cen. Athens converted the league formed to turn back the Persians into an Athenian Empire. And she used the resources of empire to make possible her golden age (461–431 B.C.). Under the leadership of Pericles she developed her democracy, empire, drama, architectural achievements of the acropolis, and other aspects of culture. Meanwhile Sparta put together a Peloponnesian league to offset the rising power of Athens. Other city-states arose to be sure, but they could not operate without reference to one or the other of the two chief powers of Hellas.

Perhaps it was inevitable that Athens and Sparta would ultimately go to war. At any rate they did; and the conflict dragged on from 431 to 404 B.C., ending in the destruction of the Athenian Empire. After a few decades of Spartan dominance in Greece, Thebes seized the hegemony temporarily. Meanwhile Macedonian power was building in the N and after 337 B.C. dominated the peninsula. Philip II did most to build the military capability of Macedon and passed on to his son Alexander an excellent army with which to launch the Panhellenic war of revenge against Persia. This had been brewing for some time because of Persian interference in Gr. affairs. For instance, Persians had provided Spartans with naval help necessary to defeat the Athenians during the Peloponnesian war. Parenthetically it should be

The Temple of Hephaestus (Vulcan) overlooking the Agora at Athens. HFV

noted that Philip employed Aristotle as tutor for the young Alexander, and Plato was partially contemporary with Aristotle.

After the assassination of his father, Alexander was left to fight the Persians. He launched the attack in 334 B.C. and within about three years conquered most of the territory of the colossus of the E. Before he could reorganize the empire, he fell victim to a fever in Babylon in 323 B.C. Sparring for power among leading members of Alexander's entourage finally led to a division of the empire into Syrian, Egyptian, and Macedonian kingdoms. Confusion reigned in Macedon after the death of Alexander, as one general after another tried to secure the throne. Finally Antigonus Gonatas, grandson of the great Antigonus of Alexander's staff, secured control over Macedon and established his dynasty there.

Although Macedon was dominant in Greece during the 3rd cen., it did not control the entire country. In central Greece Aetolian and Achaean leagues organized and in the W the kingdom of Epirus arose. King Pyrrhus of Epirus led an army to Italy to help Greeks of the S part of the peninsula take a stand against Roman efforts to unify Italy. He returned to Greece in 275 B.C. to face Macedon. After Pyrrhus was killed in battle in 272, his kingdom rapidly declined. At the end of the 3rd cen. Macedon allied with Hannibal during the second Punic war between Carthage and Rome. Naturally this act brought undying determination on the part of Rome to subjugate this new enemy in Greece.

Roman warfare in Greece lasted a half century and ended with Roman annexation of Greece and creation of the provinces of Macedonia (148 B.C.) and Achaia (146 B.C.). Now Greece was to suffer new woes, for Roman civil wars of the 1st cen. B.C. brought terrible destruction to Gr. soil. Both the decisive battles between Pompey and Julius Caesar, and Antony and Augustus Caesar were fought in Greece, as was the battle of Brutus and Cassius against Augustus at Philippi. More settled conditions under the empire after Augustus brought peace and political reorganization restored a degree of

The Temple of Apollo and Acropolis at Corinth, Mimosa

prosperity to Greece. By the time the apostle Paul came through during the middle of the 1st cen. A.D., many of the scars of war had healed. But Greece was not destined to recover the greatness of earlier centuries.

Greece as a Bible land. The claim of Greece to be a Bible land is mostly connected with Paul's second and third missionary journeys. His itinerary on his second journey is associated with Neapolis, Philippi, Amphipolis, Apollonia, Thessalonica, Berea, Athens, and Corinth (Acts 16:11–18:18). Later he addressed two epistles each to Thessalonica and Corinth and one to Philippi. Separate articles are devoted to each of these towns and epistles. After his first imprisonment in Rome Paul apparently returned to Greece briefly, and even did missionary work on Crete (*q.v.*), where he subsequently sent Titus (*q.v.*) to minister and gave him instructions in the epistle to Titus (*q.v.*).

Bibliography. M. Cary, *The Geographic Background of Greek and Roman History,* Oxford: Clarendon Press, 1949. N. G. L. Hammond, *A History of Greece to 322 B.C.,* Oxford: Clarendon Press, 1959. M. L. W. Laistner, *A History of the Greek World from 479 to 323 B.C.,* 2d ed., London: Methuen & Co., 1947. Carl Roebuck, *The World of Ancient Times,* New York: Scribner's Sons, 1966. Chester Starr, *A History of the Ancient World,* New York: Oxford Univ. Press, 1965.

H. F. V.

GREED. *See* Covetousness.

GREEK LANGUAGE. Gr. is an Indo-European language probably coming through the Sanskrit dialect, which shows a close relation to classical Gr.

The literary period began with Homer (*c.* 850 B.C.), who ushered in the classical period running to Alexander the Great (330 B.C.). This period had many dialects for the many tribes in Greece, but three chief families, Doric, Aeolic, and Ionic, emerged.

The Attic branch of the Ionic became supreme through Athens' political power by the 6th cen. B.C.; Persian wars with victories at Marathon, Salamis, and Thermopylae which prevented Greece and Europe from becoming oriental; and the 5th cen. B.C. literary giants, Sophocles, Euripides, and Aeschylus. Even after the decline of Athens, the Attic dialect continued through the writings of Plato, Aristotle, Xenophon, and Thucydides. Aristotle's pupil Alexander the Great extended the empire and pushed a program of Hellenization, making Attic Gr. a universal language even in Palestine, so that it still flourished there in Christ's time although modified to Hellenistic form since 300 B.C. Although the Hellenistic Gr. was followed by Byzantine (A.D. 550–1453) and modern (since A.D. 1453), today's Athens newspaper could no doubt be read by Plato.

Hellenistic Gr. consisted of a literary and non-literary form. Literary writers, such as Josephus, Philo, and Strabo, imitated the Attic, while the non-literary or Koine Gr. was the

Athena, patron deity of ancient Athens. Mimosa

everyday language of the masses. The literary has been found in stone inscriptions and extra-biblical literature and may appear in the NT Luke. The non-literary Koine has been found in papyri remains of letters, wills, and contracts, as well as in the ostraca (pottery fragments), and was used by the LXX and NT writers.

The Koine stressed clarity and emphasis by using the historical present tense, by piling up prepositions and adverbs before and after verbs, by using compound verbs instead of simple, and by using prepositions for simple cases and dropping the dual and optative forms. For some time many NT scholars thought the differences in vocabulary and style between biblical and classical were caused by a "Holy Spirit language" to convey divine truth, but the discovery of the papyri and ostraca in Egypt in the 1890's showed it to be the everyday living Gr. of the people, although some common words assumed new meanings or uses in the religious context of the OT and NT.

E. B. R.

GREEN. *See* Colors.

GREEN HERBS. *See* Plants.

GREETING. *See* Salutation.

GREYHOUND. *See* Animals: Fowl, Domestic, III.14.

GRIEF. Grief can be caused by many things, hence the use of a variety of words, most of which reflect the cause of the particular grief. All told, there are about 20 words in the Bible which have been translated "grief" in the KJV. In the RSV an attempt has been made to translate these in such a manner as to do credit to the root meanings.

The different words used. Such words as those listed below are to be found in both Heb. and Gr., each with its own root meaning bearing on the particular choice of the word to express a certain grief. For easy classification they are listed here alphabetically, according to their English meanings. The nature, the cause, or the motivation for grief comes out in the various words used.

1. Anger – Heb. *ḥārâ*, "to burn," "be wroth" (Gen 4:6, "Why art thou wroth"; Gen 45:5, "Now therefore be not grieved, nor angry with yourselves"; I Sam 18:8, "Samuel was very wroth"). A righteous indignation or grievance at the effects of sin in death is expressed by the Gr. *embrimaomai* ("And Jesus again boiling over within himself [*embrimōmenos*] came to the tomb," Jn 11:38, lit.). Heb. *ka'as*, "provocation," "anger," "sadness" (I Sam 1:16, "out of the abundance of my complaint and grief [my great anxiety and vexation, RSV] have I spoken"; Prov 17:25, "A foolish son is a grief to his father"; Ps 31:9, "mine eye is consumed with grief" [cf. Eccl 1:18; 2:23; Dan 11:30]). Heb. *ka'as*, "provocation," "anger" (Job 6:2, "Oh that my grief [my vexation, RSV] were throughly weighed").

2. Bitterness – Heb. *mārar*, "to be bitter" (I Sam 30:6, "The soul of all the people was grieved" ["all the people were bitter in soul," RSV]; cf. Ruth 1:13; Lam 1:20). The place where the water was bitter was called Marah (Ex 15:23; Num 33:8–9).

3. Disgust – "weariness at," Heb. *qûṭ* (Ps 139:21, "Am not I grieved with [do I not loathe, RSV] those that rise up against thee"). Gr. *prosochthizō* (Heb 3:10, "I was grieved with [provoked with, RSV] that generation").

4. Evil – Heb. *ra'*, "evil," "calamity" (Jon 4:6, "to deliver him from his grief [discomfort, RSV]"). Heb. *yēra'*, "to be evil" (Gen 21:11–12, "The thing was very grievous [very displeasing, RSV] in Abraham's sight"; cf. Isa 15:4). Gr. *kakōs*, "evilly" (Mt 15:22, "My daughter is grievously [severely, RSV] vexed with a devil").

5. Exhaustion – Heb. *lā'â*, "to be weary," "faint," "exhausted" (Prov 26:15 [cf. Job 4:2], "The slothful hideth his hand in his bosom; it grieveth him [wears him out, RSV] to bring it again to his mouth"). *diaponeo*, "to labor through," "exert oneself," "get worked up," "grieve self" (Acts 4:2, "Being grieved [annoyed, RSV] that they taught the people"; Acts 16:18, "Paul, being grieved [annoyed, RSV], turned and said . . .").

6. Frustration – Heb. *pûqâ*, "a stumbling block" (I Sam 25:31, "that this shall be no grief unto thee").

7. Pain – Heb. *mak'ōb*, "pain," "sorrow," "suffering" (II Chr 6:29, "When every one shall know . . . his own grief [affliction, RSV]"; Ps 69:26, "they talk to the grief of [afflict still more, RSV] those whom thou hast wounded"; Isa 53:3, "a man of sorrows").

8. Showing of grief – Heb. *yāgôn*, "showing of grief," "sorrow," "affliction" (Ps 31:10, "My life is spent with grief [sorrow, RSV]"; Jer 45:3, "The Lord hath added grief to my sorrow"). Gr. *lupē*, "grief," "grievance" (I Pet 2:19, "for conscience toward God endure grief [endures pain, RSV]"; cf. Heb 12:11). Gr. *lupeō*, "to grieve," "afflict" (Mk 10:22, "He was sad . . . and went away grieved [sorrowful, RSV]"; Jn 21:17, "Peter was grieved"; cf. Rom 14:15; II Cor 2:4; Mk 3:5). Gr. *stenazō*, "to groan," "sigh" (Heb 13:17, "they may do it with joy, and not with grief").

9. Sullenness – Heb. *ḥāmēṣ*, "be sour," "leavened" (Ps 73:21, "for my heart was grieved [embittered, RSV]").

10. Vexation – Heb. *'āṣab*, "to annoy or vex," "to grieve" (Ps 78:40, "How oft did they . . . grieve him"; Gen 45:5, "be not grieved [distressed, RSV]"; cf. I Sam 20:3, 34; II Sam 19:2; Neh 8:11).

11. Weakness – Heb. *ḥālâ*, "to be sick," "be weak" (Isa 57:10, "therefore thou wast not grieved [you were not faint, RSV]"; Amos 6:6, "they are not grieved"; also Jer 10:19; 14:17; 30:12; Nah 3:19). Heb. *ḥōlî*, "sickness,"

"weakness," "pain" (Isa 53:3, "a man of sorrows"; Isa 53:4, "Surely he hath borne our griefs"; also Jer 6:7; 10:19).

The causes of grief.

1. Grief over man's sin. This is seen in Isa 53 where Jesus is called a man of sorrows (v. 3).

2. Grief over our own sin. Sorrow over the consequences of what we have done when it is not accompanied by true repentance is remorse (Heb 12:15-17), in contrast to godly sorrow over the sinful act itself, that accompanies real repentance (II Cor 7:9-10; II Sam 12:13; Ps 32; 38:18).

3. Grief over loved ones who have died. David grieved over the loss of his first son by Bathsheba (II Sam 12:15-23), but was comforted by the fact that his child was in heaven and therefore said, "I shall go to him, but he shall not return to me." Mary and Martha and Christ grieved at the death of Lazarus (Jn 11:19, 35, 38). The one comfort they had was that Jesus could raise the dead—and did, in the particular case of Lazarus, right at that time, though he must have died again to await the resurrection like other men. The comfort for the Christian is that Jesus will not let him die eternally, that is, experience the second death, but will raise him at the time of the rapture (*q.v.*, Jn 11:25; I Thess 4:14-18; I Cor 15:52-55).

4. Grief over loved ones who are eternally lost. This God will Himself care for, particularly in the eternal era of the kingdom of God, in fulfillment of His promise, "God shall wipe away all tears from their eyes; and there shall be no more death, neither sorrow, nor crying" (Rev 21:4). This is to be accomplished in two ways. First, by the removal of the old heavens and the old earth so completely (Rev 20:11; 21:1, 4) that God can say, "Behold, I create new heavens and a new earth: and the former shall not be remembered, nor come to mind" (Isa 65:17). Second, there will be that direct comfort which God will give to His own. In Isa 65:18 God says, "Be ye glad and rejoice forever in that which I create: for, behold, I create Jerusalem a rejoicing, and her people a joy" (cf. Isa 51:11). He also promised to Israel to do away with death. "He will swallow up death in victory; and the Lord God will wipe away tears from all faces; and the rebuke of his people shall he take away from off all the earth: for the Lord hath spoken it" (Isa 25:8). Paul uses this verse in I Cor 15:54 as a proof of the resurrection and rapture of all believers at Christ's second coming.

See Suffering.

R. A. K.

GRIND. In Isa 3:15 "to grind the faces of the poor" means to oppress the poor still further by extortion. "Let my wife grind for another" (Job 31:10, RSV) means "let her become a slave in grinding grain for another man" (cf. Ex 11:5; Isa 47:2). In Eccl 12:3 the "grinders" that "cease because they are few" portray the teeth largely decayed in old age, whereas in v. 4 ears becoming deaf can hardly hear the noise of millstones grinding grain (cf. Jer 25:10). *See* Mill.

GRISLED, GRIZZLED. *See* Colors.

GROVE. This is a translation of two words:

1. Heb. *'ēshel,* "tamarisk." Abraham planted a grove (KJV), more appropriately "a tamarisk," at Beer-sheba (see Gen 21:33, RSV; cf. "tree" [*'ēshel*] in I Sam 22:6 and 31:13). *See* Plants: Tamarisk.

2. Heb. *'ăshērâ.* In its various forms it is rendered "grove" or sometimes "shrine" in KJV, an erroneous translation going back to the LXX. It is known now, however, that Asherah is Heb. for *athirat* (*yam*) of the Ugaritic texts of Ras Shamra. Asherah was the mother-goddess, the wife of El, who gave birth to 70 gods and goddesses including Baal. She was the foremost fertility deity of the Canaanites and she became a formidable rival to Yahweh especially during the time of Jezebel. *See* Gods, False: Asherah.

GUARD. A man or group of men who protected an important person or special object.

1. Heb. *mīshma'at,* "bodyguard," i.e., a group bound to another person by obedience. David was a bodyguard's captain under Saul (I Sam 22:14, RSV); Benaiah, the group's captain under David (II Sam 23:23).

2. Heb. *rāṣîm* (from *rûṣ,* "to run"), "guards," runners or a royal escort for Absalom (II Sam 15:1) and for Adonijah (I Kgs 1:5); the royal bodyguard who not only protected the king but also carried out his wishes (I Sam 22:17, RSV; I Kgs 14:27; II Kgs 10:25; 11:4; etc.).

3. Heb. *mishmār,* "gaol or prison" (Gen 40:3; etc.); in later times the man on watch (Neh 4:22-23) and also a guard or watchman waiting for orders (Ezk 38:7).

4. Heb. *ṭabbāh,* "guard" (lit., "slaughterer," "executioner"), exclusively of non-Israelites: of Potiphar the Egyptian over Joseph (Gen 37:36), of Nebuzaradan (II Kgs 25:8).

In the NT the RSV translation is "guard" instead of "watch" (KJV) in Mt 27:65-66; 28:11, and "executioner" in Mk 6:27.

GUARDIAN ANGELS. *See* Angels.

GUDGODAH (gŭd-gō'dȧ). An Israelite campground in the Negeb after Aaron's death (Deut 10:7), probably the same as Hor-hagidgad (*q.v.*).

GUEST. *See* Hospitality.

GUEST CHAMBER. *See* House.

GUIDANCE, GUIDE. *See* Lead, Leader.

GUILE. Three Heb words and one Gr. word are so translated in KJV. The verbal form "to beguile" represents three words in the OT and four in the NT.

The basic meaning of the word is trickery or deception, and related to attitudes held by people or actions involving people.

In Israel, taking of life "with guile" (*'ormâ*, "trickery" or "subtlety," Ex 21:14) was a crime punishable by death. (See Deissmann, LAE, pp. 214–217, on a Jewish prayer for vengeance on an ancient gravestone now in Athens.) The Lord would bless the man in whose spirit there was no guile (*r^emîyâ*, "treachery," Ps 32:2). One was to refrain from speaking guile (*mirmâ*, "deceit" or "fraud," Ps 34:13).

The verbal forms convey the idea of deceiving, as in Gen 3:13 (*nāshâ*, "lead astray" or "delude"), Gen 29:25 (*rāmā'*, "delude" or "betray") or Num 25:18 (*nākal*, "defraud"). Emphatic in these examples is wrongful behavior on the part of one or more persons.

In the NT, the single noun form is *dolos* (see, e.g., Jn 1:47; I Pet 2:22). The word referred to a "taint" in material things, as gold or silver (see MM, *Lexicon, s.v.*). By application it meant "deceit," "cunning" or "treachery" in a person's attitudes or dealings. One's motives (Acts 13:10), speech (I Pet 3:10) or actions (Mt 26:4) are so described.

The verb forms translated by "beguile" are varied. In Col 2:4 *paralogizomai* means to delude by false reasoning; in 2:18 *katabrabeuō* means to render an umpire's decision, here to rob one of his true reward. In II Cor 11:3 *exapataō* conveys the idea of being completely deceived (cf. Gen 3:13). II Pet 2:14 has *deleazō*, a fisherman's term meaning to catch by means of a bait.

See Deceit.

W. M. D.

GUILT. *See* Sin.

GULF. A translation of Gr. *chasma*, RSV "chasm," in Lk 16:26; a deep cleft separating two places. The Lord Jesus Christ lends His authority to the concept that a vast chasm has been fixed by an irrevocable decree between paradise ("Abraham's bosom," *q.v.*) and hades, in order that persons in the next life cannot cross it (cf. Heb 9:27). Gr. *chasma* may be found in other descriptions of final judgment in I Enoch 18:11; Diogenes Laertius 8:31; Plato *Republic* X.614.

GULL. *See* Animals: Cuckoo, III.8, 45.

GUM. *See* Plants: Gum.

GUNI (gū'nī), **GUNITES** (gū'nīts)

1. The second son of Naphtali, founder of the family of the Gunites (Gen 46:24; I Chr 7:13; Num 26:48).

2. Father of Abdiel and grandfather of Ahi, who was a chief man of the Gadites (I Chr 5:15).

GUR (gûr). An ascent near Ibleam, between Jezreel and Beth-haggan, where Ahaziah, king of Judah, was mortally wounded by Jehu, king of Israel (II Kgs 9:27). It is equated with Akkad. *Gurra* by Albright (BASOR, 94 [1944], 21). J. Simons, finding no ancient site in this short stretch, adopts the reading of the LXX, "at the ascent of the valley (*Gai*), which is Jeblaam" (*The Geographical and Topographical Texts of the Old Testament*, Leiden: E. J. Brill, 1959, pp. 916–918).

GUR-BAAL (gûr'bāl). A town in the Negeb, whose Arab occupants were defeated by King Uzziah (II Chr 26:7). Possibly the same as Jagur of Josh 15:21 (Khirbet Gharra), ten miles E of Beer-sheba.

GUTTER

1. The rendering of the Heb. *rahaṭ* (Gen 30:38, 41); Assyrian *râtu*, "vessel," "water container"; a depression in the trough, *shōqet* (Gen 24:20; 30:38). In Moses' time (Ex 2:16) *rahaṭ* was used alone for the watering trough. Jacob's placing peeled rods in the troughs simply was his own adherence to local superstition. Common sense dictated putting the rods where the animals would be found in largest numbers at one time. There was no biological value to the practice. God would have multiplied Jacob's herds in any event.

2. The "gutter" (*ṣinnôr*) of II Sam 5:8 almost certainly is a term for the vertical tunnel, known as Warren's shaft, in the water system of Jebusite Jerusalem. By sneaking into the spring Gihon and clambering up the 40 foot high watershaft, Joab and his men were able to enter the stronghold and take the Jebusites by surprise (see FLAP, p. 178). *See* Gihon.

H

HAAHASHTARI (hā'ȧ-hăsh'tȧ-rī). A son of Naarah and Ashur, the "father" or founder of Tekoa and a descendant of Judah (I Chr 4:6).

HABAIAH (hȧ-bā'yă). Father of one of the families of returned exiles claiming priestly descent, but put out of the priesthood since their names were not found in the genealogical register (Ezr 2:61; cf. vv. 62-63; Neh 7:63).

HABAKKUK (hȧ-băk'ŭk). Information about Habakkuk is limited to the book that bears his name. Two references ascribe the oracle which the author saw (1:1) and the prayer he prayed (3:1) to the prophet Habakkuk. The only clear historical reference in this book is to the Chaldeans (1:6), which provides the basis for dating this prophet near the close of the 7th cen. B.C.

Very likely Habakkuk witnessed the decline and fall of the Assyrian Empire. He possibly may have known about the fall of Nineveh in 612 B.C., and very likely was aware of the rising power of the Babylonians when this message was revealed to him. Conditions prevailing in Judah after Josiah's death in 609 B.C. and before the Chaldean invasion of Judah in 605 make this period a favorable time for dating the prophecy of Habakkuk.

HABAKKUK, BOOK OF. The uniqueness of this book is apparent in two distinctive features. First of all, Habakkuk records his dialogue with God in which he raises theological problems and listens to the answers. In addition, chap. 3 is a psalm with musical terms noted in the first and last verses.

In outline form the message of Habakkuk may be summarized as follows:

I. Why Does God Tolerate Violence? 1:1-4
II. Chaldeans Will Bring Punishment on Judah, 1:5-11
III. Why Should Heathen Be Used to Punish God's People? 1:12-2:1
IV. The Righteous Trust God to Do Right, 2:2-20
V. Prayer of Confidence and Praise, 3:1-19

Habakkuk (*q.v.*) appeals to God in prayer concerning the violence, injustice, destruction, and indifference to the teaching of the law that prevailed in Judah. He could not understand why a righteous God should tolerate this. When God replied, indicating that the Chaldean invaders would bring judgment on the guilty citizens of Judah, Habakkuk became more concerned. Should the Chaldeans, whose own might was their god, be allowed to punish the Jews who actually were less wicked than these pagan invaders? In response, Habakkuk is bidden to record that ultimately the unrighteous would fail but the righteous would live by his faith or faithfulness. The upright should not draw his conclusion on the basis of a limited temporal perspective, but should wait and look at the ultimate outcome. The unrighteous about him—aggressors, evildoers, murderers, deceivers, and idolators (2:6-19)—would finally perish, while the righteous would live, since the Lord is in His holy temple. Consequently all the earth should keep silence before Him (2:20). In a prayer appealing to God that in His wrath He would remember mercy, the prophet expresses his praise and thanksgiving to God. He is determined to continue this even though everything temporal should fail.

A midrash or commentary on the book of Habakkuk was found among the Dead Sea Scrolls in Qumran Cave # 1. Apparently it was written by a Jewish sectarian of Palestine interpreting the first two chapters in the light of

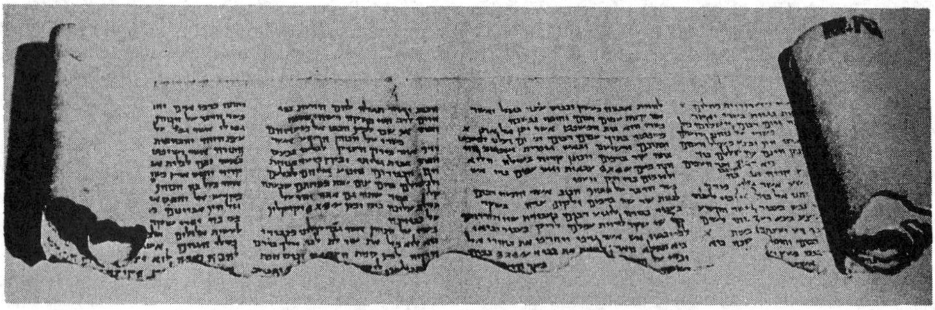

The Habakkuk Commentary. Y. Yadin and the Shrine of the Book

the history of the Qumran sect. It does not offer much insight on the meaning of the prophecy.

The theory held currently by some OT scholars is that chap. 3 was not part of the original book. The fact that the Qumran commentary does not include this chapter does not prove this theory. Since chap. 3 is a psalm, it does not lend itself to such use as was made of the first two chapters in the midrash. The probability exists that the commentary never was finished. The LXX has all three chapters. There is no evidence that disallows for the prophet to have composed a psalm of praise and thanksgiving. The writings of the prophets frequently were in highly poetic form.

Bibliography. W. F. Albright, "The Psalm of Habakkuk," in *Studies in Old Testament Prophecy*, ed. by H. H. Rowley, Edinburgh: T. & T. Clark, 1950, pp. 1–18. Gleason L. Archer, SOTI, pp. 343–346. Millar Burrows, *The Dead Sea Scrolls*, New York: Viking Press, 1955. Frank E. Gaebelein, *Four Minor Prophets*, Chicago: Moody Press, 1970. David W. Kerr, "Habakkuk," WBC, pp. 871–881. D. Martin Lloyd-Jones, *From Fear to Faith*, London: Inter-Varsity, 1953. Samuel J. Schultz, *The Old Testament Speaks*, New York: Harper and Row, 1960, pp. 406 ff.

S. J. S.

HABAZINIAH (hăb'ȧ-zĭ-nī'ȧ). Grandfather of Jaaziniah and his brothers, Rechabites, who were tested by the prophet Jeremiah in the temple (Jer 35:3).

HABERGEON (hăb'ẽr-jĕn)

1. An obsolete term for coat of mail or breastplate (II Chr 26:14; Neh 4:16) to protect the neck and shoulders, but later reaching the thighs or knees. Goliath's coat of mail (I Sam 17:5) seems to have been a coat of leather covered with bronze scales, weighing *c.* 125 pounds. A fragment of such bronze scale armor from the 15th cen. B.C. was found at Nuzu (Yigael Yadin, *The Art of Warfare in Biblical Lands*, New York: McGraw-Hill, 1963, I, 196 f.). David found Saul's coat of mail too heavy for him (I Sam 17:38). *See* Armor.

2. The term used in Job 41:26 probably denotes a pointed shaft or javelin (cf. RSV).

3. Habergeon in Ex 28:32; 39:23 translates a word of uncertain meaning, some kind of garment (cf. RSV). It may be a loan word from the Egyptian, denoting a garment used in ritual services to deck the image-statue of a god on certain festivals.

HABITATION. The translation of 20 different words in the Bible, including the ideas of temporary dwelling (sojourn), permanent home (dwelling place), fixed abode or place, and resting place.

The temple is called God's habitation (*zᵉbûl*, II Chr 6:2). The heavens also are His dwelling place (*shibtô*, from *yāshab*, Ps 33:13–14). Justice and judgment are likewise His habitation (*mākôn*, "fixed place," Ps 89:14). In the NT the Church is called the habitation of God (*katoikētērion*, "place of habitation," Eph 2:22).

Canaan was Israel's habitation (*mōshāb*, I Chr 4:33, etc.). After the Exile God promised to return Israel to her habitation (*nāweh*, "resting place," Isa 32:18; 33:20; Jer 50:19). God has also determined the limits of men's habitation (*katoikia*, "dwelling place," Acts 17:26). The Christian disciple may look forward to being received into everlasting habitations (*skēnē*, "tent," Lk 16:9).

HABOR (hā'bôr). The modern Khabur River, the eastern of the two main tributaries of the upper Euphrates, entering it from the N near Tirqah. To the Gozan district near its headwaters captives from the ten tribes were deported by Tiglath-pileser III in 732 B.C. and by Sargon II in King Hoshea's ninth year, 722 B.C. (II Kgs 17:6 and 18:11, RSV; I Chr 5:26). *See* Gozan; Halah.

HACHALIAH (hăk'ȧ-lī'ȧ). The father of Nehemiah, governor of Judea after the Captivity (Neh 1:1; 10:1).

HACHILAH (hȧ-kī'lȧ). A hill in the wilderness of Judah E of Ziph, SE of Hebron, facing the Jeshimon ("desolate") district where David took refuge when fleeing from Saul (I Sam 23:19; 26:1, 3). It is a wild area of cliffs and gorges W of En-gedi.

HACHMONI (hăk'mō-nī). Hachmoni, the "wise one," was the father or ancestor of Jashobeam (*q.v.*), the illustrious first of the mighty men of David (I Chr 11:11, lit., "Jashobeam son of *Ḥakmônî*"). In II Sam 23:8 this family name is spelled Tachmonite (KJV) or Tah-chemonite (RSV), perhaps a scribal error for "the Hachmonite." In I Chr 27:32 another son of Hachmoni is mentioned, Jehiel, who was with David's sons as their adviser. The actual father of Jashobeam may have been Zabdiel, or Zabdiel may have been the more distant ancestor (I Chr 27:2). Possibly this family belonged to the tribe of Levi, because Jashobeam is called a Korahite (I Chr 12:6, RSV).

HADAD (hā'dăd)

1. The eighth son of Ishmael (Gen 25:15, "Hadar" [*q.v.*] in Heb. and KJV; I Chr 1:30).

2. The fourth early king of Edom (in Avith) who defeated Midian (Gen 36:35 f.; I Chr 1:46 f.).

3. The eighth (and last) king of Edom (Gen 36:39; I Chr 1:50 f.), in Pau or Pai.

4. An Edomite prince whom God raised up to be an adversary against Solomon (I Kgs 11:14–25). As a child, he escaped to Egypt from Joab's slaughter in David's reign. He was sponsored by Pharaoh, giving him the queen's sister as wife and rearing his son. On David's death, he obtained release from Pharaoh and

returned to lead the Edomites in overthrowing Israel's dominance. By divine appointment, he was God's agent of punishment against Solomon by constituting a major threat and continual harassment.

5. Hadad was the name of an ancient Semitic storm-god among the Syrians and Assyrians. This name was adopted by kings, e.g., Ben-hadad (I Kgs 15:18; II Kgs 13) and Hadadezer (II Sam 10:16, 19, RSV). This deity was also called Hadadrimmon (Zech 12:11), following the identification by the Assyrians with Ramman, their god of wind and storm. *See* Gods, False.

HADADEZER (hăd'*ȧ*-dē'zẽr). Son of Rehob, Hadadezer was king of Zobah (II Sam 8:3), a Syrian region lying to the N of Damascus. In David's time Hadadezer sought with various allies to conquer Israel, but without success. II Sam 8 describes two occasions when David subdued Hadadezer, the second campaign bringing much booty of gold and brass. Solomon used this brass to make the brazen sea, the pillars, and the vessels of brass for the temple (I Chr 18:8). II Sam 10 describes a third successful campaign of David against Hadadezer, who had become allied with the Ammonites and Syrians.

HADADRIMMON (hā'dăd-rĭm'ŏn). A combination of the names of two gods, the Aramean Hadad ("thunderer") and the Akkad. Rimmon, *Ramânu* ("thunderer"; cf. II Kgs 5:18), for whom public mourning was made in the plain of Esdraelon at Megiddo (Zech 12:11). In the Ras Shamra mythology, the Canaanite Baal, same as the Amorite storm-god Hadad, was pictured as a kilted striding warrior with mace and thunderbolt, and a helmet with bull's horns. He was also the vegetation god. Mourning for Hadadrimmon, the dead Baal, and Tammuz (Ezk 18:14) are common motifs in Mesopotamian mythology. *See* Gods, False.

Hadadrimmon formerly was thought to be a place name of a locality near Megiddo where King Josiah's death was lamented after he was mortally wounded at Megiddo; but he died in Jerusalem, where the mourning took place (II Chr 35:22-25).

HADAR (hā'där)

1. Alternate form of Hadad (*q.v.*), son of Ishmael (Gen 25:15). The letters *resh* (*r*) and *daleth* (*d*) are similar in Heb. and were frequently confused. He founded a tribe of the same name, attested in cuneiform records as the *Ḫudadu*.

2. Variant for Hadad, last of the ancient kings of Edom's elective monarchy, whose city was Pau (Gen 36:39).

HADAREZER (hăd'*ȧ*-rē'zẽr). Alternate spelling of Hadadezer (*q.v.*), king of the Aramean state of Zobah, defeated by King David (II Sam 10:16, 19; I Chr 18:3, 5, 7-10; 19:16, 19; cf. spelling Hadadezer, II Sam 8:3-12).

HADASHAH (h*ȧ*-dăsh'*ȧ*). A village of Judah in the Shephelah or foothills district, possibly between Lachish and Gath (Josh 15:37).

HADASSAH (h*ȧ*-dăs'*ȧ*). The earlier name of Esther, who became queen and the wife of Ahasuerus or Xerxes I (Est 2:7). In Heb. the name means "myrtle." Possibly it could be a title given to her, derived from Akkad. *ḫaddaš-šatu,* "bride"; it was so used for Ishtar. *See* Esther.

HADATTAH (h*ȧ*-dăt'*ȧ*). Part of the name of the town Hazor-Hadattah in Judah (Josh 15:25, RSV), located in the Negeb, perhaps at el-Hudeira, S of Tuwāni, *c.* 20 miles E of Beer-sheba toward the Dead Sea.

HADES (hā'dēz). Hades is another name of Pluto the Gr. god of the underworld. The name was transferred to the realm of the dead itself. The Hades of the Greeks was in two parts. The deeper part, where souls were punished, was sometimes called Tartarus, and the place of blessed souls was called the Elysian Fields (Edith Hamilton, *Mythology,* p. 39). We must beware of importing these pagan Gr. ideas into the Christian vocabulary. Just as the Gr. word *theos,* "god," attained new meaning in Jewish-Christian thought, so Hades is not to be defined from pagan Gr. usage but from the NT.

The word *hadēs* is used some ten times in the NT. These are:

1. Mt 11:23 and Lk 10:15 (ASV, RSV). Here, as remarked in ExpB, heaven and *hadēs* are proverbial expressions for the highest exaltation and the deepest degradation.

2. Mt 16:18. The expression "gates of hell" is wholly figurative (cf. Job 38:17; Isa 38:10). Possibly the figure is of a walled city with gates and bars. The verse could possibly refer to an assault from Satan's kingdom—which will fail.

3. Lk 16:23 (ASV, RSV). This is a clear reference. *Hadēs* is used of the place of torment as distinguished from the place of bliss. Some have called this a parable, although there is no indication of that. But in any case the word is used to designate a place of punishment.

4. Acts 2:27, 31 (ASV, RSV). This passage is complicated by the fact that it is an OT quotation and its exact meaning unsure. A common view is that this refers to Christ's descent into the realm of the dead to preach to sinners or to deliver righteous ones from the upper compartment of Hades into heaven. One problem with this explanation is that Christ had already spoken of Hades as a place of torment. And elsewhere He says that at His death He was not going to such a place, but to paradise (Lk 23:43) and to be with God (Jn 16:28).

An alternative view would interpret the pas-

Dagger of Mes-kalam-dug (*c.* 2500 B.C.) with hilt of lapis lazuli and sheath of gold filigree, 14½ inches long. BM

sage by its OT original, Ps 16:10. There, the statement "thou wilt not leave my soul in hell" surely does not refer to the spiritual nature going to the netherworld. The word *nepesh* often means just the "individual." It seldom means the "spirit nature." The parallel is "neither wilt thou suffer thine holy one to see corruption." It is logical to take the first part as a synonymous parallel meaning "Thou wilt not abandon me to the grave." (See treatment in C. F. H. Henry, ed., *The Biblical Expositor,* II, 59 f.). In this case *hadēs* in this OT quotation would be used in the meaning of its Heb. original *she'ōl,* which many times means simply "grave" (*q.v.*).

5. Rev 1:18; 6:8; 20:13-14 (ASV, RSV). These verses also are figurative. In the first (Rev 1:18) Christ holds the keys of *hadēs* and death. This expression reminds one of "gates of *hadēs*" in Mt 16:18 (ASV). Hades is pictured as a walled city, in this case a prison possibly. In the next passage (Rev 6:8) *hadēs* is also linked with death and they are personified as enemies of God and men. In Rev. 20:13-14 death and *hadēs* are linked again and they deliver up the wicked dead who are in them for final judgment. This usage is reminiscent of the passage in Lk 16:23 and strengthens the idea that in the NT Hades signifies the abode of the wicked dead.

See Dead, The; Gehenna; Hell; Sheol.

R. L. H.

HADID (hā'dĭd). A town of Benjamin at the NW edge of the Shephelah, near the mouth of the Ajalon Valley, probably modern el-Ḥadīthēh, about three miles ENE of Lod or Lydda (Ezr 2:33; Neh 7:37; 11:34). An earlier town of this name is included in the Karnak list of Thutmose III.

HADLAI (hăd'lī). Father of Amasa, who was one of the chiefs of the tribe of Ephraim in the reign of Pekah (II Chr 28:12).

HADORAM (hȧ-dôr'ȧm)

1. The fifth son of Joktan (Gen 10:27; I Chr 1:21), a Shemite sixth from Noah.

2. Son of Tou (Toi), king of Hamath, who was sent with congratulatory gifts for David on his defeat of Hadarezer (I Chr 18:10; called Joram in II Sam 8:10).

3. A taskmaster to Solomon (I Kgs 4:6, called Adoniram, *q.v.*) and Rehoboam, who was stoned to death when he delivered Rehoboam's message to the ten tribes (II Chr 10:18; called Adoram in I Kgs 12:18).

HAFT. The handle of a knife or dagger, occurring only in Jud 3:22, in the account of Ehud's stabbing of Eglon, king of Moab. Translated "hilt" in RSV.

HAGAB (hā'găb). Head of a family of Nethinim who returned with Zerubbabel to Jerusalem (Ezr 2:46). The name is omitted in Nehemiah's list (Neh 7:48). A man of this name was mentioned in Jeremiah's time on Ostracon I of the Lachish letters.

HAGABA, HAGABAH (hăg'ȧ-bȧ). Founder of a family of Nethinim or temple servants that returned from Exile with Zerubbabel (Neh 7:48; Ezr 2:45). Evidently different from that of Hagab in Ezr 2:46).

Hagar in the Wilderness by Corot. MM

HAGAR (hā'gär). An Egyptian woman who belonged to Sarai, the wife of Abram. Sarai was prevented from bearing children, so she gave Hagar to Abram as a wife, hoping that she might have a child through her (Gen 16). The Nuzu tablets reveal that this practice was common, and some of the marriage contracts specify that a barren wife must provide a woman for her husband for the purpose of procreation. After Hagar conceived she looked on Sarai with contempt. Sarai, with Abram's assent, treated Hagar harshly. Hagar fled into the wilderness and was found beside a spring of water by the angel of the Lord, who instructed her to return. She was promised that her son would have innumerable descendants. After her return Ishmael was born.

Later God granted to Sarah (whose name God changed from Sarai to Sarah, and also

Abram to Abraham) a child of her own—Isaac. After the weaning of Isaac, Sarah demanded of Abraham that he send Ishmael away. According to the Nuzu tablets, such action was prohibited, and this may be the reason Abraham was so reluctant to expel Ishmael until God Himself gave him permission to do so. Hagar and Ishmael were sent away with only bread and a skin of water. The angel appeared to her again in the wilderness when she had given up hope of survival, and again promised a bright future for her son. Hagar took a wife for Ishmael from the land of Egypt.

The apostle Paul used the story of Hagar (spelled Agar in the NT) as an allegory (Gal 4:21–31). There she symbolizes the old covenant of flesh given on Mount Sinai. In contrast, Sarah the freewoman represents the new covenant of faith instituted by Christ.

R. E. H.

HAGARENES. *See* Hagarites.

HAGARITES (hăg'ȧ-rīts). Variant form of Hagarenes, Hagerites, and Hagrites (RSV).

A tribe, or confederation of tribes, dwelling in the Syrian and N Arabian desert. They were of Bedouin stock, whether Arabian or Aramean is uncertain, and their wealth consisted in livestock (I Chr 5:20–21). During the reign of Saul, the Reubenites waged war against them (I Chr 5:10). I Chr 5:18–22 indicates that the Reubenites formed a coalition with the Gadites and the half tribe of Manasseh against the Hagarites, Nodab, Jetur, and Nephish. The last two are Arab tribes and are named in Gen 25:15 as sons of Ishmael. The Ituraeans of Roman times took their name from Jetur. From the close association of the Hagarites with these Arab tribes and the similarity to the name Hagar, this people has often been assumed to be descended from Ishmael's mother (see also Ps 83:6). However, the region assigned to her descendants was near Beer-sheba. Also, both Tiglath-pileser III and Sennacherib list the *Hagaranu* (Hagarenes) with other tribes as Arameans. The Gr. geographers Strabo and Ptolemy mention the *Agraioi* as living in N Arabia. An individual Hagerite, Jaziz, was a steward of King David "over the flocks" (I Chr 27:31).

R. E. H.

HAGERITES. *See* Hagarites.

HAGGAI (hăg'ā-ī). A post-Exilic prophet who was active in Judah during the building of the second temple, 520–515 B.C. References to Haggai outside the book bearing his name are Ezr 5:1 and 6:14. His name means "festal," derived from Heb. *ḥag,* "festival." Possibly he was so named by godly parents because he was born on some major Jewish feast day. Very likely he was born in Babylonia and came to Jerusalem after Cyrus, the king of Persia, issued a decree in 538 B.C. allowing Jews to return to their homeland (II Chr 36:22–23; Ezr 1:1–4).

In his prophetic ministry Haggai was supported by the prophet Zechariah. The four messages recorded in his book are dated within three or four months in the year 520 B.C., the second year of Darius I (Hystaspes), king of Persia (521–485 B.C.). *See* Darius Hystaspes.

HAGGAI, BOOK OF. With enthusiasm the exiles, who returned after the decree of Cyrus in 538 B.C., began to rebuild the temple (536 B.C.). *See* Haggai; Zechariah. The opposition by the Samaritans was effective to the point of stopping the building efforts during the reigns of Cyrus and Cambyses until the second year of Darius in 520 B.C. (Ezr 4:4–5, 20). Marauding Persians under Cambyses en route to Egypt during this period (*c.* 525 B.C.) may have overrun Palestine to such an extent that any hope for a permanent effort to rebuild the temple was halted.

This book in the OT is unusual in being uncontested by practically all critics. There is no evidence for the conjecture that the present book is a fragment of longer writings by the prophet or a compilation of his oracles and narrative writings. Oesterly and Robinson, without recognizing the usual practice of the writing prophets, have conjectured that this collection comes from the hand of a contemporary of Haggai who wrote down the salient points of the prophet's sermons, because the third person is used for the prophet.

The book of Haggai may represent merely outlines of his messages, written under inspiration of the Holy Spirit. The Lord had spoken through him to stir up the people to a successful effort to rebuild the temple (Hag 1:12–15; Ezr 5:1–2; 6:13–15).

The conditions during this period are vividly reflected in his approach to the people. Although they were deeply engaged in private housing projects, Haggai reminded them that the Lord of hosts was the controller of the material blessings which they were lacking through drought and crop failure (1:2–11). Assuring the builders that God through His Spirit was working in their midst so that the latter glory of this temple would be greater than the former glory of the temple in Solomon's time (2:7–9, RSV), Haggai encouraged the leaders as well as the laity. To God and Haggai there was only *one* temple, not three or four (Solomon's, Zerubbabel's, Herod's, millennial); therefore this prophecy was not necessarily fulfilled before A.D. 70.

Better crops were promised (2:15–19). Zerubbabel as a representative of the Davidic throne is designated as a signet (2:23) or seal guaranteeing to God's people the fulfillment of the Davidic covenant (II Sam 7:12–16) and providing the basis for the hope that God, who shakes the heavens and the earth, will destroy the strength of the heathen nations. Consequently God's work through His chosen nation will ultimately be established (2:20–23).

The messages of Haggai may be outlined as follows:

I. Haggai Promotes Involvement, 1:1–15
II. Potential of Greater Glory in the New Temple, 2:1–9
III. Material Blessings Assured, 2:10–19
IV. God's Promise, 2:20–23

Bibliography. Charles L. Feinberg, "Haggai," WBC, pp. 889–896, with bibliography. Hobart E. Freeman, *An Introduction to the Old Testament Prophets,* Chicago: Moody Press, 1968, pp. 326–332. Frank E. Gaebelein, *Four Minor Prophets,* Chicago: Moody Press, 1970. A. Gelston, "The Foundations of the Second Temple," VT, XVI (April, 1966), 232–235, on Hag 2:18.

S. J. S.

HAGGERI (hăg'ĕ-rī). The father or ancestor of Mibhar, one of David's heroes (I Chr 11:38).

HAGGI (hăg'ī), **HAGGITES** (hăg'īts). The second son of Gad, founder of the clan called Haggites (Gen 46:16; Num 26:15). The name occurs in a Phoenician text and has been found in a number of ancient Heb. inscriptions.

HAGGIAH (hȧ-gī'ȧ). A descendant of Merari, the son of Levi (I Chr 6:30).

HAGGITH (hăg'ĭth). A wife of King David and mother of his fourth son Adonijah, who later claimed the throne (II Sam 3:4; I Kgs 1:5, 11; 2:13; I Chr 3:2).

HAGIOGRAPHA (hăg'ĭ-ŏg'rȧ-fȧ; "holy writings"). Adopted from the Gr., this is an alternate name for the last of the traditional three divisions (see Lk 24:44) of the Heb. Scriptures (*Ketûbîm,* the Writings), comprising the books not included under the Law and the Prophets. This division was so manifestly arbitrary that it was never accepted as a proper one by the Church Fathers.

The miscellaneous collection of 11 books (in Heb.) includes the following: (1) three large books of poetry: Psalms, Proverbs, Job; (2) the five scrolls or *Megilloth,* which came to be read in synagogues at five sacred occasions: Song of Solomon at Passover, Ruth at Feast of Weeks (Pentecost), Lamentations at the ninth of Ab (the anniversary of the destruction of the temple), Ecclesiastes at Feast of Tabernacles, and Esther at Feast of Purim; (3) three late narrative books: Daniel, Ezra-Nehemiah, and Chronicles. The order in our English Bibles, following the LXX and Vulgate, differs considerably from the Heb. *See* Canon of Scripture, the OT.

A. T. P.

HAI (hā'ī). Same as Ai *(q.v.),* in the vicinity of Bethel, where Abraham pitched his tent (Gen 12:8; 13:3). Here the KJV expressed the definite article (*hā*) with which Ai is always accompanied in the Heb. text (one exception, Jer 49:3).

HAIL, HAILSTONES. Hailstorms occur in hot as well as cold climates, frequently accompanying violent thunderstorms. Raindrops within the cumulonimbus cloud are carried to great altitudes where the temperature drops below 0°F; turning to ice pellets, they grow in size as they are blown up and down. Hailstones exceeding a pound in weight have been picked up after a storm. In October, 1937, roof tiles were broken by hail near Tel Aviv in Palestine.

Hailstorms affect the area along a narrow line, so that one place might suffer from the storm while an adjoining one might escape (Ex 9:26; Josh 10:11). Driving rain (Isa 28:17), storm winds (Ezk 13:11), and snow (Job 38:22) often accompanied hailstorms. An unparalleled fall of hail, the seventh judgment on Egypt, destroyed crops and trees and injured animals and men (Ex 9:18–34), becoming a prototype for the end-time judgments in the books of Ezekiel (38:22) and Revelation (8:7; 11:19; 16:21). The hailstorm over Beth-horon (Josh 10:10–11) was miraculous both in its intensity and probably in its being unseasonal, since Joshua's campaign against the Amorites seems to have been waged in the dry summer season, within a few months after Passover (Josh 5:10).

A. T. P. and J. R.

HAIR. Hair is frequently mentioned in Scripture, especially with reference to the head. The manner and customs of wearing the hair varied considerably among the nations.

Egyptians. The Egyptian men shaved their hair, except in time of mourning. Even the heads of children were shaved, leaving a few locks as a sign of youth. Slaves, when brought from other countries to serve in the court, had their heads and beards shaved. This was why Joseph, before going in to Pharaoh, shaved himself (Gen 41:14). However, the women wore their natural hair long and plaited, often reaching down in the form of strings to the bottom of the shoulder blades. Wigs sometimes were worn for disguise. The pharaoh wore a false beard as a symbol of deity.

Assyrians. The Assyrian men had the opposite custom in allowing the hair of both head and beard to grow full length. They sometimes curled the beard and added false hair to provide a headdress.

Greeks and Romans. The Greeks admired long hair on both men and women. They believed that the hair was the cheapest of ornaments. Customs varied, however, and they first wore it long, then in a knot, and at a later period short. Romans at first wore the hair long, but the men began to wear it short about three centuries B.C. Shaving was also customary, and a long beard was a mark of slovenliness. Plaiting or braiding women's hair was so elaborately done that Peter and Paul counseled against it (I Pet 3:3; I Tim 2:9).

Hebrews. The Hebrews considered the hair an important part of personal beauty for both young and old (Song 5:11; Prov 16:31). The sexes were distinguished by the long hair of the women (Lk 7:38; Jn 11:2; 12:3; I Cor 11:6) and the frequent clipping to a moderate length by the men. The ordinance for the priests, and thereby probably followed by the rest of the community, was that the hair was to be polled, i.e., neither shaved nor allowed to grow too long (Lev 21:5; Ezk 44:20). Absalom's luxuriant hair was greatly admired (II Sam 14:26). The Nazarites *(q.v.)*, for the term of their vow, wore long hair (Num 6:5). The Hebrews dreaded baldness as it was frequently the result of leprosy (Lev 13:40), and hence formed one of the disqualifications for the priesthood (Lev 21:5). Calling Elisha "bald" was therefore meant as an insult (II Kgs 2:23). In times of affliction, the hair was completely cut off (Isa 3:17, 24; Jer 7:29; 48:37; Amos 8:10). Job was bald in the day of his affliction (Job 1:20), probably as a symbol of desolation (cf. Isa 3:24; 15:2; Jer 7:29).

The usual and favorite color of the hair was black (Song 5:11). Josephus indicates that gold dust was occasionally sprinkled on the hair, but

Pharaoh Tutankhamon of Egypt with a false beard. LL

dyeing was not practiced. Pure white hair represented the divine majesty (Dan 7:9; Rev 1:14). Gray hair was considered beautiful on old men (Prov 20:29), in keeping with their age (Job 15:10; I Sam 12:2; Ps 71:18). Curls, whether natural or artificial, were considered beautiful. Jezebel attired or adorned her head (II Kgs 9:30), and Samson's hair was arranged into seven braids (Jud 16:13, 19). Sometimes ornaments were placed in the hair with combs and hairpins as mentioned in the Talmud. The hair was also profusely anointed with fragrant ointments (Ruth 3:3; II Sam 14:2; Ps 23:5; 45:7; Isa 3:24), especially for festive occasions (Mt 6:17; 26:7; Lk 7:46). Barbers *(q.v.)* have existed from ancient times (Ezk 5:1).

The beard was regarded in much the same manner as the head. With the exception of the Egyptians, most Asiatics cherished the beard as the mark of manhood. The Hebrews did not shave the beard, but trimmed it (II Sam 19:24). It was the object of an oath (Mt 5:36), shaved or plucked in mourning (Isa 50:6; Jer 41:5; Ezr 9:3), neglected during affliction (II Sam 19:24), and the object of salutation (II Sam 20:9). The shaving of the beard as well as all the hair was part of the ceremonial cleansing of a leper (Lev 14:9). The Mosaic law forbade one to "round the corners of your heads, neither shalt thou mar the corners of thy beard" (Lev 19:27; 21:5). This probably means that the hair was not to be cut from one temple to the other in a circle, as among the Arabs (cf. Jer 9:26, RSV). Also, the place where the hair and beard met was not to be shaved. Other nations may have had such customs in their idolatrous worship and as a rite of mourning or offering in behalf of the dead (Deut 14:1; Jer 16:6), and thus God prevented Israel from such by these regulations.

Figurative. The hair represented an innumerable group (Ps 40:12; 69:4), and what was of least value of a man (I Sam 14:45; II Sam 14:11; I Kgs 1:52; Mt 10:30; Lk 12:7; 21:18; Acts 27:34). White hair or the hoary head was the symbol of respect due to age (Lev 19:32; Prov 16:31). Thus God, the Ancient of Days, appears as such (Dan 7:9; cf. Rev 1:14). On the other hand, the shaving of the head signified affliction, poverty, and disgrace. "Cutting off the hair" was a figure used to denote the entire destruction of a people by God (Isa 7:20). Gray hairs here and there represent the decline of the kingdom of Israel (Hos 7:9).

The capacity of hair for continual growth made it an evidence or symbol of life; thus, letting the hair grow long was symbolic of the dedication of one's life to the Lord (Num 6:1-21; Jud 13:5; etc.). Such a vow brought God's blessing and strength, as in the case of Samson. Cutting the hair signified that the period of the vow, if temporary, was at an end (Num 6:18; Acts 18:18; 21:23 f.). Warriors anticipating battle often let their hair grow and hang loose, perhaps as a sign of dedication to their deity in a holy war (Deut 32:42, RSV; see

An Assyrian god with curled hair and beard. LM

comment on Jud 5:2 in *Wycliffe Bible Commentary*).

E. C. J.

HAKKATAN (hăk'*ȧ*-tăn). The father of Johanan, chief of the family of Azgad, who returned from the Babylonian Exile with Ezra (Ezr 8:12). The name is Katan, "little," with the definite article prefixed. The name occurs in Akkad. as *Qitinu* and *Kuṭṭunu*.

HAKKOZ. *See* Koz.

HAKUPHA (h*ȧ*-kū'f*ȧ*). The sons of Hakupha were among the post-Exilic temple servants of lower rank who returned from Babylon with Zerubbabel (Ezr 2:51; Neh 7:53).

HALAH (hā 'l*ȧ*). City or district, unidentified, in Mesopotamia, perhaps near Gozan in the basin of the Habor River to which a portion of the northern tribes of Israel were deported by the Assyrian kings in 732 and 722 B.C. (II Kgs 17:6; 18:11; I Chr 5:26). Since a city gate of Nineveh facing NE was called "Gate of the land *Ḫalaḫḫu*," Halah may have been considerably E of the other locations to which Israelite captives were taken. *See* Habor.

HALAK (hā'lăk). A mountain, named as the southern limit of Joshua's conquests and rising toward Seir (Josh 11:17; 12:7), probably Jebel Halâq in the Negeb *c*. 30 miles SW of the Dead Sea, halfway to Kadesh-barnea. Apparently Mount Halak faced Avdat and the mountainous terrain of Seir which lay S of Wadi Zin (Wadi Fuqrah), for prior to the 13th cen. B.C. expansion of the Edomites, their territory of Seir lay W of the Arabah, on the way from Horeb to Kadesh-barnea (Deut 1:2).

HALHUL (hăl'hŭl). A village in the hill country of Judah beside Beth-zur and Gedor (Josh 15:58), about three miles N of Hebron.

HALI (hā'lī). A village on the boundary of Asher, named between Helkath and Beten (Josh 19:25). Its site is unknown.

HALL. *See* Court; Praetorium.

HALL OF JUDGMENT. *See* Praetorium; Gabbatha.

HALLEL (hăl'lĕl). This term, not found in the English Bible, comes from a Heb. verb meaning "to praise" (e.g., Ezr 3:11; II Chr 7:6). It later became a Jewish liturgical term referring to certain psalms. The "Egyptian" Hallel (Ps 113–118) was sung in the homes at the Passover (Mt 26:30), in the temple, and in the synagogues at the great annual festivals and at the day of the new moon. The "Great" Hallel (Ps 120–136, or 135–136, or just 136) praises God for rain (135:1, 7) and food (136:25). *See also* Alleluia.

HALLELUJAH (hăl'ĕ-lōō'y*ȧ*). *See* Alleluia.

HALLOHESH, HALOHESH (hă-lō'hĕsh). Father of the Shallum who ruled over part of Jerusalem and helped Nehemiah rebuild the wall (Neh 3:12). He also set his seal to a covenant with Ezra and Nehemiah to worship the Lord (Neh 10:24).

HALLOW, HALLOWED. Both words (also "holy") mean basically "to be clean," ceremonially and morally, and hence "sacred." The words are used of persons and things set apart for God. The sabbath was hallowed (Ex 20:11), as well as the priests (Ex 29:1), the tabernacle and its equipment (Ex 40:9), and Solomon's temple (I Kgs 9:3). God was hallowed, and He hallowed the people (Lev 22:32) and the firstborn (Num 3:13).

See Holiness; Sanctification.

HAM (hăm)

1. A city of the Zuzim, smitten by Chedorlaomer and his allies in the time of Abraham (Gen 14:5).

2. One of the three sons of Noah (Gen 5:32; 10:6-14). His descendants, who spread also to Mesopotamia, included the civilizations of Babylon, Erech (modern Warka), Akkad, Calneh, and Assyria (Gen 10:8-12). Cush was Ham's firstborn, the ancient Cassites, followed by Mizraim, Phut, and Canaan (Gen 10:6). Cush was the father of the peoples of Arabia (Gen 10:7). Mizraim produced the inhabitants of Egypt and adjoining countries, including the Philistines (Gen 10:13-14). Canaan was the father of the peoples spread from Sihon to Gaza and to Sodom and Gomorrah.

The history of the Canaanites is foreshadowed in the dishonoring of Noah by Ham when his father lay in a drunken stupor (Gen 9:20-23). The story of Gen 9:20-25 and the genealogy of Gen 10:6, 15-20 are included to show the origin of the Canaanites and the source of their licentious practices in the days of Joshua. Since Ham was not included in the blessing of Shem and Japheth, some have argued that the curse included Ham. It was applied, however, particularly to Canaan. Historically the curse was fulfilled in the destruction of the Canaanites and their descendants the Phoenicians (*see* Phoenicia). The curse pertained in a secondary way to the religious aspect of the Hamites of the OT period in that the religions of Egypt, Canaan, and Assyria were filled with a gross, sensual polytheism. The genealogy in Gen 10 demonstrates the truth that ancestry influences morality.

H. G. S.

"HAM, THEY OF." Descendants of Ham, the youngest son of Noah, either Egyptians, Ethiopians, or more probably Canaanites (cf. Gen 10:6), who had settled in the rich pastureland of southern Palestine. Their territory was seized by the descendants of Simeon, Jacob's second son (I Chr 4:40).

HAMAN (hā'mȧn). The "son of Hammedatha the Agagite." *See* Agagite. Haman was an influential official in the court of King Ahasuerus (Est 3:1). One of the least admirable characters of the OT, this prince was the embodiment of ignoble delusions of grandeur. After his promotion his vanity was gratified by the adulation of his associates, with the exception of Mordecai who, as a Jewish monotheist, did not venerate him (Est 3:2). In his childish fury Haman determined to destroy not only Mordecai but all Jews. His plans were thwarted by the heroism of Queen Esther, and, with poetic justice, his life ended on the gallows he had prepared for Mordecai (Est 7).

HAMATH (hā'măth). KJV uses Hemath in I Chr 13:5; Amos 6:14.

A city and a state (Isa 11:11; Jer 39:5; Zech 9:2) in Syria, located just N of the ideal boundary of Israel (Num 13:21; 34:8; Josh 13:5; *see* Lebo-hamath). The present site of the city, Hama on the Nahr el-Asi (the ancient Orontes), was excavated by H. Ingholt (1932-38), who discovered 12 levels of occupation. The city was founded in Neolithic times. Level H corresponds to the age of Hammurabi of Babylon, but Hamath was uninhabited during the Hyksos period (1750-1500 B.C.). Thutmose III of Egypt captured the city (ANET, p. 242); during the Amarna period it was the capital of an Amorite kingdom. Later it flourished as a local Hittite city-state, and eventually became Aramean under an influx of immigrants or by conquest.

Located as it was on the important trade route halfway between Aleppo and Damascus, with the more powerful states of Israel and Aram as its neighbors, Hamath had to defend its independence by alliances of one sort or another. Its king Toi sought the friendship of David after the latter's victories over the Arameans (II Sam 8:9 f.). Solomon built store-cities in the land of Hamath (II Chr 8:4).

In 853 B.C. it was the third state in the coalition that faced Shalmaneser III of Assyria in the battle of Qarqar (ANET, p. 279). An inscription of its king Zakir, *c.* 800 B.C., records a successful war against a group of kings headed by Ben-hadad of Damascus (ANET, pp. 501 f.). It is possible that this Zakir was the unnamed "savior" who helped Israel against the Arameans in the time of Jehoahaz (II Kgs 13:5). Jeroboam II recaptured land from Damascus and Hamath that had once belonged to David (II Kgs 14:28).

The prophet Amos, who was active about 760 B.C., describes Hamath as being in ruins in his time (Amos 6:2), possibly as a result of the Aramean attack. Subsequently Hamath was conquered by Sargon II of Assyria *c.* 721 B.C. (as alluded to in Isa 10:9), and its inhabitants transported to other countries. Some of them were sent to repeople the cities of Samaria, where for a time they worshiped their god Ashima (II Kgs 17:24, 30).

S. C.

HAMATH, ENTRANCE OF; ENTERING IN OF. *See* Lebo-hamath.

HAMATH-ZOBAH (hā'măth-zō'bȧ). Perhaps Hamath of Zobah. It is mentioned only in II Chr 8:3 in connection with the conquests of Solomon, who is said to have conquered it. But the reference is uncertain. The site has not been identified. Some believe that Hamath-zobah refers to the neighbor kingdoms of Hamath and Zobah, or that it is identical with Hamath (*q.v.*; Num 34:8), and that Zobah is used here in a broader sense. It is perhaps better to accept it as another Hamath located in the territory of Zobah.

HAMMATH (hăm'ăth)

1. The ancestral head of the Rechabite clan (I Chr 2:55, RSV; KJV has Hemath, *q.v.*).

2. A fortified town in the territory of Naphtali (Josh 19:35). It was probably located at Hammam Tabariyeh, a village with hot springs just S of Tiberias on the W shore of Galilee. Nearly all agree that Hammoth-dor (*q.v.;* Josh 21:32) and the Hammon (*q.v.*) of I Chr 6:76 are identical with Hammath.

HAMMEDATHA (hăm'ĕ-dā'thȧ). The father of Haman, the Jews' enemy in the book of Esther (Est 3:1, 10; 8:5; 9:10, 24). His name is typically Persian, possibly from *mâh,* "moon," and *data,* "given," "given by the moon."

HAMMELECH (hăm'ĕ-lĕk). A proper name in the KJV, but the word is better rendered as the ordinary Heb. word for "the king." Jerahmeel and Malchiah are each designated as "the son of the king" (Jer 36:26; 38:6, RSV), making them royal princes.

HAMMER. Several Heb. words have been translated "hammer" in the KJV. In OT times the head of a hammer was usually of a hard stone, less often of bronze or iron. Since it was used as a cutting tool, metal tended to be too soft.

1. Heb. *pațțîsh* was the hammer of the smith used for smoothing metals (Isa 41:7), and the large hammer used in quarrying (Jer 23:29; 50:23).

2. Heb. *maqqebet* was the smaller hammer of the stonecutter (I Kgs 6:7). It was also used by artisans in the manufacture of idols (Isa 44:12; Jer 10:4), and served as a mallet to drive Jael's tent pin (Jud 4:21). The name Maccabee, "the hammerer," is traditionally derived from this word.

3. In the poetic version, Jael's feat was performed with a *halmût,* a hammer or mallet (Jud 5:26).

4. In Ps 74:6, Heb. *kêlappôt,* a loan word from Akkad. *kalapâti,* would refer to crowbars rather than hammers.

A. T. P.

HAMMOLEKETH (hă-mŏl'ĕ-kĕth). Daughter of Machir and sister of Gilead, the grandson of Manasseh. Gideon the judge was descended from her (I Chr 7:17-18).

HAMMON (hăm'ŏn)

1. A border village of Asher (Josh 19:28), possibly Umm el-'Awamîd, ten miles S of Tyre, where two Phoenician inscriptions mentioning the worship of the god Baal Hammon have been found.

2. A Levitical town in Naphtali (I Chr 6:76), probably the same as Hammath (*q.v.*).

HAMMOTH-DOR (hăm'ŏth-dôr'). A city of Naphtali, allotted to the Gershonites and appointed a city of refuge (Josh 21:32). Called Hammon in I Chr 6:76, possibly modern Hammam Tabarîyeh, the hot springs just S of Tiberias on the W shore of the Sea of Galilee, but seemingly not of sufficient antiquity. Probably the same as Hammath (*q.v.*).

Presumed head of Hammurabi. LM

HAMMURABI (hăm'ŭ-rä'bĭ). A common Amorite name in the early 2nd mil. B.C. At least two kings of Yamhad (Aleppo) and a ruler of Qurda were so named. But its most famous holder was the sixth ruler of the First Dynasty of Babylon who reigned *c.* 1792-1750 B.C. (according to Sidney Smith) or 1728-1686 B.C. (according to W. F. Albright).

Amraphel, king of Shinar, whose allies attacked Sodom (Gen 14:1 f.), formerly thought to be a Heb. rendering of the name Hammurabi, is rather to be compared with such forms as the Amorite Amud-pi-el ("enduring is the word of El") found at Mari *c.* 1750 B.C.

Hammurabi of Babylon, as all rulers of city-states in the ancient Near East, recorded the legal cases he judged. Toward the end of his reign he rendered to his deity Shamash an account of his wisdom shown in the law and order, justice and truth which he had made prevail in the land. Selected cases and new laws were inscribed on stone stelae and erected in the principal temples of Babylonia. One of these, an eight foot tall black diorite pillar taken as loot to Susa, was recovered by French archaeologists in December, 1901, and is now in the Louvre in Paris. It is likely that similar written records of legal decisions were kept by the kings of Israel and Judah (JSS, VII [1962], 161-172).

From the prologue to the laws of Hammurabi as well as from the references in numerous contemporary texts of his reign (*see* Mari), the main events of his day can be retraced. At first the king worked to establish the internal economy; then the power of Babylon was gradually extended over the southern cities of Uruk (Erech) and Isin in a series of military campaigns. The capture of cities in the Diyala region and lower Euphrates brought him into direct contact with the powerful kings of Assyria, Mari and Aleppo. One Mari letter tells how at this time Hammurabi had 10 to 15 vassal rulers under him, about half the number claimed by

Code of Hammurabi. LM

the king of Aleppo. By his thirty-eighth year Hammurabi had beaten his rival Rim-Sin of Larsa, defeated the hill tribes of the Gutians and Eshnunna, and had captured Mari on the middle Euphrates from Zimri-Lim. He had thus won an empire of an area not to be exceeded by a Babylonian king until the time of Nebuchadrezzar II (605–562 B.C.).

Hammurabi's laws (ANET, pp. 163–180), which in a large measure continued the legal tradition of his predecessors Urukagina of Lagash, Lipit-Ishtar of Isin and Bilalama of Eshnunna, were a testimony to his administrative ability. These 282 judgments and stipulations covered a wide range of subjects: marriage, divorce, adoption, apprenticeship, theft, assault, farming, trade, property and wages. The penalties imposed varied according to the status of the offender or injured party whether freeman, palace dependent or slave. Capital punishment, physical penalties *(lex talionis),* property confiscation and money fines were imposed. Women had specific rights. All this shows a definite legal tradition which, at numerous points of form and detail, offers close parallels to the OT legal sections; e.g., the law of the goring ox (Ex 21:28 ff.) or of incest (Lev 20:14). The laws of Hammurabi thus afford an extrabiblical insight into legal traditions common throughout much of the ancient Near East.

Bibliography. G. R. Driver and John C. Miles, *The Babylonian Laws,* 2 vols., Oxford: Clarendon Press, 1952, 1955.

D. J. W.

HAMONAH (hȧ-mō'nȧ; "multitude"). Symbolical name of the place near which the multitudes of Gog are to be buried after the great slaughter (Ezk 39:16).

HAMON-GOG (hā'mŏn-gŏg'). A glen previously known as the "valley of the passers-by" opposite the sea (Dead Sea?), where the hosts which Gog brings with him will be slain and buried (Ezk 39:11, 15). *See* Gog.

HAMOR (hā'môr). The ruler of Shechem at the time of Jacob's return from Padan-aram. Shechem, Hamor's son, humiliated Dinah, Jacob's daughter; and her brothers, Simeon and Levi, avenged her wrong by killing all the men of Shechem (Gen 34:1–31).

Jacob bought a parcel of land from Hamor on which to pitch his tent (Gen 33:19). Later, Joseph was buried on this parcel of ground (Josh 24:32). As late as the judges, Hamor's name was still attached to Shechem (Jud 9:28). *See* Shechem.

The name Hamor means "ass," a fact that has led some scholars to consider the term as the name of a "totem clan." However, this theory is not necessarily true. Animal personal names were common in the ancient world; for example, Caleb means "dog," and Rachel means "ewe." It is possible that Hamor was an

Amorite or a Hittite, and practiced sacrificing an ass as a part of covenant making. (Cf. Mendenhall, BASOR #133 [1954], p. 26, n. 3.)

HAMUEL (hăm'ū-ĕl). A son of Mishma, a Simeonite, of the family of Shaul (I Chr 4:26).

HAMUL (hā'mŭl), **HAMULITES** (hā'mŭ-līts). The younger son of Pharez, sôn of Judah by Tamar. Hamul was founder of a tribal family (Gen 46:12; Num 26:21; I Chr 2:4-5).

HAMUTAL (hȧ-mū'tȧl). A daughter of Jeremiah of Libnah, one of King Josiah's wives, and mother of King Jehoahaz and King Zedekiah (II Kgs 23:31; 24:18; Jer 52:1).

HANAMEEL (hăn'ȧ-mēl). Son of Shallum and cousin of Jeremiah the prophet, who purchased an ancestral field from him at Anathoth during the siege of Jerusalem (Jer 32:7-9, 12).

HANAN (hā'nȧn)

1. The son or descendant of Shashak, one of the chief men of Benjamin (I Chr 8:23).
2. One of the six sons of Azel of Benjamin (I Chr 8:38; 9:44).
3. The son of Maachah. He was one of David's mighty men (I Chr 11:43).
4. The sons or descendants of Hanan were among the Nethinim (KJV) or temple servants (RSV) who returned with Zerubbabel (Ezr 2:46; Neh 7:49).
5. A Levite active in the days of Ezra and Nehemiah. He was one of those who helped the people understand the law as it was read by Ezra (Neh 8:7). He is probably the same Levite who signed the great covenant of Nehemiah and was appointed assistant to the treasurers of the storehouses who distributed the temple revenue among the priests and Levites (Neh 10:10; 13:13).
6. One of the chiefs of the people who signed the covenant of Nehemiah (Neh 10:22).
7. Another chief who signed the covenant (Neh 10:26).
8. The son of Igdaliah; he was an officer of the temple. Jeremiah brought the Rechabites into the chamber of Hanan's sons to test their faithfulness (Jer 35:4).

P. C. J.

HANANEEL, TOWER OF (hăn'ȧ-nēl). A tower in the N wall of Jerusalem between the sheep gate and the fish gate (Neh 3:1; 12:39; Jer 31:38; Zech 14:10). Together with the Tower of Meah (*q.v.*) it was probably part of the temple fortress. King Herod later replaced these by the Tower of Antonia (*q.v.*). *See* Jerusalem: Gates and Towers 3.

HANANI (hȧ-nā'nī)

1. One of the sons of Heman who was set apart for the service of music in the sanctuary. He and his family were chosen as the 18th class in the order of service organized by David (I Chr 25:4, 25).
2. The prophet who rebuked King Asa and proclaimed God's judgment upon him because he had appealed to Syria for aid in his fight against Israel, instead of to the Lord. The angry and impenitent king put the prophet in prison (II Chr 16:7-10). He is probably the same man who was father of the prophet Jehu who condemned Asa's rival Baasha and counseled his own successor, King Jehoshaphat (I Kgs 16:1, 7; II Chr 19:2; 20:34).
3. A priest in the days of Ezra who was convicted of marrying a foreign woman and pledged himself to put her away (Ezr 10:19-20).
4. A brother of Nehemiah. It was he who led the group that informed Nehemiah of the deplorable condition of Jerusalem (Neh 1:2). After the restoration of the city, Hanani, along with Hananiah, the "ruler of the palace," was given charge over Jerusalem (Neh 7:2).
5. A priest in the days of Nehemiah, who with others played "with the musical instruments of David" at the great dedication of the completed wall (Neh 12:36).

P. C. J.

HANANIAH (hăn'ȧ-nī'ȧ)

1. A son of Heman, appointed to blow the horn for temple and royal services (I Chr 25:4-5), and head of the 16th course of Levite musicians (I Chr 25:23). *See* Heman.
2. A captain of the army under King Uzziah (II Chr 26:11).
3. The father of Zedekiah, a prince of Judah in the reign of Jehoiakim, king of Judah (Jer 36:12).
4. A son of Azur, a false prophet in the fourth year of Zedekiah, king of Judah. He falsely and publicly proclaimed in the temple that within two full years the booty Nebuchadnezzar had taken would be returned and Jeconiah and the captives restored. When Jeremiah denounced him as a false prophet, Hananiah removed the yoke from Jeremiah's neck which he had been wearing as a symbol of his counsel to submit to Babylon. Thereupon, declaring Hananiah's yoke of wood was to become iron, that is, Babylonian control would become stronger, Jeremiah predicted Hananiah's death within the year. Hananiah died two months later (Jer 28).
5. Grandfather of Irijah who arrested Jeremiah in the "gate of Benjamin" as he sought to go to Nebuchadnezzar in obedience to God's word (Jer 37:13).
6. Son of Shashak, head of a Benjamite house (I Chr 8:24).
7. The Heb. name of Shadrach, one of the three young men taken to Babylon with Daniel (Dan 1:6-7, 11, 19; 2:17).
8. A son of Zerubbabel and ancestor of Jesus (I Chr 3:19, 21).
9. A son of Bebai, a repatriot with Ezra (Ezr 10:28).
10. An apothecary who helped repair the walls (Neh 3:8).

11. Son of Shelemiah, who with Hanun helped repair the walls (Neh 3:30).

12. A ruler of the palace in Nehemiah's time (Neh 7:2).

13. A sealer of the covenant to keep God's commands (Neh 10:23).

14. A priest in the time of Joiakim, the high priest (Neh 12:12, 41).

H. G. S.

HAND. The hand is the principal organ of touch and the member of the body chiefly employed in active service. As such, it is the symbol of human action. Pure hands mean pure actions, while hands full of blood symbolize deeds of iniquity (Ps 90:17; Job 9:30; I Tim 2:8; Isa 1:15). Washing of the hands was a sign of innocence, expiation, and sanctification (Ps 26:6; 24:3-4). *See* Ablution; Hands, Washing of.

The lifting up of the hands was a sign of prayer (I Tim 2:8; Job 11:13-14). Probably with this sense in mind, the term *yad* is used of a monument (II Sam 18:18; Isa 56:5, RSV). Such a stone pillar carved with two hands uplifted to divine symbols was found at Canaanite Hazor in 1955. The raising of the right hand *(cheir)* was evidently the method of voting in assemblies (cf. *cheirotoneō:* "ordained," Acts 14:23; "chosen," II Cor 8:19). A high hand (Ex 14:8) meant a brandished fist and signified defiance (Num 15:30, RSV; Deut 32:27; Isa 10:32; Acts 13:17).

The hand, especially the right one, was the emblem of power and strength. To hold by the right hand meant protection and favor (Ps 28:2, 5). To give the hand, as to a master, was a sign of future obedience (II Chr 30:8, marg.; Ps 68:31). To kiss the hand was an act of homage (I Kgs 19:18; Job 31:27). To pour water on another's hands meant to serve him (II Kgs 3:11). To seal up the hand was to stop man's work because of the ice and snow of winter (Job 37:7). Marks or scars on the hands or wrists signified a servant. Such marks showed a heathen's devotion to false gods (Zech 13:6). To stand at one's right hand was to aid or sustain anyone (Ps 16:8; 109:31). The right hand stretched out signified immediate exertion of power (Ex 15:12) and sometimes mercy (Isa 65:2; Prov 1:24). Being at the right hand of a person was the chief place of honor, dignity, and power (Ps 45:9). Such a place of position is accorded Christ Himself and shows His pre-eminence (Ps 110:1; Rom 8:34; Heb 1:3).

The hand of God as an anthropomorphism is His instrument of power. It is that which belongs to God Himself (Job 27:11; Acts 4:28; I Pet 5:6). The hand of the Lord upon anyone denotes favor (Ezr 7:6, 28; Acts 11:21), and against anyone signifies discipline (Ex 9:3; Amos 1:8; Acts 13:11). The hand of God upon a prophet denoted the enablement of the Holy Spirit (I Kgs 18:46; Ezk 8:1). The finger of God designated His power or Spirit (Lk 11:20; cf. Mt 12:28) and spoke of a work which only God could perform (Ex 8:19).

The laying on of hands marked out an individual and set him apart for service (Num 27:18-19; Acts 8:15-17; I Tim 4:14; II Tim 1:6). A perversion of this doctrine is seen when Simon offered money to obtain such a gift for himself in order to sell it or the powers to others (Acts 8:18), hence, simony. *See* Hands, Laying on of.

E. C. J.

HANDBREADTH. The breadth of the hand at the base of the four fingers, about three inches (Ex 25:25; 37:12; I Kgs 7:26; II Chr 4:5). Six handbreadths were a cubit. Ezekiel's cubit consisted of seven handbreadths (Ezk 40:5; 43:13), as did the royal systems of Egypt and Babylon. *See* Weights, Measures, and Coins.

In Ps 39:5 a handbreadth figuratively expresses the shortness of life.

HANDKERCHIEF. This word occurs only in the NT. A cloth used for wiping away perspiration. Handkerchiefs touched by Paul were carried away to heal the sick (Acts 19:12). The same Gr. word is translated "napkin" in Lk 19:20; Jn 11:44; 20:7. *See* Napkin.

In KJV "kerchiefs" apparently refers to veils of different lengths used by false prophetesses in divination to shroud persons consulting them (Ezk 13:18, 21).

HANDLE. Found only in Song 5:5 as part of a door bolt. The greatest diversity of handles in the ancient Near Eastern world is found on clay jars: e.g., loop handles, ledge handles, pierced lug handles, and high pitcher handles being characteristic of the Early Bronze Age; and wishbone, band, and stirrup handles seen in Late Bronze ware. *See* Pottery.

HANDMAID, HANDMAIDEN. The KJV rendering of *'āmâ* and *shiphḥâ,* terms denoting female slave, bondmaid, bondwoman, or maidservant. They attended to the personal needs of the mistress of the house (Gen 16:1; 25:12; 29:24), or nursed the children (Gen 24:59; II Sam 4:4; II Kgs 11:2). They had rights under the law (Ex 21:7-11; Lev 25:6), and could even become concubines when the first wife was sterile (Gen 16:1-2; 30:3, 9). The captive slave girl acquired new rights when taken to wife (Deut 21:10-14). Heb. slaves were to be emancipated in the year of jubilee (Lev 25:40) or after serving six years (Deut 15:12-17), but foreign slaves generally were slaves for life (Lev 25:45-46).

The term was sometimes used in expressing humility and submission (I Sam 25:24; II Sam 14:12; Lk 1:38).

A. T. P.

HANDS, LAYING ON OF. This is a religious act which signifies the impartation of a special blessing. *See* Hand. It was used to set aside the Levites for their special office (Num 8:5-20) and to dedicate animals (Lev 1:4). Thus Isaac blessed the sons of Joseph (Gen 48:14-19) and Jesus the little children (Mk 10:16). Jesus healed the sick by laying His hands on them (Lk 4:40; 13:13).

The seven deacons in Jerusalem were thus set aside by the apostles (Acts 6:6), and in Antioch Barnabas and Paul (Acts 13:3) were consecrated by this means. Peter and John laid their hands on certain Samaritans "and they received the Holy Ghost" (Acts 8:14-17). At Ephesus Paul did the same, with the same result (Acts 19:6). Here the believers received the gift of tongues and prophesied. Timothy (I Tim 4:14; II Tim 1:6) received a special gift by Paul laying his hands on him. Blessing, healing, and consecration are associated with the act.

In churches today it is used in official acts of the public ministry, such as baptism, confirmation, and ordination. In the Roman Catholic church, laying on of hands is regarded as a sacrament by which the fitness for an office is conferred.

Calvin (*Institutes,* IV, 19, 6) disallowed the example of the apostolic laying on of hands, because "those miraculous powers and manifest workings, which were dispensed by the laying on of hands have ceased; and they have rightly lasted only as a time." The Lutheran Apology of the Augsburg Confession allowed it to be called "a sacrament," if it referred to teaching the gospel and administering the sacraments.

C. S. M.

HANDS, WASHING OF. Ceremonial washing of the body is universally recognized as a religious symbol or an effective sacrament for cleansing from the defilement and guilt of sin. In the OT, the brass laver was placed between the altar and the holy place of the tabernacle and temple so that the priests who were ministering unto the Lord might wash hands and feet (Ex 30:17-21). The baptism of John was a symbol of the cleansing from sins that followed repentance (Mt 3:6-11). Pilate the governor called for water and washed his hands before the multitude as though this would absolve him from the guilt of the crucifixion of Christ (Mt 27:24).

Highly decorated ablution basin at the Temple of Jupiter, Baalbek, HFV

A large ablution basin at the entrance to the Hittite temple of the storm god at Boghazköy. HFV

The Pharisees, in their zeal for the law, had deduced innumerable ways in which a person might contact ceremonial defilement, which, while not sinful, nevertheless made one Levitically unclean and unable to approach God in worship. Correspondingly, they had developed an elaborate program of washings to counteract this defilement. The discussion with Jesus in regard to the unwashed hands of His disciples had to do with this ceremonial act and not with ordinary cleansing. Jesus condemned the Pharisees because by the innumerable, burdensome details of their washings they had obscured the will as well as the Word of God. "Ye reject the commandment of God, that ye may keep your own tradition" (Mk 7:1-9). They had made a moral obligation out of what was only symbolic and ceremonial. (See Edersheim, *Life and Times of Jesus the Messiah,* II, 9 ff., for an extended treatment.)

See Ablution; Hand.

P. C. J.

HANDSTAFF. *See* Armor.

HANDWRITING. In Col 2:14 the KJV expression "handwriting" (Gr. *cheirographon*) is a hand-written document, often found in the Gr. papyri with the specific sense of a certificate of indebtedness (see NASB) or bond (RSV). In this passage the term presumably refers to the written Mosaic law. Its decrees or obligations which stood "against us" were fulfilled by Christ, and then it was cancelled and cast aside by "nailing it to His cross." *See* Writing.

HANES (hā'nēz). A city in Egypt to which Judah sent envoys (Isa 30:4), almost certainly a site just S of the Fayyum, 55 miles S of Memphis on the W bank of the Nile, still known as Ahnas. The Greeks identified the local deity

Herishef with Hercules and called the city Heracleopolis Magna. Hanes was the home of the Twenty-second Dynasty (935–735 B.C.), and remained a city of great importance. In the reign of Psamtik I (663–609 B.C., Twenty-sixth Dynasty) Hanes was the center of government of Upper Egypt. On the basis of the Aramaic targum of the passage, however, some scholars have identified Hanes with Taphanes, a fortress on the E frontier.

HANGING. *See* Gallows; Crime and Punishment.

HANIEL (hăn'ĭ-ĕl). A son of Ulla and a prince and hero of the tribe of Asher (I Chr 7:39). The name is spelled Hanniel *(q.v.)* in RSV.

HANNAH (hăn'*à*). Only one woman of this name appears in the Bible, although "Anna" (the Gr. equivalent) is the name of another woman mentioned in Lk 2:36. The name means "grace" or "graciousness."

The story of Hannah, the mother of Samuel, is found in I Sam 1–2. She was one of the two wives of Elkanah, a Levite of the line of Kohath, who lived in Mount Ephraim. Perhaps because Hannah was barren he had married Penninah, his second wife, who bore him children. Hannah was a woman of prayer and faith as well as a woman of strong desires. She begged God for a son, and promised that if God gave her one, she would give him back to the Lord. This she did when Samuel was born, taking him to the tabernacle as a small boy and leaving him in the care of Eli the high priest. She later became the mother of five more children (I Sam 2:21).

Hannah's prophetic prayer (I Sam 2:1–10) reveals much regarding her spiritual maturity and insight. She was filled with joy, she recognized God's holiness and strength, His sovereignty and grace. She spoke of His keeping power and of the fact that He would some day "judge the ends of the earth." Furthermore, she seems, however vaguely, to have foreseen the eventual establishment of God's Anointed to be King, a prophecy that began to be fulfilled in David a century later (I Sam 2:10; cf. Ps 18:50; 89:19–37).

J. A. S.

HANNATHON (hăn'*à*-thŏn). A town on the N border of Zebulun (Josh 19:14). It is mentioned twice in the Amarna tablets (EA 8:17; 245:32) of the 14th cen. B.C., where it is called Ḫinnatuni and Ḫinatuna respectively, and once in the records of Tiglath-pileser III.

Perhaps it was located at Tell el-Bedeiwîyeh, a site approximately six miles N of Nazareth. Some identify it with el-Harbaj at the S end of the plain of Acco.

HANNIEL (hăn'ĭ-ĕl)

1. The son of Ephod and a prince of Manasseh who assisted in dividing Canaan among the tribes. Appointed to superintend the distribution of the W Jordanian territory among ten tribes to be settled in that area (Num 34:23).

2. A man of Asher (I Chr 7:39, RSV). Spelled Haniel *(q.v.)* in KJV.

HANOCH (hā'nŏk)

1. Head of a Midianite clan whose ancestry is traced to Abraham through Keturah (Gen 25:4; I Chr 1:33: KJV, Henoch).

2. The eldest son of Reuben (Gen 46:9; Ex 6:14; Num 26:5; I Chr 5:3).

HANUN (hā'n*ŭ*n)

1. The son and heir of Nahash, king of the Ammonites. When David sent a message of consolation to Hanun upon the death of his father, the new king chose to interpret the act as one of espionage. The ambassadors were arrested and disgraced by having half of each man's beard shaved off and his garments cut off at the middle, before being ejected from Ammon. This insult was considered by David an act of war, and he prepared his army to invade Ammon. Hanun, anticipating the invasion, had already sent for help to the Syrians. David's army, led by Joab and Abishai, was trapped between Ammonites and Syrians, but valiantly defeated both forces. This was the beginning of a war with Ammon that went on for some time (II Sam 10; I Chr 19).

2. The sixth son of Zalaph who repaired part of the wall of Jerusalem (Neh 3:30).

3. Another Hanun who with the inhabitants of Zanoah repaired the valley gate of Jerusalem and part of the wall (Neh 3:13).

P. C. J.

HAPHRAIM (hăf-rā'ĭm). A town in Issachar mentioned as between Shunem and Shion (Josh 19:19). Spelled *ḥprm* in Shishak's list of conquered Palestinian towns. Probably located at et-Taiyibeh NW of Bethshan and seven miles NE of Jezreel.

HARA (hâr'*à*). Named in I Chr 5:26 along with Halah, Habor, and the river Gozan, to which Tiglath-pileser III of Assyria exiled the Heb. tribes of Reuben, Gad, and half of Manasseh.

In II Kgs 17:6; 18:11 where the Heb. has "cities of Media," the LXX has "mountains of Media." Perhaps the Heb. *Hārā'* in I Chr 5:26 is a corruption of this. Others have suggested Hara should be read Haran.

HARADAH (h*à*-rā'd*à*). A stopping place in the journey of the Israelites from Sinai to Kadesh-barnea (Num 33:24–25). The location is unknown.

HARAN (hā'răn). An important crossroads and commercial city of Syria, situated about 20 miles S of Edessa on the Belias (now Belikh) River, on the high road which ran from Nineveh to Carchemish and on to the shores of the

Mediterranean. Its name (Heb. *ḥārān,* Akkad. *ḫarrānu*) means "road, route, caravan." In Hittite it became *ḫarvana,* the basis of our English word caravan.

Haran is first mentioned in the Bible as the place to which Terah journeyed from Ur of the Chaldeans. Here Terah died and Abraham received the call of God to leave his kindred and go to Canaan. Abraham left with his wife and his nephew Lot, while the other members of the clan remained behind (Gen 11:31–12:4). Though it is not specifically stated, Haran was apparently the place where the servant of Abraham, seeking a wife for Isaac, met Rebekah at the well; the traditional site of this well is still shown. Later Jacob fled to his uncle Laban, who lived in or near Haran (Gen 28:10), and spent 20 years before returning (Gen 28–30).

The only other biblical reports about Haran are that it was once destroyed by the Assyrians (II Kgs 19:12) and that its merchants exported blue embroidered garments and choice carpets (Ezk 27:23–24).

Haran is frequently mentioned in sources outside the Bible. Its name appears in a letter from Mari written about 2000 B.C., close to the time of Abraham. The city was a center of worship of the moon-god Sin. The other great center of Sin worship was Ur of the Chaldeans; hence it is very probable that Haran was founded by colonists sent out from Ur. Thus it is possible that Terah made the long journey from the fertile, prosperous lands of Babylonia to the less favorable regions of Syria as the leader of such a band of colonists. In the early centuries of the 2nd mil. B.C. Haran was near the center of the Hurrian occupation, so that the patriarchs undoubtedly came in contact with this dominant social element known to us through the Nuzu tablets (*see* Horites: Nuzu). Later records show that the city passed through various vicissitudes; it was at times in the hands of Mitannians, Assyrians, and Arameans.

When the Assyrian Empire was supreme in western Asia after 730 B.C., Haran was a strong fortress and the residence of a *turtan* ("commander," usually of royal blood). According to the *Babylonian Chronicle,* when Nineveh fell to the Medes and Babylonians in 612 B.C., the turtan of Haran, Ashur-uballit II, headed a short-lived Assyrian kingdom. Haran was besieged and taken by the Babylonians, and although the Assyrians had Egyptian aid, they failed to recover it; thus ended the Assyrian Empire.

Haran appears again in the story of Nabonidus, the last king of Babylonia (555–539 B.C.), who restored the famous temple of Sin, called Ehulhul, intending it for the chief religious center of his empire. The Romans kept the town as a fortress (Carrhae); nearby the army of Crassus was annihilated by the Parthians in 53 B.C.

The present-day town marks the site of the old settlement. Ancient inscriptions have been found in Eski-haran (Turkish, "old Haran") six miles farther N, so that this may be the site of the famous temple of Sin.

Bibliography. William Hallo, "Haran, Harran," BW, pp. 280–283.

S. C.

HARARITE (hâr'ȧ-rīt). The designation of three of David's mighty men known as the "thirty," perhaps signifying each was a "mountaineer": (1) Agee (II Sam 23:11); (2) Shammah (II Sam 23:33; Shage in I Chr 11:34); (3) Sharar (II Sam 23:33; Sacar in I Chr 11:35).

HARBONA(H) (här-bō'nȧ). The third of the seven eunuchs who served as chamberlains for Ahasuerus (Xerxes) mentioned in Est 1:10. He suggested Haman be hanged upon the gallows prepared for Mordecai (Est 7:9; Harbonah in KJV).

HARDNESS OF HEART. An expression found several times in the NT describing a certain moral attitude and firm set of mind. This stubbornness, impenitence (Rom 2:5) and impenetrability of man's heart as a condition is caused by wickedness and sin (Ex 9:34; Heb 3:13). Jesus Christ was grieved at the hardness *(pōrōsis)* or callousness of the Pharisees' hearts as He was about to perform a miracle on the sabbath (Mk 3:5). This callousness or ossification often resulted in inability to understand (Eph 4:18, "blindness," KJV; "hardness," RSV; cf. the verb *pōroō,* Mk 6:52; 8:17; II Cor 3:14). Another Gr. term *(sklērokardia)* signifies the dryness or stiff, unbending quality of mind in the realms of both faith (Mk 16:14; cf. the verb *sklērunō* used in Acts 19:9; Heb 3:8, 13, 15; 4:7) and practice (Mt 19:8; Mk 10:5).

In the Bible the act of hardening is attributed both to man (Ex 8:15; Heb 3:8) and to God (Ex 9:12; Deut 2:30; Josh 11:20; Isa 63:17; Rom 9:18). Many of the passages referring to hardening the heart relate to the refusal of Pharaoh to let God's people go out from Egypt. The Heb. verbs *qāshâ,* "make sharp, hard, obstinate" (Ex 7:3; Prov 28:14; 29:1); *kāḇēd,* "be heavy, insensible" (Ex 7:14; 8:15, 32; 9:7, 34; 10:1; I Sam 6:6); and *ḥāzaq,* "make strong, headstrong, stiff, unyielding" (Ex 4:21; 7:13, 22; 8:19; 9:12, 35; etc.) are used interchangeably, both of Pharaoh's own action and of the Lord's causing the hardness. While the Lord told Moses He would harden Pharaoh's heart (Ex 4:21; 7:3), seven times it is said the king of Egypt hardened his heart himself (7:13, properly "was hardened," RSV; 7:14, 22; 8:15, 19, 32; 9:7) before God actually hardened it (9:12). Thus both in the OT (I Sam 6:6, where even the heathen recognized the Egyptians and Pharaoh were responsible for their hardness) and in the NT (Rom 9:17–18) Pharaoh's hardening is mentioned as typical.

The theological problem of who bears the responsibility for hardness of the heart is thus resolved by a close study of Pharaoh's example. Men, by acting in accordance with their own self-will, carry out God's purpose in history. The Lord finally confirmed Pharaoh's attitude, lest out of sheer human weakness the king might give in before God had fully accomplished His will in judging Egypt. Israel in the wilderness was responsible for hardening their necks (Neh 9:16–17, 29) in manifesting a lack of faith and a disobedient, rebellious spirit (Ps 95:8; Heb 3:7–4:11).

Regarding salvation, it is well to remember that God takes no pleasure in the death of the wicked and is not willing that any should perish (Ezk 33:11; II Pet 3:9; cf. I Tim 2:4). Nevertheless, the same manifestation of divine mercy softens the hearts of those who repent and find forgiveness in Christ, but hardens the hearts of those who resist and obstinately refuse to heed God's invitation. Rom 9:14–18 is not specifically speaking of the sovereign grace that leads men to salvation, but rather that chooses certain men through whom God may advance His will on earth. *See* Heart.

Bibliography. K. L. and M. A. Schmidt, "*Pachunō, . . . , Sklēras, . . . ,*" TDNT, V, 1022–1031.

J. R.

HARE. *See* Animals, II.16.

HAREPH (hâr'ĕf). A Judahite chief, descended from Caleb, who founded Beth-gader, located somewhere in the region of Bethlehem and Kirjath-jearim (I Chr 2:51).

HARETH (hâr'ĕth). A forest between Adullam and Giloh in which David hid after his sojourn in Moab (I Sam 22:5; Hereth in RSV). Possibly the scene of the incident narrated in II Sam 23:14–17; I Chr 11:16–19.

HARHAIAH (här-hā'yȧ). Father of Uzziel, who helped repair the walls of Jerusalem under Nehemiah (Neh 3:8).

HARHAS (här'hăs). Grandfather of Shallum, husband of the prophetess Huldah (II Kgs 22:14). In II Chr 34:22 the name is spelled Hasrah *(q.v.)*; the transposition of letters is probably a scribal error.

HARHUR (här'hûr). The ancestral head of a family of temple servants listed among the returned exiles (Ezr 2:51; Neh 7:53).

HARIM (hâr'ĭm)

1. The priest who was appointed by lot and thus gave his name to the third of 24 divisions or courses into which the priests were separated for service (I Chr 24:8). The 1,017 "sons of Harim" who came back from Babylon (Ezr 2:39; Neh 7:42) simply belonged to this course of Harim. Five of them took foreign wives (Ezr 10:21). The Harim who signed Nehemiah's covenant (Neh 10:5) and the priest Adna (Neh 12:15) seem to have belonged to this family. If the conjecture is correct that Rehum (Neh 12:3) is a scribal error for Harim, the name is also listed among the priests who returned with Zerubbabel from Babylon.

2. The ancestor of a large family of lay Israelites which bore his name. Accompanying Zerubbabel, 320 male members of this clan returned from Exile (Ezr 2:32; Neh 7:35). One of them was among the leaders who sealed the covenant with Nehemiah (Neh 10:27). Eight of these laymen were guilty of marrying foreign women (Ezr 10:31; cf. 10:44). One of the eight, Malchijah, helped repair the wall of Jerusalem (Neh 3:11).

P. C. J.

HARIPH (hâr'ĭf)

1. Head of a family whose 112 male members returned to Jerusalem after the Exile (Neh 7:24); apparently called Jorah in Ezr 2:18.

2. One of those who sealed Ezra's covenant (Neh 10:19).

HARLOT, WHORE. A woman guilty of illicit sexual relationships for reasons other than sexual pleasure is normally referred to in the English versions of the Bible as a whore, harlot, or prostitute, with the latter two designations being the terms normally used in the more recent versions.

In biblical times, harlotry was practiced for both mercenary and religious purposes. This fact is to be seen in the usage of the various Heb. words that refer to harlot. Heb. *zônâ,* the usual word, normally refers to a woman engaging in the practice for monetary purposes. The religious prostitute was normally called a *qedēshâ,* designating a female who belonged to a special class of religiously consecrated individuals. It was nothing unusual for the heathen religious systems of both OT and NT times to regularly employ prostitutes in their worship rituals at their idol shrines, and the Canaanite religions were no exception in this regard. It was a system which deified the reproductive organs and forces, the assumption being that reproduction and fertility in nature were controlled by sexual relations between gods and goddesses. The worshipers in the shrines of these cults would engage in sexual intercourse with the religious prostitutes (both male and female) of the shrine in the belief that this would prompt the gods and goddesses to do the same, thus bringing fertility and productivity to family, fields, and flocks. *See* Cults.

Inasmuch as the idolatrous practices of the Canaanites made inroads into the worship of the one true God, it is not at all surprising to find some indications in the OT that a syncretism of these fertility rites with the worship of Yahweh had been attempted (Amos 2:7; Hos 4:13 ff.; Jer 3:1–2).

Two other phrases occur in the Heb. of Proverbs which refer to harlots, i.e., *'ishshâ nokrîyâ* (foreign woman) and *'ishshâ zārâ* (strange woman). From the frequency of these terms in Proverbs it may be inferred that during the time of Solomon the foreign influences to which Israel was subjected caused a rise in prostitution, with many of these prostitutes being foreigners.

In the Gr. NT the one word that designates a harlot is *pornē*. Though it does not occur with great frequency in the NT, it was a common word; words related to it etymologically, two nouns and a verb, are of frequent occurrence.

The Bible consistently advocates moral purity and stands against prostitution of whatever type. Various bans are to be found in the Mosaic law (Lev 19:29; 21:7, 14; Deut 22:21). Proverbs is replete with its warnings to those who would go in to prostitutes. The same dangers confronted NT believers, for fertility cults of various types were still existent in the Roman Empire and the general moral tone in the 1st cen. was anything but high. Prohibition of prostitution would be included in those general prohibitions of illicit sexual relationships which pervade the NT. *See* Fornication.

The words for harlot and the concept of harlotry also have a significant figurative usage in Scripture in which those who are supposedly God's people, but who are also guilty of apostasy, are said to be guilty of harlotry. There is a twofold reason for this figurative usage. First, apostasy might actually involve one in the type of religious prostitution that has already been described. But the second aspect is probably the more significant. The relationship between God and His people is compared in Scripture to the marriage relationship involving union with and fidelity to one another. Thus when God's people apostatize they are in a figurative sense guilty of harlotry, for they have violated that relationship with God which is likened to marriage (cf. Num 25:1-2; Jud 2:13-17; 8:27, 33; Jer 3:1-6; Ezk 6:9; Hos 4:12; I Cor 6:15; Rev 2:21-22).

In Rev 14:8 and 17:1-19:2 the harlot named Babylon designates a future apostate religious system that is both unfaithful to and hostile to God.

Bibliography. William F. Albright, *Archaeology and the Religion of Israel,* Baltimore: Johns Hopkins Press, 1953, pp. 74-78, 93, 114 f., 158 f.; *Yahweh and the Gods of Canaan,* Garden City, N.Y.: Doubleday, 1968, pp. 119-152. Friedrick Hauck and Siegfried Schulz, "*Pornē*, etc.," TDNT, VI, 579-595.

S. N. G.

HARNEPHER (här'nĕ-fĕr). One of the sons of Zophah, a chief of the tribe of Asher (I Chr 7:36); a transliteration of the Egyptian *hr-nfr,* "Horus is merciful."

HARNESS. Found in the KJV translation of Heb. *shiryon* in I Kgs 22:34 and II Chr 18:33 where there is a marginal reading of "breastplate." The RSV translates "breastplate" in both passages. The KJV translates Heb. *nēsheq* as "harness" in II Chr 9:24; the RSV translates this as "myrrh," while the Jerusalem Bible has "armour," as in I Kgs 10:25; II Kgs 10:2; Isa 22:8.

In Jer 46:4 the expression "harness the horses" has its modern meaning of fastening animals to a vehicle, from Heb. *'āsar,* "to bind, tie," used also of the two milch cows tied or harnessed to a cart by the Philistines (I Sam 6:7, 10).

The harness of Egyptian war chariots was of leather, richly decorated and studded with gold and silver. Likewise the three horses drawing Ashurnasirpal II's royal hunting chariot were

A war chariot of King Ashurbanipal of Assyria with a good view of a harness. LM

bedecked with elaborate harness (ANEP #184).

HAROD (hâr'ŏd). A spring (not a "well," KJV) which was the site of Gideon's encampment while preparing for battle with the Midianites (Jud 7:1). Possibly the fountain where Saul made camp against the Philistines (I Sam 29:1). It has been identified by some with 'Ain Jalud, a spring located on the NW slope of Mount Gilboa, eight miles WNW of Beth-shean. The water flows out of a natural cavern into a large pool, from which Gideon's men likely slaked their thirst. It is one of the most copious springs in Palestine, an important consideration for any military movements in the neighborhood.

HARODITE (hâr'ŏ-dīt). Two of David's men (Shammah and Elika) are called Harodites in II Sam 23:25. "Harorite" (I Chr 11:27) is a common scribal error for Harodite.

HAROEH. *See* Reaiah.

HARORITE (hâr'ŏ-rīt). This term (I Chr 11:27) should probably be read Harodite (cf. II Sam 23:25) since the *r* and *d* are very similar in Hebrew. *See* Harodite.

HAROSHETH OF THE GENTILES (hă-rō'shĕth). The term occurs only in Jud 4:2, 13, 16 in connection with the confrontation between the Israelites under Deborah and Barak, and Sisera, general of the Canaanite army. If Harosheth was a city, the text calls for proximity to the Kishon River at a place near the W end of the Plain of Esdraelon where it could flood to an extent required in Jud 5:21. This would be in the Kishon pass *c.* ten miles NNW of Megiddo. The site is generally identified with either the village of *el-Ḥârithîyeh* or *Tell 'Amr* nearby, both of which are doubtful because of soundings which indicate neither are of sufficient antiquity. Some scholars prefer *Tell Harbaj,* three miles N of *el-Ḥârithîyeh.* That Sisera "dwelt" (*yôshēb,* Jud 4:2) there may mean he was (military) governor of the area, and this may explain why a specific city has been so hard to find (cf. with use of *yôshēb* in Num 33:40; Jud 4:5; 10:1, and *l.*8 of the Moabite Stone which states Omri "dwelt" in or occupied the land of Medeba, ANET, p. 320).

P. W. F.

HARP. *See* Musical Instruments.

HARPOON. Found in Job 41:7, RSV and Jerusalem Bible as the translation of Heb. *śukkâ.* KJV has "barbed irons."

HARROW. The word so translated in II Sam 12:31 and I Chr 20:3 (Heb. *ḥārîṣ*) was a sharp instrument made of iron. It may have been some kind of threshing instrument (cf. *ḥārûṣ,* Isa 28:27; 41:15; Amos 1:3) or it may have been an agricultural implement like a hoe or pick-axe drawn over plowed land to level it and break the clods before sowing the seed, and then to cover the seed which had been sown. A different word (*śādad*) used in Job 39:10; Isa 28:24; Hos 10:11 expresses the breaking of clods or fallow ground in some manner, but it is doubtful that it was the same as the modern harrow.

HARSHA (här'shȧ). Eponym of family of temple servants who returned from Babylon with Zerubbabel (Ezr 2:52; Neh 7:54).

HART. *See* Animals: Deer, II.10.

HARUM (hâr'ŭm). The father of Aharhel, listed among the posterity of Coz (I Chr 4:8) of the tribe of Judah.

HARUMAPH (hȧ-rū'măf). The father of Jedaiah, who helped repair the walls of Jerusalem in the time of Nehemiah (Neh 3:10).

HARUPHITE (hȧ-rū'fīt). The appellative of Shephatiah, one of the Benjamite warriors who joined David at Ziklag (I Chr 12:5). Possibly there is some relation between this designation and the Calebite Hareph of I Chr 2:51 or the Hariph family of Neh 7:24; 10:19, since no place of this name is known.

HARUZ (hâr'ūz). Maternal grandfather of Amon, king of Judah (II Kgs 21:19). His place of origin was Jotbah.

HARVEST. The gathering of crops was the most important season on Israel's calendar. The Hebrews were primarily dependent on their harvests for livelihood (Gen 45:6; Prov 10:5; 20:4; Jer 5:17). Events were dated from harvests (Gen 30:14; Josh 3:15; Jud 15:1; Ruth 1:22; 2:23; I Sam 6:13; II Sam 21:9; 23:13). The three principal feasts of the Jews corresponded to their main harvest seasons (Ex 23:14–17; 34:18, 22–23): (1) the Passover, April-May, early in the barley harvest (cf. II Sam 21:9); (2) the Feast of Pentecost, seven weeks later, May-June, after the wheat harvest (Ex 34:22); (3) the Feast of Tabernacles (or Booths) during the fruit harvest, September-October. (Cf. G. E. Wright, BA, pp. 180 ff., for the Gezer Calendar.)

Both in the OT and NT the harvest figure is used to teach spiritual truths. A devastated harvest signified devastation or affliction (Job 5:5; Isa 16:9; 17:11; Jer 5:17; 50:16). The "time of harvest" could mean the day of destruction (Jer 51:33; Hos 6:11; Joel 3:13). "Joy in the harvest" suggested abounding joy (Isa 9:3); "harvest of Nile," an abundant harvest for profitable commerce (Isa 23:3, ASV, RSV). "The harvest is past" meant disappointment (Jer 8:20) or lost opportunity. "A cloud of dew in the heat of harvest" (Isa 18:4-5) spoke of the calm of summer approaching harvest season, to illustrate the Lord's waiting quietly until He would annihilate the wicked. The Master frequently referred to the harvest of souls (Mt

Harvest in the Fields of Boaz at Bethlehem. MPS

9:37-38; 13:30, 39; Mk 4:29; Jn 4:35). Also He employed the term in explaining the parable of the tares, "the harvest is the end of the age" (Mt 13:39, NASB; cf. Rev 14:15).

See Agriculture.

D. W. D.

HASADIAH (hăs'ȧ-dī'ȧ). One of the sons of Zerubbabel (I Chr 3:20).

HASENUAH (hăs'ē-nōō'ȧ). The name means "the hated one."

1. A Benjamite, the father of Hodaviah (I Chr 9:7).

2. Without the definite article in Heb. the name is Senuah (KJV), a Benjamite whose son Judah was the second in command of Jerusalem (Neh 11:9). Neh 11:9 and I Chr 9:7 may refer to the same person.

See Hassenaah.

HASHABIAH (hăsh'ȧ-bī'ȧ)

1. The father of Malluch and son of Amaziah, a Levite of the family of Merari, a musician in the temple (I Chr 6:45).

2. A returned exile, the father of Azrikam and son of Bunni of the Levite family of Merari (I Chr 9:14; Neh 11:15).

3. One of the six musician sons of Jeduthun, appointed by David to head the 12th course of singers in the temple (I Chr 25:3, 19).

4. Hashabiah of Hebron, appointed by David to have oversight of Israel W of the Jordan; 1,700 men worked under him (I Chr 26:30).

5. The son of Kemuel, chief officer of the tribe of Levi in David's time (I Chr 27:17).

6. A leading man among the Levites in the days of Josiah who gave liberally for the great Passover (II Chr 35:9).

7. One of the chiefs of the Levites who went up with Ezra to Jerusalem (Ezr 8:19) and who was entrusted with the great treasure brought to Jerusalem (Ezr 8:24). He was probably the same Hashabiah who became ruler of half the district of Keilah (Neh 3:17). He was active in the days of Nehemiah, repairing the wall, sealing the covenant (Neh 10:11), and taking part in the dedication of the completed wall (Neh 12:24).

8. A Levite, son of Mattaniah and father of Bani, after the Exile (Neh 11:22).

9. The head of the priestly family of Hilkiah in the days of the high priest Joiakim (Neh 12:21), perhaps the same as 7.

P. C. J.

HASHABNAH (hȧ-shăb'nȧ). One of the chiefs of the people who with Nehemiah set their seal on Ezra's renewal of the covenant (Neh 10:25).

HASHABNIAH (hăsh'ăb-nī'ȧ)

1. Father of a certain Hattush, who helped repair the walls of Jerusalem in the time of Nehemiah (Neh 3:10).

2. One of a group of Levites who participated in a blessing offered to God during the time of Ezra as preparation for the sealing of the covenant (Neh 9:5).

HASHBADANA (hăsh-băd'ȧ-nȧ). One of the men who stood at Ezra's left when the law was read to the people at the great assembly (Neh 8:4).

HASHEM (hā'shĕm). A Gizonite, one of the 30 mighty men of the armies of David (I Chr 11:34), called Jashen *(q.v.)* in II Sam 23:32.

HASHMONAH (hăsh-mo'nȧ) One of the camping places of the Israelites in their journey from

Sinai to Canaan (Num 33:29-30), perhaps to be identified with Wadi Hashim in the vicinity of Kadesh-barnea.

HASHUB (hā'shŭb)
1. A Levite, the son of Azrikam of the family of Merari. His son Shemaiah was one of the supervisors of the temple in the days of Nehemiah (I Chr 9:14, spelled Hasshub; Neh 11:15).
2. The son of Pahath-moab, a repairer of part of the wall of Jerusalem (Neh 3:11).
3. Another who worked under Nehemiah on the wall (Neh 3:23).
4. One of the leading Israelites who sealed the covenant of Nehemiah. He could be either 2 or 3 (Neh 10:23).

HASHUBAH (hȧ-shōō'bȧ). One of the sons of Zerubbabel and a descendant of Jehoiakim, king of Judah (I Chr 3:20).

HASHUM (hā'shŭm)
1. The "children of Hashum" were among the Israelites who returned with Zerubbabel to rebuild the temple (Ezr 2:19; Neh 7:22). They are also listed among those who put away their foreign wives in the time of Ezra (Ezr 10:33).
2. One of the men who stood beside Ezra as he read the law before the people (Neh 8:4).
3. One of the chiefs of the people who signed the covenant made by Nehemiah to obey God's law (Neh 10:18).

HASHUPHA (hȧ-shōō'fȧ), **HASUPHA** (hȧ-sōō'fȧ). The ancestral head of a family of Nethinim *(q.v.)* which returned from Exile with Zerubbabel (Ezr 2:43; Neh 7:46).

HASMONEANS. *See* Maccabees.

HASRAH (hăz'rȧ). Grandfather of Shallum, the husband of Huldah, the prophetess who was consulted about the book of the law found during Josiah's reign (II Chr 34:22). Called Harhas *(q.v.)* in II Kgs 22:14.

HASSENAAH (hăs'ĕ-nā'ȧ). Identical with Senaah (Ezr 2:35; Neh 7:38) where it appears without the article. *See* Senaah. The "sons" or men of Hassenaah rebuilt the fish gate when the wall of Jerusalem was repaired after the exiles returned from Babylon (Neh 3:3). The name is probably identical with Hasenuah *(q.v.)* in I Chr 9:7 or Senuah in Neh 11:9, seemingly a personal name. But the number of sons of Senaah, nearly 4,000 (Ezr 2:35; Neh 7:38), is extraordinarily large for one family or clan. Thus Senaah may be a term for a category of persons who come from several places or families (GTT, ¶ 1035, pp. 382 f.).

HASSHUB. *See* Hashub.

HASUPHA. *See* Hashupha.

HAT. An article of clothing (Aram. *karbᵉlâ*) mentioned only in Dan 3:21. A loan word from Akkad. *karballatu,* it probably signified the high, pointed cap of a style worn sometimes by the Assyrians and Babylonians and more especially by the Cimmerians. *See* Dress.

HATACH (hăt'ȧk). A chamberlain (eunuch) of King Ahasuerus who was appointed to attend Queen Esther. Through him she learned from Mordecai of Haman's plot to have the Jews destroyed (Est 4:5-6, 9-10).

HATE, HATRED. Hatred (a strong dislike for) may be a work of the "flesh" (Rom 8:7; Gal 5:19 f.) and a sign of unregeneracy (I Jn 3:15). The unregenerate hate God (Ex 20:5; Ps 83:2; Rom 1:30), the light (Jn 3:20), the righteous (Ps 35:19; 69:4; Jn 15:25), and one another (Tit 3:3). They hate Christians as disciples of Christ (Lk 6:22; 21:17; Jn 15:18-25; 17:14).

But hatred can be a mark of spirituality. God's people must actively hate evil (Ps 97:10; 119:104, 128, 163; Jude 23). They must even hate their own lives for Christ's sake (Lk 14:26; Jn 12:25). However, hatred as a malicious attitude is incompatible with the Christian life (I Jn 2:9, 11; 3:15; 4:20). Christians must not hate others (Mt 5:43 f.; Lk 6:27 f.) except as God hates the workers of iniquity (Ps 26:5; 101:3; 139:21 f.; cf. II Chr 19:2).

Bibliography. Werner Foerster, *"Echthros, etc.,"* TDNT, II, 811-815. O. Michel, *"Miseō,"* TDNT, IV, 683-694.

HATHATH (hā'thăth). A son of Othniel, of the family of Caleb (I Chr 4:13).

HATIPHA (hȧ-tī'fȧ). Ancestral head of a family of Nethinim (temple servants) who returned from captivity with Zerubbabel (Ezr 2:54; Neh 7:56).

HATITA (hȧ-tī'tȧ). The ancestral head of a family of porters or gatekeepers (Ezr 2:42; Neh 7:45) some of whose members returned from Babylon.

HATTIL (hăt'ĭl). One of Solomon's servants, some of whose descendants returned from captivity with Zerubbabel (Ezr 2:57; Neh 7:59).

HATTUSH (hăt'ŭsh)
1. One of the sons of Shemaiah, a descendant of Zerubbabel (I Chr 3:22).
2. A descendant of David who went with Ezra to Jerusalem (Ezr 8:2). He may be the same as 1 or 3.
3. The son of Hashabniah who helped in building the wall under Nehemiah (Neh 3:10).
4. One of those who sealed the covenant of Nehemiah. He may be the same as 3 (Neh 10:4).
5. A priest who returned to Jerusalem with Zerubbabel (Neh 12:2).

HAURAN (hôr'ạn). A district of Palestine E of the Sea of Galilee, S of Damascus on the edge of the Arabian desert, N of the Yarmuk River. It was at times included in Bashan, the kingdom of Og (Num 21:33-35). In NT times the territory was practically identical with the region of Auranitis in the tetrarchy of Philip. Mainly, it is a fertile basin about 50 miles square and 2,000 feet above sea level. The area is practically treeless and is known for its production of wheat. The soil is rich because of the lava deposits. Some burned out volcanic craters remain to this day. The basin is protected from the desert sands on the E by a volcanic mountain range (Jebel Hawran). The region is still called el-Hauran. In the Bible Hauran is mentioned only by Ezekiel in his delineation of the NE boundaries of ideal Israel (Ezk 47:16, 18).

HAVEN. A port or harbor for ships (Gen 49:13; Acts 27:12). Used metaphorically of the peace and rest which come with salvation and dwell in the heart of the fully consecrated believer as he surrenders his trials and problems to God (Ps 107:30).

HAVILAH (hăv'ĭ-lȧ)

1. A land associated with the garden of Eden and cited as the source of gold, bdellium gum, and onyx stone, surrounded or drained by the river Pishon (Gen 2:11-12, ASV, RSV). Most authorities locate Havilah in central Arabia N of Yemen. The basis for this location is the association of the term with Hazarmaveth (the area now called Hadramaut) and Sheba (Gen 10:26-29), sections of S Arabia, and also the fact that the products from the area are the same as the products from central Arabia. It is probable that this area extended N for several hundred miles (I Sam 15:7; Gen 25:18). Some authorities believe that there are two places designated by this name because of the difficulty of locating the Pishon River in the Arabian peninsula, and that originally Havilah referred to the area of West Pakistan, the Pishon being the Indus River. *See* Pison.

2. A son of Cush and a descendant of Ham (Gen 10:7; I Chr 1:9).

3. A son of Joktan and a grandson of Eber (Gen 10:29; I Chr 1:23), of the family of Shem.

G. A. T.

HAVOTH-JAIR (hā'vŏth-jā'ĭr). A group of tent villages on the border of Bashan and Gilead, E of the Jordan, taken by Jair the Manassite who renamed them after himself (Num 32:41; Deut 3:14). I Chr 2:21-24 shows that Jair was a descendant of Judah, but that his grandmother was a daughter of Machir of the tribe of Manasseh. Twenty-three towns continued to belong to Jair and his descendants in Gilead. In later times, however, Geshur and Aram took those "villages of Jair" including Kenath, which were in Bashan (I Chr 2:23, RSV). This loss evidently came after the time of Solomon who ruled over the tent villages of Jair and the 60 walled cities in Bashan (I Kgs 4:13); perhaps this occurred during the reign of Hazael (II Kgs 10:32 f.). In Jud 10:3-4 there is reference to Jair the Gileadite, probably a direct descendant of the earlier Jair, as one of the judges who had 30 sons who ruled over 30 cities in the land of Gilead.

There seems to be some confusion as to the number of towns that belonged to Jair. In Deut 3:4 Moses claims that Israel had captured the 60 cities of Og in Bashan; Jair then took over the whole region of Bashan and renamed it Havvoth-Jair (Deut 3:14, Berkeley; see also Josh 13:30); Jud 10:4 says 30, I Chr 2:22 says 23. It has been suggested that the number was liable to fluctuation because the sites lay in contested land (I Chr 2:23), and because the very nature of such tent encampments was mobile and temporary.

F. B. H.

HAWK. *See* Animals, III.19.

HAY. The rendering of the KJV in Prov 27:25 and Isa 15:6 of Heb. term *(ḥāṣîr)* that occurs elsewhere in the OT as "grass." *See* Plants: Grass. The Hebrews probably did not distinguish carefully between the different grasses and grass-like herbs. Grass is not usually cut and dried for hay in the Near East.

Grass, which becomes brown during the summer dry season, is used to symbolize the shortness of man's life on earth (Ps 90:5; 103:15; Isa 51:12). Paul uses "hay" *(chortos)*, i.e., grass, figuratively to denote the inferior and non-enduring quality of the work which some men are building on the foundation of Christ (I Cor 3:12).

HAZAEL (hā'zĭ-ȧl). The ruler of Damascus during the years *c.* 843-796 B.C.; a contemporary of Joram, Jehu, and Jehoahaz of Israel. He troubled Israel often during their reigns. He is first met in the OT in I Kgs 19:15 when Elijah was commissioned to anoint him as one of God's agents in the destruction of Baal worship in Israel. At the time Ben-hadad II was ruler in Damascus. Next we hear of him when he visited Elisha, who happened to be in Damascus, to inquire on behalf of the ailing Ben-hadad whether he would recover (II Kgs 8:7-10). On that occasion Elisha wept as he told Hazael that the king would die and that he would be the next ruler and would become an oppressor of Israel (II Kgs 8:11-14). Hazael put the prophecy into effect by murdering Ben-hadad (II Kgs 8:15). Before long he was in conflict with Joram at Ramoth-gilead (II Kgs 8:28-29; 9:14-15). Joram was wounded and as he rested at Jezreel he was slain by Jehu the Israelite army captain who then seized the throne of Israel (II Kgs 9:16-26).

During the reign of Jehu (841-814 B.C.) Hazael continued to attack Israel until he overran the whole of Transjordan as far S as the river Arnon (II Kgs 10:32-33). In the time of Jehoahaz (814–798), Hazael's attacks continued (II Kgs 13:3, 22-25), and he actually penetrated into SW Palestine, capturing Gath and threatening Jerusalem. J(eh)oash, king of Judah, bought him off with the temple treasures (II Kgs 12:17–18). At one stage during Hazael's campaigns against Israel the former large chariot force of Israel was reduced to 50 horsemen and ten chariots in the days of Jehoahaz (II Kgs 13:7). Jehoahaz called upon God for deliverance, which came through a change in the international situation (II Kgs 13:4–5).

The key to Israel's deliverance lies in the activity of the Assyrians during these years. In 843 B.C. at the start of his reign, Hazael had to face renewed attacks from Shalmaneser III of Assyria and withstood a long siege in which he and his lands suffered severely. In the years that followed he was comparatively free from Assyrian attack and campaigned against Israel. But in 805–803 B.C. Adad-nirari III of Assyria attacked Hazael again, and shortly after, in 797 B.C., Shalmaneser IV followed up the assault. These repeated campaigns so weakened Hazael that Israel was able to recover towns on her northern frontier formerly lost to Hazael in the days of J(eh)oash (798–782; II Kgs 13:25). By then, however, Hazael was nearing the end of his life and he must have died shortly after J(eh)oash, perhaps in 797 or 796 B.C.

During his long reign of over 40 years he was the scourge of Israel. Even a century later Amos spoke of the rulers of Damascus as the house of Hazael and prophesied that they would yet experience the fire of God's judgment (Amos 1:4).

Hazael was known to the Assyrians and his name appears in several Assyrian texts as an opponent of Shalmaneser. He was known to be a usurper and is called on one document "a son of a nobody" (ANET, p. 280). Adad-nirari referred to him as *mari'*, lord (ANET, pp. 281 f.). A piece of ivory found at Nimrud bearing the inscription "belonging to our lord Hazael" may have been part of Assyrian spoils from Damascus.

See Syria.

Bibliography. Merrill F. Unger, *Israel and the Arameans of Damascus*, London: James Clark, 1957.

J. A. T.

HAZAIAH (hȧ-zā'yȧ). An ancestor of Maaseiah, who was a Jewish lay leader living in post-Exilic Jerusalem (Neh 11:5). Son of Adaiah and father of Col-hozeh, he was a descendant of Pharez, Judah's son.

HAZAR (hā'zȧr). A term meaning unwalled settlements (Lev 25:31; Josh 19:8). Hazar was frequently prefixed to the name of a nearby village. *See* Hazar-addar; Hazar-enan; Hazar-gaddah; Hazar-hatticon; Hazarmaveth; Hazar-shual; Hazar-susah.

HAZAR-ADDAR (hā'zȧr-ăd'ȧr). A place in the S part of Palestine near Kadesh-barnea and Azmon (Num 34:4); simply called Adar in Josh 15:3. Possibly it was modern 'Ain Qedeis, five miles SE of 'Ain el-Qudeirat (Kadesh-barnea; Y. Aharoni, *The Land of the Bible*, p. 65).

See Hazar.

HAZAR-ENAN (hā'zȧr-ē'nȧn). According to Num 34:7–10, the site at the end of the N frontier between Palestine and Hamath (cf. Ezk 47:16–17) where the border turned southward. It may be identified with the desert oasis of el-Qaryatein, half way between Damascus and Palmyra.

See Hazar-hatticon.

HAZAR-GADDAH (hā'zȧr-găd'ȧ). A city in the southern part of Judah (Josh 15:27), near Moladah and Heshmon.

HAZAR-HATTICON (hā'zȧr-hăt'ȧ-kŏn). Named by Ezekiel as the NE corner of the ultimate boundary of Israel (Ezk 47:16). Possibly it is an alternate form of Hazar-enan (*q.v.*).

HAZARMAVETH (hā'zar-mā'vĕth). Found in the Table of Nations (Gen 10:26; I Chr 1:20). One of the sons of Joktan and ancestor of a tribe in S Arabia which gave its name to the Wadi Hadhramaut. By the 5th cen. B.C. this area supported a flourishing state with its capital at Shabwa, 220 miles NE of Aden. Hadhramaut was famed for its traffic in frankincense.

HAZAR-SHUAL (hā'zȧr-shū'ȧl). A town of Simeon in the extreme S of Judah, always mentioned in close connection with Beer-sheba (Josh 15:28; 19:3; I Chr 4:28). It was reoccupied by Jews after the Exile (Neh 11:27).

HAZAR-SUSAH (hā'zȧr-sū'sȧ). A city of Simeon in the SW part of Judah (Josh 19:5). Called Hazar-susim ("village of horses") in I Chr 4:31, it perhaps contained stables where Solomon kept some of the horses he imported from Egypt and sold to Hittites and Syrians (I Kgs 4:26; 9:19; 10:29; cf. cities of horsemen in II Chr 8:6). It is possibly modern Sbalat Abû Sûsein, 20 miles W of Beer-sheba. It may be that the Hyksos or Canaanites had kept horses here. Sir Flinders Petrie discovered Late Bronze Age burial of horses which may have been sacrificed at Tell el-'Ajjul SW of Gaza on the seacoast.

HAZAZON-TAMAR (hăz'ȧ-zŏn-tā'mȧr). Hazazon-tamar is a town identified with Engedi in II Chr 20:2, but this note may only indicate the general direction. After Chedorlaomer and the other four Mesopotamian kings had subdued the cities of the plain for 12 years, the citizens of the plain rebelled and sent the once-conquering but now-defeated kings on their way. It appears that these kings attacked the small nations to the S and in the vicinity of Mount Seir, including the dwellers in Ashteroth Karnaim, in Ham, in Shaveh Kiriathaim, etc. (Gen 14:1-6). Later, they returned to Sodom and Gomorrah and en route they smote the Amorites that dwelt in Hazazon-tamar (Gen 14:7, spelled Hazezon-tamar in KJV). Engedi *(q.v.)* is an oasis below a beautiful waterfall about 25 miles up the W coast of the Dead Sea from the S end (II Chr 20:2).

Hazazon-tamar may otherwise be the Tamar *(q.v.)* fortified by Solomon to guard a trade route from the Arabah to the Negeb, located at 'Ain Hasevah near the foot of Scorpion Pass (Akrabbim, *q.v.*), according to M. Harel ("The Roman Road at Ma'aleh 'Aqrabbim," IEJ, IX, 175-179).

H. A. Han.

HAZEL. *See* Plants.

HAZELELPONI (hāz'ĕ-lĕl-pō'nī). A sister of the sons of Etam, descendants of Judah (I Chr 4:3).

HAZERIM (hȧ-zēr'ĭm). The Avim (*q.v.*) lived in unwalled villages (Hazerim) as far as Gaza until destroyed by the Caphtorim (Deut 2:23). Heb. *ḥāṣēr* often denotes a settlement or village dependent on a fortified city nearby for the protection of its inhabitants (Lev 25:31; Josh 15:45-47; 19:8).

HAZEROTH (hȧ-zē'rŏth). The camping place of the Israelites after leaving Kibroth-hattaavah (Num 11:35; 12:16; 33:17-18; Deut 1:1). It was there that Miriam and Aaron complained against Moses because of his marriage to a Cushite (Ethiopian) woman and because of his unique authority as mediator between God and the people (Num 12). The location has been identified with 'Ain Khadra, *c.* 35 miles NE of Mount Sinai (GTT, pp. 255 f.).

HAZEZON-TAMAR. *See* Hazazon-tamar.

HAZIEL (hā'zĭ-ĕl). The head of a clan of Gershonite Levites, the son of Shimei (I Chr 23:9).

HAZO (hā'zō). The fifth of the eight sons of Nahor and Milcah (Gen 22:22) and the ancestor of an Aramean tribe. The name has been identified with the mountainous region of *Ḫazû* in N Arabia or the Syrian desert, mentioned in Esarhaddon's Arabian campaign.

HAZOR (hā'zôr). The name of at least five towns mentioned in the Bible.

1. A Canaanite city ruled in the days of Joshua by Jabin (Josh 11:1). At that time Hazor was considered "the head of all those kingdoms" (v. 10), the petty city-states in N Palestine and S Lebanon. Jabin led them out with their chariots against Joshua, who almost annihilated them after surprising them at the waters of Merom, thought now to be a stream flowing S from springs in the highest mountain of Galilee. Joshua turned back and captured Hazor, killed Jabin, and burned the city with fire (vv. 10-11). Later, another Jabin (Jud 4) ruling at Hazor was considered king of Canaan; but using Deborah and Barak, God subdued and destroyed him also. Located strategically on a principal trade route from Damascus to the Mediterranean coast, Hazor was fortified by Solomon (I Kgs 9:15). Its Israelite inhabitants were carried away captive (II Kgs 15:29) to Assyria by Tiglath-pileser III on his campaign of 732 B.C.

Excavations at Hazor. Yigael Yadin

The ancient site was located by John Garstang digging in 1926 and 1928 at Tell el-Qedah on the Wadi Waqqas, five miles SW of the now-drained Lake Huleh and ten miles N of the Sea of Galilee. Hazor is mentioned in the early 18th cen. B.C. Execration texts which list potential enemies of Egypt, the 18th cen. Mari letters, records of pharaohs who conquered Palestinian cities (Thutmose III, Amen-hotep II, Sethos I), in four of the Amarna letters (14th cen.), and in the 13th cen. Papyrus Anastasi I from Egypt.

Systematic excavation of the site began with Yigael Yadin's work in 1955, who directed further seasons in '56, '57, '58, and '68-'69. Hazor consisted of two distinct areas, the 30-acre 130 foot high acropolis mound at the SW corner known as the upper city, and the huge rectangular enclosure to the N encompassing 175 acres where it is estimated 40,000 inhabitants once lived. It was by far the largest city in Palestine in OT times. This lower city was first settled before 1750 B.C., presumably by the Hyksos, who then fortified it with mighty earthen ramparts in the Middle Bronze II B and C periods (1750-1550 B.C.).

After destruction in the mid-16th cen. B.C., Hazor reached its zenith in the Late Bronze I period (1550-1400), in which the reign of the earlier Jabin would fall according to the early date of the Exodus (*see* Exodus, Date of). City gates with three pairs of pilasters and a large gate tower on either side gave access to the

Excavating the water system at Hazor. HFV

lower city. In that area the archaeologists uncovered a series of four superimposed Late Bronze Age Canaanite temples lined with basalt orthostats and revealing a floor plan similar to that of Solomon's temple. One of these temples contained a sculptured stone figure of a god seated on a throne in a raised central niche. It was found decapitated, with the head nearby. To the left in a row of stelae, the middle one depicted two hands uplifted in prayer to a sun disk within a crescent. This monument or memorial stela is probably an example of the Heb. *yad* (lit., "hand," Isa 56:5, KJV "place"; 57:8, KJV "remembrance"). The lower city was destroyed *c.* 1230 B.C. (which corresponds with the date of Deborah and Barak) and never rebuilt.

On the acropolis during the Late Bronze I period stood a large structure which most likely was the palace, and adjacent to it a 50-foot-long rectangular temple having an entrance built with orthostats. This building was demolished and abandoned by the end of Late Bronze I. The earliest stratum of the mound or upper city dates back to Early Bronze times, and continued to be occupied after Tiglath-pileser's destruction by a small undefended settlement in the 8th-7th cen., followed by Assyrian, Persian, and Hellenistic forts. Yadin excavated the gate of Solomon's city and proved it to be identical with gateways of his reign at Megiddo and Gezer (cf. I Kgs 9:15). A public building from the time of King Ahab measured 49 by 66 feet and contained two rows of stone columns, nine pillars in each row.

In the fifth season, the elaborate water system of Hazor was discovered. Evidence shows that when Ahab rebuilt the whole upper city of Hazor and refortified it to withstand long siege, his men first dug a shaft 100 feet down with a rock-cut staircase ten feet wide descending its side, and then a tunnel averaging 13 feet both in height and width and sloping down to reach the water table. Larger than comparable water systems at Megiddo, Gezer and Gibeon, this one remained in use until 732 B.C.

Bibliography. John Gray, "Hazor," VT, XVI (1966), 26–52. Yigael Yadin, Hazor articles, BA, XIX. 1 (Feb., 1956), XX. 2 (May, 1957), XXI. 2 (May, 1958), and XXII. 1 (Feb., 1959), edited as one continuous report in *The Biblical Archaeologist Reader,* Garden City: Anchor Books, 1964, pp. 191–224; "The Fifth Season of Excavations at Hazor, 1968–1969," BA, XXXII. 3 (Sept., 1969); "Hazor," TAOTS, pp. 245–263.

2. A town in the extreme S of Judah, mentioned only in Josh 15:23. Perhaps identified with el-Jebariyeh, on the Wadi Umm Ethnan, near Bir Hafir, *c.* nine miles SE of el- 'Auja.

3. Another town in the S of Judah (Josh 15:25). Possibly the same as Kerioth-Hezron. Located in Negeb district of Beer-sheba; possibly identified with Khirbet el-Qaryatein, four and a half miles S of Maon. KJV has "Kerioth and Hezron."

4. A town N of Jerusalem, inhabited by Benjamites during the restoration (Neh 11:33). The name is preserved in Khirbet Hazzur, W of Beit Hanina.

5. A region in N Arabia near Kedar (*q.v.*), inhabited by camel-riding nomads, against which Jeremiah pronounced a "doom" (Jer 49:28–33).

L. L. W.

HAZOR-HADATTAH (hā'zôr-hȧ-dăt'ȧ). A city in the extreme S of the Negeb of Judah (Josh 15:25, RSV). In KJV the words are separated, Hazor Hadattah.

HE (hā). The fifth letter of the Heb. alphabet, used as the heading of the fifth section of Ps 119, where every verse in the section begins with this letter.

HE ASS. *See* Animals: Ass, I.1.

HEAD. There are several uses of the word head.

1. It denotes the most essential part of man and beast. It is used of the serpent's head (Gen 3:15), sacrificial animals (Ex 29:10, 15, 19), and human beings (Gen 40:16–17). The head is considered the seat of the intelligence and sometimes represents the whole man (Prov 10:6). Joy and sorrow, blessing and adversity were said to come on the head of a person. Anointing the head was an emblem of joy (Ps 23:5; Heb 1:9). Hands were placed on the head of a person and blessing invoked (Mt 19:15). Cutting the hair and covering the head were signs of mourning and distress (Josh 7:6; I Sam 4:12; Lam 2:10). Bruising or smiting the head was synonymous with complete destruction (Gen 3:15; Ps 68:21). Bowing the head was a sign of humility and reverence (Isa 58:5).

2. Another meaning is the top or summit of inanimate objects such as mountains, scepters, ladders, and towers (Ex 19:20; Est 5:2; Gen 28:12; Gen 11:4). Christ is called the head-

stone or top stone (Zech 4:7; cf. 10:4, ASV, RSV).

3. Head also denotes the beginning of months, rivers, and streets (Gen 2:10; Ex 12:2; Isa 51:20).

4. It designates one in authority in the sense of foremost or uppermost. It may mean leader, prince, chief, or captain, and is used of cities, nations, men, and God. Damascus is the head or capital of Syria (Isa 7:8), and Israel is to be the head of the nations (Deut 28:13). Men of Israel are called the heads of their fathers' houses (Ex 6:14; Deut 1:15; I Chr 5:24).

5. An important NT use is the headship of Christ. *See* Head of the Church. He is the Head of His Church called His Body (Eph 4:12, 15; 5:23; Col 1:24). Believers are placed into this Body by the Holy Spirit (I Cor 12:13; cf. 12:27). The figure represents the service and manifestation of Christ through believers in union, direction, and control. *See* Body of Christ. Christ is also Head of His Church called His Bride (Eph 5:23-33). This figure shows His love and care for His Church, and looks forward to the marriage to be consummated in heaven (Rev 19:7). *See* Bride of Christ. After this example, the husband is the head of the wife and is to love and care for her (I Cor 11:3; Eph 5:23-33). Christ is also Head of the universe (Eph 1:22) and every cosmic power (Col 2:10). The head of Christ is God (I Cor 11:3).

Bibliography. J. R. Bartlett, "The Use of the Word *Rōsh* as a Title in the Old Testament," VT, XIX (1969), 1-10. Heinrich Schlier, "*Kephalē*," TDNT, III, 673-682.

E. C. J.

HEAD OF THE CHURCH. Paul presents Christ as the Head of the Church (Eph 5:32), and the individual members in the Church as parts of His Body (Eph 4:4-16; I Cor 12:12-27).

In Colossians Christ is seen as Head (Col 1:18; cf. Eph 1:21-22) in contrast to and above all principalities and powers of evil (Col 2:10; cf. Eph 6:12), and to angels (Col 2:18; cf. Heb 1:4 ff.).

In Ephesians He is seen as head of the corner, or chief cornerstone which joins together two walls in one, Jew and Gentile, breaking down the middle wall of partition between them (Eph 2:14-15, 19-20). This union, "that the Gentiles should be fellow heirs" with converted Jews (3:6), which Christ effects as their united head, was so difficult for the OT saints to grasp (Isa 9:2; 11:10; 42:6; 49:6; 60:3; 66:2, 12, 19; Amos 9:12) that it is called "the mystery . . . hid in God" (Eph 3:9).

Three main lessons are drawn. First, that we are to learn to give appropriate submission and honor to those in authority around us, even as we do to Christ (Eph 5:21–6:9). Second, even as Christ loved the Church and each one of us, we are to love our wives and others (Eph 5:25-33). Third, we are to remember we are like the members of our own body, each being gifted by the Holy Spirit in particular ways (I Cor 12:4-13; Eph 4:7 f.), and yet each needing the other (I Cor 12:14 ff.).

See Head.

R. A. K.

HEADBAND

1. KJV translation for bands or sashes around the waist (Isa 3:20). The same word (*qishshurîm*) is rendered "attire" in Jer 2:32.

2. RSV renders Isa 3:18 as "headband" (KJV "cauls"). It was probably a gold or silver head ornament.

See Dress.

HEADSTONE. This expression is found only in Zech 4:7 (KJV). ASV and RSV translate "top stone"; JerusB has "keystone." The term occurs in Zechariah's vision in which Israel is seen as a lamp of witness, fed with the oil of the Spirit by the Priest-King Messiah.

The immediate occasion was the word of encouragement to Zerubbabel that he would complete the construction of the restored temple (Ezr 5; 6:14-15) begun 14 years before and left unfinished. The urging of Haggai the prophet had initiated and carried forward the work in the second year of Darius, in the sixth, seventh, and ninth months. Zechariah's prophecies began in the eighth month, and the series of eight visions in which the vision of the candelabrum is found came on the twenty-fourth day of the eleventh month. The promised completion came four years later (Ezr 6:15). The messages of the two prophets complement each other. Haggai stirred a sluggish and self-seeking people to work; Zechariah revealed the divine power at work "not by might, nor by power, but by my Spirit, saith the Lord of hosts" (Zech 4:6). Thus the fulfillment of the prediction that Zerubbabel would finish the temple would cause the people to know that God had sent the prophet to them.

The ultimate prophetic significance of this vision is found in Jesus Christ. In almost identical words He is prefigured as "the stone which the builders rejected" who "has become the cornerstone" (Ps 118:22, RSV). Peter twice declared that Christ was the fulfillment of this concept (Acts 4:11; I Pet 2:7). Paul viewed the whole company of believers as a building of God, Christ Himself being the chief cornerstone (Eph 2:19-22). *See* Cornerstone. "In the Millennial Age, toward which the golden candlestick of Zech 4:1-7 points, Christ will be manifested also as the Headstone of the temple of His restored covenant people Israel, the golden candlestick of Zech 4:2 more specifically speaking of converted Israel as the light of the world in the Kingdom Age" (Unger's *Bible Dictionary*, p. 462).

W. B. W.

HEADY. Found in II Tim 3:4 to describe unruly or headstrong men in the last days. RSV translates the word as "reckless." The same Gr. word *propetēs* occurs also in Acts 19:36 as "rashly."

HEALING, HEALTH

Principles of Health

The Bible has much to say about healing and health. Throughout its pages may be found many sound principles for healthful living, both from the medical and the psychological standpoints. The physical strength and well-being of the body is never despised or dismissed, but is aptly summarized by the apostle's prayer: "Beloved, I wish above all things that thou mayest prosper and be in health, even as thy soul prospereth" (III Jn 2).

The law of Moses set forth specific regulations which served to prevent disease and continues to be "a model of sanitary and hygienic insight" (R. K. Harrison, "Healing, Health," IDB, II, 542). The Mosaic sanitary code provided for periodic physical rest through observance of the sabbath; dietary rules which diminished the possibility of tapeworm infestation and such diseases as trichinosis and tularemia; sexual prophylaxis and prohibitions against incestuous relationships common among neighboring peoples; cleanliness through washing the body and clothing; and sanitary procedures for armies in the field that prevented the outbreak of epidemics of infectious diseases (Deut 23:12-13).

Prevention of psychosomatic illnesses is assured by obedience to the Word of God. "Pleasant words are as an honeycomb, sweet to the soul, and health to the bones" (Prov 16:24; cf. 3:8; 4:22; 12:18; 13:17; 15:1, 4). The concept of health includes all areas of the individual's existence—body, mind, and spirit—as the psalmist suggests: "Why art thou cast down, O my soul? and why art thou disquieted within me? Hope thou in God: for I shall yet praise him, who is the health of my countenance, and my God" (Ps 42:11). Forgiveness and cleansing from sin will bring health and healing (Jer 30:12-17; 33:6-8). The redemptive work of Christ is the greatest healing force known to man; for guilt, bitterness, hatred, envy, and other negative attitudes are removed which are in themselves sickness and cause all manner of mental and physical illness. Love is recognized by psychiatrists as "the one and only antidote that can save man from the many diseases produced by the emotions of our evil nature" (S. I. McMillen, *None of These Diseases,* p. 78). Therefore the new commandment of Christ (Jn 13:34) and the various apostolic exhortations (e.g., Eph 4:25-32; Phil 4:4-8; I Pet 3:8-12) lay the foundation for physical and mental healing and health.

Divine Healing

In addition to principles of health the Bible teaches that human beings may look to God for direct healing when other avenues of help have failed. Divine healing is a subject over which differences of opinion have existed from early in the history of the Christian church. Protestants and Roman Catholics have claimed to practice it, as well as Christian Scientists and other so-called Christian cults, along with Muslims and many of the pagan mystery religions.

All Christians agree that the Bible teaches God has healed and can heal men of every kind of disease. The fact that in the OT Miriam was healed of leprosy (Num 12:10-15) and that Christ healed many lepers (Mk 1:40-44; Lk 17:12-19) proves, in view of the fact that the disease is still so difficult to handle if not still impossible to cure, that no disease is to be excepted. In proclaiming "I am the Lord, your healer," God promised the Israelites that in consequence of their obedience He would put upon them none of the diseases of the Egyptians (Ex 15:26, RSV; cf. 23:25; Ps 105:37). David could testify regarding the God-fearing man, "The Lord sustains him on his sickbed; in his illness thou healest all his infirmities" (Ps 41:3, RSV). The psalmists repeatedly prayed and thanked God for healing (Ps 6:2; 30:2; 103:3; 107:20; 147:3). Obedience to God's Word and an attitude of mercy are shown to be essential for healing and health (Ps 107:20; Prov 4:20-22; Isa 58:6-8).

Some of the healings recorded in the Bible were with means, as in the case of Hezekiah by means of a poultice of figs (II Kgs 20:2-11; cf. I Tim 5:23; Jas 5:14-15; Ex 15:23-26; Jer 8:22; I Sam 16:16; Mt 9:12). Others were without any means, as in the case of Miriam.

Certainly the Bible is not opposed to the use of means for healing, since Christ Himself considered it normal for people to go to a doctor (Mt 9:12). In the case of Asa, which has been quoted as a proof to the contrary, the "physicians" to whom Asa turned actually were equivalent to pagan magicians (II Chr 16:12). Asa's action revealed a lack of faith in God and a dependence upon men who were much like modern witch doctors. In the parable of the Good Samaritan Jesus states that oil and wine were poured on the wounds of the beaten traveler (Lk 10:34). The woman with the issue of blood suffered from a condition beyond the knowledge of the medicine of her day, and does not justify the Christian refusing proved medical remedies (Mk 5:25-26; Lk 8:43). It is significant that Paul chose Luke, a physician (Col 4:14), as his traveling companion.

There is also a class of healings in which certain additive factors have a part, though they are not of themselves actually therapeutic but rather symbolic. For example, in the healing of Naaman the leper, his stepping into the river Jordan appears to speak of faith on the part of Naaman and cleansing on the part of God (II Kgs 5:14). Also in the healing of the blind man, Jesus spit in his eyes (Mk 8:23), and for the man blind from birth, He made a salve of clay and spittle (Jn 9:6). The laying of hands upon the sick both by Jesus and by the disciples (Lk 13:11-13; Mk 6:13), and anointing the sick person with oil were symbols of the divine presence and healing power (Mk 6:13; Jas 5:14).

Various Theories of Divine Healing

These theories rest upon certain general assumptions.

1. In seeking healing we are choosing between God and the doctor. For example, A. B. Simpson wrote: "If you cannot trust the Lord, then call the doctor . . . if you can't take God's best, take God's second best" (R.V. Bingham, *The Bible and the Body*, p. 20).

The rejection of the use of remedies revealed by God to man as used in modern medicine, in favor of direct divine healing, is in itself not a reasonable act of faith in God's wonderful providence. God may lead certain individuals to glorify Him by such trust and dependence, but Scripture does not seem to indicate this need be a general rule for all believers. Many a Christian is alive today because of the discoveries of modern medicine and surgery.

2. Healing is as much a part of the salvation purchased by Christ on the cross as is the forgiveness of sins. Isa 53:4*a* and 5*c* are quoted as proof: "Surely he hath borne our griefs, and carried our sorrows . . . and with his stripes we are healed," in conjunction with Mt 8:16-17: "And he cast out the spirits with his word, and healed all that were sick: that it might be fulfilled which was spoken by Esaias the prophet, saying, Himself took our infirmities, and bare our sicknesses."

It is true that the Heb. word *ḥŏlî* translated "griefs" usually means disease or sickness, and the word *mak'ōbôth* connotes pain whether physical or mental. A. J. Gordon supported the view of healing in the atonement in *The Ministry of Healing* when he wrote: "Something more than sympathetic fellowship with our sufferings is evidently referred to here. The yoke of His cross by which He lifted our iniquities took hold also of our diseases; so that it is in some sense true that as God 'made him to be sin for us who knew no sin,' He also made Him to be sick for us who knew no sickness. . . . The passage seems to teach that Christ endured vicariously our diseases as well as our iniquities" (pp. 16-17).

Most evangelicals disagree, however, with such an exegesis. They feel the passages referred to only prove that Christ bore our sicknesses as a heavy load of sorrow. It is true that the Gr. word *bastazō* used in Mt 8:17 is used of bearing burdens (Gal 6:2; Rom 15:1) and by Galen of removing disease (Arndt, p. 137), but never of Christ's bearing imputed sin. Yet in only one other place in the NT is there any suggestion of healing in the atonement. Peter in I Pet 2:24 connects "by whose stripes ye were healed" with Christ's sacrificial death on the cross, but there is no explicit mention of physical sickness. The argument is also set forth that Christ has redeemed us from the curse of the law (Gal 3:13), of which sickness is a definite aspect (Deut 28:21-27, 59-61). Furthermore, healing as a first installment of the resurrection is promised for our mortal bodies through the indwelling Holy Spirit (Rom 8:11; cf. 6:12 *re* "mortal body").

3. That sickness is always the result of sin.

While it is true that many sicknesses are a punishment sent by God for sin; e.g., the plagues which struck Israel when they rebelled against God in the wilderness journey (Num 11:33; 14:37; 16:47; 25:8-9, 18), still some sicknesses are used by God for His own glory (Jn 9:3) and others for the good of the sufferer (II Cor 12:7-10; but *see* Thorn in the Flesh).

4. That sickness is to be attributed to the devil. Healing evangelist William Branham, for example, prayed, "Come out of him/her, thou demon of cancer." F. F. Bosworth explained disease as caused by "the oppression of the devil" (*Christ the Healer*, p. 1). He based his argument on what Peter said to the Gentiles concerning Jesus' ministry, He "went about doing good, and healing all that were oppressed of the devil" (Acts 10:38). Oral Roberts agrees with Bosworth (Oral Roberts, *If You Need Healing*, p. 16). Other passages, such as Lk 13:16, which speaks of one "whom Satan hath bound, lo, these eighteen years"; Christ's argument that He did not cast out devils by Beelzebub (Lk 11:14-23); God's permission to Satan to afflict Job with loathesome sores (Job 2:7), as well as certain references to Satan's power (Jn 12:31; Heb 2:14-15; I Jn 3:8; 5:19), are used to support the view.

While it is clear from Scripture that Satan often does inflict sickness upon men, it is equally clear that this occurs only by God's permission. God as sovereign can and does use the suffering originated by Satan and man for His own purposes and glory (Rom 8:18, 22-23, 26, 28). Many illnesses, however, stem from other causes than the direct action of Satan.

Causes of Sickness

Four main reasons for sickness can be found.

1. It is the consequence of the curse that came upon man after the Fall. In this sense, all sickness stems from man's first sin, though it does not follow that an individual's personal sickness is due to his own personal sin. The fact that there is a tree with all manner of fruits for the healing of the nations in Ezk 47:12 and Rev 22:2 does indicate sickness is the result of man's original sin, and is to be removed, even as the curse brought about by that sin will be removed (Rom 8:18-23; cf. Gen 3:18-19).

2. Ignorance and carelessness. There are many cases where sickness is caused by man's ignorance and also by his own carelessness. The high rate of deaths at childbirth until Semmelweis and Lister discovered antiseptics proves the former, and the constant sickness in the homes of some Christians, in contrast to the

wonderful health enjoyed by others, is often due to the latter. As the knowledge of medicine increases, sickness of many kinds decreases and the life span of man lengthens.

3. Individual sin. Sickness may be directly caused by man's sin, as in the spread of venereal disease, or chronic illnesses resulting from alcoholism. Or sickness may be sent by God as a punishment, as in the case of Uzziah's presumptuous sin (II Chr 26:19-20). Christ commanded one of the chronically ill men whom He healed, "Behold, thou art made whole: sin no more, lest a worse thing come unto thee" (Jn 5:14).

4. As a chastisement for the development of character. This particular use of disease and accident, in order to train and develop the child of God, cannot be ignored. It is the one whom the Lord loveth that He chasteneth (Heb 12:6). The believer is to count it all blessing when he enters into various trials and testings (which may include sickness), because if he bears them patiently, they will bring forth the peaceable fruit of righteousness, and he will receive the crown of life as a recompense (Jas 1:2-4, 12). Job was brought to recognize his pride and self-righteous attitude through his afflictions, and repented in dust and ashes (Job 40:4; 42:6). Paul saw his thorn in the flesh as something Satan could use to buffet him (II Cor 12:7), but also as something God used to keep him humble and to cause him to rely upon the Holy Spirit for grace and power (vv. 9-10), and therefore he rejoiced in it. The fact that sickness may be used of God to develop character, faith, and humility in His own children makes it impossible to maintain that it is always the immediate result of sin.

When Jesus not only healed the sick but also forgave them their sins, as with the paralytic borne of four (Mt 9:2-8; Mk 2:3-12; Lk 5:18-26), this in itself did not prove that man's sickness was due to his sin, or that the cures for sin and sickness are both in the cross, but that Christ was exercising His own prerogative as God to forgive sins. And it was in this light the scribes and Pharisees saw it (Mt 9:3; Mk 2:7; Lk 5:21). At the same time, that some are sick because of their sins, is true as seen above.

The fact that though Paul healed so many others (Acts 19:11-12) but he himself was not delivered, even when he prayed for it three times, shows it is God's will for some to suffer for their own good (II Cor 12:10). This further proves that healing does not depend on our faith in God alone; it is dependent on God's will. The "prayer of faith" that heals the sick, in James 5:15, is that prayer which God gives to His own, in which the child of God has the assurance, before or as he asks, that his request is in God's will and is going to be answered. This is made clear in I Jn 5:14-15 where we read: "This is the confidence that we have in him, that, if we ask any thing according to his will, he heareth us: and if we know that he hear us, whatsoever we ask, we know that we have the petitions that we desired of him."

The Healings of Christ and of the Early Church

Because sickness was not part of original creation but an evil thing, Jesus never hesitated to heal the sick. When a leper questioned if it would be His will to cleanse him of the disease, Jesus immediately banished the thought and healed the man (Mk 1:40-42). In His mission to undo the works of the devil (I Jn 3:8), He made every effort to cast out demons and heal the diseased. His ministry was therefore as much to the mind and soul as to the body. His goal was the restoration of the entire personality. Thus biblical healing includes the needs of the whole man.

In one sense Christ's healings must be regarded as in a special category. In them He demonstrated and proved that He was the Son of God. He performed them in His own peculiar power and that of the Holy Spirit which He possessed without measure. They confirmed His person as well as His power (Lk 4:14-21 with Isa 61:1-2; Mt 11:2-5; 15:30-31 with Isa 35:5-6).

The miracles and charismatic gifts of healing (I Cor 12:9, 28) of the disciples and the early church were similar, to the extent that they proved these men were true followers of Christ, and thus corroborated them and their ministry. Philip's miracles at Samaria, the healing of the lame beggar at the temple gate, and of the cripple at Lystra opened up doors of opportunity to testify of Christ (Acts 3-4; 8:6-8; 14:8-18).

On the other hand, neither Jesus' nor the apostles' miracles were simply signs; they were a salutary function of the kingdom of God. In His compassion the Lord brought actual relief to multitudes of sufferers who needed healing. The writings of leaders in the church of the first three centuries testify to the fact that prayer and exorcism as a means to healing continued to be effective, at least in part (see survey by A. Harnack, *The Mission and Expansion of Christianity*, pp. 120-146).

Both Christ, as in the case of the man born blind (Jn 9:1-38), and the apostles, as in the case of the lame man healed by Peter at the temple (Acts 3:1-11), healed some who initially had no faith of their own. Yet Christ and the apostles healed others on the basis of their faith (Mt 9:29; Mk 5:34; 10:52; Lk 7:50; 8:48; 17:19; Acts 14:9). The foregoing proves NT healings were only at times based on the faith of the one healed. The same should be true if there is genuine healing through the ministry of God's servants in our time.

See Aeneas; Demonology; Diseases; Miracles; Spiritual Gifts.

Bibliography. Paul E. Adolph, *Health Shall Spring Forth*, Chicago: Moody Press, 1956. Rowland V. Bingham, *The Bible and the Body*, 3rd ed., London: Marshall, Morgan and Scott, 1939. F. F. Bosworth, *Christ the Healer*, 7th ed. rev., Miami: F. N. Bosworth, 1948. C. B. Eavey, *Principles of Mental Health for Chris-*

tian Living, Chicago: Moody Press, 1956. Arno C. Gaebelein, *The Healing Question,* New York: Our Hope, 1925. A. J. Gordon, *The Ministry of Healing,* New York: Revell, 1882. Adolf Harnack, *The Mission and Expansion of Christianity in the First Three Centuries,* New York: Harper Torchbook, 1961. R. K. Harrison, "Healing, Health," IDB, II, 541-548. D. Martyn Lloyd-Jones, *Spiritual Depression: Its Causes and Cure,* Grand Rapids: Eerdmans, 1965. T. J. McCrossan, *Bodily Healing and the Atonement,* Youngstown, Ohio: C. Humbard, 1930. S. I. McMillen, *None of These Diseases,* Westwood, N.J.: Revell, 1963. Andrew Murray, *Divine Healing,* Fort Washington, Pa.: Christian Literature Crusade, n.d. A. Oepke, "*Iaomai,* etc.," TDNT, III, 194-215. T. C. Osborn, *Healing the Sick,* Tulsa: Osborn Evangelistic Assoc., 1959. A. P. Waterson, "Disease and Healing," NBD, pp. 316 ff.

R. A. K. and J. R.

HEAP

1. Heb. *gal,* designating stones rolled together. A heap or cairn of stones was sometimes placed over a slain person to serve as a reminder of his infamy (Josh 7:26; 8:29; II Sam 18:17); it seems to have been equivalent as a sign of disgrace to death by stoning. A heap or cairn of stones was used as a witness of a covenant between Jacob and Laban (Gen 31:46-52). A city which had become a heap of ruins was a reminder of God's judgment (II Kgs 19:25; Isa 25:2; Jer 9:11; 51:37).

2. Heb. *'î,* a heap of ruins (Ps 79:1; Jer 26:18; Mic 1:6; 3:12) and the cognate word *me'î* (Isa 17:1). The name of the city Ai was derived from this word.

3. Heb. *nēd* denotes a heap or wall of water as if held back by an invisible dike (Ex 15:8; Josh 3:13, 16; Ps 33:7; 78:13).

4. Heb. *'ărēmâ* signified anything piled up, whether grain (Ruth 3:7; Song 7:2; Hag 2:16) or agricultural produce (II Chr 31:5-9), rubbish or debris (Neh 4:2), or city ruins (Jer 50:26).

5. Heb. *tel,* the mound of level upon level of heaped-up ruins of a buried city (Deut 13:16; Josh 8:28; Jer 30:18; 49:2).

F. B. H. and J. R.

HEARING. *See* Ear.

HEART. The heart was considered by the Egyptians to be the central organ of physical life. Since the Hebrews likewise held this opinion instead of taking the liver as the principal internal organ as all Mesopotamian people did, here is undesigned evidence of the long stay of the Israelites in Egypt. Thus the word "heart" in both Heb. and Gr. came to mean that which is central. It is the seat of physical, mental, and spiritual life. It is seldom used of things, but when so used, it is in the sense of midst (Ex 15:8). Only rarely is "heart" used of the physical organ (II Sam 18:14; II Kgs 9:24).

As the center of physical life, the "heart" in the sense of the whole body may be strengthened by eating and drinking (Gen 18:5; Jud 19:5; Acts 14:17; Jas 5:5). As the center of

Weighing of the heart of the scribe Ani in the afterlife, a scene from the Egyptian Book of the Dead.
BM

mental and spiritual life, the term is used in a variety of ways:

1. The inner man. In this sense, the heart has secrets and is unsearchable (Ps 44:21; Prov 25:3).

2. The mental center. The heart knows (Deut 29:4; Prov 22:17), understands (Isa 44:18; Acts 16:14), reflects (Lk 2:19), considers (Ex 7:23), and remembers (Isa 42:25).

3. The emotional center. It is the seat of joy (Isa 65:14), courage (Ps 27:14; II Sam 17:10), pain (Prov 25:20), anxiety (Prov 12:25), despair (Eccl 2:20), sorrow (Neh 2:2), and fear (Deut 28:28). Fear is also expressed by being faint or wounded (Lam 5:17; Ps 109:22).

4. The moral center. God tries the heart (Ps 17:3; Jer 12:3), sees the heart (Jer 20:12), refines the heart (Ps 26:2), and searches the heart (Jer 17:10). Man may have an evil heart (Prov 26:23), be godless in heart (Job 36:13), and perverse or deceitful in heart (Prov 11:20; 17:20). However, the work of God gives him a clean heart (Ps 51:10) and a new heart (Ezk 18:31; 36:26). The heart is also the seat of the conscience (Heb 10:22; cf. I Jn 3:19-21) and that which receives the love and peace of God (Rom 5:5; Col 3:15). It is the dwelling place of the Spirit and the Lord (II Cor 1:22; Eph 3:17).

See Hardness of Heart; Mind.

Bibliography. Johannes Behm, "*Kardia,* etc.," TDNT, III, 605-614.

E. C. J.

HEARTH. The fire pit or depression in the dirt floor of poorer houses, discovered in many archaeological excavations. The pungent smoke from the burning wood, grass, or dried cow dung escaped through the door or a window.

1. A stove *('āḥ)* in which Jehoiakim burned strips of the scroll of the word of God (Jer 36:22-23). *See* Brazier.

2. A pan (*kîyyôr,* Zech 12:6). The chiefs of Judah will be the pans of coals to set on fire her enemies in days to come.

3. A place of burning (*môqēd,* Ps 102:3). The bones smoulder like the place where the fire is laid.

4. A fireplace (*yāqûd,* Isa 30:14). In breaking the earthenware jar not a sherd will be found large enough to carry coals from the hearth to start another fire.

5. An altar hearth (*'arî'el,* "hearth of God"), a square, horned altar hearth (Ezk 43:15-16). Such will Jerusalem be when she is invaded, drenched with blood, and burning with the fires of God's judgments (Isa 29:1-2, ASV marg.). *See* Ariel.

H. G. S.

HEAT. Heb. *ḥōm* is used of heat in the middle of the day in contrast to other times (Gen 18:1; I Sam 11:11; II Sam 4:5); of summer in contrast to winter (Gen 8:22; Jer 17:8); of harvest time (Isa 18:4).

Heb. *ḥōreb* refers to heat, but particularly of drought (Job 30:30; Isa 4:6; 25:4; Jer 36:30).

Gr. *kauma* means scorching heat of the sun (Rev 7:16; 16:9); *kausōn* means burning heat (Mt 20:12; Lk 12:55; cf. Jas 1:11).

One of the blessings spoken of in salvation is shielding from the heat of the sun which refers to the protection and prosperity which God grants to His own both now in this life (Ps 121:6; Jer 17:8) and in the future kingdom (Isa 4:6; Rev 7:16).

HEATH. *See* Plants.

HEATHEN. *See* Gentiles; Nations; Dispersion of Mankind.

HEAVE OFFERING, HEAVE SHOULDER. *See* Sacrificial Offerings.

HEAVEN. The word heaven, or the heavens, is used in the Scriptures in a number of different senses. In the most general of these it includes all that is distinguished from the earth. When employed this way, the words heaven and earth exclude one another; but when taken together, the two embrace all the universe of God (Gen 1:1). In this sense, the term often is used metaphorically. For example, "From one end of heaven to the other" (Mt 24:31), and "from the one side of heaven unto the other" (Deut 4:32).

In a more limited sense the word is employed to describe the atmosphere which surrounds the earth. Thus we read of the "dew of heaven" (Dan 4:15), the "clouds of heaven" (Dan 7:13), and of heaven giving rain (Jas 5:18). *See* Sky. Again, the word often includes more than just that which is comprehended within the earth's atmosphere. It is used to embrace all that is visible in the expanse of the universe above man. It would be impossible to set specific limits to the visible expanse of space which stretches away to unknown heights; but as such, the term heaven includes the vast realm in which are the sun, the moon, the planets, and the stars (Gen 1:16, 17).

From the theological standpoint, unquestionably the most important use of the term heaven is with reference to the invisible realm of which the visible may be simply the fringe nearest to man. This is the heaven which is best described as God's dwelling place. Before the Christian era, the Jews divided the heavens into seven different strata, a notion which has no basis in the Scriptures, although Paul speaks of having been "caught up to the third heaven" (II Cor 12:2). Unquestionably, the apostle is speaking of the heaven which is the abiding place of God and the blessed dead. The fact that he uses the expression "third heaven" means that he was referring either to heaven in its most exalted character, or to the heaven which is reached by the souls of the blessed when they have passed through the two lower regions of the atmosphere and of outer space containing the celestial bodies. The term "heaven of heavens" (Deut 10:14; I Kgs 8:27; Ps 68:33; 148:4) literally renders the Heb. idiom for the superlative, "the highest heaven." It may express our concept of the uttermost reaches of the universe.

When we speak of heaven as God's dwelling place, or the place where His presence is made manifest, we do not transgress the doctrine of His divine omnipresence. Though the Lord speaks of coming from heaven and going to heaven, He is infinite and therefore manifests Himself where He already was. John 1:18 implies that when the Lord was on earth He was in the bosom of the Father. We simply recognize that the description of infinite divine realities must be given to finite human minds in terms they can understand. Much of the description of heaven in this its strictest sense is given in figurative terms, because it is impossible to express heavenly things except in figurative language which is often symbolical. This language, however, does not at all mean that there is nothing literal about heaven and that it is simply a state or a condition. Jesus said, "I go to prepare *a place* for you" (Jn 14:2). Christ lives forever in His glorified resurrection body. There must be a place where He dwells with His saints. *See* Abraham's Bosom; Father's House.

Certain things are clearly revealed in the Scriptures concerning heaven. Considerable attention is given to the things which are *not* to be found there. For example, there will be no marrying or giving in marriage (Lk 20:34-36). There will be no tears, death, sorrow, crying, or pain, nothing that defiles, and no more curse. There will be no night, nor will there be need for light, because the Son of God will be the light of heaven (Rev 21:4, 27; 22:3, 5).

In addition to the negative description, certain facts are delineated concerning the inhabitants and the activities of heaven. (1) Here, God is present in a special sense, dispensing judgment, grace and glory. We pray to Him as "our Father which art in heaven" (Mt 6:9; cf. also Jon 1:9; Rev 11:13; Ps 2:4; 14:2; 102:19; 103:19; Isa 33:5; 66:1). (2) Jesus Christ descended from heaven (Jn 3:13) and He was taken up into heaven (Acts 1:9-10; 3:21). He is presently at the right hand of God, making intercession for His saints (Heb 7:25; Rom 8:34), and from this place He will come again to judge the quick and the dead (Mt 24:30). (3) Redeemed souls are presently with Christ in heaven (*see* Intermediate State). At least two OT saints, Enoch and Elijah, were translated into heaven (II Kgs 2:1, 11; Heb 11:5). All the redeemed shall ultimately be in heaven in their resurrection bodies when He comes from heaven for them (I Thess 4:16-17; Rev 19:1-4). Furthermore, their treasures and rewards await the saints in heaven (Mt 5:12; I Pet 1:4; II Cor 5:1). (4) Heaven is the dwelling place of angelic beings (Mt 18:10; Eph 1:10; Heb 12:22) and from thence they go to minister to the inhabitants of the earth (Lk 2:13-15; 22:43).

See also Eternal State and Death; Jerusalem, New; New Heavens and New Earth.

Bibliography. Calvin D. Linton, "What's So Great About Heaven?" ChT, XV (Nov. 20, 1970), 163 ff. H. Harold Mare, "The New Testament Concept Regarding the Regions of Heaven with Emphasis on II Cor 12:1-4," *Grace Journal,* XI (1970), 3-12. Wilbur M. Smith, *The Biblical Doctrine of Heaven,* Chicago: Moody Press, 1968, with comprehensive bibliography. Helmut Traub and Gerhard von Rad, "*Ouranos,* etc.," TDNT, V, 497-543.

R. G. R.

HEAVINESS. A term usually signifying grief, used to translate a number of different Heb. and Gr. words. Ezra meant by "heaviness" (Ezr 9:5) his show of humiliation and grief expressed by fasting. In Prov 12:25 the word means anxiety (RSV). The Messiah will give a garment of praise instead of a spirit of fainting or despondency (Isa 61:3, JerusB). Sorrow or grief is the connotation in Ps 119:28 and Prov 10:1 (RSV), as well as in Rom 9:2 and in II Cor 2:1, where the Gr. noun *lupē* is translated "sorrow" and the corresponding verb "make sorry" or "grieve" in the following verses (2:2-7). Trials and temptations may well cause grief and distress to the believer during this present age (I Pet 1:6).

In repenting of his sins one should turn from gaiety to a downcast look or gloomy, dejected expression (Jas 4:9). Epaphroditus was "full of heaviness" (Phil 2:26), i.e., was distressed that the Philippian church had heard that he was ill. This same Gr. verb describes the deep distress of soul that Christ endured in Gethsemane (Mk 14:33).

Our expression "a heavy heart" is found in Prov 25:20, where Heb. *ra'* means "sad," as in Gen 40:7 and Neh 2:1-2.

J. R.

HEAVING AND WAVING. *See* Sacrificial Offerings.

HEBER (hē'bẽr)

1. Son of Beriah, grandson of Asher (Gen 46:17; I Chr 7:31-32). His descendants were called Heberites (Num 26:45).

2. A Kenite of the descendants of Hobab *(q.v.),* brother-in-law of Moses (Jud 4:11). Heber had separated himself from the Kenites and had settled in the plain of Zaanaim near Kedesh when Deborah was judge of Israel. She prophesied to Barak that Sisera, captain of the Canaanitish army, would be delivered into his hand. Sisera attacked Israel, but God intervened and he was defeated by Barak. Sisera attempted to flee on foot and ran to the tent of Jael (*q.v.*), wife of Heber. While he was asleep she drove a tent pin through his temples thus killing him (Jud 4).

3. Son of Mered and Jehudijah, the founder of Socho in Judah (I Chr 4:18).

4. One of the sons of Elpaal and a chief in the tribe of Benjamin (I Chr 8:17).

See also Eber.

R. H. B.

HEBREW LANGUAGE. In the NT the term "Hebrew" is applied to language, but in the OT it is only an ethnic designation. The Hebrews are referred to as speaking "the language of Canaan" (Isa 19:18) or else "the Jews' language" (Neh 13:24). Actually, Heb. was a dialect of the Canaanites, acquired by Abraham after his migration to Canaan, and employed by most of the surrounding nations, such as the Moabites, the Phoenicians, and (probably) the Philistines.

Like other Semitic languages, Heb. is made up of three-consonant roots for the most part (although some of the commonest words were only two-consonant), and variations in meaning were indicated by the vowels inserted between the consonants. Thus *kātab* meant "he wrote"; *kātᵉbâ,* "she wrote"; *yiktōb,* "he will write"; *kôtēb,* "writing"; *niktab,* "it was written"; *hiktîb,* "he caused to write"; and so forth. In each case the three root consonants are k-t-b. Pronoun objects were simply tacked on to the end of the verb; thus, "he will write them" is *yiktebēm*. This ability to express so many words in a single word-cluster enabled Heb. to convey much thought in a few words, thereby facilitating a powerful, concentrated mode of expression admirably suited both to poetry and prophetic oratory. The frequency of long vowels gave it an impressive, sonorous character, very pleasing to the ear, and well suited to convey the mood of the poet, the preacher, or the man of prayer.

The Heb. verbal system was not concerned with expressing tenses or time values as such, but rather with the mode of action, whether a complete or single action (perfect tense or state), or an incomplete or prolonged action (imperfect tense or state). The perfect most frequently referred to past actions, and yet it could refer to certain types of present (e.g., "Thus *saith* the Lord"), or even the prophetic future. The imperfect tense usually referred to present or future actions (hence, the RSV often renders as present tense those verb forms which the KJV translated as future—either interpretation is possible, depending on the context); but it could also describe continued action in past time ("he was writing") or potential action ("in order that he may write"). More extended continuous action could be expressed by a participle with a form of the verb "to be" either expressed (in the case of past or future time) or unexpressed (in the case of present time). This lack of precision in regard to time values offers occasional perplexities to one who wishes to translate into modern European languages. It stands in considerable contrast to the Gr. of the NT in this respect. Unlike Gr., Heb. also lacks a neuter gender and treats even inanimate objects or ideas as either masculine or feminine.

The fact that Heb. was originally written in consonants only, and the vowels had to be supplied by the reader in the light of the context, meant that differences of interpretation could easily result where more than one vocalization was possible. Thus the LXX, or OT Gr. translation, vocalized the consonants of h-sh-m-n in Isa 6:10 as *hushmān* ("has been made fat"), whereas the Masoretic Jewish scribes read it as *hashmēn* ("make fat!"). Cf. Mt 13:15 (lit. trans.): "The heart of this people has been made fat," which follows the LXX rendering, in contrast to the Jewish Heb. text (which was supplied with vowel points some time between A.D. 500 and 800), which reads, "Make the heart of this people fat." Usually the Jewish tradition is to be relied upon in regard to these vowel points, but occasionally a better reading is suggested by the ancient translations into Gr., Latin, or Syriac.

All the OT was composed in Heb. except

A Hebrew alphabetic inscription of Shebna, a steward, about 700 B.C., possibly the royal steward rebuked by Isaiah (22:15–16). BM

Dan 2-6 and Ezr 3-6, which were written in Aramaic. Heb. began to fall out of common usage after the 5th cen. B.C., but was still cultivated by the Jewish scholarly class, and was occasionally revived for patriotic reasons during the Jewish revolts against Rome. Much of the Midrash and Talmud, and the rabbinic commentaries on the OT as well, were composed in a later form of Heb. With the establishment of the modern state of Israel, Heb. was reinstated as the language of the Jewish population in the Holy Land, and has been developed into a precise, versatile, linguistic medium suited to modern needs.

"Hebrew" is referred to at least ten times in the NT, but it is not clear how often this term refers to the historic Heb. language and how often the Jewish dialect of Aramaic (then the *lingua franca* of the Semitic Near East) is intended. But it is significant that in every instance where a "Hebrew" word is quoted, or a saying of Jesus is recorded in His native tongue, the quotation or term is Aramaic rather than Heb. (except where the word would be identical in both languages). Cf. Jn 5:2 ("Bethzatha" or "Bethesda"); Jn 19:13 ("Gabbatha"); Jn 19:17 ("Golgotha"); Mk 5:41 ("*talitha koum,*" best Gr. text); Mk 7:34 ("*ephphatha*"); and Mt 27:46 ("*lema sabachthani,*" best Gr. text). Thus it may be conjectured that Paul's address to the Jerusalem mob in Acts 22 was in Heb. Aramaic rather than in Heb. itself.

G. L. A.

HEBREW OF THE HEBREWS. When Paul asserted he was "a Hebrew out of Hebrews" (Phil 3:5, Gr.), he meant more than "born of" (RSV). Using a standard Semitic idiom (e.g., "holy of holies"), he indicated the superlative degree.

HEBREW PEOPLE. The first person to be referred to as a Hebrew (*'ibrî*) in the Scripture was Abraham (Gen 14:13). His descendants derived from him the ethnic designation of "Hebrews." It would appear that he derived this label from his ancestor Eber (*'ēber*), the son of Salah, son of Arphaxad, son of Shem (Gen 11:10-14). Eber was father of Peleg, grandfather of Reu, great-grandfather of Serug, who begot Nahor, Abraham's grandfather (Gen 11:16-26).

Nevertheless it is difficult to see why no other descendant of Eber was known as an *'ibrî* besides Abraham and his posterity. On the basis of ancestry alone, all the descendants of Joktan (from whom came Arabian tribes like Hadramaut and Sheba, cf. I Chr 1:19-23) could have been called Hebrews, as well as those of Peleg, Abram's forefather (to be sure) but Nahor's as well. Yet not even Terah, Abram's father, is referred to as a "Hebrew," nor his brothers, Nahor the Younger or Haran, the father of Lot. But after Abraham had settled in Canaan, he and his descendants who were of the covenant line became known to the Canaanites and Egyptians as "Hebrews." Potiphar's wife so referred to Joseph (Gen 39:14, 17), and he so regarded himself (Gen 40:15), referring to the Canaanite area as "the land of the Hebrews." Gen 43:32 affirms that the Egyptians refused to eat with Hebrews (Joseph's brothers who had come to Egypt to buy grain), because that was "an abomination unto the Egyptians"—probably because "every shepherd was an abomination to the Egyptians" (Gen 46:34).

In addition to his being a descendant from Eber, Abraham may have been called an *'ibrî* for another reason. The 2nd mil. B.C. cuneiform records refer to a class of migrant peoples as *Ḥabiru, Ḥabiri, Ḥapiru* or *'Apiru*, and these references occur as early as Warad-Sin and Rim-Sin of the Elamite Dynasty (*c.* 1800 B.C.). The Mari correspondence tells of 2,000 enemy troops of the Ḥapiru led by a certain Yapah-Adad (ANET, p. 483). Hittite and Old Babylonian texts mention them as receiving regular rations from the state, manning royal garrisons and worshiping gods invoked in suzerainty treaties (although the names of these "gods" are not given—cf. ANET, p. 206). A Nuzu tablet from about 1500 B.C. refers to a Habiru from Assyria named Mar-Idiglat ("son of the Tigris") as a volunteer slave to a local householder; another mentions a female Ḥabiru named Sin-balti ("the moon-god is my life") as a slave to a woman named Tehip-tilla (ANET, p. 220).

These names are completely pagan or idolatrous. Quite certainly none of these has any relationship to Abraham's family, and therefore could not be considered "Hebrew" in the biblical sense. The same is true of the Ḥabiri at Alalakh in N Syria, who rose to be government officials (*c.* 1450 B.C.) or chariot-owning *maryannu* in that principality.

A different situation arises in connection with the Tell el-Amarna correspondence, a file of letters addressed to Amenhotep III and Akhenaton during the 18th Dynasty (*c.* 1400-1360). *See* Amarna Letters. Invading Ḥabiri are complained of by 'Abdu-Heba king of Jerusalem as plundering all "the lands of the king" (i.e., the territory he held as a vassal of Egypt; see ANET, pp. 487 ff., Nos. 286 and 288). There are numerous other references to these invaders as *SA.GAZ* (the usual cuneiform characters for these Ḥabiri when their name was not phonetically spelled out) in correspondence from other Canaanite rulers as far to the N as Syria and Phoenicia (notably Byblos). While the book of Joshua reports no collective military operations by Joshua's troops in these northerly regions, there is nothing in the account in Joshua or Judges to discourage the supposition that after receiving their allotment (Josh 19) the northern Israelite tribes, such as Asher and Naphtali, may have launched tribal expeditions against the Phoenician territories contiguous to their borders.

It is certainly significant that no correspondence has been found at Tell el-Amarna from cities which fell earliest to Israelite power or influence, like Jericho, Ai, Bethel and Gibeon (*see* Exodus, The: Date). Most of the communications come from cities which according to the OT the Israelites were slow in conquering, namely, Megiddo, Ashkelon, Acco, Gezer and Jerusalem. Concerning Shechem, near which the Israelites solemnized their national covenant as they stood between Mount Ebal and Mount Gerizim, 'Abdu-Heba complained that Labayu of Shechem had gone over to the side of the 'Apiru (ANET, p. 489, No. 289).

In the light of the foregoing evidence it seems reasonable to conclude that the term *Ḫabiri* was a general designation originally for migrant peoples who had crossed over national boundaries (from the verb *'ābar,* "pass through, cross over," which may well have been represented by *ḫābiru,* corresponding to the participial form *'ôber*) as nomads or itinerant laborers, whatever their ethnic background may have been. As a migrant from Haran and Ur, then, Abraham would have been considered a *ḫabiru* by the Canaanites, and thus have acquired this label as a sort of surname. Presumably his descendants retained it in later generations, even through the four centuries in Egypt, and were so known at the time of the conquest under Joshua *c.* 1400 B.C.

The wider use of the term remained current as well. In 15th cen. Ugarit in N Syria, the city of Aleppo was still known as Halbu of the *'Apiru,* from which corvee labor was required for the service of the king of Ugarit. The Egyptian references to the *'Apiru* begin with the reign of Thutmose III (1504–1450 B.C.), as witness the tombs of Puyemrē and Antef (who were high officials during his reign); then in the Memphis stela of his son Amenhotep II, who claims to have captured 3,600 'Apiru in battle. Seti I encountered 'Apiru in Jarmuth or Yeroham (*c.* 1310 B.C.); Rameses III dedicated 'Apiru slaves to the temple of Amon in Heliopolis (ANET, p. 261); whereas Rameses IV mentions 800 'Apiru of the bowmen of the Antiu, which implies that they were mercenary soldiers. These Egyptian references can only be understood as immigrants into Canaan, in the more general sense of the term Ḫabiru, rather than as specifically Hebrews or Israelites.

So far as the biblical record goes, the Israelites were commonly referred to as *'ibrîm* by the Egyptians all during the Mosaic period, and the term carries with it covenantal connotations. Moses was quoted as referring to Yahweh as the God of the Hebrews (*'ibrîm*) (Ex 5:3; 7:16; 9:1, 13; 10:3). Under the law a "Hebrew servant" was to be treated with consideration, and to be granted manumission by the seventh year of his servitude (Deut 15:12; cf. Jer 34:9, where there was a move to implement this merciful provision). In the later period of the judges the Philistines are quoted as calling the Israelites by this term quite consistently; in their lips it appears as a purely ethnic designation, usually tinged with a note of contempt (I Sam 4:6, 9; 14:11; 29:3). After the division of the Solomonic domains into the northern kingdom of Israel and the southern kingdom of Judah (*c.* 930 B.C.), the term Hebrew was occasionally used by Israelites as they identified themselves ethnically in dealings with other nations. Thus Jonah, in explaining to the sailors from Joppa what his religious and national background was, said, "I am a Hebrew, and I worship Yahweh, the God of heaven, who made the sea and the land" (Jon 1:9, JerusB).

In the NT the term *Hebraisti* seems to refer to the Jewish dialect of Aramaic (thus the "Hebrew" name for Calvary is given in Jn 19:17 as Golgothā, a distinctively Aramaic formation with the final emphatic -ā; likewise *gabbathā,* the paved area on which Pilate's judgment throne was set up). Hence the consciousness of nationality was based upon a covenant commitment to Israel's God, rather than upon the language they spoke. In calling himself "a Hebrew of the Hebrews" (*q.v.*; Phil 3:5), Paul claimed to be a full-blooded Israelite, whose parents were both Hebrews (cf. II Cor 11:22).

The distinction between Jew and Gentile was occasionally expressed by this term Hebrew rather than by the usual *Ioudaioi* ("Jews"); e.g., the title of the Epistle to the Hebrews (*pros tous Hebraious*). Or it might even indicate Palestinian Jews in contrast to those of the Dispersion, as in Acts 6:1, which uses the terms *Hebraioi* and *Hellēnistai* for these two groups within the Jerusalem church. Here the term is not only ethnic, but also geographical or cultural. Yet in later times the scope of *Hebraioi* was enlarged, by some writers at least, to include even Jews of the Diaspora. Eusebius of Caesarea in the 4th cen. A.D. referred to Philo, the Alexandrian Jew, as *Hebraios* (*Eccl. Hist.* 2.4, 2), or at least as a descendant of *Hebraioi.* He likewise spoke of Aristobulus (in *Praepar. Evang.* 8.8, 34), who was a Greek-speaking scholar of the Dispersion.

The Heb. language fell into relative disuse during the post-Exilic period, during which a Jewish dialect of Aramaic prevailed among the Jews even in Palestine. Nevertheless the Heb. Scriptures were held in high esteem and were publicly read at every synagogue service—even if they had to be interpreted into Aramaic (the origin of the later written Targums). Moreover, there seems to have been some restricted use of the authentic Heb. language among scholars and students of the Bible, for only continual use as a living speech could account for the development of the Mishnaic type of Heb. found in the Dead Sea Scrolls, especially the Copper Scroll of Cave Three. The letters and legal documents from the second revolt (*c.* A.D. 135) were often couched in Heb., as might be expected in a time of intense nationalistic fervor. Interestingly enough, one such letter in Heb.

seems to have been preserved from Bar Kochba himself, the false Messiah of that unsuccessful uprising. Thus there is a sense in which the Heb. language, especially as enshrined in the sacred Scriptures, was a necessary concomitant for the Heb. people to maintain their consciousness of nationhood, despite the adoption of Aram. or Gr. as the household speech. Always they looked to the Heb. OT as the basis of their status as a covenant people, especially chosen by God to be His own. This linguistic association ultimately proved decisive in modern times, when the Heb. language was deliberately revived and enforced by the founders of modern Israel as the obligatory tongue for all of their citizens.

For history of the Heb. people *see* Nations; Patriarchal Age; Exodus, The; Israel; Israel, Kingdom of; Jew; Judah, Kingdom of; Captivity; Restoration, The. For language *see* Hebrew Language. For religion *see* Covenant; Festivals; Law of Moses; Priest, Priesthood.

Bibliography. G. L. Archer, SOTI, pp. 253–259. John Bright, "Hebrew Religion, History of," IDB, II, 560–570. E. F. Campbell, "The Amarna Letters and the Amarna Period," BA, XXIII (1960), 13–15. Moshe Greenberg, *The Hab/piru,* New Haven: American Oriental Society, 1955. M. G. Kline, "The Ḥa-BI-ru – Kin or Foe of Israel?" WTJ, XIX (1956-7), 1-24, 170–184, XX (1957), 46–70. Julius Lewy, "Origin and Signification of the Biblical Term 'Hebrew,' " HUCA, XXVIII (1957), 1-13. S. Moscati, *Ancient Semitic Civilizations,* New York: Putnam, 1960, pp. 124–166, 242 f. H. H. Rowley, *From Joseph to Joshua,* London: British Academy, 1950, pp. 45–56. Roland de Vaux, "Le Problème des Ḥapiru," JNES, XXVII (1968), 221–228.

G. L. A.

HEBREWS, EPISTLE TO THE. An anonymous epistle of the NT, placed after those identified as Pauline and before the general epistles. It is an exhortation toward a full experience of salvation, presented in a classic Gr. rhetorical style. The epistle is unique, abounding in problems and characteristics peculiar to itself. Nevertheless it contains deep theological insight into the nature of the salvation which God provided in His Son. This is predicated upon rabbinic-type argumentation from OT institutions and statements about the salvation of God. Exhortations and useful principles for the enjoyment of salvation are found throughout. The early church was for a time in a quandary as to what to do with this epistle because of uncertainty about its origin, and contemporary Christians find it an enigma because of uncertainty concerning its meaning.

Authorship and Canonicity

Uncertainty as to author resulted in slow admission to the canon. The concerted efforts of the Church Fathers to attribute it to Paul were more motivated by zeal for canonicity than nervousness about authorship. Having been admitted, however, its inspiration and authority are clearly attested by the church. Since authorship is not stated by the text, it is a matter of scholarly interest and not theological commitment.

When the Western church first mentioned the epistle, it said nothing about the epistle's authorship. Suggestions that Paul was the author came from the Alexandrian church; however, Origen of Alexandria concluded: "But as to who actually wrote the epistle, God knows the truth of the matter." The subsequent history of the question attests the wisdom of Origen's conclusion, for students of the issue up to the Reformation suggested as author, aside from Paul, Barnabas, Clement of Rome, and Luke.

Luther was the first to suggest Apollos. As biblical scholarship developed from the time of the Reformation, fewer and fewer scholars have held to Pauline authorship so that very few seriously defend it today. However, it continued to be homiletically convenient and is often so asserted uncritically. Also suggested as authors are Philip the deacon, Priscilla and Aquila, Aristion, Silas, Mark, and Jude.

Among the evidence presented for Pauline authorship is Peter's mention of a letter Paul wrote, possibly to Jews (II Pet 3:15–16); association with Timothy (cf. Heb 13:23) and Rome (cf. v. 24); an ending not unlike Paul's; and many points of theological agreement. The most frequently offered evidence, however, is simply tradition. This is, indeed, probably the strongest argument and not to be dismissed without reason. The fact is that Paul was the first widely suggested candidate, and he has been accepted by more people over a longer period of time than any other.

However, a great number of reasons have been posited to dismiss the traditional Pauline authorship. It did take the church a long time to suggest him, and the suggestion came from the part of the church least likely to know and without careful argumentation when the part most likely to know refrained from such. It was held traditional, moreover, during the time of least critical scholarship. Lack of signature and personal greetings and exclusive use of the LXX are unlike Paul's signed epistles. The style is unlike those in that it uses polished rhetoric, Hellenistic spirit, completed thoughts, and balanced sentences. There is also a distinct vocabulary and a peculiar theological viewpoint. Paul pictures Christ indwelling the believer, while Hebrews has Him at "the right hand of the Father"; Paul shows the law to be ethically impossible, while Hebrews argues that it is ceremonially impossible. Moreover, this epistle does not easily fit into the Pauline itinerary (cf. Heb. 13:23). The strongest argument against Pauline authorship is that it would appear impossible for the same man to acknowledge a secondary source of information

(2:3) and elsewhere insist upon primary and direct revelation (Gal 1:11-24).

Apollos is the apostolic character whose biblical description (Acts 18:24-28; I Cor 1:13; 3:4) comes closest to the type of man it took to write an epistle like Hebrews. He was a Jew from Alexandria who was "an eloquent man, well versed in the scriptures" and closely associated with Paul. First suggested by Luther, this has become the position of an increasingly great number of scholars which include T. W. Manson, W. F. Howard, C. Spicq, Alford, F. W. Farrar, and Hugh Montefiore. Yet this still does not account for omission of his name, and it seems strange that the Alexandrian church did not know and eagerly acknowledge Apollos as the author.

Date

Several statements indicate that the epistle was written during the second generation of the apostolic period, e.g., the process of transmission (2:1-4), time for growth (5:12), "former days" past (10:32), leaders dead (13:7), Timothy imprisoned (13:23). Yet the Jewish institutions were still in operation and the temple still standing (13:10-11) although they were soon to be gone (12:37) and persecution was imminent (10:32 ff.; 12:4). These factors seem to put the writing somewhere in the late A.D. 60's, *c.* 67-69.

Destination and Readers

It is difficult to identify the destination and readers since there are no internal or external statements. The title and OT usage have been taken as indications of a Jewish-Christian readership. But this assumption is increasingly challenged, and it has been suggested that the readers were Gentiles converted from paganism (Moffatt, E. F. Scott). Other recent scholars suggest non-Palestinian Jews (William Manson, F. F. Bruce), Essenes, or former Essenes (C. Spicq, Yadin). It is the wilderness experience of the Hebrews and the tabernacle which are featured and not the restoration state and the temple, and nothing is said of the characteristic Judaistic emphasis upon circumcision. OT quotations and references are not so obscure that they would not be understood by anyone who had studied the OT. Yet the warnings would seem to fit best Christians in danger of falling back into the practices of Judaism. Perhaps it can be assumed that, although the readers were not necessarily Jewish, they were probably Jewish or at least strongly influenced by Judaism. Rome now seems ruled out as the place of writing (see 13:24, RSV) but could be the destination.

Of greater importance than these matters, so far as interpretation of the epistle and its contemporary application, is the spiritual condition of the readers. They were converted to Christianity by those who had known Jesus (2:3 f.) and were, therefore, second generation believers. If this were not from Judaism (most likely some non-Palestinian form), they acquired a strong respect for the ancient Heb. institutions and God's promises to Israel (evidently from a study of the LXX rather than by observance of temple worship in Jerusalem). They early endured significant persecution (10:32 ff.) although not as severe as that which was imminent (12:4). The crisis created in them a practical expression of their faith in ministering to their brothers—especially those most affected by the persecution (6:10; 10:34).

Despite these early experiences, they were no longer growing (5:11–6:20) and, indeed, were beginning to go back (2:1 ff.). It was not that they were consciously rebelling against the gospel of faith or purposely turning to something else, but rather taking salvation for granted and presuming upon God's grace in the sacrifice of His Son (10:26-31). They were lethargic and sluggish in regard to their faith (3:7–4:13) and susceptible to false teachings (13:7-9). They were prone to exaggerate the importance of angels (1:5-14) and the effectiveness of the law, and to depreciate the ultimacy of Christ's sacrifice (9:11–10:31) and His perfection (4:14–5:10; 7:1–8:13), as well as the worth of the ultimate reality promised to them (11:13-16). They possessed salvation but were neglecting to live it. Therefore they were in danger not only of failing to reach the fullness of their salvation but to lose its present

A third century papyrus fragment showing Hebrews 12:1-11. BM

experience. Instead of gaining the better things promised, they might lose the good things already received and be left with only the lesser things of the past.

Purpose and Argument

This epistle makes a significant contribution to NT theology, but its main purpose is not theological. The writer calls it "my word of exhortation" (13:22, RSV), and this is its goal throughout. He writes with the compassion of one who cares about the Christians as a group and has some kind of pastoral responsibility for them. He exhorts them to a determined and active practice of their salvation so that they can achieve all that salvation was meant to give and avoid the disastrous consequences of neglecting it.

What the writer is seeking to accomplish may be seen by a collective study of the warnings and then the hortatory passages. He warns his readers of the inescapable consequence of neglecting salvation (2:1-3), about missing God's rest (3:7-19), about disqualification from the rest (4:1-11), of the impossibility of return from conscious apostasy (6:4-8), and of there being no provision for deliberate and knowledgeable sin (10:26-31). Closely related to these are his exhortations: be alert, lest you drift away (2:1-4); be careful, lest you disbelieve (3:7–4:13); go on, lest you fall back (5:11–6:20); draw near, lest you walk away (10:19-39); build up, lest you fall apart (12:12-29).

Whether his readers were Jewish or Gentile, or whether it was Judaism or paganism to which they were in danger of returning, is not as clear as their current spiritual condition and the danger in which the author found them. This he compares with neither Judaism nor paganism, but with the Hebrews wandering in the wilderness between exodus from sin's bondage and entrance into the Promised Land. That condition was as impoverished and fruitless as the wilderness. Since his readers were guilty of the same kind of unbelief and disobedience as were the Hebrews of Moses' day, they were in as much danger of dying there without ever entering into the promised rest as were the Israelites of old. They were not so much like the Jews of the synagogues overworking their religion, as they were like the Hebrews of the wilderness not exercising their salvation. The purpose of Hebrews is to exhort the Christians to become active in their present experience with God's salvation so that they possess all that God has promised while it is still "today."

Outline

An Exhortation Concerning God's Salvation

I. The Description of God's Salvation, 1:1–4:13
- A. The provision of God's salvation: God's Son, 1:1–3:6
  1. His superiority to angels, 1:1-14
  2. The reasons for His humanity, 2:1-18
  3. Consideration of Him as Apostle and Priest, 3:1-6
- B. The end of God's salvation: God's rest, 3:7–4:13
  1. Danger of missing that rest, 3:7-9
  2. Disqualification for that rest, 4:1-11
  3. The Word of God as the Christian's guard, 4:12-13

II. The Priesthood of God's Salvation, 4:14–7:28
- A. Introduction to the priesthood, 4:14–5:10
- B. Collateral instructions, 5:11–6:20
- C. Melchizedek-type priesthood, 7:1-10
- D. The perfect priesthood of Jesus, 7:11-28

III. The System of God's Salvation, 8:1–10:18
- A. The new and better covenant, 8:1-13
- B. Contrast between the earthly and heavenly tabernacles, 9:1-14
- C. The ratification of the new covenant, 9:15–10:18

IV. The Life of God's Salvation, 10:19–13:16
- A. The consequent exhortation, 10:19-39
- B. Past lives of faith, 11:1-40
- C. Our life of faith, 12:1–13:16

V. The Closing, 13:17-25

Theology

The epistle's theology is so unique that much time has been spent in comparing and contrasting it with the balance of NT theology (especially Pauline). An even greater search has been made to find ideological origins in contemporary religious and philosophic systems. The first associations were made with Philo, then Gr. Gnosticism, and more recently Jewish Essenism. In each case, impressive similarities have been outweighed by more significant divergences.

The writer shows familiarity with a variety of schools of thought, but his theology is distinctly his own. Finding an analogy in the matter-ideal dualism of Platonism, he speaks of present reality as being only a shadow of ultimate reality. Thus to the Gr. dualist Hebrews presents Christ as giving access to ultimate reality in God. Another analogy comes from the Heb. fear of God. The epistle shows that Christ has pioneered the way to God in the ultimate sanctuary of heaven by means of His own atonement "once for all." So to the Jew fearful of God, Hebrews presents Christ as giving bold access into the very presence of God.

The theological concepts of the epistle are all applications of these basic presuppositions: Christ gives access to reality and access to God. No theological concern is developed which does not make a conceptual contribution to the exhortation to live God's salvation.

Christology is important because the concept of perfection grows from soteriology which is based solidly on Christology. Salvation is great because it was provided in the person of God's Son. This epistle has one of the highest concepts of the Sonship of Christ to be found anywhere in the Bible. The Son is superior to patriarchs, prophets, and even the rabbinicly exaggerated angels. And yet the Son of God identifies Himself with man by becoming man. The believer, then, becomes a brother of the Son of God and therefore himself a son of God.

The Son became the ultimate and perfect Priest for all men (rather than exclusively on behalf of the people of the old covenant). He is the ultimate Priest because His atonement need never be repeated year after year and for the same sins, but was done "once for all." He is the perfect Saviour-Priest because He actually accomplished the real removal of sin and the redemption of the sinner rather than covering over what still remains in the consciousness. Maintaining the figure of the Day of Atonement, Jesus is pictured as a High Priest. To show His unique priesthood, the writer calls Him a Melchizedekian Priest by analogy.

The soteriology of Hebrews does not picture salvation as a goal for the lost or a possession of the believer, but exhorts the Christian to make use of his salvation. While the crucifixion and resurrection are effectively assumed and clearly implied, Hebrews focuses upon the sacrifice not as the victim is slain on the altar but as the sacrifice is carried into the holiest (the Father's right hand) and mediated by constant intercession. Salvation is described in ceremonial (ultimate priesthood) and forensic (new covenant) terms rather than ethical (Paul). Hebrews, then, shows the high priest taking the blood of the victim from the altar through the temple veil into the holiest year after year as superseded by Jesus taking His own sacrifice from the cross through the veil between imperfect reality and ultimate reality into heaven once for all.

Sanctification is described in terms highly peculiar to this epistle, and centers around a concept of perfection which is reminiscent of the Platonic dissatisfaction with the incompleteness of the present and anticipation of the ultimateness of the future. The goal of God's salvation is God's rest, which is variously spoken of as arrival at one's destination, as completion of one's task, and as peace with God. The rest of God can, then, be defined as perfect and eternal fellowship with God. But perfection and rest are conceived in dynamic terms so that the believer is always to be in the process of perfection and arriving at his rest. Perfection is not an award to be clutched but an experience to be pursued. Apostasy is to be feared because it is not the loss of a possession but of experience.

Hebrews does not debate eternal security, since the readers were thoroughly convinced of this and indeed were presuming upon it to the point of neglecting the present experience of salvation. Apostasy, he shows, is the failure to be in the process of being saved from sin. When one is not being saved from present sin, he is not experiencing salvation. If one persists in this condition long enough. he will become so hardened that he will never again return to that previous experience of being in the process of being saved.

Rather than faulting the writer with lack of appreciation for the reception of salvation, he should be credited with taking seriously its utilization. He does not teach eternal security, because it is unnecessary to do so. Rather than putting his readers at ease in regard to the end, he puts them in the wholesome tension between security about eternity and loss in the present, and this tension allows possession of the former and avoidance of the latter while assuring a full salvation from inception to culmination.

Bibliography. William Barclay, *The Letter to the Hebrews,* Philadelphia: Westminster Press, 1957. F. F. Bruce, *The Epistle to the Hebrews,* NIC, Grand Rapids: Eerdmans, 1964. Marcus Dods, "The Epistle to the Hebrews," EGT, IV, Grand Rapids: Eerdmans reprint, 1956. William Manson, *The Epistle to the Hebrews,* London: Hodder & Stoughton, 1951. Andrew Murray, *The Holiest of All,* London: Nisbet & Co., n.d. (devotional). Alexander Nairne, *The Epistle to the Hebrews,* Cambridge: Univ. Press, 1921. William R. Newell, *Hebrews Verse by Verse,* Chicago: Moody Press, 1947. John Owen, *Hebrews: The Epistle of Warning,* Grand Rapids: Kregel, 1953 (condensation of Owen's 8 vol. work). Adolph Saphir, *The Epistle to the Hebrews,* 2 vols., New York: Loizeaux Bros., n.d. (warm exposition by a Jewish Christian teacher). B. F. Westcott, *The Epistle to the Hebrews,* Grand Rapids: Eerdmans reprint, 1950. Ronald Williamson, *Philo and the Epistle to the Hebrews,* Leiden: Brill, 1970.

W. A.

HEBRON (hē'brŭn)

1. The third named son of Kohath, the son of Levi (Ex 6:18; Num 3:19, 27; I Chr 6:2, 18; 23:12). His descendants were called Hebronites (Num 3:27; 26:58; I Chr 26:23, 30–31).

2. A descendant of Caleb (I Chr 2:42–43).

3. A very old city 19 miles SSW of Jerusalem on the road to Beer-sheba via Bethlehem. It is 3,040 feet above sea level, the highest town in Palestine. It was originally called Kiriath-arba ("town of Arba" or "town of the four," referring either to a great hero of the Anakim [Josh 14:15] or, taking *'arba'* as a numeral, to the four clans living there, Anak and his three sons [Josh 15:14]). The name Kiriath-arba may have suggested a curious legend that Adam was buried here, and that Abraham, Isaac and Jacob wished to be buried alongside him. Num 13:22 speaks of Hebron as built or rebuilt seven years before Zoan (or Avaris, Ps 78:12) in Egypt. Some scholars believe that this verse implies a connection with

the Hyksos *(q.v.)*, who built their capital in the NE delta of Egypt at Avaris *c.* 1700 B.C.

The chief fame of Hebron rests in the fact that Abram dwelt much of the time at Mamre in its environs (Gen 13:18). He was living here when the confederacy of kings overthrew the cities of the plain and captured Lot (Gen 14:1-13). At Hebron his name was changed to Abraham. Here too he entertained the celestial visitors who spoke of the birth of Isaac (Gen 18:1-15). Sarah died at Hebron (Gen 23:2) and Abraham bought the cave of Machpelah nearby as a burial place (Gen 23:9). Ephron the Hittite and "the children of Heth" (Gen 23:5, 10) probably have no racial or political connection with the powerful Indo-European Hittites *(q.v.)*. Isaac lived at Hebron (Gen 35:27). Later, Joseph was sent to his brethren by Jacob from that region (Gen 37:14). Abraham, Sarah, Isaac, Rebekah, Jacob and Leah (Gen 49:31; 50:13) were all buried in the cave which Abraham had purchased near Hebron.

The 12 Heb. spies saw Hebron (Num 13:22). Joshua slew the king of the town during the period of conquest (Josh 10:3-27). Caleb claimed it as his inheritance and drove out the Anakim (Josh 14:12-15; 15:13-14). Hebron was assigned to be a city of refuge (Josh 20:7). David was well received by the Hebronites (I Sam 30:31) and reigned as king there for seven and one-half years (II Sam 5:5). Absalom's revolt began in Hebron (II Sam 15:7-12). Rehoboam fortified it as one of the bastion cities to protect his S and W frontier against Egyptian invasion such as that of Shishak (II Chr 11:5, 10; 12:2-4). Royal stamped jar handles of the 8th and 7th cen. B.C., which name Hebron among four cities, suggest that it was the key storage city for army rations in the military defense system initiated by King Uzziah (II Chr 26:10; Y. Yadin, "The Fourfold Division of Judah," BASOR #163, pp. 6-12).

Some of the Jews in the post-Exilic period preferred to live in Hebron (Kiriath-arba) and its surrounding hamlets rather than move to Jerusalem (Neh 11:25). Later the Idumeans occupied Hebron until Judas Maccabaeus captured it (I Macc 5:65). During the first Jewish revolt it was held briefly by Simon bar-Giora, but was attacked and burned by the Romans (Jos *Wars* iv.9. 7, 9).

The present town is known to the Arabs as el-Khalil ("the friend," referring to Abraham as the friend of God; cf. Isa 41:8 and Jas 2:23). It surrounds the sacred Moslem enclosure or Haram, with a large mosque over the traditional site of the cave of Machpelah. The reputation of Hebron is that of great conservatism and almost fanatical dedication to Islam.

A hill to the W of the present city, called Jebel er-Rumeideh, was the site of Hebron up to the time of the Crusades. In 1964 Phillip C. Hammond began excavations which uncovered evidence of occupation from *c.* 3000 B.C., a city wall of the entire Middle Bronze Age (*c.* 2000-1550 B.C.), material from the 15th cen. B.C., stratified remains of the Israelite period, and evidence from late Roman, Byzantine, and Islamic times (BA, XXVIII [1965], 30-32).

W. C. and J. R.

HEBRONITES (hē'brŏn-īts). A family of Levites, descendants of Hebron, the third son of Kohath (Num 3:27; 26:58; I Chr 26:23, 30-31). *See also* Hebron.

HEDGE. In the NT, a fence of any kind (Mk 12:1; Lk 14:23). The OT uses two Heb. roots, one signifying a stone wall (*gdr,* Ps 80:12; 89:40; Eccl 10:8; Nah 3:17); the other, a thorn hedge (*śûk,* Prov 15:19; Hos 2:6). Hedges were planted to protect vineyards (Isa 5:5). The verb "hedge in," "hedge about" has been used to express God's protection (Job 1:10) or His constraint (Job 3:23). *See* Fence; Plants: Hedge.

HEDGEHOG. *See* Animals, II.18.

HEEL, LIFTED UP HIS. The expression "hath lifted up his heel against me" (Ps 41:9; lit., "made great the heel against me") refers to the treachery of one's closest and most trusted friend. That some such rendering is what the psalmist meant seems clear from the LXX and from the independent translation into Gr. found in Jesus' quotation of the verse in Jn 13:18 as He applied it to Judas Iscariot. Thus Mitchell Dahood's translation of Ps 41:10 (9) in the Anchor Bible, "spun slanderous tales about me," is not a likely one.

HEGAI (hĕg'ī). The officer of King Ahasuerus in charge of the fair virgins from whom the successor to Vashti, the deposed queen, was to be taken (Est 2:8, 15). The name is also spelled Hege (Est 2:3).

HEGE (hĕg'ī). Same as Hegai *(q.v.)*.

HEGLAM (hĕg'lăm). An alternate name for Gera *(q.v.)*, a son of Ehud (I Chr 8:7, RSV). However, KJV, ASV, JerusB, and Anchor

Hebron. HFV

Bible all treat the name as a verb and translate "he removed them," "he led them into exile," etc.

HEIFER. *See* Animals: Cattle, I.6.

HEIFER, RED. *See* Sacrificial Offerings.

HEIR. *See* Inheritance.

HELAH (hē'lȧ). A wife of Ashur, a descendant of Hur (I Chr 4:5, 7).

HELAM (hē'lȧm). A town E of the Jordan River, probably on the southern border of Syria. David's commander Joab defeated the Syrian allies of Ammon here (II Sam 10:16–17). This city seems to appear in the Egyptian Execration texts (BASOR #83, p. 33), and probably is the same as the Alama of I Macc 5:26, which may be modern 'Alma in the plain of Hauran.

HELBAH (hĕl'bȧ). A town in the tribal territory of Asher (Jud 1:31). Its exact location is unknown. It is possibly Ahlab on the Mediterranean coast N of Tyre.

HELBON (hĕl'bŏn). A town in Syria *c.* 15 miles NNW of Damascus, famous in ancient times for the excellency of its wine (Ezk 27:18). It is modern Ḥalbûn, lying in a steep valley. It is still known for the extensive vineyards on its nearby slopes.

HELDAI (hĕl'dī)

1. A hero under David, Heldai was the captain over the temple services for the 12th month (I Chr 27:15). His name also appears as Heled (*q.v.;* I Chr 11:30) and as Heleb (*q.v.;* II Sam 23:29).

2. One who returned from the Exile in the time of Zerubbabel (*c.* 520 B.C.). His name also appears as Helem (*q.v.;* Zech 6:14) as well as Heldai (Zech 6:10).

HELEB (hē'lĕb). Son of Baanah the Netophathite, one of David's mighty men (II Sam 23:29). Called Heled in I Chr 11:30 (*q.v.*). *See also* Heldai 1.

HELED (hē'lĕd). Found only in I Chr 11:30. *See* Heleb; Heldai 1.

HELEK (hē'lĕk), **HELEKITES** (hē'lĕ-kīts). Second son of Gilead of the tribe of Manasseh and the founder of the family of Helekites (Num 26:30; Josh 17:2).

HELEM (hē'lĕm)

1. A great-grandson of Asher (I Chr 7:35). He is called Hotham *(q.v.)* in I Chr 7:32.

2. The same as Heldai 2 *(q.v.)*.

HELEPH (hē'lĕf). A border town of Naphtali near Mount Tabor (Josh 19:33). Its exact site is uncertain.

HELEZ (hē'lĕz)

1. A descendant of Judah of the Jerahmeelite clan (I Chr 2:39).

2. A commander over 24,000 soldiers of David's army in charge of the 7th course. He is identified as being of the tribe of Ephraim (I Chr 27:10). His village may be indicated by the adjectives "Paltite" (II Sam 23:26) and "Pelonite" (I Chr 11:27; 27:10), but neither term refers to a known village; they refer to Beth-pelet near Beer-sheba in southern Judah.

HELI (hē'lī). This is the Gr. form of the Heb. name *'Elî.*

He was the father of Joseph, the husband of Mary, according to the unpunctuated text of the genealogy of Jesus as given by Luke (3:23). The verse, however, may be translated to read: "And when He began His ministry, Jesus Himself was about thirty years of age, being supposedly the son of Joseph, the son of Heli" (NASB). R. C. H. Lenski punctuates the key phrase, "being a son (as was supposed of Joseph) of Heli." The term *hōs enomizeto,* "as was supposed," may have the sense of "according to custom." As Norval Geldenhuys comments, "Because it was not customary (among the Romans as well as among the Jews) to insert the name of a woman in a lineage list, [Luke] added the words '(as was supposed) the son of Joseph.' He was not afraid that his readers would get the impression that the genealogical tree was that of Joseph and not that of Mary, for in Luke 1 and 2 he had pointed out expressly that Jesus was solely the son of Mary and not of Joseph and Mary" (*Commentary on the Gospel of Luke,* p. 151; see also his further arguments, pp. 150–155). Thus Heli was the father-in-law of Joseph and the maternal grandfather of Jesus.

J. R.

HELKAI (hĕl'kī). A priest of the family of Meraioth (Neh 12:15), in the high priesthood of Joiakim in the early years of the 5th cen. B.C. This is probably an abbreviation of the name Hilkiah (Neh 8:4).

HELKATH (hĕl'kăth). A city of Asher on the southern border near Mount Carmel (Josh 19:25). It was assigned to the Levitical family of Gershon (Josh 21:31). The exact site is unknown. In I Chr 6:75 it is called Hukok *(q.v.)*.

HELKATH-HAZZURIM (hĕl'kăth-hăzh'ōō-rĭm; "the field of sword edges"). A field at the pool of Gibeon where David's army led by Joab met Ishbosheth's army led by Abner. Twelve men from each army killed each other in individual combat, after which David's army routed the forces of Ishbosheth (II Sam 2:16).

HELL. In common and theological usage, the place of future punishment of the wicked dead. However, since the KJV uses "hell" to signify the grave and the place of disembodied spirits.

both good and bad, care must be taken to prevent mistakes and confusion.

Hell, in the sense of a place of future punishment, is certainly distinctly taught in the Bible. Though the doctrine is not nearly so clearly expressed in the OT as in the NT, it is suggested in such passages as Isa 14:9-11 (cf. Ezk 32:21 ff.); Num 16:33; Deut 32:22; Job 24:19; Ps 9:17; Isa 33:14; Dan 12:2. In the NT it is Christ, our beloved Saviour, who gives the fullest teaching about hell. Only from the One who loved men enough to die for them can men receive this terrible truth. Paul accepts the doctrine but does not dwell upon it or expound it. The apostle John adds details in the book of Revelation (20:10, 15).

If some object that the teaching of everlasting hell fire cannot be meant to be taken literally, the least that we can conclude is that such words and descriptions as given are metaphors to express the terrible agonies of the soul as it suffers endless remorse in eternity to come, when separated from God and all that is good and confined with all that are bad. Even in this life the agonies of the mind can equal if not exceed those of the body. The biblical teaching of hell cannot be denied without assuming either that Christ knew no better, or knew better but still taught it. If He knew no better, how then does He know enough for us to trust Him to save us? If He knew better but still taught it, He used deception and was not holy enough to die for us.

The four words translated "hell" are:

1. *Sheol.* Two possible derivations of the Heb. word *shᵉʾôl* have been suggested: *shāʾal,* "to ask or inquire," and *shōʿal,* "hollow" (cf. Isa 40:12, "hollow of his hand," and Num 22:24, "the path [or hollow] of the vineyards"). In postbiblical Heb. the latter word is used for the "deep" of the sea. In the OT *sheol* is used of the grave (Job 17:13; Ps 16:10; Isa 38:10) and of the place of the dead both good (Gen 37:35; Job 14:13; Ps 6:5; Eccl 9:10) and bad (Ps 55:15; Prov 9:18). It was conceived of as a world below our world where darkness, decay and forgetfulness prevail and one is remote from God (Ps 6:5; 88:3-12; Isa 38:18).

2. *Hadēs,* the Gr. word which corresponds most closely to *sheol,* and the name of the Gr. god of the underworld. Christ taught that the realm of departed human spirits is divided into two parts: the one described as Abraham's bosom to distinguish it from the other which is called Hades and is the place of the wicked dead (Lk 16:23). The KJV translates the word as "hell" in each of the ten instances of its use (Mt 11:23; 16:18; Lk 10:15; 16:23; Acts 2:27, 31; Rev 1:18; 6:8; 20:13, 14), but the RSV and NASB use the word "Hades." It seems clear that in some instances the translation "hell" in the sense of the place of punishment is satisfactory.

In Acts 2:27, 31, however, Hades is the translation of Sheol in Ps 16:10 and refers simply to the grave or death. In the passages in Revelation Hades seems to be personified as a synonym of Death in its power over men, probably following the metaphor of Mt 16:18. The consensus of textual critics is that *hadēs* did not appear originally in I Cor 15:55.

3. *Gehenna,* the Grecized form of Heb. *gēʾ hinnōm,* the valley of Hinnom. A ravine on the S side of Jerusalem where rites of the heathen god Moloch were celebrated (I Kgs 11:7; II Chr 28:3; 33:6; Jer 7:32). Converted by Josiah into a place of abomination by the strewing of dead men's bones (II Kgs 23:13), it became the garbage and rubbish heap of Jerusalem, and as a place of continuous fires, a symbol of the place of lost spirits in torment. In every place the word is used it properly means hell (Mt 5:22, 29, 30; 10:28; 18:9; 23:15, 33; Mk 9:43, 45, 47; Lk 12:5; Jas 3:6).

4. *Tartaroō,* a Gr. verb which means "to send into Tartarus," found only in II Pet 2:4. The Greeks thought of Tartarus as a subterranean place lower than Hades where divine punishment was meted out; thus the term came to be so employed in Jewish apocalyptic literature.

Besides these four words, there are several synonyms for hell such as "unquenchable fire" (Mt 3:12); "the blackness of darkness" (Jude 13); "furnace of fire" (Mt 13:42, 50); "tormented with fire and brimstone" (Rev 14:10); "lake which burneth with fire and brimstone" (Rev 21:8); "where their worm dieth not" (Mk 9:48); the place "prepared for the devil and his angels" (Mt 25:41).

See Abyss; Dead, The; Eschatology; Eternal State and Death; Hades; Hinnom; Sheol.

R. A. K.

HELLENISTS. *See* Grecians.

HELMET. *See* Armor.

HELON (hē'lŏn). Father of Eliab, chief of the tribe of Zebulun, who was chosen to serve as an aide to Moses (Num 1:9; 2:7; 7:24, 29; 10:16).

HELP. As a verb this word means "to aid," "to assist," "to succor." Nine Heb. and six Gr. verbs are translated "help" in the KJV.

Besides its usual meaning of "assistance," a technical application is given the noun in two NT passages: (1) "Helps," Gr. plural of *boētheia,* "measures" (RSV), or a method of securing a leaking vessel by means of undergirding with chains, cables, or ropes (Acts 27:17). (2) "Helps," Gr. plural of *antilēmpsis,* "helpful deeds," one of the specific ministries in the church (I Cor 12:28), probably referring to the ministrations of the deacons, and used in the sense of "helpers" (RSV).

HELP MEET, HELPMATE. In Gen 2:18,20 the expression for the spouse for Adam consists of two Heb. words, *ʿēzor kᵉnegdô,* translated in KJV as "an help meet for him," in RSV as "a helper fit for him," and in JerusB as "a helpmate." The first word is the usual noun for "help" *(q.v.)*. The second term means "*according to what is in front of . . .* a help *corresponding to* him, i.e., equal and adequate to himself" (BDB, p. 617). Thus the idea in "meet" is "similarity as well as supplementation" (Gerhard von Rad, *Genesis,* p. 80), the sexual, social, and intellectual counterpart of Adam to complete his being. "She was to be one who could share man's responsibilities, respond to his nature with understanding and love, and wholeheartedly cooperate with him in working out the plan of God" (WBC, p. 5).

HELVE. The wooden handle of an ax. The word is found only in Deut 19:5 ("handle" in RSV).

HEM OF A GARMENT. To remind the Israelities of their obligations to God, the law directed (Num 15:37 ff.; Deut 22:12) them to attach, with blue (i.e., blue-purple or violet) thread, tassels (KJV "hem") of twisted threads to the corners of their outer garments. Pharisees ostentatiously made theirs very large (Mt 23:5). Certain sick persons exercised their faith in reaching out from the crowds to Jesus for help. When they touched even the mere hem or fringe of His garment, they were healed (Mt 9:20–21; 14:36).

HEMAM (hē'măm). Son of Lotan, a descendant of Seir and a member of a group known as Horites (Gen 36:22). In I Chr 1:39 he is called Homam *(q.v.)*. He is also called Heman in the LXX in both passages, and this spelling is used in Gen 36:22 in the RSV.

HEMAN (hē'mȧn)

1. RSV for Hemam (Gen 36:22), a Horite. *See* Hemam.

2. A wise man, one of the sons of Mahol (I Kgs 4:31), i.e., members of the orchestral guild or cantors (Jerusalem Bible). In I Chr 2:6 he is listed as a son of Zerah of the family of Judah. A superscription attributes Ps 88 to him.

3. One of the temple musicians in the reign of David. He was a Kohathite, son of Joel and a descendant of Samuel the prophet (I Chr 6:33; 15:17, 19; 16:41–42). He is called the seer of David (I Chr 25:5). The children of Heman also participated in the temple music services (I Chr 25:1–8; also II Chr 5:12; 29:14; 35:15). Perhaps "children" means the choir members under his direction.

HEMATH (hē'măth). A variant spelling in KJV of Hamath (*q.v.;* I Chr 13:5; Amos 6:14) and Hammath (*q.v.;* I Chr 2:55).

HEMDAN (hĕm'dăn). Son of Dishon (Gen 36:26). In the parallel genealogy of Chronicles (I Chr 1:41) he is called Amram (KJV) or Hamran (RSV) apparently because of a scribal error.

HEMLOCK. *See* Plants.

HEN. *See* Animals: Fowl, Domestic, III.14.

HENA (hĕn'ȧ). A city conquered by Assyria, its exact location unknown. Since the name means "low" and the city is mentioned with two other cities on the Orontes River, Hamath and Arpad, Hena probably was in the same general area (II Kgs 18:34; 19:13; Isa 37:13).

HENADAD (hĕn'ȧ-dăd). The head of a family of Levites in the post-Exilic community of Jerusalem (Ezr 3:9; Neh 3:18, 24; 10:9).

HENNA. *See* Plants.

HENOCH. *See* Hanoch; Enoch.

HEPATOSCOPY (hĕp'ȧ-tŏs'cō-py). From the genitive *hēpatos* of Gr. *hēpar,* "liver," and *skopeō,* "to look at." This was divination based on the examination of the liver of a slain animal. It was a widespread custom among the Babylonians, Greeks, and Romans by which pagan priests ascertained guidance and prognostication. The liver *(q.v.)* was considered by some to be the seat of life; by others, as an organ which reflected the universe and its history. The prognostication was probably based upon the healthiness of the liver as indicated by its depth and uniformity of color, or its unhealthiness as revealed by lack of color and by spots, together with the element of chance in choice of a particular animal for sacrifice.

Hepatoscopy is mentioned in Ezk 21:21 as having been practiced by the king of Babylon, but was never used by the Israelites except when they degenerated to paganism. Numerous clay models of animal livers, usually bearing cuneiform inscriptions to teach temple diviners this art, have been found in Babylonia and a few at Hazor and Megiddo in Late Bronze Age Canaanite levels.

See Divination; Magic.

R. A. K.

HEPHER (hē'fẽr), **HEPHERITES** (hē'fĕ-rīts)

1. The son of Gilead and father of Zelophehad of the tribe of Manasseh. His descendants are called Hepherites. Although Zelophehad had only daughters, the inheritance was continued through them as through sons, thus keeping the family alive in Israel (Num 26:32; 27:1; Josh 17:2–3).

2. A man of the tribe of Judah and a son of Ashur by his wife Naarah (I Chr 4:6).

3. The Mecherathite, one of David's mighty men (I Chr 11:36). He may be the same as Eliphelet the Maacathite who appears in the parallel list (II Sam 23:34).

4. A city in the plain of Sharon NW of Jerusalem. The king of Hepher was conquered by Joshua and the city was used by Solomon as a store city (Josh 12:17; I Kgs 4:10). It may be Tell Ibshar near the coast S of Caesarea.

HEPHZIBAH (hĕf′zĭ-bȧ)

1. Wife of King Hezekiah of Judah, mother of Manasseh (II Kgs 21:1).

2. Along with the three other feminine names having descriptive meanings in Isa 62:4 (see RSV marg.)–Azubah ("forsaken"), Shemamah ("desolate"), and Beulah ("married")–Hephzibah (KJV) is given symbolically to restored Jerusalem when God will delight in His city. Following LXX, RSV and NASB here translate the term "my delight is in her."

HERALD. One who announces or proclaims a message. The word is found only once in the KJV, referring to the one who announced the king's proclamation (Dan 3:4). The RSV uses the term three times in addition to Dan 3:4. In Isa 40:9 the term is used of Zion-Jerusalem as the "herald of good tidings," while Isa 41:27 mentions a prophet sent from God as the "herald of good tidings." In II Pet 2:5 Noah is called a "herald of righteousness." *See* Ambassador; Evangelist; Messenger; Preacher.

HERB; HERBS, BITTER. *See* Plants.

HERD. Before Joshua's time, Israel was a seminomadic people. Job, a seminomadic chieftain near the Transjordanian trade routes, owned sheep, camels, oxen, and asses (Job 1:3). Even for some time after the conquest of Canaan Israel continued to be largely a pastoral and agricultural people. Usually the herd consisted of larger animals–oxen, cattle, and asses–as contrasted with the flocks of sheep, goats, etc., as demonstrated: "Jacob divided . . . the flocks (*ṣō'n*), and herds (*bāqār*), and the camels (*gĕmallîm*). into two bands" (Gen 32:7). The word *'ēder* is translated "herd" in Prov 27:23; Joel 1:18. The cognate *miqneh* is translated "herd" in Gen 47:18, "flock" in Num 32:26, and "cattle" in a large number of places. The term "herd" also translates the Gr. *agelē*, used in connection with the drove of swine that charged down the cliff to their destruction near Gadara (Mt 8:30–32). *See* Animals: Cattle, I.6; Sheep, I.15.

A herd of sheep along the Jabbok River. HFV

HERDMAN. *See* Occupations: Herdman.

HERES (hĭr′ĭz).

1. Mount Heres was a mountain from which the tribe of Dan could not expel the Amorites (Jud 1:35). It was probably on the boundary between Judah and Dan.

2. In Jud 8:13 the RSV mentions Gideon's return from battle "by the ascent of Heres," but the KJV renders the passage as "before the sun was up." It is a mountain pass going up from the Jordan or from the Jabbok River.

HERESH (hĕr′ĕsh). A Levite mentioned among those returning from Exile (I Chr 9:15).

HERESY

1. This term originally meant choice. It is used in this sense only in the LXX.

2. A chosen way of thinking or course of action; hence, an opinion or view held by an individual (I Cor 11:19), or by a party, such as the Pharisees (Acts 15:5; 26:5), the Sadducees (Acts 5:17), or the Christians (Acts 24:5, 14; 28:22).

3. A dissension arising within the church because of a divergent view (I Cor 11:19; Gal 5:20).

4. A doctrinal departure from biblically revealed truth, or an erroneous view (Tit 3:10; II Pet 2:1). Paul says that heresies, in the sense of differing opinions, must needs arise as a necessary step in the development of true doctrine (I Cor 11:19). The great struggles which led to the councils of Nicea and Chalcedon illustrate this well.

The early church fought against certain dangerous doctrinal heresies and rejected those who taught them (cf. Tit 3:10).

The Judaizers. Paul wrote the books of Romans and Galatians to refute those who insisted Christianity must make a synthesis between the legalistic keeping of the law and faith in Christ. He urges the Galatians to stand fast in the liberty wherewith Christ has made them free, for "Christ is become of no effect unto you, whosoever of you are justified by the law; ye are fallen from grace" (Gal 5:4). Physical circumcision has been done away with by spiritual circumcision in Christ (Col 2:11; Phil 3:2–3).

The Gnostics. The books of Colossians and

Mount Hermon. ORINST

I John were written to refute their errors. They taught that Christ was a pantheistic emanation, lower than God, who only seemed to appear in the flesh. John asserts that he preaches a Christ whom he has seen, heard, and touched, and demands that the Christian test orthodoxy on the basis of a confession that Christ became incarnate in human flesh (I Jn 4:2–3). *See* Gnosticism.

The Syncretists. These attempted to make a synthesis between revelation and philosophy. Philo, prior to the time of Christ, tried to combine the Jewish religion with the Stoic concept of a Logos fashioned after Plato's "idea of ideas." Examples of later similar syncretistic endeavors are the union of neoplatonism and Christianity in the medieval church, the influences of which still appear in Roman Catholic views of evil; Hegelianism and Christianity in 19th cen. German liberalism; and Kierkegaardian existentialism and Christianity as seen wedded in modern neoorthodoxy.

R. A. K.

HERETIC. *See* Heresy.

HERITAGE. *See* Inheritance.

HERMAS (hûr'mȧs). A Christian at Rome greeted by Paul (Rom 16:14).

HERMES (hûr'mēz)

1. A Christian at Rome greeted by Paul (Rom 16:14). He is not to be confused with Hermas.

2. The Gr. god of eloquence who was the spokesman for the gods. At Lystra, Barnabas was called Zeus and Paul was called Hermes. The KJV translates the name as Mercurius, but the RSV retains Hermes (Acts 14:12). *See* Gods, False.

HERMOGENES (hĕr-mŏj'ŏ-nēz). One of the "all who are in Asia" who turned away from Paul in his troubles (II Tim 1:15). By being named, it appears that he was one of the leaders.

HERMON (hûr'mŏn). The name means "sacred mountain" or "consecrated place" (from *ḥā-ram,* in the *hiph'il,* "to devote," "consecrate"), and probably derived its name from the Baal sanctuaries located there from ancient times, prior to the Exodus (Josh 11:17). It has been called Shenir or Senir by the Amorites, Sirion by the Sidonians (Deut 3:9), Sion (Deut 4:48) and Jebel esh-Sheik by the Arabs.

Hermon formed the northern boundary of the country which Israel took from the Amorites (Deut 3:8) and is the southern terminus of the Anti-Lebanon range. The ridge of Hermon is about 20 miles long, having three peaks that cause it to be referred to on occasion as "the Hermonites" (Ps 42:6, KJV) or "the Hermons" (ASV). Two of these peaks are more than 9,000 feet above sea level, being by far the highest peaks in or near Palestine, and are covered with snow the year around. The melting snows of Hermon constitute the principal source of the Jordan River. The highest peak of Hermon is situated about 30 miles to the SW of Damascus and 40 miles to the NE of the Sea of Galilee.

Many have believed Hermon to be the site of the transfiguration of Jesus (Mt 17:1–9; Mk 9:2, 9; Lk 9:28). About a week before the transfiguration He was in the region of Caesarea Philippi just to the S of Hermon, and it has been held more likely that He went N to the slopes of Hermon rather than SW to Mount Tabor, the traditional site.

H. L. D.

HEROD (hĕr'ŏd)

Herod the Great

The most famous of those who bore the name Herod in biblical times was Herod the Great, the progenitor of a large clan. Although his name occurs in the sacred text only in connection with the historical setting for the birth of John the Baptist (Lk 1:5) and in the account of the coming of the wise men (Mt 2), his influence on Palestine during a long reign as king of Judea was so considerable that a knowledge of his career is essential for a true understanding of NT times. The fact that Josephus devotes so much space to Herod in his *Jewish Antiquities* and in *The Jewish Wars* is proof enough of the importance this historian attached to him.

Family background. Herod was an Idumean. The country of Idumea in the S of Palestine (the Negeb) became occupied by Edomites when their former territory around Petra was taken over by the Arabs or Nabataeans. They in turn were conquered by the Hasmonean rulers of the Jews and compelled to accept Judaism, including circumcision. Herod's father, Antipater, who seems to have been the head of this nation, though his official position is not delineated by Josephus, married an Arab woman. Five children were born of this union, Herod alone bearing a Gr. name. His birth can be put at 73 B.C. or thereabouts.

Before long Antipater, a man of wealth and ambition, became involved in Jewish political affairs. At this time two brothers of the royal line, Aristobulus and Hyrcanus, were struggling for power, with the former having gained the mastery. Antipater intervened to champion the cause of Hyrcanus. It was left to the Romans, however, to settle the dispute and bring to an end the period of Jewish independence.

When Pompey arrived, Herod was about ten years old. As a lad, he gained a lively impression of the Roman military might and also witnessed the sagacity of his father Antipater as he threw his support behind the Roman regime,

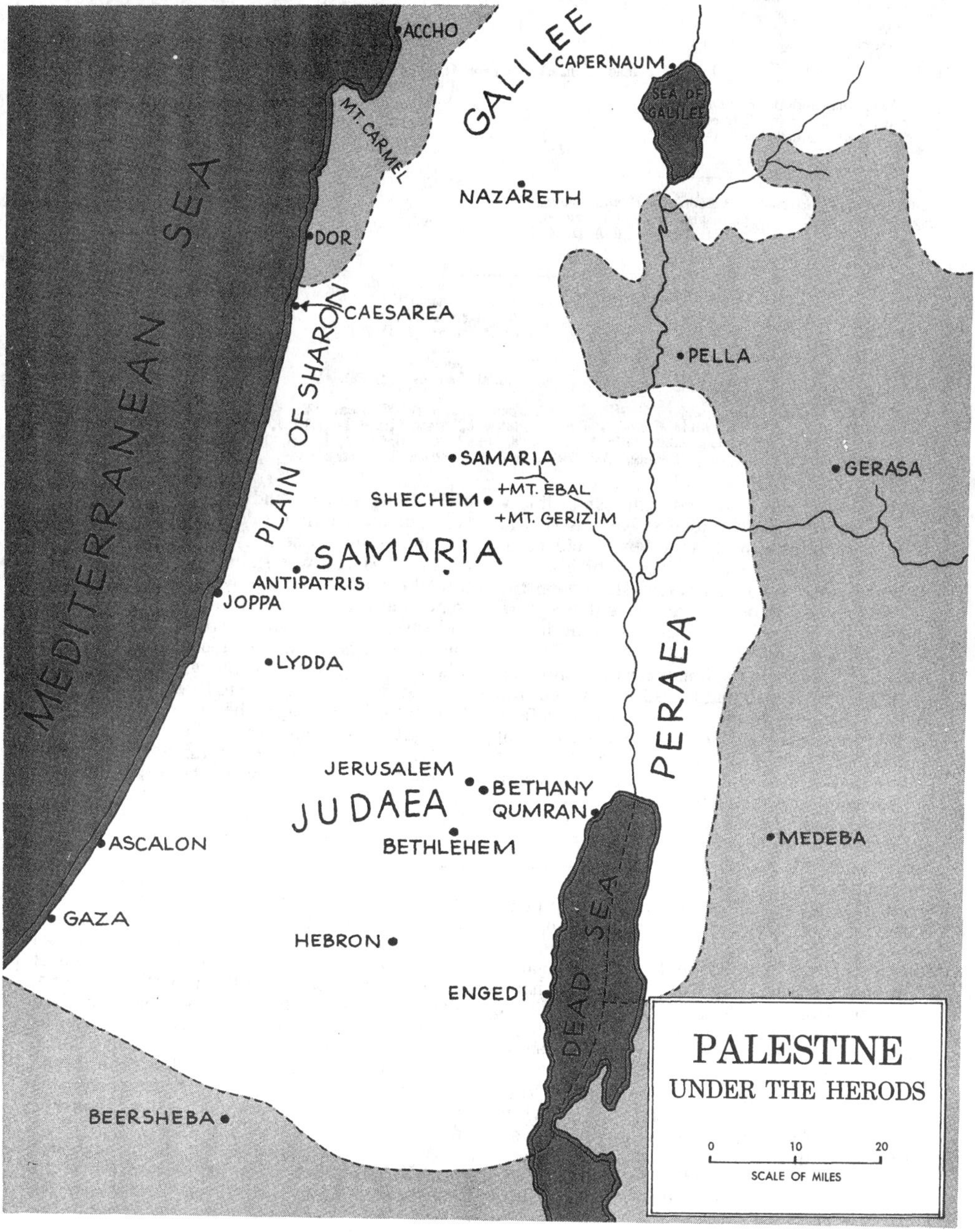

TABLE OF THE HERODIAN FAMILY

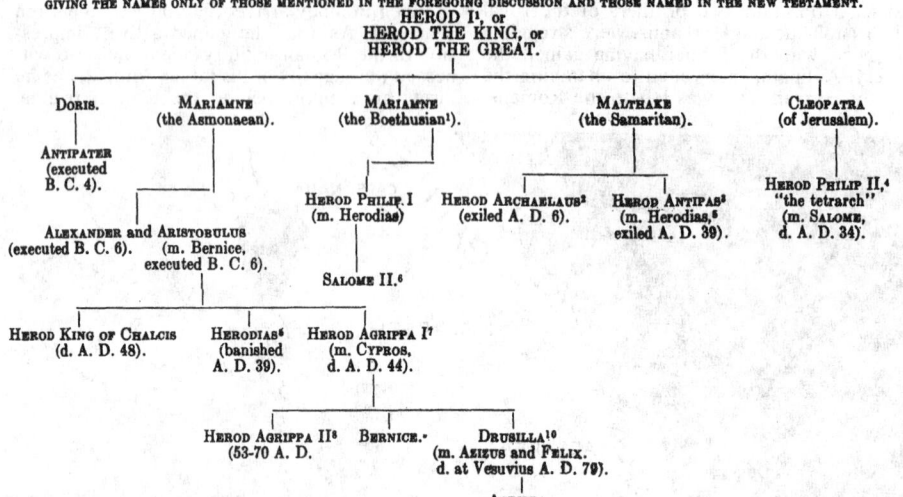

GIVING THE NAMES ONLY OF THOSE MENTIONED IN THE FOREGOING DISCUSSION AND THOSE NAMED IN THE NEW TESTAMENT.

HEROD I[1], or HEROD THE KING, or HEROD THE GREAT.

- **Doris.**
  - **Antipater** (executed B. C. 4).
- **Mariamne** (the Asmonaean).
  - **Alexander** (executed B. C. 6). and **Aristobulus** (m. Bernice, executed B. C. 6).
    - **Herod King of Chalcis** (d. A. D. 48).
    - **Herodias[5]** (banished A. D. 39).
    - **Herod Agrippa I[7]** (m. Cypros, d. A. D. 44).
      - **Herod Agrippa II[8]** (53-70 A. D.
      - **Bernice.[9]**
      - **Drusilla[10]** (m. Azizus and Felix. d. at Vesuvius A. D. 79).
        - **Agrippa** (d. at Vesuvius A. D, 79).
- **Mariamne** (the Boethusian[1]).
  - **Herod Philip I** (m. Herodias)
    - **Salome II.[6]**
- **Malthake** (the Samaritan).
  - **Herod Archaelaus[2]** (exiled A. D. 6).
  - **Herod Antipas[3]** (m. Herodias,[5] exiled A. D. 39).
- **Cleopatra** (of Jerusalem).
  - **Herod Philip II,[4]** "the tetrarch" (m. Salome, d. A. D. 34).

[1]"Herod the King," Matt. 2; Luke 1:5. [2]Herod "Archaelaus," Luke 19:12-27; Matt. 2:22. [3]"Herod" Antipas "the tetrarch," Matt. 14:1; Luke 3:1, 19; Mark 6:14. [4]Herod "Philip" "the tetrarch," Matt. 14:1, 6; Luke 3:1, 19; 9:7; Mark 6:34. [5]"Herodias," Matt. 14:3, 6; Mark 6:17. [6]Salome, Matt. 14:6; Mark 6:22, 28; Luke 3:19. [7]"Herod" Agrippa [I] "the king," Acts 12:1, 2. [8]Herod "Agrippa" II, Acts 25:13-27; 26. [9]"Bernice," Acts 25:13, 23; 26:30. [10]"Drusilla," Acts 24:24.

and as a result was rewarded with responsibility and influence in Judean affairs. Antipater, who liked to think of himself as a Jew, could point with pride to the generous favors which a later Roman leader, Julius Caesar, bestowed on the Jewish people, since in large part these were due to the help which he gave Caesar in his Egyptian campaign.

Though Hyrcanus continued as the nominal head of the Jewish nation and occupied the office of high priest, the active control of affairs passed to Antipater, who now held the rank of procurator. It was to the great advantage of Rome to have a man like Antipater at the helm, for he knew the Jews far better than the Romans did, and he could be counted on to remain loyal to his overlords. This became the keynote of Herod's own policy in later years. However, no matter how capable and how much interested in the welfare of the Jews an Indumean might be, he could never compete in the affections of the people with one of their own number, and it was bound to be held against him that he was in the service of the hated conqueror from the W (Pompey had besieged Jerusalem, killing thousands of its inhabitants, and had even dared to enter the holy of holies of the temple).

Herod as a young man. At the age of 26 he was appointed by his father as governor or magistrate of Galilee (47 B.C.), and quickly asserted himself by ferreting out nests of brigands and putting them to death. The local people were grateful, but others in the nation, resentful of Herod's success and popularity, persuaded Hyrcanus to call him to account for the taking of human life contrary to Jewish law. Accordingly Herod was summoned to appear before the Sanhedrin. But when this tall, handsome youth of athletic bearing, ornately clad and surrounded by an escort, appeared before this judicial body, its members were afraid to take action against him, though a majority favored it. Never being one to forget an indignity, Herod got his revenge when he came to power as king by taking the lives of these opponents.

Roman affairs were anything but tranquil during these closing days of the Republic. Caesar, Pompey, and Crassus had formed the first triumvirate in 60 B.C., but Crassus lost his life on the eastern frontier and the other two had a falling out. We have seen how the Jews profited from Caesar's dictatorship. After the assassination of Caesar, a second triumvirate was created by Mark Antony, Octavian (Caesar's nephew), and Lepidus. The first objective was to punish Brutus and Cassius for the murder of Caesar. Herod had loyalties in both directions, since Cassius was his friend and had promised him the kingship of Judea, whereas Antony was an even closer friend, if anything, so Herod could hardly expect less from him if he should emerge victorious. Antipater had been put to death by treachery, so Herod was next in line for promotion.

As long as a prince of the Hasmonean line was available, the spirit of revolution among the Jews could easily be stirred. One such remained, Antigonus the son of Aristobulus. Herod reasoned that if he could somehow overcome the disadvantage of alien blood by marriage with the royal line of the Jews, he might be more acceptable to the Jewish nation. With this in mind he became engaged to Mariamne, a Hasmonean princess, even though he was already married.

About this time Octavian and Antony emerged triumphant in their struggle, which brought Antony to the areas of Syria and Palestine to oversee matters there. Hyrcanus remained in his position as ethnarch (ruler of the nation) and high priest, but Herod and his brother Phasael were appointed tetrarchs and actually controlled the country, being responsible to the Roman authorities.

But Antigonus was active in fomenting rebellion. With Antony a victim of the charms of Cleopatra of Egypt, Herod soon found himself in a precarious position, especially when Antigonus gained the help of the warlike Parthians, who penetrated all the way to Jerusalem. Phasael and Hyrcanus allowed themselves to fall into a trap and were imprisoned. Shortly thereafter Phasael took his own life. Herod resorted to flight, placing his family and some others in the fortress of Masada just W of the Dead Sea, and making his way painfully to Rome in the hope of getting help there. In this hope he was not disappointed. Antony named him king of the Jews. Octavian was favorable also, and introduced this pro-Roman to the senate as one who could well lead their cause against Antigonus and their inveterate enemies, the Parthians. Without a dissenting voice, the senate proclaimed Herod king of Judea (40 B.C.).

Herod as king. At this point Herod was in the position of the man of whom Jesus spoke in the parable, "A nobleman went into a far country to receive kingly power and then return" (Lk 19:12, RSV), although the parable fits Archelaus even better than Herod. He had the title but not the kingdom. Landing at Ptolemais Herod gathered forces, rescued his family at Masada, and began the arduous task of subjugating the country. Galilee had a tendency to defect as soon as his back was turned, and the Roman generals who had been ordered to assist him were bribed into virtual inactivity by Antigonus. But finally he was able to get Roman aid in the form of two legions sent by Antony under the command of Sossius. Antigonus was shut up in Jerusalem. Feeling that the capture of the city was now a matter of course, Herod took time out to marry Mariamne at Samaria. After a siege of five months Jerusalem fell and Antigonus was slain. With him died the hopes of the Jewish nationalists for independence.

Herod's problems were not all solved by this victory. A new threat arose from the ambitions of Cleopatra, the ruler of Egypt. Antony, who had taken Asia as his sphere of influence, had fallen victim, like Caesar before him, to her beauty and blandishments. The wily queen in-

Statuary niches in facade of Herod's palace at New Testament Jericho. HFV

duced Antony to grant her several of Herod's cities and to insist that Herod undertake a war against the Arabs, hoping thereby to weaken both parties that she might the more readily gobble up their territories. After one serious reverse, Herod emerged from this conflict victorious.

Cleopatra's real objective was to erect a sovereign state in the Levant in opposition to the power of Rome in the W. When it became apparent that Antony had thrown in his lot with her, open war with Rome was inevitable. Herod, as the friend of Antony, was desirous of aiding him, and would have gone to battle at his side, but Cleopatra, ever jealous of Herod, would not permit it. In the sea battle at Actium (31 B.C.) Octavian was successful. Antony's army, stationed in Greece, was obliged to capitulate. Cleopatra sailed for Egypt, Antony accompanying her. Both eventually took their own lives.

Herod's loyalty to Antony now placed him in a precarious position with the conqueror. But instead of begging for mercy, he put on a bold front and openly admitted his friendship for Antony, giving the impression that he could be just as loyal and useful to Octavian as he had been to Antony. The tactics were effective. Octavian not only forgave him, but restored the cities Cleopatra had managed to detach from his realm, and eventually increased his territories by the addition of several areas to the E and NE of the Sea of Galilee.

Having cleared this hurdle, Herod seemed to be set for a long and prosperous reign, for the victory of Octavian (who became Augustus Caesar) made possible the *pax Romana.* The internal strife which had marred the latter days of the Republic was now at an end. But tragedy struck the household of the king of the Jews. His wife Mariamne became estranged from him due to the persistent nagging of her mother Alexandra. On top of this, Herod's sister Salome, bitterly jealous of the Hasmonean woman, sowed seeds of distrust in the mind of Herod concerning Mariamne's faithfulness. Although the charges were groundless, Herod

Temple to Augustus built by Herod at Caesarea.

came to believe them and finally had his wife put to death. Afterward he regretted his act and became ill with grief. His physicians thought he would die. Though time and diversionary activity brought healing, he was never the same thereafter, for the sunny side of his nature was gone. He was now a morose and suspicious man, more than ever an easy mark for the shafts of intrigue directed toward him by the women of his household in later days.

Herod found some relief for his spirit by plunging into a vast program of public works which would memorialize his energy and the magnificence of his regime. Foremost among these was the Jewish temple, which he rebuilt and enlarged, employing a thousand priests trained as masons, besides thousands of other workers. Begun in 20 B.C., it was still not wholly completed in the days of Christ. At the NW corner stood the castle of Antonia, named in honor of his old friend Antony. Herod's own palace was laid out on spacious lines and lavishly adorned. Its two wings were named in honor of Augustus Caesar and his minister Agrippa. Samaria was built up into a prominent city and fortress and was given the name Sebaste, the Gr. equivalent of Augustus. At Strato's Tower, on the Mediterranean Sea, the king put in a breakwater and thus provided a port, something the Palestinian coastline had lacked. Renamed as Caesarea, this city included in its construction a large amphitheater where games were held periodically. Some miles to the S Herod established the town of Antipatris in honor of his father, which served as a station on the route up to Jerusalem (Acts 23:31). Far to the N he erected a temple to Rome and the emperor at Paneion, the Caesarea Philippi of the Gospels. As a precaution against uprisings, at several points he built fortresses, one of which, near Jericho, he named Cypros after his mother.

By his munificence the king of the Jews reared temples in communities beyond the border of his realm, for despite the piety which he assumed toward the God of the Hebrews, he was a pagan at heart. To square himself with the Jews he asserted that as a king in the service of Rome he must fall in line with their practices. He also subsidized the Olympian games, which had fallen on evil days and needed help.

His liberality to foreign communities, which included Athens and Sparta, was partly to show his devotion to Hellenic culture and thus receive a measure of gratitude seldom extended to him by his own subjects, and partly to assist the Jews in the Dispersion. Pagan cities were less reluctant to permit the Jews in their midst to send sums of money for the temple in Jerusalem when they were recipients of donations from the king of the Jews.

Herod ruled his subjects with an iron hand. Josephus relates that on occasion he would dress as a private citizen and mingle with the crowds to learn what was being said of him. Any conspiracy was met with speedy retribution. On the other hand, in a year of dearth and threatened famine, the king at great sacrifice to himself brought in grain from Egypt and saved the lives of many of his people. Josephus summarizes the two aspects of his rule by saying, "He kept his subjects submissive in two ways, namely, by fear, since he was inexorable in punishment, and by showing himself greathearted in his care of them when a crisis arose."

The outward glory of Herod's reign was offset by the domestic troubles which continued to plague him. Salome, after having disposed of Mariamne, now schemed against her two sons Aristobulus and Alexander, claiming to Herod that they were plotting against him. To offset their supposed influence, the king brought Antipater, his son by his first wife Doris, into a position of favor and prominence. Malignity thickened on both sides. Herod accused the two sons of Mariamne in the presence of Augustus. Reconciliation was only temporary. Ultimately the two young men were executed. Popular resentment at Herod's treatment of his sons made his life miserable and his position less secure than formerly.

During the final decade of his life Herod became increasingly irritable and correspondingly difficult to deal with. Augustus grew cool toward him, which hurt him in many quarters. Despite all his efforts, he continued unable to gain the support of the Pharisees. Most of all, his domestic situation worsened appreciably. Herod had a total of ten wives. Salome, his sister, was an inveterate plotter who kept the pot boiling, all in Herod's interest, she thought. Antipater was busy at the same game, and in his own interest. Herod's brother Pheroras was involved, along with Antipater, in a plot to poison Herod. This plan of Antipater was foolish, since he was named in Herod's will as his successor, and was simply impatient that the old king lingered so long. One of Herod's last acts was to order the execution of Antipater and to alter his will in favor of another son, Archelaus.

Herod's massacre of the infants of Bethlehem (Mt 2:16) near the end of his reign is

HEROD

strictly in keeping with two evident facts, his bloodthirstiness, which is attested by countless episodes, and his fear of possible aspirants for his throne. His mental and physical condition in these closing days of his life made a virtual madman out of him. Proof of this is forthcoming from another act of the aging king, now nearing 70. Summoning the leading men of the nation, the elders of the various communities, to meet him at Jericho, he then had them shut up in the hippodrome, giving orders to kill them when he himself passed away, that there might be general lamentation when he died. This vicious decree of a bitter and disappointed man fortunately was not carried out.

A Roman procurator attached to Syria, Sabinus by name, went up to Jerusalem and tried to get control of Herod's records and properties, bent on personal gain. He succeeded in inflaming the populace, which was augmented by crowds attending the Feast of Pentecost. The troops of Sabinus, finding themselves in grave danger, set fire to the porticoes of the temple upon which many Jews had taken up positions for combat. Varus, the governor of Syria, answering Sabinus' call for aid, marched into Judea and found the area in dire disorder. After quelling the uprisings and crucifying 2,000 Jews, he departed, leaving behind further grievance against Rome.

Augustus had a difficult decision to make. In addition to the pleas of the claimants, he had to consider the request made by 50 men who had come from Judea, backed by 8,000 more in Rome itself, that Herodian rule be abandoned and that direct Roman rule be substituted for it. Doubtless he wished to honor Herod's desires, but felt that Archelaus was young and lacking in leadership ability. To make him king would only promote dissatisfaction and friction with the other brothers. The verdict was finally given that Archelaus should have Judea, Samaria, and Idumea, with the title of ethnarch, and might have the title king in due time if he merited it. Antipas was given Galilee and Perea. A third brother, Philip, who had followed the other two to Rome, was given Batanea, Trachonitis, Auranitis, and some additional territory.

Archelaus had the richest area, with an annual tribute equal to twice the combined revenues of the domains of his two brothers. But he proved unequal to his assignment and made some costly mistakes. For one thing, in defiance of Jewish law, he married Glaphyra, who had been the wife of his half-brother Alexander and had borne him several children. This deeply offended the Jews. By A.D. 6 his subjects had had enough, charging him with cruelty and tyranny before Caesar. Since the Samaritans joined the Jews in this, the likelihood is that the charges were well-founded. In anger Caesar sent him into exile in Gaul. Judea was placed under Roman rule, governed by a procurator, and this arrangement obtained thereafter except for a period of three years when Herod Agrippa I *(q.v.)* was made king of the Jews by a later emperor.

Herod Antipas

This man, who has been rated as the least attractive of the Herods, was the younger son of Herod the Great and Malthace. He is mentioned several times in the Gospels. The ministries of both John the Baptist and of Jesus occurred during his tenure of office as tetrarch of Galilee and Perea (Lk 3:1).

Originally Antipas made Sepphoris, between Nazareth and Cana, his capital, but later built for this purpose Tiberias on the Sea of Galilee,

Roman theater, Caesarea.
IIS

The pillared courtyard of Herod's palace at the Herodian, near Bethlehem HFV

naming it after the emperor Tiberius, who had succeeded Augustus.

On a visit to Rome Antipas became enamored of the wife of his half-brother Herod Philip, and before long married her (Mk 6:17). She insisted that he divorce the wife he had, the daughter of the king of Petra. When the wife learned of Antipas' intentions, she returned to her father's house. *See* Philip 2.

Not only were the Jews in general incensed by the conduct of Antipas, but John the Baptist, in particular, had the courage to charge him with sin. John could have stayed in the territory of Judea and Samaria and attacked Antipas at long range without fear of reprisal, but he dared to press his charges at close quarters, and for this was imprisoned (Mt 14; Mk 6).

Jesus was no more afraid of this Herod than was John, for when the tetrarch let it be known through Pharisaic channels that he was bent on killing Him, our Lord refused to be frightened off and went right on with His work. In calling Antipas a fox (Lk 13:31–32), Jesus was doubtless referring to the sly tactics of the ruler. After having dealt harshly with John the Baptist, he lacked the courage to deal thus with Jesus and hoped to frighten Him by threats.

Antipas was not on good terms with Pilate. Among other things Pilate had killed some of his subjects when they were bent on sacrificing at the temple (Lk 13:1). But the condescension of Pilate in sending Jesus to him as an interlude in the trial pleased him so much that his quarrel with Pilate was mended (Lk 23:12).

Now deaf to the voice of conscience, this ruler was soon to begin paying for his crimes. His troops met resounding defeat at the hand of the Arabs, and his subjects were quick to attribute this to divine retribution for his marital irregularities and his murder of John. Finally, prodded by his wife Herodias to seek from the emperor the title of king, which had lately been bestowed on Agrippa to the N and E of him, Antipas requested this boon of Caligula, the new emperor, only to be rebuffed and be banished to Gaul, where he ended his days.

Herod Philip

Not to be confused with the Herod Philip whose wife was taken by Antipas, this Herod remained a bachelor through most of his life. His domain, whose territories have already been noted, is partially indicated in Lk 3:1. Little is known of his reign beyond its generally satisfactory character. By moving among the people and providing justice on their behalf, he gained their admiration. Late in life he took as his wife Salome, the daughter of Herodias who danced before Antipas and his court. One of the memorials of his reign is Caesarea Philippi, built and named in honor of Caesar, with which his own name is coupled. *See* Philip 1.

Death was induced by a disease which may well have been cancer of the bowels. His funeral was a state occasion of great magnificence, the casket being carried to the fortress of Herodium for burial. From his large fortune he had arranged for a generous gift to the emperor and another to his wife, with lesser amounts going to his own relatives.

Estimate of Herod. On the whole this ruler must be credited with the achievement of an outwardly prosperous and relatively peaceful reign. As an administrator he possessed insight and initiative and seldom made a mistake in judgment. He sought to maintain the rights of non-Jews throughout his realm, and also to improve the condition of his Jewish subjects.

In personal character he is a fascinating subject for psychological study. He could be generous to a fault and also savagely cruel. He could be calm in a crisis and yet go to pieces when moods of depression or anger swept over him.

Of formal education he had little, but was humble enough to learn at the feet of his court teacher and diplomat, Nicolaus of Damascus, who had a great admiration for Herod and served him well on several occasions.

Herod's story bears testimony to his capacity for friendship. Some of the ablest and finest people of his time were in his circle, and his loyalty to them is one of his best traits.

But his sensuality and his secularism were his undoing. From the former he reaped the nemesis of jealousies, animosities, and killings that haunted his declining days. From the latter came his failure to understand the deeper significance of the religious faith to which he nominally subscribed.

Josephus in one place calls him "the Great," but only, it seems, in a relative sense, as superior in ability and achievement to others of his house who ruled after him.

Herod Archelaus

This son of Herod the Great and Malthace, a Samaritan, is mentioned only once in the biblical text, and that in connection with his accession to the rule over Judea following the death of his father (Mt 2:22). He was named for the king of Cappadocia, to whose daughter Herod and Mariamne's son Alexander had been married.

Herod made four wills altogether, and in the last one, executed shortly before his death, appointed Archelaus, then in his late teens, as his successor. When the will was read to the troops and townspeople of Jericho, the place of Herod's death, they acclaimed Archelaus king, although they were reminded that the will had to be ratified by Caesar before it could become effective. Actually the terms of the will did not award Herod's whole kingdom to Archelaus, but only Judea and Samaria. Galilee and Perea were awarded to Antipas, the full brother of Archelaus, and the rest of the kingdom, involving territories N and E of the Sea of Galilee, was to go to Philip their half-brother.

After seven days of mourning for his father, Archelaus spread a feast for his subjects in Jerusalem, then had a golden throne set on a platform, from which he received the plaudits of his subjects and addressed them graciously, promising to be kinder to them than his father had been. Sensing that the king was young and impressionable, the people began to press him for favors, including the diminution of taxes and the removal of some men honored by Herod, especially the high priest. The people turned to mourning for those lives which had been taken by Herod when they cut down a golden eagle he had set up in the temple area. Messengers sent by Archelaus were unable to disperse them, the crowds having been augmented by Passover pilgrims from far and near. To forestall any outbreak, the young king sent troops to deal with the situation. Infuriated, the crowd attacked the soldiers. More troops were called out, including the cavalry. Some 3,000 people were killed before the melee ended.

Shortly thereafter, Archelaus departed for Rome to secure the approval of Augustus concerning the arrangements made by Herod. His brother Antipas likewise made the trip to dispute the will on the ground that the previous will, made when Herod was of sound mind, gave him the succession. Caesar deferred making a decision, and in the meantime things were happening in Judea which were destined to influence the final verdict.

Herod Agrippa I

Grandson of Herod the Great and son of Aristobulus, this ruler was named in honor of Agrippa, the able minister of Augustus. His early years were spent in Rome, where he had connections with the royal family. Ambition for political power was checked by lack of appointment and frustrated by financial embarrassment. After occupying minor posts in the E for a time, he returned to Rome, where he cultivated the friendship of Gaius (Caligula). An unguarded remark to his friend to the effect that he hoped Gaius would soon be emperor was reported to Tiberius, who clapped him into prison.

After the death of Tiberius and the accession of Gaius, Agrippa was given the tetrarchy of Philip, who died in A.D. 34, and was allowed to bear the title of king. When Antipas was discredited, Agrippa took over his territory also. In the following year (A.D. 41) Gaius was murdered and was succeeded by Claudius. The new emperor, out of gratitude for help rendered by Agrippa, added Judea and Samaria to his friend's realm, so now he was king of the Jews as was Herod of old.

Posing as one ardently committed to the law and the customs, Agrippa won the favor of the Jews. He risked his position by urging Gaius to give up his plan to put a statue of himself in Jerusalem and claim divine honors. His persecution of the early church and his untimely death shortly thereafter in A.D. 44 in Caesarea are noted in Acts 12.

Herod Agrippa II

At his father's death this young man was too young, in the opinion of Claudius, to be entrusted with the kingship, so direct Roman rule was imposed once again on the Jews.

A few years later Herod succeeded to the throne of the kingdom of Chalcis in Lebanon which had formerly been ruled by a kinsman. About this time Claudius granted him the right of appointing the high priest and the supervision of the temple and its funds, so he became involved in Jewish affairs. His next move took him closer to the Holy Land, as he inherited much of the realm formerly ruled by Philip. Later, Nero added some territory around the Sea of Galilee and in southern Perea. Like his father, he was called king. It was in his presence that Paul made his defense (Acts 26).

As in the case of other Herods, he ingratiated himself with pagan Gr. cities and at the same time maintained the ordinances of Judaism. He is known to have championed the cause of the Alexandrian Jews who were suffering persecution in this period.

In particular he endeavored to stem the rising tide of nationalism among the Palestinian Jews and to dissuade them from acts of violence and insubordination against Rome, even when provoked by unworthy Roman officials. In this he was unsuccessful, and when war broke out, his troops fought with the Romans against the Jews. Josephus states that Agrippa sent him more than 60 letters with information about his part in the conflict, thus assisting Josephus in his account contained in *The Jewish Wars*. Little is known of Agrippa's later years, but he probably lived until the close of the century. With his death the dynasty of Herod came to an end.

Princesses of the House of Herod

Those whose names dot the sacred record are three in number—Herodias, Bernice, and Drusilla—and their reputation is not an enviable one.

Herodias had for her father Aristobulus, who was son of Herod the Great by Mariamne. Her mother was Bernice, the daughter of Herod's sister Salome. After being married to Herod Philip, Herodias left him to be the wife of Antipas. Her hatred of John the Baptist led to the death of the prophet (Mt 14:3-11) and the deterioration in the character of Antipas. *See* Herodias.

Bernice was daughter of Herod Agrippa I. Married first to a Jewish official of Alexandria named Marcus, and then to Herod of Chalcis, she went to live with her brother Herod Agrippa II. Ugly rumors became current of her incestuous relations with him. To allay these, she became married to a certain Polemo, king of Cilicia, but returned to her brother after a short time. In the disorders at Jerusalem which preceded the outbreak of the great war with Rome, she distinguished herself by appealing to Florus, at the risk of her own life, to call off his troops and restore peace to the holy city. In Luke's account of Paul's hearing before Agrippa (Acts 25-26), Bernice appears as accompanying her brother. *See* Bernice.

Drusilla, a full sister of Bernice and Agrippa II *(q.v.),* was slated to marry Epiphanes of Commagene, but the arrangement was called off when the prince refused to be circumcised. Azizus, king of Emesa, was willing to turn Jew to gain her hand, but the marriage did not last long because Felix, the notorious procurator who hoped to be bribed by Paul, induced her to leave her husband and marry him. Her presence with Felix is noted in Acts 24:24. *See* Drusilla.

Bibliography. Félix Marie Abel, *Histoire de la Palestine depuis la conquête d'Alexandre jusqu' à l'invasion arabe,* Paris: Gabalda, 1952, I, 287-503. F. F. Bruce, "Herod Antipas, Tetrarch of Galilee and Peraea," ALUOS, V (1963-65), 6-23. A. H. M. Jones, *The Herods of Judaea,* Oxford: Clarendon Press, 1938. Flavius Josephus, *Jewish Antiquities; The Jewish War.* Stewart Perowne, *The Life and Times of Herod the Great,* London: Hodder, 1956; *The Later Herods,* London: Hodder, 1958. E. Schürer, *A History of the Jewish People in the Time of Jesus Christ,* trans. by John Macpherson, 2nd and rev. ed., 5 vols., New York: Scribner's, 1891.

E. F. Har.

HERODIANS (hĕ-rō'dĭ-*ă*nz). The Herodians are mentioned in three passages in the Gospels, treating two incidents, the first in Galilee (Mk 3:6) and the second in Jerusalem (Mk 12:13; Mt 22:16), where they are associated with the Pharisees in their opposition to Jesus. Apart from one reference in Josephus (*Wars* i.16.6, *hoi Hērōdeio;* cf. *Ant.* xiv.15.10, "those of Herod's party"), they are not mentioned in any other ancient source, evidence that they were not a religious sect or an organized political party.

The word is of Latin formation (*Herodiani*), indicating adherents or partisans of Herod, and describes a common attitude of allegiance to Herod in a country where large numbers of people chafed under his rule. In Josephus the term clearly denotes those who were sympathizers and supporters of his cause. It is reasonable to understand the term in the Gospels in the same light. The narratives which mention the Herodians presuppose that they were influential men of standing who loyally supported Herod Antipas. From their question concerning the tribute money (Mt 22:17), it seems clear that they were also loyal to the Roman rule upon which the Herodian dynasty depended.

W. L. L.

HERODIAS (hĕ-rō'dĭ-*ă*s). Daughter of Aristobulus and Bernice. Married first to Herod Philip, a private citizen, who was the son of Herod the Great and Mariamne II (not to be confused with Philip the tetrarch of Iturea in Lk 3:1, who was the son of Herod the Great and Cleopatra of Jerusalem), she left him to marry his half-brother Herod Antipas. It was because of this marriage that John the Baptist reproved Herod Antipas and was put in prison (Mt 14:3; Mk 6:17; Lk 3:19 f.). John was finally beheaded at the request of Salome, Herodias' daughter (Mt 14:8; Mk 6:24) by her first husband.

See Herod.

HERODION (hĕ-rō'dĭ-*ŏn*). A Christian to whom Paul sent greetings. Paul called him "my kinsman," which probably meant that he was a Jew in spite of the name (Rom 16:11).

HERON. *See* Animals, III.21.

HESED (hē'sĕd). The father of Ben-hesed ("son of Hesed"), who was one of the 12 commissary officers of Solomon in charge of a district of Judah (I Kgs 4:10).

Heshbon. JR

HESHBON (hĕsh'bŏn). Built on two small hills on the Transjordan tableland, overlooking the lower Jordan Valley, Heshbon was the capital city of Sihon, king of the Amorites, who had captured it from the Moabites (Num 21:25-30). Taken by the Israelites from Sihon when he would not allow them to pass through his land (Num 21:23-24), Heshbon was among the cities rebuilt and populated by the Reubenites and Gadites (Num 32:37; Josh 13:17, 26). It was one of the cities assigned to the Levites (Josh 21:39).

Heshbon was recaptured by Mesha of Moab and held by the Moabites in the times of Isaiah and Jeremiah (Isa 15:4; 16:8-9; Jer 48:2, 34). Apparently it fell into the hands of the Ammonites during the time of Jeremiah (Jer 49:3). It was part of the Nabatean kingdom during the Hellenistic period, but later was conquered by Alexander Janneus; it was made a garrison city in Transjordan by Herod the Great (Jos *Ant.* xiii.15.4; xv.8.5). It is known today as *Ḥesbân* and is located 17 miles SW of Amman.

Excavations were begun in 1968 at *Ḥesbân,* directed by Dr. Siegfried Horn. Ruins of a Byzantine church were uncovered in addition to much pottery from Roman and Hellenistic times. Other pottery was found representing all the times Heshbon is mentioned in the OT (Late Bronze I to Iron III).

Bibliography. Yohanan Aharoni, *The Land of the Bible,* trans. by A. F. Rainey, Philadelphia: Westminster Press, 1967, pp. 187-191. Siegfried H. Horn, "The 1968 Heshbon Expedition," BA, XXXII (May, 1969), 25-41.

F. B. H.

HESHMON (hĕsh'mŏn). A town in the extreme S of Judah near Beer-sheba (Josh 15:27). The exact location is unknown.

HETH (hĕth)

1. A son of Canaan (Gen 10:15; I Chr 1:13). His descendants are identified as Hittites by the KJV (Gen 23:10), and by the RSV (Gen 23:3, 5, 7; 27:46; 49:32).

2. The eighth letter of the Heb. alphabet. The eighth section of Ps 119 is headed by this letter in the KJV.

HETHLON (hĕth'lŏn). A place mentioned by Ezekiel as situated on the future northern boundary of Israel (Ezk 47:15; 48:1). Its exact location is unknown; possibly it is modern Heitelâ, NE of Tripolis on the coast of Lebanon. The "way of Hethlon" may designate the route through the valley N of the Lebanon Mountain range to Kadesh-on-the-Orontes. Hethlon approximates the Mount Hor of Num 34:7, a northerly summit of the Lebanons (Y. Aharoni, *The Land of the Bible,* p. 67, n. 34).

HEW. Two basically different Heb. verbs are used, one in connection with wood and the other with stone. Heb. *ḥāṭab* means to chop down (a tree) or to cut and gather (firewood). Hewers of wood (Deut 19:5; 29:11; Josh 9:21, 23, 27; II Chr 2:10) were unskilled laborers, often slaves, whose task was menial and dull. On the other hand, Heb. *ḥāṣab* means to quarry and carve stone for building purposes (I Chr 22:2; Prov 9:1), to cut out a sepulcher (Isa 22:16), or to dig a watertight cistern (cf. Jer 2:13). The stonecutter was considered a skilled tradesman and was duly paid for his labor (II Kgs 12:11-12). *See* Occupations: Woodcutter.

HEZEKI (hĕz'ĕ-kī). A Benjamite (I Chr 8:17). The name is transliterated Hizki in RSV.

HEZEKIAH (hĕz'ĕ-kī*ă*)

1. A king of Judah who reigned for 29 years (cf. II Kgs 18-20; II Chr 29-32; Isa 36-39). The chronological references are best harmonized by dating his reign from 716/15 to 687 B.C. He may have been coregent with his father Ahaz beginning *c.* 729 (II Kgs 18:1, 9-10).

The Assyrian domination of the Fertile Crescent posed the major international problem for this period. Ahaz, enthroned in Judah with the support of a pro-Assyrian party, established and maintained a policy of friendship or vassalage to Assyria while Syria and the northern kingdom capitulated. Damascus was conquered by Tiglath-pileser III in 732 B.C. and Samaria by Shalmaneser V in 723/22. Sargon II, the next king of Assyria, 722-706, advanced into Philistia to conquer Ashdod in 711. The crucial time for Judah came during the reign of the Assyrian king Sennacherib, 705-681.

The heathen influence that accompanied the Judeo-Assyrian alliance may have caused a reaction during the decade before Ahaz died.

Hezekiah began his reign with the most extensive reforms in Judah's history. Keenly conscious of the fact that the captivity of the northern kingdom was caused by the breaking of the covenant and disobedience (II Kgs 18:9-12), Hezekiah removed idolatry, repaired and cleansed the temple, restored worship, and extended invitations throughout Judah and the northern tribes for an observance of the Passover that exceeded all celebrations since the time of Solomon. Religiously this reformation was a great success.

Hezekiah also was an outstanding military leader. Anticipating Assyrian attack on Judah, he concentrated on a defense program fortifying Jerusalem. By constructing a 1,777 foot tunnel through solid rock to connect the Siloam pool or cistern—the entrance to which was enclosed within the city by extending the wall—with the spring of Gihon *(q.v.)* he assured Jerusalem of an adequate water supply. This tunnel was discovered in 1880 and has ever since been an attraction for tourists. With religious and military preparations at its best, Hezekiah assembled his people in the city square and boldly expressed his confidence in God for protection (II Chr 32:1-8).

Crucial were the developments for Hezekiah personally as well as nationally in 701 B.C. That year Sennacherib advanced into the maritime plain W of Jerusalem, conquering numerous cities and exacting excessive sums of tribute from Jerusalem while he besieged Lachish (II Kgs 18:13-16). Emboldened by this submission, Sennacherib sent a large army to encircle Jerusalem and demand its complete surrender, but without success. Both the Bible (II Kgs 18:17-19:8) and Sennacherib's cuneiform records agree in essence concerning this campaign.

About this time Hezekiah became critically ill so that he anticipated death. The prophet Isaiah not only assured the king of Judah that his life would be extended 15 years, but also promised relief for the kingdom from Assyrian pressure (II Kgs 20:1-7). Perhaps the Assyrians left Jerusalem on hearing a rumor of a revolt in Babylon (II Kgs 19:7). At any rate, Assyrian records show that a year later Sennacherib was occupied with suppressing the Babylonians, which ultimately led to his destroying the city of Babylon in 689 B.C.

Probably in 688, although he left no record of such a disastrous campaign, Sennacherib turned toward Egypt, being alarmed by Tirhakah, an Ethiopian king of Egypt and Nubia, from 690 to 664 (II Kgs 19:9). By letter the Assyrian king sent an ultimatum to Hezekiah, who went to the temple to pray, confident that God would deliver him again. Once more Isaiah sent word assuring Hezekiah that the Assyrians would return the way they came (II Kgs 19:9-34). Subsequently by miraculous intervention the Assyrian army—which may have been encamped en route from Babylon across the Arabian desert to Egypt—was depleted by 185,000 troops. Sennacherib returned to Nineveh never to threaten Hezekiah again. In 681 Sennacherib was assassinated by two of his sons. *See* Sennacherib for alternate one campaign theory.

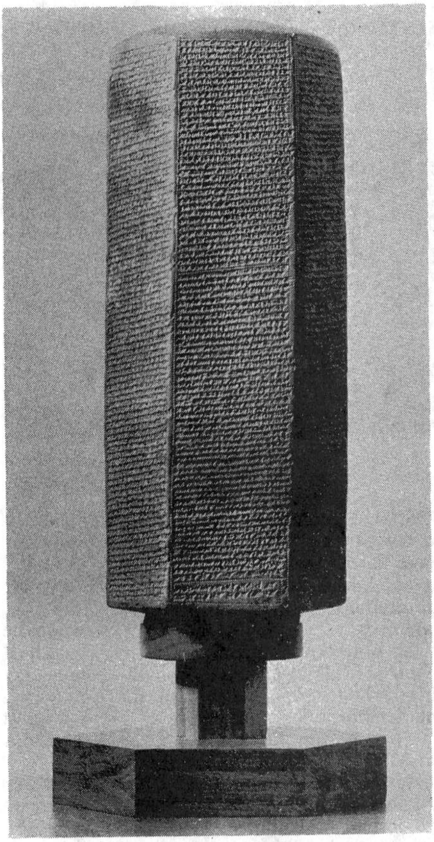

The prism of Sennacherib. ORINST

After the first crisis in 701 B.C. Hezekiah enjoyed a period of peace and prosperity. Acclaimed as the leader who had successfully withstood Assyrian aggression, Hezekiah was very likely supported politically and commercially by the surrounding nations, so that Judah enjoyed a rapid economic recovery. Hezekiah was rebuked, however, for accepting the congratulations of the Babylonians without giving witness to divine deliverance. Isaiah, who had repeatedly assured Judah of protection from Assyrian aggression, subsequently warned that ultimately the Babylonians would conquer Jerusalem, but not during Hezekiah's lifetime (Isa 39).

Hezekiah died in 686. He was succeeded by his son Manasseh, who probably had been made coregent in 696 B.C.

2. A great-great-grandfather of the prophet Zephaniah (Zeph 1:1), very likely King Hezekiah, since other prophets name only their father. (Hizkiah in KJV is spelled Hezekiah in RSV. The names are exactly the same in Heb.)

3. Ancestor of a group of exiles who returned with Zerubbabel; his Babylonian name evidently was Ater (Ezr 2:16; Neh 7:21). He is probably the same as a chief of the people who set his seal to the covenant renewal under Nehemiah (Neh 10:17; KJV, Hizkijah).

4. Son of Neariah, a descendant of the royal family of Judah (I Chr 3:23).

S. J. S.

HEZION (hĕ'zī-ŏn). The grandfather of the Syrian king Ben-hadad (*q.v.*, I Kgs 15:18).

HEZIR (hē'zĭr)

1. The head of the 17th course of priests in the time of David (I Chr 24:15).

2. The head of a family who signed the covenant in the time of Nehemiah (Neh 10:20).

HEZRAI (hĕz'rī). One of the mighty men of David. The name is found only in II Sam 23:35, but is probably the same as Hezro (*q.v.*).

HEZRO (hĕz'rō). Found only in I Chr 11:37. It is probably the same as Hezrai (*q.v.*).

HEZRON (hĕz'rŏn), **HEZRONITES** (hĕz'-rŏ-nīts)

1. The third named of the sons of Reuben, the firstborn of Jacob (Gen 46:9; Ex 6:14; I Chr 5:3). He is the ancestor of the Hezronites (Num 26:6).

2. A son of Pharez and grandson of Judah. He was the ancestor of David through whom came Jesus (Gen 46:12; Num 26:21; Ruth 4:18-19; I Chr 2:5, 9, 18, 21, 24-25; 4:1). In Mt 1:3 he is called Esrom in KJV but Hezron in RSV.

3. A city on the southern border of Judah, between Kadesh-barnea and Adar. It is also called Hazor (Josh 15:3, 25).

HIDDAI (hĭd'ī). One of David's mighty men from the wilds near Gaash (II Sam 23:30). He is called Ḥurai in the parallel passage in I Chr 11:32 (*q.v.*). The alternate spellings probably resulted from a confusion in Heb. of *r* and *d*, and of *h* and *ḥ*, letters very similar in post-Exilic Heb.

HIDDEKEL (hĭd-dĕk'ĕl). A Heb. rendering of Akkad. *Idiqlat*, the second major river of Mesopotamia (Gen 2:14; Dan 10:4). The Idiqlat was called *Diqlat* or *Diglat* in Aram., *Tigrā* in Old Persian, and Tigris (*q.v.*) in Gr.

HIEL (hī'ĕl). A Bethelite (*q.v.*) who rebuilt Jericho in the days of Ahab (I Kgs 16:34). The curse of Joshua (Josh 6:26) was understood as applying to the sacrifices of his oldest and youngest sons.

Hierapolis, appearing as a frozen waterfall.
James L. Boyer

HIERAPOLIS (hī'ĕ-răp'ŏ-lĭs). A city built on a high terrace overlooking the valley of the Lycus River in the W part of the Roman province of Asia, about six miles N of Laodicea. It was famous for its hot springs, which made it a health resort, and for the Plutonium, a crevasse in the rock which emitted poisonous gases, supposedly the domain of the Phrygian fertility goddess Leto. The church in Hierapolis was probably founded by converts of Paul, and was associated closely with the church in Colosse (Col 4:13). Legend says that Philip the evangelist and John the apostle visited this city.

HIGGAION (hĭ-gā'yŏn). Transliteration of a Heb. term appearing only in Ps 9:16 where it is a musical note or direction. The term is translated "meditation" in Ps 19:14, "solemn sound" in Ps 92:3, and "device" in Lam 3:62.

HIGH PLACE. The original meaning was simply that of a mountain or hill top (Deut 32:13; II Sam 1:19, 25). The overwhelming proportion of uses, however, indicate sanctuaries on an elevated area. These were Canaanite in origin. They may have been used for funeral rites and certainly were often the scenes of fertility rites (Hos 4:11-14; Jer 3:6; 19:5; 48:35).

Ruins of such sanctuaries are scattered throughout Canaan (as at Petra, Bab edh-Dra, Gezer, Megiddo, Hazor, *q.v.*), and were apparently located near almost every village, sometimes even inside cities (Jer 7:31; 19:13; Ezk 6:3). Every such pagan shrine included in its equipment an altar of stone or earth, stone pillars (*maṣṣēbôth*, Deut 12:3; Hos 10:1), wooden poles (*'ăshērîm*, Ex 34:13), and a basin for ceremonial washings. Some high places possessed an image like Jeroboam's golden calf or Micah's ephod; others, some sacred object such as an ark or ephod. This required a house or temple to shelter it (Jud 17:5; I Kgs 12:31). A place for groups to eat together may also be presumed for the high places (I Sam 9:13, 22; I Kgs 3:4, 15).

Steps leading to the great high place of Petra. MIS

Since the high places were the only local places of worship in early Israel after Shiloh was destroyed, they were the scenes of many religious acts. Here sacrifices were offered (I Sam 9:13; I Kgs 3:3-4; 12:32). This meant at the same time that they were the places for slaughter of all animals to be eaten for meat, for each such slaughter was at the same time a sacrifice. In earliest times this was done by the worshiper himself. Later, priests were attached to each high place to carry out these functions properly.

To the high places tithes and offerings were brought, as men came to "inquire of the Lord" through priestly oracle or prophetic word (I Sam 9:7-12). Here, as "in the gate," justice was administered in the name of the Lord. They were very likely places of asylum supplementing the six Levitical cities. Recent research suggests that they were also mortuary shrines, sometimes achieving their fame and importance as the burial place of a hero or king, or as the place where his monument (*maṣṣēbâ*) or funerary stela (*peger*) was erected (Ezk 43:7; 6:3-6; Lev 26:30).

Undoubtedly the main significance of the high place lay in its use as a local sanctuary. Official Israelitic religion consisted in the great annual pilgrimage festivals. The carryover into every week and every day religion occurred at the high place sanctuaries. They apparently emphasized an area of concern largely ignored in official Israelitic religion: that of death and life after death. By syncretizing the law (Torah) with Canaanite ideology, apostatizing Israelites became concerned with a subject actively opposed by the official religion, that of fertility. Because of these extra-orthodox concerns and the excesses for which their celebration gave occasion, they came under the severe criticism of the prophets. While the religious reform under Hezekiah (II Kgs 18:4, 22) was undone by his son Manasseh (II Kgs 21:1-6), from the time of Josiah on (II Kgs 23:4-20) the high places were summarily condemned. Ceremonial worship was allowed only in Jerusalem.

Bibliography. W. F. Albright, "The High Place in Ancient Palestine," VT, Supplement IV (1957), 242-58; CornPBE, pp. 391-94.

D. W. W.

HIGH PRIEST. *See* Priest, High.

HIGHEST

1. Superlative of the adjective "high." It is used in the KJV in the ordinary sense of elevation (Ezk 41:7; RSV "top"), and as the translation of idioms implying quality rather than elevation; e.g., *rōʼsh,* "head," translated "highest" in KJV, and "first" in RSV (Prov 8:26); *prōtoklisia,* "first couch," translated "highest" in KJV, and "place of honor" in RSV (Lk 14:8).

2. Used as a title for God in KJV (Ps 18:13; 87:5; Lk 1:32, 35, 76; 6:35). RSV translates the title as "the Most High."

The great high place or worship center of Petra. MIS

3. Used as a synonym for heaven, God's dwelling place and seat of His throne (Lk 2:14; 19:38; Mt 21:9; Mk 11:10; cf. Job 16:19), equivalent to the "third heaven" (II Cor 12:2) and the "heaven of heavens" (Deut 10:14; I Kgs 8:27; Neh 9:6; Ps 148:4).

HIGHWAY. A travel route for public use. The most frequent Heb. term used is *m^{e}sillâ* (Num 20:19; Isa 7:3; 40:3; *et al.*), which means a built-up roadway. In the NT the Gr. term *hodos* is translated "highway" three times by the KJV (Mt 22:10; Mk 10:46; Lk 14:23) and once by the RSV (Lk 14:23). *See* Commerce; King's Highway; Road; Travel and Communication with map showing the principal trade routes in ancient Palestine.

HILEN. *See* Holon.

HILKIAH (hĭl-kīʹȧ)

1. A Levite of the family of Merari, the son of Amzi and father of Amaziah (I Chr 6:45-46).

2. A Levite, the son of Hosah, a Merarite, who was appointed a doorkeeper in the temple by David (I Chr 26:11).

3. The father of Eliakim who was "over the house," that is, prime minister under King Hezekiah (II Kgs 18:18, 26, 37; Isa 22:20; 36:3, 22).

4. The son of Shallum (or Meshullam) and descendant of Zadok who was high priest in the days of King Josiah. He was also an ancestor of Ezra (I Chr 6:13; 9:11; Ezr 7:1). It was in part under his leadership that the great revival took place in the reign of Josiah. During the repair of the temple, Hilkiah discovered "the book of the law of the Lord given by Moses." This may have been a "foundation" copy, such as we now put in cornerstones, or it may have been in fact the very copy placed in the ark by Moses (Deut 31:9-26). The book was brought to the king who, after reading in it, was convicted of the great sin of his people. He requested Hilkiah and others to "inquire of the Lord" for

him. Hilkiah turned to Huldah the prophetess and through her received of the Lord the pronouncement of judgment upon Judah, but comfort and blessing personally to the devout Josiah. Hilkiah had a leading role in the reformation that followed, marked by a momentous Passover observation (II Kgs 22–23; II Chr 34–35).

5. A priest of Anathoth in Benjamin, the father of Jeremiah the prophet (Jer 1:1).

6. The father of Gemariah, who with Elasah was sent to Babylon by King Zedekiah, bearing the letter of Jeremiah to those already in captivity (Jer 29:3).

7. One of the priests who returned from Babylon with Zerubbabel. The father of Hashabiah who was priest in the days of Joiakim (Neh 12:7, 21).

8. One of the priests who stood with Ezra as he read the law of God to the people (Neh 8:4).

9. The father of Seraiah, one of the chief priests under Nehemiah and "ruler of the house of God" (Neh 11:11).

P. C. J.

HILL, HILL COUNTRY

1. The usual Heb. word for "hill" is *gib'â*, derived from a root that suggests a swelling and yields other words such as "bowl" and "humpbacked." It is peculiarly applicable to the many rounded hills in Palestine. It may refer to the elevated terrain in general of Ephraim (Gen 49:26; Deut 33:15) and the plateau of Moab (Num 23:9), or to specific heights such as the hill of Moreh (Jud 7:1) and the hill of Hachilah (I Sam 23:19; 26:1, 3). As Isa 31:4 indicates, it can be synonymous with the next term.

2. The Heb. word *har* most often refers to a range of mountains or to a particular summit, but is translated as "hill" 61 times in the KJV and once as "hill country" (Josh 13:6). The proper translation of *har* requires a knowledge of the geography of Palestine. Since the mountains of Palestine and Transjordan are seldom more than 3,000 feet in elevation, it is often preferable to refer to them as "hill country." Hence the RSV has rendered the term re-

Mount Tabor, a good illustration of one of the rounded hills of Palestine. ORINST

Holes may be seen in the base and lintel of the Lion Gate at Mycenae for the "pivot" or pole piece (hinge) of the gate. Holes may be seen for inserting bars to lock the gate. HFV

peatedly in this way when the mountainous section of an area is indicated (cf. "hill country of Seir," Gen 36:8, RSV; "hill country of Ephraim," Josh 17:15, 16, 18, RSV). The entire hill country of Judah, Benjamin, and Ephraim, and perhaps of Galilee, once inhabited by Amorites, is referred to as *hāhār*, "the mountain" (Num 13:29). On the other hand, in II Kgs 1:9; 4:27 the use of the word "hill" for *hāhār* obscures the allusion to Mount Carmel, which in other passages concerning Elijah and Elisha (e.g., I Kgs 18:19; II Kgs 4:25) has the translation "mount" correctly attached to it. *See* Palestine II.A.5; B.2.

3. Heb. *ma'ăleh* is once rendered "hill" (I Sam 9:11); better would be "ascent" or "slope" (Jerusalem Bible), the sloping ramp or roadway leading up to the city gate.

4. Gr. *bounos* is used twice in the NT and translated "hill" (Lk 3:5; 23:30).

5. Gr. *oros* is rendered 62 times as "mount" or "mountain" but three times as "hill," twice correctly (Mt 5:14; Lk 4:29). The third passage (Lk 9:37) should have "mountain" to agree with the use of *oros* in Lk 9:28.

6. Gr. *oreinos* properly is translated "hill country" in Lk 1:39, 65.

J. R.

HILLEL (hĭl'ĕl). The father of the judge Abdon (Jud 12:13, 15).

HIN. *See* Weights, Measures, and Coins.

HIND. *See* Animals: Deer, II.10.

HINGE. Two words are translated "hinge" in KJV. The Heb. word *pōt* probably means "socket" (I Kgs 7:50), and *ṣîr* refers to the "pivot" or pole piece of the ancient Palestinian door (Prov 26:14). In contrast with the gold sockets in which the doors of Solomon's temple turned (I Kgs 7:50), the sockets were more often simply a hole in the wood or stone lintel and doorsill. Stone door sockets are commonly found in Palestinian excavated sites. The pivot, to which the door was attached, was an upright beam of wood or metal fitted into the sockets.

In Prov 26:14 a sluggard turning in his bed is compared to a pivot turning in its sockets.

See Door.

Using the ancient "pole pieces," a modern gate has been installed at the north gate of Mycenae. HFV

HINNOM (hĭn'ŏm). The valley of Hinnom begins on the W side of Jerusalem at the Joppa (Jaffa) Gate, continuing S until it bends E along the southern limits of the city, joining the valley of the Kidron near the SE corner and the Dung Gate. It is a deep and narrow ravine with steep, rocky sides. *See* Jerusalem.

It is first mentioned in Scripture as a part of the boundary between Judah (to the S) and Benjamin (to the N) in the division of the land among the tribes (Josh 15:8; 18:16). Here was located Topheth, where parents had made their

Valley of Hinnom looking north toward the Jaffa Gate. HFV

children pass through the fire to the idol Molech (II Chr 28:3; 33:6). Jeremiah warned that God would punish the people so severely because of this wickedness that the place would become known as the valley of slaughter (Jer 7:31–34; 19:3–6; 32:35). King Josiah sought to bring such idolatrous abominations to an end, making the valley the dumping ground for refuse from the city (II Kgs 23:10, 13–14; II Chr 34:4–5).

The Heb. name *Gê ben-Hinnom* (Ge-Hinnom) was transliterated into Gr. as *geenna.* It becomes in the NT the word for "hell," which is found 11 times in the Gospels upon the lips of Jesus (Mt 5:22, 29–30; 10:28; 18:9; 23:15, 33; Mk 9:43, 45, 47; Lk 12:5) and once in Jas 3:6. It became known as a place of putrefaction, decay, and burning, associated with the destruction of waste, a fit symbol for the final destination of the wicked. The references in Rev 14:10; 19:20; 20:10; 21:8 to "the lake of fire" probably have their foundation in the Gehenna concept.

See Gehenna; Hell.

H. L. D. and F. B. H.

HIP AND THIGH. An idiom used in Jud 15:8 to indicate a slaughter so fierce that the bodies were mutilated.

HIPPOPOTAMUS. *See* Animals, II.20.

HIRAH (hī'rȧ). An Adullamite, a friend of Judah (Gen 38:1, 12). He was Judah's emissary to the supposed harlot (Gen 38:20 ff.). Both the LXX and the Vulgate read "shepherd" for "friend" in Gen 38:12.

HIRAM (hī'rȧm). A name that is commonly rendered Hiram in I Kings and I Chronicles but Huram in II Chronicles (*q.v.*).

1. King of Tyre. With the reign of Hiram I the great days of Tyre (*q.v.*) began. When he took the reins of government, Tyre consisted of two small islands about a half mile off the Phoenician coast. (Whether or not there was a main-

Ruins of the Roman period at Tyre, a city started on the road to greatness by Hiram. HFV

land Tyre at the time is uncertain.) These two islands he joined, and then claimed from the sea an area on the E of the larger island. The total circumference of island Tyre was now about two and a half miles. Then he proceeded to rebuild and beautify the temples, and enlarged and improved the harbor and fortifications of the city.

One acceptable chronology based on Josephus' statements (*Ant.* viii.3.1; 5.3; *Against Apion* i.17–18) pegs the 34-year reign of Hiram at 978–944 B.C. His father was Abi-baal and the remaining rulers of his dynasty include Beleazarus, seven years; Abd-Astartus, nine years; Deleastartus, 12 years; Astartus, 12 years; Aserymus, nine years; Pheles, eight months.

After David became king over all Israel, Hiram sent an embassy to David. The result was a supply of cedars of Lebanon (*q.v.*) and Tyrian carpenters and masons to provide a palace for David—on what terms we do not know (II Sam 5:11–12; I Chr 14:1–2). Later, David obtained cedar from Tyre and Sidon for the temple (I Chr 22:4).

When Solomon assumed the task of building the temple in Jerusalem, he sent to Hiram to make specific arrangements for actual construction. The correspondence between the two kings appears in II Chr 2 and I Kgs 5:1–12 (cf. I Kgs 7:13–14). The picture we get is something like this: Solomon needed wood, gold, and artisans in various trades. In exchange for the wood and skilled labor Solomon furnished agricultural products; for the gold, a section of land.

The total amount of what Solomon agreed to furnish annually for the wood and laborers was 20,000 measures (Heb. *kor* = 10–11 bushels each) of wheat, 20,000 measures of barley, 20,000 measures (Heb. *bath* = 4½ gallons each) of wine, and 20,000 measures of oil (thought to be a textual corruption; the amount is seemingly too much) (II Chr 2:10).

The fact that this payment differs from that mentioned in I Kgs 5:11 seems easily explained. The latter reference speaks of a payment of 20,000 measures of wheat and 20 measures of pure oil and says this was for "his [Hiram's] household." The II Chronicles statistics probably include receipts for public expenditures as well. For gold, Solomon gave Hiram a tract of land in Galilee; this encompassed 20 towns. Upon seeing this district, Hiram was quite unhappy and called it *cabul*. According to Josephus this word is a Phoenician term meaning "that which does not please" (I Kgs 9:10–14; Jos *Ant.* viii.5.3).

Having established an agreement for building purposes, Solomon and Hiram also seem to have drawn up a pact for joint commercial endeavor. Solomon's conquest of the Edomites gave him access to the Red Sea. There he constructed the port of Ezion-geber (*q.v.*) and built a fleet of ships for trade in eastern and southern waters (I Kgs 9:25–28). Up to this point, the Hebrews had never possessed good port facilities and had never engaged extensively in travel by sea. When constructing a port and fleet, the most natural place for the Hebrews to turn for skilled technicians was to the Phoenicians, acknowledged leaders in the field. And the Phoenicians were glad to cooperate in construction of a southern fleet because, on the one hand, such a fleet would not contest their mastery of the Mediterranean, since there was no Suez Canal. On the other hand, the Phoenicians would in this way have access to goods of Arabia and Africa for their Mediterranean trade; these products they previously had had to do without. The land of Ophir (I Kgs 9:28) was either located in SW Arabia (modern Yemen) and perhaps the adjacent coast of Africa, or possibly in western India. The Phoenicians also seem to have helped Solomon develop his copper smelting industry in the area S of the Dead Sea.

Not only did Hiram and Solomon have a public commercial alliance, they seem to have had a private tilt of shrewdness over solving riddles. Josephus relates that the two monarchs exchanged riddles or enigmatical sayings, with the understanding that the one who could not solve those submitted to him was to forfeit a money payment. At first Hiram seems to have been the substantial loser; but later Hiram, with the help of a certain Abdemon of Tyre, managed to solve the riddles. Later, Hiram proposed a number of riddles which even wise Solomon could not figure out, and Solomon paid substantial sums of money to Hiram (Jos *Ant.* viii.5.5; *Against Apion,* i.17). What relation King Ahiram of Byblos (*c.* 1000 B.C.) may have had to Hiram I of Tyre is problematical.

2. A second Hiram of Tyre (not referred to in the OT) is mentioned by Tiglath-pileser III (744–727 B.C.) of Assyria as paying tribute to the Assyrian monarch.

3. An artisan contemporary with King Hiram I, whom the king sent to Solomon to supervise casting of the molten sea (great laver), copper pillars, and other utensils for the temple (I Kgs

7:13–47). While Hiram's father was a Tyrian, his mother was either from the tribe of Naphtali (I Kgs 7:14) or of Dan (II Chr 2:14). Perhaps the discrepancy is a result of a copyist's error, or possibly Hiram's mother was descended from both tribes. Hiram was apparently a very superior craftsman.

H. F. V.

HIRE. *See* Wages.

HIRELING. The word occurs six times in the OT and always means a laborer who receives pay. Job 7:1–2 deals with the hireling's anxiety for the day's end; Isa 16:14; 21:16 refer to the hireling's tenure; Mal 3:5 warns against the mistreatment of the hireling in reference to his wages; Jer 46:21 refers to a mercenary soldier (cf. RSV, NASB; II Sam 10:6; II Kgs 7:6; II Chr 25:6).

The only usage in the NT is in Jn 10:12–13, where the hireling's neglect of the sheep is sharply contrasted with the shepherd's protection and courage. The true owner of the flock leads them to and from pasturage and lays down his life for the sheep. While there is no imputation of unfaithfulness or dishonesty necessarily conveyed by the term, nevertheless, this is usually read into the term because of Jesus' application of the word to the unfaithful shepherd.

HISS. The RSV translates the Heb. verb *shāraq,* "whistle," in the sense of calling or signaling (Isa 5:26; 7:18; Zech 10:8); KJV renders it "hiss." It is also rendered "hiss" in both KJV and RSV in the sense of expressing scorn (I Kgs 9:8; Job 27:23; *et al.*), apparently deriving this sense mimetically from the hissing of air being expelled through clenched teeth. The noun of this same root is frequently employed by Jeremiah in the same sense of derision and scorn (Jer 18:16; 19:8; 25:9, 18; 29:18; 51:37).

HITTITES (hĭt'īts). The term Hittite has a twofold use in the OT. Usually it designates a relatively unimportant ethnic group living in Palestine since the days of the patriarchs (Gen 15:19–21). These people, called the "sons of Heth," were descended from Noah's son Ham through Canaan (Gen 10:15; I Chr 1:13) and were settled in the central hills of Palestine (Num 13:29; Josh 11:3).

In a few cases, however, the term Hittite is used in the OT to designate outsiders, non-Semitic peoples living in the N, who were to be respected and feared as a great power (I Kgs 11:1; II Kgs 7:6–7; II Chr 1:17). These were the Hittites so famous from extrabiblical historical sources. Although it has been suggested that the small enclaves of Hittites in central Palestine were part of the northern Hittites who migrated S early in the 2nd mil. B.C., there need be no connection between the two groups at all, except for a coincidental similarity of name.

The Indo-European Hittites who entered Anatolia and the Near East around 2000 B.C. from the steppes of inner Asia received their name more or less by accident, by virtue of the fact that they settled in territory previously held by an earlier non-Indo-European group called Hatti-people (or Hattians). Henceforth in this article the three groups will be called "sons of Heth," "Hittites," and "Hattians" respectively, to avoid confusion.

[The red and black highly burnished Khirbet Kerah ware in Palestine is virtually identical with pottery in central Anatolia and the Kurgan homeland in Transcaucasia in the 3rd mil. B.C. This may suggest an incursion or migration of Hattians into Palestine in the 23rd cen. B.C.—Ed. See BASOR # 189 (1968), pp. 28f.]

There is no way of knowing how long the Hattians had been living in central Anatolia before the Hittites arrived *c.* 2000 B.C. Although the Hittites acquired territory and political supremacy in central Anatolia around the Halys River partly by force of arms, there was no organized conquest of the land in the manner of Israel's conquest of Palestine. The Hattians ever after formed a minority group within Hittite society, and were very influential in religious matters.

Teshub, the Hittite weather god. LM

HITTITES

Although it is possible that an earlier king, Anitta of Kussar, who subdued five rival cities and moved his capital to Nesa (Kanesh), was related in some way to the later Hittite kings, the Hittite Old Kingdom proper is usually dated (S. Smith's chronology) 1680-1460 B.C. Hattusili I (1650-1620 B.C.) raided and defeated Alalakh, Urshu, and Aleppo in N Syria. Mursili I (1620-1590 B.C.) led the Hittite army down the Euphrates to conquer Aleppo, destroy Mari, and raid and plunder Babylon itself, thus putting an end to the Babylonian dynasty founded by Hammurabi. After Mursili the power of the Hittites declined. It is possible that the first recension of the Hittite laws dates from the reign of Telipinu (1525-1500 B.C.).

Revival of Hittite power began with Tudhaliya II (1460-1440 B.C.), who in cooperation with Thutmose III of Egypt destroyed Aleppo (*c.* 1457). During the years that followed, however, the Hurrian kingdom of Mittanni established itself in N Syria, restricting the Hittites to their mountainous homeland in central Anatolia. The greatest and most famous of the Hittite kings was Suppiluliuma (1380-1340 B.C.), who reduced the kingdom of Mittanni to a vassal state and controlled Syria S to the Lebanon region. Suppiluliuma laid a solid foundation for the administration of Syrian vassal states, binding each of them to himself in suzerainty treaties, the literary form of which closely resembles that of the covenant which God gave to Israel at Mount Sinai (cf. George Mendenhall, *Law and Covenant in Israel and the Ancient Near East*).

During the reign of Muwatalli (1306-1282 B.C.) Rameses II of Egypt joined battle with the Hittite allied armies at Kadesh on the Orontes. Both sides claimed victory in their annals, but Muwatalli retained Syria and added Abina (Hobah) to his possessions. Rameses later allied himself by treaty with Hattusili III (1275-1250 B.C.) against the mutual threat of the young Assyrian state. The Hittite Empire centered in Asia Minor came to an end when barbarian hordes from Thrace swept over the western lands and *c.* 1200 B.C. destroyed the capital city of Hattusas (at Boghazköy, 75 miles E of Ankara, Turkey). Sea Peoples from the W and S may have also had a part in the collapse of the Hittites.

Entrance to the great temple of the lower city. Boghazköy. HFV

The political designation "Hatti" was carried on by a small group of N Syrian city-states, among whom were Carchemish, Aleppo, and Hamath. Hittites from these cities may have served in David's armies (I Sam 26:6; II Sam 11:3), although these may have been the sons of Heth, since Ahimelech is transparently a Semitic name and Uriah may be either Semitic or Hurrian. Semitic names in themselves, however, need not rule out a Syro-Hittite origin, since the Hittites of Syria had long since accommodated themselves to the prevailing Aramean culture.

When Ezekiel accused the profligate Jerusalem of being the offspring of an Amorite father and a Hittite mother (Ezk 16:3), he had in mind the sons of Heth, not the great empire in Asia Minor. Ephron the Hittite of Gen 23 may also have been of the sons of Heth, although some have detected traces of Hittite real estate procedure in the transaction between Ephron and Abraham (Lehmann, BASOR # 129, pp. 15-18; Tucker, JBL, LXXXV, 77-84).

The language of the Hittites was an Indo-European tongue related to early Greek, Latin, and Sanskrit. Other groups in Anatolia related to the Hittites spoke related dialects called Luwian and Palaic. The language of the Hattians was neither Semitic nor Indo-European. The laws of the Hittites, inscribed on clay tablets in cuneiform script, are very similar in form and content to contemporary law codes from Mesopotamia (ANET, pp. 188-197). But unlike Semitic law with its characteristic stress on *lex talionis,* these laws stress compensation for injuries, undoubtedly a residue of the old Indo-European *wergeld* institution.

The Hittites possessed two distinct military advantages over their foes. They were the first to smelt iron on a large scale in the Near East, which gave them superior weapons. Hittites were also in the vanguard of those who developed the breeding and training of chariot horses into a science. Among clay tablets in the Hittite archives were found an extensive series of tablets describing procedures in training chariot horses. The author of these texts was a Hurrian named Kikkuli. Solomon in later times imported fine horses from Cilicia (Kue) for his chariotry (I Kgs 10:28-29).

See Archaeology: Boghazköy.

Bibliography. Kurt Bittel, "Boghazköy: The Excavations of 1967 and 1968," *Archaeology,* XXII (1969), 276-279, O. R. Gurney, "Boghazköy," TAOT, pp. 105-116. Harry A.

Lion Gate, Boghazköy, capital of the Hittites. HFV

Hoffner, "Hittites," BW, pp. 290–294, with excellent bibliography; "Some Contributions of Hittitology to Old Testament Study," *Tyndale Bulletin,* XX (1969), 27–55. Manfred R. Lehmann, "Abraham's Purchase of Machpelah and Hittite Law," BASOR # 129 (1953), pp. 15–18. Gene M. Tucker, "The Legal Background of Genesis 23," JBL, LXXXV (1966), 77–84.

H. A. Hof.

HIVITES (hī′vīts). Numbered among the descendants of Canaan (Gen 10:17; I Chr 1:15), the Hivites were one of the ethnic groups dwelling in Canaan before the Israelite settlement (Ex 3:8; Deut 7:1; Josh 3:10). Hivite cities and settlements are known to have existed in the vicinity of Sidon and Tyre (II Sam 24:7), in the Lebanon hills (Jud 3:3), in the Hermon range and the valley leading to Hamath (Josh 11:3), and in central Palestine around Shechem (Gen 34:2) and Gibeon N of Jerusalem (Josh 9:7; 11:19). Solomon conscripted Hivites for his building projects (I Kgs 9:20; II Chr 8:7).

Since in the Heb. spelling the words "Hivite" (*ḥiwwî*) and "Horite" (*ḥōrî*) differ only in one letter (*w* and *r,* which are shaped similarly in Heb.), many scholars assume an early textual error and equate the Hivites with the Horites. Confusion of the two spellings in the course of textual transmission is evident from the Masoretic Heb. text itself, since Zibeon is called a "Hivite" in Gen 36:2 and a "Horite" in Gen 36:20. LXX reads "Horites" for MT "Hivites" in Gen 34:2 and Josh 9:7. Furthermore, Hurrians (biblical "Horites") are known to have settled in Palestine in just the areas where the biblical Hivites were located. Hurrian personal names are attested from central Palestine, Lebanon, and Syria. The prince of Jerusalem around the middle of the 14th cen. B.C., as known from the Amarna letters, bore the Hurrian personal name Abdi-Hepa.

In David's time a Jebusite prince from the Jerusalem area bore the name (or title) Araunah (II Sam 24:16; variant spelling Ornan, *'rnn,* in I Chr 21:18), which means in Hurrian "the lord." The variant spellings in II Sam 24 in the consonantal text of MT,*'wrnh* (v. 16) and *'rwnh* (vv. 20–24), have been thought to reflect dialectal differences, since "lord" was pronounced *iwri* in some Hurrian dialects and *irwi* in others. But since the term equivalent to Araunah's name is always spelled *'wrn* at Ugarit, and LXX always reads *Orna* (even at II Sam 24:20–24, reflecting *'wrnh* in the Heb. text), it is probable that MT *'rwnh* in II Sam 24:20–24 is a transpositional error for earlier *'wrnh.* The fact that Araunah with his Hurrian name or title is called a Jebusite (II Sam 24:16), along with the fact that in the stereotyped lists Hivites immediately precede Jebusites (Ex 3:8; Deut 7:1; etc.), has been construed as additional evidence that the Hivites were Hurrians (Horites). *See* Horites.

H. A. Hof.

HIZKIAH. *See* Hezekiah.

HIZKIJAH. *See* Hezekiah.

HOARFROST. *See* Frost.

HOBAB (hō′băb). The son of Raguel or Reuel the Midianite (Num 10:29), and thus the brother of Zipporah and brother-in-law of Moses (Ex 2:18, 21; 3:1). The Heb. word *ḥōtēn,* translated "father-in-law" (Num 10:29; Jud 1:16; 4:11; *et al.*), comes from the verb *ḥātan,* "to marry," and simply means a relative by marriage. Since it is no more specific than that, there is no contradiction in the passages in Judges naming Hobab as Moses' "in-law." *See* Jethro.

When Israel set out from Sinai, Moses invited Hobab to accompany them, promising that the blessing of God extended to Israel would be his also. He urged Hobab to come that he might be a guide and help to them since he was experienced in the ways of the wilderness (Num 10:29–32). The record in Numbers does not indicate whether Hobab went with them at the time or not, but people of the same Midianite family, the Kenites, are found among the Israelites from then on. In the time of the judges, Heber, the Kenite, is called a descendant of Hobab. Heber's wife Jael (*q.v.*) was the heroine who slew the oppressor Sisera (Jud 4:11 ff.).

Bibliography. William F. Albright, *Yahweh and the Gods of Canaan,* Garden City: Doubleday, 1968, pp. 38–42.

P. C. J.

HOBAH (hō'bȧ). The place to which Abram pursued the routed army of Chedorlaomer "on the left hand" (i.e., N) of Damascus (Gen 14:15). The exact site is uncertain.

HOD (hŏd). A son of Zophah of the family of Asher (I Chr 7:37).

HODAIAH (hō-dā'yȧ). Variant of Hodaviah (*q.v.*). Hodaiah is found only in I Chr 3:24, referring to a descendant of David. He was one of the seven sons of Elioenai of the descendants of Zerubbabel.

HODAVIAH (hŏd'ȧ-vī'ȧ). Variant of Hodaiah (*q.v.*). The name appears in the Aramaic letters from Elephantine.

1. One of the chief men of Manasseh, a mighty warrior, taken into exile by the Assyrians (I Chr 5:24).

2. The father of Meshullam and son of Hassenuah of the tribe of Benjamin (I Chr 9:7).

3. A Levite, ancestor of 74 who returned to Jerusalem with Zerubbabel (Ezr 2:40). In Ezr 3:9 he is called Judah and in Neh 7:43 the name is spelled Hodevah.

HODESH (hō'dĕsh). A wife of Shaharaim, a Benjamite (I Chr 8:9).

HODEVAH. *See* Hodaviah 3.

HODIAH (hō-dī'ȧ). A man of Judah (I Chr 4:19). *See* Hodijah 1.

HODIJAH (hō-dī'jȧ). The RSV consistently translates Hodiah; the KJV translates Hodiah in I Chr 4:19, but elsewhere uses Hodijah. The Heb. name has been found on an ancient seal in Palestine.

1. A man of Judah (*q.v.*; I Chr 4:19, RSV), whose wife was a sister of Naham. The word order and punctuation of the KJV give the wrong impression that Hodiah was a woman.

2. A Levite active in the days of Nehemiah. He helped the people understand the law as it was read by Ezra and led the people in prayer (Neh 8:7 f.; 9:5). He signed the great covenant of Nehemiah (Neh 10:10).

3. Another Levite who signed Nehemiah's covenant (Neh 10:13).

4. One of the chiefs of the people who signed the covenant (Neh 10:18).

HOGLAH (hŏg'lȧ). One of five daughters of Zelophehad (Num 26:33; 27:1; Josh 17:3). Since there were no sons, the daughters were to receive the inheritance provided they married within their tribe (Num 36:1–12).

HOHAM (hō'hăm). Amorite king of Hebron who joined the coalition against Gibeon. The coalition was defeated by Joshua at Beth-horon. The kings fled but were caught in the cave at Makkedah and killed (Josh 10:3 ff.).

HOLD. This term is used to refer to a stronghold (Jud 9:46, 49); to a cage or jail (Ezk 19:9; Acts 4:3; RSV "in custody"); to a den or lair (Rev 18:2; RSV "haunt"). *See* Fort.

HOLINESS, HOLY. The Heb. words *qādôsh,* "holy"; *qōdesh,* "holiness"; and the Gr. *hagios* and *hagiōsynē* mean basically separation from what is common or unclean, and consecration to God (Lev 20:24–26, RSV; Acts 6:13; 21:28). From the underlying idea of apartness or separation from the profane (Lev 10:10; Ezk 22:26) stem three derived aspects of holiness found in Scripture.

1. *Deity.* Since God is transcendent and independent of His created universe (I Kgs 8:27), He is separate from its inhabitants and feared by them (e.g., Ex 19:10–25; 20:18–21). Thus holiness becomes equivalent to true deity, separating Him from the impotence of the gods of the defeated Egyptians (Ex 15:11): "Who is like unto thee, O Lord, among the gods? who is like thee, glorious in holiness?" "Holy" in many passages is synonymous with "divine": "There is none holy [uniquely divine] as the Lord: for there is none beside thee" (I Sam 2:2; cf. Ps 99:3, 5, 9; Isa 40:25; Hab 3:3). Because He is holy, truly deity and thus infinite, there is no searching of His understanding (Isa 40:28; Ps 145:3). Holiness, then, is what characterizes God, and it includes all His other attributes.

2. *Ceremonial holiness.* While it is true that God as the "wholly other" Being "dwells in the high and holy place," yet He is "with him also that is of a contrite spirit" (Isa 57:15). That is, God shares His holiness with those in covenant relationship with Him. They too are separated from the world around them by being brought near to God (Ex 19:4–6; 33:16; Lev 11:44–45; I Kgs 8:53). Thus divine holiness is not exclusive, but God reaches out to attract others to His state and attitude of separation from the

material world which He created. Israel, therefore, is holy (Ex 19:6), and in the NT believers are called saints (Gr. *hagioi,* lit., "holy ones," Rom 1:7) and a "holy nation" (I Pet 2:9). *See* Saints.

Ceremonial objects are also classed as holy or sacred, set apart entirely for God's use. Thus the tabernacle was sanctified by God's shekinah glory (Ex 29:43-45; 40:34-35; Ps 93:5), especially the holy of holies (*q.v.*). The priests had holy garments (Ex 28:2). The spot where God appeared to Moses in the burning bush was holy ground (Ex 3:5). Such holiness possessed no essentially moral quality. As an extreme example of the root meaning of the Heb. term, the Canaanitish temple prostitute was called a *qᵉdēshâ* (Deut 23:17, RSV) because she was separated for this religious ceremonial. Wars were "sanctified" (Joel 3:9, ASV marg.), declared holy or set apart to punish the enemies of God. *See* War.

Ceremonial holiness could become fearsome, for death might follow contact with God (Ex 33:20; Jud 6:22 f.; 13:22 f.; Isa 6:5). The men of Beth-shemesh, smitten for desecrating the ark by looking into it, cried out, "Who is able to stand before the Lord, this holy God?" (I Sam 6:20, RSV). When David was bringing the ark to Jerusalem, Uzzah was struck down on the spot for merely touching the ark to steady it (II Sam 6:6-7).

As a part of the holy covenant relationship with God, Moses prescribed purifying rites, preparatory to holy ceremonies (Ex 19:14; 29:4; Lev 12-15). Some of the ceremonies and laws included (1) the dedication of the firstborn (Ex 13:2, 12 f.; 22:29 ff.) and the offering of all firstling animals and firstfruits (Deut 26:1-11); (2) the distinction between clean and unclean food (Lev 11; Deut 14); (3) regulations concerning the holiness of the priests (Lev 21:1–22:16), the Levites (Num 8:5-26), and the sacred place of worship (Deut 12); and (4) the regulations regarding the appointed feasts and holy convocations (Lev 23; *see* Festivals). The Nazarite (*q.v.*), by his vow of total separation unto the Lord, epitomized a life of ceremonial holiness (Num 6).

Comparative religionists attribute many of the *qōdesh* passages of Scripture to the primitive concept of taboo: divinely potent objects to be left alone. Superstitions like these are unworthy of the OT, but this much appears true: holy items, permanently set apart for God, were called *ḥērem,* "devoted" things; and what the Canaanites had considered *qōdesh* or taboo, God commanded Israel upon capturing them to make them *ḥērem,* "devoted" either to destruction or, if valuable in the service of the Lord, to sacred uses (Josh 6:17-19). *See* Accursed; Devote; Devoted Thing.

3. *Moral purity.* Since such ceremonial association and covenant fellowship is with the God who is also righteous and sinless, holiness acquires the meaning of separation from sin (Isa 52:11; II Cor 6:17) and conformity to God's moral standards (Lev 20:7-8; Mt 5:48; I Pet 1:15-16). From the beginning God's will has opposed sin and has sought for righteousness in the human race (Gen 6:5-6). It is God's moral wholeness or purity that leads Him to separate Himself from evil (Hab 1:13).

God's holiness, therefore, is entire freedom from moral evil on the one hand and absolute moral perfection on the other. Its greatest revelation is in the sinless character and work of Jesus Christ (*see* arts. on Christ). By the holiness of God it is not implied that He is subject to some law or standard of moral excellence external to Himself, but that all moral law and perfection have their eternal and unchangeable basis in His own nature. In this sense the saints will sing without qualification, "For thou only art holy" (Rev 15:3-4).

The punishment of man's moral infractions stems ultimately from the fact of God's holiness (Ezk 38:16, 23, RSV; Amos 4:2). The greatest loss in such punishment is his separation from the divine favor and presence. In the call of Isaiah, the prophet's natural reaction to God's holiness (Isa 6:3) was to experience conviction about his own sin and the sense of being undone (v. 5, KJV), lost (RSV, NEB), cut off or ruined (Heb. *nidmêtî*). His submission, however, eventuated in his forgiveness and the imputation to him of moral holiness through atonement ("thine iniquity is taken away, and thy sin purged [Heb. *tᵉkuppār*]," v. 7).

The NT teaches that the believer is sanctified positionally before God, with the holiness of Christ imputed to him, at the time of his conversion, by virtue of his being presented "in Christ" (I Cor 1:2, 30). He is being sanctified experientially as he keeps reckoning upon his position in Christ, refusing to yield the members of his body to sin, and presenting himself to God (Rom 6:11-13). He must deliberately "follow peace with all men, and holiness, without which no man shall see the Lord" (Heb 12:14). He will be ultimately sanctified in the sense of full conformity to Christ in glorification (Rom 8:30-31). *See* Sanctification.

Holiness, therefore, is the characteristic mark of a believer in both the OT and the NT. He that would stand in the holy place to worship God must have clean hands and a pure heart and not have sworn to a lie (Ps 24:3-4). To dwell in God's holy mountain—in His presence—one must walk with integrity and do no wrong to his neighbor (Ps 15). God "chose us in Him [Christ] before the foundation of the world, that we should be holy and blameless before Him" (Eph 1:4, NASB). Our sanctification is God's direct and perfect will for us (I Thess 4:3).

Thus every activity of life becomes sacred, for the Christian as well as for Israel. For when a man's aim is that of conformity to the will of God, who executes moral righteousness for all, life cannot be divided between the secular and the sacred. Accordingly, Christ treated the commandments as one: "Thou shalt love the Lord thy God with all thy heart . . . and thy neighbor as thyself. . . . This do . . ." (Lk 10:27-28), and illustrated His teaching with the parable of the Good Samaritan. The all-compelling motivation which determines both our religious and our ethical conduct must be one of response to the grace of God, a motivation not of reward but of gratitude.

See Example; God; Holy Spirit; Sanctification.

Bibliography. R. A. Finlayson, *The Holiness of God,* London: Pickering & Inglis, 1955; "Holiness, Holy, Saints," NBD, pp. 529 ff. Edmond Jacob, *The Theology of the Old Testament,* trans. by A. W. Heathcote and P. J. Allcock, New York: Harper, 1958, pp. 86-93. J. Barton Payne, *The Theology of the Older Testament,* Grand Rapids: Zondervan, 1962. Kenneth F. W. Prior, *The Way of Holiness,* Chicago: Inter-Varsity, 1967. Otto Procksch and Karl G. Kuhn, "*Agios,* etc.," TDNT, I, 88-115. Paul S. Rees, "Holiness, Holy," BDT, pp. 269 f. Norman H. Snaith, *The Distinctive Ideas of the Old Testament,* Philadelphia: Westminster, 1946, pp. 21-50.

J. B. P.

HOLM TREE. *See* Plants.

HOLON (hō'lŏn)

1. A village in the hill country of Judah (Josh 15:51) assigned to the Levites (Josh 21:15). Also called Hilen (I Chr 6:58).

2. A Moabite town included in the judgment upon a group of cities enumerated by Jeremiah (Jer 48:21).

HOLY. *See* Holiness; Saint.

HOLY GHOST. *See* Holy Spirit.

HOLY OF HOLIES. *See* Tabernacle; Temple.

HOLY ONE OF ISRAEL. *See* God, Names and Titles of.

HOLY PLACE. *See* Tabernacle; Temple.

HOLY SPIRIT. In the NT the Holy Spirit clearly reveals Himself as a person and is Deity. He has the attributes of personality: intellect (Rom 8:27; I Cor 2:10-13), emotions (Eph 4:30), and will (I Cor 12:11). He performs the actions of personality: teaches (Jn 14:26), testifies (Jn 15:26), directs (Acts 8:29; 13:2), guides (Rom 8:14), warns (I Tim 4:1). He is Deity because He is the Spirit of God and of Christ (Rom 8:9) and proceeds eternally from the Father (Jn 15:26; Gal 4:6).

Scripture places the Holy Spirit on a par with the Father and the Son (II Cor 13:14; Mt 28:19; I Cor 12:4-6; I Pet 1:2). Accordingly, the works of God always involve all three persons of the Trinity (*q.v.*). It was the triune God who created the world and who reveals Himself in it and by His word to man. It was the triune God who redeemed His people from their sin. Even so, some of these works are specifically the concern of the Holy Spirit. The Holy Spirit brings about the consummation of the works of the triune God.

In Creation

The Spirit hovered over the face of the deep (Gen 1:2), and by His Spirit God garnished the heavens (Job 26:13). The Spirit gives life to men (Job 33:4). He provides them with excellent gifts, both natural abilities and spiritual or charismatic powers (Ex 31:2-3; I Cor 12:8-11). When men sin, He convicts and pleads with them to return unto God (Gen 6:3; Jn 16:8-9; Rom 2:4). It is especially through the Spirit that the triune God bears witness of Himself to men.

In Revelation and Inspiration

The divine Author of God's revelation to mankind is the Holy Spirit. The prophets and apostles, the human instruments, "spake from God, being moved by the Holy Spirit" (II Pet 1:21, ASV). It is clearly stated that OT prophets received the words of the Lord by His Spirit (Zech 7:12; Ezk 2:2; Neh 9:30). A comparison of Acts 28:25 with Isa 6:9-10 teaches that the Holy Spirit is the particular person of the Trinity who delivered God's revelation in words. The Spirit of God is the One who inspired the Scriptures, i.e., taught the very words (I Cor 2:12-13) so that they are accurate, infallible, and authoritative. Jesus promised to send the Holy Spirit to teach His apostles all things and bring to remembrance all that He had said to them (Jn 14:26). *See* Inspiration; Revelation.

In Redemption

It is, however, especially when the triune God comes to redeem His people that the Spirit is clearly evident in His work of consummation.

In the Old Testament. In the period of OT revelation the Spirit prepared the people of God to yearn for their redemption through the coming Messiah. He inspired Moses and the prophets to speak of the Coming One. He broke down the attitude of rebellion in the Israel of God when they refused to obey the word of promise (Isa 63:10-14; Mic 3:8). He taught David, the sweet singer of Israel (II Sam 31:1-2), and through him many others, to say: ". . . thy spirit is good; lead me into the land of uprightness" (Ps 143:10).

Jesus and the Spirit. In the period of NT revelation the Spirit was active before the beginning of the life of Jesus (Lk 1:13-15) to the end (I Pet 3:18). Jesus was conceived by the Holy Spirit (Lk 1:35). The Spirit descended upon Christ at the time of His baptism (Mt 3:16). Then, being "full of the Holy Ghost" Jesus "was led by the Spirit into the wilderness" (Lk 4:1). The Spirit empowered and qualified the Messiah for His official task of destroying the kingdom of Satan and of establishing the kingdom of God.

Soon after His declaration of war against Satan, the Saviour "returned in the power of the Spirit into Galilee" (Lk 4:14) to preach the gospel of the kingdom. He read in the synagogue from the scroll of Isaiah about the coming Messiah: "The Spirit of the Lord is upon me. . . " (Lk 4:18) and said: "This day is this scripture fulfilled in your ears" (Lk 4:21). He told Nicodemus that "except a man be born of water and of the Spirit, he cannot enter into the kingdom of God" (Jn 3:5). By the Spirit He cast out demons (Mt 12:28, RSV). Then when the Pharisees ascribed this cleansing work of the Spirit to Beelzebub, Jesus warned them not to sin against the Spirit lest they become like Satan and their sin could not be forgiven (Mt 12:31-32). *See* Holy Spirit, Sin Against the.

Jesus promised His disciples to pray to the Father that He would give them "another Comforter," "the Spirit of truth" (Jn 14:16-17). By that Spirit the apostles would be enabled to perform their special task as teachers of the church (Jn 14:26). When Jesus would return to glory, then the Spirit would enable the apostles to set forth the full significance of all that He had come to do for His people (Jn 16:13).

Sustained by the Spirit, Jesus had set His face steadfastly to go to Jerusalem. As at the beginning, so at the end, Jesus resisted Satan's ever-present temptation to save His people and establish His kingdom by means other than that of dying in their place for their sins. He knew the prophetic word: "But he was wounded for our transgressions, he was bruised for our iniquities: the chastisement of our peace was upon him; and with his stripes we are healed" (Isa 53:5). He knew that "this day" this Scripture must be fulfilled in Him. Thus was our Saviour sustained by the Spirit in all of His redeeming work (Heb 9:14). Through the Spirit He could say: "It is finished" and could commend His spirit unto the Father.

Pentecost. It was finished indeed. Jesus died but rose again from the dead. He ascended to heaven. Now He is glorified. In accordance with His promise He sent forth His Spirit (Acts 2:3-4). *See* Pentecost.

Peter "wept bitterly" after his denial of Jesus. But from Pentecost on, filled with the Holy Ghost as the Comforter, utter victory came into his heart. Now "filled with the Holy Ghost" as the "Spirit of truth," he saw the vision of "things to come." Filled with the Holy Ghost, he boldly proclaimed that Jesus was not in the final analysis delivered unto death by the people, by the Pharisees, by Pilate, or even by Satan. It was "by the determinate counsel and foreknowledge of God" that all was done (Acts 2:23). What the "wicked hands" of men had done was now defeated. It was impossible that He should be held by the pangs of death (2:24). David the prophet had said that his soul should not be left in hell and that his flesh should not see corruption (Ps 16:10), and the Spirit taught Peter to interpret this individual as the risen Christ (Acts 2:25-36).

In the church. At Pentecost the church became the universal church. Before leaving for heaven, Jesus said to the Twelve: "But ye shall receive power, after that the Holy Ghost is come upon you: and ye shall be witnesses unto me both in Jerusalem, and in all Judea, and in Samaria, and unto the uttermost part of the earth" (Acts 1:8).

With the coming of Pentecost, the church entered upon "the last days" (Acts 2:17). Slaves ("servants") as well as free, and women ("handmaidens") as well as men, would now "prophesy" (Acts 2:18). Jews from Crete and Arabia heard in their native languages "the wonderful works of God" (Acts 2:11). *See* Tongues, Gift of. When Peter, who spoke at the occasion of Pentecost, explained how the Gentile Cornelius had turned to Christ in an absolutely convincing way, he said, "The Holy Ghost fell on them, as on us at the beginning" (Acts 11:15). The middle wall of partition between Jew and Gentile was now finally removed (Eph 2:14), and the unity of the Spirit was not only possible but should be preserved (Eph 4:3-6).

Henceforth, the "Lord *is* the Spirit" (II Cor 3:17) in the fullness of His redemption for His own. With "open face" believers now constantly behold "the glory of the Lord," the glory of Him who died for their sins and rose again for their justification. In so doing they are "changed into the same image from glory to glory, even as by the Spirit of the Lord" (II Cor 3:18). The "Spirit of life in Christ Jesus" has made them "free from the law of sin and death" (Rom 8:2). In all the days ahead they will know that they have "not received the spirit of bondage again unto fear" but "the Spirit of adoption," whereby they cry, "Abba, Father" (Rom 8:15). In the present age the Holy Spirit indwells believers (I Cor 3:16; 6:19); seals them (II Cor 1:22; Eph 1:13; 4:30); teaches them (Jn 16:12-15); guides them (Rom 8:14); helps them as they pray (Rom 8:26); and seeks to fill them (Eph 5:18).

In the world. Jesus told His disciples: "But you shall receive power when the Holy Spirit has come upon you; and you shall be my witnesses" (Acts 1:8, RSV). And through them He told all His followers the same. How will the world receive them and their witness to them? Jesus told them what their reception would be: "If they have called the master of the house Beelzebub, how much more shall they call them of his household?" (Mt 10:25). "The carnal mind is enmity against God: for it is not subject to the law of God, neither indeed can be" (Rom 8:7; cf. I Cor 2:14; Eph 2:1). But the Holy Spirit was sent to convict the world of sin and righteousness and judgment (Jn 16:7-11).

In spite of persecution nothing can stop the people of God as they "preach the unsearchable riches of Christ" (Eph 3:8). With the early Christians they can pray and be filled with the Holy Spirit and speak the word of God with boldness (Acts 4:31). With Peter they can say to the council, "We are witnesses to these things, and so is the Holy Spirit whom God has given to those who obey him" (Acts 5:32, RSV). With Paul they can exclaim, in the face of all opposition, inspired as it is by Satan: "Now thanks be unto God, which always causeth us to triumph in Christ, and maketh manifest the savour of his knowledge by us in every place" (II Cor 2:14). They know that the Gentiles walk "in the vanity of their mind, having the understanding darkened" (Eph 4:17-18). But by the renewing power of the Holy Spirit (Tit 3:5) human minds are liberated and renewed in their attitudes (Eph 4:23; Rom 12:2). Therefore the work of the Holy Spirit in evangelism is essential for men to be able to hear and receive the gospel.

Finally, the Holy Spirit, the Spirit who rested upon Christ without measure (Jn 1:32-33; 3:34) and made Him to be the faithful witness of God, will sustain those who are the last to make the good confession before men. The "seven Spirits" of God (a Semitic expression for the Spirit in seven aspects, cf. Isa 11:2) are before the throne of Christ, the Victorious One (Rev 1:4). He "who hath sealed us, and given the earnest of the Spirit in our hearts" (II Cor 1:22; cf. Eph 1:14) will seal the final witnesses of His grace when they are confronted with the climactic hatred of Satan as he inspires the Beast. Thus the Holy Spirit will witness to the world through those who are purchased unto God by the blood of the Lamb. When all is finished, the victory over Satan won, then "the Spirit and the bride say, Come" (Rev 22:17).

See Gifts, Spiritual; Holy Spirit, Filling of the; Holy Spirit, Sin Against the; Paraclete; Pentecost; Spirit; Theism; Tongues, Gift of.

Bibliography. Geoffrey W. Bromiley, "The Holy Spirit," *Fundamentals of the Faith,* ed. by Carl F. H. Henry, Grand Rapids: Zondervan, 1969, pp. 143-165. Frederick D. Bruner, *A Theology of the Holy Spirit,* Grand Rapids: Eerdmans, 1970. Lewis Sperry Chafer, *He That Is Spiritual,* Chicago: Moody Press, 1943. James E. Cumming, *Through the Eternal Spirit,* London: Partridge & Co., 1891; Minneapolis: Bethany Fellowship, reprint, 1965. Hermann Kleinknecht, *et al., "Pneuma,* etc.," TDNT, VI, 332-455. Abraham Kuyper, *The Work of the Holy Spirit,* New York: Funk & Wagnalls, 1900; Grand Rapids: Eerdmans, reprint. John Owen, *A Discourse Concerning the Holy Spirit,* London: 1674; Grand Rapids: Kregel, reprint, 1954. Rene Pache, *The Person and Work of the Holy Spirit,* Chicago: Moody Press, 1954. Charles C. Ryrie, *The Holy Spirit,* Chicago: Moody Press, 1965. John F. Walvoord, *The Holy Spirit,* Grand Rapids: Dunham, 1958; Zondervan, reprint.

C. V. T.

HOLY SPIRIT, FILLING OF THE. The Scriptures teach there is one Father, one Son, and one Holy Spirit (I Cor 12:4-6; Eph 4:4-6), and that all Christians are baptized in the Spirit into or in relationship to the Body of Christ (I Cor 12:13). Further, the Holy Spirit distributes particular spiritual gifts to each as He wills (I Cor 12:4-11). At the same time the Bible speaks of the filling of the Holy Spirit which occurs over and over again. Thus, though there is only one baptism in the Holy Spirit (Eph 4:5), there are many fillings (Eph 5:18).

The peerless example of the baptism in the Holy Spirit occurred at Pentecost in fulfillment of Christ's promise to clothe His disciples with supernatural power (Lk 24:49; Acts 1:4-5, 8; 2:1-12). Similar examples of the baptism in the Holy Spirit occurred at Samaria (Acts 8:14-17), for Saul of Tarsus when Ananias laid his hands upon him (Acts 9:17), in Cornelius' home (Acts 10:44-45), and at Ephesus to the disciples of John the Baptist (Acts 19:6). Following these initial baptisms in the Spirit there were many fillings (e.g., Acts 4:8, 31; 13:9, 52). *See* Baptism in the Spirit.

Several questions arise in regard to the filling of the Holy Spirit.

1. Did the OT believers experience this blessing? To this the answer is yes. To the extent David (II Sam 23:2) and others were inspired in their writing of the OT, they were filled "as they were moved [lit., carried along] by the Holy Ghost" (II Pet 1:21). Such was the testimony of the prophet Micah: "But as for me, I am filled with power, with the Spirit of the Lord . . . to declare . . . to Israel his sin" (Mic 3:8, RSV).

Joseph (Gen 41:38), Joshua (Num 27:18; Deut 34:9), Bezaleel (Ex 31:3), and Daniel (Dan 4:8, 18; 5:11, 14; 6:3) were recognized as being filled with the Spirit of God by their respective abilities to perform specific tasks. The Spirit of the Lord came upon other men at certain occasions to empower them to deliver God's people (e.g., Othniel, Jud 3:10; Gideon, Jud 6:34; Samson, Jud 14:6, 19; 15:14; Saul, I Sam 11:6) or to prophesy (Num 11:25, 29; I Sam 10:6, 10; II Chr 15:1; 20:14; cf. Lk 1:41, 67). In the Mosaic dispensation, however, charismatically endowed men were the exception; whereas as a result of Pentecost the Spirit has been poured out upon "all flesh," universally upon all believers regardless of race, sex, age, or social status.

2. How can the Holy Spirit dwell in the Christian and fill him when the NT teaches that the believer still has flesh or a fallen nature (Gal 5:17)? The fallen nature in the Christian is a judged thing and stands condemned, because "God sending his own Son in the likeness of sinful flesh, and for sin, condemned sin in the

flesh: that [in order that] the righteousness of the law might be fulfilled in us, who walk not after the flesh, but after the Spirit" (Rom 8:3-4). The blessed Holy Spirit can dwell beside the fallen nature because it is reckoned as crucified or dead, and thus already it stands judged and its days are numbered (Rom 6:6; Gal 2:20; 5:24).

3. If the Holy Spirit is in us, then how does the filling occur? On man's part it depends upon his opening up and surrendering every area of his life, every room in his earthly mansion to the Spirit's presence and control (Acts 5:32; Rom 12:1-2; cf. Rom 6:11-13). He must initially receive the Holy Spirit by a conscious act of faith (Gal 3:2, 5, 14). Some Bible expositors consider this reception to be God's seal or stamp of divine ownership upon the believer (Eph 1:13), even as the Father set His seal upon His Son when the Holy Spirit descended upon Him as a dove (Jn 1:30-34; 6:27). On God's part, it depends upon the Holy Spirit's occupying, enabling, and guiding in all spheres of the believer's life.

4. Is the filling then an option or a matter of indifference? No, because it is a command of the Scriptures that the believer be continuously filled with the Holy Spirit (Eph 5:18), and that he walk by the Spirit (Gal 5:16-25; Rom 8:5-13). At the same time he is warned not to grieve the Spirit (Eph 4:30) or to quench Him (I Thess 5:19).

Results of being filled with the Spirit are many and wonderful. Spirit-filled Christians were men of "good reputation" and filled with wisdom, faith, grace, and power (Acts 6:3, 5, 8, NASB). They are enabled to speak to and thus share with one another on a spiritual level, to sing joyfully praises to the Lord, to thank God for *all* things, and to submit to one another out of reverence to Christ (Eph 5:19-21). They bear the fruit of the Spirit (Gal 5:22-23) and display the manifestations of the Spirit in charismatic knowledge, wisdom, and power (Rom 12:6-8; I Cor 12:7-11; I Pet 4:10-11).

For the view that there is only one filling with the Holy Spirit without need of subsequent refillings, see Howard M. Ervin, *These Are Not Drunken As Ye Suppose* (Plainfield, N.J.: Logos, 1968).

R. A. K. and J. R.

HOLY SPIRIT, SIN AGAINST. The committing of the sin of blasphemy against the Holy Spirit, or the unpardonable sin, grew out of Christ's healing a man who was blind, deaf, and dumb because of demon possession (Mt 12:24-32; Mk 3:22-30; Lk 11:15-20; 12:10). The Pharisees accused Jesus of being in league with Satan and sought to prove it by asserting that Satan was obliging Jesus by withdrawing demons from people. The Lord's answer was twofold: such a divided kingdom could not stand; and how then did the Pharisees explain the success of their own Jewish exorcists? Then Christ declared that such an accusation as the Pharisees had leveled was an unpardonable sin against the Holy Spirit.

The sin is particularly directed against the Spirit. A similar sin against Christ the Son of Man was forgivable. The reason for this is simply that while the Pharisees might have misunderstood the claims and work of Jesus as Messiah they should have known from their OT Scriptures that the Holy Spirit was powerful enough to cast out demons. Therefore, the sin is a sin against knowledge, or a sin "with a high hand" (lit., "presumptuous," KJV) in contrast to a sin of ignorance (Num 15:30). Such a sin was unforgivable in the OT, for offerings could be brought only for sins of ignorance (Num 15:22-31).

However, in order to commit this unpardonable sin, a special situation is required. It is not simply swearing in the Spirit's name, but it is the charge that the works of Christ originate from Satan, and Christ is therefore Satan's agent. But Jesus was anointed with the Spirit at the river Jordan as God's chosen Servant, and ministered publicly in the power of the Spirit (Lk 4:1, 14). The committing of this sin presupposes the personal presence of Christ in manifestation of divine power. The incident by no means teaches that some sins can be forgiven in the age to come; rather, it emphatically teaches that eternal destiny is determined here and now.

It may be that this specific sin against the Holy Spirit cannot be committed today since the Lord is not personally present on the earth. However, one should beware of attributing the miraculous gifts of the Spirit (I Cor 12:4-11, 28) to demonic or Satanic operations; and the rejection of Christ is of course an unpardonable sin anytime (Jn 3:18). I Jn 5:16 is not speaking of an unpardonable sin, because the reference is to physical death, not spiritual death. *See* Sin unto Death.

C. C. R.

HOLYDAY. Translated "holyday" in the NT only in Col 2:16 (KJV). It was actually a festival or feast day though used for a reverent, holy purpose. In all other cases in the NT it is translated as feast day or festival (e.g., Lk 2:42; Jn 5:1; 7:2; etc.). In the OT, on the other hand, the sabbath is spoken of as a holy day in Ex 35:2, in the sense of being a sacred day.

HOMAM (hō'măm). Variant name for Hemam (*q.v.*), used in I Chr 1:39.

HOME. *See* Family; Household.

HOMEBORN. *See* Service.

HOMER. *See* Weights, Measures,and Coins.

HONESTY. Three words are translated "honest" in KJV.

1. Gr. *kalos,* that which is excellent and in this sense good. We are to provide all things honest in the sight of men (Rom 12:17), and of God and men (II Cor 8:21), and see that our conduct ("conversation," KJV) is excellent before the unsaved (I Pet 2:12).

2. Gr. *semnos,* "venerable or time-proved," "reverent." Paul urges the Christian to fill his mind with what is pure and has the reverence of age ("honest," Phil 4:8), and to live a peaceable life "in all godliness and honesty" ("godly and respectful in every way," I Tim 2:2, RSV).

3. Gr. *euschēmonōs,* "decent," "becoming." The Christian is always to act becomingly, even as he would in clear daylight (Rom 13:13), and what he does is to be decent and becoming in the sight of the unsaved (I Thess 4:12).

HONEY. *See* Food.

HONOR. Honor is the high respect or esteem shown to or received from another person, or a demonstration of such respect. The concept is expressed figuratively in the OT by words which are also translated beauty, majesty, brilliancy, preciousness, weight, and glory. The parallels are significant: glory and honor (I Chr 16:27; Ps 8:5); honor and majesty (Ps 21:5; 96:6; 104:1); honor and dignity (Est 6:3); gifts and rewards and great honor (Dan 2:6); riches and honor (I Kgs 3:13). Thus the concept is involved in worship (*q.v.*), which is *worth-ship,* recognition of worth.

God Himself deserves all honor; recognition of what He is, and ascription of praise is His due. God may also cause men to be recognized by others: "God hath given riches, wealth, and honor" (Eccl 6:2). He has commanded respect to be shown to parents (Ex 20:12) and to the elderly (Lev 19:32). A virtuous wife deserves the esteem of her husband (Prov 31:25; 11:16; I Pet 3:7). Those who honor God will in turn be honored (I Sam 2:30). The man who pursues righteousness and covenant loyalty will find honor (Prov 21:21).

A suggestion of the Lord's reason for redemptively restoring honor to men is given in Ps 8:5: God made man little less than divine. The Representative Man, Jesus, crowned with glory and honor because of His suffering of death, brings redemption and ultimate glory for His redeemed (see Heb 2:5–10). Honor as a by-product of wisdom and godliness is associated with life in a sense which could find fulfillment only in a blessed immortality (Prov 3:16; 8:18; 21:21; 22:4; cf. Rom 2:7, 10).

In the Gr. NT, words meaning weight and glory are translated honor. Ethical values are in view. Honor majestically describes that approbation and mutual esteem between Father and Son (II Pet 1:17; Heb 2:9; Jn 8:49, 54). Honor in redemptive glory is bestowed on men by God (Rom 2:10; I Pet 1:7; Jn 12:26). Men and angels give glory and honor to God (I Tim 1:17; Rev 4:9; 19:1) and to Christ (Jn 5:23; Rev 5:12 f.). Men should seek the honor or approval that comes from God instead of the approval of men (Jn 12:43). Nevertheless, we are not to deny the honor that is due others (Rom 12:10): to parents (Mt 15:4), to widows (I Tim 5:3), to masters (I Tim 6:1), and to the king (I Pet 2:17). Marriage, also, is to be held in honor by all (Heb 13:4).

W. B. W.

HOOD. The Heb. term *ṣānîp* appears in the KJV as "hoods" (Isa 3:23), and "mitre" (Zech 3:5). The RSV renders the term "turban" in both instances, which is correct as the term means "something wrapped around." *See* Dress.

HOOF. The horny casing of horses' feet (Isa 5:28; Jer 47:3), or other animals (Lev 11:3–7, 26). It is used figuratively to mean "power" or "strength" (Mic 4:13).

HOOK

1. Heb. *wāw,* a hook or ring as the head of a spike driven into wood. These were the gold (Ex 26:32; 36:36) or silver (Ex 27:10; 38:10) fasteners which held the tabernacle curtains and screens in place.

2. Heb. *ḥāḥ,* a hook or ring, such as is placed in the nose of a bull to lead it about (II Kgs 19:28) or in its jaw (Ezk 29:4; 38:4). It was a symbol of divine judgment upon Sennacherib, Pharaoh, and Gog, and upon Judah's princes (Ezk 19:4, 9, RSV). Assyrian sculpture depicts royal captives with ring in lip and attached ropes held by the Assyrian monarch (ANEP # 447), even as happened to King Manasseh of Judah (II Chr 33:11, RSV).

3. Heb. *ḥakkâ,* a hook used in fishing (Isa 19:8; Hab 1:15, RSV), mentioned in the attempts to catch leviathan (Job 41:1).

4. Heb. *ṣinnâ,* a thorn or hook, in parallel with *sîr dûgâ,* "fishhooks," a metaphor for dragging Israel captive (Amos 4:2), according to the practice described in 2.

5. Heb. *sh^ephattayim,* double or forked pegs, upon which the carcasses of beasts were hung for skinning (Ezk 40:43). The word is of doubtful meaning, however; the versions suggest edges or rims, as seen on a dressed stone sacrificial table for Apis bulls at Memphis, Egypt.

6. Gr. *agkistron,* a hook for fishing (Mt 17:27).

See also Fishhook; Flesh Hook; Pruning Hook.

H. E. Fi.

HOOPOE. *See* Animals, III.22.

HOPE. In the OT several Heb. words are translated "hope" which signify "trust," "expectation," or "prospect." In both OT and NT the object of one's hope varies according to human desires (Prov 13:12; e.g., gain, Acts 16:19; physical rescue, Acts 27:20; a husband, Ruth 1:12).

The chief theological use of the term "hope" was of trust in the supernatural, specifically in

Yahweh as the God of Israel (e.g., Ps 130:5; 146:5; Jer 17:7, 13). This trust was sometimes for safety from enemies (Ps 71:4–5; Jer 14:8–9), tending in later usage toward deliverance in the future day of the Lord (Zech 9:12). Chiefly, however, the hope of the godly Israelites was an expectation of and reliance on God's blessing and provision in the present life (Ezr 10:2; Job 11:18, 20; 14:7, 19; Ps 33:18–19, 22; 119:49–50; Lam 3:22–24).

In the NT the believer's hope is Christ (I Tim 1:1). It resides in God (Rom 15:13; I Pet 1:21), who has elected a people (Phil 1:20; Eph 1:18) and given them hope through the gospel (Col 1:23). Properly this is not merely human anticipation of better days (even salvation in one sense is "hoped for," not yet realized, Rom 8:24; 13:11), but of the final consummation of salvation in the resurrection (Acts 23:6; Rom 8:18–25) and at the revelation of Jesus (I Pet 1:13). Christ's indwelling through the Spirit becomes the Christian's "hope of glory" (Col 1:27; cf. I Jn 3:1–3). This hope is variously described: it is "laid up in heaven" (Col 1:5); it is a hope of eternal life (Tit 1:2); it is living (I Pet 1:3); and it is better than former hopes (Heb 7:19).

In the NT hope is associated with affliction and patience. Affliction is sure to come upon the faithful; it produces patience (Rom 5:3–5), and patience, hope. Such hope is an anchor for the soul (Heb 6:18 ff.). Hope in such contexts becomes virtually synonymous with trust in God, a certainty lying beyond earthly doubt (cf. Rom 5:5 with 9:33). In view of their hope Christians are to be pure (I Jn 3:3) and be ready to give their "defense" (reason) for their hope (I Pet 3:15). While living sober, upright, godly lives they are to await the fulfillment of their blessed hope, the glorious appearing of their great God and Saviour Jesus Christ (Tit 2:12–13).

Bibliography. R. Bultmann and Karl H. Rengstorf, "*Elpis*, etc.," TDNT, II, 517–535.

J. W. R.

HOPHNI (hŏf′nī). A son of the high priest Eli. The wickedness of Hophni and his brother Phinehas caused a curse to come on the house of Eli (I Sam 2:34). This curse was fulfilled at the battle of Aphek (I Sam 4:11).

HOPHRA. *See* Pharaoh-Hophra.

HOR, MOUNT (hôr). Num 20:22–29 and 33:38–39 record the death and burial of Aaron at "Hōr hā-hār" (lit., Hor the mountain), but the actual site is quite uncertain. The account in Num 20 might suggest that it lay somewhere on the E side of the Wadi 'Arabah, especially if we are right in identifying the place where Moses made the brazen serpent with the copper mining center of Punon, the modern Feinān (Num 21:6–9; cf. Num 33:42–43).

Deut 10:6, however, places the death of Aaron at Moserah, which must be the same place as Moseroth of Num 33:30. This place is equally unknown, but it was apparently somewhere in the Sinai Desert not far from Kadesh-barnea, which is usually identified with 'Ain Qadeis, close to the 1948–1967 Israeli-Egyptian boundary line. Both Mount Hor and Kadesh-barnea were thought of as being "on the border of Edom" (Num 20:14–21, 23). It seems reasonable, therefore, to look for Mount Hor in the vicinity of Kadesh-barnea. Jebel el-Hamrah has been suggested as a possible site, largely because one of the valleys running near this mountain is called Wādi Hārūniyeh, but it must be admitted that this is very fragile evidence. We are therefore driven to say that we do not know for certain where Aaron was buried.

The problem is further complicated by the difficulty that "Mount Hor" may not be a proper name at all, for *hōr* appears to be a variant of *har* (mountain), and the name may mean merely "mountain of mountains" or "the high mountain." This has some support from the fact that the same name, Hōr hā-hār, is given to a conspicuous mountain on the N frontier of ancient Israel, possibly Mount Hermon (Num 34:7). In any case the traditional identification, which goes back at least to Josephus, of Mount Hor with the towering sandstone mass of Jebel Hārūn at Petra, must with great regret be abandoned. It is too close to Sela, the ancient center of Edomite territory, into which according to the biblical account, the Hebrews were unable to penetrate during their Exodus wanderings.

D.B.

[Ed. note: Yohanan Aharoni, as a result of his explorations in the Sinai during the brief 1956–57 Israeli occupation of that region, has argued strongly for a "sacred mountain" noted first by Nelson Glueck. It is called 'Imaret el-Khureisheh, a flat-topped hill 25 acres in extent, walled about to enclose burials from the various periods of Negeb occupation. It overlooks an important road junction *c.* eight miles N of Kadesh-barnea ("Kadesh-barnea and Mount Sinai," Beno Rothenberg, *God's Wilderness,* London: Thames & Hudson, 1961, pp. 139–141.]

HORAM (hôr′ăm). The king of Gezer (*q.v.*) whom Joshua defeated and killed (Josh 10:33).

HOREB (hôr′ĕb). The name of the mountain at which Moses received the first theophany (Ex 3:1). Here also the covenant was made and the law given (Deut 5:2). The name Horeb is used synonymously with Sinai (*q.v.*). Traditionally the mountain is thought to be in the SW of the Sinai peninsula, but some modern scholars believe the site is in the S of Edom.

HOREM (hôr′ĕm). A fortified city in Naphtali (Josh 19:38). Its exact site is unknown.

HOR-HAGIDGAD (hôr'há-gĭd'găd). A campground during the Israelites' 38 years of wandering through the wilderness after their defeat at Hormah (Num 33:32-33). It is called Gudgodah (*q.v.*) in Deut 10:7. Its location is in the southern Negeb or the Sinai peninsula, but the exact site is unknown.

HORI (hôr'ī)
1. A Horite (*q.v.*), son of Lotan (Gen 36:22; I Chr 1:39).
2. The father of Shaphat, the Simeonite spy sent to Canaan by Moses (Num 13:5).

HORIM. *See* Horite.

HORITES (hôr'īts), **HURRIANS** (hōōr'ĭ-ánz)
1. The Horites (Heb. *ḥōrî*) were the inhabitants of Mount Seir (Gen 14:6) before the Edomites dispossessed them (Deut 2:12, 22). They were said to be descendants of Seir the Horite (Gen 36:20) and were governed by chieftains or clan leaders (36:21, 29-30). In one passage (Gen 36:2) the MT reading "Hivite" ("Zibeon the Hivite") seems to be a textual error for "Horite" (cf. 36:20, where Zibeon is listed as a son of Seir the Horite). The Heb. term as applied to these people is Semitic in origin, and probably means "cave dwellers" (*ḥōrîm,* cf. "holes," I Sam 14:11; Isa 42:22; Nah 2:12; "caves," Job 30:6). *See* Hivites; Hori.

According to E. A. Speiser, these Horites cannot be identified with the Hurrians because, (*a*) their personal names (Gen 36:20-30) do not conform to Hurrian patterns, but are instead Semitic (although some scholars believe Dishon and Dishan, *q.v.,* Gen 36:21, are Hurrian names); and (*b*) there is no archaeological evidence for Hurrian settlements in the Negeb (Seir) or in Transjordan ("Horite," IDB, II, 645). Such a distinction seems valid also from the standpoint of chronology, if the events of Gen 14 are to be dated *c.* 2000 B.C., too early for the known spread of Hurrians to Palestine in large numbers.

2. The LXX reads "Horites" *(Gr. chorraios)* for MT "Hivites" in Gen 34:2 and Josh 9:7. Both of these passages deal with inhabitants of central Palestine, as distinct from the Horites (see 1) of Mount Seir. Speiser pointed out in the same article that, conversely, the LXX reads *euaioi,* "Hivites," in Isa 17:9 (RSV), where the MT has *haḥōresh,* which he considers to be an evident corruption of *haḥōrî,* "the Horites."

Thus there seems to be confusion in the various texts of the OT over the matter of the Horites. These Horites in Canaan (at Shechem and Gibeon) may well be connected with the extrabiblical Hurrians, although in local usage they were commonly designated as Hivites (*q.v.*). Thus the dual use of the term "Horite" may be explained by a coincidental similarity in sound between the name of the Horites who were Semitic cave dwellers and a non-Semitic people pushing in from Mesopotamia via Syria, who are known from ancient texts as the *Ḫurru* (Akkadian), *Ḫry* (Ugaritic), and *Ḫ3rw* (Egyptian). Speiser also explored the possibility of the "children of Heth" (Gen 10:15; 23:3-19) and sometimes "Hittite" (Ezk 16:3, 45) being another biblical term for the Hurrians (E. A. Speiser, *Genesis: The Anchor Bible,* Garden City, N.Y.: Doubleday, 1964, pp. 69, 172 f.).

Various cuneiform tablets from dozens of sites reveal that the Hurrians must have lived in the Armenian or Kurdish mountains in the 3rd mil. B.C., but began to infiltrate the Tigris-Euphrates valley before 2000 B.C. By the 19th cen. B.C. Hurrian names are found in considerable numbers as far W as Alalakh near Antioch-of-Syria, at Chagar Bazar in the Habur valley (E of Haran), at Mari on the Euphrates, and as far E as Dilbat near Babylon. In Asia Minor tablets found at Boghazköy reveal that even before the 18th cen. B.C. Hurrian religious texts were translated into Hittite. It would not be anachronistic, therefore, for Jacob to have met a Hurrian family at Shechem in his day (Gen 34).

It is certain that the Hurrians shared a similar way of life with the patriarchs, who spent many years in the ancestral home region of Haran (*q.v.*). The center of the later Hurrian state, the kingdom of Mitanni, was near Haran in the middle Euphrates valley, an area which was then called Subaru.

A study of tablets found at Nuzu (Yorgan Tepe, *c.* 12 miles SW of Kirkuk in Iraq) reveals the legal customs of the Hurrians during the mid-2nd mil. B.C. Many of the unusual actions of Abraham and Jacob with regard to marriage and children can now be understood as being part of the prevailing social culture and laws that Hurrians and Babylonians alike followed for centuries in the Middle East. *See* Abraham; Archaeology; Jacob; Nuzu; Patriarchal Age.

Under Mitannian leadership the Hurrians rose to a prominent position elsewhere in Syria (as known by tablets found at Alalakh and Ugarit, and Amarna tablets sent from Qatna and Tunip), Hittite territory (Boghazköy tablets), and E Assyria (Nuzu tablets) from *c.* 1550 to *c.* 1150 B.C.

The pressure of the Hurrians on Syria and Palestine probably accounts for the Hyksos invasion of Egypt in the 18th cen. B.C. The first of these invaders were evidently Semites, who perhaps had been pushed out of their own lands. The later waves were Hurrians (*q.v.*), according to a study of the names of the Hyksos kings. Even after the Egyptians expelled the Hyksos from Egypt *c.* 1550 B.C., a strong Hurrian element remained in Canaan, which the Egyptians sometimes called *Ḫuru.* Amenhotep II (1450-1425 B.C.) claims to have brought back 36,300 Kharu or Huru as captives from a military campaign in Palestine (ANET, p. 247).

Hurrian names are found in cuneiform tablets excavated at Taanach and Shechem, dated *c.* 1400 B.C., and in the Amarna letters (*q.v.*), such as 'Abdu-Heba of Jerusalem (ANET, pp. 487 ff.). The long letter from Tushratta, king of Mitanni, to Pharaoh Akhenaton was composed entirely in classical Hurrian. The name of the Jebusite king Araunah (*q.v.*) of Jerusalem (II Sam 24:16) can be explained as a form of Hurrian *ewri-ni,* meaning "the lord." The earliest Hurrian name in the Bible may well be Arioch (*Arī-aku* or *Ari-ukku*) in Gen 14:1. The OT documents are correct, therefore, in alluding to the prevalence of Hurrians in Palestine during the 2nd mil. B.C.

Bibliography. I. J. Gelb, *Hurrians and Subarians,* Chicago: Univ. of Chicago Press, 1944. Cyrus H. Gordon, "Biblical Customs and Nuzi Tablets," BA, III (1940), 1-12. Roy Hayden, "Hurrians," BW, pp. 294-298.

J. R.

HORMAH (hôr'mȧ). A city near Ziklag. The tribes of Israel were defeated there when they tried to move into the Promised Land after the death of the ten spies sent out by Moses (Num 14:45; Deut 1:44). The city was taken later by the Israelites (Num 21:3; Josh 12:14); this feat is also attributed to Judah and Simeon (Jud 1:17). The name Hormah, "destruction," is said to come from the fall of the city formerly known as Zephath (Jud 1:17). The city is identified as being in the Negeb and belonging to Judah (Josh 15:30). David divided the spoil of the Amalekites with the city (I Sam 30:30).

HORN. Horns are mentioned in the Bible as having various uses.

1. Trumpets. A ram's horn (*qeren*) perforated at the tip was early used to sound a battle call (Josh 6:5). Similar was the *shôpār,* originally the curved horn of a wild sheep or goat, perhaps later a metal instrument in the shape of a horn which gave a loud, far-reaching note, but always translated "trumpet" (*see* Musical Instruments: Trumpet). It was used to sound an alarm (Jer 4:5, 19; 6:1, 17; Ezk 33:3-6; Joel 2:1; Amos 3:6; Zeph 1:16), to muster troops for war (Jud 3:27; 6:34; I Sam 13:3; Neh 4:18, 20; Zech 9:14) or for return from battle (II Sam 2:28; 18:16; 20:1, 22), to signal for attack (Jud 7:16-22), and to announce the beginning of religious ceremonies (Ex 19:16, 19; 20:18; Lev 25:9; Ps 81:3; Joel 2:15) or the crowning of a king (II Sam 15:10; I Kgs 1:34, 39; II Kgs 9:13). *See* Music.

Heb. *yôbēl,* "ram's horn" (Josh 6:4, 6, 8, 13), loaned its name to the year of jubilee (*q.v.*; Lev 25:8-54; 27:17-24) because the fiftieth year was opened by the blowing of the ram's horn. It is first mentioned, in Ex 19:13, as the "trumpet" blown loud and long at Mount Sinai. The *yôbēl* seems to have a religio-ceremonial significance, announcing the arrival of Yahweh as King, whether to His people to complete His covenant or proclaim release and liberty, or to His enemies to judge and smite them.

2. Containers. Being hollow and easily polished, horns have been used in ancient and modern times for drinking vessels and as flasks to hold oil or cosmetics. Ezk 27:15 describes horns inlaid with ivory and/or ebony; as such they were a much prized possession and symbol of wealth. The name of Job's third daughter reflects this usage, for Keren-happuch (Job 42:14) means "a horn of eye-paint" (jar of mascara or black antimony). The prophets used horns of this type to carry oil for anointing of kings, etc. (I Sam 16:1, 13; I Kgs 1:39).

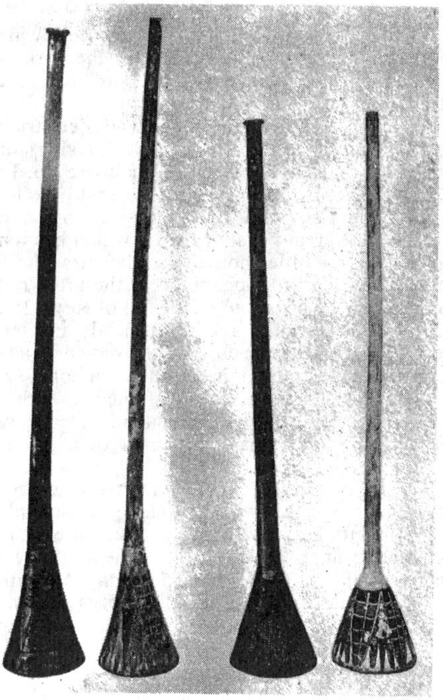

Military trumpets of copper and silver ornamented with gold. The lowest clear notes are C and D. From tomb of Tutankhamon. LL

3. Horns of the altar. Altars made of stone (the wood and brass altars disintegrated) have been found by archaeologists. The "horn" (*qeren*) on the altar (Ex 38:2) was a hornlike protrusion on each corner. In the sacrificial rites the priest put some of the blood on the horns of the altar (Ex 29:12; Lev 8:15; etc.). Even the golden incense altar had horns on its corners (Ex 30:2-3) which received the blood of the sin offering on the Day of Atonement (Ex 30:10). Since the altar stood for justice, taking hold of the horns of the altar was a sign that one claimed sanctuary from his enemy until his case could be properly adjudicated (I Kgs 1:50-51; 2:28; cf. Ex 21:14).

4. Figurative sense. The tribe of Joseph is described with horns of the wild ox ("unicorn" in KJV) to signify his strength in conquering people (Deut 33:17). Job laments that his horn is thrust into the dust (Job 16:15). Here one's horn (like that of the ram) is the symbol of his dignity, power or strength. This figurative usage of horn is apparently based on the fact that an animal's horns are its weapon of aggressive strength; animals deprived of their horns are notably more docile. Similar usage may be found in Ps 75:4-5; 89:17, 24; 92:10; 112:9; 132:17; 148:14; Jer 48:25. A certain prophet Zedekiah made horns of iron as an object lesson to encourage King Ahab to attack the Syrians (I Kgs 22:11).

In Mary's magnificat in Lk 1:69 (following Hannah's prayer in I Sam 2:1, 10), "the horn of salvation" simply means the Lord has the strength or power to deliver or save.

Prophetic passages in Daniel and Zechariah (1:18-21) use the term specifically of kings or kingdoms that have existed or shall rise up. In Dan 8 the goat with one horn (Greece) rises up against the ram with two horns (Media and Persia). The great beast of Dan 7 which has ten horns plus a little horn that devours three others is similar in appearance to the great red dragon and the beast out of the sea of Rev 12:3; 13:1, both of whom have seven heads and ten horns. Rev 17:9 reveals that the seven heads represent seven mountains and the ten horns (v. 12) are ten kings. Amos has kings in mind when he accuses Israel of boasting that they have taken horns (kings) by their own power (Amos 6:13).

The KJV in Hab 3:4 misunderstands a rarer Heb. word spelled with the same consonants *q-r-n* and translates it "horn" where it should be "ray of light." It was this same misunderstanding of Ex 34:29-30, 35 in the Vulgate which made Michelangelo put horns on his immortal statue of Moses.

E. B. S.

HORNET. *See* Animals: Wasp, III.55.

HORONAIM (hôr'ŏ-nā'ĭm). A city of Moab, site uncertain. It is mentioned in Isa 15:5; Jer 48:3, 5, 34, and on the Moabite Stone (11. 31-32). The references indicate that it was probably between the highlands of Moab and the Arabah.

HORONITE (hôr'ŏ-nīt). A title given to Sanballat, an opponent of Nehemiah (Neh 2:10, 19; 13:28). It probably indicates that he was a native of Beth-horon.

HORSE. *See* Animals, I.11.

HORSE GATE. *See* Jerusalem: Gates and Towers 13.

HORSEMAN. One who rides a horse, almost always for military purposes, i.e., a cavalryman. Israel was late among the nations to use horses and most references are to foreign armies. OT references are frequently to chariot drivers since chariotry was earlier than cavalry. The Assyrians first developed cavalry tactics, and many references to horsemen in the prophets have in mind the Assyrians, e.g., Isaiah, Jeremiah, Ezekiel, Hosea, Joel and Habakkuk. Elisha cried, "The chariot of Israel, and the horsemen thereof" (II Kgs 2:12; cf. 13:14), referring symbolically to angelic protection or to Elijah's godly influence and power in prayer. King Joram of Israel sent messengers on horseback to meet Jehu in his chariot (II Kgs 9:17-19). In the NT, Paul was escorted from Jerusalem to Caesarea by 70 horsemen (Acts 23:23-32).

Much use is made of horsemen in apocalyptic writing, e.g., in Zechariah and Revelation. Horses of white, red, black and pale have riders (Rev 6:1-8), who have come to be known as "the four horsemen of the Apocalypse." Horsemen are further pictured wearing colorful breastplates (Rev 9:17, 19). The returned Christ and His hosts are pictured as horsemen riding to victory on white horses (Rev 19:11-21).

W. A. A.

A horseman from the early Assyrian site of Halaf. BM

HORSE LEACH. *See* Animals: Leech, V. 6.

HOSAH (hō'zȧ)

1. A border city of Asher, S or SE of Tyre (Josh 19:29). The exact location is uncertain; possibly to be identified with modern Khirbet el-Hosh. Moore suggests identification with Assyrian *Usu* of Sennacherib's Taylor Cylinder (ICC, *Judges*, p. 51), which in turn may be the mainland settlement of Tyre (ANET, p. 287*b*; cf. p. 300*b*).

2. A Levite who with his family was chosen by David to be a gatekeeper to the ark of the covenant after it was moved to Jerusalem (I Chr 16:38). This family had similar assignments in the later organization of the Levites in preparation for worship in the temple (I Chr 26:10-11, 16).

HOSANNA. An indeclinable exclamation which seems to mean "help (save) now!" It occurs alone (Mk 11:9; Jn 12:13), with "to the son of David" (Mt 21:9*a*, 15), and "in the highest" (Mt 21:9*b*; Mk 11:10). The NT uses it only at the triumphal entry. The Heb. *hôshî'â nā'* and Aram. *hôsha nā'* occurred in the Hallel (Ps 113–118) and was recited ritually at the Feast of Tabernacles (Ps 118:25, "Save now, we beseech thee, O Jehovah," ASV). It is interesting to note that the Latin versions transliterated the Heb. of this expression in this verse. The Hallel was also sung at the Passover offering, the Passover supper, and the Feasts of Pentecost and Dedication (Edersheim, *Life and Times of Jesus the Messiah,* II, 371 f.). The singing was accompanied by waving palm, myrtle, and willow branches (the *Tulabh*).

Besides liturgical uses, both the Hallel and the branches were used to greet kings and visitors to festivals. The use at the triumphal entry is, therefore, probably to be interpreted as recognition (homage) paid to Jesus by the people as their anticipated promised King. The phrase was adopted by the early church as a part of its ritual (*Didache* 10:6, in the prayer of the Lord's Supper: "Let grace come and let this world pass away. Hosannah to the God of David"). From this it has passed into the modern church ritual.

J. W. R.

HOSEA (hō-zā'ə). An OT prophet of the 8th cen., the only writing prophet who lived in the northern kingdom, except possibly Jonah. His name means "salvation" and is identical with the original form of Joshua's name (Num 13:8) and that of Hoshea (*q.v.*), the last king of Israel (II Kgs 15:30).

Hosea, the son of Beeri and a younger contemporary of Amos, began his prophetic ministry before 753 B.C. when Jeroboam II died. Exactly how long his work of proclaiming God's judgment upon the sins of his country continued, is not known. Objections to treaties made with Egypt (Hos 7:11; 12:1) may refer to King Hoshea's sending messengers to the king of Egypt ((II Kgs 17:4), who would be Pharaoh Tefnakhte (726-716 B.C.). If this is the occasion to which the prophet alludes, he ministered to the very closing years of the northern kingdom. His mention of Hezekiah and his three predecessors may indicate he fled to the kingdom of Judah to close out his ministry (Hos 1:1; cf. 1:7, 11; 4:15; 5:5, 10, 12–14; 6:4, 11; 8:14; 10:11; 11:12; 12:2).

Much of what can or cannot be learned of the prophet depends on the interpretation followed in chaps. 1 and 3 of the book. For centuries these chapters have been the subject of much discussion. Basically, the various opinions can be divided into two parts.

1. The allegorical view. This view has been held by many Jewish and Christian interpreters. It maintains that all the passages dealing with Hosea's marriage and family life, such as the command to take "a wife of harlotry" (1:2), are to be understood figuratively. The God of Israel, it is thought, would not require Hosea to marry a corrupt woman, and then use that relationship to teach a lesson on faithfulness.

2. The literal view. According to this view, chaps. 1 and 3 are to be taken together and refer to the same wife. Accordingly, Hosea married a woman named Gomer and she gave birth to three children. In time Gomer proved faithless and left her husband; later, Hosea bought her from her paramour and brought her home again. This view, in spite of obvious difficulties, has commended itself to many exegetes. It is pointed out that certain details of what happened, such as the precise amount of money spent by Hosea in reclaiming his wife (3:2), do not fit an allegorical interpretation. The fact remains, also, that the incidents recorded in these controversial chapters are related as though they were actual historical events. Whatever the correct view, Hosea's personal disappointments in love certainly contributed to his tender prophetic message. In Hosea, human experience became the channel of divine revelation.

See Gomer.

N. R. L.

HOSEA, BOOK OF. The first of the Minor Prophets in the English canon and the Twelve in the Heb. canon. Although it comes from the latter half of the 8th cen. B.C. and Obadiah, Joel, Jonah, and Amos probably belonged to the 9th and early 8th cen. B.C., Hosea seems to have been placed first because it was the longest of the Minor Prophets.

The book bears the name of its author, and is the sole source of information about Hosea's life and ministry. However, more is known of Hosea's home life than of any other prophet, since it was the basis for his message to God's people (*see* Hosea). His prophecy is the only surviving writing from the northern prophet to his own people, although Amos, a southerner who ministered to the northern kingdom, has a book in the sacred canon. Snaith thinks chap. 7 of Hosea shows that the prophet was a baker. The numerous references to agricultural matters may suggest that Hosea had some connection with the soil.

Major Themes

The book of Hosea naturally falls into two parts: the prophet's domestic life (1:1–3:5) and the prophetic discourses (4:1–14:9). In the prophetic discourses there are three dominant themes: the sin of the nation (4:1–8:14; 11:12–13:16); the certainty of divine judgment for this sin (9:1–10:15; 11:12–13:16); and the ultimate bestowal of God's mercy and love on a repentant people (11:1-11; 14:1-9).

Theories of Interpretation

The first three chapters of Hosea have constituted an interpretive problem for both Jewish and Christian scholars. It appears that God commanded Hosea to marry Gomer the harlot. An order to do something so morally evil seems to impugn the righteousness and holiness of God. Hence, these various interpretations have arisen with regard to chaps. 1-3.

1. Jewish interpreters during medieval times (Maimonides, Aben Ezra, Kimchi) held that no such marriage actually took place. The whole affair was the object of a prophetic dream or vision. It was similar to Ezekiel's visit to Jerusalem (Ezk 8-11).

2. Others have argued that Hosea's marriage was a prophetic allegory. From such an allegory it would be wrong to think that one can deduce what the actual situation was. Against this view is the fact that no clear allegorical meaning can be found for Gomer's name.

3. Luther and Osiander suggested that while Gomer and her children are called adulterous, it was done for parabolic purposes, and was not actually the case.

4. Gomer was already a harlot at the time God ordered Hosea to marry her. Each step in the relationship was taken not at the prophet's impulse but at God's command. That is, the prophet's marriage, the birth of his children, the disruption of his home, and the restoration of Gomer were done deliberately as a medium whereby God could speak to Israel (e.g., Hubbard, *With Bands of Love,* p. 54).

5. Thomas Aquinas and Sebastian Schmidt sought to circumvent the problem by supposing that Gomer was a concubine rather than a wife. It is hard to see how this avoids any of the difficulties.

6. Most likely the correct interpretation was suggested by Gebhard. He held that Hosea married Gomer prior to her harlotry. It was only after the marriage and the birth of Jezreel that Gomer became unfaithful. At the time of her marriage to Hosea she had within her a spirit of harlotry (cf. Hos 4:12; 5:4, NASB), but it had not yet manifested itself. This interpretation has the advantages of preserving the historical character of the account and the holiness of God. *See also* Hosea.

Message

Whatever the difficulties of determining the correct interpretation may be, the basic message of the prophet is clear. Israel is the wife of Yahweh (2:19-20; cf. 2:2). She has entered into this holy relationship by way of a covenant (6:7; 8:1). However, like Gomer, the nation is guilty of spiritual infidelity, having been corrupted by Baal worship (2:8, 13, 17; 4:13; 11:2).

More fundamental than their idolatry is the people's lack of personal knowledge of their God (4:1, 6; 5:4; 6:6; 13:4). They have rejected a close, warm contact with His loving heart (4:6). In their return they must press on to know Yahweh (6:1-3). Coordinate to their infidelity and the spurning of His love is the absence of covenant loyalty and devotion (*ḥesed*) on their part (4:2; 6:4, 6, NASB marg.); a revival of its observance is essential (10:12; 12:6).

Even though Israel has fallen to this despicable level, Yahweh still loves her with yearning compassion (11:8-9; 14:4). If she will but repent (10:12; 12:6; 14:1) He will have mercy and restore her. Whereas Amos *thunders* against the northern kingdom, Hosea *pleads.* In Amos there is portrayed the unapproachable righteousness of God, while in Hosea there is demonstrated the unfailing love (*ḥesed*) of God. Just as Luke writes of the prodigal son, so Hosea tells of the prodigal wife.

Style and Text

The unusual style of the writer of this book poses some difficult problems for the exegete. He uses a great variety of figures of speech in achieving parallel thoughts in the usual pattern of Heb. poetry. The writer merges himself in the message he delivers, so much so that often he appears to be pleading in the capacity of God Himself. This personal vigor accounts for many of the abrupt transitions and makes it unnecessary to relegate parts of the book to later interpolations. Another difficulty is that the Heb. text of Hosea is probably more corrupt than that of any other OT book. The LXX may be used in a number of places to restore the text. Occasionally it may have preserved superior readings as well as additional phrases.

Outline

Title, 1:1

- I. The Prologue: The Message in General by Illustration, 1:2–3:5
  - A. Hosea's first marriage with harlotrous Gomer, 1:2–2:23
    1. The children born and named to symbolize Israel's rejection, 1:2-9
    2. Message of comfort to Hosea concerning Israel, 1:10–2:1
    3. Message of chastisement to Israel, 2:2-13
    4. Message of restoration to Israel, 2:14-23
  - B. Hosea's remarriage to Gomer, 3:1-5
    1. The buying back and cleansing of his adulterous wife, 3:1-3
    2. The symbolic meaning: by captivity Israel will be prepared for restoration in the latter days, 3:4-5
- II. The Treatise: The Message in Detail by Prophecy, 4:1–14:8
  - A. God's lawsuit: Israel's sin is intolerable, 4:1–6:3

1. The indictment: lack and rejection of experiential knowledge of God, fidelity, and covenant loyalty, 4:1–5:7
2. The sentence, 5:8–14
3. The prophecy of restoration, 5:15–6:3

B. God's judgment: Israel is about to be punished, 6:4–10:15
1. The character of their sins demands punishment, 6:4–8:14
2. Description of their punishment, 9:1–10:15
3. Parenthetical plea for repentance, 10:12

C. God's love: Israel shall be restored, 11:1–14:8
1. God's yearning love over Ephraim and future restoration, 11:1-11
2. Yet sinful Ephraim must first be punished, 11:12–13:16
3. Final victory of God's love, 14:1-8

Conclusion, 14:9

Bibliography. H. L. Ellison, *The Prophets of Israel,* Grand Rapids: Eerdmans, 1969, pp. 95-167. Charles L. Feinberg, *Hosea: God's Love for Israel,* New York: American Board of Missions to the Jews, 1947. J. B. Hindley, "Hosea," NBC, 3rd ed. rev., pp. 703-715. David A. Hubbard, *With Bands of Love: Studies in Hosea,* Grand Rapids: Eerdmans, 1968. John H. Johansen, "The Prophet Hosea: His Marriage and Message," JETS, XIV (1971), 179-184. G. A. F. Knight, *Hosea: God's Love,* London: SCM Press, 1960. G. Campbell Morgan, *Hosea: The Heart and Holiness of God,* New York: Revell, 1934. Charles F. Pfeiffer, "Hosea," WBC, pp. 801-818 (with good bibliography). Norman H. Snaith, *Mercy and Sacrifice,* London: SCM Press, 1953; *Amos, Hosea, and Micah,* London: Epworth, 1956. Herbert F. Stevenson, *Three Prophetic Voices,* Old Tappan: Revell, 1971, pp. 95-158. James M. Ward, *Hosea: A Theological Commentary,* New York: Harper & Row, 1966; "The Message of the Prophet Hosea," *Interpretation,* XXIII (1969), 387-407.

P. D. F.

HOSEN. Used only in Dan 3:21, where the context shows it to be wearing apparel. RSV translates the term "tunic." "Hosen" is a 17th cen. English term for a garment such as leggings or trousers covering the hips and legs. The Aramaic word *p^etash* means "undergarment, breeches" (Marcus Jastrow, *A Dictionary of the Targumim, the Talmud Babli and Yerushalmi, and the Midrashic Literature,* ii, 1155). In Daniel its obvious use is to indicate that the men were fully dressed.

HOSHAIAH (hō-shā'y*ȧ*)

1. The leader of half of the princes of Judah in the procession around the wall of Jerusalem when it was dedicated by Nehemiah (Neh 12:32).

2. Father of Jezaniah or Azariah, a commander of the forces of Judah after the fall of Jerusalem (Jer 42:1; 43:2).

HOSHAMA (hŏsh'*ȧ*-m*ȧ*). A son of Jeconiah (Jehoiachin) whom King Nebuchadnezzar carried into captivity with the 10,000 nobles in 597 B.C. (I Chr 3:18).

HOSHEA (hō-shē'*ȧ*)

1. The original name of Joshua (Deut 32:44), sometimes called Oshea (Num 13:8), but changed by Moses to Joshua (Num 13:16, RSV). *See* Joshua.

2. Son of Azaziah and a prince of the tribe of Ephraim in the time of David (I Chr 27:20).

3. The son of Elah, and the last king of Israel (II Kgs 15:30; 17:1-6; 18:1, 9–12). His reign lasted nine years (732-722 B.C.). It seems fairly certain that the anti-Assyrian demonstrations of Pekah, the preceding king, brought down the wrath of Tiglath-pileser III upon the kingdom and reduced Israel to one-third its original size. This produced a pro-Assyrian party led by Hoshea, culminating in the murder of Pekah and the enthronement of the assassin (II Kgs 15:30). But even this reacted unfavorably for Israel, for Tiglath-pileser III brought the pressure of his armed might on Hoshea so that he became a mere viceroy of a foreign power. In the annals of Assyria the monarch boasted, "They overthrew their king Pekah and I placed Hoshea as king over them" (ANET, p. 284).

Apparent chronological inconsistencies within the biblical record and amazing incongruities with contemporary Assyrian history have presented almost insuperable problems to the scholars. This has led some to conclude falsely that there was a period of nine years between the death of Pekah and the accession of Hoshea when there was no king in Israel. But once the principle for unraveling the meaning of the mysterious numbers was discovered, it was evident that the Bible contained a perfect system of chronology. Thus the dates for Hoshea's reign are *c.* 732-722 B.C. (*see* Chronology, OT).

The failure of Hoshea to display full subserviency to the new Assyrian monarch, Shalmaneser V (727-722 B.C.), heralded the end. When Hoshea failed to pay the annual tribute and instead sent envoys for assistance to the king of Egypt at So (Sais) in the western Delta (*see* So), Shalmaneser first imprisoned the king of Israel and then organized the siege of Samaria. After three years of siege the city was captured by Sargon II, the new ruler of Assyria. The northern kingdom came to an end, and thousands were carried into captivity. This was the judgment of God upon Israel (II Kgs 17:7). *See* Hosea.

4. One of the Jewish chiefs who joined in the

renewal of the covenant after the Captivity (Neh 10:23).

H. A. Hoy.

HOSPITALITY. The reception and lodging of travelers was viewed in Bible lands as a binding obligation to be conscientiously fulfilled. The stranger was to be courteously treated as a guest. In fact, the facilities of the household were placed at his disposal. After eating food with his guest, the host considered it his duty to protect him during his stay. This kind of oriental hospitality is seen in Lot's reception of the two angels (Gen 19:1-8; see also Gen 18:2-8; Ex 2:15-20). In NT times, Jesus made the 70 disciples dependent upon the hospitality of the people when He sent them out with no provisions for the journey (Lk 10:1-12). In the judgment scene of Mt 25:31-46, the criterion for judgment is the practice of hospitality toward Christ's brethren. During the Apostolic Age, apostles and itinerant teachers were supported by the hospitality of Christian people while on tour (Acts 16:15; 17:7; 18:7; 21:4-8, 16; 28:7, 14; III Jn 5-8). See II Jn 10-11 for a misuse of this practice by propagators of error. In Rom 12:13 and Heb 13:2, hospitality (*philoxenia,* "love of strangers") is treated as a Christian virtue. The corresponding adjective (*philoxenos,* "loving strangers") expresses a qualification of the bishop (I Tim 3:2; Tit 1:8) as well as a duty of all Christians (I Pet 4:9). Widows being considered for financial aid were to have been known for this quality (I Tim 5:10, "lodged strangers").

Bibliography. W. Ewing, "Hospitality," HDB rev. G. Stählin, *"Xenos . . . Philoxenia . . ."* TDNT, V, 17-25.

D. W. B.

HOST

1. Literally, Gr. *xenos,* as does Latin *hostis,* meant a stranger; then, "guest"; then, one who receives and entertains strangers, or a host such as Gaius in Rom 16:23. *See* Hospitality.

2. An innkeeper who acts as host for his guests (Lk 10:35).

3. Several Heb. words used frequently in a military sense of a large number of fighting men. *See* Army.

4. The meaning, in the plural form, of Sabaoth (*q.v.*) in the title "the Lord of Sabaoth" (Rom 9:29; Jas 5:4). It is transliterated from Heb. *ṣᵉbā'ôth,* "hosts," which occurs hundreds of times in the OT as "the Lord of hosts" and "the Lord God of hosts." God is recognized as the divine Commander of the armies of Israel on earth (Josh 5:14-15) and especially of the heavenly bodies (Isa 51:15; Jer 31:35), and of the angels in heaven (Neh 9:6; Ps 103:20-21; 148:1-6). *See* Host of Heaven.

HOST OF HEAVEN. The Heb. expression *ṣᵉbā' hashshāmayim,* "army of the skies," is found *c.* 18 times in the OT. The Heb. word *ṣābā'* occurs nearly 500 times in the OT and usually means "army."

Since the realms of the earth and heaven were closely associated in the thinking of the ancients, the heathen neighbors of Israel imagined the celestial bodies as organized in military array. The sun, moon, and stars were under the symbol of an army. The sun was the king; the moon, the viceregent; and the stars and planets, their attendants (cf. Jud 5:20), i.e., an army, the heavenly host. These creations were thought to be animated by divine spirits constituting a living army which controlled human destiny.

Although the Israelites were warned against such pagan beliefs (Deut 4:19; 17:3), they succumbed to the temptation during the Assyrian and Babylonian periods to worship the heavenly bodies (II Kgs 17:16; 21:3, 5; 23:4-5; II Chr 33:3, 5; Jer 8:2; 19:13; Zeph 1:5; Acts 7:42). Israel's doctrine of the Lord as the Creator of heaven and earth, the one who marshaled the heavenly bodies at His command, was the antidote to this pagan practice (cf. Gen 1:14-19; 2:1; Neh 9:6; Ps 33:6; 103:21; 148:2; Isa 40:26; 45:12).

The concepts of celestial bodies and angelic beings were closely related. Included in the idea of the heavenly host is that of angels (messengers). These heavenly attendants are closely related to the Lord's kingly role. They are His army. As King, He presides over His heavenly council, composed of angelic servants or "sons of God" (cf. Micaiah's vision in I Kgs 22:19; also Gen 1:26; Job 1-2; Ps 82; Isa 6). Divine messengers at intervals were dispatched from the Lord's council to accomplish His purpose (cf. the angelic host, Lk 2:13; Jacob's encounter with a band of angels, Gen 28:12 ff.).

In the OT the LORD (Yahweh) is frequently mentioned as "the LORD (Yahweh), God of hosts," i.e., the LORD God of the armies (cf. Jer 5:14; 38:17; 44:7; Hos 12:5, *et al.*). The apostles Paul (Rom 9:29) and James (Jas 5:4) use the Heb. term *sabaoth,* "hosts," as a title for the Lord. *See* God, Names and Titles of; War.

D. W. D.

HOSTAGE. Literally, the Heb. expression means "son of sureties." It occurs only in II Kgs 14:14 and the parallel passage in II Chr 25:24.

HOTHAM (hō'thăm)

1. An Aroerite, father of two of David's mighty men (I Chr 11:44). The name is incorrectly rendered "Hothan" by KJV. *See* Hothan.

2. An Asherite (I Chr 7:32). *See* Helem.

HOTHAN (hō'thăn). This name is found only in I Chr 11:44, KJV. *See* Hotham 1.

HOTHIR (hō'thĭr). A son of Heman and head of the 21st course in the temple service in the time of David (I Chr 25:4, 28).

HOUGH. The older form of "hock." In the hind leg of a quadraped it is the joint between the knee and the fetlock. The verb means "to cut the hamstring of an animal," thus permanently crippling it. The word "hough" appears in Josh 11:6, 9; II Sam 8:4; I Chr 18:4. In the RSV all of the above uses are translated "hamstring." In addition, the RSV translates the term in Gen 49:6 "hamstring," while the KJV renders it "they digged down a wall."

HOUR. *See* Time, Divisions of.

HOUSE. This is the translation of some five words in the Bible. The house (Heb. *bayit;* Gr. *oikia)* designates variously the dwelling place of a family, of the king, or the temple of God in Jerusalem. The term may also designate a nation (house of Israel), a tribe, a family (Gen 7:1, etc.).

Historical development. The earliest known dwellings were the natural caves where humans sought shelter from the elements. In the 8th mil. B.C. the cave dwellers were leaving them and moving out into the open after the heavy rains (and the glaciers farther N) of the Ice Age had ceased. Shortly thereafter began the appearance of tents and huts of sticks stuck in the ground in a circular fashion with tops secured together and covered with thatch or leaves. The ingenuity of others developed stone walls across the mouths of caves or in front of them and covered the space with poles or skins.

Reconstruction of a courtyard of a house at Ur in the days of Abraham. Family rooms were located on the second floor; the kitchen, storage, and servants' quarters on the first floor.
University of Pa. Museum

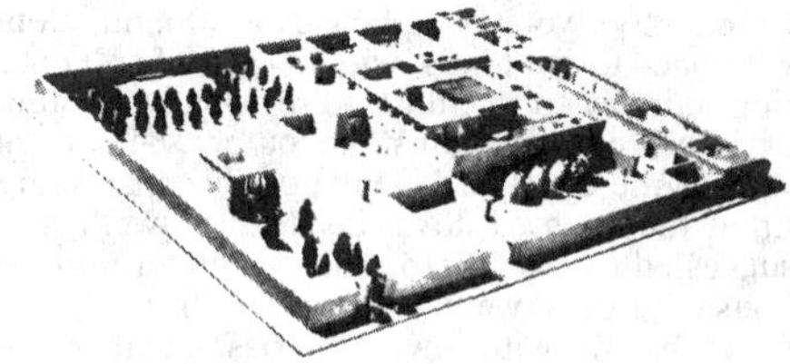

Model of a house and estate at Amarna, Egypt, *c.* 1375–1330 B.C. This is the sort of upper class home Moses would have known there.
ORINST

The evidence of huts grouped together to form houses indicates the need, in the mind of thinking men, to compartmentalize for function, privacy, and—more space. At one stage of development, some groups saw the advantage of protection in building their huts on wooden pilings in lakes, many of two or more rooms. In the European lake dwellings occurred the crossed, overlapping logs at the corners.

At what time men passed in their thinking from the consideration of houses as merely a group of dwellings to view them as a city, is not known. However, Jericho in Palestine, at present considered the oldest known walled city, goes back well before 6000 B.C., thus indicating not too long a period from the cave-dwelling era to the rise of the concept of the city. Early Neolithic agricultural villages, such as Hacilar in Anatolia, Jarmo in Iraq, and Beidha near Petra in Jordan, may slightly antedate the massive defensive wall and moat of Jericho.

In Egypt, Mesopotamia, and the lowlands of Syria and Palestine, bricks of hand-formed, sun-dried mud became the common building material. Frequently in Mesopotamia and Egypt, the seal of the reigning king was stamped upon them, helping to date the structure and to correlate it with the inscriptions of the king describing his building activities. Earlier, however, in the lowlands along the coast of Palestine and around Lake Huleh, the most available building material had been the marsh reed. The technique involved a circular floor plan in which reeds were combined with clay bricks to form beehive-like houses.

In Chalcolithic burials (4000–3200 B.C.) ossuaries, which are modeled after houses, indicate a rectangular plan, with reeds bound together and plastered solid with mud to form the roof. In other places wattle and daub houses were constructed with sticks stuck in the ground and walls formed by basket-weaving reeds (wattles) and surfaces daubed with mud to present a solid face to the weather. During the early Chalcolithic period people in the Beer-sheba plain dug subterranean dwellings in the compacted loess earth.

In the highlands of Palestine, abundance of stone determined the general building material. Frequently two-storied houses are found, along with one-storied kinds, with a flat roof and exterior stairway to it. Stairs were usually of stone or brick, placed against an outer wall or the wall of the courtyard. It is possible that sometimes they passed down inside the dwelling as suggested by Mk 13:15, "not go down *into* the house." Roofs were more often framed with wood beams with smaller cross members on which were placed small branches or straw covered with a packed clay. The OT required a parapet (Heb. *gāg*, "battlement") around the roof to prevent injury by a fall (Deut 22:8).

Ruins of the "House of the Faun" at Pompeii, an example of a Roman villa of St. Paul's day. In the front of the house was a large covered area (atrium) with a pool in the center and surrounded by rooms; in the back was an open pillared courtyard surrounded by rooms. HFV

Evidence of the use of the column reveals considerable imagination. At Neolithic Jericho a building with inner and outer chambers with six columns across the front is an outstanding example. The inner room has two wooden columns supporting the superstructure. The columns in front obviously supported a porch antedating by 3000 years the porch of Solomon's house of the forest. In an Early Bronze Age temple (*c.* 2500 B.C.) at Ai (BA, VII [1944], fig. 3) four limestone bases were found and part of a charred wooden post still *in situ*. The size of the stump and of the neatly trimmed plinths indicate heavy loads above, suggesting a second story. Later, in an Early Iron Age villa (*c.* 1200 B.C.) at the same site four hewn pillars were unearthed which supported the roof or upper story extending over one side of the courtyard. Similar plans appeared in houses dated 900 and 750 B.C. at Hazor (BA, XXI, figs. 7, 10).

As civilization developed in Egypt some of the better houses were built from stone quarried from cliffs. In Palestine from 3000 B.C. onward throughout the Canaanite period (ending *c.* 1200 B.C.), as evidence from Tell Beit Mirsim (Debir?) indicates during the Hyksos domination, houses were well constructed, and thickness of stone walls suggests a need for protection. The floor plan of the house of a patrician or Hyksos chieftain at Tell Beit Mirsim *c.* 1600 B.C. reveals six rooms on one side of a long courtyard *c.* 20 by 40 feet (Albright, *Archaeology of Palestine*, fig. 16; ANEP # 723).

In the early Israelite period, *c.* 1200–1000 B.C., rudeness of fit shows an unfamiliarity with stone construction. Later, in Solomon's time and afterward, technical advance in understanding and usage is indicated in the fine stone work of house, city wall and palace. When the need arose for monumental buildings, as the temple of Yahweh and Solomon's house of the forest of Lebanon, craftsmen familiar with this type of architecture had to be imported, the source of easiest acquisition being Phoenicia. I Kgs 6 gives some idea of what the house of Yahweh was like as to materials and techniques used. Stones were squared up by marginal drafting and then cut to shape for fitting into the wall. The roof was of timber, with the floors, interior walls and ceilings made of fir and cedar boards with carved and gold-leaf decoration.

Exact technical descriptions pertain to the enclosure wall described as of three courses of stone topped by a row of cedar beams (I Kgs 6:36; 7:12). Some light is shed on this structure by the contemporary Megiddo gate. The substructure of five courses of close-jointed limestone had bond beams four inches thick between the second and third courses. In the case of Solomon's temple, therefore, the reference to the manner of construction might refer only to the substructure.

The temple itself in plan consisted of two rooms, the holy place and the holy of holies where the ark of the covenant was placed. This reflects the familiar plan of temples found elsewhere in Palestine and other countries, indicating only the appropriateness of plan to functions and not an evolution of the worship of Yahweh. *See* Temple.

The House of the Forest of Lebanon (*q.v.*) was named for its many cedar pillars and wall boards. Four rows of pillars divided it lengthwise, and it had three rows of upper chambers of 15 each (I Kgs 7:2–5). This palace was connected to a waiting room (Hall of Pillars?) and the Hall of the Throne, and included private apartments for the king (the palace?) and for Pharaoh's daughter (I Kgs 7:6–8). It housed the golden shields, the ivory throne and precious vessels (I Kgs 10:7, 21; II Chr 9:16, 20; Isa 22:8). The palace adjoined the temple compound on the S, thus combining the house of God and His viceroy. Since no definite archaeological information exists, exact layout cannot be determined.

Plans and construction. In the cities and walled towns of Palestine and elsewhere, houses were built wall to wall. Any open courts lay within the exterior house walls and had rooms opening off them. Houses faced on the narrow streets; where city walls occurred, these commonly formed the rear house wall. When population increased as in later times, houses in Palestine usually became smaller with smaller rooms and thinner walls, and less attention was paid to urban planning. As such, city planning was known in the early history of the Sumerian city-state of Erech, whose king Gilgamesh proposed a threefold division of the town and its environs into houses, temple and fields.

In details the houses had, of course, a doorway and frequently windows. In some of the better homes, the door would be framed with wood lintel and posts. Thick doors of wood during the Bronze Age (3000-1200 B.C.) were evidenced by large threshold stone sockets; these were often absent in houses of David's day, suggestive of an effective police force to protect the inhabitants. In such cases a hanging of cloth or skin would serve as a door. Windows sometimes opened out through the city wall when the house was incorporated into the fortification (cf. Josh 2:15; Acts 9:25; II Cor 11:32-33). Windows on the street would have lattices (*q.v.*).

Storage pits for grain were dug down into the floor, sometimes lined with plaster, sometimes being large clay jars sunk into the ground. Fire pits were also dug into the floor, or sometimes built up with a low wall around to hold in the fire. Not having a chimney, the smoke found its way out through doors and windows. Such fires also heated the houses, with braziers used to supplement them. Floors were generally of beaten clay, although in the better homes plaster and even stone is found. By NT times the wealthy houses and villas often had mosaic floors, as at Pompeii and Antioch-on-the-Orontes.

Porters or doorkeepers are mentioned (I Chr 15:23-24; Jn 10:3; 18:16-17; Acts 12:13-15); in wealthier homes they determined who should be admitted to the house.

In most cities some attempt at drainage systems to carry off rain water and sometimes

A black-and-white floor mosaic from Delos. HFV

Floor mosaics of wealthy Roman homes were often elaborate and done in many colors. Here the god Dionysus is seated on a panther, from the island of Delos. Hannibal

sewage is found, usually of stone-lined and stone-covered channels, though clay pipe and open half-pipe systems are discovered.

In the Hellenistic period more evidence of city planning is found with more rectangular street plans occurring. The houses assumed a more rectangular or even square shape. Bathrooms with plumbing also occur in the homes of the wealthy. Herodian Jericho had by NT times become a garden paradise with public baths and fine homes (Lk 19:1-10). The homes of the wealthy in Roman Palestine were similar to the well-known Roman houses, with covered atrium or hall and surrounding rooms, behind which was an open court with surrounding rooms, affording utmost privacy.

Furnishings. During most of the biblical period, the house served for both dwelling and storage. Amazement occurs at the charred remains of the variety of implements, goods, animals, etc., stored in them. In very cold or severely inclement weather, the most precious animals shared its shelter (cf. II Sam 12:1-4).

The poorest families had only a few kitchen utensils and their bedding (sometimes only their cloak, Ex 22:26-27), sleeping on only a reed mat (Jn 5:8-12). If a guest room were provided, it would contain only a bed, table, chair and clay lamp (II Kgs 4:10, RSV). If beds were afforded, the rich had high bedsteads (Gen 47:31; 48:2; 49:33; Ezk 23:41); others had a sort of low cot (Ex 8:3; Lk 8:16). Some had chests for storage of clothes and bedding like the ornate boxes found in Tutankhamon's tomb. The wealthy indulged in furniture having inlaid ivory and gold leaf (Amos 6:4).

Cooking was done in good weather in outside fireplaces; in bad weather, inside. Bread ovens occur both inside and out. A pair of millstones

(Deut 24:6) provided the means for grinding grain for flour. Olive oil was stored in special clay jars. Frequently cisterns are found inside the courtyard for water storage. Cooking pots are found, wide-mouth types for stirring, smaller-mouth types for liquids. Fingers were the most usual eating "utensils." The rich provided themselves with gold and silver tableware.

See Architecture; City.

Bibliography. W. F. Albright, *Archaeology of Palestine,* Harmondsworth: Penguin, 1960. Emmanuel Anati, *Palestine Before the Hebrews,* New York: Knopf, 1963. H. Keith Beebe, "Ancient Palestinian Dwellings," BA, XXXI (1968), 38–58. A. C. Bouquet, *Everyday Life in New Testament Times,* New York: Scribner, 1954, pp. 27–38. "Cities, Israelite; Building and Houses," CornPBE, pp. 212–217. E. W. Heaton, *Everyday Life in Old Testament Times,* New York: Scribner, 1956, pp. 55–77. Otto Michel, "*Oikos,* etc.," TDNT, V, 119–159. G. Ernest Wright, *Biblical Archaeology,* rev. ed., Philadelphia: Westminster, 1962, pp. 187–190.

H. G. S.

HOUSEHOLD. This is the translation of eight words in the Bible, the most frequent OT word being Heb. *bayit,* "house." Job 1:3 has *'ăbuddâ,* "household," a set of servants for the family. Gr. *therapeia,* of similar meaning, occurs in Lk 12:42. The common Gr. *oikos,* "house(hold)," describes the families of Lydia (Acts 16:15), Stephanas (I Cor 1:16), and Onesiphorus (II Tim 4:19). An attributive form of *oikia* occurs in Mt 10:25, 36, "those of his household" (*oikiakos*).

The household is the object of the care of a virtuous woman (Prov 31:15 ff.). Members are recipients of religious instruction (Gen 18:19), rejoice together at God's mercies (Deut 14:26), and are to be evangelized (Acts 16:15; 16:33–34). Christians were numbered in the household of Caesar (Phil 4:22). Christian believers have become members of a new spiritual family, the "household of the faith" (Gal 6:10, NASB), God's household (Eph 2:19, NASB). *See* Family; Home.

HOUSEHOLDER. *See* Goodman; Household.

HOUSE OF THE FOREST OF LEBANON. A great hall of Solomon's palace in Jerusalem, named from the material imported from Mount Lebanon. It consisted of a rectangular structure 150 by 75 feet, divided by rows of pillars, possibly with an upper story of chambers distributed in rows of 15 each (I Kgs 7:2–5). It served as a royal armory and as an antechamber for audience with the king. It connected with the throne room and other public rooms of the palace, as well as with the private apartments of the king and of the daughter of Pharaoh (I Kgs 7:6–8).

References are made to the golden shields, the ivory throne, and the precious vessels that were kept in the house of the forest (I Kgs 10:17, 21; II Chr 9:16, 20; Isa 22:8).

HOUSETOP. The flat roof of a house where the family could find rest in the cool of evening, or where various activities might take place, as drying of flax (Josh 2:6) and prayer (Acts 10:9). The surface was usually a marly clay. It was kept in water-shedding condition between rains by rolling with stone rollers. Parapets were required around the housetop to prevent accidental falls (Deut 22:8). In NT times roof tiles of the curved type came into use (Lk 5:19).

HUKKOK (hŭk'ŏk). A border village of Naphtali (Josh 19:34). It may be identified with Yāqûq, a site *c.* three miles W of Chinnereth near the spot where the Waters of Merom enter the Sea of Galilee (Herbert G. May, *Oxford Bible Atlas,* p. 62).

HUKOK (hū'kŏk). A Levitical town in Asher (I Chr 6:75), an alternate name for Helkath (*q.v.*).

HUL (hūl). Son of Aram and grandson of Shem, the son of Noah (Gen 10:23). The parallel in I Chr 1:17 identifies him as a son of Shem.

HULDAH (hŭl'dȧ). The wife of Shallum, wardrobe keeper in Josiah's court, who lived in the second quarter of Jerusalem as a recognized prophetess. When Josiah felt convicted by the book of the law which had been found during the temple repair, he directed officials to inquire of God for its meaning. Although Jeremiah was contemporary, they went to Huldah, who prophesied judgment upon the nation but peace for Josiah who then began his reforms (II Kgs 22:14–20).

HUMAN SACRIFICE. *See* Sacrifice, Human.

HUMANITY OF CHRIST. *See* Christ, Humanity of.

HUMBLENESS. The term appears only once in the KJV (Col 3:12), not at all in the RSV. The Gr. word *tapeinophrosynē* is used six other times and is translated in the KJV as "lowliness" of mind (Phil 2:3; Eph 4:2), "humility" (Acts 20:19; Col 2:18, 23; I Pet 5:5). The RSV renders it "humility" (Phil 2:3; Acts 20:19; I Pet 5:5), "lowliness" (Eph 4:2), "self-abasement" (Col 2:18, 23). *See* Humility.

HUMILIATION OF CHRIST. *See* Christ, Humiliation of.

HUMILITY. A Christian characteristic, epitomized in Rom 12:3: "For I say . . . to every man that is among you, not to think of himself more highly than he ought to think." Humility (Gr. *tapeinophrosynē,* I Pet 5:5) is a mental attitude of lowliness (Eph 4:2; Phil 2:3), the opposite of pride (*q.v.*). It is that specific grace developed in the Christian by the Spirit of God wherein the believer frankly acknowledges that all he has and is he owes to the Triune God who is dynamically operative in his behalf. He then willingly submits himself under the hand of God (Jas 4:6-10; I Pet 5:5-7). Thus humility should not be equated with a pious inferiority complex. It can be pretended on the part of false teachers (Col 2:18, 23) in acts of self-abasement (NASB).

In the OT this quality is praised (Prov 15:33; 18:12; 22:4). The Heb. term *'ănāwâ* (from *'ānāh,* "be afflicted") implies that humility of spirit often results from affliction. According to this characteristic the lives of many of the kings of Judah and Israel were assessed (I Kgs 21:29; II Chr 32:26; 33:23; 34:27; 36:12). Humbling oneself is the first step in true revival (II Chr 7:14; cf. Mic 6:8), for God Himself, the high and lofty One, delights to dwell with him who has a contrite and humble spirit in order to revive him (Isa 57:15).

Jesus Christ, as the supreme example of humility (Mt 11:29), furnished His disciples with visible demonstration of it in serving them by washing their feet (Jn 13:3-16). A major Christological passage in the NT (Phil 2:5-11) finds its key in the cultivation of this trait of Jesus Christ by the believer. *See* Humbleness; Christ, Humiliation of.

F. R. H.

HUMTAH (hŭm'tȧ). One of nine cities in the hill country of Hebron inherited by Judah (Josh 15:54). Its exact location is not now known.

HUNDREDS. While the term "hundred" appears in both the OT and the NT in the normal use, where the term "hundreds" appears it usually refers to the formal grouping of society (Ex 18:21, *et al.*), soldiers (Num 31:14, *et al.*), a crowd for a specific purpose (Mk 6:40).

HUNGER. This word is used three ways in the Scriptures: (1) with reference to physiological starvation and famine (Ex 16:3; Lk 15:17); (2) with reference to the normal physiological desire for food (Rom 12:20); (3) with reference to desire for spiritual satisfaction and sustenance (Mt 5:6). See L. Goppelt, *"Peinaō,"* TDNT, VI, 12-22.

HUNT, HUNTER, HUNTING. The two most noted hunters of the Bible are Nimrod (Gen 10:9) and Esau (Gen 25:27). In the ancient Near East a hunter had special heroic standing, which reflected the non-urban life of nomadic society where men spent much time providing food by hunting, while a little agriculture was carried on by women. The very word *ṣayid* used for "hunter" and "hunting" in the OT is often translated "victuals" (Neh 13:15), "food" (Job 38:41), and "venison" (Gen 27:3, 5, 7, 19; in v. 30, "hunting").

The oldest paintings known to be done by

The Assyrian king Ashurbanipal hunting lions. BM

human hands (at Lauscaux, France; Altamira, Spain, etc.) depict prehistoric man as primarily a hunter. These amazingly life-like rock carvings and paintings have been explained as a kind of sympathetic magic whereby men sought to have good fortune in their hunting through recreating the hunt scenes with red ochre and carbon deep inside caves.

With the domestication of animals and establishment of settled agricultural communities, hunting as a necessity for livelihood became obsolete. It continued, however, in the Bible world especially as a sport for kings and nobles. This has been depicted on reliefs and murals of Egypt, Mesopotamia, Greece and Rome (ANEP # 182-190). The grand hunting scenes of the Assyrian monarchs are best illustrated by the reliefs in Ashurbanipal's palace at Nineveh.

The free and naturalistic treatment of wounded lions marks a high point in Assyrian art. The reliefs reveal that the lions were first captured and kept in cages, then released for the king to hunt down. The sporting aspect of this kind of hunting must not be interpreted in 20th cen. A.D. terms. The sport was strictly practical not for food but because it led to skill in warfare. The king, whether of Egypt or Assyria, had to be the invincible warrior, and the hunting games were used both to improve and prove his strength and accuracy with the instruments of war.

The art of these various cultures also shows the use of dogs in hunting. The Theban tomb of the Eighteenth Dynasty noble Rekh-mi-Re has a relief showing dogs attacking wild animals of the desert. Paintings from the war-like Myceneans show dogs similar to the modern greyhound assisting in a lion hunt. Palestine in OT times was infested with lions (Jud 14:5), bears (II Kgs 2:24), wild boars (Ps 80:13), etc., all of which are now extinct in that area. The Levitical statutes allowed for the taking of game in the hunt, provided the animals were clean according to the dietary laws and all blood was carefully removed (Lev 17:13). *See* Animals.

There is wide metaphorical treatment of the Heb. verb *ṣûd,* "to hunt." Jeremiah's enemies "chased" (hunted) his steps (Lam 3:52; cf. 4:18). The Lord "hunted" Job as if the latter were a fierce lion (Job 10:16). To Ezekiel, the false prophets and sorceresses hunt and capture souls (Ezk 13:18); but to Jeremiah it is the Lord who hunts out the rebellious "from every mountain, and from every hill, and out of the holes of the rocks" (Jer 16:16).

See Bow and Arrow; Occupations: Hunter.

E. B. S.

HUPHAM (hū'fåm), **HUPHAMITES** (hū'få-mīts). A descendant of Benjamin; eponymous ancestor of the Huphamites (Num 26:39). "Huppim" in Gen 46:21 and I Chr 7:12, 15 is probably a variant.

HUPPAH (hŭp'*ȧ*). A priest in the time of David in charge of the 13th course in the temple (I Chr 24:13).

HUPPIM. *See* Hupham.

HUR (hûr). Possibly an Egyptian name similar to Horus, the Egyptian god; or perhaps a pet name for a child (cf. Akkad. *ḫūru,* "child"); or a shortened form of Asshur.

1. A descendant of Judah, son of Caleb and Ephrath, and an ancestor of Bezaleel the craftsman (Ex 31:2; 35:30; I Chr 2:19-20). He is listed also as "the firstborn of Ephrathah, the father of Bethlehem" (I Chr 4:4), so the name may have been used to denote a tribe such as Hurrian or Horite (Gen 36:20).

2. Moses' assistant who in the battle against the Amalekites held up one hand of Moses while Aaron held the other until the going down of the sun and Joshua had defeated the enemy (Ex 17:10, 12). He also assisted Aaron in the rule of the Israelites while Moses was on the mount at the giving of the Ten Commandments (Ex 24:14). He may be the same as 1 and may have been the husband of Miriam, the sister of Moses, according to Josephus (*Ant.* iii.2.4). However, the OT says nothing about this.

3. Listed as one of the five kings of Midian, slain by Moses in a battle in which he killed all Midianite males, and took the women captive, while the flocks and herds were added to those of the Hebrews (Num 31:8; Josh 13:21).

4. Father of one of the officers of Solomon in the hill country of Ephraim (I Kgs 4:8).

5. Father of Rephaiah who helped rebuild the walls of Jerusalem (Neh 3:9).

A. W. W.

HURAI (hyŏŏr'ī). A mighty man of David (I Chr 11:32). In the parallel passage of II Sam 23:30 he is called Hiddai (*q.v.*).

HURAM (hyŭr'*ȧ*m). Variant of the name Hiram (*q.v.*). Huram is used by the Chronicler in every instance except I Chr 14:1.

1. Son of Bela and grandson of Benjamin (I Chr 8:5).

2. The Tyrian craftsman employed by Solomon (II Chr 4:11), called Hiram in I Kgs 7:13.

3. The king of Tyre during the reign of Solomon (II Chr 2:3, 11; cf. I Kgs 5:1 ff.).

HURI (hyŏŏr'ī). A descendant of Gad and the father of Abihail (I Chr 5:14).

HURRIAN. *See* Horite.

HUSBAND. *See* Family; Marriage.

HUSBANDMAN. *See* Occupations: Farmer, Husbandman.

HUSBANDRY. *See* Agriculture.

HUSHAH (hŏŏsh'*ȧ*). Mentioned in I Chr 4:4 as the son of Ezer of the tribe of Judah. Some accept the name as a designation of a family or a place.

HUSHAI (hŏŏsh'ī). An Archite and friend of David who aided the king during Absalom's rebellion by counteracting the sound advice of Ahithophel to Absalom (II Sam 15:32-37; 16:18-19; 17:5-14). Hushai sent word of Absalom's plans to David by Ahimaaz and Jonathan, sons of the priests Zadok and Abiathar respectively (II Sam 17:15-17), and thus David escaped Absalom's plot. Hushai apparently is to be identified as the father of Baanah, one of the 12 officers appointed to provide food for Solomon's household (I Kgs 4:16).

HUSHAM (hŏŏsh'*ȧ*m). A Temanite who succeeded Jobab as king of Edom (Gen 36:34-35; I Chr 1:45-46).

HUSHATHITE (hŏŏsh'*ȧ*-thīt). The family name of Sibbechai, one of David's 30 heroic followers (II Sam 21:18; I Chr 11:29; 20:4; 27:11); also apparently called by the name of Mebunnai (II Sam 23:27).

HUSHIM (hŏŏsh'ĭm)

1. Family name of the children of Dan (Gen 46:23), also called Shuham (Num 26:42).

2. The name given to the sons of Aher, a Benjamite (I Chr 7:12).

3. One of the two wives of Shaharaim, a Benjamite, and the mother of Abitub and Elpaal (I Chr 8:8, 11).

HUSK. *See* Plants.

HUZ (hŭz). The eldest son of Nahor by his wife Milcah (Gen 22:21). He is called Uz in the ASV and RSV. *See* Uz.

HUZZAB (hŭz'*ȧ*b). A word of doubtful meaning found in Nah 2:7. Older commentators took it as a proper noun referring to the queen of Nineveh or to a female idol such as Ishtar, or perhaps a personification of Nineveh itself; but no such name is known in Assyrian inscriptions. Another view sees it as a verb meaning "it is decreed." Others read it as "country of Zab," or "river country," designating a fertile tract of Assyria E of the Tigris River. RSV conjectures it to mean "its mistress."

HYENA. *See* Animals, II.21.

HYKSOS (hĭk'sŏs). The Hyksos were non-Egyptian rulers of Egypt who formed the 15th and 16th Dynasties in the Egyptian historical outline by the 3rd cen. B.C. priest-historian Manetho. He referred to them as "shepherd kings" and ascribed to them a rule of 511 years. The name "Hyksos" is derived from the Egyptian "rulers of foreign countries"; current chronologies assign them only some 150 years of domination in Egypt (*c.* 1730–1570 B.C.).

The Hyksos established their capital in the Nile Delta at Avaris (later Tanis; biblical Zoan). They were Asiatics who are thought to have dominated most of the Syro-Palestinian area during the Middle Bronze II period (1850–1550 B.C.) and who infiltrated Egypt, eventually gaining control of the country without warfare. The names of some of the Hyksos kings contain Semitic elements. This factor contributes to the view that Joseph, a Semitic slave, rose to power in Egypt during the Hyksos period. Josephus (*Against Apion,* i.14, 16) even confuses the Hyksos and the Israelites (FLAP, p. 95).

The Hyksos became quite Egyptianized but also made certain contributions to Egyptian culture. They left the knowledge of how to use the horse and chariot in warfare, and introduced new types of daggers and swords, and especially the strong compound Asiatic bow. The relationships of the Hyksos were widespread, for objects bearing the name of a Hyksos king have been found as far distant as Crete and Mesopotamia. Sites occupied by them usually show a typical rectangular fortification with a sloping rampart (glacis) made of beaten earth (*terre pisée*).

The native Egyptian rulers of the Theban area led by Sekenenre began the war of liberation against the Hyksos. Ahmose, his son, the founder of the 18th Dynasty, besieged Avaris and defeated the Hyksos, who fled to Palestine. Pursuing, Ahmose successfully climaxed three campaigns against them at Sharuhen W of Beer-sheba. A century later the expeditions of Thutmose III (1504–1450 B.C.) were still attributable in part to the desire to crush the Hyksos.

See Egypt; Exodus, The; Joseph.

C. E. D.

HYMENAEUS (hī-mĕ-nē'ŭs). A teacher in Ephesus (?), mentioned in I Tim 1:20 and II Tim 2:17, condemned by Paul for false teaching. He appears to have rejected the apostolic teaching and the dictates of conscience. For this Paul delivered him over to Satan (cf. I Cor 5:5) to teach him the error of blaspheming. Whether this punishment was limited to excommunication from the church only, or involved physical suffering as well (cf. Acts 5:1–11; I Cor 11:30), is difficult to ascertain. Seemingly, however, it was remedial and not simply penal in nature. (See further in Deissmann, *Light from the Ancient East,* pp. 301–303, for examples of Execration texts in antiquity.)

The second error of Hymenaeus was the affirmation that the resurrection had already taken place. Like cancer, the error was apparently spreading and doing injury to the faith of certain persons. Possibly this case was parallel to the incident in Corinth where some taught that there is no resurrection of the dead (I Cor 15:12). To the Gr. mind at least, the idea of bodily resurrection was absurd (cf. Acts 17:32).

Again, it may have been a teaching that the resurrection was spiritual in nature, referring to the regeneration of one dead in sins (see Eph 2:6; Col 3:1; Rom 6:3–4). However, both Paul (I Cor 15:4, 20–23, 51–54; Phil 3:11, 21) and our Lord before him (Jn 5:28–29) taught a bodily resurrection. This is the ordinary sense of the Gr. word *anastasis* in the NT. Some continued to spiritualize the idea, and these heretical views are recorded by 2nd cen. writers (Justin Martyr, Irenaeus and Tertullian). *See also* Resurrection.

W. M. D.

HYMN. *See* Music.

HYPOCRISY, HYPOCRITE. In the context of Gr. drama the term hypocrite was applied to an actor on the theater stage. Since an actor pretends to be someone other than himself, *hypokritēs* was applied metaphorically to a person who "acts a part" in real life, pretending to be better than he actually is, one who simulates goodness. In secular Gr. literature, therefore, *hypokritēs* may be either neutral or undesirable. In the NT, however, it is always undesirable, signifying one who works a deception by feigned piety.

This concept of pretended goodness was foreign to OT thought. The Heb. root *ḥ-n-p,* translated "hypocrisy" or "hypocrite" in the KJV, was translated in the LXX by *anomos,* "lawless," "criminal," or "godless," parallel to *ponēros,* "an evil doer" (Isa 9:17); and by *asebēs,* "godless," "irreverent" (Isa 33:14).

In the book of Job it is clear that the *ḥānēp* is one radically opposed to God, one who forgets God (Job 8:13; 15:34–35; 20:5; 27:8). The verb *ḥānap* means to pollute or corrupt (cf. Num 35:33; Ps 106:38; Isa 24:5; Jer 3:1). Theodotion's translation of Job, later incorporated into the LXX, rendered Heb. *ḥānēp* as *hypo-*

Masks used by Greek and Roman actors were made of stiffened linen. These Roman masks were made in marble for decorative purposes. BM

kritēs in two verses (Job 34:30; 36:13). Thus it seems that Greek-speaking Jews were employing *hypokrisis* in another sense in addition to its metaphorical meaning of feigning to be what one is not.

This background in the OT indicates the broader sense in which the term is used in our Lord's ministry. "Hypocrite" occurs 18 times and "hypocrisy" twice in the words of Jesus. He warned His disciples of "the leaven of the Pharisees, which is hypocrisy" (Lk 12:1). He diagnosed them as appearing righteous to men, but being full of hypocrisy and iniquity within (Mt 23:28). That He accused the Pharisees of more than mere pretending is suggested by the parallels to the reading "their hypocrisy" in Mk 12:15. In Mt 22:18 it is "their wickedness" or malice, and in Lk 20:23 it is "their craftiness." Only in Lk 20:20 does the verb *hypokrinō* retain the original Gr. meaning of pretending: the scribes and chief priests, attempting to arrest Jesus, sent spies "who pretended to be sincere" (RSV).

Outside the Gospels *hypokrisis* occurs three times. Paul rebuked Peter for "dissimulation," his deliberate inconsistency of first eating with Gentile converts at Antioch and then, fearing the circumcision party, refusing to associate with them further (Gal 2:13, verb and noun)—and this following God's vision to Peter prior to his visiting Cornelius (Acts 10). Paul reveals that in the last times there will be those who follow evil spirits and doctrines of demons and speak lies in hypocrisy (I Tim 4:1-2). The Christian himself is warned to get rid of all hypocrisy in his life (I Pet 2:1).

There are six occurrences in the NT of the verbal adjective *anupokritos,* "without hypocrisy" (Jas 3:17; also Rom 12:9, "without dissimulation"; and II Cor 6:6; I Tim 1:5; II Tim 1:5; I Pet 1:22, "unfeigned").

J. H. G. and R. A. K.

HYSSOP. *See* Plants.

I

I AM. The name God gave Himself when He commissioned Moses to deliver the Israelites from Egypt (Ex 3:14). God is the one independent, entirely self-subsistent Being in the universe. All that is, depends upon Him (Gen 1:1; cf. Col 1:17; Heb 1:3, 10). He does not need anyone or anything, since in Himself He possesses all possible relationships—the I-it or the subject-object, the I-Thou or the personal encounter, and the we-you or the social relationship (*see* Godhead; Trinity). All that exists has been created by Him for His own glory.

Christ declared Himself to be the great "I AM." In Jn 8 He maintains that He tells the truth, and supports this by claiming He is saying what He has heard (v. 26), seen (v. 38), and been taught by the Father (v. 28), and can corroborate with Him at any time (v. 29). He concludes His argument by using the expression "I am" (v. 58). The Jews realized when He said "Before Abraham was, I am," that this was a claim to deity, particularly since He was returning to the "I am" of v. 24: "If ye believe not that I am [the word "he" is not in the Gr.], ye shall die in your sins." This is why they took up stones to kill Him. He was identifying Himself, they realized, with the "I AM THAT I AM" of Ex 3:14.

Theodor Zahn found similar "I am" expressions in Jn 4:26; 9:9; 18:5; Mt 14:27; Mk 13:6; 14:62; Lk 22:70; 24:39. Greijdanus objected that in these other places a predicate is either given or implied. However, at least in Mt 14:27, as Christ came to the disciples walking on the storm-tossed waters, He announced Himself as "I am" (Gr. *egō eimi*). And again in Mk 13:6 He uses the term without any predicate saying, "Many shall come in my name, saying, I am [Gr. omits Christ]; and shall deceive many." Lk 22:70, on the other hand, has an implied predicate, and though in Lk 24:39 Christ again says "I am," He makes it clear that He is merely identifying Himself to the disciples as He adds the word *autos*, meaning "the same," "Myself."

R. A. K.

IBEX or WILD GOAT. *See* Animals, II. 22.

IBHAR (ĭb'här). A son of David, born in Jerusalem, by a wife not mentioned by name and otherwise unknown (II Sam 5:15; I Chr 3:6; 14:5).

IBIS. *See* Animals, III. 24.

IBLEAM (ĭb'lē-ȧm). A Canaanite city in northern Manasseh, whose territory extended to Issachar (Josh 17:11), and in I Chr 6:70 called Bileam (*q.v.*). However, the native inhabitants were never expelled and continued to live alongside the Israelites (Jud 1:27). King Ahaziah of Judah was slain by Jehu's men near there (II Kgs 9:27). According to LXX of II Kgs 15:10, King Zachariah of Israel was also killed there (see RSV). It is near modern Jenin, on the road from Jezreel to Dothan, now called Tell Bel'ameh. Its name occurs as *ybr'm* in Thutmose III's list of conquered towns, about 1470 B.C.

IBNEIAH (ĭb-nē'yȧ). A son of Jeroham and a chief of the tribe of Benjamin in the first settlement in Jerusalem (I Chr 9:8).

IBNIJAH (ĭb-nī'jȧ). A member of the tribe of Benjamin and the father of Reuel (I Chr 9:8).

IBRI (ĭb'rī). A Merarite Levite and son of Jaaziah in the time of David (I Chr 24:27).

IBZAN (ĭb'zăn). A judge of Israel for seven years following the death of Jephthah. He was a native of Bethlehem, whether of Judah or Zebulun is not certain. He had 30 sons and 30 daughters, all of whom took marriage partners outside his clan (Jud 12:8–10).

ICE. Frost is somewhat rare in Palestine except on the highest mountains. Three biblical references to ice or frost (Job 37:10; 38:29; Ps 147:17) stress the power of God. In a figurative sense, insincere friends are compared with brooks "which are blackish by reason of the ice" (Job 6:16).

ICHABOD (ĭk'ȧ-bōd; "no glory"). Son of Phinehas and grandson of Eli (I Sam 4:21). The shocking news of Israel's defeat by the Philistines (I Sam 4:19–22) with the consequent slaughter of Phinehas, the taking of the ark, and the death of Eli, induced labor in the pregnant wife of Phinehas and she gave birth to a son. As death laid hold upon her in this experience she named the child Ichabod, partly on account of her own personal tragedy but mainly for the national catastrophe and the loss of the ark as the visible representation of the presence of God (I Sam 4:22). Her own words of explanation of the name were, "The glory has departed from Israel" (v. 21, RSV).

ICONIUM (ī-kō'nĭ-ŭm). An ancient city of Asia Minor, now called Konya, that was visited several times by Paul on his missionary journeys. The chief city of Lycaonia in the Hellenistic period, Iconium lay on the border of the districts of Phrygia and Lycaonia. It was incorporated into the Roman province of Galatia in 25 B.C. It stood on a level plateau 3,400 feet above sea level, with 5,000-6,000 foot mountains a few miles to the W.

Paul brought the gospel there on his first missionary journey (Acts 13:51; 14:1-6, 21) and returned there on his second journey (Acts 16:2), and probably on his third as well (Acts 18:23). It was possibly to Iconium as well as the other cities in that area that Paul wrote his epistle to the Galatians to combat the inroads of the Judaizers.

IDALAH (ĭd'ȧ-lȧ). A border town of Zebulun (Josh 19:15). The Jerusalem Talmud (*Megillah*, I, 1) calls it Iralah and identifies it with Heireiah. It may be represented by the modern Khirbet el-Ḥuwārah, little more than half a mile S of Beit Lahm, the Bethlehem in Galilee.

IDBASH (ĭd'băsh). A man of Judah and one belonging to the "father" of Etam (I Chr 4:3). "Father" here probably means "founder" of the town of Etam, two miles SW of Bethlehem; Idbash was likely one of his sons.

IDDO (ĭd'ō)

1. A Gershomite Levite whom David set over the service of song (I Chr 6:21).
2. Son of Zechariah and ruler of the half tribe of Manasseh in Gilead, E of the Jordan (I Chr 27:21).
3. Father of Ahinadab, one of Solomon's 12 provisioners (I Kgs 4:14).
4. A seer (II Chr 9:29; 12:15) and prophet (II Chr 13:22) who lived in the days of Solomon, Jeroboam, and Rehoboam and recorded some of their activities. His records concerning Solomon (II Chr 9:29), Rehoboam (II Chr 12:15), and Abijah (II Chr 13:22) are unknown to us, but may form the basis for part of our Chronicles.
5. The chief of the Jews of the Captivity in Casiphia (Ezr 8:17). Ezra sent to him to requisition from the Levites and Nethinim a contingent to join his expedition to Jerusalem.
6. Grandfather of the prophet Zechariah (Zech 1:1, 7) who was contemporary with Haggai (Ezr 6:14) and author of the OT book bearing that name. Iddo was one of those who returned from the Exile with Zerubbabel, and is listed among the chiefs of the priests and heads of households (Neh 12:4, 16).

J. K. M.

IDLE. Laziness or indolence which, according to Heb. wisdom literature, leads to poverty (Prov 19:15; Eccl 10:18). Earlier Pharaoh had accused the complaining Israelites of idleness (Ex 5:8-17). The NT word *argos* (Mt 12:36; 20:3, 6; I Tim 5:13) means "inactive" or "useless."

IDOL. *See* Gods, False; Idolatry; Imagery.

IDOLATRY

Definition

This is a transliteration of the Gr. word *eidōlolatria,* which we understand to mean "the worship of idols; the worship of images as divine or sacred." *See* Imagery. This Gr. term is a compound of two. The first is *eidō* (cf. the Latin *video*), meaning "to see" and "to know"; hence it carries the basic concept "to know by seeing." On this term was formed the word *eidōlon,* "image," which came to mean specifically an image of a god as an object of worship, or a material symbol of the supernatural as such an object. The second term is *latreia,* meaning "service" or, more especially, "the service or worship of the gods."

Idolatry, then, is paying divine honors to any item of human fabrication, or the ascription of divine powers to purely natural agencies.

Description

As a time-space creature, man has been specially inclined to give adoration and worship to some sort of visible symbol of the deity. He seems to crave tangible manifestations of the divine presence. During man's history this has taken varied forms and manifestations. If he departed from the worship of the true God, he did not renounce religion but sought to substitute for the true God a false one after his own liking.

Animism was the worship or reverence of inanimate objects, such as stones, trees, rivers, springs, and other natural objects. There was also the worship of animate things: such animals as the sacred bulls or calves, symbolical of the principle of reproduction and procreation; the serpent, as a symbol of yearly renewal, since it sheds its old skin for a new one; and birds, such as the hawk, the eagle, and the falcon, as symbols of wisdom and insight. These animal forms were sometimes combined with the human as objects of worship—theriomorphism. There were the astral deities, such as the sun, moon and stars. Nature's elements and forces were also reverenced and worshiped: storm, air, fire, water, and earth; hence the vegetation gods and the *genii loci* received status.

The fertility principle was often deified as a mother-goddess (*see* Diana), as images from Ephesus indicate. This involved the worship of sex and the glorification of prostitution.

There was the common tendency toward

hero worship which also included the dead ancestors of the tribe or clan.

Totemism represented not only activity in arts and crafts, but the worship of the patron god or goddess of the clan under whatever image the deity may have been conceived. Usually this was a wild animal or a bird, or a combination of one of the animal forms with the human.

Idealism involved the worship of abstract concepts such as wisdom and justice.

Emperor worship must be included. Kings, because they had the power of life and death over their subjects, came to be deified. "*Ave Caesar*" meant more than "long live the king" or "Heil Hitler"; it was an act of worship.

The Greek goddess Aphrodite, identified with the Assyrian Ishtar. Corinth Museum, Mimosa

Man alone possesses the gift of image making. In doing so he seeks the reproduction of vanished ocular impressions or imagined sacred objects. So idolatry stands closely related to man's advance in arts and crafts. His history is filled with attempts to give material shapes to religious ideals and ideas. Once these became objectivized as concrete objects, then reverence and worship could be expressed toward them by the burning of incense, bowing the knee, kissing the image, coating it over with silver and gold, bedecking it with precious stones and jewels, or clothing it in sumptuous apparel. It was only another step to consulting it as an oracle of divine wisdom and a means of predicting one's future or the outcome of some military or political project. A cult-statue was therefore a thing of worship and delight because the visible image gave evidence of the presence of the divinity. It was customarily housed in some shrine, and an entire cultus for its worship evolved. *See* Graven Image; Imagery.

In a larger sense idolatry in theoretical forms may include the vain philosophies of men, for these detract from God's glory (Rom 1:23) and give divine honors to another. Thus naturalism, humanism, rationalism are types of idolatry. Likewise, attachment to horoscopes and any occult practices of witchcraft and spiritism must be condemned as idolatrous. *See* Magic; Sorcery.

The Idolatry of Israel's Neighbors

Heathen practices came to Israel chiefly via the Egyptians, the Canaanites and the Assyro-Babylonian nations.

Ancient Egyptian art and writing have left evidence of thousands of deities. The Pharaohs themselves were regarded to be incarnations of deity. In addition to such humans, a bull, a crocodile, a fish, a tree, a hawk, etc., might also be indwelt by a spirit and thus deified. There were many animal- or bird-headed deities with human bodies.

Among the Canaanites the many Baals with their respective fertility cults were the sponsors of orgiastic worship of nature and the productivity principle.

Chief among the deities of the Babylonians and the Assyrians was the Mesopotamian immoral goddess of lust and procreation – Ishtar. The Babylonians seemed willing to import gods from many surrounding neighbors, or from nations they had conquered and placed under tribute. Hence they had a god for almost anything: learning, war, fire, motherhood, virginity, fertility, the sky, the wind, water, earth, and the underworld, along with the usual sun, moon, and stars. The Assyrians were just as idolatrous and in addition gained the unenviable reputation of being the cruelest and most sadistic of all the ancient nations of the Near East.

The History of Idolatry Among the Israelites

Abraham lived in a world of idolatry. His westward trek was to abandon idolatrous Ur of the Chaldees and seek a new home in which to worship the one true God. It is significant that from his descendants have come the three great monotheistic religions of the world: Judaism, Christianity, and Islam.

The prohibition of idolatry is one of the few immutable absolutes in the Jewish system of ethics (along with incest and murder). The imageless worship of Yahweh announced not merely that He was greater than nature but also that He was unbounded by it. In the OT there are many Heb. terms used in derision of idolatry indicating its foulness and obscenity as well as its sheer emptiness.

All strata of Jewish law bear witness to the opposition to a portrayal of God. The first two

Altar in the Temple of Vespasian (Pompeii), sacred to the imperial cult. It portrays a sacrificing priest, a flute player, and administration of sacred oaths. HFV

commandments prohibit image worship as well as the worship of any other god (cf. Ex 20:1 ff.; Deut 5:7-8; Lev 19:4). Idolatry was classed as a state offense and savored of treason, punishable by death (Deut 17:2-7).

Heb. prophecy likewise shows an uncompromising hostility to idolatry. An image is the mere handiwork of man (Amos 5:26; Hos 13:2; Isa 2:8), an imitation of creatures (Deut 4:16 ff.) formed out of dead matter (Hos 4:12, RSV; Isa 44:9-10; Ps 115). Thus its worship is sheer folly. God alone is to be worshiped, since He alone is the living Creator of all things and a Spirit who cannot be pictured in any form. Yet among the Israelites may be noted the worship of Yahweh under the form of some image or symbol; the worship of the gods of the surrounding nations under whatever symbol was appropriate; and the worship of images and symbols themselves (the brazen serpent, II Kgs 18:4).

The story of idolatry among the Hebrews begins with the account of Rachel's stealing Laban's teraphim (Gen 31:19), which were probably statuettes of household gods. These of course were not rated on an equal basis with the God of Abraham and Nahor (Gen 31:53). Rachel may not have been interested in the teraphim for worship purposes, however, because discoveries at Nuzu indicate that with possession of the teraphim went headship of the family. She may have been trying to transfer headship of the patriarchal family from her father to her husband.

Years in Egypt resulted in Israel's infatuation with Egyptian idols (cf. Josh 24:14; Ezk 20:7-8), and thus Moses found it imperative to challenge the gods of Egypt (Num 33:4).

During the absence of Moses from the camp at the foot of Mount Sinai, the Israelites clamored for some visible representation of Yahweh (Ex 32:1). Only a mind thoroughly accustomed to the profound respect paid to the sacred bulls of Egypt could hit upon so strange a representation of Yahweh (Ex 32:4; see JerusB). Nor could any people not familiar with this Egyptian practice have responded so readily as did these Israelites. The feast that Aaron proclaimed to Yahweh (Ex 32:5), which resulted in the people singing and dancing naked before the idol (32:6, 18, 19, 25), was like the feast of Apis; it led if not publicly yet privately to indecency (the word "play," *ṣaḥēq,* in 32:6 implies sexual gestures or acts; cf. "fondling," Gen 26:8, RSV). Thus the great wrath of both the Lord and Moses is understandable (32:4, 8). Aaron called the calf Yahweh (32:5), but to represent Him thus was idolatry (Ps 106:19-20).

There was temporary apostasy at Shittim when the men of Israel, yielding to the charms of the daughters of Moab, gave way to Baalism (Num 25).

On entering Palestine, Israel came in contact with varied forms of idolatry. And though they were commanded to destroy all these (Deut 12:2-3), the command was not in all instances fully obeyed (Jud 2:12, 14).

Gideon's father had erected or had come into the possession of an altar to Baal which Gideon was obliged to destroy (Jud 6:25-32). The ephod of Gideon may have been a votive offering to Yahweh, but it became a snare to all Israel as well as his own household (Jud 8:27). No sooner was Gideon dead than Israel returned to the idolatrous worship of "Baal of the covenant" (Jud 8:33; 9:4).

The episode of Micah in Jud 17 and 18 gives evidence of secret idolatry on the part of many individuals (Jud 17:1-6). Here a Levite, of all people, becomes a priest of images (cf. Deut 27:15). Samuel, as he took over the judgeship of Israel, found it necessary to rebuke their possession of foreign gods (I Sam 7:3-4).

Solomon had already set the stage for a great apostasy to idolatry by his importation of so many foreign wives, and with them their respective forms of heathen worship, each with its false god. There was Ashteroth of the Zidonians, Chemosh of the Moabites, Milcom of the Ammonites, to mention but a few. Three of the summits of Mount Olivet were crowned with high places to these deities respectively, and the fourth was named "the Mount of Corruption" (I Kgs 11:5-8; II Kgs 23:13-14).

Solomon's son Rehoboam was of an Ammonitish mother, with whose religion was introduced some of the worst features of licentious idolatry (I Kgs 14:21-24). Jeroboam, fresh from his exile in Egypt, erected sacred bulls in honor of Yahweh at Dan and Bethel (I Kgs 12:26-33). In practice, however, the worship seems to have been directed to the animals of gold rather than to the Lord Himself (cf. Amos 4:4-5). This worship of the calves is thought of by Hosea as the "sin of Israel" (Hos 10:5-8, NASB).

One of the greatest promoters of idolatry in Heb. history was King Ahab with his Zidonian princess wife, Jezebel (I Kgs 21:25-26). He not only built a temple and an altar to Baal of the Zidonians—Melkart, but engaged in active persecution of the prophets of Yahweh (I Kgs 16:31-33). With the prophets of Baal and Asherah Elijah staged his famous contest for the vindication of the true God (I Kgs 18).

The story of the northern kingdom now becomes successively, with each of its kings, a reenactment of the sin of Jeroboam. It came to be known as "the way of the kings of Israel" (II Kgs 16:3; cf. 17:7-18). Thus there was a long line of royal apostates in the nation of Israel, which did not cease until the conquest of that kingdom by the Assyrians.

A sponsor of idolatry in the southern kingdom was King Ahaz. He built an altar after a model he had seen in Damascus, right on the site of the brazen altar of the Jewish temple (II Kgs 16:10-15). He also caused his son to pass through the fire (II Kgs 16:3) and offered sacrifices to the gods of Damascus (II Chr 28:23).

One of the longest and most idolatrous reigns in Judah was that of wicked King Manasseh, who, though he returned to the Lord just before his death (II Chr 33:10-17), could not undo the results of a lifetime of patronage of enchantments, divinations, witchcraft, profanation of the temple courts with altars to astral deities, and an image of Asherah in the holy place (II Kgs 21:1-9; Jer 32:34). Consequently, not long after his repentance and death his own son restored the altars of the Baalim and the images of Asherah.

Yet as in the days of Elijah in the northern kingdom (I Kgs 19:18), so during the reigns of the wicked kings of Judah God seems to have had a righteous remnant who refused to bow the knee to Baal.

The most deplorable type of idolatry was that led by the false prophets, who as leaders of the apostasy joined ranks with corrupt priests (II Kgs 23:5) and prophesied by Baal and followed "things that do not profit," i.e., idols with no power in them (Jer 2:8; cf. II Chr 15:3).

There seem to have been some attempts to worship the true God under idolatrous imagery and a contamination of the true worship with idolatrous rites (II Kgs 17:32; 18:22; Jer 41:5). Of course intermarriage with idolatrous nations was invariably a first step toward idolatry (Ex 34:14-16; Deut 7:3-4; Ezr 9:2; 10:18; Neh 13:23-27).

Ezekiel describes a chamber of images at Jerusalem (Ezk 8:7-12), derived no doubt from Egypt. The brazen serpent seems to have become something of an idol, with the people offering incense to it (II Kgs 18:4). Even the worship of Moloch was resorted to at times (II Kgs 17:17), though this practice of tossing their infants into the fire was basically revolting to the Heb. mind.

The Babylonian Exile came as a direct rebuke to their idolatry (Jer 29:8-10), as God had forewarned in Hezekiah's day (Isa 39:6).

In post-Exilic times, especially under Alexander and his successors, the Jews once again faced the issue of idolatry (I Macc 1:41-50, 54-64). Let it be said to the credit of many that they chose death rather than idolatry (I Macc 2:23-26, 45-48).

Later, Herod's golden eagle above one of the doors of the sanctuary aroused a storm of protest (Jos *Ant.* xvii.6.3).

Ashurbanipal, king of Assyria (*c.* 650) beginning ceremonially the work of rebuilding the temple of a god. BM

New Testament Evaluation

The early Christians unavoidably came in contact with Gentile idolatry (Acts 17:16). Thus they often had to face questions concerning the festive meals and meat offered to idols (Acts 15:20; I Pet 4:3; Rev 2:14, 20), especially at Corinth (I Cor 8, 10).

Idolater is the name given to worshipers of heathen gods and personal idols in the NT (I Cor 5:10-11; 6:9; 10:7; Rev 21:8; 22:15). Idolatry is specifically equated with covetousness which makes a god of mammon (i.e., money) and renders a man unfaithful in his stewardship (Mt 6:24; Lk 16:13; Col 3:5; Eph 5:5). The injunctions against evil concupiscence surely have a reference not only to the idolatry in the early Christian environment but also to our sex-obsessed age (Gal 5:19-20; Phil 3:19;

cf. Rom 16:18). The source of idolatry is basically an impure heart and will (Rom 1:21). Paul agrees with Isaiah that man degenerated to heathenism rather than evolved from it (cf. Rom 1; Isa 44). Therefore he commands Christians to flee from idolatry (I Cor 10:14), as does John (I Jn 5:21).

Bibliography. John Calvin, *Institutes of the Christian Religion*, Grand Rapids: Eerdmans, I, Chap. XI, 1957 reprint. E. La B. Cherbonnier, "Idolatry," *Handbook of Christian Theology*, M. Halverson, ed., New York: Meridian Books, 1958, pp. 176–183. CornPBE, "Idol Worship in Israel," pp. 398–401. John Gray, "Idolatry," IDB, II, 675–678. Gerhard Kittel, "*Eikōn*," TDNT, II, 381–397. Adolphe Lods, "Images and Idols (Hebrew and Canaanite)," Hastings' *Encyclopedia of Religion and Ethics*, VII, 138–142. McClintock and Strong, "Idolatry," *Cyclopedia of Biblical, Theological and Ecclesiastical Literature*, IV, 471–486. H. M. Schulweis, "Jewish Ethics," *Encyclopedia of Morals*, V, Ferm, ed., New York: Philosophical Library, 1956, pp. 253–265.

R. E. Pr.

IDOLS, THINGS OFFERED TO. The idea of flesh that has been offered to idols is expressed by a single Gr. word, *eidōlothyton*. The word is used ten times in the NT. It is translated once "meats offered to idols" (Acts 15:29); and "things sacrificed unto idols" (Rev 2:14, 20; cf. I Cor 10:19, 28). It refers to meat from an animal which has been slain in sacrifice to an idol. Only certain parts of the carcass were used in the sacrificial ceremony, the remainder being sold for food in the markets. Jewish law forbade the eating of this meat. The Jerusalem council (Acts 15:29) agreed that Gentile believers should abstain from meats offered to idols out of deference to their Jewish brethren. Paul urged (I Cor 8; Rom 14) Christians to consider their weaker brethren and refrain from eating such meat. *See* Expediency; Weaker Brother.

IDUMAEA (ĭd'yo͝o-mē'*à*). This term was used by the Greeks and Romans (with slightly different spellings) to refer to the region inhabited by the descendants of Esau—the Edomites of the OT. *See* Esau. The word appears once in the Bible, Mk 3:8 (the KJV uses it in Isa 34:5–6; Ezk 35:15; 36:5, but Edom is given by other translations).

The Edomites were closely associated with the Israelites in origin, culture, and language. Their primary importance in the NT is that Herod the Great's father (Antipater) was Idumaean. His mother was Nabataean, an Arab group that lived to the S of the Idumaeans (Jos *Ant*. xiv.1.3; 7.3). The Edomites (*q.v.*) are frequently mentioned in the OT. *See also* Edom; Seir.

The richest part of the land of Edom was on the eastern side of the Arabah (the continuation of the Jordan-Dead Sea cleft), but the Nabataeans had driven the Edomites westward by the 4th cen. B.C. There appears to have been an earlier migration westward, for even Hebron was probably an Edomite city by the time of Ezra and Nehemiah. Since Hebron, famous for the burial place of the patriarchs and David's one-time capital, was not mentioned as one of the cities of Judah reoccupied after the Exile, it may be assumed it was occupied by Edomites.

The Idumaean period was the last time of any greatness in the history of the Edomites, from *c.* 100 B.C. to A.D. 70. Judas Maccabaeus had defeated the Idumaeans and recaptured Hebron in 164 B.C. (I Macc 5:1–5, 65), and John Hyrcanus warred against them successfully, subjected them, and forced them to adopt Judaism and be circumcised *c.* 120 B.C. Yet it was the rise of the Herodian dynasty that lends a prominence to the Idumaeans that otherwise they never would have earned. In A.D. 66–70 they fanatically helped to defend Jerusalem over whose fall their ancestors had gloated some 600 years earlier. The last of the Idumaeans were slaughtered by Titus in A.D. 72.

D. R. S.

IGAL (ī'găl)

1. The son of Joseph of the tribe of Issachar and one of the 12 men sent out by Moses to spy out the land of Canaan (Num 13:7, 17).

2. One of David's mighty warriors, son of Nathan (II Sam 23:36), referred to in I Chr 11:38 as "Joel the brother of Nathan."

3. One of the sons of Shemaiah of the royal house of David (I Chr 3:22), called Igeal in the KJV. *See* Igeal.

IGDALIAH (ĭg'dȧ-lī'ȧ). The father of Hanan the prophet (Jer 35:4).

IGEAL (ī'gē-ȧl). One of the sons of Shemaiah of the royal house of David (I Chr 3:22), called Igal in the ASV and RSV. *See* Igal 3.

IGNORANCE. In the OT God made provision for sins committed in "ignorance" (Heb. *sh*ᵉ*gāgâ*, "error," "wandering astray") as seen in Lev 4, 5; Num 15:22–29, in distinction to sins of presumption. Such sins produced guilt. They were not necessarily done unconsciously but unintentionally, out of weakness or waywardness, and had to be atoned for. These sinners had no intent to rebel against the rule of God; but those who despised His word were to be cut off with no remedy (Num 15:30–31).

The Gr. word *agnoia* means a lack of knowledge because one is uninformed. Paul frequently wrote that he did not wish the early Christians to be ignorant in this sense (Rom 1:13; 11:25; I Cor 10:1; 12:1; etc.). Paul declared he received mercy because he acted in the ignorance of unbelief when persecuting Christians (I Tim 1:13). At Athens he preached that God overlooks the times of ignorance of the heathen (Acts 17:30; cf. 3:17). Thus we see there is special allowance both for the sins committed by the believer in ignorance, and for the ignorance of the heathen.

On the other hand, ignorance in the unconverted is linked with blindness of heart (Eph 4:18) and lust (I Pet 1:14). The heathen are without excuse in not worshiping the one true God, for what can be known about God is plain to them. Therefore their rejection of God is at heart willful and deliberate (Rom 1:18–32; II Pet 3:5; cf. Rom 10:3).

The word *idiōtēs,* meaning a private person in ordinary Gr., is used once in Acts 4:13 by the Sanhedrin of the disciples in the sense of an untrained layman: "they were unlearned [unlettered] and ignorant men [common men with no rabbinic training]."

Bibliography. Rudolf Bultmann, *"Agnoeō,* etc.," TDNT, I, 115–121.

R. A. K.

IIM (ī'ĭm)

1. The contracted form of Ije-abarim, one of the encampments of the Israelites during their exodus from Egypt (Num 33:44–45).

2. A town in the territory of Judah near Edom, the exact location of which is uncertain (Josh 15:29).

IJE-ABARIM (ī'jĕ-ăb'*a*-rĭm). An encampment of the Israelites, said to be near Moab, during their journey from Egypt to the Promised Land (Num 33:44); also called Iim (Num 33:45).

IJON (ī'jŏn). A city of Israel in the territory of Naphtali that was captured by Ben-hadad, king of Syria, at the suggestion of Asa, king of Judah (I Kgs 15:20; II Chr 16:4). Subsequently, during the reign of Pekah, its inhabitants were taken captive into Assyria by Tiglath-pileser. The city is situated about eight miles NW of Banias.

IKKESH (ĭk'ĕsh). A man from Tekoa, the father of Ira, one of David's 30 heroic men (II Sam 23:26; I Chr 11:28; 27:9).

ILAI (ī'lī). An Ahohite, one of David's mighty warriors (I Chr 11:29), also called Zalmon (II Sam 23:28).

ILLNESS. *See* Diseases.

ILLUMINATION. A theological term used to express the manner in which the Holy Spirit makes clear to man the Word of God, whether preached or in written form. Without an illumination of the Holy Scriptures, no man can understand God's divine, infallible revelation because spiritual things are only spiritually—i.e., by the aid of the Holy Spirit—understood or discerned (I Cor 2:11–14; Jn 16:13). Therefore Paul prayed that the "eyes" of our hearts might be enlightened (Eph 1:18). The Bible in its original text is the inspired, infallible Word of God. Inspiration therefore describes the work of the Spirit in the authors of the Scriptures and the Scriptures themselves; illumination, the means by which the Scriptures are made clear to the reader.

Enlightenment or illumination of the darkened mind, whether it be of Jew (Heb 6:4; 10:32) or Gentile (II Cor 4:4–6), is a necessary aspect of the salvation experience. David acknowledged that the Lord lightened his darkness (Ps 18:28). By linking this concept with the term "commandment" he implied that only as the Word of God is obeyed, does further enlightenment come (Ps 19:8).

Karl Barth and the neoorthodox theologians remove inspiration from the writer of Scripture and the Scriptures themselves and place it in the hearer or reader. Barth speaks of men being verbally inspired and means by this that the fallible, contradictory Bible becomes the Word of God as man enjoys a subjective experience of revelation. This view denies both the teaching of Christ concerning the Bible and the view which the Bible presents of itself. *See* Inspiration; Neoorthodoxy.

R. A. K.

ILLYRICUM (ĭ-lĭr'*ĭ*-c*ŭ*m). A Roman province (also called Dalmatia) lying N of Macedonia, W of Moesia and S of Pannonia, and on the E coast of the Adriatic Sea. It is approximately equivalent to the territory of modern Yugoslavia. It is only mentioned in the NT as the western limits of Paul's travels at the end of his third missionary journey (Rom 15:19).

The geographer Strabo (*Geography* VII.317) described the Illyrians as wild and given to piracy, and the land as warm on the coast but cold in the mountainous interior. Both the Greeks and the Romans carried on military campaigns against them, often not too successfully. The land was finally incorporated as a province of the Roman Empire in the first decade of the 1st cen. A.D.

IMAGE. *See* Idolatry; Imagery.

IMAGE, NEBUCHADNEZZAR'S. The only record of the golden image which Nebuchadnezzar made is in Dan 3. Images of gods and of the kings themselves were common in Babylonia, and fit in with our knowledge of religious conditions under Nebuchadnezzar. This image on the plain of Dura may have had the form of an obelisk with a nine-foot base and towering 90 feet high, plated with glittering gold. The refusal of Daniel's three friends to worship this image was readily apparent. The method of punishment by fire for those refusing to bow seems to have been common to that period (cf. Jer 29:22). Although Daniel is not mentioned, it is unreasonable to infer, on the basis of Daniel's character as portrayed in the book bearing his name, that he worshiped this image.

Possibly the great image which the king saw in his dream and which Daniel described (Dan 2:31–35) and interpreted for him, was the inspiration for the golden monument which Nebuchadnezzar created (3:1). In so doing he was defying God's express declaration that his kingdom would fall and be succeeded by other kingdoms (2:38–45).

S. J. S.

IMAGE OF GOD. Man, as created in the image of God, is distinguished from all other creatures. He is unique in that he was made for communion with and to be responsible to his Creator. God made man like Himself, as a personal being, and for Himself in an "I-Thou" relationship (Gen 1:26–27; 5:1–2; 9:6; I Cor 11:7; Eph 4:24; Col 3:10; Jas 3:9). Only in obedient response to God can man truly fulfill the purpose for which he was created. It is in Jesus Christ alone that the image of God may be perfectly seen; He is the true and perfect man (Col 1:15; II Cor 4:4).

Three aspects of this doctrine may be distinguished.

1. *The image as created by God.* The image of God bears a natural or a formal likeness to God, which consists in personality, for this is essentially what God is, a personal Spirit. It also bears a moral or relational likeness, which consisted originally in positive holiness and original righteousness. Man was not created merely in a state of innocence or moral neutrality; but his mind, affections, and will were positively directed toward God as his supreme end. As such, the first man's moral nature was a finite reflection of God's moral nature. However, he was capable of testing, probation, development and progress through the exercise of free choice in the face of temptation. His was a responsibility in freedom. It was possible for Adam to choose good or evil; his moral condition was not immutable or indefectible.

As a gift from God, man in God's image was endowed with immortality (not merely as naturally possessing endless existence in virtue of the simplicity of his soul). He was not subject to the law of death, since there was no principle of death or of sin at work in his original state of created goodness.

While God is not physical in any way, there is a sense in which even man's body is included in the image of God, for man is a unitary being composed of both body and soul. His body is a fit instrument for the self-expression of a soul made for fellowship with the Creator and is suited eschatologically to become a "spiritual body" (I Cor 15:44). There was no antagonism or contrariety between soul and body in the original state (dualism is ruled out). The body was not something to be despised as inferior to the soul or as a hindrance to the higher life of man. It was not something apart from the real self of Adam, but was essentially one with it. As such, there was a subjection of the sensuous impulses to the control of the human spirit.

Included in Adam's creation in the image of God was his dominion over the lower creation, the animals and the world of nature. This is indicative of the glory and honor with which man was crowned as the head and apex of the entire creation. Physical surroundings in the garden of Eden were fitted to bring happiness and to favor the development of the whole of nature. *See* Anthropology; on Christ as the image of God (II Cor 4:4; Phil 2:6; Col 1:15) *see* Christ, Humiliation of; Kenosis.

2. *The image as marred by the Fall.* Disobedience brought disastrous consequences to the original image of God in the first man. Sin impaired the entire natural likeness (personality), so that man's mind, emotions, and will became corrupt (total depravity). Yet man did not lose this natural likeness, however sullied it became because of sin, for it is this which constitutes him as man in distinction from other creatures. It is intrinsic to human nature and constitutes his receptivity for redemption. Even the unregenerate retain the natural image of God, otherwise they would cease to be men (rational and moral beings).

Whereas the natural likeness is still retained after the Fall, the moral image is entirely lost. Now man is destitute of original righteousness; he is dead in trespasses and sin. His affections and will are not inclined in an upward direction toward God and holiness, but in a downward, carnal direction. He has lost fellowship with God and has become an alien and enemy through the estrangement produced by disobedience (Gen 3:8–10; Rom 5:10*a*; Col 1:21*a*). Cut off from the Source of life he became a dying creature (Gen 2:17; Rom 6:23*a*).

The body is no longer such a fit instrument of the soul; it is often a hindrance to the higher life of man because it easily enters into alliance with his depraved affections and perverted will. The original subjection of the sensuous to the spiritual now seems reversed with the Fall. Adam was driven from the garden of Eden, and dominion over nature became difficult and laborious. *See* Fall of Man.

3. *The image as restored by Christ.* Through the redemption that is in Christ the believer is regenerated: he is renewed in knowledge, his affections are reorientated, his will is transformed, his body is made a temple of the Holy Spirit. The image of God is re-created in righteousness and true holiness and is restored to communion and favor with God; by faith man inherits eternal life. Indeed, through the Lord's saving work the believer has regained far more than was lost through Adam's sin (I Cor 15:44–49). The Christian is to be gradually transformed into the very image of the Son of God, which will ultimately involve not only perfect moral and spiritual likeness to Christ but also a glorified body like that of the resurrected last Adam (Rom 8:29; II Cor 3:18; I Cor 15:42 ff.). *See* New Creation.

Divergent views respecting the image of God. In Roman Catholic theology an unwarranted distinction is made between the synonymous terms "image" and "likeness." The former designates the natural image, they claim, and belongs to the very nature of man as man, including spirituality, freedom, and immortality. The latter designates the moral image, righteousness, and holiness, and is a superadded, supernatural gift given to make obedience easier in view of concupiscence, which is a natural tendency toward the lower appetites (but not itself sin, according to Catholic theology). Sometimes the "likeness" is described as a merited product of obedience, a reward for the proper use of nature, so that by it man is enabled to merit eternal life. In the Fall Adam lost only the likeness; the natural image remained unimpaired. Thus, the natural man is now in a moral condition similar to that of the unfallen Adam but before being endowed with original righteousness. This original righteousness can be regained through the sacraments of the Catholic Church.

Among other modern views is the very influential doctrine that the image of God is not at all substantial, as is personality, but is simply relational. This is the view of S. Kierkegaard, Karl Barth and a host of contemporary theologians. They teach that man stands in the image of God only when he is mirroring God's spiritual nature in his own life. This occurs when man obediently responds to God's confrontation in the point of contact between God and man which is experienced in an act of true worship. In such an experience, man at times resembles God and thus (and then) stands in the divine image.

An evolutionary view distinguishes between the image which man originally possessed and which he lost in the Fall (happiness and responsive obedience), and the image acquired by the Fall (rational powers and moral responsibility). This came about when *Homo,* or man, became *Homo sapiens,* or rational man, through the first act that involved moral accountability. In this act man lost his animal-like innocence and happiness, and gained a rational and moral nature.

Bibliography. J. Behm, "*Morphē,* etc.," TDNT, IV, 742–759. G. C. Berkouwer, *Man—The Image of God,* Grand Rapids: Eerdmans, 1962. David S. Cairns, *The Image of God in Man,* New York: Philosophical Library, 1953. Gordon H. Clark, "The Image of God in Man," JETS, XII (1969), 215–222. Carl F. H. Henry, "Man," BDT, pp. 338–342. James Gresham Machen, *The Christian View of Man,* New York: Macmillan, 1937. James Orr, *God's Image in Man,* Grand Rapids: Eerdmans, 1948. J. Schneider, "*Homoios,* etc.," TDNT, V, 186–199. A. H. Strong, *Systematic Theology,* 11th ed., Philadelphia: Judson Press, 1947, pp. 514–532. Charles L. Feinberg, "The Image of God," BS, CXXIX (1972), 235–246.

R. E. Po.

IMAGERY. Very early in human history there came to be employed various artificial representations of objects, animals, persons or gods designed to be used in worship. Some were similitudes of that which actually exists, others were pictorial representations of the imagination, and others assumed symbolic forms. Often they were employed simply for ornamental purposes, as in the tabernacle and the temple, but commonly they came to be used in idolatrous ways.

The Egyptians used images in their burial ceremonies which were distinct from their idols used in pagan worship, such as miniatures of servants, pets, foods, vehicles, etc. By means of magical formulas painted on the inside of his coffin or written on a papyrus scroll buried with the dead, the deceased was expected to bring to life these images in order to serve him in the next world.

Constantly repeated denunciations and prohibitions of images and likenesses of created things in the OT show how persistent was the tendency to idolatry among the Hebrews (e.g., Deut 5:8; 7:5; 16:22; Ps 97:7; Isa 42:17; 44:9; Jer 10:14; Ezk 7:20; Hos 10:2; Mic 1:7; Hab 2:18). Use of graven (or carved) and molten (or cast) idols and images was forbidden to Israelites by the second commandment (Ex 20:4–5), because the idol inevitably became a rival and substitute for God (not merely a symbol). Idolatry not only misrepresents the spiritual nature of God (every bodily representation is a misrepresentation), but divides or alienates devotion by placing an object between (and before) God and the worshiper. It is a root of evil; it leads to every kind of corruption of religion and morality. *See* Idolatry.

R. E. Po.

IMAGINATION. The formation of mental images by a synthesis of elements experienced separately. It presents new views and applications of ideas, events and truths already experienced. The verb "to imagine" in KJV has the meaning of "purpose, scheme, contrive." The ASV translates it "think," "meditate," "devise."

The Heb. word *sh^erîrût* (Deut 29:19; Jer 3:17; etc.) is lit., "firmness" and is generally used in the bad sense of stubbornness, as in RSV, NEB. Heb. *yēṣer* (Gen 6:5; I Chr 28:9; 29:18; etc.) means "form, conception," what is framed in the mind. The Gr. words are *dialogismos,* "thought, opinion, reasoning, design" (Rom 1:21); *dianoia,* "understanding, intelligence, mind, purpose, plan" (Lk 1:51); and *logismos,* "calculation, reasoning, reflection, reasoning power" (II Cor 10:5).

IMITATE. *See* Example.

IMLA, IMLAH (ĭm'lȧ). Father of Micaiah, the prophet of God who was consulted by Ahab and Jehoshaphat before they went to battle against the Syrians at Ramoth-gilead (I Kgs 22:8–9; II Chr 18:7–8).

IMMANUEL. *See* Emmanuel.

IMMATERIALITY. Immateriality is the negative term for which spirituality is its positive expression. It denotes the qualities of simplicity (not divisible), having no parts (not composite), indestructibility (cannot be dissolved), and incorporeality (not of the nature of matter). The Bible describes God and the human soul in terms that indicate they are immaterial.

God is pure spirit (Jn 4:24); He stands in absolute contrast to matter. God cannot be separated into parts; He is free from the limitations of time and space. He is "eternal, immortal, invisible" (I Tim 1:17; cf. 6:16). The divine immateriality is sometimes said to be the basis for God's attributes of eternity, omnipresence and unchangeableness. The fact of the immateriality of the human soul is usually used as one of the arguments for immortality.

Immateriality when used in biblical and theological language should not be understood as it is often used in ordinary language, as the quality of being unessential, flimsy or unimportant.

R. E. Po.

IMMER (ĭm'ẽr)

1. A priest, head of the 16th course of priests appointed by David (I Chr 24:14), the father of Meshillemith (I Chr 9:12) and founder of a family which was very active after the return from Exile. A total of 1,052 of his descendants returned (I Chr 9:12; Ezr 2:37; 10:20; Neh 7:40; 11:13).

2. Among those who returned to Jerusalem with Zerubbabel were some who could not prove their Israelitish descent. The record is not clear whether Immer is the name of one of their ancestors (see 1 above) or the village in Babylon from which some of them came (Ezr 2:59; Neh 7:61).

3. Father of Zadok the priest who worked on the wall of Jerusalem (Neh 3:29). If "father" here means ancestor, he may be the same as 1 above.

4. The father of Pashur the priest who had Jeremiah beaten and put in stocks because of his dire warnings (Jer 20:1). If "ancestor" is meant, he may be 1 above.

P. C. J.

IMMORTALITY. *Athanasia* ("deathlessness") and *aphtharsia* ("incorruptibility") are the two Gr. words designating immortality. *Athanasia* is found in I Cor 15:53 f.; I Tim 6:16; *aphtharsia* is found in Rom 2:7; I Cor 15:42, 50, 53 f.; Eph 6:24 (translated "sincerity"); II Tim 1:10; and the adjective *aphthartos* ("incorruptible") is found in Rom 1:23; I Cor 9:25; 15:52; I Tim 1:17; I Pet 1:4, 23; 3:4.

Immortality may be defined as that state of deathlessness and incorruptibility that resides absolutely and eternally in God and relatively and derivatively in man. This article is limited to the various aspects of man's immortality as revealed in the Scriptures.

God's eternal plan. God's plan involved not only the creation of man but also the redemption of some of fallen man's posterity through the grace of God offered to sinful men in the atoning death of Jesus Christ (Gen 1:26–28; 3:15; Isa 53:1–12; Jn 3:14–16; Rom 3:21–30; Eph 2:1–10). This plan considered man as a created being whose life would continue forever. Those of sinful man's posterity who savingly enter into God's kingdom of grace become inheritors of eternal life in Christ Jesus (Jn 17:2–3; Acts 13:48; Rom 8:28–30; Rev 13:8); but those of sinful man's posterity who reject the offer of salvation in Christ become the objects of God's eternal wrath (Mt 25:41, 46; Rom 2:5–9; 9:22; II Thess 1:8–9; II Pet 2:9; 3:7; Rev 14:9–11). It is evident, therefore, that God's decrees from eternity envisioned a creature called man whose destiny, whether in heaven or in hell, would be eternal. Thus man's immortality is an integral part of God's eternal plan.

Man's creation. The immortality of man's nature is implicit in the creation of man in God's "image" (Gen 1:26–27). Although this term is never defined as such, it is quite evident that "image" describes a kinship with God (cf. II Pet 1:4) that puts man in a category by himself among God's creatures. Even death cannot destroy man's soul (Mt 10:28; Heb 12:23; Rev 6:9–11; 20:4). Paul's interpretation of Gen 2:7 in I Cor 15:45–48 in no wise invalidates the doctrine of man's original and innate immortality, for Paul is contrasting "the image of the earthy" which we now bear as a result of our sin in Eden with "the image of the heavenly" which the redeemed will bear as a result of the resurrection of their bodies at Christ's second advent. Thus it is quite evident that the divine "image" planted in man's nature at creation included man's immortality as an integral part.

Man's apostasy. The question arises at this point whether Adam's sin in Eden (Gen 3:1–21; Rom 5:12–14) disrobed man of his essential immortality. Some believe man lost his immortality in Eden. This view finds apparent support in the fact the divine image received some serious damage as a result of Adam's sin. It is evident that man's moral nature (Rom 1:18–32; 3:9–20; Eph 2:1–3, 12; 4:18) and volitional powers (Mt 12:34; Jn 3:19; 8:43–44; II Pet 2:14) were radically affected by man's apostasy from a state of original rectitude.

It cannot be deduced, however, from these devastations upon man's original nature that man likewise lost his immortality. Such a conclusion would run contrary to three important facts: (1) the still resident image of God in man long after his fall in Eden (Gen 9:6), thus justifying the stern punishment inflicted upon the willful murderer (Num 35:33); (2) the "more than" and "much more" teaching of our Lord regarding man's intrinsic value before God (Mt 6:25–26); (3) the provision made by God in the gospel for the salvation of lost mankind (Lk 19:10; Jn 3:14–16; I Tim 1:12–16).

Moreover, the death attached to Adam's disobedience (Gen 2:17) affected primarily the *na-*

ture of his existence rather than the *fact* of his existence. This fact is confirmed by what the Bible describes as the state of spiritual death resulting from the Fall (Eph 2:1, 5; Col 2:13). Actually, Adam did not die physically on the day of his disobedience; thus the death threatened and actualized must have meant spiritual death with its eventual consequence in physical death (Rom 5:12-14). But neither of these involves the non-existence of the soul. Man did not lose his immortality when he became a sinner in the garden of Eden.

Man's redemption. Promises designed to effectuate man's recovery and restoration began to flow from the heart of God as soon as man sinned in Eden (Gen 3:15). But attached to these promises is the warning that the one who disbelieves the Son of God will "perish" (Jn 3:16, 36).

Again the question of immortality crops up, for some insist that only those who savingly believe in Jesus Christ receive immortal or eternal life (i.e., the restoration of the immortality supposedly lost in Eden), while all others perish (i.e., become non-existent at death). It is perfectly true that the Bible applies such terms as "perish" (Lk 13:3, 5; Jn 3:15-16; II Thess 2:10), "destroy" (Mt 10:28; I Cor 3:17; Jude 5; Rev 11:18), "destruction" (Mt 7:13; Rom 9:22; Phil 3:19; II Thess 1:9), "perdition" (Phil 1:28; I Tim 6:9; II Pet 3:7), "lose" (Lk 9:24-25; 17:33), and "lost" (Lk 19:10; Jn 17:12; II Cor 4:3) to those who reject Jesus Christ as their Lord and Saviour. Yet nowhere in these passages is the theory of the annihilation of the unbeliever taught or implied.

"Eternal life" is the spiritual counterpart of "eternal sin" (Mk 3:29, ASV), "eternal punishment" (Mt 25:46), and "eternal destruction" (II Thess 1:9). However, the word "eternal" in these descriptions designates not only length of existence but also the kind or nature of existence. For example, "eternal life" introduces the believer into a new kind of life—a life receiving its energy and motivation from its union with the living Lord (Jn 10:10; 17:23; Gal 2:20; Col 1:27; I Jn 5:11-12). This life continues forever (Mt 25:34; Jn 6:37-51). On the opposite side, "eternal destruction" represents a kind of life, already begun in the present world (Jn 3:36), which issues in eternal separation from the living God (Lk 16:23, 26; Eph 4:18-19; II Thess 1:9).

Thus the gospel offer of mercy in Christ does not restore to the repentant sinner an immortality which he supposedly lost in Eden; nor does this offer when rejected confirm the non-immortality supposedly brought upon man by his transgression in Eden. In other words, man's immortality as such is not affected by the acceptance or rejection of the gospel offer of mercy; but the *kind* of immortality man will experience is tremendously affected by his attitude toward Christ in the present life (cf. Mt 26:24).

The intermediate state. Both the righteous and the unrighteous die physically as a result of Adam's transgression in Eden (Gen 3:17-19; 5:1-31; Rom 5:12-14). But the Scriptures teach that the soul survives the dissolution of soul and body at physical death. The ancient patriarchs believed in the soul's continuance after death (Gen 25:8, 17; 35:29; 49:29, 33). These men looked for the City of God beyond the present life (Heb 11:10, 13-16). Job's "I know" (19:25-27) is re-echoed by Paul's "I know" (II Cor 5:1-10; II Tim 1:12; 4:18) centuries later. David believed his child (II Sam 12:23) entered a state of blessedness comparable to that state promised to the repentant thief on the cross (Lk 23:43). True, the body dies and returns to the dust (Gen 3:19); but the soul of the righteous returns to God (Eccl 12:7; Acts 7:59).

There are places in the OT revelation where the disembodied or intermediate state of the soul is described somewhat disparagingly (Ps 6:5; 30:9; 88:10-12; 115:17; Eccl 9:10; Isa 38:18). On the other hand, there are other places (Job 19:25-27; Ps 16:8-11) where faith in a life beyond the present is presented in terms prophetic of the fuller light of NT revelation (II Cor 5:1-10; Phil 1:21-23; II Tim 4:8, 18; Rev 6:9-11). This faith in the soul's immortality after death is vividly and dramatically confirmed by the appearance of Moses and Elijah with Christ on the Mount of Transfiguration (Mt 17:1-8). If further confirmation were necessary, Paul surely received it when he was transported from this world to the heavenly scene for a vision of the eternal world (II Cor 12:1-7). And still further confirmation can be found in the fact that Lazarus (Jn 11:1-44) and others (Mt 9:18-25; Lk 7:11-17; Acts 9: 36-43) were temporarily restored to the present life after the soul had left their bodies at death. Our Lord's own resurrection gives, of course, the greatest confirmation to the soul's continuance beyond the present life (I Cor 15:1-23).

The fact that the believer's state after death is sometimes called a "sleep" (Dan 12:2; Mt 27:52; Jn 11:11; Acts 13:36; I Cor 15:6, 18, 20; I Thess 4:13-18) in no wise sustains the idea that the soul enters into a state of unconsciousness after death; in fact, this very disembodied state is described as "very much better" (Phil 1:23, NASB) than the present life. There is very little in the Bible about the soul of the unbeliever after death, but there is enough to warrant the firm conclusion that he is in a state of unrelenting agony (Lk 16:22-31).

The resurrection of the righteous. The intermediate state of the soul is completed and consummated in the resurrection of the body of the redeemed at the time of Christ's return in glory (I Thess 4:13-18; I Jn 3:1-3). The beauty and grandeur of this resurrection are majestically described in the Scriptures (Job 19:25-27; Isa 25:6-8; 26:19, NASB; Mt 22:30; I Cor 15:35-49; Phil 3:20-21). There will be, of course, a generation of believers who will be ushered immediately into the next life without experiencing death (I Cor 15:51-53; I Thess 4:15, 17; 5:10).

A striking similarity exists between the immortality of the resurrected and glorified body of our Lord and the immortality of the resurrected and glorified body of the believer (Rom 8:29; I Cor 15:43, 49; Phil 3:21; Col 3:4; I Jn 3:2). A striking dissimilarity also exists in the fact that, though Christ's body did not undergo corruption (Ps 16:10; Acts 2:27; 13:35), the believer's body must return to the dust unless he is in that last generation on earth at the time of Christ's second coming (Gen 3:19; Ps 90:3; Heb 9:27-28). "The redemption of the body" is the last stage in the total restoration of the disrupted-by-sin personality of the believer (Rom 8:18-25). This blessed immortality of the redeemed shall never end (Rev 22:1-5). It is the grand and glorious climax of God's eternal plan for the salvation of some of Adam's fallen posterity (Mt 25:34; Rom 9:23-24; Heb 12:22-24; Rev 7:9-10).

The resurrection of the wicked. The Bible positively asserts that there will be a resurrection of the wicked (Dan 12:2; Jn 5:28-29; Acts 24:15; Rev 20:11-15). Their resurrection will issue in what is called "the second death" (Rev 20:6, 14; cf. 2:11; 21:8), from which state there is not the slightest hope of relief, release or restoration (Mt 10:15; 11:22-24; 25:41; II Thess 1:8-9; II Pet 2:9; 3:7; Rev 14:10 f.; 20:14; 21:8). Such terms as "perish" (Rom 2:12; II Thess 2:10), "destroy" (I Cor 3:17; Rev 11:18), and the like (see under "Man's Redemption" above) give no support to the theory of annihilationism; nor do such passages as Acts 3:21; I Cor 15:22; Eph 1:10; Col 1:20; I Pet 3:18-20 give the slightest hope, when correctly interpreted, to any theory of restorationism.

Conclusions. The following conclusions regarding man's immortality are justifiable in the light of the discussion given above: (1) Only in the Bible do we find evidence sufficient to sustain the doctrine of man's immortality; all other sources of help on this subject are vain and hopeless. (2) The biblical evidence for the immortality of the soul pervades the Scriptures from the earliest times (Job 19:23-27) and reaches its climax in the resurrection of Christ from the grave (Ps 16:8-11; Acts 2:25-28; I Cor 15:1-23). (3) This evidence is not only casual and indirect (Gen 25:8; 35:29; Ex 3:6; Mt 22:31-32) but also studied and systematic (Mt 22:29-30; Jn 5:28-29; 11:25-26; 14:1-3; Rom 2:1-11; I Cor 15:1-58; II Cor 5:1-10). (4) The Bible presents the immortality of the righteous and the immortality of the wicked with equal cogency; it is thus impossible to deny the one without denying the other (Mt 25:34, 41, 46; Lk 16:19-31).

See Anthropology; Dead, The; Eternal State and Death; Incorruption; Mortality; Resurrection.

Bibliography. Loraine Boettner, *Immortality,* Grand Rapids: Eerdmans, 1956. P. T. Forsyth, *This Life and the Next: The Effect on This Life of Faith in Another,* Boston: Pilgrim Press, 1948, reprint. W. E. Hocking, *The Meaning of Immortality in Human Experience,* New York: Harper, 1957. E. E. Holmes, *Immortality,* London: Longmans, Green, and Co., 1908. A. Kuyper, *The Shadow of Death,* Grand Rapids: Eerdmans, 1929. Carroll E. Simcox, *Is Death the End? The Christian Answer,* Greenwich, Conn.: Seabury Press, 1959.

W. B.

IMMUTABILITY. The term appears in the KJV in Heb 6:17-18: "Wherein God, willing more abundantly to show unto the heirs of promise the immutability of his counsel, confirmed it by an oath: that by two immutable things, in which it was impossible for God to lie. . . ." By the immutability of God is meant that in His essence, attributes, consciousness and will God is unchangeable.

The doctrine of God's immutability is further deduced from biblical passages such as: "They shall be changed, but thou art the same" (Ps 102:26-27); "I am the Lord, I change not" (Mal 3:6); "Jesus Christ the same yesterday, and today, and for ever" (Heb 13:8); and "with whom can be no variation, neither shadow that is cast by turning" (Jas 1:17, ASV). In such verses change is explicitly denied to God. This does not mean God is immobile, however, for He acts in history. His immutability is dynamic, not static.

Immutability is also indicated in other verses where the idea is implicit rather than explicit. For example, all those passages that teach omniscience (*q.v.*) imply immutability; for if the amount of knowledge in the divine mind increased or diminished, there would be a time in which God would not know all things (but cf. Heb 4:13). Omniscience allows no change nor temporal sequence of ideas in God's mind. God can neither forget what He now knows nor think of something additional that He never thought of before. Omniscience therefore involves immutability.

Occasionally the Bible attributes repentance or regret to God. In I Sam 15:11, 35 it is stated that God repented (Heb. *niḥam,* "feel compassion, grief, sorrow") of having made Saul king over Israel. This seems to indicate a change of mind or emotion in God. But between these two verses, in v. 29 we read that "the Strength of Israel will not lie nor repent: for he is not a man, that he should repent." God's seeming change of mind or attitude therefore should be taken as an anthropopathism, the attributing of human emotions to God, just as we understand the arms and eyes of the Lord as anthropomorphisms.

Other passages which speak of God as repenting of judgment (e.g., against Israel, Ex 32:14: Nineveh, Jon 3:10) reveal that His threats are often conditional upon human repentance (cf. Jer 18:7-10; 26:3, 13, 19). Therefore God abides by the same unchanging moral principles in all dispensations of His government. *See* Repentance.

A greater difficulty relates to the act of creating the world. All orthodox Christians admit that God eternally willed to create; but since He actually created at a particular moment, this act seems to be a change in God. Charnock, the Puritan theologian (VI, iv, 1 [p. 213]), tried to resolve the difficulty by saying, "There was no change in God by the act of creation, because . . . there was no new act of his will which was not before. The creation began in time, but the will of creating was from eternity. . . . But though God spake that word which he had not spoke before, whereby the world was brought into act, yet he did not will that will he willed not before. God did not create by a new counsel or new will, but by that which was from eternity (Eph 1:9)."

Bibliography. Thomas Aquinas, *Summa Theologica,* Book I, question IX, answers 1, 2. J. Oliver Buswell, Jr., *A Systematic Theology of the Christian Religion,* Grand Rapids: Zondervan, 1962, I, 40-71. Stephen Charnock, *Discourses upon the Existence and Attributes of God,* London: Henry Bohn, 1849, pp. 195-230. Charles A. Hodge, *Systematic Theology,* New York: Scribner's, 1872, I, v, 7.

G. H. C.

IMNA (ĭm'nȧ). A son of Helem from the tribe of Asher (I Chr 7:35).

IMNAH (ĭm'nȧ)

1. Eldest son of Asher (I Chr 7:30), also called Jimna and Jimnah (Gen 46:17; Num 26:44).

2. A Levite, the father of Kore in the time of Hezekiah (II Chr 31:14).

IMPORTUNITY. The Gr. *anaideia,* "shamelessness," "impudence," "importunity," appears only in Lk 11:8, to describe a person who is persistent in his entreaties and exemplifies perseverance in prayer (cf. Lk 18:1-8; I Thess 5:17).

IMPOSITION OF HANDS. *See* Hands, Laying on of.

IMPOTENT. *See* Diseases.

IMPRECATION. *See* Curse.

IMPRECATORY PSALMS. *See* Psalms; Prayer.

IMPRISONMENT. Imprisonment (Gr. *phylakē,* usually "watch" or "prison") was one of the trials suffered by OT believers (Heb 11:36) and by Paul and other early Christians (II Cor 6:5). Several long imprisonments were those of Joseph (Gen 39:20-41:14), Jeremiah (Jer 32:2 ff.), and Paul at Caesarea (Acts 23:23-26:32) and at Rome (Acts 28:16-31). Imprisonment (Heb. *'ᵉsûr,* from *'āsar,* "to bind") was one form of punishment imposed for disobeying the law of the Persian kings (Ezr 7:26). *See* Crime and Punishment; Prison.

Entrance to the Mamertine Prison in Rome, where Paul was presumably held when he wrote 2 Timothy. HFV

IMPURITY. *See* Ablution; Uncleanness.

IMPUTATION, IMPUTE. In the OT this concept is found in the common Heb. verb *ḥāshab,* "to think, count, be accounted" (KJV "impute," Lev 7:18; 17:4; II Sam 19:19; Ps 32:2). In the NT it is represented by the Gr. *ellogeō,* "to impute, lay to one's charge" (used only twice, in Rom 5:13 and Phm 18), and *logizomai,* "to place to the account of, reckon to, to impute" (used 41 times, KJV "impute," Rom 4:6, etc.; II Cor 5:19; Jas 2:23). The concept is beautifully illustrated when Paul writes to Philemon concerning the runaway slave Onesimus: "If he has wronged you in any way, or owes you anything, charge that to my account" (*touto emoi elloga,* Phm 18, NASB).

There are two kinds of imputation: immediate and mediate. The transmission of Adam's fallen nature consecutively to and through each following generation, from parents to their children, is mediate. For it some theologians would not even use the term imputation. They would reserve it for the three separate acts of immediate imputation: (1) the imputation of Adam's sin to his posterity (Rom 5:12; I Cor 15:22); (2) the imputation of our sins to Christ (II Cor 5:21; Gal 3:13); (3) the imputation of Christ's righteousness to us (Rom 4:1-25; I Cor 1:30). These three major imputations are fully explained in Scripture:

1. The imputation of Adam's sin to the race is clearly set forth in Rom 5:12: Death came "upon all men, for that [because] all have sinned." All died in Adam, Paul teaches in I Cor 15:22. Death reigned right from the time of Adam, and not just from the days of Moses when the Jewish law was first given—though sin is not imputed when there is no law—because Adam's sin was every man's sin (Rom 5:13-14). Because of the reconciliation (*q.v.*) which God has effected through Christ, He no longer accounts men's trespasses against them (II Cor 5:19). But this word must be preached so that men may appropriate it.

2. The imputation of the sins of man to Christ entails judicial imputation inasmuch as it is the reckoning to Christ of that which is not antecedently His own. While the theological term impute is not used to express this in Scripture, equivalent expressions are employed, such as "the Lord hath laid upon him the iniquity of us all" (Isa 53:6); "who his own self bare our sins" (I Pet 2:24); "He hath made him to be sin for us, who knew no sin" (II Cor 5:21).

3. The imputation of righteousness (*q.v.*) to the believer. The "righteousness of God" is the theme of Romans (1:17; 3:5, 21-22, 25-26). The term is used in two senses in Romans: (*a*) God's own inherent righteousness (Rom 1:17; 3:5, 25-26); (*b*) the righteousness of Christ which is imputed to the believer (Rom 3:21-22; 10:3; cf. II Cor 5:21).

Christ's righteousness is the basis of the Christian's acceptance and standing before God. God made Him to be "unto us wisdom, and righteousness, and sanctification, and redemption" (I Cor 1:30). God identifies us positionally with all that Christ did in His death, burial and resurrection, and baptizes us into Christ (Rom 6:3-6; I Cor 12:13; *see* Baptism). Thus we become recipients of the very righteousness of God, "For he hath made him to be sin for us, who knew no sin; that we might be made the righteousness of God" (II Cor 5:21). The believer is perfected in Christ (Heb 10:14), entirely complete in Him (Col 2:9-10; cf. Jn 1:16; Col 1:19), and thereby fit to appear in the presence of God (Col 1:12; Phil 3:9). As in the case of Abraham, who believed God and it was counted (Heb. *ḥāshab,* Gen 15:6; Gr. *logizomai,* Rom 4:3) to him as righteousness, so faith, not works, is the basis for receiving this righteousness (Rom 4:9-25). *See* Justification.

R. A. K.

IMRAH (ĭm'rȧ). A prominent chief of the tribe of Asher and the son of Zophah (I Chr 7:36).

IMRI (ĭm'rī)

1. A descendant of Pharez, the son of Judah (I Chr 9:4).

2. The father of Zaccur who assisted Nehemiah in the rebuilding of the wall of Jerusalem (Neh 3:2).

INABILITY. Scripture describes the unsaved man in such a way as to deny to him the ability of himself without special divine grace to turn to God, to do perfectly the will of God, or wholly to please God (Jn 1:13; 6:44; Rom 7:18; 8:7-8; I Cor 2:14; Eph 2:1). Sin has so weakened man's being and powers that he is by nature morally and spiritually unable to perform an act which is truly and entirely good in God's sight. When seen from God's viewpoint, all the works of the unregenerate are radically defective because they are not motivated by love to God and for the glory of God.

INCANTATION. *See* Magic.

INCARNATION. A term derived from the Latin version of Jn 1:14. Incarnation refers exclusively to that action by which the Son of God, often spoken of as the Second Person of the Godhead, became man. It presupposes the essential deity and eternal sonship of the Person who became incarnate. The doctrine is vitiated if it is conceived of as the beginning of existence of Him who is uniquely the Son of God. When John writes, "And the Word was made flesh" (Jn 1:14), the Word had already been identified as eternally subsistent, as eternally with God, and as Himself God (Jn 1:1-3). When Paul says that He "was made in the likeness of men" (Phil 2:7), he means that this Person was originally in the form of God and therefore on an equality with God (Phil 2:6).

The fact. The incarnation is a stupendous fact; it is the mystery of godliness, the grand miracle of the Christian faith. It means that He who never began to be but eternally existed, and who ever continued to be what He eternally was, began to be what He eternally was not. It is an event that occurred in time with reference to Him who Himself was eternal. There are, therefore, the sustained contrasts: the Eternal entered time and became subject to its conditions; the Infinite became the finite; the Immutable became mutable; the Invisible became visible; the Almighty became the weak and infirm; the Creator became the creature; God became man.

It would have been humiliation for the Son of God to become man under the most ideal earthly conditions, because of the discrepancy between the majesty of God the Creator and the humble status of the most dignified creation. But it was not into an ideal world that He came; it was into this world of sin, of misery, and of death. That He came into such a world indicates the peculiarity of the humiliation undertaken and the redemptive purpose designed. He came, therefore, "in the likeness of sinful flesh" (Rom 8:3), into the closest relation to sinful humanity that it was possible for Him to come without thereby becoming Himself sinful. *See* Christ, Humiliation of.

The mode. The mode is generally spoken of as the virgin birth. Christ was in truth born of the virgin because Mary had not yet known a man. The mode was, therefore, supernatural. Three considerations point up the supernatural character.

1. Jesus was not conceived by the conjunction of man and woman, by spermal communication from the man. He was begotten in the womb of Mary by the power of the Holy Spirit (Mt 1:20; Lk 1:35). The miracle appears first of all in supernatural begetting. In this respect it is not strictly accurate to say that Jesus was conceived by the Holy Spirit. It was Mary who conceived and our attention is expressly drawn to this fact (Lk 1:31). That is said of Mary which is said also of Elisabeth (Lk 1:24, 36). But Mary conceived only because the Holy Spirit had begotten Jesus in her womb and hence the birth was virgin. Paul reflects this doctrine in Gal 4:4 when he writes, "God sent forth his Son, born of woman" (RSV). The prophecy of Isa 7:14 foretold the supernatural manner of Jesus' birth. *See* Virgin.

2. It was not a mere baby who was conceived of Mary. It was the eternal Son of God who was conceived. Only in respect of His human nature was He formed in the womb, but it was He in this unchanged identity. The most stupendous aspect of the supernatural was the begetting and conception of this supernatural, eternal Person. Hence there is no point at which the supernatural is not present, and it is not merely in the fact of supernatural begetting that the miracle appears. It is only when this fact is overlooked that difficulty with the doctrine of the virgin birth is entertained. Natural generation would be incongruous, while supernatural generation is in perfect accord with the supernatural character of the Person.

3. The dogma of Mary's immaculate conception is an imposture; it has no warrant from the data of revelation (*see* Mary). The supernatural is evident in the preservation of the infant Jesus from the defilement that belonged to His human mother. Supernatural generation was necessary to preserve immunity to hereditary depravity, because "that which is born of the flesh is flesh" (Jn 3:6). Yet this does not appear to be of itself an adequate explanation of Jesus' spotless purity. He was made of the seed of David according to the flesh. This seed was corrupt. But Jesus was holy, undefiled, and separate from sinners.

Jesus came by a mode that was supernatural and therefore by a mode consonant with His supernatural person. He came by a mode that guaranteed His sinlessness, and therefore by a mode consonant with His divine perfection and with the redemptive design of His coming. But He came by a mode that preserved fully His genetic connection with sinful humanity. This is the meaning of conception by and birth from a virgin who herself was conceived in sin like all the other offspring of Adam by natural generation. And this belongs to the marvel and grace of the incarnation. *See* Christ, Sinlessness of.

The nature. The proposition "God became man" must not be interpreted to mean that Godhood was exchanged for manhood; it means no subtraction or divestiture. The Son of God did not cease to be what He eternally was when He became human. The incarnation was by addition. In Jn 1:14 there is no suggestion that the Word in becoming flesh surrendered that which He had been defined to be in vv. 1–3. John proceeds immediately to obviate any such conception. It is this Word, he says, who dwelt among us, and the glory beheld was the glory of the only begotten from the Father. To confirm this doctrine John adds that the revelation given by the incarnate Son was given by Him in His identity as God only begotten in the bosom of the Father (v. 18).

The idea of self-emptying, derived from a mistranslation of Phil 2:7, has no basis in Scripture. The rendering of the KJV that He "made himself of no reputation" is shown by the context and by the usage of the NT to be correct. Our Lord made no account of Himself and so He took the form of a servant and humbled Himself, becoming obedient unto death, even the death of the cross (vv. 7–8). *See* Kenosis.

The incarnation means that the Son of God took human nature in its pristine integrity, with all its essential properties and sinless limitations, into union with His divine person. The result is that human nature now belongs to His person and to His personal life and experience. He thinks and wills and acts as God, and He thinks and wills and acts as man. He possesses all divine attributes and prerogatives equally with God the Father and God the Holy Spirit. But also of Him must be predicated all that belongs to human creaturehood.

This great truth of the coexistence of both Godhood and manhood in the one divine Person was set forth in the creed of Chalcedon in A.D. 451 as follows: "We, then . . . all with one consent, teach men to confess one and the same Son, our Lord Jesus Christ . . . to be acknowledged in two natures, inconfusedly, unchangeably, indivisibly, inseparably; the distinction of natures being by no means taken away by the union, but rather the property of each nature being preserved, and concurring in one Person . . . not parted or divided into two persons, but one and the same Son, and only begotten, God the Word, the Lord Jesus Christ."

A great deal of more recent discussion has been devoted to the question, Is the man Jesus to be regarded as a human person? Catholic orthodoxy, following the Chalcedonian creed, has maintained that Jesus was one person, and that since He was divine, He was a divine person. This means that His human nature must not be regarded as personal. This is not to deny the reality and integrity of His human nature but to insist that the center of personality in His case was the deity. This doctrine reflects the witness of the NT.

In the various situations recorded in the Gospels, Jesus always recognized Himself as sustaining a unique relation to God the Father. This means that He was aware of His divine identity. And even when the limitations belonging to Him in virtue of His human nature were most in evidence (cf. Mt 24:36), He identified Himself in terms of His divine relationship. When the NT writers refer to those actions of Jesus which were performed in human nature, such as the death on the cross, they always say that *He Himself* wrought these works (cf. Phil 2:7-8; Heb 1:3; I Pet 2:24); and the personal pronoun as applied to Him has always in view His divine identity and could never be regarded as merely human.

This doctrine of one person in two distinct natures is closely related to the character and efficacy of our Lord's redemptive accomplishments. It was the God-Man who wrought salvation, and in that same capacity in His exalted glory He carries on His heavenly ministry unto the consummation of God's redemptive purpose.

See Christ, Humanity of; Christ, Sinlessness of; Jesus Christ.

Bibliography. E. C. Blackman. "Incarnation," IDB, II, 691-697. A. B. Bruce, *The Humiliation of Christ,* Grand Rapids: Eerdmans, 1955. J. Gresham Machen, *The Virgin Birth of Christ,* New York: Harper, 1932. James Orr, *The Virgin Birth of Christ,* New York: Scribner's, 1915. R. L. Ottley, "Incarnation, The," HDB, II, 458-467. H. C. Powell, *The Principle of the Incarnation,* New York: Longmans, Green & Co., 1896. W. Childs Robinson, "A Restudy of the Virgin Birth of Christ," EQ, XXXVII (1965), 198-211. Thomas A. Thomas, "The Kenosis Question," EQ, XLII (1970), 142-151. B. B. Warfield, *The Person and Work of Christ,* Philadelphia: Presbyterian and Reformed, 1950.

J. M.

INCENSE. A mixture of spices and gums used for burning in Israel's worship; sometimes the sweet odor issuing from the burning. The recipe for the incense to be used in the temple is given in Ex 30:34-38. It includes stacte, onycha, galbanum, and frankincense (*see* Plants; Spice). The use of this formula was banned for private use, and any who violated this prohibition were to be excommunicated from the congregation of Israel. The use of incense was not peculiar to Israel, and in the land of promise itself incense was offered by priests on profane high places (I Kgs 13:1-2; II Kgs 17:11, and elsewhere).

Incense was to be burned on the altar of incense which stood in the tent of meeting in the holy place directly before the inner sanctuary, the holy of holies. The priest would take pieces of coal from the altar of burnt offering on a kind of shovel, sprinkle the incense powder on the burning embers, and place the whole on the altar of incense. This was to be done morning and evening (Ex 30:7-8). Once a year, on the Day of Atonement, the high priest was to take a censer of coals within the veil into the holy of holies and sprinkle incense on the fire preparatory to sprinkling the sacrificial blood before the mercy seat (Lev 16:12-14).

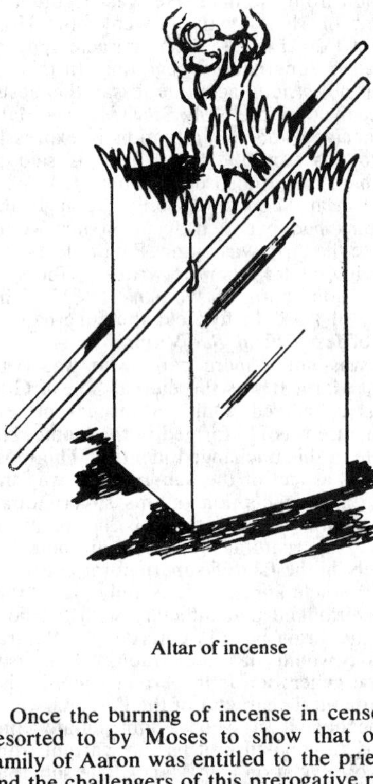

Altar of incense

Once the burning of incense in censers was resorted to by Moses to show that only the family of Aaron was entitled to the priesthood, and the challengers of this prerogative received the extreme penalty (Num 16:17 f.). Nadab and Abihu, Aaron's sons, were slain for guiltily offering incense improperly at the outset of the institution (Lev 10:1-3). King Uzziah was stricken with leprosy for presumptuously insisting on offering incense in the temple against the protests of the priests (II Chr 26:16-21). It was while offering the incense in the temple that Zacharias, John the Baptist's father, was told by the angel that he would have a son (Lk 1:8-13). The ascent of the sweet perfumed smoke appropriately signifies the prayers of God's people coming before their God (Ps 141:2; Rev 5:8; 8:3-4).

Bibliography. Gus W. Van Beek, "Frankincense and Myrrh," BA, XXIII (1960), 69-95.

N. B. B.

INCEST. The crime of cohabitation or sexual intercourse with those kin or relatives who are forbidden in the Mosaic law (Lev 18:1-18).

The list given by Moses is preceded with a warning that Israel was not to indulge in the sins of the Egyptians whom they had just left, or the Canaanites to whom God was bringing them. The list of those forbidden includes (1) mother, (2) stepmother, (3) sister or half sister, (4) granddaughter, (5) daughter of a stepmother, (6) an aunt on either side, (7) an uncle's wife on the father's side, (8) daughter-in-law, (9) sister-in-law, (10) a woman and her daughter or her granddaughter, (11) the sister of a living wife.

A daughter and a full sister are not mentioned specifically since covered by "near of kin" (v. 6). A mother-in-law is included in # 10. Those mentioned in # 1, 2, 3, 8, 10 were to be punished by the death penalty (Lev 20:11, 12, 14, 17) as accursed crimes. Those mentioned in # 6, 7, 9 were to bear their iniquity and die childless (Lev 20:19-21).

In the NT a case of incest, a man cohabiting with his father's wife, is mentioned in I Cor 5:1. Paul instructs the Corinthian church to judge this evil and "deliver such an one unto Satan for the destruction of the flesh, that the spirit may be saved in the day of the Lord Jesus" (v. 5).

R. A. K.

INCONTINENCY. Lack of self-control. Used once in I Cor 7:5 where Paul warns those who are married against withdrawing from proper regular sexual intercourse lest Satan tempt either party to extramarital relations. Since the imperative is used in v. 2: "Let every man have his own wife," both marriage and its relations are not discouraged but rather encouraged by Paul, except in certain particular cases and situations.

See Divorce.

INCORRUPTION. A term (Gr. *aphtharsia,* "perpetuity, incorruption") used by Paul in I Cor 15:42, 50, 53-54 of the resurrection body which the Christian will receive at the time of the rapture along with the departed saints, shortly before they return to reign with Christ (I Thess 4:13-18; cf. Rev 20:4-6). The Gr. word is also translated "immortality" in Rom 2:7 and II Tim 1:10, "sincerity" in the sense of incorruptibleness in Eph 6:24, and "uncorruptness" in Tit 2:7. *See* Immortality.

An eleventh century B.C. shrine model from Bethshean used as an incense burner. BM

The adjective *aphthartos* describes the incorruptible or imperishable crown the victorious believer will receive in contrast to the fading crown of laurel leaves won by the Gr. athlete (I Cor 9:25). Our heavenly inheritance is incorruptible (I Pet 1:4); so also is the Word of God viewed as seed (1:23), and the inner spirit of the godly wife (3:4). God is *aphthartos* in the sense of immortal (Rom 1:23; I Tim 1:17).

INDIA. The word is mentioned only twice in the Scriptures, both occurrences being in the book of Esther (1:1; 8:9) and referring to the extent of the realm of Ahasuerus, the Persian king. Scholars are generally agreed that the word "India" (Heb. *hōddû,* from Old Persian *hidauw* and *hinduish,* from Sanskrit *sindhu,* "stream"—i.e., the Indus River) refers not to the peninsula of Hindustan but to the territory adjoining the Indus River, i.e., the Punjab. Some identify it with the land of Havilah of Gen 2:11 and equate the Indus with the Pishon. The seafaring country of *Meluḫḫa,* mentioned often in Sumerian texts, was probably the Gujerat region of W India where the Indus civilization flourished *c.* 2000 B.C. (W. F. Leemans, *Old Babylonian Letters and Economic History*, Leiden: Brill, 1968, pp. 219–226).

INFANT BAPTISM. *See* Baptism.

INFANT SALVATION. *See* Salvation.

INFINITY. Though the Bible does not give any abstract discussion of infinity (or of the infinitesimal), yet the simple literal concept of limitlessness in certain specified aspects of being is consistently assumed. Thus, God is omnipresent in infinite space in all dimensions. Every part of all space is immediately in His presence (Ps 139:1–12). God is eternal in infinite time, both past and future (Ps 90:1–2). God is infinite in power, the Almighty (*pantokratōr,* II Cor 6:18 and frequently in Revelation). He is infinite in wisdom and knowledge, omniscient (Ps 139; Col 2:3).

On the other hand, God is never regarded as "the Infinite" without specification. Spinoza's idea that the "Infinitely Infinite" is "the All," simply means pantheism (just as "the Absolute" without specification means absolutely nothing). If God were infinite in all respects He would be infinitely evil, infinitely cruel, etc.

Modern mathematicians, such as Georg Cantor (*Contributions to the Founding of the Theory of Transfinite Numbers,* trans. by P. E. B. Jourdain, New York: Dover Publications, 1952), have developed supposed paradoxes in the concept of infinity. It is alleged that ". . . the series of odd integers can be put into one-one correlation with the complete series of integers and is therefore of the same number. This capacity to have proper parts which are equal in number to the whole can be taken as definitory of transfinite aggregates" (*Encyclopaedia Britannica,* 1967 ed., XII, 237).

The fallacy of such a paradox is in the treating of an infinite series as a whole which can be equal to another infinite whole. "Infinite whole" is a palpable contradiction.

J. O. B., Jr.

INFIRMITY. *See* Diseases.

INFLAMMATION. *See* Diseases.

INGATHERING, FEAST OF. *See* Festivals: Feast of Tabernacles.

INHERITANCE. While the OT develops the Heb. law of legal inheritance, the theological significance of inheritance is prominent in God's dealings with man in both the OT and NT.

The basic idea is settled possession of land and personal property by a stable and permanent title irrespective of how that possession has been acquired. Frequently included is the concept of the acquisition by succession of property belonging to one's forebears, the allocation or distribution of this property having been effected by God. Closely related to inheritance are the ideas of covenant (in the OT) and sonship (in the NT).

Inheritance in the Old Testament

Although statistical analysis of the Heb. words for inheritance is difficult (since the term inheritance in the English versions does not always represent the same Heb. word, nor are the pertinent Heb. words always translated inheritance), it is seen that *nāḥal* ("to give inheritance," "to receive possession") and *naḥălâ* ("inheritance") are the more relevant and frequent Heb. words. Note also: *ḥēleq* ("portion," Ps 16:5); *y^erushshâ* ("possession," "thing occupied," Jud 21:17; Jer 32:8); *môrāshâ* ("possession," "thing occupied," Deut 33:4); *yārash* ("to subdue," "occupy," "possess," "inherit," Josh 1:11).

The Promised Land, the inheritance of Israel. Material inheritance in OT law and custom cannot be understood apart from the theological significance of inheritance as derived from the Abrahamic covenant. The promise to Abraham (Gen 12:1–3; 13:14–17; etc.) had a double object: an heir (Isaac, then the nation, and ultimately Christ) and an inheritance (the land of Canaan). Israel's messianic expectancy and the gradual deepening of the inheritance theme in the OT both grow out of the Abrahamic promise.

While all the earth is God's (Ex 19:5; Deut 10:14) which He as Creator gave to man to hold, cultivate and enjoy (Ps 115:16), yet He selected a specific people for His inheritance and selected a specific portion of land to give this people as their inheritance (I Kgs 8:36). Although Israel did not initially receive Canaan from her fathers, yet, to the degree that God's promises are a reality when uttered, the land which was to be their inheritance for all generations is viewed retrospectively as an inheritance from the time of the original grant by God. Thus, the possession of Canaan, either as a whole or in its various portions, belongs to the nation Israel, or to each tribe or family or individual.

The basis of this possession is the grace of God in fulfillment of promise. God supervised the conquest by entrusting Joshua with the task (Deut 1:38) and by intervening in behalf of Israel (Josh 21:43–45). Thus, the nature of this inheritance of the land is not a simple succession from generation to generation but an inheritance which God has granted to Israel (Deut 12:9–10).

Not only did God fulfill His promise by supervising the conquest of the land which He allotted to Israel, but He also fulfilled it by directing its partitioning among the tribes, effected by lot which was regarded as a divine decision (Num 33:54; Josh 14:2). In this division, each tribe received its lot or portion in the inheritance (Josh 14:2; 15:1; 16:1; 17:1; 18:1–11). The partitioning extended to each family (Josh 15:1, 20) and to individuals (Caleb,

Josh 15:13; Joshua, Josh 19:49–50). However, the tribe of Levi had no inheritance, although assigned 48 cities (Num 35:2–8).

While God's ultimate promise regarding the land is immutable, full possession of the land by any particular generation of Israelites is conditional upon obedience to the divine commands (I Chr 28:8; cf. Deut 4:1). Punishment for disobedience includes loss of the land (Deut 4:25–26; I Kgs 14:15) as illustrated in the Babylonian captivity. Consequently, repentance is related to restoration to the land (Ezk 36:8–15; 37:21–28). The dispossession of any particular generation of Israelites because of unbelief does not invalidate God's unconditional promise, for the generation living at Christ's second advent will "inherit the land for ever" (Isa 60:21) and enjoy it in perfect happiness, a promise which will begin fulfillment in the future messianic or millennial kingdom (Deut 30:1–6). In this connection, the Davidic King is also promised the nations as His inheritance (Ps 2:8).

Israel, the land and the people, the inheritance of God. Since God gave the land, He is the ultimate Landowner and the land is viewed as His inheritance (Lev 25:23); not that He received it from someone else, but that He has chosen it for His own possession and it is His by right. Therefore, Israel is God's tenant and ought to live on the land not for itself but for God. Likewise, the people whom God has chosen are regarded as His inheritance, which He has allotted to Himself for eternal possession (Deut 4:20; 32:9). Inheritance is once more linked to covenant relationship by the formula of the covenant: "They shall be my people, and I will be their God" (Jer 24:7). *See* Land and Property.

Inheritance in Old Testament law and custom. In general, inherited property included both land and personal possessions, such as cattle, household goods, servants, and even wives. Since the land was given by God and was held in trust for Him, it properly belonged to the family and only to the individual heir as representing the family. Personal possessions, however, could be distributed among all the sons. Since given by God, the land was not to be alienated (Lev 25:23) and, though sold temporarily, the land must be returned to the original owner in the year of jubilee (Lev 25:25–34). One exception was a dwelling house in a walled city which, if not redeemed within one year of sale, did not return to the original owner in the year of jubilee (Lev 25:29–30).

The firstborn son inherited a double portion of all his father's possessions (Deut 21:17), the remainder being divided equally among the other sons. A father sometimes made disposition of his property during his lifetime (Gen 24:35–36; 25:5–6), and the patriarchal blessing seemed to function much like wills and testaments of modern times. While a father was prohibited from arbitrarily depriving his firstborn of the birthright (Deut 21:15–17), it could be taken from him because of trespass against the father (I Chr 5:1). The cases of transfer of birthright appear as exceptions which exemplify divine election (Ishmael and Isaac, Gen 21:10; cf. 21:12; Esau and Jacob, Gen 27:37; cf. Mal 1:2–3; Rom 9:13; Reuben and Joseph, I Chr 5:1; cf. Gen 49:22–26; Adonijah and Solomon, I Kgs 1:5 ff.; cf. I Chr 22:9–10).

At first a daughter could not receive the inheritance (Job 42:15 is exceptional), but a change was introduced after the death of Zelophehad so that daughters were entitled to inheritance if there were no sons in the family (Num 27:1–11). But even in this case, heiresses had to marry only within their father's tribe. If there were no direct heirs, then brothers, paternal uncles, or the next of kin could inherit. A widow had no immediate place in the succession, but if she were left without children, the nearest kinsman on her husband's side had the right of marrying her to raise up children to the name of his dead brother (Deut 25:5–10; cf. Ruth 3:12–13; 4:1 ff.). *See* Marriage, Levirate.

Other Old Testament uses of inheritance. God Himself came to be viewed as the inheritance of the righteous (Ps 16:5–6; 73:26) as He had been in a particular way the inheritance of the Levites (Deut 10:9). The law itself (Deut 33:4) and even children (Ps 127:3) are spoken of as an inheritance. Inheritance also describes the portion allotted to man in the sense of his personal destiny (Job 20:29; 27:13).

Inheritance in the New Testament

Gr. *klēronomos* (heir) and *klēronomia* (inheritance) and their cognates occur about 45 times in the NT, principally in the Synoptic Gospels, Pauline epistles (especially Galatians) and Hebrews.

While inheritance is used in the ordinary sense (Lk 12:13) and with reference to the OT usage of possession of the Promised Land (Acts 7:5; Heb 11:8), the concept of inheritance is further developed in the NT in two ways: (1) the heir is related to sonship (especially is Christ Son and Heir), and (2) the inheritance is related to the kingdom which Christ inaugurates. Both elements are present side by side in the parable of the vinedressers (Mt 21:33–46; Mk 12:1–12; Lk 20:9–19) where Jesus Christ is seen to be the Heir by virtue of being the Son (Mk 12:6–7; cf. Heb 1:2) and the inheritance is the kingdom (Mt 21:43).

Not only is Christ the Son and Heir, but in Christ believers are also sons and therefore heirs (Rom 8:17; Gal 4:7). This Pauline concept of spiritual heirship is not based on the Heb. concept of inheritance but rather upon Roman law under which all the children inherited equally. As in Roman law where the testator lived on in the group of his co-heirs, so Christ lives in believers who derive their heirship by being co-heirs with Him (Rom 8:17). While the Holy Spirit now indwells the believer

INIQUITY

as the Guarantor of his inheritance (Eph 1:14), the inheritance itself is a future one (I Cor 6:9-10; Gal 5:21; Eph 5:5; Jas 2:5; I Pet 1:3-4) into which eternal inheritance the believer will enter after resurrection (Heb 9:15).

The inheritance awaited includes the glory (Rom 8:17-18) and incorruption (I Cor 15:50-57; cf. I Pet 1:4) of resurrection life into which the believer will enter, after which he shall reign with Christ in the millennial kingdom. The inheritance of resurrected believers includes also a heavenly city in a new heaven and a new earth (Heb 11:10, 16; 12:22-24; Rev 21:1 ff.).

See also Adoption; Allotment; Family; Patrimony.

Bibliography. Francois Dreyfus and Pierre Grelot, "Inheritance," *Dictionary of Biblical Theology,* Xavier Leon-Dufour, ed., New York: Desclee Co., 1967. Werner Foerster and J. Herrmann, "*Klēronomos,* etc.," TDNT, III, 758-785. J.-Cl. Margot, "Inheritance," *A Companion to the Bible,* J.-J. von Allmen, ed., New York: Oxford Univ. Press, 1958, pp. 181-185. Merrill F. Unger, "Inheritance," UBD, pp. 525 f.

F. D. L.

INIQUITY. Sixteen Heb. and Gr. words are translated "iniquity" in the KJV. The more important are as follows: Heb. *'āwen,* "iniquity, vanity"; *'āwel,* "perversity, perverseness"; *āwôn,* "that which is crooked, perversity (most common), depravity, sin." Gr. *adikia,* "unrighteousness"; *anomia,* "lawlessness."

The Heb. *'āwôn* refers primarily to the character of an action, as seen in Isa 64:6 where iniquities are paralleled to self-righteous deeds that are like filthy rags. From this it expands to express the idea of guilt (Gen 15:16; Num 15:31; II Sam 14:32; Ps 32:5; Jer 2:22; 30:14-15, RSV), followed by punishment for guilt in the sense of Gen 4:13, "My punishment is greater than I can bear" (cf. Lev 26:41, 43, KJV, NEB; Lam 4:6, 22; Ezk 14:10).

In the NT *adikia* stresses the idea of a negative righteousness, but in the sense of actual unrighteousness as seen in the reference to the 30 pieces of silver paid to Judas as the "reward of iniquity" (Acts 1:18), and the condemnation of Simon the sorcerer's offer to buy the power of the Holy Spirit (Acts 8:23; cf. I Cor 13:6; II Tim 2:19; Jas 3:6).

The Gr. *anomia* stresses, in contrast, the rejection and breaking of God's holy law. Jesus condemns this lawlessness (Mt 7:23; 13:41; 23:28; 24:12), as well as Paul (Rom 6:19) and the writer of Hebrews (Heb 8:12; 10:17). In II Thess 2:7 we learn that the mystery of iniquity (*anomia*)—the real origin of lawlessness being the revolt of the devil and his angels, followed by the revolt of man against God—is already present and will continue right up until

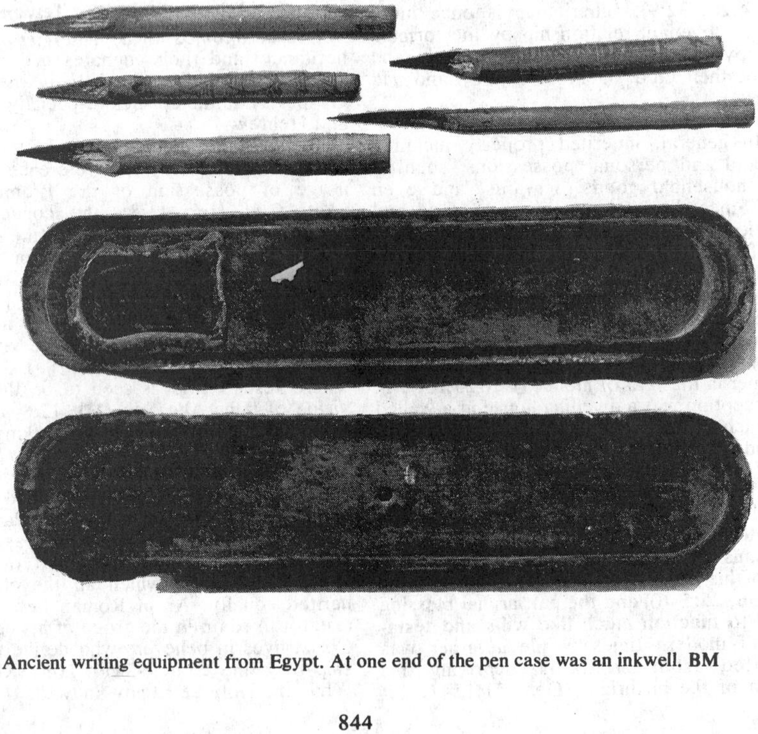

Ancient writing equipment from Egypt. At one end of the pen case was an inkwell. BM

Ruins of the traditional Good Samaritan Inn on the Jericho Road. HFV

the Antichrist is revealed and destroyed by the coming of Christ as the rider on the white horse of Rev 19:11-20.

See Evil; Sin; Wickedness.

Bibliography. W. Gutbrod, "*Anomia,*" TDNT, IV, 1085 ff.

R. A. K.

INK. Ink was used in Egypt as early as 2500 B.C. One OT reference says that Baruch wrote Jeremiah's prophecies "with ink" (Jer 36:18). The word ink occurs in the NT in II Cor 3:3; II Jn 12; III Jn 13 as the translation of Gr. *melan* (black), probably referring to lampblack carbon or soot mixed with gum (three parts to one) and water to make it adhere and have some gloss. The mass was molded into sticks and later cut off as needed and moistened for use.

Carbon's chemical inertness kept such ink black for centuries as shown by ostraca found at Lachish and Samaria from the time of the OT prophets. A rusty-brown ink of powdered nutgalls and ferrous sulfate was used in some MSS such as Codex Vaticanus and Codex Bezae. Several Egyptian papyri used a red ink (rubric) made from pulverized minerals. *See* Writing.

INKHORN. Scribes throughout the centuries have carried in their girdle a long tube or case in which they kept their pens (reeds), with a small cup or container for ink attached to the upper end. It is called in Heb. *qĕsĕth* and translated "inkhorn" (KJV, ASV). It occurs only in Ezk 9:2, 3, 11, and is translated "writing case" in RSV. The Egyptian and Syrian scribes used a palette (Egyp. *gsty*), a narrow rectangular wooden board with a long groove to hold the rush pens and circular hollows for the cakes of red and black ink. For illustrations of these palettes see ANEP, Nos. 232-234, 460. *See* Ink; Writing.

INN. The inn of Bible days was not at all like a modern hotel or motel, but is generally considered to have been similar to the Oriental caravansary or khan, which is said to still exist in rural areas of Asia. The caravansary is a large square edifice built around an open inner courtyard. In the center of the courtyard a well is provided. Often the building is two stories, with the lower one containing stalls for beasts and the upper consisting of small rooms for use of the human travelers.

The KJV terms the place where Joseph's brothers stopped (Gen 42:27; 43:21) an "inn," as well as a similar place where Moses and his family lodged (Ex 4:24). But *mālôn,* camping place for the night, was merely a resting place, not an inn in each of these references, as in Josh 4:3. On the other hand, Jewish archaeologists have discovered scores of small settlements in the Negeb and the desert of north-central Sinai, dating back to the Middle Bronze I Age or patriarchal period. These are considered to be caravan stations on the trade route to Egypt (W. F. Albright, *Yahweh and the Gods of Canaan,* Garden City: Doubleday, 1968, pp. 62-73).

The inn where there was no room for Joseph and Mary (Lk 2:7) has traditionally been thought of as a caravansary, which they found to be completely full of people and beasts, forcing them to lodge in a nearby cave used as a sheepfold. Some authorities, however, hold that the Gr. word here used (*katalyma*) refers not to a caravansary at all but to a guest chamber or lodging place in a private home, *katalyma* obviously referring to something of this kind in its only other NT usages (Mk 14:14; Lk 22:11). According to this view, Joseph and Mary planned to stay at the home of friends or relatives, but the small dwelling and its guest chamber were so full that they had to be housed in the lower portion where the animals were quartered.

The inn of the Good Samaritan parable (Gr. *pandocheion,* Lk 10:34) evidently was a caravansary between Jerusalem and Jericho, the host, or innkeeper, being a man who supplied provisions and other needs to travelers.

G. C. L.

INNER MAN. Inner or inward man is the KJV translation of *ho esō anthrōpos* in Rom 7:22; Eph 3:16; II Cor 4:16 (in last reference only *ho esō* appears, with *anthrōpos* clearly to be supplied from the immediate context). It is a Pauline expression referring to man's rational, moral and spiritual nature, that total sphere in which the Holy Spirit carries on His convicting, renewing and sanctifying work. In short, it is synonymous with man's soul. Thus it is *not* the "new man," that is, the new capacity to serve God and righteousness, which God graciously gives the sinner in regeneration. *See* New Creation.

In Rom 7:22 Paul is describing his attitude toward the divine law as a self-righteous Pharisee. (For a vindication of the view that Rom 7:14-25 describes Paul the legalistic Pharisee, cf. J. Oliver Buswell, Jr., *A Systematic Theology of the Christian Religion,* II, 115-119.) As a Pharisee, trained in and possessing a high respect for the law of God, Paul could say that even prior to his conversion he concurred with and took pleasure in God's law. But being unregenerate at the time in his life described in Rom 7, Paul had to admit that he possessed at that time no gracious enablement whereby he might obey the law in its *intended* sense. This being the case, Paul could nonetheless declare that as a highly trained religious man he respected the divine law in the "inner man."

[For the view that in Rom 7:14-25 Paul is describing his continuing experience as a believer, see Charles C. Ryrie, *Balancing the Christian Life,* Chicago: Moody Press, 1969, pp. 45-48. According to this interpretation all believers have two capacities within their being: to serve sin *and* to delight in the law of God. These two capacities remain with the Christian throughout life on earth, with the constant possibility of conflict. By his freedom of choice the believer activates either the old or the new capacity.—Ed.]

In II Cor 4:16 Paul is simply expressing his confidence that, though his physical body wear away because of the stress and strain of his work, his "inner man," that is, his soul (or spirit) would be renewed daily.

In Eph 3:16 Paul prays that the Ephesian believers might experience a fresh invigorating from the Holy Spirit in the "inner man." Here he is merely expressing his prayerful desire that they grow spiritually.

R. L. R.

INNOCENCY. In addition to this noun and its adjective "innocent" several words are used in the KJV for the idea of innocence, such as "harmless" and "blameless." Together they express the idea of freedom from corruption, taint, evil or guilt. Likewise various Heb. and Gr. terms suggest this concept. The Heb. verb *nāqâ* and its derivatives have the primary meaning of emptied out and clean, hence free from guilt, innocent (e.g., Ps 19:13; Jer 2:35). Its adjective often appears in the idiom "innocent blood" (e.g., Deut 19:10; 21:8). Its noun is translated "innocency" in Gen 20:5; Ps 26:6; 73:13; Hos 8:5. In the RSV, Heb. *ṣādîq* (*see* Righteousness) is eight times translated "innocent" (e.g., Gen 20:4; Deut 25:1; Job 9:15). The Heb. word *tāmîm* signifies wholeness, integrity and perfection (e.g., Noah, Gen 6:9; 7:1; Job, Job 1:1; David, Ps 18:23).

Absolute innocence (incapable of sinning) is an attribute of God and Christ alone (Heb 7:26, NASB) and of the saints when glorified. Adam and Eve were innocent ("very good," Gen 1:31) before the Fall, but not yet confirmed in holiness. In a relative sense those who are not morally accountable (infants and imbeciles) may be considered innocent. Innocency may also express that simplicity, childlikeness, singleness of mind and wholehearted devotion to God which our Lord requires of the citizens of His kingdom (e.g., "innocent as doves," Mt 10:16; "blameless and innocent," Phil 2:15; both RSV and NASB).

R. E. Po.

INNOCENTS, SLAUGHTER OF. This term refers to the slaughter by Herod the Great of all the male children two years old and under in Bethlehem and its environs, in his effort to destroy the Christ Child (Mt 2:16). Description of the children as "innocents" may be traced to Cyprian in the 3rd cen. Since Bethlehem was a small village, the number of children slain probably was fewer than 50 and certainly not so large a number as sometimes imagined. Matthew considered the slaughter to be a fulfillment of Jer 31:15, probably because Rachel died on the way to Bethlehem and her tomb is traditionally considered to be just N of the town. But the connection of the OT verse with Bethlehem is not clear, because Ramah was in the territory of Benjamin and Rachel was not the mother of Judah, ancestor of the inhabitants of Bethlehem. Rachel, however, *died* near Bethlehem. The primary fulfillment of Jer 31:15 is to be found in Jer 40:1.

See Ramah 1.

INSCRIPTION. *See* Writing.

INSECTS. *See* Animals, IV.

INSPIRATION. The theological concept of inspiration has reference to the fact that Holy Scripture is the utterance of the God who cannot lie and is hence the infallible Word of God. The term itself occurs seldom in Scripture (Job 32:8; II Tim 3:16).

Definition

The English word "inspiration" (Lat. *inspiratio*) alters the biblical sense somewhat by implying a merely psychological heightening of a writer's powers, rather than emphasizing the divine "inspiration" of Scripture. The Gr. adjective *theopneustos* (translated in II Tim 3:16, RSV, by "is inspired by God") has only a passive sense, affirming that Scripture was "breathed out" by God so that it is His word and oracle. Thus Scripture is what God the Holy Spirit says (Heb 3:7), as "men moved by the Holy Spirit spoke from God" (II Pet 1:21, RSV).

Inspiration is the miracle of redemptive, divine revelation by which sacred writings were called forth, the product of God's creative breath, possessing absolute divine authority. God's breath or Spirit denotes the outgoing of His dynamic power, whether in creation (Ps 33:6), preservation (Job 34:14–15), revelation (Isa 48:16), regeneration (Ezk 36:26–27), or judgment (Isa 30:28). God's breath created Scripture to be His very word in man's language.

Inspiration and Revelation

1. *Revelation a divine activity.* Inspiration needs to be understood within and not apart from divine special revelation. Inspired Scripture enjoys its dignity as the medium of, record of, and witness to divine revelation. The nature of inspiration is an aspect in the pattern of revelation. Revelation is the divine activity of self-disclosure by which the living God unveils something of His character and purposes for mankind (Deut 29:29; II Cor 4:6). Scripture is a product of that revealing activity, its linguistic residue and written embodiment. God reveals Himself on the plane of history by His saving *acts* (Acts 2:11) and on the plane of truth by His gracious *word* (Isa 55:11).

2. *Biblical balance.* The Neoprotestant understanding of revelation, under the influence of existential philosophical *a prioris*, plays down the cognitive side of revelation and refuses to recognize Scripture as written revelation. There i a shift from the propositional to the personal, and from the literary to the historical. But the two new emphases fail to observe the biblical balance. In Scripture, the personal encounter with God occurs in the context of valid knowledge (Heb 1:1 f.), and God's saving acts in history are accompanied by the prophetic interpretation (Amos 3:7). The divine acting and the divine speaking are correlative concepts of equal dignity. Act and interpretation are perfectly blended together.

3. *Purpose of revelation.* Neoprotestantism to the contrary, the *word* of God is central to the biblical idea of revelation (Jer 23:9, 16, 18, 22, 28). Pagan idols may be dumb, but the Lord is a living and a speaking God (Amos 3:8). Truth is fundamental to trust. Biblical faith means walking in the light of the divine promises. Both acts and words are divine events, forming an inseparable unity. The NT attitude to the OT is that written Scripture is a primary product of divine revelation, the locus in which the revealing activity now takes place. In Scripture God addresses the church (Mt 22:43; Acts 28:25; Heb 10:15). Thus we can say that revelation *generates* Scripture.

4. *Purpose of inspiration.* Inspiration, in other words, is the miracle of conservation whereby the truths of divine revelation have been *preserved* in an authentic and sufficient form. Scripture is nothing other than an extension of the revelation modality of the divine speaking. It exists so that the church might know God's word and distinguish it from her own sinful self-consciousness.

The purpose of Scripture is the same as that of revelation, to bear witness to the divine plan for redeeming sinners (II Tim 3:15). It is a seamless robe of truth-telling language, designed to lead men to Christ the Saviour (Lk 24:27). Christians love and reverence the Holy Scriptures because they are the locus of their confrontation and fellowship with the living Word. It contains the truths of revelation which conserve and deepen our relationship with God.

The high doctrine of biblical inspiration is not at all the result of an antiquated brand of scholastic thinking. It arises naturally out of the pattern of revelation at the heart of Christian faith. The divine activity of revelation led to the production of inspired Scripture, the written transcript of revealed truth.

The Biblical Concept of Inspiration

1. *Biblical testimony to its inspiration.* The self-attestation of the Bible to its own authority is in reality the teachings of Jesus Christ and of His apostles and prophets. Christians who have been convinced that God has revealed Himself in a historical mode culminating in Christ cannot but regard this evidence with deep seriousness. Any attempt to silence the evidence one text at a time is like trying to stop an avalanche one stone at a time.

There is a strong, pervasive, and complete testimony to the inspiration of Scripture in the biblical record. All Scripture (plenary inspiration) is of divine authorship (verbal inspiration) according to Paul (II Tim 3:16), and may be personified as God Himself speaking (Gal 3:8). Scripture records what God says (Acts 13:32–33). Peter affirms that the OT Scriptures are what the Holy Spirit spoke beforehand (Acts 1:16). Scripture is the written word of God, and cannot err because He cannot lie (Acts 4:25; Jn 10:35). Scripture was not initiated by men (II Pet 1:21). The Spirit of the Lord spoke by their tongues (II Sam 23:2).

2. *The testimony of Christ.* Jesus regarded the Scripture in its entire extent and in every part to be God-given and of indefectible authority (Mt 5:17 f.). It is the word of God (Mk 7:13), the divine commandment (Mt 19:4 f.), and had to be fulfilled in every particular (Mk 14:49).

Christ Himself constituted Christianity a religion of divine authority based on Scripture. Unless His ministry was founded upon a fallacy of no small magnitude and His divine authority an illusion, His followers are bound to His teachings in this respect. It is consistent to accept both Christ and Scripture, or to reject both; but it is neither consistent nor honest to accept one and reject the other. Where Christ is acknowledged as Lord, the matter of biblical authority is settled. What Scripture says, God says. The words of the law and the prophets are regarded as God's own speech (Ps 119; Jer 1:4, 9). The OT is a divine oracle (Rom 3:2); not merely the record of what Moses or David said, but of what God said through them (Acts 28:25). The

INSPIRATION

NT continually cites the OT as the utterance of God (Rom 9:17). Thus the testimony of the prophets, Christ, and the apostles is uniformly consistent.

3. *The divine authorship of Scripture.* While little is said regarding the mode of divine inspiration, it is clear that the role of the biblical writers was to transmit what they received. God was the primary author of Scripture, and its message is a divine creation. Scripture is a body of literature bearing prophetic witness to Christ (Jn 5:39 f.; II Cor 3:14–18) and designed to instruct believers in divine things (Rom 15:4; I Cor 10:11). The entire Scripture is a deposit of heavenly instruction, the authentic voice of God (Mt 4:4). The OT Scripture was seen as the written complement and product of old covenant revelation, called forth and generated by that divine activity. In the same way, the NT finds its validity as the witness to a new and better covenant.

4. *Attributes of the inspired Word.* On the basis of such evidence it is possible to construct a doctrinal model for biblical inspiration. Holy Scripture is God's written word to man (Mt 4:4). All its high attributes rest on this single fact. Scripture and the word of God *ought* to be identified (Mk 7:9–13). It is a *divine,* and not merely human, witness to revelation. The OT is repeatedly cited in the NT as the univocal word of God (Mt 1:22). As a consequence the Scripture is *infallible* (incapable of wandering from the truth) and *inerrant* (not guilty of mistakes or errors), fully trustworthy and authoritative (Prov 30:5–6). If the Scripture deceived its readers or erred in its teachings, it would not be *God's* word (Ps 19:7). An erring standard provides no sure measurement of truth and error.

Inerrancy is a necessary concomitant of the doctrine of inspiration. As Wesley put it, "If there be any mistakes in the Bible, there may well be a thousand. If there be one falsehood in that book, it did not come from the God of truth." Hardly a theologian of any note failed to draw this conclusion from the evidence until very recently. Divine inspiration is essentially incompatible with error. Christ's attitude to Scripture was one of *total trust* (Mt 22:29).

5. *Inspiration of the autographs.* Strictly speaking, inspiration has to do with the original text (i.e., the autographs) of Scripture, and not with the corruptions which intruded in the course of textual transmission. For instance, in reading Hamlet, it is of the greatest interest to the student of Shakespeare to know what part of the text is authentic and what is not. Textual criticism of the Bible has shown that the Heb. and Gr. texts we possess are *virtually* identical to the original, and may therefore be said to be virtually inspired as well. Inspiration terminates on *graphē* (written Scripture), not on scribal copies made from it (II Tim 3:16). Faith in the providence of God and evidence from lower criticism warrant an attitude of confidence that the text is sufficiently trustworthy so as not to lead us astray.

6. *Plenary verbal inspiration.* Inspiration is *plenary* and *verbal,* and Scripture a language deposit inspired in the whole, not merely in the parts (Rom 15:4; II Tim 3:16). Without plenary inspiration, the Bible is an equivocal authority. The control of the Spirit over the biblical writers was so complete as to ensure that they were the mouthpieces of infallible revelation.

Although many denounce verbal inspiration as a detestable theory, it is in fact the only biblical and meaningful one. Inspiration has to do with *words* and with language: "which things we also speak, not in words taught by human wisdom, but in those taught by the Spirit, combining spiritual thoughts with spiritual words" (I Cor 2:13, NASB). Scripture is the text through which God speaks to us. "And the Lord said unto me, Behold, I have put my words in thy mouth" (Jer 1:9); "thou shalt speak my words unto them" (Ezk 2:7). This word deposit is veracious, and conveys successfully the freight of divine revelation. Words signify and safeguard meaning. We get at the meaning of the Bible by the words it employs. Inspiration assures us that this verbal text is the trustworthy and sufficient vehicle of divine revelation.

7. *Dual authorship.* The authorship of Scripture is *dual,* the word of God in the words of men (e.g., Mt 2:15). In one sense the human writers contributed much to the making of Scripture (style, research, fervor), and in another sense they contributed nothing. The Spirit worked concurrently alongside the activity of the human authors (not penmen), He Himself being the principle and they the instrumental cause, with the result that their writing was both free and spontaneous on their part and divinely elicited and controlled. It is an axiom of biblical theism that divine providence can reach its ends *without* dehumanizing the agents it employs (cf. Acts 2:23).

Mechanical dictation is not involved here at all. The sacred writers retained their full individuality and made use of the full range of their capacities. They may be likened to the first violinist or concertmaster, playing with his own style, in a symphony orchestra which is directed in person by the composer of the music. Inspiration simply assured that the humanity of Scripture was not corrupted by the errancy of the human race. As Christ was truly human yet free from sin, so Scripture is truly human yet free from error. Because Scripture is the word of God, it is truthful in all that it teaches, and possesses the following properties.

8. *Inherent properties of Scripture.* The *authority* of Scripture means that it enjoys the right to rule and command our obedience. It is the *principium cognoscendi* (the beginning of knowledge) of Christian theology, and the *causa media* (intermediate instrument) of our knowledge of God. Hence, inspiration is perennially at the center of theological discussion.

The *sufficiency* and *clarity* of Scripture point to the fact that Scripture has enough light to save sinners and direct the church. All that believers need to know is contained therein (II Tim 3:17). This is not to say that Scripture contains all possible or even all actual revelation, or that a total theological system may be deduced from it, or that every text is alike clear unto all. It is nonetheless a "light shining in a dark place" (II Pet 1:19) and a lamp unto our path (Ps 119:105). There is enough clear truth in it to lead every sincere seeker to God through Jesus Christ (Jn 14:6; Acts 4:12; I Pet 3:18).

The Word of God is also *efficacious* (Heb 4:12). It possesses the capability in the presence of faith and the Spirit of convicting and converting sinners (Isa 55:11; I Pet 1:23). Therefore, it is called a "hammer" and "fire" (Jer 23:29), "seed" and "wheat" (Isa 55:10; Jer 23:28), and "spiritual milk" (I Pet 2:2). Scripture is a means of grace, a sacramental vehicle, bearing authoritative testimony to Christ who is its focus and center.

Inspiration and Authority

1. *Scripture as the source of theology*. Christian theology is the science of articulating the truth content of divine revelation. The historic church from the beginning has given the Bible a place of preeminence in providing *revelation data* for this task.

2. *The modern departure from this source*. Theologians always found it easier to accept the plenary inspiration of Scripture than to believe that Christ, His disciples, and the entire church from the first erred in their view. The reason why the doctrine was never incorporated in a formal creed may be found in the fact that scarcely anyone dreamed of challenging it. The new, higher critical views of Scripture, therefore, are a deliberate break with historic Christian opinion.

The chaos and ambiguity of so much modern theology result from the crisis in biblical authority. Suddenly, in place of a divine Word, only a human voice is heard (cf. Amos 8:11 f.). As a historical religion, Christianity depends on her historical sources. Once the strong link between divine revelation and the Hebrew-Christian Scriptures is broken, theological methodology is in shambles.

3. *The Protestant basis of authority*. Scripture is the epistemological base of theology, i.e., the foundation or grounds for our knowledge of God. Luther's motto, *Sola Scriptura* ("Scripture alone"), is the Protestant principle. Scripture constitutes, determines, and rules the entire theological endeavor. Our source of authority is the Holy Spirit speaking in the Scripture, the product of His own creative breath. In it the church has an objective check against demonic self-delusion and a resource for her correction. Scripture is the authentic map of the spiritual order. By it we encounter the living God in His gracious self-disclosure. God-talk becomes possible because grounded in ascertainable revelation data couched in human language. It is inspiring to its readers because it is in itself inspired by God.

Bibliography. Theodore Engelder, *Scripture Cannot Be Broken,* St. Louis: Concordia, 1944. Louis Gaussen, *Theopneustia, The Plenary Inspiration of the Holy Scriptures,* Chicago: Moody Press, 1949. Carl F. H. Henry, ed., *Revelation and the Bible,* Grand Rapids: Baker, 1958. James Orr, *Revelation and Inspiration,* Grand Rapids: Eerdmans, 1952. René Pache, *The Inspiration and Authority of Scripture,* trans. by Helen I. Needham, Chicago: Moody Press, 1969. James I. Packer, *'Fundamentalism' and the Word of God,* London: Inter-Varsity, 1958. Clark H. Pinnock, *A Defense of Biblical Infallibility,* Philadelphia: Presbyterian and Reformed, 1967; *Sola Scriptura,* Chicago: Moody Press, 1970. Bernard Ramm, *Special Revelation and the Word of God,* Grand Rapids: Eerdmans, 1961. Ned B. Stonehouse and P. Wooley, ed., *The Infallible Word,* Grand Rapids: Eerdmans, 1946. John F. Walvoord, ed., *Inspiration and Interpretation,* Grand Rapids: Eerdmans, 1957. Benjamin B. Warfield, *The Inspiration and Authority of the Bible,* Philadelphia: Presbyterian and Reformed, 1948.

C. H. P.

INSTANT, INSTANTLY. The KJV uses these words in translating several different Heb. and Gr. words. Although in modern English the words refer only to time, they are used predominantly in the KJV in the sense of urgency (cf. Lk 23:23; II Tim 4:2). In Isa 29:5; 30:13; Jer 18:7, 9 the concept of time is evident.

INSTRUCTION. *See* Disciple; Education; Family; Schools.

INSTRUMENT. In the OT the word "instrument" has three uses.

1. Utensils used in connection with the sanctuary of the tabernacle (cf. Num 31:6) and later of the temple. *See* Tabernacle; Temple.

2. Weapons of war (cf. I Chr 12:33). *See* Armor.

3. Musical instruments (cf. II Chr 7:6). *See* Music.

Paul refers to the members of the body as instruments to be used in the cause of righteousness whereas formerly they were used in the cause of unrighteousness (Rom 6:13).

INTEGRITY. The state or quality of being ethically sound, morally well-adjusted, from Heb. *tōm, tummâ,* "completeness, integrity." The Heb. term is used in a coordinate sense of simplicity in the phrase "a certain man drew a bow at a venture" (lit., in his simplicity or innocence, I Kgs 22:34; II Chr 18:33; cf. II Sam 15:11). It is translated "integrity" in all places where it signifies sincerity and honesty of heart (e.g., Gen 20:5; I Kgs 9:4; Job 2:3; 27:5; 31:6; Ps 7:8; 25:21; 26:1; 41:12; 78:72; Prov 11:3;

19:1; 20:7; etc.). In the plural it is used in one of the words ("thummim," *see* Urim and Thummim) on the breastplate of the high priest (Ex 28:30; Deut 33:8; Ezr 2:63; Neh 7:65) indicating possibly innocence or integrity. While the word does not occur in the NT, the concept is covered by such terms as "sincerity," "pure in heart," "single eye," and is synonymous with honesty, genuineness, sincerity.

INTENTION. The purpose, design, aim or goal which is intended by the mind or heart (Heb 4:12, NASB; "intents," KJV). It often involves the determination of the will, as in Lk 14:28. The aim or intent behind an action is most important both in ethics and in criminal law. The killing of a man when done with "malice aforethought" is murder, but when done by mistake, simply manslaughter.

Intent or purpose, however, does not of itself make an act good. It is the fault of Paul Tillich's ethics that he maintains anything done in love is thereby justified. Many serious mistakes and much evil can occur when intent and moral law are divorced, as in his theology when he denies that the laws of God and the commands of Christ apply to us today. Christ's teaching is perfectly clear that only those who have both righteous motives in the heart and do the will of God will enter the kingdom of heaven (Mt 5:17-20; 7:21). *See* Sermon on the Mount.

R. A. K.

INTERCESSION

Meaning. The Heb. word for intercede (*pāga'*) originally meant "to strike upon," and thus came to mean "to assail anyone with petitions." When such assailing was done on behalf of others this was intercession.

The Gr. word (*entygchanō*) means "to appeal or petition." The verb is used five times in the NT (Acts 25:24 [RSV "petitioned me"]; Rom 8:27, 34; 11:2; Heb 7:25). The noun occurs twice (I Tim 2:1; 4:5). In I Tim 2:1 intercession is contrasted with supplications, prayers, and giving of thanks. On the difference in meaning of these words Trench says: " 'Intercession,' by which the AV translates it, is not, as we now understand 'intercession,' a satisfactory rendering. For *enteuxis* does not necessarily mean what intercession at present commonly does mean—namely, prayer in relation to others (at I Tim 4:5 such meaning is impossible); a pleading either for them or against them ... but, as its connexion with *entugchanein,* to fall in with a person, to draw close to him so as to enter into familiar speech and communion with him ... implies, it is free familiar prayer, such as boldly draws near to God" (*Synonyms of the New Testament,* pp. 189-90). Intercession, then, highlights naturalness, boldness, and familiarity in prayer.

Illustrations of intercession. Abraham's earnest pleading for Sodom is an outstanding OT illustration of intercession (Gen 18:23-33). Moses prayed in like vein for Israel after they had made the golden calf (Ex 32:31-32). Elijah's boldness in prayer on Mount Carmel is similar (I Kgs 18:36-37). Likewise, there are many illustrations of intercession in the NT (see below).

The intercession of Christ. As Priest Christ is pictured as drawing near to God interceding for His people (Rom 8:34; Heb 7:25). This ministry has two aspects: that of advocate, pleading when we have sinned (I Jn 2:1-2), and that preventive work of keeping us from evil (Jn 17:15). This work of Christ is illustrated in His conversation with Peter in which He assured him that "I have prayed for thee, that thy faith fail not" (Lk 22:32).

The intercession of the Holy Spirit. The Spirit also intercedes on behalf of the believer (Rom 8:26) with unutterable groanings. "Thus, at the moment when the believer already feels the impulse of hope failing within him, a groan more elevated, holy, and intense than anything which can go forth even from his renewed heart is uttered within him, coming from God and going to God, like a pure breath, and relieves the poor downcast heart" (Godet, *Romans,* II, 102).

The intercession of Christians. The intercessory work of believers is in behalf of all men with a view that they might come to a knowledge of the truth of salvation in Christ (I Tim 2:1-4). In this, all believers are priests.

See Mediation; Prayer.

C. C. R.

INTEREST. *See* Usury.

INTERMEDIATE STATE. The doctrine of the intermediate state is concerned with the condition of men immediately following physical death and prior to the resurrection.

Since all Bible-believing Christians believe in the resurrection of the body and the future judgment, it follows that all believe in an intermediate state between death and the resurrection. Not all Christians, however, agree as to the condition of the dead during this interval. All recognize that it is different from the condition of those living on earth, and some believe that it is, at least in certain details, quite different from what it will be subsequent to the resurrection. The problem in the doctrine of the intermediate state, then, is the nature of the existence of the righteous and the wicked dead prior to the resurrection.

Just as the Scriptures affirm the future resurrection of both the righteous and the wicked, they also teach the continuous personal and conscious existence of both in that period immediately after death and the dissolution of the physical body. Neither the righteous nor the wicked receive bodies before the resurrection. The righteous are to receive theirs "at the last trump" (I Cor 15:52), which is identified with the personal return of the Lord (I Thess

4:16–17; cf. Rev 20:4–5). For the wicked dead there is also a resurrection (Acts 24:15; Jn 5:28–30).

The Nature of Existence in the Intermediate State

The righteous dead. Although their souls are without bodies, the intermediate state is for the righteous one of conscious joy and exaltation because they have been made perfect in holiness, are free from sin and suffering, and have passed into the presence of the Lord in glory. Their bodies, which are the Lord's, rest, or sleep, in their graves until the day of resurrection. The apostle Paul taught that believers were "confident . . . and willing rather to be absent from the body, and to be present with the Lord" (II Cor 5:8). The dying thief was told by Christ, "Today shalt thou be with me in paradise" (Lk 23:43). Being present with the Lord certainly implies conscious bliss, since Christ obviously did not sleep in unconsciousness. Although His body was taken from the cross and rested in Joseph's tomb, He had commended His spirit into God's hands (Lk 23:46).

According to the Scriptures the eternal destiny of man has been settled at his death. There is no passing from one state of existence to another after death. The parable of the rich man and Lazarus makes this clear (Lk 16:25–26; cf. Heb 9:27). It is therefore consistent with the Scripture to believe that the righteous, whose salvation has been wrought by Christ through the offering of Himself once for all, are on death immediately changed from imperfect to perfect holiness. It is this state which Paul had in view when he spoke of his "desire to depart, and to be with Christ; which is far better" (Phil 1:23). With his burning zeal for the proclamation of the gospel throughout the earth, Paul would certainly have preferred to live on and continue his labors on earth if death had held for him the prospect of unconsciousness or of inactivity. Certainly, in the presence of Christ there is "fullness of joy" (Ps 16:11) and deliverance from "every evil work" (II Tim 4:18). In the light of II Cor 12:3–4 and Heb 12:23 the "paradise" in which Christ and the righteous dead are together can only be heaven itself.

That the intermediate state for the believer does not include all of the full blessedness of the resurrection, however, is revealed by the fact that Paul hoped to avoid the period of "nakedness" for the soul and live until the rapture at the coming of the Lord (II Cor 5:2–8). The ultimate, glorious anticipation of the Christian is the resurrection. *See* Heaven.

The wicked dead. Concerning those who die in sin and unbelief, the Scriptures teach that they are in a definitely fixed and conscious state of suffering and punishment, although the degree of this punishment is not specifically identified as the same as that of the eternal state following the resurrection of the unrighteous. Eternal punishment is connected with those who are in their bodies (cf. Mt 10:28). It is spoken of in the NT in relation to a specific place, Gehenna (*q.v.*), which is a metaphorical designation of the lake of fire; and the sufferings of the intermediate state are never mentioned as occurring there. This does not mean, however, that any fundamental distinction should be made between the sufferings of hell as a place of eternal torment and the suffering which the wicked experience in the invisible world before the resurrection. *See* Hell.

Wherever the sphere of punishment in the intermediate state is localized, it is referred to in the Gr. of the NT as Hades (*q.v.*). This is the equivalent of OT Sheol (*q.v.*). It seems clear that the words Sheol and Hades do not always indicate a locality in the Scripture, but often simply denote the state of death, or the separation of the soul and body (I Sam 2:6; Ps 89:48; Acts 2:27, 31). There are also some passages in which Sheol seems merely to designate the grave in a general sense (Gen 37:35; 44:29; Job 14:13; Ps 6:5).

The principal passage in which Hades is given a localized conception is Lk 16:23. Because this is in a parable, it may be argued that the Lord in using the term did not intend to reveal any truth concerning a specific locality as distinct from Gehenna, e.g., but simply used imagery which was well known in His day. Whether this be true or not, this parable does prove that the intermediate state is for the wicked not an abiding place of a neutral character where they await the final judgment, but rather a place of conscious suffering and punishment from which there is no return. The fact that the departed are spoken of as though they were possessed of bodily organs does not mean that they actually have bodies prior to the resurrection, for God and the angels are spoken of in the same manner.

Four Common Errors

It is necessary in considering the doctrine of the intermediate state to point out the fact that the Scriptures enable us to refute four commonly held errors respecting the abode of the soul after death.

1. The doctrine that the souls of both the righteous and the wicked sleep between death and the resurrection. This view has been held by small sects since very early days in the history of the church. While it is true that the Scripture often speaks of death as a sleep (Mt 9:24; Acts 7:60; I Cor 15:51; I Thess 4:13), and there are certain passages which might seem to teach that the departed are unconscious (Ps 6:5; 30:9; Isa 38:18–19), the Scriptures never speak of the soul or the person falling asleep, but only the body. The term sleep is used because there is great similarity between a sleeping body and a dead body; and, furthermore, the sleep in death of the body is to be broken by a quickening at the resurrection.

Those passages which are thought to indicate that the dead are unconscious actually do no more than emphasize the fact that the dead are unable to take part any longer in the activity of the world of living men. The Scriptures nowhere encourage the living to seek or expect any kind of converse with the dead (Deut 18:9–12; I Sam 28:7–10; Isa 8:19–20). It should never be forgotten that the Scriptures clearly portray the righteous as enjoying conscious communion with God and with the Lord Jesus Christ immediately after their death (see section on "The righteous dead" above).

2. The doctrine that the intermediate state is one of further probation. This theory teaches that salvation through Christ is still possible in the intermediate state for certain classes of people, and perhaps for all. Some teach that this is the time when salvation will be offered to all children who die in infancy and to the heathen who never heard the gospel. The scriptures frequently used to support this theory are I Pet 3:19 and 4:6. Even though they are understood as teaching that Christ went into the underworld to preach (which interpretation is not necessary), certainly they do not prove that any offer of salvation was extended to persons there.

The Word of God uniformly represents the state of all men, whether believers or unbelievers, as completely fixed when they have died. The most important passage is Lk 16:19–31, but one should also consider Jn 8:21, 24; II Pet 2:4, 9; Jude 7–13. Furthermore, the Scriptures never represent the eternal destiny of a soul as determined by that which is done in the intermediate state (see Mt 7:22–23; Lk 12:47–48; Gal 6:7–8; II Thess 1:8; Heb 9:27).

3. The doctrine taught by the Church of Rome, that souls at peace with the church but not perfectly pure at death (and almost none are considered to be) must undergo a period of purging before they are permitted to enter into the perfect and unlimited bliss of heaven. This purifying is carried on in a place called purgatory, where all souls endure suffering for the purpose of both expiation and purification. Romanist doctrine places no limit except the final judgment on the time souls may continue in purgatory, since the extent of their suffering is determined by their guilt and impurity. They may be aided by the prayers of living saints and especially by the sacrifice of the Mass offered on their behalf.

The Roman Catholic authority for the doctrine of purgatory is almost exclusively the teaching of the Church of Rome itself. The Pope is supposed to have jurisdiction over purgatory. No proper appeal can be made to the Scripture, for as has been pointed out above, the Scriptures teach that the soul of the believer is immediately transported into the presence of Christ when he dies, just as the wicked pass into eternal torment. More than this, however, the doctrine of purgatory would destroy the clearest and most vital teachings of the gospel in the NT. The sinner's salvation rests not upon his own works or merits, but entirely upon the infinitely meritorious sacrifice of Christ to which sinners can add nothing in making satisfaction for sin (Eph 2:8–9).

There are other unscriptural doctrines which have arisen in the Church of Rome in connection with the doctrine of purgatory. For example, the doctrine of supererogation, the idea that a man may be more than perfect himself and with his superfluous merit aid those suffering in purgatory. Strangely, the Romanist believes that one human's merit can be imputed to another, yet he cannot believe that Christ's perfect righteousness is imputed to sinners. The Roman doctrine of purgatory presupposes two impossibilities: first, that any man can be better than he ought to be; and second, that man can add to the perfect work of salvation which Christ accomplished by His death and resurrection.

4. Finally, there is the error of the doctrine of annihilationism. According to this teaching, there is no conscious existence for the wicked after death. A distinction can be made between those who teach that the soul of the unbeliever is deprived of immortality by an act of God and is thus deprived of consciousness after death, and those who teach that immortality is a gift of God only to those who believe, so the soul that does not receive it simply ceases to exist.

The Scriptures are clear on the fact that the wicked as well as the righteous will live forever, and that their existence will be one of conscious suffering and punishment (Eccl 12:7; Mt 25:46; Rom 2:8–10; Rev 14:11; 20:10, 12–15).

See Dead, The; Death; Eschatology; Immortality.

R. G. R.

INTERPRET, INTERPRETER. The noun "interpreter" (Gr. *diermēneutēs,* one who explains fully or interprets) is used in the NT only in I Cor 14:28. The verb of that root occurs in I Cor 12:30; 14:5, 13, 27. In chap. 14 Paul instructs that speaking in tongues in a church assembly is to occur in an orderly manner but only when there is an "interpreter" present, for only then is it edifying. The one who speaks in a tongue ought to pray that he himself may interpret (v. 13). One purpose of the gift of tongues was that thus an unconverted man should hear a message in his own language, as did those present at Pentecost (Acts 2:8), and then hear it interpreted by another who knew not that tongue. It was thus to be a double miracle, yet one which would corroborate itself in this peculiar manner to the hearer. *See* Tongues, Gift of; Gifts, Spiritual.

The Gr. *hermēneuō* and its compound *methermeneuomai* denote interpreting by translating from one language to another (e.g., Mt 1:23; Jn 1:38, 41–42). In Ezra's time royal decrees were translated (*m*ᵉ*turgām,* Ezr 4:7), and the Aramaic translations with expositions of the Heb. Scriptures became known as the Targums or Targumim.

In II Pet 1:20 the word for "interpretation" is *epilusis,* unloosing or unfolding. Interpreting Scripture is not a matter of one's own private opinion.

In the OT Joseph acted as the interpreter (from Heb. *pāthar*) of various dreams (Gen 40-41). Daniel convinced Nebuchadnezzar of his God-given ability to give the interpretation (Aram. *pᵉshar*) or explanation of the king's dream, by first of all telling the king what he saw in the dream (Dan 2:5-45). Later Daniel gave the interpretation of Nebuchadnezzar's dream of the great tree that was cut down (4:8-27) and of the handwriting on the wall of Belshazzar's palace (5:12-28). The word *pesher,* "interpretation" (Eccl 8:1), became the standard term for the sectarian explanations or commentaries of the canonical books of the OT by members of the Qumran community. *See* Dead Sea Scrolls.

R. A. K.

INTERPRETATION OF SCRIPTURE. *See* Bible Interpretation.

IPHEDEIAH (ĭf'ē-dē'yȧ). A descendant of Benjamin, son of Shashak (I Chr 8:25).

IPHTAHEL. *See* Jiphthael.

IR (ĭr). A descendant of Benjamin (I Chr 7:12), father of Shuppim and Huppim.

IRA (ī'rȧ)

1. A chief ruler (KJV) or priest (RSV) of David (II Sam 20:26), also designated as a Jairite, perhaps a Jattirite, according to the Syriac text.

2. An Ithrite (perhaps Jattirite), one of David's mighty men and possibly the same as 1 (II Sam 23:38; I Chr 11:40).

3. Another of David's heroic followers, the son of Ikkesh the Tekoite (II Sam 23:26; I Chr 11:28).

IRAD (ī'răd). A grandson of Cain, son of Enoch, and father of Mehujael (Gen 4:18).

IRAM (ī'răm). A "duke" or chief of Edom and descendant of Esau (Gen 36:43; I Chr 1:54).

IRHAHERES (ĭr-hă-hē'rĕs). A term which appears only in the Heb. text of Isa 19:18, where it is stated that one of a certain five Egyptian cities will be called by this name or title. Though various interpretations may be found, the name usually is taken as a play on words relating to the city of Heliopolis (biblical On, Aven; Egpt. *Iwnw*), whose name means "city of the sun" (see RSV), which can be written in Heb. as *'ir haḥeres,* as the complete Isaiah scroll from Cave 1 at Qumran, *c.* 15 later Heb. MSS, Symmachus, the Vulgate, and the Talmud attest. *See* On. But the MT states that the one city will be called *'ir haheres,* "city of destruction" (KJV, NASB), possibly because the temples and other physical elements of sun-worship will have been destroyed. For an extended discussion of the textual problem see Carl W. E. Naegelsbach, *Isaiah, Lange's Commentary,* Grand Rapids: Zondervan, n.d., pp. 226 ff.

IRI (ī'rī). A Benjamite, the son of Bela (I Chr 7:7).

IRIJAH (ī-rī'jȧ). A captain of the guard who arrested Jeremiah at the gate of Benjamin during the Chaldean siege, and having falsely accused the prophet of deserting to the enemy he took Jeremiah back to the princes of Judah (Jer 37:13-14).

IR-NAHASH (ĭr-nā'hăsh). Perhaps a city founded by Tehinnah, since he is called "father" of it (I Chr 4:12). On the other hand, it could refer to a man, the son of Tehinnah.

IRON

1. *See* Minerals and Metals.

2. A fortified city in the territory of Naphtali (Josh 19:38), called Yiron in RSV. It is probably the present village of Yārûn, 10 miles NW of Hazor. Tiglath-pileser III captured Iron and took away 650 captives (ANET, p. 283).

IRPEEL (ĭr'pē-ĕl). A city of Benjamin, the identity of which is not certainly known. Some have taken it to be a site near ancient Gibeon (Josh 18:27).

IRRIGATION. This word is not found in Heb. or Gr., although the practice of irrigation for watering plants and trees is frequently implied in biblical literature (cf. Gen 13:10; Eccl 2:5-6; Isa 58:11). The term refers to artificial means of watering crops throughout biblical times in the form of aqueducts, cisterns, dams, canals, etc.

A Roman aqueduct near Caesarea. HFV

A Roman dam with a sluice gate near Samaria.
HFV

The Heb. *peleg,* translated "rivers" in KJV, often refers to irrigation canals (Ps 1:3; 46:4; Prov 21:1; Isa 30:25; 32:2). Because of inadequate rainfall, Babylonia and Egypt have always had to be supplied with water from their respective rivers. The water was conducted from the river along canals via various mechanical devices and at great cost of labor. There was less need in Palestine and Syria than in Egypt and Babylonia (cf. Deut 11:10). Generally, the winter rains were ample for the cereal crops; however, the vegetable and fruit gardens would be parched by the long summer drought. These gardens were always planted near natural supplies of water. The water was made to flow from its sources (either directly or by aqueduct, or raised from a well by an endless chain of buckets drawn by a horse or donkey, cf. Num 24:7; Isa 40:15) into little channels running through the garden. Artificial water pools for gardens are referred to in Eccl 2:6. A storage pool is an almost universal feature in such gardens. Large numbers of cisterns have been unearthed on every major site in Palestine (cf. II Chr 26:10; Neh 9:25). Before the development of watertight cisterns, the farmer had to depend entirely on springs and perennial streams, such as the Jabbok and the Wadi Qelt near Jericho, for artificial irrigation. *See* Agriculture.

D. W. D.

IR-SHEMESH (ĭr-shĕm'ĭsh). A city of Dan, apparently the same as Beth-shemesh (*q.v.*) and connected with Mount Heres (Josh 19:41).

IRU (ī'ro͞o). The eldest son of Caleb (I Chr 4:15). The word is perhaps to be read "Ir," the *-u* being the conjunction "and" belonging to the succeeding word.

ISAAC (ī'zĭk). The name, given by God before the birth of the child (Gen 17:19), signifies "he laughs" or "he who laughs." See references to laughter in Gen 17:17; 18:12-15; 21:6.

History. Isaac was born (probably in Gerar) to Abraham and Sarah when they were 100 and 90 years old respectively. He was the first to be circumcised in the normal course, when eight days old (Gen 21:4), in recognition of the covenant promise (Gen 17:2-17). The presence of Hagar and her son Ishmael was a disturbing factor in the covenant household, and by divine command they were dismissed. If the events are related in chronological order, Ishmael would be at this time about 16 or 17 years old; he is depicted in the story as an immature youth who suffered exhaustion sooner than his mother (Gen 21:15, 18). But he was old enough to be a mocker (v. 9)!

Nothing is known of the early boyhood of Isaac. We next see him big and strong enough to carry the wood for the altar fire up the mountain slope, not knowing that he himself would mount that altar. The experience of being bound as a sacrificial victim and then delivered by divine intervention must have deeply affected his whole life.

Isaac was 37 years old when his mother died in Hebron. Three years later his marriage to Rebekah took place at Lahai-roi. In this he accepted the arrangement made by his father, as evidently the ordering of the Lord.

To safeguard the inheritance, Abraham sent all his other sons away, as he had done Ishmael, making Isaac sole heir (Gen 25:1-6). This would prevent any dispute about the birthright. The death of Abraham at the ripe age of 175 brought Ishmael and Isaac together, probably for the last time.

Isaac was 40 years old when he married, and he waited 20 years for offspring. Then came the twins, Esau and Jacob, bringing new conflict into the covenant home. The favoritism of the parents fostered the struggle for power in the children, culminating in Jacob's deception by which he secured the patriarchal blessing.

In the meantime Isaac's sojourn in Gerar brought out behavior reminiscent of his father (Gen 26:6-11). Isaac passed off Rebekah as his sister, reckoning that a brother would not be in the same danger as a husband in the event of

A *shaduf,* an Egyptian irrigation "machine."
JR

someone else wanting her. His prosperity in Gerar made him unpopular, so that not only did the Philistine chief invite him to leave, but the herdsmen disputed his right to the wells which his servants dug.

The return to Beer-sheba was attended with the Lord's blessing and a renewal of the divine promise (Gen 26:23-24). But Isaac had his sorrows there too. Esau's wives distressed both him and Rebekah, but still more painful was his son Jacob's deceit, instigated by his mother. There Isaac saw his two sons part company. Isaac was already old and dim of sight when Jacob left for Padan-aram. Twenty years later, when Jacob returned, Isaac was still alive, but dwelling in Hebron, where he had buried Rebekah. There he died, at the age of 180, and there his half-reconciled sons buried him.

See Patriarchal Age.

Character. Isaac was neither as great as Abraham nor as colorful as Jacob. Yet he was great, and filled an important place between the father of the nation and the father of the tribes.

The meekness of Isaac is seen in his unresisting submission to his father in becoming the sacrifice on the altar of Moriah, and in his refusal to argue when the herdsmen of Gerar laid claim to the wells.

He was of an affectionate nature, deeply attached to his mother, grieving her passing, and then comforted in his love for Rebekah. His meditative spirit may have contributed to his outgoing affection.

He was a man in touch with God. If he did not have the dramatic visitations granted his father Abraham, he nevertheless had communication with heaven, and obeyed God's commandments. The altar, the tent, and the well symbolize the chief interests of his life.

He is included in the roster of heroes of faith in Heb 11. His benedictions upon Jacob and Esau are there declared to be acts of faith. No doubt his experience on Mount Moriah helped to make him a man of faith.

Another admirable trait in Isaac was his willingness not to hold grudges. He was treated very meanly by Abimelech and his servants, yet when Abimelech, realizing the strength of Isaac, sought a non-aggression pact, he forgave the past and gave every token of goodwill.

Like all men, Isaac had his faults. Two grave ones can be mentioned. He lacked the wisdom to avoid paternal favoritism. Perhaps it was Rebekah's manifest partiality for Jacob that induced Isaac to champion Esau. At the same time he admired the prowess and sportsmanship of Esau—and incidentally enjoyed venison! No doubt this created a feeling of inferiority in Jacob and urged him to compensate with guile.

But Isaac could lie too, like his father before him. A beautiful woman was dangerous company. A would-be suitor would give dowry to a brother in the absence of the father, but might kill a husband to gain the prize. So Isaac used the tactics of Abraham (though with less justification, for Sarah was actually half sister to Abraham), and said, "She is my sister." It was neither truthful nor heroic.

Spiritual applications

1. At the burning bush God introduced Himself to Moses as "the God of thy father, the God of Abraham, the God of Isaac, and the God of Jacob" (Ex 3:6), so establishing the covenant relationship. Our Lord took up the triple designation of God to confute the Sadducees and to confirm faith in the resurrection (Mt 22:31-32). Notice how the singular form "father" covers Abraham, Isaac and Jacob. Here is a distinction in unity and a unity in distinction not generally ascribed to men.

2. Isaac is presented in Rom 9:7 as a typical case of sovereign election. So far as the covenant was concerned, Ishmael was ruled out, as were the sons of Keturah. Natural generation does not give one a place in the kingdom of God. That is the privilege of the called, whose calling is made evident by their faith.

3. The birth of Isaac was the fruit of faith—not only Abraham's, but Sarah's (Heb 11:11). Her incredulous laughter gave place to faith, and the senile womb revived. So spiritual birth is always a miraculous operation in response to faith.

4. Abraham's faith also centered in Isaac. He believed the word of God in face of all natural impossibilities. He took a hard look at his own impotence and at Sarah's 90 years, and still believed God. It was this faith that gave Abraham a standing in righteousness before God. Isaac, therefore, was the fruit of justifying faith (see Rom 4:18-22).

The command to offer Isaac on the altar further tested Abraham's faith. How could the death of Isaac fit in with all the divine promises? Abraham had the answer of faith, that "God was able to raise him up, even from the dead." So Isaac became a figure of life from the dead, or, to give it a NT turn, the new life in Christ (see Heb 11:17-19; Rom 6:3-5). He also appears here as a prefiguration of Christ, the obedient Son, who was "obedient unto death, yea, the death of the cross."

5. The most elaborate spiritual application is in Gal 4:21-31. There the contrast is drawn between Hagar and Ishmael on the one hand, and Sarah and Isaac on the other. Historically we see the conflict between the slave girl and the wife, and between their offspring; but it was left to the apostle Paul to indicate that this feud was an allegory, pointing up the antagonisms between the flesh and the Spirit, between the bondage of the law and the freedom of grace. Any attempt at coexistence between these is bound to fail. Isaac speaks to us of "the liberty wherewith Christ hath made us free" (Gal 5:1).

J. C. M.

ISAIAH (ī-zā'*a*). The Heb. name of Isaiah is *Yᵉsha'-yahu,* meaning "Yahweh is (the source of) salvation." It is fitting that his underlying message to God's covenant nation is that salvation will come to them on the basis of divine grace and power and not by their own strength and religious works.

The fact that Isaiah is called "the son of Amoz" 13 times in the OT may mean that his father was a man of prominence. *See* Amoz. Isaiah apparently made his home in Jerusalem, since his small son Shear-jashub walked with him to meet King Ahaz outside the city (Isa 7:3). His wife was known as a prophetess, and they had another son whom the Lord commanded to be named Maher-shalal-hashbaz (8:1-4). These names were significant, constant reminders to king and to people of the prophet's message. The name of his older son means "a remnant shall return," a promise to the godly in the kingdom of Judah; the name of the younger son, meaning "swift is the booty, speedy is the prey" (Isa 8:3, NASB marg.), pointed to judgment near at hand by the king of Assyria.

It is believed that Isaiah ministered by word and pen for 60 years or more. His call to the prophetic ministry of warning and rebuke came in the year of King Uzziah's death (739 B.C.). Whether he had preached before that event is not certain. He states in the opening verse that he received revelations from God during the reigns of Uzziah, Jotham (750–731 B.C.), Ahaz (745–715), and Hezekiah (729–687). Yet he must have lived longer to be able to record the death of Sennacherib in 681 B.C. and to know the name of the succeeding Assyrian monarch, Esarhaddon (37:38). Thus Isaiah lived on into the reign of Manasseh. Whereas he had been actively engaged in the life of the court during the previous reigns (see chaps. 7, 8, 20, 22, 28–31, 36–39 and II Kgs 19:2–7, 20; 20:1–19), by now he had undoubtedly retired from public life and felt under no compulsion to list the name of the ruler whose wickedness he opposed so strongly in his later writings. II Kgs 21 is the terse historical account of the prevailing apostate worship and civil injustice that evoked from the prophet God's warning of vengeance (56:9–12; 44:9–20; 57:1–21; 58:1–4; 59:1–15; 65:2–7, 11–15). II Chr 33 indicates that Manasseh's idolatrous rampage was the worst during his early years before Esarhaddon displayed him as a vassal in chains in Babylon in 679 B.C. (II Chr 33:11; cf. ANET, p. 291). Thus the tradition that Isaiah was sawn in sunder at the order of Manasseh is credible (perhaps alluded to in Heb 11:37).

The prophets Hosea and Micah were Isaiah's contemporaries. Mic 4:1–3 is practically identical with Isa 2:2–4; which prophet quoted the other we cannot say. Perhaps they were familiar with each other's preaching. Numerous other literary resemblances may be seen between Micah and Isa 40–66, a fact which lends credence to the unity of the book of Isaiah.

Isaiah is by general consent the greatest of all the Heb. writers. His words indicate that he was a man of refinement and culture, a truly poetic soul, a lover and a profound observer of creation and of human nature, a statesman who looked upon the world as the scene of God's working, who looked upon it with fiery indignation because of its wickedness, and yet ever with a note of hope and comfort for the repentant and God-fearing remnant. So fully does he describe the person and offices of the coming Messiah, that from the time of Jerome he has been known as the "evangelist" of the OT. His reputation greatly increased after the fulfillment of many of his prophecies by the Babylonian exile, the victories of Cyrus, and the deliverance of a remnant from captivity. According to Josephus, Cyrus was induced to set the Jews at liberty by the prophecies of Isaiah concerning himself (Jos *Ant*. xi.1.2).

O. T. A.

ISAIAH, BOOK OF. In the Heb. Bible Isaiah is the first of the Latter Prophets (Isaiah, Jeremiah, Ezekiel, the Twelve).

Historical Setting

The book of Isaiah is centered in one of the most troublous and tragic periods of Jewish history. In Isaiah's day the kingdom of Judah was under five kings both good and bad—Uzziah, Jotham, Ahaz, Hezekiah, and Manasseh. It was a sinful nation. Although they were God's people, yet they were apostate and richly deserved chastisement. During Isaiah's lifetime several powerful enemies at one time or another were bent on Judah's destruction: the northern kingdom of Israel, ruled by Pekah; Syria, whose king was Rezin; and Assyria, under such warlike kings as Tiglath-pileser III, Sargon II, and Sennacherib. In addition, other neighbors such as the Philistines, the Moabites, and the Edomites harassed the tiny kingdom from time to time. Egypt was only a "broken reed" to lean upon for help against the Assyrian invader. Babylon, with whom Hezekiah made an alliance, was predicted to become the future destroyer. By revelation Isaiah foresaw Cyrus as the distant, and the Messiah as the far distant, deliverers yet to come. All of these the prophet viewed as God's instruments for the chastising and redeeming of His chosen people.

Date and Authorship

The book itself gives only scanty information about Isaiah's literary activity. According to 8:1 (RSV) and 30:8 he made notations on a tablet or writing board, but also he is commanded to inscribe a certain prophecy in a book or scroll (30:8). The divine exhortation to seek and read from the book of the Lord (34:16) implies that the entire prophecy regarding Edom has been recorded so that in the day of its fulfillment the reader may check every detail with the Scripture. Isaiah's name is specifically attached to chaps. 1, 2, and 13. This prophet is known to have been a court historian for the reigns of Kings Uzziah and Hezekiah (II Chr 26:22; 32:32). It is probable, therefore, that Isaiah wrote the words originally of II Kgs

18:13–20:19, which is essentially parallel to Isa 36–39.

Critical theories of the composition of this prophecy abound today, however, which deny that Isaiah of Jerusalem wrote all 66 chapters himself. Under the influence of deism in the late 18th cen. J. C. Doederlein published in 1789 a systematic argument that chaps. 40–66 were composed in the 6th cen. B.C. Since then it has been common for critics to speak of a "second Isaiah" who allegedly wrote in the period immediately before the end of the Babylonian Captivity (*c.* 550–539 B.C.). H. F. W. Gesenius supported this view in 1819, but Ernst Rosenmuller assigned a number of passages in chaps. 1–39 (such as chaps. 13 and 14 *re* Babylon) to the later unknown writer. Bernhard Duhm went even further in 1892 by proposing a "third Isaiah" who wrote chaps. 56–66 in Jerusalem in the time of Ezra. In 1928 C. C. Torrey in his book *The Second Isaiah* argued for a single author for chaps. 34–66 (36–39 excluded), composed by a writer who lived in Palestine near the end of the 5th cen. Some recent scholars, such as W. H. Brownlee, hold that all 66 chapters come from a circle of disciples who followed or later studied Isaiah and his oral prophecies. These writings were collected and arranged by an able practitioner of this Isaianic school, living perhaps in the 3rd cen.

Numerous evidences in refutation of these critical views may be given, arguing for the unity of the book and for its authorship by the historical Isaiah.

1. Jewish tradition. Later prophets allude to expressions in Isaiah (cf. Nah 1:15 with Isa 52:7; Zeph 2:15 with Isa 47:8, 10). In Ecclesiasticus the son of Sirach *c.* 180 B.C. speaks of Isaiah as the one who "comforted them that mourned in Zion" (48:22-25), a clear allusion to the subject matter of Isa 40–66 and to 40:1 in particular. This is the first appearance of any tradition concerning the authorship of Isaiah. Not a word is said of any later prophet of the Exile or of the time of Ezra adding to Isaiah's writings. None of the many MS copies of Isaiah found in the caves of Qumran and transcribed before and during the time of Christ give any clue to dual or multiple authorship. Nor does Josephus. The LXX has one heading for the entire book. And rabbinic tradition has remained uniform down to the period of modern rational criticism that Isaiah wrote all 66 chapters.

2. The NT witness. Christ referred to Isaiah the prophet as a distinct individual (Mt 15:7–9). The NT writers clearly regarded the author of both main sections of the prophecy to be one and the same (see Mt 3:3; 8:17; 12:17–21; 13:14–15; Mk 1:2; Lk 3:4; 4:17; Acts 8:28–32; 28:25–27; Rom 9:27–29; 10:16, 20–21). "The most conclusive NT citation is John 12:38-41. Verse 38 quotes Isa 53:1; verse 40 quotes Isa 6:9, 10. Then the inspired apostle comments in verse 41: 'These things said Isaiah, when he saw his glory, and spoke of him.' Obviously it was the same Isaiah who personally beheld the glory of Christ in the temple vision of Isa 6 who also made the statement in Isa 53:1: 'Who hath believed our report? and to whom is the arm of the Lord revealed?' If it was not the same author who composed both chap. 6 and chap. 53 (and advocates of the Deutero-Isaiah theory stoutly affirm that it was not), then the inspired apostle himself must have been in error. It therefore follows that advocates of the two-Isaiah theory must by implication concede the existence of errors in the NT" (Archer, SOTI, p. 336). It is inconceivable that the identity of so great a prophet as the author of Isa 40–66 would have been utterly forgotten by both the Jewish nation and the Christian church, by pious, God-fearing men who believed, taught, copied, and cherished the prophets as well as the law from generation to generation. It was essential among the ancient Hebrews to know the name of the prophet for his writing to be accepted and to be registered in the house of Israel (cf. Ezk 13:9).

3. Palestinian background. Rationalistic critics have asserted that chaps. 40–66 were written in Babylon, which is flat country. But both parts of the book of Isaiah tell of the rocks, mountains, valley streams, flocks and herds of Judah. If the second part had been written in Babylon, allusions to the landscape of that country would have been included. The local coloring in both parts is Judaic, showing that the entire book was written in Judah, thus pointing to the single authorship of Isaiah.

4. Historical and religious background. The fact that Babylon is mentioned in both parts of the book does not in itself necessitate a later date than Isaiah's time for those chapters. The warnings *re* Babylon *were* already relevant in his own day (see chap. 39). The events either prophesied or described in 21:9; 43:14; 46:1–2; and in part in 47:1-6, were fulfilled in history more particularly by Sennacherib's destruction of Babylon in 689 B.C. than by Cyrus' capture of the city in 539 B.C. Furthermore, the forms of idolatry condemned in Isa 57:5–9; 59:3–15; 65:3–5; 66:17 were practiced by the Jews in Judah during the reign of Manasseh (II Kgs 21:1–16), but not by the Jewish exiles in Babylon nor by the returned Jews in the post-Exilic period. Still more, the ideal completeness of the restoration of Israel depicted in chaps. 40–58 is more likely to have been written by one contemplating the return of the exiles from a distance, than by one who, as a contemporary, watched the somewhat meager results as recorded by Ezra, Nehemiah, and Haggai.

5. Language and style. All 66 chapters are written in perfectly pure Heb., without Aramaisms and Babylonian terms which characterize the known post-Exilic books. Likewise the stylistic resemblances between chaps. 1–39

One of the most important of the Dead Sea Scrolls is the complete manuscript of Isaiah (IQIs[a]) dating prior to 100 B.C. Courtesy *Biblical Archaeologist*

and 40-66 are striking. For example, the title of God "the Holy One of Israel," used but 31 times in the entire OT, is found 25 times in Isaiah; it occurs 12 times in chaps. 1-39, and 13 times in chaps. 40-66.

Another marked feature of Isaiah's style is his frequent use of the so-called prophetic perfect tense of the verb, i.e., he often speaks of future events as at hand or already come to pass (e.g., 5:13; 8:23; 9:1-7; 10:28-31); of Cyrus as already embarked on his conquering career (41:25; 45:13); or of the Servant of the Lord as having died as an offering for sin (53:1-12). The prophet could speak thus because he viewed these future events as already accomplished in the purpose of God.

This vivid way of speaking which Isaiah shares with the other prophets is especially significant in his case because of its bearing on the question of the unity of the book. Many scholars claim today that chaps. 40-66 cannot be the words of Isaiah but must come from an unknown author who lived at the close of the Babylonian Captivity (Deutero-Isaiah) or even later.

Many who accept this view fail to realize that this argument proves too much. If 41:2-4 must be the words of a contemporary of Cyrus, then chap. 53 must be the words of a witness of the crucifixion. This is of course impossible. Consequently, those who deny that Isaiah could have uttered the prophecies regarding Cyrus must either hold that the same argument does not apply to chap. 53 or they must deny that Isa 53 is a messianic prophecy, despite the clear testimony of the NT that it is fulfilled in Jesus' death (Mk 15:28; Lk 22:37; Acts 8:35; I Pet 2:22).

Back of this argument against the unity of Isaiah is of course the modern doctrine regarding prophecy, which is that the prophet was a man of his own time who spoke only to the people of his own time and not to future generations. This is a dangerous half-truth. The prophets did witness most earnestly to the men of their own day. But they also spoke about things to come, about "that day," "the day of the Lord." Without saying it in so many words, this modernistic definition of prophecy minimizes or eliminates from it the predictive element. Yet according to the clear teachings of Scripture, nowhere stated more clearly than by Isaiah himself, it is the predictions which when fulfilled are the clearest evidence that the word of the prophet is a message from God.

The denial of prediction in prophecy severs the link between the "and it shall come to pass" of the OT and the "that it might be fulfilled" of the NT (cf. Jn 12:38-41). Anti-supernaturalists deny this connection. But Bible-believers throughout the centuries have seen in predictive prophecy the clear and conclusive evidence that God has spoken. So they have rejoiced in the unity of the entire book, and have recognized Isaiah to be the "evangelist" of the OT pointing forward to a suffering Messiah as the sinbearer for all mankind.

As if to guard against the claim that Cyrus is represented as one with whom the prophet is contemporary, it is to be noted that while the prophet usually alludes to Cyrus as one present or about to appear, he introduces the name of Cyrus in the climax of a remarkable poem (44:24-28). The words "I am the Lord" are followed in the KJV by nine "that clauses," which are arranged in three groups, each group longer than the one preceding it. The first group deals with the past (v. 24*b*), the second with the present (vv. 25-26*a*), the third with the future (vv. 26*b*-28). The structure of the poem is climactic and indicates that the words, "that saith of Cyrus, He is my shepherd, etc.," refer to a future so remote that the definiteness of the prediction is to be regarded as very remarkable. Cyrus is not yet a known figure, for the prophet nowhere states his nationality.

Outline of Contents

I. Introduction, Chaps. 1-6
II. The Book of Immanuel, Chaps. 7-12
III. Oracles Concerning the Nations, Chaps. 13-23
IV. The Little Apocalypse, Chaps. 24-27
V. The Book of Woes, Chaps. 28-35
VI. The Book of Hezekiah, Chaps. 36-39
VII. The Book of Consolation, Chaps. 40-66
  A. Deliverance from sin and captivity, Chaps. 40-48
  B. The Deliverer—the Servant of Yahweh, Chaps. 49-57
  C. The delivered people and their future glory, Chaps. 58-66

Analysis of the Book

Chapters 1-6 are introductory. In the "great arraignment" (chap. 1) God's people are charged with formalism and hypocrisy, with greed and cruelty, with utter disregard of their covenant relation with their God. They deserve the fate of Sodom. But here as everywhere in the book of Isaiah there is a wonderful mingling of exhortation and comfort with denunciation and doom. "Zion shall be redeemed with judgment, and her converts with righteousness" (1:27). The glorious promise of universal peace (2:2-5) and of the Branch (4:2-6) appear amid direful threatenings. The parable of the vineyard (5:1-7) is followed by six "woes" ending with the threat of the sword, punishment at the hand of invading armies (cf. 1:20). Chap. 6 contains the call of the prophet, a vision of the holiness of God, which makes "the Holy One of Israel" Isaiah's favorite title for the God whom he serves. Whether its occurrence already in 1:4; 5:19, 24 justifies the inference that in temporal sequence Isaiah's call belongs before chap. 1 is not clear.

Chaps. 7-12, often called the "book of Immanuel," relate to the first great crisis, the Syro-Ephraimitic war, which because of Ahaz's unbelief led to the first Assyrian invasion. Isaiah's scornful references to Rezin and Pekah might, but for II Chr 28:6, lead us to minimize the greatness of this threat, which accounts for Ahaz's appeal to Assyria for help. The wonderful Immanuel prophecies (7:14; 8:8, 10; 9:6 f.; 11:1-6) end with blessing for the Gentiles (11:10) and with a song of praise to the God of Israel (chap. 12): "For great is the Holy One of Israel in the midst of thee" (v. 6).

Chaps. 13-23 contain "burdens" (weighty and grievous prophecies) against nations which threaten Israel's very existence: Babylon (and Assyria), Philistia, Moab, Damascus, Ethiopia and Egypt, Babylon, Edom, Arabia, Jerusalem (her sin makes her her own worst enemy), and Tyre. Here, as elsewhere, compassion and hope pierce the thunderclouds of wrath (14:1-3, 24-27, 32; 17:7 f.; 18:7; etc.). Especially striking is 19:23-25, where Isaiah uses his favorite figure of the "highway" to describe the future safe and friendly intercourse of ancient enemies. Egypt is called "my people" (19:25; cf. Ex 5:1); Assyria, "the work of my hands" (cf. 45:11); Israel, "my inheritance" (Zech 2:12)—a wonderful prophecy developing Isa 2:2-5.

Chap. 24 is a vision of world judgment, an apocalypse, which ends in blessing; the Lord shall reign on Mount Zion. Chap. 25, a hymn of praise, is followed by a song which like that in chap. 12 will be sung by redeemed Israel. Chap. 27 ends with a promise of deliverance.

Chaps. 28-31 contain further judgments on the nations, apparently Assyria, Babylon, and Egypt. The woe on Samaria (chap. 28), uttered probably before Sargon besieged it, is followed by the promise of the "tried cornerstone" which the Lord will lay in Zion (28:16). In chap. 29 the woe on Ariel (the hearth of God, where the altar fires are ever burning, and therefore a figurative name of Jerusalem) ends likewise with promise (vv. 22-24). It is followed by warnings against alliance with Egypt (chaps. 30-31). Yet this warning too is combined with a promise of blessing (30:18-33), and is followed in chap. 32 with the promise of a king (Messiah) who shall "reign in righteousness"; and "the work of righteousness shall be peace." Chap. 33 is directed against Assyria, "the spoiler that was not spoiled." Yet Jerusalem shall be "a quiet habitation, a tabernacle that shall not be taken down" (33:20). The terrible woe on Edom (chap. 34) is followed by a glorious picture of blessedness to come (chap. 35).

Chaps. 36-37 tell of Sennacherib's invasion, one of the most thrilling stories in the Bible. The raging bull who has blasphemed the Holy One of Israel will be led away with a hook in his nose to perish in his own land at the hand of his own sons. Hezekiah's sickness and the embassy of Merodach-baladan (chaps. 38-39) apparently belong chronologically before chaps. 36-37. These accounts are placed after them, however, in order that the ominous prophecy of 39:6 f. may be immediately followed by the great message of consolation for future generations, a deliverance which Hezekiah could only look for in his own day.

The book of consolation (chaps. 40-66) may aptly be called a prophetic sermon with Isaiah's name ("salvation of the Lord") as its theme. It has its counterpart in the words of John the Baptist and of Jesus, "Repent ye: for the kingdom of heaven is at hand" (Mt 3:2; Mk 1:15). The awfulness of human sin and the wonders of divine grace are its recurring and alternating themes. It is apparently divided into three parts by the warning words of 48:22; 57:21, and ends with the terrible words of 66:24 (cf. Mk 9:48). The major themes in these chapters are:

1. The transcendence of Yahweh. He "has made all things" (44:24; cf. 45:12), "all nations before him are as nothing" (40:17). "To whom will ye liken me?" (46:5) is His challenge to mortal men. He will "create new heavens and a new earth" (65:17; 66:22; cf. 55:9).

2. The sinful folly of idolatry, man worshiping the work of his own hands (44:9-20; 46:1-2, 6-8).

3. Israel's God, who alone can foretell future events and bring them to pass (41:22-25; 42:9; 43:9-12; 44:7; 45:21; 46:10; 48:3-5).

4. A prominent figure is Cyrus. God has raised him up "from the east" (41:2-5); he comes in righteousness (45:13); he comes as a ravening bird from a far country (46:11); he will humble Babylon (43:14; 48:14); he will cause Jerusalem to be built and the temple restored (44:28; 45:1-7).

5. A more prominent figure is the Servant of the Lord. He is called Israel (49:3), Jacob (48:20), Jacob-Israel (41:8 f.; 44:1, 21; 45:4). He is described as "deaf and blind" (42:18 f.), sinful and needing redemption (43:25; 44:22), as having a mission to Israel and the Gentiles (42:1-7; 49:1-6), as one in whom the Lord will be glorified (49:3), as one who has suffered though innocent (50:5-9), as one who has suffered vicariously for others (52:13—53:12).

The reference cannot be the same in all of these passages. Where sinfulness is attributed to the servant, he must be sinful Israel; where unmerited suffering is described and a mission to Israel and the Gentiles is referred to, the pious remnant which the Lord will use to bring blessing to Israel and the nations may be in part referred to. In chap. 53 the Servant can only be the Messiah, who in 61:1–3 speaks of His mission in words which in the synagogue at Nazareth Jesus appropriated to Himself (Lk 4: 17–21). *See* Servant of the Lord.

6. The world-embracing extent of this promised salvation is especially stressed in the closing chapters. The "every one" of 55:1 has its echo in the "whosoever will" of Jn 3:16, and the promises of 56:7 and 66:1 f. have their fulfillment in Jn 4:24.

Bibliography. Conservative: J. A. Alexander, *Commentary on the Prophecies of Isaiah,* 1846; Grand Rapids: Zondervan, reprinted 1953. O. T. Allis, *The Unity of Isaiah,* Philadelphia: Presbyterian and Reformed, 1950. Charles Boutflower, *The Book of Isaiah (Chapters I–XXXIX) in the Light of the Assyrian Monuments,* New York: Macmillan, 1930. Franz Delitzsch, *Biblical Commentary on the Prophecies of Isaiah,* 2 vols. 1866; Grand Rapids: Eerdmans, reprinted 1949. Seth Erlandsson, *The Burden of Babylon: A Study of Isaiah 13:2–14:23,* Lund: CWK Gleerup, 1970. F. Derek Kidner, "Isaiah," NBC, 2nd ed. H. C. Leupold, *Exposition of Isaiah,* Vol. I, Grand Rapids: Baker, 1968. G. L. Robinson, "Isaiah," ISBE, III, 1495–1508. E. J. Young, *Studies in Isaiah,* Grand Rapids: Eerdmans, 1954; *Who Wrote Isaiah?* Grand Rapids: Eerdmans, 1958; *The Book of Isaiah,* Grand Rapids: Eerdmans, Vol. I, 1965; Vol. II, 1969; Vol. III, 1972.

Critical or radical: B. Duhm, *Das Buch Jesaja,* 1892; 3rd ed., Göttingen, GHK, 1914. G. B. Gray, *A Critical and Exegetical Commentary on the Book of Isaiah* (Chaps. 1–27), ICC, New York: Scribner's, 1912. J. L. McKenzie, *Second Isaiah,* Anchor Bible, Garden City: Doubleday, 1968. C. R. North, "Isaiah," IDB, II, 731–744; *The Second Isaiah: Introduction, Translation and Commentary to Chapters XL–LV,* Oxford: Clarendon Press, 1964. J. Skinner, *The Book of the Prophet Isaiah,* 2 vols., rev. ed., Cambridge Bible, Cambridge: Univ. Press, 1925.

O. T. A.

ISCAH (ĭz'kȧ). A daughter of Haran, the brother of Abraham, and a sister of Milcah and Lot (Gen 11:29). Jewish tradition, with insufficient reasons, identified her with Sarah.

ISCARIOT. *See* Judas 8.

ISHBAH (ĭsh'bȧ). A member of the tribe of Judah, father of Eshtemoa (I Chr 4:17).

ISHBAK (ĭsh'băk). The name carried by the descendants of Ishbak, one of the sons of Abraham and Keturah (Gen 25:2). According to the Annals of Shalmaneser III (858–824), they seem to have settled in N Syria (ANET, pp. 277 f.).

ISHBI-BENOB (ĭsh'bī-bē'nŏb). A Philistine giant who attempted to kill David but instead was slain by Abishai, brother of Joab (II Sam 21:16–17). His name in Heb., *Yishbî-b*^{e}*nōb,* is the *Qere* reading of the text, the emendation vocalization of the Masoretes. The *Kethib* or unpointed Heb. text can also be read, "And they dwelt in Nob where there was one among the descendants of the giant, the weight of whose spear. . . ." If the latter reading is adopted the name disappears.

ISHBOSHETH (ĭsh-bō'shĕth). A Heb. name meaning "man of shame." Comparison of several OT passages indicates that this man was referred to under several names. In I Sam 14:49 the name is probably Ishvi (ASV) or Ishui (KJV), unless this is another name for Abinadab (I Sam 31:2). In II Sam 2:8 the name is Ishbosheth. In I Chr 8:33 it is Esh-baal, a compound which was probably the original name. Some think it exalts Yahweh as Lord, but was changed to Ishbosheth when the story of his shameful murder was related, in order to make it refer prophetically to the manner of his death.

When Saul and his three eldest sons were slain on the field of battle at Mount Gilboa (I Sam 31:1 ff.), Abner, the captain of Saul's hosts, took Ishbosheth, the remaining son of Saul, across Jordan to Mahanaim and there proclaimed him king over Israel (II Sam 2:8–9). Since the men of Judah acknowledged the sovereignty of David, it was inevitable that the opposing forces must meet. The first encounter was at Gibeon (II Sam 2:12 ff.). A preliminary attempt was made to settle the issue by the outcome of combat between 12 champions representing each side. All 24 fell mortally wounded. This led to full scale battle, and the resulting defeat of Abner and the death of Joab's brother Asahel. Ishbosheth was 40 years old when he was invested with sovereignty over Israel (II Sam 2:10). This was approximately 1011 B.C. Though the biblical account declares that he reigned only two years, it appears that he and his general Abner exercised combined control over Israel for a period of seven years, or until 1004 B.C., when David was crowned king over the entire nation.

Abner was alienated from Ishbosheth when the latter apprehended him in an intrigue with Saul's concubine Rizpah, and virtually charged him with an act of treason (II Sam 3:6–11). This was more than Abner could endure, and deep resentment led him to transfer his allegiance to David.

In reprisal for the death of his brother Asahel, Joab treacherously murdered Abner (II Sam 3:27). Very shortly thereafter Ishbosheth was cruelly murdered by two of his officers. Thinking to gain favor with David by this act, they were overwhelmed with denunciation and condemned to instant death (II Sam 4:5-12). Though David had no part in the misfortunes that befell Ishbosheth and his general Abner, God used these events to establish David as king over all Israel.

H. A. Hoy.

ISHI (ĭsh'ī). A term meaning "my husband," symbolizing the Israelites' relationship with God after they returned to Him from their idolatry (Hos 2:16). Ishi was also the name of four men:

1. A son of Appaim of the tribe of Judah (I Chr 2:31).
2. A man of Judah, father of Zoheth (I Chr 4:20).
3. A descendant of Simeon, father of Pelatiah, Neariah, Rephaiah, and Uzziel who fought against the Amalekites (I Chr 4:42-43).
4. Head of a family of the tribe of Manasseh (I Chr 5:24).

ISHIAH (ĭ-shī'ȧ). The KJV variant of Isshiah 4 (*q.v.*). A descendant of Issachar who is mentioned among David's valiant men (I Chr 7:3, 5).

ISHIJAH (ĭ-shī'jȧ). Son of Harim (Ezr 10:31) who along with others put away his foreign wife at the command of Ezra.

ISHMA (ĭsh'mȧ). A descendant of Hur of Judah through Etam, a brother of Jezreel and Idbash (I Chr 4:3).

ISHMAEL (ĭsh'mā-ĕl). The name means "may God hear" and is related to the experience wherein God heard the anguished prayer of Hagar in her flight from the household of Abraham (Gen 16:11).

1. The firstborn son of Abraham by Hagar, the Egyptian maid of his wife Sarah. Abraham was 86 at the time and had lived in Canaan for 11 years. Sarah, the barren wife, in keeping with the customs of her time as seen in both the Babylonian law code of Hammurabi (*q.v.*) and the Nuzu tablets, gave her slave Hagar to Abraham to produce an heir for the family.

When Abraham was 99 God renewed His covenant with him and enjoined circumcision as an external sign of membership in the covenant community (Gen 17:1-14). God also announced that He would fulfill the divine promise of a son through his wife Sarah, although Abraham looked on Ishmael with deep affection and prayed that he might be the promised heir (Gen 17:18). When Ishmael was circumcised, Abraham and all his household—those born to the men and women who had grown up in his employ and newcomers to the household through purchase from foreigners—were also circumcised. Ishmael was then 13 years old. Many Arab tribes still circumcise their youths at the age of 13.

Fourteen years after the birth of Ishmael, Isaac was born to Sarah and Abraham. The jealousy that had long separated Sarah from Hagar came to the breaking point at an anniversary celebrating the weaning of Isaac. Sarah insisted, contrary to the customs of the times as evidenced by Abraham's displeasure (Gen 21:11; cf. Nuzu legal tablet HV 67:22), that Hagar and Ishmael be sent away. Although Hagar and Ishmael left the house of Abraham and went to live in the wilderness of Beer-sheba, and later in the wilderness of Paran, there is no record of any animosity developing between Ishmael and Isaac. Both sons tended to the burial of Abraham in the cave of Machpelah (Gen 25:9). While Isaac was his sole heir, Abraham endowed the sons of his concubines (Hagar and Keturah) while he was still living (Gen 25:6). Therefore Ishmael received some of Abraham's material goods. Keturah's sons were sent away eastward, whereas Ishmael went to the SW.

Hagar took for him an Egyptian wife and he became the father of 12 sons and a daughter called Mahalath (Gen 28:9) or Basemath (Gen 36:3). She became one of the wives of Esau. The names of Ishmael's sons were Nebajoth, Kedar, Adbeel, Mibsam, Mishma, Dumah, Massa, Hadad, Tema, Jetur, Naphish, and Kedemah (Gen 25:13-15). Since most of these names occur as tribal entities of considerable influence in other places, some scholars look upon this genealogy list as ethnic rather than personal.

The epithet "a wild ass of a man" ascribed to Ishmael in Gen 16:12 (RSV, NASB) is not to be considered one of opprobrium but one of praise. The wild onager was the choicest animal on the Assyrian king's hunting list and a delicacy on the menus at royal banquets. Here it depicts the Bedouin freedom of the Ishmaelites in the southern wilderness (Gen 25:16-18).

Ishmael died at the age of 137 (Gen 25:17). His burial place is unknown. The Muslims claim that he and his mother Hagar were buried in the Ka'aba at Mecca.

In Gal 4:21–5:1 Paul interprets the narratives of Ishmael and Isaac allegorically. He uses the word "persecute" (v. 29; cf. mocking, Gen 21:9) to indicate the action of those Jews who, though clinging to the ordinances of the Mosaic law which must pass away (as Ishmael was sent away), persecute those who are the free born in Christ, the true heirs of the promise.

2. The third son of Azel, a Benjamite descendant from the family of Saul through Mephibosheth, son of Jonathan (I Chr 8:38; 9:44).

3. The father of Zebadiah, the governor of the house of Judah in the reign of Jehoshaphat (II Chr 19:11).

4. The son of Jehohanan, a captain of a "hundred." He aided Jehoiada in restoring Joash, the crown prince, to the throne of Judah (II Chr 23:1).

5. The third son of Pashur, who relinquished

his Gentile wife in the reforms of Ezra in the post-Exilic period (Ezr 10:22).

6. The son of Nethaniah, a member of the royal house of David. During Nebuchadnezzar's siege of Jerusalem he fled with many others to Transjordan and found refuge at the court of Baalis, then king of Ammon (cf. Jos *Ant.* x. 9.2). He pretended friendship with Gedaliah, the Heb. governor appointed by Nebuchadnezzar to care for the needs of those left in Judah following the sacking of Jerusalem in 586 B.C. Gedaliah's headquarters was in Mizpah, a few miles N of Jerusalem. Although Gedaliah was warned of the treacherous plot of Ishmael to slay him, Johanan volunteering to put Ishmael to death, Gedaliah refused to believe the report and held a banquet in Ishmael's honor. Ten companions of Ishmael, called princes of the king, also attended the banquet. Gedaliah, the governor of Judah, and some of the Babylonian soldiers stationed at Mizpah were murdered at the feast. Ishmael and his men escaped. So secretly was the deed accomplished that several days elapsed before anyone detected the murder. Ishmael was able to abduct King Zedekiah's daughter and several townspeople, and headed for Ammon. Johanan caught up with him at the great waters of Gibeon (Jer 41:1-12). In the ensuing battle, the abducted party was retrieved, but Ishmael and eight of his men escaped to Ammon. Nothing further is recorded of Ishmael or of his activities (II Kgs 25:25; Jer 40:7–41:18).

F. E. Y.

ISHMAELITES (ĭsh'mā-ĕ-līts). The term occurs in Gen 37:25, 27, 28; 39:1; Jud 8:24 and Ps 83:6 as a general designation for a people dwelling in the territory from Egypt to the Euphrates. According to the biblical tradition, the Ishmaelites had Egyptian as well as Semitic blood in their veins, for the mother and the wife of Ishmael were Egyptians. His descendants dwelt in a twelvefold division in settlements and in movable camps in the desert of N Arabia, in the region between Havilah, Egypt, and the Euphrates. These tribes included the Nebajoth, Kedar, Adbeel, Dumah, Massa, and Tema—all mentioned in the 8th and 7th cen. Assyrian texts; Jetur, Naphish, and Kedemah—a more or less homogeneous group; Mibsam, Mishma, and Hadar—so far not identified in any extrabiblical source. The Nabataeans (*q.v.*; the descendants of Nebajoth?) in Greco-Roman times settled permanently in Petra and in Palmyra and developed a flourishing civilization. The Muslim Arabs, following Muhammad's example, claim descent from Ishmael.

The Ishmaelite mode of life was that of itinerant caravan traders, tent dwellers, and cameleers (I Chr 27:30). They were characterized by their spirit of independence and adventurousness. They carried aromatic gum and incense from Gilead to Egyptian markets (Gen 37:25). One such caravan bought Joseph and sold him into slavery in Egypt. Following the tradition of Ishmael's skill in archery, the sons of Kedar were noted for their deftness with the bow (Isa 21:17).

II Sam 17:25 states that Amasa, commander of Absalom's army, was the son of Ithra an Israelite; according to I Chr 2:17 the father of Amasa was Jether (Ithra) the Ishmaelite. Perhaps Jether was an Israelite living in the land of Ishmael (cf. Obed-edom the Gittite).

F. E. Y.

ISHMAIAH (ĭsh-mā'yȧ). Chief of the army contingent of the Zebulunites during David's reign (I Chr 27:19).

ISHMEELITE. KJV spelling of Ishmaelite (*q.v.*) in the Genesis references and I Chr 2:17.

ISHMERAI (ĭsh'mĕ-rī). A descendant of Benjamin, son of Elpaal, and one of the chief men of the tribe (I Chr 8:18).

ISHOD (ĭsh'ŏd). A member of the tribe of Manasseh, whose mother was Hammoleketh (I Chr 7:18).

ISHPAN (ĭsh'păn). A member of the tribe of Benjamin, the son of Shashak (I Chr 8:22).

ISHTOB (ĭsh'tŏb). Ishtob is the KJV reading for "men of Tob." It was a place in Syria or Palestine, perhaps a small state, that supplied 12,000 men to support the Ammonites in their war against Joab and his forces (II Sam 10:6, 8). Jephthah had fled there from Gilead (Jud 11:3, 5). *See* Tob.

ISHUAH (ĭsh'ū-ȧ), **ISUAH** (ĭs'ū-ȧ). The second son of Asher (Gen 46:17; I Chr 7:30). The name is spelled Ishvah in the RSV.

ISHUAI. *See* Ishui.

ISHUI (ĭsh'ū-ī). Variant in KJV of Isui, Ishuai, and Jesui.

1. The third son of Asher (Gen 46:17; I Chr 7:30), his name being called Jesui and his family Jesuites in Num 26:44, with Ishvi and Ishvites being the reading of the RSV.

2. The second son of Saul by his wife Ahinoam (I Sam 14:49). His name is omitted in Saul's genealogy in I Chr 8:9 (some claim he died young) and in I Sam 31:2 his place is taken by Abinadab (*q.v.*), with whom others identify him.

ISLAND, ISLE. The Heb. word 'î is used in a much broader sense than the English, since it is based upon the idea of a mariner who sees any dry land as a place of peace from the sea and of rest, whether it be simply the seacoast or an island. Therefore the word has to be understood in context to decide whether it is to be translated island or simply coast. There are passages where an island is clearly signified (Isa

40:15), and others where it is simply the land at the coast or the coastline (Isa 20:6). It can also be used to refer to far off places of the earth in the sense of foreign shores (Isa 41:5; 66:19).

In the NT specific islands are designated by *nēsos,* and such islands are mentioned as Chios, Crete, Cyprus, Melita, Rhodes, and Samos. John was exiled to the isle of Patmos where he received "the Revelation of Jesus Christ" (Rev 1:1, 9).

R. A. K.

ISMACHIAH (ĭz'mȧ-kī'ȧ). One of the overseers in connection with the temple during the reign of Hezekiah (II Chr 31:13).

ISMAIAH (ĭs-mā'yȧ). A Gibeonite, chief of David's 30 mighty men, who came to him at Ziklag (I Chr 12:4).

ISPAH (ĭs'pȧ). A descendant of Benjamin and a son of Beriah (I Chr 8:16).

ISRAEL (ĭz'rā-ĕl). The name Israel first appears in Gen 32:28, where the Angel of the Lord bestowed it upon Jacob (*q.v.*) during His encounter with him at Peniel. Jacob had refused to let Him go until He had given him a blessing, and so God granted him the new title of Yiś-rā'ēl, stating that he had persistently struggled (*śārîtā* from *śārāh,* "exert oneself, persist") with God (*'elōhîm,* the shorter form of which is *'Ēl*) and had prevailed (i.e., in his earnest prayer). Thus it would appear that the name meant "he persists with God"; the more obvious "God persists" would not fit the circumstances of this episode very well. At any rate, this became the specific covenant name for Jacob, just as Abraham had been for Abram (Gen 17:5).

The national designation of the Heb. people was "the sons of Israel" (*benê Yiśrā'ēl*) rather than "the sons of Jacob" by the time the members of Joseph's family had multiplied (Ex 1:9, 12) and were ready to leave Egypt for the Promised Land under Moses' leadership (Ex 2:23, 25; 3:9; etc.). The expression "sons of Jacob" never appears in the Pentateuch after the book of Genesis (where it occurs only in connection with Jacob's immediate children). For the sake of brevity the "sons of" was occasionally omitted, and "Israel" by itself could refer to the Hebrews as a race. Thus the pursuing Egyptians by the Red Sea were quoted as saying, "Let us flee from the face of Israel," when they found themselves bogged down and threatened with destruction (Ex 14:25).

In surviving Egyptian records the Israelites may have been referred to by the general designation of *'Apiru* (which seems to have included other Canaanite and Semitic groups than the Hebrews alone; *see* Hebrew People). There is one reference, however, to the name of Israel in the well-known "Israel stela" of King Merneptah of the 19th Dynasty. After speaking of his military success in plundering Canaan, Ashkelon, Gezer, and Yanoam, the triumphal hymn goes on to state, "Israel is laid waste, his seed is not" (ANET, p. 378). The Egyptian spelling of the name is "Y-s-r-'-r" (Egyptian made no distinction between *l* and *r* until after the Gr. conquest), and it is followed by the man-woman-plural-strokes determinative, indicating that Israel was a tribe or nation, rather than a local city-state. The date of this inscription was about 1230 B.C., so it must refer to an Egyptian incursion which took place during the period of the judges.

Correspondingly there is only one reference to the name Israel in the Assyrian cuneiform inscriptions thus far discovered, namely, in the Balawat inscription of Shalmaneser III (ANET, p. 279) which records the battle of Karkar (853 B.C.) as fought against Hadadezer of Damascus and Ahab the Israelite (*A-ḫa-ab-bu Sir-'i-la-ai*). Otherwise the extant Assyrian records refer to Israel (and especially the northern kingdom) as "the land of Omri" (*mat Ḫumri*), apparently because it was during the reign of this dynasty that the Assyrians first came in contact with the Heb. monarchy (cf. ANET, pp. 281, 283–285). But in adjacent Moab the name "Israel" was the usual designation, if we may judge from the four or five references in the inscription of King Mesha (*c.* 840 B.C.; ANET, p. 320). In the comparatively meager collection of Phoenician inscriptions surviving to us, no reference to Israel has been found; the same is true of the Old Aramaic inscriptions.

In biblical usage, as already mentioned, the name Israel has a covenantal or theological connotation, even on the lips of Jacob himself. In Gen 49:2 he gathers his sons about him for a final blessing: "Hearken unto Israel your father." Then follows a specific characterization of each of the 12, accompanied by a prophecy of their role in the life of the future nation. In v. 28 we read: "All these are the twelve tribes of Israel; and this is what their father spoke to them as he blessed them." *See* Tribe; for the individual tribes *see* under their respective names.

In the days of Moses, Yahweh ("Jehovah") declares Himself to be the Father of Israel: "Israel is my son, even my firstborn" (Ex 4:22); in 5:1 (ASV) we read: "Thus saith Jehovah, the God of Israel, Let my people go. . . ." As "Israel" the Heb. nation was to play a special role as a theocracy governed by the specially revealed law of God, and He was to be their only King. The powerful leader Gideon reaffirmed this principle when he rejected the proposal to make him king over Israel, saying, "I will not rule over you, neither shall my son rule over you: Jehovah shall rule over you" (Jud 8:23, ASV). Even when a human king was at last anointed by the prophet Samuel, it was made clear that he was chosen and appointed by Yahweh, and was under obligation to obey His law (I Sam 10:25; 12:13–15, 24–25).

In his subsequent career, however, as the first king of Israel, Saul proved unfaithful to his trust, substituting his own will and judgment for the revealed will of God, first, in offering a sacrifice at Gilgal (I Sam 13:9–10) as if he were an ordained priest; and second, in sparing the king of the Amalekites and their cattle despite Yahweh's command to destroy them utterly (15:17–26). The result was that the Lord revoked his commission as theocratic king (I Sam 13:13–14; 15:23), and sent Samuel to Bethlehem to anoint David, the youngest son of Jesse, although under conditions of secrecy (16:13). Eventually Saul began to suspect that his valiant young harpist, the slayer of Goliath, was God's chosen successor to him and the supplanter of his dynasty (18:29), and he became obsessed with a desire to see him dead (20:31). Much of the remainder of his reign was spent in an unsuccessful attempt to capture and slay David. Finally Saul and his sons became involved in a disastrous campaign with the invading Philistines, who fatally wounded him in the battle of Mount Gilboa. After seven and a half years of intermittent civil war, Saul's youngest son, Ishbosheth, was assassinated, and the ten northern tribes acknowledged David as their king, after he had reigned over Judah and Simeon from the time of Saul's death. This confirmed the principle that Israel's king had to be chosen by God Himself, and was responsible to keep His law as His agent upon earth.

As a godly and dedicated ruler under the divine mandate David reigned over the united monarchy of Israel. He subdued not only the Philistines but also the other neighboring nations (Edomites, Moabites, Ammonites and Syrians of Damascus, and Hamath) in a long series of successful campaigns. David never experienced defeat on the battlefield. Yahweh used him to give Israel "rest" from all their enemies round about, and to take possession of the entire territory originally promised to Abraham's seed (Gen 15:18), all the way from the "river of Egypt" (the Wadi el-'Arîsh) to the Euphrates at Tiphsah (cf. I Kgs 4:24). In a sense the conquest of Canaan was not completed until Yahweh found in David a man after His own heart (I Sam 13:14). It was he who, as a dutiful theocratic ruler, subdued all of Israel's foes and took the city of Jerusalem from its heathen owners, the Jebusites, and secured a suitable permanent resting place for the Lord's sanctuary (according to the promise of Deut 12:10–11).

Yet because of his involvement in bloody warfare (which he sometimes conducted with cruel severity, cf. II Sam 8:2; 12:31), David was denied the privilege of building the temple itself (I Chr 22:8). Nevertheless, he assembled most of the costly materials necessary for its construction and devised the building plans for his son Solomon to carry out (I Chr 28:11–19). He was promised by the prophet Nathan, speaking in the name of the Lord, that Solomon would live to carry out his design and erect a beautiful structure to house the ark of the covenant and to serve as a focal point for the worship of all Israel (II Sam 7:12–13; I Chr 28:5–6).

Even more important than the temple itself was the divine promise that Solomon would be a type of the Messianic King who would some day come to establish God's kingdom upon earth (II Sam 7:13; I Chr 28:7). This promise was inherent in the angel's announcement to Mary: "The Lord God will give unto him the throne of his father David: and he shall reign over the house of Jacob forever; and of his kingdom there shall be no end" (Lk 1:32–33).

David, then, fulfilled the pattern of a theocratic king responsible to God under the covenant. But even though he received God's approval earlier in his reign, he later fell into grievous personal sin in the matter of Bathsheba (with whom he committed adultery) and in the contrived murder of her husband Uriah (II Sam 11). After the prophet Nathan privately denounced him for these sins, David broke down in grief and repentance, and was therefore forgiven and restored to fellowship with God.

Nevertheless, he had so gravely violated his role as king of Israel that the baneful consequence was pronounced: "Now therefore the sword shall never depart from thine house; because thou hast despised me. . . .Behold, I will raise up evil against thee out of thine own house" (II Sam 12:10–11). This meant that violence, cruelty and treachery would plague the dynasty of David throughout the ensuing generations. In David's own lifetime he suffered the loss of the baby first conceived by Bathsheba out of wedlock; the grief from the sordid episode of his firstborn son, Amnon, who raped his own half sister Tamar; and the subsequent revenge of Absalom, who later assassinated Amnon as a guest at his table (13:28–29). Even more serious was the rebellion raised against David by Absalom, who drove him out of Jerusalem to take refuge in Mahanaim on the other side of the Jordan (17:24). Although David's general Joab managed to defeat the pursuing forces of Absalom and put him to death, David's latter days were lived under the cloud of this sorrow.

David also brought Israel into trouble by undertaking a complete census of the 12 tribes without any divine mandate to do so (such as Moses had received in the days of the Exodus). In the resultant plague that afflicted the nation no remedy could be found until David purchased the threshing floor of Araunah the Jebusite (where the destroying angel had halted his course) and offered up sacrifice to Yahweh on the very spot which was later to be the site of the temple of Solomon (II Sam 24).

David's son by Bathsheba, Solomon the Wise, took over responsibility as Israel's theocratic king under the rule of God. His wealth, wisdom, and prosperity became proverbial, and his prestige was such that he retained control of the enlarged borders of David's empire without having to use his large and formidable chariot forces in warfare with his foes. But his most notable achievement was the erection of a beautiful temple, twice the dimensions of the Mosaic tabernacle (i.e., 60 cubits by 20 cubits, or 90 feet by 30 feet), and possessing ten times as many lampstands and tables of showbread (for the tabernacle had been furnished with only one of each). An enormous bronze altar of sacrifice replaced the smaller Mosaic one, and likewise a huge basin (15 feet in diameter) took the place of the earlier laver before the door of the temple. This structure of unparalleled beauty and costliness was solemnly dedicated to the Lord as the meeting place between Yahweh and His covenant people Israel, and the shekinah glory of God came down upon the inner sanctum once again, as it had in the days of Moses (I Kgs 8:10–11). Under Solomon's rule, then, the united monarchy of Israel enjoyed its highest degree of prosperity and glory.

Unfortunately, however, Solomon's constitutional limitations under the law (Deut 17:14–20) could not be enforced by any human authority, so absolute was his power. Thus he could violate with impunity the commandments against multiplying horses and wives, and it was the policy of permitting Pharaoh's daughter to worship her Egyptian gods in Jerusalem that first led to the introduction of idolatry. This precedent led to religious tolerance for all his other wives of heathen background, and Israel's testimony for Yahweh was greatly impaired. Extravagant building programs and costly palace expenses resulted in excessive taxation and the employment of forced labor which aroused general antagonism throughout the kingdom. Thus the way was paved for the division of Israel into the northern and southern kingdoms once Solomon had passed away, and the succession fell to his arrogant and tactless son Rehoboam, who promised his subjects an even more oppressive rule than that of his father. This marked the end of the united monarchy, and the beginning of the kingdom of the ten tribes, which came to be known as the kingdom of Israel (in contradistinction to the kingdom of Judah). *See* Israel, Kingdom of; Judah, Kingdom of; Hebrew People.

Bibliography. John Bright, *A History of Israel,* Philadelphia: Westminster, 1959. F. F. Bruce, "Israel," NBD, pp. 578–588. "Government, Authority, and Kingship," CornPBE, pp. 354–369. G. von Rad, K. G. Kuhn, and W. Gutbrod, *"Israel, Ioudaios, Hebraios, etc.,"* TDNT, III, 356–391. H. H. Rowley, "Israel, History of (Israelites)," IDB, II, 750–765. Roland de Vaux, *Ancient Israel,* trans. by John McHugh, New York: McGraw-Hill, 1961.

G. L. A.

ISRAEL, KINGDOM OF. In 930 B.C., after the death of Solomon and the accession of his son Rehoboam, the united monarchy of Israel

Tirzah. JR

broke up into two realms. Finding that the young king was determined to maintain an even more tyrannous and oppressive rule than Solomon had done (especially in his latter years), the northern ten tribes resolved to set up a new kingdom of their own, under the leadership of a promising young Ephraimite, Jeroboam the son of Nebat. But the roots of this division went back to the days of Saul and David and to the tribal jealousy that manifested itself when the leadership passed from Benjamin to Judah. For seven years after Saul's death at the battle of Mount Gilboa the northern tribes had remained loyal to Ishbosheth, Saul's youngest son, even after Judah had installed David as king at Hebron. It was only after both Abner, commander of the army under Saul, and Ishbosheth himself had been assassinated that the ten tribes resolved to submit to David's rule and enjoy the benefits of the success that invariably attended him on the battlefield.

Even in David's case their loyalty was somewhat compromised during the rebellion of Absalom against his father. After Absalom's defeat and death contention arose between Judah, whose troops had accompanied David back across the Jordan, and the forces of the northern tribes. The latter had insisted, "We have ten parts in the king, and we have also more right in David than you" (II Sam 19:43). Their resentment paved the way for a brief but abortive revolt under Sheba, a Benjamite, who declared, "We have no part in David, neither have we inheritance in the son of Jesse; every man to his tents, O Israel" (II Sam 20:1). In practically the same words the representatives of the ten tribes cast off their allegiance to the Davidic dynasty in 930 B.C. (I Kgs 12:16), feeling confident that their spokesman, Jeroboam, would be able to lead them in a successful defense of their liberties. He had been an official under Solomon in the department of public works, but after he had been proclaimed by the prophet Ahijah as the Lord's choice as ruler over the ten tribes (I Kgs 11:31–38), he fled to Egypt and there became a protégé of

Pharaoh Shishak. After Solomon's death Jeroboam returned to act as chief spokesman for the northern Israelites, and through Rehoboam's folly he became chosen as king of the revolting tribes. (Only Judah and Simeon and the southern part of Benjamin adjacent to Jerusalem remained loyal to Solomon's son.)

Jeroboam, son of Nebat, had been commissioned by God to serve as a covenant-keeping ruler obedient to the Mosaic law, in contrast to the idolatrous tendencies of Solomon's later reign (I Kgs 11:33). He was promised a long and enduring dynasty if he proved faithful to his trust. When Rehoboam massed an army of 180,000 troops to compel the submission of the ten tribes, God even restrained him through the prophet Shemaiah from attempting this invasion (I Kgs 12:21–24).

But when Jeroboam faced the problem of the yearly pilgrimages of his subjects to the temple at Jerusalem, he felt compelled by the national interest to terminate this practice (which might have eroded their loyalty to himself), and to erect new sanctuaries at Bethel and Dan where they might carry on their worship of Yahweh according to the religious calendar of the Torah. Lacking the prestigious ark of the covenant enshrined in the Jerusalem temple, he decided upon a golden calf as the focal point of worship at these new temples, and declared them to be the "gods who brought up Israel out of the land of Egypt" (I Kgs 12:28). At best this new arrangement had to be regarded as an idolatrous worship of Yahweh. The inauguration of this new cult, therefore, was attended by a divine rebuke, administered by an unnamed prophet from Judah (I Kgs 13:2), who prophesied that this schismatic altar and sanctuary would one day be destroyed by a king named Josiah (fulfilled three centuries later around 630 B.C.). Despite this solemn warning, accompanied by two miraculous signs (13:4–6), Jeroboam persisted in his religious policy, and appointed as priests any of his citizens who applied for ordination (II Chr 11:13–16), even though they were not of the tribe of Levi (most Levites having migrated to Judah after the schism).

Samaria. HFV

This evil example of the first king of Israel was subsequently followed by all his successors until the final demise of Samaria in 722 B.C. Even so zealous a worshiper of Yahweh as Jehu failed to depart from the "sins of Jeroboam the son of Nebat . . . the golden calves that were in Bethel and . . . in Dan" (II Kgs 10:29). As for Jeroboam himself, he was sternly warned by Ahijah that his line would be cut off completely, and that all ten tribes would some day be taken off into captivity to the E of the Euphrates (I Kgs 14:10, 15). His oldest son predeceased him by mortal illness, and his younger son, Nadab, did not survive him by more than two years, when he was assassinated by Baasha the son of Ahijah, of the tribe of Issachar (I Kgs 15:25–28).

After exterminating all the descendants of Jeroboam, Baasha continued a policy of hostility against Judah, fortifying Ramah as a staging area for invasion. King Asa of Judah was able to counter this move by bribing Ben-hadad of Damascus to break his treaty of alliance with Israel and attack Baasha from his rear, destroying the wealthiest cities of Naphtali (II Chr 16:2–4). While Baasha marched N to meet this threat, Asa overran Ramah and removed all of it's fortifications. Following Baasha's death in 886 B.C., his son Elah lasted barely two years before he was assassinated by his chariot commander, Zimri, during a drinking bout. After destroying all of Baasha's household, Zimri himself came under attack from Omri, the chief commander of the army, who overwhelmed him in Tirzah, the capital. Omri assumed the crown in 885 B.C. and crushed the followers of Tibni, a rival pretender to the throne (I Kgs 16:15–22).

Omri proved to be a strong and successful king, and eventually the northern kingdom came to be known abroad as "the land of Omri" (or "Ḫumri," as the Assyrians spelled it). He transferred the capital to a new site, the easily defended hill of Samaria, and acquired sufficient prestige to secure in marriage a brilliant match for his son Ahab, that is, Jezebel, the daughter of King Ethbaal of the Phoenicians. After 12 years of rule Omri passed on (874 B.C.), leaving his throne to Ahab, who was almost completely dominated by Jezebel.

As a zealous Baal-worshiper the queen persecuted the prophets of Yahweh who still adhered to the revealed faith. Only those hidden in caves were able to survive. But the prophet Elijah called for a total drought upon the entire kingdom (which affected much of Phoenicia as well, judging from the famine at Zarephath), and it lasted for three and a half years. Elijah finally came out of hiding and challenged Ahab and his followers to a contest on Mount Carmel. After Jezebel's prophets of Baal and Asherah (totaling 850) had vainly prayed all day for fire to ignite their offering, Elijah called down fire from heaven upon his sacrifice. He so con-

The Black Obelisk of Shalmaneser III of Assyria, showing Jehu of Israel paying tribute to the Assyrians in the second register. BM

vinced his countrymen of the sovereignty of Yahweh that they followed his leadership in executing all the prophets of Baal. Despite the miraculous termination of the drought by a copious rain, Elijah fled for his life because of Jezebel's grim threats, and he did not stop until he met with God on Mount Sinai.

Ahab was subjected to great pressure by Ben-hadad of Damascus, but by following the directions of some unnamed prophets of Yahweh he managed to defeat and even to capture Ben-hadad at Aphek, despite the latter's overwhelming advantage in manpower and chariotry. Yet Ahab let his captive go in return for a promise of commercial concessions, and Ben-hadad lived on to plague Israel. After the sordid affair of Naboth's judicial murder (I Kgs 21), Ahab was again confronted by Elijah as he was gloating over the confiscated vineyard, and was warned that he would die a violent death. This was fulfilled later when he died of an arrow wound at the battle of Ramoth-gilead (853 B.C.), despite his alliance with Jehoshaphat of Judah, who had come to help him against the Syrians (I Kgs 22:29-37). His son Ahaziah died two years later as the result of an accidental fall, and the crown passed to his younger son, Jehoram, who carried on the struggle against the Syrians of Damascus.

It was during Jehoram's reign that Moab regained its independence under King Mesha, despite a punitive expedition in alliance with Jehoshaphat and aided by Elisha, Elijah's chosen successor (II Kgs 3). During an interlude of peace with Damascus, General Naaman came to Samaria and was cured by Elisha of his leprosy. Nevertheless the Syrians later resumed their aggression, vainly endeavoring to capture the troublesome Elisha at Dothan (II Kgs 6:8-18), and then besieging Jehoram at Samaria, until they were miraculously chased away by a sudden panic (6:24–7:16). Upon his deathbed King Ben-hadad sent down his trusted general Hazael to seek healing from the Heb. prophet. But in the end he was smothered in bed by Hazael, just as Elisha predicted, and Hazael became an even more dangerous aggressor against Israel than his predecessor had been. It was from the battlefront at Ramoth-gilead that Jehu, Jehoram's army commander, hurried back to assassinate his king (having been anointed by an emissary of Elisha), and likewise King Ahaziah of Judah, who happened to be visiting Jehoram at the time. (As a grandson of Jezebel, Ahaziah was marked for destruction along with all other descendants of the house of Omri.)

A zealous partisan of Yahweh-worship, Jehu (841-814 B.C.) followed up the extermination of Ahab's 70 sons by a massacre of all the worshipers of Baal, whom he had craftily enticed into the great Baal temple in Samaria under guise of being a Baal worshiper himself. Yet he failed to remove the cult of the golden calves at Bethel and Dan, and forfeited divine favor by this compromise with expediency. Not only did he sustain reverses from Hazael, but in the year of his accession he even had to pay tribute to the Assyrian Shalmaneser III (who had battled Ahab and Ben-hadad at Qarqar in 853 B.C.). His son Jehoahaz (814-798) was reduced to ignominious vassalage by the Syrians (II Kgs 13:7), but his grandson Jehoash (798-782), in accordance with Elisha's dying prophecy, gained three notable victories over Hazael and regained Israel's independence. Challenged to battle by Amaziah of Judah (the cordial entente with the southern kingdom had ceased in 841), Jehoash defeated and captured him at Beth-shemesh, destroyed much of the wall of Jerusalem and rifled the treasures of its temple and palace.

Jeroboam II (782–753 B.C.), the son of Jehoash, was even more successful in battle. He succeeded in reconquering all the dominions once subject to Jeroboam I, and even subdued the Syrian kingdoms of Damascus and Hamath (II Kgs 14:28). During this military success, however, the wealthy classes in Israel secured all the booty for themselves and the poor became poorer still. It was during this period of continued moral decline that the prophets Amos and Hosea began their ministry, vainly calling for repentance and reform. Jeroboam's incompetent son Zechariah was murdered by an army officer named Shallum in 752 B.C. Shallum in turn was vanquished and killed by another general, named Menahem, within a month, and thus the achievement of Jeroboam II gave way to civil war and national enfeeblement that presaged early disaster to the whole realm.

Ominously for Israel, Menahem (752–742 B.C.) found it necessary to pay tribute to the resurgent power of Assyria under the aggressive Tiglath-pileser III (744–727 B.C.) and to follow a pro-Assyrian policy until his death. His son Pekahiah was soon cut down (in 740) by an aide-de-camp named Pekah, who had apparently claimed the throne in Gilead back in 752 (cf. II Kgs 15:27). This led to an anti-Assyrian policy which welded Pekah and King Rezin of Damascus into a defensive coalition against Tiglath-pileser. When Ahaz of Judah refused to join with them, they launched devastating invasions which smashed the Judean armed forces (II Chr 28:5–8), although they did not capture Jerusalem itself. Bribed by Ahaz, Tiglath-pileser invaded Syria with overwhelming force, storming the capital of Damascus in 732, and reducing Israel to vassalage.

That same year Pekah's assassin Hoshea was installed as king and was compelled to cede northern Galilee to Assyria. Vainly he sought Egyptian alliance against Shalmaneser V, the new Assyrian ruler. But Hoshea was arrested and imprisoned and his capital beseiged. Samaria held out for nearly three years before it finally succumbed, apparently early in 721 B.C., and was totally destroyed by Sargon II (722/1–705 B.C.). All its surviving population was removed from Israel and settled by the Assyrians in territories E of the Tigris. Only a fraction of the rural population remained behind, and these were eventually submerged by large contingents of settlers from Cuthah, Ava, Hamath, Sepharvaim (II Kgs 17:24), Babylonia, Susa, Elam and elsewhere (Ezr 4:9–10), to form the hybrid people and culture which later came to be known as the Samaritans (*q.v.*).

See Israel; Judah, Kingdom of; Chronology, O.T.

Bibliography. "Israel and Judah, Monarchies of," CornPBE, pp. 422–444. Edwin R. Thiele, *The Mysterious Numbers of the Hebrew Kings*, 2nd ed., Grand Rapids: Eerdmans, 1965.

G. L. A.

ISSACHAR (ĭs′*ȧ*-k*ȧ*r). The ninth son of Jacob, the fifth by Leah (Gen 30:17–18; 35:23). The sons of Issachar were "Tola, and Phuvah, and Job, and Shimron" (Gen 46:13), and were among those who moved to Egypt when Joseph sent the wagons from Egypt for his father Jacob and his family.

Before Jacob died he called his sons into his presence to pronounce a benediction and a prophetic utterance over each one. Jacob said, "Issachar is a strong ass couching down between two burdens" (Gen 49:14). The descendants of Issachar developed into five tribal clans, increasing in number from 54,400 at the first numbering (Num 1:29) to 64,300 at the second census (Num 26:25), and to 87,000 during the reign of David (I Chr 7:1–5).

Representatives from the tribe of Issachar stood on Mount Gerizim to bless the people (Deut 27:12). Moses predicted a joyous and quiet life for Issachar (Deut 33:18). Such notables as the judge Tola (Jud 10:1), and King Baasha (I Kgs 15:27) belonged to the tribe of Issachar. The descendants of this tribe "were men that had understanding of the times, to know what Israel ought to do," and changed their political allegiance from Saul to David at the opportune time (I Chr 12:32, 38).

At the division of the land of Canaan, the fourth lot was assigned to Issachar after the ark was taken to Shiloh. The tribe occupied most of the plain of Jezreel or Esdraelon (Josh 19:17–23). This low, fertile plain of the Kishon proved to have advantages as well as disadvantages. Its location was a disadvantage because the Canaanites long dominated that area (Jud 1:27 f.), foreign invaders often pillaged the crops (e.g., Jud 6:3–6, 33), and enemy war chariots more than once engaged in battle here, thus fulfilling Jacob's prophecy in Gen 49:15. Yet the story of Sisera indicates that this tribe possessed qualities of valor (Jud 5:15). On the positive side, the "way of the sea" passed through Issachar's allotment and became a source of lucrative revenue to its occupants (Deut 33:19).

H. A. Han.

ISSHIAH (ĭ-shī′*ȧ*). Variant of Ishiah and Jesiah (*q.v.*).

1. A Levite, the eldest son of Rehabiah and great-grandson of Moses (I Chr 24:21; cf. 23:14–17).

2. A Levite, son of Uzziel (I Chr 24:24–25; cf. 23:20, RSV).

3. One of David's mighty men whose name is spelled Jesiah in KJV (see I Chr 12:6, RSV).

4. A man of the tribe of Issachar whose name is spelled Ishiah in KJV (see I Chr 7:3, 5, RSV).

ISSUE. *See* Diseases.

ISUAH. *See* Ishuah.

ISUI. *See* Ishui.

ITALY (ĭt'ȧ-lĭ). Slashing diagonally across the center of the Mediterranean, Italy is strategically located for control of that sea, and Rome is strategically located for controlling the peninsula of Italy. The area of Italy comprises about 90,000 square miles and divides into two regions: the peninsula and the continental region. The boot-shaped peninsula stretches some 700 miles toward Africa and is never more than 125 miles wide.

The Alps extend in an irregular 1,200-mile arc across the N and the Apennines extend the full length of the peninsula in a bow-shaped range about 800 miles long. These 4,000-foot mountains have passes which do not hinder communications and which thrust out spurs to the W to divide the land into such plains as Etruria, Latium, and Campania. The rivers of Italy (except for the Po) are generally not navigable and deposit silt at their mouths to create malarial marshes.

Italy's primary source of wealth was always agricultural and pastoral. There were also notable mine fields in ancient times, especially copper and iron beds in Etruria and Elba. Marble, limestone, timber, and abundance of good clay were also available during the early centuries after Christ.

Italy figures in the NT narrative in connection with Paul's journey to Rome and imprisonment there (Acts 27:1, 6). Aquila and Priscilla had come from Italy to Corinth (Acts 18:2). The writer of the epistle to the Hebrews extended greetings from Christians from Italy (Heb 13:24), a factor in determining the place of writing and the destination of that epistle. The military unit commanded by the centurion was called the Italian cohort (Acts 10:1, NASB).

See Rome; Roman Empire.

H. F. V.

ITCH. *See* Diseases.

ITHAI. *See* Ittai.

ITHAMAR (ĭth'ȧ-mär). Fourth and youngest son of Aaron (Ex 6:23). He was consecrated to the priesthood along with his brothers (Ex 28:1 ff.), and after the death of Nadab and Abihu he and Eleazar were appointed to take their places in the priestly office (Num 3:4; I Chr 24:2). Treasurer of the offerings of the tabernacle (Ex 38:21), Ithamar was also super-

Italy at peace, and rich in crops, flocks and herds, as symbolized on the Altar of Peace of Augustus in Rome. HFV

ALPS MOUNTAINS
PO RIVER
APENNINE MOUNTAINS
ARNO R.
RUBICON R.
ETRURIA
ADRIATIC SEA
CORSICA
LATIUM
VEII
TIBER R.
ROME
OSTIA
THREE TAVERNS
APPII FORUM
CAPUA
PUTEOLI
APPIAN WAY
BRUNDISIUM
CAMPANIA
POMPEII
TARENTUM
SARDINIA
ITALY
0 25 50 100 200
SCALE OF MILES
THURII
TARENTUM GULF
MEDITERRANEAN SEA
MESSANA
RHEGIUM
IONIAN SEA
SICILY
SYRACUSE

intendent of the work of the Gershonites and Merarites (Num 4:27–28, 33). He was founder of the priestly line to which Eli (*q.v.*) belonged (I Chr 24:5–6). A descendant of Ithamar named Daniel was among the exiles who returned from Babylon (Ezr 8:2).

ITHIEL (ĭth'ĭ-ĕl)
 1. A Benjamite, the son of Jesaiah, in the time of Nehemiah (Neh 11:7).
 2. A man to whom, along with Ucal, the words of Agur were addressed (Prov 30:1).

ITHMAH (ĭth'mȧ). A Moabite, one of David's valiant men (I Chr 11:46).

ITHNAN (ĭth'năn). A town in the southern extreme of Judah, mentioned along with Kedesh and Hazor (Josh 15:23).

ITHRA (ĭth'rȧ). The father of Amasa, the commander of Absalom's rebel army (II Sam 17:25). He is called "Ithra an Israelite" in II Sam 17:25, but a better reading is "Jether the Ishmeelite" in I Chr 2:17. *See* Jether. His mother was Abigail, the sister of David.

ITHRAN (ĭth'răn)
 1. A son of Dishon, a Horite (Gen 36:26; I Chr 1:41).
 2. Son of Zophah, a descendant of Asher (I Chr 7:37).

ITHREAM (ĭth'rē-ȧm). The sixth son of David, born in Hebron. His mother's name was Eglah (II Sam 3:5; I Chr 3:3).

ITHRITES (ĭth'rīts). A family in Israel that lived at Kirjath-jearim (I Chr 2:53). Two of David's valiant warriors, Ira and Gareb, belonged to this family (II Sam 23:38; I Chr 11:40).

ITTAH-KAZIN (ĭt'ȧ-kā'zĭn). The same as Eth-kazin (RSV), a place on the border of Zebulun (Josh 19:13).

ITTAI (ĭt'ī)
 1. A Benjamite, son of Ribai, one of David's mighty men (II Sam 23:29; I Chr 11:31).
 2. A Gittite, native of Gath, thus a Philistine, who became a dear friend of David and commander of one-third of David's forces during the revolt of Absalom, serving in equal capacity with Joab and Abishai (II Sam 15:18–22; 18:2, 5). When David urged him to remain in Jerusalem rather than risk his life, Ittai refused, choosing rather to serve his king.

ITURAEA (ĭt'yo͝or-ē'ȧ). This term appears only once in the Scriptures (Lk 3:1), where it designates a portion of the territory ruled over by Philip, the son of Herod the Great and brother of Herod Antipas. It was adjacent to Trachonitis in NE Palestine, beyond the Jordan River. It received its name from Jetur, son of Ishmael (Gen 25:15–16), and after the conquest by the Israelites it was occupied by the tribe of Manasseh (I Chr 5:19–20).

IVAH (ī'vȧ). A city conquered by the Assyrians and mentioned along with Hamath, Arpad, Sepharvaim, and Hena, according to the boast of Rabshakeh, a representative of Sennacherib (II Kgs 18:34; 19:13; Isa 37:13). Although its exact location has not been determined, it apparently was in Babylonia and perhaps is to be identified with Ava (II Kgs 17:24) from which the Assyrians took people to occupy Samaria after its fall. *See* Ava.

Small ivory panel with an Egyptian scene from an Assyrian palace at Nimrud. Assyria. BM

IVORY. The Heb. word *shēn,* translated "ivory," means "tooth"; and the compound word *shenhabbîm,* also translated "ivory," means "elephant's tooth." *See* Animals: Elephant, II, 12.

Ivory is mentioned several times in the Bible, first of all with reference to Solomon's reign when he shipped it in through his Red Sea port at Ezion-geber and decorated his throne with ivory veneer or inlays (I Kgs 10:18, 22). Solomon very likely imported his ivory from Punt (Somaliland in E Africa), where the Egyptians sent trading expeditions via the Red Sea to obtain ivory. In his beautiful love song he compares the body of the bridegroom and the neck of the bride to white ivory (Song 5:14; 7:4).

Ahab is said to have built an "ivory house"

(I Kgs 22:39), undoubtedly meaning that the walls and doors of his palace and pieces of furniture were inlaid with ivory panels and carvings (cf. Ps 45:8). Amos condemned ivory houses and beds along with the other luxuries of the royalty and nobility of the northern kingdom (Amos 3:15; 6:4).

A large number of ivory pieces were found in the excavations of Samaria. They apparently date to the reign of Ahab in the 9th cen. B.C. Some are carved panels with frame and tenon on the side for attaching to woodwork. The merchants of Tyre even boasted of inlaying the decks of their ships with ivory (Ezk 27:6, RSV, NASB), which they received in the form of tusks from the Sudan by the traders of Dedan in Arabia (27:15). In Rev 18:12 articles of ivory are listed among the cargoes to be brought to the eschatological Babylon.

Both Egyptian and Assyrian texts frequently list chairs and couches decorated with ivory that were taken as booty (ANET, pp. 237, 282, 288). Archaeological excavations of many Near Eastern sites from Cyprus to Ur in lower Mesopotamia have uncovered exquisite ivory objects. A catalogue published in 1957 listed 1,271 separate pieces, such as figurines of gods and animals, plaques, combs, gaming boards, cosmetic tools, and jewel boxes (R. D. Barnett, *A Catalogue of Nimrud Ivories and Other Examples of Ancient Near Eastern Ivories;* see also ANEP, # 58, 67, 69, 70, 125–132, 203, 213–215, 290, 293, 332, 464, 566, 649, 663).

The most important collections of Palestinian ivory work have come from Samaria and Megiddo. A hoard of 383 pieces dating from 1350–1150 B.C. was discovered at the latter site. Nimrud (biblical Calah) has yielded the finest collection of all. Some of its ivories are so similar in technique to those of Samaria that it may be assumed the same Phoenician craftsmen made pieces in each group. Most of the ivory used in Assyria, Syria, and Palestine came from Asiatic elephants which inhabited the marshes along the upper Euphrates. They were hunted to extinction sometime after 850 B.C.

J. R.

IVY. *See* Plants: Ivy.

IZEHARITES. *See* Izharites.

IZHAR (ĭz'här), **IZEHAR** (ĭz'ĕ-här)

1. A Levite (Heb. *yiṣhar*), son of Kohath and father of Korah (Num 16:1), head of a tribal family called Izharites and Izeharites (see also Ex 6:18, 21; Num 3:19, 27; I Chr 6:18, 38; etc.); called Amminadab in I Chr 6:22 (*see* Amminadab 2).

2. A descendant of Judah (Heb. *yiṣḥar*), whose mother was named Helah (I Chr 4:7, RSV). The KJV renders his name Jezoar.

IZHARITES (ĭz'hȧ-rīts), **IZEHARITES** (ĭz'ĕ-hä-rīts). The descendants of Izhar, son of Kohath and the father of Korah (Num 3:27; I Chr 24:22; 26:23, 29). These Levites during the reign of David helped to supervise the treasures of the tabernacle (I Chr 26:23), and some also served as "officers and judges" (I Chr 26:29).

IZLIAH. *See* Jezliah.

IZRAHIAH (ĭz'rȧ-hī'ȧ). A descendant of Issachar and grandson of Tola, a chief of the tribe (I Chr 7:3). *See* Jezrahiah.

IZRAHITE (ĭz'rȧ-hīt). The family name of Shamhuth, one of David's heroic men and designated as "the fifth captain for the fifth month" (I Chr 27:8). The name is possibly a corruption of "Zerahite," a descendant of Zerah of Judah (I Chr 27:11, RSV).

IZRI (ĭz'rī). Apparently one of the sons of Jeduthun and also called Zeri (I Chr 25:3), leader of the fourth group of musicians in the Levitical choir during the reign of David (I Chr 25:11).

J

JAAKAN (jā'ȧ-kȧn). A descendant of a nomadic clan of the Horites (Hurrians) of Mount Seir who maintained their identity among the Edomites. He was a son of Ezer, called Jakan in I Chr 1:42 and Akan (*q.v.*) in Gen 36:27. The name also is spelled Jaakan in Deut 10:6, where it is disclosed that the Israelites had rested in the area of the wells (Beeroth) of the "children of Jaakan." Num 33:31-32 records that the Israelites pitched tent in Bene-jaakan ("sons of Jaakan"). It is to be noted that the so-called Horites have been identified with a cultured people known as the Hurrians, who migrated southward into N Mesopotamia around 2000 B.C. Later they spread over Syria and Palestine, so that by the time of Moses the Egyptians frequently called this area Kharu or Hurru.

JAAKOBAH (jā'ȧ-kō'bȧ). A descendant of Simeon (I Chr 4:36).

JAALA, JAALAH (jā'ȧ-lȧ). A servant of Solomon whose children returned from the Babylonian Exile under Zerubbabel (Ezr 2:56; Neh 7:58).

JAALAM (jā'ȧ-lȧm). A son of Esau by Aholibamah, a Hivite woman (Gen 36:5). He is referred to as a "duke" or chief (Gen 36:18).

JAANAI (jā'ȧ-nī). A chief of the tribe of Gad (I Chr 5:12).

JAARE-OREGIM (jā'ȧ-rē-ôr'ĕ-jĭm). The name given to the father of Elhanan, a Bethlehemite who killed the brother of Goliath (II Sam 21:19). The name "Jaare-oregim" may result from a scribe having inserted the word *'ōreᵊm* from the next line of the same verse (an error of dittography), since the same man is also called Jair (*q.v.*; I Chr 20:5).

JAASAU (jā'ȧ-sô). Called Jaasu in the RSV. He was a descendant of Bani and one of the Jews who put away their foreign wives upon the demand of a council headed by Ezra (Ezr 10:37).

JAASIEL (jā-ā'sĭ-ĕl), **JASIEL** (jā'sĭ-ĕl)

1. A son of Abner of the tribe of Benjamin and one of the princes of the tribe (I Chr 27:21).

2. Jasiel the Mesobaite (I Chr 11:47), one of David's mighty men. Some authorities identify the two.

JAAZANIAH (jā-ăz'ȧ-nī-ȧ). The name occurs on an agate Heb. seal, "Jaazaniah, servant of the king," found at Tell en-Nasbeh, and in one of the Lachish letters.

1. The son of Hoshaiah the Maacathite. He was one of the Jewish army officers remaining after the desolation of Jerusalem by Babylon. With the other leaders, he pledged his support to Gedaliah, and after the murder of Gedaliah, pursued and defeated Ishmael, recovering all the captives. All the commanders appealed to Jeremiah for God's guidance, but disregarded him when he counseled them to remain in the land and trust in God. Jaazaniah last appears with the other "insolent men" rejecting God's will and preparing to go to Egypt and oblivion (II Kgs 25:23; Jer 40:8; 42:1; 43:2-5). In Jeremiah the name is spelled Jezaniah, and in Jer 43:2 he is called Azariah.

2. The leader of the Rechabites (*q.v.*) in the days of Jeremiah, when the prophet tempted them with wine that they might afford Judah a symbol of faithfulness (Jer 35:3ff.).

3. The son of Shaphan, seen by Ezekiel in a vision worshiping abominable things with the other elders of Israel (Ezk 8:10-13).

4. The son of Azur, a prince of Judah, seen in Ezekiel's vision worshiping the sun with his back to the temple (Ezk 11:1-4).

P. C. J.

JAAZER (jā-ā'zẽr), **JAZER** (jā'zẽr). Jaazer occurs twice in the KJV (Num 21:32; 32:35); otherwise the name is spelled Jazer. It was a city located E of the Jordan, belonging originally to the Amorite kingdom of Sihon, captured by the Israelites (Num 21:32), and later allotted to the tribe of Gad (Josh 13:25). It furnished warriors for David (I Chr 26:31; II Sam 24:5). In the 8th cen. B.C. it was captured by the Moabites (Isa 16:8-9; Jer 48:32). In the 2nd cen. B.C. it was captured and destroyed by the Maccabees (I Macc 5:7-8). The site may be Khirbet Jazzir near es-Salt, 12 miles WNW of Amman.

JAAZIAH (jā'ą-zī'ȧ). A Levite, son or descendant of Merari, in the time of David (I Chr 24:26 - 27). However, there is a textual problem concerning this passage, with the LXX reading *Ozeiá*, which may mean Uzziah.

JAAZIEL (jā-ā'zĭ-ĕl). A Levite musician who was appointed to play an instrument at the return of the ark by David following its capture by the Philistines (I Chr 15:18). He also is called Aziel (*q.v.*; I Chr 15:20), and apparently the same man is referred to as Jeiel (*q.v.;* I Chr 16:5).

JABAL (jā'bȧl). The son of Lamech by Adah and the originator of the nomadic way of life, as well as one who raised cattle (Gen 4:20).

The Jabbok River. Richard E. Ward

JABBOK (jăb'ŏk). An E tributary of the Jordan River *c.* 60 miles long. Now called Nahr ez-Zerqa from the blue look of its water, it rises near the ancient Rabbath-Ammon, the Ammonite capital. It flows N for 20 miles or more, gradually swinging to the W, where it descends rapidly through a steep-banked gorge. This gives it a strong current, especially in the rainy season. Reaching the Jordan Valley, it flows SW to enter the Jordan River about 24 miles N of the Dead Sea.

It was a natural boundary between the kingdoms of Sihon of Heshbon and Og of Bashan before the conquest of Canaan under Joshua (Num 21:24); and it was the W boundary of the Ammonites (Deut 3:16). Later it formed the S border of the tribal territory of Manasseh (Deut 3:12 - 17).

Jacob forded the river with his family before wrestling there at night with an angel who gave him the name Israel (Gen 32:22 - 29). In memory of this event the Israelites may have named the stream, for Jabbok in Heb. is *yabbōq*, while "and . . . wrestled" (Gen 32:24) is *way-yē'ābēq*, which contains only one additional consonant, a silent aleph.

N. B. B.

JABESH (jā'bĕsh)

1. The father of Shallum, who killed Zachariah, the king of Israel, and reigned in his stead (II Kgs 15:10, 13 - 14).

2. A shortened form of Jabesh-gilead (*q.v.;* I Sam 11:1, 3, 5, 9–10; 31:12–13; I Chr 10:12).

JABESH-GILEAD (jā'bĕsh-gĭl'ē-ȧd). A town in Gilead, about ten miles SE of the ancient Beth-shan, and about two miles E of the Jordan River. The site has been identified by Glueck with Tell Abu Kharaz on the Wadi Yabis two miles E of the Jordan. Israel early put the town to the sword because its citizens would not share in the war against Benjamin (Jud 21:8 - 15). Later, Saul rescued the town when Nahash the Ammonite threatened to gouge out the right eyes of the men when they surrendered to him in return for sparing their lives (I Sam 11:1 - 11). After Saul's death at the battle of Gilboa, the Philistines beheaded his body and hung it on the fortress of Beth-shan, but the men of Jabesh-gilead nine miles away recovered the body in a daring night-long raid and gave his remains an honorable burial (I Sam 31:8 - 13). David sent them a message praising them for their action (II Sam 2:4 - 7), doubtless hoping that this would help win their support to his kingship.

N. B. B.

JABEZ (jā'bĕz)

1. Jabez was a descendant of Judah, but he can be related to no time or family. His brief record appears like a bright light in the otherwise drab genealogies of Chronicles. He had been named Jabez, "he causes pain or sorrow." In faith he laid hold upon God and sought His blessing, and that faith triumphed, for "God granted what he asked" (I Chr 4:9 - 10).

2. A town, apparently in Judah, where "the families of the scribes" dwelt (I Chr 2:55).

JABIN (jā'bĭn). According to W. F. Albright (*Yahweh and the Gods of Canaan*, Garden City: Doubleday, 1968, p. 49, n. 99), this name is an abbreviation of the longer *Yabni-Hadad*, the name of a king of Hazor in the 17th cen. B.C. It is similar to *Yabni-el*, the name of a 14th cen. prince of Lachish.

1. King of Hazor (*q.v.*) who formed a coalition with several other kings to fight against the Israelites, but who instead was defeated by Joshua and his forces near the waters of Merom (*q.v.*). After the battle Jabin was slain and Hazor burned (Josh 11:1 - 14).

2. A later king of Hazor, possibly a descendant of the former Jabin. He oppressed Israel for 20 years during the time of the judges. His forces, led by Sisera, were defeated by the Israelite forces under Barak and Deborah (Jud 4:1–24). The latest level of the great Canaanite city of Hazor may be associated with his reign. The archaeological excavations of Yigael Yadin indicate it was destroyed *c.*1230 B.C.

F. D. H.

Remains of a public building of Ahab's day at the city of Hazor. HFV

JABNEEL (jăb'nē-ĕl)

1. A town on the NW border of Judah (Josh 15:11) four miles inland from the Mediterranean Sea and nine miles NE of Ashdod. It is probably to be identified with Jabneh, a Philistine city which was captured by Uzziah (II Chr 26:6). Jabneh was called Jamnia in the Gr. and Rom. periods, and it was at this city that the Sanhedrin re-formed after the destruction of Jerusalem in A.D. 70 and that the canon of the Jewish Scriptures was confirmed (*c.* A.D. 100).

2. A town of Naphtali (Josh 19:33), identified by some with modern Kirbet Yamma, about seven miles S of Tiberias.

JABNEH (jăb'nĕ). *See* Jabneel 1.

JACHAN (jā'kăn). A Gadite chief, probably head of a father's house (I Chr 5:13; RSV, "Jacan").

JACHIN (jā'kĭn)

1. The son of Simeon, son of Jacob, who came down to Egypt when Jacob migrated there and became founder of the family of Jachinites (Gen 46:10; Ex 6:15; Num 26:12). Called Jarib (*q.v.*) in I Chr 4:24.

2. Jachin and Boaz (*q.v.*) were the names given to two enormous free-standing bronze columns that stood before the temple of Solomon (I Kgs 7:15-22; II Chr 3:17). Such free-standing twin pillars were a common feature of ancient temples from Assyria throughout the Mediterranean area, as noted in architectural ruins, on clay models, and by representations on coins and seals. Each name may be the first word of a promise of God inscribed on it; e.g., "Yahweh will establish [*yākîn*] thy throne forever," and, "In the strength [*beʿāz*] of Yahweh shall the king rejoice" (cf. Ps 21:1; R. B. Y. Scott, JBL, LVIII [1939], 143f.; P. Garber, BA, XIV [1951], 8). The tremendous pillars and their ornamented capitals (chapiter, *q.v.*) were about 35 feet high and 18 feet in circumference. The capitals were covered with sculpture in the form of flowering lilies, below which was a band of network with two rows of ornamental pomegranates (I Kgs 7:17-22).

On the basis of recent archaeological studies, Albright suggests that these were gigantic fire altars, like great torches standing before the temple of God, and reminding the people of the pillar(s) of fire and cloud that led them through the wilderness (Ex 13:21f.; Albright, *Archaeology and the Religion of Israel*, pp. 144-148). Yeivin contends that the pommel shape of the capitals prohibited their use as giant lamps, and believes the pillars signified that God was present in His sacred dwelling (S. Yeivin, PEQ, XCI [1959], 6-22). *See* Temple.

3. A priest who dwelt in Jerusalem after the return from Captivity (I Chr 9:10; Neh 11:10).

4. Head of the 21st course of priests appointed by David (I Chr 24:17).

P. C. J.

The pillars Jachin and Boaz stand before this model of Solomon's temple at the Lebanonorama near Beirut. HFV

JACINTH. *See* Jewels.

JACKAL. *See* Animals, II. 23.

JACOB (jā'kŭb). In Heb. the name *yaʿăqōb* means "heel catcher," "trickster," or "supplanter." In S Arabic and Ethiopic the word means "may God protect," from the verb *ʿaqaba,* "to guard," "watch," or "protect." The root *ʿāqab* is a general Semitic word which occurs in Arabic personal names, in Akkad. and Aram. inscriptions, as well as Syriac and Palmyrene. The noun meaning "heel" occurs in Heb. (*ʿāqēb*), Aram., Syriac, Arabic, Ugaritic, and Akkad. Jacob's name was thus an ancient member of the Near Eastern onomastica rather than a uniquely biblical name.

1. The patriarch. The younger twin son of Isaac and Rebekah; later called Israel.

Life in Palestine (Gen 25-27). The birth of Jacob and Esau is recorded in Gen 25:21-28.

Isaac married Rebekah when he was 40 years of age (see Gen 24 for this beautiful picturesque episode). Rebekah, like Sarah (cf. Gen 11:30; 16:1 - 2), was barren. Isaac's prayer for his wife was heard and rewarded. She gave birth to twin boys, who wrestled in the womb as their posterity nations did in real life (*see* Esau for the history of this long and bitter struggle). Esau, the firstborn, was so named because he was hairy. The second was named Jacob because he came forth from the womb grasping his brother's heel. Rebekah's twin sons inherited her chief characteristics: Esau, her open-mindedness; Jacob, her craftiness or guile. Esau grew into a skilled hunter, a man of the field, whom Isaac loved because Esau gave him venison to eat. In contrast, Jacob was a quiet, meditative, settled, and well-integrated man, dwelling in tents, whom Rebekah loved.

God promised Abraham that through his seed Isaac, He would make of him a great nation. This promise was renewed with Isaac. The question was through which seed, Jacob or Esau? This struggle resulted in a domestic conflict and forced Jacob to live under constant tension. Gen 25:23 states that by divine choice Jacob would be the heir of promise; but two interesting events occur to implement the divine purpose.

First, the buying of Esau's birthright (Gen 25:29 - 34). When Esau the hunter came from the field hungry and empty-handed, he desired some of that red stuff (Gen 25:30, lit.), a stew which the shepherd brother Jacob was preparing. In his famished condition Esau bargained away his birthright. Jacob insisted on an oath, considered irretractable (Gen 25:33; cf. Josh 9:19). So by shrewd foresight (as well as taking unfair advantage) Jacob lived up to the reputation of his name and gained the right of precedence which his order of birth did not give. God's intention (Gen 25:23) was working itself out with Jacob's help. However, along with Jacob's good fortune, seeds of hostility were sown that would goad Jacob in years to come (Gen 27:41). The Nuzu tablets discovered SE of Nineveh in 1926 reveal that in the prevailing culture in Mesopotamia in the first half of the 2nd mil. B.C., the birthright could be bought and sold. *See* Firstborn; Nuzu.

Second, the stealing of the covenant blessing (Gen 27:1 - 46). Aged Isaac, fearful of imminent death (137 years of age—but 43 years before his death) instructed Esau to prepare for him his favorite dish, that he might transmit to his firstborn the patriarchal blessing contained in his soul (Gen 27:4). As innocent Esau was out stalking his kill, Jacob cooperated with Rebekah's scheme to wrest the blessing for himself. He executed the deceit as outlined by his mother with boldness, and to his crass lies (Gen 27:19, 24) he added shocking blasphemy (v. 20: "Because the Lord your God granted me success," RSV). The pathos of the occasion is deepened by Isaac's blindness. Torn by suspicion and doubt (Jacob's voice but Esau's hands, 27:22), the blind father finally conveyed upon Jacob his final, deathbed benediction (Gen 27:27 - 29; cf. 24:1 - 9; 49:1 - 33). On Esau's return and Isaac's awareness of the guile, the blessing could not be recalled nor altered (27:37 - 38). So only ill-fortune remained for Esau (27:39 - 40).

Life in Haran (Gen 28 - 30). When the full import of the plot was uncovered, Jacob was sent away to his relatives in Haran. En route from Beer-sheba Jacob, as a weary, troubled, and sinful fugitive, spent his first night near the ancient Canaanite sanctuary of Luz. In a night vision God revealed Himself to this wanderer as the God of his father. He also renewed the covenant blessing (Gen 12:7; 13:14 - 17; 26:3 - 5), promised him the land, appointed him to a universal mission, and assured him of divine guidance and a prosperous life. Jacob responded with a personal vow and renamed the place Bethel (*q.v.*).

Jacob arrived in Aram-naharaim and good fortune came to his rescue again. He met Rachel at the well and it was love at first sight. She in turn brought Jacob to her father's house and introduced him to Laban, Jacob's uncle (Gen 29:10 - 11, 18, 20). Jacob's love for Rachel issued in permanent employment with Laban. Jacob worked to gain her as wife for seven years. The morning after the marriage ceremony he discovered that instead of soft-voiced Rachel, he had married weak-eyed Leah. The deceitful Laban was equal to Jacob's anger and agreed to give him Rachel after the customary one week's marriage festivities if Jacob would serve him another seven years. Jacob brought his father-in-law great prosperity (Gen 30:30), and shrewd Laban recognized a bargain when he saw one.

Jacob's fortune increased as well as his family. Twelve children were born to Jacob in Mesopotamia. Leah was the mother of Reuben, Simeon, Levi, Judah, Issachar, Zebulun, and a daughter Dinah (Gen 29:31 - 35; 30:17 - 21). From Leah's handmaid Zilpah came Gad and Asher (Gen 30:9 - 13). Rachel's handmaid Bilhah bore Dan and Naphtali (Gen 29:31; 30:1 - 2; cf. 16:2; 25:21; 30:3 - 8). Finally, God opened Rachel's womb and she bore Joseph and later on in Canaan, Benjamin (Gen 30:22 - 24; 35:16 - 18).

Jacob's preparation to return home (Gen 31). Jacob desired to return to Palestine (Gen 30:25). Realizing his prosperity came because of Jacob, Laban urged him to stay (Gen 30:27), and Jacob agreed on one condition (Gen 30:29ff.). But now the Lord instructed Jacob to go back home (Gen 31:3, 11 - 13). Jacob talked with his wives and reminded them that their father Laban had changed his wages "ten times" (Gen 31:4 - 7). They assured him that they acquiesced in his plans (vv. 14 - 16).

While Laban was shearing his sheep, Jacob with his wives and children, servants, flocks, herds, and substance departed for his fatherland (Gen 31:17 - 20). They crossed the Euphrates

Jacob Blessing Ephraim and Manasseh. Painting by Benjamin West.
Allen Memorial Art Museum, Oberlin

River and headed toward Gilead. After three days, Laban, hearing of their flight, pursued and overtook them after a seven-day chase in the mountain of Gilead, *c.* 400 miles from Haran (vv. 21 - 25). Angrily Laban leveled three charges against Jacob (vv. 26 - 30): (1) he fled in secret; (2) he kidnapped his daughters; (3) he stole Laban's household gods (teraphim; cf. G. E. Wright, *Biblical Archaeology,* p. 44). Jacob countered with the 20 years of hard service and Laban's attempt to defraud him of wages. After much haranguing, in which each sought to outdo the other in exaggeration of wrongs endured, Laban suggested a truce which was marked by setting up a pillar and a mound of stones and which climaxed in an all-night covenant feast (vv. 31-54). The next morning Laban returned to Haran and Jacob journeyed on southward.

Return to Palestine (Gen 32 -33). Twenty years had elapsed since Jacob had deceived Isaac and stolen Esau's blessing. As Jacob drew near to the land of his heart, an angelic band met him (32:1 - 2), assuring him once again of God's protection as if to welcome and congratulate him on his auspicious return. Fording the brook Jabbok (*q.v.*) to protect his family from Esau, Jacob met "a man" who wrestled with him until daybreak (v. 24). Although wounded in his hip Jacob prevailed and won from his assailant a blessing which changed his name from Jacob ("supplanter") to Israel ("he persists with God"; *see* Israel). The stranger revealed His true identity both by blessing Jacob and by changing his name – He was the Eternal Himself (cf. Gen 17:5; 35:9 - 15; Isa 65:15; Hos 2:23; 12:3 -4).

Jacob's next hurdle was to appease his wronged brother Esau. Jacob's meeting with Esau is recorded in Gen 33:1 - 16. Fearful that Esau's anger was still aflame, Jacob had dispatched messengers to spy out Esau's plans, and they reported that Esau was marching with 400 armed men. So Jacob, still the clever one, had sought both to pacify his wronged twin brother and to protect himself and his family from attack (Gen 32:3 - 8, 13 -21; 33:1 -3). In addition to this strategy, he had prayed (32:9 - 12) and petitioned the God of Abraham and Isaac who combines past events (32:9), the present need (32:11), and the promise of the future (32:12). Amid the tangled mess of human actions, Jacob recognized the need of the Lord's hand. He not only won God's favor, but Esau's in spite of his armed men. In a scene of great tenderness, Jacob met Esau, and the breach was healed at least temporarily with magnanimity and affection.

Life in Palestine the second time (Gen 33:17 – 45:5). Esau went to Seir and there sired a nation (Gen 33:16; cf. the fulfillment of the promise of Gen 25:23; 27:39 -40; 36:1 - 43). Jacob resided in Canaan to assume his inheritance. He was now indeed the patriarch.

After Esau left, Jacob remained E of Jordan and camped near Succoth; then to Shechem where he purchased ground and reconstructed an altar (Gen 33:17–20). Under God's order, he went to Bethel and there the Lord renewed the patriarchal promises (35:1–15). Jacob and his company drifted southward, and during this journey Jacob's beloved Rachel died in childbirth (during the birth of Benjamin) and was buried on the way to Ephrath (Bethlehem, 35:16–20). Jacob joined Esau at Mamre (Hebron) and there laid their father away in the cave of Machpelah, the family sepulchre (35:27–29; 49:30–31).

Jacob's latter years demonstrated Moses' later warning to Israel: "Be sure your sin will find you out" (Num 32:23). Domestic trials tracked down Jacob in the sunset of his life. First, there was severe conflict between his rash sons Simeon and Levi with the sons of Hamor at Shechem over the matter of Dinah (Gen 34:1–31). Then Deborah (Rebekah's nurse), the confidante and counselor of the family, died and the entire family was crushed (35:8). Rachel, the object of Jacob's dearest love, was taken soon afterward (35:16ff.). "Reuben went and lay with Bilhah his father's concubine: and Israel heard it" (35:22). Joseph, his favorite son, was snatched away and gray-headed Jacob was overwhelmed with grief (37:34f.). Last of all the aged patriarch was forced to expatriate himself to Egypt in order to preserve his own life and the life of his family (46:3).

The final years of Jacob. These years in Egypt (Gen 46:6—50:13) are intertwined in the Joseph story (Gen 37–50). *See* Joseph.

When seven years of famine gripped the land of Canaan, Jacob and his sons went down to Egypt. Along the way, at Beer-sheba he was assured of God's favor (46:1–4). Joseph arranged for Jacob and his company to settle in the land of Goshen where he remained until his death. At the age 130 he had an audience with the pharaoh and blessed him (47:7–10).

Before he died at the advanced age of 147 (47:28) Jacob bestowed a patriarchal blessing on Joseph's sons, Ephraim and Manasseh (48:8–20), and subsequently on his own sons (49:1–33). God's promise to Jacob was fulfilled. At his death the Egyptians paid him great homage. His sons, led by Joseph, the prime minister of Egypt, carried his body back to Canaan and buried him at Machpelah with Abraham and Isaac (49:29—50:13; cf. 25:9–10; 35:28–29), fulfilling the desire of the ancients to be buried in their homeland (cf. the Egyptian Sinuhe, ANET, pp. 20ff.). *See* Patriarchal Age.

Jacob is a typical example of God's redeeming grace. In himself he was a coarse, selfish, scheming, and passionate rogue with a capacity for business. But he had time in his heart for God. His nature was sensitive to the touch of the Lord and capable of great development. He dreamed dreams and had visions; angels visited him and he prayed. He coveted the best gifts; he developed fixed religious principles; and he finally became steady in his habits. But Jacob's life was fraught with conflict. The struggle in his soul was a long and fierce one—but grace conquered and Jacob the "overreacher" became Israel the one who "persists with God."

The use of "Jacob" in the Scriptures. The name "Jacob" appears many times in the Bible. "Jacob" occurs as an individual as a marked child of favor (cf. Mal 1:2; Rom 9:10–13), an heir of divine promise (cf. Heb 11:9), and a man of blessing (Heb 11:20–21). As the third notable patriarch, Jacob is frequently linked with Abraham and Isaac. So the God of the three renowned worthies is El Shaddai (Ex 6:3) and Yahweh (Ex 3:6, 15), faithful to His covenant (Ex 2:24; 32:13; Deut 29:12), compassionate toward Israel (II Kgs 13:23). The Jewish patriarchs dwell with Him (Mk 12:26–27), and sit at His table in the kingdom of heaven (Mt 8:11).

As the name-bearer of the nation Israel, Jacob appears frequently in the Scriptures: Israel is the "house of Jacob" (Lk 1:33); its God is the "King of Jacob" (Isa 41:21); and His temple is a habitation of the God of Jacob (Acts 7:46). The figure of Jacob (Israel) is epitomized in the title "servant of Yahweh" (Isa 41:8; 44:1–2, 21; 48:20; 49:3), of whom Messiah was the fulfillment (Isa 42:1–7; 49:1–10; 50:4–9; 52:13—53:12; Mt 8:17; 12:15–21; Mk 10:45; Lk 2:30–32; Acts 3:13, 26; 4:27, 30, NASB; 8:30–35; I Pet 2:21–25). *See* Servant of the Lord.

Bibliography. S. R. Driver, *The Book of Genesis, Westminster Commentaries,* 9th ed., London: Methuen Co., Ltd., 1913, pp. 244–401. L. Hicks, "Jacob (Israel)," IDB, II, 782–787. William S. Lasor, *Great Personalities of the Old Testament,* New York: Revell, 1959, pp. 31–39. A. R. Millard, "Jacob," NBD, pp. 593–596. John Muilenberg, "The Birth of Benjamin," JBL, LXXV (1956), 194–200. Martin Noth, *The History of Israel,* New York: Harper, 1958, pp. 1–7, 53–84, 120–126. G. E. Wright, *Biblical Archaeology,* Philadelphia: Westminster, 1951, pp. 40–68.

2. Joseph's father. The name of the father of Joseph, Mary's husband, according to the genealogy of Christ in Mt 1:15–16.

D. W. D.

JACOB'S WELL. The well, mentioned only in Jn 4:5–12, where Jesus talked to the Samaritan woman. By unanimous tradition, most probably correct, it is *Bîr Ya'qûb* lying *c.* five-eighths of a mile SW of the Arab village of 'Askar (perhaps NT Sychar, *q. v.*) and over 300 yards SSE of Tell Balatah, the site of OT Shechem. At this spot the road from Jerusalem, 40 miles to the S, forks. The W branch heads toward the Mediterranean and the city of Samaria; the E branch continues N to Tirzah and Beth-shan, which Jesus would have taken to Capernaum. One may look up directly to the W

Jacob's Well

at Mount Gerizim (*q.v.*), where the Samaritans have worshiped for over 2000 years (Jn 4:20).

Evidently the well was dug by Jacob after he purchased a plot of ground near Shechem (Gen 33:18–20) in order to have his own supply of water independent of the city. *Bîr Ya'qûb* is seven and a half feet in diameter, its upper part lined with masonry and its lower part cut through layers of limestone. G. Ernest Wright reports that after cleaning out the well in 1935 its depth was *c.* 138 feet, with the water level in summertime standing 75–80 feet below the surface (*Shechem: The Biography of a Biblical City,* New York: McGraw-Hill, 1965, p. 216). It is described both as a well fed by a spring (Gr. *pēgē,* Jn 4:6) and as a cistern (Gr. *phrear,* Jn 4:11–12) because apparently it is also fed by surface water.

The site is now surrounded by an unfinished Greek Orthodox church, built over the crypt of a Crusader church which contains the well. In the 4th cen. A.D. a cruciform church had been erected here with the well in the center of the transept.

See Sychar.

J. R.

JADA (jā'dȧ). A Jerahmeelite, the son of Onam (I Chr 2:28, 32).

JADAU (jā'dô). A son of Nebo and one of those who was compelled by Ezra to give up his foreign wife (Ezr 10:43). The name appears in the RSV as Jaddai.

JADDUA (jăd'ū-ȧ)

1. One of the chiefs of the people who set their seal to the covenant of Nehemiah to keep the law (Neh 10:21).

2. The son of Jonathan and the last of the high priests named in the OT (Neh 12:11, 22). According to the Elephantine papyri, written in the last decade of the 5th cen. B.C., the high priest in 400 B.C. was Jonathan (Johanan), the father of Jaddua. Josephus says (*Ant.* xi. 8. 3–6) that Jaddua was high priest when Alexander the Great came to Jerusalem in 332 B.C. While this is possible if Jaddua lived to be nearly 100 years old, yet it may be a second priest of the same name.

JADON (jā'dŏn). A Meronothite who worked with Melatiah the Gibeonite and the men of Gibeon and of Mizpah in repairing the wall of Jerusalem during the time of Nehemiah (Neh 3:7).

JAEL (jā'ĕl). The wife of Heber the Kenite in the days of the judges (*see* Heber). The Kenites were Midianites of the family into which Moses had married. Hobab, Moses' brother-in-law, had come to the Promised Land with Israel, and his descendants still lived there.

In the battle between Hazor and the northern tribes, Heber the Kenite was not considered one of his Israelite enemies by Jabin, king of Hazor. Therefore Sisera, Jabin's general, fleeing from his disastrous defeat at the hands of Barak, felt safe in turning aside for rest and refuge at the tent of Heber. Jael, having welcomed and given refreshment to Sisera, stood guard at the door of the tent until the exhausted man fell asleep. Then she took a tent peg and hammer and with a few vigorous strokes killed the sleeping warrior. When the pursuing Israelites arrived, Jael led them to their fallen foe. She was honored, as Deborah had prophesied, as the true heroine of the battle (Jud 4:11–5:31).

P. C. J.

JAGUR (jā'gŭr). A town in the SE part of Judah, near the border of Edom (Josh 15:21). The site is unknown; however, it may be the same as Gur-Baal, modern Tell Ghurr, eight miles E of Beer-sheba.

JAH (jä). An abbreviated form of the sacred name Yahweh. It is found in poetry, as in Ps 68:4; 118:4, ASV marg., and in various other places where it is rendered LORD in the KJV. *See* God, Names of; Lord.

JAHATH (jā'hăth)

1. The son of Reaiah of the tribe of Judah and father of Ahumai and Lahad (I Chr 4:2).

2. The son of Libni of the Levitical family of Gershom (I Chr 6:20, 43). In the genealogy of I Chr 23:9–11, Jahath is said to be the son of Shimei, Gershom's second son, but the passage is obscure.

3. The son of Shelomoth of the Levitical family of Izhar, appointed by David for service in the temple (I Chr 24:22).

4. A Levite of the family of Merari who was appointed one of the overseers of repairs to the temple in the reform of Josiah (II Chr 34:12).

JAHAZ (jā'hăz). This name occurs also in several other forms: Jahaza (Josh 13:18); Jahazah

(Josh 21:36; Jer 48:21); Jahzah (I Chr 6:78).

Jahaz was a town in the plains of Moab, where Sihon, the Amorite king, was defeated by Israel (Num 21:23; Deut 2:32; Jud 11:20). It fell in Reuben's portion (Josh 13:18) and was assigned to the Merarite Levites (Josh 21:34, 36). The area in which Jahaz was located was later lost to Israel, but Omri reconquered the land as far as Jahaz. The Moabite Stone (lines 18–20) indicates that the town was finally taken by Mesha, king of Moab, and added to his domains. It was held by Moab in the time of Isaiah and Jeremiah (Isa 15:4; Jer 48:21, 34). Jahaz was probably N of the Arnon and not far S of Heshbron, but its location is uncertain.

JAHAZA. *See* Jahaz.

JAHAZIAH (jā'ȧ-zī'ȧ). A son of Tikvah and one of the four men mentioned in connection with the controversy over "strange" (foreign) wives (Ezr 10:15). The KJV regards Jahaziah and his companions as supporters of Ezra. The RSV regards the four men as opposed to Ezra's action. The Heb. (lit., "stood against this") would seem to support the RSV rendering.

JAHAZIEL (jȧ-hā'zĭ-ĕl)

1. One of the Benjamites, mighty warriors, who deserted Saul to join David at Ziklag (I Chr 12:4).
2. A priest appointed by David to blow the trumpet before the ark after it was brought to Jerusalem (I Chr 16:6).
3. The third named of the sons of Hebron the Levite, appointed by David to serve in the temple (I Chr 23:19; 24:23).
4. The son of Zechariah of the Levitical family of Asaph. The Spirit of the Lord inspired him to prophesy a great victory by God on behalf of Jehoshaphat (II Chr 20:14–17).
5. The father of Shechaniah, a chieftain who returned with Ezra with 300 men (Ezr 8:5).

JAHDAI (jä'dī). One of Caleb's wives, or (more likely) a descendant of Caleb whose six sons are listed in I Chr 2:47.

JAHDIEL (jä'dĭ-ĕl). A leading man in the half tribe of Manasseh E of Jordan (I Chr 5:24). He is spoken of as one of the "mighty men of valor" and the head of a household.

JAHDO (jä'dō). A member of the tribe of Gad and a son of Buz (I Chr 5:14).

JAHLEEL (jä'lē-ĕl), **JAHLEELITES** (jä'lē-ĕ-līts). The third son of Zebulun and the founder of a tribal family called the Jahleelites (Gen 46:14; Num 26:26).

JAHMAI (jä'mī). Listed as grandson of Issachar and son of Tola (I Chr 7:2).

JAHZAH. *See* Jahaz.

JAHZEEL (jä'zē-ĕl), **JAHZEELITES** (jä'zē-ĕ-līts). The firstborn son of Naphtali and founder of a tribal family (Gen 46:24; Num 26:48). In I Chr 7:13 he is called Jahziel.

JAHZERAH (jä'zĕ-rȧ). A priest of the family of Immer (I Chr 9:12), and an ancestor of a priest among the returned exiles. The name parallels Ahasai in Neh 11:13.

JAHZIEL. *See* Jahzeel.

Traditional site of the prison in which Paul was kept at Philippi. HFV

JAILOR. A guard of a prison or jail (Gr. *desmophylax*). It is used once in the NT in Acts 16:23 of the keeper of the jail in Philippi. The jailer was impressed by the songs of Paul and Silas as they ached from their beating in the stocks, and by their refusal to escape after an earthquake opened their stocks. Moreover, he was terror stricken at the obvious hand of God in the events of the night. The combined effect of apostolic testimony and divine intervention brought about his conversion and baptism. His baptism involved his whole household and occurred sometime after midnight (Acts 16:25–34).

JAIR (jä'ĭr)

1. The son of Segub who was of the tribe of Manasseh on his mother's side and of Judah on his father's. During the conquest of Palestine Gilead was given to Manasseh, and Jair won for himself a number of villages in the plateau of Argob which came to be known as Havvoth-jair, "villages of Jair" (Num 32:41; Deut 3:14; I Kgs 4:13; I Chr 2:22).
2. The Gileadite who was the eighth judge of Israel and a descendant of 1 above. Although he judged Israel 22 years, nothing is known of him except that he had 30 sons and the 30 cities of Havvoth-jair (Jud 10:3–5).
3. The son of Shimei and father of Mordecai, the guardian of Esther (Est 2:5).
4. The father of Elhanan who slew Lahmi, the brother of Goliath (I Chr 20:5).

JAIRITE. *See* Ira.

JAIRUS (jā-ī'rŭs). The name of a ruler of a synagogue (Mk 5:22; Lk 8:41), probably at Capernaum. His daughter was raised from the dead by Jesus.

JAKAN. *See* Jaakan.

JAKEH (jā'kĕ). The father of Agur, the author of the proverbs recorded in Prov 30:1 (see v. 1).

JAKIM (jā'kĭm)

1. A son of Shimhi, a Benjamite (I Chr 8:19).

2. A priest and a descendant of Aaron. His family was made the 12th of the 24 courses into which David divided the priests (I Chr 24:12).

JALON (jā'lŏn). A descendant of Caleb the spy and son of Ezra (I Chr 4:17). This Ezra is called Ezrah in the RSV.

JAMBRES (jăm'brēz). *See* Jannes and Jambres.

JAMES (jāmz). At least four persons mentioned in the NT bore this name (Gr. *Iakōbos,* from Heb. *ya'ăqōb,* Jacob, *q.v.*). Two were among the 12 apostles, one was a half-brother of Jesus, and one was the father of Judas, one of the Twelve. Probably James the leader of the church in Jerusalem and James the author of the epistle were one and the same and one of the above. James the Less (Mk 15:40) may or may not have been one of the above.

1. One of the sons of Zebedee (Mt 4:21; Mk 1:19; Lk 5:10) and Salome (cf. Mt 20:20; Mk 15:40; 16:1) and the elder brother of John the apostle (James is nearly always named first, e.g., Mk 5:37). *See* John the Apostle. He was a fisherman with his brother John, netting fish in the Sea of Galilee and using the boat of their father Zebedee (Mt 4:18-22; Mk 1:16-20). Since Zebedee had hired servants (Mk 1:20) and John was acquainted with the high priest in Jerusalem so that he could enter his house unchallenged on the night of Jesus' betrayal (Jn 18:16), many have concluded that Zebedee and his sons were prosperous with some degree of social standing. James became one of the "inner three," the specially favored disciples of Christ, apparently because they understood more fully the person and work of Jesus during His ministry (Mk 5:37; 9:2; 14:33; cf. 13:3; also Peter, James and John are named first among the Twelve, Mk 3:16-19). The epithet Boanerges (*q.v.*), meaning "sons of thunder" (Mk 3:17), evidently characterized James and John as impetuous and quick to take offense (Lk 9:54-55) and to offend the other disciples by wanting the chief positions in Jesus' kingdom (Mk 10:35-41). James was the first of the apostles to suffer martyrdom, executed at the order of Herod Agrippa I *c.* A.D. 44 (Acts 12:1-2). James thus figuratively drank the cup of suffering that he and John had rashly declared they were able to drink (Mk 10:38-39).

Traditional tomb of St. James (center foreground) in the Kidron Valley, Jerusalem

2. The son of Alphaeus, one of the Twelve (Mt 10:3; Mk 3:18; Lk 6:15; Acts 1:13). Nothing else certain is known of him. Levi (Matthew) was also the son of an Alphaeus (Mk 2:14), so that James and Matthew may have been brothers.

3. The author of the epistle of James identifies himself only as "James, a servant of God and of the Lord Jesus Christ" (Jas 1:1). He could not have been the son of Zebedee and brother of John (Mt 4:21; 10:2) because that James was martyred before the epistle was written (Acts 12:2). This leaves the James who presided over the Jerusalem church as the undoubted author (Acts 15:13).

The fact that he is called "James the Lord's brother" (Gal 1:19) makes untenable the view that he was James the son of Alphaeus (Mt 10:3). Ps 69:8 makes it clear that Jesus' mother had other children, one of whom was named James (Mt 13:55; Mk 6:3).

Biographical items regarding James abound in the NT, although there are none in the epistle itself. It is assumed from I Cor 9:5 that he was a married man. He was not one of the Twelve (Mt 10:2-4). Not at first a believer (Jn 7:5), he later was probably included as one of Jesus' brothers with those who awaited Pentecost in the upper room (Acts 1:13-14). (This latter passage distinguishes between the brother of Jesus and the two apostles, James and James the son of Alphaeus.) The risen Saviour appeared to him personally after first appearing to the Twelve (I Cor 15:5, 7).

In his capacity as leader of the Jerusalem council of apostles and elders, James announced his authoritative judgment when the discussion had ended (Acts 15:13, 19). There is an undesigned coincidence in the fact that when James' decision was sent by letter from the council, he used a Gr. word rendered "greeting" in the salutation (Acts 15:23) which appears in the address of only one NT epistle, in the salutation of James 1:1.

Peter, after being miraculously released from prison, instructed the household of John Mark to report the event to James (Acts 12:17). Paul recognized "James, Cephas, and John" as pillars of the church at Jerusalem (Gal 2:9). Obviously James was the leader, for representatives who came from that church to Antioch were said to have come from James (Gal 2:12). In Acts 21:18-19 Paul reported to James the things God had wrought among the Gentiles during his third missionary journey.

Tradition describes James as very zealous for the law, combining OT righteousness with evangelical faith. He is said to have abstained from strong drink and to have refrained from cutting his hair, like a Nazarite (*q.v.*). A man of great virtue, he was called "James the Just." Because he spent so much time in prayer, he was described as having knees "hard skinned like a camel's." His epistle reveals that he spoke with an air of patriarchal authority, for its pages glow with stern and severe utterances and the fervency of his spirit. *See* James, Epistle of.

The death of James is mentioned by Josephus (*Ant.* xx. 9.1), and described by Hegesippus (Eusebius II.23), a Jewish Christian who wrote in the middle of the 2nd cen. Some time before the destruction of Jerusalem in A.D. 70, the Pharisees had him thrown down from the temple, stoned, and then beaten with a club for having faithfully witnessed to his Saviour. He is said to have died praying, "Father forgive them, for they know not what they do."

4. The father (not the "brother" as in KJV) of Judas (not Iscariot), one of the Twelve (Lk 6:16, NASB).

5. James the Less (Mk 15:40), less in stature or in age, is said to be the son of a certain Mary (*see* Mary 3) and brother of Joses or Joseph (also Mt 27:56; Lk 24:10). James the brother of our Lord also had a brother named Joses or Joseph (Mk 6:3; Mt 13:55), so that this James may be the same as 3. But it would seem strange for Mary the mother of Jesus to be identified only as the mother of James and Joses when standing near the cross, especially when Christ spoke directly to her and asked the beloved disciple to care for her (Jn 19:25-27). Some have identified James the Less with James the son of Alphaeus 2; however, there is no proof for this.

S. M. C.

JAMES, EPISTLE OF. This oldest of NT epistles is first among the General Epistles, as Eusebius termed James and Jude in the 4th cen., possibly because of their general content or readership.

Author. The writer of this epistle is generally considered to be James the brother of our Lord (*see* James 3). Since James is Jacob in the original, this may be called the Epistle of Jacob to the Twelve Tribes (1:1).

Theme. The book treats of faith demonstrated, tested, and perfected by works. This has been called the epistle of holy living, of practical Christianity, of Christian ethics, Christianity in coveralls.

Style. The style is terse, vivid, abounding in aphorisms, antithetic. Since many thoughts are grouped together in short proverbial expressions, this epistle is regarded as the Proverbs of the NT. James' imagery is drawn from nature, in contrast with Paul's which is drawn from the activities of men. Some of the terms used aptly describe the country where the author lived: near the sea (1:6), with salt springs (3:12); a place of olives, vines, and figs (3:12), burning sun and drought (1:11); early and latter rain (5:7); a place of synagogues (2:2). There is an unusual double use of words (cf. patience, perfect, 1:3-4), and a contrasting of positive and negative statements (cf. "perfect and entire, wanting nothing," 1:4).

Characteristics. James begins and ends abruptly, lacks the autobiographical data of Paul, contains more references to nature than all Paul's epistles, and more parallels to Christ's discourses than any other part of the NT. For striking similarities to the Sermon on the Mount, cf. Mt 5:34-37; 6:19; 7:1 with Jas 5:12; 5:2; 4:11-12. James is closer in style to Peter than to Paul. For similarities to I Peter cf. I Pet 1:7; 1:24; 1:23; 2:11; 5:5-6 with Jas 1:3, 11, 18; 4:1; 4:6-10.

James contains no apostolic benediction, perhaps because it sternly condemns non-Christians among its readers (4:4; 5:1-6). Although it has been criticized because it lacks such NT words as gospel, redemption, incarnation, resurrection, ascension, it does speak of the Lord Jesus Christ (1:1; 2:1), the new birth (1:18), faith (2:14-26), and the return of the Lord (5:7-8). Clearly addressed to the Jews (1:1; 2:1, 21) and reminding the reader of Matthew, the "Jewish" Gospel, James is sometimes called "Jewish," but it reveals a noticeable absence of the Jewish elements which were done away in Christ: sacrifices, circumcision, priesthood, feast days, the sabbath. In contrast, it speaks of teachers and elders in the church (3:1; 5:14).

Outline. An outline is difficult to construct because of an apparent lack of logical order. Nevertheless, a structure is clearly evident.

1. Believers and Outward Circumstances, 1:1-12
2. Believers and Inward Desire, 1:13-16
3. Believers and the Word of God, 1:17-27
4. Believers and Their Neighbors, 2:1-13
5. The Believer's Faith and Works, 2:14-26
6. The Believer's Tongue, 3:1-12
7. Heavenly Wisdom, 3:13-18
8. World, Flesh, and Devil, 4:1-7
9. God and His Law, 4:8-17
10. The Last Days, 5:1-9
11. Patience and Prayer in Trials, 5:10-20

James begins and ends with a discussion of testings, patience, the prayer of faith. Certain words occur at approximately the same distance from each end of the epistle (cf. Scripture, rich, adultery, tongue). The heart of James is the remarkable statement in 3:2 that a perfect man is one who can control his tongue. Just as an old family doctor diagnoses a disease by having his patient stick out his tongue, James diagnoses spiritual disease by examining the tongue and its manifestations. This is the most prominent theme of the epistle.

Prominent teachings. Prayer: for wisdom (1:5-7), unanswered (4:2-3), of faith (5:13-18). The Word: begotten by (1:18), receiving (1:21), obeying (1:25). Three tests of religion: self-control, love, purity (1:26-27). Trials bring perfection now (1:1-4), the crown of life later (1:12). How to make the devil flee, and bring God near (4:7-8). A definition of sin (4:17).

The charge that Jas 2:24 contradicts Rom 3:28 falls before the fact that James refers to justification before men (2:18), while Paul refers to justification before God (Rom 4:2). James deprecates only that faith which a man may *say* he has, while lacking works to demonstrate its genuineness (2:20).

Bibliography. F. J. A. Hort, *The Epistle of St. James 1:1-4:7,* London: Macmillan, 1909. Richard J. Knowling, *The Epistle of St. James,* WC, 2nd ed., London: Methuen, 1910. Joseph B. Mayor, *The Epistle of St. James,* 3rd ed., London: Macmillan, 1913. C. L. Mitton, *The Epistle of James,* Grand Rapids: Eerdmans, 1966. James H. Ropes, *The Epistle of James,* ICC, New York: Scribner's, 1916. Alexander Ross, *The Epistles of James and John,* NIC, Grand Rapids: Eerdmans, 1954. M. H. Shepherd, Jr., "The Epistle of James and the Gospel of Matthew," JBL, LXXV (1956), 40-51. R. V. G. Tasker, *The General Epistle of James,* TNTC, Grand Rapids: Eerdmans, 1956.

S. M. C.

JAMIN (jā'mĭn)

1. A son of Simeon, the second son of Jacob (Gen 46:10; Ex 6:15; I Chr 4:24). He was the founder of a tribal family called the Jaminites (Num 26:12).

2. A member of the tribe of Judah and of the family of Jerahmeel (I Chr 2:27).

3. One of the Levites who, under the supervision of Ezra, read the law to the people and helped them to understand it (Neh 8:7).

JAMLECH (jăm'lĕk). A descendant of Simeon and a prince among his people (I Chr 4:34, 38).

JANGLING. The word is used in I Tim 1:6 in the expression "vain jangling" (cf. Tit 1:10). The RSV has "vain discussion." A good translation of the word would be "chatter." Evidently it means proud, self-conceited talking against what God has revealed and against God Himself.

JANNA (jăn'*ȧ*). An ancestor of Jesus (Lk 3:24). Spelled Jannai in RSV and NASB.

JANNES AND JAMBRES (jăn'ēz, jăm'brēz). These are given by Paul as the names of the two Egyptian magicians who withstood Moses (II Tim 3:8). The reference is to the incidents described in Ex 7:11-12, 22; 8:7, 18-19; 9:11, where, however, the names of the magicians are not given nor their number. These two names appear in various forms in the Talmud, Targums, and rabbinic writings. Since in II Timothy and in the literature of the Qumran community they are referred to as familiarly known, it would seem that some Jewish apocryphon concerned with their story was in circulation in the 1st cen. B.C. This, or a Christian version of it, was known in the early Christian centuries. Certain references in Origen and the Decree of Gelasius point to the existence of a non-canonical writing describing and condemning their activities. Christian tradition is largely dependent on II Timothy, and has used them as figures symbolic of Satanic arts and opposition to truth.

J. A. R.

JANOAH (j*ȧ*-nō'*ȧ*). Variant of Janohah (*q.v.*).

A town in the northern part of Naphtali near Kedesh. It was captured by Tiglath-pileser III of Assyria in the days of Pekah, king of Israel (II Kgs 15:29). The site is uncertain.

JANOHAH (j*ȧ*-nō'h*ȧ*). A border town in Ephraim (Josh 16:6-7). It is to be identified with Khirbet Yanun, about seven miles SE of Shechem.

JANUM (jā'nŭm). A town in the hill country district of Hebron, near Beth-tappuah (Josh 15:53). It is possibly to be identified with modern Beni Na'im.

JAPHETH (jā'fĕth). The third son of Noah (Gen 10:1), father of some 14 nations forming the Indo-Germanic family, originally inhabiting the Caucasus, thence spreading E and W. His descendants erected the civilizations of the Medes and Persians, produced the Ionians of western Asia Minor, Cappadocians (including the Hittites), Cimmerians, Scythians, and the island kingdoms of the Aegean. At the time of the Flood he was married but had no children.

When his father Noah became drunken, Japheth acted to protect him. For this he was blessed by his father, under the figure of "dwelling in the tents of Shem," i.e., to find protection and deliverance (Gen 9:27). The blessing of Noah included the following points: the gospel, revealed and developed in the Jewish world, was written in Gr. and preached to the Gentiles by Paul, the Semite. The gospel went first to Asia Minor and then to Macedonia (cf. Acts 16:9), Greece, and finally Rome, and thence over all the western world, bringing myriads of Japhetic peoples into the "tents of

Shem." As was the curse of Ham, so the blessing of Japheth was essentially religious.

H. G. S.

JAPHIA (ja-fī'a)

1. The Amorite king of Lachish who joined with four other kings to oppose Joshua. They were completely routed at the battle of Gibeon and slain after they tried to hide in the cave of Makkedah (Josh 10).

2. A town on the SE border of the territory of Zebulun. It has been located as modern Yafa, a mile and a half SW of Nazareth (Josh 19:12).

3. One of the sons of David born to him in Jerusalem; his mother's name is not given (II Sam 5:15; I Chr 3:7; 14:6).

JAPHLET (jăf'lĕt). A member of the tribe of Asher and of the family of Heber (I Chr 7:32-33).

JAPHLETI (jăf'lē-tī). The descendants of a certain Japhlet, apparently not the same as the Asherite of that name. The area of the Japhleti is mentioned in stating the boundaries of the children of Joseph. The Japhletites lived in an area E of Gezer (Josh 16:3).

JAPHO (jā'fō). The KJV for Joppa in Josh 19:46. Belonging to the Philistines, it was located on the coast of the Mediterranean Sea, and bordered on the territory of the Danites. *See* Joppa.

JARAH (jâr'a). A descendant of King Saul through Jonathan (I Chr 9:42). Instead of this name, I Chr 8:36 has Jehoadah (*q.v.*).

JAREB (jâr'ĭb). The name or epithet of an Assyrian king who received tribute from Israel (Hos 5:13; 10:6). It is not safe to be dogmatic about the text and meaning. But if we adhere to the current text, we must regard Jareb as a nickname coined by Hosea to indicate the love of conflict which characterized the Assyrian king. Thus "King Jareb" is equivalent to "King Warrior" or "King Striver." The RSV rendering is "great king." Linguistic and present historical evidence is against the idea that Jareb is the proper name of an Assyrian monarch.

JARED (jâr'ĭd). An antediluvian patriarch of the line of Seth. He was the son of Mahalaleel and the father of Enoch (Gen 5:15-20; Lk 3:37). In I Chr 1:2 his name appears as Jered.

JARESIAH (jăr'ē-sī'a). A son of Jeroham and a Benjamite chief who dwelt in Jerusalem (I Chr 8:27). The name is spelled Jaareshiah in the RSV.

JARHA (jär'ha). An Egyptian slave to whom his master Sheshan of Judah, not having a living son, gave his daughter as a wife (I Chr 2:34-35; cf. v. 31). Sheshan may first have legally adopted Jarha in light of customs revealed in tablets from Nuzu (*q.v.*).

JARIB (jâr'ĭb)

1. A son of Simeon and the founder of a tribal family (I Chr 4:24). He is called Jachin (*q.v.*) in Gen 46:10; Ex 6:15; Num 26:12.

2. One of the leading men who helped Ezra in securing temple servants before the return to Palestine (Ezr 8:16).

3. A priest who had married a foreign wife and who was compelled by Ezra to give her up (Ezr 10:18).

JARMUTH (jär'mŭth)

1. A city of the Canaanites in the Shephelah whose king was defeated, captured, and slain by Joshua (Josh 10:3, 5, 23; 12:11). After its capture it was assigned to Judah (Josh 15:35) and was inhabited after the captivity (Neh 11:29). It is identified with modern Khirbet Yarmuk, about eight miles N of Beit Jibrin and about 18 miles SW of Jerusalem.

2. A town in Issachar allotted to the Gershonite Levites (Josh 21:29). It corresponds to Ramoth (I Chr 6:73) and Remeth (Josh 19:21). The site is unknown.

JAROAH (ja-rō'a). A descendant of Gad through Buz (I Chr 5:14).

JASHAR, BOOK OF (jā'shar), KJV, Jasher. The Book of Jashar (lit., "Book of the Righteous One") belongs to an ancient collection of national songs, now lost, from which the biblical writers draw some of their material (*see also* Wars of the Lord, Book of). There are two acknowledged quotes from Jashar in the Bible: Josh 10:12-13 (the event of the sun and moon standing still at Gibeon) and II Sam 1:17-27 (David's lament over Saul). A third conjectured extract appears in I Kgs 8:12-13. Other passages may be Ex 15:1 ff.; Num 21:17 f.; Num 21:27-30. The material in this book, if the dating is correct, is quite ancient. As a collection, however, it probably dates to the period 1000-800 B.C. Another view relates the Book of Jashar to the E Mediterranean Heroic Age (15th-10th cen. B.C.), its songs being used as a part of military training. II Sam 1:18 should then read, "He instructed them to train the Judeans in bowmanship, the training-poem for which is written in the Book of Jashar" (R. K. Harrison, IOT, Grand Rapids: Eerdmans, 1969, p. 670).

R. A. M.

JASHEN (jā'shēn). The father of one of David's "mighty men" (II Sam 23:32). In the parallel list in I Chr 11:34 he appears as Hashem the Gizonite. *See* Hashem.

JASHOBEAM (jȧ-shō'bē-ȧm)

1. The son of Zabdiel the Hachmonite, chief of the 30 mighty men of David. He was renowned as a great warrior who had fought with his spear against 300 at one time and had slain them (I Chr 11:11). He may also have been one of the three nameless heroes who broke through the enemy lines at Bethlehem in order to bring David a drink of water from the city well (I Chr 11:15–19). When as king David organized his army, Jashobeam was chief of the army unit of 24,000 men on duty for the first month (I Chr 27:2–3).

The Heb. of the parallel text in II Sam 23:8 is very obscure but it seems to refer to the same man. The RSV translates it "Josheb-basshebeth a Tahchemonite" who slew "eight hundred." Scribal errors in transmission have confused the text. Some MSS of the LXX at I Chr 11:11 give his name as Ishbaal, which possibly was the original form. *See also* Hachmoni; Josheb-Basshebeth.

2. A warrior who joined David at Ziklag; from the Levitical family of Korah (I Chr 12:6), residing in Benjamite territory (v. 2). Perhaps he is the same as 1 above.

P. C. J.

JASHUB (jā'shŭb)

1. One of the four sons of Issachar and the founder of a tribal family called Jashubites (Num 26:24; I Chr 7:1). He is called Job in Gen 46:13.

2. A son of Bani, who, after his return from Exile, was persuaded by Ezra to divorce his foreign wife (Ezr 10:29).

3. In Isa 7:3 it is part of the name Shear-jashub.

JASHUBI-LEHEM (jȧ-shōō'bī-lē'hĕm). A member of the family of Shelah and of the tribe of Judah (I Chr 4:22). The RSV rendering is "returned to Lehem."

JASIEL. *See* Jaasiel.

JASON (jā'sŏn). A resident of Thessalonica who entertained Paul and Silas. As a consequence the citizens mobbed his house and cast him in prison when they did not find his guests. Jason was released on security (Acts 17:5–9).

The Jason who sent greetings in Rom 16:21 was a kinsman or fellow countryman of Paul, i.e., a Jew. If the same individual as in Acts 17:5–9, Jason had by then moved to Corinth.

JASPER. *See* Jewels.

JATHNIEL (jăth'nī-ĕl). The fourth son of Meshelemiah of the house of Korah (I Chr 26:2). He was a gatekeeper at the temple.

JATTIR (jăt'ĕr). A Levitical city in the southern mountains of Judah (Josh 15:48; 21:14; I Chr 6:57). It was one of the cities which shared in David's spoil from Ziklag (I Sam 30:27). The site is identified as Khirbet 'Attir, about 13 miles SSW of Hebron.

JAVAN (jā'vȧn; Heb. *yāwān*). This name refers to one of Japheth's descendants (Gen 10:2; I Chr 1:5) from whom "the coastland peoples spread" (Gen 10:5, RSV) NW from Upper Mesopotamia and Syria (*see* Nations). Heb. *yāwān* appears as *yamānu* in the cuneiform inscriptions of Sargon II of Assyria and of Darius I of Persia, and is doubtless related to the *Iaonēs* (Ionians) of Homer's *Iliad* (xiii.685). The Ionians are referred to in Egyptian records from the time of Rameses II (*c.* 1300 B.C.). The connection of Javan (approximately Greece) with slave trade (cf. Ezk 27:13; Joel 3:6) is perhaps illustrated by a S Arabic inscription which notes *Ywnm* as one of the countries from which female temple attendants were secured (cf. ANET², p. 508). Javan (KJV, Grecia) was one of the four great empires of Daniel (Dan 8:21; 10:20; 11:2) and would one day receive a declaration of God's glory (Isa 66:19; cf. also Zech 9:13, KJV, Greece).

In Ezk 27:19, LXX reads *yyn* ("wine") for *ywn* ("Greece"; cf. v. 18 and RSV in *loc. cit.*).

R. Y.

JAVELIN. *See* Armor.

JAW. Three Heb. words are used in connection with the English word "jaw": (1) *l^eḥî*, meaning "cheek" or "cheekbone" (Jud 15:15–17, 19; Job 41:2; Isa 30:28; Ezk 29:4; 38:4; Hos 11:4); (2) *malqôaḥ*, meaning "jaw" (Ps 22:15); (3) *m^etall^e'ôt*, meaning "jaw teeth" (Job 29:17; Prov 30:14).

Jaw is used figuratively: (1) of the power of the wicked with reference to divine constraint and discipline (Job 29:17; Prov 30:14; Isa 30:28; Ezk 29:4; 38:4); (2) of human labor and trials eased by divine gentleness (Hos 11:4).

JAZER. *See* Jaazer.

JAZIZ (jā'zĭz). A Hagerite who was a royal steward and in charge of David's flocks (I Chr 27:31).

JEALOUSY. In the OT the Heb. word *qin'â* has the basic idea of deep emotional ardor. It may be the ardor (1) of jealousy (Num 5:14; Song 8:6), (2) of zeal (Num 25:11; Isa 42:13; 63:15), or (3) of anger (Ezk 35:11; 36:6). God's jealousy is that of a lover who demands the exclusive attention, worship and faithfulness of His people (Ex 34:14; Num 25:11; Deut 32:16, 21; Joel 2:18; Zech 1:14; 8:2).

In the NT the basic Gr. word is *zēlos* which may be used in the good sense of zeal (II Cor 7:11; 9:2; 11:2) or a bad sense of jealousy (RSV, Rom 13:13; I Cor 3:3). A synonym *phthonos* is always employed in the evil sense of envy (Mt 27:18; Phil 1:15). *See* Envy; Zeal.

JEALOUSY, IMAGE OF. An image mentioned in Ezk 8:3, 5. The reference may be to a "figured slab," containing cultic and mythological scenes of the type found in northern Syria, Asia Minor, and northern Mesopotamia. On the other hand, the reference could be to Tammuz (v. 14). Jealousy was not the name of the idol, but it was probably called "image of jealousy" because in a special way this particular image seems to have been drawing the people from the worship of God and therefore provoking Him to jealousy.

JEALOUSY OFFERING. The basis for this offering is to be found in Num 5:11–31. If a man had reason to suspect his wife of unfaithfulness or if a "spirit of jealousy" came upon him, a provision was made for a trial by ordeal. The man was to bring his wife to the priest along with a prescribed offering consisting of a tenth part of an ephah of barley. No oil or frankincense was to be placed upon it, thus symbolizing that the occasion was not a happy one. The object of the offering was to draw God's attention to the alleged crime so that He might render a right decision.

The woman, with hair down and the offering in her hand, was "brought before the Lord," whereupon she took an oath calling for punishment if guilty. She drank the "water of bitterness" consisting of water from an earthen vessel to which had been added dust from the temple floor and ashes from a part of the barley which had been burned. The words of the curse were written down and washed off into the water. The woman then drank the water of bitterness. If no ill effect came upon her, she was judged to be guiltless. No penalty was prescribed for a man who falsely accused his wife.

R. O. C.

JEALOUSY, WATERS OF. *See* Jealousy Offering.

JEARIM (jē'*à*-rĭm). A mountain on the northern border of Judah, and identified with Chesalon (Josh 15:10) near Kirjath-jearim. It is modern Kesla.

JEATERAI (jē-ăt'ē-rī). A descendant of Gershon, son of Levi (I Chr 6:21). In v. 41 he is called Ethni.

JEBERECHIAH (jē-bĕr'ĕ-kī'*à*). The father of Zechariah, a trusted friend of Isaiah, who lived in the time of King Ahaz (Isa 8:2).

JEBUS (jē'bŭs), **JEBUSITES** (jĕb'yŭ-sīts). Jebus refers in the OT to a name for pre-Davidic Jerusalem (Josh 15:8; 18:28; Jud 19:10; I Chr 11:4), derived from the clan name of its inhabitants who occupied the site during most of the 2nd mil. B.C. (although "Jebusite" is used also of their descendants in later times; cf. I Kgs 9:20–21; II Chr 8:7–8; Ezr 9:1).

The inhabitants of Jebus were classified as Canaanites (Gen 10:15–16; I Chr 1:13–14), but only in a geographical sense (contrast Jos *Ant.* vii.3.1), for they are elsewhere carefully distinguished from ethnic Canaanites (e.g., Gen 15:21; Ex 3:8, 17). Its ruler Adonizedek is listed as one of the five Amorite kings in league against Joshua (Josh 10:5). Melchizedek in Gen 14:18 was also an Amorite name (*Malki-ṣaduqa*). The only purely Jebusite name or title in the OT is the non-Semitic Araunah (Ornan; cf. II Sam 24:16, 18; I Chr 21:15, 18, 28; II Chr 3:1). Scholars believe Araunah is a Hurrian or Hittite title meaning "lord" or "noble." The prince of Jerusalem mentioned in the Amarna letters (*c.* 1375 B.C.) likewise had a non-Semitic Hittite name ('Abdu-Heba, ANET, pp. 487ff.). These details concur with God's statement to Jerusalem that her aboriginal population had consisted of Amorites and Hittites (Ezk 16:3, 45).

Jebus was located in the hill country (Josh 11:3) between the Kidron and Tyropoeon valleys on a long narrow spur (cf. Josh 15:8; 18:16) that extends S from the later temple area and is naturally fortified by steep descents on all sides but the N. Situated on the border between Judah and Benjamin, Jebus defended itself successfully against both tribes during the conquest period and thereafter (Josh 15:63; Jud 1:21). In spite of its vaunted strength, however, it finally succumbed to David (II Sam 5:6–9; I Chr 11:4–8) and became the capital city of his kingdom. David was lenient with the Jebusites, but Solomon subjected them to bond service (I Kgs 9:20–22). They seem ultimately to have been absorbed into the Israelite population.

R. Y. and J. R.

JECAMIAH (jĕk'*à*-mī'*à*). The fifth son of King Jeconiah, a descendant of Solomon (I Chr 3:10–18). *See* Jekamiah.

JECHOLIAH (jĕk-ō-lī'*à*). Wife of King Amaziah and mother of Azariah (Uzziah), king of Judah (II Kgs 15:1–2). In II Chr 26:3 her name is given as Jecoliah.

JECHONIAS (jĕk'ō-nī'*à*s). Jechonias is the Gr. form of Jeconiah (*q.v.*). It is found in Mt 1:11–12.

JECOLIAH. *See* Jecholiah.

JECONIAH (jĕk'ō-nī'*à*). An altered form of Jehoiachin (*q.v.*). The name is also contracted to Coniah. Jeconiah is found in I Chr 3:16–17; Est 2:6; Jer 24:1; 27:20; 28:4; 29:2.

JEDAIAH (jē-dā'y*à*)

1. The son of Shimri and father of Allon, he is listed in the genealogy of the Simeonites who settled in the valley of Gedor in Hezekiah's time (I Chr 4:37).

2. The son of Harumaph; one of those who labored with Nehemiah in rebuilding the wall of Jerusalem (Neh 3:10).

3. A priest in the time of David, the head of the second of the 24 priestly courses (I Chr 24:7).

4. The name of a priest who returned from Exile with Zerubbabel and whose descendants are mentioned down to the time of Joiakim. It is difficult to tell whether this is one or several priests with the same name (I Chr 9:10; Ezr 2:36; Neh 7:39; 11:10; 12:6, 19).

5. Another priest after the Exile. He appears in the same list as 4, but as a distinct person (Neh 12:7, 21).

6. One of the exiles taken by Zechariah as witness to the symbolic crowning of Joshua. He may be the same as 4 or 5 (Zech 6:10–14).

P. C. J.

JEDIAEL (jē-dī'ĕl)

1. One of the three sons of Benjamin. He was the ancestor of a great family, renowned as warriors and numbering 17,200 men "ready for service in war" in David's time (I Chr 7:6, 10–11, RSV).

2. The son of Shimri, he is listed as one of David's mighty men (I Chr 11:45).

3. One of the men of the tribe of Manasseh who deserted Saul and joined David at Ziklag. He may be the same as 2 (I Chr 12:20).

4. The son of Meshelemiah of the Levitical family of Korah who was appointed a doorkeeper of the temple by David (I Chr 26:2).

JEDIDAH (jē-dī'dȧ). The mother of King Josiah of the southern kingdom of Judah. She was the daughter of Adaiah of Bozcath (II Kgs 22:1).

JEDIDIAH (jĕd'ĭ-dī'ȧ). David named his second child by Bathsheba Solomon; but Nathan the prophet received word from God that the child was to be named Jedidiah, meaning "Jehovah is a friend" or "beloved of Jehovah," perhaps to indicate divine forgiveness (II Sam 12:24–25).

JEDUTHUN (jē-dū'thŭn). A Levite who was one of the great musicians of Israel. He was appointed by David along with Asaph and Heman to take charge of the temple music, and he continued to serve in the days of Solomon. Jeduthun's six sons and descendants are mentioned, some as continuing the musical heritage and others as serving the Lord in other capacities (I Chr 16:38, 41–42; 25:1, 3, 6; II Chr 5:12). Jeduthun's descendants are mentioned as active in the reformation of Hezekiah (II Chr 29:14). In the days of Josiah the liturgy of the temple arranged by the three great musicians was still being observed (II Chr 35:15). Descendants of Jeduthun ministered once more after the return from Exile (I Chr 9:16; Neh 11:17). The editorial notations to Ps 39, 62, and 77 relate them to Jeduthun.

JEEZER (jē-ē'zer), **JEEZERITES** (jē-ē'ze-rīts). The name seems to be a contracted form of Abiezer (*q.v.*; Josh 17:2). It is the name of a clan of Gilead (Num 26:30) and is called Iezer in the RSV.

JEGAR-SAHADUTHA (jē'gȧr-sā'ȧ-dū'thȧ). The word means "heap of witness" or "mound of witness," and refers to the stones raised by Laban and Jacob to be a sign of their covenant (Gen 31:47). Laban called it Jegar-sahadutha, while Jacob referred to it as Galeed. Laban's designation is Aramaic and Jacob's Hebrew. Both terms have the same meaning.

JEHALELEEL (jē-hȧ-lē'lē-ĕl). A more correct form of Jehallelel (RSV). The word means "he shall praise God."

1. The name of a Judahite (I Chr 4:16).

2. A Levite, a descendant of Merari (II Chr 29:12; "Jehalelel" in KJV).

JEHALELEL. *See* Jehaleleel.

JEHDEIAH (jē-dē'yȧ)

1. A descendant of Moses in the time of David. He was the son of Shubael (I Chr 24:20; cf. 23:16).

2. Jehdeiah the Meronothite who had charge of David's asses (I Chr 27:30).

JEHEZEKEL (jē-hĕz'ĕ-kĕl). A priest in David's time who was made 20th in course of service (I Chr 24:16).

JEHIAH (jē-hī'ȧ). One of the two gatekeepers for the ark when it was brought to Jerusalem by David (I Chr 15:24).

JEHIEL (jē-hī'ĕl)

1. The "father" or founder of Gibeon, husband of Maacah and father of a number of sons (I Chr 9:35), including Kish, the father of King Saul (vv. 36, 39).

2. The son of Hotham the Aroerite. With his brother Shama, Jehiel was one of David's mighty men (I Chr 11:44).

3. A Levite musician who was appointed with others to play music before the ark as it was brought by David to Jerusalem (I Chr 15:18, 20). Afterward he was appointed to the permanent ministry of music in the sanctuary (I Chr 16:5).

4. A Levite, son of the Gershonite Laadan. He was in charge of the treasury of the temple, an office that seems to have continued with the family (I Chr 23:8; 29:8). Also spelled Jehieli (*q.v.*) in I Chr 26:20–22.

5. The son of Hachmoni, who with Jonathan, David's uncle, "a counselor . . . and a scribe," was appointed to "attend" the king's sons, probably as a tutor (I Chr 27:32).

6. The son of Jehoshaphat. He and five brothers were slain by Jehoram when he became king (II Chr 21:2–4).

7. A Levite of the family of Heman, he dedicated himself with others for the cleansing of the temple in the time of Hezekiah (II Chr 29:14ff.). He may be the same Levite who was assigned to oversee the reception and distribution of the sacred offerings (II Chr 31:13ff.).

8. One of the chief officers (RSV) or rulers

(KJV) of the temple who contributed many sacrifices for the great Passover service of Josiah (II Chr 35:8).

9. The father of Obadiah, who with 218 of the family of Joab returned from the Exile with Ezra (Ezr 8:9).

10. One of the sons of Elam, the father of Shechaniah, who proposed that the Gentile wives who had drawn the Jews away from God be put away (Ezr 10:2). Jehiel himself was one who put away his wife (Ezr 10:26).

11. A priest of the sons of Harim who put away his Gentile wife (Ezr 10:21).

P. C. J.

JEHIELI (jē-hī'ĕ-lī). A son of Laadan the Gershonite whose two sons were in charge of the treasury (I Chr 26:22). *See* Jehiel 4.

JEHIZKIAH (jē'hĭz-kī'ȧ). An Ephraimite in the days of Ahaz who opposed making slaves of captives from Judah, declaring that God's judgment would be upon the northern kingdom if they proceeded to do so (II Chr 28:12–13).

JEHOADAH (jē-hō'ȧ-dȧ). The son of Ahaz, a descendant of Saul through Jonathan (I Chr 8:36). The same person is referred to in I Chr 9:42 as Jarah (*q.v.*).

JEHOADDAN (jē-hō'ȧ-dȧn). The wife of Joash and the mother of Amaziah, both kings of Judah (II Chr 25:1; II Kgs 14:1–2).

JEHOAHAZ (jē-hō'ȧ-hăz)

1. In contracted form, Joahaz, or Ahaziah (*q.v.*), youngest son of Jehoram, king of Judah (II Chr 21:17).

2. King of Israel, son of Jehu, who reigned in Samaria for 17 years (II Kgs 13:1–9). He was subject to Hazael, king of Syria, throughout his rule. He followed the religious practices of Jeroboam I.

3. King of Judah, son of Josiah. Although he was not the eldest, he was chosen by the people (II Kgs 23:30–31). He ruled under the tragic circumstances of the death of Josiah, which ended the hope of a great empire under the Davidic line. After only three months he was deposed by Pharaoh-Necho and taken to Egypt in chains (II Kgs 23:32–33; Jer 22:10). The people mourned his death, the first king of Judah to die in exile.

JEHOASH (jē-hō'ăsh). Alternate form of Joash.

1. The son of Ahaziah, king of Judah (II Kgs 11–12). *See* Joash 3.

2. The son of Jehoahaz and father of Jeroboam II, kings of Israel (II Kgs 13:9–14:16). *See* Joash 4.

JEHOHANAN (jē'hō-hā'nȧn)

1. The sixth son of Meshelemiah, a Levite, in the days of David. He was appointed to the office of porter or doorkeeper in the temple (I Chr 26:3).

2. One of the chief generals of the army of Judah in the days of Jehoshaphat. He commanded a corps of 280,000 (II Chr 17:15). It was probably his son, another soldier, who supported Jehoiada in overthrowing the wicked Athaliah and placing the boy Joash on the throne (II Chr 23:1).

3. An Israelite in the days of Ezra who had married a Gentile wife and put her away in the time of reformation (Ezr 10:28).

4. A priest of the family of Amariah in the days of Jehoiakim. Amariah had returned from Exile with Zerubbabel (Neh 12:13).

5. A priest in the days of Nehemiah, he is listed with those who took part in the dedication of the completed wall of Jerusalem (Neh 12:42; perhaps the same as 4).

P. C. J.

JEHOIACHIN (jē-hoi'ȧ-kĭn). Also called Jeconiah (I Chr 3:16–17; Est 2:6; Jer 24:1; 27:20; 28:4; 29:2) and Coniah (Jer 22:24, 28; 37:1). Mt 1:11–12 uses the Gr. form Jechonias.

Son of Jehoiakim, Jehoiachin became king of Judah in December, 598 B.C. He was 18 years old (the "eight years old" of II Chr 36:9 is considered a scribal error) when he began his reign, which lasted three months and ten days (II Kgs 24:8). He came on the throne when Judah was suffering from raids by neighboring people which had been incited by Nebuchadnezzar because of Jehoiakim's reckless bid for independence (II Kgs 24:1–7).

Jehoiachin's short rule gave little chance to tell what sort of king he would have made, but he is charged with doing evil as his father had done (II Kgs 24:9). When Nebuchadnezzar finished his war with Egypt, he mobilized his army to invade Judah, and Jehoiachin was forced to capitulate. A cuneiform tablet in the series of the court chronicles of the Babylonian kings states the exact date that Nebuchadnezzar took him captive, equivalent to March 16, 597 B.C. On April 22 he left Jerusalem to begin his exile in Babylon, along with 10,000 others including his mother, the leading men and women of Judah such as Ezekiel the prophet, and the royal treasures. There was only a poor and feeble remnant left behind, with no leadership or protection (II Kgs 24:10–16).

Jehoiachin was kept a captive for most of the rest of his life. At least two Babylonian tablets dated to 592 B.C. list Jehoiachin and his five sons among those who received rations from the king in Babylon (ANET, p. 308). He seems to have enjoyed a certain amount of freedom within the city at this time, but was imprisoned later, perhaps during the final siege of Jerusalem. After about 36 years Evil-merodach set him free from prison and made him eat at his table (II Kgs 25:27–30).

Jehoiachin remained a figure of nationalistic hope to his people during his long captivity, for he was the legitimate Davidic king and was even called "king of Judah." As long as he lived he kept the nationalistic spirit of his people on fire. Clay impressions of the stamp seal of his steward Eliakim have been found at Tell Beit Mirsim and Beth-shemesh in Palestine (VBW, II, 297). These suggest that while in exile Jehoiachin's royal estates were not confiscated but continued to be managed in his name by his chief steward. The time of his death is uncertain. He was the last of Solomon's line as predicted by Jeremiah (Jer 22:30), and the succession passed to the line of Nathan.

A. W. W.

JEHOIADA (jē-hoi'*ȧ*-d*ȧ*)

1. Father of Benaiah, David's general (II Sam 8:16, 18; 20:23) who succeeded Joab after serving under him (I Kgs 4:4) and under Solomon (I Chr 11:22, 24). He is probably the same one who led many Aaronites to join forces with David at Hebron (I Chr 12:27).

2. A son of Benaiah, one of David's counselors who succeeded Ahithophel (I Chr 27:33–34), and thus a grandson of the above, although some believe these to be the same.

3. The high priest during the time Athaliah usurped the throne of Judah, who overthrew her and placed the boy king Joash (Jehoash) on the throne (II Kgs 11:4–21). He made a covenant between God, the king and Judah (II Kgs 11:17) which led to some religious reforms and enabled Jehoiada to serve as the king's adviser. Jehoiada's wife was the daughter of King Joram and sister of King Ahaziah, so the priest was the uncle of the young king he aided. Jehoiada lived to be 130, and was honored for his service to the nation by burial among the kings of Judah in the old city of David (II Chr 24:15–16). His godly influence gone, Joash quickly lapsed into idolatrous ways and slew Jehoiada's son (II Chr 24:2, 17–22).

4. A priest during the time of Jeremiah who was succeeded by Zephaniah as overseer of the temple (Jer 29:26).

5. One who helped repair the old gate of Jerusalem (Neh 3:6).

A. W. W.

JEHOIAKIM (jē-hoi'*ȧ*-kĭm). King of Judah, son of Josiah by his wife Zebudah. He was first called Eliakim, but after deposing Jehoiahaz Pharaoh-Necho set him on the throne of Judah and changed his name to Jehoiakim, in the latter half of 609 B.C. (II Kgs 23:34, 36). He was subject to Egypt for four years and required to exact heavy tribute from his people. The battle of Carchemish in May-June 605 B.C. ended the rule of Egypt.

Nebuchadnezzar entered Jerusalem and received the submission of Jehoiakim (II Kgs 24:1; Jer 46:2) and took some captives including Daniel and his three friends and the golden vessels from the temple to Babylon (Dan 1:1–2, 6). Nebuchadnezzar had bound Jehoiakim in chains to take him along with the others to Babylon (II Chr 36:6), but evidently released him after receiving assurance that he would be a loyal vassal. Judah began a period of moral and religious decay. Baal and Ashtoreth were worshiped in the very gates of the temple and sacrifices may have been resumed in the valley of Hinnom. Cruelty, corruption and oppression were commonplace in the city.

Jeremiah wrote on a scroll in protest, telling how divine judgment would surely come to Judah (Jer 36), but the king, after reading a few leaves, took his knife and cut them in strips and then burned them. After three years Jehoiakim rashly rebelled against Babylonia while Nebuchadnezzar was too busy with battles elsewhere to take any action at that time.

Jehoiakim died on Dec. 10, 598 B.C. according to calculations based on the Babylonian chronicle. The people did not mourn and he was evidently given a shameful burial as Jeremiah had prophesied (Jer 22:18f.; 36:30). His young son Jehoiachin (*q.v.*) inherited his throne and all the unsolved problems.

A. W. W.

JEHOIARIB (jē-hoi'*ȧ*-rĭb). Also appears as Joiarib (*q.v.*) both in Heb. and in English. It is difficult always to tell whether the name refers to an individual or a member of the priestly course.

1. A priest, the head of the first of the 24 courses of the priesthood in the days of David (I Chr 24:7).

2. A priest who returned with the first of the exiles from Babylon (I Chr 9:10).

JEHONADAB (jē-hō'n*ȧ*-dăb). Alternate form of Jonadab (*q.v.*). The English in II Sam 13 and Jer 35 consistently calls him Jonadab, but the Heb. varies the longer and shorter forms. Jehonadab is found only in II Kgs 10:15, 23.

JEHONATHAN (jē-hŏn'*ȧ*-th*ȧ*n). A shorter form of the name is Jonathan (*q.v.*).

1. The son of Uzziah and an overseer of King David's treasuries or storehouses (I Chr 27:25).

2. One of the Levites sent out by King Jehoshaphat through the cities of Judah to teach the law of the Lord to the people (II Chr 17:8–9).

3. A priest, head of the family of Shemaiah, in the days of Nehemiah (Neh 12:18).

JEHORAM (jē-hôr'*ȧ*m). Same as Joram (*q.v.*), an abbreviated form of the name.

1. A son of Ahab (II Kgs 3:1) king of Israel, nearly contemporary with the king of Judah by the same name. He succeeded his elder brother Ahaziah. Jehoram destroyed an image of Baal which his father had made (3:2), but continued to uphold the calf worship instituted by Jeroboam I. Israel and Judah were friendly allies during his reign as a result of the alliance between Ahab and Jehoshaphat. Together they put down a revolt of King Mesha of Moab (II Kgs 3:1–27). Mesha's record of the campaign is recorded on the Moabite Stone (*q.v.*).

Jehoram must have been the unidentified king of Israel to whom Naaman was sent to be cured of leprosy (II Kgs 5:1 -8), to whom Elisha revealed the movements of the Syrian army and who sent the helpless enemy troops back to Damascus after feeding them (II Kgs 6:8 -23), and who witnessed the seige of Samaria by the Syrians (II Kgs 6:24–7:20). Wounded in the battle over Ramoth-gilead against Hazael of Syria, Jehoram went to Jezreel to seek a cure (II Kgs 8:28 -29), but instead was assassinated by an arrow from the bow of Jehu; thus ending the dynasty of Omri on the very land Jezebel had procured for Ahab by having Naboth slain (I Kgs 21).

2. Jehoshaphat's son, who served as his father's regent for about five years before succeeding him on the throne of Judah in 848 B.C. at the age of 32 (I Kgs 22:50; II Chr 21:1, 3, 5). To strengthen his father's political alliance with Israel (II Chr 18:1) he had been married to the older Athaliah, daughter of Ahab and Jezebel, who evidently influenced him to allow the worship of Baal-Melkart (II Kgs 8:18). He murdered his brothers and some of the princes of Judah (II Chr 21:4). Jehoram fought against the Philistines and Arabians (II Chr 21:16 - 17), who captured his wives and all his sons except Ahaziah (Jehoahaz). In 841 B.C. he died of a lingering, painful disease, but none mourned (II Chr 21:18–20).

3. A priest appointed by King Jehoshaphat to teach the law (II Chr 17:8).

A. W. W.

JEHOSHABEATH. *See* Jehosheba.

JEHOSHAPHAT (jĕ-hŏsh'*ă*-făt)

1. A recorder under David and Solomon, the son of Ahilud (II Sam 8:16; 20:24; I Kgs 4:3). He is listed as one of the chief officials of the kingdom.

2. One of the priests during the reign of David, appointed to blow the trumpet in front of the ark as it was brought to the city of David from Obed-edom (I Chr 15:24; Heb. *Yôshpāṭ*).

3. One of the 12 administrative officers of Solomon whose responsibility was to provide food for the king and his household for one month of each year. He was charged with the collection from the district of Issachar (I Kgs 4:17).

4. King of Judah (873 -848 B.C.), son of Asa and his successor. At the age of 35 he became coregent with his father Asa until the latter's death in 870, and ruled for 25 years (I Kgs 22:42). His mother was Azubah, daughter of Shilhi. He was contemporary with Ahab, Ahaziah, and Jehoram of Israel. He made an alliance with Israel by marrying his son Jehoram to Athaliah, the daughter of Ahab and Jezebel (II Kgs 8:18). In spite of the fact that this act opened the door to the worship of Baal in the kingdom of Judah, he was considered a good king.

In his third year he carried out some reforms to improve the religious situation, instructing his people himself as well as sending out the Levites with the book of the law to teach in the cities of Judah (II Chr 17:7 -9). The Philistines and the Arabians paid tribute (vv. 10 - 11), and he further fortified the cities of his kingdom (vv. 12 - 19).

In 853 B.C. Ahab persuaded him to join Israel in an attempt to wrest Ramoth-gilead from Syria. Ahab was mortally wounded but Jehoshaphat survived (I Kgs 22:1 -38; II Chr 18:1 -34). He was severely reproved by the prophet Jehu for having anything to do with King Ahab (II Chr 19:1 -2). Judah clearly occupied a subordinate position but the alliance was temporarily a source of strength for both kingdoms. On his return Jehoshaphat again encouraged Yahweh worship (II Chr 19:4).

He had previously strengthened the defenses of Judah and brought Edom under his control (II Chr 17:1 -2; I Kgs 22:47). This gave him command of the caravan routes from Arabia and brought him additional wealth (II Chr 17:5; 18:1). He attempted to build a fleet of ships at Ezion-geber in cooperation with Ahaziah, king of Israel, but the ships were wrecked. Jehoshaphat refused any new ventures, probably fearing encroachment on his territory and because the prophet Eliezer rebuked him for joining Ahaziah (I Kgs 22:48 -49). Jehoshaphat introduced important administrative changes (II Chr 19:5 - 11) by appointing judges in the fortified cities of Judah to replace the local elders, and establishing a final court of appeals in Jerusalem made up of Levites and priests and heads of families, with the chief priest in charge.

Once again the king of Israel, this time Jehoram, persuaded Jehoshaphat into a new venture to make Moab a tributary to Israel, but it was only partly successful (II Kgs 3:5 -7). Near the end of his reign the Ammonites, Edomites, and Moabites joined forces to invade Judah by crossing what is now the Dead Sea toward Engedi. Jehoshaphat sought the Lord and heeded the words of the prophet Jahaziel to stand still and see the salvation of the Lord on their behalf. In the confusion caused by Judah's songs of praise the enemies began to ambush one another until they destroyed themselves (II Chr 20:1 -30).

During his last five years Jehoshaphat had his son Jehoram reign with him on the throne (II Kgs 8:16 with 1:17). Jehoshaphat died at the age of 60 and was buried in the city of David (I Kgs 22:50).

5. Father of Jehu, king of Israel, he lived in the 9th cen. B.C. (II Kgs 9:2, 14).

A. W. W.

JEHOSHAPHAT, VALLEY OF (jĕ-hŏs'*ă*-făt). A valley in which the Lord will gather all nations together for judgment (Joel 3:2, 12). The name itself is significant, meaning "Yahweh judges."

It is called the valley of decision (v. 14), meaning judicial decision to determine punishment, not an opportunity to believe unto salvation. The historical event of II Chr 20: 20–26 seems to have been used here as a symbol of an eschatological event (*see* Armageddon). No actual valley bore this name in pre-Christian antiquity. Since the 4th cen. A.D. Christian tradition has commonly identified it with the Kidron Valley (between Jerusalem and the Mount of Olives). Some have identified it with the Valley of Berachah near Bethlehem. Probably neither view is correct.

The exact geographical location of the valley in which Jehoshaphat's enemies came to their destruction cannot be ascertained. It must have been somewhere in the wilderness of Judah below the heights of Tekoa (II Chr 20:20), in the direction of En-gedi (v. 2), and should probably be identified with the valley of the "ascent to Ziz" (*see* Ziz) in the vicinity of the "wilderness of Jeruel" (*see* Jeruel; II Chr 20:16).

A. F. R.

JEHOSHEBA (jē-hŏsh'ĕ-bȧ). Also called Jehoshabeath (II Chr 22:11).

Jehosheba was the daughter of King Jehoram of Judah and the sister of King Ahaziah. She was probably not the daughter of Jehoram's infamous wife Athaliah but the offspring of another wife. She was the wife of Jehoiada the high priest at the time when Athaliah attempted to kill all the heirs of the murdered Ahaziah and seize the throne. Jehosheba rescued the infant Joash and protected him for six years until the tyrant queen could be safely defied and the child Joash proclaimed king (II Kgs 11:1–3).

JEHOSHUA, JEHOSHUAH (jē-hŏsh'ū-ȧ). A peculiar spelling sometimes given to Joshua the son of Nun (Num 13:16). Another spelling adds the final "h" (I Chr 7:27). *See* Joshua.

JEHOVAH. *See* God; God, Names and Titles of.

JEHOVAH-JIREH (jē-hō'vȧ-jī'rĕ). The phrase means "Jehovah (Yahweh) sees," or "Jehovah (Yahweh) will provide." It refers to the place named by Abraham when the ram appeared in the thicket and was sacrificed instead of Isaac (Gen 22:14, KJV). *See* God, Names and Titles of.

JEHOVAH-NISSI (jē-hō'vȧ-nĭs'ī). The phrase means "Jehovah (Yahweh) is my banner," and is the name of the altar Moses built after defeating the Amalekites at Rephidim (Ex 17:15, KJV). *See* God, Names and Titles of.

JEHOVAH-SHALOM (jē-hō'vȧ-shā'lŏm). The phrase means "Jehovah (Yahweh) is peace," and is the name of the altar Gideon built at Ophrah to memorialize the words of God's message to him, "Peace be unto thee" (Jud 6:23–24, KJV). *See* God, Names and Titles of.

JEHOZABAD (jē-hō'zȧ-băd)

1. The son of Shomer (or Shimrith), a Moabitess. He was one of the two servants of Joash of Judah who assassinated the king at the house of Millo (II Kgs 12:20–21; II Chr 24:26).

2. A Levite, the second son of Obed-edom. He was appointed a doorkeeper of the temple by David (I Chr 26:4).

3. A soldier from the tribe of Benjamin. He was one of the generals of Jehoshaphat, commanding 180,000 men (II Chr 17:18).

JEHOZADAK. Alternate form of Jozadak and Josedech. *See* Josedech.

JEHU (jē'hū)

1. A servant of David born at Anathoth, one of David's chief slingers who met him at Ziklag (I Chr 12:3).

2. A prophet, son of Hanani, who prophesied against King Baasha (I Kgs 16:1, 7, 12) and later recorded events of the reign of Jehoshaphat in the chronicles of Jehu mentioned in II Chr 20:34.

3. A man of the tribe of Judah, son of Obed, descendant of Jerahmeel (I Chr 2:38).

4. A man of the tribe of Simeon, son of Joshibiah (I Chr 4:35).

5. Tenth king of Israel, son of Jehoshaphat, grandson of Nimshi (II Kgs 9:2), first king of the fourth dynasty in Israel (841–814 B.C.).

Before becoming king, Jehu played a quiet and subordinate role under Ahab, Ahaziah, and Jehoram. His earliest known military position was as a bodyguard of Ahab. In this capacity he was present at Ahab's encounter with Elijah in the vineyard of Naboth as well as the legalized murder of Naboth and his sons (II Kgs 9:25–26; cf. I Kgs 21:15–16). Under Jehoram, he was captain of the army of Israel in the defense of Ramoth-gilead (II Kgs 9:1–5). During the fighting against the Syrians in Transjordan, Jehoram was forced to return to Jezreel

Jehu doing homage to Shalmaneser III, a panel from the Black Obelisk of Shalmaneser. BM

because of wounds (II Kgs 8:28–29; 9:15), leaving Jehu in charge of the besieged city.

His anointment. The prophet Elisha recognized the strategic nature of the circumstances. He recalled that his predecessor, Elijah, had been commissioned to anoint Jehu as the future king of Israel. The reason for such a long delay is not given in the biblical record. Now conditions were ripe for a successful revolution against the house of Ahab. Elisha sent a messenger to anoint Jehu as the new king. The young messenger of wild appearance (II Kgs 9:11) secretly poured a vial of sacred oil over Jehu's head (vv. 6–10). However, the secret was short-lived as Jehu soon revealed the mission of the young prophet. Enthusiasm swept over the soldiers, causing them to throw down their garments under Jehu's feet, sound their trumpets, and proclaim him king (vv. 12–13).

His coup. Jehu wasted no time in striking against the house of Ahab. Making certain that no one would ride to warn Jehoram, he took a small group of men toward Jezreel. Jehoram, seeing the approaching troops, sent out messengers who did not return. Then he and Ahaziah, king of Judah, rode out to inquire of Jehu's business at Jezreel. Jehoram's question, "Is it peace?" was answered by Jehu's fierce denunciation of Jezebel. With positive and passionless speed, Jehu began the bloody massacre which continued for several days. Jehoram was pierced by Jehu's arrow while Jehu's men mortally wounded Ahaziah. Riding into Jezreel, Jehu ordered two servants to throw down Jezebel from the palace window. He and his men completed her demise with the wheels of their chariots (II Kgs 9:14–37).

Next Jehu challenged the leading citizens to set up one of the princes in opposition to his rulership. Once they had submitted to him, he ordered them to prove their allegiance by appearing the next day with the heads of the 70 heirs of Ahab. The heads were then piled up on either side of the gate leading into Jezreel as a reminder to anyone still inclined to resist (II Kgs 10:1–11).

The ruthless slaughter continued with the death of 42 kinsmen of Ahaziah who unluckily came from Judah for a visit at this time. The bloodbath was finally ended with the wholesale slaughter of all the worshipers of Baal who could be gathered together and the eradication of the foreign cult of Baal. Jehu showed his cunning and calculating side as he pretended to be loyal to Baal. Calling a solemn assembly and leading out in the ritual, he quietly stepped aside while 80 of his trusty guards killed everyone who had accepted his invitation (II Kgs 10:12–28).

His foreign policy. Although Jehu had ruthlessly disposed of his potential enemies, he soon found he had no friends. He had broken completely with Phoenicia by the murder of the Phoenician-bred queen mother and the overthrow of the Phoenician-inspired worship. He had destroyed all hope of close ties with Judah when he killed Ahaziah and his close kinsmen. Since Ahab had already broken the bonds with Syria and obligated his nation to Assyria, Jehu had little choice in regard to his foreign policy. During the first year of Jehu's reign, 842 B.C., Shalmaneser III directed a triumphant campaign against Hazael of Damascus. It was expedient, if not courageous, for Jehu to follow a policy of vassalage to Assyria. The Black Obelisk of Shalmaneser, found by Layard at Nimrud, describes this submission in word and picture. It tells of tribute paid by Jehu as well as the inhabitants of Tyre and Sidon—gold, silver, vessels of metal and wooden objects (ANET, pp. 280f.). It also gives an actual representation of Israelites offering their tribute to the Assyrian monarch. This is the earliest known artistic representation of an Israelite (ANEP, #351, 355).

In the years which followed, Israel was constantly threatened by Syria, as Assyria failed to keep the Syrians in check. Hazael was able to gain sufficient power to overrun all the territories of Israel E of the Jordan (II Kgs 10:32–33).

His religious zeal. The various motives behind Jehu's acts are difficult to untangle. However, a deep religious motivation is obvious since the revolution was prophet-inspired. Although Elijah was no longer on the scene, his name was associated with the movement through the memory of his words to Ahab in Naboth's vineyard. Jehu became the agent in satisfying the prophecy of Elijah as he left Jehoram's body in the vineyard of Naboth and carried out the prophetic promise concerning Jezebel. Elisha's name was inseparably connected with Jehu's rebellion by his action in ordering the anointing of the young leader.

In the final phase of his plans, Jehu linked himself with another element of Israel's religious heritage. He took Jehonadab the Rechabite with him to Samaria as his associate in eradicating the worshipers of Baal (II Kgs 9:15–16, 23). Even as he had the backing of the best in the prophetic tradition, Elijah and Elisha, he could likewise claim the sanction of the most fanatical group as well in the Rechabites.

Although there was prophetic backing of the revolution, later writers looked back with censure upon the extreme nature of Jehu's actions. The writer of II Kgs 10:29–31 views the events in the light of his toleration of the idolatrous cult instituted by Jeroboam I at Bethel and Dan. Hosea likewise decries the violence and bloodshed (Hos 1:4).

His character. Jehu was a man possessed by dominant traits of personality. In making preparation for carrying out his purposes, he was prudent, calculating, masterful, and ambitious. In executing his plans, he was bold, daring, impetuous, and stern. His zeal approached the point of ruthless fanaticism. He was seemingly lacking in the regal qualities which inspire respect, trust, and appreciation. His extreme policies alienated friend and foe, hastening the demise of Israel. The fact that he continued the identification of the sacred bulls with the Yahweh worship suggests that his prophetic zeal for God was probably leavened by his ambitious zeal for Jehu.

K. M. Y.

JEHUBBAH (jē-hŭb'ȧ). An Asherite, the son of Shemer (I Chr 7:34).

JEHUCAL (jē-hū'kȧl). Also spelled Jucal in Jer 38:1. The son of Shelemiah who was sent by Zedekiah, the king of Judah, to entreat Jeremiah to pray for him (Jer 37:3). After hearing Jeremiah, Jehucal, among others, encouraged the king to put Jeremiah to death on the grounds that his message of judgment and destruction was undermining the safety of the city (Jer 38:1-6).

JEHUD (jē'hŭd). A town in the tribal territory of Dan in the time of Joshua. Its location seems to be about seven miles E of Joppa and near the modern city of Tel Aviv (Josh 19:45).

JEHUDI (jē-hū'dī). The word refers to a man of Judah, a Jew. He was a messenger of King Jehoiakim (Jer 36:14, 21, 23) sent to Baruch to request him to bring the scroll in the presence of the king, who proceeded to cut and burn it as it was read by Jehudi.

JEHUDIJAH (jē'hŭ-dī'jȧ). The KJV lists Jehudijah as a proper name, but it is an adjective meaning "Jewess." The term is used in reference to the Jewish wife of Mered and distinguishes her from his Egyptian wife (I Chr 4:18).

JEHUSH. *See* Jeush 3.

JEIEL (jē-ī'ĕl)

1. A Reubenite chief at the time when Tiglath-pileser took into captivity the Transjordanic tribes (I Chr 5:7).
2. The founder of Israelite Gibeon, father of Ner who was grandfather of King Saul (I Chr 9:35, ASV, RSV; Jehiel in KJV).
3. The son of Hotham the Aroerite, one of David's mighty men (I Chr 11:44, ASV, RSV; Jehiel in KJV).
4. A Levite, appointed by David as doorkeeper and musician (I Chr 15:18, 21). He took part in the ministry of music before the ark as it was brought to Jerusalem (I Chr 16:5).
5. A Levite, the great-grandfather of Jahaziel who prophesied the victory of Jehoshaphat (II Chr 20:14ff.).
6. A scribe who kept account of the numbers of King Uzziah's army (II Chr 26:11).
7. A Levite, son of Elizaphan, who assisted in the cleansing of the temple under Hezekiah (II Chr 29:13, KJV; Jeuel in ASV, RSV).
8. A chief Levite who took part in the great Passover of Josiah (II Chr 35:9).
9. One of the descendants, "sons," of Adonikam who returned with Ezra (Ezr 8:13, KJV; ASV, RSV have Jeuel).
10. A son or descendant of Nebo, who had taken a foreign wife in the days of Ezra (Ezr 10:43).

P. C. J.

JEKABZEEL (jē-kăb'zē-ĕl). A city in the southern part of Judah (Neh 11:25), probably identical with Kabzeel (*q.v.*).

JEKAMEAM (jĕk'ȧ-mē'ȧm). The son of Hebron, a descendant of Levi (I Chr 23:19; 24:23).

JEKAMIAH (jĕk'ȧ-mī'ȧ). A man of Judah, the son of Shallum (I Chr 2:41). *See also* Jecamiah.

JEKUTHIEL (jē-kū'thĭ-ĕl). The son of Mered by his Jewish wife (I Chr 4:18).

JEMIMA (jē-mī'mȧ). Eldest of Job's three daughters, all of exceeding beauty, born to him after his restoration to prosperity (Job 42:14). Her name perhaps means "dove," with reference to the Egyptian turtledove.

JEMUEL (jĕm'ū-ĕl). The eldest son of Simeon (Gen 46:10; Ex 6:15). The same person is mentioned under the name of Nemuel (*q.v.*)in Num 26:12; I Chr 4:24.

JEPHTHAE. *See* Jephthah.

JEPHTHAH (jĕf'thȧ). One of the important leaders from the period of the judges (Jud 11:1-12:7). He was from the area of Gilead and was a son of a man named Gilead. His mother was a harlot, so Gilead's legitimate children drove Jephthah from home. He went to live at Tob, possibly just E of Ramoth-gilead. Here he gathered around him a band of dubious character but great courage, who lived by preying on other groups. Jephthah was himself a mighty warrior, a charismatic leader empowered by the Spirit of the Lord (11:29), but one with pride in his just and honest treatment of others.

When the area of Gilead had trouble with Ammon, its Israelite leaders could not cope with the situation. For 18 long years they smarted under the ruthless subjection of the Ammonites. Finally they begged Jephthah to help them since they had heard of his great prowess. Doubtless his brothers were in the group of elders of Gilead, for after a bitter denunciation of them he agreed to become the leader of their clan. The story suggests that they may have felt him to be especially close to God, for they may have noticed that he had taught his daughter his faith.

When Jephthah became judge he asked the tribe of Ephraim to help defeat the Ammonites, but they ignored him. Before the outcome of the battle was certain, Jephthah made a vow to sacrifice the first thing to come out his door on his return if he were successful. Some believe that this was a rash vow given in a moment of ecstacy or despair and that he little dreamed of what would actually happen. Others feel that he was quite aware of the probable consequences of his act. That he expected to make a human sacrifice is likely when one considers the alternative of an animal sacrifice. There is no reason to believe that a leader such as Jephthah would have kept in his house animals which he deemed worthy of sacrificing to fulfill his vow. The victory was important enough to him to warrant a comparably important payment, even a human life.

At any rate, he did defeat the Ammonites, and when he returned home he was greeted by his lovely young daughter. This tragedy nearly broke the heart of Jephthah, but he was loyal to his vow. His grief and her courageous faith are beautifully told by the Hebrew storyteller (11:34-40). She retired to the mountains for two months of prayer and mourning over her virginity. This may have been a delicate way of leaving the end of the story to the reader's imagination, or it might have been a way of saying she had no husband or child to come to her defense and prohibit this dreadful deed. The story may have been an acknowledgement of the fact that the pagan neighbors made human sacrifices but the Hebrews did not. Since a vow was very sacred, perhaps Jephthah did sacrifice her (II Kgs 3:27). Or he may have redeemed her with money (Lev 27:1-8) and then had her set aside to live the rest of her life in celibacy. This may have started the custom of the women of Israel setting aside four days of the year to mourn her sad fate (Jud 11:40).

Sometimes the idea is presented that Jephthah gave her to the tabernacle where she spent the remainder of her life working as a priest's servant, never marrying, for she would be devoted to the sacred duties of religion as a holy virgin (cf. Ex 38:8; I Sam 2:22). However, there is no specific OT example for the concept of the celibate female temple servant, though there were women performing various religious functions. Historically, this interpretation apparently rose from the allegorical explanation posited by the Rabbis Kimchi in the 11th and 12th cen. This interpretation was subsequently adopted by many Christian expositors but has little biblical basis.

A final campaign of Jephthah's is related, this time against the Ephraimites. They accused him of not inviting them to participate in the battle against the Ammonites (Jud 12:1-6). There seems to have been some resentment in their not being given an important place in the campaign since they claimed leadership of the northern tribes, and they considered his treatment of them a question of their honor. They demanded an immediate explanation and threatened to burn his house. He went into battle against them and won another victory. The Ephraimites were scattered, and when some of those who had escaped attempted to cross over to go home by way of the Jordan fords, they were asked by Jephthah's men if they were Ephraimites. If they said no, the famous Shibboleth-Sibboleth test was applied. If they could say the word correctly they were allowed to pass on, otherwise they were slain immediately.

Jephthah judged Israel for six years (Jud 12:7). Samuel uses him as an illustration of how God raised up a leader to deliver Israel from trouble (I Sam 12:11). He is included among the heroes of the faith in Heb 11:32.

A. W. W.

JEPHUNNEH (jē-fŭn'ĕ)

1. The father of Caleb, one of the two faithful spies of Canaan (Num 13:6). *See* Kenezite.

2. An Asherite, son of Jether (I Chr 7:38).

JERAH (jēr'*ȧ*). A son of Joktan (Gen 10:26; I Chr 1:20), presumably the origin of an Arabic tribe.

JERAHMEEL (jē-rā'mē-ĕl)

1. A son of Hezron and a grandson of Judah (I Chr 2:9).

2. A son of Kish, a Levite (I Chr 24:29).

3. One of the officers sent by King Jehoiakim to arrest Baruch (Jer 36:26).

JERAHMEELITE (jē-rä'mē-ĕ-līt). The name is a collective noun in use before the proper name. It refers to a tribe of people raided by David when he was fleeing from Saul and had taken refuge with Achish, the Philistine (I Sam 27:10).

JERED (jēr'ĕd). The son of Mered by his Jewish wife (I Chr 4:18).

JEREMAI (jĕr'ĕ-mī). One of the Hebrews whom Ezra persuaded to put away his wife (Ezr 10:33).

JEREMIAH (jĕr'ĕ-mī'*ȧ*)

1. The head of a clan in the tribe of Manasseh (I Chr 5:24).

2, 3, and 4. Three warriors who joined David at Ziklag. The second and third were Gadites (I Chr 12:4, 10, 13).

5. An Israelite resident of Libnah whose daughter Hamutal became the wife of King Josiah and mother of the kings Jehoahaz and Zedekiah (II Kgs 23:31; 24:18; Jer 52:1).

6. A Rechabite and the father of Jaazaniah, a contemporary of Jeremiah the prophet (Jer 35:3).

7. A priest who returned from Babylon with Zerubbabel (Neh 12:1, 12).

8. One of the priests who signed Ezra's covenant to keep the law (Neh 10:2).

9. An official of Judah who joined in the dedication ceremony for the Jerusalem wall under Nehemiah (Neh 12:34).

10. The major prophet during the period of the decline and fall of Judah in the 7th and 6th cen. B.C.

His birth. The latter part of the 7th cen. B.C. produced four prophets in Judah: Jeremiah the humanist, Zephaniah the orator, Nahum the poet, and Habakkuk the philosopher. The greatest of these, and the one enjoying the longest period of prophetic activity was Jeremiah.

His birthplace was Anathoth, a little village perched on a limestone ridge *c.* two miles NE of Jerusalem. Jeremiah was born *c.* 650 B.C. (Jer 1:2, 6), during the closing period of King Manasseh's reign (*c.* 695 - 642 B.C.).

About 70 years previously Samaria, the capital of the northern kingdom, had fallen, and about 65 years later Jerusalem, the capital of the southern kingdom, would fall. Immediately before Jeremiah's birth, Egypt and the small Palestinian states had formed a coalition to throw off the Assyrian yoke; so war clouds were threatening on the world's horizon. This international turmoil could be responsible for the prophet's name. Like Isaiah, there are two Heb. spellings of the English name Jeremiah—the long form *yirmᵉyāhû* and the shorter form *yirmᵉyâ* (Gr. Ieremias and Vulg. Jeremias). There are two probable meanings of the Heb. name, "the Lord [Yahweh] founds" or "establishes"; and, "whom the Lord [Yahweh] hurls" or "casts forth." If the latter interpretation is accepted, no name could be more descriptive of the character or mission of the prophet from Anathoth. Indeed, he was a spiritual missile, hurled forth in a darkened world. Hilkiah was his father's name (Jer 1:1)—a common Heb. name meaning "the Lord [Yahweh] is my portion." Both names (Jeremiah's and Hilkiah's) suggest that the family was loyal to the God of Israel during the tyrannical reign of the ungodly King Manasseh.

His formative years. Probably the family of Jeremiah descended from Eli, for Abiathar, the last of that descent to hold the priestly office, possessed an ancestral estate at Anathoth, to which he retired upon his dismissal by Solomon (I Kgs 2:26). Hence Jeremiah had a background of the finest religious traditions and grew up in the atmosphere of a pious Heb. home. Everything that was good in Heb. life was a part of his intellectual, moral, and spiritual inheritance.

Jeremiah's earliest writings reflect a thorough knowledge and insight of the prophecies of Amos, Hosea, and Isaiah. The prophet Hosea made an indelible imprint upon the young prophet (Jer 2 - 4). Yet when Jeremiah began to prophesy, he demonstrated a firsthand awareness of divine knowledge and the divine call. Like all great prophets (cf. Paul of the NT), Jeremiah shook himself free of all secondary and human sources of inspiration. He knew in his heart that God had called him, for he had heard the voice of the Lord: "Before I fashioned you in the womb I knew you, and before you were born I dedicated you; I designed you for a prophet to the nations" (Jer 1:5, Berkeley).

Anathoth, the birthplace of Jeremiah, since the time of David had been a priestly residence (Jer 1:1; 29:27; 32:7). It is known today as Ras el-Kharrubeh, *c.* two miles NE of Jerusalem, on a hill overlooking the Jordan valley. Its open range and arid landscape were a good cradle for a prophet. Jeremiah reflected his country environment: the hot desert, the village herds, the parched hills, the wild animals, etc. The city was located in the territory of Benjamin, the tribe of mad Saul and cursing Shimei. Its soil was hard and thorny, which demanded deep plowing. Frequently strong men are reared in such soil. "What," asked an English visitor to New England, surveying for the first time its rocky soil, "can you raise here?" "Here," was the proud response, "we raise men!" (G. A. Smith, *Jeremiah*, pp. 67ff.).

Since Jerusalem was less than an hour's walk from Anathoth, Jeremiah was in close touch with the heart of the nation and the pulse of the world. All the political and social news would trickle eventually to the prophet's village and the reverberations of the Assyrian, Scythian, and Babylonian campaigns sounded forth.

Jeremiah was no recluse. He was both a townsman and countryman. He had an eye for events and his sensitive soul felt the impression of the eternal God. Jeremiah possessed a knack for the commonplace. Nature made an indelible imprint on his life. He observed the farmer in the field(Jer 4:3), the children in the street (6:1), the silver refiners and the potters at their work (6:28, 30; 18:3, 6). Also he knew firsthand the strifes of debtors and creditors (15:10), the humiliation of thieves when apprehended (2:26), the lamentations for the dead (16:4), and the joy of festivals of brides and weddings (2:32; 7:34). These changing moods later were reflected in his own soul.

His call. Manasseh died when Jeremiah was about ten years old. Amon, Manasseh's son, ruled two years (642 - 640 B.C.). Then young King Josiah (640 - 609 B.C.) ascended the Judean throne at only eight years of age. Thirteen years later, 627 B.C. (Jer 1:2), during Josiah's reign, Jeremiah was drafted by the Lord to be His prophet to the nations.

The year 627/626 B.C. was an epochal year in world history. Ashurbanipal, the last great Assyrian king, died; and Nabopolassar, the first great neo-Babylonian king, came to the throne of Babylon. Ten years later the Babylonians and Medes, along with the Scythians, launched a combined attack on Nineveh. The death rattle could already be detected in the throat of the mistress of the world.

During this shaking of the nations, God's hand laid hold on Jeremiah on the quiet pathway of life, and overpowered him as recorded in chap. 1. Behind that call were inheritance, tradition, and training; but the experience itself was sudden, abrupt, and fraught with terrific weight and meaning. Also it was accompanied by a stupendous consciousness and inrush of God possessing the whole of his being. From that day, Jeremiah moved upon the stage of history as a God-possessed soul.

His apprenticeship. Jeremiah's prophetic ministry began in Anathoth, and apparently he remained there for several years as more or less an insignificant prophet. In 622 -621 B.C. a religious reformation occurred. Josiah had taken over the reigns of government and decided to restore faith in the God of Israel. In the 18th year of his reign he issued a decree to repair the temple. In the process of cleaning the debris from the temple, the book of the law was found by Hilkiah the priest. He immediately sent it to Josiah, who read it and "rent his clothes." The young king resolved to make the religious life of the nation conform to the laws of the new-found book; so he inaugurated his great reform movement, intended to bring about a national revival of the true religion. All religious worship was to be centered in the temple. All other shrines were to be destroyed.

Jeremiah probably threw himself into this revival movement and went on itinerant preaching tours. But later he broke with the movement because it failed to change the inner life of the nation. He perceived religion as an affair of the heart (see J. Skinner, *Prophecy and Religion*, pp. 89 - 107).

His arrival as a prophet. There is a strange period of silence of *c*. 13 years (621 -609 B.C.) concerning the life of Jeremiah. Evidently during this period he shifted his base of operation from Anathoth to the capital city, Jerusalem. He became the respected prophet of the state.

At the death of Josiah in 609 B.C. at the battle of Megiddo, the Judean people passed over Jehoiakim, the oldest son of Josiah, and placed Jehoahaz (who reigned only three months) on the Judean throne. He was deposed by Pharaoh-necho of Egypt, and Jehoiakim (609-598 B.C.) was set on Judah's throne as the puppet of Egypt. Jeremiah immediately clashed with this selfish, covetous, tyrannical, spoiled son of his father's harem, who paneled his roomy palace with cedar (Jer 22:13-14). The famous temple sermon (7:1–8:3) was preached during the early part of Jehoiakim's reign. As a result, Jeremiah was banned from the temple and nearly lost his life (cf. Jer 7 with 26).

In 612 B.C. Nineveh fell before the Babylonians, and in 605 B.C. at the battle of Carchemish (Jer 46:2) the Babylonians defeated a combined coalition of the remnant army of Assyria and Egypt. Now the Babylonians stepped out upon the world stage as the undisputed master.

Jehoiakim became the vassal of Nebuchadnezzar (605 -562 B.C.); Judah was reduced to a tributary vassal of Babylon. Jehoiakim remained loyal to Babylon for a few years. Then Pharaoh-necho of Egypt encouraged him to join the westland countries in a revolt. So in 598 B.C., the Judean king revolted and refused to pay annual tribute to his Babylonian overlord. The Babylonian army marched swiftly toward Jerusalem to suppress the revolt. Jehoiakim was probably slain outside the walls of Jerusalem and received an ignominious burial of an ass just as Jeremiah had predicted (Jer 22:18 - 19; 36:30). Jehoiachin, his 17-year-old son, took over the Judean throne. In three months he capitulated unconditionally to Nebuchadnezzar. The Babylonians did not destroy Jerusalem but took away about 3,000 captives, the king, the king's mother, and all the king's court to Babylonia as hostages.

Zedekiah was appointed king of Judah, and Jeremiah continued preaching his theme song that the Babylonians were God's instruments of judgment on Judah for her sins. To resist her would be futile! To submit was wisdom and the only way to survival! In Jeremiah's eyes, the Lord had ordered Babylon to invade Judah; so in the teeth of the king, priests, prophets, and people he opposed any alliance with Egypt and freely predicted the supremacy of Babylon and the destruction of the Jewish state. Also Jeremiah perceived that the hope of future Israel was wrapped up solely in the band of the Jewish captives in Babylon (Jer 31), not in Jerusalem. The leftovers in the capital city were not the true remnant.

His final years. In 588 B.C. Zedekiah, who had long been plotting against Babylon, openly revolted against his Babylonian master. Babylonian vengeance was swift and final. They marched through Judah and Jerusalem in 588 B.C. In July of 586 B.C., after a long and terrible siege of about 18 months, the city was captured. Nebuchadnezzar's patience was exhausted, so he ordered a systematic destruction of the city. The temple was pillaged and demolished. The king was carried to Riblah in chains, his sons and cabinet were slain, his eyes seared, and many Jews taken into captivity – only the poorest people were left behind to be vinedressers and husbandmen.

Jeremiah was released from the prison in Jerusalem by Nebuchadnezzar to stay with the people of the land (Jer 39:11-14). His friend Gedaliah was appointed governor of the Judean province. Jeremiah threw his influence behind the governor as he began "to rebuild" and "to replant" the nation (see 1:10).

In 581 B.C., Gedaliah was murdered by a Jewish fanatic, Ishmael, who massacred also all of Gedaliah's adherents. This brought the Babylonian army back to Palestine. In the wake of this return the people, panic-stricken over fear of Babylonian reprisal, fled to Egypt. They kidnapped Jeremiah and carried him with them (43:1 -7). There on the banks of the Nile he preached against the fanatic worship practiced by the Jewish women to the Queen of Heaven (44:15 -30). The prophet of Anathoth probably lost his life under an avalanche of stones hurled by the husbands of the female devotees.

His personality. Jeremiah is a personality of complexes—protest and agony. Our knowledge of the personal history of Jeremiah is more extensive than for any other OT prophet. Baruch, his scribe, recorded extensively Jeremiah's spiritual battles.

Also Jeremiah was an honest man, so his utterances laid bare his soul before God. Sprinkled throughout chaps. 1-20 of his book are snatches composing a spiritual diary of his inner life which are commonly termed "the confessions of Jeremiah" (Jer 1; 4:10, 19; 6:11; 11:10-23; 12:1-3, 5-6; 14:17; 15:10-21; 17:9-10; 18:18-23; 20:7-18). These prophecies reveal the conflicts which repeatedly churned within the prophet's soul as he sought to wrestle with the problems of his day.

Even though he was assured of Yahweh's strength (Jer 1:8, 17ff.) for the prophetic ministry, when he encountered persecution and abuse he stormed back with all his soul. He was a laughingstock all day long, an object of derision (20:7-8); his enemies cut him with their tongues (18:18); everyone cursed him (15:10). He was lonely and rejected by his countrymen (15:17; 16:18). Even his home townsmen plotted to assassinate him (18:18, 22; 20:10). His reaction was one of resentment and he rained down imprecations on his enemies (11:20-23; 15:15; 17:18; 20:11-12). He was haunted with apparent failure and he was a man of moods: "See, they say to me, Why tarries the word of the Lord? Let it come!" (17:15, Berkeley; cf. also 15:15; 20:8). At times his fellowship with God was a source of deep spiritual joy (15:16), but at other times he experienced deep spiritual depressions that the Lord had let him down (15:17-18). However he must go on (20:7, 9), for the Lord was stronger than he and had prevailed!

Jeremiah was a man of prayer. He said very little about prayer; he just prayed! He poured out his soul's dregs and all to the One who sees and hears in secret and rewards openly. He prayed for healing (17:14)—spiritual healing of his sick heart (17:9) and the removal of complexes which blocked him and sapped his physical energy. He prayed for relief from his adversaries, for the cause for which he was giving his life, and for vengeance on his persecutors (18:18-23). His prayers were more than petitions. They were communication with God in which his inner life was laid bare, with his frustrations, struggles, temptations, and sins. It was the exercise of his soul in which he unburdened himself of the loads and weights of life (15:15-18).

But Jeremiah was a prophet, the Lord's spokesman. Whereas Isaiah was a volunteer (he accepted his mission and sprang to it with enthusiasm), Jeremiah was a draftee. He shrank, protested, and craved leave to retire. He felt keenly his own sense of inadequacy in view of the order to be a "prophet to the nations." Yet in the midst of pressure of outward events and his own inward tumults, he was the Lord's mouthpiece—a God-possessed, God-controlled, and God-directed man. God's word was a burning fire in his heart (6:11; 20:9); he preached from an inner compulsion. He stood like a flint against the false prophets in Babylon and Jerusalem (23:9-40).

Also Jeremiah was a moral analyst, an assayer of man's thoughts, motives, and actions (5:1-5; especially 6:27: "I have made you an assayer and examiner among my people, so that you may test and analyze their actions"—Berkeley). In examining society he self-analyzed himself (12:3; 15:10, 15-18; 17:16; 18:20).

Again, Jeremiah was a crusader. What Luther was at the Diet of Worms, Jeremiah was to Israel in his famous temple sermon of 609/608 B.C. (chap. 7 for content, chap. 26 for narrative). The word of the Lord came to him, and he had to strike the fatal blow to temple superstition and empty formalism as substitutes for true religion which is an affair of the heart.

Finally, Jeremiah was an optimist. He believed that God would eventually be victorious. When he looked at the generations he was a pessimist. But when he looked at the centuries he was an optimist, and so he spoke of a new king, a good shepherd, and a Davidic righteous branch (Jer 23:5).

According to his conception of the righteousness of God, Jeremiah knew the nation was doomed, the Exile certain, and a new order was inevitable. So in the book of hope (Jer 30-33, especially 31:31ff.) a new day would dawn, a new Israel would return, and God would accomplish His purpose through the Israel of tomorrow. In that day the word of God would be written on the heart of man. Believers would have firsthand experience with the true and living God. This is the OT conception of the new birth.

Because Jeremiah so loved Jerusalem and so aligned himself with the purpose of God, there arose the tradition that Jeremiah would be raised from the dead. The Church Fathers report the belief that he was stoned to death at Tahpanhes by the Jews. He was expected by some to appear and restore the tabernacle, the ark, and the altar of incense which he supposedly had hidden in a cave (II Macc 2:1-8). So when Jesus asked His disciples for the grass roots report, "Who do people say that the Son of Man is?" they replied, "Some say . . . Jeremiah" (Mt 16:13-14, NASB).

D. W. D.

JEREMIAH, BOOK OF. The book of Jeremiah opens with the prophet's call (chap. 1) and closes with the fall of Jerusalem (chap. 52). It spans the historical period *c.* 626-581 B.C.

The Chronological Enigma

The book of Jeremiah consists of prophetic

discourses, biographical materials, and historical narratives not arranged in strict chronological sequence. A vivid illustration is chaps. 21 and 24 which are dated during the reign of King Zedekiah (597 - 586 B.C.), but chap. 25 is dated during Jehoiakim's reign (608 - 597 B.C.). Also chaps. 27 and 28 are from the reign of King Zedekiah, while chaps. 35 and 36 belong to Jehoiakim's reign. Therefore every outline of Jeremiah is somewhat arbitrary.

Since Jeremiah had a faithful secretary, Baruch, one would normally expect better order. Why all the confusion? A plausible explanation of this state of bewilderment is: the materials in the book of Jeremiah originally circulated in the form of separate scrolls, each one illustrating a Jeremianic teaching (cf. F. M. Wood, *Fire in My Bones*, pp. 9 - 11). Later these topically arranged rolls were compressed into the modern book of Jeremiah. Between the various scrolls a number of narratives have been interwoven from the biography of Jeremiah. Seven major scrolls may be detected:

1. Jeremiah's earlier prophecies, chaps. 1 - 6
2. False and true wisdom, 8:4 – 10:25
3. Messages of discouragement, chaps. 11 - 20
4. Condemnations against the kings and prophets, chaps. 22 - 29
5. The book of hope, chaps. 30–33
6. Historical section, the siege of Jerusalem through the flight into Egypt, chaps. 37 - 44
7. Oracles against the foreign nations, chaps. 46 - 51

The famous temple sermon (7:1 – 8:3) was inserted between scrolls one and two; and between the third and fourth rolls there is a narrative (chap. 21) containing Jeremiah's advice during the siege of the capital city. Three narratives (chaps. 34– 36) concerning Israel's reception of the word of the Lord provide the connecting link for scrolls five and six. Jeremiah's advice to discouraged Baruch (chap. 45) ties the historical section to the foreign prophecies. The oracles to the foreign powers appear in chaps. 46 - 51 (cf. books of Isaiah and Ezekiel for similar sections), and they are followed by a historical appendix (chap. 52), possibly lifted from II Kgs 25. Since Jeremiah spent his life in warning the city of Jerusalem, this is a fitting climax to the romantic ministry of the prophet from Anathoth. Hence this arrangement offers an explanation for the chronological maze (see C. F. Francisco, *Studies in Jeremiah*, p. 13).

The Composition

The beginning point for the writing of the book of Jeremiah is recounted in 36:1 - 8. The date for the nucleus of the roll was 605 B.C. Jeremiah was under a temple interdict from the temple sermon he preached in 609/8 B.C. In the fourth year of the reign of Jehoiakim (605 B.C.) the word of the Lord came to Jeremiah and he dictated the message to Baruch who recorded it in a roll of a book. Then Baruch took it to the temple area and read the sermon during several of the annual religious festivals. The king heard of the message and called for the scroll. After hearing its words of warning, he cut it to bits with his penknife (36:9 - 26). Baruch reported this to Jeremiah and later the Lord ordered Jeremiah to dictate another roll and add many more words to it (Jer 36:27 - 32). This second scroll, apparently the first edition of the extant prophecy, probably contained the heart of chaps. 1 - 25, i.e., the prophecies of Jeremiah which spanned the prophetic period 626 - 605 B.C.

Interspersed throughout this section are the confessions of Jeremiah (Jer 1:4 ff.; 4:10, 19; 6:11; 11:18; 12:6; 15:10– 16; 17:14 – 18; 18: 23; 20:7 - 18) which lay bare the prophet's soul. The biblical world is indebted to Jeremiah's faithful amanuensis, Baruch, for recording these passing shadows of a great soul. Later this loyal scribe, who accompanied Jeremiah step by step along his prophetic pilgrimage, added the biographies of Jeremiah (25:45) as the prophet's life unfolded during the Judean crisis, 604 - 581 B.C.

Also Baruch could have recorded chaps. 46 - 51 as Jeremiah dictated them. These oracles to the foreign nations perhaps were circulated among the neighboring peoples, in addition to being read by the Jews. This section may have been written during the siege of Jerusalem (588 - 586 B.C.). These foreign prophecies consist of oracles against Egypt (chap. 46), Philistia (chap. 47), Moab (chap. 48), Ammon (49:1 - 6), Edom (49:7 - 22), Syria (49:23 - 27), Arabia (49:28 - 33), Elam (49:34 - 39), and Babylon (chaps. 50 - 51).

It is possible that Jeremiah and his scribe Baruch revised the book more than once, so that it went through successive editions. This conclusion depends in part on the evidence of the LXX.

The Relationship to the Septuagint Text

A comparison of the Gr. and Heb. MSS reveal textual difficulties. The LXX (translated 250 - 100 B.C.) differs considerably from the Heb. Masoretic Text (MT): 2,700 words fewer than the MT, i.e., *c*. 120 verses, or four to five average chapters; the Gr. text has nearly 100 words not found in the MT. Frequently where parallel passages occur, the meaning is different.

Various explanations have been offered to explain these differences: The LXX is not a literal translation of the Heb. text. Also the MSS were often illegible; so many of the errors were unconscious mistakes of the copyists. No doubt some of the changes were intentional (see G. A. Smith, *Jeremiah*, pp. 11 - 14).

These apologies account for many of the different readings, but not the two most glaring discrepancies between the LXX and the MT: the absence of so many passages in the Gr. which appear in the MT, and the rearrangement of oracles to the foreign nations. In the LXX chaps. 46-51 are placed between vv. 13 and 15 of chap. 25. Verse 14 is absent in the Gr. version. Evidently the translators of the Gr. were using a Heb. text which differed from the present day MT.

G. L. Archer suggests that, the LXX represents an earlier edition compiled during the prophet's own lifetime and first circulated in Egypt. Then, after Jeremiah's death, Baruch made a more complete collection of his master's sermons which came into the hands of the Jews returning from Babylonian Exile—the MT (SOTI, pp. 349 f.). Others believe there were two streams of compilation which continued until *c*. 200 B.C., both coming from a parent source. Since the discovery of the Qumran scrolls, the questionable texts can be studied in light of the LXX, the MT, and the Qumran scrolls.

The Literary Analysis

The book of Jeremiah has become since 1901 a kind of happy hunting ground for the literary analysis by scholars. In that year B. Duhm assigned to Jeremiah himself only 60 short poems. He contended that Jeremiah's original words were all written in the *Qinah* poetical form (3:2 rhythm) in *c*. 280 verses. Also Baruch's biography accounts for *c*. 200 verses. Roughly speaking, then, Duhm attributed about two-thirds of the book to later editors and supplementers (see A. S. Peake, The New Century Bible, I, 48-57). Less radical scholars ascribe all but a few chapters to Jeremiah and his scribe Baruch. Happily, scholars do not destroy the message. For a more complete survey of the various critical positions, see R. K. Harrison, *Introduction to the Old Testament,* pp. 809-817. He concludes that the process of transmission from the lips of the prophet to the present form of the book was considerably less complex than the majority of liberal writers have assumed, and that it was completed by 520 B.C.

The Testimony of Scripture

The Gr. version of the OT ascribes Lamentations to Jeremiah; but the poems themselves do not claim Jeremianic authorship. Jeremiah is quoted in II Chr 36:21-23 and Ezr 1:1-2. Sir 49:6-7 reflects passages from it as well as from Lamentations. Daniel (9:2) refers to "the word of the Lord to Jeremiah the prophet" (Jer 25:12), and II Macc 2:1-8 contains echoes of the book of Jeremiah (cf. the relationship of Jer 33:15 with Isa 4:2; 11:1; 53:2; Zech 3:8; 6:12).

The NT writers show that the book of Jeremiah was held in high regard and considered canonical by often quoting and referring to it (cf. the new covenant in Jer 31:31 ff. with Heb 8:8-13; 10:15- 17; Jer 31:15 with Mt 2:17 f.; Jer 23:5 with Lk 1:32 f.; Jer 11:20 and 17:10 with Rev 2:23; Jer 51:7-9 with Rev 14:8; 17:2-4; 18:3-5; Jer 10:7 with Rev 15:4; Jer 51:6, 9, 45 with Rev 18:4; Jer 51:63 f. with Rev 18:21; Jer 25:10 with Rev 18:22 f.; Jer 9:23 f. with I Cor 1:31; Jer 7:11 with Mt 21:13; Jer 22:5 with Mt 23:38).

The Teachings

The nature and character of God. The Lord is one God, righteous and just, pure and holy, merciful and gracious, slow to anger and a punisher of evildoers for their sins.

The message of warning to Israel.

1. Israel sustains a special relation wih the Lord (Jer 2:2-3; 7:23; 11:2-5; 13:11). Hosea and Jeremiah used the metaphors of marriage and filial relation which reflect this relationship (Hos 2:2; Jer 31:9).
2. Israel was faithless and was guilty of base apostasy (Jer 2:5-8, 13, 28; 3:1; 5:12, 23-24; 6:7; 7:30).
3. The nation of Israel was self-complacent and blindly trusted in religious externals (Jer 6:20; 7:4, 9-11; 8:8, 12; 16:10-12).
4. Judgment threatened Israel because of her sin (Jer 4:3-4; 6:8; 7:16-20; 14:12; 15:1-9).

The message of hope. Future restoration was a certainty. The political nation of Judah may perish, but the chosen people of God will survive. The eternal purposes of God would be realized (cf. the book of hope, chaps. 30—33). Elements of the future glory are:

1. The preservation of a remnant (Jer 4:27; 5:10, 18; 29:11; 30:11; 46:28).
2. The return from Exile (3:12, 21-22; 16:14-15; 25:11-14; 30:7-11; 31:23).
3. The new Jerusalem (33:16, to be associated with the name "the Lord our righteousness").
4. The ideal ruler (23:4-6; 30:9, 21).
5. The new and everlasting covenant (31:31-34; 32:40; 33:8).
6. The spirituality of religion (24:7), so that the exiles in Babylon (or anywhere else), separated from the temple worship, may seek the Lord directly in prayer (29:4-14).
7. Individual responsibility as the foundation of moral character and spiritual life (31:29-30).
8. The salvation of the nations (3:17; 4:2; 16:19; 33:9).

The visible nation may fall, but true Israel would live on. In the prophecy of the new covenant of grace and forgiveness of sins (31:31 f.) Jeremiah equals the most evangelical sections of Isaiah and other OT prophets.

Bibliography. Kenneth L. Barker, "Jeremiah's Ministry and Ours," BS, CXXVII (1970), 223-231. S. H. Blank, *Jeremiah, Man and Prophet,* Cincinnati: Hebrew Union College, 1961. John Bright, *Jeremiah,* Anchor Bible, Vol. XXI, Garden City: Doubleday, 1965. F. Cawley, "Jeremiah," NBC, pp. 608-639. Clyde F. Francisco, *Studies in Jeremiah,* Nashville: Convention Press, 1961. J. P. Hyatt, *Jeremiah—Prophet of Courage and Hope,* Nashville, Abingdon, 1958. C. F. Keil, *The Prophecies of Jeremiah,* KD. Irving L. Jensen,

Jeremiah: Prophet of Judgment, Chicago: Moody, 1966. Theodore Laetsch, *Jeremiah*, St. Louis: Concordia, 1952. Elmer A. Leslie, *Jeremiah*, Nashville: Abingdon, 1954. A. S. Peake, ed., *Jeremiah and Lamentations*, The New Century Bible, Edinburgh: T. C. & C. C. Jack, 1910. George A. Smith, *Jeremiah*, 4th ed., New York: Harper, 1940. A. Stewart, *Jeremiah, The Man and His Message*, Edinburgh: Henderson, 1936. C. von Orelli, *The Prophecies of Jeremiah*, Edinburgh: T. & T. Clark, 1889. A. C. Welch, *Jeremiah—His Time and His Work*, Oxford: Blackwell, 1951. Fred M. Wood, *Fire in My Bones*, Nashville: Broadman, 1959.

D. W. D.

JEREMIAS. NT form of Jeremiah (Mt 16:14). *See* Jeremiah.

JEREMOTH (jĕr'*ă*-mōth)

1. A Benjamite, son of Beriah. He dwelt in Jerusalem, head of a father's house (I Chr 8:14, 28).
2. A Levite, son of Mushi, of the family of Merari (I Chr 23:23; called Jerimoth in 24:30).
3. A Levite, son of Heman, and head of the 15th course of temple musicians (I Chr 25:22; called Jerimoth in 25:4).
4. An Israelite of the family of Elam who put away his Gentile wife in the days of Ezra (Ezr 10:26).
5. One of the family of Zattu, another who put away his foreign wife (Ezr 10:27).
6. One of the sons of Bani who put away his Gentile wife (Ezr 10:29, ASV, RSV; KJV reads "and Ramoth").

JEREMY. NT form of Jeremiah (*q.v.*). See Mt 2:17; 27:9.

JERIAH (jē-rī'*ă*). A descendant of Levi through Hebron (I Chr 23:19; 24:23). An alternate spelling of Jerijah is used in I Chr 26:31.

JERIBAI (jĕr'ĭ-bī). One of David's "mighty men," a category used to distinguish them from the "three" and the "thirty" (I Chr 11:46).

JERICHO (jĕr'ĭ-kō). At the present stage of archaeological research OT Jericho is considered by the excavator Kathleen Kenyon to be the most ancient instance of urban civilization known to man. The site, located in the Jordan Valley about eight miles NW of the junction of the Jordan River with the Dead Sea, was supplied by a very excellent spring called 'Ayin es-Sultan and Elisha's Fountain (based on the incident in II Kgs 2:19–22). Even before pottery was used a sophisticated culture came into being near this spring. It was a walled town with solid stone structures showing an excellent architectural technique consisting of large dwellings and public buildings. The most remarkable feature of this pre-pottery neolithic culture was a number of human skulls covered with plaster molded to form the facial features, with inset shell eyes. This probably represented a form of ancestor worship, because the features resemble individual portraits; hence some concept of the spiritual nature of man was undoubtedly present. The strong fortifications and evidences of trade reveal these early people were not an isolated society. *See* Archaeology.

The following culture in Jericho was a retrogression. Sometime a little before 5000 B.C. a people using a red burnished coarse handmade pottery arrived. There was no continuity of occupation between these people and the pre-pottery culture; and though the use of pottery was a distinct advantage, the later culture as a whole was by far inferior. However, ascribed to this group is a kind of plastic art similar to, though in more ways different from, the plastered-skull art of the earlier group. A kind of idol was made with plaster smeared in a base of reeds rather than a skull. The shape is that of a flat disc on which are molded inexact features embellished with painted hair and beard and eyes again made of shell.

These people dug quarry pits into the pre-pottery level to obtain clay for their own building bricks formed in a distinctive bun shape. Little, however, is known of this 5th mil. neolithic culture because no burials have been discovered. There were two phases of this culture, the latter with a better handmade pottery which for the first time can be linked with other neolithic pottery from places like Byblos just N of Beirut and Sha'ar ha-Golan at the junction of the Yarmuk and Jordan rivers. Indeed, these crude villagers at Jericho were part of a great and wide movement of people throughout the Fertile Crescent and were making progress toward the age of metal and the dawn of history.

A well-known Chalcolithic culture called Ghassulian, which flourished throughout Palestine in the 4th mil. B.C., is completely absent at Jericho. After a period of no occupation (part of 4th mil.) Jericho came to life again *c.*3200 B.C. But the people were probably semi-nomadic because the evidence comes mostly from their rock tombs with very little from the city mound. The pottery from these tombs is of several types, each of which can be linked with separate sites in the Palestinian hill country. Hence in the late 4th mil. Palestine was receiving several new peoples. Many of them came in through Jericho from the E, a repetitive experience for this age-old city. This was a period of merging newly arrived cultures in Palestine which laid the foundation for the strong urban civilization of the coming Early Bronze Age.

During the Early Bronze Age (*c.* 2900–2300 B.C.) Jericho flourished as a fortified city. Its succession of defenses shows the constant struggle with eastern nomads and possibly the contest with other city-states like Jerusalem, Bethshan and Megiddo, which also helped to create this age of urbanization. The Early Bronze walls of Jericho give dramatic evidence of many destructions by fire. Other causes were

Airview of Old Testament Jericho

widespread erosion of the mud brick of which these walls were made and the not infrequent earthquakes to which this area is subjected. Two of these walls were thought by the 1930-36 excavators of Jericho (directed by Garstang) to be a double Late Bronze Age wall destroyed under Joshua. Kenyon's work has proved the two walls were not contemporary but both were of the Early Bronze Age.

Interesting architectural innovations appear at Jericho in this period: the use of a single and sometimes double ditch outside the walls to make them less accessible, and the abundant use of timbers in the walls for more stability but also as roof beams and roof supports in the mud brick houses. Kenyon believes this reflects the process of deforestation of Palestine which coincides with the period of major erosion at the end of the Early Bronze Age.

Perhaps the biggest change of population in Palestine came at the end of the Early Bronze Age. In the Middle Bronze Age there was a considerable technical advance in pottery through use of the fast wheel and the introduction of entirely new forms. In Jericho this change begins with a strong incursion of nomadic people whose distinctive tombs tell the story. The last Early Bronze wall was hastily built and destroyed by fire before it was completed. The newcomers usher in an intermediate period which Kenyon calls Early Bronze-Middle Bronze. At first living as nomads they built nothing, though eventually their meager building efforts were done with a unique greenish brick. Their pottery had some connection with the earlier period and was usually handmade except for the flaring necks and rims which were added on a fast wheel. Rough with no burnishing or paint, the only decoration is wavy and straight lined incisions sometimes having folded ledge handles. One house of this period seemed to be a temple with altar-like structures and an infant foundation sacrifice.

But the numerous single burial tombs make the clearest distinction with the earlier and later times. Dug into the limestone hills nearby these tombs reveal several distinct types of burial customs pointing to the separate tribes which joined to overthrow Early Bronze Age Jericho. There was the dagger tomb, a small neat type with a single dagger accompanying the articulate bones. Then there was the large roughly cut tomb where the individual was interred as a bag of bones with a batch of small pots and a four-spouted lamp set in a niche. A third square-shaft type had pots and a dagger and sometimes a javelin with curled tangs. One such tomb contained a tribal chief still wearing a copper headband. Finally there was a very large type tomb involving the removal of over 150 tons of rock simply to bury one or two individuals, who also may have been prominent personages. Though there is very little of an artistic nature about the roughly incised unburnished pottery and very utilitarian weapons of these people, yet some graffiti from a tomb shaft wall ties in with similar pottery painting of the Near East. Here are outlines of trees and desert animals with long horns like an ibex or goat, also two warriors holding javelins and small square shields.

Kenyon dates the beginning of this incursion *c.* 2300 B.C. and identifies it with that movement of nomads called in various ancient sources the Amorites.

About 1900 B.C. the Middle Bronze Age makes a full appearance at Jericho. This time the new people came from the N, perhaps pushed out of their former homes, for they came with a developed urban culture. The pottery was made completely on a fast wheel with many shapes derived from metalic prototypes. Bronze instead of copper made their tools and weapons more efficient, and building techniques reached a zenith at Jericho.

An entirely new type of defense system appears, similar to others like it in coastal Syria, Palestine and the Nile delta region. This consisted of a huge plastered embankment supported by a stone revetment at the bottom and having the town wall at the top. Such fortification is usually associated with the Asiatic invaders whom the Egyptians called the Hyksos, perhaps as a defense against new methods of warfare.

The E side of the Jericho mound yielded abundant witness to the town life of the latter part of he Middle Bronze Age. Here are ten

Major ruins of New Testament Jericho stand on the mound to the right of the mosque in right center. J. L. Kelso

strata of buildings. This Jericho came to a violent end shortly after the overthrow of the Hyksos in Egypt (*c.* 1570 B.C.). The Egyptians pursued them to Palestine and one by one destroyed many of their fortified cities such as Sharuhen, by 1550 B.C. Excavation of the last strata uncovered many houses and two steep "streets" with cobbled steps built on the E slope. One street had an underground drain; many ground level shops or storage rooms with the carbonized grain still in great jars; many clay loom-weights witnessing to a weaving industry. A single residence with dozens of querns for grinding flour was perhaps the premises of a flour merchant. Proof that this Jericho had strong contacts with Egypt comes from the presence of Hyksos-type scarabs; but also from well-preserved Egyptian-type furniture in the family tombs which were supplied with food and equipment for the after-life. The perishable items such as long, narrow wooden tables, stools, bowls, a bed, boxes, baskets, mats, etc., represent a most unusual departure for Palestinian archaeology where usually dampness puts strict limits on what is to be found. Probably volcanic gases stopped the decomposition in these sealed tombs.

On the important subject of Late Bronze Age Jericho and Joshua's conquest the Kenyon digging has produced little information. Proof of a 15th–14th cen. occupation is shown in the tombs. As to the mound, erosion is again extensive. But on the E slope erosion was stopped for 150 years by the Late Bronze town of *c.* 1400 B.C. According to Kenyon, no trace of the walls of Joshua's time remains. The reason for this seems to be that the walls were mud brick, as were most of Jericho's walls, and subject to erosion as well as to centuries of quarrying of the decayed mud brick by later peoples. The presence of the modern road over the most likely place where the wash from erosion might be found seems to be additional reason for finding sparse evidence of the Late Bronze Age. It must also be remembered that Garstang's excavations (1930–36) provided considerable uncontroverted Late Bronze material with little or no Mycenaean pottery which was entering Palestine by 1400 B.C. Yet quantities of such pottery have been found recently at Deir Allah and Tell es-Sa'idiyeh 30 miles up the Jordan. Thus Garstang dated the conquest of Jericho no later than 1385 B.C. Kenyon put the fall of Jericho to Joshua at *c.* 1350–1325 B.C. (*Digging up Jericho,* pp. 261–63). *See* Exodus, The: The Date.

Joshua's curse (Josh 6:26–27) was fulfilled on Hiel the Bethelite who rebuilt Jericho (I Kgs 16:34) in the days of Ahab (*c.* 880 B.C.). Most of this Iron Age stratum has also eroded, the earliest remains showing a prosperous community in the 7th cen. which was later destroyed by Nebuchadnezzar's army and rebuilt in the time of Ezra and Nehemiah (cf. Ezr 2:34; Neh 3:2; 7:36).

Herodian palace, New Testament Jericho. HFV

The excavations of J. L. Kelso and J. B. Pritchard in 1950 and 1951 uncovered a Roman style winter palace of Herod the Great at a town site about one and three-quarter miles SW of the OT mound. This was the Jericho where Zacchaeus (*q.v.*), the chief tax collector, lived in Jesus' time (Lk 19:1-2). It was dependent on waters brought from springs in the Wadi Qelt, up which the Roman road went to Jerusalem. Other Jews were evidently living in a village also known as Jericho but much nearer to the copious spring, for Matthew and Mark report that blind Bartimaeus (*q.v.*) was healed along the roadside as Jesus was leaving Jericho (Mt 20:29 34; Mk 10:46-52). Luke, however, states that Jesus was approaching Jericho at the time (18:35). The moving of medieval and modern Jericho a mile closer to Jordan should remind us that it was the oasis, not just the OT mound, which received the epithet "Jericho"—in its origin probably a reference to the moon-god worshiped here by the early Canaanite inhabitants.

Bibliography. John and J. B. E. Garstang, *The Story of Jericho,* London: Marshall, Morgan and Scott, 1948. Kathleen M. Kenyon, *Digging up Jericho,* London: Ernest Benn, 1957; "Jericho," TAOTS, pp. 264-275. Leon T. Wood, "Date of the Exodus," NPOT, pp. 69-73.

E. B. S.

JERIEL (jĕr'ĭ-ĕl). A man of the tribe of Issachar, the son of Tola (I Chr 7:2).

JERIJAH (jē-rī'jȧ). An alternate form of Jeriah (*q.v.*).

JERIMOTH (jĕr'ĭ-mŏth)

1. One of the five sons of Bela, son of Benjamin. He was head of his clan and a warrior in David's time (I Chr 7:7).

2. A son or descendant of Becher, son of Benjamin, head of another Benjamite clan (I Chr 7:8).

3. A Benjamite warrior who joined David at Ziklag. He could be 1 or 2 (I Chr 12:5).

4. A Levite, the son of Mushi of the family of Merari (I Chr 24:30; called Jeremoth in 23:23).

5. A Levite, son of Heman, and head of the 15th course of Levitical musicians (I Chr 25:4; called Jeremoth in 25:22).

6. The son of Azriel, chief of the tribe of Naphtali during David's reign (I Chr 27:19).

7. A son of David and father of Mahalath the wife of Rehoboam (II Chr 11:18). He is not listed among the sons of David. Jewish tradition holds that he was the son of a concubine.

8. A Levite appointed an overseer of the temple offerings by Hezekiah (II Chr 31:13).

JERIOTH (jĕr'ĭ-ŏth). One of the wives of Caleb, the son of Hezron (I Chr 2:18).

JEROBOAM (jĕr'ŏ-bō'ăm). Two kings of Israel carried this name. The name appears on a jasper seal found at Megiddo with the inscription "Shema, servant of Jeroboam," probably an official of Jeroboam II.

1. Jeroboam I (931-910 B.C.), of the tribe of Ephraim, son of Nebat and Zeruah. His energy and skill were recognized by Solomon in connection with the building of the tower of Millo, and he was put in charge of the Ephraimite draftees. The prophecy of Ahijah that Jeroboam would become king of the ten northern tribes instead of Rehoboam, the son of Solomon, came to the king's ears, and Jeroboam fled to Egypt for safety (I Kgs 11:26-40). Returning to Palestine after the death of Solomon, he headed up the delegation of the northern tribes seeking from Rehoboam an alleviation of the oppressions practiced by his father. When this was refused, the northern tribes broke away from the house of David and made Jeroboam king (I Kgs 12:2-15, 19-20).

Jeroboam rebuilt Shechem of Ephraim, which Abimelech, son of Gideon, had destroyed, and made it the royal residence. Next he built Penuel in Transjordan (I Kgs 12:25), either as a winter residence or as an alternate

Bethel, where Jeroboam set up one of his centers of calf worship. HFV

capital because of Pharaoh Shishak's campaign *c.* 926 B.C. Finally he moved his royal residence to Tirzah (*q.v.*; I Kgs 14:17), a city NE of Shechem. His training under Solomon made him a great builder. He is chiefly known as "Jeroboam, the son of Nebat, who made Israel to sin." His sin was the erecting of the calves at Dan and Bethel, establishing in Israel the calf worship which he had doubtless seen in Egypt. His purpose was political, to keep the people away from the temple in Jerusalem, where their hearts might be drawn back to the house of David. The priests and Levites whose homes were in his territory were given no place in the new worship, others being indiscriminately chosen for the priesthood. He was undeterred in his purpose by the warnings of the unnamed prophet from Judah (I Kgs 12:25–13:10, 33-34).

While his reign was prosperous, his sin brought on him the stern judgment of God, seen in the death of his young son Abijah, and in the tragic ending of his dynasty in the second generation (I Kgs 14:1-20).

2. Jeroboam II (782-753 B.C.), son of Joash, and third in succession to Jehu. The duration of his reign given in II Kgs 14:23 (41 years) includes a coregency with his father of approximately 12 years, 794-782 B.C. His reign was one of great prosperity, militarily and economically. He continued the conquests which his father Joash had begun, restoring the borders of Israel which had been overrun by the Syrians and actually subjugating Damascus. As his father had received encouragement in this from Elisha, so Jeroboam was encouraged by the prophet Jonah. It was a period of great wealth. Extravagances and luxuries abounded, as excavations at the capital city of Samaria (*q.v.*) have verified; yet the poor were oppressed, and moral standards were sinking fast. The book of Amos gives a vivid picture of the godless abandonment to pleasure in the days of Jeroboam. Outwardly prosperous, his kingdom was on the verge of disintegration. On the one hand Jeroboam was a savior of Israel (II Kgs 14:27), but on the other hand his long reign brought the nation to the brink of judgment. About 30 years after his death, the kingdom of Israel ceased to exist.

J. C. M.

The Stele of Amrith, Syria, sixth century B.C., illustrates how pagans of the eastern Mediterranean area often viewed their gods as standing on the backs of animals. Some think Jeroboam sought to have Israelites envision Yahweh invisibly standing or seated on his golden calves. LM

JEROHAM (jē-rō'hăm)

1. The son of Elihu and father of Elkanah the father of Samuel (I Sam 1:1; I Chr 6:27, 34).

2. A Benjamite, father of several sons who lived in Jerusalem after the Exile (I Chr 8:27).

3. The father of Ibneiah, a chief of Benjamin after the Exile (I Chr 9:8). Possibly the same as 2.

4. A priest whose son Adaiah resided in Jerusalem after the Exile (I Chr 9:12; Neh 11:12).

5. Jeroham of Gedor, a village in Judah. His sons Joelah and Zebadiah joined David at Ziklag (I Chr 12:7).

6. The father of Azarel, chief of the tribe of Dan in the time of David (I Chr 27:22).

7. The father of Azariah, one of the captains who helped Jehoiada restore Joash to the throne of Judah (II Chr 23:1).

JERUBBAAL (jĕr'ŭ-bāl). The name means "let Baal contend," and is the name given to Gideon by his father Joash upon his destruction of the altar of Baal (Jud 6:32; 7:1). *See* Gideon.

JERUBBESHETH (jĕ-rŭb'ĕ-shĕth). A substitute name for Gideon in place of Jerubbaal used to avoid connecting Gideon with Baal worship (II Sam 11:21). *See* Gideon.

JERUEL (jĕ-rū'ĕl). A section of the wilderness of Judah, above and W of the cliffs overlooking the Dead Sea (II Chr 20:16, RSV), between Tekoa and En-gedi.

JERUSALEM (jĕ-rū'sȧ-lĕm). This city has been aptly called the "spiritual capital of the world," a judgment underscored by the United Nations' resolution of 1947 to designate it an international holy city. To students of the Bible and of history it is perhaps the world's most fascinating community, being one of the world's best preserved medieval walled cities, and sacred to the three leading monotheistic faiths—Judaism, Christianity, and Islam.

Name

The assumption that the name came originally from Heb. *'Ir Shalēm*, meaning "city of peace," appears now to be untenable. The Amarna letters (*q.v.*) written in Akkadian cuneiform have the word *Urusalim;* the Assyrian inscriptions of Sennacherib spell it *Urusalimmu*; and Egyptian hieroglyphics (19th - 18th cen. B.C.) have the equivalent of *Urushamem*. Modern scholars take these to mean "founded by the god Shalem," a god of the Amorites meaning "prosperer" (cf. Ezk 16:2). Its ancient biblical name appears to have been Salem (Gen 14:18; cf. Heb 7:2; Ps 76:2), a form of Heb. *shālôm*, "peace." God's people are to pray for the peace of Jerusalem (Ps 122:6). In the future age God will extend peace to her like a river (Isa 66:12), and here He will give peace (Hag 2:9). The correct Gr. transliteration *Ierousalēm* (Mt 23:37), used regularly in the LXX, follows the Aram. pronunciation *yerûshelēm* (Ezr 4:8, 12, etc.). The alternate form in the Gr. NT, *Hierosolyma,* is deliberately Hellenized to make a Gr.-sounding name.

After the time of the Conquest Jerusalem was known as Jebus (Jud 19:10 - 11), named after its inhabitants the Jebusites (*q.v.*) who were descendants of Hittites and Amorites. Other names include "Ariel" (Isa 29:1), "City of Righteousness" (Isa 1:26), "The Holy City" (Isa 48:2; 52:1; Neh 11:1, 18; Mt 4:5; 27:53). Today Muslims call it *Al-Quds al-Sharīf* ("the noble sanctuary"), or simply *Al-Quds*.

Location and Topography

Jerusalem is located 33 miles E of the Mediterranean and 14 miles due W of the N end of the Dead Sea, at approximately 31° N latitude and 35° E longitude.

The ancient city was built on top of a hill (Ps 48:1 - 2; Zech 8:3) and yet was surrounded by higher hills on all sides except one (Ps 125:1 - 2). The oldest portion—the Jebusite city—lay on a rocky spur projecting S to the confluence of the Kidron and Tyropoeon Valleys. It could be easily defended, and safeguarded the only adequate spring in the vicinity. North on the same spur was the temple site, Mount Moriah. To the W, across the Tyropoeon Valley lay the "upper city," slightly higher than the eastern ridge. Thus the city was in the shape of a U with the open end facing S toward the wilderness of Judea. To the E across the Kidron lies a saddle-shaped ridge 300 feet higher, dominated by Mount Scopus to the NE and Mount Olivet directly E. The view to the W is obstructed by the watershed of the hill country of Judea *c.* 2,800 feet above sea level. *Jebel Deir abu Tor* ("the hill of evil counsel," cf. Mt 26:14 - 16) cuts off much of the view to the S, so the only distant view is to the SE overlooking the desert, a fact which may account for the city's atmosphere of rugged independence.

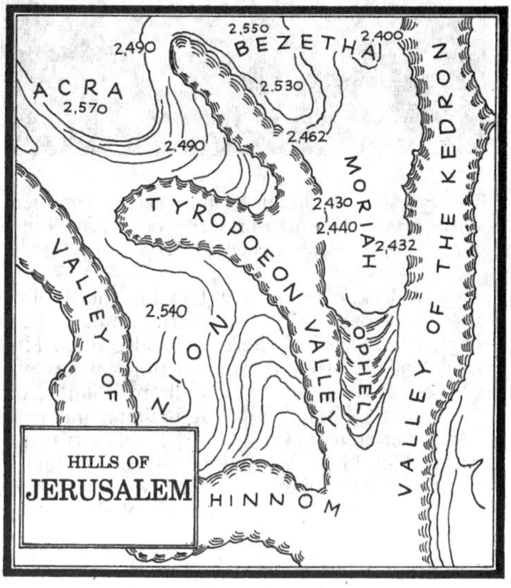

Hills of Jerusalem map

Water

The city's chief natural source of water in OT times was the spring Gihon (*q.v.*) in the Kidron Valley at the foot of the E slope of the Jebusite stronghold. It overflows intermittently three to five times a day. This is caused by underground cavities which fill up and initiate a siphoning process. Water from this source was denied to the Assyrian invaders and was made available to the besieged city by Hezekiah's famous tunnel which still conveys the water to the Pool of Siloam at the SW tip of the ridge (II Chr 32:3 - 4, 30; Isa 22:11; Jn 9:7).

The Palestine Archaeological Museum, Jerusalem, where many of the treasures excavated in Palestine have been housed. HFV

A well known as Bir Eyyub, the biblical En-rogel (Josh 15:7; I Kgs 1:9), had early been dug SE of the city where the Kidron and Hinnom Valleys meet. In Roman times water was conveyed by an aqueduct built by Pilate from "Solomon's Pools" S of Bethlehem and by a high level aqueduct (A.D. 165) from Arrub, toward Hebron. In modern times water is pumped from copious springs N of Anathoth and from Ras el-'Ain in the Shephelah to the W.

The Walls of Jerusalem

The walls originally enclosed the tiny elongated "city of David" on the SE hill. Later, they were extended to enclose the enlarged city and temple area. The main sources for present knowledge of the ancient walls are Nehemiah and Josephus. In Jesus' time, the S wall crossed the Tyropoeon Valley and embraced both David's burg and the upper city where the Church of the Dormition now stands. The first N wall in His day ran due W from the temple area. The disputed "second wall" of Josephus ran from the vicinity of the Joppa Gate N and then E to join the fortress Antonia N of the temple. The "third wall," begun, according to Josephus, in A.D. 42, either lies under the existing N wall or it may be the line of massive stones far to the N of the present wall between the American Consulate and the American School of Oriental Research. The present walls are those of Suleiman, built in A.D. 1542, and probably follow the Roman walls of Aelia Capitolina.

The Gates and Towers of Jerusalem

The gates and towers of the city wall at the time of its rebuilding during the governorship of Nehemiah are named in order, beginning with the Sheep Gate near the NE corner of the temple area, and proceeding counterclockwise around the fortifications (Neh 3). Either in connection with Nehemiah's preliminary inspection by night or with the dedication of the wall of Jerusalem most of the gates are mentioned again (Neh 2:12-15; 12:27-39).

1. *Sheep Gate* (Neh 3:1, 32; 12:39). It was on the N side of the city, between the Tower of Meah to the W and the Miphkad Gate to the E which was near the "going up of the corner," probably meaning the roof-chamber at the NE corner of the city (Neh 3:31, NEB). It is probable that the "sheep market" near the Pool of Bethesda (Jn 5:2) is actually the Sheep Gate (so RSV, NASB), the word "market" having been added by the KJV translators. Buying and selling was often done in the gateway area in ancient cities.

2. *Tower of Meah* (Neh 3:1; 12:39). Modern versions translate the name as Tower of the Hundred.

3. *Tower of Hananeel* (Neh 3:1; 12:39 ; Jer 31:38). This tower and the Tower of Meah guarded the temple area on the N, as the massive "castle" or Tower of Antonia built by King Herod did in the NT period (Acts 21:34, etc.; *see* Castle).

4. *Fish Gate* (Neh 3:3; 12:39; II Chr 33:14; Zeph 1:10). First mentioned in connection with the outer wall built by Manasseh, this gate in the N wall must have been near the present Damascus Gate, where the wall crosses the upper Tyropoeon Valley. The name probably came from the fact that fish from the Sea of Galilee were brought through it into the city, or because of a fish market located near it. This would be the Middle Gate of Jer 39:3 where the Babylonian officials sat, while King Zedekiah fled through a gate on the S side of the city (39:4).

5. *Old Gate* (Neh 3:6; 12:39). From this point onward to the Fountain Gate the line which the fortifications followed is very uncertain, for archaeologists have not yet been able to excavate sufficiently on the W hill to determine how much of it and at what periods it was enclosed within the city wall during OT times. NEB transliterates the name of this gate as the Jeshanah Gate and suggests in a footnote it was the gate of the old city. Depending on the extent of the city, it may have opened into the area called Ophel or the temple area on its W side, near the E end of Robinson's Arch. On the other hand, since Nehemiah does not mention the Corner Gate (II Kgs 14:13; II Chr 25:23; 26:9; Zech 14:10), that may be an alternate name for the Old Gate. The Corner Gate

may have been near the present citadel and Jaffa Gate, where Herod's palace stood in NT times.

6. *Ephraim Gate* (II Kgs 14:13; II Chr 25:23; Neh 8:16; 12:39). The location of this gate of pre-Exilic Jerusalem is given in II Kgs 14:13 and II Chr 25:23 as 400 cubits, or approximately 600 feet, from the Corner Gate. Because of its name it must have led out northward to the territory of Ephraim, thus serving the same purpose as the present Damascus Gate. Neh 8:16 refers to the broad place before the gate within the city walls where booths were built for the observance of the Feast of Tabernacles. Apparently this gate had been rebuilt before Nehemiah returned to Jeruslaem, since it is not mentioned in Neh 3 but is spoken of in Neh 12:39. In NT times the gate which Josephus called Gennath ("garden") stood on or near this spot (*Wars* v.4.2). Jesus may have been led out that gate, carrying His cross (Mt 27:31-32), since there was a garden near the crucifixion site (Jn 19:41).

7. *Broad Wall* (Neh 3:8; 12:38). Excavations in 1970 uncovered a 35 meter-long section of a city wall probably built by Hezekiah (*c.* 700 B.C.) on the western hill. Its unusual thickness of seven meters (23 feet) suggests that it may have been the Broad Wall, still standing in part after Nebuchadnezzar's destructions in 586 B.C. It is much farther E, however, than the present W wall built by Suleiman in A.D. 1542, the newly discovered section lying *c.* 275 meters W of the temple enclosure and *c.* 400 meters E of the Jaffa Gate (N. Avigad, "Excavations in the Jewish Quarter," IEJ, XX [1970], 129-135).

8. *Tower of the Furnaces* (Neh 3:11; 12:38). This tower may be one of those constructed during Uzziah's reign, perhaps the one to fortify the Valley Gate (II Chr 26:9). The "furnaces" or "ovens" (RSV) may refer to pottery kilns which were probably located near Jeremiah's "Potsherd Gate" (Jer 19:2, RSV, NASB), the Valley Gate.

9. *Valley Gate* (Neh 2:13; 3:13; II Chr 26:9). This is the same as the "East Gate" of Jer 19:2 (KJV), a faulty translation of Heb. *sha'ar haḥarsit*, "the Potsherd Gate" (RSV), where broken pottery from the potters' shops was thrown out into the Valley of Hinnom on the refuse heaps. The Valley Gate must have stood high on the western hill and faced SW, since it was 1,000 cubits (1,500 feet) W of the Dung Gate (Neh 3:13).

10. *Dung Gate* (Neh 2:13; 3:13-14; 12:31). It was so named because the refuse of the city was taken through it to be burned in the Valley of Hinnom. Josephus called it the Gate of the Essenes (*Wars* v.4.2). It may have been at or

Jerusalem from the Mount of Olives with the Temple area in foreground. HFV

near the S tip of the walled city, somewhat S of the Pool of Siloam, where the wall must have crossed the mouth of the Tyropoeon Valley. Remains of an ancient gate have been found here. In Jeremiah's time the gate in this section was described as "the gate between the two walls" (II Kgs 25:4; Jer 39:4; 52:7), through which King Zedekiah fled toward the Jordan Valley. Near this gate lay the "king's garden" (II Kgs 25:4; Neh 3:15).

11. *Fountain Gate* (Neh 2:14; 3:15; 12:37). This gate can be located quite closely, since it was near the Pool of Siloam or King's Pool within the city and led directly to the "stairs of the city of David" (Neh 12:37). The remains of a staircase cut in the rock, leading up from the Kidron Valley, show that the Fountain Gate was just N of the SE corner of the city. Its name may indicate that it opened to the "dragon well" (Neh 2:13), the well named En-rogel (II Sam 17:17; I Kgs 1:9), a little way down the Kidron Valley.

12. *Water Gate* (Neh 3:26; 8:1, 3, 16; 12:37). Undoubtedly this gate, which was "toward the east," provided a surface route in peaceful times to descend to the spring Gihon at the foot of the hill. When under siege the defenders walled up the mouth of Gihon, and its waters flowed through Hezekiah's tunnel to the Pool of Siloam. The gate may have been considerably N of Gihon, however, much closer to the temple, as Neh 8:1-5 might suggest. The walls between the Fountain and Water Gates must have been in an extremely bad state of disrepair, judging from the number of men who worked on rebuilding it (Neh 3:15-26).

Miss Kenyon found in her excavations that the terraces supporting houses within the pre-Exilic wall had eroded and collapsed after the Babylonian destruction of Jerusalem. She also discovered that the N wall of the Jebusite city curved from the slope not far N of Gihon and up to the top of the ridge in a northwesterly direction. The Israelite wall connecting this part of the city to the temple mount ran along the E crest on a northeasterly course, forming a right angle in the city wall where it began (cf. "the Angle," II Chr 26:9; Neh 3:19, 20, 24, 25, RSV).

Near the Water Gate was built the "great tower that lieth out" (Neh 3:27), a large projecting tower adjacent to the wall guarding the E side of Ophel, the section of the city just S of the temple area.

13. *Horse Gate* (Neh 3:28; II Kgs 11:16; II Chr 23:15; Jer 31:40). Queen Athaliah was killed at the Horse Gate, which at that time led from the temple to the palace (II Chr 23:15). By Jeremiah's time a city gate of that name marked the easternmost part of the city, probably a little N of "the corner" (Jer 31:40) where the city wall became the E wall of the temple enclosure.

14. *East Gate* (Neh 3:29). Since the East Gate is not stated to have been repaired in Nehemiah's time, it may have been the eastern gate of the temple (cf. Ezk 10:19; 11:1), which had already been rebuilt under Zerubbabel. It would have been opposite the temple building, somewhat S of the present walled-up Golden Gate. For the "east gate" of Jer 19:2 (KJV) *see* Valley Gate, 9 above.

15. *Miphkad Gate* (Neh 3:31, KJV). Other versions translate the name of this gate as "Muster Gate" (RSV), "Mustering Gate" (NEB), or "Inspection Gate" (NASB). This may have been the Benjamin Gate of Jer 20:2; 37:13; 38:7; Zech 14:10, which seems definitely to have been adjacent to the temple and near the NE corner of the city and leading to the territory of Benjamin. The "upper Benjamin Gate" where Jeremiah was imprisoned (Jer 20:2, NASB) was probably a temple gate, perhaps the same as the Gate of the Guards (II Kgs 11:19). The Miphkad Gate must have been at or near the present Golden Gate. Jesus may have come into Jerusalem through this or the East Gate in His triumphal entry. Just N of the Miphkad Gate was the corner of the city defense where the wall turned to the NW, with the Sheep Gate in that section.

16. *Gates of the temple.* In addition to the gates of the city wall certain gates of the temple are named: (1) *Gate Sur* (II Kgs 11:6)—*Gate of the Foundation* (II Chr 23:5); (2) *Gate of the Guards* (II Kgs 11:6, 19; Neh 12:39, KJV, "prison gate"; cf. Jer 20:2); (3) *Gate Shallecheth* (I Chr 26:16), on the W side of the temple area opening on the Tyropoeon Valley; (4) *New Gate* (Jer 36:10); (5) *Beautiful Gate* (*see* Gate, Beautiful; Acts 3:10), perhaps the Nicanor Gate of the Mishnaic tractate Middoth, on the E side of the court of the women (cf. Jos *Wars* v.5.3); (6) the *East Gate* (*see* 14 above).

Excavations

Captain Charles Warren, a British mining engineer, was the first man to conduct any sort of scientific investigation of Jeruslaem. In 1867-70 he excavated around the walls of the temple area, probing the four sides of the *Haram esh-Sherif* with a system of shafts and tunnels. F. J. Bliss and A. C. Dickie explored the S end of the western hill in 1894-97 and found a large wall across the mouth of the Tyropoeon Valley. While the wall has never been accurately dated, it does not seem to go back to OT times. In 1909-11 Montague Parker, with the aid of Père L.H. Vincent, explored and interpreted the maze of tunnels leading from Gihon spring, thus explaining how the Jebusites obtained water during a siege. Raymond Weill excavated parts of the SE hill in 1913-14 and demonstrated once and for all that it was the site of the Jebusite city which David captured and called Zion.

After World War I during the 1920's Weill conducted further excavations at the S tip of the old city. J. Garrow Duncan and R. A. S. Macalister investigated the ridge and along the slope above Gihon. They dated a portion of the wall to the Jebusites, but in 1961 this was proved to belong to the 2nd cen. B.C. Two other British archaeologists, J. W. Crowfoot and G. M. Fitzgerald, dug a trench from the Ophel area on the crest of the Jebusite hill down its W slope and across the Tyropoeon Valley. They uncovered a massive city gate and wall on this side of the SE hill, proving it had been encircled by walls as late as the Maccabean period. Quite far N of the walled old city E. L. Sukenik and L. A. Mayer discovered sections of a wall seemingly built by Herod Agrippa I (A.D. 40-44).

In excavations extending between 1934 and 1948 C. N. Johns carried out extensive examinations of the citadel. A city wall curved around here from the crest above the Valley of Hinnom, and then ran E toward the temple. On it were three towers, the latest Herodian and the earliest Hellenistic or early Hasmonean. Some 7th cen. B.C. pottery was found in the citadel area. A portion of a pre-Hasmonean, probably Israelite, wall built of squared but rough blocks of stone was found under the Herodian tower known as Phasael in further diggings since 1967.

After World War II and the birth of the State of Israel in 1948 no large-scale excavation in Jerusalem was undertaken until 1961. In that year and through 1967 Kathleen A. Kenyon and Pere R. de Vaux directed annual campaigns to investigate a number of areas in Jerusalem using the most up-to-date stratigraphical techniques. These excavations established with reasonable certainty the position of the earliest city and its wall. The Jebusite defenses were built well down the slope of the Kidron Valley in order to protect the entrance to the tunnel leading to the shaft above the cave of Gihon spring. From its origin *c.* 1800 B.C. the city wall was located on this course at least until the 7th cen. B.C., well into the Israelite period.

Since the Six Day War in 1967 Israeli archaeologists led by Benjamin Mazar have excavated S and SW of the temple precinct. A beautifully paved Herodian street was found running along the S and W enclosure walls of Herod's temple. The remains of the great bridge crossing the Tyropoeon Valley from the palace area on the western hill to the Royal Stoa in the temple area (connecting at "Robinson's Arch") were investigated. Instead of a series of arches, the 48-foot-wide viaduct stretched *c.* 40 feet above the street to a finely constructed pier on the W side of the valley. Four small rooms, which probably served as shops, were built into the pier and faced the Herodian avenue. Beneath the paving slabs ran a great aqueduct hewn into bedrock by Herod's workmen (BA, XXXIII [1970], 47-60). Monumental stairs were discovered leading up from the old city of David to one of the Hulda Gates in the S wall of Herod's temple. Beneath one of these gates was found a rock-cut tunnel which, according to the Mishnah, may have served for priestly access to the sanctuary.

New excavations near the Western Wall of the Temple. HFV

Other excavations have uncovered numerous Jewish tombs, including a 1st cen. A.D. cemetery N of the old city. In one of these tombs were bones of a young Jew who had been crucified (*see* Cross).

History

Jerusalem's prehistory goes back at least to the Early Bronze Age when nomadic tribes camped on the SE hill and left some of their kitchen pots and flint tools in a cave *c.* 3000 B.C. It must have been regarded as a holy city from patriarchal times, for Abraham is reported as having paid tithes to Melchizedek (*q.v.*), its unique priest-king (Gen 14:18-20). It was inhabited during the period of the Amorite influx into Palestine, listed as Aushamem in the Egyptian Execration texts (*c.* 1900 B.C.) now in the Berlin Museum (ANET, p. 329).

At the time of the Israelite invasion (*c.* 1400 B.C.) Adoni-zedec, king of Jerusalem, led a coalition which unsuccessfully challenged Joshua's advance (Josh 10:1-26). During the Amarna period its ruler 'Abdu-Heba wrote a number of letters to pharaoh begging for military assistance (ANET, pp. 487 ff.). Afterward the Israelites captured the city outside the walls and set it on fire (Jud 1:7-8); but apparently they did not occupy the citadel, for it was listed as an unconquered city of Jebusites (Jud 1:21; 19:10-12). Because of its natural defenses the Jebusites later felt strong enough to challenge David and his men. Joab and his warriors very likely gained access to the citadel through the large water tunnel leading up from the spring Gihon (II Sam 5:6-9; I Chr 11:6).

In 1867 Charles Warren discovered a vertical shaft 40 feet high within the hill. It enabled residents to draw water from a reservoir filled by means of a horizontal tunnel leading back from the spring. An erratic passage led from the top of the shaft to the surface. The entrance to the passage lay within the town wall, which was 160 feet down from the crest of the ridge and originally built in Middle Bronze Age II (*c.* 1800 B.C.).

With David's capture of the city, Jerusalem entered the realm of world history. His choice of a capital proved to be a wise one. It was a pagan city, not previously claimed by any of the tribes of Israel, and hence it could not be a source of jealousy. It was on the border line of Judah and Benjamin, adjacent to both David's tribe and that of his predecessor. In addition to these political advantages of the time there were the long-range assets of a site easily defended, a secure water supply, and a healthy climate. With an elevation of 2,600 feet it remains one of the highest national capitals in the world. Even in summer the nights are fairly cool because of the elevation and breeze.

David's first act was to strengthen the fortifications of the city by construction of Millo (*q.v.*), perhaps a fortification on the same ridge and to the N of "David's city" in the area called Ophel (Neh 3:26-27). Miss Kenyon believes the *millo* or "filling" was a series of terraces with massive substructures on the eastern slope, built to enlarge the residential area of the crowded city. With the accession of Solomon, extensive building operations transformed the hill N of Ophel into one of the architectural wonders of the world. On that hill was erected Solomon's temple, over the probable site of Abraham's sacrifice of Isaac (Gen 22) and the site of the threshing floor of Araunah the Jebusite (II Sam 24:16-25). The enormous walls built during Solomon's time are probably buried under the present *Haram esh-Sherif,* the enclosure around Herod's temple which he had enlarged to nearly twice its former size.

Jerusalem experienced numerous vicissitudes after the "golden age" of Solomon. Shishak, *c.* 926 B.C., invaded Judah and threatened Jerusalem (I Kgs 14:25-26) but was content with exacting a heavy tribute. During the reign of Jehoram the city was attacked by Philistines and Arabs (II Chr 21:16-17). When Amaziah was king, a portion of the city wall was destroyed by Jehoash of the northern kingdom, and much booty was taken (II Kgs 14:8 ff.). During the reign of Uzziah, however, the city was greatly built up and strengthened and its prestige, in a large measure, restored (II Chr 26:7-8). Another crisis in the city's history occurred when Ahaz was on the throne at the time of the Syro-Ephraimitic war (cf. Isa 7:1-9); then the nation was threatened by a coalition of Israel and Syria (II Kgs 16:5-6).

The Western Wall of the Temple (Wailing Wall). HFV

A major crisis came in 701 B.C. The Assyrians under Sennacherib invaded Judah and besieged Jerusalem (Isa 36-37). In spite of extensive precautions taken by Hezekiah—strengthening the walls and safeguarding the water supply—the city escaped destruction only by divine intervention as stated in II Kgs 18:13-19:37 (cf. Isa 22:1-14). Hezekiah's idolatrous son Manasseh further strengthened the defenses (II Chr 33:14), and it was now one of the most impregnable cities in the world.

Nevertheless, the beginning of the end may be seen in Nebuchadnezzar's occupation of the city in 597 B.C. when he carried into captivity its best citizens and its treasure (II Kgs 24:10-16). The final tragedy occurred in 587/6 B.C. with the complete destruction of the city and the transfer of most of the citizens and artifacts to Babylonia. The seriousness of this ruin can scarcely be overestimated, and the deep scar was never to be effaced (Lam 1:1-19; Ps 79:1-9). Archaeology confirms the biblical account of the thoroughness of the destruction of both city and countryside.

Hope did not die with the city, however. After the accession of Cyrus (539 B.C.) the Jewish emigrants were allowed to return and rebuild. One of their first acts was to lay the foundations of the second temple. After a 20-year period of neglect and apathy, the house of the Lord was completed and dedicated in 516 B.C. The city and environs maintained a precarious existence thereafter with only a vestige of its former glory and influence (Ezra, Nehemiah, Haggai; *see* Restoration and Persian Period).

In the 2nd cen. B.C. another major crisis arose when the Seleucids of Syria gained control of Palestine from the Ptolemies and Antiochus IV began a campaign to force Hellenism upon the Jews. In the ensuing struggle, Jerusalem was captured in 168 B.C., its temple desecrated. But it was recaptured in 165 B.C. by Jewish patriots led by the Maccabbean family of five brothers. The temple, cleansed and rededicated at the Feast of Lights, continued to serve as the focus of Jewish religious and political life until NT times.

Pompey the Roman general arrived in Jerusalem in 63 B.C. at the invitation of one of the warring factions of the Pharisees. Roman rule remained in Palestine thereafter until the Byzantine Empire became dominant. During these years Jerusalem remained the religious center of the Jews both of Palestine and of the Dispersion. Here on Passover occasions and other festivals throngs of pilgrims converged on the city. At such times it often became the scene of violence, as at the accession of Herod's successor Archelaus (when 3,000 died), at the death of Jesus, and when Paul was rescued from a mob (Acts 21:30). The temple of Herod, in Jewish thinking still the second temple although enlarged and completely remodeled, was begun in 19 B.C. and completed in A.D. 64, six years before the total destruction of the city in A.D. 70 following a four-year rebellion against Rome.

Jerusalem was leveled to the ground after the second Jewish revolt under Bar Kochba in A.D. 134 and rebuilt by Hadrian as a pagan city called Aelia Capitolina. Gradually Christians became more and more numerous in the city; Christian churches were erected there from the 4th cen. until the Muslim conquest in A.D. 637. Muslim influence has been dominant in the city from then until the present with the exception of the Latin Kingdom (A.D. 1099 - 1188) and other short intervals during the Crusades. Palestine was occupied by the Ottoman Empire for four centuries (1517 - 1917).

Since the last quarter of the 19th cen. Jewish immigration from all over the world has greatly increased the size of the city until at the present time there is a population of about 300,000 Jews and 80,000 Arabs.

After the termination of Ottoman rule in Palestine by World War I, Great Britain held a Mandate over Palestine from the League of Nations for 30 years. When this terminated in 1948 Arabs and Jews fought to a standstill along armistice lines which divided the city until 1967. After the Six Day War in 1967, Israel united the Holy City and declares she will not surrender the eastern section regardless of what decision is made on other occupied territories.

While the capitals of mighty empires—Tyre, Thebes, Nineveh, Babylon—have laid in ruins for millennia, Jerusalem survives as a commercial and political center, but most of all as a museum of the past and a symbol of hope for the future.

Bibliography. D. R. Ap-Thomas, "Jerusalem," TAOTS, pp. 276 - 295. M. Avi-Yonah, *Jerusalem,* New York: Orion, 1960. Millar Burrows, "Jerusalem," IDB, II, 843 - 866. Joseph A. Callaway, "Jerusalem," BW, pp. 309 - 323. G. Cornfeld, "Ancient Cities: Jerusalem," CornPBE, pp. 80 - 89. G. Fohrer and E. Lohse, "*Sion, Ierousalēm,* etc.," TDNT, VII, 292 - 338. John Gray, *A History of Jerusalem,* London: Hale, 1969. Joachim Jeremias, *Jerusalem in the Time of Jesus,* Philadelphia: Fortress, 1969. Kathleen M. Kenyon, *Jerusalem,* New York: McGraw-Hill, 1967; "Israelite Jerusalem," *Near Eastern Archaeology in the Twentieth Century,* ed. by J. A. Sanders, Garden City: Doubleday, 1970, pp. 232 - 253. André Parrot, *Golgotha and the Church of the Holy Sepulchre,* London: SCM Press, 1957. D. F. Payne, "Jerusalem," NBD, pp. 614 - 620. Stewart Perowne, *Jerusalem and Bethlehem,* New York: Barnes, 1965. Charles F. Pfeiffer, *Jerusalem Through the Ages,* Grand Rapids: Baker, 1967. J. Simons, *Jerusalem in the Old Testament,* Leiden: Brill, 1952. George A. Smith, *Jerusalem,* 2 vols., New York: Armstrong, 1907 - 8. Wilbur M. Smith, "Jerusalem," ZPBD, pp. 417 - 427. Hermann Strathmann, "*Polis,* etc.," TDNT, VI, 516 - 536. L. H. Vincent, *Jerusalem de l' Ancien Testament,* Paris: Gabalda, 1954-6.

G. A. T. and J. R.

JERUSALEM COUNCIL. *See* Apostolic Council.

JERUSALEM, NEW. The New Jerusalem (Rev 3:12; 21:2, 10) was looked for by Abraham (Heb 11:10, 16), promised by Christ (Jn 14:2 - 3), referred to as Zion the mountain and city of the living God (Heb 12:22), alluded to by Paul (Gal 4:26), employed as an incentive (Rev 3:12), and described in Rev 21:1 – 22:5. It is not identical with the earthly Jerusalem of the Millennium, nor is it equivalent to the new heaven. This city comes down out of heaven from God after the Millennium, and is the center of the new order. It is the habitation of Christ and the Church and is accessible to the saved nations.

The city is described first from the standpoint of its population, the Church (Rev 21:1 - 9); then from the viewpoint of its material proportions, a cube 1,500 miles each way, made of gold and precious stones (Rev 21:10 - 23); and finally from the viewpoint of its eternal provisions (Rev 21:24 – 22:5). This divine architectural achievement has material reality—the resurrected saints and Christ will inhabit it with physically real bodies, though its details symbolize great spiritual realities. *See* City of God; City, Holy; Heaven; Zion.

H. A. Hoy.

JERUSHA, JERUSHAH (jē-rū'shȧ). The mother of Jotham, the wife of King Uzziah, and the daughter of Zadok (II Kgs 15:35). The alternate spelling of Jerushah is found in II Chr 27:1.

JESAIAH (jē-sā'yȧ), **JESHAIAH** (jē-shā'yȧ)

1. A son of Hananiah, son of Zerubbabel (I Chr 3:21).

2. A Levite, one of the sons of Jeduthun. He was a harpist and appointed by David to be head of the eighth course of musicians (I Chr 25:3, 15).

3. A Levite, the son of Rehabiah. A descendant, Shelomoth, was over the treasury of things dedicated by David and the other leaders to the Lord (I Chr 24:21, Isshiah; 26:25 - 26).

4. The son of Athaliah, chief of the family of

Elam. He returned to Jerusalem with Ezra (Ezr 8:7).

5. A Levite of the family of Merari. With Hashabiah and 20 sons and brethren he joined Ezra at Ahava on the way to Jerusalem (Ezr 8:19).

6. A Benjamite, father of Ithiel, whose descendants dwelt in Jerusalem after the Exile (Neh 11:7).

JESHANAH (jĕsh'*ȧ*-n*ȧ*). One of the cities taken by King Abijah of Judah in a war with Jeroboam II (II Chr 13:19). The RSV has Jeshanah for Shen in I Sam 7:12. The most probable location is Burj el-Isaneh, about three miles N of Jifneh.

JESHARELAH (jĕsh'*ȧ*-rē'l*ȧ*). A musician among the sons of Asaph during the time of David (I Chr 25:14). He is called Asarelah in v. 2.

JESHEBEAB (jē-shĕb'ē-ăb). The head of the 14th order of priests (I Chr 24:13).

JESHER (jē'shẽr). A son of Caleb (I Chr 2:18).

JESHIMON (jē-shī'mŏn)

1. A barren place at the NE end of the Dead Sea E of Jordan ("Jeshimon," KJV; "desert," ASV, RSV). Mount Pisgah and Mount Peor look down upon it; mentioned in connection with Israel's journey to Canaan (Num 21:20; 23:28).

2. A place N of the hill Hachilah and the wilderness of Maon, and S of Hebron. Rendered "Jeshimon" in the KJV and RSV; ASV, "desert," but marg., "Jeshimon." Apparently part of the general wilderness of Judah in which David was a fugitive when Saul was hunting for him (I Sam 23:19, 24; 26:1, 3).

JESHISHAI (jē-shĭsh'ī). A member of the tribe of Gad, a descendant of Buz (I Chr 5:14).

JESHOHAIAH (jĕsh'ō-hā'y*ȧ*). A Simeonite prince (I Chr 4:36).

JESHUA (jĕsh'o͞o-*ȧ*)

1. A priest in the time of David to whom the ninth course was assigned by lot (I Chr 24:11). Descendants of the house of Jeshua returned after the Exile (Ezr 2:36; Neh 7:39).

2. A Levite appointed by Hezekiah to distribute the offerings among his brethren (II Chr 31:15).

3. A Levite whose descendants, "the children of Jeshua," returned with Zerubbabel (Ezr 2:40; Neh 7:43). Perhaps the same as 2.

4. The son of Jozadak, who returned with Zerubbabel to Jerusalem as high priest. He is of historic importance as the one under whom the temple was rebuilt and the worship restored. From him descended 14 successive high priests. Jeshua is named with the prince Zerubbabel as an equal not only in the work of the temple but in the relations of the Jews with other peoples (Ezr 2:2; 3:2, 8, 9 f.; 4:3; 5:2; 10:18; Neh 7:7; 12:1, 7, 10, 26). The word of the Lord through the prophet Haggai was addressed to Zerubbabel and Jeshua (called Joshua in Hag 1:1, 12, 14; 2:2, 4). He is used by Zechariah as a symbol of the restored, forgiven remnant, a "brand plucked out of the fire" (Zech 3:1 – 3), and also as a type of Christ, the "Branch" and the "priest upon his throne" (Zech 3:6 ff.; 6:11 – 13).

5. The father of Jozabad the Levite, appointed by Ezra as one of those to receive the treasure delivered to the temple (Ezr 8:33).

6. Of the town of Pahath-moab. His descendants are named along with Joab among those who returned with Zerubbabel (Ezr 2:6; Neh 7:11).

7. Ezer, son of Jeshua, ruler of Mizpah, helped in the repair of the wall of Jerusalem with Nehemiah (Neh 3:19).

8. A prominent Levite during the time of Nehemiah. Jeshua, son of Kadmiel, stood with Ezra as he read the law and helped explain it to the people (Neh 8:7 – 8). He took part in the great prayer of confession at the Feast of Tabernacles (Neh 9:4 – 5). He is listed among the heads of his father's houses among Levites (Neh 12:8, 24).

9. Joshua the son of Nun, called Jeshua in Neh 8:17.

10. A Levite, son of Azaniah, who sealed the covenant of Nehemiah (Neh 10:9). He is difficult to distinguish from 8.

11. A city of Judah inhabited after the Exile (Neh 11:26).

P. C. J.

JESHUAH. *See* Jeshua.

JESHURUN (jĕsh'*ŭ*-rŭn). A poetic term for Israel meaning "upright one." If the ending *-un* is a diminutive, it means "little upright one" (Deut 32:15; 33:5, 26; Isa 44:2).

JESIAH (jē-sī'*ȧ*)

1. KJV variant of Isshiah 3 (*q.v.*). One of David's mighty men when he was at Ziklag (I Chr 12:6).

2. KJV variant of Isshiah 2 (*q.v.*). A Levite, son of Uzziel (I Chr 23:20).

JESIMIEL (jē-sĭm'ĭ-ĕl). A prince of the tribe of Simeon (I Chr 4:36).

JESSE (jĕs'ī). A descendant of Obed, the son of Boaz and Ruth (Ruth 4:17, 22), in the clan of Nahshon, chief of the tribe of Judah in the time of Moses. Jesse had eight sons, of whom David was the youngest, and two daughters (I Sam 17:12). The daughters were by a different wife from David's mother. Jesse lived in Bethlehem and was supported through shepherding and goat herding

The humble status of his family is alluded to by the opprobius epithet "son of Jesse" given to David by those who disliked him (e.g., I Sam 20:27, 30; 22:7; 25:10; II Sam 20:1). Jesse sought asylum in Moab during David's flight from Saul (I Sam 22:3–4). The expression "shoot from the stump of Jesse" and "the root of Jesse" in Isa 11:1, 10 (RSV), which indicate the insignificant and lowly background of the royal line of David, became symbols of messianism.

F. E. Y.

JESTING. In the KJV the term is used only in Eph 5:4, where it means having a coarse, frivolous attitude toward serious matters. In the RSV it is used only in Gen 19:14, where Lot's sons-in-law thought he was joking about the coming destruction.

JESUI (jĕs´ū-ī). A son of Asher (Num 26:44). *See* Ishui.

JESURUN. *See* Jeshurun.

JESUS CHRIST. Jesus Christ is unique in several respects, not the least of which is the fact that in Him alone centers the gospel of the grace of God. He has changed the face of history, for in Him eternity has invaded time, God has become man, and human life has achieved through His redemption a significance that lifts it above the natural order and fits it for God's fellowship and service.

But is such a life possible? The philosopher may be inclined to deny it on the ground that the gulf between God and man is too great to be bridged in a single being and that the elements involved are too discrete to be combined in a unified personality. Yet the Gospel records present just such a personality. One has the choice between supposing a literary miracle based on fancy and accepting a historical miracle based on the sovereign action of Almighty God, adequately attested by competent witnesses. *See* Christ, Deity of; Christ, Humanity of; Christ, Humiliation of; Christ, Sinlessness of.

The historian may feel that he cannot dismiss Jesus Christ as unhistorical, in view of the substantial character of the evidence, but nevertheless acknowledges misgivings as to the factuality of many elements of the story as given in our sources. After all, the earliest of the Gospels emerged some 30 years after the latest of the events it recounts. Granted the interval exists, yet it is not an empty interval. Memories of Jesus of Nazareth lived on in scores, yes hundreds of lives, and these memories were kept vivid by frequent recollection stimulated both by meditation and by proclamation.

Though Jesus wrote nothing for posterity, He gave assurance to His closest followers that the Spirit of God would have as a peculiar part of His ministry the bringing to remembrance in the minds of these men of the things that Jesus had said (Jn 14:26). Even apart from supernatural aid the disciples could never forget the

Traditional site of the manger in which Jesus was born inside the Church of the Nativity, Bethlehem.
Giovanni Trimboli

stirring scenes that they had shared with the Master. Some incidents involved Jesus alone, such as the temptation, but there is no reason to suppose that He would have refrained from informing them of what transpired.

It is not possible to demonstrate that the materials in the Gospels are always arranged in strict chronological order. But it is clear that all the records preserve an order of events that proceeds from those that belong to the commencement of the ministry to those that mark its close, so that there is a sense of progress and also of symmetry. One does not get an impression of erratic or fanciful composition.

The setting for this greatest of all lives is the land of Palestine at a time when Rome had established her sovereignty over much of the Near East. Government officials, military men and tax gatherers were constant and unpleasant reminders that Israel was not free. Restlessness, at least among the Zealots, was gradually building up toward open revolt. In such an atmosphere it would not be easy to carry on a ministry grounded in spiritual considerations. Jesus' teaching and personal claims could be easily misconstrued. Any assertion of kingly right was bound to be distorted by some into a bid for temporal power. Any talk of freedom was all too readily lifted from its context of bondage to sin and made to apply to the current political situation. It was only with the greatest difficulty that even the Twelve were weaned from these notions. By the time this adjustment was made (Acts 1) Jesus was on the point of departure from the world. Thus even if the temporal concept of the kingdom had persisted, it would have lacked any possibility of realization, since the Master was no longer on the scene. Under the control of the Holy Spirit the church could move only along the lines laid down by Jesus—a kingdom free from worldly motives and methods. Rome need have no fears of competition from this quarter.

Although Jesus spent His days on earth under the Roman eagle, His life was far more heavily influenced by His Jewish inheritance. Born of a Jewish mother, nurtured in a home of piety and possibly of near poverty, encouraged to love the Scriptures, trained in the worship and instruction of the synagogue, He steeped His mind in the history and traditions of His people. The readiness with which He could quote Scripture and the appropriateness of His references to it testify to prolonged and thoughtful study. His boyhood development along this line is hidden from us; but this much is clear, that He turned to the Word not only for spiritual nourishment but also to find the indications of His own mission (Lk 4:18 – 19; 22:37; 24:44 -47). Lacking formal rabbinic training, He was able to assess the spiritual needs of His nation in an independent manner and could point out the various ways in which the religious leaders had led the people astray.

This ability to be in Judaism and yet to stand over against it is reflected in a certain duality that runs through Jesus' ministry, namely, loyalty to Israel (Jn 4:22; Mt 10:6; 15:24) yet admiration for the faith of those who were outside the covenant nation (Mt 8:10); compassion for His own countrymen (Mt 23:37) yet forthright prediction that others would step into Israel's inheritance (Mt 8:11 – 12). Jesus the Jew was in many ways the most unjewish of men. He was, in fact, the universal man. Perhaps that is part of what He sought to convey by calling Himself the Son of man (*see* Son of Man). To be sure, He was the son of David and the son of Abraham (Mt 1:1), but He was also the son of Adam (Lk 3:38). There is nothing surprising in this if He came to fulfill the promises made to the fathers and also to insure that the Gentiles might be able to glorify God for His mercy (Rom 15:8 -9). *See* Messiah.

Birth and boyhood. Herod the Great was still reigning at the time Jesus was born (Mt 2:1). Herod's jealous apprehension made it unwise for Jews to show any great enthusiasm over the heralded arrival of their promised King. Yet the response of the shepherds (Lk 2:8 -18) presaged a kindly reception from the common people of a godly sort even as the Magi constituted the firstfruits of the Gentiles.

A mosque at Beeroth, a day's journey from Jerusalem, where presumably Joseph and Mary discovered that Jesus was missing from the company returning from the Temple to Nazareth (Lk 2). HFV

The circumstances surrounding the conception of Jesus were such as to give rise among unbelieving Jews to ugly rumors to the effect that He was an illegitimate child. Medieval Jewish legends made much of this. Matthew's account of the nativity seems designed to answer such misrepresentations, treating the matter particularly from the side of Joseph; whereas Luke's account, probably derived ultimately from Mary herself, presents the Lord's dealings with her in a special way. Occasional insinuations may have been made against Jesus during His lifetime (cf. Jn 8:41). The nativity accounts gave to the church all it needed to know on this subject. Although the doctrine of the virgin birth took its place also in the Apostles' Creed, it was not a part of the apostolic preaching so far as the records reveal. *See* Incarnation.

Little information is given about the boyhood of Jesus, and this very fact underscores the truth that our Gospels were not intended to be biographies in the accepted sense of that word. Although they provide some materials for a life of Christ, they were not written from the biographical standpoint but rather as furnishing information leading to a better understanding of the message of the gospel. The silence concerning this period of Jesus' life is relieved by the account of the visit to the temple at the age of twelve, preceded and followed by summary statements about His development (Lk 2:40–52). In His discussions on the Scripture Jesus the lad appears as a hearer of the Word, and in His continuing obedience to His parents in the home at NazarethHe is seen as a doer of it.

Preparations for the ministry. In the providence of God Jesus had a herald who prepared the way for Him. John the Baptist, fully aware of the impact he was making on Israel, nevertheless publicly proclaimed that a greater was coming, One who was both Saviour (Jn 1:29) and Judge (Mt 3:12), and that men must repent of their sins in view of the approach of the kingdom (Mt 3:2). Similar announcements were made by Jesus Himself. Although the two were very different in appearance and habits (Mt 11:18 – 19), they were akin in possessing a large following and in creating opposition in leading circles of Judaism, an opposition that did not stop short of taking their lives (Mt 17:12).

Jesus' baptism at the hands of John marked the abandonment of the secluded life in Nazareth and the assumption of His role as the Servant of Yahweh (Mt 3:17; cf. Ps 2:7; Isa 42:1). To equip Him for this mission the Holy Spirit came upon Him and heaven acknowledged Him. The keynote of that mission was sounded in the avowed readiness of the Son to identify

Himself with the sinful nation He had come to redeem (Mt 3:15). The full implications of that identification were to become apparent in His baptism of blood at the cross (Mk 10:38; Lk 12:50).

The Son of God was not yet ready to launch out in His work, even though He had divine approval and equipment to add to His own dedication to the task. He must first be subjected to a grueling temptation at the hands of Satan. Jesus would be dealing with minds blinded by Satan, with people whose bodies were bound by him and reduced to virtual helplessness, with lives darkened and tortured by his emissaries the unclean spirits. By meeting every test of the evil one Jesus earned the right to banish the demons and deliver men from the fearful grip of the devil. He could challenge the sway of Satan's kingdom by having defeated the prince of this world, blunting every dart on the shield of faith and pinning down His opponent by means of the sword of the Spirit, the Word of God. Out of the temptation experience came a pattern of resolute dependence on God that remained a permanent feature of His ministry.

The locale and length of the ministry. A day by day chronicle of Jesus' activity is lacking. Notices of time and place are occasionally given, but they are insufficient to provide more than a sketchy outline. It is clear from the Synoptics that the bulk of the ministry took place in Galilee, with considerable itinerating among the towns and villages. Capernaum proved a suitable headquarters, because of its central location. A journey to Tyre and Sidon on one occasion took Jesus and the disciples outside the bounds of Palestine (Mk 7:24). Another trip took them through a portion of the Decapolis region consisting of a scattered group of Gr. communities to the E of the Sea of Galilee (Mk 7:31). In addition there was a withdrawal N to Caesarea Philippi (Mk 8:27) and some activity in Perea, the territory E of the Jordan (Mk 10:1).

From the Gospel according to John, on the other hand, we learn little about Jesus' work in Galilee, for most of the narrative centers around visits to Jerusalem, especially in connection with the various annual festivals of the Jews. These include Passover (Jn 2:23; 6:4; 13:1), Tabernacles (7:2), Dedication (10:22) and an unnamed feast (5:1). The Synoptics mention only one Passover, the occasion of the passion. From Acts 10:37 it is possible to assume that Jesus had a ministry in other parts of Judea than Jerusalem and vicinity.

With the help of these references to festivals in John, the duration of the ministry can be calculated roughly. It must have exceeded two years and probably approximated three. Some advocate a four year period (E. Stauffer, *Jesus and His Story*, pp. 6-7).

Jesus' teaching. The Gospel writers give many pen pictures of our Lord surrounded by large crowds and holding their attention by the fascination of His instruction. People were im-

Traditional site of the baptism of Jesus. HFV

pressed by the manner in which He spoke—with authority (Mk 1:22). He did not quote the sayings of the rabbis. He dared to put His own statements on a par with the teaching of the OT and even to supersede the authoritative declarations of the past (Mk 7:9-14; Mt 5:33-34, 38-39). In contrast to most teachers among His people, He did not become lost in a maze of inconsequential details or resort to hairsplitting, but confined His discourse to essential truths. Great simplicity marked His utterances, aided by His avoidance of technical terms and by the frequent use of illustration, especially in connection with parables. He knew how to lead people from the known to the unknown.

The teaching was carried on in various settings—on the hillside, at the edge of the lake, in homes, in the synagogues, and at the temple in Jerusalem. It was all open and public (Jn 18:20). Teaching as He did for hours at a time, He must have suffered a severe drain on His energy (Mk 4:36-38).

In His public teaching Jesus could build on the fact that His hearers were believers in God and fairly familiar with the OT. Probably for this reason He gave less formal instruction on the nature of God than would otherwise have been the case. The truth that God is Spirit was disclosed to a Samaritan rather than a Jew (Jn 4:24). Considerable attention was given to God's goodness (Mt 5:45; 7:11; 19:17), His care over His children (Mt 6:26, 30, 32), and the perfection of His love (Mt 5:46-48). Assurance was given of God's forgiveness of the trespasses of His people (Mk 11:25) and of His readiness to hear the prayer of faith (Mk 11:22-24). His righteousness is acknowledged (Mt 6:33) and His work as Judge (Mt 10:28). But above all Jesus set forth God as Father. The language of fatherhood had been used in the OT in the sense of Creator (Isa 64:8), but

Jesus conveyed to His hearers a richness of meaning hitherto unknown, especially in the area of personal relationship. Here He could speak out of immediate and intimate knowledge (Mt 11:27). He graciously welcomed His true followers into the heavenly family, which entitled them to call upon God as their Father also (Mt 6:9). *See* God.

Central to the teaching of Christ was His exposition of the kingdom of God. Those who have a part in it are not the mighty of this world or the self-righteous, but rather the poor in spirit and the persecuted (Mt 5:3, 10). In fact, Christ as King exhibits the very traits which are demanded of His subjects (Mt 11:29; 21:5). One could say He *is* the kingdom in its essence. With His coming into the world the kingdom came in an initial sense. In His teaching the principles of the kingdom stood revealed. After His departure the kingdom continued to make its appeal (Acts 28:31), and according to His prediction will be consummated in power and glory at His return (Mt 25:31-34). *See* Kingdom of God.

Jesus' evaluation of man is to be gleaned not so much from His spoken word as from His readiness to sacrifice His own life for the sake of bringing about man's redemption. Obviously mankind must in all faithfulness be pronounced evil by Him who best knows the heart (Mt 7:11). The corruption comes from within rather than from environmental influences (Mk 7:18-23).

Two blemishes on the society of that time were especially distressing to the Master. One was the result of religious factors centering in the scribes and Pharisees. By their scrupulous attention to the minutiae of the law and the traditions of the elders, to the comparative neglect of the weightier issues of justice and love, these blind leaders were strangling the religious impulses of the covenant nation. The people were like shepherdless sheep. Another distressing feature, influenced by the first, was the drift of the common man toward materialism. He was too often found serving Mammon, imagining that he could give himself to covetousness and still honor God in passable fashion. Jesus had to warn of the danger of losing one's soul in the vain attempt to gain the world (Mk 8:36-37).

No one could listen to Jesus without sensing in Him a tremendous earnestness about life and the way it should be lived. It was the vestibule of eternity. Heaven and hell were solemn realities to Him, and He challenged His hearers to consider their destiny in the light of their beliefs and practices.

Jesus' miracles. There can be no doubt that along with His teaching the mighty works of our Lord were highly influential in awakening popular enthusiasm for Him, especially at the height of His Galilean campaign. He could not be hid. Wherever He went the crowds surged about Him. It may not be possible to trace a consistent pattern of relationship between His teaching and the miracles in this matter of attracting a following; but with Mt 4:24–5:1 as a guide one may reasonably conclude that frequently the crowds were bent on securing healing for themselves and their loved ones, and when this was granted, large numbers of them remained to hear the Lord teach. Something of the same supernatural power that was unveiled in the works of healing shone forth from the teaching. The one activity complemented the other.

Modern Cana, possibly on the same location as the biblical town where Jesus performed His first miracle. HFV

Can the miracles be verified? Their very prevalence in the narratives of the Gospels makes it exceedingly difficult to treat them as pious creations of the writers. One has to ponder the fact that the early church, according to the testimony of the book of Acts and of the epistles, enjoyed similar miraculous power, which it attributed to Jesus Christ (Acts 4:10; 9:34; Rom 15:18-19; Heb 2:4). Our sources attest the spiritual transformation of a host of people, including the apostles. These are the same sources that claim miraculous power for Jesus and His followers. How is it possible to have truth and fraud jumbled together? The total picture must stand or fall in terms not of one ingredient only but of all. The transformed lives are no less marvelous than the signs and wonders, and without them the church could not have made its way in the world. It is well to remember this also, that the miracles were not doubted in Jesus' time, even by those who were counted His enemies (Mk 3:22; Mt 27:42).

A motivating purpose behind these marvelous deeds is suggested by one of the terms used for them. They were signs. This means they were intended to bear a testimony to the One who performed them or to the truth He proclaimed. They were calculated to assure those who experienced them or witnessed them that God's Anointed was at work in their midst (see Lk 4:16-21). They were counted on to add weight to the spoken word that bade men break with their sins and turn to God in penitence and faith. That this result did not always follow when miracles were performed, shows the hardness of the human heart (Mt 11:20–21). One of the Gospels openly connects the inclusion in its record of certain signs of Jesus with the expectation that as a result faith will be quickened in the heart toward Him as the Christ, the Son of God (Jn 20:30–31). It would be most extraordinary to expect such a result from the reading of this Gospel if in point of fact people had not previously been led to such faith by the witnessing of the signs during Jesus' ministry.

But to insist on this purpose as the sole reason for the miracles would be one-sided. It would hardly explain the healing of all the needy who confronted Jesus time after time. To show His power on a few would have been adequate as a demonstration of His messianic office. The plain intimations of Scripture that another motive was present cannot be ignored. Our Lord was so moved with compassion over the plight of those who flocked to Him that He could not refrain from helping them. As Peter put it, He "went about doing good, and healing all that were oppressed of the devil" (Acts 10:38). So the miracles are rightly regarded as revelations of the love of God in Christ as well as tokens of divine appointment. *See* Miracles.

Response to the ministry. This ran the gamut from bitter opposition to adoring devotion. Leading opponents were the scribes and Pharisees. At first they were content to observe Him in action, but before long they became vocal, challenging Him on a variety of counts. They took offense when He accused them of setting aside the commandments of God in favor of their traditions (Mk 7:9). His rebuke was particularly hard for them to bear because He was not trained as a rabbi, yet took the liberty of sitting in judgment on them. Friction arose also over Jesus' insistence on conducting His healing ministry on the sabbath as well as on other days (Mk 3:1–6). Delay in relieving human suffering was senseless in His eyes. But the religious leaders did not look on the matter in the same light. They became so infuriated that they determined to put Him to death. Another cause of offense was Jesus' claim to be able to forgive sins. To the opposition, this was plain blasphemy, for it meant that He was assuming a prerogative of God (Mk 2:7). This charge of blasphemy loomed large in the eyes of the Sanhedrin, especially when it involved an admission on Jesus' part of divine sonship (Mk 14:61–64).

Among the people in general the response varied from indifference to genuine faith. Perhaps the most disappointing feature to our Lord was the utterly selfish motivation governing many who followed Him. On one occasion He accused the multitude of seeking Him merely for the sake of what He could provide for them in the form of material good (Jn 6:26).

Yet there were a few in those days who gladly forsook their possessions, their gainful pursuits, their homes and their loved ones in order to become His intimate followers (Mt 19:27). It would be rash to assert that the Twelve were more devoted than any others, especially in view of the ministry of certain women (Lk 8:1–3) and the close tie that Jesus enjoyed with His friends at Bethany (Lk 10:38–42; Jn 11). Nevertheless the Gospels emphasize the fidelity of the apostles and correspondingly the attention that Jesus bestowed on them to prepare them for their future work as leaders in the church. Here was a ministry within a ministry. Jesus taught them to trust the Father and pray to Him for their needs, to look with compassion on the sufferings and trials of those about them, and to cultivate their discipleship with an ever deepening understanding of its implications. The more clearly they were able to perceive in the ministry of Jesus the outline of their own, the more meaningful became their call.

It was a shock to these men to hear from Jesus' own lips that He must go to Jerusalem and there be rejected and put to death (Mt 16:21–22). Even further instruction on this subject left them perplexed and disturbed, but they did not desert the cause. Only with difficulty did Jesus communicate to them the basic nature of His mission—obedience to the Father and self-surrender to the point of giving Himself a ransom for many (Mk 10:45).

Naturally the Twelve had difficulty in the area of humility until they had accepted their Lord's interpretation of His ministry and had adjusted themselves to it. But it was a hard lesson to learn. Even at the beginning of those sacred last hours with Christ in the upper room they were still disputing with one another as to which one of them was to be regarded as the greatest (Lk 22:24). But the sight of His bending down to wash their feet, then softly speaking of His great love for them, hearing Him pray for their unity in Himself, then seeing Him quietly submit to capture by sinners, ready to drink the cup that the Father had given Him—all this made a deep impression. Coupled with their own regrets for their numerous shortcomings, including their desertion in the hour of crisis, was their sadness over the detention, crucifixion and entombment of the Master.

Out of this abyss of penitence and sorrow came the rebirth of joy and a new usefulness to their Lord as they fellowhiped with Him in His risen state. Only the enduement with the Spirit remained to fit them for their apostolic labors. Jesus had been father and friend, teacher and critic to them. Now that He must be recognized as universal Lord as well, His faithfulness and patience in the days of their training loomed larger in their thinking. What a privilege to serve such a one as He! *See* Apostle; Disciple.

The culmination of the ministry. Even as Caesarea Philippi was a milestone in the spiritual progress of the disciples, so was it a turning point in the earthly career of Jesus (Mt 16:13–21). Here the passion was divulged, not as something tentative but as something already

Garden of Gethsemane with adjacent Church of All Nations (center) which covers traditional Rock of Agony. Giovanni Trimboli

determined and embraced. From this time on the Lord returned to the subject more than once, showing that it was engrossing His thoughts.

The transfiguration, for all the mystery that invests it on account of the visible glory that broke from the Saviour's person, must be understood in close relation to Caesarea Philippi. The divine voice with its stern admonition to the disciples to hearken to the Son (Mt 17:5), finds its explanation in Peter's audacity in rebuking Jesus for broaching the subject of the cross (Mt 16:22 - 23). Moses and Elijah talked about this very thing on the mount. The glory was there, too, as though to dramatize the truth of the resurrection and the triumphs that would follow. Most significant as binding the transfiguration to the remainder of Jesus' ministry is Luke's observation that shortly thereafter He set His face to go to Jerusalem (Lk 9:51). Jesus was already envisioning the end, no matter how much remained to fill the interim. He would hasten on to His baptism of blood (Lk 12:50).

This period between the transfiguration and the passion presents problems as soon as one tries to trace the movements of Jesus. Suffice it to say that part of this interval was spent along the border of Galilee and Samaria, and part of it in Perea. Much that is peculiar to Luke (9:51 – 19:27) belongs here. Gradually the Lord worked His way toward Jerusalem. Increasingly crowds of people thronged Him (Lk 18:36; 19:3) in a way reminiscent of His busiest days in Galilee.

Two topics seemed to dominate His teaching as the hour of His passion (Jn 12:23 -27) approached. One was His rejection by His own people, and the other His return in glory. He is the nobleman who goes into a far country to get a kingdom and returns, whose citizens hate him and insist they will not have this man to rule over them (Lk 19:14). He is the son and heir whom the tenant farmers kill that they may seize the inheritance, only to be destroyed themselves (Mt 21:33 - 41). He is the stone rejected by the builders (Mt 21:42). He is the king's son whose wedding guests spurn the invitation and go their way to other pursuits (Mt 22:2 ff.). He is the bridegroom who expects watchfulness in view of his return (Mt 25:1 ff.). He is the lord who will check the faithfulness of his servants when he comes again (Mt 25:14 ff.) and the king who will judge the nations (Mt 25:31ff.).

If the words of the Prophet from Galilee could be judged inflammatory by the Jews, His actions were no less so – the daring ride into the city accompanied by the enthusiastic acclaim of the crowd, the bold move to rid the temple area of those who commercialized its courts and ruined it as a house of prayer, and all this in broad daylight, under the eyes of the priests who were profiting from this traffic.

The questions thrown at our Lord during holy week reflect the anger and frustration of the Jewish leaders. To think that this outsider can come right into their own territory and disturb the status quo in this fashion! How exasperating! Yet they are not able to trip Him up in a verbal encounter and thus discredit Him. Desperately they confer and confess their impotence. The only course apparently open to them is to accept the dictum of Caiaphas the high priest, laid down sometime before, that this one life had better be sacrificed rather than have the whole nation thrown into turmoil and revolution. He spoke beyond his own wisdom in thus prophesying the death of the Saviour (Jn 11:49 - 51). Even so, the rulers of the Jews would have been at a loss to know how to

St. Peter's of the Cock Crowing which covers traditional site of Caiaphas' Palace. Photo courtesy of the Church

implement their decision without incurring the wrath of the people had not Judas come forward with an offer to betray the Master (Mt 26:2-5, 14-16).

Aware of Judas' intrigue, Jesus kept from him the knowledge of the place where He would meet with the disciples to eat the Passover, and in this way was able to enjoy a period of uninterrupted intercourse with His own in the upper room. The words spoken on that occasion (Jn 13-16) and the prayer offered (Jn 17) are among the most precious deposits left to us from His entire ministry. They bear the marks of the stress and pathos of Jesus' approaching "hour," but they also possess the calm assurance of the victory that He would achieve and communicate to His own for their life and service in coming days.

Then came the soul struggle in Gethsemane (*q.v.*). That Jesus should have to agonize as He did in remaining true to the Father's will is our best indication of the severity of the conflict. The cross as an instrument of torture can hardly account for it, but the cross as the focus of the sin of the ages upon the Crucified furnishes the necessary key. Only a soul with complete freedom from sin could feel the horror, as Jesus did, of taking the sins of the world on Himself.

In a matter of hours He was on the cross. The Jewish authorities, after apprehending Him in the garden, used the remainder of the night for deliberation, and in the early morning decreed His condemnation on the charge of blasphemy (Mk 14:60-64). Hurrying Him off to Pilate, the Roman governor, before the city was fully alert, the chief priests secured a verdict based ostensibly on the charge that Jesus had declared Himself King of the Jews (Mk 15:26; cf. Jn 19:21). By nine o'clock in the morning He was hanging on the accursed tree. *See* Christ, Passion of; Cross.

From His lips came no execration, but instead a prayer for His tormentors. His accusers remained hardened, but others went home beating their breasts (Lk 23:48). In awe the centurion voiced his feeling that this One could only be God's Son (Mk 15:39). One of the thieves discovered that Jesus held the key to Paradise and that his own death on a cross was no barrier to his entrance upon its joys (Lk 23:39-43). So soon did the saving power of the crucified Son of God assert itself. *See* Atonement.

As Jesus had affirmed in advance (Jn 10:18), He died a voluntary death, yielding up His spirit to God (Mt 27:50; Jn 19:30). Would He be able to make good the companion claim that He would take up His life again? The paradox is that the disciples, despite several utterances of this sort promising resurrection, were not looking for it, whereas the enemies of Jesus, with much less to go on, were determined that no basis for such a claim could be provided (Mt 27:62-66). The former group did not doubt that God *could* raise Him, but were not expecting that He would; the latter group counted

Roman steps leading to St. Peter's of the Cock Crowing, on which Jesus may have walked. HFV

only on human action, by the removal of the body, as providing a specious basis for the claim of resurrection. The one group, in joyful surprise, welcomed the resurrection because they loved the Saviour. The other group became the prototype of those who deny this great event and remain strangers to its transforming power. *See* Resurrection of Christ.

The resurrection appearances were occasions of renewed fellowship between the Lord and His own, but also gave opportunity for explanation of what had happened in terms of OT prophecy and for commissioning the apostles to preach the gospel everywhere with His universal authority (Lk 24:44-49; Mt 28:18-20). *See* Commission, Great. These appearances terminated with the ascension (*see* Ascension of Christ), which in turn opened a new era characterized by the Lord's appearance in heaven on behalf of His people (Heb 9:24). As the Head of the Church He continues to make real His presence and power on the earth ere He fulfills His promise to return and consummate all things. *See* Christ, Coming of; Eschatology; Jesus, Offices of.

Bibliography. William Barclay, *The Mind of Jesus*, New York: Harper, 1961. G. C. Berkouwer, *The Person of Christ*, Grand Rapids:

JESUS, OFFICES OF

Chapel of the Ascension on top of the Mount of Olives. HFV

Eerdmans, 1955. Alfred Edersheim, *The Life and Times of Jesus the Messiah,* 2 vols., 8th ed. rev., New York: Longmans, Green & Co., 1901. Werner Foerster, "*Iēsous*," TDNT, III, 284-293. Everett F. Harrison, *Short Life of Christ,* Grand Rapids: Eerdmans, 1968. A. M. Hunter, *The Work and Words of Jesus,* Philadelphia: Westminster, 1950. T. W. Manson, *The Servant-Messiah,* Cambridge: Univ. Press, 1953. G. Campbell Morgan, *The Crises of the Christ,* New York: Revell, 1936. A. T. Olmstead, *Jesus in the Light of History,* New York: Scribner's, 1942. A. E. J. Rawlinson, *Christ in the Gospels,* London: Oxford Univ. Press, 1944. Wilbur M. Smith, *The Supernaturalness of Christ,* Boston: Wilde, 1954. Ethelbert Stauffer, *Jesus and His Story,* New York: Knopf, 1960. James S. Stewart, *The Life and Teaching of Jesus Christ,* New York: Abingdon, n.d. Vincent Taylor, *The Names of Jesus,* London: Macmillan, 1953. Howard F. Vos, *The Life of Our Divine Lord,* Grand Rapids: Zondervan, 1958. John F. Walvoord, *Jesus Christ Our Lord,* Chicago: Moody, 1969 (with extensive bibliography).

E. F. Har.

JESUS, OFFICES OF. The offices of Christ, the Anointed of God, are threefold: that of prophet, priest, and king. These were the three offices among the Israelites in OT times whose holders were recognized by anointing with oil (prophet, I Kgs 19:16; priest, Ex 29:7; 30:25, 30; king, I Sam 9:16; 16:1, 13).

Calvin was the first theologian to recognize the importance of distinguishing the three and devoted a chapter to them in his *Institutes.* Lutheran theologians have adopted the threefold offices somewhat reluctantly and slowly. They accepted Christ's prophetical and kingly offices, but tended to reject His priestly office. Liberal theologians on the whole place such stress on Christ as a teacher that His offices lose all value. The Barthians have so reinterpreted Christ's prophetical office, with their view of existential revelation here and now through hearing or reading a "fallible, contradictory Bible" or a sermon, that the offices of Christ are largely absorbed in that of revealer.

Christ as Prophet. The office of prophet required a person to be: (1) God's spokesman, His mouthpiece to man. This ministry of the prophet is seen in Ex 7:1 where God says, "I have made thee a god to Pharaoh: and Aaron thy brother shall be thy prophet." The prophet was to hear the word of God or see a vision and declare it (Deut 18:18). His ministry was both passive, to receive; and active, to proclaim. It was not merely passive, since Abimelech, Pharaoh, and Nebuchadnezzar all received revelations but were not considered prophets. (2) A foreteller of the future. The prophet gave revelation concerning future events. He foretold the future.

Christ exercised both these functions but in such a manner that they are generally fused. His ministry as spokesman and teacher was most clearly described by Himself in John 8 where He says that He speaks what He has heard of the Father (v. 26), has seen (v. 38), been taught (v. 28), and can verify with Him (v. 29). His ministry of foretelling the future is seen in Mt 24:2-31 and 25:31-46 (cf. Lk 21:6-28).

OT Scripture foretells that the Messiah is to be a prophet (Deut 18:15; cf. Acts 3:22-23). Jesus spoke of Himself as a prophet (Mt 13:57; Lk 13:33) and claimed to bring a message from the Father (Jn 8:26-28; 12:49-50; 14:10). The people received Him as a prophet (Mt 21:11, 46; Lk 7:16; 24:19; Jn 3:2; 4:19; 6:14; 7:40; 9:17). *See* Prophecy; Prophet.

Christ as Priest. The OT foretells His priestly ministry (Ps 40:6-8; 110:4). The office of priest entails offering sacrifices (Heb 5:1-3) and making intercession (Deut 5:5; 9:18; I Sam 7:5; etc.). Both of these He does. However, the sacrifice He offered was not that of bulls and goats but of Himself, His own body (Ps 40:6-8; Heb 10:5-14; cf. Heb 9:25-28). The intercession He makes is not in an earthly temple but at the very throne of God (I Jn 2:1-2; Rom 8:34; Heb 7:25; 9:24). The OT priesthood and sacrifices were only types of Christ and His sacrifice on Calvary, and pointed to Him as the Lamb of God (Jn 1:29).

Christ as King. The third office is that of king or ruler. This office Christ already exercises over all the members of His Church, but will exercise it over the whole earth at His second coming (Zech 14:9, 16 - 17; Rev 19:6; 20:4 ff.). The order of events leading to His final rule are: (1) The promise of the Davidic covenant (II Sam 7:16; Ps 89:20 - 27; cf. Isa 11:1 - 16; 55:3 - 4). (2) His announcement and birth as a king (Mt 2:2; Lk 1:32 - 33). (3) His rejection as a king (Mk 15:12 - 13; Lk 19:14). (4) His death as a sacrifice to satisfy divine justice (Isa 53:11), and yet as a king (Mt 27:37). (5) His return in glory to reign as king in Jerusalem (Mt 24:27 - 31; 26:64; Zech 14:8 - 9, 16 - 17). His kingly reign is to last forever (II Sam 7:15 - 16; Ps 89:36 - 37; Isa 9:6 - 7; Dan 7:13 - 14).

R. A. K.

JETHER (jē'thĕr)

1. Same as Jethro, father-in-law of Moses (Ex 4:18, Heb.).

2. The firstborn son of Gideon. Exhorted by his father to kill the captive Midianite princes Zebah and Zalmunna, Jether, who was very young, declined (Jud 8:20). He probably died in the conspiracy of Abimelech in which all the sons of Gideon were murdered (Jud 9:18).

3. The father of Amasa, commander of Absalom's army, who was made captain of David's forces after the rebellion. Jether was the husband of Abigail, David's sister. In II Sam 17:25 he is called Ithra the Israelite. This is probably a scribal corruption from the correct Jether the Ishmaelite in I Chr 2:17; I Kgs 2:5, 32.

4. A son of Jada of the family of Hezron of Judah (I Chr 2:32).

5. A son of Ezrah in the genealogy of Judah (I Chr 4:17).

6. A chief prince and warrior of the tribe of Asher (I Chr 7:38, 40).

JETHETH (jē'thĕth). The chief of an Edomite clan (Gen 36:40; I Chr 1:51).

JETHLAH (jĕth'lȧ). Called Ithlah in RSV. A town of the tribe of Dan (Josh 19:42), probably in the vicinity of Aijalon.

JETHRO (jĕth'rō). Apparently also called Reuel (Ex 2:18) and Raguel (Num 10:29). He was a priest of the nomadic Midianites (*q.v.*) living near Mount Sinai (Ex 2:16; 3:1; 4:18). A descendant of Abraham by Keturah (Gen 25:1 - 2), he consequently possessed remnants of the true knowledge of Yahweh (Ex 18:10 - 12).

Moses married Zipporah, one of Jethro's seven daughters, during his 40-year stay with Jethro (Ex 2:16 - 21). She bore two sons to him (Ex 2:22; 4:20; 18:3 - 4; Acts 7:29). Moses asked for and received from Jethro permission to return to Egypt (Ex 4:18 - 20). Zipporah and her two sons accompanied Moses, but he sent them back to Jethro for some unknown reason (Ex 4:24 - 26; 18:2).

After the exodus from Egypt and while the Israelites were in the vicinity of Mount Sinai (cf. Ex 3:12 with 19:2 - 3), Jethro brought Zipporah and her two sons back to Moses (18:1 - 6). Jethro did two notable things at this reunion: (1) he initiated and observed with Israel's leaders a sacrifice of thanksgiving for the recent deliverance from Egypt (18:10 - 12); (2) he wisely counseled Moses to make certain changes in his burdensome system of judging the people, which changes were apparently instituted immediately (18:13 - 26). *See* Judge. Jethro then returned to his own land (18:27).

Jethro's further contacts with the Israelites are linked with the almost insoluble problem regarding the identity of the Hobab mentioned in Num 10:29. This man was either Jethro or Jethro's son or grandson, at any rate an in-law of Moses. The family descendants dwelt among the Israelites after the conquest of Canaan (Jud 1:16; 4:11; I Sam 15:6). *See* Hobab; Raguel; Reuel. (See also W. F. Albright, *Yahweh and the Gods of Canaan*, Garden City: Doubleday, 1968, pp. 38 - 40; Wick Broomall, "Jethro: Wise Counselor," *The Presbyterian Journal*, September 29, 1965, pp. 16 - 18.)

W. B.

JETUR (jē'tûr). One of the sons of Ishmael, founder of a tribe (Gen 25:15; I Chr 1:31; 5:19). *See* Ituraea.

JEUEL (jōō'ĕl). Listed as head of one of the families of Judah which returned to Jerusalem after the Exile (I Chr 9:6). *See also* Jeiel 7 (spelled Jeuel in RSV).

JEUSH (jē'ŭsh)

1. A son of Esau by his Hivite wife Aholibamah, born in the land of Canaan. He was one of the earliest Edomite chiefs or sheiks (Gen 36:5, 14, 18; I Chr 1:35).

2. A Benjamite, the son of Bilhan of the family of Jediael (I Chr 7:10).

3. A Benjamite, son of Eshek, a descendant of Saul (I Chr 8:39; here spelled Jehush).

4. A Levite of the family of Gershom, the son of Shimei. He and his brother Beriah were counted one "father's house" or clan because they did not have many children (I Chr 23:10 - 11).

5. The son of King Rehoboam by his second wife Abihail, daughter of Eliab the brother of David (II Chr 11:18 - 19).

JEUZ (jē'ŭz). The fifth of seven sons of the Benjamite Shaharaim and his wife Hodesh. His sons are called "heads of the fathers" (I Chr 8:10), i.e., heads of families (NEB).

JEW (jōō). Heb. *y^ehûdî* specifically refers to a descendant of Judah; the name is applied to members of the tribe of that name or to those of the country of Judah (II Kgs 16:6; 18:26, 28; 25:25; II Chr 32:18; Est 2:5; 3:6; Jer 32:12; 38:19; 52:28; etc.). I Chr 9:3 indicates that members of other tribes resided in Jerusalem in Judah. Many from the seceded northern kingdom went over to Judah to worship the true God (II Chr 11:13 - 16; 15:9; 30:1 - 18).

The Jews who finished rebuilding the temple in the reign of Darius I probably included members of various tribes, for they sacrificed twelve goats for the twelve tribes (Ezr 6:14 - 17). Therefore after the Babylonian captivity the term was used for all Israelites since Judah then formed the larger part of the returning remnant (II Macc 9:17; Mt 2:2; 27:11; Jn 4:9; Act 2:5, 8 - 10; 10:28; etc.).

As descendants of Abraham the Hebrew (Gen 14:13), the Jews were also called Hebrews; hence Paul appropriately called himself such (Phil 3:5). *See* Hebrew People; Israel.

R. A. K.

JEWELS, JEWELRY. The love of adornment has been expressed in the wearing of precious stones and the making of jewelry since the beginning of history. The practice of burying such treasures with the remains of their owners has been of inestimable help to archaeologists in tracing the history and culture of perished races and civilizations.

Jewelry of Queen Shubad of Ur, c. 2500 B.C. BM

Scriptural terms. The following words are rendered "jewel" in the KJV:

1. Heb. *ḥălî,* meaning "ornament" and probably coming from Aram. "to adorn." It is a necklace or trinket, a symbol of grace and beauty (Song 7:1; "ornament," Prov 25:12).

2. Heb. *ḥelyâ,* a piece of jewelry, probably a necklace or female ornament (Hos 2:13).

3. Heb. *k^{e}lî,* meaning an article, utensil, or vessel of any kind. When used in the sense of jewelry, it is an article of silverware or other precious metal (Gen 24:53; Ex 3:22; 11:2; 12:35; Num 31:50 - 51; I Sam 6:8, 15; Prov 20:15), money (Job 28:17), or a piece of finery in dress (Isa 61:10; Ezk 16:17, 39; 23:26).

4. Heb. *nezem,* a ring always of gold when the material is mentioned. It is generally rendered "earring" (Gen 35:4; Ex 32:2; Ezk 16:12) but also nose ring (Prov 11:22; Isa 3:21). Thus it is a specific term. However, the part of the body on which it is worn is not specified. *See* Earring.

5. Heb. *s^{e}gullâ,* a piece of valued property (Mal 3:17) or peculiar treasure, used of the choice relationship between God and His people Israel (Ex 19:5; Ps 135:4).

As indicated, only the word *nezem* is specific while the others are of general character. The KJV usually translates the specific kinds of jewelry by their specific words, such as, bracelet, necklace, earring, nose ring, etc. The term "precious stones" *('eben ye qārâ)* occurs 13 times in the OT, as well as other expressions such as "pleasant stones" (Isa 54:12) and "stones of a crown" (Zech 9:16).

Materials. The jewels and other materials used in the making of jewelry consisted of the available precious stones and metals. Many of the Heb. and Gr. terms are difficult to identify because some are foreign loan-words, and because the ancients described their gems according to color and hardness and not according to chemical structure. Pliny's *Natural History* (A.D. 77), which describes precious stones according to their Gr. names close to the very time John wrote the book of Revelation, is of inestimable help.

Agate (*sh^{e}bô,* Ex 28:19; 39:12; *kadkōd,* Isa 54:12; Ezk 27:16, "red jasper," NEB). Among the many varieties of quartz, agate is distinguished as a translucent cryptocrystalline form with certain distinctive markings, usually in the form of layers of variegated colors. The term agate is often used interchangeably with chalcedony. This material has been widely used since Sumerian times both as jewelry and as a talisman because of its supposed magical powers. Pieces of agate could be gathered in certain desert areas of Egypt. The *kadkōd,* cognate to Arabic *kadkadatu,* "bright redness," is to be used in the battlements of the future Zion. This suggests red jasper, used by the Assyrians in their buildings.

Amethyst (*'aḥlāmâ,* Ex 28:19; 39:12; *amethystos,* Rev 21:20). A clear purple variety of quartz crystal, ranging from barely perceptible tinting to an intense purple. Pliny noted its occurrence in Egypt, but the finest amethysts came from India and Ceylon.

Beryl (*tarshîsh,* Ex 28:20; Song 5:14; Ezk 1:16; 28:13; Dan 10:6; *bēryllos,* Rev 21:20). A mineral, beryllium aluminum silicate, hexagonal crystal system, hardness 8. Color distinguishes the gem varieties of this mineral: emerald–green; aquamarine–light blue; golden beryl–yellow. Only the green beryl was used in Egypt in Moses' time, the aquamarine and the yellow and white beryls not being known.

The *tarshîsh* may have been another stone, however. The Heb. name is the same as for the land of Spain, so that it may have signified the "stone of Spain." Of the various suggestions for *tarshîsh* Spain produces only "chrysolith" according to Pliny (*Natural History,* xxxvii. 43), a yellow rock crystal or citrine quartz.

Carbuncle (*bāreqet,* Ex 28:13, 17; *'eben 'eqdāḥ,* Isa 54:12). Any of several precious or semiprecious red gemstones such as red garnet. The KJV translators confused the *bāreqet* with the following *nōphek* in the list of stones in the high priest's breastplate and reversed their meanings. Therefore the *bāreqet* should have been translated "emerald," or more correctly "green beryl," because the true emerald has never been found among the many precious gems of ancient Egypt.

Carnelian (cornelian). A variety of translucent chalcedony without crystal form, usually reddish in color, though sometimes orange-red or reddish-brown. One of the gems found most frequently in Palestinian excavations, it was widely used for seals, beads, and scarabs. A richly furnished tomb of the 13th–12th cen. B.C. discovered in 1964 at Tell es-Sa'idiyeh near Succoth in the Jordan Valley held a woman's skeleton with a necklace of 670 orange carnelian beads and 72 beads of gold. The golden necklace of Queen Shubad of Ur (*c.* 2500 B.C.) was set with alternating triangles of carnelian and lapis lazuli. The NJPS version identifies it with the Heb. *'ōdem,* the sardius of the KJV (Ex 28:17; 39:10; Ezk 28:13). The deserts of Arabia and Egypt were sources of fine carnelians.

Chalcedony (Gr. *chalkēdōn,* Rev 21:19). A cryptocrystalline translucent variety of quartz. By common usage the chalcedony is milky white or light gray or blue. Specimens having special markings are more generally known as agate, while the reddish varieties are called carnelian, sardius, or sardin(e). It was much used for engraved seals and gems, especially by the Greeks in the 5th and 4th cen. B.C., and is one of the foundation stones of the walls in the New Jerusalem. Another interpretation of the Gr. word is that the stone referred to is the green dioptose (silicate of copper) from the copper mines of Chalcedon in Asia Minor.

Chrysolite (Gr. *chrysolithos,* Rev 21:20). The modern meaning of the term is the gem variety of the mineral olivine, a peridot. Its chemical composition is iron magnesium silicate, hardness 7. Peridot is valued for its hardness, transparency, and greenish to yellowish color. According to its Gr. name the ancient gem was a "gold stone," probably our topaz, or some other yellow-hued gem such as beryl or zircon. The NEB and NJPS translate Heb. *piṭedâ,* the second stone of the priestly breastplate (Ex 28:17, KJV "topaz"), as chrysolite. The Heb. name seems to be an Indian loan-word, for it is cognate to Sanskrit *pīta,* "yellow." The RSV renders Heb. *tarshîsh* as chrysolite in Ezk 1:16; 10:9; 28:13.

Chrysoprasus (Gr. *chrysoprasos,* Rev. 21:20). The modern chrysoprase is an apple-green variety of chalcedony colored by nickel oxide. Its Gr. name suggests a gold-tinted, leek-green gemstone. It may be carved into exquisite cameos, and occurs in slabs large enough to make tops for small tables. It is the 10th foundation stone of the New Jerusalem.

Coral (Heb. *rā'môt,* Job 28:18; Ezk 27:16). The solid calcareous skeleton secreted by a class of minute marine coelenterate animals. Colors range from white to red to the rare black coral which comes from the Indian Ocean and has recently been discovered in the Gulf of Aqaba. Black coral is the NEB translation of *rā'môt.* Dark pink to red coral was so highly prized in the ancient Near East that it was considered one of the precious stones. The NEB translates Heb. *peninîm* (KJV "rubies") as "coral" or "red coral" (e.g., Job 28:18; Prov 3:15). The cognate Arabic word *fananu,* "branch(es)," suggests that the Heb. means something branched, like the coral organism (Lam 4:7, NEB). Superstition held that coral worn as an amulet bestowed magical benefits upon the wearer. *See* Animals.

Crystal (Heb. *zekôkît,* Job 28:17; *qeraḥ,* Ezk 1:22; Gr. *krystallos,* Rev 4:6; 22:1). Transparent colorless quartz (silicon dioxide), hardness 7, acid resisting, does not cleave under impact. Crystal was fashioned for many different uses, such as jewelry for adornment, spheres for crystal gazing and other magical purposes, and costly utensils for table service. The Romans carved blocks of crystal into great bowls and vases as well as smaller goblets and drinking cups. Heb. *zekôkît* may not mean crystal but instead glass (RSV, NASB). The Egyptians were making colored opaque glass vases by 2000 B.C. and glass beads even earlier. The word *qeraḥ* should be translated "ice," as in Job 6:16; 37:10; 38:29; Ps 147:17. However, the sixth stone of the breastplate (Heb. *yāhălōm,* KJV "diamond") is probably a rock crystal, because the Heb. word signifies a stone hard enough to withstand the blow of a heavy hammer, yet the true diamond was unknown in the ancient Near East.

Diamond (Heb. *yāhălōm,* Ex 28:18; Ezk 28:13; *shāmîr,* Jer 17:1). A mineral composed of pure carbon, it is the hardest natural substance known, 10 on the hardness scale. Before modern times the only sources of diamond were

India and Borneo. Knowledge of them in India predates written history. The famous Kohinoor diamond is reputed to have belonged to an Indian king some 5,000 years ago. The Heb. words translated diamond mean "hard" and may refer to other hard stones (*see* Jewels: Crystal; Minerals: Adamant). The point of Jeremiah's engraving tool was almost certainly corundum (Jer 17:1). In the Mediterranean world the first sufficiently detailed descriptions to positively identify diamonds are from the 1st cen. A.D.

Emerald (Heb. *nōphek*, Ex 28:18; Ezk 27:16; 28:13; Gr. *smaragdos*, Rev. 4:3; 21:19). A transparent brilliant green variety of beryl colored by minute amounts of chromium oxide. Unflawed specimens of good color are extremely rare, which contributes to the establishment of emerald as the most precious of all gems. The most famous come from Colombia where the Incas mined them. The true emerald was probably not known in OT times, for none has ever been found in ancient tombs or ruins. Heb. *nōphek* may be compared with Egyptian *mfkȝ3t*, which is probably turquoise, the blue-green semiprecious stone mined in OT times in the Sinai peninsula; NJPS so translates *nōphek*. Some scholars believe the *bāreqet*, the third stone of the breastplate (Ex 28:17), should be translated "emerald" (NJPS) or "green feldspar" (NEB). Many of the gems called "emerald" in Egyptian jewelry are actually green feldspar, although beads and scarabs were carved from emerald matrix. Cleopatra wore emeralds from mines in Upper Egypt, so that the Gr. *smaragdos* may be a true emerald. On the other hand, the Gr. word probably included all green-hued gems from emerald to green jasper and chrysoprase.

Garnet. The garnet group of minerals contains several mineral species with a hardness of about 7. The best gem mineral in this group is pyrope, a magnesium aluminum silicate, noted for its deep wine-red color. This may be the carbuncle listed in Scripture. The garnet beads discovered by archaeologists in Egypt were fashioned from dark red or reddish-brown translucent native stone. NEB translates Heb. *nōphek*, the fourth gem of the breastplate, as "purple garnet."

Jacinth (Gr. *hyakinthos*, Rev 9:17; 21:20). The modern hyacinth is a transparent colored zircon, usually red or reddish-brown. The gem referred to in the book of Revelation was almost certainly a blue stone, possibly aquamarine, turquoise (NEB, TEV) or amethyst (Pliny, *Natural History*, xxxvii. 41).

Jasper (Heb. *yāshᵉpēh*, Ex 28:20; Ezk 28:13; Gr. *iaspis*, Rev 4:3; 21:11, 18, 19). Chalcedony rendered opaque by the inclusion of brightly colored iron oxides with shades of brown, yellow, red or green. The last in the list of stones of the breastplate is almost certainly a jasper. It was the first hard stone carved by the Babylonians and was usually green and sometimes even transparent. The jasper of the NT was "clear as crystal" (Rev 21:11), i.e., translucent at least. Therefore jade (either nephrite or jadeite), which has been suggested, is excluded as a possibility.

Necklaces of Queen Hatshepsut of Egypt, *c.* 1500 B.C., as portrayed on a wall of the Temple of Karnak, Luxor, Egypt. HFV

Ligure (Heb. *leshem*, Ex 28:19; 39:12). The identity of this stone in Aaron's breastplate is problematical. Amber or jacinth are two strong possibilities. Golden sapphire, orange zircon, turquoise, agate and opal have also been suggested. Yellow jacinth or orange zircon are the two most likely possibilities.

Onyx (Heb. *shōham*, Gen 2:12; Ex 28:9, 20; I Chr 29:2; Job 28:16; Ezk 28:13). A non-transparent variety of agate structured with parallel layers of alternating colors, as red and white, brown and white, black and white. Onyx has long been used for cutting "eye" agates, rounded forms having an eye on one or opposite sides. Cameos are carved in a manner which gives a design of one color with a recessed background of another color. As the Vulgate translates it, the eleventh stone in the breastplate was probably a sardonyx, a red and white variegated gem. NEB renders *shōham* as "(red) carnelian," a favorite stone of the ancient world which could be picked up in the deserts, as its presence in the "land of Havilah" (probably N Arabia, Gen 2:12) suggests. Both the onyx and carnelian were much used for seals, stones engraved with an inscription (intaglio carving, the opposite of a cameo). The two shoulder stones of the high priest's ephod were of this material, with the names of six of the tribes engraved on each (Ex 28:9–12).

Pearl (Heb. *gābîsh*, Job 28:18; Gr. *margaritēs*, Mt 7:6; 13:45; etc.). A dense lustrous irridescent spherical mass of calcium carbonate formed in the mantle of many species of mollusk. The best pearls have always come from a few species of pearl oyster. They have been prized through all of recorded history for their beauty, rarity, warmth of color and symmetry, and for a variety of superstitious reasons. While the *gābîsh* is more likely to be alabaster (so NEB at Job 28:18), the *pᵉnînîm* (KJV rubies) were pearls from the Red Sea, where an especially lovely pink pearl is sometimes found. *See* Pearl.

Ruby. A clear, deep red, extremely hard precious gemstone, a variety of aluminum oxide (corundum), colored by traces of chromium. A really fine ruby is so rare that it is worth more than a diamond of the same weight. Ruby in this sense was not known in the biblical world until the 3rd cen. B.C. Therefore the rubies of the OT (Heb. *p^{e}nînîm*) are more likely to have been either pink pearls from the Red Sea or red coral from the same body of water (Job 28:18; Prov 3:15; 8:11; 20:15; 31:10; Lam 4:7).

Sapphire (Heb. *sappîr*, Ex 24:10; 28:18; Job 28:16; Ezk 28:13; Gr. *sappheiros*, Rev 21:19). In modern usage a transparent gem variety of corundum of any color. The more common application of the word reserves sapphire for the dark blue gem and gives other names to other colors. The normally colorless aluminum oxide is tinted blue by traces of iron or titanium. The OT references using this word are to an opaque blue speckled stone called lapis lazuli. Job 28:6 gives the clue to the identity of this mineral which was mined out of the mountains: "and out of its rocks comes lapis lazuli, dusted with flecks of gold" (NEB); the azure-blue stone contains golden flecks of iron pyrites. It is a silicate of calcium, aluminum, and sodium.

Objects of lapis lazuli date back to 3500 B.C. in the ancient Middle East. Wooden frames of harps inlaid with lapis lazuli are among the finest treasures recovered by Leonard Woolley from the royal cemetery at Ur, dating to 2500 B.C. A golden ram standing upright by a tree had its mane, beard and horns of lapis, and thousands of beads and the queen's cylinder seal were of the same substance. A relatively soft gem stone (hardness 5.5), lapis can be carved quite easily and therefore was in great demand for inlays in furniture and caskets. The innermost gold mummy case and the gold death mask of Tutankhamen were decorated with lapis, carnelian, and turquoise, and on each the false beard was of solid lapis lazuli. Other pharaohs of Egypt also employed this prized stone on a lavish scale. Its use in highly decorated statuary is suggested in Song 5:14: "His hands are golden rods set in topaz; his belly a plaque of ivory overlaid with lapis lazuli" (NEB).

The amazing fact about this gem rock is that the only known deposit where it was mined in the ancient East is at Badakshan in N Afghanistan. Discoveries of objects made from lapis lazuli at sites in the Middle East and the Sumerian tablets both point to this source, and also testify to the extensive trading of the ancient world (V. I. Sarianidi, "The Lapis Lazuli Route in the Ancient East," *Archaeology*, XXIV [1971], 12–15; G. Hermann, "Lapis Lazuli: The Early Phases of Its Trade," *Iraq*, XXX [1968], 21–57; Joan C. Payne, "Lapis Lazuli in Early Egypt," *Iraq*, XXX [1968], 58–61).

Sardius, Sardine (Heb. *'ōdem*, Ex 28:17; Ezk 28:13; Gr. *sardion*, Rev 4:3; 21:20). The stone today called sard or sardin(e) is a clear or translucent variety of chalcedony quartz, ranging from deep orange-red to brownish-red. The sardius of the Bible probably included the blood-red jasper, the sard, and the carnelian (*see* Jewels: Carnelian). The Heb. name, *'ōdem*, signifies a reddish or ruddy-colored stone, which could vary from rich chestnut brown to blood red. Along with carnelian, the sard has been found frequently in the excavated tombs and cities of Egypt, Palestine, and Babylonia. These gems most likely were cut from pieces of chalcedony lying on the surface of the surrounding deserts. It is believed that the ultraviolet rays of sunlight produce a deeper color by affecting the iron salts included as impurities in that mineral.

Sardonyx (Gr. *sardonyx*, Rev 21:20). Parallel layers of red and white chalcedony. The eleventh stone of the breastplate (Ex 28:20, Heb. *shōham*) was probably a sardonyx (*see* Jewels: Onyx).

Topaz (Heb. *piṭ^{e}dâ*, Ex 28:17; Job 28:19; Ezk 28:13; Gr. *topazion*, Rev 21:20). The mineral now known as topaz is an aluminum fluorosilicate which forms as brownish-yellow to clear crystals of hardness 8. Topaz of the 1st cen. A.D. and earlier was some other softer material which "yielded to the file" (Pliny), possibly yellow chrysolite (*see* Jewels: Chrysolite). Pliny said the topaz came from islands of the Red Sea.

Turquoise. A greenish-blue hydrous copper aluminum phosphate mineral, hardness 6, long valued for its beauty and for certain magical benefits bestowed upon its wearer. Because turquoise was a favorite stone among the Egyptians and because it was readily obtainable from their Sinai mines, it seems very likely that one of the jewels of Aaron's breastplate would have been a turquoise. The most probable of the twelve stones to identify with turquoise is the fourth, Heb. *nōphek* (KJV "emerald"). Emeralds were unknown in the time of Moses. NEB translates the blue jacinth of Rev 21:20 as "turquoise." The famous turquoise mines at Wady Maghara and Serabit el-Khadem were worked by Egyptians from predynastic times to the 20th Dynasty. At the latter site was a temple to the goddess Hathor, with many inscriptions there and at the entrances to the mines (ANET, pp. 229 f.). Some of these are in the so-called Proto-Sinaitic alphabetic script and dated to the 15th cen. B.C.

Manufacture. The method of making jewelry depended upon the geographical location and the civilization. In Egypt, perfection in the art of manufacturing was reached very early. The elegance of the jeweled treasures of the 12th Dynasty surpasses most ancient gilt or gem-work. The jewelry found in the tomb of Tutankhamen of the 18th Dynasty was incredibly magnificent. Although most of the tombs were robbed in ancient times, large quantities of jewelry were found in this one after it was opened on Nov. 25, 1922. Among the treasures were the three mummiform coffins and death mask; exquisitely carved alabaster jars; inlaid chests containing garments, jewelry, or cosmetics; the gilded throne chair with its jeweled back panel portraying the king and queen; and many gold rings, necklaces, bracelets, etc., set with turquoise, pearls, carnelian, green feldspar, amethyst, lapis lazuli, glass, and colored frit paste. The form of Egyptian jewelry most familiar to us is the scaraboid seal of carved stone or glazed ware. Although this was useful as a signet, it had a religious purpose as well to signify belief in eternal existence.

The Canaanite Phoenician artisans in Palestine were probably itinerants with shops in the main cities (I Kgs 20:34) and selling their wares from place to place. Even today this custom may be observed in the East with the artificer making jewelry from the treasured coins of the townspeople with his portable furnace and crucible. Jewelry from the rich finds at Ugarit and in the royal tombs of Byblos, and other displays in the National Museum of Lebanon, are evidences of the Phoenician skill. A great hoard of gold and electrum jewelry belonging to the 14th - 13th cen. B.C. was found in tombs at Tell el-'Ajjul near Gaza by Petrie (ANEP, # 74 - 75).

The Assyrian and Babylonian jewelry was generally not so graceful or delicate as that of Egypt but rather was large, heavy, and showy. The gorgeous musical instruments and crowns or chaplets from Queen Shubad's tomb at Ur (2500 B.C.) are an exception, however, and many of the gold vessels are masterpieces of design and proportion. Necklaces of carnelian and lapis lazuli beads discovered at Mari illustrate the type of jewelry worn by Sarah and Rebekah. The "Chaldean cylinders" or rolling seals were popular throughout the Near East, and have been found in Palestinian excavations. These were worn largely for ornamental purposes. Herodotus mentions that they were part of the dress wardrobe for Babylonian men (cf. Gen 38:18).

The Israelites probably learned to make jewelry from those under whose dominance and influence they came. The first such people were the Egyptians. The workmanship associated with the tabernacle, especially the high priest's breastplate, was probably Egyptian in style and character. At a later period the Israelites came under Phoenician and then finally Chaldean influence.

In ancient times, stones were not cut in facets, but rather *en cabochon*, i.e., in rounded forms with smooth or polished convex surfaces. Thus, there was not the demand as today for transparent stones to give the brilliant flashing caused by the reflection and refraction of light from the numerous facets.

Uses. The Scriptures mention several different ways that jewelry was used. These include: (1) personal adornment and ornamentation (Ex 11:2; Isa 3:19 - 20); (2) gifts or tokens of friendship (Gen 24:22, 53; Ezk 16:11); (3) adornment of idols (Jer 10:4); (4) in political and religious ceremonies of foreign lands (Gen 41:42; Dan 5:7, 16, 29); and (5) as symbols of those precious to the Lord—the priestly jewels (Ex 28, 39).

Aaron's breastplate. The "breastplate of judgment" (Ex 28:15, 30, NASB) was a highly ornamented pouch to hold the sacred lots known as the Urim and Thummin (*q.v.*), by means of which judgment was given in certain cases. The "breastplate" or pectoral was made of a rectangular piece of richly woven linen. When folded in two, it formed a square of a span (nine inches) on each side. It was attached by golden cords to the two shoulder pieces of the high priest's ephod, and secured at its lower corners by a blue cord to rings on the ephod itself. On the front of the breastpiece were mounted in gold settings four rows of precious stones, three to a row. The gems were cut *en cabochon*, and each was engraved like a seal with the name of one of the 12 tribes of Israel. The KJV name, the Heb. word and its probable true meaning, and the approximate color of each stone follows:

Row 1: Sardius—*'ōdem*, carnelian or sard;orange-red
Topaz—*piṭᵉdâ*, chrysolite; yellow
Carbuncle—*bāreqet*, beryl or feldspar; green
Row 2: Emerald—*nōphek*, turquoise; blue-green
Sapphire—*sappîr*, lapis lazuli; azure blue
Diamond—*yahălōm*, rock crystal; clear, colorless
Row 3: Ligure—*leshem*, jacinth or zircon; amber yellow or orange
Agate—*shᵉbô*, agate; variegated black and white
Amethyst—*'aḥlāmâ*, amethyst; purple
Row 4: Beryl—*tarshîsh*, citrine quartz; yellow
Onyx—*shōham*, sardonyx; variegated red and white
Jasper—*yāshᵉpēh*, jasper; green

Ornaments. Besides the jewels employed in ceremonial worship, the Israelites wore a variety of types of jewelry in everyday life. Many men for business reasons wore a signet seal or ring which served as the personal signature of its owner (Gen 38:18; Song 8:6; Lk 15:22). This was generally worn on the right hand or suspended from the neck by a cord. *See* Seal, Signet. However, sometimes the position of the man (princes, etc.) required more of a display of jewelry (II Sam 12:30).

The women decorated themselves more elaborately and wore several types of ornaments (Ezk 16:10 - 13). One such type was earrings, which were universally worn by women (Ex 32:2; Ezk 16:12). They were made of bone, horn, or metal, and some that have been found have been rather large (as much as four fingers breadth in diameter). Some women would puncture the earlobe with as many openings as possible, and would then put a ring through each. *See* Earring. Nose rings were also a favorite and were used from the earliest times (Gen 24:22, 47, RSV). They were made of ivory or metal and often decorated with precious jewels.Nose rings and earrings were sometimes worn by men (Jud 8:24).

The necklace was a favorite ornament among the women. Men of rank and rulers of foreign nations also wore them (Gen 41:42; Prov 1:9; Dan 5:29). They were made of precious metal, often inlaid with gems, stones, or pearls, or of beads strung on a cord. Attached to them sometimes were other articles of finery, such as half-moons or crescents (Isa 3:18, RSV), smelling bottles (Isa 3:20, RSV), and stellated studs (Song 1:11).

Another favorite with the women from the earliest times was the armlet or bracelet (Gen 24:22, 30, 47). They were also worn by princes and nobles of rank (II Sam 1:10). These were made of ivory, precious metals, horn, cords, or chains. They could be worn on both arms, and some covered the forearm to the elbow.

The anklet was worn about the feet (Isa 3:18). These were generally so arranged that in walking a tinkling or clapping sound was made which called attention to the wearer and made her proud (Isa 3:16). Sometimes small chains were fastened from one ankle to the other in order to secure a more elegant step (Isa 3:20, NASB). Isaiah lists these as well as other articles of ornamentation in rebuking the women of Jerusalem (Isa 3:18–26). The Egyptian nobles and commoners had a profusion of such ornaments, which were demanded by the Israelite slaves as they left in the Exodus (Ex 11:2; 12:35–36, NASB). These articles of gold and silver supplied sufficient material for making the sacred utensils for the tabernacle (Ex 35:4–29). *See* Minerals and Metals.

Bibliography. Howard Carter, *The Tomb of Tut-ank-Amen,* 3 vols., London: Cassell, 1923–1933. A. Paul Davis, *Aaron's Breastplate,* St. Louis: A. P. Davis, 1960. G. R. Driver, "Jewels and Precious Stones," HDB rev., pp. 496–500. Paul L. Garber and R. W. Funk, "Jewels and Precious Stones," IDB, II, 898–905. John S. Harris, "An Introduction to the Study of Personal Ornaments of Precious, Semi-Precious and Imitation Stones Used Throughout Biblical History," *Annual of Leeds University Oriental Society,* IV (1962–63), 49–83; "The Stones of the High Priest's Breastplate," ALUOS, V (1963–65), 40–62. Ruth V. Wright and R. L. Chadbourne, *Gems and Minerals of the Bible,* New York: Harper & Row, 1970.

E.C.J., G.H.H. and J.R.

JEWESS. A female Jew by blood or conversion to Judaism. Timothy's mother was a Jewess and his father a Greek (Acts 16:1). Drusilla, the wife of Felix the Roman governor who trembled at Paul's preaching, was a Jewess (Acts 24:24). She was a descendant of Herod the Great, the offspring of converts to Judaism. *See* Drusilla.

JEWISH, JEWS'. Belonging to a Jew (Heb. *y*^{e}-*hûdîth,* adverb meaning "in Jewish," "in the language of Judah"). Used of the language of the Jews or people of Judah dwelling at Jerusalem when Hezekiah's representatives pleaded with the Assyrians not to talk with his people in their own tongue (II Kgs 18:26, 28; II Chr 32:18; Isa 36:11, 13), and again in Nehemiah of the children of the remnant that returned who could not speak their own language (Neh 13:24). Paul employed the term once when he spoke of Jewish fables (Tit 1:14).

JEWRY (jōō'rĭ). A KJV translation of Aram. *y*^{e}*hûd,* the Jewish nation, i.e., the kingdom of Judah (Dan 5:13); and in the NT of Gr. *Ioudaia,* Judea in contrast to Galilee (Lk 23:5; Jn 7:1; see RSV, NASB).

JEZANIAH. *See* Jaazaniah.

JEZEBEL (jĕz'ĕ-bĕl). The wife of Ahab, king of Israel (874–853 B.C.), and daughter of Ethbaal, king of the Zidonians. Jezebel was a devotee of Baal-Melkart, the god of Phoenecia (I Kgs 18:19). She encouraged Ahab to build shrines for worship and brought hundreds of the religion's priests and prophets to Israel. She persecuted the prophets of Yahweh and ordered those slain who spoke against her idolatrous ways (I Kgs 18:4). She seems to have had considerable influence over Ahab, who allowed her to do as she pleased. She raised her two sons to use the same practices, and her daughter Athaliah (II Kgs 8:18) even carried her ideas to Judah when she married the son of Jehoshaphat.

Jezebel's chief opponent in Israel was Elijah (I Kgs 18:21–46), who held a contest on Mount Carmel to prove who was the true God. After his success, he was threatened by Jezebel and fled to Mount Horeb. Her lack of respect for the property of others is demonstrated by the story of Naboth. Ahab at first respected Naboth's desire to keep the land of his inheritance, but Jezebel seized it ruthlessly.

When Jehu came to the throne he purged the kingdom of the house of Ahab. Jezebel was thrown from the palace tower and Jehu's chariot ran over her. Later, he sent his servants to bury her but the dogs had already eaten her, thus fulfilling Elijah's prophecy (II Kgs 9:30–37).

In Rev 2:20 the name Jezebel is given to a prophetess or a group within the church at Thyatira who encouraged idolatry and immorality. Evidently the name already was symbolic of apostasy.

A. W. W.

JEZER (jē'zẽr). The third son of Naphtali, he was head of the clan of Jezerites (Gen 46:24; Num 26:49; I Chr 7:13).

JEZIAH (jē-zī'*a*). The KJV form of Izziah. An Israelite of the family of Parosh. One of those compelled by Ezra to put away their foreign wives after the Exile (Ezr 10:25).

JEZIEL (jē'zĭ-ĕl). A son of Azmaveth, and one of the skilled Benjamite archers and slingers who defected from Saul to join David's band at Ziklag (I Chr 12:3).

JEZLIAH (jĕz-lī'*a*). ASV and RSV have Izliah. A son or descendant of Elpaal, a Benjamite who resided at Jerusalem (I Chr 8:18).

JEZOAR (jē-zō'ẽr). ASV and RSV have Izhar.

1. Son of Helah, a wife of Ashur, the father (founder) of Tekoa (I Chr 4:7). A descendant of Judah. *See also* Zohar.

2. Father of Korah (Num 16:1). A Levite, descended from Kohath, whose descendants formed a family in the tribe of Levi (Ex 6:18, 21; Num 3:19, 27; I Chr 6:18, 38); called Amminadab in I Chr 6:22.

JEZRAHIAH (jĕz'r*a*-hī'*a*). Overseer of the singers performing at the purification of the people on the occasion of Nehemiah's reforms (Neh 12:42). *See* Izrahiah.

JEZREEL (jĕz'rē-ĕl)

1. A town in the Judean hill country (Josh 15:56). It was the home of Ahinoam the Jezreelitess (*q.v.*), one of David's wives (I Sam 25:43). It is possibly Khirbet Tarrama, about six miles SW of Hebron.

2. A descendant of Judah (I Chr 4:3), who presumably may have been the eponymous ancestor of Jezreel in Judah.

3. A town of Issachar (Josh 19:18) in the southern area along the border of Manasseh's territory. It is identified with modern Zer'în about ten miles E of Megiddo, a village at the foot of the NW spur of Mount Gilboa with a commanding view of the plain of Jezreel (see 4). In ancient times it was at the intersection of trade routes from the Mediterranean coast to the Jordan Valley and those from S to N Palestine. Solomon selected it as one of his 12 administrative centers, with Baana its first resident governor (I Kgs 4:12). Ahab made it one of his royal residences since it was especially pleasant in winter (I Kgs 18:45–46). It was the place of the horrible murder of Naboth perpetrated by Jezebel (I Kgs 21). Joram fled to it after suffering wounds in a battle with Hazael of Syria (II Kgs 8:29; II Chr 22:6). It witnessed excessive bloodshed during Jehu's revolt (II Kgs 9:1–10:11). The tower of Jezreel (II Kgs 9:17) was a tower or bastion guarding the entrance of Jezreel the city.

4. The fertile plain which separated Galilee from Samaria (see Josh 17:16; Jud 6:33; Hos 1:5). It is a geological fault basin with a fairly deep alluvial covering, well watered, and thus very fertile. In some later sources, Esdraelon is designated as the western portion of this plain and Jezreel its eastern portion. The entire plain was occupied by Canaanites based principally at Megiddo before the Israelite conquest. Thus the western half is sometimes called the Valley of Har Megiddo ("mound of Megiddo") or Armageddon (*q.v.*). *See* Palestine, II.B.2.*b*.

5. The name of Hosea's first son. It was given as a symbol of the bloodshed committed by Jehu at Jezreel to grab the throne of the northern kingdom (II Kgs 9:17–10:11), as well as foretelling the divine judgment on the dynasty of Jehu for that slaughter (Hos 1:4–5).

H. E. Fi.

JEZREELITE (jĕz'rē-ĕ-līt). Applied to Naboth, a native resident of the town of Jezreel (I Kgs 21:1, 4, 6, 7, 15, 16; II Kgs 9:21, 25).

JEZREELITESS (jĕz'rē-ĕ-lī-tĭs). Used of Ahinoam, one of David's first two wives, a native

A view across the Valley of Jezreel showing the richness of the soil and its agricultural potential. IIS

Valley of Jezreel with road to Nazareth at right. IIS

of Jezreel in Judah (I Sam 27:3; 30:5; II Sam 2:2; 3:2; I Chr 3:1).

JIBSAM (jĭb'săm). The son of Tola and a grandson of Issachar (I Chr 7:2). Spelled Ibsam in RSV.

JIDLAPH (jĭd'lăf). A son of Nahor and Milcah (Gen 22:22). He became the ancestral head of a Nahorite clan.

JIMMA, JIMNAH. *See* Imnah.

JIMNITE (jĭm'nīt). Used only in Num 26:44. Descendants of Jimna or Imnah (*q.v.*), a son of Asher.

JIPHTAH (jĭf'tȧ). Called Iphtah in RSV. A town of Judah in the Shephelah region, in the same district as Libnah (Josh 15:43).

JIPHTHAH-EL (jĭf'thȧ-ĕl). This form used in KJV, but Iphtah-el used in other versions. A valley on the boundary line between Zebulun and Asher (Josh 19:14, 27). The name is perhaps found in Jotopata, the modern Tell Jefat, nine miles NW of Nazareth.

JOAB (jō'ăb)

1. The son of Zeruiah, half sister of David (II Sam 2:18), and brother of Abishai and Asahel. The only thing known about his father is that his tomb was in Bethlehem (II Sam 2:32).

The first mention of Joab's activities is the battle between David's men led by Joab and Ishbosheth's forces under Abner near the pool of Gibeon. Joab's men bested Abner's. When Abner reluctantly slew Joab's younger brother Asahel (II Sam 2:23), a blood revenge developed between the two leaders that led first to the death of Abner (II Sam 3:26–27), and second to David's pronouncement of death on Joab for killing him (a doubly heinous crime since Hebron was a Levitical city of refuge, II Sam 3:28–39).

Joab's capture of the Jebusite city of Jerusalem led to his appointment as commander-in-chief of the armies of Israel (I Chr 11:6). Nahari of Beeroth was his chief armor bearer (II Sam 23:37), and ten attendants carried his equipment (II Sam 18:15). Joab also superintended the reconstruction program of David in Jerusalem (I Chr 11:8). He led the armies of David in war against Syria, Ammon (II Sam 10:7–11:1; 12:26), and Edom (II Sam 8:13, 16). His undue cruelty toward the Edomites may be seen in his attempt to exterminate all the Edomite males (I Kgs 11:15–16). He also led the forces of David in putting down the revolts of Absalom (II Sam 18) and of Sheba (II Sam 20). His military prowess and ruthless strategy are evidenced in the manner in which he removed all barriers to the success of his master David, whom he wanted to be first, and in the severe measures he took to see to it that he, Joab, was a close second in command. Abner and Amasa, potential threats to Joab's position, were summarily executed in typical bedouin fashion.

Joab's biggest mistake was to side with Abiathar in championing Adonijah to become the next king (I Kgs 1:7, 19, 41). On his deathbed David named Solomon to succeed him, and Joab fled to the altar at Gibeon for asylum. There he was executed according to royal decree by Benaiah, chief of the royal bodyguard, the man who would succeed to Joab's position (I Kgs 2:28–35). Joab's life ended where his career began – in Gibeon!

2. Son of Seraiah, a descendant of Kenaz (I Chr 4:14; Neh 11:35), a Judahite "father" or founder of Ge-Harashim, that is, the Valley of Craftsmen.

3. The founder of a family, some of whom are listed among those who returned from the Exile with Zerubbabel (Ezr 2:6; Neh 7:11).

F. E. Y.

The pool of Gibeon where Joab's and Abner's men fought. HFV

JOAH (jō'ȧ)

1. The son of Asaph, recorder or court chronicler to Hezekiah. He was a member of the delegation that went outside Jerusalem to bargain with the Rabshakeh, emissary of Sennacherib (II Kgs 18:18, 26; Isa 36:3, 11, 22).

2. A Levite, the son of Zimmah, of the family of Gershom (I Chr 6:21); he is called Ethan in v. 42. He took part in the cleansing of the temple during the reform of Hezekiah (II Chr 29:12 ff.).

3. The third son of Obed-edom, appointed a doorkeeper of the sanctuary in the time of David (I Chr 26:4).

4. The recorder or chronicler of King Josiah, appointed one of the directors of repairs for the temple (II Chr 34:8).

JOAHAZ (jō'*ȧ*-hăz)

1. Father of Joah, the recorder under King Josiah (II Chr 34:8).

2. Alternate form of Jehoahaz (*q.v.*).

JOANNA (jō-ăn'*ȧ*)

1. An ancestor of Jesus (Lk 3:27), properly spelled Joanan in RSV.

2. Wife of Chuza, the steward of Herod Antipas, one of the women who ministered to Jesus (Lk 8:3) and who went with the other women of Galilee to the tomb of Jesus (Lk 23:55–24:10).

JOASH (jō'ăsh). Two different Heb. names appear in English as Joash. The first, Heb. *yô'ash*, means "Yahweh has given." It is a shorter form of Jehoash (*q.v.*). At least six people bear this Heb. name in the OT. The name occurs as *Y'wsh* in the Heb. Lachish ostraca. The other Heb. name is *yô'ash*, which means "Yahweh has helped." The name with this spelling occurs also on the Samaria ostraca. Heb. *yô'ash* is the actual name of 3 and 5 below; *yô'ash* is the name of the other men listed.

1. The father of Gideon of the tribe of Manasseh (Jud 6:11). Joash may have been a man of wealth and status since Gideon was in a position to command ten servants to destroy the altar of Baal and Asherah erected by his father (Jud 6:27–34).

2. A son of Shelah, of Judah (I Chr 4:21–22).

3. A Benjamite of the clan of Becher (I Chr 7:8).

4. The second in command of those who joined David at Ziklag (I Chr 12:3).

5. An official of David in charge of the storage of olive oil (I Chr 27:28).

6. A son of Ahab, king of Israel. When Micaiah prophesied before Jehoshaphat and Ahab, the latter was displeased and sent the prophet to Joash, his son, for imprisonment limited to bread and water rations (I Kgs 22:26; II Chr 18:25).

7. A son of Ahaziah, king of Judah, and his wife Zibiah (II Kgs 11:2; 12:1; II Chr 24:1); also called Jehoash. He was born during a period of excessive royal bloodshed in Judah. His grandfather Jehoram had killed six of his own brothers (II Chr 21:2–4), whereas Jehoram's other sons were killed by the Arabs, leaving only Ahaziah, who ruled but one year (II Chr 21:16 f.; 22:1 f.). When Ahaziah was killed by Jehu of the northern kingdom (II Kgs 9:27 f.), the queen mother Athaliah seized the opportunity to usurp the throne by murdering all the children of Ahaziah. The infant heir Joash, however, was saved by his aunt Jehosheba, wife of the high priest Jehoiada. The child was hidden for six years in the temple until resistance to the evil queen was well established. In the seventh year (835 B.C.), Jehoiada plotted with supporters loyal to the family of David, and they successfully proclaimed Joash king and put Athaliah to death (II Kgs 11:1–16; II Chr 22:10–23:15).

Under the guidance of Jehoiada the reign of Joash was a good and godly one. Baal worship was destroyed, the temple was repaired, and a return to Yahweh spread among the people.

On the death of the godly Jehoiada, Joash radically changed. Influenced by worldly princes he forsook the Lord and reverted to idolatry and Asherim worship. He even went so far as to have his cousin Zechariah, son of his rescuer Jehoiada, stoned to death in the temple court for rebuking him. God's judgment came upon him quickly. The Syrians under Hazael invaded the land and took Gath, and were only bribed from destroying Jerusalem with an immense temple treasure (II Kgs 12:17–18). Later, Hazael entered Jerusalem, massacring the princes and severely wounding King Joash (II Chr 24:23–24, RSV). His own servants conspired against Joash and assassinated him. In a final gesture of contempt they refused him burial with the kings (II Chr 24:23–25). The names Joash and Jehoash are used interchangeably throughout II Kgs 11–12; II Chr 23–24. He is one of the three kings omitted in the royal genealogy in Mt 1.

8. The son of Jehoahaz and father of Jeroboam II, kings of Israel. As third king in the Jehu dynasty, he ruled 798–782 B.C. Joash succeeded to the throne of Israel at a time when the nation was all but destroyed. Repeated defeats at the hands of Hazael and Ben-hadad II, kings of Syria, during the days of Jehoahaz had reduced the strength of the nation to its lowest point (II Kgs 13:1–7). It was the glory of Joash during his 16 year reign that, capitalizing on the death of the powerful Hazael *c.* 800 B.C., he restored the position and power of Israel and prepared it for its highest prosperity under Jeroboam II. Although he promoted idolatry, Joash might have done even greater things had his faith matched that of the dying prophet Elisha who exhorted him to smite the ground repeatedly with arrows in symbol of victories over the Syrian enemy (II Kgs 13:14–25).

Somewhat unwillingly, Joash also went to fight against the presumptuous and perhaps jealous king Amaziah of Judah. He thoroughly defeated Amaziah, even destroying part of the wall of Jerusalem and taking many hostages and much treasure (II Kgs 14:8–16; II Chr 25:17–24). Amaziah himself may have been among the captives. Joash died a natural death and was buried in Samaria.

According to a stela excavated in 1967 at Tell al-Rimah in Iraq, the Assyrian king Adad-nirari III (810–783 B.C.) received tribute from Ia'asu (Joash) the Samaritan (*Iraq*, XXX [1968], 139–153; VT, XIX [1969], 483 f.). This text provides the earliest known mention of Samaria by that name.

S. J. S. and P. C. J.

JOATHAM. *See* Jotham.

JOB (jōb). Although the semipoetic character of the Prologue-Epilogue of the book of Job and the poetry of the central discourses suggest that not all features of the Joban history are described with prosaic literalness, nevertheless the narrative of Job and his experiences is history, not fiction. This conclusion is required by the reference to Job elsewhere in the Bible (see Ezk 14:14, 20; Jas 5:11), and it is confirmed by the purpose of the book of Job, which is to magnify the name of God for His sovereign soteric accomplishments in history.

Job's homeland was somewhere to the E of Palestine near the border of the desert. There are several indications that he lived in the patriarchal age: the longevity of Job (he apparently lived some two centuries), the flourishing of true religion supported by special divine revelation outside the community of the Abrahamic covenant, and certain early social and ethnic features such as the still nomadic status of the Chaldeans and the patriarchal form of worship and sacrifice. Furthermore, he had a name that was borne by a number of W Semites in the earlier part of the 2nd mil. B.C., but which is not found in the 1st mil. The name occurs in the Berlin Execration texts from Egypt as Ayyabum (ANET, p. 329) and in the Amarna letters as Ayal (ANET, p. 486), as well as in Akkadian texts from Mari and Alalakh.

Materially prosperous and genuinely pious Job continued for perhaps some 70 years in the manifest favor of God and men. Then the sudden, well-nigh total reversal of all his earthly circumstances introduced the great crisis that gives Job's life special significance for redemptive history (Job 1 and 2).

Out of the agony and enigma of his sufferings arose the complaint of Job (Job 3) and a long formal discussion between him and his three philosophical friends (Job 4–31). The debate served to demonstrate the foolishness of the traditional wisdom of the world, which led the friends to the utterly false judgment that Job's sufferings were the condign consequence of a radical defection from the fear of God.

But it took the revelation of the voice of the Lord Himself out of the whirlwind, a revelation prepared for by the ministry of His young servant Elihu (Job 32–37), to bring the anguished sufferer back to the peace of a humble and trusting devotion to his Lord (Job 38:1–42:6). Thus was Job proved, contrary to the allegations of the evil Adversary, to be a trophy of divine grace.

As vindication of Job before the eyes of his human accusers, God crowned the earthly life of his servant with twofold restoration (Job 42:7–17).

M. G. K.

JOB, BOOK OF

Background

There was a rich ancient literature devoted to probing the mystery of human life and particularly to discovering the relation of cultic fidelity to material prosperity. The literary motif of the problem of the righteous sufferer was treated in Sumerian literature at least as early as 2000 B.C. A Babylonian text going back to Kassite times (1600–1150 B.C.) and entitled "I Will Praise the Lord of Wisdom" is often called the "Babylonian Job."

This theme figures prominently in the book of Job, but it is there subordinated to a grander theocentric interest, and it is treated within the biblical context of the historical realities of the Fall of man and of God's redemptive dispensation which lead to answers altogether different from those suggested in the pagan poems.

Date and Author

It is difficult to determine when the book of Job was written. Dates ranging from the Mosaic to the Persian period continue to find support among current OT scholars. Conservative scholarship has tended to associate the composition of the book with the flourishing of biblical Wisdom Literature in the age of Solomon. For the most part higher critical investigations have favored a date no earlier than the Exile, and yet a significant minority has argued for an origin in the 2nd mil. B.C.

Most scholars do not believe that one author was responsible for the entire book. Often regarded as later additions to an original work are the Elihu section, the poem on wisdom in chap. 28, and parts of the Lord's discourses. Also called in question is the integrity of the Prologue-Epilogue. The evidence for these misgivings, however, is completely subjective. On the other hand, it is compatible with the proper view of Scripture to recognize that the inspired author of the canonical book of Job made use of a (possibly quite extensive) tradition concerning the life of Job, which may have been written as well as oral.

[For the book to have been accepted in Israel as canonical, its author must have been recognized as an Israelite in the prophetic tradition. He was a poet of rare genius with a deeply sensitive soul. In order to write as he did he himself must have suffered intensely. He was well acquainted with Egypt as well as the ways of the desert, and he seems to have been familiar with the wisdom and lore of the ancient Near East. Therefore individual Israelites ranging from Joseph to Moses to Solomon, who knew Egypt well and had wide-ranging contacts and great personal ability, have been suggested as candidates for author of the book of Job. – Ed.]

Outline

I. Desolation: The Trial of Job's Wisdom, 1:1–2:10
II. Complaint: The Way of Wisdom Lost, 2:11–3:26
III. Judgment: The Way of Wisdom Darkened and Illuminated, 4:1–41:34
  A. The verdicts of men, 4:1–37:24
    1. First cycle of debate, 4:1–14:22
    2. Second cycle of debate, 15:1–21:34
    3. Third cycle of debate, 22:1–31:40
    4. Ministry of Elihu, 32:1–37:24
  B. The voice of God, 38:1–41:34
IV. Confession: The Way of Wisdom Regained, 42:1-6
V. Restoration: The Triumph of Job's Wisdom, 42:7-17

Purpose

Wisdom Literature that it is, the purpose of the book of Job is to extol God the Creator as the Lord of wisdom and, particularly, to praise the divine wisdom revealed in the redemptive might by which God delivers the slaves of Satan from the power of sin and from the hopelessness of the grave, and establishes them as His own in a triumphant service of pure devotion. As the corollary of this, the book inculcates the fear of this God of all wisdom as the true way of wisdom for man. *See* Wisdom Literature.

Content

The Prologue discloses how a demonstration of God's saving power was afforded through Job and his sufferings. God declared that Job was His servant, but Satan contradicted the divine boast. A test of strength was agreed upon to reveal whether God or Satan owned the allegiance of Job's heart. The full meaning of Job's steadfastness in his fierce temptation must be found, therefore, in the legal framework of the trial by ordeal between God and the Accuser (Job 1-2).

The doxology of Job marked the beginning of the end for Satan, but before the final bruising of Satan under foot Job was to be all but overwhelmed by the dark mystery of his experience. The arrival of his three colleagues from the ranks of the Wise precipitated a process of philosophizing which lured Job away from the simplicity of faith. Afraid now that he had lost the favor of God, Job broke into complaint (Job 3).

In their response to the complaint, Eliphaz, Bildad, and Zophar thought to defend the honor of God. But their commitment to the traditional wisdom of the world with its doctrine of proportionate sin and suffering in this life resulted in their condemnation of the sufferer and thus, in effect, in their advocacy of Satan's cause. Although Job managed to silence the three philosophers and, in the process, to attain to new insights into the ultimate beatitude of those who know God as their Redeemer, complaint continued to accompany his lament, and his longing for an immediate hearing before the great Judge became ever more consuming (Job 4-31).

A quieting of Job's inflamed spirit must precede the desired trial. Such was the service rendered by Elihu, who, anticipating the judgments of God, rebuked the friends and brought Job to silence and a humility appropriate to his imminent confrontations with God (Job 32-37).

The voice of the Almighty summoned Job to his trial, which turned out to be another trial by ordeal. It was by victory in this ordeal with Job that God purposed to perfect his triumph in his ordeal against Satan. The wrestling of God with Job took the form of a wisdom contest, and Job found himself unable to answer even one of his Creator's questions (Job 38:1–41:34).

In Job's repentant confession while still without intimation of earthly restoration, there was a final confirmation of the genuineness of his consecration. Thereby Satan was exposed as a liar still, and God's name and word were honored (Job 42:1-6).

The restoration of Job described in the Epilogue vindicated God's servant against the devil's unwitting advocates and served as a sign of the validity of that hope of ultimate justification and peace which Job had laid hold on by faith (Job 42:7-17).

Bibliography. Franz Delitzsch, *Job,* KD, 1869 (1949 reprint). E. Dhorme, *A Commentary on the Book of Job,* trans. by Harold Knight, London: Nelson & Sons, 1967. H. L. Ellison, *From Tragedy to Triumph: The Message of the Book of Job,* Grand Rapids: Eerdmans, 1958; "Job," "Job, Book of," NBD, pp. 635-637. Robert Gordis, *The Book of God and Man: A Study of Job,* Chicago: Univ. of Chicago, 1965. W. H. Green, *The Argument of the Book of Job Unfolded,* New York: Carter, 1881. A. Guillaume, *Studies in the Book of Job,* Leiden: Brill, 1968. R. K. Harrison, *Introduction to the Old Testament,* Grand Rapids: Eerdmans, 1969, pp. 1022-1046. Meredith G. Kline, "Job," WBC, pp. 459-490. Marvin H. Pope, "Job, Book of," IDB, II, 911-925; *Job,* Anchor Bible, Garden City: Doubleday, 1965. Nathan M. Sarna, "Epic Substratum in the Prose of Job," JBL, LXXVI (1957), 13-25. Elmer B. Smick, "Mythology and the Book of Job," JETS, XIII (1970), 101-108. Norman H. Snaith, *The Book of Job: Its Origin and Purpose,* Naperville: Allenson, 1968.

M. G. K.

JOBAB (jō'băb)

1. The son of Joktan of the family of Sher (Gen 10:29; I Chr 1:23).

2. The son of Zerah, one of the early kings of Edom (Gen 36:33–34; I Chr 1:44–45).

3. King of the N Canaanite city of Madon, he was allied with Jabin of Hazor against Joshua (Josh 11:1; 12:19).

4. The son of a Benjamite, Shaharaim, by his wife Hodesh (I Chr 8:8–9).

5. Another Benjamite, the son or descendant of Elpaal (I Chr 8:18).

JOCHEBED (jŏk'ĕ-bĕd). The wife of Amram (*q.v.*) and the mother of Moses, Aaron, and Miriam (Ex 6:20; Num 26:59). The faith, courage, and resourcefulness of Amram and Jochebed not only preserved the life of Moses, but his mother obtained from Pharaoh's daughter the privilege of nursing and caring for her own son (Ex 2:1–10; Heb 11:23). Jochebed was the aunt of Amram, his father's sister (Ex 6:20). Marriage of such close relations is forbidden by the Mosaic law (Lev 18:12; 20:19); but there seems to have been no law against it at the time, and even closer relatives were married (cf. Gen 20:12).

Jochebed's Heb. name, *yôkebed,* meaning "Yah is glory," reveals that the name Yahweh was known and revered by the Israelites before Moses' burning bush experience when God revealed the fuller significance of His divine name (Ex 3:1–15).

JOD. The tenth letter of the Heb. alphabet. *See* Alphabet. This letter is used in the KJV as the heading of the tenth section of Ps 119, where each verse begins with this letter.

JOED (jō'ĕd). A Benjamite living in Jerusalem during the time of Nehemiah (Neh 11:7).

JOEL (jō'ĕl). This name, meaning "Yahweh is God," was popular among the Hebrews.

1. The prophet who wrote the book of Joel (1:1; Acts 2:16). There is no reference to him in the OT historical books but his writings indicate he was the son of Pethuel and lived in Judah, probably in Jerusalem. His date depends on the dating of his book (*see* Joel, Book of), but perhaps *c.* 835 B.C. Some consider him non-historical and the name only indicative of the prophecy's theme (2:26–27). Since this is unnecessary and the NT refers to an historical character, he should be seen as historical.

2. Samuel's elder son (I Sam 8:2), father of Heman the singer (I Chr 6:33; 15:17). The KJV reads "Vashni" in I Chr 6:28, which is a transliteration of the Heb. probably meaning "and the second"; ASV and RSV so render it and correct the text by adding "Joel" on the basis of Lucian's recession of the LXX, the Syriac, v. 33 and I Sam 8:2. He and his younger brother, Abijah, were appointed by Samuel as judges at Beer-sheba. Their perversion of the office precipitated the elders' demand for a king over Israel.

3. A prince of the Simeonites who emigrated to the valley of Geder *c.* 715 B.C. (I Chr 4:35).

4. A Reubenite (I Chr 5:4, 8).

5. A chief of the Gadites in Bashan (I Chr 5:12).

6. An ancestor of 2 above and Samuel, son of Azariah and father of an Elkanah (I Chr 6:36).

7. Chief in Issachar, son of Izrahiah, in David's time (I Chr 7:3).

8. One of David's mighty men (I Chr 11:38), brother of Nathan. (In II Sam 23:36 he is called Igal and is referred to as "son.")

9. The Gershonite chief from the Levites (son of Laadan, I Chr 23:8) appointed by David to help return the ark from the house of Obed-edom (I Chr 15:7, 11) and a keeper of the temple treasury (I Chr 26:22).

10. The son of Pedaiah and David's chief over western Manasseh (I Chr 27:20).

11. A Kohathite Levite who assisted Hezekiah in the restoration of temple services (II Chr 29:12).

12. A son of Nebo listed as one of those pledging to put away their foreign wives (Ezr 10:43; also mentioned in I Esd 9:35).

13. A son of Zichri and overseer of the post-Exilic Benjamites in Jerusalem *c.* 456 B.C. (Neh 11:9).

14. The son of Bani (called Uel in Ezr 10:34 but Joel in I Esd 9:34) in the same list as 12 above.

Sometimes 4 and 5 are seen as one man, and 9 as two.

W. A. A.

JOEL, BOOK OF

Authorship

The author cannot be identified with any of the other OT persons bearing this name, and nothing is known of him outside the book. Thus identification hinges on whether the name is historical or symbolic (*see* Joel). However well his name ("Yahweh is God") expresses his message, it is usually taken as historical. He was the son of Pethuel (1:1; LXX, Bethuel), and Peter speaks of him as the author of the book (Acts 2:16).

Date

With only internal evidence, dating is the greatest problem of the book. Suggestions range from the 10th to the 2nd cen. B.C., 830 and 400 B.C. being the most common. While the earlier date is most characteristic of conservatives and the later of liberals, this lack of agreement seems to be more the result of honest uncertainty about historical possibilities rather than theological predisposition. The same data are presented in favor of both dates. Were the priests in favor (1:13 f.; 2:12–17) because they had not yet fallen into disfavor, or were they again in favor? Significantly, no king is mentioned. This implies either the regency under Jehoiada the priest early in the reign of Joash (835–796 B.C.), or the post-monarchial period after the Exile. The priests and elders as leaders could indicate either an early or a late date. A post-Exilic setting for both of these would seem more certain. No mention of Assyria or Babylon could point to a late date, but the silence regarding them can also be accounted for by proposing the early date before these nations began to harass the kingdom of Judah.

Scattered people and divided land (3:2 f.), Greeks (3:6), no mention of the northern kingdom, and alleged post-Exilic language favor the late date. None of these is conclusive, each raises additional problems, and each can be explained. Phoenicians, Philistines, Egyptians, and Edomites (3:4, 19) as early enemies, and Amos seeming to use Joel (e.g., Joel 2:2, 10; 3:16, 18 with Amos 5:18, 20; 8:8; 1:2; 9:13, respectively) are as strongly in favor of the early date. Most conclusive is the ancient position in the canon which almost obliges a cautious scholar to accept it at face value until contrary evidence compels change of opinion. It is suggested here that the evidence for the early date—while not conclusive—is sufficient to accept the ancient understanding, and that the arguments for the late date—while forceful—are not sufficient to require a departure. Joel's message, moreover, seems to make sense as an early statement which was further developed by later prophets (e.g., the day of the Lord concept, cf. Zephaniah; Joel 3:10, cf. Isa 2:4; Mic 4:3). Therefore, a date *c.* 830 B.C. seems more likely as the time when Joel wrote; thus he is one of the earliest prophets. He may have been one of the prophets mentioned in II Chr 24:19 whom God sent to warn Judah and Jerusalem after a new outburst of idolatry following Jehoiada's death.

Occasion and Purpose

While a recent locust plague and drought were surely involved as illustrations, the occasion for Joel's prophetic message is most properly seen in the spiritual conditions of the day. The people needed revival in light of the coming day of the Lord and God's climactic disposition of the universe and human society. There is none of the bitter condemnation of blatant sin and gross corruption of later prophets because the people of Judah had simply drifted in Joel's day rather than rebelled against God. While continuing to observe the mechanics of the old covenant, they had become thoughtless in their understanding and careless in their practice. They were spiritually fruitless—rather like the land after the recent locust attacks.

This condition cannot long be tolerated, Joel is convinced, because the day of the Lord is coming when God will make a final disposition of Judah. He not only draws attention to the present spiritual need and to the terribleness of the day of the Lord relative to it, but he sees a glorious future for those who will return to the Lord. The purpose of this prophecy, then, is to call Judah back to God before the day of the Lord comes, to assure the return of God's blessings, and to promise future restoration and vindication.

Structure and Style

The Heb. text is composed of four chapters so that the English 2:28–32 is chap. 3 in the Heb. and the third English chapter is chap. 4 in Heb. Moreover, the first two Heb. chapters are thought to pertain mainly to the present, while the latter two deal only with the future. Therefore, the English 2:28 is a turning point at which to divide the text in analysis, and most scholars do so.

Another way of outlining the book makes the major division before 2:18–19 where the Heb. verbs indicate a past tense. But the verb translated "I will remove" in 2:20 is in the imperfect state, indicating a future tense, so that vv. 18–19 may be interpreted as prophetic perfects foretelling a future period, as in KJV and NASB. Then everything from 2:18 to 3:21 is future in the Messianic Age.

Since the second division is markedly different from the first (apocalyptic rather than historical), many years ago the more liberal scholars began to suggest that it was written by another prophet much later. No other factor suggests dual authorship, and this is adequately accounted for by the dual aspect of God's judgment with future blessings promised for repentance after present punishment is threatened. Therefore, the face value unity of the book commends itself.

Classical among the earlier writing prophets (cf. Amos, Hosea and Micah), Joel's style includes purposeful structure, vivid illustrations, and finely polished language. The bulk of the book is metered poetry with a short prose section (3:4–8).

Outline

Superscription, 1:1

I. Decline of Judah's Prosperity, 1:2–2:11
   - A. Description of the present crisis, 1:2–20
     Assemble and cry out to the Lord because locusts have left His land without fruit and His house without offerings—and the day of the Lord is coming.
   - B. Description of the coming day of the Lord, 2:1–11
     The day of the Lord is coming with a terrible army and unparalleled destruction.

II. Return of the Lord and His Blessings, 2:12–27
   - A. The conditions for return, 2:12–17
     Let all the people return to the Lord with repentance—perhaps He will relent and provide blessings.
   - B. The Lord's response, 2:18–20
     With jealousy for His land and pity for His people, Yahweh then promised satisfying food and removal of foreign reproach and the northern enemy.

JOEL, BOOK OF

C. The prophet's song of rejoicing, 2:21–24
Be glad, for the land is productive, for the Lord has caused all the rains to fall as before.

D. Establishment of the Lord and His people, 2:25–27
"I will restore the food lost to locusts and My great army, and you will praise Me with conviction as Israel's exclusive God who has wondrously satisfied you. And My people will never again be put to shame."

III. Reconstitution of Society, 2:28–3:21

A. The Lord's Spirit and salvation, 2:28–32
"Before the day of the Lord will be cosmic upheaval, but I will first pour out My Spirit on all mankind. I will provide deliverance to those who call upon Me as I call them to escape."

B. The Lord's judgment of the nations, 3:1–15
"I will judge the nations for their oppression of Judah at the time when they will come to besiege Jerusalem."

C. The Lord's vindication of Judah, 3:16–21
The Lord acts from Zion to drive away alien nations and to guard Judah in prosperity.

The Locusts

Despite their simply instrumental function, the locusts are so dramatically described that their importance is sometimes exaggerated. The *'arbeh, gāzām, yeleq,* and *ḥāsîl* are explained as different insects, varieties or stages; but whatever, they indicate the cumulative effect of unrelenting attacks. *See* Animals, III.29. While the immediate references are to literal insects in chap. 1, it becomes difficult to be sure whether they or horses are being pictured in 2:1–11 since a locust's head resembles a horse's head in miniature. The narrative can describe equally well swarms of locusts instinctively doing as they were created, or squadrons of cavalry obediently doing as they were trained. The eschatological features of this day of the Lord passage have led many commentators to connect it with the demonic locusts of Rev 9:1–11. See Hobart E. Freeman, *An Introduction to the Old Testament Prophets,* Chicago: Moody Press, 1968, pp. 150–154 for arguments in favor of apocalyptic symbolism in 2:1–11.

The Day of the Lord

This is a major motif which is announced with alarm and described as great and dark destruction (1:15; 2:1, 11), but this negative aspect is balanced with a bright picture of restoration (3:1, 18). It is that era in which God no longer restrains the full execution of His judgment, but directly intervenes in human society and even the cosmos according to the analysis of holiness and in terms of the execution of justice. While the negative is emphasized because Judah most needed to be warned, the positive is present as an encouragement to the faithful remnant and a further motivation to those warned. However unclear the theological understanding of the time sequence of this prophecy may be, the practical implication is clear: God's judgment is coming soon; there is just enough time to repent effectively, but not enough to delay safely.

The Outpouring of the Spirit

Both Peter at Pentecost (Acts 2:21) and Paul to the Romans (10:13) quote Joel 2:32. It is Peter, however, who makes the fullest use (Acts 2:17–21) when he quotes Joel 2:28–32. In correcting those who thought the Jerusalem disciples were drunk because of their glossolalia (*see* Tongues, Gift of), Peter said, "This is that which was spoken by the prophet Joel" (Acts 2:16). The apostle may have been making specific reference only to that portion of the prophecy which speaks of the Spirit's outpouring and the consequent prophesying, for the events of the day of Pentecost do not seem to have exhausted the prophecy. The effect of the reference seems to be that this is one of the things Joel had in mind, but just the beginning of these things. From that day, the public inauguration of the Messianic Age, and onward to the day of the Lord, the promised Holy Spirit is being given to believers of every age, sex and race (Acts 2:38–39). Thus Joel is the first of the prophets to link the outpouring of the Spirit with the coming of Messiah (cf. Isa 11:2; 32:15; 42:1; 44:3; 59:21; 61:1–3; Ezk 36:27; 39:29; Zech 12:10). See Freeman, *op. cit.,* pp. 154–156 for discussion of the various views of the fulfillment of Joel 2:28–32.

The Apocalypse and the Restoration of Israel

Already indicated is that the last two Heb. chapters (2:28–3:21 in English) are clearly apocalyptic. The ultimate restoration of Israel in the land is obvious, but the exact nature and order of events is less clear. Joel's apocalypse is a significant early statement in the progression of eschatological prophecy, and one cannot formulate a doctrine of future events without inclusion of his data. This prophecy offers a needed corrective to those who are naively optimistic about world peace because of presumptions upon the promise that men will one day "beat their swords into plowshares and their spears into pruning hooks" (Isa 2:4; Mic 4:3). Joel calls upon the nations to do just the opposite (3:10) because of the day of the Lord coming upon their evil. God's promise through Isaiah and Micah, then, will only be realized after His threat through Joel has been experienced.

Significance

The contemporary and eschatological significance of Joel's prophecy is very great; the former because the people of Judah in his day were so much like Christians today; the latter because so much of his predictive prophecy remains unfulfilled. Its message should warn Christians who are beginning to drift spiritually that the consequences are already determined, but that God's blessings can be revived in their lives and that they can anticipate even fuller blessings in the days to come.

Bibliography. J. A. Brewer, ICC. J. T. Carson, "Joel," NBC, Grand Rapids: Eerdmans, 1953. S. R. Driver, *Cambridge Bible,* 1934. A. S. Kapelrud, *Joel Studies,* Uppsala: Uppsala Univ., 1948. E. B. Pusey, *The Minor Prophets,* Vol I, New York: Funk & Wagnalls, 1885. G. A. Smith, *The Expositor's Bible,* rev. ed., New York: Harper, 1928.

W. A. A.

JOELAH (jō-ē'*lȧ*). One of the sons of Jeroham of Gedor who joined David's forces at Ziklag (I Chr 12:7).

JOEZER (jō-ē'zĕr). A Korahite who joined David's army while David was exiled at Ziklag (I Chr 12:6). The name was inscribed on an ancient Heb. seal as *Yhw'zr.*

JOGBEHAH (jŏg'bĕ-*hȧ*). A fortified town of Gad (Num 32:35). Gideon passed E of the city in attacking the Midianites (Jud 8:11). This is the modern village of Jubeihât, six miles NW of Amman.

JOGLI (jŏg'lī). The father of Bukki, a Danite chief (Num 34:22).

JOHA (jō'*hȧ*)

1. A son of Beriah listed in the genealogy of the tribe of Benjamin (I Chr 8:16).
2. A Tizite included, with his brother Jediael, among David's 30 mighty men (I Chr 11:45).

JOHANAN (jō-hā'*nȧn*)

1. One of the captains of the remnant that remained in Judah after the fall of Jerusalem. He led the others in warning Gedaliah of the danger to his life from Ishmael. After the governor had been slain, Johanan led the force that pursued Ishmael and recovered the captives taken. Fearful of what the Babylonians would do in reprisal for the murder, Johanan and the other captains approached Jeremiah for advice. When he told them it was the Lord's will that they abide in the land and trust God for protection, Johanan "and all the proud men" rejected the prophet and led the remnant of people to Egypt. There Johanan passes from the record (II Kgs 25:23; Jer 40–43).
2. The oldest son of King Josiah. He probably died young as there is no further mention of him (I Chr 3:15).
3. The son of Elioenai, a descendant of Zerubbabel, after the Exile (I Chr 3:24).
4. A priest, the son of Azariah and father of another Azariah (I Chr 6:9–10).
5. A Benjamite warrior who joined David at Ziklag (I Chr 12:4).
6. A mighty Gadite warrior who joined David in the wilderness (I Chr 12:12, 14).
7. The father of Azariah who was one of the Ephraimites who insisted on returning the captives of Judah taken by Pekah (II Chr 28:12).
8. The son of Hakkatan, one of the descendants of Azgad who returned to Jerusalem with Ezra (Ezr 8:12).
9. One of the chief priests in the days of Ezra and Nehemiah. Ezra retired to the chamber of Johanan in the temple to mourn over the mixed marriages (Ezr 10:6; Neh 12:22–23).
10. The son of Tobiah the Ammonite. He married the daughter of Meshullam the priest (Neh 6:18).

P. C. J.

JOHN (jŏn). In its Heb. form *yôḥānān,* this name was once common among the Jews (*see* Johanan). At least four men named John are mentioned in I and II Maccabees. The following appear in the NT:

1. John the father of Simon Peter (Jn 1:42; 21:15–17, RSV, NASB). Jesus called Peter, Simon Bar-jona (Mt 16:17), Aram. for "son of Jonah." It is not clear whether "Jonah" and "John" represent two Gr. forms of the same Heb. name, or are two different names for Peter's father.
2. John the Baptist (*q.v.*).
3. John the apostle (*q.v.*).
4. John Mark (*see* Mark).
5. A Jewish priest who participated in the questioning of Peter and John (Acts 4:6), otherwise unknown.

JOHN, GOSPEL OF. The fourth Gospel of the NT, regarded by many as the most profound book in the NT. Simple in language and structure, it is nevertheless a deeply perceptive exposition of the person of Christ in a historical setting.

Theme

Like the Synoptic Gospels (*see* Gospels, Synoptic), the Gospel of John has as its theme the presentation of the ministry of Jesus Christ to His own nation, including the preparation for it by the work of John the Baptist, the gathering of disciples about Him, the teaching of the people, the performing of miracles, the stirring of opposition on the part of the religious leaders of Israel, and His condemnation to death by the high council, which was implemented by Pilate the Roman governor, leading to His crucifixion and resurrection, with appearances to His chosen disciples.

JOHN, GOSPEL OF

Purpose

The author's purpose in writing is plainly stated: to induce faith in Jesus as the Christ, the Son of God, so that life may come through His name (20:31). It is not life in the abstract but the divine life communicated to those willing to receive the Messiah. Because the nation as a whole was unwilling to do this (1:11; 18:35), it was left in its sins. Judaism, despite the glamour of its festivals and the enlightenment of its law and the self-confidence of its leaders, shows how pathetic is its blindness. It refused to recognize its Messiah and thereby forfeited all claim to a genuine knowledge of the God who had sent Him (chap. 8).

The appeal of the book is mainly to the Jewish Diaspora, those who because of their residence outside the land lacked the opportunity for immediate contact with Jesus. Let them see clearly the solemnity of the issues involved and choose life in the Son rather than the condemnation that belongs to those who refuse Him. It is a striking fact that despite the "whosoever" of the gospel invitation, the word Gentile does not once occur in the book—although the term "Greeks" in 7:35 apparently means Gentiles, and the Greeks who came to see Jesus (12:20) were undoubtedly Gentile proselytes.

The John Rylands Fragment of John 18: 31–33. John Rylands Library

Author and Date

Who wrote this "spiritual Gospel," as Clement of Alexandria called it? The traditional answer is John, the son of Zebedee. Irenaeus is the leading patristic writer who affirms this, and he was in a favorable position to know because of his contact with Polycarp and Pothinus, who had been associated with John in Asia Minor during the latter days of his life. Other 2nd cen. witnesses were Theophilus of Antioch, the author of the Muratorian Canon, and Clement of Alexandria.

This testimony has been widely challenged in modern times on various grounds, such as the silence of Ignatius about John when writing to the Ephesian church early in the 2nd cen., the claim that an Ephesian by the same name, John the Elder, may have written it, or that reports of the early martyrdom of John rule out the possibility of his authorship. These objections are rather easily answered.

More serious are the allegations that a fisherman could not be expected to display such a grasp of theological thought as the author of this book manifestly had (cf. Acts 4:13). It seems strange also that a Galilean would give such slight attention to Jesus' ministry in Galilee. And if the writer was a member of the apostolic circle, why did he omit a description of the transfiguration and of Jesus' agony in Gethsemane, at which he was a privileged witness?

In the face of problems such as these, many have concluded that while John may have furnished much of the material of the Gospel, another—probably one of his close disciples—actually wrote it. But it is still possible to maintain John's authorship, since no decisive argument against it has been raised, and no satisfactory alternative has been offered. The writer was familiar with Samaria (cf. 3:23; 4:5–12) and with Jerusalem prior to its destruction in A.D. 70, knowing details verified by archaeological discoveries about the pool of Bethesda (5:2) and the Pavement (19:13). He seems to have been an eyewitness of many of the events (e.g., 6:10; 19:31–35), and was conversant with the religious terminology current among pious Jews in Palestine prior to A.D. 68, according to the Qumran literature.

For many years it was popular, following F. C. Baur of the Tübingen School in Germany, to insist that the Gospel of John was a product of the mid-2nd cen. A.D. But the John Rylands fragment (P^{52}) of the text of this Gospel, found in Egypt in modern times and dated by paleographers during the first half of the 2nd cen., helps to fix the writing of the fourth Gospel by the close of the 1st cen. The use of John as an authoritative Gospel along with the other three is attested by the Egerton Papyrus 2, a harmony dated not later than A.D. 150, published in *Fragments of an Unknown Gospel and Other Early Christian Papyri*, by H. I. Bell and T. C. Sheat (1935). Furthermore, the fourth Gospel seems to have been quoted by the Gnostic writer Valentinus in his Gospel of Truth, originally composed *c.* A.D. 140 (*see* Gnosticism). Also in catacombs in Rome there are paintings of Christ as the Good Shepherd and of the raising of Lazarus that can be dated *c.* A.D. 150. Thus the origin of the Gospel of John can be placed during the last decade or so of the 1st cen., although some would make it even earlier, with Ephesus as the probable place of writing.

Outline

I. Prologue, 1:1–18
II. The Son of God Working and Witnessing Among Men, 1:19–12:50
III. The Son of God Teaching His Own, 13:1–17:26
IV. The Son of God Glorifying the Father in Death and Resurrection, 18:1–20:31
V. Epilogue, 21:1-25

Differences from Other Gospels

Though in its general nature this Gospel is similar in broad outline to the Synoptics, it differs from them in various respects. About nine-tenths of its material is not found in the Synoptics at all. Much more emphasis is put on Jesus' ministry in Judea than in Galilee. The Lord is represented as going to Jerusalem on several occasions, especially for the festivals of the Jewish year. On the basis of these, it is possible to hold that His ministry must have lasted about three years, whereas the items included in the Synoptics need not have covered more than one year, with a single Passover being mentioned.

One misses the parables that so abound in Jesus' teaching as it is reported in the Synoptics. The teaching material occurs mainly in discourses which do not center in the kingdom of God, as in the other Gospels, but in the person of Christ. It is here that the "I am" sayings are to be found. Not infrequently dialogues between Jesus and various individuals are introduced, as in the case of Nicodemus and of the Samaritan woman. A cleansing of the temple is included at an early point in the Gospel and none is mentioned at the close, where the Synoptics place it. The resurrection of Lazarus, which fails to appear in the Synoptics, is introduced in connection with the deepening of official opposition to Jesus. Much more sharply than in the Synoptics the issue of His messiahship is the focus of discussion.

In Jesus' self-revelation, as here presented, the most outstanding feature is His relation to the Father as the Son. He is conscious of pre-existence (17:5) and claims equality with the Father (10:30; 5:23). Yet along with this high claim goes an oft-repeated recognition of subordination and dependence on the Father. His words (14:24) and His works (14:10) are traced to the Father. His glorification is not merely reserved for the resurrection and what follows (12:16; 7:39), but actually includes His death (12:23; 13:31), since this fulfilled the Father's will.

That a Gospel of this character could be written in the early church and accepted by it, despite these and other differences from the Synoptics, suggests the variety and richness of the Christian tradition as it was recalled by those who had companied with the Saviour. It is wholly unlikely that this Gospel was written to replace the Synoptics since it is so different from them. While it may have been designed to supplement the other accounts, it seems to stand largely apart from them, as though springing from a source that had independent information. *See* Gospels, The Four.

Bibliography. C. K. Barrett, *The Gospel According to St. John,* London: SPCK, 1955. T. D. Bernard, *The Central Teaching of Jesus Christ,* New York: Macmillan, 1892. Raymond E. Brown, *The Gospel According to John,* Anchor Bible, 2 vols., Garden City: Doubleday, 1966, 1970. F. Lamar Cribbs, "A Reassessment of the Date of the Origin and the Destination of the Gospel of John," JBL, LXXXIX (1970), 38-55. C. H. Dodd, *The Interpretation of the Fourth Gospel,* Cambridge: Univ. Press, 1953. F. Godet, *Commentary on the Gospel of St. John,* 3 vols., 3rd ed., Edinburgh: T. & T. Clark, 1895. William Hendriksen, *The Gospel of John,* 2 vols., Grand Rapids: Baker, 1953. E. C. Hoskyns, *The Fourth Gospel,* rev. ed., ed. by F. N. Davey, London: Faber & Faber, 1940. W. F. Howard, *Christianity According to St. John,* London: Duckworth, 1943. Leon Morris, *The Gospel of John,* Grand Rapids: Eerdmans, 1971; *Studies in the Fourth Gospel,* Grand Rapids: Eerdmans, 1969. H. P. V. Nunn, *The Authorship of the Fourth Gospel,* Oxford: Blackwell, 1952. R. V. G. Tasker, *The Gospel According to St. John,* TNTC, Grand Rapids: Eerdmans, 1960. William Temple, *Readings in St. John's Gospel,* London: Macmillan, 1945. Merrill C. Tenney, *John: The Gospel of Belief,* Grand Rapids: Eerdmans, 1948. W. H. Griffith Thomas, "The Plan of the Fourth Gospel," BS, CXXV (1968), 313–323. George A. Turner and Julius R. Mantey, *The Gospel According to John,* Grand Rapids: Eerdmans, 1964. B. F. Westcott, *The Gospel According to St. John:* The Greek Text with Introduction and Notes, London: John Murray, 1908.

E. F. Har.

JOHN, I, II AND III EPISTLES OF. These are often described as catholic or general epistles, but the designation is somewhat faulty since the second and third letters are addressed to local situations and the first to believers in a limited area, probably that portion of Asia Minor that looked to Ephesus as its hub city.

I John

Purpose. This letter was written partly to instruct and encourage the readers, majoring on such fundamental terms as light, truth, knowledge (verb), belief (verb), love, and righteousness. These are not developed one after

JOHN, I, II AND III EPISTLES OF

another in systematic fashion, but are intertwined to a degree as the author repeats his themes with variations.

It is not difficult to detect along with this positive purpose a desire to warn against false teaching (e.g., 2:26). The particular error in view is Gnosticism (*q.v.*) of a Jewish type that denied that Jesus is the Christ (2:22) and that He had come in the flesh (4:2-3). The Gnostics tended to be proud and exclusive, boasting of their superior insights, and for this reason drew the fire of the writer as he insisted that genuine believers are not deficient in knowledge (2:20-21, 27). Neither must they be deficient in love, in contrast to the errorists (4:20). It is diabolical to claim superior knowledge and live on a low moral and ethical plane (3:7-8).

Author. From various references in the Church Fathers, it is known that the early church ascribed the epistle to John the apostle (*q.v.*). Agreeable to this identification is the close similarity between the introduction (1:1-4) of I John and the prologue of the Gospel of John. Much the same vocabulary is found in the two works. There are differences, of course, but these are natural in view of the diverse nature of the two writings.

Recipients. The readers of the epistle cannot be identified with certainty. If the word "idols" in 5:21 must be taken literally, then the readers were Gentile Christians. But it is perhaps more logical to understand the word in a broader sense of the fascination with false teaching and the vagaries that belong to it. At any rate, the prominence given to the confession of Jesus as the Christ (2:22) suggests that the readers were Jewish Christians (cf. Jn 20:31).

Date. The exact time of writing cannot be fixed. It was probably sometime in the last decade of the 1st cen.

Characteristics. Simplicity of language and sentence structure characterize the book. Its challenge lies in its sharply enunciated teaching on the nature of the Christian life. One is either walking in the light with God or is in darkness. To profess one thing and be another is the mark of a liar. No man can live rightly unless he is born of God (2:29; 3:9; 4:7; 5:4). The doctrinal emphasis centers mainly in Christology—the oneness of the Son with the Father (1:2-3; 2:23), His incarnation (1:2; 4:2), atonement (1:7; 2:2; 3:5), victory over the evil one (3:8), and future appearing (3:2). The Spirit is given attention also, particularly in the capacity of witness to the truth (5:7-8; cf. 4:2) and to the divine indwelling of the believer (3:24; 4:13). As in the Gospel according to John, the world, ethically considered, is pictured as evil, something to be shunned (2:15-17; 3:13; 4:5; 5:4-5, 19).

Outline

I. Introduction, 1:1-4
II. Fellowship with God (Walking in the Light), 1:5-2:28
Tested by:
1. Righteousness of life, 1:8-2:6
2. Love for the brethren, 2:7-17
3. Belief in Jesus as God incarnate, 2:18-28
III. Divine Sonship, 2:29-4:6
Tested by:
1. Righteousness, 2:29-3:10*a*
2. Love, 3:10*b*-24
3. Belief, 4:1-6
IV. The Commandment of Christian Love, 4:7-21
V. The Necessity of Christian Belief, 5:1-12
VI. The Certainties of the Christian Life, 5:13-20
VII. Concluding Exhortation, 5:21

II John

The writer makes himself known only as "the elder." This was sufficient since the recipient, identified as "the elect lady," was evidently a close friend. The elder was following the spiritual development of her children faithfully, and hoped to come in person for a visit before long. Others believe the "lady" refers to a local church or Christian community, perhaps at Pergamum, the members of which are called "her children." *See* Elect Lady.

If there was a special reason for the writing of this brief letter, it is probably to be found in the counsel not to receive visiting teachers who fail to measure up to the church's confession concerning the incarnation (vv. 7-11). The elder could not resist the urge to underscore also the need for continued love toward the saints (vv. 5-6).

Several features of this brief letter suggest John the apostle as the writer, such as the emphasis on truth and love, and especially the insistence on the incarnation. Other items looking in the same direction are the mention of Antichrist (v. 7; cf I Jn 2:18, 22; 4:3) and the word "abide" (v.9). It would be pedantic to insist that the use of "elder" rules out apostolic status (cf. I Pet 5:1). The early church generally accepted the book as emanating from John. Presumably the recipient lived fairly close to Ephesus (v. 12). The probable date is late in the 1st cen.

Outline

I. Commendation for Fidelity to the Truth, 1-3
II. Commandment of Love in Which to Walk, 4-6
III. Importance of Holding the Doctrine of Christ, 7-9
IV. Refusal of Fellowship with False Teachers, 10-11
V. Conclusion, 12-13

III John

This short missive, likewise from "the elder," is addressed to a certain Gaius who is a faithful believer (v. 3) and a leader in a local church. He had distinguished himself by his hospitality toward traveling Christian workers (vv. 5-6), in contrast to Diotrephes, who belonged either in the same church or in one close by. This man not only had refused to receive the brethren whom John had sent (apparently wishing to show his authority in the local situation by rejecting the elder's recommendation contained in his letter), but had gone so far as to put out of the church those who welcomed these visitors (v. 10). Now the elder was writing Gaius, appealing to him to help the missionaries even at the cost of bringing down upon himself the wrath of Diotrephes.

The letter bears marks of similarity to II John, not only in the person of the writer, but in the strong emphasis on the truth and the preference for a personal visit over communication by letter (v. 13).

In all probability the date of the letter is roughly the same as for II John, and the destination some spot not far distant from Ephesus.

Outline

I. Introduction, 1-4
II. Praise for Kindness to Traveling Brethren, 5-8
III. Condemnation of Diotrephes, 9-11
IV. Recommendation of Demetrius, 12
V. Conclusion, 13-14

Bibliography. Donald W. Burdick, *The Epistles of John,* Chicago: Moody Press, 1970. Robert S. Candlish, *The First Epistle of John,* Grand Rapids: Zondervan, n.d. C. H. Dodd, *The Johannine Epistles,* New York: Harper, 1946. George G. Findlay, *Fellowship in the Life Eternal,* London: Hodder & Stoughton, n.d. Robert Law, *The Tests of Life, A Study of the First Epistle of John,* Edinburgh: T. & T. Clark, 1909. Alexander Ross, *Commentary on the Epistles of James and John,* NIC, Grand Rapids: Eerdmans, 1954. Charles C. Ryrie, "I, II and III John," WBC, pp. 1463-1485. John R. W. Stott, *The Epistles of John,* TNTC, Grand Rapids: Eerdmans, 1964. B. F. Westcott, *The Epistles of John,* Cambridge: Macmillan, 1892. Reginald E. O. White, *Open Letter to Evangelicals, A Devotional and Homiletic Commentary on the First Epistle of John,* Grand Rapids: Eerdmans, 1964.

E. F. Har.

Ruins of the Church of St. John at Ephesus. HFV

JOHN MARK. *See* Mark.

JOHN THE APOSTLE. According to the testimony of the NT and of the ancient church, this John was one of the leading figures in shaping the course of Christianity, whether by his writings (the fourth Gospel, three epistles, and the Apocalypse), his missionary and pastoral labors, or his defense of the faith against the attempted inroads of Gnostic error.

Personal history. The biblical data furnish considerable information about him, at least more than is available on most of the apostles. Zebedee was his father (Mk 1:20) and Salome his mother (Mk 15:40; Mt 27:56). A comparison with Jn 19:25 makes it probable that Salome was the sister of Mary, the mother of Jesus. John was likely younger than his brother James, for, with the exception of a few Lucan passages (Lk 8:51, RSV; 9:28; Acts 1:13, RSV), he is regularly named after James. The family was engaged in the fishing business, with servants assisting the father and his sons (Mk 1:20). A partnership had been formed with another pair of brothers, Simon Peter and Andrew (Lk 5:10). Since the latter lived at Bethsaida on the northern shore of the Sea of Galilee (Jn 1:44), it may be assumed that this was John's residence also.

Whereas John is named rather frequently in the Synoptic Gospels especially in Mark, this is not true of the fourth Gospel, which merely refers to the sons of Zebedee (Jn 21:2). However, there are several references to "the disciple whom Jesus loved" (Jn 13:23; 19:26; 20:2; 21:7, 20) and to "another disciple" (Jn 18:15) who brought Peter into the court of the high priest's house. Since Peter's companion a short time afterward was the beloved disciple (Jn 20:2) and since John was closely associated with Peter both in the Synoptic Gospels and Acts, it is reasonable to infer that John was the beloved disciple. This is supported by the consideration that the absence of John's name from the fourth Gospel, in view of its prominence in the Synoptics, can best be explained on the supposition that John was the writer of the fourth Gospel, who for some reason, probably modesty, preferred to keep his name out of the record (in Jn 21:24 the writer of the Gospel is identified with the beloved disciple).

It is highly probable that John was that unnamed disciple who, in company with Andrew, spent several hours with Jesus after John the Baptist had pointed Him out (Jn 1:35-40). If so, this means that he and a number of other

JOHN THE APOSTLE

disciples of Jesus had been followers of the Baptist before transferring their allegiance to the Nazarene. However, the more definite call to discipleship came somewhat later, in Galilee, when John and his brother James were summoned from their nets to become fishers of men (Mk 1:19). Later still, when 12 men were set apart as apostles, John was included. He appears as a member of the inner circle of three (Peter, James, and John) who were with Jesus at the raising of Jairus' daughter (Mk 5:37), at the transfiguration (Mk 9:2), and at the night vigil in Gethsemane (Mk 14:33). On another occasion Andrew was present with the three (Mk 13:3). With Peter, John was delegated to prepare the Passover feast for Jesus and the Twelve (Lk 22:8).

If the reference in Jn 18:15 to the acquaintanceship between a certain disciple and the high priest really refers to John, as seems most natural, then he is not to be regarded simply as an ordinary fisherman. It is quite possible that John's family possessed means. His mother was likely a member of that group of women who ministered to Jesus of their substance (Lk 8:2–3; cf. Jn 19:25). From Jn 19:26–27 it appears that the family maintained a home in the Jerusalem area. Jesus knew that in committing His mother to John He was insuring her comfort as well as spiritual solace. Although it is only conjecture, one may conclude perhaps that it was during John's days in Judea as a disciple of John the Baptist that he secured quarters in Jerusalem and also became known to the high priest. He wanted to be near in order to keep in the closest possible touch with the new awakening that centered in the ministry of the Baptist.

Characteristics. Something of the character of John may be gleaned from the epithet given to him and his brother James by the Lord. Although "sons of thunder" (Mk 3:17) is not explained in the text, it seems to refer to the disposition or to the zeal of these brothers, or both. Fortunately, a few episodes are recorded that help to fill out the picture. On his own initiative John forbade a man to continue casting out demons in Jesus' name, on the ground that he did not belong to Jesus' chosen band of disciples. Christ would not own this narrowness, but rebuked it (Lk 9:49–50).

On two other occasions John teamed with his brother James in exhibiting undesirable traits of character. Using their mother as a go-between, they asked for the choice places of honor on either side of Jesus when His kingdom glory was achieved (Mk 10:35; Mt 20:20). They had not yet learned to crucify selfish ambition. At another time, on the way up to Jerusalem, the brothers proposed that they call down fire from heaven upon a Samaritan village that refused hospitality to their Master. Apparently it did not dawn on them that a vindictive use of miraculous power was completely alien to Him who had called them into His service (Lk 9:51–55). They were "sons of thunder" indeed.

Traditional tomb of John inside Church of St. John at Ephesus. HFV

Despite his weaknesses, and perhaps even because of them, John was given a specially close relationship to the Lord as "the disciple whom Jesus loved," leaning on His breast at supper. He was the first of the apostolic company to believe in the resurrection on the basis of what he saw in the empty tomb (Jn 20:8). It was his insight that detected the risen Lord as the one responsible for the great catch of fish (Jn 21:7). With reference to him the Lord indicated that quite a different future might unfold than that reserved for Simon Peter (Jn 21:22).

After Pentecost. Information on John for the period after Pentecost centers around his association with Simon Peter. He regularly took a subordinate role, content to let the initiative in speech and action rest with his friend. Because of his participation in the healing of the lame man (Acts 3:1, 4, 11), he was brought before the Sanhedrin, along with Peter, and almost certainly made some statement, because the boldness of both men impressed the council (Acts 4:13; cf. v. 19). These same two were deputed by the other apostles to go to Samaria to oversee the results of Philip's labors there (Acts 8:14).

Some time later, when his brother James was beheaded by order of Herod Agrippa I and his friend Peter imprisoned with a view to the same fate, John was not included in the persecution. Gradually tradition sponsored the idea that he suffered martyrdom, based mainly, one may suppose, on Jesus' prediction (Mk 10:39); but Luke knows nothing of it. This late tradition may safely be rejected. Our last glimpse of John in the Jerusalem area is furnished by Paul, who met with James the Lord's brother and Peter and John to discuss the nature of the gospel and their relation to it as servants of Christ (Gal 2:9). Here John is accounted a pillar of the Jerusalem church. It may be that John remained in the city until the troubled days prior to the siege of Jerusalem by the Roman armies under Titus, although he is not mentioned in connection with Paul's last visit (Acts 21).

Christian writers of the 2nd cen. and later tell of John's work in Asia Minor, centering in the city of Ephesus. According to Rev 1:9, John was exiled to the isle of Patmos for his testimony to the gospel. Irenaeus asserts that this occurred near the end of the reign of Domitian, which terminated in A.D. 96 (Eusebius HE iii.18.3). The same writer alleges that John lived on into the reign of Trajan, which began in the year 98 (*Against Heresies* iii.3.4).

John may well have supervised the work among the various churches in Asia Minor such as are named in Rev 2–3. Clement of Alexandria indicates a varied ministry in this area even after John's return from Patmos, when he must have been a very old man, including a moving story of his pastoral concern for a young man who fell into evil ways after his baptism. John allowed himself to be captured by the robbers over whom this young man was now chief, exhorted him, prayed with him, and brought him back to the Lord and to the church (*The Rich Man's Salvation*, p. 42).

In those days Gnosticism (*q.v.*) was gaining ground and seriously challenging the apostolic faith. John showed that he was capable not only of manifesting love for the brethren, but that he was still in measure a son of thunder. Irenaeus relates that on entering a bathhouse in Ephesus and seeing the heretic Cerinthus within, John rushed out crying, "Let us fly, lest even the bathhouse fall down, because Cerinthus, the enemy of the truth, is within" (*Against Heresies* iii.3.4).

For bibliography, *see* John, Gospel of.

E. F. Har.

JOHN THE BAPTIST. Born (*c.* 7 B.C.) of elderly parents, Zacharias and Elisabeth, both of whom were of a priestly family, John grew up in the wilderness of Judea (Lk 1:80), and there (*c.* A.D. 27) he was called to his prophetic ministry (Lk 3:2). Under what influences he lived during his formative years we can only speculate. Even if he had some association in the wilderness with the Essenes (whether those of Qumran or others; *see* Essenes; Dead Sea Scrolls), it was a new spiritual experience that launched him on his distinctive task of making ready "a people prepared for the Lord" (Lk 1:17), and this probably involved a break with his previous association. Now he rapidly gained fame as a preacher of repentance. Great numbers of Jews flocked out to the wilderness to listen to him, from Judea and the neighboring regions. Many of them received at his hands the baptism of repentance in the river Jordan, confessing their sins as they did so.

John's attitude to the Jewish "establishment" of the day was one of radical condemnation. The existing order could not be reformed; the axe was already being swung to cut down the tree at the root (Mt 3:10; Lk 3:9). The Pharisees and other religious leaders of the nation

Ein Kerem, birthplace of John the Baptist, with Church of St. John over his traditional place of birth. IIS

he denounced as a brood of vipers, trying to escape the flames of divine judgment which were overtaking them. He denied any value in natural descent from Abraham; he called for a new beginning. From the Jewish people at large he called out a loyal and repentant remnant that would make ready for the imminent advent of the greater than John who was to inaugurate the work of judgment. John spoke of himself as the preparer of the way for this Coming One, for whom he declared himself unworthy to perform even the humblest service. His own baptizing with water was to be followed by the more powerful baptism with the Spirit and fire which the Coming One would carry out.

That John's converts formed a distinct group in Israel is implied both by the fourth Gospel, with its references to the disciples of John, and by Josephus, who records that John bade his hearers "come together by means of baptism" (*Ant.* xviii.5.2). Josephus means probably that John called a religious community into being by his baptism of repentance. But when he further represents John as teaching that "baptism was acceptable to God provided that it was undergone not to procure remission of sins but for the purification of the body, when the soul had first been purified by righteousness," his account deviates from that of the Gospel writers, and probably reflects the baptismal doctrine of the Essenes, with which Josephus had some acquaintance.

To those of his disciples who sought his practical guidance, John gave some simple rules of charity and justice which demanded no such abandonment of their normal vocation as the strictest Essene code required.

Among those who received baptism from John was Jesus. After Jesus' baptism (which took place by His own request), John recognized in Him the Coming One of whom he had spoken—although later, during his imprisonment, he began to doubt this, and had to be reassured that the features of Jesus' ministry were precisely those which the prophets had said would mark the new age.

John exercised a baptismal ministry in Samaria, at Aenon near to Salim (Jn 3:23), as well as in the Judean wilderness. This ministry, which was probably of short duration, would explain certain features which emerged subsequently in Samaritan religion, and it also explains Jesus' words to His disciples in Jn 4:35–38, referring to that neighborhood: "Others have labored, and ye are entered into their labor" (ASV).

The last phase of John's career was located in the Perean region of Herod Antipas' tetrarchy. John aroused Herod's suspicion as the leader of a popular movement which might have political implications. He also incurred the personal animosity of Herodias, Herod's wife, by denouncing the illegality of their marriage. He was accordingly arrested and imprisoned in Herod's Transjordanian fortress of Machaerus (*q.v.*), where some months later he was beheaded (*c.* A.D. 29). His disciples preserved their identity for some decades after his death.

To the NT writers John's chief significance lies in his being Christ's forerunner. For a time his ministry and Christ's overlapped (Jn 3:22 f.). His imprisonment was the signal for the beginning of Christ's Galilean ministry (Mk 1:14); his baptism provided the starting point for the apostolic preaching (Acts 10:37; 13:24 f.). Jesus declared him to be the promised Elijah of Mal 4:5–6 (Mk 9:13; Mt 11:14; cf. Lk 1:17), and the last and greatest of the prophets (Lk 7:24–28; 16:16). His ministry summed up the burden of divine revelation under the old order: "The law and the prophets were until John: since that time the kingdom of God is preached." But while unsurpassed in personal stature, John was inferior in privilege, said Jesus, to the lowest in the kingdom of God. Like Moses viewing the Promised Land from Pisgah, John stood on the threshold of the new age as its herald, but did not enter it in this life.

Bibliography. W. H. Brownlee, "John the Baptist in the New Light of Ancient Scrolls," *The Scrolls and the New Testament,* ed. by K. Stendahl, London: SCM, 1958, pp. 33 ff. C. H. Kraeling, *John the Baptist,* New York: Scribner's, 1951. J. A. T. Robinson, *Twelve New Testament Studies,* London: SCM, 1962, pp. 11 ff. J. Steinmann, *Saint John the Baptist and the Desert Tradition,* London: Longmans, 1958.

F. F. B.

JOIADA (joi'*ȧ*-d*ȧ*). An abbreviation of Jehoiada (*q.v.*).

1. A son of Paseah who helped Nehemiah rebuild the wall of Jerusalem (Neh 3:6, RSV; KJV, Jehoiada).

2. A high priest and great-grandson of Jeshua (Neh 12:10, 22). One of his sons married a daughter of Sanballat, for which cause Nehemiah expelled him from the priesthood (Neh 13:28; here RSV has Jehoiada).

JOIAKIM (joi'*ȧ*-kĭm). The son of Jeshua the priest who returned with Zerubbabel (Neh 12:10, 12, 26).

JOIARIB (joi'*ȧ*-rĭb)

1. A priest in the time of David (I Chr 24:7).

2. One of the "men of understanding" or teachers sent by Ezra to Casiphia to request that ministers for the temple be sent to accompany them to Jerusalem (Ezr 8:16–17).

3. The son of Zechariah of the tribe of Judah whose descendants dwelt in Jerusalem in Nehemiah's day (Neh 11:5).

4. The father of Jedaiah and founder of one of the priestly houses after the Exile (Neh 11:10; 12:19). His name is given as Jehoiarib (*q.v.*) in I Chr 9:10.

5. One of the chief priests who returned to Jerusalem with Zerubbabel. A son Mattenai was contemporary with Joiakim (Neh 12:6, 19). Probably the same as 4.

JOINING. Two different Heb. words are translated "joining" in KJV.

1. A form of *ḥābar,* meaning "to join together, connect" (I Chr 22:3). It is translated "coupling" in ASV and "clamps" in RSV.

2. An adjective from *dābaq,* meaning "to cleave, adhere, join" (II Chr 3:12).

JOKDEAM (jŏk'dē-*ȧ*m). An unidentified town in the hill country of Judah, listed with Maon, Carmel and Ziph in Josh 15:56.

JOKIM (jō'kĭm). A son or descendant of Shelah, Judah's youngest son (I Chr 4:22).

JOKMEAM (jŏk'mē-*ȧ*m). A town in Ephraim assigned to the Kohathite Levites (I Chr 6:66, 68); perhaps the same as Kibzaim in Josh 21:22. In KJV of I Kgs 4:12 the name is incorrectly spelled Jokneam (see ASV and RSV for correction); this passage indicates Jokmeam is S of Abel-meholah in the Jordan Valley, perhaps Tell el-Mazar on the S side of the Wadi Far'ah, across from Adam (Tell ed-Damiyeh).

JOKNEAM (jŏk'nē-*ȧ*m). A royal Canaanite city (Josh 12:22) assigned to the Merarite Levites (Josh 21:34). Located on the W side of the Kishon stream at the foot of the Carmel ridge on Zebulun's boundary (Josh 19:11), it is now identified as Tell Qeimun, 12 miles SW of Nazareth and seven miles NW of Megiddo. The site guards the E end of the northernmost and lowest pass through the Carmel range, connecting the Plain of Sharon and the Valley of Jezreel. Jokneam is # 113 in the list of towns captured by Thutmose III. Jokneam in KJV of I Kgs 4:12 should read Jokmeam (as in ASV and RSV). *See* Jokmeam.

JOKSHAN (jŏk'shăn). A son of Abraham and Keturah, and the ancestor of the Sheba and Dedan tribes of Arabia (Gen 25:1–3; I Chr

1:32). The supposition that Jokshan is to be identified with Joktan (Gen 10:25; I Chr 1:20) is unsupported historically and philologically.

JOKTAN (jŏk'tăn). A descendant of Shem and the son of Eber and brother of Peleg (Gen 10:25; I Chr 1:19). He was the progenitor of 13 sons or Semitic tribal groups who inhabited the S Arabian peninsula (Gen 10:26–30; I Chr 1:20–23).

JOKTHEEL (jŏk'thē-ĕl)

1. An unidentified town in the Shephelah region of Judah near Lachish (Josh 15:38).

2. A name given to Sela(h) (now Petra) after King Amaziah of Judah captured it from the Edomites (II Kgs 14:7).

JONA (jō'nȧ). KJV form of John (Jn 1:42, RSV), used in order to harmonize with Bar-jona in Mt 16:17.

JONADAB (jō'nȧ-dăb). A shorter and alternate form of Jehonadab (*q.v.*).

1. Son of Shimeah and nephew of David (II Sam 13:3, 5, 32, 35). A crafty man, he suggested how Amnon might rape his half-sister Tamar. Later he reported the details of Amnon's death to King David. He may have been the same as or brother of the man called Jonathan son of Shimeah, who slew one of the Gittite giants (II Sam 21:21).

2. Son of Rechab and titular head of the Rechabites (*q.v.*), a clan maintaining strict principles of a nomadic life and abstinence from wine in obedience to the teachings of their father Jonadab (Jer 35:6–19). He accompanied Jehu to Samaria and participated with him in the destruction of the worshipers of Baal (II Kgs 10:15, 23). He must have been known for his piety and faithfulness to God, for Jehu invited him to go through the doomed worshipers of Baal gathered in the temple to make sure no followers of the Lord were there. Jonadab's household traced its lineage back to the Kenites (I Chr 2:55).

JONAH (jō'nȧ). The son of Amittai from Gath-hepher in Zebulun, who prophesied the restoration of Israel's borders, which was accomplished by Jeroboam II (782–753 B.C.) (II Kgs 14:25), and the hero of the book of Jonah (1:1). Since Jonah probably spoke the word concerning Jeroboam *c.* 790 B.C. during the latter's coregency with his father Jehoash, Jonah almost certainly knew Elisha (d. 797 B.C.) and may have been one of the "sons of the prophets" trained by Elisha (cf. II Kgs 6:1–7).

Most liberal scholars deny both that the events of Jonah happened and that he wrote the book. The claim is that a 4th cen. B.C. anonymous writer fabricated the story, since the early Jonah had the exclusively nationalistic spirit which was common among post-Exilic Jews and, therefore, he was a convenient illustration.

According to the book of Jonah, the Lord directed him to go to Nineveh and to "cry against it." The prophet, however, went to Joppa, where he boarded a ship scheduled to sail to Tarshish, which was either Corsica or part of Spain, as far W from Israel as Nineveh was E. When the Lord sent a great storm which endangered the ship, its captain found Jonah asleep and ordered him to pray to his deity in hope that they might be spared. The casting of lots indicated that it was Jonah whose guilt had caused the calamity. He told them to cast him overboard since he was responsible for the storm. The Lord had "prepared a great fish to swallow up Jonah" and thus to rescue him, and he stayed in it for three days and nights. After Jonah prayed a psalm of thanksgiving, the fish vomited him out on the shore, probably farther along the Syrian coast.

God again directed him to Nineveh. This time he responded and there preached: "Yet forty days, and Nineveh shall be overthrown!" Because the people repented and the king proclaimed a fast, God turned from the threatened calamity; but Jonah became very angry. It is at this point that his motive for fleeing the original order is revealed, i.e., jealousy or antipathy toward a heathen people who were the enemies of his own country. He said that he knew God, being gracious, would turn from His judgment upon Nineveh if they would repent, and asked the Lord to take his life. God caused a plant to grow up and shade the pouting Jonah as he watched the city from a distance. The next day God as quickly destroyed the plant, so that Jonah again became angry and asked once again to die. Using as an illustration Jonah's pity for the plant for which he was not responsible (in contrast to his complete lack of pity on the people to whom he had been appointed), the Lord taught him that it was morally right for Him to have pity on the people of Nineveh.

Jonah's story ends abruptly and there is no further OT record of him. It may be assumed that he learned this lesson since its story was written. Jesus Christ referred both to Jonah's three day stay in the fish and to the repentance of Nineveh (Mt 12:39–41; 16:4; Lk 11:29–32).

W. A. A.

JONAH, BOOK OF. Standing fifth among the writings of the Twelve Minor Prophets, the book of Jonah is perhaps the best known of these. It is at once one of the more appreciated, but also one of the most controversial.

Historicity

The chief critical problem of the book is its historicity. This is almost unanimously acclaimed by conservatives and denied by liberals. Upon the solution to this problem hang most others in the book. The fact is that the style and language used give every evidence of an historical narrative and both Jews (cf. Tobit 14:4 ff.; Jos *Ant.* ix.10.1) and Christians have understood it in this sense until recently. The identification of Jonah with the historical prophet (II Kgs 14:25; *see* Jonah the man) is a further indication, as is the testimony of Jesus Christ (Mt 12:38-41; 16:4; Lk 11:29-32). The historicity of Jonah's three days and nights in the fish and the repentance of Nineveh were accepted facts not only by Jesus who referred to them as such, but also by the scribes and Pharisees to whom He commended the event as a sign.

The claim that Jesus was accommodating to the historical ignorance of His audience is unconvincing, since it results from the circular argument of saying that Jesus could not have been certifying to its historicity since it could not have been historical. Moreover, this is to ignore the fact that a "sign" from fiction would hardly have been offered by Jesus as sufficient to answer the scribes and Pharisees who demanded a sign from Him. Liberals challenge the historicity, however, on the basis of miraculous elements, statements about Nineveh, language and form, and political outlook.

While the book has also been cast as mythological, symbolic, or fiction, the allegorical or parabolic character is most often suggested by the non-historicists. According to the allegorical interpretation, every feature has a corresponding element in Israel's experience. Jonah stands for the nation, his flight is Israel's avoidance of its mission to the peoples, the ship in the sea is the ship of diplomatic intrigue in the sea of the world, the sailors are the Gentiles, the storm is the power shift from Assyria to Babylon, the fish is the Exile, and the vomiting out is the return. Many liberals feel that an allegorical interpretation "depends too much upon the imaginative fancies of the interpreter" and have, therefore, claimed it to be a simple parable with more general analogy rather than precise parallelism.

Authorship

Those who recognize the historicity of the book, usually assume that Jonah was the author of his own story. While all the book except the psalm (2:2-9) is written in the third person, this may only mean, if Jonah himself did not write it, that someone else (even an amanuensis) committed it to writing, but the facts came from Jonah. More likely is the possibility that this was a literary device used by Jonah not uncharacteristic of historical narrative. (Moses always referred to himself in the third person in Exodus to Deuteronomy.) The psalm may well have been a literary unit from the prophet in which the first person was retained because of its uniquely personal nature. Many liberals, however, believe that the psalm came from an entirely different pen than that of the anonymous author of the balance. That supposed author is usually suggested as a 4th cen. B.C. writer who simply used the earlier historical figure as a peg upon which to hang his fabrication.

Date

Acceptance of the historicity of Jonah seemingly requires dating the events in the book during the reign of Jeroboam II (782-753 B.C.). The book was probably written before 745 B.C. when Assyria rebounded to dominance in the Near East under Tiglath-pileser III. R. Dick Wilson, G. L. Archer (SOTI, pp. 300 f.), and others have shown that certain unusual words and alleged Aramaisms do not prove a post-Exilic date. The non-historicist nevertheless puts most of the writing in the 4th cen. with the psalm as late as the 2nd cen. B.C. Those who deny its historicity never put it before the Exile, while those who accept such have no reason to make it later.

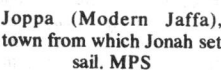

Joppa (Modern Jaffa), town from which Jonah set sail. MPS

JONAH, BOOK OF

Structure and Style

Unlike the rest of the Twelve, this book is entirely an historical narrative and not at all a collection of prophetic oracles. In point of fact, the only prophetic utterance in the book is: "Yet forty days, and Nineveh shall be overthrown!" (3:4*b*). Only the fact that Jonah was recognized as a true prophet can account for its inclusion in the canonical Book of the Twelve. The narrative is vivid but uncomplicated, and the action moves without unnecessary description. The structure is exceedingly simple with four chapters, each containing a distinct unit of thought. The only complication to the four-chapter structure is the fact that 1:17 of the English is 2:1 of the Heb. text.

Occasion and Purpose

During a time of national rebirth, Israel had to know what God's attitude was toward others. Although foreign evangelism was not the principal mission of Israel as the chosen people (see Freeman, *An Introduction to the Old Testament Prophets,* p. 163), they had to learn that the Lord still loves the other nations and wills to bring salvation to them through (or, at least, because of) His chosen people. The book was obviously addressed to the northern kingdom of Israel and takes its place with Hosea and Amos in this regard.

Outline

I. Refusal of God's Command, or Fighting God's Will, 1:1-16
   A. Flight by sea, 1:1-6
      When the Lord ordered him to cry against wicked Nineveh, Jonah boarded a ship for Tarshish to flee God's presence, only to have God threaten all aboard with a storm.
   B. Disposal into the sea, 1:7-16
      Recognizing divine retribution upon Jonah's flight, the sailors sought to escape the storm and then cast Jonah into the sea.

II. Surrendering to God's Will, 1:17–2:10
   A. Repentance, 1:17–2:1
      When Jonah was swallowed by a divinely prepared fish, he prayed to God.
   B. Prayer, 2:2-9
      "The Lord answered my cry from the depths of the sea, and I will sacrifice to Him with thanksgiving because of His deliverance."
   C. Deliverance, 2:10
      The Lord caused the fish to release Jonah.

III. Doing God's Will, 3:1-10
   A. Effective prophecy, 3:1-5
      Obeying the Lord's second order to go to Nineveh, Jonah prophesied its destruction and the people believed God.
   B. Effective repentance, 3:6-10
      The king repented and decreed, "Let every man repent"; thus God relented from the evil planned.

IV. Selfishness about God's Blessings, or Understanding God's Will, 4:1-11
   A. Jonah's objection to the Lord's compassion, 4:1-5
      Angrily Jonah prayed, "I knew You would relent," but God rebuked him and he waited outside the city.
   B. The Lord's illustration of the need for compassion, 4:6-11
      The Lord appointed a plant to shade Jonah and later destroyed it, and then asked Jonah, "How can you pity a plant but deny My pity on the people of Nineveh?"

The Problem of the Miraculous

This is often considered to be the biggest problem. The frequent mistake of theologically conservative scholars is to be too preoccupied with proving the fish-swallowing by historical parallels. While survival of such an experience is well documented relative to sperm whales, it is unnecessary since 1:17 makes clear that "the Lord had *prepared* a great fish."

There are also the miracles of Nineveh's repentance and of the plant. All three of these are involved in a complex of miracles. The reliability of any miracle depends upon the ability of God to perform it and not of man to explain it. Jonah prophesied close to the time of Elijah and Elisha in the northern kingdom, whose contacts with Phoenicia (I Kgs 17:9-24) and Syria (II Kgs 5) were likewise accompanied by miracles.

The Problem of the Psalm

The psalm (2:2-9) stands out from the prose of the book and presents not only a literary problem but also a logical problem. While many commentators cite a variety of individual psalms which may have been quoted, the words fit none well enough to conclude that these are specific quotations. More likely, many psalms were in mind and freely paraphrased to fit the particular situation and in a manner which expressed Jonah's appropriate emotions. The non-historicists, again, assigned this portion to a 2nd cen. B.C. writer who was even later than the anonymous writer of the narrative.

Even when understood as the composition of Jonah and forming a unity with the balance of the book, problems exist. Is Jonah thanking God for having delivered him from the sea by means of a fish? Could a man pray so eloquently in the midst of such a traumatic experience? Perhaps Jonah prayed from the fish thanking God for saving him from the sea and, on the basis of that initial salvation, he anticipated its completion. Moreover, the psalm as found in the text may represent his general thoughts at the moment as polished in poetic style upon reflection later.

The Problems of Nineveh

If this story be the creation of a 4th cen.

writer, he was foolishly careless when constructing his references to Nineveh because he has left himself open to many points of criticism. It is charged that a city never has a "king" (3:6); that Nineveh was never "three days' journey" in breadth (3:3); that Jonah could not have spoken their language in preaching; that it is not reasonable for such a city to have repented so easily and that there is no secular record of such. Moreover, the greatness of the city is spoken of in the past tense (3:3).

The term "the king of Nineveh" (3:6) is a metonymy with adequate precedent in the OT; e.g., there were kings of such cities as Samaria (I Kgs 21:1), Damascus (II Chr 24:23), Salem (Gen 14:18), and Zion (Jer 8:19). Furthermore, since Nineveh was not yet the capital of Assyria, the author may have used the word *melek* ("king") as a transliteration of the Akkad. *malku* meaning "governor."

The size of the city could refer to its circumference as well as diameter; the city as a metropolitan area could include its immediately neighboring cities (e.g., Calah, Rehoboth-Ir, Resen of Gen 10:11 ff.); or the "journey" could well have been a walk, preaching his message throughout the city's precincts. Aramaic was already becoming a widespread trade language (cf. II Kgs 18:26) which Jonah is likely to have known and which would have been known by enough in Nineveh to pass his message on. The question should center around what God can do rather than what the prophet could not do.

The severe plagues of 765 and 759 and the total eclipse of 763 B.C. could have been used by God to alert the people to their need; and certainly when combined with the work of the Spirit of God before and through His prophet there is sufficient cause for the great repentance recorded. The fact that this national repentance is not found in extant Assyrian annals is an argument from silence. Many other events and people known only through the Bible have only recently been confirmed by modern archaeological discoveries. That the repentance obviously did not last is not surprising and gives an added reason why the Assyrians would not have mentioned it in their official records. The past tense relative to Nineveh need mean nothing more than the fact that the events which took place there were past when the record was written.

Significance

Few OT books have more obvious application to the contemporary church. It can well be used to help the Christian overcome the barrier of his foreignness in evangelistic mission as he is assured of God's love for the world and His will to use the saved to reach all lost men. But the book of Jonah does not teach simple willingness to go to a foreign country as a missionary for the reward of being obedient. In point of fact, this is one of the deficiencies the book seeks to correct. It is not enough to be obedient to the command; one must be sympathetic with it. Evangelism is for the sake of the lost and not the evangelist. One must obey God—but for the right reason. The motive for missions is acknowledgment of God's will—but also obedience to it and agreement with it.

Bibliography. G. C. Aalders, *The Problem of the Book of Jonah,* London: Tyndale Press, 1948. J. A. Bewer, ICC. Hobart E. Freeman, *An Introduction to the Old Testament Prophets,* Chicago: Moody Press, 1968, pp. 160-171. Frank E. Gaebelein, *Four Minor Prophets,* Chicago: Moody Press, 1970. Don W. Hillis, *The Book of Jonah,* Grand Rapids: Baker, 1967. James H. Kennedy, *Studies in the Book of Jonah,* Nashville: Broadman Press, 1956. G. Herbert Livingston, "Jonah," WBC, pp. 843-850. E. B. Pusey, *The Minor Prophets,* Grand Rapids: Baker, 1960 (reprint). George L. Robinson, *The Twelve Minor Prophets,* Grand Rapids: Baker, 1962 (reprint).

W. A. A.

JONAN (jō'năn). An ancestor of Christ (Lk 3:30) who lived about 200 years after David. Jonam is the correct spelling (ASV and RSV), based on the Gr. *Iōnam.*

JONAS (jō'năs)

1. KJV form of Jonah (Gr. *Iōna*), the OT prophet (Mt 12:39-41; 16:4; Lk 11:29-32). *See* Jonah.

2. KJV form of John (Jn 21:15-17, RSV), used in order to harmonize with Bar-jona in Mt. 16:17.

JONATHAN (jŏn'ȧ-thȧn). This name occurs frequently in biblical literature.

1. The son of Gershom, son of Manasseh (Jud 18:30, KJV). The Masoretic scribes inserted an *n* (*nun*) above the line in the name of Moses, so that in the Heb. spelling it would read Manasseh (*m-n-sh-h*) instead of Moses (*m-sh-h*). Thus they thought to spare Moses the disgrace of having a grandson become an idolatrous priest. Jonathan was a Levite from Bethlehem, said to be of the tribe of Judah, probably on his mother's side (Jud 17:7). He acted as house priest in the sanctuary founded by the Ephramite Micah and later founded the priesthood which served the Danites (Jud 17-18).

2. The eldest son of King Saul of Israel.

His military prowess. After his decisive victory over the Ammonites (I Sam 11), King Saul divided his army into two divisions: about 2,000 men were stationed in Michmash under him and about 1,000 men were garrisoned under his son Jonathan about five miles S at Gibeah. Midway between the two military camps was a Philistine outpost at Geba. Jonathan killed the garrison (or, governor, NEB) there, which the Philistines interpreted as a revolt of the Israelite forces (I Sam 13:3). They decided to attack immediately, and they compelled Saul to abandon Michmash. The king withdrew to Gilgal to recoup his forces, and then returned

The mound of Beth-Shan, where the bodies of Jonathan and the rest of Saul's family were displayed for public ridicule. Remains of a great Roman theater appear at right. HFV

to the hill country to make his base at Geba (I Sam 13:16, NASB). Jonathan made a surprise attack on the Philistines who were guarding the gorge S of Michmash and slew all of them single-handedly (I Sam 14:6 - 14). God matched Jonathan's feat with an earthquake, and the Philistines fled in panic. The Israelites, fighting only with crude agricultural implements (I Sam 13:20), pursued them to complete the rout.

This victory was marred by King Saul who, seized with religious superstition, ordered all his warriors to fast until sundown (I Sam 14:24). When Jonathan unwittingly broke the command, the king ordered the prince executed. But the people remembering Jonathan's military skill and courage intervened and saved his life (I Sam 14:25 - 45).

His friendship with David. Jonathan and David's friendship is a most inspiring epic. After David slew the Philistine giant Goliath and won for himself a permanent place in the royal court, Jonathan loved the shepherd lad with all his soul. He recognized that David was a man chosen for the throne of Israel. He acquiesced to this by making a covenant and presenting to David his own princely robe and armor (I Sam 18:1 - 4).

The meteoric rise of David's military fame and his place in the people's affections were more, however, than the melancholic King Saul could take. He not only planned to slay David but attempted to press Jonathan and his courtiers to wield the javelin against this potential supplanter. Soon Saul drove David from the court. Jonathan was disgusted with his father's behavior and intervened by securing for David a temporary visa for reinstatement in the king's court (I Sam 19:1 - 7). This truce was abruptly ended when Saul suffered a fit of melancholia and threw his javelin at David; so David fled to Naioth in Ramah. During the new moon festival Jonathan discovered that his father's anger toward David was permanent and he relayed the sad news to his beloved friend by way of an arrow and lad at the appointed rendezvous (I Sam 20).

The final and romantic conference between these friends took place in the wilderness of Ziph, S of Hebron. There they made a pact that when David became the next king, Jonathan would be his prime minister, and they renewed their covenant to protect each other's posterity forever (I Sam 23:16 - 18; cf. I Sam 20:12 - 17, 42; II Sam 9:1).

His final history. During the days when Saul pursued David, Jonathan remained in the background – evidently he refused to be a party to this futile chase. The activity of the Philistines compelled Saul to terminate his hunt for David and to turn his energies to do battle with Israel's perpetual enemy. This battle was short and decisive – Saul lost! Jonathan, Saul, and his other sons, Abinadad and Malchishua, were killed in battle. Their corpses were despoiled the day following the battle and exposed by the Philistines on a wall overlooking the public square of Beth-shan (II Sam 21:12). The Jabesh-gileadites, out of gratitude to King Saul's rescuing their town at the beginning of his reign, crossed the Jordan and stormed Beth-shan, retrieved the bodies and buried them in Jabesh (I Sam 31; I Chr 10:1 - 12; cf. II Sam 2:5 - 7).

When the sad tidings of the disaster on Mount Gilboa reached David, he uttered a moving elegy lamenting the death of Saul and the loss of his true friend Jonathan (II Sam 1). David later reinterred the remains of Saul and his sons in the tomb of Saul's father Kish in Zelah of the territory of Benjamin (II Sam 21:12 - 14).

His character. Jonathan undoubtedly was one of the greatest souls of all time. He had a granite-like character. He was athletic and courageous (I Sam 14:13; II Sam 1:22 - 23). Swift as an eagle and strong as a lion, this Israelite prince inspired and led the renowned Benjamite archers in warfare. When secrecy was mandatory, he could maintain a tight lip! He could always analyze a situation, plan a strategy, and in turn act at the auspicious moment. Also he was a great lover. His unqualified love for David in the midst of adverse pressures in his father's court vindicated David's elegy: "Thy love to me was wonderful, passing the love of women" (II Sam 1:26).

His family tree. Jonathan had one son, whose name was Meribaal (Mephibosheth). He was only five years of age at the slaughter on Gilboa (II Sam 4:4). David's honoring the pledge which he forged with Jonathan assured this survivor of gaining Saul's inheritance, as well as membership in the royal court and the sparing of his head (II Sam 9; 21:7). Jonathan's posterity which passed through this lame prince lived through several generations (I Chr 8:33 - 38; 9:40 - 44; II Sam 9:12).

Jonathan's mother was Ahinoam (daughter of Ahimaaz), characterized by Saul during one of his temper tantrums as "a perverse, rebellious woman" (I Sam 20:30, RSV). Besides Abinadad and Malchishua he had another brother, Ish-baal (Ishbosheth or Ishui, a probable corruption of Ishyahu, I Sam 14:49), and two sisters, Merab and Michal. The former was promised to David but given to Adriel the Meholathite (I Sam 18:17-20); Michal instead of her sister was married to David for a dowry of a hundred Philistine foreskins (I Sam 18:20 ff.).

His family loyalty. The solidarity of the Hebraic family remained intact in Saul's family. Jonathan's independence and capacity to do his own thinking naturally collided with the impetuosity and unreasonableness of his father Saul. But in the midst of these adverse tensions, the prince struggled to conform as nearly as possible to the strong will of the king. Convinced of the high promise of David and conscious of Saul's reaction, Jonathan sought to mediate between the irresistible force and the immovable object and partially succeeded (I Sam 19:6). Filial duty was supremely tested but Jonathan's conduct toward both men is unquestionable. When Saul, under gross provocation impugned the honor of his mother and sought to kill even Jonathan, the prince's loyalty temporarily snapped. However, this estrangement was short-lived. Saul and Jonathan were one in life and one in death (II Sam 1:23)—father and son went down together!

3. A son of Abiathar, a high priest in David's cabinet who was loyal to David during Absalom's rebellion (II Sam 15:27, 36; 17:15-22). Abiathar and Zadok were dispatched to Jerusalem to assist Hushai in counteracting the betrayal of Ahithophel. As they secured valuable information from Hushai, they relayed the secrets to the couriers Jonathan and Ahimaaz, sons of Abiathar and Zadok, respectively, who were stationed at En-rogel. The young men in turn were to relay the information to King David (II Sam 15:24 ff.). When this espionage was uncovered, the couriers fled with a message of warning for David in his camp by the W bank of the Jordan (II Sam 17:15-21).

During David's latter days when his heirs were jockeying for the throne, Jonathan along with his father Abiathar joined in Adonijah's plot to snatch the Israelite throne. It was Jonathan's sad lot to bring the frustrating news to the abortive kingly sacrificial feast at En-rogel, that Solomon had been anointed in Gihon as king of Israel with the blessings and by the strong hand of David (I Kgs 1:42-48). Apparently this involvement marked Jonathan as a dispensable man, and he probably was exiled along with his father when Abiathar was stripped of the high priesthood and banished to Anathoth by Solomon (I Kgs 2:26-27).

4. A son of Shimeah, David's brother, who slew a Philistine giant who jeered the Israelites at Gath (II Sam 21:21; I Chr 20:7).

5. A son of Shage the Hararite, who was one of David's heroes (the mighty men of David, known as the "thirty," II Sam 23:32; I Chr 11:34).

6. A son of Jada and the father of Peleth and Zaza who were members of the family of Jerahmeel of the tribe of Judah (I Chr 2:32-33).

7. An uncle of David who was a wise, trusted counselor as well as a royal scribe (I Chr 27:32).

8. A son of Uzziah who had supervision of King David's storehouses in the cities, hamlets, and towns outside Jerusalem (I Chr 27:25; Jehonathan, KJV).

9. A scribe in whose house Jeremiah was imprisoned during the siege of Jerusalem by the Babylonians (588-586 B.C.), when the prophet's enemies charged Jeremiah with defecting to the enemy (Jer 37:15, 20; 38:26).

10. A son of Kareah, a Judean field captain, who settled with Gedaliah at Mizpah, after the fall of Jerusalem in 586 B.C. (Jer 40:8; KJV, NASB, NEB following Masoretic Text, list both Johanan and Jonathan; but RSV and others have only Johanan. Possibly the name Jonathan is a dittography since it is omitted by LXX and the parallel passage in II Kgs 25:23).

11. The father of Ebed who, along with 50 members of his family, returned with Ezra in 457 B.C. (Ezr 8:6).

12. A priest who descended from Melicu (KJV; others, Malluchi) during Joiakim's high priesthood (Neh 12:14).

13. A son of Joiada and one of the high priests during the post-Exilic period. His son was Jaddua, the last-named priest in the OT (Neh 12:11). The corrupted text probably should read Johanan (Ezr 10:6; Neh 12:22-23; I Esd 9:1).

14. A son of Shemaiah and father of Zechariah who was a priestly trumpeter in the thanksgiving convocation during the rededication of the walls of Jerusalem under the governorship of Nehemiah (Neh 12:35).

15. A son of Asahel, during the period of Ezra, who opposed the appointment of the marital commission in Jerusalem to investigate the Jews who had married foreign wives (Ezr 10:15).

D. W. D.

JONATH-ELEM-RECHOKIM (jō'năth-ē'lĕm-rē-kō'kĭm). This transliterated Heb. phrase in the KJV and ASV heading of Ps 56, perhaps meaning "the dove of the far-off terebinths" (cf. Ps 55:6-7), may be understood in one or all of the following ways: (1) an enigmatical reference to David among the Philistines in Gath (I Sam 21:10-15); (2) a mystical reference to Israel or God's people generally as exiles from their real home (cf. Phil 3:20; Heb 11:8-10, 13-16); (3) a technical phrase indicating the rhythm or melody to which this psalm is set (see ASV).

JOPPA (jŏp'ȧ). The modern Jaffa, it was the only seaport on the coast of Palestine between Haifa and Egypt, and is now the southern section of Tel Aviv. It is mentioned in the Tell el-Amarna letters. It was assigned to the tribe of Dan in the division of the land after the conquest of Joshua (Josh 19:46), though the Israelites may not have actually possessed it. Timber for the building of Solomon's temple was floated from Tyre to Joppa (II Chr 2:16), and also for the building of the second temple in the restoration (Ezr 3:7). In the time of the divided kingdom it was controlled by the Phoenicians. Jonah fled from Israel via Joppa (Jon 1:3).

In NT times Peter there restored Dorcas to life (Acts 9:36-43), and afterward stayed at the home of Simon the tanner, where he received the vision that summoned him to preach at the house of the Gentile Cornelius (Acts 10:1-23).

The city was built on the rocky heights above the harbor, which was formed by a natural breakwater of rocks. In the 1st cen. B.C. it was held successively by the Syrians, the Maccabees, the Romans, and by freebooters who made it a center of piracy. The harbor is too dangerous for modern shipping, and is not used extensively at present.

M. C. T.

JORAH (jôr'ȧ). The head of a family of returnees from Babylon with Zerubbabel (Ezr 2:18). Called Hariph in Neh 7:24.

JORAI (jôr'ī). One of seven Gadite chiefs who were descendants of Abihail (I Chr 5:13-14).

JORAM (jôr'ȧm). Abbrev. form of Jehoram (*q.v.*).

1. Son of Toi, king of Hamath (II Sam 8:9-10). Also called Hadoram (I Chr 18:10).
2. King of Judah, son and successor of Jehoshaphat (II Kgs 8:21-24; I Chr 3:11; Mt 1:8). Also called Jehoram (see Jehoram 2).
3. King of Israel, son of Ahab and successor of his brother Ahaziah (II Kgs 8:16; cf. 1:2, 17). Also called Jehoram (see Jehoram 1).
4. A Levite, descendant of Eliezer, son of Moses (I Chr 26:25; cf. 23:15, 17).

JORDAN (jôr'dȧn). In Heb. the name of the most famous river in the Bible is *yardēn*. Most scholars consider the word Semitic and derive it from the root *yārad,* "to descend." The name thus means "the descender," an apt description of the river. Others theorize that the word may have an Indo-Aryan origin, in which case it would mean "perennial river." The oldest form of the name is found in Nineteenth Dynasty Egyptian records as *ya-ar-du-na* (Simon Cohen, "Jordan," IDB, II, 973).

A series of gigantic faults in the crust of the earth brought about the collapse of land which now forms the Jordan Valley. From that deep trough called the Dead Sea (the Salt Sea in the OT) the earth rises both to the N and S. It ascends from 2,598 feet below sea level at the bottom of the Dead Sea to a height of plus 800 feet at one hump in the Arabah (area S of the Dead Sea) and to 9,166 foot high Mount Hermon in the N. The geological fault extends through the Red Sea deep into E Africa.

The distance by air from the sources of the Jordan to the Dead Sea is *c*. 80 miles, but the river itself is over 200 miles long on account of its circuitous course between the Galilee and Dead Seas. The valley may be said to begin in the N with the Huleh Basin, an area of about three by nine miles culminating, until recently drained, in a marsh and a shallow lake created by a dam of natural rock.

The sudden descent from about 1,600 feet in altitude at the Merj 'Ayun to 230 feet above sea level in the Huleh Basin allows two small source streams, Nahr Bareighit and Nahr Hasbani, to pour their water into the basin. The two major Jordan sources flow out of the rock as sizable streams on the slopes of Mount Hermon. The Nahr el-Leddan arises from strong springs out of the ground at Tel el-Qadi, the site of ancient Dan, the northernmost city of the land (formerly Laish, Jud 18:7, 27). The Nahr Banias originates in a large cave farther up the slope at a village called Banias (Paneas), which derives its name from the Roman god Pan. In NT times this town was called Caesarea Philippi in honor of Caesar and because it was in the tetrarchy of Philip. In this region Jesus asked His disciples, "Whom say ye that I am?" (Mk 8:27-29), and was transfigured before three of them on some part of Mount Hermon nearby (Mk 9:2). Three of these headwater streams meet about two miles S of Dan and then divide again to enter the Huleh Basin as two streams, the Tur'ah and the Jordan.

On a plateau overlooking the Huleh Basin stand the ruins of the OT city of Hazor (recently excavated) and the NT city of Chorazin (Khirbet Kerazeh). The Jordan alone flows out of Huleh for two miles to "the Bridge of the Daughters of Jacob" where travelers on the road between Galilee and Damascus forded it. After this the Jordan enters a gorge, flowing with vigor until it finally leaves these walls and gently enters the Sea of Galilee at 696 feet below sea level. The sea is really a lake surrounded almost completely by hills, but here

The Nahr Hasbani, one of the sources of the Jordan.
HFV

JORDAN

and there these hills withdraw creating some plains like the famous plain of Gennesaret on the NW shore near Capernaum. In addition to the still inhabited Tiberias, several biblical lake cities are identifiable, namely Capernaum at Tel Hum on the NW and Magdala at Majdal on the W shore at the foot of "the Valley of the Robbers." In NT times the northern part of the Jordan region was controlled by the league of ten independent cities called Decapolis. Of the cities, those in or near the Jordan Valley were Scythopolis (Beisan or Bethshan), Gadara (Umm Keis) and Pella (Fahil) across the river from Scythopolis.

The first dozen miles from the Sea of Galilee the Jordan Valley never reaches a breadth of more than four miles. Bethany beyond the Jordan where John was baptizing (Jn 1:28, NASB), or Bethabara (KJV; *q.v.*) is thought to have been in the vicinity, *c.* 12 miles S of the lake. If Elisha (*q.v.*) were living at Shunem or Mount Carmel or Dothan at the time of Naaman's visit, the Syrian general was probably sent to this stretch of the Jordan to dip seven times in its muddy waters (II Kgs 5:10, 14). At the plain of Bethshan the valley widens to six or seven miles, rising on the W side by terraces toward the level of the plain of Esdraelon.

The Jordan itself is but a groove cut into the bottom of this valley which is said to be an old seabed. Its current does not look swift but can be treacherous, the water dropping in the N about 40 feet per mile, although the average drop per mile is about nine feet. The formidable barrier created by the river is the result of other factors than the width or swiftness of the stream. Indeed, in the N the river is not so great a barrier because the distinct features of the valley are less pronounced there. The valley itself is the real barrier consisting of three interesting features: the Ghor or lowland, Qattara or sterile chalk hills, and the Zor or thicket.

The Ghor is the valley floor itself bounded by mountains or high plateaus on either side. Here are layers of alluvial deposits which need only irrigation to make rich farmland. The results of such irrigation may be seen today along the E side of the Ghor where water is available. Geological faults meet the Ghor at an angle and help form the river valleys which join the Jordan. On the E side the river has two major tributaries, the Yarmuk and the Jabbok. The Yarmuk just S of the Sea of Galilee provides almost as much water as does the Jordan itself. On the N side of the Yarmuk gorge some seven or more miles from the confluence stands the ancient el-Hammeh, a famous hot springs. A high culture flourished here from as early as the 4th mil. B.C., and its warm curative waters have been popular throughout history. Between the Yarmuk and the Jabbok nine other streams flow into the Jordan from the E. This well-watered area explains why many settlements grew up on the E side of the Ghor, towns such as Pella, Jabesh-gilead, Zaphon, Zaretan and Adam.

About 13 miles from the Sea of Galilee the river Jalud joins from the W flowing through the plain of Bethshan. Here the Ghor widens to about seven miles, only to be constricted again farther S by the hills of Samaria. Farther S the Wadi Fari'a joins from the W and the Jabbok on the E near Succoth. Here the patriarchs had entered Canaan, coming from Haran and Padan-aram far to the NE (Gen 12:5-6; 32:22; 33:17-18). Near here the Midianites must have fled across the Jordan with Gideon in pursuit (Jud 7:24; 8:4-5). The floor widens again to eight miles, from whence it continues to widen to a maximum of 14 miles at Jericho. 'Ain Fari'a at the head of its wadi, near OT Tirzah, supplies a rich quantity of water, but little of it ever reaches the Jordan. The same is true of Wadi Qelt which helps create the rich green oasis at Jericho. Such irrigation of the land has to come from the sweet water streams before they reach the Jordan because the Jordan also receives mineral salts which make its water increasingly unfit for irrigation.

The Springs of Banias which give rise to another source of the Jordan. HFV

Near Gilgal, NE of Jericho, was a well-known ford that David used in his flight from Absalom (II Sam 17:22-24) and in his victorious return (19:15-40). Perhaps this was the very spot where Elijah and Elisha crossed the Jordan prior to the former's translation (II Kgs 2:7-8, 13-14). Also in this region of the lower Jordan the two Israelite spies had swum the flooded river (Josh 2:1, 23), and soon afterward the entire nation crossed miraculously over the dry riverbed (Josh 3-4).

The Bible uses various terms to describe the Ghor. Often it is simply called the *'ēmeq*, the vale or lowland as in Josh 13:19, 27. But in Deut 34:3 the Ghor is described as "the *kikkār* even the *biq'â* of Jericho." *Kikkār* means a circuit and the *biq'â* means a broad valley. Here at Jericho the Ghor is some 14 miles across. The term *'ărābâ* meaning "a plain" is also used of the Jordan Valley. The E side of the Ghor opposite Jericho was called "the plains of Moab" (Num 22:1), an area well-irrigated and inhabited from Chalcolithic times as at Teleilat Ghassul. The Ghor was sometimes so heavily inhabited that Gen 13:10 tells us Lot beheld the "*kikkār* of the Jordan and lo, all of it was well watered (irrigated) . . . like the garden of the Lord." When one visits this region especially in summer he may be impressed with its aridity. However, it was not only one of the first settled sections of the country but at one time was one of the richest parts of all ancient Palestine. Nelson Glueck discovered at least 70 sites where people had lived and worked in the Jordan Valley S of Galilee in ancient times.

About 100 - 150 feet below the main valley floor is the depression called in Arabic the Zor through which the Jordan itself flows. The Zor can get nearly a mile wide when the river twists upon itself, though the river is only from 90 to 100 feet wide and normally ranges from 3 to 12 feet in depth. The Zor always contains the river when it floods in the spring (Josh 3:15; I Chr 12:15), but unlike the Nile, the flood is violent, carrying soil away and leaving debris, so that the rank growth of tamarisks, oleanders, willows, bushes and vines which is left is well called Zor or thicket. The OT describes the Zor as *ge'on hay-yarden*, "the jungle of the Jordan" ("Behold like a lion . . . out of the jungle of the Jordan," Jer 49:19; cf. 12:5; 50:44; Zech 11:3). Indeed, the Zor was infested with lions in ancient times and elephants in pre-historic times and was until very recently the haunt of the wild boar. Because of the twistings within the fickle snakelike route of the Jordan, the Zor jungle becomes a formidable barrier and to this barrier is added the sterile marl hills of the "qattara" separating the Ghor and the Zor.

When the OT speaks of Jordan as a barrier it certainly means the whole valley complex, not just the little river itself. Josh 22:25 expresses the fear that Reuben, Gad and half the tribe of Manasseh might become alienated by the natural border formed by the valley: "Your children might speak . . . saying, 'What have ye to do with the Lord God of Israel? For the Lord hath made Jordan a border between us and you . . . ye have no part in the Lord.' " It is curiously true that not only in OT times but even today a distinct alienation of spirit exists between those who live on either side of the Jordan Valley.

The Jordan River as it flows out of the Sea of Galilee at its southern end. HFV

The Jordan flows into the Dead Sea at about 1,290 feet below sea level. The Dead Sea is about 45 miles long and 10 miles wide. A tongue of land juts out into the E side of the Dead Sea. At one time this formed its S boundary, but the sea having no outlet has risen continuously covering erstwhile cities on its S shore, probably including Sodom (*q.v.*) and Gomorrah. The Dead Sea itself is about one-fourth to one-third mineral salts, coming largely from the many hot and cold springs which line the valley. As may be expected, the entire region is an area of above normal earthquake activity averaging about four per century. The E slopes of the sea like the wilderness of Judea are almost devoid of rain and so supply little water except from a few underground springs (e.g., 'Ain Feshkha near Qumran and Engedi, due E of Hebron).

See Arabah; Dead Sea; Galilee, Sea of; Palestine. II.B.3.*d*; River.

Bibliography. Denis Baly, *The Geography of the Bible,* New York: Harper, 1957, pp. 14 - 26, 193 - 216. Nelson Glueck, *The River Jordan,* 2nd ed., New York: McGraw-Hill, 1968. Karl H. Rengstorf, "*Potamos . . . Iordanēs*," TDNT, VI, 608 - 623.

E. B. S.

JORIM (jō̂r'ĭm). An ancestor of Christ (Lk 3:29) and descendant of David.

JORKOAM (jôr'kō-ăm). The son of Raham, and a descendant of Caleb (I Chr 2:44; Jorkeam in ASV and RSV). Two suppositions are held regarding this name: (1) that it designates a place in the tribe of Judah; (2) that it is to be identified with Jokdeam (*q.v.*) in Josh 15:56.

JOSABAD. *See* Jozabad.

JOSAPHAT. *See* Jehoshaphat.

JOSE (jō'sē). A man in Christ's ancestry not mentioned in the OT (Lk 3:29). KJV incorrectly takes the *Iōsēs* of TR as a genitive of the nominative *Iōsē*. The correct form (genitive of *Iēsous*) found in earlier Gr. MSS reads Jesus as in ASV, i.e., Joshua as in RSV and NASB.

JOSEDECH (jō'zē-dĕk). Father of Joshua, the high priest during the post-Captivity era (Hag 1:1, 12, 14; 2:2, 4; Zech 6:11). In all these verses ASV and RSV have Jehozadak. In Ezr 3:2, 8; 5:2; 10:18 and Neh 12:26 the same Heb. name is spelled Jozadak in KJV, ASV and RSV. This man, having been carried captive to Babylon by Nebuchadnezzar (I Chr 6:14 - 15), was presumably high priest during most of the Babylonian Captivity. His father, Seraiah, the last high priest who officiated in the temple before its destruction in 586 B.C., was slain by the Babylonians (II Kgs 25:18–21).

JOSEPH (jō'zĕf)

1. The eleventh son of Jacob and the first son of his favorite wife Rachel, after her sister Leah had borne Jacob six sons and a daughter. Long barren and desirous of children, Rachel named her first son Joseph (Heb. *yôsēp, yehô-sēp*), "May He (i.e., the Lord) add," as she explains, "May the Lord add to me another son" (Gen 30:24, RSV).

Joseph sold by his brethren, painted by Maggiotto. MM

Joseph was Rachel's only child at the time of the return to Palestine from the Haran area, and consequently was his father's favorite son. When Jacob went to meet Esau he put Rachel and Joseph in the safest position in the caravan. This favoritism receives comment in Gen 37:3, which states that Joseph was favored because he was the son of Jacob's old age. Joseph was a shepherd like his brothers, and incurred their hostility by bringing his father a report of their bad conduct. Jacob's partiality was demonstrated by his giving to Joseph a long robe with sleeves (lit., a robe of soles and palms). Possibly it was also a robe of patterned cloth and many colors (cf. the garments of the Asiatics, shown in the Middle Kingdom tomb of Khnumhotep II at Beni Hasan). This gift indicated that Jacob intended to make Joseph his principal heir, and further incited Joseph's brothers against him (37:4).

Fuel was added to the flames of hatred by Joseph's sharing with his brothers two dreams by which the Lord had shown him that he would rule over them. The jealousy of the brothers led them to take action against him. When Joseph was sent to check on the herding activities of the brothers, he found them at Dothan with the flocks. They planned to kill him (37:18–19), but were deterred by the eldest of them, Reuben, who wished to save him from harm (vv. 22–24). When an Ishmaelite-Midianite caravan appeared (see Kitchen, *Ancient Orient and the Old Testament,* pp. 119 f.), on its way from Gilead to Egypt, the brothers conceived the notion of getting rid of Joseph at a profit. They sold him to the traders and callously deceived Jacob into believing Joseph had been killed by wild animals; they brought to Jacob the robe, which they had dipped in the blood of a goat.

In Egypt the merchants sold Joseph to Potiphar, an officer of the king, the captain of the guard. The Lord blessed Joseph with success in his work, so that he was promoted to the office of overseer of the house, a typical Egyptian title and function. The wife of Potiphar was attracted to the young official and continually sought to seduce him (39:10). Egyptian domestic architecture, as illustrated by the excavations at Amarna, indicates that the duties of Joseph demanded his presence in parts of the estate in which he would of necessity encounter the woman. Though far from home and family, the young Hebrew was true to his ideals and rejected her propositions on the basis that his compliance would be both wickedness and a sin against God (39:9).

This interesting account (39:6–20) gives many details of Egyptian life. Novelists and popular writers have often presented an unsavory view of Egyptian morals, which seem to have been quite commendable, though proper conduct was often based on primarily practical reasons. Egyptian civilization did have its seamy side, however, and the Papyrus D'Orbiney relates a story of seduction which is common to many times and places. The story is titled "The Tale of Two Brothers" and confirms the virtuous attitude of the brothers as opposed to the immoral motives of the wife of the elder brother. Though the parallels to the biblical account are interesting, the differences are even greater (see ANET, pp. 23–25). *See* Egypt.

Potiphar accepted his wife's dramatic testimony, and Joseph was consigned to a prison for political offenders. In prison Joseph again was signally blessed by the Lord and soon rose to a position of responsibility even here. In this particular place of imprisonment he was brought into contact with officials from the royal court. He interpreted dreams which the royal butler and baker had on the same night.

The dreams contain many items of Egyptian background, for viticulture was important in ancient Egypt and a great variety of bake goods was known. Dreams were often regarded as omens in the Near East. A hieratic papyrus relating to the interpretation of dreams dates from the 19th Dynasty and may go back to the Middle Kingdom. It has the punning allusions which are typical of Egyptian literature and which occur in Gen 40 as marks of local color. Since Joseph's ability to interpret dreams was a gift from God, there is no other relationship between this papyrus and Joseph (see ANET, p. 495).

While the butler was pardoned and the baker executed, Joseph remained in prison for at least two more years (41:1). When Pharaoh's strange

Traditional tomb of Joseph at Shechem. HFV

dreams could not be interpreted by the Egyptian experts, the butler remembered Joseph, who then was summoned to the royal court. Before appearing in the presence of the king, Joseph shaved (41:14), in good Egyptian fashion (see ANET, p. 22). In Egyptian reliefs and paintings smooth-shaven Egyptians contrast markedly with bearded Asiatics; many razors have been found in excavations in Egypt. Pharaoh's dreams included the ever-present Nile, the cattle that commonly grazed along the river, and the grain which made Egypt the breadbasket of the Mediterranean world. The interpretation given by Joseph indicated that seven years of plenty would be followed by seven years of scarcity. The Nile was very regular in its annual flooding (*see* Nile). There were exceptions to this rule, however, and ancient texts preserve statements of officials who boast of providing for the needy in such lean years (see ANET, pp. 31-32).

Joseph then suggested that provision be made for the bad years by collecting one-fifth of the produce during the years of abundance. This proposal met with the approval of the king and his advisers, with the result that Joseph was given the office second only to that of the king. This office is well-known from the documents of Egypt and usually is designated by the Near Eastern term "vizier." The vizier was the chief administrative officer and his duties were quite varied; he was in charge of the treasury, justice, and the execution of all royal decrees.

Joseph was given an Egyptian name (*see* Zaphnath-paaneah) and was married to Asenath, the daughter of Potiphera, priest of On, the solar religious center better known as Heliopolis (*see* On). During the prosperous years Asenath bore two sons, Manasseh and Ephraim, who later took their place as Joseph's representatives among the sons of Jacob (Israel).

Joseph made adequate preparation for the years of famine, so that not only all Egypt but also people from neighboring lands came to buy grain from Joseph. Here the progress of the earlier prophecies of Joseph's dreams becomes apparent (42:9), for among those who came to Egypt to purchase grain were Joseph's brothers (42:5). Joseph recognized them but they did not know him (42:7-8); consequently he was able to subject them to a series of tests. He interrogated them, accused them of being spies, and finally put them in prison for three days. As proof of their honesty he demanded that they leave one of their number as a hostage and return to Canaan to get their youngest brother, Benjamin, who they said was yet in Canaan. Verses 21-23 graphically describe the workings of conscience in the reasonings of the brothers. Simeon remained in Egypt while the others returned to Palestine.

To add to the perplexity of the brothers, Joseph had their grain purchase money returned to them in their grain bags. They discovered this en route to Canaan and brought a report of their adventures to the aged Jacob, who finally was forced by circumstances to accede to the necessity for the brothers to take Benjamin with them when they again went to Egypt for grain. Every effort was made to secure the favor of the vizier, and Israel sent his sons to Egypt with his blessing and with confidence in God (43:14).

Several additional tests lay before the brothers (43:18). They were invited to eat wth Joseph, though he was served by himself, according to Egyptian custom (43:32). The final trial for the brothers lay in a framed accusation of theft, which brought them back to Egypt after they had begun their return to Palestine (chap. 44). Since the supposedly stolen silver cup was found in the grain sack of Benjamin, the most severe anxiety fell upon them.

At last Joseph arranged to disclose his identity to them. This was done with considerable emotion on his part; he wept loudly, so that all the Egyptians heard it (45:2; cf. 42:24; 43:30-31). The sensitive and understanding character of Joseph is clear from his immediate assurance to his brothers, showing that he had forgiven them and was concerned for their welfare. Beyond even this, Joseph saw the hand of God in his career, for God had designed to preserve Israel through him (45:7-8).

Joseph then made arrangements for informing his father of the good turn of events and for moving the entire family to Egypt. The titles which Joseph ascribes to himself, "a father to Pharaoh, and lord of all his house, and a ruler over all the land of Egypt" (45:8), are quite typical for an Egyptian official of his rank. Pharaoh was pleased at the report of the arrival of Joseph's brothers and personally suggested provision for bringing Joseph's family to the best part of Egypt (45:16-20). Transportation was provided in the form of the usual patient donkeys, which carried gifts and supplies, and by wagons, which were for the transport of the people. Wagons are strange to the Egyptian tomb scenes but perhaps they were a concession to the Asiatic origin of Joseph's family. Some regard the references to wagons and to chariots (41:43) as indications that Joseph was vizier during the Hyksos rule. Jacob responded favorably to the invitation and was also directed by God to go to Egypt, where God would make Israel a great nation (46:2 - 4).

Joseph went to Goshen to meet his father (46:29) and began plans to settle his relatives in that area (*see* Goshen). Because of the antipathy between cattlemen and sheep raisers, Joseph advised his family to emphasize their cattle (see 46:6) when questioned by Pharaoh about their occupation (46:31 - 34); in spite of this his brothers spoke primarily of their flocks (47:3 - 4). Pharaoh received them cordially, confirmed their locating in Goshen, and requested that capable men from among them be put in charge of his cattle (47:6). Jacob was presented before the king and in answer to Pharaoh's inquiry stated that he was 130 years old, but contrasted his age with the years of his ancestors, "few and evil have been the days of the years of my life" (47:9).

As the famine continued Joseph traded grain for land, so that the throne became the virtual possessor of Egypt, with the exception of the lands owned by the priests (47:20 - 22; see Breasted, *History of Egypt*, pp. 229, 238, 244). It is recognized that for some reason during the reign of Sesostris III (1878 - 1843 B.C.) the provincial nobles were shorn of their traditional rights and privileges and the provinces became administered by appointed officials (William C. Hayes, "The Middle Kingdom in Egypt," CAH, rev. ed., fasc. 3, pp. 44 f.). The benefactions provided for the priests by the king (47:22) are well-known from ancient documents, such as the long Papyrus Harris I, which lists the gifts of Ramses III to the temples (see ANET, pp. 260 - 62; Breasted, ARE, IV, §§ 151 - 412).

After 17 years of residence in Egypt Jacob became ill. Previously he had extracted a promise from Joseph that he would be buried in the family burial place in Canaan (47:29 - 31). He also gave a particular blessing to Joseph's sons (Gen 48) and individualized prophetic blessings to his own sons (Gen 49; for Joseph, see vv. 22 - 26). Joseph fulfilled his promise to his father, having him mummified in the Egyptian manner (50:2 - 13; *see* Embalm) and buried in the cave of Machpelah near Hebron. After Jacob's death Joseph's brothers feared that he would yet take vengeance upon them, but again he insisted that God in His providence had intended all of this for good.

Joseph died in Egypt at the ideal Egyptian age of 110 years (see ANET, p. 414, n.33). He too was mummified and placed in a sarcophagus or wooden mummy case (50:26). He had requested that when the Israelites left Egypt they should take his remains with them (50:25). This was faithfully performed by Moses at the time of the exodus (Ex 13:19). *See* Exodus, The. Joseph was buried at Shechem in a plot of ground which Jacob had acquired (Josh 24:32).

Joseph is not mentioned in the Egyptian records. It is of interest, however, that the name Joseph-El appears as a Palestinian place name in the lists of cities conquered by Thutmose III (see ANET, p. 242; J. Simons, *Egyptian Topographical Lists*, pp. 112, 118, 127 - 128). *See* Chronology, OT; Genesis; Patriarchal Age.

Bibliography. K. A. Kitchen, "Joseph," NBD, pp. 656 - 660. H. H. Rowley, *From Joseph to Joshua*, London: British Academy, 1950. J. Vergote, *Joseph en Egypte*, Louvain: Publications Universitaires, 1959. W. A. Ward, "Egyptian Titles in Genesis 39 - 50," BS, CXIV (1957), 40 - 59; "The Egyptian Office of Joseph," JSS, V (1960), 144 - 150.

2. The descendants of 1 (Gen 49:22; Deut 33:13; Jud 1:22 - 23; etc.).

3. The father of Igal, one of the spies sent out by Moses, of the tribe of Issachar (Num 13:7).

4. A son of Asaph whose name appears twice in the description of the religious services under David (I Chr 25:2, 9).

5. A man of the family of Bani (Binnui) who married a woman from outside Israel but put her away in response to a religious revival (Ezr 10:42, 44).

6. A priest in the time of Joiakim, from the family of Shebaniah (Neh 12:14).

7-9. Three men listed in the genealogy of Lk 3:24, 26 (here another reading gives "Josech," RSV), and 30.

10. The husband of Mary, the mother of Jesus. His genealogy is given in Mt 1 (cf. Lk 3:23 - 38). He was a carpenter (Mt 13:55; Mk 6:3), who lived in Nazareth (Lk 2:4), but as a descendant of David his ancestral home was in Bethlehem. He was engaged to Mary at the time Jesus was conceived by the Holy Spirit (Mt 1:18; Lk 1:27; 2:5). When he learned that Mary was pregnant he was unwilling to put her to public shame but considered divorcing or putting her away secretly. He was informed by God in a dream that Mary's conception was divine and was encouraged to marry her (Mt 1:20 - 25). To register for the imperial tax, he and Mary went to Bethlehem, where Jesus was born. Joseph is mentioned along with Mary and Jesus at the visit of the shepherds (Lk 2:16) and at the presentation of Jesus in the temple (Lk 2:27, 33). In a dream the Lord instructed Joseph to flee Herod's wrath by taking Jesus and Mary to Egypt for a while (Mt 2:13 - 15). The last mentioned participation of Joseph in the events of the Gospels relates to the annual festival visit to Jerusalem when Jesus was 12 years old (Lk 2:41 - 52). He is not included with Mary and their children in Mt 12:46 - 50; Mk 3:31 - 35; and Lk 8:19 - 21 (cf. Mk 6:3), though Jn 6:42 may indicate that Joseph was

still living during part of Jesus' ministry. Joseph does not appear at the crucifixion, when Jesus gave His mother into the care of the apostle John (Jn 19:26–27); hence it may be concluded that Joseph had died previous to this. The Jews of Jesus' time regarded Jesus as a son of Joseph (see Lk 3:23; 4:22; Jn 1:45; 6:42).

11. Joseph of Arimathea, a wealthy man (Mt 27:57), a member of the council or Sanhedrin (Lk 23:50, RSV), and a secret disciple of Jesus, for fear of the Jews (Jn 19:38). He is characterized as honorable, bold, and awaiting the kingdom of God (Mk 15:43; Lk 23:50–51). After Jesus' death Joseph went to Pilate to request the body of Jesus (Mt 27:57–58; Mk 15:43; Lk 23:52; Jn 19:38). With Nicodemus, Joseph prepared Jesus' body for burial and placed Him in the tomb which Joseph had prepared for his own use (Mt 27:60).

12. A half-brother of Jesus (Mt 13:55; some MSS read "Joses" or "John").

13. A candidate for the place of Judas among the apostles, identified as "Joseph called Barsabas, who was surnamed Justus" (Acts 1:23).

14. The original name of Barnabas (*q.v.*), a Levite of Cyprian birth (Acts 4:36, NASB). The KJV, following the Textus Receptus, calls him Joses.

C. E. D.

JOSEPHUS, FLAVIUS (jō-sē'fŭs flā'vĭ-ŭs). The life of Josephus (*c.* A.D. 37–103) is a study in contrasts. Son of a priest and reared in traditional Judaism, Josephus, or Joseph ben Matthias (his Heb. name), could boast of royal blood through his Hasmonean mother. He was so dissatisfied with the three prevailing sects of Judaism that he retired for several years to a monastery near Jerusalem under the hermit Banus. Caught up in the Jewish anti-Roman resistance movement which he had been unable to dispel, he found himself the general in charge of the Jotapata fortress in Galilee (A.D. 66). Though he refused to surrender until guaranteed his life, it was his successful prophecy that Vespasian would become emperor that brought imperial favor. He was permitted to accompany Titus to Jerusalem, but he could not persuade the besieged city to surrender.

Claiming to be a Pharisee and true patriot, he was generally thought by Romans, as well as Jews, to behave as an opportunist. He had the "abstract principles of a Pharisee, but with the principles and temper of an Herodian." Thus he later lived and wrote in despised favor at Rome.

After the destruction of Jerusalem, Josephus was given a chance to retire near Jerusalem, but he chose rather to return to Rome with Titus. Here he received Roman citizenship and was commissioned to write a history of the Jewish people.

As the Apostolic Fathers are virtually the only source for early 2nd cen. Christianity, so were it not for Josephus very little would be known of 1st cen. Judaism or its outlook on Christianity. This is the main reason for the high esteem in which his writings were held by early Church Fathers, such as Jerome.

Josephus' first literary work was his *History of the Jewish War* (against Rome), published in the closing years of the reign of Vespasian: Written first in Aramaic for the benefit of Jews in Mesopotamia and then rewritten in Gr., this is a detailed account of the futile struggle against Rome. The narrative begins in the intertestamental period with Antiochus Epiphanes and the Maccabean revolt, culminating in the insurrection against Rome and the fall of Jerusalem in A.D. 70 and Masada in 73. Josephus writes as a moderate Jew attempting to trace the faults of his compatriots to the extremities of the Zealots. While he describes the siege and fall of Jerusalem in pitiful detail, there is no explicit reference whatever to Christ or Christians in the Gr. text of this volume. The historical accuracy of much of his writing has been confirmed through various discoveries such as at Machaerus (*q.v.*).

Antiquities of the Jews is the product of Josephus' scholarly leisure under Roman patronage. He wrote it to answer his chief critic, Justus of Tiberius, and to win the favor of his pagan patrons for the Jewish religion. This may account for his naturalistic demythologizing tendency in describing OT miracles. He was also hopeful of regaining the favor of his kinsmen who distrusted him. The account ends as did *The Jewish War* with the fall of Jerusalem, but begins with the creation. Relying on the Heb. Scriptures for the earliest history, Josephus later incorporates other sources, including the Apocrypha and popular traditions but with only slight reference to the NT, except for one statement better known to the world in general than all the rest of the writings combined. The "Testimonium Flavianum" (*Ant.* xviii.3.3) is by far the most significant witness in Josephus to Christianity. Its authenticity has been seriously questioned. In this most celebrated and most debated extra-Christian testimony of antiquity, Christ is described as "a wise man, if indeed one should call him a man." Such a momentous Jewish statement not being attested by Christian writers before Eusebius (*History of the Christian Church,* i.11.7 f.) would make it appear to be non-genuine. In spite of this, however, A. von Harnack, Rendel Harris and others have championed its originality. While most contemporary scholars believe it to be spurious in its present form, some are persuaded it has a pristine Josephan ingredient.

Bibliography. Norman Bentwich, *Josephus,* Philadelphia: Jewish Pub. Society, 1914. William R. Farmer, *Maccabees, Zealots and Josephus,* New York: Columbia Univ. Press, 1956. Frederick J. Foakes-Jackson, *Josephus and the Jews,* New York: R. R. Smith, 1930. J. Rendel Harris, *Josephus and His Testimony,* Cambridge, 1931. Hugh W. Montefiore, *Josephus and the New Testament,* London: A. R.

Mowbray & Co., 1962. Henry St. John Thackeray, *Josephus, the Man and the Historian,* New York: Ktav Pub. House, 1968. Solomon Zeitlin, *Josephus on Jesus,* Philadelphia: Dropsie College, 1931.

J. H. G.

JOSES (jō'sēz). Possibly a Gr. form of Joseph, although the name *Iōsēs* is attested in Gr. inscriptions.

1. A brother of Jesus (Mk 6:3). Called "Joseph" in Mt 13:55, ASV, RSV, and NASB according to best MSS evidence.

2. A son of Mary and Cleophas (Clopas in best Gr. MSS, Jn 19:25) and brother of James the Less (Mt 27:56, KJV according to TR; called "Joseph" in RSV and NASB following a different Gr. text; Mk 15:40, 47 has the genitive of *Iōsēs* in nearly all MSS).

3. The natal name of Barnabas, a prominent missionary and early companion of Paul (Acts 4:36, KJV according to TR; called "Joseph" in ASV, RSV, NASB according to earlier Gr. MSS). *See* Barnabas.

JOSHAH (jŏsh'*ȧ*). A Simeonite chief who with others invaded the valley of Gedor in the time of King Hezekiah and destroyed the native Hamites there (I Chr 4:34–41).

JOSHAPHAT (jŏsh'*ȧ*-făt)

1. A Mithnite among David's mighty men (I Chr 11:43).

2. One of seven priests who blew the trumpet before the ark in David's time (I Chr 15:24) in accordance with the law of Moses (Num 10:8). He is called Jehoshaphat in KJV, but the Heb. text supports Joshaphat as in ASV and RSV.

JOSHAVIAH (jŏsh'*ȧ*-vī'*ȧ*). A son of Elnaam listed among David's mighty men (I Chr 11:46).

JOSHBEKASHAH (jŏsh'bĕ-kā'sh*ȧ*). A member of the house of Heman who headed the 17th course of musicians appointed by David for the sanctuary service (I Chr 25:4, 24).

JOSHEB-BASSHEBETH (jō'shĕb-bă-sē'bĕt). The name of David's most eminent warrior among his mighty men as given in ASV and RSV as a probable substitute for the meaningless "that sat in the seat" in II Sam 23:8 of KJV. In the parallel passage in I Chr 11:11 this man is identified as "Jashobeam, an Hachmonite." *See* Jashobeam.

JOSHUA(jŏsh'ū-*ȧ*). The leader of the Israelites in their conquest of the Promised Land. His full name Jehoshua (Num 13:16) means "Yahweh is salvation," and is the same as the Hellenized form of the name Jesus (Acts 7:45; Heb 4:8). His name is spelled "Jeshua" in Neh 8:17. His original name was Oshea (RSV, Hoshea, Num 13:8).

House remains of the Israelite period at Et Tell, commonly identfied as Ai. HFV

Joshua was the son of Nun, of the tribe of Ephraim (Num 13:8). After directing the allotment of tribal territories he settled in the highlands of Ephraim at Timnath-serah, where he was buried (Josh 19:50; 24:30).

Since he was over 40 when he left Egypt and seemed well-qualified to command the Israelite forces who fought off the Amalekites at Rephidim (Ex 17:8–16), it is possible that he had been trained in Pharaoh's army. During the year at Mount Sinai Joshua served as personal attendant to Moses when the latter was receiving the law and whenever he went to the tent of meeting to hear the Lord (Ex 24:13; 32:17; 33:11). Even after leaving Sinai, Moses considered Joshua to be "young" and found it necessary to rebuke him for trying to forbid two elders in the camp from prophesying (Num 11:27–29).

In addition to whatever contacts he may have had before the Exodus with Canaan and its inhabitants as they came to trade in Egypt or as he may have traveled there on an Egyptian military campaign, Joshua gained experience of that land as one of the 12 spies. He was selected as the representative from the tribe of Ephraim (Num 13:8). They scouted Canaan thoroughly from the Negeb to Rehob, near Lebo-hamath (Lebweh, 14 miles NE of Baalbek between the Lebanon ranges). As Joshua and Caleb opposed the defaming majority report and urged the Israelites to enter the "exceedingly good land" (Num 14:7) instead of rebelling against the Lord, they grew in spiritual stature. The other ten who disparaged the land died by plague (Num 14:36–38). Only Joshua and Caleb of those over 20 at the beginning of the wilderness journey remained alive at the end of the 40 years and were permitted to enter Canaan (Num 26:65; 32:12; Deut 1:34–40).

The Lord ordered Moses to give Joshua a commission as the new shepherd of His people when the lawgiver realized he would soon die

The mound of Gibeon, with whose ancient Canaanite inhabitants Joshua made a treaty. HFV

instead of crossing into Canaan (Num 27:12 - 23; Deut 3:21 - 29). Moses invested Joshua solemnly with honor or authority before Eleazar the high priest and the entire congregation, and imparted to him a spirit of wisdom as he laid his hands upon him (Num 27:18, 23; Deut 34:9). As part of Moses' final arrangements for covenant continuity he charged Joshua publicly to be strong and courageous in order to bring Israel to the land of its promised inheritance (Deut 31:3, 7 - 8). When Moses and his successor went and stood at the door of the tent of meeting, God directly commissioned Joshua (Deut 31:14 - 15, 23). After Moses' death the Lord graciously repeated this charge to Joshua privately, enlarging His promises to encourage him on the eve of the invasion of Canaan (Josh 1:1 - 9).

Encamped E of the Jordan, Joshua faced two stupendous problems, how to cross the flooded river and how to overcome the defending Canaanites. Would they be waiting with drawn swords on the opposite bank? He sent two spies to reconnoiter the bastion of Jericho and commanded them to keep their mission secret lest their report discourage the people as the ten spies had done (Josh 2; cf. Num 13; 14). God undertook for both obstacles by filling the inhabitants of the land with terror (Josh 2:9 - 11), and by stopping the Jordan when the people marched to the river in faith and at the moment the priests carrying the ark stepped in the waters (3:14 - 17).

In obedience to the Lord, Joshua had the men born in the wilderness circumcised (5:2 - 9). The nation was willing once again to walk by faith with Yahweh their God in the promises of the Abrahamic covenant and to submit to circumcision, the covenant sign. Thus God removed the reproach or disgrace of their idolatrous and sensual ways in Egypt (5:9).

Joshua exhibited great faith and discipline in obeying God's unusual tactics for reducing Jericho. He commanded the priests and people to march round the city each day and to refrain from shouts and retorts to the undoubted mockery of the defending Canaanites (6:6 - 10). Except for Achan, the Israelite troops followed his orders in not looting the ruins for their own benefit. Feeling a personal responsibility, Joshua agonized over the defeat and loss of 36 of his men at Ai, and fell on his face in desperation before the Lord (7:6 - 9).

The details of the second attack on Ai illustrate the thorough planning and strategy that went into Joshua's campaigns. He was swift and decisive in his movements, as the all-night forced march up from Gilgal to relieve the siege of Gibeon would indicate (10:9). When the Amorite ranks broke, he urged his army to follow up the victory (10:19 - 20). He had prayed for God to help him destroy in the open field the enemy's fighting potential, and after the divinely sent hailstorm he pressed his advantage as the Amorite armies fled to fortresses 20 miles away (10:10 - 14).

With blitzkrieg speed he assaulted the key southern strongholds one after another, aiming at killing their troops rather than occupying and holding the cities (10:28 - 43). He counted on divine direction and support (10:25, 30, 32, 42; 11:6 - 9, 15), on surprise and ruse, on discipline and incentive among his own troops, and on collapse of enemy morale rather than on superior weapons and numbers. Since his desert army was untrained in siege operations, he could not afford to get bogged down outside a walled city. Many Canaanites probably fled to the hills and caves, later to return and reoccupy their towns. Other cities, such as Gibeon and her allies, capitulated outright. Thus, except at Jericho, Ai, and Hazor, which Joshua burned (11:13), archaeologists can expect to find little clear-cut evidence of city destruction as a result of Joshua's incursions. He subdued the country as a whole and secured it sufficiently to enable each tribe to enter and claim its allotted inheritance. Israelite settlement and city building followed gradually during the time from the judges to David. *See* Exodus, The.

Joshua possessed the qualities of a true leader. He displayed great courage from his first battle with the Amalekites at Rephidim, grimly holding fast whenever they began to prevail, to his attack on the combined Canaanite kings at the waters of Merom. He was quick to receive and obey orders from his divine Commander-in-Chief (e.g., 5:13 – 6:5), humble enough to recognize his constant need to depend on the Lord – although he failed to seek God as to the identity of the envoys from Gibeon (9:14 - 15). He was a man of honor. He carried out the agreement made by the two spies with the household of Rahab and spared her family when Jericho fell (6:22 - 25). Nor did he abrogate the treaty made by the Israelite princes with the Gibeonites (9:18 - 26).

His finest quality was his utter devotion to the law of God. He saturated his mind and heart with the Word of the Lord. Thus the nation had confidence in his decisions (see 1:13-18; 11:12, 15; 14:1-5). In the midst of his early campaigns Joshua took time to establish Israel's covenant as the new law of the land at its very center, at Gerizim and Ebal (8:30-35). In his farewell addresses he appealed to the people to renew their covenant commitment with the Lord and exhorted them "to keep and to do all that is written in the book of the law of Moses" (23:6).

His godly example continued to influence the nation even after his death, during the lifetime of the elders who outlived Joshua (24:31).

For bibliography *see* Joshua, Book of.

J. R.

JOSHUA, BOOK OF. The sixth book of the OT, and the first of the historical books, named after its principal character, Joshua. Under God he led the nation of Israel across the Jordan, in their conquest of Canaan, in occupying their tribal territories, and in renewing their covenant allegiance to the Lord. In Jewish tradition Joshua is the first book of The Prophets, the second major division of the Heb. Bible, heading the subdivision known as the Former Prophets (Joshua, Judges, I and II Samuel, I and II Kings).

Position in the Canon

In 1792 Alexander Geddes proposed a theory that Joshua was the sixth book of a late Jewish collection which modern critics have called the Hexateuch. Developing this view along with the documentary (JEDP) theory of the Pentateuch, such scholars as Bleek, Knobel, and Nöldeke argued that there must have been a suitable conclusion to the story of Israel's beginnings described in the first five books of the OT. Since the land which God swore to give to the patriarchs is mentioned from Gen 12 to Deut 34, the fulfillment of the divine promise would not be provided without Joshua. Source analysts thought they could detect the styles of the supposed Pentateuchal sources in the sixth book.

There is no ancient Jewish tradition or MS evidence, however, that Joshua ever formed a unit with the five books of the law to constitute a so-called Hexateuch. The law was always distinguished from the other books. Josephus clearly states that the Jews of his day had five books belonging to Moses, 13 by prophets who wrote down what was done in their times from the death of Moses until the reign of Artaxerxes, and four others containing hymns to God and precepts for daily living (Jos *Apion* 1.8). Nor were any portions of Joshua ever included in the annual and triennial systems of the public reading of the law.

The strongest argument against a Hexateuch is that the Samaritans considered only the five books of Moses to be canonical, but never the book of Joshua. Yet Joshua contains various features which would aid the cause of the Samaritan sectarians. Both Mount Gerizim (Josh 8:33), where the Samaritans later worshiped, and Shechem (Josh 20:7; 24:1, 32), their home (Jos *Ant.* xi.8.6), are mentioned, with no intimation of Jerusalem becoming Israel's center of worship. Thus, since there was no reason to reject the book of Joshua and every reason to keep it, Joshua could not have been part of the Torah at the time of the Samaritan schism (see G. L. Archer, SOTI, p. 253).

More recently, Martin Noth (*Das Buch Joshua,* 1938) and others have claimed that there existed in Israel a theological history that began with Deuteronomy and continued through II Kings. While there are some similarities of style in Deuteronomy and Joshua, it must be recognized that in Jewish history Deuteronomy was always considered as part of the Torah, as one of the five books of the law. Deut 24:16 is quoted in II Kgs 14:6, indicating it was "written in the book of the law of Moses." Both Jesus and the apostles quoted or referred to portions of Deuteronomy as belonging to the law (cf. Mt 22:36-38 with Deut 6:5; Mt 19:8 with Deut 24:1-4; Acts 3:22 with Deut 18:15; I Cor 9:9 with Deut 25:4; Heb 10:28 with Deut 17:6; 19:15; Heb 10:30 with Deut 32:35-36).

Certainly no one in the early church doubted the inspiration of the book of Joshua. In Heb 13:5, Josh 1:5 is quoted as the Word of God. Numerous other references may be found in the NT to persons and events in Joshua, stamping the record of its events as authentic.

Authorship and Date

The book appears to be a literary unit, composed by a single author. Critical scholars, however, have held varying views leading to the general conclusion that it is a composite work of several late source documents, still later compiled and edited by the Deuteronomic school. Some think they find clues of the Elohist (E) and Yahwist (J) writers and claim there was a major Deuteronomic (D) revision during Josiah's reign, with Priestly (P) writers adding most of the contents of chaps. 13-22 in Ezra's time. Other liberal scholars, such as Martin Noth and John Bright (IB, II, 541-548), reject this analysis and recognize only the Deuteronomic style in the book.

Unquestionably sources were used in writing Joshua. The author specifically refers to the book of Jasher (Josh 10:13) and mentions that Joshua had ordered a description of the land to be written in a book (18:8-9). Joshua himself wrote "in the book of the law of God" the stipulations of the renewed covenant as part of the ceremony at Shechem (24:25-26).

Yet Joshua could not have been the final author of the book bearing his name since it records his death (24:29-30). Furthermore, several events are recorded which apparently did not happen until after Joshua's death: Caleb's conquest of Hebron (Josh 15:13*b*-14; cf. Jud 1:1, 10, 20), Othniel's capture of Debir

(Josh 15:15 - 19; cf. Jud 1:1, 11 -15), and the migration of the Danites to Leshem (Josh 15:17; 19:47; 24:31; cf. Jud 1:1, 17-18). The name Hormah is used for the town of Zephath (Josh 12:14; 15:30; 19:4), which was not changed until the following era (Jud 1:1, 17). But the author was a contemporary of Joshua, having participated in the Jordan crossing ("we," Josh 5:1). Also, Rahab was still alive at the time of writing (6:25).

The book gives other evidence of having been written prior to 1200 B.C. because the Philistines are barely mentioned (only in Josh 13:2 -3) and certainly were not yet considered to be a threat. The author knew them only as occupying a part of the "south," the Negeb, along with the Geshurites and the Avvim; and the territory as a whole was counted as Canaanite. Rameses III (1198 - 1166 B.C.) boasted of crushing an attempted invasion of Egypt by land and sea by the Philistines and their Aegean allies in his eighth year (ANET, pp. 262 f.). The remnants settled the Palestinian coastal plain in force from that time on. On the other hand, the phrase "all the land of the Hittites" (Josh 1:4; *not* in Deut 11:24!) in referring to Syria-Lebanon would not have been historically accurate until the Hittite king Suppiluliumas (1380 - 1346 B.C.) crushed the Mitanni in Syria *c.* 1370 B.C. Furthermore, the term may have been less significant after the treaty between Rameses II and Hattusilis III *c.* 1284 B.C. Widespread Hittite control had disappeared altogether in S Syria before 1200 B.C.

If Joshua himself did not write the major portion of the book to which a short appendix about his death was added, then a possible author might be the high priest Phinehas, the last-named person in the book (24:33). He, rather than Joshua, is the prominent person in settling the dispute over the altar built by the two and one-half tribes at the Jordan frontier (Josh 22:10 - 34). Another possibility is a nameless priest closely associated with Phinehas but who resided in Judah. The lengthy list of the borders and towns of Judah (15:1 -63) may indicate that he settled in that territory. In comparison, the borders of Ephraim and Manasseh are traced rather briefly, even though within them lay the important religious centers of Shiloh and Shechem (Josh 16 - 17). A special interest in the city of Hebron may be detected (14:6 - 15; 15:13 - 14; 21:11 - 13), suggesting perhaps the author's home.

Biblical data and archaeological discoveries provide evidence by which one may arrive at a date for the Exodus and thus the Conquest (*see* Exodus, The: Date). If Moses led the Israelites through the Red Sea *c.* 1445 B.C., 480 years before Solomon began to build the temple (I Kgs 6:1), then Joshua's invasion of Canaan took place *c.* 1405 B.C., at the close of the Late Bronze I Age (1550 - 1400). The division of the land began 45 years after Moses at Kadesh-barnea had promised Caleb an inheritance (Josh 14:1 - 10), thus *c.* 1400 B.C. After making the tribal allotments Joshua lived on until 1390 - 1380, or even later. Thus the book was probably written early in the period of the judges, *c.* 1370 - 1350 B.C. According to the late date theory of the Exodus and Conquest the Israelites would have crossed the Jordan *c.* 1250 - 1230 B.C. or even later. It would be difficult, however, to reconcile this view with a date before 1200 B.C. for the time of the writing of Joshua which seems preferable as discussed above: *c.* 1200 B.C. the Philistines came in strength to Palestine and the Hittite Empire collapsed.

Purpose

The book of Joshua seems to have been written as the official record of God's providential leading in Israel's triumph and settlement in the land He had promised their forefathers. Hence the record was undoubtedly added to the existing scrolls of the law kept beside the ark in the tabernacle (Deut 31:9, 24 -27). Samuel, for instance, wrote additional material "in the book" (I Sam 10:25, ASV marg.) and laid it up before the Lord. As part of the recognized and accepted sacred Scriptures, Joshua would be read periodically at the annual feasts and on special occasions of covenant renewal (e.g., Neh 8 -9). The book of Joshua declares the faithfulness of the Lord to His covenants with the patriarchs and with the nation as mediated to it by Moses. God is demonstrated as keeping His promises in full (Josh 21:43 -45). On their part, the future generations are inspired to renew their own covenant commitment and to imitate the faith and unity and high morale of Joshua's era.

Outline

- I. Entrance into the Promised Land, 1:1 – 5:12
  - A. God's commission to Joshua, 1:1 -9
  - B. Joshua's mobilization for crossing the Jordan, 1:10 - 18
  - C. Mission of the spies, 2:1 -24
  - D. Crossing of the Jordan, 3:1 – 5:1
  - E. Renewal of circumcision and Passover observance, 5:2- 12
- II. Conquest of the Promised Land, 5:13 – 12:24
  - A. Appearance of the divine Commander-in-Chief, 5:13 – 6:5
  - B. The central campaign, 6:6 – 8:29
    - 1. Capture of Jericho, 6:6 -27
    - 2. Repulse at Ai because of Achan's sin, 7:1 -26
    - 3. Second attack and the burning of Ai, 8:1 -29
  - C. Establishment of Israel's covenant as the law of the land, 8:30 -35
  - D. The southern campaign, 9:1 – 10:43
    - 1. Treaty with the Gibeonite tetrapolis, 9:1 -27
    - 2. Defeat and hanging of the five Amorite kings, 10:1 -27

JOSHUA, BOOK OF

3. Assault of cities and destruction of all resistance, 10:28 - 43
E. The northern campaign, 11:1 - 15
F. Summary of the conquest, 11:16 - 23
G. Appendix: Catalogue of the defeated kings, 12:1 - 24

III. Apportionment of the Promised Land, 13:1 – 22:34
A. God's command to divide the land, 13:1 - 7
B. Territory of the Transjordanic tribes, 13:8 - 33
C. Beginning of the division of Canaan, 14:1 - 15
D. Territory of the tribe of Judah, 15:1 - 63
E. Territory of the Joseph tribes, 16:1 – 17:18
F. Territories of the seven remaining tribes, 18:1 – 19:51
G. Inheritance of Levi, 20:1 – 21:42
1. Apportionment of cities of refuge, 20:1 - 9
2. Assignment of cities to the Levites, 21:1 - 42
H. Summary of the conquest and apportionment, 21:43 - 45
I. Appendix: Reconciliation with Transjordanic tribes, 22:1 - 34

IV. Final Summons to Covenant Loyalty in the Promised Land, 23:1 – 24:33
A. Joshua's farewell address to Israel's leaders, 23:1 - 16
B. The great assembly for renewal of the covenant commitment at Shechem, 24:1 - 28
C. Appendix: Death of Joshua and subsequent conduct of Israel, 24:29 - 33

Teaching and Value

Joshua is the first of the books of prophetic history that describe God's dealings with His chosen people after the death of Moses, the mediator of the Sinaitic covenant. There is a strong sense of historical continuity as God in faithfulness to His covenants with the patriarchs and the theocratic nation brings Israel into the land of blessing and settles the tribes in their promised homeland. By real and mighty acts of redemption He displays His presence and power. These acts are both actual and prophetic of the second Joshua, even Jesus our Saviour.

The era of Joshua is the high water mark of corporate faith and faithfulness in the OT. As such it is also prophetic of the faith of Israel's remnant in the end-time as they will triumph over their enemies in the day of the Lord. Likewise the book of Joshua illustrates the present-day conflict of the people of God with evil powers – with the evil kings and princes of the unseen world, the cosmic rulers of this dark age, the spirit hosts of wickedness in the supernatural sphere – and with Satan himself (Eph 6:10 - 18). Such spiritual warfare is encountered as the believer earnestly strives to possess all that God has promised to him in Christ (Eph 1:3). As in Josh 10, all strongholds must be destroyed and every thought brought captive to the obedience of Christ (II Cor 10:4 - 5). Such warfare is won by faith in the finished redemptive work of Christ and His present authority (Eph 1:19 - 22), which believers share as they are enthroned together with Him in the supernatural realm (Eph 2:6). The book of Joshua thus is filled with spiritual lessons on how the believer may live the victorious life, how he may enter the land of rest of Heb 3 - 4. In this NT passage the rest in Canaan from vain wilderness strivings is set forth as typical of the present spiritual rest as believers abide in Christ. It is He who made complete atonement and is continually interceding for the believer to enable him to conquer self and Satan.

Not only are God's faithfulness and His miraculous saving power portrayed in the book of Joshua, but also His holiness is seen in His judgment upon the iniquitous Canaanites and in His insistence that in fighting the holy war against them Israel must put away everything evil from their own use. The teaching concerning *ḥērem*, the "accursed thing" (Josh 6:17 - 21; Deut 7:2, 26), meant that every person and thing hostile to theocracy by its having been associated with another deity must be devoted to the Lord, either to be utterly destroyed or to be taken out of common use and dedicated only to sacred use.

Contents and Problems

For specific discussion of Joshua's career *see* Joshua; and of various theological, archaeological, and exegetical problems in the book *see* War on the extermination of Canaanites and holy war; Jericho; Ai; Shechem; Hazor; *see* Sun on Josh 10:12 - 14.

Bibliography. Carl Armerding, *The Fight for Palestine in the Days of Joshua,* Wheaton: Van Kampen Press, 1949. William G. Blaikie, "Joshua," ExpB. Hugh J. Blair, "Joshua," NBC. John Bright, "Joshua," IB. "Conquest," CornPBE, pp. 230 - 236. John J. Davis, *Conquest and Crisis,* Grand Rapids: Baker, 1970. John Garstang, *Joshua-Judges: the Foundation of Bible History,* New York: Richard Smith, Inc., 1931. Irving Jensen, *Joshua: Rest-Land Won,* Chicago: Moody Press, 1966. Yehezkel Kaufmann, *The Biblical Account of the Conquest of Palestine,* Jerusalem: Magnes Press, 1953. Carl F. Keil, "Joshua," KD. William S. LaSor, *Great Personalities of the OT,* Westwood, N.J.: Revell, 1959, pp. 69 - 77. George E. Mendenhall, *Law and Covenant in Israel and the Ancient Near East,* Pittsburgh: The Biblical Colloquium, 1955. F. B. Meyer, *Joshua and the Land of Promise,* London: Morgan & Scott, n.d. John Rea, "Joshua," WBC. Alan Redpath, *Victorious Christian Living: Studies in the Book of Joshua,* Revell, 1955.

J. R.

JOSIAH (jō-sī'*ȧ*)

1. Grandson of Manasseh and son and successor of Amon as king of Judah. The primary biblical information concerning him comes from II Kgs 22–23; II Chr 34–35; Jeremiah (many references); and Zephaniah. His birth was supernaturally predicted by name in the time of Jeroboam I (I Kgs 13:2). He was one of the good kings of Judah who led a reform. The "people of the land" placed him on the throne at the age of eight, and he reigned *c.* 639–609 B.C. In the eighth year of his reign (at 16 years of age) he "began to seek after the God of David, his father" (II Chr 34:3). In his twelfth year he began his reforms in Judah and Jerusalem, and evidently in northern Israel as well. (Jeremiah received his call to the prophetic ministry in Josiah's thirteenth year, *c.* 626 B.C.)

In his eighteenth year (621 B.C.) Josiah arranged for the temple repairs. It was at this time that a most important event in his reign occurred. Hilkiah the high priest found the "book of the law" in the temple. If this work is not to be identified solely as the book of Deuteronomy, it is quite certain that it at least included that book, or parts of it. This lawbook was responsible for the renewal of the covenant and further reforms, which by now certainly extended even to Bethel and Naphtali. Apparently, Assyrian control had weakened enough to allow such a widespread cleansing of the land from idolatry. In doing this, Josiah centralized public worship in Jerusalem. He also observed the Passover on the grandest scale since the days of the judges. But in spite of all this, Jeremiah (e.g., Jer 2–6, 11) makes it clear that Josiah's reform was only superficial, external, and temporary. No genuine repentance or lasting inner change of the people resulted from it.

Josiah adopted an anti-Assyrian policy and thereby met an untimely death in 609 B.C. by injudiciously leading a little army against Neco II, king of Egypt. The latter was actually on a march with his army to aid the Assyrians in making their last ditch stand against the Babylonians at Haran. At the very beginning of this encounter with the Egyptian army at Megiddo, Josiah was killed. His religious reformation was soon forgotten, and three months later the kingdom of Judah lost its political independence to Egypt.

Yet Josiah was the last good and godly king of Judah before the destruction of Jerusalem and the Babylonian captivity. The finest tribute is paid to him in II Kgs 23:25: "And like unto him was there no king before him [i.e., in the area of obedience to the law, as the following explains], that turned to the Lord with all his heart, and with all his soul, and with all his might, according to all the law of Moses; neither after him arose there any like him."

2. A son of Zephaniah who returned with other Jews from Exile (Zech 6:10).

K. L. B.

JOSIAS. *See* Josiah.

JOSIBIAH (jŏs'ĭ-bī'*ȧ*). A Simeonite (I Chr 4:35).

JOSIPHIAH (jŏs'ĭ-fī'*ȧ*). The father of a returnee to Palestine with Ezra (Ezr 8:10).

JOT. A word used in Mt 5:18 to represent the Gr. *iōta,* a letter equivalent to *i* in English. However, *iōta* was used here to designate *yōd,* the smallest letter in the Heb. alphabet, and thereby to set forth the indestructibility of the law in its smallest details. The inviolability of all of God's revelation in the Scriptures is, by implication, likewise upheld. The importance of such a minute detail as a *yōd* can be accounted for only by recognizing that Christ regarded the individual words of Scripture as inspired and authoritative, for the change of a letter might well change the whole word and its meaning.

Modern versions offer a large variety of translations of *iōta* in Mt 5:18: "jot" (ASV), "iota" (Montgomery, Moffatt, Berkeley, RSV), "smallest letter" (Weymouth, NASB), "dotting an *i*" (Goodspeed, Williams), "single dot" (Phillips), "letter" (NEB), "least point" (Today's English Version), etc.

JOTBAH (jŏt'b*ȧ*). A town where Meshullemeth, the mother of King Amon of Judah, lived (II Kgs 21:19). Its exact site is unknown, although some identify it with Khirbet Jefat, known as Jotapata in Roman times, a town near Cana of Galilee. Josephus tried unsuccessfully to defend this city against Vespasian's army (Jos *Wars* iii.7).

JOTBATH. *See* Jotbathah.

JOTBATHAH (jŏt'b*ȧ*-th*ȧ*). A place or district where Israel encamped twice during the wilderness wanderings (Num 33:33–34; Deut 10:7, Jotbath). The two references represent the beginning and the close of the period of wilderness wandering. The place is usually identified with some wady or valley (Deut 10:7, ASV, "a land of brooks of water") N of the Gulf of Aqabah, perhaps Ain el-Ghadian, 25 miles N of Ezion-geber in the Arabah. Another possible location is the luxurious oasis at Taba, six miles SW of Eilat on the western shore of the gulf (Beno Rothenberg, *God's Wilderness,* London: Thames & Hudson, 1961, pp. 163 f.).

JOTHAM (jō'th*ă*m)

1. A king of Judah who was a son of Azariah (or Uzziah) and father of Ahaz (II Kgs 15:5, 7, 30–38; II Chr 27:1–9). He was coregent with his father *c.* 750–742 B.C. because his father had leprosy and was unable to administer efficiently the affairs of the kingdom. He was sole king *c.* 742–735 B.C., continuing the anti-Assyrian policy of his father (*see* Uzziah). He abdicated the actual rulership in favor of his pro-Assyrian son Ahaz, and died in 731 B.C.

Jotham won a military victory over the Ammonites (II Chr 27:5). He was also responsible for several building projects. For example, he built the high gate of the temple (i.e., the northern gate of the inner court), fortified the wall of Ophel in Jerusalem, built cities in the hill country of Judah, and established forts and towers on the hills (II Kgs 15:35; II Chr 27:3). It may be correctly surmised from such activity that this was a period of prosperity, and this is confirmed by archaeology.

A signet ring has been found at Ezion-geber (Elath) with a seal inscribed "belonging to Jotham." This Jotham has been identified as the son of Uzziah. The fact that it was discovered at Ezion-geber evidently indicates that at that time Judah's control extended to that seaport on the Gulf of Aqabah.

2. Gideon's youngest son who escaped the massacre of Gideon's 70 sons ordered by Abimelech (Jud 9:5). After his escape, and after Abimelech was made king by the people of Shechem, he appeared on Mount Gerizim to protest their action by relating the parable of the trees selecting the bramble to be their king (which "honor" had already been declined by the cedar, the olive, and the vine). Thus he warned the Shechemites against Abimelech and pronounced a curse on them, which was fulfilled three years later (Jud 9:57).

3. A son of Jahdai and a descendant of Caleb (I Chr 2:47).

K. L. B.

JOURNEY, SABBATH DAY'S. *See* Sabbath Day's Journey.

JOY, REJOICE. Joy is inseparably connected with the life of God's people in the OT and NT (Deut 12:7, 12; Phil 4:4). It characterizes the heavenly hosts before the throne of God (Rev 19:6-7), and the consecrated life of the Christian on earth with his hope for future glory (I Pet 4:13).

In the OT joy is expressed by a number of synonyms, signifying an overflowing adoration before God, particularly in worship. This exuberant delight is often quite demonstrative in loud shouting, clapping, and dancing. God is its source and object (Ps 35:9-10). Especially in the Psalms this exultant gladness is emphasized in God's nearness (Ps 16:11), His pardon (Ps 51:8, 15), His steadfast love (Ps 31:7), His Word (Ps 119:14), and His promises (Ps 106:5). Joy is to be the characteristic of the Messianic Age and the fulfillment of Israel's hopes (Isa 35; 55:12; 65:18-19).

The chief NT words (Gr. *chara* and *chairō*) come from the same root as "grace" (*charis*). The ministry of Jesus is described as the joy of the bridegroom with his friends (Jn 3:29; cf. Mk 2:19). He Himself supplies His deep inner joy to the believer (Jn 15:11; 16:24; 17:13). His joy was a constant satisfying delight in doing the will of God (Ps 40:8), the absolute self-sacrifice of Himself to His Father. Luke particularly stresses joy in the ministry of Jesus (Lk 10:17; 13:17; 15:5, 7, 10; 19:37) and also in the preaching of the gospel ("joyous news") with its conversions (Acts 8:8; 13:48, 52; 15:3). Paul lists joy among the fruit of the Spirit (Gal 5:22), and the result of God's nearness to those whom He has graciously justified in Christ (Rom 5:20). It constantly expresses itself toward others (Phil 1:26; 2:2) in glad obedience arising from love in the fellowship of the church.

Thus joy, which comes from the indwelling of the Holy Spirit in the Christian community, is a basic characteristic of the kingdom of God (Rom 14:17; cf. 15:13; I Thess 1:6). Christian joy is lasting because it is based on a right relationship to God through Christ. Its most remarkable expression, however, is in times of suffering for Christ's sake (Mt 5:12; Acts 5:41; Rom 12:12; Col 1:24; I Pet 4:13). He went to His cross for joy (Heb 12:2). The NT opens with the angelic choruses of joy at Christ's birth and closes with the hallelujahs of His reign.

In the KJV the Gr. verb *kauchaomai*, "to boast, exult," is several times rendered "to joy" (Rom 5:11) or "rejoice" (Rom 5:2; Phil 3:3; Jas 1:9; 4:16) and the nouns *kauchēma* and *kauchēsis* as "rejoicing." This root suggests joy in the sense of proud confidence (II Cor 1:12, NASB) or glorying and boasting (II Cor 7:4; 8:24; etc.). *See* Glory.

F. P.

JOZABAD (jō'zȧ-băd)

1. A volunteer from Gederah in David's army at Ziklag (I Chr 12:4; KJV, Josabad).

2, 3. Two Manassite captains in David's army at Ziklag (I Chr 12:20).

4. A Levite overseer under King Hezekiah (II Chr 31:13).

5. A chief Levite under King Josiah (II Chr 35:9).

6. A priest who divorced his non-Jewish wife (Ezr 10:22).

7. A Levite, son of Jeshua (Ezr 8:33).

8. A priest who divorced his non-Jewish wife (Ezr 10:23).

9. A Levite expounder of the law (Neh 8:7).

10. A chief of the Levites (Neh 11:16). The same person may be represented in 7-10.

JOZACHAR (jō'zȧ-kär). A son of Shimeath and one of two murderers of King Joash of Judah (II Kgs 12:21), identified as Zabad in II Chr 24:26).

JOZADAK. *See* Josedech.

JUBAL (jo͞o'bȧl). The younger son of Lamech by Adah who first played the lyre and flute, and thus probably invented these musical instruments (Gen 4:21).

JUBILEE. *See* Festivals.

JUCAL (jo͞o'kȧl). An abbreviated form of Jehucal (*q.v.*), found in Jer 38:1.

JUDA. *See* Judah.

JUDAEA. *See* Judea.

JUDAH (jōō'dȧ)

1. The fourth son of Jacob whose mother was Leah (Gen 29:35). He married a Canaanite, a daughter of Shuah of Adullam, and they had three sons, Er, Onan, and Shelah. Because of their wickedness and contempt of God the two older sons were slain by the Lord (Gen 38:1-10). Through guile, Judah also became the father of twins (Gen 38:11-30), Pharez and Zarah, by Tamar, widow of Er. It is to be noted that Judah through Pharez became the ancestor of both David (Ruth 4:18-22) and the Lord Jesus Christ (Mt 1:3, 16).

Judah was the leader of the sons of Jacob. He proposed that Joseph be spared instead of murdering him and that he be sold as a slave to the Midianite traders who took him to Egypt (Gen 37:12-13, 18-28). Judah pleaded with the vizier of Egypt, whom he did not suspect to be Joseph, that he be kept a prisoner instead of Benjamin. This resulted in Joseph's making himself known to his brothers (Gen 44:33-34; 45:1). Jacob chose Judah to be the leader to show the way to Goshen (Gen 46:28), and bestowed the privilege of the birthright (including the ancestry of Messiah) on Judah whom he chose over his three older brothers (Gen 49:8-12).

2. The name of the tribe descended from Judah (Num 26:19-21). The men of Judah played no very important part in the Exodus from Egypt and in the wilderness wanderings except that they led in vanguard (Num 2:9). They numbered 74,600 (Num 1:26-27) in the first census at Sinai, and in the second census taken at Shittim before entering Canaan they had increased in 40 years only to 76,500 (Num 26:22). When the tribes would meet at Mount Gerizim, Judah was to stand there to bless the people (Deut 27:12).

Judah was the first tribe authorized to take possession of its assigned territory after the initial conquest of Canaan (Josh 14:6–15:63). They continued to drive out the Canaanites from their towns and from the hill country (Jud 1:1-20). Caleb, one of the 12 spies, was of the tribe of Judah, and with the help of Othniel, his nephew, he made sure his allotment. The territory that Judah occupied was one of the largest, measuring from the Dead Sea W toward the Mediterranean Sea about 30 miles. From the N border which extended from the N end of the Dead Sea W through all the mountains and hilly wilderness to include the Negeb, its length was about 80 miles. Included with that of Judah was the territory of Simeon. During the period of the judges Judah was often cut off from the other tribes by the remaining pagan peoples, such as the Gibeonites, Jebusites, etc., dwelling along the N part of their allotment.

During the latter period of the judges they were in constant conflict with the Philistines who lived along the coast and in the Shephelah (Jud 3:31; 10:7; 13:1). The men of Judah joined in the formation of the kingdom of the combined tribes of Israel. After King Saul died they turned to David and crowned him king with the capital at Hebron. *See* Judah, Kingdom of.

3. A Levite who was one of the overseers of the temple repair workmen (Ezr 3:9).

4. A Levite who put away his foreign wife (Ezr 10:23).

5. A Benjamite, second ruler of Jerusalem in the time of Nehemiah (Neh 11:9).

6. A Levite, one of the choir directors who returned with Zerubbabel (Neh 12:8).

7. One who marched in the parade at the dedication of the restored walls of Jerusalem (Neh 12:34). He may also have been a musician (v. 36).

8. An ancestor of Jesus in the line of Mary, several generations after David (Lk 3:30; KJV, Juda).

C. L. F. and E. L. C.

JUDAH, KINGDOM OF. Not until the time of David did Jacob's prophesied preeminence of Judah (Gen 49:10) begin to reach its fulfillment. After seven years and six months in Hebron (II Sam 5:5), David took Jerusalem from the Jebusites by stealth and made it his capital and center of worship. But Jerusalem and the house of David were to experience the bitterness of schism. King Solomon, in spite of all his administrative genius, only deepened the distrust between the N and S, and his son foolishly consummated the division about 931 B.C. (I Kgs 12).

The kingdoms of Judah and Israel fought for the first 60 years after the division (I Kgs 14:30) until Jehoshaphat helped Ahab with his wars against Damascus. Sadly, this resulted in the toleration of Baal worship in Judah. Under Jehoshaphat, Judah was strong enough to control Edom, but Jehoram, his son, lost both the copper mines and Elath, the seaport on the Gulf of Aqabah, to the rebellious Edomites.

This same Jehoram married Athaliah, the daughter of Ahab and Jezebel, whose treachery almost brought an end to the house of David. The son of this unholy union, Ahaziah, was caught in Jehu's purge of the house of Ahab and mercilessly slain with his cousin Jehoram, king of Israel. Athaliah used this incident to seize the throne and kill all the Davidic seed, missing only the babe Joash, who was saved by his aunt and hidden for six years. A coup lead by Jehoiada the priest brought about the demise of Athaliah, and young Joash ruled under a regency. Joash on the one hand repaired the temple but on the other gave as tribute to Hazael of Syria many of its hallowed treasures.

Amaziah who came to the throne about 800 B.C. had limited success in reviving the fortunes of Judah. With the help of mercenaries he recovered the city of Selah from the Edomites (II Kgs 14:7), but his rule was marred by a foolish challenge to Jehoash of Israel who sacked Jerusalem. Azariah (Uzziah) restored the seaport Elath to Judah and rebuilt it.

Jotham's undistinguished reign was followed by the proud Ahaz. Ahaz reacted faithlessly to a bad political situation. Rezin of Syria and Pekah of Israel were in league against him. Despite pleadings and warnings of Isaiah, Ahaz secured a treaty with the Assyrian king, Tiglath-pileser III, designed to protect him against his northern neighbors. Tiglath-pileser soon laid seige to the city of Damascus and put Samaria under heavy tribute, but then came on to Jerusalem and demanded a large ransom (II Chr 28:16-21).

Judah's good king Hezekiah brought about a spiritual revival. He eventually showed his contempt for Assyrian power when Sennacherib first came into Judah *c.* 705 B.C. Hezekiah probably paid tribute at this time, but the Assyrian king Sennacherib had troubles in many parts of his realm and left Judah. Shabako, the Ethiopian who united Egypt, and Merodach-baladan the Chaldean in Babylon, encouraged Hezekiah to slough off the Assyrian yoke. So once again in 701 Sennacherib brought his hordes into the Judean countryside. He took Lachish and many other cities and used psychological warfare against Hezekiah (II Kgs 18; Isa 36); but by divine intervention, as predicted by Isaiah (Isa 37:21-38), Sennacherib's army was so weakened that he had to give up the seige and leave again. Hezekiah engaged in missionary activities in the northern half of the land. The chronicler tells us that these met with some success in Galilee but not in Ephraim (II Chr 30:1-11).

Assyrian power was so complete it was hard for Judah to escape its influence. Consequently Manasseh, the son of Hezekiah, capitulated to the heathen forces and built altars for Baal worship. He even set up the practice of idolatry in the house of the Lord. He made his sons pass through the fire, used enchantments and dealt with familiar spirits, and tradition tells that he martyred the prophet Isaiah. Following the death of Ashurbanipal (*c.* 630 B.C.), Assyrian power began to wane.

Josiah, the new king of Judah, came to the throne with a strong instinct to bring about reform. He too extended his revival into the N, especially Galilee. In keeping with the instructions of the book of the law which Hilkiah the priest found, Josiah kept the Passover and destroyed the cult at Bethel which was in active competition with the temple. Josiah also had visions of restoring the political sovereignty of Judah over all the land. So when Pharaoh Necho marched through the land to help the dying embers of the Assyrian Empire, Josiah challenged him at Meggido, but lost his life in the battle.

Josiah's son Jehoahaz was deposed by Pharaoh Necho, who set up Jehoiakim as a puppet king. Jehoiakim became the vassal of the new Babylonian monarch Nebuchadnezzar. In due course he rebelled against the Chaldeans, but soon died, and his 18-year-old son Jehoiachin was taken into captivity by Nebuchadnezzar The Babylonians carried away 10,000 captives, all the mighty men of valor, the craftsmen and smiths, and left only the poorest of the land (II Kgs 24:14).

Nebuchadnezzar now set up Zedekiah, Jehoiachin's uncle, as king. He was destined to be the last king of the house of David. Provoked by another rebellion Nebuchadnezzar laid seige to the city of Jerusalem, and in Zedekiah's eleventh year famine prevailed so severely that Zedekiah made an attempt to escape. He was captured and witnessed the slaying of his sons before his own eyes were gouged out. The house of the Lord and all the city were burned. Not a single important city of Judah was left unburned.

At Lachish pieces of broken pottery have been found inscribed with messages from various army officials, which indicate something of the restriction of movement experienced by the Judean army during the years preceding the fall of Jerusalem (ANET, p. 321). Administrative documents found at the Ishtar gate at Babylon reveal how Jehoiachin and his five sons and other captives with him were provided for by the Babylonians (ANET, p. 308). Indeed, the post-Exilic Jewish community in Babylon fared well for many years and became a much more important Jewish community than that in Judea.

With the fall of Jerusalem in 586 B.C. Judah ceased to be a kingdom and became a small province of the Arabaya satrapy of the Persian Empire. Later, Zerubbabel, a descendant of David, became the civil ruler of this province, but never again did a Judean king of the house of David rule in Jerusalem. By NT times the messianic hope for restoration of the monarchy under the house of David ran high, but the NT teaches that this aspect of God's promise to David still awaits fulfillment (Lk 1:32-33; Acts 2:30-31; 15:15-16; Rom 11:26).

See Chronology, OT; Judah; Israel, Kingdom of.

E. B. S.

JUDAIZERS (jōō'dĭ-īz'ẽrs). An extrabiblical term for those who acted like Jews and/or sought so to influence others, based on Paul's charge that Peter's attitude would force Gentiles "to Judaize" (Gr. *'ioudaizein,* "to live like Jews," Gal 2:14, RSV).

Commentaries refer to men as Judaizers who sought to enforce Jewish circumcision and other legalisms upon Gentiles, e.g., the "false brethren" who wanted to bring the whole church into the bondage of the law (Gal 2:4), and those who taught "unless you are circumcised . . . you cannot be saved" (Acts 15:1 ff., RSV). Paul attacked Judaizers in Galatia who "would compel you to be circumcised" (Gal 6:12, RSV). In a few places (Acts 11:2; Gal 2:12; Tit 1:10) "they of the circumcision" seems to refer not to Jews generally but Judaizers specifically (cf. RSV's "circumcision party").

They may have taught that one had to become Jewishly legalistic to receive grace, and did teach that one had to live legalistically despite grace. The Jerusalem council (Acts 15; perhaps Gal 2:1 - 10?) supported Paul as over against those who carried their scruples to the extreme of Judaizing.

W. A. A.

JUDAS (jōō'dȧs). The name is so spelled in the NT after Gr. *Ioudas,* for the Heb. name Judah (*q.v.*). The latter comes from the Heb. root *yādâ* meaning "to give thanks, laud, praise."

1. Judah the son of Jacob and father of the tribe that was known by that name (Gen 35:23), called Judas in NT (Mt 1:2 - 3).

2. Judas (Jude), one of four brothers of Jesus, named along with James, Joses, and Simon as sons of Mary (Mk 6:3; Mt 13:55). Probably author of Epistle of Jude (*q.v.*).

3. Judas Lebbaeus (Mt 10:3) surnamed Thaddaeus (Mt 3:18), one of the 12 apostles, "not Iscariot" (Jn 14:22). *See* Lebbaeus. He is called "Judas of James" (Lk 6:16; Acts 1:13) which is translated "the son of James" in both the RSV and NASB.

4. A Galilean zealot who stirred up rebellion among the Jews *c.* A.D. 6 over the right of the Romans to impose a direct tax upon the Jews. He was destroyed and his followers dispersed by Cyrenius (*q.v.*), proconsul of Syria (cf. Acts 5:37; also Jos *Ant.* xviii.1.6; xx.5.2; *War* ii.8.1; 18:8; vii.8.1). Although his movement failed, there grew out of it the party of the Zealots (*q.v.*).

5. A man with whom Paul lodged in Damascus on "the street called straight" (Acts 9:11).

6. A man surnamed Barsabas and a member of the delegation sent from the Jerusalem church to the church at Antioch in Syria (Acts 15:22, 27, 32). He and Silas had the gift of prophecy with which they encouraged the brethren.

7. There are at least five men who bear this name in the Apocryphal literature.

8. Judas Iscariot. Gr. *Iskariōtēs,* meaning "inhabitant of Kerioth," derived from the Heb. *'ish,* "man," plus *qᵉrîyôt,* hence "man of Kerioth." Kerioth is probably to be identified with the modern Khirbet el-Qaryatein, located *c.* 18 miles NE of Beer-sheba, halfway between Maon and Arad, *c.* four and a half miles S of Tell-Ma'in.

He is designated by the stigma "who also betrayed him" (Mt 10:4; Mk 3:19) and "which was the traitor" (Lk 6:16; cf. Jn 18:2, 5) in the list of the 12 apostles chosen by Christ. At the same time he is also called "one of the twelve" (Mk 14:10, 20; Jn 6:71; 12:4). There is no mention of him prior to his choice by Christ.

His position. Judas was appointed treasurer for Christ and the apostolic band (Jn 12:4 - 6; 13:29). He embezzled the funds under his care and became a thief (Jn 12:6). His true character, with its avarice and covetousness, revealed itself at the anointing of Jesus by Mary with the expensive alabaster box of ointment. He pretended, along with that of the other disciples, that his concern had to do with such wastage and protested that it could have been sold for 300 pence and given to the poor (Jn 12:1 - 8; cf. Mt 26:6 - 13; Mk 14:3 - 9).

His career. Though he became a disciple and follower of Jesus, Judas did not accept Him as his Lord and Saviour. He never called Him more than Rabbi (Mt 26:25, NASB). Judas expected Christ to establish an earthly kingdom in which he would have an important position. Till that happened he was happy to enrich himself from the common funds. It undoubtedly troubled him to hear the Lord declare that His was a spiritual kingdom which none could enter except by the Father's enabling (Jn 6:44, 63 - 65). The refusal of Christ to accept an earthly kingdom angered Judas as did Christ's periodic reference to His death. The final incident which drove Judas to betray Jesus was the expensive anointing at Bethany coupled with Christ's clear declarations: "She did it for my burial" (Mt 26:12); "She is come aforehand to anoint my body to the burying" (Mk 14:8); and His admonition, "Let her alone: against the day of my burying hath she kept this" (Jn 12:7). Seeing the end of his hopes and plans, Judas determined to sell his Master for what he could get.

His responsibility. How can we reconcile Christ's knowledge of Judas' character and perfidy, together with the OT prophecies concerning Judas (Ps 41:9; 69:25; 109:8), with any true responsibility on Judas' part for his own action? Two things can be said.

First, Christ's concern. Though Christ chose Judas knowing he would betray Him, still He showed him constant compassion, gave him a complete revelation of Himself and many warnings. He humbly washed Judas' feet along with the other disciples and then said: "Ye are clean, but not all" (Jn 13:10). He sadly told His disciples at the last supper that one of them would betray Him. When they were all bewildered and asked, "Is it I?" Jesus whispered to John that it was the one to whom He should give the sop—that morsel given as an honor by the host at a feast (Jn 13:21 - 26). But this sign of love was of no avail. From none of His great messages and not even from the work of evangelism, when He sent out the Twelve (Mt 10:1 - 11:1; Lk 9:1 - 6), did Christ exclude Judas.

From time to time, even from the first, Jesus had warned Judas. For example, when many had deserted and this brought forth Peter's confession, Jesus openly said, "Have not I chosen you twelve, and one of you is a devil?" (Jn 6:67 - 70). He spoke of the dangers of avarice, covetousness and hypocrisy (Mt 6:20; Lk 12:1 - 3, 15 ff., 22 f.; Mk 7:17, 21 - 22). But it all fell upon a seared conscience. It was surely not Christ's fault that Judas refused to turn from his wicked way. Judas is an example of what sin does in the life of the unsaved unless God exercises sovereign saving grace.

Second, the true nature of prophecy and foreordination. How can Judas be condemned for what he did if it had already been foreordained and foretold (Ps 41:9; 69:25; 109:8)? Judas acted in entire freedom. He chose to steal from the common funds; he chose to betray his Master for the 30 pieces of silver paid for a slave (Ex 21:32). He should have known the prophecy of Zechariah (Zech 11:12). If he did, he ignored it. God foresaw this action on Judas' part and chose to let him act according to his fallen freedom—He foreordained it be so. There was, therefore, no curtailment of Judas' freedom or his responsibility, any more than there is of any other man's.

Judas' end. Before the supper the devil had already put it in Judas' heart to betray Jesus (Jn 13:2) and as soon as Judas took the sop "Satan entered into him" (Jn 13:27).Hurrying to the chief priests, he said that he would lead them to Christ and identify Him with a kiss. Since he knew the secret of the garden he was able to lead a great multitude with swords and staves from the chief priests, and coming up to Jesus "kissed him" (Mt 26:49; Mk 14:45). Jesus reached out in a last word of love and said, "Friend, why art thou come?" (Mt 26:50).

After Judas saw Christ condemned to be crucified, he was filled with remorse (Mt 27:3 f.), and coming to the chief priests and elders he confessed his crime, saying, "I have betrayed innocent blood" (v.4). Then he went out and committed suicide by hanging himself. When Peter says, "This man purchased a field with the reward of iniquity; and falling headlong, he burst asunder in the midst" (Acts 1:18), we can accept Edersheim's reconciliation of the two accounts in Matthew and Acts: In a figurative sense Judas bought the field, the Jews considering him the buyer in that he provided the money they used for it (*Life and Times of Jesus the Messiah,* II, 575 f.).

Many reasons have been given for Judas' actions, such as the following: (1) He was a victim of circumstances. (2) He was predestined to this course and chosen for this deed and, therefore, powerless. (3) He was a deluded soul who thought that by betrayal he could force Jesus to exert His power miraculously and take control. (4) He was a true friend of Jesus trying merely to disillusion Him of His messianic claims. (5) He was a Jewish patriot and thought it better one die than the nation perish. (6) He was a real hero who as Christ's friend tried to save Him from misguided allegiance to the God of the OT (cf. E. S. Bates, *The Friend of Jesus,* New York: Simon & Schuster, 1928). All such explanations are inadequate or in error and leave us unsatisfied.

Judas made his decisions freely, as any other man. Money is "a root of all evil," of evil of every kind (I Tim 6:10), and covetousness as his besetting sin led from thievery to hypocrisy, and finally to betrayal of the Lord of glory for a handful of money.

One thing more must be said. Karl Barth pleads for Judas' final salvation, arguing that though he sinned, he sinned no more grievously than Peter when he denied Christ thrice. After all, Barth continues, he did repent according to Scripture and this is all that is required of the sinner (*Church Dogmatics,* Edinburgh: T. & T. Clark, 1957, Vol. II, 2, 458-506). Why does Barth reason in this manner when Scripture says he went to his own place (Acts 1:25), and the psalmist pronounces upon him the most awful curse issued against the wicked recorded in the Bible (Ps 109:6-20)? According to Barth, predestination is not an individual matter. It is centered entirely in Christ. He is the rejected and the elected one, and all are both rejected and elected in Him! If Judas is lost, particularly when he "repented," then Christocentric election fails.

The traditional Aceldama or field of blood bought with Judas' betrayal money (Ac 1:19). It is located just east of Jerusalem along the Kidron. HFV

The evangelical Christian must reject such a basis for a case for Judas' salvation since it conflicts with the prophetic curse upon Judas in the psalm, removes all necessity for believing in Christ to be saved, and leads to the false doctrine of the salvation of all men, called universal salvation or ultimate reconciliation. Moreover, repentance involves a "turning" and may in Judas' case simply describe a revulsion over a reprehensible deed and need not also comprehend a personal commitment to Christ.

For the term "son of perdition" as applied to Judas Iscariot, *see* Perdition, Son of.

Bibliography. A. B. Bruce, *The Training of the Twelve,* New York: Armstrong, 1902, Chap. XXIII. Alfred Edersheim, *The Life and Times of Jesus the Messiah,* 2 vols., New York: Longsmans, Green & Co., 1901.

R. A. K.

JUDE (jōōd). Called Judas in the Gr. It is a striking fact that the writer of the last NT letter, the epistle of the apostasy, should have borne the same name as the traitor and greatest apostate, last named of the Twelve (Mt 10:4).

As "brother of James," the Lord's brother (Jude 1; Gal 1:19), Jude was also a brother of the Lord, one of His "mother's children" (Ps 69:8) who are named in Mt 13:55; Mk 6:3. He is therefore not to be confused with the Judas of Jn 14:22 (cf. Lk 6:16), who is called Thaddaeus and Lebbaeus in Mt 10:3. In cherishing the words spoken by the apostles (Jude 17), he clearly implied that he was not one of them.

Jude was characterized by humility, claiming only to be James' brother and a bondslave (lit.) of Jesus Christ; by diligence (v.3), which may have been one reason why the Holy Spirit selected him; by a knowledge of revealed truth (vv. 5-7, 11, 17), and by being chosen as the recipient of truth not previously recorded by the pen of inspiration (vv.9, 14-15).

S. M. C.

JUDE, EPISTLE OF. The last epistle of the NT was written by Judas (Gr.), the brother of James. They probably were the brothers of our Lord (Mt 13:55; Mk 6:3; *see* Judas; Jude; James). It is coincidental that the author's name, like a title, stands as the first word of the only book devoted entirely to the theme of apostasy, since Judas was also the name of the greatest apostate.

Date and Destination

[The similarity of the epistle of Jude to II Pet 2 raises the question of literary dependence. If we accept II Peter as a genuine writing of Peter (*see* Peter, Second Epistle of), then Jude is probably later, after the fall of Jerusalem (v. 17 refers to the apostles in the past). But it is not likely that Jude is directly dependent on II Peter 2. Most likely both epistles derive from a common tradition of preaching against false teachers. Two grandsons of a certain Judas (probably this Jude) were summoned by the emperor Domitian (A.D. 81-96) when he was informed that they belonged to the dynastic house of David. He dismissed them when he found they were merely poor farmers and no threat to Rome (Eusebius, Hist. Eccl. iii. 19:1–20:6). This event suggests the importance of Jude before the reign of Domitian, since he himself was not involved in the emperor's inquiry.

[It seems clear that this book was written with more regard for Jewish Christian readers than was II Peter. The Exodus (v.5) and OT figures such as Michael, Cain, and Korah's sons (vv. 9, 11) are mentioned in Jude but not in II Peter. Also, the Jewish apocalypse of First Enoch is quoted as prophecy (vv. 14-15). Thus, as Reicke (p. 191) argues, the audience Jude had in mind probably consisted of Jewish Christians. – Ed.]

Purpose

As the Acts of the Apostles begins the history of the church on earth, so Jude, in Acts of the Apostates, brings it to a close, and prepares the reader for the judgments of the book of Revelation.

The inspiration of the epistle is declared in v. 3. While the author was preparing to write about our common salvation, a divine compulsion came upon him to write instead about contending for the apostolic faith against an early antinomian form of Gnosticism (*q.v.*). The word "needful" (v. 3) is rendered "necessity" in I Cor 9:16.

Content

An astonishing sweep of revelation moves the reader from sin in the dawn of human history (v. 11) to its future judgment at Christ's return (v. 15). It speaks of the sea and the stars (v. 13), of eternal fire and everlasting darkness (vv. 7, 13), of the unseen world of angelic activity (vv. 6, 9).

New truths revealed through Jude include details about the sin of fallen angels (v. 6), Michael's dispute with the devil (v. 9), and the antediluvian prophecy of Enoch (vv. 14-15). In citing the book of Enoch and referring to Michael's contest known only from the Assumption of Moses, Jude was not endorsing pseudepigraphical literature. Rather he was employing literature used by the false teachers in question in order to silence them with their own material. Jude merely held that the passages he quoted contain remnants of truth (cf. Paul in Acts 17:28; Gal 3:19; II Tim 3:8; Tit 1:12 f.). *See* Michael.

Subject matter is clustered in orderly fashion about a common center. The salutation matches the benediction. Lest believers fear that they too may fall away from the truth, words of tender love and assurance appear in the opening and closing sentences. Salvation is the theme of vv. 3 and 23. Contending for the faith (v. 3) stands in contrast with building upon the faith (v. 20). "Remember the OT" describes the section beginning with v. 5; "remember the NT" describes the section beginning with v. 17. Apostasy in the supernatural realm (v. 9) is matched by apostasy in the natural realm (vv. 12-13).

In the heart of Jude (v. 11) appears an ancient trio of men who perfectly illustrate the three outstanding characteristics of apostasy described in vv. 4, 16, 19, which are further illustrated by three corporate examples in vv. 5-7. Verse 11 is typical of the progress of thought found throughout the epistle. Apostates enter upon a wrong way, rush headlong down that way, and perish at its end. The wrong way starts with wandering, ends with open rebellion (v.11, RSV). The *way* of Cain contrasts with Christ the way, the *error* of Balaam with Christ the truth, the *perishing* of Core (Korah, *q.v.*) with Christ the life (Jn 14:6).

The fourfold rule for Christian living given in vv. 20-21 ties Jude into other NT books. The Christian is to be building, praying, keeping, and looking. Help for soul winners is found in a threefold classification of unsaved persons (vv. 22-23, RSV). Some need compassionate tenderness because they have sincere doubts, some demand urgent boldness because they are close to the fire, some require cautious ministration lest their form of sin contaminate the believer.

In a glorious benediction, Jude suggests the rapture of the Church by suddenly passing from the possibility of present stumbling on a pilgrim pathway to the presentation of the people of God, by their Saviour and Lord, before the presence of His glory in heaven (v. 24).

Outline

I. Salutation, 1-2
II. Occasion and Purpose: Exhortation to Defend the Faith, 3-4
III. Illustrations of the Necessity of Defending the Faith, 5-16
   A. Three historic examples of judgment on corporate apostasy, 5-7
   B. Historic examplesand descriptions of false teachers, 8-16
IV. Charge to True Christians: How to Defend the Faith, 17-23
V. Conclusion: A Doxology, 24-25

Bibliography. Charles Bigg, *The Epistles of St. Peter and St. Jude,* ICC, New York: Scribner's, 1901. F. F. Bruce, "Jude, Epistle of," NBD, pp. 675 f. J. B. Mayor, *Epistle of St. Jude and the Second Epistle of St. Peter,* London: Macmillan, 1907. James Moffatt, *The General Epistles,* MNT, Garden City: Doubleday, Doran & Co., 1928. Bo Reicke, *The Epistles of James, Peter, and Jude,* Anchor Bible, Garden City: Doubleday, 1964, pp. 189-219. Robert Robertson, "The General Epistle of Jude," NBC, pp. 1161-1167.

S. M. C.

JUDEA (jo͞o-dē′*ȧ*). In Persian times Judea was a tiny province of the Arabaya Satrapy lying S of Samaria and corresponding approximately to the earlier kingdom of Judah except that the coastal cities were excluded. The term Judea (*Ioudaia*) represents the Hellenizing process which took place following the conquests of Alexander the Great. A network of Hellenistic cities surrounded the province of Judea, and little by little as the country was Hellenized cities took Greek names; many of the upper class and educated Jews encouraged this. II Macc 6:8 speaks of Hellenistic cities within the boundaries of Judea. It is not surprising, then, to find the territory itself called Judea, a Gr. equivalent of the Aram. word for Judah, *y*ᵉ*hûd*.

Geographically the territory has natural boundaries on all sides except the N. On the E is the steep ascent from the Jordan and the Dead Sea with dry chalky soil forming the barren wilderness of Judea or Jeshimon. On the W the Shephelah foothills meet the slopes of the central mountains at a moat-like depression which continues around the S end of Judea to join the chalk wilderness on the E. In the S there is a sudden drop of *c*. 650 feet about halfway between Hebron and Beer-sheba. In the days of Judas Maccabeus (165-161 B.C.) the garrison at Beth-Zur was the S frontier until he took Hebron and generally overthrew the Idumeans (I Macc 5:3, 65). The N frontier was even less defined, for here there was no protective valley. From early OT times the small tribe of Benjamin marked the N boundary of Judea (Judah).

The Maccabeans under Jonathan extended these boundaries in all directions so that when Pompey, the Roman conqueror, entered Jewish territory the northernmost town in Jewish hands was at Koraea in the Wadi Fari'a. The Romans appointed various Asmonean rulers over Judea until Herod the Great, who *c*. 40 B.C. was declared by the senate to be king of Judea. Following Herod's death Judea, until A.D. 64, was under Roman procurators (imperial governors) except for the brief reign of Herod Agrippa (Acts 26) who was proclaimed king by Claudius Caesar in A.D. 41.

The term Judea may occasionally be used to mean all the region occupied by the Jewish nation. Several of Luke's references seem to be the most conclusive, e.g., "throughout all Judea, beginning from Galilee to this place" (Lk 23:5, RSV; cf. Acts 10:37). Acts 26:20 could better be translated "the whole Jewish country," while Mt 19:1 (cf. Mk 10:1) should not be taken to imply that there was any land E of Jordan that was considered a part of Judea. This passage should be translated, "unto the territory of Judea adjacent to Jordan." The wider sense for Judea, i.e., including Samaria and Galilee, seems to be employed by secular writers of NT times, among them being Strabo, Tacitus and Philo.

See Judah, Kingdom of.

E. B. S.

The Wilderness of Judea. HFV

JUDGE, JUDGING

God As Judge

God is the supreme and absolute Judge of all the earth (Gen 18:25; Ps 94:2; Rom 3:6). God's right to be Judge is based primarily on three divine attributes: (1) God's absolute righteousness (Ps 9:8; 96:13; 98:2, 9); (2) God's infinite knowledge of the secrets of man's life (Job 34:21-28; Isa 28:17; Rom 2:16); (3) God's irresistible power to bestow rewards or inflict punishment (Ps 11:5-7; Rom 2:1-16).

God's throne is eternally set for judging mankind "righteously" (Ps 9:4, 7-8; 89:14; 97:2). His unimpeachable character makes any kind of error in His judgments utterly impossible (Gen 18:25; Deut 32:4; Job 8:3; 34:10, 12; Rom 3:5). God always judges "according to truth" (Rom 2:2). He "will render to every man according to his deeds" (Rom 2:6; Rev 20:12). His judgments are not vitiated by such human faults as favoritism (Rom 2:11; I Pet 1:17), superficial appearance (I Sam 16:7; Jn 7:24), fleshly standards (Jn 8:15), or bribe-taking (II Chr 19:7). Thus God's will, not man's, becomes the standard of all judgment. *See* Will of God.

Though the wicked may seem to escape for a while the righteous judgment of God (Ps 10; 73) as they ignore God's present goodness toward them (Rom 2:3-4; Acts 14:16-17), yet a day is inexorably set in the divine plan (Rom 2:1-16) for the judgment of all men (Mt 11:22-24; 25:31-46; Acts 17:31; II Pet 2:9; 3:7; Rev 20:11-15).

Examples of God's judgments may be seen in the following instances: (1) the judgment pronounced upon Adam and Eve and upon all mankind in Eden (Gen 3; Rom 5:12); (2) the destruction of the ancient world by flood (Gen 6-8; Lk 17:26-27; II Pet 2:5; 3:5-6); (3) the destruction of Sodom and Gomorrah (Gen 19; Lk 17:28-30; II Pet 2:6); (4) the destruction of Egypt's army (Ex 14); (5) the punishments visited upon Israel at Sinai (Ex 32), in the wilderness (Num 14; 16; 25), and at many subsequent times in her history; (6) the definitive judgment upon Israel for her rejection of her Messiah (Lk 21:20-24; I Thess 2:14-16); (7) the final punishment upon all those who reject the Lord Jesus Christ (Jn 3:36; 5:24; II Thess 1:8-9; Heb 10:26-31; 12:25; II Pet 2:1-10; 3:7).

The Judge in Israel's Judiciary System

The following stages of development may be clearly seen in Israel's history:

The patriarchal period. Judicial functions were largely in the hands of the family head during this period (Gen 21-22; 38:24). God's law, although not officially promulgated as at Sinai, was nevertheless known to the patriarchs. This knowledge was derived from the general knowledge of God's will given to all mankind (Rom 1:18-23), from God's law written upon man's heart (Rom 2:14-15), and from specific legislation given to man (e.g., Gen 9:5-6). Thus the family head became the principal agent in God's plan for transmission of concepts regarding righteousness and justice from one generation to another (Gen 18:19). Back of all this was the resident conviction that the Judge of all the earth shall do right (Gen 18:25).

The early Mosaic period. Moses, fully prepared by his extensive knowledge of worldly matters (Acts 7:21-22), was ready for the office of judge that soon was to fall upon him as leader of the people of God redeemed from Egypt. Even while in Egypt, however, he was accused of assuming this office presumptuously as he sought to render justice with his own hands (Ex 2:11-15; Acts 7:23-28, 35). Nevertheless, the exodus of the people of Israel from Egypt thrust upon them the imperative need for an authoritative judge to adjudicate lawsuits and disputes. This need was fully met by Moses, who was universally recognized by the Israelites as the mouthpiece of God, i.e., as the agent through whom the will of God was made known to the people (Ex 18:15; Num 9:8; 27:5). Thus, after the pattern of Moses, the judgeship in Israel was invested with divine rights that constituted the human judge as God's representative of justice on earth (cf. Ex 21:6, ASV; II Chr 19:6; Ps 82:1, 6; Jn 10:34).

The Jethro episode at Sinai. Jethro, Moses' father-in-law, instinctively sensing the burden that human nature could not long endure with-

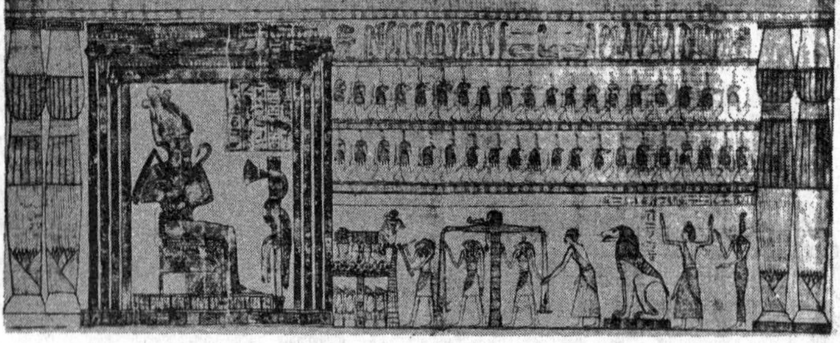

A judgment scene, "weighing of the heart" after death, from the Egyptian *Book of the Dead,* as pictured on an ancient papyrus. ORINST

out help, made some very judicious suggestions to Moses for the betterment of the legal system among the Israelites (Ex 18:17 - 26). The basic elements in Jethro's proposed revision were these: (1) a series of ascending courts; (2) an implicit "supreme court" (in Moses himself); (3) the accessibility of the courts to all the people in "all seasons"; (4) an instructional program regarding the nature and content of the laws; (5) qualifications for those entrusted with the office of judge.

Moses saw immediately the wisdom of Jethro's suggestions; they were all adopted as integral parts of Israel's system of jurisprudence. Subsequent history and legislation, even while at Sinai, simply supplied the details of Jethro's epoch-making wise counsel.

The Sinaitic legislation. The law of Sinai strengthened the revisions suggested by Jethro in the following ways: (1) by outlining more specifically the qualifications of judges (Deut 1:13 - 18; 16:18 - 20); (2) by giving preeminence to the tribe of Levi as custodians and interpreters of the law (Deut 17:8 - 13, 18 - 20); (3) by giving specific principles for the guidance of the court in rendering a verdict (Deut 19:15 - 21; 21:1 - 9; 25:1 - 3).

However, it must be admitted that there were allowable fluctuations in Israel's system of jurisprudence. There were cases, for example, when the congregation of all Israel became the absolute judge (Num 35:12, 22 - 28). At a later date, even the people could veto the unwise oath of their king (I Sam 14:24 - 46). It seems quite certain, in periods of Israel's history after Sinai, that historical and political factors influenced materially the kind of justice prevalent in any particular era.

The period of the judges. This period, graphically described in the book of Judges (*q.v.*), constitutes a transition from the rule of Moses and Joshua to the rule of kings in Israel. God raised up during this period persons especially endowed to judge a part or all of Israel (Jud 2:16 - 23; 3:9 - 10; I Sam 12:9 - 11; II Sam 7:11). The following statements may be made concerning these judges: (1) They were raised up by God in times of crisis (Jud 2:16 - 23; cf. Ps 106:43 - 45; Acts 13:20). (2) They were especially empowered by the Holy Spirit (Jud 3:10; 13:25; 14:19; cf. Num 11:25 - 29; 24:2). (3) They continued in office until the time of their death (Jud 2:19; I Sam 4:18; 7:15). (4) They rejected the temptation to establish hereditary rulership over Israel (Jud 8:22 - 23). (5) They considered their judicial functions as involving them in spiritual leadership over the people (I Chr 17:6; cf. II Sam 7:7).

The periods of the united and divided kingdoms. It is indeed difficult to trace any consistent system of jurisprudence during the long period from Samuel, the last judge, to the end of the OT dispensation. Many of the safeguards in the Sinaitic legislation against the perversion of justice were undoubtedly neglected under wicked kings or in times of religious declension.

The columned entrance to the basilica at the forum of Pompeii, where civil and commercial court cases were heard. HFV

The prophets often complain against such perversion (Isa 1:23; 5:23; 10:1 - 2; Amos 5:12; 6:12; Mic 3:9 - 11; 7:3).

Although Samuel had performed his duties as judge impeccably, and had even established a system of circuit courts (I Sam 7:15 - 16), nevertheless, his sons corrupted justice (8:1 - 3) and thus gave added weight to the people's desire to change from judgeship to kingship (8:4 - 22; 12:1 - 25).

However, even after the kings became the absolute judges, local or subordinate courts, after the precedent set by Samuel, were established by David and Solomon (I Chr 23:3 - 4; 26:29 - 32). It is to Solomon's credit that he sensed the need of divine wisdom in judging Israel (I Kgs 3:9). This wisdom was soon manifested in a most difficult case brought before him for adjudication (I Kgs 3:16 - 28). Nevertheless, some kings were notoriously wicked in the execution of justice (I Kgs 21:1 - 16; II Kgs 21:16). Lawlessness arose spontaneously in such times (Hab 1:2 - 4).

Both David (II Sam 1:15 - 16; 4:9 - 12) and Solomon (I Kgs 2:5 - 9, 13 - 46) pronounced sentences and executed offenders in a very decisive manner. The precedent set by these two notable kings probably became the standard of justice throughout most of OT history (e.g., II Kgs 11:12 - 20), even in the case of unjust judgments (e.g., I Kgs 21:7 - 16).

Jehoshaphat, it appears, was a most efficient king in the system of jurisprudence which he established throughout his kingdom (II Chr 19:4 - 11). It is even probable that the courts he placed in "the fortified cities of Judah, city by city" (v.5, ASV) were what we would call today superior courts. Jerusalem itself became, in this system, a kind of supreme court, with Amariah, the high priest, as chief justice (vv. 8 - 11). Thus Jehoshaphat finalized to a large extent the OT judicial system, a system which found its ultimate fulfillment in the Jewish Sanhedrin of NT times (e.g., Acts 5:27 - 41; 6:10 - 15; 23:1 - 10).

Christ As Judge

The various aspects of Christ's judgeship may be set forth in the following manner:

As messianically endowed. The prophets depict the coming Messiah as possessing all the attributes of a true judge (Ps 89:14; 97:2; Isa 11:1-5). This One was destined to bring in "everlasting righteousness" (Dan 9:24) in a world where justice could hardly be found (Isa 59:1-21).

As legislator of true judgment. One of the first acts performed by Christ after His mission on earth had been inaugurated was to set forth the true meaning of the law of God. This was done in His Sermon on the Mount (Mt 5-7), in which He categorically corrected the false dogmas of the Jews imposed upon the law of God. Christ's whole ministry was one of judgment upon the Jews for their perversion of God's law (e.g., Mt 15:1-20).

As non-participant in man's litigations. Christ refused to become a judge in matters affecting man's material possessions (Lk 12: 13-14). Even while before Pilate, He refrained from any involvement in the case against Him on the ground that His kingdom was "not of this world" (Jn 18:33-39).

As refiner of false judges. This implication of Christ's judgeship had prophetic antecedents (Mal 3:1-6). With all the passion of a true judge, Christ pronounced devastating judgments against the Pharisees and other leaders of the Jews as false judges "sitting in Moses' seat" (Mt 23; Lk 12:57-59; Jn 7:24).

As sent to save rather than to judge. Christ's advent to earth was designed to bring salvation to men, not to judge men (Jn 3:16-21; 12:46-47). This does not mean, however, that Christ refused to judge evil now (Jn 8:15-16). But the present time is definitely "the day of salvation" (II Cor 6:2).

As custodian of the Father's judgment. Christ plainly taught that all judgment had been committed unto Him by His heavenly Father (Jn 5:22, 30). Even now, before the future judgments, there is a decisive exercise of Christ's definitive judgment against those who refuse to accept Him as Messiah and Lord (Lk 19:41-44; 21:20-24; Jn 9:39). Such men are "judged already" (Jn 3:18; 5:24).

As final judge. Christ will be the judge of all mankind (Mt 7:21-23; 25:36-46). Christ Himself will be the righteous judge (II Tim 4:8) in that last day when His word will be the basis of man's judgment (Jn 12:48). He is the One "ordained of God to be the Judge of the living and the dead" (Acts 10:42, ASV; cf. 17:31; II Tim 4:1; I Pet 4:5).

The Christian As Judge and As Judged

The various aspects of this subject may be summed up thus:

Censorious judgment. This kind of criticism comes under the prohibition expressed by Christ in Mt 7:1-4 and Lk 6:37-42. "Judge not" (the aorist negative imperative in the Gr.) states a definitive prohibition against the pernicious habit of criticizing others while passing over our own faults (cf. Jas 4:11-12).

The Basilica Julia at Corinth, where Christians probably launched lawsuits against other Christians. HFV

Civil litigations. Two sides of this subject are presented in the NT. On the one side, Paul was certainly justified in demanding as a civil right before Roman authorities his complete vindication against the false charges of the Jews (Acts 25:9-12). This was at least a minimum benefit of his Roman citizenship (Acts 16:37-39; 22:27-29; cf. Rom 13:1-7). On the other side, Christians are urged to undergo injustice rather than to engage in lawsuits against other Christians before unbelievers (I Cor 6:1, 5-8). Paul's case before the Roman authorities was entirely different from the situation existing among believers in the Corinthian church. Paul's appeal to Caesar was thrust upon him as the only alternative to almost certain death at Jerusalem. The Christians at Corinth were in no such exigency.

Questions of conscience. The following principles may clarify this somewhat difficult area of Christian conduct: (1) The freedom of the new man in Christ must be maintained (Jn 8:32, 36; Rom 8:15; Gal 2:4; 5:1, 13; Col 2:16-23). (2) This freedom, however, must not degenerate into license or licentiousness (Gal 5:13; I Pet 2:16; II Pet 2:7, 10, 14; Jude 4). (3) The sometimes dubious or debatable area between freedom and licentiousness may be traversed by Christian love for "the weaker brother" (Rom 14:1-23; I Cor 8:9-13; 10:23-33; Gal 5:13-15), by a proper concern for one's own weakness (Gal 6:1) and proneness toward superiority (Jas 2:8-13), and by a proper application of Christ's "judge not" (Mt 7:1-5; cf. Jas 4:11-12).

Self-judgment. The Christian is called upon not only to judge or examine himself (II Cor 13:5) but also to realize that God Himself is the Examiner (I Thess 2:4; cf. Ps 139:1-6, 23). This self-judgment should be a part of the spiritual preparation for the Lord's Supper (I Cor 11:27-34). When properly conducted by the assistance of the Holy Spirit (Rom 8:26-27), this self-examination puts the Lord's Supper in its true perspective and thus obviates the divine judgment visited upon those who fail to discriminate between the ordinary meal and the Lord's Supper.

Judgments concerning faith and practice. Christians are required to "examine everything carefully" and to "hold fast to that which is good" (I Thess 5:21, NASB). They are also obligated to "test the spirits to see whether they are from God" (I Jn 4:1, NASB). Even in Christian gatherings they must "pass judgment" on what they hear (I Cor 14:29, NASB). The Corinthian Christians were commanded to pass immediate judgment on the immorality existing in their membership (I Cor 5:1-8). Even the passing stranger is not to be entertained if it is ascertained that he is not true in the faith (II Jn 10-11). And an anathema must be pronounced against those who would introduce a different kind of gospel (Gal 1:9). The principle back of all this required spiritual discrimination is that the Christian should never bring the Lord's judgment upon himself because of the things in doctrine or in practice which he approves (Rom 14:22).

The spiritual man of I Cor 2:14-15. This man is above the judgment of the unregenerate man for the simple reason that the two men are on different levels of spiritual insight and ability. The unregenerate man is a child of the devil (Jn 8:44; I Jn 3:10-12), devoid of the Holy Spirit (Jude 19), spiritually dead (Eph 2:1, 5; Col 2:13) and spiritually blind (Mt 23:16, 24; Jn 9:39-41), and a willing captive of sin (Rom 6:6, 16-23; II Pet 2:14). Thus such a person is morally unable to pass judgment on the spiritual man who has been resurrected into a new life in Christ (Col 3:1-3), indwelt by the Holy Spirit (Rom 8:11) and by Christ (II Cor 13:5), and completely transformed as a new creature (II Cor 5:17).

Judgment in abeyance. In I Cor 4:3-5 Paul speaks of three judgments: (1) by "man's judgment," i.e., by a day in any human court (NASB) or by the world's public opinion; (2) by his own conscience, which while not condemning him is still inadequate to justify (i.e., definitively approve) his stewardship; and (3) by the Lord Jesus, who at His second coming will render full judgment. Thus the believer is urged to judge nothing, i.e., to pass judgment on no one else's ministry, until that future event. All the unknown factors that now motivate man's actions will then be revealed by the Lord; and then each man, beholding the justice of the verdict rendered, will have his praise from God (cf. Jas 5:9).

The Christian and future judgments. The Scriptures reveal a threefold relationship of the believer to future judgments: (1) as one who will be judged to determine his rewards (I Cor 3:11-15; II Cor 5:10; II Tim 4:1, 8), but not concerning his salvation (Jn 3:18; 5:24); (2) as one who will participate in the judgment of the world and of angels (I Cor 6:2-3; cf. Dan 7:18, 22, 27; Mt 19:28; Rev 2:26-27; 3:21); (3) as one who will not be judged with the wicked before the Great White Throne of God, because his name is found written in the book of life (Rev 20:11-15). *See* Life, Book of; Judgments.

Bibliography. William A. Beardslee, "Judging," HDB rev., pp. 541 f. A. Marzal, "The Provincial Governor at Mari," JNES, XXX (1971), 186-217. Donald A. McKenzie, "The Judge of Israel," VT, XVII (1967), 118-121.

W. B.

JUDGE, THE. A civil judge or magistrate is first mentioned in Israel under Moses when Jethro suggested that judges be appointed to relieve Moses in his administrative responsibilities (Ex 18:13-26). Subsequently, Israel organized into units within each tribe with a qualified man as judge. These men were to judge righteously, fearlessly, and impartially (Deut 1:16 f.). Only the most important cases were brought before Moses (Deut 1:12-18; 21:2). Note also the organization of Israel in Num 1-10. Under Joshua a similar plan was followed (Deut 16:18-20; 17:2-13; 19:15-20; Josh 8:33; 23:2; 24:1; I Sam 8:1).

The era following Joshua's death portrays a modified situation as described in the book of Judges. Here the principal leaders, or judges, of the people were those who had primarily the mission of delivering the Israelites from oppressing nations (Jud 2:16). Charismatically endowed by the Spirit of God they were "saviors" (Jud 3:9, ASV), empowered to save and preserve Israel (Jud 6:34-36).

The Heb. word *shōpēṭ* translated "judge" seems to have been a term borrowed from the Canaanites. It appears in the Ugaritic literature as *spt* with the sense of "ruler" or "judge" and a synonym for "king." Later, the chief magistrates of Carthage, descendants of the Phoenicians or Canaanites, bore this title for centuries, and were known to the Romans as *suffetes*. Thus the Heb. term properly includes the concept of leader as well as arbitrator.

The oppressing invaders during the era between the Conquest and the monarchy in Israel were primarily Mesopotamians, Moabites, Canaanites, Midianites, Ammonites, and Philistines. The outstanding judges who were used to counter them were Othniel, Ehud, Deborah and Barak, Gideon, and Samson as narrated in the book of Judges. Additional judges concerning whom very little information is available were Shamgar, Abimelech, Tola, Jair, Ibzan, Elon, and Abdon. *See* individual names. Some of the judges of this era are listed in the book of Hebrews (chap. 11) as heroes of faith. The opening chapters of I Samuel (cf. 4:18) indicate that Eli served as judge of Israel for 40 years. Samuel not only led the Israelites in a successful resistance to Philistine oppression, but also established an organized circuit court. Although he appointed his sons as judges, the changing conditions marked a transition to an organized kingdom requiring the anointing of a king (I Sam 7:15–8:5).

During the monarchy the king became the supreme judge in civil matters (II Sam 15:2; I Kgs 3:9, 28). Cases were tried by the king in the palace gate (I Kgs 7:7), but local courts were likewise functioning. David assigned Levites to judicial office and appointed 6,000 men as officers and judges (I Chr 23:4; 26:29). Jehoshaphat enlarged the judicial system in Judah, appointing priests and judges in fortified cities with a supreme court in Jerusalem where religious matters were under the high priest and civil matters under the prince of Judah (II Chr 19:5-8).

Prophets frequently asserted that justice was corrupted by bribery and false witness (Isa 1:23; 5:23; 10:1; Amos 5:12; 6:12; Mic 3:11; 7:3). Kings were often unjust in their treatment of the prophet who spoke for God (I Kgs 22:26-27; II Kgs 21:16; Jer 36:26). Cf. also I Kgs 21:1-13, where the law was disregarded by Ahab and Jezebel and false witnesses were used to the advantage of the king.

See also Judge, Judging; Judges, Book of.

S. J. S.

JUDGES, BOOK OF. The title is derived from the word "judges" (*shōpᵉṭîm*, Jud 2:16), since the activities of the judges are recorded in this book. In historical sequence it covers the period of Israel's history between Joshua and Samuel.

The era of the judges was a period in which the Israelites as God's covenant people were frequently in need of divine deliverance. Through Moses the Israelites had experienced release from Egyptian bondage and received the divine revelation as recorded in the Pentateuch. Under Joshua the next generation partially conquered and occupied the land of Canaan. As subsequent generations succumbed to apostasy and idolatry which resulted in oppression, they appealed to God for deliverance. Once more the mighty acts of God were displayed as a number of judges (*see* Judge, The) responded to the call of God to lead the Israelites in military exploits to rout the oppressing nations. These religious-political cycles of sin, sorrow, supplication, and salvation occurred repeatedly, and may have been limited geographically and may have overlapped chronologically.

Purpose

Thus the purpose of the book in presenting this history is definitely didactic, to teach divine retribution upon a sinning people, God's mercy upon repentance, and the futility of man-centered and idolatrous governments.

The ministry of Eli and Samuel, recorded in the opening chapters of I Samuel, concludes this era of the judges. Religion had reached a low ebb and Israel was threatened by the Philistines in spite of Samson's exploits. Through the leadership of Samuel, who served as the law judge, came a revival so that Israel was sufficiently unified to stem the tide of Philistine aggression and occupation.

Outline

I. Conditions During the Period of the Judges, 1:1–3:6
 1. Unoccupied areas, 1:1–2:5
 2. Religious-political cycles, 2:6–3:6
II. Oppressing Nations and Israelite Judges, 3:7–16:31
 1. Mesopotamia–Othniel, 3:7-11
 2. Moab–Ehud, 3:12-30
 3. Philistia–Shamgar, 3:31
 4. Canaan (Hazor)–Deborah and Barak, 4:1–5:31
 5. Midian–Gideon, 6:1–8:35
 6. Abimelech's tyrannical career, 9:1-57
 7. Tola and Jair, 10:1-5
 8. Ammon–Jephthah, 10:6–12:7
 9. Ibzan, Elon, and Abdon, 12:8-15
 10. Philistia–Samson, 13:1–16:31
III. Appendices: Results of Apostasy, 17:1–21:25
 1. Micah's idolatry and the Danite migration, 17:1–18:31
 2. Gibeah's atrocity and Benjamite war, 19:1–21:25

Chronology

The chronology of the book of Judges is not so simple as it might appear to the casual reader. A simple addition of the years allotted to each judge totals about 410 years. Even with an early date (*c.* 1400 B.C.) for Joshua, it is impossible to include all these years before David (*c.* 1000 B.C.) and allow time for Eli, Samuel, and Saul. Consequently the careers of these judges overlapped or may even have been contemporaneous. Among numerous studies of this chronology is that of J. B. Payne (*An Outline of Hebrew History*, 1954, p. 79), which accounts for this era beginning with Othniel in 1381 B.C. and ends with the career of Samuel in 1050 B.C. Samson and Jephthah may have been contemporaneous. Scholars who advocate a date of 1300 B.C. or later for Joshua, of necessity compress the time for the judges to two centuries or less. The references in I Kgs 6:1 and Jud 11:26 seem to favor the early date for Joshua, allowing for a longer period of time between the entrance of Israel into Canaan and establishment of the kingdom.

Archaeology

Archaeology has offered significant information to provide further insights on the historical developments in Palestine during the period surveyed in the book of Judges. The initial success of Joshua in the conquest of Canaan may be reflected in the Tell el-Amarna letters written a few decades afterward. Numerous

The Valley of the Dancers, where the events of Judges 21:21 are supposed to have taken place. HFV

city-states had been defeated and they had appealed to Egypt for help. This could account for Joshua's capture of such cities as Lachish and Debir (*c.* 1400 B.C.), their reoccupation by Canaanites, and their subsequent destruction by fire (*c.* 1230 - 1200 B.C.), as indicated by archaeology. Deborah and Barak must have judged in the 13th cen., because they fought against Hazor; the occupation of the huge lower city and of Level XIII of the *tell* came to an end in the second half of that century. Abimelech, the son of Gideon, burned Shechem, and this destruction has been dated to the 12th cen. B.C. Very likely Egypt continued to control the main trade routes along the coast of Palestine and through Galilee into the 12th cen. Witness to this are the inscriptions of the name of Rameses III (1198 - 1167 B.C.) in such cities as Beth-shean and Megiddo. Garstang in his study (*Joshua-Judges,* 1931) suggests a synchronism between Egyptian control and the periods of rest as indicated in the book of Judges.

Author

The author of this book is unknown. Internal evidence points to the years after the death of Samson and after the coronation of King Saul (Jud 17:6; 18:1; 19:1; 21:25) but before the conquest of Jerusalem by David as the time of composition (*c.* 1100 - 1000 B.C.; cf. Jud 1:21; 18:1; 19:1). The assertion in Jud 1:29 that the Canaanites were still in control of Gezer dates the writing prior to the time when the king of Egypt conquered this city (*c.* 970 B.C.) and gave it to Solomon. Some of the content, such as the song of Deborah, reflects the date of composition as having been at the time of the event. It is possible that Samuel or one of his disciples may have compiled the history of this period as given in the book of Judges. *See also* Ruth.

Bibliography. Gleason L. Archer, Jr., SOTI, pp. 262 - 267. C. F. Burney, *The Book of Judges,* 2nd ed., London: Rivington, 1930. Arthur E. Cundall, *Judges,* and Leon Morris, *Ruth,* Tyndale OT Commentaries, London: IVCF, 1968. John J. Davis, *Conquest and Crisis,* Grand Rapids: Baker, 1970. John Garstang, *Joshua-Judges,* London: Constable & Co., 1931. *Joshua, Judges, Ruth,* KD. C. F. Kraft, "Judges, Book of," IDB, II, 1013 - 1023. J. Barton Payne, "Judges, Book of," NBD, pp. 676 - 679. Charles F. Pfeiffer, "Judges," WBC, pp. 233 - 265. M. B. Rowton, "Chronology: Ancient Western Asia," CAH, 2nd ed., fascicle # 4, pp. 67 ff. G. Ernest Wright, *Shechem: The Biography of a Biblical City,* New York: McGraw-Hill, 1964, pp. 123 - 128. Y. Yadin, "Hazor," TAOTS, pp. 244 - 263.

S. J. S.

JUDGMENT HALL. Judgment hall (Gr. *praitōrion*) related to the Latin word *praetorium* which originally referred to the praetor's (military officer's) tent in camp with its surroundings. The Gr. word is translated "praetorium" almost exclusively in the ASV and RSV. In the KJV it is translated "common hall" in Mt 27:27; "praetorium" in Mk 15:16; "judgment hall" in Jn 18:28, 33; 19:9; Acts 23:35; and "palace" in Phil 1:13.

The term judgment hall, or praetorium, came eventually to be applied to the residence of the civil governor in provinces and cities of the Roman Empire. More particularly, this was the part of the residence where justice was administered, or the court at the entrance to the praetorian residence. The judgment hall (praetorium) in the capital of a province was usually a large palace or palatial residence.

In Jerusalem, Pilate's judgment hall, where

Jesus was brought to trial, was either the fortified palace of Herod the Great or the Tower of Antonia. According to Josephus it was Herod's palace at the W side of the walled city, but according to some church traditions and a number of modern scholars, it was the Tower of Antonia NW of the temple. The discovery of large paving stones at the site of the latter corresponding to the Pavement of Jn 19:13 now seems to be conclusive (*see* Gabbatha; Pavement). Acts 23:35 indicates that Herod's palace in Caesarea was used as a praetorium by the Roman governor Felix.

In Phil 1:13, the Gr. word *praitōrion* is translated "palace" in the KJV but the ASV, RSV and NASB paraphrase slightly to clarify Paul's statement that the cause of his imprisonment had become well-known "throughout the whole praetorian guard and to everyone else" (NASB). Here it refers either to the guard assigned to Paul during his house arrest in Rome (Acts 28:16, 30) or, as F. F. Bruce (*The Letters of Paul: An Expanded Paraphrase,* Grand Rapids: Eerdmans, 1965, pp. 160, 165) and other scholars have suggested, to the governor's headquarters in Ephesus for the Roman province of Asia.

B. M. W.

The presumed pavement of Pilate's judgment hall (Jn 19:13). Giovanni Trimboli

JUDGMENTS. The principal words translated "judgment" are Heb. *mishpāṭ* and Gr. *krima* and *krisis*. Derived from *shāphaṭ,* "to judge," the Heb. word denotes a dynamic "right-doing" as the result of distinguishing between the right and the wrong (I Kgs 3:9).

Among God's covenant people judgment is based upon His revelation and instruction (*tôrâ*) to them. It is to be a religious activity (Mic 6:8), to punish the wrongdoer, vindicate the righteous, and deliver the weak from unjust condemnation, in order to perform real justice (Isa 1:17; Zech 8:16–17). *Mishpāṭ* is fundamental right, frequently occurring in the sense of a law, being usually translated then as "ordinance" (II Kgs 17:34, 37; Isa 58:2). God's judgment is perfectly just, not arbitrary. It is "a blend of reliability and clemency, of law and love" (Morris, *The Biblical Doctrine of Judgment,* p. 21). The judgment of the Lord is the outworking of His mercy and of His wrath, bringing deliverance to the meek (Ps 25:9; Deut 10:18; Isa 30:18 f.) as well as doom to the wicked (Deut 32:41). The OT "concept of judgment has a legal basis, arising as it does from that judicial activity of discrimination in accordance with right which separates the righteous from the wicked and takes action as a result" (*ibid.,* p. 29).

In the NT, when the two Gr. words can be distinguished in meaning, *krisis* suggests more the process of judgment, how it works (Jn 3:19), whereas *krima* denotes condemnation, the sentence pronounced by the judge (Rom 2:2–3; Jas 3:1; Jude 4).

Judgments of Men

The Scriptures teach that, under proper limitations, men should be free to form and express private judgments relative to the Word of God, to the state, and to their fellowmen. Men are to govern one another as well as to judge themselves.

1. Protestants generally hold that the Bible is a book for the people, to be read and understood by the people themselves. The OT prophets spoke to the entire nation, and the Gospels and epistles were for popular use and instruction. The Holy Spirit is the ultimate Teacher for every man (I Jn 2:20–21, 27). Roman Catholics have maintained that the church is the divinely authorized and infallible interpreter of Scripture revelation, and that the individual must submit unreservedly to the judgment of the church. Protestants claim that not tradition and formal papal decisions but the Bible alone is the only and sufficient rule of faith and practice.

2. Civil or human government is clearly recognized by the Scriptures as resting upon divine authority (Gen 9:5–6; Ex 18:13–26). Obedience to the state in general, therefore, is a commandment of God (Rom 13:1–5; I Pet 2:13–15). But it is equally clear that in order to demand obedience from citizens or subjects, the state must confine its action within its proper sphere. The function of human government is to protect life and property, and to preserve social order. All rulers and judges are to remember that they are subject to the judgment of God, and should exercise their office equitably and with due moderation. When the state, however, attempts to enforce assent to religious doctrines, or to enact laws which require disobedience to the commandments of God, then the right of private judgment must be asserted. As Peter declared, "We ought to obey God rather than men" (Acts 5:29).

3. Private, unofficial judgment of others is necessary in order to protect one's own life and character. We must constantly form estimates

of the conduct and character of others for our own guidance and safety and usefulness. For example, we are to beware of false prophets whom we shall be able to recognize by their fruits (Mt 7:15 - 20). We are to prove or examine all things, holding fast to what is good and avoiding the evil (I Thess 5:21 - 22). We need to be able to discriminate, abounding in knowledge and discernment (Phil 1:9 - 10, NEB, NASB marg.). The prohibition of judging (Mt 7:1) is not opposed to this (cf. 7:6), but refers to criticizing and condemning. We are forbidden to usurp God's place as judge, or to pass rash, unjust, uncharitable judgments on others (see "Judgment," *Unger's Bible Dictionary*, pp. 620 f.).

4. The Christian is told to examine himself (II Cor 13:5), to judge his own walk. This self-judgment refers to the believer's criticism of his own ways (I Cor 11:31 - 32), and it results in his seeing and confessing his sin (I Jn 1:7 - 9). Restoration to full fellowship through the advocacy of Jesus Christ ensues (I Jn 2:1 - 2).

Judgments of God

1. The basis of divine judgment. This depends for the unsaved entirely on their works. They are not without a knowledge of the truth for they are: (*a*) the recipients of general revelation and therefore without excuse (Rom 1:18 - 20); (*b*) they once knew God but changed what they knew into a lie (vv. 21 - 24); (*c*) they have the work of the law written in their hearts (Rom 2:15). God will judge them according to the truth (Rom 2:2); according to their deeds (v. 6); by the law if they have it, and by the work of the law written in their hearts if they do not (vv. 12 - 15).

Some will be punished with few stripes and some many, according to the degree of their responsibility and the seriousness of their sins (Lk 12:48), but none of them will be saved (Rom 2:19 - 20; Eph 2:9).

For the believers there remains only a judgment of valuation and rewards, since Christ has kept the law in their stead and suffered and died in their place (Isa 53:5, 10 - 11) under the penalty of the broken law (II Cor 5:21).

2. The description of the divine judgments. Theologians have often maintained that there is one general judgment. This is a tenet strongly entrenched in Christian theology, more the result of rationalization than of thorough biblical exegesis. But a careful inductive study of all the Scriptures involved demonstrates that there are at least seven distinct divine judgments described in the Bible.

a. The judgment of the cross. Christ as our substitutionary atonement bore the punishment for our sins on the cross (Isa 53; Heb 10:10 - 12; I Pet 2:24). He bore the curse of sin (Gal 3:13) and became our sinbearer (Jn 1:29; II Cor 5:21; Heb 9:26 - 28), and before He commended His spirit finally to God He could say, "It is finished" (Jn 19:30). When we acknowledge our sin and accept Christ as our Saviour, God identifies us with His Son and sees us as having both died in our Representative and risen in Him in newness of life (Rom 5:12 ff.; 6:3 - 5; I Cor 15:22). Because of this we read in Rom 8:1, "There is therefore now no condemnation [judgment to damnation] to them which are in Christ Jesus." As a result, the believer will never again be judged for his sins. God has put them behind His back and they shall be remembered no more (Isa 38:17; 43:25; Ps 103:12; Jer 31:34; Heb 10:17).

b. The judgment of the believer's walk. This comes in the form of divine correction and chastisement (I Cor 11:30 - 32; Jn 15:1 - 8; Heb 12:3 - 15). God inflicts it on the Christian so that he may not be judged with the world (I Cor 11:32). It may take the form of severe afflictions at the hand of Satan in order to subjugate his fleshly nature (I Cor 5:5). It may end in the removal of the Christian by death if he does not repent (I Cor 11:30). The "sin unto death" spoken of in I Jn 5:16, however, is punished by eternal death in the case of the one who deliberately continues in sin (Heb 10:26) and persistently denies the incarnation of God's Son (I Jn 2:22; 4:3; II Jn 7) or His deity. *See* Sin unto Death.

c. The judgment of the believer's works. Since his sins have already been judged in the person of his substitute, the Lord Jesus Christ (Rom 8:3; II Cor 5:21; I Pet 2:24), the Christian is not judged again for his sins along with the world (I Cor 5:5). He must, however, appear or be made manifest (ASV) before what is called the judgment seat (Gr. *bēma*) of Christ (II Cor 5:10; Rom 14:10), "that each one may receive the things done in the body, according to what he hath done, whether it be good or bad" (ASV). His works must be openly displayed at the *bēma* or judge's tribunal (cf. Acts 25:6, 10, 17, NASB), also the stand or platform in an amphitheater where awards were given, as at Caesarea (Acts 12:21). It is quite necessary that the service of every child of God be scrutinized and evaluated (Mt 12:36; II Cor 9:6; Gal 6:7, 9; Eph 6:8; Col 3:24 - 25). As a result of this judgment of the believer's works there will be reward or loss of reward. Even in the latter case, if his work is burned up, the truly born-again believer will be saved, "yet so as through fire" (I Cor 3:12 - 15).

Since we are to reign with Christ and some will be appointed rulers of five and some of ten cities in His millennial kingdom, this judgment must occur prior to the return of the saints to rule with Christ (Zech 14:5; Jude 14; Rev 20:4). It may be a continuous process, each saint being judged for his works immediately on going to be with the Lord (I Cor 3:12 - 15). Or the judgment seat may be set up in heaven after the rapture of the Church and before Christ's glorious return to earth to establish His reign at Jerusalem. *See* Judgment Seat.

d. The judgment of Israel. The Lord will judge His chosen nation Israel when He returns with all His saints, before setting up His kingdom (Ezk 20:33-44; Mal 3:2-6). This action is the final stage of His continuing judgment of national Israel, foretold so often (e.g., Deut 28:15-68; Isa 1; 3; 5; etc.; Jer 2-9) and carried out so severely in history.

e. The judgment of the nations. This is the most difficult judgment to place and define. It is spoken of in two parts. First, that poured out by Christ as He comes to punish those nations that have united under the Antichrist to destroy Israel (Joel 3:12-16; cf. Zech 12:2, 9; 14:2 f.). Such destruction is the climax of God's judgments against specific nations that harmed His chosen people Israel, as announced by the OT prophets (e.g., Isa 13-23; Jer 46-51; Ezk 25-32). Second, a judgment of all the nations after Christ's second coming (Mt 25:31-46).

The Lord cannot take up His millennial rulership over the earth without first judging the nations for what they have been doing. In Mt 25:32 the word "nations" is a translation of Gr. *ethnē,* the equivalent of Heb. *gôyim,* meaning also "peoples," "Gentiles." Here they seem to be all the civilian peoples not killed in the battle of Armageddon when their armies were destroyed (Rev 16:14, 16; 19:19-21). The basis of this judgment is to be how these peoples as individuals have treated "one of the least of these my brethren" (Mt 25:40), and refers to their treatment of both the Christian (Heb 2:11-14) and God's people Israel (Ps 22:22; 69:8).

The crux of the difficulty in deciding the nature of this judgment lies in the fact that it speaks of previously unsaved people receiving either eternal blessing or eternal condemnation on the basis of their works. Since no man can be justified by his works (Rom 3:19-20; Gal 2:16), it cannot form a part of any general judgment of the righteous and the wicked. However, for this very reason, it does fit the situation existent at Christ's second coming and describes the judgment due the "nations" for their actions toward believers and Israelites during the Great Tribulation.

The judgment seat or bema where Paul stood before Gallio at Corinth (Acts 18). HFV

The one difficulty which remains with any interpretation is the statement that while the goats "shall go away into everlasting punishment . . . the righteous [the sheep] shall go into life eternal" (Mt 25:46). If this be taken to refer merely to entry into the millennial kingdom without implying salvation, then we can understand the verdict. Or it may mean into a life which leads on to eternal life since it is one and the same with the Lord. The most likely explanation is that because the Scripture speaks of a national repentance by all Israel at that time (Zech 12:10–13:1; Deut 30:1-10; Hos 5:15–6:3; Rev 1:7), and the salvation of that nation in a day (Isa 66:8; Zech 3:9; Rom 11:26), the same will occur in those nations which did treat the Christian and the Jew well. Being permitted to enter the kingdom, they will immediately repent, acknowledge Christ and be saved, and therefore can be spoken of by Christ as going into life eternal.

f. The judgment of angels. In this the Christian is to have a part (I Cor 6:3). It would appear to occur at the time of the judgment of Satan and in connection with that of the Great White Throne (Rev 20:11 ff.; cf. II Pet 2:4; Jude 6).

g. The judgment of the wicked. There is no indication of any judgment of the wicked before Rev 20:11, except for the wicked nations in Mt 25. Only the righteous dead are to be resurrected at the beginning of Christ's millennial reign (Rev 20:4), and the second death has no power over them. All the wicked, in contrast, called "the rest of the dead," will not live again until the thousand years are finished (v. 5). They are the participants in the final judgment. Their judgment rests upon two things: their works, which alone cannot save them; and the presence or absence of their names in the book of life. All not found in the book of life are to be cast into the lake of fire (v. 15).

See Crime and Punishment; Eternal State and Death; Judge, Judging; Justice (of God).

Bibliography. F. Büchsel and V. Herntrich, "*Krinō,* etc.," TDNT, III, 921-954. Leon Morris, *The Biblical Doctrine of Judgment,* London: Tyndale Press, 1960. Norman H. Snaith, *The Distinctive Ideas of the Old Testament,* London: Epworth Press, 1944, pp. 74-77.

R. A. K. and J. R.

JUDGMENT SEAT. A step or raised place; hence a rostrum or stage for speakers. It was used of the official seat or chair of a judge in the Gr. and Rom. courts of law. The Gr. word *bēma* appears 12 times in the NT, and is translated in the KJV and ASV as "judgment seat" in ten of them (Mt 27:19; Jn 19:13; Acts 18:12, 16-17; 25:6, 10, 17; Rom 14:10; II Cor 5:10).

Generally the word designates the official seat (tribunal, judicial bench) of a judge, usually the Rom. governor or procurator (although in Acts 25:10, "of Caesar"; Rom 14:10, "of God," ASV, RSV; II Cor 5:10, "of Christ"). However, in Acts 12:21 it refers to the throne-like speaker's platform of Herod Agrippa in Caesarea. For judgment seat of Christ, *see* Judgments: Judgments of God 2, *c*.

JUDICIAL BLINDNESS. The paralysis of spiritual perception which comes on the mind and heart of one who trifles with or rejects God's gracious offer of salvation. This is a subject which occupies an important place in both OT and NT.

A judgment of God. In Ps 69:23 ("Let their eyes be darkened, that they see not"), Messiah is heard through the voice of the psalmist calling for this judgment on the people because of their sin and rebellion against the Lord's Anointed. Even more striking is God's commission to the prophet Isaiah which he is given to pronounce to the people: "Go, and tell this people, Hear ye indeed, but understand not; and see ye indeed, but perceive not. Make the heart of this people fat . . . and shut their eyes; lest they see with their eyes . . . and convert, and be healed" (Isa 6:9 – 10). While the strange-sounding "lest they turn again and be healed" must not be made to mean that God does not want Israel to truly repent, it does mean that He wants no more of the external profession in which (Isa 29:10 – 13) they "draw near with their mouth . . . but have removed their heart far from me."

Not an arbitrary judgment. In every OT passage referring to this judgment the cause is shown to be man's unbelief, rebellion, and apostasy in heart from God. Thus the judgment, far from being arbitrary, is actually a sealing of their own decision in spiritual hardness, just as Paul in Rom 1 declares that God gave men over in awful judgment to the very sins they had deliberately chosen. A further comment on the depth of this spiritual blindness and deception of heart is given by Isaiah when he describes a man worshiping a part of a piece of wood, the rest of which he burns to bake a bit of bread (Isa 44:9 – 20).

Its relation to the parables. In a parable there is a certain concealment of the truth. Jesus explained to His disciples that it was for this reason that He used this method of teaching. He was carrying out the declared judgment of God in Isaiah's prophecy by hiding God's revelation from the superficial, self-righteous rejecters of God's grace, while at the same time making it abidingly vivid to the penitent, responsive heart (Mt 13:10 – 17).

A reason for the Jewish rejection of Christ. The apostle John (Jn 12:39 -40) cites this judicial blindness as the cause of Jewish unbelief and presents the situation as a fulfillment of Isa 53:1. Paul likewise gives it as the reason for the rejection of the gospel by the Jewish leadership in Rome (Acts 28:26).

Its presentation in the Pauline epistles. In Rom 11:7 – 10 Paul shows that Israel, except for an elect remnant, has failed to obtain the promise of God, and states the cause is this blindness. God is using His rejection of Israel as a foil to win the Gentiles (11:11 – 22). In the end, after this present period of blindness or hardening on the part of Israel, the Jew himself will be saved (11:25 – 26).

In II Cor 3:14 – 16 the apostle compares this blindness on the hearts of the Jews to a veil, like the one on Moses' face. It keeps them from seeing the glory of Christ in the OT. When their hearts turn to the Lord, the veil is removed. In II Cor 4:4 Paul shows Satan's part in this blindness. He is the promoter of the superficiality, self-righteousness, and self-seeking that lead to unbelief and spiritual blindness. In this aspect the blindness is not restricted to the Jew but comes on everyone who rejects the offer of God's grace (Eph 4:18). The very darkness in which he walks in his hatred of others blinds his eyes (I Jn 2:11).

This judgment of blindness stands as a strong warning in this life against disregarding the revelation which God has given to us. In eternity the lost will be eternally conscious of the inestimable worth of that which they have rejected (Lk 16:27 – 28).

See Blindness; Hardness of Heart.

M. A. K.

JUDITH (jo͞o'dĭth). The Heb. name *y^e hûdîth* means "Jewess," and is a feminine form of *ye-hûdî* "Jew."

1\. One of Esau's wives and daughter of Beeri the Hittite (Gen 26:34); perhaps also called Aholibamah (Oholibamah in ASV and RSV) in Gen 36:2.

2\. The heroine of the apocryphal book of Judith (Jth 8:1; 9:2). Since her name means "Jewess," it suggests the personification of piety to the Mosaic law and devotion to the cause of her nation.

JULIA (jo͞ol'yȧ). A Christian woman at Rome to whom Paul sent greetings; probably the wife or sister of Philologus (Rom 16:15).

JULIUS (jo͞ol'yŭs). This centurion, mentioned half a dozen times in Acts 27, and once in Acts 28:16 according to some MSS but not in the best texts, was the man put in charge of Paul the prisoner when he was sent to Rome after his appeal to Caesar. Julius was presumably his family name. There is no certainty that he was a Roman citizen. Soldiers in Palestine were not members of the legionary forces but rather auxiliary troops recruited from the *peregrini* or provincial subjects. Julius treated Paul kindly (Acts 27:3) and spared his life when his soldiers counseled killing him prior to the shipwreck (Acts 27:42-43).

JUNIA (jōō'ni-å), **JUNIAS** (jōō'nĭ-ăs). A Christian at Rome (most probably a man, although the accusative form [Ioynian] in Rom 16:7 is ambiguous as to gender). He, with Andronicus, is greeted by Paul as a fellow Jew (cf. Rom 9:3), a fellow prisoner (during some otherwise unknown imprisonment; II Cor 11:23), a man "of note among the apostles" (using "apostles" of Christian teachers and evangelists in general; cf. Acts 14:4, 14; Gal 1:19; 2:9), and a Christian before Paul's conversion.

JUNIPER. *See* Plants.

JUPITER. *See* Gods, False.

JUSHAB-HESED (jōō'shăb-hē'sĕd). A son or grandson of Zerubbabel (I Chr 3:20).

JUSTICE (ETHICS). In two of Plato's dialogues, *The Republic* and the *Gorgias*, the subject of justice is disputed at such a fundamental level that the divergent opinions recur throughout all subsequent ages. The conflict is between those who say that might makes right and those who say that power can be either justly or unjustly used, that justice is of a higher order than utility.

In the 17th cen. Hobbes and Spinoza took a position similar to the "might makes right" view. In essence they held that the stronger party can do no injustice in serving his own interests and the weaker suffers no injustice if he is inexpedient enough to suffer when resisting the will of those who have the rule over him. For Hobbes (*Leviathan*), the word justice has no meaning until men voluntarily form a state invested with sufficient power to coerce men to submit to it who do not obey civil laws. In a natural state, according to Spinoza, nothing can be called just or unjust, but only in a civil society. Hence justice for the individual consists of keeping the laws of the state, and for the state, in enforcing whatever laws it has the power to promulgate in the interest of its own self-preservation. This is the view taken by humanists and naturalists in our own day, and graphically put into practice by the modern dictators.

The opposite view, to which all Christians together with many others subscribe, is that justice transcends and judges the will of the state. This does not deny that the preservation of justice is the task of the state. Paul stated that the governing authorities have been instituted by God (Rom 13:1-7; cf. I Pet 2:13-17). Justice is the organizing principle of the state, the bond which holds men together in civil societies, without which, as Augustine said, the state is no better than a band of robbers. The principle of justice is higher than the constitution of the state; therefore justice cannot be understood as merely right based upon might.

This second view believes that there is a natural justice which transcends the relativities of history and holds for all men everywhere. For the founding fathers of our country, this natural justice consisted in certain rights granted to all men by the Creator. These rights were inalienable in the sense that the state could guarantee them, but never deny them. The philosopher Locke (*On Civil Government*) regarded it as a self-evident axiom of reason that all men should enjoy that measure of equality and liberty which forbids injury to one's neighbor in his life, health or property. Thomas Aquinas seems to regard this natural justice as a part of the concept of natural law.

Analyzing the concept a bit more closely, thinkers who speak of justice as a natural law of human life consider it as involving the obligation to render to one's neighbor that which is due to him as his own. The idea of justice as the rendering to others what is their due lies close to the idea of fairness. This is a term employed to describe justice in economics, the exchange of goods according to an equivalent value, and the distribution of goods according to need and merit.

Aristotle in this regard employs the notion of equality, distinguishing between arithmetic (or simple) and geometric (or proportional) equality. Since arithmetic or simple justice includes remedial or corrective justice, it may involve either remuneration in kind for the loss or damage of goods, or punishment which is graded in severity to the seriousness of the crime. This is analogous to *lex talionis*, a limitation upon measureless vengeance which is expressed in the OT concept of an eye for an eye and a tooth for a tooth (Ex 21:22-25; Lev 24:17-20).

Ever since Marx wrote *Das Kapital*, much attention has been given to the special problems of economic justice. For Marx it is a self-evident principle of justice that the wealth acquired by the sale of goods should reward only the labor of the one who produced the goods. Marx also assumes that originally men possessed all things in common, and that therefore distributive justice requires a revamping of the whole order of private property in terms of public ownership of the materials and means of production to insure the laboring man the full fruits of his work. The Scriptures also say that the laborer is worthy of his hire (Lk 10:7; I Tim 5:18); but even in the early Christian community where they voluntarily had all things in common, it is clear that the right of private property was never questioned (Ananias and Sapphira did not have to sell their property and share it, Acts 5:1-4). *See* Community of Goods. Furthermore, the Marxist views of economic justice, framed in the name of equality, have proved a threat to individual liberty, and liberty has ever been, from the days of Greek Idealism, a basic co-ordinate of the concept of justice.

For the Christian, justice involves conformity to the law of God as the final and unchanging norm of right action, in contrast to the Marxist that it is determined by communistic state ownership and control, and the evolutionary view that justice is determined by social progress.

See Example; Justice of God; Law.

Bibliography. Aristotle, *Politics,* I, 6; III, 13; VI, 3; VII, 2. Augustine, *City of God,* XIX, 21. Plato, *Gorgias; The Republic,* I–II; *Laws,* IV, X.

P. K. J.

JUSTICE OF GOD. Justice is an attribute of God that manifests His holiness. Several biblical words translated "justice," Heb. *s^e dāqâ ṣedeq,* Gr. *dikaiosunē,* are more often rendered "righteousness." The Heb. words sometimes appear in conjunction after *mishpāṭ,* which the KJV renders as "judgment and justice" (e.g., II Sam 8:15) but which RSV gives as "justice and equity" or "justice and righteousness" (I Kgs 10:9; Jer 22:15; 23:5).

Assuming the uniform doctrine of the church that God is a personal Being, the statement means, "God is just," that He always acts in a way consistent with the requirements of His character as revealed in His law. He rules His creation with rectitude, He keeps His word, He renders to all His creatures their due. "Righteous art thou, O Lord, and upright in thy judgments. Thy testimonies that thou hast commanded are righteous and very faithful" (Ps 119:137–138). The justice of God is a necessary correlate of His holiness, or moral excellence. Since God is infinitely perfect, He must be impartial in His judgments and always treat His creatures with equity. "That be far from thee," says Abraham to the Lord, "to do after this manner, to slay the righteous with the wicked: and that the righteous should be as the wicked, that be far from thee. Shall not the Judge of all the earth do right?" (Gen 18:25).

The doctrine of God's justice has many ramifications but it is most often discussed in connection with man's sin, and in this connection it is close in meaning to the severity of God. Severity is the way the sinner feels the justice of God.

With the rise of German liberalism, this aspect of God's moral being was softened to the point of being emptied of all meaning. The doctrines of vicarious satisfaction and especially eternal hell were repudiated as vestigial remains of the angry God of the OT and unworthy of the heavenly Father whom Jesus revealed, who loves all His creatures and is worshiped by Christians. The Scripture, however, will sustain no such bifurcation. The God of Jesus and the apostles is the God of the OT. Jesus Himself had more to say about hell specifically, than can be found in the whole OT put together; probably more than can be found in the remainder of the NT.

As for vicarious satisfaction, this is at the heart of Paul's interpretation of the meaning of the death of Christ. As the leading theological thinker of the apostolic church, he wrote a treatise on the righteousness of God (1:16–17) to the Romans, the epistle which is justly viewed as the major exposition of the gospel from his pen. Regarding God's justice or righteousness he stated that "all have sinned, and come short of the glory of God; being justified freely by his grace through the redemption that is in Christ Jesus: whom God hath set forth to be a propitiation through faith in his blood, to delcare his righteousness for the remission of sins that are past, through the forbearance of God; to declare, I say, at this time his righteousness: that he might be just, and the justifier of him which believeth in Jesus" (Rom 3:23–26). This passage has been happily called the "acropolis of the gospel," the good news that through Christ the requirements of divine justice have been met.

Scripture does not teach that God's justice is purely remedial. It is not an expression of God's benevolence. It is that quality in God which guarantees to all His creatures that sin must be punished because of its inherent ill-desert, and that rectitude must be acknowledged and rewarded because of its intrinsic merit and worthiness.

See God; Judgments; Justification; Righteousness; Sin.

Bibliography. J. Barton Payne, "Justice," NBD, pp. 680–683.

P. K. J.

JUSTIFICATION. Justification (Gr. *dikaiōsis*) is a term that has reference to judicial judgment. It does not mean to make upright or holy, but to announce a favorable verdict, to declare to be righteous. This meaning is patent in both Testaments (Heb. *hiphil* stem of *ṣādaq,* "to declare righteous"; Gr. *dikaioō,* "to vindicate, acquit, pronounce and treat as just"). "To justify" is contrasted with "to condemn" (cf. Deut 25:1; I Kgs 8:32; Prov 17:15; Rom 8:33) and no more means to make upright than condemn means to make wicked.

It is this declarative force of the term that raises the question: how can God justify the ungodly? In God's justification of sinners there is a unique ingredient that holds in no other case of justification. This unique feature is that He causes to be the new relation which He has declared to be. This operation is expressly stated in Scripture to be the act of constituting many righteous (Rom 5:19), the bestowal of the free gift of righteousness (Rom 5:17), and making us the righteousness of God in Christ (II Cor 5:21). It is by this action that the sentence of condemnation (*q.v.*) under which we rest as sinners is changed to one of justification; there is, therefore, no condemnation to them who are in Christ Jesus (Rom 8:1). This constitutive act is properly spoken of as the imputation to us of the righteousness of Christ. It is thereby shown to have no affinity with what is inwardly wrought in us either by regeneration (*q.v.*) or sanctification (*q.v.*). Imputation is the reckoning to our account of a righteousness not our own but based on the obedience of Christ (Phil 3:9; Rom 5:17, 19). It is therefore distinguished from the forgiveness of sins, although forgiveness is necessarily included in it (Acts 13:38-39).

As the *nature* of justification is thus shown to be declarative, constitutive, and imputative, so the *ground* resides in nothing else but the accomplished work of Christ, and its *source* in the free grace of God. We are justified freely by God's grace "through the redemption that is in Christ Jesus" (Rom 3:24). This truth comes to focal expression in the designation "the righteousness of God" (Rom 1:17; 3:21-22; 10:3; II Cor 5:21; Phil 3:9). Christ's work was obedience (Rom 5:19; Phil 2:8; Heb 5:8-9). As such it was righteousness (Mt 3:15; Rom 5:17-18, 21). It was wrought by Him as the God-man and is, therefore, a righteousness with divine property, a God-righteousness contrasted not only with human unrighteousness but with all human righteousness. This righteousness alone meets the desperateness of our sinful situation and measures up to all the demands of God's holiness. It not only warrants God's justification but wherever reckoned to our account demands our justification. Grace reigns "through righteousness unto eternal life" (Rom 5:21).

As justification is of grace, it is through faith (Rom 1:17; 5:1). Faith is congruous with all the other features. This is true not because faith is the gift of God, for all grace exercised by us is the gift of God, but because the distinctive character of faith is to receive and rest upon Christ for salvation. It is the self-abandoning and self-entrusting quality of faith that makes it the fitting instrument of all else that justification involves. It is by faith we are justified and by faith alone, though never by a faith that is alone.

Justification is the basic religious question. It is not now simply the question: how can man be just with God? It is the more pressing question: how can man as a sinner *become* just with God? Justification by grace through faith is the answer.

See Faith; Forgiveness; Impartation; Righteousness; Salvation.

Bibliography. See commentaries on Romans. John A. Faulkner, "Justification," ISBE, III, 1782-1788. Leon Morris, *The Apostolic Preaching of the Cross,* Grand Rapids: Eerdmans, 1956, pp. 224-274. James I. Packer, "Just, Justify, Justification," BDT, pp. 303-308; "Justification," NBD, pp. 683-686. Gottlob Schrenk, "*Dikaios,* etc.," TDNT, II, 182-225.

J. M.

JUSTUS (jŭs'tŭs). The surname for three men of the apostolic period.

1. Joseph called Barsabas who was eliminated when Matthias was chosen to complete the Twelve (Acts 1:23).

2. Titus (or Titius), a Roman and converted God-fearer, who opened his home next to the Corinth synagogue to Paul as a meeting place when the apostle turned from the Jews (Acts 18:7). Most later Gr. MSS have only "Justus" (so KJV), but earlier MSS and versions have either "Titius Justus" or "Titus Justus."

3. Jesus (or Joshua) Justus, a Jew possibly from Colosse, who was with Paul during his first Rome imprisonment and, along with John Mark and Aristarchus, sent greetings to the Colosse church (Col 4:11).

JUTTAH (jŭt'ȧ). A town in Judah (now identified with Yatta), about five miles S of Hebron (Josh 15:55), assigned to the sons of Aaron as a refuge city (Josh 21:16). A parallel listing in I Chr 6:59 omits this town. The conjecture which equates this city with "Juda" (KJV) in Lk 1:39 is now generally rejected as linguistically indefensible.

K

KAB (kăb). A measure of capacity (cab in KJV), mentioned only in II Kgs 6:25 (RSV). *See* Weights, Measures, and Coins.

KABZEEL (kăb'zē-ĕl). A city near the border of Edom in the SE part of Judah (Josh 15:21); the home of Benaiah, a mighty man in David's army (II Sam 23:20; I Chr 11:22). It was resettled after the Babylonian Captivity (Neh 11:25, where it is called Jekabzeel). Its site has been identified with Khirbet Garreh (Tell 'Ira), nine miles E of Beer-sheba.

KADESH-BARNEA (kā'dĕsh-bär'nē-*ȧ*). Situated in the NE part of the Sinai peninsula *c.* 50 miles S of Beersheba, on the S border of the land assigned by God to Israel (Num 34:4; Josh 15:3). There are three springs or oases within a 12 mile radius ('Ain Qedeis, 'Ain Qudeirat—the largest of N Sinai, with a flow of *c.* 10,000 gal. per hr.—and 'Ain Qoseimeh), perhaps all used by the Israelites when they camped in the wilderness after leaving Horeb (Deut 1:2, 19). Kadesh-barnea apparently lay at the juncture of the Wilderness of Zin in the Negeb (*q.v.*) to the N and the Wilderness of Paran in Sinai to the S; thus it could be spoken of as lying in either of these deserts (Num 13:21, 26; 20:1; 27:14; 33:36–37).

Kadesh-barnea was to have been the base for the Israelites' invasion of Canaan. It remained their headquarters for much of the period of wilderness wandering (*q.v.*), which began when the people refused to enter the land of Canaan after hearing the report of the ten spies (Num 14:1–4, 26–34; Deut 9:23). When the Israelites attempted to invade Canaan on their own initiative, they were decisively defeated at Hormah by Amalekites and the Canaanite king of Arad (Num 14:44–45; 21:1) and retreated to Kadesh (Deut 1:44–46). It was here that Miriam died (Num 20:1) and that Moses struck the rock that water might gush out (Num 20:2–13), as he had done at Rephidim (Ex 17:5–6). This time Moses was condemned for lack of faith in not simply speaking to the rock; he was told he could not enter the Promised Land. Later, messengers were sent from Kadesh to the king of Edom asking permission to pass through his territory just to the E, and were refused (Num 20:14–21). On his S campaign Joshua conquered the kings in the Negeb "from Kadesh-barnea even unto Gaza" (Josh 10:41).

The earlier name of Kadesh-barnea was En-mishpat, "fountain of judgment" (Gen 14:7). It was on the caravan route to Shur used during the Middle Bronze I period (2100–1900 B.C.; *see* Patriarchal Age). Shur was the "wall" or series of fortifications protecting the E border of Egypt (Gen 16:7, 14; 20:1). The oases of Meribah-kadesh (KJV: "the waters of strife in Kadesh"; cf. Num 20:13; Deut 32:51) are mentioned by Ezekiel as part of the border of the future land of Israel (Ezk 47:19; 48:28).

To date no definite traces of the Israelites' stay in Moses' time have been found in this area. At that time they were living a seminomadic life. dwelling in tents and using wooden or leather implements instead of pottery which is easily breakable in travel. Trumbull surveyed the area a century ago, giving valuable descriptions. In 1914 Woolley and Lawrence excavated remains at 'Ain el-Qudeirat of one of a series of rectangular fortresses (*c.* 135 × 198 feet) with towers and casemate walls, built in the Negeb by kings of Judah (Jehoshaphat or Uzziah?) during the 9th–7th cen. B.C. Their aim was to guard the S border and the trade routes to Edom, Sinai, and Egypt. Glueck and others have identified ruins of other fortresses without towers in the same vicinity from the 10th cen. B.C. Many potsherds and ruins of dwellings in this region belong to the Middle Bronze I and the Nabataean-Roman-Byzantine periods.

Bibliography. M. Dothan, "The Fortress at Kadesh-Barnea," IEJ, XV (1965), 134–151. Nelson Glueck, *Rivers in the Desert,* New York: Farrar, Straus & Cudahy, 1959. Beno Rothenberg, *God's Wilderness,* London: Thames & Hudson, 1961, pp. 33–56, 121–125, 137–144. H. Clay Trumbull, *Kadesh-Barnea,*, London: Hodder & Stoughton, 1884. C. Leonard Woolley and T. E. Lawrence, *The Wilderness of Zin,* London: Jonathan Cape, 1936.

A. W. W. and J. R.

KADMIEL (kăd'mĭ-ĕl). A Levite family head who returned from Babylon with Zerubbabel (Ezr 2:40; Neh 7:43; 12:1, 8) and who supervised the reconstruction of the temple (Ezr 3:9). He participated in the public confession (Neh 9:4–5) and in the sealing of the covenant (Neh 10:9). He was the father of Jeshua, a chief Levite (Neh 12:24; however, see *The Pulpit Commentary* on this passage, which suggests that on the basis of the LXX it should read "and Jeshua, Binnui, Kadmiel").

KADMONITES (kăd'mō-nīts). A people mentioned only in Gen 15:19 among the nationalities whose territories God promised to the seed of Abraham. The Kadmonites, whose name means Easterners, lived somewhere in the Syro-Arabian desert. The inhabitants of this region were also called *B^ené-qedem,* "children of the last" (Jud 6:3; I Kgs 4:30; Job 1:3; Isa 11:14).

KAIWAN. *See* Gods, False.

KALLAI (kăl'ī). A priest of the family of Sallai in the time of Joiakim, the high priest (Neh 12:20).

KANAH (kā'nȧ)

1. A brook (the Wadi Qanah) running westward from near Mount Gerizim, joining the Yarkon shortly before they enter the Mediterranean N of Joppa. It formed (connecting with a line from Tappuah westward) part of the boundary between Manasseh on the N and Ephraim and Dan on the S (Josh 16:8; 17:9). See Denis Baly, *The Geography of the Bible,* pp. 134–137.

2. A city in the N part of Asher, about six miles SE of Tyre (Josh 19:28). It is now usually identified with the modern Qânah, which is not to be confused with the Cana referred to in the Gospel of John. It is mentioned in the Egyptian records of Thutmose III as *Qnw* and in the Amarna letters as Qanû.

KAPH (kăf). The eleventh letter of the Heb. alphabet, used in Ps 119 to designate the eleventh section, each verse of which begins with this letter. The Heb. word *kāp* means "palm of the hand." Its pictographic sign in the proto-Sinaitic alphabet of the 16th–15th cen. B.C. was a semicircle including two additional vertical strokes, representing four upraised fingers. *See* Alphabet.

KAREAH (kȧ-rē'ȧ). The father of Jonathan (Jer 40:8) and Johanan (II Kgs 25:23 [Careah in KJV]; Jer 40:8, 13, 15–16; 41:11, 13–14, 16; 42:1, 8; 43:2, 4–5), who were captains loyal to Gedaliah, governor of the land after the fall of Jerusalem.

KARKAA (kär'kĭ-ȧ). A place along the S border of Judah W of Kadesh-barnea (Josh 15:3; Karka in RSV). The LXX has "the [way] that is west of Kadesh." The somewhat parallel boundaries in Num 34:4 omit Karkaa. It has been tentatively identified with 'Ain el-Qeseimeh, three miles NW of the main spring known as 'Ain el-Qudeirat in the Kadesh-barnea region.

KARKOR (kär'kôr). A place or area where Gideon decisively defeated the remnants of the Midianites under Zebah and Zalmunna (Jud 8:10–11). The place, not yet definitely identified, was perhaps a small plain on the lower course of the Jabbok in E Gilead. However, some (e.g., *Encyclopaedia Biblica*) unequivocally identify it with the Karkar on the Orontes near Hamath mentioned in the inscriptions of Shalmaneser II and Sargon. Y. Aharoni, following J. Garstang in *Joshua Judges,* p. 390, believes it is Qarqar in the Wadi Sirḥan *c.* 120 miles SE of Amman (*The Land of the Bible,* p. 241).

KARNAIM. *See* Ashteroth-Karnaim.

KARTAH (kär'tȧ). A town, not yet identified, assigned to the Merarite Levities in the area of Zebulun (Josh 21:34; not listed in I Chr 6:77, a parallel passage).

KARTAN (kär'tăn). A city in Naphtali given to the Gershonite Levites when Palestine was divided by Joshua (Josh 21:32). Called Kirjathaim in I Chr 6:76, it is identified with Khirbet el-Qureiyeh, 15 miles SE of Tyre.

KATTATH (kăt'ăth). A city in Zebulun allotted at the partition of the land by Joshua (Josh 19:15); probably the same as Kitron (Jud 1:30).

KEDAR (kē'dȧr). A son of Ishmael (Gen 25:13; I Chr 1:29), and ancestor of the Arabic tribe of Kedar (Heb. *qēdār,* "black" or "swarthy"). This tribe is mentioned in the Assyrian records of Esarhaddon and Ashurbanipal as *Qidri, Qadri,* and *Qidarri,* and on a silver vessel of the 5th cen. B.C. as *Qdr.*

The Kedarites were known for their wealth in flocks (Jer 49:28–29; Ezk 27:21), and their men were famed archers (Isa 21:16–17). They lived in black tents in unwalled encampments (Song 1:5; Isa 42:11). In Isa 60:7 and also in Ashurbanipal's inscriptions they are referred to in connection with the Arabic tribe of Nebaioth (perhaps the Nabataeans) They seem to have roamed the Syrian desert E of Palestine, but in the Persian period were also found in the desert S of Palestine. At that time they were ruled by "Geshem the Arabian" (Neh 2:19), who is called "King of Kedar" on the silver vessel, already mentioned, that was discovered at Tell el-Maskhutah in the E part of the delta of Egypt (I. Rabinowitz, JNES, XV [1956], 1–9). Kedar and her confederate peoples exerted great influence from the delta region to the Syrian desert and from Sennacherib's time to the Nabataean period (W. J. Dumbrell, "The Tell el-Maskhuta Bowls and the 'Kingdom' of Qedar in the Persian Period," BASOR, #203 [1971], pp. 33–44).

S. H. H.

KEDEMAH (kĕd'ĕ-mȧ). The twelfth son of Ishmael (Gen 25:15; I Chr 1:31). The Heb. name (*Qēdmâ*) means "toward the east." It is possible that the *benê qedem,* "the children of the east" (Gen 29:1; Jud 6:3, 33, etc.). mentioned frequently in extrabiblical records, may be descendants of this Ishmaelite. *See* East, Children of the.

KEDEMOTH (kĕd'ĕ-mŏth)

1. A wilderness near the headwaters of the Arnon River, from which Moses sent messengers to Sihon, king of the Amorites, asking permission to pass through his land (Deut 2:26).

2. A city E of Transjordan assigned to the tribe of Reuben by Moses (Josh 13:18). It became a Levitical city assigned to the Merarites (Josh 21:37: I Chr 6:79). It may be identified with ez-Za'feran, eight miles SE of Medeba.

KEDESH (kē'dĕsh)

1. A well fortified Canaanite city, identified with Tell Qades, NW of the now-drained Lake Huleh and nine miles N of Hazor. It was mentioned by Thutmose III (1483–1450 B.C.) in his first list of conquered Palestinian cities as *Qdsh* and by Seti I (*c.* 1310 B.C.), according to J. Simons (*Egyptian Topographical Lists,* Leiden: Brill, 1937, pp. 35-36, 115). Its king was defeated by Joshua, and it was assigned to be a city of refuge and residence of the Gershonite Levites (Josh 12:22; 19:37; 20:7; 21:32). Its inhabitants were captured and exiled by Tiglath-pileser III during the reign of Pekah (II Kgs 15:29).

2. Kedesh-naphtali (Jud 4:6, 9–11), the home of Barak the judge, does not seem to have been Kedesh 1, the strong Canaanite city over 30 miles N of Mount Tabor. Y. Aharoni has argued convincingly for an extensive Israelite site overlooking the Sea of Galilee known as Khirbet Qedish. About two miles S of Tiberias, it has remains from the period of the judges and is only a few hours' walk from Mount Tabor (*The Land of the Bible,* Philadelphia: Westminster, 1967, p. 204).

3. A Levitical town within the borders of Issachar (I Chr 6:72), called Kishon (KJV) or Kishion (RSV) in Josh 21:28. It has been identified with Tell Abu Qedeis, two and a half miles SE of Megiddo, or with Tell Qisan at the foot of Mount Tabor. Some scholars have identified it with Kedesh 2, since the territories of the tribes sometimes overlapped.

4. A town in thē extreme S of Judah (Josh 15:23), perhaps the same as Kadesh-barnea (*q.v.*).

J. R.

KEDESH NAPHTALI. *See* Kedesh.

KEEPER. One who is responsible for the protection or maintenance of a great variety of things.

1. Most frequently as a herdsman or shepherd (Gen 4:2; 46:32, 34 47:3,6; I Sam 11:5; 17:20; 21:7), or husbandman of fields (Jer 4:17), vineyards (Song 1:6; 8:11; Isa 27:3), or orchards (Prov 27:18). Here production is most significant.

2. One who holds public trust to guard doors and threshholds (II Kgs 22:4 23:4), gates (I Chr 9:19; Neh 3:29), walls (Song 5:7), prisons (Gen 39: 21, 23; Acts 5:23; 12:6, 19), a house (Eccl 12:3, or women (Est 2:3). Protection is the emphasis here. Cain disclaimed responsibility for his brother by pleading, "Am I my brother's keeper?" (Gen 4:9).

3. Responsibility to prevent something from wrongdoing, e.g., tongue and lips (Ps 34:13; 141:3).

In all these senses the Lord is our keeper (Ps 121:3–8), our personal convoy through the dangers of all evil.

KEHELATHAH (kē'ȧ-lā'thȧ). An unidentified place at which the Israelites made camp in the journey from Egypt to Canaan (Num 33:22–23).

KEILAH (kē-ī'lȧ)

1. A fortified city in the Shephelah allotted to Judah (Josh 15:44) and mentioned in the Amarna letters as Qilti. Identified with Khirbet Qila it is situated eight miles NW of Hebron and overlooking the N-S route from the Valley of Elah to Hebron. David and his band saved the city from the Philistines who had taken it, and dwelt for a time in its fortress. Saul planned to attack it to capture David, and because he could not trust its inhabitants David departed to wander again in the wilderness (I Sam 23:1–13). In the time of Nehemiah the city had been reoccupied by Jews returning from Babylon (Neh 3:17–18).

2. A descendant of Judah called Keilah the Garmite (I Chr 4:19).

KELAIAH (kĭ-lā'yȧ). One of the Levites who were compelled by Ezra to give up their foreign wives (Ezr 10:23). *See* Kelita.

KELITA (kē-lī'tȧ). A Levite who assisted in interpreting the law when Ezra read it to the assembled people and participated in the sealing of the covenant into which the people entered (Neh 8:7; 10:10); identified with Kelaiah (Ezr 10:23).

KEMUEL (kĕm'yōō-ĕl)

1. The son of Nahor the brother of Abraham and the father of Aram (Gen 22:21).

2. A prince of the tribe of Ephraim who was responsible for the dividing of the inheritance in Canaan (Num 34:24).

3. A Levite; the father of Hashabiah who was a leader in the tribe in the time of David (I Chr 27:17).

KENAN. *See* Cainan.

KENATH (kē'năth). A Canaanite town in Gilead, at the NE border of Israel in the Hauran; for a time called Nobah, the name of one of its conquerors (Num 32:42; I Chr 2:23). Its importance in the 2nd mil. B.C. is indicated by its mention in the later Egyptian execration texts (*c.* 1825 B.C.), in a list of Thutmose III (*c.*1470 B.C.), and in the Amarna letters as Qanû (*c.*1370 B.C.). It has been identified as Qanawat, *c.* 55 miles E of the Sea of Galilee.

KENAZ (kē'năz)

1. One of the sons of Eliphaz, the son of Esau and Adah the Hittite. Kenaz became one of the chiefs or princes of the Edomite families dwelling in the Negeb or the western Arabian desert (Gen 36:11, 15, 42; I Chr 1:36, 53).

2. The brother of Caleb the Kenezite. It is possible that Caleb and his brother were descendants of the Edomite Kenaz, their more immediate ancestors joining Israel before the departure from Egypt. Kenaz was the father of Othniel, the latter being the son-in-law of Caleb and the first judge of Israel (Josh 15:17; Jud 1:13; 3:9, 11; I Chr 4:13). *See* Kenezite.

3. The grandson of Caleb and son of Elah (I Chr 4:15).

KENEZITE, KENIZZITE (kĕn'ĕ-zīt). A tribe of the land of Canaan in the time of Abraham, mentioned along with Kenites (*q.v.*), who were metalsmiths (Gen 15:19). They may have merged with a clan of the Edomites; conceivably, the name of the Edomite chieftain, Kenaz (*q.v.;* Gen 36:15, 42), was derived from his ruling over Kenezites.

Caleb (*q.v.*), chosen from the tribe of Judah to be one of the 12 spies, is called a Kenezite in Num 32:12 and Josh 14:6, 14. This relationship suggests that Kenezites joined the tribe of Judah. This occurred considerably before the Exodus, because Caleb and his father Jephunneh appear as full-fledged Judahites (Num 13:6). Caleb's relative Othniel is called the son of Kenaz (Josh 15:17) which either designates Othniel (*q.v.*) as a Kenezite or means that Caleb had a younger brother Kenaz.

In the genealogy of I Chr 4:13–15 listing the descendants of Kenaz, a certain Joab was "founder of Ge-harashim, for they were craftsmen" (v. 14, NEB). The place name means "valley of craftsmen." While the valley and the type of craft involved cannot be identified with certainty, the association of the Kenezites with the Kenites, whose name means "smiths," suggests that Joab developed a site with copper mines into a family industry.

J. R.

KENITE (kĕn'īt). A tribe indigenous to Palestine in the patriarchal age (Gen 15:19). The term "Kenite" comes from *qayin,* which originally meant "metalworker, smith," as in Aram. and Arabic. This meaning is preserved in the name of one of the sons of Lamech, Tubal-cain, "the forger of all implements of bronze and iron" (Gen 4:22, NASB).

The Kenites apparently were nomadic or seminomadic clans of smiths, who also pastured flocks and lived in tents. The famous tomb painting (19th cen. B.C.) at Beni Hasan in Egypt depicts such a group of 37 Asiatics bringing eye paint to the vizier. Two donkeys are shown, each carrying a bellows, a necessary piece of equipment for traveling metalworkers (ANEP #3).

Various OT passages report the Kenites as dwelling with the Midianites in Sinai (the father-in-law of Moses is called a Kenite as well as a Midianite, cf. Jud 1:16 with Num 10:29); among the cliffs (Num 24:21, NASB), reminding one of Petra, and probably referring poetically to the Arabah region with its many copper deposits; and in the mineral-rich Negeb S of Arad (Jud 1:16) and westward to the border of Egypt (I Sam 15:6–7). Heber the Kenite separated himself from the other Kenites and pitched his tent near the trade routes in the Plain of Esdraelon (Jud 4:11, 17). In his account of the battle of Megiddo (*c.* 1479 B.C.) Thutmose III mentions a Qina brook or valley S of Megiddo (ANET, p. 236), which possibly reflects the word "Kenite."

Through marriage Moses became related to the Kenites and subsequently invited Hobab to come with the Israelites, needing his nomadic skill to guide them (Num 10:29–32). Descendants of Moses' relatives accompanied men of Judah from the Jericho region to occupy their inheritance (Jud 1:16; I Sam 27:10). Saul spared the Kenites in his Amalekite war (I Sam 15:6), and David sent gifts from his spoils to the Kenite towns in Judahite territory (I Sam 30:26, 29). Some Kenites listed in the genealogy of Judah, who were descended from the founder of the Rechabites, formed scribal guilds ("families of scribes," I Chr 2:55).

Some OT scholars, following the documentary analysis of the Pentateuch (e.g., L. Koehler, *Old Testament Theology,* p. 45), have asserted that Moses learned the name of Yahweh from his Kenite father-in-law. Known as the "Kenite hypothesis," this theory proposes that Yahweh was originally the Kenite-Midianite tribal god and that Jethro was the chief priest of Yahweh's cult. The name of Yahweh, however, if not the full significance of its meaning, was certainly known to the patriarchs (*see* God; God, Names and Titles of; I AM). When Jethro made sacrifice to God (Ex 18:12), he was not instructing Moses how to worship Yahweh, for vv. 8–11 show Jethro being led to faith in Yahweh by Moses' testimony.

Bibliography. CornPBE, "Kenites," pp. 480 f. Y. Kaufmann, *The Religion of Israel,* Chicago: Univ. of Chicago Press, 1960, pp. 242 ff. J. A. Motyer, "Kenites,"NBD, pp. 688 f.

J. R.

KENIZZITES. *See* Kenezite.

KENOSIS (kĕ-nō'sĭs). In Phil 2:7 (RSV) Paul says that in becoming man, Christ "emptied himself." The Gr. verb used in *kenoō* from which is derived the English word kenosis.

This term has been used to describe a particular set of theories concerning the incarnation. The exact limits of the discussion are not agreed upon. The article "Kenotiker und Krypter" in Herzog's *Real-Encyklopädie* (Stuttgart, 1857) begins with the debate between Luther and the Swiss over the nature of the Lord's Supper and the presence of Christ in the elements. Berkouwer in his *The Person of Christ* refers to kenosis as a form of Christological thought influential in the 19th cen; while Donald Baillie in *God Was in Christ* declares that the kenosis theory belongs distinctively to modern times. Because of this ambiguity of meaning, all parts of the debate are briefly touched on in this article.

At the practical level of the Eucharistic controversy, the "how" of the union between the divine and the human in Christ was clearly the problem in Luther's mind, but he was not able to achieve a satisfying dogmatic formulation. The same was true of Melanchthon and his followers. But Johann Brenz of Tübingen (d. 1570), who defended the strict Lutheran position of the real presence of Christ in the element against Oecolampadius, placed stress on the fundamental thought of the complete communication of natures and their respective attributes in the person of Christ (*communicatio idiomatum*). This led to the question: how then did the humiliation of Christ differ from His exaltation? The answer given was that in the humiliation of Christ the divine majesty, which from the first moment of the incarnation belonged to His human nature, was veiled from the eyes of the world. In the exaltation of Christ, on the other hand, this divine glory, which had been completely communicated to the human nature from the beginning though hidden, was again revealed. To the questions, how could this be, how could the humanity of Christ be both glorious and yet not appear as such, Brenz answered that it was so because Scripture said so.

In the next century further questions were raised: whether Christ, in the state wherein He emptied Himself, was in His humanity present to all creatures, and whether even during His death He ruled the whole universe. Some answered yes, others no. The latter insisted that Christ's emptying Himself consisted in a real though partial renunciation of the use of the divine glory communicated to the humanity of Christ through the *unio personalis*, especially His omnipotence, omniscience, and omnipresence. But if this were so, how then could the complete union of natures and the lordship of Christ over all things be maintained? The answer was given that the hypostatic union involved, so far as these divine attributes were concerned, only the inner possession of the same, the possibility that they should be exercised, but required no necessary outward relationship to the creation. In some way Christ could be omniscient without knowing all, and omnipresent without being present to all—at least so it would seem.

Still other Lutheran theologians suggested that Christ's emptying had its seat or proper locale in His priestly office. As King, the God-man really ruled over His Church and the world even in His humiliation; but as Priest, He withdrew His divine glory insofar as this was demanded to accomplish the work of salvation, suffering poverty, pain, and death.

In the 19th cen., when the kenotic theory was taken up in British theological circles, insistence was made that the doctrine of the two natures would lead to an intolerable duality--two streams of consciousness, two sets of actions—in the life of Christ, unless the doctrine of kenosis be taken seriously. Not that the divine being was to be given up, but there must be a genuine self-limitation, an exchange of one form or mode of existence for another. But when these kenotic theologians sought to spell out their doctrine, they found themselves involved in the same untenable intricacies to which the older theologians had been driven. Some said Christ laid aside all the divine attributes; others, that He surrendered the relative but not the essential attributes. Some even went so far as to say that when God became a man His deity was transmitted into humanity. Godet reasoned from the freedom of God that He was not necessarily bound to His divine mode of existence. This of course leaves one with a theology that is quite compatible with the view of Jesus assumed in the gospel of liberal criticism. Jesus Christ becomes essentially a man. He is fully humanized. God may uniquely speak to us in and through this man, but the man who is speaking is not God.

Donald Baillie observes it is easy to see why the theory of kenosis belongs peculiarly to the modern world and seems to many of our contemporaries so promising. "It is because it apparently enables us to combine a full faith in the deity of Jesus Christ with a completely frank treatment of His life on earth as a human phenomenon, the life of a man" (*God Was in Christ*, p. 95). Baillie then observes, however, that for all its initial appeal, the doctrine of kenosis is disappointing under careful analysis and cannot possibly be harmonized with Scripture. As Charles Hodge once observed, the doctrine in all its forms is incompatible with the received Christology of the church.

In closing, consider some of the persistent problems with kenosis which have led the orthodox to reject it. If pressed consistently, the theory teaches that God became a man by ceasing to be God; God changed into a man in the incarnation. But then there is really no incarnation, no Godhead veiled in human flesh, to see. This would logically lead, as has been often pointed out, to the further conclusion that the resurrection and exaltation of our Lord should be explained as His becoming God again. If in order to become a finite man He could not exercise His distinctive divine attributes, how then can He be exalted as God over all, blessed forever, and still not be subject to the limitations of humanity? The doctrine of the kenosis really implies not an hypostatic union of the human and the divine but a succession chronologically of the divine, then the human, and then the divine again. Baur, speaking of kenosis, observes: "This complete self-renunciation is in fact the complete self-dissolution of dogma." Berkhouwer cites the Athanasian creed as explicitly condemning all thought of kenosis by asserting that the incarnation takes place not by a metamorphosis of deity into flesh, but an assumption of humanity.

But what of Paul's statement in Phil 2:7 with

which this discussion began? As Warfield and others have observed, Paul does not say, as the kenotic theorists do, that our Lord emptied Himself of anything, such as His relative attributes or His essential glory or the outward exercise of His attributes. He simply says Christ emptied *Himself*, which can hardly be taken literally, for how could He empty Himself of Himself? An expression such as this must be understood as a figurative and dramatic way of expressing the marvelous condescension of our Lord, "who, being in the form of God . . . made himself of no reputation, and took upon him the form of a servant." Only thus does the passage satisfactorily fit with the context, which is an appeal to the readers to put off rivalries, vainglory and the like and to put on the mind of Christ, which was one of humility and infinite condescension.

See Christ, Humiliation of; Incarnation; Reputation.

Bibliography. Donald Baillie, *God Was in Christ*, New York: Scribner's 1948, p. 94f. G. C. Berkouwer, *The Person of Christ*, Grand Rapids: Eerdmans, 1955, p. 27f. Charles Hodge, *Systematic Theology*, New York: Scribner, Armstrong, 1872, II, 407 ff. Charles M. Horne, "Let This Mind Be in You," BETS, III (1960), 37–44. Alva J. McClain, "The Doctrine of the Kenosis in Philippians 2:5–8," *The Biblical Review Quarterly*, XIII (1928), 506 ff.; reprinted in *Grace Journal*, VIII (1967), 3–13. Thomas A. Thomas, "The Kenosis Question," EQ, XLII (1970), 142–151.

P. K. J.

KEREN-HAPPUCH (kĕr'ĕn-hap'ŭk). The third daughter born to Jōb during the years of prosperity after his period of trial (Job 42:14). Her Heb. name means "horn of antimony," i.e., of black eye paint or mascara (cf. II Kgs 9:30; Jer 4:30).

KERIOTH (kĕr'ĭ-ŏth)

1. A city of Judah W of the southern shore of the Dead Sea (Josh 15:25), probably to be joined with the following word, forming the name Kerioth-hezron as in RSV, NASB, etc. *See* Hazor 3.

2. A city in Moab, apparently strongly fortified (Jer 48:24, 41; Amos 2:2). The Moabite Stone (line 13) refers to its sanctuary of the god Chemosh (ANET, p. 320; *see* Moabite Stone). Some have suggested to identify this city with Ar, the capital of Moab; others with Kir-heres; both identifications are doubtful, so that the site remains unknown.

KEROS (kēr'ŏs). Head of the Nethinim (*q.v.*), a family of temple servants who returned from Babylon (Ezr 2:44; Neh 7:47).

KESTREL or FALCON. *See* Animals, III. 25.

KETHIB (kĕ-thîv'). When the books of the OT were originally written, the Heb. scribes had no system for writing the vowels of their language. About the middle of the first millennium A.D. the Jewish scribes known as the Masoretes invented a method of vowel notation. However, by the time of the Masoretes, some words were traditionally read in a way at variance with the written consonants. The Masoretes, instead of altering the consonants which they found in the scrolls they copied, merely indicated the alternate reading tradition by putting the vowels of the word read (Heb. *qerê*) with the consonants as they were written (Heb. *kethîb*). These variant readings number about 1,500 in all. *See* Qere.

KETTLE. The translation of Heb. *dûd*. It is also translated "pot" and "basket." A spherical, small-mouthed cooking pot of clay or metal in which sacrificial meat was boiled (I Sam 2:14). The same word is once rendered caldron (II Chr 35:13) and might refer to vessels used for various purposes. Heb. *sîr* in Mic 3:3 is translated "kettle" in RSV and NASB; it is a shallow, wide-mouthed cooking vessel. *See* Pottery.

KETURAH (kĭ-tŏŏr'ȧ). The second wife of Abraham, who bore him six sons: Zimran, Jokshan, Medan, Midian, Ishbak, Shuah (Gen 25:1–6; I Chr 1:32–33). The marriage evidently took place after the death of Abraham's first wife, Sarah, and the marriage of Isaac to Rebekah (cf. Gen 24:67). This marriage seems to have been of lesser dignity than the first, for in I Chr 1:32–33, ASV, Keturah is classed as a concubine, probably along with Hagar. This is further established by the fact that Abraham separated Isaac, the son of promise, from the sons of his concubines (Gen 25:6), sending them to the area S and E of Palestine in northern Arabia. Midian became a prominent tribe in the area through association with Moses (cf. Ex 2:11 ff.). *See* Midian.

KEY. The instrument for raising the pins of a bolt to open a door (Jud 3:25, the only literal use of the word in the Bible). The simplest key was a short piece of wood with projecting pins. The pins fitted a corresponding pattern of slots in a bolt which dropped down into a bar to prevent its movement. The bar was held in place by cleats projecting into holes in the jamb or sill. The bar was released by putting the hand through a hole in the door and working the key by feel (Song 5:4). Metal keys with projecting fingers were also used. *See* Lock.

The word "key" is often used figuratively in Scripture to denote power and authority. The Jewish experts in the Mosaic law admittedly held the key of knowledge (Lk 11:52), which enabled men to enter the kingdom of heaven (cf. Mt 23:13). The abyss or bottomless pit where fallen angels and demons are imprisoned is locked with a key (Rev 9:1; 20:1). The word implies the royal power and authority of the

Davidic dynasty or kingdom in the expression "the key of the house of David" in Isa 22:22. In the NT this power is lodged in the risen Christ (Rev 3:7), where it is further defined as the authority to admit or to refuse admittance to heaven (cf. Mt 16:19). He also holds the "keys of" or power over death and Hades (Rev 1:18, NASB). On the "keys of the kingdom of heaven" *see* Binding and Loosing; Kingdom of God; Joachim Jeremias, "*Kleis*," TDNT, III, 744–753.

H. G. S.

KEZIAH (kē-zī'ȧ). The second daughter born to Job during the years of prosperity after his period of trial (Job 42:14). Her name means "cassis" or cinnamon.

KEZIZ (kē'zĭz). Valley of (KJV). A town of Benjamin (Josh 18:21), known as Emek-keziz (RSV, NASB), near Jericho; unidentified.

KIBROTH-HATTAAVAH kĭb'rōth-hȧ-tā'ȧ-vȧ). The first desert camp of the Israelites after they left Sinai. There the people, wearied with their monotonous diet of manna, craved flesh and God gave them quails. They overindulged and a plague resulted from which many died. Hence the name meaning "the graves of craving" (NJPS marg.) or "the graves of greediness" (NASB, marg.) (Num 11:34–35, 33:16–17; Deut 9:22).

KIBZAIM (kĭb-zā'ĭm). An unidentified city in Mount Ephraim allotted to the Kohathite Levites (Josh 21:22). Chronicles lists Jokmeam in its place (I Chr 6:68). It is uncertain whether Jokmeam is a corruption of Kibzaim or whether they are names of two Levitical cities.

KID. *See* Animals, I. 9.

KIDNEYS. The kidneys or reins, always spoken of in the plural, are situated back of the abdomen and are the organs that separate the waste materials from the blood. Because the kidneys are the most central part of the body and are surrounded with rich fat, the word is used in several ways. In the physical sense, it generally describes part of the victim of the burnt offering and signifies one of the richest parts of the animal (Ex 29:13, 22; Lev 3:4, 10, 15; 4:9; 7:4; 8:16, 25; 9:10, 19). The word was also applied to kernels of grain because of their kidneylike shape and richness (Deut 32:14).

Figuratively, the kidneys represented the inmost soul which the ancients believed was located in the internal organs and whose secrets were known to God (Jer 17:10). In the KJV "reins" is used in a physical sense (Job 16:13; 19:27; Ps 139:13; Lam 3:13) and a figurative sense (Ps 7:9; 16:7; 26:2; 73:21; Prov 23:16; Jer 11:20; 12:2; 17:10; 20:12; Rev 2:23). *See* Sacrifice; Reins; Heart.

E. C. J.

Looking South into the Kidron Valley. The walls of Jerusalem stand on the right. HFV

KIDRON (kĭd'rŏn). The name given to the deep ravine which begins N of Jerusalem near the foot of Mount Scopus; turns S to separate the E side of the city from the Mount of Olives (II Sam 15:23); and then continues in a SE direction to the Dead Sea. Modern names are varied and inconsistent for the course of the brook or winter torrent (Jn 18:1, NASB marg.) which today only rarely carries water. One of the reasons for this dry situation is that the modern bed is some 37 to 98 feet higher than the river bed of biblical times, having been filled in with occupational debris and the rubble of various destructive battles. This has also shifted the bottom of the ravine some 30 yards to the E. In antiquity, the spring of Gihon (*q.v.*) filled the brook. By means of irrigation, plush gardens and orchards were maintained along the skirts of the valley (cf. II Kgs 23:4; Jer 31:40), and in fact several royal persons and officials are known to have held real estate in the valley (*see* Shaveh, Valley of; Shebna). This brook was diverted to fill the Pool of Siloam (*q.v.*) and was enclosed to secure a water source for the city during Hezekiah's reign (II Chr 32:3–4). At least part of this valley was the site of numerous destructions and burnings of heathen images during times of reform in Judah (I Kgs 15:13; II Kgs 23:4, 6, 12; II Chr 15:16; 29:16; 30:14). Indeed, the valley was a most familiar sight to all who inhabited or frequented Jerusalem. And Jesus passed over it to Gethsemane (Jn 18:1) as well as numerous other times during Passover week.

P. W. F.

KIN. *See* Kindred.

KINAH (kī'nȧ). A city on the southern border of Judah, toward Edom (Josh 15:22). The name (*Qînâ*) suggests a settlement of the Kenites (*q.v.*; *Qênî*). The name may survive in that of the Wadi el-Qeini in the region between Arad and Sodom. It is mentioned as a fortress near Arad on an ostracon dated *c.* 600 B.C. found at Tell Arad in 1967. The commander at Ramath-negeb ordered troops to be sent from Arad and Kinah in expectation of an Edomite attack. Yohanan Aharoni suggests Kinah be identified with Khirbet et-Taiyib, three and a half miles NNE of Tell Arad ("Three Hebrew Ostaca from Arad," BASOR #197 [1970], pp. 19–27).

KINDNESS. In the OT the Heb. *ḥesed* is used of both man and God. When employed of men it may mean (1) kindness in the sense of doing favors in fulfillment of a pact or of covenant obligations (Gen 20:13; 21:23; Josh 2:12; I Sam 20:15; II Sam 9:1); (2) mercy or pity extended to needy ones (Job 6:14; Prov 20:28); (3) affection and covenant loyalty toward God (Jer 2:2); and (4) loveliness ("goodliness," Isa 40:6). When employed of God it is used to describe (1) one of His attributes (Neh 9:17; Joel 2:13), and (2) also His acts of kindness or mercy (Gen 19:19; Ps 31:21; Isa 54:8, 10).

In the NT "kindness" sometimes translates *chrēstotēs* which is employed in two senses. In one it has the meaning of uprightness ("good," Rom 3:12) and in several places it is used in the sense of kindness or generosity (II Cor 6:6; Eph 2:7; Col 3:12; Tit 3:4). *See* Goodness; Lovingkindness; Mercy; Pity.

KINDRED. The Heb. word *'āḥ*, "brother," is sometimes used for a relative or member of the same tribe or family (I Chr 12:29). The two Heb. words most often used are *mōledet*, related by birth (Gen 12:1), and *mishpāḥâ*, family (Gen 24:38, 40, 41). In the NT are found *genos*, of the same family (Acts 4:6), *suggeneia* (Lk 1:61), *phyle*, tribe, and *patria* (Acts 3:25), rendered "kindred" in KJV, but "families" in the newer versions. The term "kindred" signifies (1) relationship, kinship; (2) a group of people with relationship by consanguinity and affinity, consisting of a number of families, or even a tribe or race: When used of a number of such large groups, tribes, or races, the word sometimes appears in the plural (cf. I Chr 16:28; Ps 96:7; Rev 13:7).

Three important legal customs related to kindred were marriage, blood-revenge, and inheritance.

In the families of biblical times marriage was of utmost importance. The young woman in the case was under the control of her father, and contract had to be made with him. The romantic element usually played little or no part in the marriage contract and bargaining was often part of the procedure. A period of betrothal played an important part too. During the 2nd mil. B.C. under the prevailing Mesopotamian laws a prospective groom might render a term of service to the bride's father for her hand. Jacob served seven years for Rachel, and received Leah. Then he served seven years more for Rachel. *See* Nuzu; Patriarchal Age. Abraham sent his servant on a long journey to his former home to bring back a bride for his son Isaac (Gen 24:1–9). In this case valuable gifts were presented to the bride's family, and there is no record of a lapse of betrothal time. *See* Dowry; Family; Marriage.

Based on the command given in Gen 9:6, "Whoso sheddeth man's blood, by man shall his blood be shed," it became the recognized custom that the blood of one slain should be revenged by the nearest of kin (Num 35:19). This penalty was carried out even if a person was killed by an animal (Ex 21:28). But the motive of murder had to be carefully established. In case of accidental death, cities of refuge (*q.v.*) were provided for protection.

Laws of inheritance of land and personal property were both simple and rigid. The firstborn son received a double portion of all his father's property, other sons each a portion. Daughters shared only if there were no sons. If there were no direct heirs, the property passed to brothers or more distant kinsmen. Daughters were to marry within the tribe, for the estate must not pass out of the tribe. If land must be sold, title would be passed only until the year of jubilee, when it would again return to the original owner or heir. The Lord had said, "The land shall not be sold for ever: for the land is mine" (Lev 25:23). *See* Land and Property.

Today Christians have inheritance also as children of Abraham. "For ye are all the children of God by faith in Christ Jesus. . . . And if ye be Christ's, then are ye Abraham's seed, and heirs according to the promise" (Gal 3:26, 29). This is an eternal inheritance which nothing can take away (Col 3:24; I Pet 1:4). *See* Inheritance.

See also Kinsman; Nations.

L. A. L.

KINE. *See* Animals: Cattle, I 6.

KING. The term is used in the Bible for a ruler of the people, either Israelites or Gentiles (Gen 36:31 14:1; Mt 1:6). It is also used of God as the ruler of His people (I Sam 12:12). The meaning is "one who counsels (well)," showing that the office arose from the intellectual ability rather than from the physical prowess of the individual; the one whose counsel was consistently best became king.

Three principal concepts of kingship occurred in biblical times. The lowest degree was that of the petty king, the ruler of a city and its surroundings, such as the five kings of Midian (Num 31:8) and the kings of Jerusalem, Hebron, Jarmuth, etc. (Josh 10:3). The next degree was represented by the kings of Mesopotamia, of Assyria, and of Babylonia, who styled themselves the representative or viceregent of the deity, ordained by the gods for the political and economic good of the people. It mattered not if they came to power by revolution; they had the army to assure the imposition of their will over the people and territory. The third degree was represented by the kings of Egypt, who professed to be and were represented as deity. Alexander the Great does not seem to have claimed to be a god, although an oracle at a desert temple in Egypt said he was the son of Zeus-Amon. But during the Hellenistic period, some of the Seleucid kings in Syria professed to be reigning deities and assumed appropriate titles such as Theos and Epiphanes.

Kingship developed slowly in Israel, coming to full flower only when the people began to lose faith in God and to ape the manners and customs of their neighbors. Though Moses exercised the powers of a king, giving forth the laws of God and giving counsel (Ex 20:1 ff.; 18:16 ff.), he did not assume the title. He predicted only that that time would come later, and that when the people chose a king (Deut 17:14 ff.) they must be careful to receive the man whom God selected (cf. I Sam 8:7*b*; 9:16; 16:1 ff.). In seeking as king a man after God's own heart (e.g., David), there is intimated the holy character of the Messiah-Christ, Redeemer of God's elect, who one day will reign as *chosen* King of all God's creation. This emphasis on God's will in the selection was claimed as the basis for the authority exercised by Mesopotamian kings and Israelite rulers (Deut 17:15).

Occasional petty kings arose in Israel before Saul, as Jephthah (Jud 11:9) and Abimelech (Jud 9:6). In the days of Samuel the threat of the Philistines aroused apprehension in Israel, leading them to ask for a king. Saul was given to the people but was an example of what a king was not to be. David was the outstanding example of the Lord's king, who sought God's will and governed the people with His wisdom and grace (II Sam 23:1-5).

God promised to David an eternal dynasty (II Sam 7:16). In his day the Hittite vassal treaties provided this benefit of perpetuity when the vassal was a relative of the sovereign ruler. In David's instance, the relationship was not physical but spiritual. IIIIts full significance worl out in Christ and has benefits for all humanity in that Christ is the God-man (Isa 9:6-7). By His incarnation, death, and resurrection, He brings all who believe in Him as the risen Son of God into the eternal relationship of sons, who shall live and reign with Him forever. *See* David.

Bibliography. CornPBE, "Government, Authority, and Kingship," pp. 354-369. H. Kleinknecht, G. von Rad, Karl G. Kuhn, Karl L. Schmidt, "*Basileus*, etc.," TDNT, I, 564-593.

H. G. S.

KINGDOM OF GOD, KINGDOM OF HEAVEN

The Terms

The first question which must be considered is, are the two terms "kingdom of God" and "kingdom of heaven" synonymous? Some premillennialists insist they are different, and say the kingdom of heaven refers to the earthly physical kingdom promised Israel in the OT, while the kingdom of God refers to the spiritual rule of Christ within the heart of those who are saved (L. S. Chafer, Arno C. Gaebelein, William Kelly); other premillennialists maintain their identity (George E. Ladd, J. O. Buswell, Jr.). All amillennialists and postmillennialists would identify the terms.

King Ramses II of Egypt pictured as slaying prisoners of war. From a temple wall at Abu Simbel. LL

A study of the use of the two terms reveals that Matthew uses the term "kingdom of heaven" 34 times but "kingdom of God" only four times. Matthew uses "kingdom of heaven" four times where Mark, Luke, and John use "kingdom of God" (Mt 4:17, cf. Mk 1:15; Mt 10:7, cf. Lk 9:2; Mt 5:3, cf. Lk 6:20; Mt 13:11, cf. Mk 4:11; Lk 8:10). Evidently, Matthew had a reason for his preference. He was a Jew writing to his own race and respected their custom of using the name of God as little as possible and therefore spoke of the kingdom of heaven. On the other hand, to speak of the kingdom of heaven to the Gentiles and the heathen would have been to suggest concepts which for them implied polytheism, while to speak of the kingdom of God would have stressed monotheism. This apparently is the reason the other three Gospel writers do not speak of the kingdom of heaven. Those who feel that Matthew uses "kingdom of heaven" for theological reasons and means to distinguish it from the "kingdom of God" should note that Matthew uses the latter five times (Mt 6:33; 12:28; 19:24; 21:31, 43). In the case of the rich young ruler he uses both terms together Mt 19:23-24), demonstrating their interchangeability for his purposes.

Aspects of the Kingdom

There are two aspects of the kingdom, present and future.

1. *Present.* The present invisible phase is set forth in the Gospels in the call to repentance by John the Baptist and Christ (Mt 3:2; 4:17, 23: Lk 4:43; cf. Mt 10:7); in Christ's teaching on sanctification as an aspect of the Christian life as in the Sermon on the Mount (Mt 5-7); and in the revelation of the mysteries of the kingdom particularly of the hidden start, growth, and development of the kingdom during the Gospel Age until its open manifestation in the Millennium (Mt 13:19, 24, 31, 33, 44-45, 47, 52; Mk 4:30).

Passages in the epistles reveal that the rule of God on earth today is effective only among those who have been delivered from darkness and transferred into the kingdom of His Son (Col 1:13). The kingdom exists at present where Christians are living in subjection to the will of God, where His power is producing changed lives (I Cor 4:20). The kingdom of God is not a matter of getting what one wants to eat and drink, but a matter of upright conduct, peace and harmony with other believers, and joy inspired by the Holy Spirit (Rom 14:17). Paul was apparently opposing the materialistic ideas which the Jews of his day held concerning the expected messianic kingdom.

2. *Future.* The future visible aspect of the kingdom when Messiah will reign over the earth from Jerusalem is foretold in many passages in the OT (Deut 30:1-10; Ps 2; 72; 89:19-29; 110; Isa 11:1-16; 65:17-66:24; Jer 32:36-44; 33:4-18; Joel 3:17-21; Zech 14:9-17). For this visible kingdom the Jews were looking. The parables of the kingdom (Mt 13) were given to reveal the mystery that the kingdom must first develop spiritually and unobtrusively in the Gospel Age. But this was not enough! On His last visit to Jerusalem Christ gave the parable of the pounds to teach that the future earthly kingdom was still far away, "because they thought that the kingdom of God should immediately appear" (Lk 19:11).

The very last question asked by the disciples of the Lord concerned the future aspect of the kingdom. "Lord, wilt thou at this time restore again the kingdom to Israel?" (Acts 1:6). Christ did not tell them there was to be no earthly kingdom or restoration of the kingdom to Israel. Since He never said anything before nor at this last meeting to change their concept and conviction concerning a millennial reign of the Son of David over His own, evidently they were correct about the nature of the kingdom, even if still confused about its timing. To draw any other conclusion is to claim that they were wrong, that we know more than they, and that Christ departed purposefully leaving them holding a mistaken idea. The premilliennialist cannot accept such conclusions. For further discussion of the future phase of the kingdom *see* Millennium. *See also* Eschatology; King; Theocracy.

Bibliography. Louis Berkhof, *The Kingdom of God,* Grand Rapids: Eerdmans, 1951. John Bright, *The Kingdom of God,* Nashville: Abingdon, 1953. J. O. Buswell, Jr., *A Systematic Theology of the Christian Religion,* Grand Rapids: Eerdmans, 1963, II, 346-361. L. S. Chafer, *Systematic Theology,* Dallas: Dallas Seminary Press, 1947. George E. Ladd, *Crucial Questions About the Kingdom of God,* Grand Rapids: Eerdmans, 1952; *The Gospel of the Kingdom,* Grand Rapids: Eerdmans, 1959; *Jesus and the Kingdom,* New York: Harper and Row, 1964. Alva J. McClain, *The Greatness of the Kingdom,* Chicago: Moody, 1968. George Peters, *The Theocratic Kingdom,* 3 vols., Grand Rapids: Kregel, 1952. John F. Walvoord, *The Millennial Kingdom,* Findlay: Dunham, 1959.

R. A. K.

KINGDOM OF ISRAEL. *See* Israel, Kingdom of.

KINGDOM OF JUDAH. *See* Judah, Kingdom of.

KINGLY OFFICE OF CHRIST. *See* Jesus, Offices of.

KINGS, I and II. These two books originally were one book or scroll in Heb. The division into two volumes in the Heb. text appeared first in a mid-15th cen. MS and then in Daniel Bomberg's printed Heb. Bible in A.D. 1516-17. Since the Gr. text, however, required twice as much space as the Heb. in which vowels were not introduced until after A.D. 600, the translation of the book of Kings into Gr. for the LXX had precipitated centuries earlier a division using two scrolls instead of one. The books of Samuel and Kings in the Gr. and Latin Bibles are regarded as one continuous history in four volumes. In some Gr. texts, however, the end of David's reign (I Kgs 2:11) or the beginning of Solomon's reign (I Kgs 2:46*a*) marks the division between the books of Samuel and Kings. The division between I and II Kings seems to be quite artificial.

Although Josephus regarded the books of Samuel and Kings as two volumes, the Alexandrian Jews considered these as books "of kingdoms" (*basileiōn*) forming four books. The Latin Vulg. identified these as books of "kings" introducing the current designation as I and II Samuel and I and II Kings for this historical account.

Chronologically the events of I and II Kings cover a period of more than four centuries beginning with the reign of Solomon, *c.* 971 B.C., to the release of Jehoiachin from Babylonian Captivity, *c.* 562 B.C. In addition to offering a continous survey of the Davidic dynasty, it also narrates the contemporary developments in northern kingdom from its beginning in 931 B.C. to the fall of Samaria in 722 B.C.

Sources for Writing

This volume was obviously written by an author who used historical sources. Documents actually named are "the book of the acts of Solomon" (I Kgs 11:41), "the book of the chronicles of the kings of Judah" (I Kgs 14:29), and "the book of the chronicles of the kings of Israel" (I Kgs 14:19). In addition, Isa 36-39 very likely provided the source for the account of the Judo-Assyrian relations in the days of Hezekiah and Sennacherib. It may well be that prophets, who lived in the border area of the northern and southern kingdoms during the four centuries following Solomon's death, kept records which were available to the author who made the final composition shortly after the fall of Jerusalem.

Author

Talmudic tradition (Baba Bathra 15a) asserts that Jeremiah was the author. The literary ability and prophetic perspective reflected throughout these books greatly favor Jeremian authorship, with the final chapter probably added by a resident of Babylon after Jehoiachin's release in 562 B.C.

The influence of Deuteronomy reflected throughout these books has been used by some OT scholars as the basis to ascribe the final authorship to Deuteronomists who were active about 550 B.C. This theory assumes that the book of Deuteronomy was written during Josian times. However, if Moses wrote Deuteronomy, his influence as the greatest of all prophets would naturally permeate the subsequent history of Israel beginning with Joshua and continuing through the books of Judges, Samuel, and Kings.

Outline

I. The United Kingdom under Solomon, I Kgs 1:1–11:43
  - A. Solomon established as king, 1:1–4:34
  - B. Temple built and dedicated, 5:1–9:25
  - C. International relations, 9:26–10:29
  - D. Apostasy and death, 11:1-43

II. Tension and Warfare after Division, I Kgs 12:1–16:28
  - A. Rehoboam and Jeroboam, 12:1–14:31
  - B. Abija, Asa, and the northern kings, 15:1–16:28

III. The Era of Alliance, I Kgs 16:29–II Kgs 8:29
  - A. Kings Ahab and Jehoshaphat and the prophet Elijah, 16:29–22:53
  - B. Elijah, Elisha, and the allied kings, II Kgs 1:1–8:29

IV. The Jehu Dynasty and Contemporary Developments, II Kgs 9:1–15:12
  - A. Jehu's revolt and purge of Baalism, 9:1–10:31
  - B. The reform of Joash and Syria's ascendancy, 10:32–13:9
  - C. Israel's emergence as the stronger kingdom, 13:10–15:12

V. The Era of Assyrian Domination, II Kgs 15:13–21:26
  - A. The decline and fall of Samaria, 15:13–17:41
  - B. The threat to Hezekiah, king of Judah, 18:1–20:21
  - C. The wicked reigns of Manasseh and Amon, 21:1-26

VI. The Decline and Fall of Judah, II Kgs 22:1–25:30
  - A. Revival under Josiah, 22:1–23:30
  - B. Conquest by Babylonia, 23:31–25:26
  - C. Jehoiachin's captivity and release, 25:27-30

Theme

The admonition to covenant allegiance is the theme of these two books of Kings. Faithfulness to their covenant with God was essential for Israel's welfare as a nation. The author measured each ruler by his conformity to the Mosaic law. Outstanding secular achievements by kings were often minimized or omitted, whereas covenant responsibilities were significantly emphasized. Beginning with the Davidic and Solomonic kingdom when Israel reached the height of international fame and wealth – a period never exceeded since then – the author seeks to account for the division and decline of the kingdom which terminated in the fall of Jerusalem.

Throughout these centuries of decline, prophet after prophet reminded the kings and citizens of their failure to love and serve God wholeheartedly, and warned them about God's judgment because of their social injustice. The destruction of Jerusalem with its temple reduced to ashes was accompanied by Israel's captivity, which was the greatest judgment on God's people in OT times. In this manner the first commonwealth of Israel was terminated.

Difficulties in the Books

The problems of correlating the statistical data given throughout the books of Kings are numerous. A marked advance in scholarship offering a solution to many of the chronological difficulties is the volume by E. R. Thiele (cf. bibliography). A proper understanding of the dating systems used in the northern and southern kingdoms at various times and of the matter of coregencies has made it possible to account for most of the problems in the biblical accounts. Secular sources from the Assyrian eponym lists covering the history of that empire from 893 to 666 B.C. and the Gr. canon of Ptolemy giving the reigns of Babylonian kings from 747 B.C. onward into the Graeco-Roman period provide a basis of comparison and correlation.

Tablets read and published by Donald J. Wiseman have provided more specific information for dating the Chaldean kings in the period 626-566 B.C. Consequently the dates for the fall of Samaria in 722 B.C. and the fall of Jerusalem in 586 B.C. are accepted as fixed dates with a variable of a year or so. The year 931 B.C. as the date for the division of the

The King's Highway and the mountains of Gilead. HFV

kingdom after the death of Solomon has excellent historical support according to E. R. Thiele, although suggested dates by various scholars vary from 937 to 922 B.C.

Bibliography. Gleason L. Archer, SOTI. Sh. R. Bin-Nun, "Formulas from Royal Records of Israel and of Judah," VT, XVIII (1968), 414-442. John J. Davis, *The Birth of a Kingdom*, Grand Rapids:Baker, 1970. Roland Kenneth Harrison, *Introduction to the Old Testament*, Grand Rapids: Eerdmans, 1969. James A. Montgomery, *A Critical and Exegetical Commentary on the Books of Kings*, ed. by Henry S. Gehman, ICC, 1951. Samuel J. Schultz, *The Old Testament Speaks*, New York: Harper and Row, 1960. Edwin R. Thiele, *The Mysterious Numbers of the Hebrew Kings*, Grand Rapids: Eerdmans, 1966. Donald J. Wiseman, *Chronicles of Chaldean Kings (626-556 B.C.) in the British Museum*, London, 1956.

S. J. S.

KING'S DALE. The king's dale (King's Valley, RSV) is equated with the valley of Shaveh (*q.v.*) near Salem (Jerusalem) in the account of Abraham and Melchizedek (Gen 14:17). The only other mention is made in II Sam 18:18 in regard to a monument Absalom erected in honor of himself in the king's dale. Josephus (*Ant.* vii. 10.3) mentions that this monument stood two furlongs (*c.* 400 yds.) from Jerusalem. Absalom's monument (not the Hellenistic tomb on SE of city) no longer stands, and thus positive identification is unlikely. However, the areas most likely are: (1) NW of the "old city" toward the Russian compound; or, (2) the junction of the Kidron and Hinnom valleys (by virtue of royal real estate holdings there).

KING'S GARDEN. *See* Jerusalem: Gates and Towers 10.

KING'S HIGHWAY. A major commercial arterial trade route along the length of the Transjordanian plateau from Ezion-geber through Karnaim to Damascus. A branch, perhaps leaving the main route at Bozrah and crossing the Arabah near Tamar, traversed the Negeb to Kadesh-barnea and perhaps on to Egypt through territory controlled by the Edomites in Moses' time (Num 20:17). Mentioned by this name only three times in the Bible (Num 20:17; 21:22; Deut 2:27), various segments were also called "the way of the wilderness of Moab" (Deut 2:8) and "the way of Bashan" (Num 21:33; Deut 3:1). As such, it served as major competition to the via Maris in the W along the coastal plain.

On the southern plateau of Transjordan there is a double watershed, each with a caravan route. One runs about 15 miles E of the Arabah and is marked by the present-day railroad track. Because of the deep canyons cut by the Zered and Arnon Rivers, the track must go out another 10 to 15 miles E into the desert to cross these valleys. Marauding nomads of the desert cause settlements along this route to be spotty if not absent. The second watershed is farther W. This marked the main route of the large import trade of spices and perfumes from Arabia. Sites along this route were occupied during the patriarchal and Israelite periods of biblical history.

In all probability, this road was used in the invasion of the kings from Mesopotamia (Gen 14:5–6) and certainly must have played an important role in the economics and military campaigns of the kingdom period (cf. II Kgs 10:33; 16:6). At Rabbath-ammon the two lines merged to continue N toward Damascus and points beyond. Therefore, Rabbath-ammon was one of the more important cities on the route, along with Bozrah and Sela in Edom, Kirhareseth in Moab, Heshbon in Ammon, Ramoth-Gilead and Gerasa in Gilead, and Ashtaroth and Karnaim in Bashan.

See Travel and Communication: Road, Highways and Sea Lanes.

P. W. F.

KING'S HOUSE. *See* Palace.

KING'S MOTHER. *See* Queen.

KING'S POOL. The pool called by this name only by Nehemiah on his inspection tour of the city walls (Neh 2:14) is located to the SE of Jerusalem in connection with the King's Garden in the Kidron Valley where it may have served for irrigation. *See* Jerusalem.

KING'S SEPULCHER. *See* Tomb.

KINSMAN. In the OT the word is most often used of Heb. *gō'ēl*, the one who has the right to redeem. Three obligations were his: (1) to redeem his brother and his inheritance, if poverty had caused him to go into slavery or dispose of his land (Lev 25:25, 47–49); (2) to avenge his blood if he were slain (Num 35:19); (3) to raise up a successor to his brother if he had died childless (Ruth 3:13).

In the NT Gr. *suggenēs* may refer to a family relative (NASB at Mk 6:4; Lk 1:36,58 [KJV, "cousin"]; Lk 2:44; 14:12; 21:16; Jn 18:26; Acts 10:24). In a broader sense the term may be a fellow countryman, a fellow citizen of the same race or nation (Rom 9:3; 16:7, 11, 21).

The outstanding picture in the Bible of the kinsman-redeemer is the beautiful story of Ruth and Boaz. In the time of the judges, Naomi with her husband Elimelech and two sons left Bethlehem ("house of bread") and went into Moab because of famine. Only Naomi and Ruth, the Moabite widow of one of the sons, returned to Bethlehem ten years later, at the time of barley harvest. Taking advantage of Heb. law, Ruth gleaned in the field of Boaz, kinsman of Naomi. Boaz, in accordance with Jewish law, acted as *gōʼēl,* and married Ruth. Thus she became the ancestress of David and of Christ.

Spiritually our great Kinsman-Redeemer is Jesus Christ, who Himself came to Bethlehem over a thousand years after the time of Ruth and Boaz. To act as our *gōʼēl,* like Boaz He had to have the right, the power, and the will to redeem.

See Blood, Avenger of; Kindred; Levirate Marriage; Redeemer.

L. A. L.

KIR (kĭr)

1. The place from which the Aramaeans migrated to Syria (Amos 9:7). King Tiglath-pileser III of Assyria deported the Aramaean inhabitants of Damascus back to it as captives (II Kgs 16:9; Amos 1:5). Its militia is represented as allied with Elam against Judah (Isa 22:6). The place has not yet been attested in ancient Near Eastern records, and remains unidentified.

2. A city of Moab mentioned along with Ar in Isa 15:1. Kir is probably the same as Kir-haraseth (*q.v.*), located at Kerak, 11 miles E of the southern bay of the Dead Sea.

KIR-HARASETH (kĭr-hăr'*ȧ*-sĕth). Commonly identified with Kir of Moab, a chief city in the southern part of the Moabite kingdom, probably to be identified with Kerak, a city which figured significantly in the Crusades. It is alternately spelled Kir-hareseth (Isa 16:7), Kir-haresh (Isa 16:11), Kir-heres (Jer 48:31, 36), and simply Kir (Isa 15:1), in which passages the prophets of Judah foretold the destruction of the city.

Here King Mesha (*q.v.*) of Moab offered his son as a sacrifice on the walls while the city was being besieged by the Israelites (II Kgs 3:25–27). It may be the city Qarhoh which Mesha rebuilt with the labor of Israelite captives, according to his Moabite Stone inscription (ANET, p. 32). It lies on "the King's Highway," 17 miles S of the Arnon. Its 12th cen. A.D. castle is still conspicuous on its precipitous hill dropping over 300 feet to the valleys on the three sides. About 10,000 people live in el-Kerak today.

Bibliography. George M. Harton, "The Meaning of II Kings 3:27," *Grace Journal,* XI (1970), 34–40. In a short note Ph. Derchain argues that Mesha's son was sacrificed by dropping him from the battlement (VT, XX [1970], 351–355).

G. A. T.

KIRIOTH. *See* Kerioth.

KIRJATH (kĭr'jăth)

1. A city of Benjamin (Josh 18:28); sometimes identified with Kirjath-jearim.

2. A prefix of several site names. *See* Kirjathaim, Kirjath-arba, Kirjath-baal, Kirjath-huzoth, Kirjath-jearim, Kirjath-sepher.

KIRJATHAIM (kĭr'j*ȧ*-thā'ĭm)

1. A city in Transjordan identified with Khirbet el-Qureiyat *c.* six miles NW of Dibon. It was formerly occupied by the Emim (Shaveh Kiriathaim, *q.v.,* "the plain of Kirjathaim," Gen 14:5). The Reubenites received it as part of their inheritance (Num 32:37; Josh 13:19). Later it was part of the Moabite kingdom (Moabite Stone, line 10, *q.v.;* Jer 48:1, 23; Ezk 25:9).

2. A Levitical city of Naphtali (I Chr 6:76) which appears in Josh 21:32 as Kartan (*q.v.*). The site is unknown.

KIRJATH-ARBA (kĭr'jăth-är'b*ȧ*). An old name for the city of Hebron, where Abraham established his home (Gen 23:2; 35:27). A city in the hill country of Judah (Josh 15:54; Jud 1:10), Caleb captured it from the Anakim for whose hero Arba, the father of Anak, it had been named (Josh 14:15). It became a city of refuge (Josh 20:7) and a Levitical city (Josh 21:11). It was reoccupied after the Exile (Neh 11:25). *See* Hebron.

KIRJATH-ARIM. *See* Kirjath-jearim.

KIRJATH-BAAL (kĭr'jăth-bāl). The same as Kirjath-jearim (Josh 15:60; 18:14). Its name means "city of Baal," indicating that it may have been a center for Baal worship in the city-state of the Gibeonites during the Late Bronze Age. It was located at the SW corner of the boundary between Judah and Benjamin, seven miles from Jerusalem, and belonged to the tribe of Benjamin.

KIRJATH-HUZOTH (kĭr'jăth-hū'zŏth). The Moabite city to which Balak and Balaam first went when Balak employed Balaam to curse Israel and he blessed her instead (Num 22:39). The location is uncertain.

KIRJATH-JEARIM (kĭr'jăth-jē'*ȧ*-rĭm). A town

in Judah (Josh 15:9, 60), now represented by Deir el-'Azar, overlooking the modern village of Abu Gosh. Its other ancient names were Kirjath-baal (Josh 15:60; 18:14), Baalah (Josh 15:9, 11), or Baale (II Sam 6:2; cf. I Chr 13:6). Joshua encountered it as a member of the Gibeonite league (Josh 9:17). After the settlement of the land it stood at the boundary juncture between Judah, Benjamin and Dan (Josh 15:9; 18:14–15), but it was occupied by Judah (Josh 15:60; Jud 18:12).

The ark of the covenant remained there in the house of Abinadab for 20 years after its return by the Philistines (I Sam 6:19–7:2). Shishak may have besieged this town on his march through Palestine if the reading *qdtm* of No. 25 in his list may be amended to *qrtm*, Heb. *qiryataim* (*r* and *d* are quite similar in Egyptian hieratic script from which the scultor must have copied). The town receives no further mention until after the Babylonian Captivity at which time some of its citizens returned to Judah (Neh 7:29; cf. Ezr 2:25 where the town is written Kirjath-arim).

Bibliography. Joseph Blenkinsopp, "Kiriath-jearim and the Ark," JBL, LXXXVIII (1969), 143–156.

A. F. R.

KIRJATH-SANNAH (kĭr′ĭ-ăth-săn′ȧ). The reputed name of a city in the hill country of Judah (Josh 15:49); the same as Debir (*q.v.*). It is possible that this is a third name for Debir (in addition to Kirjath-sepher), although no satisfactory explanation has been given as to its meaning. However, the LXX evidently had the reading Kirjath-sepher here, so the name in the Masoretic Text may be a scribal error caused by confusion with the preceding name, Dannah.

KIRJATH-SEPHER. *See* Debir.

The Kishon currently is a much smaller stream than in biblical times because its waters are used for irrigation. HFV

KISH (kĭsh)

1. A Benjamite, a descendant ("son") of Jeiel and father of King Saul (I Sam 9:1–3; 10:11, 21; 14:51; II Sam 21:14; I Chr 8:30, 33; 9:36, 39; 12:1; 26:28). Kish was a man of considerable means, having a number of servants and donkeys (I Sam 9:3). Saul's description of his family as the least of all the families in Benjamin must be taken as an example of Oriental modesty (I Sam 9:21).

2. A Levite in David's time, of the family of Merari (I Chr 23:21–22; 24:29).

3. A Levite, son of Abdi, of the family of Merari who assisted in cleansing the temple at the time of Hezekiah's revival (II Chr 29:12).

4. An ancestor of Mordecai (Est 2:5).

KISHI. *See* Kushaiah.

KISHION (kĭsh′ĭ-ŏn). A city on the border of Issachar (Josh 19:20), identified with Kh. Qasyûn about a mile and a half S of Mount Tabor, given to the Gershonite Levites (Josh 21:28).

KISHON (ki′shon). The main stream of the valley of Jezreel for which it provides the western drainage. Its sources lie in the N and W slopes of Mount Ephraim, the W slopes of Mount Tabor, and the S slopes of lower Galilee. The name means "crooked" and aptly describes the stream's course to the sea. Shihor-libnath (Josh 19:26) may be a special name for the Kishon's mouth on the Gulf of Acco or Bay of Acre, the second element, -libnath, possibly being the ancient name of Tell Abu Huwam. The river flows in the dry summer season only in its last seven miles, receiving water from springs at the base of Mount Carmel. Because of its slight fall as it crosses the level plain the stream becomes swollen during heavy rains and may flood much of the valley.

Two dramatic events in biblical history took place in connection with the Kishon. (1) The victory of Barak and his troops over the chariotry of Sisera is ascribed not only to the valor of the troops but to the aid rendered by the stars and by the torrent Kishon (Jud 5:19–21). Apparently a flash flooding of the river caused Sisera's chariots to bog down in mud. (2) The 400 priests of Baal who lost their contest with Elijah (*q.v.*) were executed on the Kishon's S bank (I Kgs 18:40).

A. F. R.

KISON. *See* Kishon.

KISS. In the Bible the word is used in at least eight different ways.

1. The kiss of relatives, which may have been the origin of kissing (Song 8:1): Isaac and Jacob (Gen 27:26–27); Jacob and Rachel (Gen 29:11); Esau and Jacob (Gen 33:4); Joseph and his brothers (Gen 45:15); Jacob and Joseph's sons (Gen 48:10); Joseph and his father (Gen 50:1); Aaron and Moses (Ex 4:27); Moses and Jethro (Ex 18:7); Naomi and her daughters-in-law (Ruth 1:9, 14); David and Absalom

(II Sam 14:33); Elisha and his parents (I Kgs 19:20); the father and the prodigal son (Lk 15:20).

2. The kiss of friendship and affection: David and Jonathan (I Sam 20:41); Absalom and those who came to him (II Sam 15:5); David and Barzillai (II Sam 19:39; cf. kiss of an enemy, II Sam 20:9; Prov 27:6); Paul and the Ephesian Christians (Acts 20:37).

3. The kiss of love: true love (Song 1:2); feigned love (Prov 7:13).

4. The kiss of dedication: of a king (I Sam 10:1).

5. The kiss of homage: that due the Messiah (Ps 2:12).

6. The kiss of adoration: the woman with the alabaster box (Lk 7:38, 45).

7. The kiss of idolatry (I Kgs 19:18; Hos 13:2; Job 31:27 f).

8. The "holy kiss" of NT Christians, the *philema* commanded by Paul and Peter (Rom 16:16; I Cor 16:20; II Cor 13:12; I Thess 5:26; I Pet 5:14).

The weaker term (*phileō*) is used three times in the NT by Judas to the council (Mt 26:48; Mk 14:44) of his purpose to use a kiss as a means of identification and betrayal (Lk 22:47). However, when Judas accosted Christ he kissed Him again and again, increasing his perfidy (*kataphileo*, Mt 26:49; Mk 14:45).

R. A. K.

KITCHEN. A term not appearing in the KJV or NASB, but found in Ezk 46:24 in the RSV, Berkeley, and NEB, used in connection with the four small subcourts at the corners of the outer court of the future temple. In these "boiling places" (NASB) were hearths where the sacrifices of the people could be boiled (vv. 21–24), separate from the place where the priests cooked the guilt, sin, and grain offerings (vv. 19–20).

KITE. *See* Animals, III. 26.

KITHLISH (kĭth'lĭsh). An unidentified town in the Shephelah of Judah near Eglon (Josh 15:40).

KITRON (kĭt'rŏn). A city in the area allotted to Zebulun from which they failed to drive out the inhabitants (Jud 1:30); probably the same as Kattath.

KITTIM. *See* Chittim.

KNEAD. *See* Food.

KNEE. The Heb. word as a verb means "to kneel down" (II Chr 6:13) as well as "to bless" or "to pronounce a blessing," because the person blessed kneels. Thus it is used in reference to making camels bend the knee to take rest (Gen 24:11). It is used of men blessing God (Gen 24:48; I Kgs 1:48); God blessing men (Num 23:20), and men blessing men (Gen 14:19; 27:4).

The word also signifies "to salute," which is connected with blessing (I Kgs 1:47; Ps 49:18; 62:4). To bow the knee or kneel on the knees was an act of worship (I Kgs 8:54; 19:18; Ezr 9:5). Kneeling was a posture of prayer (Dan 6:10; Lk 22:41; Acts 9:40; 20:36; 21:5; Eph 3:14). However, Elijah put his face between his knees in prayer (I Kgs 18:42).

Bodily weakness often shows up first in the knees: "thou hast strengthened the feeble knees" (Job 4:4; cf. Isa 35:3; Ezk 7:17; 21:7; Heb 12:12). The new-born babe was placed upon the knees of the father (Job 3:12, RSV, "Why did the knees receive me?") or of the legal wife (Gen 30:3) or of an adopting relative (Gen 50:23; Ruth 4:17) to signify legal parentage, since the knees were as close as possible to the source of life.

See Worship.

E. C. J.

KNIFE. A sharp hand instrument for cutting. Ancient languages give imprecise designations and there is little consistency in the half dozen Heb. words translated "knife," "sword," "razor." The purpose to which the instrument was put and the manner of operation seems more helpful in deciding with which modern word to translate.

Knives were made first of stone, especially flint (Josh 5:2 f., RSV), and then of bronze and iron. A typical knife was a straight blade six to ten inches long with handle and blade as one piece.

The principal uses were domestic (for butchering and food preparation, not eating, Gen 22:6), professional ("a scribe's knife," Jer 36:23, JerusB), and ritual (Josh 5:2; I Kgs 18:28). Only once is knife used metaphorically (Prov 30:14), the sword being the usual figure.

KNOP

1. Heb. *kăphtôr:* a part of the golden lampstand in the tabernacle. It seems to have been a support for the branches and for the ornamental flowers (Ex 25:31–36; 37:17–22). In Amos 9:1 (NASB) the same Heb. word means the crown or capital of a column (KJV, "lintels").

2. Heb. *p^eqā'îm* ("gourds," NASB): associated with open flowers in the cedar work of the walls of Solomon's temple (I Kgs 6:18) and under the rim of the "molten sea" (I Kgs 7:24).

KNOW, KNOWLEDGE. *Biblical terms.* The verb "to know" is used in English both of becoming acquainted and familiar with an object by experience and of gaining theoretical or general understanding in a scientific sense. In the OT the latter sense is almost entirely absent. The most common Heb. verb, *yāda'*, found more than 900 times, basically means to know by experience. The noun *da'at* is derived from it and is often nearly synonymous with wisdom, occurring often in the books of wisdom (e.g., Job 15:2; 33:3; Prov 1:4; 1:7 with 9:10; Eccl 1:16, 18; 2:21, 26). The verb *nākar* means to know, discern, perceive, or recognize (e.g., Gen

KNOW, KNOWLEDGE

37:33; 42:7–8; Ruth 3:14; I Sam 26:17; Job 2:12).

In the NT there are two basic verbs translated "to know." The first, *ginōskō*, has a wide range of uses but seems to emphasize gaining or having knowledge grounded on personal experience (Jn 17:3; Eph 3:19; Phil 3:10). The other, *oida*, the perfect tense of *eidō*, "to see," means to know by seeing or observation and can signify a purely mental perception (e.g., Jesus' knowing the thoughts of the Pharisees or of His disciples, Mt 12:25; Lk 6:8; 11:17; Mk 12:15; Jn 6:61). It is often used of knowing a familiar fact or truth (e.g., Mt 20:25; Mk 4:13; 10:19; Jn 9:29, 31). Another verb, *epistamai*, means to understand or be intelligent (Acts 10:28; I Tim 6:4; Jas 3:13). The noun *gnōsis* is the general Gr. word for knowledge. The verb *epiginōskō* and its noun *epignōsis* imply full, complete, or real knowledge (Lk 1:4; Col 1:9; II Pet 1:2–3, 8).

Definitions. Knowledge is, according to Webster (*New Collegiate Dictionary*, 1958): "1. Familiarity gained by actual experience; practical skill. 2. Acquaintance with fact . . . 3. The act or state of understanding; clear perception of truth . . . . 4. That which is gained and preserved by knowing; enlightenment; learning." James Orr defines the term as follows: "Knowledge strictly is the apprehension by the mind of some fact or truth in accordance with its true nature; in a personal relation the intellectual act is necessarily conjoined with the element of affection and will" (ISBE, III, 1816).

The nature of man's knowledge. Both the senses and the understanding have their part: the senses are the channel for data upon which knowledge may be based; the understanding is the seat of all knowledge gained and the source of knowledge attained by reason. Knowledge is to be distinguished from opinion by its greater certainty.

The nature or character of knowledge varies with its object. Knowledge of outward objects and appearances comes through the senses; that of principles governing these appearances comes through the intellect; and moral knowledge comes through both revelation and the God-given ability to distinguish between right and wrong. The most fundamental knowledge of all, that which explains the origin and relation of the world and man to their Creator, God, comes through revelation (*q.v.*). This knowledge demands spiritual enablement from God (I Cor 2:10–14). It is of this knowledge the Scriptures particularly speak.

The attainment of some knowledge entails simply the perception of facts, e.g., events in history; other requires comprehension and understanding; and again, other needs perception, comprehension and personal acceptance. General revelation supplies man with a sufficient knowledge of God, through comprehension and understanding, to make him without excuse (Rom 1:19–20). Special revelation gives man enough knowledge that through comprehension and understanding he may know about God and His plan of salvation for man. But only with personal acceptance of such knowledge can he truly know God through Jesus Christ as his Redeemer and experience eternal life (Mt 11:27; Jn 17:3).

The element of personal participation in knowledge appears prominently in the use of the Heb. *yāda'* and the Gr. *ginōskō* to express sexual relations. Nevertheless it is dangerous to argue from this, as Paul Tillich did, that therefore all knowledge consists in a union with the person or thing known. Even though Christ prayed for His disciples "that they may be one, as we are" (Jn 17:11) and "that they also might be one in us" (Jn 17:21), this does not mean there must always be union with the object of knowledge in order for knowledge to exist. What about knowledge of what is evil? It was the lie of Satan that Adam would be like God, knowing good and evil, if he acted evilly and united with Satan against God (Gen 3:5).

No man who unites with evil knows it properly; only the one who avoids all appearance of evil and knows it only by understanding, knows it as does God. Thus there is a false knowledge as well as a true (Isa 47:10). Furthermore, intellectual knowledge as opposed to moral and spiritual knowledge can cater to one's pride. The desire for and use of knowledge should be motivated by love, for "knowledge puffeth up" (I Cor 8:1; cf. 13:2). The great attraction of Gnosticism (*q.v.*) in the early church was its promise of esoteric knowledge hidden from the common worshiper of God (cf. I Tim 6:20, NASB, "the opposing arguments of what is falsely called 'knowledge' "; Col 2:8, 18).

The contrast with God's knowledge. The Scriptures speak of our knowledge as only partial (I Cor 13:9, 12). Yet it is real knowledge even if not complete. Only God has perfect comprehensive knowledge. His knowledge embraces all things past, present, and future. It extends to all things, even to the thoughts and interests of man's heart (Ps 139:1–24), as did that of Jesus Christ (Mt 9:4; Jn 2:24–25; cf. Jn 6:64). Thus we speak of the omniscience (*q.v.*) of God. His knowledge is infinite (Ps 147:5) and eternal. He was never ignorant and does not have to learn. His knowledge may be said to be intuitive, distinguished from both the reasoning and the empirical learning of man (BDT, pp. 314 f.).

Coordinate to a man's saving personal knowledge of Jesus Christ and thus of God as our heavenly Father, there is God's election (*q.v.*) and personal knowledge of the believer as His child (II Tim 2:19; Jn 10:14; I Cor 8:3; Ps1:6; Jer 1:5—cf. JerusB; cf. Mt 7:23) and of Israel as His covenant people (Amos 3:2).

The condition of knowledge. In order for man to have the highest knowledge (*epignosis*) possible for a finite creature, knowledge of God Himself and of His Son Jesus Christ (Hos 6:6; Eph 1:17; 4:13; Phil 1:9; Col 1:10; II Pet 1:2–3, 8) and of His will (Col 1:9), two conditions must be met: (1) faith, believing that God exists and that He is the rewarder of those who diligently seek Him (Heb 11:6); and (2) obedience or willingness to know and submit to His will (Jn 7:17).

Bibliography. Rudolf Bultmann, "*Ginōskō,* etc., TDNT, I, 689–719. Stephen Charnock, *Discourses upon the Existence and Attributes of God,* London: Henry Bohn, 1849, Discourses VIII and IX (pp. 259–396). Gordon H, Clark, "Knowledge," BDT, pp. 314 ff. Otto A. Piper, "Knowledge," IDB, III, 42–48 (with extensive bibliography).

R. A. K.

KOA (kō'*ȧ*). This is one of the minor nations identified with the Kutu or Ku of slightly earlier Assyrian records. It was situated E of the Tigris River. Koa would combine with the Chaldeans, men of Pekod (the Puqudu) and Shoa (the Sutu), and Assyrian remnants, all mercenaries of Babylon, to punish Aholibah, the shameless harlot who personified Jerusalem (Ezk 23:22–23).

KOHATH (kō'hăth). One of the three sons of Levi who went down with Israel into Egypt (Gen 46:11). The sons, or more probably descendants, of Kohath were Amram, Izhar, Hebron, and Uzziel. Amram, who married his father's sister Jochebed, was the father of Moses and Aaron; thus the later priestly line of Israel comes from Kohath through Aaron (Ex 6:1–18). The rest of the descendants of Kohath were numbered among the other Levites and given the highest privilege, the care of the sacred vessels of the sanctuary (Num 3:27 ff.; 4:2 ff.; 7:9).

KOHATHITES (kō'hă-thīts). Descendants of Kohath (*q.v.*), the second son of Levi; the branch of the family to which Moses, Aaron, and Miriam belonged (Num 26:57). When they were numbered at Sinai there were 8,600 males (Num 3:27–28), 2,750 from 30 to 50 years of age (Num 4:34–37). With the other Levitical families, they were placed near the tabernacle in the organization of the camp of Israel (Num 3:29). They were in charge of the ark, table, lampstand, altars, sacred vessels, and screen (Num 3:31). When the Israelites journeyed, the Kohathites were responsible for the movement of these most holy things. This was done with the most careful reverence, approaching them only after the objects had been covered by Aaronand his sons (Num 4:1–20; 10:21).

In Canaan, the Kohathites were given 13 priestly cities in Judah, Simeon, and Benjamin, and ten Levitical cities in Ephraim, Dan, and Manasseh (Josh 21:4, 5, 10, 20; I Chr 6:54). Certain Kohathites were appointed by David to bring the ark to Jerusalem (I Chr 15:4–5), and for the music ministry (I Chr 6:33 ff.). Some were performing a ministry of praise in the time of Jehoshaphat (II Chr 20:19). The Kohathites joined the other Levites in cleansing the temple in Hezekiah's and Josiah's reforms (II Chr 29:12; II Chr 34:12). After the return from Exile, some were responsible for the preparation of the showbread (I Chr 9:32). *See* Korahites.

R. S.

KOLAIAH (kō-lā'y*ȧ*)

1. A Benjamite whose descendants lived in Jerusalem after the Exile (Neh 11:7).

2. Father of the false prophet Ahab (Jer 29:21).

KOPH. The nineteenth letter of the Heb. alphabet. *See* Alphabet. This letter is used in the KJV as the heading of the nineteenth section of Ps 119, where each verse begins with this letter.

KORAH (kôr'*ȧ*)

1. A son born to Esau and Aholibamah, his Hivite wife; he became a tribal chieftain (Gen 36:5, 14, 18; I Chr 1:35).

2. One of the "chiefs" descended from Esau and his Hittite wife Adah through their son Eliphaz (Gen 36:16).

3. One of the sons of Hebron, included in the tribe of Judah (I Chr 2:43).

4. A descendant of Levi through Kohath and Izhar and younger contemporary of Moses (Ex 6:16, 24; Num 16:1 ff.; I Chr 6:22) who was a leader in a rebellion against the leadership of Moses and Aaron. He was related to Aaron and Moses, whose father was Amram; Korah's father was Izhar, both Amram and Ishaz being sons of Kohath.

The revolt was inspired by envy, according to the account in Num 16, 17. Korah was joined by Dathan and Abiram (sons of Eliah), other Levites, and On of the tribe of Reuben in his revolt, together with 250 representatives of the tribes. The followers of Korah accused Moses and Aaron of separating themselves from the congregation and claiming a "holiness" limited to themselves. They argued that the entire congregation was "holy" and not two men alone; they stood for the "priesthood of all believers" insisting that the entire assembly was a "holy priesthood" (cf. Ex 19:6). Moses counter-charged that God would vindicate existing leadership. More specifically, he charged Korah and the Levites with an ambition to become priests. He argued that they should be content with the high privilege of being Levites rather than aspiring to the priesthood which had been assigned to Aaron alone (Num 16:5–11).

A second accusation was made by Dathan and Abiram when they refused Moses' summons to stand forth. They accused him of incompetence, breach of promise, and selfishness, leading the nation from security into a deadly desert, failing to give them a land "flowing with milk and honey," and making himself a king (Num 16:12–14).

On the following day they assembled for the trial to determine whose incense God would accept. Meanwhile Korah and enlisted the sympathy of the entire congregation so that Moses and Aaron were virtually alone. When Yahweh purposed to smite the entire assembly, Moses and Aaron interceded for them; consequently the Lord directed Moses and Aaron to isolate the rebels from the congregation as a whole (Num 16:20-24).

Apparently there were four groups in this dramatic confrontation: Moses and Aaron were joined by the 70 elders of Israel; Korah, Dathan, and Abiram with their families were separate from all the rest; the 250 Levites with rival censers were in a group by themselves; and the rest of the congregation stood in the distance looking on. The challenge was for God to vindicate by divine judgment those who were on His side. Suddenly the earth opened up and "swallowed" the three rebel leaders and their families; then fire from the Lord consumed the 250 rebels with censers (Num 16:28-35).

Eleven of the psalms (Ps 42, 44-49, 84, 85, 87, 88) were dedicated to the sons (or descendants) of Korah, who are described as singers in the temple choir (II Chr 20:19). *See* Korahites.

G. A. T.

KORAHITES (kôr'ȧ-īts). A family of the Kohathite clan of the Levites. Genealogical data are given in I Chr 6:22-38; 9:19-32; 26:1-19; Ex 6:24; Num 26:58. To their ranks belonged such famous men as Samuel the prophet and Heman the singer (I Chr 6:22, 28, 33).

Korathites from Benjamin joined David at Ziklag as expert warriors (I Chr 12:6). Korathites were doorkeepers in the tabernacle and temple (I Chr 9:17 ff.; 26:1 ff.). They belonged to an elaborate organization for the temple musical services beginning with David's preparation (I Chr 6:31 ff.; 15:17 ff.; II Chr 20:19 ff.; 29:13 ff.). Their name appears in the heading of eleven psalms (42, 44-49, 84, 85, 87, 88). *See* Kohathites.

An ostracon found at Arad (*q.v.*) in 1967 mentions the "sons of Korah" along with names of other families and numerals. This appears to be a list of donations to the Israelite temple at the military base of Ara (Y. Aharoni, "Arad: Its Inscriptions and Temple," BA, XXXI [1968], II. See also J. Maxwell Miller, "The Korahites of Southern Judah," CBQ, XXXII [1970], 58-68).

R. S.

KORATHITES. *See* Korahites.

KORE (kôr'ĭ)

1. A Levite of the house of Korah whose sons were gatekeepers of the sanctuary (I Chr 9:19; 26:1, 19).

2. A Levite appointed over the freewill offerings during the reign of Hezekiah (II Chr 31:14).

KORHITES. *See* Korahites.

KOSMOS. *See* World.

KOZ (kŏz)

1. A Judahite (Coz in I Chr 4:8, KJV).

2. Alternate form in KJV of Hakkoz, omitting "ha," the Heb. definite article; a descendant of Aaron. His descendants were unable to establish their genealogy after the return from Exile and so were barred from priestly service (Ezr 2:61 f., Neh 7:63 f). Evidently it was eventually established, for they had a priestly assignment in the rebuilding of the walls (Neh 3:4, 21).

KUSHAIAH (ko͝o-shā'yȧ). One of the sanctuary singers in the time of David; a Merarite Levite (I Chr 15:17). In I Chr 6:44 called Kishi.

L

LAADAH (lā'ȧ-dȧ). A descendant of Judah, the second son of Shelah, and the "father" or founder of Mareshah (I Chr 4:21).

LAADAN (lā'ȧ-dȧn)

1. The son of Tahan and father of Elishama. Elishama was prince of Ephraim in the time of Moses and the grandfather of Joshua (I Chr 7:26).

2. The first named of the two sons of Gershom, son of Levi. He established one of the clans of the Gershonites by which genealogies were traced through the centuries (I Chr 23:7-9; 26:21). In I Chr 6:17 he is called Libni.

LABAN (lā'bȧn). The son of Bethuel; grandson of Nahor, Abraham's brother; and uncle of Jacob. He lived in Haran of Padan-aram in Mesopotamia (Gen 24:15; 28:2; 29:4-5). When Abraham sent a servant to Laban's country to find a bride for Isaac, Laban looked with covetous eyes on the gold rings and bracelets bestowed as gifts on his sister Rebekah. He encouraged the proposed marriage, and then shared in the additional gifts that the servant presented to the family (24:22, 29, 30, 53).

Many years later Jacob fled from Esau to Laban's home in Haran. Laban welcomed him and employed him to tend his flocks for seven years in return for Rachel, Laban's daughter

(29:18). But Laban then tricked Jacob into receiving Rachel's older sister Leah as his wife (29:21–26). Although Jacob was permitted to marry Rachel a week later, Laban made Jacob work seven more years for her (29:27–30). Jacob then wished to return to his old home, but Laban did not want to lose him, believing God had blessed him through Jacob's presence (30:25–27). When Laban allowed Jacob to propose his wages, it was settled that certain flocks would accrue to Jacob by an arrangement which Laban thought would be profitable to himself. However, Jacob succeeded in outwitting him. Laban became resentful and Jacob started for home after 20 years of service (31:41). He took his now numerous flocks and children with his wives, who felt that their father had used them unfairly.

Laban pursued Jacob with a party, but God warned him not to harm Jacob (31:22–24). Upon catching up with Jacob, Laban accused him of cheating him and forcing Leah and Rachel to leave with him. Laban further accused Jacob of stealing his household gods. Jacob was innocent of this; Rachel had taken them secretly and had hidden them, because their possession gave inheritance rights according to the prevailing culture of that period. Laban made a covenant with Jacob in which they agreed to respect each other's rights, and they peacefully parted.

Laban was a shrewd and covetous man. He gave recognition to the God of his relative Abraham, but he mingled this with idolatrous reverence for household gods (teraphim).

N. B. B.

LABOR. The English translation of a variety of Heb. and Gr. words used to indicate an even greater variety of functions (physical, mental, spiritual). All, however, are somehow related to the regular activity (both in the sense of maintenance and productivity) of fulfilling the purpose of one's being. The emphasis is not on activity which is difficult, burdensome, or necessary, but on that which is real, productive, and worthwhile.

The biblical concept of man's labor in the world is predicated on the statement of God's labor in creating and sustaining the world and man in it. God's creative activity is spoken of as "all his work which he had done in creation" (Gen 2:2–3, RSV). While He rested from the labor of initial creation which was then "accomplished," God is spoken of as still laboring creatively not only in the active sustaining of His creation (Heb 1:3), but in His providential responsibility for the dynamic quality of self-propagation with which He invested His creation (Ps 19:1 ff.; 104:24; Isa 61:11).

After God had created the universe, it is observed that "there was no man to till the ground" (Gen 2:5), and so "Yahweh God planted a garden in Eden . . . and there he put the man he had fashioned" (v. 8, JerusB) "to cultivate and take care of it" (v. 15). It is important to note that this appointment of man to labor follows close upon his creation, and this, in turn, is directly related to the need for labor. Not only is man necessary to complete the creation, but man's labor is also necessary. His labor is as reflective of and as derived from God's labor as is his being and, therefore, is as important and honorable. Since labor is an integral element of God's constitution of man as the lord of His creation, labor is the result of creation and not of sin.

It was when man sought to escape human labor and seize divine status that he sinned. The effect of sin upon labor was not to create it (for it had been given before the Fall), but to frustrate its performance and to impoverish its rewards. Man who was told in regard to the ground "to till it and keep it" (Gen 2:15) is now told, "Cursed is the ground because of you; in toil you shall eat of it" (3:17) and "In the sweat of your face you shall eat bread . . ." (v. 19, all RSV). The essence of labor, then, becomes freighted with accidents from sin.

The word "labor" is used in all these senses: Heb. *āṣēb* (Isa 58:3) and *'eṣeb* (Prov 5:10) are grievous burdens, and *'āmāl* (Deut 26:7; 20 times in Ecclesiastes; etc.) is hard toil. Heb. *y^{e}gîa'* (Job 39:11; Hag 1:11) is the product of working, or acquired property; *ma'ăśeh* (Ex 23:16) is work done. Heb. *melā'kâ* (Neh 4:22; 126 times as "work") is one's occupation, business or work; *'ăbôdâ* (Ex 1:14; 39:32; Lev 23:7; Ps 104:23) is slave labor or one's daily task. Heb. *p^{e}'illâ* (Prov 10:16; Ezk 29:20) usually is found in the plural as "deeds" or "wages." The LXX uses Gr. *kopos* to render *'āmāl,* and the NT uses it to express the labor of the righteous in accomplishing the will of God (Jn 4:38; Heb 6:10). It is a characteristically Pauline term (I Cor 3:8; 15:58; etc.). Those who labor wearily to the point of exhaustion (*kopiaō*) in order to bear the yoke of the law and fulfill its demands are invited by Jesus to come to Him (Mt 11:28). The NT also uses the general Gr. term for work or business (*ergon*) in this special sense of a man's work or labor (I Cor 3:13–15).

The Hebrews always held labor in high respect (Prov 22:29) and, contrary to the Greeks and Romans, respected manual labor: "He that gathereth by labour [lit., by hand] shall increase" (Prov 13:11). In the Talmud are such sayings as the following: "He who does not teach his son a craft is, as it were, bringing him up to robbery"; and, "Labor is greatly to be prized, for it elevates the laborer, and maintains him." The apostles labored with their hands (Acts 18:3) and taught such (I Thess 4:11; II Thess 3:10 ff.). *See* Laborer; Occupations; Service; Wages.

W. A.

LABORER. Adam as keeper of the garden of Eden was from the beginning a laborer, working to preserve and increase that which was entrusted to his care. God made man's labor a stewardship during his lifetime of the valuable things to be found in the earth, with physical and spiritual products the reward, and with physical and spiritual death the results of misuse (Gen 2:9–17). When Cain and Abel offered the products of their labor as gifts for God, they were accepted only when they were offered in faith (Gen 4:3–5; Heb 11:4).

The Scriptures reveal the divine supervision of all human labor (Jas 5:4). When Laban arbitrarily changed Jacob's wages many times, God intervened to protect Jacob (Gen 31:29, 42). After the Mosaic law was given, the rights of laborers in Israel were protected in many ways. To a slave, opportunity was given to earn complete freedom or at least an exercise of choice (Ex 21:2–6). Oppression of a hired laborer was strictly forbidden (Deut 24:14–15), and the prophets cried out against it continually.

Jesus' parable of the vineyard (Mt 20:1–2) and His statement that "the laborer is worthy of his hire" (Lk 10:7) made fulfillment of an agreement about wages a principle. Paul rebuked those "that work not at all" and called upon them to earn "their own bread" by becoming laborers (II Thess 3:10–12).

See Labor; Occupations.

J. W. W.

LACE. A thread or ribbon, such as the blue "lace" (KJV) that fastened the high priest's breastplate to the rings of the ephod (Ex 28:28; 39:21) and the plate of gold to Aaron's turban (Ex 28:37; 39:31). The Heb. word *pathil* also refers to the gold threads in the ephod (Ex 39:3); flammable strand of flax yarn (Jud 16:9); a measuring line of flax (Ezk 40:3); a fastening for attaching a lid (Num 19:15); the cord around the neck used to suspend the signet ring (Gen 38:18, 25).

Mound of Lachish. HFV

LACHISH (lā'kĭsh). Lachish (Tell ed-Duweir) was the most important city of the Shephelah, the low rolling foothills between Philistia and the highlands of Judah. The summit of the tell covers 18 acres, equal to Gezer and larger than OT Jerusalem or Megiddo. It lies 30 miles SW of Jerusalem and 15 miles W of Hebron.

Sennacherib's siege of Lachish. BM

Many 18th Dynasty scarabs reveal its importance to Egypt. But by Joshua's time Egyptian influence in Palestine was fading fast, and he captured Lachish in the campaign which gave him all of S Palestine except the coastal plain (Josh 10:1–43, esp. vv. 31–33). He did not leave a garrison in the city, however (*see* Exodus, The; Joshua). The city was allotted to Judah (Josh 15:39).

Lachish is mentioned as an important city-state a number of times in the Amarna tablets (ANET, pp. 488 ff.). Its rulers are accused of plotting against the pharaoh and of favoring the 'Apiru (*see* Amarna Letters; Hebrew People). G. E. Wright believes that during the Late Bronze Age Lachish was protected by a series of small fortress towns whose ruins appear today as cone-shaped tells (BA, XXXIV, 80–85). Three superimposed Canaanite temples (1500–1200 B.C.) built over a Hyksos fosse or defensive ditch show something of local cultic practices as well as the history of the site (ANEP #150, 731). The earliest of these buildings was demolished, with no trace of burning, and replaced by Structure II during the reign of Amenhotep III (1417–1379 B.C.). A broken bowl inscribed in Egyptian hieratic characters mentions "year four . . . ," almost certainly the fourth year of the reign of Merneptah (1236–1223 B.C.). A scarab of Rameses III (1198–1166) suggests that Canaanite Lachish was not destroyed until early in the 12th cen. B.C.

The excavations of the Wellcome-Marston expedition (1932–38) indicate that David or Solomon made Lachish an important city. Rehoboam refortified it (II Chr 11:9), probably after Shishak's invasion. King Amaziah was assassinated here after trying to escape his Jerusalem conspirators (II Kgs 14:19).

According to the Bible the most dramatic event in the city's history was Sennacherib's invasion in 701 B.C. From Lachish he sent a deputation to demand Hezekiah's surrender of Jerusalem (II Kgs 18:13–19; 36; Isa 36:1–37:38)). Jerusalem was spared by a miracle, but Sennacherib claimed that 46 cities were destroyed, including Lachish (ANET, p. 288). In his palace at Nineveh he portrayed the Lachish episode, depicting the attack on the city, its capture, and its inhabitants led out to death by torture or to captivity (ANEP #371-374). A pit on the NW slope of the tell contained bones of at least 1,500 human bodies intermixed with broken pottery and desecrated further by a covering layer of pig bones. These may have been corpses swept out of the city by the victorious Assyrians.

A new double-walled city was built and became the second city of the kingdom of Judah. It fell to Nebuchadnezzar in 597 B.C. but was not destroyed. In quelling Zedekiah's revolt ten years later (Jer 34:7) Nebuchadnezzar completely annihilated the city. In the ruins of its massive double gateway the archaeologists found 21 potsherds inscribed in ink, the now famous Lachish letters (ANET, pp. 321 f.; ANEP #273). These demonstrate by means of the similarity in vocabulary and grammar that the canonical writings of Jeremiah and his contemporary prophets are genuine literary works of this date.

A Lachish letter. Wellcome Archaeological Expedition

The city was reoccupied in the post-Exilic period (Neh 11:30). The archaeologists uncovered the villa or palace (ANEP #728) of the Persian governor, who may have been Geshem the Arabian (Neh 6:1; *see* Geshem). A small temple (the "solar shrine") near this villa, thought to have been contemporary, was proved in diggings in 1966 and 1968 to be Israelite, constructed *c.* 200 B.C. Two levels beneath this building was found a 10th cen. B.C. (Israelite?) temple with smashed cult objects including a horned stone altar, four incense burners, lamps and juglets (AJA, LXXIV [1970], 188 f.; *see* Arad for another unauthorized Israelite temple). This gives new meaning to Micah's charge that Lachish was "the beginning of sin to the daughter of Zion, for in you were found the transgressions of Israel" (Mic 1:13).

Bibliography. CornPBE, pp. 89-94. Anton T. Pearson, "Lachish," BW, pp. 343-349. D. Winton Thomas, *"The Prophet" in the Lachish Ostraca,* London: Tyndale Press, 1946. Olga Tufnell, "Lachish," TAOTS, pp. 296-308. G. Ernest Wright, "Judean Lachish," BA, XVIII (1955), 9-17; "A Problem of Ancient Topography: Lachish and Eglon," BA, XXXIV (1971), 76-86.

J. L. K. and J. R.

LAD. In the OT the Heb. *na'ar* usually designates a young person, boy, or child (Gen 21:12; 22:5; Jud 16:26; I Sam 2:11, 26; 20:21; etc.). It may also be used of a married man, however, as of Benjamin in Gen 43:8; cf. 46:21; of a servant (II Kgs 4:19, KJV "lad," RSV "servant"; Num 22:22; II Kgs 4:25, "Gehazi his servant"), and of young men of outstanding military prowess (I Chr 12:28). The term *na'ar* ranges in age from a baby such as the infant Moses (Ex 2:6; cf. NASB marg.) and the newborn Ichabod (I Sam 4:21) to the veteran officers of the Assyrian army (II Kgs 19:6, "servants"; cf. 18:17, 28). In the NT the equivalent Gr. words are *paidarion* (Jn 6:9) and *pais* (Acts 20:12, RSV "lad," KJV "young man").

See Family.

LADANUM. *See* Plants.

LADDER. Direct reference to a ladder is found only in Gen 28:12. The Heb. *sullām,* from a verb meaning "to raise or heap up," is used only here in the OT. H. C. Leupold states that the word "is well established in its meaning 'ladder' " (*Exposition of Genesis,* p. 772). D. Kidner (*Genesis,* pp. 158 f.), E. A. Speiser (*Genesis,* Anchor Bible, p. 218), and KB, p. 660, however, believe that "stairway" is a better translation. There is a cognate Akkad. word in the story of Nergal and Ereshkigal in which divine messengers ascend "the long stairway [*summiltu*] of heaven." Furthermore, a heaped-up stairway of the ziggurat type would allow many angels at a time to traverse it.

An evident allusion to Jacob's vision is found in Christ's words recorded in Jn 1:51. The ladder or stairway is shown by this statement to represent Jesus Christ Himself, the One who connects heaven and earth. "When He comes the second time to take His great power and reign, the words of this text shall be literally

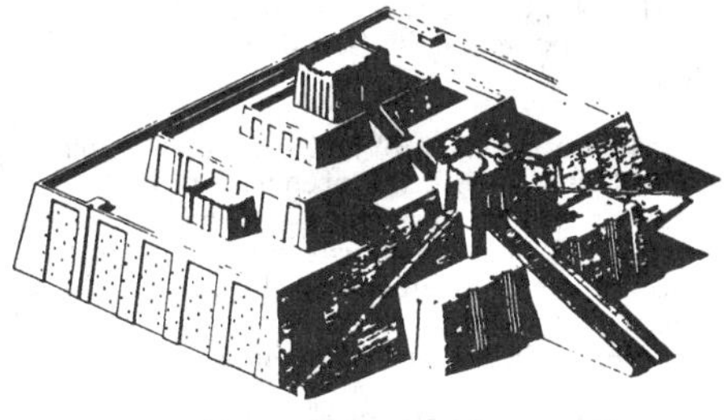

The wide stairways of the ziggurat at Ur may help to illustrate Jacob's ladder. University of Pennsylvania Museum

fulfilled" (J. C. Ryle, *Expository Thoughts on the Gospels*, III, 87).

A few verses, without calling them by name, apparently allude to scaling ladders used to climb the walls of besieged cities (Prov 21:22; Joel 2:7).

G. C. L.

LAEL (lā'ĕl). The father of Eliasaph, a Gershonite Levite (Num 3:24).

LAHAD (lā'hăd). A man of Judah, son of Jahath (I Chr 4:2).

LAHAI-ROI. *See* Beer-lahai-roi.

LAHMAM (lä'măm). A village in the Shephelah of Judah (Josh 15:40); possibly to be identified with Khirbet el-Lahm, two and a half miles E of Lachish.

LAHMI (lä'mī). The brother of Goliath the Gittite, slain by Elhanan the son of Jair in one of David's wars (I Chr 20:5). The parallel passage in II Sam 21:19 reads, "Elhanan . . . killed Goliath the Gittite" (NASB). While the text has been considered by some as corrupt in one of the passages, it is possible there was another giant called Goliath from Gath besides the one slain by David (WBC. p. 304).

LAISH. *See* Dan, City of.

LAKE. The Gr. word *limnē* comes from *leibō*, "to pour out," and expresses the concept of water poured out from a river to form a fresh water sea or lake.

The more common term for the Lake of Gennesaret (Lk 5:1-2; 8:22-23, 33) is Sea of Galilee (about 30 times), which uses the Gr. word *thalassa*, following Heb. *yām*.

The book of Revelation speaks of the "lake of fire" as it describes the final place prepared for the devil and his angels and the doom of all who are unsaved (Rev 19:20; 20:10, 14-15; 21:8). *See* Gehenna.

LAKE OF FIRE. *See* Gehenna.

LAKKUM (lăk'ŭm). A border city in Naphtali (Josh 19:33), probably Khirbet el-Mansurah, near the outlet of the Sea of Galilee W of the Jordan.

LAMA (lă-mä'). Heb. and Aram. interrogative *māh*, "what," with the preposition *le*, "to," together meaning "For what reason?" "To what purpose?" The evangelists quote and translate into Gr. Jesus' utterance on the cross, "Eli, Eli, lama sabachthani" (Mt 27:46; cf. Mk 15:34). *See* "Eloi, Eloi, Lama Sabachthani."

LAMB. *See* Animals: Sheep, I. 15.

LAMB OF GOD. Three Gr. words in the NT are translated "lamb": *amnos*, "lamb" (Jn 1:29, 36; Acts 8:32; I Pet 1:19); *arnos*, "lamb" once (Lk 10:3); *arnion*, "little lamb" (Jn 21:15; Rev 5:6, 8, etc.)

Lambs and young rams formed an important part of OT sacrifices (Num 6:14; Lev 4:32). *See* Sacrifice. A study of the whole concept of the sacrificial lamb and the Paschal lamb as it is developed throughout the entire Bible can alone do justice to the theme of the Lamb of God.

The lamb in the OT. The first mention of lamb in the Bible is found with the offering of the firstling of the flock by Abel and its acceptance by God (Gen 4:3-5). The Passover lamb of Ex 12 was to be slain and eaten on the night of the Passover and its blood was to be sprinkled on the doorpost. It was the Jewish Passover feast with which Christ associated the Lord's Supper (Mt 26:17-19; Lk 22:14-30), thus typifying that Christ is our Passover (I Cor 5:7).

The lamb to be offered was to be without spot or blemish (Ex 12:5; cf. I Pet 1:19), and not a bone was to be broken (Ex 12:46; Num 9:12; Ps 34:20; Jn 19:36), thus signifying the fact that not a bone would be broken in Christ's death on the cross.

The concept of the Lamb of God was developed in Isa 53 so fully that it was clear to the OT saints that He was none other than the Servant of Yahweh. To no other chapter in the Bible perhaps can more cross references be found in the NT than to Isa 53.

The Lamb of God in the NT. John, in the first chapter of his Gospel, records how John the Baptist points to Jesus as "the Lamb of God that taketh away the sin of the world" (Jn 1:29, 36). Peter, in his first epistle, says that Christ was the lamb foreordained before the foundation of the world (I Pet 1:19-20). Thus the OT concept of the sacrificial lamb unfolds typically and prophetically God's plan to offer Christ as the propitiatory sacrifice for man's sins.

The Lamb in the book of Revelation. Christ is referred to 28 times as the *arnion*, "the little lamb," in the book of Revelation. In this book the future history of the Lamb is unveiled (5:9; 7:14). He is the God-Man who has offered the propitiatory sacrifice of Himself, and therefore who alone can open the book of the last times (5:2-5). He will make His servants kings and priests of God, and they will reign with Him on the earth (5:10). The 144,000 Jews of the 12 tribes of Israel will be sealed with His name, and they will witness during the time of the Great Tribulation (7:3-8; 14:1-5). He has the book of life (13:8) and will conduct the final judgment of the Great White Throne (Jn 5:22; Rev 20:11-15).

Satan, the one who offers counterfeits of all that God does in order to deceive mankind, will present his own "lamb" during the ascendancy of the Antichrist (Rev 13:11). The marriage supper of the Lamb, the final uniting of Christ with His Church, is to take place after the rapture of the saints (I Thess 4:13-18; Rev 19:7-8). Throughout all the eternities to come the most wonderful name which Christ will

bear will be that of the Lamb (Rev 22:3).
See Animals: Sheep, I.15.

Bibliography. Joachim Jeremias, "*Amnos*, etc.," TDNT, I, 338–341.

R. A. K.

LAME. A man who was lame was disqualified to act as priest lest he defile the altar (Lev 21:18). A lame animal might not be offered in sacrifice (Deut 15:21; Mal 1:8, 13). Mephibosheth, son of Jonathan, who was made a member of David's household for friendship's sake, was lame from an accident on the day of Jonathan's death (II Sam 4:4; 9:3–13).

Allusions to the lame are frequent; for instance, in Job's happier days he was "feet . . . to the lame" (Job 29:15); a parable in the mouth of fools is like the legs of a lame man, hanging loose (Prov 26:7). Healing of the lame was among the miraculous works of Jesus and His disciples (Mt 11:5; 15:30–31; 21:14; Lk 7:22; 14:13). *See* Diseases.

LAMECH (lā'mĭk)

1. The son of Methushael, a descendant of Cain, who was the first polygamist having married Adah and Zillah (Gen 4:18–24). His sons were Jabal (father of tent-dwellers and cattle-keepers), Jubal (father of lyre and pipe players), and Tubal-cain (forger of iron and bronze instruments). Lamech sang to his wives, boasting of having killed men who wounded or struck him. This boast is usually understood to be confidence in his son's metal weapons as over against trust in God. These sons appear to make him the father of nomads, musicians, and metalsmiths.

2. The son of Methuselah who, at age 182, became the father of Noah, and lived to be 777 years old (Gen 5:25–31). At his son's birth he expressed the longing that in Noah, the curse of Adam would be ended: "Out of the ground which Yahweh has cursed this one shall bring us relief from our work and from the toil of our hands." He is included in Jesus' genealogy (Lk 3:36).

The liberal documentary theory sometimes claims the son of Methushael to be of the J document, the son of Methuselah to be of the P document, and the son of Lamech to be distinct from these two. The three sources were then edited to form the present narrative. The Genesis Apocryphon of the Qumran scrolls and the Book of Jubilees contain traditions which expand upon the biblical account.

W. A.

LAMED (lä'mĕd). The twelfth letter of the Heb. alphabet translat d into English as "L." It is the character for the number "30." In the KJV it stands at the head of the 12th section of Ps 119, in which section (vv. 89–96) each verse in the original begins with this letter.

LAMENESS. *See* Diseases.

LAMENT. *See* Mourning.

LAMENTATIONS, BOOK OF. The book consists of five separate poems, similar in style, all dealing with the desolation of Jerusalem and the sufferings of the Jews brought about by the overthrow of the city by Nebuchadnezzar in 586 B.C. Each of the poems consists of 22 stanzas or verses, the number of the Heb. alphabet. The first four chapters are alphabetical (acrostic) in arrangement. In chap. 3, which has 22 stanzas of three verses each (66 verses in all), each verse in the stanza begins with the same letter of the Heb. alphabet. The meter peculiar to the Heb. elegy characterizes the book—the long line, a slow, solemn movement.

The poems are anonymous. The tradition that attributes them to Jeremiah can be traced to the LXX where Jeremiah's authorship is directly stated, but the date of translation is about 400 years after the prophet. It is possible that the translators had some documentary authority or trusted tradition for affixing Jeremiah's name. Much modern scholarship rejects his authorship on the basis of stylistic differences with the book of Jeremiah. The author, however, seems to have been an eyewitness of the horrors at the time of the fall of Jerusalem. Similar imagery and the same causes for the destruction may be found in Jeremiah and Lamentations, so that many commentators still favor the prophet Jeremiah as the author.

The lament is not simply that Jerusalem is destroyed and the people devastated; it is that the catastrophe is God's act, executing merited punishment. Those who should have been the responsible leaders have not led aright and the people have willingly followed. God is punishing Israel for her sin. But the adversity is not only punitive, it is also corrective. God's covenant love and purpose have not failed.

R. S.

LAMMERGEIER. *See* Animals, III. 27.

LAMP

Translation. The words rendered "lamp" in English versions are Heb. *lappîd* and *nēr*, and Gr. *lampas* and *lychnos*. Heb. *lappîd* means "torch" (BDB, p. 542), and is translated in the LXX (Gen 15:17) by Gr. *lampas*, the basic meaning of which is "torch" (Arndt, p. 466). Heb. *nēr* means "lamp" (BDB, p. 632), and is translated in the LXX (Ex 25:37) by Gr. *lychnos* which basically means "lamp" (Arndt, p. 484). These words uniformly designate a small vessel containing olive oil burned by means of a flax or linen wick, never a wax candle (which was unknown in biblical times) as *nēr* and *lychnos* are sometimes incorrectly rendered in the KJV.

In the ASV, e.g., *lychnos* is consistently translated "lamp" in the 14 places where it occurs (Mt 5:15; 6:22; Mk 4:21; Lk 8:16; 11:33, 34, 36; 12:35; 15:8; Jn 5:35; II Pet 1:19; Rev 18:23; 21:23; 22:5), but *lampas* is translated "lamp" (Mt. 25:1, 3, 4, 7, 8; Rev 4:5), "torch" (Jn 18:3; Rev 8:10), and "light" (Acts 20:8). Trench feels it would be better to translate *lampas* "torch" and *lychnos* "lamp" throughout (Trench, p. 165). Even in the parable of the ten virgins (Mt 25:1 ff.), the *lampades* need not be designated "lamps" simply because they used oil "since in the East the torch, as well as the lamp, is fed in this manner" (Trench, p. 166; cf. NBD, p. 709). However, other authorities believe the Gr. term *lampas* is ambiguous, so that a true lamp is signified in Mt 25:1-8 (BA, XXIX [1966], 4-7).

Other associated terms include Gr. *phanos* (Jn 18:3), "lantern"; and Heb. *m*ᵉ*nôrâ* (Ex 25:31; *et al.;* Zech 4:2, 11, RSV), and Gr. *lychnia* (Mt 5:15; Rev 1:12, *et al.,* RSV), "lampstand" (*q.v.*).

Form. There is no indication in the Bible as to the form of the lamps mentioned. Their shapes varied with the periods of history along with other types of pottery. In Abraham's time (Middle Bronze I Age, 2100–1900 B.C.) lamps often held four wicks. During the period of the conquest of Palestine the Hebrews adopted the single-wicked Canaanite lamp for common use: "A saucer for oil which had a pinched lip to hold the wick" (BA, II [1939], 23). This type with variations was used for well over a thousand years. Seven-spouted lamps have also been found in tombs and in the remains of Canaanite temples, apparently used in religious ceremonies. Thus the concept of a seven-fold lamp for sacred use in the Mosaic tabernacle was not anachronistic, as OT critics used to claim.

Babylonian lamps of a smaller type with a closed tube for the wick are known to have found their way into Palestine in the 6th cen. B.C. Though these were more economical with oil and probably gave more light than the Canaanite saucer lamp, they were not widely used in Palestine because they were not well known to the Heb. potters. In the 4th cen. B.C. the beautiful, compact, Grecian lamp was widely imitated in Palestine. This was small and could be carried without spilling the oil. During the short period of intense national interest in the 2nd cen. B.C. the Jews rejected all foreign influence and used again the saucer lamp. However, with the coming of the Romans in the 1st cen B.C. all new lamps were either of foreign make or designed from foreign models (BA, II [1939], 24).

Lamps were made almost entirely of clay until metal became plentiful. Then they also appeared in copper, bronze, and gold. *See* Lampstand; Oil; Pottery.

At least one lamp was kept burning day and night in the ancient home, both to provide light in the often windowless rooms and to keep a means of lighting the fire at hand. Lamps were often placed in niches in the wall of the house as well as in the sides of tombs and of tunnels descending to the town water supply.

Figurative. The word "lamp" or "torch" is frequently used in the Scriptures in a figurative way to indicate: (1) the Word of God (Ps 119:105; Prov 6:23; II Pet 1:19, RSV); John the Baptist as the prophetic voice of God was "the lamp that was burning and was shining" (Jn 5:35, NASB); (2) the guidance of God (II Sam 22:29; cf. Ps 27:1); (3) the human conscience: "The spirit of man is the lamp of the Lord" (Prov 20:27, NASB); (4) salvation (Isa 62:1, lit., "torch"); (5) life as opposed to death, the realm of darkness (Job 18:5-6; 21:17; Prov 13:9; 20:20; 24:20); this concept accounts for the almost universal practice of placing lamps in tombs, showing belief in an existence after death; (6) blessing and prosperity (Job 29:3); and (7) posterity, or the lasting existence of one's family line or dynasty (I Kgs 11:36; 15:4; II Kgs 8:19; Ps 132:17); God ordained a series of descendants of David, culminating in Messiah the Light of the world.

Bibliography. R. W. Funk and I. Ben-Dor, "Lamp," IDB, III, 63 f. Robert H. Smith, "The Household Lamps of Palestine in Old Testament Times," BA, XXVII (1964), 1-31; ". . . in Intertestamental Times," ibid, 101-124; ". . . in New Testament Times," BA, XXIX (1966), 1-27. G. E. Wright, "Lamps, Politics, and the Jewish Religion," BA, II (1939), 22-24.

J. McR.

LAMPSTAND. Not "candlestick" as in KJV but an instrument for elevating a lamp for the wider diffusion of light (Mt 5:15).

In the OT, although seen in a private home (II Kgs 4:10), the Heb. *m*ᵉ*nôrâ* mentioned is usually the sacred lampstand, either the single seven-branched variety in the tabernacle (Ex 25:31 ff.; Num 3:31; 8:4) or the ten lampstands of Solomon's temple (I Kgs 7:48-49; II Chr 4:7; Jer 52:19), or the *m*ᵉ*nôrâ* of Zecharish's vision (Zech 4:2).

In the NT the Gr. *lychnia* is depicted as an object on which the light of a lamp is diffused (Mt 5:15; Mk 4:21; Lk 8:16; 11:33). In Heb 9:2 it represents the OT tabernacle lampstand. The seven churches are represented as seven lampstands (Rev 1:20).

A variety of Palestinian lampstands of cylindrically shaped pottery and bronze stands with a single upright shaft have been excavated (Lawrence E. Toombs, "Lampstand," IDB, III, 64 ff.). Inscribed seven-branched *m*ᵉ*nôrâ* have been found or depicted in Asia Minor, Alexandria, Rome (Titus Arch), and elsewhere (see *Lychnia,* MM).

W. H. M.

LAMPWICK. *See* Wick.

LANCE. An offensive weapon used in battle (Jer 50:42). The Heb. *kîdôn* is translated "spear" in five other passages in the KJV. In the War Scroll from Qumran Cave I the *kîdôn*

A Hittite soldier from Carchemish with lance (8th cen. B.C.). Hittite Museum, Ankara

is a sword. The Heb. *rōmah* is more correctly our light spear or lance. *See* Lancet; Armor, Arms.

LANCET. The word appears in the KJV at I Kgs 18:28, an older form of the word "lance" (KJV, NASB, etc.), translating Heb. *rōmah*. This weapon began to supplant the heavier spear (*ḥănît*) in the 1st mil. B.C., although the *rōmah* was in use in Moses' time (Num 25:7, KJV "javelin") and during the period of the judges (Jud 5:8, KJV "spear"). *See* Armor, Arms.

LAND. *See* Agriculture; Earth.

LAND AND PROPERTY. Patterns of land tenure as reflected in the Bible can generally be divided into three periods: the patriarchal age, the age of the tribal confederacy, and after the establishment of the monarchy in Israel.

The Patriarchal Age

From two examples in the patriarchal narratives we observe that land was directly purchased, and thereby permanently taken from the former owner. Abraham purchased land from a local resident Hittite in order to provide a burial plot for Sarah (Gen 23), and Jacob bought a portion of a field from the Shechemites (Gen 33:19). The fundamental contract for such a sale was merely verbal, made in front of witnesses (Gen 23:17-18). Some parallels have been drawn between Abraham's purchase from the Hittites and certain customs of land exchange noted in the Hittite law code (Manfred R. Lehman, "Abraham's Purchase of Machpelah and Hittite Law," BASOR #129 [1953], pp. 15-17).

The view that permanent alienation of land through sale was a common feature of Canaanite life in Palestine, in spite of only two examples from patriarchal narratives, may be reinforced by comparison with Canaanite sources from neighboring Syria. Tablets from Alalakh dating from the 18th cen. B.C. document a number of land sales or purchases by private citizens as well as members of the royal house (D. J. Wiseman, *The Alalakh Tablets,* British Institute of Archaeology in Ankara, 1953, p. 103 *et passim*). Many sale documents from Ugarit, although stemming from the 14th and 13th cen. B.C., may be taken to show that permanent land sales were ordinary.

Possession of property by inheritance is best understood by comparison with the pertinent Mesopotamian customs. Only those holding the legal status of sons were eligible to succeed to landed property. Wives and daughters were afforded some degree of economic security, as reflected in the code of Hammurabi (par. 138-150, ANET, p. 172), but only sons were regarded as heirs of real estate. The legal status of sonship was all-important in this matter. Paragraphs 170-171 of the Hammurabi code regulate the allotment of a deceased father's estate among his surviving sons. Each son of his wife was to receive a share. If the father had also begotten male children by a slave woman or concubine, and if he had ever legitimized them by a formal declaration of their sonship, then the sons of the slave woman and the sons of the wife shared equally in the inheritance, except that the firstborn of the wife received a preferential share. If the children of the slave woman had never been legitimized, they were not permitted to share in the paternal estate.

This legal aspect is stressed in the Bible concerning Abraham's succession. Abraham had a male child by the slave woman Hagar whom he never formally legitimized, although he seems to have expressed a willingness to do so (Gen 17:18). Abraham's offspring by Keturah likewise were denied sonship and accordingly were sent away with gifts of movable property, while the landed estate was preserved for Isaac alone (Gen 25:1-6). That Isaac was the sole claimant to the inheritance is emphasized in Gen 22:12, where he is called Abraham's only son (*yaḥîd*).

Inheritance of property was sometimes accomplished through adoption. Mesopotamian documents show that this method of conveying property was resorted to by those who had no children of their own to care for them, and who sought to insure for themselves by this means a sustenance in their old age; since the adopted party was obliged to provide for the needs of the adopting one during his lifetime (Ephraim A. Speiser, "New Kirkuk Documents Relating to Family Law," AASOR, X [1930], 36 f.).

A few biblical texts illustrate this means of conveying property. Abraham seems to imply that his slave would inherit his estate through adoption unless a natural son should be born to him (Gen 15:2–4). Jacob adopted two grandsons, the first two sons of Joseph, as his sons (Gen 48:5–6). Jacob claimed Ephraim and Manasseh exclusively; any other offspring should be reckoned to Joseph and should succeed Ephraim and Manasseh in the inheritance. The incident explains why the two sons of Joseph are reckoned among the sons of Jacob as heads of tribes.

Preferential treatment of the firstborn son in the inheritance was normally in force. Although a clear statement that a double portion belonged to the firstborn does not appear until Deut 21:15–17, the variations to this pattern noted in the patriarchal narratives show that the custom was generally observed. Esau's sale of his birthright to Jacob (Gen 25:29–34) and the subsequent attainment by Jacob of Isaac's blessing through deceit (Gen 27) meant that Jacob had become the "firstborn" insofar as inheritance and privileges were concerned. Jacob in his turn, set aside Reuben, his firstborn, and denied him the preeminence (Gen 49:3–4). He put in that place Joseph (I Chr 5:1–2) and accordingly gave him a special gift of land in preference to his brothers (Gen 48:22). The sons of Joseph likewise experienced the younger replacing the elder in preferred status (Gen 48:13–20). The text makes it clear that this was contrary to the norm, for Joseph protested the action of Jacob on the basis that the elder should have the more prominent position.

The preferential treatment of Joseph may be assigned to the fact that he was the first son of Jacob's favorite wife. Such a practice is paralleled by a clay document from Alalakh in Syria which records a marriage contract. The tablet states that a woman named Naidu is betrothed to a certain noble of the city. In case Naidu does not bear a son, a second wife is specified for the noble. Should the second wife bear a son and thereafter Naidu bear a son, the son of Naidu shall be the superior. Thus the status of the wife would give preference to her son over sons born to the husband by another wife, even though they might have been born first (Wiseman, *Alalakh Tablets,* No. 92, pp. 54 f.). Abundant evidence from Mesopotamia and Syria shows that preferential treatment of the firstborn was usual, but that exceptions occurred.

The Law of Moses

The system of land tenure set up by Moses and persisting through the period of the judges had its own distinctive features, but nonetheless resembled the customs of Mesopotamia more than other regions of the Near East. The land appropriated by Israel through conquest was apportioned according to two principles: it was to be by lot (grants of land were made by drawing lots at Nuzu), evidently to maintain impartiality; and it was to be according to the numerical strength of the unit of tribe or family (Num 26:53–56; Josh 18:2–19:48). Within the units of tribe and clan, individual allotments, "portions," were given to every male of military age and capability.

Inheritance regulations were designed to prevent land from passing out of the control of the tribe to which it had been allotted. In most cases no problem would arise, since normally only the sons participated in the division of the landed estate; but daughters were permitted to inherit land in the event that there were no sons (Num 27:1–11). However, in order to retain this right, such daughters were required to marry within their own tribe. Their successors to the land would therefore retain the land within the tribe (Num 36:3–11).

The custom of levirate marriage (Deut 25:5–10) appears also to work toward the retention of land within the tribe. A widow evidently did not inherit her deceased husband's estate, but her sons were reckoned the heirs. If she were childless, the brothers of her deceased husband inherited the property (Num 27:9). However, custom called for a brother of her deceased husband to take her as his wife and to generate a son by her who would inherit the property in the name of the deceased husband (cf. Deut 25:7 with Ruth 4:5, 10).

Redemption rights also regarded the proprietorship of land within the framework of tribal ownership. If an impoverished man was forced by circumstances to sell agricultural land, he or a kinsman had the right to redeem it (Lev 25:24–34). Actually, only the use of the land was sold or leased for the number of years until the next jubilee, when it would revert to the seller or to his heirs (Lev 25:10, 13–16). On redeeming the land, the redeemer refunded what amounted to rent pro-rated according to the number of years remaining until the next jubilee. The main purpose of the custom was to keep the land within the control of the tribe and family. The Lord directed Jeremiah to follow this law regarding his cousin's field at Anathoth. The prophet bought the land and had a sealed and an open copy of the deed of purchase signed in the presence of witnesses (Jer 32:6–15, RSV). Mesopotamian parallels to the custom are well established (e.g., "The Laws of Eshnunna," No. 39, ANET, p. 163). Houses in non-Levitical walled cities were not considered as being so closely connected with the land. If a man sold such a house and did not redeem it within a whole year, it became the purchaser's in perpetuity (Lev 25:29–34, RSV).

Proprietorship of all Israelite land by Yahweh as the principal owner was the most significant feature of land tenure under the Mosaic economy. Even though God "gave" the land to the Israelites (Josh 1:2; 23:15; *et al.*), He retained ultimate title for Himself (Lev 25:23). Continuing possession by the tribes was conditional on their faithful fulfillment of the covenant obligations (Lev 26:27–35; Deut

4:25-26; 11:13-17, 22-25; 30:16-18).

Since God was the ultimate owner, an Israelite was not to alienate his land. He could sell the produce of the land, and he could sell the use of the land for a limited number of years, but he could not sell the land itself in perpetuity (Lev 25:23, RSV). Parallels to this concept of the inalienability of land are known from the Mesopotamian community of Nuzu, where numerous documents record adoptions as a sort of legal fiction to circumvent the rule against sales (Speiser, AASOR, X, 14-17).

The Israelite's relation to his land was that of a fiefholder to his king. The Lord was his king and ultimate owner of his land. The Israelite could use the land and subsist from it, and pass it on to his male heirs, but he was not to dispose of it. A condition for holding land was willingnese to perform military service in conquering the land, and thereafter defending it (Num 32:5-6, 16-33; Deut 3:18-20; Josh 1:12-15). The census lists of Num 1 and 26 showw that only men of military age and capability were numbered, and it was to these that the land was later to be apportioned (Num 26:52-56).

Some similarities to these concepts are seen from Mesopotamia. At Larsa crown land apportioned to soldiers could not be sold, but was inherited by male heirs, and entailed military or other services (F. Thureau-Dangin, "La correspondance de Hammurapi avec Samas-Hasir," RA, XXI [1924], 3-4; cf. code of Hammurabi, par. 27-41, ANET, pp. 167 f.). At Mari administrative letters discuss the census of troops and the allocation to them of land by the king or his viceroy (*Archives royales de Mari,* I, Nos. 91, 7, 6; III, 21; IV, 4; *et. al.*).

The jubilee law of Israel also related to the ultimate ownership of the land by the Lord, and the vassalage of the landholder to Him (Lev 25:8-55). A landholder was permitted to sell the use of his land until the next jubilee, an event which was supposed to recur at 50 year intervals. The arrangement could be viewed as a sort of loan or mortgage without interest, since the buyer (creditor) had the use and custody of the property, with the production of the property supplying the place of interest payments and constituting also a gradual amortization of the principal. By the time of the jubilee the creditor was evidently repaid, since the amount paid for the field was always adjusted at the time of the sale according to the number of years remaining until the jubilee. The same is implied by the manner in which the price of redemption was computed. Customs comparable to the jubilee in Mesopotamia of the 2nd mil. B.C. are known from Nuzu, Hana and Babylon (Julius Lewy, *Eretz Israel,* V, 21-31; J. J. Finkelstein, *Journal of Cuneiform Studies,* XV, 91-104; Speiser, AASOR, X, 9, 12).

In general it may be said that land tenure laws in the Pentateuch reflect the non-urbanized Amorite milieu as reflected in the tablets of Mari, Nuzu, Hana, etc., of the 2nd mil. B.C.—but not of Babylon, a great city. The Mosaic property laws do not reflect the background of the monarchy or post-Exilic period.

The Period of Israelite Kings

Establishment of the monarchy brought far-reaching changes in the socio-economic life of Israel and a break with the Mosaic pattern of landholding. Samuel foresaw that the king would eventually usurp the prerogatives of God in treating the land as his own, disposing of it at his will, and granting it as fiefs to his vassals (I Sam 8:4-17). He had only to look at the neighboring Canaanite states to realize what conditions would develop (I. Mendelsohn, "Samuel's Denunciation of Kingship in the Light of the Akkadian Documents from Ugarit," BASOR #143 [1956], pp. 17-22). Saul anticipated some possibility of this if the rule should shift to David (I Sam 22:7-8).

David evidently did take over Saul's estate when he succeeded him (II Sam 12:8), and felt free to dispose of it as it pleased him. He restored property to Mephibosheth, Saul's descendant, as an act of grace, not of right (II Sam 9:7-10), and later gave the same property to Ziba, Mephibosheth's servant (16:1-4). Still later he divided the property between the two of them (19:24-30). His actions make it clear that land granted in this way was held contingent upon loyalty to him personally. David seems to have amassed a large estate (I Chr 27:25-31), either through confiscation, conquest, purchase or otherwise.

According to the Alalakh documents there was wholesale buying and selling of villages by the crown. Solomon gave King Hiram of Tyre 20 "cities" in Galilee in exchange for 120 talents of gold (I Kgs 9:10-14, RSV). When Solomon married an Egyptian princess, the pharaoh gave her the city of Gezer as a dowry (I Kgs 9:16), similar to the dowry of seven towns that Agamemnon, king of Mycenae, offered to his daughter (Iliad, 9:149-152).

The role of Israel's king as a feudal lord granting land to faithful subordinates can be inferred from the development of war chariot forces in Israel in emulation of the neighboring states. Solomon had 1,400 chariots (I Kgs 10:26), and Ahab is reported to have sent 2,000 chariots into the battle against Shalmaneser III at Qarqar (ANET, p. 279). The nobles who manned and maintained the chariots were doubtless supported as they were in the Canaanite states, with grants and special privileges.

The development of a landed aristocracy and the reduction of the peasant class is documented by the ringing denunciation of the prophets. Isaiah proclaimed woe to those who joined house to house and field to field (Isa 5:8); to those who devoured vineyards and took the spoil of the poor, who crushed the people, grinding the faces of the poor (3:14-15). Micah denounced those who exploited the poor and appropriated a man's inheritance portion simply because they had the economic power to accomplish it (Mic 2:1–2). Elijah condemned the action of Ahab and Jezebel (I Kgs 21:17–24) when they conspired to kill Naboth and confiscate his vineyard which he had refused to sell, trying to adhere to the old tradition of the inalienability of his inheritance (21:1–15).

The Mosaic legislation would ideally have established a society of free landholding agriculturalists who were in obligation to no one but the Lord, from whom they held their land. The monarchy saw the abandonment of that ideal and the assimilation of Canaanite customs of land tenure which permitted permanent alienation of property and the growth of a landed aristocracy.

Neh 5 shows that there was a brief effort in the post-Exilic age to reverse the trend and return to the old traditions, but the effort was evidently only briefly effective. Tenant farming was unknown to Israel in OT times. Matthew (21:33–41) gives the first reference to the renting of lands in Jesus' parable of the vineyard and its wicked tenants.

See Agriculture; Festivals: Jubilee; Inheritance.

Bibliography. "Property, Land, and Its Conveyance," CornPBE, pp. 607–610. Roland de Vaux, *Ancient Israel,* trans. by John McHugh, New York: McGraw-Hill, 1961, pp. 68–74, 164–177.

S. H. B.

LANDMARK. Much Near Eastern culture was oriented to real property. This is clearly the case in Israelite culture as indicated by the importance placed upon keeping a tract of land within the clan (Num 27:1–11; 36:7; cf. I Kgs 21; Ezk 46:18) as well as the legal injunctions against tampering with the boundaries of such property (Deut 19:14; 27:17). In the ancient Near East property was commonly marked off with small pillar-like stones with elaborate verbal and pictorial inscriptions. In Heb., the term *gebûl,* usually translated "landmark," literally means "boundary." This term was used for the stone markers or even furrows which indicated a boundary. Solomon denounced the anarchy of some who dared to infringe on these rights and so disobey the divine injunctions against such practice (Prov 22:28; 23:10).

A wall with piles of stones serving as a landmark near Samaria. HFV

A boundary stone from Babylon dating *c.* 1200 B.C. LM

LANE. A narrow passage between buildings in a town. "Lane" is the translation of Gr. *hrumē* in Lk 14:21 in distinction from "street," but this Gr. word is otherwise translated "street" (Mt 6:2; Acts 9:11; 12:10).

LANGUAGES. The three languages of the Bible are Hebrew, Aramaic and Greek (*q.v.*). In addition, several other languages are important in biblical studies. One of these is Akkadian, a Semitic language spoken by the ancient peoples of Mesopotamia. Its two chief dialects are Babylonian and Assyrian. Since both the Babylonians and Assyrians play important roles in the history recorded in the Bible, the cuneiform texts which have been found in the Akkadian dialects have shed a flood of light on both the historical and cultural background of the Bible. In Turkey, Egypt (at Amarna), Syria (at Mari), and Assyria (at Nineveh, etc.) outstanding finds of clay tablets written in Akkadian have been made. A knowledge of Akkadian is a *sine qua non* for a serious OT scholar.

LANGUAGES

Another language of particular importance to OT studies is Ugaritic, a NW Semitic dialect. This Canaanite language, like Akkad., uses the cuneiform method to inscribe tablets, but unlike Heb. it is written from left to right. It is unlike Akkad. with its syllabic signs, for Ugaritic was written with an alphabet of 30 characters. The Ras Shamra tablets (discovered since 1929 at Ugarit on the Syrian coast), inscribed in Ugaritic, have had a tremendous influence on OT studies. A study of Ugaritic has shed much light on the nature of Heb. poetry, on the religion of the Canaanites, a ritual system similar to that of the Hebrews, and on various Heb. words and phrases. In fact, few aspects of OT study have been unaffected by the discoveries at Ugarit. *See* Ras Shamra.

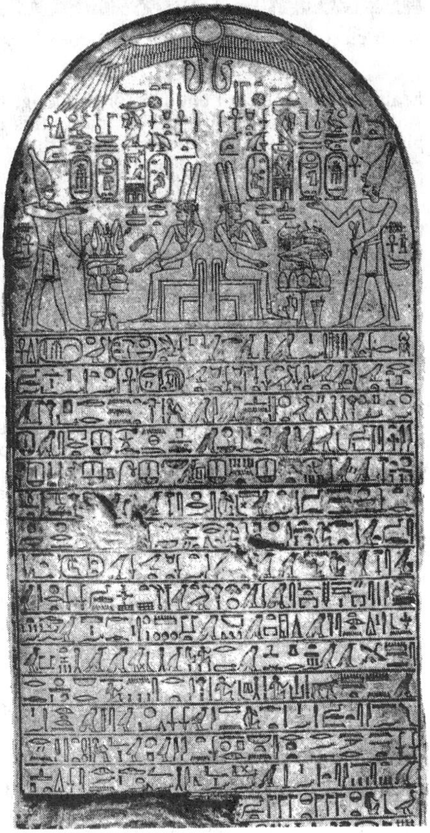

Limestone stela of King Ahmose I, *c.* 1600 B.C., showing Egyptian hieroglyphic script. LL

Egypt too played an important role in OT history. Its language (Ancient Egyptian) is of mixed origin. It is basically Hamitic (i.e., related to the languages on the N coast of Africa),

A late Hittite inscription from Carchemish, Syria. Hittite Museum, Ankara

but before the dawn of history it became thoroughly mixed with a Semitic language. Five distinct stages (with some overlapping) are evident in its history: (1) Old Egyptian (3rd mil. B.C.); (2) Middle Egyptian (2200–1300 B.C., the language of most Egyptian classical literature); (3) Late Egyptian (16th to 8th cen. B.C.); (4) Demotic (8th cen. B.C. to Roman times); (5) Coptic (Roman-Byzantine times). Interesting close literary parallels exist between certain of the Heb. Psalms and Egyptian hymns (e.g., Akhenaton's "Hymn to Aten" and Ps 104), and between the Heb. Proverbs (Prov 22:17–24:22) and Egyptian wisdom sayings ("Instruction of Amenemope"). The Egyptian sayings of Amenemope seem to have been translated from a Heb. original source (*see* Proverbs, Book of).

In addition to the biblical languages, Syriac and Latin are important in the study of the NT. Syriac is a northeastern dialect of Aramaic (the Palestinian dialect), which began to be spoken about the beginning of the 2nd cen. in Edessa. It subsequently became the literary language of the Christian writers of northern Syria and western Mesopotamia and was referred to as "Christian Aramaic." Early versions of the NT were in Syriac (the *Diatessaron* of Tatian and the Old Syriac versions).

Although Latin was not spoken in the eastern half of the Roman Empire, a considerable number of Latin terms found their way into the NT (transliterated into Greek). Some of these are *denarius* (Gr. *denarion,* "penny," Mt 18:28; etc.); *centurio* (Gr. *kentyrion,* "centurion," Mk 15:39, 44–45); *legio* (Gr. *legion,* "legion," Mt 26:53; etc.); *libertinus* (Gr. *libertinos,* "freedman," Acts 6:9, RSV); *speculator* (Gr. *spekoulator,* "executioner," Mk 6:27). Some of the earliest versions of the NT were translations into Latin. *See* Alphabet; Writing.

W. W. W.

LANTERN. The English word is used only once in the Bible (Jn 18:3) where it is recorded that Judas led a band of soldiers carrying lanterns, torches, and weapons into the garden of Gethsemane to capture Jesus. There is no real distinction to be made between the Gr. word *phanos* used here and *lampas,* "lamp" (A-S, p. 466). Perhaps a windbreak of some kind was attached to a lamp (*q.v.*) to make a lantern. The word *phanos* originally meant "torch." "Lamp" and then "lantern" were later developments in the use of the word (Arndt, p. 861).

LAODICEA (lā-ŏd'ĭ-sē'ȧ). A city of the Roman province of Asia in the area of Phrygia. Laodicea stood on an 850-foot hill ten miles from Colosse up the broad valley of the Lycus, a tributary of the Meander. It was *c.* 90 miles E of Ephesus by road on the great commercial route from the coast into the interior of Asia Minor. Laodicea was founded by the Seleucid King Antiochus II (261–246 B.C.), who named it for his sister and wife, Laodice. He settled it with Syrians and Jews brought from Babylonia.

The city's great wealth came from its commerce and its production of a fine quality world-famous black wool. Laodicea was so prosperous that it refused an imperial subsidy when a disastrous earthquake leveled it in A.D. 60. Its citizens rebuilt their city with their own resources. The Lord scored the members of the church at Laodicea for their trust in riches (Rev 3:17), and encouraged them to anoint themselves with a (spiritual) eyesalve that they might really see (Rev 3:18). The latter is no doubt an allusion to "Phrygian powder," a medicine for the eyes which seems to have come through Laodicea into general use among the Greeks.

Laodicea obtained its water from hot springs some distance away through pipes made of cubical blocks of stone three feet across, bound and cemented together. By the time the water reached the city it was not hot enough for health baths, nor cool enough for drinking, but suitable only for an emetic. For many, this explains the reference in Rev 3:16, "So then because thou art lukewarm, and neither cold nor hot, I will spew thee out of my mouth."

The north gate of Laodicea. HFV

Water pipes made of cubical blocks of stone (center) at Laodicea. HFV

A church already existed in Laodicea by the time Paul wrote his epistle to the Colossians, although he had not personally visited the city (Col 2:1). Epaphras' great concern for the Christians there suggests he may have founded the church (Col 4:13). Paul requested the Colossian believers to greet the brethren in Laodicea and to exchange letters from him with them (4:15–16). Paul's epistle to Laodicea was probably lost, as were some others of his letters (cf. I Cor 5:9), although certain devout scholars have argued that the canonical book of Ephesians was originally sent to the Laodiceans (*see* Ephesians, Epistle to). The last of John's letters to the seven churches of Asia was sent to Laodicea (Rev 2–3). By the time he wrote the congregation had become largely apostate (Rev 3:14–22).

The ruins of the city, covering hundreds of acres, began to receive the attention of excavators in 1961.

H. F. V.

LAODICEANS, EPISTLE TO THE. *See* Ephesians, Epistle to the; Epistles, Spurious; Laodicea.

LAP. As a noun, this word refers to the fold in the garment in which articles were carried (Prov 16:33; Neh 5:13). The two top corners of the upper garment were joined together. After the loop was placed over one shoulder, the formed apron was used to carry herbs, loaves, grain, and other articles (Ps 129:7). One of the sons of the prophets gathered "wild gourds his lap full" (II Kgs 4:39). The psalmist prays that God would "render unto our neighbours sevenfold into their bosom their reproach" (Ps 79:12; cf. Lk 6:38). *See* Dress (of Men).

LAPIDOTH (lăp'ĭ-dŏth). The husband of Deborah the prophetess (Jud 4:4). His name means "torches" (cf. Jud 7:16; 15:4) or "lightning flashes" (cf. Ex 20:18).

LAPIS-LAZULI. *See* Jewels.

LAPPED, LAPPETH. To drink by licking up the liquid with the tongue as dogs and cats do. Gideon was instructed by God to use this as a test for diminishing the number of his soldiers, so that the Israelites would not later boastfully claim they had won the victory over the Midianites by their own human strength (Jud 7:2–7). A separation was made between the 9,700 who "bowed down upon their knees to drink" water and the 300 who "lapped, putting their hand to their mouth," i.e., bringing the water to the mouth in the hand and then lapping it. The Bible does not state why the 300 who lapped were chosen as superior to the rest. It is commonly supposed that by this action they showed alertness and watchful vigor in contrast to carelessness and indolence on the part of the majority. The same Heb. word is also rendered "lick" in the record of the dogs licking up the blood of wicked Ahab (I Kgs 21:19; 22:38).

G. C. L.

LAPWING. *See* Animals: Hoopoe, III. 22.

LASCIVIOUSNESS. The Gr. *aselgeia* ("not affecting pleasantly, exciting disgust") means unbridled lust, debauchery, licentiousness, wantonness, shamelessness. Included by Christ in the list of evil things which proceed out of the heart or from the fallen nature of man, it apparently covers fornication and adultery (Mk 7:22; cf. Rom 13:13). It is used in the general sense of excess and licentiousness in I Pet 4:3 and Jude 4, and of sensuality in II Cor 12:21; Gal 5:19; Eph 4:19; II Pet 2:2, 7, 18 (see NASB).

LASEA (lȧ-sē'ȧ). Mentioned in connection with Paul's voyage to Rome, the text (Acts 27:8) requires that the town of Lasea be located on the S side of the island of Crete. The many variants in the NT Gr. MSS, the Vulgate, and Pliny and its absence from onomastica, etc., seem to indicate the place was not commonly known. Because of its proximity to Fair Havens (*q.v.*), it is usually identified on the promontory midway on the S coast of Crete.

LASHA (lā'shȧ). A city included along with Sodom and Gomorrah in the Canaanite boundary description of Gen 10:19. Jerome mistakenly followed Jewish tradition in identifying Lasha (meaning lit., "bursting forth") with the hot springs later known as Callirrhoe on the E side of the Dead Sea near Machaerus. Its location remains unknown, but it must have been near the S end of the sea.

LASHARON (lă-shâr'ŏn). This town is included among the list of city-states conquered W of the Jordan (Josh 12:18). Some suggest it is to be identified with the district of Sarona (Eusebius' *Onomasticon*) in Lower Galilee *c.* five miles NW of Mount Tabor. If in fact Lasharon is a district, it seems most probable that the name (lit., "of" or "in the Sharon") modifies Aphek, which is indeed in the Plain of Sharon (necessary since there are several Apheks). Such usage is not unprecedented (cf. v.22; annals of Thutmose III) and in the Amarna texts the king of Sharon is equated with the king of Aphek (EA #241).

LAST DAY. *See* Judgments.

LAST SUPPER. *See* Lord's Supper.

LAST TIME. *See* Eschatology.

LATCHET. The leather strap or thong which secured the sandal to the foot (Gen 14:23; Isa 5:27; Mk 1:7; Lk 3:16; Jn 1:27). The earliest portrayal of the sandal and latchet is found in the Benihasan tomb paintings in Egypt (19th cen. B.C.), showing a strap either crisscrossed up around the ankle or just wound around it. In the 9th and 8th cen. B.C. in N. Syria, shoes built up around the heel were secured with a strap over the arch of the foot and one over the toes. The thongs or straps were fastened through holes in the edges of the leather or wood soles.

John the Baptist's unworthiness to unloose the latchet of Christ's "shoes" is to be understood as his evaluation of himself in comparison to Christ, even though John held an exalted position (Jn 1:27). Abraham would not take even a sandal strap from the king of Sodom because he did not want the king to have any influence over him (Gen 14:23). Isaiah describes the readiness of God's avenging nations in which not the smallest detail escapes their attention (Isa 5:26–27). *See* Sandals; Shoes; Thong.

H. G. S.

LATIN. The language of Rome. Its Palestinian use was limited to legal, military, and governmental communications, since Greek was spoken more widely. The title of the cross "was written in Hebrew, and Greek, and Latin" (Jn 19:20; Lk 23:38 marg.).

LATTER RAIN. An expression translating Heb. *malqôsh* and referring to the spring rain. The KJV also so translates Gr. *opsimos* in Jas 5:7, while newer versions have "late rain" (RSV, NASB) or "spring rains" (NEB).

In Palestine the early or autumn rain (mid-Oct. to mid-Dec.) softens the ground for plowing and waters the freshly seeded fields. The latter or spring rain (late Feb. to early Apr.) brings the grain to full growth. God promised the Israelites before they crossed into Canaan that if they would obey His commands, "I will give the rain for your land in its season, the early and late rain, that you may gather in your grain and your new wine and your oil" (Deut 11:14, NASB; cf. Jer 5:24; Prov 16:15; Zech 10:1). A few verses before his prophecy of the outpouring of the Spirit, Joel tells that God will pour down the early and the latter rain as before (Joel 2:23).

In a beautiful prophecy of the coming of the Lord, Hosea exhorts God's people: "So let us know, let us press on to know the Lord. His going forth is as certain as the dawn; and He will come to us like the rain, like the spring rain watering the earth" (Hos 6:3, NASB). James seeks to prepare his readers for the return of Christ in 5:1-11 of his epistle. After warning nominal Christians who have cheated in business (vv. 1-6), he urges the godly believers to exercise patience while they await the coming of the Lord, just as a farmer does while he waits for his field to get the early and late rains.

See Rain.

J. R.

LATTICE. The rendering of several words in the OT.

1. The Heb. word *'eshnāb*, "lattice," "casement" (Jud 5:28; Prov 7:6), denoting a small window with grating through which one could look without being seen.

2. Heb. *ḥărakkîm*, "lattices" (Song 2:9), meaning the window enclosure which provided for sight through it.

3. Heb. *sᵉbākâ*, "lattice" (II Kgs 1:2), carries the thought of network as ornamentation on pillars (I Kgs 7:17), or an animal snare or net (Job 18:8). *See* Checker Work.

4. Heb. *'ărubbâ*, "window," denoting a latticed opening for a smoke vent (Hos 13:3, RSV), openings of a dovecote (Isa 60:8), or sluices of sky in destructive rainstorms (Gen 7:11; Mal 3:10).

5. Heb. *hallôn*, "window" (Gen 8:6; Josh 2:15; I Sam 19:12; Joel 2:9; I Kgs 6:4; etc.), the common word for a window in the outside wall of a building, large enough for a man to crawl through.

Archaeological remains often show recessed windows with lattices of crossed bars or simply vertical bars (see ANEP #131). It must be remembered that window glass was unknown in biblical times and not so necessary with Mediterranean temperatures. *See* House.

H. G. S.

LAUGHTER. An emotional response to supposedly humorous situations. It is a part of life (Eccl 3:4), often accompanying festive occasions (Eccl 10:19) with various amusements (cf. Ex 32:6; Jud 16:25, JerusB).

Laughter expresses such emotions as true joy (Lk 6:21), amused incredulity (Gen 17:17; 18:12-15), contempt (Neh 2:19), scorn (II Chr 30:10), and utter unbelief (Mt 9:24).

Some laughter is commendable (Gen 21:6; Ps 126:2), and some is censurable (Prov 17:5). The ultimate laughter and joy of the righteous will be radically different from the present selfish frivolity, feasting and laughter of the wicked (Job 5:22; 8:20-22; 22:17-19; Prov 10:23; Lk 6:21, 25; Jas 4:8-9).

Christ never spoke merely to amuse people; however, some of His remarks undoubtedly prompted a smile or laughter among His hearers (cf. HDCG, *s.v.* "Laughter"). God Himself mocks or laughs in derision at man's pride and rebellion (Ps 2:4; 37:13; 59:8; Prov 1:26).

LAUREL. *See* Plants: Ash, Bay Tree.

LAVER. *See* Tabernacle.

LAW. The word law is used to translate Heb. *tôrâ* (meaning "instruction") and the Gr. *nomos* (meaning "established custom"). *See* Torah. Fundamentally, both *tôrâ* and *nomos* designate some rule or regulation imposed upon man or nature by a higher power. The lawgiver reserves the right to punish all disobedience.

Those invisible forces resident in nature and productive of order and design in the universe are usually called *the laws of nature*. The Bible rarely speaks of such laws in the abstract. The reason often given is that the Bible is not a textbook on science. However, though not a textbook on science, the Bible has much to say about scientific laws as revelatory of the nature of God. Such verbs as "make" (Job 36:27-33), "direct" (37:3), "command" (37:12; 38:12), "cause" (37:13, 15; 38:26-27), "guide" (38:32), and such nouns as "way" (38:24), "ordinances" (38:33), "time" (39:1 f.), all indicate in non-technical language God's control over nature by the laws He has established. It is impossible to posit actual conflict between these laws of nature and the laws that God has established in other realms of His universal government.

On another level are found *God's laws written in the hearts of men*. A twofold distinction must be made here. On the one hand, God's laws are written in the hearts of all men as a result of the image of God planted in man at creation (Gen 1:26 f.). These laws, as ineradicable as the color of one's skin, make even pagan Gentiles "do by nature the things contained in the [Mosaic] law" (Rom 2:14). The evidence of such laws is manifested in conscience (2:15) and confirmed by nature (Rom 1:26 f.; I Cor 11:14). *See* Conscience. On the other hand, God's laws are written on the hearts of believers in the new covenant (Jer 31:31-33; Ezk 11:19 f.; 36:25-27; II Cor 3:3, 7-8). These laws implanted by the "new creation" (II Cor 5:17) are evidenced by the Spirit's fruit (Gal 5:22 f.) and confirmed by "perfect love" (I Jn 4:17 f.).

On yet another level are *the laws of the state* instituted as agents of God in human society (Rom 13:1-7; I Pet 2:13-15). (For collections of laws and legal documents from ancient Mesopotamia, Egypt and Asia Minor, see ANET, pp. 159-198, 212-222.) There are times, however, when the state, inspired by Satanic Hostility to God's truth, makes laws which must be disobeyed by God's true children (Dan 3:8-30; 6:1-28; Acts 5:26-29, 40-42). Unjust laws enacted in the reign of the Antichrist will bring persecution and death to the followers of the Lamb (Rev 13:1-17; 20:4). The believer's ultimate obedience must always be to God rather than man (Acts 5:29; Rev. 1:9; 12:11).

At a higher level still are *those laws instituted by God for man's present stage of existence.* They may be classified as judicial and ceremonial. The judicial, based largely on the Ten Commandments (*q.v.*), deal with those relationships in society where restrictions must be placed upon the evil propensities of human nature (Rom 7:6; Gal 3:19). These laws still have validity in the Gospel Age insofar as they represent basic relationships of life where sin and righteousness are involved. The ceremonial laws, however, were intended by God to be typical representations of gospel truths embedded in the OT. Now that Christ has fulfilled the types by His death on the cross, they have no further validity (Mt 27:51; Gal 5:1-9; Heb 9:1-28; 10:1-22).

At the highest level of all laws are *God's moral laws as summarized in the Ten Commandments.* These laws are of eternal validity because they are based on the unchangeable nature of God. The believer will eventually pass into a realm of glory where disobedience to God's laws will be not only unthinkable but also impossible. These laws of God enunciated in the Ten Commandments and reinterpreted in terms of absolute love to God and to our neighbor (Mt 22:36-40; Rom 13:8-11; Gal 5:14) find their present fulfillment and realization in the believer's life now and then final consummation in his life and fellowship in the heavenly city throughout the ages of an endless eternity.

In summary, the following distinctions may be made: (1) laws made by God (Ex 20:1-17) and laws made by man (Dan 6:6-9); (2) laws of temporary significance (Heb 10:1-4) and laws of eternal duration (II Sam 7:12-16; Ps 1-4); (3) laws written on tablets of stone (Deut 5:22) and laws written on the hearts of men (Heb 8:10; cf. II Cor 3:3); (4) laws intended for the Jews only (Acts 15:1, 10) and laws designed for all mankind (Gen 1:28; 9:5-7).

See Law of Moses; Law, Administration of.

Bibliography. H. Kleinknecht and W. Gutbrod, "*Nomos,* etc.," TDNT, IV, 1022-1091. G. Quell and G. Schrenk, "*Dike,* etc.," TDNT, II, 174-225. A. N. Sherwin-White, "Roman Public Law," HDB rev., pp. 855-859.

W.B.

LAW, ADMINISTRATION OF. The ninth commandment indicates the existence of a system of jurisprudence at an early date in Israel. Perjury, or bearing false witness in a legal trial (Ex 20:16), is here viewed as destructive of this essential aspect of society.

The first biblical reference to the administration of law is in Ex 18:13-27. To avoid feuds in the fledgling nation, the people came to the judgment seat of Moses, who sought to render a decision that would accord with the statutes of God. However, there were too many cases for Moses to hear, and justice was delayed.

For the sake of Moses' well-being and national serenity, Jethro suggested that Moses appoint a series of rulers or judges of various levels of authority. These men could handle the lesser cases. The cases of significant import could be brought to Moses' attention. This was the beginning of the administration of civic law in Israel. The prosperity of the nation depended on prompt justice by men who were trained for their task.

The judges were appointed by someone in authority such as Moses (Ex 18:25) or Samuel (I Sam 8:1). At a later time it became a royal function (II Chr 19:5). The men chosen were usually priests (Deut 17:8-13; Ezk 44:24).

Under the reign of Jehoshaphat after the oppression of Asa, the king stationed judges throughout the land. These men were in the service of God, and would be aided by Him in their judging. They were reminded that they, too, would be judged by the Judge. He was to be their example. Judgment was to be given impartially, and honestly (II Chr 19:5-7).

After the Exile, Artaxerxes commanded Ezra to appoint magistrates and judges to judge all the people and to teach them the laws of God (Ezr 7:25-26). Artaxerxes put a premium on speedy justice. After all, it was the serious delay in the administration of justice that gave Absalom his opening wedge to separate the loyalties of the people from David (II Sam 15:4).

Moses gave instructions for the establishment of a higher court. The day would come when he would not be there, so a court of Levites, priests, and a judge was to be established at a place that the Lord would choose. The findings of this higher court were obligatory (Deut 17:8-13).

In the wilderness, the entrance to the tabernacle was the location of the court. Deut 16:18 looks forward to the city life of Canaan and prescribes that judges be appointed "in all thy gates." Thus the gate of the city became in practice the site of the courts of Israel (Ruth 4:1-2, 11; Amos 5:15).

Samuel was a circuit judge, who went from place to place holding court (I Sam 7:16). This he did in addition to judging Israel at a central location in Ramah (I Sam 7:17).

In the administration of law, the Bible forbids those acts which would pervert justice. The avoidance of covetousness on the part of judges was essential (Ex 18:21). Favoritism or partiality was to be shown neither to the poor nor the rich (Lev 19:15). Bribery is condemned, since it is an offense to God and jeopardizes the nation's existence (Ps 26:9-10; Prov 17:23; Isa 33:15; Amos 5:12; Mic 3:11; 7:3). Perjury is likewise not to be tolerated (Prov 6:16, 19;

21:28; 24:28; 25:18; Zech 8:17; Mal 3:5). Its punishment is mandatory (Deut 19:16-19).

Another essential involved was the requirement of two witnesses for conviction (Deut 17:6). The witness of one was insufficient to cause punishment, since personal malice could be the motivating factor.

Ex 22:9 prescribes the right of both parties to be heard. A fair hearing for all is necessary to the administration of justice (Deut 1:17).

Ex 21:24 declares "eye for eye, tooth for tooth" (cf. Lev 24:20; Deut 19:21). This is a good principle of jurisprudence and was one which guided the administration of justice in Israel. The punishment was to fit the crime. Such a principle acknowledges the seriousness of the crime, but prevents excessive punishment.

The OT encourages the settlement of disputes by legal means rather than by personal vendettas.

That there was corruption in the court system of Israel is clear from the denunciations of such by the prophets. Amos condemns the taking of bribes by those who sit in the gate, preventing justice in behalf of the needy (Amos 5:12, 15; Mic 3:1, 9-11). Thus the courts became at times the instruments of oppression, rather than the dispensers of justice.

In the NT the concept of Christian forgiveness is to play a role in the seeking of justice from the courts. While a Christian is to abide by the decisions of the courts (Rom 13:1-3), he is not to seek satisfaction from them. Jesus counsels that the Christian go the second mile (Mt 5:38-41). If the Christian is the offender instead of the offended, he is to seek to make amends (Mt 5:23-24), so that recourse to a court of law will not be necessary.

In I Cor 6:1-7, Paul is scandalized by the frequent recourse to the courts by Christians to settle disputes among themselves. Disputes between believers are to be settled within the circle of the church. The use of the courts can only bring shame upon the name of Christ.

The trial of Jesus offers an example of legal technicalities being observed while justice is denied. He was not executed by the Jews, for the Romans alone had the legal power so to do. Since Jesus was a Galileean, Herod Antipas as ruler of Galilee was given opportunity to rule in the case of one of his subjects. Pilate offered the release of a prisoner at the feast according to custom, but the innocent one still died.

Acts offers several examples of the administration of law. In Philippi Paul and Silas were imprisoned and beaten on the charges of the owners of the demon-possessed girl. When the magistrates sought to release them quietly, Paul insisted on his rights as a Roman citizen. A Christian may properly stand for his legal rights (Acts 16:35-39).

The town clerk in Ephesus quelled a riot that could have erupted into tragedy by appealing to the orderly functions of the courts. If Demetrius had a complaint against Paul, the courts would settle the matter properly (Acts 19:35-40).

It is finally a legal technicality that sent Paul to Rome and execution. Having been found innocent by Festus and Herod Agrippa, he could have been released. However, he had appealed to Caesar to hear and settle his case. Such an appeal by a Roman citizen could not be denied, nor could it be avoided once made.

See Law: Law of Moses.

R. B. D.

LAW OF MOSES

The Law of Moses Explained

The various aspects of the law of Moses may be set forth in the following distinctions:

(1) Some parts of the law state commands as categorical imperatives (illustrated in the Ten Commandments, Ex 20:1-17); other parts of the law deal with specific cases and are introduced usually by "if" (illustrated in Ex 21-22). The former state the basic principles of all law (apodictic or categorical laws). The latter apply these principles, along with the laws of conscience and society, to specific cases (casuistic or case-laws). This is the dominant form of law known from the ancient Near East (see ANET, pp. 159-198).

(2) The changes made in the laws originally given in Exodus as found in Deuteronomy have raised a problem for many. The differences that exist between the law given at Sinai and that renewed 40 years later in the plains of Moab by Moses in Deuteronomy are to be explained by the change in circumstances, and consequently in specific laws required as Israel moved from the simpler, less complex nomadic life in the desert to the more complex conditions which accompanied fixed abode in the Promised Land. Attention has also been drawn to what appears to many to be a difference between the attitude toward the law of Moses in the Synoptics and in the Gospel of John. They are legalistic in tone – "This do, and thou shalt live" (Lk 10:28), while the Gospel of John is said to be all love and grace. This problem is resolved when we see that the law is expressed in two ways in the Scriptures: negatively in the Ten Commandments, since they were given to a rebellious people; positively in the two great commandments of the law, "Thou shalt love the Lord thy God with all thine heart, and with all thy soul, and with all thy might" (Deut 6:5; cf. Mt 22:37), and "Thou shalt love thy neighbor as thyself" (Lev 19:18; cf. Mt 22:39). In the Synoptics the negative aspect of the law is stressed more than the positive; in John the positive more than the negative. That neither is to be seen as excluding the other is evident as we see Christ bringing the two together as He quotes the summarizing commandments of the two tablets of the law and says, "On these two commandments hang all the law and the prophets" (Mt 22:40).

(3) A very common distinction has been

LAW OF MOSES

made between the moral, the civil (or judicial), and the ceremonial legislation embedded in the Pentateuch. The moral is summed up in the Ten Commandments; the civil is found in the many amplifications or applications of the moral law to specific cases (as in Ex 21-22); and the ceremonial is contained in the numerous rites concerning the priesthood and the sacrifices (as seen in Ex 25:1–31:17; 35-40; all of Leviticus; and Num 1:1–10:10; 15; 17-19; 28-36). This distinction receives a fuller treatment below under "The Christian and the Law of Moses."

(4) A distinction may be made between laws originating apart from a specific case (as in the giving of the Ten Commandments) and laws arising clearly out of a specific situation (as in Num 27:1-11; 36:1-12).

(5) Another distinction is seen in laws antedating Sinai, such as circumcision (Gen 17:9-27) and the Passover (Ex 12:1-28); and, on the other hand, laws originating as completely new regulations at Sinai (such as the ceremonial legislation referred to above).

(6) A distinction may be seen also between laws dealing primarily with non-Israelites, usually called "strangers" (*gerîm*, Ex 23:9; Lev 19:10; etc.), and laws dealing primarily with Israelites (as in Ex 20-23).

(7) Finally, a distinction may be made between laws dealing almost exclusively with priests and Levites (as in Lev 1-10) and laws dealing with all Israel (as in Deut 19-26). It must not be supposed, however, that any of the distinctions enumerated involve contradictions or non-Mosaic authorship.

The Preeminence of the Ten Commandments

The moral law given on Mount Sinai assumes a preeminent place in biblical revelation. (1) This law alone was written by the finger of God, and therefore it was received by Israel as the foundation of her theocracy (Ex 24:12; 31:18; 32:15-16; Deut 5:22; 9:10-11). (2) This law alone was placed in the ark of the testimony where it continuously represented the basic covenant between God and Israel (Deut 10:1-5; I Kgs 8:9). (3) This part of the law is probably referred to in those places depicting the saint's delight in God's law (Ps 1; 119). (4) This part of the law was probably in the minds of the prophets as they spoke of God's law as written upon the heart in the new covenant (Jer 31:31-34; Ezk 11:17-20; 36:25-27; 37:24-28).

(5) In questions and controversies about God's law the Ten Commandments (*q.v.*) are cited as comprising the essence of His law (Mt 19:16-20; Lk 10:25-28; Rom 2:17-23; 7:7; 13:9-10; I Tim 1:7-10). (6) It is this part of the law which Paul describes as "holy, and just, and good" (Rom 7:12) and "spiritual" (7:14). This is the law that reveals sin to man (7:7). (7) Christ had the Ten Commandments primarily in mind in His restoration of the true intent of the law as requiring obedience of heart rather than external conformity only (Mt 5:21-48; cf. Rom 13:9-10).

The Critical and Conservative Views of the Law of Moses Contrasted

In the last century or so the traditional or conservative view of the Mosaic authorship of the law has been opposed by what is commonly called the critical view. The radical differences between these two views may be set forth thus: (1) Conservatives maintain that the legislation of Sinai (Ex 10-Num 9) and of the plains of Moab (Deuteronomy) originated in the time of the historic Moses; liberal critics deny that this legislation arose in the time of Moses, insisting rather that it was produced by authors or schools (commonly called J, E, D, and P) over a period of history extending down to the return from the Exile in Babylon. (2) Conservatives believe in the historicity of the events related in the Pentateuch; critical scholars question or deny leading events of the Pentateuchal history, implying rather strongly that these events have been embellished and glamorized by tendentious writers of a later age.

(3) Conservatives accept the miraculous events of the Mosaic era without question; liberal critics, however, question such events, subtly insinuating rather that these "miracles" are more the invention of a late writer or writers than the sober account of a contemporary historian. (4) Finally, conservatives maintain the uniqueness and superiority of the Mosaic legislation over all similar laws originating in ancient times (such as the famous Code of Hammurabi, ANET, pp. 163-180); liberal scholars, grudgingly admitting certain superiorities, seek rather to "average up" Israel's laws with her pagan predecessors or contemporaries, even to the extent of asserting boldly that certain rites were actually borrowed from the Canaanites and other non-Israelites. *See* Canon of Scripture, The OT; Covenant; Pentateuch.

The Law in the History of Israel

The wide prevalence of the Mosaic legislation in the history of Israel will be readily recognized in the brief survey given here. (1) The provisions of the law were scrupulously performed by Joshua in the generation that followed Moses (Josh 1:13-18; 4:10; 8:30-35; 11:12, 15, 20, 23; 14:1-14; 17:4; 20:2; 21:2, 8; 22:2, 4-5, 9; 23:6). (2) The injunctions of the law calling Israel to obedience are cited on important occasions (I Kgs 2:1-3; I Chr 22:11-13; 28:8-9; 29:19). (3) Legislation given to the law is appealed to on specific occasions (II Kgs 14:6 [cf. Deut 24:16]; I Chr 15:15 [cf. Num 4:1-15; 7:9]; I Chr 23:13 [cf. Ex 28:1; 29:33-37, 44; 30:6-10; Num 6:23-27; 18:3-8]; II Chr 8:13 [cf. Ex 23:14-17; Lev 23:37]; II Chr 23:18 [cf. Num 28:1-31]; II Chr 24:6-9 [cf. Ex 30:12-14]; II Chr 30:16-20 [cf. Num 9:1-14]; Ezr 3:1-4 [cf. Num 29:16; Deut 12:5-7]; Ezr 6:18-22 [cf. Num 3:6-13; 8:6-19]; Ezr 9:11-12 [cf. Lev 18:24-30; Deut 7:3]; Neh 13:1-3 [cf. Deut 23:3-5]).

(4) Punishments attached to disobedience of the law are cited as fulfilled in events of Israel's history (II Kgs 18:11-12 [cf. Deut 29:24-28]; II Kgs 21:8-15; II Chr 34:24-25, 30-32 [cf. Deut 28:15-68]; Neh 1:7-9 [cf. Deut 30:1-6]; Neh 9:13-38; Dan 9:11-13 [cf. Deut 32:15-43]). (5) Throughout OT history the law is always assigned to Moses (Josh 1:7; 22:5; 23:6; Jud 3:4; I Kgs 2:3; II Kgs 18:6, 12; II Chr 8:13; 34:14; Ezr 6:18; 7:6, 10; Neh 1:7-8; 9:14; Mal 4:4). (6) Institutions of Israel (such as the sabbath and the tabernacle worship) are ascribed to the Mosaic era (I Chr 21:29; II Chr 1:3; Neh 9:14). (7) The prophets are spoken of as confirmers of the testimony of the law (II Kgs 17:13, 23; Dan 9:10-14).

The Latent Spiritualization of the Law in the OT

That the law of Moses is neither an end in itself nor the ultimate in man's worship is evident even to a casual reader of the OT. The brief survey that follows shows how the law, rightly understood, prepared the way for the NT revelation. (1) The Mosaic legislation contains references showing that the law can be fulfilled only by a radical change in a person's nature (Deut 10:16; 30:6; cf. Jer 6:10; 9:25-26). (2) In OT history and prophecy obedience to God is described as vastly more important than the observance of rites and ceremonies (I Sam 15:21-23; Ps 40:6-8; Isa 1:11-17; Hos 6:6). (3) Man's inability to fulfill the law often became a burden in the confessions of God's people (Neh 9:13-38; Ps 51:1-9; Dan 9:4-19).

(4) So corrupt did the outward observance of the law become that the prophets often contrast the outward form with the inner obedience (Isa 1:11-17; Jer 7:21-28; Amos 5:21-24; Mic 6:6-8). (5) The inability of the law to justify is tacitly set forth in the example of Abraham (Gen 15:6 [cf. Rom 4:1-25; Gal 3:9-29]), in the affirmation of David (Ps 32:1-2), and in the declarations and symbols of the prophets (Isa 53:11-12; 60:21; 62:1-2; Jer 33:15-16; Hab 2:4; Zech 3:1-10). The "gospel" was thus set forth before the law was given (cf. Gal 3:6-8). (6) Consequently, the prophets look forward to the time when the law will be inscribed on the regenerated heart rather than on tables of stone (Jer 31:31, 33; Ezk 11:19-20; 36:24

(7) So extensive and far-reaching is the prophetic anticipation connected with the Messiah's advent that they envision a complete transformation of worship. The Jerusalem temple will be restored at Messiah's advent (Ezk 40-48). In it the Gentiles will participate and offer sacrifices of praise (Isa 2:1-4; 56:3-8; Zech 6:13, 15; Mal 1:11; cf. Rom 15:9-12; Eph 2:11-22). (8) With such a glorious hope before them the prophets speak of a law going forth from Jerusalem, which law, in the light of the NT, must be the gospel sent forth into all the world by the risen Christ (cf. Isa 2:3; 51:4-5 with Lk 24:47; Acts 1:8; 13:46-48; Rom 10:18). Thus the law introduces the gospel (cf. Gal 3:19-25).

Jesus and the Law of Moses

The manifold relations of Christ to the Mosaic legislation may be succinctly set forth in the following manner: (1) "Born under the law" (Gal 4:4). "Under" here indicates that He was subject to the ceremonial observances of the law (Lk 2:21-27), that He observed the basic rituals of the law (Mk 1:21; 14:12), and that He taught others to observe these rituals (Lk 5:14; 17:14). These OT ceremonies and rites were valid up until the cross (Mt 27:51). (2) The Purifier of the law. Jesus purified the moral law of perversions attached to it by the Jews (Mt 5:27-48), and purified the ceremonial law of similar perversions (Mt 15:1-11). This was in line with His predicted mission (Mal 3:1-4). (3) The Defender of the law. Jesus taught that the law was of divine authority (Mt 5:18; Lk 16:17); He put the law on the same level as His own words (Jn 5:45-47). He saw in the law predictions concerning Himself (Lk 24:27, 44; Jn 5:45-46). (4) The Interpreter of the law. Jesus summed up the law in absolute love to God and to our neighbor (Mt 7:12; 22:34-40; Mk 12:28-34; Lk 10:25-37).

(5) The Fulfiller of the law. Jesus fulfilled the ceremonial law by observing its rites (Lk 2:21-27); He fulfilled the civil (or judicial) law by obeying Roman law (Mt 17:24-27; 22:17-22); and He fulfilled the moral law by perfectly obeying God's commandments, by which obedience He became the sinner's perfect rightousness for the broken law (Dan 9:24; Mt 3:15; Rom 10:3-4; II Cor 5:21; Gal 4:4-5). (6) The Abolisher of the ceremonial law. Christ's death on the cross abolished the ceremonial legislation (Mt 27:51); but even before that event Christ made statements that prepared the way for the simplified worship of the Gospel Age (Mk 7:15, 19; Lk 11:41; Jn 4:23-24; cf. Acts 10:15; 11:9; Rom 14:1-12; Col 2:16; Heb 13:9-16).

The Law and the Gospel

The relationship of the law to the gospel has given rise to many errors and misunderstandings in Christian teaching and practice from the days of the apostles down to the present day. It is well, therefore, to set forth some aspects of this relationship in the light of God's total revelation in the Bible.

(1) The law given at Sinai did not alter the promise of grace given to Abraham (Gen 12:3; 18:18-19; 22:18; 26:4-5; Acts 3:25-26; Rom 4:11-18; Gal 3:5-9, 16-18). The law was given to magnify human sin against the background of God's grace (Rom 7:7-11; Gal 3:19-25). It should ever be remembered that both Abraham and Moses and all the other OT saints were saved by faith alone (Heb 11:1-40). (2) The law in its essential nature was written on man's heart at creation and still remains there to enlighten man's conscience (Rom

2:14); the gospel, however, was revealed to man only after man had sinned (Gen 3:15; Jn 3:16; Rom 16:25-26; Eph 3:3-9). The law leads to Christ, but only the gospel can save (Gal 3:19-25).

(3) The law pronounces man a sinner on the basis of man's disobedience (Rom 3:19-20; 5:20); the gospel pronounces man righteous on the basis of faith in Jesus Christ (Isa 45:24-25; 54:17; Jer 23:6; 33:16; Rom 3:22-28; 4:6-8, 22-24; 5:19; I Cor 1:30; II Cor 5:21; Phil 3:9). (4) The law promises life on terms of perfect obedience (Lev 18:5; Lk 10:28; Rom 10:5; Gal 3:10, 12; Jas 2:10), a requirement now impossible to man (Acts 13:39; Rom 3:20; Gal 2:16); the gospel promises life on terms of faith in the perfect obedience of Jesus Christ (Isa 53:10-12; Dan 9:24; Rom 5:18-19; Phil 2:8; Tit 3:4-7; Rev 7:9-17).

(5) The law is a ministration of death (Rom 7:9-11; II Cor 3:6-9; Heb 12:18-21); the gospel is a ministration of life (Jn 10:10, 28; 17:2-3; 20:31; Rom 5:21; 6:23; I Jn 5:11-13, 20). (6) The law brings a man into bondage (Acts 15:10; Rom 8:15; Gal 4:1-7, 9-11, 21-31); the gospel brings the Christian into liberty in Christ (Jn 8:36; II Cor 3:17; Gal 2:4; 3:23-26; 5:1, 13).

(7) The law writes God's commandments on tables of stone (Ex 24:12; 34:1, 4, 28); the gospel puts God's commandments in the believer's heart (Jer 31:31, 33; Ezk 11:19-20; 36:24-27; Rom 7:6; 8:1-10; II Cor 3:3, 7:12; Gal 5:22-23; H b 8:10; 10:16). (8) The law sets before man a perfect standard of conduct, but it does not supply the means whereby that standard may now be attained (Rom 7:21-25); the Gospel supplies the means whereby God's standard of righteousness might be acquired by the believer through faith in Christ (Mt 5:20; Rom 8:1-4; 10:3-10; Gal 2:21; Phil 3:9). (9) The law puts men under the wrath of God (Rom 2:1-29; 3:19; 4:15); the gospel delivers men from the wrath of God (I Thess 1:10; 5:10; Eph 2:3-6). *See* Gospel.

The Christian and the Law of Moses

What really is the proper relation of the Christian today to the law of Moses? This is a question that has been debated interminably. Opposite and extreme positions have been taken; the solution of one party will be rejected by another party. No solution is adequate, however, if it lumps all the Mosaic legislation together without distinction. As indicated above under "The Law of Moses Explained," there is a valid distinction between the moral, the civil or judicial, and the ceremonial legislation given through Moses. This threefold distinction brings certain issues into their proper focus.

The moral law. The Christian's attitude toward this part of the law of Moses may be summed up thus: (1) No one can be saved by keeping the Ten Commandments. This fact is not only taught plainly in the NT (Acts 13:39; Rom 3:20; Gal 2:16) but is also accepted by most Christians. (2) These commandments are still valid, however, in discovering to the Christian the nature and power of sin. This truth is taught by Paul (Rom 3:20; 5:20; 7:7; Gal 3:19) and is acknowledged by Christians universally. (3) Because the law is "holy" (Rom 7:12), it is a source of spiritual delight to the child of God. This approach to the moral law, still valid for the Christian today, is beautifully described in Ps 119:97: "O how love I thy law! it is my meditation all the day." (4) It is also a norm for the Christian life, because nearly every one of the Ten Commandments is repeated specifically or in principle as applicable to the believer (Mt 5:21-48; Rom 7:7; 13:9; I Cor 8:1-6; 10:14-22; Eph 5:3-5; 6:1-3). Only the commandment to keep the sabbath is lacking in the NT. Thus the moral law of the OT acts as a guide to know the will of God and is part of the pattern for our sanctification. At the same time the requirement of the law is fulfilled only by the Holy Spirit as He works in and through the believer (Rom 8:3-4).

The civil or judicial law. The relationship of this legislation to the Christian's life is more difficult to explain. How far, for example, shall the Christian go today in observing the laws concerning dietary restrictions (Deut 14:1-21), dress (22:5), mixing seeds (22:9-11), military service (24:5)? If such laws are extensions or applications of the Ten Commandments, they are still valid in principle. Paul's appeal to the law of nature in a parallel case (I Cor 11:14) would surely justify the observance of Deut 22:5 in our modern world. Spiritual discrimination saturated in the NT will guide the sincere Christian and keep him from the extremes of either legalism or licentiousness. It should be remembered that these specific laws were given primarily to ancient Israel; their application to the Christian life today must be governed by basic principles laid down in the NT.

The ceremonial law. Here the Christian will observe certain truths easily discernible in the light of the NT. (1) The Levitical rites and ceremonies had their validity up until the death of Christ (Mt 27:51); since that time they have no validity in the Christian's life (Gal 5:1-12; Col 2:16-23). These rites were imposed upon Israel as figures of the coming salvation through the Messiah (Heb 9:9-10); now, by His death, they are taken away completely as valid instruments of worship (Heb 10:8-10). To resort to such things (as is done by Rome in her dress for the clergy) is utterly contrary to the spirituality of NT worship (Jn 4:23-24; Phil 3:3).

What of the question of the return to animal sacrifices predicted, if we take Ezk 40-48 literally, for a future age (Ezk 40:39-43; 42:13; 43:19-27; 45:15-25; 46:2-24; Zech 14:21)? Many argue that this passage must be taken figuratively. Certainly the words of Heb 10:18 must be carefully regarded and in no way nullified: "Now where remission of these is, there is no more sacrifice for sin." Two answers are possible. Perhaps Ezk 40-48 is to be taken figuratively. However, many feel such a drastic action may be unnecessary. God may have chosen, in His infinite wisdom, to reinstitute animal sacrifices during the millennial reign of Christ. If He has, that is His privilege and must be right. Yet certainly from Heb 10:18 we can conclude such would then be merely commemorative.

(2) The Christian must not neglect the vast spiritual and typical significance of the Levitical legislation. He will now understand that Christ is the true Paschal Lamb (Jn 1:29; I Cor 5:7); that he, the believer, as a priest (I Pet 2:5, 9; Rev 1:6) now offers "sacrifices" acceptable to God (Mal 1:11; Rom 12:1; Phil 4:18; Heb 13:15-16).

See Covenant; Law; Ten Commandments.

Bibliography. H. J. Brokke, *The Law Is Holy,* Minneapolis: Bethany Fellowship, 1963. J. Oliver Buswell, Jr., *Systematic Theology,* Grand Rapids: Zondervan, 1962, I, 385-418. "Law of Israel," CornPBE, pp. 487-496. W. D. Davies, "Law in the New Testament," IDB, III, 95-102. Roland de Vaux, *Ancient Israel,* trans. by John McHugh, New York: McGraw-Hill, 1961, pp. 143-163. P. Fairbairn, *The Revelation of Law in Scripture,* Edinburgh: T. & T. Clark, 1869. R. V. French, ed., *Lex Mosaica, or The Law of Moses and the Higher Criticism,* London: Eyre and Spottiswoode, 1894. W. J. Harrelson, "Law in the Old Testament," IDB, III, 77-89. Archibald M'Caig, "Law in the New Testament," ISBE, III, 1844-1852. S. M. Paul, *Studies in "the Book of the Covenant" in the Light of Cuneiform and Biblical Law,* Leiden: E. J. Brill, 1970. W. S. Plumer, *The Law of God as Contained in the Ten Commandments,* Philadelphia: Presbyterian Bd. of Educ., 1864. Ulric Z. Rule, "Law in the Old Testament," ISBE, III, 1852-1858. A. van Selms and J. Murray, "Law," NBD, pp. 718-723. E. C. Wines, *Commentaries on the Laws of the Ancient Hebrews,* New York: Putnam, 1853.

W. B.

LAWGIVER. "One who gives a law" (Heb. *meḥōqēq,* Gr. *nomothetēs*). The Heb. word is applied to the Messiah (Gen 49:10), to the territory of the tribe of Gad (Deut 33:21), to Judah as the messianic tribe (Ps 60:7; 108:8), and to God Himself (Isa 33:22). The Gr. term is applied only to God (Jas 4:12). The plural is used in Jud 5:14 ("governors").

In Gen 49:10; Num 21:18; Ps 60:7; 108:8 the RSV and other versions render *meḥōqēq* as "ruler's staff, mace, or scepter," the symbol of the commander or ruler. Gen 49:10 is especially important as indicating prophetically that the Messiah will come of the tribe of Judah (cf. Heb 7:14; Rev 5:5) and that He will be the final Lawgiver, as predicted in Isa 2:3.

LAWLESS ONE. *See* Man of Sin.

LAWLESSNESS. *See* Iniquity.

LAWYER. *See* Occupations: Lawyer.

LAYING ON OF HANDS. *See* Hands, Laying on of.

Traditional tomb of Lazarus at Bethany. HFV

LAZARUS (lăz'ȧ-rŭs). An abbreviated form of the Heb. name Eleazar (meaning "God has helped").

1. In the story of the rich man (Lk 16:19-31) the beggar is named Lazarus, who died and went to Abraham's bosom, whereas the unnamed rich man departed to Hades. The story teaches that one must settle his destiny before death and that this destiny is not determined by outward circumstances such as wealth.

2. A brother of Mary and Martha of Bethany who was raised from the dead by Christ (Jn 11:1-44) and was later present at a dinner given in Jesus' honor (Jn 12:1-3). Although Christ had raised Jairus' daughter (Mk 5:22-43—Jesus said she was sleeping, v. 39) and the widow's son at Nain (Lk 7:11-18) from the dead, it was only Lazarus that had been buried, and that for four days. This was the greatest miracle of Christ before His death, and it was so convincing of Jesus' person and work

that the Pharisees wanted to put to death both Jesus (Jn 11:47-57) and Lazarus (12:9-11).

Because of the omission of this miracle in the Synoptic Gospels, some critics have questioned its authenticity. The Synoptic authors may have omitted it because enemies wanted to kill Lazarus, or it did not fit within the scope and purpose of their miracles.

Its authenticity is substantiated by the following facts: (1) the story is recorded as by one who had witnessed it; (2) it is a vivid and lifelike description, e.g., "Jesus wept" (Jn 11:35), rather than a fanciful exaggeration of apocryphal stories; and (3) nothing of Lazarus is recorded as far as his experiences during the four days of burial or after his resurrection, or that he had become some sort of hero before, during or after Jesus' passion.

H. W. H.

LEAD. *See* Minerals and Metals.

LEAD, LEADER. The concept of leading and guidance pervades the Scriptures. It is found not only in the many words meaning to lead and to guide and their derivatives, which occur over 150 times in the KJV, but also in passages speaking about the will of God, God's way, wisdom, prayer, man's ways, paths, and steps, and verses using such verbs as to bring, to carry, to direct, to rule, to show, and to teach.

Divine Leadership

The Word of God is insistent that man needs God to be his leader. Jeremiah testified, "I know, O Lord, that a man's way is not in himself; nor is it in a man who walks to direct his steps" (10:23, NASB). "Man's steps are ordained by the Lord; how then can man understand his way?" (Prov 20:24, NASB). Therefore man needs to humble himself to depend on the Lord for guidance and teaching (Ps 24:4-5, 9).

God the Father (I Thess 3:11) is presented in many different passages and by various metaphors as the leader of His people. He led Israel out from Egypt, through the wilderness, and into the promised land (Ex 6:6-8; 13:17-21; 15:13; Deut 4:38-39; 8:2, 15; 11:29; 29:5; Isa 63:7-14; Amos 2:10; Heb 8:9). As a father to Israel He will bring them back from the remote parts of the earth (Jer 31:7-9). As their Saviour He lifted and carried them all the days of old (Isa 63:8-9). He leads us as a shepherd leads his flock (Ps 23; 77:20; 78:52-53; 80:1; Isa 40:11; 49:10). He will be our guide even unto death (Ps 48:14).

Christ the Son, according to OT prophecy and NT declaration, is revealed as our Leader. The One who fulfills the Davidic covenant is stated to be our Leader (Heb. *nāgîd*, Isa 55:4). It is the same word as "prince" in the expression "Messiah the Prince" (Dan 9:25). In the NT Jesus is called in Gr. the *archēgos*, chief leader; in the KJV in Acts 3:15, the "Prince" of life (cf. Acts 5:31); in Heb 2:10, the "captain" of our salvation; in Heb 12:2, the "author" of our faith. He calls Himself "the good shepherd" (Jn 10:11, 14) who leads His sheep out to pasture and they follow Him (Jn 10:3-4, 27; cf. Heb 13:20; I Pet 2:25). He has gone ahead to pioneer the way to heaven for us, acting as our forerunner (Heb 6:20; cf. 4:14). He can lead us because He is the light of the world (Jn 8:12) and the way (Jn 14:6), both as the truth (the reality and the content) and the life (the actual experience). He acts with the Father in directing the believer.

The Holy Spirit also leads and guides the child of God (Rom 8:14). The Spirit was with the Israelites to instruct them on their wilderness journey (Neh 9:20; Isa 63:10-11; cf. Ps 143:10, NASB), and led Jesus into the wilderness (Mt 4:1; Lk 4:1). He guides into all the truth as He unfolds the meaning of the gospel to the believer (Jn 16:13-15; cf. 14:26; 15:26). By submitting to the leading of the Spirit, the Christian is liberated from the hold of the law and is enabled to overcome his fleshly desires (Gal 5:16, 18). The Holy Spirit gives direction by inner prompting of one's thoughts as He renews the mind (Rom 12:2; Eph 4:24; Tit 3:5; e.g., Acts 8:29), and by words of prophecy (Acts 13:4; perhaps 16:6-7).

Knowing our human frailty and ignorance, God leads us because He is kind (Rom 2:4, RVS) and compassionate (Isa 49:10, NASB). His purpose is to direct us into His love and into the steadfastness manifested by Christ (II Thess 3:5, NASB), into righteousness (Ps 5:8; 23:3; 25:8-10), into the way of peace (Lk 1:79; cf. Isa 59:8), and in the way everlasting, the way to eternal life and peace (Ps 139:24; cf. Ps 16:11; Jer 6:16)—all for His name's sake (Ps 31:3). He gives guidance in answer to prayer (Gen 24:12-14, 27, 48; Jer 42:2-22; Lk 6:12-13).

God can lead directly by an angel (Ex 23:20-23; Isa 63:9; Acts 12:7-11; *see* Angel); by His appointed servants (e.g., Nathan sent to lead David to repentance, II Sam 12); by dreams and visions (Mt 1:20; 2:12, 13, 19, 22; Acts 10:3, 10-16); by instruction and teaching found in the written Word (Josh 1:7-8; Ps 19:7-9, 11; 119:35, 105); by granting wisdom and knowledge of His truth (I Kgs 4:29; Prov 2:1-12; 8:20-21; Jas 1:5; Ps 25:5; 43:3); by arousing or stirring up one's spirit (e.g., Cyrus, Ezr 1:1; Zerubbabel, etc., Hag 1:14), i.e., planting a thought, desire, or ambition in the heart or mind (cf. Phil 2:13); and by a personal, external, audible voice (I Sam 3:10; Isa 30:21), which may be loud or soft like a gentle whisper (I Kgs 19:12, LB).

God often leads indirectly in a providential way, i.e., through circumstances. In the course of necessity and duty (gleaning to get food for Naomi and herself) Ruth "happened" (NASB) to come to the field of Boaz (Ruth 2:3), which led to her divinely blessed marriage. One may be assured that his guidance has come from God and not from Satan or from his own imagination when he senses the peace of Christ which acts as arbiter deep in the heart (Col 3:15, NASB marg.).

In seeking and praying for guidance from God, one must be willing to forsake his own desires and to depend on the manner, direction, and timing of the leading which God gives. He should expect three signal lights to line up perfectly and wait until they do. These are: (*a*) the Word of God (the objective standard), (*b*) the Holy Spirit (the subjective, inner witness), and (*c*) circumstances (arranged by divine providence). The biblical principle is that a matter is established or confirmed by two or three witnesses (Deut 17:6; 19:15; Mt 18:16; II Cor 13:1; I Tim 5:19; Heb 10:28; cf. Jn 5:31-39). Asking for a specific sign should not be the primary method of obtaining guidance. Gideon's purpose in using the fleece was not to ascertain God's will but to gain assurance of it (Jud 6:36-40).

Much of God's guidance for the believer's life is conditional. It is conditioned by his willingness to obey (Jn 7:17). The following, therefore, are hindrances to guidance: selfishness or lack of compassion (Isa 58:10-11); stubbornness (Ps 32:8-9; Jer 11:6-8), grumbling and disobedience (Num 14:2-3, 27, 36, 39-45; Isa 48:17-18), insincerity or deceitfulness in wanting only God's approval on one's predetermined way (Jer 42), impatience (Hab 2:3; I Sam 13:8-14), and pride in one's own wisdom and self-sufficiency (Prov 3:5-7). The secret of obtaining guidance is to have the attitude of David: "I delight to do thy will, O my God: yea, thy law is within my heart" (Ps 40:8). This was also the attitude of Jesus Christ (Heb 10:7, 9), as His own words reveal, "My food is to do the will of Him who sent Me, and to accomplish His work" (Jn 4:34, NASB; cf. Lk 22:42). *See* Authority; Will of God; Wisdom.

Human Leadership

There are many examples in Scripture of men whom God appointed to lead others. Some of these are Moses (Ex 6:13, 26-27; 32:34), Joshua (Num 27:18, 23; Deut 34:9; Josh 1:1-9), David (I Chr 11:1-3; Ps 78:70-72), David's mighty men (I Chr 11:12), Christ's apostles (Mk 3:13-19; 6:7-13, 30-31), Paul (Acts 26:16-18; 13:1-3; Eph 3:2, 7-10; Col 1:23-29), Timothy (Phil 2:19-23; I Tim 4:12; II Tim 2:2), Epaphroditus (Phil 2:25-26), and Epaphras (Col 1:7-8; 4:12).

In addition to these individuals Christ has given numberless other persons as "gifts" to the church, consisting of apostles, prophets, evangelists, and pastor-teachers (Eph 4:7-13). He calls and appoints the person (II Tim 1:9-11; Jn 15:16) and then *makes* him to become a leader (a fisher of men, Mk 1:17). The elders and deacons are also God-ordained leaders (*see* Deacon; Elder). In fact, in the sense that every Christian is to be a witness representing Christ to others and making disciples of them and teaching them Christ's doctrines (Acts 1:8; Mt 29:19), he is to be a leader (*see* Commission, Great). Ideally, each believer as he grows to maturity becomes a leader of younger, newer Christians.

The Christian leader is to be obeyed and respected in his position of responsibility (Heb 13:7, 17, 24, NASB; I Thess 5:12-13; I Tim 5:17; *see* Obedience). Obviously it is not wrong or sinful to desire to be a leader, for Paul writes to Timothy: "To aspire to leadership is an honourable ambition" (I Tim 3:1, NEB). He who rules (or leads, NASB) must perform his tasks with diligence (Rom 12:8). The leader acts as a spiritual shepherd, leading the flock by his example and not by lording it over them (I Pet 5:2-3). Paul lived such an exemplary life that he could encourage others to imitate him and follow his example (I Cor 4:16; 11:1; Phil 3:17; 4:9; I Thess 1:6; II Thess 3:9). Therefore most of the qualifications of elders and deacons concern their personal life (I Tim 3:1-13; Tit 1:5-9).

The goal of all Christian leadership is to bring people into vital contact with God. Therefore the leader must be a man of faith himself (Acts 6:5; 11:24). He must teach others to know Christ experientially and how to worship and have fellowship with God. Other responsibilities are to guide and make decisions (Acts 15:2, 6-30), to defend the faith (Tit 1:9; Jude 3; Acts 20:28-31), and to "admonish the unruly, encourage the fainthearted, help the weak" (I Thess 5:14, NASB).

Paradoxically, the leader must be a servant even while he is a ruler and a teacher (Mt 20:26-27). The words referring to the different leadership functions and offices imply service and loving care, never dictatorial or self-seeking power. He must love people and learn to know his followers individually and be ready to give them proper recognition for their development and accomplishments (e.g., how Paul complimented Timothy, Phil 2:19-23). Above all else, the leader must be a man "full of the Holy Ghost" (Acts 6:3).

See Bishop; Deacon; Disciple; Elder; Minister, Ministry; Pastor; Service; Teach.

Bibliography. Melvin L. Hodges, *Grow Toward Leadership*, rev. ed., Chicago: Moody Press, 1969. Derek Prime, *A Christian's Guide to Leadership*, Chicago: Moody Press, 1966. J. Oswald Sanders, *Spiritual Leadership*, Chicago: Moody Press, 1967. Kenneth Gangel, *Leadership for Church Education*, Chicago: Moody Press, 1970.

J. R.

LEAF. This English word is used in the KJV in a threefold way: (1) the foliage of a tree or vine (see below); (2) the wing of a folding door (I Kgs 6:34; Ezk 41:24; *see* Door); (3) the column of a scroll (Jer 36:23; *see* Scroll).

Heb. *'āleh* ("leaf, leafage") is translated in KJV six times "branch" (Neh 8:15 [five times]; Prov 11:28) and 12 times "leaf" (Gen 3:7;

8:11; Lev 26:36; Job 13:25; Ps 1:3; Isa 1:30; 34:4; 64:6; Jer 8:13; 17:8; Ezk 47:12 [twice]). The Heb. *terep* ("prey, food, leaf") is translated "leaf" in Ezk 17:9. The Aram. *'ŏpî* is rendered "leaves" in Dan 4:12, 14, 21. The Gr. *phyllon* is translated six times as "leaves" (Mt 21:19; 24:32; Mk 11:13 [twice]; 13:28; Rev 22:2).

The leaves of the following trees or vines are mentioned: fig (Gen 3:7; Mk 11:13), olive (Gen 8:11; Neh 8:15), wild olive, myrtle, palm (Neh 8:15, ASV), oak (Isa 1:30), grape (Jer 8:13; cf. Isa 34:4). *See* Plants.

Leaves are described as sprouting (Ezk 17:9, RSV), green (Jer 17:8), fair (Dan 4:12, 21), plucked off (Gen 8:11), shaken off (Dan 4:14), driven (Lev 26:36; Job 13:25, both in ASV), not withered (Ps 1:3; Ezk 47:12, RSV), fallen (Isa 34:4, RSV), faded (Isa 1:30; 64:6; Jer 8:13), and healing (Ezk 47:12; Rev 22:2).

Leaves convey such truths, either literal or figurative, as these: (1) man's sinful state: his guilt indicated by the desire to cover his bodily nakedness (Gen 3:7; cf. 2:25), fearfulness (Lev 26:36), deadness (Isa 1:30), mortality (Isa 64:6), worldly glory (Dan 4:12, 14, 21), pompous religiosity of the king or nation of Israel represented by a vine or fig tree (Ezk 17:9; Mt 21:19; Mk 11:13); (2) man's redeemed state: fruitfulness (Ps 1:3; Prov 11:28, RSV; Jer 17:8), eternal life (Ezk 47:12; Rev 22:2); (3) man's cosmic relations: to the earth (Gen 8:11), to God's judgments (Isa 34:4; Jer 8:13), to Christ's return (Mt 24:32–36).

W. B.

LEAGUE. *See* Covenant.

LEAH (lē'*ȧ*). The elder daughter of Laban, married to Jacob through deception after he had served seven years for the hand of Rachel, the younger daughter. Leah became the mother of six sons and a daughter: Reuben, Simeon, Levi, Judah, Issachar, Zebulun, and Dinah (Gen 29:16–35; 30:17–21). She was buried in the family burial cave at Machpelah in Hebron before Jacob's migration to Egypt (Gen 49:31). The Mosque of the Patriarchs now stands over this cave. *See* Jacob.

LEASING. An obsolete word for lying (*q.v.*), used twice in the KJV (Ps 4:2; 5:6) but not at all in the ASV, RSV, or NASB.

LEATHER. In the preparation of leather, the hair was removed from skins, usually sheep or goat skins, by the use of lime or a substitute. The skins were then dried in the sun and treated with sumac pods, pine or oak bark, or leaves. For fine leather, alum was used. Sometimes the skins were dyed. Various grades of leather were employed in producing articles of clothing for civilians and soldiers, bottles for water and wine, fittings for chairs, beds, and chariots, and also some luxury items like pouches made of porpoise skin.

LEAVEN. *See* Food: Leaven.

LEBANA, LEBANAH (lē-bā'n*ȧ*). The head of a family of Nethinim returning from Babylon with Zerubbabel about 538 B.C. (Ezr 2:45; Neh 7:48).

LEBANON (lĕb'*ȧ*-nŏn). Lebanon probably comes from a Semitic word meaning "to be white," a name suggested either by the gleaming limestone cliffs of the mountains of the region or the snow that covers some of the peaks during much of the year. The modern state of Lebanon approximately encompasses the geographical area and is approximately 3,500 square miles, about half the size of Wales or a little less than that of the state of Connecticut.

Lebanon is part of a geological structure that

The Dog River, Dog River Pass, and Lebanon Mountains. Photo Sport

Cedars of Lebanon on the slopes of the Lebanon Mountains. HFV

extends from the Taurus range of Asia Minor to the Gulf of Suez. Basically this structure involves a coastal plain, a western mountain ridge, a fertile valley, and an eastern mountain ridge. In Lebanon the coastal plain averages about a mile and a quarter in width. Behind this plain stand the Lebanon Mountains. Some 105 miles in length, they have many peaks as high as 7,000 to 8,000 feet and in the N reach a maximum height of more than 10,000 feet. Their width varies from 35 miles in the N to six in the S.

The fertile valley between the Lebanons and Anti-Lebanons, the Beqa'a, averages about six miles in width and extends 75 miles N and S. This valley lies at an average altitude of 3,000 feet and at Baalbek rises to 3,600 feet. Near Baalbek is the watershed from which the Orontes River flows northeastward and the Leontes or Litani flows southwestward.

The eastern mountain range, the Anti-Lebanons, parallel the Lebanons in almost equal length and height. This mountain complex is divided into two parts by the plateau and gorge of the Barada or Abana River. The southern part of this eastern range, Mount Hermon, rises to a height of about 9,200 feet and is one of the highest and most majestic peaks of Syria. The Anti-Lebanons collect their waters and send them southward into the Jordan system and eastward into the channels of the Barada or Abana and the Pharpar or Awaj, by which they create the Damascus oasis.

The people who inhabited the Lebanon region during biblical times, the Phoenicians (*q.v.*), prospered by means of their commerce, which was in part based on production of purple (*q.v.*) dye from murex shellfish and in part on sales of cedar (*q.v.*) wood to Egyptians, Hebrews, Persians and others.

The beauty and prosperity of the Lebanon region often inspired biblical writers (e.g., Deut 3:25; Ps 72:16; 92:12; Song 4:15; 5:15; Isa 35:2; 60:13; Hos 14:5). *See also* Phoenicia; Hiram; Tyre; Sidon.

H. F. V.

LEBAOTH. *See* Beth-lebaoth.

LEBBAEUS (lĕ-bē'ŭs). The name of one of Jesus' apostles, based on a variant reading of the Western text (D) and chosen by Textus Receptus in Mt 10:3, instead of the better attested reading *Thaddaios* given in the Gr. text of Nestle and Souter. Matthew, however, may have remembered the Heb. name of Thaddaeus. Mark (3:18) lists the name of this disciple as Thaddaeus, and later copyists seem to have made a composite reading in Mt 10:3 by including both names: "and Lebbaeus, whose surname was Thaddaeus" (KJV). Luke designates him as Judas (the brother or son) of James (Lk 6:16; Acts 1:13). Both Luke and John (14:22) carefully distinguish him from Judas Iscariot. The two names, Lebbaeus and Thaddaeus, may be descriptive designations of this apostle, introduced to avoid confusion with the traitor. The first name may be derived from Heb. *lēb,* "heart," and the second from Aramaic *thad,* a mother's "breast," both then signifying a beloved child. *See* Thaddaeus; Judas 3.

R. A. K.

LEBO-HAMATH (lĕ'bō-hā'măth). The name of a place marking the ideal northern boundary of Israel (Num 34:8; Josh 13:5; Jud 3:3; Ezk 48:1, NASB). Other versions have usually rendered the expression as "the entrance of Hamath" or "the entering in of Hamath."

Egyptian and Assyrian texts make clear that L^{e}*bô'* does not mean "entrance" but is the name of a town in S Syria, the modern Lebweh, *c.* 15 miles NB of Baalbek and 20 miles SW of Kadesh on the Orontes River, near Riblah. Since it commands the watershed between the Orontes and the Leontes Rivers in the broad valley between the Lebanon and Anti-Lebanon Mountains, it at one time must have acted as a fortress guarding the S route to the great city of Hamath. Thus it could be translated "Labo of Hamath."

The 12 men sent out by Moses spied out the land as far N as Lebo-hamath (Num 13:21, RSV). David assembled Israelites from as far as this site when he brought the ark to Jerusalem (I Chr 13:5). Solomon's kingdom extended from Lebo-hamath to the brook of Egypt (Wadi el-'Arish) in the Sinai (I Kgs 8:65; II Chr 7:8). Jeroboam II once again pushed the border of the kingdom of Israel N to Lebo-hamath (II Kgs 14:25), but God warned that enemies would afflict them from there to its S border (Amos 6:14).

J. R.

LEBONAH (lĕ-bō'nȧ). A village situated in a saddle-shaped depression in the hill country of Ephraim, three miles WNW of Shiloh and ten miles S of Shechem (Jud 21:19). The site, known by the Arabic name Lubbân Sharqiya, lies just W of the highway from Bethel to Shechem.

LECAH (lē′kȧ). Mentioned only in I Chr 4:21, as a son of Er, a descendant of Judah. He should probably be regarded as the founder of an otherwise unknown village in the territory of Judah.

LEECH. *See* Animals, V. 6.

LEEKS. *See* Plants.

LEES. The dregs (*sh^{e}mārîm*) or sediment that collected in the bottom of winejars or wineskins during the second or slower stage of fermentation. After about 40 days it was necessary to change containers and to strain off the lees, otherwise the wine became flat in taste and lost its strength. Thus wine on its lees is "good" wine up to a certain point or time; after this, left on its lees, it turned into poor quality wine. In the former sense it is used symbolically of a divine feast for the nations (Isa 25:6). In the latter sense it is a figure of Moab's situation (Jer 48:11) and of Judah's condition (Zeph 1:12). Experiencing full execution of divine judgment is described in Ps 75:8 as draining a cup of wine, drinking even the dregs (NASB). *See* Dregs.

LEFT. The word is used chiefly in connection with the word "hand." Geographically the term is used as a synonym for N; when a person faced E, the N would be to his left (Gen 14:15; Ezk 16:46; Acts 21:3). The left hand was usually considered weaker than the right. It was likewise considered of ill omen, this still being reflected in the English use of its Latin counterpart, "sinister." In all respects the left was the exact opposite of the right. *See* Right.

LEFT-HANDED. Strictly, one who is unable to use his right hand skillfully, although it may be used to mean one who is equally capable in the use of both hands. The ability to use both hands equally was highly prized among the ancients, especially in time of war (Jud 20:16).

Although it is not expressly stated, both Ehud (Jud 3:15, 21) and Joab (II Sam 20:9-10) employed the left hand in an act of deceit and stealth. *See* Right-handed.

LEG. This word is used in the following ways:

1. Anatomically, of the pedal extremities of man (Deut 28:35; I Sam 17:6), of animals (Ex 12:9), and of insects (Lev 11:21).
2. Ceremonially, of the parts of animals used in the Levitical sacrifices (Ex 29:17; Lev 1:9, 13; 4:11; 8:21; 9:14).
3. Metaphorically, of man's weakness (Ps 147:10), of the uselessness of a fool's proverb (Prov 26:7), of a city's degradation (Isa 47:2; see below), of strength and fortitude (Song 5:15), and of a remnant rescued (Amos 3:12).
4. Prophetically, of a period in world history (Dan 2:33), the legs of iron interpreted by many to signify the Roman Empire with its eventual divisions centered in Rome and Constantinople; and of a fulfilled detail in Christ's crucifixion (Jn 19:31-36; cf. Ps 34:20). The leg bones of crucified persons were usually broken to hasten death. *See* Cross.

"Leg" in Isa 3:20 (KJV) should be "armlet" (RSV). In Isa 47:2 (KJV) "leg" should be "robe" (RSV), and "thigh" should be "legs" or "leg" (RSV, NASB).

W. B.

LEGEND. The prevailing view of liberal scholarship is that the Bible contains legends which may or may not have an historical nucleus and which are not to be depended upon for basic historical reliability. (A typical example of this approach may be found in the article on "Legend" by Sigmund Mowinckel in IDB, III, 108-110).

In saying that the Bible contains legends, the liberal scholar is generally accepting the meaning attached to "legend" that literary critics in general attach to the word, and that meaning is very wide. Fairy tales are regarded as legends. They are tales in which fairies, elves, trolls, demons, animals, or plants are the acting persons, and Balaam's ass that spoke is identified as one such fairy tale in the Bible. The reader must distinguish between legend and the literary device known as the fable or parable deliberately used, such as the story of Jotham about the trees (Jud 9:7-20).

Folktales are also broadly classified as legends. Some five or six basic types of folktales are identified, but essentially they are all tales connected with some factual person, thing, event, locality, or sociological or cultural relation. Here then is a kernel of fact, but to this kernel tradition has attached all sorts of fairy tales and poetical decorations. Many of the OT accounts about Noah, Abraham, Isaac, Jacob, Moses, the judges, Saul, David, etc., are classified as one of the five or six types of folktales.

Myths are also sometimes classified broadly as legends, though they are usually dealt with in detail as a separate category. Myths are tales in which the actions and deeds of God are especially prominent, particularly His saving deeds as retold and reexperienced by the cult. Of course the liberal critic would not agree that God had actually acted in the ways described in the myth; the myth, rather, was the way in which the cult expressed its faith in God and His work.

The term "legend" is also used in a more narrow sense alongside such terms as "myth" and "fairy tale." In this more narrow sense a legend is a devotionally edifying story about some great religious hero or saint from the past in which the activity of God plays a prominent role. Though legends may have an historical nucleus, their tendency is to glorify the individual so as to arouse admiration and imitation of his religious and moral virtues.

To say that ordinary literature contains legends in the manner described above is an obvious and incontrovertible fact. However, to say that Scripture contains them is controvertible. Though legends may have a nucleus or kernel of historical fact, basically they are not historically reliable. Yet the results of archaeological work in the 20th cen. have consistently tended to substantiate the historical notations contained in the Scriptures. Liberal scholars who assert the presence of legends in the Bible seem to ignore the implications of the growing body of evidence for the Bible's historicity. And while they assert the presence of legends in Scripture they seem to ignore the great diffierence between those accounts they call "legends" in Scripture and legends as found outside the Bible. That is, the stories in the Bible are sane, consistent, reasoned, logical accounts. They do not tend to glorify the hero (quite the opposite at times!); they do not incline toward the fantastic; they do not give evidence of being creations of flights of poetic or religious imagination. The difference between the legends of popular folklore and the biblical accounts is so great that is should be apparent to all.

In view of these two considerations, why does liberal scholarship persist in the assertion that the Bible contains legends? Apparently because this type of scholarship is controlled by an antisupernatural bias. The Bible quite obviously contains many references to God and His work in human history. Indeed, the Bible claims to be the Word of God written—an inscripturated revelation. The Bible's orientation is consistently and thoroughly supernatural (though not in the manner of popular religious folklore). Thus, the mind that is controlled by presuppositions that reject the supernatural quite naturally relegates those elements of Scripture that do not fit this pattern of thinking to the realm of legend. In other words, it is not literary analysis or historical research that has determined that there are legends in the Bible; it is rather the antisupernatural presuppositions of the liberal scholar which predetermine the rejection of the historicity of so much of Scripture and classify it as legendary.

S. N. G.

LEGION. The main unit of the Roman army in NT times, ordinarily numbering 6,000 men. The legion was divided into ten cohorts, each composed of three maniples, which in turn were made up of two centuries. In the NT the term is only used to refer to demons (Mk 5:9, 15; Lk 8:30) or to angels (Mt 26:53). *See* Cohort; Army.

LEHABIM (lĕ-hā'bĭm). The third son of Mizraim (Gen 10:13; I Chr 1:11). Scholars have differed as to the correct spelling of the word, some preferring to see it as a misspelling for *Lûbîm* (II Chr 12:3); others believe the spelling to be *Lu'bim.* The LXX transcribes the word *Labiēim* which would reflect *Lûbîm.* However, there is little textual evidence for either identification. They appear to have been neighbors of the ancient Egyptians on the basis of the groupings in Gen 10 and I Chr 1.

LEHI (lē'hī). An elevated place in Judah meaning "jawbone" (Jud 15:9) to which the Philistines came to seize Samson. It received its name from either a series of jagged crags resembling a jawbone or from Samson's use of a jawbone as a weapon. It is referred to as Ramath-lehi, "height of the jawbone" (Jud 15:17). It was probably located a few miles NW of Bethlehem near Malhah.

LEMUEL (lĕm'ū-ĕl). The name means "belonging to God." Lemuel is mentioned in Prov 31:1–9 as writing the apothegms or oracles taught him by his mother. Nothing is known of him, but the rabbinical commentators identified him with Solomon; others (as Gesenius) think the name refers to some petty Arabian prince; still others (as Grotius) would identify him with Hezekiah. The RSV (see marg.) leaves the word "oracle" (also ASV, NASB) after his name and translates it "king of Massa" (Gen 25:14).

LEND. *See* Loan.

LENTILS. *See* Plants.

LEOPARD. *See* Animals, II. 24.

LEPER, LEPROSY. The precise meaning of leprosy in both OT and NT is still in dispute. It is a vague comprehensive term that may possibly have included modern leprosy.

In the OT Heb. *ṣāra'ath,* translated "leprosy," connotes (1) a scaly condition of human skin and of inanimate objects; and (2) a human disease, sometimes serious, and sometimes a sign of divine displeasure entailing ceremonial uncleanness and exclusion from the community. In some contexts, *ṣara'ath* indicates an enervating or prostrating infirmity. The emphasis is not on its clinical manifestations or contagiousness (though this latter may be implied), but on its ritual significance. Medical and ceremonial words are used indiscriminately in different passages.

Heb. *ṣāra'ath* as used by doctors and laity in modern Israel connotes any repulsive skin condition, including leprosy. In widely scattered lands, true leprosy has for centuries evoked deep-seated emotional reactions attributable to diverse elements (guilt complex, taboo violation, fear of deformity or of divine punishment, dread of contracting a supposedly highly contagious disease). Regrettably, such an attitude may result from or be reinforced by the misidentification of biblical "leprosy" with true leprosy.

Leprosy is a feebly contagious disease caused by a germ (*Mycobacterium leprae*) described in 1874 by Hansen (hence, "Hansen's disease" to denote leprosy), and affecting principally the limb nerves and the skin. Leprosy was clinically differentiated from other diseases as recently as 1847 by Daniellsen and Boeck. It has a lengthy latent period of up to 15 years. It is never hereditary, but susceptibility to leprosy may be inherited.

No evidence of leprosy is found in inscriptions, skeletal remains or mummies from dynastic Egypt, or from Palestine. The earliest written records (*c.* 600 B.C.) are from India, and the earliest skeleton with leprosy lesions is dated to the 5th cen. A.D.

OT references. The details given in Lev 13 and 14 to help priests distinguish between *ṣāra'ath* and benign conditions are of no diagnostic value today, the exact meaning of the Heb. words in Lev 13:2–10, 30 translated "rising, scab, bright spot, quick raw flesh, scall" being doubtful. The signs of *ṣāra'ath* (central depression, whiteness of skin and hair, scaliness, infection of the scalp) are not typical of leprosy. Conversely, the hallmarks of true leprosy (nodules, lionlike face, anesthetic skin patches, plainless ulceration of extremities) are not mentioned.

In Leviticus "leprosy" could be a localized infection of the skin (13:3); erysipelas adjacent to a boil (v. 18); complications of a burn (v. 24 RSV): a ringworm or sycosis of scalp or beard (v. 29); a pustular dermatitis (v. 36); a favus or desert sore (v. 42); a mildew of garments or leather (vv. 47–59); a fungus growing on stone walls (14:34). The priest could order exclusion from the camp, a temporizing measure (not quarantine) pending the appearance of indubitable signs. True leprosy changes perceptibly in only one or two weeks.

Moses' hand became "leprous as snow" (Ex 4:6); "Miriam became leprous, white as snow" (Num 12:10); and Gehazi became "a leper as white as snow" (II Kgs 5:27). True leprosy lesions, however, are never achromic, but "as snow" may characterize flakiness rather than whiteness. References to a leprosy victim as "one dead" whose "flesh is half consumed" (Num 12:12) cannot indicate the benign "white leprosy" (vitiligo, leucoderma) of medieval Europe and modern India.

The instructions in Num 5:2 and Deut 24:8 place "leprosy" on a ritual par with sexual pollution and contact with a corpse. The nature of Naaman's *ṣāra'ath* (II Kgs 5:1–14), which did not render him socially "unclean" or unfit for public office, is unknown; it was possibly scabies, for which the sulphur-containing baths of Rabbi Mayer, near Tiberias, are a reputed cure to this day, sufferers still being exhorted to "dip seven times."

The transmissible disease that suddenly afflicted Gehazi could also have been scabies, contracted from the garments he coveted (v. 27). The four leprous men of Samaria (II Kgs 7:3) were living outside the city, but were mobile. King Uzziah's (Azariah's) forehead lesion (II Chr 26:19–21), possibly true leprosy, became more noticeable during red-faced anger.

NT references. A similar imprecision regarding leprosy occurs in the NT. The LXX translates *sara'ath* by Gr. *lepra,* a comprehensive term embracing any scaly condition of the skin. True leprosy was known to Aristotle (345 B.C.) as leontiasis or satyriasis. Alexandrian physicians in the 3rd cen. B.C. described true leprosy, calling it elephantiasis. Galen (A.D. 133–201) described it under the name *elephantiasis Graecorum.* The disease was introduced into Italy and the Mediterranean littoral (including Palestine) by Pompey's returning soldiers (62 B.C.).

The evangelists refer to *lepra* (Mt 10:8; 11:5; 26:6; Mk 1:40–44; 14:3) and not to the current Gr. *elephantiasis Graecorum.* In Lk 4:27 the reference to Naaman has a diagnostic imprecision reminiscent of II Kgs 5:1–27. Similarly imprecise are references to the "man full of leprosy" (Lk 5:12), and ten lepers (Lk 17:11–19), and Simon "the leper" (Mk 26:6; Mk 14:3).

The disappearance of leprosy was usually associated with cleansing, emphasizing the ceremonial aspect. "Heal" is once used in NT (Lk 17:15) and in respect to a non-Jew. However, the neutral phrase "the leprosy departed from him" (Mk 1:42; Lk 5:13) is used of Jews, and the word "cleansed" of a non-Jew (Lk 4:27).

Extravagant exegesis invested Job and Lazarus the beggar (Lk 16:20–21) with leprosy. Lazarus of Bethany also was, on no discoverable grounds, pronounced a leper and became the patron saint of those thus afflicted (hence, lazar-house, lazaret, lazarine leprosy).

The belief once widely held that our Lord had leprosy may be traced to Jerome's (A.D. 383) Vulgate mistranslation of Heb. *nāgûa'* ("stricken" [of God]) in Isa 53:4 by "leprosum," which the version of John Wycliffe (d. 1384) renders "leprous." Wycliffe followed Jerome's transliteration of Gr. *lepra* in the NT, anticipating other versions in most European languages. This use of "leprous" is in keeping with medieval terminology: "leprosy" included mangy conditions of animals, blight of growing or stored crops, plague, smallpox and indigence. "Leprosy" was used with the definite or indefinite article, and could be singular or plural.

Because of its implied connotation of ceremonial uncleanness and divine punishment, and because of the terrible accompanying social stigma, the word "leper" should not be used today to designate those suffering from true leprosy. Similarly, its figurative use in a pejorative sense is to be deprecated. Our Lord showed practical compassion toward the ceremonially unclean and the socially ostracized when He "put forth his hand and touched" (Mk 1:41) those suffering from leprosy. *See* Diseases.

S. G. B.

LESHEM (lē'shĕm). The city (also called Laish, *q.v.*) taken by the Danites and renamed after

Dan, their ancestor (Josh 19:47). Situated in the Huleh Basin on the SW side of Mount Hermon along one of the tributaries in the headwaters of the Jordan River, it was on the E border of the tribal settlement of Naphtali.

LETTER. This is the translation of five Heb. and two Gr. words. The Heb. words and Gr. *epistolē* refer to an epistle or letter written to one person or a group of persons. The use of Gr. *gramma* is much more diversified: (1) A letter of the alphabet. Paul writes, "See with how large letters I write unto you with mine own hand" (Gal 6:11, ASV). (2) A document, record or bill (Lk 16:6-7). (3) An epistle or letter (Acts 28:21). (4) The Scriptures (II Tim 3:15; cf. Jn 5:47). (5) Learning or letters, e.g., a man of letters. "How knoweth this man letters" (Jn 7:15); i.e., how could Jesus be so learned when He had never been educated in the rabbinic schools.

Figurative. Paul contrasts Pharisaic legalism and the Spirit-filled keeping of the law in II Cor 3:6-18 as he writes, "The letter killeth, but the spirit giveth life" (II Cor 3:6; cf. Rom 2:27-29). He shows that the law of Moses is a ministration of death and condemnation when merely externally kept, but a means of liberty (cf. Jas 1:25; 2:8-12) when kept not by man in his own strength but by the presence and power of the indwelling Holy Spirit in the life of the believer (Rom 8:1-4).

R. A. K.

LETUSHIM (lē-tōō'shĭm). A tribe (Gen 25:3) descended from Abraham and Keturah through Dedan the progenitor of the Asshurim (*q.v.*) and Leummim (*q.v.*).

LEUMMIM (lē-ŭm'ĭm). One of the three Semitic tribes descended from Abraham and Keturah through Dedan (Gen 25:3). Not positively identified but possibly located in Transjordan or Arabia (cf. Gen 25:6).

LEVI (lē'vī)

1. The third son born to Leah and Jacob. The word probably is related to the verb *lāvāh*, "to be joined to." When the boy was born, Leah declared that perhaps her husband might be disposed to draw even nearer to her (Gen 29:34). The brothers of Levi were Reuben, Simeon, Judah, Issachar, and Zebulun. His sister was Dinah.

Levi acquired the reputation of being a merciless adversary through tragic experience following Dinah's disastrous visit to Shechem (Gen 34). The treacherous revenge of Levi and Simeon brought on a general feud-war with the Shechemites and stirred the righteous indignation of Jacob. The old patriarch did not forget the shameful details of that ugly encounter with a neighboring tribe. His heart was still bitter when he gave his last statement to his sons before his death in Egypt. This attitude explains why he bypassed Simeon and Levi and gave the blessing to the firstborn, which Reuben had forfeited, to his fourth son Judah (Gen 49:1-12).

The sons of Levi who became heads of clans were Gershon (or Gershom, I Chr 6:16), Kohath, and Merari (Gen 46:11; Ex 6:16; etc.). These men went down to Egypt with Jacob and his descendants and died in the land of Goshen. The name Levi attained unusual stature because of the choice of the man and his family to be the priestly family (e.g., Ex 32:25-29; Deut 33:8-11). *See* Levites.

2. Another Levi (Mk 2:14; Lk 5:27-32; Mt 9:9; 10:3) is presented as a disciple of Jesus and is usually identified as the apostle Matthew (*q.v.*).

3, 4. Two descendants of David, otherwise unknown, who appear in Luke's genealogy of Jesus (Lk 3:24, 29).

K. M. Y.

LEVIATHAN. It is one thing to discover the literal significance of the term Leviathan (*see* Animals, V. 7); it is quite another to determine figurative or symbolic usage. There seems to have been a widespread reference in the mythology of the Mediterranean peoples to a great sea monster capable of devouring on a large scale. A many-headed creature, it also had serpentine features. Somewhat parallel to the many-headed Leviathan of Ps 74:14 is the Canaanite seven-headed Lotan of Ras Shamra or Ugaritic literature, dating *c.* 1700-1400 B.C. (ANET, pp. 137f.).

While Job 41:1 and Ps 104:26 do not seem to have any symbolic significance, possibly Ps 74:14 and certainly Isa 27:1 do liken Leviathan to forces of evil (or even specially to Satan), in the latter case to be destroyed by the power of God at the judgment day. Isaiah's words ("Leviathan the fleeing serpent, Leviathan the twisting serpent . . . the dragon that is in the sea," RSV) call to mind the similar phraseology of the Ugaritic Baal epic: "When thou hast smitten Lotan, the fleeing serpent (and) hast put to an end the tortuous serpent, the mighty one with seven heads" (Charles F. Pfeiffer, "Lotan/Leviathan from Ugarit to Patmos," *Bulletin of the Near East Archaeological Society*, VIII [1965], 4). The OT prophet was referring to poetic imagery known to his people just as Christian writers allude to Graeco-Roman mythology without encouraging belief in the pagan deities. *See also* Rahab 1.

The NT reflects the figure of Leviathan in Rev 12:9, where Satan is called "the great dragon" and "that old serpent" (*see* Animals, II. 11, "Dragon").

Bibliography. Nicolas K. Kiessling, "Antecedent of the Medieval Dragon in Sacred History," JBL, LXXXIX (1970), 167-177). Howard Wallace, "Leviathan and the Beast in Revelation," BA, XI (1948), 61-68.

H. F. V.

LEVIRATE MARRIAGE. *See* Marriage, Levirate.

LEVITES (lē'vīts). The progeny of Levi, the son of Jacob, and therefore members of the tribe made up of descendants of Levi. The OT treats them in this light.

There is a view, however, advanced by Julius Wellhausen in 1878, which considers the author(s) of the Pentateuch and the Chronicler to be in full agreement, but Ezekiel as out of step with those idealized, fictional estimates of the priests and the Levites. For a century, scholars have tended to split the Pentateuch into a number of fragments and to declare that the Chronicler cannot be trusted to present an accurate picture of the Levites. They make Ezekiel a prominent link in a study of the development of Levitical life. The crux of the relationship between priest and Levite for Wellhausen was God's demotion of the Levites from priests to temple servants (Ezk 44:6-16). Modern higher criticism would describe the Levites as professional priests who originally chose that way of life because of their likes and aptitudes. In Wellhausen's reconstruction there was no connection with Levi, the son of Jacob. Instead, the Levites are considered an "artificial tribe" of professional cultic officials called in to guard the ark on its journey, who later attached themselves to local sanctuaries. Reference is made to Minean inscriptions of Arabia, and the inference is that the Levites came into being as a class to carry out the demands of the S Arabian cultic ritual.

It seems wise, rather, to accept the biblical presentation and regard these people as descendants of Levi, chosen of God in the wilderness during the days of Moses, assigned to specific duties in connection with the Heb. tabernacle, and, while forbidden to minister before the sacred sanctuary, claimed as special servants of God in holy matters. They were to teach the Torah to the people (Deut 33:10; II Chr 17:7-9), and to assist the priests in all matters connected with the worship at the sanctuary. They were given no inheritance in the new land when Joshua made the official allotment of territory (Josh 21; cf. Num 18:20-24; Deut 10:9; 12:12). God was their inheritance. Forty-eight cities and towns were set apart as places for them to live. *See* Levitical Cities.

The three sons of Levi, Gershon, Kohath, and Merari, were listed as the ones through whom the divine blessings flowed. In the early days of national life these families were assigned the task of caring for and transporting the tabernacle (Num 3:5ff.). When Aaron and his family were chosen as priests, it became necessary to set up a group of helpers for them (Num 8:19). The entire tribe found itself set apart as a sacred group to perform the duties connected with priestly rites and functions. When the tabernacle was built at Sinai, men were selected from this honored tribe to work as porters, builders, and helpers in every phase of the work. It seems clear that they transported the materials of the tabernacle on the long journey to the Promised Land (Num 4:1-33). They served the priests as they were needed, leaving the priests free for the work at the altar. The Lord's original purpose for the Levites is summarized in Num 1:50: "They shall bear the tabernacle, and all the vessels thereof; and they shall minister unto it, and shall encamp round about the tabernacle."

The Levites were assigned an appropriate position in the camp as the nation journeyed across the wilderness. Placed as they were immediately around the tabernacle, they were considered special protectors who could be relied on to give their own lives to protect the holy house of God. Because they were set apart as God's own special possession (Num 8:14-19; 18:6), they were regarded as His in place of the firstborn of Israel who, but for them, would have been forfeited to God. Because of the position of the Levites around the tabernacle no wrath would come upon the community (Num 1:51, 53).

Thus their position was between the priests and the people. Much of their work was hard and menial. They could not go in to see the holy altar nor touch the sanctuary lest they die (Num 4:15). They were servants of the priests and spent their lives doing the ordinary things that made the holy services possible. For their work they were to receive one-tenth of the income of all Israelites. In turn they were to give a tithe of their income to the priests (Num 18:21-28; Deut 14:27-29).

It is evident that the duties assigned to the Levites would change as living conditions altered. When the tribes of Israel were settled in Palestine, the descendants of Levi found themselves placed in all areas of the land, on both sides of the Jordan, but not for the most part in close touch with the central sanctuary at Shiloh (Josh 21). The duties and responsibilities usually associated with the members of this tribe were not to continue exactly as in the days of the desert wanderings. No doubt those stationed nearest Shiloh were assigned to some of the responsibilities of the worship and sacrificial system, but the work of dismantling and transporting the tabernacle was no longer demanded of them. Those not otherwise engaged functioned chiefly as teachers in the towns where they were settled (cf. Deut 12:18-19; 14:27, 29; II Chr 17:7-9; 35:3; Neh 8:7).

After David removed the ark to Jerusalem and set up a more elaborate program of worship, it became necessary to have a larger number of helpers in the capital (cf. I Chr 15:1-15, 25-28; II Sam 15:24). When the temple was completed and provision made for the singers and members of the orchestras, even more Levites were needed (I Chr 6:16-31; 15:16-24; 16:1, 4, 37-42). With so many available all over the land it seems reasonable to expect them to have made their way to the central place.

LEVITES

When Jeroboam took over the ten tribes in the N, he made it clear that Levites and priests were not acceptable in his plans for the religious life of his nation. He used men of his own choosing at his two places of religious observance (II Chr 13:9–10). This radical move practically drove out the remaining Levites from all his realm. It would be difficult to estimate the effect of this change in the development of the religion of Israel. The Levites had been charged with the task of exercising the preservative power of salt among the people. If all this "salt" were removed, the results must have been disastrous. The Levites had also been charged with the task of teaching the things about the Lord (e.g., II Chr 35:3). Without this teaching it is no wonder that Jeroboam's people turned more and more toward paganism and godless behavior.

During the reign of Jehoshaphat in Judah the Levites were assigned the task of going throughout the kingdom with "the book of the law" and pausing long enough in every locality to teach the people concerning God and His Word (II Chr 17:7–9). It would be difficult to overestimate that religious program and its effect upon God's people. Jehoshaphat also erected a court in Jerusalem "for the judgment of the Lord, and for controversies" (II Chr 19:8–10). Selected Levites were chosen to sit on that body of godly counselors.

When Jehoiada the high priest sought to eliminate the influence of Baalism which Athaliah had brought into Jerusalem, he was aided by the heroic efforts of the Levites and the wicked usurper was deposed and executed. Joash was placed on the throne in Judah (II Chr 23:1–21). The Levites were used to help repair the temple.

In the reformation instituted by Hezekiah the Levites were in the forefront of the movement which reinstated the Davidic program for spiritual worship (II Chr 29:12–16). They were responsible for the restoration of the choir program, which had much to do with the revival that set in. David's plans and suggestions were carried out to the letter (II Chr 29:25–30). Some Levites composed psalms during this period.

When Josiah came to the throne he found it reasonably easy to project the forces that guaranteed his reformation because the Levites had prepared the ground for it with unusual faithfulness (II Chr 34:12–13). The reform movement was already under way because of the effective teaching of the Levites (II Chr 35:3). David's full program was in operation. Singers, teachers, porters, keepers of the threshold, and cooperative helpers had specific parts to play in the rapidly unfolding drama. It *ould not do, however, to minimize the influence of the priests and of Huldah and Jeremiah. Josiah's powerful aggressiveness also proved a big factor in the reformation.

No dependable word comes about the work and life of the Levites during the Exile. For more than 50 years in a foreign land without the temple the captives waited for the promised deliverance. Daniel and Ezekiel exerted unusual influence upon these only exiles. What about the priests and Levites? The answer must wait. During this time the idea of the synagogue was born, psalms were written, manuscripts were copied and preserved; thus probably the teaching program of the Levites moved forward. When Zerubbabel led the people back to Jerusalem, very few Levites were listed as members of the returning band (Ezr 2:40, 70; 3:8–18; 6:16–20). The number who returned with Ezra was still disappointingly small, but was a larger percentage than in the first contingent (Ezr 7:7, 13; 8:15–20, 33; cf. Neh 11:18). Before the end of Nehemiah's work in Jerusalem the old program which David had set up had been restored and the work moved forward more acceptably (Neh 12:8, 27, 30, 44–47; 13:10–31).

Under Ezra's direction the Levites were given increasing responsibilities. They were at his disposal and entered heartily into his teaching program. Ezra's exceptional interest in the manuscripts required much labor in preserving and copying these previous documents. The Levites did much in that area and proved helpful as instructors. They took over almost all the teaching responsibilities in the second temple. It is conceivable that their duties extended into the work at the synagogues.

The Chronicler, living about 400 B.C., gave much prominence to the Levites and presented them as highly favored instruments of God. He portrayed them as the special keepers of the ark of the covenant who were the only ones allowed to carry it (I Chr 15:2). When the ark was to be moved, the Levites were called in for that special work. Later, chosen Levites were assigned the task of ministering before the sacred place (I Chr 16:4) and of lifting praises to God in public worship services. It was a far cry from the old days when menial tasks characterized their assignments. Gradually the more specialized duties of teaching and exhorting were added to their work and they were relieved of the more onerous duties. It became an honorable ministry with many delightful fringe benefits. It was a joy to serve before the holy sanctuary of the Lord.

In describing their peculiar fitness to minister before God it was said: "The Levites were more upright in heart than the priests in sanctifying themselves" (II Chr 29:34, RSV). Thus the descendants of Levi became the purveyors of culture and religion. The divine plan had been that the whole nation should be a "kingdom of priests" and hence a holy people. The priests and the Levites became the mediators of that sacred covenant. *See* Levi; Priest.

Bibliography. R. Abba, "Priests and Levites," IDB, III, 876–889. Roland de Vaux, *Ancient Israel,* trans. by John McHugh, New York: McGraw-Hill, 1961, pp. 358–371.

K. M. Y.

LEVITICAL CITIES. Instead of apportioning land to 13 tribes, the tribe of Levi was singled out to live in 48 cities scattered throughout Palestine (Num 35; Josh 20, 21; I Chr 6:54–81). These towns and the surrounding pasture land were under the control of the members of Levi's tribe. Of these 48 cities, six were designated as "cities of refuge," where unintentional killers might find refuge. These "cities of refuge" were situated in separate areas of the land (Deut 4:41–43; 19:1–10; Josh 20:1–9). *See* Cities of Refuge.

Since the Levites received their income from the tithes of the other people of the land, they did not depend on this property to bring in income for their living expenses (Num 18: 20–24; Deut 10:9). The cities were strategically placed so that the Levites as spiritual leaders were near to help other Israelites at all times. They were to be God's men and He was their inheritance. They were placed according to the divine will to exert the kind of influence that would please God. Thus the landless Levites were set to serve in every part of Israel. *See* Levites.

It is quite clear that not all these cities were taken over right away from the warlike inhabitants of Palestine. It is also true that many of the sons of Levi were not disposed to take their assignment in undesirable areas. Many became wanderers who moved about over the land to find work or income where it became available (e.g., Jud 17:7–13). While the ideal arrangement of 48 cities on both sides of the Jordan in which the people of Levi could be placed would seem to be unusually attractive, to bring the people to work it out practically was another matter. In many instances it was impossible to provide "employment" for a large number of Levites. Even when these cities became available, many other people lived in them. It is not clear how the Levitical members of the population adjusted themselves to the life of the municipality. The rules that were given in the wilderness were still in force (e.g., Lev 25:32–34), but the conditions found in the new land had much to do with the actual working out of the rules in the lives of the Levites. In it all God was preparing a chosen group of the descendants of Levi to lead His people in the worship and sacrificial exercises.

W. F. Albright assigns to the time of David the completed allocation of these cities. The plans set in operation in the days of Joshua were worked out as conditions allowed progress to be made. Some of the ancient holy cities of the land were made a part of the religious system of Israel (e.g., Bethel and Gilgal, Hos 4:15; 12:11; Amos 4:4–5; 5:5; Gibeon, I Kgs 3:4).

The Levitical system was based on the doctrine that God was the real owner of all property and that His chosen ones were selected to enjoy the land as His tenants and servants (Lev 25:23, 55).

K. M. Y.

LEVITICUS, BOOK OF. The third book of the OT, so named by the Greek and Latin versions because of its emphasis on the Levitical priesthood. The Heb. title is *wayyiqrā'*, "And He called," the first word of the book. An integral part of the Pentateuch, the narrative of chaps. 8–10 and chap. 16 continue from Ex 40 and are resumed in Num 1. Events move from the building of the tabernacle, past the ordination of the Aaronic priests and the Day of Atonement, to the census and reorganization of the people. Between these appear four collections of instructions and laws.

Chaps. 1–7 contain the only technical treatment of the sacrificial system of the OT. This section fittingly appears between the completion of the tabernacle and the priests' ordination.

Besides sacrifice, the priests were to give instruction concerning ritual purity. The delineation of clean and unclean is taught in chaps. 11–15. This most complete and authoritative treatment was the foundation of the instruction which the prophet Haggai sought from the priests after the Exile (Hag 2:10–14).

The words "You shall be holy, for I am holy" in chaps. 17–26 (Lev 19:2; 20:7, 26; 21:6–8) have given that section the name holiness code. Lev 19:1–17 seems to contain a version of the Decalogue within this code. Compare covenant code (Ex 21–23) and Deuteronomic code (Deut 12–26). All three balance strictly religious demands with those of personal and social morality. Leviticus stresses their inseparable relation to the holiness required of the people in whose midst God will dwell. The phrase "I am Yahweh [the Lord]" is also typical. These demands are required by the very nature of God.

Chap. 27 is an appendix of laws concerning vows.

Outline

I. Instructions for Sacrifice, Chaps. 1–7
II. Ordination of the Aaronite Priesthood, Chaps. 8–10
III. Instructions Concerning Clean and Unclean, Chaps. 11–15
IV. The Day of Atonement, Chap. 16
V. The Holiness Code, Chaps. 17–26
VI. Appendix Concerning Vows, Chap. 27

This priestly material, although in a reasonable order, is only loosely related. It is tied together by the repeated introduction for narrative and law: "And the Lord [Yahweh] said to Moses." Yahweh is the source of Israel's knowledge of the covenant and all its institutions, and Moses is the mediator of His will at the fountainhead of Israel's existence as a covenant people. Each of the so-called codes as found in Exodus, Leviticus, and Deuteronomy, whether concerning priests, sacrifice, or general legislation, claims Mosaic, and beyond that God's, authority.

The basic theme of Leviticus is holiness: the gap between God's holiness and man's, even within the covenant. The tabernacle, sacrifice, and priesthood limit contact between God and His people to prevent the difference from becoming unbearable, yet they do provide for the minimum of contact necessary to life within the covenant. Atonement and rites of cleansing witness to God's willingness to remove elements inimical to holy fellowship. The law with its exhortations reveals God's will for His people to be truly holy in a moral sense as well. The NT references to Leviticus in Rom 3:25, Hebrews, and Mk 12:31 show the values of Leviticus for the Christian in expounding atonement for sin and its fruits in holy living.

J. D. and W. W.

Authorship and Date

The question of the authorship and date of the book of Leviticus is an integral part of the criticism of the Pentateuch. *See* Canon of Scripture, the OT; Law of Moses; Pentateuch. The critical school has usually dated Leviticus to the time of Ezra. W. Möller has shown, however, that many passages in Deuteronomy presuppose the existence of Leviticus, so that even according to the documentary hypothesis of Wellhauser, Leviticus must have been put in written form before the Exilic or post-Exilic period (ISBE, III, 1878). The book of Deuteronomy, e.g., takes into account different kinds of sacrifices (cf. Deut 12:6, 11, 17, 26, 27) such as are described in Lev 1-7. It mentions the priests' due from the people (Deut 18:3-5) as offerings with which the Israelites should already be familiar (see Lev 7:32-34). Deut 24:8 refers directly to the laws concerning leprosy, which are found in Lev 13-14. The regulations not to eat the blood even of wild game but to pour it out on the ground (Deut 12:15-16, 22-25; 15:22-23) can only be understood in the light of Lev 17:10-14.

Furthermore, undesigned references in the laws of Leviticus point to a time when Israel was living in a camp (Lev 4:12; 13:46; 14:3, 8; 17:3) in the midst of a desert (Lev 16:10, 21, 22). All the people could easily bring any animal they slaughtered to the tent of meeting or tabernacle to offer it first to the Lord (Lev 17:3-9). In contrast, regarding the eating of meat, provision was made in Deuteronomy for the time when people would not all be able to come to the central place of worship (Deut 12:15, 20, 21).

R. K. Harrison has argued for an early (Mosaic) date for Leviticus from a comparison with the priestly and religious texts of ancient Sumer and Egypt. The scribal practices of those lands indicate that liturgies and rituals were very early committed to writing and treasured for many succeeding centuries. They were not transmitted from one generation to another in an oral form before finally being written down. The Sumerian literature was passed on in verbatim copies, unmodified by any later compilers or commentators (*Introduction to the Old Testament*, pp. 591ff.).

The names of offerings similar to those described in Lev 1-7 have been discovered in the Ugaritic (Canaanite) literature from the 14th -13th cen. B.C. found at Ras Shamra (Archer, SOTI, pp. 149, 163). Excavations at Lachish unearthed three Canaanite shrines (1500-1200 B.C.), with a refuse pile containing large quantities of animal bones. Most of these were of the right foreleg or shoulder (cf. Lev 7:32-33), disproving the claim of the higher critics that the Levitical sacrifices were necessarily a late institution. Legal documents from Ugarit which are conveyances of property often have a formula, similar to the term "for ever" in Lev 25:23, 30, which indicates that the transfer was made in perpetuity (J. J. Rabinowitz, VT, VIII [1958], 95). These discoveries go far to negate the claim that the terminology of Leviticus requires a late date, a whole millennium after the time of Moses.

J. R.

Bibliography. Oswald T. Allis, "Leviticus," NBC. Andrew A. Bonar, *A Commentary on the Book of Leviticus,* 1851; 5th ed., London: Nisbet, 1875 (Zondervan, 1959 reprint). A. T. Chapman and A. W. Streave, *The Book of Leviticus,* Cambridge: University Press, 1914. Charles R. Erdman, *The Book of Leviticus,* Westwood, N.J.: Revell, 1951. Roland K. Harrison, *Introduction to the Old Testament,* Grand Rapids: Eerdmans, 1969, pp. 589-613. A Jukes, *Law of Offerings in Leviticus I-VII,* London: Nisbet, 1870. Samuel H. Kellogg, *The Book of Leviticus,* ExpB, 3rd ed., London: Hodder & Stoughton, 1899. Wilhelm Möller, "Leviticus," ISBE, III, 1870-1880. Charles F. Pfeiffer, *The Book of Leviticus, a Study Manual,* Grand Rapids: Baker, 1957, and literature listed there.

LEVY. Taxes or forced service imposed upon a people by a government. The Heb. word *mas* is translated "levy" five times in KJV (I Kgs 5:13 [twice], 14; 9:15, 21). It is also translated "tribute" and "tributary" frequently in the KJV and "forced labor" in the RSV. All references cited below contain *mas;* read them in ASV and RSV.

A levy of conscripted or enslaved labor is seen on the following occasions: (1) Israel in Egypt under Pharaoh (Ex 1:11; the "taskmasters" were lit. "directors of task workers or slave gangs"); (2) conquered Canaanite peoples (Deut 20:11; Josh 16:10; 17:13; Jud 1:28, 30, 33, 35); (3) David's "forced labor" department (II Sam 20:24, RSV); (4) Solomon's conscripted Israelites (I Kgs 5:13-14; cf. 11:28; 15:22) and "forced levy of slaves" from conquered peoples (I Kgs 9:15, 21; II Chr 8:8, RSV). Samuel warned that future kings of Israel would demand unpaid service from the people (I Sam 8:10-18).

Such labor is often called "corvée," a period of unpaid work required of a vassal by his feudal lord, as opposed to permanent enslavement. In the Amarna letters (*q.v.*) and other tablets from Alalakh and Ugarit are references to corvée work for the local king. An ostracon excavated in 1960 S of Joppa was a 7th cen. B.C. Heb. letter written to the governor of a district in Josiah's kingdom of Judah by a free-born peasant. He complained that although he had fulfilled his assigned quota of reaping on the royal estate, the supervisor had confiscated his garment, perhaps to punish him for suspected idleness (BASOR #167 [1962], pp. 31-35).

Paradoxically, the people who began their national life as forced laborers in Egypt (Ex 1:11), and who themselves forced their defeated foes into that same kind of life (I Kgs 9:15, 20-21), ended their national life with their chief city described as a "vassal" (Lam 1:1, RSV).

W. B.

LEWD, LEWDNESS. The Heb. word *zimmâ* means a plan, purpose or scheme shading off into a wicked thought or device, especially with reference to sexual unchastity (Jud 20:6; Jer 13:28; Ezk 16:27, 43, 58; 22:9, 11; Hos 6:9).

Gr. *ponēros* means evil in the sense of physical or moral evil. It is rendered once in the NT as "lewd" (Acts 17:5, KJV), though "evil" or "wicked" would be a better translation.

LIBATION. In antiquity libation referred to a liquid or a mixture of liquids poured upon a sacrificial offering as part of the sacrifice. Among the Hebrews, the amount of this libation was designated as the fourth part of a hin—a little more than two pints (Num 15:5). The libation usually consisted of unmixed wine, but sometimes the wine was mixed with honey and water. It was customarily poured upon the victim on the altar after it was killed (Lev 9:4; II Kgs 16:13). *See* Altar; Sacrifice; Offering.

LIBERALISM. Liberalism or, as it is more popularly called, modernism is a system of religion which, rejecting the Bible as the infallible Word of God and disparaging objective, intellectual truth, is based on subjective, emotional, personal experience.

Schleiermacher (1768-1834) was its founder. He held that the ideas of creation, miracles, the virgin birth, etc., are scientifically untenable, and that therefore religion should be reconstructed so as not to lose the allegiance of educated people.

Pietism had already prepared the way by its rejection of intellectual theology in favor of emotional experience. Whereas the reformers had held that Christian experience is the result of belief based on reasonable evidences—he that cometh to God must (first) believe that He is—Schleiermacher denied the necessity of a verbal revelation that gives knowledge, and removed the need of grace by asserting that religion is essentially a matter of feeling. Grace is not necessary because everyone has an innate capacity for religion. These feelings are natural, and by them man realizes his inherent possibilities.

In Schleiermacher's system, the particular doctrines of his dogmatics are obtained by analyzing one's feelings. Feelings of course are subjective; they do not reflect the objective character of the environment, but rather they reflect the inner feelings of the person experiencing them. Dogmatics to him, therefore, was not a knowledge of God but a description of one's emotions. Thus for biblical or systematic theology Schleiermacher substituted the psychology of religious experience.

Philosophically Schleiermacher was a sort of pantheist. But to maintain his reputation as the preeminent Christian preacher in Germany, he disguised his actual views as much as possible and used conservative language.

A later important development of liberalism is found in Albrecht Ritschl (1822-1889). Even more convinced than Schleiermacher that the Bible is scientifically and historically in error, he sought to preserve the essential kernel of Christianity by discarding its husks. Science and biblical criticism, he held, deal with facts. They are objective. They state things that are. But religion consists exclusively in value-judgments. In talking about the Godhead of Christ, the predicate Godhead or Deity may be retained, but only as expressive of the revelatory worth of Christ, i.e., His religious value. To say that Christ is God is not an intellectual proposition referring to the essence or nature of Christ, but a subjective, emotional evaluation of the term Christ as applied to the worshiper's experience. Likewise the term miracle expresses the religious value of an event but says nothing as to its scientific status. Thus orthodox terms can be retained without retaining their ordinary meaning. Religion is all value and no facts; science is all facts and no value; therefore neither can disturb the other.

Since according to these views religion develops out of a natural human capacity, the biblical doctrine of the total depravity of man was replaced by that of man's essential goodness. As a result Herbert Spencer wrote on the evanescence of evil, and churchmen urged the politicians to build the kingdom of God on earth by means of socialism and pacificism. The pervasive theme of many sermons soon became the universal Fatherhood of God and the universal brotherhood of man.

These ideas spread to America. Popular modernism in the 1920's produced such results as Harry Emerson Fosdick's attack on the virgin birth; his sermons on "The Peril of Worshipping Jesus" and "Shall the Fundamentalists Win?"; and the Auburn Affirmation, a document signed by more than 1,200 Presbyterian ministers who repudiated the truthfulness of the Bible and declared that the virgin birth, the atonement, and the resurrection are unessential to Christianity. These followed more profound men like Walter Rauschenbusch of Rochester Theological Seminary, who in 1907 published his influential work on *Christianity and the Social Crisis*. These sociological emphases led to a disinterest in heaven (later and more crudely:

pie in the sky) and in God. The term God was of course retained but H. N. Wieman of the University of Chicago defined God as "that character of events to which man must adjust himself in order to attain the greatest goods and avoid the greatest ills." God therefore is a part or aspect of the world.

Humanists have accused the liberals of inconsistency and dishonesty in their use of orthodox terminology and have urged them to espouse naturalism openly.

The liberal hope of ushering in the kingdom of God by socialism was shaken in Europe by World War I. World War II then weakened American optimism. And no one should now fail to see that socialism, either Hitler's national socialism or communism's international socialism, or any form of "big government," serves only to give greater scope to human depravity. Man needs to be guided not by emotions or subjective value-judgments, but by an objective divine message. He needs not the development of inherent natural capacities, but a supernatural regeneration. He basically needs not economic and political action, but the theology of salvation from sin through the Lord Jesus Christ.

See Existentialism; God Is Dead Theology; Neoorthodoxy; Theology.

G. H. C.

LIBERALITY. The words lie at the base of this concept: (1) Gr. *haplotēs,* unaffectedness, simplicity, mental honesty, openness of heart, generosity. It is used in the latter two senses in II Cor 8:2 (cf. 9:11, 13, NASB). (2) Gr. *charis,* grace or benevolence, in the sense of something done beyond what is required, as in sending a gift (RSV, NASB) to Christians in need elsewhere (I Cor 16:3).

LIBERATION. Liberation, deliverance or liberty cover the biblical idea of freedom from bondage, enslavement or imprisonment. Heb. *y^{e}shû'â* (three times) and *t^{e}shû'â* (five times), "safety," deliverance"; *p^{e}lêtâ* (five times), "escape," "deliverance"; Gr. *apolutrōsis,* "loosing," "deliverance" (once, Heb 11:35); *aphesis,* "sending away," "deliverance" (once, Lk 4:18). These words are supplemented by a study of the words denoting freedom: Heb. *ḥophshî,* "free," used 12 times for freedom from slavery and four times for other freedoms; Gr. *eleutheros,* "free," used 18 times to express the NT concept of freedom.

In the OT three kinds of liberation or freedom are spoken of:

1. Liberation from bondage in Egypt to become a peculiar people unto God, a kingdom of priests and a holy nation (Ex 19:3-6; cf. I Pet 2:9; Rev 1:6; 5:10). It was God in His sovereign grace who brought about this liberation (Ex 20:1-2). This deliverance from oppression and want in Egypt to freedom and plenty in Palestine (Ex 3:8; Deut 8:7) was not to a freedom of libertinism. It was from servitude to Pharaoch to the service of God (Lev 25:55). Each of these phases of Israel's liberation from Egypt is found in the NT. Believers are freed from the bondage of Satan and the world (Eph 2:1-3; Rom 6:16) to be a kingdom of priests (I Pet 2:9) and bondslaves of the Lord (Mt 10:24; Lk 17:10; Rom 1:1).

2. Liberation of slaves. The dignity of man was maintained in the laws for the liberation of slaves every seventh year or in the year of jubilee, whichever came first, and in their humane treatment (Ex 21:2-11; Lev 25:39-55; Deut 15:12-15; Jer 34:8-11, 14).

3. Liberation of Israel. If Israel obeyed God they would enjoy peace and freedom (Deut 28:1-14). but rebellion and idolatry would lead to bondage to other nations (Deut 28:15-69). However, a glorious deliverance was promised with the coming of the Messiah (Isa 61:1). This proved to be in two parts, Christ quoting and fulfilling the first part, "The Spirit of the Lord is upon me" down to the words, "to preach the acceptable day of the Lord" (Lk 4:16-20) at His first coming (v. 21), while the second, "the day of vengeance of our God," remains to be fulfilled just before His second advent. With His millennial return He will usher in the greatest liberation of all, and one in which both Israel and the Church will share (Joel 2:32; Amos 9:11 [cf. Rom 11:26]; Obad 17; Zech 14:1ff. [cf. Rom 4:16; Heb 11:39-40]).

In the NT, liberation takes on a much more theological nature. It speaks of deliverance from spiritual rather than physical bondage. Christ quoted Isa 61:1, as mentioned, and spoke of its fulfillment with His coming (Lk 4:16-20; cf. Jn 8:34-36, 41-44) and the judgment of Satan (Jn 12:31; 16:11; Mk 3:27; cf. Lk 10:17). This covers deliverance from: (1) Sin and its power. If we reckon ourselves dead to sin, it is not to have dominion over us (Rom 6:6-7, 11-23). (2) Satan and demonic powers (Lk 10:17; Col 1:13; cf. Eph 6:10-18). (3) The law as a means of justification (Rom 6:14; 7:5-25, 8:2-4; Gal 4:21 ff.; 5:1-2). (4) The ceremonialism which goes with the law is done away with (Gal 2:5; 5:3-6; Heb 10:26; 12:27). (5) Death and the fear of death; not in the sense the Christian will not die, but that the fallen nature will be removed and he will have a resurrection body (Rom 6:9-10; 8:18-23; Heb 2:14-15). (6) Pagan superstitions. The believer is no longer in bondage to the polytheistic ideas and practices of paganism (I Cor 10:23; Rom 14:1ff.).

The spiritual liberation taught in the Scriptures guards against two extremes. First it forbids libertinism: "Let us do evil, that good may come" or "that grace may abound" (Rom 3:8; 6:1-2). Second, it does not teach legalism, that is, justification by works, by perfectly keeping the law. Christ alone could and did fulfill the law for our justification; and all law-keeping done by man in self-justification is therefore condemned (Rom 3:19-20; Gal 5:4). The believer's liberty is one that is maintained in a life of progressive sanctification which occurs within the bounds of the law (Mt 5:17-19, 21, 27,

43, 48; 22:35–40; Rom 13:8–10). When we live according to its precepts we have freedom, therefore it is called "the perfect law of liberty" (Jas 1:25), "the royal law" (Jas 2:8) and "the law of liberty" (Jas 2:12).

R. A. K.

LIBERTINES. Only in Acts 6:9 does this word occur in the KJV. "The synagogue of the Libertines" is in some versions rendered "synagogue of the Freedmen." This evidently was a synagogue in Jerusalem composed not of free-thinkers in religion or of persons advocating release from conventional morality, but probably of persons descended from those Jews who had been taken captive by Rome a century earlier and later released. It is uncertain whether the synagogue of the Freedmen included in its membership some from Cyrene and Alexandria, and some from Cilicia and Asia, or whether there were two or more synagogues which entered into a debate with Stephen. In any case, men from the synagogue of the Freedmen argued with Stephen and accused him of blasphemy against God and Moses, and of denouncing the temple and the law. They, with others no doubt, eventually succeeded in bringing about the martyrdom of Stephen.

During excavations at Jerusalem in 1914 an inscription was discovered that may have come from this synagogue. The highly legible words in Gr. capitals mention that the building was for the use of Jews from the Dispersion:

"Theodotus the son of Vettenus, priest and ruler of the synagogue, son of a ruler of the synagogue, son's son of a ruler of the synagogue, built the synagogue for the reading of the law and for teaching of the commandments, also the strangers' lodging and the chambers and the conveniences of waters for an inn for them that need it from abroad, of which (synagogue) his fathers and the elders and Simonides did lay the foundation" (DeissLAE, p. 440).

The term libertine is sometimes used in theology to refer to one who puts no check on indulgence of fleshly lusts, rejecting all standards of morality. *See* Liberty.

J. A. S.

LIBERTY

The OT concept of liberty. The Heb. term *d^e^rôr* always implies a liberation from slavery or imprisonment (e.g., Jer 34:8–17). It is cognate with Akkad. *andurârum* signifying a release, in legal documents from the kingdom of Hana. The LXX translates it by *aphesis,* a Gr. term for release or exemption from taxes as found on the Rosetta Stone (1.12; inscribed in 196 B.C.) and in papyri of the Ptolemaic period (Deiss BS, pp. 100f.). In the OT economy it was exemplified in the freeing of all slaves who were fellow Israelites every seventh year, unless they chose to stay on permanently with their masters (Deut 15:12–18). Again, in every fiftieth year, which was called the year of jubilee, Heb. slaves were to be released and all patrimonial agricultural lands were to be restored (Lev 25:10; Ezk 46:17). Jeremiah spoke out against the citizens of Jerusalem who had covenanted with King Zedekiah to free their slaves and then had put them in bondage a second time (Jer 34:8–22). Thus liberty meant "the happy state of having been released from servitude for a life of enjoyment and satisfaction that was not possible before" (NED, p. 732).

The NT concept of liberty. When He spoke in the synagogue at Nazareth, Jesus Christ selected the passage in Isa 61:1ff. foretelling liberty for the captives and freedom for the downtrodden and imprisoned. Then He declared, "This day is this scripture fulfilled in your ears" (Lk 4:16–21). He had come to liberate the slaves of sin and Satan (Jn 8:34–36, 41–44).

Two kinds of liberty were envisioned by Christ: spiritual liberty, which began in its fuller sense after Calvary; and complete political liberty, which would come only with the inauguration of the millennial kingdom. Paul speaks of the spiritual liberty (Gr. *eleutheria,* from *eleutheros,* "free") inaugurated by the cross, declaring that it frees a man from all legalism and self-justification (Rom 8:21; Gal 5:1ff.). It will culminate in "the glorious liberty of the children of God" when all of creation will be set free from its slavery to corruption (Rom 8:21).

Some feel that this freedom did not exist in any real sense before the cross, while others are convinced that it existed already in the OT and that this is proved in that the Israelites were saved by grace on the basis of faith alone. The latter find their proof in Rom 4 in which Abraham is said to have been justified by faith before the law was given, David after the law was given and under it. These do, however, see the cross as making a real difference in the sense that it freed the Holy Spirit to perform a fuller ministry in the NT than in the OT.

Paul insisted upon absolute liberty from the law-system of Moses as the result of justification through faith in Christ (Rom 7:1–6; I Cor 10:29; II Cor 3:17; Gal 2:4; 4:21–31; 5:1, 13). At the same time he warned against using this liberty as grounds for license (I Cor 6:12; 10:23; Gal 5:13; cf. I Pet 2:16), or allowing it to become a stumbling block to a weaker brother (Rom 14:1–23; I Cor 8:7–13).

R. A. K.

The exercise of Christian liberty with reference to law. The Christian's liberty is subject to a great deal of misunderstanding because the concept of law is often inadequately understood. Without qualifying words or phrases attached, the concept of law has reference to teaching or instruction which issues in rules or principles for conduct. Law is a norm for living. God's law is the norm for living which He has delivered for instruction in His will. In the progress of divine revelation God has seen fit to set forth different norms or systems of rule which vary according to time, people, and the divine purpose. A proper view of two of these economies is especially important in relation to the question of Christian liberty and law.

The law of Moses, also commonly called the OT law, contains the revelation of God to Moses. Though the Ten Commandments are usually thought of as practically synonymous with the Mosaic law, this law-system, by the most common Jewish court, is divided into 613 commandments which covered every area of Jewish life and worship. While it is possible to divide this Mosaic law-system into different categories, such should never be allowed to obscure the fact that the law of Moses is a unit, and it stands or falls as a unit. To say that one part of the Mosaic law remains in force today (such as the Decalogue) is to ignore its unitary nature (cf. Charles Ryrie, *The Grace of God*, Moody Press, 1963, pp. 98-105).

Besides being unitary in nature, the Mosaic law is distinctly Jewish; that is, the intended recipients were the Israelites. Both Testaments are clear on this point (Lev 26:46; Rom 2:14; 9:4).

As a rule of life for the believer, the Mosaic law came to an end in Christ, this by virtue of the fact that Christ met its demands and was its fulfillment and goal (Rom 7:4; 10:4; Gal 3:10-13; II Cor 3:7-11; Heb 7:11-12). Those who would take sections of the law of Moses (such as the Decalogue or dietary laws) and insist that they are in force today, whereas other elements came to an end with Christ, ignore the fact that when the Mosaic law came to an end, it came to an end as a unit, a system, a whole. The believer today is not bound by the Mosaic law-system.

This is not to say that the Mosaic law has no use or value today. It does, "if a man use it lawfully" (I Tim 1:8). In part this use would seem to consist in pointing out the character of sin to the unrighteous (I Tim 1:7-10) and in bringing the unbelieving to the point of seeing their condemned and helpless condition (Rom 3 and Gal 3).

Furthermore, it should be recognized that embodied in the Mosaic law are moral and spiritual principles (such as nine of the Ten Commandments, sabbath keeping being excluded) which have an abiding and universal validity that transcends the temporary and Jewish character of the Mosaic law-system. To such timeless principles the believer should consider himself responsible, not because embodied in the Mosaic law as such, but because of their timeless character as indicated by their essential inclusion in NT revelation.

However, the fact that the Christian is free from the Mosaic law (Rom 7:6) does not mean that he is free from law, i.e., norms of life. That is not the nature of Christian liberty; for besides the believer's freedom from the Mosaic law, the believer is also free from slavery to sin (Rom 6:17-23). This hardly implies lack of norms; in fact, this same passage speaks of the believer's new status as that of a slave of righteousness and a slave of God (Rom 6:19, 22).

This new norm to which the Christian is subject is perhaps best referred to as the law of Christ (Gal 6:2; I Cor 9:21). The essence of the law of Christ is love for God and neighbor (Lk 10:27; Mt 22:35-40; Jn 13:34; Mt 5:44) with all the other NT imperatives for which the believer is responsible being implied in and flowing out from this love ethic (Rom 13:8-; cf. I Cor 13; Gal 5:14, 22-23; Col 3:14). While the law of Christ is not codified in the same sense as the Mosaic law, nevertheless its precepts fall into three general categories, i.e., positive commands, negative commands, and non-specific principles of conduct.

Christian liberty with reference to license. The doctrines of grace and liberty have often been abused and misused by those looking for an excuse to gratify their sinful desires. Grace and liberty clearly do not justify one's indulgence of the flesh (Rom 6:1-2; Gal 5:13). Libertinism or license is not only categorically repudiated (as in Rom 6:1-2 and Gal 5:13) but its impropriety for the Christian is clearly implied by the believer's responsibility to the law of Christ as explained above. But three things are especially important in this connection. Christian liberty is limited by love (Gal 5:13-14). Christian liberty is in a sense a new slavery (Rom 6:16-22). Christian liberty is to be exercised under the control of the Holy Spirit (Gal 5:13-22).

Christian liberty with reference to the Holy Spirit. Without the ministry of the Holy Spirit the believer will fall into either libertinism or legalism. The Spirit preserves from libertinism by providing the direction for the exercise of liberty through His written Word and through the control which He desires to exercise within the believer by His indwelling presence (I Cor 6:19-20). This control is described by such concepts as walking in the Spirit (Gal 5:16, 25), walking after the Spirit (Rom 8:4), being led by the Spirit (Rom 8:14), and being filled with the Spirit (Eph 5:18).

On the other hand, the Holy Spirit's manner of control prevents legalism. Rather than the precepts of the NT being objects of fear, they are objects of delight; for the Spirit produces the life, power, and motivation that makes obedience to Christ and His precepts a matter of love rather than mere legalistic necessity. For this reason the Christian graces are called "the fruit of the Spirit" (Gal 5:22-23).

See Freedom; Law.

S. N. G.

Bibliography. Ch. Biber, "Freedom," *A Companion to the Bible*, ed. by J. J. von Allmen, New York: Oxford Union Press, 1968, pp. 129-132. J. I. Packer, "Liberty," NBD, pp. 732ff. Charles C. Ryrie, *The Grace of God*, Chicago: Moody Press, 1963, pp. 92-113, 121-126. Heinrich Schlier, "*Eleutheros*, etc.," TDNT, II, 487-502.

LIBNAH (lĭb'nȧ). A town in the Shephelah or foothills of Palestine, on the border of Judah and Philistia. Its name, which means "whiteness," may be derived from nearby white cliffs. It was one of the towns taken by Joshua in his conquest of Canaan (Josh 10:29-32). Libnah was in the territory of Judah (Josh 15:42), one of the cities assigned to the Levites (Josh 21:13). The city revolted against Joram at the time he was attacked by the Edomites (II Kgs 8:22), but apparently was subsequently recovered by Judah, as it is mentioned as being beseiged by Sennacherib (II Kgs 19:8). Hamutal, the daughter of Jeremiah, wife of King Josiah and mother of Jehoahaz and Zedekiah, was a native of Libnah (II Kgs 23:31; 24:18). The site is uncertain; it may be either Tell Bornat (*c.* 25 miles SW of Jerusalem) or Tell es-Safi (now thought to be Gath, *q.v.*).

S. C.

LIBNI (lĭb'nī), **LIBNITES** (lĭb'nīts)

1. The eldest son of Gershon and grandson of Levi (Ex 6:17; Num 3:18, 21; I Chr 6:17, 20); also the progenitor of the Libnites, a family of Gershonites (Num 3:21; 26:58). Identified as Laadan in I Chr 23:7-9; 26:21. *See* Laadan 2.

2. A Levite descendant of Merari (I Chr 6:29).

LIBYA (lĭb'ĭ-ȧ). A nation represented in the Table of Nations (Gen 10; I Chr 1) as Phut, a descendant of Ham.

The Libyans were fair complected people who inhabited the N coast of Africa. They have been designated by several names in ancient Egyptian texts: Tehenu (Old Kingdom), Temehu (Middle Kingdom), Meshwesh (18th Dynasty), *Rbw* (Lîbu, 19th-20th Dynasty). Three distinct Heb. words are translated by "Libya" or "Libyans" in the various versions: (*a*) *kûb*, KJV "Chub," LXX *Libues*, followed by RSV, etc.; (*b*) *lûbîm* (always in the plural form), LXX *Libues*, KJV "Lubim"; (*c*) *pût*, LXX *Phout*, *Phoud*, or *Libues*, KJV "Phut," "Put." Put may refer to the region of Libya called Cyrenaica by the Romans, which lies beyond the inhospitable desert W of the delta. *See* Chub; Lubim; Phut.

Apparently the influence held by the Libyans over N Africa and Egypt waxed and waned throughout antiquity. This is implied by the fact that they had to be subdued *c.* 1230 B.C. by Mer-ne-Ptah of Egypt. Then in the 10th cen. the Libyans reestablished dominion over Egypt and rules until *c.* 730 B.C. from the delta city of Bubastis. The first king of the 22nd Dynasty, Shishak, sided with Jeroboam I in the Israelite civil war *c.* 926 B.C. and invaded Judah (I Kgs 14:25-26).

Jews from Libya were in Jerusalem on the day of Pentecost (Acts 2:10). These probably came from Cyrenaica, which had been united with Crete as one province in 67 B.C. Cyrene was its capital. From there came Simon, who carried Jesus' cross when He fell (Mt 27:32), some early Christians at Antioch (Acts 11:20; 13:1), and Jews who argued with Stephen (Acts 6:9).

P. W. F.

The Nile River with Libyan hills rising to the west.
HFV

LICE. *See* Animals: Louse, IV. 24.

LIE. A false statement or piece of information deliberately given as being true; anything meant to deceive. *See* Deceit.

Satan authored "the lie" (*to pseudos*) in his original apostasy (Jn 8:44; cf. Isa 14:12-20; Ezk 28:1-19). Man in his apostasy likewise preferred "the lie" (*to pseudos*) to God's truth (Rom 1:25; cf. Gen 3:1-7). In the final apostasy, just before the second advent, the world will receive "the lie" (*to pseudos*) of the Antichrist (II Thess 2:11-12; cf. I Jn 2:22; 4:3; Rev 13:1-18). False prophets (*q.v.*) readily become Satan's dupes (cf. II Cor 11:13-15) by deceiving people with lies against God's truth (Isa 9:15-16; 30:9-10; Jer 23:14, 25-26, 32). Unregenerate men, like their spiritual father (Jn 8:44), speak lies from their birth (Ps 58:3), making them their refuge (Isa 28:15, 17; 59:3-4) until they settle among liars forever (Rev 21:27; 22:15). The lot of liars of every kind, along with other incorrigible sinners, will be in the lake of fire (Rev 21:8).

God, of course, cannot lie (Num 23:19; Tit 1:2). His truth is incompatible with a lie (I Jn 2:21, 27). Lying was forbidden by the law of Moses (Ex 20:16; Lev 19:11). Christians must, like God (Prov 6:16-19; 12:22), utterly detest lying (Eph 4:25; Col 3:9; cf. Ps 31:6; 119:29, 163; Prov 13:5).

Lying is illustrated in the lives of Cain (Gen 4:9), Jacob (27:19), Joseph's brothers (37:31-32); Gehazi (II Kgs 5:20-27), Peter (Mt 26:69-75), and Ananias and Sapphira (Acts 5:1-11).

W. B.

LIEUTENANTS. The translation of Heb. *'ăḥashdarpenîm*, Persian satraps, princes or governors of provinces of the Persian Empire mentioned in Ezra (8:36) and Esther (3:12; 8:9; 9:3).

LIFE. *In the OT* life is primarily referred to by *nephesh* and *ḥay*. Basically *nephesh* means "breath," "soul," "life with individual existence," "self." In connection with life it signifies: (1) the life principle, that which breathes (Gen 9:4-5; 35:18; Lev 17:11; I Kgs 17:21-22); (2) physical life (I Sam 22:23; 23:15); (3) living animals (Gen 9:10, 12); (4) human beings (Gen 36:6; 46:15-27). Heb. *hay* in the singular usually refers to animal life (KJV "beasts," Gen 7:14; Ex 23:11; Lev 11:2; 26:6, 22; Job 5:23). The plural form is almost always used for human life. Intensity or the varied aspects of life seem to be involved.

In the OT life is associated with a right relationship with God. Apart from this, true life is impossible (Deut 8:3; 30:15, 19-20). God is sovereign in life (Gen 2:7; Num 16:22). The OT anticipates a resurrection life (Job 19:25-27; Ps 16:10; Isa 26:19; Dan 12:2).

In the NT three basic words are employed. The most common is *zoe*, which basically looks at the life principle (cf. Jn 6:63). It may refer to: (1) physical life (Acts 17:25; I Cor 15:19); (2) God's life (Jn 5:26; Eph 4:18; Rom 5:10); or (3) the life of Christ in the believer (II Cor 4:10-11; Col 3:4). This new life (Rom 6:4) is a present possession (Jn 5:24), is eternal (Jn 6:51), has a future manifestation (Rom 5:17; II Cor 5:4; I Tim 4:8), and is received by faith (Jn 3:16). Jesus Christ Himself is our life (Jn 11:25; 14:6; Col 3:4; I Jn 5:11-12, 20). *See* Eternal Life; Resurrection.

The second NT word is *bios* which basically considers the external aspects of life in this world. It or a cognate describes our present earthly life as to its: (1) duration (I Pet 4:2-3); (2) functions (Lk 8:14; I Tim 2:2; II Tim 2:4); (3) conduct (Acts 26:4); (4) means of subsistence (Mk 12:44; Lk 8:43; 15:12, 30; I Jn 3:17). It is never used of eternal life.

The third word is *psychē*, often translated "soul," which corresponds to Heb. *nephesh*. Fundamentally it describes natural life. With respect to life this many-faceted word may refer to: (1) the breath (Latin *anima*) or vital force which animates the body, the life principle which leaves the body when death occurs (Lk 12:20; Acts 20:10; Rev 8:9); (2) physical life (Mt 2:20; Mk 10:45; Lk 12:22); (3) that which possesses life whether human or animal (I Cor 15:45; Rev 16:3); (4) the center of the personality (Lk 12:19; Jn 12:27); (5) man's inner being which can be saved, lost, tempted and sanctified (Jas 1:21; Mk 8:36; I Pet 2:11; III Jn 2).

Bibliography. Rudolf Bultmann, *et al.*, "*Zaō*, *Zōē*, etc.," TDNT, II, 832-875; David Hill, *Greek Words and Hebrew Meanings*, Cambridge: Univ. Press, 1967.

S. D. T.

LIFE, BOOK OF. In the NT the book of life is the register which contains the names of those who are saved and will inherit eternal life. It is called by this designation in Phil 4:3; Rev 3:5; 13:8; 17:8; 20:12, 15; 21:27 (22:19 should read "tree" of life, not "book" of life). The concept is also found in Lk 10:20 and possibly Heb 12:23. The phrase also occurs in the OT (Ps 69:28; cf. Ex 32:32-33; Dan 12:1). But in the OT the concept seems to be that of a list of those living in this present world, though some would say that it denotes a list of the heirs of salvation in the OT also. If the former is correct, when the OT speaks of being blotted out of the book of life, it refers to physical death and extinction of the family line.

Rev 3:5 also speaks of being blotted out of the book of life, meaning here the list of the saved. Some say that such a blotting out is possible and implied. But that a saved person could thus lose his salvation is felt by many to contradict those passages which teach the security of the believer in Christ. Consequently, these interpreters have taken one of the following approaches: (1) Rev 3:5 does not explicitly say that anyone's name will be blotted out; (2) this register originally has everyone's name on it, but when a person finally rejects Christ his name is blotted out; (3) the book of life in Rev 3:5 is the register of profession from which some names will be erased, whereas the Lamb's book of life (Rev 13:8; 17:8; 20:12, 15; 21:27, referring to the Lamb's book of life though not specifically so called in every verse) contains only the names of genuine believers from which no names can be erased. *See* Perseverance.

S. N. G.

LIFT. The English translation of 16 or more Heb. roots and of six Gr. roots. It is exclusively the rendering of verb forms, never of nouns. It therefore conveys the idea of raising or elevating action. It is used with respect to many situations, either literally or figuratively.

The verb translated most frequently "lift" is *nāśâ*, "to lift up," "bear," "carry away," as in Isa 53:4, 12. It is used of the eyes for greater or clearer vision (Gen 13:10); of the voice in cries of anguish and distress (Num 14:1); of the soul or hands lifted up to the Lord in prayer or in presenting offerings (Ps 25:1; 28:2; 63:4; 86:4; I Tim 2:8).

More difficult idioms for the Western mind to grasp are:

1. To lift up another's head (Gen 40:13, 19 f.; II Kgs 25:27; Ps 3:3; 27:6; Jer 52:31), meaning to raise from an enslaved condition.

2. To lift up the horn (Ps 75:4, 5, 10; Zech 1:21; I Chr 25:5; I Sam 2:1, 10), i.e., to exalt someone else or to assume a superior attitude, the figure being taken from a fighting bull brandishing its horns.

3. To lift up one's hand (Gen 14:22; Ex 6:8, ASV marg.; Deut 32:40; Ezk 20:5; Rev 10:5-6), the sign of taking an oath. But to lift up one's hand *against* another is to attack or fight him (II Sam 18:28; 20:21; I Kgs 11:26), or perhaps to take an oath to oppose him.

4. To lift up one's face toward another (Gen 4:4-7, ASV; II Sam 2:22, RSV; Ezr 9:6; Job 11:15; 22:26f.), meaning to dare to be confident or glad in his presence.

5. When one's heart is lifted up (Deut 8:14; II Chr 25:19; 26:16; 32:25; Ezk 28:2, 5, 17; Dan 5:20; 11:12), he becomes very bold, usually with resultant pride in self, but occasionally with godly courage by trusting in the Lord (II Chr 17:6).

H. E. Fi. and J. R.

LIGHT

The Origin of Light

The first recorded words of God are, "Let there be light" (Gen 1:3). Thus light came into being by the direct command of God. It was acclaimed as "good," was divided from the darkness, and was called "day" (Gen 1:4-5).

It is to be noted that light existed before the creation of the lightbearing sun, moon, and stars on the fourth day (Gen 1:14-19). "Something akin, possibly, to the all pervasive electro-magnetic activity of the aurora borealis penetrated the chaotic night of the world. The ultimate focusing of light . . . in suns, stars, and solar systems brought the initial creative process to completion, as the essential condition of all organic life" (ISBE, III, 1891).

It is significant that God who is light (I Jn 1:5) initiated His creative design with light. Before His command the earth was without form (Gen 1:2). The act of producing light formed a direct and personal association of the Creator with His creation. Parallels to this may be noted in God's direct association with the Israelites as He led them by the pillar of fire (Ex 13:21-22), and by the manifestation of the Shekinah glory in the completed tabernacle (Ex 40:34-38) and the Solomonic temple (I Kgs 8:11; II Chr 5:13-14).

The full personal association of God with His creation began when the Second Person of the Trinity, the light of the world (Jn 3:19; 8:12), became flesh and dwelt among us. It is to be further noted that in the new creation there is no need for either the light of candle, moon, or sun (Rev 22:5; 21:23), for "the glory of God did lighten it, and the Lamb is the light [lit., lamp, or light giver] thereof" (Rev 21:23; cf. Isa 60:19-20).

Words Translated "Light"

The KJV translates "light" in the sense of illumination for 12 Heb. words (five different roots) and six Gr. words (four different roots). The common Heb. word is *'ôr,* translated "light" 108 times throughout the OT. It occurs 28 times in Job, 23 times in Isaiah, and 18 times in the Psalms, with all other occurrences spread through 17 other OT books. The second most common Heb. word translated "light" is *mā'ôr* (same root as *'ôr*), which literally means "light giver," occurring 17 times, 11 in Genesis and Exodus. All other Heb. words translated as "light" occur only 14 times.

The most common Gr. word is *phōs,* translated "light" 64 times and found throughout the NT. It occurs most often in the writings of John (23 times in the Gospel and five times in the first epistle) and the second most often in the Acts (ten times). The second most common word is *lychnos* meaning "lamp" or "light giver," occurring six times. The other four Gr. words are translated "light" only eight times.

Biblical Usages of the Word "Light"

The concept of light is used both literally and metaphorically in Scripture. In the OT the usage is about equal, but in the NT the metaphorical outweighs the literal by about four to one. In addition to these two usages there are some distinctively miraculous instances of light.

Literal. OT usage: Light is used (1) of the primal luminescence created by God (Gen 1:3-5); (2) of the light givers: sun, moon, and stars (Gen 1:14-16); (3) of the dawn (Job 7:4); (4) of the light of sun, moon, and stars (I Sam 14:36; Isa 30:26; Ezk 32:7; Eccl 12:2); (5) of the light from fire (Isa 50:11); (6) of lamps (Ex 25:6; Lev 24:2); and (7) of lightning (Job 36:32), RSV).

NT usage: Light in the NT is used (1) of the primal luminescence created by God (II Cor 4:6; cf. Jas 1:17); (2) of lamps (Acts 20:8; II Pet 1:19; Rev 18:23); (3) of the light of day (Jn 11:9; Rev 22:5); (4) of that which is illuminated by light (Eph 5:14); and (5) in a semi-literal sense of the eye as an organ of light (Mt 6:22-23; Lk 11:34-35).

Metaphorical. OT usage: In a figurative or symbolic sense light is used in the OT (1) as an image of good fortune or prosperity (Job 22:28; Est 8:16); (2) of life itself (Job 3:16, 20; Ps 56:13); (3) of doctrine or instruction (Isa 2:5; 49:6; 51:4); (4) of the guidance of God (Job 29:3; Ps 112:4; Isa 58:10); (5) of the illuminating power of the Scriptures (Ps 119:105); (6) of wisdom (Dan 2:22; 5:11, 14); (7) of cheerfulness, sereneness (Job 29:24); (8) of favor shown by God, king, or influential man (Ps 4:6; Prov 16:15; (9) of progeny (I Kgs 11:36; II Kgs 8:19; II Chr 21:7); and perhaps (10) of the glory of an individual (II Sam 21:17).

NT usage: Metaphorically light is used in the NT (1) of the nature of God (I Jn 1:5); (2) of the glory of God's dwelling place (I Tim 6:16; cf. Ps 104:2); (3) of Jesus Christ as the illuminator of men (Jn 1:4, 5, 9; 3:19; 8:12); (4) of the gospel of salvation (Mt 4:16; Acts 26:18; Col 1:12; I Pet 2:9; II Cor 4:4, 6); (5) of truth to be obeyed (I Jn 1:7; Jn 12:36; Eph 5:8; Rom 13:12; I Jn 2:9-10); and (6) of those bearing truth (Mt 5:14, 16; Acts 13:47; Jn 5:35; Phil 2:15; cf. Rom 2:19).

Instances of miraculous light. Scripture notes several instances of light in a miraculous sense. (1) The Israelites had light in their houses while the Egyptians were in thick darkness (Ex 10:21-23). (2) The "pillar of fire" which led the Israelites at night (Ex 13:21; 14:20; Ps 78:14). (3) The supernatural brightness of Christ's garments at His transfiguration (Mt 17:2). (4) The light that was brighter than noonday at Paul's conversion (Acts 9:3; 22:6;

26:13). The implication of each of these instances is clearly of the immediate presence and glory of God.

The Contrast of Light and Darkness

A quick concordance study will demonstrate how often the concepts of light and darkness (*q.v.*) are employed in contrast. A modified ethical dualism between light and darkness, i.e., good and evil, may be noted throughout the Bible. Light and darkness have been mutually exclusive ever since the creation when "God divided the light from the darkness" (Gen 1:4-5, 18; II Cor 4:6). To the degree that light is present, to that degree darkness is dispelled or constrained. Though the contrast is employed in a literal sense (Eccl 2:13; Ps 139:12; II Cor 4:6*a*), it is more often in the metaphorical sense. "Darkness is the universal symbol and condition of sin and death; light the symbol and expression of holiness" (ISBE, III, 1891). *See* Holiness.

When we read that "God is light, and in him is no darkness at all" (I Jn 1:5), we understand this figuratively, that God is altogether good with no trace of evil. "By his light I walked through darkness" (Job 29:3) is understood to mean a life guided and protected through difficult and evil times (cf. Isa 42:16). Those that "put darkness for light, and light for darkness" (Isa 5:20) are men who call evil good and good evil. Judgment is pictured as a time of darkness from which one is restored (to light) (Amos 5:18; Mic 7:8).

Similarly in the NT, men are pictured in the darkness of despair and death to whom the light of hope is offered (Mt 4:16; II Pet 1:19; Jn 1:5). And though men love the darkness of wickedness rather than the light of truth in Jesus Christ (Jn 3:19-20), and though they resist the light, the darkness cannot extinguish the light (Jn 1:5, LB). Men are exhorted to walk while they have the light lest darkness overtake them (Jn 12:35). Believers are called the "children of light" who are "not of the night, nor of darkness" (I Thess 5:5; cf. Col 1:13). They who have been called "out of darkness into his marvelous light" (I Pet 2:9) are to "walk in the light" (respond to the truth) (I Jn 1:7), and those who "do not the truth" are they "who walk in darkness" (I Jn 1:6; cf. Lk 11:35).

Believers are exhorted to be careful in their associations with those who reject the truth, "for what fellowship hath righteousness with unrighteousness? and what communion hath light with darkness?" (II Cor 6:14). At times this may prove difficult to discern, for Satan, the prince of the "rulers of the darkness of this world" (Eph 6:12), is himself "transformed into an angel [messenger] of light [truth]" (II Cor 11:14). Yet the duty of believers is clear—putting on the "armor of light" (Rom 13:12; cf. Eph 6:14) they are to "shine as lights in the world" (Phil 2:15; cf. Mt 5:14), to turn men "from darkness to light" (Acts 26:18; cf. II Cor 4:4).

Light as a Symbol in the Writings of John

Of the Gospel writers, John makes the greatest use of symbols, light being the chief of these. It is not without significance that the Gospel that opens with "in the beginning" should echo Genesis in the coming of light. John probably reflects his Jewish-Hellenistic background in his extensive reference to light, though it is not necessary to trace his concept of light to the Hellenistic mysticism, in which light is identified with God. John seems rather to have been influenced by some of the ideas and language of the Qumran sect, perhaps through John the Baptist who must have known of the sectarians' teaching. Thus John the apostle may be indebted to the Dead Sea community for the particular way he gives expression to the idea of the struggle between light and darkness (Morris, *Studies in the Fourth Gospel*, pp. 321-358; *see* Dead Sea Scrolls; John, Gospel of).

With one exception (Jn 5:35, *lychnos*, a lamp, and referring to John the Baptist), John's word for "light" is *phōs*, radiance. It occurs 23 times throughout the first 12 chapters of the Gospel. In only one instance (11:9) does it clearly refer to physical light. In one case it refers to those who have responded to the truth (12:36, "children of light," cf. I Jn 1:7; 2:8-10). The other 21 usages are either directly to Jesus Christ or to the truth brought by His coming.

Jesus is the "true [real] light" (Jn 1:9), the true revelation of God. As such He is distinct from any other man, even one as great as John the Baptist (1:7-8; cf. 5:35). He came as "the light of men" (1:4), and as the "light of the world" (8:12; 9:5; 12:46). In rabbinic tradition the phrase "light of the world" had been applied to the Torah and temple, and did not amount to a claim to deity. But for John it implies that Christ is the true light, the real light, the ultimate reality. As the light that "shineth in darkness" (1:5) He came for every man (1:9; cf. 12:36), but many rejected the light because it exposed their evil (3:19-21). To those who accept Him He becomes the "light of life" (8:12; cf. 12:36). Those who reject Him lose purpose and truth, for they walk in darkness (11:10; 12:35).

It is more than a coincidence that the last occurrence of the word "light" in John's Gospel comes at the end of chapter 12, for it is at this point that Christ's offer of Himself to the world reached its conclusion. Beginning with chapter 13 Jesus' ministry is turned to His disciples in private instruction. What is the purpose of further light to the world when light already given has been rejected?

For the believer, since the appearance of the light displays God's love, true life in the light involves keeping Jesus' commandments, especially in loving one's brother (I Jn 2:8-11) and in doing the truth (I Jn 1:6-7). *See* Life; Love; Truth.

Jesus Christ as the Light

It was predicted that the Messiah would be

"for a light of the Gentiles" (Isa 42:6; 49:6), and the aged Simeon saw in the child Jesus that fulfillment (Lk 2:32). As the "dayspring" or rising sun, He was to "give light to them that sit in darkness and in the shadow of death" (Lk 1:78-79). The eternal Word (Jn 1:1-3), who Himself commanded "Let there be light" (Gen 1:3; cf. Col 1:16), became Himself the "brightness of [God's] glory" (Heb 1:3), "the true light, which lighteth every man that cometh into the world" (Jn 1:9). He called Himself "the light of the world" (Jn 8:12; 9:5; 12:46). Isaiah had prophesied that "the people that walked in darkness have seen a great light: they that dwell in the land of the shadow of death, upon them hath the light shined" (Isa 9:1-2); and when Jesus initiated His preaching in Galilee it was to fulfill that prophecy (Mt 4:12-16). On the occasion of His transfiguration, the visible glory of God, hidden beneath the lowliness of flesh, broke through to a few choice witnesses. His face shone and His garments were brilliant as light (Mt 17:1-2). This was a foreview of His risen and ascended state. In His glorified resurrection body He appeared to Paul in a shining light (Acts 9:3; 22:6; 26:13) and to John in a vision (Rev 1:12-18).

Jesus' primary revelation of Himself as the light of the world was in His works and words. His cures of the blind have particular significance here as demonstrations of His ability and desire to heal man's greater spiritual blindness (Mk 8:22-26; Jn 9:5; cf. Jn 8:12; 12:46). "Instead of the intermittent manifestations of the heavenly light characteristic of the old aeon, in which light and darkness alternate, as in the natural order, the light is now permanently present in Jesus Christ" (IDB, III, 132). But in the confrontation of light with darkness (Jn 3:19), men rejected that light, so that at the time of His arrest Jesus declared, "This is your hour, and the power of darkness" (Lk 22:53). But the powers of darkness could not contain Him, and He rose from the dead to "show light unto the people, and to the Gentiles" (Acts 26:23). That light continues today in the gospel, "For God, who commanded the light to shine out of darkness, hath shined in our hearts, to give the light of the knowledge of the glory of God in the face of Jesus Christ" (II Cor 4:6; cf. 4:4-5; Eph 5:13-14). Christ's coming brought the dawn of a new day which will never be followed by night (Rev 21:23; 22:5). *See* Jesus Christ.

Bibliography. J. A. MacCulloch, *et al.,* "Light and Darkness," HERE, VIII, 47-66. Leon Morris, *Studies in the Fourth Gospel,* Grand Rapids: Eerdmans, 1969. O. A. Piper, "Light, Light and Darkness," IDB, III, 130-132. Dwight M. Pratt, "Light," ISBE, III, 1890-92.

H. D. F.

LIGHTNING. Lightning is most often the translation of Heb. *bārāq* and Gr. *astrapē,* and is used figuratively and symbolically as well as literally.

Actual lightning occurs in Palestine and nearby desert areas in the spring and autumn. It is accompanied by thunder, wind squalls, and clouds of dust in fierce electrical storms. Heavy rains and occasional destructive hail may follow (Ex 9:23-24, JerusB; cf. Ps 105:32). Lightning is viewed as a manifestation of God's command over nature (Job 28:26; 36:32 [RSV]; 37:3-4; 38:35; Ps 77:18; 97:4; 135:7; Jer 10:13). Ps 29 describes in poetic fashion a great storm over the Lebanon Mountains with lightning striking the cedars: "The voice of Yahweh cleaves with shafts of fire" (v. 7, Anchor Bible). Lightning is also an instrument of God to destroy His enemies (Ps 18:14; 144:6; Zech 9:14; cf. Hab 3:11; Deut 32:41, lit., "the lightning of my sword," RSV marg.).

In his visions John saw flashes of symbolic lightning which were representative of the glory and majesty of God (Rev 4:5; 8:5; 11:19; 16:18), a figure probably derived from the lightnings which lit up Mount Sinai when God descended to give Moses the law (Ex 19:16, 18; 20:18). Lightning is a symbol of speed (Ezk 1:14; Nah 2:4) and of the supernatural brightness of Deity and angels (Dan 10:6; Mt 28:3). Jesus used the idea of lightning (Mt 24:27; Lk 17:24) to depict the conspicuousness and universality of His return. He also applied the figure of lightning to the spent power of Satan as a result of his fall (Lk 10:18).

It is quite reasonable that the "fire of the Lord" which fell on Elijah's sacrifice and consumed it as well as the stones of the altar (I Kgs 18:38) was lightning. Jon Ruthven argues for this interpretation because (1) lightning could result from cloudless turbulence produced by a cool, moist Mediterranean breeze meeting the hot, dry air over Mount Carmel; (2) the altar was on a height, and the water wetted its stones, making them better attractors of lightning; (3) lightning has been known to melt rocks; and (4) the contest was between Yahweh and Baal, the reputed god of thunder and lightning ("A Note on Elijah's 'Fire From Yahweh,'" JETS, XII [1969], 111-115).

See Rain; Thunder.

J. Ma.

LIGN-ALOES. *See* Plants: Aloes.

LIGURE. *See* Jewels.

LIKENESS. *See* Image of God.

LIKHI (lĭk'hī). Mentioned only in I Chr 7:19, as the third of four sons of Shemidah, a descendant of Manasseh. Apparently he was a member of the half tribe of Manasseh living E of the Jordan.

LILITH. *See* Gods, False.

LILY. *See* Plants.

LILY-OF-THE-VALLEY. *See* Plants.

LILY WORK. *See* Jachin 2.

LIME. *See* Minerals and Metals.

LINE. The rendering of several Heb. and Gr. words in the Bible.

1. Heb. *qaw,* "line," the commonest word, refers to the builder's measuring line (Job 38:5; Jer 31:39; Zech 1:16). It came to designate that a site was measured for judgment (II Kgs 21:13; Isa 28:17; 34:11). Some uses (I Kgs 7:23; II Chr 4:2; Ezk 47:3) indicate something of the modern surveyor's chain. Its use in Ps 19:4 is a separate problem. Perhaps *qaw* designates the line of the horizon denoting the heaven's total encompassing of the earth; thus, the limitless expansion of the testimony of creation. Or *qaw* may be derived from a different Heb. root, meaning a call (Dahood, *Psalm* 1, Anchor Bible, pp. 121f.). Laird Harris argues convincingly that the LXX preserves the original Heb. reading, "their voice" (*qlm* instead of *qwm*), which Paul correctly chose to quoootte Rom 10:18 (*Inspiration and Canonicity of the Bible,* Grand Rapids: Zondervan, 1957, p. 69).

2. Heb. *hebel,* "cord," is the line or measuring cord used to mark off portions of land (Ps 16:6; Amos 7:17), or the parts or portions themselves (Josh 17:5).

3. Heb. *hûṭ,* "line," "cord," "thread" (I Kgs 7:15; Song 4:3; Jer 52:21).

4. Heb. *tiqwâ,* "line," "cord." The derivative of *qaw,* denoting a certain kind of line (Josh 2:18).

5. Heb. word *śered,* "stylus," "pencil," "red chalk" (Isa 44:13), an instrument or material to make a line or mark.

6. Gr. *kanōn,* "line" (II Cor 10:16), a custom or standard which governs activity. *See* Weights and Measures.

H. G. S.

LINEAGE. A term meaning family (Gr. *patria*) found only in Lk 2:4 (KJV). Lineage enumerates the links in a person's ancestry. It serves to give the sequence of history (Gen 5); to insure priestly rights (Ex 6:14–27; I Chr 15:1–15; Neh 7:61–65); to secure a place on David's throne (I Chr 3:10–15); and, most importantly, to fulfill Scripture regarding the Messiah's linkage with Judah's tribe (Gen 49:10; Heb 7:13–14) and with David's seed (Isa 9:7; Mt 1:1–25; Lk 1:32–33, 69). *See* Genealogy.

LINEN. Thread or cloth made from flax. The word linen represents several Heb. and Gr. words. The material designated by them in general is the product of the flax plant (Ex 9:31). It is an annual, cultivated mainly for its fiber. The long, silky fiber is separated from the wood-like stem by rotting or "retting" in water. After the stem is beaten, the fiber is drawn out by a comb-like instrument (Isa 19:9, RSV) and spun into thread for the weaving of cloth. Hemp is closely associated with flax. *See* Occupations: Weaving; Plants: Flax.

Both the Gezer calendar (ANET, p. 320; *see* Calendar) and the story of Rahab indicate that flax was cultivated in Canaan (Josh 2:6). The people of Palestine manufactured linen, for loom weights and dyeing vats have been found in many excavated towns, and simple linen cloths were wrapped around some of the Dead Sea scrolls. Balls of flax thread and linen cloth from the Chalcolithic period and the revolt of Bar Kokhba were discovered in isolated caves near Engedi in 1960 and 1961.

Spinning was a woman's task (Ex 35:25; Prov 31:13, 19). It was at times a family occupation (I Chr 4:21). However, the finest linen came from Egypt as noted (Gen 41:42; Ezk 27:7; Prov 7:16). Egyptian documents, such as the Story of Wen-Amon (ANET, p. 28), reveal that linen was exported from Egypt to Phoenicia during many centuries. In general, linen was used for all kinds of clothing, sacking,

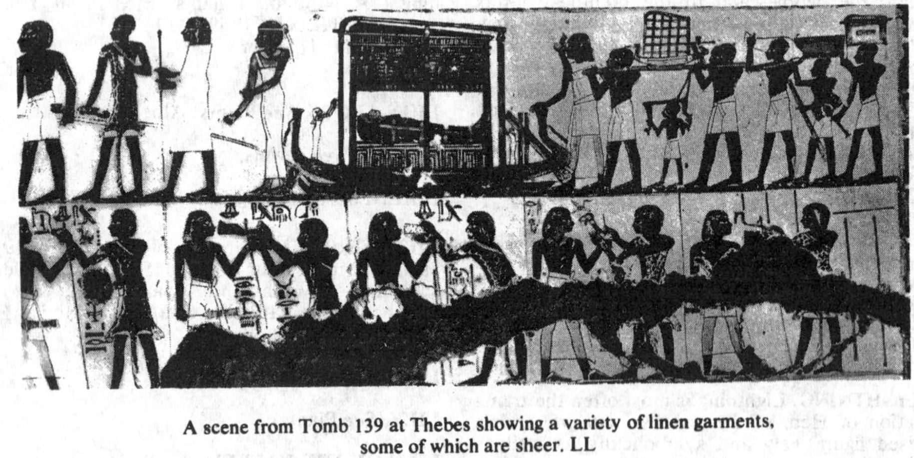

A scene from Tomb 139 at Thebes showing a variety of linen garments, some of which are sheer. LL

wrappings for the dead, sails, and curtains. Linen garments were cooler than woolens and especially desirable in hot weather.

The four common Heb. words translated "linen" in KJV are:

1. Heb. *pishteh.* This may refer to the flax as the raw material (Josh 2:6; Jud 15:14; Prov 31:13; Isa 19:9; Ezk 40:3; Hos 2:5, 9) or to the product linen (Lev 13:47; Deut 22:11, *et al*). Such linen was used for men's girdles or kilts (Jer 13:1) and for priestly dress (Ezk 44:17-18). *See* Dress.

2. Heb. *bûṣ;* Gr. *byssos, byssinos.* This is apparently a late word for fine white linen, the cloth of the finest and most precious garments worn by kings, priests and people of distinction and honor. (*a*) Royalty (David's robe, I Chr 15:27) and men in high position, as Mordecai (Est 8:15) and the rich man (Lk 16:19). Fine linen, white and pure, will clothe the Bride of the Lamb (Rev 19:8) as well as the armies in heaven (Rev 19:14), being symbolic of the righteousness and purity of the saints. (*b*) The Levitical singers (I Chr 15:27; II Chr 5:12). (*c*) In the temple such linen was used for the veil (II Chr 3:14), and for the cords to fasten the hangings in the palace garden at Susa (Est 1:6). It was a valuable article of trade both in OT (Ezk 27:16) and NT times (Rev 18:12, 16).

3. Heb. *bad.* This meant a part, a piece of cloth, usually plain linen. The linen breeches or underpants of the priests were made of this more durable type of linen (Ex 28:42; 39:28; Lev 6:10), as well as his white linen working garments worn on the Day of Atonement (Lev 16:4, 23). The ephod or kilts worn by Samuel and David were made of *bad* linen (I Sam 2:18; II Sam 6:14), as well as the clothing of the angel in Daniel's vision (Dan 10:5; 12:6-7). The official garments of the Egyptian priests were always of pure white linen.

4. Heb. *shēsh* (Egyp. *sś*). This was Egyptian linen of peculiar whiteness and fineness, as in the garb of Joseph (Gen 41:42). The Israelites gave as offerings for the tabernacle construction and priestly garments the finely woven linen (Ex 25:4; 26:1; 28:5; 35:6, 23), undoubtedly handed over to them by the frightened Egyptians on the night of the Passover (Ex 12:35-36). Egyptians wrapped mummies in linen, at times using as much as 100 yards in one bandage.

The Jews in NT days followed this custom of swathing the corpse in spices and linen wrappings (Gr. *othonion,* Lk 24:12; Jn 19:40; 20:5-7, NASB), without, however, further embalming the body. The dead was then wrapped in a linen sheet or shroud (Gr. *sindōn,* Mt 27:59; Mk 15:46; Lk 23:53).

Other words referring to flax or linen are Heb. *'etûn,* a red linen from Egypt (Prov 7:16); *sadîn,* a luxury cloth made by the virtuous housewife (Prov 31:24) and prized by Jerusalem women (Isa 3:23), and thirty lengths of linen promised by Samson (Jud 14:12-13, NEB); Gr. *othonē,* a linen sheet or cloth, as the

An inscribed lintel mentioning Augustus Caesar in the agora at Ephesus. HFV

one Peter saw in a trance (Acts 10:11; 11:5); and Gr. *linon,* the smoking wick (Mt 12:20) and the clothing of the seven angels (Rev. 15:6).

I. R.

LINTEL. The horizontal beam forming the top of a door frame. Before the Passover the wooden lintel (Heb. *mashqôp*) and doorposts were smeared with blood (Ex 12:22-23). In I Kgs 6:31 the word for "lintel" (Heb. *'ayil*) may mean the projecting framework with sideposts of the entrance to the innermost sanctuary (cf. Ezk 41:3); or it may refer to a gabled lintel with a peaked "roof," making the entire doorway pentagonal (RSV). Heb. *kaphtôr* in Amos 9:1 and Zeph 2:14 is the capital of a column, not a door lintel.

LINUS (lī'nŭs). One of several persons joining Paul in sending greetings to Timothy (II Tim 4:21). He is otherwise unknown except for the identification made by Irenaeus (*Against Heresies* III. iii. 3) and confirmed by Eusebius (*Church History* III. 2; V. 6) that he was the first bishop of Rome (cf. Blunt, s.v. "Popes, Catalogue of"). Supposedly he wrote two tracts on the martyrdoms of Peter and of Paul (detailed fully in *A Dictionary of Christian Biography,* III, 726-729). Other writings are also ascribed to him (cf. HDB, III, 126). He is commemorated on September 23 in the Roman church.

The place of Linus in the Roman controversy over the primacy of Peter is amply documented from original sources in "A Treatise of the Pope's Supremacy," in *The Works of Isaac Barrows, D.D.* (New York: John C. Riker), 1845, III, 124-129.

LION. *See* Animals, II. 25.

LIQUOR. As referred to in the Bible, liquor should not be understood in the ordinary modern sense of a distilled or spirituous beverage (brandy or whiskey). Nor should it necessarily be applied to a fermented beverage (wine or beer), but may refer to any liquid substance.

fruit juices in general (Ex 22:29), or specifically grape juice (Num 6:3). In the latter reference, unfermented grape juice seems clearly indicated. The only other occurrence of liquor in the KJV is Song 7:2, where some sort of juice that might be drunk seems to be indicated.

LITTER. The translation of a Heb. word that appears only in Isa 66:20; in a compound form it is rendered "covered wagons" in Num 7:3. Litter was a portable couch or chair often covered and curtained, which might be carried by men or animals. Litters were in common use throughout the ancient Near and Far East.

A covered chair from Ur mounted on a sled, *c.* 2500 B.C. BM

LITTLE OWL. *See* Animals, III. 36.

LIVER. The Heb. word *kābēd* basically means "heavy," and thus the liver was considered the heavy organ par excellence of the body. Piercing the liver of a man by an arrow was considered fatal (Prov 7:23). An animal's liver was an important part of the sacrificial offering (Ex 29:13, 22; Lev 3:4, 10, 15; 4:9; 7:4; 8:16, 25; 9:10, 19). *See* Caul.

The liver was considered the most important organ in the heathen custom of divination by the entrails and is referred to in connection with a heathen prince (Ezk 21:21). *See* Divination; Hepatoscopy; Magic.

The liver was also regarded as the seat of the emotions, and therefore is figurative for joy, grief, etc. (Ps 16:9, "glory," KJV, ASV; Lam 2:11).

LIVING CREATURES. The four "living creatures" (Heb. *hayyôth,* from *ḥāyâ,* "to be alive") of Ezekiel (1:5-25; 3:13; 10:15-22) are probably the four living beings (Gr. *zōa*) of Rev 4:6-9, incorrectly translated "beasts" in the KJV. In Ezk 10 they are equated with the cherubim (*q.v.*), each having four faces—of a man, an ox, a lion, and an eagle—and four wings, although one face of the cherubim was cherubic (10:14) instead of ox-like (Ezk 1:10) or calf-like (Rev 4:7). The beings of Rev 4:8 have six wings each. In figurative language they are represented as the guardians of God's throne. Together with the four wheels (Ezk 1:15-21), they symbolize the omni-directional mobility of His throne and the power and intelligence of His rule.

One interpretation sees each living creature as the emblem of three tribes of Israel, as the 12 tribes were placed in threes N, S, E, and W of the tabernacle in the wilderness. As the four emblems or standards flanked God's abode in the tabernacle in Israel, so the four corresponding "living ones" surround His throne in heaven.

The rabbinic interpretation taught that the four faces represented God's dominion over man, over wild beasts (whose king is the lion), over domesticated animals (of which the ox is the most powerful), and over the birds of the air (ruled by the eagle). God is thus depicted as Ruler of all life, as well as the Creator.

R. A. K.

LIZARD. *See* Animals, IV. 21.

LIZARD, DABB. *See* Animals, IV. 22.

LOAF. *See* Food: Bread.

LO-AMMI (lō-ăm'ī). The Heb. name of Hosea's third child by Gomer (Hos 1:9), meaning "not my people," is to be understood as a symbolic contrast to Ammi, "my people" (Hos 2:1, 23). The name designates the northern kingdom called Israel. Symbolically, therefore, Israel as "not my people" is contrasted with Judah, the chosen tribe (Hos 1:6-7; cf. Gen 49:10; Heb 7:14), and with the faithful remnant in natural Israel (Hos 1:9-10; Isa 10:21-22; Zech 13:9; Rom 9:27-29). *See* Lo-ruhamah; Ruhamah.

LOAN. In the economy set up by the law of Moses, loans were on a charitable rather than a commercial basis. They were to help those in an essentially agricultural economy who faced a time of stress, poverty, or need. The commercial loan system practiced in Babylon did not exist in Israel, nor was it encouraged by God. The Israelite was enjoined to lend to the poor (Lev 25:35-37; Deut 15:7-11). He was forbidden to charge a fellow Israelite any interest (Ex 22:25; Lev 25:36; Deut 23:19), though he could charge a foreigner (Deut 15:3; 23:20). The only profit he could expect on loaning to another Israelite was the promised blessing of the Lord in all his other undertakings (Deut 15:10; Prov 19:17). Lending to the poor was a mark of the godly man (Ps 37:26; 112:5).

Though the laws of lending were gracious, the results of failure to repay were very stringent. One might be forced to sell his children into slavery or the children might be seized for unpaid debts (II Kgs 4:1; Neh 5:5, 8), or the debtor and his wife might be forced by their debts to become slaves (cf. Ex 21:2–11; Lev 25:39–43; Deut 15:12–18), or one might voluntarily choose to become a slave to another.

The law offered liberty (*q.v.*) from debts every seventh year (Deut 15:1–3, 7–10), and from slavery after six years' service (Ex 21:2 f.; Deut 15:12; Jer 34:14). The near approach of this "year of release" was not to affect one's willingness to give a loan to the poor (Deut 15:9–11). Also, there was the year of jubilee which came once every 50 years (Lev 25). In it not only were debts to be cancelled and slaves freed, but land, whether farm or unwalled village property which had become alienated because of debts and had not been redeemed, was to be returned to its former owner (Lev 25:28). Property within a walled city, however, was redeemable for only a year and did not come under the provisions of the year of jubilee (Lev 25:30).

Pledges on loans. There was no prohibition on pledges except for the primary necessities required by the poor: (1) An outer garment taken in pledge must be returned by sunset (Ex 22:26). (2) A widow's garment (Deut 24:17) and one's millstones, or even the upper (smaller) one alone, might not be taken in pledge, for these were the debtor's very means of subsistence (Deut 24:6). (3) No creditor could enter a man's home to possess a pledge—the borrower must bring it out to him (Deut 24:10–11). (4) Though bondage was not excluded, it was limited to six years (Ex 21:2; Lev 25:39–42; Deut 15:9).

By the time of Solomon's widespread commercial enterprises, many Jews must have been making loans after the pattern of the Phoenician merchants. Thus in Proverbs severe warnings are stated about the danger of posting surety for another man's debt (Prov 6:1–5; 11:15; 17:18; 20:16; 22:26). Gross injustices must have been practiced against debtors toward the close of the Judean monarchy because God classed taking interest along with the sins of idolatry, murder, and robbery (Ezk 18:13; cf. vv. 8, 17; Jer 15:10).

New Testament economy. While Christ exhorted liberality in giving to the needy and lending without seeking usury (Lk 6:32 ff.), yet in the commercial economy which had arisen by that time He recognized a fair rate of interest, and in His parables of the talents and of the pounds He encouraged sound investment (Mt 25:27; Lk 19:23). *See* Borrow; Debt; Land and Property; Mortgage; Surety; Usury.

Bibliography. H. Gamoran, "The Biblical Law Against Loans on Interest," JNES, XXX (1971), 127–134.

R. A. K.

LOCK

1. A "twist" or tuft of hair, from Heb. *ṣîṣit,* "lock" (Ezk 8:3), denoting a loose style of hair arrangement; *maḥlāphôt,* "braided locks" (Jud 16:13, 19), a style of hair arrangement still practiced by some Arab peoples; *pera',* "locks," "part of hair," "tresses" (Num 6:5; Ezk 44:20); *ṣammāh,* "lock of hair," or a woman's veil (Song 4:1; etc.); *q^{e}wuṣôt,* "locks of hair" (Song 5:2, 11).

2. The Heb. *man'ûl,* "lock," refers to the device on a door, which when released permitted withdrawal of the bar(s). Neh 3:3, 6, 13–15 and Song 5:5 (actually, "bolt") indicate that in some cases a hand-hole existed, providing for the passage of hand and key to operate from outside, the lock on the inside. A common example of a lock had an upright piece with a number of small pins which dropped into a bar that passed through cleats. The proper key displaced the pins (modern "tumblers") and allowed the bar to be withdrawn. The possible variations in the number and in the length of individual pins in the key permitted all the variations needed for locking house doors in any ancient city of Israel. Called in England the Egyptian lock, it is still in use in Syria. *See* Key; Bolt.

H. G. S.

LOCUST. *See* Animals, III. 29.

LOD (lŏd). Named Lydda (*q.v.*) in the NT, Lod is located on the E edge of the Philistine plain along the Via Maris between Gath and Aphek, 11 miles SE of Joppa. It apparently was ruled by a rebellious vassal king in the late 19th or early 18th cen. B.C., as it occurs in the Execration texts used in an Egyptian ritual cursing of rebellious satellite city-states in Canaan. It was subdued by Thutmose III in the 15th cen.

Lod obviously had a strategic location as it overlooked the plain of Ono (Valley of the Craftsmen, cf. Neh 11:35) where the Via Maris intersected the Way-of-Beth Horon, the main road leading up into the hill country. I Chr 8:12 indicates the city was built and inhabited by people of Benjamin in the periods of the judges and the monarchy. The city was reinhabited by Benjamites during the restoration (Neh 7:37; Ezr 2:33), but it later fell to the Samaritans; then included in the area suggested by Sanballat to be a no-man's-land. It was not considered Jewish real estate in Judea until 145 B.C. (cf. I Macc 10:30; 11:34; Jos *Ant.* xiii.4.9).

P. W. F.

LO-DEBAR (lō-dĕ-bär'). A place in Gilead where Machir (II Sam 9:4–5; 17:27) lived and where Mephibosheth stayed after Jonathan's death, also called Debir (*see* Debir 3). Amos sarcastically makes a pun against those who "rejoice in Lo-debar" (Amos 6:13, RSV, NASB), for the name literally means "a thing of nought" (KJV). While the site is not certain, it has been identified with *Umm ed-Dabar, c.* eight miles S of the Sea of Galilee.

LODGE. The verbal forms (Heb. *lûn, lîn;* Gr.

A watchman's stone hut in a field near Samaria. HFV

katuluō) usually signify "taking up lodging to pass the night," in contrast to *shākan* meaning "to settle down, abide or dwell" (Gr. *katas-kēnoō*, used of birds nesting in the branches; Mt 13:32); e.g., Lot's invitation for the angels to lodge all night in Sodom (Gen 19:1-2), Jacob at Bethel (Gen 28:11), the two spies at Jericho (Josh 2:1), and the disciples' recommendation concerning the multitude (Lk 9:12). It denotes also the lodging of animals, as the wild ox in its crib (Job 39:9); or inanimate objects, as food remaining from the Passover meal (Ex 34:25), the dew (Job 29:19), or a dead body (Deut 21:23). Figuratively it expresses righteousness residing in Jerusalem (Isa 1:21); the seat of strength (Job 41:22); or a temporary emotional occurrence (Ps 30:5).

The nouns (Heb. *malôn m^{e}lûnâh;* Gr. *katáluma*) denote a lodging place for the night, as Israel's camp (Josh 4:3) or Assyria's (Isa 10:29); a watchman's hut or shelter (Isa 1:8); an inn (Gen 42:27; Jer 9:2) or a guest chamber (Lk 22:11; cf. 2:7). In modern Heb. *mālôn* signifies a hotel.

The Gr. verb *xenizō* (KJV "lodge," Acts 10:6, etc.; 21:16; 28:7) more accurately means to receive and entertain as a guest. Paul asked Philemon to prepare him a guest room (Gr. *xenia*, Phm 22, RSV), and he invited the Jews of Rome, who came in large numbers as his guests (Acts 28:23, NEB).

H. E. Fr.

LOFT. In I Kgs 17:19, translated "upper chamber" in RSV, or "upper room" in NASB. Loft refers to a small room built on the flat roof of a Palestinian house. It was a permanent room as compared with tents (II Sam 16:22) or booths (Neh 8:16) that might be temporarily constructed on a rooftop. The loft of Acts 20:9 refers to an upper story of a building.

LOG. *See* Weights, Measures, and Coins.

LOGOS (lŏg'ŏs)

Historical Background

In order to understand the controversy surrounding the Logos doctrine, it is necessary to note briefly the early history of the concept. Probably the germ of the concept comes from the teachings and writings of the Gr. philosopher Heraclitus (*c.* 490 B.C.), who pictured the universe as fashioned by a fiery element, the all-penetrating reason, of which the souls of men are a part. Anaxagoras of Athens (*c.* 500–428 B.C.) went a step further in teaching that a shaping mind (Gr. *nous*) acted in the ordering of matter and yet was independent of it. Plato (430–348 B.C.) used the word *logos* to describe the Divine Force from which the world arose. Aristotle (384–322 B.C.) posited that in man there exists a divine spark, or Logos, which he shares with God.

Probably the Stoics were responsible for the first systematic statement of a Logos concept. Stoicism (in vogue *c.* 300 B.C. on) modified Heraclitus' fire idea and called the Logos the intelligent, self-conscious world-soul, an all-indwelling reason of which our reason is a part. It was a sort of all-pervading, all-ruling divine wisdom. They said man had a god within which one can follow. If man had divinity inside him, then, said the Stoics, "We too are thy offspring."

Straddling the bridge of time from B.C. to A.D. was the Jewish philosopher Philo of Alexandria, who taught that between God and the world were a group of divine powers, the highest being the Logos. He flowed out of the being of God and is the agent through whom God created the world and from whom all other powers flow. Through the Logos the ideal man was created, "of whom actual man is a poor copy, the work of lower spiritual powers as well as of the Logos. Even from his fallen state man may rise to connection with God through the Logos, the agent of divine revelation" (Williston Walker, *A H story of the Christian Church*, New York: Scribner's, 1947, p. 17).

New Testament Concept

Many scholars have argued that the apostle John had this philosophical development in the back of his mind when he wrote the prologue to his Gospel and that he actually tried to impart some of these concepts. For a long time many have contended that the background of the fourth Gospel was essentially Hellenistic rather than Hebraic. In dealing with such an assertion we may note that studies in the Dead Sea scrolls have tended to confirm the traditional conservative position that the cultural orientation of the Gospel of John was Hebraic. Moreover, we must observe that John was a simple fisherman from Palestine. While he did come to live in the sophisticated city of Ephesus, probably after the fall of Jerusalem in A.D. 70, there is no evidence that he imbibed any of that city's Gr. philosophical orientation. If he intended to be philosophical in the first few verses, he certainly was not anywhere else. We may argue that John used the word "logos," which was common in the language of the day, in its ordinary meaning and poured into it a spiritual significance.

Logos simply means "word" or "expression." Jesus is then the expression or revealer or unveiler of God the Father. Words are the vehicles for the revelation of the thoughts and intents of the mind to others. In the Person of the Logos incarnate God has made Himself fully known to us. Christ as the Word constitutes the complete and ultimate divine revelation. "In the beginning was the Word" (Jn 1:1) implies eternity; "the Word was God" (1:1) declares deity—He is identical in essence with God. "And the Word became flesh" (1:14); the Logos became incarnate to reveal God to men (in v. 18 "declare" lit. is "show Him forth") and to accomplish their salvation. Moreover, in further emphasis on Christ's deity the passage declares that the Logos was creator of the visible universe ("All things were made by him," v.3) and He is the source of the intellectual, moral and spiritual life of man ("In him was life; and the life was the light of men," v. 4).

The first verses of John's Gospel provide a simple, straightforward and unphilosophical but profound description of Jesus as the complete and ultimate revelation of God to men. Only in and through this divine-human Logos could God fully "express" Himself. *See* Word.

Bibliography. J. N. Birdsall, "Logos," NBD, pp. 744 f. A. Debrunner, *et al., "Legō, Logos,* etc.," TDNT, IV, 69–143. C. H. Dodd, *The Interpretation of the Fourth Gospel,* Cambridge: University Press, 1953, pp. 263–285. Merrill C. Tenney, "The Meaning of the Word," *The Bible: The Living Word of Revelation,* Grand Rapids: Zondervan, 1968, pp. 11–27. Andrew F. Walls, "Logos," BDT, pp. 327f. See also commentaries on John, Gospel of.

H. F. V.

LOINS. The rendering of several Heb. words, the most important of which are *ḥălāṣiyim* and *mothnayim* (the two sides of the back), both dual forms, and of the Gr. *osphus,* "loin," or lower part of the back.

The loins are the part of the back and side between the hip and ribs, forming as it were the pivot of the body. The word is used in the physical sense primarily as the place for the girdle (Ex 12:11; II Kgs 1:8; Ezk 23:15; Mt 3:4). The loins are also the region of the reproductive organs: "And kings shall come out of thy loins" (Gen 35:11; cf. I Kgs 8:19; Heb. 7:5, 10).

Figuratively, the loins were considered the seat of strength (Deut 33:11; Job 40:16; Prov 31:17; Nah 2:1), and were said to be affected by pain or terror (Deut 33:11; Ps 38:7; 69:23; Dan 5:6). The loins were girt with sackcloth in token of mourning (Gen 37:34; I Kgs 20:31–32; Amos 8:10).

The expression "Gird up the loins" (I Kgs 18:46; II Kgs 4:29; 9:1; I Pet 1:13) came from the need to gather the long and flowing dress of Orientals closely at the waist before engaging in any exertion or enterprise.

E. C. J.

LOIS (lō'ĭs). Grandmother of Timothy, and undoubtedly the mother of Eunice, Timothy's mother. She is mentioned but once (II Tim 1:5). Apparently the family lived at Lystra, where Paul was stoned. Lois had a genuine faith in God, in which she was joined by Eunice and Timothy, although Eunice's husband was a Greek, and evidently an unbeliever (Acts 16:1). It seems probable she was a godly Jewess before Paul's first visit to Derbe and Lystra, and that she, her daughter, and her grandson all became converts to Christianity through Paul's ministry. Perhaps the circumstances surrounding the stoning of Paul and his recovery contributed to their conversion. *See* Timothy.

LONGSUFFERING. The Heb. expression *'erek 'aph* means lit. "long of nose" or "long of breathing," since anger is accompanied by rapid, violent breathing through the nostrils; hence the possible translations "long of anger," "slow to wrath" and "longsuffering." It is applied to God (Ex 34:6; Num 14:18; Ps 86:15; cf. Neh 9:17; Joel 2:13; Jon 4:2; Nah 1:3 where KJV translates it "slow to anger").

The Gr. *makrothymia* (lit., long of spirit or rage) is applied to God in regard to His patience with sinners and slowness in bringing judgment upon them (Rom 2:4; 9:22; I Pet 3:20; II Pet 3:9; cf. I Tim 1:16; II Pet 3:15). Since it is a quality of God, it is also a fruit of the presence, guidance and enabling of the Holy Spirit in the believer (Gal 5:22) aiding him to endure trials (Col 1:11; II Tim 3:10; 4:2) and to be patient (Eph 4:2; Jas 5:7). *See* Forbearance; Patience, translations of this Gr. word found in many modern versions.

Bibliography. J. Horst, *"Makrothymia,"* TDNT, IV, 374–387.

R. A. K.

LOOKING GLASS. *See* Mirror.

LOOPS. Probably of goat's hair cord dyed blue, loops were to be fastened to the linen curtains of the tabernacle to make it possible for the tent to be one piece of cloth. Ten curtains or pieces of cloth, each 28 by four cubits (a cubit = *c.*18 inches), were to be fastened together, forming a surface 28 by 40 cubits. This joining was made possible by sewing 50 loops on each of the long sides of a curtain. The loops were then coupled together by clasps to make one piece of cloth. See Ex 26 and 36.

LORD. This is the translation of several Heb., Aram. and Gr. words. In the list below, sample Scripture references are not usually given because the words are of such frequent occurrence. The primary words are:

1. *YHWH.* This is to be vocalized and pronounced Yahweh (contracted or abbreviated as Yah). It is usually represented in the KJV, ERV, RSV, NEB and NASB by LORD (sometimes by GOD) and in the ASV by Jehovah (see below). It means "He is," i.e., "He is the eternally self-existent One," the absolute, unchanging One. The name connotes the underived and independent existence of God. As an extension of this idea, in usage it conveys the additional thought that God is present to save, help, deliver, redeem, bless and keep covenant. It is used in the OT as a proper name of God. All other words are generic terms (e.g., *Elohim*) or appellative titles (e.g., *Adonai*). It would have been preferable for the translators to have retained it as a proper name. God Himself calls it His name in Ex 6:3. But it is not sufficient to stop with the statement that Yahweh is His name, for the word "name" itself possesses far-reaching implications in Semitic usage. Thus, when God speaks of His name as Yahweh, He means that Yahweh is His nature, essence, being, or character.

In the Heb. Bible the Jews wrote the consonants of the tetragrammaton *YHWH,* but out of reverence for this sacred name of God, vocalized and pronounced it as Adonai (which meant "lord"; see below). It is unfortunate, then, that the name was transliterated into German and English as Jehovah (which is the way the name is represented in the ASV), for this conflate form represents the vowels of Adonai superimposed upon the consonants of Yahweh and it was never intended by the Jews to be read as Yehowah (or Jehovah). By the same token, to use LORD to represent *YHWH* is also not quite accurate since LORD represents the word the Jews pronounced instead of Yahweh.

The meaning assigned to Yahweh above reflects an understanding of the name as an earlier form of the Qal imperfect of the Heb. verb *hāyāh,* sometimes written *hāwāh* (the actual original root was *hwy*). However, the form has also been analyzed (e.g., by W. F. Albright, *From the Stone Age to Christianity,* Garden City: Doubleday Anchor Books, 1957, pp. 15–16, 259–261) as the Hiphil imperfect of the same verb, meaning "He (who) causes to be," i.e., "He (who) creates, brings into existence." Ex 3:14 ("I am who I am") may be of some assistance in deciding between these two views. It is my opinion that this verse is a divine commentary on or exposition of the meaning of Yahweh (v. 15). If this is true, then obviously it favors the former view.

As to the common expression "the Lord (Yahweh) of hosts," the hosts have been variously defined as the army (or people) of Israel, angels and stars. This problem of interpretation has never been solved to the satisfaction of even a majority of scholars. It should simply be noted in passing that these views are not necessarily mutually exclusive.

A problem has been imagined in Ex 6:3 because of the words, "By My name, Yahweh, was I not known to them' ' (i.e., the patriarchs). Yet there are several references to Yahweh in the patriarchal narratives. Derek Kidner points the way to one solution: "In Ex 3:14 the divine exposition, 'I am . . .' introduces and illuminates the name given in 3:15, and this remains the context for 6:3 as well . . . . The name, in short, was first *known,* in any full sense of the word, at its first expounding" (*Genesis,* London: Tyndale Press, 1967, p. 19; cf. also Edmond Jacob, *Theology of the Old Testament,* New York: Harper, 1958, pp. 48–54).

Another approach is to let the emphasis fall on the personal, intimate, experiential sense in which "know" is usually employed. In effect, God would be saying, "By My name Yahweh I was not intimately and experientially known to the patriarchs. Their experience of Me was largely as El Shaddai. But now, beginning with the exodus and deliverance from Egypt, I am about to fully and personally reveal Myself in the experience of My people Israel in that aspect of My character signified by Yahweh, i.e., as the God who is ever present with His people to help and redeem them and to keep covenant with them" (cf. Ex 6:4–8).

For a valuable and generally valid treatise on the use of the divine names Yahweh and Elohim, cf. U. Cassuto, *The Documentary Hypothesis,* trans. by I. Abrahams, Jerusalem: Magnes Press, 1961, pp. 15–41.

2. *'Ādôn,* "lord," "sovereign," as one having power or strength. There is also the form *'Adōnai,* regarded by many as the plural of *'ādôn* with the suffix "my"; hence, "my lord." The plural is the honorific plural or intensive plural of rank. This is the word the Jews read in place of Yahweh. For this reason, some take Adonai and its variants simply as variations of the Masoretic pointing to distinguish the divine reference from the human.

3. *Ba'al,* "lord," as owner, master or husband. This Heb. word is used of God, human beings, and the Canaanite god Baal.

4. *Mārē',* "lord, master." This is an Aram. word occurring in the Aram. section of Daniel. Cf. "Maran-atha" (I Cor 16:22), Aram. for "Our Lord, come!"

5. *Kurios,* properly a Gr. adjective meaning "having power or authority"; used as a noun, it means "lord, master, owner." This is the standard word for "lord" in the LXX and the NT. It was the exact equivalent of Adonai, and also was used in the LXX to translate Yahweh because the rabbis read Adonai in place of the divine name. It is applied to Jesus by the NT writers as a divine title.

All the above words except the first are applied to human beings as well as to God.

See God; God, Names and Titles of.

Bibliography. J. A. Motyer, *The Revelation of the Divine Name,* London: Tyndale Press, 1959. G. Quell and W. Foerster, *"Kurios,"* TDNT, III, 1039–1098. William C. Robinson, "Lord," BDT, pp. 328 ff. W. E. Vine, *An Ex-*

pository Dictionary of New Testament Words, Westwood, N.J.: Revell, 1952, III, 16 ff.

K. L. B.

LORD OF HOSTS. *See* God, Names and Titles of, 6, *i.*

LORD'S DAY. The term is found only in Rev 1:10, though the adjective (*kuriakos*) is used in connection with the Lord's Supper in I Cor 11:20. Most commentators explain the expression as meaning "the day consecrated to the Lord," not the future eschatological day of the Lord. The fact that Paul uses "the first day of the week" in I Cor 16:2 seems to show that "the Lord's day" was not a widely used expression in the Apostolic Age. In post-apostolic literature it is used in Ignatius *To the Magnesians* ix. 1; Gospel of Peter vv. 35, 50; Epistle of Barnabas 15:9.

The origin of the term "the Lord's day" is traceable to its association with the day of Christ's resurrection. It was also marked off by Christ's appearance to the disciples on Sunday (Jn 20:26) and the sending of the Spirit on the first day of the week (Acts 2:1). Although daily gatherings of Christians were held in Jerusalem at first (Acts 2:46), gradually Sunday became the day of worship (Acts 20:7; I Cor 16:2). Thus the phrase was probably the defiant Christian replacement of "the Emperor's day," by which the first day of the month was known in Egypt and Asia Minor, in honor of the Roman emperor. Though the NT nowhere presents the Lord's day as a fulfillment of the Jewish sabbath, many in the Christian church regard its observation as the present fulfilling of the fourth commandment. *See* Sabbath.

The account in Acts 20:7 shows that the observance of the Lord's Supper was evidently a distinctive feature of worship on the Lord's day. The collection was also a part of the activities of that day (I Cor 16:2). Justin (A.D. 150) describes its activities as including reading the letters of the apostles and prophets, exhortation, prayer, the Lord's Supper, the collection (Apology i. 67). Earlier the *agapē* (love feast, *q.v.*) had been a part of the services (I Cor 11:33–34) but was evidently discontinued by Justin's time.

Bibliography. Paul K. Jewett, *The Lord's Day,* Grand Rapids: Eerdmans, 1971. C. C. Richardson, "Lord's Day," IDB, III, 151–154. Willy Rordorf, *Sunday: The History of the Day of Rest and Worship in the Earliest Centuries of the Christian Church,* trans. by A. A. K. Graham, Philadelphia: Westminster, 1968.

C. C. R.

LORD'S PRAYER. This occurs in a longer (Mt 6:9–13) and a shorter (Lk 11:2–4) form in the NT, each evangelist having recorded that form which was currently used in worship in the church center from which he wrote. The essential elements of the prayer occur in both forms. The differences between the two may be explained in terms of liturgical tradition (e.g., the longer Matthean address is paralleled in many Jewish prayers; the shorter Lucan form is more typical of Hellenistic piety) and alternate translation of an originally Semitic prayer (e.g., the conception of sin as debt reflects a variant translation of the Aramaic *hôbā'*).

The context in which the prayer is introduced is also dissimilar. Matthew introduces the prayer as a pattern for true praying in a context dealing with the three pillars of Jewish piety, almsgiving (Mt 6:2–4), prayer (6:5–15), and fasting (6:16–18). Luke appears to have preserved the original occasion for the prayer, recording a disciple's request to be taught how to pray as John the Baptist had taught his disciples (Lk 11:1). It is possible that Jesus Himself gave different versions of the prayer as He taught it on separate occasions.

Both Matthew and Luke see the Lord's prayer as a pattern for all prayer, as well as a specific devotional piece for individual or corporate use. In focusing prior attention upon God and His kingdom, and then upon human concerns, it furnishes a summary of the matter of prayer.

The prayer is best interpreted in an eschatological sense, for throughout there is a tension between the future fulfillment and present experiences which anticipate that fulfillment. In the initial petitions of the prayer there is requested a sovereign affirmation of God's dignity, which can have its fullest response only at the consummation. Prior to the consummation the prayer is a missionary request for the extension of God's sovereignty over the lives of men. This tension should not be resolved but consciously sustained. In the later petitions there is also an eschatological note sounded. Notice the request for "the bread of the coming day" which will be most fully answered in the kingdom of God, as well as the prayer to be delivered from the final, overwhelming test that heralds the Lord's return, and from the power of the evil one.

While the doxology which is found in many later MSS of Matthew (6:13) is an addition patterned after I Chr 29:11, and occurs in more than one form (cf. Didache 8:2), it furnishes an appropriate response to the petitions of the prayer. God will establish His sovereignty and preserve intact His people, for to Him alone belongs the Kingdom, the power, and the glory.

It is possible that when Paul describes all prayer as a saying "Abba, Father" (Rom 8:15; Gal 4:6) and that when Peter speaks of invoking God as Father (I Pet 1:17), it is the Lord's prayer to which reference is made.

See Prayer.

Bibliography. J. Jeremias, *The Lord's Prayer,* Philadelphia: Fortress Press, 1964. J. Lowe, *The Interpretation of the Lord's Prayer,* Evanston: Seabury-Western, 1955.

W. L. L.

LORD'S SUPPER. The term most commonly used by the Reformation churches for the taking of bread and wine in accordance with Christ's institution. Other meaningful names are the holy communion and the Eucharist.

The Lord's Supper, along with baptism, is one of the two ordinances or sacraments enjoined by the Lord Himself. It is thus observed by all Christian bodies apart from a few groups such as the Quakers. Even in Roman Catholic theology with its seven sacraments, priority is accorded to baptism and the Lord's Supper.

Meaning. The origin of the Lord's Supper is recounted in the Synoptic Gospels (Mt 26:26-29; Mk 14:22-25; Lk 22:14-20) and in I Cor 11:23-26. Particular attention should be paid to the paschal and convenantal setting. The apostle Paul clearly states that Christ our Passover (Gr. *pascha*) has been sacrified (I Cor 5:7). John the Baptist had earlier identified Jesus as the true Lamb of God (Jn 1:29), anticipating that His broken body and shed blood would be offered for the redemption of His people. In the upper room Christ introduced the new symbols of bread and wine in remembrance of His sacrificial death, which is to be commemorated in the fellowship of believers.

The paschal work of Christ, furthermore, is in fulfillment of the divine covenant of redemption. *See* Covenant. The eating and drinking together has the significance of a covenant meal in which the two parties had fellowship and pledged their loyalty to each other (cf. Gen 26:28-30; 31:44, 46, 54; Ex 24:1-11). The new covenant between the Lord and His people (Jer 31:31-34) was thus ratified by our Saviour in the communal meal before His death.

In instituting the communion supper Jesus emphasized the messianic and eschatological aspects of the Passover meal. At this feast pious Jews looked forward to another deliverance like that from Egypt (cf. Isa 51:9-16). Now it is the Messiah who has come in person to this paschal feast, taking the cup of judgment and salvation which means deliverance for God's people. Yet the meal also anticipates the final messianic banquet (Isa 25:6; cf. Lk 14:15-24) when the divine work of salvation is consummated and there is a fulfillment of fellowship with the Lord (Mt 26:29).

Although John gives no account of the Last Supper, there is little doubt that the miracle of feeding the multitude at the Passover season and the ensuing discourse (Jn 6) provide understanding of the sacramental significance of the Last Supper. Christ is here the true bread prefigured by the manna of Moses' time (Jn 6:31-35, 48-51). Jesus gave His life for us, so that eternal life is by participation in Him (vv. 40, 47, 51-58). This is possible, however, only in the Spirit and by saving faith in response to His word (v. 63). Applied to His broken body and shed blood, this gives us a clue to the proper use and understanding of the supper.

The Lord's Supper is the re-enactment in sign of the reality of Christ's self-offering. The sacrifice itself is not repeated. Rather, it is remembered, and it gives assurance that God Himself has remembered His people in fulfillment of the covenantal promise. No fresh atonement is made, e.g., for the temporal guilt of post-baptismal sin or for offenses against the church, as Romanism claims. The one sacrifice of Christ needs neither repetition nor supplementation; and the notion that the eucharistic sacrifice derives repeated efficacy from the re-enactment of the one offering is unfounded theologizing. The sign brings this one sacrifice vividly before us in an action. It overcomes the barrier of time and furnishes an active sign of our participation in Christ's death.

Like baptism, the supper is thus an enacted preaching of the gospel, a visible word (Augustine). Yet it does not work magically. Its force is derived in the Spirit from its meaning. It is thus to be accompanied by the declaration of its meaning in the Word read and preached. Its specific function is to stress the historicity of what took place and its present relevance. Hence there is action on both sides. The divine action is recalled and presented, the demand of the gospel for human, living participation fulfilled. Without the Word the action would degenerate into magic, as in the Middle Ages when the Word remained only in a mere formula approximating to a conjuration. On the other hand, without the action the Word might well involve intellectualist abstraction in which the gospel is only a system, faith only an intellectual assent and perhaps a compensating emotional experience, and the sacrament only a superflous ordinance to be fulfilled simply because it is commanded.

In the Lord's Supper the stress falls on the continuing significance of what was done once, i.e., on abiding fellowship and nurture. Note Paul's question: "The cup of blessing which we bless, is it not a participation in the blood of Christ? The bread which we break, is it not a participation in the body of Christ?" (I Cor 10:16, RSV). The great importance attached to taking and receiving makes nonsense of the non-communicating mass and the arbitrary Roman Catholic denial of the cup to the laity. It is also a reproach, however, against too infrequent communion in many Protestant churches, in contrast to the regular administration in the early church.

The participation involved is a participation by faith (Jn 6:35). Thus the physical eating is no guarantee of genuine spiritual nourishment by Christ or fellowship with Him. The sacraments cannot be made instruments to control the divine operation. If they are means of grace, the grace itself is God's free and sovereign favor to separate individuals in Jesus Christ. Therefore to take the bread and wine is not necessarily to receive Christ and His benefits. Nor are we to say on the basis of I Cor 11:29 ("he that eateth and drinketh unworthily eateth and drinketh damnation to himself") that an unbeliever still receives Christ, but to perdition. This is unthinkable: "unworthily" is not in the best Gr. MSS, and "damnation" simply means "judgment"; see RSV, NASB.

On the other hand, with genuine faith there may be genuine expectation of genuine nourishment of the new life in the power of the Spirit. The sacrament is no mere observance with only psychological effects. But by its evangelical proclamation it can be used by the Spirit to strengthen faith, to evoke love, to promote sanctification, to confirm fellowship with the Lord and with Christian brethren.

Participation implied communion. It thus raises the question of Christ's presence. Obviously Christ was present in His incarnate body at the original supper. He was also present in His risen body at the post-resurrection meals. On the other hand, He has not been present since His ascension in this form, for He is now at the right hand of the Father until the day of His coming again. Does this mean that He is absent? Does it mean that we have fellowship only in a mental or abstract or derivative sense? This question has been a source of confusion in many circles and thus claims some attention.

It is hardly conceivable that Christ should be entirely absent when He says plainly, "This is my body," and when it is on Him that we feast and with Him that we have fellowship. Yet it is obviously quite unbiblical to see a presence similar to that of His incarnate life or of the 40 days. Three alternatives remain.

First, we can try to split Christ, e.g., into substance and accidents, as in transubstantiation (the Roman Catholic view that the wine and wafer actually become the blood and body of Christ), or into deity and humanity, or perhaps into spirit and body, arguing for the presence of the former aspect but not the latter. In the form of transubstantiation especially, this procedure is speculative, obscure, unbiblical and dangerous in connotation.

Second, we can try to conceive the presence only in a mystical, subjective, or figurative way. This is equally devoid of secure biblical foundation and threatens to dissolve the reality of God and His present action.

Third, we can accept what seems to be the plain teaching of Scripture, that Christ is now present with His people by the Holy Spirit, the third Person of the Trinity. Hence Christ is indeed the Host at His table. He gives Himself to be the abiding sustenance of His people. We have fellowship with Him, and with one another in Him. But we are neither ensnared in a false literalism nor in an equally false subjectivism. The reality and mystery of His presence are the reality and mystery of the Spirit.

In fulfillment of its covenantal signification, the Lord's Supper has a further aspect. Our participation in the Lord and His work implies response of thanksgiving and self-dedication, a biblical sacrifice of praise. It expresses both the glorifying of God for what He has done and commitment to what He calls us to do. It is a feast of joyous love in which the love of Christ for us evokes, confirms, and demands our love for Him and for one another. The proclamation of the gospel carries with it the evangelical obligation of service to God and of service to the brethren who are common suppliants and recipients at His bounteous table. The foretaste of the heavenly feast, in which we are as it were lifted up in the Spirit to the presence of God, stimulates the upward look of hope. We are not to set our affections on the things of the world, but to believe and love and work as those who await the final marriage feast of the Lamb when the supper will be needed no more.

When the richness of its meaning is thus brought out in the Word, and when the relevance of the Word is brought home by the act of personal response, the Lord's Supper may be indeed a true means of grace. Through the sacred meal Christ's saving work is once more presented, we experience the enjoyment of His abiding and sustaining fellowship in the Spirit, and we are confirmed in our Christian life and our commitment to Christian service in faith and love and hope.

G. W. B.

Date. Christian scholarship generally accepts the traditional view that the day of the crucifixion was Friday because the day following was the sabbath (Mk 15:42; Lk 23:54; Jn 19:31), and because the women visited the tomb the next day after the sabbath, the first day of the week or Sunday (Mt 28:1; Mk 16:2; Lk 24:1; Jn 20:1).

Assuming that Friday was the actual day of Christ's death, the problem is in trying to determine whether or not the Last Supper was a Passover meal. The Synoptic Gospels state that the meal which Jesus and His disciples ate on Thursday evening was the Passover (Mt 26:17–20; Mk 14:12–17; Lk 22:7–16). However, the picture in John is that the Passover meal of the Jews occurred on Friday evening, after the death and burial of Christ.

There are basically two arguments for this: (1) John 19:14 states that the day of Jesus' trial and execution was "the day of preparation for the Passover" (NASB), implying that the Passover was the next day. The term "preparation" both in the Synoptics (Mt 27:62; Mk 15:42; Lk 23:54) and in John (19:31, 42) always has reference to the day before the sabbath, i.e., to Friday. So in the present passage the "preparation for the Passover" may simply be interpreted as "Friday of the passion week." (2) John 18:28 states that the Jewish accusers of Jesus "did not enter the praetorium, so that they might not be defiled, but might eat the Passover" (RSV). In conclusion, then, the Synoptics present the picture that the Last Supper was the Passover meal, whereas John gives the idea that the Passover was not celebrated by the Jews until after Jesus' death and burial.

An alternative in which Jesus and His disciples ate the Passover meal earlier than most of the Jews is worth consideration and may well be the answer to the problem. There are several approaches within this basic solution. Some feel that Jesus arranged for an early Passover meal because He foresaw that His death would occur at the time of the official Passover sacrifice. Others think that Jesus and His disciples followed the Qumran calendar and ate their Passover on Tuesday evening (FLAP, p. 297) while mainstream Judaism had it on Friday. Regarding these two views, however, it is difficult to understand why the priests at the temple would have slain a lamb especially for Jesus' disciples before the official time.

Finally, others think that the Galileans and/or the Pharisees ate the Passover on Thursday night (Nisan 14) and the Judeans and/or the Sadducees ate the Passover on Friday night. Hence, Jesus and His disciples were among those who ate the Passover on Thursday. Since a great number of people would be eating the Passover on Thursday evening, the priests would accommodate them (as in other years) with an earlier Passover sacrifice. Mark (14:12) literally says, "when they were sacrificing [Gr. *ethuon,* imperfect tense] the Passover," that Jesus' disciples asked Him where to prepare to eat the Passover.

H. W. H.

See Covenant; Festivals: Passover; Ordinances, Christian; Sacrament.

Bibliography. William Barclay, *The Lord's Supper,* Naperville: SCM Book Club, 1967, pp. 16-34. Johannes Behm, "*Klaō,* etc.," TDNT, III, 726-743. Matthew Black, "The Arrest and Trial of Jesus and the Date of the Last Supper," *New Testament Essays: Studies in Memory of Thomas Walter Manson,* ed. by A. J. B. Higgins, Manchester: Manchester Univ. Press, 1959, pp. 19-33. Geoffrey W. Bromiley, *Sacramental Teaching and Practice in the Reformation Churches,* Grand Rapids: Eerdmans, 1957. A. J. B. Higgins, *The Lord's Supper in the New Testament,* Chicago: Regnery, 1952, pp. 13-23. Joachim Jeremias, "*Pascha,*" TDNT, V, 896-904; *The Eucharistic Words of Jesus,* trans. by Norman Perrin, Oxford: Blackwell, 1955. George Ogg, "The Chronology of the Last Supper," *Historicity and Chronology in the New Testament,* London: SPCK, 1965, pp. 75-96; *The Chronology of the Public Ministry o*

205-242. Massey H. Shepherd, Jr., "Are Both the Synoptics and John Correct About the Date of Jesus' Death?" JBL, LXXX (1961), 123-132. David Smith, *The Days of His Flesh,* London: Hodder, 1910, Appen. VIII, pp. 534-540. Ethelbert Stauffer, *Jesus and His Story,* trans. by Richard and Clara Winston, New York: Knopf, 1960, pp. 93-98.

The Destruction of Sodom (Corot). MM

LO-RUHAMAH (lō'rōō-hā-mȧ). A daughter, born to Gomer, Hosea's wife (Hos 1:6) whose Heb. name means "not pitied." As in the case of Hosea's other children, Jezreel and Lo-ammi, the name Lo-ruhamah symbolizes the spiritual condition of Israel (the northern kingdom) in the time of Hosea. This kingdom had reached such a stage of apostasy, exemplified in the lives of all the kings following Jeroboam, that God's mercy now had reached its end. However, as illustrated in the case of Lo-ammi (*q.v.*), the faithful remnant in the nation becomes Ruhamah, "pitied" (Hos 2:1, 23). *See* Ruhamah.

LOT (lŏt). Abraham's nephew, who moved with the family from Ur of the Chaldees, and then continued with Abraham from Haran in Mesopotamia into Canaan (Gen 11:31; 12:4-5). Later he went to Egypt with Abraham (13:1), and returned with him.

When the flocks of Lot and Abraham increased, their herdsmen disputed over living space. Abraham generously let Lot choose first what land he should occupy, and Lot took the well-watered Jordan valley toward the Dead Sea near Sodom. But it is noted that the people of Sodom were exceedingly sinful (Gen 13:5-13). The NT declares that Lot was vexed by the open wickedness around him in Sodom (II Pet 2:7 f.).

A group of kings from Mesopotamia defeated the kings of Sodom and Gomorrah and their allies in a fight, and carried off Lot, his household and his goods (Gen 14:12). The faithful Abraham routed the enemy with a force of men in a night battle which took them as far as Damascus. Lot and his party and property were recovered (14:15-16).

God later mercifully rescued Lot and his wife and two daughters by angelic intervention when He was about to destroy the cities of Sodom and Gomorrah (Gen 19). The evil attempt against Lot's visitors by the men of Sodom illustrates the depravity which called down the divine judgment, and Lot's attempt to pacify the citizens shows the harmful effects of the city upon him (vv. 4-9). Lot and his relatives were warned not to look back when they fled, but Lot's wife did so and became a pillar of salt (19:26; cf. Lk 17:28-32). In the hill country afterward, Lot's daughters caused him under the influence of wine to father by them two sons who became the ancestors of the Moabites and the Ammonites (Gen 19:30-38).

N. B. B.

LOTAN. *See* Leviathan.

LOTS. The casting of lots was a widely used method of coming to a decision in the ancient world, and especially, as among the Jews, to ascertain God's will. The exact nature of the objects cast is not certain, though they probably were some kind of marked stones.

A momentous decision was made by lot in Persia (Est 3:7), and Roman soldiers cast lots for Christ's garment at the cross (MT 27:35). In Israel Lots were cast to decide the choice of goats on the Day of Atonement (Lev 16:7-10), and to divide the territory after the conquest of Canaan (Num 26:55 f.; Josh 14:2; 18:8; 19). The guilty Jonah was discovered by lot (Jon 1:7), and Saul the first king of Israel was so chosen (I Sam 10:21-22). Duties at the temple were assigned by lot when the service was organized under David (I Chr 24:5 *et al.*).

Apparently the Urim and Thummim were sacred lots placed in the pouch called the ephod *(q.v.)*, which was attached to the breastplate of the high priest (Ex 28:30). Joshua was to be guided in his judgments by this method (Num 27:21). The ephod was brought to David to get answers to his questions when he was fleeing from Saul in the wilderness (I Sam 23:9-12). Evidently the lot indicated a simply yes or no answer. The Urim and Thummim were used in casting the lot to decide between Saul and Jonathan (I Sam 14:41 f.). Sometimes the Lord gave no response even when the Urim was used (I Sam 28:6).

The disciples used lots to decide upon Judas's successor, and the choice fell to Matthias (Acts 1:26). There is no record of any further use of lots in the NT. Apparently after Pentecost the church relied upon the Holy Spirit to lead them through other means.

Bibliography. W. Foerster, "*Klēros*, etc.," TDNT, III, 758-766.

N. B. B.

LOTUS. *See* Plants: Lily.

LOUSE. *See* Animals, IV. 24.

LOVE. In KJV the noun is often "charity" (*q.v.*). The principal Heb. verb for love is *'āhēb* (*c.* 225 times in OT), though some 18 other words of similar meaning occur (less than 30 total occurrences). The usual LXX rendering of *'āhēb* is *agapaō* (195 times). Classical Gr. words for love varied: (1) *erao, eros,* "sexual desire, passionate longing" (noun in LXX twice, verb none; neither in NT); (2) *phileō, philia,* "affection of friends or kinsmen" (noun in LXX eight times, verb 26 times; noun in NT once, verb 25 times); (3) *philadelphia,* "love of the brethren" (not in LXX, NT six times); (4) *philanthrōpia,* "love for mankind" (LXX once, NT twice); (5) *stergō, storgē,* "affection, familial love" (not in LXX or NT, but see *astorgos,* Rom 1:31; II Tim 3:3; *philostorgos,* Rom 12:10); (6) *agapaō, agapē, agapētos* (noun in LXX 20 times, verb some 250 times; NT has noun over 100 times, the verb some 140 times, the adjective over 60 times).

In the LXX there seems to be little difference between the ideas translated by *phileō* and *agapaō,* both being used to translate the idea of love for food, pleasure, a woman, and sleep. *Eros* (whence our adjective "erotic"), though spiritualized by Plato, does not figure in the NT. Both the Heb. and Gr. words are concerned with the feeling of desire and are personal in nature.

The comparison of OT (*'āhēb-agapaō*) and NT (*agapaō*) uses shows how diverse are the objects of love; e.g., (1) husband-wife (Gen 24:67; Eph 5:25), (2) neighbor (Lev 19:18; Mt 5:43; 19:19), (3) money (Eccl 5:9; II Pet 2:15), (4) a friend (I Sam 20:17—David and Jonathan; Jn 11:5—Jesus-Martha), (5) a city (Ps 78:68; Rev 20:9).

The theological uses in both covenants concern the love of (1) God to man, (2) man to God, and (3) man to man.

1. The OT representation of God's love to man is seen in His concern for all men (Deut 33:3), but especially in His choosing Israel (His elective love, *'ahăbâ*, Deut 7:7-8; 10:15; Isa 63:9; Hos 11:1; Mal 1:2) and His constantly renewed covenant pledge to them (His covenant love, *ḥesed,* "mercy," Deut 7:9; I Kgs 8:23; Neh 9:32; "kindness, Isa 54:5-10; *see* Lovingkindness). This love secures for Israel God's protection and redemption (Isa 43:25; 63:9; Deut 23:5) and is extended to each individually (Prov 3:12; Ps 41:12).

The NT repeats God's love for all creatures (Mt 5:45) but emphasizes the particular manifestation of Himself in Christ and Calvary (Jn 3:16; Rom 5:8; 8:31-39), events which procure eternal life for the believer. God is revealed as loving because He is love itself (I Jn 4:8, 16). It is His very essence; love is the other term along with "light" (I Jn 1:5) which describes the moral quality of His being. *See* God.

2. The love of man to God in the OT is the total response of man (Deut 6:5, "with all the heart") to Israel's gracious God (Deut 6:5-9; Ex 20:1-17; Ps 18:1; 116:1). Love to God is expressed ethically especially in keeping the law and fearing Him (Ex 20:6; Deut 5:10; 10:12; Isa 56:1-6). This concept of total response is repeated in the NT by Jesus (Mk 12:29-30; see also Mt 6:24; 10:37-39; Lk 9:57-62; 14:26-27). However, the response is to a new set of events—the incarnation (Jn 4:10, 19, 25-29, 39-42), the cross (Rom 6:3-11; Gal 2:20; 5:24; 6:14), the resurrection

(Phil 3:10-11; Col 3:1-2), and the second coming (II Tim 4:8). The equation of love and obedience is also repeated (Jn 14:15, 21; I Jn 4:21–5:3). Love is not a mere sentiment but a voluntary self-dedication to the point of self-slavery.

3. The love of man to man in the OT is founded on the previous love of God and is demanded especially for neighbors (Lev 19:18) and for foreigners living in Israel (Deut 10:19; Lev 19:34). Even the enemy is to be treated kindly (Ex 23:4-5; Prov 25:21). Jesus set forth love between men (chief NT usage) as the second commandment (Mt 22:39), the unfailing sign of discipleship (Jn 13:34-35), of sonship (I Jn 4:7), and of new life (I Jn 3:14). It must be expressed "in deed" (I Jn 3:17-18). It is emphasized by the oneness of the body (Eph 4:1-4; Rom 12:16; Phil 1:27; 2:1-2; 4:2) and the stress on the heinousness of the sin of faction (Gal 5:19-21; I Cor 1:10-13; 3:3-8; 11:18-22). Jesus taught that love must include one's enemy (Mt 5:44), just as Paul taught that practical love was to include all men (Gal 6:10).

This love, which must be distinguished from erotic and romantic affection, is the logical counterpart of the divine love toward man (I Jn 4:11), and without it the claim to love God is seen as inconsistent (I Jn 4:20-21). It is also seen as the effect of the Holy Spirit poured out in our hearts (Rom 5:5; cf. Gal 5:22). It is a conscious imitation of God's love even to those who do evil (Mt 5:43-45; Jn 13:34; 15:12; Rom 15:7). The Christian's duty to counter evil with good rather than retaliation (Rom 12:17-21) is probably to be thought of as a cooperation with God's scheme to lead men to repentance (Rom 2:4; 12:20-21). So central is this concept of creative lofe (*agapē*) that it may be considered the distinctive Christian ethic.

The greatest definition of love (*agapē*) in human relationships ever penned is that of the apostle Paul in the hymn of I Cor 13: "Love is patient, love is kind, love knows no jealousy, love is never boastful. Love puts on no airs, never acts dishonourably, never places her own interests first, and never loses her temper. Love never imputes evil motives, never feels glad when others go wrong, but rejoices in everything that is right and true. Love conceals the faults of others, always believes the best, never despairs, and remains steadfast to the end. Love never fails, though everything else may fail . . ." (vv. 4-8*a*, F. F. Bruce, *The Letters of Paul, an Expanded Translation,* Grand Rapids: Eerdmans, 1965, p. 107). In short, love is fellowship between persons, based on acts of self-sacrifice. Such love is willed, deliberate kindness, extending even to enemies for whom one has no personal affection.

See Friend(ship); Kindness; Lovingkindness; Mercy.

Bibliography. Edwin M. Good, "Love in the Old Testament," IDB, III, 164-168. George Johnston, "Love in the New Testament," IDB, III, 168-178. C. S. Lewis, *The Four Loves,* New York: Harcourt, Brace & World, 1960. Anders Nygren, *Agape and Eros,* trans. by Philip S. Watson, Philadelphia: Westminster, 1953. Gottfried Quell and Ethelbert Stauffer, "*Agapaō,* etc.," TDNT, I, 21-55. Norman H. Snaith, *The Distinctive Ideas of the Old Testament,* London: Epworth Press, 1944, pp. 94-142.

J. W. R.

LOVE APPLE. *See* Plants: Mandrake.

LOVE FEAST. Known as *agapē* (from the Gr. word meaning love). Strictly, in the NT *agapē* is used in the special sense of "love feast" only in Jude 12 (except for a variant reading in a few MSS in II Pet 2:13) where warnings are given as to its misuse. All else about love feasts in the NT must be derived from possible implications from such passages as Acts 2:42, 46; 6:1; I Cor 11:20 ff.

If I Cor 11:20 ff. indicates both an *agapē* feast (vv. 20-21) and the Lord's Supper (Eucharist) celebrated together, they are distinct parts with different emphases. In the communal meal the believers were lovingly to share their food with the poor and the widows, not to gorge themselves.

The *agapē* feast is found separated from the Eucharist by sometime in the 2nd cen. (Tertullian, *Apology* 39:16), although earlier writings are unclear (Ignatius, *Smyrnaeans* 8:2; *Didache* 9, 10).

Tertullian's description (*Apology* 39:16) of elements of a Christian *agape* feast show great similarity to early Jewish feasts (cf. the Talmudic *Berakoth* tractates; Philo, *Contemplative Life* 10-11; DSS, *Manual of Discipline*) in which are included prayer, eating, religious conversation, washing of hands, lighting lamps, singing (cf. Acts 2:42, 46; Eph 5:19; Col 3:16).

It can be concluded that the early church, developing from a Jewish background, had fellowship *agape* feasts similar to feasts of the surrounding Jewish communities, but with a Christo-centric emphasis.

See Agape; Lord's Supper.

W. H. M.

LOVINGKINDNESS. In the KJV Heb. *ḥesed* is translated "lovingkindness" *c.* 30 times, very often as "mercy," "kindness" 38 times, and "goodness" 12 times. The RSV often renders it "steadfast love." The Heb. word was early used "to denote that attitude of loyalty and faithfulness which both parties to a covenant should observe toward each other" (Snaith, *Distinctive Ideas,* p. 99).

When *hesed* is used of God it generally denotes: (1) God's *ḥesed* to His covenant people Israel (Ps 136; cf. Deut 7:12; II Sam 7:15; Isa 55:3). In keeping with this the KJV translates *ḥesed* by "lovingkindness" 23 times in Psalms, twice in Isaiah, four times in Jeremiah, and once in Hosea (2:19). In His unswerving love

God determines to keep His *ḥesed* commitment to His covenant nation in spite of their apostasy; thus His *ḥesed* becomes unmerited love, "lovingkindness." (2) "The divine love condescending to His creatures, more especially to sinners, in unmerited kindness" (Delitzsch). It is frequently translated "mercy" in the KJV and connected with forgiveness (Ex 20:6; 34:6–7).

Since it is a quality of God *ḥesed* should also characterize His people; therefore it is called for in them ("mercy," Mic 6:8; Zech 7:9; cf. Hos 4:1; 12:6). On their part it is loyalty to His covenant expressed in obedience and acts of mercy and compassion toward their fellows.

The Gr. word is *chrēstos,* kindness, friendliness, generosity. It is used of God, e.g., in Rom 2:4; Eph 2:7; and of men, e.g., in Gal 5:22 (a fruit of the Spirit); II Cor 6:6. According to I Cor 13:4, love is "kind" (*chrēsteuetai*). *See* Kindness; Love; Mercy.

Bibliography. Nelson Glueck, *Ḥesed in the Bible,* trans. by A. G. Gottschalk, Cincinnati: Hebrew Union College Press, 1967. Norman H. Snaith, *Distinctive Ideas of the Old Testament,* London: Epworth Press, 1944, pp. 94–130.

R. A. K.

LUBIM (lū'bĭm). A people of Libya, probably descended from the Lehabim (*q.v.*; Gen 10:13), an early tribe of the Nile delta. They first appear in biblical history in the army of Shishak (II Chr 12:3), when he spoiled Solomon's temple of its gold shields in the time of Rehoboam. The Lubim were included in the army of Zerah, the Ethiopian leader of Egyptian troops, which army Asa destroyed (cf. II Chr 16:8 with 14:9-12). They came to the aid of No (No-Amon-Thebes) when Ashurbanipal sacked the Egyptian city (Nah 3:9) and were allied with Phut (*q.v.*) there. In the future the Lubim will follow in the train of the king of the N (Dan 11:43).

The name occurs as *Rbw* (=Lîbu) in Egyptian texts of the 13th-12th cen. B.C., referring to a hostile tribe W of the delta (Gardiner, *Ancient Egyptian Onomastics,* I [1947], 121 f.). On the Egyptian monuments the Libyans were depicted as tall, light complexioned, well-built people. Seti I, Rameses II and III record their strong invasion attempts, warded off with difficulty. Later, because of their prowess, they became Egyptian mercenaries; later yet, privileged Egyptian soldiers. Shishak, a Libyan, after having been a general in the Egyptian army, seized the throne c. 950 B.C. and at Bubastis in the Nile delta began the 22nd or Libyan Dynasty, which lasted over 200 years.

See Libya; Phut.

H. G. S.

LUCAS. *See* Luke.

LUCIFER (Heb. *hêlēl,* "the shining one"). The term is used only once (Isa 14:12). It is specifically directed to the king of Babylon. However, this particular prophecy so far transcends anything that can be said of any earthly king that it is very generally accepted as referring to Satan, the "prince of this world." The same literary phenomenon is to be found in the description of the king of Tyre in Ezk 28, and in that of Babylon the Great, the woman riding on the Beast in Rev 17.

It has been well pointed out that in Isa 14:12 Satan is called "son of the morning," while Christ is called "the bright and morning star" (Rev 22:16), and that this in itself reveals both the original power and the beauty of this greatest angel ever created by God prior to Satan's rebellion and fall (Ezk 28:12-19). A study of such passages as Dan 10:13; II Cor 11:14 ("an angel of light"); Eph 6:12; Rev 12; 13; 17 divulges something of the presence and activity of Satan and his demonic powers in the conduct of religions and secular governments in this age. *See* Day Star; Devil; Satan.

For the view that Lucifer is only the proud but now fallen king of Babylon, see Robert L. Alden, "Lucifer, Who or What?" BulETS, XI (1968), 35-39. For a mythological explanation, see J. W. McKay, "Helel and the Dawn Goddess," VT, XX (1970), 451-464.

R. A. K.

LUCIUS (lū'shŭs)

1. Lucius of Cyrene, one of five men in the Antioch church called "prophets and teachers" (Acts 13:1).

2. Lucius at Corinth, one of Paul's "kinsmen" or fellow Jews who sent greetings to Christians in Rome (Rom 16:21).

1 and 2 may represent the same person; but it is quite unlikely that Luke, a Gentile (Col 4:11, 14), is to be identified with either one.

LUD (lŭd), **LUDIM** (lū'dĭm)

1. The fourth son of Shem (Gen 10:22; I Chr 1:17). Josephus (*Ant.* i.6.4) refers to the Lydians of SW Asia Minor as his descendants, but they did not speak a Semitic language. Nothing is actually known of Semitic Lydians, unless they can be identified with the country of Lubdi, mentioned in ancient cuneiform records as lying between the upper Tigris and Euphrates rivers.

Herodotus (1.7) reports the tradition that the name Lydia derived from the name Lydus, son of Atys, but that the land was previously named Maeonia (Iliad, ii, 865, etc.). It is probable that the Lydians, a tribe to the N of the Maeonians, conquered them and thus gave their name to the land. The name Luddu appears in the 7th cen. Assyrian inscriptions of Ashurbanipal (see Rassam Cylinder, II, 95) and *c.* 175 B.C. in the Maccabees' time (I Macc 8:8).

In Isa 66:19 Lud is listed with Tubal and Javan (Ionia). Here the area from the Aegean to the Caspian Sea is included, seeming to settle the question of Lydia's location.

Lydian walls at Sardis. HFV

Lydians were employed as mercenaries by the Egyptians (Jer 46:9; Ezk 30:5). King Gyges (*c.* 662 B.C.) sent Lydian troops to Psammeticus of Egypt (663-609 B.C.) against the Assyrian armies (Rassam Cylinder II, 114-115), who were described by Herodotus (i, 79) as "good soldiers" in pre-Persian times. Lydia was a prosperous kingdom with its capital at Sardis (*q.v.*). Cyrus of Persia conquered their last king, Croesus, in 546 B.C. The area continued to be known for its purple dye and woolen fabrics.

2. In Gen 10:13; I Chr 1:11, the first son of Mizraim (Egypt). According to some scholars these people were located W of Libya (Phut, *q.v.*). However, they have not been certainly identified. These Lydians may have migrated from N Africa very early in their history. At any rate, Lydians are known on the plain of Sardis in W Asia Minor before 1500 B.C. They may have become the mercenaries of Gyges (see 1 above). In Isa 66:19 the LXX has Put for Pul, which with Lud would agree with Nebuchadrezzar's account of his war in his 37th year with Amasis, king of Egypt, in which he mentions a people of Put-Iaman (Put-Ionia). Isaiah certainly shows the contact between Greek-Ionians and Egypt some time before Psammeticus.

H. G. S.

LUHITH (lū'hĭth). An unidentified town of Moab which was slated for doom along with the other towns of Moab. Apparently Luhith was located on a height or hillside of some sort and offered temporary refuge to those fleeing from invasion (Isa 15:5; Jer 48:5).

LUKE (lo͝ok). The author of the third Gospel and the Acts of the Apostles is mentioned by name in three passages of the NT (Col 4:14; Phm 24; II Tim 4:11). It may be inferred from these verses that Luke or Lucas KJV, Phm 24, from Gr. *Loukas*) was a physician and a fellow worker of Paul. He accompanied the apostle in his first imprisonment in Rome and was Paul's sole companion during the second and final imprisonment. In Col 4:11, 14 Luke is distinguished from the men of the circumcision. Nevertheless W. F. Albright has argued from the Aramaic form of his name in Gr. and the Heb. idioms in the three poems of Lk 1, 2 that Luke was a converted Jew (*New Horizons in Biblical Research,* London: Oxford Univ. Press, 1966, pp. 49f.). From the "we" sections of Acts, it may be deduced that the writer traveled with Paul from Troas to Philippi (Acts 16:10-12), Philippi to Jerusalem (Acts 20:5-21:17), and on the voyage to Rome (Acts 27:1-28:16).

The 2nd cen. Anti-Marcionite Prologue to Luke's Gospel claims that Luke was a Gentile of Antioch in Syria, lived a single life, and died in Bithynia (some MSS have "Boeotia," in Greece) at the age of 74 years. A "we" section in Codex Bezae at Acts 11:28, plus the large amount of material in Acts dealing with the church in Antioch, has also been thought to point to an Antioch residence. Some, however, have felt that a tendency to confuse Luke with Lucius of Acts 13:1 gave rise to the tradition. Sir William Ramsay argued that the "we" sections begin just before Paul goes to Philippi; that Luke remained in Philippi; that he shows pride in the place in his phrase "the first of the district" (Acts 16:12, ASV); that therefore Luke was a native of Philippi. About this question there can be no certainty.

From the 2nd cen. on the early church attributed both the third Gospel and the Acts of the Apostles to Luke. He is probably the only Greek to whom a book of the NT is traced. Lk 1:2 makes it unlikely that he was an eyewitness of the Gospel events. Some scholars believe that he collected the data for his Gospel, and perhaps wrote it, while Paul was imprisoned in Caesarea for two years. *See* Luke, Gospel of.

J. P. L.

LUKE, GOSPEL OF

Outline

I. Preface, 1:1-4
II. Birth Narratives, 1:5-2:52
III. Mission of John the Baptist, 3:1-20
IV. Jesus' Ministry in Galilee, 3:21-9:50
V. Travel Narrative, 9:51-19:44
VI. Jerusalem Ministry, 19:45-21:38
VII. Passion Experiences, 22:1-24:53

Introduction

Evidence from the 2nd cen. for the recognition of Luke as one of the four Gospels is seen in the Muratorian Canon, in Tatian's *Diatessaron,* in Irenaeus, and in Tertullian. A mutilated form of it was used by Marcion. (Texts are collected in D. Theron, *The Evidence of Tradition.*) The earliest known MSS of Luke are the Bodmer (P^{75}) and the Chester Beatty (P^{45}) papyri from the 3rd cen.

The unanimous tradition of the early church is that both the third Gospel and Acts were written by Luke the physician, who was the companion of Paul. *See* Luke. Acts was intended to be a part of a larger work (Acts 1:1). Both books are addressed to Theophilus, and the vocabulary and style show similarities. These two books together fffform the largest block of material by any one NT writer.

Discussions of the date of the book raise a complicated problem involving the assumption of dates previously assigned to Mark and Acts, and the question of whether the statements in Lk 19:43f. and 21:20-24 reflect a knowledge of the fall of Jerusalem in A.D. 70. The prologue implies that some time had passed in which other accounts had been written. Hence, the book was likely written sometime in the second half of the 1st cen.

The writer was not an eyewitness of the events he narrates (Lk 1:1-2). Nothing definite is known about Theophilus, to whom the book is addressed, except the title given him, which implies he was an official of high rank (cf. Acts 23:26). Luke probably wrote for Gentile readers since his book is comparatively free from OT quotations.

That the Gospel was written in Achaia, as the Anti-Marcionite Prologues affirm, cannot be either substantiated or denied. Some have felt that the interest of the writer in the movement of the gospel toward Rome makes that city a more likely place of composition. In the absence of data, there can be no certainty in these matters.

Luke wrote an orderly account of events to confirm the minds of those who had already believed the truth of what they had been taught. Some have thought Luke's secondary purpose was to demonstrate that Christianity was not politically dangerous. These purposes are revealed when the writer parallels gospel events with contemporary history (1:5; 2:1-2; 3:1-2), and when he repeatedly makes clear that apostolic men, though accused by the mobs, were acquitted by the authorities.

It has been observed that Luke emphasizes the privileges of the poor. He is concerned with the outcasts of society: the sinful woman, the publican, the prodigal, the Samaritan. He attempts to demonstrate that the life, death, and teaching of Jesus form a message of salvation addressed to all men: the revelation is given to Gentiles (2:32); guests from highways and hedges are compelled to come in (14:23); preaching is to be done to all nations (24:47). Considerable interest is shown in the part that women played in the Saviour's life. Luke is also interested in the role prayer had in the devotions of Jesus. In the Synoptic Gospels Jesus prays 15 times, 11 of which are narrated in Luke. The third Gospel places great emphasis on the Holy Spirit, a characteristic likewise of Acts.

The writer of the third Gospel began his book with a classical prologue. He was skillful in Greek and had a versatile vocabulary. He used 312 words unique in the NT to his book. While he used Gr. phrases rather than the Heb. names and Aramaic phrases found in Mark, and while "verily" is preferred to "amen," Hebraisms are frequent: "It came to pass"; "And behold." These are especially frequent in the birth and infancy sections as though the writer consciously imitated the Semitic style of the LXX. Paul Winter in a number of articles has sought to demonstrate that Luke used a source of Jewish Palestinian origin written in Heb. for chaps. 1-2, by showing the Jewish character of various expressions in this section (e.g., "On the Margin of Luke I, II," *Studia Theologica,* XII [1958], 103-107.

Luke is characterized by the long narratives of the birth of John and Jesus (1:5-2:52) and by the long travel narrative (9:51-19:44), which are not found in the other Gospels. A number of significant parables and miracles are included in the latter section. Eighteen of Jesus' parables are peculiar to Luke. The Sermon on the Plain (6:20-49) is much briefer than the Sermon on the Mount in Matthew, but other sayings of Jesus which are paralleled in the Sermon on the Mount are scattered throughout Luke. Only Luke tells of Christ eating when He appeared to the ten apostles (24:36-43). He alone records the appearance to the Emmaus disciples (24:13-31).

See Luke under Gospels, The Four.

Bibliography. H. J. Cadbury, *The Making of Luke-Acts,* New York: Macmillan, 1927; "The Tradition," in F. J. Foakes-Jackson and K. Lake, *The Beginnings of Christianity,* II, 200-264. Earle E. Cairns, "Luke as a Historian," BS, CXXII (1965), 220-226. J. M. Creed, *The Gospel According to Luke,* London: Macmillan, 1953. J. Norval Geldenhuys, *Commentary on the Gospel of Luke,* Grand Rapids: Eerdmans, 1956; "Luke the Evangelist," "Luke, Gospel of," NBD, pp. 755-759. Frederic Godet, *A Commentary on the Gospel of Luke,* trans. by E. W. Shalders and M. D. Cusin, 3rd ed., New York: Funk & Wagnalls, 1887. A. Harnack, *Luke the Physician,* London: Williams and Norgate, 1909. I. Howard Marshall, *Luke: Historian and Theologian,* Grand Rapids: Zondervan, 1971. A. Plummer, *The Gospel According to Luke,* ICC. A. T. Robertson, *Luke the Historian in the Light of Research,* New York: Scribner's, 1923. Ned B. Stonehouse, *The Witness of Luke to Christ,* Grand Rapids: Eerdmans, 1951. Vincent Taylor, "Luke, Gospel of," IDB, III, 180-188. Merrill C. Tenney, "Luke," WBC, pp. 1027-1070.

J. P. L.

LUNATIC. *See* Demonology; Diseases.

LUST. The English word lust as employed in the KJV covers a wide range of desires. It was not restricted in A.D. 1611 to the modern sense of sexual passion.

1. Strong desire. It may be a keen desire (Heb. *nephesh*), as that of the Egyptian army to overtake and destroy Israel at the Red Sea (Ex 15:9), or of merchants with eagerness (*epithumias*) to gain the profits of their commercial

ventures (Rev 18:14); or simply a desire (Gr. *epithumia*) for other things (Mk 4:19).

2. Execessive desire, strong craving, lust in the sense of excess (Heb. *ta'ăwa,* Num 11:4, 34; Ps 78:30). Many good things when done in excess for self-gratification become lusts, as for example overeating, too much time spent on pleasure (Rom 13:14).

3. Consuming desire for what is good, namely, zeal for what is right. The Gr. *epithumia,* when used for what is truly godly zeal, has been translated as "desire" in Lk 22:15; Phil 1:23; I Thess 2:17. This use of the Gr. term clearly shows that it is either the object of one's desire or one's motivation, not its intensity, which makes that desire right or wrong.

4. Lust as a craving for that which is forbidden. This is the most common use of the term. Paul reveals that God has given fallen man over to his own lusts (*epithumiais,* Rom 1:24). He quotes the OT commandment, "Thou shalt not covet" (Ex 20:17; Deut 5:21) in Rom 7:7, showing that to covet what is not one's own is a form of lust. This was apparently Paul's own besetting sin with which he had most strenuously to wrestle after his conversion (Rom 7:7–25).

Lust (*epithumia*), James declares, is a root cause of sin (Jas 1:14–15), which in turn leads to death. The downward path of lust is depicted graphically in Rom 1:24–32. James also uses another word, Gr. *hēdonē,* in 4:1, 3 (KJV "lusts"; RSV "passions"; NASB "pleasures") to explain that the quarrels and conflicts among believers result from the lust-for-pleasures within their own bodily members. The word also occurs as "pleasures of this life" in Lk 8:14 and in "enslaved to various lusts [*epithumiais*] and pleasures" in Tit 3:3, NASB.

See Covet; Sin.

Bibliography. Friedrich Büchsel, *"Thumos, Epithumia,* etc.," TDNT, III, 167–172. Gustav Stahlin, *"Hēdonē,"* TDNT, II, 909–926.

R. A. K.

LUZ (lŭz)

1. The earlier name of Bethel (Gen 28:19; 35:6; Josh 18:13; Jud 1:23). The name Luz ("almond tree") also appears in Gen 48:3; Josh 16:2.

The texts of Josh 16:2 and 18:13 deserve special attention. A problem is posed by the earlier reference, for the text speaks of the boundary of the descendants of Joseph as in part reaching from Bethel to Luz. If the terms are interchangeable, why this distinction? Various answers have been proposed: (1) The occurrence of Luz in Josh 16:2 is perhaps an explanatory gloss (BDB, p. 531). (2) It should be noticed that both the Heb. MT (Josh 16:2) and the LXX (v. 1) allow the translation "Beth-el-luzah" (see August W. Knobel, *Kritik des Pentateuch und Josua* [*Exegetic. Handbuch,* Part XIII]; quoted in *Lange's Commentary on the Holy Scriptures,* Joshua, pp. 142, 154). It is pointed out, however, that such a construction is contrary to the normal usage in the book of Joshua. (3) Bethel may have been the name which Abram had given to "the place" (Gen 28:11, 19, Heb.) where he had erected an altar, E of the town (cf. Gen 12:8). As a holy place, its name may have ultimately been used of both that site and the town (W. Ewing, "Luz," ISBE, III, 1942). (4) Josh 18:13 may provide the solution. This passage speaks of "the side of Luz, which is Bethel." The word *kātēp,* translated "side," means "shoulder," and by usage "mountain slope" (cf. Num 34:11; Josh 15:10). The LXX uses *nōtos* meaning "back" for this Heb. word. Is this a reference to a ridge, a rocky height? In any case, Luz and Bethel are intimately related in location, and Bethel replaced Luz in common usage. *See* Bethel.

2. The name of a city built in the land of the Hittites after the Canaanite city was captured by the Israelites (Jud 1:26); not yet identified.

W. C.

LYCAONIA (lĭk'ĭ-ō'nĭ-ȧ). A region of southern Asia Minor subject to varying boundaries. In the 1st cen. A.D., however, it was part of the Roman province of Galatia (except for a small sector in the eastern extremity).

In Acts 14:5–6, Lystra and Derbe are called "cities of Lycaonia." While the Gr. language was widely used in Asia Minor, the local tongue did not die out, as Acts 14:11 indicates, and the missionaries were unable to understand their speech.

There seems to have been little Jewish influence in this area, as Paul and Barnabas found no synagogue, and the people seem to have been warlike and primitive.

LYCIA (lĭsh'ĭ-*ȧ*). This Roman province occupied the SW tip of Asia Minor. A rather mountainous region, its chief importance lay in its harbors, of which two are mentioned in the NT. Paul touched at Patara in the course of his last journey to Jerusalem, where he changed ships, presumably to make faster time (Acts 21:1–2). Later, on his journey to Rome as a prisoner, his ship touched at Myra and there he was transferred to a grain ship bound for Italy (Acts 27:5–6). Lycia became Roman territory in 188 B.C., but was not organized into a Roman province until Claudius ordered it in – a.d. 43.

LYDDA (lĭd'*ȧ*). A town in the old tribal area of Benjamin, about 11 miles SE of Joppa. Its OT name was Lod (I Chr 8:12) and today is known as Ludd. The church in Lydda may have been started by Philip as he evangelized northward after meeting the Ethiopian eunuch (Acts 8:40). Peter healed the palsied man Aeneas there, miracle that turned many to the Lord (Acts 9:32–35). *See* Lod.

LYDIA (lĭd'ĭ-*ȧ*). A woman called Lydia who was living in Philippi when Paul arrived there on his second missionary tour (Acts 16:14). She was a merchant (perhaps a widow), a seller of purple or dyed goods, a convert to the ethical monotheism of Judaism (she "worshiped God").

While Lydia was a personal name, it may also be an adjectival form, "the Lydian" (cf. *pros tēn Lydian,* v. 40). The city of her origin, Thyatira (*q.v.*), was in Lydia, renowned for its purple dyes (*see* Lud).

When Paul came to Philippi Lydia received the gospel as God opened her heart. After being baptized, she invited the missionary party to her home. Following the prison experience of Paul and Silas and their release, they returned to her house before leaving the city (Acts 16:40).

LYING. *See* Lie.

LYRE. *See* Music.

LYSANIAS (lĭ-sā'nĭ-ȧs). A tetrarch of Abilene (Lk 3:1), a region of Anti-Lebanon, NW of Damascus. Luke named him along with others of the year A.D. 26–27 (or 28–29) to date the beginning of the preaching of John the son of Zacharias.

Josephus (*Ant.* xv.4.1) refers to an earlier Lysanias, king of the Itureans (a region to the W of Abilene), who was executed by Mark Antony in 36 B.C. Whether this person or Luke's Lysanias is the one mentioned on coins inscribed "Lysanias tetrarch and high priest" is uncertain. The name does appear on an inscription (*Corpus Inscriptionum Graecarum,* 4521) of the period A.D. 14–29 in the phrase "Lysanias the tetrarch."

The history of Abilene is not clear and, while Josephus gives further references to this region (see *Ant.* xix.5.1; xx.7.1), the problem of specific identification of Lysanias remains. *See* Abilene.

LYSIAS (lĭs'ĭ-ȧs). A Roman officer in Jerusalem at the time of Paul's arrest. He is called "the chief captain" (Acts 21:31–33,37), or "military tribune" (ASV marg.). The Gr. word *chiliarchos* is, literally, "a ruler of a thousand,"

Mound of Lystra. Robert Cooley

thus he commanded a cohort (about 1,000 men).

His longer name, Claudius Lysias (the latter probably signifying Gr. birth), is given in Acts 23:26. He had purchased his Roman citizenship (Acts 22:28). In Jerusalem he was stationed in the "castle" (Acts 21:34), the tower of Antonia at the NW corner of the temple area, a place of ready access by a stairway to the confines of the temple itself.

LYSTRA (lĭs'trȧ). A city about 18 miles SW of Iconium in the Roman province of Galatia where Paul established a church on his first missionary journey and which he visited on his second and third journeys (Acts 14:6–20; 16:1–5; 18:23). Here he and Barnabas were hailed as Jupiter and Mercury, but Paul was later stoned and left for dead. At Lystra or Derbe Paul met Timothy. Founded as a Roman colony by Augustus about 6 B.C., for the purpose of training and regulating the mountain tribes on the southern frontier of the province of Galatia, Lystra was a place of some importance under the early emperors. J. R. S. Sterrett in 1885 fixed the location by means of an inscribed altar standing on the site and bearing the Latin name Lystra.

M

MAACAH, MAACHAH (mā'*ȧ*-k*ȧ*)

1. One of the four children of Nahor, born to him by his concubine Reumah. There is no indication of whether it was a son or daughter (Gen 22:24).

2. The daughter of Talmai, king of Geshur. She was married to David and was the mother of Absalom (II Sam 3:3; I Chr 3:2).

3. A city and small Aramaean kingdom N of the Sea of Galilee, near the SW slope of Mount Hermon. It was allied with other Syrians in fighting David (II Sam 10:8; I Chr 19:6–7), but later some of its men were in David's army. *See* Maachathites.

4. The father of Achish, king of Gath (I Kgs 2:39), called Maoch in I Sam 27:2. Two of Shimei's servants ran away to the Philistine king. In earlier days Achish had befriended David. *See* Achish.

5. The wife of Rehoboam and mother of King Abijam (Abijah). She was the granddaughter of Absalom (Abishalom, I Kgs 15:2), the daughter of Uriel (II Chr 13:2, where she is called Michaiah) and evidently of Tamar, Absalom's only daughter (II Sam 14:27). Because Maachah was the favorite wife of Rehoboam, he appointed her son chief prince in order to insure his being the next king (II Chr 11:20–22). In I Kgs 15:10, 13 she is called the "mother" of King Asa. This term probably signifies "queen mother," which position she must have retained after her son's death. Thus Asa deposed his grandmother from the influential position of queen or queen mother because of her idolatry (II Chr 15:16; I Kgs 15:13).

6. The concubine of Caleb son of Hezron who bore several children (I Chr 2:48).

7. The wife of Machir, prince of Manasseh in the time of Moses. It is not clear whether Machir also had a sister named Maacah, or his wife Maacah was the sister of Huppim and Shuppim (I Chr 7:15–16).

8. The wife of Jeiel (Jehiel) who was the "father," i.e., "founder" of the Israelite settlement of Gideon, and the great-grandfather of King Saul (I Chr 8:29; 9:35).

9. The father of Hanan, one of David's mighty men (I Chr 11:43).

10. The father of Shephatiah, ruler of the tribe of Simeon in David's time (I Chr 27:16).

P. C. J.

MAACHATHI (mā-ăk'*ȧ*-thī), **MAACHATHITES** (mā-ăk'*ȧ*-thīts). The inhabitants of the small Aramaean kingdom of Maac(h)ah which lay N and W of Geshur in the territory once captured by Jair (Deut 3:14; II Sam 10:8; I Chr 19:6–7). *See* Maacah 3. The territory of Israel in Joshua's day was usually described as "unto the border" of the Maachathites (Josh 12:5; 13:11, 13). Maachathites joined other Aramaeans in opposing David when his army came to avenge the insult given his ambassadors by Hanun the Ammonite (II Sam 10:6–8; I Chr 19:6–7). Later, Maachathites are found among the mighty men of David (II Sam 23:34). Eshtemoa the Maachathite was a descendant of Caleb (I Chr 4:19). A Maachathite was the father of Jaazaniah, one of the leaders remaining after the fall of Jerusalem (II Kgs 25:23; Jer 40:8). It is possible that the name had come to designate a warrior class rather than a nationality.

MAADAI (mā'*ȧ*-dī). An Israelite of the family of Bani who agreed to give up his foreign wife in the days of Ezra (Ezr 10:34).

MAADIAH (mā'*ȧ*-dī'*ȧ*). A priest who returned from the Exile with Zerubbabel (Neh 12:5). Maaziah (Neh 10:8) and Moadiah (Neh 12:17) are likely variants of the same name.

MAAI (mā'ī). A musician who took part in the dedication of the Jerusalem wall after its rebuilding (Neh 12:36).

MAALEH-ACRABBIM. *See* Akrabbim.

MAARATH (mā'*ȧ*-răth). A village located in the hill country of Judea mentioned in Josh 15:59. Possible identifications are Khirbet Qufin or Beit Ummar in the vicinity of Beth-zur about seven miles N of Hebron.

MAASEIAH (mā'*ȧ*-sē'y*ȧ*). A name common in Israel and attested on ancient Heb. seals.

1. According to several Heb. MSS and the LXX, an ancestor of Asaph (I Chr 6:40), spelled Baaseiah (*q.v.*) in all English versions following the MT.

2. One of the Levitical musicians who accompanied David when he brought back the ark from the house of Obed-edom (I Chr 15:18, 20).

3. One of the captains who aided Jehoiada at the coronation of Joash (II Chr 23:1).

4. An officer who assisted Jeiel the scribe in organizing the army of King Uzziah (II Chr 26:11).

5. A royal prince slain by the Ephraimite Zichri in the invasion of Judah by Pekah, king of Israel (II Chr 28:7).

6. A governor of Jerusalem under Josiah (II Chr 34:8) appointed by him to cooperate with Shaphan and Joah in repairing the temple.

7. One of the sons of the priests who had married a Gentile wife and who had put her away after the order of Ezra (Ezr 10:18).

8. A son of Harim who put away his Gentile

wife (Ezr 10:21). Thought to be the one referred to as a member of the chorus that sang when the city walls were completed (Neh 12:42).

9. A priest of the sons of Pashur who divorced his Gentile wife (Ezr 10:22). Perhaps one of the trumpeters who celebrated the completion of the walls of Jerusalem (Neh 12:41).

10. A member of the family of Pahath-moab who put away his Gentile wife after the Exile (Ezr 10:30).

11. Father of Azariah, one of the builders of the city wall after the return from Babylon (Neh 3:23).

12. One who stood at Ezra's right hand during the reading of the law (Neh 8:4).

13. One of the priests who expounded the law to the people as it was read by Ezra and helped the people to understand (Neh 8:7).

14. One of the "chiefs of the people" who took part in the sealing of the covenant under Nehemiah's direction (Neh 10:25).

15. A Judahite inhabitant who lived in Jerusalem after the Captivity (Neh 11:5); thought to be the person called Asaiah (I Chr 9:5). *See* Asaiah 4.

16. A Benjamite son of Ithiel whose descendants lived in Jerusalem after the Captivity (Neh 11:7).

17. A priest in Zedekiah's reign and father of Zephaniah who interviewed the prophet Jeremiah during the invasion of Nebuchadnezzar (Jer 21:1; 29:25; 37:3).

18. Father of the false prophet Zedekiah who prophesied a lie to Judah (Jer 29:21).

19. A son of Shallum and a keeper of the temple threshold in the reign of Jehoiakim (Jer 35:4).

20. The father of Neriah and grandfather of Baruch and Seraiah (Jer 32:12; 51:59, spelled Mahseiah in RSV, NASB, etc.).

R. H. B.

MAASIAI (mā-ăs'ĭ-ī). One of the priests living at Jerusalem after the return from the Babylonian Captivity. He is mentioned only in I Chr 9:12.

MAATH (mā'ăth). The son of Mattathias and father of Nagge in the genealogy of Jesus (Lk 3:26). Since the name does not appear in any OT genealogies, it has been thought an accidental interpolation of Matthat from v.24, but this seems an unnecessary explanation.

MAAZ (mā'ăz). The eldest son of Ram, a descendant of Judah. He is mentioned only in I Chr 2:27.

MAAZIAH (mā'*ȧ*-zī-*ȧ*)

1. The head of the 24th division of priests as arranged by David (I Chr 24:18).

2. One of the priests who signed the covenant with Nehemiah (Neh 10:8). Apparently each name represented "heads of families" as the lists in Chronicles and Nehemiah seem to indicate.

MACCABEES (măk'*ȧ*-bēz)

The Name

The derivation of the name is uncertain. *Makkabaios* was originally the surname or nickname of Judas, one of five sons of a Jewish priest named Mattathias and leader of the Jewish war for independence that began in 168 B.C. Each of the sons had such a nickname (cf. I Macc 2:2–5), but since Judas was the first and greatest of the family heroes, his name was used to designate the whole family. *Makkabaios* is most commonly related to the Heb. *maqqebeth,* "hammer," so that Judas' nickname would coincide in meaning with that of Charles Martel, grandfather of Charlemagne. The *maqqebeth,* however, is not an instrument of battle, but a common workman's tool (cf. Jud 4:21; I Kgs 6:7; *et al.*), and it should be remembered that Judas apparently received this nickname before his prowess in war had been demonstrated. Although some (e.g., Zeitlin) have traced this designation to the shape of Judas' head, it is at least as likely that the term came from Judas' skill as a boy in carpentry. For a list of many other etymologies and interpretations of the name, see R. H. Pfeiffer, *History of New Testament Times,* pp. 461 f. The final solution to this problem may come when more light is shed on the obscure nicknames of the other four brothers.

The Maccabean Revolution

The major source for this period in Jewish history is the apocryphal book of I Maccabees. Additional information is supplied by II Maccabees and by Josephus (*Ant.* xii.5–xiii. 7, and *Wars* i.1–ii.2). The background of the war was the conflict between Judaism and Hellenism that came to a head early in the 2nd cen. B.C. The initiative for Hellenization seems to have come from "lawless men" among the Jews themselves who built a Gr. gymnasium in Jerusalem and repudiated circumcision and the covenant (I Macc 1:11–15). At the same time there was a bitter and shameless struggle between two claimants to the high priesthood, Jason and Menelaus, and their followers (II Macc 4:7–5:10).

Antiochus IV Epiphanes, Gr. king of the Seleucid Empire (at that time comprising Babylonia, Phoenicia, Syria, and Palestine), interpreted these disorders as an open revolt against his rule. He returned from a campaign in Egypt to sack Jerusalem and desecrate the temple, stripping it of its golden altar and candlesticks and all the silver and gold adornments. Two years later, Antiochus carried out a massacre in Jerusalem and established a citadel (the *Acra*) over against the temple, "a place to lie in wait against the sanctuary, and an evil adversary to Israel" (I Macc 1:36). Jewish worship and circumcision were forbidden, idolatry was commanded, and all copies of the law that could be found were burned (I Macc 1:41–64). Upon the Jewish altar of burnt offering was erected a smaller heathen altar, which the writer of I Maccabees regarded as an "abomination of desolation" (1:54), the fulfillment of Dan 9:27; 11:31; 12:11.

The response of the pious Jews to these blasphemies began to take shape at the small town of Modin, NW of Jerusalem. A priest named Mattathias defied the king's emissaries by refusing to sacrifice to idols. When another Jew started to comply with the royal edict, Mattathias slew him on the altar and fled to the mountains with his five sons (I Macc 2:15-28).

At this point, the pious in Israel faced a struggle with conscience. A thousand of them were killed because they refused to defend themselves on the sabbath. But pacifism and quietism soon gave way to a dedication to the concept of "holy war" and to self-defense even on the sabbath day (I Macc 2:29-48). Judas the Maccabee assumed leadership at the death of his father. He was celebrated as one who "was like a lion" in his deeds, who "pursued the wicked" and "turned away wrath from Israel" (see I Macc 3:1-9).

Judas' campaign of guerrilla warfare paid quick and rich dividends. While Antiochus was occupied in Persia, Judas and his outnumbered army won a succession of victories over the Seleucid forces, so that by 165 B.C. he was able to regain Mount Zion and to restore and rededicate the temple. The edict proscribing Judaism was rescinded; religious freedom had been regained, and the initial purposes for the revolt had been achieved (I Macc 4:36-61; II Macc 10:1-8; 11:13-33). This victory is commemorated by the Feast of Hanukkah, or the Dedication (Jn 10:22). Many of the "pious" (Chasidim) then laid down their arms, but Judas and his brothers felt that the war had to continue for the sake of political independence. Judea was still under Seleucid rule, and Jews were still a persecuted minority in many cities; even in Jerusalem the *Acra* continued to stand as a symbol of Gentile domination.

The rest of I Maccabees narrates the Maccabaean war as it developed under Judas (5:1–9:22) and his brothers Jonathan (9:23–12:53) and Simon (13:1–16:16). Judas won many notable battles, culminating in the great victory over the Seleucid general Nicanor in 161. But in the same year Judas died fighting against the forces of the new king Demetrius.

Jonathan's period of leadership was marked by extensive involvement in the struggle for the Seleucid throne between Demetrius and a pretender named Alexander Balas. Jonathan strengthened his hand by an alliance with Balas, even receiving from him appointment as high priest in Jerusalem (I Macc 10:1-21). Such activity, however, was not without risk. Jonathan was finally betrayed and executed by Tryphon, a new pretender to the throne.

Simon made an alliance with Tryphon's rival, Demetrius II, and finally regained the *Acra* (13:51) which had resisted the attacks of Judas (6:18 ff.) and Jonathan (11:20 ff.). This event marked the attainment of independence. Documents came to be dated from "the first year of Simon the high priest" (142 B.C.), the year that saw "the yoke of the heathen . . . taken away from Israel" (13:41 f.). The period of independence that extended from 142-63 B.C. is called the Hasmonean era after Ḥashmōn (Gr. *Asamōnaios*), one of the ancestors of Mattathias (Jos *Ant.* xii.6.1; xiv.16.4).

Interpretations of the Maccabean War

Two partially conflicting interpretations of the Maccabean revolt are represented in I and II Maccabees. Despite their names, these books do not stand in sequence. While I Maccabees covers the whole of the Maccabean period, II Maccabees extends only to Judas' victory over Nicanor in 161 B.C., thus paralleling in time I Macc 1–7.

First Maccabees is a fine piece of historical writing, extant in a Gr. text that is apparently a translation of a Heb. original. The concluding words of the last chapter suggest that the reign of John Hyrcanus may not have been over: "The rest of the acts of John . . . are written in the chronicles of his priesthood . . ." (16:23-24). It is unlikely that the writer would have ignored the achievements of John's later years if he had known of them. In fact, I Maccabees may be the work of a Hasmonean court historian, writing midway through the reign of Hyrcanus. Although his history is remarkably objective for the time, the author's sympathies are clearly with the Maccabees. The trouble that came upon Israel is entirely the fault of the "wicked root" Antiochus Epiphanes (I Macc 1:10) and the lawless men who followed him. It is a war of good against evil, and the family of Mattathias are the divinely chosen instruments to bring about the triumph of good. When two of Judas' lieutenants attack the Gentiles on their own initiative, the author attributes their failure to the fact that "they came not of the seed of those by whose hand deliverance was given unto Israel" (5:62). Simon especially, the founder of the Hasmonean dynasty, is to be obeyed (2:65; 14:41-45). The continuity between the Maccabees and the great biblical heroes of the past is frequently stressed.

It is not certain, however, that the author actually believed "holy history" was being made. He avoids any direct mention of the name of God. He seems to believe that prophecy has ceased (4:46; 14:41), and he records no physical miracles. But these points are not conclusive. The biblical book of Esther also lacks direct references to God, while both in Esther and in I Maccabees the providential working of God is very evident. And even in the biblical period there are indications that certain modes of priestly revelation had ceased (cf. I Macc 4:46 and 14:41; Ezr 2:63 and Neh 7:65). Though there is no evidence that the author of I Maccabees thought he was writing scripture, he did have a firm conviction that the God of the OT was still at work and that the Maccabees were just as certainly His chosen vessels in putting down His enemies as Moses or Joshua had been.

Second Maccabees, though less reliable historically, is of far more theological interest than I Maccabees. Of Alexandrian provenance and uncertain date, it consists of (*a*) two prefixed letters from Jews in Palestine to Jews in Egypt urging the observance of the Feast of the Rededication of the temple (1:1–2:18); (*b*) an epitome of a five-part history by a certain Jason of Cyrene (3:1–15:39; see the author's preface in 2:19-32). The five divisions of Jason's work seem to be marked by summary statements at 3:40; 7:42; 10:9; 13:26; 15:37.

It is not possible to determine which of the theological ideas come from Jason and which from the Epitomist, but the differences from I Maccabees are quickly apparent. The name of God is used frequently, and there are miracles and supernatural manifestations in abundance (e.g., 3:23 ff.; 5:1 ff.; 10:29 f.; 11:8 ff.), as well as a belief in resurrection (7:9 ff., 23; 14:46), and even prayer for the dead (12:43 ff.). Most striking, however, is II Maccabees' distinctive interpretation of the revolt. The cause of Israel's trouble is not simply the wickedness of the Gentiles; it is the sin of God's people themselves. A section unparalleled in I Maccabees tells of a threat to the temple from a certain Heliodorus several years prior to the pogrom of Antiochus IV (II Macc 3:1-39). This attack was crushed by immediate divine intervention (vv. 23 ff.). Then Jason (or the Epitomist) describes in some detail the vicious intrigues and bickering over the high priesthood between Jason and Menelaus (4:7–5:10).

Second Maccabees is probably correct historically as well as theologically in tracing Antiochus' desecration of the temple to these events, also unrecorded in I Maccabees. The author comments: "Antiochus was elated in spirit, and did not perceive that the Lord was angered for a little while because of the sins of those who dwelt in the city . . . . But if it had not happened that they were involved in many sins, this man would have been scourged and turned back from his rash act as soon as he came forward, just as Heliodorus was" (II Macc 5:17-18, RSV). Though the temple was "forsaken in the wrath of the Almighty [it] was restored again in all its glory when the great Lord became reconciled" (5:20, RSV). The sufferings of the people were for chastening, not for destruction such as awaited the heathen (6:12-16). The "reconciliation" came in the expiatory deaths of the martyrs, typified by a mother and her seven sons in chap. 7. The last of the sons tells his tormentors: "We are suffering because of our own sins. And if our living Lord is angry for a little while, to rebuke and discipline us, he will again be reconciled with his own servants" (7:32-33, RSV). He intends, "through me and my brothers to bring to an end the wrath of the Almighty which has justly fallen on our whole nation" (7:38, RSV). Significantly, in chap. 8 Judas begins his resistance, and "the Gentiles could not withstand him, for the wrath of the Lord had turned to mercy" (8:5, RSV).

Second Maccabees is concerned less with the wickedness of the heathen and the glory of the Hasmonean house, and more with the theological problem of sin and its remedy. Though the author at times reassures himself that the "holy war" was necessary (as when he depicts Jeremiah, of all people, presenting to Judas in a dream a "holy sword" to "strike down your adversaries," 15:15 f.), he lacks the militant nationalism of I Maccabees. He probably speaks for the Pharisees (*q.v.*) whose spiritual ancestors, the Chasidim, had broken with the Maccabees, but who later accepted independence as a *fait accompli* and a gift of God. His emphasis upon retribution, resurrection, and angelic appearances would bear this out.

A third interpretation of Maccabean history may be reflected in the Dead Sea Scrolls. Many scholars believe that the Qumran community arose out of a total disillusionment with the Hasmoneans on the part of some of the Chasidim. The increasing involvement of Jonathan and Simon in Seleucid power politics and their usurpation of the high priesthood may have occasioned the withdrawal into the wilderness. In fact, the "wicked priest" of the Qumran literature is most frequently identified either with Simon Maccabeus, John Hyrcanus, or John's successor, Alexander Jannaeus.

Third Maccabees has nothing to do with the Maccabees, but deals with Jews under the Ptolemies of Egypt in the 3rd cen. B.C.

Fourth Maccabees is a Hellenistic Jewish moral discourse on the Maccabean martyrs, to be dated perhaps near the beginning of the Christian era. It develops the concept of the martyrs' death as an atonement.

Bibliography. W. H. Brownlee, "Maccabees, Books of," IDB, III, 201-215. R. H. Charles, ed., *The Apocrypha and Pseudepigrapha,* Oxford: Clarendon Press, 1913, I, 59-154. CornPBE, pp. 370-377.W. R. Farmer, *Maccabees, Zealots, and Josephus,* New York: Columbia Univ. Press, 1956. H.M. Orlinsky, "Maccabees, Maccabean Revolt," IDB, III, 197-201. R. H. Pfeiffer, *History of New Testament Times,* New York: Harper, 1949. S. Tedesche and A. Zeitlin, *The First Book of Maccabees,* New York: Dropsie College, 1950; *The Second Book of Maccabees,* New York: Harper, 1954. C. C. Torrey, *The Apocryphal Literature,* New Haven: Yale, 1945. A. F. Walls, "Maccabees," NBD, pp. 762 ff.

J. R. M.

MACEDONIA (măs'ĕ-dō'nĭ-*á*). Macedonia, a kingdom whose boundaries varied over the centuries, was located at the NW corner of the Aegean. Its capital was Pella, 24 miles NW of Thessalonica. Under Philip II (359-336 B.C.), Macedonia came to include Thrace and to dominate all of Greece. Under Alexander the Great it conquered the entire Persian Empire.

When Macedonia became a Roman province in 148 B.C. and throughout most of the 1st cen. A.D., the boundaries of the territory were quite well fixed. The Macedonia in which Paul ministered had a border line which stretched from a point near the Nestos River in eastern Greece to the Adriatic at approximately the latitude of Tiranë, modern capital of Albania; then S to the northern border of Epirus, which it skirted to its southern end and turned E to the Gulf of Volos (ancient Pagasaeus). Thus it may be seen that the province included not only most of the northern part of modern Greece, but also portions of Bulgaria and Yugoslavia and about half of Albania. Macedonia was an important land route between Asia and the W. Cities of this area included in the Pauline itinerary were Neapolis, Philippi, Amphipolis, Apollonia, Thessalonica (the capital), and Berea.

H. F. V.

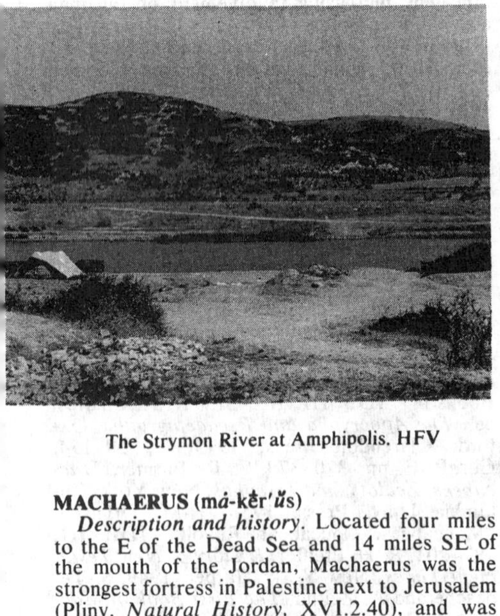

The Strymon River at Amphipolis. HFV

MACHAERUS (**mȧ-kẽr'ŭs**)

Description and history. Located four miles to the E of the Dead Sea and 14 miles SE of the mouth of the Jordan, Machaerus was the strongest fortress in Palestine next to Jerusalem (Pliny, *Natural History,* XVI.2.40), and was the scene of the imprisonment and execution of John the Baptist, according to Josephus (*Ant.* xviii.5.2). The citadel was built by Alexander Jannaeus on a natural ridge that rises about 3,500 feet above the Dead Sea and is inaccessible on three sides (Jos *Wars* vii.6.1 ff.). After it was destroyed by Gabinius, Herod the Great restored it and built a magnificent palace there. As Machaerus is not mentioned by name in the Gospels, the presence of the nobles from Galilee (Mk 6:21) has caused some to think that Herod's birthday party was held at Tiberias in Galilee and not at Machaerus (cf.,

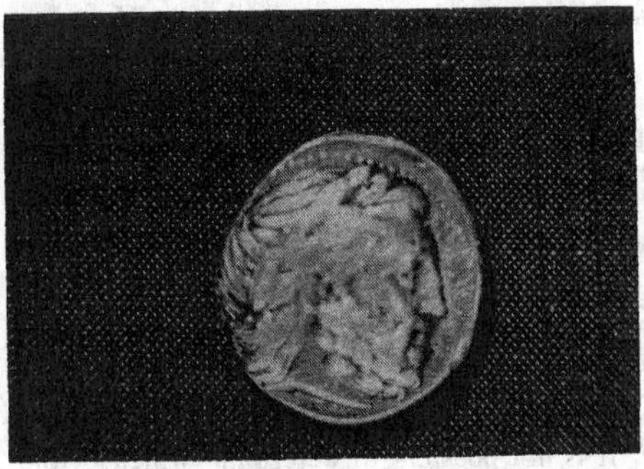

Coin of Philip II of Macedon. Gleason Archer, photo by W. LaSor

however, A. H. M'Neile, *The Gospel According to St. Matthew,* p. 210).

During the Jewish-Roman War, Machaerus along with Herodium and Masada (*q.v.*) continued to resist even after the fall of Jerusalem. The Jewish defenders finally surrendered (*c.* A.D. 72) because they could not bear to see their heroic compatriot named Eleazar crucified before them by the besieging Romans (Jos *Wars* vii.6.4).

Apart from the disputed mention of *Makwar* in rabbinic literature, Machaerus was forgotten until V. J. Seetzen rediscovered it in 1907. The ancient name is preserved in the village of Mukâwer, half a mile E of the summit, called today Qaṣr el-Mishneqeh.

For an early description of the site, see H. B. Tristram, *The Land of Moab* (New York: Harper, 1873, pp. 271 f.; plan, p. 274). For a photograph of Machaerus see Denis Baly, *The Geography of the Bible* (New York: Harper, 1957, p. 251).

E. M. Y.

Excavations. In June, 1968, Jerry Vardaman began archaeological work at Machaerus, sponsored by the Antiquities Department of Jordan and the Southern Baptist Theological Seminary. The excavations concentrated on the very summit of the fortress. The expedition surveyed the fortress and noted traces of the circumvallation wall, the Roman camps, and the *agger* (siege ramp) built by the Tenth Legion under Sextus Lucilius Bassus.

An aqueduct system was discovered, including large reservoirs on top of the mountain and the lower slopes (SW and NE) of the fortress as well. The water impounded in the reservoirs on the lower slopes had first been filtered in a sediment basin located on a hill SE of Machaerus. From there it flowed in a 600-foot-long aqueduct, constructed 60 feet higher than the saddle which linked these two points together. Thus, for the first time since Josephus, who alludes briefly to these details, the method of supplying the fortress with water and of its storage became clear.

Josephus furthermore described the Zealot occupation of Machaerus, and it is significant that 19 ostraca (written in Gr., Aram., Heb. or Latin) were discovered, many of which mention the personal names of the Zealots who defended the mountain against Bassus. The names of these Zealots (e.g., John, Zebedee, Simeon, Joseph, Isaac, Eleazar and Shallum) harmonize beautifully with personal names of the Jews known from the 1st cen. A.D. from such sources as Josephus, papyri, the NT, ossuaries, etc.

One text refers to "[Beth-]Peor," the first time that such epigraphical documentation concerning this biblical site has been discovered. Another document mentions an "Eleazar (=Lazarus) son of Joseph," but it cannot be certain whether this person is the Eleazar whose capture was referred to by Josephus. One abbreviated text seems to refer to the "(Tenth?) Legion," which, along with other traces discovered of the Roman offensive (including a fire layer all over the top of the mountain and many ballistic missiles, some of which weighed as much as nine pounds), gives clear evidence that Josephus' statements concerning the fall of the fortress to Bassus were highly accurate.

Such striking confirmation of Josephus' account of Machaerus' capture by Bassus certainly adds weight to his record of John's imprisonment and death at this isolated place. Josephus was obviously drawing from information about the history of Machaerus entirely independent of the NT authors. Therefore I am convinced that Josephus' references to the Baptist are basically genuine, and that the Gospel narratives of John's imprisonment and death can be reconciled with Josephus' records, whose historical sources were practically contemporaneous with the NT records.

E. J. V.

MACHBANAI (măk'bá-nī). One of the mighty men of war from the tribe of Gad who joined David at Ziklag while David was in exile in Philistine territory (*c.* 1015 B.C.), before he became king at Hebron (see I Chr 12:13). ASV and RSV spell the name Machbannai.

MACHBENAH (măk-bē'ná). Son of Sheva, named in the genealogical list of Judah and more particularly of the family of Caleb (I Chr 2:49). Some identify the name as a place rather than a person, and observe that it is from the same root as Cabbon (Josh 15:40), a town near Eglon, possibly modern Khirbet Hebrah.

MACHI (mā'kī). The father of Geuel, whom Moses appointed to represent the tribe of Gad to spy out the land of Canaan before the Hebrews entered in force (Num 13:15). He was among the majority of ten who advised against trying to enter because of the power of the inhabitants and their fortifications (*c.*1440 B.C.). See Num 13:26–33.

MACHIR (mā'kĭr)

1. The oldest grandson of Joseph and Asenath, the son of Manasseh and the Syrian concubine (I Chr 7:14; Gen 50:23). The name is always connected with the idea of strength and daring and wild exploits. Machir's descendants became strong fighters and ferocious leaders among the clans of Manasseh. They lived on both sides of the Jordan and seemed to constitute a strong unit in the northern confederacy. In the war with Jabin, the sons of Machir became valiant fighters and distinguished themselves for their bravery and courage under fire (Jud 5:14). It is possible that Machir's descendants moved across the river to become the dominant power in Gilead (Num 32:39–40; I Chr 2:21–23). In fact, the record speaks of Machir as being the father of Gilead (Num 26:29; I Chr 7:14*b*). *See* Machirites; Gilead; Manasseh.

2. Another Machir is mentioned in David's day as a loyal follower who brought food and refreshment to the old king when he was pursued by Absalom (II Sam 17:27–29). His home was at Lo-debar near Mahanaim (II Sam 9:4–5).

K. M. Y.

MACHIRITES (mā'ká-rīts). The warlike descendants of Machir, the eldest son of Manasseh, Joseph's son. These Machirites were powerful warriors who possessed qualities that helped them overrun neighboring tribes and rule peoples in wide areas. They formed the aggressive and leading clan in Joseph's line. Since they were warlike men, they were successful in subduing and holding the territory of Gilead and Bashan (Josh 17:1). Reuben and Gad also had been given that good grazing land (Josh 12:6; 13:15–31; cf. Deut 3:15–17) and had sought to hold it for themselves. Machir's men defeated them and the Amorites, for they had taken on something of the spirit that characterized their father. The Machirites were invincible and for generations held sway in SE Palestine. In Num 26:29 it is recorded that "Machir begat Gilead." In other passages it is said that the children of Machir "went to Gilead, and took it, and dispossessed the Amorite which was in it. And Moses gave Gilead unto Machir the son of Manasseh; and he dwelt therein" (Num 32:39–40; cf. Josh 17:1, 3; I Chr 2:21, 23; 7:14–17; Deut 3:15; Josh 13:31). The descendants of Machir became the dominant Manassite family. *See* Machir.

K. M. Y.

MACHNADEBAI (măk-năd'ĕ-bī). A son of Bani, who heeded the call of Ezra to put away his non-Jewish wife during the extensive effort of Ezra (458–457 B.C.) to prevent the Jews who had returned from Captivity from being engulfed by a pagan and non-Jewish population (Ezr 10:40).

MACHPELAH (măk-pē'lá). A field with trees and a cave near Mamre, purchased by Abra-

The mosque at Hebron over the traditional site of the cave of Machpelah. HFV

ham from Ephron, a Hittite, as a burial place for his wife Sarah (Gen 23:9, 17,19). It is now located in the center of the modern city of Hebron. Abraham was buried here by his sons Isaac and Ishmael (Gen 25:9–10). The cave was once covered by a Christian church but it was later converted into a mosque by the Muslims. Arab control of this area long made it impossible for Christians to visit this ancient shrine. This restriction was finally broken when, on April 7, 1862, the Prince of Wales was permitted to visit what is now known as the Mosque of the Patriarchs.

The mosque is surrounded by an ancient wall containing masonry typical of that which remains around the temple area in Jerusalem from the period of Herod the Great. Inside the mosque near the NW side is a round opening in the floor which leads to the cave below where it is said the patriarchs are buried. Cenotaphs in honor of those buried below (Abraham, Sarah, Isaac, Rebekah, Leah, Jacob, Gen 49:31) have been erected on the floor of this mosque. One of these is dedicated to Joseph, although he was buried at Shechem (Josh 24:32).

H. A. Han.

MAD. *See* Madness.

MADAI (mā'dī). Third son of Japheth (Gen 10:2; I Chr 1:5). The descendants of Madai were the Medes, an Aryan people, first mentioned by Shalmaneser III *c.* 886 B.C. Adad-Nirari III (*c.* 800 B.C.), Tiglath-pileser III (743 B.C.) and Sargon II (716 B.C.) conquered their land. Allied with the Babylonians, led by Nabopolassar, they helped destroy Assyria in 612 B.C. They maintained their empire to the E of Babylonia during the days of Nebuchadnezzar (605–561 B.C.) and became part of the Persian Empire after the rise of Cyrus the Great in 559 B.C. *See* Elam (Country); Media.

MADIAN. *See* Midian.

MADMANNAH (măd-măn'*ȧ*). A Calebite town in the S of Judah near Ziklag (Josh 15:31; I Chr 2:49), perhaps identical with Beth-marcaboth (Josh 19:5). It is probably modern Umm Deimneh *c.* ten miles NE of Beer-sheba.

MADMEN (măd'mĕn). A town in Moab whose destruction was foretold by Jeremiah (Jer 48:2). There may be a word play here giving the idea "thou city of silence [Heb. *madmēn*]shalt be brought to silence [from *dāmam,* to be silent]." It has been tentatively identified with Khirbet Dimneh, eight miles N of Kerak.

MADMENAH (măd-mē'n*ȧ*). A town N of Jerusalem, mentioned only in Isaiah's description of the Assyrian advance on Jerusalem (Isa 10:31). The site is unknown.

MADNESS. In addition to its common biblical usage for lunacy, the concept of madness had a variety of applications. It was frequently used of temporary conditions or acts to which one would hardly apply the term except in some colloquial sense, e.g., the practical joker of Prov 26:18; the fury of the wicked against the good (Ps 102:8). Mental disease of a chronic nature was not uncommon in the ancient Near East, though comparatively few instances of insanity are recorded in Scripture. *See* Diseases.

In antiquity the madman was held in universal dread, for his insanity was believed to be the result of special contact with a deity, generally through demon possession. As a consequence no one interfered with him and all contact was carefully avoided, as reflected in the attitude of Achish toward David's feigned madness (I Sam 21:12–15). Madness was regarded as divine judgment meted out to those who disobeyed God's law (Deut 28:28). It was also attributed to a spirit sent by God (I Sam 16:14; 18:11; 20:30–34; 28:20) and accompanied demon possession (Lk 8:2, 29–30). Classic examples of madness in Scripture are Saul and Nebuchadnezzar (*q.v.*). *See* Demonology.

H. D. F.

MADON (mā'dŏn). A royal city of the Canaanites in the N whose king Jobab was confederate with Jabin, king of Hazor. Both kings were killed in the battle with Joshua at the waters of Merom (Josh 11:1; 12:19). It has been identified with Qarn Ḥaṭṭin ("the horns of Hattin") on the heights five miles NW of Tiberias. The LXX, however, has *Marrōn,* which may rather indicate that Merom (*q.v.*) is meant.

MAGADAN. *See* Magdala.

MAGBISH (măg'bĭsh). An unidentified town in Judah, 156 inhabitants of which are said to have returned from Exile with Zerubbabel (Ezr 2:30). Some think, however, the name is that of a man and refers to a family of returning exiles.

MAGDALA (măg'd*ȧ*-l*ȧ*), **MAGDALENE** (măg'd*ȧ*-lēn). A town mentioned only once in the

NT, in Mt 15:39 (KJV) where the important Gr. MSS Aleph, B, and D and most of the ancient versions have Magadan (ASV, RSV, NASB) or an alternate spelling. The parallel passage in Mk 8:10 calls the place Dalmanutha (*q.v.*). Magadan seems to have been the name of the *locality* or "region" (RSV) on the W shore of the Sea of Galilee to which Jesus crossed after feeding the 4,000, and it probably included the town of Magdala.

Magdala, whose Gr. name was Taricheae, stood on the W shore of the lake at the S end of the fertile Plain of Gennesaret, *c.* three and a half miles NNW of Tiberias. Its site is presently known as Mejdel, strategically located at the junction of the road along the lake from Tiberias and the road from Nazareth coming down through the hills following the Valley of Robbers. The name Magdala derives from the Heb. *migdal,* "tower." Apparently the town was so named because it once served as a fort. In the Talmud the city is called Migdal Nunya, "fish tower" (Pesahim 46*a*). Taricheae was a flourishing city in the 1st cen. A.D., an important fishing, fish-curing, ship-building, and trading center (Jos *Wars* ii.21.3–9; iii.9.7–10.5). The majority of its population was Gentile, as evidenced by the presence of a hippodrome or stadium (Jos *Wars* ii.21.3; iii.10.10). During the Jewish revolt against the Romans, Josephus strongly fortified the city on its landward sides.

"Magdalene," a person from Magdala, is the frequent term in the Gospels used to designate one of the women of Galilee who followed Jesus (Mt 27:56,61; 28:1; Mk 15:40, 47; 16:1; Lk 8:2; 24:10; Jn 19:25; 20:1, 18). *See* Mary 2.

J. R.

Ruins on the site of Magdala. HFV

MAGDIEL (măg'dĭ-ĕl). The name of a chief or duke of Edom, descended from Esau (Gen 36:43; I Chr 1:54).

MAGI (mā'jī). A class of learned men originating in Persia or Babylonia, who were experts in the lore and science of their day and in the interpretation of dreams. Because they dealt with occult learning, their name gained the connotation of the modern term "magician." They were not primarily tricksters. Herodotus, an early Gr. historian, states that they were a class or caste of the Medes, who exercised priestly functions, and who were renowned for their learning. They are included among the wise men of Babylon in the LXX translation of Dan 2:2, 10, where the English parallel is "enchanters" (ASV, RSV).

The title became a general term descriptive of all who professedly possessed extraordinary or occult knowledge. In the book of Acts it is applied to Simon in Samaria (Acts 8:9–24), who sought to purchase from Peter the power of working miracles, and to Elymas, a Jew at Paphos in Cyprus, who endeavored to win the patronage of the Roman proconsul, Sergius Paulus (Acts 13:6–11). Not all magi were charlatans, for in several instances writers of antiquity, like Cicero (*On Divination* I . 91) and Philo of Alexandria (*Every Good Man Is Free* 74), indicate that they were truly scientific in temper and genuinely learned. *See* Magic, Magician.

The Magi connected with Matthew's account of the birth of Jesus were probably strangers from Mesopotamia or Arabia who knew the OT predictions of a coming Messiah, and who watched the skies for some astral phenomena that would foreshadow His advent. Possibly they were aware of Balaam's prophecy: "I see him, but not now; I behold him, but not nigh: there shall come forth a star out of Jacob, and a scepter shall rise out of Israel, and shall smite through the corners of Moab, and break down all the sons of tumult" (Num 24:17, ASV), which they applied literally to the appearance of a special star to herald the birth of a king. It is more likely, however, that this interpretation arose later among Christians rather than with the Magi.

The consternation which the visit of the Magi produced in Jerusalem may be explained by the fact that Parthia, which controlled the East in that day, was Rome's chief rival. Between Rome and Parthia war was constantly imminent, and on at least two occasions the Parthian archers had crushed Roman invasions. Herod, as king of Judea, a buffer state on the borders of Rome and Parthia, had double cause to fear when delegates from the East came asking, "Where is he that is born King of the Jews?" (Mt 2:2). To Herod their question would imply a successor not of his own line who would deprive his sons of their heritage, and who might seek a Parthian rather than a Roman alliance. Herod, an Idumean by birth, knew that he was hated by the Jews, and he feared that if they had a king they might initiate a revolution with the support of Parthia. The Magi had political as well as academic influence, and may even have been the official emissaries of the Parthian court to investigate the advent of a new Jewish power.

The legend that the Magi were three kings named Caspar, Melchior, and Balthazar, whose mummified bodies were preserved in Constantinople until they were transferred to Cologne Cathedral, is baseless. Matthew states that they returned to their own country and tells nothing of their subsequent fate. In the literature of the Gospels they represent the reaction of the learned pagan class to Jesus as the shepherds of Luke represent the reaction of the Judean peasantry. Although numerous legends have grown around the Magi, their visit was undoubtedly historical.

See Astronomy; Star.

M. C. T.

MAGIC, MAGICIAN. These words come from the name of a priestly class in ancient Media, "the Magi" or "wise men" (Mt 2:1, 7), who were not only sacrificial priests but men who interpreted the meaning for human affairs of heavenly phenomena and dreams. *See* Magi.

Magic, divination, sorcery, enchantment, and witchcraft are all connected with belief in superhuman or occult powers, and are ways by which men have sought to obtain knowledge of the future and assistance in the affairs of life, either benefit to themselves or harm to their enemies.

Classes of professional diviners and magicians abounded in Egypt (Gen 41:8, 24; Ex 7:11, 22; 8:7, 18-19; 9:11) and in Babylon (Dan 1:20; 2:2, 10, 27; 4:7, 9; 5:11). Magic was also practiced by the Canaanites and other peoples, as is indicated by wands, amulets (Isa 3:20, RSV), and other objects common to the magical arts, found in Palestinian excavations. Ezekiel reports of women "who sew magic bands upon all wrists, and make veils for the heads of persons of every stature, in the hunt for souls" (13:18, RSV). There were also snake charmers (Ps 58:4-5; Eccl 10:11; Jer 8:17) as well as spiritist mediums who sought to charm familiar spirits (Isa 19:3; cf. 8:19). *See* Astronomy; Belomancy; Demonology; Divination; Enchantment; Familiar Spirit; Necromancer; Sorcerer; Teraphim.

The attitude of the Bible toward magic is distinctly hostile (Deut 18:9-14; II Kgs 21:6; Acts 8:9-24; 13:6-12). Babylon was mocked for her trust in her sorceries and magical spells or enchantments (Isa 47:9, 12-13). Jewish magicians or sorcerers, such as Simon (Acts 8) and Elymas (Acts 13), were considered to be in the bondage of iniquity and an instrument of the devil.

In Ephesus as a result of Paul's ministry of exorcism "many of those who practiced magic brought their books together and began burning them in the sight of all" (Acts 19:19, NASB). The value of their books of magical incantations was extremely high, 50,000 pieces of silver, probably equivalent to that many days' wages. *See* Curious Arts.

Paul lists *pharmakeia,* "magic," "sorcery" (RSV, NASB), or "witchcraft" (KJV), immediately after idolatry in Gal 5:20, thus classing it among the chief sins of the flesh. Those who continue in sorcery will have their end in the lake of fire (Rev 9:21; 21:8; 22:15).

Bibliography. CornPBE, "Magic, Divination and Superstition," pp. 503-509. G. Delling, "*Magos,*" TDNT, IV, 356-359. Kurt E. Koch, *Christian Counseling and Occultism,* Grand Rapids: Kregel, 1965. Merrill F. Unger, *Biblical Demonology,* 2nd ed., Wheaton: Van Kampen Press, 1953. J. Stafford Wright and K. A. Kitchen, "Magic and Sorcery," NBD, pp. 766-771. Roy B. Zuck, "The Practice of Witchcraft in the Scriptures," BS, CXXVIII (1971), 352-360.

S. F. B. and J. R.

MAGISTRATE. The rendering of a variety of Heb. and Gr. terms in the KJV which refer to a public civil official.

Behind its use in Jud 18:7 stands a somewhat obscure phrase probably meaning "possessing authority" (ASV). In Ezr 7:25 "magistrates" (also RSV) translates a word (*shāpeṭîn*) normally rendered "judges." It is also the RSV rendering (Dan 3:2-3) of *tiptāyē',* KJV "sheriffs."

In Lk 12:11 "magistrates" (RSV "rulers") represents the general Gr. word (*archē*) for ruling powers whether human (Tit 3:1) or divine and demonic (Rom 8:38; Eph 3:10; Col 2:10). Similarly at Lk 12:58 "magistrate" (also RSV) translates the Gr. *archōn* (one who rules), a word used for various types of officials; e.g., civil judges (Acts 16:19); a ruler of the synagogue (Lk 8:41); influential Jews (Lk 14:1; 24:20); the high priest (Acts 23:5). Christ is so designated (Rev 1:5), translated "prince" in KJV, and likewise Satan (Mt 9:34). The same root is involved with Tit 3:1 where *peitharchein* (KJV "to obey magistrates") would better be translated simply "to be obedient" (Arndt, p. 644).

The principal use of "magistrates" in the KJV and the RSV is in Acts 16 for *stratēgoi,* also designated "rulers" (*archontas*) in 16:19. The Gr. term *stratēgos* more properly designates the "commander of an army" but in the NT it is limited to civic officials. In Philippi (Acts 16:20, 22, 35, 36, 38) these were the highest officials of the Roman colony and possessed the power to administer justice in lesser cases. They were usually two in number, more exactly called in Latin *duumviri* or *praetores.*

F. G. C.

MAGNIFICAT. *See* Poetry.

MAGOG (mā'gŏg). A descendant of Japheth (Gen 10:2; I Chr 1:5). According to Ezk 38:2 a people whose territory will be ruled in a future time by Gog (*q.v.*); literally 38:2 reads, "set your face toward Gog of the land of the Magog . . ." Josephus (*Ant.* i.6.1) identified Magog as the Scythians, a savage, wandering people whom Herodotus mentioned as living N of the Crimea. Gog will lead the northern hordes in an invasion of Israel (Ezk 38:8-12), but the Lord will turn back his armies (39:2) and will send a hail of fire on the land of Magog and the surrounding areas (39:6). *See also* Rosh.

After the millennial reign of Christ Satan will be released from imprisonment in the abyss. The move of his rapidly gathered armies to besiege "the beloved city," and the consequent supernatural destruction by fire, are likened to the episode of Gog and Magog (Rev 20:7-9).

MAGOR-MISSABIB (mā'gŏr-mĭs'ȧ-bĭb). A name meaning "terror on every side," given by Jeremiah to Pashhur, son of Immer, a temple official and priest, who caused Jeremiah to be beaten and put in the stocks after the prophet had predicted the fall of Jerusalem. Pashhur, whose name means "largeness on every side," was to become "terror on every side" (Jer 20:1-6). The same expression is used in several other passages, though not as a proper name (Ps 31:13; Jer 6:25; 20:10; 46:5; 49:29; Lam 2:22).

MAGPIASH (măg'pĭ-ăsh). One of the chiefs of the people who sealed the covenant with Nehemiah (Neh 10:20).

MAHALAH. *See* Mahlah.

MAHALALEEL (mȧ-hăl'ȧ-lēl)

1. An early patriarch in the line of Seth, apparently the great-grandson of Seth (Gen 5:12-17; I Chr 1:2; Lk 3:37).

2. Ancestor of Athaiah, one of the descendants of Judah who dwelt in Jerusalem after the return from Exile (Neh 11:4).

MAHALATH (mā'ȧ-lăth)

1. One of the wives of Esau and daughter of Ishmael (Gen 28:9), called Basemath in Gen 36:3.

2. One of the 18 wives of Rehoboam and granddaughter of David (II Chr 11:18).

3. A musical term found in the titles of Ps 53 and Ps 88, the meaning of which is uncertain.

MAHALI. *See* Mahli.

MAHANAIM (mā'ȧ-nā'ȧm). The name given by Jacob to the place where he saw the angels of God (Gen 32:1-2). It probably lay to the S of the Jabbok, a little S of the border between Gad and Manasseh (Josh 13:26, 30; 21:38), several miles S of Peniel (Penuel, Gen 32:22-31), at Tell el-Hajjaj on a height overlooking the Jordan Valley. The exact location, however, is unknown. Joshua appointed it as a residence for some of the Merarite Levites (Josh 21:34-38; I Chr 6:77-80). After the death of Saul, Mahanaim became the seat of the brief reign of his son Ishbosheth (II Sam 2:8, 12, 29). David fled here from the revolt of Absalom (II Sam 17:24, 27; 19:32; I Kgs 2:8). It is last mentioned as the residence of the seventh commissary officer of King Solomon (I Kgs 4:14).

MAHANEH-DAN (mā'ȧ-nĕ-dăn'). "Camp of Dan." An unidentified place behind, i.e., W, of Kirjath-jearim which the 600 Danites who camped there before setting out for Laish, named (Jud 18:12). Here also, between Zorah and Eshtaol, the Spirit of the Lord began to move Samson (Jud 13:25). This may have been Samson's burial site (Jud 16:31).

MAHARAI (mā'ȧ-rī). One of David's "mighty men" (II Sam 23:28; I Chr 11:30). He was one of the 12 monthly captains in David's reign, serving in the tenth month (I Chr 27:13). He was one of the family of Zerah, and came from Netophah in Judah.

MAHATH (mā'hăth)

1. A descendant of Kohath the son of Levi and an ancestor of Samuel the prophet, and of Heman, a Levitical singer in the time of David (I Chr 6:35).

2. A Levite and an overseer of the tithes and dedicated things in the temple in the reign of Hezekiah (II Chr 31:13). Probably he should be identified with Mahath in II Chr 29:12, the son of Amasai, a descendant of Kohath, since both references are to the time of Hezekiah.

MAHAVITE (mā'ȧ-vīt). The designation given to Eliel, one of David's mighty men (I Chr 11:46), perhaps to distinguish him from the Eliel in the following verse. The term is plural in Heb., and unknown in meaning.

MAHAZIOTH (mȧ-hā'zĭ-ŏth). One of the 14 sons of Heman set over the service of song in David's reign and leader of the 23rd course of the temple singers (I Chr 25:4, 30).

MAHER-SHALAL-HASHBAZ (mā'ĕr-shăl'ăl-hăsh'băz). A symbolic name meaning "Swift is the booty, speedy is the prey," given to one of Isaiah's sons to signify the speedy destruction of the combined power of Rezin of Damascus and Pekah of Samaria by the king of Assyria (Isa 8:3-4). Isaiah had been directed to display these words on a public tablet and have them witnessed several months before he was told to give them as a name to his second son (Isa 8:1-2), thus providing double attestation to the certainty of the doom of Judah's two enemies.

MAHLAH (mä'lȧ)

1. The eldest of five daughters of Zelophehad. Because her father, a descendant of Joseph's son Manasseh, had no sons, she and her sisters successfully claimed their father's inheritance by marrying their uncles' sons (Num 26:33; 27:1; 36:11).

2. Another descendant of Manasseh whose mother's name was Hammolecheth (I Chr 7:18, Mahalah).

MAHLI (mä'lī)

1. A son of Merari and grandson of Levi (Ex 6:19; Num 3:20; I Chr 6:19, 29; 23:21; 24:26; Ezr 8:18). He founded a tribal family (Num 3:33; 26:58). His grandsons married their cousins, apparently to prevent the extinction of any of the family name (I Chr 23:22).

2. A son of Mushi, Mahli's brother, bears the same name (I Chr 6:47; 23:23; 24:30).

MAHLITES (mä'līts). Descendants of Mahli (*q.v.*), a son of Merari (Num 3:33; 26:58).

MAHLON (mä'lŏn). Elder son of Elimelech and Naomi (Ruth 1:2). He was the first husband of Ruth the Moabitess and died in Moab childless (Ruth 1:5; 4:9-10).

MAHOL (mā'hŏl). The father of three men, Heman, Chalcol, and Darda, noted for their wisdom, though surpassed in this respect by Solomon (I Kgs 4:31). Some describe the wise men mentioned above as "sons of dance," since the word *māḥôl* is found in Ps 149:3; 150:4, where it is translated "dance." In this case their wisdom may have consisted primarily in their skill to compose songs accompanied by dance. According to the JerusB they may have acted as cantors or leaders of the sacred chants.

MAID, MAIDEN. The KJV translates several Heb. and Gr. words by "maid" or "maiden," in most cases the word favoring a more specific idea than the mere feminine gender.

1. Heb. *'āmâ* conveys the idea of servitude, and thus is rendered "handmaid" or "maidservant" in Gen 20:17; Ex 20:10; Deut 5:14; Jud 19:19.

2. Heb. *bᵉthûlâ* carries the idea of the bloom of womanhood, sexual ripeness or maturity which usually implies virginity (cf. *bᵉthûlîm* which signifies "tokens of virginity"), and thus is rendered "maid," "virgin" (Gen 24:16; Ex 22:16; Deut 22:28; Jud 21:12). But in Joel 1:8 the Heb. word refers to a young widow; and figuratively the nation of Israel was often referred to as the "virgin" or "virgin daughter" (Isa 23:12; 37:22; Jer 14:17; Amos 5:2), yet guilty of spiritual adultery (Jer 18:13; 23:14). The word is even applied to the "virgin daughter of Babylon" (Isa 47:1).

3. Heb. *na'ărâ* (feminine of the common *na'ar*, "boy") covers merely the generic idea of the feminine, and thus is rendered simply "maid" or "maiden" (Ex 2:5; Ruth 2:8; I Sam 9:11; II Kgs 5:2).

4. Heb. *'almâ* signifies the idea of sexual chastity and virginity, of one not married (cf. 2 above), and is rendered "maid" in Ex 2:8 and Prov 30:19, but (rightly) "virgin" in Gen 24:43; Song 1:3; 6:8; Isa 7:14. *See* Virgin.

5. Heb. *hipḥâ* carries, like 1 above, the idea of servitude, and thus is rendered "maid," "handmaid," and "maidservant" in many contexts (Gen 16:2; 24:35; 33:6; Ps 123:2; Eccl 2:7).

6. Gr. *doulê* conveys the idea of servitude, and thus is rendered "handmaiden" in Lk 1:38, 48; Acts 2:18.

7. Gr. *korasion* refers to a young woman, and thus is rendered "maid" in Mt 9:24-25 and "damsel" in Mt 14:11; Mk 5:42; 6:22, 28.

8. Gr. *pais* (with feminine article) signifies basically the feminine gender and is rendered "maid, maiden" (Lk 8:51, 54).

9. Gr. *paidiskê* is the diminutive of 3 above and is rendered "maid" in Mk 14:66, 69; Lk 12:45; 22:56.

R. L. R.

MAIL, COAT OF. *See* Armor.

MAIMED. *See* Diseases.

MAINSAIL. *See* Ship.

MAKAZ (mā'kăz). One of the towns in the NW of Judah from which Ben-deker, an officer of Solomon, drew supplies to provide victuals for the king and his household one month in the year (I Kgs 4:9). It has tentatively been identified with Khirbet el-Mukheizin, six miles NW of Beth-shemesh, two and a half miles S of Gezer.

MAKHELOTH (măk-hē'lŏth). An unidentified encampment of the Israelites in the wilderness between Sinai and Kadesh-barnea, their 21st station from Egypt (Num 33:25-26).

MAKKEDAH (mȧ-kē'dȧ). A Canaanite royal city which lay in the Shephelah of Judah (Josh 15:41) near Azekah (Josh 10:10), *c.* 20 miles SW of Jerusalem. It is listed by Thutmose III among his captured cities (ANET, p. 243) and probably by Shishak. Joshua captured the city and utterly destroyed its inhabitants, doing to the king as he had done to the king of Jericho (Josh 10:28; 12:16). Here the five kings of the Amorites fled from Joshua and sought refuge in the cave of Makkedah, where at Joshua's command they were blocked in with great stones. Later, the royal prisoners were brought out, slain, hanged on the trees until sunset, and then cast back into the cave which was again blocked up with stones (Josh 10:16-27). The site of Makkedah is uncertain, but that of Khirbet el-Kheishum, two miles N of Azekah, accords well with the location stated by Eusebius. Alternate suggestions are the nearby Tell Maqdûm, and Tell es-Safi, which has been identified by others with Libnah or Gath seven miles farther W.

S. F. B.

MAKTESH (măk'tĕsh). A locality in Jerusalem where foreign merchants congregated, presumably so named (*maktesh* means "mortar, trough") because it was basin-shaped (Zeph 1:11). It is mentioned in connection with the Second Quarter (Heb. *mishneh*) and the Fish Gate (v. 10), both W of the temple area. Most authorities think that it refers to a part of the Tyropoeon Valley where the silver traders and silversmiths conducted their business. Because of the high value of silver, very likely their shops were inside the walls of the city, not outside the Fish Gate (in the area of the present Damascus Gate) as some have supposed.

MALACHI (măl'*ȧ*-kī). This is the last of the Heb. prophets, as well as the last book of the English OT. The prophecy represents a call to Israel for repentance and obedience, with a stern warning of judgment on the disobedient and rebellious. The book places considerable emphasis on the "day of the Lord" (3:2, 17; 4:1, 3, 5), closing the OT period with a final promise of the advent of the Messiah.

Author

The name Malachi appears nowhere else in Scripture, thereby leading critical scholars to surmise that the term *mal'ākî*, which in Heb. means "my angel or messenger," is an appellative and not a proper name (cf. 3:1), and the book an anonymous prophecy. This theory, as well as the conjecture by the Targum that Malachi is a pseudonym for Ezra, is weakened by the fact that this would constitute the only exception in the prophetic literature, since every other prophetic book bears the author's name to authenticate it. No doubt Malachi is a contraction from *mal'ākîyâh*, "messenger of Yahweh," just as the name Abi represents a contracted form of Abijah.

Malachi's style is direct and concise. A marked characteristic is his frequent use of the rhetorical question and answer (e.g., 1:6-7; 3:7-8). The unity of the book has never been seriously questioned, although some critics, without any justification, have conjectured slight editorial additions (viz., 2:7, 11-12; 4:4-6).

Date

On the basis of internal evidence, the book is clearly post-Exilic. The Jews were under a Persian governor (1:8); the temple had been rebuilt and Levitical worship restored (1:6 ff.; 2:1 ff.; 3:1, 8, 10); and the moral and religious offenses which were condemned, as well as the reforms urged, portray the period of Ezra-Nehemiah. A date between the coming of Ezra (457 B.C.) and before the second visit of Nehemiah (432 B.C.) is most likely.

Outline

I. God's Love for Israel, 1:1-5
II. Denunciation of Priests, 1:6–2:9
III. Denunciation of Ungodly Divorces and Marriages, 2:10-16
IV. God's Coming Judgment, 2:17–3:18
V. The Day of the Lord, 4:1-6

Content

Three chapters in the Heb. Bible are divided into four in the LXX and Vulg. versions, and hence in the English. The book reflects a dismal scene of creeping spiritual decay. It opens with a declaration of God's love for Israel, demonstrated in His electing choice of Jacob over Esau (1:1-5). However, Israel has been unfaithful in her response, while the priests have been foremost in offending the Lord by polluting His altar and offering unworthy sacrifices (1:6–2:4). Furthermore, they have led the people astray by giving faulty instruction in the law and by perverting justice (2:5-9). The men were guilty of profaning the Mosaic covenant by divorcing their wives and marrying idolatrous heathen (2:10-16).

Chap. 3 (which really begins with the charge and questions of 2:17) presents God as coming in judgment. The people have been complacent in their sins, which included skepticism, complaint, and neglect of tithes and offerings. The Lord will send His messenger to prepare His way before Him, after which He will come suddenly and unexpectedly to His temple. He will punish the wicked and execute swift judgment on transgressors, sparing only those written in "the book of remembrance," and thereby He will purge His land. The prophet concludes with a final admonition to repentance and obedience to the law before the coming of the great and terrible day of the Lord in which the wicked will be consumed as stubble but the righteous will be delivered (chap. 4).

H. E. Fr.

MALCHAM (măl'kăm)

1. A Benjamite, one of the sons of Shaharaim by his wife Hodesh (I Chr 8:9).

2. A Heb. form which may mean "their king" and is so translated in KJV of Amos 1:15; Jer 49:1,3. In Jer 49:3 (NASB) it evidently refers to a false god, as it does in Zeph 1:5. Malcham was a god of the Moabites and Ammonites, possibly identical with Molech. *See* Gods, False.

MALCHIAH (măl-kī'*ȧ*), **MALCHIJAH** (măl-kī'j*ȧ*)

1. A Levite, descendant of Gershom, ancestor of the singer Asaph (I Chr 6:40).

2. A priest, father of Pashur who was prominent in the days of Jeremiah. His descendants returned to Jerusalem in the days of Nehemiah (Jer 21:1, KJV Melchiah (*q.v.*); 38:1; Neh 11:12; I Chr 9:12).

3. A priest in the time of David, head of the fifth course (I Chr 24:9).

4. An Israelite, descendant of Parosh, in the time of Ezra who put away his Gentile wife (Ezra 10:25).

5. Another descendant of Parosh who divorced his Gentile wife (Ezr 10:25).

6. A son of Harim who helped Nehemiah with the rebuilding of the wall, and also put away his Gentile wife (Ezr 10:31; Neh 3:11).

7. The son of Rechab, ruler of part of the Judean village of Bethhaccerem. He was responsible under Nehemiah for repairing the dung gate of Jerusalem (Neh 3:14).

8. The goldsmith's son who repaired part of the wall of Jerusalem (Neh 3:31).

9. One of those who stood beside Ezra as he read the Scripture before the people of Jerusalem (Neh 8:4).

10. A priest who sealed the covenant made by Nehemiah (Neh 10:3).

11. One of the priests appointed to sing the thanksgiving at the dedication of the rebuilt wall of Jerusalem. Possibly the same as 10 (Neh 12:42).

P. C. J.

MALCHIEL (măl'kĭ-ĕl). Son of Beriah and grandson of Asher (Gen 46:17; Num 26:45; I Chr 7:31), and founder of a tribal family (Num 26:45).

MALCHIRAM (măl-kī'răm). A son of Jeconiah (King Jehoiachin) and therefore a descendant of David (I Chr 3:17-18).

MALCHI-SHUA (măl'kī-shū'ă). One of the sons of Saul (I Chr 8:33; 9:39), killed by the Philistines on Mount Gilboa (I Sam 31:2; I Chr 10:2). The name is spelled Melchi-shua in the KJV in I Sam 14:49; 31:2.

MALCHUS (măl'kŭs). A slave of the high priest Caiaphas (Jn 18:10, NASB). Being foremost among those who seized Jesus in the garden of Gethsemane, he was wounded by the sword of the apostle Peter who cut off his right ear. All four Gospel writers mention the incident (Mt 26:51; Mk 14:47; Lk 22:50) but John includes more of the personal details surrounding the incident and the man. Only he calls Malchus by name (Jn 18:10). John tells us that he was somehow acquainted with Caiaphas (18:15). Only John identifies the swordsman as Peter. Malchus had a relative who later questioned Peter about his connection with Jesus (Jn 18:26). Perhaps John, writing near the end of the 1st cen., felt free to cite the names without embarrassment, both Peter and Malchus being by that time deceased. However, only Luke the physician records the fact that Jesus "touched his ear, and healed him" (Lk 22:51). From this wording some conjecture that the ear was not entirely severed, but this is debatable. It was the last miracle of healing our Lord performed. We are curious to know if this unusual incident made any lasting spiritual impression on Malchus, but Scripture is silent on his subsequent history.

G. C. L.

MALE. A word referring to the masculine gender of human beings and of animals, occurring more than 70 times in the OT and four times in the NT. The Heb. word used predominantly in the OT is *zākār* from the verb *zākar*, "to remember." A possible meaning of the word *zākār* is "he through whom the *memorial* of parents is continued," or, "he who is competent to *remember* or call upon the deity in worship."

MALEFACTOR. Two Gr. words are used in Scripture: *kakopoios*, "a bad doer," i.e., evildoer, criminal (Jn 18:30; I Pet 2:12, 14; 3:16-17; 4:15), and *kakourgos*, "a wrongdoer" (Lk 23:32-33, 39; II Tim 2:9). "The former describes the subject as doing or making evil; the latter as creating or originating the bad, and hence designates the more energetic, aggressive, initiating type of criminality" (ISBE). The word is often associated with the two crucified with Christ on the cross, of whom the stronger Gr. word is used, though only Luke refers to them as malefactors. Matthew and Mark call them "thieves"; John says "two other." The penitent one was saved at the eleventh hour by faith in the Saviour. *See* Evildoer.

MALELEEL. *See* Mahalaleel.

MALICE, MALICIOUSNESS. These words, representing "the very essence of badness lying in the heart" (Crabb), are the translations of Gr. *kakia* (Rom 1:29; I Cor 5:8; 14:20; Eph 4:31; Col 3:8; Tit 3:3; I Pet 2:1, 16) and of *ponēria* (Mt 22:18, RSV). The expression "malicious [*ponērois*] words" occurs in III Jn 10. RSV also uses "malice" for *sheʼāṭ* ("despite, contempt") in Ezk 25:6, 15; and for *raʻ* ("evil") in Ps 41:5; 73:8. Unregenerate men are not only "filled with" malice (Rom 1:29) but they also "live in" it (Tit 3:3). On the other hand, Christians are exhorted to "put away" decisively (aorist tense) this inborn evil (Eph 4:31; Col 3:8; I Pet 2:1). *See* Sin; Wicked.

MALIGNITY. A word meaning "bad character, depravity of heart and life" (Thayer, p. 320, *kakoētheia*), used by Paul to describe the nature of the Gentiles who refused to have God in their knowledge (Rom 1:29). This characteristic is especially manifested in malicious subtlety and craftiness, with intense ill will and desire to harm others or see them suffer.

MALLOTHI (măl'ŏ-thī). One of the 14 sons of Heman set over the service of song in David's reign. By lot he became the leader of the 19th course of singers (I Chr 25:4, 26).

MALLOW. *See* Plants: Mallow.

MALLUCH (măl'ŭk)

1. A Levite of the family of Merari, and an ancestor of Ethan, a musician in David's day (I Chr 6:44).

2. One of the family of Bani who put away his Gentile wife after the return from Babylon (Ezr 10:29).

3. One of the sons of Harim who divorced his foreign wife (Ezr 10:32).

4. A priest who sealed the covenant of Nehemiah (Neh 10:4). It seems incredible that he could be the same priest who returned with Zerubbabel (Neh 12:2), yet the possibility is suggested by the inclusion of some of the same names in both lists.

5. One of the chiefs of the people who signed the covenant of Nehemiah (Neh 10:27).

MAMMON (măm'ŏn). The term occurs four times (Mt 6:24; Lk 16:9, 11, 13). It is a transliteration of Aramaic *māmôn* meaning "property," "earthly goods," "wealth" or "money." Mt 6:24 and Lk 16:13 are parallel, in which Christ teaches that mammon demands one's heart and service; consequently one cannot do service to both God and mammon. In Lk 16:9, 11 it is further described as "mammon of unrighteousness," having the idea of acquiring possessions dishonestly which corresponds to the actions of the unjust steward in the parable. In conclusion, mammon is gathered by man, sometimes by unjust means, for the erroneous purpose of security (cf. Lk 12:15), since the result is enslavement to it rather than to God.

Bibliography. F. Hauck, "*Mamōnas,*" TDNT, IV, 388–390. J. Jeremias, *The Parables of Jesus,* 6th ed., trans. by S. H. Hooke, New York: Scribner's, 1963, pp. 45–48.

MAMRE (măm'rē)

1. One of three Amorite brothers who were allied with Abraham in the fight in which they freed Lot and others from their captors (Gen 14:13, 24).

2. A place two miles N of Hebron (*q.v.*), today called Ramet el-Khalil. Abraham lived there in a tent (Gen 13:18; 14:13). The word translated "plain" in the phrase "the plain of Mamre" in the KJV is better rendered "oaks" as in the RSV. The spot seems to have taken its name from Mamre the Amorite, the owner at the time (Gen 14:13). Abraham was visited at Mamre by three heavenly messengers who promised him a son (Gen 18:1 ff.). East of there he bought a burial place in Machpelah where he buried Sarah (Gen 23:17–19; 49:30; 50:13).

Isaac spent his last years at Mamre, where Jacob came to visit him (Gen 35:27), and evidently died there. Because of its patriarchal associations Israelites built a shrine there whose pavement dating to the 9th–8th cen. B.C. has been uncovered. Herod the Great erected an enclosure which was destroyed in A.D. 70 and rebuilt by Hadrian. A venerable oak and a well are pointed out today as belonging to Abraham.

N. B. B.

MAN, MEN. *See* Anthropology.

MAN OF SIN, MAN OF LAWLESSNESS. The phrase occurs in the NT only in II Thess 2:3. The MS evidence is rather equally divided between *anomias* ("man of lawlessness") and *hamartias* ("man of sin"). He is further described in vv. 3–4 as the "son of perdition" or "destruction" (cf. Jn 17:12) and "the one who sets himself against, and makes himself superior to, all that is called God or is worshipped."

The well of Abraham inside the temple of Hadrian at Mamre. HFV

Paul teaches that before the day of the Lord (or, Christ, KJV on basis of some later Gr. MSS) arrives there must first be a falling away (apostasy, NASB, vv. 2–3), the removal of God's restraining force (i.e., lawful government, Holy Spirit, etc.) against the full exercise of iniquitous power (v. 7), and the appearance of the satanically inspired man of sin (v.3) whom the Lord will destroy (v. 8).

Interpretation of the man of sin as Antiochus Epiphanes, Roman emperors (as Caligula, Nero) or the papacy do not satisfy the eschatological viewpoint of the NT. Rather, the man of sin is an individual embodying anti-God power who is still to arise before the future day of the Lord. *See* Antichrist; Beast; Iniquity *re* Lawlessness.

W. H. M.

MAN, SON OF. *See* Son of Man.

MANAEN (măn'ȧ-ĕn). One of the five prophets and teachers in the church at Antioch and "foster-brother" (*syntrophos*) of Herod the tetrarch (Acts 13:1), i.e., Antipas (4 B.C.–A.D.37). The latter designation may mean that he was brought up (NASB) and educated with this Herod. Some have speculated that he was the son, or at least a relative, of Manaen the Essene who predicted to Herod the Great, when a child, that he would become king of the Jews. When the prediction was fulfilled, Herod held Manaen the Essene and his sect in high regard (Jos *Ant.* xv.10.5). Possibly Manaen of Acts 13:1 was adopted by Herod the Great and made a companion to one of his sons. The term *syntrophos,* however, may mean simply an intimate friend or "member of the court" (RSV; cf. NEB).

MANAHATH (măn'ȧ-hăth)

1. One of the sons of Shobal and grandson of Seir the Horite (Gen 36:23; I Chr 1:40).

2. A place in Judah, mentioned in the Amarna letters (*q.v.*) as *Manḫate,* to which certain Benjamites of Geba were carried captive

(I Chr 8:6). It may be that the sons of Salma, of the family of Caleb, of the tribe of Judah formed half the population of Manahath (I Chr 2:54). The LXX adds the name of this town to the Heb. text of Josh 15:59, thus placing it in the hill country. It may then be identified with Malḥa, a modern village three miles SW of Jerusalem.

MANAHETHITES. *See* Manahath 2.

MANASSEH (mǎ-năs'ǎ). The name Manasseh means "one who causes to forget." Joseph's use of it for his firstborn reflects the effect the child's birth had on his attitude toward his trials in Egypt (Gen 41:51). Later use was merely as a name drawn from the list of ancestors, so far as records indicate.

1. *The firstborn son of Joseph.* Gen 48:8-22 recites the blessing of Jacob upon both of Joseph's sons. He gave the chief blessing to Ephraim, but he adopted both of them, putting them on the same level as his own sons. Many modern interpreters explain this account as etiological and unhistorical. On the other hand, it should be remembered that this description of Jacob's blessing is in harmony with Abram's blessing of Isaac above Ishmael, with Isaac's blessing of Jacob above Esau, and with Jacob's blessing of Judah and Joseph above Reuben. The common practice of giving the chief blessing to the firstborn was broken repeatedly in the line of the patriarchs by making faith in God and obedience to Him the determining factors in the blessing. Manasseh the firstborn was to receive a lesser blessing than Ephraim because his service would be less.

2. *The tribe of Manasseh.* At Sinai and in the journeys through the wilderness, Manasseh was one of the 12 tribes, according to Num 1:34-35; 2:20. In allotting territory to the 12 tribes Moses granted a portion E of Jordan to one-half this tribe under descendants of Machir, the firstborn of Manasseh (Deut 3:13, 15). To the other half, Joshua granted a portion W of Jordan (Josh 22:7). The eastern portion covered part of Gilead and all of Bashan, and later Jair extended it northward (Deut 3:14). The western portion lay N of Ephraim and S of Zebulun and Issachar (Josh 17:1-12). Five sons of Manasseh still living received their inheritances there. The sixth son, who had died during the wilderness journeys, was represented by five daughters of his son Zelophehad. God had directed through Moses that they should receive his portion. This action initiated an entirely new set of laws controlling the inheritance of possessions belonging to one who died without a male heir (Num 27:1-11). Within this western portion lay strong Canaanite cities, including Megiddo, Taanach, Ibleam, and Bethshean. These were never destroyed, though forced eventually to pay tribute. In the days of the judges, leaders for the fighting men of Israel arose from Manasseh at various times. Gideon came from the western portion (Jud 6:15), and Jephthah from the eastern (Jud 11:1).

The genealogies in Num 26:28-34; Josh 17:1-3; I Chr 2:21-23; 7:14-19 cannot be reconciled as they stand. They can, however, if these suggestions by R. J. A. Sheriffs ("Manasseh," HBD) concerning I Chr 7:14-15 are accepted: "It is probable that the words 'Huppim and Shuppim' are glossed into verse 15 from verse 12, and possible that the word 'Asriel' is a dittograph." The greater portion of this tribe went into captivity in Assyria. *See* Machirites.

3. *The king of Judah.* Manasseh, the son of Hezekiah and Hephzibah (II Kgs 21:1; II Chr 33:1), became king at 12 years of age and reigned 55 years. E. R. Thiele (*The Mysterious Numbers of Hebrew Kings,* pp. 154 ff.) reckons these years as 696-642 B.C. with the first ten spent as coregent with his father.

Manasseh reversed the policies of Hezekiah concerning idolatry. He went so far as to place an idol in the temple itself and to offer human sacrifices (II Kgs 21:1-9). His abominations were cited by the prophets as the climactic cause for God's sealing the judgment of Judah by captivity (II Kgs 21:10-15). Moreover, Manasseh is said to have "shed innocent blood very much" (II Kgs 21:16).

According to II Chr 33:10-11 Manasseh's stubborn refusal to heed rebukes of the prophets led to his deportation to Babylon. Repentance and prayer to "the Lord his God" are credited with bringing about his restoration (II Chr 33:12-13). Some interpreters have doubted this account of repentance (cf. "Manasseh" in HBD). The finding of his name in recent years, however, in records of Esarhaddon and of Ashurbanipal as one of 22 tributaries of Assyria (ANET, pp. 291, 294), and a parallel in Ashurbanipal's capture and release of Necho I, king of Egypt (ANET, p. 295), give strong support to the biblical account. Reforms credited to him, however, were not lasting (II Chr 33:17). He could not stem the tide of corruption his influence had released (II Kgs 21:19-21; II Chr 33:21-23).

J. W. W.

MANDRAKE. *See* Plants.

MANEH. A weight among the Hebrews (Ezk 45:12, KJV, NASB), spelled mina in many modern English versions. Sixty manehs made one talent. In Babylonia and Assyria 60 shekels made a maneh, while in Palestine a maneh consisted of 50 shekels. *See* Weights, Measures, and Coins.

MANGER. In Lk 2:7, 12, 16, it is the place the infant Jesus was laid and in Lk 13:15 it is the stall where the ox and ass were kept. In classical Gr. the meaning of the word was "stall." The NT meaning is an open courtyard enclosed by a fence where the cattle were shut up for the night. The people in the East fed their beasts of burden out of nose-bags of haircloth and not from what is known in this country as a manger. *See* Crib; Stall.

MANNA. *See* Food; Plants.

MANOAH (*mä*-nō'*ä*). Best known as the father of Samson; indeed, in Scripture every mention of him is in connection with either the birth, life, or death of Samson (Jud 13:2–16:31). Zorah, a border city between Dan and Judah, was his home, and he was a member of the tribe of Dan (Jud 13:2). He lived in a time of spiritual declension in Israel for which God had punished the nation by allowing it to become tributary to the Philistines.

It was in this situation that the Angel of the Lord appeared to Manoah's previously barren wife to reveal to her that she was to bear a son who was to be raised as a Nazarite and who would become Israel's deliverer. At Manoah's request, the messenger reappeared with instructions concerning the child's upbringing. Samson, the son that was born to Manoah and his wife, judged Israel 20 years and was buried on his death with his father (Jud 16:31). Manoah is depicted as a God-fearing man who believed in prayer and who sought to dissuade his son from marrying a heathen woman outside the covenant (Jud 14:3).

S. N. G.

MANSERVANT. *See* Service.

MANSION. This word appears only once in the KJV at Jn 14:2, where it is an apparent carry-over from the Latin Vulg., *mansiones,* meaning "abiding places." With the passage of time mansion has come to have an idea of grandiosity not intended by the original Gr. nor the Lat. translation. The true meaning of the Gr. term (*monai*) is "abiding places," "abodes," or "dwelling places" (NASB). The apparent teaching is that there is plenty of room for the disciples in the Father's house. Perhaps the RSV translation "rooms" is to be preferred, for in the Father's house there will be an abundance of rooms for all believers in the life to come.

MANSLAYER. A person who commits homicide, directly or indirectly, which is at least partially justifiable. Such a person would be involved in the following cases: (1) death by a blow in a sudden quarrel (Num 35:22; cf. Hittite Laws 1 and 2, ANET, p. 189); (2) death by a stone or missile thrown at random (Num 35:22–23) or by the blade of an axe flying from its handle (Deut 19:5); (3) death by falling from a roof not provided with a parapet or guard rail (Deut 22:8); (4) death by assault when killer didn't lie in wait (Ex 21:12–13; cf. Hittite Laws 3 and 4); (5) death by goring by an ox not previously known by its owner to be vicious (Ex 21:28–32; cf. Hammurabi's code 250–1, ANET, p. 176; the Laws of Eshnunna 54–55, ANET, p. 163); (6) death in act of stealing at night at the hands of an owner of property (Ex 22:2; cf. Laws of Eshnunna 12–13, ANET, p. 162, for day and night distinction); (7) death at hand of enemy in battle (II Sam 2:18–23; 3:26–30; I Kgs 2:5).

In determining manslaughter as opposed to murder, it was important to take into consideration the weapon (Num 35:16–18) and the intention (Num 35:15). In order to protect the person who was a manslayer but not a murderer, from the avenger of blood, cities of refuge (*q.v.*) were designated at different locations throughout the land, where he might flee and be safe from his pursuers.

H. A. Hof.

MANTLE. *See* Dress.

MANUSCRIPTS, DEAD SEA. *See* Dead Sea Scrolls.

MANY, THE. This term, both with and without the definite article, has important theological significance in several biblical passages (e.g., Isa 53:11–12; Dan 9:27; 12:3; Mt 20:28; 22:14; 26:28 and parallels; Rom 5:15, 19; Heb 9:28).

The Semitic usage of (ha-)*rabbîm* can mean the whole community comprised of many members, so that the term becomes all-inclusive, not partitive. NT writers, with the Heb. text in mind instead of the LXX, sometimes used Gr. *polloi* in the comprehensive sense of all mankind (Joachim Jeremias, "*Polloi,*" TDNT, VI, 536–545).

In our Lord's statement, "Many are called but few are chosen" (Mt 22:14), Jeremias argues that "many" must be inclusive, i.e., all are called (cf. Jn 1:9; 12:32). If "many" were exclusive, it would mean that there was a selection in both cases.

Interpreting "many" in the comprehensive sense, we may conclude that the Servant of Yahweh bore the sin of all mankind (Isa 53:12; Heb 9:28). Likewise the Son of Man came to give His life a ransom and shed His blood for "many," not merely for some but for all (Mt 20:28; 26:28). Paul, using a term more in keeping with Gr. thinking, says that the man Christ Jesus "gave Himself a ransom for all" (*pantōn*) (I Tim 2:6).

The expression *hoi polloi,* "the many" (NASB) occurs four times in Rom 5:15, 19. Once in each verse it has reference to the many who were made sinners and died because of Adam's sin; according to Rom 3:9, 23; 5:12; II Cor 5:14 "the many" must mean all men. Therefore when Paul states that the grace of Jesus Christ abounds to "the many" (Rom 5:15) and that "the many" will be "made" righteous (Rom 5:19; cf. Isa 53:11), even as justification of life resulted to all men (Rom 5:18), the theologian must decide whether in the latter case "the many" means the entire human race or merely all who are in union with Christ.

J. R.

MAOCH (mā'ŏk). Father of Achish, king of the Philistine city of Gath. David fled to Achish and sojourned with him when trying to escape from Saul (I Sam 27:2).

MAON (mā'ŏn)

1. A city in the hill country of Judah (Josh 15:55) and the home of Nabal, the great flockmaster (I Sam 25:2). The site is now called Tell Ma'în, eight miles S of Hebron. It was in the wilderness of Maon E of the town where David and his men were hiding when their presence there was revealed to Saul by the Ziphites (I Sam 23:24–25). Only a raid by the Philistines delivered David from Saul at that time.

2. A descendant of Caleb, son of Shammai, founder of Beth-zur (I Chr 2:45).

MAONITES (mā'ŏ-nīts). A people mentioned as oppressors of the Israelites before the time of Jephthah (Jud 10:12). They can hardly be the same as the Calebites of Maon in Judah, who were too few to figure as dangerous enemies. The word should probably be vocalized as Meunim (*q.v.*), an Edomite tribe from the territory of Ma'an in the region of Mount Seir; possibly it should read Midianites, with the LXX.

MARA (mâr'ȧ). The new name meaning "bitterness, sadness, grief" in Heb., which Naomi chose for herself on her return to Bethlehem to express the bitterness of her experiences in Moab (Ruth 1:20).

MARAH (mâr'ȧ). An oasis pool of bitter water in the wilderness of Shur which the Israelites reached in three days after their crossing of the Red Sea (Ex 15:23; Num 33:8–9). When the people murmured against Moses, he cast a tree into the waters and the waters were miraculously, although temporarily, sweetened. On the traditional route to Mount Sinai, the oasis of 'Ain Hawarah is usually identified with Marah, *c.* 47 miles SE of Suez. Its spring gives brackish water because of salts in the soil of the vicinity.

MARALAH (măr'ȧ-lȧ). A city on the W border of Zebulun (Josh 19:11).

MARANATHA (măr'ȧ-năth'ȧ). The word appears once (I Cor 16:22). The Aramaic from which it comes is made up of two words which may be divided as *maran atha* or *marana tha*. The first possibility means "our Lord came" or "has come," thus referring to the incarnation and serves as a refutation that Messiah had not yet come. The second possibility means "our Lord, come!" In view of the context in which the word occurs with the preceding anathema or curse and in view of the belief of the early church in the imminent hope of Christ's return, the latter meaning is preferred. The reminder, therefore, is that when the Lord, the righteous Judge, comes, the anathema will be carried out.

MARBLE. *See* Minerals and Metals.

MARCUS. *See* Mark.

MARDUK. *See* Gods, False.

MARESHAH (mȧ-rē'shȧ)

1. The first fortress city N of the great citadel of Lachish. Josh 15:44 enumerates it among the cities of the Shephelah of Judah. The earlier Amarna tablets knew it as a Canaanite city. Rehoboam fortified the site after Shishak's invasion (II Chr 11:5–8), and Asa defeated Zerah the Ethiopian near here (II Chr 14:9–10). It was the home of the prophet Eliezer who predicted the destruction of the merchant fleet created by Jehoshaphat and Ahaziah at Ezion-geber (II Chr 20:37). Micah predicted the capture of Mareshah (Mic 1:15).

Early in the intertestamental period, under the name Marisa, it became one of the capitals of the Idumeans. It was later colonized by the Sidonians and subsequently captured by John Hyrcanus. Pompey restored it to the Idumeans, but Caesar returned it to the territory of Judea. The Parthians were its ultimate destroyers in 40 B.C.

The site is now known as Tell Sandahannah. The most interesting archaeological period excavated here was the intertestamental city which gave an excellent example of a small Hellenistic city with its painted tombs. A new city Eleutheropolis (Beit Jibrin) less than two miles to the N replaced Mareshah.

2. The name Mareshah in I Chr 2:42 and 4:21 presents difficult exegetical problems which have not yet been solved. Both passages occur in genealogies of Judah. In the former, Mareshah seems to be a person, the father or settler of Hebron. In 4:21 Laadah is said to be the father or settler of Mareshah.

J. L. K.

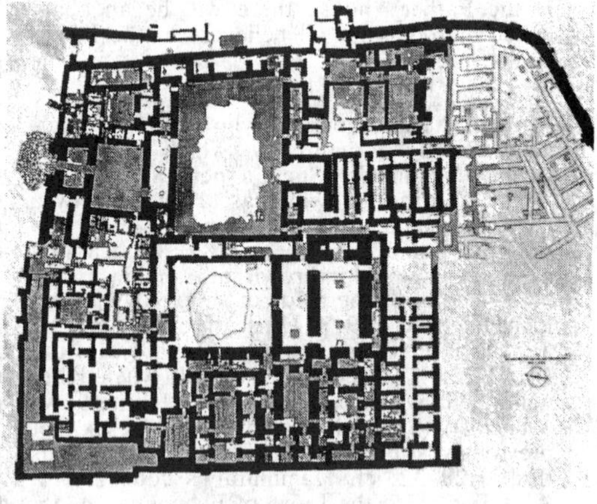

Mari palace plan. JR

MARI (mä'rē). The ancient city of Ma-ri (modern Tell Hariri) lies near the Euphrates River seven miles NNW of Abu-Kemal, by the border of Syria and Iraq. A. Parrot of the Louvre, Paris, excavated there 1933–64, uncovering temples, including those of the god Dagan (*see* Gods, False: Dagon) and the goddess Ishtar, and an immense palace of more than 270 rooms covering 15 acres, as well as earlier remains and a temple-tower. More than 20,000 inscribed clay tablets, a quarter of which are letters, from the Old Babylonian period (*c.* 1750 B.C.) illustrate the patriarchal narratives.

While Mari is not mentioned in the OT, the finds, and especially the texts, help to explain many customs of the patriarchal period and are written in a NW Semitic dialect "virtually identical" with that spoken by the Hebrews of Gen 12–35. Treaties or covenants were ratified by the killing of an ass, as in the pact between the Shechemites (B^{e}nê Ḥamor, "sons of an ass," Josh 24:32) and Jacob (Gen 33:19; 34:1–3; ANET, pp. 482–3). Other treaties show the form of OT covenants and practice (M. Noth, *Mari und Israel,* 1953) as well as the procedures of international diplomacy.

Semi-nomadic tribes roamed freely between the large cities as did Abraham, and it is striking that the Sutu, Habiru (*see* Hebrew People) and Ben-Yamini ("Benjamites") are mentioned, though these are not necessarily the same as their biblical counterparts. Among place names in Palestine, only Hazor is mentioned; but villages near Harran (biblical Haran), such as Nahur (Nahor), Turahi (Terah) and Sarug (Serug) are named (cf. Gen 11:23–24). The tablets indicate that at Harran there was a temple of the moon-god Sin, probably one of the pagan deities worshiped by Terah (Josh 24:2). West Semitic personal names include Ariukku (Arioch, Gen 14:1) and forms like Abraham and Jacob. The occurrence of Dawidum ("chief") is now doubted, being perhaps a word for "defeat" rather than a forerunner of the name of David (BA,XI,2; cf. JNES, XVII [1958], 130). Tribal land, as with the Hebrews, was inalienable and inheritance was only through members of the family.

At Mari the census was of religious and ritual as well as political and economic significance (cf. II Sam 24). The letters tell of the activities of the diverse classes of officials and priests. A god had his prophet, a man whom he sent to make proclamations in his name. When Zimri-Lim failed to report regularly to his god Dagan at Terqa, he was told by a dream-revelation that had he done so the god would have delivered the Benjamites into his hand.

The texts give a detailed view of the everyday life and customs of the area as well as of the history of the city. The earliest reference to Mari is in the 3rd mil. B.C. when the first Semitic inscriptions are found. It was conquered by Sargon of Agade *c.* 2250 B.C., and thereafter ruled by governors dependent on Ur until freed by the Amorite Ishbi-Irra. Yahdun-Lim ruled until murdered in a palace revolution. The throne was seized by Shamshi-Adad I of Assyria who handed Mari to his son Yasmah-Adad. On his father's death he was, however, driven out by Zimri-Lim, a son of Yahdun-Lim, who governed there until Hammurabi of Babylon captured the city in 1761 B.C. Two years later Mari was destroyed. Throughout these reigns there was constant correspondence between the kings of Aleppo, Qatna, Carchemish, Assyria and Babylonia. *See* Archaeology; Patriarchal Age.

Statuette of a worshiper from Mari, third millennium B.C. LM

Bibliography. Herbert B. Huffmon, "Prophecy in the Mari Letters," BA, XXXI (1968), 101–124. George E. Mendenhall, "Mari," BA, XI (1948), 1–19. J. M. Munn-Rankin, "Diplomacy in Western Asia in the Early Second Millennium B.C.," *Iraq,* XVIII (1956), 68–110.

D. J. W.

MARINER. *See* Occupations.

MARISHES. The KJV word is an archaic form of marshes in Ezk 47:11. *See* Marsh.

MARK (PERSON). Son of Mary (Acts 12:12), cousin of Barnabas (Col 4:10, RSV), companion of Paul (Phm 24) and Peter (I Pet 5:13), and author of the second Gospel. Like many other Jews of his day, he had assumed a Latin surname (Marcus, "a large hammer") in addition to his Heb. name John. His father is not mentioned in the NT, but his mother appears to have been a prominent and somewhat well-to-do member of the Jerusalem church (Acts 12:12). It has been conjectured that Mark was the youth who fled from the scene of Christ's arrest (Mk 14:51–52), and that he was the man with the pitcher whom the disciples were to follow (Mk 14:13).

Mark came to Antioch with Paul and Barnabas (Acts 12:25) and subsequently accompanied them on their first missionary journey as far as Perga in Pamphylia (Acts 13:5, 13). Whatever the cause of Mark's desertion, Paul considered it grounds for refusing to take him on his second missionary journey (Acts 15:37–39). Instead, Barnabas stood by him even as he had Paul earlier (Acts 9:26–27) and took Mark to Cyprus. About ten years later, during Paul's house arrest in Rome, Mark appears again as Paul's fellow laborer (Phm 24), who apparently was about to travel to the province of Asia (Col 4:10). When Peter wrote his first epistle (5:13), Mark was with him in Babylon (Rome, if understood cryptically). By the time of Paul's second imprisonment (*c.* A.D. 66–67), Mark, who was then in Ephesus, had so proved his usefulness that Paul requested that he come to Rome (II Tim 4:11).

It seems reasonably certain from statements of the Church Fathers that Mark served as Peter's "interpreter," that he was in Rome with Peter and Paul, and that he wrote the second Gospel there. *See* Mark, Gospel of. Less reliable tradition makes him the founder and bishop of the church in Alexandria, where he is said to have been martyred in Nero's eighth year (A.D. 61–62).

D. W. B.

MARK (SIGN). Used in the KJV to translate five Heb. and three Gr. words. These eight words can be readily placed in two general categories: a mark to be aimed at, or a mark as a sign. In the first category are the Heb. *maṭṭārâ*, a target (I Sam 20:20; Job 16:12); Heb. *miphgā'*, an object of attack (Job 7:20); and Gr. *skopos*, a goal (Phil 3:14).

It is the second category, a mark as a sign, or identification, that is the more common, of which four distinct uses may be observed. (1) Heb. *'ôth*—a special mark, e.g., upon Cain (Gen 4:15). What this was is not specifically known, but it was certainly some identification visible or otherwise which indicated either infamy or protection. (2) Heb. *tāw*—a seal or sign of ownership. This was the symbol for protection put upon the foreheads of the righteous (Ezk 9:4, 6; cf. Rev 7:2–3; 14:1; 22:4). It is translated "signature" in the RSV of Job 31:35. (3) Heb. *qa'ăqa';* Gr. *stigma*—a mark or brand, cut or burnt. Branding was not uncommon in biblical times. Cattle, slaves, and even soldiers were branded with the name of their master. Israelites were forbidden to brand or mark (tattoo) themselves (Lev 19:28). According to III Macc 2:29 Jews were branded with the fig leaf of Dionysius by Ptolemy Philopater. Paul, viewing himself as the bondslave of Jesus Christ, saw his bodily scars as the sign of ownership by his Lord (Gal 6:17; cf. II Cor 11:23–27). (4) Gr. *charagma*—the technical term for the official seal of commercial documents inscribed with the details of the reigning emperor. As a sign it could be withheld or rejected. The term is used eight times in the book of the Revelation and always for the mark of the beast. It is some visible sign received in the right hand or on the forehead by those who worship the beast (Rev 13:16). Without the sign, buying and selling are impossible (Rev 13:17), but it will be a curse bringing judgment upon the bearers (Rev 14:9–11; 16:2).

H. D. F.

MARK, GOSPEL OF. The second Gospel according to the order in the English Bible.

Author

Although the Gospel is anonymous, there is adequate reason to ascribe the book with certainty to John Mark, the attendant of Peter. The Marcan authorship finds its earliest attestation in the writings of Papias from the early part of the 2nd cen., and is further confirmed by Irenaeus, Clement of Alexandria, Origen, Jerome, and the Anti-Marcionite Prologue. Internal evidence reveals the author's familiarity with Palestine (11:1); with Aramaic, the language of Palestine (5:41; 7:34); and with Jewish institutions and customs (1:21; 7:2–4). These items suggest authorship by a Palestinian Jew, such as Mark was (Acts 12:12). Furthermore, the striking similarity between the general outlines of the second Gospel and of Peter's sermon in Caesarea (Acts 10:34–43) harmonizes with NT indication that Mark and Peter sustained a close relationship (I Pet 5:13).

Date

The majority of recent interpreters date this Gospel between A.D. 65 and 70. The best basis for dating the book is information from the Church Fathers. Irenaeus and the author of the Anti-Marcionite Prologue place the writing of Mark after the death of Peter and Paul, which would require a date later than A.D. 67, the probable year of Paul's martyrdom. On the other hand, the silence concerning the destruction of Jerusalem in fulfillment of Mk 13 may point to a date prior to A.D. 70. The most probable date, therefore, for the writing of the Gospel would seem to be A.D. 67–70. Statements of the Anti-Marcionite Prologue, Clement of Alexandria, and Irenaeus indicate Rome as the place of origin.

Characteristics

It has been an almost unanimous opinion that

the Gospel was directed to the Roman mind. The Marcan habit of explaining Jewish terms and customs points to Gentile readers (5:41; 7:2-4). That they were Romans is indicated by the occurrence of certain Latinisms in the book, as well as by the statement of Clement of Alexandria that Roman Christians who heard Peter preach were the ones who requested the writing of the Gospel.

Several striking peculiarities of Mark's account make it unique among the Gospels. The manner of writing has been described as graphic, forceful, and dramatic. A vivid realism characterizes both Mark's style and his unvarnished reporting of the facts. Events are described without alteration or extensive interpretation, and their presentation is marked by an on-the-spot quality found in the reports of eyewitnesses. A vigor and a note of urgency may be sensed in almost any portion of the writing. The characteristic word of this Gospel of action is *euthys,* which occurs 41 times and is translated "straightway," "immediately," "forthwith," "anon." Gr. tenses and words of unusual forcefulness are used with dramatic and graphic effect.

Outline

I. Title, 1:1
II. Preparation for Christ's Ministry, 1:2-13
III. Christ's Ministry in Galilee, 1:14-6:30
IV. Christ's Withdrawals from Galilee, 6:31-9:50
V. Christ's Ministry in Perea, 10:1-52
VI. Christ's Concluding Ministry in Jerusalem, 11:1-13:37
VII. Christ's Passion and Resurrection, 14:1-16:20

See Gospel of Mark under Gospels, The Four.

Bibliography. R. A. Cole, *The Gospel According to St. Mark,* TNTC, Grand Rapids: Eerdmans, 1961. "Mark, Gospel of," NBD, pp. 781-785. Ralph Earle, *The Gospel According to Mark, The Evangelical Commentary on the Bible,* Grand Rapids: Zondervan, 1957. *Mark: The Gospel of Action,* EBC, Chicago: Moody, 1970. R. C. H. Lenski, *The Interpretation of St. Mark,* Columbus: Wartburg, 1946. G. Campbell Morgan, *The Gospel According to Mark,* New York: Revell, 1927. James Morison, *A Practical Commentary on the Gospel According to St. Mark,* 6th ed., London: Hodder & Stoughton, 1889. A. T. Robertson, *Studies in Mark's Gospel,* New York: Macmillan, 1919. H. B. Swete, *The Gospel According to St. Mark,* 3rd ed., London: Macmillan, 1927, and Grand Rapids: Eerdmans, 1956 (reprint)—probably the best technical and most thorough commentary on Mark, Greek text with notes. Vincent Taylor, *The Gospel According to St. Mark,* London: Macmillan, 1952.

D. W. B.

MARKET. In the OT, a place for selling merchandise (Ezk 27:13, 17, 19, 25. KJV; 27:15, RSV, NASB). It was often located in the open place just inside the city gate where streets converged. Here people also would gather to exchange information and opinions and to mingle socially. In Palestine the sick were laid in the marketplace for Jesus to heal them (Mk 6:56, RSV); children played games there (Mt 11:16-17), and idlers stood around (Mt 20:3). Scribes and Pharisees would love to strut and be greeted "Rabbi" in the marketplace (Mt 23:6-7); and after being there they felt it necessary to purify themselves ritually before eating (Mk 7:4).

Remains of Trajan's Market, Rome. Trajan was Roman emperor A.D. 98-117. HFV

While among Jews a market was rather strictly a commercial center, among Gentiles it was associated with other functions of public life. A Greek agora or Roman forum was an open area surrounded by commercial buildings, temples, a hall of justice, and government buildings (senate, public records, etc.). A rostrum or bema also stood there, from which public officials could harangue assembled crowds and even render judgments (e.g., Paul stood before Gallio in Corinth, Acts 18:12-16; and before officials at Philippi, Acts 16:19). In Athens Paul reasoned in the marketplace with those who were willing to talk with him (Acts 17:17-18).

N. B. B. and H. F. V.

MAROTH (mâr'ŏth). A town in Judah mentioned only in Mic 1:12, in a passage containing plays on the meaning of the place names. Its name means "bitter fountains." The site is unknown, although some identify it with Maarath (*q.v.*).

MARRIAGE. That most intimate of unions into which, by personal consent, one man and one woman enter on the basis of mutual love and fidelity. It is nourished by sexual intercourse and perfected in a lifelong partnership of united endeavor.

The Nature of Marriage

1. It is a part of the very order of creation. God revealed to man his need for a wife (Gen 2:18) and a woman's need for a husband (Gen 3:16). He created woman for man and man for woman at the very beginning (Gen 1:26–27). From the start man realized that it was God's will that he have one wife, "bone of my bones, and flesh of my flesh" (Gen 2:23), and to love and cherish her as his very own. Paul writes, "So ought men to love their wives as their own bodies. He that loveth his wife loveth himself. For no man ever yet hated his own flesh; but nourisheth and cherisheth it, even as the Lord the church" (Eph 5:28–29).

2. Marriage is a sacrament of society. In marriage, and in sexual communion in particular, man and woman enjoy and demonstrate in outward manifestation what is an inward grace. Ordained of God (cf. I Tim 4:3), it is the highest expression of mutual affection, the deepest human communion, so that God Himself has used marriage to express the unfathomable depths of His own love to us.

3. Marriage is a solemn covenant entered into by one man and one woman in perfect freedom, in which they pledge their love and fidelity, one to the other, in joy and in sorrow, in health and in sickness, in prosperity and in adversity, so long as they both shall live. It is terminable in God's sight only by death, or by gross infidelity, or by separation on the part of an unbelieving spouse (Mt 5:32; 19:9; Rom 7:2–3; I Cor 7:15). Such a covenant should be made only between two persons of like mind and faith, for "what has a believer in common with an unbeliever?" (II Cor 6:14–15, RSV).

4. Marriage is a vocation, a calling of God to demonstrate the highest form of love to each other and thus to the world (Gen 2:23–24; Eph 5:21 ff.). It is also to propagate children (Gen 33:5; 48:4; Deut 28:4; Josh 24:3–4; Ps 127:3), and to nourish them physically and spiritually, teaching them the Word of God (Deut 6:7–20; 11:18–21; Prov 22:6) and training them to be good citizens (Prov 13:24; 19:18; 22:15; 23:13; 29:15, 17).

The Purposes of Marriage

1. The propagation of the human race. It is the God-ordained way to develop a species called mankind. In the case of angelic beings, God created each of them as separate individuals; but in the case of humanity, He created one male and one female and the whole race is descended from the first pair. God could have redeemed the separately created fallen angels only by Christ's dying individually for each one, but He could redeem the race of Adam by Christ's dying once, since it could be represented by one federal head. It is in the light of this fact that I Cor 15:22 takes on its meaning: "As in Adam all die, even so in Christ shall all be made alive."

God has chosen to beget spiritual children who will love Him because of His sovereign saving grace, and to bring them into physical being through the marriage relationship. The sacramental and the propagational aspects of marriage thus become united, and the begetting of children becomes holy and for the very glory of God.

2. God's way to rear children. Children need a home and parents in that home. In the home they receive both shelter and nurture. From their parents' lives they learn what real love is by being the objects of the love of both parents, and by seeing real love reciprocated between their parents. Only from their parents can they most fully learn about deep abiding conjugal love, and thus be prepared to wait and seek for such for themselves. It is at this point that marital discord and broken homes have the most devastating effects upon children. The child who has not seen real love demonstrated in his own home is not ready to face life on his own. God intended also that the demonstration of real love between the parents, and between parents and children, should be the basis for the understanding of His love in sending His Son to die for our sins (cf. Eph 5:25–32).

3. God's way to instill in children the principles of justice and responsible government. Parents are to deal patiently and justly (Eph 6:4; Col 3:21), and thus teach their children what is just and fair. They are to illustrate responsibility and good government in the divinely ordered economy of the household (cf. I Tim 3:4–5, 12; Tit 1:6). The father as the head of the wife and head of the home, while conferring fully with his wife in a really democratic manner, is the one responsible for all decisions. This teaches submission to authority and a sense of real responsibility (Eph 5:21–24).

4. Marriage is God's pedagogical means to teach children of Himself. God calls Himself our Father and demonstrates His love to be as wonderful as the love of a father (Ps 103:13; Jn 3:16), as tender as that of a mother (Isa 49:15; 66:13; Mt 23:37), as intimate as that of husband and wife (Eph 5:25 ff.). Thus every relationship within marriage and the family has its place in demonstrating and teaching what God is and what is the nature of His love. *See* Family.

The Place of Sex

While sex has as its God-given goal the begetting of children to populate the earth, and thus indirectly to fill heaven with born-again children of God, it also fills very important personal and family needs. The husband needs the wife and the wife needs the husband, because man is so made that the tensions of life are relieved through conjugal love (I Cor 7:1–5). At the same time, in this act of intimate love creative energies are released in the lives of both husband and wife.

That God has thus made man and woman for their real enjoyment and mutual fellowship can best be seen in the Song of Solomon, in which the intimacies of conjugal love and enjoyment are depicted in the most beautiful and yet the most pure manner. In intercourse all the love expressed in act and word is consummated in communion and union. It is an expression of love which can be exercised with only one person, because of its holy nature. Each keeps this experience of his deepest love for the other, and for the other alone. In this sense it typifies the exclusive relationship which is to exist between the individual Christian and his Lord, and into which no other person or god is to be allowed to enter (Ex 20:3; cf. Eph 5:25 ff.).

A marriage based upon a full, stable sex life is a happy, well-balanced one, providing this aspect of life is the expression of the deepest love and not the satisfaction of merely fleshly desires. It is most important to the children as well as to the husband and wife, because here they see not only a stable marriage but also the wonder of it, the purity, the beauty, and the deep satisfaction. They in turn can be taught that sex is given of God and is truly beautiful and wonderful when used as God intended. The guards which God has set upon the sexual act enable children to keep themselves pure by using sex as God intended it be used, and to see that man's fullest freedom and joy in marriage really come by living within the framework of the seventh commandment (I Thess 4:3-8, Phillips; Heb 13:4, RSV).

How God Speaks of Marriage

First of all God uses it as a metaphor to express Christ's relationship to the Church, likening Christ to the bridegroom and the Church to the bride (Eph 5:24-32; Rev 19:7-9). Both the individual believer and the church at large are always looked upon in the sense of being the bride, the female, in relation to Christ (II Cor 11:2). The Virgin Mary's complete submission to the guidance and empowering of the Holy Spirit as she said, "Behold the handmaid of the Lord; be it unto me according to thy word" (Lk1:38), is an analogy of the relationship which should exist between the Holy Spirit and the Christian. For the fruit of the Spirit must be brought out in the life of the believer (Gal 5:22-23), even as Christ was brought forth as the fruit of the Spirit in Mary's womb (Lk 1:42).

In Ps 45 Christ is Himself foreseen in all His majesty and beauty along with His queenly Bride the Church to represent the purity which God desires of His children. The Bride is greatly to be desired because of her beauty (v.11) both outwardly and inwardly. Her raiment is fine and beautiful down to the smallest detail.

Monogamy

While polygamy was practiced for some time in the OT, it was only permitted as a temporary measure. It denied the principle of husband and wife being one flesh (Gen 2:24; Mt 19:5) and led to many marital problems. Both Abraham and Jacob had much sorrow because of this (Gen 21:9 ff.; 30:1-24), and David and Solomon were led astray through their pagan wives (II Sam 5:13; I Kgs 11:1-3). Only in monogamy is it possible to escape family jealousies and to correctly illustrate the relationship of Christ to the believer (Eph 5:23 ff.). *See* Concubine.

Marriage and Divorce

Divorce has always presented a serious problem. Christ's teaching is found in Mt 5:31-32; 19:3-9; Mk 10:2-12; Lk 16:18. He revealed that it was only because of the hardness of men's hearts that Moses allowed a bill of divorcement, and that this could actually cause adultery (Mt 19:8-9). Marriage is to be annulled only for fornication (Mt 5:31-32; 19:9). This means that a divorce could be allowed only when there had been intercourse with another person other than the betrothed either in premarital sex or afterward in marriage. Christ pointed out that a man could commit adultery just as well as a woman, by forcing an unjust divorce. This was contrary to the views of the Jews, who saw the woman as the only possible offender.

There are differences of opinion, but most churches consider that a divorce is to be permitted in case of willful desertion. If so, there are two biblical grounds, fornication and desertion. The Scriptures do, however, allow that a higher law may be applied to the divorced, namely, that of forgiveness where there is true repentance from sin. Hosea forgave and took back his adulterous wife because he loved her, even as God is ready to forgive and take back His adulterous Israel (Hos 2:1-2; 3:1 ff.; 14:1-8). *See* Divorce.

R. A. K.

Marriage Customs and Ceremonies

1. Choice of the bride. No restrictions are stated in the Bible relative to the proper age for marriage. It seems certain that girls were married quite young, in their youth (Prov 2:17; 5:18). In Isa 62:5 the young man who marries is termed a *bāḥûr*, a choice, stalwart fellow in the prime of his strength (cf. I Sam 9:2; Isa 40:30; Amos 8:13); and the virgin a *b^{e}tûlâ*, a young maiden attractive and sexually mature, and hence ready for marriage (cf. Joel 1:8; Jer 2:32). In the Talmud the rabbis set the minimum age for marriage at 12 years for girls and 13 years for boys.

Because of the strong influence of tribal and clan unity in the patriarchal society, fathers considered it their duty and prerogative to secure wives for their sons (Gen 24:3; 38:6). Normally the prospective bride and bridegroom simply acquiesced to the arrangements made in the interests of family and tribal loyalty. Not surprisingly, parents often arranged a marriage between first cousins, e.g., Isaac and Rebekah. Marriage with foreign women was discouraged (Gen 24:3; 26:34-35; 27:46; 28:8) and later on banned (Ex 34:16; Deut 7:3; Ezr 10:2-3, 10-11) because of the danger of turning to their idolatrous practices. Mixed marriages were tolerated only in the case of exiles (e.g., Joseph, Gen 41:45; Moses, Ex 2:21) and of kings for political reasons.

On the other hand, there was opportunity in Israel for marriages based on courtship. The young man could state his preference (Gen 34:4; Jud 14:2). Michal fell in love with David (I Sam 18:20). In OT times women were not kept secluded as in Muslim lands and went out unveiled (cf. I Sam 1:13). They tended sheep (Gen 29:6; Ex 2:16), carried water (Gen 24:13; I Sam 9:11), gleaned in fields (Ruth 2:3), and visited in other homes (Gen 34:1). Thus young men could themselves look for prospective brides.

2. The betrothal. The selection of the bride was followed by the espousal (*q.v.*) or betrothal. It was a formal proceeding and far more binding than our engagement. The men who were to marry Lot's daughters were already considered to be his sons-in-law (Gen 19:14, RSV). A betrothed man was deferred from military service so he could take (i.e., marry) his wife and live with her in his house for a year (Deut 20:7; 24:5). Sexual immorality with a betrothed girl was just as serious a crime as adultery (Deut 22:23-27 with 22:22). Inscriptions from the ancient Near East also indicate that betrothal was a recognized custom with definite legal consequences.

The betrothal was ordinarily undertaken by a friend or legal representative on the part of the bridegroom (I Sam 25:39 f.) and by the parents on the part of the bride. It was confirmed by oaths ("Thou shalt this day be my son-in-law," I Sam 18:21*b*). The amount of the "gift" (Heb. *mōhar; see* Dowry) was discussed with the girl's parents at this time and was paid at once to her family if money was the medium of compensation.

In both ancient Mesopotamia and Israel marriage was a purely civil contract, not formalized by any religious ceremony. While the OT does not specifically mention a written marriage contract, such contracts were stipulated in the Code of Hammurabi. Several marriage contracts are among the papyri from the Jewish colony at Elephantine in the 5th cen. B.C., and the practice is mentioned in the Book of Tobit (Tob 7:13). The Talmudists in the Mishnah term such a contract a *k^e^tûbâ* and gave minute directions as to the use and keeping of the *mōhar* sum. The term "covenant" (*b^e^rît*) in Prov 2:17 and Mal 2:14 may allude to a written contract.

3. The marriage ceremony. The essence of the marriage ceremony or festivities was the taking of the bride from her father's house and bringing her to the house of the bridegroom or his father. Thus there was literal truth in the Heb. expression "to take" a wife (e.g., Gen 4:19; 12:19; 24:67; 38:2; Num 12:1, marg.; I Sam 25:39-42; I Kgs 3:1; I Chr 2:21, marg.).

Wearing a stately turban (Isa 61:10, KJV "ornaments") or a nuptial crown (Song 3:11), the bridegroom set forth accompanied by his friends (Jn 3:29) or attendants (Mt 9:15, NASB) with tambourines and a band (I Macc 9:39). Since the wedding procession (cf. Song 3:6-11) was usually at night, many would carry torches or lamps (Mt 25:1-8). Their mirth and gladness (Jer 7:34; 16:9; 25:10; Rev 18:22 f.) announced their approach to townspeople waiting in houses along the route to the bride's house and on their return to the home of the groom (Mt 25:5-6).

The bride was beautifully dressed and adorned with jewels (Ps 45:13 f.; Isa 61:10; Rev 19:8). For the occasion she wore a veil (Gen 24:65; Song 4:1, 3; 6:7, RSV), which she would not remove until she was alone with her husband in the darkened nuptial chamber (cf. Gen 29:23-25).

The bridegroom escorted the whole wedding party, now including the bride and her companions (Ps 45:14*b*), to his own or his father's house for the "marriage supper" (Rev 19:9). All the friends and neighbors were invited to the wedding feast (Gen 29:22; Mt 22:3-10; Lk 14:8; Jn 2:2), which was normally given by the father of the groom (Mt 22:2, NASB). To refuse an invitation to such a feast was a gross insult (Mt 22:5; Lk 14:16-21). The festivities normally lasted a week (Gen 29:27 f.; Jud 14:10-12, 17), but the marriage was consummated on the first night (Gen 29:23). The guests were provided by the host with fitting robes (Mt 22:11). Riddles (Jud 14:12-18) and other forms of amusement added to the gaiety of the feast.

The last act in the ceremony was the conducting of the bride to the nuptial chamber (Heb. *ḥeder*, Jud 15:1; Song 1:4; Joel 2:16). In this room a canopy (Heb. *ḥuppâ*, Ps 19:5, "chamber" KJV; Joel 2:16, "closet" KJV) was prepared over the bridal couch or bed (Song 1:16). Then the bridegroom "went in" to the bride (Gen 16:2; 30:3; 38:8). The blood-stained linen of this wedding night was kept to prove the bride's virginity (Deut 22:13-21).

4. Marital status. The relative status of the husband in Israel is seen in the fact that in Heb. he is called the *ba'al*, the master or lord of his wife (Ex 21:22; Deut 21:13; 22:22; II Sam 11:26; Prov 12:4; 31:11, 23, 28). This provides the double meaning for the prophecy of Hos 2:16, "In that day, says the Lord, you will call me, 'My husband,' and no longer will you call me, 'My Ba'al' " (RSV). The wife's acceptance of her dependent role is illustrated in Sarah's speaking to her husband Abraham as "my lord" (*'adōnî*, Gen 18:12; I Pet 3:6).

For the duty of a man to beget a child for his deceased brother by the widow, *see* Marriage, Levirate.

J. R.

Bibliography. Nathan W. Ackerman, *The Psychodynamics of Family Life,* New York: Basic Books, 1958. Ray E. Baber, *Marriage and the Family,* New York: McGraw-Hill, 1953. Roland de Vaux, *Ancient Israel,* trans. by John McHugh, New York: McGraw-Hill, 1961, pp. 24-38, 521 f. Ralph Heynen, *The Secret of Christian Family Living,* Grand Rapids: Baker, 1965. Dean Johnson, *Marriage and Coun-*

selling, Englewood Cliffs: Prentice Hall, 1961. J. Kenneth Morris, *Premarital Counselling,* Englewood Cliffs: Prentice Hall, 1960. John Murray, *Principles of Conduct,* Grand Rapids: Eerdmans, 1957, pp. 45-81. Marc Oraison, *Man and Wife,* New York: Macmillan, 1958. John R. Rice, *The Home, Courtship, Marriage and Children,* Wheaton: Sword of the Lord, 1945. C. W. Shudder, *The Family in Christian Perspective,* Nashville: Broadman, 1962. Dwight H. Small, *Design for Christian Marriage,* Westwood, N.J.: Revell, 1959. E. Stauffer, "*Gameō,* games," TDNT, I, 648-657. Charles William Stewart, *The Minister as Marriage Counsellor,* New York: Abingdon, 1961.

MARRIAGE, LEVIRATE. The term "levirate" is derived from Latin *levir,* a husband's brother. The marriage of a childless widow to her husband's brother was an ancient custom in practice at the time of the patriarchs (Gen 38:8), and later incorporated into the law of Moses (Deut 25:5-10). Such a legal custom was known in Assyria according to Nuzi Tablet #441 (BA, III [1940], 10), and it was proper for a father-in-law to enter into levirate marriage according to Hittite law (ANET, p. 196).

Since levirate marriage could take place only after the death of the first husband, it does not contradict the purpose of Lev 18:16; 20:21. These passages forbade marriage to a brother's wife as a general rule, but this was to be annulled when the first brother had died childless, in order that his family name might be maintained by another of his family. Either a brother or the nearest male kin was required to raise up seed to the name of the deceased. If the obligation was repudiated, the widow was to put him to open shame.

Ruth's marriage to Boaz is an illustration of this law. Boaz offered the opportunity of redemption to the nearest of kin, and upon his refusal, Boaz redeemed the inheritance himself (Ruth 4:1-10).

A double violation of the levirate law is found in Gen 38. Judah had three sons, Er, Onan and Shelah. Er married a woman named Tamar and died without child. Judah then gave Tamar his second son Onan in levirate marriage, but Onan refused to have a child by her and died. Judah, who had now lost two sons, would not give the third son in marriage to Tamar, so she took the matter into her own hands. Dressed as a harlot she seduced Judah and had a child by him. Confronted by proof of his sin, Judah acknowledged his wrong in the matter (Gen 38:1-26).

The Sadducees referred to this custom in scorn in Mt 22:23-30 since they did not believe in resurrection or life after death. They asked Jesus which of seven brothers would be the real husband of a woman married to the seven in succession in order to perpetuate the first husband's name in the life to come.

See Marriage.

***Bibliography*.** Millar Burrows, "The Ancient Oriental Background of Hebrew Levirate Marriage," BASOR #77 (1940), pp. 2-15. D. R. Mace, *Hebrew Marriage,* New York: Philosophical Library, 1953, pp. 95-118. E. Neufeld, *Ancient Hebrew Marriage Laws,* London: Longmans, 1944, pp 23-55. Thomas and Dorothy Thompson, "Some Legal Problems in the Book of Ruth," VT, XVIII (1968), 79-99.

R. A. K.

MARRIAGE OF THE LAMB. The great celebration when Christ and His Bride the Church are united (Rev 19:7-9). *See* Bride of Christ.

Differing views are held as to those who will be wedded to Christ at that time. Dispensational Bible teachers suggest that only the members of the NT Church from Pentecost to the rapture will comprise the Bride, because John the Baptist seems to exclude himself from the Bride (Jn 3:29), and because Israel is not called a bride but a wife, while God pictures Himself as a husband to Israel and not as a bridegroom (Jer 31:32; Hos 2:1-23). Others consider that believers of all ages will make up the Bride, since saints of the NT times are to partake of the promises along with the saints of the OT (Rom 4:16; Heb 11:39 f.). Since Paul in Rom 4 proves that all, both in OT and in NT times, are saved by simple faith, and goes on to say that all believers partake of the promise given to Abraham of the heirship of the world (Rom 4:13-16), the Reformed theologians have always spoken of the unity of the covenant of grace in both Testaments, and have taught that therefore all believers of both Testaments will be equal partakers of the marriage supper of the Lamb.

Both in the Bible and in the Middle East today there are found many variations of wedding customs. Hence it may be rash to speculate on the basis of the imagery found in the parables and other passages foretelling the coming marriage of Christ, what will be the exact nature and order of events in connection with it. Nevertheless, three basic steps are known to have existed in an oriental marriage of the 1st cen. A.D.: (1) the marriage contract, often concluded by the parents when one or both of the parties to the marriage were still children, with the presentation of a dowry to the bride and compensation gifts to her family by the groom to seal the covenant and bind the two families together (cf. Gen 34:6-12); (2) a procession, when the couple had reached a suitable age, in which the bridegroom went to the house of the bride to escort her to his home (Mt 25:1-13); and (3) the marriage feast, to which guests were invited, held after the groom had brought his bride to his home (Jn 2:1-12). As John F. Walvoord has pointed out (*The Revelation of Jesus Christ,* p. 271), the marriage symbolism is beautifully fulfilled in the relationship of Christ to His Church. The marriage covenant is implemented at the time the members of the Church are redeemed. Christ the Bridegroom comes to receive His Bride at the rapture (*q.v.*). The third phase then will follow, i.e., the wedding supper.

Rev 19:6–9 is actually a prophetic hymn anticipating the marriage of the Lamb and His Bride *after* He has begun to reign, and He will not begin His reign on earth until He has conquered the kings of the earth led by Antichrist (George E. Ladd, *The Blessed Hope,* pp. 99–102). Will the wedding supper take place, then, in heaven or on earth in Jerusalem, Christ's millennial capital of the world? Should it be identified with the messianic banquet foretold in Isa 25:6–9 (cf. Lk 14:7–24)? While upon occasion the marriage feast could be held in the bride's home (Gen 29:22; Jud 14:10), it was usually at the home of the groom (Mt 22:2f.; Jn 2:9) and often at night (Mt 25:6). There is no indication, however, of two suppers, one in the bride's house and another furnished by the bridegroom.

Does the term "marriage supper" (Rev 19:9) indicate an actual future event, a single ceremonial banquet? Or is the concept of a wedding feast merely symbolic of the close fellowship that the resurrected saints shall continually enjoy with their heavenly Bridegroom, as Jesus suggested in saying that He would drink the fruit of the vine with us in His Father's kingdom (Mt 26:29; cf. Lk 13:28 f.)? Is the Church consistently and only represented as the Bride in parables about the forthcoming messianic marriage, or does the figure vary freely so that upon occasion NT believers are also seen as companions of the Bridegroom ("sons of the bridechamber," Mt 9:15, ASV), as virgin attendants (Mt 25:1–13), or as wedding guests (Mt 22:1–14; Rev 19:9)? The Bride is described as arrayed in "fine linen, clean and white," interpreted as denoting the righteous deeds of the saints (Rev 19:8, RSV). Thus whatever the exact nature of the believers' future fellowship with the Lord, their present conduct is of the utmost importance as a means of pleasing the heavenly Bridegroom.

R. A. K.

MARROW. This English word occurs five times in the KJV as the translation of four Heb. words and one Gr. word. It is the soft, fatty material that fills bone cavities (Heb 4:12) to strengthen and nourish the bones (Job 21:24; Prov 3:8). Therefore it signifies the inmost, choicest, or essential part of one's being. "Marrow" also is a synonym for "fatness," and is used figuratively of those things which alone can satisfy the human soul (Ps 63:5; Isa 25:6). The abundance or richness of the satisfaction seems to be implied also.

MARS HILL. *See* Areopagus.

MARSENA (mär-sē'nȧ). One of the seven princes of Persia and Media, "who saw the king's face, and sat first in the kingdom" (Est 1:14), indicating that they were counselors of Ahasuerus (Xerxes).

MARSH. A translation of Heb. *gebe',* from an unused root which means "to gather together, to collect" (water). In Isa 30:14 this Heb. word, following the meaning of its Akkad. cognate *gubbu,* is translated "cistern" in the ASV, RSV, and NASB, and "pit" in the KJV. In Ezk 47:11, however, it is translated "marshes." For the most part Palestine is rocky and dry, but some marshes are found near the mouths of some of the rivers, as the Kishon, at various places along the course of the Jordan, and about the Dead Sea. According to Ezk 47:11 the "miry places and the marshes" around the Dead Sea will not be healed by the life-giving river, but will be left for salt. The synonym *biṣṣâ,* "miry place" or "swamp" (RSV, NASB) also occurs in Job 8:11 (KJV, "mire") and 40:21 (KJV, "fens") with the meaning of "marsh" (RSV, NASB). In Jer 38:22 a similar Heb. word, *bōṣ,* means the "mire" of a swamp.

S. F. B.

MART. *See* Market.

Bethany with Church of St. Lazarus in foreground and adjacent location of home of Martha and Mary.
HFV

MARTHA (mär'thȧ). Mentioned by name only in Luke and John, Martha was a member of the famous family group which included, besides herself, her sister Mary and her brother Lazarus. Martha figures in three incidents, in each of which our Lord also appears. In Lk 10:38–42 she is placed in contrast to Mary. Martha appears as the active sister, mistress of the home apparently, busily engaged in preparing and serving the food, while Mary sat at Jesus' feet hearing His words. When Martha complained, the Lord gently admonished and soothed her.

In Jn 11, the two sisters were mourning the death of their brother. When Jesus came, Martha told Him that if He had been there her brother would not have died. The Lord assured her that Lazarus would rise again, which he did.

Jn 12:1–11 says of Martha merely that she served at a supper given for the Lord. Probably Martha was the eldest of the three. Evidently she was given to hospitality, and gladly ministered to the Lord as she was able.

J. A. S.

MARTYR. In the KJV the word occurs only in Acts 22:20; Rev 2:13; 17:6. The Gr. word *martus*, from which the English word "martyr" comes, is usually translated "witness" in KJV. A witness, in this sense, is one who bears record or testifies. This is the literal meaning. In Acts 22:20 and Rev 2:13, ASV reads "witness" instead of "martyr," but in Rev 17:6 "martyrs" is retained. LXX renders the Heb. word *'ēd* for "witnesses" by *martyres*, as for example in Isa 43:10. *See* Witness.

The three NT passages above apparently form the basis for the shift in meaning from "witness" to "martyr." A martyr to us is a witness for the Lord who gives his life because of his testimony, as did Stephen (Acts 22:20) and Antipas (Rev 2:13) and other "martyrs of Jesus" (Rev 17:6).

MARVEL. This English word in verb form occurs three times in the KJV of the OT (Gen 43:33; Ps 48:5; Eccl 5:8) and comes from the Heb. *tāmah* which means "to wonder" or "to be astonished." The Heb. verb *pālā'*, "to be difficult, extraordinary, wonderful, marvelous," is once translated "I will do marvels" in Ex 34:10, and many times is translated as the adjective "marvellous" (e.g., I Chr 16:12, 24; Mic 7:15) or the adverb "marvellously" (e.g., Job 37:5; II Chr 26:15). In the KJV of the NT "marvel" or "marvellous" occurs 37 times, coming from the Gr. word *thaumazō* which means "to admire, wonder." *See* Wonder, Wonderful.

MARY (mâr'ĭ). This name is found in the NT as Maria or Mariam, Gr. forms of the Heb. name Miriam. In the LXX the name of the sister of Moses appears as Mariam (*see* Miriam).

1. Mary the mother of Jesus

Biblical references. The first reference to the mother of the Messiah is the *protevangelium* in Gen 3:15 indicating that the destroyer of Satan would be the seed of "the woman." Isa 7:14 is interpreted by Matthew (1:22–23) as a prediction that the messianic birth should come about through a virgin. The incarnation (*q.v.*) of God by means of a virgin birth was promised to the house of David as a miraculous sign. The fulfillment of these prophecies was effected in Mary of Nazareth, a virgin betrothed to a carpenter named Joseph (Lk 1:26–27). Though she was frightened when the angel announced that she would become pregnant before she had known her espoused Joseph, she accepted the overwhelming dignity with humility (Lk 1:38). The royal genealogy of Mary is given in Luke (3:23 ff.). Her various rare appearances during the life of her Son reveal the graciousness but imperfection of her character as she failed to comprehend her 12-year-old's actions (Lk 2:41 ff.). Later she presumed on His authority and judgment (Jn 2:3), and elicited a tender rebuke for her presumption (2:4); but was lovingly committed to the apostle John's care by the dying Christ (Jn 19:25–27), and is last mentioned joining with the disciples in awaiting the outpouring of His Spirit (Acts 1:14).

Ecclesiastical tradition. While the biblical narrative is as reserved as Mary herself, ecclesiastical Mariology can be only technically distinguished from Mariolatry. On the other hand, early Christian teaching about Mary began with a zeal for the glory of her Son and throughout all its traditional development has incidentally extolled the deity of Christ.

(1) Gr. *theotokos.* When in the 4th cen. Nestorius, shrinking from Nicene orthodoxy, wished to deny the deity of Christ at the incarnation, he insisted on calling Mary *Christotokos* (bearer of Christ) but not *Theotokos* (bearer of God). Cyril of Alexandria and other orthodox men recognized that Mary herself *conceived* only the humanity of her child but (since the incarnation took place at the same time) *carried* the God-man and was therefore *Theotokos*.

(2) Gr. *aeiparthenos.* Once the orthodox *theotokos* doctrine was clearly established, certain deductions began to be made. Since Mary was the "mother of God," in the proper sense of that expression, it began to be felt incongruous for her to have subsequently had ordinary children by ordinary generation. As a result of this Manichean strain of thought, she was declared *aeiparthenos* (ever virgin) and the other children (the *adelphoi* of Mt 13:55–56) were forcibly construed as "cousins" of Jesus.

(3) Sinlessness and the immaculate conception. It seemed necessary for Mary to be virgin and sinless not only henceforth after the incarnation but prior to that event as well. This had to begin with her sinlessness at birth; hence the immaculate conception doctrine was advanced. While Duns Scotus in the 13th cen. argued for this doctrine for this reason, for a different reason Aquinas and the Dominicans opposed it. Christ, Thomas Aquinas said, could not be the Saviour of the whole world, including Mary, if she were without sin and not in need of salvation. By the 16th cen. these objections were outgrown and the dogma was officially promulgated. For some reason, or lack of it, it has never seemed necessary to the Roman church to argue for the sinlessness of Mary's parents. However, if it were necessary for Mary to have been sinless if Christ were not to be contaminated, why would not the same be true of Mary's parents?

(4) The bodily assumption. A tradition about the assumption of Mary's body has been known in the church from the earliest times; in fact, two traditions, one favoring assumption from death and one from life. But only after the immaculate conception, perpetual virginity and

The reconstructed traditional home of the Virgin Mary at Ephesus. HFV

sinless perfection had been defined, did the Roman Catholic church dogmatize about Mary's death. Nor is it clear in Pius XII's papal bull *Munificentissimus Deus* (November 1, 1950) whether she is thought to have died before being raised, though the implication of the following words seems to favor this: ". . . when the course of her earthly life was finished, (she) was taken by body and soul into the glory of heaven."

(5) Co-redemptrix. After developing a full Mariology of her life and character, the Roman church, at Vatican II, defined Mary's role in the economy of salvation, her relation to the church and her veneration. According to the Vatican Council, Mary "far surpasses all creatures," is "a preeminent and singular member of the Church" and "mother of men, particularly of the faithful" (VIII, 53–54). Because of her acceptance of the divine birth in her and her being "full of grace and truth" she "contributed to life" as Eve had contributed to death (p. 57). Her life is interpreted as perfectly sinless. The rebuke of Christ is construed as a compliment—construing those who do the will of God as being Christ's mother, as "those who heard and kept the Word of God, as she was faithfully doing (cf. Lk 2:19, 51)."

Following this comes the formulation of Mary's mediation. First, the council makes an evangelical insistence on the sole mediatorship of Christ so that "all the salvific influence of the blessed virgin on men originates not from some inner necessity, but from divine pleasure and from the superabundance of the merits of Christ." Her own "salvific influence" appears in her cooperation with Christ on earth and the continuance in heaven of her intercession for men. Therefore she is invoked as "advocate, auxiliatrix, adjutrix, and mediatrix. This, however, is to be so understood that it neither takes away from, nor adds anything to, the dignity of efficaciousness of Christ the one Mediator" (p. 62). Others also participate in a "manifold cooperation." The church herself becomes a virgin spouse to Christ imitating His virgin mother (p. 64).

We notice that the term "mediatrix" is used in spite of opposition at the council and that pains are taken to indicate that the term does not mean what it appears to teach. Insistence is made that Christ is sole Mediator although Mary is also mediatrix. It is not clear why Rome, if she desired to teach that there is only one mediator between God and man, did not deliberately avoid using the term "mediatrix" of Mary rather than stubbornly, in spite of opposition within and without the council, applying it to her.

Mariolatry. In 1955 Father Kenneth Dougherty of Washington's Franciscan Friars of the Atonement sent a questionnaire to 270 ministers of 17 denominations in 29 states and the District of Columbia. Of the 100 who answered, 64 percent said they did not believe Mary is the Mother of God, the Episcopalians being most in favor and the Presbyterians most opposed. The reasons for unbelief in the doctrine was the presumed attempt to "divinize" Mary. Father Dougherty felt those opposed were overlooking Rome's distinction between *latreia* (worship) and *douleia* (veneration). Those in opposition must recognize that Mary has been declared sinless though all men have fallen in Adam. She is not only called the Mother of God but sometimes the very word "genetrix" is used, and when it is not, care is seldom taken to explain in what sense Mary is not the Mother of God. She is now called redemptrix, is able to intercede with the Son unfailingly, is prayed to, adored and called upon in many cases more commonly, frequently and urgently than is Christ Himself. The only argument against this being a deifying of Mary is that a certain word (*latreia*) is not used. What is in a word when all that is in a word is contained in alternative expressions and rituals?

It is true that according to Roman Catholic theology sacrifice is offered to God only; to no one else, even Mary. This, however, is derivative from Roman liturgical practice rather than determinative of it and also virtually implies that in other matters of redemption there is no essential distinction.

Protestants generally and historically have held aloof from the Mariological development in Rome. They are probably under-appreciative of the mother of the Lord by virtue of over-reaction. Present ecumenical discussion reveals a slight moderating of Roman dogma by Protestant influence on the one hand (cf. Vatican II), and on the other a greater Protestant concern for Mariology (cf. H. Asmussen).

[The Latin prayer to Mary known as the Ave Maria is a combination of the salutations recorded in Luke and the later worship of Mary as the mother of God. Translated into English, it reads: "Hail Mary full of grace, the Lord is with thee. Blessed art thou among women, and blessed is the fruit of thy womb, Jesus. Holy Mary, mother of God: pray for us sinners now and in the hour of our death." The first two parts, echoing the greeting of Gabriel and Elisabeth (Lk 1:28, 42), first appeared in the *Liber Antiphonianus* attributed to Gregory the Great, and were authorized to be taught with the Apostles' Creed and the Lord's Prayer about A.D. 1198. The third part was added in the 15th cen. and was authorized by Pope Pius V in 1568. The Gr. words of Lk 1:28, in the KJV "Hail, thou that art highly favored," are translated in the Vulgate: "*Ave, gratia plena*" (Hail, full of grace). Roman Catholic expositors take this to mean that Mary is full of gifts of grace and accordingly appears between God and man as mediator to dispense gifts. The context, however, clearly favors the interpretation that Mary is the recipient of the favor of God in being chosen to be the mother of Jesus. —W. B. W.]

2. Mary Magdalene, identified with the flourishing but corrupt city of Magdala (*q.v.*), which guarded a road juncture in the plain of Gennesaret. She is mentioned in Lk 8:2 as one from whom seven demons had been driven. This together with her identification (though without any evidence) with the nameless woman of Lk 7:37–50 is the basis for the questionable assumption that she was a prostitute. In any case, after her conversion her devotion to Christ was evident as she appears during His ministry and passion (Lk 8:1–3; Mk 15:40–41; Jn 19:25). She was the first to see the risen Lord (Lk 24:1 f.; Jn 20:11–18).

3. Mary the mother of James the Younger and Joses, who followed Jesus in Galilee and contributed to Him (Mk 15:40–41). She is mentioned in connection with all the events centering around the death, burial and resurrection of Christ, but little else can be said about her with confidence.

4. Mary the wife of Cleophas, who also stood by the cross at Jesus' death (Jn 19:25). The correct spelling of her husband's name is Clopas (NASB), not the Cleopas of Lk 24:18.

5. Mary of Bethany, the sister of Martha and Lazarus (Jn 11:1–46), who preferred the "better part" and sat at Jesus' feet enthralled by His teaching (Lk 10:39–42). She is mistakenly believed to have been the one who anointed Christ in a Pharisee's house in Capernaum as recorded in Lk 7:36–50; but is the Mary who similarly ministered to Jesus at Bethany (Jn 12:1–8; Mk 14:3–9).

6. Mary the mother of John Mark, at whose house many were gathered for prayer when Peter, being released from prison, came there (Acts 12:12 ff.).

Bibliography. H. Asmussen, *Maria die Mutter Gottes,* 3d Auflage, Stuttgart, 1960. Donald A. Attwater, *Dictionary of Mary,* New York: Kenedy, 1956. W. Grayson Birch, *Veritas and the Virgin; or Jesus, the Son of God and the Children of Joseph and Mary,* Berne, Ind.; Berne Witness, 1960. Walter J. Burghardt, *The Testimony of the Patristic Age Concerning Mary's Death,* Westminster, Md.: Newman Press, 1957. *De Ecclesia, The Constitution on the Church of Vatican Council II,* foreword by Abbot B. D. Butler, O.S.B., commentary by Gregory Baum, O.S.B., Glen Rock, N.J.: 1965, pp. 52–60, 177–190. J. G. Machen, *The Virgin Birth of Christ,* New York: Harper, 1930. Thomas A. O'Meara, *Mary in Protestant and Catholic Theology,* New York: Sheed & Ward, 1966. J. Orr, *The Virgin Birth of Christ,* New York: Scribner's, 1908. Karl Rahner, *Mary, Mother of the Lord,* New York: Herder & Herder, 1963. A. T. Robertson, *The Mother of Jesus, Her Problems and Her Glory,* New York: Doran, 1925. Edward Schillebeeck, *Mary Mother of the Redemption,* trans. by N. D. Smith, New York: Paulist Press, 1964.

J. H. G.

MASADA (mȧ-sā'dȧ). A high "ship-shaped" rock formation converted into a fortification by the high priest Jonathan sometime after 152 B.C. It is located opposite the Lisan (broad sandy peninsula jutting into the Dead Sea from the E) on the W side of the Dead Sea between the shore line and the cliffs surrounding the Dead Sea basin. The nearly vertical faces of the rock drop *c.* 820 feet on the E and 600 feet on the W to the surrounding terrain. Masada is not mentioned in the Bible, but its dramatic history is part of the fulfillment of Jesus' prophecy in Mt 23:37–38.

In later years Herod the Great built a wall around the rim of the mesa of Masada (flat top of the rock) and dug cisterns in the side of the cliffs for water supply. After Jerusalem fell to the Parthians (*c.* 40 B.C.) Herod fled to Masada with his mother and sister, his betrothed Mariamne and her mother and brother Joseph.

Herod furnished the fortress as a place of refuge for himself in the face of danger from the Jewish people and Cleopatra, queen of Egypt. Herod's wall around the top (total length about 4,300 feet) was about 20 feet high, 13 feet thick and had 37 towers, each about 90 feet high. The meager soil on top of the rock was used to cultivate grain and vegetables.

Large storehouses for wheat, wine, oil, beans, and dates were erected. The fortress contained enough weapons and materials, including ingots of iron, brass and lead, to supply an army of 10,000 men.

After Herod's death the fortress was manned by a Roman garrison until A.D. 66. During the Roman War (A.D. 66–73) the fortress, captured by a ruse, was in possession of the Zealots under the direction of Eleazar the "Tyrant of Masada."

Masada became the last Jewish stronghold to withstand the Romans. In A.D. 72, two years after the fall of Jerusalem under Titus, the Roman governor, Flavius Silva, marshaled a formidable army against the fortress. Before attack he encircled the entire rock with a retaining wall to prevent escape. A siege ramp was built on the W side, and on this platform of stones almost 100 feet high and 100 feet wide the Romans raised a siege tower, clad in iron, about 120 feet high. From its top engines of war shot

Masada. IIS

arrows, flaming torches, and stones at the defenders. A battering ram broke a breach in the wall, whereupon the defenders erected a secondary wooden wall. Silva's men attacked the wooden wall with torches. During the night Eleazar persuaded his followers to commit suicide rather than surrender to the Romans. Of the 960 men, women, and children, only two women and five children survived. Silva surveyed the ruins the next morning and then returned to Caesarea (Jos *Wars,* vii. 8.1 – 9.2).

Large scale excavations at the site were conducted in 1963-65 as a joint venture of the Hebrew University, the Israel Exploration Society, and the Israel Government Department of Antiquities, all under the leadership of Yigael Yadin. The historical account of Josephus was remarkably confirmed. Archaeologists found fragments of 12 1st cen. A.D. scrolls at Masada, containing passages from Genesis, Leviticus and other biblical and apocryphal books. See especially Yigael Yadin, *Masada,* New York: Random House, 1966.

H. A. Han.

MASCHIL (măs'kĭl). A Heb. term found in the title of 13 psalms (Ps 32, 42, 44, 45, 52, 53, 54, 55, 74, 78, 88, 89, 142), indicating the type of psalm, i.e., a didactic poem. The same Heb. word is found in Ps 47:7 where in the KJV it is translated "understanding" (NASB, "a skillful psalm"). It is probably based on a Heb. verb meaning "to attend, to turn the mind to, to be understanding or prudent." On the other hand, the term may indicate a special kind of musical performance.

MASH (măsh). One of the four sons of Aram and a descendant of Shem (Gen 10:23). In the parallel passage in I Chr 1:17 the name Meshech is used instead of Mash. The LXX has Meshech in both passages. In Gen 10:2 Meshech is listed as a son of Japheth. This may indicate an intermingling of the lines of Japheth and Shem in Meshech. On the other hand, Mash may refer to Mount Masius and its inhabitants (identified either as the Lebanons [ANET, pp. 88–89] or as a range on the N boundary of Mesopotamia) or to a region and people in the Syro-Arabian desert equivalent to the "desert of Mash" of the Assyrian inscriptions (ANET, pp. 283–284, Mas'a, Mas'ai). *See* Nations.

MASHAL (mā'shȧl). A town in Asher with its suburbs given to the Gershonite Levites (I Chr 6:74). It is also called Mishal (*q.v.*) in Josh 19:26; 21:30.

MASON. *See* Occupations: Mason.

MASREKAH (măs'rĕ-kȧ). Home town of an ancient Edomite king, Samlah (Gen 36:36; I Chr 1:47). Its site is uncertain.

MASSA (măs'ȧ). One of the sons of Ishmael and descendant of Abraham (Gen 25:14; I Chr 1:30). According to the RSV, Agur (Prov 30:1) and King Lemuel (Prov 31:1) may have belonged to this Arabic tribe. There are references to Massa (Akk. Mas'a), Tema, and Nebajoth (cf. Gen 25:13-15) in the Assyrian inscriptions of Tiglath-pileser III (ANET, pp. 283 f.).

MASSAH (măs'ȧ). One of the names (meaning "testing, trial") given by Moses to the place where the Israelites tested the Lord saying, "Is Jehovah among us, or not?" (Ex 17:7, ASV). The other name was Meribah (*q.v.*), meaning "quarreling, dissension." The incident occurred at Rephidim (*q.v.*) near the beginning of the desert wanderings en route to Mount Sinai. There was no water to drink and the people murmured and strove against Moses. At the command of God Moses smote the rock in

Horeb and water came forth out of it (cf. Deut 6:16; 9:22; 33:8; Ps 95:8, ASV, RSV, NASB).

In Ex 17:7 and Ps 95:8 the names Massah and Meribah occur together and apply to the same event. In all other passages the terms refer to two separate events or places. The waters at Kadesh-barnea were also called Meribah, because once again Israel strove (contended, NASB) with the Lord. In this instance Moses angrily accused the people of rebelling against him and Aaron, and then struck the rock twice, thus rebelling against God's command (Num 20:13, 24; cf. 27:14; Deut 32:51; Ps 106:32). In Deut 33:8, then, both events are in view, God proving the tribe of Levi (as well as all the others) at Massah and striving with them in the person of Moses their leader at the waters of Meribah.

J.R.

MAST. *See* Ship.

MASTER. This word in Scripture designates in general one who is superior to others, either in power, authority, knowledge, or in some other respect.

Several words are rendered "master" in KJV. The most frequent Heb. word, *'ādôn,* means "sovereign" or "lord." The literal meanings of the various Gr. words range from "instructor," *didaskalos,* as in Mt 10:24, to "despot," *despotēs,* as in I Pet 2:18. Another Gr. word rendered "master," *epistatēs,* means "one appointed over" others, as in Lk 5:5. Still another Gr. word is really Heb.—"rabbi," meaning "my master" (or "superior," or "teacher"), as in Jn 4:31, ASV. A fifth Gr. word for "master" is *kurios,* which is ordinarily rendered "lord" throughout the NT. This word means "supreme" (in authority). In the highest sense, the title applies only to the Lord. There are still other Heb. and Gr. words having different shades of meaning which are translated "master."

Two of the Gr. words for "master" occur in Mt 23:8-10. "But be not ye called rabbi (*rhabbi,* "my master" or "teacher"): for one is your Master (*kathēgētēs,* "leader," "teacher"), even Christ; and all ye are brethren. And call no man your father upon the earth: for one is your Father, which is in heaven. Neither be ye called masters (*kathēgētēs,* "leaders"): for one is your Master (*kathēgētēs* again), even Christ." *See* Rabbi; Education; Teach.

J.A.S.

MASTIC. *See* Plants: Balm.

MATHUSALA. The Gr. form of Methuselah (*q.v.*; Lk 3:37).

MATRED (mā'trĕd). According to the Heb MT, the mother-in-law of Hadar (Genesis) or Hadad (Chronicles), the last of the ancient kings of Edom (Gen 36:39; I Chr 1:50). In the LXX and Peshitta of Genesis, Matred is the son of Me-zahab rather than the daughter.

MATRI (mā'trī). A family of the tribe of Benjamin from which Kish and his son Saul came (I Sam 10:21).

MATRIMONY. *See* Marriage.

MATTAN (măt'*ă*n)

1. A priest of Baal who was killed by the people of Judah when Jehoiada led the revolution against the wicked usurper Athaliah on behalf of her grandson Joash, the rightful heir to the throne (II Kgs 11:18; II Chr 23:17).

2. The father of Shephatiah (Jer 38:1). The latter, together with some others—all princes apparently (v. 4)—requested the execution of Jeremiah on the ground that his utterances were unpatriotic and harmful to the people's welfare. Jeremiah was imprisoned but not executed.

MATTANAH (măt'*ă*-n*ă*). A campground of the Israelites N of the Arnon, between Beer and Nahaliel, in their journey through Moab (Num 21:18-19). It has been tentatively identified with Khirbet el-Medeiyineh, 12 miles SE of Medeba and 11 miles NE of Dibon.

MATTANIAH (măt'*ă*-nī'*ă*)

1. Original name of Zedekiah (*q.v.*), king of Judah. His name was changed when Nebuchadnezzar put him on the throne replacing his nephew Jehoiachin. He reigned 11 years in Jerusalem and was an evil king (II Kgs 24:17-20).

2. A descendant of Asaph (I Chr 9:15), leader of the temple choir (Neh 11:17; 12:8). One of the porters at the threshold of the gates (Neh 12:25), and ancestor of one of the trumpeters (Neh 12:35). He lived in one of the villages with the rest of the "sons of the singers" who had built villages for themselves around Jerusalem (Neh 12:28-29). Possibly the descendant of Asaph is not identified with the musician.

3. One of the sons of Heman whose office it was to blow the trumpet in the temple service instituted by David. He had charge of the ninth division of 12 Levites who were proficient in songs of the Lord (I Chr 25:4, 16). He may have been the father of Jeiel, descendant of Asaph, and ancestor of Jahaziel the Levite in the reign of Jehoshaphat (II Chr 20:14).

4. A descendant of Asaph who assisted in the purification of the temple when Hezekiah vowed to cleanse the house of the Lord (II Chr 29:13).

5. One of the sons of Elam who put away his Gentile wife after the Captivity (Ezr 10:26).

6. A descendant of Zattu who put away his Gentile wife after the Captivity (Ezr 10:27).

7. An inhabitant of Pahath-moab who divorced his Gentile wife in obedience to the demand of Ezra (Ezr 10:30).

8. A descendant of Bani who put away his

Gentile wife in obedience to Ezra's order (Ezr 10:37).

9. A Levite, father of Zaccur and grandfather of Hanan, who was one of the treasurers of the tithes of corn and wine and oil which the people of Judah brought to the house of God. It was their duty to distribute it to their brethren. They were men who "were counted faithful" (Neh 13:13).

R. H. B.

MATTATHA. *See* Mattathah.

MATTATHAH (măt'tȧ-thȧ). One of the sons of Hashum who had taken a foreign wife in the time of Ezra (Ezr 10:33).

MATTATHIAS (măt'ȧ-thī'ȧs). The name of two ancestors of Jesus (Lk 3:25-26). If there are no omissions in the genealogy given in Lk 3, the first of these was eight generations before Jesus, and the second 14. It is remarkable how many men in this line have names similar to this one. In v. 24 there is Matthat, in v. 26 Maath, in v. 29 Matthat again, and in v. 31 Mattatha.

The name Mattathias is a common one in the OT Apocrypha. The most notable person of that name was the father of Judas Maccabaeus and his four brothers. It was this Mattathias who was the initial leader of the Jewish revolution against Antiochus Epiphanes and his successors in the 2nd cen. B.C.

In Neh 8:4, the first named man who stood beside Ezra when he read from the book of the law of Moses is called Mattithiah (*q.v.*), the Heb. equivalent of Mattathias. His time would have been somewhat earlier than either of the ancestors of Christ.

J. A. S.

MATTENAI (măt'ȧ-nī)

1. One of the sons of Hashum who had taken a foreign wife in the days of Ezra (Ezr 10:33).

2. One of the sons of Bani who likewise had taken a foreign wife in the days of Ezra (Ezr 10:37).

3. A post-Exilic priest in the days of Joiakim, son of Jeshua, and representative of the house of Joiarib (Neh 12:19).

MATTHAN (măth'ăn). A legal ancestor of Jesus through Joseph (Mt 1:15), perhaps the grandfather of Joseph.

MATTHAT (măth'ăt). The name of two ancestors of Jesus, one near (perhaps the grandfather of Mary, Lk 3:24), and the other remote (Lk 3:29).

MATTHEW (măth'ū). One of the 12 apostles whose name occurs seventh in the list in Mk 5:18 and Lk 6:15, but in eighth place in Mt 10:3 and Acts 1:13.

Outside the mention of his name in the lists, only two episodes are related of Matthew. The first, his call from his tax office near Capernaum, is the only individual call of a single disciple related in the Synoptic Gospels. Matthew was probably in the service of Herod, tetrarch of Galilee, and as a publican (*telōnēs*) would have been literate. The second episode is the feast given by Levi to which many "publicans and sinners" were invited (Lk 5:29).

The name Levi (*q.v.*) does not occur in the lists of apostles and no Gospel uses both names. Yet Levi, son of Alphaeus, and Matthew are to be identified, as is made likely by the fact that the call of Matthew from the tax office and the account of the feast in Mt 9:9–13 are told of Levi in Mk 2:14–17; Lk 5:27–32. The information available is not sufficient to determine his relationship to James the son of Alphaeus (cf. Mk 2:14; 3:18).

Of the post-Pentecost activities of Matthew, the NT tells nothing. The early church believed that Matthew wrote the first Gospel. Papias and Eusebius related a tradition that after a ministry among the Jews, Matthew, on the verge of going to others, wrote his Gospel for Jews in the Heb. dialect (Euseb. HE III. 24.6; 39.16). Various stories carry him to Ethiopia, Macedonia, Syria, Persia, Parthia, and Media. One line of tradition has him die a natural death in Ethiopia or Macedonia. The Gr. and Rom. churches, on the other hand, celebrate his martyrdom. These latter legends cannot be proved historical.

Bibliography. E. J. Goodspeed, *Matthew, Apostle and Evangelist*, Philadelphia: John C. Winston, 1959.

J. P. L.

MATTHEW, GOSPEL OF

Introduction

The first Gospel was the most widely used of the Gospels in the 2nd cen. A.D. church. Its initial popularity has continued, for today Matthew is still probably the most widely read Gospel.

Matthew has a number of indications of having been originally written in Gr. Its quotations are most often from the LXX; it contains plays upon Gr. words. For these reasons some scholars do not think that Papias' statement (Euseb. HE III. 39.16), "Matthew wrote the *logia* in Hebrew," can describe this Gospel. Various efforts have been made to identify Papias' *logia* with a collection of OT passages or with a collection of sayings of Jesus, but none are entirely satisfactory. To this extent Papias' statement remains a mystery. However, Matthew was clearly written for Jews rather than Gentiles. *See* Gospels, The Four.

Date

Matthew was written between the time of the resurrection and the time of Ignatius, i.e., A.D. 30–115. Efforts to date the book more specifically usually stem from presuppositions about the relationship of the book to Mark and the relationship of Mt 24:15 and 22:7 to the fall of Jerusalem in A.D. 70. Early tradition claimed that the book was written before Matthew left Judea to preach elsewhere, and during the ministry of Peter and Paul in Rome (Euseb. HE III.24.6; Iren. *adv. Haer.* III.1). The phrase "until this day" (Mt 27:8; 28:15) would indicate that some time had elapsed since the death of Jesus. The book was known at an early time in Antioch of Syria, but Streeter's effort to prove that it was written there cannot be said to have succeeded. Others feel that the general area of Syria is more suitable. There can be no certainty in these matters.

Outline

I. Birth Stories, 1:1–2:23
II. John the Baptist, 3:1-17
III. Galilean Ministry, 4:1–18:35
  A. Preparation, 4:1-25
  B. Sermon on the Mount, 5:1–7:29
  C. Miracles and teaching, 8:1–18:35
IV. Activities in Jerusalem and Judea, 19:1–25:46
V. Passion, 26:1–27:66
VI. Resurrection, 28:1-20

Content

The Gospel relates the life of Jesus from His birth to the giving of the Great Commission in Galilee. The story is told with marked emphasis on the fulfillment of OT prophecy. Thirteen times the phrase "that it might be fulfilled which was spoken by the Lord through the prophet" is used. Out of a total of about 40 proof texts mainly centering on the birth, infancy, and passion of Jesus, 36 are based on a defined Scripture. Twenty of these are peculiar to the Gospel of Matthew. Jesus' genealogy is traced back to David and Abraham, both of whom are important in OT promises (Gen 12:3; II Sam 7). An audience of Jewish background seems to have been anticipated.

Jesus is depicted as the new lawgiver who had come to fulfill the law given by Moses. He is the great teacher.

Out of 35 miracles of Jesus related in detail in the Gospels, Matthew tells of 20. Three of these: two blind men healed (9:27-31), the dumb demoniac healed (9:32-33), and the shekel in the fish's mouth (17:24-27), are unique to Matthew. There are also numerous summaries of miraculous activities (4:23; 9:35; 15:30-31; 19:1-2). *See* Miracles.

Twenty-one parables are related in Matthew out of a total of some 51 parabolic passages in the Gospels. Eleven of these are peculiar to Matthew: the tares (13:24-30, 37-43); the hid treasure (13:44); the pearl of great price (13:45-46); the drag net (13:47-50); the unmerciful servant (18:23-35); the laborers in the vineyard (20:1-16); the two sons (21:28-32); the marriage of the king's son (22:1-14; cf. Lk 14:16-24); the ten virgins (25:1-13); the talents (25:14-30); the sheep and the goats (25:31-46).

Matthew has organized his material into blocks of teaching separated by blocks of deeds. Five sections of teachings are seen, each ending with a statement such as, "when Jesus had finished these sayings": (1) the Sermon on the Mount (5:1–7:29); (2) the mission of the disciples (9:35–11:1); (3) parables of the kingdom (13:1-53); (4) discipleship (18:1–19:1); (5) last things (24:1–26:1). To describe Christ's denunciation of the Pharisees (23:1-39) as the sixth discourse would wreck the analogy often made with the five books of Moses.

Other evidences of schematic arrangement are to be seen in the genealogy, which is divided into three sections of 14 generations each; in the seven parables of chap. 13; in the seven woes upon the Pharisees in chap. 23 (v. 14 is not found in the earliest Gr. MSS). Miracles in chaps. 8 and 9 are in groups of three. There are three men in the parable of the talents (25:14-30) and three parables in that chapter. Plummer lists a total of 38 instances of groups of three in the book. There are also groups of two: the blind men (20:30); the false witnesses (26:60).

Marked peculiarities are to be seen in the material Matthew has given. Four women: Tamar, Rahab, Ruth, and Uriah's wife, are mentioned in the genealogy. The term "kingdom of heaven," which is not found in any other book, is used 32 times; frequently the other Gospels use "kingdom of God." Matthew is the only Gospel in which the word church occurs (16:18; 18:17). Several passages offer direction in church situations. The Sermon on the Mount (chaps. 5-7) is three times as long as Luke's Sermon on the Plain (6:20-49) though they are similar in beginning with beatitudes and ending with builders.

Matthew has an unusual number of items in common with rabbinic literature which are not stressed in the other Gospels. For this reason, as well as for its continuous appeal to OT Scriptures, it has been thought of as the "most Jewish of the Gospels."

Bibliography. W. C. Allen, *A Critical and Exegetical Commentary on the Gospel According to St. Matthew,* Edinburgh: T. and T. Clark, 1912. Floyd V. Filson, *The Gospel According to St. Matthew,* New York: Harpers, 1960. A. H. McNeile, *The Gospel According to St. Matthew,* London: Macmillan, 1955. A. Plummer, *An Exegetical Commentary on the Gospel According to St. Matthew* (1910), Grand Rapids: Eerdmans, 1956 (reprint).

J. P. L.

MATTHIAS (mă-thī′ȧs). The disciple chosen to replace Judas as the twelfth apostle. Peter led the company of about 120 disciples to take this step in the interval between Jesus' ascension and Pentecost (Acts 1:15-26). Two men who met certain conditions were proposed. These conditions were that they should have accompanied the disciples during Jesus' whole ministry, from the baptism by John until Jesus was taken into heaven, and they should therefore be able to witness to Jesus' resurrection. After prayer, lots were cast and the choice fell to Matthias, "and he was enrolled with the eleven apostles" (Acts 1:26, RSV). It is quite possible that, as the early historian Eusebius wrote, he was one of the 70 chosen by the Lord (Lk 10:1). Nowhere else does the NT refer to him.

Some writers have felt that Peter was presumptuous in moving to replace Judas—that he and the others should have awaited the Lord's own choice, namely, the apostle Paul. However, the disciples assumed that the Lord would lead them following prayer. The lot was an approved method derived from the OT (e.g., Lev 16:8; Prov 16:33). *See* Lot (casting lots). There is no hint of criticism of this action anywhere in the NT. Paul himself writes that Jesus appeared to "the twelve" after His resurrection, apparently including Matthias in that number as the one eventually enrolled with the 11 others (I Cor 15:5). If Matthias falls into obscurity after this, it is a destiny he shared with others among the Twelve.

Various traditions attach to his name. One has him preaching in Judea and stoned by the Jews. Another says he evangelized in Ethiopia. A spurious Gospel is attributed to him.

N. B. B.

MATTITHIAH (măt'*á*-thī'*á*)

1. A Levite, son of Shallum of the family of Korah, responsible for offerings "baked in pans" (I Chr 9:31).

2. A Levite, appointed doorkeeper in the time of David, who was also a musician, playing before the ark and in the tabernacle (I Chr 15:18, 21; 16:5). Probably the same as the son of Jeduthun (I Chr 25:3), head of the 14th course (I Chr 25:21).

3. An Israelite of the sons of Nebo who put away his Gentile wife after the Exile (Ezr 10:43).

4. One of the prominent men who stood with Ezra as he read the law (Neh 8:4).

MATTOCK. The translation of three Heb. words in the KJV.

1. In Isa 7:25 Heb. *ma'der* means "hoe"and refers to an instrument (something like a pickaxe) which was used in digging and loosening the ground.

2. In I Sam 13:20–21 Heb. *maḥărēshâ* refers to a metal agricultural instrument with an edge, and perhaps denotes the plowshare.

3. In II Chr 34:6 the Heb. word *ḥereb* can mean sword or some other cutting instrument, e.g., a knife, a razor, a graving tool, an axe, which might be used to lay waste or to destroy. The verse, however, is obscure in the Heb.

In most of the modern versions in I Sam 13:20–21 "mattock" is the translation of *'et,* which the KJV renders "coulter."

MAUL. The Heb. *mēpîṣ* comes from a root which means to break in pieces, and hence refers to a weapon, e.g., a hammer, a mace, or war club (Prov 25:18). In Jer 51:20 "battle axe" (*q.v.*) translates a similar Heb. word, *mappēṣ.*

MAW. The rough stomach of animals that chew the cud, e.g., the ox or sheep, which, along with the shoulder and cheeks, was to be the priests' share of any sacrifice brought by the Israelites (Deut 18:3).

MAZZAROTH (măz'*á*-rŏth). This word is found only in Job 38:32. Some interpret it as "the signs of the Zodiac" (NEB) and equivalent to the word *mazzālôth,* "planets," in II Kgs 23:5. Others feel that the parallel passage in Job 9:9 suggests that the *mazzārôth* are a constellation (NASB) or cluster of stars in the southern sky.

MEAH, TOWER OF. *See* Jerusalem: Gates and Towers 2.

MEAL, MEALTIME. *See* Food.

MEAL OFFERING. *See* Sacrificial Offerings.

MEARAH(mē-âr'*á*). A town, district, or place which belonged to the Sidonians and which yet remained to be possessed by the Israelites in Joshua's old age (Josh 13:4). The Heb. word *m*[e]*'ārâ* is found frequently in the OT as a common noun meaning "cave" (e.g., Gen 19:30; I Sam 24:3,7). Therefore Mearah is probably to be identified with the caves called Mughar Jezzin, E of Sidon.

MEASURE. *See* Weights, Measures, and Coins.

MEASURING LINE. *See* Weights, Measures, and Coins.

MEASURING REED. *See* Weights, Measures, and Coins.

MEAT. *See* Food.

MEAT OFFERING. *See* Sacrificial Offerings.

MEBUNNAI (mē-bŭn'ī). One of David's 37 mighty men (II Sam 23:27). Elsewhere he is named Sibbechai (II Sam 21:18; I Chr 11:29; 20:4; 27:11) and is mentioned as the slayer of a Philistine giant and as captain of the eighth of the 12 monthly courses that served the king.

MECHERATHITE (mē-kĕr'*á*-thīt). Related to Mecherah by birth or residence; but such a person or place is unknown. This is the description of Heper, one of the mighty men of David's armies (I Chr 11:36). Some think this is a misreading of "Maacathite" in II Sam 23:34.

MEDAD (mē'dăd). A man associated with Eldad who received the Spirit of the Lord without formal ordination. When informed that Medad was prophesying without being officially approved, Moses did not object but expressed a wish that all of the Lord's people might prophesy and "that the Lord would put his Spirit upon them" (Num 11:26-29).

MEDAN (mē'dăn). A son of Abraham by Keturah and brother of Zimran, Jokshan, Midian, Ishbak, and Shuah, who became ancestors of desert tribes (Gen 25:2; I Chr 1:32). The Heb. word for "Medanites" occurs in Gen 37:36, but most of the English versions translate it "Midianites." Medan is unknown elsewhere in the Bible. Since the consonants "m" and "b" are often interchanged in Arabic, possibly the tribe of Badana, conquered by Tiglath-pileser III of Assyria (ANET, pp. 283 f.), can be identified with Medan.

MEDE. *See* Madai.

MEDEBA (mĕd'ĕ-bȧ). A city E of the Dead Sea in Moab, *c.* 15 miles ESE of the mouth of the Jordan, 20 miles SSW of Amman (ancient Philadelphia), the capital of modern Jordan. The Israelites took it from Sihon, the Amorite king, who had earlier seized the town from Moab (Num 21:21-30).

The territory allotted by Moses to the tribe of Reuben included all the tableland of Medeba (Josh 3:9, 16). The claim to this land was often disputed by the Reubenites, the Ammonites, and the Moabites. Reuben, however, soon vanished from the scene, and after the time of Joshua the tribe is mentioned only three times.

In David's day the city seems to have been in Ammonite hands, for the Syrian allies of the Ammonites encamped there before their defeat by Joab (I Chr 19:7). The Moabite Stone *(q.v.)* says the Israelite King Omri had retaken Medeba probably from Moab, and Israel dwelt there in his time and in half of his son's time, 40 years. King Mesha of Moab recaptured and rebuilt it, along with the cities of the area (ANET, pp. 320 f.). Isa 15:2 implies that Medeba was still held by the Moabites in the 8th cen. B.C. *See* Mesha; Moab.

Modern Madaba (ancient Medeba) became very famous when in the process of building operations in 1896 a number of mosaic pavements of churches of the 5th and 6th cen. A.D. were found. The most famous was a large mosaic map of the Holy Land, with the principal cities marked and the plan of Jerusalem being shown in great detail. At that time Medeba was the seat of a bishopric. No remains earlier than the Byzantine period have been discovered so far.

L. L. W. and D. C. B.

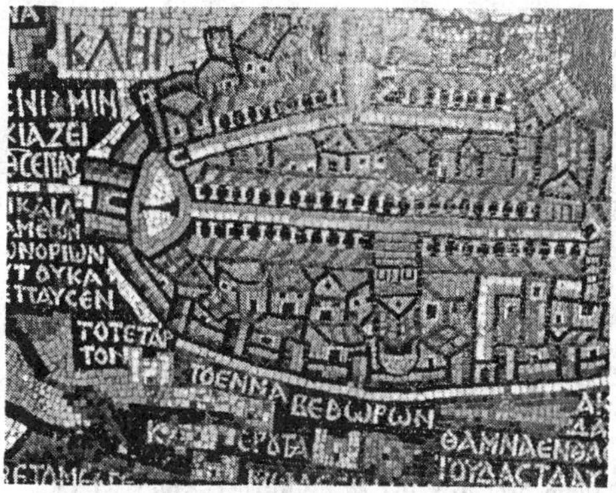

The Medeba map. Sisters of Zion, Jerusalem

MEDES (mēdz), **MEDIA** (mē'dĭ-ȧ). The Aryan people of the high plateau E of the Tigris River S of the Caspian Sea, who are called Madai (*q.v.*) in Gen 10:2, ruled the kingdom of Media. Their homeland was E and S of Lake Urmia.

One of the first extant references to the Medes in ancient documents comes from the annals of Shalmanezer III who reports that he received tribute from them in 836 B.C. A certain Deioces was the first chieftain to unite the nomadic tribes of Madai into a nation. Later their ruler Cyaxares I paid tribute to Sargon II, who consummated the fall of Samaria and deported thousands of Israelites to Media (II Kgs 17:6; 18:11). Sargon in his annals also states that he took horses as tribute from the Madai, who were known for their fine horses.

Median imperialism did not begin until the time of Phraortes (675-653 B.C.) who made the Persians his vassals and formulated a strong anti-Assyrian policy. His son Cyaxares II (635-585) allied himself with Nabopolassar the Chaldean, and with the aid of the Scythians they captured the mighty Assyrian capital of Nineveh in 612 B.C. Cyaxares II gained control over the Assyrian homeland and moved on to help defeat the remnants of Assyria at Haran. He then marched into Anatolia to fight the Lydians, but was forced to make a treaty at the Halys River.

The son of Cyaxares, Astyages (585-550 B.C.), gave Amyitis, one of his daughters, in marriage to the famous Nebuchadrezzar II, who built for her the Hanging Gardens of Babylon. He married his other daughter, Madane, to the Persian Cambyses I, and their son Cyrus II became the greatest conqueror of them all. In 550 the Persians rebelled against Median overlordship and Cyrus II, king of Anshan, became ruler of Medo-Persia. Following the death of Alexander the Great, Media at first came under Seleucid rule, but eventually became part of the Parthian Empire (Acts 2:9).

Isa 13:17-18 and Jer 51:11, 28 predict the part the Medes would play in the fall of Babylon, though at that time the Persians would be dominant. Daniel also attributes to the Medes a key role in the fall of the city of Babylon (Dan 5:30-31). Perhaps the armies of Cyrus the

Great in 539 B.C. were led by one Darius the Mede who "took the kingdom, being about three score and two years old" (v.31). This Darius the Mede is difficult to identify. J. C. Whitcomb, Jr. believes it was Gubaru of the Nabonidus Chronicle (*Darius the Mede*, Grand Rapids: Eerdmans, 1959).

The Median kingdom is mentioned symbolically in Dan 8:3-7, 20 where the first horn of the two-horned ram refers to Media. The second horn is Persia, which came up later and was bigger; so indeed the Persian Empire eclipsed Media and became dominant in the biblical world until the time of Alexander the Great. On a foundation tablet from Persepolis the Persian king Xerxes (485-465 B.C.) puts Media first in a list of countries "over which," he says, "I am king under the shadow of Ahuramazda, over which I hold sway, which are bringing their tribute to me . . . and abide by my laws" (ANET, p. 316). *See* Persia.

E. B. S.

MEDIAN (mē'dĭ-ăn). An inhabitant or a native of the country of Media. In this form the word occurs only in Dan 5:31, and is translated "Median" only in the KJV. Other versions translate it Mede. *See* Darius the Mede; Medes, Media.

Head of a Mede, Persepolis. ORINST

MEDIATION, MEDIATOR. Though the word mediator (Gr. *mesitēs*) occurs in only six biblical references (Gal 3:19-20; I Tim 2:5; Heb 8:6; 9:15; 12:24), the theme of mediation runs through all of Scripture. A mediator is one who stands between two parties in order to establish friendly relations. This usually presupposes that the situation existing between the two parties is one of alienation which the mediator then attempts to overcome. The concept of mediator appears in the Heb. participle *môkîaḥ*, "daysman" (Job 9:33, KJV), "umpire" (RSV, Berkeley), or "arbiter" (JPS, JerusB); cf. vv. 32-35. The same verb (*hiphil* of *yākaḥ*) occurs in Gen 31:37; Job 16:21; Isa 2:4; 11:3-4 in contexts which may include the idea of arbitration.

Such is the situation as it has existed between God and man as a result of the Fall. Man's sin aroused the enmity of the holy God, and man's fellowship with God was broken off. Man, who had revolted, needed to be reconciled to God and to be delivered from the power and effects of sin. God, whose wrath had been aroused by man's violation of His holiness in sinning, required satisfaction. (Modern views of the atonement which deny its objective and substitutionary character will view mediation differently; cf. Edwin C. Blackman, "Mediator, Mediation," IDB, III, 320-331.)

There were preliminary and incomplete forms of mediation between God and man in the OT—angels and prophets who spoke for God to man, priests who represented man before God, kings who ruled over men for God. Of all these Moses perhaps best illustrated the work of a mediator in receiving the law from God for Israel (Ex 20:19-22; Deut 5:4-5; Gal 3:19) and later in interceding for Israel (Ex 32:11-14, 30-34).

However, not one of these was able fully to perform his own mediatorial function nor to combine in himself the manifold functions demanded of an effectual mediator between God and man. A mediator was needed who could himself represent both God to man and man to God. Furthermore, he must be sinless; otherwise he himself would stand in need of a mediator and would thus be disqualified from fulfilling his office. And finally, an individual was needed who had all the powers to do whatever was necessary to effect the restoration of relations between the estranged parties, God and man.

It is only in Jesus Christ, God incarnate, the God-man, that these qualifications are to be found. Thus Paul says that there is one mediator between God and man, the man Christ Jesus (I Tim 2:5; the same thought is implied in the passages in Heb). The aspects of His mediatorial functions are seen to be inseparably connected with His person, work, and offices. As God (Jn 1:1), He can represent and reveal God to man (Jn 1:18; Heb 1:1-2), thus fulfilling His office as Prophet. As sinless man (Heb 4:15; 7:26; I Pet 2:22) He can represent man to God, and He can do it effectually just because He is also God. Thus He performs His priestly office with all that it involves with reference to sacrifice, substitution, reconciliation, propitiation, satisfaction, and present intercession (Heb

9:15; 7:21–25; 2:11–18; 4:14–16; Jn 3:16–17; Rom 5:1–11; Eph 1:7; Col 1:20; I Jn 4:9). In short, as the God-man Christ alone can act as mediator in effecting man's salvation and consequent restoration to fellowship with God. Finally, as the God-man, He is *the* one who is qualified to reign as mediatorial King over man in world history as it will be consummated in the Millennial Age (Ps 2; Rev 19:6–20:6). Thus, the God-man considered as Mediator fulfills the offices of Prophet, Priest, and King. *See also* Atonement; Intercession.

Bibliography. Louis Berkhof, *Systematic Theology,* Grand Rapids: Eerdmans, 1959, pp. 282f. Lewis Sperry Chafer, *Systematic Theology,* Dallas: Dallas Seminary Press, 1948, VII, 234f. Charles Hodge, *Systematic Theology,* Grand Rapids: Eerdmans, n.d., II, 455–543. Leon Morris, "Mediation, Mediator," BDT, pp. 346f. John F. Walvoord, *Jesus Christ Our Lord,* Chicago: Moody Press, 1969, pp. 136 f., 240–250.

S. N. G.

MEDICINE. *See* Diseases.

MEDITATION. The terms for meditation in the original languages of the Bible are found almost exclusively in the Psalms and the NT. The main Heb. verbs are *hāgâ* and *śîaḥ*. The first has a variety of meanings, but is used in such passages as Josh 1:8; Ps 1:2; 63:6; 77:12; 143:5; Isa 33:18 in the sense of "to meditate" (properly, "to speak with oneself") or "to mutter." The second term appears in such passages as Ps 119:15, 23, 48, 78, 148; 143:5 in the sense of "to meditate on divine things" (*see* Muse). The noun based on the first of the above verb roots appears in such passages as Ps 5:1; 19:14; 49:3, whereas the noun based on the second of these verb roots appears in Ps 104:34; 119:97,99.

The two NT instances are Lk 21:14, where the Gr. term is *promeletaō* with the basic idea of "premeditation" or "to take care beforehand"; and I Tim 4:15, where *meletaō*, "meditate," carries the basic idea "to attend to carefully" or "to be diligent in." Related passages such as Phil 4:8 and Col 3:2 should not be overlooked. The passage in Philippians gives not only a clear enumeration of the items deserving a place in meditations, but uses the term *logizomai*, "think," which carries the further meaning "to reckon inwardly," "to weigh the reasons of," "to deliberate," "to meditate on." The passage in Colossians uses the term *phroneō*, meaning both "to direct the mind to" and "to strive for."

Careful study of Scripture encourages meditation on God, God's law, God's works, and things that are heavenly and elevating to the soul.

R. E. Pr.

MEDITERRANEAN SEA. *See* Great Sea.

MEEK, MEEKNESS. The OT noun "meekness" (*ʿănāwâ*) comes from a verb stem meaning "to be bowed down, afflicted," which in turn comes to mean "to be lowly, submissive." The meek are the poor and afflicted persons who are often pushed aside by the rich or the leaders (Amos 2:7; cf. Ps 147:6; Isa 11:4). The noun occurs in II Sam 22:36; Ps 18: 35; 45:4; Prov 15:33; 18:12; 22:4; Zeph 2:3. The use of this feminine noun in the OT shows that it is very similar in meaning to humility, although the concept of patient submission is included at times. Moses demonstrated great meekness in being attacked personally without resentment or countercharge (Num 12:1–3).

In the NT "meekness" is the translation of *prautēs* and *praotēs*, which occur 11 times. It carries the basic idea of the inward attitude of submission to God and His Word (Jas 1:21). While the noun also conveys the idea of gentleness expressed in outward action, it does not include timidity. Meekness does not mean weakness; rather it suggests controlled and bridled strength. Other adjectives describing this quality are "considerate," "unassuming," "courteous," and "humble." It has the idea of submission without struggle, a holy gentleness in the face of wrath or in situations where one is experiencing mistreatment or an injustice. Thus the meek are extolled in the Beatitudes (Mt 5:5). A good illustration is seen in II Cor 10:1 where Paul refers to the meekness of Christ. The Lord, who was "meek and lowly" (Mt 11:29; cf. 21:5), obviously possessed great authority; yet when He experienced grave injustices He held His power in check (cf. Mt 12:14–21). During His trial He stood before His accusers without a word of threat or self-justification.

S. D. T.

MEGIDDO (mĕ-gĭd'ō), **MEGIDDON** (mĕ-gĭd'ŏn)

Site and location. Megiddo (modern Tell el-Mutesellim) gave its name to the famous battlefield of Armageddon (a Gr. transliteration of Heb. *Har-Megiddô*[n], "Mount of Megiddo"). Its mound consists of a citadel of *c.* 13 acres (ANEP #708, air view), and a lower terraced area during the Middle and Late Bronze Ages of another ten acres (IEJ, XVII [1967], 121). It stands on the SW edge of the Esdraelon plain, adjacent to the Carmel ridge at the intersection of the main N-S pass which constituted a part of the dominant route between Mesopotamia and Egypt. This strategic position caused the city to become an important trade and military center throughout the Bronze and Iron Ages.

Biblical references. Megiddo's place in the Scriptures is small in comparison with the prominence of other biblical cities where events of great theological importance took place. Nevertheless, the biblical references to the town underscore its role as a strategic military fortress city and administrative center.

The king of Megiddo is included among the

Solomon's stables at Megiddo. ORINST

31 kings conquered by Joshua (Josh 12:21). The name of nearby Taanach was associated with it in this same passage, as it is in Josh 17:11, where Taanach and Megiddo and their dependent towns are assigned to the tribe of Manasseh, in spite of the inability of the Israelites to drive the Canaanites out (Jud 1:2; I Chr 7:29). In the days of Deborah and Barak, the Canaanite military strength under Jabin, king of Hazor, was gathered in the vicinity of Megiddo, and the battle of Taanach, "near the waters of Megiddo" (Jud 5:19, NASB), was celebrated in their famous song.

It was in the early monarchy, however, that Israelite supremacy at Megiddo became an accomplished fact. The city shared with Taanach the honor of administrative capital of one of the 12 districts of Solomon, which extended as far as Beth-shan (I Kgs 4:12).

The most interesting reference to Megiddo is found in I Kgs 9:15-19, where the extensive building activities of King Solomon are mentioned. Megiddo is listed as one of his garrison towns and cities for chariots and horses. It thus formed, along with Hazor, Gezer, Beth-horon the lower, Baalath, and Tamar in the wilderness, a line of chariot cities containing the core of Solomon's standing army for the purpose of defending the essential Israelite territory.

When Jehu was anointed to be king of Israel in 841 B.C., he immediately went to Jezreel and slew Jehoram, the reigning Israelite king. The Judean King Ahaziah, on a state visit to Jehoram, was wounded near Ibleam, fled to Megiddo and died there (II Kgs 9:27).

The valiant but foolish King Josiah tried to intercept Pharaoh-necho at Megiddo in 609 B.C. Necho was on his way to assist the Assyrians and, hopefully, prevent their imminent collapse. Josiah reckoned that Judah would be safer once the Assyrian power was finally crushed, but he was killed in the first encounter in the plain before the city (II Kgs 23:29-30; II Chr 35:22-24).

The last OT reference to Megiddo is a mere literary allusion without prophetic significance (Zech 12:11), but the ensuing passage does refer to an apocalyptic encounter. The eschatological battle of Rev 16:16 is related to the plain of Megiddo or Armageddon (*q.v.*), which becomes the gathering place for the final battle between Christ and the Beast (Rev 17:11-14; 19:11-21).

These brief biblical notices tell only part of the story of Megiddo's lengthy career. Fortunately for our reconstruction of biblical history, plentiful new information has been provided by the extensive archaeological investigations carried out at the site, and by Egyptian historical texts and letters (see refs. in ANET).

Egyptian references. The earliest and most famous battle fought at Megiddo was the first battle in history to be recorded in such detail that its tactics can still be studied today. About the year 1482 B.C., Thutmose III (1504-1450), one of the greatest Egyptian conquerors, launched a campaign to subdue his vassals in *Retenu* (Palestine). The kings of Kadesh and Megiddo stood at the head of the rebels. After a march of ten days from Shur to Gaza, and another eleven days to Yehem in the Plain of Sharon, the Egyptians stood ready to advance on Megiddo. The Canaanites, apparently thinking that the enemy would arrive by one of the logical routes via Taanach or Jokneam, had divided their army into northern and southern wings and prepared chariot ambushes, but had left the narrow pass through the Wadi 'Arah leading directly to Megiddo undefended.

When Thutmose, in a bold move against the advice of his officers, moved through the defile and surprised the city, the campaign turned into a rout. The fleeing Canaanites were pursued so closely by the Egyptians that the gates of Megiddo could not be opened. Instead they had to be drawn up over the walls in haste. The Egyptians took 924 chariots as part of the booty. All of this is recorded in an inscription on the walls of the temple of Karnak (ANET, pp. 234-238).

A few years later Amenhotep II also mentioned Megiddo in his military campaigns, and it appears that the city became an Egyptian administrative center for most of the 15th cen. B.C. Not quite a hundred years after Thutmose's conquest, Pharaoh Amenhotep IV (Akhenaton) gradually released the Egyptian grasp on Palestine by failing to be attentive to the desperate pleas for help from his vassals. Biridiya, king of Megiddo, sent six letters to the Egyptian king (cf. ANET, p. 485), calling for, among other things, 100 soldiers to help protect the city. These letters were written in Akkadian (the diplomatic language) on clay tablets, and were found in the Pharaoh's palace at Tell el-Amarna in 1887. *See* Amarna Letters.

The importance of Megiddo as a military base has been repeatedly demonstrated throughout ancient times, continuing right up to this century, when British and Turkish armies met there in World War I. Subsequently, Arab and Israeli forces have made use of the area's strategic capabilities.

Archaeological evidence. The tell was first

excavated by G. Shumacher for the Deutsche Orient-Gesellschaft from 1903 to 1905. One of his important finds was the seal of "Shema, the servant of Jeroboam" (ANEP #276), probably belonging to an officer of King Jeroboam II.

The Oriental Institute of the University of Chicago began a lengthy series of campaigns in 1925. C. S. Fisher directed the first two seasons' work but was forced to withdraw from the field due to ill health. He was succeeded by P. L. O. Guy, who continued until 1935, followed by Gordon Loud, the latter remaining until the excavations ended in 1939.

The resources of the Oriental Institute allowed a more comprehensive work to be achieved at Megiddo than at any other Palestinian tell. This fact, together with the utilization of the Tell Beit Mirsim chronology developed by Albright, has made the city the classic archaeological type site for Palestine.

The excavators divided Megiddo's history into 20 periods corresponding to the 20 major strata found from the top of the mound to bedrock. The city was occupied from the Chalcolithic period (prior to 3300 B.C.) down to the end of the Iron Age III (*c.* 350 B.C.) when the Persian dominance over Palestine was ending and the Hellenistic period had not yet begun.

In Stratum XVII (*c.* 2500 B.C.) a Canaanite temple with a high circular altar was found. The huge altar was rebuilt, in Stratum XVI, of uncut stones but with a flight of steps (cf. Ex 20:25); it is over 25 feet in diameter. To the period *c.* 1150 B.C. was dated the fabulous underground water system, consisting of a deep shaft inside the city and a tunnel in the bedrock extending to the spring outside the fortified area. Other finds of significance included inscribed Egyptian monuments and 282 fragments of ivory carvings from the 13th cen.

It was Stratum IVB, however, which produced the discoveries of greatest interest for biblical history. A gateway having three chambers on each side, similar to the eastern gate of the temple described in Ezk 40:6-13, was found and dated to the time of Solomon (ANET #721). Gateways of the same type were subsequently discovered at Hazor and Gezer, two of the other Solomonic chariot cities. Casemated walls, a "palace" area, and most significantly, two series of buildings described as stables were also attributed to the same period. Each "stable" seemingly could house 24 horses, for an estimated total of 450. Altogether, the evidence presents a vivid picture of a fortress city and administrative complex of the early monarchy which served as a base for the deployment of chariotry from the time of Solomon onward.

The date of the structures termed "Solomonic" by the excavators has been disputed by the Israeli archaeologist Yigael Yadin since his soundings at the site in the late 1950's. Inasmuch as Stratum IV covers the period 1000-800 B.C., he has attempted to date the principal structures to the time of Ahab rather than of Solomon. In the ensuing controversy, another Israeli archaeologist, Yohanan Aharoni, has vigorously defended the original conclusion of the Chicago excavators. The matter is still unclear, but the weight of the evidence from the biblical text favors the interpretation that the gate, walls, palace, and stables were indeed from Stratum IVB and were built in the reign of Solomon. The explicit statement of I Kgs 9:15-19 clearly supports this view. To ignore its testimony is to fail to make full use of the historical sources. Apparently these structures continued in use despite Shishak's invasion, until the time of Ahab, less than a century later.

Recently J. B. Pritchard has challenged the view that the ruined structures interpreted as stables were stables. He suggests that horses were always kept in open enclosures, and that the buildings in question were possibly storehouses or barracks ("The Megiddo Stables: A Reassessment," *Near Eastern Archaeology in the Twentieth Century* [Glueck Festschrift], J. A. Sanders, ed., Garden City: Doubleday, 1970, pp. 268-276). The similarly shaped storerooms found by Y. Aharoni next to the city gate at 8th cen. B.C. Beer-sheba may support this contention (BA, XXXV [1972], 122 f.).

The great Canaanite altar at Megiddo. HFV

Stratum IV A was probably destroyed by Tiglath-pileser III during his invasion *c.* 732 B.C. (II Kgs 15:29; cf. 16:9). The next level has ruins of a differently planned city with a central court of the Assyrian style. This must have been the seat of the Assyrian governors who administrated an Assyrian province from here for about a century. One of these governors was named Ishtu-Adadaninu who ruled Megiddo (Akkad. *Magidu*[*nu*]) in 679 B.C. Stratum II was unwalled, but had a large fortified residence probably dating to the time of King Josiah (640-609).

To the Oriental Institute official excavation publications of two volumes of text, one of plates, and one monograph each on the tombs, the water system, the Megiddo ivories, and the Megiddo cult, can now be added a vast corpus of scholarly material, only selections of which can be listed below.

Bibliography. C. S. Fisher, *The Excavation of Armageddon,* Chicago: Univ. of Chicago Press, 1929. P. L. O. Guy, *New Light From Armageddon,* Chicago, 1931. R. S. Lamon, *The Megiddo Water System,* Chicago, 1935. H. G. May, *Material Remains of the Megiddo Cult,* Chicago, 1935. P. L. O. Guy, *Megiddo Tombs,* Chicago, 1938. G. Loud, *The Megiddo Ivories,* Chicago, 1939. R. S. Lamon, G. Shipton, *Megiddo I,* Chicago, 1939. G. Loud, *et al., Megiddo II,* 2 vols., Chicago, 1948.

Yohanan Aharoni, "The Stratification of Israelite Megiddo," JNES, XXXI (1972), 302–311. R. M. Engberg, "Megiddo—Guardian of the Carmel Pass," BA, III (1940), 41–51; IV (1941), 11-16. J. N. Schofield, "Megiddo," TAOTS, pp. 309–328. Yigael Yadin, "New Light on Solomon's Megiddo," BA, XXIII (1960), 62–68; "Megiddo of the Kings of Israel," BA, XXXIII (1970), 66–96.

J. E. J.

MEHETABEL (mē̇-hĕt'ȧ-bĕl)

1. Wife of Hadar or Hadad, an Edomite king, and daughter of Matred (Gen 36:39; I Chr 1:50).

2. Grandfather of that Shemaiah who was hired by Tobiah and Sanballat to give deceitful advice to Nehemiah in order to terrify him (Neh 6:10, KJV Mehetabeel).

MEHIDA (mē̇-hī'dȧ). Father or founder of a family of Nethinim who returned to Jerusalem from the Babylonian Captivity (Ezr 2:52; Neh 7:54).

MEHIR (mē'hĭr). A descendant of Judah and son of Chelub and nephew of Shuhah (I Chr 4:11).

MEHOLATHITE (mē̇-hō'lȧ-thīt). An inhabitant or native of Meholah. Adriel, the son of Barzillai, who married Merab, the daughter of King Saul, was so designated (I Sam 18:19; II Sam 21:8). Meholah may have been the same as Abel-meholah *(q.v.),* the home town of Elisha I Kgs 19:16), identified by some with Tell-el-Maqlûb, 13 miles SE of Beth-shan and E of the Jordan, and by others with Khirbet Tell el-Ḫilu or Tell el-Hammi, S of Beth-shan and W of the Jordan.

MEHUJAEL (mē̇-hū'jā-ĕl). A descendant of Cain through Enoch and Irad (Gen 4:18).

MEHUMAN (mē̇-hū'mȧn). One of the seven chamberlains (eunuchs) who ministered in the presence of Ahasuerus, the king of Persia (Est 1:10).

MEHUNIM. *See* Meunim.

MEJARKON (mē-jär'kŏn). A site or geographical feature in the territory of Dan near Joppa (Josh 19:46). It probably is the name of the river called Nahr el-'Auja in Arabic which flows into the Mediterranean *c.* four miles N of Joppa, rising at Ras el-'Ain (*see* Antipatris; Aphek 3) ten miles inland. It is one of five perennially flowing streams draining the plain of Sharon, turning greenish-yellow at certain times from the soil which it carries and thus explaining its name *yarqôn* ("pale green").

The Yarkon River, north of ancient Joppa, today flows into the Mediterranean on the outskirts of Tel Aviv. HFV

MEKONAH (mē̇-kō'nȧ). A town with daughter villages, near Ziklag, which was reoccupied after the return from Babylonian Captivity by some of the children of Judah (Neh 11:28); not identified. Also spelled Meconah.

MELATIAH (mĕl'ȧ-tī'ȧ). A Gibeonite who helped to repair the wall of Jerusalem under Nehemiah's leadership (Neh 3:7).

MELCHI (mĕl'kī). The name of two ancestors of Jesus, according to Luke's genealogy. One was in the fourth generation before Joseph and Mary (Lk 3:24); the other was in the third generation before Zerubbabel (Lk 3:28).

MELCHIAH (mĕl-kī'ȧ). The name appears only once in the KJV in this form (Jer 21:1). Here it is the name of the father of Pashur, who along with Zephaniah the priest was sent by King Zedekiah to the prophet Jeremiah to inquire of the Lord regarding the siege of Jerusalem. The same person appears in Jer 38:1, but the spelling of the name is Malchiah (*q.v.*) or Malchijah.

MELCHISEDEC. *See* Melchizedek.

MELCHI-SHUA. *See* Malchisua.

MELCHIZEDEK (mĕl-kĭz'ĕ-dĕk). Melchizedek (Heb. *malkî-ṣedeq,* "king of righteousness") is mentioned in Gen 14:18; Ps 110:4; Heb 5:6, 10; 6:20; 7:1, 10, 11, 15, 17. In Genesis he is the Canaanite priest-king of Salem (Jerusalem) who blessed Abraham as he returned from rescuing Lot, and to whom Abraham tithed the spoil of battle. Because of the mystery surrounding his sudden appearance on the stage of history and his equally sudden disappearance, he has been identified with an angel (Origen), the Holy Spirit (Epiphanius), Christ (Ambrose), Enoch (Calmet), Shem (Targums, Jerome, Luther), *et al.*

As to his religion, he was "priest of God Most High" *('ēl 'elyôn)*. The Ras Shamra texts have verified the fact that Canaanite cities had high priests in the first half of the 2nd mil. B.C., and Idrimi, king of Alalakh in N Syria *c.* 1500 B.C., was the personal representative of his god and the one who officiated in the shrine. Thus the Genesis account need not be anachronistic. There is not agreement as to whether Melchizedek was a worshiper of Yahweh or Baal. In a Ras Shamra liturgy, Baal is referred to as the "God Most High," the supreme deity in the Canaanite pantheon. Therefore, some understand Melchizedek as blessing Abraham by the Baal whom he regarded as the highest god of the city-state of Salem (Eric Voegelin, *Israel and Revelation,* London: Oxford Univ. Press, 1956, pp. 191 f.; Ralph H. Elliott, *The Message of Genesis,* Nashville: Broadman, 1961, pp. 115 f.). Gerhard von Rad *(Genesis,* trans. by J. H. Marks, London: SCM Press, 1961, p. 175) says the divinity referred to is probably the Canaanite "Baal of heaven," known particularly in Phoenicia but also far abroad, and that in Melchizedek's veneration of "God Most High, maker of heaven and earth," he came close to believing in the one God of the world whom Israel alone knew. The traditional view has been that Melchizedek was a true worshiper of Yahweh (Josephus, Irenaeus, Calvin, KD, Leupold, *et al.).* If Abraham is correctly dated *c.* 2000 B.C., Melchizedek lived prior to the displacement of El as the chief god of the Canaanites. The worship of Baal-hadad was established by the invading Amorites early in the 2nd mil. B.C. (*see* Gods, False: Baal).

Some scholars regard the other OT reference, Ps 110:4, as a Maccabean psalm (F. Buhl, SHERK, VII, 286f.; R. H. Charles, *Religious Development Between the Old and New Testaments*, London and New York: Home Univ. Library, 1914, p. 78; *et al.*), and the subject of it is variously interpreted as Jonathan, Hyrcanus the son of Simon, or Simon the Maccabee. Others, however, regard the psalm as Davidic in authorship with a reference either to David himself or to a king of his lineage, or they restrict it to a messianic prophecy of Jesus Christ. The problem is solved when we note that in Mt 22:43 Jesus ascribes the psalm to David and the reference to Himself as Messiah.

The passages in the book of Hebrews interpret it similarly. The author is arguing the superiority of Christ's priesthood to Aaron's priesthood. Melchizedek and his priesthood are a type of Christ and His priesthood. Melchizedek's priesthood was not limited to any race or tribe, hence it was universal. His kingship was not inherited from father or mother (cf. disclaimers of human parentage by Gudea and Ashurbanipal, and Amarna letters 286, 287, 288, the correspondence of 'Abdu-Heba, king of Urusalim, to Amenophis IV, king of Egypt: "It was not my father and not my mother who set me in this place; the arm of the mighty king [Pharaoh] brought me into the house of my father"—ANET, p. 487). Nor was it transmitted to offspring; thus it was eternal. Therefore, Melchizedek is a type of Christ and His universal and eternal priesthood.

Also, Melchizedek was superior to Aaron in that: (1) Abraham, Aaron's ancestor, paid tithes to Melchizedek; (2) Melchizedek blessed Abraham; (3) Levitical priests were subject to death, but there is no mention made of Melchizedek's death. Therefore, Christ and His priesthood are superior to Aaron and his priesthood. See O Michel, "Melchisedek," TDNT, IV, 568–571.

According to fragments found in Cave XI, Melchizedek was considered to have an exalted status in the heavenly realm in Qumran theology. He is associated with the deliverance of divine judgment, with a day of atonement that is connected with the last jubilee, perhaps referring to Daniel's 70th week (9:24–27). Such a contemporary view of Melchizedek makes it more understandable how the author of Heb 7 could argue for the superiority of Jesus by appeal to such a figure (Joseph A. Fitzmeyer, "Further Light on Melchizedek from Qumran Cave 11," JBL, LXXXVI (1967), 25–41.

E. W. C.

MELEA (mē'lē-*ȧ*). A descendant of David and an ancestor of Jesus (Lk 3:31).

MELECH (mē'lĕk). A son of Micah and great-grandson of Jonathan, the son of Saul (I Chr 8:35; 9:41).

MELICU. *See* Malluch.

MELITA (mĕl'ĭ-t*ȧ*). Commonly known as Malta (Acts 28:1, NASB), this tiny island (95 square miles) about 60 miles S of Sicily, was the site of Paul's shipwreck. During his three months' stay he healed sick people, was considered a god, and won a number of converts (Acts 28:1–10). Today many churches there honor St. Paul.

Occupied by Phoenicians as early as the 10th cen. B.C., the island later became a Roman province. The inhabitants apparently did not speak Greek (see Acts 28:4, "barbarians").

MELODY. *See* Music.

MELON. *See* Plants: Melon.

MELZAR (mĕl'zăr). In the KJV this is a proper name, but in the ASV and RSV it is a title meaning "steward." It refers to the person whom the prince of the eunuchs appointed over

St. Paul's Bay, Malta, where the shipwreck of Acts 28 occurred. Malta Government Tourist Board

Daniel and his three friends (Dan 1:11, 16). To him was entrusted the nurture and education of these Heb. youths who were to serve in the court of Nebuchadnezzar on completion of their training.

MEM (mĕm). The 13th letter of the Heb. alphabet. It is used to introduce the 13th stanza of Ps 119, every verse of which section begins with this letter in the original Heb. As a numeral it stands for 40. From this is derived the Gr. *mu*, from which comes the Latin and English *m*. The wavy line pictograph of this letter in proto-Sinaitic Heb. was a representation of water. Taking the Egyptian hieroglyphic character for water, by application of the acrophonic principle the inventor(s) of the Semitic alphabet used the sign to represent only the initial consonant of the Heb. or Semitic word *mayim* meaning "water." *See* Alphabet.

MEMBER

1.Any part or organ of the body, such as a limb, hand, or eye (Deut 1:25; Job 17:7; Mt 5:29–30; Rom 6:13, 19; 7:5, 23; 12:4; I Cor 12:12, 14–23; Col 3:5; Jas 3:5–6; 4:1).

2. One of the persons composing a society or community (Rom 12:5; I Cor 12:12–17; Eph 4:25; 5:30), as in the case of the Church which is considered as the body of Christ. *See* Body of Christ 3; Church.

Bibliography. J. Horst, *"Melos,"* TDNT, IV, 555–568.

MEMORIAL. A memorial in biblical terminology usually has to do with the worship of God. There was the Heb. *'azkārâ*, a handful of meal as a memorial offering which was burnt before the Lord (Lev 2:2, 9, 16). The remainder of the meal offering was for the priests to eat. In the case of the showbread, pure frankincense was also set on the table to be offered by fire as a memorial portion, while the bread was eaten by the priests (Lev 24:7–9). In a broader sense the whole Passover was reckoned as such a memorial (Heb. *zikkārôn*, Ex 12:14).

In the NT the ordinance of the Lord's Table, the communion, is called "a remembering again" (Gr. *anamnēsis*, "remembrance," I Cor 11:24–25). In Acts 10:4 Cornelius' prayer and alms giving are declared by the angel as having gone "up for a memorial before God." In Ex 3:15 and Hos 12:5 that special covenant name by which the Lord was known to the Israelites, Yahweh, is called God's memorial (Heb. *zēker)* to the people. In all these verses and others, the subject is worship in which the Lord is being remembered by His people through acts of worship, use of His name, in prayer and deeds of love to others. To remember their past servitude and God's saving acts and His covenant was a key commandment to Israel, as found in Deuteronomy.

There are two sides to this truth about remembrance. God's people remember Him because He first remembered them (Gen 8:1; 19:29; Ex 2:24; 6:5; Ps 9:12). It is the story of God's abiding love and human response.

E. B. S.

MEMPHIS (mĕm'fĭs). The first capital of united Egypt. It was founded by the traditional first king of Egypt, Menes (*c.* 3200 B.C.), on the W side of the Nile, S of the apex of the Delta and about 20 miles S of modern Cairo. Originally called "The White Wall," the city was later associated in name with the pyramid of Pepi I of the Sixth Dynasty (Men-nefer-Pepi) and from this name the Coptic and Gr. forms originated.

The kings of the archaic period were in particular worshipers of Horus, but the chief god of Memphis, Ptah, was prominent in the long history of Egypt. According to Memphite theology, Ptah was the creator of the universe. Apis, the bull of Memphis, was a manifestation of Ptah and subsequently was combined with Osiris to form the deity Serapis. In the necropolis of Sakkarah, just W of Memphis, is the well-known burial place of the Apis bulls, the Serapeum.

The only references to Memphis in the Bible appear in the prophetical writings (usually called Noph (*q.v.*). Hosea foresaw a return of Israelites to Egypt and mentioned Memphis (Heb. *nōph*) in this connection (Hos 9:6). The fulfillment of his prophecy is described by another prophet, Jeremiah, who was among those Jews who went to Egypt after the murder of Gedaliah (cf. Jer 41:16–18). Memphis became a residence of the refugees (Jer 44:1). Both Jeremiah and Isaiah had foreseen the fateful results of an alliance between Judah and Egypt and both referred to Memphis (Jer 2:16; Isa 19:13).

The destruction of Memphis was predicted by Jeremiah (cf. Jer 46:14, 19); Ezekiel later spoke of distresses in Memphis (Ezk 30:16) and made the specific declaration that the Lord

Newly excavated remains at ancient Memphis. HFV

would "destroy the idols, and put an end to the images, in Memphis" (30:13, RSV), a prophecy which has been dramatically fulfilled. Much of the stone of Memphis was carried off during the Middle Ages and used for the building of Cairo. Today all that the visitor to the area can see are a large fallen statue of Rameses II, a sphinx and some column bases and other stones scattered in the cornfields. For over a century excavations have been conducted in the Memphis area. Digging by German archaeologists has been progressing on the site of the city itself during the last few decades, but finds are as yet not fully interpreted or published.

C. E. D.

Entrance to the Serapeum at Memphis. HFV

MEMUCAN (mē-mū'kăn). One of "the seven princes of Persia and Media, who saw the king's face, and sat first in the kingdom" (Est 1:14). He was regarded as one of the wise men who understood the times and knew law and justice. When this group was asked by King Ahasuerus as to the proper treatment of Queen Vashti, who had refused to do the bidding of the king, Memucan became the spokesman of the council and advocated that Vashti be permitted to come no more before the king and that her royal estate be given to another (Est 1:16–21). Memucan's advice was followed by the king.

MENAHEM (mĕn'ȧ-hĕm). The son of Gadi, and the sixteenth in the line of kings in Israel (II Kgs 15:14-22), reigning only ten years, from 752 to 742 B.C., according to Edwin R. Thiele's studies in chronology (*The Mysterious Numbers of the Hebrew Kings,* rev. ed., Grand Rapids: Eerdmans, 1965). A stele of Tiglath-pileser III found in Iran and published in 1972, however, lists Menahem of Samaria as a tributary. A date of 737 B.C. is argued for this stele, which would indicate Menahem was still on the throne or at least king in name in that year (Louis D. Levine, "Menahem and Tiglath-pileser: A New Synchronism," BASOR #206 [1972], 40–42).

The murder of King Zechariah in Samaria by Shallum was the occasion for Menahem as commander of royal forces in Tirzah to slay Shallum and reign in his stead. With unusual strength he ruled as absolute monarch over his realm, beginning by subjugating the inhabitants of Tiphsah and the regions about Tirzah, even murdering women with child. Later, when threatened by King Pul of Assyria (identified as Tiglath-pileser III in I Chr 5:26), Menahem accepted the only alternative to surrender, namely, paying a heavy tribute of 1,000 talents of silver and passing the financial burden on to his wealthy citizenry. In this way he retained right to the throne, though now as a vassal, till the end of his life. Menahem's policy proved to be a disastrous one for Israel, for it led eventually to a complete Assyrian takeover of the nation. He died a natural death, and was the last king of Israel to be succeeded by his son (Pekahiah).

H. A. Hoy.

MENAN (mē'nȧn). A descendant of David (great-grandson) and an ancestor of Jesus (Lk 3:31). The ASV and the RSV have "Menna."

MENE, MENE, TEKEL, UPHARSIN (mĕ-nā',tĕ-kāl',ū-făr-sĭn'). Aramaic words inscribed on the palace wall during Belshazzar's feast which could be interpreted only by Daniel (Dan 5:25). Two problems relate to the explication of the baffling inscription: form and meaning ("*read* this writing and show its interpretation," 5:7).

Form. Perhaps the characters were unfamiliar to the Chaldeans or they were set down in an unusual arrangement; e.g., in anagram style, each word consisting of three consonants. It may be significant that the specific words are not mentioned until Daniel offers the interpretation.

Meaning. If the characters were legible, then the enigma lay in the meaning alone. The three words may designate weights and money: *m^e^nē'*, a mina; *t^e^qēl*, a shekel; *parsîn* (from Bab. *parisu*), the plural for half-shekel. (The *u* is the conjunction "and.") The resultant translation is "a mina, a mina, a shekel and half-shekels." Using other vowels (to be supplied in all Heb. and Aram. words), the nouns become verbs meaning, respectively, "numbered," "weighed," and "divided." Wealth and pride of person, esteemed by Belshazzar, become reasons for judgment. Accordingly, Daniel applies the verbal ideas to the king who is about to fall under the judgment of God (vv. 26–28), with his kingdom to be *divided* between the Medes and the Persians.

Attempts have been made to equate the four words with four Babylonian kings. Daniel applies them all to the incumbent. *See* Daniel; Weights, Measures, and Coins.

J. D. Y.

MENI. *See* Gods, False.

MENSTEALER. An enslaver of men, a slave dealer, a kidnaper (I Tim 1:10). The word could refer as well to one who unjustly reduces free men to slavery (cf. Ex 21;16; Deut 24:7) as to one who steals the slaves of others and sells them (cf. Rev 18:13). Paul contends that law is made for such. *See* Crime and Punishment.

MEONENIM (mē-ŏn'ĕ-nĭm). The name of a place which could be seen from the gate of Shechem (Jud 9:37). The KJV speaks of "the plain of Meonenim"; the ASV has "the oak of Meonenim"; the RSV and NASB translate "the Diviners' Oak." Apparently it was a sacred tree under which soothsayers, enchanters, or diviners sat and practiced their magic arts. *See* Divination.

MEONOTHAI (mē-ŏn'ŏ-thī). A descendant of Judah and father of Ophrah (I Chr 4:14). According to the LXX and Vulg., Meonothai was reckoned also as a son of Othniel (I Chr 4:13, RSV).

MEPHAATH (mĕf'ā-ăth). A former Amorite city in Transjordan allotted to the tribe of Reuben by Moses (Josh 13:18) and named along with Kedemoth and Kirjathaim. Along with its suburbs, it was designated a Levitical city and assigned to the families of the children of Merari (Josh 21:37; I Chr 6:79). Apparently it became a possession of Moab later, because it is referred to as a Moabite town in Jer 48:21, where the prophet of God pictures judgment coming upon it. It has been tentatively identified with Tell ej-Jawah, six miles S of modern Amman.

MEPHIBOSHETH (mĕ-fĭb ŏ-shĕth)

1. Son of Saul by his concubine Rizpah, daughter of Aiah. David delivered him up to the Gibeonites to be hanged (II Sam 21:8 f.).

2. Son of Jonathan, grandson of Saul, nephew of Mephibosheth 1. Disaster and disappointment marked his life. He was a lad of five when the news came from Jezreel of the death of his father and grandfather. As his nurse fled in haste, the boy fell and became lame in both feet (II Sam 4:4). He was taken to Lo-debar in Gilead where he was cared for by Machir, son of Ammiel (II Sam 9:5). Later Mephibosheth, also called Merib-baal ("Baal contends" or "Baal's fighter"; I Chr 8:34; 9:40), had a son named Micha (II Sam 9:12).

When David had established himself as king, he inquired if there were any of Saul's family to whom he might show kindness for Jonathan's sake. Ziba, a servant of Saul's house, informed him of Mephibosheth. Immediately David sent for him, gave him Saul's property, made Ziba his servant, and permitted Mephibosheth to eat daily at the king's table (II Sam 9).

When David fled from Absalom, Ziba met David with much-needed provisions, and falsely accused Mephibosheth of desiring the kingdom. David believed the lie and gave Ziba all that belonged to Mephibosheth (II Sam 16:1-4). Ultimately, the innocent Mephibosheth had opportunity to vindicate himself. When David returned after the death of Absalom, Mephibosheth met the king. He had been in deep mourning for David as evidenced by the fact that he had not bathed, nor washed his clothes, nor trimmed his beard. When David asked why he had not gone with him, Mephibosheth told him of Ziba's deception—he had asked for an ass to be saddled that he might go, but Ziba had left him behind. David believed him but refused to do more than divide the property between the two (II Sam 19:24 ff.).

Later, Mephibosheth was spared by David when seven members of Saul's family were delivered to the Gibeonites to expiate a wrong of Saul, and to end a famine caused by it (II Sam 21:1-9).

E.W.C.

MERAB (mē'răb). The elder daughter of Saul. According to the report in camp (I Sam 17:25), the king's daughter would be given to the hero who killed Goliath. This seems not to have happened, but Saul did promise David that he would give him Merab as his wife if he would continue to fight valiantly against the enemy (I Sam 18:17). Saul's purpose was to expose his young rival to danger and thus dispose of him. When this plot failed, Saul broke his promise and Merab was married to Adriel (I Sam 18:19). When the country later suffered God's judgment because Saul had broken the treaty with the Gibeonites, the five sons of Merab were put to death for the sin of their grandfather (II Sam 21). (The Heb. text reads Michal for Merab in II Sam 21:8, an ancient scribal error.)

MERAIAH (mē̇-rā'yȧ). One of the priests under Joiakim (Neh 12:12).

MERAIOTH (mē̇-rā'yŏth)

1. A priest, son of Zerahiah, who lived and served while the ark of God was in Shiloh (I Chr 6:6-7, 52). He was in the lineage from Aaron to Ezra, according to Ezr 7:3-4.

2. A priest whose father was Ahitub and whose son was Zadok (I Chr 9:11; Neh 11:11). He apparently served about a half century before the Exile. These may designate the same individual placed in a different chronological sequence in diverse sources.

3. The name survived the Exile and appears as a priest "in the days of Joiakim" and as head of a household. He was perhaps a descendant of the foregoing (Neh 12:15).

MERARI (mē̇-rär'ī). Third son of Levi, younger brother of Gershon and Kohath (Gen 46:11; Ex 6:16; Num 3:17; I Chr 6:1). Through his sons Mahli and Mushi (Ex 6:19; Num 3:20; I Chr 6:19) were descended the Merarites, one of the three great divisions of the Levites.

In the wilderness the Merarites carried the frames, bars, pillars, and sockets of the tabernacle and the pillars, sockets, pegs, and cords of the court (Num 3:33-37). Those who actually served (age group 30-50) numbered 3,200 (Num 4:42-45). In the land they were assigned 12 cities in the territories of Reuben, Gad, and Zebulun (Josh 21:7).

Merarites were present when David brought the ark to Jerusalem (I Chr 15:3, 6). Some became singers in the temple headed by Ethan, also called Jeduthun (I Chr 6:31, 44; 25:1, 3); others were gatekeepers (I Chr 26:10-19). Merarites helped cleanse and repair the temple during the reforms of Hezekiah and Josiah (II Chr 29:12; 34:12), and some served under Ezra and Nehemiah (Ezr 8:18-19; Neh 11:15 with I Chr 9:14).

L.L.W.

MERARITES. *See* Merari; Levites.

MERATHAIM (mĕr'ȧ-thā'ĭm). Only used in the dual. In Jer 50:21 it is a play on a name applied to S Babylon, *mât marrâti,* land of "double rebellion," a designation of Babylonia.

A Greek mercenary soldier hired by Seleucids, found at Sidon. Istanbul Museum

MERCENARY. Soldiers whose only concern in a conflict was the money paid them. Gr. soldiers had a reputation as fighters and, when not engaged in their own wars, they hired out to other nations. Greeks were mercenaries in the Egyptian armies during the time of Cambyses. Alexander had 5,000 in his pay (*Encyclopaedia Britannica,* 9th ed., II, 561, 564). *See* Soldier.

MERCHANDISE, MERCHANT. *See* Commerce; Occupations: Merchant.

MERCURIUS, MERCURY. *See* Gods, False: Hermes.

MERCY. "Mercy" in the NT renders Gr. *eleos* "pity, compassion, mercy" (see its use in Lk 10:37; Heb 4:16), and *oiktirmos,* "fellow sympathy" (see use in Phil 2:1; Col 3:12; Heb 10:28).

In the OT (KJV "mercy") it represents two distinctive roots: *reḥem,* softness(?), "the womb," hence motherly compassion (I Kgs 3:26, KJV "bowels"); and *ḥesed,* enduring strength (Ps 59:16; 62:12; 144:2), "the mutual liability or solidarity of related parties," hence loyalty (KB). The former expresses God's goodness, particularly toward those in trouble (Gen 43:14; Ex 34:6). The latter expresses His bond of faithfulness, or "belongingness" with His own, His steadfast love (RSV) which lies behind and comes to expression in the *b^e rît,* "covenant, testament" (Ex 15:13; Deut 7:9; Ps 136:10–24). *See* Kindness; Loving-kindness.

Bibliography. R. Bultmann, *"Eleos,* etc.," TDNT, II, 477–487. J. Barton Payne, *The Theology of the Older Testament,* Grand Rapids: Zondervan, 1962, pp. 161–164.

MERCY SEAT. For the mercy seat in the OT, *see* Tabernacle. The term occurs only once in the NT. The KJV, ASV, RSV, and NASB translate Gr. *hilastērion* as "mercy seat" in Heb 9:5 but "propitiation" in Rom 3:25. *Hilastērion* in the LXX translates the Heb. *kappōreth* (mercy seat) as in Lev 16:15. Heb 9:5 is clearly a reference to this golden lid on the ark of the covenant. Rom 3:25 presents a problem. Most commentators agree that *hilastērion* (a neuter adjective) should not be rendered simply "propitiation" since the noun form *(hilasmos)* could have been employed (cf. I Jn 2:2; 4:10). The three common interpretations are that it refers either to a propitiatory place (i.e., the cross), a propitiatory act (i.e., sacrifice), or a propitiatory person. *See* Propitiation.

MERED (mĭr'ĕd). One of the sons of Ezra, a descendant of Judah through Caleb, a son of Jephunneh. Mered married Pharaoh's daughter (I Chr 4:17–18).

MEREMOTH (mĕr'ē-mōth)

1. A priest who returned to Palestine with Zerubbabel, *c.* 536 B.C. (Neh 12:3). On the basis of the LXX and Syriac, some read Meremoth instead of Meraioth in Neh 12:15.

2. A priest in the time of Ezra and Nehemiah whose family was traced to Hakkoz (see Ezr 2:61; Neh 3:4, ASV). After his priestly lineage was established, he was able to take the leading role in weighing the returned temple treasures (Ezr 8:33). During the reconstruction of the wall of Jerusalem, Meremoth assisted in rebuilding the Fish Gate (Neh 3:3–4). He also worked with Baruch son of Zabbai and others of the house of Eliashib the high priest (Neh 3:20–21) in finishing another part of the wall. He was apparently among those who set their seal on the renewed covenant (Neh 10:5).

3. A son of Bani. A "son of Israel" or of the laity who was among those who had married foreign women and who pledged to put away their non-Israelitish wives as a result of Ezra's reform (Ezr 10:36).

H.E. Fi.

MERES (mĭr'ēz). One of the seven princes and counselors of Ahasuerus, king of Persia and Media, who "saw the kings's face" freely and sat first in the kingdom (Est 1:14; HDB III, 346).

MERIBAH (mĕr'ĭ-bȧ)

1. The second of two names given by Moses to a place near Rephidim as Israel journeyed to Sinai. Having no water, the people strove with Moses until God provided water as Moses struck the rock. The place was called Massah, "tempting," and Meribah, "strife" (Ex 17:7), or "provocation" (Heb 3:8). *See* Massah.

2. At Kadesh near the close of the wilderness wanderings Israel again strove with Moses because of no water. Though Moses acted in rebellion, water was provided, called "waters of Meribah" (Num 20:1–13), distinguished by the addition of Kadesh (Num 27:14; Deut 32:51). Yet Moses and Aaron were punished for their sin (Num 20:12, 24). *See* Kadesh-barnea.

MERIBAH-KADESH. *See* Meribah.

MERIB-BAAL. *See* Mephibosheth.

MERODACH. *See* Gods, False: Marduk.

MERODACH-BALADAN (mĕr'ō-dăk-băl'ȧ-dȧn). This name is generally written Merodach-baladan (Isa 39:1) but in II Kgs 20:12 is given as Berodach-baladan, which may be a copyist's misspelling for Merodach or represent the approximation of sound between *m* and *b* in Akkadian. The name in Assyrian means "god has given a son."

Merodach-baladan was a Chaldean, the son of Baladan, and a petty king, a strong and courageous leader of his people living in the marsh lands of southern Iraq. His capital was Bit Yakin. In 722 B.C. he rebelled against Sargon II, king of Assyria, and was recognized by him as king of Babylon. He reigned for 11 years.

In 710 B.C. he sent an embassy to Jerusalem to congratulate Hezekiah on recovering from his serious illness (II Kgs 20:12–19; Isa 39:1–8). The real purpose of the embassy was to enlist Hezekiah in a plot with other nations against Assyria. Sargon II learned of it, captured Babylon and demoted Merodach-baladan to his small kingdom of Bit Yakin. After Sargon

II died (705 B.C.), in 703 B.C. he retook Babylon, but did not rule long, for Sennacherib, Sargon's son and successor, drove him from Babylon. He fled to Elam for refuge. Though he had failed to continue his rule of Babylon, his people, the Chaldeans, became the ruling caste in Babylon (cf. Ezr 5:12; Dan 2:2, 10; 5:7).

V.G.D.

MEROM (mē'rŏm). By the waters of Merom Joshua defeated the combined armies of Galilee (Josh 11:5, 7). The location of this battle is in dispute. The term "waters of Merom" does not indicate the former Lake Huleh but rather a flowing spring (cf. Josh 15:7, 9; 16:1; 19:46; Jud 5:19). It must refer to the water source of the city Merom where Jabin assembled his Canaanite forces. The place appears in Egyptian records as *mrṃ* (No. 85 of Thutmose III) and *mrm* (Rameses II). The Assyrian form of the name was *Marum* (Tiglath-pileser III). The village of Meirun is usually suggested as the site of Merom, but the settlement is not ancient enough, and chariots could not possibly have been used there. Present evidence favors Tell el-Khirbeh, a bit farther N, at the foot of Jebel Marun. It was a very important Bronze Age town, and the Wady Fara nearby is known for its many springs. The plain on its E side would have been a fitting scene for the battle. The site lies *c.* seven miles WNW of Hazor.

The LXX has *Marrōn* both for Merom and for Madon (Josh 11:1–12; 12:19), whose king also came out to this war. It is likely therefore that Madon should be identified with Merom rather than with Khirbet Madin on the slopes of Qurn Hattin W of the Sea of Galilee.

Bibliography. Yohanan Aharoni, *The Land of the Bible*, Philadelphia: Westminster, 1967, pp. 205, 206, 210.

A. F. R.

MERONOTHITE (mĭ-rŏn'ŏ-thīt). An inhabitant of a place called Meronoth, not otherwise mentioned in the OT. The context of Neh 3:7 suggests that it was in the neighborhood of Gibeon and Mizpah. Two persons are called "the Meronothite": Jehdeiah, who was in charge of David's asses (I Chr 27:30); Jadon, one of the repairers of the wall under Nehemiah (Neh 3:7).

MEROZ (mĭr'ŏz). A town N of Mount Tabor near the Lake of Merom. Meroz did not come to the aid of Israel against the Canaanites and was cursed by the prophetess Deborah (Jud 5:23). It is suggested that since the Canaanites were given refuge by Meroz, the town was a Canaanite community living in a covenant relationship with Israel.

MESECH. *See* Meshech.

MESHA (mē'shă)

1. A king of Moab in the reigns of Ahab, Ahaziah, and Jehoram, kings of Israel. In the days of Omri and Ahab he had been subject to Israel, but after Ahab's death, he rebelled (II Kgs 1:1; 3:4–5) and eventually threw off the Israelite yoke when Jehoram succeeded to the throne after Ahaziah's short reign. When Jehoram king of Israel, Jehoshaphat king of Judah, and the king of Edom combined forces to invade Moab, Mesha sacrificed his own son on the wall of Kir-hareseth *(q.v.)* during the siege of that Moabite city (3:9–27).

In 1868 the Moabite Stone *(q.v.)* was discovered at Dibon, the Moabite capital. Evidently it was erected *c.* 830 B.C. It contains an inscription of Mesha and is written in a Canaanite dialect similar to Heb. Mesha mentions Omri's humbling Moab many years and an attempt by his "son" to do the same, but Mesha triumphed over him and his house (i.e., family or dynasty). As F. M. Cross and D. N. Freeman explain (*Early Hebrew Orthography*, New Haven: American Oriental Soc., 1952, pp. 39–40, footnote), "son" here must mean "grandson," as frequently elsewhere, because the Bible plainly states that the revolt took place after Ahab's death.

2. Firstborn son of Caleh (I Chr 2:42).
3. A Benjamite (I Chr 8:9).
4. One of the limits of the territory of the Joktanites (Gen 10:29–30).

K. L. B.

MESHACH (mē'shăk). The name given to Mishael, one of Daniel's three companions, by the chief of Nebuchadnezzar's eunuchs (Dan 1:7; 2:49; 3:12–30). His Heb. name means "Who is what God is?" Thus it is conjectured that his Akkad. name may have been *Mishaaku*, "Who is what Aku [Sumerian moon-god] is?" No Babylonian name of this form is known, however. Name changes such as this were not uncommon and usually signified the beginning of a new state of life. Apparently no dishonor was intended. *See* Abednego; Shadrach.

MESHECH (mē'shĕk)

1. A son of Shem (I Chr 1:17), probably a scribal error for Mash (*q.v.;* Gen 10:23).

2. Sixth son of Japheth (Gen 10:2; I Chr 1:5), and ancestor of a people mentioned by Ezekiel and in Ps 120:5. The Mushki of the Assyrian inscriptions, first mentioned by Tiglath-pileser I (*c.* 1100 B.C.) and then by Shalmaneser III (859–824 B.C.) (see *Western Asiatic Inscriptions,* I, 60 ff.; Luckenbill, *Ancient Records of Assyria and Babylon,* II, 61), were located between Cilicia and the Caspian Sea. By the time of Sargon II (722–705 B.C.), they had moved to Phrygia *(q.v.)* in N Anatolia and were formidable enemies whose King Mita is mentioned in Sargon's annals. A century later Meshech (Phrygia) is mentioned along with Javan (the Greeks) and Tubal as traders in the markets of Tyre in slaves and bronze vessels (Ezk 27:13). They are listed as the Moschoi in the 19 satrapies of Darius (Herodotus iii. 94).

In Herodotus' time they moved to the mountains to the SE of the Black Sea. In Greco-Roman times they dwelt between the Cyrus and Phasis Rivers (Strabo, xi,2,14,16).

In Ezk 38:3 and 39:1 this country is predicted to be allied with Gog *(q.v.)* and Magog against Israel and to share in destruction by fire (Ezk 39:6).

H. G. S.

MESHELEMIAH (mĭ-shĕl'ĕ-mī'*á*). The name of a member of the Korahite tribe whose son Zechariah was a gatekeeper of the tabernacle (I Chr 9:21; 26:1). He was also called Shelemiah (I Chr 26:14).

MESHEZABEEL (mĭ-shĕz'*á*-bēl)

1. A descendant of Meshullam who helped to repair the wall at Jerusalem (Neh 3:4).
2. A person or family who sealed the covenant with Nehemiah (Neh 10:21).
3. The father of Pethahiah, an official, who served the king (Neh 11:24).

These may be two or three persons, or a single individual.

MESHILLEMITH (mē-shĭl'ĕ-mĭth). An ancestor of the priest Adaiah (I Chr 9:12).

MESHILLEMOTH (mĭ-shĭl'ĕ-mŏth)

1. An Ephramite whose son and three other chief men of the tribe opposed making slaves of the captive Jewish people (II Chr 28:12).
2. A priest named Azarel is called "son of Ahzai, son of Meshillemoth, son of Immer" (Neh 11:13, RSV).

MESHOBAB (mĭ-shō'băb). One of the Simeonites listed in I Chr 4:34 who were called princes in their families and occupied a settlement in Ham near Gerar.

MESHULLAM (mĭ-shŏŏl'*á*m)

1. The grandfather of Shaphan, the scribe who was sent by King Josiah to Hilkiah to administer the money brought to repair the temple (II Kgs 22:3).
2. The first named son of Zerubbabel (I Chr 3:19).
3. A chieftain of the tribe of Gad dwelling in Bashan in the time of Jotham and Jeroboam II (I Chr 5:13).
4. A Benjamite, descendant of Elpaal, who dwelt in Jerusalem after the return from Babylon (I Chr 8:17).
5. A Benjamite, the father of Sallu who dwelt in Jerusalem after the return. He was the son of Joed (Neh 11:7), or Hodaviah (I Chr 9:7).
6. Another Benjamite, the son of Shephathiah, who lived in Jerusalem after the Captivity (I Chr 9:8).
7. A priest, the son of Zadok, whose descendants lived in Jerusalem after the return (I Chr 9:11; Neh 11:11). He is probably the same as Shallum, the ancestor of Ezra. *See* Shallum.
8. The son of Meshillemith and ancestor of Adaiah. He was a priest after the return from Babylon (I Chr 9:12).
9. A Levite of the family of Kohath, an overseer of the repairs to the temple in the time of Josiah (II Chr 34:12).
10. One of the chief Levites who was sent by Ezra to Casiphia to gather Levites and Nethinim for the return to Jerusalem (Ezk 8:16 f.).
11. A chief man, probably a Levite, in the days of Ezra who helped in the problem of dissolving the marriages of Jews to Gentile wives. Possibly the same as 10 (Ezr 10:15).
12. One of the family of Bani who put away his Gentile wife in the time of Ezra (Ezr 10:29).
13. The son of Berechiah who worked at the building of the wall under Nehemiah. His daughter married Johanan, son of Nehemiah's enemy, Tobiah the Ammonite (Neh 3:4,30; 6:18).
14. The son of Besodeiah who helped repair the old gate of Jerusalem (Neh 3:6).
15. One of the chief men in the time of Ezra who stood with him as he read the law to the people (Neh 8:4). Probably the same man who sealed the covenant of Nehemiah (Neh 10:20).
16. A priest who signed the covenant of Nehemiah (Neh 10:7).
17. A priest, head of the house of Ezra, in the days of the high priest Joiakim (Neh 12:13). He may be the man who took part in the dedication of the wall (Neh 12:33), but there were so many of the same name that there is no way of determining.
18. Another priest of the days of Joiakim, head of the house of Ginnethon (Neh 12:16).
19. A Levite with the responsibility of being porter at the temple gates (Neh 12:25).

P. C. J.

MESHULLEMETH (mĭ-shŏŏl'ĕ-mĕth). The feminine form of Meshullam. The daughter of Haruz of Jotbah (II Kgs 21:19), she was the wife of Manasseh and mother of Amon, king of Judah.

MESOBAITE (mĭ-sō'bĭ-īt). Jasiel, one of David's heroic men, is designated as the Mesobaite (I Chr 11:47). Because there is no community known in the OT by the name of *Meṣob*, perhaps the term means "the man from Zobah."

MESOPOTAMIA (mĕs'ŏ-pŏ-tā'mĭ-*á*). The English word Mesopotamia derives from the Gr. meaning "between the rivers." The rivers were the Tigris and Euphrates. In the OT the word is used only five times; it goes back to the Heb. expression *'ărām nahărayim* (see Ps 60, title), which means literally "Aram of the two rivers." The people called *'ărām* in the Heb. are called Syrians in the English translations.

There were a number of enclaves where Syrians or Arameans lived, but one most important area was in the region N and E of the Euphrates, whence the name "Aram of the two

Austen H. Layard, pioneer Mesopotamian archaeologist, in Bakhtiyari costume, from a portrait in his *Early Adventures.*

rivers." Indeed it is this area that is usually in mind when the OT uses the term Mesopotamia. Here lived the ancestors of Abraham in the region of Haran (Gen 11:31*b*), and hither went Abraham's servant to the city of Nahor to the house of Laban to obtain Rebekah for Isaac (Gen 24:10). Balaam, the false prophet of Num 22–24, came from Pethor in Mesopotamia (Aram-naharaim, Deut 23:4, see ASV marg.). In the NT the Gr. term has a wider meaning, covering all the territory of ancient Babylonia and Sumer, including Ur of the Chaldees (Acts 7:2) as well as Syria. The "dwellers in Mesopotamia" present in Jerusalem for the Feast of Pentecost (Acts 2:9) would include Jews from Babylon, Nippur, Ctesiphon and other nearby cities with Jewish communities.

Mesopotamia had a very complicated history involving many ethnic groups. Generally, tribes of Semitic bedouin from the S and W settled in the fertile land between the rivers, while non-Semitic (largely Indo-European) nomads moved into the same area from the N and E. These cultures merged in the region called Mesopotamia. Jud 3:8–10 reflects a time when such a non-Semitic element ruled over Mesopotamia. Chushanrishathaim was probably a Kassite king whose people had ruled "the land between the rivers" for many centuries by the time of the judges. But the Kassites were a people who were culturally inferior to those who preceded them, such as the Amorites under their famous king Hammurabi.

Mesopotamia may be divided for convenience into southern, middle and northern regions. In the S the non-Semitic Sumerians were the first people in historic times to rule the land. They left a permanent mark on all the cultures to follow by inventing the system of writing, which continued to prevail in Mesopotamia throughout the biblical period. *See* Sumer. A people of lesser importance who influenced S Mesopotamia were the non-Semitic Elamites (*q.v.*). In the N the non-Semitic Hurrians (*see* Horites), Kassites, Urartians, and Protohattic people prevailed at different times. But it was left to the Semites to develop the strongest kingdoms and provide the dominant culture of Mesopotamia over most of its history.

This began with the rule of the Akkadians, who appeared in the region about 2500 B.C. and adopted much of the Sumerian culture. The Amorites (or Proto-Arameans) came in from the Syro-Arabian desert around 2000 B.C. These people spoke a W Semitic language similar to Aramaic and Hebrew. They are known from the thousands of clay documents from the middle Mesopotamian city of Mari (*q.v.*; *see also* Amorites). From an amalgamation of these and other elements there emerged in Mesopotamia the people who came to be known as Babylonians, this name deriving from the name of their capital city Babylon in the S, and the people called Assyrian from their capital city on the northern Tigris and chief god's name, Asshur. *See* Assyria; Babylonia.

About 1000 B.C. a tribe of Semites emerged called the Chaldeans (*see* Chaldea). At first they only made trouble for their Assyrian overlords, but eventually this group helped to overthrow the Assyrians. In this they were joined by nomads from the N called Scythians and two Aryan tribes from the E called the Medes and the Persians. Following a somewhat

A lion in enameled brick from the Ishtar Gate, Babylon. LM

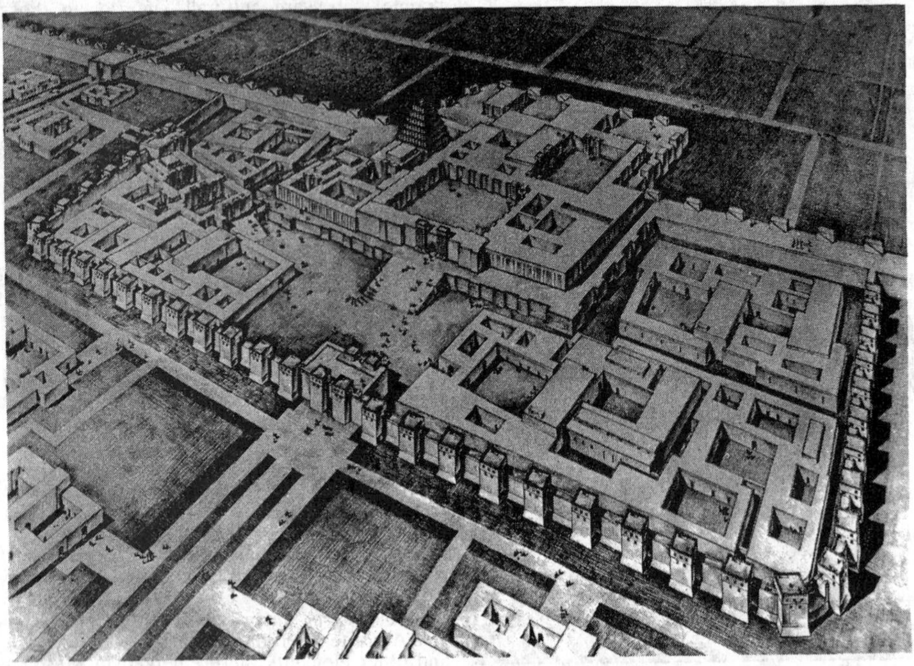

Reconstruction drawing of the palace of Sargon II of Assyria at Khorsabad. ORINST

short-lived Neo-Babylonian kingdom ruled by Chaldeans in the 6th cen. B.C., these Persians under Cyrus the Great in the latter part of the 6th cen. established themselves as the supreme rulers not only in Mesopotamia but throughout the Near East until the conquests of Alexander the Great. *See* Nations.

Bibliography. J. J. Finkelstein, "Mesopotamia," JNES, XXI (1962), 73-92. Roger T. O'Callaghan, *Aram Naharaim*, Rome: Pontificium Institutum Biblicum, 1948. A. Leo Oppenheim, *Ancient Mesopotamia,* Chicago: Univ. of Chicago Press, 1964. Georges Roux, *Ancient Iraq,* New York: World, 1964.

E. B. S.

MESS. *See* Food.

MESSENGER. Although the Heb. term *mal'āk* is translated *aggelos* in the LXX, it is rendered "messenger" about 100 times in the KJV. Most often it is used with reference to a messenger from God. It also refers to one sent by a human being, or even by Satan. Only once does the OT refer to a prophet as a messenger (Hag 1:13), but the name of the prophet Malachi means "my messenger." In the NT *apostolos* is translated as "messenger" (II Cor 8:23; Phil 2:25) in the KJV and RSV. The NT Gr. word *aggelos* (angel) is translated "messenger" in reference to John the Baptist (Mt 11:10); John's messengers (Lk 7:24); those sent by Christ (Lk 9:52); and the spies as received by Rahab (Jas 2:25). *See* Herald; Angel.

MESSIAH. The word "Messiah" as a transliteration of the Heb. word *māshîach* comes through the Aram. *māshîchā* and the Gr. *messías*. Its Heb. source is found in the verb *māshach,* "to anoint," and is most often translated in English versions as "the anointed." In the KJV "Messiah" as a transliteration appears only in Dan 9:25-26 and Jn 1:31; 4:25. *Māshîach* occurs 37 times in KJV as "the anointed." Of these 37 occurrences, four refer to the high priest as God's anointed (Lev 4:3,5,16; 6:22) because the anointing oil was poured out upon the high priest at his consecration, and 33 refer to the king. The biblical references to the king as "the Lord's anointed" seem to stem from David's deep respect for the king as the representative of Yahweh. Most of the early occurrences of the word come from David's references to Saul, and more of the subsequent occurrences refer to David himself than to any one other person, though it is used of other kings, even of Cyrus of Persia (Isa 45:1), and of the patriarchs in retrospect (Ps 105:15; cf. I Chr 16:22).

In the intertestamental literature the word "Messiah" is not found in the Apocrypha but occurs in a number of the pseudepigraphical books (Pss of Sol 17:32; 18:5,7; Enoch 48:10;

52:4; II Esd 7:28,29; 12:32; II Bar 38:7; 40:1; 70:9; 72:2). References also occur in the Qumran literature, the Aramaic Targums, the Talmud, and in some ancient Jewish prayers.

In the NT the Gr. word *Christos* has the same meaning of "anointed one" as does the Heb. *māshîach*.

The messianic idea in the OT associates itself not especially with the contemporarily reigning king, though the word is often used this way, but with an eschatological king and a kingdom of utopian character. The ideas of the Messiah and his messianic roles are much wider than the use of these terms, though the ideas certainly center around the thought of the Davidic kingship as the ideal for a greater and more perfect king and kingdom of the future. The source, or sources, of the messianic concepts lie behind David, but in his kingship the expectations of God's special provident blessings for His people find a center around which they can concretely be expressed. The prophecy of Nathan (II Sam 7:4–17) formed a solid basis for the expression of the eschatological promises and expectations in the Davidic line.

The idea of the Messiah cannot be confined strictly to that teaching which relates to the eschatologically oriented anointed king. The term Messiah has been descriptive of all the streams of prophecy in the OT which speak of one who was to come from God to fulfill the promises of deliverance and the promises of a new state of divine blessing. The nature of this deliverance, the nature of the state of divine blessing, and the nature of the Messiah vary greatly in the several streams of expectant hope which appear in the OT. So greatly, in fact, do the prophecies vary that Messiahs of several sorts with a variety of descriptive names were expected by those who adhered to these differing conceptions in both intertestamental and NT times, as well as in the whole Christian era. The term Messiah enveloped other prophetic figures in the OT, such as Moses' Prophet "like unto me," Isaiah's suffering Servant, Jeremiah's Branch, Daniel's Son of Man, and other figures, including the coming of the Lord Himself as the deliverer of His people.

The story of the messianic promises as the Scriptures present it begins with the recorded statement of God to the serpent and to Eve in the garden of Eden regarding their respective offspring. The fall of Adam and Eve from their pristine state and the advent of sin in the garden through the seductive suggestions of the serpent produced a division between the forces of good and the forces of evil which eventually was to result in victory over evil by the offspring of Eve. This victory over evil and a consequent return to blessed existence, whether on spiritual or physical levels, underlies all messianic representations and concepts. The time when victory would come to pass is often referred to as the day of the Lord.

A very early messianic prophecy is found in the blessing of Jacob when he says: "The sceptre shall not depart from Judah, nor a lawgiver from between his feet, until Shiloh come; and unto him shall the gathering of the people be" (Gen 49:10). Regardless of the meaning of "until Shiloh come," which has been variously rendered, here a ruler from the tribe of Judah is prophesied. Since Shiloh means "rest," many think the passage speaks of a dynasty in Judah until the rest giver comes. With a change of vowels (which were not in the original text) this phrase might be translated "until he come whose it is." On any account, a climax is to come in some supreme person. The seer Balaam also saw a coming and triumphant king, as recorded in Num 24:17, 19: "There shall come a Star out of Jacob, and a Sceptre shall rise out of Israel . . . Out of Jacob shall come he that shall have dominion . . . ."

Most of the prophecies of the messianic king grew out of the idea of the Davidic king and kingdom as ideal; they are, therefore, national and political in form, though national dominance was seen to be universal.

Isaiah saw the dawn of a new day coming by means of a child of peace with extraordinary names that belong to God, who would have an eternal government of unlimited expansion from the throne of David (Isa 9:2–7). The characteristics of peace, spirituality, beneficence, righteousness, and universality with which this root, stem, and Branch of Jesse would be endowed are beautifully emphasized in Isa 11.

Jeremiah also refers to the Messiah as the Branch: "Behold, the days come, saith the Lord, that I will raise unto David a righteous Branch, and a King shall reign and prosper, and shall execute judgment and justice in the earth" (Jer 23:5). In the next verse the coming one is called "the Lord our righteousness." Micah refines the messianic coming still further by prophesying that the ruler shall come from Bethlehem (Mic 5:2) and also refers to Him as the Breaker (*q.v.;* Mic 2:13), while Ezekiel sees "David" coming as a shepherd and prince (Ezk 34:23–24), and Zechariah portrays Him as "just, and having salvation; lowly, and riding [into Jerusalem] upon a colt" (Zech 9:9).

Especially notable in the many messianic references are Ps 2, 45, 72, and 110. The Davidic covenant promised a unique sonship to the kingly line of David, which could not have real fulfillment until his dynasty eventuated in a king who embodied this unique relationship of sonship to God (II Sam 7:14). Ps 2 emphasizes this relationship: "Thou art my Son; this day have I begotten thee" (v. 7). The whole psalm portrays the universal character of the messianic reign and the Messiah's power in quelling revolt. Ps 45 shows the messianic king as greater than Solomon, as Ps 2 represents Messiah as greater than David. This psalm, too, is in a direct line with the Davidic covenant. The main emphasis of vv. 6–7 is the eternal duration of the throne of this righteous King who is called God. The original source of the idea of eternal reign is II Sam 7:13, 16.

MESSIAH

Parallel with the statements of Ps 45 are those in Ps 89:4, "Thy seed will I establish forever, and build up thy throne to all generations"; in Ps 89:36–37, "His seed shall endure forever, and his throne as the sun before me. It shall be established forever as the moon. . ."; in Ps 72:5 (ASV), "They shall fear thee while the sun endureth, and so long as the moon, throughout all generations"; and in Isa 9:7, "Of the increase of his government and peace there shall be no end. . . ." The same marks of eternal duration and righteous rule, which are everywhere marks of the Messiah who was promised as the culmination of the Davidic line, are here evident in the psalm of the God-King.

In Ps 72 the sublime character of the righteous, compassionate King-Messiah and His reign with its universal dominion and eternal duration are brought together to make a picture of a utopian rule and ruler.

Ps 110 presents the eternal reign of a priest-king. The psalmist sings an oracle which Yahweh will fulfill when the Davidic covenant comes to its fruition in King-Messiah. The Messiah will be placed at the right hand of Yahweh, where He will remain until all who oppose Him will be prostrated before Him. An entirely new element is here added to the messianic picture. This all-powerful king is also to be an everlasting priest. He shall have eternal dominion in both governmental and ecclesiastical offices.

Isaiah introduces another stream into the river of messianic prophecy in the Servant of the Lord passages (42:1–9; 49:1–6; 50:4–9; 52:13–53:12) which find their culmination in Isa 53. Here the Servant of the Lord is a rejected, suffering leader who dies a substitutionary death for His people and yet prolongs His days and prospers.

Daniel provides yet another tributary to this swelling stream as he tells of his visions of the end time. In a crucial vision he sees a figure "like the Son of man" coming on the clouds of heaven and receiving from the Ancient of Days a glorious, universal, everlasting, and final kingdom (Dan 7:13). The vision contains the paradoxical elements of humanity and deity in the phrases "like the Son of man" and "coming on the clouds of heaven," since Son of man means human being, and the clouds of heaven were considered to be the vehicle of God.

While some insist this figure is a personalization of the saints of the Most High who later are said to possess the kingdom (vv. 18,22), this conclusion is unwarranted because elsewhere in the Danielic visions both king and kingdom are referred to in the same figures (7:17; cf. v. 23). The differences between the representation of the Son of man vision and the Davidic king lie in the characteristics of apocalyptic prophecy. The Davidic king was to be born as a child in the Davidic line on the earth; the Son of man comes from above, out of heaven. The Davidic king was to experience normal growth as a human being and extend His sway over the earth; the Son of man comes suddenly, cataclysmically, out of heaven. Both kingdoms were to be universal and eternal. In the intertestamental period the figure of the Son of man appears especially in I Enoch where the characteristics of the Danielic vision are evident.

Another stream of messianic prophecy starts with God's promise to Moses as recorded in Deut 18:15, where a prophet "like unto me" is promised. The Samaritans especially used Deut 18:15 as a messianic proof text, so it is not surprising that the woman of Samaria to whom Jesus spoke, said that the Messiah would "teach us all things" (Jn 4:25).

The coming of the Lord Himself contributes to the messianic stream. In Isaiah especially reference to Yahweh as the one who comes as Saviour and Redeemer adds to the messianic portrayal (Isa 35:4; 40:10; 59:20). It is the way of Yahweh which is to be prepared in Isa 40. It is the Lord God who is to come to rule and feed and care for His flock (Isa 40:3,4,9–11). Malachi predicts also the coming of the Lord Himself after His messenger had prepared the way before Him (Mal 3:1).

From the intertestamental literature, including certain of the Qumran writings, and from the NT it is evident that this rich and varied presentation of one who was to come to usher in the day of the Lord issued in the notion of different Messiahs. Not before Jesus of Nazareth guided these tributaries into one stream did anyone find it possible to harmonize in one person all the messianic hopes. Occasionally in one simple statement our Lord brought two or more themes of OT messianic prophecy together, as, for instance, in the saying, "For the Son of man came not to be ministered unto, but to minister, and to give his life a ransom for many" (Mt 20:28; Mk 10:45). Here the Danielic apocalyptic Son of man and the Isaianic prophetic Servant of the Lord (Isa 53) are brought together.

In post-resurrection appearances especially, Jesus is said to have taught His disciples how the OT predictions were fulfilled in Himself (Lk 24:27, 44–47; Acts 1:3).

Many of these prophecies are declared by the NT writers to be fulfilled in Jesus' first advent. Others are by Jesus Himself related to the current period between the two advents or to the time of His return; if not for their initial fulfillment, certainly for their culmination. So the Son of man prophecy is related to a later time than that of His first advent in His words to Caiaphas (Mt 26:63–64) and in His message to His disciples in Mt 24.

The burden of the NT is to show that Jesus is the Messiah promised in the OT, and that He Himself gave the clues of OT interpretation to His disciples. The New English Bible reports Jesus as saying to the disciples on the Emmaus road: "This, he said, is what is written: that the Messiah is to suffer death and to rise from the

dead on the third day, and that in his name repentance bringing the forgiveness of sins is to be proclaimed to all nations" (Lk 24:46–47).
See Jesus Christ.

Bibliography. A. Bentzen, *King and Messiah,* London: Lutterworth Press, 1955. Charles A. Briggs, *Messianic Prophecy,* New York: Scribner's Sons, 1886; *The Messiah of the Gospels,* Edinburgh: T. & T. Clark, 1894; *The Messiah of the Apostles,* Edinburgh: T. & T. Clark, 1895. A. Edersheim, *Prophecy and History in Relation to the Messiah,* London: Longmans, Green and Co., 1885. T. F. Glasson, *Moses in the Fourth Gospel,* Naperville: Alec R. Allenson, Inc., 1963. E. W. Hengstenberg, *Christology of the Old Testament,* Washington, D. C.: William H. Morrison, 1836. S. Mowinckel, *He That Cometh,* New York: Abingdon, n.d. Edward Riehm, *Messianic Prophecy,* Edinburgh: T. & T. Clark, 1876. H. Ringgren, *The Messiah in the Old Testament,* Chicago: Alec R. Allenson, Inc., 1956. H. H. Rowley, *The Relevance of Apocalyptic,* London: Lutterworth Press, 1944; *The Servant of the Lord and Other Essays on the Old Testament,* London: Lutterworth Press, 1952. Wilhelm Vischer, *The Witness of the Old Testament to Christ,* London: Lutterworth Press, 1949. Edward J. Young, *The Messianic Prophecies of Daniel,* Grand Rapids: Eerdmans, 1954.

E. S. K.

MESSIANIC PSALMS. The ancient rabbis listed 26 psalms as having messianic portent (A. Edersheim, *Life and Times of Jesus the Messiah,* Appen. IX in Vol. II, pp. 716–20). These were psalms they could use to encourage Israel to unity and devotion promising help from God through His Anointed One. Ps 2, 16, 45, 72, 89, and 110 have definite messianic significance. Some of the others have been counted messianic because of strained interpretations. *See* Psalms, Book of.

MESSIAS. Gr. form of Messiah (*q.v.*).

METALS. *See* Minerals and Metals.

METALWORKERS. *See* Minerals and Metals; Occupations: Goldsmith, Refiner, Silversmith, Smith.

METEYARD. *See* Weights, Measures, and Coins.

METHEG-AMMAH (mē'thĕg-ăm'*à*). The ASV translates the word in II Sam 8:1 as "the bridle of the mother city." This would mean Gath, the capital of the Philistines. A number of problems are connected with II Sam 8:1. There is a possibility that the name simply fell into disuse. The NASB, however, interprets the passage as follows: "David took control of the chief city from . . ."

METHUSAEL (mē̇-thōō'sĕ-ĕl). A son of Mehujael, a descendant of Cain, and father of Lamech (Gen 4:18).

METHUSELAH (mē̇-thōō'zĕ-l*à*). The father of Lamech, grandfather of Noah, and son of Enoch. He died when 969 years of age (Gen 5:25–27), in the year of the Flood.

MEUNIM (mē̇-ū'nĭm). The LXX equates the Meunim (Heb. *me'ûnîm*) with the Mineans, who constituted the ancient S Arabian kingdom of Ma'în. Certain recent writers would seek the home of the Meunim in Maon (*q.v.*), modern Tell Ma'în, eight and a half miles S of Hebron. However, their OT associations point rather to Ma'ân, 12 miles SE of Petra, as their capital. Always enemies of the Heb. people, they were first defeated by Israel in the pre-monarchy period (Jud 10:12, where they are called "Maonites"), and subsequently by Jehoshaphat (II Chr 20:1, where "Meunites" is to be read instead of "Ammonites"; cf. ASV marg., RSV), by Uzziah (II Chr 26:7), and by Simeonites during Hezekiah's reign (I Chr 4:41, ASV, RSV). The sons of the Meunim listed among the Nethinim (RSV, "temple servants"), who returned to Palestine with other exiles during the early Persian period (Ezr 2:50; Neh 7:52), were apparently descendants of captives taken during the aforementioned battles.

R. Y.

MEZAHAB (mĕz'*à*-hăb). Grandfather of Mehetabel, wife of Hadar, the eighth king of Edom (Gen 36:39; I Chr 1:50). Some suggest that it is more likely the name of a place than a person (HDB 3.357) and that it may possibly be identical with Dizahab (ISBE 3.2045).

MEZUZAH. *See* Phylacteries.

MIAMIN (mī'*à*-mĭn). *See* Mijamin.

MIBHAR (mĭb'här). One of David's heroic men, the son of Haggeri (I Chr 11:38). The parallel passage (II Sam 23:36) reads: ". . . of Zobah, Bani the Gadite."

MIBSAM (mĭb'săm)
1. A son of Ishmael (Gen 25:13; I Chr 1:29).
2. A descendant of Simeon (I Chr 4:25), possibly named for the Ishmaelite Mibsam.

MIBZAR (mĭb'zär). A chief of Edom listed in Gen 36:42; I Chr 1:53. Eusebius (ISBE, Driver, Dillman) connects Mibzar with Mibsara, a large village (ISBE III.2045).

MICAH (mī'k*à*). The name Micah, meaning "Who is like Yahweh?" was common among the Hebrews.
1. An Ephramite living in the time of the judges (Jud 17–18). His mother had 200 she-

kels of silver recast as an image for a shrine eventually captured by a group of Danites.

2. Head of a family of Reuben (I Chr 5:5).

3. A son of Mephibosheth and grandson of Jonathan (I Chr 8:34-35; cf. II Sam 9:12).

4. A Levite of the family of Asaph (I Chr 9:15). In Heb. the name is Micha (*q.v.*). Perhaps he is the same as 3.

5. A Kohathite (I Chr 23:20; 24:24-25).

6. The father of Abdon whom Josiah sent to inquire of the Lord when the book of the law was found (II Chr 34:20). He is called Michaiah in II Kgs 22:12.

7. A prophet, author of the book bearing his name (Mic 1:1; Jer 26:18). He lived at Moresheth-gath (Mic 1:1, 14), a town in Judah near the Philistine city of Gath, and at one time possibly under the rule of Gath. The town was 20 to 25 miles SW of Jerusalem. Eusebius and Jerome quote tradition which placed the site not far to the E of Eleutheropolis, which has been identified with Beit Jibrin, located in a valley which leads from the coastal plain to the Judean highlands about Jerusalem. The prophet thus lived where he was able to view the great road along which invading armies had passed for centuries, as well as caravans for trade and pilgrims.

Micah was a contemporary of Isaiah. He preached during the reigns of Jotham (*c.* 742-735 B.C.), Ahaz (*c.* 735-715 B.C.), and Hezekiah (*c.* 715-687 B.C.), kings of Judah, and served both the northern as well as the southern kingdom, addressing himself to Samaria and Jerusalem.

The title of the book (1:1) has been disputed, but the contents confirm both the date assigned to the prophet and the objects of his ministry, the capitals of Israel and Judah. Whereas Isaiah ministered in Jerusalem, Micah supposedly prophesied among the lowly classes of the nation. But he could easily have prophesied in the capital also, for he denounced the leaders of the kingdom and made Jerusalem in large measure the center of his messages.

Evidence is lacking to substantiate the position that Micah was merely a man of the country because he resided in a town of the Judean lowland. He mentions places in the lowland (1:10-15), but also places elsewhere in both kingdoms (2:12; 4:8; 5:2; 7:14). His style does not show him as a rustic. His rapid transitions from one theme to another show only that his was a vivacious spirit, and that he possessed a certain boldness in speech. Traditions concerning his origin, death, and burial originate in part from confusing him with Micah the son of Imlah, the contemporary of Ahab, king of Israel (I Kgs 22:8).

It has been conjectured from 2:2 that he was a farmer, and may have had his property taken from him by violence. But Micah was capable of directness of speech and strong indignation. He was a writer of great ability, some of his tender and sublime utterances (6:1-8) rivaling those of Isaiah. It cannot be doubted that Micah, as well as Isaiah, greatly influenced King Hezekiah in his reformation of the spiritual life of the realm (see Jer 26:18).

Micah was a man of great sympathies for the downtrodden, sensitive to the sufferings of his countrymen, and met opposition with evident courage. His language shows him to have been a man of great emotional force and lofty moral ideals.

C. L. F.

MICAH, BOOK OF. Micah is the sixth of the minor prophets. The style of the prophecy is simple and forceful. The prophet is fond of questions, and employs metaphor, play on words, and irony. Micah has given only a condensation of his preaching, but what he has recorded shows him to be a worthy contemporary of Isaiah in forthright denunciation of the sins of the nation and its leaders, and in the glowing fervor of messianic prediction. Ministering in the 8th cen. B.C., he saw that the threatening power over Judah was Assyria, the empire that had destroyed the northern kingdom of Israel (5:5ff.). Micah witnessed the fall of Samaria in 722 B.C.

Micah's prophecy bears a number of resemblances to the book of Isaiah. The most remarkable parallel is the passage in Mic 4:1ff., which is almost word for word with what is found in Isa 2:2ff. Explanations have ranged from ascribing the prediction to Isaiah, to Micah, or to an older prophet, but no argument has satisfied a majority of interpreters.

Some scholars have assigned certain portions of the book to other writers than Micah. These arguments are purely subjective, and have been ably answered by defenders of the traditional position, namely, that the entire book was written by one author, Micah the Morasthite.

Outline

I. First Oracle, Chaps. 1-2
  A. Denunciation, 1:2-16
  B. Threat, 2:1-11
  C. Promise, 2:12-13
II. Second Oracle, Chaps. 3-5
  A. Denunciation, 3:1-11
  B. Threat, 3:12
  C. Promise, 4:1–5:15
III. Third Oracle, Chaps. 6-7
  A. Denunciation, 6:1-5
  B. Threat, 6:6–7:6
  C. Promise, 7:7-20

Contents

Nearly all interpreters divide the book into three sections indicated by the introductory words "Hear ye." The first address covers chaps. 1 and 2, and its theme is judgment on Samaria and Jerusalem, the capitals of both kingdoms. Judgment is approaching for the sins of the nation (1:2-5), which will overtake Samaria for its idolatrous ways (1:6-7). But Judah will be devastated and her people exiled for the same offenses (1:8-16), the punishment being depicted under the figure of a desolating army. Destruction and captivity are in store for the leaders who have oppressed the people with unrighteous and unjust dealings (2:1-5), and the false prophets are equally blameworthy in their predictions which indulge the people and lull them to sleep in their moral complacency (2:6-11). There follows a promise of ultimate blessing for a remnant of Israel which will return (2:12-13).

The second oracle dilates on the sins of the princes, the false prophets, the unfair judges, and wicked priests. Again, the political and religious leaders of the nation are rebuked for their utter disregard of the right and for their concern for personal gain (3:1-11). Consequently, the Lord was to deliver Zion to her enemies (3:12). So potent was this last oracle that it was remembered a century later (Jer 26:18). The latter part of the second prophecy (chaps. 4-5) reveals that God's kingdom will be realized in power, peace, and plenty (4:1-8). In the meantime only distress and captivity await the nation because of the people's inveterate sinning (4:9-10), but their visitation will be followed by God's judgment on their enemies (4:11-13). There is a climax in the announcement of the birth in Bethlehem of the Messiah who liberates Zion from Assyrian domination and shepherds His flock (5:1-6). The remnant will not only be preserved from hostile attack, but will be a dread to the inimical nations (5:7-9). The Messiah will establish a kingdom of peace (5:10-15).

The third prophecy presents God's way of redemption under the figure of a legal controversy between the Lord and His people. The questions introduced at the outset are among the most striking in all prophetic literature. The plea is based on the many tokens of God's blessing on Israel and their ingratitude for them seen in their prevailing sins (6:1-5). The basic requirements for blessing are set forth (6:6-8), and then Micah shows that these requirements are absent among them (6:9–7:6). He concludes with a prediction of future blessing because of God's faithfulness to the Abrahamic covenant (7:7-20). Ultimately, the nation in its conviction of sin will turn with penitence and confession to the Lord. By trusting the Lord, Israel will experience His compassion, His reestablishment of Zion with the subjugation of every foe, and the renewal of His supernatural acts on its behalf. The book closes with praise for the grace of God (7:18-20).

Bibliography. Gleason L. Archer, "Micah," NBC. B. A. Copass and E. L. Carlson, *A Study of the Prophet Micah,* Grand Rapids: Baker, 1950. J. Marsh, *Amos and Micah: Introduction and Commentary,* London: S.C.M. Press, 1959. Norman H. Snaith, *Amos, Hosea and Micah,* London: Epworth, 1956. A. S. van der Woude, "Micah in Dispute with the Pseudo-Prophets," VT, XIX (1969), 244-260.

C. L. F.

MICAIAH (mī-kāy'yȧ). Sometimes the name is contracted to Mica or Micah (*q.v.*). In the KJV it is generally spelled Michaiah.

1. Mother of King Abijah (II Chr 13:2), also spelled in the ASV Maacah, or Maachah in the KJV (II Chr 11:20).

2. Father of Achbor (II Kgs 22:12), called Micah in II Chr 34:20. *See* Micah 6.

3. One of five princes sent by Jehoshaphat to teach God's law throughout Judah (II Chr 17:7).

4. Ancestor of Zechariah, who was a trumpeter at the dedication of the wall (Neh 12:35).

5. One of the priestly trumpeters at the dedication of the wall (Neh 12:41).

6. One who reported to the princes Baruch's reading of Jeremiah's prophecy (Jer 36:11-13).

7. Son of Imlah and a prophet in Israel during the days of Israel's King Ahab. The one event of his ministry specifically described is his prediction regarding the death of Ahab and the defeat of Israel at the hands of the Syrians (I Kgs 22:4-28; II Chr 18:3-27). Having made an affinity with Ahab, Jehoshaphat, the king of Judah, agreed to fight with Israel against Syria over Ramoth-gilead. First, however, Jehoshaphat wanted to know the will of the Lord in the matter. Thereupon Ahab summoned 400 prophets, distinctly called "his prophets" (II Chr 18:21-22). These unitedly predicted God's blessing of victory for Ahab. Yet Jehoshaphat was not satisfied and requested a prophet of Yahweh. Reluctantly Ahab called Micaiah (whose name means "Who is like Yahweh?") after declaring his hatred of him because he had always prophesied evil. Urged by the messenger to agree with the 400 prophets, Micaiah at first in a spirit of irony did, but then predicted disaster. Ahab attributed this to Micaiah's personal hatred of him. Therefore Micaiah affirmed as the word of the Lord that Yahweh had permitted a lying spirit to speak through Ahab's prophets. Zedekiah, evidently a leader of the false prophets, smote Micaiah on the cheek and Ahab ordered him to prison, defiantly declaring that Micaiah's prophecy would not occur. Micaiah, true to Deut 18:20-22, publicly staked all on its fulfillment. Nothing more is heard of Micaiah in the Scriptures, but Ahab learned that Yahweh's word through Micaiah was true. In spite of Ahab's disguising himself, "a certain man drew a bow at a venture" and the arrow found its mark through the joints of the king's armor and he died at sundown.

C. J. W.

MICE, GOLDEN. When the Philistines had possession of the ark of the covenant, they felt that they were being punished because of it. Part of the offering along with the return of the ark was to include golden mice (I Sam 6:1-5,11,18). It is thought that perhaps mice had overrun the country as part of the plague. Gesenius suggests that the word is taken from two words which indicate eating corn; thus he believes that field mice are meant. *See* Animals, IV. 27.

MICHA (mī'kȧ). A variant of Micah and Micaiah.

1. A son of Mephibosheth, the crippled son of Jonathan (II Sam 9:12; called Micah in I Chr 8:34). *See* Micah.

2. A Levite who sealed the covenant with Nehemiah (Neh 10:11).

3. A Levite who was a descendant of Asaph (Neh 11:17, 22; cf. I Chr 9:15). The full name "Michaiah" is used in Neh 12:35, 41. *See* Michaiah.

MICHAEL (mī'kĕl). The Heb. name of 11 biblical personages, meaning "Who is like God?"

1. The archangel Michael who in the OT is mentioned by name in Daniel. He is there designated as "one of the chief princes" (10:13), as "your prince" (10:21), as "the great prince" (12:1), and probably as "the prince of the host" (8:11). In all these passages Michael appears as a warrior angel acting as the guardian and heavenly champion of Israel in its conflict with the godless powers of Greece and Persia. In Jewish apocalyptic literature (Enoch 9 and 40) Michael is depicted as the first of the "four presences that stand before God" (Michael, Gabriel, Raphael, and Phanuel or Uriel). Other apocryphal writings list seven as the number of archangels, Michael being one of them (Tob 3:17; 12:15; II Esd 4:1).

In the NT Michael is described as "contending with the devil . . . about the body of Moses" (Jude 9). Some scholars find,the source for Jude's statement in the pseudepigraph the Assumption of Moses which ascribes the burial of Moses to Michael and the angels. In the Targum of Jonathan on Deut 34:6 a similar legend is found. A more likely interpretation of the passage in Jude is that which stresses the appropriateness of the archangel as the guardian of Moses' body, since probably Michael was the angel who spoke to Moses on Mount Sinai (Acts 7:38). The basic thrust of the passage is to show that fallen angels such as the devil retain from their first condition a status and dignity, so that even their unfallen former associates may not speak against them in unbridled terms, but must leave the final condemnation to God. *See* Jude, Epistle of.

Michael last appears in Scripture in Rev 12:7 as leading the angelic armies against the dragon and his angels. Cast again in his warrior role, Michael is said to defeat Satan and to hurl him from heaven to the earth. According to some Protestant scholars, Michael is to be identified with the preincarnate Christ. They cite for support the juxtaposition of the "man child" and Michael in Rev 12, as well as the title and attributes of "prince" in the book of Daniel. *See* Angel.

F. C. K.

2. Father of the spy representing the tribe of Asher (Num 13:13).

3 and 4. Two men of Gad, one the descendant of the other (I Chr 5:11, 13, 14).

5. A Levite and ancestor of Asaph (I Chr 6:39-40).

6. A chief of the tribe of Issachar (I Chr 7:3).

7. A descendant of Benjamin (I Chr 8:16).

8. A Manassite warrior with David (I Chr 12:20).

9. A man of Issachar whose son David appointed to govern that tribal territory (I Chr 27:18); perhaps the same as 6.

10. One of the seven sons of King Jehoshaphat, slain by his brother Jehoram (II Chr 21:2-4).

11. Father of a leader of 80 returnees from Babylon (Ezr 8:8).

MICHAH. *See* Micah.

MICHAIAH. *See* Micaiah.

MICHAL (mī'kȧl). Saul's younger daughter, given as wife to David because of his notable exploit against the Philistines (I Sam 14:49; 18:20-25). She helped David escape the murderous plot of Saul (I Sam 19:11-17). Saul gave Michal to Phaltiel for a wife when David was in flight (I Sam 25:44), but David recovered her after Saul's death (II Sam 3:13-15). She lost favor with David because she was contemptuous of his dancing before the ark when it was brought to Jerusalem. She bore him no children (II Sam 6:16-23).

MICHMASH (mĭk'măsh), **MICHMAS** (mĭk' măs). A town of Benjamin near Geba (*q.v.*), seven miles N of Jerusalem, where the Lord saved Israel in battle with the Philistines (cf. I Sam 14:23). At first 2,000 men were with Saul in Michmash and 1,000 with his son Jonathan in Gibeah (I Sam 13:2). The Philistine army then came in force and occupied Michmash. A Philistine garrison was positioned to command the gorge of the Wadi es-Suwenit to the S of Michmash. Without knowledge of his father, Jonathan and his armor bearer climbed the steep cliff between two sharp rocks, Bozez and Seneh (I Sam 14:4), surprised the garrison, and slew 20 men. Aided by their valor and by an earthquake, Israel's army routed the Philistines that day.

Later reference to this pass appears in latter day prophecy, "at Michmash he hath laid up his carriages" (Isa 10:28). Exiles from the Captivity, 122 men returned to Michmash with Zerubbabel (Ezr 2:27; Neh 7:31, here spelled Michmas). In the Maccabean period, Jonathan Maccabaeus had the seat of his government at Michmash (I Macc 9:73). In modern times the spot is marked by the village of Mukhmas. Visible are some ancient foundations, large stones, and a vaulted cistern.

L. A. L.

MICHMETHAH (mĭk'mĕ-thȧ). A town on the boundary between Ephraim and Manasseh, W of Jordan and E of Shechem (Josh 16:6; 17:1). It is suggested that the article ("the Michmethah") may indicate that it is not a proper name but an appellative relating to some feature of the landscape. Others suggest it is a corruption of Mukhanah and refers to the plain E of Shechem.

MICHRI (mĭk'rī). A Benjamite, whose descendants lived in Jerusalem (I Chr 9:8).

MICHTAM (mĭk'tȧm). The meaning may be "golden poem," or "a mystery," "a song of deep import." Ps 16, 56–60 are so designated.

MIDDAY. *See* Time, Divisions of.

MIDDIN (mĭd'ĭn). A city in the desert of Judah, one of six wilderness cities (Josh 15:61) whose site has not been definitely established. If the word is a corruption for Mârâd, the site of Khirbet Mird on a plateau SW of Jericho may be its location. Or the LXX posits Madon as the correct reading, placing the city in the valley of Achor where it would be identified with modern Khirbet Abu Tabaq, four miles W of Qumran.

In 1965–66 three Iron Age sites were discovered along the W shore of the Dead Sea, halfway between Qumran and En-gedi; one of these may possibly have been Middin (*see* Nibshan).

Cast of inscription found by Clermont-Ganneau on the Middle Wall of Partition. Palestine Archaeological Museum

MIDDLE WALL OF PARTITION. A Pauline figure of speech to signify the removal of enmity between the Jew and the Gentile, bringing about the unity of the Body of Christ, the Church (Eph 2:14). Literally, it refers to an actual wall in the temple of Jerusalem beyond which no Gentile might safely pass (see Jos *Ant.* xv.11.5; *Wars* v.5.2). That such an allusion should have occurred to Paul appears natural, if we remember that he was falsely accused of bringing in Trophimus, the Ephesian, past the barrier, and thus polluting the sacred precincts of the temple proper (Acts 21:29; 24:6). This misunderstanding almost cost the apostle his life.

The middle wall of partition was constructed of marble, highly decorated. In 1871, as a result of Clermont-Ganneau's excavations, one of the limestone blocks of this wall was unearthed, bearing the following Gr. inscription: "No one of another nation is to enter within the fence and enclosure around the temple, and whoever is caught will have himself to blame that his death ensues" (cf. Deiss LAE, pp. 79ff.). The wall was thus the separating barrier between national Jews and (mere) pious Gentiles.

J. F. G.

MIDIAN, MIDIANITES (mĭd'ĭ-ȧn, mĭd'ĭ-ȧ-nīts). Midian, whose name means contention or strife, was the fourth of the six sons of Abraham by Keturah (Gen 25:2; I Chr 1:32). He, along with the other sons of the concubines, was sent away with gifts into the wilderness to prevent a contest over the inheritance of Isaac (Gen 25:1–6).

Midian was also an area in the northern Arabian desert beyond the Jordan in eastern Moab and Edom, E of the Gulf of Aqabah, and in the eastern part of the Sinai Peninsula. The OT references to this region are many. Its heartland lay along the E shore of the Gulf of Aqabah and was bordered by Edom to the NW. After killing the Egyptian, Moses fled to the land of Midian (Ex 2:15). W. J. Dumbrell, however, questions whether Midian was ever a territorial term, believing the name in the Late Bronze Age (Moses' time) to have been that of a large league of nomadic peoples ("The Midianites and Their Transjordanian Successors," Th.D. Dissertation, Harvard Univ., 1970, summarized in HTR, LXIII [1970], 515f.).

The Midianites were desert people who lived in tents like nomads (Ex 3:1; Num 10:29–31). Five Midianite clans traced their ancestry to the sons of Midian (Gen 25:4). The Ishmaelites and the Midianites were sometimes so closely associated that it is hard to distinguish them. Evidently all the exiled children of Abraham intermarried. Some of the merchants in the company of Ishmaelites from Gilead were Midianites who bought Joseph and took him to Egypt (Gen 37:25–28). According to Ex 3:1, Moses' father-in-law, Jethro, was a priest of Midian. Moses kept his sheep for 40 years (Acts 7:30). The Midianites on one occasion became partners with the Moabites as they hired Balaam to pronounce a curse on the Israelites. Israel then waged war on them and succeeded in killing five of their kings and many of their people (Num 22:4–6; 25; 31).

W. F. Albright believes that the Midianites were one of several tribes which controlled the donkey caravan trade that began between S Arabia and the Fertile Crescent *c.* 1400 B.C. or perhaps a little earlier (JBL, LXXXVII [1968], 389f.). Note the large number of donkeys

(61,000) and no camels in the spoils taken from the Midianites (Num 31:34).

Judges 6 and 7 record the seven-year oppression of the Israelites by Midian. Because of Israel's sin of idolatry, God permitted the Midianites to wage an effective warfare against them. When the divine protection was withdrawn from Israel, the Midianites joined with the Amalekites and the children of the E to fight against Israel. Their oppression was directed primarily against the harvest fields, the crops, and those who had sown them. God raised up Gideon to deliver his people who had repented. The enemies of God and of Israel suffered complete defeat, and their two princes and two kings were killed (Jud 7:23-8:35; Ps 83:11; Isa 9:4; 10:26; Hab 3:7). While they continued to exist (see Isa 60:6), never again are Midian and the Midianites mentioned as oppressors of Israel.

R. P. L.

MIDNIGHT. *See* Time, Divisions of.

MIDRASH (mĭd'răsh). A Jewish term from the Heb. verb *dārash,* "to search," and therefore, to expound. This is a body of Jewish literature that embraces the exegesis, exposition, and homiletical interpretations of Scripture, beginning in the rabbinical schools in ancient Israel during the periods of the *Sôpherîm* (400-180 B.C.) and *Zûgôt* (2nd and 1st cen. B.C.). Other materials were at later dates.

There are two types of Midrash: the *halakâh* that treats the legal materials of Scripture, and the *haggadâh* which handles all the nonlegal parts (e.g., ethics, theology) and is homiletical. Ezra used it in the public reading of the law (Neh 8), and it became the basic work for the *Targûmîm* (Aramaic paraphrases of Scripture) and the mainline expression of Judaism (*Mishnâh, Talmûd).*

The principal use of the Midrash is that it gives the exegete of Scripture a greater insight into interpretation from a people closer to the original appearance of the OT books, as well as an understanding of the text across history by Jewish people. *See* Talmud.

L. Go

MIDWIFE. *See* Occupations: Midwife.

MIGDAL-EL (mĭg'dȧl-ĕl'). A fortified city in Naphtali near Yiron and Horem (Josh 19:38 RSV). Its location is a matter of dispute. Some suppose that it is Magdala of the NT on the W side of the Sea of Galilee.

MIGDAL-GAD (mĭg'dȧl-găd'). Mentioned only in Josh 15:37 along with 15 other cities in various parts of Judah. Its location is unknown.

MIGDOL (mĭg'dŏl). The place name Migdol is related to the common Heb. noun *migdāl,* "tower," and is regarded as indicating a fortified site. Usually the biblical references are taken to apply to two separate places in Egypt, both in the Delta, but some authorities refer all to one city (BDB, p. 154; cf. GTT, pp. 239-240, 447-448). Migdol appears as a loan-word in Egyptian; it occurs in the New Kingdom (1570-1085 B.C.) in hieroglyphic and later in Coptic (A. Erman and H. Grapow, *Wörterbuch der Aegyptischen Sprache,* II, 164).

1. The Exodus account mentions a Migdol NW of the Red Sea, in connection with a stopping place of the Israelites (Ex 14:2; Num 33:7). It was near Migdol that they crossed the sea and entered the Sinai Peninsula. This tower must have been one of the guardposts or checkpoints built by the Egyptians to protect the NE frontier against Asiatic incursions. As early as the Middle Kingdom (2160-1785 B.C.) such stations or posts are referred to in the story of Sinuhe (ANET, p. 19; a later reference to the Migdol of Seti Mer-ne-Pṭah, *ibid.,* p. 259).

2. An Egyptian city named Migdol appears twice in the prophecies of Jeremiah concerning Egypt and the Jewish refugees who fled from Palestine after the murder of Gedaliah (Jer 44:1; 46:14).

3. In the predictions of Ezekiel against Egypt, Migdol is referred to as the northernmost place in that country, "From Migdol to Syene" (Ezk 29:10; 30:6, RSV). It was situated in the extreme NE part of the Delta and is identified as the modern Tell el Heir, near Pelusium (*Westminster Historical Atlas,* p. 126; E. Kraeling, *Bible Atlas,* p. 482; Gardiner, JEA, VI [1920], 109-110).

See Tower; Fortress; Exodus, The: The Route.

C. E. D.

MIGHTY MAN (MEN). A phrase occurring more than 150 times in the KJV, translating mainly the Heb. *('îsh) gibbôr. Gibbôr* derives from the Heb. root *gbr* (Akk. *gapru),* "to be superior, strong, mighty, to prevail over." Thus *('îsh) gibbôr* is "mighty man."

The phrase connotes normally nothing of a supernatural power about the person, although certain mighty men definitely received help from God in their exploits. It simply denotes a man who, like David (I Sam 17:8), carries himself proudly, a bold, courageous warrior (particularly in conjunction with *ḥayil,* "valor"), occasionally a tyrant (Gen 6:4).

The most notable are David's mighty men (II Sam 23:8-39; I Chr 11:10-47) "who strengthened themselves with him in his kingdom, and with all Israel, to make him king, according to the word of the Lord concerning Israel" (I Chr 11:10). Apparently there were originally 30 such men who attached themselves to the charismatic David, who in turn assigned them to command his troops. This supposition is based on the fact that they are referred to as "the thirty" even though the listing in II Samuel contains 32 names and the Chronicles listing adds 16 more to the group. It is equally plausible that as certain ones of them were killed in battle or died, others would take their places, thus swelling the number of the original 30 while the group still retained the elite name "the thirty."

David's mighty men are divided by the listings themselves into two groups: (1) the three most renowned champions: Jashobeam (Adino?), Eleazar, and Shammah (II Sam 23:8-12; I Chr 11:10-14); and (2) "the thirty," led by Abishai and Benaiah (II Sam 23:18-39; I Chr 11:20-47). Ishmaiah and Amasai were also leaders of the thirty (I Chr 12:4, 18, RSV) at one time or another. Joab may have been among them before becoming commander-in-chief. In II Sam 23:39 the total given is 37; apparently the last seven names were those of foreign officers (e.g., Uriah the Hittite) over mercenary units in David's army. The three mighty men of the thirty who hazarded their lives for David (II Sam 23:13-17; I Chr 11:15-19) are unnamed. To equate them with Jashobeam, Eleazar, and Shammah is mere conjecture, although such an equation is entirely possible. *See* Army; War.

Like Kish (I Sam 9:1), Boaz (Ruth 2:1), David's ancestor, was a "mighty man of valor [wealth]." Perhaps they were courageous warriors, but more than likely in the contexts the phrase is intended to describe them as wealthy land owners.

Bibliography. Roland de Vaux, *Ancient Israel,* New York: McGraw-Hill, 1961, pp. 219ff. B. Mazar, "The Military Elite of King David," VT, XIII (1963), 310-320.

R. L. R.

MIGHTY WORKS. *See* Miracles; Signs.

MIGRON (mĭg'rŏn). The probable site is Tell Miryam, located halfway between Michmash and Geba. Saul and his army of 600 stationed themselves there preparatory to a battle with the Philistines (I Sam 13:23–14:5; read perhaps "Geba" for "Gibeah" in 14:2). It was on the line of march of the Assyrians, who attacked Jerusalem from the N in the days of Isaiah (Isa 10:24-34).

MIJAMIN (mĭj'ȧ-mĭn). KJV twice spells the name Miamin (Ezr 10:25; Neh 12:5).

1. A descendant of Aaron and head of the sixth of the 24 courses into which David organized the priests (I Chr 24:9).

2. A member of the family of Parosh who had married a foreign wife in the post-Exilic period (Ezr 10:25).

3. A priest who signed the covenant with Nehemiah (Neh 10:7).

4. A priest who returned from Babylonia with Zerubbabel and Jeshua (Neh 12:5, 7).

MIKLOTH (mĭk'lŏth)

1. A son of Jeiel, a Benjamite. By comparing I Chr 8:32 and 9:37-38 it appears that the words "and Mikloth" have been dropped at the end of 8:31. Both are in 9:37 in the MT and LXX.

2. An officer in the second division of the guard appointed by David (I Chr 27:4).

MIKNEIAH (mĭk-nē'yȧ). One of the harpists whom the chief of the Levites chose upon request of David (I Chr 15:18, 21). In the KJV it appears that he may have been a porter also; the ASV designates him as a doorkeeper for the ark. The RSV speaks of him only as a musician.

MILALAI (mĭl'ȧ-lī). A musician involved in the ceremonies in the dedication of the wall of Jerusalem (Neh 12:36).

MILCAH (mĭl'kȧ)

1. The daughter of Haran and the wife of Nahor, Abraham's brother. She was the mother of eight children, among whom were Bethuel, the father of Rebekah and Laban (Gen 11:29; 22:20,23; 24:15,24,47).

2. The fourth of the five daughters of Zelophehad of Manasseh at the time of the Exodus. The five daughters had no brother and their case set a legal precedent in Israel when they received the same inheritance as sons (Num 26:33; 27:1 ff.; Josh 17:3 ff.). They were restricted to marriage within the tribe (Num 36:6 ff.). *See* Zelophehad.

MILCOM. *See* Gods, False: Molech, Moloch.

MILDEW. The Heb. *yērāqôn* (cognate with Arabic *yērākân,* "jaundice") signifies a yellowness or pallor. It always appears with *shiddāphôn,* "blasting," which means to dry up or scorch the grain or fruit. The term mildew can refer to any of several species of fungus that appear on plants and live on them until they kill them (Deut 28:22; I Kgs 8:37; II Chr 6:28; Amos 4:9; Hag 2:17). *See* Blasting.

MILE. *See* Weights, Measures, and Coins.

An aqueduct and Byzantine church, Miletus.
ORINST

MILETUM. *See* Miletus.

MILETUS (mī-lē'tŭs). A city which lay on the S shore of the Latonian Gulf, which penetrated Caria in SW Asia Minor and which received the waters of the Maeander River. A commercial and cultural center during the 7th and 6th cen. B.C., Miletus led the Ionian revolt against Persia in 499 B.C. and was destroyed by Persia. Rising again, she became a thriving city of some 100,000 during the 1st cen. A.D. At the end of his third missionary journey, Paul spent some days at Miletus waiting for and meeting with the Ephesian elders (Acts 20:15–38). Later he returned briefly, probably after release from his first Roman imprisonment, and was forced to leave Trophimus there ill (II Tim 4:20). The waters of the Maeander have silted up the Latonian Gulf, and Miletus is now five miles from the sea in the midst of a malarial swamp. Excavations beginning in 1899 have laid bare much of the city Paul would have known.

H. F. V.

MILK. Milk and milk products (cheese, curds, and butter) furnished a large part of the Hebrew's diet from earliest times (cf. Gen 18:8). The term for milk is used more than 40 times in the OT and five times in the NT—predominantly in the figurative sense. Goat's milk was most common (Prov 27:27). However, we read also of milk from human mothers (Isa 28:9), cows, asses, sheep (Deut 32:14; I Cor 9:7), and camels (Gen 32:15). Milk was milked into pails (Job 21:24, ASV) and preserved in skins (Jud 4:19, RSV; "bottle," KJV). *See* Food: Milk.

Metaphorically, milk is used to describe the fertility of the land of Canaan, "a land flowing with milk and honey" (18 times). Egypt (Goshen) is described by the same expression by the embittered Israelites in the wilderness (Num 16:13). Elsewhere in the OT milk is used as a symbol for abundance (Deut 32:14), including that of the eschatological age (Isa 55:1; Joel 3:18); for the whiteness of teeth (Gen 49:12) or skin (Lam 4:7); for Israel's vindication ("You will also suck the milk of nations," Isa 60:16, NASB); and for the excellencies of loved ones (Song 4:11; 5:12). In the NT milk is used to refer to rudiments of instructions for new converts (I Cor 3:2; I Pet 2:2); however, Paul (I Cor 3:2–3) and the writer of Hebrews (Heb 5:12–13) reprimand their readers for not being more mature.

The strange prohibition against boiling a kid in its mother's milk (Ex 23:19; 34:26; Deut 14:21) is probably directed against a Canaanite sacrificial ritual. References to such a fertility rite have been found in the Ras Shamra (*q.v.*) tablets: "Over the fire seven times the sacrificers cook a kid in milk" (G. R. Driver, *Canaanite Myths and Legends,* Edinburgh: T. & T. Clark, 1956, p. 121; cf. p. 23). On this prohibition in the Heb. Bible is built the Jewish dietary law forbidding the eating of milk and meat at the same meal.

Millstones in a bakery at Pompeii. HFV

R. L. S.

MILL, MILLSTONE. Two stones so combined as to rub against each other and grind grain into flour. The method has a long history and is still used in places in Palestine today.

From neolithic times onward the lower stone was usually rectangular in shape, varying greatly in size, hollowed out to leave a turned-up lip at each end. The upper stone was cylindrical or convex to rub back and forth over grain sprinkled on the stationary lower stone. Small enough to carry easily, the upper stone was sometimes demanded as a pledge by a creditor (Deut 24:6), and made a convenient missile to drop on a besieging enemy (Jud 9:53). The captured Samson was used by the Philistines to grind at the prison mill (Jud 16:21), a task normally delegated to a slave girl (Ex 11:5; Isa 47:2). The noise of the basalt stones being rubbed against each other before dawn each day typified normal peaceful conditions (Eccl 12:4; Jer 25:10; Rev 18:22).

By NT times the lower or nether millstone was commonly circular, the upper side more or less conical or convex in shape. The upper millstone was also circular and concave in the interior lower section so that it fitted over the lower cone to establish good grinding contact. The upper stone would have a funnel-like hole in the top through which the grain could be poured in. Grinding with the small household mill was ordinarily the work of two women, one to turn the upper stone and the other to pour in the grain (e.g., Mt 24:41). In the larger forms of this combination, the upper stone would be shaped so that from the side view it would look like an hour glass. A pole parallel to the ground could be attached to the upper stone so that an animal, such as a donkey, could be used to turn it (Mt 18:6; Mk 9:42, NASB marg.).

N. B. B.

MILLENNIUM. This word comes from the Latin *mille*, "a thousand," and *annum*, "year," "a thousand years," and is a theological term based upon the thousand years spoken of in Rev 20:2-7. It is a time of special blessing during which Satan is bound and the gospel will go forth without hindrance. Three main views are held.

Postmillennialism. Christ's second coming will occur after the Millennium. The preaching of the gospel by the church will bring about a time of peace and prosperity, and the knowledge of the Lord will fill the whole earth. The length of this period is generally regarded as approximately a thousand years. This theory was first promulgated in England by the teaching of Daniel Whitby (1638–1726). It was quite popular until World War I disillusioned men to realize that all would not eventually accept the gospel and that mankind is not making moral progress. It has been revived recently, by Loraine Boettner in particular (*The Millennium*).

Amillennialism. There will be no literal period of a thousand years of peace. Neither will there be a physical millennium during which Christ will reign on the earth. The passages which speak of an earthly kingdom are to be interpreted as applying to the Church and the blessings which the gospel brings as it is preached in the world during the Gospel Age (Hamilton). The binding of Satan is considered to have occurred either at the cross, at the time of Constantine the Great, or at some later period. Many amillennialists regard Rev 20:4 ff. as referring to the blessed state of those saints who have died and have gone to be with the Lord during the Gospel Age (Kuyper, Bavinck). Christ's second coming is regarded as ushering in a final general judgment of both the good and the wicked.

Premillennialism. The Millennium is the period of the literal reign of Christ over the earth for a thousand years. Christ must come before the Millennium can begin (Rev 19:11 ff.; 20: 4 ff.). No general judgment of both the believers and the unbelievers can occur, since the judgment of the wicked occurs after the thousand years (Rev 20:5-6, 11 ff.).

A comparison of the three views. A thorough evaluation of the three views is beyond the scope of this article. Three positions are possible regarding the two lines of prophecy found in the Bible concerning a ruling, reigning Messiah, and a suffering, sacrificial Messiah. (1) The prophecies concerning the ruling, reigning Messiah can be accepted literally, and those concerning the suffering, sacrificial Messiah can be spiritualized or interpreted symbolically (e.g., as many Jews do). (2) Those concerning the suffering, sacrificial Messiah can be accepted literally, and those of the ruling, reigning Messiah can be spiritualized or interpreted figuratively or mystically (e.g., the postmillennialists and the amillennialists). (3) Both can be taken literally (e.g., the premillennialists).

Though certain problems are connected with each view, when studied in systematic theology the premillennial view finds strongest support in biblical theology. It is difficult to justify a change from the literal interpretation of prophecy concerning Christ's first coming to a metaphorical interpretation of His second coming.

Description of the Millennial Age

Fulfillment of the covenants. The Millennium is the period in which all of God's unconditional covenants with the nation Israel will be fulfilled (*see* Dispensations). The promises covenanted to Abraham (Gen 12:1-3) concerning the land and seed will be fulfilled, for Israel will possess Palestine, and Abraham's seed will occupy it. The promises covenanted to David concerning his house, his throne, and his kingdom (II Sam 7:16) will be fulfilled, for one of David's lineage will occupy David's throne and will rule over David's nation. The promises covenanted to Jeremiah (Jer 31:31-34) concerning the writing of God's law upon men's hearts will be fulfilled, for Israel will be converted, will receive a new heart, will experience the forgiveness of sin, and the fullness of the Spirit. The promises covenanted to Moses (Deut 30:1-10) concerning the regathering of Israel will be fulfilled in that Israel will be blessed in the land of Palestine.

Ideal conditions on earth. A number of characteristics of the Millennial Age are given in Scripture. It will be a time of peace, for all nations will be subjected to Christ's authority (Rev 11:15; cf. Isa 9:6-7). Consequently war will be abolished. It will be a time of joy (Isa 65:18–19). Holiness will characterize the kingdom and its subjects (Zech 14:20-21). The glory of the Lord will be manifested throughout the earth (Isa 35:2). Comfort will be administered by the King (Isa 66:13). Perfect justice will be administered by the King (Isa 9:7). Through the teaching of the Holy Spirit knowledge of divine truth will be widespread (Isa 11:2; cf. Jer 31:33-34). The effects of the curse will be lifted from the earth (Isa 11:6-9; Rom 8:17-23). Physical infirmity and sickness will be removed (Isa 35:3-6; Ezk 47:12). Longevity of life will be restored (Isa 65:20). There will be a perfect social order (Isa 65:21-23) and economic abundance (Isa 30:23-26; Amos 9:13). The whole earth will join in the worship of Jehovah (Isa 45:22-24; Zech 14:16 f.). Divine empowerment will continue to be imparted by the Spirit to obey the commands of the King (Joel 2:28-32).

The course of the Millennium. At the time of the second advent, Jesus Christ will put down all organized rebellion against His authority (Rev 19:11-21; cf. Ps 2:9). Satan will be bound (Rev 20:2-3) so that the external source of temptation will be removed. The saints of the present Church Age who are to reign with Christ (Mt 19:28; Lk 19:12-17; 22:30; Rev 3:21; 5:10; 20:4) will demonstrate the fullness of salvation by having not merely the "earnest of salvation" which is the Holy Spirit (Eph 1:13-14; Rom 8:23), as now, but also their resurrection bodies which are free of the fallen Adamic nature. The earth with all in it will be a revelation of salvation in that it will be freed from the curse (Isa 11:6-9; 65:25; Ezk 34:25; Rom 8:17-23).

Yet in proof of the exceeding sinfulness of sin, multitudes will not believe in Christ for salvation but merely render lip service. As a result, when Satan is loosed at the end of the thousand years they will follow him and attack the Lord and the camp of His saints (Rev 20:7-9). Having finally proved the incorrigibility of the sinner and the exceeding sinfulness of sin in the rejection of His grace under the law, the gospel, and the kingdom, God will righteously judge the world. The final destruction and judgment of Satan and the wicked will follow (Rev 20:10-15). At the end of the thousand years Christ will surrender the kingdom to the Father that He may be all in all (I Cor 15:24-28).

The divine purposes of the Millennium. At the time of creation it was God's purpose to subject creation to a man who would be a theocratic ruler (Gen 1:26). This purpose was never realized because of Adam's sin (Heb 2:8), but will be accomplished during the Millennial Age when all things will be subjected to Christ (I Cor 15:25, 27). It will thus be the time of the fullest unveiling of God's Son ever known in world history, for Jesus Christ will reign in person in righteousness and peace.

A future Millennium is clearly not a denial of the wonders or present efficacy of the gospel. Only in the Millennial Age will the full effects of Christ's redemption appear in the removal of the fallen human nature from resurrected believers, of the curse upon nature, and of the effects of physical death. Today men can reject Christ because they fail to see what salvation means, and they stumble at what is still offensive, such as the fallen nature in Christians, the curse on nature, and the mortality of the body. Then, they will not be able to excuse themselves because of these objections. To prove His righteousness and love, God will consign no one to eternal and final hell until He has shown to all that man is so sinful that he will not believe—even in the Millennium—except by sovereign grace.

See Day of the Lord; Eschatology; Kingdom of God; Prophecy, Fulfillment of.

Bibliography. Loraine Boettner, *The Millennium,* Philadelphia: Presbyterian and Reformed, 1958. Charles L. Feinberg, *Premillennialism or Amillennialism?* 2nd ed., Wheaton: Van Kampen, 1954. Floyd E. Hamilton, *The Basis of Millennial Faith,* Grand Rapids: Eerdmans, 1942. Alva J. McClain, *The Greatness of the Kingdom,* Chicago: Moody, 1959. J. Dwight Pentecost, *Things to Come,* Findlay: Dunham, 1958. Charles C. Ryrie, *The Basis of the Premillennial Faith,* New York: Loizeaux, 1953. John F. Walvoord, *The Millennial Kingdom,* Findlay: Dunham, 1959.

J. D. P.

MILLET. *See* Plants: Millet.

MILLO (mĭl'ō). The term means "filling" and probably was an artificial embankment, terrace, or tower. From II Kgs 12:20 (cf. II Sam 5:9; I Kgs 9:24) some have guessed that "the house of Millo" (Beth-millo) was a Jebusite temple. In Shechem the term may refer to a clan or dynasty associated with Abimelech (Jud 9:6, 20); or it may be identical with the "tower of Shechem," the Migdal-Shechem (9:46-49), the filled and raised sacred area of the fortress-temple excavated in 1955–66 by G. Ernest Wright (*Shechem,* New York: Mc-Graw-Hill, 1965, p. 126).

In Jerusalem the contexts indicate that Millo was a fortress, probably incorporated into the wall. It was in existence in the time of David (II Sam 5:9; I Chr 11:8) and rebuilt by Solomon, perhaps to guard the palace on the S and the temple on the N (I Kgs 9:15). Hezekiah "strengthened the Millo in the city of David" (II Chr 32:5, RSV) in preparation for the advance of Sennacherib.

Excavations by R. A. S. Macalister and J. G. Duncan in 1923–4 S of the temple area uncovered masonry going back to David's time tentatively identified as the Millo. Masterman's conclusion that it stood on the Syria Akra between the temple area and the city of David (Ophel) to the S, before that hill was lowered by the Hasmoneans (Jos *Wars* v.4.1), would place it near the present *Al Aksa* Mosque. In 1964 Kathleen Kenyon excavated a massive supporting wall for a terrace on the E slope of Ophel. Its large stones may well have been the filling

The fortress temple of Shechem, possibly the house of Millo. HFV

of David's Millo, and subsequent rebuildings the repairs of Solomon and Hezekiah (PEQ, XCVII [1965], 13 f.). *See* Jerusalem.

G. A. T.

MILLSTONE. *See* Mill.

MINA. *See* Weights, Measures, and Coins.

MINCING. Used to describe the walking of children. The women of Israel were reproached by Isaiah for walking in this affected manner because it symbolized their haughty spirit (Isa 3:16).

MIND AND ATTITUDES. This subject is well summarized in Phil 2:5: "Let this mind be (from *phroneō*) in you, which was also in Christ Jesus," in which context Paul also refers to the *intellect* ("He thought [from *hēgeomai*] it not robbery to be equal with God," v.6), the *will* ("He emptied himself," from *kenoō;* "He humbled himself," from *tapeinoō,* vv. 7-8), *attitudes* of lowliness of mind (*tapeinophrosunē,* v.3), and consideration of others (v. 4), and *emotions* (love, compassions, and mercies, vv.1-2). This entire epistle teaches much about right attitudes (see 3:15, NASB).

A number of Heb. and Gr. words involving mind or thought include the concept of rational mental activity, and frequently such words may carry in their meaning both the concepts of thinking (the rational process) and feeling (the emotional factors).

In the Heb. OT *lēb* or *lēbāb* is often translated "mind" or "understanding" (as in Job 12:3; I Kgs 3:12, RSV; I Chr 22:7; Lam 3:21), although these words properly mean "heart" (cf. Ps 27:3; Deut 6:5), and refer to the center of man's personality, involving the intellect (Prov 15:14), will (I Sam 7:3), affections (Ex 4:14), and moral character (I Chr 29:17).

Likewise referring to the inner man and at times conveying the concept "mind" are Heb. *nephesh* (soul) as in Ps 139:14; II Kgs 9:15, and *ruaḥ* (spirit, wind), as in Ex 28:3.

An important NT word unit for mind and thinking is the base *phrone-*, from which comes the verb *phroneō,* "to hold an opinion" (and thus think, I Cor 13:11), "set one's mind on" (Rom 12:16*b*), and "have thoughts or attitudes" (be minded, Phil 2:5). The companion nouns *phronēma* (Rom 8:6*a*, 7) and *phronēsis* (Lk 1:17; Eph 1:8) indicate a way of thinking or understanding, while the cognate verb *sōphroneō* means "being in control of one's mind and life" (Mk 5:15; Lk 8:35; II Cor 5:13; Tit 2:6). A verb of another base, *merimnaō* (cf. also the noun *merimna),* adds the additional dimension of anxiety in the meaning, "have anxious thought" (Mt 6:25; Phil 4:6).

Another NT word unit for mind and thought, *no-*, has the noun form *nous,* a classical Gr. philosophical concept, used almost exclusively by Paul in the NT (except Lk 24:45; Rev 13:18; 17:9) carrying the idea of ability to reason (Lk 24:45; Rom 1:28) and make moral judgments (Eph 4:23), the *nous* being able to be corrupted (Rom 1:28; Col 2:18; I Tim 6:5; II Tim 3:8) and be renewed (Rom 12:2) so that it is practically equivalent to character. The spiritual man has "the mind of Christ" (I Cor 2:16). The cognate nouns carry a similar concept, *noēma* indicating thought, mind (Phil 4:7) and purpose (II Cor 2:11); *ennoia,* insight (I Pet 4:1); and *dianoia,* intelligence or mind with ability to reflect (Mt 22:37), while the verb *noeō* means "perceive" or "understand" (Mt 16:9).

Kardia, used often for affections (Lk 24:32), may indicate mind (Rom 1:21; Eph 1:18), as may also occasionally *pneuma* (spirit, II Cor 2:13), *psuchē* (soul, Phil 1:27), and *nephros* (kidney, Rev 2:23).

The proper Christlike attitude which the apostles exhort each believer to maintain is one of humility (Rom 12:3, 16; Phil 2:3,5,8); unity, cooperation and harmony with his brethren in the common cause of the gospel (Phil 1:27; 2:2; 4:2; Rom 15:5; II Cor 13:11; I Pet 3:8); willingness to suffer or die for Christ (I Pet 4:1); concern for others (Phil 4:10); and spirituality (Rom 8:5-7; Col 3:2), the opposite of a worldly, self-indulgent attitude (Phil 3:19; cf. Mt 16:23). *See* Heart.

Bibliography. Johannes Behm and E. Wurthwein, "*Noeō, Nous,* etc.," TDNT, IV, 948-1022.

W. H. M.

MINER. *See* Mining.

MINERALS AND METALS. A mineral is any naturally occurring inorganic compound or element characterized by distinctive chemical and physical properties. In ancient usage all matter was classified as belonging to either the animal, vegetable, or mineral kingdom. The list below includes a number of entries which are not mineral in the strict sense of the word, but are mineral in the more general sense of belonging to the mineral kingdom.

Mankind has always used minerals as the raw material for manufactured products ranging from flint tools to spacecraft. Some minerals are valued as a source for chemicals; others are used as ores for metals; still others have value because of special properties; and some, like salt, are used in food. Another long established use of minerals is for gemstones. Factors which contribute to the value of gems are beauty, rarity, durability, tradition, quality, and a variety of magical effects which superstitious people have attributed to certain stones (*see* Jewels).

At least six metals and three alloys were used in antiquity. The first metals to be worked by man appear to be those found in their natural state—gold, copper, and meteoric iron. Gold may have been the very first, but copper enjoyed the greatest practical importance from earliest times until the wide introduction of iron. By the time of Moses these additional metals were being used to a lesser or greater extent: silver, electrum (gold-silver alloy), lead, tin, and bronze (copper-tin alloy); and brass (copper-zinc alloy) by NT times. *See* Mining.

1. **Adamant.** The KJV translation of Heb. *shāmîr* in Ezk 3:9; Zech 7:12. It is derived from the Gr. *adamas* meaning "hard" or "invincible," or the Latin *adamas* meaning the hardest metal. This word has evolved through Middle English *adama(u)nt* to give us "diamond." Hence it was so rendered in Jer 17:1 by the KJV translators. Since the diamond was unknown in Bible lands during the OT, the biblical references figuratively compare the stubborn foreheads or hardened hearts of the Jews to other hard stones, such as emery (NASB) or corundum, which is even harder than flint (Ezk 3:9).

Corundum is a mineral composed of aluminum oxide, hexagonal crystal system, hardness 9. Only diamond is harder. Clear red crystals are ruby; all other colors, especially blue, are sapphire. In addition to its value as a gem stone, corundum is used as an abrasive for grinding hard materials. Engraving on other stones can be done with a corundum point.

2. **Agate.** *See* Jewels: Agate.

3. **Alabaster.** The massive compact variety of gypsum, hydrous calcium sulfate, hardness 2. Some if not most "alabaster" (Heb. *shayish* or *shēsh*) of ancient times was marble (I Chr 29:2; Est 1:6), composed of calcite, hardness 3. Being soft these materials are easily carved and were much used for making statuary (Song 5:15, NASB) as well as jars (RSV), cruses (ASV), flasks (ASV marg.), boxes (KJV), or vials (NASB) for perfume or ointment (Mt 26:7; Mk 14:3; Lk 7:37). *See* Box.

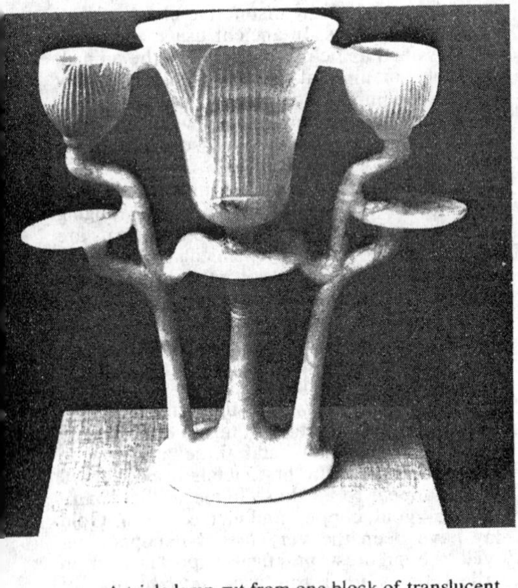

A triple lamp cut from one block of translucent alabaster, from Tutankhamen's tomb. LL

The alabaster vessels imported from Egypt were prized because of the darker veins in the light creamy color. Other such vessels were made locally from stone quarried in the Jordan Valley. Many beautiful alabaster treasures were discovered in the tomb of King Tutankhamen.

4. **Amber.** Fossil resin from prehistoric pine trees, valued for its transparency, brilliance, and attractive yellowish or brownish-yellow color. The primary source of amber in ancient times was the Baltic region. In the 2nd mil. B.C. traders brought it to Knossos in Crete and Mycenae in Greece. Phoenician traders continued to import it in the 1st mil. B.C. According to the KJV Ezekiel refers to the color of amber (1:4, 27; 8:2); modern versions, however, translate the Heb. word *ḥashmal* as "gleaming bronze" (RSV), "glittering brass" (NEB), or "glowing metal" (NASB, which suggests electrum in the marg.). The LXX has *ēlektron* and the Vulg. has *electrum*, referring to the brilliant alloy of silver and gold.

5. **Amethyst.** *See* Jewels: Amethyst.

Antimony was commonly used for darkening eyelids in ancient Egypt. Here are properly made-up eyes from Tutankhamen's tomb. LL

6. **Antimony.** A metallic element (Latin *stibium*) with the appearance of tin or lead. The word occurs as the translation of Heb. *pûk* in modern English versions of Isa 54:11, "I will set your stones in antimony" (RSV, NASB), and as one of the materials King David provided for the temple (I Chr 29:2, RSV, NASB). The ancients ground *pûk* into a black powder which was used both for making a black cement to outline precious stones in bold relief when setting them, and for darkening eyelids (II Kgs 9:30; Jer 4:30). *See* Eye; Eyes, Painting the.

Antimony occurs in nature usually as stibnite, an attractive mineral of lead-gray color which forms interesting crystals. The earliest written mention of it is in the hieroglyphic inscription accompanying the painting in the tomb of Khnum-hotep at Beni Hasan in Egypt (*c.* 1890 B.C.). Ibsha, the leader of a caravan of 37 Asiatics, is depicted bringing a gift of costly antimony for eye paint for the nobleman—or his wife (ANEP #3).

7. **Asphalt.** *See* 10. Bitumen.

8. **Bdellium.** Identification of this word in Gen 2:12 and Num 11:7 is not certain. It has been variously interpreted to mean a precious stone, opal, pearl, gum, or resin. The plant product now seems to be the most likely interpretation (*see* Plants: Bdellium).

9. **Beryl.** *See* Jewels: Beryl.

10. **Bitumen.** A viscous black hydrocarbon obtained in ancient times from natural oil seeps and used for mortar and caulking.

Asphalt, mortar, pitch, slime, and tar are other translations given to the Heb. terms *ḥēmār, kōper*, and *zepet*. *Ḥēmār* perhaps means "covering." Moses' mother took her "chest of papyrus reeds and covered it with the 'covering' [KJV, 'slime'] and the pitch . . . and set it in the rushes by the edge of the Nile" (Ex 2:3, orig. trans.). The ziggurat at Ur, for example, was of trampled clay with layers of brick set in asphalt on the outside (cf. Gen 11:3). Others derive *ḥēmār* from the Heb. verb *ḥāmar*, "to boil up," indicative of the bubbling action in the tar pits.

With the invasion of the kings from the East, the rulers of Sodom and Gomorrah fled to "the valley of the Siddim [which was] pits, pits of bitumen," where "they fell" (Gen 14:10, lit.). There was much bitumen at the S end of the Dead Sea and, indeed, it was also called Lake Asphaltitis. But the greatest supplies were in the Tigris-Euphrates Valley near Kirkuk in Assyria and at Hit along the Euphrates.

God told Noah to make the ark and "cover" it inside and outside with the "covering" (Gen 6:14). The word for pitch or "covering," *kōper*, perhaps is derived from a Semitic root *k-p-r-*, "to smear." More likely, however, it is a loanword from Akkad. *kupru*, "asphalt." In the Gilgamesh Epic Utnapishtim, the Babylonian hero of the Flood, used *kupru* and *ittu* (asphalt and pitch) in caulking his ship (Tablet XI, 11. 65-68, ANET, p. 93).

According to Ex 2:3 Moses' mother covered his basket both with tar or bitumen and with "pitch" (Heb. *zepet*). Apparently derived from Akkad. *ṣippatu*, the word most likely describes the resinous product of fir or pine trees. It is a fluid and a highly flammable substance. Thus Isaiah pronounced a curse on Edom with its scattered pine forests on the Transjordan heights, prophesying that its streams and land would be turned to burning pitch (Isa 34:9).

W. G. B.

11. **Brass.** *See* 13. Bronze.

12. **Brimstone.** The native element sulfur. This may also refer to lava or falling ash from a volcanic eruption which would emit stifling sulfurous gases, especially sulfur dioxide. The nauseous odor of brimstone pervaded the atmosphere and tarnished brasswork on ships in the area for weeks after the volcanic destruction of Krakatoa Island in 1883.

The word "brimstone" occurs 14 times in the Bible and is used in every instance to indicate punishment and devastation for sin, probably because of its brilliant flame. Evil men and their land would be covered with brimstone (Deut 29:23; Ezk 38:22; Job 18:15; Ps 11:6). In the day of God's vengeance His breath would become as brimstone (Isa 30:33), as would the dust (Isa 34:9). Sodom (*q.v.*) and Gomorrah were thus destroyed (Gen 19:24; Lk 17:29). John saw idolaters and those who worshiped the Beast destroyed by fire and brimstone (Rev 9:17–18; 14:10; 19:20). The devil and the wicked will be cast into the lake of fire and brimstone (Rev 21:8; 20:10).

Bronze doors of the ancient senate building of Rome. HFV

13. **Bronze.** The Bible rarely makes a clear reference to bronze as an alloy of copper and tin, for the Heb. and Gr. words translated "brass" or "brazen" in the KJV primarily mean copper. But brass, an alloy of copper and zinc, was not known until perhaps Roman times. Alloying of copper and tin was introduced into Palestine probably by invading Amorites at the close of the Early Bronze Age (*c.* 2200 B.C.), to harden copper for tools and weapons before the advent of iron and to make objects formed by casting. Chemical analyses of ancient bronze objects show from 2 to 16 percent of tin. The only clear biblical reference to such an alloy is the use of *chalkolibanon* (lit., "white copper")

in Rev 1:15 and 2:18 where it is translated "fine brass" (KJV) or "burnished bronze" (RSV). Copper and zinc ore minerals do occur mixed in the natural state, with the result that brass was sometimes accidentally produced during the smelting process. The chemical distinction between zinc and tin was not recognized until modern times.

The Heb. term *nᵉḥōshet* and its derivatives as well as the Gr. *chalkos* refer to pure copper or bronze from which every kind of sacred and profane instrument or vessel was made, including brazen altars, gates overlaid with bronze plates (Isa 45:2), fetters (II Chr 33:11, RSV, NASB), daggers, helmets (I Sam 17:5), household and sacred vessels (Rev 18:12), idols, musical instruments (I Cor 13:1), mirrors (Ex 38:8), pins, and even coins (Mt 10:9).

The Heb. term is frequently employed in a figurative sense where it may refer, for example, to strength as in Job 40:18 (bones of hippopotamus), or obstinacy as in Isa 48:4 (the brow of Israel); or it may be the pitiless sky (Deut 28:23) or the unproductive earth (Lev 26:19).

The terms Early (3100–2100 B.C.), Middle (2100-1550), and Late (1550–1200) Bronze Ages continue to be used for convenience in the study of Palestinian archaeology, even though Early Bronze Age is largely a misnomer for that land. It is thought that the art of making bronze was discovered in Armenia or Anatolia early in the 3rd mil. B.C. Bronze objects have been found at Ur dating from *c.* 2500 B.C.

See 22. Copper; 55. Tin.

E.B.S.

14. **Carbuncle.** *See* Jewels: Carbuncle.

15. **Carnelian.** *See* Jewels: Carnelian.

16. **Chalcedony.** *See* Jewels: Chalcedony.

17. **Chalkstone.** A soft, white or buff-colored powdery limestone formed from the calcareous shells of single-celled marine animals. Chalk is an abundant mineral in many parts of the world including Israel. When used for building stone, the softer varieties would weather and disintegrate in a few years. In Isa 27:9 the word "chalkstones" is used as a symbol of brittleness. The altars of idols were to be as easily pulverized as if made of chalkstone.

18. **Chrysolite.** *See* Jewels: Chrysolite.

19. **Chrysoprasus.** *See* Jewels: Chrysoprasus.

20. **Clay.** Any of more than 60 different layer silicate minerals which occur as dust-sized particles. Mud is composed largely of clay minerals. Particles of most clay minerals have strong cohesion in a dried mass. This property has been utilized since before recorded history in the manufacture of mud bricks. Clay particles will fuse in strong heat, which property is used to make fired brick, pottery, and fine china.

To make bricks or pottery, clay was mixed with water in a pit where it could be trampled (Ps 40:2; Isa 41:25; Nah 3:14). The Egyptians had learned that letting straw soak in water made the clay more pliable and cohesive (cf. Ex 5:7, 12; *see* Brick). One ready source of clay in Palestine was the district in the Jordan Valley between Succoth and Zarthan (I Kgs 7:46). Job 38:14 (RSV) mentions the ability of a clay tablet while still soft to receive the impression of a seal. Jesus, by spitting on dirt, formed a clay poultice which He used in His healing of the man born blind (Jn 9:6, 11, 14–15). Most frequent are the references to clay as the potter's material used in his craft (Isa 29:16; Jer 18:4, 6). Often it is in a figurative sense, likening the Creator to a potter and people to the clay (Job 10:9; 33:6; Isa 45:9; 64:8). *See* Pottery.

21. **Coal.** Glowing wood embers or charcoal (Lev 16:12; Ps 120:4; Prov 25:22; 26:21; *et al.*). There is no evidence that scriptural references to coal meant mineral coal, i.e., the fossilized organic substance which has been so greatly used for fuel in modern times. *See* Coals.

22. **Copper.** A ductile, malleable, reddish-brown metallic element. It was named after the island of Cyprus, where copper was mined for export as early as the 18th cen. B.C., according to the Mari economic archives. With the exception of gold from pure nuggets and meteoric iron, copper was the first metal used by man. The primary ores available to the Hebrews were the bright green malachite, the bright blue azurite, and small amounts of cuprite (a natural red copper ore).

In the Near East copper is known to have been used as early as 4500-4000 B.C. The oldest copper object yet found in Palestine is from Jericho Level VIII. A Chalcolithic Age (4500–3100 B.C.) settlement at Tell Abu Matar on the outskirts of Beer-sheba gives evidence of the earliest known copper-workers in Palestine. They had to obtain ore from at least 60 miles away to the S. Its preliminary reduction was in open fireplaces. Then it was melted in ovens 12 to 18 inches in diameter with thick walls of earth mixed with straw. After further refining in crucibles the copper was evidently cast in molds to make such objects as mace-heads, pins, rings, and other ornaments (K. A. Kenyon, *Archaeology in the Holy Land,* London: Benn, 1960, pp. 79 f.). From this same period a remarkable hoard of *c.* 430 copper cultic objects was discovered in 1961 in a cave near En-gedi (*q.v.*). At that site a Chalcolithic Age open-air sanctuary was excavated by Israeli archaeologists.

Copper was the most useful metal to early man for several reasons: (1) It could be produced by the simple process of heating malachite ore in a wood or charcoal fire; (2) it could be shaped and hardened by hammering either hot or cold; (3) it could be annealed by reheating in order to make it less brittle; (4) it could be melted at 1083° C in order to cast it in molds (1200° C was about the maximum temperature obtainable in ancient furnaces); and (5) its malleability allowed it to be sharpened over and over again by hammering. Bronze, the copper-tin alloy, has the initial hardness of ham-

Copper panel from Sumerian temple lintel at 'Obeid (2600 B.C.), showing the god Im-du-gud and stags. BM

mered copper; when a bronze blade is hammered its cutting edge can approach the hardness of mild steel. Bronze is superior for molding because it makes a much cleaner cast than does copper and at a lower temperature. *See* 13. Bronze.

Copper seems to have remained relatively scarce among the Canaanites throughout the Early Bronze Age. With the influx of people from the N (probably the Amorites) *c.* 2000 B.C. bronze was introduced and copper became more abundant. Itinerant smiths such as the Kenites (*q.v.*) undoubtedly worked the mines in the Arabah and Sinai (*see* Mining) during politically unstable times. *See* Occupations: Coppersmith. A Late Bronze Age copper smelting operation has been discovered at Tel Zeror S of Caesarea, other such furnaces of the Philistines at Tell Qasile N of Tel Aviv (ANEP #134), Tell Jemmeh S of Gaza, and Bethshemesh, and numerous smelting sites in the Arabah (formerly dated to Solomon's time but now assigned a date some 300 years earlier). *See* Smelting.

23. **Coral.** *See* Animals, V.1; Jewels: Coral.

24. **Crystal.** *See* Jewels: Crystal.

25. **Diamond.** *See* Jewels: Diamond.

26. **Emerald.** *See* Jewels: Emerald.

27. **Emery.** *See* 1. Adamant.

28. **Flint.** A hard, tough, cryptocrystalline variety of quartz. Excellent conchoidal fracture with sharp edges as well as hardness made this an ideal material for the manufacture by early man of stone tools and weapons, such as arrowheads, knives, scrapers, chisels, and sickle blades. When struck against another hard object such as steel or another flint, it can yield a hot spark, so that it has long been used to ignite fire. Flints continued to be used long after the introduction of metals, both because flint was readily obtainable and because metal remained expensive for the common man. Also flint knives seem to have been preferred for the rite of circumcision (Ex 4:25; Josh 5:2-3, both NASB). Flint is used in poetic references to the rock which Moses struck to obtain water for Israel (Ps 114:8; Deut 8:15; cf. Ex 17:6) and to the rocky ground of Canaan in general (Deut 32:13). In Isa 5:28 (NASB) horses' hoofs seem like flint, and in Ezk 3:9 adamant (*see* 1. Adamant) is harder than flint. Flint symbolizes the steadfastness of the Servant of the Lord (Isa 50:7).

29. **Garnet.** *See* Jewels: Garnet.

30. **Glass.** A liquid which has such high viscosity at ordinary temperatures that it behaves essentially as a solid. Quartz sand (silicon dioxide) is the principal ingredient of most glass used in commerce. Additives, such as soda, lime, and metallic oxides, impart special properties and colors to glass. It cools without crystallization, and is generally translucent or transparent.

The art of using glaze on brickwork and beads originated in prehistoric times, but glass itself first appears *c.* 2600 B.C. A cuneiform tablet from Nineveh records a 17th cen. B.C. formula for glassmaking using sand, alkali from salt-marsh grasses, and lime from limestone deposits. By the 18th Dynasty (1570-1320 B.C.) a glass factory at El-Amarna in Egypt was producing small unguent vessels by winding drawn glass rods around a sand core and reheating. Imitation gemstones made of frit (colored glass pastes) were given high value, equated with gold by the writer of Job 28:17 (RSV, NASB).

Egyptian faience, made by mixing natron with ground quartz and heating, was the most famous glazed material in ancient times. A word for glaze, *spsg,* occurs in a Ugaritic text and helps explain the Heb. words translated "silver dross" in Prov 26:23 (BASOR #98

MINERALS AND METALS

[1945], pp. 21, 24). On the basis of this discovery RSV renders the line, "Like the glaze covering an earthen vessel." Transparent flat glass was never produced in biblical times, so that the "looking glasses" of Ex 38:8 and "glass" of I Cor 13:12 and Jas 1:23 refer to mirrors of polished bronze.

The Phoenicians may be credited with inventing the method of blowing glass in the 1st cen. B.C. Much of this was translucent and some even transparent (Rev 21:18, 21).It often had a lustre like highly polished glaze, perhaps giving rise to the expression "sea of glass" in Rev 4:6; 15:2 (*see* Sea of Glass).

By the time of Bar-Kochba's rebellion (A.D. 132–135) glass vessels had replaced many pottery styles, according to those found in the hideout caves of his Jewish partisans. A glass factory was operated by Jews at Beth-shearim E of Haifa *c.* A.D. 352–382.

See Glass.

31. **Gold.** A soft metallic yellow mineral which occurs as a native element. Therefore it was probably the first metal known to man (cf. Gen 2:11–12). It melts at 1063° C and is easily worked, being the most malleable and ductile of the available metals. Pure gold does not tarnish. Gold was obtained as scales and dust particles (Job 28:6), occasionally nuggets, from alluvial placer deposits (cf. Job 22:24) in Nubia (modern Sudan), Egypt in the desert E of the Nile, Sinai, the W coast of Arabia, Asia Minor, and other places such as Ophir (*q.v.*).

The mineral usually occurs alloyed with small amounts of silver (a natural alloy called electrum), and possibly with other elements such as copper. In the native state its purity may be from as little as 700 fine to as much as 950 fine (1,000 fine is pure gold). Much ancient gold was melted and used directly without benefit of purification. Other gold needed only to be refined by simply melting it and removing the dross without further metallurgical processes (I Chr 28:18; Prov 27:21; Mal 3:3).

Gold is mentioned hundreds of times in the Bible. In Heb., in addition to qualifying adjectives, there were at least six terms for it: *zāhāb* (over 360 times), *beṣer* (Job 22:24-25), *ḥārûṣ* ("fine gold," Prov 3:14; Zech 9:3; *et al.*), *ketem* ("fine gold," Job 31:24; Prov 25:12; Lam 4:1; Dan 10:5; *et al.*; "pure gold," Job 28:19), *s^egôr* (Job 28:15), and *pāz* ("fine gold," nine times).

Until the Persian period when Chronicles and Daniel were written, usually silver precedes gold when the two are mentioned together in the OT (e.g., Gen 13:2; 24:35; Ex 3:22; Josh 6:19; I Kgs 7:51). Therefore it is believed that before 500 B.C., when more silver became available on the market, gold was surpassed by silver in value. Only in the reign of Solomon was silver considered less valuable (I Kgs 10:21, NASB), when it is said he made silver as common as stones in Jerusalem (10:27).

The art of working gold is of great antiquity. A fascinating scene from the 6th Dynasty (2350–2200 B.C.) tomb of Mereru-ka in Egypt depicts goldsmiths weighing and recording the raw gold, blowing through long tubes into a furnace to melt it for casting, and fashioning the ornate molded objects (ANEP #133). Fabulous items of jewelry and personal adornment were discovered by Sir Leonard Woolley in the royal tombs of Ur (*c.* 2500 B.C.). The solid gold mesh and the innermost coffin in the burial of King Tutankhamen, not to mention the great wealth of pectorals, rings, and bracelets, are among the most famous treasures of all time. Sir Flinders Petrie found a hoard of gold and electrum jewelry at Tell el-'Ajjul near Gaza, belonging to the 14th or 13th cen. B.C. (ANEP #74–75).

A glazed brick griffon from the palace at Susa, biblical Shushan. LM

A gold helmet of Mes-kalam-dug from Ur, *c.* 2500 B.C. BM

The OT speaks of the numerous methods of working the precious metal: beating or hammering it into the desired shape (Ex 25:18, 31, 36); overlaying with gold leaf or thin plating on wood, stone, or baser metal (Ex 25:11; I Kgs 6:20-22, 32, 35); casting such objects as rings (Ex 25:12) and perhaps molten idols (Ps 115:4); cutting gold sheets into threads to be woven in material for the tabernacle hangings (Ex 39:3) or royal garments (Ps 45:13); making filigree settings for jewels and chains of twisted cordage work (Ex 28:11, 20, 22, NASB); and engraving a plate of pure gold (Ex 28:36).

Aaron formed the golden calf by pouring into a mold gold obtained by melting the gold earrings of the people, and fashioning it further with an engraving tool (Ex 32:2-4). The "wedge" of gold which Achan took from Jericho (Josh 7:21) was a bar or ingot (Heb. "tongue"). Macalister unearthed a gold bar 10 × 1 × ½ inches at Gezer, and a similar wedge is mentioned in Amarna letter #29, l. 39. This, along with large thick rings and disks, was one of the forms in which gold was shaped to be used as money. The earliest gold coins known to the Jews would have been the thick gold *daric* which portrayed King Darius I kneeling with bow and spear (Ezr 2:69).

32. **Iron.** A silvery-white, malleable, ductile, metallic element. The various iron ores—principally hematite (dark red), limonite (yellowish brown), and magnetite (black)—are more widely distributed than copper. But iron is much more difficult to work than copper because of its high melting point (1535°C). Iron smelting therefore requires a greater heat for a longer time and also a stronger air blast than copper. Furthermore, it must be reheated to forge it, whereas copper and bronze can be hammered cold. All of this requires much greater expenditure of fuel. Thus iron was expensive to produce.

In OT times ironworkers were unable to make a furnace hot enough to produce molten iron for casting. The product from the furnace was a "bloom," a spongy mass of iron, slag, and cinders. This had to be hammered to remove the slag and air bubbles. Then the blacksmith forged and reforged it into wrought iron (Ecclus 38:28). But relatively pure iron is too soft to make good cutting tools. While the ancients could not produce a uniform steel, they learned how to carburize the edges of iron weapons by placing these in a charcoal furnace where the iron absorbed enough carbon to harden and strengthen it (*see* 53. Steel). About 900 B.C. they began to quench the forged iron to obtain a better cutting edge, but tempering was not common until Roman times. Apparently whetstones were used to sharpen tools (Eccl 10:10), and iron (an iron file?) was used to sharpen iron (Prov 27:17).

The earliest iron known and used by man came not from ore but from meteors. Thus iron was sometimes called the "metal of heaven." Meteoric iron can be easily identified by its nickel content of 4 to 30 percent. Nickel rarely occurs in terrestrial iron, and then only in minute amounts. Beads were made of meteoric iron in Egypt as far back as predynastic times (before 3000 B.C.). Tubal-cain, the first metalsmith (Gen 4:22), may have used iron from meteors. On the other hand, his primitive knowledge of metallurgy may have been completely forgotten as a result of the Flood and of the confusion of languages at the Tower of Babel. *See* Dispersion of Mankind.

While iron did not begin to become common in the Near East until the middle of the 2nd mil. B.C., it is wrong to conclude that all iron objects prior to that time were made from meteors. Iron in small quantities was produced from ores in the 3rd mil. B.C. The trace of rust from an iron dagger blade with a copper handle was found at Eshnunna (Tell Asmar, 50 miles NE of Baghdad) dating from *c.* 2700 B.C. Another iron dagger (*c.* 2450 B.C.) comes from Dorak in NW Anatolia. A piece of a rusted iron tool was found embedded in the Great Pyramid (*c.* 2600 B.C.) of Egypt, although it could have been left there by a later tomb robber. None of these showed traces of nickel. Other iron implements were discovered in the early levels of Tell Chagar Bazar and Mari in Mesopotamia.

In addition, 18th cen. Babylonian cuneiform texts and the Amarna letters reveal that iron was used in the Near East from the times of the patriarchs down to the judges. A magnificent iron-bladed dagger in its sheath was included in the treasures of Tutankhamen's tomb (*c.* 1350 B.C.). While the evidence is somewhat meager, it goes far to counter the charge that the references to iron in Num 31:22; 35:16; Deut 3:11; 27:5; Josh 6:19, 24; 22:8 are anachronistic, implying that these books were written much later, in the Iron Age. The Canaanites' "chariots of iron" (Josh 17:16, 18; Jud 1:19; 4:3, 13) were not made completely of iron or armored with iron plates but evidently had some iron fittings and ornamentation. Compare the annals of Thutmose III at Karnak where he described the chariots of the defenders of Megiddo as "chariots of gold and silver and of painted work," and listed with the booty was "1 chariot worked with gold, with a body of gold" (ANET, p. 237).

It is quite certain that the Hittites of Anatolia were the ones who discovered or at least developed the technique of smelting and working iron *c.* 1500 B.C. This view is supported by the fact that the Heb. word *barzel,* Akkad. *parzillu,* and Ugaritic *bršl* are all apparently derived from Hittite *barzillu.* A letter of King Hattusilis III (1275-1250 B.C.) states that his men need more time to produce the good iron asked for by the addressee of the letter (O. R. Gurney, *The Hittites,* 2nd ed., Harmondsworth: Penguin, 1954, p. 83). Jeremiah preserves an interesting recollection of the northern origin of iron in the question, "Can anyone smash iron, iron from the north, or bronze?" (15:12, NASB).

An iron stove from Pompeii. HFV

Iron deposits exist in the vicinity of Palestine (Deut 8:9; Job 28:2), in Midian E of the Gulf of Aqabah, in the Lebanons, and in Gilead and the Arabah (*see* Mining). The Israelites, however, did not at first know how to obtain this iron. When the Philistines came in great numbers *c.* 1200 B.C., they evidently brought the art of smelting with them (cf. I Sam 17:7) from contacts with the Hittites. But they monopolized the iron industry to prevent the Hebrews from making up-to-date weapons (I Sam 13:19-22). By conquering the Philistines and other nations David amassed great quantities of bronze (II Sam 8:8), and presumably iron as well, from the booty and tribute. From his reign onward iron became more plentiful and could be used by commoners (II Kgs 6:5-6) as well as by kings in their royal building projects (I Chr 22:3; 29:2; I Kgs 6:7). Strong iron crossbars were a great boon for holding shut the heavy bronze-plated city gates (Ps 107:16; Isa 45:2); this is probably the meaning of "iron gate" in Acts 12:10.

In metaphors iron is used as a symbol of hardness and strength and durability (Deut 33:25; Job 40:18; Jer 1:18; Dan 2:40). A neck with iron sinews signified obstinacy (Isa 48:4); a sky like iron and the earth like bronze, hopelessness (Lev 26:19; cf. Deut 28:23); and an iron yoke (Deut 28:48; Jer 28:13-14) and iron chains (Ps 105:18; 107:10; 149:8), harsh servitude and imprisonment. Messiah will rule the earth with a rod of iron (Ps 2:9; Rev 2:27; 12:5; 19:15), a just rule that will allow no opposition.

33. **Jacinth.** *See* Jewels: Jacinth.

34. **Jasper.** *See* Jewels: Jasper.

35. **Lead.** A heavy blue-gray soft metallic element which melts at 327.5°C. Its principal ore, called galena (lead sulfide), was mined in Egypt, Asia Minor, and Spain (Tarshish; AJA, LXXVI [1972], 139; Ezk 27:12). Because of its low melting point man early discovered the rendering of lead to be quite easy. Yet it was usually a by-product from the smelting of silver ore often found with galena (cf. Ezk 22:18, 20). The presence of lead actually helped produce the silver, for the heated lead oxidized and carried off the impurities (Jer 6:29-30). *See* 51. Silver.

Galena was pulverized for eye paint in predynastic Egypt, before 3400 B.C. By Moses' time it was used in weights for fishnet sinkers, the basis for his reference to Pharaoh's troops in his song of victory: "Thou didst blow with thy wind, the sea covered them; they sank as lead in the mighty waters" (Ex 15:10). It was part of the spoils of war taken from the Midianites (Num 31:22). Job wished that his words might be engraved forever in rock with an iron stylus and with lead to fill the carved letters (Job 19:24), as in the Behistun inscription of Darius I. It was incised on a prepared vertical face high on the side of a mountain, some of the characters having been filled with lead to retard erosion and enhance legibility. Lead was also used for heavy lids (Zech 5:7-8) and for the weight on the end of a plumbline (*q.v.*; Amos 7:7-8). The Romans were the principal users of lead in the biblical world. Among other things they made lead coins and even pipes to carry water. The Latin *plumbum* means lead and from it is derived our word "plumber," one who lays water pipes.

36. **Ligure.** *See* Jewels: Ligure.

37. **Lime.** A white powdery substance obtained by burning calcite (calcium carbonate) to

change it to calcium oxide. It is obtained by roasting limestone in a kiln which consisted of a pit three or four feet deep. Alternate layers of fuel and crushed limestone were placed in it, the fuel ignited, and the pit covered but with an opening to provide a draft. Lime could also be produced by calcining gypsum (calcium sulfate) in the same manner.

Lime (Heb. *śîd*) was used in plastering walls, floors, cisterns, etc. *See* 44. Plaster. The Israelites were to coat large stones with lime (as we would use whitewash) after they entered Canaan, to prepare the pillars for writing on them the law (Deut 27:2–4, NASB). The lime of Isa 33:12; Amos 2:1 came from the burning of human bones as a mark of thoroughgoing destruction and humiliating defeat.

A marble panel from the Parthenon at Athens. BM

38. **Marble.** A metamorphic rock composed of calcite or dolomite. It is hard enough to withstand weathering in a dry climate, yet soft enough to work easily. Its crystalline forms can receive a high polish. It comes in attractive colors, white, light brown, and light gray. For these reasons it was the favored stone for buildings and statuary in the ancient world (I Chr 29:2; Est 1:6; Song 5:15; Rev 18:12).

Alabaster gypsum has also been called marble and used in its place; however, being softer and not nearly so resistant to weathering, alabaster is not as durable (*see* 3. Alabaster). Jurassic limestone, a type of marble, was quarried in Lebanon for Solomon's temple (I Kgs 5:13–18). The Persian monarchs obtained marble locally in Elam for their palaces in Susa and Persepolis. The famous snow-white Gr. statuary marbles came from the island of Paros and Mount Pentelikon N of Athens. Perhaps John knew of Carrara marble from the quarries at Carrara in Italy.

39. **Mortar.** *See* Mortar.

40. **Niter.** A highly soluble white mineral known also as saltpeter or potassium nitrate. It burns vigorously when ignited on charcoal, and is explosive when mixed with combustible substances. This mineral is sometimes found as a crust left by evaporating water in desert areas. It is used in preserving meat, and in medicine.

The KJV word "nitre" (Heb. *neter*), however, must refer to natron, sodium carbonate. This mineral is an alkali or soda and will react to vinegar which is acidic, whereas niter or saltpeter will not (Prov 25:20). Natron, imported from the alkaline lakes NW of Cairo in Egypt, was mixed with oil to make a soap (Jer 2:22).

Another kind of soap was made from lye (a liquid) or potash (potassium carbonate, a salt), products obtained by leaching wood ashes; this is the Heb. *bōrît* of Jer 2:22; Mal 3:2, and *bōr* of Job 9:30. Potash (*bōr*) was also used as a flux in the refining of metals (Isa 1:25, NEB), and in the making of some kinds of glass as well as glaze for ceramics.

41. **Onyx.** *See* Jewels: Onyx.

42. **Pearl.** *See* Jewels: Pearl; Pearls.

43. **Pitch.** *See* 10. Bitumen.

44. **Plaster,** KJV "plaister." A pasty substance used for coating surfaces such as walls. It is produced by calcining or roasting gypsum (calcium sulfate). A product remaining after the evaporation of bodies of water, gypsum is available in the Jordan and Dead Sea valley. Plaster

The "Priest-King," painted in wet plaster on the wall of the palace at Knossos, Crete. HFV

MINERALS AND METALS

may also be made by mixing water with lime obtained from limestone. *See* 37. Lime.

The poorer peoples of Palestine often used only clay or mud, sometimes mingled with straw, as their mortar or plaster. Lev 14:42–43, 48 do not give a hint as to what materials were used in the mortar but refer merely to what was daubed on the stones or smeared on the wall. Deut 27:2,4 and Dan 5:5, however, do give definite indication that lime was a part of the plaster. In the former case the word has in view the boiling effect produced when lime is slaked with water, and in the latter case the word indicates what is burned in a furnace or kiln. The monuments of Deut 27 would require a good grade of mortar since they stood in the weather. The building in Dan 5 was a royal palace where the finest materials and workmanship would be expected.

45. **Quartz.** A mineral, silicon dioxide, forming in the hexagonal crystal system, hardness 7. It is the most widespread mineral in the crust of the earth. More than 1,000 named varieties of quartz have been described; among them quartz crystal, chalcedony, agate, jasper, onyx, flint, and amethyst, which are mentioned in the Bible. Many of these varieties are beautiful and rare, therefore valued as semiprecious gems. *See* Jewels.

46. **Ruby.** *See* Jewels: Ruby.

47. **Salt.** Mineral salt is sodium chloride, essential as a nutrient in the food of animals and also used in seasoning and preserving food. Sodium chloride is the most abundant compound dissolved in the sea. Salt of inferior quality is readily obtainable from the salt flats and the rock salt mountain Jebel Usdum, at the S end of the Dead Sea (Zeph 2:9, "salt pits"). It contains a high percentage of impurities, however, such as clay and gypsum. The word "salt" is used in a number of idiomatic expressions in the Bible (*see* Salt).

48. **Sapphire.** *See* Jewels: Sapphire.

49. **Sardius, Sardine.** *See* Jewels: Sardius.

50. **Sardonyx.** *See* Jewels: Sardonyx.

Jebel Usdum at the south end of the Dead Sea. IIS

51. **Silver.** A lustrous whitish-gray metallic element which occurs as a native mineral as well as the metallic component in a number of other minerals such as argentite. It does not tarnish in a pure atmosphere and is the brightest of all metals, able to take a mirror-like polish. Its melting point is 961°C.

The Egyptians lacked native supplies of silver ore, so that they prized it more highly than gold. They obtained it from Asia by barter and by conquest and tribute (ANET, pp. 237, 239, 249). Much of the silver of the ancient Near East was mined in Asia Minor. According to the Cappadocian tablets from Kanesh (modern Kultepe), Assyrian merchants exported silver and lead ore to Ashur the capital of Assyria as early as the 20th cen. B.C. Later, the Hittites controlled this silver market.

In the Near East silver was often found in conjunction with galena, the principal ore of lead. The OT has many references to the smelting and refining of silver. Jeremiah speaks of the lead being consumed by the fire in the attempt to get pure silver (6:29). The impure mineral was placed in a cupel, a porous vessel of bone ash (the "fining pot" of Prov 17:3; 27:21), and heated in a furnace. A blast of air intensified the heat. Ezekiel mentions the baser metals of copper, tin, iron, and lead as the dross of silver (22:18–22; cf. Jer 6:27–30). These were oxidized and absorbed in the porous cupel. The process could be hastened by adding an alkali flux, as Isa 1:25 indicates: "I will smelt away your dross as with lye, and will remove all your alloy" (NASB). For even purer silver the ingots would be further refined. The words or promises of the Lord are likened to silver "refined in a furnace on the ground, purified seven times" (Ps 12:6, RSV).

In Heb. the word for silver is *kesep*, which occurs over 400 times. More than 100 times it is translated "money," because both among the Israelites and the peoples of Syria and Babylonia silver was the principal medium of exchange. Abraham paid silver for his household slaves (Gen 17:13) and for the cave of Machpelah (23:16). He received indemnity for Sarah in silver (20:16) and was very rich in silver as well as in cattle and gold (13:2; 24:35). Joseph was sold for 20 pieces of silver (37:28). By Moses' time the price of a slave had increased to 30 shekels of silver (Ex 21:32). Silver, not gold, was the standard for fines, wages, and prices in the time of Hammurabi as well, according to his famous law code (ANET, pp. 175 ff.). A pyxis jar was found in a Late Bronze Age tomb at Dothan containing strips and bits of silver, undoubtedly used as money.

The use of silver was similar to that of gold (*see* 31. Gold). Silver, however, cannot be beaten into such thin sheets as gold, so that it was employed less in decorating woodwork and furniture. Joseph's drinking cup (Gen 44:2); a royal crown (Zech 6:11); jewelry (Gen 24:53; Ex 3:22; 11:2; 12:35; Song 1:11); idols (Jud 17:4; Ps 115:4; Isa 30:22; 31:7; *et al.*); and many

A silver mirror with obsidian handle from tomb of a princess of ancient Egypt. LL

objects for the tabernacle, such as the trumpets (Num 10:2), hooks and fillets (Ex 27:10–11), and platters and bowls (Num 7:13 ff.), were made of silver. Silver coins were common in the NT period. *See* Weights, Measures, and Coins.

52. **Slime.** A viscous substance, possibly mud or asphalt tar (Gen 11:3; Ex 2:3). *See* 10. Bitumen.

53. **Steel.** A hard, strong, malleable alloy of iron and carbon, usually containing between 0.2 and 1.5 percent carbon. It is doubtful that steel as such is mentioned in the Bible or that it was regularly produced in OT times. *See* 32. Iron. The word occurs four times in the KJV as the rendering of Heb. *n^{e}ḥûshâ* and *n^{e}ḥōshet* (II Sam 22:35; Job 20:24; Ps 18:34; Jer 15:12), and in every case should be translated "bronze." *See* 13. Bronze.

54. **Sulfur.** A soft yellow native element. When it burns it emits suffocating fumes of sulfur dioxide. *See* 12. Brimstone.

55. **Tin.** A soft, silver-colored metallic element used to coat other metals to prevent corrosion and to form part of various alloys such as pewter and bronze (*see* 13. Bronze). Its melting point is 232°C. Its chief source is the ore cassiterite (tin oxide), which the ancients mined somewhere in Caucasia or the Zagros Mountains E of Assyria. The Midianites, whose camps were plundered by Israel, seem to have been middlemen in the trading of metals, including tin (Num 31:22). Later on, the Phoenicians imported tin along with silver, iron, and lead from Tarshish in Spain (Ezk 27:12). It is known that their sailors went as far as Cornwall in the British Isles to secure the tin and brought it first to Gades (modern Cádiz) in SW Spain beyond Gibraltar. Here they transshiped it to the various Mediterranean ports.

56. **Topaz.** *See* Jewels: Topaz.

57. **Turquoise.** *See* Jewels: Turquoise.

Bibliography. L. Aitchison, *A History of Metals,* Vol I, London: 1960. R. J. Forbes, *Metallurgy in Antiquity,* Leiden: Brill, 1950. P. L. Garber, "Silver," IDB, IV, 355 f. J. L. Kelso, "Ancient Copper Refining," BASOR #121 (1951), pp. 26–28; "Metallurgy," BW, pp. 382–388. A. Lucas, *Ancient Egyptian Materials and Industries,* 4th ed., London: Edw. Arnold & Co., 1962. A. Leo Oppenheim, *et al., Glass and Glassmaking in Ancient Mesopotamia,* Corning: Corning Glass Center, 1972. A. Stuart, "Mining and Metals," NBD, pp. 823–825. F. V. Winnett, "Bronze," IDB, I, 467; "Iron," IDB, II, 725 f.; "Metallurgy," IDB, III, 366–368. R. V. Wright and R. L. Chadbourne, *Gems and Minerals of the Bible,* New York: Harper & Row, 1970.

G. H. H. and J. R.

MINGLED PEOPLE. Jer 25:20–22 lists the people of Uz, Philistine, Edom, Moab, etc., as "the mingled people" (KJV). The RSV translates *hā'ereb* as "foreign." In Ezk 30:5 RSV translates the word as "Arabia." Webster defines the Arabs as "intermixed with other native races."

MINIAMIN (mĭn'yȧ-mĭn).

1. A Levite who distributed tithes and offerings in the time of Hezekiah (II Chr 31:15).

2. A priest who took part in the ceremonies of dedication of the walls (Neh 12:17, 41). *See also* Mijamin.

MINING. In ancient literature frequent mention is made of various types of metals and minerals. Mining details, however, are obscure since few mining sites have been archaeologically excavated. Apparently in most cases minerals were obtained by surface mining, the usual method until the Greco-Roman period when shaft mining was widely introduced. The mined ore was processed in two main steps: the crushing of earth or stone and washing with water to separate the mineral (placer technique); and the smelting (*q.v.*) process of breaking down the ore through "roasting" in furnaces.

The ancient sources of Mesopotamian copper and iron (Anatolia and Armenian-Transcaucasian regions) have been forgotten or obliterated by modern activities. Thus the four major complexes known to us are situated in the southern area of the Fertile Crescent and in Egypt and Cyprus.

1. Iron (cf. Deut 8:9) seems to have been mined in OT times in Gilead, where several deposits of iron ore are known. Og, king of Bashan, had an iron "bedstead" (Deut 3:11), and a wealthy supporter of David from Gilead was named Barzillai ("iron man," II Sam 17:27). In Wadi Arabah (S of the Dead Sea) copper (and iron?) ore was collected at smelting centers such as Khirbet en-Nahas, el-Gheweibeh, and el-Jariyeh, 16 to 20 miles S of the Dead Sea, and given initial smelting before transportation to population centers. One exception is Khirbet Feinan (*see* Punon) where both mining and smelting were practiced as early as 2000 B.C. Near Feinan was discovered the one shaft mine in this area (Umm el-ʻAmad). In the 1960's was discovered a mining center operated at Timnah by the Egyptians with local Bedouin (Edomite or Midianite?) laborers. An Egyptian temple, dated to the reigns of Seti I and Rameses III, was surrounded by smelting camps.

2. Mining from predynastic times took place intermittently in Sinai, according to artifacts and inscriptions dating from the Egyptian Old, Middle, and New Kingdoms (2800–1100 B.C.). Magharah and Serabit el-Khadem produced turquoise and copper, while Wadi Nasb and Kharit only the latter. Sinai mines and methods are comparable to those in the Wadi Arabah, but the ores averaged only 5 to 15 percent copper.

3. In Upper Egypt gold mines are divided into three areas: Coptos, in the mountainous region N of Thebes and parallel to the Red Sea, which also had quarries of alabaster, breccia, and diorite; Wawat, Wadi Allagi, and Cabgaba S of Elephantine and Aswan; Kush, along the Nile from Buhen to Sabu. The latter two probably were not worked before the Middle Kingdom (*c.* 2000–1800 B.C.), their peak being during Dynasty XVIII.

4. So extensive was the export of copper from Cyprus in ancient times that copper obtained its name from the name of Cyprus. The English word "copper" is derived from the Gr. name of the island, *Kypros*, through the Latin *cuprum*. Produced as early as the 3rd mil. B.C., copper has continued to be mined extensively there until recently.

The biblical passage which most clearly describes ancient mining practices (Job 28:1–11, NASB) is usually associated with Sinai or the Wadi Arabah. It, however, mentions various types of minerals and thus suggests that no particular place was implied. Other brief references to digging for valuable metals are Deut 8:9, "a land whose stones are iron, and out of whose hills you can dig copper" (RSV), and Prov 2:4, "if you seek her as silver, and search for her as hidden treasures" (NASB).

See Minerals and Metals.

R. A. M.

MINISTER, MINISTRY. The Heb. and Gr. words for minister are used to designate officials of a civil and religious nature. From the etymology of the words and from the context it is clear that these are positions of responsibility rather than privilege.

In the OT the usual word for minister is *m^eshārēt*. This is the piel participle of the verb *shārat*. The expression may indicate one who attends a person of high rank, such as Joshua did Moses (Ex 24:13; Josh 1:1) or Elisha did Elijah (I Kgs 19:21). In the later writings it came to refer to royal officers (I Kgs 10:5; II Chr 22:8), even to the angels of God (Ps 104:4). However, by far the most characteristic use was in connection with the ministration of the priests in the temple (Deut 10:8; 17:12; 21:5; Isa 61:6; Ezk 44:11; Joel 1:9, 13; Ezr 8:17; Neh 10:36).

The NT Gr. employs three terms for minister. *Leitourgos* is the first word and is used for *m^eshārēt* in the LXX. It referred to a public servant, possibly a wealthy citizen, who would offer his services to the state (cf. Rom 13:3–6). In due time it took on the distinctively religious flavor which it enjoyed in the LXX (Rom 15:16). Thus Christ is the minister in the heavenly temple (Heb 8:2), and Paul is such in bringing the gospel to the Gentiles (Rom 15:16).

Hypēretēs is a Gr. compound meaning an under-rower in a galley. It came to signify anyone in a subordinate position or one who was a personal attendant or helper to a superior (Lk 1:2; Acts 13:5; 26:16; I Cor 4:1). This term translated *ḥazzān*, an attendant in the synagogue whose duty it was to open and close the building, care for the books used in the services, and assist the priest or teacher in worship (Lk 4:20).

Finally, the most characteristic NT word for minister is *diakonos*. It was used of those who waited on tables (cf. Lk 12:37; 17:8). This word emphasizes the lowliness of Christian service (Mt 20:26; Mk 10:43). The apostles and their helpers are called ministers of God (II Cor 6:4; I Thess 3:2); of Christ (II Cor 11:23; Col 1:7; I Tim 4:6); of the gospel (Eph 3:6-7; Col 1:23); of the new covenant (II Cor 3:6); and of the church (Col 1:24-25). In Acts 6:2–3 seven were chosen to assist the apostles in the serving of tables. These men served as the prototype of the deacon, the later church officials mentioned in Phil 1:1 and characterized in I Tim 3:8ff. While *diakonos* is usually associated with the Christian ministry, the expression is also used of Satan's ministers (II Cor 11:13) and possibly ministers of sin (Gal 2:17).

In the OT the ministry referred primarily to the religious services performed by the priests and Levites. However, after the death of Christ, the NT speaks of each believer as functioning as a priest before God (Rev 1:6; I Pet 2:9). According to Rom 12:6-8; I Cor 12:28; Eph 4:11 those in the body of Christ have been endowed with charismatic gifts by the Holy

Spirit to the end that they might be involved in the ministry. It is further clear that no matter how insignificant that gift might be, it is to be exercised "for the perfecting of the saints" and "for the edifying of the body of Christ" (Eph 4:12).

Alongside the priestly function of the individual believer, the NT marks the development of a professional Christian ministry. During our Lord's ministry on earth, He trained and sent out the Twelve (Mt 10:1 ff.; Mk 6:7 ff.; Lk 9:1 ff.). After Christ's death, Matthias was chosen to take part in the ministry of the apostles (Acts 1:23ff.). The seven deacons were added to help with the serving of the tables (Acts 6:1–8). By the time of the Jerusalem council (Acts 15) the term apostle seems to have had a broader reference. An apostle was one who had witnessed the resurrection and had received a direct commission from the risen Christ to preach (cf. I Cor 9:1 ff.). By the close of Paul's ministry the leadership of the local church was in the hands of bishops, elders, and deacons. The exact interrelationship that existed among these leaders has long been a matter of dispute. Lightfoot, along with Harnack, takes the bishop and elder to be one in the NT. The title bishop emphasizes the function of oversight, while elder characterizes the dignity of the office. Later the two became separated, and the bishop became a distinct order, higher than that of the elder. Sohm and Lowrie, on the other hand, contend that the two were always separate, although this distinction became more pronounced with the passing of time. At first not all elders were bishops, but all bishops were elders.

The doctrine of apostolic succession first appeared in the 1st cen. Letter of Clement. By the close of the 2nd cen. the teaching seems to have crystallized. However, from the very beginning orthodox fathers, notably Irenaeus (*Heresies* 3:3–4), rejected this claim by appealing to the teaching of the NT.

See Lead, Leader; Service.

Bibliography. G. Henton Davies, "Minister in the Old Testament," IDB, III, 385f. Adolf von Harnack, *The Constitution and Law of the Church in the First Two Centuries*, trans. by F. L. Pogson, New York: Putnam, 1910. J. B. Lightfoot, "The Christian Ministry," *Saint Paul's Epistle to the Philippians*, London: Macmillan, 1885 ed., pp. 181-269. Walter Lowrie, *The Church and Its Organization in Primitive and Catholic Times*, New York: Longmans, Green & Co., 1904. Thomas W. Manson, *The Church's Ministry*, Philadelphia: Westminster, 1948. Leon Morris, "Minister, Ministry," BDT, pp. 355f. John K. S. Reid, *The Biblical Doctrine of the Ministry*, Edinburgh: Oliver & Boyd, 1955. Massey H. Shepherd, Jr., "Ministry, Christian," IDB, III, 386–392. H. Strathmann and R. Meyer, "*Leiturgeō*, etc.," TDNT, IV, 215-231.

P. D. F.

MINNI (mĭn'ī). In Jer 51:27 the Lord summons the nations of Ararat, Minni, and Ashkenaz (KJV, Ashchenaz) for the destruction of Babylon. Since Ararat (Assyrian *Urarṭu*, Armenia) and Ashkenaz (Assyrian *Aš̌guzāya, Išhkuzāya*, the region of the Scythians) are well-known areas which were located E of the Black Sea, Minni must be the *Mannāy(a)* or Manneans of the 9th through the 7th cen. B.C. Assyrian sources, a people who lived in Kurdistan S of Lake Urmiah and E of the Zagros Mountains. That they are to be equated with the Armenian Minyas (Jos *Ant*. i.3.6) is questionable. They were related linguistically to the Urartians and the Hurrians of N Mesopotamia. Although they had been frequently invaded by Assyria in earlier times, they came to the Assyrians' assistance in 616 B.C., but were defeated by Nabopolassar of Babylon (ANET, p. 304). Since they later belonged to the Medo-Persian Empire, they apparently took part in Cyrus' war against Babylon, as Jeremiah had prophesied.

According to Urartian and Assyrian texts the Mannean capital was Izirtu, not yet discovered but thought to be near Saqqiz. At nearby Ziwiye a hoard of gold objects (*c*. 700 B.C.) was found in 1947. In 1956 excavations began at

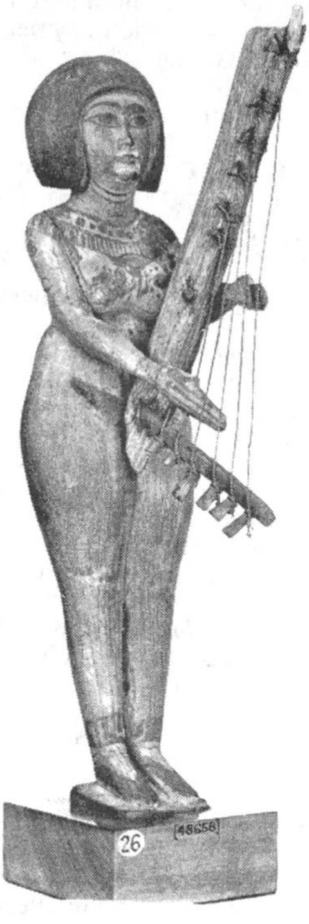

An Egyptian harpist of about 1200 B.C. BM

Hasanlu Tepe overlooking the plain S of Lake Urmia. In the 9th cen. B.C. it was a Mannean stronghold under Assyrian influence and evidently sacked by the Urartians *c.* 800 B.C. A magnificent gold bowl with Hurrian representations as early as 1200 B.C. and a tall silver cup were found in the ruins of the 60 acre citadel (Robert H. Dyson, Jr., "Hasanlu and Early Iran," *Archaeology,* XIII [1960], 118–129; "Ninth Century Men in Western Iran," *Archaeology,* XVII [1964], 3–11).

R.Y. and J.R.

MINNITH (mĭn'ĭth). One of the cities named in Jephthah's conquests (Jud 11:33). Ezekiel speaks of wheat of Minnith as among the merchandise of Tyre (Ezk 27:17). Eusebius connects Minnith with a Maanith on the road from Rabbath Ammon to Heshbon. El Yadūdeh has been suggested as the site (Kraeling, *Biblical Geography,* p. 16).

MINSTREL. In the OT a player upon a stringed instrument, common in the royal courts of Assyria, Egypt and Palestine. David played his harp to soothe King Saul (I Sam 16:23), and Elisha called for a minstrel, perhaps to quiet his mind to receive God's message (II Kgs 3:15).

One occurrence in the NT (Mt 9:23) is rendered "flute-players" in the ASV. For those who could afford it, as would have been true of the ruler of the synagogue, these professional mourners were called in to play their dirges and laments as an expression of grief for loss of the deceased. *See* Music.

MINT. *See* Plants.

MIPHKAD GATE. *See* Jerusalem: Gates and Towers 15.

MIRACLES

Nature of the Miraculous

Since the term miracle is popularly applied to unusual events even by those who profess not to believe in the supernatural, it is not always easy to give the word its true biblical significance. Probably the simplest definition is, "an interference with nature by supernatural power" (C.S. Lewis, *Miracles,* p. 15). Also, a definition by Machen is helpful: "A miracle is an event in the external world that is wrought by the immediate power of God" (J. Gresham Machen, *The Christian View of Man,* p. 117). By this he means that a divine work is miraculous when God "uses no means but puts forth His creative power as He put it forth when He first made all things of nothing" (*loc. cit.*). In other words, a miracle occurs when God steps in to do something beyond what could be accomplished according to the laws of nature as we understand them, and which actually may be in violation of them. Moreover, a miracle is beyond man's intellectual or scientific ability.

Four Gr. words appear in the Gospels to describe the supernatural works of Jesus: *teras* (translated "wonder") speaks of their extraordinary character; *sēmeion* ("sign") symbolizes heavenly truths and indicates Christ's immediate connection with a higher spiritual world; *dynamis* ("power") describes an exercise of divine power and demonstrates the fact that higher forces have entered into and are working in this lower world of ours; *ergon* ("work") refers to miraculous deeds which Christ came to do. The first three of these terms are brought together in Acts 2:22: "Jesus of Nazareth, a man approved of God among you by miracles [*dynamesi*] and wonders [*terasi*] and signs [*sēmeiois*], which God did by him in the midst of you, as ye yourselves also know." (See W. Graham Scroggie, *A Guide to the Gospels,* pp. 203–204.)

The Purpose of Miracles

Some tend to view miracles as isolated events in the lives of the prophets or of Jesus Christ. Presumably the dire straits of an individual, the seriousness of a situation, or the initiative of an Elijah or Elisha dictated whether or not a miracle was to be performed. But miracles are not scattered helter-skelter throughout the Bible. Four periods in biblical history are characterized by them: the days of Moses and Joshua, of Elijah and Elisha, of Daniel, and of Christ and the early church. In each case miracles served to accredit the message and the messenger of God at critical junctures in the development of the Hebrew-Christian tradition. They also preserved the truth of God from extinction.

Moses was a stranger to his people and needed some means to demonstrate that he had been sent by God to lead them from bondage. Moreover, he needed a way to persuade Pharaoh to release the enslaved Israelites. And, of course, once God led the Israelites out of Egypt, He had to exercise miraculous power to bring millions of them through the wilderness and into Canaan.

Elijah and Elisha ministered to Israel in a day when calf worship and Baal worship threatened to exterminate faith in the true God. Miraculous acts showed that the message of the prophets was true and worthy of belief, and that their God was the only true God. This fact is made especially clear in Elijah's confrontation with the prophets of Baal on Mount Carmel.

Daniel and his associates were thrust into positions of leadership in a day when the temple and Heb. political power had been destroyed, and when a large percentage of the leading members of the Heb. community were exiled from their homeland. Numerous questions must have rushed through the minds of the exiles. Did God any longer exist? Was He through with them? Were the Assyrians and Babylonians right when they taunted that their gods had greater prowess than the God of the Hebrews? Was the Heb. God a local god able

MIRACLES

to protect His worshipers only in Palestine? Did God have power now that His temple was gone and He had no house in which to dwell? Were Daniel and his associates mistaken in their view of God and His power? The miracles performed in Babylon gave ringing answers to all of these questions. The God of heaven was the one true God, universal in His power and loving in His tender watchcare over His own. He honored the testimony of His faithful servants; He showed that the image of Nebuchadnezzar was nothing compared to His power; He struck down Belshazzar at the precise moment he dared to desecrate the holy vessels of the temple and make fun of the Heb. deity. A people torn from their homeland and their customary worship patterns needed such a demonstration of power to carry them through the days of captivity. The fact that the Hebrews were not assimilated into the Mesopotamian population but maintained their distinct nationality is a miracle in itself. It is even more remarkable that so many of those people who came to Mesopotamia as prisoners of war and slaves rose to prominence in Babylonian and Persian society. Archaeological discoveries wonderfully attest that fact.

During Jesus' earthly ministry, He used miracles to demonstrate His deity, to prove that He was sent from God, to support His messiahship, to minister in compassion to the needy multitudes, to lead His followers to saving faith, to give evidence of an inner spiritual rejuvenation (as in the case of the healing of the paralytic, Mk 2:10–11), and as an instructional aid to help prepare His disciples for the ministry they were to perform (e.g., Mk 8:16–21). And, of course, the miracles of the incarnation, the resurrection, and the ascension are part and parcel of the divine provision of salvation for mankind.

After Christ ascended to heaven, His disciples began to preach in His name, to interpret the events of His life and especially of His death, and to write authoritative messages to their converts. Therefore the question of authentication once more arose. Were they truly God's messengers, interpreting correctly the message and work of His Son? Were their pronouncements to be treated as inspired? Miraculous acts helped answer these questions in the affirmative.

The Plausibility of Miracles

Men living in the age of science frequently have difficulty accepting the miraculous. From our earliest days at school we are impressed with natural law—with the constancy or uniformity of operations in the universe. As we grow older and begin to develop a world and life view for ourselves, a conflict arises between this outlook on nature and the supernatural. How shall we resolve the problem? Can we accept the miraculous?

Basic to any solution of the problem is an adequate view of God. One way to begin to arrive at such a concept is through the philosophical arguments for the existence and nature of God. The first of these is the *ontological* argument, which, simply stated, reasons that man has within him the idea of a perfect being. If this being is perfect, he must exist because perfection includes existence. Some philosophers have held it impossible to argue from abstract thought to real existence; but Hegel, among others, felt that the ontological was the supreme argument for the existence of God.

Kant, on the other hand, believed that the *moral* argument was the most important. Starting with the "ought" or categorical imperative in man, he argued for the existence of a being who had the absolute right to command man—a lawgiver and judge. Others express this argument differently and hold that the wide divergence between the conduct of men and their present prosperity demands a righting of the balances in the future, which in turn demands a righteous judge. Yet others who use the moral argument emphasize that the soul or religious spirit in man demands a personal object who is infinite, ethical, and knowable.

A third argument is called the *cosmological* or the argument from causality. Every part of the universe is contingent on something else. Even the universe is not eternal but is an event and so must have a cause. The argument goes back through the cause-effect relationship to the uncaused cause, to the self-existent One. As we think of the cause of the universe, we conclude that: (1) whatever caused it is a real something; (2) it is a great cause that might be infinite; (3) it must be free or self-determined; (4) it must be a single or unified cause; if many gods, they are working together.

A fourth argument is the *teleological*. There is order, adjustment, design everywhere visible in the universe. There is evidence of a designer of the universe. From this argument we may conclude that: (1) this designer must have great power; (2) he must have great intelligence; (3) personality and self-consciousness may possibly be inferred from such great intelligence.

By careful reasoning, we can further arrive through these theistic arguments at the possibility, probability, even a high probability of a full theism: a belief in a personal, supernatural, omnipotent God. Although we might arrive at moral certainty, we could not arrive at true intellectual certainty so that there would remain no intellectual doubt on the part of the individual. Intellectual certainty as to a personal, ethical God can be attained only through the facts of Christian revelation and conclusively only through an inner experience with God. It is unreasonable to conclude that an omnipotent designer of the universe would be without power to reveal Himself or without interest in revealing Himself to His creatures (i.e., through the written Word or the Living Word).

Once we admit the existence of God, we

MIRACLES

cannot deny supernatural activity in the space-time universe. Comments Boettner: "If opposition to the supernatural is consistently carried out, it cannot stop with the denial of miracles, but must carry the person straight over into agnosticism or atheism. It is the height of inconsistency for the modernist to admit the existence of God and yet to deny the miracles recorded in Scripture on the ground that they are opposed to natural law. A little reflection should convince anyone that the whole theistic conception of the universe is at stake in the denial of miracles" (Loraine Boettner, *Studies in Theology*, p. 53).

But many find little or no help in the theistic arguments for the establishment of the miraculous. Then take another approach; look at the laws of nature themselves. What are they? Do they preclude the possibility of miracles? As to the character of the laws of nature, Boettner observes, "They are not themselves forces in nature, but are merely general statements of the way in which these forces act so far as we have been able to observe them. They are not powers which rule all nature and force obedience to themselves, but rather mere abstractions which have no concrete existence in the external world" (*ibid.*, p. 61).

In the same vein, C. S. Lewis concludes, "We are in the habit of talking as if they caused events to happen; but they have never caused any event at all. . . . They produce no events: they state the pattern to which every event—if only it can be induced to happen—must conform, just as the rules of arithmetic state the pattern to which all transactions with money must conform—if only you can get hold of any money. Thus in one sense the laws of nature cover the whole field of space and time; in another, what they leave out is precisely the whole real universe—the incessant torrent of actual events which makes up true history. That must come from somewhere else. To think the laws can produce it is like thinking that you can create real money by simply doing sums" (Lewis, *op. cit.*, p. 71).

It should be clear, then, that the laws of nature are merely observations of uniformity or constancy in nature. They are not forces which initiate action. They simply describe the way nature behaves—when its course is not affected by a superior power. On the human plane, we observe constant introduction of new factors or forces to interfere with the normal course of nature. It is contrary to the laws of nature for immense steel ships to float or for airships weighing many tons to fly. Other factors have been introduced. According to the laws of nature, chemicals mixed in certain quantities will produce a commodity beneficial to man. If another force, such as heat or another chemical is introduced, the result may be an explosion or a deadly poison.

Man is constantly performing "miracles" as he interferes with nature. Thousands of his inventions violate the laws of nature. Is God less than man? Lewis well concludes, "The more certain we are of the law, the more clearly we know that if new factors have been introduced the result will vary accordingly. What we do not know, as physicists, is whether supernatural power might be one of the new factors. . . . Miracle is, from the point of view of the scientist, a form of doctoring, tampering, (if you like) cheating. It introduces a new factor into the situation, namely, supernatural force, which the scientist had not reckoned on" (*ibid.*, pp. 70–71).

There need not be any basic conflict between science and religion. "Science. . . . has for the most part now clearly seen that to seek to *describe* an order in nature does not imply the denial of a ground of nature" (C. J. Wright, *Miracle in History and in Modern Thought*, p. 178). Increasingly there is a tendency to recognize that science is one thing and religion another. Science seeks to describe phenomena and to develop new inventions in the physical world. It seeks to answer the question "How?" Religion seeks to describe phenomena and broaden horizons in the spiritual world. It seeks the reasons behind the phenomena. It endeavors to answer the question "Why?" The two can be reconciled by an intelligent approach to the problem. That a reconciliation is possible is clear from the fact that a number of outstanding scientists in our day are thoroughgoing supernaturalists—believers in miracles. The difficulty comes when men "proceed upon the hypothesis that miracles are impossible. Thus a nontheistic world view is made the criterion of history. Instead of examining the world to obtain a world view, the unbelievers use their world view to construct the history of the world. And the history they construct is self-contradictory" (Gordon H. Clark, "The Resurrection," *Christianity Today*, April 15, 1957, p. 19).

A defense of the miraculous in the late 20th cen. requires an understanding of modern thought and opinion. For some time there has been a tendency to abandon the extreme position of a denial of miracles. At the turn of the century Adolf Harnack, a great liberal, could write, "Much that was formerly rejected has been reestablished on a close investigation, and in the light of comprehensive experience. Who in these days, for example, could make such short work of the miraculous cures in the Gospels as was the custom of scholars formerly?" (Adolf Harnack, *Christianity and History*, p. 63). Since his day an even greater trend in this direction has set in. The old liberalism has had no message for a world convulsed by two world wars, the nuclear arms race, the cold and hot wars between East and West and in the Middle East, and the challenge of the space age. Gradually the bulwarks of the old liberalism have crumbled before worlds in collision and the onslaughts of neoorthodoxy or neosupernaturalism. Einstein's law of relativity and other factors have modified the old Newtonian concept of the universe, and other variables have been introduced which open the door to a return to the conservative position on miracles.

This does not mean that the world is being converted to conservative Christianity, but a belief in the miraculous is much more intellectually respectable than it used to be. We may conclude, then, that a belief in the miraculous is not only plausible in our day but is the only hope for a humanity caught in the maelstrom of power politics and imminent atomic warfare. Without the miraculous element Christianity would have no message, no solace for our age. A Jesus who is merely a martyr for the truth, a prince of philanthropists, a paragon of ethical teachers could present to men only a threadbare idealism. The only answer to the choppy seas of life is a Saviour who can say, "Peace, be still." The only hope for victory over Satanic power is through the One whom the demons recognized and obeyed. The only hope for the body in this life and the next lies in the One who is Lord of life and death. The only hope for the soul rests in the One who died for our sins and rose again and ever lives to make intercession for us.

Suggestions for the Study of Miracles

Miracles are easily passed over as interesting and dramatic phenomena. But a careful investigation of them will provide information of real value to the Bible student and will contribute to his knowledge of methodology in Bible study. Following are a few possible ways of approaching them.

1. Classify the miracles. For instance, they may be organized according to whether they display power over nature, demons, sickness and disease, or physical deformity.

2. Study them as a teaching device. What point did the miracle worker try to get across in connection with the miracle?

3. Note their apologetic value. For instance, consider them as an evidence of the deity of Christ. Recognize the fact that in almost every instance the wonders Jesus performed were humanly impossible.

4. See what they reveal about the person of the miracle worker. Some facts gleaned from Christ's miracles are His power, compassion, love, attitude toward Judaism, toward government, and toward respect of persons.

5. Note the method or procedure followed in performing miracles. Jesus *spoke* to the three whom He raised from the dead. He *touched* a leper. He *put clay* on the blind man's eyes.

6. See what they reveal about the individual upon whom the miracle is worked. What do they tell about his economic position, social position, religious outlook, and his gratitude? What about the effect on him psychologically and spiritually?

7. Note the relative need of the beneficiaries of the miracles.

8. Visualize the drama of the occasion. Develop a sanctified imagination. For instance, imagine Jairus nervously fidgeting in the background as Jesus turns from his request to deal with the woman with the issue of blood who touched the hem of His garment. Perhaps the thought flashed through Jairus' mind that his daughter might not have died if the Master had made greater haste.

The Question of Miracles Today

The question is often raised whether the modern church may enjoy the same power of performing miracles as the NT church did. It must be granted that God is omnipotent and can enable His own to perform miracles today. While it is clear from history that God generally ceased to work through "sign" miracles at the end of the NT period, such miracles have occurred occasionally. Well authenticated occurrences of miraculous healing have taken place in our day (*see* Healing, Health). Among tribal peoples such miracles have served to attest the message and messenger on first presentation of the gospel. In those same tribes miracles apparently did not occur after a church had been established. This is not to imply that miracles have not occurred or will not occur under other conditions.

The gift of performing certain kinds of miracles is often related to the spiritual condition of the church, and it is asserted that if the 20th cen. church were more spiritual, it could exercise gifts as the 1st cen. church did. Note, however, that the Corinthian church was exercising those gifts while in a carnal condition. Moreover, I Cor 12 makes it clear that gifts of miracles, tongues, and interpretation of tongues are not given to all, but different members of the Body of Christ are given a variety of gifts. Apparently gifts are bestowed according to the sovereign will of God and not necessarily in relation to the spirituality of the recipient (*see* Gifts, Spiritual). It should be remembered that some of the most spiritual men in the Bible—e.g., Abraham and John the Baptist (who was filled with the Spirit from birth)—did not perform miracles. And the apostle Paul did not always perform miracles; he left Trophimus at Miletus sick.

It is clear from Scripture that in general the performance of miracles is related to a divine program or timetable. It may well be that another widespread manifestation of miracles will occur in the last days before Christ's return. In the Olivet Discourse Christ prophesied that false Christs and false prophets would perform miracles which would be so clever as almost to deceive the very elect (Mt 24:24). Further indications to the same end appear in II Thess 2:9 and Rev 13:12-15 (cf. Mt 7:21-23). If these wonders are to be counteracted, presumably God will permit believers a new display of divine signs and wonders.

Non-Christian Sources of Miraculous Power

It has just been noted that in the end times

miracles will be performed by demonic power. Presumably the work of Simon Magus and Elymas the sorcerer should be placed in the same category (Acts 8:9–24; 13:6–12), as well as the acts of the Egyptian magicians in their contest with Moses (Ex 7–8). For a discussion of this subject see M. F. Unger, *Biblical Demonology*.

The Miracles of the Bible

The miracles performed by Moses and Joshua may easily be found and studied in the early chapters of Exodus and subsequent chapters of the Pentateuch and the book of Joshua. The wonderful works of Elijah are described in I Kgs 17–II Kgs 2, and of Elisha in II Kgs 2–8. The miracles of Daniel's period are recorded in his prophecy.

Since the miracles of our Lord are scattered through four Gospels and since some of the miracles are mentioned in more than one Gospel, it may be useful to provide a complete list in one place. Miracles performed by leaders in the early church may be found in the book of Acts, beginning in chapter 3.

The Gospels record 35 separate miracles performed by Christ. Of these Matthew mentions 20; Mark, 18; Luke, 20; and John, 7. It should not be concluded, however, that these are all the miracles of our Lord. Matthew, for instance, alludes to 12 occasions when Jesus performed a number of wonderful works (4:23–24; 8:16; 9:35; 10:1, 8; 11:4–5; 11:20–24; 12:15; 14:14; 14:36; 15:30; 19:2; 21:14). Obviously the Gospel writers merely selected according to their purpose from the large number which the Lord performed. There are many ways of arranging the individual miracles noted in the Gospels, depending on the purpose of the commentator. It may be of value to list them in the order of their occurrence, as nearly as that order can be determined.

1. Turning water into wine (Jn 2:1–11)
2. Healing a nobleman's son at Cana (Jn 4:46–54)
3. Healing a lame man at the pool of Bethesda (Jn 5:1–9)
4. First miraculous catch of fish (Lk 5:1–11)
5. Delivering a synagogue demoniac (Mk 1:23–28; Lk 4:31–36)
6. Healing Peter's mother-in-law (Mt 8:14–15; Mk 1:29–31; Lk 4:38–39)
7. Cleansing a leper (Mt 8:2–4; Mk 1:40–45; Lk 5:12–16)
8. Healing a paralytic (Mt 9:2–8; Mk 2:3–12; Lk 5:18–26)
9. Healing a man with a withered hand (Mt 12:9–13; Mk 3:1–5; Lk 6:6–10)
10. Healing a centurion's servant (Mt 8:5–13; Lk 7:1–10)
11. Raising a widow's son (Lk 7:11–15)
12. Healing a blind and dumb demoniac (Mt 12:22; Lk 11:14)
13. Stilling a storm (Mt 8:18, 23–27; Mk 4:35–41; Lk 8:22–25)
14. Delivering the Gadarene demoniacs (Mt 8:28–34; Mk 5:1-20; Lk 8:26–39)
15. Healing a woman with an issue of blood (Mt 9:20–22; Mk 5:25–34; Lk 8:43–48)
16. Raising Jairus' daughter (Mt 9:18–19, 23–26; Mk 5:22–24, 35–43; Lk 8:41–42, 49–56)
17. Healing two blind men (Mt 9:27–31)
18. Delivering a dumb demoniac (Mt 9:32–33)
19. Feeding the 5,000 (Mt 14:14–21; Mk 6:34–44; Lk 9:12–17; Jn 6:5–13)
20. Walking on the water (Mt 14:24–33; Mk 6:45–52; Jn 6:16–21)
21. Delivering a Syrophoenician's daughter (Mt 15:21–28; Mk 7:24–30)
22. Healing a deaf mute in Decapolis (Mk 7:31–37)
23. Feeding 4,000 (Mt 15:32-39; Mk 8:1–9)
24. Healing a blind man at Bethsaida (Mk 8:22–26)
25. Delivering a demon-possessed boy (Mt 17:14–18; Mk 9:14-29; Lk 9:38–42)
26. Finding the tribute money (Mt 17:24–27)
27. Healing a man born blind (Jn 9:1–7)
28. Healing a crippled woman on the sabbath (Lk 13:10–17)
29. Healing a man with dropsy (Lk 14:1–6)
30. Raising of Lazarus (Jn 11:17–44)
31. Cleansing ten lepers (Lk 17:11–19)
32. Healing blind Bartimaeus (Mt 20:29–34; Mk 10:46–52; Lk 18:35–43)
33. Cursing the fig tree (Mt 21:18–19; Mk 11:12–14)
34. Restoring Malchus' ear (Lk 22:49–51; Jn 18:10)
35. Second miraculous catch of fish (Jn 21:1–11)

See Diseases; Gifts, Spiritual; Healing, Health; Jesus Christ: Jesus' Miracles; Sign; Wonder, Wonderful; Works of God.

Bibliography. Frank G. Beardsley, *The Miracles of Jesus*, New York: American Tract Society, 1926. John H. Best, *The Miracles of Christ*, London: SPCK, 1937. Alexander B. Bruce, *The Miraculous Element in the Gospels*, London: Hodder & Stoughton, 1886. John Laidlaw, *The Miracles of Our Lord*, London: Hodder & Stoughton, 1890. C. S. Lewis, *Miracles*, New York: Macmillan, 1947. H. van der Loos, *The Miracles of Jesus*, 2nd ed., Leiden: Brill, 1968. Richard C. Trench, *Notes on the Miracles of Our Lord*, Westwood, N.J.: Revell, n.d. H. Wace, "Miracle," ISBE, III, 2062–2066.

H. F. V.

MIRAGE. "An atmospheric phenomenon in which the air appears to move in ascending waves like those above a heated metal" (Webster). A phenomenon in which an image is mirrored in the heated air. It is usually a distant image, often distorted, and frequently found in the desert.

MIRIAM (mĭr'ĭ-ăm)

1. A descendant of Ezra through Mered (I Chr 4:17, RSV).

2. The daughter of Amram and Jochebed and the sister of Moses and Aaron (Ex 15:20; Num 26:59). No doubt she was the Miriam who protected the ark of bulrushes in which the infant Moses was hidden. She is mentioned by name for the first time and is called a prophetess in connection with the jubilant celebration which she led after the crossing of the Red Sea (Ex 15:20–21). She sinned when she was insubordinate to God's will and incited Aaron against Moses and then led in the obvious rebellion against Moses. She and Aaron objected to his prominence and respected position. As a result of her involvement and leading of the rebellion, God judged her by smiting her with leprosy. Moses prayed for her recovery and God answered his prayer. During her time of recovery no progress was made by Israel in their journey (Num 12:1–16). She died in Kadesh-barnea and was buried there (Num 20:1).

R. P. L.

MIRMA (mûr'mȧ). A son of Shaharaim, a Benjamite (I Chr 8:10).

A bronze mirror, *c.* 450 B.C. in the Archaeological Museum, Athens. Mimosa

MIRROR. Three NT passages (I Cor 13:12, II Cor 3:18; Jas 1:23) which speak of a "mirror" in ASV are translated "glass" in the KJV. In addition the ASV translates "mirror(s)" for "looking glasses" in Ex 38:8 and for "looking glass" in Job 37:18. The meaning of the Heb. in Isa 3:23 is uncertain, the KJV and ASV translating it to mean mirrors, whereas the RSV (following the LXX) reads "garments of gauze."

The mirrors of Bible times were not made of glass (glass mirrors were not available until late Roman times) but of brightly polished metal, usually bronze. The laver of bronze was made of the mirrors of the Israelite women (Ex 38:8; cf. "molten mirror" of Job 37:18, ASV). Though at first they were rare objects outside of Egypt, the Hellenistic culture made their use widespread. Round mirrors both plain and artistic, which had handles of wood, metal, and stone, have been found in the biblical lands. The metal tended to tarnish, making rubbing with a sponge and powdered pumice necessary. The indefinite image produced by a tarnished or imperfect mirror is probably alluded to in I Cor 13:12.

H. D. F.

MIRY PLACE. *See* Marsh.

MISGAB (mĭs'găb). A lofty place affording shelter and safety. The KJV transliterates it as a town. The RSV translates it "the fortress" (Jer 48:1).

MISHAEL (mĭsh'ā-ĕl)

1. A son of Uzziel, descendant of Kohath son of Levi (Ex 6:16, 18, 22). With Elzaphan he carried out the bodies of Nadab and Abihu from the tabernacle outside the camp (Lev 10:1–4).

2. One who stood by Ezra at the reading of the law when the former captives in Babylonia returned to Jerusalem (Neh 8:4).

3. Heb. name of Meshach, companion of Daniel, of the tribe of Judah (Dan 1:6–7). With Hananiah and Azariah, he was put under the charge of Melzar who provided their food. With Daniel the trio refused the king's food as ceremonially tainted. The diplomatic entreaty of Daniel for a test and its successful conclusion, secured them a special diet of vegetables (pulse). Mishael and the other two were entreated to pray with Daniel for the solution to Nebuchadnezzar's dream (Dan 2:17–18). They successfully defied the king later before his golden image, and though cast into the roaring furnace, emerged unharmed through the intervention of God (Dan 3:8–27).

H. G. S.

MISHAL (mī'shȧl). Also spelled Misheal and Mashal. A Levitical town in the tribe of Ashur (Josh 19:26; 21:30; I Chr 6:74). The site is unknown.

MISHAM (mī'shăm). A Benjamite, son of Elpaal. Also eponym of a family of Benjamin (I Chr 8:12).

MISHEAL. *See* Mishal.

MISHMA (mĭsh'mȧ)
1. A son of Ishmael. An Arab tribe called *Benee Mesma* is said to exist to this day (Gen 25:14; I Chr 1:30).
2. A descendant of Simeon (I Chr 4:25).

MISHMANNAH (mĭsh-măn'ȧ). A member of the Gadite tribe who joined David at Ziklag as a part of the "mighty men" (I Chr 12:10).

MISHNAH. *See* Talmud.

MISHRAITES (mĭsh'rȧ-īts). One of the post-Exilic families who lived at Kirjath-jearim, from whom came the Zareathites and the Eshtaulites (I Chr 2:53).

MISPAR. *See* Mispereth.

MISPERETH (mĭs'pĕ-rĕth). An exile who returned with Zerubbabel (Neh 7:7). A variant spelling is Mizpar (Ezr 2:2).

MISREPHOTH-MAIM (mĭz'rē-fŏth-mā'ĭm). A place near the Mediterranean Sea to which Joshua chased the Canaanites after defeating them at the waters of Merom (Josh 11:8). Several places at the northern end of the Plain of Acco *c.* 12 miles S of Tyre still recall this name, but the exact location is uncertain. On the basis of its being listed along the northern boundary of Israel with Sidon (Josh 13:6), Yohanan Aharoni has suggested that it is the Litani River which flows into the Mediterranean five miles N of Tyre (*The Land of the Bible*, Philadelphia: Westminster, 1967, p. 216).

MISSION OF THE CHURCH. *See* Commission, Great; Witness.

MIST. Water vapor as a fog or cloud enveloping a person, territory, or land.
1. Mist, vapor (Heb. *'ēd*). The first mentioned moisture for vegetation after creation (Gen 2:6) and a stage of the rain cycle (Job 36:27, RSV, NASB; KJV, "vapour"). It was the source of water supply before the Flood (*q.v.*), as in the tropics where mist and dampness abound. On the other hand, E. A. Speiser derived *'ēd* from Sumerian and Akkad. *edû*, an underground flow of fresh water (BASOR #140 [1955], pp. 9–10; and R. Laird Harris believes it denotes an inundation (Bul ETS, XI [1968], 177 ff.).
2. The RSV translation of Heb. *'ānān* in Isa 44:22; Hos 13:3 (KJV, "cloud").
3. The RSV translation of Heb. *n^{e}s'îm* in Jer 10:13; 51:16 (KJV, "vapours").
4. A mistiness (Gr. *achlus*) or condition of darkness caused by the Lord so that it blinded Elymas (Acts 13:11).
5. Thick darkness, blackness (Gr. *zophŏs*, also found in Heb 12:18; II Pet 2:4; Jude 6, 13). The apostle Peter describes the fate of unstable people or false teachers as those to whom "the mist of darkness is reserved for ever" (II Pet 2:17).
6. The RSV translation of Gr. *atmis* (KJV, "vapour") in the description of the brevity of life (Jas 4:14).
See Rain.

J. R.

MITE. A small bronze or copper coin (Gr. *lepton*, Mk 12:42; Lk 12:59; 21:2) used in Palestine in Jesus' day, and was so translated because it was the least of all coins, only half a farthing. It is hard to equate it with American currency, but it was worth only a small fraction of a cent. *See* Weights, Measures, and Coins.

A mite dating to the reign of Pontius Pilate.
G. L. Archer; photo by W. LaSor

MITHCAH (mĭth'kȧ). The stopping place for the Israelites on their way from Egypt, lying some distance from Sinai in rocky Arabia. Its name possibly is derived from the fact that its waters were almost free from impurities (Num 33:28–29).

MITHNITE (mĭth'nīt). Joshaphat, one of David's men, was called a Mithnite (I Chr 11:43). This would imply that there was a place called Methen, but there is no evidence of the existence of such a place.

MITHREDATH (mĭth'rē-dăth)
1. The treasurer of Cyrus, who was in charge of restoring to Sheshbazzar the vessels taken from the temple in Jerusalem (Ezr 1:8; cf. I Esd 2:11).
2. A Persian officer who governed Samaria. Together with Bishlam and Tabeel he wrote in Aramaic to Artaxerxes Longimanus, protesting the rebuilding of the walls of Jerusalem by the Jews (Ezr 4:7; cf. I Esd 2:16).

MITRE. A head covering or turban of linen, made for the high priest (except in Ezk 21:26 where the word translated "diadem" in KJV and "turban" in RSV refers to the headpiece worn by the prince of Israel). The mitre was worn by the high priest on the Day of Atonement (Lev 16:4).
See Turban; High Priest, Dress of.

MITYLENE (mĭt'ĭ-lē'nĭ). The leading city of Lesbos, an island lying off the NW coast of Asia Minor not far from Pergamum (on the E) and Alexandria Troas (on the N). It was early populated by Aeolian Greeks, and in Roman times enjoyed the status of a holiday resort. Paul stopped here briefly on his way from Greece to Miletus (Acts 20:14). An earthquake later destroyed the city (A.D. 151–152). During the Middle Ages the name was given to the entire island.

MIXED MARRIAGE. Marriage between Israelites and Canaanites was forbidden by the Mosaic law (Deut 7:3–4). Earlier, Abraham had been concerned lest Isaac take a daughter of the Canaanites as a wife. Jacob married the daughters of Laban, his kinsman. Judah, however, married one of the Canaanite women (Gen 38:2), and Joseph married the Egyptian priest's daughter (Gen 41:45). His descendants, however, were commanded not to marry outside the tribe. On the other hand, the Deuteronomic law permitted soldiers of Israel to bring women home from conquered nations to be their wives. They were not permitted to sell them in slavery (Deut 21:10–14).

In the restoration Ezra mourned when he learned that the sons and daughters of other nations had married sons and daughters of Israel (Ezr 9:1–15). He cited Ex 23:32 as forbidding intermarriage. But the passage does not explicitly forbid intermarriage as such. Nehemiah, referring to the same incident, rejoices that every foreign thing had been cleansed out of Israel. Ezra had resolved the "sin" by forcing the men to put away their wives and children (see Ezr 10:18–44).

The basis of this prohibition was the fear that intermarriage would lead to corruption and sin. The experiences of Solomon and Ahab, whose wives led Israel away, were warning enough to these leaders. There was no argument here for "purity of blood" as such. It was rather a policy to avoid corrupting influences from idolatrous people. *See* Marriage; Divorce.

L. Ga.

MIXED MULTITUDE. A designation (Heb. *'ēreb,* "a mixture") given primarily to that heterogeneous company who attached themselves to the Israelites at the time of the Exodus from Egypt (Ex 12:38). They proved a snare to the Israelites in that they "fell a lusting" at Kibroth-hattaavah (Num 11:4).

The identification of this group has posed a difficult problem. In the Targum the phrase is rendered "many foreigners." Some have therefore suggested that these people were remnants of the Hyksos or other alien Asiatics who departed Egypt with the Hebrews; others, that they were native Egyptians, themselves oppressed by the new Pharaoh. Still others suggest a hybrid race is meant, the progeny of marriages contracted in Egypt during the oppression between Israelites and the native Egyptians (see Lev 24:10–11).

Mitylene Harbor

The phrase is also significantly found in Neh 13:3. A public reading of the law was held and it was found written that no Ammonite or Moabite should come into the congregation of God. The Jews responded with prompt obedience and separated the "mixed multitude" from them. The same Heb. term is translated in Jer 25:20; 50:37 as "mingled people" (*q.v.*).

D. K. C.

MIZAR (mī'zär). A positive identification of this hill, named only in Ps 42:6, is not presently possible. Some suggest the psalmist used the names Hermon and Mizar only symbolically. A more reasonable assumption would seem to be that it is a hill in proximity to both Mount Hermon and the Jordan, e.g., in upper Galilee. Another possibility is that it simply means "small hill," and refers to Mount Zion.

MIZPAH, MIZPEH (mĭz'pȧ). Heb. *miṣpâ* or *miṣpeh* means a watchtower or lofty place from which one can see far and wide whether men have built a tower there or not (Isa 21:8; II Chr 20:24). It is always used with the definite article except at Hos 5:1.

1. A heap of stones which Jacob set up in Gilead as a marker of the covenant between Jacob and Laban, making a boundary between the two (Gen 31:45–49). Jacob called it Galeed, but Laban, Jegar-sahadutha ("heap of witness"), and they further explained it as the Mizpah, i.e., the watchtower, saying, "May the Lord watch between you and me. . . ."

2. A town or site in Gilead, headquarters of Jephthah (Jud 10:17; 11:11, 34), called Mizpah of Gilead (11:29). It was probably also known as Ramath-mizpeh (Josh 13:26), the Ramoth in Gilead which was a city of refuge (Josh 20:8; 21:38; I Kgs 22:4). Nelson Glueck identified it with Tell Rāmîth, *c.* 30 miles E of Bethshan (BASOR #92 [1943], pp.10 f.). *See* Ramoth-gilead.

3. The land of Mizpeh (Josh 11:3, 8), a valley at the foot of Mount Hermon in N Palestine.

4. A place in Moab to which David took his parents for safety (I Sam 22:3).

Mizpah of Benjamin, Tell en-Nasbeh. HFV

5. A town in the Shephelah (foothills) of Judah (Josh 15:38).

6. A city of Benjamin (Josh 18:26), in the vicinity of Geba and Ramah (I Kgs 15:22) and Gibeon (Jer 41:12, 16). On several occasions Mizpah served as an assembly point for the tribes of Israel (Jud 20:1-3; 21:1; I Sam 7:5-6; 10:17), and here Samuel came annually to judge Israel (I Sam 7:17).

King Asa fortified Mizpah and Geba against the northern kingdom of Israel, using stones and timber with which Baasha had built up Ramah (I Kgs 15:22). Mizpah served as the governor's seat of Gedaliah, appointed to rule the territory of Judah by Nebuchadnezzar after the destruction of Jerusalem in 586 B.C. (II Kgs 25:22-25; Jer 40:6-13). There Gedaliah was assassinated by Ishmael, who soon afterward slaughtered 70 pilgrims from Shechem and threw their bodies into the government cistern Asa had built (Jer 41:1-9). It is probably this Mizpah which was resettled after the Exile and some of whose inhabitants assisted in rebuilding the wall of Jerusalem (Neh 3:7, 15, 19).

Its location has been disputed by scholars, with two identifications remaining as the chief possibilities. The first is Nebi Samwil, a prominent hill five miles NW of Jerusalem, 2,935 feet above sea level, and the traditional burial place of Samuel.

The more likely site is Tell en-Naṣbeh, eight miles N of Jerusalem and only 2,570 feet above sea level but beside the main N-S road running from Jerusalem to Shechem and Samaria. It was excavated under the direction of W. F. Badè from 1926 to 1935. One of the strongest walls (over 13 feet thick) yet found in Palestine was built around it *c.* 900 B.C., with nine or ten rectangular towers strengthening the wall at turns or long stretches. Its city gate with massive tower was on the NE side of the tell. From Tell en-Naṣbeh comes a seal belonging to Jaazaniah (probably the man of II Kgs 25:23; Jer 40:8), showing a fighting cock. Also 86 jar handles with the royal stamp *lmlk* were found, proving this was a Judean city. No such impressions have been discovered at Bethel, only three miles farther N and across the border between Judah and Israel. Most of the jar handles date to the period of King Josiah and his successors (640-586 B.C.).

Bibliography. D. Diringer, "*Mizpah,*" TAOTS, pp. 329-342. C. C. McCown, *et al., Excavations at Tell en-Nasbeh* (2 vol.), New Haven: ASOR, 1947.

J. R.

MIZPAR. *See* Mispereth.

MIZPEH. *See* Mizpah.

MIZRAIM (mĭz'rā-ĭm). Mizraim Heb. *miṣrayim*) is a name whose form and derivation are not certain. It is the common biblical designation for Egypt, and consequently the word usually is regarded as a dual, reflecting Egyptian expressions for the "Two Lands" of Egypt, Upper and Lower Egypt. Equivalent names for Egypt are found in a number of Semitic languages: in Ugaritic, *mṣr;* in Akkadian, *Muṣur, Misri* (e.g.. in the Amarna tablets); in Arabic, *Masr,* the present name for Cairo and for Egypt.

In the Bible the name has several usages.

1. It first appears in the Table of Nations (Gen 10), where Mizraim (Egypt, RSV) is list-

A palette commemorating a victory of Narmer, possibly to be equated with Menes, the king given credit for uniting ancient Egypt. LL

ed as a son of Ham (v.6; cf. I Chr 1:8). In Gen 10:13–14 he is named as the father of the following peoples: "Ludim, Anamim, Lehabim, Naphtuhim, Pathrusim, Casluhim (whence came the Philistines), and Caphtorim" (RSV; cf. I Chr 1:11–12). Along with his brothers, Cush (also a name for Ethiopia) and Phut (Libya), Mizraim is associated with NE Africa. The mention of the Philistines and Caphtorim (Cretans) is also of interest in view of the relations between Egypt and Crete. *See* Nations.

2. *Miṣrayim* is the usual Heb. name for Egypt in the Bible and is always translated thus in the RSV. (*a*) It occurs more than 500 times as a name for the land of Egypt, and hence is important as a geographic term. In Isa 11:11 and possibly Jer 44:15 the term may be used of only Lower Egypt, since in these passages the name Pathros, "Upper Egypt," also is found. (*b*) Heb. *miṣrayim* is used also in an ethnic and political sense for Egypt and Egyptians (e.g., Gen 41:55; Isa 19:23, 25).

3. In a few references where horses are prominent (I Kgs 10:28–29; II Kgs 7:6; II Chr 1:16–17), some commentators, following Hugo Winckler, take the Heb. name as referring to a land called Muṣri or Muṣur in N Syria or SE Asia Minor, but most prefer Egypt. *See* Egypt.

C.E.D.

MIZZAH (mĭz'*ȧ*). A son of Reuel; a descendant of Esau and Bashemath, the daughter of Ishmael, and chief of a clan not yet identified (Gen 36:13, 17; I Chr 1:37).

MNASON (nā'sŏn). An early disciple (ASV, RSV) mentioned only once (Acts 21:16). He came from the island of Cyprus, as did Barnabas. When Paul and his companions left Caesarea for Jerusalem after Paul's third missionary tour, Mnason was evidently living in Jerusalem, and Paul and the others were lodged with him there.

MOAB (mō'ăb), **MOABITE** (mō-*ȧ*-bīt'). A country and people E of the Dead Sea.

The Name

The derivation and etymology of the name is not given in the Bible. On the basis of Gen 19:30–38 a popular etymology is suggested because the LXX text of v. 37 adds, "saying, from my father," after the name "Moab" which on the basis of its consonants may be made to read according to some scholars, "from my father." This is the only reference in the Bible where the name "Moab" refers to a person. Everywhere else the name refers to a people.

The Land

Moab occupied the plateau about 4,500 feet above the Dead Sea which was its western border and 3,200 feet above the Mediterranean Sea. On the E Moab was bounded by the Arabian Desert and on the S by the canyon of the Zered (Wadi Hesa), with the land of Edom beyond. Its northern border varied at different periods from the Arnon River to an uncertain boundary N of Heshbon. The length of the country from N to S varied with her political fortunes from about 35 to 60 miles, while her width E to W was about 25 miles. The plateau is well watered and produced the crops of grain and grapes which were the basis of Moab's prosperity. The economy was also supported by the raising of sheep.

Flood time near the Pyramids. LL

The People

According to Gen 19:30–38 the Moabites descended from Moab, son of Lot, who was a nephew of Abraham, as the result of an incestuous relationship with the elder of Lot's two daughters. The narrative therefore indicates that the Israelites and the Moabites were Semites and kinsmen, and this is confirmed in a measure by the fact that the language of the Moabites is closely related to that of the Hebrews. The characters of the inscription of 34 lines on the Moabite Stone (*q.v.*) correspond to the characters of Hezekiah's Siloam inscription and show that both languages are of the same Semitic stock. Similarity of some customs also indicate the same kinship. Moab is represented in Ex 15:15 as already a powerful people when Israel fled from Egypt.

The land which came to be known as Moab was, as far as we are able to learn, originally inhabited by a people famed for their great stature and in the Bible called Rephaim (Deut 2:10–11). They were referred to by the Moabites, who dispossessed them, as the "Emim," the "terrible" or "frightful ones." They are mentioned in Gen 14:5 and are said to be inhabitants of Shaveh Kiriathaim.

Religion

The religion, and consequently the culture, of the Moabites were very similar to that of the Canaanites. The fertility of Moab, its wealth in wine and grain, the temperate climate, and the enervating heat provided the conditions which determined the form of the cult. Consequently, fertility cult nature-worship prevailed with all of its impure rites. Sexual orgies were a ceremonial expression of the worship of Baal of Peor (Num 25:1-6). Mesha's allusion in the Moabite Stone to Ashtar-Chemosh (line 17), a compound deity, has led to the view that there was a corresponding female consort, which would be natural and expected in the fertility cult. Fertility figurines of the mother-goddess Astarte found in Moab are similar to those of the Canaanite figurines. The kinship of Moabite and Canaanite fertility cult practices is further illustrated in names like Bamoth-baal (Num 22:41, RSV), Beth-baal-meon (Josh 13:17), and Beth-peor (Josh 13:20). *See* Peor.

Sacrifices of oxen and sheep were common on the altars of the high places and were followed by sacrificial meals (Num 22:40–23:2; 25:1–3; cf. Rev 2:14). Human sacrifice was practiced, and lines 11 and 12 of the Moabite Stone describe how all the people of Ataroth were sacrificed to the god Chemosh. Chemosh, the national deity of the Moabites, frequently appears as an element in their names. The names Chemosh-ṣedeq and Chemosh-yeḥi are especially interesting. In the fertility cult compound name Ashtar-Chemosh, he is related to Ashtar, the Canaanite god of the morning star. The sun disk is used occasionally on seals with the name Chemosh. The name also appears in Babylon inscriptions, all this indicating its use in the wider Semitic pantheon. Although Chemosh was a god of war, he was also thought of as being involved in the common experiences of the individual's life to bring blessing or cursing. *See* Gods, False.

History

Archaeological explorations in Moab have shown that until the end of the Early Bronze Age, i.e., *c.* 2000 B.C., the country was inhabited by a highly civilized agricultural people. Their towns were walled and strategically located for purposes of defense. An extensive fortified cemetery with as many as 20,000 tombs belonging to the Early Bronze Age has been excavated in part at Bab edh-Dhra (*q.v.*), E of el-Lisan (the tongue of land protruding into the Dead Sea). The pottery produced by these people resembles that made by the Canaanites. The important trade route was the King's Highway running the entire N-S length of the country. This was the route taken by Chedorlaomer (Gen 14:5–7), and the destruction left by his invasion of the country may have been the cause of the elimination of the Emim who were the predecessors of the Moabites in the area (Deut 2:10–11).

Shortly after the beginning of the Middle Bronze Age the sedentary life of the area S of the river Jabbok gave way to a more nomadic culture. The country was invaded by seminomadic elements, usually identified with the Amorite migrations, who accomplished the destruction of the cities and brought the Bronze Age civilization largely to an end. It appears that a predominantly nomadic type of life continued for some centuries. One of these groups was known to the Egyptians as the Shutu in the Execration texts of *c.* 1900 B.C. (ANET, p. 329), and suggests the "sons of Sheth" in Num 24:17. The absence of strong population centers in Moab in this period is an evidence, according to some scholars, for the late date of the Exodus. *See* Exodus, The: Date.

Near the close of the Late Bronze Age, in the 13th cen. B.C., the nomadic life was supplanted by a more sedentary population and the establishment of the kingdom of Moab. The earliest reference to Moab in extrabiblical sources is in the lists of Ramses II (1304–1237 B.C.) at Luxor (ANET, p. 243).

Before the arrival of the Israelites in the area of Transjordan after the Exodus the Amorite king Sihon had defeated the Moabites (Num 21:26) and occupied their territory as far S as the Arnon River. Sihon was the king of Heshbon and controlled the area from the Jabbok to the Arnon at the time of the coming of the Israelites (Num 21:27–30). The Israelites were able to defeat Sihon, and later divided the former Moabite territory between the tribes of Reuben and Gad (Deut 2:24–36; Num 32:2–5, 34–38; Josh 13:8–10, 15–23).

The Israelites, now in a position to attack Canaan, encamped in the plains or lowlands (NEB) of Moab across the Jordan from Jericho (Num 22:1 ff.). Balak, king of Moab, sent his envoys to Balaam at Pethor to induce him to curse Israel (Num 22–24). The result was a blessing of Israel instead of the curse wanted by the Moabite king (*see* Peor). It was during this period of encampment in the plains of Moab that the Israelites became involved in illicit relations with Moabite women and their gods (Num 25:3). The tribes of Reuben and Gad rebuilt many of the Moabite cities (Num 32:34–38). Moses died and was buried "in the valley in the land of Moab opposite Beth-peor" (Num 27:12–23; Deut 32:48–52; 34:1–8, RSV).

During the period of the judges of Israel when Israel was weak, the Moabites pushed northward from the river Arnon to several miles N of the northern end of the Dead Sea, and even across the Jordan River to Jericho. The Israelites were oppressed by Eglon king of Moab for 18 years until he was assassinated by Ehud the judge (Jud 3:12–30). The campaigns of King Saul in Transjordan included the defeat of Moab (I Sam 12:9). When David fled from Saul he brought his parents to the king of Moab for protection. Perhaps the latter was sympathetic to David because of Ruth, David's Moabite great-grandmother. Throughout the reigns of David and Solomon Moab was under the domination of Israel.

The most important historical period of Moab coincided with the period of the existence of the northern kingdom of Israel, i.e., from 931 B.C., when Israel became a divided nation, until 722/1 B.C., when the northern kingdom was destroyed by the Assyrians. The weakness of Israel following the division of the monarchy enabled Moab to gain her independence, but she was again brought under the domination of Israel during the reign of King Omri, *c.* 876 B.C. (II Kgs 3:4). Moab was subject to Israel until the death of King Ahab to whom Mesha of Moab had paid tribute. Mesha then staged a rebellion (II Kgs 3:5 ff.), which was successful, and Moab became independent of Israel. Later, however, Israel, Judah, and Edom formed a coalition to attack Moab. In desperation Mesha took his oldest son and sacrificed him on the wall. This act prompted the allies to give up the battle (II Kgs 3:27), perhaps in fear of retribution from the god Chemosh (G. M. Harton, "The Meaning of II Kgs 3:27," *Grace Journal,* XI (Fall, 1970, #3, pp. 34–40), and Mesha claimed the victory. In subsequent years marauders from Moab frequently pillaged Israel (II Kgs 13:20).

It would appear that later, in the time of Jeroboam II, Moab was independent (Amos 2:1–3) but may have felt the military might of the king of Israel as he extended his borders to the Dead Sea (II Kgs 14:25). Moab apparently never again attained full independence, falling next under the control of the Assyrians.

The invasion of Tiglath-pileser III into Israel in 734–733 B.C. brought Moab, together with other states in Transjordan, under the control of the Assyrian Empire. There was no serious attempt on the part of the states of Transjordan to free themselves of Assyrian rule, because of the economic prosperity they enjoyed as part of the great empire.

The coming of the Babylonians to rule Transjordan did not involve a significant change in the status of Moab. Moabite troops were in the Babylonian army when the revolt of Jehoiakim of Judah was crushed (II Kgs 24:1–2; cf. Ezk 25:6–8). But in the fourth year of the reign of Zedekiah, the last king of Judah, the king of Moab participated in a conspiracy against Babylon (Jer 27:3). There is no evidence that the Moabites actually participated in the fighting in 586 B.C. when Jerusalem and the temple were destroyed.

In 581 B.C. another punitive expedition against Judah and Transjordan was undertaken by the Babylonians. Josephus says that in that year the Babylonian army moved against Syria, Ammon, and Moab (*Ant.* x.9.7; cf. Jer 40:11; 48:7). There is no evidence that Moab ever again became an independent or even semi-independent kingdom after the period of Babylonian rule. Ezr 2:6 seems to indicate that Moab became a province of the Persian Empire following the defeat of the Babylonians by Cyrus the Persian.

In the following period of decline Moab, too weak to resist, suffered from the nomads who raided Transjordan. Many Moabites were driven from the region S of the Arnon and were scattered in surrounding countries. The population that remained in the land was assimilated among the Arabian tribes who took possession of the area. The coming judgment pronounced by Ezekiel (25:4–10; 35:15) upon the nations of Transjordan is attested to by archaeological researches in the area and foreshadows the coming of shepherds and nomads from the east. Moab experienced another period of prosperity in the Hellenistic and Roman periods, but by that time had been taken over and absorbed by the Nabateans (*q.v.*). The area was eventually incorporated into Provincia Arabia. The Pentateuchal lament on the destruction of Moab (Num 21:27–35) is reflected in Isa 15–16 and Jer 48.

Archaeology

Very few major excavations that relate to the Moabites themselves have been carried out in Moab. The two exceptions are at Dibon (*q.v.*), where the results were disappointing because no definite stratification could be established, and at Heshbon (*q.v.*), where the digging had at time of publication not yet reached Moabite levels in any sizeable area. In other places such as Madeba, Elealeh, Adar, Balu'ah, and Kir-Moab (Kerak) explorations and minor soundings have found some traces of Moabite occupation.

The earliest archaeological find attributable to the Moabites is the Balu'ah stele (ANEP #488), a black basalt stone standing six feet high and carved with three human figures. A king with beard and headdress typical of the Shasu-Bedouin is standing between a god and a goddess with characteristic Egyptian insignia. It may be dated *c.* the 12th cen. B.C. An illegible four-line inscription at the top appears to be proto-Sinaitic in style and may be much earlier. Another stone relief *c.* 40 inches high was found E of the Dead Sea in 1851. It depicts a warrior (?) clothed only in a short kilt and holding a spear (ANEP #177).

Bibliography. W. F. Albright, *The Archaeology of Palestine,* Baltimore: Penguin, 1960; *The Biblical Period from Abraham to Ezra,* New York: Harper & Row, 1963. Michael Avi-Yonah, ed., *A History of the Holy Land,* Toronto: Macmillan, 1969. CornPBE, pp. 528–532. Nelson Glueck, *The Other Side of the Jordan,* New Haven: ASOR, 1940; "Transjordan," TAOTS, pp. 445–450. William H. Morton, "Dibon," "Moab, Moabites," BW, pp. 200–202. 392–396. F. W. Winnett and W. L. Reed, *The Excavations of Dibon (Dhiban) in Moab,* AASOR, XXXVI–XXXVII, New Haven: ASOR, 1964. A. H. van Zyl, *The Moabites,* Leiden: Brill, 1960.

A.C.S.

MOABITE STONE (mō-*à*-bīt'). A black basalt stela, or memorial tablet, three feet ten inches high, two feet wide, and ten and a half inches thick, with a flat base but a rounded top. It was found at Dhiban (biblical Dibon) in Moab in 1868 by a German missionary, the Rev. F. A. Klein.

It was set up by Mesha (*q.v.*) the king of Moab toward the end of his reign (*c.* 830 B.C.), to celebrate his liberation of Moab from the Israelite yoke and his subsequent rebuilding of many cities in his land. Mesha states that Omri king of Israel had reduced Moab to a state of vassalage during the reign of Mesha's father, and that he, Mesha, successfully revolted against Israel and liberated Moab.

The Moabite Stone is the longest historical inscription of OT Palestine discovered thus far. It tells the Moabite side of the events recorded in II Kgs 3. For a translation of its 34 lines of text see ANET, pp. 320 f.

The Moabite Stone is also important because it forms a link in the study of the development of the alphabet and of Heb. paleography. Its language is closely akin to the Heb. of the OT. Fifteen of the place names mentioned by Mesha are to be found in the OT. It reveals something of the Moabite belief in their god Chemosh, and mentions Yahweh as the deity of Israel. *See* Moab; Dibon.

D. C. B.

The Moabite Stone. LM

MOABITESS (mō'ȧb-īt'ĕs), **MOABITISH** (mō'ȧb-īt'ĭsh). A person from Moab. Ruth was called "the Moabitess" (Ruth 1:22; 2:2; etc.). Some of Solomon's wives were called Moabites (I Kgs 11:1). The mother of Jehozabad who conspired with Zabad to kill Joash (II Chr 24:26) was a Moabitess. *See* Moab.

MOADIAH. *See* Maadiah.

MODERATION. The limitation of one's appetite, actions, or emotions. The word usually refers to being temperate, meaning that one does not go to excess even in normal habits such as eating. The word does not appear in the OT and only in the NT at Phil 4:5. The Gr. word is *epieikes* which means "mildness," "gentleness," "forbearance" (ASV, RSV), "moderation" (KJV). It expresses that considerateness that looks humanely and reasonably at the facts of a case.

MODERNISM. *See* Liberalism.

MOLADAH (mŏl'ȧ-dȧ). A town in the Negeb of Judah (Josh 15:26), mentioned among the settlements of Simeon (Josh 19:2; I Chr 4:28). It was also occupied during the Persian period (Neh 11:26). The usual identification had been with Tell el-Milḥ (now considered to be the site of Bronze Age Arad), 12 miles E of Beer-sheba. However, the Arab name was derived from Heb. *Malḥātâ*, which is preserved in the Gr. *Malatha* (Jos *Ant.* xviii.6.2) and *Malaatha* (Eusebius, Onom., 14:3; 88:4; 108:3). Khureibet el-Waṭen, five miles E of Beer-sheba, seems to be a translation of Moladah, "birthplace." Sherds of Iron Age and later have been found there, making its identification with Moladah possible.

MOLE. *See* Animals: Mole Rat, IV. 25.

MOLE RAT. *See* Animals, IV. 25.

MOLECH, MOLOCH. *See* Gods, False.

MOLID (mō'lĭd). A descendant of Jerahmeel, grandson of Phares, son of Judah (I Chr 2:25–29).

MOLLUSK, PURPLE. *See* Animals, V. 8.

MOLTEN IMAGE. *See* Calf, Golden; Imagery.

MOLTEN SEA. *See* Tabernacle: Laver.

MOMENT. *See* Time, Divisions of.

MONEY. *See* Weights, Measures, and Coins.

MONEY CHANGERS. The Jews of NT times, abhorring idolatry, could not use coins in religious service that had the head of a "divine" Caesar or other symbol of paganism. When it came to the payment of the yearly temple tax

(Mt 17:24 ff.), based by the rabbis on the census half-shekel of Ex 30:13, offices of exchange were opened in the towns in Adar (March) for ten days. Also at Passover money might be changed to Tyrian silver coins or Jewish copper coinage right in the temple. For Jews and proselytes from a distance it would be needed also to pay for sacrifices and offerings: lambs, bulls, wine, oil, salt, incense. For convenience, in Jesus' day, the sons of Annas, the former high priest, had sales in the outer court of the temple through which one passed to ascend toward the altar. The money changers normally charged perhaps 12 percent exchange for the proper coins. *See* Weights, Measures, and Coins.

A sesterce of Augustus. G. L. Archer; photo by W. LaSor

Mk 11:15 (parallel to Mt 21:12) calls these bankers by the Gr. term *kollubistai,* from *kollubos,* for "bit," "small coin," or "small fee." Jn 2:13-15 uses this word and another rarer term *kermatistai,* also from a word for "small coin" (*kerma*).

Early in His ministry the Lord Jesus, as Messiah and Prophet-Reformer, demanded the removal of such merchandising from His Father's house, and poured out the coins and upset the tables where the brokers sat (Jn 2:15). But the greedy merchants, under protection of ex-high priest Annas, came back. Therefore later in His ministry Jesus again cleared the place (Mk 11:15-16; Mt 21:12; Lk 19:45-46). The animals and supplies, the buying, the barter, the exchange could all be done elsewhere. It was far too distracting to have in a temple, where there must be no trader (Isa 56:7; Zech 14:21, RSV) who would hinder Gentiles from praying in their outer court. But also Christ evidently believed the money changers were demanding an excessive charge, for He accused them of making the temple a den of robbers (Mk 11:17; cf. Jer 7:11). The Mishna reports that on one occasion the profiteering on the sale of sacrificial doves drove the price up to an outrageous figure.

See Occupations: Banker.

W. G. B.

MONEY, LOVE OF. Gr. *philarguria,* lit., "the love of silver." Paul exhorts the Christian to be content with what he has because, first, he brought nothing into the world at birth and will take nothing away at death (I Tim 6:7 f.); second, riches bring many temptations. The love of money is a root or cause (not "the root") of all kinds of evil. The rich young ruler had this as his besetting sin and turned from Christ (Lk 18:23 f.). Judas Iscariot sold his Lord for "thirty pieces of silver" (Mt 26:15). Barnabas, in contrast, "having land, sold it, and brought the money, and laid it at the apostles' feet" (Acts 4:37). He took no chance that his wealth might become a snare. Scripture does not condemn the possession of wealth, but views the believer having wealth as a steward rather than owner of riches. He is to dispense what he has for the glory of God and with proper regard for the needs of others—both believers and unbelievers (I Tim 6:17-19; Gal 6:10; Phil 2:4).

R. A. K.

MONEY, PIECE OF. *See* Weights, Measures, and Coins.

MONKEY. *See* Animals: Peacock, III. 40.

MONSTERS. In Lam 4:3 the KJV translates *tannîn* as "sea monsters." The RSV translates "jackals": "Even the jackals give the breast. . . ." In Gen 1:21 (KJV) the word is translated "whales" and in the RSV, "sea monsters." *See* Animals, II.23; V.13.

MONTH. *See* Calendar; Festivals; Time, Divisions of.

MOON. At least 34 references are made to the moon in the OT and nine in the NT, with emphases on the cosmogonical, worshipful, and eschatological passages. The most common Heb. term is *yārēaḥ,* of which the meaning is obscure but it may come from the verb root *'rḥ,* "to travel, wander." The same word occurs in other Semitic languages, e.g., Akkad. *(w)arḫu,* Ugaritic *yrḫ,* and Phoenician *yrḥ.* In poetic passages *lᵉbānâ,* "white one," is used of the moon in Song 6:10; Isa 24:23; 30:26. The NT word *selēnē* occurs in Mt 24:29; Mk 13:24; Lk 21:25; Acts 2:20; I Cor 15:41; and in the Apocalypse.

Its cosmogonical usage. The moon is first mentioned in the Mosaic account of creation (Gen 1:14-16). It was formed as a part of the firmament on the fourth day with the purpose of illuminating the night and regulating the seasons. It appeared simultaneously with the sun, although independent of it, "for signs and for seasons, and for days and years." With the sun, it was to distribute light and to divide between day and night. It was considered to be inferior to the sun (Gen 1:16; Isa 30:26), and to be controlled by God in its functions (Ps 104:19; 136:9).

The Heb. calendar (*q.v.*), like that of most

A Kassite boundary stone, showing Melishipak presenting his daughter to the moon goddess Nanna. LM

ancient peoples, was based on the regular phases of the moon in its repeated circuit around the earth. Therefore the Heb. word for month, *yeraḥ*, is closely associated to *yārēaḥ*. The first day of each month, the "new moon," was set apart as a special day for worship and feasting (Num 10:10; 28:11-15; I Sam 20:5; II Kgs 4:23; Ps 81:3; Ezk 46:1, 3), and ordinary labor and commerce were suspended (Amos 8:5).

Its importance in worship. Moon worship was fairly common in the ancient Near East (cf. Job 31:26-27) and inevitably affected the Israelites. Pagan cults regarded the moon as a deity to whom sacrifices were made, e.g., called *yrḫ* at Ugarit (ANET, pp. 152, 155, Yarikh). Personal names with the name of the moon-god as one element appear in the Mari documents. The moon as Khonsu (ANEP, #563) received the reverence of all of Egypt, which may have necessitated the Mosaic warning to Israel against being drawn into moon worship (Deut 4:16-19; 17:3). In Mesopotamia the Sumerian moon-god Nanna, called Sin in Akkadian, was worshiped at Ur as the chief god of the city, and at Harran in Syria. The once widely accepted association of the Assyrian moon-god Sin with Sinai and the Wilderness of Sin is now disputed because of lack of any evidence of the use of that deity's name in Canaan or by Semitic nomads.

The city of Jericho (*y^{e}rîḥô*) was evidently named for the ancient Semitic moon-god. At Hazor (*q.v.*) in Galilee a small Canaanite shrine (*c.* 1300 B.C.) was discovered in 1955 which contained among other cultic objects a basalt stele depicting two hands lifted as in prayer to a crescent moon (BA, XIX [1956], 10-12).

Following the Mosaic injunction against moon worship, apparently the greatest OT violations had arisen by the times of Kings Manasseh and Josiah. Even in Isaiah's day the women wore crescent ornaments (Isa 3:18, NASB), probably associated in some way with moon worship (cf. Jud 8:21, 26). Manasseh actively promoted moon worship as part of worshiping "all the hosts of heaven" (II Kgs 21:3-5). This form of idolatry seems to have been practiced widely in Judah, although Josiah attempted to extinguish moon worship as a part of the short-term revival (II Kgs 23:5). But Jeremiah particularly made several references to the widespread influence (Jer 7:18; 8:2; 44:17), including picturing families cooperating in worship of and offerings to the moon. This may have included unusual rooftop ceremonies (Jer 19:13; Zeph 1:5).

Its eschatological importance. Generally the NT references to the moon, along with several from the OT, have futuristic meaning. Attention turns to the moon in connection with the return of Christ. The moon will be darkened (Isa 13:10; Mt 24:29; Mk 13:24) and will turn to blood (Joel 2:31; Rev 6:12), a reference to impending judgment. The moon of Rev 12:1 under the feet of the woman seemingly points to the future glory of Israel with the symbolism possibly following that of Joseph's dream in Gen 37. During the millennial reign of Christ, His glory will outstrip that of both the sun and moon (Isa 60:19-20).

J. Ma.

MOON, NEW. *See* Festivals.

MORALITY. *See* Example.

MORASTHITE (môr'ăs-thīt). A gentilic adjective to designate the prophet Micah (Mic 1:1; cf. Jer 26:18). Possibly derived from Moresheth-gath (*q.v.*), the town where Micah was born. *See* Micah.

MORDECAI (môr'dĕ-kī). The name (from Akkad. Marduk, god of Babylon) given to two biblical characters.

1. A leader among the exiles who returned from Babylonia to Jerusalem with Zerubbabel (Ezr 2:2; cf. Neh 7:7).

2. One of the Heb. exiles who occupied a position of high responsibility in the Persian

Empire, as told in the book of Esther. He was a Benjamite, the descendant of a certain Kish, who was deported to Babylonia along with Jeconiah in 597 B.C. (Est 2:5-6). He flourished during the reign of Ahasuerus or Xerxes I (*c.* 486–465 B.C.) and was perhaps 50 years of age at the time of the events recorded in the book of Esther, i.e., the "third year of his reign" or *c.* 483 B.C. (Est 1:3). (Some scholars read Est 2:5-6 as though the "who" of v. 6 refers to Mordecai in v. 5 rather than to Kish, and conclude that the story is fictional because Mordecai would have been about 150 years old!)

The account states that Mordecai had reared as his own daughter an orphan cousin named Hadassah or Esther (Est 2:20). He must have been a eunuch, for no mention is made of a wife or children of his own (2:7), and he had access to the harem or women's quarters (2:11). His influence over Esther continued after she became queen, implying his strong and virtuous character.

While Mordecai was watchman at the gate he overheard a plot to take the king's life. He reported the plot to Queen Esther and she relayed it to the king. The two would-be assassins were hanged, and the incident was recorded in the royal archives.

Mordecai's troubles began when one of the court officials by the name of Haman was promoted by the king. Mordecai refused to join the sycophants who bowed in reverence to this ego-maniac, perhaps because such an act could not be distinguished from worship. Haman's vanity would not tolerate this affront, and he determined to get rid not only of Mordecai but of all the other Jews as well. Haman succeeded in persuading the king to issue a decree for the massacre of all Jews throughout the provinces of the empire.

To attract attention to the plight of the Jews, Mordecai boldly put on sackcloth and publically lamented this decree. Through a messenger he urged Esther to intercede with the king for their people. When Esther indicated the dangers of such an unprecedented undertaking, Mordecai insisted that it was worth the risk. He pointed out that even Esther would not escape if she were too timid to intercede. His faith in divine providence is indicated in his statement that if Esther failed, deliverance would arise from some other source. He emphasized, however, that failure on her part to act courageously would bring her and her family into disgrace. He further challenged her with the thought that perhaps her selection as queen was to make possible this deliverance. In this message the reader gets his clearest insight into Mordecai's thought (Est 4:7-17).

While Haman was arranging for Mordecai's execution, the king, during a sleepless night, was reminded of Mordecai's unrewarded service of reporting the plot against the king's life (6:1-3). The public honors which Haman had assumed were intended for himself were then given to Mordecai by Haman at the king's request (6:10-12).

After Haman's death, on the special gallows prepared for Mordecai, the king gave to the latter the position held by Haman. In response to Esther's second request, the king authorized Mordecai to write letters in the king's name to all provinces authorizing the Jews to defend themselves. Thus began the day on the Jewish calendar known as Purim (lot), and Mordecai came to be second only to the king himself in authority (10:1-3).

See Esther; Esther, Book of.

An undated cuneiform document, found at Borsippa (near Babylon), mentions a Mardukâ who was a high official at Susa in the court of Xerxes I; his title, *sipîr,* indicates he was an influential counselor. Ctesias (xiii.51) lists three men who were important figures early in Xerxes' reign. Among them was Matakas who "was the most influential of the eunuchs." J. Stafford Wright argues that both these references may be equated with Mordecai ("The Historicity of the Book of Esther," NPOT, pp. 44 ff.). Mordecai is also a featured hero in the Apocrypha; in II Macc 15:36 the Feast of Purim is referred to as "Mordecai's Day."

G. A. T.

MOREH, HILL OF (môr'ĕ). Located at the E end of the Jezreel valley (also called valley of Esdraelon or valley of Armageddon; *see* Jezreel 4), 12 miles W of the Jordan River and five miles WSW of Mount Tabor in lower Galilee. The hill is mentioned in the Bible in connection with the Midianite encampment which stretched out into the valley to the W of the hill (Jud 6:33; cf. 7:1). Gideon's troops were mustered at 'Ain Harod (modern 'Ain Jalud) at the foot of Mount Gilboa, about five miles to the SE. Rising some 500 meters over the valley floor, the hill of Moreh occupied a strategic position over the link between the Jezreel valley and the valley of Beth-Shean (*q.v.*). Though not mentioned by name again, the hill did play a larger role in biblical history in that the villages of Endor (*q.v.*), Shunem (*q.v.*), and Nain (*q.v.*) were located on its slopes.

MOREH, OAK OF (môr'ĕ). As Abraham entered the land of Canaan, he stopped first at Shechem (Gen 12:6). It was there at the oak of Moreh (Heb. *'ēlôn môreh;* KJV "plain of Moreh" is incorrect) that the Lord began the unfolding of His covenant promise, and near it Abraham built his first altar. The site cannot be precisely identified, but must be regarded as in proximity to Shechem itself.

This oak, a terebinth which normally grows as a solitary tree, was already famous and probably sacred to the local Canaanites, for its name means "the teacher's oak." It probably was the same tree under which Jacob buried his family's idols (Gen 35:4). It is mentioned as a landmark in Deut 11:30. Under it Joshua made an open-air sanctuary with a stone to mark Israel's

The Dome of the Rock covers the traditional site of Moriah. HFV

renewal of their covenant with Yahweh (Josh 24:26), and there Abimelech was made king of Shechem (Jud 9:6; cf. also 9:37).

For the significance of the oak or terebinth in ancient Near Eastern culture *see* Plants: Oak.

P.W.F.

MORESHETH-GATH (môr′ĕ-shĕth-găth). The home of the prophet Micah (cf. Jer 26:18; Mic 1:1), one of the 8th cen. B.C. writing prophets. *See* Micah. The city is referred to in the pun-section of Micah (cf. Mic 1:14). Ancient Moresheth is identified with modern Tell ej-Judeideh, *c.* 20 miles SW of Jerusalem (*c.* two miles N of Beit Jibrin or Eleutheropolis). Gath may have been added to indicate that this was the Moresheth which is near Gath in the Shephelah.

Morasthite is the gentilic adjective of a shortened form of the name Moresheth. Pseudo-Epiphanius claims that Micah was buried in his home near the Anakite cemetery in the vicinity of Eleutheropolis.

MORIAH (mō-rī′*ȧ*). The term was applied to the *region* where Abraham offered Isaac (Gen 22:2) and to the *site* of Solomon's temple (II Chr 3:1). Some have challenged this identification because of textual variants at II Chr 3:1 and because of its short distance from Beer-sheba. However, with a loaded donkey Abraham could have taken three days to travel the 50 miles to Moriah (Gen 22:4). There are no rival claimants and no adequate reason to doubt that Mount Moriah (Gen 22:2), the Jebusite threshing floor (II Sam 24:16 ff.), and the site of Solomon's temple (II Chr 3:1) are practically identical. *See* Jerusalem.

MORNING. Eight different Heb. words are translated "morning" in the KJV of the OT. By far the most common (180 times) is *bōqer*, which means "the breaking forth of the light" or "the splitting or penetrating of the darkness." The second most frequently used word is *shaḥar*, which means "dawn." In the NT *prōi* and *prōia* both mean "early," but are translated "morning," or "in the morning," or even "early in the morning" (*prōi* twice). They normally refer to early dawn. *Orthros* is translated "early in the morning" in all three of its occurrences (Lk 24:1; Jn 8:2; Acts 5:21). The Orientals were normally early risers. *See* Time, Divisions of.

Figuratively, the "morning" may indicate the direction of E (Ps 139:9, "If I take my flight to the frontiers of the morning," NEB). The beauty of dawn is an apt simile for the beloved (Song 6:10), and its sudden and widespread appearance for the rapid invasion of a great army (Joel 2:2). "The eyelids of the morning" or dawn (Job 41:18), in the sense of the red glow surrounding the rising sun, describe the reddish eyes of the submerged crocodile appearing above the surface. The coming of the Lord is said to be as sure as the dawn (Hos 6:3, RSV).

R.E.

MORNING SACRIFICE. *See* Sacrifice.

MORNING WATCH. *See* Watch.

MORSEL. A piece of bread or loaf of small quantity (Gen 18:5; Jud 19:5; Ruth 2:14; I Sam 2:36; 28:22; I Kgs 17:11; *et al.*).

MORTAL, MORTALITY. Mortal has the connotation of "certain to die" (Job 4:17), and so is the opposite of immortality, which is without death. Mortality occurs only in the KJV in II Cor 5:4, translating the adjective *thnētos* ("mortal," "liable to death").

In Rom 6:12; 8:11; II Cor 4:11, where *thnētos* also occurs, translated "mortal," Paul connects the word with "body" and "flesh." In these passages the special situation of believers is in view. Regenerated and destined for glory, they are nevertheless still "in the flesh," in a body liable to death, decaying (II Cor 4:16), characterized by sinful practices and tendencies (Rom 6:8), humiliated and degraded (Phil 3:21). In spite of all this, the challenge and exhortation is to refuse to let sin reign as king, assured that this body will be made alive, has even now been released (Rom 6:8) so that it need no longer serve sin, and will be made like the glorified body of Christ.

In the Gr. text of I Cor 15:53–54 and II Cor 5:4, *thnētos* does not have an accompanying noun expressed which it would normally modify, but its appearing in the neuter gender would naturally suggest the neuter noun *soma* (body). In both passages it seems that resurrection from death is not in view but the instantaneous transformation of believers living at the parousia of Jesus Christ.

In I Cor 15 Paul treats of resurrection in a compact outline of eschatology (vv. 20–28). In v.50 an important reason for resurrection is announced: flesh and blood cannot inherit the kingdom of God. The dead must be raised incorruptible. Living believers must also be changed so as to "put on" incorruption and immortality (*see* Immortality). The special case of living believers is in view in I Cor 15:53–54; II Cor 5:4; I Thess 4:17. In the instantaneous transformation of the living is found the fulfillment of Isa 25:8: death is swallowed up in victory. As shown by the confirmatory parallel quoted from Hos 13:14, the meaning is that death has not had even a temporary victory: some have not been in the grave, but have been "swallowed up" in "[resurrection] life."

Yet it is not to be forgotten that another change must take place at the same time. Heb 12:23 speaks of the "spirits of just men made perfect," completely sanctified at death. These are the righteous dead who will rise from their graves first. At the moment of "swallowing up," this change also is to be experienced by those that are alive and remain to the parousia.

See Dead, The; Eschatology; Life.

W. B. W.

MORTAR

1. A hollowed-out stone (usually basalt) vessel in which wheat or some other substance is pounded with an implement called a pestle (*q.v.*). It is said the Israelites beat the manna in such a vessel (Num 11:8). A like process is alluded to in Prov 27:22. It has a beneficial result in the separating of the husk from the grain, but a fool will still cling to his folly even though "brayed [or beaten] in a mortar."

2. A substance used to fasten building materials such as stones or bricks together. This word is spelled morter in KJV but mortar in ASV. "Slime" or "bitumen" (ASV marg.) was used as mortar by the builders of the tower of Babel (Gen 11:3). The Heb. word *ḥōmer* literally refers to clay used for cement. Ex 1:14 mentions such mortar being used by the Israelites in their Egyptian bondage; and Nah 3:14 warns the Ninevites to use it in the rebuilding of their fortifications. Isa 41:25 prophesies that Cyrus shall "come upon princes as mortar," meaning that he will tread them underfoot, as clay seems to have been mixed with water in this way to prepare mortar.

Another Heb. word, *tāphēl,* is used several times in Ezk 13 and 22:28, being translated "untempered mortar." The reference is to the false prophets who soothingly predicted peace when the true man of God was warning of judgment soon to fall upon Jerusalem. One builds an unsound "wall" based on vain hopes and then the others smear it with "untempered mortar" (Ezk 13:10). Mortar here probably refers to a light coating of something like whitewash or stucco which would tend to conceal the structural defects of the wall. The Lord promises that He will break down this wall.

"Mortar" in Lev 14:42,45 represents the Heb. word *'āphār* for "dust," which is probably its true meaning in these verses as elsewhere.

G. C. L.

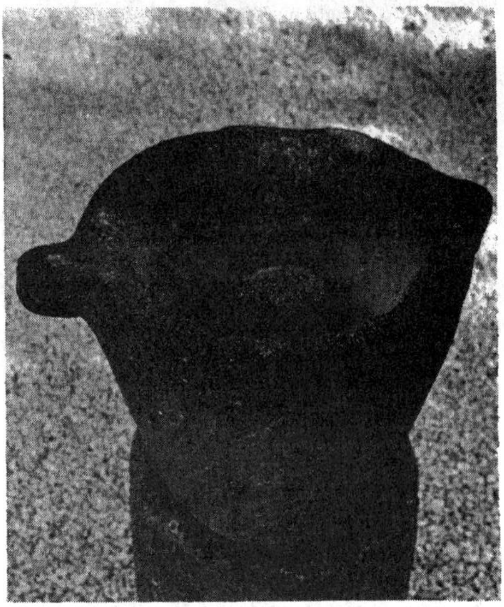

A mortar and pestle from Capernaum. HFV

MORTGAGE. A rendering of Heb. *'ārab,* "to take or give in pledge," "exchange," "to give a lien on real estate" (Neh 5:3; cf. Prov 17:18). The poor in Nehemiah's day as a last resort had temporarily mortgaged their lands and houses. Hearing that these had been signed over in order to be able to buy food and to secure money for "the king's tribute," Nehemiah demanded the nobles and local rulers to return the properties. He then called on the priests to witness their promises that they would correct the abuse (5:6–13). *See* Loan; Surety.

Infant Moses in Pharaoh's Palace painted by Bonifazio. MM

MORTIFICATION. The verb "mortify" occurs in the KJV of Rom 8:13 (Gr. *thanatoō*) and Col 3:5 (Gr. *nekroō*). The ASV, NASB, and NEB render Rom 8:13 as "put to death" or "putting to death." The ASV and NEB render Col 3:5 in the same manner. The NASB renders Col 3:5 "consider . . . as dead." The word "mortify" was used at one time with this meaning (e.g., "Christ was mortified and killed in dede, as touchynge to his fleshe," Erasmus, *Commune Crede,* 81), but this meaning is obsolete in modern English. The expression "put to death" renders the meaning of the Gr. words far better. Both Gr. words were used (as verbs or nouns) in the sense of physical death (e.g., Mt 8:22; 26:59; Mk 14:55).

In the two passages mentioned the usage is clearly metaphorical. In both passages the context goes to the heart of Paul's doctrine of the believer's union with Christ. What is true positionally, identification with Christ in death to the old life (cf. Rom 6:6–7; 7:4), is to be made actual, the believer himself responding to God's act and "putting to death" the deeds of the body. It is the breaking of cooperation with sin, a hostility toward it, a strong resistance to the evil desires which work in the body, and is accomplished in the power of the Holy Spirit (Rom 8:13; 6:11–13).

H. D. F.

MOSERA (mō-zē'rȧ). The stopping place between Beeroth Bene-jaakan and Gudgodah near where Aaron died and was buried (Deut 10:6–7). Mosera may be identified with the plural form Moseroth (Num 33:30–31). It was in the vicinity of Mount Hor (*q.v.*) where Aaron died, according to Num 20:25–28; 33:38; Deut 32:50.

MOSEROTH (mō-zē'rŏth). One of the stopping places of Israel in the wilderness after they had passed Sinai (Num 33:30–31). *See* Mosera.

MOSES (mō'zĕz). The great leader and lawgiver of the Hebrews, under whose hand God brought the Israelites from Egypt to the borders of the Promised Land. Moses was the greatest figure in the OT dispensation, for he was its human founder and as such was a type of Christ (cf. Heb 3:1–6).

The name. In Ex 2:10 a pun is made on the name of Moses. The child was so named because "I drew him out [m^e*shîtî-hû*] of the water." There is an exegetical question concerning the subject of who named Moses. If it was his mother, possibly the word is to be explained as related to *māshâ* ("to draw out"), the Semitic adaptation of an Egyptian form. On the other hand, most scholars think that Pharaoh's daughter named him and that the word is actually Egyptian, although there are philological difficulties in such a view.

The life. According to Ex 2:1 the parents of Moses were descendants of Levi, although we cannot tell how many generations intervened between Levi and Moses. The story of Moses' childhood is well-known. Defying the king's order to cast every male child into the river, the parents hid the baby Moses in an ark, a small basket of reeds that was caulked with pitch. *See* Ark of Bulrushes. Pharaoh's daughter, having come down to the river to bathe, saw the ark, and took compassion upon the infant. Moses' sister who was present arranged to have the child's mother care for him. Thus God graciously saved his life.

Concerning his life at the Egyptian court practically nothing is known, save that, according to Heb 11:24, Moses refused to be called the son of Pharaoh's daughter. We do know that he was raised in "all the wisdom of the Egyptians" (Acts 7:22). We know also that when he was grown he showed an interest in the welfare of his own people. Seeing an Egyptian smiting one of the Hebrews, Moses intervened and slew the Egyptian. On the second day, when Moses attempted to intervene in the dispute between two Hebrews, one of them reproached him and referred to the murder of the previous day. Moses realized that his deed was known and he fled into Midian, a district of Arabia. Pharaoh had heard of his action and sought to slay him.

At the same time Moses did not fear the king's wrath (Heb 11:27), but defied it. In Midian he helped the daughters of Reuel (Jethro) water their flocks and exhibited the nobility of his character in defending them from other shepherds. He married Zipporah, one of Jethro's daughters. Concerning his shepherd life in Midian little is told, for the purpose of Scripture is not so much to focus attention on the details of Moses' life as to show his place in the work of deliverance and in the carrying out of God's purposes.

In the wilderness God appeared to Moses in the burning bush, for the work of the covenant-God in redemption is surrounded with the miraculous. This event had all the characteristics of a true miracle; it was a work performed by the supernatural power of God in the external world. God caused the bush to burn so that Moses would see it. It seems to have been contrary to God's ordinary providential working, and so it fits the requirements of the term *niflaoth* ("wonders," those things which are distinct). Furthermore, the event was designed to be a sign. It pointed to the presence of God as a consuming fire revealing His presence with His people. It showed that He would deliver them from bondage and that He had not forgotten His promises to the patriarchs. *See* Burning Bush.

Moses was somewhat hesitant about returning to Egypt to meet Pharaoh, and in loving fashion God dealt with him, assuring him that He would be with him. He permitted Moses' brother Aaron to act as intermediary or prophet, declaring Moses' word—a message which God gave him—to Pharaoh.

The encounter with Pharaoh was extremely interesting. In the last analysis it amounted to a contest between Yahweh, the God of Israel, and the "divine" Pharaoh, a representative of the powers of darkness. At first Moses simply requested that the Israelites be permitted to make a short journey into the wilderness to worship their God. Because this was refused, God showed His signs and wonders to Pharaoh. The plagues were designed to convince the Egyptians and the Israelites that the God of Israel was the God of all power. The plagues culminated in the death of the firstborn of Pharaoh.

The account of the Exodus is told in a simple, straightforward manner. When the Israelites arrived at Sinai, God revealed that He had chosen them to be His people and gave them His holy and unchangeable law. Moses was to be a mediator between the nation and God. The Scriptures relate the journeyings of the Israelites until they came to the borders of Palestine, but Moses was not permitted to enter the land. He died and was buried in Mount Nebo, his grave being unknown. For historical setting and date of Moses' life *see* Egypt; Exodus, The.

The significance. The above sketch of Moses' life reveals the significance of this great man. His true greatness is brought out, however, in connection with an episode which took place after the Israelites had left Sinai. Miriam and Aaron had exhibited jealousy over the fact that God had given revelations to Moses. "Hath he not spoken also by us?" they asked (Num 12:2). Moses could not enter into a defense of himself because of the exalted position which he occupied in the divine economy. He had been humble in the high position into which he had been placed by God, so that to have engaged in a personal defense would have deflected attention from his position and drawn that attention to himself personally. For this reason the Lord intervened suddenly and made clear the proper relationship of Moses to Aaron and Miriam. To true prophets God made Himself known in dreams and visions, but to Moses, who was His servant and faithful in all His house, He spoke plainly and without the cloak of ambiguity.

The same thought is in Heb 3 where a comparison is made between Moses and Christ. In this passage it is clear that Moses was the most exalted man in the OT dispensation, and that this dispensation looked forward to fulfillment in Jesus Christ. Whereas Moses as a servant was faithful in all God's house, Christ as a Son is over that house. The OT is largely the account of the *Mosaic* dispensation. The prophets, therefore, and all others such as Miriam and Aaron, were under Moses. This is the reason the sin of Miriam and Aaron was so heinous. Miriam, who doubtless was the instigator, was punished with leprosy.

Moses, the man who occupied this exalted position in the divine economy of the OT, was a man of true greatness. He lived by faith in God (cf. Heb 11:27*b*), and possessed a deep concern for the honor of the God whom he served (cf. Num 14:13 ff.). This concern also manifested a genuine desire that the purpose of God should be fulfilled. A careful reading of Heb 11 shows that Moses realized he was a servant of God in the carrying out of His purposes of redemption. Moses was willing to be blotted out of God's book if only his people might be saved (Ex 32:32).

Only a man of such deep devotion could have served in Moses' several capacities. He showed himself to be a true leader of his people. Although he sinned, and at times exhibited weakness, nevertheless he stayed with his task until he had brought the people to the borders of the land of promise. At the time of their great defection in the incident of the golden calf, he vigorously asserted his leadership. The same was true in the rebellion of Korah, Dathan and Abiram (Num 16). Only a man of the greatness of Moses could have brought the nation out of Egypt to the Promised Land.

Moses was also a lawgiver, and in this respect he will always be remembered. "The law was given by Moses" (Jn 1:17). More was given to Israel than a code of laws such as the law-code of Hammurabi, for in reality Moses was the mediator of a covenant. A study of covenant treaties made by the ancient Hittites indicates that in giving the covenant to Israel, God employed a form that was well understood at the time, the so-called suzerainty treaty. Between this type of covenant and the covenant of Israel there are formal similarities. *See* Covenant.

However, as far as content is concerned, there is a profound difference. The Hittite suzerains imposed a set of conditions which their conquered peoples were to obey. Between the king and the people there was no particular love or affection. In the case of Israel, however, all was different. Israel was to hear God's voice and to obey it, for God was truly sovereign. Furthermore, God had manifested His love to Israel in choosing and in redeeming her. From among all the nations on the face of the earth Israel was the one God had elected. She was to be His peculiar people, and the closeness of her relationship to God was shown in that He redeemed her from the bondage of Egypt. Israel was not to render an obedience based upon force, but as a holy nation, indeed, as a kingdom of priests, was to serve her God out of love. To Israel God revealed Himself as Yahweh, the God of the covenant, the God of redemption. The man who was honored of God as the mediator of the covenant was Moses.

Moses and the Law (window of Abbey of Flairgny, Lorraine, 16th century). MM

Moses also showed his greatness in his literary productions. As the mediator of the covenant, the servant faithful in God's house, Moses was the author of the law, the five books which speak of the establishing of the theocracy. The question of Mosaic authorship, then, is fundamentally a theological one. These books of Moses stand apart from all other books of the OT as the product of the mind of that man whom God chose to mediate the covenant, the mind of the lawgiver.

This does not suggest that Moses composed these books out of whole cloth. Doubtless he employed written documents which had been handed down from early times; doubtless he employed his tremendous erudition, for he had been brought up in all the wisdom and learning of the Egyptians (Acts 7:22). Yet we must not forget that the five books of the law are Scripture and hence, in writing them, Moses served as a prophet who delivered God's words to the people. He was to be the pattern for all true prophets who followed, culminating in Jesus the Messiah (Deut 18:15, 18). As a writer of Scripture, he was under the superintendence of the Holy Spirit so that what he wrote was God-breathed (II Tim 3:16; II Pet 1:21). Thus the five books of Moses, whose human author was the servant of God, are also the Word of God.

Moses and the smiting of the rock. After the long journey through the wilderness, Moses was not permitted to enter the Promised Land. The reason given is that he smote the rock at Kadesh. This was an act of disobedience in which God was not given the glory. Smiting the rock was also an act of disbelief on the part of Moses. Here the great leader faltered; here he in effect renounced all that he had stood for, and exhibited disbelief in the word of God. For this reason he was not permitted to enter the land. This episode stands out as a dark blot on the record of the faithful and trusting servant of the covenant-God.

Bibliography. Oswald T. Allis, *God Spake by Moses,* Philadelphia: Presbyterian & Reformed Pub. Co., 1951; *The Five Books of Moses,* Philadelphia: Presbyterian & Reformed Pub. Co., 1943. Martin Buber, *Moses,* 2nd ed. rev., Heidelberg: Verlag Lambert Schneider, 1952. Jack Finegan, *Let My People Go,* New York: Harper & Row, 1963. Joachim Jeremias, "*Mōusēs,*" TDNT, IV, 848-873. Melvin G. Kyle, "Moses," ISBE, III, 2083-2091. F. B. Meyer, *Moses, the Servant of God,* Grand Rapids: Zondervan, 1953. Henry S. Noerdlinger, *Moses and Egypt,* Los Angeles: Univ. of So Calif. Press, 1956. Gerhard von Rad, *Moses,* London: Lutterworth Press, 1960. Edward J. Young, *An Introduction to the Old Testament,* Grand Rapids: Eerdmans, 1958, pp. 45–154.

E. J. Y.

MOSES, BOOKS OF. *See* Moses; Pentateuch.

MOSES, LAW OF. *See* Law of Moses.

MOST HIGH. The Heb. term *'elyôn* in the title *'El 'Elyôn,* "most lofty," "most high God," used of Yahweh as supreme in the OT (Gen 14:18; Ps 7:17; 9:2; Isa 14:14; etc.). According to the Ugaritic tablets the cognate name *'Aliyy* was given to Baal by the Canaanites (ANET, p. 148), and the term was used in the plural as a synonym for their gods. When Nebuchadnezzar used the Aram. *'illāy* in referring to the God of the Hebrews (Dan 3:26; 4:2, 17, 34), he was acknowledging Him as the greatest of all gods, although not necessarily as his own god. The Aram. word occurs also in Palmyrene and Nabataean inscriptions.

This was the highest title (Gr. *hypsistos,* "highest," "most exalted") given to God in the NT (Acts 7:48; 16:17; Heb 7:1). Jesus Christ is named the Son of the Most High (Mk 5:7; Lk 8:28), even as His conception resulted from "the power of the Most High" overshadowing Mary (Lk 1:35). The Greeks applied this term to Zeus, the supreme deity of their pantheon. *See* God, Names of.

MOST HOLY. *See* Holy.

MOTE. The word occurs in KJV only in Mt 7:3–5; Lk 6:41–42. The Gr. word *karphos,* which signifies "something withered or dried up," is rendered "splinter" or "speck" in some translations. The contrast intended by our Lord seems to be basically that between a small piece of straw, chaff, or wood such as a chip or splinter, and a beam or log. He warns against criticizing or attempting to correct a brother's insignificant fault or blemish when one has a much more glaring or serious one himself. If he does attempt to do so, Jesus says, he is not merely a hypocrite but in addition is unable to see clearly enough to help his brother.

MOTH. *See* Animals, IV. 26.

MOTHER. The Scripture gives a much higher position to women, especially mothers, than the religions of most Eastern lands. OT women sometimes held important positions, as did Miriam and Deborah. Father and mother were classed and honored together. Rebekah's advice seems to have carried more weight with her son Jacob than did Isaac's. The child who struck or cursed his father or mother was punished by death (Ex 21:15, 17). The last chapter of Proverbs pictures the honor and reverence accorded the faithful and virtuous mother. "Her children arise up, and call her blessed; her husband also, and he praiseth her" (Prov 31:28).

In the NT the same high standards were upheld. When Christ was born of the Virgin Mary who was overshadowed by the Holy Spirit, the place of motherhood was lifted even higher. Even the grandmother is sometimes mentioned. Paul in II Tim 1:5 calls to remembrance "the unfeigned faith that is in thee, which dwelt first in thy grandmother Lois, and thy mother Eunice; and I am persuaded that in thee also."

Jerusalem is referred to as "the mother of us all" (Gal 4:26), and the love of God is likened to that of a mother (Isa 66:12–13; cf. Mt 23:37).

Jesus refused to give Mary any higher place than that of other believers (Mt 12:46–50; cf. Jn 2:4), a fact which should be an important warning against the elevation of the Virgin Mary and mariolatry. Still, when suffering on the cross, He thought of His mother, and provided a home for her with John, the beloved disciple. "And from that hour that disciple took her unto his own home" (Jn 19:27).

In the Bible mother might refer to stepmother (Gen 37:10), grandmother (I Kgs 15:10), a female ancestress (Gen 3:20), or a benefactress (Jud 5:7).

See Family; Marriage; Parent; Woman.

L.A.L.

MOTIONS. A 16th cen. word frequently found to mean "spiritual or mental impulse or agitation" (HDB III, 451). In the NT it is found in Rom 7:5, where it means "motive or impulse." The Gr. word *pathēmata* used in this passage means "passions" or "desires" that lead to sins (cf. Gal 5:24).

MOTIVE. *See* Intention.

MOULDY. A term describing the dried out bread brought by the Gibeonite envoys to Joshua. In Josh 9:5, 12 the KJV, ASV, and RSV translate "mouldy," but the Heb. *niqqudîm* is better rendered "and has become crumbled" (NASB). The same Heb. word appears as "cracknels" in I Kgs 14:3, referring to hard biscuits or, perhaps, crumb cakes. *See* Bread.

MOUNT. *See* Mountain.

MOUNT EPHRAIM. *See* Ephraim.

MOUNT HOREB. *See* Horeb.

MOUNT OF BEATITUDES. The mountain plateau where Jesus preached the Sermon on the Mount has often been referred to as the Mount of Beatitudes. Delitzsch has called the Mount of Beatitudes the "Sinai of the New Testament." No one knows the exact location of this mountain. It was most likely somewhere N (or perhaps W) of Capernaum, in the Galilean highlands as distinct from the shore region. G. E. Wright and F. V. Filson state that none of the rival sites appear to be more than early guesses (*Westminster Historical Atlas to the Bible,* rev. ed., 1956, p. 94). Current Christian tradition has settled on a hill 368 feet higher than Capernaum a couple of miles to the NW. Here the Italian Franciscans have built a convent and chapel. There is an old tradition dating from about the time of the Crusades that identifies the Mount of Beatitudes with the Horns of Hattin W of Magdala. On the plain just below these horns (small peaks) the Crusaders suffered their decisive defeat at the hands of Saladin, the Saracen leader, in A.D. 1187.

D. R. S.

MOUNT OF CORRUPTION. *See* Corruption, Mount of.

MOUNT OF OLIVES. The term is sometimes applied to the four hills E of Jerusalem which form a ridge running in a N-S direction. Popularly, it refers only to the central pair of these hills directly E of the temple area. The northernmost of the four hills is Mount Scopus. The southernmost is S of the road to Jericho and is called the Mount of Offense. It was the place of houses and idol temples of Solomon's foreign wives (II Kgs 23:13), if they were not on Olivet proper.

The two central hills, with a slight dip between, have an elevation of 2,723 feet. Jerusalem's elevation is 2,550 feet. The climb up from the Kidron Valley takes one's breath and the buses grind slowly up in lowest gear. From the name of the hill it is inferred that the slopes were once wooded. Now they are rocky and eroded because of the deforestation of the two world wars with only a few trees on the W slope and fewer yet to the E. The Arabic name for the hills is Jebel ez-Zaitoun (Mount of Olives) and Jebel et-Tur. The Dead Sea is visible to the E and an imposing view of Jerusalem opens to the W.

On the northern of the two hills stands the Lutheran Augusta Victoria Hospital with its high tower for a landmark. On the S hill rises the tower of the Russian Church of the Ascension and other buildings marking the traditional site of Christ's departure. In the saddle between is the Galilee Convent. To the E, the road runs down to Bethany and to the Jericho road. On the W face are three old roads, possibly all of Roman times, on which Christ would have walked. The Church of Dominus Flevit (The Lord Wept) is halfway down the hill. The Church of All Nations, with a traditional Gethsemane rock and a garden of olive trees hoary with age, is near the bottom. Many famous churches have been built on the summit and the remains of some of these have been uncovered and identified.

The Mount of Olives is named in connection with David's flight from Absalom (II Sam 15:30) and in Zech 14:4, which speaks of the Lord's coming when the mount will split from E to W. It is referred to as a stage in the departure of God's presence from Jerusalem in Ezekiel's day (Ezk 11:23). In the NT it is mentioned as the favorite resort of Christ as He withdrew from Jerusalem. It was the start of His triumphal entry (Mt 21:1), the scene of His weeping over Jerusalem (Lk 19:37–41), His eschatological instruction (Mt 24–25), His agony in Gethsemane (Mt 26:30), and His ascension (Acts 1:9–12). It will be the mount of His return (Acts 1:11; cf. Zech 14:4). *See* Ascension; Gethsemane; Kidron.

R.L.H.

MOUNT OF THE AMALEKITES (ȧ-măl′ ĕ-kīts). Called "hill country of the Amalekites" in Jud 12:15 (RSV). The Amalekites are usually connected with the Negeb where Kadesh-barnea was located (Num 14:25), but appear from Jud 5:14 to have had a settlement in the hill country of Ephraim. *See* Amalekites.

The Mount of Olives seen through the facade of the Temple area. HFV

MOUNT OF THE CONGREGATION. *See* Congregation, Mount of the.

MOUNT OF THE VALLEY. A peculiar expression found in Josh 13:19. Apparently a prominent hill or elevation (Heb. *hār*) overlooking the Jordan or Dead Sea Valley (Heb. *'ēmeq*, the same term used in 13:27 for the Jordan Valley). On it was built the town of Zareth-shahar (*q.v.*), "Zereth of the dawn," a site which could catch the first rays of the rising sun.

MOUNT SEIR. *See* Seir, Mount.

MOUNT TABOR. *See* Tabor, Mount.

MOUNTAIN. Two Heb. terms and their Gr. equivalents are often translatd "mountain" in the KJV: *gib'â* (Gr. *bounos*) and *hār* (Gr. *oros*), best rendered "hill" and "mountain," respectively. The former refers to more gradual slopes and lesser elevations and applies to parts or the whole of the kind of terrain running N-S as the central ridge of Palestine. The latter usually describes the more severe, higher kind of elevated terrain and is used interchangeably for a single mountain, a mountain range, or even a mountainous area. *See* Hill, Hill Country; Palestine: II. A.5; B.1.*c*.

The frequent references to mountains and hills are both literal and figurative. God calls the entire land of Israel "My mountains" (Isa 14:25; 65:9). Mountains were often chosen as the place for worship or a divine revelation; e.g., Sinai (Ex 19:18-20; 24:9-18), Moriah (Gen 22:2), Zion (Ps 2:6; 48:1-2), Carmel (I Kgs 18:19-39). Heathen high places were frequently erected on open hilltops (Deut 12:2).

Mountains are a place to extend one's vision (Deut 3:27; cf. Lk 4:5). They influence rainfall and thus are related to productivity (Ps 29:3-9; Deut 33:15; Joel 3:18). They are symbols of permanence (Hab 3:6) and stability (Ps 30:7; 125:1-2; Isa 54:10). They are personified to give expression to human emotions: shuddering because of the terrible judgments of God (Ps 18:7; 97:5); rejoicing at the event of Israel's redemption (Ps 98:8; Isa 44:23; 49:13; 55:12); leaping in fear to escape God's wrath (Ps 29:6; 114:4, 6); being called to witness God's controversy with His people (Mic 6:2); etc.

Mountains are also symbols of calamities on life's journey (Jer 13:16) and humanly insurmountable obstacles (Zech 4:7; Mt 21:21). But these may be moved by faith, little though it be, placed in the Almighty God (Mt 17:20).

Bibliography. Werner Foerster, "*Oros*," TDNT, V, 475-487.

H. E. Fi.

MOUNTAIN OF THE AMORITES. A general term referring to the hilly or mountainous region inhabited by the Amorites in the time of Moses and Joshua (Deut 1:7, 19-20; cf. Num 13:29; Josh 10:6). The area is roughly that dominated by the five kings of the Amorite league of Josh 10:3-5. It must have included the mountains rising in the Negeb to the N of Kadesh-barnea (Deut 1:20) and all of the central ridge of Judah and Benjamin and perhaps southern Ephraim. *See* Amorites.

The Lebanon Mountains and Dog River. HFV

MOURN, MOURNING. The expression of grief, occasioned by calamity or tragic loss such as the death of a relative or friend, is as universal as death itself. In the Near East, violent weeping has always been a part of mourning, though it often accompanied any strong emotion, e.g., that of Joseph when he revealed his identity to his brothers (Gen 45:2, 14-15). Abraham lamented and wept because of the death of his wife Sarah (Gen 23:2). Jacob wept, believing the false report that Joseph had been killed (Gen 37:35), and later Joseph wept when Jacob died (Gen 50:1). David and his men wept when they learned of the death of Saul and Jonathan (II Sam 1:12). The widows of Joppa wept as they displayed the handwork of their deceased friend Dorcas (Acts 9:39). We cannot fail to be moved by the sympathy of Jesus, who wept at the death of Lazarus, sharing the sorrow of His friends (Jn 11:33-35). See also Ps 6:6-7; Lam 1:16; 3:48.

Often the mourning was loud and uncontrolled, with wailing, lamentation, and loud cries accompanying sobbing and shedding of tears (Gen 23:2; II Sam 1:12; 3:31-34; 11:26; 19:4). Professional mourners were hired to add to the volume of mourning (possibly Jer 9:17 ff.; Amos 5:16). Perhaps these were included among the true mourners at the house of Jairus, for when Jesus came "he saw a tumult, and people weeping and wailing loudly" (Mk 5:38, RSV), and Matthew mentions the flute players (Mt 9:23; cf. singers, II Chr 35:25) who quite certainly were engaged for this occasion.

Personal deprivation or neglect or abuse of one's person often characterized rites of mourning. Ornaments were put aside (Ex 33:4-6); mourners tore their clothing as a symbol of grief (Gen 37:34; II Sam 3:31). Frequently associated with the rending of garments was the putting on of sackcloth, which represented both grief and humility (I Kgs 21:27; Est 4:1; Jer 4:8). Dust or ashes were put upon the head (Josh 7:6; Lam 2:10; Ezk 27:30). The beard and the hair of the head were plucked (Ezr 9:3) or cut off (Isa 15:2; Jer 7:29). Fasting was observed (II Sam 1:12; Neh 1:4; Zech 7:5). Some mourning practices were expressly forbidden to Israel, probably because they were heathen rites. Israelites were not to cut themselves nor "make any baldness" on their foreheads for the dead (Lev 19:28; Deut 14:1). The rules for priests were particularly stringent (Lev 21:1-5, 10-12).

The literature of other lands of the Bible gives some concept of sorrow in Mesopotamia and Egypt. The Epic of Gilgamesh portrays the bitter mourning of the hero for his companion Enkidu, "crying bitterly like unto a wailing woman" (Tablet VIII, col. ii, line 3; see ANET, p. 87). In his sorrow he roamed over the desert and confessed that he was afraid of death (IX, i, 1-5; ANET, p. 88). He pulled out his hair and took off his beautiful garments and threw them down.

From Egypt the literary remains and the tomb scenes combine to present the depths of sorrow (e.g., ANEP, Nos. 634, 638). This is true especially because of the religious psychology of these people, who as perhaps no other people tried to escape the reality of death. Part of that attempt was to emphasize the present life; part was to try to make adequate preparation for death, including the depiction of proper funeral services on the tomb wall. Here grieving relatives are seen weeping copiously and gesturing wildly with their arms. Professional mourners exhibited grief with abandon. Women were especially demonstrative; they daubed their faces with mud; with garments torn, they wept and wailed, threw dirt upon their heads, waved their arms, and beat themselves upon their heads.Despite the ritual, the consciousness of loss and separation was inescapable and the poignant texts vividly convey this reality (Pierre Montet, *Everyday Life in Egypt in the Days of Rameses the Great,* New York: St. Martin's Press, 1958, pp. 322 f.; Herodotus, ii, 20, 85).

The time devoted to mourning varied; the longest mourning period mentioned in the Bible is the 70 days during which the Egyptians wept for Jacob (Gen 50:3), a period customary among the Egyptians. At the time of the burial of Jacob the Egyptians lamented at the threshing floor of Atad "with a very great and sorrowful lamentation," which impressed the Canaanites by its intensity. Here Joseph mourned for his father seven days (Gen 50:10-11). Thirty days of weeping were observed for Aaron (Num 20:29) and for Moses (Deut 34:8). The men of Jabesh-gilead fasted for seven days after cremating and then burying the remains of Saul and his sons (I Sam 31:13).

See Burial; Dead, The; Funeral; Tomb.

Bibliography. Gustav Stählin, "*Thrēneō,* etc.," TDNT, III, 148-155; "*Kopetos,* etc.," TDNT, III, 830-852.

C. E. D.

MOUSE. *See* Animals, IV. 27.

MOUTH. This physical organ, which most often expresses the intents of the heart, is used in a variety of ways. It is the organ for eating and drinking (Jud 7:6; I Sam 14:26-27; Prov 19:24). The earth and Sheol are pictured as having mouths (Gen 4:11; Isa 5:14). The word also refers to an opening (Josh 10:18, 22, 27).

However, the mouth is generally the organ of speech (Gen 45:12; Isa 9:17) and many idiomatic phrases are used of it. Heavy-mouthed means slow of speech (Ex 4:10) and smooth-mouthed signifies a flattering speech (Prov 26:28). To speak mouth-to-mouth means to speak in person (Num 12:8). "With one mouth" means with one voice or consent (Josh 9:2; I Kgs 22:13). To put words into one's mouth is to suggest what one shall say (Ex 4:15; II Sam 14:19). To lay the hand upon the mouth signifies to be silent (Jud 18:19; Job 21:5). To inquire at the mouth of the Lord is to consult Him (Josh 9:14). To set the mouth against the heavens means to speak arrogantly and blasphemously against God (Ps 73:9). For a being or thing to come out of the mouth of another signifies that it is the minister or servant of the other (Rev 16:13-14; 9:18-19; 11:4-5; 12:15). The term mouth is also used in the sense of mouthpiece (Ex 4:16; Jer 15:19). *See* Speech.

Bibliography. Konrad Weiss, "*Stoma,*" TDNT, VII, 692–701.

E. C. J.

MOWING. The crop resulting from mowing a field or meadow. The Heb. noun *gēz* (Ps 72:6; Amos 7:1) is also translated "fleece" in Deut 18:4 and Job 31:20, coming from the verb *gāzaz,* "to shear."

This activity which began the long anticipated harvest must be understood as hand cutting with a short sickle. This instrument was first made of pieces of sharp flint set in wood or bone (often the jawbone of an animal), later of bronze and iron. An act common to an agricultural people (Ps 72:6; 129:7; Amos 7:1; Jas 5:4), the figure of putting in the sickle was used as a picture of the beginning of judgment (Joel 3:13).

MOZA (mō'zá)

1. The second son of Caleb by his concubine Ephah (I Chr 2:46).

2. Son of Zimri, a descendant of Saul and Jonathan (I Chr 8:36-37; 9:42-43).

MOZAH (mō'zá). A town in Benjamin listed after Mizpah and Chephirah (Josh 18:26), probably represented by Khirbet Beit Mizzeh. The site is by the Arab village of Qaluniya, four and a half miles WNW of Jerusalem, near the modern highway to Tel Aviv. The name of Mozah (Heb. *m-ṣ-h*) was stamped on jar handles excavated at Jericho and Tell en-Nasbeh from the Iron Age, suggesting that a royal pottery was located there.

MUFFLER. An article of women's apparel the exact nature of which is not known. The Mishnah uses a cognate word to refer to a veil (ISBE, III, 2093). Evidently the muffler (KJV) or scarf (RSV) was costly and overly decorative (Isa 3:18–19). *See* Dress.

MULBERRY. *See* Plants.

MULE. *See* Animals, I. 12.

MUPPIM (mŭp'ĭm). A son of Benjamin, Jacob's youngest son (Gen 46:21) who went down to Egypt with Jacob. He is also called Shephupham (Num 26:39, ASV, RSV), Shuppim (I Chr 7:12, 15), and Shephuphan (I Chr 8:5). His family was afterward reckoned with the sons of Bela (I Chr 7:7, 12). *See* Shupham.

MURDER. The following observations cover the essential facts concerning the biblical teaching about murder.

1. A person who murders another must die because he has destroyed God's "image" in another man (Gen 9:6). Human government has the right to exact the death penalty (Num 35:33; Jn 19:10 f.; Rom 13:1–4).

2. Premeditated murder must be distinguished from the unintentional slaying of a man. This distinction involves three criteria of investigation: (*a*) a prior state of enmity (Num 35:20 f.; Deut 19:11–13); (*b*) a search for the intended victim (Num 35:20; Deut 19:11); (*c*) the use of a murderous instrument (Num 35:16–18). The murderer must have no provided refuge (Lev 24:17; Ex 21:12, 14), but the manslayer who kills another man unintentionally must flee to one of the cities of refuge provided for him (Ex 21:13; Num 35:9–15; Deut 19:1–13; Josh 20:1–9).

3. The killing of an enemy in war does not constitute murder. The sixth commandment (Ex 20:13) does not prohibit war. A nation has the right to defend itself against aggressors. God commanded Israel to fight righteous wars (Ex 17:8–16; Jud 6:33–40; I Sam 7:3–13). The Lord taught David how to fight (Ps 18:34; 144:1). The state has the right to use the sword (Rom 13:1–4).

4. The killing of a man in self-defense does not constitute murder (Gen 4:23 f.; II Sam 2:19–23). Even an ethnic group may defend itself (Est 9:1–10). There is no guilt in killing an intruder at night, but there is guilt when he is killed after sunrise (Ex 22:2 f.).

5. A man is a murderer when his animal, known to be vicious, kills a person (Ex 21:29). However, the death penalty may be commuted by the payment of a fine (Ex 21:30–32).

6. A murderer's guilt does not involve his children (Deut 24:16; II Kgs 14:6; Jer 31:29–30) unless they knowingly and willingly participate in the same crime (Josh 7:24 f.; Est 9:7–10; Mt 23:34–36; 27:25).

7. A nation can become guilty of corporate murder. The death of Jesus Christ at the hands of the Jewish leaders made the Jewish people "murderers" (Acts 7:52; cf. Acts 2:23, 36; 3:15; 5:28). This guilt is sometimes recognized (Mt 27:25); at other times providential circumstances bring it to a nation's attention (II Sam 21:1–14).

8. Satan is the original murderer (Jn 8:44). Man's kinship with Satan makes every man who possesses a spirit of hatred an actual (I Jn 3:15) or a potential murderer (Mt 5:21 f.). Such murderers have no place in God's kingdom either now (Gal 5:20 f.) or hereafter (Rev 21:8). *See* Crime and Punishment.

W. B.

MURMUR. The English verb "to murmur" translates several Heb. and Gr. words (*gogguzō, diagogguzō, embrimaomai;* also a Gr. noun, *goggusmos*). In general the words mean to grumble or mutter in subdued, perhaps semi-articulated, speech. Involved in the murmuring may be such elements as discontent, complaint, dissatisfaction, disagreement, anger, opposition, and rebellion. Though this is not always the case (cf. Acts 6:1), God is usually the object of the murmuring that is mentioned in Scripture. For instance, in Ex 15–17 and Num 14; 16–17 the discontented Israelites murmured against God as they traversed the wilderness; indeed, they murmured against Moses and Aaron also, but God regarded this murmuring against His servants as being in reality directed against Himself (cf. Ex 16:2, 7–8; Num 14:2, 27).

The attitudes and actions of murmurers are a manifestation of a corresponding type of unbecoming character; e.g., the complaining and rebellion of the Israelites in the wilderness, the self-righteousness of the scribes and Pharisees, the unbelief of the remaining Jews who rejected Christ's teachings and claims, the resentment of the hired men in Christ's parable who objected to the householder's generosity to others, and the ungodliness of the apostates in Jude's epistle. Further, it was the first threat to the unity of the early church, an actual division being avoided by the appointment of the seven deacons to administer goods to widows in an equitable way (Acts 6:1–6). Obviously murmuring is completely out of character for the people of God. Indeed, Paul twice warns believers of this pitfall—don't murmur as the Israelites did (I Cor 10:10) and do all things without murmurings (Phil 2:14).

Bibliography. K. H. Rengstorf, "*Gogguzō*, etc.," TDNT, I, 728–737.

S. N. G.

MURRAIN. *See* Diseases.

MUSE. Heb. *śîaḥ* means "to talk or speak" (Job 12:8; Prov 6:22), and "to talk to oneself," "complain," "commune" (Ps 77:3-6); "to meditate" (Gen 24:63; Ps 119:15; 145:5, RSV). It is translated "muse" in Ps 143:5. Another word, from Heb. *hāgâ*, is translated "musing" (KJV) or "mused" (RSV) in Ps 39:3. *See* Meditation.

MUSHI (mo͞o'shī), **MUSHITES** (mo͞o'shīts). A son of Merari, son of Levi (Ex 6:19; Num 3:20; *et al.*). His descendants were called Mushites (Num 3:33; etc.).

MUSIC

History of Music

Music is as old as the human race, and from the earliest days it has been employed in the service of religion. The Israelites regarded music as a proper vehicle for the expression of the gratitude and devotion which they felt to God. They were not, however, the only people who used music in worship. Among the most ancient extant specimens of heathen literature, particularly those in the primitive Sumerian language, there are hymns in praise of the gods.

The origin of vocal music is not known, but according to the Pentateuch instrumental music had its origin with Jubal, one of the three sons of Lamech (Gen 4:21). It is clear from the words of Laban, Jacob's father-in-law (Gen 31:27), that instruments of various kinds were in common use at an early date among the ancient peoples who lived beyond the Euphrates and from whom the Heb. nation came. With their instrumental music these peoples combined singing and dancing. *See* Dance; Games.

The Heb. people put an emphasis on music above the other arts. Besides poetry, it is the only art which they developed to a high degree. Throughout their history they emphasized the importance of music, especially in their worship. Most of their poetry was cast in the form of sacred lyrics or psalms.

While the Pentateuch does not specifically mention sacred singers or musicians in connection with the general instruction for the sacrifices and festivals of the tabernacle, the Lord did command Moses to have two silver trumpets made which should be used for the calling of the assembly together and for sounding alarms (Num 10:1 ff.). The use of instruments was nothing new, nor was the use of sacred song, for it is evident that the Israelites had barely stepped on the far shores of the Red Sea when Moses and Miriam led the people in a triumphant song of praise to God. The beautiful hymn which was sung on that occasion (Ex 15) was not the work of a novice, nor was it a primitive expression of a people to whom sacred music was a still undeveloped art. It indicates a skill which could have been reached only through many years of cultural development.

As the Israelites established their national home in Canaan, their customs and traditions in worship became more pervasive. With the erection of the temple, music took a firm position as an integral part of the worship of Yahweh, the God of Israel. More and more attention was given to perfection of performance, and elaborate preparations were made for the impressive worship ceremonies which occurred frequently during the year. *See* Worship.

What has been called by Delitzsch the "golden age of Hebrew music" was the period from Samuel through Solomon. During this time, King David contributed more than any other individual to raising music to its exalted position in the national life. David was born both a musician and a poet. His was a genius, the like of which the world has never known. To his natural gifts he added a deep devotion to the Lord, and when he became king he brought music to the highest place of honor in the service of worship (I Chr 15:16-28; 25; Neh 12:24). David was also an inventor of musical instruments (I Chr 23:5; Neh 12:36).

Our knowledge of the nature of Heb. music is so meager that it is impossible to arrive at any satisfactory conclusions about it. Whether the Israelites ever possessed a system of musical notation is not known. It is probable that they did not. Those scholars who have attempted to construct a note system from the accents of Heb. poetry have failed to add anything to our knowledge of Heb. notation. We know nothing about their scales nor their intervals. The method by which they tuned their instruments, and the pitches to which they were tuned are unknown.

To assume, however, as some have done, that because we have no knowledge of the tonal system of the Hebrews, it was therefore extremely rude and unrefined is to make a serious error. Music which had not advanced beyond a monotonous rudimentary stage could hardly have had such remarkable effects as Heb. music had, for example, in restoring tranquility to the troubled mind of Saul.

But there are certain characteristics of Heb. music about which we are quite sure. It was played or sung in unison. The theories of harmony and counterpoint were unknown to the nations of antiquity. For musical effect, Heb. musicians depended not only upon their melodies, but also upon the contrasts in tone quality afforded by the different singers (men, boys, women) and by the various instruments.

Israel specialized in choral music, and from the earliest days it was sung antiphonally. The first recorded illustration of this style of singing is that of Miriam and the women of Israel singing responsively to Moses and the men (Ex 15). Antiphonal singing is also clearly indicated in many of the psalms (e.g., Ps 107 and 136). It was used at the dedication of the new walls of Jerusalem when, under the direction of Jezrahiah, the singers were placed in two great companies or choirs in the house of God and sang loudly (Neh 12:31, 40-42). This type of singing, with appropriate orchestral accompaniment, would provide the variety required to make the unisonal music moving and beautiful. It is quite probable that the word "selah," occurring so often in the Psalms, was used to indicate an orchestral interlude in the choral singing. At such times there may also have been a change of key, although this is uncertain. *See* Singer; Song.

Musical Instruments

Heb. musical instruments may be divided into three groups: strings, wind instruments, and percussion.

Strings. Perhaps the most numerous and most important in the OT were the stringed instruments. The common name in Heb. is *n^{e}gînôth* (from a root *nāgan,* "to touch or strike"), but there was a great variety of species of stringed instruments. The two principal groups were the harp or lyre (Heb. *kinnôr),* and the psaltery or lute (Heb. *nēbel*).

The harp was the instrument invented by Jubal and referred to by Laban (Gen 4:21; 31:27). It was used by the sons of the prophets in their schools (I Sam 10:5). The *kinnôr,* having from three to 12 strings either strummed with the fingers or with a plectrum, was the instrument of which David was a master and upon which he played with such telling effect (I Sam 16:16, 23). Whether this instrument was a true harp with the strings free on both sides, or a kind of lyre with strings which were in part carried over a sounding board and therefore played from only one side, is not known. It makes little difference, for the lyre is only a modification of the harp, and the name may have been used for both types of instruments.

There were small harps for individual use. These were light and portable and were played while carried. Larger harps, used often in ensemble for the temple service, were intended to stand on the ground when played. These yielded a much more powerful tone. The numerous illustrations of harps found on Egyptian and Assyrian monuments, and the actual instruments in Egyptian tombs, make it clear that the harps of the ancient nations were exceedingly varied in their size, style, and power.

The LXX often translates *kinnôr* by Gr. *kithara,* the cithara, with ten to 20 strings, which closely resemble a harp or lyre. The Gr. *lyra,* as known from ancient Gr. vase paintings, consisted of a horseshoe-shaped frame with a bar across the open end to hold its five or more strings. The *kithara* is uniformly translated "harp" in its NT occurrences (I Cor 14:7; Rev 5:8; 14:2; 15:2).

The psaltery is difficult to identify exactly. Some have insisted that it was a lute; others are equally convinced that it was a dulcimer. The best evidence seems to point to its being an instrument quite similar to the harp. Josephus says that it had 12 strings, but mention is made in Ps 33:2 and Ps 144:9 of a variety which had only ten strings. In ancient times the strings were made from the small intestines of a sheep or other animal. The strings were played by plucking (Isa 23:16, NASB), never with a bow.

Some Heb. words have been considered by

Ancient Egyptian harps and flute. BM

Orpheus and the Beasts, mosaic from Tarsus, 3rd century A.D. HFV

certain scholars to be names of musical instruments; e.g., *gittît, māḥălat,* and *ʿălāmôt.* These words are found in the titles of psalms (e.g., Ps 81; 53; 46, respectively) and other places in the OT. It is generally agreed that they were not actually instruments, but either designations of well-known tunes or else keys in which the songs were to be sung.

Dan 3:5, 7 gives a list of musical instruments with their Aramaic names. Some of these are stringed instruments. The *qaythrôs* (KJV "harp") was either a zither or the same as the Heb. *kinnôr.* The Aram. *p^{e}santērîn* (KJV "psaltery") was in all probability the same as the Heb. *nēbel,* but perhaps more like a dulcimer. A third stringed instrument in the list is the "trigon," Aram. *sabb^{e}ka',* wrongly translated "sackbut" (a wind instrument) in the KJV; instead it was an instrument of triangular shape with the strings carried over a bridge. This distinguishes it from the dulcimer, which had no bridge for its strings. The dulcimer, however, was the more common instrument in the ancient countries of the Near East.

All the stringed instruments were used to accompany vocal music (I Kgs 10:12). They also were played both in orchestral combinations and as solo instruments. The strings were especially popular because only upon them and the flutes could melodic lines be played. Such instruments often provided music at banquets (Isa 5:12; Amos 6:4-5). Their sound was associated with joy and rejoicing (Isa 24:8; II Chr 20:27-28). When the Hebrews were in captivity in Babylon, they refused the request of their captors to play their harps but in their sorrow hung them on the willows (Ps 137:1-4).

Wind instruments. These were divided into two general classes: the pipes or flutes, and the trumpets. The Heb. word translated "pipe" in Gen 4:21 (RSV, NASB; KJV "organ"), which also appears in Job 21:12; 30:31; Ps 150:4, is the word *ʿûgāb,* undoubtedly a general term for instruments of the flute variety. Specific instruments of this kind were the *ḥālîl,* possibly a primitive clarinet (I Sam 10:5; I Kgs 1:40; Isa 5:12; 30:29), capable of producing plaintive tones (Jer 48:36); the *mashrôqîtā* (KJV "flute") found in Dan 3:5 which may have been a type of woodwind; and the *sûmpōnyāh* (KJV "dulcimer" is incorrect), also found in Dan 3:5, which was possibly a bagpipe (NASB). The Gr. *aulos,* mentioned in I Cor 14:7 as a "pipe" (KJV) or "flute" (RSV), was similar to the *ḥālîl.*

Flutes were made from wood, bone, cane, and ivory. They were sometimes single and sometimes had double pipes with a single mouthpiece. They were exceedingly popular instruments, partly because they were easy to make. They were used not only in the worship of the Lord, but also for domestic enjoyment (Mt 11:17; Lk 7:32). At funerals the "minstrels" (KJV) or "flute players" (RSV) rendered accompaniment to the customary wailing women (Mt 9:23; cf. Jer 9:17).

Of almost equal antiquity to the flutes were the trumpets or horns with curved-up ends (Heb. *yôbēl* and *shôphār*). In Josh 6:4–5 the two expressions *shôphār hayyôbēl* and *qeren hayyôbēl* are used interchangeably, showing that they refer to the same instrument. The *qeren* was the natural horn of the wild ox, goat (Dan 8:5), or ram (Gen 22:13). The *yôbēl* (Ex 19:13) was a horn specifically from a ram. The word *shôphār* also originally meant the curved horn of a ram or ibex, but in the OT always refers to a musical instrument. Its chief use was in warfare, to give an alarm or signal (Jud 7:8, 16; Job 39:24-25; Hos 8:1). Four times it is translated "cornet" in the KJV. At first the *shôphār* was made from the horn of an animal, but later was imitated in various metals, especially bronze or brass. These instruments had a beautiful, clear tone and were used to announce special events such as the beginning of the year of jubilee (Lev 25:9).

A scene from the tomb of Nakht, an official under Pharaoh Thutmose IV, (*c.* 1450 B.C.), showing a harp, a double flute and a lutelike instrument. LL

There were also the long, straight trumpets with flaring ends (Heb. *ḥăṣoṣerôt*). When they appear with the *shôphār,* the latter is translated "cornet" (KJV) or "horn" (RSV, NASB) to distinguish it (I Chr 15:28; II Chr 15:14; Ps 98:6; Hos 5:8). These instruments were always made of metal. Those which Moses made for the priests were of beaten silver (Num 10:2). *See* Horn.

At first trumpets were used only on special days of solemn sacrifice, but during the time of David and Solomon their use was greatly enlarged. At the dedication of Solomon's temple, at least 120 priests blew upon these trumpets during the time of sacrifice (II Chr 5:12; 7:6).

The trumpet (Gr. *salpigx*) referred to in the NT was most likely the *shôphār,* since it always appears in a martial or apocalyptic rather than a liturgical setting. RSV and NASB translate it "bugle" in I Cor 14:8 (G. Friedrich, "*Salpigx,* etc.," TDNT, VII, 71–88).

Bacchic dancers with cymbals on a mosaic from Seleucia, port of Antioch of Syria. Antioch Museum

Percussion. The Israelites used three principal types of percussion instruments. The first was the timbrel, tabret, or tambourine (Heb. *tōph*), which was a circle of wood covered with a tight piece of skin, behind which some thin metal disks or bells were hung loosely. The Arabs today have an instrument they call the *doff* which is of exactly the same nature. In Heb. society this instrument was chiefly played by the women and was used to mark the time in dancing or in solemn processions (Ex 15:20; Jud 11:34; I Sam 18:6; Jer 31:4; Ps 150:4; *et al.*). The Egyptians and Assyrians had drums which more nearly correspond to the drums in use in the Western world today. These may have been used by the Hebrews as well, but there is no specific proof that they were. The *tōph* is the only drumlike instrument known to have been in common use.

The second type of percussion instrument was the pair of bronze or silver cymbals (Heb. *ṣelṣelîm* or *meṣiltayim*). The name is found only in the plural or dual form, which indicates that the instrument consisted of more than one part. In Assyrian art two kinds are depicted: the large metal disks held horizontally, familiar to us; and the smaller conical-shaped cups, each with a stick handle, held vertically.

Cymbals are first mentioned in II Sam 6:5. Some other references to them are in I Chr 15:16, 19; 16:5; Ps 150:5. The latter passage indicates that there may have been two kinds, larger louder ones and smaller higher-pitched ones. They were probably used to beat time for the Levitical choir.

The artistic representations of ancient Egyptian cymbals which have been discovered on the monuments and in tomb paintings indicate that they were very similar to modern cymbals. In addition to the bronze gong known in rabbinic literature, Paul makes reference to the cymbal in I Cor 13:1. The KJV translation here is unfortunate, for he actually referred to clanging or clashing cymbals, rather than to tinkling ones. The word "clashing" gives an idea of their resounding tone quality which was more noisy than expressive.

The third percussion instrument which the Hebrews used was the sistra (Heb. *mena'an'îm*), mentioned only once in the Scripture (II Sam 6:5). It was apparently an oval or U-shaped instrument of agitation 16 or 18 inches long. It consisted of a handle attached to a loop-shaped metal frame through which two or three loose cross-rods were passed with movable rings made of the same metal as the instrument. When the instrument was shaken, these rings produced a piercing, jingling noise. The KJV translation "cornet" is inaccurate as a designation for this instrument. While the RSV and NASB rendering of "castanets" is closer, it is not exactly correct either.

A sistra or sistrum from ancient Egypt. BM

Music in the New Testament

There is no record in the NT of the use of instruments in the musical worship of the Christian church. In this regard, early believers followed the practice of Heb. synagogue music. Singing the praise of God continued to be a prominent part of every worship service. Jesus Himself sang a hymn (the Hallel—Ps 113–118) with His disciples at the close of the first communion service.

The apostle Paul, writing by inspiration of the Holy Spirit, urged the Christians to admonish each other "with psalms and hymns and

The Odeion or music hall at Ephesus, capable of seating an audience of about 1,500. HFV

spiritual songs, singing with grace in [their] hearts to the Lord" (Col 3:16). It has been suggested that these three categories of song were directed to each of the members of the Trinity. "Psalms" were OT odes; "hymns" were new expressions of faith in Christ, many of which can be found in the epistles; and "spiritual songs" were possibly ecstatic songs in unknown languages, improvised in the worship experience, and thus related to the singing in tongues or in the Spirit (I Cor 14:15).

Bibliography. CornPBE, pp. 537–542. Curt Sachs, *The History of Musical Instruments,* New York: W. W. Norton, 1940. O. R. Sellers, "Musical Instruments of Israel," BA, IV, Sept., 1941. Howard F. Vos, "The Music of Israel," BS, Oct.–Dec., 1949, and Jan.–Mar., 1950. Eric Werner, "Music," IDB, III, 457–469; "Musical Instruments," IDB, III, 469–476.

R. G. R.

MUSICIAN. *See* Occupations: Musician; Music; Minstrel.

MUSTARD. *See* Plants.

MUSTER GATE. *See* Jerusalem: Gates and Towers; Miphkad.

MUTTER. The Heb. word is used of a lion growling over his prey (Isa 31:4), of low thunder (Job 37:4), of the mutter of enchanters, etc. Only the context can give the word the meaning of "mutter." Isa 59:3 is perhaps better translated "murmur." In Isa 8:19 *hāgâh* describes the tone of voice used by the necromancers in uttering their formulations: "Who chirp and mutter" (RSV). It was probably a subdued, restrained tone of voice. *See* Magic; Necromancer; Wizard.

MUZZLE. The humanitarian provision of Deut 25:4 prohibits muzzling an ox threshing grain. The apostle Paul used the analogy in referring to the support of the ministry (I Cor 9:9; I Tim 5:18). Note NT figurative uses of terms for "muzzle" meaning silencing or being silent; e.g., Mt 22:12; Mk 4:39; I Pet 2:15, and Ezk 39:11 (KJV "stop").

MYRA (mī'rȧ). A city in Lycia on the S coast of Asia Minor, where Paul transferred to a grain ship from Alexandria on his voyage to Rome (Acts 27:5). Myra was located two miles from the sea on a navigable river. A large theater, 360 feet in diameter, and beautiful tombs mark its site today. In Paul's day its port (now called Andriaki) was an important stop for Egyptian grain ships that sometimes sailed directly to Myra before July 20, that is, before the westerly winds became northwesterly. Myra is inserted into the text by Codex Beza at Acts 21:1; it is omitted entirely by the Vulgate.

MYRRH. *See* Incense; Plants: Myrrh.

MYRTLE. *See* Plants.

MYSIA (mĭsh'ĭ-ȧ). A district of NW Asia Minor. Its borders never clearly defined, Mysia was mountainous and heavily forested. In 133 B.C. it became part of the Roman province of Asia and included such cities as Troas (*q.v.*), Assos and Pergamum. The name occurs only in Acts 16:7–8 in the Bible.

MYSTERY. This significant term (Gr. *mystērion*) appears 27 times in the NT, 20 uses of which are Pauline. Considerable debate exists concerning its background, with some arguing for a pagan and others for a Jewish source. It would seem, however, that both influences can be seen in the NT usage of the word. In the mystery religions the term described the esoteric teachings revealed only to those initiated into the cult.

While the word "mystery" does not appear in the English OT, the related word "secret" (Heb. *sôd;* Aram. *rāz*) occurs a number of times, and *mystērion* is used in the LXX of Dan 2:18–19, 27–30, 47. The OT concept of the secret is that of the counsels of God which He reveals to His people. The Pseudepigrapha and the Qumran literature add the ideas of cosmic mysteries and mysteries of evil, which likewise can only be known by divine revelation.

From this varied background springs the NT concept of the "mystery" as a divine truth, formerly hidden but now supernaturally revealed to men, which can be fully understood only by the saved individual through the illumination of the Holy Spirit. The NT uses the term to refer to the gospel, sometimes in its most comprehensive sense including God's age-long redemptive plan (Rom 16:25–26; I Cor 2:7; 4:1; Eph 1:9–10; 6:19; Col 1:26–27; 4:3; I Tim 3:9; Rev 10:7). It is also applied to specific aspects of the gospel: the incarnation (Col 2:2,9; I Tim 3:16); the Church as the Body of Christ including both Jew and Gentile (Eph

3:3–6, 9; 5:32); characteristics of the present spiritual kingdom (Mt 13:11; Mk 4:11; Lk 8:10); the temporary blindness of Israel (Rom 11:25); and the believer's transformation at Christ's return (I Cor 15:51). The term is also used to refer to any hidden truth which must be supernaturally understood (I Cor 13:2; 14:2), to truth symbolically portrayed (Rev 1:20; 17:5,7), and to the as yet unrevealed mystery of the influence of Antichrist (II Thess 2:7).

Bibliography. Raymond E. Brown, *The Semitic Background of the Term "Mystery" in the New Testament,* Philadelphia: Fortress Press, 1968. G. Bornkamm, "*Mystērion,*" TDNT, IV, 802–827.

D. W. B.

MYTH, MYTHOLOGY. The Gr. word *mythos* occurs five times in the KJV of the NT, translated as "fable" (I Tim 1:4; 4:7; II Tim 4:4; Tit 1:14; II Pet 1:16). *See* Fable. In koiné as well as in classical Gr. the term signifies that which is fictitious, as opposed to the term *logos,* which connotes what is true and historical. In modern parlance mythology is the folklore of pagan tribes and nations which has been handed down from generation to generation. "A story, the origin of which is forgotten, ostensibly historical but usually such as to explain some practice, belief, institution, or natural phenomenon" (Webster, 5th ed.). The most extensive mythology is that found in the Graeco-Roman stories of heathen gods and goddesses.

It is now known that much of early Gr. myth and ritual had its roots in the still earlier mythology of the Near East as rediscovered in Mesopotamian, Egyptian, Hittite, and Canaanite literature. Several references to mythological motifs are to be found in the OT, used as illustrative material in poetic passages (e.g., Yahweh's primordial battle with a monster variously termed Leviathan, Ps 74:14; Rahab, Job 26:12, RSV; Isa 51:9; Tannin—i.e., "dragon," Ps 74:13; or Yam—i.e., "sea," Hab 3:8). Because of these occurrences the question must be asked if myth is ever used in Scripture as a straightforward means of conveying truth in a non-poetic passage.

In contemporary theological discussion the term myth has achieved special prominence, largely because of Rudolf Bultmann's demand for the "demythologization" of the NT. On the one hand, in the writings of Bultmann the mythical refers to that which is miraculous or supernatural. In another sense a myth is a literary device or symbolism by which eternal truth or revelation from God has been expressed in terms understandable to man. Some neo-orthodox theologians confine it to the revelation given in the Bible (Barth, Brunner); others extend it to cover progressive revelation in and through all religions (Tillich).

Theories of the Origin of Myth

1. Neoorthodox scholars maintain that eter-

Ruins of the hall of initiation of the Eleusinian mysteries at Eleusis, Greece. HFV

nal truth—truth revealed by God—cannot be transmitted directly from God to man. They see God and His knowledge as timeless and spaceless, in contrast to man and his knowledge which is confined to time and space and must be expressed in time-space categories. Since man has no categories or thought-containers in which to receive God's transcendent truth, when it comes to him in revelation he forces it into his own finite concepts. Thus man has to express such a truth as the Fall of mankind as occurring at a definite place on earth, namely, in the garden of Eden, and at a certain time, that is, the beginning of the human race. Karl Barth, seeing that there is a danger in interpreting all myths as the vehicle of religious truth, confines revelation through myth to the Bible. He does not mean that the Bible directly dispenses truth, but that man receives truth through the Bible as he reads it.

2. Myths and mythology, according to Paul Tillich, reveal the evolution of religion from ancient times to our day. The pagan myths were simply an earlier, more primitive development than that found in the Bible. Tillich explained the phenomenon of myth as the result of a revelation which wells up in the "depth of reason" in man. He maintained that the same phenomenon explains the content and message found in art, music, and other expressions of culture. He believed that "sign-events" or media of revelation, such as historical happenings, groups, or individuals, occur only *within* the orderly processes of nature. Thus he specifically excluded the possibility of any supernatural event as being a means of revelation.

The orthodox Christian agrees that myths and mythology do reveal much concerning the conditions and faith of the primitive and the pagan. Myths do not in any sense, however, convey propositional truth itself, i.e., truth from God as expressed in direct statements. Paul speaks of man as not willing to retain the knowledge of God which he receives from the world around him in general revelation, and therefore as making images of himself, of birds, and animals, and creeping things, and then worshiping these (Rom 1:18–23). Man sets up a god whom he has fabricated in his own fallen image, and then worships this projection of himself. This is the biblical analysis of paganism.

The answer which the Bible gives to the theory presented by Fichte and adopted by Communism—that man sets up an image of himself in the Christian religion and worships it as if it were God—is that the God worshiped by the Christian is absolutely holy and perfect. Therefore He can be fully known only by His directly revealing Himself to man, whereas the mythical gods projected by the heathen are beings fashioned in the mind of man after his own fallen nature with all of man's lusts and frailties. The reason for this is that man turns from the true God, who condemns him by His perfection and purity, in order to set up a myth, a god after his own likeness, so that he might relieve himself of real moral responsibility.

Demythologization

In 1941 Rudolf Bultmann of Marburg, Germany, published an essay, "Neues Testament und Mythologie." In it he stated that the NT does contain the saving *kerygma* or gospel of Christ. In preaching this message and later in recording it the early church used thought-patterns current in that day. By means of Form Criticism he discovers these, usually in the form of Jewish apocalyptic myths or Gr. Gnostic redemption myths. He believes that this "cosmology of a pre-scientific age" must be discarded because it is incredible and unacceptable to modern man, an offense to him, because the concept of the universe has changed so radically since the first century, so that no one now can honestly believe in a world of spirits above and below. He accordingly finds it necessary to eliminate such obviously (in his view of the world as a closed system, governed by fixed natural laws) mythical elements as the preexistence of the Son of God, the virgin birth, Christ's deity and sinlessness, His bodily resurrection and ascension, His glorious return, and the personality and power of the Holy Spirit. "It is self-evident that this process of demythologization, when carried through with the thoroughness Bultmann displays, mutilates the Christianity of the NT in so radical a manner as to leave it unrecognizable" (P. E. Hughes, "Myth," BDT, p. 369).

Bultmann recognizes that all mythology expresses a truth, though in an obsolete way. To preserve the theological essence of the Christian faith—i.e., the announcement that God came in divine grace through Christ to man's soul or self in order to accomplish a radical change in a person's "existence"—it is necessary to strip off from the gospel message the descriptions of all supernatural events taking place in time and space. Inside will be found the original *kerygma*. Existential philosophy, the science of human existence, is the means whereby the *kerygma* can be uncovered.

As Otto A. Piper concludes, "By denying the incarnation and ascribing to Jesus but an incidental role in the formation of the gospel, Bultmann ignores the particular emphasis all the NT writers place upon the necessity of a divine redemption through the agency of an individual man" ("Myth in the NT," *Twentieth Century Encyclopedia of Religious Knowledge*, Baker, 1955, II, 781).

The fundamental difference, then, between mythology and the Bible is that the former is *man's* attempt to narrate in story form his experience with the forces of nature. The latter is the Word of *God*. It is the revelation given by the Creator Himself, the One who also chose to act in history to redeem the people with whom He had made a covenant. Yahweh the God of Israel has no mythology. He is the one true living God. There is no polytheism. No nature myths appear in narrative sections to explain the existence of the supernatural (G. E. Wright, *The Old Testament Against Its Environment*, Chicago: Regnery, 1950, pp. 16–29). The account of the creation and the Fall of man in Gen 1–3 is not fanciful, imaginative, or mythical; it is revealed truth about actual events, stated rationally in simple terms that are comprehensible to people of all ages.

See Bible Interpretation; Leviathan; Miracles; Revelation.

Bibliography. Edwyn Bevan, "The Religious Value of Myths in the Old Testament," in S. H. Hooke, *In the Beginning*, Oxford: Clarendon Press, 1947. B. S. Childs, *Myth and Reality in the Old Testament*, London: S. C. M. Press, 1960. E. Dinkler, "Myth in the New Testament," IDB, III, 487 ff. G. R. Driver, *Canaanite Myths and Legends*, Edinburgh: T. & T. Clark, 1956. T. H. Gaster, "Myth, Mythology," IDB, III, 481–487. S. H. Hooke, *Middle Eastern Mythology*, Harmondsworth: Penguin, 1963. G. Stahlin, "*Mythos*," TDNT, IV, 762–795.

R. A. K. and J. R.

N

NAAM (nā'ām). A son of Caleb, son of Jephunneh (I Chr 4:15).

NAAMAH (nā'ā-mā)

1. The daughter of Lamech and Zillah who were descendants of Cain, and sister of Tubal-cain, the inventor of cutting tools (Gen 4:22).
2. The Ammonitess wife of Solomon and the mother of King Rehoboam (I Kgs 14:21, 31; II Chr 12:13).
3. A city assigned to Judah in the Shephelah region of Palestine (Josh 15:41), possibly located at Khirbet Fered, NW of Timnah.

Cleansing of Naaman, Flemish tapestry, fifteenth century. MM

NAAMAN (nā'ā-măn). The name occurs in Ugaritic as *N'mn* and in an Egyptian text from the time of Thutmose III.

1. A Benjamite and founder of a clan (Gen 46:21).
2. A son of Bela, son of Benjamin (Num 26:40; I Chr 8:4). Some scholars equate this man and No. 1 as the same person.
3. A son of Ehud, grandson of Benjamin (I Chr 8:7).
4. A Syrian captain in the army of Ben-hadad, king of Damascus. This able commander-in-chief was cured of leprosy through the ministry of Elisha the prophet (II Kgs 5; Lk 4:27).

The exact nature of Naaman's leprosy is unknown, since the Heb. term (*ṣāra'at*) is used for various types of skin diseases (cf. Lev 13–14). Evidently it was not dangerously contagious, for neither Naaman nor Elisha's valet, Gehazi, was isolated from society (II Kgs 5:27; 8:4). The biblical account is loaded with drama about the Syrian general who was afflicted with this dreaded disease. With death stalking him, Naaman heard, through a little Israelite slave girl in his household, of the wonder-working power of a Heb. prophet in Palestine. Armed with a letter, which was couched in somewhat preemptory terms, from his Syrian king to the king of Israel, Naaman came to Samaria and requested healing. The king of Israel immediately became suspicious and alarmed over the demands of the letter and rent his clothes in despair. The prophet Elisha heard of the king's dilemma and sought to reassure the frightened monarch. So Elisha sent word to Naaman that he must bathe himself seven times in the river of Jordan. At first the Syrian general haughtily spurned his miscalculated humiliation, and rejected the remedy. But his attendants persuaded him to yield to the treatment, and he was cured.

On being cleansed of the leprosy, Naaman insisted that Elisha accept gifts of silver, gold, and clothing, but the prophet graciously refused. Naaman confessed that the God of Israel is the one and true God and requested two mule loads of Canaanite earth (II Kgs 5:15–17). This could have been an indication of his belief that the Lord (Yahweh) was limited to Palestine and could be worshiped *only* on His soil (Ex 20:24). Also he reflected the contemporary pagan idea of religious syncretism when he raised the question with Elisha of worshiping in the house of Rimmon (v. 18). Elisha was strangely silent. The idea that Yahweh was viewed as the God of the whole world, but that He performed some historical events through the members of His heavenly council, and that the gods of the surrounding nations were these lesser heavenly beings (Deut 32:8–9; I Kgs 22:19, 22; Ps 82) is an unsatisfactory explanation of this enigma.

Cured of his leprosy and possessing a new faith, Naaman departed for his fatherland. But he was apprehended enroute by the opportunist Gehazi, Elisha's servant, who, under false pretense and motivated by greed, requested some of the gifts which Elisha had refused. Naaman graciously and liberally responded. On Gehazi's return to Elisha's house, his falsehood was exposed and Naaman's leprosy fell upon him.

International exchange of medical hospitality appears to have been prevalent in the ancient world as shown by the Egyptian king Rameses

II who offered medical aid to a Hittite princess. Also, *c.* 1275 B.C., a physician and exorcist was dispatched by the Babylonian king to the Hittite king Hattusilis.

Jos (*Ant.* viii. 15.5) refers to a Jewish tradition which equates Naaman with the man who "drew a bow at a venture" and killed King Ahab (cf. I Kgs 22:34). Again this is probably wishful thinking.

The miracles of Christ and those of Elisha (*q.v.*) are strikingly similar. Jesus in Lk 4:27 singles out the healing of the Syrian officer as an example of God's concern for the Gentiles. Naaman's healing stands as an immortal testimony that the power of God cannot be bought with the mundane!

D. W. D.

NAAMATHITE (nā'*ȧ*-m*ȧ*-thīt). Zophar, one of Job's friends, was called a Naamathite (Job 2:11; 11:1; 20:1; 42:9). It is a Gentile name, possibly of a town in Edom.

NAAMITE. Mentioned in Num 26:40. *See* Naaman 2.

NAARAH (nā'*ȧ*-r*ȧ*)

1. One of the two wives of Ashur of the tribe of Judah who founded Tekoa. She bore Ashur four sons (I Chr 4:5–6).

2. A town on the border of Benjamin and Ephraim, between Bethel and Jericho (Josh 16:7), which the KJV transliterates as Naarath. In I Chr 7:28 the town is called Naaran. Josephus called it Neara and said Herod Archelaus diverted half of its water supply to irrigate the palms at his palace in NT Jericho (*Ant.* xvii.13.1). Nelson Glueck identified its site with Khirbet el-'Ayâsh, near Wadi el-'Auja, *c.* five miles N of Jericho in the Jordan Valley (BASOR, XXV–XXVIII, Part I [1939], 412 f.).

NAARAI (nā'*ȧ*-rī). One of David's heroic men called Paarai the Arbite in II Sam 23:35 but Naarai in I Chr 11:37.

NAARAN. Spelling for Naarah (*q.v.*) in I Chr 7:28.

NAARATH (nā'*ȧ*-răth). A city of Benjamin or Ephraim near Jericho (Josh 16:7). *See* Naarah 2.

NAASHON. *See* Nahshon.

NAASSON (nā-ăs'sŏn). The NT spelling of Nahshon. An ancestor of Christ, he was the son of Amminadab (Mt 1:4; Lk 3:32). *See* Nahshon.

NABAL (nā'b*ȧ*l). A wealthy rancher living SSE of Hebron. He resided in a town named Maon (not the Maon near Petra) and pastured his flocks on the border of Judah at Carmel (not Mount Carmel) at a place now known as el-Kurmul. He is mentioned in biblical history because of a confrontation with David and his 600 free-booters who found refuge from King Saul in the same vicinity. While there, David's men protected Nabal's livestock from the raids of neighboring Bedouin and maintained good relations with his shepherds (I Sam 25:15). Because of his need for supplies, David sent ten staff members to Nabal at the time of sheep shearing to seek a gratuity in return for his restraint from pillaging and for protection rendered to Nabal's herdsmen.

Nabal professed never to have heard of David and insinuated that he was only a runaway slave. This insult so enraged David that he gave orders to his men to move against Nabal 400 strong. Nabal's servants informed Abigail (*q.v.*), the attractive and resourceful wife of Nabal, in time to avert catastrophe. Abigail hastened to load a large stock of provisions on asses, and, unknown to her husband, accompanied the peace offering to the camp of David. Her generosity, graciousness, and beauty were sufficient to dissuade David from his purpose, thus saving her husband from assassination and David from blood-guiltiness. In her lengthy and eloquent intercession she appealed not only to David's mercy but to his self-interest (I Sam 25:24–31). Out of deference to her and her gifts, and out of a desire to avoid a blot on his record, David reconsidered and called off the attack.

Both the servants of Nabal (whose name in Heb. means "foolish," intellectually and morally senseless) and his wife agreed as to the meanness of their master. When Abigail returned to the ranch, she found her husband eating and drinking like a king. He was so drunk that she did not tell him of his narrow escape until the next day when he had become sober. After hearing of the danger to which he had been exposed, he suffered a heart attack, or perhaps a stroke, and "became as a stone." Ten days later "the Lord smote Nabal" and he died. David regarded his death as an act of God by which David was avenged and kept from shedding blood himself.

Shortly thereafter David sent servants to ask the widow's hand in marriage. Abigail graciously and without hesitation consented, agreeing to "wash the feet of the servants of my lord." On her second trip to David's camp she was accompanied by her personal effects and five servant girls, in order to remain with David as his second wife. She later went with David to Hebron and to Jerusalem as his queen.

This story bears every earmark of authenticity. The area S of Hebron is best suited for grazing and thus agrees with the nature and scope of Nabal's grazing operations. The churlishness of Nabal is also characteristic of many a "self-made man" who is concerned only with his own affluence.

G. A. T.

NABATAEANS (năb'*ȧ*-tē'*ȧ*ns). The Nabataeans were a Semitic tribe coming from NW Arabia who began to settle in the area falling between the Dead Sea and the Gulf of Aqaba sometime during the 6th cen. B.C., invading the greater part of the territory occupied by the Edomites. Their name may appear for the first time in 646 B.C. when a people called the Nabaiate revolted against Ashurbanipal, the king of Assyria, who took seven long years to subdue them. From their first appearance, they seem to have been engaged in trade and in the protection of the caravan routes between Arabia and the Fertile Crescent for which they levied exorbitant fees. Prosperity gradually followed and eventually made possible the sculpture of the magnificent monuments which still call for the admiration of modern visitors. *See* Arabians.

The Nabataeans are next heard of in 312 B.C. when Antigonus the One-Eyed, one of the generals of Alexander the Great, sent an expedition against their capital, Petra (*q.v.*), in his advance on Egypt. His troops captured the city and looted it, but they were waylaid by the Nabataeans on the way back, and completely annihilated in a surprise night attack. The Nabataeans later profited from the turmoil prevailing in the Seleucid kingdom and extended their power over all Transjordan, penetrating as far N as Damascus. During the 1st cen. B.C. they became involved in a war with the Maccabaean king Alexander Jannaeus, whom they defeated, and again with the last Seleucid king Antiochus XII, whom they captured.

With the coming of the Romans, the Nabataeans assumed a more subservient role, and they are often found assisting the Romans in their wars in the Near East. Aretas III sent a cavalry force of 40 horses to assist Julius Caesar in the battle of Alexandria, and Aretas IV sent a contingent to help Varus against the Jews. It was this Aretas who was ruling Damascus at the time of Paul's escape from the city (II Cor 11:32). Eventually the Romans, under Trajan, annexed their kingdom and converted it into the Third Province of Arabia in A.D. 106.

The Nabataeans were pagans who worshiped a multiplicity of gods at the head of which was Dhu Shara (Dusares). Worship at high places appears to have been very popular with them, and among their monuments at Petra there were two high places, one of which consisted of an altar and two obelisks nearby, all carved out of the rock. They buried their dead in rock-cut chambers, adorned on the outside either with a stepped pattern, or in the Hellenistic style, with columns and friezes. Their most famous monuments are the Khazneh and the Deir. The former is cut out of the many colored sandstone rock of the region, and is situated at the end of a narrow gorge leading into the city, while the Deir stands at the top of a steep ravine. Besides these, there are numerous other tombs around their city. *See* Petra.

In addition to their buildings at Petra, the Nabataeans have left a number of forts and outposts which lie on the old caravan route between Hedjaz and Damascus. The remains of their dams and cisterns in the Negeb indicate their great engineering skill and intensive agricultural programs which brought the population of that area to its greatest point in history. They made remarkably thin pottery, beautifully decorated with floral designs. All these mute remains attest to the high degree of their civilization.

Bibliography. CornPBE, pp. 542–554. Nelson Glueck, *Deities and Dolphins, The Story of the Nabataeans,* New York: Farrar, Straus and Giroux, 1965.

D. C. B.

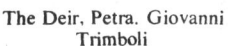

The Deir, Petra. Giovanni Trimboli

NABONIDUS (năb'ŏ-nī'dŭs). The last Neo-Babylonian king (556–539 B.C.) and the father of Belshazzar (*q.v.*). The fact that Belshazzar, not Nabonidus, is mentioned as the king of Babylon in the book of Daniel has caused some scholars to question the accuracy of Daniel. Recently published cuneiform texts reveal Nabonidus as an intriguing person and give a basis for understanding Belshazzar's prominence at Babylon in his father's place.

It was not until Sidney Smith published a "Persian Verse Account" of Nabonidus in 1924 that scholars took seriously the intimation that the king had spent several years in the Arabian desert. In 1929 Dougherty published *Nabonidus and Belshazzar,* which marshaled all the pertinent cuneiform and non-cuneiform evidence for the reign of Nabonidus and his son. In 1956 D. S. Rice discovered three stelae at Harran, which were reused as thresholds by the Moslems in their mosque. These important inscriptions, which describe the death of Nabonidus' mother, were published by Gadd in 1958. In 1956 Milik published some Aramaic fragments from Qumran which deal with Nabonidus. See ANET, pp. 305–306, 308–316.

These discoveries force us to revise the older view of Nabonidus as a scholarly antiquarian who was not interested in administration. We find that Nabonidus was an able monarch, whose fault as a ruler lay in his fanatical devotion to the moon-god, Sin. This devotion had been kindled in Nabonidus by his mother, a remarkable woman who lived to be 104 years old. When Nabonidus came to the throne in 556 B.C. he must have been in his 50's.

Early in his reign Marduk revealed to him in a dream that Sin was angry because the Ummanmanda (the Medes) had destroyed his temple at Harran. Nabonidus resolved to suspend the New Year festival until he could rebuild Sin's temple. His devotion to Sin did not endear him to the priests of Marduk. When Cyrus turned against the Medes, Nabonidus was able to rebuild the temple at Harran in 553 B.C. From a campaign in Lebanon, where he fell sick and recovered, Nabonidus proceeded S to Edom, and then still farther S to the oasis of Tema (*q.v.*) in NE Arabia. In an unprecedented decision, Nabonidus chose to remain in Arabia, leaving Babylon in the hands of Belshazzar. It was formerly thought that the king stayed in the desert for seven to eight years. The new Harran texts show that he stayed even longer, ". . . ten years I went amongst them, (and) to my city Babylon I went not in." His exile lasted possibly from the fifth to the fifteenth year of his reign, 552–542 B.C. He still retained the title of king, however, and gave orders from Tema. Food was brought by camel from Babylon 500 miles away. He established outposts at five other oases, including Yathrib (Medina, the refuge of Muhammad), 250 miles S of Tema.

Among the various reasons postulated for Nabonidus' strange decision are the following: (1) Economic. The Medes and the Persians controlled the trade routes to the N and E; the S remained open to Babylon. (2) Military. The need for Arab allies against the growing power of Cyrus may have been a factor. (3) Hygienic. The climate may have appealed to the aged and sickly king. The true reason presents itself from the new Harran texts which relate that "the sons of Babylon, . . . priests (and) people of the capitals of Akkad, against his great divinity (Sin) offended. . . . treason and not loyalty, like a dog they devoured one another; fever and famine in the midst of them. . . ." The king refused to return to Babylon, a city which had been punished by Sin for the disrespect shown to the deity, until the people repented of their attitude. His alienation was so strong that he did not return to Babylon for the funeral of his mother, who died in his ninth year. As a consequence of his absence the New Year's rite was suspended in Babylon.

Nabonidus, however, had not abdicated. He was still called *šarru* or "king," and gave orders from Tema to Belshazzar, who was called *mâr šarri* or "the king's son." Before leaving for Tema, Nabonidus had "entrusted kingship" (*šarrutam*) to his son. Dougherty demonstrates that Belshazzar exercised regal power and is associated with Nabonidus in a variety of inscriptions. He concludes that Daniel's depiction of Belshazzar as king in Babylon is an accurate one. The elevation of Daniel as the "third ruler" (Dan 5:29) also seems to be a recognition of the situation.

Shortly before the capture of Babylon by the Persians in 539 B.C., Nabonidus returned to the city and celebrated the New Year's rite. He tried to gather the gods of the various other cities in Babylon, but Borsippa, Cuthah, and Sippar refused to send theirs. Many of the Babylonians indeed welcomed Cyrus as a king who would do more honor to Marduk than Nabonidus. According to Gr. sources, his life was spared and he was made a governor of Carmania (cf. the similar story of Croesus).

Many biblical scholars have accepted the thesis that the story of Nebuchadnezzar's madness in Daniel is a distorted reflection of Nabonidus' exile in Arabia (see Genouillac, Von Soden). Among other objections to this theory is the point that this was based on Smith's rendering of a line in the Persian Verse Account: "an evil demon (*šedu*) had altered him." According to this rendering, Nabonidus went to Arabia because he was mad. Oppenheim now renders this line: "(his) protective deity became hostile to him" (ANET, p. 313).

According to "The Prayer of Nabonidus," the recently published Aram. text from Qumran, Nabonidus (not Nebuchadnezzar, as in Dan 4) was afflicted with a disease for seven years at Tema by God. After praying in vain to the gods of silver, wood, stone, etc., a Jewish exorcist (Daniel?) healed him. Milik and Freedman believe that this story is earlier than that of Daniel's; Dupont-Sommer believes otherwise. It does show that the Jews were familiar with

Nabonidus, though he is not mentioned by name in Daniel. *See* Nebuchadnezzar.

Bibliography. Raymond P. Dougherty, *Nabonidus and Belshazzar,* Yale: Yale Univ. Press, 1929. C. J. Gadd, "The Harran Inscriptions of Nabonidus," *Anatolian Studies,* VIII (1958), 35–92. Henri de Genouillac, "Nabonide," RA, XXII (1924), 71–81. Hildegard Lewy, "The Babylonian Background of the Kay Kâûs Legend," *Archiv Orientální,* XVII (1949), 28–109. Julius Lewy, "The Late Assyro-Babylonian Cult of the Moon . . . at the Time of Nabonidus," HUCA, XIX (1946), 405–489. J. T. Milik, "Prière de Nabonide," RB, LXIII (1956), 407–415. D. S. Rice, "From Sin to Saladin," *Illustrated London News* (Sept. 21, 1957), 466–469. H. H. Rowley, "The Historicity of the Fifth Chapter of Daniel," JTS, XXXII (1931), 12–31.

E. M. Y.

NABOPOLASSAR (năb'ŏ-pŏ-lăs'*ȧ*r). The Babylonian king (626–605 B.C.) who founded the Chaldean Dynasty, and father of Nebuchadnezzar II. He assumed the title of king of Akkad (ANET, pp. 303 ff.). He was part of a coalition with Cyaxares, ruler of the Median Empire, that overran Nineveh in 612 B.C. A series of Babylonian texts in the British Museum's collection mentions all but years four to nine of Nabopolassar's reign and his campaigns against the Assyrians and their former vassals in Syria and Cilicia.

NABOTH (nā'bŏth). A citizen of the northern kingdom of Israel who had a vineyard in Jezreel next to the country palace of Ahab and Jezebel (I Kgs 21:1; II Kgs 9:21, 25). Ahab summoned him to Samaria and tried to buy the land. Naboth refused because it was a part of his family inheritance, and therefore its title was never to be transferred to anyone outside his tribe (Lev 25:23; Num 36:7; cf. Ezk 46:18). When Jezebel heard how much the pouting Ahab wanted to annex the vineyard, she unhesitatingly wrote letters in Ahab's name to the city officials in Jezreel, and ruthlessly had Naboth stoned to death with his children on the false conviction of blasphemy (I Kgs 21:8–14).

Ahab and Jezebel were condemned by Elijah for this crime (I Kgs 21:17–24), who prophesied that dogs would lick up the king's blood and eat Jezebel's flesh just as they had lapped up Naboth's blood after his stoning. The prophecy had a dual fulfillment, with dogs licking up Ahab's blood when his chariot was washed by the pool of Samaria (I Kgs 22:38), and other dogs eating Jezebel's trampled corpse outside the gate of Jezreel (II Kgs 9:30–37).

According to Francis I. Andersen, Jezebel's purpose may have been to claim that Naboth had actually promised to sell the vineyard to Ahab, but later reneged. She sent a spurious deed of sale, sealed with the king's seal, among her "letters" to the elders of Jezreel. At the trial the two false witnesses testified Naboth had invoked the name of Yahweh in an oath to formalize the supposed transaction ("The Socio-Juridical Background of the Naboth Incident," JBL, LXXXV [1966], 46–57).

A. W. W.

NACHON (nā'kŏn). A Benjamite at whose threshing floor Uzzah was smitten for touching the ark (II Sam 6:6). He is also called Chidon (I Chr 13:9).

NACHOR (nā'kôr)

1. The brother of Abraham (Josh 24:2).
2. The grandfather of Abraham (Lk 3:34).

The name is also spelled Nahor (*q.v.;* Gen 11:22–29; 22:20, 23).

NADAB (nā'dăb)

1. The firstborn son of Aaron (Ex 6:23). With Moses, Aaron, the elders of Israel, and his brother Abihu, Nadab was present on Mount Sinai when God revealed Himself (Ex 24:1–9). The consecration of Aaron and his four sons to the priesthood with their distinctive vestments is described in Ex 28:1–43. Because he and his brother Abihu presumed to offer "strange fire" upon the altar of incense inside the tabernacle, they were slain (Lev 10:1–3). Since the prohibition of wine is mentioned after this incident (Lev 10:8–9) some have concluded that their sin was drunkenness. Others believe the manner of presenting the burning incense was unlawful because only one priest at a time was allowed in the holy place. It is further suggested that the two were intending to proceed into the holy of holies when God's fire killed them. Nadab left no descendants (Num 3:4).
2. A descendant of Jerahmeel, a son of Shammai and the father of Seled and Appaim (I Chr 2:27–30).
3. One of the sons of Jeiel, the first Israelite settler in Gibeon of the tribe of Benjamin (I Chr 8:29–31; 9:36, NASB).
4. Son and successor of Jeroboam I, who reigned over Israel for two years (I Kgs 14:20; 15:25–26). He followed the precedent of his father in "causing Israel to sin" by fostering the worship of the calf-idols at Bethel and Dan. During his short reign he besieged Gibbethon, a Philistine city, at which time he was attacked by a rebel of his own army named Baasha. In the ensuing conflict Nadab was slain and Baasha reigned in his place (I Kgs 25:27–31). With his death the dynasty of Jeroboam I came to an end as had been predicted by the prophet Ahijah (I Kgs 14:7–16).

G. A. T.

NAGGE (năg'ī) (or **NAGGAI**). Listed in Lk 3:25 as one of the ancestors of Jesus.

NAG HAMMADI. *See* Chenoboskion.

NAHALAL (nā'h*ȧ*-lăl). A Levite city in Zebulun near Kattath and Dimnah (Josh 19:15; 21:35). Israel was unsuccessful in driving out the Canaanites, possibly because it was an open country better adapted to Canaanite warfare.

NAHALIEL (nȧ-hā'lĭ-ĕl). A stopping place of the Israelites in the wilderness between Mattanah and Bamoth. It lies near the wilderness of Kedemoth, N of Moab, and was on the last part of the journey (Num 21:19). Since its name means "brook of God," it may be either a N tributary of the Arnon River, the large Wadi Wala, or the Wadi Zerqa Ma'in, which enters the Dead Sea *c.* 11 miles S of Mount Nebo.

NAHALLAL. *See* Nahalal.

NAHALOL (nā'hȧ-lŏl). Another form of Nahalal (*q.v.*), found only in Jud 1:30. It was one of the Canaanite cities, lying within the territory of Zebulun (Josh 19:15), which was given to the Levitical family Merari (Josh 21:35). The Cannanites were not driven out but were made tributary. Tell en-Nahl, just E of Haifa in the plain of Acre, is the probable modern site.

NAHAM (nā'hăm). A Judahite, the brother-in-law of Hodiah (I Chr 4:19, NASB).

NAHAMANI (nā'hȧ-mā'nī). One of the 12 leaders of the tribe of Judah who returned from the Babylonian Captivity with Zerubbabel (Neh 7:7). He was omitted from a parallel listing in Ezr 2:2.

NAHARAI. *See* Nahari.

NAHARI (nā'hȧ-rī). A man from Beeroth in Benjamin; he was numbered among David's 30 mighty men as an armor bearer to Joab, commander-in-chief of David's army (II Sam 23:37; I Chr 11:39).

NAHASH (nā'hăsh)

1. An Ammonite king who besieged Jabesh-gilead after Saul had been anointed king by Samuel (I Sam 11:1-2; 12:12). Nahash's term of surrender included his gouging out the right eye of every man of Jabesh in order to incapacitate him for further warfare. R. W. Corney suggests that Nahash desired to gain greater glory by defeating a larger enemy, and therefore permitted the defenders to send for help; but he miscalculated the size of the army that Israel could send ("Nahash," IDB, III, 497). Saul's stunning victory paved the way for his acceptance as king by the Israelites (I Sam 11:6-15). Probably this is the Nahash who was kind to Saul's enemy David (II Sam 10:2; I Chr 19:1-2), and whose son Shobi brought supplies to David at Mahanaim (II Sam 17:27).

2. The father of Abigail, and apparently of Zeruiah her sister (II Sam 17:25). Since Abigail and Zeruiah are said in I Chr 2:13-16 to be the sisters of David and his brothers, it is possible that they were the stepdaughters of Jesse; their sons were about the same age as David. Nahash conceivably was the Ammonite king of 1; David's friendship with that ruler then would have been based on a close family relationship.

J. R.

NAHATH (nā'hăth)

1. A grandson of Esau by Bashemath, Ishmael's daughter, through their son Reuel (Gen 36:13, 17; I Chr 1:37).

2. A descendant of Levi through his son Kohath (I Chr 6:26); probably the person elsewhere called Toah (I Chr 6:34) and Tohu (I Sam 1:1). He was an ancestor of Samuel.

3. A Levite who, in the reign of Hezekiah, assisted in the oversight of the temple tithes and offerings (II Chr 31:13).

NAHBI (nä'bī). The representative from the tribe of Naphtali chosen to spy out Canaan (Num 13:14).

NAHOR (nā'hôr)

1. The son of Serug, father of Terah and grandfather of Abraham; he lived 148 years (Gen 11:22-25).

2. The son of Terah and brother of Abraham. He married Milcah, the daughter of his brother Haran, by whom he had eight children. Among them was Bethuel the father of Rebekah and Laban (Gen 11:26-29; 22:20, 23; 24:10, 15, 24, 27; 29:5). When Abraham left Ur, his whole family went with him to the region of Haran. Nahor's idolatrous faith is suggested in the covenant between Laban and Jacob when they swore by the God of Abraham and the god of Nahor (Gen 31:53, Anchor Bible, p. 243; cf. Josh 24:2).

The "city of Nahor" (Gen 24:10) was formerly considered to be Haran. It may, however, have been a nearby settlement, perhaps founded by Nahor. The Mari tablets (18th cen. B.C.) frequently mention *Naḫur* as a city E or S of Haran.

NAHSHON (nä'shŏn). The prince of the tribe of Judah at the time of the Exodus. As head of the tribe he appears in the numbering of the people (Num 1:7), in the designation of encampments (Num 2:3), and in bringing the offering of the tribe with the other princes at the dedication of the tabernacle (Num 7:12, 17). His sister Elisheba was the wife of Aaron (Ex 6:23; Naashon, KJV). He died with his generation in the wilderness, but from his descendants came David (I Chr 2:10-11; Ruth 4:20-22) and the Lord Jesus Christ (Mt 1:4; Lk 3:32; Naasson in Gr.).

NAHUM, BOOK OF (nā'*ŭ*m)

Place in the Canon

Nahum is seventh in order of Minor Prophets in the second division of the Heb. canon. The LXX places it immediately after Jonah since both inveigh against Nineveh, the capital of Assyria.

Authorship

Nahum the author came from Elkosh, an unknown village variously identified as Elkesi of Galilee or as Capernaum (lit. "village of Nahum") or as Elcesei of Judah.

Nahum's authorship of the book was not questioned until the 19th cen. when critics assigned a post-Exilic date on the following groundless bases: that the presence of an acrostic poem (1:2–10) indicated a later editor (Pfeiffer), or that this is a prophetic liturgy made up of four liturgical poems (Haupt), or that it is a cult-motif clothed in historical form (Mowinckel) both celebrating Nineveh's fall. The only way an acrostic could be construed is by grossly emending the text. The text destroys the liturgical and cult-motif theories because its message looks to the future and not to the past downfall of Nineveh.

Date

The prophecy can be dated fairly accurately from 3:8 ff. to the second half of the 7th cen. B.C. Nah 3:8 refers to the destruction of No-Amon, the Thebes of Upper Egypt, by the king of Assyria in 663 B.C. And since Nineveh's fall is prophesied as yet in the future, the date of Nahum lies between 663 and 612 B.C., the date of the Assyrian capital's overthrow determined by the Babylonian Chronicle.

Title and Theme

"The Lord's Judgment upon a Nation (Nineveh) for Her Sins of Pride, Oppression, Adulteries, and Witchcraft." The theme is well expressed in 1:2 that the Lord takes vengeance on His adversaries. Nahum was just as deeply concerned with the justice and power of God in history as Amos and Isaiah were. The greatest military power of his day would soon be destroyed with no recovery.

Outline and Comments

I. The Character and Majesty of the Lord in Relation to His Judgment, Chap. 1
II. The Siege and Fall of Nineveh, Chap. 2
III. Reasons for Nineveh's Downfall, Chap. 3

The prophecy begins with a burden (Heb. *maśśā'*, 1:1), which is a threatening oracle about the just and jealous God who will avenge Nineveh for the oppressive cruelty toward His people.

Chap. 2 vividly portrays the siege and the overthrow of Nineveh by scarlet-coated men in chariots who would storm the city's gates. They were helped by heavy rains that carried part of the city away as the remarkable prediction in 2:6 indicates would happen. So the Medes and Babylonians captured a city partially inundated with water.

Chap. 3 reveals that Nineveh had fallen because of her cruelties, harlotries, impenitence and witchcraft. As No-Amon (Thebes) fell, so would the Assyrian capital, and neither her fortifications nor her officials and nobles could be looked to for deliverance.

Bibliography. Oswald T. Allis, "Nahum, Nineveh, Elkosh," EQ,XXVII (1955), 67–80. W.J. Deane, *Nahum, The Pulpit Commentary*, ed. by H. Spence and J. Exell, London and New York: Funk & Wagnalls, 1913. Charles L. Feinberg, "Nahum," WBC, pp. 863–869. Hobart E. Freeman, *An Introduction to the Old Testament Prophets*, Chicago: Moody Press, 1968, pp. 225–231. A. Haldar, *Studies in the Book of Nahum*, Uppsala: Lundequistska, 1947. R. K. Harrison, *Introduction to the Old Testament*, Grand Rapids: Eerdmans, 1969, pp. 926–930. Walter A. Maier, *The Book of Nahum, A Commentary*, St. Louis: Concordia, 1959.

D. S.

NAIL

1. Fingernails (Heb. *ṣippōren*) are mentioned only three times in the OT: Deut 21:11–13, where a captive woman was to pare or cut her nails as part of her month-long lament for her parents and her purification before entering Israel, symbolizing the end of the former life and the beginning of the new; Dan 4:33 and 7:19, referring to claws of animals.

2. Wooden tent peg (Heb. *yātēd*), the weapon by which Jael slew Sisera (Jud 4:21–22; 5:26). Nails were driven into the wall for hangers (Ezr 9:8). When placed in sound material, it provided adequate, trustworthy support (Isa 22:23).

3. Nail or pin (Heb. *masmēr*), the ordinary carpenter's nail (Jer 10:4; Isa 41:7). Metal nails have frequently been found in archaeological work in Palestine. The earliest were made of bronze. After 1200 B.C., when iron smelting became known, the larger nails were of iron, the smaller still of bronze. Iron spikes as long as nine inches have been found at Samaria. Nails usually were square of shaft and had more taper than modern nails. David prepared in abundance such nails of iron for the temple (I Chr 22:3). Solomon used gold nails in interior decorative work of the temple (II Chr 3:9). Similar nails from Nuzu (*q.v.*) and Tell Abu Hawam near Haifa had broad, flat-domed heads and were sheeted with gold foil or silver.

The type of nail (Gr. *hēlos*) used to fasten Christ to the cross (cf. Jn 20:25) was an iron spike five to seven inches long. In 1968 Israeli archaeologists discovered 15 ossuaries from the period A.D. 7–70 in burial caves a mile N of Jerusalem's Damascus Gate. One contained the bones of a child and of a young adult named Yehohanan. The latter had been crucified, for the man's heel bones were still penetrated by the rusty remains of a seven inch nail. Both legs had been broken, apparently to hasten death (cf. Jn 19:31–36). The positioning of the nail has enabled an anatomist to reconstruct a typical crucifixion: the nails were driven through the forearms below the wrists to provide greater support, and the victim's legs were twisted to one side and folded up. This seemingly unnatural position would have enabled the victim to continue breathing and thus prolonged his life and his agony (N. Haas, "Anthropological Observations on the Skeletal Remains from Giv'at ha-Mivtar," IEJ, XX [1970], 38–59). *See* Cross.

4. The verb "nailed" (Gr. *prosēloō,* Col 2:14). God cancelled the certificate-of-debt consisting of the Mosaic decrees against us, having nailed it to Christ's cross.

H. G. S. and J. R.

NAIN (nān). The town where Jesus raised the widow's son from the dead, stopping the funeral procession and restoring the young man to his mother (Lk 7:11). The town is on the northern slope of the ancient Hill of Moreh (Jud 7:1), about six miles SE of Nazareth and is still called Nein. Today there is a small sanctuary here called "The Place of Our Lord Jesus," which commemorates the visit.

NAIOTH (nā'yōth). Apparently a section of Ramah, not a separate village. Because the word means something like "dwelling places," it may have referred to the common living place or monastery of the band of prophets to whom Samuel gave inspiration and leadership. Cf. a similar settlement or school under the direction of Elisha (II Kgs 6:1–7). Reference to Naioth is confined to I Sam 19:18–20:1. David joined Samuel there when he fled from Saul. Saul sent messengers to capture David, but they began to "prophesy" under the influence of the company of prophets, as did Saul himself when he followed his men to Naioth. David then fled from there to meet Jonathan (I Sam 20:1).

NAKED. This term frequently refers to being physically nude (Gen 3:7; Job 1:21; Eccl 5:15). In the Levitical laws the word identifies indecent, unacceptable exposure of certain parts of the body (Lev 18:6; 20:11). It refers also to improper exposure of the lower leg and of the foot during holy rites (Ex 20:26; etc.). The word describes tattered, torn garments (Isa 58:7; Mt 25:36). The destitute, bedraggled condition was that which Isaiah apparently used to portray the coming captivity of Egypt and Ethiopia (Isa 20:2–3). It is applied to the resources of a land which had been stripped or made bare (Gen 42:9, 12), the result of judgment upon a transgreesing nation (II Chr 28:19). Thus the word was applied to the condition of a nation in downfall (Nah 3:5; etc.). In Jn 21:7, Peter had been working in his undergarment only, having taken off his outer clothing.

NAME(S). In Scripture a name is often an expression of the nature of its bearer, describing his character, position, function, some circumstance affecting him, or some hope or sorrow concerning him.

Terminology. Heb. *shēm* meaning "name," "memorial," "majesty" (Ps 54:1), "renown" (Gen 6:4); and *zēker* meaning "remembrance," "memorial," "name" (Ps 30:4); Gr. *onoma* (for *shēm), mnēmē* (Ps 30:4), *mnēmosynon* (Ex 3:15), and *mneia* (Isa 26:8). In the NT Gr. *onoma* is also used to indicate persons (Acts 1:15; Rev 3:4; 11:13, NASB), rank (Mt 10:41), authority (Mt 21:9), the person and character of God (Jn 17:6, 26).

In the ancient Semitic world a name had much more religious, personal, family, historical or geographical significance than in our Western culture. The extensive genealogical tables in Scripture are indicative of the historical importance the Hebrews attached to ancestral origins and development regarding the names of individuals, families, tribes, and nations; thereby establishing inheritance rights, and substantiating pedigrees, lineage, and royal succession, especially of the Davidic Messiah (e.g., Gen 5; 10; 11; 46; I Chr 1–9; Mt 1:1–17; Lk 3:23–38).

Since the name was considered to be descriptive of the essential nature of the person or thing, there was a conception of identity between the name and its bearer (Gen 2:19–20). To cut off one's name from the earth signified to remove him or his descendants from existence (Josh 7:9; II Sam 14:7; II Kgs 14:27; Ps 83:4). To act or speak or write in someone's name was to act as that person's representative, with his inspiration and power and authority (Ex 5:23; Deut 18:19; I Sam 17:45; I Kgs 21:8). Thus the literal expression "call one's name over or upon" a people or place indicated a claim to possession or ownership (II Sam 12:28; Isa 43:7; Jer 7:10). The recipient might not use the name, but was made subject to the name's authority and was provided protection (II Chr 7:14; Prov 18:10; Isa 4:1; Jer 14:9).

Declaring one's name was a chief means of revealing or manifesting oneself (Ex 9:16; Josh 9:9). Notice how solemnly God revealed the meaning of His own name to Moses on various occasions (Ex 3:2–15; 6:2–8; 33:13–34:7). The name by paronomasia (a play on words) is what is known of the person; e.g., Naomi ("pleasant") changing her name to Mara ("bitter") in her bereavement (Ruth 1:20); and Nabal ("fool"): "As his name is, so is he; Nabal is his name, and folly is with him" (I Sam 25:25). The names prophesied of the coming Messiah depict aspects of His character and ministry (Isa 7:14; 9:6).

A new or second name is given when there is a change in one's personality or function or in his experience or circumstances (e.g., Simon to Cephas or Peter, Jn 1:42), and when regeneration produces a new character (Isa 56:5; 62:2; 65:15; Rev 2:17; 3:12; 14:1). On the basis of his covenant relationship Abram ("exalted father") was changed to Abraham ("father of a multitude"). Jacob ("supplanter") became Israel ("he perseveres with God") after his encounter with God at the Jabbok (Gen 32:28). See Otto Eissfeldt, "Renaming in the Old Testament," *Words and Meanings,* ed. by P. R. Ackroyd and B. Linders, Cambridge: University Press, 1968, pp. 69–79.

Personal names. These were generally bestowed on the child at or shortly after birth. Before the Exile the name was often given the child for the significance attached to it, but after the Exile it was customary to name the individual after a relative, frequently the grandfather.

Many Bible names are Heb. in origin, but some place-names of Palestine may be other than Heb., such as the non-Semitic word Ziklag. Gr. and Lat. names, such as Antipatris (Acts 23:31), Caesarea Philippi (Mt 16:13), and Ptolemais (Acts 21:7), also occur.

Heb. names may be composed of one element, such as Jacob ("supplanter") and Nabal ("fool"); several elements such as Penuel ("face of God") and Emmanuel ("God with us"); or even a whole sentence, as Jehoshua ("Yahweh is salvation"), Jehoshaphat ("Yahweh has judged"), and Elijah ("my God is Yah[weh]"). G. B. Gray listed 135 names with *El* and 157 with one of the abbreviations of *Yahweh.*

Personal names were used to identify or say something about:

1. Personal, physical, or spiritual factors, such as Esau ("hairy") and Peter ("rock").

2. Faith and gratitude to God. Godly parents reflected their piety by compounding their children's names with elements of the two chief names for God, either El (from Elohim) or Jah or Yah (from Yahweh), e.g., Joel ("Yahweh is God"), Daniel ("El is my Judge"), Abijah ("Yahweh is my Father"), Nathanael ("El has given"), and Ishmael ("El hears").

3. Association with animals and plants, as Jonah ("dove"), Rachel ("ewe"), Peninnah ("coral"), and Tamar ("palm tree"), as a term of endearment or expression of a wish that the child might have the peculiar quality of said animal or plant.

4. Something important to the parent, as Jacob named his last son Benjamin ("son of the right hand"), although the dying Rachel had called him Ben-oni ("son of my sorrow").

5. Historical events at the time of birth, as Ichabod ("inglorious"), because the mother said, "The glory is departed from Israel, for the ark of God is taken" (I Sam 4:21–22).

6. Prophecy concerning work to be done, as Jesus ("He shall save His people," Mt 1:21).

7. Relationship to a quality and/or a place, as Melchisedek ("king of righteousness"), king of Salem ("peace," Heb 7:2). and Zerubbabel ("begotten in Babylon").

8. Tribal names, such as Cushi (Cushite tribe, II Sam 18:21).

9. Events prophesied to occur, as in the names of Isaiah's children: Shear-jashub ("a remnant shall return," Isa 7:3) and Maher-shalal-hashbaz ("swift is the booty, speedy is the prey," Isa 8:3, NASB marg.); and in the names of Hosea's children: Jezreel ("God sows"; so named with dual significance because of past events and future blessing, Hos 1:4-5, 11; 2:22–23), Lo-ruhamah ("not pitied," Hos 1:6) and Lo-ammi ("not My people," 1:9).

10. Function, as the name Eve ("life") was suggested to Adam because she was to be "the mother of all living" (Gen 3:20), and in such names as Obil ("camel driver," I Chr 27:30) and Onesimus ("useful," as a slave, Phm 10–11).

Names for towns, places, and things. Geographical names may denote a number of different things, such as:

1. Physical conditions involved, such as the Salt Sea (Gen 14:3), Lebanon ("white," because of its snow-covered summit), Jericho ("fragrance of palms, rose gardens, and balsams"), Engedi ("spring of the kid").

2. Qualities, as Joppa ("beauty"), Shiloh ("tranquility") and Salem ("peace").

3. Shape, as Chinnereth ("harp-shaped," i.e., Sea of Galilee, Num 34:11), Shechem ("shoulder of a mount").

4. Occupation, as Gath ("winepress"), Bethlehem ("house of bread").

5. Deity or religious custom, as Beth-dagon (Josh 15:41), Ashtaroth (Deut 1:4), Beth-shemesh ("sun temple," Josh 19:22).

6. Important historical events, as Ebenezer ("stone of help," I Sam 7:12), Bethel ("house of God," Gen 28:16–19).

7. Connection with a person or tribe, as Gibeah-Saul (I Sam 11:4), Dan (Jud 18:29).

8. Animals and plants, as Aijalon ("deer field"), Bethhoglah ("house of the partridge"), Valley of Elah ("oak" or "terebinth").

Divine names and titles. It was considered all-important to learn the name of the divine being who appeared to one (e.g., Jacob, Gen 32:29, and Manoah, Jud 13:6, 16–21). Knowing His names and titles, such as Yahweh, Elohim, and Lord, made God living and real to His people. Sometimes the very concept "name" of God stood for the person of God Himself (Lev 24:11, RSV; Mt 12:21). To know and believe God's name or that of Christ is equivalent to knowing and believing in God or Christ Himself (Ps 9:10; 91:14; Isa 64:2; Mal 3:16; Jn 1:12; 2:23; 3:18; I Jn 3:23; 5:13). *See* God, Names of, for the various single and compound names which manifest His attributes and character to men.

The name of Jesus. The early Christians placed no magical value on the name of Jesus but used it as their forefathers had employed the names of God in OT times. Jesus had taught His disciples that to do something for His name's sake was to do it for Him (Mt 19:29; cf. 10:22). His name represented His power and authority, e.g., in working miracles (Mt 7:22; Acts 4:7,10). People were exhorted to call on His name for salvation (Acts 2:21; 4:12), and sinners were justified in or through His name (I Cor 6:11; Acts 10:43). The gospel was to be preached in His name (Lk 24:47), and eternal life comes in or through His name (Jn 20:31). Jesus instructed His followers to pray to the Father in His name, i.e., on His authority (Jn 16:23–24). "The name" alone is even used to refer to the Lord Jesus Christ ("His name," KJV, Acts 5:41; III Jn 7).

The meaning of baptism in the name of Jesus varies slightly according to the Gr. preposition used. In Acts 2:38 Peter exhorted the Jews to repent and be baptized in or upon (*epi*) the name of Jesus Christ, resting upon His authority and being devoted to Him. Later Peter instructed Cornelius to be baptized in (*en*) the name of Jesus Christ, acting on His authority. Three passages use *eis* (Mt 28:19; Acts 8:16; 19:5) plus the parallel phrase "baptized into Christ" (Rom 6:3; Gal 3:27). A study of these verses along with the verb *baptizō* and *eis* in I Cor 1:13; 10:2; 12:13 indicates that the one baptized is identified with Christ (or Paul or Moses) and passes into new ownership or partnership with Him, with new loyalty and fellowship.

Bibliography. Raymond Abba, "Name," IDB, III, 500–508. Hans Bietenhard, "*Onoma,* etc.," TDNT, V, 242–283. John D. Davis, "Names, Proper," ISBE, IV, 2113–2117. George Buchanan Gray, *Studies in Hebrew Proper Names,* London: 1896 (the most comprehensive work in English on this subject). H. Michand, J. J. Von Allmen, *et al.,* "Name, Names," *A Companion to the Bible,* ed. Von Allmen, New York: Oxford Univ. Press, 1958, pp. 278–300. W. L. Walker, "Name," ISBE, IV, 2112 f.

W. H. M. and H. E. Fr.

NAMES OF GOD. *See* God, Names of.

NAOMI (nā-ō'mĭ). The wife of Elimelech the Ephrathite of Bethlehem-judah who, because of a famine, migrated into the land of Moab. During the ten years in that land, her husband and two sons died, whereupon she returned to Bethlehem accompanied by Ruth, one of her daughters-in-law. Having arrived home, Naomi guided her daughter-in-law in the procedure to follow in obtaining Boaz to be her husband. Upon the birth of Obed, their first child, Naomi became the nurse for the child (Ruth 1:1–4:17). *See* Ruth; Elimelech.

NAPHISH (nā'fĭsh). The eleventh son of Ishmael (Gen 25:15; I Chr 1:31) and founder of a clan with which the Israelite tribes E of the Jordan made war and subdued. Also spelled Nephish in I Chr 5:19 (KJV). This clan is not mentioned in later records, nor is positive identification possible.

NAPHTALI (năf'tȧ-lī). The sixth son of Jacob and second of the two sons by Bilhah, Rachel's maid (Gen 30:4–8; 35:25). Dan was his older full brother. Naphtali was given his name, which may be interpreted as "my wrestling," because Rachel had wrestled about her sister Leah bearing children while she herself remained barren (Gen 30:8). Naphtali went down into Egypt as part of his father's patriarchal family and with four sons of his own (Gen 46:24; I Chr 7:13).

Jacob prophesied only one statement about Naphtali in the days to come (Gen 49:21): "Naphtali is a doe let loose, he gives beautiful words" (NASB). The translation and meaning are both debated, although the "goodly words" (KJV) may anticipate the song of Deborah and Barak (Jud 5), the latter coming from Naphtali.

When the first census was taken in the wilderness, the tribe of Naphtali numbered 53,400 fighting men (Num 1:43; 2:30), ranking as sixth. At the second census taken after the plague (26:1–2) the number of males 20 years old and upward numbered 45,400 (26:50), ranking eighth. The tribe occupied the position on the N of the tabernacle along with Asher, the two being on either side of Dan (Num 2:25–31). When the Israelites marched, the camp of Dan came in the rear (2:31).

The territory allotted to Naphtali was in N Palestine (Josh 19:32–39). The E border was the Sea of Galilee and the upper reaches of the Jordan, the S border that of Issachar and Zebulun, and the W border Zebulun and Asher (19:34). Nineteen fortified cities are mentioned (19:35–38), including Hazor (*q.v.*), the largest city in Palestine at the time. Three cities were given to the Levite family of Gershon, Kedesh in Galilee, Hammothdor and Kartan (Josh 21:6, 32; I Chr 6:62, 76), the former also being a city of refuge (Josh 20:7). Naphtali did not drive the Canaanites out of two cities, Beth-shemesh and Beth-anath, but did subject them to taskwork (Jud 1:33).

During the period of the judges the Naphtalites fought under Deborah and Barak, Barak himself of Kedesh-Naphtali (Jud 4:6, 10), and were praised for valor in Deborah's song (5:18). They also responded to Gideon (6:35; 7:23). Thirty-eight thousand came to David at Hebron to aid him in the contest with Ish-bosheth (I Chr 12:34, 40).

Naphtali was ravaged by Ben-hadad, king of Syria (I Kgs 15:20; II Chr 16:4). Its inhabitants were the first W of the Jordan to be carried into captivity by Tiglath-pileser III, king of Assyria (II Kgs 15:29).

Isaiah alludes to these calamities and promises them in darkness a great light (Isa 9:1 ff.). This was fulfilled when Jesus came and dwelt in Galilee in the borders of Zebulun and Naphtali (Mt 4:12–17). In this passage and in Rev 7:6 in the KJV, the people of Naphtali are referred to as Nephthalim.

G. W. K.

NAPHTUHIM (năf'tū-hĭm). The fourth son of Mizraim, the son of Ham, listed only in the genealogical records as a part of the Hamitic family division which occurred after the Flood (Gen 10:13; I Chr 1:11). Various suggestions have been made to account for the name, but positive identification continues to be impossible. In all probability this tribal family settled in Egypt or a little W of it.

NAPKIN. A transliteration of the Latin word

which means "to perspire." Hence, the word is applied to the cloth used in wiping the perspiration from the face, corresponding to our word handkerchief (*q.v.*). The word is translated napkin three times in the NT, once for the cloth used in preserving a servant's pound (Lk 19:20), twice as the cloth which was wrapped around the head of the dead person for burial (Jn 11:44; 20:7). The same Gr. and Latin word is translated handkerchief (pl.) in Acts 19:12.

NARCISSUS (när-sĭs'ŭs). In Rom 16:11 Paul greets Christians who are of the household of Narcissus. Although the name was common at that time in Rome, it may be that this was the very rich and prominent freedman who served the emperor Claudius and was put to death by Nero shortly before the epistle to the Romans was written. If so, it is an indication that Christianity was getting into the households of the highest officials.

NARD. *See* Plants: Spikenard.

NATHAN (nā'thȧn)

1. Son of Attai and father of Zabad of the clan of Jerahmeel in the tribe of Judah (I Chr 2:36).

2. The third child of David who was born to him and Bathsheba after beginning his reign in Jerusalem (II Sam 5:14; I Chr 3:5; 14:5). He is one of the forefathers of Christ (Lk 3:31). His branch of the Davidic family seems already to have been recognized as important by the time of the prophet Zechariah (Zech 12:12).

3. An inhabitant of Zobah who was father of Igal and brother (LXX has "father") of Joel. Both Igal and Joel were mighty men in David's army (II Sam 23:36; I Chr 11:38).

4. A prophet and courtier in the reigns of David and Solomon. Two of his sons, Azariah and Zabud, were prominent in the court of Solomon (I Kgs 4:5), on the supposition that the Nathan of that verse is the prophet. This Nathan played an important role at three critical junctures.

a. Concerning a house for the Lord (II Sam 7:1-17; I Chr 17:1-15). David confided in Nathan his desire to build the Lord's house as a permanent place for the ark of the covenant. Nathan's response was enthusiastic and encouraging, but that night the Lord gave the prophet a message for the king, which can be summed up in two statements: You will not build My house, but I shall build your house; and you will not build My house, but a son of yours will. The messianic element in the message cannot be overlooked. The house of David which God promised to build was the messianic "house" in the sense of line or dynasty, for certainly II Sam 7:16 looks beyond the reign of Solomon.

b. Concerning the sin of David (II Sam 12:1-15). David's double sin of adultery with Bathsheba and the murder of her husband Uriah "with the sword of the children of Ammon" called for rebuke. Nathan was the chosen messenger. His parable stirred David's sense of justice, so that the application was clear. David's repentance secured divine forgiveness, but the dire effects of the deed could not be avoided. There was, however, an amelioration of the effects for Bathsheba in that one of her sons, Solomon, was appointed heir to the throne. II Sam 12:25 seems to signify that God sent Nathan to David to bestow the name Jedidiah ("beloved of Yahweh") upon Solomon.

c. Concerning the succession of Solomon (I Kgs 1:5-48). David was near death and had not officially announced the succession to his throne. Adonijah, Solomon's half-brother, plotted a coup, about which Nathan received word. He sent Bathsheba to the ailing king to remind him of his promise to appoint Solomon as his successor. While she was in audience, Nathan joined her to tell the king of Adonijah's plan. The king then gave orders for the anointing and enthronement of Solomon at the hands of Nathan the prophet and Zadok the priest. Thus the prophet showed himself a man of action as well as a conveyor of the divine message.

Nathan also played a part in the development of the temple music (II Chr 29:25) and wrote a history of the reign of David (I Chr 29:29) and at least of a part of Solomon's reign (II Chr 9:29). Therefore portions of his court chronicles may have been included in the canonical books of Kings and Chronicles.

5. The father of Azariah, a high official of Solomon (I Kgs 4:5). He may be identical with Nathan the father of Zabud, a priest and Solomon's confidant (I Kgs 4:5, RSV), and possibly with 3 or 4 above.

6. A chief man sent by Ezra from his camp on the Ahava River to a colony of Jews at Casiphia to obtain ministers for the house of God (Ezr 8:16). It is possible that he is the Nathan who put away his Gentile wife (Ezr 10:39).

E. M. B. and J. C. M.

NATHANAEL (nȧ-thăn'ĭ-ĕl). Considered traditionally to have been one of the Twelve, though an apostle by this name does not appear in the lists given in the Synoptic Gospels (Mt 10:1-4; Mk 3:16-19; Lk 6:13-16). In John's Gospel (Jn 1:45-49) Nathanael is directed to Jesus as the promised Messiah by Philip. In John the name Bartholomew, one of the Twelve by Synoptic reckoning, is never encountered. Nathanael has been commonly identified as Bartholomew (son of Talmai), this perhaps being the surname; hence, Nathanael Bartholomew after the pattern of Simon Bar-jona. The two names are used interchangeably in the Church Fathers. Remembering the association of Philip with Nathanael in John, it is also to be noted that Bartholomew is named by each of the first three evangelists immediately after Philip, and in Luke he is joined with Philip in the same manner that Simon is joined with his brother Andrew, and James with his brother John.

Nathanael's encounter with Jesus is most significant and unusual in the evangelist's record. The reluctance to accept one from Nazareth as the Messiah has been charged to the petty jealousy between Nazareth and Cana, presumably Nathanael's home town. It would seem rather, in light of the full response to Jesus which follows, that his hesitation was occasioned by the fact that Nazareth is not mentioned in the OT and was certainly not the expected place of origin for the Messiah. Jesus praised the integrity of the man and received in consequence of the discussion, which in several respects is mysterious, the fulsome designation "Son of God" and "King of Israel." *See* Bartholomew.

Other men are mentioned in the OT under the Heb. form Nethaneel (*q.v.*).

H. L. D.

NATHAN-MELECH (nā'thăn-mĕl'ĭk). A Judean official (chamberlain, i.e., eunuch) before whose quarters at the temple entrance King Josiah removed the horses which previous kings of Judah had dedicated to the sun (II Kgs 23:11).

NATIONS. The English Bible has a number of synonyms for "nations" such as "Gentiles" (*q.v.*), "heathen," "pagans," and "peoples." When the various Heb. and Gr. words occur in the plural, "nations" is usually the most accurate translation. The term "people" is found very frequently in the singular referring to the nation or people of Israel.

In the Scriptures God declares repeatedly that He has chosen Israel to be "a holy people . . . a people for His own possession out of all the peoples who are on the face of the earth" (Deut 7:6; 14:2, NASB; cf. 26:18–19; *et al.*). Israel was to be a holy nation set apart and consecrated as priests to all other peoples (Ex 19:5–6). The first book of the Bible lists 70 nations or ethnic groups (Gen 10), while the last book foretells that in the end time a vast throng from every nation and all tribes and peoples and languages will stand before the throne of God (Rev 7:9). This interest in surrounding nations indicates the importance of history in the Bible as a vehicle of revelation. The fact that its historical data is uniformly accurate is unique in the world's sacred literature.

Terminology

In the OT two main Heb. words are rendered "nation" in the KJV. The most frequent (557 times in Heb., 373 times in KJV) is *gôy* (plural, *gôyim*), "people, nation, the whole population of a territory" (KB, p. 174). This word stresses the impersonal political and social aspects rather than kinship bonds. It is the state, the institution of nationhood, the masses of humanity. To the Jew it came to mean specifically the Gentiles, the heathen, in contrast to Israel or Judah. Israel is called a *gôy* after it became a nation with laws and government at Mount Sinai, but implied is a similarity to the idolatrous Gentiles in their disobedience to God and backsliding (Deut 32:28; Jud 2:20; Isa 1:4).

The Heb. word *'am* occurs 17 times in the KJV as "nation" and 1,835 times as "people." The term originally stressed close family relationships as in a clan. In Heb. it ranges in meaning from the people around an individual (Gen 32:7; II Sam 15:30; II Kgs 4:41), to the people of a town (Ruth 4:9), to a tribe (II Sam 19:40), to a nation (Ex 9:15, 27), to all mankind (Gen 11:6; Isa 42:5). Heb. *'am* suggests a group of *individuals*, of *persons* with common blood ties, not a regimented organization (E. A. Speiser, " 'People' and 'Nation' of Israel," JBL, LXXIX [1960], 157–163). Soon after the Exodus the term *ha'am*, "the people," was applied almost exclusively to Israel as the chosen people of Yahweh. Thus *'am* and *gôy* became nearly opposite terms, Israelites and non-Israelites, as in rabbinical literature.

The biblical phrase *'am hā'āreṣ*, "people of the land," in pre-Exilic times meant the qualified male citizens of the locality (Gen 23:13), the men who crowned the king (II Kgs 11:19; 23:30), who were specially taxed for the tribute to Egypt (II Kgs 23:35), and who owned slaves (Jer 34:8–19). In the post-Exilic period this term was applied by those returning from Babylon to those already residing in the land of Judah (Ezr 4:4).

In the NT Gr. *ethnos* is translated "nation" 64 times and "Gentiles" 93 times in the KJV. The latter word is used when the reference is to non-Jewish nations (Mt 20:19, 25; Acts 4:27; 9:15). "Nations" is employed when the reference is to all nations including the Jews (Mt 24:9, 14; 28:19; Mk 11:17; Rev 7:9). Gr. *laos* (143 times) is always rendered "people"; in the LXX it is the equivalent of Heb. *'am* in the singular. Another Gr. word, *ochlos*, "crowd" or "multitude," is translated 83 times as "people" in the KJV. *Demos.*, "populace, people," occurs in Acts 12:22; 17:5; 19:30, 33.

Biblical Lists of Nations

The Table of Nations. This title is often given to Gen 10 and I Chr 1:5–23, which furnish an ethnic list of the descendants of Noah through his three sons Japheth, Ham, and Shem. The record seems to be limited to nations and peoples of the middle of the 2nd mil. B.C. in the Near East with whom the Israelites might have some contact. Inscriptions of ancient Egypt and Mesopotamia reveal that a person educated in the court of Egypt *c.* 1500 B.C., as Moses was (Acts 7:22), could have known of most of these nations. Furthermore, the Heb. term *tôl^edōth*, "generations," in Gen 10:1, 32 suggests that the author of Genesis was using records or histories of family origins. These may have been handed on to him via the patriarchs that had come from Ur or its vicinity *c.*

2000 B.C. This could explain the mention of Accad and Erech (10:10) as important cities in the land of Shinar, for they had lost their preeminence by the end of the 3rd mil B.C. and by Hammurabi's reign (1792–1750), respectively.

There are certain indications in the table that it was compiled around the middle of the 2nd mil B.C. At that time the Hittites (*q.v.*) controlled much of the area from Carchemish on the Euphrates to Hamath on the Orontes and W to the Mediterranean coast, this explaining Heth (Gen 10:15) as part of the population group in Canaan-Syria. W. F. Albright has observed that nearly all the names of the tribal descendants of Aram (10:23) and Joktan (10:26–29) are archaic, not occurring in 1st mil B.C. inscriptions from Assyria and S Arabia. Also several of the names belong to types known as personal names only in the early 2nd mil, though they may have long continued as tribal names ("The Old Testament and Archeology," *Old Testament Commentary*, ed. by Alleman and Flack, Philadelphia: Muhlenberg Press, 1948, p. 139).

In Gen 10 the peoples and lands of the then known world are divided into three main lines: the descendants of Shem in Mesopotamia and Arabia, the descendants of Ham in NE Africa and within the sphere of Egyptian influence, and the descendants of Japheth in the northern and Mediterranean lands, with all of them meeting and overlapping in Canaan or Palestine, the land promised to Abraham. Included are some of the royal cities and important centers of the day in the Fertile Crescent.

The names of the descendants in Gen 10 are not derived from any *one* of the several principal characteristics that distinguish a people. In some cases they seem to be racial groups, in others linguistic entities, and in others geographical or political units. In Gen 10:5, 20, and 31 (NASB) note the phrases "according to their families" (racial), "according to their languages" (linguistic), "by their lands" (geographical), and "by their nations" (political).

By recognizing this multiple basis of distinguishing the nations one may understand why Canaan is listed as a son of Ham and not of Shem, although the Canaanites of 2000 B.C. and onward spoke a W Semitic dialect. Canaan may have been considered Hamitic either because it had been brought under Egyptian sway by the early 18th Dynasty kings, or because the tribes which had conquered Palestine at the start of the early Bronze Age (3100–2100 B.C.) may have been Hamitic but which later succumbed to the influence of Semitic-speaking invaders.

Three names have double appearances in the table: Sheba (vv. 7, 28), Havilah (vv. 7, 29), and Lud (vv. 13, 22) as descendants of both Ham and Shem. Probably Sheba and Havilah were originally Semitic by race in N Arabia (cf. Gen 25:3, 18) and then moved to S Arabia in the Yemen region where Sheba (Heb. *sh^{e}bā'*) was known as Saba, the S Arabic name of the

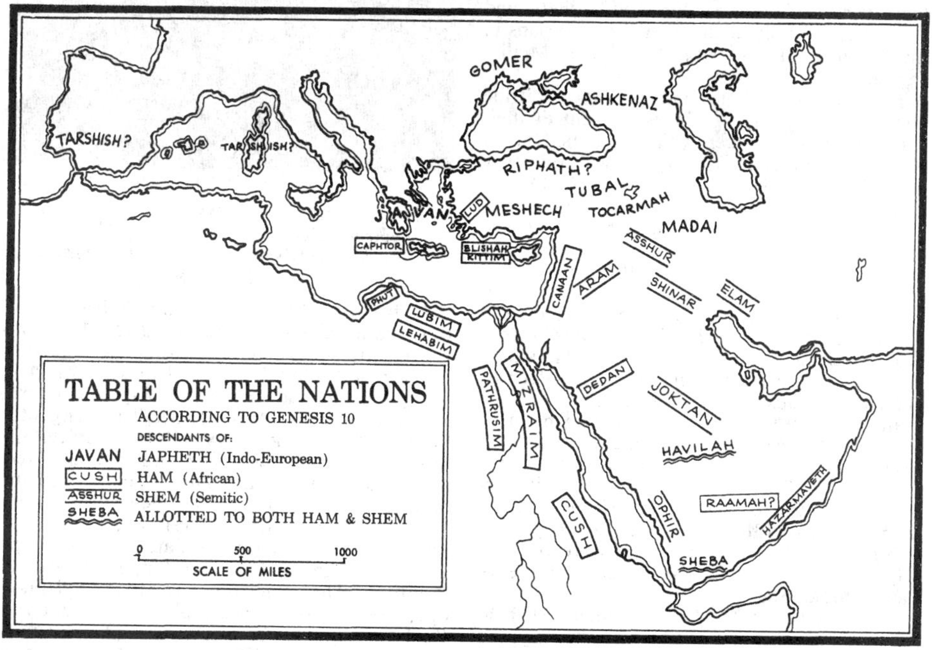

Sabean kingdom (IDB, IV, 144 f.). Some, however, crossed into Africa as traders and colonists in Ethiopia (Cush) and intermixed with Hamitic groups, where they were known as Seba ($s^e b\bar{a}$') to the Hebrews (cf. Ps 72:10; Isa 43:3; 45:14). The identity of Lud and the Ludim is not yet clear. The name Cush also involves a problem, because it is applied in the OT and in extrabiblical records both to Nubia or the Sudan (KJV "Ethiopia"; *q.v.*) and to the land of the Kassites in Babylonia (*see* Cush). Perhaps Hamitic Cushites came from the land of Shinar (or Sumer), where Nimrod made them rulers. There is evidence from before 3000 B.C. both in the Negeb and in Egypt that those early inhabitants had affinities with the Sumerians. Thus Sumerian traders traveling either overland through Palestine and up the Nile Valley or by ship to E Africa may have settled in the Sudan area and imposed their name on that district. Regarding the events of Gen 10:8-12 and their probable historic setting in the Ubaid period (3800-3500 B.C.) *see* Nimrod.

Data from ancient inscriptions regarding the names in Gen 10 are now discussed in order.

1. Japheth. Most of the ethnic groups in vv. 2-4 were of Indo-European stock. Gomer has been identified with the Gimirrai, who no later than the 8th cen. B.C. had fled into Cappadocia via the Caucasus from the Scythians. Magog may possibly appear as the far northern land of Gagaia in Amarna letter No. 1 (1. 38). From Madai descended the Medes, who roamed the semi-arid uplands E of the Zagros Mountains. Nomads of Indo-Iranian stock from S Russia, they were skilled horsemen and archers and became formidable enemies of the Assyrians in the 9th and 8th cen. B.C. *See* Medes, Media; Persia.

Javan undoubtedly is a name for the Gr. tribe known as the Ionians. The equivalent of their name occurs in 14th cen. Ugaritic texts. Known also as the Mycenaeans, they began to destroy the Minoan civilization in Crete *c.* 1400 B.C. Homer's *Iliad* dramatizes their famous expedition against Troy 150 miles N of Ephesus *c.* 1200 B.C. *See* Javan; Greece. From the steppes of Russia came both the Tabali, descendants of Tubal who settled in E Anatolia, and the Mushki, stemming from Meshech and dwelling E of the upper Euphrates. Both warred against Tiglath-pileser I *c.* 1100 B.C. Tiras may be the same as Turasha, one of the Sea Peoples named by Rameses III *c.* 1190 B.C.

In the line of Gomer, Ashkenaz may be identified with the Ashkuz who made a league with Esarhaddon (681-669 B.C.) of Assyria. Also known as the Scythians, they too came from S Russia. Togarmah appears in Hittite texts of Suppiluliumas (1380-1342 B.C.) as Tegarama (ANET, p. 318) and in Assyrian records as Tilgarimmu, mentioned as a people of the N Taurus Mountains.

Those linked with Javan include Elishah, known as Alashiya, an early name for Cyprus in records from Mari, Alalakh, Ugarit, Amarna letters No. 33-40, and Hattusas (Hittite capital at site of Boghaz-koi); Tarshish, the name for the areas in Spain and/or Sardinia colonized by the Sea Peoples and then by the Phoenicians and called Tartessos in Gr.; Kittim, *Kit* or *Kiti* of the Phoenician inscriptions, modern Larnaka on the SE coast of Cyprus; and Dodanim (Rodanim, I Chr 1:7, NASB), the people of the island of Rhodes.

2. Ham. The descendants of Cush (v. 7) are the peoples of the shores of the Red Sea and S Arabia. Seba, Havilah, and Sheba have been discussed above. Sabtah has been equated with Sabota, the chief city of the land of Hadhramaut (Hazarmaveth, v. 26) on Arabia's S coast. Raamah points to the Rhammanites (Strabo xvi. 4. 24) and their city of Ra'amah near Ma'in in SW Arabia. Dedan was a tribe controlling caravan routes between S and N Arabia, centering around the oasis el-'Ula 150 miles N of Medina.

Tomb inscriptions are typical of the ancient Egyptians. Here Ra-hetep, a priest at Memphis, is seated before a table of offerings, c. 2600 B.C. BM

Mizraim (v. 13), another Hamite listed in v. 6, is the usual Heb. name for Egypt. It means "two districts," a reference to the two sections of the Nile Valley, Upper and Lower (the Delta) Egypt. The name appears in Ugaritic as *mṣr* and in Akkad. as *Muṣur* or *Miṣir* (*see* Egypt). Several of the names in vv. 13-14 are uncertain or otherwise unknown. The Lehabim are often identified with the Libyans. The Naphtuhim may have been people of the Delta or of oases W of the Nile (NBD, p. 865). The Pathrusim, known to the Assyrians as Paturisi (ANET, p. 290), were the inhabitants of Upper Egypt (*see* Pathros). The Philistim are the Philistines (*q.v.*), one of the Sea Peoples. They and the Caphtorim came from Caphtor (Amos 9:7), from either Crete or the islands of the Aegean

NATIONS

Sea. The Philistines migrated in various waves to the Palestinian coast and eventually built five city-states after they came in force and even attempted to invade Egypt *c.* 1190 B.C. But the Philistines of Moses' time were probably Minoan merchant colonists from Crete, having continuity with the rather peaceful Philistines whom Abraham and Isaac met (Gen 21; 26). At the time of the Exodus the Israelites avoided the coastal route known to them as the way of the Philistines (Ex 13:17) because of small Philistine settlements between Wadi el-Arish and Gaza. The reason, then, for mentioning them with Mizraim may be purely geographic, in that they had been settling along the coastal highway which Egypt usually controlled as far as Gaza (cf. Gen 10:19).

Phut (v. 6) or Put (RSV, NASB) probably is the region of Cyrenaica along the coast of Libya, called Puta in records of Darius I (NBD, p. 1066).

Canaan and Sidon are clearly related, according to v. 15. Historically, the Canaanites of Lebanon and Syria came to be called Phoenicians by Gr. traders *c.* 1200 B.C. (*see* Phoenicia; Purple). Sidon became their chief city at that time, Byblos (Gebal) having been taken over by the Hurrians and Hittites midway through the 2nd mil. B.C. The term Sidonians continued to be the OT equivalent of Phoenicians down to the time of Ezekiel (32:30).

As discussed above, Heth is listed as one of the peoples with Canaan. While Heth may point to the historically powerful Hittites, who spoke an Indo-European language and ruled a large part of W Asia from their capital in Anatolia, it is equally possible that the "children of Heth" of Gen 23 are in view. These were either Hattians (proto-Hittites), some of whom entered Canaan in small numbers in the Early Bronze Age and are associated with the distinctive Khirbet Kerah pottery; or they may have been an early Hurrian enclave, part of the people who were so prominent in the Near East in the middle of the 2nd mil. B.C. (E. A. Speiser, *Genesis,* Anchor Bible, p. 69). The Jebusites, inhabitants of the Jerusalem city-state until David captured it, were very likely Hurrians.

The Amorites, according to Sumerian texts from before 2000 B.C., were seminomads of the N Syrian steppe and mountains near Palmyra. They spoke a W Semitic dialect. A powerful group of tribes, they established kingdoms early in the 2nd mil. B.C. from the Orontes to the Tigris valleys. They controlled Mari *c.* 2000 B.C., and by 1800 they ruled in Babylon (the dynasty of Hammurabi). These kingdoms had all been destroyed by Moses' time, however. Therefore in the Table of Nations they are listed on a geographical basis with greater Canaan, the one area where they were still a prominent part of the population (*see* Amorite).

The Girgashites are unknown as a people outside of the Bible. Personal names such as *Grgs* and *Grgsy* in texts from Ugarit and Carthage, however, suggest that the Girgashites

The Phoenicians were great mariners of the ancient world. Here is the Phoenician harbor at Sidon. HFV

were related to the Canaanites and later Phoenicians. Although the racial origin of the Hivites is not known, they are linked with Canaan geographically, since their center was in the Lebanon Mountains (Jud 3:3). Many believe that "Hivite" is an alternate spelling of "Horite" and that both are biblical names for the Hurrians (*q.v.*). Migrating from the Caucasian Mountains, the non-Semitic Hurrians became influential in the upper Mesopotamian region before the mid-2nd mil. B.C. The patriarchal narratives of Genesis reflect many customs and laws practiced by the Hurrians as revealed in the Alalakh and the Nuzu (*q.v.*) tablets. Canaan was often called Huru by the 18th Dynasty pharaohs, and the ruler of Jerusalem in the Amarna letters has a Hurrian name, Abdu-Heba (ANET, pp. 487–489). Because of their prominence one would expect the Hurrians to be listed in some way in Gen 10.

The Arkites, Arvadites, and Zemarites (vv. 17–18) lived in towns (Irqata, the island city of Arwada, and Sumur) just N of Tripoli on the Lebanese coast. Thutmose III captured these seaports on his campaigns prior to 1450 B.C. The name of the Sinites survives in Nahr as-Sinn and Sinn ad-Darb along the coast of Lebanon, and may be the Phoenician *Usnu,* Akkad. *Siannu* (ANET, p. 282), and Ugaritic *'sn.* The Hamathites were centered in Hamath-on-the-Orontes, an Amorite city-state in the Amarna period.

It is significant that the Sumerians, who had developed the world's first great civilization by 3000 B.C. (*see* Sumer), are not listed as one of the peoples of the time. The reason for their absence is that their last great city-kingdom, the Ur III dynasty, fell before the attacking Elamites and Amorites *c.* 2000 B.C. Thus the Sumerians were no longer considered a nation, even though their language continued to be used until the 3rd cen. B.C.

3. Shem. In this branch of humanity only a few names can be identified with reasonable certainty. Elam was the eastern neighbor and rival of the kingdoms in Mesopotamia since the

NATIONS

dawn of history. Although the Elamite language was not Semitic, Elam is included here for political and geographic reasons. The Semitic king Sargon of Agade conquered Elam *c.* 2200 B.C. and settled some of his Semitic-speaking troops there (Archer, SOTI, p. 203). Asshur is familiar to us as the nation of the Assyrians. Linguistically they belonged to the E branch of the Semitic language family. They became politically important soon after 2000 B.C. By 1900 merchants from Asshur the capital had established a number of trading colonies in distant Anatolia. The Assyrian kingdom of Shamshi-Adad I (*c.* 1800 B.C.) soon afterward fell to Hammurabi of Babylon, and the influence of Assyria was at a low ebb in the days of Moses.

The Assyrians stationed great winged bulls at the gates of their palaces. This one is from the palace of Sargon II at Khorsabad. ORINST

The name of Babylonia is strangely absent in Gen 10, unless it appears in the last three Heb. letters of the etymologically difficult name Arpachshad (v. 24, RSV). The name may be analyzed as *Arip* (a Hurrian name) plus *kasd* (the Kasdim or Chaldeans, i.e., the Babylonians; see IDB, I, 231). The absence of Babylon, however, may be explained by the Hittite destruction of the city *c.* 1600 B.C. and by the subsequent takeover of the whole territory for the next few centuries by the Kassites. Thus Babylon was not a politically independent nation when the Table of Nations was written.

Aram is known through the Arameans, a group of tribes in the middle Euphrates district. They had occupied Haran by the time of Abraham. Laban spoke Aramaic, a W Semitic language, *c.* 1900 B.C. (Gen 31:47), although the first Aram. words to appear in extrabiblical texts occur in 15th cen. B.C. Ugaritic tablets. A settlement called Arami in the E Tigris region E of Assyria and NW of Elam is mentioned in Sargonid and Ur III inscriptions (2300-2000 B.C.), corresponding to the grouping of Aram with Elam and Asshur in Gen 10:22. *See* Aram, Arameans.

Uz (v. 23) was located somewhere in the Syrian or N Arabian desert N of Edom and S of Damascus. Mash was situated on the E side of that desert, known in Assyrian records as *Mas'a* (ANET, pp. 283 f.).

The genealogy from Shem to Peleg (vv. 24-25) is repeated with more detail in Gen 11:10-17. Regarding Eber as the so-called eponymous ancestor of the Heb. people and the possible relationship between Eber and the Habiru, *see* Eber 1; Hebrew People. The reference to the division of the earth in the days of Peleg (v. 25), when the nations were "separated on the earth after the flood" (v. 32, NASB), seems definitely to be to the confusion of languages that occurred at the Tower of Babel (Gen 11:1-9; *see* Dispersion of Mankind; Tongues, Confusion of).

Lists of Non-Israelite Nations. The OT contains 22 lists which name from two to ten of the peoples who occupied Palestine prior to the Israelite conquest under Joshua. The most frequent listing has seven "nations": the Amorites, Canaanites, Hittites, Perizzites, Hivites, Jebusites, and Girgashites. The first two are the well-known ethnic groups of those names. The Hittites were either remnants of the Hattians or Indo-European Hittites if there were Hittite enclaves or commercial colonies in Palestine. The Hivites may be the better known Hurrians. The Perizzites could hardly have belonged to a major people since they are not named in Gen 10. Yet they were still a distinct tribe in Solomon's reign (I Kgs 9:20-21). They may have been Hurrian, because a Hurrian messenger of the Mitannian King Tushratta bore the name Pirizzi (Amarna letters Nos. 27, 28). The last two names are discussed under the Table of Nations.

Gen 15:18-21 lists the largest number of peoples and tribes, placing them geographically between the Nile and the Euphrates. In addition to the others already discussed are the Kenites, Kenizzites, Kadmonites, and Rephaim. The Kenites were a tribe of Canaan who seem to have intermarried with the Midianites, because Jethro is called a Kenite as well as a Midianite (cf. Jud 1:16 with Num 10:29). Some of them may have been itinerant coppersmiths since Heb. *qayin* can mean "smith." The Kenizzites were an obscure tribe, perhaps related to the Kenites, with which Caleb (Num 32:12) and Othniel (Josh 15:17; I Chr 4:13) had some connection. The Kadmonites (*qadmōnî*) are synonymous with the "children of the east" (*bᵉnê qedem;* Gen 29:1; Jud 6:3, 33; I Kgs 4:30; Job 1:3). The latter term covers the nomadic tribes which roamed the area E and NE of Canaan (Jer 49:28; Ezk 25:4, 10). *See* East, Children of the. The Rephaim were a strong people, as tall as the Anakim (Deut 2:20-21, NASB), who

NATIONS

lived in Transjordan (Gen 14:5; Deut 2:11; 3:11).

OT literature abounds in descriptive and poetical references to the nations with which Israel had contact during its history (e.g., Ps 83; Isa 11:11-16; 60:1-9; 66:18-20; Jer 25:12-33; Ezk 27). Many of the prophetic messages are oracles of judgment against the hostile peoples who took advantage of the tiny kingdom of Judah (Isa 13–23; Jer 46–51; Ezk 25–32; Amos 1:3–2:3; Obadiah; Nahum; Zeph 2:4-15). At no point can it be demonstrated that either in the names of the peoples or of their rulers, or of the events or customs associated with them, is there a clear-cut historical or factual error.

The Jews of the Diaspora. Acts 2:9-11 lists the various countries where Jews were living in their dispersion after the time of Alexander the Great. From those lands the Jews came as pilgrims to Jerusalem for the annual Feast of Weeks or Pentecost. The foreign Jews were amazed at each one hearing the Galilean Jews praising God, not in their native Aramaic, but in his language or dialect (Gr. *dialektōs*) to which he was born. They had come from Persia and Mesopotamia, Asia Minor, Egypt, N Africa, and Rome, and from islands (Cretans) and desert regions (Arabians) as well. Most of the pilgrims would have spoken as a second language one used commonly in Jerusalem, either Greek or Aramaic (the Parthians, Medes, Elamites, and residents of Mesopotamia would be more familiar with the latter).

Divine Concern for the Nations

The responsibility of Israel. Under the Abrahamic and Mosaic covenants the Jews had a God-given responsibility toward the nations. God had chosen their father Abraham (Isa 51:2) and made a covenant with him for the blessing of all the nations of the earth (Gen 12:3; 18:18; 22:18; 26:4; 28:14). This promise became the basis for the covenantal relationship with the redeemed Israelites at Mount Sinai: "Now then, if you will indeed obey My voice and keep My covenant, then you shall be My own possession among all the peoples, for all the earth is Mine; and you shall be to Me a kingdom of priests and a holy nation" (Ex 19:5-6, NASB). "A kingdom of priests . . . among all the peoples"—thus did God consecrate Israel for service to bear a witness among the nations and to bring them to worship Him.

Repeatedly through the prophets the Lord reminded the nation of Israel of His purpose. In spite of this, Jonah as a prophet and the people as a whole were deaf to their covenantal responsibility (Isa 42:19). Nevertheless God kept on calling: "You are My witnesses, . . . and My servant whom I have chosen" (Isa 43:10). He foretold that He would pour out His Spirit on all mankind (Joel 2:28), and that He would restore the fallen house of David so that His people might possess all the nations who are called by His name (Amos 9:11-12). God announced His coming to gather all nations in order to see His glory, and that He would send His remnant to distant nations which had not heard His fame to declare His glory among them (Isa 66:18-19). Zechariah (2:11) and Malachi (1:11) among the post-Exilic prophets continued to publish the Lord's desire to make all the nations to be His people as well as Israel. *See* Dispersion of Israel.

The mission of the Church. Isaiah prophesied of Messiah that God would give Him to be a light to the nations so that His salvation might reach to the end of the earth (Isa 49:6; cf. 42:1-6). When Jesus came He clearly stated: "I have other sheep, which are not of this fold; I must bring them also . . . and they shall become one flock with one Shepherd" (Jn 10:16, NASB). He taught His disciples that the gospel would be preached in the whole world for a witness to all nations before the end would come, and that all the nations would be gathered before the Son of Man for judgment (Mt 24:14; 25:31-33).

After His resurrection Christ on several occasions commissioned His followers to go and make disciples of *all* nations (Mt 28:19; *see* Commission, Great). It took the outpouring of the Holy Spirit at Pentecost in fulfillment of Joel's prophecy to empower the early Christians so that they could obey Jesus' command (Lk 24:49; Acts 1:8; 2:4, 16-18). Peter announced that the promised gift of the Holy Spirit was for the Jews present at Pentecost and their descendants, "and for all who are far off, as many as the Lord our God shall call to Himself" (Acts 2:38-39, NASB). The expression "far off" is a term describing the spiritual position of the Gentiles (Isa 57:19; Eph 2:13, 17).

The Holy Spirit led the apostles and early Christians to follow the order of Christ's strategic plan in Acts 1:8. Paul recognized its directive as he wrote of his obligation "to the Jew first and also to the Greek" (Rom 1:16). His final words to the Jewish leaders in Rome clearly declare that the salvation of God has been sent to the Gentiles, and that they will respond (Acts 28:25-28).

John foresaw the day when members of every nation upon earth will be assembled around the throne of God in triumph and praise (Rev 5:9; 7:9). The nations will be healed (22:2), and they will walk by the light of the glory of God and the Lamb, with the kings of the earth bringing the glory and the honor of the nations into the holy city (21:24, 26).

Bibliography. G. L. Archer, Jr., "Peoples of Bible Times," *The Holy Bible,* Family Heritage ed., Cleveland: World Publ. Co., 1968, pp. 27-32. J. M. Grintz, "On the Original Home of the Semites," JNES, XXI (1962), 186-206. E. J. Hamlin, "Nations," IDB, III, 515-523. T. C. Mitchell, "Nations, Table of," NBD, pp. 865-869. John Rea, "Nations," ZPBE (forthcoming). K. L. Schmidt, "*Ethnos*, etc.," TDNT, II, 364–372. J. Simons, GTT, 1959. E. A. Speiser, "Man, Ethnic Divisions of," IDB, III, 235–242; *Genesis*, Anchor Bible, Garden City: Doubleday, 1964. H. Strathmann and R. Meyer, "*Laos*," TDNT, IV, 29–57.

J. R.

NATIVITY OF CHRIST. *See* Christmas; Incarnation; Jesus Christ.

NATURAL, NATURE

1. Heb. *lēaḥ*, "freshness," "moistness," "the suppleness of youth." In Deut 34:7, in its single occurrence in the OT, this word is translated "natural force" in the phrase "his eye was not dim, nor his natural force abated." Though he was 120 when he died, Moses' vitality still had not waned.

The word *lḥ* has been found twice in Ugaritic tablets with the meaning of vigor or life-force (cf. ANET, p. 150, col. 1, l. 30).

2. Gr. *genesis*, "origin," "birth," "coming into being," "natural," in the course of nature with its cycle of development. Used of viewing the face of one's birth or nature in a mirror and seeing his age reflected (Jas 1:23), and of (our) life as a progressive cycle (Jas 3:6).

3. Gr. *psychikos*, "natural," "sensual," having the nature and characteristics common to animal life. Thus we have the natural body contrasted with the spiritual (I Cor 15:44, 46) and equivalent to flesh and blood (v. 50). In I Cor 2:14 it is used to express the unsaved, unregenerate man in contrast to the redeemed. "The natural man receiveth not the things of the Spirit." He is subject to his own appetites and passions and cannot grasp divine truth.

4. Gr. *physis*, "nature"; *physikos*, "that produced by nature," "natural" (Rom 11:21, 24). Some men are Jews by natural birth (Gal 2:15). Paul speaks of both men and women departing from the normal role of sex found in nature (Rom 1:26–27), Peter and Jude of those who act like animals (II Pet 2:12; Jude 10). There is an implanted moral law in Gentiles which they follow instinctively or "by nature" (Rom 2:14). Yet all men by nature or in their natural condition are "children of wrath," subject to the dreadful judgment of God (Eph 2:3). In Christ we become partakers of the divine nature, sharing in the very being of God (II Pet 1:4). Thus we are set free from those beings which in their nature are no gods (Gal 4:8, NEB), merely inferior spirits or demons (v. 9).

R. A. K.

NAUGHTINESS. Heb. *rōaʻ*, "evil, badness, wickedness of heart" (I Sam 17:28); *hawwâ*, "mischief, evil, naughtiness" (Prov 11:6; 17:4). Gr. *kakia*, "evil, wickedness, malice" (Jas 1:21).

NAUM (nā'ŭm). The only NT reference (Lk 3:25) includes him in the ancestry of Christ as the son of Esli and the father of Amos. *See* Nahum.

NAVE. The word is used in two ways in English translations of the Bible.

1. In I Kgs 7:33 (only occurrence for this usage) the KJV has "nave" in the plural, meaning the central part or hub of the wheel into which the spokes fit on the side and the axle in the middle; NEB has "hubs." The Heb. word is *gab*, meaning "hollow" or "curved." The ASV, NASB, RSV, and Berkeley have rendered this Heb. word as "felloes" or "rims" of the wheel (cf. Ezk 1:18; 10:12), and have rendered another Heb. word *ḥishshûq* (the only occurrence in Heb. OT) in I Kgs 7:33 as "nave" or "hub."

2. The RSV and NASB use the word "nave" in the sense of the *hall* of the temple, the holy place distinguished from the inner sanctuary, translating Heb. *hêkal* (cf. I Kgs 6:3, 5, 17, 33; 7:50; Ezk 41:1, 4, 15, 21, 23, 25; the word is translated elsewhere as temple or palace). The RSV similarly renders Heb. *bayit* (cf. II Chr 3:4, 5, 13; 4:22; Ezk 41:17; which word has the general meaning "house"); and finally "nave" is supplied as the meaning of the suffix designation in Ezk 41:2 (KJV and ASV, "length thereof"; "length of the nave," RSV and NASB).

G. W. K.

NAVEL. The depression or scar in the middle of the abdomen which marks the umbilical connection of the fetus with the mother; used to convey food to and remove waste from the fetus (Ezk 16:4; Job 40:16; Prov 3:8; Song 7:2).

NAVY. Used in the sense of a fleet of ships (I Kgs 9:26). The only references in the Bible are applied to Solomon's navy, which was based at Ezion-geber and which brought luxury goods from Africa and Asia for exchange with Phoenicia (I Kgs 10:22). *See* Ships.

NAZARENE (năz'ȧ-rēn). A NT designation translates Gr. *nazarēnos* and *nazōraios*, used a number of times of Jesus and once (Acts 24:5) of His followers. Except in Mt 2:23 and Acts 24:5, it is always used with the name Jesus (in the KJV always "Jesus of Nazareth"; in the ASV "Jesus the Nazarene" six times). It was used fearfully by demons (Mk 1:24; Lk 4:34), contemptuously by His enemies (Mt 26:71; Mk 14:67; Acts 6:14), and favorably by His followers (Lk 18:37; 24:19; Acts 2:22; 3:6; 4:10), by the resurrection messenger (Mk 16:6), and by the risen Lord Himself (Acts 22:8). Mt 2:23 associates the name with His residence in Nazareth. While *nazōraios* is often regarded as referring either to the "Branch" (*nēṣer*) of Isa 11:1 or to the Nazarite (*nāzîr*), Matthew's indefinite "the prophets" (2:23) suggests not a specific prediction but a prophetic theme, i.e., that He was despised.

Bibliography. H. H. Schraeder, "*Nazarēnos*, etc.," TDNT, IV, 874–879.

NAZARETH (năz'ȧ-rĕth). The village of Nazareth, secluded among the surrounding hills of Lower Galilee, was not a significant place until it became famous in NT times as the boyhood home of Jesus. The ancient town is represented by the modern site of en-Nâzirah, and the general location is one of the most beautiful in Palestine.

Nazareth is not mentioned in the OT, the Talmud, nor by the historian Josephus. The oldest known literary references to the place appear in the NT. It was the residence of Mary and Joseph (Lk 1:26–27; 2:39), and the place where the angel announced the Messiah's birth to Mary (Lk 1:26–28). Joseph brought the child and His mother there after the sojourn in Egypt (Mt 2:19–23), and it was the place where Jesus grew to manhood (Lk 4:16) and spent about 30 years of His life (Lk 2:39–51). There He taught in the synagogue (Mt 13:54; Lk 4:16), and experienced rejection on the part of the hometown people. Although His birthplace was in Bethlehem, His long association with the village caused Him to be called Jesus of Nazareth (Lk 18:37), and His disciples to be known as Nazarenes. The reputation of Nazareth was not the best; the people there had established a bad name in morals and religion (Jn 1:46).

Before 1948 Nazareth was a town of about 22,000, composed chiefly of Muslims and Christians. By 1970 its population had increased to 33,000.

P. S. H.

Nazareth with dome of Church of the Annunciation in distant center. HFV

NAZARITE (năz'ȧ-rīt), **NAZIRITE** (năz'ĭ-rīt). A lay person of either sex who was bound by a special vow of consecration to God's service for a defined period of time or for life (Num 6:1–5). His abstinence was an individual matter, not as a member of a group such as the Rechabites (*q.v.*). Ordinarily the vow was made voluntarily, but occasionally the parents made the dedication for the child for life, as in the cases of Samson (Jud 13), of Samuel (I Sam 1:9–11), and of John the Baptist (Lk 1:15, 80; Mk 1:6).

A Nazarite (1) could not partake of the fruit of the vine; (2) had to leave his hair uncut (*see* Hair); (3) had to remain free from all impurities including the touching of dead bodies (Num 6:3–8). In case of defilement a ritual of purification was prescribed (Num 6:9–12). At the end of the period of separation the Nazarite followed a specified procedure for release from his vow, which included appearing before the priest with certain prescribed offerings and shaving his head and burning the hair (Num 6:13–21).

During the monarchy God charged that apostate men were forcing Nazarites to drink wine (Amos 2:11–12). When in Corinth Paul had made a temporary Nazarite vow, perhaps for divine protection in that city; its period ended when he was in Cenchrea and there he cut his hair (Acts 18:18). Later he was persuaded to purify himself as a Nazarite along with four Jewish believers in Jerusalem and to pay for the terminating sacrifices of their vow (Acts 21:18–26).

E. M. B.

NEAH (nē'ȧ). One of the northern border towns of Zebulun (Josh 19:13) of which there is presently no positive identification. Some have suggested the word may be a corruption of Neiel (*q.v.*; Josh 19:27) which is mentioned in the delimitation of Asher.

NEAPOLIS (nē-ăp'ŏ-lĭs). The "new city," modern Kavalla in N Greece, which served as the port of Philippi, situated ten miles inland. An ancient aqueduct and other remains indicate its past importance. It is located on a neck of land between two bays of the Aegean Sea. Paul

Neapolis. HFV

landed here from Troas on his second missionary journey (Acts 16:11), after his call to Macedonia.

NEARIAH (nē'*ȧ*-rī'*ȧ*)

1. One of the six sons of Shemaiah, and father of Elioenai, Hezekiah, and Azrikam; listed in the royal family of Judah after the captivity (I Chr 3:22–23).

2. A Simeonite captain, a son of Ishi who together with his brothers and 500 other Simeonites, successfully conquered the Amalekites near Mount Seir in the days of Hezekiah (I Chr 4:42).

NEBAI (nē'bī). One of the chiefs of the people who helped Nehemiah sign the covenant after it had been read to the people at the completion of the rebuilding of the walls of Jerusalem (Neh 10:19).

NEBAIOTH (nē̂-bā'yŏth), **NEBAJOTH** (nē̂-bā'jŏth). The eldest son of Ishmael and brother of Kedar (Gen 25:13; I Chr 1:29) and ancestor of a pastoral tribe named after him (Isa 60:7). Esau, Isaac's eldest son, married Nebajoth's sister (Gen 28:9; 36:3). On the problem concerning her name *see* Bashemath 2; Mahalath 1. It is doubtful whether this Arabic tribe of the Syrian desert together with the people of Kedar are the forerunners of the Nabateans (*q.v.*) who conquered and occupied Petra in the 4th cen. B.C. The Nebaioth Arabs seem to have been the *Nabaiati*, mentioned in Assyrian records by Tiglath-pileser III, and along with the *Qidri* (Kedar) by Ashurbanipal (ANET, pp. 298–300). But the later Nabateans spelled their name with a *ṭ* (teth), not the *t* (tau) of the Nebaioth of the OT.

NEBALLAT (nĭ-băl'*ȧ*t). A town located in the low hills of Ephraim about four miles NE of Lod (Lydda). It was one of the listed cities occupied by the Benjamites following the Babylonian Exile (Neh 11:34). Identified with modern Beit Nebala.

NEBAT (nē'băt). The father of Jeroboam, the first king of the ten northern tribes (I Kgs 12:2; *et al.*). He is said to have been an Ephrathite of Zereda in the Jordan Valley (I Kgs 11:26). His name is probably used to distinguish his son from Jeroboam the son of Joash (II Kgs 14:23).

NEBO (nē'bō)

1. The Babylonian deity Nabu (Isa 46:1). *See* Gods, False.

2. A mountain of the Abarim range in Moab opposite Jericho (Num 33:47; Deut 32:49; 34:1). It affords a view of much of the land of W and E Palestine. It was on Mount Nebo, the summit of Pisgah (*q.v.*), that Moses overlooked Canaan and then died without entering the Promised Land (Deut 34:1–8).

The most probable location is Jebel en-Neba, a prominent spur or headland of the Moabite plateau. About 2,700 feet above sea level, it drops off sharply toward the N end of the Dead Sea 4,000 feet below and 12 miles due W. An early Christian tradition identified Mount Nebo with the slightly lower Ras es-Siyaghah, separated by a "saddle" from the summit of en-Neba, where ruins of Byzantine churches were excavated from 1933 to 1937 by the Franciscans of Jerusalem. The view from either spot is superb. On a very clear day one can see the snow-capped peak of Mount Hermon far to the N. He can discern the towers on the Mount of Olives to the W, and see as far S as En-gedi on the W shore of the Dead Sea. The twin peaks of Ebal and Gerizim are visible to the NW.

3. A town in Moab E of the Jordan, occupied and rebuilt by the tribe of Reuben (Num 32:3, 38; I Chr 5:8). On the Moabite Stone (*q.v.;* lines 14–16, ANET, p. 320) Mesha king of Moab tells how he conquered the town of Nebo and took from there a cult object of Yahweh. The town may have been retaken by Jeroboam II along with other cities of Moab, but still later Nebo was again in Moabite hands (Isa 15:2; Jer 48:1, 22). It has been tentatively identified with Khirbet Mekhayyet, *c.* two miles SE of Ras es-Siyaghah, where there are ruins of an ancient fortress and large quantities of Moabite (Iron Age I–II, 1200–585 B.C.) potsherds.

4. A town mentioned after Bethel and Ai in the lists of Israelites who returned from the Babylonian Captivity (Ezr 2:29; Neh 7:33). Nehemiah calls it "the other Nebo," perhaps to distinguish it from the town of that name in Moab (3 above). Its site may be modern Beit Nuba, near Aijalon, *c.* 12 miles NW of Jerusalem.

5. The ancestor of seven Jews who had married foreign wives during or after the Exile (Ezr 10:43).

J. R.

NEBUCHADNEZZAR (nĕb'*ŭ*-kȧd-nĕz'*ȧ*r), **NEBUCHADREZZAR** (nĕb'*ŭ*-kȧd-rĕz'*ȧ*r)

The name. The throne-name *Nabû-kudurrī-uṣur* ("Nebo, Protect My Frontier!") was adopted by four Babylonian monarchs, only one of whom (Nebuchadnezzar II) is mentioned in the Bible, though with a frequency and emphasis that witness to his important role in redemptive history. Of the two English transcriptions of his name found in our standard versions the one with *r* (Heb. *Nebûkadre'ṣṣar* in Jeremiah and Ezekiel) most faithfully represents the Akkad. original (cf. above). The spelling with *n* (Heb. *Nebûlukadne*[']*ṣṣar* in II Kings, I and II Chronicles, Ezra, Nehemiah, Esther, Daniel and occasionally in Jeremiah; Aram. *Nebûlukadneṣṣar* in Ezra and Daniel; LXX *Nabouchodonos*[*s*]*or*) is the result of a dialectal dissimilation.

Sources of information. Over 500 administrative and contract tablets dated according to the days, months and years of Nebuchadnezzar's reign have been excavated. Also there are about 30 building and honorific inscriptions mostly on stone cylinders and bricks, but including the important East India House Inscription, a black basalt stela with 621 lines of script describing his fortifying Babylon and restoring the old palace and the building of a new one. The 720 line Wadi Brissa inscription in Syria (ANET, p. 307) records his conquest of Lebanon and transport of its cedars to Babylon. D. J. Wiseman has recently published tablets of the year-by-year Babylonian Chronicle dealing with the first 12 years of his reign. Other sources include the OT books of II Kings, II Chronicles, Jeremiah, Ezekiel and Daniel, and fragments of later historians cited by Josephus and Eusebius.

Political history. Nebuchadnezzar II was unquestionably the greatest of the rulers of the short-lived Neo-Babylonian Empire (626–539 B.C.), over which he reigned for 43 years (605–562). His father was Nabopolassar who, defying the armies of weakened Assyria, was enthroned as king of Babylon on November 23, 626. Upon the destruction of Nineveh in 612 by a Medo-Babylonian alliance, Assyria moved her capital westward to Harran which, in 610, was occupied by Nabopolassar without a struggle. We hear no more of Assyria after 609.

The immediate result of Assyria's fall was a brief assertion of Egyptian hegemony over Judah. Pharaoh Necho II (609–593 B.C.) deposed and enthroned Judahite monarchs at will until the defeat of the Egyptian forces at Carchemish. The credit for the Babylonian victory goes to Nebuchadnezzar, the crown prince, who had been sent by Nabopolassar to lead the Babylonian army.

Recently published tablets of the Babylonian Chronicle enable us to date the battle of Carchemish rather precisely (May–June, 605). Both Jeremiah (Jer 46:2–12) and Jos (*Ant*.x.6) recognized something of its significance, marking as it did the removal of Egypt from any further important role in Palestinian affairs, as well as the rise to power of Nebuchadnezzar. On August 16, 605, Nabopolassar died, and Nebuchadnezzar halted his pursuit of the retreating Egyptians to return home to assume the Babylonian throne. His coronation took place on September 7, after which he returned to his army in the W and resumed his advance into Syria.

By 603 B.C. Nebuchadnezzar was master of the whole of Syro-Palestine. Jehoiakim had transferred his fealty, if only temporarily, to Nebuchadnezzar (II Kgs 24:1). Ashkelon in Philistia was destroyed by Nebuchadnezzar before his return to Babylonia in February, 603. Saqqara Papyrus Number 86984 (Cairo Museum), an Aram. letter appealing to the Pharaoh for assistance, was apparently written from Ashkelon just before its destruction.

In 601, Nebuchadnezzar once again marched toward Egypt and engaged the forces of Necho in a pitched battle near the Egyptian border. Both sides suffered heavy losses, and the encounter ended in a stalemate. At this point Jehoiakim, evidently convinced that his chance had come, rebelled against Babylonia and withheld tribute (II Kgs 24:1). But though caught off balance for the moment, Nebuchadnezzar had no intention of permitting Judah to secede from his empire. For the time being he harassed the tiny kingdom with marauding bands of troops, assembled from his own armies as well as from mercenary contingents (24:2).

Nebuchadnezzar returned with the main Babylonian army against Judah (II Kgs 24:10–11) in December, 598. The laconic scribe of the Babylonian Chronicle, reporting the events of 597, states simply that Nebuchadnezzar "encamped against the city of Judah [i.e., Jerusalem] and on the second day of the month Adar [i.e., March 16] he seized the city and captured the king [i.e., Jehoiachin]. He appointed there a king that pleased him [i.e., Zedekiah]." Jehoiakim had mysteriously died in the same month in which the Babylonian army had set out against Judah. In view of the fact that his son Jehoiachin (II Kgs 24:6) ruled for three months and ten days (II Chr 36:9; the "three months" of II Kgs 24:8 is intended only as an approximation) before the capture of Jerusalem, the exact date of Jehoiakim's death was December 7, 598. Jehoiachin's stated age in II Chr 36:9—eight years old—seems to be a copyist's error for the 18 years old of II Kgs 24:8.

Nebuchadnezzar, following the example of his Mesopotamian predecessors since the time of Tiglath-pileser III (*q.v.*), deported the king (Jehoiachin) and his retinue, as well as all the other Jerusalemites who might be expected to foment rebellion (II Kgs 24:12–16; II Chr 36:10; Jer 22:24–30; 52:28). Though Nebuchadnezzar had demanded to take to Babylon some hostages including Daniel and his three friends and part of the vessels of Solomon's temple immediately following the battle of Carchemish (Dan 1:1–7; cf. also II Chr 36:5–7), the deportation of 597 B.C. constituted the first major phase of what has been traditionally referred to as the Babylonian Captivity (cf. Mt 1:11). As before, though on a much grander scale, Nebuchadnezzar plundered Solomon's temple and carried off an enormous booty. He installed Jehoiachin's uncle, Mattaniah, on the Judahite throne (II Kgs 24:17; in II Chr 36:10 "brother" is better rendered "kinsman"), renaming him Zedekiah to demonstrate his own suzerainty.

Zedekiah would doubtless have proved a docile vassal of Nebuchadnezzar had not several factors beyond his control disturbed the political situation. A considerable number of Judahites, both in Jerusalem and in Babylonia, still considered Jehoiachin the legitimate claimant to their throne. Ezekiel, e.g., betrayed his true feelings by reckoning dates from "king Jehoiachin's captivity" (Ezk 1:2; etc.).

Furthermore, even after her defeat at Carchemish, Egypt, though seriously weakened, continued to exert some influence in Near Eastern affairs. In addition, dissension against Ba-

NEBUCHADNEZZAR

A reconstruction of Babylon in Nebuchadnezzar's day with the Ishtar Gate in foreground and hanging gardens at right. ORINST

bylonia was rife not only in Jerusalem (witness the unavailing efforts of Jeremiah to keep his countrymen from overt rebellion) but among Nebuchadnezzar's own people as well. In 595/4 Nebuchadnezzar found it necessary to remain in Babylonia to suppress a local rebellion there. In the following year Hananiah, a false prophet in Jerusalem, publicly foretold the return from exile, within two years, of all whom Nebuchadnezzar had carried away to Babylonia (Jer 28:1-4). Perhaps Hananiah had received word of the Babylonian insurrection and interpreted it as a sign of more widespread dissension. At any rate, Jeremiah denounced such undue optimism and advised the exiles to adopt a philosophy of "life-as-usual," for the Lord had revealed that their stay in Babylonia would be a prolonged one (Jer 29:1-23).

For a time Zedekiah remained convinced of the wisdom of Jeremiah's counsel. Jer 51:59 would seem to indicate that in the very year of Hananiah's ill-advised prophecy, and indeed perhaps as a result of it, Zedekiah was summoned by Nebuchadnezzar to Babylon for an interview to determine the extent of his loyalty. Nebuchadnezzar was evidently satisfied with Zedekiah's answers, for he permitted him to remain on the throne of Judah. Succeeding years, however, found Zedekiah increasingly less able to withstand the pro-Egyptian, anti-Babylonian element of Judah's population. Finally, contrary to the advice of Jeremiah (II Chr 36:12; Jer 21:1-7; 37:3-10, 17-20; 38:14-23), he rebelled (II Kgs 24:20; II Chr 36:13-16; Jer 52:3).

By January of 588 Nebuchadnezzar and his army were besieging Jerusalem (II Kgs 25:1; Jer 39:1; 52:4; Ezk 24:1-2). The Babylonian army had been capturing the fortified cities of Judah one by one, so that by the time the siege of Jerusalem was well under way only Lachish and Azekah remained (Jer 34:6-7). The Lachish letters, a cache of 21 ostraca found at modern Tell ed-Duweir (the biblical Lachish, *q.v.*) in 1935 and 1938, illustrate the consternation that reigned in Judah during the final days of her national existence (see ANET, pp. 321 f.). The only glimmer of hope in an otherwise hopeless situation was a temporary withdrawal of the Babylonian forces from Jerusalem to deal with an advancing Egyptian army (Jer 37:5, 11), probably under Pharaoh Apries (589-570; *see* Pharaoh-Hophra). The relief in Jerusalem was short-lived, however, for the Babylonians quickly forced the Egyptians to retreat and resumed the siege.

The city held out for a total of 30 months, but the superior Babylonian forces finally breached its walls in July, 586, in the 19th year of Nebuchadnezzar (II Kgs 25:2-4, 8; Jer 39:2; 52:5-7, 12). Zedekiah and a number of his troops, attempting to flee during the night, were overtaken near Jericho. The king was brought before Nebuchadnezzar at Riblah on the Orontes, where he was forced to watch the execution of his sons. He was then blinded and carried off in chains to Babylonia (II Kgs 25:5-7; Jer 39:4-8; 52:8-11) as one of the exiles in the second major phase of the Babylonian Captivity (Jer 52:29). Subsequently *Nabû-zēr(a)-iddina* (Nebuzaradan, *q.v.*), captain of Nebuchadnezzar's guard, arrived in Jerusalem to complete the razing and plundering of the city and temple as well as the deportation of the population, leaving behind only the poorer elements (II Kgs 25:8-17; II Chr 36:17-20; Jer 39:9-10; 52:12-23).

Following the destruction of Jerusalem, Nebuchadnezzar appointed as governor over Judah Gedaliah (*q.v.*), who soon fell into disfavor with the remaining anti-Babylonian elements of the Judahite population. Awaiting a suitable opportunity, they assassinated him at Mizpah together with a number of his Jewish and Babylonian companions (II Kgs 25:22-25; Jer 40:7–41:3). The instigator of the plot, one Ishmael, escaped to Ammon with eight of his lackeys (Jer 41:15), while another group of Judahites, fearing Babylonian reprisals, fled to Egypt (II Kgs 25:26; Jer 41:16-18), taking Jeremiah with them (Jer 43:5-7). The third and final phase of the Babylonian Captivity occurred in 582 (Jer 52:30) and was apparently the aftermath of a punitive expedition sent by Nebuchadnezzar to Judah following the murder of Gedaliah.

The blind Zedekiah, meanwhile, languished in prison, there eventually to die (II Kgs 25:7; cf. Ezk 12:13). His predecessor, Jehoiachin, was considerably more fortunate; in 562 Amēl-Marduk (Evil-merodach, *q.v.*), the son and successor of Nebuchadnezzar, released him from prison and made him a ward of the Babylonian court (II Kgs 25:27-30; Jer 52:31-34). Prior to that time Jehoiachin's needs had also been amply supplied, as is clear from a number of administrative documents, found in Babylon and dating from Nebuchadnezzar's reign, which refer to Jehoiachin as *Ya(k)ukīn(u)*, king of *Yaḫ/kūdu* (Judah; ANET, p. 308).

Nebuchadnezzar's western expeditions after 586 B.C. were anticlimactic from the standpoint of Judah. His campaigns against Tyre (585-572) are alluded to in Ezk 26–28; 29:18, while a battle against the troops of Amasis of Egypt in 568/7 (ANET, p. 308) seems to have been foreseen by Ezekiel (29:19). Nebuchadnezzar died in 562, just 25 years after the capitulation of Jerusalem.

Buildings. While justly famed as a brilliant military strategist and administrator, Nebuchadnezzar II also merits recognition as a great builder. The archaeological expeditions of the Deutsche Orientgesellschaft under the direction of Robert Koldewey beginning in 1899 have shown that Nebuchadnezzar rebuilt Babylon into a magnificent city (cf. Dan 4:30), at once strengthening and beautifying it. In Borsippa and Babylon he restored more than 20 temples, while in Babylon itself he constructed a raised street with its Ishtar gate for the procession of

Tablet relating accession of Nebuchadnezzar to the throne of Babylon and his capture of Jerusalem in 597 B.C. BM

Marduk and his colossal and ornate palace (cf. Dan 1–4 for glimpses of Babylonian court life during Nebuchadnezzar's reign). There also he erected one of the so-called seven wonders of the ancient world, the fabulous hanging gardens, a terraced arboretum designed to compensate his Median wife, Amytis, for the loss of her mountainous childhood home. To judge from a number of Nebuchadnezzar's royal inscriptions which were composed in an archaic Babylonian script and dialect, a different kind of nostalgia gripped him–a poignant longing for the better days of a bygone era.

[*Lawgiver*. A tablet in the British Museum published in 1965 by W. G. Lambert and A. R. Millard extols the virtues as lawgiver and judge of a certain king who can only be Nebuchadnezzar II. A code of laws is ascribed to him, as well as regulations for his city (which is obviously Babylon) and his own royal office. Justice was enforced by beheading a criminal in one case, and in another by condemning an accused murderer and his accuser to the river ordeal (*Iraq*, XXVII, 1-11).

[*Religion*. The inscriptions of Nebuchadnezzar reveal that he was a very religious man who sought to observe all the ceremonies connected with the worship of the Babylonian deities. The longer texts usually contain two hymns and close with a prayer. Frequent mention is made of his elaborate offerings to the gods.

[*References in Daniel*. In light of a fragmentary Aram. scroll from Qumran Cave 4, known as the "Prayer of Nabonidus," many scholars who hold to a Maccabean date for the writing of the book of Daniel have recently suggested that the Scripture is in error in representing Nebuchadnezzar as the king who was afflicted with a strange disease for seven years (D. N. Freedman, BASOR #145 [1957], pp. 31 f.; J. T. Milik, *Ten Years of Discovery in the Wilderness of Judaea*, Naperville, Ill.: Allenson, 1959, pp. 36 f.). Instead, according to the Qumran text, Nabonidus (*q.v.*) the father of Belshazzar is meant. The malady described in Dan 4:33 was a mental illness or paranoia, and may be diagnosed as lycanthropy or boanthropy, a clinically recognized if rare form of monomania in which the king imagined himself to be a bull or an eagle, and acted accordingly (Harrison, IOT, pp. 1114–1117). But the sickness mentioned in the "Prayer of Nabonidus" had to do with the inflammation of the tissues or a malignant disease, certainly a different affliction from insanity. R. K. Harrison concludes that the Qumran text is legendary material, similar in origin to the stories of Bel and the Dragon and of Susanna, and even closer in form and content to the apocryphal Prayer of Manasseh (IOT, pp. 1117-1120).

[Column VIII of the East India House Inscription, which dates to the latter half of Nebuchadnezzar's reign, gives some reason to believe that he may have been removed from power for at least four years. The significant portion is translated as follows: "For four years the seat of my kingdom in my city . . . did not rejoice my heart. In all my dominions I did not build a high place of power, the precious treasures of my kingdom I did not lay out. In the worship of Marduk my lord, the joy of my heart in Babylon, the city of my sovereignty, I did not sing his praises and I did not furnish his altars, nor did I clear out the canals" (IDB, I, 851). One could scarcely expect a proud Oriental monarch to refer to his own calamity, especially madness, more specifically than this. Furthermore, very few other records come to us from this part of his reign. R. Dick Wilson suggests that the "seven times" (Dan 4:16, 23, 25, 32) may have been months, not years (ISBE, IV, 2128), so that the extreme stage of the illness may have lasted much less time than the four years of the above inscription.

[None of Nebuchadnezzar's inscriptions mention any of his dreams, although the annals of other rulers (e.g., Ashurbanipal, Nabonidus, Xerxes) indicate that importance was attached to dreams and their interpretation. We know from his records that Nebuchadnezzar once made an image of his royal person (ISBE, IV, 2128). Six miles SE of Babylon J. Oppert found remains of a massive square brick platform (46′ × 46′ × 20′) on which the image of gold described in Dan 3:1 may have stood. As to the "fiery furnace," R. Dick Wilson states that Ashurbanipal, king of Assyria, recorded that his brother Shamash-shumukin was burned in a similar furnace (ISBE, IV, 2129).–J.R.]

See Babylon; Babylonia; Daniel, Book of.

Bibliography. W. F. Albright, "King Joiachin in Exile," BA, V (1942), 49–55. J. Bright, "A New Letter in Aramaic, Written to a Pharaoh of Egypt," BA, XII (1949), 46–52. D. N. Freedman, "The Babylonian Chronicle," BA, XIX (1956), 50–60. W. G. Lambert, "Nebuchadnezzar King of Justice," *Iraq,* XXVII (1965), 1–11. Stephen Langdon, *Building Inscriptions of the Neo-Babylonian Empire,* Paris, 1905. G. R. Tabouis, *Nebuchadnezzar,* New York: McGraw-Hill, 1931. R. Dick Wilson, "Nebuchadnezzar," ISBE, IV, 2127 ff. D. J. Wiseman, *Chronicles of Chaldean Kings (626–556 B.C.),* London: British Museum, 1956.

R. E. Y.

NEBUSHASBAN (nĕb'ū-shăs'băn). One of the Babylonian princes who occupied the office of Rab-saris (i.e., chief of the eunuchs), whom Nebuzaradan, Nebuchadnezzar's guard captain, sent to protect Jeremiah during the siege of Jerusalem in 587 B.C. (Jer 39:13). He probably succeeded Ashpenaz, whose office and title were identical (Dan 1:3).

NEBUZARADAN (nĕb'*ŭ-zȧ*-rā'dȧn). The captain of Nebuchadnezzar's bodyguard who played a prominent role in the capture of Jerusalem. His Babylonian name *Nabu-zir-iddina* means "Nebo-has given- a posterity." He was responsible for the burning of the temple, the palace, and the great houses, for the deportation of the population to Babylon, and for the removal of the sacred vessels from the temple (II Kgs 25:8 ff.; Jer 39:9 ff.). Together with other Babylonian officers he was entrusted with the care of Jeremiah. He granted the prophet an allowance of food and a gift, and gave him the choice of going to Babylon with the exiles or of staying in Judah (Jer 40:1 ff.).

The name is listed as *Nabû-zêr-i-din-nam rab-nuhtimmu* in a list of Nebuchadnezzar's officials found at Babylon, published by Eckhard Unger in *Theologische Literaturzeitung,* L (Oct. 17, 1925), 482–86. The phrase *rab-nuhtimmu* means "chief of the bakers" and may correspond to the biblical phrase associated with Nebuzaradan, *rab-ṭabbāḥîm*. The latter is usually rendered "guards"; literally it means "slaughterers," and may also mean "cooks." The "baker" and the "butler" (or cupbearer) were no menial servants, but rather trusted and honored officials (cf. Samuel Feigin, "The Babylonian Officials in Jeremiah 39:3, 13," JBL, XLV (1926), 149–55.

E. M. Y.

NECHO. *See* Pharaoh.

NECK. This word denotes a part of the physical frame (Gen 46:29; Acts 20:37), and is used figuratively many times. It sometimes signifies gracefulness (Song 4:4; 7:4). To lay down the neck means to hazard one's life (Rom 16:4). To reach even to the neck was to approach the point of overwhelming destruction (Isa 8:8; 30:28), and to put the feet upon the neck was to conquer (Josh 10:24). Because beasts of burden bore the yoke upon the neck, the yoked neck signified service. Thus Christ invites all to take up His yoke (with neck understood, Mt 11:29). Persons with a stubborn and rebellious attitude were characterized as stiffnecked (*q.v.;* Ex 32:9; Acts 7:51).

NECKLACE. A chain or ornament for the neck (Heb. *rābîd,* Gen. 41:42; Ezk 16:11). Made sometimes of gold or silver (Ex 35:22; Song 1:10), sometimes of beads or jewels on a string and hanging down to the breast or girdle. Amulets and golden crescents (Isa 3:18; Jud 8:26; both RSV) may often have been attached. *See* Jewels.

NECROMANCER. The term of Gr. origin meaning "one who calls up ghosts to reveal the future." The word occurs once in the English translation (Deut 18:11). The original Heb. is a phrase, lit., "one who seeks to the dead." Moses uses the expression in a list of eight terms describing related occult practices (Deut 18:10–11), all of which are "abominations of the nations" (v. 9). Necromancy was practiced by Manasseh (II Kgs 21:6), and was common in the religion of the Babylonians (Isa 47:9–14). A letter on a clay tablet found at Taanach in Palestine, and written *c.* 1450 B.C., mentions a wizard or spiritist medium (BASOR #94, p. 18).

The only instance of necromancy given in the Bible is Saul's experience. God did not answer him in the usual way, by dreams, urim of the high priest, or prophet. Therefore the king went by night to the Endor medium (KJV, "witch") and asked her to bring up Samuel, who had been dead for some time. She said she saw what seemed to be a god or superhuman being coming out of the earth, appearing as an old man wrapped in a robe (I Sam 28:6–14). From such an appearance Saul really should not have expected to learn anything. God's will was given by the office of a spokesman for God, as Moses makes clear in Deut 18:15–22 (cf. Isa 8:19 f.). All else would normally be mere deception (Jer 27:9 f.; Rev 18:23) and usually came with pagan immorality (Isa 57:3). In Saul's case, however, God made an exception and enabled the spirit of Samuel actually to speak to the terrified king and to pronounce his doom (I Sam 28:15–20). *See* Familiar Spirit; Divination; Magic; Mutter.

W. G. B.

NEDABIAH (nĕd'*ȧ*-bī'*ȧ*). The last named son of King Jeconiah (Jehoiachin), a descendant of David through Solomon (I Chr 3:17–18).

NEEDLE. Gr. *rhaphis,* a needle used for sewing. Used three times in Jesus' parabolic saying, "It is easier for a camel to go through the eye of a needle, than for a rich man to enter into the kingdom of God" (Mt 19:24; Mk 10:25; Lk 18:25, TR). The best Gr. MSS show that Luke, a physician, employed the medical term *belonē*, a needle used in surgical operations. The proverb is similar to a form of words found in rabbinic writings to express the unusual or impossible. Some have suggested that the "eye of a needle" refers to a small pedestrian gate in Jerusalem which a camel could enter only on its knees, but this lacks historic evidence.

NEEDLEWORK. *See* Occupations: Embroiderer, Needlework.

NEEDY. *See* Poor.

NEESINGS. An obsolete Anglo-Saxon word which occurs in Job 41:18; II Kgs 4:35 (1611 ed. only) and is translated "sneezings" in the ASV. It is used in Job in the description of the leviathan or crocodile, who inflates himself and then discharges through his nostrils a moist, heated vapor which sparkles in the sunlight. This act is neither a sneeze nor a snort. The force intended by the KJV translators is uncertain, but the word is sufficiently descriptive.

NEGEB (nĕg'ĕb). Translated "the South" in about 40 places in both the KJV and the RSV. The Negeb is comprised of about 4,500 square miles of desert which composes the southern part of Judah and constituted nearly half the area of modern Israel before the 1967 war.

The northern boundary of the Negeb may be drawn S of the Gaza-Beer-sheba road and then due E to the Dead Sea. The southern boundary, which used to be thought of as extending into the highlands of the Sinai Peninsula, is now drawn from the Kadesh-barnea area to the head of the Gulf of Aqabah. Most OT references to the region of the Negeb are found in the pre-Exilic writings.

Explorations by Nelson Glueck and others have revealed that there were numerous settlements in the Negeb in the Middle Bronze I Age (2100–1900 B.C.). Therefore when Abram traveled to and from Egypt, he was able to obtain sustenance for his large household of servants and animals (Gen 12:9–13:1). W. F. Albright argued that the settlements were the frequent stopping points needed for the flourishing trade between Egypt and Syria by means of donkey caravans.

The region was important because of the location of copper in the E Negeb; because of Israel's trade with Arabia; and, from Solomon's day on, because of Ezion-geber, the copper-shipping port established by Solomon with the aid of Phoenician technicians. The occupation of this area by the Amalekites and Edomites in tent encampments, and the Canaanites in cities such as Arad (*q.v.*) along the N edge, from before the entrance of Israel into the Promised Land, and their strong entrenchment there (Num 13:29; 20:14–21; 21:1), led to numerous wars between them and Israel (e.g., Jud 6:3, 33; I Sam 14:48; 15:1-9; 27:8-10; 30:1-20; I Kgs 11:15 f.; I Chr 4:39-43). Uzziah established fortified settlements in the N Negeb to strengthen his southern flank (II Chr 26:10). The Negeb was a convenient place for migrants to resettle after being forced out of the Fertile Crescent by population pressures.

The "way of Shur" (*see* Shur) crossed the Negeb coming from Egypt and N central Sinai, and heading NE to Beer-sheba and Hebron (Gen 16:7; 20:1; 25:18; Ex 15:22). It was undoubtedly followed by the patriarchs (Gen 13:1; 24:62), Hadad the Edomite (I Kgs 11:14, 17), possibly by Jeremiah (Jer 43:6–12), and by Joseph and Mary (Mt 2:13–15). The course of the road, at least in Palestine, was dictated by available wells (Gen 16:7; 21:19; Josh 15:18–19; Jud 1:14–15).

The modern Israelis have made intensive explorations and studies of ancient settlements in the Negeb, especially of the Nabateans (*q.v.*), in order to learn how towns could flourish there in the past. By means of water piped from the Galilee region they are causing the desert once again to "blossom as the rose" (Isa 35:1).

Bibliography. Y. Aharoni, "Forerunners of the Limes: Iron Age Fortresses in the Negeb," IEJ, XVII (1967), 1–17; "The Negeb of Judah," IEJ, VIII (1958), 26–38; "The Negeb," TAOTS, pp. 385–404. Denis Baly, *Geography of the Bible,* New York: Harper & Bros., 1957, pp. 74–75, 260–266. Nelson Glueck, *Rivers in the Desert,* New York: Farrar, Straus and Cudahy, 1959. Benno Rothenberg, *God's Wilderness,* London: Thames and Hudson, 1961.

R. A. K.

NEGINAH (nĕg'ĭ-nȧ), **NEGINOTH** (nĕg'ĭ-nŏth). A term meaning "stringed instrument," occurring in the titles of many psalms (e.g., Ps 4, 6, 54, 55, 61, 67, 76). *See* Psalms.

NEHELAMITE (nē-hĕl'ȧ-mīt). A name applied in Scripture only to the false prophet Shemaiah as Jeremiah pronounced God's judgment upon him (Jer 29:24, 31–32). The appellative would seem to be either a family or a city name identifying Shemaiah, but no person or place of that name is known either in Scripture or elsewhere. While it seems rather dubious, it has been suggested that the name is a punning epithet, describing the false prophet as "the dreamer." In Heb. the radical or root letters for "dream" and Nehelamite are the same, *ḥlm* (L. Yaure, "Elymas-Nehelamite-Pethor," JBL, LXXIX [1960], 297–314).

NEHEMIAH (nē'ĕ-mī'ȧ)

1. A returnee with Zerubbabel in 538 B.C. who had been carried away by Nebuchadnezzar (Ezr 2:2; Neh 7:7).

2. Ruler of Bethzur, son of Azbuk, who gave aid to Nehemiah, the governor, in rebuilding the walls of Jerusalem (Neh 3:16).

3. Governor of Judah, son of Hachaliah

NEHEMIAH

King Solomon's Pillars in the Negeb. IIS

(Neh 1:1; 8:9; 10:1; 12:26, 47; probably a Judahite). A descendant of those carried into Babylonian Captivity, Nehemiah gained prominence after the Persians defeated the Babylonians. He attained the influential position of personal cupbearer to the Persian king, Artaxerxes I Longimanus (465-424 B.C.). This was a place of utmost trust in that he alone passed on the wine given to the king. While serving in this capacity, word reached Nehemiah about conditions in Jerusalem. The walls were still in ruins, the gates were charred remains, and there was no defense against enemy attacks.

Nehemiah was able to receive permission from Artaxerxes to restore the dignity of his ancestral home. After being appointed governor of the province surrounding Jerusalem, he was given letters of safe conduct to the satraps along the way and authority to secure the necessary materials from the king's forests. Arriving in Jerusalem in 444 B.C., he began his vital work by secretly surveying the remains of the walls toppled by Nebuchadnezzar (Neh 2:11-16).

The work of rebuilding the walls was constantly thwarted by the selfish interests of Sanballat of Samaria, Tobiah of the Ammonites, and Geshem of Arabia. These men, though powerful and crafty, were no match for the resourcefulness of Nehemiah. They attempted insult and mockery; they planned armed attacks; they tried to lure Nehemiah out where they could seize him; and they sent charges of rebellious intentions to Artaxerxes in the hope of discrediting Nehemiah. Although they were successful in hindering and stopping the work for a time, Nehemiah continually demonstrated his powerful leadership qualities and organizational abilities. According to the book of Nehemiah (6:15) the work was completed in 52 days, although Josephus used the figure of two years and four months.

The duties of Nehemiah went beyond his original purpose in rebuilding the walls. He was able to awaken a sense of national honor and to restore dignity to Jerusalem. He appointed officers to whom authority was delegated for better government. He corrected many abuses, settled difficult grievances, and established law and order. He revived worship by encouraging the reading of the law, celebrating the Feast of Tabernacles, observing national fasts, and renewing the covenant. He protected Jerusalem by ordering that one of ten must reside in the city walls. He further separated mixed multitudes, purified the temple, improved the support of the priesthood, and revitalized the observance of the sabbath.

There is some difficulty in establishing the length of Nehemiah's governorship. He was originally appointed for a definite period of time, beginning in the 21st year of Artaxerxes I. However, this time limit was undoubtedly extended owing to the pressing need at Jerusalem. In the 32nd year of Artaxerxes, he again applied for leave to go to Jerusalem. It appears that he was officially governor during the intervening years, though not always on hand. The fact that many abuses had to be corrected immediately upon his second arrival in Jerusalem suggests that the "after certain days" in Neh 13:6 may have been a considerable time. The mention of "Darius the Persian" (Darius II Nothus, 423-404 B.C.) in the book of Nehemiah (12:22) further suggests that Nehemiah continued for some time in active leadership at Jerusalem. Although some scholars would extend his tenure to 405 B.C., an Aramaic letter from Elephantine in Egypt refers to Bagoas as governor of Jerusalem *c.* 407 B.C. (ANET, p. 492).

The character of Nehemiah is almost without blemish in the material available. He was as gifted and accomplished as any man of post-Exilic times. His deep and intense patriotism was contagious, causing men to leave their harvests in order to journey to Jerusalem for work on the walls. His strict integrity, coupled with kindly humility, makes him stand out as an outstanding example of lay leadership. His unselfish practice of refusing any pay for his services (5:14-18) must have left an indelible impression upon the poor of Jerusalem. His intense faith in God and genuine piety were evidenced in his zeal for both the ethical and ceremonial side of religion. Above all, his devotion to duty, his untiring energy, and his determined persistence swept forward a group of men who had all but given up. Nehemiah was a man of action, not one to sit down and wait for God to cause some supernatural event to pass. The desperate position of his people called for rather extreme measures without delay. Viewing the work of Nehemiah as a whole, he was truly God's man of the hour.

See Ezra; Restoration, The, and Persian Period.

K. M. Y.

NEHEMIAH, BOOK OF. The book bearing Nehemiah's name appears in early MSS combined with Ezra as a single book. Certain Gr. MSS separated the two prior to the time of Origen and Jerome, but Heb. MSS combined them until A.D. 1448. Their union in the major codices (Vaticanus, Sinaiticus, and Alexandrinus) point to their being one originally in the LXX.

Contents

I. Nehemiah's Administration of Judah, 1:1–12:47
  - A. Arrival in Jerusalem, 1:1–2:20
  - B. Rebuilding the wall, 3:1–7:4
  - C. Registering the returnees, 7:5-72
  - D. Renewing the covenant, 7:73–10:39
  - E. Census of Jerusalem and neighborhood, 11:1-36
  - F. List of priests and Levites, 12:1-26
  - G. Dedication of the wall, 12:27-47

II. Nehemiah's Second Visit to Jerusalem and Final Reforms, 13:1-31

Sources

As in the case of the book of Ezra, several distinct sources are easily recognized which demonstrate the composite character of the book as it now stands.

1. Personal memoirs of Nehemiah (1:1–2:20; 4:1–7:5; 10:28–11:2; 12:27–13:31). These passages are written in the first person.

2. Third person narratives (7:73–9:38). These passages may have been adapted from Nehemiah's memoirs but more probably come from temple records.

3. Lists and genealogies

a. Builders (3:1-32), from Nehemiah's memoirs.

b. Returned exiles (7:6-73), from the same source as Ezr 2:1-70.

c. Covenant sealers (10:1-27), from Nehemiah's memoirs or from temple records.

d. Residents of Jerusalem and area (11:3-36), from temple records or state archives.

e. Priests, Levites, high priests (12:1-26), from temple records.

Authorship

The book has long been linked with the name of Ezra in Hebrew-Christian tradition. Its close ties with I and II Chronicles in style, language, outlook, and purpose point to one work originally embracing Chronicles, Ezra and Nehemiah. That Chronicles once stood first in the series is shown by the repetition of the closing verses of II Chronicles at the beginning of Ezra. Chronicles was probably placed last by virtue of later acceptance in the Jewish community. In the LXX, other variant arrangements are evident, such as part of Neh 8 being transferred to follow Ezr 10:2. The composite nature of these works and their close similarities has given the name "Chronicler" to the author or editor. The Talmud (*Baba Bathra* 15*a*) names Ezra as the principal author and Nehemiah his contemporary as the one who completed the record.

The extended use of personal memoirs from the hand of Nehemiah certainly makes him a substantial author of the material now bearing his name. The material comes from a document much like a personal diary. Some believe that Nehemiah never intended for it to be published, because the events and emotions associated with the events are reported so frankly and vividly. These first-hand observations are tremendously important in shedding light on the political history of the Jews during the Persian period.

See Nehemiah; Ezra; Ezra, Book of.

Bibliography. S. E. Anderson, *Nehemiah the Executive*, Wheaton: Van Kampen, 1954. A. E. Cundall, "Ezra and Nehemiah," NBD, rev. (1970). G. Coleman Luck, *Ezra and Nehemiah*, Chicago: Moody, 1961. Jacob M. Myers, *Ezra, Nehemiah*, Anchor Bible, Garden City: Doubleday, 1965. John C. Whitcomb, Jr., "Ezra, Nehemiah," WBC. J. Stafford Wright, *The Building of the Second Temple*, London: Tyndale, 1958.

K. M. Y.

NEHILOTH (nē'ĭ-lŏth). A musical term used in the title of Ps 5 meaning wind instrument, which is interpreted by some to be a flute (RSV). *See* Music.

NEHUM (nē'hŭm). One of the 12 leaders who returned from the Babylonian Captivity with Zerubbabel (Neh 7:7). In Ezr 2:2 his name appears as Rehum (*q.v.*).

NEHUSHTA (nē-hŭsh'tȧ). The daughter of Elnathan of Jerusalem, wife of Jehoiakim and mother of Jehoiachin. She is mentioned in connection with the latter's short reign as king of Judah (II Kgs 24:8), and as accompanying her son who was taken prisoner to Babylon by Nebuchadnezzar (vv. 12, 15).

NEHUSHTAN (nē-hŭsh'tȧn). The bronze serpent destroyed by King Hezekiah during his reform of the temple worship (II Kgs 18:4). It had been made by Moses centuries earlier. The name can mean "a piece of bronze" (NASB marg.), and it was probably so named by Hezekiah in contempt. *See* Brazen Serpent; Animals, IV.30.

K. R. Jones ("The Bronze Serpent in the Israelite Cult," JBL, LXXXVII [1968], 245-256) lists various archaeological discoveries which have demonstrated that in Mesopotamia before the time of Abraham the serpent was a common symbol of fertility and the return of life. Apparently it was the Hyksos who brought the serpent symbol into Palestine, where at least seven cultic bronze serpents have been found in excavations dating to the Middle and Late Bronze Ages (1650-1200 B.C.). Representations of serpents together with fertility goddesses on plaques and cult standards were frequent in the ancient Near East (ANEP, #470-474, 585, 590, 591; BA, XX [1957], 43 (fig. 8). The fertility symbolism most likely was transferred to the bronze serpent made by Moses during the reign of Solomon, who imported many forms of idolatry (I Kgs 11:1-8).

J. R.

NEIEL (nē-ī'ĕl). One of the frontier villages designated as a border division for the tribe of Asher. It was located between the valley of Jiphtah-el and Cabul (Josh 19:27). Some have suggested the village is identical with Neah (v. 13), but Neah is on the NE sector of Zebulun's border. More likely it may be associated with modern Khirbet Ya'nîn, with Late Bronze and Iron I Age remains, on the E edge of the Plain of Acco, eight and a half miles ESE of Acco.

NEIGH. Used figuratively to describe the lustful actions of the men of Jeremiah's time toward their neighbors' wives (Jer 5:8), and given as one of the reasons for God's judgment upon Judah. (Also see Jer 8:16; 13:27; 50:11, ASV and RSV).

NEIGHBOR. The translation of three Heb. and two Gr. words. In the present day we think of a neighbor as one living near by. In OT times he was one of the same kin, tribe or country. Moral obligation of the Israelite to his neighbor is stated in Lev 19:18, "Thou shalt love thy neighbour as thyself." Generally statements in regard to such moral attitude are given in negative terms (Ex 20:17; Ps 15:3; Prov 24:28; Zech 8:17). In the NT Christ gave as the second great commandment of the law, "Thou shalt love thy neighbour as thyself" (Mt 22:39). And He showed in the parable of the Good Samaritan (Lk 10:30–36) that a neighbor may be anyone who has a need, or meets a need of someone else, regardless of race, religion or social status.

Bibliography. H. Greeven and J. Fichtner, "*Plēsion*," TDNT, VI, 311–318.

NEKEB (nĕk'ĕb). One of the frontier towns, midway between Mount Tabor and Tiberias, included in the division for the tribe of Naphtali (Josh 19:33). In the ASV and RSV it is connected with the preceding word, making it Adami-nekeb. *See* Adami.

NEKODA (nē-kō'dȧ)

1. One of the Nethinim or temple servants whose descendants returned to Judah and Jerusalem with Zerubbabel after the Babylonian Captivity (Ezr 2:48; Neh 7:50).

2. The head of one of the families who, after the Babylonian Captivity, came from various settlements in Babylonia and presented themselves to the governor for registration but could not prove their Israelite descent (Ezr 2:58–60; Neh 7:62).

NEMUEL (nĕm'yōō-ĕl), **NEMUELITES** (nĕm'-yōō-ĕ-līts)

1. A Reubenite, son of Eliab and brother of Dathan and Abiram (Num 26:9). He was numbered among the Israelite men 20 years of age or over who were fit for military service.

2. The eldest son of Simeon (I Chr 4:24), called Jemuel (*q.v.*) in Gen 46:10. His descendants, the Nemuelites, were numbered among the men fit for military service (Num 26:12).

NEOORTHODOXY. Neoorthodoxy, Barthianism, dialectical theology, or the theology of the Word came into existence because of the failure of modernism (*see* Liberalism).

First, modernistic theology lacked a sense of sin, understood evolution as a "fall" upward, and optimistically expected to establish the kingdom of God on earth in a decade or two. Second, modernism, at least in its more advanced and consistent form, had no place for a transcendent God. Under Hegelian influence the stress on God's immanence virtually amounted to a disguised pantheism. Then, third, biblical criticism and "the quest of the historical Jesus" required a constant alteration of one's religious faith with the ever changing conclusions of scholarly investigations.

War and brutality in 1914–18 shattered the liberals' optimistic picture of man. Hegelian pantheism was no better than atheism, which indeed it explicitly became in Feuerbach and Marx. In addition it volatilized the human individual into abstract concepts. And, finally, the instability of historicism could lead only to skepticism and despair in a world of constant danger.

By the end of World War I a group of German and Swiss theologians discovered the writings of the heretofore unrecognized Sören Kierkegaard (1813–1855). He had stressed the existential individual in opposition to abstract concepts, defined trûth as subjective passion, and destroyed the uniformity of Hegelian pantheism by a radical dialectic between time and eternity. *See* Existentialism. Karl Barth and Emil Brunner then saw man as a sinner who needs a divine revelation that biblical criticism cannot shake.

[Neoorthodoxy, then, is the name given to the theology developed by Barth and Brunner on the basis of Kierkegaard's existentialism. It has adopted Kierkegaard's theory of indirect communication in revelation, his views of time, original sin and salvation. Though called a neo, or new, orthodoxy, it is closer to a neomodernism in that it accepts the conclusions of higher criticism but rejects the position of evangelical Christianity and fundamentalism with regard to inspiration, the infallibility of the Bible, sin, the Fall and regeneration. Its position on Christ and the Trinity is weak and varies with its different proponents. The doctrine of the Trinity particularly suffered at the hands of Barth, who presented a Christomonism which proves to be pure modalism, while it disappears altogether in Tillich, who transformed the Trinity into a Hegelian dialectic within the Absolute or Being. In his earlier writings when he desperately tried to rescue theology from historicism by an emphasis on eternity, Brunner would have nothing to do with the temporal life of Christ at all; later he admitted the crucifixion as essential.

[Sören Kierkegaard faced a crisis early in his life over a guilt problem, the loss of faith in the infallibility of the Bible, and the insistence of Immanuel Kant that God is timeless and spaceless (*see* Time). Ready to completely discard the Bible, which appeared to him to be filled with the absurd, the contradictory and the paradox, Kierkegaard suddenly saw a solution. It is because God is timeless and spaceless, and man is in time and space, that the Bible presents so many problems. Man has no categories, no mental containers in which to receive timeless-spaceless eternal truth. There is a disjunction, a Chinese wall betwēen God and man. Whatever gets through, man perverts and forces into his own categories. He clothes eternal truth in the garments of time and locates it in space. For example, the Fall, the fact that every man sins—that I am Adam and you are Adam—is pictured in the Bible as occurring as an event in time and space. It is depicted as at the beginning of man's life on the earth, and as happening at a particular place, the garden of Eden. Thus revelation comes only indirectly through such myths, i.e., by indirect communication.

[According to Kierkegaard, several things follow as consequences. If God is beyond created time, then He lives in an "eternal now" in which past, present and future are one homogenous present. In the existential experience of revelation, the way in which man receives eternal truth, through and in spite of the fallibility of Scripture, he experiences contemporaneity with God and all He has done through Christ in redemption. Thus revelation is identical with salvation. This is the cure for the guilt complex. How were the OT saints saved? In a similar way. As part of the eternal now, a primal history or *Urgeschichte,* Christ has always died and, therefore, the OT believers are contemporaneous with His death in the experience of revelation. Though much is said of their *Erwartung* or expectation of that event, it means little in the light of contemporaneity.

[What is the Christian answer? First of all, it is necessary to see that the Bible is the inspired, infallible Word of God (*see* Inspiration). Then it is necessary to consider the biblical view of time and understand the fallacy of Kant's three infinities (*see* Time; Theology). God works in creation and redemption entirely within time. Time is not a category or quality merely of creation and the finite, but a relationship which finds its existence first in God and then in creation. The same holds true for space. If this were not so, the creation would add to God by offering new relationships to Him, and thus become both a necessity for Him, if He is to be fully God, and also a limitation to Him in the sense He cannot be fully God without its existence.

[Kant's argument about the three infinities is fallacious. One infinity does not necessarily rule out another, particularly one of another kind. Infinite time does not rule out infinite space, nor either of these an infinite God. If infinities which are alike, such as an infinite number of infinite lines and infinite time and infinite space, do not exclude each other, how much more infinites which are different, such as the relationships of time and space on the one hand and God on the other. When we add to this the fact that relationships are not material in nature, we clear time and space of their finite dimensions.—R. A. K.]

Though the neoorthodox recognize the sinner's need of a revelation which scholarship cannot overthrow, they do not precisely equate it with the Bible. God speaks in the Bible, to be sure; but Brunner dallied with the notion that God also speaks in the Koran and the Vedas. In any case, God need not speak the truth because "God can, when he wants to, speak his Word to a man even through false doctrine" (*Wahrheit als Begegnung,* p. 88; *Divine-Human Encounter,* p. 117).

Barth finds the Word of God in three places: the weekly sermon, the Bible, and the revelation-event. The Bible is not infallible, for "the prophets and apostles as such, even in their office, even in their function as witnesses, even in the act of writing down their witness, were . . . actually guilty of error in their spoken and written word" (*Church Dogmatics,* I, 2, p. 529). *See* Illumination; Inspiration.

Barth's revelation-event, corresponding to Brunner's divine-human encounter, seems to be a wordless, unintelligible experience. If the apostles could not avoid error in relating their experience, it is doubtful that anyone else can find in it a credible and stable theology of salvation. It would seem therefore that neoorthodoxy has not solved the problems it inherited from modernism.

Bibliography. Karl Barth, *Church Dogmatics,* Edinburgh: T. & T. Clark, 1936 (later volumes still appearing in English). G. C. Berkouwer, *The Triumph of Grace in Theology of Karl Barth,* Grand Rapids: Eerdmans, 1956. Gordon H. Clark, *Karl Barth's Theological Method,* Philadelphia: Presbyterian and Reformed, 1963. Paul K. Jewett, *Brunner's Concept of Revelation,* London: James Clarke & Co., 1954. Klaas Runia, *Karl Barth's Doctrine of Holy Scripture,* Grand Rapids: Eerdmans, 1962.

G. H. C.

NEPHEG (nē'fĕg)

1. One of the sons of Izhar and a great-grandson of Levi. He was listed among the heads of the Israelite homes at the time of the exodus from Egypt (Ex 6:21).

2. One of King David's sons born in Jerusalem (II Sam 5:15; I Chr 3:7; 14:6).

NEPHEW. The rendering of Heb. *bēn,* normally "grandson" (Jud 12:14); Heb. *nĕkĕd* (Job 18:19; Isa 14:22); Gr. *'ekyonas,* "to be born of," "offspring," "descendant," "grandson" (I Tim 5:4). In the ASV (OT) the word is translated "son's son" and (NT) "grandchildren."

NEPHILIM (nĕf'ĭ-lĭm). This word is translated "giants" in the KJV but is retained in the ASV and RSV. It is used of a group of antediluvian beings thought by some to be the result of the intermarriage of the sons of God with the daughters of men (Gen 6:4).

The second OT usage describes the sons of Anak, men of gigantic stature, whom the Israelite spies declared occupied the land of Canaan, causing them to refuse to enter the land (Num 13:33). *See* Giants; Anak.

NEPHISH. *See* Naphish.

NEPHISHESIM. *See* Nephusim.

NEPHTHALIM. *See* Naphtali.

NEPHTOAH, WATERS OF (nĕf-tō'*á*). Usually identified with modern Lifta, about three miles NW of Jebusite Jerusalem, six miles E of Kirjath-jearim, and SW of Gibeah. It was a spring of gushing water that served as a marker on the boundary line between Judah and Benjamin (Josh 15:9; 18:15). Other possible identifications include Ain Karem, the spring of Philip (Ain Haniyeh), the well of Job in the W end of the Wady Aly. These latter attempts to identify Nephtoah have little if any sound basis.

NEPHUSIM (nĭ-fū'sĭm). The head of a family of Nethinim or temple servants who returned with Zerubbabel from the Babylonian Captivity (Ezr 2:50); also spelled Nephishesim (Neh 7:52).

NER (nûr). A Benjamite, the son of Abiel and the father of Kish and Abner, the latter being King Saul's army commander (I Sam 14:51; I Kgs 2:32; I Chr 8:33; *et al.*). Ner was therefore the grandfather of Saul. As E. R. Dalglish makes clear ("Ner," IDB, III, 537), in I Sam 14:50 the designation "Saul's uncle" must refer to Abner, not to Ner. The Kish of I Chr 9:36 must be another man of the same name in addition to the Kish who was Ner's son and Saul's father (I Chr 9:39). *See* Kish.

NEREUS (nĭr'ĭ-*ŭ*s). A member of the church in Rome, who with his sister was saluted by the apostle Paul (Rom 16:15).

NERGAL. *See* Gods, False.

NERGAL-SHAREZER (nûr'găl-sh*á*-rē'zĕr). The Babylonian name *Nergal-šar-uṣur* (Gr. *Nērigli-saros*) means "Nergal, protect the king." In Jer 39:3 the name occurs twice in a list of princes of Babylon who were with Nebuchadnezzar at the capture of Jerusalem, the second time with the title Rabmag (*q.v.*). The repetition may be due to a copyist's error, or may indicate that there were two persons by the same name.

A broken clay prism of Nebuchadnezzar lists some of his court officials, among whom is Nergal-shar-uṣur prince of Sin-magir. On the basis of this cuneiform text the NEB and JerusB have regrouped the name elements in Jer 39:3 to read "Nergalsarezer of Simmagir, Nebusarsekim the Rabsaris, Nergalsarezer the Rabmag, and all the other. . . ."

Nergal-sharezer was probably the army commander who occupied the Babylonian throne in 560 B.C. upon the murder of Amel-Marduk (Evil-Merodach), known in history as Meriglissar. He was married to Bel-šum-iškun, a daughter of Nebuchadnezzar. He may have succeeded to the throne as the result of a revolution or as the legitimate successor to his brother-in-law. Some 35 years prior to his accession he appears in contracts as a wealthy landowner with properties at Babylon and Opis, and as Nebuchadnezzar's appointee over the business affairs of the sun-god's temple at Sippar. During the early part of his short reign he was active in the restoration of the Esagila temple at Babylon and the Ezida temple at Borsippa, the reconstruction of an old palace as his residence, and the repair of the canals around Babylon.

A fragment of the Babylonian Chronicle reveals an interesting campaign which Neriglissar conducted in 557 B.C. The king led his army to the far NW of his realm into Cilicia to repulse the invasion of Appuašu, king of Pirindu (W Cilicia and Tracheia), who had crossed over into Hume (E Cilicia). In spite of the difficult mountainous terrain, Neriglissar and his forces were completely successful in repulsing Appuašu and even in chasing him back deep into his own territory. The Chronicle reports that the trails were so narrow that the soldiers had to march in single file for about 100 miles! They also succeeded in taking the rocky island of Pitusu, which was garrisoned with 6,000 soldiers. After the death of Neriglissar in 556, his son Labasi-Marduk was able to reign for only nine months before being killed by Nabonidus, the last of the Chaldean kings. (See D. J. Wiseman, *Chronicles of the Chaldaean Kings,* London: British Museum, 1956. pp. 37 ff).

E. M. Y.

NERI (nēr'ī). A son of Melchi and father of Salathiel, included in the genealogical list as an ancestor of Jesus (Lk 3:27–28). He is an important link in the royal messianic line through David's son Nathan because Solomon's line was cut off from the throne after Jeconiah.

NERIAH (nĭ-rī'*á*). The son of Maaseiah and father of Baruch, Jeremiah's scribe (Jer 32:12, 16; *et al.*), and Seraiah, the chief chamberlain who accompanied Zedekiah into Babylonian Captivity (Jer 51:59).

NERO (nē'rō). Named Nero Claudius Caesar Drusus Germanicus, the adopted son of the emperor Claudius (A.D. 41–54), he ascended the throne of Rome when 17, ruling from A.D. 54 to 68. During his early years he was aided by his mother, Agrippina, the Stoic philosopher Seneca (brother of Gallio, see Acts 18:12–17), and the capable soldier Burrus.

After several years he rid himself of the three and embarked on a career marked by cruelty and self-indulgence. His genuine abilities, mainly artistic, were often marred by his atrocities and excesses. Finally, when revolt against him became widespread (in Africa, Spain and Gaul), he fled Rome and committed suicide on June 9, 68. (Some report he lost his nerve and ordered one of his soldiers to finish his life.)

His name does not occur in the NT, but his title and activities appear, and during the years 59–68 his career directly touched the early church. Paul appealed to him for a fair trial (Acts 25:10–12) and spent two years in Rome awaiting a hearing (Acts 28:30). Whether his case was ever heard is unknown, although some see reference to it in II Tim 4:16–17. References in the Pastoral Epistles to Paul's activities seem to indicate that he was released by Nero from his first Roman imprisonment. However, after a period of freedom and renewed activity, Paul was imprisoned again, presumably in Rome under Nero. For a description of the ruins of Nero's palace, see WHG, pp. 548 f.

Nero. Gleason Archer; photo by W. LaSor

Then came the fire of A.D. 64. The Roman historian Tacitus recorded the details in his *Annals*, XV, 44. Rome was severely damaged by flame, evidently the emperor's way of clearing ground for his new palace complex, and Nero came under suspicion. Blaming "a class of men, loathed for their vices, whom the crowd styled Christians," he instituted a series of cruel and ingenious punishments against these people. Thus came the first official Roman persecution of the church, local but severe.

According to tradition, Peter and Paul were martyred in Rome under Nero, and there may be a reflection of the period in certain of the NT writings, principally the Gospel of Mark, I Peter and according to some the book of Revelation.

Bibliography. Robert M. Grant, "Nero," IDB, III, 537 ff. Merrill C. Tenney, *New Testament Times*, Grand Rapids: Eerdmans, 1965, pp. 282–293.

W. M. D.

NEST. Heb. *qēn* is the OT word for "nest," and the verb *qānan* means "to make a nest." The word used by our Lord in Mt 8:20 and Lk 9:58 is Gr. *kataskēnōsis*, which connotes a pitching of tents, an encampment, or dwelling place. The contrast drawn with His own homelessness is very forceful.

Various uses of *qēn* in the OT include the term for the cubicles or "rooms" of the ark in Gen 6:14; several allusions to fortifications (e.g., Num 24:21); Job's expression for permanence and security ("die in my nest," 29:18); one for hiding places of fugitives (Jer 48:28); and a forsaken nest (Isa 16:2, lit.) as an expression for "scattered nestlings" (RSV, NEB, NASB), a picture of the fleeing Moabites.

NET The OT words for "net" are Heb. *hērem* ("perforated" or "slit"), *mikmār* or *makmōr* and *mikmōreth* or *mikmereth* ("dragnet, seine"), a group of words from the root *ṣûd* ("to hunt, lie in wait"), *reshet* (root *yārash*, "to possess"), *śābāk* and *śᵉbākâ* ("interwoven"). Several of these are also translated "snare" in the KJV, and the common snare (*paḥ*) may also have been a net. In the NT, the *amphiblēstron, diktyon*, and *sagēnē* were all nets used for fishing.

Nets made of cords of various types of fiber seem to have been used from prehistoric times in the Near East. The OT speaks of their use in trapping land animals (Isa 51:20; Ezk 19:8) and birds (Prov 1:17; Hos 7:12; cf. the "snare of the fowler," Ps 91:3) as well as fish (Eccl 9:12; Isa 19:8). In the NT, *diktyon* seems to be a general term for "net," while the other two terms distinguish the casting net (*amphiblēstron*) and the dragnet or seine (*sagēnē*). The round casting net forms a cone in the water; the long dragnet is drawn at both ends, either toward the shore or into a circle. *See* Occupations: Fishing.

The terms for "net" and "network" (*q.v.*) are also used to describe some decorative grating on the altar (Ex 27:4; etc.) and on the two pillars flanking the entrance to the sanctuary (I Kgs 7:17; Jer 52:22). The net is used figuratively for the plots of the wicked (Ps 140:5; 141:10), for the heart of an evil woman (Eccl 7:26), and for divine retribution (Ezk 12:13; 17:20).

W. R. L. McL.

NETHANEEL (nē-thăn'ē-ĕl). The name is spelled Nethanel in all modern English versions.

1. The son of Zuar of the tribe of Issachar, prince of the tribe in the time of the Exodus (Num 1:8; 2:5; 7:18, 23; 10:15).

2. The fourth son of Jesse and brother of David (I Chr 2:14).

3. One of the priests who blew trumpets before the ark as it was brought from the house of Obed-edom to Jerusalem (I Chr 15:24).

4. A Levite, father of the scribe Shemaiah, in the time of David (I Chr 24:6).

5. The son of Obed-edom, appointed as doorkeeper of the temple by David (I Chr 26:4).

6. One of the princes sent out by Jehoshaphat to teach the law in the cities of Judah (II Chr 17:7).

7. A chief Levite who took part in the great Passover under Josiah (II Chr 35:9).

8. A priest of the family of Pashhur who had married a Gentile wife in the days of Ezra (Ezr 10:22).

9. A priest of the family of Jedaiah in the time of Joiakim after the Exile (Neh 12:21).

10. A Levite who took part in the dedication of the wall of Nehemiah (Neh 12:36).

P. C. J.

NETHANIAH (nĕth'*á*-nī'*á*)

1. A musician in the time of David, one of the four sons of Asaph. He was leader of the fifth division of temple singers and musicians (I Chr 25:2, 12).

2. One of the Levites sent out by Jehoshaphat to teach the law in the cities of Judah (II Chr 17:8).

3. Father of Jehudi who brought the prophecy of Jeremiah to the princes and later read it before King Jehoiakim (Jer 36:14).

4. The son of Elishama of the royal family of David. He was the father of Ishmael, the fiercely nationalist prince who slew the governor Gedaliah after the fall of Jerusalem (II Kgs 25:23, 25; Jer 40:8, 14–15; 41:1 ff.).

NETHINIM (nĕth'ĭ-nĭm). The KJV and ASV term Nethinim(s) is a transliteration of Heb. *n*[e]*tînîm,* literally meaning "those given," which occurs 17 times in the OT. The translation "temple servants" (RSV, NEB [servitors], Berkeley, NASB) describes their function.

They are said specifically to be those "whom David and the princes had appointed for the service of the Levites" (Ezr 8:20), thus indicating both their realm of activity and their historical origin. In most of the occurrences they are listed with and after the Levites (cf. I Chr 9:2; Ezr 7:7; Neh 7:73).

Because of this reference to the activity of David and their being joined with Solomon's servants (Ezr 2:58; Neh 7:60; cf. I Kgs 9:21) and the foreign names that they bear, it has been thought that they were foreigners, mostly captives of war, put into this service. For example, Mehunim (Ezr 2:50; Neh 7:52) may refer to those overcome by Uzziah (II Chr 26:7). Nephusim (Ezr 2:50; Neh 7:52) may refer to the Hagarite clan of Naphish (Gen 25:15; I Chr 5:19). Because of the similarity of duty, some have sought their background in the Gibeonites, "hewers of wood and drawers of water for the house of my God" (Josh 9:23, 27) and also in the Midianites (Num 31:30, 47). The correlation is probably no more than that of similarity of service, not direct relationship. Whatever may be the roots of their origin, they were treated as part of the people of God, at least as proselytes (Neh 10:28 ff.).

They are mentioned by name in the OT in post-Exilic times. From Babylon 612 returned, 392 with Zerubbabel (Ezr 2:58; Neh 7:60; a count which includes "the children of Solomon's servants") and 220 with Ezra (Ezr 8:20) as "ministers for the house of our God" from the place Casiphia (Ezr 8:17) "in the seventh year of Artaxerxes the king" (Ezr 7:7). Like other sacred ministers, they were exempted from taxation (Ezr 7:24).

The Nethinim dwelt in the Levitical cities (Ezr 2:70) and in the Ophel area of Jerusalem near the water gate (Neh 3:26; 11:21; see 3:31, "the house of the Nethinim"). Their own leaders were Ziha and Gispa (Neh 11:21).

The passage I Esd 5:29 ff. (cf. Jos *Ant. xi.* 5.1) parallel to Ezr 2:43 ff. and Neh 7:46 ff. designates the same group as "the servants of the temple" (Gr. *hierodoyloi*). The Talmudic writers speak of them in very low terms (Mishna, *Kiddushin,* iii. 12; iv. 1; *Jebamoth, ii,* 4).

See Service.

G. W. K.

NETOPHAH (nĭ-tō'f*á*). A Judean town near Bethlehem to which 56 men of the Babylonian Captivity returned and settled (Ezr 2:22; Neh 7:26). *See* Netophathites.

NETOPHATHITES (nē-tō'f*á*-thīts). Dwellers in Netophah, a village now identified with Khirbet Bedd Faluh, three miles S of Bethlehem. The inhabitants were of the tribe of Judah and are first mentioned when two of them are listed among the mighty men of David (II Sam 23:28–29; I Chr 11:30; 27:13–15). Seraiah and the sons of Ephai were Netophathites who were leaders of the remmant left after the fall of Jerusalem (II Kgs 25:23; Jer 40:8).

Inhabitants of the village are also mentioned among those who returned after the Exile (Ezr 2:22; Neh 7:26; 12:28).

NETTLE. *See* Plants.

NETWORK

1. Used of the brass grate around the altar of burnt offering, which was kept in place by four brass rings on each of four corners. Its exact position and purpose are uncertain (Ex 27:4; 38:4). *See* Altar.

2. Applied to the plaited work around Jachin and Boaz, the two court pillars of the temple, made by Hiram of Tyre and destroyed by Nebuchadnezzar (I Kgs 7:13, 18, 20, 41–42).

3. The general name for cotton fabrics, or different types of byssus made in Egypt (Isa 19:9). *See* Cotton.

NEW BIRTH. *See* Born Again; New Creation; Regeneration.

NEW CREATION. The term itself occurs in Gal 6:15 (RSV, NASB) and II Cor 5:17 (RSV). This subject is associated by the Scriptures with the original general creation recorded in Gen 1 and 2, as in the case of Isa 40:26–31 and Isa 42:5–7 (the God who created all things will redeem and strengthen His people); and II Cor 4:6 (the God who brought the light into existence at creation has enlightened the minds and hearts of His people; cf. II Cor 5:17).

Also the new creation is compared by Scripture to the original creation of man as is seen in Eph 4:24 (the new man in Christ is created after God in righteousness and holiness) and in

Col 3:10 (the new man is being renewed in knowledge according to the image of God who created him).

The subject of the new creation centers around two major themes: the new spiritual creation of man and the implications following therefrom; and the new physical-material creation to be brought into being in the events involving the second coming of Christ.

Both the OT and NT speak in similar terms of the new creation of man based on the redeeming work of Christ accomplished on the cross. Christ is the Head of this new creation both as its Creator and as the firstfruits, the first to be resurrected in this new life (Col 1:18–20; I Cor 15:20, 23). These concepts include:

1. A new covenant in connection with which God's Word becomes a vital part of the redeemed individual's life (Jer 31:31–34; Mt 26:28; Mk 14:24; Lk 22:20; Heb 8:8–12; 9:15); it demands a new and different sign or seal—baptism.

2. The new divine creative work of the new birth or regeneration (*q.v.*) produced by God and His Spirit (Ezk 36:26–27; Jn 1:12–13; 3:3–5; Rom 7:6; Tit 3:5) brought to fulfillment through the redemptive work of the incarnate Christ (Isa 42:5–9; Eph 2:10).

3. A new spiritual enlightenment as to the importance of Christ and His salvation (Isa 42:6; Lk 2:32; Jn 1:4–5, 9; 3:19; 8:12; 12:35–36, 46; I Jn 1:5–6; 2:8–11).

4. A new heart and life (Ezk 36:26–27; Rom 6:4; II Cor 5:17; Eph 2:10).

5. A new or renewed personal relationship to God (Jer 31:32–33; Eph 2:11–22; Hos 2:23).

6. A renewal in the image of God like that in which man was originally created (Gen 1:26–27) with respect to knowledge, righteousness, and true holiness (Ezk 36:26; Eph 4:24; Col 3:10).

7. A new commandment to love one another even as Christ has loved us (Jn 13:34).

8. A new revived walk and freedom in the way of the Lord (Ezk 36:27; Gal 4:5–7; 5:1, 13; Rom 8:2; Eph 2:10).

9. A projected millennial situation when all of God's people will in fact know the Lord (Jer 31:31–34; Heb 8:8–12; cf. Rev 20:4–6).

The Gr. words used for this new creation in the NT are *ktizō* ("to create") and *ktisis* ("creation"), one of the word types, along with *poieō* ("to make") used by the LXX instead of *dēmiourgeō* ("to work at," "fabricate") (cf. LSJ and HR) which word may have been thought by the Jewish translators of the Heb. OT into Gr. as suggesting depreciation of God's creative power (cf. B. W. Anderson, "Creation," IDB, I, 731).

Of the new creation's theme concerning the new physical-material creation of the future, both the OT and NT suggest that God's covenant promises involve a millennial milieu of peace and harmony in the physical and animal creation (Isa 11:1–9; Hos 2:18–23; Rom 8:19–23) at the time in which Christ shall come to reign on earth with His saints (Rev 20:4). Also both Testaments present a future newly created heaven and earth in which there will be no sin nor evil (Isa 65:17–18; 66:22–24; II Pet 3:13; Rev 21:1–8). It will have a new capital, the New Jerusalem (Rev 3:12; 21:2, 10).

W. H. M.

NEW HEAVENS AND NEW EARTH. The final consummation and goal of the kingdom of God will be created by God after the thousand year millennial reign of Christ. His reign on the earth with His saints (Rev 5:10; 20:4 ff.) ends with the final loosing of Satan, the rebellion of Gog and Magog, and God's punishment of Satan and the rebellious nations (Rev 20:7–10). This is followed by the judgment of the Great White Throne—which is the final judgment of the unsaved of all ages—and the destruction (Rev 20:11; 21:1) or renovation (II Pet 3:11–12) of the present heavens and earth. The new heavens and the new earth are spoken of twice in the OT (Isa 65:17; 66:22) and twice in the NT (II Pet 3:13; Rev 21; 22).

Two main views are held by orthodox theologians.

1. The new heavens and the new earth appear immediately after the second coming of Jesus Christ. This view takes two forms. First, that held by both amillennialists and postmillennialists who believe that the final judgment of the Great White Throne will occur at the second coming of Christ and that the new heavens and the new earth will immediately follow this.

The difficulty with this view is that, in the case of amillennialists, it requires the spiritualization of the many prophecies given to Israel in the OT concerning a land and a kingdom, and also of the clear teaching of Rev 20:4–10. In the case of the postmillennialists, it requires an identification of those prophecies of Christ in Mt 24, which foretell the conditions preceding the actual second coming of Christ, with those in Lk 21:5–24, which foretell the fall of Jerusalem in A.D. 70. Many amillennialists also make this identification. One difficulty with such an identification is that it leaves unanswered the second and third parts of the question asked by the disciples in Mt 24:3: When shall these things be (destruction of the temple)? What shall be the sign of Thy coming? What shall be the sign of the end of the age? Further, it does violence to Mt 24:15 ff. to force it into agreement with Lk 21:5–24.

Second, that held by some premillennialists who identify the creation of the new heavens and the new earth with the beginning of the thousand year millennial reign of Christ. These premillennialists are impressed by two things: that in Isa 65:17 we read, "Behold, I create new heavens and a new earth," and in Isa 65:18 we read, "Behold, I create Jerusalem a rejoicing." Since the new heavens and the new earth are mentioned along with the re-creation of Jerusalem at the second coming of Christ, they feel that the two must be contemporaneous.

The difficulty is that this identification conflicts with the order given in Rev 20–21 where the new heavens and the new earth are specifically said to come after the Millennium is finished. The answer to Isaiah's placing of the creation of Jerusalem and of the new heavens and the new earth in juxtaposition is to be found in Isa 66:22, "As the new heavens and the new earth, which I will make, shall remain before me, saith the Lord, so shall your seed and your name remain." Since here it is used merely as a comparison, the same can well be the case in Isa 65:17–18. Just as the Holy Spirit in Isa 65:17 compares the renewal of Jerusalem in the time of the Millennium to the creation of an entirely new heavens and new earth, so in Isa 66:22 He compares the unending permanence of Israel to the permanence of the new heavens and new earth. Interpreting Isa 65:17 in the light of Isa 66:22 brings what Isaiah says into harmony with what Rev 20 reveals.

Hodge has wisely said that the less clear passages ought to be interpreted in the light of the more clear, and this is a good example. It should further be pointed out that according to Isa 65:20 there is both sin and death in the millennial kingdom, while in the final estate of the blessed in the new heavens and the new earth these are no more (Rev 21:4). This should be conclusive evidence that they cannot be identical.

However, one other passage remains to be reconciled. Not only do the amillennialists and the postmillennialists, but also the premillennialists mentioned above, see II Pet 3:11–13 as identifying the new heavens and the new earth with the time of the Millennium. Peter speaks of the new heavens and the new earth appearing in the day of the Lord. The answer to this is that the day of the Lord in the OT includes not only the second coming of Christ but also the Millennium, and that at its end will come the creation of the new heavens and the new earth (cf. Zech 14:1 ff.).

How does this fit into what Peter says? He begins by saying, "One day is with the Lord as a thousand years, and a thousand years as one day" (II Pet 3:8). In other words, he indicates that the day of the Lord is actually one thousand years in length—which is the exact length of the Millennium in Rev 20:4–6. In that day, Peter says, first the Lord will come as a thief in the night (v. 10; cf. Rev 16:15; I Thess 5:4); but also within that day—at its end according to Rev 20:11—"all these things shall be dissolved" (II Pet 3:11) or as Rev 20:11 puts it, "the earth and the heaven fled away."

Again when we apply Hodge's rule that the less clear be interpreted in the light of the more clear, and II Pet 3:10–13 is interpreted in the light of Rev 20, the passage in II Peter is seen as reconcilable with Rev 20.

2. The new heavens and the new earth are created at the end of the millennial reign of Christ. In the Millennium the believers of both Testaments will reign with Christ in resurrection bodies (Dan 12:2, 13; Rev 20:4, 6). In spite of the fact that mankind will then for the first time see clearly that full or completed salvation means a new nature, removal of the fallen nature, a resurrection body, and the removal of the curse from nature, still men will not believe in Christ except through the sovereign grace of God because of their total depravity and the exceeding sinfulness of their sins. As soon as Satan is loosed, once more they follow him. Having proved through the different dispensations the total sinfulness of man, God will now close the Gospel Age, judge the wicked of all ages at the Great White Throne, and create "new heavens and a new earth, wherein dwelleth righteousness" (II Pet 3:13).

In the last two chapters of the Bible the New Jerusalem is described in detail, giving a glorious picture of the final dwelling place of God's redeemed in a great city sent down from God out of heaven and situated in the new heavens and the new earth.

See Eschatology; Millennium.

Bibliography. Robert D. Culver, *Daniel and the Latter Days*, Chicago: Moody Press, 1954. John F. Walvoord, *The Revelation of Jesus Christ*, Chicago: Moody Press, 1966. J. Dwight Pentecost, *Things to Come*, Grand Rapids: Dunham, 1958.

R. A. K.

NEW JERUSALEM. *See* City of God; Jerusalem, New.

NEW MAN. *See* New Creation.

NEW MOON. *See* Festivals; Sacrifices.

NEW NATURE. *See* New Creation.

NEW TESTAMENT. The name given to the second part of the Bible, comprising 27 documents written by eyewitnesses of Christ or by their contemporaries. The title implies a contrast with the OT, the sacred Scriptures which the church inherited from Judaism. The name New Testament (Gr. *hē kainē diathēkē*) can better be translated "new covenant," and denotes an agreement established by God which man can either accept or reject, but cannot alter. The term was first used by Jesus in instituting the eucharistic meal to define the new basis of communion with God which He intended to establish by His death (Lk 22:20; I Cor 11:25). The essence of this new covenant lay in its fulfillment of the old covenant by the provision of a sacrifice adequate to remove all sin (Heb 9:11–15) and operative on inner motivation rather than on being merely a regulation of outward conduct (Jer 31:31–34; Heb 10:14–25). The amplification of this new method of God's dealing with man is recorded in this collection of writings, and the name "New Testament" was applied to them by metonymy.

Content

The books of the NT may be divided into four general sections: first, the historical books, including the four Gospels and Acts; second, the 13 epistles of Paul; third, the general epistles, two by Peter, one by James, one by Jude, and four which have no definite name attached to them. Three of these are generally attributed to John, since they bear a marked resemblance to the Fourth Gospel in vocabulary and style, and the book of Hebrews' authorship has been disputed since the early centuries. Fourth, the book of Revelation is prophetic and apocalyptic, describing in symbolic terms the achievement of the divine purpose for the world. All these books may be dated within the first century, though the exact order in which they were written is still debatable.

The Gospels provide the chief sources for knowledge of the life of Christ, though no one of them is a complete biography. Matthew stresses the royal and prophetic character of Jesus' work; Mark emphasizes His acts of moral and spiritual authority; Luke deals with His humanitarian ministry; John presents His claim to deity and the meaning of belief in Him. The book of Acts records the movement of missionary preaching from Jerusalem to Rome in the middle third of the first century, centering on the life of Paul. The epistles are the inspired and authoritative letters of the correspondence of Paul and the other writers with churches or individuals who needed teaching and counsel. Revelation is a dramatic pictorial presentation of the state of seven typical churches of Asia, and of "the things which must shortly come to pass hereafter." Written about A.D. 95 in the reign of Domitian, it reflects the conflict of the church and the Roman Empire, and presages the ultimate struggle that will precede the return of Christ.

Several of the Pauline epistles, such as Galatians, Thessalonians, and Corinthians, antedate the writing of the Gospels, and reflect the knowledge and the history of the church concerning Christ prior to the reduction of that information to permanent record. The entire NT grew out of the necessity for instruction.

Growth of the Canon

From the beginning, most of the writings of the NT were accepted as authoritative by Christians, and as time progressed the books considered doubtful were either fully acknowledged or rejected by the church as a whole. The canon, or collection of books, was not arbitrarily created or decided upon by a group of leaders, but was gradually recognized by the individual churches and by councils. The four Gospels and the epistles of Paul were collected at a very early date, probably before A.D. 100, and were circulated widely among the churches.

About A.D. 140 Marcion, a Gnostic teacher from Asia Minor, came to Rome. He repudiated the authority of the OT as a "Jewish" book, and proposed a canon consisting of the Gospel of Luke, revised to remove all Jewish influence, and ten epistles of Paul. His proposal evoked strong reaction. The church leaders were compelled to define their own canon and to defend it. The early anti-Marcionite lists, such as the Muratorian canon (*c.* A.D. 170), contain the Gospels, Acts, 13 epistles of Paul, Jude, two epistles of John, and the Apocalypse.

Irenaeus, bishop of Lyons, of contemporary date with the Muratorian canon, quoted the Gospels, Acts, all of Paul's epistles except Philemon, I Peter, I and II John, Jude, James, and Revelation. He probably knew Hebrews, though the quotations are not clear. The absence of Philemon, III John, and II Peter from his NT quotations may indicate that these small works contained no material apposite to his immediate needs, or else that they were not in circulation in the quarter of the world where he lived.

Tertullian (*c.* A.D. 150–220) is the first writer to use the term "New Testament" in the sense of a collection of authoritative writings. In it he includes the four Gospels, the 13 letters of Paul, Acts, Revelation, I John, I Peter, and Jude.

In A.D. 367 Athanasius listed the "books that are canonized and handed down to us and believed to be divine"; without hesitation he named, after the books of the OT, all 27 books of our NT canon.

The regional councils of Hippo (A.D. 393) and Carthage (397) and the ecumenical council of Chalcedon (451) reaffirmed the full canon of 27 books, after which it was generally accepted by the church at large.

See Canon of Scripture, the NT; Bible; Bible Manuscripts; Gospels, The Four; Gospels, Synoptic; Paul; Epistles, General; articles on the individual books; Apocrypha, for non-canonical books of NT era.

M. C. T.

Bibliography (recent books). Glenn W. Barker, William L. Lane and J. Ramsey Michaels, *The New Testament Speaks,* New York: Harper and Row, 1969. Everett F. Harrison, *Introduction to the New Testament,* Grand Rapids: Eerdmans, 1964. Bo Reicke, *The New Testament Era: the World of the Bible from 500 B.C. to A.D. 100,* Philadelphia: Fortress Press, 1968. Merrill C. Tenney, *New Testament Survey,* rev. ed., Grand Rapids: Eerdmans, 1961; *New Testament Times,* Grand Rapids: Eerdmans, 1965.

NEW YEAR, FEAST OF TRUMPETS. *See* Festivals.

NEWNESS. A term occurring twice in the KJV and NASB translating Gr. *kainotēs,* "freshness," "newness." The new state of life into which the Holy Spirit introduces the believer in Christ by regeneration. Paul states that all who have been baptized into Jesus Christ are united with Him in His resurrection so that we might "walk in newness of life" (Rom 6:4–5). We are to serve God in "newness of spirit" rather than in the letter of the law (Rom 7:6). This occurs in the Spirit-filled life as the Holy Spirit keeps the law in and through us for our sanctification (Rom 8:3–4). Christ has already fulfilled the law for us in His life and borne its penalties in our stead in His death for our justification (II Cor 5:21; I Pet 2:24); therefore we do not serve God in the deadness of the letter, which condemns and kills, but in the power of the new life given us by the Spirit in regeneration. *See* New Creation.

R. A. K.

NEZIAH (nĭ-zī'*ȧ*). One of the Nethinim whose descendants accompanied Zerubbabel from the Babylonian Captivity and were listed in the genealogical record (Ezr 2:54; Neh 7:56).

NEZIB (nē'zĭb). A town in the Shephelah of Judea which was included in the division of Canaan by Joshua for the tribe of Judah (Josh 15:43). It is identified with modern Khirbet Beit Nesib.

NIBHAZ. *See* Gods, False.

NIBSHAN (nĭb'shăn). A town in the Judean wilderness on the shore of the Dead Sea N of En-gedi, which was included in the division of land by Joshua (Josh 15:62). F. M. Cross, Jr., and J. T. Milik have identified Nibshan with Khirbet el-Maqari, a site going back only to the Iron Age, in the Buqe'ah region (the Valley of Achor) SW of Jericho (BASOR #142 [1956], p. 16). But Nibshan and its five sister cities were large enough to have outlying villages, so that a larger site dating at least as early as the Late Bronze Age should be sought.

In 1965–66 three sites dated by pottery to the 8th–7th cen. B.C. were investigated along the W shore of the Dead Sea, halfway from Qumran to En-gedi. They lie near several fresh water springs just N of a wadi flowing down from Bethlehem, and are known as Ramad, Ain Turabi, and Ain Ghuweir. These may be the sites of Nibshan, Middin, and Secacah (Ian Blake, "Dead Sea Sites of 'The Utter Wilderness,' " ILN, March 4, 1967, pp. 27–29).

J. R.

NICANOR (nī-kā'nôr). One of the seven men chosen as deacons to look after the needs of the Greek-speaking widows in the church in Jerusalem (Acts 6:5).

NICODEMUS (nĭk'ŏ-dē'mŭs). A Pharisee, a ruler of Jews (*archōn,* "ruler," often used as a title for a member of the Sanhedrin, cf. Jn 7:50, "he . . . being one of them"), a teacher of Israel, and probably a very wealthy man (Jn 3:1, 10; 19:39). His nocturnal visit to Jesus was the occasion for the discourse on the new birth recorded in Jn 3:1–10.

Nicodemus is mentioned (in the NT) only in the Gospel of John. (1) He sought out Jesus by night and was taught the doctrine of the new birth (Jn 3:1–10); (2) he defended Jesus before the chief priests and Pharisees—the Sanhedrin (Jn 7:46–52; (3) he assisted Joseph of Arimathea in the preparation of Jesus' body for burial (Jn 19:38–42).

Nothing is known with certainty about his family or background. Attempts have been made to identify him with the Nicodemus ben Gorion mentioned in the Talmud. After his participation in the burial of Jesus, Nicodemus disappeared from the NT narrative, but in an apocryphal narrative of the passion and resurrection of Christ, variously entitled Gospel of Nicodemus and Acts of Pilate, further references are made to him.

Although the NT does not state that Nicodemus later became a Christian, there is a strong probability that he did. In Christian legend, he is represented as having been baptized by Peter and John, suffered many hardships at the hands of hostile Jews, deprived of his office in the Sanhedrin, and banished from Jerusalem because of his faith in Christ.

B. M. W.

NICOLAITANS (nĭk'ŏ-lā'ĭ-tȧnz). The mention of this name in connection with the reference to Balaam (Rev 2:14–15) may well indicate the antinomianism of this group. Eating meat which had been sacrificed to idols and committing fornication are specifically mentioned as the current evidence of the teaching of Balaam. The phrase "in like manner" (Rev 2:15, ASV) would imply the parallel in Nicolaitanism.

Such an understanding of the meaning of the term is confirmed in the writings of the early Church Fathers. Ignatius (*c.* A.D. 110) speaks of them as "lovers of pleasure" and "given to calumnious speeches" (*Epistle of Ignatius to the Trallians,* chap. 11), and defines the term: "A Nicolaitan . . . a corrupter of his own flesh" (*Epistle of Ignatius to the Philadelphians,* chap. 6). Irenaeus (*c.* A.D. 180) says, "They live lives of unrestrained indulgence" (*Against Heresies,* I.26.3). Clement of Alexandria characterizes them as self-indulgent (*Stromata* II.20). Tertullian (*c.* A.D. 200) speaks of their eating things sacrificed to idols and of their committing fornication (*On Proscription Against Heretics,* chap. 33). Hippolytus (*c.* A.D. 200) writes: "John reproved them in the Apocalypse as fornicators and eaters of things offered to idols" (*The Refutation of All Heresies,* VII.24).

The references of Irenaeus and Hippolytus to Nicolas, a proselyte of Antioch (Acts 6:5), as the founder of the Nicolaitans should be viewed with suspicion. The general testimony indicates that the Nicolaitans were guilty of antinomianism.

W. C.

NICOLAS (nĭk'*ȧ*-lȧs). The name, meaning "conqueror of the people," is mentioned only in

Acts 6:5. He was one of the seven men (sometimes thought of as the first "deacons") chosen to take over the "daily ministration" and "serve tables" (Acts 6:1-2) when the task became burdensome to the apostles. His home town was Antioch and he was originally a Gentile convert to Judaism, as he is called "the proselyte of Antioch."

Epiphanius (c. A.D. 315-403), bishop of Salamis claimed that this Nicolas later became disgruntled and started the heretical sect of Nicolaitans (Rev 2:6, 15), but this seems extremely doubtful. Clement of Alexandria (c. A.D. 150-220) defends the character of Nicolas. With the other six deacons, Nicolas evidently fulfilled the qualifications laid out by the apostles: "seven men of honest report, full of the Holy Ghost and wisdom" (Acts 6:3).

NICOPOLIS (nĭ-kŏp'ō-lĭs). In his letter to Titus Paul informs Titus of his plan to spend the winter in Nicopolis (Tit 3:12). Although there are small cities by this name in Thrace and Cilicia, Paul undoubtedly referred to that "city of victory" founded by Augustus in Epirus on the W coast of Greece. It was a large, flourishing city and Paul called Titus from Crete to help him there. It was in this city that Paul was probably arrested and taken to Rome for his last imprisonment.

NIGER. *See* Simeon.

NIGHT. The unit of time designating the period from sunset to sunrise, including the morning and evening twilight. Figuratively, the term is used to designate a period of trouble or distress (Isa 21:11-12), the time of death or the grave (Jn 9:4), a time of ignorance and helplessness (Mic 3:6), and the depraved condition of mankind (I Thess 5:5-7). *See* Time, Divisions of.

NIGHTHAWK. *See* Animals: Goatsucker, III.17.

NIGHT MARCHES. To escape the desert heat or to avoid enemies, the Israelites sometimes marched in the nighttime as they journeyed from Egypt to Canaan (Ex 13:21; 14:19-23; Num 9:21). Joshua led his army on an exhausting all-night march up from Gilgal to relieve the besieged Gibeonites at dawn (Josh 10:6-9). Abram rescued Lot by pursuing the Mesopotamian kings at night (Gen 14:15). Gideon attacked and chased the terrified Midianites at night (Jud 7:9-22). Other night marches are described in Jud 9:32 ff.; I Sam 14:36; 31:11 f.; II Sam 2:29, 32; 17:16, 22; II Kgs 6:14; 8:21; Acts 23:23, 31.

NIGHT MONSTER. A translation of Heb. *lîlît*, which occurs only in Isa 34:14. Its various translations are as follows: LXX *onokentayroi;* Symmachus *lamia;* Vulg. *lamia;* screech owl, KJV; night monster, ASV, NASB, Berkeley, JPS; Lilith, ASV and NASB marg.; night hag, RSV; nightjar, NEB.

Two essential views are taken (see translations above and also commentaries) as to the meaning of this word in its biblical setting: (1) some form of real night creature (cf. Alexander, and G. R. Driver, "Lilith," PEQ, XCI [1959], 55-57, who argues that it is a desert bird called a goatsucker or nightjar which inhabits desolate places); (2) a demon (BDB, Young). If the latter, a mythological name is used to express vividly and figuratively the reality without giving credence to the myth. A major consideration for deciding between the two alternatives is whether the other creatures mentioned are real or demonic, e.g., the "wild goat" or "satyr" (Heb. *śā'îr*).

NIGHT WATCH. *See* Watch.

NILE (nīl). The Nile River is one of the great river systems, the second longest in the world (after the Amazon), and one of the few that run from S to N. From its sources at the equatorial lakes of E Africa it flows more than 4,000 miles to empty into the Mediterranean Sea. Beginning at Lake Victoria, it moves through Lake Kioga, plunges down Murchison Falls, and passes through Lake Albert. Eventually the waters spread out in a vast swamp where vegetation obscures the channels and makes navigation almost impossible. The luxuriant growth, the sudd, was the curse of early explorers, though it contributes to the fertility which characterizes the Nile.

The tributaries of the Nile are few in number and almost all of them enter from the E carrying waters from the Abyssinian highlands. The main stream, the White Nile, is joined by the Sobat near Malakal. At Khartoum the White Nile meets the Blue Nile, which plays an important role in the annual inundation. The triangle formed by the White and Blue Niles, the Gezira ("island") is a rich agricultural area specializing in cotton. Below Khartoum the last tributary, the Atbara, is a dry stream bed most of the year but a raging torrent when in flood. The Nile continues N some 1,500 miles to the sea without another tributary. Between Khartoum and Aswan the river passes through six cataracts, which are numbered from N to S in the order of discovery. In this region were the areas of Cush and Nubia.

The Egyptians were active in the Nubian section as early as the Old Kingdom (c. 2700-2200 B.C.). During the Middle Kingdom (c. 2000-1775 B.C.) they built forts and trading posts as far S as the Second and Third Cataracts. A number of Egyptian temples were situated in Nubia in the New Kingdom (c. 1580-1100 B.C.), with Abu Simbel the best known.

Just above the First Cataract at Aswan stands the island of Philae, with the famous temples of later date. At Aswan, ancient Syene, is the island of Elephantine, which had a Jewish community that was in contact with Palestine in the 5th cen. B.C. From Aswan to Cairo the valley is relatively narrow, a strip of land two to 30 miles in width, hemmed in by cliffs and rocky desert.

Below Cairo the fan-shaped Delta opens up, about 125 miles long by 115 wide. In classical times the Nile here branched into seven channels, but today there are two main branches, the W or Rosetta, which debouches near Alexandria, and the E or Damietta, which reaches the sea W of Port Said, the N terminus of the Suez Canal. In the time of the Nineteenth Dynasty (*c.* 1300 ff.) much building was done in the NE part of the Delta by Rameses II, who had his royal residence and capital at Tanis (*see* Zoan).

Since the Nile was the source and supply of life in Egypt—without it much of NE Africa would not be habitable—the Egyptians recognized a god of the river, Hapi, who was represented as a hermaphroditic being with pendulous breasts. The river provided many of the necessities of life: water for irrigation, drinking water, washing and bathing facilities, food such as fish and fowl. Along its banks were the reed pastures where cattle were raised (Gen 41:1-4). It was the avenue of commerce; the northbound current facilitated downstream traffic and the prevailing N wind provided sail-power for travel S (upstream). Boating, fishing, and hunting along the river furnished sport and recreation for the nobles.

Twin statues in black granite representing the Nile god Hapi stand behind altars on which are fish, flowing water, and aquatic plants. LL

The Nile at Luxor with Lybian hills in the background. HFV

The annual inundation was the basis of the agriculture of the country. This life-giving flood began in equatorial Africa with the seasonal rains. These increased the volume of the White Nile, which consequently overspread large tracts of the swamplands and accumulated much organic material. It is the rains of the Ethiopian mountains, however, which contribute the most to the annual flood. Since the rivers that originate there have much more fall than the White Nile, they rush down at great velocity and carry quantities of soil for alluvial deposit. The Blue Nile in flood even holds back the waters of the White Nile.

In the latitude of Memphis (near modern Cairo) the beginning of the inundation occurred in June, with a pronounced increase which took place about July 19. The rising waters were carefully observed by officials and were measured by Nilometers at various checkpoints. An optimum flooding was of great importance: too little water spelled agricultural disaster, with ensuing shortages of food; too much meant catastrophe from water damage. During October the waters attained their greatest height and by December the river was again in its normal channel.

Attempts to control the waters for irrigation date back to ancient times, for most of the water has gone to sea unused. In the Middle Kingdom water control was effected by use of the Fayyum depression. Currently there are dams (barrages) at a number of places. The Aswan Dam was completed in 1902 and has twice been increased in height. The new High Dam (Sadd el Aali), begun in 1960 and officially dedicated Jan. 15, 1971, creates the huge Lake Nasser. The dam is expected to provide an additional 2,500,000 acres of agricultural land and to supply a tremendous increase in electrical power.

In antiquity the inundation influenced the calendar of Egypt in several respects. The flooding determined the practical calendar of agriculture, which was the basis of the economy of the country. The appearance of the Dog Star (Sirius, Sothis) on the E horizon at dawn at the July 19 date gave rise to a cycle of 1,460 years, the Sothic cycle, which has been useful in working with the chronology of ancient Egypt. *See* Egypt.

In the Bible, references to the Nile are fairly frequent in the latter part of Genesis and the early section of Exodus. These marks of local color accurately reflect firsthand acquaintance with Egyptian life and therefore support the traditional view of the Mosaic authorship of those books. The term *y^{e}'or*, "stream, watercourse," is the ordinary designation of the Nile in Heb. This is a loan-word from Egyptian; *itrw*, like *y^{e}'or*, was used for the mainstream of the river, its branches in the Delta, and even for canals, which of course derived their water from the river. Usually the Heb. word is accompanied by the definite article, "the river," which expresses a clearly Egyptian point of view. In the RSV the term is regularly translated "the Nile"; the name "Nile" does not appear in the KJV. In Heb. the Nile is also called *shîḥôr* in several passages (Isa 23:3; Jer 2:18). Care must be taken not to confuse the Nile and the "River of Egypt," which in most instances is the Wadi el-Arish, the SW boundary of Palestine. *See* Egypt, River of.

In the Joseph narrative Pharaoh dreamed that he stood by the Nile (Gen 41:1, 17); the cattle of his dream fed along the river (Gen 41:2-3, 18). In the period of oppression in Egypt it was ordered that all Heb. male infants should be disposed of at birth by throwing them into the river (Ex 1:22). The baby Moses was placed in a watertight basket and hidden in the reeds at the river's edge (Ex 2:3), where he was discovered by the princess and her attendants (Ex 2:5-6). The first plague was directed against the Nile (Ex 7:14-25; cf. Ps 78:44). The plague of frogs also was associated with the river (Ex 8:3, 5, 9, 11).

In the writings of the prophets the Nile figures in predictions against Egypt. It was prophesied that the Nile would dry up (Isa 19:5-10; 37:25; Ezk 30:12; Zech 10:11). The harvest of the Nile is mentioned as part of the revenue of the merchant city of Tyre (Isa 23:3), and an allusion to the inundation may be found in Isa 23:10. Nahum refers to the city of Thebes, "that sat by the Nile, with water around her, her rampart a sea, and water her wall" (Nah 3:8, RSV).

Bibliography. Georg Gerster, "Threatened Treasures of the Nile," *National Geographic*, CXXIV (Oct., 1963), 587-623 and Atlas Pl. 56. Irving and Electa Johnson, *"Yankee* Cruises the Storied Nile," *National Geographic*, CXXVII (May, 1965), 583-633 and Atlas Pl. 58.

C. E. D.

Nilometer on the island of Elephantine at Aswan, used for measuring the Nile flood. HFV

NIMRAH (nĭm′rȧ). A city on the E side of Jordan which was included in the tribal division for the tribe of Gad (Num 32:3). It is identical to Beth-nimrah (*q.v.*; v. 36) and is located at Tell el-Bleibil in the Wadi Sha'îb. Not far away is the Wadi Nimrin, preserving the ancient name of the waters of Nimrim (*q.v.*). Both are about eight miles N of the Dead Sea at the E edge of the Jordan Valley.

NIMRIM (nĭm′rĭm). A name still to be found in Wadi en-Numeirah SE of the Dead Sea. These waters were cursed in oracles against Moab (Isa 15:6; Jer 48:34).

NIMROD (nĭm′rŏd). A descendant of Ham through Cush who early distinguished himself throughout the region of Mesopotamia (Gen 10:8-12). He is described as "a mighty one in the earth" (v. 8) and "a mighty hunter before the Lord" (v. 9), probably signifying that he was one of the first recorded potentates in history and a tyrant (a hunter of men, cf. Jer 16:16). According to v. 10 he founded a kingdom in the land of Shinar (*q.v.*), i.e., in southern Iraq, consisting of Babel, Erech, and Accad, "even all of them" (see JBL, XC [1971], 99-102). Then he went forth into Assyria and built—or rebuilt—Nineveh, Rehoboth-Ir, Calah, and Resen (vv. 11-12, NASB).

Archaeologically speaking, Nimrod may have been the leader of the Ubaid movement from S to N Iraq, *c.* 3800-3500 B.C. That is the only period prior to the time of Abraham (*c.* 2000 B.C.) when a non-Semitic culture came from the S and left significant remains in the early levels of the Assyrian cities. Sargon of Akkad or Agade (*c.* 2300 B.C.), who conquered all of Mesopotamia by marching from his capital near Babylon, was a Semitic ruler.

In Mic 5:6 Assyria is called the land of Nimrod. To the present day his name is attached to ruined cities: the site of Calah (*q.v.*) is called *Nimrûd,* and the site of ancient Borsippa in Babylonia is called *Birs Nimrûd.*

J. R.

NIMRUD. *See* Calah.

NIMSHI (nĭm'shī). The grandfather of Jehu (II Kgs 9:2, 14), who is usually designated as the son of Nimshi (I Kgs 19:16; II Kgs 9:20; II Chr 22:7).

NINEVE. Gr. translation in Lk 11:32 of Nineveh (*q.v.*).

The mound of Kuyunjik, Nineveh. JR

NINEVEH (nĭn'ĕ-vĕ). Opposite the modern town of Mosul on the E side of the Tigris River stand two mounds called in Arabic Kuyunjik (the castle of Nineveh) and Nebi-Yunus (the presumed burial place of the prophet Jonah). The latter is still inhabited. They were part of a building complex surrounded by a seven-and-a-half-mile brick wall with 15 city gates which comprised ancient Nineveh.

Jonah, who was sent to preach to this Assyrian city in the early 8th cen. B.C., described it as "an exceeding great city of three days' journey" (Jon 3:3). By this, apparently, he meant it took three days to reach all parts of the city on a preaching mission. One may judge the size of the population from the statement in Jon 4:11 which says Nineveh's innocent population, that is, children not old enough to know the difference between their right hand and their left, was 120,000, suggesting a total population of 600,000. Perhaps Jonah had in mind a "greater Nineveh," since such major cities often consisted of a walled fortress plus many outlying hamlets for miles around, which in Heb. parlance was called a city and her daughters (Josh 15:45, 47).

Others, however, regard the expression of Jon 4:11 as metaphorical, designating the entire population, whom God considered to have an imperfect knowledge of good and evil. A total population of 120,000 accords well with the recorded number of 69,574 persons accommodated in Calah, a city of less than half the size in 879 B.C.

Nineveh did not become the capital of Assyria until the reign of Sennacherib (705–681 B.C.). Nevertheless, various kings before him built palaces in Nineveh and added public buildings and temples. Ashurnasirpal II (884–859) and Shalmaneser III (859–824) used Nineveh as their residence city for portions of their reigns (ANET, pp. 277 ff.). It is possible to interpret the word "king" (Heb. *melek*) in Jon 3:6–7 in the Akkad. sense of *malku,* meaning "prince, governor," so that the book of Jonah is not historically inaccurate (*see* Jonah, Book of).

The two mounds, separated by the rivulet known today as the Khosr, have received the archaeologist's spade many times since the excavation began at Kuyunjik under P. E. Botta and A. H. Layard in the mid-19th cen. In 1903 L. W. King was joined by R. C. Thompson, who used modern archaeological techniques on this site in extensive diggings from 1927 to 1932. While Nebi-Yunus has houses and a mosque containing Jonah's supposed tomb, Layard did some underground digging in this mound, and in 1954 the director general of antiquities of Iraq uncovered part of the palace of Esarhaddon.

Excavations have shown that Nineveh went back to late neolithic times (*c.* 5000 B.C.). *See* Archaeology. This is in keeping with the biblical tradition which mentions Nineveh in the Table of Nations (Gen 10) along with another Assyrian capital, Calah. Both cities were built by Nimrod, who invaded the region later called Assyria, coming from the land of Shinar. Perhaps this occurred *c.* 3500 B.C., for an early level at Kuyunjik has Ubaid-type pottery known to have originated in S Mesopotamia. Nimrod's name has persisted among the local populace, who call the site of Calah Tell Nimrud even today.

Nineveh is mentioned in cuneiform documents as early as the 22nd–21st cen. B.C. Tablets found at the Assyrian commercial colony at Kultepe in ancient Cappadocia from early in the 2nd mil. B.C. name the city and indicate that it was a center of Ishtar worship. This is confirmed by a document from the time of Shamshi-Adad (1748–1716 B.C.) which says the Ishtar temple was built by Manishtusu (2295–2281 B.C.), the son of Sargon of Akkad. A later temple of Ishtar, the goddess of fertility and war and identified with the planet Venus, was unearthed on Kuyunjik along with a temple of Nabu, the god of arts and crafts.

However, the greatest discovery at Nineveh was the palace of Sennacherib (705–681 B.C.), the Assyrian king who did most to glorify the great city. Sennacherib's palace at the SW tip of the 90-foot-high mound of Kuyunjik was cleared first by Layard in 1849–51. There were two large halls, each some 7,000 square feet and more than 9,000 feet of walls, decorated with inscribed annals and pictures of the king's exploits in low relief. Many winged bulls and sphinxes weighing as much as 30 tons guarded the entrances. Sennacherib also built a 30-mile aqueduct to bring fresh water into the city. To Nineveh, which he called "my lordly city," he brought the tribute and captives from Jerusalem and other Palestinian cities (ANET, p. 288).

While no temple of Sennacherib's god Nisroch, in which he was murdered (II Kgs 19:37), has been discovered, the temple of Nabu from his period yielded about 1,000 cuneiform tablets, evidently a part of a royal library. But a greater and well-arranged library was discovered at the NE end of the mound, for here King Ashurbanipal (669–631 B.C.) stored nearly 100,000 tablets which he had his scribes collect or copy from many sources ancient in his day. The discovery of this library in the 19th cen. gave the original impetus to the study of cuneiform. Much of this material has been published in the series entitled *Cuneiform Texts from Babylonian Tablets in the British Museum.* The most startling of these texts when they were finally translated were the seven tablets of the Babylonian creation epic (ANET, pp. 60–72) and the 12 tablets of the epic of Gilgamesh containing a Babylonian account of the Flood (ANET, pp. 72–99). *See* Flood; Genesis.

A creation tablet from Ashurbanipal's library, Nineveh. BM

Excavations at Calah, suburb of Nineveh. JR

After the reign of Ashurbanipal Assyria began to lose power. Babylon became independent and was joined by the Medes. Together they succeeded in first taking the ancient capital called Ashur. Then with the help of nomadic hordes of Scythians, Cyaxares the Mede and Nabopolassar the Chaldean began their assault on Nineveh. For three months the allies delivered unsuccessful assaults on the city. Finally it fell before this coalition of power which had been trained in siege warfare by the Assyrian kings themselves. The Babylonian Chronicle records that Nineveh fell in the fourteenth year of Nabopolassar, which chronologists have computed to be the year 612 B.C. (ANET, pp. 303–305).

The fall of Nineveh closed Assyrian history, though the final destruction of the Assyrian army did not come until 609 B.C. when their remnants were destroyed in the capture of Harran by the Babylonians and Scythians. Nineveh became an utter desolation and its palaces and temples were torn down. The words of the prophet Zephaniah give a remarkable description of what happened to Nineveh: "And he will make Nineveh a desolation, a dry waste like a desert. . . . This is the exultant city that dwelt secure, that said to herself, 'I am and there is none else.' What a desolation she has become, a lair for wild beasts" (Zeph 2:13, 15, RSV).

The prophet Nahum devoted his oracle to the overthrow of Nineveh. His mood is one of exultation because a bitter scourge would soon be brought to an end, and the Assyrian atrocities were exactly that. Nahum sings at the end of the first chapter: "Keep your feasts, O Judah, fulfill your vows, for never again shall the wicked come against you, he is utterly cut off" (RSV). How true this was, for all the major Assyrian cities were destroyed. Thus deurbanized, only a primitive civilization continued there until the 1st cen. A.D. when a people re-emerged as a vassal kingdom of the Parthians. It is perhaps one of the ironies of history that the royal house of this kingdom of Adiabene was converted to Judaism and contributed to the building up of Jerusalem.

Bibliography. C. J. Gadd, *The Fall of Nineveh,* London: Oxford Univ. Press, 1923. André Parrot, *Nineveh and the Old Testament,* trans. by B. E. Hooke, London: SCM Press, 1955. R. C. Thompson and R. W. Hutchinson, *A Century of Exploration at Nineveh,* London: Luzac, 1929.

E. B. S.

NINEVITES (nĭn'ē-vītz). Residents of Nineveh, used in the Bible only in the plural (Lk 11:30). *See* Nineveh.

NIPPUR (nĭ-po͞or'). One of the major cities of ancient Mesopotamia located *c.* 95 miles SE of Baghdad, Nippur occupied a unique position because of its extraordinary religious status. Though never a political capital, so far as we can tell, Nippur figured prominently throughout the entire recorded history of Mesopotamia. It was the special city of Enlil, chief of all the gods of the various cities of Babylonia and Assyria, and his temple known as the Ekur was located there. Accordingly, from early Sumerian times down to and including the Neo-Assyrian Empire every ruler confirmed his authority by making a journey to Nippur and "seizing the hands" of Enlil. In fact, the name Nippur is written by means of a Sumerian logogram *EN.LÍL.KI* which means "the place of the god Enlil."

The original occupation of Nippur, however, precedes the time of the Sumerians. Early Ubaid-type sherds indicate that it existed at virtually the beginning of settled occupation in southern Iraq. It was more or less continuously occupied down to the Parthian period, a span of nearly 4,000 years. At its largest extent the city proper covered an area of about 180 acres. But the population was scattered over a much wider area outside the walls, and the village of Puzris'-Dagan six miles farther S served as Nippur's cattle market.

The first significant excavations were undertaken by the University of Pennsylvania for four seasons under the scientific guidance of Professor Herman V. Hilprecht from 1888–1900. Most of the time John Henry Haynes supervised the actual digging. This was the first full-scale American expedition to the Near East following the lead of the British and French.

Perhaps the most important discovery was the large collection of nearly 6,000 clay tablets and fragments originally supposed to have come from a temple library. Subsequent study has shown that they actually came from the private homes of professional scribes and were used in the process of teaching apprentices the art of writing Akkadian and Sumerian in the cuneiform script. These tablets are described generally as school texts and include many different classes from exercise tablets containing separate wedges or simple signs to copies of such literary compositions as proverbs, epical poems, and hymns. Interestingly enough, both the Sumerian literature and the key to it came from the same collections of school texts; for without the data from the vocabularies and grammatical paradigms used long ago to teach Sumerian, modern scholars would have been unable to translate the literary documents.

Recent excavations have been conducted by the Oriental Institute of the University of Chicago together with the University of Pennsylvania from 1948–52 and subsequently for several seasons by the former institution alone. They have turned up nearly a thousand additional tablets and fragments containing these unique "school texts." Also discovered and excavated was the great temple of Inanna, the Sumerian counterpart to Babylonian Ishtar, goddess of love and war. This temple dates from early dynastic times and played a large part in the religious and economic life of Nippur.

Much still remains to be recovered, however, for literary references to many other deities indicate that they too had temples at Nippur which have not yet been discovered.

See Babylonia; Sumer.

F. R. S.

NISAN (nī'zăn). The first month of the Jewish sacred calendar (Neh 2:1; Est 3:7), called Abib (*q.v.*) in the Pentateuch. It denotes the month of flowers during which the Passover occurred and corresponds to our March–April. *See* Calendar.

NISROCH. *See* Gods, False.

NITER. *See* Minerals and Metals.

Hypostyle Hall, temple of Karnak, Thebes.
HFV

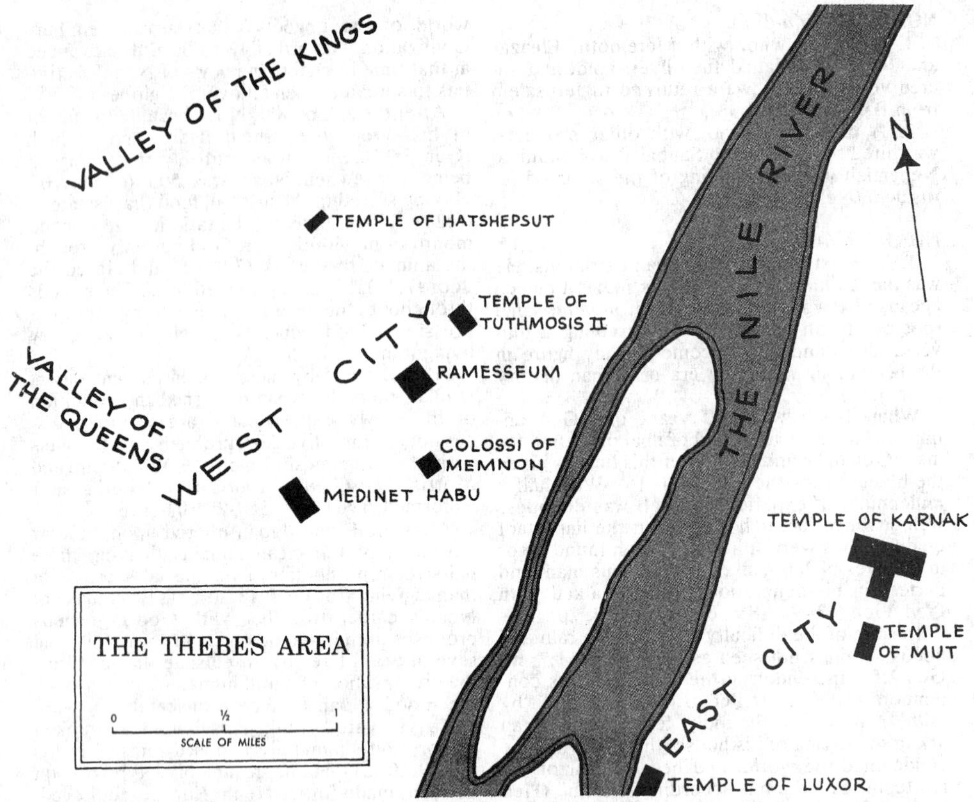

NO, NO-AMON (nō-ăm'ŏn). The Heb. place-name meaning "town of Amon" derived from the Egyptian *niwt,* "village," "town," and designating the Egyptian city which the Greeks called Diospolis, Diospolis Magna, or Thebes. The Egyptian name translated Thebes is *Waset,* applied both to the village on the E bank of the Nile and to the fourth nome of Upper Egypt. In general use the town name Thebes came to mean Karnak, Luxor, and the necropolis area W of the river.

No achieved its greatest glory during Dynasty XVIII (1570–1329 B.C.), when it was the capital of Egypt. It was nicknamed "the city of a hundred gates." The cult-center of the triad of Amon, Mut, and Khonsu, the name No-amon indicates the relationship between the city and its principal god. The priests of Amon became increasingly powerful and assumed the kingship after the death of Tutankhamon. No was plundered when the Assyrian Ashurbanipal captured it in 663 B.C. (cf. Nah 3:8). The Persian Cambyses marched through the city on his way to Nubia in 525 B.C. It suffered great destruction by the hand of the Roman prefect Cornelius Gallus for participating in a revolt against excessive taxation after Cleopatra's suicide in 30 B.C.

Numerous evidences of the glory of Egypt may still be seen at Thebes, including the great temples of Luxor and Karnak on the E bank of the Nile. On the W side are vast mortuary temples such as the Ramesseum, Medinet Habu, and Deir el-Bahri, and magnificent tombs of the Pharaohs in the Valley of the Kings. Paintings in numerous rock-cut tombs of nobles depict native life and customs in the time of Moses.

Especially impressive among the ruins of the temple of Karnak is the Hypostyle Hall, one of the great architectural achievements of the world. Here 134 columns supported the roof; the central avenue has columns 70 feet high, the tallest in the world. Rameses II of the 13th cen. was largely responsible for this construction.

In the Bible Thebes appears only in contexts of judgment. Jer 46:25 (RSV) states that the Lord will punish Amon of Thebes; Ezk 30:14–16 declares various judgments on the city; and in Nah 3:8 ff. (ASV) the fate of No-amon serves as an object lesson for her Assyrian conquerors.

Bibliography. Charles F. Nims, *Thebes of the Pharaohs,* New York: Stein and Day, 1965.

C. E. D.

NOADIAH (nō'ȧ-dī'ȧ)

1. A Levite who, with Meremoth, Eleazar and Jozabad, weighed the silver, gold, and sacred vessels which were returned to Jerusalem from Babylon (Ezr 8:33).

2. A prophetess who, with other prophets, was hired by Tobiah and Sanballat to intimidate Nehemiah in the rebuilding of the walls of Jerusalem (Neh 6:14).

NOAH (nō'ȧ)

1. The last of the antediluvian patriarchs. He was named *nōaḥ* in Heb. by his father Lamech because he would comfort (Heb. *nāḥam,* same root as "Noah") mankind by surviving a universal flood and thus become the key figure in the beginnning of a new era of human history (Gen 5:29).

When Noah was 480 years old, God announced a 120-year period of final probation for man (Gen 6:3), and soon after this he was given the blueprint for the ark (6:14–16). With half a millennium of experience, Noah was doubtless well qualified for such a task; but the important qualifications were spiritual: "Noah found favor in the eyes of Jehovah . . . a righteous man, and perfect in his generations: Noah walked with God (Gen 6:8–9, ASV; cf. Ezk 14:14, 20).

In spite of the difficulty of imagining rain and floods ("things not seen as yet," Heb 11:7; cf. Gen 2:5), and enduring the scoffing of his contemporaries (cf. II Pet 3:4–6), Noah "by faith . . . moved with godly fear, prepared an ark to the saving of his house; through which he condemned the world, and became heir of the righteousness which is according to faith" (Heb 11:7, ASV). While "the longsuffering of God waited in the days of Noah, while the ark was a preparing" (I Pet 3:20, ASV), the great patriarch, as a "preacher of righteousness" (II Pet 2:5), was no doubt constantly explaining the terrifying significance of his project to "the world of the ungodly" that surrounded him. Civilization was probably sufficiently advanced at that time to enable the news of Noah's activities to spread to men all over the globe.

After the age of 500, Noah became the father of his three sons, Shem, Ham, and Japheth (Gen 5:32). Shem was probably the youngest, being born when Noah was 503 (cf. 11:10). Having stored in the ark "all food that is eaten" (6:21), Noah entered the ark in the second month of his 600th year. God not only brought the animals to the ark (7:9, 15) and closed the door (7:16), but also provided for all their needs throughout the Flood (implied by the expression: "God remembered Noah, and every living thing . . . in the ark," 8:1).

After a year, by means of birds sent out at regular intervals, Noah discerned the condition of the newly exposed land areas. For a discussion of the olive leaf problem and parallels with the Gilgamesh Epic, see Whitcomb and Morris, *The Genesis Flood* (Presbyterian and Reformed, 1961), pp. 38–40, 104–106.

After the Flood, Noah offered upon an altar one each of the clean animals (leaving three pairs for reproduction) as a special sacrifice of thanksgiving to God (8:20). This climax of Noah's career (together with God's gracious promises in the Noahic covenant) was followed several years later by an episode that confirms the preservation of sinful human nature through the Flood. Noah became a husbandman, planted a vineyard, drank himself into a drunken stupor, and shamefully exposed himself in his tent (9:20–21). Ham, presumably led by his son Canaan, made fun of Noah. For this foul deed, Canaan was cursed and Ham received no blessing. On the other hand, Shem and Japheth showed due respect to their father (9:23) and received rich blessings for their descendants.

Noah lived 350 years after the Flood, dying

Temple of Rameses III, Medinet Habu, Thebes. LL

at the age of 950. He was truly one of the greatest men in history.

See Antediluvians; Ark; Flood.

J. C. W.

2. One of the five daughters of Zelophehad (Num 26:33; 27:1; 36:11; Josh 17:3). In Heb. her name was *nō'â*.

NOB (nŏb). A town of priests in the time of Saul (I Sam 22:19), just N of Jerusalem in Benjamin near Anathoth, probably on Mount Scopus. Ahimelech, the priest at the tabernacle, innocently gave David the sacred bread and the sword of Goliath in his desperate need when hiding from Saul (I Sam 21:1-9). At Saul's command Doeg the Edomite slaughtered Ahimelech and 85 priests with the sword after Saul's guard refused to do so. He then killed every living thing in Nob (I Sam 22:17-19). Assyrian invaders later halted there confronting Jerusalem (Isa 10:32). Nob was inhabited after the Exile (Neh 11:32).

Nob. HFV

NOBAH (nō'bȧ)

1. An Israelite who was probably a son of Machir of the tribe of Manasseh. In conquering the land on the E side of Jordan, he took the town of Kenath with the surrounding villages and gave it his own name (Num 32:42).

2. A town E of Gilead mentioned in Gideon's pursuit of the Midianites (Jud 8:11).

NOBAI. *See* Nebai.

NOBLES. *See* Princes.

NOD. *See* Eden.

NODAB (nō'dăb). A Hagarite clan which, along with Jetur and Nephish, suffered defeat in the war with the Reubenites, Gadites, and the half tribe of Manasseh (I Chr 5:18-20).

NOE. *See* Noah.

NOGAH (nō'gȧ). One of the sons of David born to him by one of his wives other than Bathsheba after he had established his throne in Jerusalem (I Chr 3:7; 14:6).

Recent excavations on the site of ancient Memphis. HFV

NOHAH (nō'hȧ). The fourth son of Benjamin, the youngest son of Jacob (I Chr 8:2). He is not included in the list of those who accompanied Jacob into Egypt (Gen 46:21), so he was probably born later. Some have identified him as Shupham (*q.v.;* Num 26:39).

NON (nŏn). An Ephraimite through Beriah, who was born to Ephraim after the Gathites slew some of his sons (I Chr 7:20-23, 27, RSV). He was the father of Joshua (Josh 1:1). *See* Nun.

NOON. *See* Time, Divisions of.

NOPH (nŏf). The Heb. name of the Egyptian city Memphis (Hos 9:6), the capital of lower Egypt, located on the W bank of the Nile, S of Cairo. It was probably the capital of the Pharaohs in the time of Joseph and the Exodus. *See* Memphis.

NOPHAH (nō'fȧ). A Moabite city which, together with Heshbon, Dibon, and Medeba, was occupied by the Amorites and subsequently captured by the Israelites en route to the Jordan River (Num 21:30). It is probably the same as Nobah (*q.v.;* Jud 8:11), NW of Amman, presently called Nowakis.

NORTH. The common word for north in Heb., *ṣapôn,* means "hidden" or "secret," perhaps because the mountains that lay far to the N bordering the Mesopotamian valley were the end of the world as the people of early days knew it. *See* Zaphon. Out of those mysterious lands came sudden and violent incursions of aliens. Although Babylon, Assyria, *et al.* are not strictly N of Palestine by the compass, they are called nations and kings of the N because this was the direction by which they came to the conquest of Palestine (Zeph 2:13; Jer 1:14; 46:6; Ezk 26:7). The "king of the north" in Dan 11 refers to the king of Syria, who came down into Palestine in the 2nd cen. B.C.

Another Heb. word for north used in Job 37:9 (RSV) literally means "scattering," referring to the cold N wind that scattered the clouds.

NOSE, NOSTRILS. This is the organ through which we breathe (Num 11:20). Thus, God breathed into man's "nostrils the breath of life" (Gen 2:7). The nose is also the organ for smelling (Ps 115:6; Isa 65:5). It was the place of the ornament ring (Gen 24:47, RSV; Isa 3:21; Ezk 16:12, RSV) and the captive's ring or hook (II Kgs 19:28; Isa 37:29).

The same Heb. word is used to denote the face, since the nose is the most prominent feature of the face (Gen 19:1; Num 22:31; I Kgs 1:23, 31). The word also signifies anger since this is sometimes shown by hard breathing (Gen 27:45; 49:6-7; Ex 32:12; Deut 9:19; Prov 22:24).

NOSE, FLAT. *See* Diseases.

NOSE JEWEL. A ring worn, usually by the women, in or on the nose as an ornament; generally made of gold or silver (Gen 24:47, ASV, RSV; Isa 3:21). It was about one to three inches in diameter and was passed through the right nostril. *See* Amulet; Jewels; Ring.

NOSE RING. *See* Nose Jewel.

NOVICE. The word is found in the LXX of Job 14:9 and Isa 5:7 as "newly planted." It occurs only once in the NT (I Tim 3:6), where it refers to a new convert or one not yet matured in Christian experience.

NUMBER, NUMEROLOGY

The Construction of Numbers

The basic method of counting in Israel, as in Assyria, Egypt, Greece, and Rome, was the decimal system. In Assyria, however, the sexagesimal system was also popularly used. The numbers appearing in the Heb. text of the OT are always written out in word form. The same is true for the text of the NT with the exception of the occurrence of the Gr. letters *chi* (600), *xi* (60), *zēta* (6) for 666 in some MSS at Rev 13:18. At Ugarit, the numbers in literary texts are generally spelled out, except in administrative documents where they are written ideographically with Sumero-Akkadian symbols. While special signs for numbers were used by Israel's neighbors, there is little evidence that Israel used such signs in its literature to any great extent until the time of the Exile. Symbols were employed for certain numbers on ostraca from Samaria (8th cen. B.C., ANET, p. 321) and strokes or symbols on inscribed stone weights found in Iron Age levels of cities of Judah (*see* Weights, Measures, and Coins).

The number one in Heb. is an adjective while the numbers two to ten are nouns. The numbers eleven to nineteen are formed by placing the unit before the ten. The *waw* conjunctive is not employed and the two words remain separate (e.g., *'aḥad 'āśār,* "eleven"). The tens are denoted by the plural of ten (*'eśer*).

The Uses of Numbers

The conventional use of numbers. This is that use concerned with the mathematical value of the number. Numbers so employed are designed to denote either a specific or a general mathematical quantity. Only a few arithmetical processes can be illustrated from the Bible. Addition is used in Gen 5:3-31 and Num 1:20-46; subtraction in Gen 18:28 ff.; multiplication in Lev 25:8 and Num 3:46 ff.; and division in Num 31:25-41. The Bible demonstrates a remarkable degree of accuracy in its use of fractions, which was not always the case in contemporary documents. The practice of rounding out numbers is common to the Bible and extrabiblical literature. Frequently the writers of Scripture felt it unnecessary to include exact, official, detailed enumerations or sums, but only a rounded estimate of the total. Battle statistics many times take this form.

One of the crucial problems related to the conventional use of numbers is what appears to be excessively high numbers. The large numbers given for the size of the Exodus (Num 1, 26); the number of men in David's census (1,300,000 in II Sam 24:9 or 1,570,000 in I Chr 21:5); the 7,000 sheep sacrificed in Jerusalem (II Chr 15:11); the large numbers of chariots used in the hill country (30,000 in I Sam 13:5) have caused some to question the historicity of the text at this point. Scholars have attempted to resolve the problem by making the Heb. term *'elep* mean something other than "thousand" in these problem passages. W. M. Flinders Petrie proposed that it meant "group" or "family" in connection with the size of the Exodus, thus reducing the size of the Exodus to about 20,000 people including women and children. R. E. D. Clark later proposed that *'elep* probably meant "captain" or "mighty men" in military statistics. Mendenhall suggests the term has reference to a military unit.

It is, of course, true that *'elep* is used in these ways in the OT (cf. Jud 6:15; Mic 5:2; Num 1:16; I Sam 10:19). However, it does not appear that these proposals will work in the census lists relating to the Exodus for at least three reasons: (1) Most of the numbers include hundreds as well as thousands. (2) The tribe of Gad numbered 45,650 (Num 1:25), indicating a threefold numerical declension; namely, thousands, hundreds and fifties (cf. Ex 18:21). (3) The totals for the census lists were added up on the basis of *'elep* meaning "thousand," not "tribe," "captain," or "military unit" (Num 1:46; 2:32; 26:51). It should be observed that the large numbers relating to the Exodus refer to the military *potential* of the tribes, not necessarily to the size of a mobilized army. Such is probably the case with many of the large figures related to the size of armies in the OT. *See* Census.

The rhetorical use of numbers. A very important use of numbers in both the OT and NT is that for rhetorical or poetic effect. Whenever numbers are so used, they are not intended to be taken either literally or symbolically. The intention of the writer is to express concepts such as "a few," "many," or perhaps to intensify or emphasize a thought. The arrangement of a numeral with its sequel within the same clause is a common literary device in NW Semitic poetry. The actual value of such numbers is not significant. An excellent example of this phenomenon is found in Amos 1:9, "For three transgressions of Tyrus, and for four, I will not turn away the punishment thereof." It is evident that the prophet is not attempting to total the sins of Tyrus in this verse, but to emphasize their sins (cf. also Prov 30:18). This literary device is common in Ugaritic literature as well as in the OT (cf. Epic of Baal and Anath II, iii, 16–21, ANET, p. 132; II, vii, 9–12, ANET, p. 134).

The symbolic use of numbers. Number symbolism was not limited to Israel, for it is found in many contemporary documents. Its origin, however, appears to lie with priestly scribes in Egypt and Babylon and not with the Bible writers. The number seven seemed to be widely used for symbolic purposes among many peoples of the ancient Near East. It was not until the age of Pythagoras (6th cen. B.C.) that number symbolism received systematic treatment. He based his philosophy upon the postulate that number was the source of the various qualities of matter and was the basis for meaningful knowledge of the universe. This led him to dwell upon the mystic and symbolic properties of numbers and their relationships. The followers of Pythagoras expanded his ideas and methods giving detailed theological significance to numbers. This practice became popular among Jewish writers of the intertestamental period and was later employed by many of the Church Fathers.

Of importance is the question, Did Bible writers use numbers symbolically and if so, to what extent? It is quite clear that some numbers are used symbolically in the Bible, notably, the number seven. Some scholars have argued that all numbers are used symbolically and have theological values associated with them. For example, one is supposed to stand for "unity"; two, "division" or "separation," etc. However, one encounters a serious problem at this point, for with every writer there are major differences of opinion as to the theological intention of the numbers. This is the case because the Bible nowhere ascribes theological values to any number. The Bible does use numbers symbolically to represent ideas, such as "completeness," "a few," etc., which is a common phenomenon in all ancient Near Eastern literature. The system which attributes theological values to numbers, therefore, appears to be a development of Pythagorean and Gnostic practices.

It is strange indeed that not one NT writer ever pointed back to the theological significance of a symbolic number occurring in the OT. Many other symbols are cited by NT writers and are interpreted. It appears, therefore, that while the Bible uses numbers schematically and symbolically to convey general ideas, such as "completeness," "few," "many," etc., it never ascribes mystical or theological concepts to numbers.

The mystical use of numbers. The theory of mystical numbers is that system of interpretation which endeavors to seek out hidden truths by means of numerical phenomena. Gematria, the system of mystical numbers or Bible numerics, operates on two basic assumptions: (1) there is design in the use of numbers in Scripture, and (2) there is theological significance connected with the numerical patterns found in the Bible. In this system letters of the Gr. and Heb. alphabets are given numerical value which enables the interpreter to "discover" hidden meanings in the biblical text which would otherwise be obscure. The system actually has its origin with Pythagorean thought and was developed by Jewish writers in Palestine during and after the Alexandrian conquests.

[The only authentic example of a mystical number in the Bible is the number of the name of the Beast, 666 (a variant reading is 616), in Rev 13:17–18. It is obvious that the apostle John knew it had a hidden meaning, for he wrote, "Here is wisdom. Let him who has understanding calculate the number of the beast, for the number is that of a man, and his number is six hundred and sixty-six" (v. 18, NASB). Various interpretations have been suggested. By gematria the number 666 has been identified with the numerical values of the names of various prominent persons from the Roman emperors Caligula, Nero, and Trajan onward, and with such concepts as the chaos monster. The most probable of the historical personages is Nero(n) Caesar (in Heb. letters): *n-r-w-n q-s-r*, 50 + 200 + 6 + 50 + 100 + 60 + 200 = 666. –Ed.]

The same system was used by the Gnostics as an apologetic for their theories. This method of interpretation was taken over by the Church Fathers and given a Christian slant. The whole theory rests on the premise that the alphabet always had numerical values attached to it. So far as the evidence is concerned, Pythagoras was the first to employ a system of this kind in the 6th cen. B.C. There is no evidence that the writers of the OT had knowledge of it.

For a full discussion of the development of this system of interpretation and an evaluation, see John J. Davis, *Biblical Numerology* (Grand Rapids: Baker, 1968), pp. 125 ff. For articles giving more credence to symbolical or theological significance see R. A. H. Gunner, "Number," NBD, pp. 895–898; Marvin H. Pope, "Number, Numbering, Numbers," IDB,

NUMBERS, BOOK OF

III, 561-567; "Seven, Seventh, Seventy," IDB, IV, 294 f.; "Twelve," IDB, IV, 719.

J. J. D.

NUMBERS, BOOK OF. This fourth book of Moses' Pentateuch is described more accurately by the name it bears in the Heb. Bible, *bemidbar*, "in the wilderness." The events take place in the wilderness (e.g., Sinai, 1:1; Zin, 20:1) and at the oases adjoining the wilderness, as, e.g., Kadesh-barnea (*q.v.*) in the wilderness of Paran (13:26).

The name Numbers is derived from the mustering of the army (described in chaps. 1-4 and chap. 26) which was done in preparation for the military exploit on entering the Promised Land. The first attempt from the S ended in failure because of disobedience to God (14:41-45). The second mustering (chap. 26) creates the logical division of the book since the material following it (chaps. 27-36) is more closely associated with Deuteronomy and the last few months of preparation before entering the land from the E; having such subject matter as the law of inheritance (27:1-11), appointment of Moses' successor (27:12-23), and division of the land (33:50–34:29).

The Balaam story (chaps. 22-24) is an interlude between these two parts; it forms a kind of literary hinge since it described events completely outside Israel's camp, though its purpose is to show God's sovereign blessing upon His chosen people. In alternating sections the historical sequences are supplemented by various religious directives and ceremonial details. For example, 5:1–10:10 may be considered as somewhat of a unit of priestly material. Following this comes the journey from Sinai to Paran, the story of the spies and the futile attempt to enter the land (10:11–14:45); then comes a second priestly "scroll" involving many ceremonial details and the rebellion of Korah (15:1–19:22). This is followed by a narrative of the final events of the years of wandering whence they come through the wilderness of Sin to the steppes of Moab (20:1–22:1). The time involved in Numbers covers a period beginning with the last 19 days at Sinai (1:1; 10:11) and ending after 40 years of wandering with the arrival of a new generation in the plains of Moab in the Jordan Valley opposite Jericho.

Outline

I. Israel in the Wilderness, 1:1–22:1
   1. The first census, at Sinai, 1:1–4:49
   2. First section of priestly material, 5:1–10:10
   3. Journey from Sinai to rebellion at Kadesh, 10:11–14:45
   4. Second section of priestly material, 15:1–19:22
   5. Journey from Kadesh to Abel-shittim, 20:1–22:1

II. The Balaam Story, 22:2–25:18
   1. Balaam hired by Balak to curse Israel, 22:2-41
   2. Balaam's oracles, 23:1–24:25
   3. Appendix: the sin of Baal-peor, 25:1-18

III. Israel's Preparation for Entering Canaan, 26:1–36:13
   1. Arrangements for conquest and apportionment of the land, 26:1–27:23
   2. Third section of priestly material, 28:1–30:16
   3. War against Midian, 31:1-54
   4. Tribal inheritances in Transjordan, 32:1-42
   5. Summary of journeys from Egypt to Jordan, 33:1-49
   6. Directions for settlement in Canaan, 33:50–36:13

Numbers is highly supernaturalistic. This fact has prejudiced its case as trustworthy in the minds of critics of the Bible. In addition to Israel's being led (10:11-13) and cared for supernaturally (11:8-9), there is the basic "problem" of the vast numbers of people involved; an army of more than 600,000, which implies that a nation of at least two million had to be sustained in the wilderness for nearly 40 years. If this were an account of ordinary history, one could well question such a circumstance; but this is redemptive history and its reliability is asserted by Christ Himself in Luke 24:44.

The old higher critical documentary view which held Numbers to be mostly the work of priests of the 6th or 5th cen. B.C. (P document) has now been seriously called into question. In its place some modern critical scholars believe Numbers came into being gradually by many authors, editors and redactors but that it was based on a Mosaic oral tradition which has preserved some "valid" history.

A conservative view in keeping with the doctrine of inspiration sees Moses making use of one or more scribes (cf. Num 11:16 where the "officers," Heb. *shōṭerîm*, were scribes), which would explain the use of the third person regarding Moses. God revealed directly to Moses some parts of the book, such as directions for settlement in the land and for the ceremonies. But Moses and his scribe(s) kept records (1:20-46; chap. 7; 26:3-51; chap. 33) and had access to documents (21:14) and knew many oral traditions (22-24). Num 32:34-42 may have been added by Joshua or a scribe in the settlement period. The Spirit of God kept the writers from error of fact, doctrine, or judgment.

See Canon of Scripture, the OT; Census; Law of Moses; Pentateuch; Wilderness Wandering.

Bibliography. Roland K. Harrison, *Introduction to the Old Testament*, Grand Rapids: Eerdmans, 1969, pp. 614-634. Irving L. Jensen, *Numbers: Journey to God's Rest-Land*, Chicago: Moody Press, 1964. A. A. MacRae,

"Numbers," NBC, 1953. Elmer B. Smick, "Numbers," WBC, 1962. J. A. Thompson, "Numbers," NBC[2], 1970.

E. B. S.

NUN (nŭn)

1. Father of Joshua (Ex 33:11; *et al.*), the military leader of the Israelites when they entered Canaan. Nothing is known of Nun's life. *See* Non.

2. The 14th letter of the Heb. alphabet (Ps 119). The English *N* has the same origin and represents the anglicized Heb. names. Nun can also be used for the number 50.

NURSE. Two kinds of nurses are mentioned in the Heb. OT. The *mêneqet* (from *yānaq,* "to give suck") was a wet nurse as in the case of Deborah who apparently had suckled Rebekah when an infant (Gen 24:59; 35:8), of Moses' mother (Ex 2:7–8), and of Joash's nurse (II Kgs 11:2; II Chr 22:11). Suckling continued usually for two years. The *'ōmenet* (from *'āman,* "to support," "be faithful"), in contrast, was a children's nurse and is used of Naomi (Ruth 4:16) and the governess of the five year old Mephibosheth (II Sam 4:4). The nurses of both kinds were of great importance and were trusted family servants (cf. Deborah, Gen 35:8).

The term "nurse" is used figuratively in both Testaments. Moses is spoken of as a "nursing father" of Israel (Num 11:12), kings and queens as nursing mothers to the returning Jews at the beginning of the Millennium (Isa 49:23; cf. 60:16), Israel as nursed of God 40 years in the wilderness (Acts 13:18, KJV and NASB marg.). Paul treated his new converts as gently as a nurse (Gr. *trophos,* "nourisher") does children (I Thess 2:7).

See Occupations: Nurse.

R. A. K.

NURTURE. The Gr. word *paideia,* "child training," "instruction," "nurture," is used three times in the NT. It covers the whole cultivation of the mind and morals of a child, and the employment of commands and admonitions, reproof and punishment to attain this goal (Eph 6:4). When applied to adults, it speaks of that which develops the soul by correcting mistakes and controlling passions through "instruction" in righteousness (II Tim 3:16) and child training or "chastisement" (Heb 12:5, 7, 11; cf. Prov 3:11–12; 15:5).

NUTS. *See* Plants.

NUZU (nū'zū). An administrative center and military outpost of the Hurrians during the Mitanni kingdom, this ancient city was identified in 1925 by Dr. Edward Chiera. Tablets excavated at Yorghan Tepe gave the Hurrian name of the site as Nuzu (known for a long time by the genitive form Nuzi). The much eroded mound is about 200 meters on a side rises about five meters above the plain, and lies about ten miles SW of modern Kirkuk in Iraq and some 150 miles N of Baghdad.

Earliest occupation seems to begin with the prehistoric Halaf period. Levels X–XII, however, are predominantly Obeid. Levels VII–IX are chiefly Uruk. During the occupation of levels III–VI the city had a different name. At this time it was known as Gasur and it flourished under the empire of the great dynast Sargon of Agade. After a considerable period of decline, if not complete abandonment, it was resettled by the Hurrian invaders of Mesopotamia and received the name Nuzu (levels I and II). The final stage of occupation covers the Partho-Sassanid period. All in all this totals nearly 5,000 years.

The most interesting and important period in the history of this site is the time it was inhabited by Hurrians and called Nuzu. Most of what is known of Hurrian social and economic life has come from a study of the twenty-some thousand clay tablets excavated from Nuzu, since the Mitannian city-state of Arrapkha (modern Kirkuk) has not been studied, and the Mitannian capital Washshukanni, somewhere E of Haran, has never been located with certainty.

Furthermore, details of Hurrian social life appear to parallel conditions in Padan-aram and Palestine during the time of the patriarchs Abraham, Isaac and Jacob, and hence shed considerable welcome light on biblical events at that time.

The Nuzu-type tablets were first acquired from dealers in the bazaars, having been dug up by Arabs. Later, others were found in the vicinity of Kirkuk. Finally, following hints from local Arabs, the mound Yorghan Tepe was selected as a likely spot for more tablets and excavations began in 1925. Five seasons were spent there down to 1931 involving at different times the Iraq Museum, Harvard University, the University of Pennsylvania, and throughout the whole time the American Schools of Oriental Research.

The first site chosen, a smaller mound about 300 meters from Yorghan Tepe, proved to be the remains of the private houses of Shukri-Tilla and Tehip-tilla, prominent and wealthy citizens of Nuzu. Later excavations at the main mound uncovered many private dwellings and also a large "palace" and temple. The so-called "palace" was in all likelihood the dwelling and office of the local mayor (*hazannu*) named Kushshiharbe. Tablets found therein reveal the fact that such a high public official could be and was sued for bribes, theft and even kidnapping.

It is the private archives, however, which contribute data regarding the background of the patriarchal period in the Bible. Parallels have been noted to the adoption of Eliezer by Abraham, the arrangements between Jacob and Laban, and the significance of the teraphim or gods of Gen 31:19, 30–35. See ANET, pp. 219 f.

Additional evidence of Hurrian culture and its influence that extended throughout the eastern Mediterranean area and Hittite territory, even as far as the Aegean, may be noted in the artifacts found at Nuzu. The cylinder seals have certain peculiar motifs, and "Mitannian ware" pottery is distinctive wherever it is found, especially the typical button-based beaker with geometric and animal designs painted in white on a red or dark brown background. *See* Archaeology; Assyria; Horites.

In 1967-69 Tell al-Fakhar, a site 18 miles SW of Nuzu, was excavated. Here a large palace 200 by 100 feet was found dating to the mid-2nd mil. B.C. and presumably destroyed by Assyrian armies. It contained at least a thousand tablets—business contracts and documents related to land lease, land purchase, adoption, and barter— all throwing more light on the Hurrian-Mitannian culture.

Bibliography. FLAP, pp. 47-48, 65-67 for fuller bibliography. Cyrus H. Gordon, "Biblical Customs and the Nuzu Tablets," BA, III (1940), 1-12. E. A. Speiser, *Oriental and Biblical Studies,* ed. by J. J. Finkelstein and M. Greenberg, Philadelphia: Univ. of Pennsylvania Press, 1967, pp. 62-82, 89-96, 126 ff., 132-137, 151-156, 244-269, 542-545. C. J. Mullo Weir, "Nuzu," TAOTS, pp. 73-86.

F. R. S.

NYMPHAS (nĭm'fȧs). A prominent believer at either Colosse or Laodicea, whose house was used for worship, to whom Paul sent greetings (Col 4:15). The name occurs in the accusative form *Nymphan,* so that it is not certain whether it represents the male name Nymphas (KJV, ASV) or the female name Nympha (RSV, NEB, NASB). The pronoun "his" occurs in Codex D and other Gr. MSS, while "her" is found in Codex B, in the phrase "and the church which is in his [her] house."

O

OAK. *See* Plants: Oak, Terebinth. For worship under oak trees, *see* Plants: Terebinth.

OAR. *See* Ship.

OATH. An appeal by word or act to confirm the truth of one's statement or the fulfillment of a promise (Gen 21:23, 30; 31:53; Gal 1:20; Heb 6:16). Oaths in Scripture are of two kinds, those made by God and those made by men.

God's oaths are solemn asseverations to His covenant people of the absolute truth of His word (Num 23:19) in order that they may put implicit trust in His word (Isa 45:20-24). His oath-confirmed promises were made to the patriarchs (Gen 50:24; Ps 105:9-11), the nation of Israel (Deut 29:10-13), the Davidic dynasty (Ps 89:35-37, 49), and the messianic Priest-King (Ps 110:1-4; Heb 7:15-22). The Guarantor of all the divine promises is Jesus Christ in whom they find their fulfillment (II Cor 1:19 f.).

An oath sworn by men is a solemn appeal to God to confirm the truth of their word, carrying the express implication of punishment in case of failure to speak the truth or fulfill their promise. In Scripture oaths played an important part in legal trials (Ex 22:11; Lev 6:2-5) and national transactions (I Kgs 18:10; II Kgs 11:4; Ezk 17:16), as well as in domestic and religious affairs (Gen 24:37; Jud 21:5; I Kgs 2:43; Ezr 10:5). The oath of a virgin was binding if her father did not disallow it (Num 30:3-5); likewise the oath of a married woman if her husband did not object (Num 30:6-15).

The Mosaic law emphasized the binding nature of oaths (Num 30:2, NASB), and decreed punishment for a perjurer, one swearing a false oath (Deut 19:16-19; I Tim 1:10). The false oath of a witness or a false asseveration concerning a pledge or a thing found required a sin offering (Lev 5:1-6; 6:2-6). The law stressed the seriousness of oaths (Ex 20:7; Lev 19:12; Zech 8:16-17) and forbade swearing by false gods (Josh 23:7; Jer 12:16; Amos 8:14).

The Scriptures cite some grossly sinful oaths, such as the reckless oath of Herod Antipas (Mt 14:6-10), the blasphemous oath of Peter (Mt 26:72), and the hate-prompted oath of Paul's enemies (Acts 23:12-15).

Oaths were commonly made by lifting the hand to God (Gen 14:22; Ezk 20:5 f., Heb.; Rev 10:5), and in exceptional cases by placing the hand under the "thigh" or scrotum of him to whom the oath was taken (Gen 24:2 f.; 47:29). This was a solemn way of signifying that if the oath was violated, one's descendants would avenge the act of disloyalty (WBC, p. 28; *see* Thigh).

Oaths were sometimes taken before the altar (I Kgs 8:31; II Chr 6:22). Solemn covenant oaths were often accompanied by some sevenfold action (Gen 21:27-30), or by dividing an animal into two parts and passing between the pieces (Gen 15:8-18).

Oaths were made by the life of the person addressed (I Sam 1:26; 17:55; II Sam 11:11), by one's own head (Mt 5:36), by Jerusalem (Mt 5:35), by the temple or its different parts (Mt 23:16–22), by earth or heaven (Mt 5:34 f.), by God's throne (Mt 5:34), or by God Himself (Jud 8:19; I Kgs 18:15). Various formulas were used, such as, "God is witness between me and thee" (Gen 31:50), or more commonly, "As Yahweh lives" (Jud 8:19; Ruth 3:13; Jer 38:16). Usually the penalty invoked for violation was only suggested (Ruth 1:17; II Sam 3:9; II Kgs 6:31), but at times it was expressed (Jer 29:22).

Christ condemned the indiscriminate, light, or evasive use of oaths prevailing among the Jews (Mt 5:33–37; 23:16–22). He taught that men should be so transparently honest in their speech that oaths between them were unnecessary (Mt 5:34–37). In His kingdom the honesty of its members should eliminate the use of oaths (cf. Jas 5:12).

See Adjure; Covenant; Curse; Vow.

Bibliography. Marvin H. Pope, "Oaths," IDB, III, 575–577. Johannes Schneider, "*Omnuō*," TDNT, V, 176–185; "*Horkos*, etc.," TDNT, V, 457–467.

D.E.H.

OBADIAH (ō'bȧ-dī'ȧ). At least 12 men bear this name in the OT.

1. A descendant of David (I Chr 3:21).
2. One of the chief men in the tribe of Issachar (I Chr 7:3).
3. A Gadite who joined David at Ziklag (I Chr 12:9).
4. A Benjamite, descendant of Saul and Jonathan (I Chr 8:38; 9:44).
5. A Levite (I Chr 9:16), apparently identical with Abda (Neh 11:17), who was founder of a family of porters (Neh 12:25).
6. A Zebulonite (I Chr 27:19).
7. One of Jehoshaphat's princes who taught the law in the cities of Judah (II Chr 17:7).
8. A Levite who supervised the workmen repairing the temple under Josiah (II Chr 34:12).
9. An Israelite leader, descendant of Joab, returning from Babylon (Ezr 8:9).
10. A priest who sealed the covenant in Nehemiah's time (Neh 10:5).
11. A steward or governor in charge of the palace of Ahab and Jezebel (I Kgs 18:3–16). From his youth he was a God-fearing man. During Jezebel's persecution of the prophets, Obadiah hid 100 prophets in two caves. Sent out by Ahab to search for grass for the royal horses and mules, Obadiah was met by Elijah. Subsequently Obadiah arranged for Ahab to meet Elijah on Mount Carmel where the prophets of Baal were slaughtered. An ancient seal with the Heb. text "To Obadiah servant of the king" may have reference to this servant of Ahab. Obadiah's identification in the Babylonian Talmud (Sanhedrin 39*b*) with the prophet Obadiah is dubious.
12. A prophet who is best known for the book bearing his name. No information is available about him personally. His book seems to indicate that he was a citizen of Judah. It is very doubtful that he can be identified with King Ahaziah's captain (II Kgs 1:13–15), as does Pseudo-Epiphanius in *The Lives of the Prophets*. Nor is it probable that the talmudic tradition is correct in identifying him as a proselyte of Edomitic origin. For dating Obadiah *see* Obadiah, Book of.

S. J. S.

OBADIAH, BOOK OF. In the present arrangement of the Heb. Bible this book is listed as the fourth of the Minor Prophets. The LXX order has it in fifth place.

Author

See Obadiah 12.

Theme

The distinctive theme of this book is the prophet's rebuke of the Edomites for their pride as they rejoiced over the misfortunes that befell Jerusalem.

Outline

Being the shortest of the OT books it has but one chapter divided into 21 verses.

I. The Fall of Edom from Its Stronghold, vv. 1–9
II. Pride the Cause of Edom's Doom, vv. 10–14
III. God's Judgment on Edom, vv. 15–16
IV. Israel's Ultimate Superiority, vv. 17–21

Date

No specific data is given to offer a definite date for the activity of Obadiah. It seems to be definitely related to a time when a terrible misfortune befell the city of Jerusalem and the Edomites gleefully prided themselves in the fact that they, because of their geographical location, were immune to such a fate. The crucial question is the dating of Jerusalem's calamity described in vv. 11–14.

Significant invasions to which Jerusalem was subjected during OT times were by (1) Shishak during Rehoboam's reign (I Kgs 14:25–26); (2) Philistines and Arabians while Jehoram was king (II Chr 21:16–17; II Kgs 8:20); (3) King Joash of Israel while Amaziah ruled in Jerusalem (II Kgs 14:13–14); (4) Edomites attacking Judah during the reign of Ahaz (II Chr 28:17); (5) Nebuchadnezzar who not only invaded Judah but reduced Jerusalem with its temple to ruins during the years 605–586 B.C. (II Kgs 24:1 ff.).

The content of Obadiah, according to the general concensus of current scholarship, seems to reflect more particularly either the conditions during Jehoram's reign, *c.* 848–841 B.C., or the time of the actual destruction of Jerusalem in 586 B.C. Most crucial are the interpretations of vv. 11–14. Does this reflect a complete devastation and terminal destruction of Jerusalem, or does it refer to an invasion, plunder, and looting which did not result in its destruction nor an exile that terminated the kingdom of Judah? Such an invasion in which the Edomites participated seems to be best dated in the reign of Jehoram. This view has been held by Delitzsch, Kleinert, Orelli, Kirkpatrick, and Archer (cf. bibliography).

The literary relationship between Ob 1–9 and Jer 49:7–22 also deserves serious consideration. Although they could have used a common source, it seems quite probable that Jeremiah in his extended passage reflects knowledge of Obadiah. This would favor an early date for Obadiah. It has also been suggested that Joel in his book reflects acquaintance with Obadiah in the following references: Joel 3:19, cf. Ob 10; Joel 3:3, cf. Ob 11; Joel 1:15; 2:1; 3:4, 7, 14, cf. Ob 15; Joel 3:8, cf. Ob 18. This would likewise point to an early period for Obadiah.

Bibliography. Gleason L. Archer, *A Survey of Old Testament Introduction,* Chicago: Moody Press, 1964. Frank E. Gaebelein, *Four Minor Prophets,* Chicago: Moody Press, 1970. Theodore Laetsch, *Bible Commentary on the Minor Prophets,* St. Louis: Concordia, 1956. Samuel J. Schultz, *The Old Testament Speaks,* New York: Harper and Row, 1960.

S. J. S.

OBAL (ō'bȧl). A son of Joktan the brother of Peleg and founder of an Arabian tribe in the line of Shem (Gen 10:25–29). He is called Ebal (*q.v.*) in I Chr 1:22.

OBED (ō'bĕd)

1. The son of Boaz and Ruth the Moabitess. He was the father of Jesse, grandfather of David, and ancestor of Jesus (Ruth 4:17, 21–22; I Chr 2:12; Mt 1:5; Lk 3:32).

2. The son of Ephlal, son of Zabad, one of David's mighty men. He was of the tribe of Judah, descending through Sheshan's only remaining child, a daughter who was married to an Egyptian slave in order to preserve the family line (I Chr 2:34–38).

3. One of David's mighty men (I Chr 11:47). Nothing further is known of him.

4. One of the sons of Shemaiah, the son of Obed-edom. Although he is listed as a gatekeeper of the temple, he is also called, with his brothers, a mighty man of valor, and could be the same as 3 (I Chr 26:6–7).

5. The father of Azariah, one of the captains who followed Jehoiada in restoring Jehoash to the throne of Judah (II Chr 23:1).

OBED-EDOM (ō'bĭd-ē'dŏm)

1. Obed-edom, the Gittite, was possibly a Levite whose birthplace was Gath-rimmon, a Levitical city in Dan (Josh 19:45). At the death of Uzzah, when David sought to move the ark from the house of Abinadab, the sacred vessel was put in the house of Obed-edom near Jerusalem to its W, for three months (II Sam 6:1–11; I Chr 13:13). When God manifestly blessed this house, David took heart and, this time acting in accord with the law, brought the ark to Jerusalem (II Sam 6:12 ff.; I Chr 15:25). Perhaps this was the same Obed-edom who was of the Korahite family appointed as gatekeepers to the temple (I Chr 15:24; 26:4, 8, 15). It is specifically stated that God had indeed blessed him (26:5) perhaps with reference to I Chr 13:14. Since he was gifted as a musician, he and some of his sons were also appointed as temple musicians (I Chr 15:16, 18; 16:5, 38).

2. The son of Jeduthun, a Levite appointed gatekeeper in the temple (I Chr 16:38).

3. The treasurer or steward of the vessels of the temple in the days of Amaziah. He was taken captive by Joash of Israel (II Chr 25:24).

P. C. J.

OBEDIENCE. The Heb. and Gr. words translated by "obey" or "obedience" are usually *shāma'* and cognate forms of *akouō,* both of which carry the basic meaning of "hearing." In fact, many times when the translator confronts these words and their cognates it is very difficult to determine whether "hear" or "obey" is the most appropriate rendering. This difficulty, however, gives an insight into the basic biblical concept of obedience, a concept which holds for both the OT and NT.

Although obedience expresses an action which can exist in ordinary human relationships (such as servants to masters or children to parents), its most significant reference is to a relationship that should exist between man and God. God reveals Himself to man by His voice and words. Words are intended to be heard. This obviously involves a physical reception of the words with a presumed mental apprehension of their meaning.

But in terms of man's reception of God's revelation, this in itself is not true hearing. True hearing is faith which receives the divine Word and translates it into action. It is a faith-response. It is a positive, active response, not merely passive listening and consideration. To hear is to act. In other words, to really hear God's Word is to obey God's Word. In the NT the idea of putting oneself under responsibility to obey the heard Word is clearly emphasized by *hupakouō,* a compound of "under" and "hear."

Many passages referring to hearing and obedience obviously have this matter of positive, active response in view. "He who has ears to hear, let him hear" (Mt 11:15; cf. 13:9, 43; Rev 2:7, 11, 17, 29; 3:6, 13, 22; 13:9, NASB). *See* Ear. The wise man is the one who "hears these words of Mine, and acts upon them" (Mt 7:24). "My sheep hear My voice . . . and they follow Me" (Jn 10:27). With regard to the revelation he had received on Patmos, John said, "Blessed are . . . those who hear the words of the prophecy, and heed the things which are written in it" (Rev 1:3, NASB). There is to be no dichotomy between hearing and obedience. True hearing is obedience. Faith itself involves obedience, and Jesus, Paul, and James make it quite clear that true faith issues in obedience.

S. N. G.

In the OT, because Abraham believed God and obeyed His voice, all the nations of the earth are blessed (Gen 15:6; 22:18; 26:4-5). Obeying God's voice is equivalent to keeping His covenant (Ex 19:5; cf. 23:20-22); therefore the Israelites promised to be obedient when the Book of the Covenant was ratified with the sprinkling of blood (Ex 24:7-8). The rededication of the people to obey the law was a basic part of covenant renewal ceremonies (Deut 27:1-10; 30:2, 8, 20; Josh 24:24-27).

In castigating King Saul for his incomplete obedience, Samuel taught the great truth that to obey is better than sacrifice (I Sam 15:22). In later centuries the nation was repeatedly warned of its disobedience to God and His law (Isa 42:24; Jer 3:13; 7:23-28; Zeph 3:2; Neh 9:17, 26). Obedience, or the lack of it, may be either inward, from the heart (Prov 3:1), or merely outward, in the sense of enforced obedience (Ps 72:8-11).

In the NT Paul speaks of "obedience to the faith" (KJV) on the part of Christians (Rom 1:5; cf. Acts 6:7). The phrase in Gr. is the same as in Rom 16:26, however, where he writes that the gospel leads to "obedience of faith." He is evidently referring to God's desire that the Gentiles, when they hear the gospel, will obey it in the sense of receiving it by faith and trusting in its terms (cf. I Pet 1:2, 22; I Jn 3:23). Paul warns of the terrible punishment awaiting those who refuse to obey the gospel of our Lord Jesus (II Thess 1:8; cf. Rom 2:8; I Pet 2:7-8). He commends the Corinthians for their obedience to their confession of the gospel of Christ (II Cor 9:13, NASB).

As an example of obedience Paul and Peter both point to the Lord Jesus Christ "who humbled Himself by becoming obedient to the point of death" (Phil 2:8, NASB; cf. I Pet 2:18, 21) Paul speaks of the obedience of Christ in mak ing atonement for sinners, in contrast to the disobedience of Adam and his descendants (Rom 5:19). The statement in Heb 5:8, "He learned obedience from the things which He suffered" (NASB), must mean that Christ made the experience of obeying the Father actual As He did so, He fulfilled the eternal purpose of the Godhead in living His whole life as our representative, obeying and suffering in our stead and for our sakes, and satisfying the whole law in all its relations (J. O. Buswell, Jr., *A Systematic Theology of the Christian Religion,* Grand Rapids: Zondervan, 1962, II, 111 f.). *See* Obedience of Christ.

The Word of God exhorts servants (slaves) to obey their masters (Eph 6:5-8; Col 3:22; I Tim 6:1; Tit 2:9); Christians to obey their leaders (Heb 13:17); wives to obey their husbands (Tit 2:5; Eph 5:22-24; I Pet 3:1-6); and children to obey their parents (Eph 6:1; Col 3:20; cf. Prov 6:20; 23:22; 29:15). Therefore believers as a whole are characterized as "obedient children" (I Pet 1:14; cf. Rom 6:16-17; Heb 5:9). Disobedience to parents is considered to be a mark of human depravity (Rom 1:30) and a sign of the last days (II Tim 3:2). Christians are taught to compel every human thought to surrender in obedience to Christ (II Cor 10:5, NEB).

The highest realm of obedience for the Christian is that of doing the will of God from the heart (Rom 6:17), not of mere outward compliance. He possesses a spirit of obedience that creates within him the desire to obey in areas of thought and attitude that are unenforceable (e.g., Mt 5:28, 44; 19:21-22). He has the mind of Christ (Phil 2:5), for the Word of God is within his heart and he delights to do God's will (Ps 40:8; cf. Heb 10:5-9).

See Example.

J. R.

OBEDIENCE OF CHRIST. This includes Christ's willing acceptance of the incarnation when God the Father spoke with the Son in eternity past as recorded in Ps 40:6-8 (cf. Heb 10:5-10). His life of perfect obedience to the Father is shown in that He was "made of a woman, made under the law" (Gal 4:4), and kept the law perfectly. He fulfilled the will of God in His birth (Lk 2:21-22, 39), His boyhood (Lk 2:52), His baptism (Mt 3:15), His temptation in which He triumphed over Satan in contrast to Adam who fell (Mt 4:1-11; Lk 4:1-13), and throughout His entire life (Jn 4:34; 6:38; 8:29, 46; 15:10; 17:4; Acts 3:14; II Cor 5:21; Heb 4:15). None could convict Him of disobedience to God or His law (Jn 8:46; Heb 5:8-9). Though He struggled with the awfulness of His coming condemnation when He was made sin for us and bore our sins in His own body on the tree (II Cor 5:21; I Pet 2:24), still He submitted Himself in obedience to death on the cross (Phil 2:8).

It is customary to divide Christ's obedience into two phases: His life of active obedience, and His suffering and death or His passive obedience. His active obedience then becomes the basis of the righteousness imputed to us, and His passive obedience, the atonement for our sins and our forgiveness. The division is not entirely satisfactory, however, since His suffering occurred even before the cross, and the merit of His sacrificial death rests upon His sinless, holy life (I Pet 1:18-19).

Christ and Adam stand in antithesis (Rom 5:12-19). Through the first Adam, sin and death entered the world; through the second, righteousness and life (vv. 12, 17). By the disobedience of one, all became sinners and died spiritually; through the obedience of the other, all who are in Christ are made righteous and alive (v. 19; cf. I Cor 15:22). The perfect obedience of the Saviour is to be our example (Heb 12:1–2; I Pet 2:21).

See Obedience.

R. A. K.

OBIL (ō'bĭl). An Ishmaelite camel driver who was appointed supervisor over King David's camels (I Chr 27:30).

OBLATION. An offering freely brought to God. The word is frequently found in the KJV in Leviticus and the major prophets. It is used to translate three Heb. words: *minḥâ*, the general word for offering; *tᵉrûmâ*, often translated "heave offering"; and *qorbān*, used in connection with a meal offering. The Heb. terms include offerings of all kinds, from the peace offering to vessels of gold and silver or even land dedicated to the Lord (Ezk 48:12). in Num 31:50 it has a distinct note of propitiation, but its usual emphasis is a general acknowledgment of God's high honor and goodness.

At times the oblation may express a consciousness in the offerer that he himself belongs to God. Since the accomplishment of Christ's once-for-all offering, the believer now brings as his obligation such offerings as his body ("a living sacrifice," Rom 12:1), "the sacrifice of praise" (Heb 13:15), and gifts for the Lord's work (Phil 4:18).

See Sacrifices.

M. A. K.

OBOTH (ō'bŏth). One of the desert camps of the Israelites, the first after leaving Punon (*q.v.*; modern Feinan), and near the border of Moab (Num 21:10–11; 33:43–44). A possible identification is 'Ain el-Weiba on the W side of the Arabah. Nelson Glueck, however, suggested et-Telah, 15 miles N of Feinan (*The Other Side of the Jordan*, p. 50).

OBSCURITY. In the English dictionary this word generally denotes a state of not being easily perceived, faint, undefined, not easily understood. When accompanied by a word such as "total," it denotes absence of all light. In the KJV only the latter concept is found, as "obscurity" translates the following Heb. words: (1) *'ōpel*, "dusk," "darkness," denotes the gloom of blindness (Isa 29:18); (2) *ḥōshek*, "darkness," "ignorance," equates obscurity with darkness (Isa 58:10; 59:9); (3) *'îshôn*, the reading of Kethib in Prov 20:20, together with *ḥōshek* means the "pupil" or center of darkness, i.e., "utter darkness" (RSV); the Qere reading, *'ěshûn*, means "time of darkness" (NASB).

OBSERVATION. The Gr. word *paratērēsis*, meaning "intense or careful watching," "observation," is used once, in Lk 17:20, "The kingdom of God cometh not with observation." God's kingdom does not develop in the Gospel Age in such a way that it can be visibly observed. It is already present (Mt 12:28; Mk 1:15; Lk 11:20) in its first stage in the hearts of men. It will enter its visible stage with the second coming of Christ (Mt 6:10; Rev 20:4).

OBSERVER OF TIMES. A fortune-teller or soothsayer who sought to foretell events by interpreting signs in the clouds, the rustling of leaves, the hum of insects, and other omens. The Canaanites (Jud 9:37, NASB) and Philistines (Isa 2:6) depended heavily on such divination (*q.v.*). Manasseh the king of Judah (II Kgs 21:6; II Chr 33:6) and the kings of the surrounding countries (Jer 27:3, 9) followed this practice, even though it had been forbidden in the law of Moses (Lev 19:26; Deut 18:10, 14) along with all other forms of sorcery and witchcraft. At Philippi Paul commanded a spirit of divination in the name of Jesus Christ to come out of a girl soothsayer (Acts 16:16–18).

See Magic.

OCCUPATIONS. The various arts and crafts, professions and trades of Bible times were not so clearly delineated as in our modern society. There were fewer specialists and more jacks-of-all-trades. In the prevailing agricultural society the majority of the people lived in small towns comparable to the villages of medieval Europe. Each community was a group of farm families who daily went to their fields, grew their own food, and manufactured virtually all their tools, clothing and other necessities.

But Palestine lay astride the international trade routes of the day. The residents had a natural desire for the luxuries obtainable only in Egypt or Phoenicia or Babylonia. Therefore some began to produce more crops or make more objects than they needed locally in order to have goods for barter. The Israelites learned many of their skills from their contact with their Canaanite and Phoenician neighbors. Specialization developed, especially in and near the larger cities. Families employed in the same craft formed clans that later grew into guilds (e.g., Neh 3:8). Children naturally followed in the trade of their father. Members of these guilds tended to live and work in their own settlements (e.g., I Chr 4:14, 21, 23) or in certain quarters and on certain streets of the cities (Jer 37:21).

The Hebrews were virtually the only people of the ancient Near East who viewed work for themselves as dignifying rather than debasing. The Egyptians considered shepherds as abomination (Gen 46:34), but from this humble occupation Moses learned invaluable lessons of leadership and David rose to sit on the throne. Nehemiah was a cupbearer to the king, while Amos earned his living as a lowly herdsman and tender of sycamore fig trees. Over and over again idleness is condemned in the Proverbs, and men are exhorted to learn industry from the ant (Prov 6:6–11). The sabbath was designed to attest to the dignity of labor by giving man a well-earned rest on the seventh day (Walter Duckat, *Beggar to King*, pp. xv–xxiii).

In addition to the text of Scripture itself, our knowledge of the arts and crafts of the biblical world has reached us in several ways. First is the tremendous hoard of written records from Mesopotamia, Syria, and Egypt. It is estimated that 95 percent of the cuneiform tablets in the Sumerian and Akkadian languages are economic in content, mentioning scores of crafts and trades. Second are the extremely realistic and detailed tomb paintings and models of servants attending their occupations found in many of the Egyptian tombs. Third are the artifacts themselves, the very tools and products attesting to the skill, or the lack of it, of the ancient tradesmen (*see* Tools). The work of the potter is especially illuminated by the myriads of potsherd and whole vessels found in the excavated cities and tombs of Palestine. Upward to a hundred of these occupations are mentioned specifically in the Bible or alluded to by the effects of their work.

Apothecary. The translation in the KJV of all six occurrences of Heb. *rōqēaḥ* (Ex 30:25, 35; 37:29; II Chr 16:14; Neh 3:8; Eccl 10:1). It should be more properly translated "perfumer" (*q.v.*).

Artificer. *See* Occupations: Engraver.

Baker (Heb. *'ōpeh*). There are 11 occurrences of the word for baker in Scripture, seven of them concerning the experience of Joseph in prison with Pharaoh's butler and baker (Gen 40:1–41:13). In his dream the chief baker saw three baskets of white bread on his head, with the top basket containing all sorts of baked foods (40:16–17). Egyptian bakers are known to have made as many as 38 varieties of cake and 57 of bread. They were compelled to render strict accounts of their supply of materials to their lord's overseer of granaries. The 12th cen. B.C. tomb of Rameses III depicts royal bakery scenes.

In ordinary life the women usually did the baking for their families (Lev 26:26; but see Gen 19:3). Girls were often drafted by the feudal kings of Canaan to serve as bakers, a pattern which Samuel warned that the kings of Israel would follow (I Sam 8:13). However, a town often had a man who baked for the community, and the Levites baked the bread for the tabernacle.

Dough was prepared by mixing flour with boiling water and then kneading. A small piece of yesterday's dough was crumbled into the water before mixing to act as yeast or leaven. Baking was done in one of three ways. The most primitive method was to make a fire over large flat stones, rake off the ashes, place a flat piece of dough on the heated stones, and cover it with ashes (I Kgs 19:6). A second way was to bake the dough on a griddle or pan (Lev 2:5; 6:21; I Chr 9:31; 23:29). A fire was built in a pit to form hot coals over which the griddle was placed (Isa 44:19). The most desirable method was to use an oven (*q.v.*) with coals in the bottom from a fire made the night before. The baker desisted from stirring up his fire during

Flat "loaves" of bread baked at Pompeii, A.D. 79. HFV

the night while the leaven was taking effect in the kneaded dough. The coals smoldered all night, thus heating the oven thoroughly, and would burst into flame in the morning when the baker opened the oven door (Hos 7:4, 6, NASB). He removed the coals and either applied the flat dough to the hot walls or placed it on a baking tray. During the process the cake would have to be turned to assure thorough baking (cf. Hos 7:8). God described Israel as an adulterous nation whose people in their lusts were as hot as a bread oven (Hos 7:1–6).

While Jeremiah was in prison God gave him favor with King Zedekiah, who ordered that he should receive bread daily from the bakers' street, the public supply, until it was exhausted (Jer 37:21). The bakers' guild presumably had located near the W side of Jerusalem, perhaps near the Tower of the Ovens (Neh 3:11, RSV; *see* Jerusalem: Gates and Towers).

See Food: Bread, Cooking; Occupations: Cook.

Banker. Banking as a system of exchange, credit, and interest developed in Babylonia, among the Phoenicians, and in the Gr. cities of the Near East. The Sumerians gave promissory notes and kept records of loans issued by their temples before 2000 B.C. In Hellenistic Egypt there was a state bank in Alexandria, and branch banks in villages which loaned money to private individuals and received taxes and made payments on treasury accounts similar to the banks in Gr. cities.

Jews were forbidden by the law of Moses to take interest from other Jews, though permitted to do so from Gentiles (Deut 15:3). For the safekeeping of treasures, their rulers depended on the palace and temple (I Kgs 14:26), while ordinary men kept theirs privately (Gen 24:25), deposited them with neighbors (Ex 22:7), or buried them (Josh 7:21).

Nevertheless, simple banking services performed by individuals for other individuals do appear. (1) "Money changers" (Mt 21:12; Mk 11:15) in the Court of the Gentiles of the temple exchanged foreign money into the half-shekels required of each Jew on the Day of Atonement (Ex 30:11–15). Furthermore, in Jesus' day, ideally, Jewish coins were the only ones fit to be presented for offerings. Roman coins with their heads of the deified emperors were considered particularly offensive. Because of the absence of silver money with Heb. inscriptions, however, the half-shekel was paid in Tyrian silver coins. The tables of these money changers were overthrown by Jesus because they were dishonest and charging exorbitant fees (Mt 21:13). (2) "Bankers" (Mt 25:27, ASV, RSV; KJV "exchangers") were described by Jesus as making a practice of paying legitimate interest on sums deposited with them (cf. Lk 19:23).

See Bank; Money Changer.

Barber (Heb. *gallāb*). The noun (Ezk 5:1) comes from a Heb. root meaning "to shear away or shave." This profession was well known in early Egypt and Mesopotamia as seen in archaeological inscriptions and drawings. The ancient barbers used as their instruments straight razors, combs, and shears, some of which have been found in Egyptian tombs (ANEP #80–83). The Egyptian was required to keep his hair cut and his beard shaven, because the beard was a symbol of divinity and only the pharaoh was permitted to wear a (false) beard. Therefore Joseph shaved himself before he was brought into Pharaoh's presence (Gen 41:14). *See* Hair.

Brickmaker. The first account of brickmaking in the Bible concerns the Tower of Babel (Gen 11:3). On the flat alluvial plain between the Tigris and Euphrates Rivers both sun-dried brick for the inner core of walls and kiln-burned brick for the outer facing have been used "for stone" from the earliest times.

It is said the Egyptians regarded brickmaking as an unhealthy occupation. Ex 5 records the bitter experiences of the Israelites as slaves in Egypt when they were compelled to make bricks. First using straw provided to them as binder, they were later ordered to gather their own straw, and finally stubble (Ex 5:7, 11–12).

Criticism was formerly raised regarding this account in that it was claimed the Egyptians did not use straw; but archaeological evidence is sufficient to prove the biblical account to be true. Joseph P. Free quotes an ancient Egyptian document, the Papyrus Anastasi, which contains the lament of an officer who had to erect buildings on the Egyptian frontier. He could not work, saying, "I am without equipment. There are no people to make bricks and there is no straw" (*Archaeology and Bible History,* pp. 91–92). Naville in 1883 unearthed the store pits of Tell el-Maskhuta on the edge of the land of Goshen. He identified the place as Pithom where the Israelites made bricks. The walls were made of courses of sun-dried bricks, some made with straw and some without.

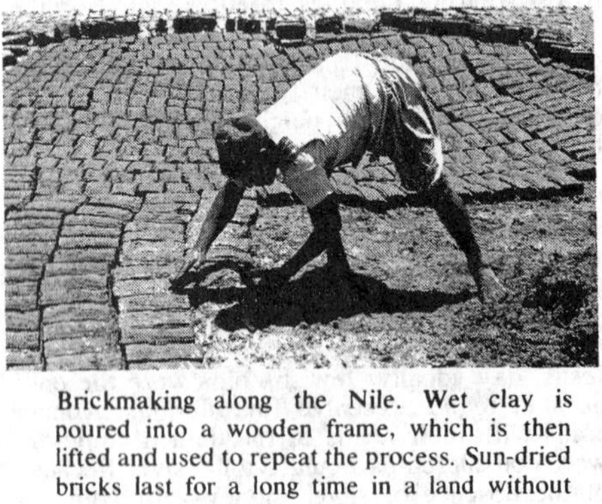

Brickmaking along the Nile. Wet clay is poured into a wooden frame, which is then lifted and used to repeat the process. Sun-dried bricks last for a long time in a land without rain. HFV

Egyptian bricks varied in size from 14 to 20 inches long, 6½ to 8½ inches wide, and 4½ to 7 inches thick. These were formed in wooden molds after the clay was thoroughly soaked and mixed with straw or other vegetable matter (cf. Nah 3:14, RSV). An expert brickmaker in Egypt in recent times has been known to turn out 3,000 bricks a day.

The Jews learned the art of brickmaking from the Egyptians and for the most part followed their method of drying them in the sun, although a brick kiln is mentioned in the time of David (II Sam 12:31). Brickmakers often developed great artistic skill, producing beautifully decorated glazed tiles for pavements, facings, and altars.

See Brick.

R. H. B.

Builders. In OT days buildings were usually constructed of stone or mud brick with wooden roof beams. The construction of Israelite homes was often crude prior to the Solomonic period. Canaanite and Hyksos builders, however, had demonstrated outstanding engineering and architectural ability in the construction of massive city walls and fortified gates. Bezaleel (*q.v.*), Aholiab, and others had learned the skills of the Egyptian craftsmen and were further endowed by the Spirit to be the builders of the tabernacle (Ex 31:2–11; 35:30–35; 36:1–4, 8). Solomon employed master Phoenician builders to superintend his workmen in the building of the temple (I Kgs 5:18). From time to time builders were needed to repair the temple (II Kgs 12:11; 22:6), and to rebuild it after the Exile (Ezr 3:10; Neh 4:5, 18). *See* Architecture; Occupations: Brickmaker, Carpenter, Mason.

The figurative usage of the Heb. and the Gr. words is significant. God is spoken of as the divine builder by establishing Israel (Ps 69:35; 102:16; Jer 12:16); building David's throne (Ps 89:4); rebuilding Israel (Isa 58:12; 61:4; 65:21; Jer 31:4, 28; 42:10; Ezk 36:10; Amos 9:11); rebuilding Jerusalem (Ps 147:2); choosing the cornerstone which the builders rejected (Ps 118:22–23). This is quoted in the NT and refers to Christ (Mt 21:42; Mk 12:10; Lk 20:17; Acts 4:11; I Pet 2:7). Christians are said to be built on Christ as the foundation (I Cor 3:9–11; I Pet 2:5 f.; Acts 9:31, RSV; Rom 15:20; Eph 2:20). The Christian is to build upon Christ (I Cor 3:11), and is to be built up in the faith (Acts 20:32; I Cor 8:1, RSV); he is also to build using doctrine as the material (Gal 2:18; I Cor 3:10). Rewards are to be given to the faithful builder (I Cor 3:14).

R. H. B.

The interior of the Temple of Bacchus at Baalbek, Lebanon, shows the ability of stone masons of the Roman period. HFV

Butcher. *See* Occupations: Cook.

Butler. An officer in the household of a king or other dignitary having charge of wines and other potables (lit., one who gives drinks; Gen 40:1–23; 41:9). The translation "cupbearer" is used in other scriptures (I Kgs 10:5; II Chr 9:4; Neh 1:11). *See* Occupations: Cupbearer.

Calker. The calker's task was to fill the seams in wooden boats so as to make them waterproof (Ezk 27:9, 17). The first step in his work was to separate and untwist the strands in rope made of hemp. These were picked and beaten into a soft and pliable tow (Heb. *neʿōret,* Jud 16:9; Isa 1:31), called oakum today. The oakum was driven and packed tightly by chisels made of wood or metal into the seams between the boards. Afterward they were smeared with melted pitch to keep them waterproof. *See* Occupations: Shipbuilder.

Carpenter. The Heb. *ḥārāsh* is a general term for any shaper of wood, including the cabinetmaker, joiner, maker of coffins, and woodcarver, as well as the carpenter *per se.* Because of the lack of good native timber the Egyptian carpenters became masters in their craft. The stubby acacia grows in the deserts along the Nile, but cedar, cypress, fir, and pine had to be imported from the Lebanon, and ebony and other tropical woods from central Africa. Consequently considerable labor was expended to obtain the desired effect with a minimum amount of wood. Boards were cut, planed, and shaped by bronze saw, adze, and chisel, and smoothed by a lump of sandstone. They were fastened by hardwood pegs and mitre joints (W. C. Hayes, "Daily Life in Ancient Egypt," *Everyday Life in Ancient Times,* Washington: National Geographic, 1951, p. 108; see also ANEP #123).

Except for those who built the tabernacle and its furniture, Israel had few if any skilled carpenters until later in its history. David arranged with King Hiram of Tyre to send Phoenician carpenters and masons to build his palace, and later the temple (II Sam 5:11; I Kgs 5:18; I Chr 14:1; 22:15). By the time of Kings Jehoash and Josiah, however, Judah had carpenters able to repair the temple (II Kgs 12:11; 22:6; II Chr 24:12; 34:11). In 597 B.C. a thousand skilled carpenters and smiths were taken from Jerusalem along with King Jeconiah and other royalty as captives to Babylon (Jer 24:1; 29:2; cf. II Kgs 24:14–16). Ezr 3:7 suggests that Phoenician masons and carpenters were hired to help rebuild the temple after the Exile.

In the NT only Joseph (Mt 13:55) and Jesus (Mk 6:3) are called carpenters. The Gr. *tektōn* has broad meaning including "builder" as well as "wood-worker," but according to Justin Martyr Jesus made plows and yokes (*Trypho* 88).

Various tools of the carpenter are mentioned throughout the OT. The axe (*q.v.*) of Deut 19:5 had an iron head and wooden handle (cf. II Kgs 6:5–6). The tool of Jer 10:3 was probably an adze or chisel (NEB). A hatchet is mentioned in Ps 74:6 (RSV). By Jeremiah's time carpenters used stone hammers and nails (Jer 10:4) as well as dowel pegs and mortised joints. The saw was wielded by one man (Isa 10:15), made either of flint blades with serrated edges, mounted in a frame, or of bronze and later of iron. Holes were bored with a drill rotated back and forth by a bow and string. Isa 44:13 describes how an idol-maker marks out and measures his piece of wood with measuring line, chalk or scriber, and compass or calipers. Numbers of such tools belonging to the OT period have been found at Gezer and other sites in Palestine.

See Craftsman.

J. R.

Carving. Carving in wood and ivory (*q.v.*; ANEP #125–132) of high artistic quality was done by peoples surrounding the Israelites. Amorite inhabitants of Jericho, Canaanites in Phoenicia, and especially Egyptian craftsmen displayed such skill. The influence of Yahweh worship, however, eliminated from Israelitish art images that were idols and lascivious motifs born of idolatry. The work of Bezaleel and Aholiab in the tabernacle (Ex 31:1–5) and of others in the temple (I Kgs 6:18, 29–35) revealed art that was pure as well as beautiful. Sculptured walls and doors, carvings of lotus buds and fleur-de-lis, olive-wood furniture covered with gold, and cherubim designed to symbolize the presence of Yahweh fitted into patterns of worship that pointed to God as Spirit and that taught conduct which was righteous. The KJV uses such terms as artificer, engraver, and graver to refer to craftsmen of this type.

See Occupations: Engraver.

Reconstruction drawing of an ivory plaque. Megiddo

Ceramics. The art of molding, modeling, and baking clay, or the things made of baked clay. This is one of the oldest arts in man's experience. *See* Pottery; Occupations: Potter.

Chamberlain. In the OT "chamberlain" is the translation of the Heb. *sārîs,* meaning "eunuch," or officer in charge of the private quarters of a king or noble. In KJV the Heb. is translated "chamberlain" in II Kgs 23:11; Est 1:10, 12, 15; 2:3, 14–15, 21; 4:4–5; 6:2, 14; 7:9. In the RSV "chamberlain" is used only in II Kgs 23:11 and Est 1:10. Frequently, male officials in ancient palaces were emasculated since they had access to the women's quarters. Potiphar, though married, was termed a eunuch of Pharaoh (Heb. *sārîs*; LXX *spadōn*) in Gen 37:36; 39:1. This perhaps explains his wife's designs on Joseph as well as his personal rage against one whom he supposed to be a philanderer who took advantage of an unfair situation.

In the NT "chamberlain" is used twice. Acts 12:20 reads: "*ton epi tou koitōnos,*" "the one in charge of the bedchamber." W. Dittenberger (*Orientis Graeci Inscriptions Selectae* [1903–5], No. 256, 5) cites an inscription dated *c.* 130 B.C. which mentions an official who was "in charge of the bedchamber of the queen." Thus Blastus was doubtless a highly trusted and influential official. Erastus (*q.v.*) is called "the chamberlain [Gr. *oikonomos*] of the city" (Rom 16:23; "city treasurer" in RSV). *See* Occupations: Treasurer.

E. J. V.

Chancellor. *See* Chancellor.

Clerk. *See* Town Clerk.

Confectionary. *See* Occupations: Perfumer.

Cook. In the home cooking was usually performed by the women of the family (Gen 18:6; 27:9; II Sam 13:8; Mk 1:31; Lk 10:40; Jn 12:2). Men, however, also knew how to cook (Gen 25:29; Jud 6:19; II Kgs 4:38). In wealthy homes a slave or servant usually prepared the one main meal of the day, in the evening (Lk 15:22–23; 17:8). Cooking included the task of slaughtering and butchering, since the Heb. word *ṭabbāḥ* for "cook" means "slaughter." There were no professional butchers in the towns of Israel, however, because the average person ate meat only on festal days or other special occasions.

Professional male cooks were employed at religious centers in Israel, as in the case of Samuel's cook who prepared a leg of meat for Saul (I Sam 9:23–24). Doubtless they worked in the royal court (cf. I Kgs 4:22–23). Kings also would conscript female cooks in conformity with the Canaanite social system, as Samuel warned (I Sam 8:13). *See* Occupations: Baker.

Egyptian tomb models represent such kitchen scenes as slaughtering, grinding grain, and making beer. Scenes on monuments and tomb paintings depict attendants supplying their master and his wife with provisions including a hind quarter of beef (VBW, II, 125). Gen 40:20 records Pharaoh's birthday feast for all his servants. The earliest known royal menu appears on the stele of Ashurnasirpal II in which he describes his feast given to 69,574 persons at the dedication of his new palace at Calah in 879 B.C.

Cooking was usually done over an open fire in the courtyard of the house. When meat was roasted, an entire animal normally was placed directly on the coals or on a spit, well cooked

Oven and grindstone of a bakery at Pompeii.
V. Carcavallo

so that the meat could be easily pulled off and eaten with the fingers. Many people, however, preferred to boil or stew their meat in a pot (Jud 6:19; Jer 1:13; Ezk 11:3, 7; 24:3-5; Mic 3:3). Jesus' disciples enjoyed eating broiled fish (Lk 24:42; Jn 21:9). *See* Food; Pottery.

J. R.

Coppersmith. A worker in metal, usually called a coppersmith or brazier. Metal workers with brass (bronze or copper) and iron were among the first specialists in ancient history (Gen 4:22). The Israelites early came in contact with the Kenites (*q.v.*), considered to have been a tribe of seminomadic coppersmiths. The most famous craftsman in copper and bronze was a half-breed Jew, Hiram of Tyre, whom Solomon brought, because of his outstanding skill and ingenuity, to manufacture the bronze objects for the temple (I Kgs 7:13-46). Paul mentions that a coppersmith by the name of Alexander had done him great harm (II Tim 4:14). *See* Minerals and Metals: Copper.

Counselor. This term is employed in the following senses: (1) of a state official, a justice (Dan 3:2-3); (2) of a court official, an adviser of the king (II Sam 15:12; Isa 19:11); (3) in general of a wise person who gives advice (Prov 11:14; 12:20; 15:22; 24:6); (4) of the Messiah, indicating His wisdom (Isa 9:6); (5) of a member of the Sanhedrin (Mk 15:43).

Kings in ancient times gathered numerous counselors around themselves, just as rulers today have their advisers and cabinet members. David had the trusted Ahithophel (*q.v.*), who was succeeded by Jehoiada and Abiathar. In addition, Jonathan (David's uncle), Hushai the Archite, and Joab often acted in an advisory capacity (I Chr 27:32-34). Nebuchadnezzar kept many high officials as counselors in his court (Dan 3:24, 27; 4:36). King Artaxerxes of Persia had seven counselors (Ezr 7:14-15, 28; 8:25). *See* Occupations: Cupbearer.

The danger of immature counselors may be seen in the case of Rehoboam (I Kgs 12:6-19) and of outright wicked counsel, in the case of Ahaziah (II Chr 22:2-4).

Craft, Craftsman. A craft is an occupation done with the hands which requires some special skill. Those who do such work are called artisans or craftsmen.

The Heb. term *ḥārāsh* indicates especially one who carves wood or engraves metal (*see* Occupations: Carpenter, Engraver). In Bible times craftsmen often worked in families and groups (I Chr 4:14). They congregated together as members of guilds after the Exile (Neh 3:8, 31, RSV), but earlier most crafts were performed in the home by both men and women. There was a fellow feeling among craftsmen (Isa 41:6-7). During the first centuries after the Heb. people came back to Palestine from Egypt, they had little technical skill (cf. I Kgs 5:6), but they learned from the Canaanites and Phoenicians (II Chr 2:7, 14). Three centuries later a thousand craftsmen and smiths were taken captive along with King Jehoiachin to Babylon (II Kgs 24:14, 16).

Shops were kept by craftsmen such as the potter (Jer 18:2). Often sections of the cities were occupied by shops of the same craft, with wood-carvers in one section, carpenters in another, smiths in gold and silver in another, etc. People in Jerusalem could buy bread on the bakers' street (Jer 37:21).

In the NT the Gr. terms *technē* (trade, craft, skill; Acts 17:29, "art"; 18:3; Rev 18:22) and *technitēs* (craftsman, artisan, designer; Acts 19:24, 38; Heb 11:10, "builder") have a wide range of meaning, from tentmaker and silversmith to architect (Heb 11:10, NASB).

The list of crafts and craftsmen is a long one. *See* under separate occupations.

A. W. W.

Cupbearer. The word occurs three times in KJV, once in the singular and twice in the plural. The Heb. term *mashqeh* occurs more often, however. Pharaoh's "butler" was a cupbearer (Gen 40:1-41:13). Solomon had cupbearers (I Kgs 10:5; II Chr 9:4). The only cupbearer mentioned by name is Nehemiah, cupbearer to Artaxerxes (Longimanus), in Neh 1:11. His first duty, described in Neh 2:1, apparently involved responsibility to guard against poison in the king's cup, perhaps even to tasting it first himself. Hence, the king's life lay in his cupbearer's hands who, obviously, would be a trusted man, and presumably of high rank and able to advise the king in matters of state. *See* Occupations: Butler, Counselor.

Diviner. *See* Divination.

Doctor. The Gr. term *didaskalos* (Lk 2:46) actually means "teacher" and *nomodidaskalos* (Lk 5:17; Acts 5:34) "teacher of the law." From Lk 5:21 it is clear that Luke's "doctors" were scribes (*see* Scribe) or professional expositors of the laws of Judaism. They took special training and had to pass rigid examinations before being recognized officially. Later their traditions, along with those of other prominent teachers, were recorded in the Talmud. Saul of Tarsus was taught by one of these doctors,

Egyptian mummies in the Louvre. LM

Gamaliel (*q.v.*), who belonged to the liberal school of Hillel within the Pharisaic party. *See* Doctor; Rabbi; Occupations: Lawyer.

Dyer. Israelites were familiar from earliest times with dyed stuffs even though the process is not described in the OT. Dyes of purple, blue, crimson and scarlet were used on cloth. Purple was a symbol of royalty (Mk 15:17 f.). Only kings could afford it, because it was claimed to be worth its weight in silver.

The Canaanites traded in purple (*q.v.*) as early as 1500 B.C., according to texts and remains of a dyeing establishment found at Ugarit in Syria. Phoenicians (Ezk 27:7, 16, 24) kept secret their art of making purple and blue dyes from shellfish. The pigment was removed from a gland of the mollusk, and after treatment became light or dark purple, depending on exposure and the addition of other ingredients. Lydia, from Thyatira, was a dealer in purple dye (Acts 16:14). Crimson and scarlet dye was obtained from the kermes or cochineal insect which feeds on a certain species of live oak in Turkey and southern Europe. Rams' skins dyed red were used in building the tabernacle (Ex 25:5; 26:14). Such dye is still used in Syria in the making of slippers and other leather articles.

Solomon requested King Hiram of Tyre to send him a skilled man to work "in purple, and crimson, and blue" (II Chr 2:7). Israelites later acquired the secret of dyeing from the Phoenicians and gained a monopoly on the art in some sections. Several Palestinian towns apparently were centers of the dyeing guild (cf. I Chr 4:21). At Tell Beit Mirsim an estimated 30 homes had rooms with two round stone dye vats. Each vat had a small opening on top through which thread was dipped, and a channeled rim to catch splashed dyes. A Jewish guild of purple dealers is mentioned on a tombstone at the textile center of Hierapolis near Colosse.

See Occupations: Fuller.

C. K. H

Embalmer. The Egyptians employed professional embalmers because they desired to preserve the corpse from decay. According to Gen 50:2 those who embalmed Jacob's body were court physicians. *See* Embalm; Occupations: Physician.

Embroiderer. In embroidery the design is sewn upon the finished fabric purely for ornamentation. Brocade is a heavy fabric interwoven with a raised design. Because Heb. *rāqam* simply means to make variegated (cloth), it is not certain which exact product is meant.

The curtains for the tabernacle and the high-priestly garments were embroidered (Ex 26:36; 27:16; 28:39; cf. 35:35; 38:23). The royalty and nobility of all of Israel's neighbors enjoyed embroidered clothing, from the Canaanites in Deborah's time (Jud 5:30, RSV, NASB) to the Phoenician sea-kings (Ezk 26:16) who obtained it through trading with Egypt (Ezk 27:7), Syria (v. 16), and various centers in Assyria (v. 23). Ps 45:14 describes the royal princess coming in embroidered work (NASB) to be wedded to the king. Israel is figuratively pictured as being adorned by the Lord God with embroidered cloth (Ezk 16:10, 13, 18).

Monuments from Assyria and Babylonia depict royal garments with embroidered designs, and 8th cen. B.C. Assyrian bas-reliefs imitate in detail the intricate patterns of embroidered covers (W. Corswant, *A Dictionary of Life in Bible Times,* New York: Oxford Univ. Press, 1960, p. 110).

See Occupations: Needlework, Weaver.

Engraver. This artist-craftsman was adept in carving or chiseling various hard substances such as stone, gems, ivory, bone, and metals. He produced seals and scarabs, statues and images in the round (cf. Acts 17:29), plaques in bas-relief, and inscribed steles. Hiram from Tyre was a master engraver, along with his other skills (II Chr 2:7; I Kgs 7:36). With an engraving tool (*ḥereṭ*) or stylus (cf. Isa 8:1) Aaron sculptured the details of a golden calf or young bull on the rough cast form he had made (Ex 32:4). Writing upon stones is also referred to in the KJV as graving (Ex 32:16; 39:6, 30; Job 19:24; Jer 17:1; cf. Isa 49:16). *See* Graven Image; Jewels; Occupations: Carving; Seal, Signet.

Farmer. While this term does not appear in the KJV, which regularly translates Gr. *geōrgion* as "husbandman" (*see* Occupations; Husbandman), it is found in most modern English versions at II Tim 2:6 and Jas 5:7. The NASB has "farmer" also in Isa 28:24; 61:5; Jer 14:4; 31:24; 51:23; Joel 1:11; Amos 5:16, and "farming" in Gen 9:20. Other terms that describe the farmer are "plowman" and "thresher" (I Cor 9:10, RSV), "vinedresser" (Jn 15:1, RSV), and "vine-grower" (Mt 21:33 ff., NASB; marg., "tenant farmer").

The prevailing economy in ancient Israel was agricultural. The majority of the people therefore lived in villages or walled towns near their

OCCUPATIONS

fields and went out by day to farm them. Since much of the land is hilly, very early the inhabitants built terraces with the overabundant rocks to extend their arable land.

Wealthy landowners could afford extra farm hands (Lk 15:17, 19). These were either slaves or hired laborers (Lev 25:6; Job 7:1-2). Day laborers in Israel were to be paid at the end of each day's work (Lev 19:13; Deut 24:14; Mt 20:1-16), and their wages were not to be withheld (Mal 3:5; Jas 5:4). An Israelite who sold himself as an indentured servant to another Israelite was not to be treated as a slave but as a hired man, whose term of service would end in the year of jubilee (*q.v.*; Lev 25:40, 50, 53).

For the agricultural seasons, methods of farming, and farm products *see* Agriculture.

J. R.

Finer. *See* Occupations: Refiner, Metalsmith.

Fishing. This was an industry pursued by many in Palestine, especially in the Sea of Galilee, in the former Lake Huleh, in the Jordan, and in streams near the Mediterranean coast. Much fishing was also done in Egypt in the Nile and its marshes (Num 11:5; Isa 19:8), where the pharaohs and nobles often fished for sport. The Phoenicians fished at Sidon and Tyre (Ezk 26:5, 14), and exported fish to such cities as Jerusalem (Neh 13:16), where there was a fish gate and probably a fish market (II Chr 33:14). *See* Animals, V.4.

Various methods were used by ancient fishermen. Job 41:7, 26 mentions fishing spears or barbed harpoons. Angling was a favorite sport, then as now, according to Assyrian and Egyptian art. Rods were not used, simply a line with fishhook (*q.v.*), as in Isa 19:8; Mt 17:27.

King Tutankhamon of Egypt harpooning fish or marine animals in the Nile. LL

Fishing boats and nets at ancient Tyre. HFV

The principal commercial methods employed nets (*q.v.*). These were of two main types: (1) The cast net or round throwing net (Heb. *ḥērem,* used also in hunting; Gr. *amphiblēstron*), mentioned in Ezk 26:5; 32:3; 47:10; Hab 1:15-17; Mk 1:16. It is a circular net with fine meshes, about 15 feet in diameter, with leaden sinkers loaded on the margin (cf. Ex 15:10). Holding a long line attached to the center of the net in his left hand, the fisherman gathers the net in his right hand and casts it by a broad sweep of the arm over an area of shallow water near the shore, where he has observed a school of fish. Drawing up the center of the net, he wades into the water to secure the catch. (2) The dragnet or seine (Heb. *mikmeret;* Gr. *sagēnē*), mentioned in Isa 19:8; Hab 1:15-16; Mt 13:47. Half the dragnet is loaded in one boat, and the other half in another. The boats then separate, paying out the net as they go to enclose a large area of water. Having sailed toward the shore, the two crews then begin to pull in their respective ends of the net, thus enclosing the various fish and bringing them to land on the beach (Mt 13:48). Or the two crews may enclose a circle in the water and drag the fish into their boats (Lk 5:4-9).

Recent studies help to explain the reason for Peter's protest in Lk 5:5. It has been discovered that at night fish in the Sea of Galilee gather below the steep eastern bank, or in those deep parts of the lake where mineral springs bubble forth. Toward morning, the fish swim to shallow water, either near the mouth of the Jordan where they find much food in the water entering the lake, or near the Seven Springs at Bethsaida near Capernaum. Therefore fishermen use dragnets at night in deep waters, but employ their throwing nets in shallow water during the day. Such information clearly indicates that the great catch of fish of Lk 5:6-9 was indeed miraculous.

In addition to catching the fish, the job of the fisherman included salting and marketing the fish, as well as mending nets and keeping the boats in repair (Ezk 26:5; Mk 1:19). Some scholars have suspected that the Zebedee fami-

OCCUPATIONS

ly, which was able to employ hired servants (Mk 1:20), had a concession for selling fish in Jerusalem. This in turn might explain why the other disciple with Peter, whom many think to be John, would have been known to the high priest (Jn 18:15–16).

In the OT the concept of fishing is used metaphorically to illustrate judgment (Eccl 9:12; Ezk 29:4; Hab 1:14–17). Throughout history since the days of the prophets God has been sending many "fishers" and many "hunters" to "catch" and judge the children of Israel (Jer 16:16). In the NT, on the other hand, the idea of fishing is taken by Jesus to portray the entire mission of the church: "Follow me, and I will make you fishers of men" (Mt 4:19; Mk 1:17; Lk 5:10). Cf. Wilhelm H. Wuellner, *The Meaning of "Fishers of Men,"* Philadelphia: Westminster Press, 1967. Thus the symbol of the fish used by the early church is consonant with our Lord's commission to be fishers of men. In addition, the five Gr. letters of the Gr. word for "fish," *ichthus,* as an anagram, suggest the confession *Iēsous Christos Theos Uios Sōter* ("Jesus Christ, God, Son, Saviour").

J. R.

Founder. *See* Occupations: Refiner, Goldsmith, Silversmith.

Fuller. A fuller was a person, man or woman, engaged in cleaning cloth (Isa 7:3; Mal 3:2; Mk 9:3). The work of the fuller was of two kinds, depending on whether he dealt with new cloth from the loom or with soiled garments that had already been worn. He cleaned dirty clothing by steeping and treading them in water mixed with an alkaline substance obtained from plant ash (translated "soap" in Mal 3:2). Hence the fuller was characteristically called a "treader" or "trampler" (from Heb. *kābas*). Because of the foul odor involved, such work was carried on in a "field" or place outside the city where water, stones on which the garments might be trampled, and space for drying and bleaching them by the sun were available (II Kgs 18:17; Isa 7:3; 36:2). *See* Fuller's Field. A cleansing agent sometimes used by the fuller was natron (saltpeter) imported from Egypt and mixed with white clay (Prov 25:20; Jer 2:22).

Newly woven material (the "unshrunk cloth" of Mt 9:16; Mk 2:21, RSV) had to be cleansed of natural oils or gums before dyeing. The cloth was thoroughly steeped, stamped in order to felt it, then bleached with fumes of sulphur, and finally pressed in the fuller's press. *See* Occupations: Dyer.

The cleansing, bleaching, or whitening accomplished by the fuller gave occasion for descriptions of the purified character produced by forgiveness of sin (Ps 51:7; Jer 4:14). Thus, in Zech 3:4, the removal of the "filthy garments" of Joshua the high priest symbolized God's taking away his iniquity. Isa 1:18 describes the forgiveness of the Lord as imparting a character "white as snow."

J. W. W.

Gardener. Used only in Jn 20:15, the Gr. word *kēpouros* (lit., "garden-watcher") evidently refers to the watchman (*q.v.*); cf. the "keeper of the vineyards" (Song 1:6; cf. 8:11, "caretakers," NASB). During the season while the fruit was ripening the keeper would normally rest in a "booth" (Job 27:18) or "lodge" (Isa 1:8), a shelter or hut in the field. He guarded the crop from human thieves and predatory animals such as foxes (Song 2:15). He was not expected to do manual labor in the garden.

In Egypt and Mesopotamia gardeners in the modern sense of the word were commonly employed by the royalty and nobility. Often these were knowledgeable slaves. The 14th cen. B.C. palace of the Canaanite kings of Ugarit had a garden court. Neh 2:8 mentions the keeper or overseer of the royal "forest" (Heb. *pardēs,* a word of Persian origin signifying an enclosed park or orchard; *see* Plants: Forest).

See Plants: Garden.

J. R.

Gold pitcher and goblet from Alacahuyuk, Turkey, *c.* 2200 B.C. Ankara

Goldsmith. An artisan who fashions vessels, ornaments, and jewelry of gold. One of the most ancient arts, the craft of refining and shaping gold was practiced by the early Sumerians and pre-dynastic Egyptians (i.e., before 3100 B.C.). Therefore it is not surprising that Abraham's servant could give Rebekah a gold ring and two gold bracelets (Gen 24:22). Neh 3:8, 31–32 suggests that after the Exile the goldsmiths in Jerusalem had grouped themselves into a guild.

During the Middle Bronze Age (2100–1500 B.C.) goldsmiths developed a technique known as "granulation," by which tiny globules of gold arranged in designs were soldered onto a gold object. The OT reveals other processes used by goldsmiths: (1) casting idols ("molten images," Num 33:52; etc.) and other objects of solid gold such as the rings for the ark (Ex 25:12); (2) making figures such as the cherubim and lampstand of beaten or hammered gold (Ex 25:18, 31, 36); (3) plating or overlaying with extremely

Gold death mask from Mycenae, *c.* 1400 B.C. Mimosa

thin sheets of gold, i.e., gold leaf (Ex 25:11; I Kgs 6:20; Isa 40:19); (4) soldering (Isa 41:7); (5) making gold thread by cutting sheet gold into narrow wires (Ex 39:3); (6) engraving images (Jer 10:14, ASV); and (7) mounting jewels in gold filigree settings (Ex 28:20; 39:6, 13, 16, RSV).

See Jewels; Minerals and Metals: Gold; Occupations: Smith.

J. R.

Governor. *See* Governor.

Graving. *See* Graven Image; Occupations: Engraver.

Herdman. The word "herdman" (KJV) or "herdsman" (modern versions) generally means the keeper or shepherd of domesticated animals (sheep, goats, etc.) which travel in flocks, herds, or droves (cf. Gen 13:7-8; 26:20). Jacob's sons, Saul, and many others kept cattle. The herdmasters of Saul, David, and later kings were among the chief officers of the state (I Sam 21:7; I Chr 27:29; II Chr 26:10; 32:27-29). The herdsman generally did not own the flock, but was a hireling. Three Heb. words are translated herdman in the Bible.

1. Heb. *rō'ēh* is the general word for any kind of herdsman (Gen 13:7-8; etc.).

2. Heb. *nôqēd* occurs only twice in the OT (Amos 1:1; "sheepmaster," II Kgs 3:4). According to one view, it means "one who spots or marks the sheep," since spotting the wool with different dyes is the method used for distinguishing between the sheep of different flocks. Another view is that *nôqēd* is a shepherd of a special variety of sheep called in Arabic *naqad* and noted for its stubby legs, peculiar shaped head, and excellent wool (federq sheep). A third view is that *nôqēd* signifies a member of a guild of shepherds or sheep breeders and dealers. The verb *nqd* is used of King Mesha on the Moabite Stone (1.30). The noun appears in tablets of Ugarit, where shepherds had guild status, and the Akkad. *nakidu* likewise indicates a guild of shepherds. Modern Scandinavian scholars question the traditional interpretation that the Amos passage suggests that the prophet was of lay origin and the king of Moab was wealthy, holding that the term *nôqēd* suggests priestly origin for both Amos and Mesha. *See* Occupations: Sheepmaster.

3. Heb. *bôqēr* is the term used in Amos 7:14 as the prophet describes his occupation prior to his prophetic call. *See* Occupations: Shepherd.

D. W. D. and J. R.

Hewer of Wood. *See* Hew; Occupations: Woodcutter.

Hunter, Hunting. After their settlement in Canaan few if any Israelites engaged in hunting as a vocation. The patriarchs, however, lived as seminomads, and Esau "became a skillful hunter, a man of the field" or outdoor man (Gen 25:27, NASB; cf. 27:5, 30) in a time when deer and other wild game were plentiful in Canaan. The term "hunter" is used metaphorically of military tyrants, as in the case of Nimrod (*q.v.*; Gen 10:9) and that of the oppressors of the Jews (Jer 16:16). *See* Hunt.

A Hittite hunting scene from Carchemish. Ankara Archaeological Museum

Husbandman, Husbandry. A cultivator of the soil (Gen 9:20; Mt 21:33; *et al.*), in modern terms, a farmer. "Husbandman" is not used in the RSV, which renders the biblical term as "tenants" in Jesus' parable of the vineyard (Mt 21:33-41; Mk 12:1-9; Lk 20:9-16), because the farmers did not own the vineyard. In II Chr 26:10 (KJV) it is said that King Uzziah loved "husbandry." The Heb. word *'ădāmâ* literally means the ground or soil, an idiomatic way of expressing his liking for agriculture.

Figuratively, God is described in Jn 15:1 (KJV) as a husbandman (*geōrgos,* lit., a "worker of the soil") or "vinedresser" (RSV). A Christian congregation is said to be "God's

OCCUPATIONS

husbandry" (I Cor 3:9), His cultivated land or farm. *See* Agriculture; Occupations: Farmer.

Jailor. The keeper of a prison (Acts 16:23, 27, 36). *See* Jailor; Prison.

Jeweler. *See* Jewels; Occupations: Goldsmith, Silversmith.

Judge. *See* Judging; Occupations: Lawyer.

Laborer. *See* Labor; Laborer; Service.

Lawyer. Eight of nine NT usages of Gr. *nomikos* refer to those versed in religious law. Lawyers are regularly associated with the Pharisees (Lk 7:30; 11:44, 46; 14:3). A lawyer was also called scribe, rabbi, and doctor, and was practically identical with a scribe (*q.v.*). His task was to study, interpret, and teach the written and oral law of Israel, as well as to decide questions concerning it.

The lawyers' commitment to salvation by the law was such that they rejected John the Baptist's preaching of the counsel and purpose of God for themselves (Lk 7:30). They also tested Jesus with difficult questions (Mt 22:35; Lk 10:25).

Jesus condemned the lawyers for increasing the burdens of the people and hiding the key of knowledge (Lk 11:45-52), and did not hesitate to challenge them (Lk 14:3).

Paul mentions Zenas, a Christian lawyer (Tit 3:13), perhaps a secular jurisconsult who had made a profession of faith.

See Occupations: Doctor; Rabbi; Scribe.

R. B. D.

Magician. *See* Magic, Magician.

Mariner. The Heb. word *mallāḥ* is derived from *melaḥ*, "salt," and in Ezk 27:9, 27, 29 and Jon 1:5 has the idea of "sailor" (NASB) or one who helps to navigate a ship. Another Heb. word, *shāṭîm*, is found in Ezk 27:8 and means "rowers" (RSV). The Israelites were primarily a pastoral and agricultural people and had few encouragements to follow a seafaring life. The Phoenicians were the great seamen of OT times; hence, the references in Ezk 27 to "mariners" in the lamentation over Tyre.

Egyptian model boat with rowers, *c.* 2000 B.C.
BM

Egyptian sailors traveled up and down the Nile and plied the waters of the Mediterranean and Red Seas. The Story of the Shipwrecked Sailor goes back to the Middle Kingdom period (Adolf Erman, *The Ancient Egyptians,* New York: Harper Torchbook, 1966, pp. 29-35), and an 11th cen. B.C. papyrus tells of the voyage of Wen-Amon to procure lumber in Phoenicia (ANET, pp. 25-29).

In the NT sailors are mentioned as viewing the destruction of end-time Babylon (Rev 18:17-19). The sailors or "shipmen" (KJV) handling the storm-tossed ship on which Paul was being taken prisoner to Rome took soundings, cast anchors, and then tried to escape in the ship's boat (Acts 27:27-30).

See Ship.

S. F. B. and J. R.

A Corinthian capital and column base from Epidaurus, Greece. Stone masons required great skill to carve these capitals. Mimosa

Mason. The mason was a "worker of stone" (I Chr 22:15), one skilled not only in digging out or quarrying stones and hewing them to shape (I Chr 22:2), but also in building walls (II Kgs 12:12; 22:6, where "masons" lit. were "wall-builders").

In the hill country of Palestine soft limestone is plentiful. It provides an excellent building material for public structures and the homes of the wealthy. The citizens of ordinary means, however, could ill afford a cut stone house because of the time and expense involved in quar-

Typical Herodian masonry with a "frame" around each block appears in the Western Wall of the Temple, Jerusalem. MIS

rying, transporting, and hewing the stone. Thus there were no experienced masons in Israel at the beginning of the monarchy, and David (II Sam 5:11; I Chr 14:1) and Solomon (I Kgs 5:18) had to obtain expert artisans from King Hiram. Because quarrying required less skill, Solomon sent relays of conscripted Israelites to the Lebanon Mountains to dig out and haul the stone for his temple (I Kgs 5:13–17).

A large metal sledgehammer was used in quarrying for repeated pounding of the rock (Jer 23:29). The stonecutter could also hammer in wooden wedges and soak them until they expanded and split the rock. He shaped stones into building blocks with a pick-axe or adze (I Kgs 6:7). This was the type of tool employed in cutting Hezekiah's tunnel (II Kgs 20:20; II Chr 32:30) from both ends toward the middle, as the workmen tell in their famous Siloam inscription. A good mason could hew stones so accurately that no mortar was needed in laying up his wall. The wise masterbuilder took pains to prepare a solid foundation (Mt 7:24–27; I Cor 3:10–13). The builders (Ps 118:22) worked from a prepared plan or "blueprint" (I Chr 28:11), using a line of flax and a measuring rod or reed (Ezk 40:3) and a plumb line (Amos 7:7; Zech 4:10). *See* Architecture; House.

In Palestine masons also carved out tombs in the natural caves or drove shafts into the limestone cliffs (Isa 22:16). Often side chambers were excavated beyond the entrance room (*see* Grave; Tomb). Stonecutters dug deep cisterns, stairways, and underground water tunnels at Gibeon, Hazor, Lachish, Megiddo, and other cities. During the monarchy many buildings had large stone pillar bases. Masons also chiseled out stone vessels, dye vats, and rollers for mud roofs, as well as monuments for royal inscriptions such as the Moabite Stone (*q.v.*). One of the bronze bands from the gates of a palace of Shalmanezer III at Balawat depicts a stonemason with chisel and hammer carving a royal image (ANEP #364).

See Architecture; House; Cornerstone; Headstone.

J. R.

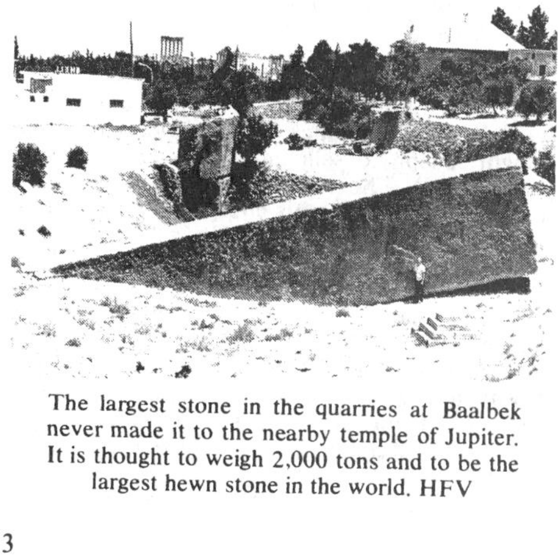

The largest stone in the quarries at Baalbek never made it to the nearby temple of Jupiter. It is thought to weigh 2,000 tons and to be the largest hewn stone in the world. HFV

A wine merchant's shop at Pompeii. HFV

Merchant. Many of the oldest cuneiform texts from Mesopotamia deal with the trade between the Sumerians and their neighbors. Assyria and Babylonia became one of the greatest commercial areas of antiquity (cf. Isa 47:15; Nah 3:16). In Akkad. the merchant was called a *tamkārum*. He was a free citizen who bought and sold goods or loaned money on his own account. His trade was regulated by civil laws, such as the code of Hammurabi, and by certain statutes of public law pertaining to transport permits and taxes. As early as 1950 B.C. the Assyrians had established a number of merchant colonies or trading stations in Cappadocia, 500 miles to the NW of Asshur (W. F. Leemans, *The Old Babylonian Merchant*, Leiden: Brill, 1950). In the next centuries tablets from Mari in E Syria tell of trade missions taking shipments of tin to Aleppo and to Hazor in Palestine. The Amarna letters (*q.v.*) contain much evidence of the international trade between Egypt, Canaan, and Mesopotamia in the 14th cen. B.C.

In the 2nd mil. B.C. the merchant almost invariably traveled about with his own goods. The three Heb. roots forming words for merchant and trader (*sāḥar, rākal, tûr*) all mean to go about or explore. Even in NT times the Gr. word *emporos* (Mt 13:45; Rev 18:3; etc.) signifies a traveling merchant, as distinct from a *kapēlos*, a purely local peddler (cf. II Cor 2:17, RSV). For mutual protection merchants often went in caravans, such as the Midianites who bought Joseph to sell him as a slave in Egypt (Gen 37:25). The trader carried his merchandise either directly to his customers or to public markets at city gates (II Kgs 7:1; Neh 13:15-21). Frequently he purchased his wares from the one who made them at home (Prov 31:24), so that no middleman was involved.

Not until the time of Solomon did foreign trade become big business in Israel. Even then it was a royal monopoly. Solomon obtained assistance from Hiram of Tyre in building and manning a commercial fleet based at Ezion-geber (I Kgs 9:26-28; 10:11, 22). His merchants bartered the copper ingots smelted at mines in the Arabah and the chief agricultural products for export—olive oil, grain, and wine—for the gold and exotic goods of Arabia and beyond. Solomon also traded with desert caravans (I Kgs 10:15). It is thought that the queen of Sheba journeyed the 1,200 miles to Jerusalem in order to visit the court of Israel on a trade mission (I Kgs 10:1-10). Her purpose presumably was to acquire an agreement covering the barter with Israel of incense and spices (cf. Song 3:6), gold and gems, and the export of these items to other peoples through Solomon's territory. His agents also bought horses in Kue (Cilicia) and chariots in Egypt and then resold them to the rulers of the Syro-Hittite city states (I Kgs 10:28-29, NASB).

After the capital of the northern kingdom moved to Samaria, Israel established close trade relations both with Phoenicia and with the Arameans. King Ahab signed a commercial agreement with Ben-hadad of Damascus so that their merchants could set up bazaars ("streets," KJV, NASB) in each other's city (I Kgs 20:34, JerusB). From the 9th to the 7th cen. B.C. the Phoenician sea merchants were in their heyday. Isaiah in his oracle concerning Tyre refers to the ships of Tarshish—merchant ships that sailed to Sardinia and Spain— to Tyre as the market of nations and the grain of the Nile valley as her revenue, to her practice of colonizing distant places, and to her merchants as princes (Isa 23:1-8, NASB). In even more detailed prophecies Ezekiel lists the nationalities and products that contributed to Tyre's wealth (Ezk 27:1-27; 28:4-5,18).

Jesus, reared in busy Nazareth astride the trade routes through Galilee and the valley of Esdraelon, grew up with an awareness of merchant life. He likened the kingdom of heaven to a pearl merchant who on one of his journeys found one of great price, perhaps in an Arabian shop or in the hand of a diver along the Red Sea (Mt 13:45). He told of an invited wedding guest who would not come because of attending to his merchandise (Gr. *emporia*, Mt 22:5). The master who went on a long journey and entrusted his possessions to his servants expected them to gain a profit for him by trading (Mt 25:14-16).

See Commerce; Travel and Communication; Weights, Measures, and Coins.

J. R.

Metalsmith. *See* Minerals and Metals; Occupations: Smith.

Metalworkers. *See* Minerals and Metals; Occupations: Coppersmith, Goldsmith, Refiner, Silversmith, Smith.

Midwife. A woman who assists mothers at childbirth. In the biblical period, at the time of delivery women kneeled or crouched upon a birth stool or a pair of stones called in Heb. *'ābnayim* (I Sam 4:19; Ex 1:16). According to 2nd mil. B.C. medical papyri from Egypt, the midwife seized the infant, cut the umbilical cord, and washed the newborn child. Statuettes indicate the midwife holding a horn-like object with a hook or spoon-like appendage, probably a primitive obstetrical instrument (H. Rand, "Figure-Vases in Ancient Egypt and Hebrew Midwives," IEJ, XX [1970], 209–212). According to Ezk 16:4 she would have rubbed the baby with salt as an antiseptic and wrapped it in cloths, and then seen to getting someone to inform the father (Jer 20:15).

The only two women whose names are recorded who are specifically designated as midwives in the Bible are Shiphrah and Puah (Ex 1:15–21). However, a midwife attended Rachel during her severe labor giving birth to Benjamin (Gen 35:17), and another assisted Tamar when she delivered her twins (Gen 38:28). Naomi and other women of the community were present when Ruth bore Obed (Ruth 4:13–17). Women were standing by when Phinehas' wife died in childbirth (I Sam 4:20).

Miner, Mining. *See* Minerals and Metals; Mining.

Money Changer. *See* Money Changer; Occupations: Banker.

Mourner. In Bible times professional mourners were hired to eulogize and to lament the death of the deceased (Amos 5:16, NASB; see also II Chr 35:25; Eccl 12:5; Jer 9:17–20). Because they tend to be more emotional and more intense in their expressions, most of these professional mourners were women (Jer 9:17, 20). During the lament and loud wailing (Mk 5:38)

A muse playing a cithara, 2nd cen. B.C. Istanbul Archaeological Museum

flutes were usually played, as at the death of Jairus' daughter (Mt 9:23). The high, plaintive notes of the flute contributed to the mournful attitude of the moaning hearts (Jer 48:36). *See* Mourn, Mourning.

Musician. Professional musicians played in the courts of ancient Egypt, Assyria, and Babylonia, and were known among the Canaanites and Phoenicians as well. It seems that King David introduced professional singers and instrumentalists to the palace and the temple of Israel (II Sam 19:35; Ps 68:25; Eccl 2:8). The temple musicians were appointed from the ranks of the Levites (I Chr 15:16–22). While singing at the dedication of Solomon's temple, they were clothed in fine linen and were stationed E of the altar (II Chr 5:12). Many of the titles of the psalms indicate that the psalms were written for the chief musician (KJV, ASV) or choir director (NASB). Likewise Habakkuk stated that his prayer in chap. 3 was "For the choir director, on my stringed instruments" (Hab 3:19, NASB).

There is some evidence for musical guilds in ancient Israel. In I Kgs 4:31 the well known wise men Ethan, Heman, Chalcol, and Darda are called "the sons of Mahol"; but in I Chr 2:6 they are listed as the sons of Zerah, a Judahite. In Heb. Mahol means "dance," so it is thought that these men were members of an orchestral or dancing guild (IDB, III, 227). In the ancient Near East music and wisdom were often associated.

See Music; Minstrel.

J.R.

Needlework. Work of the embroiderer (Heb. *ma'ăśēh rōqēm*); embroidery (Heb. *riqmâ*). This was done with linen, woolen, and even metal threads of gold or silver (Ex 39:3), sometimes woven or plaited, sometimes stitched. This was probably so in the case of the intricate design of the cherubim (Ex 26:1). Such fine embroidery and needlework formed the appropriate dress of kings and queens (Jud 5:30; Ps 45:13f.), but was also found on the dress of poor Near Easterners. It was much used in the tabernacle hangings (Ex 26:36; 27:16; 36:37; 38:18) and in the garments of the priests (Ex 28:39; 39:29). Appliqué work of colored pomegranates interspersed with bells was probably used in the hem of the priest's skirt (Ex 28:33). Both the Babylonians and the Egyptians were skilled in such work, hence the origin of Israel's skill. In addition, God gifted certain Israelites "with the spirit of wisdom" so that their skill surpassed natural ability (Keil and Delitzsch on Ex 28:3).

See Occupations: Embroiderer.

R. A. K.

Nurse. Nursing was not a formal occupation in Bible times, but the tender care of parents for their children has been known since the creation of man (Num 11:12; I Thess 2:7). A nursemaid was sometimes employed to care for another woman's child (II Sam 4:4; II Kgs 11:2). On occasion she might remain with her charge for life, as in the case of Rebekah's nurse (Gen 24:59; 35:8). In the event of the death of the mother, real or supposed, a wet nurse had to be found to suckle the infant (Ex 2:7-9). *See* Nurse.

Perfumer (Heb. *rōqēaḥ*). The words ordinarily used to describe a perfumer, either man (KJV "apothecary") or woman (KJV "confectionary") meant one who compounded an ointment. The ingredients were oils (Eccl 10:1), spices, gum, resin, or other substances extracted from roots, bark, leaves, or blossoms by boiling or cooking; and they were mixed to produce odoriferous ointments and attractive cosmetics. Flowers were crushed by compressing in a bag and soaked in olive oil or dipped in hot fat or oils at 65°C. After burning spice roots or bark and reducing to a powder, it might be used in dry form, as a sachet (Song 3:6), or kept in a pouch (Song 1:13). Widespread desire for ointments and perfumes made the art of the perfumer to be highly respected.

Special appointees served the priesthood and produced the holy anointing oil by blending myrrh, sweet cinnamon, sweet calamus, and cassia in olive oil (Ex 30:22-33). The sacred incense consisted of four perfumes: stacte, onycha, galbanum, and pure frankincense (vv. 34-35). Egyptian incense and anointing oils had as many as 16 ingredients. The court of the king required similar service (I Sam 8:13). The great palace at Mari (18th cen. B.C.) had its own perfumers who supplied ointments and perfumes in abundance to the royal family, officials, and soldiers. In the days of Nehemiah, perfumers were organized in a guild and helped repair the wall of Jerusalem (Neh 3:8).

Perfumers also compounded spices which were used in burying the dead (II Chr 16:14). According to the Egyptian process of embalming, spices and perfumes were undoubtedly employed in the burial of Jacob and of Joseph (Gen 50:2-3, 26; *see* Embalm). Perfumes were applied to furniture and garments as well as persons at festivals and royal banquets (Ps 45:8; Prov 7:17; Song 4:11).

See Perfume; Ointment; Incense; Plants, the individual ingredients; Spice.

J. W. W. and J. R.

Physician. Both the Heb. *rōpē'*, from *rāpā'*, "to heal," "to repair," and the Gr. *iatros*, signify a healer, physician, equivalent to what we call a doctor today (Ex 15:26; Jer 8:22). Doctors were highly esteemed in Egypt from the time of Imhotep in Dynasty III onward, and have left several ancient papyri describing their medical and surgical practices. The code of Hammurabi *c.* 1750 B.C. indicates a high level of medical organization in Babylonia, as well as other texts giving a record of prescriptions for mineral and animal drugs in addition to herbs.

Physicians are mentioned for the first time in the OT in the embalming of Jacob for burial (Gen 50:2). Asa was condemned for seeking physicians rather than the Lord, in the first place, because he had not put his main and real trust for healing in God; and, in the second place, probably because they were pagan and more magicians than physicians (II Chr 16:12). Job speaks of his comforters metaphorically as physicians of no value (Job 13:4).

Christ uses the term proverbially twice, once of Himself (Lk 4:23), and once of His ministry (Lk 5:31; cf. Mt 9:12; Mk 2:17). The miracle of the healing of the woman with the issue of blood was all the more wonderful since she had been to many physicians and was now bankrupt financially (Mk 5:26; Lk 8:43). Because of His healing ministry, Christians today often refer to Jesus as the Great Physician. Paul called Luke "the beloved physician" (Col 4:14), suggesting that Luke may have had similar training to that of Galen (*c.* A.D. 130-200), the Gr. anatomist, physiologist, and physician.

See Diseases; Healing, Health.

R. A. K.

Plowman. *See* Agriculture; Occupations: Farmer, Husbandman.

Porter. The OT word *shô'ēr*, "porter," in the sense of gatekeeper, is almost exclusively found in Chronicles, Ezra, and Nehemiah. The LXX and NT use *thyrōros*, "doorkeeper," and the Vulg. *portarius*, "janitor."

Levites were assigned to various posts in the temple to guard it day and night (I Chr 9:17-26; 26:1-19; II Chr 8:14; 31:14; 35:15; Ezr 2:42; Neh 7:1-3; 12:25, 45). No less than 4,000 such gatekeepers are mentioned (I Chr 23:5) to prevent unauthorized persons from entering the holy court and profaning it. When he was planning the coup against wicked Queen Athaliah, Jehoiada the priest took the precaution to appoint extra gatekeepers from Levites brought in from the other towns in Judah (II Chr 23:1-7, 19).

Gates of the city (II Sam 18:26; II Kgs 7:10-11), public buildings, private houses (Mk 13:34), and even sheepfolds (Jn 10:3) were carefully guarded for the safety of all concerned. This responsible trust also was given to women of maturity and judgment. Women at the gate are seen in two experiences of Peter: at the time of his denial of Christ (Jn 18:16-17), and later, his release from prison (Acts 12:13).

See Doorkeeper; Occupations: Watchman.

R. V. U.

Potter. Clay vessels molded by a potter around 5000 B.C. have been found at Jericho. About 2000 B.C. the use of a potter's wheel, although somewhat earlier in Egypt and Sumer, was begun in Palestine. This wheel consisted of a pair of stone discs (Jer 18:3, NASB marg.), one above the other. The lower was turned by the foot of the potter, and the upper on which the clay was placed was turned by the disc underneath. The wheel required rapid use of the hands in shaping a vessel from a revolving

Mycenaean pottery, Rhodes Museum. Mimosa

lump of clay instead of working with a rigid form. Thus the potter developed greater ability, design, and variety. Because of their skill, certain families were placed in special service of the kings (I Chr 4:23).

Carefully made shapes and designs were used quite regularly at any given time and locality. Often these designs were fixed by decree in form and decoration. The finished vessel was burnished or painted, then placed in a kiln to harden. Because pottery styles changed frequently and because the pieces of broken pots are virtually indestructible, archaeologists use potsherds to date finds according to a scientifically worked out pottery chronology.

See Pottery.

J. W. W.

Priest. *See* Priest, Priesthood; Priest, High.

Prophet. *See* Prophet; Seer; Sons of the Prophets.

Publican. A tax collector for the Roman government. *See* Publican.

Purifier of Silver. *See* Minerals and Metals; Occupations: Refiner, Silversmith.

Rabbi. A title of respect for a Jewish scholar and teacher of the law. *See* Rabbi; Occupations: Lawyer.

Refiner. The process of securing a pure metal or liquid was called refining. This idea is presented by the Heb. words *ṣārap* and *zāqaq*. Unger (*Bible Dictionary*, pp. 915 f.) is of the opinion that a fairly uniform distinction was observed here, the former word referring to metal smelting and the latter to purification of liquids by filtering, but that in time *zāqaq* came to be used also of gold and silver (I Chr 28:18; 29:4).

The earliest smelting was done by placing the ore directly on the fuel of a bonfire. Later, various types of furnaces were invented to intensify the heat (Ezk 22:22). In refining, the metal was reheated to a liquid state in a crucible (Prov 17:3; 27:21, NASB) and the dross or impurities removed through the use of a flux or solvent such as alkali (Isa 1:25). Bellows were used by the refiner (Jer 6:29). Usually the goldsmith and silversmith did their own refining, whereas slaves were used in smelting.

Figuratively, God is the refiner of men's hearts (Isa 1:25; 48:10; Zech 13:9; Mal 3:2-3).

See Minerals and Metals; Occupations: Goldsmith, Silversmith.

B. C. S.

Sailor. *See* Occupations: Mariner; Ship.

Schoolmaster. Neither the word "schoolmaster" (Gal 3:24–25) nor "instructor" (I Cor 4:15) is adequate as a translation of the Gr. word *paidagōgos*. Paul's metaphor was much more apt than the common English translation indicates. The *paidagōgos* (lit., boy-leader) was not an instructor nor tutor but a servant whose responsibility it was to have oversight of the boy of the house. He would not only conduct him safely to and from school, but he was charged to see that he had the right companions and that he would grow up in the proper moral and ethical environment. This, Paul says to the Galatians, was the role of the law. It was the servant of God that was to guide men and keep them from evil ways until they were brought to the Saviour.

See Education; Schools, Hebrew.

Scribe. *See* Scribe; Rabbi; Occupations: Doctor, Lawyer.

Secretary. The verb *sāpar* in Heb. means to write or count; the derived noun *sōpēr* is ordinarily translated "scribe." These men were professional writers and recorders, and in a day when few knew how to read or write their place was essential. *See* Scribe.

In a number of places in the OT the common name is misleading since the office described is more exalted. The RSV has marked this distinction by translating "secretary" in a number of cases. Such men as Seraiah, Sheva, Shebna, and Shaphan (II Sam 8:17; 20:25; II Kgs 18:18; 22:8) were important members of the king's council and might bear such a title as Secretary of State. It has been suggested that Ezra, although a scribe in the religious sense, might well be titled Secretary of State for Jewish affairs (Ezr 7). Jeil was in charge of the muster of all Uzziah's troops (II Chr 26:11), and the scribe of II Kgs 12:10 was a financial secretary or treasurer.

Baruch is spoken of as the private secretary of Jeremiah, very much as in modern days (Jer 36:4). Silvanus (I Pet 5:12) served Peter and perhaps Paul (I Thess 1:1) in the same way.

P. C. J.

Sentry. Irijah, the sentry (RSV) at the Benjamin gate who arrested Jeremiah, bears the title, literally, of "lord of oversight" which the KJV renders "captain of the ward" (Jer 37:13). The Heb. title describes the function of the man whose supreme duty was to watch and guard. The word "sentry" rather than "keepers" (KJV) would better describe the soldiers in Acts 5:23; 12:6, 19, as well as the officers in II Kgs 11:5; 22:4; I Chr 9:19, men posted to guard and keep the gates. Abner and his men were on sentry duty guarding King Saul, but fell asleep at the time David stealthily took away Saul's spear and jug of water (I Sam 26:7-16). Likewise the soldiers guarding Christ's tomb acted as sentries (Mt 27:66; 28:4, 11).

Servant. One who renders service, voluntary or involuntary, to another person. Four principal words in Heb. express this relationship: (1) *na'ar,* a young man, an attendant (Num 22:22), who donated his service or was entitled to remuneration, as Gehazi thought he was (II Kgs 4:12; 5:20–27); (2) *meshārēt,* a minister of the temple (Joel 1:9, 13) or officer of the king (II Chr 17:19; Est 1:10) or a domestic servant of higher standing (I Kgs 10:5); (3) *śākîr,* a hired servant (Ex 12:45; Job 7:1), who therefore could refuse to perform a task; and (4) *'ebed,* a slave (Deut 5:15) or servant who performed menial work. By usage the latter term was extended in meaning to refer to the angels (Job 4:18), the prophets (Jer 7:25), and all true worshipers of God (Isa 54:17; 56:6) as His servants.

In the NT a number of Gr. words for servant are found: (1) *doulos,* the exact equivalent of *'ebed;* (2) *pais,* like Heb. *na'ar,* also means "boy," "youth," or "servant"; (3) *diakonos,* a servant or helper, hence a deacon; (4) *oiketēs,* a domestic or household servant (Rom 14:4; I Pet 2:18); (5) *hypēretēs,* lit., "underrower," an assistant, subordinate (I Cor 4:1, NEB), or minister, often of fairly high rank such as a magistrate (Mk 14:54, 65, NASB).

In the Israelite economy the slave was usually a domestic servant in a royal or wealthy family rather than an agricultural or industrial worker. Laws regarding such slaves are recorded in Ex 21; Lev 25; and Deut 15:12–18; 23:15–16. There is, however, a vast amount of data concerning slavery in the ancient Near East to be found in the law codes and private economic documents. The latter extend from the earliest Sumerian records in Mesopotamia through tablets from Hittite cities, from Alalakh and Ugarit in Syria, down to the Aramaic papyri from Elephantine (*q.v.*) in Egypt. *See* Service.

When addressing one higher in rank or authority, a person by custom would refer to himself as a servant or slave of the superior, thus expressing submission (Gen 50:18; II Kgs 1:13; Lk 2:29; Acts 4:29). Therefore Paul frequently referred to himself as a bondservant of Jesus Christ (Rom 1:1; Phil 1:1; Tit 1:1). Even Jesus considered Himself a servant of His Father in that He came to do His will and accomplish His work (Jn 4:34; 5:30, 36; 8:28–29).

See Servant of the Lord.

J. R.

Sheepmaster. The Heb. term *nôqēd* is used both for a shepherd or herdsman such as Amos (1:1), and of a great master breeder and owner, or dealer, such as the king of Moab (II Kgs 3:4). The term later came to be used of the owner of a superior breed of sheep. *See* Occupations: Herdman.

Shepherd. The term is used in its natural sense in a number of biblical passages to refer to persons engaged in the tending of sheep. Sometimes the owner cared for his own sheep (Gen 4:2); others committed their flocks to sons (I Sam 17:34); others used servants or hirelings (Jn 10:12–13). In general, shepherds fell into three classes: (1) the nomads who wandered with their sheep wherever they could find grass and water (e.g., the Amalekites, I Sam 30:1, 17,20); (2) the settled shepherds who always grazed their sheep in the same general area (Gen 29:2–13); and (3) the shepherds who drove the flocks of a wealthy owner from pasture to pasture (Gen 37:12–17).

It was the duty of the sheepherder to lead his flock to pasture and fresh water (Ps 23:2). In some instances this necessitated long treks across the countryside. In Bible lands it was the custom for the shepherd to lead his sheep rather than to drive them (Jn 10:4). Another necessary task was that of protecting the flock from wild animals (I Sam 17:34–35) and robbers (Jn 10:1). At night the shepherd led his sheep to a place of shelter and protection, such as a fold or a natural enclosure (*see* Sheepcote), where he counted them to see that none had strayed (Jer 33:13; cf. Lk 15:3–7). At lambing time the shepherd gave special care to the ewes and the lambs (Isa 40:11).

The equipment ordinarily needed for the work of the shepherd included a rod or club (Heb. *shēbeṭ,* cf. Ex 21:20) to smite predators, and a staff with a crook at one end (Ps 23:4). The latter cane-like instrument served a number of purposes from supporting himself (cf. Ex 21:19; Zech 8:4) to managing the flock. A sling was also a standard weapon for the shepherd (I Sam 17:40). Other items were a bag (I Sam 17:40) to carry smaller possessions, a cloak, and sometimes a musical instrument with which the shepherd passed the time. In many instances one or more dogs accompanied the flock (Job 30:1).

Inasmuch as shepherd life in so many aspects is parallel to spiritual relationships, biblical writers use it repeatedly as an apt illustration of experiences in the spiritual realm. Throughout the ancient Near East rulers were accustomed to picturing themselves as the shepherds of their people. The earliest known use of the term in this sense was by Kudur-Mabug, king of Elam (*c.* 1900 B.C.). After recounting a military exploit he ended with the prayer that he might become a "dear shepherd."

In the OT the Lord is the Shepherd of His people (Gen 49:24; Ps 23; Isa 40:11). Faithless shepherds ("pastors," KJV) have scattered the Lord's flock, but when Christ returns He will gather them again from the ends of the earth and set faithful shepherds over them (Jer 23:1–6; Ezk 34:11–16, 22–31). In that day Israel and Judah shall be united under one Shepherd, the Messiah (Ezk 37:24). The unscrupulous shepherds who led God's people astray fall under His condemnation (Ezk 34:2–10).

In the NT Christ declared Himself to be the good Shepherd who laid down His life for His sheep (Jn 10:11), who is known by His sheep (v. 14), and who will someday be Shepherd over the united fold of all God's redeemed (v. 16; see also Heb 13:20; I Pet 2:25; 5:4). Like

Various stages of shipbuilding as pictured in the tomb of Ti at Sakkara, Egypt. LL

their Master (Jn 10:1–14), the leaders of NT churches are to do the work of a shepherd, to feed and to protect the flock (Acts 20:28–31). The same commission is repeated by Peter (I Pet 5:1–4), who by referring to Christ as the Chief Shepherd suggests that elders are under-shepherds. The same idea is preserved in the English term pastor, which means shepherd.

See Animals, I. 15.

D. W. B.

Shipbuilder. No shipbuilders appear in the early history of Israel because of the smooth and limited coastline with few ports and little occasion for trade by sea. Egypt, however, used ships for trade along the Mediterranean coast as far as Byblos long before 2500 B.C. The annals of Senefru (*c.* 2650 B.C.) refer to some 40 ships, each *c.* 179 feet long. David (*c.* 1000 B.C.) made an alliance with Hiram of Tyre to bring material for the temple from Phoenicia (II Sam 5:11). Solomon with Phoenician aid built "ships" on the Red Sea and traded even to Ophir (I Kgs 9:26–28). No doubt these ships were designed by Phoenicians, like their merchant ships sent to distant Tarshish (*q.v.*) in Spain (I Kgs 10:22). These may have had from 30 to 50 double-banked oars extending from the lower decks, with a single mast and sails above. Jehoshaphat attempted to reopen the Red Sea trade (I Kgs 22:48). Later Tyre dominated these shipping routes (Ezk 27). Judas Maccabeus prepared a harbor at Jaffa (I Macc 14:5); the Romans did so at Caesarea.

The design of the ship was probably laid out by a master ship's carpenter. He and his assistants used such tools as saws, planes, scrapers, and hammers. The shipbuilders of Tyre obtained fir trees from Senir for the planks, cedar from the Lebanon Mountains for masts, oaks from Bashan for oars, boxwood from Cyprus for the deck—which they ornamented with ivory inlay—fine embroidered linen from Egypt for the sails, and blue and purple dye from Elishah (Cyprus) to color the awnings (Ezk 27:4–7, NASB). The seams were calked with pitch, which needed to be replaced from time to time (Ezk 27:9, 27).

See Ship.

J. W. W. and J. R.

Silversmith. The only person specially designated in the Bible as a silversmith is Demetrius, who made silver shrines of the goddess Artemis at Ephesus (Acts 19:24). He apparently belonged to a guild of silversmiths or craftsmen in that city.

In addition to refining his metal and manufacturing silver vessels and jewelry, the silversmith repaired silverware. He used a very hot fire to heat the object until it became sufficiently softened for reworking. After he had soldered on any missing parts such as legs or handles, he filled in holes and cracks with silver solder. Also he could hammer out any deformities or dents. Like most other craftsmen he usually performed his work while squatting on the ground.

See Minerals and Metals: Silver; Occupations: Metalsmith, Purifier of Silver, Refiner.

Singer. *See* Minstrel; Music; Occupations: Musician.

Slave. *See* Occupations: Servant; Service.

Smelting. When Isaiah (1:25) speaks of purging away dross and taking away tin, he is referring to a refining or smelting process of separating a metal from its ore by heat. Likewise, references are made in Job 28:1–2 to the refining of gold and to the smelting of copper from the ore. Such metals as gold, silver, copper, lead, tin, and iron were refined and used in Palestine during OT times. *See* Minerals and Metals; Occupations: Refiner.

Smith. When iron as well as copper became abundant in Palestine (after 1200 B.C.), metal workers became smiths in the sense of blacksmiths. Before Saul's and David's victories the Philistines prevented the Israelites from having their own blacksmiths and making up-to-date weapons. Consequently, when the Hebrews

A scene from a metal worker's shop, showing six men blowing on the fire to increase its intensity. The man at the right pours out liquid gold or silver. Tomb of Mererula, Sakkara. LL

needed to sharpen or repair their tools, they were forced to go down to Philistine smiths (I Sam 13:19–22, NASB).

Because the smith used bellows made of leather and blew air through clay pipes onto the coals with which he melted his metals, he was called "one who blows" (Isa 54:16). Because he used hammers and anvil to shape the iron after it was smelted, he was also called "he who smooths metal with the hammer" and the one "who beats the anvil" (Isa 41:7, NASB). The process of casting and grinding iron had not yet been developed in OT times. Therefore all iron tools had to be produced and sharpened by pounding: "The man shapes iron into a cutting tool, and does his work over the coals, fashioning it with hammers, and working it with his strong arm" (Isa 44:12, NASB). The implements produced for work, warfare, and home life were quite varied and too numerous to mention here. *See* Minerals and Metals: Iron; Occupations: Coppersmith, Goldsmith, Refiner, Silversmith.

Soldier. The nation of Israel did not have an organized army or professional soldiers until the beginning of the monarchy under King Saul. Before that, in a time of emergency a military leader, such as Gideon, called the people to arms by sounding a trumpet or by sending out messengers (Jud 6:34–35). Other nations, however, had standing armies centuries earlier.

In Babylon, according to the code of Hammurabi, many of the soldiers in the regular army were of the landed gentry and were called away from their feudal obligations for one or more years to serve the king. Others were conscripted or hired (illegally) as substitutes to go on foreign campaigns (§§26–41, ANET, pp. 167 f.).

At Ugarit the soldiers in the garrison received regular wages in silver. Canaanite city-states maintained small armed forces consisting of foot soldiers (recruited from the common people) and professional warriors. The latter were chosen from the hereditary aristocratic class, and were known by the Indo-European name of *maryannu*. These were the charioteers. Owing to their superior military equipment, which they were responsible to maintain at their own expense, they occupied a highly privileged position in Canaanite semi-feudal society. Only the king could elevate a commoner to the rank of *maryannu*, roughly equivalent to a "knight" (I. Mendelsohn, "Samuel's Denunciation of Kingship in the Light of the Akkadian Documents from Ugarit," BASOR #143 [1956], pp. 18 f.). Samuel warned Israel that a king would initiate such a class, and it became a reality during Solomon's reign (I Kgs 9:19; 10:26).

From David onward the nation had several categories of soldiers. Foremost was an elite corps of warriors who constituted a kind of general staff for the king. These were David's hand-picked heroes, his famous Thirty Men (II Sam 23:8–35). In the standing army was a second class, foreign mercenaries (e.g., II Chr 25:6). The Cherethites and Pelethites, commanded by Benaiah (II Sam 20:23; 23:22 f.), were of this category; they acted as a special force of up to 600 men to guard the palace, David's "servants" (II Sam 15:18). In the third category were the soldiers of the national army under Joab's command (II Sam 8:16; 20:23), the army of the people, who were drafted into service only when needed. Fourth were the garrison troops in occupied territory (as in Edom, II Sam 8:14) and those who manned the fortresses (II Chr 11:5–12), such as the citadels recently excavated at Arad (*q.v.*) and Beersheba.

In the NT Roman soldiers are frequently mentioned. Because the province of Judah was under a military governor or procurator by the time of Jesus' ministry, the legions of Rome were continuously present in the country. Their duty was to keep order in the streets in case of rioting, to guard prisoners, and to execute crim-

Bronze gladiator's helmet, 2nd cent. A.D. BM

A contingent of Egyptian soldiers. LM

inals. For this reason many troops were on hand in Jerusalem at the time of the Passover, because Pilate could always expect trouble from the swollen crowds during the Jewish festivals. It is believed that Rome had four regular legions (from 3,000 to 6,000 men each) stationed in Palestine when Pontius Pilate was governor. In addition to these, three others were brought into Syria early in the reign of Nero.

See Army; War.

J. R.

Sower. *See* Agriculture; Occupations: Farmer.

Spinning. Women spun the blue, the purple, the scarlet, the fine linen, and the goat's hair (Ex 35:25-26) for curtains for the tabernacle. Spinning apparently was one of the many household activities of the worthy woman (Prov 31:13-19). The lilies of the field possess beauty without toil and without the need for spinning (Mt 6:28; Lk 12:27).

There is both literary and archaeological evidence for understanding that spinning and weaving were developed early in all areas of the ancient Near East. The vegetable fibers principally used were cotton and flax; the animal fibers, mainly wool, goat's hair, and camel's hair. The fibers were wound on the distaff (Prov 31:19*a*, RSV), or balls or roves of fibers were contained in spinning bowls. From either of these the threads to be twined or spun were formed by the left hand as the fibers were turned between the thumb and first two fingers. The right palm twirled the spindle (Prov 31:19*b*, RSV) by means of the round whorl affixed to its shank, thus twisting the spun yarn on the spindle. Spinning was the necessary preparatory step to weaving. *See* Cloth; Distaff; Occupations: Weaving; Spindle.

H. E. Fi.

Steward. An administrator of the affairs, household, and property of a person of means. The steward's duties usually included such responsibilities as the oversight of meals, household finances, servants, children of the family, flocks and herds, and the tilling of the fields. An OT example is Eliezer, the steward of Abram (Gen 15:2). In the NT the most common Gr. word for steward is *oikonomos* meaning "ruler or manager of a house" (Lk 12:42; 16:1, 3, 8). Because of its apt illustrative value, the term is used of Christian leaders such as bishops and apostles (Tit 1:7; I Cor 4:1-2). It is also applied to Christians in general (I Pet 4:10).

Stonecutter. *See* Occupations: Mason.

Tanner. The process of tanning skins by the use of lime, the juice from certain plants, or the bark or leaves of certain trees was an ancient art. The Israelites learned the art of tanning from the Egyptians who were highly skilled. It was one of the most important trades of Egypt, where leather was extensively used for ornamental work. The demand for skins was so great there that they were unable to supply enough and one form of tribute exacted from subject nations was a supply of skins.

Tanning developed from the necessity of changing a hide or skin from something which would easily decay to a material which would last almost indefinitely. This is done by soaking the skin in a liquid containing tannic acid. In ancient Palestine and Syria tanners' houses were usually on the seashore for ease of disposal of unpleasant liquids and convenience of obtaining the salt water used in the tanning process. Vats were made of stone masonry and plastered. Sheep and goat skins were smeared on the flesh side with slacked lime, folded, and allowed to stand until the hair loosened. After the hair and fleshy material had been removed, the skins were again treated with lime and fermenting bran. They were usually tanned with sumac. After drying, they were blackened on one side by rubbing with a solution of vinegar and pieces of copper. Oak chips were used around Hebron in making leather bottles (Josh 9:4, 13; Mt 9:17).

Tanning was not held in favor among the Jews. It was accompanied by unpleasant odors and was ceremonially defiling because dead animals were regarded as unclean. Simon the tanner found fellowship among Christians. This would not have been granted by other Jews (Acts 9:43; 10:6, 32). Peter stayed in Simon's home in Joppa.This indicates that Peter was developing a more liberal attitude toward ceremonial rules.

C. K. H.

Tax Collector. *See* Publican.

Teacher. *See* Education.

Tentmaker. The most eminent tentmaker in history was the apostle Paul (Acts 18:3). Both men and women (e.g., Aquila and Priscilla) engaged in this trade. They first had to weave the tent cloth on their looms. In Palestine camel and goat hair was used, which gives a dark brown, almost black material (Song 1:5). Then the long, narrow loomed strips were sewn together. Cords were attached which would be tied to stakes when pitching the tent (Isa 54:2).

Since Paul came from Tarsus in Cilicia, he undoubtedly was trained in making tents of the wool or hair of Cilician goats. This material was called *cilicium* in Latin; it was superior in its ability to shed the most drenching rains. Being somewhat stiff, however, the fabric was more difficult to cut and assemble than other cloths, so that this activity came to be a distinct trade. On the basis, however, of the earliest Latin version of Acts 18:3, which reads *lectarius* for the Gr. *skēnopoios,* some have thought that Paul was rather a leather worker.

See Tent.

J. R.

Trader. *See* Commerce; Occupations: Merchant.

Treasurer. Treasurers held very important posts in Bible times. In Israel there were three such offices: (1) a sacral treasurer who had the oversight of the treasury of the house of the Lord (cf. Josh 6:24; I Kgs 7:51; I Chr 9:26; II Chr 5:1; Neh 13:12–13; Ezr 2:68 f.; Jn 8:20; Mk 12:41–43; Lk 21:1; Mt 27:6); (2) a royal treasurer who supervised the treasury of the king's house (I Kgs 14:26; 15:18; II Chr 32:27); and (3) provincial treasurers of the crown who had the custody of the royal stores outside Jerusalem (I Chr 27:25).

The sacral treasurer in the time of David was Shebuel who was the chief officer in charge of the temple treasuries as a whole (I Chr 26:24). (In I Chr 26:20 the confusing reading "Ahijah" is best rendered as "their brethren" in accordance with the LXX.) Under Shebuel were Jehiel and his sons (cf. I Chr 26:22 with 23:8) who were in charge of the income and expenditure of the funds (I Chr 29:8), the holy utensils, and the provision for the temple sacrifices; and Shelomoth (or Shelomith, I Chr 26:28), assisted by his brethren, who was in charge of the votive gifts which had been dedicated from the war booty (I Chr 26:20 ff.).

The sacral treasuries were located in the chambers of the temple (I Chr 28:11). The treasury over which Jehiel and his successors had charge included precious metals and stones, frankincense, vessels, grain, wine, oil, and priests' garments (II Kgs 14:14; I Chr 29:8; Ezr 2:69; Neh 7:70; 13:5). The treasury in charge of Shelomoth and his successors embraced the spoils won in battle which had been dedicated by Joshua, Samuel, various kings and officers in the army (Josh 6:18–19; I Kgs 7:51; II Kgs 12:18; I Chr 26:26 ff.; II Chr 5:1). This wealth was to be used for the maintenance of the temple (I Chr 26:27). The four chief gatekeepers of Jerusalem were charged with the security of the sacral treasuries (I Chr 9:26 ff.).

The role that Jehiel and his sons performed was assumed by Shelemiah the priest and certain Levites in the time of Nehemiah. He appointed them as treasurers over the storehouses in Jerusalem and charged them with the collection of the tithe of grain, wine, and oil, and their distribution to the Levites and singers (Neh 13:10 ff.; cf. 10:38; 12:44). In the time of the Maccabees the dual structure of the sacral treasury appears to have been maintained since mention is made of accounts belonging to the temple sacrifices, deposits of wealth for safe custody in the temple, and preservation of significant records (I Macc 14:19; II Macc 3:6 ff.).

The royal treasurer in the administration of David was Azmaveth, who was over the crown treasury in Jerusalem (I Chr 27:25). Jonathan the son of Uzziah was in charge of the provincial treasuries of the king in the country, cities, villages, and towers outside of Jerusalem. The royal treasury in Jerusalem was situated in the king's house and preserved precious stones and metals, armor and shields, precious oils and spices, grain, and wine (II Kgs 20:13; II Chr 32:27). The royal treasuries in the urban and rural areas outside of Jerusalem appear to be regional storehouses particularly adapted for the conservation of cattle, sheep, and agricultural produce.

A certain Shebna is described in Isa 22:15 as the "treasurer" who was "over the [royal] house" (KJV). However, the term *sôkēn* is more correctly rendered by "steward" (RSV, NASB). His position was that of the governor or major-domo of the palace.

Treasurers (Aram. *gedābrayyā'*) are mentioned among the various Babylonian officials who were summoned by Nebuchadnezzar to attend the dedication of the golden colossus (Dan 3:2 f.). Cyrus the Persian king ordered Mithredath, the royal treasurer (Heb. *gizbār*), to remove from the house of his gods the vessels that had been taken from the temple at Jerusalem by Nebuchadnezzar and to deliver them to Sheshbazzar, the prince of Judah (Ezr 1:7-11). Artaxerxes I (465-425 B.C.) promulgated a decree to all the treasurers (Aram. *gizbar,* a loan-word from Persian *ganzabara*) in the province "beyond the river" to assist Ezra with needful provisions for his journey to Jerusalem (Ezr 7:21 ff.; cf. Est 3:9; 4:7).

In the NT there is mention of a certain Erastus, the city treasurer (Gr. *oikónomos*) of Corinth, who sends along his greetings to the church at Rome in the concluding salutations of the epistle to the Romans (Rom 16:23). The Ethiopian eunuch is described as "a minister of Candace the queen of the Ethiopians, in charge of all her treasure" (Acts 8:27, RSV). *See* Occupations: Chamberlain, Steward.

E. R. D.

Vinedresser. *See* Occupations: Farmer, Husbandman; Plants: Vine.

Watchman. A sentinel or guard. Such watchmen were stationed like policemen in the streets of the city (Song 3:3; 5:7), upon the walls of fortified cities (II Sam 18:24; II Kgs 9:17-20; Isa 62:6), in wilderness watchtowers (II Kgs 18:8; II Chr 20:24), or on some commanding hill (Jer 31:6). In Ezk 3:17-21 and 33:2-9 the prophet is appointed as a watchman to warn Israel of her wickedness and spiritual danger. Habakkuk took his stand upon the spiritual ramparts of his nation to see what God would speak to him about the coming judgment (Hab 2:1). *See* Occupations: Sentry.

Weaver, Weaving. Weaving is the making of cloth or matting by interlacing thread, yarn, or reeds. The spinning of yarn was the necessary first step in the production of the coarser types of cloth most frequently used in Bible times. Yarn was made from wool and flax (linen) fibers (Lev 13:47), from goats' hair (Ex 35:26), and from camels' hair (Mt 3:4).

The loom was the weaver's principal piece of equipment. The word "loom" does not occur in the KJV, but appears in the RSV and NASB twice (Jud 16:14; Isa 38:12). The purpose of the loom is to facilitate the interlacing of the woof or weft strands back and forth at right angles to the warp strands. Three kinds of looms were in common use around the ancient Mediterranean world – the horizontal or ground loom, and two varieties of the upright loom. The first of these was already known in pre-dynastic Egypt, and is still the most common among nomadic peoples because it is easy to transport. The ground loom is undoubtedly the kind Delilah had when she wove into the warp the locks of hair of the sleeping Samson (Jud 16:13-14, NASB).

The warp (Heb. *sh^etĥı,* Lev 13:48-59) threads are stretched between two wooden poles held apart by stakes driven into the ground. The even-numbered warp threads are run through loops of string attached to a cross-rod. In the first position this rod is raised to lift the even-numbered threads and form a shed over the odd-numbered ones. Through the "shed" is passed the shuttle with the weft thread wrapped around it like a spool. This strand of the weft is "beaten" together with the previous weft strands by a removable flat lath or stick (the "pin" or "beater" [NEB], Heb. *yātēd,* of Jud 16:14) in order to make the cloth tight or firm. In the second position the cross-rod is allowed to lie loosely on the warp, and the weaver pulls forward toward himself the "beam" (Heb. *mānôr,* I Sam 17:7), which is under the odd threads and above the even ones. This action forms a new shed with the odd threads now on top. The weft is run through by means of the shuttle, and again beaten into place. The resultant product before it is cut off from the loom (Isa 38:12, NASB) is called the "web." The adept weaver passes his shuttle back and forth very swiftly, a vivid figure for the rapid but monotonous repetition of the seemingly endless days of the invalid (Job 7:6). The width of the cloth was limited by the length of the weaver's arm for pushing the shuttle through the warp.

In the older type of upright loom the strands of the warp, singly or in bundles, were suspended from a horizontal pole on two upright posts, and were held taut by numerous small weights made of stones or baked clay. The weft had to be beaten upward. The weaver could move about, and therefore he could make much wider fabrics. Since loom weights are found in the excavation of nearly every Iron Age city in Palestine, it is evident that this form of loom was common in Israel. Several towns in Judah seem to have been centers of the cloth industry, from the presence of large numbers of loom weights and dyeing vats. The OT indicates that a guild of linen weavers had developed during the monarchy (I Chr 4:21).

The other vertical loom had two horizontal poles, a warp pole at the top and a cloth pole at the bottom, capable of revolving in order to roll up the web as it was made. Two weavers stood, one on each side of the loom, and passed the shuttle back and forth through alternating sheds, beating the weft down. While this type of loom was already in use in Egypt during the 12th Dynasty, it became common in Palestine only by NT times (Louisa Bellinger, "Cloth," IDB, I, 650-655).

The weaver produced patterns in the web by (1) using different colored warp threads; (2) alternating the colors in the weft or woof; (3) a combination of (1) and (2) to form "checkered work" (Ex 28:39, NASB); and (4) running special weft threads through only a portion of the warp (James A. Patch, "Weaving," ISBE, V, 3077 f.). In order to obtain heavier or stronger fabrics several threads were twisted together (Ex 26:1, 36; etc.).

See Dress; Occupations: Dyer, Embroiderer, Spinning, Tentmaker.

J. R.

Woodcutter. Called a "hewer of wood," the woodcutter in Israel was normally a captive or slave since the work of chopping wood for fires was considered a menial task. Forced to serve the whole community of Israel, the Gibeonites became woodcutters and water carriers (Josh 9:21, 23, 27; cf. Deut 29:11). The hewers of King Hiram who cut timber in the Lebanon Mountains to supply lumber for Solomon's temple were experienced woodsmen, however, and needed to be paid for their labor (II Chr 2:10). The judgment to be inflicted on Egypt by Nebuchadnezzar is likened to an army of woodcutters coming with axes to cut down a forest (Jer 46:22-23, NASB). Usually they worked two by two, with the consequent possibility of accidental injury or death from his partner's flying axehead (Deut 19:5). *See* Hew.

Bibliography. Walter Duckat, *Beggar to King: All the Occupations of Biblical Times,* Garden City, N.Y.: Doubleday, 1968, with extensive bibliography. R. J. Forbes, *Studies in Ancient Technology,* 9 vols., Leiden: E. J. Brill, 1955-1964. Madeleine S. and J. Lane Miller, "Arts and Crafts," "Professions and Trades," *Encyclopedia of Bible Life,* New York: Harper, 1944, pp. 88-118, 332-356. James A. Patch, "Crafts," ISBE, II, 734-737. Roland de Vaux, *Ancient Israel,* trans. by John McHugh, New York: McGraw-Hill, 1961. Donald J. Wiseman, "Arts and Crafts," NBD, pp. 89-93.

J. R.

OCRAN (ŏk'ran). The father of Pagiel, the prince of the tribe of Asher, whom Moses and Aaron were instructed to select while at Mount Sinai (Num 1:13; 2:27; 7:72-77; 10:26).

ODED (ō'dĭd)

1. The father of Azariah, a prophet in the reign of Asa of Judah (*c.* 911-869 B.C.), who met Asa on his return from defeating the Ethiopians (II Chr 15:1-7). However, in v. 8 the prophecy is ascribed to Oded.

2. A prophet of the Lord in Samaria who lived (*c.* 735 B.C.) in the reign of Pekah, king of Israel, and Ahaz, king of Judah (II Chr 28:9). Pekah invaded Judah and took 200,000 persons back to Samaria. Oded met the victorious army with the prisoners and warned them of God's anger. In this protest Oded was joined by some of the chiefs of Ephraim. The captives were well-treated and were set free at Jericho.

ODOUR. In the OT Heb. *beśem,* "sweet odour" (II Chr 16:14; Est 2:12), means the fragrance emanating from balsam oil (Isa 3:24, NASB marg.) or sweet cinnamon (Ex 30:23). Heb. *nîḥôaḥ,* also translated "sweet odour" (Lev 26:31; Dan 2:46), refers to the soothing aroma from a sacrifice which appeases the Lord (Gen 8:21; Lev 1:9, NASB). In the KJV Gr. *osmē* is translated "odour" in Jn 12:3, speaking of the fragrance of Mary's ointment, and in Phil 4:18, referring figuratively to the fragrant aroma (NASB) of the Philippians' gift to Paul. It is also used metaphorically in II Cor 2:14-16, "We are unto God a sweet savour of Christ," and refers to Christ's offering Himself to God as a "sweet smelling savor" (Eph 5:2).

OFFENSE. Singular and plural, the word occurs often in the NT, but seldom in the OT. There seem to be two basic ideas—any stumbling or slipping of one's own, and any occasion of the stumbling or slipping of another. Hosea speaks of the Lord chastising Ephraim and Judah until they "acknowledge their offence" (Hos 5:14-15). Paul, quoting from Isa 8:14, speaks of "a stumbling stone and rock of offence" (Rom 9:33), referring to Christ as the rock over which Israel stumbled. Paul also warns the Corinthians not to give any offense, or be the occasion of anyone's stumbling (I Cor 10:32). *See* Stumbling Block.

Bibliography. G. Stahlin, "*Skandalon,* etc.," TDNT, VII, 339-358.

OFFERING. *See* Sacrifices; Sacrificial Offering; Libation.

OFFICE. A translation in the KJV of six Heb. words covering such things as place of service or post (II Chr 7:6, NASB), duty or responsibility (I Chr 23:28), position (Gen 41:13; Num 4:16; I Chr 24:3; II Chr 23:18; Ps 109:8). In the NT the word designates the rank or position of Paul (Rom 11:13, *diakonia*), the duty or responsibility of Christians in action (Rom 12:4, *praxis*), the office of bishop or overseership (I Tim 3:1, *episkopē*) in a local church, and the position of priest (Lk 1:9; Heb 7:5, *hierateia*).

OFFICER. In general the term designates a royal court functionary, such as a prince, steward, chamberlain, overseer, deputy, and others.

1. Heb. *niṣṣāb* (I Kgs 4:5; etc.) refers to deputies appointed by Solomon to administer newly established administrative centers. It was also used of an interim ruler of Edom (I Kgs 22:47).

2. Heb. *sārîs* denotes a eunuch in a foreign court (Gen 37:36) or in Israel's court (I Kgs 22:9; etc.).

3. Heb. *pāqîd* means an overseer appointed by another in higher authority (Gen 41:34; Jud 9:28; II Chr 24:11; etc.). Moses appointed such persons to maintain the needed organization among the traveling Israelites (Num 31:14, 48).

4. The Heb. word *rab* means a "great person," or one having authority by virtue of his relationship with the king in the Persian court (Est 1:8).

5. Heb. *shōṭēr* refers to persons who filled offices of a secondary nature, such as those under taskmasters in Egypt (Ex 5:6, 14; etc.); associates of the elders in Mosaic times (Num 11:16; etc.); adjutants in time of war (Josh 1:10; etc.). Originally they may have been

scribes or secretaries since the word root is cognate to Akkadian *šaṭâru*, "write."

6. Heb. *śar* refers to a prince or one of the royal family or of the royal cabinet (I Kgs 4:2; Ezr 7:28; etc.), often serving as an officer of the army (II Chr 32:3; Neh 2:9*b*, RSV). *See* Officials.

7. Gr. *praktōr* means an under officer of a court of justice, such as a bailiff or constable (Lk 12:58).

8. Gr. *hypēretēs* originally meant an assistant or "under-oarsman." By the 1st cen. A.D. the word meant a prison guard (Mt 5:25, RSV). John uses the term to designate the deputies or magistrates of the Sanhedrin sent by the chief priests to arrest Jesus (Jn 7:32, 45 f.; 18:3, 12, 18, 22), who had the right to accuse Him in court (Jn 19:6; see also Acts 5:22, 26).

H. E. Fi.

OFFICIAL. A person occupying an office, a position of authority; an officer. In the Bible such a position was generally obtained either by inheritance or appointment. *See* Officer.

OFFSCOURING. Heb. *s^{e}ḥî* found in Lam 3:45, means scrapings or refuse; Gr. *peripsēma* means what is wiped up, scrapings, scourings. Offscouring is a figurative expression for what is useless, worthless and vile, used by Paul to express the view held of Christians by unbelievers in his day (I Cor 4:13).

OG (ŏg). An Amorite king of Bashan, whose domain, embracing 60 cities from the Jabbok River to Mount Hermon, was conquered by Moses and the Israelites (Num 21:33–35; Deut 3:1–5). The inhabitants, except the king, were exterminated (Deut 3:6–11), and his territory was occupied by the half tribe of Manasseh (Deut 3:13; 29:8).

Og was the last of the Rephaim (*q.v.*) or giant race of that district and had an iron bedstead nine cubits long and four cubits wide which was preserved at Rabbath-ammon (Deut 3:11). His "bedstead" has been interpreted as an iron-trimmed sarcophagus, an iron-decorated couch to be placed in his tomb for his corpse as in Jericho tombs, or a dolmen of basalt (iron-bearing) blocks, found frequently in Transjordan. *See* Giant.

OHAD (ō'hăd). The third named son of Simeon (Gen 46:10) and head of one of the tribal families (Ex 6:14–15). His name is missing from the list in Num 26:12–14.

OHEL (ō'hĕl). One of the seven sons of Zerubbabel (I Chr 3:20).

OHOLAH. *See* Aholah.

OHOLIAB. *See* Aholiab.

OIL. Mineral oil or petroleum was unknown in biblical times.

Olive oil, however, was an important product in the OT economy and also for people of NT times. The olives were picked before ripening fully. While some might fall early, the main crop would be harvested in September and October. After gathering the fruit by shaking and beating the branches (Deut 24:20; Isa 17:6), the oil was pressed out, either by treading on the olives with the feet (Mic 6:15), by using a pestle and mortar (Ex 27:20; 29:40; Lev 24:2), or by grinding in a stone press with its accompanying vat (Joel 2:24). At many places in Palestine such as near Taanach, Megiddo, and Jerusalem, olive presses have been discovered which were hewn out of the solid rock. Having to produce oil within the city walls where there would be room for no such press was a sign of oppression (Job 24:11).

Oil was used in many ways. *Trade*. Solomon gave Hiram of Tyre oil in payment for help in construction of the temple (I Kgs 5:11; cf. Ezr 3:7; Ezk 27:17). The Israelite officials received oil, along with grain and wine, in payment of the taxes levied on the citizens. These commodities were kept in royal storehouses (I Sam 8:14–15; II Chr 11:11; 32:28). Egypt, whose climate prevents olive culture, imported much Palestinian oil (Hos 12:1). Oil will be included in the cargoes of end-time Babylon (Rev 18:10–13).

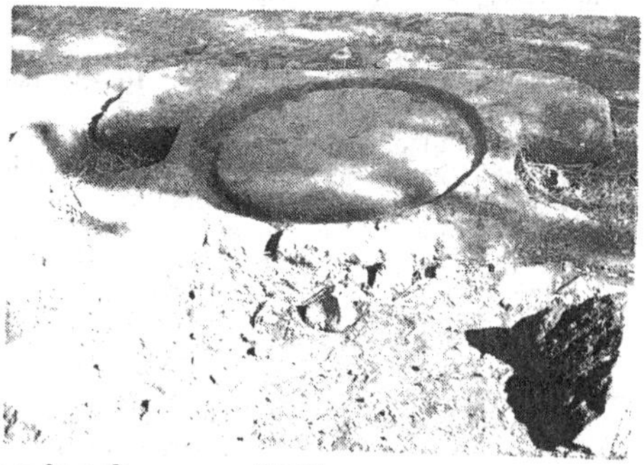

Two kinds of ancient oil presses from Capernaum. HFV

Food. Olives and olive oil are a staple part of the diet even today in Mediterranean lands. It was considered a necessity in OT times (I Kgs 17:12; II Kgs 4:2). Oil is mentioned with fine flour and honey as a symbol of good dining (Ezk 16:13, 19). Its possession was considered a mark of prosperity (Joel 2:19).

Cosmetics. Oil was used for the anointing of the body after a bath and for the hair (Ruth 3:3; II Sam 14:2; Amos 6:6; Mt 6:17). The head of a guest was often anointed with oil as he was seated (Ps 23:5; 92:10; Lk 7:46).

Funerals. The body of the deceased was washed and anointed with oil or other ointments (*q.v.*) by the Greeks and Romans and also, it appears, by the Jews.

Medicinal. Oil was used by the Jews and Romans for massage, for baths, and on wounds (Isa 1:6, NASB; Lk 10:34). The disciples used it as a symbol of healing in the miraculous cures they performed (Mk 6:13). Its use was likewise enjoined by James as a symbol along with prayer for the sick (Jas 5:14).

Light. Oil was generally burned to produce light, as in the tabernacle (Ex 25:6; Lev 24:2). The flame was lit on a flax wick held in the spout of an oil lamp. An extra bottle of oil was sometimes carried on the wrist on a thong. This practice appears to be the background of the parable of the foolish and the wise virgins (Mt 25:8 f.; cf. Lk 12:35). *See* Lamp.

Ritual. Oil was to be mixed with flour in the daily or continual burnt offering (Ex 29:40), the meal or grain offering (Lev 2:1–10), the Nazarite's offering (Num 6:15), the leaders' dedication offerings (Num 7:13; etc.), and the guilt offering of a cleansed leper (Lev 14:10–32). It was also a part of the offering of the firstfruits (Lev 2:14–16). Oil was not to be used in the sin offering (Lev 5:11) or the offering of jealousy (Num 5:15), because oil signified joy and gladness (Ps 45:7; Heb 1:9).

Tithing. Oil was to be tithed (Deut 12:17; II Chr 31:5; Neh 10:37, 39; 13:12; Ezk 45:14).

Consecration. Oil was used in the consecration of kings and priests (Ex 29:7; I Sam 10:1; I Kgs 1:39).

Figurative. An ample supply of oil was indicative of joy and gladness (Job 29:6; Isa 61:3; Joel 2:19). Its lack signified sorrow or humiliation (Deut 28:51; Joel 1:10). In both Testaments it is used also as a symbol for consecration and the endowment with the Holy Spirit (Lev 8:12; I Sam 10:1, 6; 16:13; Isa 61:1; Lk 4:18; Acts 10:38; II Cor 1:21). " 'To suck honey out of the rock, and oil out of the flinty rock' (Deut 32:13) is a figure . . . [which] suggests the most valuable production out of the most unproductive places, since God so blessed the land that even the rocks and stones were productive" (*Unger's Bible Dict.*, p. 806).

See Anoint; Ointment; Plants: Olive.

R. A. K.

OIL, HOLY ANOINTING. The ceremony of using oil for the anointing of a person or object to be set apart for religious or civil service was very common in ancient times (e.g., Lev 8:12). However, specific instructions were given for the preparation of a special anointing oil used solely in the consecration of the priesthood and the tabernacle (Ex 30:22–33). The preparation of the first anointing oil was supervised by Bezaleel (Ex 37:1, 29). *See* Oil; Ointment; Priest, High.

OIL TREE. *See* Plants.

OINTMENT. The rendering of several different words in the original. (1) Heb. *shemen,* "oil" (II Kgs 20:13; Ps 133:2; Prov 27:9, 16; Song 1:3; 4:10; Isa 1:6; 39:2; 57:9; Amos 6:6). (2) Heb. *mirqaḥat,* "mixed compound" (Ex 30:25; I Chr 16:14; Job 41:31). (3) Gr. *myron,* "myrrh," "aromatic balm," but invariably rendered "ointment" in KJV (Mt 26:9, 12; Mk 14:3–4; Lk 7:37–38, 46; 23:56; Jn 11:2; 12:3, 5; Rev 18:13).

Unguent preparations were widely used throughout the world of the Bible. Ointment was generally compounded from several different ingredients using olive oil or olive oil and calves' oil as a base, with the addition of myrrh, nard, cassia, or other spices. Such preparation required the special skill of an apothecary or perfumer (Ex 30:25–35; 37:29; Neh 3:8; Eccl 10:1).

Ointment had several uses. *Cosmetic.* In the hot climates the problem of extreme perspiration led to a stress on special perfumes (*see* Perfume) just as deodorants are important today. Jews, Greeks, and Romans anointed the head and clothes on festive occasions (Ruth 3:3; Est 2:12; Eccl 7:1; 9:8; Prov 27:9, 16). Egyptian art shows servants placing small cones of perfumed ointment on the foreheads of guests on arrival. Ointment was extremely costly, as witnessed in the anointing of our Lord's feet by Martha's sister Mary (Mt 26:6–13; Mk 14:3–9; Jn 12:2–8; cf. Lk 7:37–38). According to Pliny, alabaster proved to make the best containers for preserving ointments. The perfume itself was very strong (Jn 12:3) and in some cases has retained its scent for over 3,000 years. (Alabaster vials exist which retain traces of the ointment contained.)

Funereal. Ointments and oil were used to anoint dead bodies and the clothing in which they were wrapped (II Chr 16:14; Mt 26:12; Mk 14:3, 8; Lk 23:56; Jn 12:3, 7; 19:40).

Medicinal. Ointments were used in medical treatment (Isa 1:6). The balm (*q.v.*) of Gilead mentioned in Jeremiah appears to have had healing properties (Jer 8:22; 46:11; 51:8), as well as the eyesalve in Rev 3:18 (cf. Jn 9:6).

Ritual. Moses was instructed in the preparation of a very special ointment for the anointing of the tabernacle, its furnishings, the ark of the testimony, and Aaron and his sons (Ex 30:22–33), and also of what appears to be a perfumed powder (Ex 30:34–38). The formula for the ointment was to be regarded as so holy that it was to be used for ritual purposes alone (v. 32), never made by any except the priests, nor placed upon any ordinary Israelite or any stranger on pain of excommunication (v. 33). *See* Anoint; Occupations: Apothecary; Oil; Perfume; Spices.

R. A. K.

OLD. *See* Elders.

OLD GATE. *See* Jerusalem: Gates and Towers 5.

OLD MAN. *See* Carnal; Flesh; New Creation.

OLD TESTAMENT. This is the first of the two major divisions of the Bible. It consists of the "holy scriptures" (II Tim 3:15) or "sacred writings" (NASB) of the Jewish people. It was written largely in Heb., with sections of Daniel and Ezra, a verse in Jeremiah, and various words elsewhere in Aramaic. The word "testament" is an unfortunate translation of the Gr. term *diathēkē* and would be better rendered "contract" or "covenant."

In the English Bible the OT appears as 39 books—from Genesis to Malachi— in the following arrangement: (1) five books of law (Genesis to Deuteronomy); (2) 12 books of history (Joshua to Esther); (3) five books of poetry (Job to Song); and (4) 17 books of prophecy (Isaiah to Malachi). The latter section is sometimes subdivided into five books of major prophets and 12 books of minor prophets. This arrangement is derived from the Latin Vulgate, which in turn was derived from the LXX.

In the Heb. Bible, however, there are three main divisions—the Law, the Prophets, and the Writings. The Law is made up of "the five books of Moses," the Pentateuch. The Prophets are composed of two subdivisions: the Former Prophets, including Joshua, Judges, Samuel, and Kings; and the Latter Prophets, comprising Isaiah, Jeremiah, Ezekiel, and the Twelve (the minor prophets). The Writings contain all the rest of the books. As counted by the Jews, the total number of books is 24, but in this enumeration the 12 minor prophets are counted as one book, and also Samuel, Kings, Chronicles, and Ezra-Nehemiah as one book each.

The old covenant was made with the Israelites at Sinai through the agency of Moses as mediator (Deut 5:1–5; Gal 3:19). The new covenant was made with Christians through Jesus Christ as mediator (Heb 8:6–13; I Tim 2:5). Thus the basic structure of the Bible hinges on the idea that God has made two main covenants with His chosen people, and that the new covenant has displaced the old for those believing in Jesus Christ.

While Christians are under a better covenant, this fact in no way invalidates the OT Scriptures. They remain part of the inspired Word of God and are "profitable for teaching, for reproof, for correction, for training in righteousness; that the man of God may be adequate, equipped for every good work" (II Tim 3:16–17, NASB). God continues to reveal Himself and to provide wisdom that leads to salvation (II Tim 3:15) through these Scriptures even today.

See Bible; Bible Manuscripts; Canon of Scripture, the OT; Covenant; Inspiration; New Testament.

N. R. L.

OLD TESTAMENT CANON. *See* Canon of Old Testament.

OLD TESTAMENT CHRONOLOGY. *See* Chronology of Old Testament.

OLIVE. *See* Plants.

OLIVE YARD. *See* Plants: Olive.

OLIVES, MOUNT OF. *See* Mount of Olives.

OLIVET. *See* Mount of Olives.

OLYMPAS (ō-lĭm′pȧs). One of the saints in Rome to whom Paul sent greetings (Rom 16:15). He may have been of the household of Philologus who is also mentioned in the greeting.

OMAR (ō′mär). The second son of Eliphaz, Esau's firstborn by his wife Adah (Gen 36:11; I Chr 1:36). He is listed as one of the chiefs of the land of Edom (Gen 36:15), and it is supposed that his name survives in Amir, an Arab tribe E of the Jordan.

OMEGA (ō-mĕg′ȧ, ō-mē′gȧ). Omega is the last letter of the Gr. alphabet as Alpha is the first. In its use metaphorically the meaning would be "the end" or "the last." The Jewish custom was to use the first and last letters of the Heb. alphabet, Aleph and Taw, as a symbol of the totality of anything. John follows this usage in Revelation when he speaks of God as "Alpha and Omega, the beginning and the ending" (Rev 1:8). The phrase is used again in Rev 21:6 with the sense that God is the beginning and ending not only of all time and all creation but of all meaning in existence. It is of extreme importance for the Christology of the NT to notice that exactly the same phrase is applied to Christ in Rev 22:13, and also the phrase "the first and the last" in Rev 1:17; 2:8; 22:13.

P. C. J.

OMER. *See* Weights, Measures, and Coins: Dry Measures.

OMNIPOTENCE. This is a theological term which refers to God's unlimited power, although the noun is not found in the English Bible. While there is no word in Heb. which exactly corresponds, in the OT *El Shaddai* or *Shaddai* (48 times) is translated Almighty God (Gen 17:1; Job 5:17; etc.). It probably means "God of the mountain(s)," mountains signifying majesty or strength, and being the place where God displays His power in great storms (Ps

29:4–6). *Yāhweh Ṣᵉbā'ôt* and *'Elōhê Ṣᵉbā'ôt* perhaps come closest to the meaning of the term, referring to the Lord of hosts or the God of hosts (Ps 24:10; Isa 2:12; 6:3, 5; 8:13; Jer 35:17; 38:17). Since in ancient times potentates were known by the ranks and numbers of their retinues and armies, it was a very suitable designation of God to the OT people.

In the NT the Gr. word *pantokratōr* is found ten times, though only once translated "omnipotent" in the KJV (Rev 19:6). It is used in the LXX to translate *Yāhweh Ṣᵉbā'ôt,* Lord of hosts. Its literal meaning is "all powerful" or "omnipotent."

God's omnipotence does not mean that He can do anything whatsoever, since His omnipotent power is governed by His will, and this in turn is governed by His character. He cannot will to do anything contrary to His character (e.g., God cannot lie, Tit 1:2, or deny Himself, II Tim 2:13). At the same time His will cannot be identified with His power. This would deny both His personality and His character.

The Scriptures speak of God's omnipotence in several ways. There is nothing too hard for Him (Gen 18:14; Jer 32:17); none can hinder His purpose (Isa 43:13); with God all things are possible (Mt 19:26; Mk 10:27; Lk 18:27). God's omnipotence is also shown indirectly in the fact that "all things are possible to him that believeth" (Mk 9:23), and, "nothing shall be impossible unto you" (Mt 17:20). Nothing can escape from His power either in nature (Isa 43:13; Dan 4:35; Amos 9:2–3; cf. Mt 10:30; Lk 12:7), or in history (Isa 10:5, 15; 28:2; 45:1; Jer 25:9; 27:6; 43:10).

A distinction should be made between God's *potentia absoluta,* His absolute direct power, e.g., when He wills and the world is created, or Christ speaks and a man is healed, or Christ walks upon the water; and God's *potentia ordinata,* when He works through secondary causes.

See God.

R. A. K.

OMNIPRESENCE. Though neither the noun omnipresence nor the adjective omnipresent are found in Scripture, the Bible presupposes God's presence everywhere. In order to guard against pantheism—the idea God is all and all is God—and so as not to confuse God and the world, it is advisable to define omnipresence by saying that everything is equally present to God and equally under His power and authority (I Kgs 8:27; II Chr 2:6; Ps 139; Isa 66:1; Acts 17:28). He is exempt from all the limitations of space, both subjectively and objectively. He is both transcendent to the world and immanent in it. Liberalism places all its stress upon the immanency of God and ignores His transcendence; neoorthodoxy stresses His transcendence to the neglect of His immanence. At the same time we must be on our guard against theories that suggest God is merely present as either will or power and thus deny Him full personality (Jer 23:24, omnipresence and omniscience; cf. Ps 139:2, 9f., 13f.; I Kgs 8:27; Isa 66:1).

The theophanic appearances do not establish the localization of God in one place to the exclusion of another, but only that He chose to reveal Himself in a particular form at a certain place. The altars and places where God dwells (Num 10:35; I Kgs 8; Jn 1:14; Col 2:9; Jn 14:23; Eph 2:21–22; Rev 21:3) do not constrict Him to particular places, but are rather appointed places of worship. This doctrine is of great comfort to the believer, since it assures him of the personal presence of God to protect him from every temptation, foe, and danger (Isa 43:2; Dan 3:25, 27).

R. A. K.

OMNISCIENCE. This term does not appear in Scripture in either its nominal or its adjectival form, yet the Bible teaches God's complete knowledge of all things. God knows to an infinite degree all that is both actual and possible. His knowledge of the actual is seen in knowing when the sparrow falls (Mt 10:29); numbering the hairs of our head (Mt 10:30); knowing the thoughts and intents of the heart (Ps 139); foretelling the future, particularly that of His people Israel (Deut 30:1–8; Isa 65–66; Mal 3:16–4:6).

God's knowledge of the possible is seen in revelations of what could have been (Isa 48:18; Mk 11:21). God's knowledge is eternal (Acts 15:18); incomprehensible (Ps 139:6; Rom 11:33); and all-wise (Ps 104:24; Eph 3:10).

The question as to whether there are time and space for God, or whether these categories or classifications exist only for finite man, has long been argued in theology. With the appearance of neoorthodoxy and its teaching that there is no time or space for God, and that therefore eternal truth, which is timeless and spaceless, cannot come directly to man but must come indirectly as myth, symbol, or saga, the issue has become acute. Suffice it to say that if there is no time or space for God, this pertains to God in His essence. Since we do not know Him thus, the question is something which does not affect His relationship to us. Further, it is unnecessary that God be timeless and spaceless. His omnipresence makes space no problem, and His omniscience removes the shackles of the problems of time.

R. A. K.

OMRI (ŏm'rī)

1. A Benjamite, son of Becher (I Chr 7:8).
2. A Judahite, son of Imri (I Chr 9:4).
3. Chief of the tribe of Issachar in the reign of David, and son of Michael (I Chr 27:18).
4. Sixth king of Israel, founder of the Omride dynasty (I Kgs 16:15–28). Omri appears first as an army commander under Elah, engaged in the siege of the Philistine city of Gibbethon. Before the siege was completed, word reached the Israelite camp that Zimri, another army officer, had assassinated Elah and claimed

the kingship. The army in the field immediately proclaimed Omri king. He at once abandoned the siege in order to move against Zimri at Tirzah. The rivalry lasted only seven days, as Zimri chose to perish by burning down his headquarters. However, another rival appeared in the person of Tibni, son of Ginath. Omri, supported by the army and the prophetic party, struggled against Tibni, who maintained much popular support for four years. The civil war was finally ended with the death of Tibni.

Omri was undoubtedly a more capable and important ruler than the biblical record indicates in its brief mention of his reign (I Kgs 16:23–28). Since his father's name is not given, while Tibni's father is recognized, he may well have been a non-Israelite who gained prominence through his military abilities. This may explain the popular support given to Tibni and the lack of recognition for Omri in Judean circles.

Among Omri's accomplishments, the strategic choice of the hill of Samaria as his capital is most obvious. This hill, purchased for two talents of silver from Shemer, was unusually well situated for easy defense. Its strategic worth is evidenced by its repeated defiance of Syrian and Assyrian invasions. It was finally captured by Sargon in 721 B.C., but only after a three-year siege.

Omri demonstrated strong leadership abroad as well as at home. Although he lost ground to the Syrians during the days of civil strife at the beginning of his reign, he recouped these losses in other areas. He developed extensive trade with neighboring nations and saw Samaria become an important part of the caravan routes. His alliance with the Phoenicians made many economic advantages possible. Although the marriage of his son Ahab to Jezebel was to bring disastrous results later, new areas of trade and foreign contacts strengthened Israel for the moment. Omri was able to subdue Moab and exact heavy tribute from her inhabitants. Details of this are given in the famous Moabite Stone (*q.v.*) which was set up in commemoration of Moab's later deliverance in the days of Ahab. The Assyrian records further attest the importance of Omri's reign, referring to Israel as the "Land of the House of Omri" for the next 100 years. Omri was thus responsible for placing Israel on the world map. *See* Samaria.

Although Omri added great wealth and prestige to Israel, he failed to build on strong spiritual foundations. The later Judean evaluation of his reign stated that he "dealt wickedly above all that were before him" (I Kgs 16:25–26, ASV). Ostraca discovered in Samaria bear testimony of his syncretism and apostasy by the use of the names of both Baal and Yahweh.

K. M. Y.

ON (on)

1. The son of Peleth, who joined the rebellion of Korah against Moses (Num 16:1).

Part of the unfinished palace of Omri, which he started at Tirzah before moving to Samaria.
HFV

2. The Egyptian city of On, known to the Greeks as Heliopolis. It was located at the present site of Matariyeh, a suburb to the NE of Cairo. Though important as a religious center, On never achieved political prominence. The city was noted for its worship of the sun, associated with the gods Re-Harakhte, Atum, and Khepri, and represented by the phoenix and the Mnevis bull. Re became important from the Fifth Dynasty on; from that time the name of the god was made part of the titulary of the king, "son of Re" being one of the five royal titles. The theology of On later influenced the doctrines of Atonism. On seems to have been called Per-Atum, "the House of Atum," and hence may be the Pithom (*q.v.*) of Ex 1:11 (Eric P. Uphill, "Pithom and Raamses: Their Location and Significance," JNES, XXVII [1968], 292–299; XXVIII [1969], 32–39). *See* Egypt; Exodus, The.

Joseph married Asenath, an Egyptian woman whose father was the priest of On (Gen 41:45, 50; 46:20). Because of its connection with sun-worship, On is referred to in Jer 43:13 as "Beth-shemesh, that is in the land of Egypt" (KJV). The RSV here reads, "Heliopolis," whose meaning, "city of the sun," approximates the Heb. Beth-shemesh, "house of the sun." The passage states that Nebuchadnezzar "shall break the obelisks of Heliopolis" (RSV). Obelisks were emblems of sun-worship and a sole obelisk, erected by Sesostris I (1971–1928 B.C.), is the only remnant at On testifying to the ancient religious importance of the city.

In Ezk 30:17 a prophecy against Egypt pronounces that the young men of On shall fall by the sword and that captivity shall befall the survivors. Here the Masoretic Text reads *'āwen,* "idolatry," for *'ôn*. The KJV gives Aven, but the margin says "Heliopolis or On"; the ASV and RSV read "On." There is a possibility that On was also intended in Isa 19:18, where it is said that a city in Egypt will be called Ir-haheres (*q.v.*). The Heb. text as it stands is translated in the KJV "the city of destruction" (*q.v.*); reading *ḥeth* for *he,* as is often suggested here, gives in the RSV "the city of the sun," equivalent to Heliopolis. In later times the Gr. historian Herodotus reported that the priests of Heliopolis were said to be the most learned Egyptian antiquarians (II, 3).

A local tradition makes Heliopolis a stopping place for the Holy Family at the time of the flight from Bethlehem. A sycamore tree called the Tree of the Virgin is the magical resort of women who hope to obtain fertility. Nearby is a well whose sweet water contrasts with the brackish quality of other wells in the vicinity. Tradition attributes this distinction to an early miracle of the infant Jesus.

C. E. D.

ONAGER or HALF ASS. *See* Animals, II. 29.

ONAM (ō'nȧm)

1. One of five sons of Shobal, a son of Seir the Horite (Gen 36:23, 20; I Chr 1:40, 38).

2. Son of Jerahmeel of the tribe of Judah by his second wife Atarah; father of Shammai and Jada (I Chr 2:26, 28; cf. 2:25, 3-5).

ONAN (ō'nȧn). The second son of Judah whom the daughter of Shua, a Canaanite, bore to him (Gen 38:2-4; I Chr 2:3). Onan, by practicing *coitus interruptus* (whence the term "onanism") thereby refusing to enter into a proper levirate marriage relationship with his dead brother's widow, was thereafter slain by the Lord (Gen 38:6-10) in the land of Canaan (Gen 46:12; Num 26:19). *See* Marriage.

ONESIMUS (ō-nĕs'ĭ-mŭs). He was Philemon's runaway slave in whose behalf Paul wrote the epistle to Philemon. Col 4:9 connects him with Colosse. Escaping from his master, perhaps having also robbed him, Onesimus fled to Rome, hoping to escape detection amid its teeming population. He there somehow met Paul, through him was converted, and proved himself "profitable" and dear to Paul. Refusing to retain his services without his master's knowledge and consent, Paul returned Onesimus under the protection of Tychicus (Col 4:7-9), sending along also his masterly epistolary plea for his spiritual child. That Philemon granted Paul's plea need not be doubted.

See Philemon, Epistle to.

ONESIPHORUS (ŏn'ē-sĭf'ō-rŭs). A Christian friend from Ephesus who not only ministered to the apostle Paul there but, while he was in Rome during Paul's second imprisonment, sought him out and cared for him (II Tim 1:16-18). In Paul's second epistle to Timothy, Onesiphorus is one of the recipients of Paul's greetings (II Tim 4:19).

ONION. *See* Foods; Plants.

ONLY BEGOTTEN. Gr. *monogenēs* means "single of its kind," "only," "unique," "only begotten" (KJV). This term is used of an only child in the NT (Lk 7:12; 8:42; 9:38; Heb 11:17). It is used of Christ in the sense that He is the only Son of God (Jn 1:14, 18; 3:16, 18; I Jn 4:9). The root of the Gr. word, careful lexigraphical experts now see, is not *gennaō*, "to beget or generate," but *genos*, and therefore its meaning is "the only one of its kind" rather than the only one born. The orthodox defenders of the faith against Arius at the Council of Nicea appear not to have grasped this, and therefore argued from Christ's eternal existence rather than from what the word signifies, namely, His unique existence always as the Son. The light thrown on the controversy when it is seen the word comes from *genos*, raises the question as to whether it is necessary any longer to teach the difficult doctrine of eternal generation (see J. O. Buswell, Jr., *Systematic Theology*, I, 110-111).

Bibliography. F. Buchsel, "*Monogenēs*," TDNT, IV, 737-741.

R. A. K.

A limestone pedestal urn of the Herodian period from Ophel. Palestine Archaeological Museum

ONO (ō'nō). A city rebuilt along with Lod (Lydda) by Shamed a Benjamite (I Chr 8:12). The fact that its name appears as *'Unu* or *'Inw* in the Karnak records of Thutmose III shows that Ono was founded before the settlement of the tribes in Joshua's time. After the Exile its Jewish inhabitants, together with those of Lod and Hadid, numbered about 725 persons (Ezr 2:33; Neh 7:37). The valley in which the city was located was known as "the plain of Ono." It was here that Sanballat and Geshem tried to inveigle Nehemiah into a conference (Neh 6:2). It is probably the same as "the valley of craftsmen" (Neh 11:35). It is generally identified with modern Kefr 'Ana, which lies NW of Lydda.

ONYCHA. *See* Animals, V. 9; Plants.

ONYX. *See* Jewels.

OPAL. *See* Jewels.

OPHEL (ō'fĕl). As a proper name the term is translated "hill" (Isa 32:14, RSV), "forts" (Isa 32:14, KJV), or "stronghold" (Mic 4:8). Sometimes it is a common name and other times a proper name, as it should be with regard to a district in the capital city of Samaria (II Kgs 5:24).

The name is frequently associated with a section of ancient Jerusalem fortified by the early kings. It appears to have been the high ground on the eastern hill located to the N of the primitive city of David and just to the S of the present walled city of Jerusalem (S of the temple area). King Jotham fortified it (II Chr 27:3), as did Manasseh (II Chr 33:14). Later it became the residence for servants of the temple (Neh 11:21).

OPHIR (ō'fĩr)

1. A descendant of Shem through Eber and Joktan (Gen 10:29; I Chr 1:23).

2. The territory occupied by the descendants of Ophir was located in the SW Arabian peninsula or in neighboring Somaliland in Africa, just across the narrow Gulf of Aden. India and Africa have also been suggested as possible locations. Jerome and Josephus apparently located it in India (Jos *Ant.* viii. 6.4). It was probably a way station for ships of Solomon trading between India and the Israel seaport of Ezion-geber (I Kgs 9:26-28). There are many references to the fine gold that comes from this area (I Kgs 9:28; Job 22:24; 28:16; Ps 45:9; Isa 13:12). The only non-biblical reference to Ophir is on a sherd found at Tell Qasileh N of Jaffa. The 8th cen. B.C. inscription reads, "Gold of Ophir for Beth-horon, thirty shekels." Other products of this area were almug trees, silver, precious stones, ivory, monkeys, and similar oriental luxuries. *See* Gold.

G. A. T.

OPHNI (ŏf'nī). One of the cities numbered among the 12 given to the tribe of Benjamin by Joshua (Josh 18:24). General agreement identifies this town with modern Jifna, or Jufna, two and one-half miles NW of Bethel off the Nablus road.

OPHRAH (ŏf'ra̍)

1. A town in Benjamin (Josh 18:23) once exposed to Philistine raiding parties (I Sam 13:17-18). It is probably to be identified with the modern et-Taiyibeh, five miles N of Michmash and four miles E of Bethel (Beitin). *See* Ephraim, City of.

2. The hometown of Gideon (Jud 6:11, 24; 8:27, 32) of the clan of Abiezer, located in the territory of Manasseh, probably at the S edge of the plain of Esdraelon, at the foot of Mount Gilboa. Gideon received his call, built an altar to Yahweh, lapsed into idolatry (Jud 8:27), and was buried here (Jud 8:32).

3. A son of Meonothai of the tribe of Judah (I Chr 4:14), a descendant of Kenaz and Othniel.

ORACLE. In itself an oracle was a divine message, often given to man through a prophet as an answer to man's request. The Heb. word *neʼum,* literally, "the utterance, declaration of," is employed hundreds of times to designate such messages (e.g., Gen 22:16; Isa 14:22; 49:18; 54:17; 56:8). In II Sam 16:23 the KJV translates the Heb. *dābār* as "oracle." Here the oracle of God is the place or person where the Word of God is to be heard, but the passage says nothing about how the oracle was made known to man. It is supposed that in some cases the Urim and the Thummim were employed (*see* Urim). In a number of passages (cf. Jer 23:33-40, NASB), particularly in headings such as Isa 13:1; 14:28; Hab 1:1, "oracle" is accepted in nearly all English versions since 1950 as a translation of the Heb. *maśśā'*, rendered "burden" in the KJV. In such passages, however, the rendering "burden" is still preferred by some recent scholars.

In the KJV the term "oracle" is also used 16 times to translate the Heb. *debîr,* which term designated the most holy place in Solomon's temple (I Kgs 6:5, 16, 19-23; etc.). In some temples of antiquity the inner shrine or chamber was the place where the oracles were delivered. But the translation "oracle" rests upon an incorrect etymology, for the word *debîr* is not immediately connected with *dibber,* "to speak," but rather with a root signifying "to be behind

Theater at Delphi and Temple of Apollo which was the center of the famous oracle of Delphi.
HFV

or beyond." The error in translation was caused by following the rendering of Aquila, Symmachus, and the Vulgate. The most holy place of the temple, however, was not a place where oracles were delivered.

Heathen oracles abounded in Palestine and were a snare to trap and deceive God's people. King Ahaziah sent from Samaria to inquire of the god of Ekron whether he would recover from his disease (II Kgs 1:2). Other oracular means were the ephod of Gideon (Jud 8:27), the ephod and the teraphim or silver idols in the shrine of Micah (Jud 17:4–5), and the wooden and stone idols consulted by Israel and Judah (Hos 4:12; Hab 2:19).

In the NT the Gr. *ta logia* is translated consistently, "the oracles" (four times), and each instance refers to utterances of God (Acts 7:38; Rom 3:2; Heb 5:12; I Pet 4:11). The oracles were from God, and bore His absolute authority; hence, they required implicit obedience upon the part of man.

See Prophecy; Prophet.

E. J. Y

ORATION. *See* Orator.

ORATOR

1. Found once in the OT (Isa 3:3) as a rendering in the KJV of the Heb. *laḥash* ("a whispering," "charming") which is more appropriately rendered by the ASV as "enchanter."

2. The translation in Acts 24:1 by the KJV, ASV, NASB marg. and Berkeley of the Gr. *rhētōr* (RSV "spokesman," NEB "advocate," NASB "attorney"). The term literally means a public speaker, or orator, one using a special style and accomplished in presentation. In Acts 24:1 it indicates the professional speaker in a court, i.e., Tertullus, who acted as the advocate of the Jewish persecutors of Paul before Felix (for this usage see MM and Arndt). Paul specifically refused to use the style and technique of the orator (cf. I Cor 2:1, 4, 5).

3. The KJV, ASV and RSV use the word "oration" in Acts 12:21 to indicate the public address Herod made to the people. The Gr. verb *dēmēgoreō,* here only in the NT, means "to speak to an assembly" (probably from *dēmos,* "people," *agoreuō,* "harangue").

G. W. K.

ORCHARD. *See* Plants.

ORDAIN. This term means to invest with ministerial or sacerdotal functions (Ex 28:41; 29:9, 33, 35); to introduce into the office of the Christian ministry by the laying on of hands (*q.v.*) or by some other form; to set apart by the rite or ceremony of ordination (*q.v.*). The word also means to establish, order, constitute, appoint, enact.

Again, it is used of the decrees and counsels of God as a synonym of "to predestinate" or "to destine." Jesus Christ was ordained by God to be the Judge of the living and the dead (Acts 10:42). Those ordained to eternal life in Antioch believed because of Paul's sermon (Acts 13:48). God ordained victories for Jacob (Ps 44:4, RSV), for what He ordains comes to pass (Lam 2:17; 3:37). Paul states that the law was ordained by angels through a mediator (Gal 3:19) in order to point up his emphasis on salvation by grace alone. Peace is ordained for those who put their trust in God, knowing that God works their good works in them (Isa 26:12).

C. S. M.

ORDINANCE. Six Heb. words are translated "ordinance," the most important of which are: *ḥuqqâ,* "statute," "decree" (Ex 12:14, 17, 43; Lev 18:3; Ezk 43:11; etc.); *mishpāt,* "judgment" (Ex 15:25; I Sam 30:25; Ps 119:91; etc.); *ḥōq,* "statute," "decree" (Ex 12:24; 18:20; Ps 99:7; Mal 3:7; etc.).

Five Gr. words are used: *diatagē,* "precise arrangement" (Rom 13:2); *dikaiōma,* "a judicial requirement" (Lk 1:6; Heb 9:1, 10); *dogma,* "dogma," "declaration," "edict" (Eph 2:15; Col 2:14); *ktisis,* "a legal institution," "a judgment that is made" (I Pet 2:13); *paradosis,* "a tradition which has been handed down" (I Cor 11:2).

There are several different kinds of ordinances.

1. A decree or regulation, such as a statute and an ordinance made by Moses at Marah (Ex 15:25); the ordinance of the Passover (Num 9:14); the ordinance proclaimed by the priests' trumpets (Num 10:8); the ordinance regarding the stranger (Num 15:15); the ordinance granting priests charge of offerings and hallowed things (Num 18:8); an ordinance proclaimed by David (I Sam 30:25); general reference to the ordinances or requirements of God (Isa 58:2; Lk 1:6); government designated as an ordinance of God (Rom 13:2); the laws of nature regulating natural phenomena (Job 38:33; Jer 31:35); human laws as ordinances of man to be obeyed (I Pet 2:13).

2. A religious rite, specifically the Passover (Ex 12:24, 43; 13:10; Num 9:14).

3. In plural the term in certain passages refers to the legal commandments and the ceremonial regulations which were done away with for the believer by the coming of Christ (Eph 2:15; Col 2:14, 20 [cf. vv. 14–23]; Heb 9:1, 10 [cf. vv. 1–12]).

4. In post-biblical times the term is used of institutions of divine authority found in the church: baptism (*q.v.*) and the Lord's Supper (*q.v.*); and in some denominations the office of the public ministry, hearing the Word, prayer with fellow believers, and praise and thanksgiving.

See Law; Law of Moses; Sacrament.

R. A. K. and C. S. M.

ORDINATION. The act whereby sacred office is conferred. In the OT priests were ordained by laying on of hands (Ex 28:41; 29:9, 33;

Num 3:3); the ceremony was solemnized with the sacrifice of a ram (Ex 29:22–34; Lev 8:22–33). Ordination in the NT, likewise symbolized by the laying on of hands, was conferred on deacons (Acts 6:6), elders (Acts 14:23), and missionaries (Acts 13:3).

In the Roman Catholic church it is regarded "truly and properly a sacrament, instituted by Christ the Lord" (Council of Trent, sess. VII, Can. 9). Ordinarily ordination is performed only by a bishop, who says: "Receive the Holy Ghost."

John Calvin condemned "the ceremony itself" (*Institutes,* IV, xix, 29), but if divested of its abuses ("provided it be not turned to superstitious abuse"), beneficial for the dignity of the office, a warning to the one ordained "that he is no longer a law unto himself, but bound in servitude to God and the church" (*Institutes,* IV, iii, 16). He cited with approval the decree of the Council of Nicea which called for ordination by all the neighboring bishops (*Institutes,* IV, iv, 14). In the calling and election of ministers, ordination should be used, according to the Second Helvetic Confession (Chap. XVIII); it adds: "We do here, therefore, condemn all those who run of their own accord, being neither chosen, sent, nor ordained."

The Lutheran Apology of the Augsburg Confession (Art. XIII) permits the designation "sacrament" for the rite of ordination, "if ordination is interpreted in relation to the ministry of the Word." The Smalcald Articles (Pt. III, Art. X) invoke the example of the ancient churches and the Fathers for ordaining suitable persons. In the "Treatise on the Power and Primacy of the Pope," the assertion that the bishop of Rome has the ultimate right to ordain is denied. It is not ordination by a bishop, it declared, that makes a valid ordination; ordination is the confirmation of the election to the ministerial office. The Lutheran Confessions do not speak of any apostolic succession through ordination.

The Anglican communion makes much of ordination and many among them of apostolic succession. Free churches, Anabaptist, Pentecostal, and other groups minimize ordination, frequently making it only a ceremony of "laying on of hands."

C. S. M.

OREB (ôr'ĕb). One of two Midianite princes (*see* Zeeb) beheaded by men of Ephraim in Gideon's army (Jud 7:25) near the Jordan. Isa 10:26 calls this the "slaughter of Midian at the rock of Oreb." Gideon was of the tribe of Manasseh. Manasseh and Ephraim were both sons of Joseph. When the men of Ephraim later found fault with Gideon because he had not called them to the earlier battle, their anger was abated when he replied, "God hath delivered into your hands the princes of Midian, Oreb and Zeeb: and what was I able to do in comparison of you?" (Jud 8:3).

OREB, ROCK OF. The place where Gideon's army cut off the head of the Midianite prince Oreb (Jud 7:25; Isa 10:26) and brought it to Gideon. The exact location is a matter of debate but it is somewhere near the Jordan. *See* Oreb.

OREN (ôr'ĕn). The third mentioned son of Jerahmeel, the firstborn of Hezron of the tribe of Judah (I Chr 2:25).

ORGAN. *See* Music.

ORIGINAL SIN. *See* Fallen Man.

ORION (ō-rī'ŏn). An outstanding southern constellation near the equator early imagined to resemble the form of a hunter. In ancient mythology Orion the hunter was killed by the goddess Diana and placed in the sky as a constellation. He is imagined to be standing braced for an attack by Taurus (the Bull), the neighboring constellation which contains the Pleiades.

Four of the seven most prominent stars form a huge quadrangle; the other three bright stars lie in a diagonal line in about the center and are referred to as a belt or bands. The giant red Betelgeuse forms the top-left corner of the quadrangle and Rigel, a blue-white star of first magnitude, the bottom right.

Translators modern and ancient (e.g., LXX has *ho orion* at Isa 13:10 and Job 38:31; Jerome *Orion* at Amos 5:8; Job 9:9) have correctly taken the Heb. singular form *k^esîl* to

Persians portrayed on the stairway of the palace of Darius at Persepolis, showing bracelets, armbands, and a gold neckband. ORINST

refer to this constellation at Job 9:9; 38:31; Amos 5:8. This identification is evidenced by the context which refers to the heavens and also in each case refers to the nearby constellation, the Pleiades (Heb. *kîmāh*). The plural form occurs in Isa 13:10 and probably indicates Orion and other constellations. *See* Astronomy; Pleiades; Star.

G. W. K.

ORNAMENT. According to Occidental taste, Orientals generally adorn themselves excessively. With the exception of those in the poorest class, men wore seal rings (Gen 38:18; *et al.*), which were also useful in business, or a gold chain around their neck (Gen 41:42). Some Oriental men wore earrings (Jud 8:24). A greater variety of ornaments was to be found among the women. Beads, pearls, articles of gold, silver, and brass represent the types of materials worn (Song 1:10–11; I Tim 2:9). Earrings, nose rings, pendants, necklaces, chains, brazen mirrors, armlets, bracelets, finger rings, and anklets are representative articles generally worn (Gen 24:22, 47; 35:4; Ex 35:22; Num 31:50; Isa 3:18–23; *et al.*). Ornaments were laid aside during times of mourning (Ex 33:4–6). *See* Amulet; Dress; Jewels.

ORNAN (ôr'năn). Another name for Araunah (*q.v.*; II Sam 24:16), a Jebusite prince who owned the threshing floor on Mount Moriah which David purchased for the erection of an altar to Jehovah (I Chr 21:15–28), and upon which Solomon later erected the temple (II Chr 3:1).

The Orontes River at flood stage in the center of Antioch of Syria.

ORONTES (ō-rŏn'tēz). The largest river in W Syria. It rises in the Biqa' Valley between the Lebanon and Anti-Lebanon Mountains, flows N for approximately 250 miles, and then turns W, emptying into the Mediterranean Sea at the site of Seleucia, the port city of ancient Antioch (modern Antakya). Barnabas and Saul (Paul) must have walked along its bank as they began the first missionary journey (Acts 13:1, 4). The Orontes was too shallow to be navigable, but the valley in which it cut through the mountain range E of Antioch became a highway for the caravans that plied between Antioch and the hinterland of Asia Minor on the way to the Far East.

Three important cities of the OT period, Riblah, Hamath, and Kadesh, stood by the Orontes. Riblah was the scene of Pharaoh-necho's defeat of Jehoahaz II of Judah, whom he took captive (II Kgs 23:33–35), and of Nebuchadnezzar's deposition of Zedekiah (II Kgs 25:6–7). Hamath was the northernmost city of Israel at the height of its prosperity (I Kgs 8:65). Kadesh was the site of an historic battle between the Egyptians under Rameses II and the Hittites *c.* 1297 B.C. The Egyptian advance was halted, but the two nations signed a non-aggression treaty afterward, and agreed to respect each other's territory (ANET, pp. 255–258, 199–203).

See Antioch 1; Lebanon; Syria.

M. C. T.

ORPAH (ôr'pȧ). A Moabitess, wife of Chilion, son of Elimelech and Naomi (Ruth 1:4). Unlike her sister-in-law Ruth, when Naomi decided to return to Bethlehem after the death of her husband and two sons, Orpah gave Naomi the farewell kiss and returned to her people and unto her gods (Ruth 1:14–15).

ORPHAN. Heb. *yātôm* is translated "orphan" once in Lam 5:3, but elsewhere in the KJV "fatherless" (Ex 22:22; Isa 9:17; Jer 49:11). This Heb. word (Gr. *orphanos*) and the Gr. verb *aporphanizō* are used figuratively of one without a teacher, guide, or guardian (Hos 14:3, NASB; Jn 14:18; I Thess 2:17).

God expresses great concern for those bereft of their immediate relatives, such as the fatherless and widows. The care of the fatherless is particularly enjoined in the first promulgation of the law of Moses, the covenant code (Ex 22:22), and the second, the Deuteronomic code (Deut 16:11, 14; 24:17). A part of the tithe was to be devoted to their support (Deut 26:12) and their inheritance rights protected. God is concerned for them (Ps 10:14, 18; 68:5; 146:9; Hos 14:3; cf. Jn 14:18), promises His aid to them (Ex 22:23; Deut 10:18), and condemns those who oppress them (Deut 27:19; Mal 3:5). That the Israelites failed in their duty to them is attested by the cry of the prophets (Job 24:3, 9; Ps 94:6; Isa 1:23; 10:2; Jer 5:28).

R. A. K.

OSEE (ō'zē). The Gr. name of the prophet Hosea (Rom 9:25). *See* Hosea.

OSHEA. *See* Joshua.

OSNAPPER. *See* Asnapper; Ashurbanipal.

OSPREY. *See* Animals: Vulture, Black, III. 52.

OSSIFRAGE. *See* Animals: Lammergeier, III. 27.

OSSUARY. *See* Burial.

OSTIA (ŏs'tĭ-ă). Ostia was the seaport for the city of Rome. Like many of the great cities of ancient times, Rome was not on the coast but upriver some 14 miles from Ostia. It was into this port that the wealth of the world was poured as tribute to sovereign Rome. When the ancient port was excavated in 1914–16, a vast amount of material illustrating the life of the first Christian centuries was brought to light From Ostia to Rome ran the famous Ostian Way, and according to strong Christian tradition it was on this way, a mile or so from Rome, that Paul was brought out to die and there was buried. *See* Paul; Rome.

A view across the ruins of ancient Ostia. HFV

OSTRACA. The plural of the Gr. word *ostrakon,* a broken piece of pottery. Pottery fragments or potsherds were widely employed in the ancient world for writing purposes. As a writing surface, they were much less expensive than papyrus sheets and were often used by the poor for letters, receipts, accounts, etc. Potsherds are mentioned in the Scriptures (Job 2:8; Ps 22:15; Isa 30:14), but not as writing materials.

Thousands of ostraca have been unearthed in Egypt and in Palestine, some of which have considerable significance for the OT period. From the royal palace at Samaria (*q.v.*) 75 ostraca, dealing with supplies of oil and wine, have been excavated, and are dated from the time of Jeroboam II (*c.* 770 B.C.). From the town of Lachish (*q.v.*) have come 21 ostraca; they are dated *c.* 589 B.C. and thus would be contemporary with the prophet Jeremiah. Jewish archaeologists have found more than 50 ostraca at Arad (*q.v.*), a border fortress in the Negeb. Ten or so are from the 4th cen. B.C., the remainder are pre-Exilic. Excavations at Hazor yielded a few from the 8th cen. B.C., and one was discovered in the Ophel area of Jerusalem. The inscribed potsherds from these sites are important because of the welcome light they cast on the Heb. language and writing style in that time. A number of ostraca also have been recovered in Egypt that relate to NT research. The most noteworthy of these contain lines of the Gospel texts, attesting the interest of the common man in Holy Scripture.

N. R. L.

OSTRICH. *See* Animals, III. 34.

OTHNI (ŏth'nī). One of the sons of Shemaiah, a Korahite Levite, and gatekeeper of the tabernacle in the days of King David (I Chr 26:7).

OTHNIEL (ŏth'nĭ-ĕl). A son of Kenaz, and either a younger brother or a nephew of Caleb (Josh 15:17; Jud 1:13; 3:9; I Chr 4:13). Othniel earned the hand of Caleb's daughter Achsah in marriage by capturing Kirjath-sepher (*q.v.* ; Josh 15:15–17; Jud 1:11–13). The Lord used him to deliver the Israelites from the eight-year oppression of Cushan-rishathaim, and his leadership and spiritual influence continued to give a measure of civil peace to the Israelites for 40 more years (Jud 3:8–11). Therefore Othniel is considered the first of the "judges" (*see* Judge). According to the early date of the Exodus (*c.* 1446 B.C.) Othniel's judgeship may be dated *c.* 1375–1335 B.C. It is quite probable that he is the Othniel whose descendant is mentioned as a captain during the reign of David (I Chr 27:15).

OUCHES. Settings or holders for precious stones (Ex 28:11, 13–14, 25; 39:6, 13, 16, 18). These settings in the ephod for Aaron were not solid fillings but were made by interweaving thin wires of beaten gold (cf. Ex 39:2–3) into a lacy mesh or netlike pouch which might then be threaded into the cloth of the ephod.

OUTCASTS. The word is sometimes used of heathen nations (Jer 49:36), but most frequently of Israel and God's rejection of her in the figurative sense of a wife put away by her husband (Jer 30:17; cf. Isa 62:4); of Israel as scattered among the nations (Isa 11:12; Ps 147:2); and of her regathering when Christ returns at the second coming (Isa 27:13; Mic 4:6; Zeph 3:19). In the NT Paul considers Israel's position as an outcast under the figure of the natural branches broken off the good olive tree. While converted Gentiles have been grafted into their place and benefited thereby, Israel will be regrafted in (Rom 11:15–24) and will all be saved at the second coming of Christ, because "the gifts and calling of God are without repentance" (vv. 25–29).

OUTLANDISH. The common Heb. word for "foreign" or "strange person" is translated "outlandish" in Neh 13:26 and "strange" in 13:27. The word "outlandish" has the meaning of an "out-lander," a person who is of another country.

OUTRAGEOUS. In the KJV the Eng. word carries the sense of "going beyond the ordinary" (Prov 27:4). The idea expressed by the Heb.

word for flood is that anger is as destructive and uncontrollable as a flood. The ASV "anger is overwhelming" is a more precise translation.

OVEN. A hot-air chamber or small furnace for the baking of bread (Lev 2:4; 26:26). In Egyptian and Assyrian pictorial representations it was a round pottery structure two or three feet in diameter with a layer of pebbles in the bottom on which a fire was built. Beehive shape ovens with a side opening for fuel or for putting in the bread also have been found. The oven was heated with thorns, grass (Mt 6:30), or dung mixed with straw. When the oven was sufficiently heated, the ashes were scooped out and the dough either stuck to the sides or laid on the pebbles to bake.

Such heating processes would blacken the interior of the oven (Lam 5:10). The hot oven (Hos 7:4, 6-7) denotes the readiness of those mentioned to pursue their evil ways, just as the hot oven is ready for the bread dough. The destructive or consumptive power of God is symbolized by the oven (Mal 4:1).

The Tower of the Ovens (Neh 3:11; 12:38, RSV) was the tower in Jerusalem near which the public bakers did their bread baking. Ovens are found in houses on floors or on platforms, in the yard, or grouped in some corner of the village.

H. G. S.

A fishmonger's shop in ancient Ostia, Italy. A tank for fresh fish appears in the center and an oven for baking fish at right. HFV

OVERSEER. A person who superintends a household, such as Joseph (Gen 39:4-5); a superintendent or foreman of workmen (II Chr 2:18; 34:12-13, 17); of the Levites (Neh 11:22); of the singers (Neh 12:42). The use of the NT term *episkopos* in this sense (Acts 20:28) is to be distinguished from its more technical use for an elder in such passages as Phil 1:1; I Tim 3:2; Tit 1:7; I Pet 2:25. *See* Bishop.

OVERSHADOW. The Gr. *episkiazō* basically refers to a cloud casting a shadow. It is used in the NT of a man's shadow (Acts 5:15); to express the presence of the glory of God at the transfiguration of Christ (Mt 17:5; cf. Mk 9:7; Lk 9:34); and of the presence and power of the Holy Spirit at the miraculous virgin conception (Lk 1:35).

OWL. *See* Animals, III. 35-38; Night Monster.

OX. *See* Animals: Cattle, I. 6.

OX GOAD. *See* Goad.

OX, WILD, or UNICORN. *See* Animals, II. 30.

OYSTER, PEARL. *See* Animals, V. 10.

OZEM (ō'zĕm)

1. The sixth son of Jesse the Bethlehemite (I Chr 2:15).

2. The fourth named son of Jerahmeel (I Chr 2:25).

OZIAS (ō-zī'ȧs). The name of a king of Judah (Mt 1:8-9). Ozias is the Gr. equivalent of Uzziah (cf. Isa 1:1, LXX). *See* Uzziah.

OZNI (ŏz'nī), **OZNITES** (ŏz'nīts). Ozni was one of the sons of Gad (Num 26:16), also called Ezbon (Gen 46:16). He was the eponymous ancestor of the "family of the Oznites."

P

PAARAI (pā'ȧ-rī). The name of one of David's 37 mighty men (II Sam 23:35, 39). In I Chr 11:37 his name is given as Naarai (*q.v.*).

PACE. *See* Weights, Measures, and Coins: Linear Measure.

PADAN (pā'dȧn). An abbreviation (Gen 48:7) for the country of Padan-aram (*q.v.*).

PADAN-ARAM (pā'dȧn-âr'ȧm). It is a region which lies largely E and N of the upper Euphrates River as it flows S and then turns E. The district lies opposite the NE corner of the Mediterranean Sea, E of the Orontes River. Haran, its chief city, was the home of Abraham from which he emigrated to Canaan. He sent a servant to Padan-aram (also called Mesopotamia or Aram-naharaim, Gen 24:10) to obtain a wife for Isaac (Gen 25:20). Jacob fled there from the anger of Esau (Gen 28:2, 5). He married his cousins Rachel and Leah and, after prospering, returned to Canaan (Gen 31:18; 35:9, 26; 46:15; 48:7). The language spoken there was Aramaic (Gen 31:47) and the inhabitants, Arameans (Gen 25:20; 28:5; 31:24; Deut 26:5). *See* Mesopotamia; Aram.

PADDLE. A sharp implement with which one might loosen enough earth so as to cover personal human excrement for sanitary purposes (Deut 23:13).

PADON (pā'dŏn). One of the Nethinim whose descendants returned from Babylon under the leadership of Zerubbabel (Ezr 2:44; Neh 7:47).

PAGIEL (pā̆'gĭ-ĕl). A son of Ocran who was chosen head of the tribe of Asher to take a census of that tribe's fighting men in the days of Moses (Num 1:13; 2:27; 7:72–77; 10:26).

PAHATH-MOAB (pā̆'hăth-mō'ăb)

1. The ancestral head of a large family, many of whose members returned from Babylon (Ezr 2:6; 8:4; Neh 7:11). One of them helped rebuild the wall of Jerusalem (Neh 3:11), and a number of them had married foreign wives (Ezr 10:30). Pahath-moab is a title meaning "governor of Moab," suggesting that he had been an officer or governor in Moab, perhaps in the reign of David when Israel ruled Moab (cf. II Sam 8:2).

2. A man who set his seal to the renewal of the covenant, evidently representing the clan of Pahath-moab 1.

PAI. *See* Pau.

PAIN. *See* Sorrow.

PAINTING. No examples of painting on walls by the ancient Hebrews have been referred to in the Bible or discovered by archaeologists. Paintings of this kind were common, however, in the temples and palaces of Egyptians, Amorites, and Assyrians. Lack of evidence indicating anything of this kind in Israel appears to point to significant differences in faith and culture.

Abraham at Ur and possibly while stopping at Mari on the way to Haran had opportunity to observe wall paintings. Israelites saw many such murals in Egypt. Moses had been educated in the associations of painted figures and symbols with religion, life, and government (Acts 7:22).

The Hebrews certainly possessed the pigments for painting, for their perfumers were artists in making cosmetics out of them. Men like Bezaleel produced many representative figures, such as cherubim from wood, cloth, gold, silver, and bronze for adornment of the tabernacle, the temple, and the palaces of their kings. They did not lack, therefore, artistic taste

The priest-king, a fresco painting from the palace at Knossos, Crete, dating c. 1500 B.C. HFV

or talent. They also turned at times to their neighbors for material such as the cedars of Lebanon and for aid from experienced artisans like those sent by Hiram of Tyre when Solomon appealed for cooperation in building the temple.

The Heb. artisans learned much from their neighbors, as may be detected in the architecture and pottery of the period of the Israelite monarchies. In Level V at Ramat Raḥel (biblical Beth-haccerem, Jer 6:1) a painted jar fragment in black and red was found. It depicts a bearded king seated on his throne. It may be dated to the time of King Jehoiakim, who built a new and luxurious palace with cedar paneling and bright red painted walls (Jer 22:13-15, NASB; BA, XXIV [1961], 107-108, 118).

Then why were there so few painters like those who produced the remarkable figures seen on the walls of temples and palaces of Egypt, Mesopotamia, and Syria? The second commandment appears to furnish the clue. Prohibition of the making of "any likeness of anything that is in heaven . . . or . . . earth . . . or in the water . . ." (Ex 20:4) did not condemn art, but it did condemn the worship of objects of art. Images and pictures as used in idolatrous places generally not only blasphemed God but seduced the people by association with sacred prostitution in the temples and by morally corrupt influences of many kinds (Ezk 8:10; 23:14-17).

See Occupations: Painting.

J. W. W.

PAINTING THE EYES. *See* Eyes, Painting of the.

PALACE. The translation in KJV of a number of words in the original, some rendered differently in RSV and NASB.

1. Heb. *'appeden*. A loan-word: Old Persian *apa-dāna*, Akkad. *appadân*, "treasury, armory." This word appears only in Dan 11:45 concerning the apocalyptic "king of the north":

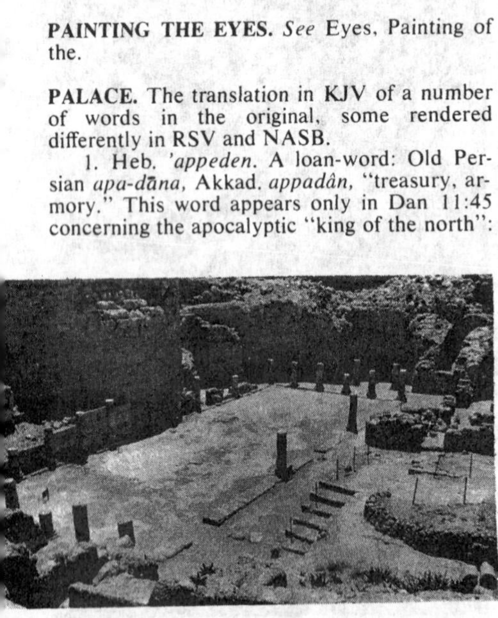

The open courtyard or peristyle garden from the palace of Herod the Great at the Herodium, near Bethlehem. HFV

"tabernacles of his palace" (KJV); "his palatial tents" (RSV).

2. Heb. *'armôn*, "citadel, castle, palace, stronghold." "A dwelling-tower or fortified building of small square base with several stories" (KB, p. 88). This word is found frequently in the prophets, especially Amos and Jeremiah, referring to the buildings usually the object of attack during war (BDB, p. 74). Royal buildings of the Israelites and of other peoples: "palace" in KJV and RSV: II Chr 36:19; Isa 23:13; 25:2; 32:14; Jer 6:5; 9:21; 17:27; 30:18; 49:27; Lam 2:5, 7; "citadel" in RSV: I Kgs 16:18; II Kgs 15:25; Ps 48:3, 13. "Strongholds" in RSV: Isa 34:13; Hos 8:14; Amos–7 times (1:4; etc.). In Mic 5:5 KJV reads: ". . . shall tread in our palaces"; NASB, ". . . tramples on our citadels"; RSV, however, renders the LXX: ". . . and treads upon our soil." *See* Citadel.

3. Heb. *bîrâ*, "fortress, palace"; a loan-word, cf. Akkad. *bîrtu*. It is used of the proposed temple (I Chr 29:1, 19); of a building in a city (Ezr 6:2; however, cf. RSV); and of a ruling city or the capital–*shûshan hab-bîrâ* (Neh 1:1; Est 1:2, 5; etc.; Dan 8:2). A part of the temple (Neh 2:8; "fortress" in NASB) and the residence of the governor of Jerusalem (Neh 7:2; "castle" in RSV; "fortress" in NASB), where the Tower of Antonia later stood (Acts 21:34).

4. Heb. *bayit*, lit. "house." Translated "palace" once in KJV: ". . . the king's palace" (II Chr 9:11; cf. "the king's house," RSV). "House" or "household" in KJV but "palace" in RSV: I Kgs 4:6; II Kgs 10:5; 11:6; 16:18; II Chr 2:1 (Heb. 1:18); 2:12 (Heb. 2:11).

5. Heb. *bîtān*, "palace"; a loan-word: Akkad. *bitânu* (KB, p. 126). Used in referring to Ahasuerus' royal garden (Est 1:5; 7:7-8).

6. Heb. *hêkal* or *hêkāl*, "temple, palace"; Ugaritic *hkl;* Akkad. *ekallum*, "palace" from Sumerian *E-GAL*, "great house"–temple (BDB, p. 228). Used most frequently of the central place of worship (I Sam 1:9; I Kgs 6:3; etc.–77 times; only 11 times for the royal residence). The place or building in Jezreel near Naboth's vineyard (I Kgs 21:1); a place with ivory decorations and stringed instruments (Ps 45:8, 15); its stateliness a figure for stateliness of character (Ps 144:12); where even the small but wise creatures may be found (Prov 30:28); whose pleasant features will be turned to desolation and to the abode of howling animals (Isa 13:22; see RSV); in Babylon where the sons of Hezekiah would serve as eunuchs (Isa 39:7; cf. II Kgs 20:18); the building in which Daniel served and gained respect in Babylon (Dan 1:4; 4:4, 29; 5:5; 6:18).

7. Heb. *harmôn*, "palace" (KJV). Found only in Amos 4:3. The meaning is dubious (BDB); unexplained (KB, p. 243). It is best understood as a proper noun, a place whose location is forgotten (BDB, p. 248; cf. RSV, NASB).

8. Heb. *ṭîrâ*, "encampment"; "the circular

encampment of nomadic tribes" (BDB, p. 377); "encampment (protected by stone walls)" (KB, p. 352). "Palaces" in KJV, but "encampments" in RSV in Ezk 25:4 (cf. Gen 25:16; Num 31:10; Ps 69:25). Used figuratively of correcting the unattractiveness of a plain maiden in Song 8:9 – "palace" in KJV and "battlement" in RSV and NASB.

9. Gr. *aulē*, "court, palace." Used almost exclusively of the high priest's residence in Jerusalem (Mt 26:3, 58, 69; Mk 14:54, 66; Jn 18:15) – in RSV "court" or "courtyard." The residence of a strong man (Lk 11:21).

10. Gr. *praitōrion*, the praetor's court or *praetorion*, mentioned in connection with Paul's imprisonment (Phil 1:13; RSV, "praetorian guard"). *See* Praetorium.

A number of elaborate royal buildings have been excavated in Egypt (at Amarna, Thebes), in Syria (Mari, Ugarit, Alalakh), in Iraq (Babylon, Calah, Khorsabad, Nineveh), and in Turkey (Boghaz-koi, the ancient Hittite capital). In Persia the ruins of Ahasuerus' palace at Susa have yielded much illuminating data, while many of the walls and columns of Darius I's treasure city of Persepolis are still standing. For a description of Nero's *Domus Aurea* ("Golden House") *see* Rome.

In Palestine remains of royal Israelite buildings or of administrative centers have been unearthed at Arad, Dan, Dothan, Gibeah, Hazor, Megiddo, Lachish, Ramat Rahel, and Tirzah. The most noteworthy palace remains from the OT period, however, have been excavated at Samaria. Herod the Great built a number of palaces throughout Palestine, two of which have been excavated and partially restored, at Masada W of the Dead Sea and at Herodium near Bethlehem. Another of his, at Machaerus, E of the Dead Sea, has also been explored.

The residences of the kings of Israel and Judah were essentially like those of their neighbors both in construction (*see* Architecture) and in groundplan. Such palace complexes usually consisted of public rooms or halls approached from an outer courtyard, and private living quarters for the king and his harem arranged around an inner courtyard.

Built with the help of Phoenician craftsmen, Solomon's palace seems to have been similar in style to the *bit-ḫilani* palaces of the Syrian, Phoenician, and Neo-Hittite kingdoms of the 9th and 8th cen. B.C. One entered the palace from the "great court" (I Kgs 7:12) through a portico supported by two or more large pillars (v. 6*b*), forming one of the long walls of the entrance hall, the "porch (hall, NASB) of pillars," 75 × 45 feet (v. 6*a*). After crossing the width of this hall the visitor came into one end of the adjoining main hall, parallel with it but somewhat longer. At the far end stood the great ivory throne with its six steps (I Kgs 10:18–20), from which Solomon meted out judgment (I Kgs 7:7). In front of the throne there was probably a hearth or brazier for a fire in wintertime (Jer 36:22). Another doorway

Substructure of the palace of Domitian (Rome), the emperor who sent the apostle John to the Isle of Patmos. HFV

opened from the throne room to the "other court inward from the hall" (I Kgs 7:8, NASB), which in turn gave access to Solomon's "house" or living quarters.

The "house of the forest of Lebanon" (*q.v.*, I Kgs 7:2–5) may have been a separate building, serving as the royal armory or storehouse (I Kgs 10:17, 21; Isa 22:8), accessible from the great court. The palace compound was undoubtedly located S of the courtyard of Solomon's temple.

Bibliography. Geoffrey Turner, "The State Apartments of Late Assyrian Palaces," *Iraq*, XXXII (1970), 177–213. D. Ussishkin, "King Solomon's Palace and Building 1723 in Megiddo," IEJ, XVI (1966), 174–186.

H. E. Fi. and J. R.

PALAL (pā'lăl). A son of Uzai who helped repair the walls of Jerusalem under the leadership of Nehemiah (Neh 3:25).

PALESTINA. *See* Palestine.

PALESTINE

I. The Geology of Palestine

A. *Geological strata*

The tiny area of Palestine exhibits a great variety of geological formations. The basic strata of exposed stones are, in order from the most ancient to the most recent: Nubian sandstone, Cenomanian limestone, Turonian limestone, Senonian chalk, Eocene limestone, and volcanic basalt.

1. The oldest rocks. Granite classified as pre-Cambrian lies exposed N of the Gulf of Elath. Strata of Nubian sandstone, which may be seen in Transjordan, especially in Edom, have been estimated to be 2,500 to 3,000 feet thick.

2. The Cretaceous period. Many geologists believe that in the so-called Cretaceous age there were several transgressions of the sea which even extended to E of the Jordan. During these periods marls, limestones, and chalk

PALESTINE
0 5 10 20 30 40 50
SCALE OF MILES
SIDON
PHOENICIA
LEBANON
MOUNTAINS
DAMASCUS
MT. HERMON
TYRE
DAN
ROSH HA-NIQRA
LAKE HULEH
HAZOR
GALILEE
BASHAM
PLAIN OF ACRE
ACCHO
CHORAZIN
CAPERNAUM
SEA OF GALILEE
TIBERIAS
BROOK KISHON
MT. CARMEL
YARMUK RIVER
NAZARETH
PLAIN OF ESDRAELON
MT. TABOR
MEGIDDO
JORDAN RIVER
CAESAREA
PLAIN OF SHARON
MT. GILBOA
MEDITERRANEAN SEA
THE GREAT SEA
SAMARIA
GILEAD
SAMARIA
MT. EBAL
SHECHEM
MT. GERIZIM
JABBOK RIVER
YARKON RIVER
EPHRAIM
JOPPA
PHILISTIA
BETHEL
EKRON
JERICHO
AMMON
JERUSALEM
MT. NEBO
VALLEY OF ELAH
ASHDOD
BETHLEHEM
ASHKELON
DEAD (SALT) SEA
GATH
LACHISH
PLAIN
HEBRON
GAZA
SHEPHELAH
ARNON RIVER
JUDEA
MOAB
BEERSHEBA
ZERED RIVER
WADI EL-ARISH
NEGEV
EDOM
PETRA

were formed by marine deposition, covering especially areas of the N and W. These Cretaceous rocks are the most important elements in Cis-Jordan, i.e., the area W of the Jordan.

a. Cenomanian. Cenomanian limestone, which is hard and resists erosion, is found in thick strata totaling about 2,000 feet in N and central Cis-Jordan and in strata of 1,000–1,500 feet in S Cis-Jordan. It is thin in N Transjordan and altogether lacking in S Transjordan. It is found, for example, in upper Galilee and forms the headland of Mount Carmel and the central backbone of Samaria and Judea.

b. Turonian. Turonian limestone is also a hard rock, but it is more easily quarried than the Cenomanian. In Jerusalem numerous tombs were carved out of Turonian limestone. This stratum is to be found in the W foothills of Samaria and along the central spine of Judea.

c. Senonian. The soft chalk laid down in the Senonian period has had a profound influence upon the history of Palestine. As the chalk is exceptionally porous and weathers into infertile soil, it is very poor for agriculture. In Jerusalem the Kidron Valley demarcates the boundary between the Turonian to the W and the Senonian to the E. The barren wilderness of Judea to the E of Jerusalem is composed almost entirely of Senonian strata. On the other hand, because Senonian valleys wear into smooth thoroughfares which are dry even in the winter, they form some of the most important passageways in Palestine. The Megiddo and Jokneam passes through Carmel are Senonian, as well as numerous valleys in Samaria. The important Aijalon Valley leading up to Jerusalem and the thin "moat" separating the Shephelah from Judea are also Senonian.

3. Eocene. Eocene limestone is another hard stone which resists erosion. The most prominent Eocene areas are the so-called Carmel Shephelah between the Jokneam and Megiddo passes, parts of Samaria, the Judean Shephelah, and in Transjordan the area S of the Yarmuk River. In Cis-Jordan Eocene deposits are from 650 to 1,000 feet thick, and in Transjordan only 300 feet thick. Large areas of the Negeb lowlands consist of *hamadas* (stony deserts) of Eocene limestone.

4. The Oligocene to the Pleistocene eras. From Oligocene times onward the coastal plain and the Jordan Valley both subsided, while the central mountain areas were raised upward, resulting in different patterns of sedimentation. In the Jordan Valley, sedimentation took place in brackish water and under arid conditions. More than 3,000 feet of rock salt with intercalated sandstones and dolomites were laid down in the Dead Sea area during the Oligocene and early Miocene periods. This was followed by the deposition of more than 2,000 feet of shales and sandstones during the late Miocene and Pliocene times. In the middle Pleistocene times, a single inland sea extended from the Sea of Galilee to the Dead Sea.

5. Recent alluvium. The coastal plains, the Esdraelon Valley, the Jordan River Valley, and the Arabah Valley S of the Dead Sea are covered for the most part with recent alluvium. A few miles inland from the coast the Sharon and the Philistine plains are dotted with longitudinal strips of "kurkar," which is hard Pleistocene sandstone formed from the solidification of ancient sand dunes. More recent sand dunes composed of Nile sediment deposited by the Mediterranean current have penetrated three to four miles inland along the Philistine coast.

B. *Geodynamic phenomena*

1. Volcanoes. The Miocene, the Pliocene, and especially the Pleistocene eras have left traces of volcanic eruptions in N Palestine. The youngest flows of lava in this area have been dated to about 2000 B.C. Volcanic basalt covers large areas NW and SW of the Sea of Galilee and the areas to the E of the sea known as Bashan and Hauran. Volcanic craters and cones may be seen in the area of Hauran. In Galilee the Horns of Hattin and in Esdraelon the Hill of Moreh are of volcanic origin. Patches of basalt also occur E and SE of the Dead Sea and NW of the Gulf of Elath.

2. Hot springs. On the W shore of the Sea of Galilee hot springs are found at Tiberias, and others on the N bank of the Yarmuk River. Hot springs occur along both shores of the Dead Sea. It was at the hot springs of Callirhoe on the E shore that Herod the Great sought relief during his fatal illness. Nearby in the gorge of the Zerqa Ma'in is a spectacular steaming waterfall.

3. Faults. The Jordan Rift Valley is part of a major fault system that extends beyond the Red Sea into Africa. Transverse faults running E and W are numerous in Galilee and include the scarp formation which separates upper Galilee from lower Galilee. Oblique or hinge faults trending NW-SE mark the S boundary of the Esdraelon Valley and are also responsible for the Wadi Far'ah which flows from Samaria into the Jordan.

4. Earthquakes. In a land characterized by numerous fault systems it is not surprising that earthquakes have been recurring phenomena. The destruction of Sodom and Gomorrah (Gen 19) did not result from volcanic activity, as none is attested in this area for that period, but was probably caused, as Harland has suggested, by a great earthquake accompanied by lightning which ignited the gases and asphalt seeping from the Dead Sea. At the time of Jonathan's foray at Michmash a quake threw the Philistine camp into a panic (I Sam 14:15). David discerned the anger of the Lord in earthquakes (Ps 18:7; cf. Job 9:5–6). A memorable earthquake took place in the 8th cen. B.C. in the days of Uzziah (Amos 1:1; Zech 14:5). One of the most disastrous quakes ever recorded in Palestine was that which occurred in 31 B.C. and killed numerous cattle and from 10,000 to 30,000 persons (Jos *Ant.* xv. 5.2; *Wars* i. 19.3). Striking evidence of this quake has been

Beersheba, southern boundary of Palestine in biblical times. IIS

unearthed in the excavations at Qumran. Some 60 years later the crucifixion of Christ was accompanied by an earthquake (Mt 27:51–54). In 1837 an earthquake claimed 4,000 victims at Safed and 600 at Tiberias. A serious quake occurred in 1927, destroying 175 houses in Jerusalem and killing 500 victims.

C. *Geomorphic products*

1. Stones and minerals. The Nubian sandstones of Edom and the Arabah contain copper deposits (Deut 8:9) which were mined by Solomon. The ancient miners extracted the metal from lumps of copper sulphide, containing 40 to 45 percent copper. The modern Israeli plant at Timnah in the Arabah is able to extract the metal from chrysocolla ore containing only 2 percent copper. The Cenomanian and Turonian strata provided an abundant supply of limestone and marble for building purposes. In parts of Galilee, as at Chorazin and in the Hauran, volcanic basalt was also used in buildings. The Dead Sea provided the ancients with salt and asphalt. Its bromine, phosphate, and potash have been exploited only since the days of the British Mandate.

2. Soils. The basalt of Galilee and Bashan has weathered into black and brown soils of proverbial fertility. The dark alluvium that floors the Esdraelon Valley is also a rich soil. Terra rosa, a reddish soil which originates from the Cenomanian and Turonian limestones, covers much of the central hill country. It is a soil which may be poor in humus and which tends to be washed away from the slopes unless it is terraced. Soil derived from the Eocene rock is less fertile than the terra rosa. Senonian rock easily erodes into a light gray, infertile soil. On the Sharon plain is a bright red to orange clayey sand which is used today for the raising of citrus fruits, but which was useless for agriculture in antiquity. In the area around Beer-sheba one encounters loess, a fine yellow-brown dust carried by desert winds, which is fertile if irrigated and cultivated. Closer to Gaza the loess is mixed with alluvium, and this mixture forms a fertile soil for the growth of cereals. Much of the area between the Dead Sea and the Gulf of Elath is covered by parched arid soils and stony deserts.

3. Erosion. The erosion of the soil is a process which was known in biblical times (Job 14:18–19; cf. Prov 28:3). Many areas of friable soils are affected by a combination of violent winter storms, high rates of evaporation, extremes in temperature, strong winds, and vulnerable vegetation. Man has aggravated the situation by his destructive invasions: the prolonged grazing of goats, and the cutting of trees for charcoal.

II. The Geography of Palestine

A. *Prolegomena*

1. Designations. The name Palestine, originally derived from the name of the Philistines, was first used by Herodotus (5th cen. B.C.), who included in this designation the area of Phoenicia to the N. Josephus used the Gr. word *Palaistinē* for the area of the Philistine coast (Jos *Ant.* i. 6.2). After the Jewish revolt of A.D. 135 the Romans replaced the Latin name *Judaea* with the Latin *Palaestina* as their designation of this province. The OT often speaks of the land as Canaan (*q.v.*).

Tell Dan, at the northern boundary of Palestine in biblical times. HFV

2. Boundaries. In current practice the term Palestine is generally used to designate the territory allotted to the 12 tribes of Israel only to the W of the Jordan. It is convenient to distinguish between the area W of the Jordan as Cis-Jordan and the area to the E as Transjordan. The proverbial N and S limits were the cities of Dan and Beer-sheba (Jud 20:1; I Sam 3:20), *c.* 150 miles apart. More extensive boundaries are envisioned in the description of Canaan given to Moses in Num 34, where the S boundary is placed at Kadesh-barnea, 45 miles SSW of Beer-sheba (Num 34:4). In this passage the N boundary is placed at the "entrance of (*Lebo-*) Hamath" (Num 34:8, RSV). This may either be at the entrance to the Beqa' Valley between the Lebanon and Anti-Lebanon Mountains or farther N at modern Lebweh, 14 miles NNE of Ba'albek. In many periods the N border fluctuated and was in any case ill-defined.

3. Distances. To modern man accustomed to rapid transportation the distances involved in measuring the length and breadth of Palestine seem quite short. Speaking in terms of air miles the greatest distance would be the 300 miles from Dan to Eilat; from Dan to Beer-sheba measures but 150 miles, and from Nazareth to Jerusalem 60 miles. It is 45 miles from Jaffa on the coast to Jericho, with the country narrowing to the N of this axis and broadening to the S. Of course, travel by even modern roads involves greater distances. By road from Dan to Beer-sheba it is 198 miles, from Nazareth to Jerusalem 85 miles, and from Jaffa to Jericho 62 miles.

4. Size of areas. The historical importance of Palestine is out of all proportion to its tiny size. As Cis-Jordan from Dan to Beer-sheba is 150 miles long and averages a little over 40 miles in breadth, it is a little more than 6,000 square miles in area. The largely vacant triangle of the modern Negeb extending to the Gulf of Elath adds 3,200 square miles. The area of Transjordan under Israelite control stretched 90 miles from the Yarmuk River to the Arnon River. This area is from 25 to 60 miles wide and comprises about 4,000 square miles. Cis-Jordan without the Negeb triangle is therefore a little larger than Connecticut and Rhode Island put together. Cis-Jordan and Israelite Transjordan, covering 10,000 square miles, is a little larger than Vermont and somewhat smaller than Belgium.

5. Elevations. Apart from snow-capped Mount Hermon (9,232 feet), which lies outside of its boundaries though it is visible from N Palestine, most of the mountains in Palestine are not very high. The highest peak in Cis-Jordan, Jebel Jarmuq, NW of the Sea of Galilee, reaches nearly 4,000 feet. In Samaria Mount Ebal stands at 3,084 feet and Mount Gerizim at 2,890 feet. Jerusalem itself averages 2,460 feet above sea level (2,435 feet at the site of the temple). The hills around Hebron are about 3,300 feet. There are higher summits in Transjordan: the many peaks of Jebel Druze (Mount Bashan, Ps 68:15, RSV) on the E edge of the Haurah region tower up to 6,000 feet; the mountains of Edom reach in parts 5,700 feet.

Palestine has the distinction of the lowest elevations in the world in the Rift Valley. Whereas Lake Huleh, now drained, stood about 220 feet above sea level, the Sea of Galilee, about ten miles to the S, is located at 686 feet below sea level. Jericho stands at −820 feet. The traveler going from Jericho to Jerusalem has to ascend 3,280 feet in about 20 miles. The ancient traveler normally took two days for the arduous climb. The lowest spot in the world is the Dead Sea at 1,280 feet below sea level. Death Valley contains the lowest point in the W Hemisphere, only −280 feet.

B. *Regional analyses*

It is amazing to find in such a small area the proliferation of geographical variations that the

Modern Jaffa and ancient ruins. IIS

land possesses. It has been aptly remarked that one reason the Bible is intelligible in all parts of the world is that it so nearly runs the gamut of the earth's living conditions. Palestine may be divided into four major longitudinal strips: (1) the coastal plains; (2) the central highlands (Cis-Jordan); (3) the rift regions; and (4) Transjordanian plateau.

1. The coastal plains

a. Harbors. The deposition by the Mediterranean current of silt from the Nile River has made the Palestinian coast a flat sandy shore without good harbors for nearly 200 miles. The few anchorages on this coast were far inferior to the famous harbors of the Phoenicians to the N. Although there are some references to the maritime interests of Zebulun (Gen 49:13) and of Dan and Asher (Jud 5:17), fearful references to the raging sea (Ps 107:23–29; Isa 57:20) seem to be more typical. As G. A. Smith has remarked, the sea was a barrier and not a highway for the Israelites.

Examining the coast from N to S, the first harbor is the bay of Acco, which was exposed to the SW storms. Much of the nearby area was marshy. Excavations have revealed a nameless ancient port at Tell Abu Hawam at the mouth of the Kishon brook which empties into the Haifa Bay. Fifteen miles S of the Carmel headland was the port of Dor, the major port in Israelite hands. It was, however, somewhat isolated by the Sharon marshes. Eight miles S of Dor King Herod the Great created the artificial harbor of Caesarea in the 1st cen. B.C.

At the N limit of modern Tel Aviv, excavators have uncovered a port at Tell Qasileh near the mouth of the Yarqon brook. Immediately S of Tel Aviv, the ancient site of Joppa (modern Jaffa) was an important port created by the projection of a rocky bluff and some low reefs (associated with the release of Andromeda by Perseus). It was from Joppa (Jon 1:3) that Jonah set sail on a ship of Tarshish. Near the small site of Tell Mor, which served as a port for the Philistine city of Ashdod, the Israelis have built a modern harbor. To the S the Philistine city of Ashkelon lay immediately on

PALESTINE

Antiquities park, Ashkelon, one of the towns of ancient Philistia. IIS

the coast on a line of low cliffs which interrupted the sand dunes. Unfortunately for the Israelites, with the Philistines in control of the area S of Joppa and the Phoenicians in control of Acco, many of even these inadequate harbors listed here were not under their control for much of their history.

b. Plain of Asher. Phoenicia proper began with the white headland of Ras en-Naqurah, the "Ladder of Tyre," which shuts off land traffic along the coast. The plain S of it and N of Mount Carmel along the coast was the allotment of Asher, who, however, failed to keep it (Jud 1:31). The port of Acco was to achieve fame as the Roman Ptolemais (Acts 21:7) and the Crusader Acre, but the region does not play a major role in the OT.

c. Mount Carmel. The famous steep promontory is but the extremity of a range of hills extending inland SE from the sea. Its maximum height is 1740 feet. As there is but a narrow beach of 200 yards at its base along the shore, Carmel would have effectively blocked all land traffic were not the range pierced by the Jokneam and Megiddo passes. The mountain was forested (Song 7:5) and thinly populated. The traditional scene of Elijah's contest with the prophets of Baal (I Kgs 18) is located some 20 miles inland on a crest of Carmel above Jokneam.

d. Coast of Dor. The coastal plain of Dor is a small triangular area 20 miles long, hemmed in by the Carmel range to the NE and by the marshes of the Nahr ez-Zerqa or the Crocodile River to the S. From the Egyptian narrative of Wenamon we learn that *c.* 1100 B.C. Dor was in the hands of the Tjeker, one of the Sea Peoples who had migrated from the Aegean-Anatolian areas. In NT times Dor was not included in the area given to Herod the Great by the Romans, but was affiliated with Ptolemais under the governor of Syria.

e. Sharon plain. The Sharon plain extends from the Crocodile River in the N southward to the 'Auja (called by the Israelis the Yarqon) stream, which marks the N edge of modern Tel Aviv. It is a narrow plain, ten miles wide and 50 miles long. Low kurkar ridges blocked the drainage of the five streams that flowed through the Sharon to the sea, creating marshy areas. Moreover the rich Mousterian red sand of the Sharon supported an impenetrable oak forest; the LXX in fact translates the word Sharon by *drumos* or "forest." The area was therefore not heavily settled by the ancient Israelites but was used primarily for pasturage (I Chr 5:16; 27:29; Isa 65:10). The "rose of Sharon" (Song 2:1) was a delicate flower in the midst of towering trees. The region assumed great importance with the construction of Caesarea by Herod. The important *Via Maris* (Isa 9:1), the trunk road from Egypt by way of Philistia which led through Galilee ultimately to Damascus, skirted the marshes of the Sharon on the low foothills to the E and penetrated the Carmel range through the Megiddo pass.

f. Philistia. The Philistine coast and plain extending S of the Sharon is so named for the Philistines, an Aegean Sea People who became predominant there *c.* 1200 B.C. This area is characterized by gently rising land and wide valleys. It is rich in ground water fed by aquifers from the Hebron hills. The decrease of rain as one approaches the deserts in the S and the more rapid run-off from the higher slopes prevented the formation of marshes here. The *Via Maris* therefore no longer has to cling to the dry inland slopes as in Sharon but follows the coast. Along the coast itself sand dunes have blanketed much of the area, but the Philistines were able to locate three of their five major cities on the coast in breaks in the dunes: Ashdod, Ashkelon, and Gaza. Gaza as the southernmost city before the long eight-day march to Egypt has played a crucial role throughout history. G. A. Smith has called Gaza "the outpost of Africa, the door of Asia." The exact locations of the two other cities of the Philistine Pentapolis, Gath (Tell es-Safi?) and Ekron (Khirbet el-Muqanna'?), is in dispute.

2. The central highlands

a. Galilee. It is customary to divide this region into upper Galilee and lower Galilee, with the division marked by a steep escarpment running along a line between Accho and Safed. The area to the N, upper Galilee, is characterized by hills that range from 2,600 to 3,000 feet; to the S, lower Galilee is characterized by hills less than 2,000 feet and broad valleys. Upper Galilee is further subdivided into a forested area in the S and a lower, spacious tableland to the N which was thickly settled. The latter area is now in the modern state of Lebanon. With few exceptions, such as Kedesh Naphtali (Josh 20:7), upper Galilee played almost no role in the OT.

Galilee is favored by a cool climate, heavy rains, and rich soil. It supported a large population living in many small villages. Lower Galilee, famed for its prominence in the NT, is in particular an attractive and fertile area of gentle slopes suited to settled life and farming.

Certain areas of Galilee were also exposed to the international influences of the traffic on the *Via Maris* to Damascus. To the NW were the heathen Phoenician "coasts" and to the SE the Gentile cities of the Decapolis. Nazareth, the city of Jesus, is located on a ridge 1,200 feet above sea level. On its S is a steep scarp overlooking the Esdraelon Valley (Lk 4:29).

b. Esdraelon-Jezreel Valley. The name Esdraelon is simply the Gr. spelling of the Heb. Jezreel, "God will sow" (cf. Hos 2:22–23). It is the name of "the valley" par excellence lying between the Carmel range and the hills of lower Galilee. The Kishon stream which drains it flows through a narrow pass in the NW. A rainstorm turned the little Kishon and the surrounding plain into a quagmire, enabling Barak to defeat the chariots of Sisera (Jud 5:20–21). The Esdraelon plain proper forms an equilateral triangle, with sides about 20 miles long. Four fortress cities at intervals of about five miles guarded the entrances from the Carmel range into the plain: Jokneam, Megiddo, Taanach, and Ibleam. The most important was Megiddo which guarded the pass through which the *Via Maris* turned inland. This is a route with an easy gradient. Thutmose III (15th cen. B.C.) was well aware of its importance when he said: "The capturing of Megiddo is the capture of a thousand towns." So many battles have been fought by the site (e.g., II Chr 35:22) that its name has become a symbol of the future conflict with the kings of the world (cf. Gr. *'Armagedōn* with Heb. *har megiddō,* Rev 16:16). The Jokneam pass was serviceable for anyone traveling between Acco and Dor. The Taanach pass was the least attractive as it was a narrow and steep path. The Ibleam pass, S of Jenin, leads to the fertile Dothan valley. The Midianites who took Joseph to Egypt were traveling this route (Gen 37).

At the E end of the Esdraelon plain is an area between the volcanic Hill of Moreh to the N and the limestone spur of Mount Gilboa to the S; it served as a battleground between Gideon and the Midianites (Jud 7:1), and between Saul and the Philistines (I Sam 31:1). At the foot of Gilboa is the city of Jezreel, the winter

Dothan in Samaria. JPF

Nazareth in Galilee, with the Valley of Jezreel in the background. IIS

capital of the Omrides, where Jezebel was slain by Jehu (II Kgs 9:30–37). Also at the base of Gilboa is the spring of Harod, where Gideon tested his troops and selected his corps of 300 (Jud 7:1–7). The little Jalud River flows from 'Ain Harod eastward through a narrow but fertile corridor to the plain of Beth-shean on the edge of the Jordan Valley, 400 feet below sea level. The men of Jabesh-Gilead crossed the Jordan at this point by the easy ford to Gilead in order to rescue the body of Saul from Beth-shean (I Sam 31:11–12). In NT times Beth-shean was known as Scythopolis and was the only member of the Decapolis on the W side of the Jordan.

c. Samaria. The region of Samaria stretches 50 miles S of the Esdraelon Valley and extends 40 miles E and W, covering an area of 2000 square miles. The region was apportioned to the tribes of the two sons of Joseph, Manasseh taking the area from Shechem northward, and Ephraim the smaller area S to Bethel. The Cenomanian limestone of Ephraim has weathered into terra-rosa soil which supports extensive vegetation and a sizeable population. The area of Manasseh is largely Eocene with large areas of Senonian chalk, resulting in rounded hills with broad valleys rich in alluvium. Although the Senonian stratum does not form good agricultural soil, it provides roadways in all directions. A major longitudinal highway ran on the watershed of the Samaria hills from Jerusalem N through Bethel and Shiloh to Shechem (Jud 21:19). Shechem lay at the foot of the twin Eocene peaks of Ebal and Gerizim, where the Samaritans worshiped (Jn 4:20). At Shechem the road branched to the NE and the NW. The NE road led to Tirzah, the early capital (I Kgs 14:17; 15:21, 33) at the head of the Wadi Far'ah. The NW road led to the new capital of Samaria established by Omri in the 9th cen. (I Kgs 16:24).

What constituted both the strength and the weakness of Samaria, especially of Manasseh, was its openness to foreign traders and invaders. The Assyrians finally swept down and destroyed the city of Samaria in 722 B.C.

PALESTINE

The Via Dolorosa, traditional route that Christ took to Calvary. MIS

(II Kgs 17:3 ff.), deporting great numbers of the ten tribes of Israel and importing strangers from Mesopotamia. The mixed population which resulted formed the Samaritans.

d. Judah. The small area of Judah or Judea, which has played the most important historical role, was in some respects the least desirable. From its N frontier it stretched 50 miles S to Beer-sheba. About 30 miles broad, it encompassed an area of about 1,500 square miles. On the W slopes it had some rich but patchy areas of terra rosa which could sustain crops if terraced. Its relative isolation from the international trade route meant that commerce was routed around Judea and not through it. The fact that it was easily defended on all sides

Beth-Shemesh in the Judean hills. IIS

but the N helped it to maintain a political stability which Samaria did not enjoy.

The N boundary of Judah was finally set at Geba (I Kgs 15:22; II Kgs 23:8), only five miles S of Bethel. The land between Geba and Bethel was a no-man's-land (II Chr 13:19; I Kgs 15:17) fought for by the kings of Judah and of Israel. As there was no natural barrier in this direction, a powerful foe in control of the N like the Assyrians could advance unopposed upon Judah (Isa 10:28–32).

The most important cities of Judah were on the watershed running along the spine of the Judean hills. Jerusalem, whose towers can be seen from Bethel ten miles N, was chosen by David to unite the southern and the northern tribes. Its position also commands the E-W road which leads down to Jericho and the last ford across the Jordan N of the Dead Sea. Hebron, David's earlier capital which lies 18 miles S of Jerusalem, is closer to the center of Judah. The area S of Hebron is a region of the broad open hills of Ziph, Maon, and Judean Carmel (I Sam 25:2), suitable for pasturing flocks. The Judean plateau comes to an end about 15 miles S of Hebron, grading off into steppe land and desert. Beer-sheba, which is 28 miles SW of Hebron, is at a level of but 1,000 feet above sea level and is at the border between the steppe land and desert.

To the E of the central spine about a third of Judah consists of the Judean wilderness, a forbidding area whose major uses were defense and refuge. This wilderness begins a short distance E of the Mount of Olives and continues for over ten miles to the edge of the Jordan Valley. It extends 50 to 60 miles from the latitude of Bethel all along the cliffs on the W side of the Dead Sea. The soft Senonian chalk and the fact that this area lies in the rain shadow have contributed to its desolation. Only in the wettest of winters does grass grow on the slopes of the wilderness. In the Bible there are some 17 names for the region, including the "wilderness of Judah" (Jud 1:16) and Jeshimon or "Desolation" (I Sam 23:24). Except for the oasis at En-gedi on the W shore of the Dead Sea, about the only inhabited places were religious communities as at Qumran, caves for refugees, and fortresses like Masada.

Judah could be approached from the W through several routes, but these ascents could be defended. These passes which lead up from Philistia through the Shephelah into Judah have been the scenes of many battles. Considering these routes from N to S, first is the Aijalon Valley which leads up from Lod (Lydda) by an easy ascent past upper and lower Beth-horon. A traveler could then turn NE to Bethel or SE by way of Gibeon to Jerusalem. The Valley of Aijalon is a wide and fertile down-faulted basin and was both the easiest and most important passage into Judah from the W. It was through this valley that Joshua chased the Amorites (Josh 10:10–12), and that Saul and Jonathan pursued the Philistines (I Sam 14:31). Farther

S of Aijalon the Sorek Valley approaches Jerusalem directly from the W and leads to the Vale of Rephaim SW of the city, where David twice defeated the Philistines (II Sam 5:17–25). The Sorek Valley with its sites of Timnah (Jud 14:1), Eshtaol and Zorah (Jud 13:24–25; 16:31) was the arena for many of the exploits of Samson. Still farther S the Valley of Elah leads to Bethlehem five miles S of Jerusalem. It was down this valley that the young David came to challenge the Philistine Goliath between Socoh and Azekah (I Sam 17:1–2). The route into S Judah and Hebron was guarded in the W by the great fortress city of Lachish (II Kgs 18:13–17).

e. Shephelah. The Shephelah ("lowland") was that part of the Judean realm which lay between the Judean hills and the Philistine plain. It is an area 40 miles long and up to eight miles wide, rising in height from 300 to 1,300 feet above sea level. This rocky plateau is an outcrop of Eocene limestone separated from the Cenomanian limestone of the Judean mountains by a narrow valley of Senonian chalk. It is an area of wide valleys, fertile alluvial soils, olive and sycamore groves (I Chr 27:28). Because of its desirability and its position, it was always an object of contention between the Philistines and the Israelites (II Chr 28:18).

A wadi in the Negeb. IIS

f. Negeb. The biblical Negeb or "Southland" (lit., "dryland") encompassed only the small area of a strip about 30 miles wide from N to S centered at Beer-sheba. This is the habitable sector, the Negeb proper. It is a fairly level area of up to 800–1,000 feet above sea level receiving an annual rainfall which is marginal for agriculture (four to 12 inches). There are in this area long periods of drought resulting in the lack of permanent settlements except under a strong and interested government. When flash floods do occur (Ps 126:4), most of the water drains off uselessly in broad wadis to the Mediterranean. It is, however, along the beds of these wadis that springs are to be found and that wells may be dug. In the eastern Negeb the important cities of Arad and Hormah were located along the Wadi Meshash.

As rainfall was so capricious, some areas of the Negeb were able to support crops even while other areas were experiencing drought. This may explain the movement of the patriarchs to Gerar in the W Negeb (Gen 20–21, 26). By the careful conservation of water the Nabataeans of the Roman period and the later Byzantine monks were able to support agriculture in the higher Negeb tablelands 30 miles S of Beer-sheba.

Because of its long frontier with the desert areas the Negeb has constantly faced incursions from the Bedouins, such as the Amalekites (Num 13:29; I Sam 30:1). The vast triangular area stretching S to Elath, which is the modern Negeb of Israel, was known in the Bible as the wilderness of Zin and of Paran. The important route to Sinai and Egypt, known as the way of Shur (Gen 16:7), went SW from Beer-sheba past the oasis of Kadesh-barnea in this region.

3. The rift regions

a. Mount Hermon and the sources of the Jordan. Majestic and snow-capped Mount Hermon towers 9,232 feet above sea level. Its melting snows feed the several sources of the Jordan River. One of these sources is the Nahr Leddan which arises near Dan. Another source is the stream which arises from the Baniyas spring, three miles E of Dan. Baniyas, which is named after the Gr. god Pan, was known in NT times as Caesarea Philippi (Mt 16:13 ff.).

b. Lake Huleh. Some seven miles S of the confluence of the headwaters of the Jordan masses of basaltic overflow created a small lake three miles long and two miles wide and but nine to 16 feet deep, known as Lake Huleh. This lake, which Josephus called Lake Semechonitis, does not appear in the Bible. The basin of Lake Huleh was a warm area which supported an abundance of animals, wild fowl and papyrus plants in the marshy waters. It was, however, an unhealthy region for humans because of malaria. The Jews, who purchased the area during the British Mandate, have since then drained the lake, creating a wild life preserve and fish ponds in its place.

Southwest of the lake stood the important fortress of Hazor (Josh 11:10), guarding the major ford of the Jordan at the site of the Bridge of Jacob's Daughters. Below this ford the Jordan enters a narrow basalt gorge where cliffs rise 1,200 feet above the surface of the stream. As Lake Huleh was located about 220 feet above sea level and the Sea of Galilee some ten miles S lies around 690 feet below sea level, the Jordan plummets over 900 feet between these two points.

c. Sea of Galilee. Perhaps the most storied body of water in the world, the lovely Sea of

The Sea of Galilee. IIS

Galilee takes the shape of an ancient harp or lyre 13 miles long and seven miles wide. Its fresh waters rich with fish reach a depth of over 150 feet. It is known in the Bible by various names: the Sea of Chinnereth ("harp," Num 34:11); the Sea of Galilee (Mt 4:18); the Lake of Gennesaret (Lk 5:1); and the Sea of Tiberias (Jn 21:1). Surrounded by mountains on all sides, its placid waters could be transformed into a boiling caldron by sudden tempests (Mk 4:35–41). The broadest level area along its shores is the small plain of Gennesaret in the NW. Between this plain and the entrance of the Jordan in the N lay the city of Capernaum, the scene of so much of Jesus' ministry. The most important city of the lake was that of Tiberias (Jn 6:23) on the W shore, founded *c.* A.D. 20 by Herod Antipas. It was a largely Gentile city which Christ seems not to have entered.

d. Jordan River. The straight-line distance of the Jordan from the Sea of Galilee to the Dead Sea is 65 miles; its sinuous course, however, triples its actual length to 187 miles. From the Sea of Galilee it descends about 600 feet to the Dead Sea, or about ten feet per mile. The Jordan's swift current, whirlpools, cascades, and sharp bends are an obstacle to river traffic. Moreover, its waters lay too far below the cultivable plain for use in irrigation in antiquity. The Jordan, which is from 90–100 feet wide and but three to ten feet deep, is not a majestic river but a muddy torrent (II Kgs 5:10–12).

The Jordan Valley increases from a width of three miles to a maximum of 14 miles just before it reaches the Dead Sea. The Arabs divide the valley into two levels: the *Ghor* or "Depression" of the main valley, and separated from it by a slope of 150 feet the deeper *Zor* or "Thicket" of the flood plain itself. The area between the Zor and the Ghor is characterized by *qattaras,* badly eroded marl hills. The Zor is a lush region of dense, tangled vegetation from 200 yards to a mile broad—a veritable jungle which was inhabited by jackals, wolves, and lions (Jer 12:5; 49:19; 50:44; Zech 11:3, RSV, NASB).

The Jordan is fed by a number of tributaries, the more important of which flow from the E. On the W it is fed by the Jalud stream flowing past Beth-shean, by the Wadi Far'ah flowing from Tirzah in Samaria, and by the Wadi el-Qelt flowing past NT Jericho. The most important tributary from the E is the river Yarmuk, joining the Jordan just below the Sea of Galilee. Though it carries an equal if not larger volume of water than the Jordan, it is not named in the Bible, unless it is Elijah's "brook Cherith" (I Kgs 17:3–7). Some 20 miles below the Sea of Galilee the Wadi el-Yabis flows into the Jordan from the E, and 15 miles farther S the larger Jabbok River enters the Jordan near the city of Adam (by the present Damiya Bridge). This is an area where landslides have blocked the course of the Jordan several times in recorded history (cf. Josh 3:16).

The surveys of N. Glueck indicate that there were 35 areas of settlement in the Jordan Valley in the Israelite period. On the E bank N of the Wadi el-Yabis were located Jabesh-gilead (I Sam 11), and Pella, the city to which the Jerusalem Christians fled in A.D. 70. Between the Wadi el-Yabis and the Jabbok River lay Succoth and Zarethan. Excavations suggest that the latter may be identified with Tell es-Sa'idiyeh where objects of metal tend to confirm the biblical description of the site as a center of metallurgy (I Kgs 7:46). Aharoni, however, believes this *tell* was Zaphon (Jud 12:1, RSV). On the W bank, in addition to the oasis city of Jericho, Herod the Great built a number of fortresses to the N: Archelais, Phasaelis, and Alexandrium.

The Jordan River as it flows out of the Sea of Galilee. HFV

e. Dead Sea. The Dead Sea was known by other names in antiquity. In the OT it was known as the "Salt Sea" (Gen 14:3), the "Eastern Sea" (Ezk 47:18, RSV), and the "Sea of the Arabah" (Deut 4:49, RSV). The Romans called it the "Asphalt Sea." The term *Mare Mortuum* or "Dead Sea" was used from the 2nd cen. A.D. To the Arabs it is known as the Sea of Lot.

The floor of the Dead Sea is a trough within a trough. The lowest spot in the world with its surface being about −1,280 feet (this has varied somewhat depending on intake and rate of evaporating), its deepest point is another 1,300 feet below its surface. It is approximately 50 miles long and ten miles wide. The S third of the sea is a shallow bay of recent origin which is only about 15–35 feet deep. This is set off from the main body of water by the marl peninsula of the Lisan ("tongue") jutting out from the E coast. The water between the tip of the Lisan and the W coast is only two and a half miles broad, and could be forded as late as 1846. Dead branches of submerged trees in the S bay reveal that part of this area was dry land in recent times, and measurements show that the level of the sea has been rising steadily.

Not only is the Dead Sea the earth's lowest body of water, it is also one of the saltiest. Because of the tremendous heat, the rapid rate of evaporation, and the lack of rain in the area, its waters contain a 25 percent concentration of common salt, bromide, magnesium chloride, and calcium chloride. Fish swimming into the sea from the Jordan are killed instantly.

The steep cliffs, especially on the E side, prevent a passage around the sea. On the NW shore the Essene monks maintained a monastery at Qumran near the spring of 'Ain Feshkha. Farther S on the W shore was the oasis of En-gedi famed for its henna (Song 1:14, RSV) and opobalsamon plant. At the SW corner of the sea is a salt mountain known as Jebel Usdum, which is popularly associated with the fate of Lot's wife (Gen 19:26). The actual sites of Sodom and Gomorrah are believed to be hidden now under the shallow waters of the S part of the sea. The classical authors Diodorus Siculus (ii. 48.7-9), Strabo (*Geography* xvi. 2.42–44), Tacitus (*History* v. 6.7), and Josephus (*Wars* iv. 8.4) describe visible remains of burned cities S of the Dead Sea of their day.

f. Arabah. The continuation of the Jordan rift S of the Dead Sea is known as the Arabah, a word which is also a synonym for desert land. The Arabah Valley is 105 miles long and between three to nine miles wide. The elevation of the valley floor rises from the depths of the Dead Sea region to a height of 750 feet and then descends to sea level at Elath. The main significance of the area lay in its copper deposits. The major ancient copper works which have been discovered are at Punon and Ir-nahash 30 miles S of the Dead Sea, and at Timnah 15 miles N of the Gulf of Elath. Ezion-geber near Elath (I Kgs 9:26) served as the port for Solomon's trading missions to Arabia, Africa, and possibly to India.

4. The Transjordanian plateau. The area of the Transjordan is a mountain tableland mainly of Cenomanian and Senonian limestone, with basalt to the E and NE of the Sea of Galilee and with Nubian sandstone and pre-Cambrian rocks in Edom. The elevations of Transjordan are higher on the average than those of Cis-Jordan. The height of the plateau averages 2,000–2,500 feet with peaks of more than 3,000 feet at many points and over 5,000 feet in Edom. One marked difference from Cis-Jordan is the fact that Transjordan is not bounded by the sea but by a vast desert. Its E highlands blend into the Syrian-Arabian Desert, and are therefore exposed both to the winds and to the nomads of the desert.

a. Bashan. OT Bashan is the plateau N of the Yarmuk and E of the Sea of Galilee, extending N to the foot of Mount Hermon. Its proximity to Damascus made this region a constant battleground between Syria and Israel. This is an area of wide open plains between 1,600–2,300 feet above sea level. As its basalt has weathered into fertile soil and as the low hills of Galilee to the W permitted rain to penetrate inland, the well-fed bulls of Bashan were proverbial (Ps 22:12; Amos 4:1; Ezk 39:18). Bashan also served as an important granary for the Roman Empire. In the time of Herod the region immediately NE of the Sea of Galilee was known as Gaulanitis (cf. the modern Golan Heights).

b. Hauran. Between Bashan and the desert is the area of Hauran, a treeless plain 50 miles by 20. At the E edge of the Hauran is the great volcanic mass known as Mount Bashan or the Jebel Druze, which was famed for its oaks (Ps 68:15; Isa 2:13; Ezk 27:6; Zech 11:2). Because of its height the area is well-watered but also bitterly cold in the winter. The region N of the Jebel Druze is known as el-Leja ("the refuge") for here refugees and robbers can maintain an existence independent of the control of Damascus to the N. In the NT period the general area of Hauran was known as Auranitis, and the region of el-Leja as Trachonitis. These two areas together with Gaulanitis and Batanaea were ceded to Herod Philip (Lk 3:1).

c. Gilead. The region S of the Yarmuk, E of the Jordan, and down to the latitude of Rabbath-ammon (modern Amman) but not including the latter, was known as Gilead. This is a high upland region of rugged mountains reaching 3,000 and even 4,000 feet. It covered an area 35 miles long and 25 miles wide between the Jordan and the desert. Geologically the Gilead dome is an upwarp of Cenomanian limestone, which has been split by the Jabbok River. The divisions were known as Half-Gilead (Josh 12:2, 5). As the region because of its height receives 24–28 inches of rain, it was and still is thickly forested (II Sam 18:6, 8; Jer 22:6). Its balm was proverbial (Jer 8:22; 46:11); the Ishmaelite caravan which took Joseph to Egypt was bearing balm from Gilead (Gen 37:25).

Gilead was settled by the Israelite tribe of Gad and the half tribe of Manasseh. In times of trouble it served as a place of refuge, e.g., for David fleeing from Absalom (II Sam 17:22). During the NT period the part of Gilead bordering the Jordan was known as Perea and fell under the jurisdiction of Herod Antipas, who also controlled Galilee.

d. Ammon. The small territory of Ammon centered about the city of Rabbath-ammon and extended E but did not reach W to the Jordan until the post-Exilic period. This is a high and fertile plateau, though more arid than Gilead and sparse in trees. Rabbath-ammon is located on a S bend of the upper course of the Jabbok and is almost on the desert fringe. The city dominated the King's Highway leading N to Damascus.

e. Moab. Moab was the region S of Ammon and Gilead, E of the Dead Sea, and N of the Zered (Num 21:11-12; Deut 2:13), which flows into the SE corner of the Dead Sea. It is a high tableland (2,000-2,400 feet) of Cenomanian limestone resting on Nubian sandstone. Just as Gilead is divided, Moab is divided in two by the deep gorge of the Arnon. The so-called "river" Arnon (Deut 2:24; Josh 12:1) is a veritable canyon two and a half miles wide at the top of cliffs which rise 1,650 feet above the floor of the stream.

When the Moabites were weak the Arnon acted as their N border (Num 21:13, 15). In times of Moabite strength no natural border existed in the N between Moab and Ammon, or between Moab and the Israelite holdings in the Transjordan. The approximate boundary was a line from the N end of the Dead Sea between Heshbon and Medeba. The area of Moab N of the Arnon, the *Mishor* or "tableland" (Deut 3:10; 4:43, RSV), was for centuries disputed between Israel and Moab. The Moabite King Mesha (II Kgs 3:4) seized this area from the Israelites in the 9th cen. B.C. as he tells in his important inscription, the Moabite Stone. The major cities of Moab were located on the King's Highway: Medeba in the N, Mesha's capital Dibon, and Aroer which guarded the highway as it crossed the Arnon (Josh 12:2).

Moab S of the Arnon was higher land up to the 4,000 feet range. Little is known about any cities in this area except for Kir-hareseth or Kir of Moab (II Kgs 3:25). This is identified with modern Kerak, located on a rocky hill 3,370 feet above sea level, overlooking the S end of the Dead Sea 11 miles away.

f. Edom. The vast area S of Moab and of the Dead Sea and E of the Arabah is known from the time of King Saul and onward as Edom. Its name, which means "red," befits the red Nubian sandstone which is so prominent in its W areas. As a result of Edom's elevation, its W slopes receive an adequate rainfall in the winter. Edom has therefore enjoyed a thick shrub forest, which was preserved until recent times. Its wood was important for use as fuel in the copper smelteries of the Arabah. Edom fought with Israel and Judah not only for control of the copper mines and the port of Elath, but also for control of the King's Highway which ran through its territory. Amaziah (II Kgs 14:7), and his son Uzziah (II Kgs 14:22) were able to conquer much of the Edomite area. For the most part, however, Edom enjoyed its independence and trusted in its well-defended strongholds. It was this fierce pride of Edom which Obadiah the prophet condemned.

Roman theater in modern Amman, ancient Rabbath-Ammon. HFV

Edom had a few notable cities: Teman near Petra was renowned for its wisdom (Jer 49:7; cf. Job 2:11). Bozrah is located between Sela and Punon in the N, 25 miles S of the Dead Sea, and Sela a short distance NW of Bozrah. Some scholars, however, would place Sela 50 miles to the S of the Dead Sea at the site which was later to be transformed into Petra, the capital of the Nabataeans. After the conquest of Judah by the Babylonians in 587 B.C., the Edomites took advantage of the situation and moved into the area of Hebron. With the incursions of the Nabataean Arabs into the area of Petra *c.* 300 B.C. the Edomites left Transjordan altogether and occupied the area known as Idumaea, which included S Judah and the Shephelah. Herod the Great was an Idumaean.

III. The Climate of Palestine

A. *Meteorological factors*

Several factors affect the characteristic weather of Palestine. The country lies between 33° 15′ at Dan and 31° 15′ N at Beer-sheba, which is the same latitude as the southernmost section of California. It is therefore on the N margin of the subtropical zone. The Mediterranean to the W, and the deserts to the S and the E play a major role, as does the great variety of topographical features. The following regional generalizations may be made: (1) Temperature decreases with height and increases with depth below sea level. (2) The temperature ranges increase as one moves away from the moderating influence of the sea. (3) Rain tends to decreases from N to S. (4) Rain decreases from W to E. (5) Rain increases as heights are encountered. (6) As the prevailing moisture-bearing winds are from the W, rain precipitates on the W slopes, leaving the E slopes in a rain shadow.

1. Temperatures. (All figures are cited in Fahrenheit.) The sea breeze has a moderating effect on the temperatures on the coast, but humidity makes the summer quite oppressive here. The mean minimum-average-maximum temperatures at Haifa in January are 47-56-65, and in August 76-83-90. Winter frosts along the coast are rare. The ranges of temperature in the Samaria and Judean hills are much greater. Summer nights are comfortable, but winter nights are cold and frosts are not uncommon. The minimum-average-maximum temperatures in Jerusalem in January are 42-48-54, and in August 65-75-85. In the Rift Valley tempera-

Roman street in Petra

tures are much hotter all year, making these regions comfortably warm in the winter and unbearably hot in the summer. Jericho, which enjoys a range of 68 to 84 in January, served as Herod's winter palace. In July maximum temperatures at Jericho reach 114. Summer at Elath is also torrid with temperatures ranging from 80 to 104. The Transjordanian plateau suffers from blistering desert winds that are extremely hot or extremely cold.

Extremes of temperature are noted in the Bible. The burning midday sun caused the death of a lad in Elisha's day (II Kgs 4:18–20; cf. Ps 32:4). King Jehoiakim sat in his winter house before a brazier (Jer 36:22). Even in April it was necessary for the high priest's servants to warm themselves around a charcoal fire at night (Jn 18:18). The poor suffered from the cold because of inadequate clothing (Job 24:7).

2. Winds. During the summer Palestine lies midway between a monsoon low over the Persian Gulf and a high pressure area in the Atlantic. It therefore enjoys steady NW Etesian winds and a sunny almost rainless summer, as there are no frontal storms of cold air clashing with warm air masses. In the winter, however, cold maritime air pushes S into the Mediterranean basin clashing with the warm tropical air masses and creating wet and stormy weather (Job 37:9). A partial tabulation at Jerusalem from May to October indicates the frequency of the various types of prevailing winds: from the NW 78.8 days, from the W 27.5 days, and from the N 26.5 days. During the rainy months the winds come from the W and SW on 60.7 days, from the NE, E and SE 67.4 days.

a. West winds. During the winter season the moisture bearing winds from the W and SW precipitate rains as they encounter colder land and air masses (I Kgs 18:44; Lk 12:54). During the summer the drier NW winds encounter only warm land and air masses and do not precipitate any rain. The winds do, however, mitigate the heat of the day for Cis-Jordan at least. The westerly winds reach the Transjordanian plateau about 3:00 P.M., after the heat of the day. These regular winds are used for the winnowing of grain (Ps 1:4) even to this day.

b. North winds. North winds are relatively rare. There are two types. Chiefly in October a cold dry wind seeps over the mountain barriers from central Asia (Sir 43:20). In March a surge of polar air across the Balkans may produce heavy rains (Prov 25:23, RSV).

c. East and south winds. The scorching desert wind (*sirocco, khamsin*) from the E, SE, or S was and still is a dreaded phenomenon. It strikes for three to four days in the transitional seasons between the rainy season and the summer, i.e., in the spring from April to the middle of June, and in the autumn from the middle of September to the end of October. A sirocco will produce the hottest temperatures of the year, often 20 degrees above the average (Jer 4:11). Even worse, it is an exceedingly dry wind, dropping relative humidity by 30–40 percent, fraying tempers, debilitating energies, and causing dehydration. The air is filled with a fine yellowish dust which veils the sun and reduces visibility. The siroccos of the spring are particularly devastating, withering the winter vegetation in a few hours (Ps 103:15–16; Isa 40:6–8; Ezk 17:10; 19:12; Hos 13:15; cf. Jon 4:8). The fullest fury of the sirocco is experienced in the Transjordan, the Negeb, and the Rift Valley. In certain coastal regions the sirocco winds may pour down the slopes at 60 miles per hour, shattering ships off the coast (Ps 48:7; Ezk 27:26).

B. *Precipitation*

1. The rainy season. The exact commencement of the rainy season is not predictable, but in general it runs from mid-October to mid-April, with perhaps a day or two in May with some rain. The rainy season includes but is also more extensive than our winter months (cf. Song 2:11). In this season three to four days of heavy rain alternate with dry days during which cold desert winds blow from the E.

2. The early and the latter rains. The Bible refers repeatedly to the early (RSV "autumn") and the latter (RSV "spring") rains (Deut 11:14; Jer 5:24; Joel 2:23), giving rise perhaps to the impression that rains fall only at the beginning and the end of the rainy season. As a matter of fact, much of the heaviest rains fall in January and February in the middle of the season (Lev 26:4; Ezr 10:9, 13). These initial and final rains are stressed because they were crucial for agriculture. The early rains come in late October, softening the ground for plowing and sowing. The latter rains fall in March and April, and are needed to make the grain swell for a good harvest (Hos 6:3; Zech 10:1).

3. Drought and unseasonable rains. If the high pressure areas over Europe and Asia in the N linked up with the high pressures over Africa and Arabia, this would block cyclonic storms from arriving through the trough of low pressure in the Mediterranean. In that case rain would sometimes be delayed until as late as December, or in some years rain would amount to only 50–75 percent of the average. A drought that lasted three and one-half years is

recorded in Elijah's day (I Kgs 17:1; Lk 4:25; Jas 5:17; cf. Deut 28:23–24; I Kgs 8:35; Jer 14:3–6). If the thermal difference between the warm and cold air masses was not great, rainless clouds would float by (Prov 25:14; Jude 12). On rare occasions a late surge of cold Atlantic air would penetrate into the area of Palestine in summer, bringing unseasonable rain (I Sam 12:17; Prov 26:1).

4. The distribution of precipitation. As Amos 4:7 indicates, there are considerable local differences in the distribution of rainfall. Galilee receives the greatest amount of rain, from 28–40 inches. Haifa on the coast receives 24 inches, Tiberias 16–18 inches, and Beth-shean in the Jordan rift only 12 inches. In Judea the foothills receive 16–22 inches; the rainfall at Jerusalem fluctuates from 17–28 inches, with an average of 25 inches. Jericho receives an average of 4–6 inches; in the very wet winter of 1944 it recorded 13 inches. The S end of the Dead Sea receives only 2 inches. The steppe region around Beer-sheba receives between 8–12 inches; areas to the S which receive less than 4–8 inches are considered desert and thus beyond the Negeb proper. In the Transjordan Gilead and Bashan receive from 20–28 inches; Moab about 16 inches. Amman is in the steppe zone and receives but 13 inches.

5. Dew. The summer drought is not caused by the lack of humidity, which is in fact twice as intense in the summer as during the rest of the year. The lack of rain storms results from the absence of frontal clashes between warm and cold air masses. The summer humidity manifests itself in the dew that condenses as the ground cools during the night. At Gaza with its extremes of temperature dew may form as many as 250 nights a year. On the coast dew forms five out of six nights during August and September. Gideon was able to collect a bowl full of water from dew on the fleece which he had set out (Jud 6:38). Dew is vital for the growth of grapes during the summer (Zech 8:12). It was indeed a calamitous drought when not even dew was available (II Sam 1:21; I Kgs 17:1; Hag 1:10). Its value may be seen in the numerous comparisons of God's grace and goodness to the benefaction of dew (Gen 27:28; Isa 18:4; Hos 14:5; Mic 5:7; Sir 43:22). When the sun appears the moisture from the dew rises like a thick mist in the valleys (Hos 13:3).

6. Hail and snow. In contrast to dew which is a blessing, hail which falls in thunderstorms in the winter and in the spring is always a calamity. It beats down the standing grain and destroys the tender vines (Ps 78:47; Isa 28:2; 30:30; Ezk 13:11, 13; Hag 2:17). There were even occasions when hailstones were large enough to slay men (Josh 10:11).

Snow, which falls occasionally on the hills in the rainy season, brought misery to many whose houses were not built for warmth (Ps 147:16–17). The virtuous wife was not afraid of the snow because she had provided her family with warm clothes (Prov 31:21). In David's time Benaiah slew a lion, which had come up from the Jordan Valley on a memorable day when snow fell (II Sam 23:20). During the Maccabean revolt a heavy snow frustrated the invasion of Trypho (I Macc 13:22). Records kept for Jerusalem during a period of 22 years show that there were in this period eight years without snow, five years with snow only in February, and other years with a little snow also in other months. A very heavy snow occurs about once in 15 years. In 1920, 29 inches of snow fell; in 1968 heavy snow broke the branches of many trees in Jerusalem. The snow that does fall in Judea does not remain; snow that falls in Transjordan remains for a few days. The Jebel Druze is covered with snow every year from January to March. The snow of Mount Hermon (Sirion) and of the Lebanon Mountains was a symbol of permanence (Jer 18:14, RSV).

7. Drainage and springs. About half the water that falls in the hills is lost by evaporation. Much of the rest drains rapidly through the porous Cenomanian and Turonian limestone and the Senonian chalk until it reaches the level of harder rocks and emerges at the foot of hills as springs. Though Palestine did not have rivers suitable for irrigation like Egypt and Mesopotamia, she had her springs (Deut 8:7). It has been estimated that there are an average of nine springs per square kilometer in upper Galilee; seven to eight per square kilometer in Samaria, and two to three per square kilometer in Judah. Because of the especially porous nature of the Senonian chalk of the Judean wilderness, some very strong springs appear at its eastern edge, e.g., 'Ain es-Sultan at Jericho.

Bibliography. F. M. Abel, *Géographie de la Palestine,* 2 vols., Paris: J. Gabalda, 1933, 1938. Y. Aharoni, *The Land of the Bible,* Philadelphia: Westminster Press, 1967. M. Avi-Yonah, *The Holy Land,* Grand Rapids: Baker, 1966. M. Avnimelech, "The Influence of Geological Conditions on the Development of Jerusalem," BASOR, #181 (Feb., 1966), 24–30. Denis Baly, *The Geography of the Bible,* New York: Harper & Bros., 1957. E. M. Blaiklock, ed., *Zondervan Pictorial Bible Atlas,* Grand Rapids: Zondervan, 1969. N. Glueck, *The Other Side of the Jordan,* New Haven: ASOR, 1940; *The River Jordan,* Philadelphia: Westminster Press, 1946; *Rivers in the Desert,* New York: Grove Press, Inc., 1959; "Transjordan," TAOTS, pp. 429–453. L. H. Grollenberg, *Atlas of the Bible,* London: Nelson, 1963. G. Lankester Harding, *The Antiquities of Jordan,* London: Lutterworth, 1959. J. P. Harland, "The Destruction of the Cities of the Plain," BA, VI (1943), 41–52. Martin Noth, *The Old Testament World,* Philadelphia: Fortress Press, 1966. C. F. Pfeiffer and H. F. Vos, *The Wycliffe Historical Geography of Bible Lands,* Chicago: Moody Press, 1967. G. A. Smith, *The Historical Geography of the Holy Land,* London: Collins, 1966, reprint of 1931 ed. Z. Vilnay, *The New Israel Atlas,* Jerusalem: Israel Universities Press, 1968. *Maps:* 1-100,000 Map of Palestine (1956); 1-100,000 Map of Israel (1968); 1-250,000 Map of Israel (1967); 1-250,000 Geological Map of Israel (1965); 1-250,000 Archaeological Map of the Kingdom of the Jordan (1950).

E. M. Y.

PALLU (păl'ōō), **PALLUITES** (păl'ōō-īts). Pallu was a son of Reuben who went to Egypt with Jacob (Ex 6:14; Num 26:5, 8; I Chr 5:3; "Phallu" in Gen 46:9). The Palluites were descendants of Pallu (Num 26:5).

PALM. *See* Plants.

PALM AND HANDBREADTH. *See* Weights, Measures, and Coins: Linear Measure.

PALM TREES, CITY OF. *See* Jericho.

PALMERWORM. *See* Animals: Locust, III. 29.

PALMYRA. *See* Tadmor.

PALSY. *See* Diseases.

PALTI (păl'tī). A Benjamite who was chosen to represent that tribe as one of the 12 spies sent to reconnoiter Canaan for Moses (Num 13:9). Other Heb. spellings are Phalti and Phaltiel (*q.v.*).

PALTIEL (păl'tĭ-ĕl). A "prince" of Issachar chosen to represent that tribe in the division of Canaan (Num 34:26). Phaltiel is another spelling for this Heb. name in II Sam 3:15.

PALTITE (păl'tīt). A descendant of Palti (*q.v.;* II Sam 23:26).

PAMPHYLIA (păm-fĭl'ĭ-*a*). The region of Pamphylia consisted of a plain 80 miles long and 20 miles broad at its widest, lying on the S coast of Asia Minor between the Taurus Mountains and the Mediterranean (Acts 27:5). It was bordered on the E by Cilicia and on the W by Lycia. The plain was shut in from N winds but was well watered by springs from the Taurus ranges.

Very likely Dorians came to Pamphylia at the time of the Dorian migrations and mingled with the aborigines. The region was subject successively to Lydia, Persia, Alexander the Great, the Seleucids, Pergamum, and Rome. Pamphylia does not seem to have benefited greatly from civilizing influences and long remained a rough and rather dangerous area. The port of Side is said to have earned its prosperity as the market of Cilician pirates.

About 102 B.C. Rome established the province of "Cilicia" (merely a series of posts along the Pamphylian coast) to deal with the Mediterranean pirates. When Pompey took Cilicia after his tilt with the sea brigands (67 B.C.), Pamphylia became part of the province of Cilicia and remained such until 36 B.C., at which time Antony gave it to Amyntas of Galatia. It was probably not detached from Galatia until A.D. 43 when Claudius took away the freedom of the Lycians and added them to the province of Pamphylia. Under Nero the Lycians were freed, and in 69 Pamphylia and Galatia were put under one governor. Vespasian took away the Lycians' freedom and reunited Lycia and Pamphylia. In A.D. 74 the Roman province of Pamphylia was extended to include the mountainous area to the N, properly known as Pisidia. Besides Perga, the chief cities of Pamphylia were Attalia (*c.* 12 miles SW of the metropolis) and Side (more than 30 miles SE of Perga).

When Paul traversed Pamphylia it was part of the combined province Lycia-Pamphylia (Acts 13:13; 14:24; 15:38). According to his custom, he must have been concerned for the Jews of Pamphylia. That there were some Jews there is demonstrated by the fact that representatives from the province were present in Jerusalem on the day of Pentecost (Acts 2:10). Although introduced by Paul and Barnabas, Christianity was slow in being established there.

H. F. V.

PAN. *See* Frying Pan.

PANNAG. *See* Plants.

PAP. *See* Breast.

PAPER. *See* Writing; Papyrus; Gebal.

PAPHOS (pā'fŏs). A city on the W end of Cyprus. It was the capital of Cyprus during the Roman administration. When Paul and Barnabas had evangelized Cyprus from Salamis at the E end to Paphos in the W, they preached to the governor, Sergius Paulus. In spite of the oppo-

Traditional site of the landing of Venus near Paphos after the goddess was born at sea.
HFV

Papyrus bundle columns of Amenhotep III, Luxor Temple. LL

sition of the magician Elymas, called Bar-jesus, the governor was won to faith in Christ.

Old Paphos, seven miles away, was settled by Phoenicians, but the new Paphos of Paul's day was Gr. as it is to this day under its modern name, Baffa. The city was a famed center of worship of the goddess Aphrodite. From Paphos, Paul and his companions set sail for the mainland at Perga (Acts 13:6–13).

PAPYRUS. This term applies to an aquatic plant of the sedge family (*Cyperus papyrus*), to the "paper" prepared from its pith, and to the manuscript(s) made by attaching these individual sheets together.

The plant is designated in the Heb. OT by the word *gōme'* in Ex 2:3; Job 8:11; Isa 18:2; 35:7. KJV has "bulrushes" or "rush(es)"; some modern translations have "papyrus" (ASV marg. except Isa 18:2, in text; RSV and NASB at Job 8:11 and Isa 18:2). The LXX, at Job 8:11 only, uses the Gr. word *papyros* (from which is derived "papyrus," "paper"). The Gr. NT only once refers to papyrus paper with another Gr. word, *chartēs* (II Jn 12; usually translated "paper").

The plant in antiquity grew predominantly in Egypt and in the northern reaches of the Jordan. Growing in the mire (Job 8:11), it was used by Isaiah as an indication of luxuriant growth (35:7). The long triangular stems, averaging three to ten feet, ended in open bell-shaped flowers. The plant was used for making various items, including boats (Ex 2:3, the basket in which Moses was set afloat; Isa 18:2 refers to sizeable boats used to transport the envoys of Cush). Because of the scarcity of wood, Egyptians made skiffs or rafts of papyrus reeds lashed together and waterproofed with pitch. They were also used for fishing and hunting in the marshes and as ferries across canals.

The paper was formed by cutting the inner stem into thin strips, placing them side by side, and then placing over these at right-angles another series of strips which were then joined together by some adhesive and some form of pressure. The side having horizontal strips (the recto) was usually written on first; the back side with vertical strips is the verso.

Pasted end to end these sheets formed papyrus rolls of different lengths. About 20 sheets was standard. The Egyptian Papyrus Harris I (*c.* 1160 B.C.) in the British Museum is the longest known, being 133 feet long. The height varied from a maximum of 18½ inches to seven inches and sometimes less. A roll was usually made long enough to permit an entire composition, such as a book of the Bible, to be inscribed on it. *See* Writing.

Papyrus was used from as long ago as 3000 B.C. in Egypt (e.g., The Wisdom of Ptah-hatep) and continued in use until the 7th cen. A.D. or later. Papyrus was exported to Syria-Palestine as indicated by the Wen-Amon papyrus which relates that 500 rolls were sent to Byblos (ANET, p. 28). Papyri have been found in dry areas where they have not deteriorated, such as Italy, Egypt, and the Dead Sea area.

The oldest Heb. papyrus is the Wadi Murabba'at palimpsest with a list of personal names (7th or 8th cen. B.C.). Until the Qumran discoveries, the earliest extant Heb. OT MS was the Nash Papyrus (part of Deut 5–6, *c.* 2nd cen. B.C.). The Elephantine (*q.v.*) papyri (5th cen. B.C.) are the most notable Aramaic papyri. The oldest Gr. OT MS is the John Rylands Library Papyrus Greek 458 (fragments of Deut 23–28, 2nd cen. B.C.). Of the apocryphal and noncanonical papyri, the most notable are the *Logia* or Sayings of Jesus found at Oxyrhynchus, Egypt, in 1896 and 1897 (2nd and 3rd cen. A.D.), and the Gospel of Thomas found near Nag Hammadi in 1946.

There are more than 241 Gr. NT papyri. Some of the most important are the Chester Beatty Papyri ($P^{45, 46, 47}$), PP^{52}, the famous

Cultivated papyrus at the Cairo Museum. HFV

John Rylands fragment (three and one-half by two and one -half inches) of Jn 18:31-33, 37-38, early 2nd cen. A.D. and thus the oldest NT MS, and P[66], the Bodmer papyrus II of most of the Gospel of John.

The papyri have played an important role in NT studies. The oldest NT document (P[52]) bears on the date and authorship of John's Gospel (*see* John, Gospel of). The papyri in correlation with the great uncial vellum codexes influenced the principles of textual criticism and provided significant evidences for particular textual decisions. The papyri documents in general, especially the large number of non-literary ones, have given insight into the linguistic milieu (the *koinē*) in which the NT belongs and have aided particularly in the realms of vocabulary and style (cf. among others the works of Deissmann and especially Moulton and Milligan, *The Vocabulary of the Greek Testament*).

See Bible Manuscripts; Versions, Ancient and Medieval; Writing; Plants: Reed; Archaeology.

G. W. K.

PARABLE

Meaning of the term. The word parable is derived from the Gr. *parabolē* which etymologically means "a placing of things side by side," usually for the purpose of comparison. Since in the LXX *parabole* was used to translate the Heb. word *māshāl,* some of the diverse meanings of *māshāl* have been attached to *parabolē*. Thus in the NT, figurative sayings, similes, and metaphors are all called parables. The parable proper, i.e., the short, simple story from which some teaching point can be derived, is an extended simile or metaphor. A. M. Hunter suggests the following definition: a parable is "a comparison drawn from nature or daily life and designed to illuminate some spiritual truth, on the assumption that what is valid in one sphere is valid also in the other" (*Interpreting the Parables,* p. 8).

Jesus, of course, did not invent the parable. Parables are found in the OT (cf. e.g., II Sam 12:1-14; Isa 5:1-7) and in the rabbinical writings. A careful comparison between the use of the parable in the OT and the rabbinical writings with that of Jesus reveals many striking similarities. The differences, however, are even more striking. The rabbis used the parable to illuminate truth already known from Scripture. Jesus utilized the parable to proclaim the kingdom of God which came in His own person and ministry. The originality, forcefulness, and artistry of Jesus' parables have no parallel in either the OT or the rabbinical writings.

Classification of parables. Approximately one-third of the teaching of Jesus is cast in parabolic form. This fact is particularly striking since He is the only person in the NT who uses parables at all. There are no parables in the NT epistles, although of course many metaphors and similes occur. The total number of parables in the Gospels will differ according to how one defines a parable, but between 50 and 60 is an approximate number. Luke's Gospel is richest in this form of Jesus' teaching, having about 24, of which 15 occur only in that Gospel. Matthew has 20, of which 11 are peculiar to him; and Mark has eight, only two of which occur only in Mark. Although the word *parabole* does not occur in John's Gospel, Jesus uses many figures and allegories of Himself; e.g., the Good Shepherd, the Vine, the Bread from Heaven, etc.

The range of subjects dealt with in the parables are relatively few. Jeremias puts them into eight basic groupings, whereas Hunter reduces these to four: the coming of the kingdom, the grace of the kingdom, the men of the kingdom, and the crisis of the kingdom. This is probably an oversimplification, but it emphasizes the point that the parables are inextricably bound up with the person and work of Jesus Christ. *See* Parables of Jesus.

Purpose of parables. The obvious purpose of Jesus' use of parables was to make spiritual truth clear and compelling. "Everybody loves a story," and thus He told fascinating stories taken from nature (e.g., the sower, Mt 13:3-23; the mustard seed, Mt 13:31-32) and the vicissitudes of life (e.g., the lost coin, Lk 15:8-10; the wise and foolish virgins, Mt 25:1-13) to drive home spiritual truth to the minds of His hearers.

Mk 4:11-12, however, seems to suggest that Jesus spoke in parables in order to obscure the truth: "To you has been given the secret of the kingdom of God, but for those outside everything is in parables; so that they may indeed see but not perceive, and may indeed hear but not understand; lest they should turn again, and be forgiven" (RSV).

Many solutions have been offered for this *crux interpretum.* The older interpreters saw in the passage the exercise of divine sovereignty, arbitrarily choosing whom it would and hardening whom it would. Others, rejecting such an idea as unworthy of the teaching of Jesus, took the saying from Him and assigned it to the developing theology of the early church. Since, however, there is good evidence that the saying is authentic (it agrees with the Targum and contains several Aramaisms), other alternatives have been suggested. The most attractive is to take the purpose clause (*hina*) as a result clause (*hoti*, cf. Mt 13:13), and to understand the passage as a description of the hardening effect that the teaching of Jesus has on those who reject Him. Jesus' parables are not nice stories with a simple moral at the end. They summon men to decision. This decision relates not only to the truth of the parable but to the Person who is teaching by this means. If the hearer refuses to respond, the heart is further hardened. This process is described in Mk 4:11–12, a passage which instead of being described as the purpose of parables should be called the result of failure to respond to the teaching of Christ's parables.

Interpretation of parables. No other segment of Christ's teaching has suffered so much at the hands of the interpreter as have the parables. Origen interprets the parable of the good Samaritan as follows: "The man who fell among thieves is Adam. As Jerusalem represents heaven, so Jericho, to which the traveler journeyed, is the world. The robbers are man's enemies, the devil and his minions. The priest stands for the law, the Levite for the prophets. The good Samaritan is Christ Himself. The beast on which the wounded man was set, is Christ's body which bears the fallen Adam. The inn is the church; the two pence, the Father and the Son; and the Samaritan's promise to come again, Christ's second advent." Similar examples of this astonishing kind of interpretation can be found in the writings of Tertullian, Augustine, and others. Inevitably a reaction set in, led by the Antiochene Fathers (notably Theodore of Mopsuestia and John Chrysostom); but despite their efforts the allegorizing method generally prevailed.

During the Reformation significant advances were made in biblical studies, and these were reflected in the understanding and interpretation of the parables. Allegorizing was generally rejected. If Luther and Calvin erred in interpreting the parables, it was only because of their eagerness to find "Reformation doctrine" everywhere in Scripture, including the parables of Jesus.

The next great step in understanding the parables was made by Adolph Jülicher by the publication of his now famous two volume work, *Die Gleichnisreden Jesu*, in 1888 and 1889. Jülicher dealt the death blow to all allegorizing of the parables. He insisted that each parable had one and only one truth to teach, and that all the other details of the parable were just so many trappings. Jülicher performed an important function. He eliminated the subjective, allegorical interpretation of the parables that had so long prevented an adequate understanding of them. However, he made two errors. First, he pressed too far his "one truth" theory. Some parables in fact have allegorical elements in them. Second, he was mistaken in his assertion that the parables teach only moral truth – the more general the better.

Jülicher's corrective came in the publication of C. H. Dodd's *The Parables of the Kingdom* in 1935. Dodd's great contribution was that he placed the parables in their life setting, viz., the great eschatological [or redemptive – Ed.] act of God realized in the person, ministry and teaching of Jesus Christ. In Him the kingdom of God had come, and the parables are to be understood in the setting of that kingdom now realized.

More recent studies (e.g., Jeremias, *The Parables of Jesus*, 1954) assert that the parables in their present form as found in the Gospels have suffered a radical modification. Their original settings in the life of Jesus have been lost. By studying the way in which the transformation of a parable from the life setting of Jesus to that of the early church came about, one can reconstruct what the original setting was. Such an approach is highly subjective and the results tentative, although it is doubtless true that in some instances the precise historical circumstances of the parables have been lost. Instead, the redemptive mission of Christ, i.e., "the presence of the kingdom of God in the person, ministry, and teaching of Jesus" (cf. George E. Ladd, "The Life Setting of the Parables of the Kingdom," JBR, XXXI [1963], 197), provides the general life situation of all of Jesus' parables. It is in these terms that they are to be understood and not in terms of general moral and religious truth.

See Bible Interpretation.

Bibliography. C. H. Dodd, *The Parables of the Kingdom*, London: Nisbet, 1935. F. Hauck, "*Parabolē*," TDNT, V, 744–761. A. M. Hunter, *Interpreting the Parables*, London: SCM Press, 1960. Joachim Jeremias, *The Parables of Jesus*, London: SCM Press, 1954. Adolph Jülicher, *Die Gleichnisreden Jesu*, 2 vols., Leipzig: J. C. B. Mohr, 1888, 1889. Neil R. Lightfoot, *Lessons from the Parables*, Grand Rapids: Baker, 1965. G. Campbell Morgan, *The Parables and Metaphors of Our Lord*, Westwood, N.J.: Revell, 1943. W. O. E. Oesterley, *The Gospel Parables in the Light of Their Jewish Background*, New York: Macmillan, 1936. Richard C. Trench, *Notes on the Parables of Our Lord*, 14th ed. rev., London: Macmillan, 1882.

W. W. W.

PARABLES OF JESUS. For an introductory statement on the parables of Jesus *see* Parable. An attempt is made here to list, classify, and provide some guide to interpretation of those parables. Scholars vary widely in the number of parables they discover in the Gospels. Their lists range from about 30 to 80, depending on whether they include seeming parables not described by the term "parable" and whether they include shorter parables and parabolic illustra-

PARABLES OF JESUS

tions. A total of 52 are noted here. These are arranged in nine categories; in a few cases assignment of a parable to one of these categories is somewhat arbitrary. In each case the story of the parable is not told but merely intimated in conjunction with the interpretation. Scripture references are noted in every instance so that the reader can follow with an open Bible.

I. The Message of God in the World

A. *Nature of the message.* The patched cloth and the wine skins (Mt 9:16–17; Mk 2:21–22; Lk 5:36–38). New cloth is not yet shrunk and when an old garment is patched with it, skrinkage tends to make the tear worse. New wine placed in old wine skins will cause the skins to burst because they already have been stretched about as far as possible with a previous fermenting process. The point of the parable is that Christ has come with a new message of grace, as opposed to the old legal order; this new message requires a new approach and new forms.

B. *Proclamation of the message.* The sower (Mt 13:3–9, 18–23; Mk 4:1–9, 13–20; Lk 8:4–15). According to the parable, the seed of the good news of the kingdom is sown on various soils with varying results; a majority of people do not, for one reason or another, receive the truth of God unto salvation.

C. *Growth of the truth (kingdom) in the world.*

1. The seed growing secretly (Mk 4:26–29) describes the imperceptible growth of the kingdom in the world.
2. The mustard seed (Mt 13:31–32; Mk 4:30–32; Lk 13:18–19) portrays the rapid and unexpected growth of the kingdom. Though the seed is small (Palestinian mustard seed is black and small as a petunia seed or smaller), it grows quickly to great height (in Palestine 12 to 15 feet or more).

D. *Corruption of the message and work of God*

1. The leaven (Mt 13:33; Lk 13:20–21). Leaven in Scripture standardly speaks of evil and presumably does here also; so reference would be to corruption of the doctrine of the kingdom by false doctrine. Some prefer to see it in this case as signifying that gospel truth will permeate evil society.
2. The parable of the wheat and tares (Mt 13:24–30, 36–43) teaches that Satan counterfeits the gospel with his own brand of religion, and there grow up together in Christendom both professors and real possessors of the truth; these will be separated at the judgment.

II. Salvation and Forgiveness of Sin

1, 2, 3. The lost sheep, the lost coin, and the prodigal son (Lk 15) were aimed at Pharisees who criticized Jesus for His association with publicans and sinners and who sought to justify themselves before men. Apparently Jesus likened the 99 sheep, the nine coins, and the elder brother to the Pharisees who considered themselves spiritually safe; He turned instead to the publicans and sinners (the hundredth sheep, the lost coin, and the prodigal son) who recognized their need of a Saviour.

4. Pharisee and the publican (Lk 18:9–14). Jesus again hits the self-righteous Pharisee. The publican was justified because he came in humility, recognizing his sin and resting in divine provision.
5. Sons called to work (Mt 21:28–32). The one son represents the publicans and harlots, who at first had no sympathy with John the Baptist and his ministry and message, but later repented and believed. The other represents the chief priests and elders who as religious men professed initial interest in John but did not receive his message in their hearts.

6, 7. The hid treasure and pearl of great price (Mt 13:44–46) illustrate the value of believers for whom Christ made the supreme sacrifice. The field must represent the world as it does in the first two parables of Mt 13. The man who gave up all to buy the field and its treasure and the merchant man who bought the pearl can be none other than Christ, who made the supreme sacrifice to pay the sin-debt of the whole world. Within the world of sinners are those who would believe on Him—treasure and pearl.

8. The marriage of the king's son (Mt 22:1–14) tells first of the religious leaders who refuse the King's invitation, resulting in God's turning from the Jews to the Gentiles; second, it tells of Gentiles who dare to come before the King in their own way; they do not have the wedding garment—His robe of righteousness.
9. The great supper (Lk 14:16–24). Similar in nature to the foregoing, this parable involves three groups: those who at first received the invitation and refused; the poor,maimed, halt and blind; those among the highways and hedges. It would appear that the first group represents the scribes and Pharisees; the second and third groups (which respond) represent Jewish publicans and sinners, and Gentiles, respectively.

10, 11. The barren fig tree (Lk 13:6–9) and the strait gate and shut door (Lk 13:23–30) speak of the salvation of God and His judgment for failure to receive His grace.

12, 13. The door of the sheep (Jn 10:1–10) and the good Shepherd (Jn 10:11–18, 25–30). The former parable declares that Jesus is the way through whom one becomes a member of this new spiritual family (flock). Those who refuse to come by way of the door (such as the Pharisees) and seek salvation by means of their own righteousness are classed as

PARABLES OF JESUS

thieves and robbers and are outside the fold. As the good Shepherd, Jesus lay down His life for His sheep and chooses sheep from among both Gentiles and Jews and makes of them one flock ("fold" in the KJV is an incorrect translation).

14, 15. Defilement from without (Mt 12:43–45; Lk 11:24–26) and from within. In these parables Jesus made it clear that there was no middle ground between acceptance and rejection of the Saviour. In the former parable, a certain evil spirit left a man, and later finding the man without sufficient moral defense entered his life with seven more wicked spirits. So it is not enough merely to live a good life—to be negative about evil. One must be full of good, must possess positive righteousness which is available through Christ alone. In the second parable, the source of difficulty is described not as coming from without but from within. Not only does an individual have to combat the work of the evil spirits, but he has a fallen nature within. His heart is desperately wicked and the source of all kinds of defilement.

16. Inward light (Mt 6:22–23; Lk 11:34–36). As the physical body is lighted with the eye, so the soul has an "eye." Those whose spiritual sight has not been darkened by impenitence understand the significance of spiritual developments occurring around them because they belong to the Saviour.

17. Under the figure of two roads (Mt 7:13–14) Jesus pictures the alternate moral courses open to man in this life.

18. The builders (Mt 7:24–27; Lk 6:46–49). There are two classes of men as builders. One wisely builds his life and character on a faith rooted in Christ; the other foolishly tries to build a life and character without being effectively established in Christ.

III. Treatment of Christ

At least two parables deal with this theme: the wicked husbandmen (Mt 21:33–41; Mk 12:1–9; Lk 20:9–16) and the rejected stone (Mt 21:42–46; Mk 12:10–11; Lk 20:17–19). In the first parable Christ's enemies are likened to vinedressers who failed to fulfill their responsibility of keeping the vineyard (Israel) for their landlord (God). In fact, they maltreated the servants (prophets) of the landlord when they came with messages from their master. Finally, they even slew the son (Jesus Christ) of the landlord; for this God would destroy them. In the second parable the Pharisees appear as builders who cast away a certain stone (Christ) as unfit for the structure they were building. But this stone became head of the corner and also became a powerful weapon in the hand of God for destroying opponents of the Messiah.

IV. Fellowship with God

Those who have in faith appropriated the work of Christ and experienced the new birth have the privilege of fellowship with the Father and the Son. Jesus expressed this truth in several parables.

A. *Prayer.* Two, on prayer, are closely related: the importunate friend (Lk 11:5–8) and the unjust judge (Lk 18:1–8). Both demonstrate that God will certainly hear His children, but that prayer should be importunate and persevering. However, these two parables differ slightly in that the former demonstrates that prayer is never out of season, and the latter that it is sure to bring blessing and not a curse.

B. *Gratitude.* The parable of the two debtors (Lk 7:41–43) seems to teach that the gratitude of sinners depends on *their* estimate of the amount remitted to them.

C. *Christ's relationship with His disciples.* The parable of the bride and the bridegroom (Mk 2:19–20; Lk 5:34–35) describes Christ's joyous relationship with His disciples and His coming departure.

D. *Spiritual fellowship and nourishment.* The parable of the vine and the branches (Jn 15:1–11) concerns the ministry of Christ to and through His disciples, and the conditions for fruitbearing.

E. *Supply of temporal needs.* The story of the rich fool (Lk 12:16–21) teaches that the abundant life for the believer does not depend on wealth, and even life itself cannot be secured by wealth. The accompanying exhortation in v. 31 is especially important here: "Seek ye the kingdom of God; and all these things shall be added unto you."

V. Witness or Discipleship

1, 2. Just as a man who prepares to build a tower first counts the cost to determine whether he can finish it (Lk 14:28–30), and as a king estimates his military resources before going to battle (Lk 14:31–32), so the disciple of Christ should count the cost of discipleship and prepare himself to live a life of complete self-renunciation.

3, 4. A disciple without the spirit of self-abnegation is likened to salt which has lost its savor (Mt 5:13; Mk 9:50; Lk 14:33–35), in which condition it is good for absolutely nothing. Effective Christians, like good salt, have a preservative and cleansing effect and give a good flavor to society. The parable of a Christian as a lighted lamp (Mt 5:15; Mk 4:21; Lk 8:16–17; 11:33) focuses on the diffusion of his testimony.

5. If a disciple desires the most effective testimony, he must constantly engage in self-judgment. Such is the message of the parable on offending members (Mt 5:29–30; Mk 9:43, 45, 47). In fact, no sacrifice is too great if it promotes a cor-

PARABLES OF JESUS

rect spiritual condition and a good testimony on the part of the believer.

VI. Relations with Others

A. *A forgiving spirit:* the unmerciful servant (Mt 18:23–35). Jesus dealt here with the hatefulness of an unforgiving spirit and conveyed the idea that if God forgave us so much, we should be willing to forgive all who sin against us.

B. *Neighborliness:* the good Samaritan (Lk 10:30–37). Have a spirit of divine concern and altruism; be a neighbor to him who has no natural claim upon you.

VII. Rewards

The parable of laborers in the vineyard (Mt 20:1–16) teaches that God will reward work well done, but He will reward according to His sovereign will. No one has a right to demand rewards for service to God. A similar parable of service appears in Luke 17:7–10, the main thrust of which is that a servant of God can make no *just claim* for having done more than was due.

VIII. The Return of Christ

Six parables deal with the theme of Christ's return. Others, noted in the next section, deal with judgment in connection with His return. In Lk 12:35–38 Jesus teaches the duty of loyal vigilance concerning His return. Just as servants should be prepared to meet their master at whatever hour a wedding feast breaks up and he returns to his home, so believers are to be ready for Christ's return at any time. Under another figure of speech—the breaking in of a thief—He presents a similar message (Lk 12:39–40; Mt 24:43–44). The householder is exhorted to constant watchfulness lest while he sleeps, the Lord comes as a thief in the night. In an effort to underscore further the matter of watchfulness, Jesus again changes the figure—this time to a servant in the house awaiting the return of his master (Mt 24:45–51; Lk 12:42–46). While there may have been some uncertainty as to whether or not a thief would break in, there is no uncertainty that the master will return. The parable of the householder and the porter (Mk 13:34–37) exhorts watchfulness in view of the return of Christ and is self-explanatory.

Our Lord further emphasizes the importance of preparedness for His coming and for the next life in the parable of the unrighteous steward (Lk 16:1–13). Many have been the difficulties in interpreting this parable; most of them come from pressing the interpretation of unimportant details. The main point is that Jesus is simply trying to teach His disciples that even the unrighteous men of their generation used present opportunities to prepare for the future. Believers could take a lesson from unbelievers in this respect and by being faithful stewards now could prepare to give a good account at the end of their service.

While in the previous parables Christ ex-

Ruins of the Good Samaritan Inn on the Jericho Road. HFV

horted watchfulness in view of His return because the time was uncertain, He did pause to give signs indicating the nearness of that return. In the parable of the sprouting fig tree (Mt 24:32–35; Mk 13:28–31; Lk 21:29–33) He teaches that as the budding of the fig tree indicates the coming of summer, so the existence of certain conditions are sure signs of His coming again.

IX. Judgment

When Jesus returns again at the end of the Tribulation, there will be a judgment of all people then living. The parable of the fish net (Mt 13:47–50) speaks of this judgment in general terms.

Three other parables pertain to the post-Tribulation judgment of Christ. Two are similar but apparently not identical: the ten pounds (Lk 19:11–27) and the ten talents (Mt 25:14–30). A careful study will reveal a whole list of differences between them. In the former, the nobleman going into a far country seeking a kingdom must be none other than our Lord Himself. His servants would then be the disciples or other believers, and the citizens who hated him would be Christ-rejecters. The latter are to be slain (cast into the place of condemnation) at His coming. The disciples are to be rewarded according to their service during His absence. The parable of the talents likewise demonstrates the importance of faithfulness in the light of Christ's return. Perhaps there is an intimation in v. 30 that faithlessness indicates a lack of regenerating experience. Therefore faithless ones are cast into perdition.

Another parable of judgment and one which has been the subject of much debate is that of the ten virgins (Mt 25:1–13). Of course it is superficially obvious that Jesus sought to teach in this passage the importance of watchfulness in the light of His return. The following is offered as a tentative interpretation. The parable describes the judgment of Israel. The ten virgins refer to the professing remnant of Israel after the Church has been taken up by the rapture. The five wise virgins represent the believing remnant; the foolish virgins, the unbelieving who profess to be looking for Messiah's coming in power. The marriage of the bridegroom to the bride (the Church) has already taken place in heaven and the parable alludes to the wedding feast which takes place on earth. The bridegroom's coming is the return of the Lord in glory at the end of the Tribulation. Entrance into the marriage feast corresponds to entrance into the kingdom of heaven on earth (the Millennium). Lack of space prevents a detailed defense or a discussion of the facets of this interpretation.

A last parable on judgment has to do with individual judgment, which occurs whenever a person departs his earthly life: the rich man and Lazarus (Lk 16:19–31). Some would prefer to call this a historical incident rather than a parable; in either case the message is not greatly changed. For the significance of this passage, we need to remember the context. Preceding is the parable of the unjust steward, which seeks to show the benefits following a wise use of present advantages. The rich man, instead of taking advantage of his opportunities to do good on earth, made wealth his highest good. His riches became a stumbling block to a virile faith in God and a life of blessing to others. He forfeited his chance to lay up treasure in heaven. Lazarus, however, maintained a faith in God during his years on earth; for this he was rewarded in the next life.

Bibliography. G. Campbell Morgan, *The Parables and Metaphors of Our Lord,* Westwood, N.J.: Revell, 1943; *The Parables of the Kingdom,* Westwood: Revell, 1907. Alfred Plummer, *A Critical and Exegetical Commentary on the Gospel According to St. Luke,* 4th ed., Edinburgh: T. & T. Clark, 1913. W. Graham Scroggie, *A Guide to the Gospels,* London: Pickering and Inglis, 1948. Richard C. Trench, *Notes on the Parables of Our Lord,* 10th ed., London: Macmillan, 1866.

H. F. V.

PARACLETE (păr'ȧ-klēt). The Gr. word *paraklētos* (from the verb *parakaleō,* "to call alongside for the purpose of helping, to exhort, to console, to encourage") occurs five times in the NT, all in John's writings. Jesus called the Holy Spirit "another Paraclete" (Jn 14:16), which means that He too is a Paraclete. When Christ was on earth He was a helper to His followers. Christ continues to be our Paraclete in heaven, in the sense of our "advocate" with the Father if we should commit an act of sin (I Jn 2:1). *See* Advocate.

In Christ's absence the Spirit carries on this work of helping. With reference to the Spirit the word *paraklētos* is rendered variously: Comforter (KJV, LB), Helper (Williams, NASB, TEV), Advocate (Weymouth, NEB), Counselor (RSV). The work of the Spirit as Paraclete is (1) to convict and give to the world demonstrable proof of the truth of sin, righteousness, and judgment (Jn 16:7 ff.); (2) to abide forever with the disciples of Christ in order to help, exhort, and encourage them (Jn 14:16); (3) to testify or bear witness concerning Christ (Jn 15:26); (4) to aid the disciples in remembering the words of Christ (Jn 14:26). This term applied to the Holy Spirit and the work of the Spirit associated with its occurrences become strong arguments for both the deity and the personality of the Spirit.

Beginning *c.* A.D. 150 in Phrygia, Montanus and his followers emphasized the present supernatural work of the Holy Spirit. In reaction to the increasing rigidity of the organized church he and two women announced themselves as prophets and claimed the period to be the age of the Paraclete in which new revelations from God were to be given. They emphasized the nearness of the end and insisted on very high and strict moral standards in their followers. Montanism was officially rejected, however, because of its insistence on additional revelation apart from the Scriptures.

See Holy Spirit; Trinity.

Bibliography. Johannes Behm, *"Paraklētas,"* TDNT, V, 800–814. Johnstone G. Patrick, "The Promise of the Paraclete," BS, CXXVII (1970), 333–345. O. Schmitz and G. Stahlin, *"Parakaleō,* etc.," TDNT, V, 773–799.

C. C. R.

PARADISE. A place of happiness and bliss. The Heb. word *pardēs* is translated "forest" in Neh 2:8 and "orchard" in Eccl 2:5; Song 4:13. It is derived from an Old Persian word *pairidaeza* meaning a garden with a wall. *See* Plants: Orchard. Nowhere in the OT is the word *pardēs* used in an eschatological sense.

By NT times, however, the Jews considered the region of the dead (Hades or Sheol) to be in the heart of the earth; the wicked dead in "a place of torment," and the righteous dead in "a place of blessedness" (paradise).

Christ used the word only once, to the thief on the cross: "Today shalt thou be with me in paradise" (Lk 23:43). Yet in the story of the rich man and Lazarus He used an alternate term, "Abraham's bosom" (*q.v.;* Lk 16:22). In II Cor 12:4 Paul speaks of being "caught up into paradise, and heard unspeakable words . . . not lawful for a man to utter." In v. 2 he calls it "the third heaven." Many have thought that when Christ rose from the dead He changed the location of this paradise to the upper heavens, as suggested in Eph 4:8–10.

The garden of Eden was very early considered to have been the first paradise. The LXX translates *gan 'ēden* in Gen 2:8 by *paradeisos.* There Adam and Eve had fellowship with God. Rivers flowed peacefully through the garden. There they had access to the fruit of many trees, but because of disobedience they lost the right to "the tree of life" (Gen 3:24). There God gave the first promise of a Redeemer from sin before they were driven out of the garden (Gen 3:15).

A new paradise for the redeemed sinner appears in the last book of the Bible (Rev 2:7; cf. 22:2). In his final vision of the future eternal state John saw "a river of the water of life, clear as crystal, coming from the throne of God and of the Lamb, in the middle of its street. And on either side of the river was the tree of life, bearing twelve kinds of fruit, yielding its fruit every month; and the leaves of the tree were for the healing of the nations" (Rev 22:1-2, NASB).

Bibliography. Joachim Jeremias, *"Paradeisos,"* TDNT, V, 765-773.

L. A. L.

PARAH (pâr'*ȧ*). A city in SW Palestine which was included in the territory of Benjamin in the division of the land under the leadership of Joshua (Josh 18:23).

PARALYTIC. *See* Diseases.

PARAMOUR. A male lover or concubine (Ezk 23:20). In all other instances the Heb. word *pîlegesh* used in this verse is translated "concubine" (*q.v.*) and refers to a female lover or "half-wife."

PARAN (pâr'*ȧ*n). A desert region somewhere in the extreme S of Palestine, near Kadesh-barnea. Most scholars place it in the NE region of the Sinai Peninsula. Others identify it with Et Tih, the great central plateau of Sinai. Beno Rothenberg in *God's Wilderness* (pp. 165-170) argues convincingly that Paran was the original name by which the entire Sinai Peninsula was known in biblical times. Deut 33:2 and Hab 3:3 speak of God coming from Mount Paran to help His people, and associate Paran with Seir and Teman. In Jud 5:4 God is described as coming from Seir and Edom, and therefore all these must have been names for the same general region.

Until David's subjugation of the Edomites (II Sam 8:13 f.), the latter lived chiefly in and W of the Arabah. They had constructed fortresses along their eastern border in the heights of Transjordan in the 13th cen. B.C., but in Moses' time their land lay entirely within the Negeb and overlapped Paran.

Chedorlaomer conquered as far as "El-paran on the border of the wilderness" (Gen 14:5-7, RSV), and Ishmael lived in the Wilderness of Paran after his expulsion by Abraham (Gen 21:21). Later the Israelites crossed this region during the Exodus (Num 10:12; 12:16). It was from Paran that spies were sent out by Moses to explore the land of Canaan (Num 13:3). In Num 13:26 it is said that they returned to the "wilderness of Paran, to Kadesh." Deut 1:19-22 says definitely that the spies were sent from Kadesh, and if this is correctly identified with 'Ain Qudeirat on the present Israeli-Egyptian border, then Paran must have been on the western side of the Arabah, the great rift valley. After leaving Midian, Hadad the Edomite traversed Paran on his flight to Egypt (I Kgs 11:18).

D. B.

PARBAR (pär'b*ȧ*r). A place name for a section of the temple area (I Chr 26:18). A similar Heb. word (*parwarîm*) is translated in II Kgs 23:11 as "suburbs" (KJV) or "precincts" (RSV, NASB). The NEB translates both Heb. terms as "colonnade." It seems to refer to an enclosed area on the W side of the temple area, where horses dedicated to the sun were stabled during Manasseh's wicked reign.

PARCHED CORN. *See* Food.

PARCHED GROUND. The Heb. word used in Isa 35:7 is akin to the Arabic word for mirage, and pictures a land burned by summer heat until a wavy, mirage-like effect is produced over it. Isaiah used a striking contrast taken from desert phenomena to present his confidence that a day would come in which the ideals of righteousness and peace in a golden age, which are now only shimmering hopes, would become abundantly satisfying realities.

PARCHED PLACES. Stretches of land that are dry, cracked, and scorched by the burning sun (Jer 17:6).

PARCHMENT. *See* Writing.

PARDON. *See* Forgiveness; Justification.

PARE THE NAILS. *See* Nail.

PARENT. Although the words "father" and "mother" occur many times in both Testaments, the word "parent" is found only in the NT. Jesus' parents brought Him as a young child to the temple to present Him to the Lord (Lk 2:27), and again at the feast of the Passover when Jesus was 12 years of age (Lk 2:41-42). Other references to the parents of Jesus in the Gospels use the words "father" and "mother."

Great stress is laid in the NT on obedience and respect toward parents. This is doubtless part of Christianity's heritage from the religion of the OT, where to honor one's father and mother is the first commandment with promise (Ex 20:12; cf. Deut 5:16; Prov 1:8; 6:20; etc.). Paul specifically mentions children's responsibilities toward parents in Eph 6:1 and Col 3:20, and includes disobedience to parents among the most despicable of sins (Rom 1:30; II Tim 3:2).

Paul likewise stresses parents' responsibility toward children. They are to provide for their children, not children for their parents (II Cor 12:14). Further, they (fathers, particularly) are not to provoke their children, "lest they be discouraged" (Col 3:21), but are to "bring them up in the discipline and instruction of the Lord" (Eph 6:4, RSV).

See Children; Family; Father; Mother.

W. W. W.

PARLOUR. Rendering of three Heb. words in the OT.

1. Heb. *ḥeder,* i.e., chamber (I Chr 28:11),

the inner rooms of Solomon's temple, probably the holy place and the holy of holies. It is also rendered "innermost part" and "inward part."

2. Heb. *lishkâ*, rendered "parlour" once (I Sam 9:22), otherwise "chamber"; in the former it is probably not the best translation. It designates a room for scribes (Jer 36:12), storerooms in Zerubbabel's temple (Ezr 8:29), priests' cells, etc. (Ezk 40:17 ff.), and rooms in Solomon's temple (Jer 35:2 f.), all translated "chamber."

3. Heb. *'ălîyâ*, roof chamber (Jud 3:20–25) where Eglon was keeping cool in summer. In some cases such a shelter may have been a tent, but the room on top of Eglon's palace was substantially constructed, with doors and a vestibule or porch.

PARMASHTA (pär-măsh'tȧ). One of the ten sons of Haman (Est 9:9).

PARMENAS (pär'mĕ-nȧs). One of the seven deacons chosen by the people and appointed by the Twelve to supervise the daily distribution of goods to the Christian widows in Jerusalem (Acts 6:5). *See* Deacon.

PARNACH (pär'năk). The father of Elizaphan, the representative of Zebulun in the dividing of the land of Canaan (Num 34:25).

PAROSH (pâr'ŏsh). A man whose descendants returned from captivity partly with Zerubbabel (Ezr 2:3) and partly with Ezra (Ezra 8:3, KJV, Pharosh). Some descendants took foreign wives (Ezr 10:25), some entered into the covenant Nehemiah presented (Neh 10:14), and one, Pedaiah (*q.v.* 4), helped repair the wall of Jerusalem (Neh 3:25).

PAROUSIA. *See* Christ, coming of; Presence.

PARSHANDATHA (pär-shăn'dȧ-thȧ). One of the ten sons of Haman (Est 9:7).

PARTHIANS (pär'thĭ-ȧnz). The Parthians are mentioned in the Bible only in Acts 2:9 as the nationality of some of the Diaspora who gathered in Jerusalem on the day of Pentecost. But this people played a significant role in the biblical world. The homeland proper of the Parthians lay to the SE of the Caspian Sea, corresponding to modern Khurasan. They are mentioned by Darius I in the Behistun inscription, but it was not until after Alexander the Great that they emerged as a strong kingdom. In 250 B.C. their king Arsaces I, who claimed descent from the royal Persian family, revolted against the Seleucid king Antiochus II and established a dynasty which lasted for five centuries. The Parthian kings Artabanus I, Phraates I and II, and Mithridates I and II continued aggression against the Seleucids and won an acknowledgment of their independence. Thus the Seleucids finally gave up their attempt to subdue the Parthians.

Phraates III made an alliance with the Roman general Pompey in 66 B.C., but Crassus, who took the eastern third of the Roman Empire, attempted to subdue Parthia in 53 B.C. His army was destroyed, Crassus killed, and the coveted Roman eagle standards were taken. Parthia became a rival to Rome for three centuries.

In 40 B.C. Pacorus, king of Parthia, invaded Syria, deposing Hyrcanus in Palestine and putting Antigonus on the throne of Judea. Three years later the Romans drove them out. Caesar Augustus wisely restored a captive Parthian king, Tiridates, without asking ransom, and by this secured a peace and recovered the eagle standards Crassus had lost. This peace lasted for about 130 years when Trajan arrogantly invaded Mesopotamia despite attempts of the Parthians to pacify him. Peace was restored again by Emperor Hadrian, who gave back conquered provinces. In A.D. 162 the Parthians again overran Syria, but this time were too weak to resist Roman punishment. Both Severus and Caracalla sent armies which eventually took the capital city, Ctesiphon. After a brief revival of strength in A.D. 217 when the Roman Macrinus had to pay the Parthians indemnity, the empire fell to the Sassanid Persians who revolted in A.D. 226.

The Parthians were noted for their use of cavalry in battle. They would pretend to flee or would ride circles around the enemy and shoot their arrows from the side or even from behind. They left no native literature. Indeed, the advanced phases of their culture were borrowed largely from the Semites and Greeks.

See Persia.

E. B. S.

PARTIALITY

1. The inclination of mind to favor a person or party and thus act in a biased manner (I Tim 5:21).

2. In Jas 3:17, the Gr. adjective *adîa-kritos* indicates a confused state of mind when making moral decisions. The same Gr. word is used in a phrase in Jas 1:6 where the translation is "nothing wavering" or "doubting." The ASV marg. gives "without doubtfulness." The sense of Jas 3:17 thus might be stated positively as "single-mindedness."

PARTITION, MIDDLE WALL OF. *See* Middle Wall of Partition.

PARTRIDGE. *See* Animals, III. 39.

PARUAH (pȧ-rōō'ȧ). The father of Jehoshaphat, who was a tribal officer charged with supplying Solomon with foodstuff from the tribe of Issachar (I Kgs 4:17).

PARVAIM (pär-vā'ĭm). An unidentified place from which Solomon obtained gold for his temple (II Chr 3:6). A cognate word in Sanskrit means "eastern," and some such idea as "oriental regions" may have been intended.

PASACH (pā′săk). One of the three sons of Japhlet, and a great-great-grandson of Asher (I Chr 7:33).

PAS-DAMMIM (păs-dăm′ĭm). An abbreviated form of Ephes-dammim (*q.v.;* I Sam 17:1). A place in western Judah, literally, "boundary or edge of blood," perhaps from the red color of the earth in the area (I Chr 11:13).

PASEAH (p*á*-sē′*á*)

1. A descendant of Judah named in I Chr 4:12 as the son of Eshton.

2. The head of a family of Nethinim (Ezr 2:49; Neh 7:51, Phaseah), who returned from the captivity with Zerubbabel. His son, Jehoiada, helped repair the old gate when Nehemiah rebuilt the wall of Jerusalem (Neh 3:6).

PASHUR (păsh′*ŭ*r). A name of probable Egyptian origin meaning "the son of Horus" (S. Ahituv, "Pashhur," IEJ, XX [1970], 95 f.).

1. A son of Immer; a priest who served as "chief officer" in the temple during the days of Jeremiah (Jer 20:1-6). He beat Jeremiah and put him in stocks because the prophet had prophesied against Jerusalem and the temple. When he released Jeremiah the next day, Jeremiah renamed him Magor-missabib, "Terror on every side," and predicted that he would go into captivity and die in the land of Babylonia. He is not mentioned again.

2. Son of Malchiah (or Malchijah), and one of the high officers of Zedekiah's court (Jer 21:1; cf. 38:1). He and Zephaniah, a priest, went to Jeremiah for a word from the Lord concerning Nebuchadnezzar's siege of Jerusalem. Jeremiah told them that the Lord would not spare the city but would deliver it into the hands of the Babylonians (Jer 21:1-10). Pashur also was among those who wanted to put Jeremiah to death (Jer 38:1-6). His descendant was among the priests of Nehemiah's time (Neh 11:12; cf. I Chr 9:12).

3. The father of Gedaliah who also was among those who wanted to kill Jeremiah (Jer 38:1).

4. Father or ancestor of one of the main families of the post-Exilic priests who returned to Judah (Ezr 2:38; Neh 7:41). Possibly the Pashur of Neh 11:12.

5. A priest who participated in sealing a covenant under Nehemiah (Neh 10:3).

H. E. Fi.

PASSAGE

1. The ford of a river (Jud 12:5-6; Jer 51:32).

2. The pass in a mountain range (I Sam 14:4; Isa 10:29). In Josh 22:11 the translation "region" or "side" is more exact, and a better reading is "on the side that pertaineth to the children of Israel" (ASV). In Jer 22:20 the translation should be "and cry from Abarim" (*q.v.*).

PASSENGER. The active verbal idea is of persons passing by or through (Prov 9:15; Ezk 39:11, 14-15). "Passenger" is used in the KJV and "pass by" and "pass through" in ASV and RSV.

PASSION. The sufferings and crucifixion of Jesus Christ (Acts 1:3). *See* Christ, Passion of.

PASSIONS, LIKE. "Passion" indicates strong emotions arising from a condition of mind; "like passions" means "of the same human nature." In Acts 14:15 the missionaries disclaim divinity, and in Jas 5:17 special reference is probably made to Elijah's human emotional infirmities.

PASSOVER. The festival instituted by God for Israel at the time of the Exodus in order to commemorate the night when Yahweh spared all the firstborn of the Israelites but struck dead all those of the Egyptians (Ex 12:1-30, 43-49).

The Heb. word *pesaḥ* (Gr. *pascha*) is of uncertain origin. G. E. Mendenhall relates it to the Akkadian *pašḫu* which appears in Amarna letter 74:37 to describe the peace or security resulting from the formation of a covenant (BASOR, #133 [1954], p. 29). B. Couroyer suggests that it is a transliteration of two Egyptian words *p3 šḫ*, "le coup" (the blow, the striking), with reference to Yahweh's smiting the land of Egypt in the tenth plague. He believes that the Egyptian expression has been placed beside a Heb. root composed of the same consonants, *pāsạh*, meaning to skip or leap (over), as in I Kgs 18:26 (KJV "leaped"). By its connection with the sparing of the Israelite firstborn, *pesaḥ* came to have the sense of Yahweh's merciful bypassing of the houses where the blood was applied ("L'origine égyptienne du mot 'Pâque,'" *Revue Biblique,* LXII [1955], 481-496).

The verb *pāsaḥ* occurs in Ex 12:13, 23, 27 where it obviously means that the Lord skipped over or passed over and thus spared the Israelite homes when He smote the Egyptians. (Another verb with the same radicals means to limp or to be lame [II Sam 4:4].) The only other occurrence in the sense of sparing or protecting is in Isa 31:5 where *pāsạh* is in parallel with three verbs meaning "protect," "deliver," and "rescue" (NASB). It is possible that in Isaiah the meaning may have been set by its usage in Ex 12, rather than reflecting the original meaning of the root. Therefore it is not certain whether or not the noun *pesaḥ* was derived from the verb *pāsạh* and originally meant a passing over.

For the ceremonial observance of the Passover festival in the OT *see* Festivals; Sacrifices; Worship.

In the NT reference is made to Moses' observing the first Passover with the sprinkling of blood so that the Israelite firstborn might not be touched (Heb 11:28). Many other references are to various Passover festivals during the life

Samaritan Priests celebrating the Passover.
Richard E. Ward

of Jesus. As a boy He went every year with His parents to Jerusalem for the Feast of the Passover (Lk 2:41). In the fourth Gospel three Passovers during the ministry of Christ are definitely mentioned (Jn 2:13, 23; 6:4; and 11:55; 12:1; 13:1; 18:28, 39; 19:14), and it is believed that the feast of Jn 5:1 was a fourth Passover.

In the time of Christ the Passover lamb (usually a year-old male sheep, but see Ex 12:5) was ritually slaughtered in the temple area. The meal, however, could be eaten in any house within the city. A communal group, such as Jesus and His disciples, could keep the Passover together as though they formed a family unit. As many as 120,000–180,000 Jews were present in Jerusalem for this and other annual feasts, the great majority of whom might be pilgrims from the countries of the Diaspora (J. Jeremias, *Jerusalem in the Time of Jesus*, Philadelphia: Fortress, 1969, pp. 58–84). After the destruction of the temple in A.D. 70 the provisions for sacrificing an animal in ritual manner utterly ceased, and the Jewish Passover became simply a family observance, a meal with no shedding of blood. Today only the Samaritans (*q.v.*) in their annual observance of the Passover on Mount Gerizim slaughter young rams in fulfillment of Ex 12.

One last passage in the NT clearly develops the typological significance of the Passover and Feast of Unleavened Bread for the Christian. Paul urges the Corinthians to clean out the leaven of malice and wickedness and daily to keep festival, "for indeed our Passover has been sacrificed—Christ Himself!" (I Cor 5:7, orig. trans.). Thus Paul directly declares Christ to be "our paschal lamb" (RSV) in keeping with the Baptist's pronouncement that Jesus is "the Lamb of God who takes away the sin of the world" (Jn 1:29). Because of this and similar teaching, the church early came to realize that the Lord's Supper (*q.v.*) replaces the Passover observance completely.

Bibliography. H. Danby, ed., *The Mishnah*, tractate "Pesaḥim," Oxford: Univ. Press, 1933, pp. 136–151. Alfred Edersheim, *The Temple, Its Ministry and Services*, Grand Rapids: Eerdmans, 1950 (reprint), pp. 208–248. J. Jeremias, "*Pascha*," TDNT, V, 896–904. K. E. Keith, *The Passover in the Time of Christ*, rev., London: Church Missions to the Jews, 1958. J. B. Segal, *The Hebrew Passover from the Earliest Times to A.D. 70*, London: Oxford Univ. Press, 1963.

J. R.

PASTIMES. *See* Games.

PASTOR. The KJV renders Heb. *rōʿeh* ("shepherd") as "pastor" in Jer 2:8; 3:15; 10:21; 12:10; 17:16; 22:22; 23:1–2. This Heb. word is translated elsewhere in Jeremiah as shepherd (23:4; 25:34, 35, 36; 31:10; 33:12; 43:12; 49:19; 50:6, 44; 51:23) and elsewhere in the OT from Genesis to Zechariah. Those passages rendered "pastor" in the KJV are usually translated by "shepherd" in modern versions (e.g., ASV, RSV, NEB, with "ruler" for Jer 2:8 being an exception); the ASV and RSV do not use "pastor" at all in the OT. The term in the KJV designates the leaders of government and rulers of the people of God and in every case but two (Jer 3:15; 17:16) regards them as false or unfaithful.

The Gr. word *poimēn* is uniformly translated "pastor" at Eph 4:11 as a designation of the minister in the church. Elsewhere in the NT this word is translated "shepherd" (*q.v.;* Mt 9:36; 25:32; 26:31; Mk 6:34; 24:27; Lk 2:8, 15, 18, 20; Jn 10:2, 11, 12, 14, 16; Heb 13:20; I Pet 2:25).

See Pastor, Christian.

G. W. K.

PASTOR, CHRISTIAN. The word pastor literally means "shepherd." It is used of Christ several times in the NT (Heb 13:20; I Pet 2:25) and of the Christian pastor only once (Eph 4:11). In this passage it is listed as a spiritual gift to be exercised, not an office to be occupied. Actually, any Christian who guides, guards, and generally functions as a shepherd in relation to other believers is exercising the spiritual gift of pastor. However, the word has come to stand for an office occupied by one who formally feeds the flock, administers the ordinances, leads the worship, and guards the truth (Heb 13:17; I Pet 5:2). The Pastoral Epistles furnish guidelines for the duties of those who occupy officially designated places of leadership as pastors among God's flock (II Tim 4:1–5). In addressing the elders of the church at Ephesus (Acts 20:17), Paul called them overseers or bishops (v. 28) and enjoined them to feed (or pastor) the flock (v. 28).

C. C. R.

PASTORAL EPISTLES. A name given to three NT letters, I Timothy, II Timothy, and Titus, because their contents consist of advice regarding the administration of the local church. The title "Pastoral Epistles" became common after the publication of a work by Paul Anton in 1726. Even though the addressees may not have been pastors in the modern sense of the term, the title is appropriate because these are the only NT letters to deal with many church problems from the administrator's viewpoint. Addressed to two of Paul's trusted associates, they nevertheless went beyond the merely personal, and were to be regarded as official communications from the writer to churches at Ephesus and Crete, as indicated by the plural "you" in the closing salutation of each letter.

Early Historical Testimony

The question of Paul's authorship of these three letters has been more hotly debated than that concerning any of the other Pauline epistles. Yet evidence of acquaintance with and acceptance of the Pastoral Epistles as canonical writings is early and abundant in church history. In the well-known discussion of the canon by Eusebius in the early 4th cen., the Pastorals were accepted as Paul's and classed with the Homologoumena (Acknowledged Books).

Long before this, however, Clement of Alexandria (e.g., *Stromata,* II, 6) and Tertullian (e.g., *On Prescription Against Heretics,* chap. 25) made many citations from these epistles, attributing them to "the apostle" or else to Paul by name. The Muratorian Canon (*c.* A.D. 170) includes the Pastorals in its list of accepted NT books. Irenaeus, writing before the end of the 2nd cen., quotes or alludes to every chapter of the Pastorals except Tit 1 (e.g., *Against Heresies,* II, 14.7). Hegesippus (*Memoirs Concerning the Martyrdom of Symeon*), Theophilus of Antioch (*To Autolycus,* III, 14), *Epistles of the Churches of Vienne and Lyons,* Athenagoras (*A Plea for the Christians,* sect. xvi, xxxvii), Justin Martyr (e.g., *Dialog with Trypho,* sect. vii. xxxv), *Epistle of Barnabas* (e.g., sect. xii), and Ignatius *Epistle to Polycarp,* sect. iii. iv) are examples of historical notices well within the 2nd cen. The citations in Polycarp's Epistle to the Philippians (*c.* A.D. 110) are numerous and clear and were so early that there was not time for a fraudulent composition to have gained sufficient stature to be used without question by this man who had known the apostle John (e.g., sect. iv, viii, xii). To argue, as does J. C. Baker in his article "Pastoral Letters, The" (IDB, III, 670) that both Polycarp and the author of the Pastorals used a common source, appears utterly gratuitous. Even Clement of Rome (A.D. 95) reveals possible awareness of I Tim (e.g., *First Epistle to the Corinthians,* sect. xxxvii).

The only dissenting voices regarding canonicity of the Pastorals were such heretics as Basilides, Marcion, and Tatian, whose rejection was based upon doctrinal disagreement with their contents. Yet this very rejection focused attention on the matter of canonicity, so that their acceptance by the church as a whole becomes the more impressive. This unanimity of opinion prevailed until the 19th cen.

Problems of Authorship

The widespread critical rejection of the Pauline authorship of the Pastorals usually rests upon one or more of the five problems discussed below. In spite of the trend, many scholars have continued to accept the genuineness of the Pastorals, including Guthrie (1957), Hendriksen (1957), Jeremias (1953), Spicq (1947), Schlatter (1936), Lock (1924), White (1910), Ramsay (1909), Zahn (1906), and Godet (1893).

1. *Chronological setting.* The problem is caused by inability to fit the chronological data of the Pastorals into the framework of Acts. If the imprisonment demanded by II Timothy is the Roman imprisonment of Acts 28, then the freedom reflected in I Timothy and Titus must precede Acts 21. A place must be found where Paul leaves Timothy in Ephesus while he departs for Macedonia (I Tim 1:3). The closest one can come to solution on this premise is to note that Paul went from Ephesus to Macedonia on his third journey (Acts 20:1), but Timothy either accompanied him or joined him soon after (Acts 20:4). This becomes difficult to harmonize with I Tim 3:14. Furthermore, the tasks laid upon Timothy in the epistle would take considerable time to effect.

Inasmuch as Acts ends without stating the outcome of Paul's case, it is gratuitous to insist that Acts 28 was his final imprisonment. The historian Luke has consistently left the impression that no serious charge had been filed against Paul (Acts 25:26–27; 26:31–32). Paul himself expected release from this imprisonment (Phm 22; Phil 1:23–25; 2:24). For Acts to end as it does with no hint that Paul's prospects were not realized is inexplicable. Early historical testimony, including Clement of Rome, the Muratorian Canon, and Eusebius, tells of a trip by Paul to Spain, and thus argues for release from the first Roman imprisonment, a period of renewed missionary activity, and then a later imprisonment which was final. The so-called historical problem against Pauline authorship is a problem only if one assumes that Acts tells the whole story of Paul's life. Such an assumption is both unnecessary and unwarranted.

2. *Ecclesiastical complexity.* It has been objected that the Pastorals reflect a state of organization in the church too advanced for the days of Paul. Thus a 2nd cen. date is posited. Attention is called to the various grades of clergy, and the detailed descriptions regarding their qualifications, salary, and discipline. Yet the same two officers are found in the undisputed letters of Paul (Phil 1:1), and even the Jerusalem church had deacons and elders (Acts 6; 15:2–6). Interchangeability of the titles "bishop" (Gr. *episkopos*) and "elder" is a clear 1st cen. usage. Plurality of elders was Pauline policy (Acts 14:23; Phil 1:1), and remuneration of elders was taught by Paul in I Cor 9:7–14. The existence of female deacons is paralleled by the case of Phoebe (Rom 16:1), and the enrollment

of widows had a much earlier instance in Acts 6.

The examples of organization are much more at home in the 1st cen. than in the 2nd cen. church of Ignatius. The Qumran sectarians well before A.D. 70 had an overseer or superintendent (*m*^{e}*baqqer,* the ordinary Aram. and Heb. word for overseer and exact equivalent of Gr. *episkopos,* Manual of Discipline 6:12–14; see Frank M. Cross, Jr., *The Ancient Library of Qumran,* Garden City, N.Y.: Doubleday, 1958, pp. 175 ff.).

3. *Doctrinal viewpoint.* Sometimes it is argued that the Pastorals reflect a lowered theology from Paul. The author is supposed to be a sincere Paulinist (thus accounting for certain similarities to Paul's teaching), but Paul's basic doctrines are missing, and even some of his terminology is allegedly used in a different way.

However, God is presented as Father (I Tim 1:2), who chose the redeemed from eternity past (II Tim 2:10), and became their Saviour through Christ's mediation (I Tim 1:1; 2:5–6). Salvation is based on God's grace, not man's works (Tit 3:5). The Holy Spirit is the One who warns believers (I Tim 4:1). The purpose of the epistle dictated its scope, and hence it is not legitimate to expect exhaustive treatment of theological truths in this manual of procedure for church administration.

4. *Linguistic peculiarities.* Since the appearance of P. N. Harrison's *The Problem of the Pastoral Epistles* in 1921, this argument has had great influence. Harrison pointed to the large number of words which occur only once in the NT (*hapax legomena*), and argued that the proportion of new words per page in the Pastorals is significantly higher than in the ten Paulines. Other peculiarities are the absence of characteristic Pauline words and certain word groups. Affinities have been claimed with 2nd cen. vocabulary and style.

However, if the comparison of new words to total vocabulary is made, the result is quite different, and the Pastorals have only a slightly higher percentage than Romans. Of the words that occur in the ten Paulines but not in the Pastorals, 80 percent of them appear in one letter only, thus missing from the other nine as well as the Pastorals. Of the 175 *hapaxes* in the Pastorals, 80 of them are found also in the LXX. Of the *hapaxes* which are found in the writings of 2nd cen. Church Fathers, all but a few were known prior to A.D. 50. Thus a case for 2nd cen. authorship has hardly been established. The total length of the Pastorals and of the other ten Paulines is much too small to allow any rigid conclusions based on statistical analysis. A difference in subject matter calls for different vocabulary. It may also be noted that these alleged linguistic differences apparently never caused suspicion in the early church.

5. *Heretical opposition.* The heresy under attack in the Pastorals is alleged by some to have been 2nd cen. Gnosticism. References in I Tim 1:4; 4:1–5; 6:20 have been appealed to as demanding this conclusion. However, the author's use of the common word *antithesis* in I Tim 6:20 is no proof that Marcion's treatise of that name was in view. Further, nowhere in Gnostic literature are *aeons* called "genealogies" (I Tim 1:4). It is better to regard them as Jewish, as a similar reference in Tit 1:14 clearly implies, as well as the context in I Timothy.

The discovery of Coptic codices of Gnostic treatises originally written in Gr. in the 2nd cen. A.D. confirms the testimony of Irenaeus and Hippolytus about Gnostic origins. The Gnostics were specifically Christian heretics who quoted widely from the authentic NT books. The movement began in Palestine and Syria within two decades after Pentecost in direct opposition to the gospel. Thus reaction against the radical ideas of the Gnostics could be expected in the later NT epistles (W. F. Albright, *History, Archaeology and Christian Humanism,* New York: McGraw-Hill, 1964, pp. 39–42, 277, 295). *See* Gnosticism.

Date and Order

The traditional view of Pauline authorship places the writing of I Timothy and Titus during the period of release following the first Roman imprisonment. Assuming that Paul's expectation of soon release was fulfilled, one may reconstruct the ensuing events as follows: Paul first traveled eastward, visiting Crete (Tit 1:5), Colosse (his hope in Phm 22), Ephesus (I Tim 1:20), and Macedonia (I Tim 1:3) including Philippi (his expectation in Phil 1:25; 2:24). At this time (A.D. 62 or 63) he wrote I Timothy, sending it to Ephesus in anticipation of his own revisit (I Tim 3:14). At about the same time he wrote to Titus, asking him to join him in Nicopolis for the winter (Tit 3:12). The last of the three to be written was II Timothy, penned during the apostle's final imprisonment in Rome which culminated in his death sometime between A.D. 64 and 68.

Bibliography. Glenn W. Barker, William L. Lane and J. Ramsey Michaels, *The New Testament Speaks,* New York: Harper & Row, 1969, pp. 233–247. Donald Guthrie, *The Pastoral Epistles,* Grand Rapids: Eerdmans, 1957. P. N. Harrison, *The Problem of the Pastoral Epistles,* London: Oxford Univ. Press, 1921. William Hendriksen, *Exposition of the Pastoral Epistles,* Grand Rapids: Baker, 1957. Walter Lock, *A Critical and Exegetical Commentary on the Pastoral Epistles* (ICC), New York: Scribner's, 1924. E. K. Simpson, *The Pastoral Epistles,* Grand Rapids: Eerdmans, 1954. Newport J. D. White, *The First and Second Epistles to Timothy and the Epistle to Titus* (ExpGT), Grand Rapids: Eerdmans, reprinted.

H. A. K.

PASTURE. *See* Occupations: Shepherd.

PATARA (păt'ȧ-rȧ). A seaport of Lycia on the SW coast of Asia Minor, *c.* 60 miles E of

Rhodes. It was situated *c.* six miles E of the mouth of the Xanthus River. The city was said to have been founded by Patarus, son of the god Apollo. Worshiped as Apollo Pataraeus, his temple and oracle were famous. Extensive remains of a theater, baths, walls, etc., are still in evidence. A triumphal arch contains the inscription, "Patara, the capital of the Lycian nation." In this port Paul changed ships on his voyage to Jerusalem at the close of his third missionary journey (Acts 21:1–2).

PATH. In addition to the literal use (Gen 49:17), the word is frequently employed in a figurative sense. (1) With reference to God's ways of dealing with men (Ps 25:10; Mt 3:3) and God's standards for worship and conduct (Ps 25:4). (2) With reference to man's ethical conduct (Prov 4:18; Heb 12:13) and man's destiny or lot in life (Job 8:13). "Paths" in Ps 23:3 translates the Heb. word which means sheep or wagon "tracks."

PATHROS (păth'rŏs). The Heb. name for Upper Egypt (*see* Egypt; Isa 11:11; Jer 44:1, 15; Ezk 29:14; 30:14).

PATHRUSIM (pȧ-thro͞o'zĭm). The descendants of the fifth son of Mizraim, a son of Ham. They were the inhabitants of Pathros (*q.v.;* Gen 10:14; I Chr 1:12).

PATIENCE. This word is for the most part a NT term, being found only three times in the OT. In Ps 37:7 and 40:1 the Heb. words *ḥûl* and *qāwâ*, respectively, are translated "wait patiently," and in Eccl 7:8 *'ārēk,* "long," is employed to describe one who is patient in spirit.

In the NT, four Gr. terms are translated by some form of the word patience. Gr. *makrothumia* is the quality of long-suffering endurance (Mt 18:26, 29). According to Chrysostom *makrothumia* describes the man who is fully able to revenge himself, but refuses to do so. It is also rendered "long-suffering" as a quality of God (Rom 2:4; II Pet 3:9) and as the fruit of the Holy Spirit (Gal 5:22).

Gr. *hypomonē* is described by William Barclay, in *A New Testament Wordbook* (London: SCM Press Ltd., 1956, p. 59), as "one of the noblest of NT words." Its basic meaning is that of endurance (Heb 12:1), the quality which enables a man to bear up under trial (Rom 12:12). Whereas *makrothumia* more correctly concerns persons, *hypomonē* speaks of patience in regard to difficult circumstances. The word does not depict a passive, submissive patience which resigns itself hopelessly to its unhappy lot; instead it is an active endurance marked by hope and assurance (I Thess 1:3). Barclay further describes it as "the quality which keeps a man on his feet with his face to the wind" (p. 60). A good example of this kind of patience is Job, who endured the afflictions sent upon him (Jas 5:11).

The Monastery of St. John crowns the Isle of Patmos. HFV

The third word translated as "patient" by the KJV is *epieikēs* (I Tim 3:2–3), which describes an attitude that is gentle, yielding, reasonable, and conciliatory, one that does not insist on its rights (Barclay, p. 38 f.).

The fourth term, *anexikakos* (II Tim 2:24), literally means "bearing up under evil," and thus is the kind of patience which puts up with evil without resentment (Arndt).

See Forbearance; Long-suffering; Steadfastness.

D. W. B.

PATMOS (păt'mŏs). An island of the Dodecanese in the Aegean, SW of Samos, eight miles long and five miles across the northern coast. The crescent shape provides a protected harbor on the E side of the isthmus between the northern and southern parts. While banished to the island, John the apostle received the visions of Revelation (1:9). Clement of Alexandria (*Rich Man* 42), Tertullian (*Prescription* 36), Eusebius (*Church History* III. 18), and Jerome (*Lives* 9) testify to the apostle John's exile to Patmos under the emperor Domitian. The volcanic hills rising over 800 feet and the surrounding sea may have influenced the imagery of Revelation. *See* Revelation, Book of.

PATRIARCH. Head or founder of a family or tribe, as used of Abraham (Heb 7:4) and of Jacob's 12 sons (Acts 7:8–9). The word is applied to David (Acts 2:29) because he founded the line of messianic descent (II Sam 7:11–16). *See* Abraham; Patriarchal Age.

PATRIARCHAL AGE

The Patriarchs

The Gr. term *patriarchēs* is sometimes used in the LXX and the NT in a loose sense, as in Acts 2:29 of David and in Acts 7:8–9 of the 12 sons of Jacob. It has, however, become more common to restrict the word "patriarchs" to the founding fathers—Abraham, Isaac, and Jacob. The Patriarchal Age is therefore the period in

PATRIARCHAL AGE

Israelite history of these three initial generations. *See* Genesis.

Critical Skepticism

Until the breakthrough of archaeological discoveries, most biblical critics viewed the stories of the patriarchs with considerable skepticism. S. R. Driver explained the patriarchs as personifications of tribes. The Pan-Babylonian scholars H. Winckler and J. Jeremias interpreted them as reflections of Babylonian astral deities. Others, including E. Meyer, R. Weill, G. Hölscher, and C. A. Simpson (in 1948), regarded them as transformed Canaanite deities. H. Gunkel considered them as figures of folk poetry. More recently M. Noth and O. Eissfeldt have conceded that they were real persons, but have at the same time discounted the stories about them as unhistorical.

Archaeological Discoveries

In the last 40 years a steadily increasing flow of archaeological evidence from Mesopotamia and Syria-Palestine has convinced all except a few holdovers of the authenticity of the patriarchal narratives. The geographical notices, the names, the social customs and political conditions reflected in the stories ring true to the purported date of the patriarchs. With a few exceptions (the so-called "anachronisms" discussed in the last section below), these elements accord with a date in the 2nd mil. rather than a date in the 1st mil. B.C. This is in sharp contrast with Wellhausen's view that "we attain to no historical knowledge of the patriarchs, but only of the time (the first millennium B.C.) when the stories about them arose in the Israelite people. . . ."

The Date of the Patriarchs

The exact date of the patriarchs is differently estimated by scholars. Ex 12:40 speaks of the sojourn in Egypt from the time of Jacob's entry to the Exodus as lasting 430 years (the LXX makes the 430 years cover both the stay in Egypt and the previous sojourn in Canaan).

The Plains of Mamre, near Hebron, figure prominently in the narratives of Abraham and Isaac. HFV

The date of the entrance of Jacob then depends on one's date of the Exodus (*q.v.*). Conservative scholars who prefer a 15th cen. B.C. date for the Exodus place Abraham in the 21st cen. and Jacob's descent to Egypt in the 19th cen. Many scholars on the basis of archaeological data have preferred the 20th-18th cen. for Abraham—e.g., W. F. Albright, R. de Vaux, S. Yeivin. H. H. Rowley has espoused a date in the 17th cen. for Abraham. C. H. Gordon arguing from the parallels to the 15th cen. Nuzu texts suggests a date close to the 14th cen. Amarna age. On other grounds, O. Eissfeldt also favors the 14th cen.

The overall evidence would seem to indicate that the early 2nd mil. B.C. fits in well with the background of the patriarchal narratives, in particular the period known as the Middle Bronze Age I (M.B. I), dated to 2100-1900 by Glueck and to 2000-1800 by Albright.

A number of sites associated with the patriarchs are known to have been occupied at this date. Shechem is mentioned in the 19th cen. Egyptian Execration texts, and remains of this period have been found in excavations by G. E. Wright. After a gap of a millennium Bethel is first reoccupied in this period. P. Hammond has found remains of the M.B. I at Jebel er-Rumeideh, the site of ancient Hebron. Surveys by N. Glueck and B. Rothenberg have turned up evidence for seasonal occupation at sites in the Negev associated with the patriarchs. These sites were occupied in the M.B. I period, and not for about a millennium before and a millennium after.

Archaeologists do not as yet agree as to the terminology and the limits of the Middle Bronze Age in Palestine. B. Mazar dates the M.B. I period to 2200-2000, and calls the period from 2000 to 1800 the M.B. IIA period. Albright calls the period from 2200 to 2000 Early Bronze IV, and the period from 2000 to 1800 M.B. I. Kathleen Kenyon, the excavator of Jericho and early Jerusalem, calls the period from 2300 to 1900 the Intermediate E.B.-M.B. period, and the short half century from 1900 to 1850 the M.B. I period. She further ascribes the seminomadic settlements of the Intermediate E.B.-M.B. period to the Amorites and the period thereafter to the Canaanites. Some recently published evidence relates some of the early Hebrew names with the Amorite tribes from Syria who established the First Dynasty at Babylon in the 19th cen. B.C.

The picture of the patriarchs moving about in the hill country of central Palestine fits in well with the population patterns of the early centuries of the 2nd mil. B.C. They would have avoided the larger settlements of the coastal plains and the valleys in their search for pasturage for their sheep.

Personal Names

Many of the personal names of the patriarchal narratives have been found in the texts of the early 2nd mil. B.C., particularly in the 18th cen. archives of Mari. Abraham in trav-

PATRIARCHAL AGE

eling from Ur in southern Mesopotamia to Harran (Haran, Gen 11:31 f.) in northern Mesopotamia may very well have passed Mari on the Euphrates some 200 miles SE of Harran.

Similar to the name Abram is the name *Aba(m)rama* from Dilbat, and comparable to Abraham is the name *'Aburahana* from the 19th cen. Egyptian Execration texts. Similar to the name Terah, Abraham's father, is the name of *Turakhi,* a place near Harran. Similar to the name of Abraham's grandfather Nahor (Gen 11:25) and to a city by the same name (Gen 24:10) is the name *Nakhur* found at Mari. The name of Abraham's great-grandfather Serug is found in *Sharugi* near Harran. Ishmael's name may be compared with the name *Yasmakh-el* from Mari. Names similar to Jacob have been found, as in *Ya'qub-il* from Chagar-Bazar. The name Laban has been found at Mari. Similar to Benjamin is the name *Binu-* (or *Maru-*) *yamina,* meaning "son of the right," i.e., "son of the south," also recorded at Mari.

It should be noted that none of these examples should be interpreted to mean that any of these names refers to the actual biblical figures themselves. However, the attestation of such names from the time and the area associated with the patriarchs is valuable evidence for the authenticity of the narratives.

Travel, Trade and Nomadism

Freedom and wide scope of travel (*see* Travel and Communication) is especially attested for the Near East in the Old Babylonian period (19th-16th cen. B.C.). Abraham's migration from Ur to Harran was a move from one great trade center to another. The name Harran means "Caravan City." It is perhaps not accidental that both Ur and Harran were also centers of the worship of Sin, the moon-god, as Terah's name may be related to the moon cult (cf. Josh 24:2).

The career of Abraham has been understood by Gordon in the light of the *tamkarum* or traveling Mesopotamian merchant, and by Albright in the light of his interpretation of the *'Apiru* or *Habiru* (*q.v.*) as donkey caravaneers (*see* Animals, I. 1, Ass). On the other hand, other scholars, including Y. Aharoni, M. Greenberg, K. Kitchen, and R. de Vaux, regard the patriarchal mode of life as that of the semi-nomad or shepherd-nomad who pastured his flocks and engaged in seasonal agriculture (cf. Gen 26:12-14). The patriarchs moved about in the hilly and forested areas of the country in seeking pasture for their flocks. The story of Joseph's search for his brothers indicates how far the shepherds took their flocks in search of pasture. Joseph went from the valley of Hebron (Gen 37:14) 50 miles to Shechem, and then found that his brothers had gone to Dothan (Gen 37:17), 20 miles farther N. As in modern times, there were clashes between herdsmen and townspeople over water sources (Gen 21:25 ff.; 26:17-32).

Bethel, significant in the lives of Abraham and Jacob. HFV

Social Customs

It is especially the finds from Nuzu (*c.* 1500 B.C.) which have cast much light on the social customs of the patriarchs. Abraham's probable adoption of Eliezer of Damascus (Gen 15:2) can be illustrated from the Nuzu texts, which show that it was the custom for childless couples to adopt a man to be their heir. If, however, a son were later to be born, the adopted person would have to yield to the real son (Gen 15:4). The incident in Gen 16:1-2 which tells of Sarah presenting her handmaid Hagar to Abraham to beget a child is illustrated by a Nuzu tablet of adoption which stipulates that a barren wife must provide a slave girl to her husband to beget offspring (cf. Gen 30:1-13). This particular tablet and the Hammurabi law code require that the slave's child be kept—a rule which was preempted by the divine permission to send away Hagar and Ishmael (Gen 21:10-12). Esau's sale of his birthright to Jacob is paralleled at Nuzu by a man's transfer of his inheritance regarding a grove to his brother for three sheep.

The story of Jacob and Laban (Gen 29-31) has been richly illustrated by the Nuzu texts. It seems that Laban, who had no male heir at the time, may have adopted Jacob and given him his daughters, Leah and Rachel. The Nuzu texts show that Rachel's theft of the family gods or teraphim (Gen 31:34) was evidently not prompted by sentimental reasons. The possession of these objects insured title to the family inheritance, and in some cases to the leadership of the clan.

The explanation for the striking similarities between the patriarchal stories and the Nuzu texts may be explained in part by their common Hurrian cultural heritage. The inhabitants of Nuzu were largely Hurrians, who had migrated into northern Mesopotamia and Syria-Palestine from the area of Armenia in the 2nd mil. They were also prominent at Harran where Abraham and, later, Laban lived.

PATRIARCHAL AGE

The Raid of the Four Eastern Kings

In addition to the general parallels of social customs there is a specific incident in the life of Abraham that can be set in the early 2nd mil. This is the invasion of the four kings of the E—Amraphel, Arioch, Chedorlaomer, and Tidal—against the kings of Sodom and Gomorrah, recorded in Gen 14.

Some critical studies, including an article by Albright in 1918, questioned the historicity of the story. Noth in 1948 rejected it as a late scholastic reconstruction. T. Nöldeke had earlier rejected it on the basis that there was no route of march E of the Jordan River as described in the narrative. Such a route has now been found by N. Glueck, who notes that the route is lined with M.B. I cities that were destroyed at the end of the 19th cen. with only a few of them having ever again been reoccupied. Glueck would in fact attribute their destruction to the onslaught of the four kings.

The Mari letters indicate that it was only in the period *c*. 2000–1750 B.C. that the system of power alliances attested in this passage holds true. The names of the eastern kings are foreign and have an authentic ring. Amraphel can no longer be identified with Hammurabi, as was once popular, but the name accords well with several Amorite or Akkadian combinations. Arioch is the same name as *Arriwuk*, a contemporary of Hammurabi. The form is rare and is not attested after the middle of the 2nd mil. The name Chedorlaomer contains tangible Elamite components (Elam was in SW Persia). Some scholars believe that Tidal represents the Hittite name *Tudkhaliya*. The Heb. word which is used for Abraham's armed retainers (*hanîkîm*, Gen 14:14), is found in the 19th–18th cen. Execration texts from Egypt. Speiser, who believes that Gen 14 comes originally from a non-Israelite source, concludes that this passage is clear evidence that Abraham was a very real person and not a nebulous literary figure. Albright has also become a strong advocate of the account's historicity.

Patriarchal Religion

The patriarchs worshiped a God who appeared to each of them personally. God's covenant with Abraham (Gen 12, 15, 17) is a promise that God would bless Abraham and his posterity, and the nations of the earth through them. The promise of God was received by faith at a time when Abraham was childless and Sarah past the age of bearing children (Acts 7:5; Rom 4:16–22). By his unwavering faith Abraham became the prototype of all his spiritual children who are likewise saved by faith (Gal 3:7–29). Moreover, Abraham's faith was not a dead faith but an obedient trust (Jas 2:21–23).

Abraham seemed to be on such intimate terms with his God that he is called the "friend" of God in the Scriptures (Isa 41:8; II Chr 20:7; Jas 2:23). Isaac's name for his God is to be rendered either "Fear" or "Kinsman" (Gen 31:42). Jacob's name for his God is the "Mighty One" (Gen 49:24). The concept of the patriarchal "God of the fathers" is paralleled from the Old Assyrian tablets of the 19th cen. B.C. found in Cappadocia.

Critics have been accustomed to attribute the genesis of Heb. monotheism to the Mosaic period. The Scriptures themselves, however, speak of the monotheistic faith of the patriarchs. The extrabiblical parallels to various elements in the patriarchal narratives have recently convinced Speiser, Cross, and Albright that not only the social traditions but also the religious traditions of the patriarchs in the Scriptures are to be regarded as ancient and trustworthy.

Alleged Anachronisms

Although many elements in the patriarchal stories have been shown to be authentic, there are also certain features which are regarded by some scholars as late and anachronistic. The mention of camels (*q.v.*) is questioned because widespread domestication of camels seems not to have occurred before the end of the 2nd mil. B.C. Though camels are not often mentioned in the early texts, there is indeed evidence for the domestication of camels in the Patriarchal Age from art and from actual remains (Kitchen, *Ancient Orient and Old Testament*, pp. 79 f.). *See* Animals, I. 5, Camel.

One of the more controversial issues concerns the Hittites (*q.v.*) or "children of Heth" in the narratives; in Heb. the terms are respectively *ḥittî* and *b*^{e}*nê ḥēt* (Gen 15:20; 23:3). On the one hand, M. Lehmann has called attention to what appear to be striking parallels between the Hittite law code and Abraham's transactions for the cave of Machpelah with Ephron the "Hittite" in Gen 23. On the other hand, there is no evidence from the Hittite records themselves of any penetration of the Hittites S of Syria into Palestine, and very little archaeological evidence to support the claim that Hittites were in this area. Gene Tucker has shown that Gen 23 also has parallels with Neo-Babylonian sale documents ("The Legal Background of Genesis 23," JBL, LXXXV [1966], 77–84). This does not mean, as he argues, that the patriarchal narratives are therefore late. When both early and late parallels exist, neither can be used as the sole evidence for dating the stories.

Harry Hoffner has argued that the biblical *ḥittî* were an ethnic group that was unrelated to the Anatolian Hittites, and that the similarity in names is simply accidental. Speiser has suggested that the biblical term may actually refer to the Hurrians inasmuch as the LXX and the Masoretic Text confuse the Hurrians, Hittites, and Hivites more than once. There is considerable evidence to indicate that the Hurrians penetrated into Palestine.

The references to Aramaeans (translated "Syrians" in the KJV) in connection with the story of Laban have been regarded by some scholars as anachronistic. It is held that the name of this Semitic group which spread E from Syria is attested only in the 11th cen. B.C. at the time of Tiglath-pileser I. A related nomadic tribe, the *Akhlamu,* is mentioned in the 14th cen. De Vaux would consider the earlier Amorites of Syria as "Proto-Aramaeans." Although some scholars would dispute the identification with the later nomadic and semi-nomadic Aramaeans, A. Dupont-Sommer has pointed out that the names "Aram" and "Aramu" are already found at the end of the 3rd mil. B.C. As an indication that Laban's designation as an Aramaean is not a later gloss is the fact that he is shown speaking Aramaic (Gen 31:47).

The designation of Abraham's city of Ur in lower Mesopotamia as Ur "of the Chaldees" is, however, best explained as a gloss. The Chaldaeans are not mentioned in Mesopotamian texts until the 11th cen. B.C.

The references to the Philistines (*q.v.*) in the patriarchal stories constitute a well-known difficulty. The first historical references to the Philistines are in the texts of Rameses III (*c.* 1190 B.C.), though they are pictured in their typical "feather" or "horsehair" headdresses in slightly earlier reliefs of the Sea Peoples who attacked Egypt. Some scholars have maintained that the term "Philistine" in the narratives concerning Abimelech of Gerar and Abraham (Gen 20–21), and a later king of Gerar with the same name and Isaac (Gen 26), may be intended to denote an earlier migration of people from the Aegean than that of the Philistines. Amos 9:7 describes the Philistines as coming from Caphtor, which is usually interpreted as Crete, but which may perhaps by extension have included the Aegean area influenced by the Minoan civilization of Crete.

The actual term "Philistine" in the patriarchal narratives may have been a later gloss which was substituted for an earlier no longer comprehensible term. Perhaps the basis of the scribal substitution could have been the fact that the kings of Gerar belonged to a stock which was related to the area later dominated by the Philistines.

Bibliography. William F. Albright, "Abram the Hebrew: A New Archaeological Interpretation," BASOR, #163 (1961), 36–54; "The Patriarchal Background of Israel's Faith," *Yahweh and the Gods of Canaan,* Garden City, N.Y.: Doubleday, 1968, pp. 53–109. Millar Burrows, "The Complaint of Laban's Daughters," JAOS, LVII (1937), 259–276; "Patriarchs—in Genesis and in History," CornPBE, pp. 559–568. Frank M. Cross, "Yahweh and the God of the Patriarchs," HTR, LV (1962), 225–259. Roland de Vaux, "Les patriarches hébreux et les découvertes modernes," RB, LIII (1946), 321–343; LV (1948), 321–347; LVI (1949), 5–36; "Les patriarches hébreux et l'histoire," RB, LXXII (1965), 5–28; "Method in the Study of Early Hebrew History," and responses by George Mendenhall and Moshe Greenberg in *The Bible in Modern Scholarship,* ed. by J. Philip Hyatt, Nashville: Abingdon Press, 1965, pp. 15–43. A. Dupont-Sommer, "Sur le débuts de l'histoire araméenne," *Supplements to Vetus Testamentum* (1953), pp. 40–49. J. C. L. Gibson, "Light from Mari on the Patriarchs," JSS, VII (1962), 44–62. Nelson Glueck, "The Age of Abraham in the Negeb," BA, XVIII (1955), 2–9; *Rivers in the Desert,* New York: Grove Press, 1959. Cyrus H. Gordon, "Biblical Customs and the Nuzu Tablets," BA, III (1940), 1–12; "The Patriarchal Age," JBR, XXI (1953), 238–243; "The Patriarchal Narratives," JNES, XIII (1954), 56–59. M. Haran, "The Religion of the Patriarchs: An Attempt at a Synthesis," *Annual of the Swedish Theological Institute,* IV (1965), 30–55. Harry A. Hoffner, "Some Contributions of Hittitology to Old Testament Study," *Tyndale Bulletin,* XX (1969), 27–55. John M. Holt, *The Patriarchs of Israel,* Nashville: Vanderbilt Univ. Press, 1964. Kathleen Kenyon, *Amorites and Canaanites,* London: Oxford Univ. Press, 1966; *Palestine in the Middle Bronze Age,* Cambridge: Univ. Press, 1966. K. A. Kitchen, *Ancient Orient and Old Testament,* Chicago: Inter-Varsity Press, 1966; "Historical Method and Early Hebrew Tradition," *Tyndale Bulletin,* XVII (1966), 63–97. Manfred R. Lehmann, "Abraham's Purchase of Machpelah and Hittite Law," BASOR, #129 (1953), 15–18. Herbert G. May, "The God of My Father—A Study of Patriarchal Religion," JBR, IX (1941), 155–158. Benjamin Mazar, "The Historical Background of the Book of Genesis," JNES, XXVIII (1969), 73–83; "The Middle Bronze Age in Palestine," IEJ, XVIII (1968), 65–97. Andre Parrot, *Abraham and His Times,* Philadelphia: Fortress Press, 1968. H. H. Rowley, "Recent Discovery and the Patriarchal Age," *Bulletin of the John Rylands Library,* XXXII (1949–50), 44–79. Ephraim A. Speiser, *Genesis,* New York: Doubleday, 1964. Gerhard von Rad, "History and the Patriarchs," ExpT, LXXII (1961), 213–216. Donald J. Wiseman, *The Word of God for Abraham and To-day,* London: Westminster Chapel, 1959. Samuel Yeivin, "The Age of the Patriarchs," *Rivista degli Studi Orientali,* XXXVIII (1963), 227–302.

E. M. Y.

PATRIMONY. An inheritance or inherited estate. The Heb. word (lit., "the fathers," Deut 18:8) is used only here in the OT and is probably an abbreviation of a larger phrase, "possession of the fathers." *See* Law of Moses: Inheritance, Property.

PATROBAS (păt'rŏ-bȧs). One of the Roman Christians to whom Paul sent greetings in the epistle to the Romans (16:14).

PATTERN. *See* Type.

PAU (pô, pā'ū). The royal city of Hadar or

Hadad (Gen 36:39), one of the early kings of Edom. The same city is mentioned in I Chr 1:50 as Pai.

PAUL (pôl)

Background

Modern studies of Paul once again are emphasizing the fact of his Jewishness. Of the various strands within his cultural milieu, this seems basic. Writers such as W. D. Davies, *Paul and Rabbinic Judaism* (1948); J. Munck, *Paul and the Salvation of Mankind* (1959); H. J. Schoeps, *Paul: The Theology of the Apostle in the Light of Jewish Religious History* (1961); and R. N. Longenecker, *Paul: Apostle of Liberty* (1964), have made major contributions in scholarly works which have established this thesis for the present. (The situation up to 1960 has been concisely surveyed in E. E. Ellis, *Paul and His Recent Interpreters.*)

Paul's own testimony seems certainly to look in the same direction. A circumcised Israelite, of the tribe of Benjamin, speaking the Aramaic language in his home, inheritor of the tradition of Pharisaism, a strict observer of the requirements of the Torah, and advancing in Judaism beyond many of his contemporaries, he was first and foremost a Jew (Phil 3:5–6; Gal 1:14). So deeply ingrained upon his soul were these qualities, that even near the end of his life he could speak with honest appreciation of that heritage. More than 20 years after his Christian conversion he could cry out, "I am a Pharisee, a son of Pharisees; I am on trial for the hope and resurrection of the dead" (Acts 23:6, NASB). Even some time after this he claimed that he served "the God of our fathers, believing everything that is in accordance with the Law, and that is written in the Prophets" (Acts 24:14, NASB).

Yet he was a Jew of the Dispersion, born in Tarsus (*q.v.*) of Cilicia, a place that he called "no insignificant city" (Acts 21:39). As a child he lived in the midst of Greek culture, a place of education and commerce. It was "the city whose institutions best and most completely united the oriental and the western character" (Ramsay, *Cities,* p. 88).

Such an environment would likely have posed certain problems for a Jew. First, he would be a member of a minority, and to some extent, a despised group. His tenacious loyalty to the ideas of his religion would invite the taunts of the Tarsians (cf. Schonfield, *The Jew of Tarsus,* p. 33). It is not without reason to assume that the highly developed defensiveness of Paul, so often evident in his epistles, had its roots in these early days. Second, a Jew would be faced with the problem of social relationships with Gentiles. Pharisees in particular, among the Jews, were sensitive, although not by any means necessarily hostile, to such meetings. This whole area of life so often emphasized in the letters must eventually have been carefully thought through by Paul. And it is to his credit that he developed a spirit of kinship with these "outsiders." He learned to understand them and to "become all things to all men" (I Cor 9:22).

Common enough has been the idea that Paul grew to at least late adolescence in this environment before going to Jerusalem to be educated under Gamaliel (Acts 22:3). But in recent years a serious blow has been dealt to this conjecture by the careful study of van Unnik, *Tarsus or Jerusalem: The City of Paul's Youth* (1962). According to this work, the triad of words: (1) "born," (2) "brought up," and (3) "educated" (Acts 22:3), was "a fixed literary unit" (see also Acts 7:20–22), indicating that, while the birthplace of Paul was Tarsus, his upbringing, both in the home and under teachers, was in Jerusalem. Buttressing this conclusion with a wealth of evidence from ancient literature, van Unnik ventures the supposition that the move from Tarsus "took place quite early in Paul's life, apparently before he could peep round the corner of the door and certainly before he went roaming on the street" (p. 54).

Does all this mean that Paul had little opportunity to really learn of the Greek world in which he was born? Not at all. It means, rather, that at this early stage he had ingrained upon his mind certain basic attitudes toward life. After his conversion Paul spent a period of eight to ten years in Syria and Cilicia (see Gal 1:21–2:1; cf. Acts 9:30), a time during his adult years when he would be deeply aware of the world culture about him. These were years of preparation for that ministry in which he was known as "the apostle to the Gentiles."

In addition to these aspects of his life, one other is emphasized directly in Acts, and is implicit in the letters. He was a Roman citizen (Acts 16:37–39; 22:25–28). This was a prized possession, for it has been estimated that from one-third to two-thirds of the population of the Roman Empire were of the slave classes, and thus without Roman citizenship. Paul recognized the value of both his Tarsian citizenship (Acts 21:39) and his Roman citizenship (Acts 22:25–28). It is interesting to notice the difference in the estimate of these respective citizenships in the eyes of the Roman captain Claudius Lysias. The first only established the fact that Paul was not an Egyptian (Acts 21:38); the second gave him immunity from scourging.

Paul apparently inherited his Roman citizenship from his father: "I was actually born (a citizen)." The father may have had it conferred upon him for some service to the Roman government. Some of the privileges contained therein were (1) the guarantee of a trial (before Caesar if requested, cf. Acts 25:11) in cases of accusation; (2) legal immunity from scourging before condemnation (contrast the case of Jesus, Mt 27:24–26); and (3) immunity from crucifixion, the worst form of capital punishment, in case of condemnation.

In his letters, Paul not only strongly advocated the maintenance of law and order (the very foundation of Roman government), but also referred frequently to citizenship. Believers in Christ were "no longer strangers and aliens, but . . . fellow-citizens with the saints" (Eph 2:19). Their "citizenship" was in heaven (Phil 3:20). The word occurs again in Phil 1:27, which reads literally, "Perform your duties as citizens" (Lightfoot). Such an emphasis was particularly meaningful to the recipients of the letter to Philippi, for the city was a Roman colony (Acts 16:12), and they doubtless would recall that Paul had here appealed to his own Roman citizenship.

Conversion

In his letter to Galatia, Paul referred to his "former manner of life in Judaism," and how he "used to persecute the church of God beyond measure, and tried to destroy it" (Gal 1:13). At that time he had believed that in pursuing such a course he was serving God and maintaining the purity of the Law. Gal 1:15 shows no indication of a break in this endeavor to please God at the time of his conversion. And in Phil 3:6 he indicated his "blamelessness" in regard to "the righteousness which is in the law."

While the narratives in Acts, as well as the notes in the letters, seem to indicate the "suddenness" of the conversion, some have argued that certain experiences must have prepared him beforehand. The death of Stephen, at which Saul "was in hearty agreement" (Acts 7:58–8:1); the heat of his house-to-house campaign against those of the Way (Acts 8:3; 9:1–2; 22:4; 26:10–11) could hardly leave him unaffected; and his furious journey toward Damascus represented the climax of his efforts.

In any case, there are two elements in the story which are clear. First, Paul was convinced that he had seen the risen Lord; and, second, his life was radically changed from that day forward. The basis of his claim to apostleship lay in that experience. Once and again he insists upon it (see I Cor 9:1; 15:8–15; Gal 1:15–17; cf. Acts 9:3–8; 22:6–11; 26:12–18). Since he was not one of the Twelve, since he had no claim on Jesus, and since he had persecuted His followers, the necessity of the personal revelation of Christ to Paul seems apparent.

The change was first indicated by Paul's response to the heavenly voice: "What shall I do, Lord?" (Acts 22:10). Thomas Chalmers (1780–1847) preached a great sermon entitled "The Expulsive Power of a New Affection." That seems to fit the case of Paul. In Gal 2:20 Paul shows that he had a new relationship with Christ (cf. II Cor 5:16–17).

Second, the change was evidenced by the message Paul began to preach in the synagogues of Damascus (the very place he intended to visit in order to arrest the disciples of Jesus, cf. Acts 9:1–2): "He [Jesus] is the Son of God" (Acts 9:20). Now he assumed the task of "proving that this Jesus is the Christ" (Acts 9:22). Only a short time before he had thought that he "had to do many things hostile to the name of Jesus of Nazareth," even attempting to force His followers to blaspheme (i.e., to say that "Jesus is accursed," cf. I Cor 12:3), pursuing them like a wild animal (Acts 26:9–11).

Third, there was a change in his sense of mission. He was convinced that God had called him to "preach Him [God's Son] among the Gentiles" (Gal 1:16). In fact, this was the means by which Israel would ultimately be restored and blessed of God (cf. Rom 11:25–27).

Finally, there was a change in Paul himself. This was indicated in many ways. See, e.g., Phil 3:7–14, for a change in his sense of values. Or I Cor 13, a "hymn of love" written by one who had hated so bitterly. Or the Epistle to Philemon, written in tones of tenderness and tact, rather than his once forceful and demanding demeanor.

The conversion experience has been explained in a number of ways. Some attribute it to the effect of disease, such as epilepsy (cf. J. Klausner). Others attribute it to hallucinations or some similar psychological phenomenon. But the remarkable transformation of Paul's personality and life looks in the other direction. Whatever the means employed, Christ had appeared to him—just as surely as He had appeared to others after His resurrection (cf. I Cor 15:5–8).

East gate, Damascus, leading into Street called Straight, which figure in the Pauline narrative after the Apostle's conversion. HFV

"St. Paul's Window," Church marking traditional site where Paul was lowered over wall of Damascus. HFV

A helpful, popular treatment of the problem will be found in E. White, *St. Paul: The Man and His Mind* (1958), pp. 20-36.

Post-Conversion Activities

Following the conversion experience, Paul's life can be divided into several general periods: (1) the relatively silent years, probably extending over ten to 12 years; (2) the work at Antioch; (3) the missionary journeys; and (4) the imprisonments.

The silent years. Information about this period is scant. What little is known comes from the facts recorded in Gal 1:15-24; II Cor 11:32-33 (and probably most of the data in II Cor 11:23-27); and Acts 9:19*b*-30 (together with the parallels in Acts 22 and 26). An outline of the period would include at least the following points:

Preaching in Damascus (briefly), Acts 9:20-22
Journey into Arabia, Gal 1:17
Return to Damascus, Gal 1:17
Flight to Jerusalem, Gal 1:18; II Cor 11:32-33; Acts 9:23-26
Meeting with Peter and James in Jerusalem, Gal 1:18-19
Return to Syria and Cilicia (Tarsus), Gal 1:21-24; Acts 9:30

The scant nature of the data has left many questions unanswered for the modern student of Paul's life. Where was "Arabia"? And, what did he do there? Why was Aretas' ethnarch desirous of taking Paul prisoner in Damascus? What was the purpose and nature of his visit with Peter and James? Why did he drop out of sight for so many years before beginning his public ministry? And, further, why was he continually on the run?

One is impressed with the energy of the man. He was indeed zealous (lit., "bubbling" or "boiling") in whatever he undertook. For this reason alone one might suppose that the silent years were not years of inactivity or repose. The indications seem otherwise. He began "immediately" to preach Jesus as the Son of God (Acts 9:20); he went "immediately" into Arabia (Gal 1:16-17); his preaching in Jerusalem aroused the fury of some (Acts 9:28-29); and reports filtered back to Judea that in Syria and Cilicia he "is now preaching the faith which he once tried to destroy" (Gal 1:21-23).

The work at Antioch. While Paul was in Tarsus (and other places in Syria and Cilicia), the gospel had been spread from Jerusalem to Syrian Antioch (Acts 11:19-21). Barnabas had been sent to see what had happened there, and was instrumental in enlarging the number of converts. But when the work grew too large for him, "he left for Tarsus to look for Saul" (Acts 11:25). Together the two worked in Antioch "for an entire year."

This was a crucial point in the life of Paul, for it may well have been here that his vision of taking the gospel to the Gentile world crystallized. At any rate, it was while he was active in Antioch that "the Holy Spirit said, 'Set apart for me Barnabas and Saul for the work to which I have called them' " (Acts 13:2). Thus were launched the missionary travels of the apostle Paul.

The missionary journeys. Covering a period of about ten years, Paul's work was chiefly in four provinces of the Roman Empire: Galatia, Macedonia, Achaia, and Asia. In each of these he concentrated on the key cities, the centers of population. Once his work was begun, he reached out into the surrounding countryside, usually by employing the native converts (cf. Col 1:7-8; 4:12).

Paul's methods of founding and establishing churches assumed a fairly regular pattern, at least where conditions permitted. A summary is stated in Acts 14:21-23: (1) preaching the gospel (*evangelism*); (2) strengthening and encouraging believers (*edification*); and (3) appointing elders in every church (*organization*). Much the same approach is intimated (or assumed) in Philippi (Acts 16:40; cf. Phil 1:1), Corinth (Acts 18:4, 11; cf. I Cor 16:15-16), and Ephesus (Acts 19:8-10; 20:17, 28).

1. The first journey (Acts 13:1–14:28). This was a "mission to the Gentiles" (see 14:27). Like each of Paul's periods of travel, the point of departure was Antioch (in Syria), a place which had assumed the role of the center of Gentile Christianity. Sailing from the port of Seleucia, Paul and his companions landed on Cyprus at its eastern end. From Salamis they traversed the entire length of the island, preaching first in the synagogues of the Jews. Indeed, this was their point of contact with Gentiles, some of whom were adherents to Judaism, others merely curious onlookers. Also, the first meeting with Roman officialdom occurred in Paphos, the capital city and residence of the proconsul Sergius Paulus. Despite opposition from his Jewish magician (13:6-12; cf. 8:9-11), the proconsul believed the message of Paul.

Putting out to sea, the party next came to Perga in Pamphylia. Up to this point Barnabas had been the leader, Paul the main speaker, and John Mark (the cousin of Barnabas) the apostles' helper. But leaving Cyprus (which was Barnabas' home, Acts 4:36), Paul assumed the leadership, whereupon Mark left (lit., deserted) them and returned to Jerusalem (13:13). The timing seems hardly accidental. Was he jealous? or offended? or just homesick?

Moving northward, the pair entered the province of Galatia, and their visits extended to four cities: Antioch (in Pisidia), Iconium, Lystra, and Derbe. The events may be briefly summarized thus:

In Antioch, Paul preached in the synagogue, discoursing on the history of Israel and the fulfillment of God's promises in the coming of the Saviour, Jesus. His closing emphasis was upon forgiveness of sins and justification through faith in Christ (13:38-39), a note sounded again later on in the Epistle to the Galatians. When the Jews opposed him, Paul said, "We are turning to the Gentiles" (13:46), a usual procedure in Paul's ministry in various cities (see also 18:6; 28:28).

Driven out of Antioch, they came next to Iconium, one of the most beautiful sites in the ancient world, and repeated the familiar pattern (14:1-6). One new note was added: the Lord bore witness to His word by "granting that signs and wonders be done by their hands" (14:3; cf. Gal 3:5; Heb 2:4).

The third center was Lystra, a city in which there was no synagogue, probably a sign that few Jews resided there. It was rather a native settlement, peopled mainly by Lycaonians of the region of central Anatolia. The worship of Zeus and Hermes (14:12) was popular there, and the language was principally Lycaonian rather than Greek (14:11). After Paul healed a man "lame from his mother's womb," the people began to worship them as gods, reminiscent of the story of Baucis and Philemon found in Ovid's *Metamorphoses* (viii), a tale which provides a background for appreciating the reaction of the people (cf. Gal 4:8-15). Even after order had been restored, the peace was short-lived, for "Jews came from Antioch and Iconium" and Paul was stoned and left for dead.

Miraculously, he rose to his feet soon after, and the next day he and Barnabas set out on the 60-mile journey to Derbe (SE of Lystra). There the journey reached its terminal point, from which they returned through the cities establishing their converts (14:21-23), coming eventually to Antioch in Syria.

Concerning the time relationship of Paul's Epistle to the Galatians with the council of the church at Jerusalem (Acts 15), *see* Galatia; Galatians, Epistle to the.

2. The second journey (15:36–18:22). This was intended to be a revisit of "every city in which we proclaimed the word of the Lord" (15:36), according to Paul's statement to Barnabas. But the pair, disputing over whether to take John Mark who had deserted them the first time, decided to go their separate ways, and Paul, taking Silas with him, traveled by the land

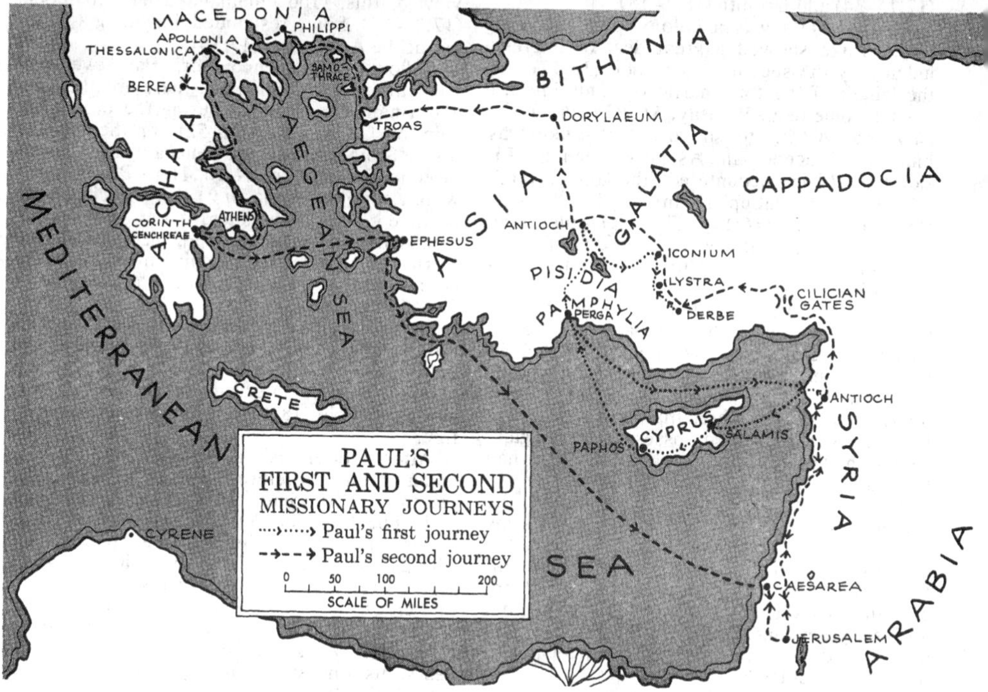

PAUL'S FIRST AND SECOND MISSIONARY JOURNEYS

Mars Hill with a bronze plaque at right bearing Paul's Acts 17 speech. HFV

route northward through Syria and Cilicia, and thus began his second visit to Galatia in Derbe.

But the center of interest became Macedonia and Achaia rather than Asia Minor. Taking Timothy with them as they passed through Lystra (16:3), the travelers came at last to the port city of Troas on the Aegean Sea. In response to a vision, the company embarked for Macedonia (16:6-10), thus inaugurating the work on European soil.

In Macedonia, the work centered in three key centers: Philippi (16:12-40), Thessalonica (17:1-9), and Berea (17:10-14), while in Achaia, two cities were visited: Athens (17:15-34) and Corinth (18:1-18).

Philippi (*q.v.*) was a colony, and a city in which Luke showed a great deal of interest, judging by the specific description (16:12) and the length of the total narrative. This interest has led some (e.g., Ramsay, *St. Paul the Traveller*, pp. 201 ff.) to suppose that Luke was himself a Macedonian. As in Antioch (in Pisidia), Paul had encountered "the God-fearers" (13:43), so in Philippi he met Lydia, "a worshiper of God" (16:14). These Gentiles who had been "prepared" were often the first to respond to the gospel of Christ, and to be saved (cf. 16:31-34).

Further, in this city Paul felt the sting of anti-Semitism. He and his companions were accused of "being Jews" as opposed to the citizenry "being Romans" (16:20-21), a charge sufficient to stir up trouble and result in their imprisonment. It was here that Paul appealed to his Roman citizenship, a possession that legally should have prevented the beating that had been administered (16:22-24, 37-39).

Thessalonica (*q.v.*) was the capital of the province of Macedonia, a free city, possessing the right of self-government. Luke's use of the Gr. title *politarchas* (17:6, 8) is another illustration of his historical accuracy. It does not appear in other Gr. literature, but is known from 19 inscriptions dated between the 2nd cen. B.C. and the 3rd cen. A.D., most of them related to Macedonian cities.

Here Paul began in the synagogue, and "reasoned with them from the scriptures" (17:2, the first time the term "to reason" occurs in Acts). It is significant that in his entrance into the heart of the Gr. cities, this word describes Paul's approach (see also 17:17, Athens; 18:4, Corinth; 18:19; 19:8, Ephesus), for such was the way of the Gr. mind.

The missionaries were accused here of sedition (against Caesar), "saying that there is another king, Jesus" (17:7). The charge was adequate to force their expulsion from the city, and they traveled southward to Berea, a place of short stay before Paul went on alone to Athens (17:10-15).

Now Paul entered the province of Achaia ("Greece") and found himself in the most famous city of the Gr. world, Athens (*q.v.*). It was a "city full of idols" (17:16), a place where "it was easier to find a god than a man." Meeting with people both in the synagogue and the marketplace, he soon encountered the Epicurean and Stoic philosophers (see the separate articles on these schools), who regarded Paul as a collector and dispenser of scraps of knowledge ("this idle babbler," lit., "a seedpicker," 17:18). To them his message of "Jesus and the resurrection" seemed like the extolling of two strange gods. Thus he was brought before the council of Athens (the Areopagus [*q.v.*], a name also given to the meeting place of the tribunal which judged affairs affecting the welfare of the city). Here he expounded the doctrine of a living, personal God who had created the world, sustained it, and would one day judge it. In view of this, God commanded men to repent (17:22-31). Some responded, including a member of the Areopagus (17:34).

Following this encounter, Paul went to Corinth (*q.v.*) and remained there about a year and a half. His visit fell during the proconsulship of Gallio (A.D. 51-52), brother of the noted Stoic philosopher Seneca who was adviser to the emperor Nero. Here Paul resided with a couple, Aquila (*q.v.*) and Priscilla, who became his fast friends and fellow workers (cf. Rom 16:3-5*a*), made tents for his support, and carried on an extended teaching ministry. From here he sent two letters to the infant church in Thessalonica.

He was accused by the Jews of teaching men "to worship God contrary to the law," and brought before Gallio for trial. The wise Roman judge refused to intervene in the Jewish religious squabble (18:15, 17*b*), and Paul was set free.

After a brief visit to Ephesus (18:19-21), and a promise to return later "if God wills," he returned to the home base of Antioch.

3. The third journey (18:23–21:14). Traversing once again the Galatian region and Phrygia, Paul spent some time in follow-up work, strengthening his disciples in the Galatian cities. Then he pursued his journey westward, coming into Asia and to its key city Ephesus. Here he spent between two and three years, his longest stay in any single place (see Acts 19:8-10; 20:31).

Prior to Paul's visit, Apollos of Alexandria (18:24-28) had spent some time preaching and teaching in Ephesus. Together with the labors of Priscilla and Aquila, left there by Paul earlier (18:18-19, 26), his work may be considered to have laid the foundation for Paul's extended ministry in that city.

At this point in history, Ephesus was the leading center of the Roman province of Asia (*see* Ephesus). A number of the institutions and practices which characterized its life are reflected in Luke's account in Acts 19, and represented challenges to Paul's program: (1) the Jewish synagogue (19:8-9); (2) the practice of exorcism and magical arts (19:13-19); and (3) the guild of silversmiths (19:24-41).

In spite of these opposing influences, some significant results have been recorded by Luke: "All who lived in Asia heard the word of the Lord, both Jews and Greeks" (19:10); and "the word of the Lord was growing mightily and prevailing" (19:20).

Thus the greatest of Paul's churches took its rise, and the careful student of the NT should take notice of its subsequent history. It is the only church in the NT whose history is traced in various stages from the time of its founding to the end of the Apostolic Age. See, along with Acts 18-20, the Epistle to the Ephesians, I and II Timothy (cf. I Tim 1:3), and Rev 2:1-7. During these days three great leaders were responsible for its welfare: Paul, Timothy, and John.

Following his departure from Ephesus, Paul traveled northward through Troas (see II Cor 2:12-13); then into Macedonia and Greece, where he spent three months (Acts 20:3). While at Corinth he wrote his Epistle to the Romans. Returning through Philippi and Troas, he stopped at Miletus and met with the elders of the church of Ephesus (20:17-35). Here he rehearsed his ministry among them, and charged them with their sober responsibilities, while also warning them of dangers that would arise after his departure (Acts 20:28-31; cf. I Tim 1:3-4, 18-20; 6:3-5, 20-21; II Tim 2:16-18).

Wishing to be in Jerusalem for the Feast of Pentecost (Acts 20:16), Paul made his way through Tyre and Caesarea (21:3-6, 8-16), where he was warned of the dangers awaiting him. But willing "even to die at Jerusalem for the name of the Lord Jesus" (21:13), he pursued his course. With him was the money he had collected for the needy saints in Jerusalem (cf. I Cor 16:1-4; II Cor 8-9; Rom 15:25-27). While he was warmly received by James and the elders, certain Jews from Asia, present in Jerusalem for the Feast of Pentecost, accused Paul of defiling the temple area (see Acts 21:27-36). A riot followed and the incident led to his arrest by the Roman captain in the city.

The imprisonment period (Acts 21:15-28:31). At first sight it appears strange that Luke should have given so large a section of his narrative to Paul's imprisonments, when it was the missionary expansion of the early

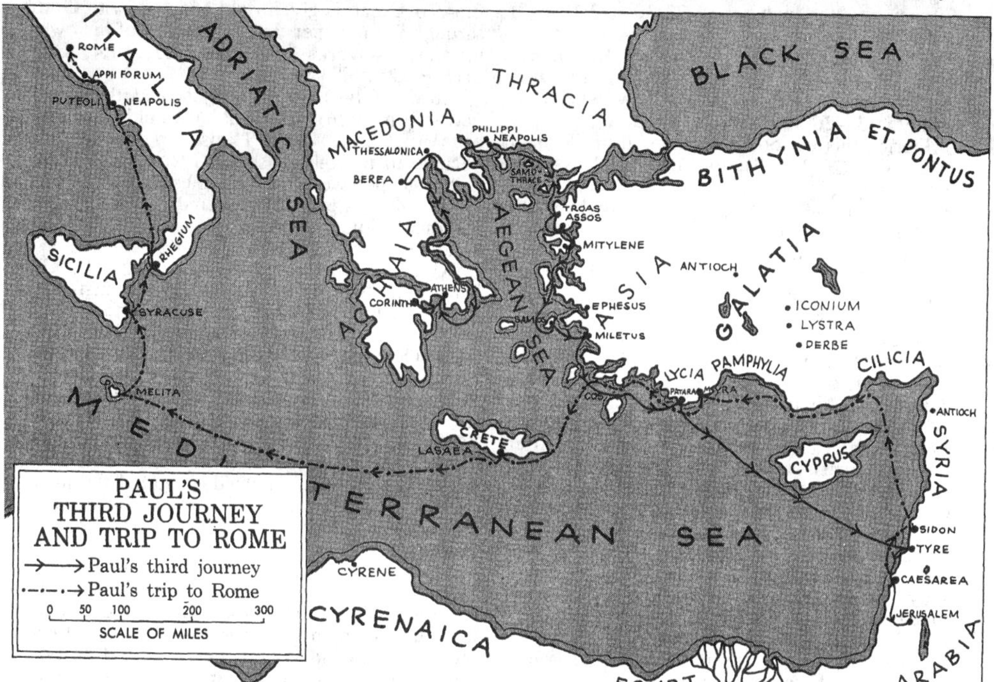

PAUL

The great theater at Ephesus where the mob scene of Acts 19 took place. HFV

church that had occupied him up to this point. But it was one large part of his apologetic for early Christianity that he was able to show that this "prisoner" had been unjustly accused, and that the church had not violated Roman law (cf. Acts 23:26-30; 25:23-27; 26:30-32; 28:30-31).

Concerning this period of Paul's life, it will be well to study Paul's relations with the following persons and groups: (1) James and the Jerusalem elders (Acts 21:18-26); (2) Claudius Lysias, the captain of the Roman garrison in Jerusalem (21:31-39; 22:22-30); (3) the Jewish mob in the temple area (21:40–22:22); (4) the council (or the Sanhedrin, the supreme governing body of Judaism in Jerusalem, consisting of 70 men plus the high priest, 22:30–23:10); (5) Felix, the procurator of Judea (24:1-27); (6) Festus, successor to Felix (25:1-12); and (7) Herod Agrippa II, Roman-appointed king over certain territories adjacent to and within Palestine (25:13–26:32).

During this period, Paul claimed his Roman citizenship (22:25-28), appealed to Caesar for a fair trial (25:10-12), and was judged to be innocent of the charges against him by both Festus and Agrippa (26:31-32). His voyage to Rome eventuated in a two-year period of unhindered preaching and teaching, practically on Caesar's doorstep (28:30-31)! There the story penned by Luke comes to its end.

What happened to Paul then? Did he ever appear before Nero? If so, was he condemned and executed, or released? If the latter, what did he do following that time? The only further information in the NT comes from the Pastoral Epistles, indicating that Paul was released after his (first) imprisonment (II Tim 4:16-17), traveled to such places as Crete (Tit 1:5), Nicopolis (Tit 3:12), Troas (II Tim 4:13), Miletus, and Corinth (II Tim 4:20); and then was arrested the second time and executed (II Tim 4:6-8, 18). Tradition places his death along the Ostian Way outside the city of Rome (*see* Ostia) sometime between A.D. 64 and 68, toward the end of Nero's reign. (See the volumes listed in the Bibliography for discussion of various viewpoints on the latter years of his life.)

Main Teachings

Paul's thought was complex. The problem of understanding his ideas is further complicated by the lack of systematic development. The Jews knew nothing of a systematic theology approach, as even a cursory look at, e.g., the Mishnah will make clear, and as one recognizes the almost total lack of agreement on issues by leading Jewish scholars of any period.

The letters of Paul exhibit the same tendency. Even the "logical treatise" called the Epistle to the Romans is no exception. While it is organized, it is not developed beyond the barest minimum. Rather, Paul often brings together an astonishing number of profound ideas and leaves them for the reader to plumb their depths. In many cases, of course, either he had spent long months (or even years) in the oral instruction of his converts, or he could assume that the traditional teachings of the early church would be known to his converts. His letters, then, were written against this background.

Attempting to garner from his writings key ideas, the following merit particular discussion.

The doctrine of justification by faith. This great truth had first been experienced by Paul himself (cf. Gal 2:16), had formed the core of his missionary message (cf. Acts 13:38-39), and had become foundational in his letters to his churches. Particularly is it central in such letters as Galatians (3-4) and Romans (3:21–5:21), and even where not repeatedly elaborated is assumed to be basic to Christian experience (e.g., I Cor 6:11; II Cor 5:16-21; Eph 2:8-9). A man is given right standing with God through faith, rather than as a result of his own meritorious works (cf. Rom 3:22; 10:4; Gal 2:16; 3:22; Phil 3:9).

How is God able to "be just and the justifier" (Rom 3:26)? It is, Paul would say, because of Christ who is Himself righteous. He became to us righteousness (I Cor 1:30). And in the gospel we have that message declared. God's good news is centered in the faith-response of one who is unrighteous to One who is righteous (cf. I Jn 2:1).

It has been affirmed by some (e.g., C. G. Montefiore, G. F. Moore) that Paul, in insisting on the demand of God's law for perfect obedience else one is condemned (as in Gal 3:10), has neglected a whole (and basic) area of Jewish teaching, viz., that of repentance. Critics of Paul have noted the paucity of occurrences of the term in his epistles (Rom 2:4; II Cor 7:9-10; cf. Acts 17:30; 20:21). But it might be argued that Paul used the more comprehensive word "faith," which, indeed, included the idea of repentance. If a man believes in God, he has changed his mind (repented) about a number of things.

The concept of being in Christ. Judging by the frequent occurrence of this phrase in Pauline writings, more than 160 times, it must have formed an important part of the apostle's thought. It included both personal and corporate points of reference, and served to be a unifying factor within his churches. Sanday and Headlam (*Romans*, p. 160) called the phrase "one of the main pillars of St. Paul's theology."

Its meaning has been variously understood. A. Deissmann (*Paul*, pp. 138–140) equated "in Christ" with "in the (Holy) Spirit," both being nuptial formulae. A. Schweitzer (*Mysticism of Paul*, pp. 122 ff.) regarded the phrase as a concise statement for "being partakers in the mystical Body of Christ," and furnished a contrast with expressions such as "in the body," "in the flesh," "in sin," "in the Spirit," and "in the law." R. Bultmann (*Theology*, I, 311) understands the words as "primarily an ecclesiological formula," meaning to be a part of the Christian church, and, in the eschatological sense, to be "a new creation."

Even such a limited sampling brings out two differing types of approaches. One looks in the direction of a personal, mystical relationship. The Lord and the individual believer have been joined together, a union of spirits has been established. The other emphasizes the corporate aspect. All believers have been united in a fellowship, in a Body, of which Christ is the Head. Thus the Church is in view. (For a concise sampling and discussion of the problem, see R. N. Longenecker, *Paul: Apostle of Liberty*, pp. 160–170.)

But there is another facet to be considered. For Paul, to be "in Christ" meant to be liberated from the bondage of sin and the Law. A powerful example of this truth is found in Rom 6–8. One is made "alive to God in Christ Jesus" (6:11); he receives "eternal life in Christ Jesus our Lord" (6:23); no longer is there condemnation for those "who are in Christ Jesus" (8:1); and there is nothing that can separate us from God's love, "which is in Christ Jesus our Lord" (8:39). All this stands in contrast to being "in the flesh" (8:8) and experiencing bondage to sin "which indwells me" (7:17). The corollary truth is that Christ is in us by His Spirit to give this victory (8:9–11).

Paul's eschatological viewpoint. The classic exposition of NT studies in eschatology is that of A. Schweitzer, *The Quest of the Historical Jesus* (1910). According to this work, Jesus expected His messianic *parousia* in the near future, and this vivid hope determined His conduct. This same expectancy was evidenced by the early disciples (cf. Acts 1:6–11; 3:19–21), and by Paul as well.

"From his first letter to his last Paul's thought is always uniformly dominated by the expectation of the immediate return of Jesus, of the judgment, and the messianic glory" (A. Schweitzer, *The Mysticism of St. Paul*, p. 52).

Yet many have reacted against the excesses of this viewpoint. Not only was there a shift of emphasis from the *parousia* hope to present blessedness, as A. M. Hunter (*Paul and His Predecessors*, rev. ed., 1961) sees it, but there was also "a gradual shift from apocalyptic to nonapocalyptic eschatology," according to H. M. Shires (*The Eschatology of Paul in the Light of Modern Scholarship* [1966], p. 41).

Possibly the distinction between eschatology and apocalyptic serves a purpose here. Paul, indeed, firmly believed in the second advent of Christ as is evident from many passages in his letters (e.g., I Thess 4:13–5:11; II Thess 1–2; I Cor 15; Rom 13:11–12). Yet he realized the danger in excessive enthusiasm, an unrestrained attitude toward the *parousia*. Unless a control was exercised, how could his churches survive in a society such as that of the 1st cen. Roman Empire? The Romans were suspicious of any movement that appeared to threaten their control and the stability of the existing order. And, as a matter of fact, so were the Sadducean rulers of Palestine. Paul early realized this problem.

Thus he said in effect, "It will occur—but not yet." In the meantime, the believers were to occupy themselves with honest industry, with attention to the responsibilities of everyday life. "If anyone will not work, neither let him eat" (II Thess 3:10) was a potent reminder of attention to daily obligations. There was to be a witness to Christ borne in the midst of the toils of life, not through a nervous and detached "apocalyptic temperament." They were to be people of good report, not deluded visionaries who contributed nothing to the society of their day.

One further thought might be added here, an idea emphasized by J. Munck. Paul envisioned the salvation of the Gentiles as a necessary preliminary to the ultimate salvation of Israel. Contrary to Jewish eschatological belief, in which the order was reversed (Israel, then the Gentiles), Paul taught that "the wild olive branches" would first be grafted in, and later on "the natural branches" would be grafted into their own olive tree (Rom 11:13–27). Then, even "thus," all Israel will be saved.

Paul looked forward to the second advent as a logical result of the resurrection of Christ. Even as He became "the first fruits of those who are asleep" (I Cor 15:20) by being raised from the dead, even so He shall raise His own from the dead at His coming (15:23). In that day, all enemies will be abolished, including death, and God's purpose to "sum up all things in Christ" (Eph 1:10) will have been realized.

Bibliography. W. Barclay, *The Mind of St. Paul*, New York: Harper, 1958. W. J. Conybeare and J. S. Howson, *The Life and Epistles of St. Paul*, London: Longmans, Green, and Co., 1898. W. D. Davies, *Paul and Rabbinic Judaism*, London: SPCK, 1962. A. Deissman, *Paul*, trans. by W. E. Wilson, New York: Harper, 1957. C. H. Dodd, *The Meaning of Paul for Today*, New York: George H. Doran Co., n.d. E. Earle Ellis, *Paul and His Recent Interpreters*, Grand Rapids: Eerdmans, 1961; "Paul," NBD, pp. 943–955. W. Ward Gasque and Ralph P. Martin, eds., *Apostolic History* *and the Gospel* (F. F. Bruce Festschrift), Exeter: Paternoster, 1970. T. R. Glover, *Paul of Tarsus*, New York: George H. Doran Co., n.d. A. M. Hunter, *Paul and His Predecessors*, London: SCM Press, 1961. J. Klausner, *From Jesus to Paul*, trans. by W. F. Stinespring, Boston: Beacon Press, 1961. R. N. Longenecker, *Paul: Apostle of Liberty*, New York: Harper & Row, 1964. J. G. Machen, *The Origin of Paul's Religion*, Grand Rapids: Eerdmans, 1947. F. B. Meyer, *Paul: Servant of Jesus Christ*, Fort Washington, Pa.: Christian Literature Crusade, 1953. J. Munck, *Paul and the Salvation of Mankind*, trans. by F. Clarke, Richmond: John Knox Press, 1960. A. D. Nock, *St. Paul*, New York: Harper, n.d. W. M. Ramsay, *St. Paul the Traveller and the Roman Citizen*, Grand Rapids: Baker, 1949 (reprint); *The Cities of St. Paul*, Grand Rapids: Baker, 1960 (reprint). H. Ridderbos, *Paul and Jesus*, trans. by D. H. Freeman, Philadelphia: Presbyterian and Reformed Publ. Co., 1958. A. T. Robertson, *Epochs in the Life of Paul*, New York: Scribner's, 1956. S. Sandmel, *The Genius of Paul*, New York: Farrar, Straus & Cudahy, 1958. J. Stalker, *Life of St. Paul*, Grand Rapids: Zondervan, n.d. J. S. Stewart, *A Man in Christ*, New York: Harper, n.d. W. C. van Unnik, *Tarsus or Jerusalem: The City of Paul's Youth*, trans. by G. Ogg, London: Epworth Press, 1962. E. White, *Saint Paul: The Man and His Mind*, London: Marshall, Morgan & Scott, 1958. R. E. O. White, *Apostle Extraordinary*, Grand Rapids: Eerdmans, 1962.

W. M. D.

PAULUS. *See* Sergius Paulus.

The presumed "pavement" of John 19. Sisters of Zion

PAVEMENT. Although the word occurs several times in the OT, chief interest centers in a single NT reference (Jn 19:13). The Gr. word used here means "paved [lit., strewn] with stones." Its Semitic name is given as Gabbatha (*q.v.*), which means ridge or elevated area. The location was uncertain until Père Vincent uncovered an extensive area at the Castle of Antonia on the NW corner of the temple precincts, finding large slabs of stone a yard square. On the assumption that this is the correct site, the name Gabbatha becomes intelligible, for this spot is raised considerably above the level of the surrounding terrain.

PAW. In Lev 11:27, the Heb. word is "palm" and is intended to distinguish the animals which have padded feet from those which have hooves. The noun "paw" in I Sam 17:37 is literally "hand," and is used in the figurative sense of "power" or "control."

PE (pē). The seventeenth letter of the Heb. alphabet, commonly given as *P*. When used numerically, it stands for the number 80. Pe heads the seventeenth section of Ps 119 where every verse begins with this letter.

PEACE. Represented in the Heb. OT chiefly by the root noun *shālôm* and in the Gr. NT by the root noun *eirēnē*. In both OT and NT the word has a wide range of meanings. The general idea of well-being (Isa 48:18, NASB) embraces most of the nuances and gives the dimension of the more general and quite acceptable translation "peace."

The word occurs in the general greeting or salutation "Peace to you," equivalent to our perfunctory question, "How are you?" (Gen 43:23; Jud 19:20). It is also used where the reality is present (I Sam 1:17) and where it is a vain and false hope (Ps 28:3), especially in the words of the false prophets (Jer 6:14; 8:11; Ezk 13:10, 16). With the power of reality, it is the usual greeting of the risen Lord (Jn 20:19, 21, 26) and the opening salutation and/or closing blessing of apostolic epistolary writers (all except James and I John).

Peace is also used to designate interpersonal relationships (Gen 26:29; Josh 9:15). Thus one may speak of the relations between men (Prov 16:7) or nations (I Kgs 5:12). It may designate the good relations that have existed (Jud 4:17; Acts 24:2) or are about to be entered into; the cessation of hostility or war on the basis of the surrender of one party, as in the case of the Gibeonites to Joshua (Josh 10:1; cf. II Sam 10:19; I Chr 19:19; Lk 14:32); and the state of tranquility and prosperity that prevails (I Kgs 4:24) or is prayed for (Ps 122:6–9; Acts 12:20). *See* War.

The well-being, health, and prosperity of an individual's situation also merits the designation of peace. One's progress on a journey or departure from someone (Ex 4:18), and in general, the way one lives (Isa 38:16–17; I Cor 7:15) and dies (Gen 15:15; II Kgs 22:20) with equanimity, all may be designated under the nomenclature of peace. Economic prosperity and safety (Ps 147:14; Jer 29:11; Lk 11:21), ecological health (Lev 26:4–6; Zech 8:12), military and political security (II Kgs 20:19; Eccl 3:8), and freedom from persecution (Acts 9:31) are all aspects of peace.

In the entire sweep of the biblical usage, peace is understood as the gift of God (Isa 45:7) who Himself is designated as the God of peace (Rom 15:33; II Cor 13:11; Phil 4:9; II Thess 3:16), who gives peace (Num 6:26; Lev 26:6), and who has made a covenant of peace (Isa 54:10; Ezk 34:25; 37:26). Our appropriation of the peace He grants is conditional upon our trust in Him (Isa 26:3) and love for His Word (Ps 119:165) and the work of His righteousness (Isa 32:17; cf. Jas 3:13–18). The blessing of peace is as broad as God's providence (Jer 29:7; I Tim 2:2, *hesychios*) but comes to particular expression as the fruit of the messianic work of redemption (Isa 9:7; Zech 9:10; Mic 5:5).

Both the OT and NT indicate that the promised Messiah who is designated the Prince of Peace (Isa 9:6) will bring a personal (Isa 53:5) and cosmic peace (Ezk 34:25; 37:26). His birth is announced in terms of peace on earth for men with whom God is pleased (Lk 2:14, NASB). His resurrection appearances bring that announcement in the power of His death and resurrection (Jn 20:19, 21, 26). By Christ's death, the hostility and barrier between God and man has been removed so that He who is our peace brings the covenant of peace to men and makes peace with God through the blood of His cross (Col 1:20; Eph 2:11–22). [*See* Atonement; Reconciliation.] That same transaction also removes the barriers between Jew and Gentile, and in the community of grace and peace, the church, makes of all men in Christ by faith one new man dwelling in peace (Eph 2:14–16). This double-sided reality of peace with God (Rom 5:1) and with other men demands a corresponding response.

The man made at peace with God must pursue that peace in the increase of sanctification (I Thess 5:23; Heb 12:14; Col 3:15; I Pet 3:11) by the work of the Spirit, who gives as a particular fruit peace itself (Rom 8:6; 15:13; Gal 5:22). He must not live in fear and anxiety, because the treasure of Christ's legacy of peace has been deposited in his heart (Jn 14:27). His serenity of mind and inner tranquility in Christ will not depend upon or be shaken by the fact that he will have tribulation in this evil world (Jn 16:33). Being at peace with his fellow Christians through the indicative of God's grace, he will strive with that motivation to keep the unity of the Spirit in the bond of peace (Eph 4:3; II Cor 13:11; I Thess 5:13).

The Christian will pray and act for peace for the community and nation in which he lives (Jer 29:7; I Tim 2:2, *hēsychios*) and thus beseech the providential blessings of the present rule of Christ upon all men (Eph 1:22–23). The Christian will do this not for his or their selfish desires, but especially so that it might provide the occasion for the peaceful proclamation of that message which announces and brings God's peace to men in Christ (I Tim 2:2; Acts 10:36; Eph 6:15). With seeming contradiction that message will bring a sword not peace, as it evokes either men's hostility or their submissive trust and thus divides men against one another (Mt 10:34–36; Lk 12:51–53). This division must not be the occasion for the Christian to return hostility, but rather for the attempt to live peaceably with all men as much as he is able (Rom 12:18).

The completeness of the victory of God's peace will only come in the triumph of the messianic reign which will follow Christ's return. Then the peacemakers who are the sons of God (Mt 5:9) will in Christ be used by the God of peace to crush Satan under their feet (Rom 16:20). Then shall the peace which the Christian has personally enjoyed be the condition of the whole universe (cf. Rom 8:20–22). See J. Barton Payne, *The Theology of the Older Testament*, Grand Rapids: Zondervan, 1962, pp. 479–504.

The peace of God which keeps the heart of the Christian surpasses the mind's attempt at full comprehension (Phil 4:7). It does so because to have the peace of God is to have the God of peace (Phil 4:7, 9). Thayer (p. 182) has laid hold upon the essence and breadth of its meaning when he says of the peace distinctly peculiar to Christianity that it is "the tranquil state of the soul assured of its salvation through Christ, and so fearing nothing from God and content with its earthly lot, of whatsoever sort that is" (cf. II Thess 3:16).

Bibliography. Werner Foerster, "*Eirēnē*, etc.," TDNT, II, 400–420.

G. W. K.

PEACE OFFERING. *See* Sacrifices.

PEACEMAKERS. Those who through personal work and preaching bring about or effectuate peace between God and the sinner. God is now propitious to the sinner because Christ has "made peace through the blood of his cross" (Col 1:20), but the Christian still needs to plead with the sinner to be "reconciled to God" (II Cor 5:20). That it is making peace between man and God and not the reverse, between God and man, is proved by the fact God has already made His peace through Christ at the cross. That it is not peace between nation and nation, but between man and God, is proved by the fact the peacemakers are called the children of God, those who are His by the new birth. Theirs is the ministry of the Great Commission in Mt 28:19–20.

PEACOCK. *See* Animals, III. 40.

PEARLS. Since ancient times pearls have been highly prized for beauty of form and color. They consist of interstratified layers of mineral matter and animal membrane which form in several species of molluscan shellfish. *See* Animals, V. 10.

While the Israelites were probably acquainted with pearls at least from the time of Solomon, it is uncertain that pearls are specifically mentioned in the OT. The Heb. term *p^enînîm*, used in Job 28:18; Prov 3:15; 8:11; 20:15; 31:10, has been translated "precious stones," "rubies," "coral," "crystal," and "pearls."

Jesus spoke of pearls (Gr. *margaritēs*) as a symbol of the purity, beauty, and value of His truth and kingdom when He exhorted His disciples not to cast their pearls before swine (Mt 7:6). The interpretation of His parable of the pearl of great price (Mt 13:45–46) is less certain. Some expositors explain the one pearl to be the Church, which Christ as the merchant purchased at the supreme cost of His life; others take the pearl to be Christ for whom each of His followers must be willing to sell out completely in order to gain Him, even as Paul testifies that he did (Phil 3:7–10).

Paul recommended that women not use pearls in personal adornment (I Tim 2:9). And the Revelator included them among the prized earthly treasures of the great harlot and of commercial Babylon (Rev 17:4; 18:12, 16). The gates of the heavenly Jerusalem are portrayed as 12 individual pearls (Rev 21:21).

See Jewels.

D. R. R.

PECULIAR. An archaic term in the KJV translating Heb. *segullâ*, a special treasure, valued property (cf. Eccl 2:8; I Chr 29:3, "a treasure of my own," RSV); Gr. *periousios*, beyond the ordinary, especial; *eis peripoiēsin*, for acquisition, for (one's own) possession.

By sovereign grace Israel was chosen of God to be His peculiar people (Deut 14:2), not because of their number but because the unchangeable God loved them and intended to keep His oath to Abraham the friend of God (Gen 12:1–8; Deut 7:6–8). The conditions upon which the promise rested that Israel would be a peculiar treasure to the Lord were two: obedience to His voice and His revelation, and faithfulness in keeping His covenant (Ex 19:5; Deut 26:18).

Israel was a "peculiar" people through the separation made between them and the pagan world of the Gentiles by the establishment of a personal covenant for each male Israelite. This was made by the parents and sealed by the rite of circumcision (Gen 17:9–14). In contrast, Christian believers in the NT are circumcised in Christ by being buried or identified with Him in their baptism (Col 2:10–13). Israel was a peculiar treasure (Ex 19:5; Deut 26:18; Ps 135:4), and a holy people even as believers are (Deut 14:2; I Pet 2:9). Many theologians equate baptism with circumcision on the basis of Col 2:11–12: "In whom also ye are circumcised . . . buried with him in baptism." To them baptism, as the distinguishing mark of covenantal relationship, is considered to be the outward mark of God's precious possession today.

R. A. K.

PEDAHEL (pĕd'*ȧ*-hĕl). A "prince" of Naphtali chosen to represent that tribe in the division of Canaan when the land was conquered (Num 34:28).

PEDAHZUR (pĕ-dä'zŭr). The father of Gamaliel, who was head of the tribe of Manasseh during the Exodus (Num 1:10; 2:20; 7:54–59; 10:23).

PEDAIAH (pĕ-dā'y*ȧ*).

1. An Israelite from the city of Rumah. He was the father of Zebudah who was the wife of Josiah and mother of Jehoiakim (II Kgs 23:36).

2. He is called the son of Jeconiah (Jehoiachin), captive king of Judah, and the father of Zerubbabel (I Chr 3:18–19). Since Zerubbabel is everywhere else called the son of Shealtiel (*q.v.*; Ezr 3:2, 8), Pedaiah may have been his actual father, having married the widow of Shealtiel according to the Levirate law (*q.v.*).

3. The father of Joel who was ruler of the half tribe of Manasseh dwelling W of the Jordan (I Chr 27:20).

4. The son of Parosh who took part in rebuilding the wall of Jerusalem under Nehemiah (Neh 3:25).

5. A Levite appointed by Nehemiah with others over the temple treasury with the responsibility of distributing to their brethren. He is probably the one who stood with Ezra as he read the law to the people (Neh 8:4; 13:13).

6. The son of Kolaiah of Benjamin and ancestor of one who returned from Babylonian Exile (Neh 11:7).

P. C. J.

PEDIGREE. Heb. *yālad*, a special use of this Heb. verb meaning "to beget" or "to bear," translated "declared their pedigrees" (KJV) in Num 1:18.

PEEP. In Isa 10:14, the word describes the sound made by a nesting bird, a "chirp." In Isa 8:19, it describes faint, unintelligible sounds uttered by a sorcerer who is claiming to receive messages from the dead.

PEKAH (pē'k*ȧ*). The son of Remaliah (II Kgs 15:25–32, 37; 16:1, 5–6; II Chr 28:5–15; Isa 7:1–16). By murder which advanced him from cavalry officer to king, Pekah became the eighteenth king and the eighth dynasty in Israel. Serious problems of chronology appear in the biblical account of his reign. It is recorded in II Kgs 15:27 that his reign lasted 20 years. But other data relating to the time of his accession and demise make it clear that his actual reign could not have lasted more than eight years (740–732 B.C.). The solution rests in the policy of usurpers dating their reigns from the earliest point of the ruling house thus dethroned. Pekah dated his reign from 752 B.C. when Menahem came to the throne (Edwin R. Thiele, *The Mysterious Numbers of the Hebrew Kings*, 1951, p. 115).

The most important event of Pekah's short

reign was his alliance with Rezin, king of Syria, designed to force Judah to join in a coalition of Palestinian states to check the rising power of Tiglath-pileser III. Two invasions of Judah developed within a short period. A careful examination of all the parallel passages reveals the fact that the first invasion succeeded overwhelmingly (II Chr 28:5–8). It resulted in the slaughter of 120,000 men, a multitude being deported to Damascus, and 200,000, women and children being carried to Samaria. The fiery words of Oded the prophet resulted in the return of the women and children (II Chr 28:9–15). The threat of a second invasion led Ahaz, even against the counsel of Isaiah the prophet, to appeal to the Assyrian monarch for help (II Kgs 16:5–10; Isa 7:1–16). Tiglath-pileser III marched westward, defeated Syria, and slew Rezin. By this time, six and one-half tribes of Israel were in captivity, and Hoshea conspired against and assassinated Pekah (II Kgs 15:29–30). *See* Pekahiah.

H. A. Hoy

PEKAHIAH (pĕk'*ȧ*-hī'*ȧ*). He succeeded to the throne of Israel upon the death of his father Menahem in the fiftieth year of Azariah (or Uzziah) in Judea (II Kgs 15:23–26). Pekahiah's two-year reign (742–740 B.C.) was characterized by weakness and sin. Since Israel had no settled law of succession, Pekahiah experienced the fate of six other kings before him when his chief cavalry officer, Pekah (*q.v.*), murdered him, his two bodyguards, and 50 Gileadites.

PEKOD (pē'kŏd). In Jer 50:21 Pekod (lit., "having been visited in judgment") is a reference to the Chaldeans in general terms, symbolizing them as judged and deserving of punishment by God. In Ezk 23:23 the word probably refers to a small, little-known country lying E of the Tigris River.

PELAGIANISM. The doctrine developed *c.* A.D. 400 by the British monk called Pelagius concerning the original condition of man, the Fall, and its consequences in the life of Adam's posterity.

Original Man

According to Pelagius, man was created in a neutral condition, neither sinful nor holy, and with a capacity for either good or evil. His will was free and entirely undetermined. He was mortal from the beginning and subject to the law of death. When he sinned it was not because of antecedent evil in his nature, but because he chose to do so. The first man's fall injured no man who was to follow, but only himself. It was therefore not transmitted either as a sinful nature or as guilt to his posterity.

Each succeeding man is born in the same condition as Adam before the fall, and is therefore free from guilt or pollution at birth. Man has no evil tendencies or desires which would inevitably lead to sin. The difference between those born after Adam and Adam himself is that they have his evil example before them. Sin consists, according to Pelagius, not in evil thoughts and desires but in evil actions brought about through separate acts of the will. No man need therefore sin, since he is endowed with free will as was Adam. This is proved, for Pelagius, by the fact that God commands man to do what is good, and he argues that God would not command what is impossible. Man's responsibility is governed by the measure of his ability. If sin is universal, as it appears to be, then this is the result of wrong education, bad example, and a long established habit of sinning. When man turns from sin it is not because of God's sovereign grace, for even sin does not produce total depravity, but because of man's use of his rational endowments, God's revelation in the Scriptures, and the example of Christ.

The Errors of the System

These can only be understood when the system is viewed in contrast with the Augustinian view of man, based upon an inductive study of the Scriptures. According to the Bible, man was created in a state of holy innocency. God made man and woman as the crowning act of His creation and they were "very good" (Gen 1:31). Man could either develop through a period of probation to that place where his character was itself a holy character, as was the case with the holy angels, or he could choose to rebel against God and sin and fall, as did Satan and the wicked angels. Man came into the world under a covenant, called by the Reformed theologians the covenant of works. When man sinned it was not because he had been made prone to sin and to fall, any more than had any of the angels, but that he himself chose to sin in full responsibility.

At the same time Adam was different from his posterity, other than the Lord Jesus Christ, in that he was the head and representative of a race. When he fell, because he was man's representative in God's sight, all mankind fell in him. As a result all his posterity were born totally depraved, guilty of the sin of Adam, and inheriting a sinful fallen nature. Therefore no man can turn from his sin and live a righteous life unless he is first brought to a saving knowledge of Jesus Christ through God's sovereign grace, and enabled to fulfill the works of God's law by the presence and power of the indwelling Holy Spirit (Rom 8:3–4; Gal 2:20; 5:22–23).

Semi-Pelagianism

This is a position between the views of Pelagius and those of Augustine, which teaches that man's will has been weakened and his nature diseased, but that he is not totally depraved as a result of the fall. Fallen man retains a measure of freedom by virtue of which he can cooperate with God's grace. Regeneration then is a product of man's will and God's grace, instituted by man and not by God. This is the view held by Roman Catholicism today. In A.D. 416 Pelagianism was condemned at the Synods of Milene and Carthage, and finally in 431 at the Council of Ephesus and in 529 at the Council of Orange. Nevertheless, the church gradually drifted into semi-Pelagianism.

See Arminianism; Calvinism.

R. A. K.

PELAIAH (pĕ-lā'yȧ)

1. A son of Elioenai of the family of David (I Chr 3:24).

2. One of the teachers who assisted in the instruction of the people in Ezra's reform movement (Neh 8:7), who later gave public sanction to the covenant Nehemiah presented (Neh 10:10).

PELALIAH (pĕl'ȧ-lī'ȧ). A priest whose grandson Adaiah was a leader among the 242 priests who returned to Jerusalem to perform priestly duties other than "the work of the house" (Neh 11:12-13).

PELATIAH (pĕl'ȧ-tī'ȧ)

1. The son of Hananiah, a descendant of David through Shealtiel, after the return from Babylon (I Chr 3:21).

2. The son of Ishi of the tribe of Simeon. In the days of Hezekiah, he and his brothers led a large band of men against the remnant of Amalekites dwelling in Mount Seir (I Chr 4:42-43).

3. One of the chiefs of the people who signed the covenant of Nehemiah (Neh 10:22).

4. The son of Benaiah, one of two princes of the people seen in a vision by Ezekiel and called by God "men who devise iniquity and who give wicked counsel" (Ezk 11:1-2, RSV). As Ezekiel prophesied, he saw, still in the vision, Pelatiah fall dead (Ezk 11:13).

PELEG (pē'lĕg). A son of Eber of the family of Shem in whose days the peoples of the world were divided (Gen 10:25). The verb form, *pâlag*, is used in the same verse and is translated "divided." *See* Dispersion of Mankind.

PELET (pē'lĕt)

1. A son of Jahdai of the family of Caleb the son of Hezron (I Chr 2:47; cf. I Chr 2:18).

2. A son of Azmaveth and one of David's men who could hurl stones or shoot arrows with either hand (I Chr 12:2-3).

PELETH (pē'lĕth)

1. A Reubenite whose son On rebelled against the leadership of Moses and Aaron (Num 16:1). His name may also be spelled Pallu (*q.v.*).

2. A son of Jonathan, a descendant of Jerahmeel (I Chr 2:33).

PELETHITES (pĕl'ĕ-thīts). A choice company of soldiers (II Sam 8:18) who were David's bodyguards with the Cherethites (*q.v.*). They were probably from Beth-palet (*q.v.*). Some believe that the Pelethites and Cherethites refer to Philistines (*q.v.*) and Cretans, respectively. As such, they were foreign mercenary troops who would not become involved in domestic politics and would therefore remain loyal to David.

PELICAN. *See* Animals, III. 41.

PELONITE (pĕl'ŏ-nīt). An inhabitant of Palon, an obscure and unknown place from which two of David's mighty men came (I Chr 11:27, 36). Pelonite may be a variant spelling for Paltite (*q.v.*; cf. II Sam 23:26).

PEN. *See* Writing.

PENCE. *See* Weights, Measures, and Coins.

PENCIL. *See* Writing.

PEN-CONTAINER. *See* Writing.

PENIEL. *See* Penuel.

PENINNAH (pĕ-nĭn'ȧ). The second wife of Elkanah, Samuel's father (I Sam 1:2-4).

PENITENCE. *See* Repentance.

PENKNIFE. A knife (Jer 36:23) used by a scribe in making the writing point on a reed pen.

PENNY. *See* Weights, Measures, and Coins.

PENTATEUCH. This designation, derived from two Gr. words, *pente*, "five," and *teuchos*, "volume," and meaning five volumes or books, is applied to the first five books of the Bible. Later Jews designated these books "the five fifths of the law." Evidence for this fivefold division is as early as Philo and Josephus. In itself, however, the division is a natural one, and probably derives from the original author, Moses. In the Heb. OT, the Pentateuch is designated the Torah (Law), a term which lays emphasis upon the legal element that forms a large portion of the work.

Content

The purpose of the Pentateuch is to recount the grace of God in forming Israel into a nation and giving to it His law. Thus the work begins with the creation of the world and traces the history of mankind, emphasizing the formation of the theocratic nation and relating its history to the point where it is ready to enter the Promised Land.

Broadly speaking, the Pentateuch can be divided into two parts. Gen 1–Ex 19 is historical, in that it recounts the various steps by which Israel was brought to the point where it could be constituted the theocracy. Ex 20–Deut 34 is legal, containing the Ten Commandments and the legislation concerning the tabernacle, sacrifices, priesthood, etc. The first section is an obvious preparation for the second; it was necessary that the people of God be first drawn apart from the world in order that, as the organized theocracy, they might receive the laws of the divine government. *See also* introduction to Genesis.

Genesis recounts the creation of the world and of man, man's fall into sin and expulsion from the garden, and the rapid growth of sin demanding the destruction of man by a flood. In Noah, the race was kept alive, and a new beginning, as it were, was made. Once more, however, corruption and wickedness became powerful, so that it was necessary for God to call His people out to be separate from the sinful world. This was done in the call of Abraham to leave Ur of the Chaldees and to be the father of the faithful. Genesis relates his obedience and recounts his wanderings, showing that even with weak men God remained true to His promise of salvation.

Samaritan high priest and Samaritan Pentateuch

Exodus begins with the descendants of Jacob in Egypt and relates their mighty deliverance under Moses. It tells how at Mount Sinai God formed them into a nation, giving the Ten Commandments and ratifying the covenant. Directions are then given for the erection of the tabernacle, for God may now dwell in the midst of His people.

Leviticus gives the various laws requisite for worship. Sacrifices are required, for the defilement which separates man from God must be removed, and fellowship between God and man must be restored.

Numbers recounts the arrangements of the camp, the preparations for departure, and the journeyings of the people from Sinai to the plains of Moab with mention of various incidents that occurred on the way.

Deuteronomy contains the last addresses of Moses to the nation and prepared them for entrance into Canaan. The book is cast in the form of a covenant document, and in a formal sense is arranged similarly to the suzerainty treaties of the Hittites. The entire Pentateuch is a unit, and contains one essential theme.

Authorship

That Moses was the human author of the Pentateuch is the view of Scripture and is strongly supported by all the evidence. There are six passages in the Pentateuch which specifically claim Mosaic authorship (Ex 17:14; 24:4–8; 34:27; Num 33:1–2; Deut 31:9, 24–26; 31:22, 30–32:43). Three of these references have to do with legislative sections and three with historical. These six sections are integral parts of their context, so that the references cited probably attribute to Moses the authorship of a good bit of the context in which they occur.

With respect to Genesis, no specific statement of authorship is found in the book itself. But Genesis is an integral part of the Pentateuch. Its narrative leads up to the events related in Exodus, and without it Exodus would not be understandable. Exodus clearly presupposes Genesis; indeed, its first Heb. word, *w^e*, usually translated "and," shows that it is to be connected with what precedes in Genesis. If Moses was the author of the last four books of the Pentateuch, he was the author of Genesis also.

Throughout the last four books of the Pentateuch Moses is the principal character. He was the mediator through whom God spoke to the nation of the giving of the law. To him God made known the directions for the building of the tabernacle, and to him the laws concerning worship were revealed. Over and over we read such phrases as, "And the Lord spake unto Moses, saying," "As the Lord commanded Moses," etc. When we come to Deuteronomy we are in the same atmosphere. The book begins with, "These be the words which Moses spake." In the entire book of Deuteronomy Moses stands out as the leading figure.

In the remainder of the OT the Pentateuch is uniformly regarded as the work of Moses. It is correct to say that the only authoritative law that is recognized in the OT is the law of Moses. The same is true of the NT. Quotations from the Pentateuch are so made as to attribute authorship to Moses (cf. Mt 19:8; Mk 10:3–5; Lk 24:27, 44; Jn 5:46–47; 7:19; Acts 3:22;

Rev 15:3; etc.). Both OT and NT regard Moses as the human author of the law.

In the 18th cen. the view appeared that the Pentateuch was not entirely the work of Moses. The presence of different divine names in Genesis was thought to be a mark of different authors. It came to be assumed finally that Genesis consisted of three principal documents which had finally been pieced together by a redactor. These three documents, or parts of them, were thought to be found also in Exodus, Leviticus, and Numbers, Deuteronomy being attributed to a different source. The documentary hypothesis, as it is called, although held by many scholars, nevertheless destroys the true unity and harmony of the Pentateuch. It is a theory which the facts do not support and hence must be abandoned. *See* Genesis.

Purpose

The Pentateuch is the foundation upon which the remainder of Scripture builds. It contains the basic law of the theocracy upon which the prophets base their messages. It tells of Moses, the great lawgiver, the greatest figure of the OT, who was a witness of the future, even of Christ the Son of God.

See Canon of Scripture, the OT; Law of Moses; Priest, Priesthood.

Bibliography. G. Ch. Aalders, *A Short Introduction to the Pentateuch,* London: Tyndale Press, 1949. Oswald T. Allis, *The Five Books of Moses,* Philadelphia: Presbyterian and Reformed, 1943; *God Spake by Moses,* Philadelphia: Presbyterian and Reformed, 1951. David A. Hubbard, "Pentateuch," NBD, pp. 957-964. W. J. Martin, *Stylistic Criteria and the Analysis of the Pentateuch,* London: Tyndale Press, 1955. Nicholas H. Ridderbos, "Reversals of Old Testament Criticism," *Revelation and the Bible,* Carl F. H. Henry, ed., Grand Rapids: Baker, 1958, pp. 335-350. Moses H. Segal, *The Pentateuch: Its Composition and Its Authorship and Other Biblical Studies,* Jerusalem: Magnes Press, 1968 (rejects the documentary theory).

E. J. Y.

PENTECOST (pĕn'tē-kôst). Pentecost was the second of the three great festivals of Israel (Deut 16:16). The main passages for the feast are Ex 23:16; Lev 23:15-22; Num 28:26-31; Deut 16:9-12. The Gr. word Pentecost (*pentēkostē*) means "the fiftieth," referring to the fiftieth day after the offering of the firstfruit of a sheaf of grain during the Feast of Unleavened Bread (Lev 23:16; Tob 2:1; II Macc 12:32; Jos *Ant.* iii. 10.6; Acts 2:1; 20:16; I Cor 16:8).

Other titles by which this festival is known are Feast of Weeks (Ex 34:22; Deut 16:10, 16; II Chr 8:13), which refers to seven weeks after the offering of the firstfruits; Feast of Harvest (Ex 23:16), referring to the conclusion of the grain harvests; day of firstfruits (Num 28:26), speaking of the firstfruits of a completed harvest; and later Jews called it a solemn assembly (Mishnah: Arakhin ii.3; Hagigah ii.4; Rosh ha-Shanah i.2), which was applied to the closing festival, hence the closing festival of the harvest season.

Although the Scriptures do not specifically state its historical significance, they seem to indicate it was basically a harvest festival. Possibly the earliest designation, a Feast of Harvest in Ex 23:16, is significant. The reckoning time for Pentecost is the fiftieth day from "the morrow after the sabbath" (Lev 23:11, 15), a phrase that is chronologically problematic. The Pharisees took this sabbath as meaning "festival day," i.e., the first day of the Passover (Mishnah:Hagigah ii.4) regardless of what day of the week it fell. On the other hand, the Sadducees (or Boethuseans) and the Karaites since the 8th cen. A.D. felt that the phrase had to be taken literally. Therefore "the morrow after the sabbath" would be the day following the first sabbath (i.e., Sunday) after the Passover and not necessarily the second day of the feast (Mishnah:Hagigah ii.4; Menahoth x.1-3). Hence, if one accepted the Sadducean interpretation, it would mean that the waving of the firstfruit of a sheaf of grain would occur the day after the first weekly sabbath during the Feast of Unleavened Bread and that Pentecost, being fifty days of seven weeks completed (Lev 23:15-16), would always come on the morrow after the sabbath, that is, on Sunday.

At the time of the firstfruits the Israelite would bring the first few sprigs of ripe grain and give them to the priest, who would offer them to the Lord by waving the sheaf (Lev 23:9-14; Num 18:12-13; Deut 26). This seems to have been a thank offering with anticipation of God's blessing on the harvest. At Pentecost, 50 days after the firstfruits, the priest would wave two loaves baked with leaven as a thanksgiving offering to the Lord for the harvest, and this would mark the conclusion of the harvest. The other ceremonies in connection with this feast are described in Lev 23:15-22. In Num 28:26, Pentecost is called both the Feast of Weeks and the Feast of the Firstfruits. This Feast of Firstfruits is not to be confused with the firstfruits offered during the days of unleavened bread. *See* Festivals; Firstfruits.

Pentecost in the NT is in connection with the gift of the Holy Spirit (Acts 2:1-4). Christ rose as the firstfruit of resurrection (I Cor 15:23), and 50 days afterward came the outpouring of the Holy Spirit as the beginning of the fulfillment of Joel's prophecy (Joel 2:28-32). The suddenness of the manifestation and the accompanying signs (*see* Tongues, Gift of) indicated the supernaturalness of the endowment. The gift of the Spirit was the firstfruits (Rom 8:23; Eph 1:13-14) of the spiritual harvest procured through the work of Christ. There were 3,000 who became Christians, i.e., the firstfruits of all the believers after Christ's death who were presented as a wave offering to the Lord (cf. Jas 1:18). Pentecost is regarded as the birthday of the Church. Since Christ's resurrection fell on Sunday, Pentecost also fell on the first day of the week—the day on which Christians worshiped and continue to worship (Acts 20:7; I Cor 16:2).

Some Jews of the post-biblical period believed that Pentecost commemorated the giving of the law at Sinai, which was calculated to have occurred on the fiftieth day after the Exodus (Ex 19:1). Modern Jews accept the tradition, and spend the previous night in reading appropriate Scripture.

Bibliography. Roland de Vaux, *Ancient Israel: Its Life and Institutions*, trans. by John McHugh, New York: McGraw-Hill, 1961, pp. 493–495. Alfred Edersheim, *The Temple: Its Ministry and Services*, London: Religious Tract Society, n.d., pp. 256–267. M. Lohse, *"Pentēcostē,"* TDNT, VI, 44–53. G. T. Purves, "Pentecost," HDB, III, 739–742. J. C. Rylaardsam, "Weeks, Feast of," IDB, IV, 827–828.

H. W. H.

PENUEL (pē-nū'ĕl), **PENIEL** (pē-nī'ĕl)

1. The place of Jacob's struggle along the Jabbok (Wadi Zerqa). Since there he wrestled with God as it were face to face (cf. Hos 12:4), Jacob named it Peniel, "the face of God" (Gen 32:30). The alternate spelling Penuel (v. 31) may give the original pronunciation using an old nominative case ending *u*, later dropped in Heb.

Later on, a city was built there whose tower Gideon destroyed (Jud 8:8–9, 17). Jeroboam I enlarged or rebuilt it (I Kgs 12:25), perhaps as a winter residence or as an alternate capital, hoping it would be less vulnerable than Shechem. But Shishak of Egypt probably mentions it as *Pernoual* in his list of conquered cities of Judah and Israel. It appears as *Panili* in the Assyrian records. It is to be identified with the twin mounds *Tulul edh-Dhahab* along the Jabbok, four miles E of Succoth.

2. A member of the tribe of Judah and "father" or founder of the town of Gedor (I Chr 4:4).

3. A Benjamite, son of Shashak (I Chr 8:25).

H. E. Fi.

PEOPLE. *See* Nations.

PEOPLE OF GOD. *See* Children of God.

PEOPLE OF THE EAST. *See* East, Children of the.

PEOR (pē'ôr)

1. A mountain of Moab NE of the Dead Sea overlooking the desert wasteland (Num 23:28, NASB). From its top Balaam could also see the tribes of Israel in their tents at Shittim in the Jordan Valley (Num 24:2; 25:1). While encamped there many of the Israelites were seduced into worshiping the Baal of Peor (Num 25:1–5; Josh 22:17). The location of the mount is not certainly identified.

2. A pagan deity (Num 25:18; 31:16), more fully called Baal-peor (Num 25:3, 5; Deut 4:3; Ps 106:28; Hos 9:10), considered to be the local manifestation of Baal or perhaps the Moabite god Chemosh (*see* Gods, False).

PERAZIM, MOUNT (pĭ-rā'zĭm). A place near the valley of Rephaim (Isa 28:21), remembered for the victory by David over the Philistines (II Sam 5:20) at Baal-perazim (*q.v.*).

PERDITION. This English word never appears in the OT. The Gr. word *apōleia* appears 19 times in the NT and is translated by six different expressions in the KJV: damnable, damnation, destruction, perdition (eight times), pernicious way, waste. The word basically means destruction, the direct antithesis of salvation (*sōtēria*) and its blessedness (Phil 1:28). It has special reference to the wicked, either as to their expected fate (Jn 17:12; Phil 1:28), or their present lost and ruined condition (I Tim 6:9; Heb 10:39), or the time of their judgment and destruction (II Pet 3:7), or the place where ruined humanity is finally confined (Rev 17:8, 11).

The term "son of perdition" appears twice in the NT, once of Judas Iscariot (Jn 17:12), and once of Antichrist (II Thess 2:3). Some identify the two, but this seems wholly unnecessary. The phrase "the son of" is a well-known Heb. or Gr. idiom, followed by the trait or quality or destiny it embodies. In this case it is that of a ruined character (Jn 6:70; II Thess 2:3), which produces ruin in others (Jn 18:2–3; II Thess 2:9–12), eventually experiencing destruction (Acts 1:18; II Thess 2:8) and a final casting into eternal damnation (Acts 1:25; Rev 17:8, 11). The name thus portrays the progress of both these individuals from evil character to the place of eternal loss.

H. A. Hoy

PEREA. *See* Palestine: II.B.4.*c*.

PERES (pē'rĕs). The Aramaic word means "divided" and refers to a division in the sense of military defeat and dissolution of power over a kingdom (Dan 5:28). *See* Mene, Mene, Tekel, Upharsin.

PERESH (pĭr'ĕsh). A grandson of Manasseh from an Aramitish concubine (I Chr 7:14, 16).

PEREZ. *See* Pharez.

PEREZ-UZZA(H) (pĕr'ĕz-ŭz'ȧ). A place between Kirjath-jearim and Jerusalem; not identified. Its name, meaning "a break-through of Uzza" (NASB marg.), was given it by King David after Uzzah was smitten there by God for having touched the ark while it was being conveyed to Jerusalem (II Sam 6:8; I Chr 13:11).

PERFECT, PERFECTION. The terms in the biblical sense usually connote that which is complete, conformed to a standard or pattern, and represent normally the translation of Heb. *tām* and Gr. *teleios*. In an absolute theological sense, perfection can be seen in the Triune God alone. Often His attributes are called perfections, for they are aspects of His very Being.

In a relative sense, perfection as completeness or maturity is ascribed to believers in Jesus Christ (Phil 3:15), and yet paradoxically is also held forth as the goal for the Christian (Phil 3:12–14). The seeming paradox is explained by a recognition of at least two aspects of perfection, comparative and evangelical (MSt, VII, 942). Comparative perfection applies to the Christian who is advanced in progressive sanctification. Evangelical perfection is applicable to every Christian, regardless of the degree of growth in sanctification. Through evangelical perfection the believer is viewed as complete or perfect in Christ, and accepted by God in this positional sense (Col 2:10). Though the creature-Creator relationship of man to God is never violated, still Jesus sets forth the goal for His disciples in Mt 5:48, "Be ye therefore perfect, even as your Father which is in heaven is perfect." This is clearly an appeal to excellence in Christian growth, greater and greater conformity on a finite level to the biblical standard of completeness in Jesus Christ. *See* Vocation.

Theologically, the question of perfection has issued in debate as to the ability of the Christian to attain in this life to sinless perfection within the confines of practical sanctification. Adherents of the belief that the Christian can reach sinless perfection claim scriptural ground for a higher life of Christian perfection, free from all sin. Opponents to this position cite the creature-Creator relationship as a refutation of this, and such Scripture as I Jn 1:8, 10. *See* Sanctification.

Bibliography. G. Delling, "*Telos*, etc.," TDNT, VIII, 49–87.

F. R. H.

PERFUME. The Israelites, like other peoples of the Near East and the Orient, made extensive use of perfumes manufactured from a variety of aromatic organic substances. Reduced to powder, perfume might be carried on the person as a sachet (Song 1:13; 3:6; Isa 3:20, RSV). Aromatic extracts were combined with oils as ointment or anointing oils, a necessity for the care of the skin in the dry, hot climate of Palestine (Song 1:3).

Mary anointed the feet of Jesus with a costly ointment of nard (Jn 12:3; cf. Mt 26:7; Mk 14:3; Lk 7:37; many such alabaster ointment jars have been found in excavated sites, particularly in Egypt). Perfume was also applied to the clothing (Ps 45:8; Song 4:11). The harlot sought to entice to a bed "perfumed . . . with myrrh, aloes, and cinnamon" (Prov 7:17). Myrrh and aloes were used in wrapping the body of Jesus for burial (Jn 19:39–40); however, the hundred pounds used was small compared to the amount used for the funeral of Herod the Great. requiring 500 slaves to carry it (Jos *Ant*. xvii.8.3).

The attractiveness of the bride in Song 4:9–15 is expressed in terms of the fragrance of a variety of aromatic spices and is a fairly complete catalogue of those in common use: nard, saffron, calamus, cinnamon, frankincense, myrrh, and aloes. Ex 30:24, 34 adds cassia, stacte, onycha, and galbanum.

Large alabaster vase for perfumed ointments from the tomb of Tutankhamon. LL

Perfumes compounded according to the special formulae of Ex 30:22–38 were restricted to worship purposes. They included anointing oil for consecratory rites and incense for burning on the golden altar of the tabernacle and temple. The large number of incense altars found in Palestinian excavations testify to extensive use in local pagan sanctuaries apart from the official temple rituals of Judaism.

This wide use of perfumes, not only in Israel but in the whole Near East, made spices of major importance in the commerce of that part of the world. Some were available in the Jordan Valley, but most had to be imported from Arabia, the E coast of Africa, Ceylon, and India. Commercial empires were built on the trade involved. This trade was one of the main factors in Solomon's wealth as well as that of Jeroboam II. The Queen of Sheba brought great quantities of spices as a gift to Solomon

(I Kgs 10:2, 10). The gifts and tribute of other rulers likewise included spices and myrrh (I Kgs 10:25). Control of the routes for the spice trade, whether overland by caravan or by water (cf. Solomon's navy, I Kgs 9:26-28; 10:11-12), was essential to commercial success and so conditioned both the political and military history of the time.

See Anoint; Ointment.

R. V. R.

PERFUMER. *See* Occupations: Perfumer.

PERGA (pûr'gȧ). Perga was the capital of the district, later the Roman province, of Pamphylia on the southern coast of Asia Minor, located on the Cestrus River, 12 miles inland from its port city of Attalia. On Paul's first missionary journey, he seems to have passed through Perga without stopping as he made his way up into the mountains of the interior. It has been suggested that at that time of year, malarial conditions in the lowland city had emptied it of most of its inhabitants and Paul himself may have had the fever (Acts 13:13-14; cf. Gal 4:13). At the close of the first missionary journey, on his way back to Syrian Antioch, Paul stopped and preached the Word in Perga (Acts 14:25). Perga was never much influenced by the Greeks, but remained oriental in character with worship centered in the Artemis of Perga. It would seem that Paul's ministry had little effect in Perga, for there is no mention of the city until centuries later when it became the center of a metropolitan bishopric.

P. C. J.

PERGAMOS. *See* Pergamum.

PERGAMUM (pûr'gȧ-mŭm). Pergamum, capital of Asia, was situated on a hill about 1000 feet high and commanded the fertile valley of the Caicus River in southern Mysia. The city stood opposite the island of Lesbos about 18 miles from the Aegean and communicated with the sea via the Caicus, which was navigable by small craft. Pergamum was also located on the great N-S road which ran from Ephesus to Cyzicus on the Propontis or Sea of Marmara.

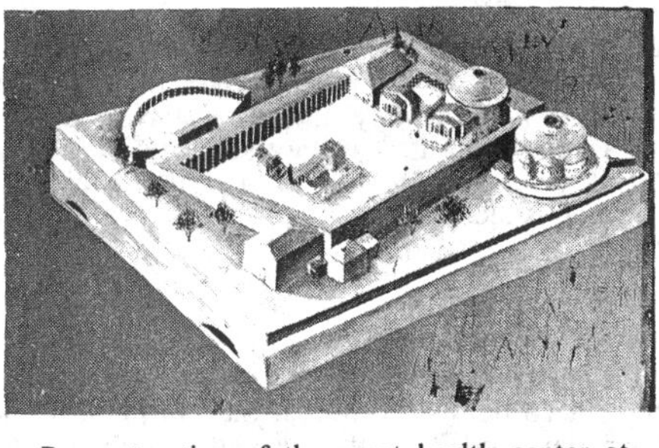

Reconstruction of the great health center at Pergamum. HFV

The city's real history began in the 3rd cen. B.C. under the Attalid dynasty, when it became the capital of a Hellenistic kingdom of considerable importance. Attalus III willed his kingdom to Rome at his death in 133 B.C., when it became the province of Asia. The Pergamene kings owed their power to expand to their skillful management of the country's natural wealth, which they bestowed freely as patrons of the arts and made Pergamum one of the greatest and most beautiful Gr. cities. It was laid out in terraces on a hillside. A city also developed at the foot of the hill; there was located a famous health resort dedicated to the god Asclepius. Pergamum was renowned for its school of sculpture.

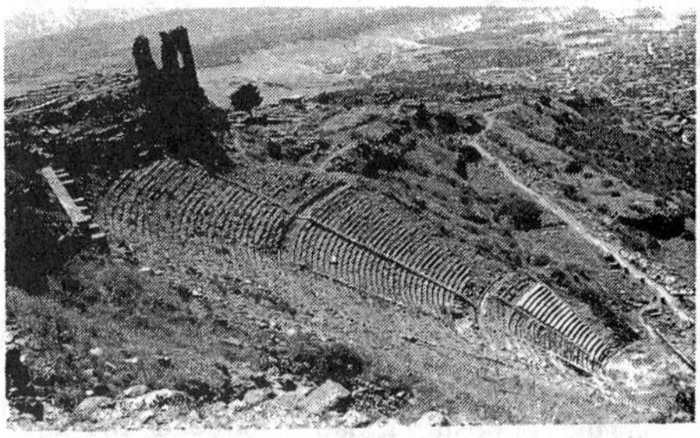

Theater of the acropolis of Pergamum seating 15,000. HFV

Excavations at Pergamum began in 1868 and have now uncovered some 60 percent of the city. The great sculptured altar of Zeus there (125 × 115 feet) has been identified by some as "Satan's throne" (Rev 2:13, RSV). In his letter to the church of Pergamum John scored the doctrines of Balaam and the Nicolaitanes. The former apparently had to do with Christians marrying pagans, and the latter with the belief that since heathen gods did not exist anyway, Christian participation in idolatrous feasts couldn't hurt them. *See* Archaeology.

H. F. V.

PERIDA. *See* Peruda.

PERIZZITES (pĕr'ĭ-zīts). One of the six "tribes" of the Canaanites who dwelt in the land as early as the time of Abraham (Gen 13:7; see also Gen 15:20; Ex 3:8; Deut 7:1; Josh 3:10; etc., for enumeration with other groups). Jacob feared reprisal from them after the slaughter of Shechem by his sons (Gen 34:30), reflecting their alliance with Canaanites. The tribes of Judah and Simeon battled them in the vicinity of Jerusalem (Jud 1:1-7). They were inhabitants of the "hill country" (Josh 9:1; 11:3; 12:8) in the territory of the tribes of Ephraim, Manasseh, and Judah. The term Perizzi may come from *perāzâ*, "hamlet," "village," so that the Perizzites are villagers in the hills of Canaan, rather than an ethnic group.

God commanded Israel to exterminate them (Deut 7:2), and not enter into marriage with them (7:3) because of their sins, which if adopted by Israel would cause God's people to fall away from Him (7:4). Archaeology has revealed the gross sexual practices to which these people gave themselves, and by their self-corruption brought destruction upon themselves.

The Israelites did not utterly exterminate them and did intermarry with them (Jud 3:5-6), bringing idolatry into Israel. For this the Israelites were brought into bondage from which the judges delivered them. Solomon made the Perizzites bondservants (I Kgs 9:20-21; II Chr 8:7-8).

In the time of Ezra (Ezr 9:1) the Perizzites were still in the land and were a peril to the returned exiles.

H. G. S.

PERJURY. *See* Oath.

PERSECUTION. K. S. Latourette has described the movement of the church in history, beginning with the Acts of the Apostles, as "advance through storm." No sooner had the Christian enterprise been launched at Pentecost than the apostolic leaders Peter and John were summoned before the Sanhedrin (Acts 4:1-22). Soon the opposition had produced the first Christian martyr, Stephen (Acts 6:8–8:1). Before his conversion, Paul persecuted Christians to death (Acts 9:1 ff.). The Jerusalem community as a whole was both persecuted and spread by persecution (Acts 12:1-25). On the missionary journeys that fill the remainder of the book of Acts persecution constantly recurred, Paul and his associates being pursued from city to city.

Other books of the NT reveal this same burning bush pattern (the church always in the fire of persecution but never being consumed). Thus in his first letter to the Thessalonians Paul reminded them, "And you became imitators of us and of the Lord, for you received the word in much affliction" (I Thess 1:6, RSV). Paul sent Timothy to them "that no one be moved by these afflictions. You yourselves know that this is to be our lot" (I Thess 3:3, RSV). Peter also encouraged his readers to "rejoice, though now for a little while you may have to suffer various trials, so that the genuineness of your faith, more precious than gold . . . may redound to praise and glory and honor at the revelation of Jesus Christ" (I Pet 1:6-7, RSV).

The last book of the canonical NT is an apocalyptic of a suffering church which is yet being avenged and delivered. Typical are the souls "under the altar who had been slain for the word of God . . . they cried out with a loud voice, O Sovereign Lord, holy and true, how long before thou wilt judge and avenge our blood?" The answer is, not "until the number of their fellow servants and their brethren shall be complete, who were to be killed as they themselves had been" (Rev 6:9-11, RSV). [Ed. note: While some interpreters understand such passages in Rev 4-22 to refer to a suffering church, others view them as descriptive of what is yet to take place in the future tribulation in which the true Church is not present. This futurist position, however, does view the churches in Rev 2 and 3 as representative of churches in the present age of the church. Conditions as described in these seven letters indicate that Christians in John's day were undergoing persecution. God's sovereignty in the climactic events of history following the Church Age (Rev 4-22) serve as a tremendous reassurance now to the church of God's sovereign rule in all events, including persecution.]

The Bible not only presents the church as suffering but develops a theology of persecution as well—its source, aim and effect. The source of persecution is sinful man's hatred of God. Paul calls unreconciled men God's "enemies" (Rom 5:10). The love of the world is enmity to God. "No man can serve two masters" (Mt 6:24). "The light is come into the world, and men loved the darkness rather than the light" (Jn 3:19, NASB). "The mind that is set on the flesh is hostile to God; it does not submit to God's law, indeed it cannot" (Rom 8:7, RSV).

Christ assures His followers that the disciple is not greater than his Lord. "If they persecuted Me, they will persecute you" (Jn 15:20). In the world disciples are to expect tribulation, but are to beware when all speak well of them. They are to rejoice when men speak ill of them (Mt 5:11-12). Men will do more than speak against the Name, they will kill the disciples, thinking themselves to have done God service thereby (Jn 16:2).

Nor is this anything new. On the contrary, says Paul, "Now we, brethren, like Isaac, are children of promise. But as at that time he who was born according to the flesh persecuted him who was born according to the Spirit, so it is now" (Gal 4:28-29, RSV). "The insults of those who insult thee have fallen on me" complains the psalmist (Ps 69:9, RSV). In fact, the Psalms abound in records of complaints of persecution. "How long, O Lord" is the lament of the OT believer, to which the complaining of the souls under the altar is the NT counterpart.

If the source of Christian persecution is hatred of God, its aim is to destroy Him. Someone has well said, "If men were able to kill God, His life would not be safe for a moment." Not being able to reach God, they did by wicked hands crucify and slay His Son (Acts 2:23). In killing Christ they shed the "blood of God" (Acts 20:28). A ghastly "deicide" was accomplished as the Prince of Life was put to death.

Now that Christ has broken the bonds of death and is alive forevermore in the transcendent heavenlies, the insatiable malice of men must wreak its cruelty on His representatives here below. Although Saul in persecuting Christians did it ignorantly and in unbelief, he nonetheless was persecuting Jesus in persecuting His followers (Acts 9:4). Christ sends His followers out as lambs among wolves to be the victims of their rapacity (Lk 10:3). Every day they are accounted as sheep for the slaughter (Rom 8:36). As Christians suffer, they are the victims of man's inhumanity to God.

The result of persecution is to remove hypocritical and nominal believers, reveal and confirm the genuine ones, spread the church and glorify God. Christ defined a disciple indeed as one who continued in His word (Jn 8:31), one who endured to the end (Mt 24:13). In a statement which Calvin says makes "our hair stand on end," Christ teaches that fearing him who can destroy our body exposes us to the wrath of Him who can destroy body and soul in hell (Mt 10:28). Those who under persecution do not confess Christ before men, He will not confess before God to be His disciples (Lk 12:8-9; Mt 10:32-33). Those who receive Him with joy but go back as soon as trouble appears, do not permit the seed of the kingdom to grow in them (Mt 13:20-21).

It is no coincidence that the NT word for witness, *martus*, becomes our word for martyr. A witness is a martyr. He stands ready to die following the orders of the Captain of his salvation. He does not count his life "of any value" (Acts 20:24). He loves Christ more than his own soul. He rejoices and is exceeding glad (Mt 5:12). He counts it all joy (Jas 1:2). He rejoices in tribulation (I Pet 1:6). Thus persecution reveals the true believer in the world, confirms his faith to himself, and Christ sees His offspring and is satisfied (Isa 53:10-11).

This wrath (*orgē*) of men does not of itself work the righteousness of God (Jas 1:20), but God makes it to praise Him (Ps 76:10). He makes the blood of martyrs become the seed of the church, as Tertullian put it. The storm advances the church. The early church seemed serenely aware of God's strange way of extending His kingdom, and when the Christians saw the Jewish leaders preparing to destroy them, they prayed not for protection but for courage (Acts 4:24-30).

Persecution glorifies God. An evil world relentlessly and perpetually attacks a defenseless little flock. What is the result? The result is that the world destroys itself and increases the church! The wolf attacks the lamb, but the lamb lives and the wolf dies! Who but God could make the very wrath of men, which ever strives to destroy Him and His, to praise and glorify Him? *See* Tribulation.

This biblical theology of persecution was needed in the early post-apostolic church. Christ's promise of tribulation for the disciples in this world was abundantly fulfilled and joyously met. The first physical persecution of the church by Rome occurred under Nero (A.D. 64-68) in the capital city as Tacitus reported, but a more determined and general persecution arose in various parts of the empire in the reigns of Trajan (98-117) and Hadrian (117-138), which was not to reach its climax until the Decian and Diocletian persecutions of the 3rd and 4th cen. Ignatius, bishop of Antioch, wrote his letters while being taken to Rome for probable martyrdom *c.* 115, and Polycarp was burned at the stake during a local persecution in Smyrna in 155.

In 248 Rome was celebrating the thousandth anniversary of its founding. Such a recollection of the brilliant past made the present appear the more alarming. To make matters worse, the barbarians were becoming ever more threatening. What was wrong? The gods were not worshiped as they used to be. Why not? Because the Christians refused to do so and were persuading others also to become irreligious. What could be done? Only one thing—wipe out the Christian "atheists" and return to the true worship of the gods. Any alert emperor devoted to the perpetuation of the empire on its presumed foundations must recognize the danger. Decius (249-251) was such an emperor. He issued an edict requiring all Christians to offer sacrifice. Those who did not suffered loss of property, imprisonment, torture, exile and even death for their faith. In spite of the severity and the extent of this persecution, the church endured it and the one that followed under Gallus (251-253).

Nevertheless, the increased secularization of the church was also revealed as many professing Christians denied their faith. Some did it by sacrificing to the gods as they were commanded by Caesar and forbidden by Christ. These were called *sacrificati*. Others securing falsified certificates, pretended to have sacrificed to satisfy the authorities but avoided doing it to satisfy their own consciences (*libellatici*). This was done by bribing officials to place their names on the list of those who had actually sacrificed.

Feeling that a concentration of severe persecution on the Christian leaders would be a more effective way of uprooting Christianity, Valerian (253-260) resumed the attack by his edicts of 257 and 258. He not only demanded of the clergy that they should sacrifice to the gods, but also forbade them to worship their God publicly, or even visit Christian cemeteries. Many bishops, presbyters and deacons were put to death. Men and women of high social or political rank were subjected to heavy punishments and even death if they refused to offer the required sacrifices. "Now blood flowed in streams." The very frightfulness and extensiveness of this ordeal made it impossible to pursue it long. Soon came the peace which was to last 40 years as Gallienus (260-268) retracted the edicts of his father and Christians were again unofficially tolerated.

Following this period of practical tolerance, Christianity faced its most severe final persecution under Diocletian and Galerius. Once again it was the case of a "conscientious" emperor spelling doom for the children of God. Diocletian (284-305), too, wished to see again the glory of Rome which had departed. In point of extent, duration and severity his persecution was the worst. It was so obviously the decisive struggle between the church and the empire that it could not have been otherwise. In 295 Christian soldiers were ordered to sacrifice. In 298 a commander was killed and persecutions multiplied in the army. By 303 they became general as three edicts were issued in rapid succession. Even Diocletian's Christian wife and daughter were required to sacrifice. Christian buildings were ordered destroyed. Bishops and presbyters were imprisoned. Scriptures were burned. Christians lost all legal rights and all were to be tortured. This lasted until 305 in the West, until 311 in the East, especially in Palestine and Egypt, which suffered most severely.

In this great tribulation many Christians were martyred, but others denied their faith or handed over their Bibles (*traditores*). This persecution revealed the futility of trying to eradicate Christianity. The empire might fall, but not the church. No alternative was now left for the empire but to come to terms. This it was soon to do. *See* Rome, Roman Empire.

These early "killing times" produced two different reactions in the church – recantation and martyrdom. Capitulation was justified by devious methods. Some insisted that the duty to higher powers included recantation when required. Others handed over the Scriptures while observing that Christ had said that those who denied Him would be denied by Him. Many, with no particular rationalization, followed in the footsteps of Peter to deny their Lord. But on the whole a great chapter in martyrdom was written. Agnes, a noblewoman of Sicily, died for her faith. Carpus, a Thracian bishop, could say, "I saw the glory of the Lord, and I was glad, and at the same time I was freed from you and am not a party to your misdeeds." He was nailed to the stake. Cyprian, bishop of N Africa, was beheaded in 258. A whole body of Asiatic Christians presented themselves to their proconsul, Arrius Antonius, for martyrdom, to show him what a bath of blood he must wade through to destroy Christ's church.

But still the church grew. Imprisoned and tortured confessors of the 3rd cen. might have uttered Martin Niemoller's words: "I believe my incarceration [under Hitler] is an instance of God's holy humor. They laugh scornfully, 'At last we have got him,' and arrest eight hundred more. But what is the result? Full churches with praying congregations. It would be utter ingratitude to become bitter in the face of such facts." With Constantine, Christianity achieved full toleration.

While this article is not meant to extend beyond the early church, one postscript may not be out of order. These Roman persecutions which came to dreadful proportions in the 3rd cen. have hardly been paralleled until the present century when they have been greatly exceeded. The church is suffering more now than ever in her history. And if Christ does not soon return, it appears that worse persecution is yet to come. Once again the true Christian may be revealed as what he in spirit always is – the martyr.

Bibliography. E. M. Blaiklock, *The Christian in Pagan Society*, London: Tyndale Press, 1951. E. H. Broadbent, *The Pilgrim Church*, London: Pickering & Inglis, 1945. Leon H. Canfield, *The Early Persecutions of the Christians*, New York: Columbia Univ., 1913. John Foxe, *Foxe's Christian Martyrs of the World*, Chicago: Moody Press, n.d. W. H. C. Frend, *Martyrdom and Persecution in the Early Church*, Garden City: Anchor Books, 1967. Heinrich Schlier, "*Thlibō*, etc.," TDNT, III, 139–148. Herbert B. Workman, *Persecution in the Early Church*, London: C. H. Kelly, 1906.

J. H. G.

PERSEVERANCE. This word has both a biblical and theological usage. In the strictly biblical significance it is used in the KJV to render the Gr. noun *proskarterēsis* in Eph 6:18. The verbal form *proskartereō* is more common, being found in the LXX (Num 13:20), classical Gr., and papyri as well as the NT. In each instance the primary thought is the steadfast continuance in something, whether it be described as the waiting of a boat (Mk 3:9), the continual care of personal servants and bodyguards (Acts 10:7), or steadfastness (*q.v.*) in the Christian way of life (Acts 1:14; 2:42, 46; 6:4; 8:13; Rom 12:12; 13:6; Col 4:2).

The more prevalent theological usage is associated with the fifth point of Calvin's soteriology. The doctrine of the perseverance of the saints is to the effect that those on whom God has bestowed special grace can neither totally nor finally fall from that state. This doctrine was first explicitly taught by Augustine. However, it was Calvin and the reformers who set it forth with consistency. They cited in support of this teaching scriptural statements (Jn 10:27–29; Rom 8:31–39; 11:29; Phil 1:6; II Tim 1:12; I Pet 1:5) and necessary inferences from such doctrines as election, regeneration, justification, union with Christ, and sanctification.

Arminians find this teaching objectionable at three points. First, it is their contention that the perseverance of the believer is dependent upon his will. They quote Bible passages teaching the necessity of striving (Lk 13:24; Col 1:29; II Tim 2:5), and the possibility of falling away (Lk 9:62; I Cor 9:27; Gal 5:4; Heb 6:3 ff.). Second, it is maintained that such certainty about final salvation can only lead to immorality and indolence. Third, such teaching is inconsistent with human freedom.

With reference to the passages Arminians cite, Calvinists reply that the context frequently is against the Arminian understanding and that in any event such passages must be interpreted in harmony with the doctrine of perseverance as it is clearly taught and implied elsewhere.

Some of the passages cited are to be taken as warnings to those who have had a close and lengthy association with the truth of God, but as yet have never come into vital relationship with it (cf. Heb 6:3 ff.). Others serve as warnings to believers that they *are* responsible to live according to God's will. Moreover, the claim that assurance of salvation leads to immorality and indolence is based upon a misconception of the doctrine of perseverance. The saint perseveres in holiness not unholiness. He is saved *from* sin not *to* sin. Such assurance of success, rather than leading to idleness, is the strongest incentive to activity in the fight against sin. Finally, the doctrine of perseverance is consistent with human freedom when the nature of freedom is properly understood. True freedom exists only in the power to choose in the direction of holiness. Therefore, man is never more free than when he consciously chooses that which is God's will. He perseveres as he abides in the grace of Christ (see F. Hauck, "*Menō*, etc.," TDNT, IV, 574–588).

See Security.

P. D. F.

PERSIA. The Assyrian kings were the first to mention Persia in their annals. Shalmanezer III received tribute from the kings of Parsua in 836 B.C., Tiglath-pileser III invaded Parsua in 737, and Sennacherib fought them at Halulina in 681. Achaemenes (Hakhmanish in Persian) was the eponymous ancestor who founded the Persian dynasty. Teispes, the son of Achaemenes, and two grandsons, Ariyaramnes and Cyrus I, and a great-grandson, Cambyses, ruled the homeland but were subordinate to their more powerful cousins to the N, the Medes. The homeland of these Indo-European-speaking people was called Parsa by them, but they called themselves Airyana from the Sanskrit word *ārya* meaning "noble," hence the present Iran. The country lay E of Elam from the Per-

The Apadama, or Audience Hall, palace at Persepolis. ORINST

sian Gulf to the Great Salt Desert. These people moved across the Iranian plateau and occupied this region early in the 1st mil. B.C.

After the fall of Nineveh in 612 B.C. the Medes controlled all of N Mesopotamia. Cambyses' marriage to the daughter of the Median king Astyages resulted in the birth of Cyrus II. This leader united the Persian tribes and joined forces with Nabu-na'id (Nabonidus) of Babylon in a revolt against the Medes. It was not long before all that Media controlled fell to Cyrus the Great, and he moved on to victory over Croesus, the Lydian king of western Anatolia in 547 B.C.

Taking advantage of the dispute between the moon-worshiping Nabu-na'id and the priests of Marduk, Cyrus was able to take Babylon without a siege and marched into the city as a deliverer in 539. Apparently the citadel where Belshazzar, the king's son, held out had to be taken by force (Dan 5:30).

Cyrus did not change things radically as he took over the reins from the Chaldeans, but he did institute reforms. He put the temple in Babylon under his own administration, but used an enlightened attitude toward religions other than his own. The exiled Jews were not the only ones who were given religious freedom and allowed to return to their homelands. The Neo-Babylonian Empire had been lax in administration. In contrast, Cyrus set up "the king's messenger," a system of inspection which checked on officials. In 530 B.C., nine years after he took Babylon, Cyrus was slain while fighting his enemies E of the Araxes River. His tomb may still be seen near his home capital at Pasargadae.

Cambyses II (530–522 B.C.) distinguished himself by using Gr. mercenaries and Nabatean camels to defeat the Egyptian army at Pelusium in 525 B.C., thus adding Egypt to the empire. Before his suicidal demise a rebellion broke out. It was led by one Gaumata who claimed to be Smerdis, a brother whom Cambyses had already murdered.

The empire might have broken up had not a great leader come forth in the person of Darius I (521–486 B.C.). It took a few years for Darius to put down all rebellions and establish his authority. He then divided the empire, which extended from the Black Sea to the Indus River and from the Araxes River to the Nile, into some 20 provinces over which he placed Median or Persian governors as satraps. It is believed that Darius was converted by Zoroaster, a prophet who reformed the original religion of the Iranians which was closely allied with the Indian Vedas. Though this reformation was great, the resultant religion was not monotheistic but a system of dualism in which all creatures were either under the power of the All Wise Ahura-mazda, god of light, or Ahriman, the destroying mind. As Zoroastrianism developed, the popular deities became something like evil spirits, though Darius himself said that "Ahura-mazda and the other gods that are" helped him.

Darius continued the enlightened policy of Cyrus on foreign religions. This is evidenced by his decree to allow the Jews to finish the rebuilding of their temple in Jerusalem (Ezr 6). Haggai and Zechariah date their messages to the second year of Darius' reign (520 B.C.). Ezr 6:15 states that the temple was completed on the third day of the month Adar, in the sixth year of the reign of Darius, i.e., the year 515 B.C.

In this same year Darius used a pontoon bridge to march his army across the Bosporus and on into Europe. But before he could fight the Greeks he had to strike at the homeland of the Scythians on the N coast of the Black Sea. In this campaign the Persians even crossed the Danube, but provisions were short for such an extensive expedition, so Darius annexed Thrace and went home. His later attempt to annex Greece and his defeat at Marathon in 490 B.C. are a part of Gr. history.

Darius' greatest achievement was his organization of the empire. Each of the 20 or more satraps had a secretary who made confidential reports to the king. Also, a military commander who was placed in each satrapy was directly responsible to the king. Close contact with these officials was possible by an extensive system of roads from one end of the empire to the other and by relay messengers for fast delivery of official mail. Darius continued Cyrus II's institution called "the king's eye," by which a near relative of the sovereign traveled throughout the empire checking on the loyalty of officials.

The empire had many capital cities. There was Ecbatana (Ezr 6:2, RSV; Achmetha, KJV), the original Median capital where the Persian kings resorted in order to escape the summer heat of their homeland. Susa (Shushan of Esther), the ancient Elamite city, became an administrative center. Babylon was continued as the capital over Mesopotamia. But the old ancestral capital at Pasargadae was eclipsed by a gleaming new show capital not far away called Persepolis. Artisans and architects from many areas produced buildings and sculptures showing the combined influences of Greece, Egypt, and Mesopotamia. Though destroyed by fire at the command of Alexander the Great, Persepolis is still the show place of Persian remains today. Darius and his successors built and embellished this monumental city. Darius himself left a great carving high on the side of a mountain at Behistun. Picturing himself and his captives with inscriptions in Old Persian, Elamite, and Akkadian, Darius thus sought to immortalize his conquests. But only 100 years later the Gr. philosopher Plato knew Darius not as a builder and conqueror but as a great lawgiver. His "Ordinance of Good Regulations"

A sphinx in low relief from the palace of Darius at Persepolis. BM

shows that Darius' scribes were very dependent on the code of Hammurabi which was over 1,200 years old by this time.

Stimulation of trade was another of this monarch's achievements. He brought about new explorations of the water route from Egypt to India, and restored and completed the canal which connected the Nile with the Red Sea. He wrote on a red granite stele placed on the bank of the canal: "I commanded this canal to be dug from the river, Nile by name, which flows in Egypt, to the sea which does from Parsa. Afterward this canal was dug as I commanded, and ships passed from Egypt through this canal to Parsa as was my will" (A. T. Olmstead, *History of the Persian Empire*, p. 146). Commerce was helped by a uniform system of weights and measures throughout the empire and an official coinage was adopted. The latter was a new idea, and many places continued to barter and pay in kind.

In 486 B.C. Xerxes I ascended the throne. He is considered to be the Ahasuerus of Ezr 4:6 and the book of Esther. He came to the throne in a time of rebellion and had to punish Babylon by destroying the temple of Marduk. The Asian empire was secured, but Xerxes suffered severe defeat at the hands of the Greeks, who destroyed his Phoenician navy and drove his army from the Gr. homeland. In 464 Xerxes was murdered and his son Artaxerxes I became king. Called Longimanus ("the long-handed one"), he is known by biblical students primarily for his dealings with the Jews in the days of Ezra and Nehemiah. The latter was a high official at the Persian court, the cupbearer of Artaxerxes. Nehemiah persuaded the ruler in the second half of his reign to send him to Jerusalem with a mandate to rebuild its walls. According to the traditional view, Ezra had been there on a spiritual mission earlier in Artaxerxes' time.

Because of additional reverses with the Greeks, Artaxerxes was forced to agree to the peace of Callias in 449 B.C. All cities allied to Athens in western Anatolia were conceded their freedom and the Persian army had to stay E of the Halys River. Under Darius II and Artaxerxes II the empire was again in peril with rebellions on all sides. Even the younger brother of Artaxerxes II gathered 13,000 Gr. mercenaries in an attempt to overthrow the king. Their retreat from Babylonia back to the Black Sea is immortalized in Xenophon's *Anabasis*. Artaxerxes III with ruthless ferocity destroyed his enemies and reasserted dominion from Persia. He even brought an end to Egyptian independence.

In 336 B.C. Darius III came to the throne, the same year Alexander, the son of Philip of Macedon, began to rule in Greece. The two met first at the Battle of Issus in 333, when the Persian army was routed, but the Persian king escaped, only to meet disaster before Alexander again at Arbela in 331. Thus ended the Persian Empire of the Achaemenids and Persian history so far as the biblical period is concerned. *See* Medes.

See Restoration and Persian Period; Archaeology: Persepolis.

Bibliography. CornPBE, pp. 573–578. M. J. Dresden, "Persia, History and Religion of," IDB, III, 739–747. Richard N. Frye, *The Heritage of Persia,* Cleveland: World Pub. Co., 1962. R. Ghirshman, *Iran,* Harmondsworth: Penguin, 1954. A. T. Olmstead, *History of the Persian Empire (Achaemenid Period),* Chicago: Univ. of Chicago Press, 1948. Donald N. Wilber, *Persepolis: The Archaeology of Parsa, Seat of the Persian Kings,* New York: Crowell, 1969 (with excellent bibliography).

E. B. S.

PERSIS (pûr'sĭs). A Christian woman in Rome to whom Paul sent greetings (Rom 16:12). She is characterized as one who had "labored much in the Lord."

PERSON, PERSONALITY. The Heb. language had no word denoting the concept of personality, that which constitutes and characterizes a person. Various words, however, have been translated "person" in the KJV. The more frequent are: Heb. *nephesh,* that which breathes, soul, person (e.g., Lev 27:2; Num 5:6; 35:30); *'îsh,* a man, an individual person (I Sam 9:2); *'ādām,* man, human being (Prov 6:12); *pānîm,* face, person (Deut 10:17).

In the NT are found two Gr. words: *prosōpon,* face, person (II Cor 1:11); *hypostasis,* foundation, substance, person (Heb 1:3). The

Tombs of the Persian kings, Naksh-i-Rustam. ORINST

Heb. *pānîm,* "face," corresponds to the Gr. *prosōpon* in the sense of that which I see opposite me, the face. Gr. *hypostasis* gives the idea of that which forms the basis, the final reality; thus it may refer to the essential substance of either God or man, namely, spirit or soul.

Two questions arise:

What constitutes a person? A person can be defined as that living being which possesses intellect, will, and emotion; is capable of self-consciousness and self-determination; and has a moral nature. Psychologists have difficulty with the concept because some of them claim to find something of the first four qualities in animals, while many of them deny the presence of a moral nature in man. But according to Scripture it is the possession of a moral nature which distinguishes man from the rest of sentient creation on earth. Because man is a moral being, God has placed in his heart a standard, the work of the law (Rom 2:15). Man has personality because he is essentially a spirit clothed with a material body, made in the image of God who is spirit (Jn 4:24). *See* Anthropology; Soul; Spirit.

Is God a person? He is a trinity of persons. The Shorter Catechism says, "There are three persons in the Godhead, the Father, the Son, and the Holy Ghost; and these three are one God, the same in substance, equal in power and glory." Each one of the members of the Trinity possesses intellect, will, emotion, is self-conscious, and has a moral nature; therefore each is a distinct person. The concept of person also includes that of substance, not in the sense of material substance, but of that which forms essential identity. For example, when man dies his soul continues to exist because it is a spiritual substance. It is in this sense orthodox Christians speak of God as personal and substantial. *See* God.

In recent theology the concept of God as a person has been attacked by Paul Tillich from two angles. First, he reasons, if God is a person or an object, or exists, then He is limited by other objects and persons which also exist. This is an argument formulated first by the early Gr. skeptics, quoted by Fichte, and reproduced by Tillich. Charles Hodge answered it in his *Systematic Theology* in 1875 (I, 191 ff.). It rests upon a mistaken definition of infinity, and God's in particular, as immensity. God is infinite in His being, wisdom, power, holiness, goodness, justice, and truth, and not in a material sense.

Second, Tillich insists the Gr. word for person really means "mask" instead of "person," and therefore is inapplicable to God. This argument fails when it is seen that while both the Gr. *prosōpon* and the Latin *persona* were used of masks worn in plays, the Gr. word literally means that which one sees opposite, or faces, and does not primarily refer to a mask. Actually this was one of its less common meanings and it is not found used in this sense in the NT. In any case, the use of the word in the NT sets the scriptural meaning (Mt 22:16; Mk 12:14; Lk 20:21; II Cor 1:11; 2:10; Gal 2:6) and not its use by pagan playwrights.

R. A. K.

PERSON OF CHRIST. *See* Jesus Christ.

PERUDA (pĭ-rōō'dȧ). One of Solomon's servants whose descendants returned to Jerusalem with Zerubbabel (Ezr 2:55). Another spelling is Perida (Neh 7:57).

PESTILENCE. *See* Diseases.

PESTLE. A blunt tool of wood or stone used for crushing or powdering wheat into a flourlike meal (Prov 27:22). *See* Mortar.

PETER (pē'tẽr). One of the earliest and most prominent disciples of Jesus. Several names are given him: the Heb. name Simeon (Acts 15:14) and Gr. Simon, after a son of Jacob whose descendants became one of the tribes of Israel; Cephas (Jn 1:43) and Peter, both meaning "rock." *See* Simeon; Simon; Cephas.

Origin and Early Life

Peter's original home was Bethsaida, a fishing village on the northern shore of the Sea of Galilee not far from Capernaum (Jn 1:44). His father, Jonah, was probably a fisherman (Jn 1:42), an occupation which Peter and his brother Andrew both followed. According to present standards, his education was limited, but he would have been able to read and write Aram. and to speak some Gr. which was widely used in the cities of the Decapolis, though with the guttural Galilean accent (Mt 26:73). Peter and Andrew were partners in the fishing business with Zebedee and his sons James and John (Lk 5:7, 10). During his association with Jesus, Peter made his home in Capernaum (Mk 1:21, 29). He was married (Mk 1:30), and in his later ministry his wife traveled with him (I Cor 9:5).

Peter and his partners were followers of John the Baptist, who first called their attention to Jesus. When Peter was introduced to Jesus by his brother Andrew, Jesus renamed him Cephas (Aram.) or Peter (Gr.), meaning "rock," to signify that instead of having the inconstant and violent temper of a Simeon (Gen 49:5-7), he would become as steady as a rock (Jn 1:42).

Peter with the other disciples accompanied Jesus from the scene of John the Baptist's ministry back to Capernaum (Jn 2:1-2, 12). In all probability they returned to their fishing for a brief time, although the Gospels do not state so directly. The Synoptic Gospels indicate that He summoned them from their fishing boats to accompany Him on His tours in Galilee, in order that He might train them as His assistants (Mk 1:16-20). The Lucan narrative in particular depicts the call as a spiritual crisis for Peter, who was keenly aware of his sinfulness and uncertain of his ability to follow the Lord. Jesus encouraged him, and from that point onward

Newly excavated fisherman's quarters at Capernaum. HFV

Peter devoted himself completely to the service of Christ.

From the large number of disciples who followed Him, Jesus later chose 12 to be His intimate companions. In the four lists given (Mk 3:16-19; Lk 6:14-16; Mt 10:2-4; Acts 1:13-14), Peter's name always appears first. He acted as the spokesman for the group, expressing both their problems and their hopes. His great confession, "Thou art the Christ, the Son of the living God" (Mt 16:13-20) and the parallel in Jn 6:67-69, crystallized the disciples' attitude to Jesus as they entered upon the road to the cross.

The motives of Peter in following Jesus were initially as much personal as spiritual. Knowing that Jesus was recommended by an influential figure like John the Baptist, and seeing in Him a potential Messiah for the nation, Peter sought to enhance his own status by attaching himself to Jesus. He reminded Jesus that he and the others had left their homes and businesses to follow Him (Mk 10:28; Lk 18:28), and that they expected to be properly recompensed for their sacrifice. Even at the last supper they were still arguing over the place of precedence in the coming kingdom (Lk 22:24).

Jesus' education of Peter is illustrated by a number of episodes. The great crisis of Peter's career was Jesus' challenge, asking the disciples for their estimate of Him. When Peter responded, "Thou art the Christ, the Son of the living God," Jesus pronounced a blessing on him, and assured him that the revelation of this truth had come to him from God. Jesus informed Peter that He would give him the keys to the kingdom of heaven, the right to admit men into the kingdom as he proclaimed the truth (Mt 16:13-20). Peter was the first to preach the new message to the Jews on the day of Pentecost (Acts 2:14), and to the Gentiles in the household of Cornelius (10:34 ff.). Jesus' promise contained a play on words: "I tell you, you are Peter [a piece of rock], and on this kind of rock [a ledge] I will build my church, and the gates of Hades shall not prevail against it." Christ did not build the church on Peter, but on the rocklike regenerate nature that He proposed to create in His disciples.

Jesus began to teach Peter a new mode of life. In response to Peter's question concerning the payment of the temple tax, Jesus assured him that the true Israelites should be free from taxation, and then supplied enough money to pay for Himself and for Peter also. When Peter asked Jesus whether he should forgive an annoying enemy for more than seven offenses, Jesus replied that he should forgive 70 times seven (Mt 18:21-22)—an injunction that Peter would find hard to obey. Peter's surprise over the withered fig tree implies some incredulity concerning Jesus' power. Jesus promptly reminded him that he needed more faith (Mk 11:20-22).

Peter became especially prominent in the last hours of Jesus' life. He and John were assigned the task of arranging for the final meal in Jerusalem (Lk 22:8), probably because Jesus considered them to be the most faithful and stable of the disciples. Peter objected to letting Jesus wash his feet, but when Jesus told him that it was a necessary condition of friendship, Peter revealed his real attitude by asking for a bath. He did not want to be severed from Christ (Jn 13:6-9). When Jesus announced the impending betrayal, Peter asked John to inquire the identity of the traitor, and had he learned his name at that time, Judas might not have survived to complete his evil bargain with the priests. Peter was one of the three chosen to watch with Jesus in Gethsemane, but fell asleep from weariness and sorrow (Mt 26:37-46; Mk 14:33-42; Lk 22:45). When the arresting party came, Peter attempted to defend Jesus with weapons, and was sternly rebuked (Jn 18:10-11). Bewildered by Jesus' unusual response, and perhaps hurt by the rebuke when he might have expected thanks for risking his life, Peter fled from the garden with the other disciples.

Having regained his equanimity in some measure, Peter with John appeared at the house of the high priest after following the arresting party at a discreet distance (Jn 18:15). Upon being admitted to the courtyard, he was warming himself by the fire when one of the servants questioned whether he were a disciple of Jesus. Alarmed by the latent hostility around him, three times he vigorously denied any connection with Jesus (Mt 26:58, 69-75; Mk 14:66-72; Lk 22:54-62; Jn 18:15-18, 25-27). Convicted instantly of his failure by the glance of Jesus, he left the high priest's house and repented in tears. He may have witnessed the crucifixion (I Pet 2:21-24; 5:1), though the Gospels do not mention his presence at Calvary.

When Mary Magdalene reported early on the resurrection morning that the tomb was empty, Peter and John ran to investigate it, and noted the fact that the grave clothes were still in place, while the body was absent (Jn 20:1-10). Later on the same day Jesus appeared to Peter

(I Cor 15:5; Lk 24:33–34). When the disciples returned to Galilee, Peter proposed that they resume their trade of fishing, and when the Lord appeared again and repeated the miracle of the catch of fish (Lk 5:5–8), Peter was the first to welcome Him (Jn 21:7). Jesus restored him to favor, and charged him again with responsibility for leadership in His work (Jn 21:15–19).

Peter in Jerusalem

After the ascension of Jesus the disciples were gathered in an upper room for prayer, awaiting the promised gift of the Holy Spirit. Peter proposed that one be chosen to take the place of Judas so that the apostolate might be complete. On the day of Pentecost he preached the initial message to the crowd that gathered, declaring that they must repent and be baptized in the name of the Lord Jesus. Approximately 3,000 were converted, and the church was begun (Acts 2:14–42).

During the early years of the church in Jerusalem, Peter was the acknowledged leader. He performed notable miracles (Acts 3:1–10; 5:12–16), defended the cause before the Sanhedrin (4:5–12), and disciplined offenders like Ananias and Sapphira (5:1–11). Although he removed from the city after the persecution under Herod in A.D. 44 (Acts 12:1–17), he returned to Jerusalem to participate in the council concerning Gentile liberty (15:6–11). He agreed with Paul against the legalists that the Gentiles should not be compelled to obey the ceremonial law as a condition of salvation in addition to faith in Christ.

Peter's Ministry Outside Jerusalem

When persecution against the church broke out after the controversy over Stephen, Peter extended his ministry to new fields. Summoned with John to Samaria where Philip had gathered a large number of new converts, he instructed them in the work of the Holy Spirit. He ministered in the coastal cities of Lydda and Joppa, where he healed Aeneas and raised Dorcas from death (Acts 9:32–43), and preached through the maritime plain of Sharon. In response to a vision given to him while staying at Joppa, he initiated the evangelization of the Gentiles by preaching in the house of Cornelius, a Roman centurion stationed at Caesarea (Acts 10:1–45). For entering a Gentile's house he was criticized by the Jewish party in the church, and was obliged to justify his conduct when he returned to Jerusalem (Acts 11:1–18).

Peter's Later Ministry

The council of Jerusalem marked the mid-point of the 1st cen. (*c.* A.D. 48–50). Just prior to the council Peter visited Antioch, if the episode recorded in Gal 2:11–21 belongs to this period of the church's development. His disagreement with Paul was resolved, for he stood with Paul at the council, and later spoke of him as "our beloved brother" (II Pet 3:15).

Between A.D. 50 and the close of the NT period little is said about Peter. Paul alludes to his travels (I Cor 9:5), and the fact that a group in the Corinthian church said, "I am of Cephas" (I Cor 1:12), seemingly indicates that he may have been known personally there. The destination of I Peter (1:1) implies that he may have preached in the synagogues of the Dispersion in northern Asia Minor, and the second epistle hints that he anticipated a sudden and perhaps a violent death (II Pet 1:12–15) in accord with Jesus' prediction (Jn 21:18–19).

In I Peter he refers to himself as the elder who was responsible for tending the flock of God (I Pet 5:1–2). His epistles show that he was active in preaching until the time of his death, and that he had exercised a wide ministry in the Roman world.

Whether Peter ever reached Rome or not is debatable. There is no evidence whatever for the claim of the Roman church that he founded the church there and served it for a quarter of a century until his martyrdom. Had he been living in Rome between the years A.D. 55 and 65 it is inconceivable that Paul would have written to the Romans without mentioning him, or that there would have been no allusion in Acts to his presence if he had been in the city when Paul was there.

The tradition that Peter was the first bishop of Rome is not supported by any biblical text, and even his martyrdom in Rome depends upon late testimony. Irenaeus (*c.* A.D. 180) says that Peter and Paul preached at Rome and laid the foundation of the church (*Adv. Haereses* III.1.1). Tertullian (A.D. 200) refers to the martyrdom of Peter and Paul at Rome (*De Praescriptione* XXXVI), but in language which sounds as if he were quoting tradition rather than citing documentary evidence. Origen asserted that Peter finally visited Rome and was crucified head downward (Eusebius *Historia Ecclesiae* III.1.2). A careful analysis of these

St. Peter's Church, a Crusader construction that encloses a cave at Antioch of Syria where early Christians met in secret. HFV

traditions shows that while there may be some reason for believing that Peter may have been in Rome, he neither founded the church nor was its bishop for any appreciable length of time; nor can it be incontrovertibly asserted where he was buried. It is possible that the Church Fathers from the time of Irenaeus onward merely repeated with additions the central legend that he had died in Rome, without having investigated the evidence independently.

The Character of Peter

Peter was distinctly a rural type—vigorous, strong, straightforward, impulsive, and an extrovert. He was usually talkative and curious, somewhat emotional, hot-tempered, loyal to his friends and violent against his enemies, and quite self-confident. He possessed great natural capacity for leadership because of his warm and enthusiastic nature. His rather precipitate disposition led him into inconsistencies and vagaries from which occasionally he had to extricate himself by apology or repentance. His preaching shows that he was an exhorter rather than a logician. His affectionate nature, utter devotion to Christ, and courageous ministry made him an outstanding leader in the first few years of the church's existence.

Bibliography. Oscar Cullmann, *"Petros, Kēphas,"* TDNT, VI, 100–112. E. Schuyler English, *The Life and Letters of St. Peter,* New York: Our Hope Publications, 1942. F. J. Foakes-Jackson, *Peter: Prince of Apostles,* New York: George H. Doran Co., 1927. W. H. Griffith Thomas, *The Apostle Peter,* Grand Rapids: Eerdmans, 1946.

M. C. T.

PETER, FIRST EPISTLE OF

Authorship

The First Epistle of Peter not only carries the name of the apostle, but also reflects in some degree his temperament and experience. The author calls himself "an apostle of Jesus Christ" (1:1) and a fellow-elder (5:1). He alludes to the new hope given him by the resurrection of Christ (1:3) and to the sufferings of Christ (1:11; 2:21–24; 3:18; 4:13), and his language recalls Jesus' injunction to "tend my sheep" (5:2; cf. Jn 21:16, ASV, RSV). Some of the phrases of this epistle are echoed in Polycarp's Epistle to the Philippians (*c.* A.D. 125), in the Epistle of Barnabas (*c.* A.D. 135), and in the writings of Justin Martyr (*c.* A.D. 150). The Second Epistle of Peter implies the existence of a previous epistle (II Pet 3:1) which may well be this one. From the time of Irenaeus (*c.* A.D. 170) the genuineness of I Peter seems to have been well-established in the church.

Date

Because I Peter mentions Silvanus (5:12) and Mark (5:13), it was probably written after these two had become prominent in the church. If they are the same two who were associated with Paul, it belongs to the period after Silvanus (Silas) left Paul and before Mark joined him during Paul's first Roman imprisonment (Col 4:10; Phm 24), unless Mark was associated with Peter before Paul's second imprisonment (II Tim 4:11). The epistle could not have been written earlier than the last part of the sixth decade, nor later than the middle of the seventh decade of the 1st cen. when Peter was martyred. Probably a safe date for I Peter would be about A.D. 63/64.

Place

The epistle was sent from Babylon (5:13), but whether this was the literal Babylon on the Euphrates River where there was a fairly large Jewish settlement, or whether Babylon was a figurative designation for Rome (cf. Rev 17:5; 18:10), is still debated by scholars. It is more likely that Peter would have met Silvanus and Mark in Rome than in Mesopotamia.

Destination

Peter wrote to the Christians on the northern border of Asia Minor where Paul had not preached. Although he directed the epistle to the members of the Dispersion, who were Jews, he refers to the past in which they "wrought the desire of the Gentiles" (4:3, ASV) as if to imply that they, or at least some of them, had been Gentiles. Perhaps he was referring to proselytes who in company with Jews had become believers.

Outline

I. Thanksgiving for the Revelation of God's Love in Christ, 1:1–12
II. A Charge to Holy Living, 1:13–2:10
III. Christian Ethics in the Household, 2:11–3:12
IV. A Good Testimony a Defense Against Slander, 3:13–4:11
V. Counsel to the Church, 4:12–19
VI. Counsel to the Elders, 5:1–9
VII. Benediction and Greetings, 5:10–14

Purpose

First Peter was written to encourage a church that was threatened with persecution (4:12–19). Therefore the keynote of the epistle is the relation of suffering to salvation. Suffering, says Peter, is inevitable, but it is not abnormal, for it is the way to perfection (5:10).

Bibliography. Francis W. Beare, *The First Epistle of Peter,* 2nd ed. rev., New York: Macmillan, 1959. Charles Bigg, *Commentary on the Epistles of St. Peter and St. Jude,* ICC, Edinburgh: T. & T. Clark, 1901. George H. Cramer, *First and Second Peter,* EBC, Chicago: Moody Press, 1967. Bo Reicke, *The Epistles of James, Peter, and Jude,* Anchor Bible, Garden City: Doubleday, 1964. Edward G. Selwyn, *The First Epistle of St. Peter,* 2nd ed., London: Macmillan, 1947. Alan M. Stibbs, *The First Epistle General of Peter,* TNTC, Grand Rapids: Eerdmans, 1959.

M. C. T.

PETER, SECOND EPISTLE OF. This letter was designed to warn its readers against the peril of apostasy, as I Peter was a preparation for suffering. Like the first epistle, it bears the name of Peter, and it refers to a previous letter by the same author, which may well be I Peter (II Pet 3:1).

Authorship

The external evidence for the Petrine authorship of II Peter is much inferior to that for I Peter. There are occasional allusions in the Shepherd of Hermas (*c.* A.D. 140) and the Teaching of the Twelve Apostles (*c.* A.D. 150) which resemble it, but there is no direct reference to II Peter in the sub-apostolic literature until Origen (*c.* A.D. 220), who remarked that there was some doubt concerning the authorship of II Peter. Eusebius of Caesarea, the noted church historian of the 4th cen., classed it among the disputed books of the canon rather than among those of unquestioned apostolic origin.

In favor of its early acceptance, however, is its manner of inclusion in P^{72} (first published in 1959). This manuscript, which contains I and II Peter and Jude, was copied by Coptic Christians in Egypt in the late 3rd cen. The scribe has added a decorated border around the appended title of II Peter, not used for the other two books. Marchant A. King concludes that this extra care indicates II Peter was in use and highly respected in the 3rd cen. ("Notes on the Bodmer Manuscript," BS, CXXI [1964], 54-57).

The internal evidence for the Petrine authorship is stronger than the external evidence. The writer calls himself "Simon Peter, a servant and an apostle of Jesus Christ" (1:1). He claims to have witnessed Christ's transfiguration (1:16-17), an event at which Peter was present (Mk 9:5-7), and declares that the Lord had predicted his death (1:14; cf. Jn 21:18-19). He identifies himself as one of the apostles of the Lord (3:2). In alluding to the writings of Paul he calls him "our beloved brother," a title of familiarity that would probably be used only by a contemporary associate (3:15).

The resemblance of II Pet 2 to the Epistle of Jude is so close that the literary relationship between the two can hardly be accidental. One writer must have known the work of the other. Although the brevity and compactness of Jude may be used as an argument for its priority, his reference to "the apostles of our Lord Jesus Christ" (Jude 17) seems to imply that he was following the lead of some apostolic writer or writers. Since the author of II Peter claims to be an apostle (II Pet 1:1), it is more likely that Jude was stimulated to compose his epistle by Peter's missive than that a pseudonymous document was copied from Jude and published under Peter's name. The fact that II Peter predicts apostasy (2:1), whereas Jude announces that the declension has already begun (Jude 4) may indicate that II Peter belongs to an earlier stage in the history of the apostolic church. *See* Jude, Epistle of.

The vocabulary and style of II Peter differ from those of I Peter, but in writing the first epistle Peter had the aid of Silvanus, who had been Paul's secretary (I Pet 5:12; I Thess 1:1), whereas late in his life he may have had no assistance. The second epistle is much less like Paul's in structure, and more like Peter's forthright bluntness in expression.

Date and Place

Since II Peter was written close to the end of Peter's life, it was probably composed between A.D. 64 and 68. According to tradition, Peter died at Rome, and the epistle may have been written there.

Destination

Inasmuch as the author refers to an earlier letter sent to the same group (3:1), it is likely that II Peter was addressed to the provincial churches in Asia Minor (I Pet 1:1). In the interval between the two letters conditions had changed. Peter foresaw that the advent of religious agitators who would pervert the moral life of the church would constitute a greater threat than persecution. Their immorality (II Pet 2:2), greed (2:3), cynical impudence (2:10), boastfulness (2:18), and advocacy of false liberty (2:19) would endanger the very existence of the church. Peter was endeavoring to avert the danger of such deceptive leaders.

Outline

The Salutation, 1:1-2

I. The Nature of True Knowledge, 1:3-21
   1. A gift from God, 1:3-4
   2. A growth in experience, 1:5-11
   3. The grounds of this knowledge, 1:12-21
      a. Peter's own experience and testimony, 1:12-18
      b. The prophetic word, 1:19-21

II. The Peril of Abandoning True Knowledge, 2:1-22
   1. The invasion of false teachers, 2:1-3*a*
   2. God's judgment on false teachers, *2:3b*-10*a*
   3. The excesses of false teachers, *2:10b*-17
   4. The danger of false teachers, 2:18-22

III. The Hope Belonging to True Knowledge, 3:1-18*a*
   1. The promise upheld against scoffers, 3:1-7
   2. The promise a challenge to believers, 2:8-13
   3. The exhortations in view of the future hope, 3:14-18*a*

The Doxology, 3:18*b*

Content

The keynote of II Peter is *knowledge*. The words *know* and *knowledge* occur 16 times in the three chapters, six of which refer to the knowledge of Christ. In contrast to the empty knowledge offered by the apostate libertarians, Peter stressed the experiential knowledge which could bestow grace and peace (1:2), fruitfulness (1:8), freedom (2:20), and opportunity for growth (3:18).

The epistle may be divided conveniently by chapters. The first chapter deals with the sufficiency and reliability of God's revelation in Christ and in the Scriptures, which supplies the standard for moral conduct and eschatological hope. The second chapter contains a warning against the false prophets who will corrupt the church by their destructive teachings. The third chapter reiterates the promise of the coming of Christ, assuring the readers that "the Lord is not slack concerning his promise . . . not wishing that any should perish, but that all should come to repentance" (3:9).

The total thrust of this epistle may be summed up in Peter's words in 1:10–11, ASV.

Bibliography. E. M. B. Green, *2 Peter Reconsidered,* London: Tyndale, 1961. Donald Guthrie, *New Testament Introduction,* Downers Grove, Ill.: Inter-Varsity Press, 1970, pp. 814–863. E. I. Robson, *Studies in the Second Epistle of St. Peter,* Cambridge: Univ. Press, 1915. B. B. Warfield, "The Authority and Canonicity of Second Peter," *Southern Presbyterian Review,* XXXIII (1882), 45–75.

M. C. T.

PETHAHIAH (pĕth'*ȧ*-hī'*ȧ*)

1. A priest appointed chief of the nineteenth course of priests in the days of David (I Chr 24:16).

2. A Levite in the days of Ezra-Nehemiah who put away his foreign wife (Ezr 10:23), and who later led the people in the public confession and covenant (Neh 9:5).

3. A son of Meshezabeel, descendant of Judah, whom the king of Persia used in public matters concerning the people in general (Neh 11:24).

The great high place at Petra

PETHOR (pē'thôr). A city on the W bank of the Euphrates River in the land of Amaw (Num 22:5, RSV) in northern Mesopotamia (Deut 23:4), the home of Balaam, the hireling prophet. To this city Balak, king of Moab, sent messengers to hire Balaam to curse Israel. *See* Amaw.

This city is possibly to be identified with the site of Tell Ahmar, 12 miles S of Carchemish. The *Annals* of Shalmaneser III (859–824 B.C.) stated that its name (Pitru) was the Hittite name, which he renamed Ina-Ashur-utir-asbat ("I settled it again for Asshur"). His record locates Pethor "on the other [western] side of the Euphrates, on the river Sāgūr [modern Sajūr]," and suggests its importance for 9th cen. B.C. Assyria by the fact that there he received tribute from the kings of the districts of Carchemish, Commagene, Melitene, Hattina, and Gurgum (ANET, p. 278).

PETHUEL (pĭ-thōō'ĕl). The father of the prophet Joel (Joel 1:1).

PETITION. *See* Prayer.

PETRA (pē'trȧ). It is not certain that Petra is a biblical site, but a considerable number of scholars identify it with OT Sela (meaning "rock"; cf. II Kgs 14:7–10; II Chr 25:11–12; Isa 16:1; Jer 49:16–17; Obad 3–4). *See* Sela. The LXX translates Sela as *Petran* and the Latin Vulg. translates it *Petram,* all meaning the same thing, "rock." The Arabic *sela* designates a rock cleft, which is an especially appropriate name for Petra, which is entered through the Siq, a long twisting cleft in the mountains. Whether or not the OT refers to Petra, the NT indirectly refers to it. Aretas, king of Petra (9 B.C.–A.D. 40), ruled Damascus during the days of Paul's conversion and sought to apprehend the apostle there (II Cor 11:32–33). According to Josephus (*Ant.* iv.7.1) Petra was called Rekem by the Arabs, named after the Midianite king of Num 31:8.

Petra was located *c.* 50 miles S of the Dead Sea in the highlands of Transjordan at an altitude of 2,700 feet. The town lay in a basin surrounded by mountains and its principal entrance was through the narrow, twisting Siq between cliffs towering 500 feet high. The site is about a mile long and a half mile wide. Its dominant natural feature is the 950-foot acropolis known to the Arabs as Umm el-Biyara ("the mother of cisterns"). Petra was the capital of a trading empire and was advantageously located on the trade route linking Solomon's seaport at Ezion-geber on the Gulf of Aqaba with Ammon and Damascus, and at the junction where the Gaza-Beersheba road joined the N-S road just mentioned. Its immense commercial wealth provided resources for cultivating much more of the semi-arid lands of the area than an agricultural economy would have permitted.

Paleolithic remains in the Petra area go back to about 10,000 B.C. But the Chalcolithic and Bronze Ages are as yet archaeologically un-

The theater at Petra

known. Some Iron Age (7th cen. B.C.) pottery, walls, and cisterns have been uncovered on the top of Umm el-Biyara, during which time the town served as an Edomite fortress and capital. In 1966 the seal of Qos Gabr, an Edomite king who reigned *c.* 650 B.C. was found on Umm el-Biyara (ILN, Apr. 30, 1966, pp. 30–31; cf. ANET, pp. 291, 294, "Qaushgabri"). *See* Edom. Its great days date to the Nabataean and Roman periods, however. During the 4th cen. B.C. the Nabataeans (*q.v.;* an Arab tribe) established their power in this region, and in A.D. 106 the Roman emperor Trajan added Petra to the Roman Empire. After Palmyra became a great caravan city and Roman power declined in the 3rd cen. A.D. Petra sank into insignificance.

Exactly when Christianity came to Petra is not known, but an inscription dating in the year 447 refers to the consecration of a chapel by the bishop of Petra. Evidently several Nabataean structures were converted to Christian usage. The Arabs took Petra in the 7th cen., and in the 12th cen. the Crusaders built a fort there. When Saladin destroyed this Crusader outpost in 1189 Petra seems to have disappeared from history.

In fact, it was virtually unknown, in the W at least, until the Swiss explorer Johann Burckhardt rediscovered it in 1812. Systematic excavation did not begin until 1929, when a British expedition under the leadership of George Horsfield undertook to unlock the secrets of the ancient site. The Melchett Exploration Fund supported excavations there during the 1930s; William F. Albright, Nelson Glueck, and others worked at Petra during that decade. In 1958 the British School of Archaeology began work there under the leadership of Peter J. Parr, and the following year an American team joined them under the leadership of Philip C. Hammond.

Petra is a striking place even in ruins. Some of its structures are rose-red and others of a dark red ochre shade of sandstone with bands of yellow, gray, and white. These buildings and tombs are almost all cut into the rock cliffs of the area. Among the most exciting remains at Petra are the Khazneh (often called "the Treasury"), probably a tomb of a Nabataean king, carved into the rose-red cliff; a wide colonnaded street laid out in Roman style; a Roman theater capable of seating 4,000; the Palace Tomb; Ed Deir, a temple with a facade 165 feet wide, 148 feet high, and a door 23½ feet high; the Great High Place, an ancient Nabataean worship center of the god Dushara; and the natural fortress of Umm el-Biyara.

Bibliography. C. M. Bennett, "The Nabataeans in Petra," *Archaeology,* XV (1962), 233-243. G. A. Larue, "Petra," BW, pp. 443–446, with extensive bibliography to 1962. W. H. Morton, "Umm el-Biyara," BA, XIX (1956), 25–36.

H. F. V.

PEULTHAI (pē-ŭl'thī). A Korahite, the eighth son of Obed-edom, who was one of the gate keepers of the tabernacle in the days of David (I Chr 26:5).

PHALEC (fā'lĕk). The Gr. form of Peleg (*q.v.*; Lk 3:35).

PHALLU. *See* Pallu.

PHALTI (făl'tī). Son of Laish to whom Saul gave his daughter Michal, David's wife (I Sam 25:44). The name is also spelled Phaltiel (II Sam 3:15). Another Heb. spelling is Palti (*q.v.*).

PHALTIEL (făl'tĭ-ĕl). Another Heb. spelling for Phalti (*q.v.*).

PHANUEL (fȧ-nōō'ĕl). The father of the aged Jerusalemite prophetess Anna (Lk 2:36).

PHARAOH (fâr'ō) (Heb. *par'ô*; Gr. *pharaō;* Akkad. *pir'u, pir'ū*; Egyptian *pr—*", "the great house"). In the Old Kingdom period, as early as *c.* 2500 B.C., the palace was called "the great house." It was not until the time of the 18th Dynasty, *c.* 1500 B.C., that it became the title of the person living in the palace, similar in function to our term "his majesty." In the ensuing years it became the practice to use it with a monarch's personal name or to use it alone to refer to him.

In the OT "pharaoh" occurs frequently in Genesis and Exodus; it is only in a few instances in other OT books that the personal name is combined with "pharaoh." The occurrences of "pharaoh" in the OT allude to rulers of several of the 30 dynasties listed by Manetho.

1. *Pharaohs in Genesis.* When Abram went to Egypt because of a famine in Palestine, pharaoh took Sarai into his house (Gen 12:15). Another pharaoh is mentioned frequently in incidents of Joseph's life and of Jacob's later years (Gen 37:36; 40:1 ff.). In identifying these pharaohs at least two considerations are important: the Bible does not give their personal

names; the date of Abraham and consequently that of the other patriarchs cannot be fixed precisely. W. F. Albright places Abraham's migration from Ur to Haran and westward sometime during the 20th or 19th cen. B.C. (*Archaeology of Palestine,* Harmondsworth: Penguin Books, 1960, p. 83). It is possible only to state that the time of the patriarchs coincided with that of several of the pharaohs of the 12th Dynasty (1991–1786 B.C.).

Amenhotep II, possible pharaoh of the Exodus according to the earlier chronology. ORINST

Interesting discussion has developed concerning the pharaoh of Joseph's time, whether he was one of the later rulers of the 12th Dynasty or one of the early rulers of the Hyksos period (*c.* 1720–1570 B.C.). If the earlier date for the Exodus is correct, a strong case can be made for his being Sesostris III (1878–1843 B.C.; see James R Battenfield, "A Consideration of the Identity of the Pharaoh of Genesis 47," JETS, XV [1972], 77–85). *See* Patriarchal Age.

2. *Pharaohs in Exodus.* Pharaoh "who did not know Joseph" (RSV) instituted very oppressive measures against a growing Israel (Ex 1:8 f.). A later pharaoh continued the oppression and sought to execute Moses for killing an Egyptian taskmaster (2:15). His successor (see 2:23) was pharaoh of the plagues and of the Exodus (4:21–14:31). The oppression and Exodus took place in the reigns of certain pharaohs of the New Kingdom (Dynasties XVIII–XX; *c.* 1580–1100 B.C.). According to an earlier chronology (*c.* 1445 for the Exodus), pharaoh of the oppression was Thutmose III (*c.* 1482–1450 B.C.), and pharaoh of the Exodus was Amenhoteop II (*c.* 1450–1425). According to a lower chronology (*c.* 1280 for the Exodus), pharaoh of the oppression was Seti I (*c.* 1318-1304), and pharaoh of the Exodus was Rameses II (*c.* 1304–1237). The earlier chronology is sometimes called a biblical or Masoretic chronology because it is structured around certain chronological statements in the OT; e.g., I Kgs 6:1; Jud 11:26. The later view, making use of biblical references also, has its basic support in present understanding of archaeological evidence concerning the travels of Israel around Edom and Moab and the Conquest of Canaan. *See* Exodus, The: Date.

3. *Pharaohs unnamed in other OT passages.* Solomon (*c.* 971–931 B.C.) married pharaoh's daughter (I Kgs 3:1), the marriage apparently the basis for a political alliance. Also, pharaoh gave Gezer as a dowry to his daughter (I Kgs 9:16). These two passages apparently refer to Siamun (*c.* 974–957), the next to the last king of the weak 21st Dynasty. A triumphal relief-scene found at Tanis depicts this ruler smiting a foreigner, apparently a Philistine, and a scarab bearing his name comes from Tell el-Far'ah (Sharuhen) in S Palestine. These details agree with the pharaoh of Solomon's early reign marching into Canaan as far as Gezer as an ally of the Israelite king. (*See* KD on I Kgs 3:1; cf. Alan Gardiner, *Egypt of the Pharaohs* [Oxford: Clarendon Press, 1961], p. 446).

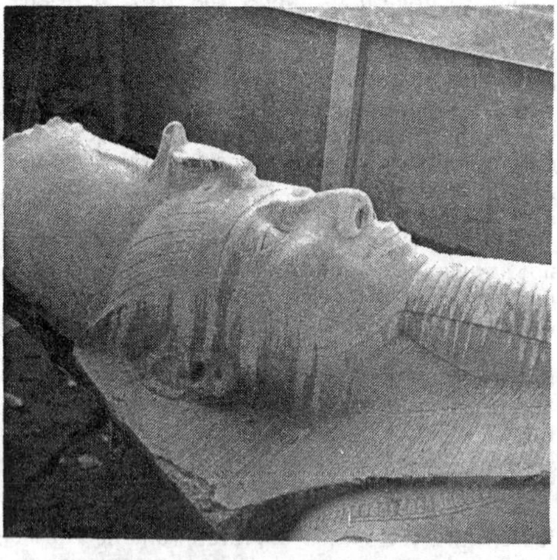

Head of a great fallen statue of Rameses II, possible pharaoh of the Exodus according to a lower chronology. Herbert Lockyer, Jr.

Pharaoh to whom the young prince Hadad of Edom had fled as a refugee from David (I Kgs 11:17–18) was either Amenemope or Siamun of the 21st Dynasty. Pharaoh who gave the sister of his queen Tahpenes to Hadad as wife could either have been Psusennes II (957–945) or Shishak (945–924), the first king of the 22nd Dynasty. Pharaoh of Hezekiah's time (II Kgs 18:21) was one of the 25th (Ethiopian) Dynasty.

Pharaohs mentioned by personal name are Shishak (I Kgs 14:25; etc.); So (II Kgs 17:4, but now recognized as a place name); Tirhakah

(II Kgs 19:9); Pharaoh-nechoh (II Kgs 23:29–30); and Pharaoh-hophra (Jer 44:30). *See* individual articles on these rulers; Egypt: History.

H.E.Fi.

PHARAOH-HOPHRA (fâr'ō-hŏf'rȧ). The fourth king of the 26th Dynasty of Egypt (Jer 44:30), who ruled at Sais in the Delta (588–569 B.C.), called Apries by the Greeks. Hophra continued the anti-Babylonia policy of his predecessors, and early in his reign marched to the assistance of King Zedekiah of Judah, causing the Babylonian army to lift its siege of Jerusalem temporarily (Jer 37:5–11; Ezk 17:15, 17). He was accompanied by his fleet (Herodotus ii.161), but the effort failed.

In 587 B.C. Ezekiel prophesied several times against this pharaoh (Ezk 29:1–16; 30:20–26; 31:1–18), and again in 585 B.C. (32:1–32). After Nebuchadnezzar destroyed Jerusalem, a number of Jews fled to Egypt, taking Jeremiah with them, but against his warning (Jer 42:7–43:7). They settled around Tahpanhes, where Hophra maintained a royal residence (Jer 43:9). Jeremiah prophesied (44:30) Hophra would die at the hand of his enemies; and he was later killed in a revolt led by his coregent Ahmose (Amasis).

See Egypt: History.

J.R.

Temple of Rameses II at Abu Simbel. LL

PHARAOH-NECHO (fâr'ō-nĕ'kō). Pharaoh of Egypt (609–594 B.C.), generally designated Necho II, son and successor of Psammetichus I (664–609) who founded the 26th Dynasty at Sais in the Delta. The KJV employs the spelling Necho in II Chr 35:20, 22; 36:4; Jer 46:2 and Nechoh in II Kgs 23:29, 33–35; newer versions usually adopt Neco as the spelling.

Following his father's policy of maintaining a balance of power in Asia by aiding the hard-pressed Assyrians against Babylon, in 608 B.C., Necho marched N to recapture Carchemish (II Chr 35:20). This he did to assist Ashur-uballit II, last king of Assyria (II Kgs 23:29,

Fifty-foot statues of Pharaoh Amenhotep III—the famous Colossi of Memnon. HFV

RSV, NASB), who was besieged at Harran. Necho captured Gaza en route (Jer 47:1), but had to battle the anti-Assyrian King Josiah of Judah at Megiddo. This delay of Egyptian help for the Assyrians sealed their fate, but cost Josiah his life (II Chr 35:20–24).

After Necho had consolidated his power over Syria and Phoenicia, he summoned Jehoahaz, Josiah's anti-Assyrian son, to his Syrian headquarters at Riblah. He deposed Jehoahaz and deported him to Egypt, enthroning instead Eliakim (renamed Jehoiakim) to be a tribute-paying vassal king in Jerusalem (II Kgs 23:33–35; II Chr 36:3–4).

For a few years Necho was successful in the N, but in May/June 605 B.C. the Babylonian army commanded by the crown prince Nebuchadnezzar (*q.v.*) crushed his forces at Carchemish (*q.v.*) and escaped back to Egypt (Jer 46:1–12). Nebuchadnezzar's pursuit as far as the river of Egypt (II Kgs 24:7) was halted only by the sudden death of his father in August, for he had to rush back to Babylon to assume the throne. Not until 601 B.C. did Nebuchadnezzar return against Egypt, according to the Babylonian Chronicle. Necho met him in battle, and both sides must have suffered heavy losses. This setback to Babylonian dominance of the area apparently encouraged Jehoiakim to rebel against Nebuchadnezzar (II Kgs 24:1), but Necho no longer dared give aid.

According to Herodotus (ii.158; iv.42), Necho granted trading concessions to Gr. merchants and undertook the digging of a canal through the Wadi Tumilat from the Nile to the Red Sea, completed by Darius I of Persia. He sent out a fleet with Phoenician sailors that circumnavigated Africa.

See Egypt: History.

J.R.

PHARES. Gr. spelling of Pharez (Mt 1:3; Lk 3:33). *See* Pharez.

PHAREZ (fâr′ĕz). The name, meaning "breach," refers to the peculiar manner of his birth as the firstborn of the twin sons of Judah by his daughter-in-law Tamar (Gen 38:27–29; RSV, ASV, Perez). Judah had violated both the law and the custom of levirate marriage (*q.v.*) by refusing to permit his third son Shelah to marry Tamar, who had been widowed by his two older sons. Disguised as a sacred prostitute, Tamar had approached Judah and had conceived by him (Gen 38:6–26). Pharez was acknowledged as the son of Judah and in all the genealogies his name is prominent (Gen 46:12; Num 26:20–21; I Chr 2:4–5). He is the direct ancestor of David and through him of the Lord Jesus Christ (Ruth 4:12, 18; Mt 1:3; Lk 3:33). A large number of the descendants of Pharez (Perez) dwelt in Jerusalem after the return from Babylon (Neh 11:4, 6).

PHARISEES (făr′ĭ-sēz). The term Pharisee is believed to be derived from the Heb. verb *pārash*, "to divide or separate." Hence, the Pharisees were the "separated ones," but the origin of this Jewish group and of the name they bore is uncertain. The "separation" of which their name speaks could be separation in general from uncleanness or from the world, or it could be connected with some particular historical situation. For example, the Pharisees could have arisen as an expression of the strict avoidance of heathen customs in the time of Ezra and Nehemiah (*q.v.*), or of the refusal to adopt Gr. ways under threat of death in the time of Antiochus Epiphanes (*q.v.*), or of the break that occurred after the recapture of the temple in 165 B.C. between the Maccabees (*q.v.*) and the "pious ones," or Chasidim, who were willing to fight for religious freedom but not for political independence. All these possibilities have been put forth as theories and all may be said to embody some aspects of the Pharisaic spirit; but the evidence is not conclusive for any one of them.

The Pharisees are first mentioned as an existing party in Israel during the reign of John Hyrcanus (135–104 B.C.). According to Josephus, they had at this time great influence with the masses. Hyrcanus was at first one of their disciples, but because of a misunderstanding broke with them and joined the Sadducees (*Ant.* xiii. 10. 5 f.). As a foreboding note, Josephus adds: "Out of this, of course, grew the hatred of the masses for him and his sons" (*ibid.*). Hyrcanus is also said to have set aside certain "regulations" which the Pharisees had established for the people. Josephus explains that "the Pharisees had passed on to the people certain regulations (*nomima*) handed down by former generations and not recorded in the laws (*nomoi*) of Moses, for which reason they are rejected by the Sadducean group" 10.(xiii.6).

This account underlines the key factor in any definition of Pharisaism—the concept of *tradition*, of the continually expanding oral law. It also indicates that by the time of Hyrcanus, Pharisaism was already a flourishing movement with great popular influence. Moreover, the reference to passing on regulations that had been handed down by former generations suggests some continuity with the past. Therefore, those who have sought to trace the Pharisees back to the Chasidim who fought beside Judas Maccabeus until the rededication of the temple (I Macc 2:42 ff.; 7:13 ff.; II Macc 14:6) may be close to the truth. Although some of its features may have roots that go back much earlier, Pharisaism as we know it from available sources seems to have come into being as one Jewish response to the challenge of Gr. culture in the early 2nd cen. B.C. At a much later time, when Pharisaism had become the normative expression of Judaism, the historical gaps were filled in so that the oral law was believed to have come from Moses himself, via Joshua and the elders, the prophets, the men of the Great Synagogue founded by Ezra, and such men as Simeon the Just and Antigonos of Socho (3rd and 4th cen. B.C.), down to the "pairs" (*zūgoth*) of authoritative teachers (e.g., Shemaiah and Abtalion, Hillel and Shammai), and the rabbis that followed them (see the tractate of the Mishna known as *Pirke Aboth*, chap. 1). It is noteworthy that the "pairs" begin at approximately the same time the Pharisees begin to appear in our sources, Most probably the Maccabean era does mark their real beginning, even though they claimed as their spiritual ancestors such men as Ezra who had upheld and expounded the Torah. They may even have possessed some oral traditions that went back to early post-Exilic times.

After their break with the ruling Hasmonean house represented by John Hyrcanus, the Pharisees' political fortunes fluctuated. They became the leaders of continual popular opposition to Hyrcanus' successor, Alexander Janneus (103–76 B.C.), so that on his deathbed, impressed by the influence they had with the masses, Alexander urged his wife, Alexandra Salome (76–67 B.C.), to work more closely with them (Jos *Ant.* xiii. 15. 5). The traditional "regulations" handed down from "the fathers" were reintroduced, and the Pharisees became the power behind the throne, free to avenge wrongs they believed had been done to them by Alexander (*ibid.*, xiii. 16. 1; cf. *Wars* i.5.2 f.). In the power struggle that followed the death of Alexandra, the Pharisees seem to have been that third party which supported neither of her two sons; they petitioned the Romans for abolition of the Jewish kingship (which the priests had usurped after the Maccabean revolt) and a return to the older type of priestly rule (*Ant.* xiv.3.2). This hope was not realized, but the Romans did finally put an end to the factional strife when Pompey captured the temple, entered the holy of holies, exiled one of Alexandra's sons, and retained the other (Hyrcanus II) as high priest and figurehead king. Political independence, gained so nobly a century before, was lost again as the Jewish people passed under Roman rule in 63 B.C.

The Psalms of Solomon are the finest expression of pre-Christian Pharisaic piety, and date from the troubled period that followed Pompey's conquest. They articulate the Pharisees' righteous anger against the "sinners" in Israel whose deeds had brought from God such terrible judgment (i.e., the last Hasmonean rulers and the Sadducees who supported them), and against the Gentiles who had overstepped the bounds that God had imposed upon them in chastising His own people (Ps Sol 2:16–29). The unknown author of these psalms sketched the situation clearly ("Alien nations ascended Thine altar, they trampled it proudly with their sandals," 2:2), and rejoiced in the subsequent violent death of Pompey in 48 B.C. ("God showed me the insolent one slain on the mountains of Egypt," 2:30). The Pharisees found illustrated here one of their classic themes, the concept of retribution: God's vindication of the "righteous" (i.e., the Pharisees themselves) and His punishment of "sinners." The doctrine of a future resurrection so uniformly attributed to the Pharisees (cf. Acts 23:6 ff.; Jos *Ant.* xviii.1.3 f.; *Wars* ii.8.14) is simply the product of their consistent application of this retribution principle (cf. Ps Sol 3:16).

The messianic hope of the Pharisees is beautifully set forth in the latter part of Ps of Sol 17. The Lord is to "raise up unto them their king, the son of David" (17:23) who shall "destroy the godless nations with the word of his mouth" (v. 27). Of him it is said that "he shall be a righteous king, taught of God, over them, and there shall be no unrighteousness in his days in their midst, for all shall be holy and their king the anointed, the Lord" (vv. 35 f.). While the king and the kingdom for which the Pharisees looked was earthly, it was also spiritual, and not to be gained by "trust in horse and rider and bow" (v. 37).

From Pompey's conquest on, the Pharisees were for the most part political quietists. Although some of the Zealots came out of their number, the Pharisees as a group sought to avert conflict with Rome, and were finally drawn into the ill-fated revolt of A.D. 70 only wth great reluctance. After the destruction of Jerusalem, it was the Pharisees who undertook to pick up the shattered pieces of Jewish faith and life and to reconstruct Judaism as we know it in the rabbinic writings. The situation was analogous to that which prevailed after the Babylonian Exile; there was no Jewish nation, and the unity of the people was expressed through the law and the synagogue and good works. Eschatological hopes were pinned not on revolutionary activity but on God's intervention, and that in His own good time. Thus, Judaism since A.D. 70 is the direct outgrowth of what had previously been just one party among several—the Pharisees.

If the Psalms of Solomon show Pharisaism at its best, the NT exposes it at its worst. At the time of Jesus, the Pharisees seem to have been a group of laymen (i.e., not priests), some of whom were especially trained in the study of Scripture. These were the scribes and it was against the scribes and Pharisees that Jesus directed some of His most scathing denunciations. He did not take sharp issue with their synagogue teachings; they sat in Moses' seat and their words were to be kept (Mt 23:2 f.). But they were hypocrites because they did not live up to their own high standards of righteousness. They laid burdens upon others which they themselves were unwilling to bear (Mt 23:4). They used casuistry to evade the spirit of the law while carrying out its letter (Mt 23:16–22; cf. Mk 7:9–13). They gloried in their own righteousness and did good works only to be seen by men (cf. Mt 23:5–12; 6:1–6, 16–18; Lk 18:9–14). John the Baptist had called them a "brood of vipers" who rested complacent in their Abrahamic sonship (Mt 3:7 f., RSV). Jesus seconded this verdict (Mt 23:33), adding that they were "whitened sepulchres" (23:27), and sons not of the "prophets and righteous" (like Abraham) for whom they had built elaborate tombs, but of those who had slain those same prophets and the righteous, even from Abel to Zechariah (23:29–36). They were "blind leaders of the blind" who sought many proselytes but in reality kept men out of the kingdom of heaven (Mt 15:14; 23:13–15).

This strand in the NT is well known, but it should not be forgotten that on occasion Pharisees are seen in a somewhat more favorable light (e.g., Lk 7:36 ff.; 13:31 f.). To Gamaliel (*q.v.*) are attributed some of the same good qualities that Josephus saw in the Pharisees—moderation, avoidance of harsh punishments, and awareness of divine sovereignty as well as human responsibility (Acts 5:33–39; cf. Jos *Ant.* xiii.5.9; 10.6; *Wars* ii.8.14). Paul was a Pharisee before his conversion, and apparently regarded this party as the highest expression of the "righteousness which is in the law" (Phil 3:4–6; cf. Gal 1:14). Nor should it be forgotten that even as Jesus denounced the Pharisees, so the Pharisees themselves were on occasion capable of searching and severe self-criticism. The Talmud humorously lists seven classes of Pharisees. Among them were the "shoulder Pharisee," who carried his good works on his shoulder to be seen of men; the "pestle Pharisee," whose head was bent like a pestle in a mortar in false humility, as well as the truly God-loving Pharisee, who was like Abraham (see, e.g., Ber. 9, 14b; Sot. 5, 20c; Sot. 22b, most conveniently set forth in C. G. Montefiore and H. Loewe, *A Rabbinic Anthology,* p. 1385).

A definition of Pharisaism might begin by stressing that it was legalistic but not literalistic. It was a religion that "built a fence around the law" (*Pirke Aboth* 1:1), by taking the legal regulations of the OT, many of which were intended for the Levitical priests, and making them relevant and applicable to every Jew. This the

Pharisees did by their system of oral tradition and interpretation. They brought the law within the reach of every man, so that in a sense quite different from Martin Luther, Pharisaism stood for the "priesthood of the believer." The law was no dead letter to the honest Pharisee; as expounded and interpreted by the scribes, it was his very life.

Why then did Jesus denounce Pharisaism? Partly because of the hypocrisy of some of its representatives who "say, and do not" (Mt 23:3), but partly also because Pharisaism, in its sincere attempt to adapt the eternal law of God to the changing conditions of men, had compromised God's absolute and righteous demand (Mt 15:3). While laying external burdens upon themselves and their followers, they had actually made righteousness an easier way, a goal that was attainable by certain observances, so that when these acts had been performed the Pharisee might think he had done all that was required of him. Against this attitude Jesus said that when all such requirements had been carried out, the servant of God could still not rest secure. The ethical demand was still there; he was still an "unprofitable servant" (Lk 17:10). Therefore, Jesus told His disciples that "unless your righteousness exceeds that of the scribes and Pharisees, you will never enter the kingdom of heaven" (Mt 5:20, RSV).

Bibliography. I. Abrahams, *Studies in Pharisaism and the Gospels,* New York: Ktav Pub. House, 1967. W. D. Davies, *Introduction to Pharisaism,* Brecon: J. Colwell and Sons, 1954. A. Finkel, *The Pharisees and the Teacher of Nazareth,* Leiden: E. J. Brill. 1964. L. Finkelstein, *The Pharisees,* 3rd ed., Philadelphia: Jewish Pub. Society, 1962. R. T. Herford, *The Pharisees,* Boston: Beacon Press, 1962. Joachim Jeremias, *Jerusalem in the Time of Jesus,* Philadelphia: Fortress Press, 1969, pp. 246–267. J. Z. Lauterbach, *Rabbinic Essays,* Cincinnati: Hebrew Union College Press, 1951. G. F. Moore, *Judaism in the First Three Centuries of the Christian Era,* Cambridge: Harvard Union Press, 1932–40. Jacob Neusner, *The Rabbinic Traditions About the Pharisees,* Leiden: Brill, 1971.

J. R. M.

PHAROSH. *See* Parosh.

PHARPAR (fär'pär). A river of southern Syria near Damascus (II Kgs 5:12).

PHARZITES (fär'zīts). The descendants of Pharez (*q.v.*; Num 26:20).

PHASEAH. *See* Paseah.

PHEBE (fē'bē). A common Gr. name, *Phoibē,* "radiant," "bright," found in Gr. mythology and attested in inscriptions; spelled Phoebe in all modern versions. The woman of Rom 16:1–2 was a deaconess (NASB marg.; "servant") of the church at Cenchraea, the eastern port of Corinth. Paul recommended her to the Christians at Rome, and may have committed the delivery of his Roman epistle into her care. Paul asked for her all the assistance that believers in Rome could render in her activities there. There is a debate over whether Phebe's title of "deaconess" should be considered in a non-technical sense as one rendering service or as holding a formal office in the church. *See* Deaconess.

Paul also called Phebe a "succourer" of many, including himself. The Gr. word *prostatis* means "patroness," "protectress," suggesting she was a wealthy woman who looked after the needs of less fortunate persons. In Athens the masculine term designated the office of a man who represented people without civic rights. Under Roman law such a patron could represent foreigners.

J. R.

PHENICE (fē'nĭs). A harbor on the S coast of Crete (Acts 27:12; spelled Phoenix in all modern versions) which those in charge of Paul's ship wanted to reach for wintering. Ancient writers including Strabo and Ptolemy mention it. It is undoubtedly near modern Loutro in the Cape Mouros area, the only harbor on the southern coast that provides safe all-year anchorage for larger ships such as the Alexandrian grain ship with its 276 persons aboard. The ancient name is perpetuated by Phinikia, a modern town on the plateau 2,000 feet above the harbor.

Luke describes the harbor as being "exposed southwest and northwest" (NEB; the RSV and NASB texts are incorrect, but see margins). Loutro, however, faces E, with a narrow peninsula separating it from a poorer harbor facing W. Very likely the western bay was once much better protected, but earthquake disturbance has apparently changed the coastline there. A harbor facing W would have afforded the protection needed from Euroclydon (Acts 27:14), the ENE wind which caused the eventual shipwreck (A. F. Walls, "Phoenix," NBD, p. 994).

J. R.

PHENICIA. *See* Phoenicia.

PHI-BESETH. *See* Pi-beseth.

PHICHOL (fī'kŏl). Chief captain of the army of the Philistine king Abimelech in the days of Abraham (Gen 21:22, 32) and Isaac (Gen 26:26).

PHILADELPHIA (fĭl-*á*-dĕl'fĭ-*á*)

1. A city of Lydia (modern Alasehir) 26 miles E of Sardis by the Roman road. It stood on a broad hill 800 feet in altitude on the imperial post road which came from Rome via Troas and led eastward through Phrygia. Location on an important trade route and control of a great grape-growing district contributed greatly to

Philadelphian prosperity. Though a Lydian town stood on the site much earlier, the importance of Philadelphia dates from *c.* 150 B.C. when it was refounded by Attalus II of Pergamum. The earthquake of A.D. 17 destroyed the city; Tiberius gave large sums for its rebuilding. John addressed the church in Philadelphia (Rev 3:7–13). Without the help of an excavation there, it is impossible to recreate a view of the city as the apostle knew it.

2. The name given to ancient Rabbath-ammon (modern Amman), 20 miles E of the Jordan, by Ptolemy Philadelphus early in the 3rd cen. B.C.

H. F. V.

PHILEMON (fī-lē'mŏn). With the help of the Epistle to the Colossians it can be determined with reasonable certainty that Philemon was a resident of Colossae. Onesimus, whose relation to Philemon is revealed in Paul's letter to him, is said to be of that community (Col 4:9), and Archippus, who shares in the address of the Philemon letter, receives a charge from Paul in Col 4:17. From the fact that a church met in Philemon's house it may be concluded that he was a leader among the believers and possibly a man of some means. He had at least one slave, Onesimus. Paul's letter to him gives ground for judging that he must have been a Christian gentleman of high calibre.

PHILEMON, EPISTLE TO (fi-le'mon)

Occasion and Purpose

This briefest of Paul's letters was precipitated by two things: the flight of a slave Onesimus (*q.v.*) from his master Philemon (*q.v.*), who resided at Colossae in the Lycus Valley of Asia Minor, and the conversion of Onesimus through the instrumentality of Paul. The apostle writes to effect a reconciliation, so that the truant slave will be received by his master and forgiven for his desertion.

It is not certain whether Onesimus knew the whereabouts of Paul when he left Colossae and deliberately hunted for him, or whether, knowing of his reputation through having heard of him in the home at Colossae, he sought him out when he accidentally learned that Paul was in the same city where he himself was staying. It may be that a combination of financial need, fear of detection, and prickings of conscience for the wrongs he had perpetrated, moved him to seek for Paul and to appeal to him for help. The apostle was able to send him back a new man in Christ Jesus.

The address of the letter is somewhat peculiar in that the members of Philemon's family are included and even the church which met in his house (v. 2). Surely the intent of this was to acquaint all these people with the request that the apostle was making of Philemon, calling for forgiveness and possibly even for manumission (v. 21), so that he would have to make his decision in the light of the fact that others knew

A pillar of the Church of St. John rises above a modern roof in Philadelphia. HFV

of the situation. It would be hard to deny Paul's request anyway, but doubly hard to resist the pressure of family and friends besides.

Place and Time of Composition

The most likely place is Rome shortly after A.D. 60. Here Paul was accessible to visitors (Acts 28:30–31). Onesimus was probably safer from detection among the large floating population of the great city than in some smaller place in the Near East. Some have adopted Ephesus as the point of origin of the letter, but there is no clear evidence of Paul's imprisonment in that city. Verse 22 might be regarded as favorable to the Ephesian hypothesis, but for all we know Paul may have abandoned his plan to go from Rome to Spain or else postponed it in favor of a quick return to the E following his release by the imperial court. The letter is thought to have been carried, along wth Paul's epistle to the Colossians, by Onesimus when Paul sent him back to Philemon.

Outline

I. Salutation, vv. 1–3
II. Thanksgiving for Philemon, vv. 4–7
III. Appeal for Onesimus, vv. 8–21
IV. Conclusion, vv. 22–25

Value

This is twofold. For one thing, we get a glimpse of Paul's inner life as we see it laid bare to the gaze of his close friends. The letter is a marvelous blend of confidence in Philemon that he would comply with the apostle's request, and the irresistible approach of a suppliant. Paul refuses to take advantage of his friendship by keeping Onesimus to aid him in his own situation (vv. 11–14). He even offers to make up any deficiency caused by the slave's thievery (vv. 18–19). No less impressive is Paul's love for Onesimus, whom he has begotten in his bonds (vv. 10, 12).

A second value is the insight into the attitude of early Christianity toward slavery. While it was impossible to campaign for abolition, it was possible to love the slave and treat him as a brother in Christ.

Bibliography. G. W. Barker, W. L. Lane, and J. R. Michaels, *The New Testament Speaks*, New York: Harper & Row, 1969, pp. 210–217. P. R. Coleman-Norton, "Paul and the Roman Law of Slavery," *Studies in Roman Economic and Social History in Honor of A. C. Johnson*, Princeton: Univ. Press, 1951, pp. 155–177. J. Knox, *Philemon Among the Letters of Paul*, Chicago: Univ. of Chicago Press, 1935. J. J. Muller, *The Epistle to the Philippians and to Philemon*, Grand Rapids: Eerdmans, 1955. T. Preiss, "Life in Christ and Social Ethics in the Epistle to Philemon," *Life in Christ*, Chicago: Allenson, 1954, pp. 32–42.

E. F. Har.

PHILETUS (fĭ-lē′tŭs). Mentioned but once in the Bible (II Tim 2:17). Paul warns against him and Hymanaeus whose teachings undermined the faith. They were Gnostics and their specific error was the Gnostic teaching that there is no future resurrection of the body—the body is entirely evil and therefore irrelevant—but only a "spiritual experience" which occurs at salvation. Thus they were saying that those who have spiritual enlightenment have already enjoyed the real blessing of resurrection. This Gnostic denial of the bodily resurrection was destroying the faith of some in Paul's day.

PHILIP (fĭl′ĭp). Four men bear this name ("lover of horses") in the NT.

1. Philip the tetrarch, brother of Herod Antipas and ruler of Ituraea and Trachonitis (Lk 3:1). He was son of Herod the Great by his fifth wife Cleopatra of Jerusalem. Appointed by Augustus, he reigned for 37 years (4 B.C.-A.D. 34). Josephus (*Ant*. xviii. 4.6) reported that Philip's benevolence and justice earned him the favor of his subjects and also marked him out from his family (!). He built Caesarea Philippi (Mt 16:13) and called Bethsaida "Julias" (in honor of the daughter of Augustus). Salome, daughter of Herodias, became his wife. His Roman sympathies are well-known. *See* Herod: Herod Philip.

2. Philip (Herod), son of Herod the Great and Mariamne; first husband of Herodias (Mk 6:17). He did not actually reign, but lived as a private citizen in Rome. His half-brother Herod Antipas married Herodias after divorcing his own wife. Nothing else is known of him from the NT, and Josephus only refers to him as Herod.

3. Philip the apostle, one of the 12 disciples of Jesus. He is mentioned only formally in the first three Gospels and Acts (Mt 10:3; Mk 3:18; Lk 6:14; Acts 1:13), fifth in the list of apostles. It is in John's Gospel that he occupies a more prominent and symbolic role (in keeping with John's method of illustration).

He came from Bethsaida, the same town as Andrew and Simon (Jn 1:44). It is said that Jesus "found" him; he in turn found Nathanael, told him of Jesus and invited him to "come and see" (Jn 1:43, 45–46). Next, he was questioned by Jesus as to a source of bread to feed the multitude (Jn 6:5). His reply marked him as a practical, realistic person (Jn 6:7), and one who did not yet fully understand Jesus' power. Then he was approached by "certain Greeks" who wanted to see Jesus (Jn 12:20–21). It may have been only a coincidence, or they may have known of his Greek name (Philippos). His response was to tell Andrew who in turn told Jesus. Finally, he requested of Jesus to see the Father (Jn 14:8). Here, as in 6:7, he used the word "suffice" to characterize his statement. Thus, it seems he thought in "down-to-earth" categories, carefully calculating before he spoke. The early Church Fathers apparently confused him with Philip the evangelist. *See* below.

4. Philip the evangelist, a resident of Caesarea (Acts 21:8) and father of four virgin daughters who prophesied in the early church (21:9). Along with Stephen, he was one of the most prominent of the seven deacons appointed originally to care for needy widows (Acts 6:1–6) in the church in Jerusalem. He is described as one of good report, full of the Spirit and of wisdom.

During the persecution under Saul of Tarsus Philip was forced to flee Jerusalem and went down to Samaria, proclaiming the Christ ("Messiah") to the Samaritans (Acts 8:5). He had a successful ministry there, even influencing Simon Magus to believe and receive Christian baptism (8:9–13). Later he went down toward Old Gaza and led an Ethiopian official to faith in Jesus (26:38). Thus as a Hellenistic (Greek-speaking) Jew he formed an important link between the Jerusalem church and outlying regions.

References in the Church Fathers, especially in Eusebius and Clement of Alexandria, seem to show a confusion of Philip with the apostle (above). Luke, however, takes care to distinguish the two both by locale (Acts 8:1, "except the apostles") and title (1:13; 21:8).

W. M. D.

PHILIPPI (fĭl′ĭ-pī). A town of Macedonia 13 miles inland from the Aegean served by its port Neapolis. Philippi was founded by and named after Philip II of Macedonia in 360 B.C. It was significant to the Macedonian as the chief mining center in the Pangaeus gold fields; these were largely exhausted by the time Macedonia came under control of Rome in 168 B.C. The Romans settled a colony (Acts 16:12) of Roman veterans at Philippi after 42 B.C., when Octavius and Antony defeated Brutus and Cassius there.

Paul evangelized there on his second missionary journey, speaking first to some devout Jews at a prayer meeting by a riverside (Acts 16:13), the Gangites. Lydia of Thyatira was the

PHILIPPIANS, EPISTLE TO THE

first convert (Acts 16:14), and the conversion of a "fortune teller" led her exploiters to stir up a riot against Paul and Silas. The 300-by-150 foot agora where the judgment scene took place prior to Paul and Silas' imprisonment has been completely excavated by the French School at Athens. Through the agora ran the Egnatian highway which connected Rome with Asia. On the N side of the agora stood the podium where magistrates rendered judgment. Above that towered the 1000-foot acropolis of the town, on the E slope of which was a large Gr. theater. None of the remains of churches now known as a result of excavations at Philippi dates before A.D. 400. *See* Archaeology.

The church at Philippi was the first established in Europe, and it was very liberal with its founder, sending gifts to him on various occasions (Phil 4:14–17; II Cor 11:9). The Epistle to the Philippians is in part at least a thank you note for this kindness. Later Paul visited Philippi and kept the Passover with the brethren there (Acts 20:6).

H. F. V.

Ruins of a fifth-century church at Philippi. The entrance, the center aisle, and two side aisles may be clearly seen. HFV

PHILIPPIANS, EPISTLE TO THE. A hortatory letter written by the apostle Paul and addressed to the church at Philippi. Together with Colossians, Ephesians, and Philemon, it forms the fourfold cluster of the Prison Epistles.

Background and Date

The Epistle to the Philippians finds its historical framework of reference against Acts 16:12–40. Paul and Silas, having advanced as far as Troas, paused there to await the further leading of the Holy Spirit, who had already debarred the way of their entrance into the province of Asia (v. 7). At Troas Paul saw a vision of the "man of Macedonia," imploring them to "come over and help us" (v. 9). Immediately they responded and went to Philippi.

Their first convert proved to be Lydia of Thyatira, a seller of the expensive purple dye (Acts 16:14). She then became their hostess. Next in order, as a result of delivering a demonized girl, they were falsely accused and cast into prison (vv. 16–23). Being of great courage,

Possible site of the prayer meeting Paul attended at Philippi. HFV

they changed the dismal character of their surroundings into a place of song. An earthquake ensued and the jailer was converted (vv. 24–33). Paul and Silas were subsequently released, but not until reparations had been made in the form of apologies for offending Roman citizens (vv. 35–40).

In regard to the book itself, Epaphroditus had come to Paul from Philippi bearing gifts for the aging apostle (Phil 4:10–19). The reference to "Caesar's household" in Phil 4:22 seems to indicate Rome as the place of origination, as does the passage in Phil 1:13, where the writer mentions the "praetorian guard" (RSV, NASB; KJV, "palace"). The epistle was thus evidently penned from Rome toward the climax of Paul's first imprisonment there (cf. Acts 28:30–31). It is consequently dated *c.* A.D. 60.

On the other hand, certain scholars, including evangelicals such as F. F. Bruce (*The Letters of Paul,* Grand Rapids: Eerdmans, 1965, pp. 160 f.), have suggested that Paul must have been imprisoned in Ephesus when he wrote to the Philippians. They believe there would not have been sufficient time for all of the traveling back and forth indicated in the epistle, if Paul were in Rome. The letter would then have been written a few years earlier.

Outline

I. Christ the Believers' Joy, 1:1–30
   - A. Identification and salutation, vv. 1–2
   - B. Joy inspiring prayer for the Philippians, vv. 3-11
   - C. Joy despite suffering and pretenders, vv. 12-18
   - D. Joy despite the possibility of approaching death, vv. 19–30

II. Christ the Believers' Example, 2:1–30
   - A. An appeal for unity, vv. 1–4
   - B. An appeal for humility, vv. 5–11
     1. Christ's humiliation, vv. 5–8
     2. Christ's exaltation, vv. 9–11
   - C. A call for positive Christian living, vv. 12–18
   - D. Paul commends his co-workers to the church, vv. 19–30

III. Christ the Believers' Hope, 3:1–21
  A. A warning against legalism, vv. 1–3
  B. Paul's description of his life before and after conversion, vv. 4–14
  C. A personal example of proper attitude, vv. 15–19
  D. The true believer's destiny, vv. 20–21

IV. Christ the Believers' Sufficiency, 4:1–23
  A. A call to rejoicing, vv. 1–4
  B. An exhortation to commit the affairs of life to Christ, vv. 5–7
  C. The Christians' formula for right thinking and action, vv. 8–9
  D. A note of thanks to the Philippians, vv. 10–20
  E. Benediction and closing words, vv. 21–23

The great theater at Philippi. HFV

Occasion and Purpose

The book engages in no harsh censure, although Paul lovingly reproaches Euodia and Syntyche for their lack of harmony (4:2). This apparently was a root cause of disunity in the church, necessitating Paul's call to agreement (1:27; 2:1-4, 14). With its many references to individuals it is certainly one of his most personal letters. It may be regarded as an inspired thank-you letter for the gift which the church at Philippi had sent Paul (4:10–20), as well as an epistle of commendation for his fellow workers Timothy and Epaphroditus.

Highlights of the Epistle

Valuable contributions of this epistle are (1) the "Kenosis" passage (2:5–11, *see* Kenosis); (2) Paul's autobiographical note (3:4–9), apart from which significant data regarding him would be lacking; (3) the ultimate resurrection of believers based on present experiential knowledge of Christ (3:10–11); (4) "heavenly citizenship" (3:20–21); (5) a Christian standard for meditation and life (4:8–9); (6) Paul's overall emphasis on joy and rejoicing, the word "joy" and its cognate forms occurring 16 times in the epistle.

Bibliography. F. W. Beare, *A Commentary on the Epistle to the Philippians,* New York: Harper, 1959. J. B. Lightfoot, *St. Paul's Epistle to the Philippians,* London: Macmillan, 1868 (1903 ed. reprinted by Zondervan, 1968). Ralph P. Martin, *The Epistle of Paul to the Philippians,* TNTC, Grand Rapids: Eerdmans, 1959; *An Early Christian Confession: Philippians ii.5–11 in Recent Interpretation,* London: Tyndale, 1960. H. C. G. Moule, *Philippian Studies,* 6th ed., London: Hodder & Stoughton, 1908. J. J. Muller, *The Epistles of Paul to the Philippians and to Philemon,* NIC, Grand Rapids: Eerdmans, 1955. A. T. Robertson, *Paul's Joy in Christ,* New York: Revell, 1917. John F. Walvoord, *Philippians: Triumph in Christ,* EBC, Chicago: Moody Press, 1971.

J. F. G.

PHILISTIA. *See* Palestine: II.B.1.*f;* Philistine.

PHILISTINE (fĭ-lĭs'tĭn, fĭl'ĭstēn). A Gentile people of Cretan (Aegean) origin who resided on the S coastal plain of Palestine.

Philistia. The name of their occupied territory has various designations in the OT: "land of Philistines" (Gen 21:32, 34; Ex 13:17), "the regions of the Philistines" (Josh 13:2, RSV), and "Philistia" (Ex 15:14, NASB; Ps 60:8; 87:4). Palestine derived its name from the Philistines.

The Philistine territory at most was a small section. The land was early marked as extending 60 to 70 miles from Sihor (or the brook of Egypt) to the boundary of Ekron N (Josh 13:2–3). The E border ran along the Judean foothills on the line of Beth-shemesh with the sea on the W. It was extremely fertile in spite of the threat of sand dunes along the coast. Its territory enclosed many populous towns and villages, its important cities being the "Big Five," Gaza, Ashdod, Ashkelon, Gath and Ekron.

Etymology. The Egyptian form *prst* is the first reference to the Philistines as one of the "peoples of the sea" who invaded Egypt during the eighth year of Rameses III (*c.* 1200 B.C.). The name occurs in Assyrian sources as both *Pilisti* and *Palastu.* The Heb. is *pelishtim.* This is probably an ethnic adjective based on the territorial designation *pelesheth* since there remains no acceptable Semitic etymology for this name; it could even be of Indo-European origin.

Origin. The Philistines "came out from" Casluhim who were descendants of Mizraim, the son of Ham (Gen 10:14; I Chr 1:12). They came into Palestine, probably by way of Cyprus, from Caphtor (Heb. name for Crete; cf. Jer 47:4; Amos 9:7; Deut 2:23). *See* Caphtor. In the latter half of the 2nd mil. B.C. groups called in Egyptian records "peoples of the sea" ravaged the Hittite country, the Cilician and N Syrian coast, Carchemish, and Cyprus. Excavations in Anatolia and Syria reveal the destruction of many cities (e.g., Ugarit and the

Hittite capital Khattushash) at the end of the Late Bronze Age (*c.* 1200 B.C.).

These elusive bands attempted to invade Egypt during the reigns of Merneptah and Rameses III. Some fell back on Palestine. One group settled at Dor in the plain of Sharon (cf. the Egyptian story of Wen-Amon, ANET, pp. 25–29). South of Gerar there settled another group called Cherethites (I Sam 30:14; Ezk 25:16; Zeph 2:5). By far the most important of the sea peoples in Palestine was the Philistine group clustering around their pentapolis of Gaza, Ashkelon, and Ashdod on the coast; Gath in the W Shephelah; and Ekron *c.* six miles inland. The Greeks gradually applied the name Palestine to all of Canaan.

Language. No certain documents in the Philistine language are extant. A few biblical words may be Philistine loanwords (cf. *seren,* "lord"; *kôba',* "helmet"; *'argaz,* "coffer, box," I Sam 5:8; 6:8; 17:5). The language soon coalesced into a Canaanite dialect, and later this in turn subsided in favor of the Aramaic (cf. Neh 13:24, "the language of Ashdod"). Some believe that Minoan Linear A from Crete is akin to Philistine. In 1964 at Deir 'Alla in the Jordan Valley three inscribed tablets dated to the 13th cen. B.C. were found. The script is similar to the Linear A syllabary (see BA, XXIX [1966], 73 f.).

Religion. Since the Philistines were uncircumcised, they naturally would be despised by the Israelites (Jud 14:3; 15:18; I Sam 17:26; 18:25). Yet the names of their known gods were Semitic (cf. the temples of Dagon in Gaza and Ashdod, Jud 16:21–30; I Sam 5:1–5; one of Ashtoreh in Ashkelon, Herodotus I, 105; one to Baalzebub in Ekron, II Kgs 1:2–6). Here is further indication that the Philistines were largely engulfed by the Canaanite culture which surrounded them. Some of these temples still existed in the Hellenistic age (cf. I Macc 10:83; Diodorus Siculus 11:4). The Philistines also possessed reputable soothsayers (Isa 2:6).

Military. Until King David (*c.* 1010–971 B.C.) crushed them, the Philistines resided chiefly in their five cities ruled by *serānîm,* "lords" (or "tyrants"). These lords composed a council which could for the common good override the decision of any single lord (cf. I Sam 29:1–7). After their defeat, the term "king" replaced this "lordly" council (cf. Jer 25:20; Zech 9:5). In their heyday the Philistines mustered impressive numbers of well-armed troops of foot soldiers, archers and charioteers (cf. I Sam 13:5; 29:2; 31:3). Also they pressed into military service subjected captives and hired mercenaries (cf. David in I Sam 27–29; the Rephaim in II Sam 21:18–22). Likewise, individual giants (cf. Goliath in I Sam 17:4–10) and shock troops ("spoilers" or "raiders," cf. I Sam 13:17–18; 14:15) were employed.

Archaeology. Documents discovered at Ugarit reveal that this N Canaanite city imported textiles from Ashdod in the 14th and 13th cen. B.C., as well as traded with Ashkelon and Accho.

Brook in Vale of Elah where David may have gathered stones to kill Goliath. HFV

Beginning in 1962 large scale excavations have been carried out at Tell Ashdod in Philistine territory. The earliest stratum yielded locally made pottery very similar in shape and painted designs to Late Mycenaean III C (1230–1050 B.C.) ware found in Cyprus. Several seals have been unearthed engraved with signs resembling the Cypro-Minoan script, in use in the 13th and early 12th cen. B.C.; this is the first written evidence from a definite Philistine context. Also, eight lentoid Minoan seals from the end of the 2nd mil. B.C. were found in the Gaza area earlier this century. Discoveries at adjacent sites such as Tell Jemmeh, Tell Qasileh, Ain Shems (Beth-shemesh), Tell Jezer (Gezer), and Tell el-Far'ah help fill in the gap.

Bas relief scenes at Medinet Habu in Egypt show that the Philistines used wagons, chariots, and ships. Their type of ship was unique, with its carved keel, high stern and bow, and straight mast rising from the middle of the ship. The warrior wore an Aegean type kilt, with plumed helmet fastened with chin straps, like the feathered headdress of the Phaistos Disk (dated *c.* 1700 B.C.) found in southern Crete. I Sam 17: 5–7 depicts Goliath as armed to the teeth. His weapons of iron were undoubtedly made by one of the Philistine ironsmiths, who possessed a monopoly on this profession (cf. I Sam 13:19–21). Smelting furnaces for iron have been uncovered at Tell Qasileh, Tell Jemmeh, and Ain Shems.

Evidence for earlier settlers coming from the Aegean by way of Cyprus has been noted in bilobate ("two-lobed") chamber tombs at Tell el-Far'ah in the S, Lachish, and Cyprus, all from the period c.1600-1525 B.C. (AJA, 74 [1970], 139–143). Hittite texts reveal that armies of Ahhiya (Achaean) soldiers and charioteers were invading Hittite territory in the interior of Anatolia before 1400 B.C., and that Cyprus was being attacked by these Aegean peoples well before the Amarna period (AJA, 75 [1971], 169).

Finds at Beth-shan, Tell el-Far'ah, and Lachish reveal 12th cen. B.C. clay coffins, each with a face molded in relief at the head end. These are attributed to the Philistines and are connected with similar anthropoid coffins in Egypt (at Tell Yehudiyeh in the Delta).

Biblical history. The Philistines long were a thorn in the side of the Israelites. The Scriptures allude to numerous incidents.

Patriarchs. Abraham and Isaac came in contact with the Philistines under Abimelech, the king of Gerar, and his general Phicol (Gen 20–21, 26). While the later Philistines were extremely aggressive, Abimelech was a reasonable man. He practiced the policy of coexistence by appropriating many Canaanite customs, using a Semitic name, and making covenants with Abraham and Isaac. When or how these earlier Philistines reached Palestine, present scholarship finds it hard to explain. Evidence presently available suggests they were Minoan merchants who were already establishing trading colonies at various points in the eastern Mediterranean world early in the 2nd mil. B.C.

Exodus and Judges. When the Israelites left Egypt, the Philistines were so spread out along the coastal strip between Egypt and Gaza that Moses had to detour inland to avoid "the way of the land of the Philistines" (Ex 13:17). The adjacent section of the Mediterranean Sea was known as the sea of the Philistines (Ex 23:31). The Philistines in this area were probably the Caphtorim of Deut 2:23.

The Israelites did not do battle with the Philistines during the Conquest, but in Joshua's old age they were firmly established in their five fortified cities (Josh 13:1–3). Again and again in subsequent history these sea people were used by the Lord to goad and chastise the Israelites (Jud 3:2–3). Shamgar temporarily repulsed them (Jud 3:31), but they constantly pressed inland and the Israelites even adopted their gods (Jud 10:6–7). The Philistines captured the ark *c.* 1070 B.C. in a disastrous battle at Aphek and destroyed the shrine at Shiloh (I Sam 4).

The modern Israeli city of Ashdod rises at the ancient Philistine site. IIS

Samson was the great Israelite judge-hero of the latter period of the judges (Jud 13–16). Philistia and Israel evidently were coexisting during his youth because he married a Philistine wife. Later he had relations with Delilah (probably a Philistine or possessing a close affinity with them). His suicidal destruction of the temple at Gaza with many of their leaders (Jud 16:27–30) *c.* 1050 B.C. may well have paved the way for the Israelite victory under Samuel at the second battle of Ebenezer (I Sam 7:7–14).

Saul and David. In spite of Samuel's success, the Philistines soon again controlled Esdraelon, the coastal plain, the Negeb, and much of the hill country. They also controlled the distribution of iron, keeping useful weapons from the Israelites (I Sam 13:19–22). This continuous pressure called for a strong leader among the Israelites. So Saul was anointed king by Samuel.

Early in his reign King Saul won a smashing victory at Michmash and drove these "tyrants" into the hill country. His reign of folly, however, permitted the Philistines again to harass Israel. They challenged Israel at Ephes-dammim and there David slew Goliath (I Sam 17–18). Foolishly, Saul turned on David and forced him to become an outlaw and eventually a vassal of Achish, king of Gath (I Sam 27). David was not required to fight in the battle of Mount Gilboa when King Saul and his sons lost their lives (I Sam 29).

When David assumed the rule of Israel he coexisted with Gath at least. In fact, he maintained a personal Philistine bodyguard (*see* the Cherethites and Pelethites). Finally, David drove the Philistines out of the hill country and struck heavy blows in Philistia itself (II Sam 5:25), clipping the wings of the Philistines as a serious enemy.

Divided monarchy. The Philistines continued to goad the Israelites throughout the monarchy. After the death of King David and the subsequent weakening of the kingdom, the Philistine cities (except Gath, II Chr 11:8) won their independence and there were skirmishes again on the frontier (II Chr 17:11). However, under Jehoram the border town of Libnah asserted her independence (Isa 9:8–12). After the Philistines invaded Judah during the reign of Ahaz (II Chr 28:18), King Hezekiah dealt them a stinging defeat (II Kgs 18:8). In chap. 47 Jeremiah prophesied their coming destruction by the might of Nebuchadnezzar's armies. The last time they are referred to in the Scriptures is in Zechariah (9:5–6), after the return from Exile.

Inscriptions. The Philistines are first mentioned in Rameses III's annals (*c.* 1200 B.C. and subsequent years). They appear on his temple at Medinet Habu near Thebes in which he describes his campaign against an invasion of Libyans and other "peoples of the sea" (ANET, pp. 262 f.). These sea peoples also are mentioned in the inscriptions of Merenptah in the 13th cen. B.C. The Assyrians refer to Philistia as frequently being in revolt. Inscriptions of Adad-nirari III (810–783 B.C.) mention Philistia among other states (including Israel) as paying him tribute. Later Tiglath-pileser III, Sargon II, Sennacherib, and Esarhaddon refer to suppressing Philistine rebellion (ANET, pp. 282–291). A group of cuneiform documents found at Babylon from the time of the Exile record the issue of rations to expatriates, among whom are the Philistines.

Philistine pottery from Gezer. Archaeological Museum, Istanbul

The Assyrian references (*c.* 735–586 B.C.) complement the biblical history of the monarchy. The Philistines during Ahaz' reign once again raided Judah and appropriated cities in the Shephelah and Negeb (II Chr 28:18; Isa 9:11; 14:28–30). But this occupation was short-lived. During the Syro-Ephraimitic war (735–732 B.C.), Tiglath-pileser III (745–727 B.C.) stormed Ashkelon and Gath for disloyalty and replaced Mitinti of Ashkelon. Hanno of Gaza fled to Egypt, but Sargon II (722–705 B.C.) captured him in 720 B.C. and deported him to Assyria. In 713 B.C., when Azuri of Ashdod refused to pay tribute, Sargon II replaced him with Azuri's brother Ahimiti. But the Ashdodeans deposed him and placed a usurper, Iamani, on the throne, who in turn spearheaded an alliance against Assyria, including Philistia, Judah, Edom and Moab. Sargon II stamped out the revolt and converted Ashdod into an Assyrian province (Isa 20:1) and raided Gath, Gibbethon and Ekron.

Hezekiah invaded Philistia and attacked Gaza (II Kgs 18:8). The populace of Ekron handed their pro-Egyptian king, Padi, over to him. In 701 B.C., Sennacherib (705–681 B.C.) invaded the W land and captured the cities of Beth-dagon, Joppa, Banai-barqa, and Azuru. During the reign of Esarhaddon (681–668 B.C.) the Philistine cities (especially Ashdod) felt the strong pressure of Egypt (cf. Herodotus II, 157). They were overrun by the Scythians, who plundered the temple of Astarte in Ashkelon (Herodotus I, 105). Later they were overrun by Pharaoh-necho, who captured Gaza (*c.* 609 B.C.; cf. Herodotus II, 159; Jer 47:1).

Aramaic letters found at Saqqarah from Adon to Pharaoh, pleading for help during Nebuchadnezzar's attack upon Ashkelon in 604 B.C., reveal that the Philistines were allied with Egypt during the final struggle. Following the battle of Carchemish, Nebuchadnezzar stamped out any remaining sparks of Philistine independence by deporting both rulers and people (see D. F. Weidner, *Mélanges syriens offerts à M. René Dussand,* Paris: Paul Geuthner, 1939, II, 923–935; also Jer 25:20; 47:2–7; Zech 2:4–7; Zeph 9:5–6).

The last glimpse of the cities Ashdod (Azotus), Ashkelon (Ascalon), and Gaza comes during the Hellenistic period; then the cities were composed of extremely mixed population. Today only the word Palestine connects them with the once glorious and powerful Philistine empire.

Bibliography. CornPBE, pp. 580–585. Moshe Dothan, "Ashdod of the Philistines," *New Directions in Biblical Archaeology,* ed. by D. N. Freedman and J. C. Greenfield, Garden City: Doubleday, 1969, pp. 15–24. Trude Dothan, "Archaeological Reflections on the Philistine Problem," *Antiquity and Survival,* II (1957), 151–164. V. Hankey, "Late Mycenaean Pottery at Beth-shan," AJA, LXX (1966), 169–171. James E. Jennings, "The Problem of the Caphtorim," *Grace Journal,* XII (Spring, 1971), #2, pp. 23–43. R. A. S. Macalister, *The Philistines, Their History and Institutions,* London: 1913 (reprint, Chicago: Argonaut, 1965). T. C. Mitchell, "Philistia," TAOTS, pp. 403–427. Hayim Tadmor, "Philistia Under Assyrian Rule," BA, XXIX (1966), 86–102. G. Ernest Wright, "Philistine Coffins and Mercenaries," BA, XXII (1959), 53-66; "Fresh Evidence for the Philistine Story," BA, XXIX (1966), 70–86.

D. W. D.

PHILO JUDEUS (fī'lō jo͞o-dē'ŭs). A Jew of Alexandria, Philo (*c.* 20 B.C.–*c.* A.D. 50) was the only Jew of his time from outside Palestine whose writings survive in full length. If Josephus would try to turn pagans to Judaism by his historical and apologetic works, Philo attempted the same but was most famous for his philosophical (*De Aeternitate Mundi, De Providentia*) and biblical writing (*Legum, Allegoriae, De Vita Mosis*). Again, like Josephus, he joined an embassy to Rome on behalf of his kinsmen. Like Josephus, too, his influence was specially strong among Christians, beginning in Philo's case with the Alexandrians (Clement and Origen) of the late 2nd cen. and early 3rd cen. A.D.

Most of the Gnostic elements later to appear in Christianity are already present in Philo. He represents the synthesizing tendency between Jewish and Hellenic culture as it went on in the ancient melting pot of Alexandria and elsewhere among the Jews of the Dispersion (*see* Dispersion of Israel). If "Plato was only Moses speaking Greek" (Carrington), Philo, on the other hand, found much Gr. philosophy in the OT. It was, for example, the Logos who spoke in the burning bush and was represented in the high priest.

Philo's writings, while numerous, are not systematic, being mainly commentaries on the OT. In these he exhibits the allegorizing for which he is famous and by which he was able to conjure up the Gr. spirit from the Heb. text. By this same device he was able to demythologize the creation, to reinterpret Jonah's whale, and to honor the Jewish law while making it palatable to the Gentiles.

God, for Philo, is transcendent and indefinable, lacking knowable attributes. He is described mainly by the *via negativa,* explaining what He is not. God is pure being apprehended by intuition alone. Matter (Gr. *hule*) is utterly other than and separated from God. The intermediary beings between God and *hule* in this system are *logoi,* chief among which is the *Logos,* or Mediator, who is agent at once of creation and revelation. This presumably is the means by which the transcendentally Other becomes the Father of providence. Only implicit and impersonal in Philo at most, this teaching is explicit and personal in the Johannine doctrine of the incarnation.

Gnostic ethics are usually either libertine or ascetic, depending on whether matter is to be yielded to as irresistible or eschewed as of no worth. Philo's system is ascetic. The following of stern self-denial is designed to lead to ecstatic experience (Gr. *ekstasis*), the only means of communion with the being of the unknowable God. The fundamental element in ecstasy, as conceived by Philo, is the relacement of the human reason by the Divine Spirit, who takes complete possession of the human personality and uses it for higher divine ends (H. A. A. Kennedy). In this we notice far greater dissimilarity than resemblance to the Pauline doctrine of the communion of Christ and believers.

Philo lived and died as a Jew, apparently never hearing of Jesus. Yet he was to have more influence on the Christian religion than perhaps on his own, for Christian writers after the 2nd cen. often used the allegorical method of interpretation on the OT in an attempt to discover Christian truth in the OT; and sometimes the method was used on both OT and NT to try to bring them into harmony wth Gr. philosophy (as Origen did).

Bibliography. Norman Bentwich, *Philo-Judaeus of Alexandria,* Philadelphia: Jewish Pub. Society, 1940. P. Borgen, *Bread From Heaven: An Exegetical Study of the Concept of Manna in the Gospel of John and the Writings of Philo,* Leiden: E. J. Brill, 1865. James Drummond, *Philo Judaeus,* 2 vols., London: Williams, 1888. Erwin R. Goodenough, *An Introduction to Philo Judaeus,* New Haven: Yale Univ. Press, 1940. Donald A. Hagner, "The Vision of God in Philo and John: A Comparative Study," JETS, XIV (1971), 81–93. Philo, *Works,* 10 vols. trans. by F. H. Colson, G. H. Whitaker and R. Marcus, New York: Loeb, 1929 ff. Sidney G. Sowers, *The Hermeneutics of Philo and Hebrews,* Richmond: John Knox Press, 1965. Harry A. Wolfson, *Philo. Foundations of Religious Philosophy in Judaism, Christianity and Islam,* 2 vols., Cambridge: Harvard Univ. Press, 1947.

J. H. G.

PHILOLOGUS (fĭ-lŏl′ŏ-gŭs). A Roman Christian whose wife or sister was Julia and who, along with others, formed a congregation or group of worshipers in the Christian community in Rome (Rom 16:15).

PHILOSOPHY. The Gr. word *philosophia,* "love of wisdom," covered search for all kinds of wisdom. In Col 2:8 it designates the teaching of certain Jewish ascetics who busied themselves in speculations concerning the angels (Col 2:18) and taught a ritualism even stricter than the law of Moses (Col 2:20–23). On the Areopagus at Athens Paul encountered mem-

Marble statuette of Socrates. BM

bers of the two leading philosophies of his day, Epicureanism and Stoicism (Acts 17:18 ff.).

Paul discusses the Gr. search for wisdom, clearly referring to their love of philosophy, in I Cor 1:18 ff., and contrasts it to the real wisdom of God which is revealed in the sending of Christ and the preaching of the cross. While the gospel is so simple that the unlearned can accept it and believe to eternal life (I Cor 1:26 f.), it is so complex and reveals such depths of reason that the wisest can never fully fathom its depths (I Cor 1:24-25; cf. Rom 11:33-36).

Should, then, a Christian be concerned with philosophy as the term is used today? The answer is dependent on the current meaning of philosophy. A good definition is hard to find. B. A. G. Fuller describes it as "a reflective and reasoned attempt to infer the character and content of the universe, taken in its entirety and as a single whole, from an observation and study of the data presented by all its aspects" (*A History of Philosophy,* New York: Holt, 1952). This statement is good insofar as it defines the need to study reality inductively and to define and explain it, but it says nothing about offering an explanation of the origin or the destiny of man and the world.

The following definition is brief but adequate: A fully developed philosophy offers an explanation for the origin of man and of the universe, a view of reality, just what it is and how it works, and a description of the goal or destiny of both man and the universe. Many philosophers, and some philosophical systems, confine themselves to reality (empiricism, positivism, logical positivism); some give some explanations of origin also (materialism), but a fully developed philosophy also adds destiny (Platonism, Neo-Platonism, Ontologism, e.g.; Paul Tillich).

In that the Christian offers an explanation of the origin of the world and man, of reality and what it is (dualistic realism—the world is real and I have a reliable knowledge of it), and of destiny, based upon the Scriptures and coordinated with a study of science and reality, he is a philosopher, the one philosopher who presents the most comprehensive analysis and answer. When the Christian enters the philosophical arena he need make no excuses for his position since it rests upon two solid pillars; scientific observation and divine revelation.

R. A. K.

PHINEHAS (fĭn'ē-ăs)

1. Son of Eleazar (*q.v.*). After Aaron, he was the most noteworthy priest of the OT, the third high priest of the Aaronic line, gaining the position after the fatal Nadab-Abihu incident (Lev 10:1-3). Mentioned often in genealogies (Ex 6:23, 25; I Chr 6:4, 50; 9:20; Ezr 7:5; 8:2), and remembered for his zeal and mighty deeds, he was a priest with a prophet's *charisma,* for it is written of him: "The Lord was with him" (I Chr 9:20). He acted decisively in slaying Zimri and Cozbi at the time Israel was suffering under a plague as a result of many yoking themselves to Baal of Peor (Num 25:7-15). On the "plains of Moab by the Jordan at Jericho" (Num 31:12, RSV), in an official priestly capacity he accompanied the 12,000 men Moses sent against Midian to avenge Israel (Num 31:5-6). He was chief spokesman and arbitrator during an explosive situation that developed because of the altar built by the returning Transjordan warriors (Josh 22:13, 30-32).

His name was apparently used for a village, the burial place of Eleazar his father (Josh 24:33).

2. Son of Eleazar, chief priest before the ark at Bethel during the time of the Benjamite war. His oracle from the Lord for the inquiring Israelites was that they should go against Benjamin and that the Lord would give them victory (Jud 20:27-28). A helpful suggestion concerning the mention of "Phinehas, the son of Eleazar, the son of Aaron" in this passage is that of W. F. Albright: "This is not necessarily a late, erroneous insertion. Rather, the names Phinehas and Eleazar are characteristic of the Aaronic line; this Phinehas may be considered Phinehas II, perhaps the predecessor of Eli" (see "Excavations and Results at Tell el-Ful," AASOR, IV [1924], 47-50).

3. A son of Eli (I Sam 1:3; 2:34). One of the two sons of Eli who had the responsibility of caring for the ark at Shiloh (I Sam 4:4). He lost his life accompanying the ark into a second battle between Israel and the Philistines (I Sam 4:17).

4. Father of Eleazar, a priest in the second temple, who assisted in weighing the silver and gold vessels (Ezr 8:33).

H. E. Fi.

PHLEGON (flĕg'ŏn). A Roman Christian to whom Paul sent greetings (Rom 16:14).

PHOEBE. *See* Phebe.

Lebanon Mountains. HFV

PHOENICIA (fē-nĭsh'*à*), **PHOENICIANS** (fē-nĭsh'ĭnz). Phoenicia apparently comes from a Gr. word which in its singular form is *phoinix*. It probably means "dark red" or "purple," and seems to refer to the extensive production and export of reddish-purple dye obtained from Tyrian sea snails.

Phoenician sarcophagi, Roman and Crusader ruins, Byblos. Photo Sport

Geography. During most of her history, Phoenicia occupied a strip of the Syrian coastal plain roughly encompassed by the present N and S boundaries of Lebanon (*q.v.*). But at her height she extended her control S to Mount Carmel and N to Arvad—a distance of some 200 miles. Nowhere is this coastal plain—opposite the Lebanon Mountains—more than four miles wide,and it averages little over a mile.

This small area is cut up by spurs which jut out from the Lebanons and almost reach the sea, as well as by torrential streams with deep gorges. Each of the ancient city-states of Phoenicia rose in an area situated between a pair of such gorges or mountain spurs. Thus the plain of Sidon was about ten miles in length and the plain of Tyre about 15 miles; neither was more than about two miles in width. *See* Lebanon.

While the Lebanon Mountains were not part of Phoenicia, they did play an important part in her history. Virtually impassable, with peaks rising to more than 10,000 feet, they shut the inhabitants up to the sea. They provided the Phoenicians with some of the most valuable timber of antiquity for use in shipbuilding and in international trade. Along with cedar (*see* Plants: products Cedar), the Phoenicians exported dye made from the murex (sea snails) found in abundance along her coasts, and wines from the grapes produced on her well-watered plains. In addition, the Phoenicians manufactured metal goods and glass, and became prosperous middlemen between East and West and between Mediterranean communities.

History. While paleolithic remains have been found in the area, Phoenicia did not begin to assume a position of any importance in international affairs until the 3rd mil. B.C. Its rise occurred under the Canaanites, who occupied the Lebanese Littoral about 3000 B.C. According to the Table of Nations, Sidon was the firstborn of Canaan (Gen 10:15). The city he founded gradually assumed domination of the Phoenician coast and maintained it for several centuries, finally losing it to Tyre (*q.v.*).

The Phoenician Canaanites are often called Semites, even though they are listed in Gen 10 as descendants of Ham. The explanation for this switch is that at an early date an admixture of Semites and Canaanites took place in Phoenicia, with the result that the Semites became predominant. Semitic ascendancy occurred as a result of a great Amorite invasion of Phoenicia, Syria, and Palestine a century or two before 2000 B.C.

Earliest known contacts between Phoenicia and a foreign power occurred with Egypt, before 3000 B.C. The Phoenician trading capital of those days was Gebal (Gr. Byblos), 25 miles N of Beirut. So great was the volume of papyrus rolls that Egyptian merchants brought into Gebal, that the Gr. word (*byblos*) for a papyrus stalk became synonymous with a papyrus scroll or "book," and the name was given to the city where the Gr. traders first saw "paper books." Thus our word Bible ("the book") perpetuates the name of the ancient port.

Throughout the Old Kingdom of Egypt (*c.* 2700–2200 B.C.) Egyptian influence in Phoenicia reigned supreme. Though that influence and commerce declined during Egypt's First Intermediate Period, it was thoroughly rehabilitated during the Middle Kingdom (*c.* 2050–1800). Egyptian Pharaohs now exercised greater suzerainty in Phoenicia, as well as in Syria and Palestine.

Subsequently the Hyksos controlled Phoenicia, along with Syria, Palestine, and at least part of Egypt. But when the Egyptians overcame the Hyksos and extended their empire northward after 1570 B.C., they occupied Phoenicia and exercised a military control there not previously exerted. Though this control slipped during the Amarna Age (*c.* 1400–1360), it was generally effective until about 1200 B.C.

The period of Phoenician independence (*c.* 1200–880 B.C.) is characterized by the rise of Tyre (*q.v.*), especially under the leadership of Hiram I (*q.v.*). Allied with David and Solomon, Hiram furnished cedar for David's palace and for the palace and temple during the reign of Solomon. He also helped Solomon build his navy and seaport at Ezion-geber (1 Kgs 9:26–28).

Hiram's place in Tyrian advance is significant. He is given credit for joining the two small islands on which the original city of Tyre was located, for rebuilding the city's temples, for constructing or enlarging the northern (Sidonian) harbor and the southern (Egyptian) harbor, and sometimes is given credit for constructing the city's breakwaters and fortifications. Whether or not there was a mainland Tyre at the time is not now certain.

To a large degree the development of Phoenicia during her period of independence was made possible by the fact that Assyria was quiescent. Although Tiglath-pileser I (*c.* 1114–1076 B.C.) gave promise of building a formidable empire, his successors for some 200 years were not at all of his mettle and posed little threat to surrounding lands. Everything changed with the reign of Ashurnasirpal

II (883–859 B.C.), however. He developed the Assyrian army, campaigned in the westland, and received tribute from Arvad, Byblos, Tyre, Sidon, and other nearby towns.

Though under Assyrian suzerainty, Phoenician towns enjoyed a considerable amount of local autonomy and achieved their height of prosperity during the 8th cen. It should not be supposed, however, that Phoenicia accepted subject status with good grace. Numerous revolts flared there during the great Assyrian period, and at times some of the Phoenician city-states enjoyed virtual independence.

During the Assyrian period, partly because of commercial advantage and partly because of Assyrian oppression, Phoenicians established numerous colonies in the western Mediterranean. The best known was at Carthage, but others were located in Spain, and on Sicily, Sardinia, Corsica, and the Balearic Islands.

During this same period the Phoenicians transmitted the alphabet to the Greeks (probably about 750), who improved upon it and passed it on to the Western world. While the Phoenicians are sometimes given credit for invention of the alphabet, that is apparently too great a claim. *See* Alphabet; Writing.

About the same time, the Phoenicians also exported the worship of Baal (*see* Gods, False: Baal) to the Hebrews with the marriage of Jezebel of Tyre to Ahab of Israel and her daughter Athaliah to Jehoram of Judah. Elijah exerted his greatest energies to keep Baal worship from exterminating the worhip of Yahweh in Israel.

Phoenician harbor, Sidon. HFV

After the fall of Nineveh (612 B.C.), the Assyrian Empire was replaced by the Neo-Babylonian. The Babylonian Nebuchadnezzar was forced to meet determined resistance to his rule in greater Syria. He besieged Tyre for 12 years (585–572 B.C.) before destroying the mainland city and Tyrian prosperity. But without a navy he could not force capitulation of the island city of Tyre.

When Babylon fell to the Persians in 539 B.C., Phoenicia passed under Persian rule quite peacefully and remained docile for a century or

Crusader Castle, Sidon. HFV

more. During the entire period Sidon was the predominant city. But in the 4th cen. the Phoenicians grew increasingly restless. In 352 B.C. a general revolt flared during which the Phoenicians were aided by Egypt. When the Persian army stood before the city of Sidon, the leaders defected to save their own skins. Robbed of all protection, the people determined to set fire to their homes and to perish with them. It is said that more than 40,000 died in the flames. Other Phoenician towns had no heart to continue the struggle.

When Alexander the Great came through Phoenicia, none of the cities offered resistance except Tyre, which withstood siege for seven months in 332 B.C. Hope of Tyrian success was not ill-founded. Their city was located on an island a half mile from shore and was well defended by fortifications and a navy. But Alexander hit upon unexpected tactics. He resolved to construct a causeway out to the island, on which he could plant his siege engines. Ruins of mainland Tyre furnished material for the causeway. Though they fought heroically, the Tyrians were eventually worsted and their city utterly destroyed. The population was for the most part either killed or sold into slavery. The terrible prophecies of Ezk 26 had been abundantly fulfilled.

Although Phoenician cities were rebuilt and attained a degree of prosperity during the Hellenistic and Roman periods, the old glory was gone. The Romans incorporated Phoenicia along with Palestine and Syria into the province of Syria. The cities of Aradus, Sidon, Tyre, and Tripolis were given rights of self-government. Phoenician industrial and commercial activity again became widespread; purple, wine, and linen were among the chief exports of the city-states.

Christianity came to Phoenicia shortly after Pentecost. The persecution accompanying the stoning of Stephen scattered believers to Phoenicia, among other places (Acts 11:19). Barnabas and Saul preached there briefly on the way back to Jerusalem from their period of ministry in Antioch (Acts 15:3). At the close of Paul's third missionary journey he stopped at Tyre for

Phoenician temples at Byblos. HFV

a week while his ship unloaded her cargo. There he seems to have contacted a considerable number of believers (Acts 21:2-7). The apostle stopped briefly at Sidon on his way to Rome and met certain friends there (Acts 27:3).

Cultural Importance

While men tend to judge the importance of a country by its size or its ability to control its neighbors, Phoenicia cannot be so judged. If she did not invent the alphabet she at least developed it and passed it on to the Greeks. She made significant developments in production of both molded and blown glass; some would credit her with having invented these processes. Having learned from Babylonian astronomers to use the stars as a guide to navigation, she passed this knowledge on to Greeks and Romans, and thus revolutionized navigation. Phoenician ships controlled the Mediterranean for almost half a millennium and the Aegean for some three centuries.

In her merchant role she bartered ideas as well as goods, bringing ideas of the East to the West and vice versa. Thus she sped the progress of culture in the ancient world. The Bible student is also alert to Phoenician impact on Heb. cultural and religious development. So notorious is the latter involvement that the name Jezebel has become a byword in Western Christian culture—both as the wife of wicked Ahab and as a synonym for a shameless woman.

Bibliography. W. F. Albright, *Yahweh and the Gods of Canaan,* Garden City: Doubleday, 1968, pp. 208-264. Dimitri Baramki, *Phoenicia and the Phoenicians,* Beirut: Khayats, 1961. John P. Brown, *The Lebanon and Phoenicia: Ancient Texts Illustrating Their Physical Geography and Native Industries, Vol. I, The Physical Setting and the Forest,* Beirut: American Univ. of Beirut, 1969. Lionel Casson. *The Ancient Mariners,* New York: Macmillan, 1959. Georges Contenau, *La Civilisation phénicienne,* Paris: Payot, 1926. CornPBE, "Phoenicia and Its Cities," pp. 585-592. Frederick C. Eiselen, *Sidon,* New York: Columbia Univ. Press, 1915. Wallace B. Fleming, *The History of Tyre,* New York: Columbia Univ. Press, 1915. Donald Harden, *The Phoenicians,* New York: Praeger, 1962. Philip K. Hitti, *Lebanon in History,* London: Macmillan, 1957. Sabatino Moscati, *The World of the Phoenicians,* New York: Praeger, 1968. E. A. Speiser, "The Name Phoinikes," *Oriental and Biblical Studies,* Philadelphia: Univ. of Pennsylvania Press, 1967, pp. 324-331.

H. F. V.

PHOENIX. *See* Phenice.

Phrygian pitcher from Gordion, c. 700 B.C. Archaeological Museum, Ankara

PHRYGIA (frĭj′ĭ-ȧ). A large mountainous area in central Asia Minor, the boundaries of which are difficult to determine, as the following historical discussion demonstrates.

The Phrygians moved across the Hellespont from what is now European Turkey about 1200 B.C. and gradually spread over Asia Minor, destroying Hittite rule in many areas. They established a kingdom with considerable power, governed from Gordium, some distance to the W of modern Ankara. Gradually other powers encroached upon their territory in Asia Minor—Greeks in the W, Bithynians in the NW, Assyrians in the E. Shortly after 700 B.C. the Cimmerians, a Thracian people, destroyed the Phrygian kingdom but later passed out of existence. During the Lydian period there was a Phrygian revival, but these people experienced decline under Persian rule.

About 275 B.C the E part of Phrygia came under the control of Celtic invaders from the Danubian area and was renamed "Galatia." At approximately the same time the Pergamene kingdom took over W Phrygia, which was their undisputed possession after the Roman victory at Magnesia in 190 B.C. expelled the Seleucid kings from Asia Minor and forced the Celts to settle in Galatia. When the Pergamene kingdom became the province of Asia in 133 B.C., most of Phrygia came under control of Rome.

By that time Phrygia in a narrower sense was considered to be that interior tableland of Asia Minor (*c.* 3,000–5,000 feet in altitude) roughly bordered by the Sangarius River (modern Sakarya) on the N and NE, the upper Hermus River on the W, the upper Maeander River on the S and SW, and Galatia on the E. It was a region best suited to grazing. Most of the area of Phrygia in Paul's day was part of the province of Asia, but a small portion of it lay in the province of Galatia. Iconium and Antioch (of Pisidia) were cities of Galatian Phrygia. The apostle Paul ministered in Phrygia on all three of his missionary journeys (Acts 16:6; 18:23). Jews from Phrygia were in Jerusalem at the time of Pentecost (Acts 2:10).

H. F. V.

PHURAH (fyŏŏr'*ȧ*). Gideon's armor bearer, who went with him to scout the camp of the Midianites (Jud 7:10–11). Another spelling is Purah.

PHUT (fūt), **PUT** (pūt). The third son of Ham (Gen 10:6; I Chr 1:8), "brother" of Cush, Mizraim, and Canaan. Josephus (*Ant.* i.6.2) identifies their country as Libya. Jeremiah (46:9, ASV, etc.) describes the men of Put as skillful with the shield. Ezekiel predicts the nation's fall as an ally of Egypt to Nebuchadnezzar (30:5; KJV, Libya), and as allied with Persia in the eschatological rebellion (38:5; *see* Magog). Phut was allied to Tyre as "men of war" (Ezk 27:10). As allied to No (Thebes) in Egypt, they were not able to prevent its sack by Ashurbanipal in 663 B.C. (Nah 3:8–10).

Phut was certainly in Africa. Egyptologists had formerly equated Heb. *pût* with *Pw(n)t,* Punt (Somaliland) of the Egyptian texts. But in Darius' inscription at Naqsh-i-Rustam and in that of Xerxes at Persepolis, a *Putaya* is listed, once with Ethiopia and once with Carians and Ethiopians, as a province of the Persian Empire. If *Putaya* were Somaliland, then Libya would be missing from these province lists of the Persian Empire. But it is known that Libya and Cyrene submitted to Cambyses *c.* 525 B.C. In the description of his campaign against Egypt in his 37th year, Nebuchadnezzar refers to a city of *Putuyāman,* i.e., *Puṭu* of the Ionians which suggests a more exact identification of Put with Cyrene (ANET, p. 308). *Pûṭ* of the Heb. MT is often translated in the LXX by "Libyans," and Tyre would hire Libyan rather than Somali mercenary troops. Thus Libya seems to be a correct identification for Phut. *See* Libya.

H. G. S.

PHUVAH (fū'vȧ). The second son of Issachar (Gen 46:13), described as an ancestor of the Punites in the census taken by Moses (Num 26:23; KJV, Pua; ASV, RSV, Puvah); also spelled Puah (I Chr 7:1).

PHYGELLUS (fī'jĕ-lŭs).This name, along with Hermogenes, is mentioned in II Tim 1:15 as one who repudiated or turned away from the apostle. The exact circumstances are unknown. When Paul states that "all" of the Asiatics had deserted him, he does not refer to all Asian Christians, but probably to those Asians in Rome at the time of his trial, led away by Phygellus. When needed, they deserted him. The Asians subsequently returned home, and Timothy possibly heard from them of Paul's arrest. The help of Onesiphorus is contrasted to the shameful behavior of Phygellus (II Tim 1:16–18).

PHYLACTERIES. The Gr. designation *phylaktērion* for the Jewish prayer reminder is inappropriate, for the Gr. meaning is "safeguard" or "amulet," and has the idea of warding off ill fortune. But this word has been universally adopted, passing through the many ancient versions and arriving in the English versions as the Gr. equivalent. The Aram. term used by the rabbis, *tᵉphillîn,* literally means "prayers," i.e., prayer cases.

Phylacteries are first mentioned in the pseudepigraphal Letter of Aristeas (*c.* 100 B.C.). Josephus also makes reference to them (*Ant.* iv.8.13). They are mentioned once in the NT in Christ's diatribe against the Pharisees, "But they do all their deeds to be noticed by men; for they broaden their phylacteries" (Mt 23:5, NASB). In defense of the Pharisaic practice, the rabbis interpreted Deut 28:10, "So all the peoples of the earth shall see that you are called by the name of the Lord" (NASB), by linking it to the "phylactery of the head" (*Berakot* 6*a*). A head phylactery was found in one of the Qumran caves along with the appropriate Scripture passages and Decalogue, confirming the NT indication of the use of such reminders in the 1st cen. A.D.

The term "phylacteries" is applied to two black leather cubes about one and a half inches on a side. Each of the cubes has long leather straps passing through hollow extensions protruding from the back of the phylactery cases.

One cube, called *shel yad,* "of the hand," is placed on the left arm facing the heart; the other cube, *shel rôsh,* "of the head," is placed on the center of the forehead. The word *Shaddai,* "Almighty," one of the names of God in the OT, is represented on both phylacteries by various combinations of inscribed letters and curious formations of the straps.

The head phylactery has four small compartments. The following four Scripture passages: Ex 13:1–10; 13:11–16; Deut 6:4–9; 11:13–21, are each written on a separate piece of parchment, tied, and inserted in its particular compartment. The hand phylactery has only one compartment, in which are placed the four paragraphs on one piece of parchment.

The scriptural basis for the custom of wearing phylacteries is found in the above four passages of Scripture. In each of these occurs the almost identical phraseology requiring the Jewish person to put "these words" for "a sign upon your hand, and a frontlet between your eyes" (Deut 6:8).

The context of the Exodus passage treats the Feast of the Unleavened Bread and the redemption of the firstborn. Therefore both of these institutions were to be a sign on the hand and a memorial (Ex 13:9), and also a sign on the hand and phylacteries (frontlets) between the eyes (v. 16).

The other passages in Deuteronomy describe the same procedure that treats a wider body of material to be kept in mind. In Deut 6:8 the reference to the sign on the hand and frontlets on the forehead is generally taken to stress vv. 4 and 5, Israel's confession of the one true God, the *Sh^{e}ma'*. The phraseology of sign and frontlets of Deut 11:18 has reference to the law in general. In the Deuteronomy passages the emphasis is on a perpetual remembrance of these words. It should be noted that for the word "memorial" in Ex 13:9, the other three passages use "frontlets" (or phylacteries, Heb. *ṭôṭafōt*). The meaning of this Heb. word is not that certain, but this word is translated *tephillîn* by the *Targumîm* and rendered later by Mt 23:5 as "phylacteries." Therefore the four basic scriptures speak of signs, frontlets, and memorials as figures of the words of the revelation of God.

The wearing of phylacteries was also intended to stress a sanctity and provide for a serious frame of mind. In this way all levity would be prevented when involved in prayer or devotion before God.

To "broaden the phylacteries" (Mt 23:5, NASB) meant that the parchments were made larger, thus requiring that the phylactery cubes be made correspondingly larger. Some have also referred this to the straps attached to the phylactery boxes being made wider. Jesus therefore rebuked the Jewish leaders for deliberately attracting attention by wearing phylacteries broader and fringes or tassels longer than necessary.

Orthodox Jews also seek to fulfill the requirement of Deut 6:9 and 11:20 in a literal fashion. A piece of parchment bearing Deut 6:4-9 and 11:13-21 written on 22 lines, called a *mezuzah,* is rolled up in a case and fastened to the doorpost of their home as the identifiable symbol of a Jewish resident. No Gentile, no matter how friendly or charitable toward the Jews, would be apt to do it.

See Dress; Frontlets.

L. Go.

PHYSICIAN. *See* Occupations: Physician.

PI-BESETH (pī-bē'sĕth). A town on the Pelusiac arm of the Nile River (Ezk 30:17; LXX, Boubastis), whose name is derived from Egyp. *Pr-B'stt,* "House of (the goddess) Ubastet." The site, Tell Basta, near modern Zagazig 40 miles NE of Cairo, was excavated in 1886-87. The town dates back to the 4th Dynasty (*c.* 2600 B.C.) and was the residence of the 22nd Dynasty Egyptian kings, including Sheshonk I (biblical Shishak). The city was practically destroyed by the Persians *c.* 350 B.C. Its significance in Ezekiel is probably to be connected with its worship of Ubastet (the cat), from whence it derived its name. Later, in Greek (Herod. 2:59, 137), the cat goddess was given the compound name Bubastis or Bubastos.

Because it was situated at the W end of the territory of Goshen (*q.v.*), the pharaoh of the Exodus may have resided here temporarily in a temple guest house during the time of the plagues (cf. Ex 7:20-23; 9:33). *See* Exodus, The: Biblical Account.

A. K. H. and J. R.

PICTURES. This word in the KJV stands for Heb. *māśkît* (Num 33:52; Prov 25:11) and *s^{e}kîyyâ* (Isa 2:16). These terms may refer to visual imagery in general. Drawing and painting of pictures on pottery and walls are very ancient. The Egyptians in particular were notable for their fine pictures and tasteful use of color. *See* Painting.

The biblical Israelites left little archaeological evidence of their own development along these lines. Later Jewish artistic skill is attested by the pictures of the Dura-Europos synagogue (3rd cen. A.D.).

PIECE OF GOLD, MONEY, SILVER. *See* Weights, Measures, and Coins.

PIETY. Gr. *eusebeia* means reverence or respect toward men; piety or godliness (*q.v.*) toward God (e.g., Acts 3:12; I Tim 2:2; 3:16; II Pet 1:3, 6; 3:11). This Gr. word is translated once in KJV as "piety" (I Tim 5:4), but a better translation would be "respect," since it speaks of teaching children the proper attitude toward their parents as required by the fifth commandment.

Bibliography. W. Foerster, "*Eusebēs,* etc.," TDNT, VII, 175-185.

PIG. *See* Animals, I. 14.

PIGEON or DOVE. *See* Animals, III. 42.

PI-HAHIROTH (pī'hȧ-hī'rŏth). A place near the head of the Red Sea in sight and E of Baal-zephon (*q.v.*), where the Israelites camped before crossing over the sea (Ex 14:2, 9; Num 33:7-8). Perhaps it was part of the swampy land along the western shore of the Bitter Lakes, with Baal-zephon on a height of Jebel

Murr or Jebel 'Ataqah overlooking the whole area from the W.

PILATE, PONTIUS (pŏn-shŭs pī'lăt). Called "governor" (Gr. *hēgemōn*) of Judea in the NT and once in Josephus (*Ant.* xviii.3.1). Josephus also refers to him as *epitropos* (*Wars* ii.9.2), as does Philo (*Embassy to Gaius* 38). The latter Gr. term served as the equivalent of the official Roman title of procurator (cf. *Ant.* xx.6.2; *Wars* ii.8.1). The Latin term "procurator" is applied to Pilate by the Roman historian Tacitus in his *Annals* xv. 44. Another title, "prefect" (*praefectus*), is now attested by an inscription found at Caesarea in 1961 that speaks of "Pontius Pilate, Prefect of Judea" (see J. E. Vardaman in JBL, 81 [1962], pp. 70 f.). There is no evidence of any difference in meaning among these terms; the new inscription may simply indicate that the terminology for such offices was not as technical as had been supposed.

An inscription found at Caesarea mentioning Pilate. Gleason Archer

Pilate assumed his office in A.D. 26, during the reign of Tiberius Caesar. At about this time Sejanus, a notorious anti-Semite, had considerable influence with the emperor. Philo indicates that Sejanus was dedicated to the obliteration of the Jewish people (*Embassy to Gaius* 24; Eusebius, *Ecclesiastical History* II. 5). The policies of Pilate and of his contemporary Flaccus, procurator of Egypt, suggest that they shared Sejanus' anti-Semitic viewpoint and may even have been his proteges (see Philo, *Flaccus* 1).

Pilate's procuratorship consisted largely of a series of provocations against the Jews. First he broke with the custom of former procurators by bringing into Jerusalem ensigns that bore the image of Caesar. This was a deliberate offense against the Jewish law, and when the people petitioned for the removal of the effigies, Pilate surrounded them with his soldiers and threatened immediate death. Josephus (*Ant.* xviii.3.1; *Wars* ii.9.2, 3) tells how the Jews threw themselves to the ground to show their willingness to die rather than transgress the law. Pilate was so impressed by their zeal that he ordered the ensigns to be removed and taken to his headquarters at Caesarea. But his basically callous attitude to the Jewish religion did not change (cf. also the incident of the gold shields in Philo, *Embassy* 38).

The next clash came when Pilate appropriated the funds of the temple treasury to construct an aqueduct. Again the populace protested. Disguised as civilians Pilate's soldiers wrought havoc among the multitude that had gathered, killing many unarmed Jews with concealed weapons (*Ant.* xviii.3.2; *Wars* ii.9.4). Jesus in the Gospel of Luke speaks of certain "Galileans, whose blood Pilate had mingled with their sacrifices" (Lk 13:1). This incident, unrecorded in Josephus, nevertheless coincides with what we know of Pilate from that historian.

Pilate's removal from office was brought about by a similar outrage, this time against the Samaritans. Pilate heard that a group of them were planning to gather on their holy mountain to view some sacred vessels allegedly put there by Moses. He sent his troops to ambush them, killing or capturing some and putting others to flight. The Samaritans promptly appealed to Vitellius, the legate of Syria, who ordered Pilate to Rome to give account of his actions to the emperor (*Ant.* xviii.4.1.2). This was the end of Pilate's procuratorship, and nothing is known of his subsequent career. A later tradition of uncertain value states that he committed suicide (Eusebius, *Ecclesiastical History* II.7). Philo attributes to Herod Agrippa I a summary description of Pilate as "naturally inflexible, a blend of self-will and relentlessness . . ." (*Embassy* 38).

In the light of this background, Pilate's weakness and vacillation at the trial of Jesus, and his willingness to please the Jews, hardly seems in character. The reason may be that he already felt his own position to be in danger. There are hints in Philo that Sejanus may have come to a bad end, and that after his death Tiberius took strong measures against any repressive anti-Semitism in the empire (*Embassy* 24; *Flaccus* 1 and 21; see note by F. H. Colson in the Loeb edition, X, 403).

The statement of the Jews to Pilate in Jn 19:12 ("If you release this Man, you are no friend of Caesar," NASB) is a thinly veiled threat. A complaint to Tiberius could cause Pilate to lose his official status as the king's "friend" (*Amicus Caesaris*), and with it his procuratorship and his very life. Fear of such consequences could have transformed the "inflexible" Pilate into the double-minded person set forth in the Gospels. But even in this precarious situation, Pilate the anti-Semite could not resist a final cut at his enemies in the ironic inscription over the cross, "The King of the Jews" (Mk 15:26; Jn 19:19). What a sorry race of people this was, whose "king" hung upon a cross!

None of the Gospels suggest that Pilate had any desire to execute Jesus. But because the legal authority to pass the death sentence belonged to the Roman governor (Jos *Wars* ii.8.1) and not to the Sanhedrin, the chief priests and elders of the Jews delivered Jesus to Pilate (Mk 15:1; Jn 18:31). The charge was that Jesus claimed to be a king, stirring up the people and forbidding taxes to be paid to Caesar (Lk 23:2, 5). Pilate asked Jesus whether He was indeed claiming to be "king of the Jews," and received the reply, *Su legeis,* "It is as you say" (Mk 15:2, NASB). He marveled at Jesus' refusal to answer the charges brought against Him (Mk 15:5). Pilate was not convinced that Jesus posed any threat to Roman rule. According to Luke and John he pronounced Jesus innocent three times (Lk 23:4, 14, 22; Jn 18:38; 19:4, 6), while Matthew relates that Pilate's wife had been warned in a dream against prosecuting "that innocent man" (Mt 27:19).

Pilate's actions clearly indicate his reluctance even to prosecute Jesus. Executing an innocent man would not enhance his own prestige and could have serious repercussions. Yet, although he knew that Jesus had been arrested out of envy (Mk 15:10), he could not afford further to antagonize the Jewish leaders by dismissing the case. Therefore because Jesus was a Galilean, Pilate sent Him to Herod Antipas, the tetrarch of Galilee. On a previous occasion Pilate had encroached upon Herod's authority by his ruthless murder of Galileans (Lk 13:1), and probably for this reason the two men had been at odds with one another. Pilate did not wish to make the same mistake again, for he needed all the friends he could find. His attempt at reconciliation was successful, and Herod returned Jesus to Pilate's jurisdiction (Lk 23:6–12). The Christians found in this alliance a symbol of the united Gentile and Jewish rejection of Jesus as the Christ, in fulfillment of Ps 2:1 ff. (cf. Acts 4:26 f.).

Pilate tried unsuccessfully to appease the aroused multitude, first with the choice between Jesus and the rebel leader Barabbas (Mk 15:6 ff.), then with an offer to chastise Jesus and release Him (Lk 23:16, 22; cf. Jn 19:1 ff.). Finally he yielded to the mob, even while carrying out an empty ritual of absolving himself of all responsibility (Mt 27:24 ff.).

The fourth Gospel supplements the Synoptic accounts with two significant dialogues between Pilate and Jesus (Jn 18:33–38; 19:8–11), stressing the fact that Jesus and His kingdom are not "from this world" (18:36 f.; cf. 19:9), but "from above," the very place that was the source of Pilate's own authority (19:11; cf. 3:27). It is John also who depicts Pilate's dramatic "coronation" of Jesus and his famous words "Behold the man" (19:5) and "Behold your king" (19:14). He attributes to Pilate awe at the mystery of Jesus' person (19:7 f.), and represents Pilate's guilt as being less than that of the Jewish leaders (19:11; cf. Acts 3:13). Neither in John, however, nor anywhere else in the NT is there basis for the later legends that transform Pilate into a kindly magistrate of justice, or into a Christian saint and martyr (see E. Hennecke and W. Schneemelcher, *New Testament Apocrypha* I, 444–484).

Pilate's name is remembered today chiefly because of the words of the Apostles' Creed, "suffered under Pontius Pilate," a phrase whose roots go back to Ignatius (*Trallians* 9:1) and to Paul (I Tim 6:13).

Bibliography. Paul L. Maier, *Pontius Pilate,* Garden City: Doubleday, 1968. Jerry E. Vardaman, "Pilate, Pontius," BW, pp. 455–458.

J. R. M.

PILDASH (pĭl'dăsh). A nephew of Abraham, the sixth son of Nahor (Gen 22:22).

PILEHA (pĭl'ĕ-hä). One of the Levites who accepted the covenant Nehemiah presented (Neh 10:24). Also spelled Pilha (ASV, RSV).

PILGRIM. One who comes from a foreign country to dwell by the natives of a city or land, a stranger (I Pet 1:1), sojourner. Since heaven is the home of the Christian, the NT speaks of Abraham and other believers as pilgrims while on earth (Heb 11:13; I Pet 2:11; cf. Gen 23:4; Ps 39:12). *See* Foreigner.

PILGRIMAGE. Both the Heb. *māgûr* and the Gr. *paredēmos* stress the idea of a foreign residence rather than of travel. Jacob calls his whole life of 130 years a pilgrimage (Gen 47:9). God speaks of Canaan as the land of the patriarchs' pilgrimage (Ex 6:4). David refers to God's statutes as his songs in the land of his pilgrimage (Ps 119:54). Altogether the concepts of pilgrim and pilgrimage stress the fact that life on earth is only temporary and heaven is the believer's true home.

PILLAR. The designation of gravestones, memorials, columns, altars, and formations of cloud, smoke, or fire.

1. Heb. *'ōmᵉnôt,* "pillars" (better, "supports") at temple doors, overlaid with gold which Hezekiah stripped off for the enemy (II Kgs 18:16), probably the door frames. Emphasis is on function.

2. Heb. *mis'ād,* "support"; made of almug wood for the house of Yahweh (Solomon's temple) from trees brought from Ophir (I Kgs

10:12). Emphasis is on function, though exact arrangement of these pillars in not known.

3. Heb. *muṣṣāb,* "pillar"; a casual reference to a commonly known pillar near Shechem, which could have been used in some sort of worship (Jud 9:6). A standing stone is denoted, with its nearby oak or terebinth tree (NASB).

4. Heb. *n*^{e}*ṣîb,* "pillar"; the natural shape of Lot's wife after being overwhelmed by the eruption that destroyed Sodom (Gen 19:26).

5. Heb. *tîmerôt,* "pillars" (of smoke). Root of the word for date palm (*tāmār*) is used, because the shape of the shaft and head of the smoke column is similar to that of a date palm (Song 3:6; Joel 2:30).

6. Heb. *'ammûd,* the most common word for pillar or column in the OT. It designates a supporting column of a building (Jud 16:25; I Kgs 7:1 ff.); the pillars Jachin (*q.v.*) and Boaz of the temple (I Kgs 7:15; II Kgs 25:16); the silver uprights or posts of Solomon's sedan chair (Song 3:10); and the Shaft of the column of Cloud or fire of the wilderness wanderings (Ex 13:21; etc.).

7. Heb. *maṣṣēbâ* denotes a stone set up on end to act as a marker. In Palestine and Syria there was a predominance of these plain stones with no inscription or carving in relief, whereas in Egypt and Mesopotamia the sculptured and/or inscribed stele was the rule. Such a plain pillar was used in worship of Yahweh by Jacob (Gen 28:18); a memorial of an agreement between Jacob and Laban (Gen 31:45); a memorial to the covenant Yahweh made with Jacob (Gen 35:14); Absalom's pillar which he erected to preserve his name because he had no son (II Sam 18:18). The Heb. term is variously used to designate a gravestone (Gen 35:20), a cultic image (Ex 23:24; Lev 26:1; II Kgs 3:2; 10:26–27), or to commemorate an event or covenant (Ex 24:4). Stone pillars have been found in the Canaanite and Israelite levels of numerous city sites in Palestine and Syria. Whether to be denoted as cultic, commemorative, or structural pillars depends on their location in the plan of the city or building of which they were a part. Some were obviously supporting posts; others had no structural purpose and were clearly markers. The cultic function is often indicated by the position of a standing stone near the entry of a holy place (Gen 28:16–18, 22) or by being set up beside the altar (Ex 34:13; Deut 7:5; Hos 3:4; 10:1–2) to mark the presence of the deity. Israel was commanded to smash these sacred pillars, no doubt because they were equivalent to images of male deities (Ex 23:24; Deut 7:5; 12:3; 16:22).

Sacred pillars (*massebô*) at the Gezer high place. HFV

Stone pillars for roof support, from the Israelite period at Hazor. HFV

Clear examples of *maṣṣēbôt* have been found at Petra, Hazor, Arad, and in conjuction with the temple of Baal-berith at Shechem (Jud 9:4, 46). Rows of standing stones have been excavated at Bab edh-Dra', Byblos (Gebal), Gezer, Hazor, and near the copper mines at Timna. At Gezer ten huge uneven stones, several over ten feet tall, were erected simultaneously *c.*1600 B.C. Graesser suggests these were legal *maṣṣēbôt,* "erected to mark a treaty or covenant relationship between ten groups, either clans inhabiting Gezer or cities in a wider league in the area" (BA, XXXV, 57).

Terms used figuratively are:

8. Heb. *māṣûq,* a molten pillar supporting the earth (I Sam 2:8), symbolic of the power of God whereby "he hangeth the earth upon nothing" (Job 26:7).

9. Gr. *stylos,* "pillars," the title applied to James, Peter, and John as church leaders (Gal 2:9); the church as upholding or supporting the truth (I Tim 3:15); believers as overcomers are to be memorials to God's power (Rev 3:12); the feet of the angel as pillars of fire, signifying judgment to come (Rev 10:1).

Bibliography. W. F. Albright, "The High Place in Ancient Palestine," *Supplement to Vetus Testamentum,* IV, Leiden: Brill, 1957, pp. 242–258. Carl F. Graesser, "Standing Stones in Ancient Palestine," BA, XXXV (1972), 33–63. A. R. Millard, "Pillar," NBD, pp. 998 f. Ulrich Wilckens, "*Stylos,*" TDNT, VII, 732–736.

H. G. S. and J. R.

PILLAR OF FIRE AND OF CLOUD. This succinct phrase occurs only in Ex 14:24. There are a number of occurrences of separate phrases as "pillar of cloud" and "pillar of fire" (cf. Ex 13:21-22; Num 14:14; Neh 9:12, 19; Ps 99:7).

Symbols of divine presence. The Israelites encountered the pillar at the edge of the wilderness and it served as their guide through the crossing of the desert. The cloud by day and the pillar of fire by night advanced in front of the Israelites, revealing to them continuous and perpetual guidance (Ex 13:21-22). When Israel was approached by their enemy, the pillar of cloud moved from the front to the rear of the Israelites' camp, separating the Egyptians from the Israelites (Ex 14:19-20). This phenomenon protected the Israelites and blinded the Egyptians.

The various phenomena. There are varying phenomena in the Pentateuch of the cloud as an indication of the divine presence. In one place, the Lord led the people continuously by moving in front of them in a column of cloud by day and fire by night; this pillar "departed not" (Ex 13:22, ASV) until they arrived in Canaan (Ex 40:38; Num 14:14). A cloud also accompanied the theophany at Sinai as the Lord descended in it and conversed with Moses (Ex 34:5). In another place, the fiery appearance of the cloud is not mentioned and it was not a guide going in front of the people. It came down periodically and stood before the "tent of meeting" (RSV), which was pitched outside the camp (Ex 33:7-11; the Heb. verbs are frequentatives signifying reiterative action; cf. Num 11:25; 12:5, 10; Deut 31:15). Also, Deut 1:33 refers to the cloud on the mountain (Ex 19:16; Deut 4:11; 5:22). In still another place, the account begins with the appearance of a cloud enveloping the glorious presence of the Lord at Mount Sinai (cf. Ex 24:16-18). It appeared in the camp only at the completion of the tabernacle, when it overshadowed the tent of meeting. It continually covered the dwelling until the journeys were completed (Ex 40:34-38; Num 9:15 ff.), and gave the signal for moving the camp by rising above the dwelling (Num 9:17-23; 10:11 ff.). However, these various appearances supplement each other just as the Gospels do the life of the Master.

Influence of natural phenomena. The possibility should be considered that natural phenomena may have influenced the biblical account. In early times braziers containing burning wood were carried at the head of an army or caravan; the fire indicated by night the line of march, as illustrated by Alexander's march through Babylonia and by the general practice of the Persians. This custom is still prevalent in Arabian caravans. Also, during festivals the two pillars (or fiery cressets), Boaz and Jachin, emitted clouds of smoke and flame by day and night. The difference is that this is an account of a theophany. God supplied the light for Israel that men must provide for Alexander. The pillar of cloud and the pillar of fire are symbols of the protective presence of God. Later references occur in Neh 9:12; Ps 78:14; 105:39; cf. I Cor 10:1 ff. Also, further spiritual insight comes as we remember that the phenomenon of "a cloud and smoke by day, and the shining of a flaming fire by night" will be seen over Jerusalem when the Lord dwells there in the Millennium (Isa 4:5).

Bibliography. A. H. McNeile, *The Book of Exodus,* London: Methuen & Co., 1908. J. Pedersen, *Israel,* London: Oxford Univ. Press, 1926, III-IV, 1940. J. C. Rylaarsdam, "Exodus," *The Interpreter's Bible,* New York: Abingdon-Cokesbury Press, 1952. R. de Vaux, *Ancient Israel,* trans, by J. McHugh, New York: McGraw-Hill, 1961.

D. W. D.

PILLOW. The KJV rendering of:

1. Heb. *m^{e}ra'ashōt* (from *rō'sh,* "head"), which literally means a "head-place," as in the NASB margin of Gen 28:11, 18. The term occurs also in I Sam 19:13, 16; 26:7, 11, 12, 16; I Kgs 19:6, referring to the close vicinity where a sleeping man lays his head.

2. Heb. *k^{e}sāthôt* (from Akkad. *kasū,* "to bind"), magic wrist bands (Ezk 13:18, 20; see RSV, NEB, NASB).

3. Heb. *k^{e}bîr,* probably a woven quilt or shawl of black goats' hair (I Sam 19:13, 16). Michal so folded one and covered it as to simulate a man's head with a bit of his black hair showing.

4. Gr. *proskephalaion,* the sailor's or rower's leather-covered cushion on which Jesus slept in the stern of the boat (Mk 4:38).

PILOT. Used by Ezekiel for the leaders of Tyre, either because it would be appropriate as a metaphor for the chief men of a seafaring city, or because sea captains were in such positions. "Pilot" is used in Ezk 27:8 and "shipmaster" in Jon 1:6.

PILTAI (pĭl'tī). One of the leading priests in the days of Joiakim (Neh 12:17).

PIM. A Heb. weight in I Sam 13:21, RSV. *See* Weights, Measures, and Coins.

PIN. Though not mentioned in the Bible, a most common artifact to the Palestinian archaeologist is the pin to fasten clothes; in the early form as a toggle pin (straight) and later a fibula (safety pin). The bronze pegs or tent pins of the tabernacle form the largest usage of the term in the Bible (Ex 27:19; 35:18; 38:20, 31; 39:40; Num 3:37; 4:32). There was also the tent pin of Jael with which she smote Sisera (Jud 4:21; 5:26). Ezk 15:3 mentions the wall peg on which vessels were hung.

The word *yātēd* is also used in Deut 23:13 (RSV) as a spade for digging, and in Jud 16:14 as a stick for beating up the woof in the loom. The term is applied to Zion under the figure of a tent in Isa 33:20 and 54:2, and figuratively of Judah's ruler as pin or perhaps kingpin in support of the nation (Zech 10:4). A similar figurative use is reflected in Isa 22:23–24 where Eliakim is likened to "a nail fastened in a sure place," and in Ezr 9:8 where the remnant's security from the Lord is like a nail in the holy place.

E. B. S.

PINE TREE. *See* Plants.

PINNACLE. A part of the temple mentioned in the temptation of Christ (Mt 4:5; Lk 4:9). Since the definite article is used in the Gr. and not the indefinite as in the KJV, probably there was only one such place. Since it entailed a fearful drop, it would seem most likely to have been located somewhere near the present SE corner of the temple area overlooking the Kidron Valley, where the drop is greatest and the view most extensive. Yet because the Gr. word *pterygion* means "little wing" followed by the Vulg. *pinnaculum,* also meaning "little wing," opinions vary. It might have been the roof of "Solomon's porch" or portico (Jos *Ant.* xv.11.5; *Wars* v.5.1, "cloister"), perhaps at the top of the SE corner of the enclosure found by Herod's covered colonnades (*see* Solomon's porch); one of the battlements on the portico as required in the Mosaic law for any high place (Deut 22:8); or one of the two winglike projections of the front of the temple building which Josephus called "shoulders" (*Wars* v.5.4).

R. A. K.

PINON (pī′nŏn). One of the chiefs of Edom of the family of Esau (Gen 36:41; I Chr 1:52). The word could be the name of the town of which he was the chief. *See* Punon.

PIPE. *See* Music.

PIRAM (pī′răm). The king of Jarmuth, one of the five Amorite kings in the confederacy to repel the invasion by Joshua (Josh 10:3).

PIRATHON (pĭr′ȧ-thŏn), **PIRATHONITE** (pĭr-ȧ-thŏ-nīt). Pirathon was a village in the hill of the Amalekites in the land of Ephraim, where Abdon the son of Hillel was buried (Jud 12:15). Benaiah, a chief captain of David's army, was a Pirathonite, evidently from this village (II Sam 23:30).

PISGAH (pĭz′gȧ). Sometimes identified with Mount Nebo and sometimes with Ras es-Siaghah, a headland connected with Nebo and extending to the NW. Pisgah may, however, refer to the entire peninsula-like ridge which is part of the Abarim Mountains and which extends from the high Moabite plateau toward the NE corner of the Dead Sea. Nebo, about ten miles E of the mouth of the Jordan, is its highest peak. The top (Heb. *ro'sh,* "head") of Pisgah is said to look toward (literally, "overhang") Jeshimon, the wasteland at the N end of the Dead Sea (Num 21:20). This fits exactly the headland of Ras es-Siaghah. There Moses would have a fine vantage point for surveying the Jordan Valley and the mountains of Canaan (Deut 3:27; 34:1). On a clear day one can see Mount Hermon to the N and the towers of the Mount of Olives and Bethlehem to the W.

At the field of Zophim on the top of Pisgah Balaam built seven altars in an attempt to get the Lord to curse Israel (Num 23:14). From this headland, steep slopes drop 2,600 feet into the Jordan-Dead Sea valley (Deut 3:17). Ashdoth-pisgah, "the slopes of Pisgah"(translated "the springs of Pisgah" in Deut 4:49), also marked the S limits of the territory of Sihon, king of the Amorites (Josh 12:3) and was allotted to the tribe of Reuben as part of its inheritance (Josh 13:15, 20–21).

See Nebo 2.

S. M. H.

PISHON. *See* Pison.

PISIDIA (pĭ-sĭd′ĭ-ȧ). This district was about 120 miles long (E-W) and 50 miles wide and was entirely filled by ranges of the Taurus Mountains. It had always been a wild country infested by brigands. Alexander the Great had to fight his way through them as he tried to conquer the interior of Asia Minor. The emperor Augustus, about 25 B.C., determined to reduce these bandits by establishing a chain of posts which included Antioch and Lystra on the northern side. Apparently the Romans felt they had achieved their aim by A.D. 74 when Pisidia was linked to the Pamphylian plain in the province of Pamphylia. Formerly Pisidia had been treated as part of Galatia.

The area of Pisidia was still very dangerous when Paul came through on his first missionary journey (Acts 13:14; 14:24). It is thought that Paul had the journey through Pisidia in mind when he made his autobiographical comment about "perils of robbers" in II Cor 11:26. It is often suggested, too, that the dangers in further missionary activity to the N of Perga caused John Mark to turn back, and for this reason Paul refused to take the young man with him on his second missonary journey (Acts 13:13; 15:37–39). Of course there is no way of knowing whether either supposition is correct.

H. F. V.

PISON (pī′sŏn). One of the four rivers named in connection with Eden (Gen 2:11) and described as draining the land of Havilah (*q.v.*). Another spelling is Pishon (ASV, RSV). If the Gihon River (Gen 2:13) were the Nile, it has been suggested the Pison might have been the Indus in W Pakistan with its early Harappan civilization. Most likely, the Pison was equivalent to a large wadi which now drains the N Arabian desert. *See* Eden.

PISPAH (pĭs′pȧ). A son of Jether named among the men of war in the tribe of Asher (I Chr 7:38). Another spelling is Pispa (ASV, RSV).

PISTACHIO. *See* Plants: Nuts.

PIT. Fifteen different words are translated "pit" in the Bible. Reference is often to cisterns (Gen 37:20; Ex 21:34; Zech 9:11). The Vale of Siddim was full of "slime pits," lit., "bitumen wells" (Gen 14:10). Pits were dug, covered, and baited to trap animals (Ps 7:15; Prov 28:10; Ezk 19:4, 8). Pits might be used as dungeons (Jer 38:6) or as tombs (II Sam 18:17). They were a menace to animals (Mt 12:11) and the blind (Mt 15:14; Lk 6:39). Just such a pit (Lk 14:5) became the awe-inspiring reservoir of apocalyptic judgments (Rev 9:1-2).

One word, *sheʼôl*, which specifically means the abode of the dead (usually rendered "hell" in the KJV and transliterated "sheol" in RSV), is three times rendered "pit" in the KJV (Num 16:30, 33; Job 17:16). Most of the terms were also used metaphorically for the grave or sheol (Ps 28:1; 30:3; Job 33:24; Isa 14:15). *See* Cave; Den; Grave; Sheol.

PITCH. *See* Minerals and Metals: Bitumen.

PITCHER. The translation of three words in the Bible designating containers for liquid.

1. Heb. *kad*, translated improperly as "barrel," four times as "pitcher." Rebekah used the *kad* to water the servant's camels (Gen 24:14-20, 43 ff.). Gideon used pitchers to shield his torches, and the breaking of them indicates they were clay jars (Jud 7:16 ff.). In Eccl 12:6 breaking the pitcher symbolizes the termination of life.

2. Heb. *nēbel*, "storage jar," is used in a figure of the cheapness with which the chiefest sons of Israel will be held in the time of destruction by the sword (Lam 4:2; cf. Jer 48:12).

3. Gr. *kerámion*, "pitcher," "a water container or jug," was the sign of the man who owned the upper chamber (Mk 14:13; Lk 22:10).

See Pottery.

PITHOM (pī'thŏm). One of the two store-cities (Ex 1:11) built for the Egyptians by Israelite forced labor (cf. LXX, which adds, "On, that is Heliopolis"), mentioned only once in the Bible. *See* City, Treasure. The OT does not give specific information to aid in locating the site. Pithom has been sought in the Delta because of its association with Rameses (*q.v.*) which has always been considered a city of Lower Egypt, and because the land of Goshen, the Israelite center in Egypt, was in the eastern part of the Delta. The name is a Hebraized form of the Old Egyptian *pr-itm* (Pi-Tūm), "the house of the god Atum." Since the cult center of Atum was Heliopolis (*see* On), religious association may also suggest a Lower Egyptian site for Pithom.

Various identifications of Pithom have been proposed but none is certain. Edouard Naville excavated at Tell el-Maskhutah in the Wadi Tumilat and was convinced that this was Pithom (see also J. Simons, *Geographical and Topographical Texts of the OT*, p. 245). At present, a common identification, supported by A. H. Gardiner and W. F. Albright, is Tell er-Retâbeh, situated about eight miles W of Tell el-Maskhutah, which now is regarded by many as Succoth (*q.v.;* see JEA, V [1918], 267-269; X [1924], 95-96; ANET, p. 259).

C. E. D.

PITHON (pī'thŏn). A grandson of Meribbaal, another name for Mephibosheth (*q.v.*), Jonathan's son (I Chr 8:34-35; 9:40-41).

PITY. Pity is to be distinguished from compassion. One who is weak or defenseless is pitied; one who is reduced to want or is suffering from a misfortune receives compassion. God expects His children to show pity, particularly to the poor (Prov 19:17; cf. Mt 5:7). The rich man in Nathan's parable, David judged worthy of death since he had no pity (II Sam 12:5-6). God shows pity to those who fear Him (Ps 103:13; cf. Ezk 36:21).

Yet there were sins which God considered so serious He forbade Israel to show pity, such as idolatry (Deut 7:16), particularly among their own children (Deut 13:8), and murder (Deut 19:13, 21; cf. 25:12). There were times when God withdrew His pity because of Israel's sin (Jer 13:14; Lam 2:2; Ezk 5:11; etc.). *See* Compassion; Kindness; Mercy.

R. A. K.

PLACE. In general a locale defined by the context. Certain places have assumed especial importance in redemptive history because of the action of God or His people. The "place" of Eden (Gen 2:8) is not known geographically, but it is very significant theologically because of the Fall. Yahweh said He would choose a place (*maqôm*) to put His name, i.e., designate a place for His temple (Deut 12:5), Moriah being that place. Jesus was crucified significantly enough at the "place [*topos*] of the skull" (Mt 27:33). Judas, who betrayed Christ, went to his own place (*topos*) as his proper abode, i.e., Hades. According to His promise in Jn 14:2-3, Christ is preparing a place (*topos*) for His own, called "mansions" (dwelling places).

Bibliography. Helmut Köster, "*Topos,*" TDNT, VIII, 187-208.

PLAGUE. A plague may be any form of trouble or harassment, but the term most often has reference to evil, or to disease of pestilential proportions, epidemic in its occurrence and fatal in its effects.

In Bible times there were sudden epidemics such as leprosy (Lev 13:14; Deut 24:8). A common plague which came with great suddenness and caused death in from half a day to three days appears to have been the bubonic plague. Some think this was the cause of the death of the firstborn in Egypt (Ex 11:1; cf. I Sam 4:8), though the biblical event appears to be too selective for this. It does seem, however, to account for several instances of plagues experienced on the wilderness journey, such as in Num 11:33 which is synchronous with the flight of the quails. Such birds would have been able to carry the plague to the Israelites.

Other instances of God's use of a plague to punish unbelief and sin were at the return of the spies with their evil report on the land (Num 14:37), at the destruction of Korah and his followers (Num 16:47), and at Baal-peor (Num 25:8–9, 18; 26:1; Josh 22:17; Ps 106:29–30; cf. I Sam 5:6; 6:5; II Sam 24:15; I Chr 21:12). Sennacherib's army was destroyed by a sudden plague (II Kgs 19:35; Isa 37:36). In I Cor 15:55 Paul quotes Hos 13:14 concerning the plagues (Heb. *deber*) of death.

The book of Revelation speaks of many plagues in the last days (Rev 9:20; 11:6; 15:1, 6, 8; 16:9, 21; 18:4, 8; 21:9; 22:18). Zech 14:12, 15, 18 foretell a plague in the Millennium which God will use against those nations that are disobedient to the Messiah and fail to come and worship Him.

R. A. K.

The plagues of Egypt combine all aspects of biblical plagues. These events are elucidated by an examination of the Heb. terms applied to the plagues. Several of the words are derived from the root *nāgap,* "strike, smite," and indicate the plagues as a smiting by God as punishment or judgment. Heb. *negep* is a "blow, striking," used as a term of judgment. It is found in connection with the Egyptian plagues only in Ex 12:13, which concerns the death of the firstborn. Heb. *maggēpâ* also is "blow, slaughter, plague, pestilence" (BDB, p. 620), applied to the plague only in Ex 9:14, which is a general reference to these events.

From the root *nāga',* "touch, reach, strike," comes *nega',* "stroke, plague," which is used metaphorically of disease as divine chastisement. In the Exodus narrative it appears only in 11:1, where it refers to the smiting of the firstborn. These terms indicate the direct action of God in judgment; other biblical terms and statements show that these acts testified to the power and unique deity of God (cf. Deut 4:34–35).

Ps 78:43 and 105:27 call the plagues "signs" and "wonders," or "miracles" (RSV). The word *'ôt,* "sign," has a variety of meanings, such as "pledge, token, memorial, reminder, symbol." Here it means "signs, miracles, as pledges or attestations of divine presence and interposition" (BDB, p. 16. See also Ex 4:8–9, 17; 7:3; 8:19; etc.). A "wonder, miracle, sign, portent" is *môpēt,* applied to wondrous displays of the power of God (Ex 4:21; 7:3; 11:9–10; Ps 105:5; etc.).

The extensive use of such terms demonstrates that the plagues were primarily works of God intended to exhibit His deity and to enforce His will. In summarizing what He was doing in these events, God called them "signs and wonders" and "great acts of judgment," with the declared result that "the Egyptians shall know that I am the Lord, when I stretch forth mine hand upon Egypt, and bring out the children of Israel from among them" (Ex 7:3–5).

An immediate effect of the plagues was to get the Israelites out of Egypt and on their way back to the land of promise. In the providence of God, Israel had been sent to Egypt; now the time for the Exodus had come and was conditioned on the human level by an intensity of affliction that caused the Israelites to cry for help (Ex 2:23–25; 3:7–8). To carry out His plan, the Lord secured their release by sending ten great plagues upon their Egyptian oppressors.

The Nile god Hapi represented as a bull. LM

1. *Water to blood* (Ex 7:14–25; Ps 78:44; 105:29). Water is essential to life everywhere, but the awareness of this dependence is particularly acute in a land such as Egypt, where the Nile is its life stream (*see* Nile; Egypt). God instructed Moses to strike the water with his rod and the water would become blood.

Naturalistic interpreters point to the color of the Nile at inundation time and state that organic material in the water gives the river a reddish or blood-like appearance. The text, however, does not indicate that this event occurred during the inundation. The statement that the Egyptians "dug round about the Nile for water to drink" (Ex 7:24, RSV) indicates that the stream was in its normal channel. The reference to canals, ponds, etc., in Ex 7:19 also shows that the inundation was not in progress, for at flood time the whole land is a sheet of water. Furthermore, the color of the Nile during flood is brown rather than red and can hardly be described as like blood in appearance. Ex 7:19 extends the plague to rivers, canals, ponds, pools of water, and even to the vessels in which water was carried and stored. The solely natural explanation of this plague flies in the face of the text. The Egyptians normally drank the water of the river; now it was impossible for them to do so. The death of the fish (Ex 7:21) also

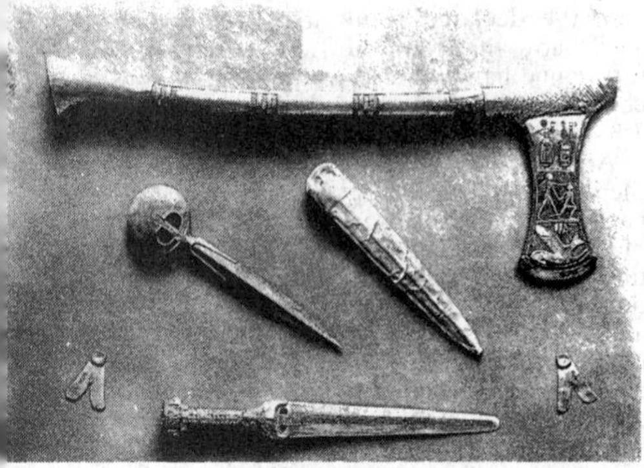

Egyptian military decorations in the form of flies appear in the lower corners. LL

shows that something unusual had happened to the water. If the strange color of the Nile were a matter of annual occurrence, it would not have impressed the Egyptians, who were close observers and measurers of the river.

The magicians, wise men, and sorcerers opposed Moses and Aaron (Ex 7:11–12; cf. II Tim 3:8) and they successfully imitated this plague by their magical arts (Ex 7:22). The extent of their success is not told, but it was sufficient to impress Pharaoh. The fact that drinking water could be obtained by digging near the river to get percolated water shows God's tempering of the plague.

Various gods are associated with the river. A deity who symbolized the beneficent nature of the Nile was named Hapi and was represented as a man with pendulous breasts carrying in his hands tokens of the fruitfulness of the river. This plague, then, served also to destroy the reputation of the river deities.

2. *Frogs* (Ex 8:1–15; Ps 78:45; 105:30). Seven days after Moses struck the Nile he appeared before the king with another ultimatum. When this was rejected, Moses extended his rod over the waters and frogs appeared everywhere. The magicians also produced frogs (Ex 8:7), but the king was not impressed, for he was concerned with the riddance not the production of frogs. The number of frogs compelled Pharaoh to make a temporary agreement with Moses and Aaron. The departure of the frogs was effected at a set time (Ex 8:9–11). It is impossible that such a widespread killing of frogs could be predicted and accomplished on schedule by wholly natural means. When the plague ceased, Pharaoh changed his mind and hardened his heart.

The frog-headed goddess Heket is often mentioned in connection with this plague. She was a relatively insignificant divinity and no mention of her appears in the Bible.

3. *Lice* (Ex 8:16–19; Ps 105:31). The meaning of the Heb. *kinnîm* is uncertain, though the LXX, Vulgate, and most commentators give "gnats" or "gnat-swarm" rather than "lice." They were small insects that plagued man and beast. Moses was not told to forewarn Pharaoh of the coming of this scourge. The magicians were not able to bring forth gnats. This was their first recorded failure and they confessed that the plague was "the finger of God" (Ex 8:19).

Some commentators have sought a natural association between the insects and the dead frogs; v. 17 associates the plague with the dust of the ground. The text makes no statement concerning the cessation of this plague. Residents in Egypt may feel that this is significant, but one must conclude that this plague was lifted as were the others.

4. *Swarms* (Ex 8:20-32; Ps 78:45; 105:31). The Heb. *'ārov* is usually taken as "swarm," and is generally assumed to be swarms of flies. The swarms could have consisted of beetles (*scarabae*), which represented one of their chief gods, Khephera. This plague is the first instance of separation between the Israelites in Goshen and the Egyptians in the rest of the land. The king was willing to let the people go, but again retracted when the swarms were removed. It is of interest to note that amulets or ornaments in the form of flies, sometimes of gold, are fairly frequent in various periods of Egyptian history.

5. *Pestilence affecting the livestock* (Ex 9:1–7). The Heb. *dever* refers to a form of pestilence, and since it is restricted here to cattle or domestic animals, it is termed a "murrain" in the KJV. A time was specified for the beginning of this plague, and again a distinction was made between Israel and Egypt. Pharaoh checked to see if this difference really existed, but he refused to let the Israelites go. Several Egyptian deities were represented by domestic beasts—Apis the bull-god, Hathor the cow-goddess, Khnum the ram-god, and Mnevis the bull-god.

6. *Boils* (Ex 9:8–12). Moses and Aaron were instructed to take ashes from the kiln and to throw it into the air. After they did this, sores and boils broke out on man and beast. The affliction on the magicians receives singular

The temple of Hathor, the cow-goddess, at Denderah, Egypt. LL

PLAGUE

mention; they were not able to stand before Moses (Ex 9:11). Pharaoh had hardened his heart many times; now the Lord confirmed his attitude and we read that "the Lord hardened the heart of Pharaoh" (Ex 9:12).

7. *Hail* (Ex 9:13–35; Ps 78:48; 105:32–33). The prediction of this plague was prefaced by a repeated statement of the great purpose of the plagues: "to show you my power, so that my name may be declared throughout all the earth" (v. 16, RSV). The hail was predicted to affect all of Egypt except Goshen, but in this case the Egyptians were warned to put their cattle within shelter. This is another evidence of the Lord's tempering judgment with mercy. The Egyptians who had come to fear the word of the Lord preserved their cattle (Ex 9:20), but there was nothing that could be done to save the crops.

When Moses stretched out his hand toward the sky, the storm began, including heavy hail, thunder and lightning. Everything unprotected from the storm was destroyed; men and animals were killed and all plants were destroyed. In any agricultural country the impact of this devastation was very great. Also it was a distinct blow to faith in the sky-goddess Nut.

On this occasion the king sent for Moses and Aaron to confess that he had sinned this time and to ask them to entreat the Lord to end the storm. Along with this he agreed to let the people go. Moses told him that the Lord would stop the storm as soon as Moses had gone outside the city (9:29). With the halting of the storm, Pharaoh again changed his mind. In this plague there is indication of the time of year by agricultural references. The storm occurred early in the calendar year, for the barley was headed and the flax was in bud. The wheat and spelt were not injured, however, for they were not up as yet (9:31–32).

8. *Locusts* (Ex 10:1–20; Ps 78:46; 105:34–35). Locusts are a frequent threat to crops in many parts of the Near East, but this was "such a dense swarm of locusts as had never been before, nor ever shall be again" (Ex 10:14, RSV). They consumed all that was left after the hail. The goddess Isis was considered to be the protectress against locusts. Pharaoh hastily summoned Moses and Aaron and again confessed his fault and asked forgiveness and the removal of "this death," as he described the locust invasion. The Lord used an E wind to bring the locusts and a very strong W wind to drive them into the Red Sea.

9. *Darkness* (Ex 10:21–29; Ps 105:28). In response to Moses' outstretched hand, the Lord without warning sent upon Egypt an intense darkness, "a darkness to be felt" (Ex 10:21–22, RSV), which continued for three days. All activity stopped among the Egyptians, but the Israelites had light in their part of Egypt. This was a judgment against the numerous sun-gods of Egypt, Re, Khepri, Harakhte, Atum, etc. Pharaoh was so moved by this phenomenon that he was willing to let the people go, but he stipulated that they must leave their flocks and herds behind. When Moses rejected this condition, Pharaoh refused to let the people go.

Horus (left), Osiris (center), Isis (right). Isis was supposed to protect against locusts. LM

10. *Death of the firstborn* (Ex 11:1–10; 12:29–32; Ps 78:51; 105:36). Moses next announced to Pharaoh that the firstborn of both men and cattle were to be slain at about midnight. As a result of many deaths, a great cry would go up throughout Egypt (*see* Mourn). The distinction between Egypt and Israel was very pronounced; though every Egyptian household would suffer a death, not a dog would growl against man or beast of Israel. The Israelites had an obligation of obedience laid upon them, for the celebration of the Passover was inaugurated on this occasion. The blood of a slain lamb must be applied to the doorways of their houses as a symbol of identity, for God was to pass through Egypt to smite the firstborn and to execute judgment on all the gods of Egypt (Ex 12:12). The great sorrow and loss which reached every Egyptian household included the royal palace; the royal heir died that night. Pharaoh again called Moses and Aaron and permitted the Israelites to leave Egypt at last.

General. The relation of the plagues to the Egyptian scene is often pointed out, sometimes to show their local color and the historicity of the narrative, and sometimes to attempt to explain away their divine origin. The flora, fauna, climatic, and seasonal phenomena, and even religious and social features of Egypt are accurately represented. The text makes it clear that the Egyptians recognized (1) in the intensity and severity of the plagues that these were more than natural occurrences. The supernatural character of these events is also shown by their (2) progression in severity and by (3) the fact that they came and went at the command, prayer, or prediction of God's spokesman. (4) The designed sparing of the Israelites also demonstrated that the plagues were under God's control.

In addition, the plagues revealed the inadequacy or non-existence of the Egyptian gods, for these divinities were powerless to protect themselves or anything else from the omnipotence of the only true God (Ex 12:12). In certain of the plagues the religious significance of the act is immediately apparent; in others it is not possible to associate some great god of the vast Egyptian pantheon. In every case, however, there was a violation of a very important principle in Egyptian religion and world view. Basic to the Egyptian understanding was the idea of *ma'at,* "truth, right," which probably is to be understood as "the right and proper order in the universe." Since the plagues were disturbances of this order, they affected the basic psychology of the people. The cumulative effects, physical, emotional, and economic, exercised an irresistible influence on the Egyptians, and eventually even the proud king, regarded as himself divine, was forced to submit to God's will for His people.

C. E. D.

On the throne of King Tutankhamon appears the sun-disk with life-giving rays, symbol of the god Aton. LL

PLAIN. The most important plains in Palestine are the coastal plain, the plain of Esdraelon or Jezreel or Megiddo, and the Jordan Valley. Much of the best agricultural trade and military routes passed through them.

Scripture also mentions the plain of Shinar (Gen 10:10; 11:2; *et al.*), and applies the term

The Jordan River wends its way through the plain of the Jordan. MPS

to the greater part, if not the whole, of Babylonia.

"Plain" is the KJV translation of:

1. Heb. *'ābēl,* "meadow," transliterated by RSV as part of the name Abel-keramim (Jud 11:33).

2. Heb. *'ēlôn,* "oak," rightly so translated by RSV in Gen 12:6; 13:18; Jud 4:11; 9:6, 37; *et al.*

3. Heb. *biq'â,* "broad plain," the plain near Babylon (Gen 11:2); the plain of Ono, part of the coastal plain (Neh 6:2); the plain of Megiddo (II Chr 35:22, RSV; KJV "valley").

4. Heb. *kikkār,* "circle," the plain containing Sodom and Gomorrah, probably S of the Dead Sea (Gen 13:12, RSV "valley"); the plain near Jericho (Deut 34:3, RSV "valley").

5. Heb. *mîshôr,* "level land," the tableland or plateau of Moab (Deut 3:10, RSV).

6. Heb. *'ărābâ,* "steppe" or "wilderness," the western slopes of Moab (Num 22:1); as a name for the Jordan Valley often transliterated Arabah by RSV (Deut 3:17).

7. Heb. *shepēlâ,* "lowland," especially of the low hill country or foothills between the coastal plain and the central ridge of Palestine, often transliterated Shephelah by RSV (e.g., Ob 19).

8. Gr. *pedinos* (Lk 6:17), RSV "level place" in Galilee, perhaps on the side of the mountain where Jesus preached (Mt 5:1).

Bibliography. D. Baly, *Geography of the Bible,* New York: Harper, 1957. E. Robinson, *Physical Geography of the Holy Land,* Boston: Crocker and Brewster, 1865, pp. 125–142. G. A. Smith, *Historical Geography of the Holy Land,* 25th ed., London: Hodder and Stoughton, 1931. A. R. Stanley, *Sinai and Palestine,* New York: Widdleton, 1865, pp. 478–485.

J. A. T.

PLAINS OF PALESTINE. *See* Palestine.

PLAISTER

1. A poultice of figs (Isa 38:21) for medicinal purpose. This was a plaster of fig paste laid over Hezekiah's boil to soften it and draw it to a head.

2. *See* Minerals and Metals.

PLAITING. *See* Hair.

PLANE. *See* Chisel.

PLANE TREE. *See* Plants: Chestnut.

PLANK. A thick board, slab of wood, or joist, used in the floor of Solomon's temple (I Kgs 6:15), and on the floor and porch of the temple in Ezekiel's vision (Ezk 41:25–26). ASV uses plank to describe pieces of the ship used as life preservers in Paul's shipwreck (Acts 27:44).

Four other Heb. words for plank are used in Ex 26:15; I Kgs 7:36; I Kgs 6:36; I Kgs 6:9.

PLANTS. The lands of the Bible present vast extremes both of climate and geography. Conditions range from the snow-covered tops of the Lebanon Mountains to the deserts of Sinai and Arabia. The lush undergrowth of the Jordan Valley lies but a few miles from the high, fertile plateau of Gilead, while the sandy coastal plain of Sharon rises up into the foothills that lead the way to the mountains around Jerusalem. Within these lands there is an amazing variety of vegetation, about 2,300 different species.

This article treats only of the flora named in the Bible, a very small percentage of the trees, flowers, and vegetables actually to be found in the Near East. Since the Bible is concerned with spiritual not botanical truth, plants are seldom mentioned in connection with the historical narrative, but the interest and love of nature of the ancient people appears on every page. They lived a life very close to nature and their thoughts are expressed in terms of the living world about them.

Attempt is made here to identify the different trees and plants as well as to indicate their uses and values in Bible times. Such identification is not always possible or certain. Sometimes the original word is simply descriptive, e.g., "white tree" or a general term like "thorn." The botanist attempts to identify from the context by the stated use of the plant or by its description just which of a number of possible species is intended. This means that different authorities will often come to different conclusions. In addition, the English versions of the Bible have been inconsistent, translating the same word in several different ways, or different words in the same way. On many identifications the versions disagree considerably among themselves. In spite of all the difficulties, most of the biblical flora have been identified with a fair degree of certainty.

It should be remembered that the Holy Land in particular has undergone tremendous changes since the days of Abraham. Great cultures have risen and fallen. Where once great forests existed, there are now only bare hillsides. What was once intensely cultivated with fields and orchards has been for centuries barren waste. Since the restoration of the state of Israel in 1948 extensive reclamation has been done. Reforestation programs, irrigation, and the application of modern agricultural knowledge to the ancient land is making much of it blossom as the rose. Palestine may again appear as it did to the ancient Israelites, a land flowing with milk and honey.

In this comprehensive article on the plants of the Bible, *q.v.* refers to other listings within the article.

Almonds in blossom in February in the Valley of Jezreel. IIS

Acacia. *See* Plants: Shittah, Shittim.

Algum (Heb. *'algûmmîm*). Although many commentators assume that the algum is the same as the almug tree (*see* Plants: Almug), the Scripture, at least in II Chr 2:8, suggests that it is different. Here it is not an import but a tree from Lebanon to be used in Solomon's temple. It has been identified with the Grecian juniper, *Juniperus excelsa,* a great pyramidal-shaped tree that grows to the height of 65 feet.

Almond (Heb. *shāqēd*). The Heb. name means "awakening" and the almond tree, *Amydalus communis,* was welcomed in Palestine as the harbinger of spring (Jer 1:11–12). The beautiful pink and white blossoms that cover it in January and February were a promise of new life and a symbol of hope (VBW, I, 217). In the era of the Maccabees when Israel seemed to have a new national beginning, the almond was pictured on the shekel. As early as the time of Jacob (Gen 43:11) the nuts are mentioned as one of the products of the land, and Jordan almonds and their oil are still a well-known export. The rod of Aaron that budded and bore fruit as a sign of the blessing and choosing of the Lord was an almond (Num 17:8). The almond flower was an artistic decoration on the seven-branched lampstand (Ex 25:31–38). The tree is slightly larger than a peach tree and grows from Spain to China, the best being found in Syria.

Almug (Heb. *'almûggîm*). This costly wood, imported from Ophir by Solomon (I Kgs 10:11–12), is probably the red sandalwood, *Pterocarpus santalinus.* This tree, which grows up to 20 feet in height, is a native of India and Ceylon, and its fragrant, beautifully grained red wood is still widely used there. It would be unsuitable for the great beams of the temple (*see* Plants: Algum), but is still used for musical instruments such as were made for Solomon. Also from almug wood his craftsmen made supports (RSV) or stools (NEB, I Kgs 10:12) and steps (RSV following LXX), floorboards (JerusB), or stands (NEB, II Chr 9:11) for the temple.

Aloes (Heb. *'ăhālôth;* Gr. *aloē*). Although translated alike in English, the OT and NT refer to different species.

1. The OT references are to the lign aloe or aloes tree, probably the *Aquilaria agallocha* or eaglewood. This is a great tree towering 100 to 120 feet; therefore it was thought of as being planted by the Lord (Num 24:6). A native of India and Malaya, the inner wood as well as the resin is fragrant and widely used in perfumery (Ps 45:8; Prov 7:17; Song 4:14). It is called paradise wood because according to legend Adam brought a shoot from the garden of Eden. In ancient times it was literally worth its weight in gold.

2. Although identified by some with 1, the NT aloes is probably the true or "bitter" aloes, *Aloe succotrina,* a native of the island of Socotra in the Indian Ocean. This is a succulent plant with thick fleshy leaves. From the leaves is pressed aloin, a bright violet liquid which was mixed with water and added to sweet-smelling spices for use in embalming (Jn 19:39). The bitter juice was also condensed and used as a purgative. The imported drug was, of course, very expensive.

Anemone. *See* Plants: Lily.

Anise (Gr. *anethon*). The anise known today was rare if known at all in Bible times. The plant meant is the common garden herb, dill (RSV), *Anethum graveolens.* The brown, hard, oval seeds were used then as now for flavoring food. It was also used medicinally. In their excessive zeal for the law, the Pharisees tithed even these tiny seeds (Mt 23:23). *See* Plants: Cummin, Dill.

Apple (Heb. *tappûaḥ*). Although excellent apples are now produced in Palestine, most authorities agree that this is not the fruit called in Heb. *tappûaḥ*. In ancient times apples were small, hard, and bitter, much like the crab apple. The fruit described as "apples of gold in pictures of silver" (Prov 25:11) and enjoyed for its fragrance (Song 7:8) was most likely the apricot, *Prunus armeniaca.* This orange colored, delicious fruit (Song 2:5) is still called "golden apple" in Gr. Some writers suggest the quince and others the citron (cf. Plants: Goodly Trees), but the latter is a green, hard, bitter fruit and is not at all suitable. The orange, proposed by others, was not known in Palestine in ancient days. It is only a popular legend that the apple was the forbidden fruit of Eden. Even so, the apricot fits the description better (Gen 3:6). The apricot tree is 12 to 20 feet tall with dense foliage on its spreading branches (Song 2:3; 8:5; Joel 1:12—all NEB).

In the expression "apple of the eye," apple (lit., "little man") probably refers to the tiny image a man sees of himself reflected in the pupil of another person's eye (Deut 32:10; Ps 17:8; Prov 7:2). *See* Eye.

Apricot. *See* Plants: Apple.

Ash (Heb. *'ōren*). Mentioned only in Isa 44:14 (KJV); the RSV calls it "cedar" while the LXX and Vulg. translate "pine." Modern authorities agree that it was an evergreen and most identify it as a pine. Zohary contends that it was the laurel (cf. Plants: Bay Tree).

Balm, Balsam (Heb. *ṣ^eri, ṣorî*). Balm is a medicinal gum or resin used from earliest times (Jer 8:22; 46:11; 51:8). Two trees native to Palestine have been suggested for the references in Gen 37:25; 43:11: the Jericho balsam, *Balanites Aegyptica,* and the lentisk tree, *Pistachia lentiscus.* The former is an evergreen shrub, nine by 15 feet in height that bears a green apple-like fruit that turns purple when ripe. A sweet oil extracted from the crushed fruit as well as the resin from the bark was used as an ingredient in medicine until the 17th cen. A.D., and is still sold by monks in Jericho as the true "balm of Gilead." Because *Balanites* abounds in Egypt as well as Palestine, some authorities believe that the balm brought to Egypt must have been the *Pistachia lentiscus.* This shrubby evergreen exudes a fragrant sap known commercially as "mastic." The better grades of the resin, astringent and aromatic, are used in medicine and the hardened drops are the universal chewing gum of the East. Oil from the berries was used both for food and illumination by the Arabs, and the light, flexible twigs are used in basketry. *See* Plants: Terebinth.

The *Commiphora opobalsamum,* also called *Balsamodendron opobalsamum,* is indigenous to S Arabia, especially Yemen. According to Josephus, it was introduced into Palestine by Solomon who received it as a gift from the Queen of Sheba. When the bark of this small straggly evergreen is pierced, it bleeds a gum very costly and highly prized in ancient times. This may be the balm mentioned in Jer 8:22; 46:11; Ezk 27:17 as being brought from Gilead or Israel. Apparently it was an article carried by the trading caravans from Arabia which had to come through Gilead at that particular time in history.

Barley (Heb. *s^e'ōrâ*; Gr. *krithē*). The Heb. name means "long hair" and aptly describes the long spiny hairs on the barley heads. Several varieties of *Hordeum* are found in Palestine and have been cultivated from antiquity. Barley was the chief grain food for horses, mules, and donkeys, oats being unknown. It was also the food of the poor, ground and made into bread. The famine conditions of II Kgs 7:1, 16 are marked by the high price of barley flour, and it was with this bread of the poor that Jesus fed the multitudes (Jn 6:9). Barley was sown in Palestine in October to November and harvested at Passover time, thus making it the earliest of the grain harvests.

Bay Tree. The translation of Ps 37:35, "like a green bay tree," is misleading because no specific tree is mentioned. The NASB, "like a luxuriant tree in its native soil," is a more correct version. Various authorities have tried to determine which particular green tree best fits the context, so the RSV following the LXX says "cedar of Lebanon." Since the word *'ezraḥ* means literally "a native tree" the majority of authorities seem to agree that the *Laurus nobilis,* called the bay laurel, sweet bay, rose laurel, etc., was meant. This is an evergreen rising 40 to 60 feet, a towering rather than a spreading tree. The leaves have a sweet spicy fragrance, and an extract for perfumed oil was made from them. The Greeks and Romans made chaplets of bay leaves for their heroes and victors. The roots and bark are still used medicinally. An attractive and useful tree, it would be a good symbol for prosperity. *See* Plants: Ash.

Bdellium (Heb. *b^e^dōlaḥ*). Bdellium is referred to only twice; as a product of the land of Havilah in Gen 2:12, and in Num 11:6–7 to describe the appearance of manna. It is probably the odoriferous gum resin of the African bdellium, *Commiphora africana.* When the bark of this tree is incised it exudes a gum that forms into white pearl-like beads about the size of an olive. These beads become transparent and waxlike and give a delightful perfume. Women in biblical times carried the perfumed drops around in little bags like a sachet. Moffatt denies that bdellium is a plant at all and translates the word "bedolach-pearls."

Beans (Heb. *pôl*). The beans of Palestine were the horse bean, *Faba vulgaris.* They were widely cultivated by the Egyptians, Greeks, and Romans, and were either cooked in the pods or shelled like white or lima beans. Eaten chiefly by the poor in earlier days, the horse bean is now grown chiefly for cattle fodder. Beans are mentioned as part of the food brought by Barzillai to David fleeing from Absalom (II Sam 17:27–28) and as a component of the strange bread Ezekiel was to prepare (Ezk 4:9).

Bitter Herbs. This descriptive term can be applied to many plants. The Hebrews were to eat "bitter herbs" in connection with the Passover to remind them of the bitter slavery from which God redeemed them (Ex 12:8; Num 9:11). According to rabbinic tradition in the Mishnah (Pesahim 2:6), the herbs were wild lettuce, chicory, pepperwort, snakewort, and dandelion. Other herbs with a sharp or bitter taste grow in Palestine and have been suggested, such as endive, water cress, and *Centaurea,* the century plant which grows in the desert. The legal statement of the rabbis, however, probably preserves ancient tradition.

Box Tree (Heb. *t^e^'ashshûr*). The box tree is mentioned in Isa 41:19; 60:13 along with the fir and pine. While some authorities contend that it is unlikely that the box tree would be listed with such towering evergreens, Moldenke *et al.* identify it as the Syrian box, *Buxus longifolia.* This hardy evergreen found in northern Palestine, Galilee, and Lebanon, is a slender tree, not more than six to eight inches in diameter and 15 to 20 feet in height. The wood is very hard with a fine grain that takes a fine polish and is much used for wood carving and turning. The RSV calls it "pine."

Bramble, Briers. *See* Plants: Thorns.

Branch. *See* Branch.

Broom Tree (Heb. *rōtem*). Translated "juniper" in I Kgs 19:4–5; Job 30:4; Ps 120:4, but "broom tree" in RSV. This is a desert shrub providing scant but welcome shade. It makes excellent charcoal, which burns with intense heat for a long time. *See* Plants: Juniper.

Bulrush. *See* Plants: Reed.

Bush

1. God manifested Himself to Moses by the wondrous sight of a bush that burned with fire and yet was not consumed (Ex 3:2). No particular plant is designated and it is apparent that this was a miraculous event. Nevertheless many have sought to find some type of bush that naturally fits the description. Most often suggested is the gas plant or fraxinella, *Dictamnus alba,* a shrub covered with tiny oil glands that produce a volatile gas. The gas might burn without consuming the bush, and conceivably God might have used such a bush. It has even been suggested that what Moses saw was simply the glowing red berries of the mistletoe, *Loranthis acaciae,* which covered the bush. This impugns the intelligence of Moses as well as the credibility of the report. In Ex 3:2–4 and Deut 33:16 Heb. *s^e^neh* and in Mk 12:26; Lk 20:37; Acts 7:30, 35 Gr. *batos* refer to the same event and simply mean a bramble or thorn bush. The Gr. word also occurs in Lk 6:44. *See* Burning Bush.

2. The Heb. word *śîaḥ* is a general term for any bush or shrub found in a dry country (Gen 2:5, NASB). Under such a bush Hagar put Ishmael (Gen 21:15). Job describes the famished among the bushes (Job 30:4, 7).

3. The Heb. *nahălōlîm,* from the verb *nāhal,* to lead to a watering place, is found in Isa 7:19 and translated "bush" in KJV, and "pasture" in ASV and RSV. As to the regular meaning of the noun it should be translated "watering places."

Calamus (Heb. *qāneh*). The words "sweet cane" and "sweet calamus" are the same in Heb. (Ex 30:23; Jer 6:20) and are probably the same as "calamus" (Song 4:14; Ezk 27:19). This sweet-smelling cane was probably ginger grass, *Andropogon aromaticus,* one of a whole group known as Indian grass oils, including citronella, *A. nardus,* and *A. schoenanthus* which are also known to have been used in biblical times. It was a constituent of the sacred anointing oil (Ex 30:23) and used in connection with sacrifice (Jer 6:20). This grass or cane from India was indeed from a "far country" (Jer 6:20). Tyre exchanged her merchandise with traders from Arabia for calamus (Ezk 27:19). The bruised leaves give a fresh, gingery

Cedars of Lebanon. HFV

smell that was much relished in the East. *See* Plants: Sweet Cane.

Camphire (Heb. *kōpher*). This is not to be confused with the camphor tree, native to China and unknown in Bible times. The camphire or henna plant is *Lawsonia innermis,* a small shrub or tree reaching about ten feet in height. In Palestine it is found in the tropical region of En-gedi and Jericho. It bears cream-colored flowers that hang in clusters like grapes and are very highly scented with a fragrance like a rose. It is the lovely fragrance referred to in Song 1:14; 4:13. Although not mentioned in the Bible, the reddish-orange dye, known as henna and obtained from the leaves, was widely used by both men and women to dye the hair as well as the fingers and nails and the soles of the feet. The tree is widely scattered through Palestine, Arabia, Egypt, and N Africa.

Cane. *See* Plants: Calamus, Sweet Cane.

Caperberry (Heb. *'ăbîyônâ*). This word is found only in some modern translations of Eccl 12:5, and is usually translated "desire" (KJV, RSV). The actual reference is to the caperberry, *Capparis spinosa,* a spiny, trailing plant growing in clefts in the rocks and old walls (VBW, IV, 176). "Capers," the pickled buds of the plant, are still used as a condiment or appetizer. The caperberry was supposed to be an aphrodisiac or stimulant to sexual desire, and the point of the reference is that in old age even "the caperberry is ineffective" (NASB).

Carob. *See* Plants: Husks.

Cassia (Heb. *qiddâ, qeṣî'â*). Although some hold that the two words translated cassia refer to the same thing, there is probably a distinction.

1. Heb. *qiddâ* means "peeled." This ingredient of the holy anointing oil (Ex 30:24), one of the exotic items of ancient Tyrian merchandise (Ezk 27:19), is *cassia lignea,* strips of bark from the fragrant tree, *Cinnamomum cassia*. Cassia has the flavor and aroma of true cinnamon (*see* Plants: Cinnamon) but is less delicate. It was used as a spice and the buds were used like cloves in cooking.

2. The Heb. word *qeṣî'â* occurs in Ps 45:8. If it is not the same as 1, as many authorities contend, then the cassia that perfumed the garments of the king may be the Indian orris, *Saussurea lappa*. The roots of this strong, thistle-like plant are still dried and shipped in great quantities from the Kashmir region of India. It is used medicinally and as an aphrodisiac, but chiefly in perfume and incense.

Cedar (Heb. *'erez*). The Heb. word indicates a strong, firmly rooted tree. Two or three different trees have been identified because of the varying contexts in which the word is used.

1. Since the true cedar does not grow in the wilderness of Sinai, it has been suggested that the cedar to be used for purification (Num 19:6; Lev 14:4, 6, 49, 51 ff.) was the brown berried juniper, *Juniperus oxycedrus,* or the savin juniper, *Sabina vulgaris*. These are low growing, shrub-like straggly trees, 15 to 20 feet tall, common in the craggy mountain wastes and deserts of Palestine and Syria (VBW, III, 113). *See* Plants: Heath.

2. The "cedar trees beside the waters" of Num 24:6 are thought not to be cedars because they do not ordinarily grow near water. No identification has been made.

3. The cedar usually referred to, often by name, is the cedar of Lebanon (Ps 29:5), the great *Cedrus libani,* one of the noblest and most beautiful of all trees. These giant trees grow to a height of 120 or more feet with a circumference as much as 40 feet. They are often dome-shaped, with long, contorted, spreading branches, evergreen needles, and cones three to five inches long. See VBW, I, 190; III, 190.

The vast cedar groves that once clothed the Lebanons have long since disappeared, for Tyre was lumber merchant to all the ancient world. The worst ravaging, however, took place during the four centuries under Turkish rule beginning in A.D. 1516. During World War I the trees were cut to fuel their iron furnaces and locomotives. Individually owned trees were heavily taxed, and goats were allowed to forage on the mountains and eat any new growth. There are still some scattered trees growing on the slopes, however, and one main grove of 400 trees varying in age from 200 to 1000 years old.

The wood from the trees is a warm red and free from knots. It is not only beautiful and fragrant but almost indestructible. The cedar was widely used in ships (Ezk 27:5), idol-making (Isa 44:14), palaces (II Sam 5:11; 7:2; Jer 22:14), and buildings of all sorts, and is particularly mentioned in the construction of the temple and palace of Solomon (I Kgs 5:5-10; 6:9-20, 36; 7:1-12). The logs were floated as large rafts along the coast from Lebanon to Joppa (I Kgs 5:9; II Chr 2:16; Ezr 3:7).

Predynastic and First Dynasty tombs in Egypt reveal objects of cedar wood imported from Gebal (Byblos) in Lebanon. The Egyptian official Wen-Amon reported on his mission to Byblos to procure cedar lumber for the ceremonial barge of the god Amon at Karnak, *c.* 1100

B.C. (ANET, pp. 25–29). Like many other ancient monarchs, Nebuchadnezzar captured the Lebanon region in order to send back cedar logs to his capital for his palaces and temples (ANET, p. 307).

The majestic cedar is often used in Scripture as a symbol of longevity, earthly dignity, and power (II Chr 25:18 ff.; Ps 92:12; Isa 2:13; Ezk 17:22–23; 31:3–18), and some commentators believe that it was the true cedar, a symbol of life, that was fittingly used in preparation of ashes for the cleansing from the pollution of death (Num 19:6 ff.).

Chaff (Heb. *mōṣ;* Gr. *achyron*). The husks and stem of the grain which are blown away by the wind when the grain is threshed and flung into the air to be winnowed (Isa 17:13; Hos 13:3). In Isa 5:24 the KJV incorrectly translates "chaff"; it is the Heb. word *ḥăshash,* correctly called "dry grass" in the RSV. Scripture uses chaff in a figurative sense to depict the worthlessness and final doom of evil men (Job 21:18; Ps 1:4; Mt 3:12). *See* Plants: Straw, Stubble.

Chestnut (Heb. *'armôn*). The chestnut (Gen 30:37; Ezk 31:8) is not found in Palestine and modern scholars, following the LXX, identify this as the plane tree, *Platanus orientalis.* The Heb. word means "naked" and refers to the fact that the bark of the plane tree peels off every year. The plane is a tall (reaching a height of 70 to 90 feet), stately tree with smooth trunk, spreading branches, and large vine-like leaves of a rich glossy green (VBW, I, 83). It is named along with the cedar and fir in Ezk 31:8 as among the most beautiful of trees. It grows wild in Syria and Palestine along watercourses, and is cultivated as a shade tree where there is sufficient soil moisture to sustain it. *See also* Plants: Pine.

Cinnamon (Heb. *qinnamôn*). The inner bark of the cinnamon tree, *Cinnamomum zeylanicum,* was prized as a spice both for perfumery and for cooking, as it is today. It is a 25 to 30 foot high tree of the laurel family. It is native to the islands of Ceylon and Java, but cultivated in other tropical lands, and the spice was a costly import in Bible times. It was used in the holy anointing oil (Ex 30:23). Its fragrance perfumed the bed (Prov 7:17) and described the beauty of the beloved in Song 4:14. Cinnamon appears in Rev 18:13 as one of the luxury items purveyed by fallen Babylon.

Citron. *See* Plants: Apple, Goodly Trees.

Cockle (Heb. *bo'shâ*). Cockle is mentioned only in Job 31:40, KJV. As the Heb. name means "bad," "evil smelling," it might better be translated "foul weeds" as in the RSV. The name fits any number of plants in Palestine: goose weeds, stink weeds, arum, henbane, mandrake (*q.v.*), and even the deadly nightshade. Moldenke favors the ordinary corn-cockle, *Agrostemma githago,* because it seems to fit the context in Job. It is a beautiful, sturdy plant, three to four feet tall, with vivid rose-pink flowers marked with black. It is, nevertheless, a noxious weed, growing among the grain in the fields; its seeds are poisonous to the human system.

Coriander (Heb. *gād*). The *Coriandrum sativum* is an umbelliferous plant of the carrot family with leaves like parsley. The seeds or fruit are rounded and gray, the size of a peppercorn with a sharp, pleasant aroma. It grows wild in Egypt and Palestine, and both seeds and oil were very early esteemed both for flavoring foods and medicinally as a carminative. The Bible mentions it only to describe the appearance of manna (Ex 16:31; Num 11:7), but it must have been familiar and widely used.

Corn. The word "corn" is used in the KJV and NEB as a generic term for different cereal grains. *See* Plants: Wheat, Barley, Millet, etc., for the various grains covered by this term. "Corn" is never used in the Bible to mean maize or Indian corn as it is in the United States, since this grain was unknown until the discovery of the New World. *See* Plants: Grain. For "parched corn" *see* Food: Parched Corn.

Cotton. This word does not appear in the KJV, but there is a possibility that the Heb. word *karpas* (borrowed from Sanskrit *karpasa*) in Est 1:6, translated "green" by the KJV, is correctly given as "cotton" by the RSV. The word *ḥôrâ* translated "white cotton" in the RSV of Isa 19:9 (KJV "networks," *q.v.*) is more likely white linen or "white cloth" (NASB). The common cotton plant, *Gossypium herbaceum,* was cultivated from time immemorial in India, but was not known in Egypt and Europe until introduced by Alexander the Great in 330 B.C. The Jews would become acquainted with it in Persia after the conquests of Darius I, for his great empire stretched from the Mediterranean to India.

Crocus. *See* Plants: Rose 2.

Cucumber (Heb. *qishshu'îm*). Although mentioned only two or three times in Scripture, the familiar garden vegetable must have been as well known and relished throughout Palestine and Egypt as it is today. It provided an important part of the diet of the poor and its juicy coolness was much appreciated in those hot lands. No wonder the Israelites in the hot, dry wilderness dreamed of the cucumbers of Egypt (Num 11:5). While they ripened on the vine, a fragile lodge of sticks and leaves was thrown up to protect a watchman guarding the cucumber field (Heb. *miqshâ*) against pillaging birds and beasts. Isaiah compares desolate Judah to such a forlorn and deserted lodge (1:8). The same Heb. word appears in Jer 10:5 describing the futility of idols, "like a scarecrow in a cucumber field are they" (NASB; KJV, "They are upright as the palm tree"). Contrary to most authorities, Zohary believes that cucumbers were not known and that the reference is to muskmelons. *See* Plants: Melon.

Cummin (Heb. *kammōn;* Gr. *kuminon*). The aromatic and carminative seeds of the *Cuminum cyminum* were used universally in Bible times both medicinally and in cooking. The use of cummin has now been superseded by caraway seed which it much resembles. Although it does not grow wild in Palestine, it has been cultivated from earliest times. The round dry seeds were harvested by beating with a stick (Isa 28:25–27). Tithing of such tiny seeds was used by Jesus to point out the excesses of Pharisaic legalism (Mt 23:23). Deut 14:22–23 required the tithing of grain, etc., and the Mishna (Ma'as, IV.5) includes dill and cummin in the category of "grain."

Cypress (Heb. *tirzâ*). The cypress of Isa 44:14 (KJV) is translated by the Vulg. *ilex*, the evergreen oak, and followed by the RSV with "holm tree." Most authorities now agree that the tree probably meant is the evergreen cypress, *Cupressus sempervirens*. This is a massive evergreen of which some ten species are to be found in the mountains of Bible lands. Formerly it thrived on the cloud-covered heights of Mount Hermon (Sir 24:13; 50:10). Today they are frequently planted in cemeteries in Palestine. See VBW, III, 222. The wood is hard and fragrant, of a reddish hue and almost indestructible. Two doors in St. Peter's cathedral made of cypress wood have lasted for 600 years. Cypress was widely used in ancient times wherever strong enduring wood was needed: wine presses, rafters, joists, the decks of ships. Although the word *tirzâ* is found only in Isa 44:14, the RSV and NASB translate "cypress" instead of "fir" (*q.v.*) for Heb. *b^e^rôsh* in I Kgs 6:15; etc.; II Chr 2:8; 3:5, following Herodotus who says that King Hiram of Tyre offered to Solomon "fairest cedars and cypress" for the building of the temple. The "gopher wood" from which Noah built the ark (Gen 6:14), although otherwise unknown, has been identified as either cypress or cedar (*q.v.*).

Dill. The RSV rendering of Heb. *qeṣaḥ* (KJV "fitches," *q.v.*) in Isa 28:25, 27, and of Gr. *anēthon* (KJV "anise," *q.v.*) in Mt 23:23. It is a parsley-like plant (*Anethum graveolens*) with oval-shaped seeds similar to caraway, used for seasoning food. *See* Plants: Rue.

Dove's Dung (q^e^rē, *dibyonîm;* k^e^thîb, *ḥărê yônîm*). Although Josephus claims that the "dove's dung" used by the starving Israelites during the siege of Samaria (II Kgs 6:25) is to be taken literally and was used like salt, most scholars believe that the Scripture refers to a plant called Star of Bethlehem, *Ornithogalum umbellatum*. This is a bulb that produces a lovely white flower and it grows abundantly in Palestine. The bulbs are dried and roasted or ground to flour and mixed with meal for bread. They are still eaten in Italy roasted like chestnuts.

Ebony (Heb. *hobnîm*, a loanword from Egyp. *hbny*). Ebony is the very hard black, close-grained heartwood of the date-palm or ebony tree, *Diospyros ebenaster*. The tree grows in tropical India, Ceylon, the East Indies, and perhaps E Africa. It was brought to ports along the Persian Gulf or on the S coast of Arabia from where the caravans or fleets brought it to Palestine. The costly wood was used then as now for inlays or for such exalted items as scepters and other staffs of office. Ezekiel speaks of ebony, along with ivory tusks, as one of the precious wares of the Tyrian merchants (27:15).

Elm (Heb. *'elâ*). The KJV translates *'elâ* as "elm" in Hos 4:13, elsewhere as "oak." The correct rendering is "terebinth" (*q.v.*), which the RSV, NEB, and NASB employ in Hos 4:13. The elm is not native to Palestine.

Fig, olive, and grape, three basic plants of the Mediterranean world, grow together in the Forum at Rome. HFV

Fig (Heb. *te'ēnâ*; Gr. *sykē*). The fig tree was one of the most valuable and beloved of trees in Bible times. It is the first of fruit trees to be named in the Bible (Gen 3:7) and appears often throughout Scripture until Rev 6:13. *Ficus carica* is not a tall tree, rising to about 25 feet, but it is wide-spreading and was greatly appreciated for its thick shade (cf. I Kgs 4:25; Mic 4:4; Jn 1:48, 50). The fruit was eaten as it still is both fresh and dried, often pressed into cakes and sold commercially (Neh 13:15). Fig syrup is still in use as a purgative, while a fig poultice was a common remedy (II Kgs 20:7).

This bountiful tree provides a double or even triple yearly crop. About the end of March the new leaf buds appear. At the same time or even beforehand tiny figs begin to grow at the juncture of the old wood and the new buds. These figs (called *taqsh* by the Arabs) grow to the size of a cherry but fall to the ground with every wind that blows (Isa 34:4). These "green" (Heb. *paggîm*, Song 2:13) or "untimely" (Gr. *olynthoi*, Rev 6:13) figs are eaten with relish and even sold in the market. Those that remain on the tree reach their ripeness and are harvested in June, the "first ripe figs" (Heb. *bikkûrâ*) of Isa 28:4, RSV; Jer 24:2; Hos 9:10; Mic 7:1, RSV; Nah 3:12. These are known as *dafūr* to the Arabs, who enjoy them especially for their delicate flavor. While the winter figs are maturing, buds of a second crop start on new twigs of the current year. These are the summer or autumn figs (Heb. *t^e^'ēnâ*), harvested in August or September (Jer 8:13; 24:1-8; Num 13:23). Undoubtedly they were included in Amos' basket of summer fruit (Amos 8:1-2). The Gr. term is *sykon* (Mt 7:16; Lk 6:44; Jas 3:12), the main harvest from a healthy tree. See VBW, III, 121; V, 68.

So valuable a tree was widely cultivated and became a symbol of safety and prosperity (I Kgs 4:25; Isa 36:16; Zech 3:10), while the failure or destruction of the tree was considered complete disaster (Hos 2:12; Joel 1:7, 12; Hab 3:17). The fact that the fig tree puts forth green figs at the same time or even before the leaves (at Passover season early in April) gives meaning to Jesus' cursing of the fig tree which by its leaves gave promise of a fruit it failed to produce (Mt 21:18-21). The application of this incident to Israel's own failure to produce fruit for God would naturally occur to the disciples, for the fig had more than once been used as a symbol of Israel (Isa 34:4; Jer 24:1-8; Hos 9:10; Lk 13:6-9).

Perhaps because Adam and Eve tried to cover their nakedness with fig leaves (Gen 3:7), some traditions claim that the fig was the forbidden fruit in Eden. Other traditions, with as little reason, hold that it was from the fig that Judas hanged himself (Mt 27:5). Cf. C. H. Hunzinger, "*Sukē*, etc.," TDNT, VII, 751-759.

Fir (Heb. *b^e^rôsh, b^e^rôth*). Although translators cannot agree on what to call the *b^e^rôsh*, whether fir, pine, cypress, *et al.*, botanical authorities seem to agree that it is generally the Aleppo pine, *Pinus halepensis*. A veteran grows in the yard of the Rockefeller Museum in Jerusalem. Through the ages the tall, straight pine, rising to a height of 60 feet or more, has been favored by builders for beams, rafters, masts, etc. The Scripture agrees with this usage, classifying the "fir" (KJV) or "pine" (NEB) with the cedars of Lebanon as the major lumber used in their building projects (I Kgs 5:8, 10; II Kgs 19:23; II Chr 2:8; Isa 37:24). Moldenke (p. 46) thinks that in Hos 14:8 the reference is to the stone pine, *Apinus pinea*, because it has an edible, nut-like seed. In I Kgs 6:15, 34; II Chr 2:8; 3:5 the RSV translates "cypress" (*q.v.*), feeling that the pine would not be so suitable for flooring and doors. For Heb. *tidhār* (Isa 41:19; 60:13) as being the true fir, *Abies cilicica, see* Plants: Pine.

Fitch (Heb. *qeṣaḥ*). Although translated "fitch" by the KJV in Isa 28:25-27 (RSV "dill"), this has nothing to do with the true fitch or vetch. It is correctly identified as the nutmeg flower, *Nigella sativa*, a member of the buttercup family which grows wild in most Mediterranean lands. The plant, about two feet high with bright blue flowers, produces seed pods which, as Isaiah says, are threshed with a light staff or cane. The tiny black seeds are very hot and pungent and were used like pepper long before pepper was known, and in seasoning bread, along with the larger cummin seeds. *See* Plants: Dill.

Another Heb. word, *kussemet*, is translated "fitches" in Ezk 4:9 (KJV), but should be rendered "spelt." This is an inferior kind of wheat, the chaff clinging to the grain. It was used in Egypt for bread (Herodotus, II.36). *See* Plants: Rye.

Flag

1. Heb. *'āḥû*, originally an Egyp. word, denotes any growth in a marshy place where water is present (Job 8:11). In Gen 41:2 it is translated "meadow" in KJV and "marsh grass" in NASB.

2. Heb. *sûp* is translated "flags" in Ex 2:3 and Isa 19:6. The same word is used in speaking of a reed or rush, or a seaweed (Jon 2:5).

See Plants: Reed.

Flax (Heb. *pishtâ*). Flax is the most ancient of all textile fibers and botanists have named it most accurately *Linum usitatissimum*. Until the time of the Exile when cotton (*q.v.*) was introduced in Persia, flax and wool were the sources of all cloth in the Middle East and Egypt (Ex 9:31). In early times the plant, which grows about three feet high, was pulled up by the roots and laid out to dry, often on the flat housetops (Josh 2:6). The stems were steeped or retted in water for several weeks until the outer bark decayed; then the inner fibers were combed (Isa 19:9, RSV, NASB), spun into thread, and woven into cloth. The raw fibers or tow (*q.v.*) were twisted and used for wicks in the oil lamps (Isa 42:3). The widespread use of flax is evident from the various grades of linen, distinguished by distinct names in Scripture. *See* Linen. Modern uses of flax for twine or rope, linseed oil from the seeds, and the use of seeds for cattle fodder were not known in biblical times.

Flowers. The blossoms of trees, shrubs, and other plants. Of the many hundreds of varieties of flowers known to grow in Palestine, only about 15 are mentioned specifically in the Bible. The rich use of Heb. words to describe the varieties indicates the interest and appreciation of the people for them. Yet gardens strictly for flowers are not mentioned, and it is doubtful that they were known. *See* Plants: Garden.

Live flowers are referred to in the KJV of Song 5:13 (Heb. *migd^e^lôt*, "banks" of sweet-scented herbs, NASB) and of Song 2:12 as simple blossoms or flowers that appear on the earth after winter is ended. A flower is associated with fruit of the vine which develops before the harvest (Isa 18:5), or is blown from the olive tree before maturing (Job 15:33).

Flower patterns were used to adorn the branches of the golden lampstand (Ex 25:31-34), as well as carvings of flowers to decorate the walls and doors of Solomon's temple (I Kgs 6:18, 29, 32, 35). The brief period of a flower's beauty before fading often signifies the brevity of life on this earth (Job 14:2; Ps 103:15; Isa 28:1, 4; 40:6-7; Jas 1:10-11; I Pet 1:24). *See* Flower. See individual varieties of flowers under their respective names in this article.

Fodder (Heb. *b^e^lîl*). This word designated a

mixture of several kinds of grain, as "wheat, barley, vetch, and other seeds" (Gesenius), used in feeding stock. The idea "mixed together" is indicated in the word. Sometimes the animals were given salted fodder (Isa 30:24, RSV). It is translated "fodder" in all versions of Job 6:5, and in the NASB at Job 24:6 (KJV "corn") and at Isa 30:24 (KJV "provender").

Forest. In ancient times trees and large forests were far more common in the Near East than at present. For example, the Bible speaks of the forest of Hareth, Lebanon, Carmel, Arabia (I Sam 22:5; Jud 9:15; II Kgs 19:23; Isa 21:13), and no doubt others flourished in the area. The great thicket-like jungle in the Zor or river bottom land of the Jordan and known as the "pride of the Jordan" (Zech 11:3) was an almost impenetrable forest. Modern governments, however, are attempting by reforestation to preserve the moisture in the soil and to restore the land as nearly as possible to its former beauty and usefulness. In patriarchal times (the Middle Bronze Age, 2100–1550 B.C.) and earlier, the central N-S ridge (the hill country) and its W slopes were covered with trees, shrubs, and thickets. Invading peoples had to chop down forests to clear land for agriculture (Josh 17:15, 18). Wild animals such as lions still frequented the forests of Palestine during the time of the prophets (Isa 56:9; Jer 5:6; 12:8; Amos 3:4; Mic 5:8).

The word most frequently used for forest is Heb. *ya'ar* (I Sam 22:5; II Kgs 19:23; Ps 80:13, RSV; Mic 3:12; *et al.*). Another word is *ḥōresh* (II Chr 27:4; cf. I Sam 23:15–19). A third word is *pardēs* (Neh 2:8), from which is derived our "paradise"; it refers to a royal forested park or botanical garden (*see* Orchard). Gr. *hylē,* "forest," in Jas 3:5 (RSV), is used figuratively. Cf. M. B. Rowton, JNES, XXVI (1967), 261–277.

Frankincense (Heb. *l^ebônâ*; Gr. *libanos*). Frankincense is the pungent gum resin obtained from three species of the genus *Boswellia,* a tree (Song 4:14) native only to S Arabia (Isa 60:6; Jer 6:20, RSV) and Somaliland. The bark is peeled back a few inches and the resinous sap exudes, forming globules or lumps called "tears." Frankincense was one of the most highly valued of all ancient incense gums, and the limited source of supply made it very costly and one of the most lucrative items in the great land and sea caravans that came from the East. The gum has a fragrant, balsamic odor and was used alone or with other materials for incense. It was one of the ingredients of the holy incense to be used only in Israel's tabernacle (Ex 30:34), and was placed on the meal offering of first fruits (Lev 2:15–16) and on the showbread (Lev 24:7). Later it was also used as an element in cosmetics and perfume (Song 3:6). Frankincense was extensively used throughout the Greco-Roman world as an incense and was also used medically, although there is no mention of this in Scripture. Its primary use among the Jews in worship makes the presentation of frankincense to the infant Jesus a very significant act (Mt 2:11). Cf. "Frankincense and Myrrh" by Gus W. Van Beek, BA, XXIII (1960), 69–95. A native Palestinian "frankincense tree" is considered under Balm (*q.v.*). *See* Incense.

Fruit. To this day, the ordinary diet in the East contains comparatively little meat. It consists largely of fruits and vegetables. Fruits such as figs, dates, grapes, etc. (*q.v.*) were not only relished for their flavor and refreshment, but were a staple part of the diet. A good share of the agriculture of Israel was devoted to vineyards and orchards. Although grown now in Palestine, oranges, bananas, and such apples as we now have, were not known in biblical days. *See* Fruit for figurative usages.

Galbanum (Heb. *ḥelb^enâ*). Galbanum is mentioned only as an ingredient of the holy incense reserved for the worship of God (Ex 30:34). It is obtained from the Ferula, a strong rooted perennial of the carrot family, nine species of which are found in Palestine. When the stem of the plant is cut, a milky juice flows out which hardens into a fetid, yellowish gum with a pungent odor, disagreeable when burned. From related Persian and Indian species asafetida is obtained. At present galbanum is used medicinally and in the preparation of varnish.

Gall (Heb. *rō'sh;* Gr. *cholē*). Of the two words for "gall" in the OT, *m^erorâ* is not vegetable but refers to the bile, the bitter secretion of the gall bladder (Job 16:13; 20:14, 25). *See* Gall. The other word, *rō'sh,* means "head" and suggests that it is a plant from whose head comes a bitter product. This has been identified as the opium poppy, *Papaver somniferum,* and as the wild colocynth (*see* Plants: Gourd). The poppy thrives in Palestine and juice from the seed heads provides the bitter narcotic opium, a valuable but dangerous drug. Many commentators believe that the wine mingled with gall (Gr. *cholē*) offered to Jesus in Mt 27:34 was a drugged wine provided by the women of Jerusalem to ease the suffering of crucified criminals. Whether colocynth or poppy, the word "gall" is often used in the Bible to symbolize the bitterness of life (Deut 29:18; Jer 8:14; Lam 3:5, 19; Acts 8:23). Usually the RSV translates *rō'sh* as "poison" or "poisonous" (Deut 29:18; 32:32; Ps 69:21; Jer 8:14; 9:15; 23:15; Hos 10:4; Amos 6:12). *See* Plants: Hemlock, Wormwood.

Garden (Heb. *gan, gannâ, ginnâ*; Gr. *kēpos*). From the garden planted by God in Eden to the garden of Gethsemane, gardens are often mentioned in the Bible. Most of them were functional gardens of spices (Song 6:2), vegetables and herbs (Deut 11:10; I Kgs 21:2), vineyards, or fruit and nut orchards (Song 6:11; Jer 29:5, 28; Amos 4:9; 9:14). They were usually enclosed by a stone wall or thorny hedge (Song 4:12) with water for irrigation (Num 24:6; Song 4:15; Isa 58:11; Jer 31:12; cf. Isa 1:29–30). Sometimes gardens were the extensive parks or pleasure grounds of the kings (II Kgs 21:18;

25:4; Eccl 2:4–6; Est 1:5; Jer 39:4; 52:7). See Dorothy B. Thompson, "Parks and Gardens of the Ancient Empires," *Archaeology,* III (1950), 101–106. Gethsemane was a "garden" (Gr. *kēpos,* Jn 18:1) or olive orchard, and Jesus' tomb was also in a garden near Calvary (Jn 19:41). Royal burials in the OT period were also sometimes in gardens (II Kgs 21:18, 26). Throughout the Near East gardens and groves of trees were chosen as places of idol worship (Isa 65:3; 66:17), and the prophets repeatedly condemned Israel for worshiping "under every green tree" (Deut 12:2; II Kgs 16:4; 17:10; Jer 3:6, 13). Although generally planted for their product of vegetables and fruit, gardens were situated outside the walls of the crowded towns and made a cool and welcome place of refreshment and retreat much appreciated in that hot climate (cf. Song 4:16). *See* Plants: Orchard.

Garlic (Heb. *shûm*). The familiar, onion-like garlic, *Allium sativum,* was a favorite article of diet in the ancient world as it is in much of the modern. Although mentioned only in Num 11:5 as one of the longed-for pleasures of Egypt, there can be no doubt that Israel cultivated garlic extensively in Palestine. Post records 67 different varieties of onion and garlic to be found in Bible lands, and Pliny asserted that divine honors were paid to the garlic and that it was added to the deities of Egypt. According to Herodotus (II.125), an inscription on the great pyramid at Gizeh listed garlic among the larger food supplies for the builders.

Goodly Trees. In the directions for celebrating the Feast of Tabernacles (Lev 23:40) the Israelites are told to take "the fruit of goodly trees" (RSV) and rejoice before the Lord. Although the specific fruit is not mentioned, long tradition and actual practice identifies it as the citron, *Citrus medica.* Therefore the NEB translates ". . . take the fruit of citrus-trees. . . ." The shrub-like citron tree is only about ten feet in height with thick, straggly branches (VBW, I, 196). Although a native of India, it has been cultivated in Palestine for centuries. The fruit is large as a cucumber and green with many knobs and bumps. It cannot be eaten raw as it is hard and bitter. After being cooked and candied it is a delicacy used both in cooking and as a confection. For some reason, it has been believed to be the forbidden fruit of Eden and has been given the name *pomum Adami,* Adam's apple. *See* Plants: Apple.

Gopher Wood. Gen 6:14. *See* Plants: Cypress, Cedar.

Gourd (Heb. *qîqāyôn, paqqu'ôt*). The two words translated "gourd" are not identified with certainty. Because *qîqāyôn* means "nauseous," Celsus long ago identified it with the castor oil plant, *Ricinus communis,* also known as the Palma Christi from its large palm-shaped leaves. Many modern authorities concur. The castor oil plant grows very swiftly from ten to 12 feet in height, and its broad leaves would afford the welcome shade described in Jon 4:6–10 (VBW, III, 254). The bottle gourd, *Cucurbita lagenaria,* fits the description equally well because of its ability to grow over booths and trellises and its tending to wither rapidly. Other scholars, following the LXX *kolokynthē* say that it was the pumpkin, *Concurbita pepo,* and others claim the globe or prophet's cucumber, *Cucumis prophetarum.* Since the gourd in the story of Jonah was miraculous in its overnight growth, it is questionable whether it can be identified.

The second word, *paqqu'ôt,* is the wild gourd of II Kgs 4:39 that poisoned the food. This has been identified with the wild colocynth, *Citrullus colocynthis.* These are extensive vines, trailing along the ground and at times growing so luxuriantly that they cover the ground for miles. It bears a fruit the size and color of an orange, which is bitter and highly toxic, although used medicinally as a strong purgative (VBW, II, 260). The Heb. name is derived from the verb root *pāqa',* "to burst," perhaps because these gourds readily burst open when ripe. The same word is used in I Kgs 6:18; 7:24 (KJV "knops") to describe the shape of the ornamentation in Solomon's temple (RSV "in the form of gourds"). *See* Plants: Gall.

Grain. Several different Heb. and Gr. words are associated with the biblical references to grain. The KJV uses the word "corn" (*q.v.*) to translate these words, but none of them denote the Indian corn of the Western Hemisphere. The main kinds of grain grown in biblical days were millet, wheat, barley, and emmer or spelt. Jesus on several occasions used grain or seeds to illustrate spiritual truth (e.g., Mt 13:3–38; Mk 4:26–29; Jn 12:24). Paul used a kernel of grain such as wheat as an illustration in His teaching on the resurrection body (I Cor 15:37). Grain as a source of food was so important to the ancient world that fertility cults originated to insure abundant harvests. Archaeologists have discovered grain storage jars and pits used as granaries at numerous sites in Egypt and Palestine. *See* Garner; Storehouse.

Grape. *See* Plants: Vine.

Grass. The four words used in Heb. (*yereq, ḥāṣîr, deshe', 'ēseb*) and translated "grass" in the OT and Gr. *chortos* in the NT are all generic terms meaning plants, vegetation, vegetables, herbs, green growing things. The KJV usually renders the word *deshe'* as "grass" (Gen 1:11), "green herb" (II Kgs 19:26), or "tender herb" (Job 38:27). The RSV varies its translation to "vegetation" (Gen 1:11), "grass" (Isa 66:14), "new growth" (Prov 27:25; Isa 15:6), "vegetables" (Deut 11:10; cf. Rom 14:2, Gr. *lachanon*).

Grass (*ḥāṣîr*) is frequently an illustration of the shortness of man's life on earth (Ps 37:2; 90:5; 103:15; Isa 40:6–8; 51:12; cf. Jas 1:10–11; I Pet 1:24). The Gr. word *botanē* appears once (Heb 6:7) as "herbs" (KJV) or "vegetation" (RSV).

Grove. This is the translation of two words.

1. Heb. *'ēshel,* "tamarisk." Abraham planted

a grove (KJV), more appropriately "a tamarisk," at Beer-sheba (Gen 21:33).

2. The KJV has repeated references to the "groves" of idolatrous worship (Ex 34:13; Jud 6:26, 28; I Kgs 14:15; II Kgs 13:6; *et al.*). While it is true that very often the heathen worship was held in groves ("under every green tree"), it is now known that the Heb. word *'ăshērâ*, translated "grove" by the KJV, is actually the name of a goddess or of the image worshiped in her name. The RSV has correctly changed the translation to Asherah (*see* Gods, False: Asherah; Idolatry; Trees, Sacred).

Gum (Heb. *n^ekō't*). The Heb. word is translated "spicery" in KJV, "gum" in RSV, "gum tragacanth" in NEB, and "aromatic gum" in NASB of Gen 37:25; 43:11. It denotes the resin of an herb or shrub, probably *Astragalus tragacantha.*

Hay. Hay in its modern sense of grass cut and dried to be used for fodder for cattle was unknown to the Israelites. The words so translated, *ḥāṣîr* and *chortos* (Prov 27:25; Isa 15:6; I Cor 3:12), are very general terms for green herbs or grass. *See* Plants: Grass, Straw.

Hazel (Heb. *lûz*). Although it is not the ordinary Heb. word for "almond," most authorities agree that the "hazel" of Gen 30:37 is actually the almond (*q.v.*).

Heath (Heb. *'ar'ār, 'ărô'ēr*). The words translated "heath" in Jer 17:6; 48:6 do not in all probability refer to the true heaths which occur seldom in Syria and Lebanon and not at all in Palestine. The desert vegetation to which Jeremiah refers is believed by most authorities to be the savin or brown-berried cedar, probably the latter (*see* Plants: Cedar 1). *Juniperus oxycedrus,* the brown-berried cedar, is a low lying tree, 15 to 20 feet in height, found in the almost inaccessible wastes and the lonely crags of mountains. It is a fitting symbol for the loneliness described by Jeremiah. The RSV, following the reading of Aquila's Gr. translation, interprets the reference of Jer 48:6 "a wild ass"; but NASB has "juniper."

Hedge. The biblical hedges were not ornamental but protective. In addition to stone walls (Ps 80:12; Eccl 10:8 – both RSV), the Israelites used to take the abundant thorny shrubs and briers (*see* Plants: Thorns) to make protective barriers around their vineyards, orchards, sheepfolds, etc. (Prov 15:19; Isa 5:5; Mt 21:33). These hedges also became an apt symbol for God's protective care and discipline (Job 1:10; 3:23; Hos 2:6; Ps 89:40).

Hemlock. Two words are translated "hemlock" in the KJV, *rō'sh* in Hos 10:4 (*see* Plants: Gall) and *la'ănâ* in Amos 6:12. Both references apply to some bitter, poisonous plant, but it is unlikely that it is the European hemlock, *Conium maculatum,* whose most famous victim was the philosopher Socrates. In all probability it was one of the species of wormwood, *Artemisia* (*see* Plants: Wormwood).

Henna. RSV translation in Song 1:14; 4:13. *See* Plants: Camphire.

Herbs. *See* Plants: Grass.

Holm Tree. A small holly-like evergreen oak, *Quercus ilex.* Holm tree is the RSV translation for Heb. *tirzâ* in Isa 44:14; KJV, ASV, NASB more correctly have "cypress" (*q.v.*).

Husks. Although the OT uses the word "husks" in the ordinary sense of the skin or outer covering of grapes (Num 6:4; in II Kgs 4:42 Heb. *ṣiqlôn* probably means "sack," as in RSV), in Lk 15:16 the reference is altogether different. The "husks" which the prodigal son was feeding to the pigs and would have eaten himself are called in Gr. *keration,* and are the edible pods of the carob tree. *Ceratonia siliqua.* This evergreen tree, widely cultivated in Palestine, produces a flat horn-shaped pod six to ten inches long and one to one and a half inches wide (VBW, V, 124). The pods contain many pea-like seeds embedded in a sweet mucilaginous pulp. Although usually fed to cattle, they are even now eaten by the very poor and may be purchased in some health food stores in the United States. They have been called "St. John's bread" from the notion that the "locusts" that John the Baptist was said to have eaten (Mt 3:4) were the carob pods rather than the insect. This is probably an error since locusts are an accepted article of diet in the East.

Hyssop (Heb. *'ezôb; Gr. hyssōpos*). Moldenke writes that "Of all the words in the Bible referring to plants, 'hyssop' is undoubtedly the most controversial" (p. 222). He cites Celsius as devoting 42 pages and discussing 18 plants without coming to a conclusion. One conclusion seems valid, that the common garden hyssop, *Hyssōpos officinalis,* is not the biblical plant, for it was unknown either in Egypt or Palestine. Most modern authorities are agreed that the word may refer to several different plants. They also concur in the belief that the OT hyssop, used for sprinkling the sacrificial blood, is probably not the same as the NT "hyssop" (Jn 19:29) which in Mt 27:48 and Mk 15:36 is called a "reed." In Heb 9:19, however, *hyssōpos* must refer to the OT plant because it speaks of the Mosaic ritual of sprinkling with blood.

The OT plant is commonly held to be the Syrian and Egyptian marjoram, *Origanum maru.* This plant of the mint family has stiff, hairy branches and thick hairy leaves that would serve well to sprinkle. The caperberry (*q.v.*) has also been suggested, but its smooth leaves would hardly serve the purpose.

The hyssop was used as a means of applying the sacrificial blood at the Passover (Ex 12:22), at the ceremonies connected with the cleansing of the leper (Lev 14:4, 6, 49, 51–52), and in connection with the ceremonial cleansing of one defiled by touching a dead body (Num 19:6, 18). It is spoken of as a common, easily obtainable plant in that part of the world (I Kgs 4:33). The application of the blood speaks of the personal appropriation of God's provision. "The sprinkling with hyssop meant the application of the blood, speaking of that faith which appropriates the death of Christ as a personal matter. Sprinkling of blood therefore meant faith in Christ's atoning death" (J. H. Todd, *Prophetic Pictures of Christ*, p. 63). David used hyssop by metonymy for the atoning blood by which the sinner is cleansed (Ps 51:7).

The NT hyssop by which wine was brought to the lips of the crucified Jesus has been identified by many as the sorghum, *Sorghum vulgare*. This is a tall, corn-like plant with a strong stem, six feet or more in height. The grain appears in a thick brush-like head and is sometimes known as "Jerusalem corn"; it is ground and baked into a coarse bread.

Ivy. The plant mentioned in II Macc 6:6-7 as forming the wreaths which Jews were compelled to wear at pagan festivals is the *Hedera helix*, an evergreen climber with rich, glossy leaves and creamy green flowers. It was commonly used by the Greeks and Romans for chaplets worn as a symbol of rejoicing. *See* Crown.

Judas Tree. Legend has it that the tree upon which Judas hanged himself (Mt 27:5) was the "Judas tree," *Cercis siliquatrum*. This medium-sized tree, familiar even in the United States, grows to about 30 feet and has heart-shaped leaves. The most striking feature is the clusters of purple flowers that appear in the spring on both old and new branches and sometimes on the trunk. These blood-red blotches on the tree inspired the legend which, of course, has no biblical basis.

Juniper (Heb. *rōtem*). The KJV "juniper" is not a juniper at all but a species of 'broom" as it is translated by the RSV. The white broom, *Retama raetam*, is an almost leafless shrub four to 12 feet high, which provides a welcome shade in the desert regions where it grows (I Kgs 19:4-5; VBW, II, 242). The Heb. name *rōtem* means "to bind," and the pliant branches were used as withes or ropes for binding. The roots of the broom tree provide an excellent fuel and are used extensively in the East for making charcoal (Ps 120:4).

Job 30:4 speaks of utterly destitute people eating "juniper" roots. This is unlikely since the roots are bitter and nauseous, and even poisonous. It has been suggested that what was eaten was a parasitic fungus that grows on the roots of the broom tree and is edible. The station called Rithmah (derived from *rōtem*) in Num 33:18-19 probably received its name from the abundance of broom shrubs in that part of the Sinai desert.

Ladanum. *See* Plants: Myrrh.

Laurel. *See* Plants: Ash, Bay Tree.

Leaf. *See* Leaf.

Leeks (Heb. *ḥāsîr*). Although this word is usually translated "grass" (*q.v.*) or "green herb," in Num 11:5 the particular herb mentioned along with the melons and onions and garlic has been identified as the leek, *Allium porum*. The leek has a creamy white bulb from which it sends up a stem about eight inches. Both the onion-like bulb and the leaves are used for food. Leeks are still grown in great quantities in the East and are familiar in the diet of the West as well. In ancient days it was also used medicinally and Pliny mentions 32 remedies in which it was an ingredient.

Lentils (Heb. *'ădāshîm*). The lentil, *Lens esculenta*, is a small, pea-like plant related to the vetch which thrives in poor soil unsuitable for other crops (cf. II Sam 23:11). The reddish brown lentil beans are still widely used as food, as they were in David's time (II Sam 17:28). They are made into a reddish soup (Gen 25:29-34) and also mixed with flour for an inferior kind of bread (Ezk 4:9).

Lign Aloes. *See* Plants: Aloes.

Lily (Heb. *shôshan*). Although only one Heb. word is used, a number of flowers have been suggested for the "lily." It is probable that the Heb. term covered a wider range of flowers than our modern "lily." The primary clue as to the particular flower meant is the context of each passage.

1. Song 5:13 compares the red lips of the beloved to a rare and beautiful flower, and the scarlet or Martagnon lily, *Lilium chalcedonicum*, a native of Palestine though rare, with flowers the color of glowing flame, seems to fit the description.

2. The "lily of the valley" (Song 2:1, 2, 16; 4:5) is not the fragrant flower known to us by that name, as it does not occur in Palestine. Some scholars suggest the brilliant *Anemone coronaria*, while others hold it to be the violet, jasmine, buttercup, *et al.* Moldenke believes that the deep-blue, fragrant *Hyacinthus orientalis* is most likely (p. 114). It is altogether possible that the flower is the well known Madonna or Easter lily, as was believed by many ancient and medieval writers, and that appears

The lotus lily growing in Egypt. HFV

often in Christian art. Although long believed to be a stranger to Palestine, there is now evidence that it grows there and was perhaps even more abundant in the past (VBW, III, 221). At least, this may be the garden lily of Song 6:2.

3. The lily described as flourishing by the water (Hos 14:5; Sir 39:14; 50:8) is probably the iris, which has also been suggested for other "lily" contexts. Although more than 50 kinds of iris are to be found in Palestine, the most likely one is the yellow *Iris pseudacoris* which grows in shallow water and on the margins of streams and pools.

4. Unquestionably one of the lilies of the Bible is the beautiful lotus or water lily. This was a favorite flower in Egypt and appears in much of their art (ANEP #93). The description of the decoration in Solomon's temple as being of "lily work" (I Kgs 7:19, 22, 26; II Chr 4:5) certainly refers to the rose-like many-petaled water lily, either the great white lotus of Egypt, *Nymphaea lotus,* called "Bride of the Nile," the blue *N. caerulea,* or the simple white *N. alba.*

5. The Gr. *krinon* of the NT is also difficult to identify. The "lily of the field" compared by Jesus to Solomon in all his glory (Mt 6:28–29) has seemed to many to be the *Anemone coronaria* (cf. 2). It is more brilliant than the other anemones or wild flowers, shading from glowing crimson to deep purple. The little flower, rising not more than six inches from the bulb, grows abundantly throughout Palestine and seems perfectly suited for Jesus' illustration. Others have felt that the chamomile, *Anthemis palaestina,* a common white daisy-like flower, easy to overlook and yet perfect in its delicate beauty, is a better possibility. The tulip, gladiolus, asphodel, and others have also been suggested.

Lotus. *See* Plants: Lily.

Love Apple. *See* Plants: Mandrake.

Mallow (Heb. *mallûaḥ*). The Heb. name means "salted" and with this as a guide the plant has been identified as the saltwort, *Atriplex,* of which some 21 varieties grow in Palestine. *A. halimus,* the sea purslane or shrubby orach is the most likely. It needs salt sea air to grow and is found along the shores of the Mediterranean, the Gulf of Aqaba, and the Dead Sea. The perennial bushy shrub, related to the spinach, grows as high as five to ten feet with small purple flowers. Its thornless twigs and thick fleshy leaves, although unpleasant in taste, can be eaten if necessary (Job 30:4). The Talmud says that the Jews who returned to restore the temple (520–516 B.C.) had to eat mallows in their dire poverty. Following the LXX, RSV has "like the mallow" in Job 24:24, instead of "as all other" (KJV).

Mandrake (Heb. *dûdāim*). The Heb. name means "loving" and suggests the nature of the mandrake or love apple. *Mandragora officinarum* is a narcotic plant of the potato family that has been esteemed for ages as an aphrodisiac or love philter (cf. Gen 30:14–16). The wide, dark green leaves of the mandrake form a large flat rosette on the ground, with purple flowers at the center (VBW, I, 81). The fruit is small and bright red, shaped like a tomato but soft, pulpy, and somewhat poisonous. The plant has an enormous root, brown and rugged, which with some imagination looks like a human body. It has a heavy smell that may have been pleasant and even exhilarating to Orientals (Song 7:13). Many fantastic legends attend the mandrake in addition to its supposed power over love: that it shrieks when pulled from the ground, grows only under a gallows, etc.

Manna (Heb. *mān*). The Heb. word means simply "what?" and expresses the wonder of the Israelites at God's strange provision of food (Ex 16:15, 31–35; Num 11:6–9; etc.). The Scripture makes it plain that this was a miraculous provision, appearing only on six days, worthless if kept till the morrow except on the sabbath. The words of Jesus in Jn 6:32, that it was God who provided this "bread from heaven," affirms this miraculous character. Nevertheless, scholars have persisted in trying to identify some natural source of the manna. The Sinai manna, *Alhagi maurorum,* the manna tamarisk, *Tamarisk mannifera,* and the flowering ash, *Fraxinus ornus,* all produce a sticky gum that hardens and is edible. The shrub-like manna tamarisk is invaded at times by a small scale insect that pierces the stem and causes a honey-like liquid to exude which hardens and falls in drops from the tree. Made into cakes, these drops are eaten by the Arabs and sold to tourists as the original manna. None of these gummy mannas have the qualities of the scriptural food, including the fact that the manna appeared without fail for 40 years no matter where the Israelites might be.

See Food: Manna.

Mastic. *See* Plants: Balm.

Melon (Heb. *'ăbaṭṭiḥîm*). Like the cognate Arabic word *baṭîḥ,* the Heb. word was probably used for both watermelon, *Citrullus vulgaris,* and the cantaloupe or muskmelon, *Cucumis melo.* Both of these melons were enjoyed in Egypt in ancient times, as well as today, for their delicate taste and for their cooling refreshment. No wonder Israel longed for the melons of Egypt in the hot and dry wilderness (Num 11:5).

Millet (Heb. *dōḥan*). The millet is said to be a native of India but it has been cultivated in Bible lands for ages. The *Panicum miliaceum* now raised in Palestine and Egypt was probably the same variety as in ancient days. The seeds are small, the size of mustard seed, but each head produces multitudes of them. They are made into porridge or a rather unpleasant tasting bread, which explains why Ezekiel used them in symbolizing the siege and famine of Jerusalem (4:9). An annual grass, it is cut in the United States for hay and the seeds used for bird feed.

Mint (Gr. *hēduosmon*). The Gr. word translated "mint" in Mt 23:23; Lk 11:42 is a generic term for the fragrant herbs cultivated for flavoring in salads and cooking. Three varieties are found in Palestine: pennyroyal, peppermint, and garden mint. *Mentha longifolia,* the "horse mint," is probably the one referred to by Jesus. The Jews of old used to strew the floors of the synagogues with mint to perfume the air, while Pliny names 41 remedies made from the plant. Although mint is used today as one of the "bitter herbs" for Passover, it was probably not so enployed in Bible times. *See* Plants: Bitter Herbs.

Mulberry (Heb. *bākā'*). The word translated "mulberry" by the KJV in II Sam 5:23-24; I Chr 14:14-15 means "weeping, distilling" and was probably a tree from which sap or resin was distilled (RSV, "balsam"). *See* Plants: Balm, Willow. The "sycamine" (*q.v.*) of Lk 17:6 is probably the black mulberry and is so translated in RSV, NEB, JerusB, and NASB.

Mustard (Gr. *sinapi*). This seed and plant described in the parables of Jesus (Mt 13:31; 17:20; Mk 4:31; Lk 13:19; 17:6) is the familiar mustard, *Sinapis arvensis,* a staple condiment to this day. Both the black and white mustard were cultivated in Palestine, and the seeds, ground into powder, were used both in cooking and medicine, while the greens were cooked as a vegetable. The tiny seeds the size of petunia seeds or smaller, that could produce a great plant the size of a small tree ten feet or more in height, furnish an illustration of the growth of the kingdom of God as well as the tremendous potential of even a minute faith in the omnipotent God.

This Palestinian mustard "tree" towers over a six-foot man. HFV

On the problem of the mustard seed actually not being the smallest known seed (Mt 13:32; Mk 4:31) see W. Harold Mare, "The Smallest Mustard Seed—Matthew 13:32," *Grace Journal,* IX (1968), # 3, 3-11. He explains that the Gr. *mikroteron* is comparative and can mean "a smaller example out of all the seeds," especially in the group of the garden herbs or vegetables (Gr. *tōn lachanōn*).

Myrrh. Two words are translated "myrrh" in the KJV. The first, *lōṭ* (Gen 37:25; 43:11) refers to a product of Palestine and should properly be called "ladanum" (Akkad. *ladunu,* Arabic *ladan*), an exudation from the rockrose *Cistus,* three species of which are found in Palestine. A fragrant but bitter gum is obtained from the stems and leaves of this shrub, which was formerly used medically but is now chiefly valued as a fixitive in perfumery. This was the "myrrh" carried down into Egypt.

The true myrrh (Heb. *mōr;* Gr. *smyrna*) is an exotic gum resin from the low thorny shrub *Balsamodendron myrrha,* native only to the rocky or mountainous terrain of S Arabia and Somaliland. The resin is obtained by incising the bark, and the gum is a soft yellowish liquid which hardens quickly when it drops off the plant. Along with frankincense (*q.v.*), which comes from the same area, myrrh formed the base of a vast and lucrative trade in spices and perfumery that enriched the Arabs and made this one of the most important commercial ventures of the ancient world. *See* Incense; Spice.

Myrrh was used in incense but less so than frankincense. Its chief use was in the holy anointing oil (Ex 30:23) and in cosmetics and perfumery (Est 2:12; Ps 45:8; Prov 7:17; Song 1:13; 3:6; 5:5). It was, of course, very costly and only rulers and the very wealthy could afford it (Mt 2:11). It was also used medically, and perhaps it was to deaden pain that the mixture of wine, myrrh, and aloes was offered to Jesus on the cross (Mk 15:23). In Palestine as well as in Egypt (Herodotus, II.86) it was part of the preparation for burial of the bodies of royal and distinguished persons (Jn 19:39). Cf. G. W. Beek, "Frankincense and Myrrh," BA, XXIII (1960), 70-94.

Myrtle (Heb. *hădas*). The beautiful and familiar evergreen shrub *Myrtus communis* was a favorite in the ancient world (VBW, I, 196). Its fragrant leaves and white or pale pink flowers were used to perfume rooms and made into wreaths for the nobility in their banqueting. Its edible but astringent bluish-black berries were swallowed to sweeten the breath. The myrtle was sacred to Venus, and this may explain the change of the Heb. *Hadassah* to the pagan *Astarte* as the name for Esther (Est 2:7). The Israelites took fragrant branches of the myrtle to make their booths for the Feast of Tabernacles (Lev 23:40; cf. Neh 8:15). Zechariah saw the angel of the Lord standing among myrtle bushes as symbolic of Israel in his first vision (Zech 1:8–11). The myrtle will supplant the brier in the eschatological age (Isa 41:19; 55:13).

Nard. *See* Plants: Spikenard.

Nettle. Two words are translated "nettle" in the KJV.

1. Heb. *ḥārûl* in Job 30:7; Prov 24:31; Zeph 2:9 is hardly the true nettle, for even the wretched folk described by Job would not gather for shelter "under the nettles." If the word is not simply generic for desert shrubbery or "scrub" (NEB), it may refer to the *Acanthus.* This is a strong-growing perennial whose curling spiny leaves have for ages served as models for the beautiful scroll work of the artist and architect, as on the capitals of Corinthian columns. Both *A. spinosus* and *A. syriacus* are common as weeds through the East.

2. Heb. *qîmôsh* in Isa 34:13 and Hos 9:6 is the true nettle, *Urtica,* of which several species are found in Palestine. The nettle has strong, stinging hairs and in addition secretes a burning liquid that adds to the discomfort. The eastern variety is even more stinging than the western.

Nuts. Nuts are mentioned just twice in the Bible.

1. Heb. *boṭnîm,* the nuts sent as a gift by Jacob to Egypt (Gen 43:11), are unquestionably the pistachio (RSV). The familiar *Pistachia vera,* with its thin dry shell, pale green kernel, and oily taste, is still relished for food and flavoring. Betonim, a town of Gad E of the Jordan (Josh 13:26), may have been named because of pistachio orchards there.

2. The nuts of Song 6:11 are *'ĕgôz,* walnuts, *Juglans regia.* The handsome widespreading walnut tree provides a deep and welcome shade as well as the rich, flavorful nuts. From the hard rind in which the nuts are enclosed, a deep brown dye is obtained. The tree is native to Persia and the Caucasus, being widely planted in Syria, Galilee, and on the slopes of Lebanon and Hermon.

Oak (Heb. *'ēlâ, 'allāh, 'allôn, 'êlîm*). The various words translated "oak" in the OT are believed by some to mean simply a large, sturdy tree. On the other hand, there are a number of kinds of oak in Palestine and Syria, and the words may indicate different species. About all modern scholars can do is recognize that there are various oaks and trust to the context to determine the specific one. It is too warm in the valleys; therefore most of the 24 species of oak are found on the hills and mountain sides. On Mount Carmel, e.g., the kermes oak, *Quercus coccifera,* forms nine-tenths of the vegetation. The holly oak, *Q. ilex,* whose leaves resemble holly, always grows in solitary majesty on firm, dry ground. Perhaps at the foot of such a giant, Rachel's nurse was buried (Gen 35:8; VBW, I, 92).

The oak of Isa 2:13; 44:14; Ezk 27:6; Zech 11:2 has been identified as the Valonia oak, *Q. aegilops,* still abundant in Bashan. The Valonia produces abundant acorns on which swine and sometimes men may feed. From the acorns is also made a strong black dye. Galls on the trunk and branches caused by insect bites contain allic acid and tannin from which ink was made.

The oaks of Carmel, Bashan, and Gilead also include *Q. sessiliflora* and other evergreen oaks.

The "plain" of Moreh and of Mamre (Gen 12:6; 13:18; 14:13) where Abraham camped is correctly translated "oak" in the RSV. Both *coccifera* and *Palaestina* are found here.

Some authorities believe that the *'ēlâ,* one of the "oaks" of the KJV, is actually a terebinth (*q.v.*), but the terebinth does not compare in size and strength with the oak and does not fit the context of all passages with that word.

The sacred groves on the high places where pagan worship was carried out (Isa 57:5; Ezk 6:13; II Kgs 16:4) may have been for the most part groves of oak (Hos 4:13; Isa 1:29). Even today groves of venerable oak trees are to be found throughout the Holy Land. The oak signified strength (Amos 2:9) and permanence, and when it failed this signified utter disaster (Zech 11:2).

Oil Tree (Heb. *'ēṣ shemen*). This name is found several times in Scripture, but whether it can be identified is a question. The pine, olive, and oleaster have all been suggested. The name indicates a tree rich in resinous sap, and its use for the doors and cherubim of the temple (I Kgs 6:23, 31–33) demands a good-sized tree with hard wood. The olive tree does not meet the specifications. In Neh 8:15 the Jews are directed to go to the mountains and fetch branches of the oil tree (KJV, "pine"; RSV, NASB, "wild olive"). I Chr 27:28 also speaks of the oil tree in the Shephelah or foothills.

If the tree is to be identified at all, perhaps the narrow-leaved oleaster or Jerusalem willow, *Elaeagnus augustifolia,* best fits the description. Although not a large tree, its wood is hard and fine grained, suitable for carving. Its fruit, though not related to the olive, yields an inferior oil used in medicine. Zohary prefers the *Pinus halapensis* (*see* Plants: Fir), which is being widely used in Israel today for reforestation.

A Ugaritic tablet lists 140 pieces of *šmn* and 140 pieces of *tišr,* both apparently kinds of timber which could be bought at equal prices. The latter is the Heb. *t^e'ashshûr,* the "box tree" (*q.v.*) of Isa 41:19; 60:13. Thus the "oil tree" is probably a variety of pine (*q.v.*; cf. JNES, XXIX [1970], 56).

Olive (Heb. *zayit;* Gr. *elaia*). One of the most beautiful, and certainly one of the most valuable of all Bible trees, is the olive, *Olea europaea.* It is the emblem of peace and prosperity (Ps 52:8; Jer 11:16; Hos 14:6) and speaks of the blessing of the Lord, from the olive leaf that marked the end of the Flood (Gen 8:11) to the two "olive trees," witnesses who prepare for Christ's second coming (Rev 11:4; cf. Zech 4:3, 11–14). Throughout the Mediterranean world the olive is a familiar sight on the hill-

PLANTS

sides; the ancient gnarled trunks (VBW, I, 261, 293), sometimes almost completely hollow, the gray-green leaves with their silver sheen, proclaim peace and blessing. The trees are planted in orchards or groves enclosed by a hedge or stone wall and called "oliveyards" (Josh 24:13; I Sam 8:14; II Kgs 5:26; Neh 5:11; 9:25).

It is the fruit of the tree, however, that is its chief virtue. Olives are picked green and preserved in brine, or allowed to ripen to a dark purple or black (VBW, II, 93). In the latter case they are harvested in September and October by shaking or striking the branches with long poles (Isa 17:6; 24:13). Olives are still a prime article of diet throughout the East, and the chief crop of many places. When crushed by treading (Mic 6:15) or pressed between stones, they produce the olive oil without which one cannot imagine any Mediterranean woman cooking. In Bible times the oil took the place of butter, and in addition was used as an ointment (Mic 6:15) and universal remedy for all sorts of ills (Isa 1:6; Lk 10:34). *See* Oil. Because the cultivation of the olive requires much time, toil, and patience, the Israelites were forbidden to harm them in time of war (Deut 20:19–20) and the destruction or failure of the olive was regarded as the utmost disaster (Deut 28:40; Hab 3:17). Its chief natural enemy is the locust (Amos 4:9, RSV). The trees were not to be harvested in the sabbatical (every seventh) year (Ex 23:11).

The olive appears in all Israel's activity: the Promised Land was described in terms of the olive (Deut 6:11; 8:8); both kings and priests were anointed with the oil (I Sam 10:1; Ps 45:7; Lev 8:10, 30), as well as guests (Ps 23:5; 92:10); and God was worshiped with sacrifices upon which oil had been poured (Lev 2:1–7, 15). Israel itself was symbolized as a domesticated olive tree, while Paul likened Gentiles to wild olive branches (Rom 11:17–24). Christians are instructed to anoint the sick with (olive) oil when praying for their recovery (Jas 5:14). *See* Anoint; Hands, Laying on of. It seems most fitting in keeping with the symbolism of the tree, that Christ, the Saviour and Prince of Peace, should suffer in Gethsemane (the "Olive press") and that He should ascend from the Mount of Olives.

Olive trees are grown from slips that are grafted on an old trunk or a wild tree when the shoots or suckers are about three feet long (*see* Graff, Graft). Also new shoots may spring from the roots or stump of an old parent tree (Ps 128:3; Isa 11:1). There is no fruit for three to four years, and no plentiful harvest for 17 to 18 years. All this time the tree requires careful attention, the soil plowed and fertilized each spring and faithfully watered. When the tree begins to bear, it must still be carefully tended or it will stop producing, but properly cared for, a full-sized tree will produce a half ton of oil a year and continue until it reaches incredible age. See W. M. Thomson, *The Land and the Book* (Grand Rapids: Baker, 1954 ed.), pp. 51–57.

An ancient olive tree in the Garden of Gethsemane. HFV

Onion (Heb. *beṣel*). One of the most common and widely eaten vegetables in the world today, the onion was equally familiar in Bible times. Although mentioned only in Num 11:5, it was a universal food. In addition, some 26 remedies to be obtained from the onion are found in ancient lists of medicines.

Onycha (Heb. *sh^{e}hēleth*). The onycha used in preparation of the holy incense (Ex 30:34) is somewhat of a mystery. Some consider it an aromatic gum resin and identify it with other biblical gums. *See* Plants: Balm, Bdellium, Myrrh, Storax. Others believe it to be the product of a marine animal, obtained from the claw-like operculum or horny shell cover of a mollusk of the genus *Strombus*.

Orchard (Heb. *pardēs*). A royal park (RSV) or forest preserve (Neh 2:8) such as the ones the Preacher (Solomon?) planted with all kinds of fruit trees (Eccl 2:5), including pomegranates and spice trees (Song 4:13–14). The Heb. word is borrowed from the Persian, and from it we get our word paradise (*q.v.*). The ancient kings often imported exotic trees from faraway lands (cf. *Archaeology*, III [1950], 101–106).

Palm (Heb. *tāmār*; Gr. *phoinix*). The palm tree of Scripture is the stately, beautiful date palm, *Phoenix dactylifera*. Coconut palms do not grow in the Near East. The long slim trunk 80 to 100 feet in height, crowned with long compound leaves, is almost as familiar to northern peoples through pictures as it is to people of

Date palms on the shore of the Sea of Galilee. IIS

Mediterranean lands where it grows. The trees are long lived, normally 100 to 150 years, and an extremely long tap root enables them to flourish even in the midst of the desert (VBW, I, 55, 148, 237, 248). The name "Tamar" was a favorite one for girls, who it was hoped would display the grace and beauty of the palm (Gen 38:6; II Sam 13:1; 14:27).

The tree is one of the most useful imaginable, every part of it being employed by man. The fruit itself (VBW, I, 260) is a staple food in the East, particularly because the dates can be preserved for long periods. From the spathe surrounding the flowers a syrupy liquid is obtained which is called "honey," and it is this rather than bee honey that the Bible often refers to (Gen 43:11; I Sam 14:25; Ps 19:10). The liquid is fermented to make "palm wine," called *arak* by the Arabs. Some authorities think this is the "strong drink" of the Bible (Lev 10:9; Num 6:3; Prov 20:1; *et al.*). Herodotus says that the palm produces bread, wine, and honey, and the Arabs say that it has as many uses as the days of the year. Other products are sugar, oil, resin, tannin, and dyestuff. The strong fibers of the leaves provide thread for sewing, and the leaves themselves are used in innumerable ways for roofs, fences, baskets, etc. Even the seeds are used for necklaces or ground into fodder for cattle.

Palms made Elim (Ex 15:27; Num 33:9) a welcome place on the way to Sinai. Elath (Deut 2:8) at the northern end of the Gulf of Aqaba, where palms are abundant today, may have been so named because of its "lofty trees" (II Kgs 14:22; 16:6; also Eloth in I Kgs 9:26; II Chr 8:17). From earliest times palms have grown abundantly in Jericho, called the "city of palms" (Deut 34:3; Jud 1:16; 3:13; II Chr 28:15).

Palms are also mentioned in connection with religious settings and activities. In the OT the fronds were used at the time of the Feast of Tabernacles (Lev 23:40; Neh 8:15). They were carved in relief on doors and walls of Solomon's temple (I Kgs 6:29) and of Ezekiel's visionary temple (Ezk 40:16; etc.).

Palm Sunday will always remind Christians of the palm branches brought to symbolize victory and thus honor Christ entering Jerusalem (Jn 12:13). Even in heaven, according to the vision of John, palm fronds will be waved to signify final victory (Rev 7:9).

Pannag (Heb. *pannag*). A word of uncertain meaning, but almost certainly not a place name as the KJV would imply (Ezk 27:17). The LXX suggests a spice, "cassia," and the ASV marg. following the Targum "a kind of confection." Generally speaking, pannag was some kind of marketable sweet delicacy produced in Palestine, perhaps made from early figs (RSV). The NASB uses "cakes," which seems to be the most likely translation, based on the cognate Akkad. *pannigu*, a variety of baked goods.

Papyrus. *See* Papyrus; Writing; Plants: Reed.

Pine Tree (Heb. *tidhār*). Only in Isa 41:19 and 60:13 does the KJV correctly speak of the pine. J. C. Trever, however, believes this is the true fir, *Abies cilicica,* which at present grows best in high alpine regions like the Lebanon Mountains (IDB, II, 268). It is probable that many other passages refer to pine as well. *See* Plants: Ash, Chestnut, Fir, Oil Tree. Evergreens of every sort abound on the hills and mountains of Palestine-Syria, but it is unlikely that authorities will agree in any one passage on the particular species meant. For the reference to "pine" in Neh 8:15 (KJV) *see* Plants: Oil Tree.

Pistachio. *See* Plants: Nuts.

Plane Tree. *See* Plants: Chestnut.

Pomegranate (Heb. *rimmôn*). One of the favorite fruits of the Mediterranean and now enjoyed worldwide is the pomegranate, *Punica granata,* the "apple with grains." The fruit is spherical, about the size of an apple, turning maroon when ripe. The rind is woody and astringent but within are multitudes of clear, ruby-colored seeds or "grains" full of delicious juice. The fruit grows on a small, thickly branched tree with dark green leaves and large orange-red blossoms (VBW, IV, 148).

The word "*rimmon*" found in many place names (*see* Rimmon; En-rimmon) in the Bible refers to a pagan deity (II Kgs 5:18), and the name may have been given to the fruit as his symbol. The pomegranate was cultivated in Egypt (Num 20:5), and is listed as one of the fruits of the Promised Land (Deut 8:8). It appears, probably as a symbol of fruitfulness, on the hem of the high priest's robe (Ex 28:33–34) and in the carvings of Solomon's temple (I Kgs 7:18, 20). The fruit was enjoyed raw, and also made into wine and sherbets (Song 8:2). The rind and flowers yield a red dye used in tanning the famous red Morocco leather. Legend makes the pomegranate the "tree of life" in the garden of Eden (Gen 2:9; 3:22).

Poplar (Heb. *libneh*). The Heb. name simply means "white tree," and it is not certain which tree is meant. Some follow the LXX (Gr. *styrakinos*) in Gen 30:37 and accept the storax whose leaves and flowers are white (*see* Plants: Stacte). But the storax is a scrubby tree with short branches, not to be classed with the oak and elm as in Hos 4:13. Most modern authorities hold that it is the white or silver poplar, *Populus alba,* so called because of the white underside of the leaves. The poplar provides a dense shade and is very much appreciated in the East.

Pottage. *See* Plants: Lentils; Food: Pottage.

Pulse (Heb. *zērō'îm*). The word "pulse" in Dan 1:12, 16 (KJV) is an enigma to scholars. The word literally means "seeds" and the most probable guess is that it is a general term for some leguminous vegetables like peas, beans, or lentils. The RSV, NASB, and NEB simply translate it "vegetables." "Pulse" in II Sam 17:28 was supplied by the KJV translators to suggest a second type of parched food; NASB has "parched seeds."

Purslane. This is the RSV rendering of Heb. *ḥallāmût* in Job 6:6, referring probably to the sea-purslane or mallows (*q.v.*) which have a thick, slimy juice. Most authorities go along with the KJV and take it to mean the slime or "white" of an egg. In either case the idea is clear, one rejects what is insipid or loathsome to him.

Raisin. *See* Food: Raisins; Plants: Vine.

Reed (Heb. *'āḥû, sûp, 'agmôn, gōme', qāneh, 'ārôt;* Gr. *kalamos*). The six Heb. words translated in terms of various marsh plants, cane, flag, reed, rush, etc., are used with little or no consistency by translators, and almost no agreement. To a large degree any attempt to identify specific plants either by word or context is arbitrary. It may be that all of these words are general terms to describe the many types of plants growing in or by the water. The following arrangement distinguishes certain usages.

1. The word *'agmôn* in Isa 58:5 is the "bulrush" with bending head (cf. 9:14; 19:15). It is derived from *'ăgam*, a marshy pond or pool (Isa 14:23; Ex 7:19) or the reeds thereof (Jer 51:32). In Job 41:2 the "hook" (KJV) is better translated a "rope" of rushes (NASB and marg.). In Job 41:20 the "caldron" (KJV) should be "burning rushes" (RSV).

2. Heb. *qāneh* is equivalent to the English "cane" and is properly translated "reed" or "cane." The Persian reed, *Arundo donax,* a gigantic grass growing eight to 18 feet high, is common throughout Syria, Palestine, and the Sinaitic peninsula, and is probably the plant usually meant by the terms "reed" or "bulrush."

3. Cattle could not feed upon the huge Persian reed, so Moldenke suggests that in Gen 41:2 (RSV) what is meant is one of the 15

kinds of bulrush or clubrush, *Scirpus*, to be found in Egypt, or perhaps one of the 21 kinds of rush, *Juncus*. Others suggest that it was the water gladiole or flowering rush, *Butomus umbellatus*. The word *'āḥû*, translated "meadow" in the KJV but "reed grass" by the RSV, is an Egyptian not originally a Heb. word. This term also occurs in Job 8:11 as "flag" (KJV) or "rushes" (NASB).

4. Pens for writing with ink on papyrus were usually made from the stems of the common reed, *Pragmites communis*, found in marshes and swamps throughout the Holy Land. The end of the reed was pounded so that the fibers became separated and resembled a fine brush (III Jn 13; perhaps Jer 8:8; Ps 45:1).

5. In connection with pens is the papyrus reed, *Cyperus papyrus*. From this most famous of reeds (Heb. *gōme'*) came man's first paper. The triangular stems, eight to 16 feet high, with a plume of feathery stalks, were split and the pith rolled flat and the strips glued together. *See* Papyrus; Writing. Papyrus reeds formerly grew in the marshes (Job 8:11, RSV, NASB) of Egypt and now-drained Lake Huleh in northern Israel (VBW, IV, 109). Vessels of papyrus (Isa 18:2, RSV) are still made of bundles of these reeds, lashed and woven together to form a little boat (cf. Job 9:26, NASB; ANEP # 124). Of this material the "ark" or basket for the baby Moses was constructed (Ex 2:3).

6. The OT *qāneh* and NT *kalamos* refer to the *Typha latifolia* or *T. angustata*, the familiar cattail reed found abundantly in Palestine. These long reeds were often cut to size and used as measuring sticks (Ezk 40:3, *et al.*; Rev 11:1). Such a reed was handed to Jesus as a mock scepter and then used to beat Him (Mt 27:29-30). The "reed" with which drink was raised to Jesus' lips on the cross was probably sorghum rather than a true reed (*see* Plants: Hyssop).

The reed is often used figuratively to suggest insecurity or frailty (Isa 36:6; 42:3; I Kgs 14:15; Mt 11:7; 12:20).

Rolling Thing (Heb. *galgal*). The expression "rolling thing" in Isa 17:13 and possibly the "wheel" of Ps 83:13 have been interpreted as references to a plant of which two have been suggested. *Anastatica hierochuntica*, the rose of Jericho, looks like a dry, withered ball blown about the desert, but with a little moisture it puts down roots and soon produces green leaves and tiny flowers. This remarkable renewal of life has given it the name "resurrection plant" and many seek it as a souvenir of the Holy Land. Other scholars (JerusB, marg. of RSV, NASB at Ps 83:13) prefer the true tumbleweed of which there are 30 species in Palestine, the most common being *Gundelia tournefortii*. These plants, when the seed pods have been formed, break loose from their roots and are blown about by the wind, thus spreading their seeds. For these two references the NEB has "thistledown," the seed of which turns round and round as it flies.

Root. *See* Root.

Rose (Heb. *ḥăbaṣṣelet*). Two flowers go by the name of "rose" in the KJV.

1. The "rose of Sharon" (Song 2:1) is generally believed by scholars to be not a rose but a bulb-rooted plant, since this may be the meaning of the Heb. name. There is little agreement, however, on the particular bulb; and crocus, lily, anemone, narcissus, and tulip all have their champions. The modern Rose of Sharon is a hibiscus originating in China and unknown in Palestine. Perhaps the most likely is the tulip, either the mountain tulip, *T. montana*, or the glowing red *T. sharonensis*, common to the plain of Sharon.

2. The rose of Isa 35:1 ("crocus" RSV, NASB) is believed on the basis of the Targum to be the dazzling yellow-green polyanthus narcissus or asphodel (NEB), *N. tazetta*, that grows abundantly on the Judean hills. The Akkad. cognate, however, suggests that the meadow saffron, genus *Colchicum*, also called autumn crocus, may have been meant.

3. Sir 24:14; 39:13 speaks of a rose growing by the brooks, which most authorities agree to be the *Nerium oleander*, a poisonous evergreen shrub that grows by water. In the spring it is covered with masses of white or pink rose-like flowers, and Moldenke calls it "the most gloriously beautiful of all the woody plants" (p. 123).

4. There are seven species of true rose native to Syria-Palestine. The most widely distributed is the *Rosa Phoenicia*, a very fragrant pink rose, like the wild roses of the West. This was cultivated extensively in Damascus for its essential oil, attar of roses, used in perfume. It may be this rose that is referred to in II Esd 2:19; Wis 2:8.

Rue (Gr. *pēganon*). The common garden herb, rue, was well known in Bible times. It has gray-green leaves and yellow clusters of flowers and emits a strong, penetrating odor, rather disagreeable to Western senses. It was used for seasoning and medicinally; Pliny mentions 84 remedies using rue. The African rue, *Ruta chalepensis* or *R. graveolens*, is most common in Palestine. Lk 11:42 classes rue with the other herbs in the rigorous tithing practices of the Pharisees, although the parallel passage in Mt 23:23 has dill (*q.v.*).

Rush. *See* Plants: Reeds.

Rye, Rie (Heb. *kussemeth*). The modern cereal grass, rye, was unknown in early days. Various other grains have been suggested but the "rie" (KJV) of Ex 9:32; Isa 28:25 (also translated "fitches" in the KJV of Ezk 4:9) is considered by some scholars today as spelt (so RSV), *Triticum aestivum*, var. *spelta*, an inferior kind of wheat. Although not to be found now in Palestine, it was common in Egypt from the earliest times and was probably grown also in the Holy Land. More likely is the inferior grain known as emmer, *Triticum dicoccum* which still grows in the area (IEJ, XII [1962], 217). It appears in a Ugaritic tablet as *ksmm* in poetic parallelism with wheat (ANET, p. 148*a*). The identification of "rye" as the fitch (*q.v.*) is no longer held.

Saffron (Heb. *karkōm*). Saffron is a condiment, coloring material, and perfume which is a product of several species of crocus, especially the saffron crocus, *Crocus sativus*. The stigmas of this flower, which are narrow, thread-like and a vivid orange, are dried and pressed into small cakes. The stigmas are so small that it takes 4,000 of them to make one ounce. Cake saffron has a peculiar aromatic odor and a bitter taste. It was widely used medically as well as a cosmetic and flavoring. The petals in ancient times were used to perfume banquet halls and the clothes of guests. Solomon compared his bride to a garden in which were planted saffron and other fragrant spices and trees (Song 4:14).

Saltwort. *See* Plants: Mallow.

Sandalwood. *See* Plants: Almug.

Seed. *See* Seed; Agriculture.

Sheaf (Heb. *'ălummâ, 'āmîr, 'ōmer, 'ărēmâ*). In farming, a bundle of cut stalks of grain bound together for ease in handling. The first Heb. word is derived from the verb *'ālam*, "to bind" (Gen 37:7; Ps 126:6). The second and third signify a swath or row of cut grain (e.g., Jer 9:22, RSV; Deut 24:19; Ruth 2:7, 15). The fourth (Neh 13:15) speaks of the heaped-up grain before or after threshing (Ruth 3:7; Song 7:2; Hag 2:16). The dry sheaves were highly inflammable (Zech 12:6). They were carried on donkeys or camels or in carts (Amos 2:13) to the village threshing floor (Mic 4:12) where the sheaves were untied and spread about for the threshing operation. Forgotten sheaves were to be left for the gleaners (Deut 24:19; Job 24:10; cf. Ruth 2:7, 15-17). The word *'ōmer* is used in the OT in connection with the Levitical offerings (Lev 23:10-12, 15), e.g., to "wave the sheaf before the Lord" (v. 11), as a sign of thanksgiving.

Shittah, Shittim. The Heb. words simply transliterated in the KJV are now generally accepted as referring to the acacia trees that are found throughout the wilderness of Sinai and around the Dead Sea, both *Acacia seyal* and *tortilis*. These thorny trees, about 20 feet high, grow in dry places with remarkable luxuriance. They are picturesque with gnarled trunks sometimes two feet in diameter and twisted branches (VBW, I, 161). The wood was not only quite suitable for use in the tabernacle but also readily obtainable (Ex 25:5, 10; 26:15, 26; 27:1, 6). It is a hard, heavy wood almost indestructible from insects; it also has a fine close grain and orange color that finishes very beautifully. The sap of the acacia furnishes the gum arabic used both in industry and medicine. Some think that the "acacia" of Isa 41:19 must be some other tree, since the desert would not be transformed by planting the acacia there. There is no good reason, however, for changing the name. For places named after this tree *see* Shittim.

Shock (Heb. *gādîsh*). A small stack or heap of reaped grain in contrast to standing grain (Jud 15:5; Job 5:26). The Heb. word also appears in Ex 22:6 where the KJV has "stacks" of corn and the RSV "stacked" grain.

Shrub (Heb. *śîaḥ*). A general word in Gen 21:15 (KJV) and Gen 2:5 (NASB) meaning "bush" (*q.v.*).

Spelt. *See* Plants: Rye.

Spice (Heb. *beśem, bōśem, sam, n*e*kō't;* Gr. *arōma*). The words for "spice" in the Bible are probably generic terms and cannot be identified any further. They include plants such as balm, storax, etc. (*q.v.*). The "beds of spices" (Song 5:13; 6:2) seem to mean some low growing herb rather than the trees. Some authorities believe that the term may refer to such fragrant herbs as lavender, rosemary, thyme, sage, marjoram, all of which grow in Palestine. Probably Heb. *n*e*kō't* (Gen 37:25; 43:11) is the gum tragacanth, also called thorny astragal. *Astragulus tragacanthus, A. gummifer,* and 18 or more other varieties are found in Syria-Palestine. This formidable dwarf shrub about two feet high is covered with hundreds of sharp thorns. The gum that exudes from the branches is not actually a spice but a fragrant perfume. *See* Spice, Spicery.

Spikenard, Nard (Heb. *nērd;* Gr. *nardos*). It is generally agreed that spikenard is an aromatic oil extracted from a perennial herb of the valerian family, the nard plant, *Nardostachys jatamansi.* This was an exotic plant in Palestine (Song 4:13-14) imported from India, native to the mountains of Nepal and Tibet. From the roots and lower hairy or woolly stems comes a perfume (Song 1:12) that was highly prized in ancient times, but is rather strong for today's tastes. The Hebrews and Romans used it chiefly in preparation of the dead for burial. As can be imagined, the remote source and long, difficult journey from the East made this an extremely costly perfume. It was commonly stored in alabaster boxes which had to be broken in order to obtain the perfume (Mk 14:3; Jn 12:3).

Stacte, Storax (Heb. *nāṭāph*). The ingredient of incense called "stacte" in Ex 30:34 and "storax" in Sir 24:15 comes from the storax tree, *Styrax officinalis.* This beautiful shrub, that sometimes reaches the size of a small tree, is covered in the spring with white or yellow blossoms like a fall of snow (VBW, III, 209). For this reason the LXX and others have identified the "white tree" of Gen 30:37 as the storax. *See* Plants: Poplar. The Heb. name means "drops" and refers to the resin that gathers in drops when the bark is incised. The gum was highly prized as a perfume.

Strange Vine. It is not at all necessary that the "strange vine" to which God likens Judah in Jer 2:21 should be a specific plant. Some, however, identify it as the *Vitis orientalis.* This bushy and sometimes climbing plant with dark green leaflets and bright red berries like currants is prolific on the mountains of Palestine. It is handsome and free from pests but absolutely useless to man.

A sycamore tree at Jericho. HFV

Straw (Heb. *teben*). The stalks of grain left after threshing were cut up into one-half to two foot lengths and mixed with chaff. This straw took the place of hay, which was unknown in ancient farming (Gen 24:25, 32; Jud 19:19; I Kgs 4:28; Isa 11:7; 65:25). The chopped stalks were used by the Israelites for making bricks in Egypt (Ex 5:7–18). *See* Brick; Straw.

Stubble (Heb. *qash*). Although the stalks of grain were often pulled up by the roots in ancient harvesting, the sticks, weeds, straw, etc., that were left on the field (Ex 5:12) provided subsistence for the flocks and herds through the summer.

The expression is used figuratively of the brief existence and worthlessness of the wicked who are destroyed by God's judgment and wrath, just as stubble is sometimes burnt off a field (Ex 15:7; Ps 83:13; Isa 5:24; 33:11; 40:24; 47:14; Joel 2:5; Ob 18; Nah 1:10; Mal 4:1). The Gr. *kalamē* is actually straw (I Cor 3:12) in contrast to *chortos*, "grass," "hay," "fodder." *See* Plants: Chaff, Straw.

Sweet Cane, Sweet Calamus (Heb. *qāneh*). The "sweet cane" of Isa 43:24 is now generally regarded as the sugar cane, *Saccharum officinarum*. Although the Hebrews knew nothing of sugar making, the cane was used for sweetening food and was chewed as a confection. The reference to "sweet cane" in Jer 6:20 and Ezk 27:19 (NASB) means a sweet smelling cane and probably is the sweet calamus. *See* Plants: Calamus.

Sweet Storax. *See* Plants: Stacte.

Sycamine (Gr. *sycaminos*). The "sycamine" of Lk 17:6 is the black mulberry, *Morus nigra*. The small decorative trees produce a fruit that looks like a blackberry but has a decidedly different, acid flavor. The white mulberry, upon which the silk worms feed, is now also cultivated in Palestine, but silk was not known there until the 7th cen. B.C. The first unquestionable mention of silk in the Bible is Ezk 16:10, 13. *See* Plants: Mulberry.

Sycamore (Heb. *shiqmâ*; Gr. *sycomōraia*). The biblical sycomore (KJV) or sycamore is not to be confused with the western sycamore which is a species of maple. The biblical tree is a fig, *Ficus sycomorus*, a strong, widespreading tree, 30 to 40 feet in height, with a great trunk having a circumference up to 20 feet (VBW, III, 241; V, 126). Twisted and gnarled branches fork outward in every direction and make it very easy to climb (Lk 19:4). The fruit, borne directly on trunk and branches, is yellowish with black spots and is inferior in taste to the true fig (*q.v.*). Three or four days before harvest, the figs must be cut or pierced or they will not properly ripen. This menial task was an occupation of the prophet Amos, who calls himself "a dresser of sycomore-figs" (7:14, NEB). The wood is soft and porous but very durable, and is much used for furniture, boxes, etc. Mummy cases of sycamore are still in good condition after 3,000 years.

Sycamore fruit. HFV

Tamarisk (Heb. *'ēshel*). The word "grove" in Gen 21:33 and "tree" in I Sam 22:6; 31:13 are translations of the Heb. *ēshel*, correctly rendered by the RSV and NASB as "tamarisk." There are eight species of tamarisk found in Palestine. It grows in arid, desert places where few other trees grow, and furnishes welcome shade for the traveler with its long, feathery branches and minute, scale-like leaves (VBW, I, 65).

Tares (Gr. *zizanion*). The tares (RSV "weeds") referred to in our Lord's parable (Mt 13:25 ff.) are without doubt the bearded darnel, *Lolium temulentum*. This destructive weed is almost indistinguishable from wheat in its early growth. At harvest time its true nature is disclosed and the farmer (or his women and children) separates the weed, poisonous both to man and beast, from the good wheat.

Teil. An obsolete name for the lime or linden tree; properly in Isa 6:13 the terebinth (*q.v.*).

Terebinth (Heb. *'ēlâ*). In the KJV the Heb. word is erroneously translated "elm" in Hos 4:13 and "teil" in Isa 6:13. The tree identified as the terebinth or turpentine tree (Sir 24:16) by modern authorities bears one of the Heb. names usually translated as "oak" (*q.v.*). Yet there is a distinction as the RSV and NASB of Isa 6:13 and Hos 4:13 clearly reveal where both *'ēlâ* and *'allôn* occur in the same passage. The NASB has "terebinth" in the margin at Gen 12:6; 13:18; 14:13; 18:1; 35:4; Deut 11:30; Jud 4:11; 6:11, 19; I Kgs 13:14; Isa 1:29–30; 57:5. The NEB uses it in the text at these references, plus in Josh 24:26 and Ezk 6:13.

The Palestine terebinth, *Pistacia terebinthus,* var. *Palaestina,* is a deciduous tree with great straggly boughs, and in its leafless condition does resemble the oak. It grows 20 to 25 feet high, generally solitary on the lower slopes of the hills, usually in an area too warm for the oak which it replaces. Its compound leaves, a rich coppery green, resemble those of the ash. The "turpentine" that flows from any part of the tree when it is cut, is a fragrant resinous juice like jasmine. It has been suggested that the "spicery" carried from Palestine to Egypt (Gen 37:25; 43:11) may have been obtained in part from the terebinth. *See* Plants: Balm. The valley of Elah where David fought Goliath may have been so called from terebinths that grew there (I Sam 17:2).

Tamarisk tree. Photo Leon

In ancient times a terebinth was often considered a sacred object and a favorite place for heathen worship (Isa 1:29–30; Hos 4:13; cf. Isa 57:5; Ezk 6:13). Jacob buried the family idols under such a tree (Gen 35:4). Joshua placed a great stone under a terebinth near the ancient sanctuary at Shechem as a memorial of God's covenant with Israel (Josh 24:26). A terebinth made a fine shade tree for rest and private conversation (Jud 6:11, 19; I Kgs 13:14). While the Heb. word *'ēlâ* is used, most scholars believe that it was in the branches of an oak that Absalom's hair, of which he was so proud, became entangled before his death (II Sam 18:9–10, 14), because oaks are larger, grow in forests, and are more common to Gilead.

Thicket (Heb. *s[e]bak, s[e]bōk*). These two related Heb. words have for their meaning the dense, interwoven undergrowth such as might catch a ram by its horns (Gen 22:13), or provide a lair for a lion (Jer 4:7), or simply refer to the dense growth of a forest (Isa 9:18; 10:34). The corresponding verb speaks of "entangled" thorns in Nah 1:10 (RSV). Another word, Heb. *'āb,* is a thicket to which citizens of Judah will flee (Jer 4:29). Heb. *ya'ar* normally means "forest" (*q.v.*), but in Isa 21:13 (RSV, NASB) it must speak of the bushes or "scrub" (NEB) of Arabia; and in Mic 3:12; Jer 26:18 ("forest") it foretells the "thicket-covered heights (overgrown with bushes and trees)" (BDB, p. 420) of Jerusalem after its forthcoming destruction.

Thorns, Thistles, Brambles, Briers. At least 22 Heb. and Gr. words are used to describe the thorny, prickly plants so well known to all men, and they are rather indiscriminately used by translators to mean thistles, thorn, brambles, or briers. Since there are 50 genera and some 200 species of thorny plants in Syria-Palestine, it is impossible to know exactly which plant the writer had in mind. Although hardly any two authorities agree, Moldenke is followed in the divisions below:

1. The thorn of Isa 7:19; 55:13; Jud 8:7; Mt 7:16 is the Syrian Christ-thorn, *Zizyphus spina-christi.* This is actually a small tree, nine to 15 feet tall, with strong curved unequal spines (VBW, V, 151). It grows in great, impenetrable thickets on the plains of Syria, Lebanon, and Palestine. For Heb. *na'ᵃṣûṣ* in the two Isaiah references the NEB has "camel-thorn," a spiny desert shrub.

2. The "pricks" of Num 33:55 is a true bramble; both the Palestinian and elm-leaf brambles, *Rubus sanctus* and *R. ulmifolius,* are prickly evergreen shrubs.

3. The thorns of Gen 3:18; Ps 58:9; Prov 15:19; Isa 7:23–25; 10:17; 33:12; Ezk 2:6; Mic 7:4 are the Palestine buckthorn, *Rhamnus palaestina,* a shrub or small tree, three to six feet tall, with velvety thorny branches. It grows in thickets on the hillsides from Syria and Lebanon through Palestine to Sinai and Arabia. It is much used for hedges and fuel.

4. Gen 3:18 and Hos 10:8 (Heb. *dardar*) and Mt 7:16 and Heb 6:8 (RSV) (Gr. *tribolos*) are the true thistles of which there are some 125 varieties in the Holy Land. They grow from one to six feet high and are a painful and undesirable weed. When the spines are removed, however, they are edible and even nutritious. Moldenke also includes the *ḥôaḥ* of

PLANTS

Jehoash's allegory (II Kgs 14:9) as a thistle, but elsewhere it is a thorn, so that the NASB translates "thorn bush." The NEB renders Gr. *akantha* as "thistle" in the parable of the sower (Mt 13:7, *et al.*) because it is more apt to be found in a grain field.

5. Considerable discussion has gone on for ages concerning the thorns from which the mocking crown was made for Christ (Mt 27:29; Jn 19:2), and many plants bear the title. Moldenke chooses the *Paliurus spina-christi* with its slender sharp spines because it is a low growing shrub easy for the soldiers to gather; but it does not grow naturally in the Judean hill country and must be sought in the valleys of N Palestine. Zohary prefers the *Poterium spinosa* because it grows near Golgotha. It is a low shrub of the rose family with thorny branches.

6. Isa 34:13 and Hos 9:6 speak of a thorn which grows in ruined buildings. Moldenke suggests the burrweed, *Xanthium spinosum*, which in addition to its thorny fruit has long yellow spines.

7. Heb. *'āṭād*, the "bramble" in Jotham's fable (Jud 9:14-15, KJV, RSV, NASB), is now considered as referring to the European boxthorn, *Lycium europaeum*, a thorny bush six to 12 feet tall common throughout the Holy Land; therefore the NEB has "thorn-bush." It is widely used in hedges in Palestine (see VBW, II, 93).

Many other thorny plants are common in Palestine fulfilling the judgment of God because of man's sin (Gen 3:18). Included are the Syrian thistle, hawthorn, spotted golden thistle, Palestinian nightshade or brier, the pricking brier, and blackberry.

For Paul's "thorn in the flesh" (II Cor 12:7) *see* Thorn in the Flesh.

Thyine (Gr. *thyinos*). Thyine or citron wood was highly prized in the ancient world for cabinet work. Native to the Atlas Mountains of NW Africa, it is a large tree of the cypress family, *Tetraclinis articulata*, also called *Callitris quadrivalvis*. The wood is reddish brown, extremely hard and fragrant. It has a whitish-yellow resin, sandarac, used for incense and in making varnish. This "scented wood" (RSV) is listed among the luxury articles of Babylon the Great (Rev 18:12), and it was literally worth its weight in gold.

Tow (Heb. *n^{e}'ōret*). The term means the refuse of the flax (*q.v.*) produced in the manufacture of linen and occasioned by the processes of pounding and carding the fibers. Its highly flammable nature was proverbial (Jud 16:9) and was used as an effective emblem of the speedy disintegration of the unrighteous (Isa 1:31). The KJV of Isa 43:17 uses "tow" to render the Heb. *pishtâ*, but it is more correctly translated as "flax" (RV) or as "wick" (ASV, RSV).

Tree. The trees, both fruit and shade, outnumber all other plant groupings of the Bible. Their variety, beauty, and usefulness impressed the Heb. mind, and there are numerous references in Scripture to the part trees had in their thinking as well as their living.

The olive, fig, almond, pomegranate, and others were widely used for food. Since they required long cultivation and years of care before their produce was available, it was a command of God that even in times of war such trees were not to be cut down, an act of vicious inhumanity (Deut 20:19).

Trees played an important part in the pagan worship of Palestine to which the Israelites apostatized, and one of the most familiar charges of the prophets is that Israel worshiped its idols "under every green tree" (Deut 12:2; I Kgs 14:23; Jer 3:6). *See* Trees, Sacred.

The trees found their way into the language as metaphors for beauty, majesty, righteousness, and sin. The great height and grandeur of some trees reminded the people of important public figures, and they are used to symbolize kings and rulers (Ezk 17; Dan 4). The fruitfulness of a well-watered tree symbolized for Israel the life of the righteous man, sustained by God (Ps 1; Jer 17:8). The swift and luxuriant growth and beauty of some trees also spoke to them of the "sinner" flourishing for a season in his unrighteousness (Ps 37:35).

Two of the most mysterious of trees are found in the garden of Eden, the tree of life and the tree of the knowledge of good and evil (*q.v.*; Gen 2:17; 3:22). Whether these are to be taken purely metaphorically or as a sacramental reality has puzzled the interpreters for ages. The tree of life also appears in Rev 22:2 and probably in Ezk 47:12. *See* Trees of Knowledge and of Life.

Turpentine Tree (Sir 24:16). *See* Plants: Terebinth.

Vine (Heb. *gephen;* Gr. *ampelos*), **Vineyard** (Heb. *kerem*). The grapevine, *Vitis vinifera*, is the most common, best known, and best loved of all plants of the Bible (VBW, I, 102, 227; III, 169, 217; IV, 142). The Scripture speaks of it from the days of Noah (Gen 9:20-21) until the days before the return of Christ (Rev 14:18). It is the constant parable of prophet, psalmist, and apostle. Israel was the vine planted by the Lord (Isa 5:1-7; Ps 80:8-16), and Jesus was the true vine (Jn 15:1 ff.).

The cultivation of the grape in the favorable soil and climate of Palestine began at least as early as the Early Bronze Age (3200-2100 B.C.), so that wine was a common product by Abraham's time (Gen 14:18). The spies sent out by Joshua to explore the Promised Land witnessed to its richness with great bunches of grapes (Num 13:20 ff.). The choice grapes of Palestine were famous for their size, some as big as plums. Huge clusters of grapes weighing 12 to 16 pounds are recorded. Israel is again becoming a land of vineyards to rival the past.

The vineyard was usually planted on a hill too steep for growing grain (Isa 5:1; Joel 3:18), and was surrounded by a protective wall made of stone or bushes (Isa 5:5; Ps 80:8-13). At harvest time the grapes were processed in the winepress on the premises of the vineyard (Isa 5:2; VBW, V, 61). Vineyards were cultivated by their owners (Lev 19:10; 25:3-5; Prov

PLANTS

24:30-31) or by hired hands (Song 1:6; 8:11; Mt 20:1-16; Lk 13:7). At times a large land owner rented out his vineyard on a share crop-per basis (Mt 21:33-43). That the vineyard played a large part in the life of Israelites may be seen from the law making a person who had planted a vineyard exempt from the military service (Deut 20:6). Many people had no other financial resources than their vineyards.

The harvest or vintage of grapes in late summer or early fall was a joyous occasion for the people (Jud 9:27; Isa 16:10; Jer 48:33). The poor were permitted to glean grapes that were missed during the vintage (Lev 19:10; Isa 24:13; Mic 7:1). The grapes were eaten when ripe (Num 6:3; Deut 23:24), dried into raisins, made into juice (Deut 32:14) and wine, or boiled down into a syrup like honey (Heb. *debash,* cf. Arabic *dibs,* "grape syrup"). *See* Drink; Food: Banquet, Honey, Raisins; Wine. Cf. J. P. Brown, "The Mediterranean Vocabulary of the Vine," VT, XIX (1969), 146-170.

Vine of Sodom. The "vine of Sodom" in Deut 32:32 may be only a literary figure for the deadly fruit of corruption, but some have interpreted the phrase as a reference to an actual plant. The apple of Sodom, *Solanum sodomeum,* is a plant about four feet high, its widespreading branches armed with short, sharp thorns. It bears an appetizing looking tomato-like fruit which is full of hard black seeds and silky hairs like ashes. It is completely inedible. Since the apple of Sodom is not a vine, other scholars propose the wild colocynth, an equally disappointing fruit. *See* Plants: Gourd.

Weeds (Heb. *sûph*). The word translated "weed" in Jon 2:5 is one of the common words for "reed" (*q.v.*). Since in this context it is found at the bottom of the sea, perhaps "seaweed" or "eelgrass" would be proper. For the term "sea of weeds" (Heb. *yam sûph*) *see* Exodus, The: Route. For the weeds of Mt 13:25-30 (RSV) *see* Plants: Tares.

Wheat (Heb. *ḥiṭṭâ*; Gr. *sitos*). Wheat, *triticum compositum,* is the most widely sown of all grains. Its origin as a cultivated crop is so ancient that there is no definite trace of it. Charred kernels have been discovered in Neolithic Age levels of Jericho and other early sites. As flour and bread it has been the "staff of life" (Ps 105:16) for countless generations of mankind. Five varieties of wheat grow wild in Palestine, and there are eight others which are cultivated. See VBW, I, 260; V, 47, 85. Wheat is sown in November to December and harvested in April to June. The term "corn" (*q.v.*) of the KJV, although used for other cereals, is in most cases wheat. *See* Plants: Grain; Agriculture; Food: Bread.

Wild Gourd. *See* Plants: Gourd.

Wild Vine, Wild Grapes. The wild grape or vine of Isa 5:2-4 has been taken to be simply a true grape that has degenerated, even as Israel had degenerated from being the planting of the Lord. Some authorities believe it to be the native wild fox-grape, *Vitis orientalis* (*see* Plants: Strange Vine). Since the fox-grape does not now grow in Palestine and some believe it never did, this identification is a question. Others have suggested the deadly nightshade or Jericho potato, a poisonous weed which does not at all resemble the grape.

Wheat carved on marble at the sanctuary of the Eleusinian mysteries near Athens. Wheat was sacred to the cult. HFV

Willow (Heb. *'ărābâ, ṣapṣāpâ*). The two words translated "willow" in the OT are always spoken of in connection with water. There is no doubt that in some references these are true willows, of which 21 varieties are found in Palestine growing along all the water courses. The willows of Palestine, particularly *Salix safsaf,* the most common, are shrubs, or small trees, not the size of the European willow (Job 40:22; Isa 44:4; Ezk 17:5). They have the same pliable twigs and branches, however, and have been used from time immemorial for basketry. The green withes with which Samson was bound (Jud 16:7-9) were probably willow.

In spite of the name, *Salix Babylonia,* and the legend, the weeping willow is of Chinese origin and was not known in Bible lands in earlier days (Ps 137:2). Although all authorities are not agreed, some believe that the "willow" of Lev 23:40 and Ps 137:2 is the Euphrates poplar or aspen, *Populus euphratica,* found along the shallow streams from Syria to Arabia (VBW, III, 172). The stiff, rustling leaves of the aspen have given them the name of "weeping" and they may also be the trees called "mulberries" (ASV) in II Sam 5:23-4 (RSV "balsam").

Wormwood (Heb. *la'ănâ*; Gr. *apsinthos*). There are many species of wormwood, *Artemisia,* all of which have a strong, bitter taste. *A. herba alba* and *A. judaica* are probably the ones referred to in Scripture. From one species the liquor absinthe is made, which not only intoxicates but drugs and brings stupor and even death (Lam 3:15, 19). The references to wormwood in the Bible are usually metaphorical for the bitterness of sin and judgment (Deut 29:18; Prov 5:4; Jer 9:15; Amos 5:7; Rev 8:10-11). *See* Plants: Hemlock, Gall.

Bibliography. A. W. Anderson, *Plants of the Bible*, London: Lockwood, 1956. R. K. Harrison, "Plants," NBD, pp. 1003-1007; *Healing Herbs of the Bible*, Leiden: Brill, 1966. Alastair I. MacKay, *Farming and Gardening in the Bible*, Spire Book, Old Tappan, N. J.: Revell, 1970. H. N. and A. L. Moldenke, *Plants of the Bible*, Waltham: Chronica Botanica Co., 1952. G. E. Post, *Flora of Syria Palestine and Sinai*, 2nd ed., 2 vol., 1932-1933. M. B. Rowton, "The Woodlands of Ancient Western Asia," JNES, XXVI (1967), 261-277. John C. Trever, articles on the individual plants, IDB. Gus W. Van Beek, "Frankincense and Myrrh," BA, XXIII (1960), 69-95. Winifred Walker, *All the Plants of the Bible*, New York: Harper, 1957. E. R. Yarham, "The Cedars of the Lord," *American Forests*, LXXV (1969), 24-26, 59. M. Zohary, "Flora," ISBE, II, 284-302.

P. C. J.

PLASTER. *See* Minerals and Metals.

PLATTER. A flat dish or plate, usually of wood, mentioned in Jesus' rebuke to a certain Pharisee (Lk 11:39). The Gr. word *paropsis* in Mt 23:25-26 is one which is more commonly used to describe a serving tray or side dish. *See* Pottery.

PLAY. *See* Games; Music.

PLEASURE, GOOD. *See* Will of God.

PLEDGE. *See* Loan.

PLEIADES (plē'*á*-dēz). A cluster of stars poetically referred to as the "seven stars" in Amos 5:8 (cf. Job 9:9; 38:31). *See* Astronomy; Orion.

PLEROMA. *See* Fulness.

PLOW, PLOWSHARE. After the sickle, which was made by placing sharpened flints like wedges in a bone or wooden haft, the plow was the most important agricultural instrument invented by primitive man. Proper instruction for the productive use of these instruments was considered to come from God (Isa 28:23-29). Plowing was done in the autumn (Prov 20:4), after the early rains softened the ground following the summer dry season (cf. Jer 14:4).

According to descriptions in postbiblical literature, the ancient Heb. plow did not differ greatly from plows used by many peoples in biblical lands today. The body or stock was a pole of tough wood, holm oak or the like. The heavy end was bent downward at the rear to form the share (an iron tip being added in later times, Isa 2:4; Joel 3:10; Mic 4:3), or bound by thongs to a crosspiece, the upper end of which served as the handle and the lower end as the share. There was only one handle. One hand of the plowman was free to use the goad. The plow in biblical times did not turn large furrows as do modern plows, but merely scratched the soil to a depth of three or four inches (Ps 129:3).

The yoke was pinned to the stock of the plow at its lighter end. Each end of the yoke was part of a frame fitted to an animal's neck. Animals pulled by throwing their weight against this yoke. Naturally the yoke needed to be very smooth for it to be "easy" and the burden "light" (cf. Mt 11:29-30). This was borne usually by two animals of the same kind, two oxen (Amos 6:12; Job 1:14) or two asses (Isa 30:24). The mixing of kinds of draft animals, which increased the difficulty for one by reason of difference in size, height, or nature, was forbidden by the law (Deut 22:10). *See* Yoke.

Wealthy landowners could afford to hire plowmen (Lk 17:7; Job 1:14-15; cf. Isa 61:5), and Elisha seems to have had eleven plowmen working with him (I Kgs 19:19). Plowing became a figure for judgment (Mic 3:12), as well as for committing sin with the inevitable consequences to follow (Job 4:8; Hos 10:13; cf. Gal 6:7).

See Agriculture.

J. W. W.

PLOWMAN. *See* Agriculture; Occupations: Farmer, Husbandman.

PLUMBLINE, PLUMMET. The etymological use of *anâku*, "lead" or "tin," in Akkad. suggests that Heb. *'anak* (Amos 7:7-8) can mean "plummet" as well as "plumbline." The corresponding word "plummet" in other passages is the Heb. *mīshqōlet*, meaning a level or leveling instrument (KB). Still another word associated with plumbline and plummet is "stone" (Heb. *'eben*). The plumbline was a line or cord to which was attached a weight called a plummet, a piece of stone, clay, lead or tin. Masons used the device to insure that the walls they built would be vertical. By means of the plumbline, horizontal accuracy could also be ascertained. A somewhat similar usage today is the line and plummet under a surveyor's level. The plummet is mentioned very early in Egyptian and Mesopotamian literature.

In symbol, Israel was considered as a wall or building, and the act of applying a plumbline or plummet was to test Israel's straightness and see whether the nation was in line with the revelation of God. In situations of judgment, God was said to set a plumbline (Heb. *'anak* in the midst of Israel (Amos 7:7-8), for they did not measure up concerning their integrity. One of the prophets pointed out that the Lord would stretch over Jerusalem the measuring line of Samaria and the plummet of Ahab's house, thereby noting that Jerusalem figuratively was lacking on the level of basic righteousness (II Kgs 21:13). Isaiah (34:11) also spoke of the measuring line of confusion and the stones (Heb. *'eben*) of emptiness, a graphic description of an indictment concerning the land of Israel. The stone (Heb. *'eben*) or weight of tin in the hand of Zerubbabel was the indication of being engaged in the work of erecting a building

(Zech 4:10). Concerning the future establishment of the kingdom in Israel, God says that He will make justice the measuring line and righteousness the plummet (Isa 28:17).

L. Go.

PNEUMATOLOGY. The study of the doctrine of the third person of the Trinity, the Holy Spirit. The most important aspect of the doctrine concerns the true personality and deity of the Holy Spirit. That the Holy Spirit is a person and is an equal member of the Godhead seems to be the teaching of the NT. For example, Christ told the disciples to baptize in the name of the Father, and of the Son, and of the Holy Spirit, ascribing the same individuality and personality to the Spirit that He did to Himself and the Father (Mt 28:19). *See* Holy Spirit.

The doctrine of the Holy Spirit, while always accepted by the Christian church, developed somewhat more slowly than the doctrine of the Son. In fact; the split between the church of the East, which became the Greek Orthodox, and that of the West, which later became the Roman Catholic, was caused partly by disagreement over the procession of the Holy Spirit. At the Council of Nicea it was agreed that the Son proceeded from the Father by eternal generation. The Eastern church, on the basis of Jn 15:26, insisted that the Spirit proceeded from the Father alone, while the Western church, fearing the teaching that the Son is subordinate to the Father, and the Spirit subordinate to both, said that He proceeded from both the Father and the Son. The two churches finally separated in 1054.

Modalism and Patripassianism (Latin *pater*, father; *passio*, suffering) were 3rd cen. A.D. errors that denied the existence of the actual trinity of three persons in the Godhead. Modalism taught that the Father and the Son and the Holy Spirit are only names, expressions or modes of the one individual being, God Himself. Patripassianism taught that only the Father exists and that it was He who became man and suffered on the cross for the sins of the world. Karl Barth has adopted what is essentially the view of Modalism but has modified it to the extent that he says all of God is in each of the modes of His revelation as Father, Son, and Holy Spirit. The Father is the revealer, the Son is revelation, and the Holy Spirit is revealedness. Any denial, however, of the true personality of the Holy Spirit is subject to all of the philosophical and scriptural errors which belong to all antitrinitarianism. *See* Trinity.

R. A. K.

POCHERETH (pŏk'ĕ-rĕth). The head of a family returning to Palestine under Zerubbabel (Ezr 2:57; Neh 7:59). He was included in a group called the "children of Solomon's servants." In Heb. *pokereth* appears with *ṣebāim* ("gazelles"), and the name thus means "binder of the gazelles." Several of the modern versions simply transliterate the whole expression as Pochereth-hazzebaim (RSV, NASB, and Berkeley).

POET. This word occurs only in Acts 17:28, although the Gr. word *poiētēs* which it translates is used several other times. The expression is used by Paul to refer to pagan writers in his famous Mars Hill address. Paul seems to allude to Epimenides of Crete in his statement, "In him we live, and move, and have our being." More certain is the quotation, "For we are also his offspring," taken from the beginning of the *Phaenomena* by Aratus, a 3rd cen. B.C. poet born in Cilicia. Paul should not be understood as seeking direct support for his teaching from Gr. paganism.

POETRY. In poetry man expresses his deepest and highest thoughts and emotions. In its imagery and swelling rhythm he sings of his love, his adoration, his pain, his sorrow, and his hope. It would be strange indeed if the Bible, which lays bare the very heart of man and of God, should not also be a book containing sublime poetry. Indeed the Bible, particularly the OT, is one of the greatest of all poetic books. Although the nature of its poetry has often been obscured by the form in which it appears in translations, the poetic passages of the Bible have not only revealed God to man but have been the expression of man's love and adoration toward God.

Old Testament Poetry

History of interpretation. Until about 200 years ago, much of the poetry of the OT was unrecognized as such. Books such as Job, Psalms, and Proverbs were obviously poetic, but ignorance of Semitic poetic style and the mistaken assumption that poetry should conform to the canons of classical literature had obscured the fact that more than a third of the OT was poetry. A great part of the messages of the prophets was given originally in poetic form, not only for greater vividness and appeal, but that it might remain longer in the memory. Even in the books of law and history there are many poetic passages, such as the song of Lamech (Gen 4:23-24), the blessing of Jacob (Gen 49:2-27), the victory songs of Moses and of Miriam (Ex 15:1-21), the prophecies of Balaam (Num 23:7-10, 18-24; 24:3-9, 15-24), the song of Deborah (Jud 5), and the prayer of Hannah (I Sam 2:1-10).

In 1753 the first great book on the subject of biblical poetry began a new era of understanding for much of the Bible. Robert Lowth, after careful study, had rediscovered the basic nature and laws of Heb. poetry and published his findings in *De Sacra Poesi Hebraeorum*. Since that time many studies have been made and outstanding books have been produced, such as Herder's *The Spirit of Hebrew Poetry* and G. B. Gray's *The Forms of Hebrew Poetry*.

POETRY

Of particular value to the study of Heb. poetry has been the discovery by archaeologists of the vast literature of the ancient world contemporary with the Bible. The literature of Egypt, Assyria, Babylonia, and Canaan forms a background for the biblical writing as it is a part of the same culture and thought world. The discovery of the Ugaritic literature at Ras Shamra (*q.v.*), belonging to a Semitic culture very near the time of Moses, has greatly facilitated our understanding of the poetry of Scripture and our exegesis of the biblical message. Consider how great a difference in meaning is involved if such a line as "Behold, the Lord's hand is not shortened that it cannot save" (Isa 59:1) is construed as sober prose instead of poetic imagination!

The clay tablets from Ugarit have supplied philological data which have served to illuminate many obscure expressions in biblical poetry. In both Ugaritic and Heb. poetry the dominating principle is the same, one of balance or symmetry of ideas. Scholars have also discovered considerable similarity in diction between the Canaanite epics and OT poetry, so much so that long lists have been made of fixed pairs of synonyms or related words common to Ugaritic literature and various books of the Bible (Mitchell Dahood, *Psalms I*, Anchor Bible, Garden City: Doubleday, 1966, pp. xv–xliii; *Psalms II*, 1968, pp. xv–xvii).

Characteristics. The most striking difference between Heb. and Western poetry is found in the fact that rhyme and meter which are so important in Western literature are incidental or non-existent among the Hebrews. While Heb. poetry has the natural rhythm and flexibility that marks all true poetry, its chief distinguishing feature is found not so much in form as in content. Heb. poetry is marked by the correspondence in thought that appears in successive lines. This is called "parallelism," a symmetry of ideas, and appears in several variations:

1. Synonymous—the same thought is repeated in a slightly different way; e.g., Ps 12:1:

"Help, Lord; for the godly man ceaseth;
For the faithful fail from among the children of men."

2. Antithetical—the thought of the first line is contrasted in the second, sometimes by the completely opposite thought. This is found most frequently in the book of Proverbs; e.g., Prov 1:7:

"The fear of the Lord is the beginning of knowledge;
But fools despise wisdom and instruction."

3. Synthetic—the second line furthers or completes the thought of the first. This is sometimes continued in a third line, and by some scholars is classified as another form of parallelism, climactic; e.g., Ps 92:9:

"For, lo, thine enemies, O Lord,
For, lo, thine enemies shall perish;
All the workers of iniquity shall be scattered."

4. Chiastic—a development of the basic synonymous parallelism, in which four lines are used, the first and fourth being parallel and the second and third; e.g., Ps 137:5–6, RSV:

"If I forget you, O Jerusalem,
let my right hand wither!
Let my tongue cleave to the roof of my mouth,
if I do not remember you."

Recognition of these forms, which are clearly marked in most modern translations such as the ASV, RSV, and NASB, not only adds to the enjoyment and appreciation of the Bible, but is a distinct aid to understanding. One line throws light on the meaning of another as the same or opposite things are said in slightly different ways.

While balance of thought is the primary principle of Heb. poetry, meter also appears, but on a different basis than in Western languages. The meter is determined not by syllables but by tonal stress or accent on important words, as it is to some degree in our music. No attempt is made to produce a uniform number of intervening syllables. Although as long ago as Josephus it was declared that Moses like Homer had written in hexameters, most scholars today are agreed that whatever rhythm is found is not set in a strict metrical pattern. Many commentaries by critical scholars are weakened by their attempts to emend the Heb. text in order to make it conform to some metrical form.

The question of strophes or stanzas has also been raised, and it would appear that the Hebrews did use stanza divisions. Like the individual lines, the stanzas were determined by the content of the words, and a change in thought would bring a new strophe. While some stanzas are clearly marked, such as the alphabetically divided sections of the great acrostic Psalm 119, they do not follow any apparent pattern and are not always to be determined. The attempt to establish strophic structure for various types of poetry is very inconclusive. The emendations and conjectural changes in the Heb. text to fit these assumed patterns is a questionable practice.

Heb. poetry delights in certain other characteristics which are found to some extent in our own literature. Assonance, the use of words that sound alike, is found in many places, and seems to be used particularly by certain authors such as Isaiah, e.g., Isa 53:1–9. Alliteration is also commonly found, in which a succession of words begin with the same sound.

The figurative and exalted language that is the mark of all true poetry is found in the Bible in abundance. Simile, metaphor, personification, and hyperbole enliven and beautify the literature. Because the Heb. language does not have many abstract words, its images are concrete and very vivid. It abounds in descriptions in which the whole created world is employed to express the emotion and passion of love, hate, adoration, praise, warning, or exhortation. Notice the bewildering array of objects with which the lovers in the Song of Solomon compare one another. Instead of saying that God is omnipotent and omniscient, Isaiah describes His creative powers (40:12 ff.), and Job depicts the mighty creatures whom God has made (chap. 40–41). In Heb. poetry "the heavens declare the glory of God" (Ps 19:1) in a most literal way.

New Testament Poetry

The NT contains comparatively little poetry, and what is there is usually either quoted from the OT or modeled upon it. The *Magnificat* of Mary (Lk 1:46-55) and the *Benedictus* of Zechariah (Lk 1:68-79) are almost completely made up of OT lines. The *Gloria* (Lk 2:14) and the *Nunc Dimittis* (Lk 2:29-32) are also in the style of the psalms. The wonderful hymns of the book of Revelation are Heb. in both form and matter, not Gr. Other passages not usually thought of as poetry, as seen through Jewish eyes, might very well be listed as such, e.g., the Beatitudes and the Lord's Prayer (Mt 5:2-10; 6:9-13), the Prologue of John's Gospel (1:1-18) and the hymn of love (I Cor 13). It is thought that Eph 5:14 and I Tim 3:16, and perhaps Phil 2:6-11 are portions of early Christian hymns.

In these passages is found the same general style of parallelism and descriptive language as in the OT. The change from Heb. to Gr. has simply given a much greater vocabulary of conceptual words. It is doubtful that any of the NT writers observed the laws of Gr. prosody.

See Music; Psalms, Book of.

Bibliography. "Poetry, Hebrew," CornPBE, pp. 593-596. Stanley Gevirtz, *Patterns in the Early Poetry of Israel*, Chicago: Univ. of Chicago Press, 1963. Norman K. Gottwald, "Poetry, Hebrew," IDB, III, 829-838. George B. Gray, *The Forms of Hebrew Poetry*, London: Hodder & Stoughton, 1915. T. H. Robinson, *The Poetry of the Old Testament*, London: Duckworth, 1947.

P. C. J.

POISON. The English word appears several times in the sense of snake venom, being a translation of the Heb. *ḥēmâ* and *rō'sh*, and the Gr. *iós*. In the song of Moses reference is made to "the poison of serpents" and "the poison of dragons" (Deut 32:24, 33). Job's response to Eliphaz speaks figuratively of poisoned arrows (Job 6:4), while Zophar describes the fate of the wicked in terms of sucking the poison of asps (Job 20:16). The evil influence of the wicked is compared to the poison of a serpent in Ps 58:4; and Ps 140:3, quoted by Paul in Rom 3:13, is to the same general point. The idea that the writers of the Bible thought that the serpent's tongue was the poison-bearer is sheer fancy. On the other hand, James states figuratively that the human tongue is "full of deadly poison" (Jas 3:8). *See* Animals, IV.8, 30, 34.

POLE. The KJV word translating Heb. *nēs* (usually "banner," "ensign," or "standard") in Num 21:8-9. Modern versions normally render it here as "a standard." The suggestion that the account in Num 21 refers to a pole sharpened at the top and which transfixed the brazen serpent is an attractive one. The NT sees in this event a type of Christ's death (Jn 3:14).

The so-called "groves" of pagan worship were not such at all, but were sacred pillars or poles called *'ashērâ*, which represented the goddess Asherah (*see* Gods, False).

POLITENESS. A quality becoming to Christians at all times. It is constantly to be seen in the manner in which Christ dealt with all who were earnest seekers, such as the rich young ruler whom He challenged rather than reproved (Lk 18:18-22); the young lawyer whom He treated likewise (Lk 10:25-37); Nicodemus (Jn 3:1 ff.). The OT prophets showed respect and courtesy to those with whom they dealt, such as Nehemiah with Artaxerxes (Neh 2:3); Daniel with Nebuchadnezzar (Dan 2:37). Paul did likewise with Ananias (Acts 23:1-5).

POLL. The noun is from the Heb. *gulgōlet*, which means "skull." The connection of this with "poll" is probably to be understood as a synecdoche, analogous to such expressions as 25 head of cattle. The numbering of people was to take a census for military or labor purposes or for taxation (Num 1:2, 18, 20, 22; 3:47; I Chr 23:2, 24).

The verbal idea is expressed by three Heb. words whose distinctions are not at all clear: (1) *gāzaz* (Mic 1:16) in participial form means "sheepshearer"; (2) *gālaḥ* (II Sam 14:26) is definitely connected with shaving parts of the human body, e.g., Samson in Jud 16:17, 22; (3) *kāsam* occurs only in Ezk 44:20 (twice), where it refers to the priests and Levites cutting their hair.

POLLUTION. Rare in KJV, although "pollute" and "polluted" frequently occur. In Ezk 22:10 the word is used in connection with the sins of the people of Jerusalem just before its destruction. In Acts 15:20 James speaks of the "pollutions of idols"; and in II Pet 2:20 Peter refers to the "pollutions of the world." The word means "defilement," whether physical or moral or spiritual. If a person or thing is good or clean, it is possible to pollute or defile it by contaminating it with evil. Idol worship constitutes a pollution of the idol worshiper, and worldliness brings pollution to any believer.

POLLUX. *See* Gods, False: Castor and Pollux.

POLYGAMY. *See* Marriage.

POMEGRANATE. *See* Plants.

POMMEL. A bowl or oil vessel, named *gullâ* for its roundness (II Chr 4:12-13, KJV). Its root is the Heb. *gālal* meaning "to roll." In the parallel passage in I Kgs 7:41 the term is translated "bowls." The word is now obsolete in the sense discussed. In the passages above it appears to be a rounded ornament of a sort, on the capitals of the two pillars in front of Solomon's temple. The NEB combines the words "the pommels and the chapiters" to form the rendering "the two bowl-shaped capitals."

PONTIUS PILATE. *See* Pilate, Pontius.

PONTUS (pŏn'tŭs). An ancient kingdom of Asia Minor founded *c.* 302 B.C., on the Black Sea lying between Armenia and the Halys River, originally part of Cappadocia. It attained its greatest influence under Mithridates VI (111-63 B.C.) remaining a threat to Roman rule until defeated by Pompey in 66 B.C. For the next 130 years the western portion of the region was under Roman control, but the eastern sections were still under independent chieftains or puppet kings. It was finally made a senatorial province by Nero in A.D. 64. The area was mountainous on the E and S with large fertile plains.

Jews from Pontus were present in Jerusalem on Pentecost (Acts 2:9). Aquila was a native of Pontus (Acts 18:2). Peter addressed Christians in this province in his first epistle (I Pet 1:1).

One of the so-called pools of Solomon, dating to the first century A.D.

POOL, POND. These words in the OT are the translations of three Heb. words. (1) Heb. *'ăgam,* "pond," properly, muddy marshes or stagnant pools formed by the flooding of a river such as the Nile (Ex 7:19; 8:5; Isa 14:23; 19:10; 42:15). (2) Heb. *berēkâ,* "a pond," "pool" (II Sam 2:13; 4:12), from the root *bārak,* "to bend the knee" or "kneel"; an artificial tank where, for example, camels would kneel to drink. (3) Heb. *mikweh,* "a gathering together" or "collection" of waters (Gen 1:10; Ex 7:19; Lev 11:36). The NT word is *kolumbēthra* meaning "a swimming pool," "a place of diving" (Jn 5:2, 4, 7; 9:7, 11).

Pools (*berekôth*) were large open receptacles fed either by springs or by rainwater. Ordinarily

A pool or stepped cistern at Qumran. Robert Unmack

they were carved out of the natural rock or were enclosed by masonry walls, or both. These were all carefully lined with cement or lime plaster so as to hold water. As in the case of cisterns, a crack in the wall by earthquake or other causes, leading to loss of water, was considered a great calamity (Jer 2:13). Other pools were formed by dams built across narrow valleys much like the system of the American farmer. This was especially practiced by the inhabitants of the Negeb such as the Nabateans (*q.v.*), where it was essential to conserve the water of flash flood.

Although the *berēkâ* was an artificial tank, it differed from the *bôr,* "cistern," in that it was of large construction and excavated to a considerable depth, for the use of the entire population, whereas *bôr* was properly a small domestic tank closely associated with a person's house. A good example of the former are the three so-called pools of Solomon near Bethlehem. They were built one below another on a sloping hill so as to catch the overflow, and connected by drainage pipes. These large rectangular pools still in use today, with an estimated capacity of 44 million gallons, were part of the system of Pontius Pilate to bring water to Jerusalem by means of conduits (*q.v.*).

Larger fortified towns often had an underground pool or reservoir for the main city water supply. This was fed through a tunnel leading from a covered spring outside the defense to ensure water in time of siege. It was reached by a sloping passage or steps descending in a tunnel as in Jebusite Jerusalem and Canaanite Gezer, or by a circular staircase in an open shaft as at Gibeon, or by a combination of both as at Megiddo and Hazor.

In the NT era, pools were often adorned with beautiful porticoes or stoae as, for example, the pool of Bethesda (Jn 5:2). Named pools appearing in Scripture are the pool of Samaria (I Kgs 22:38), the pool of Hebron (II Sam 4:12), the pool of Gibeon (II Sam 2:13), the pool of Siloah (Neh 3:15), the pool of Heshbon (Song 7:4), and the pool of Siloam (Jn 9:7). *See* names of specific pools; Water.

R. V. U.

POOR. The Heb. *'ebyôn,* often parallel to *'ānî,* means "afflicted, wretched, distressed, needy," i.e., one ill-treated or suffering social distress. Heb. *dal* means "weak, feeble, thin," i.e., impoverished or reduced in means but not necessarily without property. Heb. *rûsh* means "to be poor, impoverished, to suffer want," and its cognate *rîsh* or *rē'sh* distinctively gives the idea of poverty. The LXX usage is *penēs,* and the NT uses *ptōchos,* meaning "poor, miserable, impotent, beggar."

The poor were those deprived of life's basic necessities. Early Israelite law protected the poor from unlawful usury charges (Ex 22:25; Lev 25:36). The corners of the field were not to be reaped or the vineyards stripped of their fruit, thereby leaving provisions for the needy (Lev 19:9-10; 23:22). Whatever grew spontaneously in the fields during the sabbath year was to be left unreaped for the benefit of any who would gather (Lev 25:5). Again, individuals were allowed to pluck grain or eat grapes belonging to another, provided they carried nothing away (Deut 23:24-25). Poverty as a rule was the result of invasions and war, drought and crop failure, or slothfulness and enslavement.

Numerous scriptures portray God as on the poor man's side (Prov 14:21; Ps 12:5; 41:1; 107:41; Isa 3:15; Amos 2:6-7), as well as reveal the Christian's duty for caring for him (Mt 6:2-4; Acts 9:36; 10:4; II Cor 8:1-7; 9:1-6; Jas 2:15-16). *See* Alms.

The phrase "poor in spirit" (*q.v.;* Mt 5:3 and other scriptures, e.g., Ps 34:6; 37:14; 40:17; Zeph 3:12; Zech 11:7, 11) speaks of poverty in a spiritual sense. Poverty is never eulogized for poverty's sake; rather voluntary self-denial and service is the ideal (Lk 9:23-26; 14:26-33). Jerusalem and Judea, where Jesus had the most association with poor people (Mt 20:30; 26:9, 11; Mk 10:21, 46; 12:42-43; 14:5; Lk 14:13, 21; 18:22, 35; 19:8; 21:3; Jn 12:5-8; 13:29) are contrasted with a more materially prosperous Galilee.

Bibliography. Israel Abrahams, "Poverty and Wealth," *Studies in Pharisaism and the Gospels,* Cambridge: Univ. Press, 1924, I, 113-117. Ernst Bammel, "*Ptōchos,* etc.," TDNT, VI, 885-915. Kaufmann Kohler, "Charity," JewEnc, III, 667-671. R. E. Nixon, "Poverty," NBD, pp. 1016 f. C. U. Wolf, "Poor," IDB, III, 843 f.

R. V. U.

POOR IN SPIRIT. The Gr. word *ptōchos,* "poor," means reduced to beggary, lowly, lacking in something, as "poor in spirit" (Mt 5:3). According to Thayer (*Greek-English Lexicon,* p. 557), Jesus declared those blessed who were lacking in or destitute of the wealth of higher learning and intellectual culture of His day. The kingdom of heaven is made up of such. The Jewish authorities marveled that Peter and John could have such success and speak so boldly, for they knew these followers of Jesus to be "uneducated and untrained men" (Acts 4:13, NASB). It was from such that Christ obtained most of His disciples, though not all. Paul is the chief exception, for he was educated under Gamaliel, a famous Jewish scholar (Acts 22:3). Yet Paul points out that "not many wise men after the flesh, not many mighty, not many noble, are called" (I Cor 1:26). Thank God there have been some such as Paul himself, Augustine, Calvin, Luther, etc. But the principle remains that "God hath chosen the foolish things of the world to confound the wise . . . that no flesh should glory in his presence" (vv. 27-29).

The term "poor in spirit" may also be interpreted to mean those who recognize their own spiritual poverty or bankruptcy. They humbly realize, as Paul did, that in themselves, in their old fleshly nature, "dwelleth no good thing" (Rom 7:18). *See* Flesh. Once having confessed their utter lack, they become blessed because they cast themselves upon the mercy of the Lord. The term, then, is the opposite of proud in spirit. The attitude of pride is a principal reason why men do not seek the great Physician in their deep spiritual need (Mt 9:10-13).

See Poor.

R. A. K.

POPLAR. *See* Plants.

PORATHA (pō-rā'thȧ). One of the several sons of Haman (Est 9:8). He was slain in Shushan by the Jews in their effort to save their own lives (vv. 6-10).

PORCH. The OT word *'êlām* or *'ûlām* means a "hall" or "vestibule." So indicated is the entrance porch on the E side of Solomon's temple (I Kgs 6:3; 7:6; II Chr 15:8), and the temple's inner or outer vestibule in Ezekiel's vision (Ezk 40:7, 48; 41:15). The other OT word *misd^erôn* appears only in Jud 3:23 where it refers to a balcony porch with pillars or balustraded railing.

In the NT three distinct words occur. (1) Gr. *proaulion* is a covered passageway or exterior vestibule leading from the court of a house to the street. In such a forecourt, Peter's denial occurred (Mk 14:68). (2) Gr. *pylōn* ordinarily means "gate," "gateway, entrance" (Lk 16:20; Acts 10:17; 12:13; 14:13; Rev 21:12 f.); in Mt 26:71 (KJV "porch") it must refer to the same architectural feature as *proaulion* in the Mark passages, i.e., the "gateway" (NASB) or entrance vestibule. (3) Gr. *stoa* is a covered "colonnade," "cloister," or "portico." Five such porches surrounded the two sections of the pool of Bethesda (the fifth running between the sections) to provide shelter (Jn 5:2). The colonnade of Herod's temple known as Solomon's porch was a covered walk 30 cubits wide with two rows of pillars 25 cubits high along the E side of the court of the Gentiles (Jn 10:23; Acts 3:11; 5:12; Jos *Ant.* xv.11; xx.9.7).

The purpose of the porch was not only to connect a house to a street, but, as remains in Athens and Corinth illustrate, to give shelter from the rain and burning heat. The school of Tyrannus where Paul taught at Ephesus is thought to have met in such a *stoa* (Acts 19:9).

See Architecture; Temple.

R. V. U.

PORCIUS. *See* Festus.

PORCUPINE. *See* Animals, II. 31.

PORPOISE. The translation in NASB of Heb. *tahash* (Ex 25:5; Num 4:6; *et al.*, KJV "badger"). *See* Animals: Dugong, V.3.

PORT. An obsolete English word meaning "gate" (Heb. *sha'ar*). The English word appears only in Neh 2:13 (KJV) in the phrase "dung port."

PORTER. *See* Doorkeeper; Occupations: Porter, Watchman.

PORTION. This word commonly denotes less than the whole of anything. A special use or destiny of the part as distinguished from the whole is sometimes in view.

A portion may be a parcel of ground (II Kgs 9:10, 36, 37; Ezk 48:21), one's family inheritance (Gen 31:14; Deut 21:17; Lk 15:12), an allowance of clothing or a serving of food (Gen 14:24; Neh 8:10, 12; Dan 1:8–16). It may refer to one's lot or destiny in life (Job 20:29; 31:2; Isa 17:14; Ps 11:6).

Figuratively, portion may refer to one's spiritual heritage or experience in this life or to his destiny in the life to come. This varies from a passage like II Chr 10:16 ("What portion have we in David?"), where strong tribal overtones exist, to passages like Ps 16:5; 73:26; 119:57; Lam 3:24, where pure religious ideas are in view. God is presented as the satisfying possession of believers, while condemnation and judgment are the lot of the wicked (Mt 24:51; Lk 12:46).

See Allotment; Inheritance.

J. K. M.

POSSESSION. *See* Inheritance.

POSSESSION, DEMON. *See* Demonology.

POST

1. An architectural feature meaning either the doorjamb or a pilaster. The Heb. *'ayil*, "post" (Ezk 40:9 ff.; RSV, "jamb"), refers to a part of the framing or ornamentation at the portal. It derives from *'ûl* meaning "to project." Thus, it could be a projecting piece of wall or a pilaster forming the jamb of the opening, or a true pilaster on the wall beside the opening.

Heb. *'ammâ*, "post" (Isa 6:4), is properly "pivots" or "foundations" (RSV), thus, "door sockets." The Heb. *m^ezûzâ* means the members forming the jambs of the door (Ex 12:7).

Part of the framing of a gate at Mycenae, Greece, dating to the thirteenth century B.C. Note holes above and below where a post could be inserted on which to hang a door.
HFV

That they were separate members and detachable is shown by Jud 16:3. In some cases they were square (Ezk 41:21), indicating that usually they were round and possibly made of wood. Heb. *saph* (II Chr 3:7) is actually "threshold," "sill." It is the stone member at the bottom of the door spanning the opening between the jambs. *See* Door.

2. Heb. *rûṣ*, "letter carriers"; actually members of the king's guard, available for any service (II Chr 30:6, 10). The characteristic speed of the courier is the base of Job's metaphor (Job 9:25). The Persian couriers rode horses (Est 8:10, 14).

H. G. S.

POT. A general word for a cooking container. "Pot" expresses a number of Heb. words, the most frequently used of which is *sîr*. Before the divided kingdom, such pots were usually wide-mouthed and rather shallow, often with no handle. They were used both domestically and as ritual vessels, and were often of metal. The term is used in such references as Moab is a "washpot" (Ps 60:8) and Jerusalem is a copper "caldron" (Ezk 11:3; cf. 24:3, 11). The Gr. *xestēs* (Latin, *sextarius*) was a liquid measure of about one pint; hence any small pot (Mk 7:4). The *stamnos* was an earthen jar designed especially for wine. Since the LXX used this word in Ex 16:33 to refer to the jar in which manna would be kept before the Lord, the writer to the Hebrews employs this term to speak of the golden pot or urn for the manna in the tabernacle (Heb 9:4). *See* Pottery.

POTASH. A term found in the NEB at Isa 1:25, translating Heb. *bōr* (KJV "purely"; RSV, NASB "lye"). The Heb. word also occurs in Job 9:30, where RSV, NASB, and NEB all have "lye" (the KJV translators did not understand the Heb. word). Potash is potassium carbonate, so called because of evaporating in iron pots the lye obtained by leaching wood ashes. One use is as a flux in the refining of silver (Isa 1:25). *See* Minerals and Metals: Silver; Occupations: Refiner.

POTENTATE. The Gr. *dynastēs* is translated thus in I Tim 6:15 (KJV) in a description of Jesus Christ as "the blessed and only Potentate." It means "ruler" or "sovereign." The Gr. word appears also in Lk 1:52 as "mighty" with reference to human rulers, and in Acts 8:27 in the phrase "of great authority," speaking of the Ethiopian court official. It is clear that it may refer to other than God, and is designed to express the idea of sovereign authority or power.

POTIPHAR (pŏt'ĭ-fär). The Egyptian officer, "the captain of the guard," to whom Joseph was sold when brought to Egypt by the Midianites (Gen 37:36). The mention of his being "an Egyptian" (Gen 39:1-2) may indicate that Joseph lived during the Hyksos period. Potiphar made Joseph "overseer of his house," but later had him imprisoned upon a false accusation by Potiphar's wife (Gen 39:19-20), after her attempts to seduce Joseph had been frustrated. The name of Joseph's father-in-law, Potipherah (Gen 41:45; 46:20), is regarded as a longer form of Potiphar. Various interpretations of the name have been made; often it is translated "he whom Re has given." *See* Potipherah.

POTIPHERAH (pŏ-tĭ'fĕ-rà). The name of the priest of On who became the father-in-law of Joseph (Gen 41:45, 50; 46:20). He is generally believed to have been a pagan priest of the Egyptian sun-god *Re'* or *Ra* in On (*q.v.*). It is known that a temple to *Re'* existed at On (Gr. Heliopolis) as early as the Old Kingdom period. Potipherah (Heb. *pôṭî-pera'*) is universally recognized as being Egyp. *P'-di-P'R'*, "he whom *P'Re'* [the sun-god] has given." While this exact form of the name is found only in late inscriptions (*c*. 1000-300 B.C.), the name type is known from the New Kingdom or Empire period (1570-1200 B.C.). K. A. Kitchen believes it may have been simply a modernization in Moses' time of the older form *Didi-Re'*, with the same meaning, of a name-pattern which was particularly common in the Middle Kingdom and Hyksos periods (1990-1570 B.C.) ("Potipherah," NBD, p. 1012). *See* Potiphar.

POTSHERD. A piece of broken pottery, a sherd (Heb. *ḥereś*). Potsherds are practically indestructible and show up in large quantities in nearly every archaeological excavation in the Near East. Even a sherd reveals something of the original vessel, and is invaluable to the archaeologist for dating a stratum.

The scales on the underside of Leviathan were compared to "sharp potsherds" (Job 41:30, RSV; "sharp stones," KJV), similar to the cutting teeth on the underside of a threshing sledge. Potsherds are used also as a symbol of the dryness or physical impotence that afflicts the sufferer of Ps 22:15.

However, even potsherds normally had their domestic uses, such as taking live coals from a hearth or dipping water from a cistern (Isa 30:14); but Isaiah was comparing Judah to a pot on which judgment will be so totally disintegrating that what remains is altogether worthless.

Sherds on which messages were written in ink are called ostraca (*q.v.; see also* Writing). Job, sitting on a refuse heap, scraped his body with one of the potsherds he found there (Job 2:8), even as the Romans later scraped their skin clean with a metal strigil.

In Ezk 23:34 the sherds seem to be the sherds of the cup of God's wrath which, having been drained by the harlot sisters, Aholah and Aholibah (Samaria and Jerusalem), will be "gnawed" (Heb., cf. NASB, RSV marg.) by them in their madness and desolation. However, the text is not entirely clear.

See Pot; Pottery.

R. V. R.

POTSHERD GATE. The Heb. name *ḥarsît* (ASV, "Harsith," RSV and NASB "Potsherd Gate," KJV "east gate") apparently is derived from the Heb. *ḥereś*, "potsherd." It was probably so named because of the pieces of pottery from the potters' shops cast out of the city there as refuse. Some have related this gate to the Valley Gate located on the western side of Jerusalem (Neh 2:13; 3:13; II Chr 26:9) that led to the upper end of the Valley of Hinnom. This could correspond to the present Jaffa Gate. However, the Targum relates it to the Dung Gate that led southward from the city toward the Potter's Field (*see* Akeldama). *See* Jerusalem: Gates and Towers.

POTTAGE. *See* Food; Plants: Lentils.

POTTER. *See* Occupations: Potter.

POTTER'S FIELD. A field purchased by the members of the Sanhedrin with the money that Judas threw into the sanctuary (Mt 27:3-10). The priests had counseled among themselves that they would not refuse unlawfully gained money for sacred things. Since the money should have been returned to Judas according to the law, but he continued to insist on donating it, they decided it should be spent for charitable purposes. By a quirk of the law, the money still belonged to Judas (Acts 1:18), and with the priests as his legal executors, they used the money to purchase a potter's field for burying foreigners, i.e., pilgrims from the Diaspora who died in the Holy City.

J. Jeremias believes that when the priests refused Judas' repayment of the money, he brought it to the temple treasury as a means of revoking the "sale" of Jesus (*Jerusalem in the Times of Jesus*, Philadelphia: Fortress, 1969, pp. 138–140). The field came to be known as "the field of blood" (Aram. *ḥăqēl dᵉmā'*, Acts 1:19, English, "Aceldama," *q.v.*), probably for two reasons: because the money to purchase the field was blood money, and because Judas hanged himself there. Tradition has located the field at the E end of the Valley of Hinnom and on the S slope. Apparently it was near the potters' dump outside the Potsherd Gate (Jer 19:2, RSV). *See* Jerusalem: Gates and Towers.

Matthew related this purchase (Mt 27:9–10) as a fulfillment of an OT prophecy (cf. Zech 11:12 f.), but ascribed it to Jeremiah. A number of reasons have been suggested for this. Edersheim (*Life and Times of Jesus the Messiah*, Grand Rapids: Eerdmans, 1950, II, 572) seems to have the most plausible explanation: "And so St. Matthew, targuming this prophecy in form as in its spirit, and in true Jewish manner stringing to it the prophetic description furnished by Zechariah, sets the event before us as the fulfillment of Jeremiah's prophecy" (Jer 18:2–12; 19:1–5; 32:6–9).

In his full treatment of Mt 27:9 Edward J. Young reaches the same general conclusion, that Matthew referred to two OT prophets and mentioned Jeremiah as being the older and greater of the two and the one who speaks of the purchase of a field, the basic point of the reference (*Thy Word Is Truth*, Grand Rapids: Eerdmans, 1957, pp. 172–175).

L. Go.

A potter working at his wheel on the island of Rhodes. HFV

POTTER'S GATE. *See* Potsherd Gate.

Iron age pottery from Dothan, Palestine

POTTERY. Because kiln-fired earthenware vessels are very resistant to weathering, they constitute a vital link with the past. Sherds by the thousands may be seen on every ancient mound in Palestine. Through careful scientific study of the various forms, composition, coloring, sizes, etc., the archaeologist may reconstruct an amazing sequence of ancient cultures. Pottery in each land has had a definite evolution, and the person familiar with it is able to trace the stages of the local civilization. The nature of the pottery material, its binder, rim forms, handles, painted decorations and shapes, all tell an eloquent story of the past. The periods of antiquity covering Bible times are usually divided into Neolithic, Chalcolithic, Early Bronze, Middle Bronze, Late Bronze, Iron, Persian, Hellenistic and Roman periods.

The word pottery is not found in the Bible, but there is an abundance of particular terms which refer to specialized products of the potter. In modern usage the term pottery may refer to a potter's workshop as well as to his ware.

The substance of the potter's ware is described by an Aramaic term *ḥăsap*, which appears in Dan 2:33 as part of the account of Nebuchadnezzar's dream image. To translate this "clay" is most confusing and without warrant since the reference is not to raw clay but brittle, baked pottery or earthenware. All pottery work was wrought by hand until the introduction of the potter's wheel, after 3000 B.C. in Palestine. Some of these ancient methods prevail even to this day. The potter's wheel varied somewhat in basic design, but fundamentally it consisted of a flat, round bed of stone centered atop a nearly vertical shaft; near the lower end of the shaft was another wheel which was rotated by kicking with the foot. Great skill was developed in this art.

Care must be exercised in defining precisely the kind of vessel or utensil any given word may describe. The general word for "vessel" is *k^e^lî*, appearing nearly 150 times in the Heb. OT. Some of the more specific terms are used only a few times, and there is insufficient evidence to be certain of too-neat distinctions. The following are some of the major ceramic terms:

Heb. *kad* means pitcher or jar (I Kgs 18:33, RSV) and was the vessel customarily carried by women to bring water from the well or river (Eccl 12:6), as in the account of the choosing of Rebekah (Gen 24:14–20). The "waterpot" (Gr. *hydria*) was the equivalent vessel in NT times (Jn 4:28).

The *sappaḥat* was a pottery canteen or lens-shaped traveler's flask with two handles, popular from *c.* 1400 to 700 B.C. ("cruse," I Sam 26:11 ff.; I Kgs 19:6). It was hardly large enough to be a household container for olive oil, but the poor widow evidently had never had a large supply of cooking oil before Elijah came (I Kgs 17:12–16).

A *pak* was a small juglet for holding perfumed oil. This is reflected in the translation "vial" in I Sam 10:1, KJV, RSV, but very inappropriately as "box" in II Kgs 9:1, 3, KJV. It occurs only in these accounts of the anointing of Saul and Jehu.

The OT word *kôs* is regularly translated "cup" in most versions, and finds extensive use in describing a small individual wine bowl, sometimes literal (II Sam 12:3; Prov 23:31; Jer 35:5) and sometimes figurative (Isa 51:17, 22; Jer 25:15).

The Heb. word *sîr* occurs 28 times. It was a wide-mouthed, round-bottomed cooking pot used especially by the poor over an open flame (Eccl 7:6). The Israelite slaves stewed meat in such pots in Egypt (Ex 16:3). It could be large enough to boil herbs for vegetable soup for all the sons of the prophets under Elisha (II Kgs 4:38).

Pottery from Ur dating to about 2200 B.C. BM

A *baqbûq* was an expensive, artistically made earthenware water decanter or bottle with a narrow neck. This name may originate from the gurgling sound which it makes when emptied. Its use in Jer 19:1, 10–11 fittingly illustrates the care God took in forming the people of Jerusalem as well as the fact that He could break them in judgment.

A large painted Mimoan storage jar (about four feet high) from Crete, dating c. 1500 B.C. HFV

The *gābîa'* (bowl) has extended associations with wine. It was the larger vessel from which the *kôs* was filled. The fact that *gābîa'* describes Joseph's silver cup in Gen 44:2, 12, 16–17 might appear to controvert this, but not necessarily so. A fairly large vessel could be hidden in a bag. The "bowls" (KJV) of the golden lampstand (candlestick) in the tabernacle are described by this term (Ex 25:31, 33, 34; 37:17, 19–20). It also appears in that interesting account of the Rechabites in Jer 35:5, and is translated by the KJV as "pots," while the Berkeley and RSV use "pitchers." Probably here at least the *gābîa'* was pottery. These vessels were similar in function and shape to the pitcher or water jug carried by the owner of the house of the upper room (Mk 14:13).

The word *maḥabat* may refer to a flat baking plate or grill, composed either of pottery or metal. It is translated "pan" in Lev 2:5; 6:21; 7:9; etc. The Heb. *dûd* seems to have a double meaning, expressing the idea of a caldron or kettle in I Sam 2:14; II Chr 35:13; Job 41:20; and of a basket in II Kgs 10:7; Ps 81:6 (RSV); Jer 24:1–2. The pottery vessel of this name was probably a deep spherical cooking pot with small mouth and two small handles.

Heb. *kiyyôr* usually refers to a deep bronze basin; in Zech 12:6 it may be made either of metal or earthenware, a "fire-pot" (cf. RSV) or brazier. It is the word selected to describe the bronze laver (Ex 30:18; 38:8; 40:7, 11, 30; Lev 8:11). The word *nēbel* originally meant a wine-skin (I Sam 1:24; 10:3; 25:18, RSV). As a large pottery vessel it was like our jug or pitcher or was used as a household storage jar holding five to ten gallons (Isa 22:24, "flagons"; 30:14, "vessel"; Lam 4:2, "pitcher"). When made for storing wine (Jer 13:12; 48:12) it was called an *amphora* by the Greeks. The *sap* was a wooden or clay bowl or basin (Ex 12:22; II Sam 17:28; Zech 12:2) or of metal for the temple (I Kgs 7:50; II Kgs 12:13).

As far as other Gr. words for specific vessels are concerned, the NT has the following:

Potērion is always rendered as "cup" in the 30 times it appears (Mt 10:42; Lk 11:39; I Cor 10:16, 21). *Phialē,* "vial," represents a shallow bowl of gold or clay and is found only in the judgment scenes of Revelation (Rev 5:8; 16:1, 2, 3; 17:1). A *tryblion* was a large dish made of metal or pottery from which all could take food (Mt 26:23).

See Basin; Bowl; Dish; Lamp; Pot; Potsherd; Occupations: Potter.

Mycenaean jars from Rhodes, dating c. 1300 B.C. Mimosa

Bibliography. Ruth Amiran, "The Story of Pottery in Palestine," *Antiquity and Survival,* II, Nos. 2-3 (1957), 187-207; *Ancient Pottery of the Holy Land,* New Brunswick: Rutgers Univ. Press, 1970. CornPBE, pp. 597-601. H. J. Franken and J. Kalsbeek, *Excavations at Tell Deir 'Alla, Part I: A Stratigraphical and Analytical Study of the Early Iron Age Pottery,* Leiden: Brill, 1969 (reviewed by Paul W. Lapp, VT, XX [1970], 243-256). Vronwy Hankey, "Pottery Making at Beit Shebab, Lebanon," PEQ, C (1968), 27-32 and Pl VII–XVII. James L. Kelso, *The Ceramic Vocabulary of the Old Testament,* BASOR Supplementary Studies, Nos. 5-6, 1948. John Rea, "Pottery," *Zondervan Pictorial Bible Dictionary,* Grand Rapids: Zondervan, 1963, pp. 674-678.

B. C. S.

POUND. *See* Weights, Measures, and Coins.

POVERTY. *See* Poor.

Red tinted Attic vases from Rhodes, fifth century, B.C. Mimosa

POWDERS. The only occurrence of this word in Scripture is Song 3:6 where the Heb. *'ăbqâ* is so translated by the KJV and ASV. It is likely a collective that refers to pulverized aromatic spices. The RSV translates it "fragrant powders," the NEB "powdered spices," and the NASB "scented powders."

POWER. The Heb. language, like the English, has many words which convey the concept of power. The two most common words appear in the well-known passage, "Not by might nor by power, but by My Spirit, says the Lord of hosts" (Zech 4:6, NASB). Heb. *ḥayil,* the word for "might," can mean physical strength or valor, as of warriors (Josh 1:14; 8:3; 10:7) and therefore military power (I Chr 20:1); the armed forces or army itself (Ex 14:4, 28; I Kgs 20:19, 25; Jer 32:2); ability or efficiency, often involving moral worthiness (Ex 18:21, 25; Gen 47:6; Prov 12:4; 31:10; Ruth 3:11); and wealth or economic influence (Gen 34:29; Deut 8:17-18; Prov 28:8; Ruth 2:1, NASB).

The word for "power" is Heb. *kōah,* which can also mean physical strength (e.g., Samson, Jud 16:5; Saul, I Sam 28:20; strength to weep, I Sam 30:4; burden bearers, Neh 4:10), as well as ability (Gen 31:6; Ezr 2:69; Deut 8:17-18) and mental power ("strength of understanding," Job 36:5, RSV). Heb. *geḇûrâ* signifies strength or might (overmastering power), as of a war horse (Job 39:19), the sun (Jud 5:31), or a king (II Kgs 14:28). The arm *zeroa'* and the hand (*yād*) are used as metaphors of power and so translated (Ezk 22:6 and Job 1:12, respectively; cf. Ezk 20:33-34). Heb *'ōz* is another frequent synonym for strength and power (Lev 26:19; Ps 62:11; 63:2; 66:3).

In the OT the exercise of all true power rests in the hand of God alone, and forever (Ps 66:7; 72:11). He is the One who gives political power to whom He pleases (Jer 27:5; Dan 2:20-21; 4:17), and strengthens those who wait on Him (Isa 40:29-31). God revealed His power in creation (Jer 10:12-16; 51:15-19) and in the upholding of the world and creation (Job 26:12; Ps 65:5-8; Isa 40:26; cf. Col 1:17). Therefore there is nothing too hard for Him (Jer 32:17).

God delegates some of His authority to mankind (Gen 1:26-28; Ps 8:5-8). At times He lets man exercise it on His behalf, as with Moses (Ex 7:1), Elijah (I Kgs 17:1), and Micah (Mic 3:8). At times He intervenes with special displays of His power, as before and during the Exodus (Ex 6:6; 7:3-5; 15:6; Deut 5:15), at the entrance to the Promised Land (Josh 3:14-17; 6:20; 10:10-14; cf. Ps 111:6), at the time of Elijah and Elisha, at the time of Christ, and in the early days of the church (Heb. 2:4). *See* Miracles; Works of God.

In the NT, *dynamis* represents ability (II Cor 8:3) or strength (Eph 3:16), such as the power to perform miracles (Rom 15:19), the power exhibited in Christ's resurrection (Eph 1:19-20; Phil 3:10), the power of the gospel (Rom 1:16; I Cor 1:18, 24), and the power of the Holy Spirit in Christ (Lk 4:14) and as He came at Pentecost (Acts 1:8). See W. Grundmann, "*Dunamai*, etc.," TDNT, II, 284-317.

Gr. *exousia* designates right and power in the sense of derived authority. Jesus speaks of all authority being given to Him (Mt 28:18), such as authority to forgive sins (Mk 2:10, NASB). Jesus gave both power and authority to the Twelve in order to exorcise demons and heal diseases (Lk 9:1). The person who believes in Christ has the "power" or right (NASB) to become a son (child, ASV) of God (Jn 1:12). *See* Authority. Gr. *kratos* expresses more the idea of strength to do things and is used of God's power (Eph 1:19; 6:10; Col 1:11; I Tim 6:16; Rev 5:13) and the devil's (Heb 2:14).

The power of the keys refers to the power either to loose and forgive or to retain sins, announced by Christ to Peter at the time of his confession in Mt 16:18-20. That this power was not to be Peter's alone, or even to be delegated by Peter to the church, as claimed by Roman Catholicism, is proved by the fact that Christ declared it to be applicable to all the disciples and all believers (Mt 18:18). How is this power administered by believers? In two ways, the Reformed theologians say. First, through the teaching and preaching of the Word of God so that men may believe or refuse to believe. Second, through the discipline by the church of those who have sinned (see Calvin on I Cor 5).

R. A. K.

PRAETORIUM. This originally Latin term comes from *praetor*, "leader," "head," "chief," and appears in later Gr. First it signified the tent of the praetor (general) in a Roman army camp (Livy, *Hist.* vii.12; x.23). Then it denoted the general's officers who assembled in his tent as a council (Livy, *Hist.* xxvi.15; xxx.5; xxxvii.5). Later it referred to the official provincial residence of a governor (Cicero, *in Verr.* II.iv.28; II.v.35) or of a procurator (Jn 18:28). Finally it designated the imperial troops acting as bodyguards (Tacitus, *Hist.* ii.ll.24; iv.46; Suetonius, *Nero*, 9). See G. T. Purves, "Praetorium," HDB, IV, 32 f.

In the KJV the word appears only in Mk 15:16, but in the Gr. text it occurs in Mt 27:27; Jn 18:28, 33; 19:9; Acts 23:35 as "common hall" or "judgment hall," and in Phil 1:13 as "palace." Disagreement continues on the location of Pilate's Jerusalem headquarters (praetorium) for the trial of Jesus (i.e., whether Herod's palace or the Antonia fortress). *See* Judgment Hall; Antonia. In Caesarea, however, certainly Herod's magnificent palace served as the procurator's praetorium and Paul's place of imprisonment (Acts 23:35). The phrase *en holō tō praitōriō* (Phil 1:13) best refers to "the whole praetorian guard" in Rome rather than to the "palace" or residence of Caesar on the Palatine hill. The palace in Rome was never called "praetorium."

R. V. U.

PRAISE. The principal Heb. words for praise are *hillēl* from the root *hālal*, and *hôdâ* from *yādâ*. The former is familiar in the word hallelujah, "Praise ye the Lord (Yahweh)." The Heb. title of the book of Psalms is "praises" (*tᵉhillîm*), while Ps 113-118 are known as the Hallel psalms, and are used at the Jewish feasts. The "hymn" sung before Jesus' exit from the last supper may have been the second part of the Hallel, Ps 115-118 (cf. Mishna Pesaḥim 10:6 f.). *Hôdâ*, while common in the OT, is now most familiar from the sectarian hymns (*Hodayoth*) found at Qumran.

Praise of God is one of the most characteristic features of biblical piety. As early as the song of Moses (Ex 15:1-19), Yahweh is praised for His redemptive acts, but the systematization of Israelite praise is attributed to David. The books of Chronicles record in detail his institution of the Levitical temple musicians and gatekeepers (I Chr 23:1–26:32, especially 23:5, 30; cf. chap. 6), and the ascription of many of the psalms to David or to his musicians (e.g., Asaph, the sons of Korah, Heman, or Jeduthun) bears out this tradition.

When Judah went into exile, temple worship was impossible; thus, praise centered in the synagogue. It took on some of the characteristics of sacrifice in that times were appointed for it, and special merit was attached to "ceaseless" praise (or prayer, *q.v.*), i.e., praise before dawn or all through the night (see, e.g., Psalms of Solomon 3:1 ff.; Qumran *Hodayoth* xii. 1-11).

Praise as sacrifice (Heb 13:15) and as a continual duty and privilege (I Thess 5:16 ff.; cf. Rev 4:8) is also a NT theme, The NT hymns of praise center around redemption in Christ (e.g., Lk 1:46-55, 68-79; 2:13 f.; Eph 1:3-14; Col 1:18-20; Rev 5:9-14; 7:10-12), although God's being (Rev 4:8) and creative work (Rev 4:11; Col 1:15-17) are not forgotten. Moreover, Christians are encouraged to make their whole lives and conduct a form of praise to God (Eph 1:12; Phil 1:11; 4:8; I Pet 1:7; 2:9). *See* Worship.

J. R. M.

PRAYER

Biblical Vocabulary

The terminology of prayer in the Bible is rich and varied. The general Heb. noun is *tepilla*, from a form of the verb *pālal*; the Gr. is *proseuchē*, with the middle deponent very *proseuchomai*. The root idea in the Heb. term is intercession, and in the Gr., a vow; but the etymologies are no longer determinative for the meaning. Both words can be used comprehensively for any kind of petition, intercession, or thanksgiving. (*See* Supplication.)

Prayer is described as "calling upon the name of the Lord " from the days of Seth (Gen 4:26) up to that time when the "Lord" was revealed as Jesus Christ (cf. Joel 2:32 with Rom 10:9, 12-13). Christians are identified as those who call upon His name (I Cor 1:2). Other OT expressions are to "entreat" or "seek the favor" of Yahweh (*pi'el* of *ḥālà*, lit., "to make his face pleasant"), "to bow in worship" (*shāḥà*), "to draw near" (*nāgash*), "to fall upon" or "meet" for entreaty (*pāga'*), "to cry out" (*zā'aq*) for the redress of a wrong, "to ask" (*shā'al*), "to supplicate" (*'āthar*), or "to appear before the face of the Lord." In addition to *proseuchomai*, the NT writers use the terms "beseech" (*deomai*), "request" (*aiteō*), and simply "ask" (*erotao*), in reference to prayer. Unlike *proseuchomai*, these are not distinctively "religious" words but may denote petitions addressed to men as well as to God. Among the more specialized NT words for prayer are *entygkanō*, "intercede"; *proskyneō*, "worship"; and *eucharisteō*, "to give thanks."

Old Testament

There was no one posture required for the exercise of prayer. Most often prayer was made standing (e.g., I Sam 1:26); the great prayer of the Jewish synagogue was to be called the "standing prayer" (*Amidah*). On occasion, however, one might pray kneeling (I Kgs 8:54), or prostrate (I Kgs 18:42), with hands spread out (I Kgs 8:22, 54; Isa 1:15) or lifted up (Ps 63:4; cf. I Tim 2:8). Those praying often faced the temple because it was the place where God had caused His name to dwell (I Kgs 8:29-30). When the temple was destroyed prayer was sometimes made toward Jerusalem (Dan 6:10). Nevertheless, Solomon had recognized at the beginning that "the highest heaven cannot contain Thee, how much less this house which I have built!" (I Kgs 8:27, NASB). Not the posture nor the "geography" of prayer, but the prayer itself and the needs that called it forth, were the primary concern of the Heb. writers.

Prayer in the OT can be appropriately described in terms of the great men of Israel, who often appear as great intercessors standing before God on behalf of the people. In this capacity they manifest remarkable boldness and persistence. Abraham pleads with God for wicked Sodom, persistently bringing down the minimum number of righteous for whose sake the city can be spared (Gen 18:22-33). Jacob wrestles with the angel (Gen 32:24-32), an experience interpreted within the OT itself in terms of prayer (Hos 12:4). Moses asks that his own name might be blotted out of the book of life if God would forgive those who worshiped the golden calf (Ex 32:31 ff.; cf. Num 14:13-19). Made in a similar spirit of intercession but with more emphasis on humility, confession, and repentance are the prayers that focus around the experience of the Exile: the prayers of Daniel (Dan 9:3-19), Ezra (Ezr 9:5-15), and Nehemiah (Neh 1:5-11). The great covenant prayer of Neh 9-10 rehearses the holy history from Abraham to Ezra with its pattern of sin and confession, forgiveness and renewal, and vows faithfulness to God's law.

In this later period prayer also takes on communal aspects. The book of Psalms is the prayer book of the OT, encompassing every conceivable type of prayer—praise, petition, intercession, blessing, confession, thanksgiving. Probably most of the psalms were originally composed as expressions of individual piety, but they were soon adopted into the corporate worship of the Israelite community. Their overall title is *tᵉhillîm*, "praises" (*q.v.*), although some of them are called "prayers" (*tᵉpillîm*, see, e.g., Ps 72:20, ending Book II of the Psalms), and many others can be classed as prayers in a broad sense.

Of particular note are the so-called imprecatory psalms, in which the suffering righteous so identifies his own interests with those of God that his outcry for vindication is accompanied by its corollary, a prayer for the downfall of his enemies. This "intercession in reverse" can be seen in such psalms as 109, 137, and 140. Such psalms are simply a special instance of the plaintive cries for deliverance that accompany the plight of those who suffer unjustly throughout the Bible (cf. the phrases "to wait on the Lord," 27:14; "How long, O Lord, how long?" 13:1; and "Awake, why sleepest thou, O Lord?" 44:23). It is this type of prayer which forms the background of NT eschatological prayer (cf. Lk 18:7; Rev 6:10).

At the other end of the spectrum are the penitential prayers in which the righteous become more aware of their own sins than of their external enemies, and plead for divine forgiveness, often with a similar, almost eschatological urgency (e.g., Ps 32, 38, 51). It has been truly said that when men have been sinned against, they petition for justice; but when they have sinned, their prayer is for mercy. The OT answer to both prayers is the same, however; the "righteousness" (*ṣedeq*), the "steadfast love" (*ḥesed*), the "faithfulness" (*'ĕmûnâ*), and the "truth" (*'emet*) of Yahweh.

New Testament

1. *Jesus in the Synoptics*. The synoptic life of Jesus is a life of prayer, especially in Luke. Jesus' habit was to withdraw to a lonely place and pray, often before sunrise or even all night

(Mk 1:35; Lk 5:16; 6:12). Luke mentions prayer in connection with the great crises of Jesus' ministry: the baptism (3:21-22), the calling of the Twelve (6:12 ff.), Peter's confession (9:18 ff.), and the transfiguration (9:28 ff.). Jesus' last days in Jerusalem before His passion are divided between daily teaching in the temple and nightly prayer on the Mount of Olives (Lk 21:37 f.). In Luke the eschatological discourse is given as a sample of the former (21:20-33) and the agony in the garden as an illustration of the latter (cf. 22:39 ff.).

This pattern became the model for the primitive Christian community (cf. Acts 1:14, 24; 2:42, 46; 5:20-21, 42; 6:4, 6; 10:9; 12:5 ff.; 16:25; 20:7 ff.). Jesus Himself became the great example to the believer of vigilant and faithful prayer (cf. "Watch and pray," Mk 14:38; Lk 21:36). Even two of the Lucan words from the cross are prayers—words of intercession (23:34) and of trust (23:46). The latter, based on Ps 31:5, corresponds with a prayer commended in the Talmud to faithful Jews before going to sleep each night ("Into thy hands I commend my spirit," *Berakoth 5b*).

At first Jesus seems not to have taught His disciples to share in His prayer life, contrary to the custom of John the Baptist and other religious teachers (Lk 5:33). But when they asked Him (Lk 11:1), He gave them the "our Father" prayer that has come to be called the "Lord's Prayer" (Mt 6:9-13; Lk 11:2-4). Although most of this prayer can be paralleled from the Jewish synagogue worship (e.g., the Mourner's *Kaddish:* "Magnified and hallowed be His great name in the world which He created according to His will. May He establish His kingdom in your lifetime . . . speedily and in a near time . . ."), the direct address "Father" (Lk 11:2) makes the whole prayer uniquely Christian. It is not a prayer that unites men of all faiths, but is distinctively a prayer of those who are "sons of God" through Jesus Christ (cf. the Aramaic form of the address "Abba" in the two great "adoption" passages, Rom 8:15 and Gal 4:6). Thus, Jesus' unique consciousness of God as Father is transferred to His disciples and becomes the basis for their every petition (cf. Jn 20:17). His own prayer in Gethsemane echoes the "Father" prayer at several points (e.g., "Abba," "temptation," "Thy will be done").

Jesus warned against hypocrisy, incoherence, and long-windedness in prayer (Mt 6:5-8), but not against boldness or persistence. Even though He stressed that "your Father knows what you need before you ask him" (Mt 6:8, RSV; cf. v.32), Jesus counseled importunity in two of His parables (Lk 11:5-13; 18:1-8), especially with relation to the realities of the Holy Spirit (11:13) and to final vindication (18:7 f.). The earnest longing for the consummation, enunciated in Jesus' "Thy kingdom come," is echoed in the *maranatha* of I Cor 16:22 and the equivalent "Come, Lord Jesus" of Rev 22:20. *See* Lord's Prayer, The.

Other memorable emphases in Jesus' teaching on prayer are (*a*) His exclusion of all anxiety about material things (Mt 6:11, 19-34); (*b*) His sweeping assurance that believing prayer will be answered (Mt 7:7; 18:19; Mk 11:23 f.); and (*c*) His inseparable linking of prayer with forgiveness (Mt 6:12, 14; 7:1-12; 18:15-22; Mk 11:25; cf. Mt 5:23 ff.). Man's relation to God in prayer is interdependent upon his relation to other men; forgiveness comes by prayer, and without mutual forgiveness, prayer itself is ineffective.

2. *Acts.* If Luke is the Gospel of prayer, its companion volume, Acts, shows the primitive church as a praying community. The disciples pray as they wait for the Holy Spirit (Lk 24:53; Acts 1:14), and after the Spirit comes the cardinal practices of the young church are summed up as "teaching," "sharing of goods," "breaking of bread," and "prayers" (2:42-45). Luke describes this early prayer life as "steadfast" and "with one accord" (e.g., 1:14; 2:42, 46). As in Luke's Gospel, prayer accompanies crises of decision (Acts 1:24) or deliverance (4:24 ff.; 12:5; 16:25) or trust (7:60). It is also associated at times with the laying on of hands and the coming of the Holy Spirit on individuals or groups (6:6; 8:14-17).

3. *Paul.* The Pauline contribution to the NT theology of prayer is the apostle's great emphasis on thanksgiving. The fact that all of Paul's epistles except Galatians and Titus have a thanksgiving or a blessing to God immediately or soon after the salutation can hardly be explained as a mere epistolary form, but is rooted in the Pauline theology. Paul believed that all prayer should include thanksgiving (Phil 4:6; Col 4:2); for thanksgiving (*eucharistia*) caused glory to ascend to God for the grace (*charis*) that had descended to us in Jesus Christ (cf. II Cor 1:11; 4:15; 9:11 f.).

Thanksgiving was that Spirit-led response in the heart of man to God's great redemptive acts (e.g., "our Amen," II Cor 1:20-22, NASB). Along with it, Paul spoke of that aspiration in prayer by which the believer, living between the firstfruits and the harvest, looked forward to that total redemption that Christ would yet accomplish (Rom 8:15-25). Sometimes these prayers were unspoken, but were formed within the heart by the Spirit of God (Rom 8:26-27); sometimes they were in "tongues," intelligible only to God or to others when accompanied by the gift of interpretation (I Cor 14, especially vv.2, 14-15).

The extent of Paul's interest in prayer can be seen in the way it serves to bind him in spirit with his churches (even in a matter of discipline, I Cor 5:3 ff.). The most general of all his epistles, Ephesians, is set within a framework of prayer and praise (cf. Eph 1:3-14, 15-23; 3:1, 14-19, 20-21) that becomes the vehicle for his most profound statements about the church. Paul's general teaching on prayer is well summarized in I Tim 2:1-9.

4. *Hebrews* is important not because of direct teaching that is given about prayer, but

because of its doctrine of Christ as the great High Priest who, by His intercession with the Father, makes Christian prayer possible.

5. *James* is concerned with the right and wrong use of the tongue (3:1 ff.). The wrong use includes false teaching (3:1), cursing (3:9), complaining (4:11; 5:9), and oaths (5:12); the right use includes prayer for wisdom (1:5 f.), for justice (5:4-8), and for healing and forgiveness (5:13-20). James recognizes that there is such a thing as "asking amiss" (4:3); he warns against that double-mindedness that pretends to submit to God while actually seeking its own end (1:7 f.; 3:8 f.; 4:4, 8 ff.). He teaches that prayer offered in faith, when it is "effective" (Gr. *energoumenē*, inwrought and energized by the Holy Spirit), will accomplish much (5:15-16, NASB).

6. *John.* Jesus lived in such close communion with God that the first of His prayers that John was inspired to record is a thanksgiving that the Father had already heard Him (Jn 11:41 f.). When He prays, "Father, glorify thy name," the answer comes, "I have both glorified it and will glorify it again" (12:28). The prayer at the tomb of Lazarus in chap. 11 and the voice from heaven in chap. 12 are not recorded to magnify Jesus in Himself, but to show that His power and glory are not His own; they belong to the One who sent Him (11:42; 12:30) and must be invoked by prayer. Those who accuse John of denying Christ's humility and humanity ignore Jn 12:27 ("What shall I say?") in which Jesus exhibits the full weakness of human nature that He has taken upon Himself (cf. Rom 8:26).

In His farewell discourse Jesus gives to His disciples several assurances of answered prayer (14:13 ff.; 15:7, 16; 16:23 f.). Such prayer is "in Jesus' name" (cf. "according to his will," I Jn 5:14), and is one of the blessings that is made possible because Jesus "goes to the Father" (14:12*b*; 16:24-28). The promise is not a form of magic by which man manipulates his god according to his own whim, but it is always qualified by the will of God or the name of Jesus Christ. Paul and Jude would have added that it concerns a prayer that is worked within the believer by the Spirit (Eph 6:18; Jude 20).

The most extensive NT prayer is Jn 17. Jesus prays again for that glorification that comes in the cross (vv. 1-5), for His disciples (vv. 6-19), and for the Christian church that would come into being (vv. 20-25). It is a prayer for unity, but the goal of that unity is the world mission of the church which is "sent" and gathered into one "so that the world may believe that thou hast sent me" (see vv.17 f., 21, 23). Thus, the whole life and work of the church in this age is established and girded about by the prayer of her Lord and High Priest who sanctified Himself in death for her sake.

See Intercession; Supplication; Thanksgiving; Worship.

Bibliography. William E. Biederwolf, *How Can God Answer Prayer?* New York: Revell, 1910. Heinrich Greeven, "*Euchomai*, etc.," TDNT, II, 775-808. O. Hallesby, *Prayer,* Minneapolis: Augsburg, 1931. James Hastings, *The Christian Doctrine of Prayer,* New York: Scribner's, 1915. Friedrich Heiler, *Prayer,* London: Oxford Univ. Press, 1932. A. Maillot, "Prayer," *A Companion to the Bible,* ed. by J. J. von Allmen, New York: Oxford Univ. Press, 1958, pp. 329-334. J. G. S. S. Thomson, *The Praying Christ,* Grand Rapids: Eerdmans, 1959; "Prayer," NBD, pp. 1019-1023.

J. R. M.

PRAYER, LORD'S. *See* Lord's Prayer.

PREACHER, PREACHING. The common motif which runs through all the biblical references to preaching is that of public proclamation. The most characteristic word in the NT is *kērussō* (more than 60 times), which means "to proclaim as a herald." In the ancient world the herald was a key figure in making known official information and all royal decrees. A second word, *euaggelizomai* (more than 50 occurrences), emphasizes the quality of the message as good (from the primitive *eus*) or joyful news.

The nature of biblical preaching depends upon its specific content and the audience to which it is addressed. In the epistles the content of preaching is normally said to be "the gospel" (Rom 1:15; 15:20; I Cor 1:17) or some variant, such as "Christ" (I Cor 15:12), "Christ crucified" (I Cor 1:23), or "the word of faith" (Rom 10:8). This is the message to the non-Christian world.

However, Paul and his companions also preached to the assemblies of believers. This consisted of a blend of catechetical instruction, ethical exhortation, and eschatological encouragement. In current biblical studies this latter type of public address is called *didachē* (teaching) and is usually distinguished rather sharply—although opinion is now changing—from *kērygma* (preaching). While this differentiation is valid, it should not be pressed too strenuously. The Synoptics evidence an overlapping of terms (cf. Mt 4:23 with its parallels), and in Acts 15:21 James refers to the weekly synagogue reading of the Torah as preaching.

It is perhaps more helpful to subdivide preaching in terms of the audience. When a preacher stands over against his listeners he proclaims the death, resurrection, and exaltation of Christ. This answers to C. H. Dodd's definition of preaching as "the public proclamation of Christianity to the non-Christian world" (*The Apostolic Preaching and Its Developments,* New York: Harper, 1949, p. 7). It is what we mean today by "evangelistic preaching." When the preacher stands with his listeners, the message takes the form of *didachē,* corresponding to the usual Sunday morning sermon.

On this basis the first type has little background in the OT. Prophetic oracles against Israel's enemies (e.g., Obadiah) and the ministry of Jonah in Nineveh are in a sense forerunners. Preaching as instruction and exhortation may be traced to Ezra, who read the Scriptures and then interpreted freely so that the people would understand (Neh 8:8). By NT times this had developed into an important part of the synagogue service. Philo indicates that the content of such sermons was "what is the best and sure to be profitable," and the purpose, to "make the whole of life grow to something better" (*de specialibus legibus,* ii.62). Jesus' Nazareth sermon (Lk 4:16 ff.) took place on such an occasion, as did many of Paul's sermons (cf. Acts 13:14 ff.).

One of the more important advances in recent NT scholarship has been the crystallization of the primitive apostolic proclamation—the *kērygma* as it is now designated. (The transliteration from Gr. should not lead us into the misunderstanding that *kērygma* was its technical name *at that time.*) Professor Dodd of Cambridge led the way. Following his approach (comparing the early speeches in Acts with the pre-Pauline fragments embedded in the epistles), but altering the emphasis slightly, we understand the apostolic *kērygma* to have been "a proclamation of the death, resurrection, and exaltation of Jesus that led to an evaluation of His person as both Lord and Christ, confronted man with the necessity of repentance, and promised the forgiveness of sins" (R. H. Mounce, *The Essential Nature of New Testament Preaching,* Grand Rapids: Eerdmans, 1960, p. 84).

This proclamation was delivered with a driving sense of urgency (I Cor 9:16), appealed to every man's conscience by the open statement of truth (II Cor 4:2), and more often than not met with opposition (cf. II Cor 11:23–28). Since it demanded faith from the hearer, it was careful not to obscure its message with lofty words or eloquent wisdom (I Cor 1:17; 2:1–4).

The *kērygma,* or NT gospel message, came into being in what might be called three stages. First, John the Baptist appeared on the scene as a messianic herald proclaiming, "Repent ye: for the kingdom of heaven is at hand" (Mt 3:2). To him fell the task of preparing the nation for the coming of the One who would baptize with the Holy Spirit (Mk 1:8). Then came Jesus heralding the arrival of the kingdom of God. Thaf long awaited time, foretold by prophets of old, had now broken in upon history. The "acceptable year of the Lord" (Lk 4:19) had come. The kingdom was a present reality (Lk 11:20; 16:16). This basic truth is the foundation of all the teaching of Jesus.

A change of terminology may be noted in moving from the Gospels to the Acts and epistles. The message of the "kingdom of God" has suddenly become "Christ crucified" (I Cor 1:23), "Christ . . . raised" (I Cor 15:12), or "Christ Jesus as Lord" (II Cor 4:5). However, the continuity of the message remains undisturbed because Christ *is* the kingdom. It is in and through the great redemptive act which centered in Jesus Christ that God has established His sovereignty in history. Although the kingdom now exists in mystery form, the day will come when it will be openly manifested to all creation (Phil 2:9–11). For this we are told to pray (Mt 6:10).

This great event is still the burden of biblical preaching. It is not a demythologized *kērygma* that brings redemption but the Spirit-compelled proclamation of the Christ of the *kērygma.* Fidelity to this essential message marks the true herald of God in our contemporary scene.

In the OT "preacher" or "preach" is used in two special senses: (1) In Eccl 1:2 it translates a word meaning "assembler," one who addresses a public assembly. (2) In Neh 6:7 Sanballat accused Nehemiah of "appointing prophets to preach of thee at Jerusalem"; this involves proclaiming or heralding Nehemiah as king.

Bibliography. H. H. Farmer, *The Servant of the Word,* London: Nisbet, 1950. G. Friedrich, "*Kērux,* etc.," TDNT, III, 683–718. J. Knox, *The Integrity of Preaching,* Nashville: Abingdon, 1957. B. Reicke, "A Synopsis of Early Christian Preaching," *The Root of the Vine,* London: Dacre Press, 1953. J. M. Robinson, "Preaching," HDB rev., pp. 789–791. L. J. Tizard, *Preaching: The Art of Communication,* London: Oxford, 1959. G. Wingren, *Living Word,* Philadelphia: Muhlenberg, 1960.

R. H. M.

PRECIOUS STONES. *See* Jewels.

PREDESTINATION. *See* Election; Sovereignty of God.

PREPARATION. In the sense of the time of being mustered or prepared for battle this word appears in Nah 2:3. In Prov 16:1 it represents the Heb. *ma'ărāk* and refers to mental dispositions or plans (see RSV). The Gr. *hetoimasia,* "preparation," "readiness," occurs in Eph 6:15 where it is part of the translation "the preparation of the gospel of peace."

The Gr. *paraskeuē,* found in all four Gospels in the narration of the last days of Christ, refers to the day before the sabbath, the "preparation" for the weekly sabbath (Mk 15:42) and not for the festival of Passover. To interpret John in this way (Jn 19:14, 31, 42) maintains a noncontradictory relation with the Synoptics (Mt 27:62; Mk 15:42; Lk 23:54). The phrase in Jn 19:14, "the preparation of the passover," then means the weekly day of preparation during the Passover, i.e., Friday of Passover week. This interpretation is in accord with Jewish usage, as Josephus reveals in quoting an edict of Caesar Augustus that Jews be not obligated to go before any judge "on the Sabbath-day, nor on the day of the preparation to it, after the ninth hour" (*Ant.* xvi.6.2). The matter is thought by some to have a bearing on whether Jesus and His disciples ate the Passover meal at the time of the Last Supper (*see* Lord's Supper; FLAP, pp. 328, 559, 596 f.).

B. C. S.

PRESBYTERY. The group or order of elders which ordained young Timothy (I Tim 4:14), of which Paul appears on that occasion to have occupied the chair (II Tim 1:6). Even as the Israelite nation had its elders, the Jewish synagogues their elders, and the Sanhedrin its elders together with the priestly party and scribes, with the high priest in NT times as chairman, so Paul set up churches under ruling bodies of elders (Acts 14:23; 16:4; Tit 1:5; cf. Acts 15:4, 6, 23; 20:17, 28). In today's churches, particularly in those with the Presbyterian form of government, the group of elders in a local church is called a session, while those that meet as representatives of the churches in a larger area or district are called a presbytery. It is impossible to say whether the elders mentioned in I Timothy were of one or more churches.

PRESENCE. This word requires little comment in its ordinary usage (usually the Heb. *'ayin,* "eyes," and *pānîm,* "face," in the OT), but in its application to God it involves rich theological concepts. In addition to the glory cloud of the tabernacle (Ex 25:8), the OT speaks of the Angel of the Lord, the bread of the presence (showbread), the ark of the covenant, etc. All these are symbols of God's presence.

Gr. *parousia* in certain cases conveys the idea of presence (II Cor 10:10; Phil 2:12). NT truth centers in Christ as the living presence of God. The consistent biblical emphasis is on the ever-present God. The word *parousia* as an eschatological term signifies the moment of arrival of the returning Christ plus His subsequent presence with His redeemed people (I Thess 2:19; 3:13; 4:15; 5:23; etc.). It was an official term for the visit of a king or emperor to one of his provinces. *See* Christ, Coming of.

B. C. S.

PRESENCE, BREAD OF THE. *See* Bread of Faces.

PRESENT. *See* Gift.

PRESIDENT. Daniel's exalted position in Medo-Persia after Belshazzar of Babylon had been vanquished is described as that of a "president" (KJV, RSV) or "commissioner" (NASB). There were three such offices, but that held by Daniel was more authoritative (Dan 6:2-3). The references in Dan 6:2, 3, 4, 6, 7 are translations of Aram. *sārak*. The word "president" is contrasted in context with the provincial governors (satraps), and obviously refers to a high governmental official. Daniel's appointment occasioned a jealous plot thwarted by God.

PRESS. A wide variety of ideas is conveyed by this verb in different contexts. It refers to God's judgment (Ps 38:2), the strong urging of another person (Gen 19:3; Jud 16:16), and the crowding of a mob (Gen 19:9; Mk 3:10). The idea of forcible entry into the kingdom of God is expressed by the verb "press" in Lk 16:16 (KJV). The agonized straining of a runner as expressive of Paul's own ministry is rendered by this word in Phil 3:14. It is significant that he describes the tribulations of Christian service in such terms (II Cor 1:8).

As a noun in the OT "press" is a shortened form of winepress. In the KJV it translates three different Heb. words: *gat,* the actual place of treading the grapes (Joel 3:13); *yeqeb,* the trough or vat hollowed out in the rock to receive the juice trodden out in the *gat* (Prov 3:10; Isa 16:10; Hag 2:16); and *pûrâ,* a measure of juice from one filling of the vat (Hag 2:16). *See* Oil; Winepress. The NT noun in the KJV signifies a large crowd (Mk 2:4; 5:27, 30; Lk 8:19; 19:3).

B. C. S.

PRESUMPTUOUS, PRESUMPTUOUSLY. In religious matters, presumption is a daring defiance of God's commandments while still expecting His mercy. Biblical terms expressing presumptuous attitudes and actions are:

1. To presume (Heb. *'āpal,* "to be heedless, proud"), as the rebellious Israelites who heedlessly ascended the mountain (Num 14:44; cf. Deut 1:43).

2. To act proudly (Heb. *zûd,* lit. "to boil, seethe," as in Gen 25:29, RSV; figuratively "to feel boiling anger, to be arrogant, haughty"), applied to those who premeditatively disobey God's commands (Ex 21:14; Deut 1:43; 17:13; 18:20).

3. Arrogant, proud (Heb. *zēd,* "insolent, haughty"), as in Ps 19:13 when speaking of "presumptuous sins" which spring from proud self-reliance. Such rebels were to be severely punished. *Zēd* is found in Ps 86:14; 119:21, 51, 69, 78, 85, 122; Prov 21:24; Isa 13:11; Jer 43:2; Mal 3:15; 4:1, and often means "proud, godless, insolent."

4. Arrogance (Heb. *zādôn,* "pride, presumptuousness"), as personified in Babylon who acted arrogantly against God in burning His temple and taking His people captive (Jer 50:31-32; see NASB marg.). Cf. Deut 17:12; 18:22; I Sam 17:28; Prov 11:2; 13:10; 21:24; Jer 49:16; Ezk 7:10; Obad 3, where the same Heb. word expressing pride (*q.v.*) occurs.

5. Presumptuously (Heb. *beyād rāmâ,* "with a high hand") in Num 15:30 means "defiant," open rebellion against God. Such persons were to be cut off (cf. Gen 17:14) with no provision of atonement allowed, because they had despised the word of the Lord (Num 15:31).

6. Bold, daring (Gr. *tolmētēs,* "a bold, daring one"), applied to headstrong persons who despise and resist authority (II Pet 2:10).

Presumptuous sins must ever be distinguished from sins of ignorance and of infirmity. Sins are presumptuous when committed knowingly (Jn 15:22), premeditatively and deliberately (Prov 6:14; Ps 36:4), rebelliously (Jer 44:16; Deut 1:43), and repeatedly (Ps 78:17). *See* Sin.

D. R. R.

PRETENCE. The Heb. *sheqer* in Jer 3:10 is translated "in pretense" by the RSV (KJV "feignedly"), and usually carries the idea of "deception," "a lie," or "falsehood." In the NT the word "pretence" (Gr. *prophasis,* "pretext," "excuse") means the "ostensible reason" for which a thing is done, usually a false reason as contrasted with a true one (MM). Paul uses it to refer to hypocritical preaching (Phil 1:18), and in Mt 23:14 and Mk 12:40 it describes insincere praying.

PRETORIUM. *See* Praetorium; Antonia.

PREVENT. A word appearing 17 times in the KJV in the obsolete sense of "precede" or "go before." In the OT it was frequently used to translate Heb. *qādam,* "to meet," "confront," "anticipate." In II Sam 22, e.g., the terrors of death (v. 6) and the enemies of the psalmist "confronted" him (v. 19, NASB). Sinners may boast that calamity will not "confront" them (Amos 9:10, NASB). The knees of Job's mother "received" him after his birth (Job 3:12, RSV). God "meets" the righteous king with blessings (Ps 21:3, RSV; cf. 59:10; 79:8). He calls upon the Dedanites to "meet" the fugitive with bread (Isa 21:13-14, RSV). The psalmist's prayer "comes before" God in the morning (Ps 88:13, RSV). He "anticipates" the dawn (Ps 119:147, NASB marg.) as well as the night watches (v.148, NASB).

In the NT the best known verse using this archaic term is I Thess 4:15, stating that living Christians will not "precede" (Gr. *phthanō*) the believers who have died, in being caught up to meet their returning Lord. In Mt 17:25 Jesus anticipated what Peter was going to say and "spoke to him first" (from Gr. *prophthanō*).

J. R.

PREY. *See* Spoil.

PRICE. A rather broad range of meanings is given to the word "price." The Heb. *yeqâr* (Zech 11:13) means "honor" or "precious thing"; *meḥîr* and *meker* may mean respectively "price" (as an inducement, II Sam 24:24) and "value" (Prov 31:10). Heb. *'ērek* (Job 28:13) is sometimes rendered as "estimation" or "valuation" (BDB). The Heb. *sākār* (Zech 11:12) is translated usually as "wages," "fare," or "reward." The most frequently used word is the NT *timē,* expressed as "honor," "price" (e.g., Mt 27:6, 9; Acts 4:34; 5:2), or "sum." The context must always be relied upon to guide to the specific meaning of each word.

PRICK. As a verbal, it means "to pierce" or "transfix." In Acts 2:37 the word is *katanussō,* and as a figure of speech points to the conviction which fell upon the people. As a substantive, it can translate *sēk* ("thorn," BDB), as in Num 33:55. The Gr. *kentron* means "a cattle goad," and its most notable usage is in Acts 9:5 in the account of Paul's conversion. The whole phrase is probably spurious there, but does appear in Paul's testimony before Agrippa in Acts 26:14. It is rendered "sting" in I Cor 15:55-56.

PRIDE. An attitude of self-exaltation which, in its conceit of superiority, arrogantly tramples on others and, in its independence of spirit, self-sufficiently rebels against God. The OT usage of nine Heb. words indicates the universality, nature, effects, and condemnation of pride (cf. Young's *Analytical Concordance to the Bible*).

The NT revelation concerning pride is conveyed by three Gr. words which indicate much about the nature and operations of pride. They occur together in an alternate form in Rom 1:30.

1. Gr. *alazoneia* (boastful in *words*) refers to the pretension and arrogance of the *alazōn* ("boasters," Rom 1:30; II Tim 3:2), the proud and pretentious braggart who peddles words for his own profit, promising what he cannot perform. It describes the man who ignores the sovereignty of God by attempting to control his own present life (I Jn 2:16) and to shape his own future (Jas 4:16).

2. Gr. *hyperēphania* (proud and overbearing in *thoughts*) describes the man who exalts himself above others, not in outward blustering actions but in inward attitude of heart by erecting an altar to himself in his heart and worshiping there ("proud," Rom. 1:30; II Tim 3:2; Lk 1:51; Jas 4:6; I Pet 5:5; cf. Mk 7:22).

3. Gr. *hybris* (insolent and injurious in *actions*) is the pride which makes a man act with violent, wanton insolence against both God and man. Regarding God, *hybris* leads man to forget his creaturehood and to exalt himself against God. Regarding the insolent treatment of other men, *hybris* allows the passions to rule so that superiority to others is achieved by injuring them (II Cor 12:10). In Mt 22:6 *hybris* refers to man's insolent rejection of God's invitation. (The noun form occurs in Rom 1:30 as "despiteful," and in I Tim 1:13 as "injurious"; the verb is found in Mt 22:6; Lk 11:45; 18:32; Acts 14:5; I Thess 2:2; Tit 1:11.) See Georg Bertram, "*Hybris,* etc.," TDNT, VIII, 295-307.

The believer is taught in Scripture that pride was the sin of Satan (I Tim 3:6); that it deceives the heart (Jer 49:16) and hardens the mind (Dan 5:20); that it is an abomination to God which He hates (Prov 16:5; 6:16-17) and which He will bring into judgment (Prov 16:18). Thus he should realize the absolute necessity for the Holy Spirit to impart to him the mind of Christ, who is the supreme example of humility and who is free from every form of evil pride in word, in thought, and in action.

F. D. L.

PRIEST, PRIESTHOOD. A priest is an authorized minister in sacred things, especially one who offers sacrifices at the altar and acts as mediator between men and God.

Purpose

The Heb. priesthood constituted one of the dominant characteristics of OT religion and life. This is seen not only by the multiplied references in the Scriptures, as noted below, but in the very construction of OT religion with its special representative class of priests and in the importance of religious relations and functions to all of life.

The Heb. view of the world and of life in the world was completely controlled by and impregnated with the supernatural. The necessity of acceptable relations with God, which were not natural to man, made the priests and their ministrations of highest priority. These were essential for the preservation of Israel's continuing contact with God. The Israelite was related to God through a unique national covenant, which covenant involved the priesthood because of its essential mediatorial and representative service. Therefore the priest operated between God and the people to preserve the covenant relationship.

The success of this priestly religion depended heavily on the meaning and spirit of its operation, especially on the part of the people themselves. Priestly effectiveness, because of its highly representative character, can readily slip into the barren activity of the ritualistic pattern without the meaning and spirit of the ritual. This in turn eliminates any real, personal involvement of the people represented. The ritual becomes rigidly important and the meaning evanesces. This very largely became the history of the Heb. priesthood. In the OT the prophets often lifted up their voices against the departure on the part of the people from God who spoke to them through Moses. By the time of the NT a sharp cleavage existed between the Pharisee with his meticulous adherence to the ritual and physical aspects of the OT pattern, as he saw it, and Jesus Christ with His emphasis on the inner meaning and spiritual interpretation of all elements of life.

The cardinal components of the gospel which fulfilled the OT forms by Christ's redemptive acts are typically represented in the Heb. priesthood. This priesthood, therefore, which was of supreme importance in OT times as the means of securing and retaining acceptable standing and fellowship with God, becomes in the NT the ground for understanding the mediatorial and redemptive ministry of Jesus Christ.

Terminology

The Heb. words *kōhēn, kahēn* (an Aramaized form), translated generally as "priest," and *kehunnâ*, "priesthood," together with the verb form *kāhan,* "to be priest" or "to minister" or "execute the priest's office," occur about 775 times in the OT. Levite, the term for the priestly tribe, occurs 280 times. The Heb. plural designation *kemārîm* is used three times for idolatrous priests (II Kgs 23:5; Hos 10:5; Zeph 1:4). The term first appears *c.* 2000 B.C. in records from the Assyrian colonies of Cappadocia.

More than one-third of the OT references to priests are found in the Pentateuch. Leviticus, with approximately 185 references, can rightly be called the handbook of the priests. More references are found in the books of Chronicles than in the books of Kings, as the character of I and II Chronicles would lead us to expect. Only Leviticus has more references to priests than II Chronicles. Priests are mentioned, however, in all the books of the OT except Ruth, Esther, Job, Ecclesiastes, and several of the so-called Minor Prophets.

In the NT the Gr. forms *hiereus,* "priest"; *archiereus,* "high priest" or "chief priest"; *hierōsynē, hierateia,* "priesthood"; *hierateuma,* "the office of priest" or "order of priests"; *archieratikos,* "high priestly"; *hierateuō,* "to be a priest" or "to serve as priest," occur about 165 times, approximately 30 of these occurrences being *hiereus,* "priest," and 125 being *archiereus,* "high priest," signifying the importance of the high priests in the Gospel narratives. Almost all these NT references to priest and high priest are confined to the Gospels, Acts, and Hebrews. Levite occurs only three times in the NT.

The term *kōhēn* occurs as a designation not only of the Heb. priesthood but also of Egyptian priests (Gen 41:45, 50; 46:20; 47:26), Philistine priests (I Sam 6:2), and priests of Dagon (I Sam 5:5), Baal (II Kgs 10:19), Chemosh (Jer 48:7), and Baalim and Asherim (II Chr 34:5).

The source of *kōhēn,* though unknown, is generally thought to be from *kāhan* as allied to *kûn,* "to stand," referring to the priest as one who stood before God as a servant or as a representative of the people, and also as one who stood before the people as a representative of God. Priestly service is so represented (Num 16:9; Deut 10:8; 17:12; 18:5) though the word used is not *kûn* but *'āmad.*

Background and History

Prior to the Heb. priesthood established by Moses, the Bible mentions the priesthood of Melchizedek (Gen 14:18), of the Egyptians (Gen 41:45; 46:20; 47:22, 26), and of the Midianites (Ex 2:16; 3:1; 18:1). The priests referred to in Ex 19:22, 24 are thought to be either Midianite priests or priests in Israel prior to the Levitical establishment. Moses' act of choosing young men as priests to confirm the covenant (Ex 24:5) seems to indicate at least the propriety of making priests in Israel prior to the Levitical priesthood, if not the existence of such priests on other earlier occasions.

Priestly functions had been carried on from earliest patriarchal times by heads of families. The activities of Noah, Abraham, and Job, among others, exemplify the patriarchal priestly functions of heads of families. After the Flood

Samaritan priests at the Samaritan Synagogue at Nablus. Giovanni Trimboli

Noah is said to have built an altar upon which he sacrificed burnt offerings which were acceptable to God (Gen 8:20–21). Abraham built altars at Bethel, Mamre, and Moriah. Though no sacrifices are mentioned as offered on these altars, except the requested sacrifice of Isaac and that of the ram caught in a thicket, which was offered in his stead, Isaac's question, "Where is the lamb for a burnt offering?" indicates the practice of sacrifice at these altars (Gen 12:7; 13:4, 18; 22:1–13). The prologue to Job represents the patriarch as continually acting as priest on behalf of his erring children (Job 1:5).

After the organization of the Heb. priesthood, others who were not priests at least occasionally engaged in priestly ministrations. Gideon (Jud 6:24–26), the men of Beth-shemesh (I Sam 6:14–15), Samuel (I Sam 7:9), David (II Sam 6:13–17), and Elijah (I Kgs 18:23, 37–38) are illustrative of this practice. These activities were not disapproved. The men of Beth-shemesh were smitten by the Lord not because they sacrificed burnt offerings but because they looked into the ark of the Lord. Other usurpations of priestly functions were strongly disapproved on the basis of the impropriety of the person so engaged, or the priestly action involved, or the god to whom the activity was directed. The line of demarcation between proper and improper participation in priestly operations by those who were not Aaronic or Levitical priests is not always easily discerned.

Ordination

According to divine instructions, Aaron and his sons, Nadab and Abihu, Eleazar and Ithamar, were established as priests by Moses (Ex 28:1, 41; 29:9, 29–30). Since Nadab and Abihu died when they "offered strange fire before the Lord," the priesthood as descended from Aaron was limited in the time of Moses and Aaron to the lines of Eleazar and Ithamar (Lev 10:1–2; Num 3:4; I Chr 24:2).

However, all persons born into the family of Aaron could not become priests. Not only was the priesthood not subject to human choice, but it also was to be holy. Certain physical deformities evidently were judged not to be compatible with the representation of the perfection of holiness (Lev 21:17–23). Ceremonial impurity, as well, prohibited a priest from performing the duties of his office. Though no rules for disbarment nor procedures for reinstatement are given in Leviticus, ceremonial prohibitions are listed (Lev 21:1–15).

The seven-day consecration ceremony of Aaron and his sons was most solemn, picturesque, and meaningful (Ex 29:1–37; Lev 8). In addition to being chosen of God and marked by holiness, the consecration narratives enunciate the priestly characteristics of hereditary continuity and representative appearance and activity. Noteworthy in the event were the investiture of the priestly garments, and the consecration sacrifices and ceremonies. The holy garments of Aaron were considerably more elaborate than those of the other priests (Ex 28:2–39). All priests had special coats, girdles, and headgear, but Aaron was arrayed also in a breastplate and in an ephod in addition to more elaboration of the other parts of his clothing.

On two onyx stones placed on the shoulders of Aaron's ephod were inscribed the names of the tribes of Israel, six names to each onyx stone on either shoulder. On the breastplate made of gold, blue, purple, scarlet, and fine twined linen cloth, as in the ephod, there were to be 12 precious stones imbedded. Inscribed upon each stone was the name of one of the 12 tribes. These stones with their inscriptions portrayed the representative character of the priesthood. The priest bore the names of the tribes before the Lord for a memorial. Aaron's mitre or headdress had upon it a gold plate on blue lace engraved with the words, "Holiness to the Lord." Upon this was a holy crown. *See* Priest, High: Dress.

In the order of the consecration, Aaron and his sons were first washed with pure water. Then Aaron's holy garments were put upon him and an anointing oil was poured on his head. Finally his sons were clothed with their priestly garments and the sacrifices were offered. Aaron and his sons were to identify themselves with the young bullock and a ram of the offerings by placing their hands upon the animals. This action made the value of the animals' sacrifice accrue to the benefit of Aaron and his sons, purifying them for their priestly roles.

The bullock as a sin offering, one ram as a sweet savour offering, and another ram as a consecration offering were required for the sacrifice. Blood of the ram of consecration was put upon the tip of the right ear, upon the thumb of the right hand, and upon the great toe of the right foot of Aaron and of each of his sons. The blood of this ram of consecration was sprinkled also upon the altar, uniting the altar and the priests in the consecrating rites. Blood from the altar mingled with anointing oil was sprinkled also upon Aaron, his sons, and their garments.

PRIEST, PRIESTHOOD

The ceremonies and sacrifices of consecration were repeated for seven days to insure their complete effectiveness.

Undeniably, this elaborate ritual of installation set the Heb. priest apart from the people as a holy person, one who was chosen of God, consecrated to God, and representative of the people before God, as well as representative of God to the people. The blood upon the right ear would signify the priest's inclination to the voice of God both to hear and obey His injunctions. The blood-marked hand indicated the consecration of his occupation as priest in the sanctuary to act before God as a holy person on behalf of the people. The blood on his great toe demonstrated his consecration to the hallowed precincts of the tabernacle (and later temple) where unconsecrated persons were not allowed to enter. Perhaps the idea that one's walk related to all one's behavior as is seen elsewhere in the Scriptures (Prov 28:6, 18; Gal 5:16) was also in mind. These actions certainly were to show that consecration to the priesthood involved the whole man and all his behavior. He was to be God's man, a representative of God to the people portraying holy separation from ceremonial impurity and sin (Lev 10:8-11), and as a representative of the people to offer acceptably the sacrifices on their behalf and officiate in the prescribed services as instituted by God through Moses. Thus the priest acted as the official mediator between God and man.

Secondary Functions

The priests also were to minister as teachers of the law (Lev 10:10-11; Deut 33:10; II Kgs 17:27-28; II Chr 15:3; 17:7-9; Jer 18:18; Ezk 7:26; 44:23; Mal 2:6-7), a task which they did not always rightly perform (Mic 3:11; Mal 2:8). As pedagogues they were limited media of revelation in certain areas of health and jurisprudence, including the discerning and cleansing of various types of leprosy (Lev 13-14), the cleansing of men and women and articles of furniture touched by any issues from the bodies of men and women (Lev 15), the trial of jealousy (Num 5:11-21), controversies and punishments for uncertain murder (Deut 21:5), and other civil matters (II Chr 19:8-11; Ezk 44:24).

Classification

The Heb. priesthood included three basic classes: the high priest, the priests, and the Levites. The Levites (*q.v.*) as a subsidiary servant class to the priests are not always easily distinguished, because Aaron and his sons were not counted among the tribes of Israel as a tribe, but were themselves appointed to the service of the tabernacle in the wilderness especially in relation to moving it (Num 1:47-53; 3:6 ff.; Deut 11:8-9). Originally the Levites were distinguished carefully from the priests. This is clearly illustrated in the rebellion of Korah, Dathan, and Abiram whose lives and those of their families were forfeited because as Levites they sought to invade the priest's office (Num 16:1-33). Subsequent to this experience, God reaffirmed the choice of Aaron and his sons as priests out of all the tribes, and reasserted the servant status of the Levites by the budding of Aaron's rod while the rods of the princes of the rest of the tribes remained sterile (Num 17:1–18:6). In Chronicles, in addition to their duties in connection with the physical care of the sanctuary as porters, the Levites are musicians and treasurers (I Chr 6:31-32; 9:19; 16:4-5, 7; 25:1-7; 26:1, 20; II Chr 8:14).

Sustenance

The priests and the Levites were assigned no landed inheritance in Palestine as were the other tribes of Israel. Their recompense and livelihood came from certain parts of the sacrifices, and from free will offerings and tithes (Num 18:3-32). Some property ownership was possible, however. To the Levites were given 48 cities for their dwelling, 13 of which were for Aaron's sons, the priests (Num 35:1-8; Josh 21:4, 13-19). During the monarchy individual priests could own land (I Kgs 2:26; Jer 32:6-8; Amos 7:17), and in later years priests were given property in Jerusalem and environs (Neh 11:3, 10-23, 36).

The first fruits of the field, the firstborn of all clean domestic animals, and redemption money paid for firstborn sons of Israelites and for the firstborn of unclean beasts were to be the recompense of the priests (Ex 13:12-13; Num 18:12-19). From the other offerings and the sacrifices the priests were to receive the bread of the presence (Lev 24:5-9), the majority of the meal offerings (Lev 2:3-10; 6:16; 7:9-14; 10:12-13; Num 18:9), the majority of the sin offerings (Lev 5:13; 6:26; Num 18:9), the breast and thigh of the peace offerings (Ex 29:26-28; Lev 7:30-34; 10:14-15), and the majority of the trespass offerings (Lev 7:1-8). A tithe of the Levites' tithe from all the people was also to be given to the priests (Num 18:26-28).

The 35 Levitical cities—which remained after the priests' 13 cities were subtracted from the original 48—along with the surrounding pasture lands and the tithe (minus the priest's tithe) provided for the sustenance of the Levites (Num 18:21, 24-28; 35:1-8).

Levitical Service

The years for service of the Levites varied from time to time. When the Levites were first numbered and chosen instead of the firstborn of all Israel, "to do the work in the tabernacle of the congregation" (Num 4:3, 23, 30, 35, 39, 43, 49), they were to be from 30 to 50 years of age. At the time of the initial consecration of the Levites by the sprinkling of the water of purifying, the shaving of all their flesh, the washing of their clothes, and the offering of a bullock as a burnt offering of atonement (Num 8:5-14), the age of specific service was given as 25 to 50 years (Num 8:24-26). David, according to the Chronicler, changed the time for the beginning of Levitical service at the end of his regime to the age of 20 with no terminal date mentioned (I Chr 23:24, 27; cf. 23:1–3).

The number of Levites listed for service under Moses and Aaron was 8,580 (Num 4:46–48). This number increased, according to Chronicles, to 38,000 at the end of David's reign; 24,000 being workers of the house of the Lord, 6,000 officers and judges, 4,000 porters, and 4,000 musicians (I Chr 23:3–5). Ezra lists only 74 Levites among the exiles who returned with Zerubbabel (Ezr 2:40), though 973 priests were with him (Ezr 2:36). Persons, however, in activities elsewhere ascribed to Levites are given in additional numbers: 128 singers, 139 children of porters, and 392 Nethinim (*q.v.*) and children of Solomon's servants (Ezr 2:41–42, 58). There is no mention of Levites returning with Ezra. Later, however, 38 Levites and 220 Nethinim joined him (Ezr 8:15–20) after express invitation, in order that ministers for the house of God be provided.

Failures in the Priesthood

That the priestly code of Moses was not scrupulously followed through Israelite history is evident from the narratives of Judges and Samuel especially, as well as in the history of later times. The variations from the Mosaic norm have led some critics to deny the existence of the norm, but this is certainly neither a necessary nor a natural conclusion. The OT abounds with its own criticisms of the Israelites for their failure to follow the ways of the Lord their God. It is not surprising that lapses from rigorous and exact application of the Mosaic codes regarding the priesthood occurred.

A certain Micah established one of his sons as family priest (Jud 17:5) until a Levite, Jonathan, appeared and was made priest instead of the son. Evidently the son officiated in place of the father under the old patriarchal practice. Since he was of the priestly tribe, the Levite was judged to be more fitting for this position, though in the law of Moses Levites were not fully qualified priests.

Some have thought that Samuel, on the basis of I Sam 1:1, was an Ephraimite. In I Chr 6:16–28, however, Samuel is listed as a Levite. Elkanah, then, was a Levite living in the hill country of Ephraim when Samuel was born. Moreover, it is suggested that Samuel was too young to do any priestly service, during the time of the early part of I Sam (I Sam 1:27–28; 2:11, 18; 3:1) and that the meaning of the phrase, "ministered to the Lord," must refer to some simple servant tasks. In later times, however, it appears that Samuel did offer sacrifices (I Sam 7:9–10; 10:8; 16:2, 5).

Saul with the disapproval of Samuel acted as priest (I Sam 13:8–13); but David (II Sam 6:12–19) and Solomon (I Kgs 8:22–53) without recorded disapproval also served as priests on certain occasions.

At the separation of the northern kingdom from Judah, Jeroboam I appointed priests regardless of their tribal descent (I Kgs 12:31; 13:33) and himself served as priest (I Kgs 12:32–33). Ahaz' offering of sacrifices upon his Damascene-type altar (II Kgs 16:10–16) obviously would not have been approved by Isaiah (Isa 7) and other men of God. II Chr 26:16–20 tells of Uzziah's leprosy as a judgment of God because of his usurpation of the priest's office. In Ezr 6:19–20 (cf. II Chr 29:34; 35:11–14) the Levites killed the Passover lambs, a responsibility of the priests alone under Moses' law.

Because of the failure of his sons in the priest's office, a certain prophet predicted to Eli that his descendants would lose the priestly office (I Sam 2:27–36). In David's last days, Abiathar the priest joined Adonijah in his attempt to secure the throne, and so brought upon himself the displeasure of Solomon who was anointed king by Zadok. Abiathar, deposed from the office of priest, was banished to Anathoth. The priestly line from this time on was confined to the Zadokites. This action was declared to be the fulfillment of the prophecy to Eli (I Kgs 2:27). The Chronicler stated that Zadok was a descendant of Aaron through his son Eleazar (I Chr 6:8, 53; 24:3; 27:17). *See* Zadok.

Importance of the Priesthood

The relative position of high priest or chief priest, priests, and Levites does not seem to have been consistent throughout Israelitish history. Plainly the presentation in Exodus, Leviticus, and Numbers indicates the relative position of Aaron and his sons, with Aaron as the superior priest. The Levites were given to Aaron and to his sons, the priests, to be their helpers in definitely limited service (Num 1:50; 3:28, 32; 8:15; 31:30, 47; cf. I Chr 23:25–32). In Deuteronomy the Levites appear to be equated with the priests in the use of the terms "the priests the Levites" or "the priests the sons of Levi" (Deut 17:9, 18; 18:1; 21:5; 24:8; 27:9; 31:9). Perhaps the use of these terms simply indicates the tribe to which the priests belonged and does not include all the Levites, but rather, only those Levites who were priests.

Moses' final blessing on the tribes (Deut 33:8) reckons the Thummim and Urim to be the property of Levi, the care of which was certainly a priestly function belonging to Aaron the priest (Ex 28:30). Here also the use of the name Levi indicates only that this power was resident in the tribe, because it was in the care of Aaron and his successors as high priests. It is not necessary that the statement imply that every Levite could handle the sacred means of determining the Lord's will.

The priesthood had a place of highest importance in the theocracy, though Moses, not Aaron, remained leader during his lifetime, while Joshua and the judges succeeded Moses. In the transition period of Eli and Samuel some leader-priest amalgamation existed, though this was not by divine sanction as a system of government. In Samuel's time the monarchy was established with the priesthood in a secondary role at best. Throughout the monarchy the influence of certain prophets often seems to have been in ascendancy over the priesthood. The idea of a governing priesthood became prominent in Ezekiel's time, with the Zadokite priests in dominant position because they only remained true to the Lord when the Israelites went astray (Ezk 44:10–16).

After the return from Babylonian Exile in the days of Haggai and Zechariah, the offices of governor and high priest seem to have been of equal importance. The word of the Lord through Haggai was said to be unto Zerubbabel the governor, and Joshua the high priest (Hag 1:1, 12, 14; 2:2, 4), both of whom were also prominent in Zechariah (chaps. 3–4. In the intertestamental period the two offices eventually became one with the dominance of the high priests under the Hasmoneans and later. After Maccabean rule, the higher governmental rule reverted to foreign rulers until the extermination of the Jewish state in A.D. 70.

Varying views of the priesthood were held in intertestamental and NT times. Evidently the Qumran sectaries by the Dead Sea had priests who did not sacrifice animals, according to what Philo and Josephus wrote concerning the Essenes. By NT times the high priesthood no longer was held for life by the incumbent, so that several persons carried the name high priest, though only one officiated during a given period (Mt 26:3, 65; cf. Jn 18:13, 24). The high priestly office remained the dominant religious and political office held by a Jew in Palestine in NT times.

Among the most noteworthy priests in the Bible were Aaron, Nadab, Abihu, Eleazar, Ithamar, Hophni, Phinehas, Ahijah, Ahimelech, Abiathar, Amaziah, Jehoiada, Urijah, Hilkia, Ezekiel, Ezra, Zacharias, Caiaphas, Annas, and Ananias.

The NT Priesthood of Christ and the Church

The doctrinal relationship between the OT economy and NT Christianity relative to the priesthood is most clearly portrayed in the Epistle to the Hebrews. The OT priesthood of Aaron and his successors is declared never to have been effective for the removal of sin. Because of the necessity of repetition of both priests (because they did not live forever) and sacrifices, the OT priesthood is shown to be incapable of making the worshiper perfect (Heb 7:23; 10:1–4). The Aaronic priesthood as such was not even the best type of Christ in His high priestly redemptive acts and occupation. Melchizedek, because of his royal status and the lack of recorded beginning or ending of his life, office and service, becomes the better type of Christ as provider and purveyor of an everlastingly active and effective saving ministry (Heb 4:14–5:10; 7:1–28).

However, the Aaronic priesthood and sacrificial system in broad outline and in certain specific ways is typical of the saving work of Christ as the fulfillment of the priesthood and the sacrificial system. Included in the typical aspects of the Aaronic priesthood fulfilled in Christ according to the Epistle to the Hebrews are: (1) the idea of the high priesthood itself (Heb 4:14); (2) the priest as chosen of God (5:4); (3) the priest identified with the people (5:1–3); (4) the priest a holy person (7:26); (5) the priest consecrated to his office (7:28); (6) the priest as one who offers sacrifices (7:27; 8:3; cf. 9:12–14); (7) the priest as serving a sanctuary (8:2; 9:6–7; cf. 9:11); (8) the priest operating under a covenant (8:6).

In the OT the nation was to be a kingdom of priests (Ex 19:5–6; Lev 11:44–45; Num 15:40), but this was only realized in the priesthood as being representatively holy for the multitude. In the NT Christ becomes the fulfillment of all that the OT priesthood signified in person and activity. In the NT the Church, as the nation in the OT, is a kingdom of priests. The Church, however, has not only an imputed holiness but a developing personal holiness because of the sanctifying work of the Holy Spirit (Rom 8:2–13; I Pet 2:5, 9; Rev 1:6; 5:10; 20:6).

All in Christ are priests, though not called priests individually. This priesthood is severely limited in action to intercession, because all being priests no representative functions remain except on the part of Christ in His redemptive acts and continuing mediatorial ministry. As the priests of the OT washed at the laver before being consecrated for their work in the holy place, all Christians are urged to draw near to God having "hearts sprinkled from an evil conscience, and bodies washed with pure water" (Heb 10:22; cf. Ex 29:4; Lev 16:4). The Heb. priesthood, then, though it is for the most part fulfilled in Christ in the NT, in a limited sense is also fulfilled in the NT Church. The ephemeral priesthood of Aaron and his sons fades into uselessness when Christ comes as the perfect intermediary and intercessor, as well as the perfect sacrifice for His people and their sins.

With the destruction of the Jewish state and the temple in A.D. 70, the OT Heb. priesthood vanished from history. Attempts were made for a while subsequent to that date to continue some parts of the priestly and sacrificial system, but these proved unsuccessful and they soon ceased completely.

Critical Theory of the History of the Priesthood

During the last 200 years scholars have sought to analyze the OT by literary criticism and historical reconstruction. Their efforts brought into ascendancy in the last half of the 19th cen. what has been popularly called the Graf-Wellhausen theory of Jewish history and of the formation of the OT. It is so called because of the work of Karl Heinrich Graf (1815–1869) and Julius Wellhausen (1844–1918), who brought the former studies to a climax. In general, the Graf-Wellhausen reconstruction asserted that the priestly institution of the OT did not have its inception in the time of Moses but rather in the time of Ezra. An evolutionary development was thought to have occurred from the times of Israel's early allegedly naturalistic religion, in the periods of the judges and early kings, to the reform under Josiah. During his reign religious activities supposedly for the first time became centralized in the Jerusalem sanctuary because of the influence of the newly discovered book of the law (II Kgs 22:8-10; thought to have been the book of Deuteronomy). Ezekiel, it was averred, was an innovator with high notions of the priesthood preceding the Levitical legislation. This accounted for the differences between the priestly arrangements of Ezekiel's prophetic picture and the Mosaic legislation which was said to have appeared in Ezra's time.

While almost as many variations of the basic scheme of the Graf-Wellhausen structure appeared as there were writers, the twin ideas of historical religious evolutionary progress and a divisive literary formation of the OT have been widely accepted. The Jehovist, Elohist, Deuteronomist, and Priestly (JEDP) writers or schools of writers were supposed to have written or edited most of the OT. This reconstruction of OT history and writing is obviously not that of the OT as it stands or of Jewish and Christian tradition. It suggests not only a major variance in the OT picture of the priesthood concerning the time when it appeared but, what is much more important, a major variance in the source of its genius and therefore in its value. This is true both for OT religion and for its NT fulfillment. *See* Canon of Scripture—OT; Law of Moses; Pentateuch.

No adequate historical reason exists for the denial of the establishment of the Aaronic priesthood by Moses. On the contrary, many features of the OT sacrificial system have been found to have existed in Palestine at the time of Moses. Though certain broad outlines of the Graf-Wellhausen theory of OT formation and history still are held by many OT scholars, current knowledge of the social structure not only of ancient Israel but also of the whole ancient Middle East has to a great extent destroyed the fabric of this reconstruction. The Pentateuchal presentation of the Aaronic priesthood, the corresponding system of Levitical sacrifices, and the tabernacle as Mosaic institutions has been largely vindicated and substantiated by the knowledge gleaned from archaeological findings. *See* Sacrificial Offerings; Tabernacle.

Bibliography. G. C. Aalders, "Priests and Levites," *A Short Introduction to the Pentateuch,* London: Tyndale, 1949, pp. 66-71. R. Abba, "Priests and Levites," IDB, III, 876-889. Oswald T. Allis, "Priestly Religion in the Post-Exilic Period," *The Five Books of Moses,* Philadelphia: Presbyterian and Reformed, 1943, pp. 183-199. W. Baudissin, "Priests and Levites," HDB, IV, 67-97. A. Cody, *A History of Old Testament Priesthood,* Rome: Pontifical Biblical Institute, 1969. G. Cornfeld, ed., "Priesthood, Priests and Levites," CornPBE, pp. 602-607. Alfred Edersheim, "The Officiating Priesthood," *The Temple, Its Ministry and Services* (1874), Grand Rapids: Eerdmans, 1950 (reprint), pp. 82-104. George B. Gray, "The Hebrew Priesthood: Its Origin, History, and Functions," *Sacrifice in the Old Testament,* Oxford: Univ. Press, 1925, pp. 179-270. David A. Hubbard, "Priests and Levites," NBD, pp. 1028-1034. Joachim Jeremias, *Jerusalem in the Time of Jesus,* Philadelphia: Fortress Press, 1969, pp. 147-221. Y. Kaufmann, *The Religion of Israel,* trans. by M. Greenberg, Chicago: Univ. of Chicago, 1960, pp. 175-200, 258-260, 301-304. G. F. Oehler, *Theology of the Old Testament,* trans. by George E. Day, Grand Rapids: Zondervan, n.d. (reprint), pp. 203-214. James Orr, *The Problem of the Old Testament,* New York: Scribner's, 1926, pp. 180-192, 285-329. J. Barton Payne, *The Theology of the Older Testament,* Grand Rapids: Zondervan, 1962, pp. 274-284, 372-378. G. Schrenk, "*Hierus,* etc.," TDNT, III, 257-283. Roland de Vaux, *Ancient Israel,* trans. by John McHugh, New York: McGraw-Hill, 1961, pp. 345-405.

E. S. K.

PRIEST, HIGH. In Israel, as in many other states with historical priestly religions, a hierarchical system of graduated powers and responsibilities existed with a chief or high priest at the head of the organization. For over a millennium before Moses, each of the larger temples and religious centers in Egypt had its high priest. The land of Ugarit had a high priest (*rabbu kâhinîma,* "chief of the priests") in the 14th and 13th cen. B.C. (W. F. Albright, *Archaeology and the Religion of Israel,* 3rd ed., Baltimore: Johns Hopkins, 1953, p. 108).

Terminology

In the OT the high priest is referred to as *hak-kōhēn,* "the priest"; *hak-kōhēn ham-māshîaḥ,* "the anointed priest"; *hak-kōhēn hag-gādôl,* "the high priest" (the great priest); *kōhēn hā-rō'sh,* "the high priest." In the LXX reference is made to *ho hiereus,* "the priest"; *ho hiereus ho christos,* "the anointed priest"; *ho hiereus ho megas,* "the high priest" (the great priest); *ho hiereus hēgoumenos,* "the high priest" (the chief priest). In the NT the high priest is called *ho hiereus,* "the priest," in Acts 5:24 but elsewhere 56 times he is called *archiereus,* "the high priest." The high incidence of "high priest" in the NT in comparison to its infrequency in the OT indicates how important this office had become in NT times.

Ordination

Moses, according to the Pentateuch, was directed of God to install his brother Aaron and Aaron's sons as priests. Aaron is most often simply called the priest, as were his sons. In Leviticus he is four times referred to as the anointed priest (Lev 4:3, 5, 16; 6:22). Once in

Leviticus and twice in Numbers Aaron is called the great or high priest. It seems evident from Num 35:25 that the term "high priest" (lit., "the great priest") was not originally a technical term, else there would be no necessity for the further description "which was anointed with the holy oil." The position of responsibility and the dress of his office, rather than the name of his office, most often distinguished Aaron as the high or superior priest.

As early as the call of Moses, Aaron was designated by God to be His spokesman (Ex 4:14-16; 5:1; etc.). The first intimations that Aaron should be the leading priest, however, appeared when Moses asked Aaron to lay up an omer of manna in a pot before the Lord (Ex 16:32-34) and when Aaron was accorded a special place with Moses to meet God (Ex 19:24; 24:1, 9-11). The first specific order making Aaron the priest was received by Moses on Mount Sinai after instructions for the building of the tabernacle had been given (Ex 27:21; 28:1; 29:9, 44). Not even Aaron's part in the worship of the golden calf discredited him from becoming the first person to hold the office of high priest.

In the ordination service establishing the priesthood, the position of Aaron as high priest was clearly differentiated from the other priests (his sons) by the ceremonies of consecration and the variations in garments (Ex 28:1, 29; Lev 8). During his ordination Aaron was anointed by the pouring of the oil upon him in a special rite (Ex 29:7; Lev 8:12) to make him holy. Though later the anointing oil mingled with blood was sprinkled upon Aaron, his sons, and upon their garments (Ex 29:21; Lev 8:30), the pouring of the anointing oil in abundance upon the *head* was reserved for the high priest alone (Ex 29:7). On this account, the high priest was called the anointed priest or the priest that was anointed (Lev 4:3, 5, 16; 6:22; 21:10; Num 35:25). The consecration of Aaron's successors was to follow the same pattern (Ex 29:29-30). The pouring of the anointing oil upon Aaron's head and running down to the very edges of his robe became a symbol of unity (Ps 133:2).

The composition of the anointing oil was unique and holy. He who compounded this mixture or used it in any other than the specified ways was to be cut off from his people (Ex 30:23-33). The apothecaries mentioned by Nehemiah may have been the priests who manufactured the anointing oil as well as other mixtures. *See* Oil; Oil, Holy Anointing.

Dress

The holy garments of Aaron as high priest were also distinctive in relation to the simpler priestly garments which consisted of a coat or tunic, a girdle or sash, a bonnet or skullcap, and breeches (Ex 28:40, 42). The Jews considered the high priestly garments as composed of eight parts; though, because of a difference of opinion on the eighth part, they might be counted as nine. The breastplate, the ephod, the robe of the ephod, and the mitre or turban (instead of the cap) with the golden plate were distinctive of the high priest. But if this be so, what of the "curious girdle" of the ephod (Ex 28:8, 27-28)? If this curious girdle or "skillfully woven band" (RSV) was in addition to the girdle of the coat rather than instead of it, and the engraved plate on the headdress be considered an additional accoutrement, then there were nine rather than eight actual parts to the high priest's habiliments, five of these being in addition to those of the other priests.

The Hebrew high priest

According to Ex 28:2 these garments were for glory and beauty. That they were also significant of holiness and priestly representation is seen from their consecration (Ex 29:21; Lev 8:30), their designation as holy garments (Ex 28:2, 4; 29:29; 31:10; 35:19, 21; 39:1, 41; 40:13), and the function of the onyx stones on the shoulders of the ephod and the precious stones of the breastplate (Ex 28:9-12, 17-21, 29).

In the order of dress, the high priest's garments included:

1. The breeches, a pair of short-legged linen trousers as an undergarment. These breeches were held on by a cloth band made and used much like a modern belt (Ex 28:42).

2. The "coat," an undertunic (for the high priest) or long shirt of fine linen woven with a pattern and with sleeves and a tie around the neck much like the tie around the waist of the breeches (Ex 28:4, 39).

3. The girdle, a long embroidered linen sash, which was wound around the middle of the body several times before tying in front so that the ends hung down to the bottom of the coat (Ex 28:39).

4. The robe of the ephod, a shorter, outer coat of woven work, blue in color, sleeveless, but with openings in the material as arm holes and a hole with a border for the head. This garment is believed to have been longer than the ephod but shorter than the undertunic. The bottom of the robe of the ephod was adorned with alternating pomegranates, in blue and purple and scarlet, and bells of gold (Ex 28:31–34). The sound of the bells was to tell when the high priest went into the holy place and when he came out (Ex 28:35). The son of Sirach adds that the bells were "to remind the sons of his people" (Sir 45:9). This may be a misplaced reference to the biblical statement concerning the breastplate (Ex 28:29).

5. The ephod, consisting of two aprons, one covering the front of the body and the other the back, fastened together with a shoulder piece on either shoulder to which was attached a large onyx stone (Ex 28:6–14). Each stone was inscribed with the names of six tribes of Israel. These two aprons were united around the middle by the "curious girdle" of the ephod of gold, blue, purple, scarlet, and fine-twined linen cloth. Linen ephods were also worn on certain occasions by Samuel (I Sam 2:18), David (II Sam 6:14), and the priests of Nob (I Sam 22:18). Ephods were also used by other Israelites in improper worship (Jud 8:27; 17:5). *See* Ephod.

6. Breastplate of judgment, a cloth piece fitted on the ephod, skillfully made two spans long and one span wide, but folded in the middle so that the resultant form was square (Ex 28:15–30). The breastplate was fastened at the top by two rings and chains of gold to the shoulder pieces of the ephod, and by like rings and chains with a lace of blue it was fastened at the bottom corners of the breastplate to the front of the ephod. To represent the 12 tribes of Israel, 12 precious stones of differing sorts were set on the breastplate (*see* Jewels). On each stone was engraved the name of one of the tribes. These stones were fixed on the breastplate in four rows of three stones each. The order of the names is not known. It has been conjectured that the order was either chronological or according to the arrangement of the tribes for the camps in the wilderness.

Placed in the breastplate were the Urim and Thummim, the nature of which no one knows with certainty. The two most likely explanations either identify the Urim and Thummim with the stones of the breastplate, or suggest them to be symbolic objects used by the priests to determine by some kind of inspiration the judgment of God. The Heb. words mean "lights" and "perfections"—or, what seems more likely, light and perfection, the plural forms being those of fullness or intensity. In favor of the former view which the LXX, Josephus, and many others hold, is the fact that the same statements are made of Urim and Thummim in Ex 28:30 as are said of the breastplate in v. 29 preceding. In favor of the second of these suggestions is the form of the first phrase of v. 30, "and thou shalt put in the breastplate of judgment the Urim and the Thummim . . ." The words "thou shalt put in" certainly seem to suggest something additional being put into some sort of pocket in the breastplate (cf. Lev 8:8). No such pocket, however, is mentioned.

Regardless of the exact nature of the Urim and Thummim, their use is not simply magical but illuminative or revelative of God's judgment on the question brought to the priest for decision. The possession of Urim and Thummim involved the teaching of the ways of the Lord. In Moses' blessing on Levi (Deut 33:8), and at the return from Captivity, it was apparently the sure badge of priestly authority (Ezr 2:63; Neh 7:65), or of the priestly power of receiving direct answers from God, a power which was involved in the original use of Urim and Thummim, but which did not return after the Captivity. Moses' reference to the Urim and Thummim belonging to Levi does not suggest that all Levites had recourse to the Urim and Thummim, but rather simply suggests that Aaron and his successors as high priests were of the tribe of Levi. *See* Urim and Thummim.

7. The bonnet, a cap of linen differing from the other headgear of the high priest. Apparently it was a skullcap like an inverted bowl.

8. The mitre or turban of the high priest, larger than the headdress of the priests. On the front of it was a gold plate upon which was engraved "Holiness to the Lord." This gold plate was fastened to the mitre by means of a ribbon of blue. Josephus describes also a golden crown (*Ant.* iii.7.6) which was fitted over the mitre at the forehead. The crown mentioned in Lev 8:9 appears to be identical with the golden plate upon which were the words "Holiness to the Lord." This golden plate was to be on Aaron's forehead in order that he "may bear the iniquity of the holy things . . . and . . . that [the children of Israel] may be accepted before the Lord" (Ex 28:38). Evidently the words "Holiness to the Lord" indicated the high priest's representative sanctity so that he could bear the iniquity of the people by making their sacrifices acceptable and, therefore, rendering the people acceptable to God. Of the wearing of all the garments on the part of Aaron and his sons, Ex 28:43 declares this necessary "that they bear not iniquity and die." The priests' clothes invested them with a ceremonial purity which saved them from the death which other persons would incur from contact with the holy things

of the tabernacle and from engaging in its holy ministries.

On the annual Day of Atonement other garments of white linen are specified for the high priest. These Day-of-Atonement garments were to be worn only during the ceremony of atonement. They were to be put on before the high priest entered the holy of holies and taken off in the tabernacle of the congregation after the atonement had been made in the holy of holies or "the holy place" as it is called in Lev 16:4, 23. These clothes had none of the ornate character of the high priest's usual regalia. They included only breeches, coat, girdle, and mitre, all of white linen. This variation in clothing signified the extraordinary solemnity and importance of this ceremony of atonement. The simplicity and whiteness of the garments as well as their use only during that ceremony indicated the purity and holiness necessary for entrance into the holy of holies where God dwelt between the cherubim. *See* Festivals: Day of Atonement.

Duties

Though the high priest officiated in regular priestly tasks, certain unique responsibilities appertained to his office. Only the high priest could enter the most holy place and that only during the ceremony of the Day of Atonement once a year. He also was the only priest who was authorized to officiate on the Day of Atonement. On other special days, such as new moons and great feasts, the high priest would serve as priest.

The term of the high priest's service determined applications of the law regarding manslayers. A person who committed manslaughter, killing a person unaware, could flee to any of the cities of refuge where he would find asylum. His asylum was inviolate as long as he remained within the city of refuge or until the congregation had judged his action as murder. If the manslayer was judged by the congregation as having killed accidentally, then the manslayer was protected from the avenger of blood as long as he remained in the city of refuge and as long as the incumbent in the high priest's office was alive. At the death of the high priest, which served as our statute of limitations does, all manslayers were free to return to the lands of their possession (Num 35:25, 28).

By Josiah's time, a priest next in line to the high priest was called the second priest. This second priest apparently officiated in certain functions as high priest when the high priest was absent (II Kgs 23:4; 25:18).

Regulations

The high priest was not to mourn for the dead by uncovering his head nor rending his clothes nor going in to a dead body nor going out of the sanctuary to attend a funeral (Lev 10:6; 21:10-12). A widow, a divorced woman, or one profaned by harlotry was not to be taken by a priest as wife. Only a Jewish virgin was eligible to become wife to the high priest (Lev 21:14).

Persons with certain physical blemishes were excluded from the priesthood. Moses lists 12 specific blemishes which eliminated one from the high priestly and priestly office: blindness, lameness, a flat nose or disfigured face, a deformed limb, a broken foot, a broken hand, a crooked or hunch back, dwarfed, an eye blemish, scurvy or eczema, scabs, and crushed testicles (Lev 21:17-20, NASB).

History

Being dependent upon the date of the Exodus, the length of the history of the high priesthood is not a matter of general agreement (*see* Exodus, The: Date). The estimates vary from a low chronology of about 1,300 years to Josephus' impossibly high chronology of 1,793 years (*Ant.* xx.10). Of course to those who believe that the priesthood was not established by Moses as the Bible declares, but rather was established during the time of Ezra, the length of the temporal history of the high priesthood is very much shorter.

According to Josephus, 83 high priests ruled from Aaron to Phannias who was made priest during the war ending with the destruction of the Jewish state in A.D. 70 (*Ant.* xx.10). Not even all those who are said by Josephus to have ruled during biblical times are found in the Bible. From the time of Moses until David seven high priests are named in the Scriptures: Aaron, Eleazar, Phinehas, Eli, Ahitub, Ahiah, and Ahimelech (Jud 20:28; I Sam 1:3, 9; 14:3 [where Eli and Phinehas seem to be inverted]; 22:11-12). From the time the Philistines destroyed Shiloh where Eli had served as high priest and the ark was taken by the Philistines, the high priests had a very limited service.

Two leading priests served simultaneously during David's reign. Zadok apparently officiated at Gibeon where the tabernacle and the brazen altar were located and where they remained until the time of Solomon (I Chr 16:39-40; II Chr 1:3-5), while after the ark was removed to the tent which David pitched in Jerusalem, Abiathar served there until Solomon deposed him (II Sam 8:17; I Kgs 2:35; I Chr 16:1-7) in fulfillment of the prophecy against Eli (I Sam 2:30-36; I Kgs 2:26-27). Following the deposition of Abiathar, the descendants of Zadok controlled the high priesthood.

A comparison of I Chr 6:8-15 with the biblical historical books produces 17 names of high priests from Zadok to the Captivity. Josephus says 18 priests reigned during this interval though he gives only 17 names. These names, however, are in a corrupt list with variations from the biblical list (*Ant.* xx.10). Between the time of the high priest Amariah in the reign of Jehoshaphat (II Chr 19:11) until the high priesthood of Hilkiah in the reign of Josiah (II Chr 34:9), a period of about 240 years, the genealogy in I Chr 6 gives the names only of

Ahitub, Zadok, and Shallum. The books of Kings and Chronicles supply, in addition, Jehoiada in the reign of Athaliah and Joash, Zechariah his son in the reign of Uzziah, Urijah in the time of Ahaz, and Azariah in the period of Hezekiah.

At the return after the Captivity in Babylon, Joshua (Jeshua), the son of Jozadak (I Chr 6:15, Jehozadak), who had been taken into captivity, carried on the Zadokite line of high priests (Ezr 3:2; etc.). The successors to Joshua were Joiakim, Eiiab who was a hindrance rather than a help to Nehemiah, Joiada, Johanan who, Josephus says, murdered his own brother, and Jaddua. Josephus states that there were 43 priests from Joshua to the burning of the temple (*Ant*. xx.10).

The high priesthood during the intertestamental years increased in power and decreased in spiritual, moral, and ethical behavior. Under the Maccabeans the kingship and the high priesthood were for a while combined (if the political leaders of the time could be called kings). During the intertestamental period the high priesthood often became the pawn of ruling authorities. As the highest ruling office among the Jews, the high priesthood was the subject of purchase and intrigue. Gradually its life tenure was lost so that more than one high priest was alive at a given time though only one officiated as the highest officer (Lk 3:2). In the NT three high priests are mentioned by name: Annas, who was high priest when John the Baptist ministered and was put to death (Lk 3:2); Caiaphas, who ruled at the time of Jesus' trial and crucifixion (Jn 11:49-51; 18:13), and who gave letters to Paul to pursue Christians in Damascus; and Ananias, before whom Paul was later tried (Acts 23:1-10).

The Heb. priesthood ended with the destruction of the Heb. state in A.D. 70.

Christ as High Priest

In the Epistle to the Hebrews, Jesus is shown to be the fulfillment of the priestly office and all the priestly activities of the OT. Jesus the Son of God is declared to be the true high priest, having accomplished in the perfection of His person and redemptive acts all that the OT priesthood, centered in the high priestly person and office, could not do because of its natural and spiritual limitations. The term high priest in some relation to Christ is used 17 times in the epistle. The writer of the epistle shows that the Aaronic priesthood and animal sacrifices are no longer needed because Jesus has completed the work of salvation as the high priest "consecrated for evermore" (Heb 7:28).

See Priest, Priesthood.

E. S. K.

PRINCE, PRINCESS. The word prince occurs frequently in the OT, while the word princess is used less frequently. There are nearly 20 different Heb., Aram., and Gr. terms translated

Prince Xerxes (husband of Esther) stands behind his father, Darius the Great, on a relief at Persepolis. ORINST

"prince" in the KJV. The meanings correspond to the various uses of the English word.

In the Bible a prince is a ruler, a leader, an official, a magistrate, an exalted person with authority. With the exception of Abijah (II Chr 11:22, ASV, RSV) it is never used to denote royal parentage (cf. I Chr 29:24). The term often indicates actual royal or ruling power, together with royal dignity and authority. As a rule, the title is given to human beings (Num 1:16; Josh 9:15; I Kgs 14:7); in a few instances it is applied to God and Christ (Josh 5:15, ASV), to angels (Dan 12:1), and to the devil (Jn 12:31). The Messiah is the Prince of Peace (Isa 9:6), of life (Acts 3:15), of the kings of the earth (Rev. 1:5).

The use of "princess" (*śārâ*) apparently is meant to call attention to royal character. (1) The wives of Solomon are called "princesses" (I Kgs 11:3). Heb. *śārâ* may also mean (2) a queen (Isa 49:23), (3) wife of a prince (Est 1:18, ASV), (4) daughters (NASB) or attendants (KJV, RSV) of the mother of the army commander Sisera (Jud 5:29).

R. L. D.

PRINCIPALITIES. The term is used of the authority or position both of rulers and governments to which the Christian is to be subject (Tit 3:1; cf. Rom 13:1-7; Heb 13:17), and of the angels and demons (Eph 3:10; 6:12). Christ created all things "whether they be thrones, or dominions, or principalities, or powers" (Col 1:16). The Christian wrestles not primarily with sinful fallen men, but chiefly with evil principalities and powers still located in "heavenly places," i.e., in the spirit realm (Eph 6:12; cf. Rom 8:38). Yet victory is assured because Christ disarmed these evil powers at the cross (Col 2:15). In view, then, both of creation and redemption, Christ has been established as head over all principality and power (Col 2:10; cf. Eph 1:20-22). Christ's full work of salvation will finally be complete when He has abolished all other rule and authority and power (I Cor 15:24). *See* Angels; Demonology.

PRINCIPLE. Two Gr. words translated "principles" in the KJV are used in close conjunction in Heb 5:12 (*stoicheion*) and Heb 6:1 (*archē*). The Hebrews were spiritual babes who needed to be taught again the elementary principles, the fundamental or beginning teachings of Christianity. They needed to turn from difficult doctrines to the fundamental principle of saving faith (Heb 5:8-12). In Gal 4:9, Paul made reference to the "weak and beggarly elements" (*stoicheia*) which characterized the pre-Christian background of his converts. *See* Elements; Rudiments.

PRINT. The history of modern printing is of particular interest to the Bible student. The invention in Europe of a practical way of duplicating a text without having to copy it by hand opened the way for the great movement to make the Bible widely available in the language of the people. Though an inscribed clay disk from ancient Phaestos in Crete appears to have been impressed with moveable type, it is unique in the ancient world, and modern printing dates from the middle of the 15th cen. Gutenberg's Bible was one of the first books to be printed.

In Lev 19:28 the prohibition against printing marks upon the body refers to tattooing. The meaning of Job 13:27*b* is probably that God marks out a clear-cut limit for the soles of Job's feet. The reference in Jn 20:25 is obviously to the visible scars left by the nails in the hands of the risen Lord.

PRINTED. *See* Writing.

PRISCA. *See* Priscilla.

PRISCILLA (pri̇-sil'*ȧ*). The wife of Aquila (*q.v.*). While Luke calls her by this familiar name (Acts 18:2), Paul prefers to give her the more formal name of Prisca (Rom 16:3, ASV, RSV; I Cor 16:19, ASV, RSV; II Tim 4:19). The name belonged to a noble Roman family, the *gens Prisca*. Both Luke and Paul usually mention her before her husband; this may reflect her higher social status or (more probably) her more impressive personality. Adolf Harnack and others have credited her with the authorship of the Epistle to the Hebrews.

PRISON. No less than eight Heb. terms appear in the OT for prison, of which two are the most common: (1) *bêth sōhar,* "round house, tower house, house of the fortress," and (2) *maṭṭārâh,* "place of a guard, prison, jail." The NT uses five words, *phylakē,* "watch, guard, prison," being the most frequent.

Flagrant crimes as well as sabbath breaking (Num 15:34) resulted in confinement. OT examples of imprisonment are Joseph (Gen 39:20), Pharaoh's two officials (Gen 40:3), Joseph's brethren (Gen 42:17, 19), Samson (Jud 16:21), Jeremiah (Jer 37:15), conquered kings (II Kgs 17:4; 25:27), and others.

Cities of refuge afforded asylum for those persons guilty of accidental homicide (Num 35:25-28). Special prison buildings were unknown in Israel; rather, incarceration occurred in designated portions of fortresses, temples, or palaces. Jeremiah at first was flogged and put in an underground vaulted cell in a house converted into a prison (Jer 37:15-16, NASB). Next the king committed his imprisonment to the court of the guardhouse (37:21), but his enemies cast him into a dungeon or cistern where he sank into the mud and would have died a lingering death of starvation (38:6-10). Prisoners were often kept in chains (Jud 16:21; Jer 52:11; Acts 12:6; 21:33; 28:20) or their feet placed in stocks (Jer 20:2; Acts 16:24).

Periods of internment before trial were common (Lev 24:12; Num 15:34), but long imprisonments as criminal punishment were rare. The usual penalty for crime was scourging, fine, banishment, or death. *See* Crime and Punishment; Imprisonment; Punishment.

NT personages imprisoned were John the Baptist, Peter, Silas and Paul (Mt 14:3; Acts 12:5; 16:23; 22:19; Eph 3:1; 4:1; Phil 1:13). *See* Jailor.

Jesus taught His disciples to visit those in prison (Mt 25:36, 39), a practice which Onesiphorus carried out when Paul was in the Mamertine prison in Rome (II Tim 1:16-17).

Metaphorically, "prison" is used of the disobedient spirits confined in Noah's day (I Pet 3:19 f.) and the binding of Satan in the abyss (Rev 20:2-3).

R. V. U.

PRISONER. *See* Punishment.

PRIVILY, TO PUT AWAY. *See* Divorce.

PRIZE. An award to a victor in the games (I Cor 9:24; Phil 3:14). It is closely connected with the crowns mentioned as rewards for Christian conduct and service: of righteousness for those who love and prepare for Christ's second coming (II Tim 4:8); of life for those who patiently bear the tribulations of training (Jas 1:12; Rev 2:10); of glory for the faithful pastor (I Pet 5:4); of rejoicing for those who win souls (I Thess 2:19; cf. Phil 4:1). *See* Rewards.

PROCHORUS (prŏk'ō̆-rŭs). The name appears in the list of some early disciples, commonly referred to as deacons (Acts 6:5). Tradition reports him to have become bishop of Nicomedia. The apocryphal *Historia Prochori Christi Discipuli* contains many legendary accounts of this man. On the strength of his name (*prochoros,* "leader of the dance," Thayer), it is widely believed that he was a Hellenist. Byzantine art depicts him as the amanuensis of John the apostle in the writing of the Gospel of John. A life of John appearing in the latter half of the 5th cen. A.D. represents him as the author (H. H. Platz, "Prochorus," IDB, III, 892).

PROCLAMATION. An official announcement set forth publicly. It is ordinarily used of the authoritative announcements of a king or other high government official. In the Bible it is used of the supreme proclamation of the will of God. There are a number of words used in Heb., most of them with the idea of lifting up the voice, causing the word to be heard. The ancient proclamations were made by an official herald calling aloud in some public place (e.g., Ex 34:5; Lev 25:10; Jud 7:3; Isa 61:1–2; Ezr 1:1).

The NT word is the ordinary word for a "herald" (Gr. *kērux,* from *kērussō*). It is used almost exclusively to speak of the glorious proclamation of the gospel. Although the English translations are not consistent, the word is found in numerous passages, e.g., Mt 3:1; 26:13; Mk 6:12; Lk 24:47; Acts 8:5; 10:42; I Cor 1:21, 23; II Cor 11:4; Rev 5:2. *See* Herald.

PROCONSUL. *See* Deputy.

PROCURATOR. *See* Governor.

PRODIGAL SON. The parable of the prodigal son (Lk 15:11–32) has aptly been called "the gospel within the gospel" and "the crown and pearl" of all Christ's parables because of its lucid portrayal of gospel truth. In response to the grumbling of the scribes and Pharisees (15:1–2) Christ structured a parable around the Jewish custom whereby a father could assign his possessions to his heirs during his lifetime. He might actually hand over the allotment (cf. the younger son, 15:12); or he might present the share but retain the right to usufruct (cf. the elder son, 15:31). The attitudes and actions of the parable's personae then depict the various facets of the gospel: (1) The younger son (15:12–20)—the tax-gatherers and sinners whom Jesus received (NB the prodigal's sin, misery, and repentance). (2) The father's joyful and enthusiastic reception of the returned prodigal (12:20–24)—God's welcome to the repentant sinner. (3) The annoyance and bitterness of the elder brother (15:25–28)—the grumbling discontent and spiritual poverty of the scribes and Pharisees, who thought that salvation was a matter of meritorious works and outward piety. Possibly one could say there were *two* prodigal sons!

S. N. G.

PROFANE. To treat a holy person, place, or institution with irreverence, as if it were "common," i.e., not holy (Lev 19:8). The thought behind the Heb. word *ḥālal* is to untie, open, and make accessible and common what is sacred, since holy things were not open to the people. Thus, anything may be profaned by disregarding God's laws regarding its proper use: a sanctuary (Lev 21:12; Acts 24:6); the sabbath (Ex 31:14; cf. Mt 12:5); the altar (Ex 20:25); the covenant (Mal 2:10); a father's bed (Gen 49:4).

Prophets and priests may be defiled or polluted (Jer 23:11). Because Yahweh commands His people to be holy as He is holy (Lev 20:22–26), profanation in any of these realms is basically an attack on the holiness of God, a case of profaning His holy name (Lev 19:12; 21:6; Ezk 22:26; Amos 2:7; Mal 1:11–12).

Esau, because he despised and sold his birthright, was called "profane" (Gr. *bebēlos*) in the sense of being godless and materialistic (Heb 12:16). Old women's fables are termed profane or worldly (I Tim 4:7, NASB), as well as vain babblings or empty chatter (I Tim 6:20; II Tim 2:16). Ritually unclean food was considered common or unholy (Acts 10:14; see NASB marg., "profane"). *See* Clean; Holiness.

J. R.

PROGNOSTICATOR. The expression "the monthly prognosticators" (Isa 47:13, KJV) is translated in the NASB as "those who predict by the new moons." *See* Moon; Magic.

PROMISE. While referring occasionally to a man's word, the characteristic use of "promise" in Scripture is concerning what God declares He will bring to pass. Though we may infer promises between the Father and the Son before creation, God's first great promise to man is in Gen 3:15 inaugurating the succession which, in growing clarity and detail right down to the annunciation, tells of the coming Messiah-Deliverer. A wide range of promises is connected more or less directly with this great central promise, including the new covenant (Jer 31:31–34), the outpouring of the Spirit (Joel 2:28 f.), the restoration of Israel (Deut 30:1–5), and ultimately, new heavens and earth (Isa 65:17; 66:22).

Paul demonstrates that God's "promise" has the quality of a covenant, because every word of God is sure, yet free from legalism and dependence on man's efforts (e.g., in Rom 4:13–16; Gal 3:16–18; cf. Heb 11:40). The technical term *epangelia,* then, designates God's whole gracious commitment, expressed especially to Abraham, to perform His full redemptive work in Messiah, in whom "all the promises of God are yea and Amen" (II Cor 1:20).

Bibliography. Otto Michel, "*Homologeō*, etc.," TDNT, V, 199–220. Paul S. Minear, "Promise," IDB, III, 893–896. J. Schniewind and J. Friedrich, "*Epaggelō*, etc.," TDNT, II, 576–586. Wilbur M. Smith, "Promise," BDT, pp. 422 f.

M. A. K.

PROMISED LAND. *See* Canaan; Joshua, Book of.

PROPERTY. *See* Land and Property; Law of Moses.

PROPHECY. In the OT a prophetic oracle or message to be delivered to the people was conceived of as a "burden" (Heb. *maśśā'*) on the soul of the prophet until he could utter it (Prov 30:1 and 31:1, NASB marg.; cf. Isa 13:1; Hab 1:1; Zech 9:1; etc.). Also the word *nᵉbû'â* related to *nābî'*, "prophet," is used (II Chr 9:29; 15:8; Ezr 6:14; Neh 6:7). The NT term is Gr. *prophēteia,* which can refer to prophetic activity or "prophesying" (Rev 11:6, RSV); to the gift of prophecy or prophesying (Rom 12:6; I Cor 12:10; 13:2, 8–9; 14:1–6; etc.); and to prophetic utterances (Mt 13:14; I Thess 5:20; I Tim 1:18; etc.). *See* Gifts, Spiritual.

Functions of Prophecy

1. *Forthtelling.* The prophets were first of all forthtellers and spokesmen for God (*see* Prophet). Abraham, as he received and announced the covenant which God had made with him concerning his seed, was such (Gen 12:1–3; 15:1; 22:15 f.). Moses, as the greatest of all the prophets, was to receive the word directly from God's mouth and pass it on to Aaron who was to be his spokesman (Ex 7:1–2). Since Moses was to be Pharaoh's "god," Aaron's ministry demonstrates perfectly the ministry of the spokesman. All who act in the capacity of proclaiming the Word of God are His spokesmen. It is in this sense that the NT believer may prophesy when directed and empowered by the Holy Spirit.

In the designation of the OT as the Law and the Prophets (Mt 11:13; 22:40; Lk 16:16), the writers of all the books subsequent to the Pentateuch are classified as "prophets." They were prophets in the sense that they recounted history, manifested God's glory in praise and song, revealed His wisdom, and delivered His warnings of judgment and promises of restoration, all as God's inspired spokesmen.

2. *Foretelling.* Though not all foretold the future, many prophets did so. Abraham, as the first man named a prophet, was both a forthteller and a foreteller. He delivered to Isaac and his descendants a prophecy concerning Israel which revealed the promise of the first coming of Christ as the seed (cf. Gal 3:8, 16) and also the setting up of a kingdom. Though the details in the Abrahamic covenant were meager and still indistinct, they formed the framework to which the Mosaic covenant added a revelation of Israel's apostasy and rejection, followed by her repentance, regeneration, and restoration to the Promised Land (Deut 27:12–30:20). The certainty of this restoration was attested by God's personal oath (Jer 31:27–37; 32:27, 36–44; 33:2–26; cf. Heb 6:17–18; 8:8–13). It was also revealed through David, the prophet-king, in the Davidic covenant that his "house" or dynasty would endure forever (II Sam 7:16). Therefore a greater David, even Christ, would reign in this restored kingdom (Jer 33:15–17; Ezk 34:23–24; 37:24–28).

At the same time another and even more vital thread of prophecy had already been revealed right after the Fall. In Gen 3:15 Adam and Eve were told that the seed of Eve would destroy Satan. "It shall bruise thy head, and thou shalt bruise his heel." The seed therefore referred to in the Abrahamic covenant had already been revealed to Adam. Thus Gen 3:15 and 22:18 both point to the cross.

Throughout the OT three lines or strands of prophecy were developed:

One line concerning the suffering, sacrificial Messiah and Christ's first coming (Gen 3:15; 22:18; cf. Gal 3:8, 16; Gen 49:10–11; Isa 7:14; 9:6; 53; Ps 16; 22; 69).

A second strand concerning the reigning Messiah and Christ's second coming as promised in II Sam 7, and delineated in such great passages as Isa 11; 66; Hos 1:10–11; Amos 9:11; Zech 12–14. The prophets explain in detail both the second coming of the Lord and the conditions of peace and prosperity which shall accompany His reign (Isa 66:15; Zech 12-14).

A third strand intertwines with the prophesies of the first and second coming of Christ. It has to do with certain historical events which are not connected with either the first or second coming of Christ but are prophecies of particular historical events given to steady God's people in times of great trial and distress. They sketch out beforehand certain happenings in secular history. Examples are the revelation of the time to be spent by Israel under oppression in Egypt, namely, 400 years (Gen 15:13; cf. Ex 12:40; Gal 3:17), and 70 years of captivity in Babylon (Jer 25:11–12; cf. Dan 9:2), and the delineation of the events between Daniel's day and the time of Antiochus Epiphanes (Dan 11:1–21). *See* Prophecy, Fulfillment of.

3. *Ethical and social teaching.* This ministry of the prophet has been all too often ignored in the studies of evangelical scholars. Moses' first attempt to help his brethren was in the social sphere (Ex 2:11). Later, he was guided of God to set up the great theocratic principles of social and economic justice found especially in Exodus and Deuteronomy. Amos was the OT prophet who stressed this function of prophecy in particular as he revealed the social injustices in the northern kingdom. Hosea reflects similar teaching, as does also Isaiah. Our Lord fulfilled this responsibility particularly in the Sermon on the Mount and in some of His parables.

4. *Political influence.* This is also often overlooked. Moses received a commission to demand the release of Israel by Pharaoh (Ex 6:11; 9:13). Nathan was to appear before David (II Sam 12). Isaiah confronted King Ahaz and advised Hezekiah (Isa 7; 37). Jeremiah was commanded to appear before the king at different times (Jer 22:1; 34:2; 37:7). Daniel appeared before Nebuchadnezzar and Belshazzar (Dan 2:19, 25; 5:17). Amos' message reached the king through one of his ministers (Amos 5:15–17).

5. *A soteriological message.* The most important ministry performed by the prophet was that of giving a message of salvation. In this

respect the minister of the gospel follows in his footsteps. Constantly the prophets warned the people of their sins and urged them to repent. We find such examples as Joshua calling upon Israel to choose whom they would serve (Josh 24:15). Moses gave the blessings and curses, followed by a plea to repent—which would only be fulfilled finally as God led them to repentance at Christ's second coming (Deut 28:1 ff.). Jonah called on Nineveh to repent within 40 days (Jon 3:4). Ezra prayed for those who had returned from the Exile, to confess their sins and put away their foreign wives (Ezr 9:5–10:11). And John the Baptist exhorted Israel to prepare a highway in their hearts for the coming of their King (Lk 3:4-6).

Modes of Communication

1. *Direct proclamation.* The prophet proclaimed in simple, bold language (Jon 3:4) the message which God had given to him. It was communicated either, as in Moses' case, "mouth to mouth" (Num 12:8, though he alone was permitted to talk with God face to face, Deut 34:10), or through a dream or vision (Jer 1:11 ff.). But always it was by direct inspiration of God so that the prophets could again and again write "Thus saith the Lord."

2. *Figurative language.* As a rule the prophecies of the OT are clear and direct, though some are certainly purposely figurative. The main reasons for the figurative are two: (*a*) To convey more effectively and expressively some fact or truth (cf. Isa 66:12-13; Amos 9:13). (*b*) To express a knowledge of future events in such a form that it could not be fathomed by the unbeliever, on the one hand, but could be understood by the believer, on the other hand, only after most careful study. God does not cast all His pearls before swine.

In general, however, the figures of speech are readily understandable when examined in the context of OT culture. For example, when Isaiah says, "Prepare ye the way of the Lord, make straight in the desert a highway for our God" (Isa 40:3-5), the metaphoric imagery is that of preparing a highway for the coming of a king. The voice speaking this in the wilderness turned out to be that of John the Baptist as he preached repentance preparatory to the coming of the Messiah (Lk 3:1–18). When Isaiah speaks of a birth without travail and asks can a nation be brought forth all at once (Isa 66:8, NASB), the picture is easily recognizable as the same as that given in Zech 12–14, where the whole nation repents at Christ's second coming.

3. *Dramatic presentation.* Sometimes the Lord directed the prophet to dramatize the message. Jeremiah was to make yokes and put them on his neck (Jer 27:2), Ezekiel to set up a drawing of the city on a tile and lay siege to it (Ezk 4:1 ff.). Ezekiel was also to shave his head and his beard, and to burn a third of the hair in the city, strike a second third with a sword, and scatter the last third to the wind, etc., to illustrate Jerusalem's approaching fate (Ezk 5:1–12). God called upon Hosea to marry a harlotrous woman and redeem her from slavery as a picture of His undying love for Israel (Hos 1:2; 3:1).

Development of Prophecy

Prophecy in the Bible opens with the declaration of the protevangelium in Gen 3:15. This belongs to the first prophetic strand which announces the first coming of Christ as the suffering, sacrificial Messiah. The second thread, that of the ruling, reigning Messiah, appears so closely intertwined with this first thread in the Abrahamic covenant that they are at first almost indistinguishable. The third, namely, that line of prophecies which foretell historical events needed to strengthen the faith of the believer in dark, difficult days, appears first of all in Gen 15:13 with the announcement that Israel will remain in Egypt for 400 years.

Though Abraham was a prophet, it was Moses who most fully exemplified all the ministries of the OT prophet. He was so far above the other prophets, both in character and in administration, that God compares Christ to him (Deut 18:18). In contrast, the NT writer compares him to Christ as the lesser to the greater (Heb 3:1–6). In the times of the judges there was sporadic political and military but little real spiritual leadership. Word from the Lord was rare in those days and visions were infrequent (I Sam 3:1, NASB). This continued until the days of Samuel.

This prophet appears to have started a school of the prophets, which died out, only to be revived again by Elijah and Elisha (II Kgs 2:3) during the time of apostasy and idolatry in the northern kingdom (I Kgs 18:18). It was to be expected that great spiritual leaders, such as Samuel and Elijah, would attract to themselves young men keen to follow in their footsteps.

Two prophetic movements remain to be described: that of Amos and Hosea to warn the northern kingdom of their sin and coming captivity, and that of Isaiah, Jeremiah, *et al.* to warn the southern kingdom of Judah of her sin, judgment, and coming exile. There is a close resemblance between the prophetic messages to the north and to the south. Passages of warning against sin and threatened punishments are interspersed with promises of future restoration, peace, and blessing. As these passages are sorted out and fitted into the pattern given in the Mosaic covenant in Deut 27–30, a marvelous picture emerges of the future promised to Israel and of the millennial kingdom in which all believers will have a part. The kingdom promises add details to the revelations given in the covenants.

It is Daniel, however, who gives the most extensive prophetic outline of history. He starts by interpreting Nebuchadnezzar's dream of the great human statue (Dan 2), and later the visions of the lion, the bear, the leopard, and the terrible beast with ten horns which "brake in pieces and stamped the residue with its feet"

(Dan 7:1-7). These visions reveal the history of those great nations which were to affect Israel's history until the second coming of Christ. Daniel ends by foretelling the abomination of desolation, the Great Tribulation, and the resurrection of the saints of the Most High (Dan 9:27; 12:1-2).

In the NT Christ is both the fulfillment of prophecy as the sacrificial, suffering Messiah and a prophet in His own right (Mt 21:19; Lk 24:19; Jn 4:19; 7:40). He announces that the kingdom of God is at hand and speaks of its dynamic existence during the Church Age in the hearts of those who have accepted Him as their Saviour (Lk 17:21). He teaches that the kingdom has become a living reality at His first coming, but that its full development awaits His return from heaven to take over its rulership (Mt 22:33-44; cf. Dan 2:35, 43-44; 7:9-14).

Christ put His hand directly on Daniel's prophecy of the "abomination of desolation" and identified it as the sign which would immediately precede the Great Tribulation (Mt 24:15), thus dispelling all speculation as to the terminal point of Daniel's prophecies in Dan 2; 7; 9; 11-12. Once this point has been established, the terrible beast of Dan 7 and its counterpart in Rev 13 and 17 can be seen as identical. The key has thus been given by Christ to Daniel's prophecy, and by Daniel's prophecy to the book of Revelation. Daniel's last beast is then the kingdom reigning at the time of Christ's second coming.

Methods of Interpretation

1. *Orthodox views.* The interpretation of that strand which concerns Christ's first coming is agreed upon by all orthodox theologians. They also agree that Christ will return. However, there is much disagreement surrounding the details of His second coming, and especially on the matter of the kingdom.

Very simply stated, the problem is this: can prophecies about the kingdom and the second advent of Christ be accepted and understood in the same literal manner as the prophecies which foretold His first coming? Certain prophecies in the OT, e.g., foretell the presentation of animal sacrifices in the eschatological temple (Ezk 43-46; Zech 14:21). Because of the theological problems raised by blood sacrifices subsequent to Christ's all-sufficient atoning death, some feel these and other prophecies concerning an earthly kingdom must be spiritualized. They are applied either to the presentation of the gospel in the present Church Age, or else to the future eternal state in some spiritualized sense. But is it permissible to depart from the normal grammatical-historical method of interpretation?

The strand of prophecy which deals with Christ's second coming is interpreted in three different ways. (1) the postmillennialist considers that the kingdom promises and the thousand years of Rev 20 refer to a golden age which will be ushered in as a result of the preaching of the gospel and occur before Christ's second coming. (2) The amillennialist identifies the kingdom promises and the thousand years (Rev 20) either with the progression of evangelism through the church (O. T. Allis, *Prophecy and the Church*), with the intermediate state of the redeemed as they await the end of the world when Christ returns to resurrect the dead and judge His enemies, or with the time of the new heavens and the new earth (Herman Ridderbos, *The Coming of the Kingdom*). He sees no kingdom for Israel and the believer on the earth as it now exists. (3) The premillennialist observes the identification of Mt 24:15 with the abomination of desolation in Daniel, and the beast of Dan 7:7-8 with that of Rev 13 and 17, and identifies the start of the Millennium in Rev 20 with Dan 12:2-3, 13. He sees the kingdom as beginning on earth with the second coming of Christ and lasting for a thousand years, according to the prophecy of Rev 20:4-7, and the new heavens and the new earth succeeding this in Rev 21:1–22:5.

While this article cannot go into the merits of the arguments for each of the above views, the premillennial view has the great advantage that it applies the same method of interpretation to all three strands of prophecy mentioned above. Besides this, it builds upon a fully developed theology of the covenants. The premillennialist develops progressively the details given in the Abrahamic covenant which point to an earthly kingdom under the rulership of the Messiah. He follows them through the Mosaic and Davidic covenants, adding the details of eschatological truth revealed in Isaiah to Malachi (A. J. McClain, *The Greatness of the Kingdom*). He accepts the view expressed by Jesus' disciples, and not corrected by Him, that God will finally restore the kingdom to Israel (Acts 1:6).

The premillennial view extends the grace of God to the fullest limit of all the views mentioned, in that it allows a thousand years for man to repent, with the Saviour Himself reigning over the earth. Furthermore, it proves the total sinfulness of sin in that even with Christ here on earth and Satan bound, man still refuses to believe except by the sovereign grace of God (Rev 20:9). *See* Millennium.

2. *Neoorthodox view.* Of several other views which could be considered, the most important for our day is the neoorthodox. This teaches that all eschatology refers to supra-history, i.e., to the so-called "eternal now" of heaven in which a timeless, spaceless God exists, and not to actual future events on the earth. At death man will enter this transcendent sphere of contemporaneity where past and future are present, so that the past, present, and future are all one grand homogenous "now."

This view must be rejected by evangelicals because it is part of a philosophy of revelation which denies the possibility of direct communication between God and man, and rules out all possibility of propositional revelation, namely, of God speaking directly to man, and of true verbal inspiration.

PROPHECY, FULFILLMENT OF

Bibliography. O. T. Allis, *Prophecy and the Church,* Philadelphia: Presbyterian and Reformed, 1945. W. J. Beecher, *The Prophets and the Promise,* New York: Crowell, 1905. C. A. Briggs, *Messianic Prophecy,* New York: Scribner's, 1886. J. O. Buswell, Jr., *A Systematic Theology of the Christian Religion,* Grand Rapids: Zondervan, 1963, Vol. II, Part IV. A. B. Davidson, *Old Testament Prophecy,* Edinburgh: Clark, 1903. F. E. Hamilton, *The Basis of Millennial Faith,* Grand Rapids: Eerdmans, 1953. G. E. Ladd, *Jesus and the Kingdom,* New York: Harper & Row, 1953. A. J. McClain, *The Greatness of the Kingdom,* Chicago: Moody, 1968. C. Von Orelli, *Old Testament Prophecy,* Edinburgh: Clark, 1885. H. Ridderbos, *The Coming of the Kingdom,* Philadelphia: Presbyterian and Reformed, 1962. Wilbur M. Smith, *A Preliminary Bibliography for the Study of Biblical Prophecy,* Boston: Wilde, 1952. For additional books *see* Prophet.

R. A. K.

PROPHECY, FULFILLMENT OF. Fulfilled prophecy is one of the strongest evidences available for the divine origin of Christianity and the Bible. The precise fulfillment of various prophecies of both the OT and the NT, in some cases uttered many centuries before they come to pass, proves beyond reasonable doubt the divine inspiration of the Scriptures, and their supernatural authority and veracity.

Biblical Warrant

The Bible itself sets up a structure of Christian evidences. In Deut 18 the difficulty created by the appearance of false prophets is discussed. The Israelite will ask, "How shall we know the word which the Lord has not spoken?" The answer follows: "When a prophet speaks in the name of the Lord, if the thing does not come about or come true, that is the thing which the Lord has not spoken. The prophet has spoken it presumptuously; you shall not be afraid of him" (vv.21-22, NASB). The corollary follows that if the prophetic utterance does come to pass, the prophet speaks from the Lord.

The apologetic value of fulfilled prophecy is developed further in Isaiah. How could the Israelite differentiate the true God from the so-called gods of the surrounding nations? In poetic device Yahweh challenges the heathen deities to present evidence of their reality: "Let them bring forth and declare to us what is going to take place; as for the former events, declare what they were, that we may consider them, and know their outcome; or announce to us what is coming. Declare the things that are going to come afterward, that we may know that you are gods" (Isa 41:22-23, NASB). The structure of the apologetic is this: if a god does not know the future, he is of no account (v.24); if he knows the future, he is the true God. Even more emphatically, the Lord later on says: "I am God, and there is no other; I am God, and there is no one like Me, declaring the end from

In fulfillment of prophecy the city of Tyre was destroyed. Here are ruins of a very unusual rectangular amphitheater at the site. HFV

the beginning and from ancient times things which have not been done, saying, 'My purpose will be established, and I will accomplish all My good pleasure' " (Isa 46:9-10, NASB). Daniel learned this lesson well, for in his worship he acknowledged that only the God of his fathers could reveal the profound and hidden things of the future course of world history (Dan 2:20-23).

The Lord is eager for His people to *know* that He is the living God. More than 50 times in Ezekiel God says that He will foretell the future or act in judgment so that Israel may know that He is the Lord their God (e.g., 6:10, 14; 7:27; 12:16; 39:28). Therefore He chooses to manifest His omnipotence in miracles and His omniscience in declaring the future. As Bernard Ramm says, man feels his limitations of knowledge most keenly when he faces decisions which seem to require detailed knowledge of future events which do not exist as yet. Therefore the God of Israel is the living God because He knows what shall be. This omniscience differentiates Him from false gods, and the prophet of Israel from false prophets, and the religion of Israel from false religions (*Revelation and the Bible,* p. 262).

When the early Christians began to preach they boldly declared that God had acted in history through the coming, ministry, and atoning death of Jesus of Nazareth, the Messiah, God's Servant and Son, to obtain forgiveness of all sins (Acts 2:22-23; 3:13-15; 10:34-43; 13:22-30). They always supported these remarkable claims with proof that the claims were true. They appealed to two facts: they had witnessed Jesus alive after God had miraculously raised Him from the dead, and the events which transpired in connection with His life and death had been supernaturally predicted in the OT (Acts 2:25-35; 3:18, 22-25; 8:32-35; 13:30-37). They considered such proofs to be sufficient for them to command men to repent and acknowledge Jesus as both Lord and Messiah (Acts 2:36-40; 3:19-20; 4:10-12; 17:30-31). These proofs produced such assurance in the apostles and their followers that they risked their very lives for the sake of the gospel.

It is highly instructive for the Christian apologist to note how each of the following appealed to the OT prophets for validation of the gospel message. Christ Himself after His resurrection spent much time explaining to His disciples "the things concerning Himself in all the Scriptures" and berated them for not believing in all that the prophets had spoken (Lk 24:25–27, 44–47, NASB). Peter referred to David as a prophet (Acts 2:30) and quoted from Ps 16 and Ps 110 to prove to the Jews that Jesus whom they had crucified was the predicted Messiah. Later he again boldly proclaimed Christ, arguing from the twofold evidence of a present miracle performed in the name of Jesus (Acts 3:12–16) and fulfilled prophecy: "The things which God announced beforehand by the mouth of all the prophets, that His Christ should suffer, He has thus fulfilled" (3:18, NASB; cf. his further appeal to the prophets in vv. 21–25). Note also Peter's statement in Acts 10:43: "Of Him all the prophets bear witness" (NASB).

Paul likewise used prophecy in the synagogue of Antioch of Pisidia to produce evidence for the truthfulness of his preaching (Acts 13:27, 29, 32–37). At Thessalonica for three sabbaths he reasoned with the Jews from the Scriptures, "explaining and giving evidence" that the Messiah had to suffer and rise again from the dead, and saying, "This Jesus whom I am proclaiming to you is the Christ" (Acts 17:3, NASB). His defense before Agrippa and his evangelistic appeal to that ruler were based largely on the prophets (Acts 26:22, 23, 27). The eloquent Apollos could powerfully refute the Jews in public because, knowing the OT Scriptures so well, he could demonstrate by them that Jesus was the Messiah (Acts 18:28).

Essential Features

The biblical prophecies that have already been fulfilled can be shown to have some distinctive characteristics. These then are undoubtedly true of all prophecies. They are not mere sage remarks and educated guesses, or scientific predictions based on laws of nature. Neither do they reflect a humanly controlled situation wherein the prophet or his followers bring about the fulfillment. They must be predictions of the future which only God could foreknow and bring to pass.

There is also a degree of obscurity in many of the prophecies. In telling of the "sign" that His resurrection would be to His generation, Jesus did not clearly say He would die, that His body would be buried, and that three days later He would be raised, leaving a tomb empty. Rather He made an enigmatic reference to Jonah's experience in the "whale's belly" and indicated that He would have a similar experience in the "heart of the earth," i.e., in an underground tomb (Mt 12:40). When Christ predicted His resurrection in connection with His cleansing the temple, He said, "Destroy this temple, and in three days I will raise it up" (Jn 2:19). As Robert D. Culver points out, no one on earth except Jesus Himself really understood those predictions until after Christ's resurrection; and then only with considerable reflection did His disciples remember what He had said, and understand it and believe (Jn 2:20–22). Only when prophecy becomes history can one see unmistakably what the Lord is speaking about (cf. Jn 13:7, 19). Culver concludes that if this obscurity were not initially present, a prophecy either could actually produce its nonfulfillment through efforts of those who might desire to oppose God's plan, or its evidential value could be destroyed by the bungling efforts of other too-helpful friends who might try to bring it to pass ("Were the OT Prophecies Really Prophetic?" *Can I Trust My Bible?* p. 99).

On the other hand, biblical prophecies are not ambiguous and trivial like the prognostications of the French astrologer Nostradamus (A.D. 1555) or the responses of the pagan oracles of Greece and Rome. One answer would agree with several, and sometimes directly opposite, events. When King Croesus of Lydia consulted the Delphic oracle as to whether he should proceed against the Persians, the reply was: "By crossing Halys, Croesus will destroy a mighty power." Instead of the kingdom of Cyrus it was his own that fell. The Bible, however, contains prophecies of amazing detail. Cyrus' very name was foretold well over a century before his rise to fame (Isa 44:28; 45:1). The 11th chapter of Daniel is so detailed that it forced the Neo-Platonist philosopher Porphyry in the 3rd cen. A.D. and many critics since then to argue that the passage was written after the events transpired. Therefore the book of Daniel is dated by them *c.* 165 B.C. and Isa 40–66 in the time of Cyrus or later, in order to evade the argument from fulfilled prophecy. It must be emphasized that no prophecy of the Bible can be proved to have failed to come to pass. This factor stands in bold contrast to the frequent misses of the prognosticating efforts of Jeanne Dixon and other modern so-called prophets.

Along with the evidential value of fulfilled biblical prophecies is their spiritual value. Divination, fortune telling, and other occult practices have as their goal merely the satisfaction of the curiosity and selfish interests of man. Biblical prophecy, on the contrary, always contains a preview of God's wisdom, omniscience, and sovereignty. In disclosing the future the Lord reveals something of Himself and prepares us to meet Him by giving both warnings and encouragements. The prophetic figure of the Messiah, e.g., surpassed the understanding and even the expectations of God's chosen nation. But the very prophecies that so portrayed Him helped to prepare the hearts of many of these people to receive Him. And when we see the fulfillment of a prophetic word it strengthens our faith (Jn 13:19; 14:29; 16:4).

OT Prophecies of Christ

It has been estimated that several hundred prophecies concerning Jesus Christ have been fulfilled in His first advent. Arthur T. Pierson (1837-1911) stated that there are 332 references to Christ in the OT which are expressly cited in the NT, either as predictions fulfilled in His life and ministry, or as previsions of His character (*Many Infallible Proofs*, II, 13). According to the law of mathematical probability there would be one chance in 84 followed by 98 zeros that all these predictions would occur in the case of a single individual; this is assuming that each one had an even possibility of success, whereas if they were mere guesses most are highly improbable. Needless to say, such a "chance" is so remote that only an omniscient and omnipotent God could predict accurately so many events and details and then bring them to pass.

Some of the more important prophecies fulfilled in Jesus Christ are listed here:

Gen 3:15 – the seed of a woman [of a *man* in normal births] and the conqueror of Satan.

Gen 12:1-3, 7 – the seed of Abraham, in whom all the families of the earth will be blessed; cf. Gal 3:16; Acts 3:25.

Gen 49:9-10 – Shiloh, who came from the tribe of Judah just before all authority to govern was taken from Judah; cf. Rev 5:5.

II Sam 7:16 – the descendant of David who would reign forever over the house of Jacob; cf. Lk 1:31-33.

Ps 16:10 – God's Holy One whose body would not undergo decay in the tomb; cf. Acts 2:27-32; 13:35-37.

Ps 22:1, 6-8, 11-18 – the God-forsaken cry and the portrayal of the scoffing and crucifixion suffered by one greater than David; cf. Mt 27:46, 39, 43, 35.

Isa 7:14 and 9:6-7 – the opening and closing words of a single prophetic oracle predicting that a virgin would bear a son whose very character would be divine; cf. Mt 1:18-25; Lk 1:30-35.

Isa 42:1-7; 49:1-7 – the first two of the Servant Songs, about the obedient Man formed from the womb for the purpose of serving the Lord, who would not incite violence or political revolution, but would establish a new covenant of salvation for both Jew and Gentile; cf. Mt 12:18-21.

Isa 50:4-9 – the third Servant Song, about the One who gave His back to the smiters; cf. Mt 26:67; 27:26, 30; Jn 19:1.

Isa 52:13 – 53:12 – the fourth and last Servant Song, the most amazing prophecy of all time. Every statement in these 15 verses is directly predictive of Jesus Christ. Depicting in detail the humble background and the substitutionary atoning work of our Saviour and His burial, and even intimating His resurrection (53:10), this passage must be studied in depth even to begin to discover all of its apologetic, let alone its theological, value. The American Bible Society Greek NT (eds. Aland, Black, Metzger, and Wikgren) lists 41 quotations by NT writers of portions of this passage. To destroy the force of this prophecy unbelievers have claimed that the NT writers invented a literary career for Jesus deliberately to correspond with the prophecy even though His actual life and death were far different.

Isa 61:1-3 – the anointing of the Messiah and His ministry of deliverance; cf. Lk 4:17-21.

Dan 9:25-26*a* – the only prediction of an actual date for the Messiah's advent: 69 weeks (of years, i.e., 483 years) from the decree to rebuild the walls of Jerusalem in the reign of Artaxerxes (Ezr 7:11-13, 18, 25; cf. the results, Ezr 4:12; 9:9; or Neh 2:1-8; 3:1) until Messiah would come to Jerusalem as Prince (cf. Jn 12:12-15).

Joel 2:28-29 – the outpouring of the Holy Spirit which began at Pentecost and which the risen Christ promised to send after His ascension; cf. Acts 1:4-5; 2.

Mic 5:2 – the exact birthplace of Messiah foretold, extremely unlikely of fulfillment considering the fact that His mother lived a hundred miles to the N in Nazareth; cf. Mt 2:4-6; Lk 2:1-7.

Zech 9:9 – the triumphal entry of the humble King of Jerusalem; cf. Mt 21:4-10.

Zech 12:10 – the piercing of the Son of God; cf. Jn 19:37.

Zech 13:7 – the smiting of the Shepherd and scattering of His flock or disciples; cf. Mt 26:31; Mk 14:27.

Mal 3:1 – the preparatory work of John the Baptist and the coming of the Lord to His temple; cf. Mt 11:3, 10.

Prophecies of the Nations of Antiquity

Among the prophecies of the Bible are dozens concerning the future of cities, nations, kings, and dynasties. Some of the most interesting are listed here:

1. The fall of Babylon (Isa 13; Jer 51:36-58).
2. The total destruction of Nineveh (Nahum; Zeph 2:13-15).
3. Egypt's decline, loss of her fisheries, and dread of the land of Judah (Isa 19:1-17); her desolation wrought by Babylon, Persia, and Rome (Ezk 29-30).
4. The destruction in 572 B.C. of the mainland city of Tyre by Nebuchadnezzar after a 13-year siege (Ezk 26:1-11; 29: 17-20), and the eventual capture of its island fortress in 332 B.C. by Alexander the Great after he used the mainland rubble to build a causeway across the channel (Ezk 26:12-21).
5. The progression of the four main empires in the Near East from Babylon to Rome, with the first three actually being named (Dan 2:36-45; 7:3-7; 8:1-8, 19-22; 10:20).

6. Alexander's invasion of Phoenicia and Philistia (Zech 9:1-8; Jos *Ant.* xi.8.3-5).

Prophecies of the Jewish People

The most remarkable case of the fulfillment of prophecies concerning a nation is that of the Jews. A few of the great number of these are given here:

1. Their captivity and dispersion in many foreign lands and their eventual return (Deut 28:36-68; Lev 26:33-45).

2. Judah's 70 year captivity in Babylon (Jer 25:11-12; 29:10; cf. Dan 9:1-2), from Nebuchadnezzar's first deportation of captives in 605 B.C. until the return of the first exiles led by Zerubbabel *c.* 536 B.C.

3. The survival of the Jews as a distinct people after the total defeat of their nation, in contrast to the other great peoples of antiquity (Jer 31:35-37; 33:24-26).

4. The destruction in A.D. 70 of Jerusalem and the second temple (Herod's), as foretold by Jesus (Mt 24:1-2).

5. The regathering of the Jews in Palestine and reestablishment of an independent political state in 142 B.C. (I Macc 13:36-42) and A.D. 1948, the only people ever to stage such a national comeback, and not only once but twice (Isa 11:11-16; Jer 16:14-16; Ezk 36:8-12, 24; 37:11-14, 21-22*a*).

6. The Negeb desert blossoming like a rose and being resettled (Isa 35:1-2; 51:3; 61:4; Jer 32:43-44; 33:13).

7. The rebuilding of modern towns in Israel at Ashkelon and Ashdod after the lapse of many centuries (Zeph 2:4-7), in contrast to the sparse population in the areas of Chorazin, Bethsaida, and Capernaum in keeping with Christ's "woe" or curse (Mt 11:20-24).

Even by employing the most extreme measures it is impossible to date many of these OT passages so late that they may be considered mere historical accounts rather than true predictions. Having been assured that these (and many other prophecies not listed here) are genuine, we gain confidence that other prophecies yet future will be fulfilled with like exactitude. It becomes folly not to pay heed to the prophetic warnings of the Word of God. For the Bible bears its own evidence that it is the Word of the omniscient God who declares the end from the beginning and will bring to pass what He has purposed (Isa 46:10-11).

See Prophecy; Prophet.

Bibliography. Robert D. Culver, "Were the Old Testament Prophecies Really Prophetic?" *Can I Trust My Bible?* Chicago: Moody, 1963. George T. B. Davis, *Bible Prophecies Fulfilled Today*, Philadelphia: Million Testaments Campaigns, 1955. Floyd E. Hamilton, *The Basis of Christian Faith,* 3rd ed. rev., New York: Harper, 1946, pp. 296-317. Alexander Keith, *The Evidence of the Truth of the Christian Religion Derived From the Fulfillment of Prophecy,* London, 1832. René Pache, *The Inspiration and Authority of Scripture,* Chicago: Moody, 1969, pp. 282-285. Arthur T. Pierson, *Many Infallible Proofs,* 2 vols., Grand Rapids: Zondervan reprint, n.d. Bernard Ramm, *Protestant Christian Evidences,* Chicago: Moody, 1953, pp. 81-124; "The Evidence of Prophecy and Miracle," *Revelation and the Bible,* Carl F. H. Henry, ed., Grand Rapids: Baker, 1958, pp. 253-263. Wilbur M. Smith, *The Supernaturalness of Christ,* Boston: Wilde, 1940, pp. 73-80, 190 f.; *Egypt in Biblical Prophecy,* Boston: Wilde, 1957. Hawley O. Taylor, "Mathematics and Prophecy," *Modern Science and Christian Faith,* Wheaton: Van Kampen, 1948, pp. 175-183. John Urquhart, *Wonders of Prophecy,* rev. ed., London: Pickering & Inglis, 1939. John F. Walvoord, *The Nations in Prophecy,* Grand Rapids: Zondervan, 1967.

J. R.

PROPHET. The English word is derived from the Gr. *prophētēs,* "one who speaks forth," a proclaimer and interpreter of the divine revelation (Arndt, p. 730). It generally refers to one who acts as a spokesman. At times also it is practically synonymous with "seer" or "inspired person." Often it bears the connotation of a predictor or revealer of future events. English usage determines the sense in which the word is to be understood.

Terminology. In the Heb. OT several words are found the precise significance of which is to be determined by usage rather than by etymology. Among these the one of most frequent occurrence is *nābî'*. Various learned attempts have been made to discover the etymological significance of the word (cf. *My Servants the Prophets,* pp. 56-57), but these are not satisfactory. Usage, however, does show what the force of the word was. Thus in Deut 18:18*b* God states that the prophet (*nābî'*) will declare all that God commands him. Again in Ex 7:1 the word has the same significance. Other passages are Ex 4:15-16; Jer 1:17*a*; 15:19; etc. In all these passages, and indeed throughout the OT, the *nābî'* appears as one who declares a message on behalf of a superior.

The OT does not place its emphasis on the manner in which the divine revelation is received, but on the proclamation of the message. The divinely revealed religion of the OT in this respect is seen to be very practical in nature. In many pagan cultures, on the other hand, what is prominent is the manner in which the seer obtains his message. Not the proclamation but the dark background of mystery seems to receive the greater emphasis. At this point the OT presents a marked contrast to the pagan world. It is clear that the prophetic message was not of human but of divine origination (II Pet 1:20-21), and for that reason the OT prophet was not similar to the heathen soothsayer or diviner of antiquity. Whereas the soothsayer might have received his "message" or omens by methods of human devising, the prophet's words came to him by dreams and visions sent from God. Micah claimed that he was full of power—with the Spirit of the Lord—to make known to the nation of Israel its sin (Mic 3:8).

Two other words, *rô'eh* and *ḥôzeh,* both being participles denoting one who sees, are used practically as synonyms. In both of these words stress falls upon the method of receiving the revelation, namely, seeing. The *rô'eh* and the *ḥôzeh* were men who saw the message which God gave them. Whether this seeing was with the physical eye or a seeing in vision, or whether the word may refer to a metaphorical seeing such as supernatural insight, is difficult to tell. Possibly the seer was simply a man who with the inner eye saw in vision the truth which God gave him. At the same time, it is clear from a comparison of the principal passages in which the words occur (e.g., I Sam 9:9; Isa 30:9-10) that the *rô'eh* and the *ḥôzeh* were spokesmen for God. Their function was the same as that of the *nābî'*. By way of summary we may say that the OT prophet, by whatever name he may have been designated, was a man in whose mouth God had placed His words and who spoke those words to the people.

The prophet and Moses. For an understanding of the divine origin of the prophetic institution, the key passage is Deut 18:9-22. As a counterpart to the continuous activity of the Canaanite soothsayers and diviners, God promised to give to Israel His prophets. Israel, therefore, would not be compelled to resort to mere human means of obtaining information about life and death. Instead she was to listen to the prophets who would declare to her the very words of God. The prophet, therefore, like Moses was to be a mediator between God and the nation. Just as the priest represented the people before God, so also did the prophet represent God before the people. Nevertheless, none of the prophets was an exact counterpart to Moses, and only with the coming of Christ did there appear that great Prophet who was truly like unto Moses, whom the Lord knew face to face (Deut 34:10; cf. Num 12:8).

In Heb 3:1-6 a contrast is made between Moses and Christ. *In* God's house, i.e., the divine economy or dispensation, Moses was faithful as a servant, but Christ is *over* the house as a Son. The OT or Mosaic age is set forth here as a witness of the NT period. In this sense the entire Mosaic dispensation may be said to be typical of and preparatory for the new age. And in that dispensation of type and preparation, Moses was the greatest figure. The only one who was truly like unto Moses was Christ.

One may ask why there was need of other prophets to follow Moses the lawgiver. When the Israelites entered the Promised Land they discovered that there were many situations about which the law of Moses did not speak in detail. To meet the needs caused by such situations, further revelation, often of a specific and detailed nature, was necessary. This information constituted the subject matter of prophecy. The prophets built upon the law of Moses; they did not contradict it or abrogate it.

Moses, however, stood above all the prophets, not as the first among equals, but as the faithful servant under whom the prophets were to labor. The position which Moses occupied in the economy was unique and was not shared by any of the other prophets. This uniqueness appears, for one thing, in the manner in which God spoke to the prophets. To Moses He spoke mouth to mouth, plainly, not in dark or enigmatic sayings, and He permitted Moses to see His form. On the other hand, God spoke to the other prophets by means of dreams and visions, and the Scripture implies that He might also have spoken in riddles (Num 12:1-6). To the prophets God gave revelations in a manner less clear and distinct than that in which He spoke to Moses. It is for this reason, therefore, that we may find in many of the prophetic utterances a certain measure of obscurity and even ambiguity. The prophetic language cannot be interpreted as though it were merely normal prose. In the interpretation of prophecy one must always consider the nature of prophetic language, as well as the fact that much of what the prophets spoke was typical.

The prophets, then, were men whom God raised up to declare His will to the nation. They themselves were an integral part of the OT economy. Like the age of which they were a part, they were types, pointing forward to the coming of One who should embody in its fullest and most complete sense the ideals of the prophetic institution. When He would come in finality there would be no further need of prophecy, for then the dispensation of preparation would have given way to the dispensation of completion and fulfillment (cf. I Cor 13:8-12). In the deepest sense, therefore, just as prophecy itself was a preparation for Christ, so also was the individual prophet in the entirety of his ministry a witness to and a type of Christ, the Prophet par excellence.

Schools of the prophets. During the period of Samuel we find mention of bands of prophets. About these bands very little is known, although they have been the subject of much speculation. It would seem, however, that they aided Samuel in ministering to the spiritual needs of the country. The work of the theocracy had proved to be too great for Moses, and hence 70 elders were chosen to assist him in his arduous task. In the period of Samuel the work again proved to be too much for one individual. This was a particularly crucial period, for the days of the judges were coming to a close and the times of the monarchy were beginning. There was need that the Spirit be poured out, not merely upon Samuel, but also upon those of lesser stature.

About the organization of these groups we know practically nothing. They are described as a "band" (RSV) or "company" (*ḥebel*); they engaged in prophesying and praising God in accompaniment to music (I Sam 10:5, 10). Probably the group was organized by Samuel, but Scripture does not explicitly state this as a fact.

After the division of the monarchy a prophetic body again appears, this time designated "sons of the prophets" (*q.v.*). The sons of the prophets were found only in the northern kingdom in connection with the ministry of Elijah and Elisha. At this time the nation had not only been divided, but there was present the additional danger of the influence of Phoenician Baal worship. Hence these prophets stood in a closer spiritual relationship to Elijah and Elisha than did the band of prophets to Samuel. For that reason they are designated "sons," i.e., spiritual sons of prophetic masters. These men may have been married (cf. II Kgs 4:1) and may have had a common dwelling place (cf. II Kgs 6:1-2). With the completion of the work of Elijah and Elisha they disappear from the scene, except for an obscure reference on the part of Amos that he was not the son of a prophet (Amos 7:14).

The prophet and the theocracy. It was practically an axiom of the higher critical school of Wellhausen that a great cleavage existed between the priest and the prophet. The priest was the representative of the formal, official religion, whereas the prophet supposedly called for a more spiritual type of religion. A reaction against this false disjunction has set in, and scholars now generally hold that the prophetic and priestly emphases were not necessarily antagonistic. Indeed, there are some (e.g., A. R. Johnson) who even speak of cultic prophets and who maintain that the prophet was often an employee of the cult.

From the biblical-theological standpoint we may say that the prophet was a guardian of the theocracy. In accordance with the custom of the times, he had ready access into the presence of kings. When the theocratic kings were in need of encouragement or rebuke, the prophet was present to offer his help (e.g., Isa 7:3 ff.; 37:5-7, 21-35). It was his duty to point out the course of action which God desired the nation to take. The prophets, therefore, were not merely political figures as such, but spoke out on political issues because these could affect the future course of the theocracy.

True and false prophets. It was to be expected that true prophecy would be opposed by imitators (Deut 13:1-5). Some men spoke in the name of other gods, but some spoke falsely in Yahweh's name. An outstanding example of the latter was Hananiah who falsely prophesied concerning the Exile (Jer 28).

To distinguish the true prophet from the false ones who claimed to speak in God's name there was the test of fulfillment versus nonfulfillment (Deut 18:20-22; cf. Jer 28). In the case of those prophets who foretold events which were so far in the future that they could not be evaluated by the test of fulfillment, they were to be judged by their doctrine, plus any events which fell within their lifetime (cf. Jer 25:12; Dan 4:19-37).

Sometimes false prophets were merely deceived men (Lam 2:14; Ezk 13:2-7), but often they were drunken men whose principal concern was the money and gain that they could acquire (e.g., Isa 28:7; Mic 3:5-11).

The prophet and the Messiah. The entire prophetic movement must be understood as a preparation for the coming of the Messiah. Had there been no Fall, there would have been no need for a Messiah or for the prophets. According to the prophets, the Messiah was One who was to perform a threefold work of prophet, priest, and king. There are certain essential elements in the messianic picture which the prophets present.

1. The coming of the Messiah is supernatural. The Messiah is not merely a human figure whose appearance on the scene of history is accidental. He is truly a human figure, but His coming brings God Himself (e.g., "Immanuel," Isa 7:14; Mic 5:2; Zech 6:12).
2. The Messiah Himself is a divine person. Such passages as Isa 9:6-7 show that He is truly God.
3. The coming of the Messiah is eschatological. It ushers in the end times (Mal 3:1-4; Hag 2:6-9).
4. The Messiah is a King who will rule in perfect righteousness and justice (Jer 23:5; Isa 11:1-5; Zech 6:13).
5. The Messiah is a prophet who will declare the Word of God with a clarity and fullness that was unequalled (Deut 18:9-22).
6. The messianic work is soteric (Isa 53:5-6, 10-12; Zech 12:10; 13:1). The heart of the Messiah's task is to save His people from their sins. The Messiah is a Saviour.

If one will compare the content of this picture of the Messiah with that of our Lord's own messianic consciousness, he will be struck by the remarkable identity. The elements here mentioned are essential to the full picture of the Messiah contained in the OT. Remove any one of them and the picture suffers. It goes without saying that not every one of these elements may be found in each of the messianic prophecies. Rather, in a given prophecy, certain of these elements may be emphasized more than others. For example, in Isa 53 the soteric element is paramount, whereas the regal element is more or less obscure. It is when one takes the total picture presented in the OT that he sees these six elements as six necessary constituent parts of the total messianic portrayal.

In the nature of the case it must be clear that the OT does not present these elements in systematic form. Rather, in the revelation concerning the Messiah there is a remarkable progression of unfolding. Whereas the word "messiah" itself is of infrequent occurrence, nevertheless the picture of salvation accomplished by the Lord through a human agent appears frequently; and where any of the above-

PROPHET

mentioned essential elements occur, a genuine messianic prophecy is in evidence.

The first messianic prophecy was uttered by God Himself and was addressed to the serpent. It speaks of the Seed of the woman bruising the serpent's head (Gen 3:15). In this verse God refers to a human being, descended from Eve, who will deliver a capital blow against the serpent. Inasmuch as this blow is the culmination of enmity between the woman and the serpent, an enmity extending also to their respective seeds, it is a blow which defeats the enemy of mankind and so delivers man from his power. Here the soteric element stands out most clearly.

As time progressed God revealed more and more about the Messiah to His servants and prophets. Always at the heart of the revelation lay the wondrous work of salvation which the Messiah was to perform. The peak of messianic prophecy is reached in Isa 53 which clearly teaches that the substitutionary death of the Messiah would accomplish salvation. As the Servant of the Lord, the Messiah performs this wondrous feat. *See* Messiah.

Evaluation. In order properly to evaluate the prophetic movement of the OT, there are three fundamental considerations which must be taken into account.

1. The psychological conviction on the part of the prophets that God had spoken to them. In proclaiming their messages the prophets were convinced that the God of Israel, Yahweh, whom they believed to be the God of heaven and earth, had spoken to them. They did not present a message in their own name or in the name of the body of prophets, but only in the name of the Lord. Furthermore, they were convinced that the very words which they declared were God-given and God-originated words. It is clear that the prophets did not regard themselves as men who worked out or expanded upon a message which God had given them, but as the bearers of the actual message of God Himself.

2. The continuity of the prophetic movement. For a period of over 1000 years the ministry of prophecy was nearly continuous in Israel. Living hundreds of years apart, the prophets nevertheless asserted that God had spoken to them. All recognized the same God, Yahweh, believing that He was the author of the messages which they in turn proclaimed. This is a phenomenon without parallel in the world's history.

3. The content of prophecy. Although scattered widely throughout Israel's history, the prophets did not proclaim heterogeneous, unrelated, and conflicting messages. Uniting their ministry was a teleological purpose, the proclamation of the Messiah to come. The prophets were men belonging to the OT dispensation, the age of type, and as such they spoke of the redemption to come. Although their messages often had to do with local matters, nevertheless at the heart of their ministry lay a message which pointed to the future. In a very real sense, therefore, the prophets did utter predictive prophecy. They spoke of the One who was to come to save His people from their sins.

It is in this light that prophecy must be understood. In their own knowledge the prophets could not have predicted the future, but God revealed to them His purposes, and hence they spoke of the coming salvation (I Pet 1:10-12).

Prophecy is a gift of God, not given to enable us to predict the future, but to point us to Christ (Rev 19:10*b*). Prophecy is filled with edification, consolation, and comfort; it presents the will of God on many practical problems that vex and perplex (I Cor 14:3). But above all it fixes our eyes on Him who took up in Himself the redeeming offices of prophet, priest, and king.

[*Prophets in the church.* Prophets continued to play an important role in the NT church. Paul writes that God's household, the church, has been "built upon the foundation of the apostles and prophets" (Eph 2:20), and that the mystery of the equal position of Gentiles in the Body of Christ was "revealed to His holy apostles and prophets by the Spirit" (Eph 3:5). There were men known as "prophets," specially set apart for a regular, ongoing ministry of prophecy (Eph 4:11). Next to the apostles themselves, they were the highest ranking ministers in the early church (I Cor 12:28).

[Such prophets are in evidence throughout the book of Acts. Their ministry was the customary dual one of forthtelling (proclamation) and foretelling (prediction). Note how Agabus on two separate occasions foretold future events in order to allow the Christians to prepare for a coming emergency (Acts 11:27-30; 21:10-14). They provided spiritual direction to the church at Antioch, because evidently through one of them the Holy Spirit gave orders regarding future evangelistic work for Barnabas and Saul (Acts 13:1-4). The work of two other prophets was that of exhorting ("encouraging," NASB) and strengthening the brethren (Acts 15:32), similar to the functions of prophecy listed in I Cor 14:3, viz., edification, exhortation, and comfort or consolation.

[In a church meeting a prophet might be granted a revelation to share with the assembled believers (I Cor 14:30). As J. A. Motyer says, "This could take the form of spontaneous utterance, and is associated with the activity of the Spirit of God (cf. I Thess 5:19). . . . It is some perception of the truth of God intelligibly made to the assembly" (NBD, p. 1045).

[Paul instructed that the prophets speak forth their messages in an orderly fashion, explaining that it is right "for prophets to control prophetic inspiration, for the God who inspires them is not a God of disorder but of peace" (I Cor 14:32-33, NEB). Their messages were to be tested, first of all, by the other prophets present (14:29), and secondly, by the teaching of the apostles, the full deposit of the Word of God (14:36-38). Therefore it does not seem that the

NT prophets were apart from the apostles' sources of new doctrinal truth to the church. Mark, Luke, and Jude, e.g., may have been prophets who wrote their books under the guidance of one or more of the apostles, as well as by the direct inspiration of the Holy Spirit. *See* Canon of Scripture–NT.–J. R.]

See Prophecy; Prophecy, Fulfillment of; articles on the individual prophets.

Bibliography. R. D. Brigg, "More Babylonian 'Prophecies,'" *Iraq,* XXIX (1967), 117-132. John Bright, *Jeremiah,* Anchor Bible, Garden City: Doubleday, 1965, pp. xv-xxvi. Alfred Edersheim, *Prophecy and History in Relation to the Messiah,* New York: Randolph, 1885. H. L. Ellison, *Men Spake from God,* Grand Rapids: Eerdmans, 1958; *The Prophets of Israel,* Grand Rapids: Eerdmans, 1969. Patrick Fairbairn, *The Interpretation of Prophecy,* New York: Carlton & Porter, 1866 (Banner of Truth, 1964 reprint). Hobart E. Freeman, *An Introduction to the Old Testament Prophets,* Chicago: Moody, 1968. E. W. Hengstenberg, *Christology of the Old Testament,* 4 vols., Grand Rapids: Kregel, 1956 (reprint). Abraham J. Heschel, *The Prophets,* New York: Harper & Row, 1962. H. B. Huffman, "Prophecy in the Mari Letters," BA, XXXI (1968), 101-124. A. R. Johnson, *The Cultic Prophets in Ancient Israel,* Cardiff: Univ. of Wales, 1944. H. Kramer, *et al., "Prophētēs,* etc.," TDNT, VI, 781-861. J. Lindblom, *Prophecy in Ancient Israel,* Philadelphia: Fortress, 1963. E. H. Merrill, "Name Terms of the Old Testament Prophet of God," JETS, XIV (1971), 239-248. J. A. Motyer, "Prophecy, Prophets," NBD, pp. 1036-1046. B. D. Napier, "Prophet, Prophetism," IDB, III, 896-919. H. M. Orlinsky, ed., *Interpreting the Prophetic Tradition,* New York: Ktav, 1969. Samuel J. Schultz, *The Prophets Speak,* New York: Harper & Row, 1968. Edward J. Young, *My Servants the Prophets,* Grand Rapids: Eerdmans, 1952.

E. J. Y.

PROPITIATION. Three important Gr. words are used to present the teaching of propitiation. They are *hilasmos* (I Jn 2:2; 4:10), *hilasterion* (Rom 3:25; Heb 9:5, "mercyseat"), and *hilaskomai* (Lk 18:13; Heb 2:17). The need for propitiation arose because of the holiness of God on the one hand, and the sin of man on the other. The emphasis in the meaning of the word is upon satisfaction. The NT usage indicates clearly that Christ's death fully satisfied the demands of the offended holiness of God. In the OT the place where the holy God met sinful man was at the mercyseat where the blood was sprinkled. In the NT the cross becomes the place where God would meet man through the blood of Christ. Thus John could say that Christ is the propitiation, the satisfaction, for the sins of believers and also for the sins of unbelievers (I Jn 2:2).

The doctrine of propitiation clearly teaches that Christ's death on the cross was a substitution for sin. His death satisfied the righteous demands of God the Father incurred by man's sin. As a result of that propitiation God was satisfied and the relation of the entire world to God was altered. The propitiatory sacrifice of Christ was the basis for the reconciliation of the world to God Himself (II Cor 5:19). Reconciliation has to do with the fact that the world has changed in relation to God through the death of Christ. Propitiation relates to the satisfaction brought to God as a result of the death of Christ. God was the one offended by man's sin, and it is He who must be satisfied with the payment for that sin.

The judicial work of Christ in propitiation must, of course, be appropriated by faith by the individual sinner before it will be of any benefit to him. God need not be begged and persuaded to be propitious or "merciful" as the publican tried to do (Lk 18:13). The work has been done now. God has already been propitiated. He is satisfied with the work of Christ. Now man is invited to enter by faith into that completed work. *See* Atonement; Christ, Passion of; Expiation.

Bibliography. J. Herrmann and F. Büchsel, "*Hilaskomai,* etc.," TDNT, III, 300-323. David Hill, chap. on *hilaskesthai, Greek Words and Hebrew Meanings,* Cambridge: Univ. Press, 1967. Leon Morris, *The Apostolic Preaching of the Cross,* Grand Rapids: Eerdmans, 1960, Chaps. IV, V.

R. P. L.

PROSELYTE (prŏs'ĕ-līt). The word is derived from Gr. *prosēlytos,* a newcomer or visitor, the usual rendering in the LXX of the Heb. *gēr.* In the OT *gēr* meant a stranger or alien, a member of a community from which he did not originate. In a progressive use of the term, the Mishnah of the second temple period used *gēr* to define the convert to Judaism, and the NT *prosēlytos* has the parallel meaning pointing to some form of conversion. Therefore the OT meaning of the word is different from rabbinic and NT usage, and this difference indicates some of the progressive changes that took place in the history of Judaism leading to the NT procedure of preaching and calling for conversion.

Legal Specifications under the Law

Beginning with the Exodus (Ex 12:38, 48-49), there were strangers or aliens living among the Israelites, soon to be protected by the law. Because the Israelites themselves had once been sojourners in Egypt, they in turn were not to mistreat sojourners in their midst (Ex 22:21; 23:9). In fact, Israelites were to treat these displaced persons and aliens with consideration, love, and even as equals with full privileges and blessings (Lev 19:34; Deut

10:18–19). With such an acceptance among the Israelites, it would not be difficult to see how the *gēr* would eventually be regarded in some status of religious convert.

When strangers desired to enter the first commonwealth (pre-Exilic period), the law made provisions for their acceptance by means of circumcision. Aliens who did not become Israelites were still fully protected under the law. If aliens wanted to live among Israelites, they could not do anything basically contrary to Israelite practice, such as idolatrous worship (Lev 20:2), blaspheming the name of the Lord (Lev 24:16), working on the sabbath (Ex 20:10), or eating leavened bread during the Passover season (Ex 12:19). Further serious spiritual restrictions forbade the alien from eating blood (Lev 17:10, 14), from withholding burnt offerings for personal gain (vv.8–9), or from defiling himself by eating the flesh of dead animals. Aliens were to respect the morals and ethics of a supernatural revelation by carefully avoiding immoral acts of indecency (Lev 18:26).

Aliens in need could share with the poor, the widows, and the orphans in the third year tithe for those in poverty (Deut 14: 28–29). The aliens were many times classed with hired servants and thus might be regarded as laborers (Lev 25:6, 40), but occasionally an alien could become a wealthy man (Lev 25:47). The alien was not to be oppressed (Deut 24:14) nor was improper judgment to be rendered against him (Deut 27:19). *See* Foreigner.

The Early Pre-Exilic *Gēr*

The most significant group to join with Israel prior to the entrance of Canaan was the Kenites, descendants of Moses' father-in-law. At the recital of the blessings and curses at Mount Ebal and Mount Gerizim, the presence of aliens was noted (Josh 8:33). During the period of the Conquest, it would have been difficult to attract or encourage the presence of Canaanite strangers. Rahab was an exception. The Gibeonites were another, being allowed to live among the Israelites in a capacity between that of outright slaves and free immigrants. They enjoyed full protection, and Israelites were severely judged when the Gibeonites did not receive this care (II Sam 21:1 f.). Ruth the Moabitess was still another exception, in this case to the exclusion placed upon Ammonites and Moabites (Deut 23:3).

Within the Monarchy Period and Exile

In the time of the monarchy many strangers, while not mistreated, were subject to the mandatory labor system. David gathered aliens to prepare stone for the temple (I Chr 22:2). Solomon took a census of the strangers and numbered them at 153,600; more than half of these worked in the labor force building the temple (II Chr 2:17–18). No doubt most of these were descendants of the Canaanites, and they did have rights under the law which the prophets championed. Naaman the Syrian was a notable instance of a foreigner who came for healing by the God of Israel and then became a worshiper (II Kgs 5:15–19).

The dispersion of Israelites began to have a profound influence on the missionary spirit. After the Assyrian conquest, many people of the northern kingdom were deported to various parts of the Assyrian Empire (722/21 B.C.; II Kgs 17:6). The Babylonian deportations between 605 and 586 B.C. also took many Judeans to the Mesopotamian valley. Trade, politics, and commercial relations had also led Israelites from their homeland to heathen countries (I Kgs 9:26; 10:28). In the 5th cen. B.C. Jewish people lived in a colony at Elephantine in Egypt with their own temple, according to the Elephantine papyri (*q.v.*). As a result of the Exile in Babylon, Jewish people were scattered in the provinces of the Persian Empire (Est 3:8). Among these God was preserving a faithful remnant, resistant to heathen practices and corruption. Therefore through this dispersion monotheism spread, with its attendant emphasis on an ethic and moral far surpassing that of the pagan religions. Jewish people in their fellowship within the law began to attract many Gentiles to enter Jewish ranks to find what was not possible in pagan religions. Solomon had long before prayed at the temple dedication that the Lord would hear the request of the foreigner when he came to worship Israel's God (I Kgs 8:41–43).

Post-Exilic and Intertestamental Periods

The post-Exilic prophets and writers opposed the intermarriage of Israelites and foreigners. It was not the intermarriage with foreigners *per se* which alarmed the leaders, but rather, with foreigners who had not come within the second commonwealth of Israel through conversion (Ezr 9–10; Neh 13). The action which was taken by the Jewish authorities probably hastened the decisions of many of the foreigners to become Israelites. However, many outsiders were attracted of their own volition to Judaism, and intermarriage played an important part in the conversion of Gentiles to Judaism.

The Hellenism of Alexander the Great and the subsequent struggle for power between the Seleucids and Ptolemies (3rd and 2nd cen. B.C.) brought about a further dispersion of Jewish people. In the movements of Jewish people which followed, Hellenism and Judaism had opportunity to exchange ideas. While many Jewish people were Hellenized, there was also a movement in the opposite direction as many Greeks, Egyptians, and later on Romans adopted the faith of Judaism in varying degrees. During the years of Alexander the Great (*c.* 333–323 B.C.) a Jewish colony was established in Alexandria in Egypt. In the onslaught by Antiochus IV of Syria (175–163 B.C.), Onias, son of Simon, being one of the high priests, received permission from Ptolemy VI to build a temple in the city of Leontopolis. As a result many Jews emigrated from the conflict in Israel to settle in what came to be called Onion (Jos. *Ant.* xiii.3.1; *Wars* vii.7.2). Of course, the Jewish community had its influence on the Gentile subjects of Ptolemy's kingdom.

This movement of Jewish people out into the Gr.-speaking world during the latter half of the intertestamental period also necessitated a Gr. version of the OT for use by Gr.-speaking Jews. The work of translation was done in Egypt and probably finished about 100 B.C. (*see* Versions, Ancient and Medieval: Septuagint). This was a period when Jewish proselytism in the Hellenistic world was already a procedure well known, judging from the LXX's translation of the Heb. *gēr*.

Jewish scholars of the later intertestamental period and 1st cen A.D., because of the pagans' fascination for Jewish belief and practice, developed rules for accepting converts. This was necessary in order to have a measure of conformity for directing the missionary zeal of Judaism, as seen in the statement in the NT concerning the Pharisees, ". . . you travel about on sea and land to make one proselyte" (Mt 23:15, NASB). The rabbis of this period distinguished between the full convert (*gēr ṣedeq*) and the person who accepted monotheism and Noachian laws but not all the other commandments of ritual, e.g., dietary laws (*gēr tûshāb*). The latter was not classified as a heathen, but he had no formal membership in a Jewish congregation, although he could attend the synagogue and mix with Jewish people. The Noachian laws supposedly given prior to the Flood which the partial convert was to observe prohibited (1) idol worship, (2) blasphemy, (3) murder, (4) adultery, and (5) theft; (6) they were to establish courts of justice (*Genesis Rabbah* 16:9; 24:5). A seventh commandment was added after the Flood, not to eat flesh cut from a living animal. All these laws were considered to be binding on all mankind, in contrast to laws applicable to Israelites only (*Tosefta Abodah Zerah* 9:4).

Both Philo and Josephus mention the zealous success of Jewish missionary activities. In the latter half of the intertestamental period the number of partial and full adherents grew at a fast pace. Note examples of many Gentile converts in Philo (*Embassy to Gaius,* xxxvi, 281–82) and Josephus (*Ant.* xi.7.2; xviii.3.5; xx.8.11).

New Testament Period

The increasing trend of Gentile conversion to Judaism continued at an accelerated pace in the 1st cen. A.D. Numerous mentions of proselytes can be found in the Midrash, the Mishnah, the Pseudepigrapha, and especially the NT. Luke (7:2–5) speaks of the centurion at Capernaum who loved Israel and had built the synagogue. Because he deferred to the Jewish elders, he could hardly have been a full convert. However, Jesus spoke of his great faith which He did not find in Israel, indicating that the centurion probably could have been a partial adherent (*gēr tûshab*), even though the religious persuasion of the centurion was not designated in any way.

Jerusalem was host to many visitors during the pilgrimage festivals. In Acts 2:10–11 the multitude of visitors are referred to as Jews and proselytes. Here the proselyte could be a loose term applied to the two kinds of proselytes. That there were partial adherents is seen by the visit of the Ethiopian eunuch to Jerusalem who was puzzled by basic passages of Scripture (Acts 8:31).

The missionary journeys of Paul give evidence of the many proselytes in the Diaspora synagogues. On his first journey, while speaking in the synagogue of Antioch in Pisidia, he referred to his audience as "men of Israel, and you that fear God" (Acts 13:16), "brethren, sons of the family of Abraham, and those among you that fear God" (v. 26, RSV) and "Jews and . . . God-fearing proselytes" (v. 43, NASB). The term God-fearers probably refers to both the partial and the full adherents.

On the second missionary journey, Paul's audience at the Thessalonian synagogue, besides the Jewish people, also included "devout" or God-fearing Greeks (Acts 17:4). In Athens there were also devout persons (v. 17). Lydia was styled a "worshiper of God" (Acts 16:14, NASB), no doubt a partial adherent. After preaching in the synagogue in Corinth, Paul entered the house of Titius Justus, termed a "worshiper of God" (Acts 18:7, NASB), again probably a partial adherent.

The essential difference between the partial and full adherent was the fact of circumcision (*q.v.*). Jewish authorities were content not to discriminate against the partial adherent, and the latter was permitted to worship along with the other Jewish people in the synagogue. When the message of the NT burst on the 1st cen. A.D. world, and as Paul carried the message to the synagogues of the Diaspora, he found a ready audience among the partial adherents who would listen intently to this new message. The strict ethic was there in the preaching of Paul, as well as a message of salvation which did not require circumcision in order to become full members of God's family. One can imagine the favorable impact on partial adherents as well as the consternation among Jewish people and full proselytes. The preaching of the gospel served as a wedge between the synagogue and the partial adherents, and the possibility of gaining new converts for the synagogues was seriously impaired once the church began to grow.

The Heb. Christian leaders at Jerusalem eventually had to face the problem of circumcision. Most of the leadership and assembly in Jerusalem, already knowing the practice required for partial adherents in the Noachian laws, formulated a minimum ethic for Gentile believers, and the message was sent to the Antioch assembly (Acts 15:20–29; 21:25). It did *not* mean a low moral or ethic in relation to

God's Word; certainly the NT practice insisted on the highest quality of life for both Jewish and Gentile believers.

Bibliography. B. J. Bamberger, *Proselytism in the Talmudic Period,* Cincinnati: Hebrew Union College, 1939. S. Baron, *A Social and Religious History of the Jews,* New York: Columbia Univ., 1951. W. G. Braude, *Jewish Proselytizing in the First Five Centuries,* Providence: Brown Univ., 1940. W. D. Davies, *Invitation to the New Testament,* New York: Doubleday, 1965. Louis Finkelstein, "The Institution of Baptism for Proselytes," JBL, LII, 203-221. K. G. Kuhn, *"Proselytos,"* TDNT, VI, 727-744. G. F. Moore, *Judaism in the First Five Centuries of the Christian Era,* Cambridge: Harvard Univ. Press, 1927. E. Schuerer, *The History of the Jewish People in the Times of Jesus Christ,* New York: Scribner's, 1890.

L. Go.

PROSTITUTE. *See* Harlot.

PROVENDER. Chopped grasses, grains, and straw mixed together and used for feeding domestic animals. Proper hospitality demanded such provision for the asses or camels of the traveler (Gen 24:25, 32; 43:24; Jud 19:21). A person traveling in isolated areas must carry his own (Gen 42:27; Jud 19:19). To express the graciousness and largesse of God's provision when once His people have returned to Him, the prophet speaks not only of "rich and plenteous" produce and "large" pastures but of "salted" provender for oxen and asses (Isa 30:23-24, RSV). The latter is fodder (*q.v.; see also* Plants) mixed with salt or aromatic herbs.

PROVERB. This word is used in the English versions to translate two Heb. and two Gr. words. Aside from Hab 2:6, where *ḥîdâ* is translated "proverb," every other instance of "proverb" in the OT translates *māshāl,* noun or verb. In the NT "proverb" represents *parabolē* once and *paroimia* four times.

Heb. *māshāl* has a wide range of connotation, but is translated by either "proverb" or "parable." *Māshāl* refers to poems of various kinds, a similitude or parable, a by-word, a prophetic discourse, or sentences of ethical wisdom. The Gr. word, with few exceptions, chosen to translate *māshāl* in the LXX was *parabolē,* readily recognized as the familiar "parable" of the NT, though *parabolē* in the NT is only once rendered "proverb," as noted above. Hence the LXX indicated a general equivalence between Heb. *māshāl* and Gr. *parabolē*. *Māshāl* in the OT is translated "proverb" about 19 times. Nearly all the remaining occurrences of *māshāl* are rendered "parable." The verb related to *māshāl* is translated "use a parable," etc. (Num 21:27; Ezk 12:23; 16:44). BDB notes that *māshāl* usually refers to "sentences constructed in parallelism." This feature may be the family resemblance in the connotations of *māshāl* for which the most appropriate English words are "proverb" or "parable." Thus proverb in the OT belongs to the genus *māshāl.*

The idea of by-word is appropriate in Ps 69:11; Deut 28:37; I Kgs 9:7; II Chr 7:20; Jer 24:9; Ezk 14:8. In I Sam 10:12; 24:13; Ezk 12:22-23; 18:2-3 the idea of a proverbial saying is uppermost. In I Kgs 4:32; Prov 1:1, 6; 10:1; 25:1 the references are to the sentences of ethical wisdom attended by Solomon. In Isa 14:4 a taunting utterance is meant. Occurrences of the related verb are found in Num 21:27; Ezk 12:23; 16:44, where "proverb" appears in the translation.

Lk 4:23 is the only place where *parabolē* is translated "proverb." "Physician, heal thyself" obviously fits well the idea of a true statement of popular wisdom. *Paroimia* is translated "proverb" in II Pet 2:22, where there is a citation from Prov 26:11. The remaining occurrences of *paroimia* translated "proverb" are found in Jn 16:25 (twice) and 29. Here the idea of parable is apparent.

The richest implications of the word "proverb" are found in the book so named. All aspects of moral and ethical instruction are included, but in general it may be said that the special interest is in the walk and character of the godly. The "upright" and "righteous" are referred to over 50 times in the portion of Proverbs (chaps. 10-29) especially labeled as Solomon's. The general truth emerges that the upright life and righteous walk reveal the righteous standing of their possessor. That the purpose of the proverb is to bring faith and instruction is well illustrated in Prov 22:17-21.

There are several citations from Proverbs in the NT. Prov 3:11-12 is quoted in Heb 12:5-6 as of direct applicability to all believers. The relation of the righteous and wicked to God is shown in Jas 4:6 as quoted from Prov 3:34 (LXX). Characteristic of the force of the proverbial ethical teaching is Paul's use of Prov 25:21-22 in Rom 12:20. Perhaps the most outstanding and frequently cited aphorism of Proverbs is found in 24:12: "Shall not he render to every man according to his works?" The doctrine of judgment thus taught is reiterated in Mt 16:27; Rom 2:6; II Tim 4:14; Rev 2:23; 20:12; 22:12.

It has been mentioned above that our Lord's teaching in parables would, in Bible usage, be included in the range of teaching in proverbs, as indicated by the choice of the LXX translators of *parabolē* to render *māshāl.* The character of many other utterances of Christ shows their proverbial nature. The sharp aphoristic saying: "Let the dead bury their dead" (Mt 8:22), and many like it, were designed to sink into the memories of the hearers and, on reflection, produce action. A whole field of ethical endeavor is revealed in the pregnant words: "It is more blessed to give than to receive" (Acts 20:35). The effect in Paul's life is illustrative of the powerful impetus of this type of teaching.

The teaching of the Lord Jesus Christ is the

māshāl—proverb type. Ps 78:2, where "parable" is *māshāl* in Heb., is cited in Mt 13:35 to characterize Jesus' teaching in parables.

It should be noted that the proverb type of utterance, the cryptic saying, the epigrammatic, crisp, gnomic verse was designed often to conceal truth sufficiently to intrigue the mind and demand reflection and inquiry before the full meaning could be grasped. *See* Proverbs, Book of; Riddle; Wisdom Literature.

Bibliography. F. Hauck, *"Paroimia,"* TDNT, V, 854–856.

W. B. W.

PROVERBS, BOOK OF. The name of this book of Scripture is taken from the first verse, "The proverbs of Solomon the son of David, king of Israel." The Heb. word for proverb is *māshāl* which means a comparison, similitude, representation, or generalization. A biblical proverb is therefore a brief, pithy, and pointed saying expressing widsom, a condensed parable or fable (I Sam 24:13; Jer 31:29; Ezk 18:2; Lk 4:23).

The proverb was sometimes presented with the lesson clearly taught, but sometimes it was made obscure so that its very difficulty might stimulate the desire to understand and so impress the lesson more indelibly on the mind. The proverb might be a "dark saying," requiring an interpretation; e.g., "The fining pot is for silver, and the furnace is for gold: but the Lord trieth the hearts" (Prov 17:3). In Prov 1:17, however, the proverb, "Surely in vain the net is spread in the sight of any bird," is given without any interpretation and is capable of many applications. *See* Proverb.

Individual proverbs are found in the OT much earlier than the time of Solomon. The saying, "Wickedness proceedeth from the wicked," passed as a "proverb of the ancients" in the days of Saul (I Sam 24:13). The campaigning Israelites under Moses overheard the proverb sung about Heshbon (Num 21:27–30). The book of Job is full of maxims of the proverb type, one of which became the theme of the book of Proverbs, "The fear of the Lord, that is wisdom; and to depart from evil is understanding" (Job 28:28). When Solomon came into contact with "the children of the east country" (the *b^e^nê qedem,* I Kgs 4:30), whose wisdom clothed itself in this form, it was only natural that he should express himself in and become the patron of such maxims, precepts and condensed parables ("Proverb," UBD, p. 896). Such Wisdom Literature that ignored national boundaries was known throughout the ancient Near East, from Egypt to Mesopotamia.

Canonicity

The book of Proverbs is included in all the Jewish lists of the scriptural writings and is also quoted or referred to in the NT (Prov 1:16 and Rom 3:15; Prov 25:21–22 and Rom 12:20; Prov 3:11–12 and Heb 12:5–6; Prov 3:34 and Jas 4:6; Prov 10:12 and I Pet 4:8; Prov 11:31 and I Pet 4:18; Prov 3:34 and I Pet 5:5; Prov 26:11 and II Pet 2:22). The book is considered along with Job and Ecclesiastes as part of the so-called Wisdom Literature of the OT.

Authorship and Date

On the basis of internal evidence the bulk of the Proverbs may be attributed to Solomon (cf. 1:1; 10:1; 25:1). Delitzsch affirms that one historical background is displayed throughout Prov 1–29 corresponding only to the conditions of Solomon's reign. Prov 30 is attributed to Agur and Prov 31 to King Lemuel, individuals concerning whom we have no information.

The fact of Solomonic authorship for the major part of this book is also in keeping with the historical accounts of this man as the embodiment of wisdom. In I Kgs 3–4 it is revealed that he began his reign with a prayer for wisdom and that this request was granted by God. It is also recorded of Solomon, "And he spake three thousand proverbs . . ." (I Kgs 4:32).

Some scholars have supposed that "the words of the wise" in Prov 22:17–24:22 were taken from the Egyptian work, "The Instructions of Amen-em-opet" (ANET, pp. 421–424) because of close verbal resemblances. But careful study of the two texts reveals that the Egyptian writing must be a translation from a Heb. original (K. A. Kitchen, "Egypt," NBD, p. 348; SOTI, pp. 457 f.).

Any discussion of date must distinguish between the time of the writing of the Proverbs and the time when they were collected and edited. A date of approximately 950 B.C. may be posited therefore for the writing, whereas the men of Hezekiah "copied out" or collected and added other Solomonic proverbs about 700 B.C. The words of Agur and Lemuel were no doubt added at this time also. There seems to be no valid reason therefore why the book could not have been complete in its present form around 700 B.C.

The presence of supposed Aramaisms does not automatically require a late date for the book of Proverbs. Indeed, these may be early NW Semitic terms (K. A. Kitchen, *Ancient Orient and OT,* 1966, p. 145). It is now known that the inscription of Zakir, the Syro-Hittite king of Hamath, was written shortly after 800 B.C. largely in Old Aramaic with a sprinkling of NW Semitic (Canaanite-Heb.) expressions (ANET, pp. 501 f.; VBW, II, 263). Conversely, the presence in Proverbs of poetic forms known in Ugaritic literature but totally absent from the Aramaic wisdom literature of the 7th cen. B.C. as represented by the *Sayings of Aḥīqar,* serve to date the contents of Proverbs well before that period (Archer, SOTI, pp. 456 f.).

Contents

A book of diversified contents, Proverbs treats such themes as wisdom, folly, sin, goodness, wealth, poverty, the tongue, pride, humility, justice, vengeance, strife, gluttony, love, lust, etc. There is a comprehensiveness of outlook so that no phase of human relationship seems to have been overlooked. The tone is definitely universalistic, the word "Israel" not being found in the book. Its teaching is therefore applicable to all men everywhere. This is not to deny, however, that the outlook is essentially in keeping with the OT emphasis on earthly hopes and material prosperity.

Outline

The book scarcely lends itself to formal analysis; however, the following divisions may be observed:

Prologue, 1:1-7

I. Proverbs of Solomon Extolling Wisdom, 1:8–9:18

II. Proverbs of Solomon Extolling Practical Morality, 10:1–24:34

III. Proverbs of Solomon Compiled by Hezekiah's Scribes, 25:1–29:27

IV. Appendices: Proverbs of Agur and Lemuel, 30:1–31:9

Epilogue, Alphabetical Poem on the Virtuous Wife, the Personification of Wisdom, 31:10-31

The prologue or introduction (1:1-7) identifies the author, states the purpose of the book and its theme. The first major division (1:8–9:18) contains a dozen or more addresses which discuss the path of wisdom. The second division (10:1–24:34) contains, for the most part, single detached proverbs, many of which are antithetical in form. The third division (25:1–29:27) contains the proverbs "copied out" of the mass of Solomonic proverbs by the "men of Hezekiah" possibly including Isaiah and Micah. They are mainly set forth in the form of couplets. Final appendices (30:1–31:9) contain the words of Agur, which are striking in form and content, and the words of King Lemuel. The book closes with an allegory which consists of an acrostic or alphabetic poem in praise of a virtuous woman, as a description of Wisdom personified.

See Wisdom; Wisdom Literature, OT.

Bibliography. Charles Bridges, *Exposition of Proverbs,* Evansville: Sovereign Grace Publishers, reprinted, 1959. Franz Delitzsch, *The Proverbs of Solomon,* Grand Rapids: Eerdmans, reprinted, 1950. Julius H. Greenstone, *Proverbs with Commentary,* Philadelphia: Jewish Publication Society, 1950. R. Laird Harris, "Proverbs," WBC. Derek Kidner, *Proverbs, Tyndale OT Commentary,* London: Tyndale Press, 1964. R. B. Y. Scott, *Proverbs, Ecclesiastes,* Anchor Bible, Garden City, N.Y.: Doubleday, 1965.

D. K. C.

PROVIDENCE. "God's works of providence are His most holy, wise and powerful preserving and governing of all His creatures and all their actions" (Shorter Catechism). Moment by moment the world continues because of Christ's "upholding all things by the word of His power" (Heb 1:3) and because "by Him all things consist" (Col 1:17; cf. Neh 9:6). At the same time God not only sustains but governs all the world and mankind: the nations (Ps 47:7; Dan 2:21; 4:25; Isa 10:5-7); individuals (I Sam 2:6-9; Isa 45:5; Prov 16:9; Ps 75:6-7; Acts 27:24); the free acts of man (Prov 16:1; 21:1).

Providence is not a continuation of creation but rather the preservation and purposeful direction of what God had first made. It is most important to realize that it was only after creation was complete that sin entered God's universe, because this leads us to the further conclusion that any theory which teaches that God constantly recreates the world makes Him the renewer of both that which is good and that which is evil, and thus the author not only of good but also of evil.

Besides establishing the difference between providence and creation, we need to see that the doctrine of providence excludes all the following:

Pantheism. This either absorbs the world and man into God (Spinoza), or sees both the world and man as partaking, in some manner, directly of God Himself (Tillich).

Deism. This sees God after the analogy of a watchmaker and a watch (as a watchmaker He wound up the watch and left it running), since it removes Him entirely from the world which He has made. Scripture replies with such passages as Ps 33:13, 15; Isa 45:7; Acts 17:24-28.

Dualism. God is only one of two principles or powers, the one good and the other evil. This makes God finite. The Scriptures teach that only God existed at the beginning and that all which God created was good (Gen 1:4, 10, 12, 18, 21, 25, 31); that sin and moral evil were originated by the creature (Ezk 28:15; Gen 3:1-7).

Indeterminism. This maintains there is no planned control of anything.

Determinism. This assumes such absolute control of all that happens that man is robbed of all free will and responsibility.

Chance. This sees any controlling force as irrational.

Fate. This sees events as uncontrollable and entirely without any element of benevolent purpose.

God's Sovereignty Shown

The doctrine of providence rests upon God's divine sovereignty and the revelation that He is King over all and orders everything according to His own will. His will, however, is entirely subject to His character, and therefore to be described not as arbitrary but as perfect and holy.

1. *Providence and the natural order.* Providence includes all things both great (Ps 145:9-17; Isa 41:2-4) and small, such as the course of an arrow (I Kgs 22:34), the birds of the air (Mt 6:26), a dream (Mt 27:19), the fifth sparrow thrown in to make a bargain (Mt

10:29; cf. Lk 12:6-7), a rumor (Acts 23:16), and the fall of a lot (Prov 16:33).

Providential acts, for the purpose of further analysis, can be divided into general, or those which apply to the world and mankind at large; and particular, or those that happen to both unsaved individuals and to God's elect nation and those He has chosen to redeem. Under His special providence then comes Israel (Amos 3:1; Mal 1:2; Acts 15:14-16; Rom 11:26-29), the Church (Eph 5:25-27), and individual believers (Ps 91:11; 147:9, 20; Mt 6:26; Acts 14:16-17; Rom 8:28-39).

2. *Providence and history.* God controls and guides the entire course of history from beginning to end. He chose one nation, Israel (Amos 3:2), and made it the means of His self-revelation; gave it His word in the Scriptures of the OT; promised the Messiah through it (Deut 18:15-19; cf. Acts 3:22-23; II Sam 7:8-16; Isa 7:14; Mic 5:2); and covenanted to preserve it and to bring it through every trial into His millennial kingdom (Deut 30:1-10; II Sam 7:16; Isa 65-66; Hos 1:10-11; 2:16-23; Joel 3:17-21; Amos 9:11-15; Zech 14:1-21).

At the same time He broke down the middle wall of partition between Jew and Gentile (Eph 2:14) as He revealed the mystery of the expansion of His Church (Eph 3:1-11) by the death of Christ to include both. The theme of the whole Bible is God's plan to save His elect and set up His kingdom, in its first phase in the millennial reign of Christ (Rev 5:10; 20:4-6), and in its second and final one in the New Jerusalem (Rev 21-22). Nothing can thwart God's final consummation of His plan (Isa 40:15; Ps 2:4; Acts 4:25-28).

3. *Providence and personal experience.* God promises to prosper the righteous (Lev 26:3-13; Deut 28:1-14). Why then, cries the believer, do the wicked also prosper? Why do they so often go unpunished? The inspired answer of the psalmist is twofold: their affluence is only temporary, and God will finally judge their wickedness and vindicate His own holiness (Ps 37:16-22; 73; 91:8; Mal 3:13-4:3). At the same time God delays His judgment in order that the wicked may have an opportunity to come to repentance (Rom 2:4; II Pet 3:9; Rev 2:21).

But why must the believer suffer so much adversity and tribulation? (*a*) It can be for his development (Ps 94:12; Prov 3:11; Heb 12:5-13). (*b*) It may be as testing before the opening of greater fields of service (I Cor 16:9; Jas 1:2-12). (*c*) It will bring glory to God if well borne (Job 1; 2; 42). (*d*) It is a part of the vocation of the Christian church (Mt 10:24 f.; Jn 15:18; 16:33; Acts 9:16; 14:22; Rom 5:3-5; Phil 3:10; I Pet 4:12-19).

4. *Providence and personal freedom.* God rules over the hearts and actions of all (Prov 21:1), though they do not necessarily know it (Gen 45:5-8; 50:20; Isa 10:5-12; 44:28-45:4; Jn 11:49-52; Acts 2:23; 13:27-29). Yet He does it in such a manner that their actions are those of free agents and they therefore remain responsible for them (Isa 10:12; Rom 1:24-32). Thus He permits the wicked to act according to their own nature (Ps 81:12 f.; Rom 1:24 ff.; Acts 14:16), but will finally punish them (Lk 22:22; Acts 3:13-19). At the same time He prompts His own to do His commandments (Phil 3:12-13), even though this is possible only through the indwelling power of the Holy Spirit (Rom 8:3-4; Gal 5:22-23).

Bibliography. L. Berkhof, *Systematic Theology*, Grand Rapids: Eerdmans, 1949, pp. 165-178. G. C. Berkouwer, *The Providence of God*, Grand Rapids: Eerdmans, 1952. Charles Hodge, *Systematic Theology*, Grand Rapids: Eerdmans, 1952, I, 575-616.

R. A. K.

A Roman aqueduct (see arches) brought water into the gate area of Caesarea, capital of Roman Palestine. HFV

PROVINCE. The province was the basic unit of administration in the Roman Empire. In earliest usage it was the general term referring to the magistrate's sphere of administrative action. After Roman authority was extended beyond Italy, the term began to signify the rule of the governor and the region entrusted to his care. After some time, the geographical sense became the dominant one. Thus, Sicily became the first Roman province (227 B.C.). At this time, four praetors were selected. From the time of Sulla, those designated as proconsuls were sent to more important provinces, and those called propraetors to less important ones.

Under Augustus (27 B.C.), the Act of Settlement divided all provinces into two types. One was the senatorial province, where a governor called a proconsul was sent out for a term of one year (Acts 13:7, Cyprus; Acts 18:12, Achaia). In these areas, life was normal and stable; military forces were at a minimum, and military action was unlikely.

The great marble street of ancient Ephesus, de facto capital of the Roman province of Asia. HFV

The second type of province was under the direct control of the emperor and was designated an imperial province. His power was delegated to legates (prefects) and procurators. The term of office in these was not uniform but usually extended for more than one year. Military forces were kept in considerable numbers in these provinces. Rule was left to the emperor under the pretext of sparing the Senate and people the trouble of managing them, but actually, so that the emperor could keep the army under his control.

In 27 B.C. there were 12 imperial and ten senatorial provinces. All new provinces came under the direct control of the emperor. Syria was such an imperial province. Changes could be made in alignment depending upon conditions. However, Egypt was so vital to the empire, mainly because of its grain supply, that it always remained the personal domain of the emperor.

Judea became part of the province of Syria in 63 B.C. It was made part of Herod's kingdom in 40 B.C., but came under provincial rule again in A.D. 6 and remained so except for the period of A.D. 41–44, when it was part of the kingdom of Agrippa I. The procurator (e.g., Pontius Pilate) lived in Caesarea and was under the authority of the governor of Syria.

C. K. H.

PROVOCATION. This term represents several original words. Heb. *ka'as,* used of certain kings, means "vexation, cause of anger"; e.g., Jeroboam in his "provocation" provoked the Lord to anger (I Kgs 15:30). Another Heb. word is used somewhat technically in Ps 95:8 and quoted in Heb 3:8, 15: "Harden not your hearts, as in the provocation." This is emphatically *m^{e}rîbâ,* "the provocation." Rephidim (*q.v.*), where the Israelites irritated God before reaching Mount Sinai, was named Massah and Meribah; for there they demanded that Moses give them water, and were about ready to stone him for not doing so. They challenged the Lord saying, "Is the Lord among us, or not?" (Ex 17:1–7). This provocation and another like it at Kadesh-barnea (Num 20:13, 24) are referred to in Num 27:14; Deut 6:16; 9:22; 32:51; 33:8; Ps 81:7; 106:32. *See* Meribah. Israel repeatedly provoked God to anger by their idolatry in later generations (Jud 2:12; I Kgs 14:9, 15; II Kgs 17:11, 17; Isa 65:3; etc.).

PRUDENCE, PRUDENT. The Heb. *'ārûm* is used both in the good sense of sensible (e.g., Prov 14:8, 15, 18; 15:5) and in the bad sense of shrewd or crafty (Gen 3:1; Job 5:12–13; 15:5; Ps 83:3). Heb *bîn* and Gr. *synetos,* on the other hand, stress an intelligent decision (Prov 16:21; 18:15; Isa 29:14; Mt 11:25; Acts 13:7; I Cor 1:19). *See* Wisdom.

PRUNING HOOK. A small knife with a curved blade. The Heb. word *mazmērôth* appears only in this plural form. The Bible refers to making such knives out of spears, and there is nothing unrealistic in this possibility. The expression is intended to portray settled and peaceful conditions, where a man could concern himself with the business of horticulture instead of the grim concerns of war. The word appears four times (Isa 2:4; 18:5; Mic 4:3; Joel 3:10), with the idea reversed in the last text. An iron blade made like a heavy sickle, with rivet holes in order to be attached to a handle, was discovered at Tell Jemmeh by Flinders Petrie. He dated it *c.* 800 B.C. *See* Hook.

PSALMIST. *See* Music; Poetry; Psalms, Book of.

PSALMS, BOOK OF (säms)

Name of the Book

The book of Psalms is a collection of Heb. songs, hymns, and poems taken from various periods in the history of Israel. The book itself furnishes no title, nor is such a title found anywhere else in the OT. The nearest approach to a title is seen in Ps 72:20, "The prayers of David the son of Jesse are ended." The later Jews gave the book the title *sēpher t^{e}hillîm,* "Book of Praises." The LXX entitled it "The Book of Psalms." The Gr. word "psalm" was used to translate the Heb. word *mizmôr* and probably means a song sung to the accompaniment of stringed instruments. It is interesting to note that *tᵉhillîm* occurs in the title of only one psalm (145, feminine pl.), while *mizmôr* is found in 57 titles.

Perhaps one reason ancient Israel left this book without a title was the fact that an appropriate one would be very hard to find. One writer says, "Why call it praises? They prayed and begged much more than they praised. They lamented and confessed more than they thanked. They queried and complained and even cursed and meditated more than they adores" (Samuel Terrien, *The Psalms and Their Meaning for Today,* p. 37). Many different moods and attitudes are expressed in the book. One title could scarcely have covered them all.

Number and Arrangement

The Heb. Bible contains 150 separate psalms. The LXX version has an extra psalm (151) which relates how David was chosen by Samuel the prophet over his brothers. Although the Masoretic and LXX versions contain essentially the same psalms, they are not numbered the same. In the LXX Ps 9 and 10, and 114 and 115 are merged into one psalm, whereas Ps 116 and 147 are divided into two separate psalms. The difference in numbering between the Heb. and the LXX can be seen in the following chart:

Hebrew	*LXX*
1-9	1-9:21
10	9:22-39
11-113	10-112
114-115	113
116:1-9	114
116:10-19	115
117-146	116-145
147:1-11	146
147:12-20	147
148-150	148-150

The psalms as they now stand are divided into five groups or books: 1-41, 42-72, 73-89, 90-106, 107-150. Each of these books ends in a doxology. Ps 150 was probably intended to be a doxology for the entire Psalter. The first three divisions are natural and mark successive stages in the early growth of the Psalter. However, the division between 106 and 107 is arbitrary. This fivefold division antedates the LXX, and its purpose according to Jewish tradition was to make the collection of psalms correspond to the five books of the Torah.

Early in 1956 a leather scroll of psalms all written in Heb. was found in Cave 11 near Qumran. It was unrolled, edited, and published by J. A. Sanders of Union Seminary, New York. The scroll, along with four separate leaves, contained 36 psalms or portions of psalms from the Heb. Bible, plus Ps 151 known previously from the LXX. In addition to these 37 psalms, the scroll contains six other psalms, two of which had been known in a Syriac version. Four were completely new. The scroll also contained a prose section giving the total number of David's musical compositions as 4,050. The 36 or 37 canonical psalms are not in the same order as they appear in the Masoretic text. They fall in the following sequence: 105, 146, 148, 121-130, 132, 119, 135, 136, 118, 145, 139, 137, 138, 93, 141, 133, 144, 142, 143, 149, 150, 140, 134, 151. (Cf. J. A. Sanders, *The Psalms Scroll of Qumran Cave 11,* 1965).

Titles

All but 34 psalms have titles or superscriptions. It is generally agreed that these titles were not a part of the original psalms but were added later by an editor or collector. The titles are not identical in the Heb. and Gr. versions. The Syriac versions do not have these titles at all, but include some completely different, which were created under the influence of Theodore of Mopsuestia (A.D. 350-428).

The titles contain a number of technical terms, the meanings of which have been lost. The titles might denote: (1) an author, collector, or one to whom the psalm was dedicated, such as David, Solomon, Moses, sons of Korah; (2) the type of psalm such as a song, *shîr;* a psalm, *mizmôr;* one of praise(s), *tᵉhillîm;* a prayer, *tᵉphillah;* a *miktām;* a *maskîl;* and *shiggāyôn;* (3) some musical note such as "to the chief musician," "for the maidens," or perhaps a hymn tune such as "according to the hind of the dawn" (22:1, RSV); (4) the cultic use of some of the psalms by later Israel such as Ps 30, "a song for the dedication of the temple," and Ps 92, "a psalm for the sabbath day."

Date and Authorship

The date and authorship of the canonical psalms have been the object of scholarly research for centuries. The findings of the scholars have varied also with the centuries. The titles refer 73 of the psalms to David (88 in the LXX); 12 others are connected with Asaph, 12 with the sons of Korah, two with Solomon, one with Ethan, and one with Moses. Since the titles at best, however, represent only a very old tradition and cannot be taken as a part of the original inspired text, the psalms are left as "pictures without frames" (cf. Artur Weiser, *The Psalms,* p. 9). Evidently many of the Jews in NT times, largely on the basis of the titles, regarded David as the author and editor of most of the psalms. His name came to be identified with the Psalter as the name of Moses was related to the law, and Solomon to the Wisdom writings. There is reason to believe that David was an outstanding musician and probably wrote many psalms, but it is obvious that he could not have written such psalms as 74 and 137.

With the rise of scientific study of the Bible, the Davidic authorship of the book of Psalms was largely abandoned and, on the basis of an evolutionary view of Israel's religion, most of them were assigned to a post-Exilic period. Julius Wellhausen said, "The question is not whether the Psalter contains any post-Exilic psalms, but whether it contains any which are pre-Exilic." T. K. Cheyne maintained that only parts of Ps 18 were pre-Exilic, and Duhm assigned most of the psalms to the Maccabean period. The modern trend, however, influenced by form criticism, is to bring the psalms back to a relatively early date. Engnell, a Scandinavian scholar, has said that only one psalm (137) is post-Exilic.

Classification

A new trend in the study of the psalms was begun with the work of Hermann Gunkel. His commentary on the book of Psalms was published in 1926. Gunkel believed that much of Israel's religious tradition grew out of her worship at the various sanctuaries and that these traditions were preserved and repeated orally by priests and people. In the reciting of these traditions, certain set forms were used for different types of religious experience. For example, a lament took on a special form, as did a hymn or a thanksgiving. Gunkel believed that the form of each of these types might have been very old, some of them even having been used by Egyptians, Babylonians, and Canaanites for centuries. It must be acknowledged that parallels in form have been found in ancient Egyptian, Babylonian, and Canaanite (Ugaritic) materials. But this is not to say that the content is the same. The form and to some degree the vocabulary may be the same, and the content or message quite different (cf. Ringgren, *Faith of the Psalmists,* pp. 115 f.). *See* Poetry.

Gunkel classified, on the basis of their form and situation in life, the canonical psalms into five major categories: hymns, communal laments, royal psalms, individual laments, and individual songs of thanksgiving. In addition to these five major categories, Gunkel had a number of minor classes such as songs of pilgrimage, communal songs of thanksgiving, wisdom poetry, and liturgies.

Gunkel has been followed in his method of studying the psalms by such scholars as Sigmund Mowinckel, Artur Weiser, Hans-Joachim Kraus, Claus Westermann, and Elmer Leslie. Most of these scholars have seen some cultic festival as the background for many of the psalms. Mowinckel posits a new year festival or an enthronement festival behind many of the psalms. Weiser believes the festival is a covenant renewal festival. Kraus believes that the festival was a royal Zion festival commemorating God's covenant with David and Jerusalem. Westermann believes that all of these men have gone too far in reconstructing a festival and that scholars need to turn their attention back to the psalms themselves. Therefore recent evangelical writers have insisted that the most reasonable basis for classification is the character of the religious ideas found in each psalm (J. G. S. S. Thomson, "Psalms, Book of," NBD, p. 1056; R. K. Harrison, *Introduction to the Old Testament,* pp. 996 f.).

Those psalms generally classified as hymns are: 8, 19:1-6; 29, 33, 65, 100, 103, 105, 136, 145-150. Psalms which have as their theme the enthronement of Yahweh as the Lord of the universe are: 47, 93, 96-99. Psalms which refer to Jerusalem as the chosen city of God (songs of Zion) are: 46, 48, 76, 86. A number of psalms seem to have been written for some special event in the life of the king. Such psalms are referred to as royal psalms and are: 2, 18, 20, 21, 45, 72, 89, 101, 110, 132, 144. A similar classification more often used by evangelical scholars is that of messianic psalms, which wholly or in part predict the sufferings and the reign of a future divine-human king. Those psalms usually so designated are (at least) 2, 8, 16, 22, 40, 45, 69, 72, 110, 118. Jesus' own testimony in Lk 24:44 and quotations from these psalms by NT writers as applying to Christ tend to confirm such analysis.

The best examples of national laments are: 44, 74, 79, 80, 137. The laments of the individual are the most numerous type in the Psalter. The personal involvement expressed in them probably has had much to do with the continuing appeal of the psalms to this day. Individuals, though always recognizing themselves as members of the covenant community, faced the trials of sickness, imminent death, false accusation, imprisonment, and personal enemies. They protested their innocence. They prayed for God to curse their enemies. They confessed their sins and prayed for God's forgiveness and cleansing. The most typical examples of the individual laments are: 3, 5, 7, 13, 22, 42-43, 51, 54-56, 88, 120, 130, 141-142.

The prayers which appeal to God to pour out His wrath are often called imprecatory psalms. We must remember that the psalmists lived under the old covenant before Jesus came to teach us to love our enemies and pray for those who mistreat us (Lk 6:27-38) and before the indwelling of the Holy Spirit. On the other hand, even the NT teaches us to permit God to be our Vindicator (Rom 12:19-20).

Songs of thanksgiving are much fewer than laments. The national thanksgiving psalms are: 67, 75, 107, 118, 124; and individual thanksgiving psalms are: 30, 32, 34, 41, 66, 92, 116, 138. Those generally classified as wisdom psalms are: 1, 19:7-14; 37, 49, 73, 112, 119, 127, 133, 139. Psalms which have obvious liturgical use with an antiphonal arrangement of various speakers or singers are classed as liturgies; Ps 14 (53), 15, 24, 50, 75, 82, 126 are examples.

The Theology of the Psalms

To make an adequate statement about the theology of the psalms is difficult because the psalms are not systematic theological treatises. They are the expressed response of the people to God's saving acts or the lack of them. Again, the psalms were not all written by one person or at the same time, but were produced by sufferers, supplicants, worshipers, and wise men, over a period of many centuries. However, all the psalmists were members of the covenant community and had a common trust in the Lord.

One basic element of Israel's faith which all

the psalmists shared is that God reveals what He is by what He does. The great acts of God are often referred to in the psalms (cf. 77:11-15; 78:3-4; 103:7; 136:1-26). There is more said in the psalms about creation than in any other book in the OT with the possible exception of Isaiah. The most important passages in the psalms relating to creation are 8:3-5; 24:1-2; 36:6; 74:12-17; 89:9-12; 96:5; 102:25; 104:1-30; 115:15-16; 121:2; 124:8; 134:3; 136:5-9; 146:6.

Another doctrine which is basic and prominent in the psalms is that of election, along with the related idea of the covenant between God and Israel. According to the psalms God chose Abraham (104:6, 9), Israel (33:12; 105:6; 106:5; 135:4), Israel's land (147:4), Zion (78:68; 132:13), Judah (78:68), David (78:70; 89:19), and Moses and Aaron (105:26; 106:23). Election is one of Israel's most distinct doctrines. On this foundation all religious life in Israel rested, for it explained her origin, her position, and her mission.

Closely related to the doctrine of election is the doctrine of redemption. Israel believed that she was a part of a sinful race (51:5) that had rebelled against God (58:1-5). However, God had chosen Israel and redeemed her. He had brought her up "out of the land of Egypt" (81:10; cf. 66:6; 68:7-10; 78:13; 80:8; 105:37-44). Israel had been "saved" at the exodus. She remained in the saving relationship by keeping the covenant. However, many of the psalmists were aware that the covenant had been broken by the people as a whole and by individuals (78:8-11, 17-20, 32, 36-37, 40-42, 56-58).

Salvation in the psalms can also refer to deliverance from trouble—personal or national. Many of the individual laments call for God to save them from their enemies. Many of the psalmists' troubles were the result of their sins. Seven of the psalms (6, 32, 38, 51, 102, 130, 143) have been called penitential psalms. But references to sin are also found in many other psalms. Sin for the psalmist was a willful act of rebellion against a personal God. The psalmists believed that God was gracious and merciful and would forgive sins (51:1-2; 78:38; 86:15), but they also believed that God was Judge and would ultimately judge all unconfessed sin in heaven and on earth (49:3-5, 21-22; 58:1, 11).

From the Christian standpoint the theology of the psalms is weak in at least two points: (1) the view of life after death, and (2) lack of emphasis on Israel's mission to the nations. Sheol, or the pit, is the dominant conception of the abode of the dead in the psalms (9:17; 18:4, 5; 55:15). Ordinarily Sheol is thought to make communion with God impossible (6:5; 30:9; 88:10-12; 115:17). However, one psalmist insists on the presence of God even in Sheol (139:8). It is possible also that some psalmists anticipated eternal life in the presence of God (16:10-11; 17:15; 49:15; 73:24).

Instead of praying for the conversion of his enemies or the heathen, the average psalmist prayed either for victory over them or for their destruction (109:6-19; 137:7-9). The strongest "missionary" passages in the psalms are to be found in the "enthronement psalms." Here God's universal reign is proclaimed. All people are called upon to clap their hands and praise God, for he is "King over all the earth" (47:1-2). He is proclaimed as King of the whole earth, and the time is spoken of when "the princes of the people gather as the people of the God of Abraham" (47:9). David says in Ps 22, "All the ends of the earth shall remember and turn to the Lord; and all the families of the nations shall worship before Him. For dominion belongs to the Lord, and He rules over the nations" (22:27-28, RSV).

The Use of the Psalms

In the OT period the psalms were used to express the petitions, praise, and gratitude of worshipers to God. In the NT they are quoted more than any other OT writings. Satan quoted Ps 91:11 in his temptation of Jesus. Jesus probably sang the great Hallel (118) at the last supper. He quoted 22:1 and 35:5 on the cross. The hymns Paul and Silas sang in the Philippian jail were probably psalms. The early church used them in public worship and in the homes (Eph 5:19; Col 3:16; I Cor 14:26).

In the 5th cen. A.D. the psalms were repeated in the monasteries at least twice a week. St. Patrick of Ireland and St. Benedict recited the psalms daily. A council of the church and the capitularies of an emperor provided that no one should be raised to any ecclesiastical dignity who could not recite the psalms. The psalms have sustained martyrs, comforted the sorrowing, and strengthened the weak. With their words on their lips, men have gone to be burned at the stake, to be tried by councils, and to be missionaries to dark continents. Today the psalms are read, chanted, or sung by more people than any other sacred writing.

R. L. S.

Bibliography. Conservative: Joseph A. Alexander, *The Psalms Translated and Explained,* 2 vols, 6th ed., New York: Scribner, Armstrong, 1873. Arthur G. Clarke, *Analytical Studies in the Psalms,* Kilmarnock: Ritchie, 1949. A. Cohen, *Psalms,* Hindhead, Surrey: Soncino Press, 1945. Franz Delitzsch, *Biblical Commentary on the Psalms,* trans. by Francis Bolton, 3 vols., Grand Rapids: Eerdmans, reprint, 1949. Herbert C. Leupold, *Exposition of the Psalms,* Columbus: Wartburg Press, 1959. Alexander Maclaren, *The Psalms,* New York: Funk and Wagnalls, 1908. G. Campbell Morgan, *Notes on the Psalms,* New York: Revell, 1947. J. J. Stewart Perowne, *The Book of Psalms,* 2 vols., London: G. Bell, 1892. Johannes Vos, "The Ethical Problem of the Imprecatory Psalms," WTJ, IV (1942), 123-138. Robert Dick Wilson, "The Headings of the Psalms," PTR, XXIV (1926), 1-37, 353-395.

Liberal and other: Charles A. and Emilie G. Briggs, *The Book of Psalms,* 2 vols., ICC, Edinburgh: T. & T. Clark, 1907. T. K. Cheyne, *The Book of Psalms,* London: Kegan Paul, Trench, Trubner & Co., 1904. Mitchell Dahood, *Psalms,* 3 vols., Anchor Bible, Garden City, N.Y.; Doubleday, 1966, 1968, 1970. W. T. Davison, *The Psalms I–LXXII,* and T. Witton Davies, *The Psalms LXXIII–CL,* Century Bible, Edinburgh: T. C. & E. C. Jack, 1906. Frederick C. Eiselen, *The Psalms and Other Sacred Writings,* New York: Methodist Book Concern, 1918. Hermann Gunkel, *Die Psalmen,* Gottingen: Vanderhoeck & Ruprecht, 1926. Fleming James, *Thirty Psalmists,* New York: Putnam's, 1938. Aubrey R. Johnson, "The Psalms," *The Old Testament and Modern Study,* H. H. Rowley, ed., Oxford, 1951, pp. 162–209. A. F. Kirkpatrick, *The Book of Psalms,* 3 vols., *The Cambridge Bible for Schools and Colleges,* Cambridge: Univ. Press, 1902. E. A. Leslie, *The Psalms,* New York: Abingdon-Cokesbury, 1949. W. Stewart McCullough and William R. Taylor, "The Book of Psalms," IB, Vol. 4. John E. McFayden, *The Psalms in Modern Speech and Rhythmical Form,* London: James Clark & Co., 1926. Sigmund Mowinckel, *The Psalms in Israel's Worship,* A Translation and Revision of *Offersang og Sangoffer,* by D. R. Ap-Thomas, 2 vols., Oxford, 1963. W. O. E. Oesterley, *A Fresh Approach to the Psalms,* New York: Scribner's, 1937; *The Psalms,* London: SPCK, 1939. John Patterson, *The Praises of Israel,* New York: Scribner's, 1950. John H. Patton, *Canaanite Parallels in the Book of Psalms,* Baltimore: Johns Hopkins, 1944. John D. Peters, *The Psalms as Liturgies,* New York: Putnam's, 1922. Helmer Ringgren, *The Faith of the Psalmists,* London: SCM Press, 1963. Theodore H. Robinson, *The Poetry of the Old Testament,* London: Duckworth, 1947. J. A. Sanders, *Discoveries in the Judaean Desert of Jordan, IV: The Psalms Scroll of Qumran Cave 11,* Oxford: Clarendon Press, 1965. David C. Simpson, *The Psalmists,* London: Oxford Univ. Press, 1926. Norman H. Snaith, "The Psalms," *Twentieth Century Bible Commentary,* New York: Harper, 1955; *Studies in the Psalter,* London: Epworth Press, 1926. Samuel Terrien, *Psalms and Their Meaning for Today,* New York: Bobbs-Merrill, 1952. Rollin H. Walker, *The Modern Message of the Psalms,* New York: Abingdon-Cokesbury, 1938. Artur Weiser, *The Psalms: A Commentary,* trans. by H. Hartwell, OT Library, London-Philadelphia: SCM Press, 1962. Claus Westermann, *The Praise of God in the Psalms,* Richmond: John Knox, 1965.

PSALTERY. *See* Music.

PTOLEMAIS. *See* Accho; Acre.

PUA (pū'*á*). The Heb. name *puwwâ* occurs in Num 26:23 and refers to one of the sons of Issachar, whose descendants were called Punites (*q.v.*). The name (with the same Heb. spelling) also appears as Phuvah in Gen 46:13, and in a longer Heb. form (*pû'â*) in I Chr 7:1.

PUAH (pū'*á*). Two persons in the OT had this name, but the Heb. spelling is different.

1. One of the Heb. midwives (Ex 1:15, Heb. *pû'â*). Along with Shiphrah she was commanded by Pharaoh to kill all male Israelite infants at birth. This gruesome order was intended to curb a steadily rising Heb. population which seemed to pose a threat to Egyptian security. *See* Occupations: Midwife.

2. The father of Tola, the judge (Jud 10:1, Heb. *pû'â*).

PUBLICAN. A subordinate collector of tax or customs for the Romans. The NT publicans, mentioned only in the Synoptic Gospels, are to be distinguished from the Roman *publicani,* who never appear in the NT. The *publicani,* generally living in Rome, were capitalists who, individually or jointly, purchased at auction the revenues of a region or province by paying a definite sum into the public treasury (*in publicum*), whence the name.

Roman taxes were of two sorts, direct and indirect. By NT times the direct taxes, on land and persons, were no longer farmed out but were collected by the regular imperial officers. But the indirect taxes, import and export dues, road money, bridge tolls, harbor dues, etc., were still farmed out to the highest bidders. The actual collection was usually performed by native employees. Native subcontractors may have been used. Zacchaeus, called "a chief publican" (*architelōnēs*), may have been the contractor for the revenues of Jericho, having collectors under him. At least he supervised a collecting district.

Most of the NT publicans, like Levi (Mt 9:9; Mk 2:14; Lk 5:27), were customhouse employees. They might have their "place of toll" (ASV) at city gates, on public roads, or bridges. Levi's post (*telōnion*) at Capernaum apparently was near the sea on the important trade route entering Galilee from Damascus.

The publicans were hated and despised by the scribes and people alike. The hostility is evident in the expressions "publicans and sinners" (Mt 9:10 f.; 11:19; Mk 2:15 f.; Lk 5:30; 7:34; 15:1), "publicans and harlots" (Mt 21:31), and their equation with Gentiles (Mt 18:17). This antagonism came from several circumstances. They were victims of the ingrained human dislike of paying taxes. Customhouse officials are never popular. The very nature of their work offered many opportunities for extortion, their chief sin as recognized by John the Baptist (Lk 3:12 f.). Since the payment of taxes to a foreign power was hateful and commonly regarded as unlawful (Mt 22:17), the publicans were regarded as traitors to their nation, willing tools of their oppressors. This ha-

Publius showed hospitality to Paul after his shipwreck here in St. Paul's Bay, Malta. A statue of Paul stands on the island in background. Malta Government Tourist Board

tred of publicans was also strengthened by religious considerations. Since their work threw them into constant touch with Gentiles, they were considered ceremonially unclean, hence, to be shunned.

Christ's association with the publicans was not intended to clear their character altogether of current evaluations (cf. Mt 5:46 f.; 18:17). Their extortion and oppression was as abhorrent to Him as the formalism and hypocrisy of the self-righteous scribes and Pharisees. They too stood in need of His salvation (Lk 19:9 f.). Although to eat with them was regarded incompatible with the character of a rabbi, Jesus justified His association with the publicans on the basis of their need (Mt 9:12; Mk 2:17; Lk 5:30 f.). The bitterest complaints were hurled against Him because of this association (Lk 7:34; 15:1 f.). Christ found them refreshingly free from the hypocrisy and self-righteousness of the Pharisees (Lk 18:9-14). Whatever morality they had was real, not conventional. His choice of Matthew as one of His disciples made a deep impression (Mk 2:14-17), although there is no trace of offense among the disciples at the call. Abhorred by others, the publicans were attracted to Jesus because He showed Himself "a friend of publicans" (Lk 15:1 f.; cf. 7:34).

Bibliography. Otto Michel, "*Telōnēs*," TDNT, VIII, 88-105.

D. E. H.

PUBLIUS (pŭb'lĭ-ŭs). The "chief [first] man" on the island of Malta who showed generous hospitality to Paul and his shipwrecked companions (Acts 28:7-10), whose father Paul healed of a fever and dysentery. He was probably the leading official under the governor of Sicily responsible for any Roman soldiers and their charges who might land there. Tradition asserts he was the first bishop of the island and later became bishop of Athens. Jerome records a tradition that Publius was martyred (*On Illustrious Men*, XIX).

PUDENS (pū'dĕnz). A Christian in Rome during the writing of II Timothy. His name is Roman, and he, along with Eubulus, Linus, and Claudia, sent greetings to Timothy (II Tim 4:21). Lock in HDB gives a sevenfold listing of possible identifications of this man. As this is his only NT reference, nothing certain is known of his history. Since his is a familiar Roman family name, the most common guess hazarded is that Pudens may have been either a soldier to whom Paul was chained, or a senator commemorated by the church of S Pudentiana.

PUHITE (pū'hīt). The KJV form of Puthite (RSV). It was a family name from the line of Caleb of a clan in Kirjath-jearim (I Chr 2:53).

Pul or Tiglath-pileser III. BM

PUL (po͝ol)

1. Another name for Tiglath-pileser III (also Tilgath-pilneser), king of Assyria. Both names are mentioned in I Chr 5:26 and II Kgs 15:19, 29, implying that they were separate monarchs. However, the two names probably refer to the same person who ruled over strife-torn Babylon (729-727 B.C.) as Pul, and over Assyria as Tiglath-pileser. The Babylonian King List A shows "Pulu" to be equivalent to Tiglath-pileser (*q.v.*).

2. A geographic location (Isa 66:19). LXX has Put (*phoud*); thus, Pul should likely be considered in the Masoretic Heb. Text as a misspelling of Put (*q.v.*), an Egyptian term for Libya.

PULPIT. Apparently a high wooden platform capable of accommodating at least 14 persons (Neh 8:4; cf. II Chr 6:12-13; II Kgs 23:2-3).

PULSE. *See* Plants.

PUNISHMENT

Biblical Definition of Punishment

Punishment may be defined as the measure of pain or suffering justly inflicted on the sinner or criminal as a retribution for his wrongdoing. Punishment always implies a standard or law that sets forth both what is right and what is wrong. God's law, according to divine revelation, is the only absolute standard in determining the guilt of a sinful act. Practically all the categories of punishment described in the Bible fall within the scope of the following observations:

Fundamentally, punishment is *the revelation of God's wrath* against the creature's transgression of God's will or law. This punishment involves the angelic world (II Pet 2:4; Jude 6), man (Gen 3:16–19; Ps 90:9; Jn 3:36), and the natural world (Gen 3:17–19; Rom 8:19–22).

Punishment follows a threefold sequence in time: first, upon Adam and his posterity because of the sin of Eden (Gen 3:1–24; Rom 5:12); second, upon Israel (Lev 26:14–46; Jer 25:1–14; Lk 21:20–24; I Thess 2:14–16), the nations (Gen 19:1–28; Jer 25:15–38; Nah 3:1–19), and individuals (Gen 4:9–16; I Cor 5:1–5) because of their transgressions of God's laws; third, upon Satan, the apostate angels, and the impenitent among men because of their rebellion against God (Rom 2:5, 8–9; Acts 17:31; II Thess 1:8–9; Rev 20:11–15).

Punishment sometimes assumes the form of *revenge inflicted upon another*. This revenge belongs essentially to God alone (Deut 32:35, 43; Ps 94:1–3; Nah 1:2–3; Rom 12:19; Heb 10:30); but it is delegated to the state as God's agent (Rom 13:4; I Pet 2:14). The Mosaic legislation permitted "the revenger of blood," under prescribed regulations, to perform this function (Num 35:19–27; Deut 19:2–13; Josh 20:1–9). David was sovereignly hindered from taking vengeance (I Sam 25:21–39); but the Jews under Esther and Mordecai were sovereignly allowed to take vengeance (Est 8:11–13; 9:1–16). Personal vengeance is prohibited both in OT times (Deut 32:35; Prov 20:22; 24:29) and in the NT age (Rom 12:19; I Thess 5:15; I Pet 3:9).

Scarcely any consideration is given in the Bible to punishment as a *reformatory or remedial measure* designed to rehabilitate the transgressor. On the contrary, punishment must be executed swiftly and without mercy (Deut 13:6–9; 19:13, 21; Heb 10:28). No opportunity, for example, was given either to Achan (Josh 7:10–26) or to Ananias and Sapphira (Acts 5:1–11) to redress their wrongs before judgment fell upon them. Not even Israel's apparent repentance at Kadesh mitigated God's punishment upon that rebellious generation (Num 14:26–45). Moses' act of striking the rock twice unalterably kept him from the Promised Land (Num 20:1–13).

However, there are cases where punishment is modified (II Chr 33:10–19) or delayed (II Chr 34:23–28) after the transgressor has repented; and there are other cases where punishment, though modified or delayed by man, is finally executed in all its fury (I Sam 15:1–35; II Sam 21:1–14). Shimei, pardoned and given parole (II Sam 16:5–14; 19:16–23), is summarily executed when his incorrigible nature reappears (I Kgs 2:8–9, 39–46). Israel, punished in exile, returns practically unchanged (cf. Isa 1:1–31 with Mal 1:6–14).

However, on a higher level, God does use correctional measures for *the rectification of His regenerated children*. The heavenly Father chastens them in order to purify their lives of earthly dross (Prov 3:11 f.; Heb 12:5–14). Such chastisements are sometimes very severe (I Cor 5:5; 11:27–32). There is, however, no basis in Scripture for the notion that purgatorial flames will consummate their purification in the world to come (Jn 14:1–3; II Cor 5:1–10; Phil 1:21–23; Rev 14:13). Nor does the Bible support the idea that the impenitent in hell will finally respond to correctional means supposedly employed for their salvation (Lk 16:19–31; Rev 14:9–11). Their punishment is clearly stated as being eternal (Mt 25:44, 46).

Finally, punishment becomes *retaliatory* in the "eye-for-eye" principle (the *jus talionis* of Roman law) incorporated in God's law (Ex 21:23–25; Lev 24:19 f.; Deut 19:21). Actually this statute was instituted to limit the severity of redress to punishment no more than equal to the crime. Israel's 70-year captivity in Babylon is, for example, an exact repayment in kind for her failure to keep the sabbatical law (II Chr 36:21; Jer 29:10; Dan 9:2). Yet Christians are forbidden to retaliate in kind (Mt 5:38–42); they are encouraged to return good for evil (Lk 6:27–30; Rom 12:20–21; I Pet 3:9), even as God does in His long-suffering and grace (Mt 5:44–45).

However, in Christ's death on the cross God exacted in full and in kind the punishment incurred by the sinner but borne by the sinner's Substitute (Isa 53:4, 11; Mt 20:28; 27:46; I Pet 2:24; 3:18). And that same principle of full legal retribution will measure the unrepentant sinner's punishment in hell when the day of grace is past (II Thess 1:8; Rev 14:10–11; 18:6–7, 20).

Premises on Which Punishment Is Founded

The theological premises which justify punishment are never enunciated as such in the Mosaic legislation. Nevertheless, they constitute the basis and background of every punishment prescribed in this legislation.

1. The concept of man as created in God's image (Gen 1:26 f.; 5:1; 9:6). Though never once specifically mentioned, this concept of man's nature undergirds the law of Moses. If a man maliciously murders another man, the law requires that the murderer be put to death (Ex 21:12, 14 f.; Num 35:16–21; Deut 19:11–13). Only thus can the guilt of the land be removed (cf. II Sam 21:1–14). A crime against man is essentially a sin against the "image" of God in man. This fundamental premise justifies the

severity of the punishments inscribed in the Mosaic code.

2. The concept of man as a sinner. Though the residual "image" of God still remains in man's nature, man is now a sinner and a rebel against the authority of God (Deut 1:26, 43; 9:6 f., 13, 23 f.; 31:27). Israel's leaders poignantly recall how God's punishments fell repeatedly upon the nation because of disobedience to divine laws (II Chr 36:11-21; Neh 9:5-38; Dan 9:1-19). [But no law, even with severe penalties attached, can completely deter the evil inclinations and passions of human nature. Man needs a change of heart (Deut 10:16; Jer 4:4). This change will prompt man to obey God's laws because of love rather than because of the penalties of disobedience (Deut 6:5 f.; 10:12 f.; 11:13; 30:6).] Thus, punishments in the Mosaic law become a necessity resulting from the unregenerate human nature. The "new covenant" provided for the writing of God's laws upon the hearts of the redeemed (Jer 24:7; 31:33; 32:39-40; Heb 8:10).

3. The concept of Israel as a theocracy. At Sinai Israel became a theocratic government. In this kind of government it is God who gives the laws (Ex 20:2 ff.) and specifies the penalties for disobedience to His laws (20:22–23:19). Israel's acceptance of the theocracy (19:8; 24:3-8) is never qualified with the condition that either the nation or individual Israelites may change the laws or the punishments received at Sinai. The rectitude of God's laws and the justice of God's punishments must be obediently accepted by the nation and by the individual. For because of the absolute holiness of the divine nature Israel's God-given laws are founded on absolute righteousness; therefore, as a logical consequence, punishments prescribed in these laws must be absolutely just.

Ten Commandments Illustrative of Punishments in Mosaic law

Since the Ten Commandments (Ex 20:1-17; Deut 5:6-21) constitute the legal core of Israel's judicial system, these commandments are illustrations of the way in which, in the amplified judicial legislation (Ex 20:22–23:19; etc.), punishments are prescribed for their infraction. The subsequent history of Israel will in most cases add further illustrations. In the Ten Commandments themselves only the second and the third attach a penalty.

1. No other gods. This commandment is basic to the religion of the Bible (Deut 6:4 f., 14; Ps 81:9 f.; Isa 45:21 f.; Mt 4:10; I Cor 8:4, 6). Penalties against those who break this fundamental commandment are among the most terrible of the Mosaic legislation. The episode at the foot of Mount Sinai while Moses was receiving the law illustrates how strong Israel's propensity was toward other gods and how terrible God's punishment had to be to break the nation of this propensity (Ex 32:1-35). But Israel's idolatry, in spite of repeated warnings and punishments (Deut 13:1-18; Josh 24:14 f, 20; Jud 2:11-23), was only broken by the severity of the Babylonian Captivity, which came upon the nation as a result of breaking this first commandment (Jer 25:4-11).

2. No graven images. The second commandment is really an extension of the first commandment. The dire consequences of breaking the second one are set forth in the Mosaic legislation in all their utter awfulness (Deut 4:23-28). God's punishments upon the nations of Canaan on account of their idolatry were designed to safeguard His own people against similar idolatry (Ex 23:20-28; 34:11-16; Deut 7:1-6; Josh 23:12 f.). But these illustrative punishments proved ineffectual in Israel's history until God finally sent the nation into exile in Babylon (Jer 7:21-34; 25:4-11). The justice of God's punishment was never questioned by later interpreters of Israel's history (Neh 9:6-38; Dan 9:1-19).

3. Taking God's name in vain. The third commandment comprises all kinds of disrespect manifested toward the divine name. Repeatedly the Sinaitic legislation emphasizes the dignity of God's name (Ex 34:5-7; Lev 18:21; 19:12; 20:3; 21:6). The profanation of the divine name brings quick judgment upon the offender (Lev 24:10-16). Even an Assyrian king is destroyed, as later history records (II Kgs 18:13–19:37), because he blasphemed the name of God. The ultimate climax of this sin is revealed in what Christ calls "the blasphemy against the Spirit" (Mt 12:22-37), which is "an eternal sin" (Mk 3:28-30, RSV).

4. Sabbath-breaking. The fourth commandment sets off a portion of man's time for rest and divine worship. The Sinaitic legislation is replete with stern warnings concerning the sanctity of the sabbath (Ex 23:12; 31:12-17; 35:2 f.). A summary execution of an offender graphically reminds Israel concerning the inviolability of God's laws (Num 15:32-36). Later prophets in Israel's history held up sabbath-keeping as a standard for the people's faithfulness to the Lord (Isa 56:2-7; 58:13 f.; Hos 2:11; Amos 8:5). Israel's long period of disobedience to God's sabbatic law was eventually punished with 70 years in exile in Babylon in order to make up for the prior 490 years of disobedience (II Chr 36:20-21; Jer 25:12; 29:30).

5. Honor to parents. The fifth commandment begins that section in the Decalogue dealing with man's relationship to his fellowman. It is amplified in the Mosaic code in those places where the sentence of death is pronounced against revilers of parents (Ex 21:17; Lev 20:9; Deut 27:16). The heinousness of this sin is vividly set forth in the law recorded in Deut 21:18-21. The proverbs of Israel duly amplify the magnitude of this crime (Prov 19:26; 20:20; 30:11, 17).

6. Murder. The sixth commandment reiterates the basic statement found in Gen 9:6. Nothing in the Sinaitic legislation is more pro-

nounced than the law forbidding a man to kill another man (Ex 21:12-14; Lev 24:17, 21). This legislation makes a clear distinction between the manslayer (Num 35:9-15, 22-28; Deut 19:1-10) and the murderer (Num 35:16-21, 29-34; Deut 19:11-13). The murderer must be slain by "the avenger of blood"; the manslayer must flee to one of the cities of refuge for protection and for adjudication of his case. Israel's subsequent history shows how the law concerning murder was sometimes ignored or modified by men but finally executed by God (II Sam 3:27-39; cf. I Kgs 2:31-34; II Sam 21:1-14; II Chr 24:20-22, 25). In fact, Christ uses the murder of Abel (Gen 4:8-15) and the murder of Zechariah (II Chr 24:21) as examples of the punishment yet awaiting Israel for the slaughter of innocent men (Mt 23:32-36).

7. Adultery. The seventh commandment prohibits sexual relations outside of marriage. The Mosaic code stipulates death as the penalty for those who break this commandment (Lev 18:20; 20:10). Two unusual events recorded by Moses set forth the abomination of adultery. The first event centers around Israel's moral looseness at the foot of Sinai while Moses was receiving the law. This moral laxity brought instant punishment at the hand of Moses and the Levites (Ex 32:6, 25-28; I Cor 10:7). The other event centers around Israel's licentious relation with the Midianites. This perversion was instantly punished by Phinehas (Num 25:1-18; I Cor 10:8). In the proverbs of Israel the sin of moral looseness is set forth with all its devastating effects on the mind and the body (Prov 5:3-23; 7:5-27; 9:13-18; 23:27-28; 29:3). David's adultery with Bathsheba shows that such transgression is inexcusable even when a king commits it (II Sam 11:2-5; 12:7-23; Ps 51). Capital punishment in his case was averted only because of his genuine, heartfelt confession and repentance.

8. Stealing. The eighth commandment prohibits the unlawful taking of another's property. The Mosaic code amplifies this commandment with various details (Ex 21:16; 22:1-4; Lev 19:11, 13, 35-37; Deut 24:7; 25:13-16). In some cases the prescribed punishment was very severe (Deut 24:7). Later proverbs vividly describe the heinousness of this sin (Prov 11:1; 28:24; 29:24).

9. Bearing false witness. The ninth commandment forbids any kind of false statement or accusation. The Mosaic code sternly rebukes and severely punishes those who are guilty of this sin (Ex 23:1, 7; Lev 19:11, 16; Deut 19:15-21). In later periods of Israel's history it was condemned by precepts (Prov 6:16, 19; 12:17; 14:5; 19:5, 9, 28; 21:28; 24:28; 25:18) and by example (Jer 37:11-21).

10. Coveting. The last commandment forbids all unlawful desires. Israel's "lusting" is illustrated not only by the evil physical desires of the people (Num 11:4-6; Ps 78:18; 106:14 f.) but also by the evil desires of certain Levites for the priesthood (Num 16:1-40). In later times this subtle sin is exemplified in Achan's transgression (Josh 7:10-26). It is also condemned in various proverbs (Prov 1:19; 15:27; 28:16).

Conclusions

The most obvious conclusion regarding the punishments prescribed in the Mosaic law is that these punishments are not only holy and just in the sight of God but are also acceptable to all men indwelt by the Spirit of God. God will legislate what is right. A further conclusion is that the believer has no fear that the punishment of the Mosaic law will ever fall on him personally. He knows that this punishment has been borne once and for all by Christ.

See Crime and Punishment; Chastisement.

W. B.

PUNITES (pū'nīts). The descendants (Heb. *pûnî*) of Pua, one of the sons of Issachar (Num 26:23). The ancient versions suggested that the correct reading should be *pû'î*, which would be translated Puites (NEB).

PUNON (pū'nŏn). One of the stations in the wilderness journey of the Israelites after the exodus from Egypt (Num 33:42 f.). It was situated on the eastern side of the Arabah about 25 miles S of the Dead Sea. Located at the junction of two wadis, it is modern Khirbet Feinan, a large well-watered site with potsherds from 2200-1800 and 1250-700 B.C. occupations below remains of the Nabataeans who resumed mining and smelting operations there. It was possibly the home of one of the lords of Edom (Gen 36:41, where Pinon is listed, which is conceivably the same name as Punon). Eusebius stated that Christians were forced to work in the mines and smelters at Punon (*phinōn, phainōn*), which had been a penal colony where convicts were sent to mine copper.

Here the main Transjordanian trade route (the King's Highway, Num 20:17; 21:22; Deut 2:27) branched and one fork turned westward to *'Ain Ḥuṣb* (Tamar?) and up through the rugged hills of the Negeb. Punon is five miles S of another copper mine at Khirbet en-Naḥas (Heb. *nāḥāsh* means "serpent"), so that it is very possible that the spot where Moses made and elevated the bronze or copper serpent (Num 21:9) was in this vicinity. Punon was the encampment just before Oboth (Num 33:43), and Oboth was the next stop after the punishment by poisonous snakes (Num 21:6-10).

J. R.

PUR. *See* Purim.

PURAH. *See* Phurah.

PURGATORY. According to Roman Catholic doctrine, only the souls of those who are perfectly pure at death are immediately admitted to heaven. But the great majority of those who die in justifying grace are still burdened with the guilt of venial sins and have not endured the temporal punishment for their mortal sins by fulfilling the works of penance during life on earth. These must endure a time of expiatory suffering as a process of cleansing before they may experience the beatific vision of God in heaven. The place where this intermediate suffering and cleansing takes place is called purgatory.

Roman Catholics generally agree that purgatory is a place of punishment and cleansing by fire, and that the time spent there might vary from hours to thousands of years, though no one in this life knows how long he himself or one who has already died might have to spend. Actually, the only ones who are certainly known not to be in purgatory are the canonized saints. The duration and intensity of suffering depend on the degree of purification and the amount of temporal punishment still lacking at the time one dies. These can be shortened and alleviated by the prayers and good works of those on earth, especially by masses and the granting of papal indulgences by which the benefits of the treasury of merit (consisting of the works of supererogation by Christ and the saints) might accrue to the dead in purgatory.

The Roman Catholic doctrine of purgatory has absolutely no basis in Scripture, and so Protestants have not accepted it. Roman Catholics appeal to II Macc 12:39–45, a book which Protestants do not accept as canonical. Some passages of Scripture are cited as justification (Isa 4:4; Mic 7:8; Zech 9:11; Mal 3:2–3; Mt 12:32; I Cor 3:13–15; 15:29), but only the most forced eisegesis can read purgatory into these verses. Even the contemporary Roman theologians Rahner and Vorgrimler (*Theological Dictionary,* p. 391) admit the paucity of scriptural evidence for the doctrine. The doctrine of purgatory is an integral part of the Roman view of salvation and satisfaction for sin with the place it gives to man's works and supposed merits. To Protestants, this seems directly contrary to the Pauline teaching of grace (cf. Eph 2:8–10) and Christ's words in Jn 3:36 and 5:24.

If the source of this doctrine of purgatory is not to be found in Scripture, where did it come from? In Session XXV, the Council of Trent decreed that the existence of purgatory and the detention of souls there is "taught by the Holy Spirit from the sacred writings and the ancient traditions of the Fathers." As a result, the church taught it in earlier holy councils and in this ecumenical synod (meaning the Council of Trent). Teaching of the purgative cleansing by fire existed as early as Origen, Cyprian, and Augustine. It is found in Gregory the Great and it developed in medieval theology. The teaching of purgatory was formally affirmed at the Council of Lyons (1274), Council of Florence (1439), and finally at the Council of Trent (1545–1563) (cf. Sessions VI and XXV). However, the magisterium has never given a detailed definition on the exact nature or duration of purgatory.

S. N. G.

PURGE. *See* Uncleanness.

PURIFICATION. *See* Uncleanness.

PURIFIER OF SILVER. *See* Minerals and Metals: Silver; Occupations: Refiner, Silversmith.

PURIM (pūr'ĭm). A feast of the Jews that is observed on the 13th and 14th of the month Adar (March) in celebration of the deliverance of the Jews from the wicked plot of Haman. The story is recorded in the book of Esther (9:24–32). Haman had obtained permission from the king and had proclaimed that on the 13th of Adar throughout Persia the Jews were to be exterminated (Est 3:13). Through the intervention of Esther and Mordecai, the plot was stopped and the days that were to have marked Jewish destruction became days of victory and celebration (Est 8:1–12).

The name Purim comes from the plural of the word *pur,* a term that may be cognate to Akkad. *pūrū* used of the casting of lots to obtain oracles. The name was given because of Haman's casting of lots by which the original evil day was determined (Est 3:7; 9:24). Although the feast is not mentioned by name in the NT, Josephus says that it was observed annually (*Ant.* xi.6.13), as it is to our own day. In II Macc 15:36 it is called quite appropriately "Mordecai's Day." *See* Festivals: Post-Exilic Festivals.

P. C. J.

PURITY. Purity permeates the message of the Scriptures. Its range of reference sweeps from the quality of being not diluted (e.g., oil for the golden lampstand, Ex 27:20), through ceremonial cleanness as in the priests (Ezr 6:20) and the condition of being redemptively cleansed (e.g., the Christian's mind, II Pet 3:1), to the very quality of God in His holiness in whose sight even "the stars are not pure" (Job 25:5). So too, purity is ascribed to the Scripture as inspired of God (Ps 12:6; 19:8; 119:140). The "pure in heart" are blessed because cleansed by the blood of Christ (I Jn 1:7), and kept undefiled by love of self or evil things through the Spirit's continuing work, they can truly love God.

See Clean; Chaste; Holiness, Holy; Sanctification.

PURLOINING. The Gr. word *nosphizomai* is so translated in Tit 2:10 (KJV, ASV). Paul stresses the need for the Christian servant (*doulos*) to refrain from talking back and "purloining." The word means "to steal" or appropriate something unlawfully, "to pilfer" (NASB), as Achan did at Jericho (Josh 7:1, LXX). The same Gr. verb is used in Acts 5:2–3, where Ananias misappropriated, or kept back for himself, a part of the selling price of a piece of property.

PURPLE. Ordinarily "purple" in the Bible refers to thread or cloth dyed purple. Heb. *'argā-*

mān and the related Aramaic *'argewān* (II Chr 2:7; Dan 5:7, RSV) are of uncertain shade, but doubtless refer to a reddish-purple color, inasmuch as the color violet or blue-purple is expressed by another Heb. word, *tekēlet*.

This most valued of ancient dyes was obtained from a species of shellfish common in the Mediterranean Sea known as *Murex trunculus*. The dye seems first to have been manufactured from this source by Canaanites in the area of Phoenicia. The Hurrians (see Horites) coined an adjective *kinaḫḫe(na)* from the name Canaan (*kna'n*) to refer to the Canaanites' characteristic product, "Canaanite dye" or "dyed cloth." The name Phoenicia comes from the Gr. *phoinos*, "red-purple." The cognate word to Heb. *'argāmān* appears in Ugaritic as *'rgmn*; both seem to be loanwords of Anatolian origin. Clay tablets reveal that wool dyed purple could be had in Ugarit *c.* 1500 B.C. The people of ancient Sumer had a word for purple, and commoners of that civilization were prohibited from wearing purple garments.

To make purple dye the shell of the mollusk was broken so that a small gland in the neck might be extracted and crushed. The gland then would exude a few drops of a milk-like fluid that turned reddish-purple on contact with the air. Hundreds of shellfish were necessary for a tiny amount of dye. Hence only the wealthy (Lk 16:19) and royalty (Jud 8:26; Est 1:6) and persons of high rank (Est 8:18; Prov 31:22) could afford garments dyed with such costly substance. The *Murex* shells can still be seen in piles along the shore at Tyre and near the ancient dye-works of Athens and Pompeii. In Ezekiel's day purple was obtainable from Cyprus (Elishah, Ezk 27:7). *See* Animals, V.8.

Purple dye was used for some of the tabernacle furnishings (Ex 26:1, 31; etc.; Num 4:13) and the high priestly garments (Ex 28:4-6; 39:1-2, 28-29) as well as for the veil of the temple (II Chr 3:14). Solomon employed a Phoenician craftsman from Tyre who was skillful in the use of purple dye (II Chr 2:14), and had a palanquin whose seat was covered with purple (Song 3:10, RSV). The heathen enshrined their idols with purple drapes (Jer 10:9).

In the NT, Jesus was forced to wear a purple cloak in order to mock His claim to be king of the Jews (Mk 15:17, 20; Jn 19:2, 5). Lydian purple dye, which Lydia of Thyatira sold (Acts 16:14), was not made from shellfish but from the madder root, and was a bright red. Eschatological Babylon is described as being clothed in purple (Rev 17:4; 18:16).

See Colours; Dress.

J. R.

PURPOSES OF GOD. *See* Election; Sovereignty of God.

PURSE. Found but once in the OT (Prov 1:14). It translates the Heb. *kîs*, which is usually rendered "bag." The Gr. *balantion* occurs in the commissioning of the 70 (Lk 10:4), where they are prohibited from taking a purse. LSJ suggest "pouch" as a translation. The Gr. *zōnē* was the girdle or belt which both bound the loose garments together and held various articles. In the instructions to the 12 (Mt 10:9), Jesus does not say not to take a purse (*zōnē*), for this was part of their clothing. He tells them rather not to take *in* it any money.

PURSLANE. *See* Plants.

PURTENANCE. A rather unsatisfactory rendering of *qereb* in Ex 12:9. ASV translates "inwards" and the RSV "inner parts." The notion of "entrails" (NASB) is clearly intended. A study of the more than 100 occurrences of this word, usually rendered "midst" or "inwards" in the KJV, reflects how strange its handling in Ex 12:9 really is.

PUT. *See* Phut.

PUTEOLI (pū-tē'ō-lī). The harbor on the Bay of Naples where Paul landed after the long, almost disastrous journey from Palestine. The city was on one of the best harbors on the Italian coast and had been established centuries earlier by the Greeks. Because it was a great trading center, many Jews lived there; and a Christian church was already established when Paul arrived (Acts 28:13-14). A part of the pier where Paul may have landed is still to be seen in the modern Pozzuoli. After seven days, Paul and the others set out to walk to Rome.

PUTIEL (pū'ti-ĕl). The father-in-law of Eleazar, Aaron's son (Ex 6:25). The Heb. name *pûṭî'ēl* is a combination of an Egyptian element *pu-di*, "the one given by," and the Heb. *'el*, "God." His name indicates that Putiel was undoubtedly born in Egypt.

PUVAH. *See* Phuvah.

PYGARG. *See* Animals: Antelope, II.1.

The wharf-breakwater where Paul landed at Puteoli is built into the modern wharf there.
HFV

Q

QERE. An Aramaic term, *qerê*, meaning "that which is to be read." A marginal notation which the scribes made in the Heb. text when the oral tradition or private interpretation differed from the authoritative written text (the *Kethîb, q.v.*). They were forbidden to alter the text itself, but made more than 1,300 such notes.

QESITAH. *See* Weights, Measures, and Coins: Weights.

QOPH (kōf). The 19th letter of the Heb. alphabet, corresponding to the English "q," but transliterated as Koph in the KJV (*q.v.*). It is used to introduce the 19th section of Ps 119 (vv. 145–152), every verse of which in Heb. begins with the letter.

QUAIL. *See* Animals, III. 43.

QUARRIES. "The quarries" are mentioned in the KJV of Jud 3:19, 26. Since the Heb. is *happesîlîm*, "sculptured stones" (RSV) is a more accurate translation. Elsewhere the KJV translates the term as "graven image" or "carved image" (Deut 7:5, 25; 12:3; Jud 17:3; 18:14, 30; II Chr 33:22; 34:3; etc.). The reference may be to a pre-Israelite circle of carved stone idols (LXX, Vulg. read "idols") at Gilgal, from which the site originally derived its name; for it is not stated that Joshua and his men carved the stones they carried to Gilgal from the Jordan riverbed (Josh 4:8, 20). *See* Gilgal.

In the RSV of I Kgs 6:7 it is said that the temple was built with stone prepared at "the quarry" (Heb. *massā'*), a noun based on the verb root *nāsa'*, "to pull out," "remove." A form of this verb means "to quarry," as in I Kgs 5:17; Eccl 10:9 (both RSV). The RSV has "quarried" stone (*maḥṣēb*) for "hewn" stone (KJV) at II Kgs 12:12; 22:6; etc. This latter verb root appears in the expression *ḥōṣēb bāhār* (II Chr 2:2, 18), and is understood by the RSV to mean "to quarry in the hill country." It is possible, however, that the reference is to woodcutters (as in KJV). The RSV renders "hole of the pit" as "quarry" in Isa 51:1. The huge cavern under the present N city wall of Old Jerusalem is popularly called "Solomon's quarries." Its size, *c.* 325 by 650 feet, suggests that limestone blocks cut here were for a state project, although probably not so early as for Solomon's temple. In the ancient Near East, stones were quarried by cutting deep grooves with iron picks on all four sides and then prying, wedging, or splitting the stone loose with a sharp blow.

Some scholars have taken the name Shebarim (Josh 7:5) as "quarries," but the word can also signify broken places or defiles in the cliffs overlooking the Jordan Valley.

J. R.

The Syene quarry at Aswan furnished much of the best granite for Egyptian construction. A large cracked obelisk was left in the quarry thousands of years ago. HFV

QUARTUS (kwôr'tŭs). Mentioned only in Rom 16:23. He was one of several residents of Corinth (presuming that Paul wrote the Epistle to the Romans from that city) whose greetings were sent to the Roman Christians. His name was evidently derived from the Latin and signified "fourth." "The ordinal numbers were employed by the Latins as proper names" (W.G.T. Shedd, *Commentary on Romans,* p. 435). Probably he was Italian by birth and had friends in Rome. All else we know about him is that he was a believer in Christ, for Paul calls him "a brother."

QUARTZ. *See* Minerals and Metals.

QUATERNION. A squad of four soldiers, such as was detailed to guard Peter while in prison in Jerusalem (Acts 12:4; cf. Mt 27:65). Four of these "squads" (RSV) were assigned, one for each watch or quarter of the night. Two soldiers were chained to Peter in the cell, and two stood guard outside the door.

Queen Nefertiti, wife of Akhenaton, who possibly ruled Egypt while the Hebrews wandered in the Sinai wilderness. LL

QUEEN. The term is used in the Bible to translate four or five Heb. and Gr. terms and has a number of applications.

1. The queen mother or dowager queen (*g^e^bîrâ*). As a rule the queen mother was much more powerful and influential than the king's wives. Polygamy naturally lessened the influence of the king's wives, whose hold on his affection was shared by others and was at best precarious. But the queen mother shared a fixed position of dignity; she took rank almost with the king.

When Bathsheba, the mother of Solomon, desired to plead the cause of his half brother Adonijah, it is written that Solomon "arose to meet her, bowed before her, and sat on his throne; then he had a throne set for the king's mother, and she sat on his right hand" (I Kgs 2:19, NASB). King Asa's mother, Maachah, was removed from her position of *g^e^bîrâ* because of her idolatry (I Kgs 15:13). Nehushta (II Kgs 24:8), the mother of King Jehoiachin, is referred to twice by this term (Jer 13:18; 29:2). The political importance of the dowager queens is illustrated by the fact that in the book of Kings, with two exceptions, the names of the Heb. kings are recorded together with those of their mothers.

2. The wife of a king (*malkâ*, queen consort). In the book of Esther this is the title given to Vashti, the deposed queen of Ahasuerus of Persia (Est 1:9), and this is the title used for Esther, the Jewess successor to Vashti (2:22). With wisdom and courage Esther used her position to save her people.

3. This term (*malkâ*) may also refer to a female ruler or sovereign. There was the Queen of Sheba who came to inquire after the wisdom of Solomon (I Kgs 10:1–13). Christ referred to her as "the queen of the south" (Mt 12:42). *See* Sheba 7. In the NT there is the reference to Candace, the queen (*basilissa*) of the Ethiopians (Acts 8:27).

4. The queen of heaven (*m^e^leketh ha-shāmayim*), the moon or the starry heavens being idolatrously worshiped by the people of Judah (Jer 7:18; 44:17, 19, 25). She is to be identified with Assyrian Ishtar and the Canaanite Astarte. The worship itself was of a grossly immoral character. Because of such idolatry Jeremiah warned of the wrath of God which "shall burn, and not be quenched" (Jer 7:20).

5. Metaphorically the term queen is used (Rev 18:7) to refer to "Babylon the Great, the Mother of Harlots" (17:5) who represents the apostate church of the times just prior to Christ's second coming (Rev 17–18).

R. L. D.

QUEEN OF HEAVEN. *See* Gods, False; Queen 4.

QUEEN OF SHEBA. *See* Queen 3; Sheba 7.

QUICK, QUICKEN. These are old English expressions for giving life. God is the judge of "the quick and the dead" (Acts 10:42; I Pet 4:5). The Word of God is spoken of as "quick," or alive and "powerful" (Heb 4:12). Even as God raises the dead and quickens (gives life, RSV), so Christ quickens whom He will (Jn 5:21; Rom 4:17; 8:11). The third person of the Trinity quickened Christ as He rose from the dead (I Pet 3:18), and quickens the believer as he is regenerated (Jn 6:63; Eph 2:5; Col 2: 13). *See* Resurrection; Life.

QUICKSANDS. The only occurrence of this term is in the KJV of Acts 27:17, where the Gr. *syrtis* appears. A sandbank in the Mediterranean is meant, specifically the Syrtis (Major and Minor) off the coast of Libya. *See* Syrtis.

QUIRINIUS. *See* Cyrenius.

QUIVER. *See* Armor.

QUMRAN. *See* Dead Sea Scrolls.

R

RAAMAH (rā'ȧ-mȧ)

1. The fourth son of Cush, eldest son of Ham, and father of Sheba and Dedan (Gen 10:7; I Chr 1:9).

2. A tribe associated with Sheba (Ezk 27:22), believed by some to be Regma, a city in SE Arabia (following LXX). More likely the identification is with the Rhammanites in SW Arabia (Strabo xvi.4.24). Ezekiel refers to them as a people who traded spices, gold, and gems with Tyre. The name is also mentioned in an ancient S Arabic inscription that praises the local deity for rescuing the Minaeans from attackers on the way from Ma'in to Ra'amah.

RAAMIAH (rā'ȧ-mī'ȧ). The name refers to one of the leaders who returned from Captivity with Zerubbabel (Neh 7:7), the equivalent of Reelaiah in Ezr 2:2.

RAAMSES. *See* Rameses.

Amman citadel. JR

RABBAH (răb'ȧ)

1. A city of Judah in the hill country named along with Kirjath-jearim (Josh 15:60). Aharoni equates Rabbah with Rubute of the Amarna letters and locates it at Khirbet Bîr el-Ḥilû five miles E of Gezer on the road to Jerusalem (VT, XIX [1969], 137–141).

2. The chief city of the Ammonites (*q.v.*). Lying E of the territory assigned to the tribe of Gad (Josh 13:25), it is frequently known in the OT as "Rabbah of the children of Ammon" to distinguish it from other towns of the same name. The famous iron bedstead of Og king of Bashan was kept in Rabbah (Deut 3:11, RSV). It was the Ammonite capital until the reign of David, and here Uriah the Hittite was killed on David's orders (II Sam 11:1, 15). Joab finally captured the city, and David subjected the Ammonites to forced labor (II Sam 12:27–31; I Chr 20:1–3, RSV). The prophets referred to Rabbah as if it were the only important city in the territory, describing it as a fertile valley (Jer 49:2; Ezk 21:20; 25:5; Amos 1:14). It lay astride the King's Highway (*q.v.*) in E Gilead.

The city under Ptolemy Philadelphus (285–246 B.C.) regained its importance and became a leading city of Decapolis under the name Philadelphia. During Byzantine rule in the 4th cen. A.D. it ranked in importance with Gerasa (Jerash) and was strongly fortified. It became the seat of a bishopric but was apparently destroyed, perhaps at the time of the Muslim conquest.

In recent years Rabbah has regained its ancient splendor. It is now called Amman, the capital of Jordan's Hashemite kingdom with some 565,000 inhabitants. Well-watered in fertile environs, the city's location on the Hejaz railway is strategic. At its airport, one of Jordan's three air fields, ruins of a square temple from the Late Bronze Age (*c.* 1400-1200 B.C.) were discovered in 1955. It is supposed that this building, 15 meters square, served a group of tribes in league with another (BA, XXXII [1969], 104–111). Its existence, in addition to recently found pottery and walls on the citadel of Amman from the same period, furnish clear evidence that the area was settled in the time of Moses and Joshua. *See* Ammonites.

Ruins from the Roman period are rather extensive, including a large amphitheater, a citadel on the acropolis, baths, and an odeum. A recently built museum adds to the site's interest for Bible students.

G. A. T.

RABBI. The word rabbi is a transliteration of the Heb. word, used as a term of respect and honor. The word literally means "my great one" or "my master." Although it was originally used as a mark of respect, after the 1st cen. A.D. it had become a title given to religious teachers and leaders and largely lost its original meaning. It has been in continuous use through the Christian era and is used today to designate the ordained ministers among the Jews. Although later schools among the Jews attempted to use a gradation of titles from "rab," an ordinary teacher, to "rabbi," and then "rabboni," there does not seem to have been any consistency in usage in Jesus' time.

In the NT the term rabbi was applied to Jesus on a number of occasions, probably more as a word of honor than in the later technical sense (Jn 1:38, 49; 3:2, 26; 6:25). The word rabboni used by Mary in addressing the risen Lord (Jn 20:16) is the Aram. form of the same word. On one occasion Jesus forbade the use of the term among the disciples because of the pride and self-exaltation with which it was used by the Pharisees (Mt 23:7-8).

See Education; Master; Occupations: Doctor, Lawyer; Scribe; Synagogue; Talmud.

Bibliography. CornPBE, pp. 615ff. Edward Lohse, *"Rabbi, Rabboni,"* TDNT, VI, 961-965. W. Harold Mare, "Teacher and Rabbi in the New Testament Period," *Grace Journal,* XI, #3 (Fall, 1970), 11-21. Roy A. Stewart, *The Earlier Rabbinic Tradition,* London: Inter-Varsity Fellowship, 1949; *Rabbinic Theology,* Edinbugh: Oliver & Boyd, 1961.

P. C. J.

RABBITH (răb'ĭth). The name of a town in the territory of Issachar (Josh 19:20 only). Its site is unknown.

RABBONI. *See* Rabbi.

RABMAG (răb'măg). The title of an officer in the army of Babylon, or of a royal office (Jer 39:3, 13), presumably held by Nergalsharezer (*q.v.*). The English word is simply transliterated from the Heb. An origin from Akkad. *rab-mûgi* ("great prince") has been suggested, but the exact meaning of the title is unknown.

RABSARIS (răb'sȧ-rĭs). A title meaning "chief of the eunuchs." The title is used of (1) one of the three Assyrian officials sent by Sennacherib to Hezekiah (II Kgs 18:17); (2) Sarsechim, one of the Babylonian princes who judged in the gate of Jerusalem after Nebuchadnezzar had captured it (Jer 39:3, RSV); (3) Nebushashban, one of the Babylonian officers who took Jeremiah from prison and committed him to Gedaliah (Jer 39:13).

The precise formula *rab sārîs* is attested in Aram. on an Assyrian document from Nineveh (cf. the similar Heb. phrase *śar hassārîsîm* in Dan 1:7). The phrase and the Heb. word *sārîs* for "eunuch" may be derived from the Assyrian title *ša rêši,* which means "one who (stands) at the head" of the king. This appeared regularly in the Middle Assyrian laws as a euphemistic designation for officials who were eunuchs (G. R. Driver and J. C. Miles, *The Assyrian Laws,* p. 463).

Eunuchs enjoyed positions of great responsibility, not only as harem overseers but as governors (cf. Acts 8:27; Herodotus VIII, 105).

Since its significance was not understood, "Rabsaris" was misrendered as a proper name by the LXX, the Vulg. and the KJV.

E. M. Y.

RABSHAKEH (răb'shȧ-kĕ; Heb. *răb-shâqēh*). The title of the Assyrian officer who was spokesman for the group Sennacherib sent to demand that Hezekiah surrender Jerusalem (II Kgs 18:17–19:8; Isa 36:2–37:8; see RSV). He systematically but unsuccessfully derided all the defenders' hopes of deliverance. The KJV and ASV improperly treat "Rabshakeh" as though it were a proper name, but the Akkad. *rab-shaķû* literally means the "cupbearer-in-chief" (JerusB).

RACA (rä'kä). A transliteration of the Gr. *hraka* in its only occurrence in the NT in Mt 5:22. The meaning is "empty" or "senseless." It is a vernacular word of comparatively mild abuse (MM). The RSV too freely translates the passage "whoever insults his brother." It is not as extreme a term as *mōros* which means "foolish" or "fool," and this idea is substantiated by noting the progressive intensity of expressions in Mt 5:22. Raca seems to cast reflection on a man's intellectual capacity, i.e., "you ignoramus!" This concept must not be pressed exclusively, as we are warned by JewEnc. It does at times refer to lack of morals as well.

Bibliography. J. Jeremias, *"Raka,"* TDNT, VI, 973-976.

RACE. *See* Games.

RACHAB. *See* Rahab.

RACHEL (rā'chĕl). The wife of Jacob and mother of Joseph and Benjamin. She was the younger daughter of Laban, the brother of Jacob's mother, thus making Rachel and Jacob cousins. After Jacob cheated his brother Esau out of his birthright, Isaac commanded him to seek a wife from among their own ancestors in Padan-aram near Haran (Gen 28:1-2).

When Jacob arrived at the old home place he was attracted immediately by Rachel's beauty and fell in love with her (Gen 29:10ff.). Jacob agreed to work for Laban seven years in order to obtain Rachel's hand in marriage. The narrative states that it "seemed unto him but a few days, for the love he had for her" (Gen 29:20). When the veiled marriage ceremony was concluded, Jacob discovered that he had been tricked into marrying the less attractive and older daughter Leah. When Jacob objected, Laban agreed to give him Rachel also after Leah's bridal week was over, if he would serve seven more years.

Jacob was distressed when he discovered that "Rachel was barren" (Gen 29:30-31), while Leah bore him children. In her jealousy Rachel employed the expediency to which Sarah resorted under similar circumstances (Gen 16:2ff.). According to Hurrian custom which prevailed around Haran at that time, a woman of high social standing at her marriage might be assigned a slave girl who could be employed to bear legal offspring if the young wife were found to be barren (*see* Horite; Nuzu). Thus Rachel urged Jacob to have a child for her by her handmaid Bilhah (Gen 30:3). Dan and Naphtali were born of this union. Nevertheless Rachel prayed desperately that she herself could have children. Her prayer was answered and she gave birth to Joseph (Gen 30:22-24).

Tomb of Rachel. HFV

Jacob prospered greatly while working for Laban, all the while increasing his herds and family. When Jacob's relationship with Laban became strained, he fled with his herds and family, only to discover later that Rachel had taken her father's teraphim, possibly thinking that by securing her father's "household gods" their continued prosperity would be assured (Gen 31:19). When God summoned him back to Bethel, Jacob instructed his household to "put away the strange gods" (Gen 35:2).

En route to Canaan Jacob assigned to Rachel the place of greatest safety (Gen 33:2). While traveling between Bethel and Ephrath (Bethlehem) she gave birth to her second son, Benjamin, and died shortly thereafter (Gen 35:16ff.). Tradition says she was buried about one mile N of Bethlehem on the road to Jerusalem. Jacob erected a pillar, or monument, over her grave. At present there stands near Bethlehem what is now called the "Dome of Rachel"–a small mosquelike building controlled by the Muslims. However, Samuel mentioned Rachel's tomb at Zelzah (I Sam 10:2), a town in Benjamin whose location is uncertain. The prophet Jeremiah also refers to Rachel and it would seem that the place he had in mind is Ramah, about five miles N of Jerusalem (Jer 31:15). His prophecy found fulfillment in the slaughter of the innocents at Bethlehem (Mt 2:18).

H. A. Han.

RADDAI (răd'ī). One of David's brothers (I Chr 2:14), the fifth of Jesse's seven sons.

RAFT. In the RSV and NASB of I Kgs 5:9 the word "raft" appears as a translation of Heb. *dōbrôt*. Berkeley renders it "floats" and this is much to be preferred. The RSV and NASB also translate *rapsōdôt* as "raft" in II Chr 2:16. Since neither Heb. word appears in any other context, it is difficult to see any distinction between them. Both refer to a number of cedar logs, probably roped together in some fashion, which were floated down to Solomon by Hiram of Tyre. There is no clear example of the word raft in the OT in the sense of a water conveyance.

RAGAU (rā'gô). A name transliterated from the Gr. of Lk 3:35. It appears in a genealogy that is likely that of Mary, the mother of Jesus. The name should more properly be translated Reu as in the ASV, RSV, and Berkeley. Reu is obtained by a comparison of the context with Gen 11:18–20, which is a list of Shem's descendants. Reu is the first-mentioned progeny of Peleg in the passage which is background for the Abrahamic narrative. Even though the genealogies above operate in reverse to each other, it is clear that Ragau is the NT equivalent of Reu.

RAGUEL (răg'yoo-ĕl). The name of Moses' father-in-law which means "friend of God." He bears this name in Num 10:29, but several modern versions change it to Reuel (ASV, RSV, Berkeley). The name Jethro (*q.v.*) is also ascribed to this man (Ex 3:1; cf. Ex 2:18). It is likely that Jethro was his official title (Jos *Ant.* ii. 12.1). For one person to bear more than one name can hardly be called uncommon among the Hebrews. Raguel was the prince-priest of Midian and father of Zipporah. Attempts to solve the problem of the multiplicity of names by seeing a more elastic sense in the Heb. *ḥōthēn,* "father-in-law," or *'āb,* "father," or *bat,* "daughter," cannot be said to be very satisfactory.

RAHAB (rā'hăb)

1. The name (Heb. *rahab*) of a sea monster, used as a figurative expression for pride, as in Job 9:13; 26:12 (ASV, RSV). Elsewhere it is a symbolic name for Egypt, proud, boasting, pierced with divine judgments, as in Ps 87:4; 89:10; Isa 30:7 (ASV, RSV); 51:9. See N. K. Kiessling, "Antecedents of the Medieval Dragon in Sacred History," JBL, LXXXIX (1970), 167–177.

2. An inhabitant of Jericho at the time of Israel's invasion of Canaan. Her story is told in Josh 2:1–22; 6:17–25, and reference is made to her in Jas 2:25, and in Heb 11:31 where her salvation is ascribed to her faith.

Rahab (Heb. *rāḥāb*) is generally referred to as the harlot (*q.v.*). The word so translated (*zônâ*) may simply mean a woman who has dealings with men (KB, p. 261). Hence it is conjectured that the term can also mean an innkeeper, and this is favored by some commentators (on the basis of Jos *Ant.* v.1.2), especially by those who hold that she became the wife of Joshua. According to the code of Hammurabi (*q.v.*) the tavern or inn (*bît sabītu*) was a place where visitors could lodge or assemble, though the presence of outlaws had to be reported to the palace (ANET, p. 170, ¶108–111). The *sabītu* was the woman wine seller and thus the innkeeper in charge of the establishment, to whom foreigners would resort but not necessarily in an immoral way. The *sabītu* or ale-wife plays a similar role in conversing with her guest Gilgamesh in the epic of that name (ANET, pp. 90-91). Thus it is assumed that the Heb. expression *bêt 'îshâ zônâ*, "the house of a woman, a harlot" (Josh 2:1) is equivalent to the Babylonian term. However, the references to Rahab in Hebrews and James use the Gr. word *pornē*, which definitely means "harlot," and that is decisive for those who hold the plenary inspiration of the Scriptures.

Another question is whether the Rahab of Mt 1:5 is the Rahab of Jericho. There is no mention in the OT of Rahab's marriage to Salmon, but there would seem to be no point to the mention of her name in the genealogy if it belonged to some other Rahab totally unknown in the OT record. The whole tone of Josh 6:17-25 indicates that she was accepted into the camp of Israel with every honor, and it is therefore not too strange that she should marry into an honorable family. There is no problem with the time factor. We take it, therefore, that the Rahab of the genealogy of Jesus is Rahab the harlot of Jericho.

While accepting the designation "harlot" on the strength of the NT reference, this does not rule out the possibility of Rahab's house being an inn, which indeed may explain the spies' choice of that place for a lodging. It may not have been the best security measure to go to a place open to the public, but it was a convenient place, right on the wall. Evidently Rahab's establishment was under "police" surveillance, and it was not long before the presence of the spies was reported to the king. The demand of the king that she surrender her guests stirred her to action. Hiding the men under stalks of flax on the roof in case of a search, she threw the king's messengers off the track, sending them to the fords of Jordan in pursuit of the men on her rooftop.

Then it was that Rahab made her great confession of faith in the God of the Hebrews, based on the reports of His wonderful deliverance of His people from Egypt and the conquest of the kings E of the Jordan. She revealed the terror that had seized the hearts of the Canaanites, and made her plea for her own life and that of her family. The spies gave their promise, which later was honored by Joshua, their leader (Josh 6:17, 23, 25). They agreed on a token of good faith, namely, a cord made of scarlet yarn to be hung in her window (2:18). Then she lowered them through that window by a rope to make good their escape. If her lying to the king's messengers (Josh 2:3-6) disturbs us, let us remember that she was only emerging out of heathendom, and had much to learn regarding the character of God. That this woman should become "a mother in Israel" and an ancestor of Christ after the flesh is another mark of the grace of God.

It is interesting that both the writer to the Hebrews and James should bear witness to Rahab, the one to emphasize the faith which inspired her deed, and the other to stress the deed as the necessary expression of faith.

J. C. M.

RAHAM (rā'hăm). One of the descendants of Caleb, a son of Shema, and father of Jorkoam (I Chr 2:44). By some, Jorkoam is regarded as a place of which Raham was the prince or founder.

RAHEL (rā'hĕl). This is the spelling accorded Rachel in Jer 31:15. The Heb. word is the same as that which is regularly translated Rachel (*râḥēl*). All the modern versions translate this word as Rachel (*q.v.*).

RAIL. The idea of uttering abusive, reproachful language is conveyed by the Heb. *ḥārap* ("taunt"). Typical usages would be the insulting letters of Sennacherib to Hezekiah (II Chr 32:17), and the ridicule of the psalmist's enemies (Ps 42:10). The Heb. *'îṭ* expresses the idea of a swooping bird of prey (I Sam 25:14; cf. 14:32 [*qere*]; 15:19). The NT *blasphēmeō* and kindred forms are in close parallel to the above (Mk 15:29; Lk 23:39), and have come to convey the idea of irreverence toward God, a meaning not inherent in the words themselves. An even sharper word is *loidoria*, "railing" or "insult" (I Pet 3:9; cf. I Cor 5:11). *See* Reproach; Revile.

RAIMENT. *See* Dress.

RAIMENT, CHANGE OF. *See* Change of Raiment.

RAIN. Rainfall was of particular importance to the peoples living in the land of the Bible. Drought (*q.v.*), with consequent famine, was a frequent and much-dreaded calamity. Not all were so fortunate as the Egyptians, who could depend upon the annual inundation of the Nile. The spring and fall rainy periods in Palestine are referred to as the "latter rain" (Heb. *malqôsh*) and "former rain" (*môreh, yôreh*), respectively. Between them is the hot, dry summer.

The Heb. *geshem* may mean a heavy rain (I Kgs 18:45; Ezr 10:9, 13), and occurs in the flood account (Gen 7:12; 8:2). More frequently found is *māṭār*, the common word for rain (e.g., II Sam 23:4; Prov 26:1; Isa 4:6). The Gr. *brochē* in Jesus' account of the two foundations (Mt 7:25, 27) means a torrential rain or violent storm. The usual Gr. word for rain is *huetos* (e.g., Acts 28:2).

The uniform recognition of the Bible is that God controls the weather and gives or withholds the rain (Lev 26:4; Deut 11:14, 17; 28:12, 24; I Sam 12:17-18; I Kgs 8:35-36; 17:1, 14; 18:1; Job 5:10; 28:26; 37:6; Ps 147:8; Isa 30:23; Amos 4:7; Zech 10:1; Mt 5:45; Acts 14:17; Heb 6:7; Jas 5:18; Rev 11:6). The OT writers had a simple understanding of the cycle of evaporation that forms the clouds to give rain and fill the rivers and the seas (Job 36:27-29, NASB; 38:25-28, 34-38; Ps 135:7; Prov 3:20; Jer 10:13; 51:16).

According to Gen 2:5 (cf. 7:4) the earth may not have experienced rain, as we know it today, before the Flood (*q.v.*). Instead, a mist (*q.v.*) used to rise from the earth and water the whole surface of the ground (Gen 2:6, NASB). Some have explained this phenomenon as the result of a vapor canopy that enveloped the earth.

See Palestine, III.B; Bow in the Clouds; Hail, Hailstones; Latter Rain; Lightning; Storm; Thunder; Water.

B. C. S.

RAINBOW. *See* Bow in the Clouds.

RAISIN. *See* Food; Plants: Vine.

RAKEM (rā'kĕm). A descendant of Manasseh, son of Sheresh (I Chr 7:16). This is another form of Rekem (*q.v.*).

RAKKATH (răk'ĭth). The name of a city in Naphtali (Josh 19:35). It was located W of the Sea of Galilee and was formerly believed by some Jewish authorities to have been the site on which Tiberias was built. It is now tentatively identified with Tell Eqlatiyeh, also called Tell Raqqat, by a perennial spring *c.* one and a half miles NW of Tiberias on the lakeshore.

RAKKON (răk'ŏn). The name of a city in Dan, not far from Joppa. It is referred to in Josh 19:46 as *hāraqqôn*. The fact that it is not found in the text of the LXX has led some to think that it is a repetition in part of a preceding word (*me-jarkon*). It is difficult to evaluate this opinion with any degree of conclusiveness. The current tendency is to identify Rakkon with Tell er-Reqqeit, *c.* two miles N of the mouth of the Yarkon River.

RAM. *See* Animals: Sheep, I.15.

RAM, BATTERING. *See* Armor, Arms.

RAMA. *See* Ramah 1.

RAMAH (rā'mȧ). Ramah means "height" and was frequently used as a place name.

1. A town in the tribal area of Benjamin (Josh 18:25) in the vicinity of Bethel (Jud 4:5), Gibeah (Jud 19:13), and Beth-aven (Hos 5:8). Robinson's identification of Ramah with er-Ram, five and a half miles N of Jerusalem, still stands.

Baasha of Israel began to fortify it against Asa of Judah (I Kgs 15:16-17), but an attack by Syrians from the N forced him to abandon the project. Asa then dismantled the fortifications of Ramah and used the stones to build two forts of his own at Geba and Mizpah (I Kgs 15:18-22; II Chr 16:1-6). Thus Ramah's proximity to the border between those rival kingdoms is clearly seen.

Church of the Virgin Mary, Ramah of Naphtali. IIS

Ramah stood in the line of Assyrian advance toward Jerusalem in Isaiah's oracle (Isa 10:29) when one column of Sennacherib's army advanced through the hill country in 701 B.C. Jeremiah describes it as the scene of Rachel's weeping for her children (Jer 31:15; cf. Mt 2:18, KJV "Rama"; *see* Innocents, Slaughter of). Some of its citizens were among the post-Exilic returnees (Ezr 2:26; Neh 7:30). Its appearance in the list of settlements (Neh 11:33), some of which were outside the territorial bounds of the Judean province, may mean that a truly Judean population had remained there throughout the period of exile.

2. A town in the hill country of Ephraim, doubtless to be equated with Ramathaim-zophim (I Sam 1:1, 19; 2:11), where Samuel's parents lived. It was not only Samuel's birthplace, but after the destruction of Shiloh he made it his main headquarters on his judicial circuit (I Sam 7:17; 8:4; cf. 15:34; 16:13). To this place David fled from the wrath of Saul (I Sam 19:18-23; 20:1). Samuel was buried there (I Sam 25:1; 28:3).

Since Elkanah, Samuel's father, was a member of the Levitical Zuphites (I Sam 1:1; I Chr 6:33-35), who had apparently received their inheritance in the territory of Ephraim (Josh 21:5; I Chr 6:22-26, 35, 66ff.), it was probably at Ramah in the land of Zuph that Saul first met Samuel (I Sam 9:5-6, 18). Samuel's directions for Saul's return journey from there (I Sam 10:2-8) need not be taken as an indication that the land of Zuph was S of Gibeah, especially if the tomb of Rachel (*q.v.*) is located at Ramah 1 above (cf. Jer 31:15). Grollenberg identifies Ramathaim-zophim with modern Rentis (*Atlas of the Bible*, p. 160), halfway between Joppa and Shiloh. Other suggestions are Beit Rimah (12 miles NW of Bethel) and Ramallah (nine miles N of Jerusalem). A person returning S from any of these locations would surely come near to Ramah 1 before approaching Gibeah. In NT times its name seems to have been Arimathea (*q.v.*).

3. A fortified town in the territory of Naphtali (Josh 19:36). It may be identified with Khir-

bet Zeitun er-Rama, about two and a quarter miles SW of the modern village of er-Rama. The potsherds collected in this site testify to its existence from the Early Iron Age until the Persian period. In the Hellenistic age the village was apparently moved to its present location at er-Rama.

4. A town on the border of Asher's tribal inheritance (Josh 19:29). Its location will be determined by one's interpretation of the boundary described in Josh 19:28–29. Since this border extended N as far as "Sidon the Great" even though it had to bend back S to reach the sea at the "fortified city of Tyre," one should look for Ramah somewhere between Sidon and Tyre rather than at er-Ramia, which is about 13 miles SSE of Tyre.

5. One of Simeon's villages (Josh 19:8); the same as Ramoth of the Negeb (I Sam 30:27), also known as Baalath-beer.

6. An abbreviation for Ramoth-gilead (*q.v.*) used twice (II Kgs 8:29; II Chr 22:6).

A. F. R.

RAMATHAIM-ZOPHIM (răm'*ȧ*-thā'ĭm-zō̆'fĭm). *See* Ramah 2.

RAMATHITE (rā'm*ȧ*-thīt). This term appears in I Chr 27:27 in connection with Shimei, the overseer of the vineyards of David. Since several towns were designated Ramah it is impossible to say from which of them he came.

RAMATH-LEHI (rā'măth-lē'hī). A place mentioned in connection with Samson's slaughter of a thousand Philistines (Jud 15:17). It was known simply as Lehi (*q.v.*), but was called the longer name by Samson. The name means "high place of the jawbone." It was situated a few miles NW of Jerusalem.

RAMATH-MIZPEH (rā'măth-mĭz'pĕ). A city in Gad (Josh 13:26) not far from the Jabbok River in Gilead, the name meaning "high place of the watchtower." It is possible that this site was the location of an earlier sanctuary where Laban and Jacob made their covenant (Gen 31:44–55). Laban called this place Jegar-sahadutha, but Jacob named it Galeed, Mizpah. It is held by some that these locations are identical with Ramoth-gilead. *See* Mizpah 1.

RAMATH OF THE SOUTH (rā'măth). The KJV form of this name, which appears as Ramah of the Negeb in RSV of Josh 19:8. In the apportionment at Shiloh of the territory of Canaan (Josh 18:10), this town is designated as Simeon's (Josh 19:9). The name suggests that it was in the extreme S, and is possibly another name for Baalath-beer. Ramath of the South does not appear in the list of Judah's holdings (Josh 15:21–32), nor the Simeon list in I Chr 4:28–33. It is likely the same as south Ramoth of I Sam 30:27 (Ramoth of the Negeb, RSV).

In 1967 an ostracon was found at Tell Arad urging the commander of Arad (*q.v.*) to send men from the various border forts to help defend Ramath-negeb against an anticipated Edomite attack (*c.* 598 or 587 B.C.). On the basis of this letter Ramath-negeb has been identified with Khirbet Ghazzeb (today called Horvat 'Uzza) *c.* six miles SSE of Tell Arad, at the head of Wadi el-Qeini which descends toward the Dead Sea (Y. Aharoni, "Three Hebrew Ostraca from Arad," BASOR #197 [1970], 16–28).

B. C. S.

RAMESES (răm'*ĕ*-sēz). Also called Raamses. An Egyptian city located in the NE section of the Delta. The name is also applied to an area of the Delta in which Joseph settled his father and brothers when they migrated from Palestine in time of famine (Gen 47:11). Rameses was one of the two store-cities built for Pharaoh by Israelite slave-labor (Ex 1:11; the LXX adds a third, "On, which is Heliopolis"). From Rameses Israel set out on the Exodus (Ex 12:37; Num 33:3, 5), making Succoth the first stop.

The city of Rameses has not been identified with certainty. Often it is taken to be identical with the city named "House of Rameses," built by Rameses II. "House of Rameses" is identified by Montet and Gardiner as the present San el Hagar, also recognized as Avaris, Tanis, and biblical Zoan. Hamza, Habachi and Uphill have supported the site of Qantir, *c.* 11 miles S. Gardiner earlier had concluded that Rameses was Pelusium, an identification which is not compatible with the topographical information of Exodus since Pelusium is at the edge of the wilderness, while Tanis is correctly two days' journey from "the edge of the wilderness" (Num 33:5–6). (For Pelusium, see Alan H. Gardiner, JEA, V [1918], 127–138, 179–200, 242–271. For San el Hagar, see Gardiner, JEA, XIX [1933], 122–128; *Ancient Egyptian Onomastica,* II, 169, 171–175, 278–279; *Egypt of the Pharaohs,* p. 258. For Qantir, see M. Hamza, ASAE, XXX [1930], 31–68, esp. 64–68; Labib Habachi, ASAE, LII [1954], 443–562; Eric P. Uphill, "Pithom and Raamses: Their Location and Significance,"

Ramah of Benjamin. HFV

JNES, XXVII [1968], 291–316; XXVIII [1969], 15–39.

The name of the city undoubtedly is associated with that of a royal builder or renovator. Rameses was the most common royal name of Egyptian Dynasties XIX and XX. Of the kings who bore the name, Rameses II, a very energetic egotistic monarch, was extremely active as builder, restorer, and usurper of the monuments of his predecessors. Ruling in the 13th cen. B.C., he has often been identified as the Pharaoh of the Oppression or of the Exodus, in spite of chronological incongruities with OT data. If the Gen 47 reference is related to the kings of Dynasties XIX-XX, the name must be a substitution for an earlier name of the area. Proponents of the 15th cen. date of the Exodus must regard the name of the city as a name predating those dynasties or as a renaming. In the latter instance they must identify as Raamses a site which was occupied during both the 15th cen. (or earlier) and the Ramesside period.

See Exodus, The; City, Treasure.

C. E. D.

RAMIAH (rȧ-mī'ȧ). One of the sons of Parosh (Ezr 10:25). He was among those who put away their pagan wives at the command of Ezra.

RAMOTH (rā'mŏth)

1. A city in the territory of Gad, also called Ramoth-gilead (*q.v.*). Citations are found in Deut 4:43; Josh 20:8; 21:38; I Chr 6:80.

2. A city of Issachar (I Chr 6:73), for which Josh 21:28–29 substitutes Jarmuth (*q.v.*).

3. A town in the Negeb (I Sam 30:27, RSV, NASB). *See* Ramath of the South.

4. A Jew who had married a foreign wife (Ezr 10:29, KJV); called Jeremoth in RSV, Jeramoth in NASB.

RAMOTH-GILEAD (rā'mŏth-gĭl'ē-ȧd). An important town in Gilead near the border of Syria. Located 25 or 30 miles E of the Jordan River on a line roughly parallel with Jezreel and Megiddo, it is identified by Nelson Glueck with the modern Tell Rāmîth. Moses designated it a city of refuge for the tribe of Gad (Deut 4:41–43). The region had good pasture land, and Solomon stationed one of 12 district officers there to secure food for the large royal household (I Kgs 4:7, 13).

Because of its strategic importance Ramoth-gilead was the object of frequent battles between Israel and Syria and changed hands a number of times. King Ahab was killed in a battle for it after he refused to heed the prophet Micaiah's warning (I Kgs 22:1–40). Joram, his grandson, was wounded in a later battle there (II Kgs 8:28–29). Elisha sent his agent to Ramoth-gilead to anoint Jehu, a commander stationed there, to succeed Joram as king of Israel (II Kgs 9:1–10). From there Jehu drove to Jezreel to lead a successful but bloody revolt.

It may be identical with Ramath-mizpeh (Josh 13:24, 26), perhaps the same as Mizpah, the home of Jephthah (Jud 11:34). *See* Mizpah 2.

N. B. B.

RAMPART. The outer wall of a fortification, or, by figure, the area between the inner and outer wall. It is a translation of the Heb. *ḥēl* or *ḥêl* which appears about ten times. It bears such translations as "trench," "wall," "host," "bulwark," and "army." The KJV translates it as "rampart" in Lam 2:8 and Nah 3:8, and the RSV adds several more (II Sam 20:15; Nah 2:1; Ps 48:13).

RAM'S HORN. *See* Music.

RAMS' SKINS. The skins of male sheep were utilized in the construction of the tabernacle (*q.v.*) after proper preparation by dyeing or tanning. They are first mentioned in Ex 25:5 where God instructs Moses to advise the people to bring such skins for work on the tabernacle. Rams' skins were to be the inner layer, the outer being the so-called badger (KJV) or porpoise (NASB) skins (Ex 26:14). The usual Heb. phrase is *'ōrōt ēlim me' oddāmîm*, "rams' skins dyed red."

RANGE. As a verb, the word "ranging" is used once in the KJV to translate the Heb. *shāqaq*, which describes a charging bear (Prov 28:15; cf. RSV). As a noun, range may mean a "range" of mountains (Job 39:8, KJV; Heb. *y^etûr*), or possibly he who ranges the mountains (RSV). The OT *s^edērâ* is used of a row or rank of soldiers (II Kgs 11:8, 15). As a cooking term the *kîrayim* in Lev 11:35 is probably a hearth for supporting two pots (NASB marg.).

RANSOM. This term normally carries the connotation of deliverance from some sort of bondage by the payment of a price. The following basic meanings may be noted for the biblical words referring to this concept.

1. *Covering*. The Heb. *kōper* means a "cover," and expresses the idea of obliteration. This concept, in fact, may be rooted in its connection with the Aramaic *k^epar* ("to wash away"), if the opinion of W. Robertson Smith is correct (cf. Ex 30:12; Job 33:24; 36:18).

2. *Freedom.* This use is illustrated by the Heb. *pidyôn* in Ex 21:30, where it refers to what is purchased, i.e., liberty. The verbal idea to free is expressed by *gā'al*, which is used to describe the deliverance from Egypt (Isa 51:10), and the buying back of a field (Ruth 4:4, "redeem").

3. *Price*. The Gr. *lytron* was the release price for a slave. Jesus used this word of His own death (Mt 20:28). Approximately the same significance is conveyed by *antilytron* (I Tim 2:6), except that the idea of exchange is stressed. As ransom, Christ redeems sinners

from the bondage of sin and the condemnation of the law.

See Atonement; Redemption; Salvation.

B. C. S.

RAPHA, RAPHAH (rā'fȧ)

1. The fifth son of Benjamin (I Chr 8:2), but not mentioned in the list of Gen 46:21.

2. The first son of Binea and father of Eleasah, the eighth in descent from Jonathan of Saul (I Chr 8:37). He is called Rephaiah in I Chr 9:43. The Heb. word *rāpâ* or *rāpā'* is translated "the giant" in II Sam 21:16, 20, 22 and I Chr 20:4, 6, 8. ISBE suggests that the name in these passages is an eponym. Berkeley substitutes the name Raphah (except in I Chr 20:4 where the plural form is rendered Rephaim).

RAPHU (rā'fū). The father of Palti, the Benjamite spy sent into Canaan by Moses (Num 13:9).

RAPTURE, THE. The NT teaches that the believer will be removed from the earth by Christ prior to the outpouring of the wrath of God which precedes the second coming of Christ to reign over the earth (I Thess 4:14–17; 5:9; cf. I Cor 15:51–53). There are three main views as to the time of the rapture.

1. Pretribulation rapture theory. This teaches that Christ can come to take away His own at any time, maintaining that this event is preceded by no specific signs (Mt 24:36, 42ff., 50; 25:13; Rev 3:3). The rapture will be succeeded by a seven year period during which the Antichrist will make a treaty with Israel, only to break it after three and a half years. The last three and a half years of the Antichrist's reign will be the time of the Great Tribulation spoken of by Christ in Mt 24:21. This will be followed by the return of Christ with His saints to rule the world in righteousness (Zech 14:3–5; Jude 14).

2. Midtribulation rapture theory. According to this view (cf. J. Oliver Buswell, Jr., *Systematic Theology,* II, 456), believers will be taken away halfway through the seven year period of the covenant made by the Antichrist with Israel. Christ will come "as a thief in the night," that is, suddenly and unexpectedly as far as the unbeliever is concerned (Mt 24:43; I Thess 5:4; Rev 16:15), but not as far as the believer is concerned because there will be signs. The world will appear to be at peace (I Thess 5:3), the temple will have been rebuilt (Mt 24:15), a truce will have been made already for three and a half years by the Jews with a great dictator. Then the temple will suddenly be desecrated (Mt 24:15; cf. Dan 9:27). The Christian will escape the Great Tribulation.

3. Posttribulation rapture theory. According to this view, near the end of the Great Tribulation, and just prior to the pouring out of the seven vials of God's wrath, the rapture occurs. The reasoning behind this view is: (*a*) Paul says that the Christian is not appointed to wrath even as others (I Thess 5:9). (*b*) The mention of Christ's coming as a thief in the night is found very late in the book of Revelation, in fact, between the sixth and seventh vials of wrath (Rev 16:15; cf. Mt 24:43; I Thess 5:4). (*c*) The Christian has never escaped tribulation and persecution at any earlier time in history, and why should he do so at the end times? (*d*) Christ speaks in Mt 24:15 ff. in such a way as to imply the believer will enter the Tribulation when He says, "When ye . . . see the abomination of desolation . . . flee into the mountains."

Wise premillennialists agree to differ with those holding other views, since this concerns a matter of minor importance compared with the whole question as to whether there will be a millennial kingdom on the earth or not. The postrapturists stress that there would be no harm in hardening the Christian and preparing him to face the Great Tribulation even if he does not go through it, but there would be great damage in softening him if he is to have to go through it. The prerapturist, especially, would stress the distinction between Israel and the Church, maintaining that the Great Tribulation period concerns only Israel.

See Coming of Christ; Eschatology.

R. A. K.

Reception hall at the palace, Ras Shamra. JR

RAS SHAMRA (räs-shäm'rȧ). The present-day name of Ugarit, an ancient seaport **c.** seven miles N of modern Latakia in Syria (***q.v.***). It was the closest mainland city to Cyprus. Archaeological findings there have been so important that the French under C. F. A. Schaeffer have conducted about 25 seasons of digging, beginning in 1929. *See* Archaeology. The Bible student's interest in Ras Shamra is primarily a result of the Canaanite mythological texts uncovered there. Now for the first time scholars know Canaanite religion through its own literature (ANET, pp. 129–155), although it has long been known through such things as temples and cult objects.

The various views of older liberal scholars

could be paraphrased in the statement, "Israelite theology was simply the cream of Canaanite religion." The Ras Shamra texts, however, demonstrate that Canaanite mythology and Israelite theology are as far apart as east and west (*see* Myth, Mythology). The Canaanite literature only strengthens the archaeological evidence that the Canaanites had the most depraved of all ancient religions. El was formerly the head of the Canaanite pantheon, but he was being replaced by the young, dynamic Baal, a storm-god similar to Zeus but more depraved. There were three major goddesses, Ashtaroth (in OT nomenclature). Anath (after whom Jeremiah's home town of Anathoth was named), and Asherah. The last is best known in Scripture as the goddess in the episode of Elijah on Mount Carmel (I Kgs 18:19, RSV, NEB). The other goddesses shared the power of war, love, and fertility. *See* Gods, False.

Technical terms used in the Canaanite sacrificial system were similar to those in the Israelite, but the meanings of the two systems of worship were in striking contrast. Canaanite literature has also helped OT linguistic studies by opening up new features of vocabulary, grammar, and syntax. There are Canaanite poetic patterns similar to the early poems of the Bible. Some of the Canaanite legal practices, such as adoption within the family, are matched in Scripture, as Jacob's adoption of Ephraim and Manasseh.

J. L. K.

The Canaanite religious epics were recorded on clay tablets written in previously unknown cuneiform characters. After decipherment it was recognized as an alphabet of 30 signs, the Canaanite or NW Semitic language used at Ugarit (*see* Alphabet). These texts were discovered during the first season of excavation in the library of the official building where the chief priest had lived. It was situated on the highest part of the mound between two Canaanite temples, one dedicated to the worship of Baal and the other to that of Dagon. These buildings and the tablets belonged to the uppermost level, which may be dated to the 14th and 13th cen. B.C. The city seems to have been destroyed, and never rebuilt, shortly after 1200 B.C., probably by the invading Sea Peoples who ravaged the Syro-Palestinian coast at that time.

Resuming excavations in 1948 after World War II, Claude F. A. Schaeffer and his team uncovered the great palace in a number of successive seasons. It is nearly 400 feet long N-S and 270 feet wide E-W. In it were discovered the royal archives with administrative, legal, and economic documents. They were largely written in the international language of that period, the Akkadian (the same as the language of the Amarna tablets, *q.v.*). From these texts a large amount of historical data has been gleaned, for they mention the names of at least 12 kings of Ugarit, and cover the 18th to the 13th. cen. B.C.

Schaeffer has recognized five main levels of occupation, beginning with a Neolithic culture (stratum V). The next dates to the Chalcolithic period (*c.* 4000-3500 B.C.). Level III (*c.* 3500-2100) reveals by the pottery styles much influence from Mesopotamia, at a time when there were known military campaigns to the Mediterranean and trading contacts. Level IV includes the Middle Bronze Age ruins (2100-1500), the time of the 12th Dynasty ambassadors from Egypt, the Hyksos, the Hurrians, and the early Hittites. The final period (stratum I, 1500-1150) is the one best known, both from the evidence from Ras Shamra and from inscriptions found in Egypt and elsewhere. Thutmose III (1504–1450) stationed an Egyptian garrison in Ugarit. Later the Hittite monarch Suppiluliumas conquered the area and made the king of Ugarit his vassal. An earthquake shook the city and its port in the 14th cen., so that Ugarit never regained its former splendor. Nevertheless Mycenaean merchants from Greece seem to have established a trading colony there which helped to maintain its importance.

See Canaan, Canaanites.

Bibliography. William F. Albright, *Yahweh and the Gods of Canaan,* Garden City: Doubleday, 1968. George R. Driver, *Canaanite Myths and Legends,* Edinburgh: T. & T. Clark, 1956. John Gray, *The Legacy of Canaan: The Ras Shamra Texts and Their Relevance to the Old Testament,* Leiden: Brill, 1957; "Ugarit," TAOTS, pp. 145–167. Arvid S. Kapelrud, *Baal in the Ras Shamra Texts,* Copenhagen: G. E. C. Gad, 1952; "Ugarit," IDB, IV, 724–732; *The Violent Goddess: Anat in the Ras Shamra Texts,* Oslo: Universitetsforlaget, 1969. Charles F. Pfeiffer, *Ras Shamra and the Bible,* Grand Rapids: Baker, 1962.

J. R.

RAVEN. *See* Animals, III. 44.

RAVIN, RAVENING. In its verbal form ravin comes from *ṭārap,* which is especially descriptive of the rending and tearing of wild beasts (Gen 37:33). Jacob employed this word in his description of the character of Benjamin (Gen 49:27). It also portrays those who will eagerly await the death of the Crucified One (Ps 22:13), and the prophets and princes of apostate Judah (Ezk 22:25, 27).

The word may also be applied to the object of prey as in Nah 2:12. The KJV translates *harpagē* and *harpax* as "ravening" (Lk 11:39 and Mt 7:15, respectively). Thayer suggests "rapine" or "pillage" as a translation of the former, while Deissmann believes "swindler" to be a good equivalent to the latter when the adjective is used as a noun in Lk 18:11. Actually, it is difficult to improve on the KJV and ASV rendering of "extortioner."

RAZOR. *See* Hair; Occupations: Barber.

REAIAH, REAIA (rē-ā'yȧ)

1. The son of Shobal and father of Jahath, descendants of Caleb (I Chr 4:2), apparently called Haroeh in I Chr 2:52.

2. The son of Micah and father of Baal, descendants of Reuben (I Chr 5:5; KJV, Reaia).

3. One of the families of the Nethinim or temple servants (Ezr 2:47; Neh 7:50).

REAPING. The act of harvesting the ripened crop, performed by cutting the grain stocks with a sickle (Mt 4:29) usually of flint in OT times. Sometimes used figuratively, as reaping a harvest of people for Jesus Christ (Jn 4:36–38), or as a picture of judgment (Mt 13:30, 39; Rev 14:15–16).

REBA (rē'bȧ). A Midianite king or prince who was slain by Israel in the plains of Moab. He was involved in the moral treachery that reduced Israel to lewd idolatry (Num 31:8; Josh 13:21).

REBECCA. *See* Rebekah.

REBEKAH (rĕ-bĕk'ȧ). A daughter of Bethuel, sister of Laban, wife of Isaac, and mother of Esau and Jacob. A servant of Abraham was sent to obtain a wife for Isaac (Gen 24). When he arrived at the well outside the city of Nahor in Padan-aram, he asked for a sign that he might make the proper choice. When Rebekah came with her pitcher, she offered to draw water for him and his camels. He took this as the requested sign. She was beautiful and her conduct indicated that she was generous and hospitable. He gave her expensive presents which he had brought, asked her name and if he could lodge at her father's house. When he was welcomed in her home, he would not accept the father's hospitality until he had explained his errand. When Rebekah's father and brother heard his story, they allowed her to decide whether she would leave home, go to a strange country, and marry a man she had never met. That she was given a choice indicates a custom in upper-class patriarchal families. She left her home and became Isaac's wife (Gen 24:66–67), and shared his prosperous life near Beer-sheba

A similar story to that of Abraham and Sarah tells of Isaac passing Rebekah off as his sister in the court of Abimelech (Gen 26:1–16). He was reproved when the king discovered their true relationship.

After 20 years of barrenness (Gen 25:21, 26), Rebekah bore twin sons, Esau and Jacob. When he was grown, Esau married two Hittite women in spite of the disapproval of his parents. Jacob was the favorite of his mother and she approved his purchase of the birthright from his brother. Even then she did not leave things entirely in God's hands, but persuaded Jacob to obtain the blessing by deceit. When Jacob had to flee from the wrath of Esau, Rebekah urged him to go to her people in Padan-aram, and she presumably died before his return. She was buried in the cave of Machpelah near her mother-in-law Sarah (Gen 49:31).

A. W. W.

RECEIPT OF CUSTOMS. All three occurrences of this phrase in the NT are found in connection with the call of Jesus to Matthew the publican (Mt 9:9; Mk 2:14; Lk 5:27). "Levi" is used in the last two passages. The Gr. word involved is *telōnion,* and refers in the NT to "the place of toll" (ASV). The same word may indicate the tax itself, but this is not the case in the NT. "Tax office" is suggested by Thayer and followed by RSV and NASB, while MM give "revenue office." NEB has "custom-house."

RECEIVER. One who tested gold or silver by weighing it was known as a receiver (Isa 33:18). The Heb. *shāqal* is employed a number of times in the OT to express various particular applications of the idea of weighing, both literal (II Sam 14:26, of Absalom weighing his hair), and figurative (Job 6:2, of Job crying out for someone to measure his grief). In Isa 33:18 the point seems to be that ultimately great effort will be required to recall the dangers presently threatening.

RECHAB, RECHABITES (rē'kăb, rĕk'ȧ-bīts)

1. One of the sons of Rimmon, a Beerothite of the tribe of Benjamin. He was one of the captains of Ishbosheth in his war with David. After the death of Abner, Rechab and his brother Baanah murdered Ishbosheth and brought his head to David. David had them executed for their brutal murder of an innocent man instead of rewarding them (II Sam 4:2–12).

2. The father of Jonadab (*q.v.*) and founder of the family of Rechabites. Rechab may have been from one of the Kenite families that came into Palestine with the Israelites (I Chr 2:55). In the days of the divided kingdom, Rechab determined that it was the Palestinian culture that was the cause of the apostasy and immorality of the people, and commanded his sons to return to the old nomadic way of life in all its simplicity. Jonadab, the leader of the Rechabites in the days of Jehu, assisted that king in his destruction of Baal worship (II Kgs 10:15, 23). In the days of Jeremiah, the prophet used the Rechabites as an object lesson. He brought them to the house of the Lord and offered them wine. They refused because of their loyalty to their ancestor Rechab and his command. Jeremiah used their faithfulness as a rebuke to the unfaithfulness of Israel to Yahweh. The Lord promised that because of their faithfulness they should "not want a man to stand before me forever" (Jer 35:19). Rab Judah is said to have recorded that Rechabite daughters married Levites and thus the promise was fulfilled. Hegesippus said that "Rechabite priests" interceded for James, the brother of Christ, but failed to save his life (Eusebius, *History,* ii.23).

3. Malchiah, the "son of Rechab," repaired the dung gate of Jerusalem under Nehemiah (Neh 3:14). He may have been the head of the Rechabites after the Exile.

P. C. J.

RECHAH (rē'kȧ). A city in Judah mentioned in I Chr 4:12. Eshton and Tehinnah are said to be "men of Rechah." In the Targum of Rabbi Joseph they are called "the men of the great Sanhedrin," which may be explained by reading *răbbâh* for *rēkâh*. If a city is meant, its location is not known to date. The RSV uses the form "Recah" as does the Berkeley.

RECOMPENSE. *See* Punishment; Rewards; Wages.

RECONCILIATION. Words in the NT signifying reconciliation are all based on the Gr. root *allag,* with different prepositional prefixes, most common of which is *kata.* The etymological meaning is "change," but the usage always includes the bringing together of two or more parties by the removal of grounds or causes of disharmony. Reconciliation is necessary to do away with existing enmity.

The doctrine of reconciliation has to do with the restoration of fellowship between man the sinner and God the holy Creator, through Christ the Redeemer. Because of his evil deeds man is declared to be an enemy of God (Rom 5:8; Col 1:21; Jas 4:4). Liberal theologians who deny the penal, propitiatory, substitutional satisfaction of divine justice by the objective provision of the atonement point out that in the NT God is never the object of reconciliation. They deny need for vindication of divine justice, and insist that all that is necessary for reconciliation between God and man is a change in man. They object to Wesley's great hymn "Arise, My Soul," especially to the words "My God is reconciled."

The fact that the sinner is the one to be reconciled to God (II Cor 5:20) constitutes no argument against the need of propitiation (*q.v.*) toward God. This should be evident from one of the NT passages in which the word is used in a nonsoteriological sense. In Mt 5:23-24 the one whom Christ commanded to be reconciled to his brother was the offender, against whom the brother had a grievance. The only reconciliation possible was through the objective removal of the grievance or the satisfaction of justice.

That there is a change in God's attitude when a sinner is reconciled to Him is abundantly evidenced by the many scriptures which declare God's wrath toward the unregenerate sinner, and the removal of His wrath when the sinner is justified (see, e.g., Jn 3:36).

Perhaps one reason the biblical writers speak of man as the object of reconciliation is that in changing from wrath to favor, God's love and His ethical character do not change. His holy nature is immutable.

Central passages setting forth the doctrine of reconciliation are Rom 5:8-11; II Cor 5:18-21; Eph 2:16-18; Col 1:20-22. In each case the objective, propitiatory nature of the atonement is clearly indicated.

See Atonement; Christ, Passion of; Forgiveness; Wrath.

Bibliography. F. Büchsel, "*Katallassō,*" TDNT, I, 254-258. James Denney, *The Christian Doctrine of Reconciliation,* London: Hodder & Stoughton, 1917. Leon Morris, *The Apostolic Preaching of the Cross,* Grand Rapids: Eerdmans, 1956, pp. 186-223.

J. O. B.

RECORDER. An office of Israel's royal cabinet. Originated by David (II Sam 8:16), the office of recorder continued to be significant throughout the period of the monarchy (II Kgs 18:18). In developing his court, David apparently followed a pattern established in Egypt. This particular office was the equivalent to the Egyptian royal herald. A public relations office, he arranged royal ceremonies, scheduled appointments of other officers with the king, and prepared for the king's travels.

RED. *See* Colors.

RED HEIFER. *See* Sacrifices; Uncleanness.

RED SEA. Contrary to its name, this sea is as blue in color as any other part of the ocean surface. The origin of the word "red" in this name is not certain. There are several possibilities: (1) Surface reflections of the red granite mountains which surround parts of the sea. (2) The copper skinned Edomites, Himyarites, and Phoenicians who once inhabited areas along its shores. (3) The reddish corals which are to be found along its shores.

The Red Sea proper is about 1,500 miles long with an average breadth of about 150 miles. At the N end it terminates in a "Y" formation—each branch forming a gulf. The E prong is about 100 miles long and is known as the Gulf of Aqabah and joins the Arabah (valley leading to the Dead Sea). Saudi Arabia borders it on the E and the Sinai Peninsula on the W. On its N end stood the town of Elath, which is now undergoing modern development by the state of Israel. It is a petroleum pipe line terminus and a freight dock for heavy cargo. On the border near Ezion-geber (*q.v.*), a few miles to the E in Arab Jordan, are the archaeological remains of Solomon's seaport. Elath and Ezion-geber were both port cities for Solomon's ships (I Kgs 9:26).

The W prong (180 miles long and 20 miles broad) is known as the Gulf of Suez and forms the S terminus for the Suez Canal. In prehistoric times it extended much farther N and probably included what is now known as Lake Timsah and the Bitter Lakes. The shores of both lakes abound in reeds and may account for the Heb. term *yam sûph,* often translated "sea of reeds."

The sea was crossed by the Israelites under the leadership of Moses (Ex 14:15 ff.). It is quite possible that the point of the crossing has now been covered by the ever-shifting sands. The opinion of many scholars, however, is that the Red Sea crossed by the Israelites was the Gulf of Suez, but probably in the vicinity of the Bitter Lakes to which the gulf then extended. At the present time a strong wind blows from the N to the S for about nine months of the year. Therefore the E wind that parted the sea for Moses was unusual, truly an act of God (Ex 14:21). *See* Exodus, The.

H. A. Han.

RED SEA PASSAGE. *See* Exodus, The.

REDEEM. *See* Redeemer; Redemption.

REDEEMER. Only one Heb. word is translated "redeemer" in the KJV, the participial form *gō'ēl.* It is used 18 times in all, 13 times in Isaiah, usually with a pronoun suffix.

The verb from which this noun comes occurs frequently, and is related in meaning to OT and NT words signifying redemption, ransom, and atonement (*q.v.*).

The essential meaning of the word *gō'ēl* is "kinsman-redeemer." The functions of the *gō'ēl,* as indicated by the usage of the corresponding verb, include all kinds of actions whereby persons or properties were bought back or restored from alienation to their proper position and relationship. *See* Kinsman.

In every case in which the verbal noun *gō'ēl* is translated "redeemer," God (sometimes specifically the Messiah) is the Redeemer referred to; and always in His saving, protecting, and preserving activities. Most of the references are general. In several instances (Jer 50:34; Isa 43:14; 47:4; 48:17; 49:26) restoration from Babylon is mentioned or implied. Isa 59:20–21, as interpreted in Rom 11:26–27, is definitely eschatological (see also Isa 60:16; 63:16) and promises a future restoration of Israel by the Messiah.

The LXX several times translates *gō'ēl* by *lutrōtēs* or some form from the same root, indicating the payment of a ransom. In eight passages in Isaiah the word is translated by *ruomenos* or some related form, meaning one who rescues. In the one NT passage where *gō'ēl* is directly translated (Rom 11:26–27; from Isa 59:20–21) Paul uses *ruomenos,* which presents the Messiah as the rescuer.

From Paul's use of the word for "rescue" in Rom 7:24, as well as from the common NT use of "ransom" (Mt 20:28) and "redemption" (Heb 9:12), it is clear that Christ as our Redeemer is the One who makes atonement for our sin.

Of special significance is Job's appeal to his *gō'ēl* (19:25) in supreme confidence that his eternal future is in the hands of his Redeemer.

See Redemption.

J. O. B.

REDEMPTION. Deliverance from some form of bondage on the basis of the payment of a price by a redeemer (*q.v.*). Redemption is a concept basic to the biblical view of salvation.

In the OT redemption is integrally related to the family, social, and national life of Israel. The individual Israelite could function as a redeemer by paying a ransom for the release of a slave (Lev 25:48 ff.), to regain a field (Lev 25:23 ff.), in lieu of sacrificing a firstborn male (Ex 13:12 ff.), and on behalf of someone who would otherwise be condemned to death (Ex 21:28 ff.).

Early in the OT God revealed Himself as acting redemptively on behalf of man. Jacob called on God as the One "which hath redeemed me from all evil" (Gen 48:15–16). God declared His intention to deliver Israel from bondage in Egypt, saying, "I will redeem you with a stretched out arm" (Ex 6:6). In the majority of instances in the OT where reference is made to the redemptive activity of God, the deliverance effected is physical rather than spiritual in nature (e.g., the deliverances of Israel from Egypt and Babylon). Even these deliverances, however, carry a spiritual significance in that deliverance indicated God had forgiven the sin or sins which either directly or indirectly occasioned the calamity. In at least one instance (Ps 130:8) the redemption referred to is clearly spiritual in nature, i.e., it is a redemption from sin.

In the NT redemption is strictly a divine activity which is effected by and through Jesus Christ (Eph 1:7; Gal 3:13; 4:5). Though the redemptive activity of Christ has its physical manifestations (e.g., healing), its primary significance is the spiritual ransom of sinners from their bondage to sin (Mk 10:45). The deliverance of the sinner is secured on the basis of the ransom price paid to God the Father by Jesus Christ in His death on the cross (Tit 2:14; Heb 9:12; I Pet 1:18–19). *See* Atonement; Christ, Passion of; Propitiation; Ransom; Reconciliation; Salvation.

The perfection of Christ's redemptive work is clearly stated in the NT (Heb 9:25–28). However, the redeemed individual's experience of redemption will not be complete until the second advent of Christ (Lk 21:28; Rom 8:23; Eph 1:14).

Bibliography. Friedrich Büchsel, *"Agorazō,* etc.," TDNT, I, 124–128. David Hill, *Greek Words and Hebrew Meanings,* Cambridge: Univ. Press, 1967. Leon Morris, *The Apostolic Preaching of the Cross,* Grand Rapids: Eerdmans, 1956, pp. 9–59. John Murray, *Redemption–Accomplished and Applied,* Grand Rapids: Eerdmans, 1955. Roger Nicole, "The Nature of Redemption," in *Christian Faith and Modern Theology,* Carl F. H. Henry, ed., New York: Channel Press, 1964, pp. 193–222. B. B. Warfield, *The Person and Work of Christ,* S. G. Craig, ed., Philadelphia: Presbyterian and Reformed, 1950, Chap. IX.

W. M.

REED
1. *See* Plants: Reed.
2. *See* Weights, Measures, and Coins.

REELAIAH (rē'ĕ-lī'ȧ). One of the important men who returned to Palestine with Zerubbabel (Ezr 2:2), called Raamiah in Neh 7:7.

REFINE, REFINER. *See* Minerals and Metals: Silver; Crucible; Occupations: Refiner.

REFORMATION. This word occurs in the English Bible only in the phrase "until a time of reformation" (Heb 9:10, NASB). The Gr. word *diorthōsis* means an "improvement," "reformation," "new order"; lit., a making straight.

The context of the epistle to the Hebrews assumes that the audience, or some among them, did not realize that the blood of bulls and goats could not take away sin, nor change the conscience (Heb 10:1-4). This reliance for salvation on sacrifices and ritual is sacramentarianism—salvation by sacrament. The epistle argues that it is, and always was, wrong to use sacrifice in this manner. This the author does by showing that the ritual coexisted with a heavenly and eternal priesthood and therefore must take a subsidiary and temporary place; hence, it was not a proper object of faith for salvation. But the ritual was not only temporary but also weak and unprofitable, i.e., inadequate intrinsically. This is shown by pointing out that the Levitical ritual cannot cleanse the conscience (Heb 9:14; 10:2).

This author declares that there is a disannulling or setting aside of the Levitical priesthood (and its system of commandments) because of its weakness and unprofitableness. For the law perfected nothing, i.e., did not in itself bring salvation and peace of conscience. On the other hand, Ps 110:4 declares there will be a new priesthood, according to the order of Melchizedek, which means there will be the introduction of a better hope through which we may draw nigh to God (Heb 7:11-19).

It is this erroneous conception of the efficacy of the law and its sacrifice which is the object of the reformation or correction. The central proof is that Jesus was the Christ—that He offered Himself to God as a sacrifice for sin. Since the OT itself postulated a greater priesthood, it could not be denied that Christ was that greater Priest, perfectly fulfilling the requirements of priesthood as He did, and demonstrating by His resurrection that He is a Priest forever. Resurrection is not openly asserted until Heb 13:20, but is assumed throughout the epistle.

From the proof that Jesus was the great and eternal Priest follows the inference that any other way of salvation is contrary to the Scriptures. His coming and the full revelation of the one way of salvation brings a reformation or a setting straight of the place and function of the Mosaic law. Thus reformation appears to be parallel to the "change" of Heb 7:12, where a change of relationship is contemplated. The change is a bringing of the Levitical ritual into the correct subordinate relationship to the eternal priesthood.

W. B. W.

REFUGE, CITIES OF. *See* Cities of Refuge.

REFUSE. The Heb. word *mā'as* and its kindred forms convey the idea of rejection. In Ps 78:67 it describes God's action toward men in His rejecting the tribe of Joseph as the site for His sanctuary, while in Amos 5:21 it means rejecting in the sense of despising and hating. In Lam 3:45 "refuse" is a noun formed from this root, whose appearance with "offscouring" makes its significance clear. The verbal idea may be thought of as opposite to *bāḥar*, "to choose."

Heb. *mappāl* means "fallings" and may refer to the bran or unfilled grains which go through the sieve (Amos 8:6). The Gr. *perikatharmata* means "offscouring" (I Cor 4:13) or "refuse," being connected with *perikathairō* ("to cleanse on all sides"). Metaphorically it refers to the basest of men (Thayer).

REGEM (rē'gĕm). A Calebite, a son of Jahdai (I Chr 2:47).

REGEM-MELECH (rē'gĕm-mē'lĕk). The name appears in Zech 7:2 where a group of men is sent into the temple to inquire concerning a day of national mourning. It is treated as a proper name in most versions, but there are those who hold that it should be thought of as a descriptive phrase modifying Sherezer, thus: "Sherezer, the friend of the king." This is an interesting possibility but unlikely, and it is best to retain the more customary rendering as in KJV, ASV, RSV, and NASB.

REGENERATION. This subject is not prominently presented in the OT, though it can be seen in such scriptures as Isa 57:15 and Ps 51:10. However, it can also be inferred from those passages which speak of a national regeneration. Passages that speak of the salvation of all Israel when Christ returns at the second coming indicate the regeneration of the surviving Israelites (Jer 24:7; 31:31 ff.; 32:38 ff.; Ezk 11:19; 36:24-27; 37:14; Rom 11:26). Zech 12:10-14 and 13:6 refer to the repentance of individual Jews.

In the NT, *palingenesia* is used of the eschatological restoration (Mt 19:28) of all things. In Titus, the only other time the word is used, it refers to the salvation of the individual (Tit 3:5). Other NT expressions are used for the same truth, but all have in common the idea of a dramatic change likened to and called a new birth, hence, to be born again or born from above (Jn 3:3; I Pet 1:23), born of God (Jn 1:13), being begotten (I Pet 1:3), made alive (Eph 2:5; Col 2:13). *See* Born Again. This renewal comes about by the power of the Holy Spirit (Jn 3:5; Tit 3:5) and makes the man a new creation (*q.v.*; II Cor 5:17; Eph 2:5; 4:24).

Regeneration is to be distinguished from justification. Justification changes the believer's relationship to God, regeneration affects his moral and spiritual nature and changes his nature. Justification removes his guilt; regeneration, his spiritual atrophy, so that he passes from spiritual death to spiritual life. Justification brings forgiveness of his sins; regeneration, the renewal of spiritual life so that he can function as a child of God.

Regeneration is also to be distinguished from sanctification (*q.v.*). Sanctification, or the life of progressive growth in grace, begins only after regeneration and continues on till a believer goes to be with Christ. Yet sanctification is spoken of in similar terms to regeneration. The Christian is exhorted to be transformed by the renewing of his mind (Rom 12:2), to put on the new man (Eph 4:22–24; Col 3:9–10), and to count himself dead to sin and alive unto God (Rom 6:3–11). These passages show that he begins the period of sanctification with his regeneration.

The Reformed theologians make a further distinction and place regeneration before faith, pointing out that the Holy Spirit must bring new life before the sinner can by God's enabling exercise faith and accept Jesus Christ. However, this does not mean that regeneration can occur without faith immediately succeeding thereto, because they belong together (Eph 2:8). Neither occurs without the other.

The Roman Catholic and Anglican churches teach a form of baptismal regeneration, and some Reformed churches even have spoken of regeneration occurring "before, at, or after baptism." The Scriptures do not, however, teach baptismal regeneration of any sort.

Though Peter does speak of baptism saving the believer (I Pet 3:21), he also says regeneration is brought about by the Word of God (I Pet 1:23), as does James (Jas 1:18). It seems clear that what Peter means is that Spirit baptism saves, the actual application of Christ's blood by the Holy Spirit to our sins in regeneration. Christ places such stress on the act of faith in accepting Him as Saviour (Jn 3:16, 36; 5:24) that any regeneration without a rational knowledge of Him and a personal acceptance, is ruled out. The objections in Scripture to circumcision and to law-keeping as a means of regeneration show that any teaching of an *ex opere operato* efficacy of baptism is also out of place. The Word of God gives the content of what one must believe to be saved, and baptism signifies and confesses the cleansing power of the blood of Christ to wash away sins; but saving faith, given as a gift to man at the moment of regeneration, is the condition. *See* Baptism.

Bibliography. Billy Graham, "The New Birth," in *Fundamentals of the Faith,* Carl F. H. Henry, ed., Grand Rapids: Zondervan, 1969, pp. 189–208. Herman A. Hoyt, *The New Birth,* Findlay, Ohio: Dunham, 1961. Robert D. Knudsen, "The Nature of Regeneration," in *Christian Faith and Modern Thought,* Carl F. H. Henry, ed., New York: Channel Press, 1964, pp. 307–321.

R. A. K.

REGISTER. *See* Genealogy.

REHABIAH (rē'*ȧ*-bī'*ȧ*). This name appears in two Heb. forms which differ only slightly. The reference is to the oldest son of Eliezer, the son of Moses. Several passages may be noted: I Chr 23:17; 24:21; 26:25. He was a leader among the families of Levites who had special temple responsibilities. He had numerous offspring (I Chr 23:17).

REHOB (rē'hŏb)

1. Father of King Hadadezer of Zobah (II Sam 8:3, 12).

2. A Levite who joined in sealing Nehemiah's covenant document (Neh 10:11).

3. A town in Lebanon near Lebo-hamath (Num 13:21). *See* Beth-rehob.

4. A town along the NE border of Asher (Josh 19:28); site unknown.

5. Another city assigned to the men of Asher (Josh 19:30), but the tribe was unable to drive out the Canaanite inhabitants (Jud 1:31). It was among the towns allotted to the Levites (Josh 21:31; I Chr 6:75). The city was probably located at Tell el-Gharb (also known as Tell Berweh), about seven miles ESE of Acco. The site controls a junction of the coastal route and a road to the interior of Galilee, with occupational remains from most of the 2nd mil. B.C. and the Hellenistic-Roman period. Rameses II marched northward through Rehob after leaving Dor.

REHOBOAM (rē'ŏ-bō'*ȧ*m). The only son of Solomon, as far as we know, by Naamah the Ammonitess. Rehoboam succeeded Solomon on the throne in 931 B.C. and reigned for 17 years till the day of his death in 913 B.C. (I Kgs 11:43; 14:21, 31). Judah and Benjamin displayed no apparent opposition to him at his accession, but the northern tribes were manifestly dissatisfied. Before the coronation ceremonies scheduled at Shechem, the chief city of northern Israel, the people stated the conditions under which they would serve him as king. In short, they demanded lighter taxation (II Chr 10:4–5).

Determined to pursue the course of his father, Rehoboam rejected the counsel of the experienced advisers for the wild and merciless schemes of the young men (II Chr 10:6–15). The response of Jeroboam (just returned from Egypt, II Chr 10:2–3) and the people was swift and decisive. The ten tribes openly rebelled. When Rehoboam sought to enforce his authority by sending his taskmaster to quell the disturbance, Hadoram was stoned to death. Rehoboam realized the peril to his own life and fled ignominiously back to Jerusalem (II Chr 10:16–19). He mobilized an army of 180,000 men against Israel, but civil war was averted by the stern words of the Lord through Shemaiah the prophet (II Chr 11:1-4). Nevertheless throughout the period of his reign "there were wars between Rehoboam and Jeroboam continually" (II Chr 12:15). Scripture traces all these unfortunate events ultimately to the sin of Solomon (I Kgs 11:1-13).

Subsequent developments reveal the underlying causes for disruption. Under Jeroboam spiritual defection among the northern tribes grew intolerable (I Kgs 12:25-33), causing priests and Levites to return to Judah (II Chr 11:13-17). Judah, too, soon fell into open idolatry under the direction of Rehoboam (II Chr 12:1; I Kgs 14:21-24). Like his father, he practiced polygamy, taking to himself 18 wives and 60 concubines, and actually promoted the same thing among his sons (II Chr 11:18-23).

Left with but two tribes, Rehoboam turned to the building of defenses in southern Judah for protection against invasion from the S (II Chr 11:5-12). The test soon came in his fifth year (926 B.C.) when Shishak (Sheshonk I, the first king of the XXII or Bubastite Dynasty of Egypt; see Shishak) invaded the land. He destroyed the fortified cities and besieged Jerusalem. Advised by Shemaiah, Rehoboam humbled himself for the moment under the hand of the Egyptian potentate and thus escaped utter destruction. It was necessary to surrender the temple and palace treasures to Shishak, and even the golden shields which Solomon had made (II Chr 12:1-12).

H. A. Hoy.

REHOBOTH (rē-hō'bōth)

1. A city of Assyria (Gen 10:11), founded by Nimrod in Asshur (ASV, RSV, NASB, which call it Rehoboth-Ir). Nothing certain is known of its position, but it was probably a suburb of Nineveh and became a part of "Greater Nineveh."

2. The home of a certain Saul or Shaul, one of the early kings of Edom (Gen 36:37; I Chr 1:48). The affix "by the river" usually denotes the Euphrates, but some think it here refers to the "River of Egypt" or some other. At any rate, the site of the city is unknown.

3. The third of a series of wells dug by Isaac after leaving Gerar (Gen 26:22). The Gerar herdsmen did not allow Isaac to keep the first two. Now his good will had overcome their evil and God had made room for all, so he named the well Rehoboth ("broad spaces"). Ruheibeh, *c.* 19 miles SW of Beer-sheba with its numerous ruins of cisterns cut in solid rock, is the probable site.

R. L. D.

REHUM (rē'hŭm). The name occurs in the Aramaic papyri from Elephantine, Egypt.

1. An Israelite, of "the people of the province," who came to Jerusalem with Zerubbabel (Ezr 2:2). In Neh 7:7 he is called Nehum (*q.v.*).

2. A Persian official in Samaria about the time of Nehemiah. In the days of Artaxerxes, Samaritan leaders, alarmed at the indications of a restoration of the power and influence of Jerusalem, urged Rehum, the "chancellor" (KJV) or "commander," to write to the king and have all work on Jerusalem stopped. Rehum did so, dictating the letter to his scribe Shimshai, and the royal reply directed him to use haste and cause the work to cease. Not until Nehemiah came was the work completed (Ezr 4:7-24).

3. A Levite, the son of Bani, who worked on the wall with Nehemiah (Neh 3:17).

4. One of the chiefs of the people who signed Nehemiah's covenant (Neh 10:25).

5. One of the chiefs of the priests who came to Jerusalem with Zerubbabel (Neh 12:3).

P. C. J.

REI (rē'ī). One of the men who refused to join in Adonijah's rebellion against David (I Kgs 1:8). He is listed with Shimei and David's mighty men as having no part in the uprising. The name is a problem, and has been understood by some to mean "friend" and made it modify Shimei. In the belief that it is really a proper name, others have connected him with Ira the Jairite, David's private priest (II Sam 20:26, RSV). Perhaps he was a member of the royal bodyguard, for the weight of evidence favors the proper name interpretation.

REINS. The usual OT word for reins is *k^{e}lāyôt*, which is used primarily in the poetical books and Jeremiah. It refers to the kidneys (*q.v.*) and, in figure, to the inward, secret parts and affections of the soul. In the NT the word appears only in Rev 2:23. The Gr. word is *nephros*, used in the LXX to translate *k^{e}lāyôt*, and may be assumed to have the same general range of meaning. The designation "reins" is a more typical OT way of expressing the idea of emotions than is the word "heart" (*q.v.*).

For the rope or leather strap used to control a horse, *see* Bridle.

REJOICE. *See* Joy, Rejoice.

REKEM (rē'kĕm)

1. A Midianite king slain by Phinehas (Num 31:8; Josh 13:21). God brought vengeance upon Midian for corrupting Israel in pagan worship and unlawful sexual union (cf. Num 25). According to Josephus (*Ant.* iv. 7.1) the "Arabian nation" (Nabataeans, *q.v.*) called its capital city Arekem after this king, the city called Petra (*q.v.*) by the Greeks.

2. The son of Hebron and father of Shammai (I Chr 2:43-44).

3. A city in Benjamin as noted in Josh 18:27. Identification is uncertain, although el-Burg near Nebi Samwil has been suggested.

RELEASE

1. In ancient Israel a device to control slavery and personal debt (Deut 15:1-3, 9; 31:10). Every seventh year (Ex 21:2) the slave was to

be freed, and if he chose not to go free, his ear was pierced as a sign of perpetual servitude (Ex 21:5 ff.). Likewise in the seventh year the debtor was to go free, and the debt was not to be collected by any means from neighbor or brother (Deut 15:2). The debt could be "exacted" only from foreigners, so that there would be no poor among the Israelites (Deut 15:3-4, NASB). This clearly indicates the injunction's control over personal debt and the abuse of debts to impose slavery. *See* Festivals: Year of Jubilee.

2. The Persian king Ahasuerus made a "release" to all the province in honor of his marriage to Esther, probably declaring certain debts or taxes void, and freeing certain prisoners (Est 2:18; cf. RSV).

3. In the NT the only "release" spoken of is that of Barabbas, preferred to the release of Christ (Jn 18:39-40).

H. G. S.

RELIGION. The Gr. word *thrēskeia* is used four times in the NT (Acts 26:5; Col 2:18; Jas 1:26-27). In Col 2:18 it is translated "worshipping" of angels (KJV). The Gr. verb *latreuō* (II Tim 1:3; Heb 12:28) and the noun *latreia* are also used to express the same idea of worship and service of God (cf. Rom 9:4; Heb 9:1).

The English word "religion" raises certain problems. There are diverse opinions concerning its root and origin. Cicero connected it with *religare*, "to read again," "to consider," "give attention to the divine." Lactantius and Augustine translated *religare* "to bind back," and saw the idea of obligation in the word. The NT *thrēskeia*, as seen above, speaks merely of religious worship, particularly in its external form.

In philosophy and in common use the word has been used with a variety of meanings. Schleiermacher defines it as "the feeling of absolute dependence," Kant as "the observance of the moral law as a divine institution." In general, a religion may be said to be any system of faith and worship of God.

The classic passage on religion in the NT is Jas 1:26-27. Here the terms used (*thrēskos* and *thrēskeia*) definitely refer to outward expression. The contrast is drawn between one whose religion consists of formal ceremonies that have no support in heart devotion, and the one whose religion consists of deeds of mercy, because it flows from a right heart attitude to God.

See Worship.

R. A. K.

RELIGIOUS PROSELYTES. *See* Proselytes.

REMALIAH (rĕm-ȧ-lī′ȧ). The father of Pekah, king of Israel. Pekah gained the throne by assassinating Pekahiah (II Kgs 15:25-37; 16:1, 5; II Chr 28:6; Isa 7:1-9; 8:6). Each time the name Remaliah occurs it is to identify his infamous son. Possibly the phrase, "Pekah, the son of Remaliah," was intended as a contemptuous reflection on the background of Pekah (ISBE).

REMETH (rē′mĕth). A border town of the territory of Issachar (Josh 19:21). In I Chr 6:73 it is called Ramoth (*see* Ramoth 2), and Jarmuth in Josh 21:29 (*see* Jarmuth 2). It has tentatively been identified with Kokab el-Hawa, on a height overlooking the Jordan Valley seven miles N of Beth-shan.

REMEMBRANCE. *See* Memorial.

REMISSION. *See* Forgiveness.

REMMON. *See* Rimmon.

REMMON-METHOAR. *See* Rimmon 3.

REMNANT. In the OT four Heb. roots (*yāthar, pālaṭ, śārad, shā'ar*) express the concept of a remnant. With their derivatives they occur more than 600 times. The NT word for remnant (*leimma*) with its derivatives occurs less than ten times. In both Testaments the idea of the remnant is "those being left" or "having escaped," especially a portion of a community which has escaped a devastating calamity and will form the basis for a new community.

The thought possibly goes back to Deut 4:27-31; 28:62-68; 30:1-10, where Moses warns that God will disperse Israel among the nations, after which He will regather a remnant. This warning speaks not only of the Assyrian and Babylonian captivities and the return from those captivities, but also, and ultimately, of the time when Messiah will establish His kingdom. The prophets develop the concept of the remnant; it figures prominently in their warnings to Israel of impending judgment. Isaiah names one of his sons Shear-jashub, "a remnant shall return" (Isa 7:3; 8:18), and in 10:21 specifically states that a remnant will return. In 11:10-16 he speaks of a second return; this points to the time when Messiah will set up His kingdom, since it is given in a messianic context (cf. Rom 15:12).

Isaiah's contemporary, Micah, also says much about the regathering of a remnant after judgment (2:12; 4:7; 5:3, 7-8; 7:18). Jeremiah discusses three remnants: (1) the group left after Jerusalem's destruction who later fled to Egypt (24:8; 39:9; 40:11-15); (2) those who would return after the Babylonian Captivity (24:5; 50:20); and (3) those whom Messiah will gather (23:3; 31:7). The other pre-Exilic prophets elaborate in the same vein. The post-Exilic books speak of the return after the Captivity (Hag 1:12-14; 2:2; Zech 8:6, 11-12; Ezr 9:8, 14-15; Neh 1:2-3) and of a remnant that will be present at the time of the messianic kingdom (Zech 12:10–13:1; 13:8-9; 14:2).

The number of the remnant is always small. In Zech 13:8 it is a third of all; in Isa 6:13 it is only a tenth of the total; and in Ezk 5:3 the remnant is pictured as only a few hairs wrapped in a fold of a garment.

In the NT the concept of the remnant is the same; it still revolves around those Israelites who will enter the millennial kingdom with Messiah, though Rom 11:5 does speak of a remnant who are present in this dispensation. In Rom 11:23-27 Israel is pictured as being grafted back into the olive tree. At the second advent of Christ she will be saved by the power of Messiah, fulfilling God's covenants with her. This is the ultimate fulfillment for which Messiah and the remnant have waited.

In summary, the future remnant is pictured as that small number of Jews that will ultimately abide with Messiah Himself. In setting up His kingdom He will regather and cleanse this remnant and consequently fulfill God's covenant promises with Israel.

Bibliography. J. C. Campbell, "God's People and the Remnant," *Scottish Journal of Theology,* III (1950), 78-85. R. Laird Harris, "Remnant," BDT, pp. 442-443. E. W. Heaton, "The Root *sh'r* and the Doctrine of the Remnant," JTS, III (1952), 27-39. E. Jenni, IDB, IV, 32-33. G. Schrenk and V. Herntrich, *"Leimma,"* TDNT, IV, 194-214.

H. W. H.

REMPHAN, REPHAN. *See* Gods, False.

REND, RENT. Heb. *qāra'* is the usual word for tearing one's garments in grief (Gen 37:29, 34). The prophet advises the people to rend their hearts and not their garments (Joel 2:13). *See* Mourn, Mourning.

The NT uses forms of *diarhēgnymi* as, e.g., the rending of the garments of the high priest (Mt 26:65). Paul and Barnabas tore their garments to dissuade the people of Lystra from worshiping them (Acts 14:14). The tearing of demonic oppression is expressed by *rhēgnymi* and *sparassō* (Mk 9:18 and Mk 9:26, respectively). Gr. *schizō* is used of the rending of the thick veil of the temple at the time of Jesus' death (Mt 27:51).

REPENTANCE. The most common Heb. words for repentance are from the root *naḥam* and signify a change of mind or purpose, or sometimes, being sorry. The NT concept, however, is more nearly expressed by the Heb. verb *shûb,* which means "to turn," or "return," and is sometimes translated "repent" (Ezk 14:6; 18:30). It is the verb "return" in the classic OT text on repentance, Isa 55:6-7. In the NT repentance is usually signified by Gr. *metanoia,* "change of mind" and its related verb; though *metamelomai,* "to change attitude," is used five times and a related adjective twice.

The doctrine of repentance is most clearly set forth in the NT by the noun *metanoia* and its related verb. Wherever this noun or verb occurs there is an invitation to men to turn from sin unto the grace of God, or a record of or reference to such turning. The repentance may be that of professing Christians (II Cor 7:9-10; Rev 2:5, 16, 21-22; 3:3, 19), although the appeal for repentance is usually addressed to unbelievers.

There is a definite development of the use of the word in the NT. John the Baptist (Mt 3:2, 8, 11; Mk 1:4; Lk 3:3, 8) sounded the note of repentance for all the Jewish people, in view of the advent of the Messiah. His ministry is summarized in the words of Paul, "John baptized with the baptism of repentance, saying unto the people that they should believe on him that should come after him, that is, on Jesus" (Acts 19:4, ASV; see also 13:24).

For many of the Jews, as probably for the 12 men of Ephesus (Acts 19:1-7), the baptism of John may have represented the time of their definite *believing,* in the OT sense of saving faith. Yet many had doubtless been believers, and John's baptism for them like the "many baptisms" (Heb 9:10) would have represented an act of repentance and reconsecration. We may suppose that many of those who sincerely repented at John's preaching were among the thousands who came into the church at Pentecost and subsequently.

The Lord Jesus picked up the thread of John's message in the very same words (Mt 4:17; Mk 1:15). Repentance had a prominent place in the preaching of Jesus and His disciples (see Mk 6:12; Mt 11:20-21 with Lk 10:13; Mt 12:41 with Lk 11:32). Luke gives much more emphasis to the preaching of repentance in the ministry of Jesus than do the other Gospel writers. Passages peculiar to Luke are 5:32; 13:3, 5; 15:7, 10; 16:30; 17:3-4; 24:47.

In the book of Acts the fully developed gospel message of repentance and faith is presupposed from beginning to end. On the day of Pentecost (2:38) and soon thereafter (3:19), repentance for salvation from sin was the predominating theme. The exaltation of Christ means the gift to Israel of repentance for the remission of sins. A great advance in understanding is indicated in 11:18, "They glorified God, saying, 'So God has granted repentance unto life to the Gentiles also!' " Paul preached repentance to the philosophers in the Areopagus (17:30). In the clearest of all the references in Acts, Paul summarizes his ministry in the words ". . .testifying to Jews and to Greeks *repentance toward God, and faith toward our Lord Jesus Christ*" (20:21); and again "among the Gentiles I preached that they must repent and turn back to God and practice activities consistent with repentance" (26:20, Berkeley). In writing to Corinth Paul indicates the proper function of sorrow when it turns a person to God and produces repentance that leads to salvation, for the hopeless grief of the pagan world leads only to bitterness and spiritual death (II Cor 7:9-10).

From these and other passages we may formulate a definition of repentance such as that of

Carl G. Kromminga: "*Metanoia* can be said to denote that inward change of mind, affections, convictions, and commitment, rooted in the fear of God and sorrow for offenses committed against Him, which, when accompanied by faith in Jesus Christ, results in an outward turning from sin to God and His service in all of life" ("Repentance," BDT, p. 444).

There are terrible warnings for those who will not repent (Heb 6:6; Rev 9:20–21; 16:9, 11). The most winsome of all the references to repentance is Rom 2:4, "The goodness of God leadeth thee to repentance" (cf. also II Pet 3:9).

See Confession; Forgiveness.

Bibliography. J. Behm and E. Würthwein, "*Metanoeō*, etc., "TDNT, IV, 975–1008. Harry A. Ironside, *Except Ye Repent,* New York: American Tract Society, 1937. J. P. Ramseyer, "Repentance," *A Companion to the Bible,* J. J. von Allmen, ed., New York: Oxford, 1958, pp. 357–359.

J. O. B.

REPETITION. In the Sermon on the Mount (Mt 5–7), Jesus warns against externalism and vain repetitions in our prayers (Mt 6:7). The Gr. *battologeō* is the root and means "to stammer." The context supplies the parallel phrase "for their much speaking." Is Jesus' thrust against repetitiousness, undue length, or overanxious concern for earthly matters? All of these ideas have been advanced, but on the strength of the parallel phrase and Jesus' words in Mt 23:14, it is best to stress the first two suggestions.

REPHAEL (rĕf'ĭ-ĕl). One of the course of gate keepers (I Chr 26:1). He is mentioned in I Chr 26:7 as the son of Shemaiah who was the son of Obed-edom. He is described with others as a man of valor and is traditionally believed to have been consecrated to this work by David.

REPHAH (rē'fȧ). The son of Beriah who was of Ephraim. He became an ancestor of Joshua (I Chr 7:25).

REPHAIAH (rĕ-fā'yȧ).

1. A post-Exilic descendant of David in the line of Zerubbabel (I Chr 3:21).

2. One of four captains of a Simeonite band of 500 who destroyed the Amalekite inhabitants of Mount Seir and settled in their lands (I Chr 4:42–43).

3. Second son of Tola, son of Issachar, famed as a warrior (I Chr 7:1–2).

4. A descendant of Saul, king of Israel, of the tribe of Benjamin (I Chr 8:37, spelled "Rapha," KJV; "Raphah," RSV; but "Rephaiah" in I Chr 9:43).

5. A leader in the repair of the wall of Jerusalem under Nehemiah (Neh 3:9). He was "ruler of half the district of Jerusalem" (NASB), i.e., one-half of one of the districts into which Judah was divided after the Exile.

REPHAIM (rĕf'ā-ĭm)

1. A race of people inhabiting Palestine mentioned with the Zuzim and the Emim as having been defeated by Chedorlaomer (Gen 14:5; cf. 15:20). The LXX translates the term as "giants" (Josh 12:4; I Chr 11:15; 14:9; 20:4). Og king of Bashan, who belonged to the remnant of the Rephaim, was an unusually large man, according to the dimensions of his iron bedstead (Deut 3:11; *see* Og). His size tends to confirm that the Rephaim were much taller than the other peoples of Canaan. It is conjectured that these may have been the people who erected the dolmens (*q.v.*) in Palestine, which were built of colossal slabs of rock. *See* Giant. The Rephaim apparently occupied a wide section of Palestine at the time of the conquest. They inhabited at the time both the E and W banks of the Jordan (Deut 2:11, 20–21). *See* Anakim.

2. Inhabitants of the underworld (Job 26:5, NASB marg.; Ps 88:10; Prov 2:18; 9:18; 21:16; Isa 14:9; 26:14, 19). As used in these passages it is roughly an equivalent of the term "ghosts," "shades" (RSV), or "departed spirits" (NASB). In other words, they are the inhabitants of Sheol (*q.v.*). The term is found in Ugaritic literature referring to ghosts and minor gods. *See* Dead, The; Rephaim, Valley of.

G. A. T.

REPHAIM, VALLEY OF (rĕf'ā-ĭm). A valley in the vicinity of Jerusalem but toward Bethlehem (II Sam 23:13–14; Jos *Ant.* vii.4.1); probably the valley now called the Baqa', through which a modern railroad approaches from the SW. That it was not NW is clear from the description in Josh 15:8; 18:16. There David won two victories over the Philistines, who apparently invaded the hill country by this route in order to sever communications between Jerusalem and Hebron (II Sam 5:18–22; I Chr 14:9; II Sam 23:13–14; I Chr 11:15). Its rich grain crop was proverbial (Isa 17:5).

REPHAN. *See* Gods, False: Remphan.

REPHIDIM (rĕf'ĭ-dĭm). The last stopping place on the journey before the Israelites reached Mount Sinai. The exact site is uncertain, and various places have been suggested, usually in the southern Sinai Peninsula, e.g., Wadi Refayid, or less probably Wadi Feiran. At Rephidim the people found fault with Moses because they had no water to drink, and so the place was called Massah and Meribah. Here also Joshua defeated the Amalekites while Moses held up his hands, supported by Aaron and Hur. After the victory Jethro persuaded Moses to appoint "able men" to help him judge the people (Ex 17:1, 7–13; 19:2; Num 33:14–15). The name may either mean "rests" or "resting-place," or "expanses," referring to the oasis that stretches out for several miles in its lush valley. Undoubtedly the Israelites were anticipating cool water from melted snow on the 8,000 foot

Palm trees in Wadi Feiran. JR

mountains surrounding Rephidim, but in a drought year there was none.

See Exodus, The: Route; Massah; Sinai.

D. B.

REPROACH. In Heb. this idea is usually expressed by the verb *ḥārap* and its noun *ḥerpâ*, lit., to say sharp things against. A number of applications of this idea may be found. In the sense of revile or curse, Ps 42:10; Isa 51:7; Zeph 2:8 are illustrative. When reviling is directed toward God, it becomes blasphemy (II Kgs 19:4, 22–23; Ps 69:9; 74:22). It stands for the scorn and taunting (I Sam 17:26, NASB) and defying words of an enemy (I Sam 17:10, 25–26, 36, 45; Heb. *ḥārap*).

Sexual shame or disgrace is expressed by *ḥerpâ* in I Sam 13:13; Prov 6:33; Ezk 16:57. There was also reproach connected with uncircumcision (Gen 34:14) and with barrenness and widowhood (Gen 30:23; Isa 54:4; Lk 1:25). A land was disgraced by famine (Ezk 36:30) and ruined cities (Neh 1:3; 2:17). The Israelites were disgraced by their apostasy in the wilderness and by the shame of their idolatry and lustfulness stemming from Egypt (Josh 5:9; see WBC, p. 211). Often the word indicates that one has become an object of reproach to his neighbors or his accusers (Ps 31:11; 79:4; 109:25; Jer 24:9; etc.).

The concept of insult or dishonor is found in Heb. k^{e}*limmâ* (Job 20:3; Mic 2:6, NASB), while *kālam* conveys the idea of humiliation in Ruth 2:15 and Job 19:3.

In the NT Gr. *oneidizō* and *oneidismos* have a similar range of meanings. Like Moses of old, believers today must endure reproach and ridicule for following Christ (Heb 11:26; I Pet 4:14).

B. C. S.

REPROBATE, REPROBATION. The word "reprobate" appears once in the OT (KJV), translating *mā'as*, "to reject," when Jeremiah compares "reprobate" silver ore with Israel, rejected by God because of corruption (Jer 6:30). Six times in the NT "reprobate" is the rendering of the Pauline adjective *adokimos*, "not standing the test, disqualified." The apostle wishes none to fail to evidence genuine Christianity, for Jesus Christ dwells in them unless they "fail the test" (II Cor 13:5–7, NASB). The wicked are reprobate, "unfit" for good deeds (Tit 1:16), "disapproved" in respect to the faith (II Tim 3:8), and therefore "subject to rejection" (Rom 1:28) or theological reprobation.

Theologically, then, reprobation is the condemnation of the lost to eternal separation from God. The teaching of reprobation has been greatly misunderstood. If one means by it that God ordained to save some men and to condemn the rest to reprobation, then the doctrine has been stated in such a form that it is incompatible with God's just and holy character. However, if the doctrine is more fully and carefully expressed, as in infralapsarianism, then it expresses as evident truth of Scripture: (1) that God ordained to create the world and man; (2) that He ordained to permit the fall of man; (3) that God ordained to send Christ as Redeemer and to save the elect but to pass by and reject those who refuse His grace.

The decrees of election and of reprobation, according to the above view, are not symmetrical and equal. God does not will reprobation in the same sense that He wills election. They are, of course, both according to the good counsel of God's will, and therefore not arbitrary but nonetheless certain. The will to save the elect is efficacious and based upon the exercise of God's sovereign grace; the will to permit the unbelieving to be lost is permissive.

A further distinction must be made. In His efficacious grace God is the credible cause of the salvation of the elect. He is not, however, the cause of the wicked being lost, for they are the chargeable cause of their own reprobation. They are "vessels of wrath who have fitted themselves for destruction" (Rom 9:22, lit. trans.). Man is held responsible by God for his sin and for his rejection of God's way of salvation. God is not, however, obligated to overcome man's total depravity and to save him by efficacious grace, because that is an unmerited favor given by God only to those whom He chooses.

See Fall of Man; Sin.

R. A. K.

REPUTATION. The term reputation, which in modern English usage frequently denotes ostensible character, in the KJV indicates prominence. The KJV uses it to translate several Gr. words. In Acts 5:34 *timios* ("of great price," "prized," "honorable") indicates the people's respect for Gamaliel. Paul uses a related term, *entimos* ("valuable," "honorable") in Phil 2:29 to enjoin esteem of all who serve as did Epaphroditus. The term *dokeō* (frequently meaning "to think, seem, or appear") describes the esteem accorded both political leaders (Mk 10:42) and religious leaders (Gal 2:2, 6, 9).

The KJV says in Phil 2:7 that Christ "made himself of no reputation." A clearer translation is "emptied himself" (ASV, RSV, NASB). Paul is referring to Christ's laying aside the manifestation of His divine glory and to His voluntary nonuse of certain divine attributes during the period of His earthly life. In no sense did He empty Himself of deity or cease to be God. Paul mentions the self-humiliation of Christ here to support an exhortation for believers to exercise humility toward one another. *See* Christ, Humiliation of; Incarnation; Kenosis.

F. D. L.

RESEN (rē'sĕn). An ancient Assyrian city built by Nimrod between Nineveh and Calah (Gen 10:12). Assyrian sources do not list any major town of this name. Possibly it is the village Resh-eni located NE of Nineveh which Sennacherib mentions in connection with his efforts to supply Nineveh with water.

RESERVOIR. Rainfall in Palestine comes abundantly in the winter season from November to April. From May to October, however, hardly a drop falls, and the earlier rains have run off the stony hills which form so much of the country. Very few streams and perennial springs are to be found, and most ancient cities, such as Jericho and Jerusalem, were situated near such water supplies. In some parts of the country it was possible to dig wells and find water. Most of the people, however, were dependent upon the rain, and a system of preserving the water was essential.

From ancient times until today, cisterns and reservoirs have been the chief water supply of Israel. Every house of any distinction had its own cistern to catch the rainwater running from the roof or off the side of the hill. The cities had great reservoirs, not only for daily use but particularly for the emergencies of war. Some of these were simply holes lined with rocks; others were cut into solid rock. Cisterns were lined with waterproof plaster even before the time of Abraham, according to one discovered at the Early Bronze Age town of Bab edh-Dhra (*q.v.*). A deep shaft and cistern at Taanach *c*. 1500 B.C. was similarly plastered (BASOR # 195 [1969], p. 33). The Israelites put this practice to good use in settling the central ridge of Palestine, as they lined their pools and cisterns with slaked lime plaster to make them waterproof (W. F. Albright, *Archaeology of Palestine,* Harmondsworth: Penguin, 1960, p. 113).

Some of the pools mentioned in Scripture are natural ones, but many of them are great reservoirs made by man; e.g., the recently excavated great pool at Gibeon (II Sam 2:13), and the pool of Hezekiah which collected the water of Gihon brought by a tunnel through 1,700 feet of solid rock (II Kgs 20:20; II Chr 32:30). This pool is called a "reservoir" in Isa 22:11, RSV and NASB (KJV "ditch"). By Roman times Jerusalem received additional water through aqueducts from the so-called "Pools of Solomon" S of Bethlehem. Three in number, these huge reservoirs are *c*. 200 feet in width, and the largest is almost 600 feet long and 50 feet deep.

See Cistern; Pool; Water.

P. C. J.

RESH (rāsh). The 20th letter of the Heb. alphabet. It serves as a numeral for 200. Its earliest pictographic sign pictured a "head" (Heb. *rō'sh*). It is placed at the head of the 20th section of the acrostic psalm, Ps 119, where each verse of the section begins with this letter.

RESHEPH (rē'shĕf). A Heb. name meaning "flame." The term, lit. translated as "sons of resheph," in Job 5:7 refers to sparks from the fire. In Song 8:6 it is "coals" or "flashes" of fire. Other meanings include "inflammation," "fever," or "plague" (Deut 32:24; Hab 3:5), and "bolts of lightning" (Ps 78:48, NASB).

1. The name of a member of the tribe of Ephraim, the son of Rephah and the father of Telah (I Chr 7:25).

2. Reseph also refers to a Canaanite deity generally thought of as the god of plague or mass destruction. *See* Gods, False.

RESPECT OF PERSONS. God does not show respect of persons in His judgment (Rom 2:11; Heb 6:10; Col 3:25; cf. I Pet 1:17), nor are we to do so in our treatment of others (Jas 2:1, 9). God commanded His judges to show no favoritism in the OT (Lev 19:15; Deut 1:17; 16:19; cf. Prov 24:23; 28:21).

REST. This word often has special meaning in Scripture. For instance, God is said to rest from His creative activity on the seventh day (Gen 2:2-3). The sabbath as instituted for Israel was to be a day of rest (Ex 31:15). Rest was promised to the Israelites if they would obey (Deut 3:20). The Promised Land was to be allowed to rest every seventh year (Lev 25:4). The temple was to be the Lord's resting place among His people (I Chr 28:2; Ps 132:8, 14).

The writer of Hebrews gives the fullest exposition of rest in its special theological sense. In his second parenthetical section (3:7–4:13) he warns against the dangers of unbelief (which he equates with disobedience). Having alluded to Israel's failure to enter the land of rest at Kadesh-barnea because of unbelief, he warns professors to make sure that they also do not respond in unbelief to the good news preached to them (3:7–4:2). The author then goes on to make these points: (1) Believers are presently in the process of entering into rest (4:3*a*). (2) This rest has yet to be attained inasmuch as the Israelites in the wilderness failed to attain it, and even Joshua did not lead them into its fullness. (3) This rest, the fullness of which is yet to be realized, is analagous to the sabbath rest of God (Heb 4:3-4, 9-10). As God ceased

Grand stairway at the palace, Persepolis capital of the Persian Empire. ORINST

from His work on the seventh day, even so the believer has ceased from those works intended to earn salvation. Thus it is seen that unbelief (reliance on one's own efforts instead of faith in Christ) will be the cause of failure to enter into rest now, even as it was with the Israelites. This concept of rest in Hebrews is related to Mt 11:28 and Christ's promise of rest to those who come to Him. The rest He offered was in contrast to the heavy burdens of works righteousness imposed by the legalistic teachings of the Pharisees. (4) Finally, believers who complete their earthly labors enter into rest (Rev 14:13; cf. Isa 57:1-2; II Thess 1:7; Rev 6:11).

S. N. G.

RESTITUTION. *See* Restoration, Restitution.

RESTORATION AND PERSIAN PERIOD. OT books and passages referring directly or prophetically to events in the restoration and Persian period are Isa 44:26–45:1; II Chr 36:22-23; Daniel, Ezra, Nehemiah, Esther, Haggai, and Zechariah. Malachi, probably written about 440 B.C., indirectly indicates a rebuilt temple (1:7, 10; 3:1) and a foreign (Persian) governor (1:8).

The Babylonian Captivity began in 605 B.C., when Nebuchadnezzar deported the first Jews from the kingdom of Judah (II Chr 36:2-7; Dan 1:1-3). In a second and a third campaign, dated 598-597 B.C. (II Kgs 24:10-16) and 588-586 B.C. (II Kgs 25:2-21), he took many more Jews captive to Babylon. This exile lasted for approximately 70 years, during which the Jews in Babylon yearned for Jerusalem (Ps 137). *See* Captivity.

In 539 B.C. Cyrus invaded Babylonia with the Medo-Persian army. On October 10 his general Ugbaru took Sippar (30 miles N of Babylon), the temporary headquarters of Nabonidus the king of Babylon. Two nights later Ugbaru's troops entered Babylon and killed Belshazzar the crown prince (Nabonidus Chronicle. ANET, p. 306; Dan 5). Nabonidus was arrested when he returned to Babylon. Cyrus entered the city in triumph on October 29, presenting himself to the people as a gracious liberator and benefactor.

In 538-537 B.C. Cyrus decreed that Jews return to Jerusalem to rebuild the temple (Ezr 1:1-4; 5:13). He restored the temple vessels (Ezr 1:7) and supplied funds for the work (Ezr 3:7). The period of restoration, during which Zerubbabel, Ezra, and Nehemiah were key leaders, was important, for in it the people as a nation turned back to God, and the development of the synagogue and Jewish religious parties began.

Cyrus II (the Great) ruled from 550 to 530 B.C. His successful revolt against Astyages, the Median king, in 550 B.C. established the Achaemenid dynasty (cf. Herodotus I, 107) and the Persian Empire, which was the world power from 539 to 330 B.C. In taking Babylon (539 B.C.), Cyrus II became God's instrument for punishing the Babylonians for oppressing the Jews (cf. Jer 50:33–51:64).

II Chr 36:22-23; Ezr 1:1-4, and Ezr 6:3-5 also record Cyrus' decree to rebuild the Jerusalem temple in accord with Isaiah's prophecy (44:26–45:1). Cyrus' magnanimity extended to all his subject peoples, not merely to the Jews. He restored religious sanctuaries and idols ruined by the wars of his predecessors and returned deported peoples to their "habitations" (Cyrus Cylinder, ANET, pp. 315 f.).

Following Cyrus' decree, close to 50,000 exiles and slaves returned to Jerusalem under Sheshbazzar (Zerubbabel?) and Jeshua. This remnant built the altar of the Lord and laid the foundation of the temple (Ezr 1:1–3:13), but stopped working on it because of opposition from neighboring peoples (Ezr 4:1-5, 24). They resumed work as a result of the prodding of the prophet Haggai, and finished the temple between 520 and 516 B.C. in the reign of Darius I (Ezr 5-6). Ezra made the 900 mile journey to Jerusalem with more exiles in 457 B.C. during the reign of Artaxerxes I (Ezr 7-8).

For the needs of the temple in Jerusalem Ezra took with him gifts of silver and gold from the king and freewill offerings of the Jews remaining in Babylon. He was made responsible for Jewish affairs in the province of Syria and Palestine (Ezr 7:25). He aimed at a revival of religious life under the Mosaic covenant and law given at Mount Sinai (Ezr 7:10; Neh 8). To achieve reform he demanded dissolution of the foreign marriages which many of the previous returnees had contracted. This edict, renewed by Nehemiah, was resented by some of the Jews and stirred up the Samaritans and others of the non-Jewish population against God's people (Ezr 9-10; Neh 10:30; 13:23-30).

The Talmud (*q.v.*) credits Ezra with the reintroduction of the law of Moses and also ascribes to him and his associates many other ancient statutes. Traditionally, he was the founder of the Jewish Great Synagogue or Assembly (*k*[e]*nēset g*[e]*dôlâ*), the body of Jewish scholars who expounded the law during the 5th–3rd cen. B.C.

In 445 B.C. Nehemiah, the adviser (cupbearer) to King Artaxerxes I, had obtained permission from him to go to Jerusalem to rebuild the city walls. He succeeded in this reconstruction despite foreign opposition led by Sanballat the Samaritan, Tobiah the Ammonite, and Geshem the Arab (Neh 1-6). The wall was completed in record time (Neh 6:15) and dedicated a short time later (Neh 12:27–13:3). Nehemiah made a second trip to Jerusalem in 433 B.C. to correct various abuses of the law (Neh 13:4-31). Apparently during the interval between his two visits, the last of the canonical prophets, Malachi, delivered God's message to His covenant nation. Little is known of Jewish history for the next 200 years.

The Achaemenid kings of the restoration and the Persian period were:

1. Cyrus II (the Great) (550-530 B.C.).

2. Cambyses II (529-522 B.C.), who conquered Egypt (522 B.C.).

3. Pseudo-Smerdis (or Gaumāta) (522 B.C.), who forcibly took the throne.

4. Darius I, Hystaspes (521-486 B.C.), who defeated Gaumāta and other revolters (cf. the Behistun inscription on the cliff in Iran). By military genius he extended his kingdom from India to N Africa and Thrace. The Greeks defeated him at Marathon (490 B.C.). Under his order the Jerusalem temple was completed in 520-516 B.C. (Ezr 5:1; 6:1-12; Hag 1:1; Zech 1:1).

5. Xerxes I (486-464 B.C.), who made war against the Greeks and lost decisively in the sea battle of Salamis (480 B.C.). He was no doubt the Ahasuerus of the book of Esther (cf. his position between Darius and Artaxerxes in the order of Persian kings, Ezr 4:4-7).

6. Artaxerxes I, Longimanus (464-423 B.C.), who quelled revolts in Egypt and made peace with the Athenians (Peace of Callias, 449 B.C.). It was under this king that Ezra went to Jerusalem in 457 B.C. (Ezr 7:1-26); construction on Jerusalem's walls ceased for a time (Ezr 4:7-23); and Nehemiah made his trips to the Holy City, one in 445 B.C. (Neh 2:1-6) and the second in 433 B.C. (Neh 13:6-7).

Succeeding kings in the Persian period not mentioned in OT history were:

7. Darius II, Nothus (423-404 B.C.), who is mentioned in the Aramaic papyri from Elephantine in Egypt including the so-called Passover Papyrus of 419 B.C. (ANET, p. 491).

8. Artaxerxes II, Mnemon (404-359 B.C.), who defeated his rebellious brother Cyrus in 401 B.C. (cf. Xenophon, *Anabasis*).

9. Artaxerxes III, Ochus (359-338 B.C.).

10. Darius III, Codomannus (336-330 B.C.), whom Alexander the Great conquered.

Cyrus II divided the Persian Empire into relatively autonomous administrative units (at least 20) called satrapies. Later Darius developed the system further. Tatnai, the governor (Aram. *peḥa*), was no doubt some sort of satrapy official (Ezr 5:3, 6; 6:6, 13), as Nehemiah may also have been (Neh 5:14-18).

See Esther; Ezra; Nehemiah; Persia; Samaritans; Synagogue.

Bibliography. CornPBE, pp. 617-622. R. K. Harrison, *Old Testament Times,* Grand Rapids: Eerdmans, 1970, pp. 271-289. A. T. Olmstead, *History of the Persian Empire,* Chicago: Univ. of Chicago Press, 1948. Charles F. Pfeiffer, *Exile and Return,* Grand Rapids: Baker, 1962.

W. H. M.

RESTORATION, RESTITUTION. In the Bible these terms refer to property, to persons, and to the total theocratic economy. The Mosaic law provided for the return or replacement of stolen property, with various prescribed fines and compensations for damages or injury (Ex 22:1-15; Lev 6:1-7; 24:18-21; *see* Crime and Punishment). In the light of such requirements Zacchaeus offered to restore fourfold (Lk 19:8). One of the Heb. verbs meaning to restore or make restitution is *shālam* (*see* Peace), "to make whole," "to make good," "to complete" (Ex 22:3, 5-6, 12). It is used of the restoration of comfort to those who are sick and grief stricken (Isa 57:18), and of productivity to a land ravaged by locusts (Joel 2:25-26).

Heb. *shûb* in the Hiphil stem means to cause to return, to bring or give back, to restore, with reference to a wife to her rightful husband (Gen 20:7, 14), one's office (Gen 40:21; 41:13), property (Deut 22:2; Jud 11:13), stolen money (Jud 17:3-4), spiritual blessings such as joy (Ps 51:12), rebuilding a ruined city (Dan 9:25).

The Bible contains frequent reference to the restoration of the backslider (Job 22:23; Prov 1:22-23; Jer 3:12, 14, 22; Hos 14:1, 4; Joel 2:12-13; Jas 5:19-20). The responsibility of restoring (Gr. *katartizō*) a sinning Christian rests upon spiritually minded believers who are to perform their duty in a gentle manner (Gal 6:1). The Gr. verb means to put in order, restore to its former condition, as fishing nets by mending and cleaning (Mt 4:21; Mk 1:19). Paul exhorted the Corinthians to "be perfect" (*katartizesthe,* II Cor 13:11), telling them to put themselves in order (NASB marg.) or mend their ways, to adjust and equip themselves spiritually.

In one sense, the Bible from Gen 3:9 onward is the record of God's program to restore fallen man to fellowship with Himself. A prominent and integral part of that program is the restoration of the nation Israel, for it is through Israel that salvation is brought to the world (cf. Gen 12; Rom 11). Because of her disobedience Israel was punished by the breakdown of the theocracy, the dispersion, and accompanying hardships. But restoration was in God's plan for the nation. A remnant returned from Babylon after 70 years. But it was no real restoration; indeed, after this partial return, promises of full restoration were still to be made. *See* Restoration and Persian Period.

Only an interpretation that violates the normal use of language can avoid the impact of the OT prophecies of Israel's literal restoration (cf. Isa 65:17-25; 66:22; Jer 23:1-8; 27:22; Ezk

34:11-31; 36:1-37:28; Hos 3:5; Zech 2:1-12; 8:1-8, 20-23; 9:10-17; 10:9-12; 12:1-14:21). Nor did Christ spiritualize the OT promises of Israel's restoration (Acts 1:6-7), though in fulfillment of OT prophecy He provided the spiritual basis of full restoration not only for Israel but for all believers. Israel's restoration will be accomplished in connection with the return and reign of the messianic King. But at that time, restoration is not confined to Israel alone, for all believers will have entered into the full realization of their salvation and the heavens and the earth themselves will undergo "restitution" (Acts 3:21; cf. Isa 65:17-25; 66:22; II Pet 3:7-13; Rev 21:1-4). Our Lord spoke of that future time as "the regeneration" (Mt 19:28), the consummation of the ages.

It is important to note that in Acts 3:21 the passage should be read "until the period of restoration of all things about which God spoke by the mouth of His holy prophets from ancient time" (NASB, omitting the comma after "things"). Peter's statement, therefore, is not a declaration of universal salvation or ultimate reconciliation, but of the fulfillment of the promised blessings for national Israel prophesied in the OT. In v. 23 Peter warns that everyone who does not heed God's final Prophet (the Messiah) will be utterly destroyed (see James I. Packer, "The Way of Salvation, Part III: The Problems of Universalism," BS, CXXX [1973], 3-11).

Bibliography. A. Oepke, *"Apokatastasis,"* TDNT, I, 389-393.

S. N. G.

RESURRECTION OF JESUS CHRIST. The miracle of Easter is the heart of the Christian faith and message. The resurrection and the cross are the main themes of Acts and of the epistles. Peter speaks of the One "whom God hath raised up, having loosed the pains of death," in his speech at Pentecost (Acts 2:24). The phrase "whom God hath raised from the dead," or its equivalent, recurs again and again in Acts (3:15; 4:10; 5:30; 10:40; 13:23, 30, 37; 26:8) and in the same manner in the epistles of Paul (Rom 8:11; 10:9; I Cor 6:14; 15:15; II Cor 1:9; 4:14; Gal 1:1; Eph 1:20; I Thess 1:10; cf. I Pet 1:21). Christ's atoning death and the empty tomb are mentioned together by our Lord in what can be called a redemption complex. He associated the two together in His teaching (Mt 16:21; 20:18-19; Mk 8:31; 9:31; 10:33-34; Lk 18:32-33; Jn 10:17-18). Peter does the same (I Pet 1:2-4; 3:18 f.).

The Garden Tomb, Jerusalem. Photo Leon

Theology of Christ's Resurrection

The resurrection is the miraculous proof that Christ has atoned for sin (Acts 2:24, 38; 13:37-38; Rom 1:4) and overcome death (II Tim 1:10; Rev 1:18). Through it He has been declared to be Lord and Christ (Acts 2:32-36) and the Son of God with power (Rom 1:4; Phil 2:6-11; cf. Acts 13:33). As the firstborn from the dead He has been declared Head of the Church and Sovereign of the universe (Col 1:16-18; Eph 1:19-23; cf. Heb 1:3). He Himself is the resurrection, the dispenser of eternal life (Jn 11:25). When He was raised from the dead and ascended on high, He sent forth the Holy Spirit (Acts 2:33, 38; cf. Jn 15:26; 16:7).

It is the resurrected Lord who, as our High Priest, has presented His sacrificial blood to God the Father (Heb 10:19-22; cf. 8:3; 10:10-14), now makes intercession for us (Rom 8:34; I Jn 2:1), and is fitted and ordained to unseal the judgments at the end of the age (Rev 5:1-7) and to be the final judge of man (Jn 5:21-22; Acts 10:42; 17:31).

Soteriology of the resurrection. In order that man's sin be atoned for, there must be a perfect life of righteousness lived in complete obedience to God's holy law to be offered "without blemish"; this Christ accomplished in His life (Rom 5:19; 10:4; Heb 4:15; 5:8-9). There must also be a satisfactory atonement for man's sins and the broken law which demands the death penalty (Rom 6:23), and this He provided by submitting to death as our substitute. God showed His absolute satisfaction with Christ's active and passive obedience by raising His Son from the dead and thus attesting that His work to achieve our justification was approved and accepted (Rom 4:25).

Eschatology of the resurrection. The resurrection bespeaks the final complete victory over death and sin and over their effects upon both man and creation. Because Christ arose, believers shall also arise in resurrection bodies (I Cor 15). Because He arose, nature too will be freed from the curse. This is the explanation of the fact that the resurrection of the believer, or the manifestation of the sons of God through "the redemption of our body," and the removal of the "bondage of corruption" at Christ's second coming, are spoken of as occurring simultaneously in Rom 8:18-23 (cf. Isa 11:6-12; 65:25; Zech 14:5).

Denials of the Resurrection

Several theories have been suggested which deny the bodily resurrection of Christ.

Fraud theory. His disciples stole His body from the tomb and hid it somewhere. This view fails to explain how cowards became brave men overnight, and also ignores the fact of the Roman guard. It assumes that the lie of the soldiers is to be accepted instead of the testimony of the believers in Christ. A variation of this view is that Christ's enemies stole the body and hid it. Why then did they not produce it later to refute the claims of the disciples that the Lord had risen?

Hallucination theory. The disciples only thought they had seen Jesus. This fails to account for the fact that they felt His hands and His feet, talked to Him, and ate with Him and He with them (Lk 24:42–43). A variation of this is Richard Niebuhr's historical reason theory, that the disciples had such a vivid historical memory of Christ they thought and spoke of Him as risen. This view fails for the same reasons as the hallucination theory. Besides, as with the former, it must deny the empty tomb.

Objective vision theory. God granted Jesus' followers actual visions to assure them that the spirit of Jesus survived. This view likewise cannot account for the empty tomb nor for His tangible body in His appearances.

Transformed spiritual body theory. In order to attempt to explain how the graveclothes were left intact and how the risen Christ passed through a closed door, some have claimed on the basis of a mistaken interpretation of I Cor 15:44 that Jesus rose with a "spiritual," non-material body. But He ate food in the presence of His disciples.

Swoon theory. Christ was only in a swoon and His disciples spirited Him away from the tomb and revived Him. This view involves the disciples in fraud. Deceivers do not risk their lives later in righteous causes as did the disciples. It fails to do justice to the examination and pronouncement of the Roman soldiers that Jesus was dead. It is most derogatory to the founders of the early church.

Mistaken tomb theory. Kirsopp Lake suggests the women went to the wrong tomb and encountered a stranger, from whom they fled. This is a somewhat desperate attempt to explain a phenomenon which Lake has ruled out as *a priori* impossible, namely, the miracle of a resurrection. It fails to explain both the experience of the soldiers guarding the tomb in which Jesus was buried and the fact that the tomb from which the women fled was empty.

Proofs of the Resurrection

The validity of the resurrection of Christ rests upon the certainty of Jesus' death and burial and sealing of the tomb, the displaced stone and empty tomb, the undisturbed condition of the graveclothes, and on the record of ten different physical appearances of the risen Jesus. The appearances are attested in six accounts—in all four Gospels, in Acts, and I Cor 15:

1. To Mary Magdalene (Jn 20:11–18).
2. To the other women (Mt 28:9–10).
3. Privately to Peter (I Cor 15:5; Lk 24:34).
4. To Cleopas and his companion on the road to Emmaus (Lk 24:13–35).
5. To ten of the apostles in a locked room (Jn 20:19–25; Lk 24:36–43).
6. To Thomas and the others a week later (Jn 20:26–29).
7. To over 500 disciples on one occasion (I Cor 15:6). Presumably this was in Galilee in fulfillment of Mt 28:7–8; Mk 16:7. It may have been the same occasion as Jesus' giving the great commission to His followers (Mt 28:16–20).
8. To James the Lord's brother (I Cor 15:7).
9. To seven disciples by the Sea of Galilee (Jn 21:1–23).
10. To the apostles and perhaps others in Jerusalem at the time of His ascension (Lk 24:50–52; Acts 1:4–9).

Other such appearances are alluded to in Acts 1:3.

Christ's resurrection is historically attested by: (1) the fact of the sudden change in the lives of the apostles—the 11 were cowards at the crucifixion but men ready to give their very lives 50 days later at Pentecost: (2) the descent of the Holy Spirit on the day of Pentecost, in fulfillment of Jesus' promise (Jn 14:16; 15:26; 16:7; cf. 7:37–39; Acts 2:32–33); (3) the changing of the day of worship from the Jewish sabbath to the first day of the week, as a testimony to the day upon which Christ arose; (4) the sudden and amazing growth of the Christian church; (5) the existence of the NT, whose very message hinges upon the authenticity of the resurrection.

The bodily resurrection of Jesus Christ is the best attested event in ancient history. And as Merrill C. Tenney sums it up: "The resurrection is relevant to the human need for purpose and assurance. . . .The event is fixed in history; the dynamic is potent for eternity" (*The Reality of the Resurrection,* p. 19).

See Resurrection of the Body.

Bibliography. William Milligan, *The Resurrection of Our Lord,* London: Macmillan, 1894. Frank Morrison, *Who Moved the Stone?* London: Faber & Faber, 1930. Richard R. Niebuhr, *Resurrection and Historical Reason,* New York: Scribner's, 1957. J. Orr, *The Resurrection of Jesus,* Cincinnati: Jenning and Bryan, 1909. Elmer E. Parsons, *Witness to the Resurrection,* Grand Rapids: Baker, 1967. A. M. Ramsey, *The Resurrection of Christ,* Philadelphia: Westminster, 1946. Merrill C. Tenney, *The Reality of the Resurrection,* Chicago: Moody, 1972 (with extensive bibliography).

R. A. K.

RESURRECTION OF THE BODY. The resurrection of the body is a distinctly biblical idea. The Greeks, and Gr. philosophy in general, had little respect for the body, considering it to be a hindrance, and taught only the immortality of the soul. The Bible sees man as created with both body and soul and as incomplete, therefore, during the intermediate state until he receives his resurrection body. The NT adds to the mere idea of a resurrection of the body the revelation that the Christian will have a glorified body like that received by Christ (Phil 3:21; I Jn 3:2).

Resurrection in the OT. The doctrine of a bodily resurrection is clearly taught in the OT, particularly in Job (14:13-15; 19:23-27), the Psalms (16:9-11; 49:14 f.), Isaiah (26:19), and Daniel (12:2). The conscious existence of the soul between death and the resurrection is also clearly stated. The fact that more is said of the condition of the wicked than of the righteous in the intermediate state does not detract from the fact that the dead remain conscious, even if their bodies sleep in the grave (Isa 14:9-20; Ezk 32:17-32).

Job in 14:14 asks, "If a man die, shall he live again?" and answers: "All the days of my appointed time will I wait, till my change come. Thou shalt call, and I will answer thee. . . ." In chap. 19 he takes up the subject again. Job knows his Redeemer lives and will stand upon the earth in the latter days, and he is sure that, even though worms destroy his body in the grave, yet "from" his flesh and with his own eyes he will see God at that time (Job 19:25-27). The translation "from my flesh" (RSV) rather than "in my flesh" (KJV) is preferable on the basis of the Heb. *mibbeśārî* (*min,* "from"; *bāśār,* "flesh"; see BDB: *min,* "the place out of which," p. 579*a*). Both the LXX and Jerome support the view that Job is referring to his future resurrection.

Ps 16:9-11 gives the promise, "Thou wilt not leave my soul in hell; neither wilt thou suffer thine Holy One to see corruption," which Peter points out in his sermon at Pentecost applies to the Greater David, Christ (Acts 2:25-31). This is the most important mention of the resurrection in the Psalms, though it is referred to at least in Ps 49:14 f.

In Dan 12:2 there is a very important prophecy of the resurrection. A literal translation of the Heb. would be, "Many from among those who sleep in the dust of the earth shall awake, these to everlasting life but those to shame and everlasting contempt." The translation "many from among those who sleep" is justified by the Heb. words *rabbim miyy'eshērê* (see JFB, which bases such a translation on data from Tregelles). The translation "these . . .but those" is a better rendering of the Heb. *'ēlleh. . . 'ēlleh,* than the "some. . .some" of the KJV. This passage is very important, since when translated literally it teaches two resurrections, one of the righteous and a second of the wicked, as found in Rev 20:4-6 (cf. Jn 5:28-29).

The prophet Zechariah foretells the final siege of Jerusalem along with the repentance of Israel at the second coming of the Lord, and writes, "The Lord my God shall come, and all the saints with thee," showing that the believers who have died are with the Lord and will return to reign with Him on the earth (Zech 14:5; cf. Rev 5:10).

Some have criticized the OT for its lack of information on the immortality of the soul, and have suggested that even what is given only appeared quite late. Both of these criticisms are unjustified. The NT also does not go into any detail about the state of the soul immediately after death, that is, the intermediate state. God has concentrated His revelation both in OT and NT upon the resurrection and the blessings of the kingdom.

It is difficult to prove that the idea oι immortality appears only late in the OT. Many consider Job to be very early, and this book is very clear both on immortality and bodily resurrection. Be that as it may, the patriarchs believed in a future life. Enoch did not even die but went directly to be with God (Gen 5:24; Heb 11:5). Abraham "looked for a city which hath foundations, whose builder and maker is God" (Heb 11:10). The OT saints all looked forward to the kingdom (Heb 11:13-16; cf. Lk 13:28-29) from the days of the Abrahamic covenant on, not only for their distant descendants but also for themselves.

Resurrection in the NT. In the NT the Gr. *anastasis* refers to the rising to life of the dead body. Only in Lk 2:34 is the word translated otherwise, and even there resurrection may be the correct translation. This does not have to be a particle-by-particle regathering and reconstitution of the old body of flesh, since the resurrection body is one with entirely different qualities from the old body; but it does mean the constitution of a body like that received by Christ (Phil 3:21) and suitable to the soul's eternal state.

The NT clearly teaches an order or series ın the resurrection. Paul reveals in I Cor 15:20-24 that it is to be "every man in his own order: Christ the firstfruits; afterward they that are Christ's at his coming. Then cometh the end. . . ." This agrees with what Christ had Himself said in Jn 5:28 f.: "Marvel not at this: for the hour is coming, in the which all that are in the graves shall hear his voice, and shall come forth; they that have done good, unto the resurrection of life; and they that have done evil, unto the resurrection of damnation." Daniel, as seen, indicates two resurrections, and Rev 20:4-6 speaks of a first resurrection of the saints as distinct from a second of "the rest of the dead," the unsaved, and says the second is separated from the first by a thousand years. In I Thess 4:16-17 it is only the dead in Christ who are raised at His coming, and these are immediately snatched, raptured, to heaven (cf. Christ's warning to be ready for the rapture, Mt 24:40-44; Mk 13:28-29; Lk 21:29-31).

The resurrection body. It is revealed that the believer shall be like his Lord (Phil 3:21; I Jn 3:2), having a tangible body "like his glorious body." The identity will be retained between the mortal body and the new resurrection body, even though this does not necessitate a reconstitution from the same atoms. Even in this life the materials of the body change constantly. They are entirely replaced in a progressive manner within the span of a few years.

Christ arose in the body in which He had suffered, leaving an empty tomb. His new body had "flesh and bones," and yet, though He was absolutely recognizable, its qualities were gloriously changed. The believer's new body is not to be "flesh and blood," for this is the nature of his mortal body. He will be like the angels in that he will neither marry nor give in marriage (Mt 22:29-30). This new body is described in I Cor 15:35-50.

Spiritual and moral implications. Man is a bipartite creature composed of body and soul. He is part of a race. Only because he is, can he know the federal headship of the first Adam in which he fell and was lost, and can enter into the benefits of the federal headship of the last Adam, Jesus Christ, and be saved. "As in Adam all die, even so in Christ shall all be made alive" (I Cor 15:22). Christ redeemed not only the soul but also the body, as proved in the resurrection of His own body.

The believer's body is the temple of the Holy Spirit and is to be kept pure (I Cor 6:19-20), and finally miraculously changed to suit the eternal needs of the sons of God. Because of the important function of the body he is neither to despise it, nor to destroy it by licentious living.

See Dead, The; Eschatology; Eternal Life; Eternal State and Death; Immortality; Life; Resurrection of Christ.

Bibliography. Norman H. Camp, *The Resurrection of the Human Body*, Chicago: Bible Inst. Colportage Assn., 1937. Albrecht Oepke, *"Anistēmi,* etc.," TDNT, I, 368-372. Irwin Reist, "The OT Basis for the Resurrection Faith," EQ, XLIII (1971), 6-24. Elmer Smick, "The Bearing of New Philological Data on the Subject of Resurrection and Immortality in the OT," WTJ, XXXI (1968), 12-21. Wilbur M. Smith, "Resurrection," BDT, pp. 448-456.

R. A. K̦.

RETRIBUTION. *See* Death; Eschatology; Eternal State and Death; Hell.

RETURN OF CHRIST. *See* Christ, Coming of.

REU (rē'ū). A descendant of Shem; the son of Peleg and father of Serug (Gen 11:18-21; I Chr 1:25; Lk 3:35, RSV). After him a Mesopotamian tribe or its territory may have been named, for there is an island in the Euphrates with the Akkad. name of Ra'ilu.

REUBEN (rū'bĕn)

1. The oldest son of Jacob by his wife Leah (Gen 29:31-32; 35:23; 46:8; I Chr 2:1; 5:1). Reuben had four sons, Hanoch, Phallu, Hezron, and Carmi (Gen 46:8-9; Ex 6:14; I Chr 5:3).

Reuben lived under the cloud of his gross sin of lying with Bilhah, his father's concubine (Gen 35:22). Many of his later acts were more noble. When his brothers plotted to kill Joseph, he persuaded them to put Joseph in a well instead, with the hope that he could later liberate him. Reuben was not with his brothers when Joseph was sold to the Midianites (or Ishmaelites), and he was greatly distressed to find the pit empty (Gen 37:21-29).

When the brothers were in Egypt buying grain, Reuben immediately associated their peril and anxiety with a judgment from God upon them for what they had done to Joseph (Gen 42:22). Reuben was ready to pledge his own two sons to assure his father of Benjamin's safe return (Gen 42:37).

On his deathbed Jacob seemed to commend Reuben for his strength and "excellency of dignity," but in the next breath he told him that he was as "unstable as water" and declared that he should not be the leader because of his incestuous act with Bilhah (Gen 49:1-4).

2. The tribe of Reuben was divided into four clans, or divisions. Elizur was their "prince" or chief at the beginning of the journey from Egypt (Num 1:5; 2:10; 7:30-35; 10:18). The first census showed the number of fighting men to be 46,500 (Num 1:20-21), while at the second numbering it had decreased to 43,730 (Num 26:7). The tribal standard of Reuben flew over three tribes—Reuben, Simeon, and Gad—totaling 151,450 fighting men (Num 2:10, 16). When the 12 spies were sent out, Shammua, son of Zaccur (Num 13:4), was selected to represent the tribe.

Three men of Reuben—Dathan, Abiram, and On—joined Korah's revolt against Moses and Aaron (Num 16:1-50; 26:9; Deut 11:6). At the end of the war with Sihon and Og, Reuben, Gad, and half the tribe of Manasseh petitioned Moses to allow them to settle on the E side of Jordan. Moses approved their request on the condition that they send a sizable group of fighting men across the Jordan to help their brethren in wresting the W side from the Canaanites (Num 32:1-42; Josh 18:7). They fulfilled this agreement, taking part in all of Joshua's campaigns (Josh 4:12), and afterward returning to their own territory. It lay almost entirely E of the Dead Sea. It extended from Heshbon and Beth-jeshimoth S to the Arnon River (Josh 13:15-20; Num 32:37-38).

In their patriotic enthusiasm the men of Reuben, Gad, and Manasseh erected a testimonial altar on the W side of the Jordan (Josh 22:11, NASB) which, through a temporary misunderstanding, almost caused civil war (Josh 22:1-34). When war came with Sisera a century and a half later, the Reubenites took no part and were reproached in Deborah's song (Jud 5:15-16). Reuben, Gad, and the half tribe of Manasseh waged a successful war against the

Hagarites (*q.v.*) during the reign of Saul, and lived in their territory until the Assyrian captivity (I Chr 5:10, 18–22). But the Moabites occupied the towns in the land of Reuben by the 9th cen. B.C. according to the Moabite Stone (see also Isa 15; 16; Jer 48). It was Tiglath-pileser III (747-725 B.C.) who carried Beerah, the last leader of the Reubenites, into exile (I Chr 5:6; II Kgs 15:29).

Ezekiel assigned Reuben a portion in his reconstituted Israel (Ezk 48:6, 31), and John mentioned the tribe in his list of the 144,000 witnesses (Rev 7:5).

H. A. Han.

REUBENITE (rōō'bĕn-īt). The tribe or family of Jacob's eldest son (Num 26:7; I Chr 5:1–8; Deut 3:12). They settled E of the Jordan River (Josh 13:15–23). Their land was the southernmost of Israel's inheritance in Transjordania, and was constantly menaced by adjacent peoples. The tribe played no important part in Israelitish affairs subsequent to the invasion, and in all probability ceased to function as a tribe following the reigns of Omri and Ahab. The Reubenites were taken into exile by Tiglath-pileser III to upper Mesopotamia (I Chr 5:26). *See* Reuben.

REUEL (rōō'ĕl)

1. A descendant of Esau and of Ishmael (Gen 36:2–4, 10, 13, 17; I Chr 1:35, 37); his genealogy points to an early close relationship between the Edomite and Arabian tribes.

2. Moses' father-in-law (Ex 2:18, 21), spelled Raquel in the KJV in Num 10:29 following the LXX; also called Jethro (*q.v.*). The name Reuel (Heb. *re'û-'ēl)* means "friend, companion of El," suggesting that Jethro and the Midianites were worshipers of El, the chief deity of the early Semites, the God of the patriarchs and of Melchizedek (Gen 14:18–22). Therefore original El worship may have continued unrivaled in desert areas, where Jethro lived, long after it died out in Canaan (Ulf Oldenburg, *The Conflict Between El and Ba'al in Canaanite Religion,* Leiden: Brill, 1969, p. 170). W. F. Albright believes Reuel is the clan name of Jethro and Hobab *(Yahweh and the Gods of Canaan,* Garden City: Doubleday, 1968, pp. 38 ff.).

3. A Gadite, father of Eliasaph (Num 2:14), same as Deuel (*q.v.*).

4. A Benjamite (I Chr 9:8).

J. R.

REUMAH (rōō'mȧ). Nahor's concubine (Gen 22:24). Her four sons were probably the ancestors of the Aramean tribes generally located N of Damascus and related secondarily to the Israelites.

REVELATION. The Heb. and Gr. verbs pertaining to revelation (*gālal, apokalyptō)* express the idea of uncovering or revealing something which has been hidden and unknown.

History of revelation. The history of revelation began in the garden of Eden when man had direct communication with God. The Fall brought in sin, the exclusion of man from his former life of blessedness, and the end of direct communion with God. Ever since that time there have been two means or kinds of revelation: general and special. General revelation continued as before, but special revelation henceforth depended upon the sovereign grace of God. Through God's intervention in the life, first of the patriarchs and then in the chosen nation of Israel, special revelation was given. Israel alone of all nations was chosen to receive this blessing (Deut 4:7–8; Ps 147:19–20; Amos 3:2), not because of their greatness or goodness, but by God's grace (Deut 7:7–8; 9:4–6). They did not receive it for themselves alone, but that through them all the nations should be blessed (Gen 12:2–3; 17:4-6, 16; 18:18; 22:18; cf. Rom 4:13–18). The revelation given to Israel included covenants and promises which culminate in Christ, as first the suffering, sacrificial Messiah, and then, the ruling, reigning Messiah. When Christ came, His life, actions, and words were all a revelation. The book of Revelation, given some years later to John and introduced by the words "the Revelation of Jesus Christ," only completed this revelation that began with His incarnation.

The relationship between general and special revelation. General revelation is adapted to man as man, and directed to all intelligent creatures; special revelation is to man as a fallen, sinful creature, and directed to that particular class of sinners to whom God has chosen to make Himself known. General revelation is sufficient to reveal to man God's eternal power and Godhead (or deity). It makes man responsible, as a rational creature made in the image of God, to recognize His existence, power, and deity. It renders him inexcusable if he fails to do so (Rom 1:19–20).

But general revelation is not sufficient to bring man to heaven. Since man is a fallen creature and a sinner, he needs to know a way of salvation. This, special revelation alone supplies. There is, therefore, no question, even if a natural theology is possible through general revelation, whether special revelation is necessary or not. Jesus said to His followers, "Ye believe in God, believe also in me" (Jn 14:1). A belief in God without a belief in Christ, brought about through a special revelation, cannot save.

While general and special revelation are to be distinguished, still they belong together. Each is incomplete without the other. Revelation in its most general sense has to do with the creation of the world and man, and man's relationship to the world and to God. The Fall, destroying the direct communication between man and God, necessitated the new mode of special revelation.

Theological controversies over revelation. Several controversies in particular have arisen in recent theology.

1. Existential versus propositional revela-

tion. Sören Kierkegaard introduced the idea of existential, personal, subjective, here-and-now revelation. Karl Barth, Emil Brunner, and the other neoorthodox theologians have propagated the view that as man reads a faulty, contradictory Bible, he may receive Christ, who is revelation and the Word of God, and thus may experience revelation. Inspiration and revelation are transferred from the writer of Scripture and the time when he wrote, to the reader and hearer and the time he has his experience. In doing this, the neoorthodox confuse and transpose the inspiration of the writer and the illumination of the hearer. At the same time, they deny that there is such a thing as propositional revelation, that is, statements of revealed truth, to be found in the Bible. This denial of propositional truth cannot be reconciled with the statements of the apostles about Scripture (II Tim 3:16-17; II Pet 1:19-21) and the teachings of Christ concerning the infallibility of the Bible (Mt 5:17-18), or with His own claim concerning the truth of what He teaches as that which He has heard (Jn 8:26), seen (v. 38), and been taught (v. 28) by God the Father.

2. Denial of general revelation. This is not a general characteristic of neoorthodoxy. It concerns a difference of viewpoint between Karl Barth and Emil Brunner in particular. Fearing that the acceptance of any truth such as general revelation must inevitably lead to the formation of a natural theology—as in Roman Catholicism—Barth violently opposes any view of general revelation. The heavens are "dumb" and Ps 19 and Rom 1:18-20 are only the confessions of a regenerated man, Barth claims. Man is dead in sins and God must create a point of contact in man before he can receive any revelation. Brunner, on the other hand, teaches general revelation. Man is still man and has the image of God even if that image is marred.

For the evangelical the argument of Rom 1:18-20 is clear and conclusive: man definitely can know of God's existence, His power, His deity, and His glory (Ps 19:1 ff.), and is without excuse when he holds down the truth in unrighteousness and represses general revelation.

The modes of special revelation. Throughout history God has revealed Himself in several different ways. He appeared and conversed with man in the theophanies of the OT. To Moses and to him alone He spoke not by dream or vision, but mouth to mouth (Num 12:8). To others He revealed Himself in visions or dreams. Again, He spoke through the prophets, or in a concursive operation guided the thought and hand of the prophets and psalmists. However, between these different modes no discrimination or gradation in value is ever made. They all form parts of the one great unified body of progressive revelation of which Christ's teachings form the capstone. Jesus Christ Himself as the Son of God is God's supreme revelation to man (Heb 1:1-3).

See Inspiration; Prophecy.

The barren isle of Patmos, where John probably wrote the Revelation. HFV

Bibliography. Carl F. H. Henry (ed.), *Revelation and the Bible,* Grand Rapids: Baker, 1958; "Revelation, Special," BDT, pp. 456-459. Albrecht Oepke, "*Kalyptō, . . . Apokalypsis,*" TDNT, III, 556-592. J. I. Packer, "Revelation," NBD, pp. 1090-1093. Clark H. Pinnock, *Biblical Revelation,* Chicago: Moody, 1971. Bernard Ramm, *Special Revelation and the Word of God,* Grand Rapids: Eerdmans, 1961. Merrill C. Tenney (ed.), *The Bible—The Living Word of Revelation,* Grand Rapids: Zondervan, 1968.

R. A. K.

REVELATION, BOOK OF THE. This concluding book of the NT reveals the final and permanent victory that is obtained by the King of kings and Lord of lords. It shows heaven's rule, the establishment of righteousness, and an unveiling of the heavenly home in its infinite glory and beauty. The book of Revelation is the perfect, inevitable conclusion to divine revelation.

"Revelation" is a Latin word from the verb *revelare,* meaning "to reveal or unveil that which has previously been hidden." Revelation is the title of this book in the Latin Vulgate and the English translations. The Gr. title is Apocalypse, taken directly from the first word of the Gr. text *apokalypsis.* As a verb, it is frequently used in the NT, particularly in reference to God's special revelations to man in Jesus Christ (Lk 17:30; Rom 8:18; II Thess 1:7; I Pet 1:7, 13). *See* Apocalypse.

Author and Date

It was the unanimous verdict of the early church, and generally though not exclusively of biblical scholars since then, that the author was the apostle John, the writer of the fourth Gospel. He inserted his actual name four times in this book (Rev 1:1, 4, 9; 22:8). A majority of conservative scholars today are agreed that John wrote this book on the island of Patmos, to which he had been banished by Emperor Domitian (A.D. 81-96).

Characteristics

It is interesting that of the 916 different words found in the Gr. text of Revelation, 416 of them are also found in the fourth Gospel, 98 occur only once elsewhere in the NT, while 108 are not found anywhere else in the NT. Words meaning "to see," "to perceive," etc., occur nearly 150 times in this book. Sometimes John records what he hears, but generally what he sees. It is estimated that in its 265 verses there are 550 references to OT data, including 79 to Isaiah. The book itself often closely parallels and supplements the prophecies of the book of Daniel.

The first three chapters of Revelation relate to the seven churches of Asia as they existed toward the end of the 1st cen. The vision of heavenly activity recorded in chaps. 4 and 5 does not have a specific time factor. Beginning with chap. 6, however, events are prophesied which have not taken place on this earth. Whatever may have been the attempts of different commentators, e.g., to identify the locusts coming out of the bottomless pit in chap. 9, no such world catastrophe has yet occurred involving "armies of the horsemen twice ten thousand times ten thousand" (9:16, ASV). The rule of Antichrist in chap. 13 is not to be identified with any past event, nor is the battle of Armageddon. This is a book, therefore, that has to do principally with events that are yet to come, with the terrible destructions and tribulations at the end of this age, with the second coming of Christ, the Millennium, the judgment of the Great White Throne, and our eternal home in heaven.

Revelation above every other book of the Bible is a book of one world. Frequently such phrases occur as "many peoples, and nations, and tongues, and kings" (10:11; 11:9; 17:15). When kings are introduced they are often referred to as "the kings of the whole world" (16:14; 17:2, 18; 18:9; 19:19). Of Satan it is said that he is "the deceiver of the whole world" (12:9). The beast of the sea is given "authority over every tribe and people and tongue and nation" (13:7-8, ASV). Christ will ultimately reign over "the kingdom of the world" (11:15).

Remains of a Byzantine church, Sardis, one of the seven churches of Rev. 1-3. HFV

REVELATION, BOOK OF THE

While the book of Revelation is one of ultimate glorious, permanent victory, it is at the same time a book of constant conflict to the very end of its prophecies. It is significant that such words as "king," "kingdom," "rule," "throne," "conquer," "power," "war," "slay," "kill" are used both in reference to Christ, and to Satan and Antichrist and the other enemies of God. While there are 38 references to the throne of God from 1:4 to 22:3, yet Satan has a throne (2:13; 13:2), and the beast has a throne (16:10).

The word "kill" (Gr. *apokteinoō*) occurs more frequently here than in all the rest of the NT combined. The rider on the pale horse killed with the sword, with famine, and with death (6:8, 11; see also 9:15, 18). The witnesses in Jerusalem were killed by the beast (11:7); but toward the end of the book, at the battle of Armageddon, "the rest were killed with the sword of him that sat upon the horse, even the sword which came forth out of his mouth" (19:21, ASV). In the latter part of the book mention is made of a war in heaven (12:7); of a beast who had great military power (13:4); of the kings of the earth who war against the Lamb (17:14); and of Christ Himself on a white horse, and "he that sat upon him was called Faithful and True, and in righteousness he doth judge and make war" (19:11). Sometimes the enemies of God overcome the saints of God (11:7; 13:7; etc.). But these powers are ultimately overthrown, and to all believers of every age is given the promise, "They overcame him by the blood of the Lamb, and by the word of their testimony" (12:11).

In studying this book and attempting to separate its various periods and types of activity, note that there is here an alternating sequence of scenes in heaven and on earth. Thus the description of the Son of God in heaven in chaps. 4 and 5 is followed by the judgments of the six seals on earth. The second scene in heaven (7:9–8:5) is followed by the judgments of the seven trumpets. The voice from heaven recorded in chap. 10 is followed by the fearful events of chaps. 11–13. This sequence of activity in heaven followed by judgments on earth emphatically presents two great truths: that heaven foreknows what will take place on earth, and what is decided in heaven is what must occur on earth. Throughout the book the fact is continually emphasized that it is God who "did put in their hearts to do his mind, and to come to one mind, and to give their kingdom unto the beast, until the words of God should be accomplished" (17:17, ASV).

Within the context of these heavenly scenes are a series of 14 remarkable hymns sung in heaven (4:8; 4:11; 5:9-10; 5:12; 5:13; 7:10; 7:12; 11:15; 11:16-17; 14:3; 15:3-4; 19:1-2; 19:3-5; 19:6-8). These hymns are sung by different groups, concerning varying themes, sometimes addressed to God, sometimes to Christ, and sometimes to both.

Methods of Interpretation

Different from any other book of the NT, Revelation has given rise to four major schemes of interpretation. From the days of Augustine down to the present time, some have insisted that the purpose of the book is not to teach about future events but rather to encourage Christians with basic spiritual principles, especially the power of God and the ultimate victory of Christ. It is true that the book does have such a message, but certainly it is a book of prophecy, with such specific events as the appearance of Antichrist, the battle of Armageddon, etc.

The second scheme of interpretation is known as the preterist, which insists that primarily the author was only referring to contemporary events occurring within the Roman Empire, a view that has been held by Moffatt, Simcox, etc. These scholars insist, e.g., that the ruler with the deadly wound refers to Nero, and the beast of chap. 13 refers to Domitian, but, as Milligan has well said, "The whole tone of the book leads to the opposite conclusion. It treats of much that was to happen down to the very end of time. . . .The Apocalypse bears distinctly upon its face that it is concerned with the history of the church until she enters upon her heavenly inheritance."

The third scheme of interpretation is known as the historicist, which sets forth the view that, especially in the judgment of the seals, the trumpets and the bowls, the book predicts specific events relating to the church, occurring from the 1st cen. down to modern times. Many holding this view claim that the trumpet judgments extend from A.D. 495–1453. Some say that the earthquake of 11:19 refers to the French Revolution, etc. But such a system of interpretation allows freedom for those holding it to identify any event they wish with any major section of the book of Revelation. None holding this view agrees in general as to the specific events which are indicated by any one of these 21 periods of judgment represented by the seven seals, the seven trumpets and the seven bowls.

Ruins of the Church of St. John, Ephesus, one of the seven churches of Rev. 1-3. Esat Balim

The fourth group, known as futurists, believe that the visions of this book, from the events of chap. 6 down to the appearance of the Holy City, are all to be placed in the future. Some of the outstanding contributors to an understanding of the book of Revelation belonging to this school have been Joseph Seiss, S. P. Tregelles, William Kelly, Nathaniel West, Henry Alford, Theodore Zahn, William G. Moorehead, Walter Scott.

There is some truth in each of these systems of interpretation; e.g., there are great spiritual truths throughout the book, and the first three chapters must be interpreted historically; but for the most part the prophecies of the Apocalypse still await their fulfillment.

Since the invention and use of atomic bombs and the creation of hydrogen bombs, many interpreters are willing to consider the future view. Many writers have begun to refer to this era as "an apocalyptic age," because the dreadful possibilities of mass destruction by the enormous powers under the control of godless and unmoral governments seem similar to the havoc to be wrought on this earth by the judgments prophesied in the Apocalypse.

Outline

There have been a number of different proposals made in attempting to outline the book of Revelation, but the following contains at least the major subjects of the book in the order of their presentation.

Prologue, 1:1–8

I. The Vision of the Glorified Christ and His Letters to the Seven Churches of Asia, 1:9–3:22

II. The Opening of the Seven-sealed Book in Heaven and the Earthly Events It Announces, 4:1–6:17

III. The Condition of Redeemed Saints on Earth and in Heaven, and the Judgments Announced by Seven Trumpets, 7:1–9:21

IV. The Rule of Antichrist, the Darkest Hour in World History, 10:1–13:18

V. The Preparatory Announcements from Heaven and the Seven Bowls of Judgment, 14:1–16:21

VI. The Fall of Babylon and the Battle of Armageddon, 17:1–19:21

VII. The Millennium; the Last Judgment; the New Jerusalem and Eternity, 21:1–22:5

Epilogue, 22:6–21

Bibliography. Henry Alford, *The Greek Testament,* 2 vols., Chicago: Moody Press, 1958. J. Oliver Buswell, Jr., *Systematic Theology,* Grand Rapids: Zondervan, II (1963), 424–538. Robert Govett, *The Apocalypse Expounded,* London: Thynne and Jarvis, 1929. G. H. Lang, *The Revelation of Jesus Christ,* London: Paternoster, 1945. J. P. Lange, *Commentary on the Holy Scriptures,* Vol. XXIV, New York: Charles Scribner's Sons and Armstrong, 1874, especially notes by E. R. Craven. R. C. Lenski,

The Interpretation of St. John's Revelation, Columbus: Wartburg, 1943. William Milligan, *The Book of Revelation,* New York: Armstrong, 1889. William C. Moorehead, *Studies in the Book of Revelation,* New York: Revell, 1908. William R. Newell, *The Book of the Revelation,* Chicago: Grace Publications, 1941. Ford C. Ottman, *The Unfolding of the Ages,* New York: Baker and Taylor, 1905. Walter Scott, *Exposition of the Revelation of Jesus Christ,* London: Pickering and Inglis, n.d. Joseph A. Seiss, *The Apocalypse,* Grand Rapids: Zondervan, n.d. J. B. Smith, *A Revelation of Jesus Christ,* Scottdale, Pa.: Herald Press, 1961. Wilbur M. Smith, "Revelation," *Wycliffe Bible Commentary,* Chicago: Moody, 1962. Henry Barclay Swete, *The Apocalypse of St. John,* 3rd ed., London: Macmillan, 1909. M. C. Tenney, *Interpreting Revelation,* Grand Rapids: Eerdmans, 1957. John F. Walvoord, *The Revelation of Jesus Christ,* Chicago: Moody, 1966.

W. M. S.

REVELLING. The KJV translation of Gr. *kōmos* (Gal 5:21; I Pet 4:3). The word also occurs in Rom 13:13 as "rioting" (KJV), "reveling" (RSV), or "carousing" (NASB). It denotes excessive feasting, which often accompanied the orgiastic festivals in honor of such gods as Dionysus and Zeus (as implied by Wisd 14:23; II Macc 6:4 where the Gr. word occurs). It came to mean a riotous procession of drunken fellows who paraded through the streets at night after a feast with torches and loud music (Thayer, *Greek-English Lexicon,* p. 367).

REVENGE, REVENGER. These words are used in the sense of righting or avenging a wrong, or of the one who avenges a wrong. The revenger of blood (*gō'ēl haddām;* cf. "avenger of blood," ASV and RSV) was a near relative who by ancient law was permitted to slay the murderer of a member of his family (Num 35:19–21; II Sam 14:11). However, he was not permitted to kill a manslayer who remained in a city of refuge (Num 35:22–27). *See* Blood, Avenger of.

The psalmist prayed that there might be the revenging of the shed blood of God's servants (Ps 79:10; cf. "avenging," RSV). Jeremiah faced acquaintances who desired to take revenge on him (Jer 20:10). The Philistines had dealt revengefully (Ezk 25:15; cf. "acted revengefully," RSV). In the last two passages the wrong, spiteful spirit is evident, which God will punish.

"The beginning of revenges [*p^erā'ôt*] upon the enemy" (Deut 32:42) appears to be a mistranslation in the KJV. "From the long-haired heads of the enemy" (RSV) is an attempt to make the passage more meaningful. Yet the overall meaning of Deut 32:39–43 is clear that God takes vengeance on His adversaries (cf. Nah 1:2).

As the concept of revenge in the NT is studied it is clear that this hateful attitude or a vindictive, resentful feeling against the offender is absent. The civil magistrate is called by Paul "the minister of God, a revenger to execute wrath upon him that doeth evil" (Rom 13:4). In II Cor 7:11 he says the church in Corinth is guiltless in its disciplinary zeal and revenge or punishment meted out to the incestuous person. He writes further that he is ready to "revenge" or punish all disobedience when their obedience is fully shown (II Cor 10:6). *How* he intended to carry out this avenging is not stated; he might do it by excommunication, by giving the offenders over to the power of Satan (as in I Cor 5:5), or by a certain exercise of a charismatic gift with apostolic authority.

In no case does God, or His servant Paul, ever display resentment. This rises up in the mind immediately upon being injured; but godly revenge may wait years after the offense is committed. Revenge in the vindictive sense is forbidden by the commands to love our enemies and to return good for evil.

Paul suggested that an aspect of the life in Christ is that of having a readiness to revenge disobedience (II Cor 10:6).

H. E. Fi.

REVENUE. *See* King; Taxes; Tribute.

REVERENCE. The respect shown to some important or distinguished person: to a king (II Sam 9:6; I Kgs 1:31); to the son in the parable of the vineyard (Mt 21:37; Mk 12:6; Lk 20:13); to a father (Heb 12:9); to a husband (Eph 5:33). Israel was to respect God's sabbath and His sanctuary (Lev 19:30; 26:2). We are to reverence and respect God with a sense of awe and godly fear (Ps 89:7; Heb 12:28).

REVILE. The English term appears in Mt 27:39 where the Gr. is *blasphēmeō,* "to blaspheme" or "to speak reproachfully," "to rail at," or "to calumniate." This term is indicative of the contemptuousness of sheer irreverence for either God or sacred things (cf. Lk 23:39; Tit 3:2; Jas 2:7). In Mk 15:32 the term *oneidizō* appears, meaning "to reproach," "upbraid," or "revile." The verb *loidoreō* is used to describe the abusive attack on Jesus by His persecutors (I Pet 2:23). These terms show the utter lack of reverence for the suffering Saviour expressed by those who mocked Him. Paul was accused of this in his answer to the high priest (Acts 23:2–4). And Paul lists it in the catalog of evildoers given in I Cor 6:10.

Jesus has given by precept (Mt 5:11–12) and example (I Pet 2:23) the Christian's correct response to such verbal abuse, as has the apostle Paul (I Cor 4:12). "We do not return revilings, persecution, defamation: nothing but blessing" (John Wesley, Notes, 416).

R. E. Pr.

REVIVE, REVIVAL. Revival may be defined as the reawakening of religious faith and spiritual

REVIVE, REVIVAL

life and activity. While the English word "revive" does not occur frequently in the Bible, a number of revivals can be traced and the reviving work of God's Spirit described. The two principal words are Heb. *ḥāyâ*, "to live, recover, come to life" (*Qal*, stem); "preserve alive, quicken, revive" (*Pi'el*); "cause to live, restore to life, revive" (*Hiph'il*), and Gr. *anazaō*, "to be alive again, come to life again, spring into life, revive."

In the KJV "revive" sometimes means literally to come back from the dead to physical life, as in the case of the widow's son (I Kgs 17:22), the man buried in the tomb of Elisha (II Kgs 13:21), and Christ (Rom 14:9). It may describe restoration from grief and discouragement (Jacob, Gen 45:27) or from physical weakness (Samson, Jud 15:19). In Rom 7:9 it speaks of how sin sprang into life in Paul when the commandment regarding coveting convicted him.

Ezra thanked God that He was granting the Jews "a little reviving," a spiritual and political restoration from their bondage and exile in Babylonia (Ezr 9:8-9). This was in answer to prayers for national revival such as Ps 80:18 (NASB) and 85:6, and to the prophecy of Hosea that God would revive His people when they would earnestly seek Him and return to Him (Hos 5:15-6:2; cf. 14:7). In Ezekiel's vision of the dry bones, national resurrection, i.e., the rebirth of Israel politically and spiritually, is depicted by the reconstruction of the human skeletons and then by the breath of the Spirit on them so that they "come to life" (Ezk 37:5, 9, 14, NASB; Heb. *ḥāyâ*). Habakkuk calls upon the Lord to revive His work of redemption in the prophet's own day, such as God had demonstrated long ago in judging Egypt and delivering Israel (Hab 3:2; cf. Ps 44:1-8; 77:12-15).

Passages dealing with personal reviving include those which use "quicken" in the KJV, often translated "revive" in the newer versions. David beseeches the Lord to revive him and bring his soul out of trouble (Ps 143:11), and in another psalm he voices his confidence that God will revive him (or, keep him alive) and save him from his enemies (138:7). In Ps 119 the psalmist repeatedly asks the Lord to "quicken" or revive him, according to His word (vv. 25, 107, 154; cf. vv. 50, 93), in His ways (v. 37), through His righteousness (v. 40), according to His lovingkindness (vv. 88, 159), and according to His judgments or ordinances (vv. 149, 156). The exalted, eternal, holy and transcendent God is the One who delights to dwell with the man broken and humbled in spirit, in order "to revive the spirit of the humble, and to revive the heart of the contrite ones" (Isa 57:15). The father's cry regarding his prodigal son is the epitome of revival: "This my son was dead, and is alive again" (Gr. *anezēsen*, Lk 15:24). Paul reminds Timothy to "rekindle" the gift which God had given him (II Tim 1:6, RSV). But in Ps 71:20 the aged believer seems to go beyond mere hope for revival when he expresses his confidence that God will "quicken me again, and . . . bring me up again from the depths of the earth"; here resurrection from the grave is in view.

In addition to the periodic times of repentance in the era of the judges, at least eight large-scale revivals are described in the OT: the revival at Mount Sinai (Ex 32-34), the revival at Mizpah under Samuel (I Sam 7), the revival on Mount Carmel (I Kgs 18), the revival in Judah during Asa's reign (II Chr 15), the revival in Nineveh (Jon 3), the revival led by Hezekiah (II Chr 29-31), the revival under young King Josiah (II Chr 34-35), and the post-captivity revival (Ezr 9-10; Neh 8-10). The NT records how the early Christians in Jerusalem were revived when they prayed for new boldness and all were filled with the Holy Spirit to witness concerning the resurrection of Jesus (Acts 4:29-33). The sin of Ananias and Sapphira was sovereignly judged, and none of the unbelieving populace dared to associate with the Christians, while multitudes were being saved and healed (5:1-16).

Out of these revivals great spiritual leaders came to the fore, whether they were the human instruments or the products of them. Nevertheless genuine revivals following the biblical patterns are the sovereign work of God. There is always a divine or miraculous element about them (Ex 34:29-35; I Sam 7:10; I Kgs 18:38; Jon 2:10; II Cor 14:11-12; 30:20; 34:14; Neh 8:10, 17; Acts 4:31; 5:5, 10). "No human being can kindle the interest, quicken the conscience of a people, or generate that intensity of spiritual hunger that signifies revival" (F. Carlton Booth, "Revival," BDT, p. 460). Yet great revivals never are sent apart from prayer and intercession and confession of sin (Ex 32:30-32; I Sam 7:5-9; I Kgs 18:36-37; Jon 3:5-9; II Chr 34:26-27; Ezr 9:5-10:1; Neh 9:2-3). The prophetic word (II Chr 15:1-8) or the written Word (II Chr 34:18-21; Neh 8) are vital elements.

God-sent revival produces spiritual revolution and emotional fervor. Great fear (Acts 5:11) or weeping (Joel 2:12; Ezr 10:1; Neh 8:9) or joy (II Chr 30:21-26; Neh 8:17) usually result, along with singing (II Chr 29:30). Above all there is a return to the Lord Himself and to moral righteousness and godly living. II Chr 7:14 remains the greatest revival promise of the Word of God: "[If] My people who are called by My name humble themselves and pray, and seek My face and turn from their wicked ways, then I will hear from heaven, will forgive their sin, and will heal their land" (NASB).

See Quicken; Restore, Restitution.

Bibliography. C. E. Autrey, *Revivals of the Old Testament*, Grand Rapids: Zondervan, 1960. James Burns, *Revivals, Their Laws and Leaders*, 2nd ed. with two chapters by Andrew W. Blackwood, Grand Rapids: Baker, 1960.

J. R.

REWARDS. The OT outlook was that God rewarded the obedient with earthly prosperity and visited the wicked with retribution (Lev 26; Deut 28). In the NT obedience is irrespective of reward (Lk 17:9–10), for obedience is due to God to whom believers owe their whole life. Good works are never viewed as meritorious in the strict sense of the word, for they can be performed only in the strength and grace which God Himself imparts (Rom 8:1–4; I Cor 15:10; Phil 2:13), and even then the Christian's best deeds are always imperfect in this life.

Thus, when God rewards the believer for his works, it is because of His gracious promise and covenant faithfulness, which reckons the deeds as praiseworthy and rewardable because of the motive and end for which they were performed rather than for their actual intrinsic value and worth. Reward does not flow from divine justice or righteousness but from grace and mercy (II Cor 4:17; I Pet 1:4; Rev 21:7).

Reward is used in the Bible also in a negative sense as the punishment for sin (Ps 91:8; 103:10). It is used in the merely human or natural sense of receiving something for something done (Gen 44:4; I Kgs 13:7; Ps 35:12; Mt 6:5). Rewards can be lost (II Jn 8).

There is no question that the NT gives a legitimate and even prominent place to rewards as a motive for the Christian, but rewards are predominantly described in moral and spiritual terms rather than in earthly or material terms (Mt 10:42; 25:45–46; Lk 6:22–23; Heb 11:26), and they are never the chief motive for the believer. *See* Crowns; Prize.

Bibliography. H. Preisker and E. Würthwein, "*Misthos,* etc.," TDNT, IV, 695–728.

R. E. Po.

REZEPH (rē'zĕf). A city in E Syria, an oasis *c.* 80 miles N of Palmyra, or a site in the Jebel Sinjar N of the Euphrates and 100 miles W of Asshur. It is listed with Haran and Gozan (modern Ras-el-'Ain). Sennacherib's commander, in a message to Hezekiah (II Kgs 19:12; Isa 37:12), mentioned it as an example of cities captured by the Assyrians. The city at the time of this message had been in Assyrian hands for at least a century. It was probably incorporated as a part of Assyria by Shalmaneser III after his campaign in that region in 838 B.C. It appears frequently as Raṣappa in Assyrian records between 839 and 737 B.C., which show it to have been an important trading center and the seat of an Assyrian governor (ANET, p. 274).

REZIA (rē-zī'*ȧ*). An Asherite, a son of Ulla (I Chr 7:39), spelled Rizia in RSV and NASB.

REZIN (rē'zĭn)

1. The last king of the Aramaean state of Damascus. Coming from Hadaru, 32 miles SW of Damascus, Rezin probably usurped the throne (ANET, p. 283). "Tabeal" in Isa 7:6 is not the father of Rezin, as had been conjectured earlier, but an Aramaean site. (Cf. W. F. Albright, "The Son of Tabeel," BASOR #140, 34–35.) The death of Jeroboam II of Israel (746 B.C.) gave Rezin the opportunity to bring Damascus back to power again. Early in his reign Rezin is listed as *Raḫianu* in the annals of Tiglath-pileser III along with Menahem of Israel (745–738 B.C.) as being among those paying tribute to the Assyrian. In 734 B.C. Rezin joined Pekah of Israel in attacking Ahaz of Judah to coerce him into joining an anti-Assyrian coalition (II Kgs 15:37; 16:5; Isa 7:1 ff.). At this time Rezin attacked Elath and gave it back not to "Syrians" as in the KJV, but to the Edomites to induce them into the same coalition. (In II Kgs 16:6 there has evidently been a copyist's error in substituting the root *'rm,* "Syria," for *'dm,* "Edom." It is not, however, necessary to delete Rezin's name from the verse as the RSV does.) Pressed on all sides, Ahaz in desperation sought the aid of Tiglath-pileser against the advice of Isaiah. The Assyrian first swept down the Philistine coast, and then attacked Israel. In 732 B.C. he succeeded in taking Damascus, a feat the Assyrians had not been able to accomplish for a half-century, and killed Rezin, deporting the people of Damascus to Kir (II Kgs 16:9).(See Merrill F. Unger, *Israel and the Aramaeans of Damascus,* pp. 95–101.)

2. The ancestor of certain Nethinim (*q.v.*), who returned with Zerubbabel from the Exile in Babylon (Ezr 2:48; Neh 7:50). The Nethinim have usually been interpreted as temple slaves, but have more recently been explained as the members of a service guild. (See Baruch A. Levine, "The Netînîm," JBL, LXXXII, 207–12.)

E. M. Y.

REZON (rē'zŏn). Son of Eliadah, who had fled from Hadadezer, king of Zobah (I Kgs 11:23). When David defeated Hadadezer (II Sam 8:3), Rezon gathered a force about him and established himself as king of Damascus (I Kgs 11:23–25). From this position at Damascus, Rezon harassed Israel during the reign of Solomon, for "he was an adversary to Israel all the days of Solomon . . . and he abhorred Israel, and reigned over Syria." Scholars are of the opinion he was Hezion, who was the founder of the dynasty of the Syrian kings so well known in the history of Israel at this period (I Kgs 15:18). Rezon may have reigned about 30 years, probably *c.* 960– *c.* 930 B.C.

RHABDOMANCY. "The art of using a divining rod for discovering something hidden" (*Encyclopaedia Britannica,* 11th ed.). In the medieval period it was practiced particularly by the use of a forked stick shaped like a large tuning fork, the individual holding the two prongs firmly, one in each hand, with the palms turned outward. He claimed that he felt a pull on the short cropped main stem as he held this over a place where there was water or minerals.

Its use spread from Germany to England. It was used in the 17th cen. in France to track criminals. The practice is referred to in Hos 4:12: "My people inquire of a thing of wood, and their staff gives them oracles" (RSV), and in Ezk 8:17: "Lo, they put the branch to their nose." The twin magical art of shaking arrows, belomancy, is mentioned in Ezk 21:21, RSV. *See* Belomancy; Divination; Magic; Necromancer; Teraphim.

R. A. K.

RHEGIUM (rē'ji-ŭm). A city on the "toe" of the "boot" of Italy. It lies opposite Messina in Sicily. Here Paul's ship stopped on his way to Rome (Acts 28:13). The name means "breach," which is a reference to the ancient belief that Sicily was rent from the continent by an earthquake. Other early writers believed the name was derived from *regium,* the Latin word for "royal." Because of its strategic location, Rhegium has played a prominent role in history. It is now called Reggio, and is the capital of Calabria.

RHESA (rē'sȧ). A son of Zerubbabel and ancestor of Jesus (Lk 3:27).

RHODA (rō'dȧ). A servant girl in Jerusalem who answered Peter's knock at the gate of Mary (the mother of Mark) after his release from prison by angelic intervention (Acts 12:13). The term *paidiskē* indicates she was probably a slave (see its use in Mt 26:69; Jn 18:17; Acts 16:16; Gal 4:22-23, 30-31). Her Gr. name *Rhodē,* "rose," suggests she may not have been a Jewess. Whether she was attached to Mary's household, or was one of the believers gathered to pray for Peter, is not known. Her joy at recognizing Peter's voice (Acts 12:14-15) reveals that she knew the apostle and points to her being a Christian.

St. Paul's Bay, Rhodes. HFV

Temple of Athena, acropolis of Lindos, Rhodes. HFV

RHODES (rōdz). One of the largest islands of the Aegean-Mediterranean area, lying SW of Asia Minor toward Crete, it covers an area of 545 square miles. Its capital, a city of the same name, was built at the NE tip of the island. Because of its natural location astride the E-W shipping routes, it was always an important commercial center. During the 2nd cen. B.C. Rhodes was at her zenith, the leading Greek republic; but by the time Paul visited (Acts 21:1), that day was past, for she had fallen out of favor with Rome because of her Macedonian sympathies.

Here in her harbor once stood the great Colossus of Rhodes, one of the seven wonders of the ancient world. A statue of the sun-god, over 100 feet high, it held a javelin in its right hand and a torch in its left. Destroyed in 225 B.C., restored by the Romans, it was finally done away with by the Muslims in the 7th cen. A.D.

Bibliography. G. Konstantinopoulos, "Rhodes: New Finds and Old Problems," *Archaeology,* XXI (1968), 115-123.

W. M. D.

RIBAI (rī'bī). The father of Ittai, who was one of David's valiant men known as the "Thirty." He was from Gibeah of the Benjamites (II Sam 23:29; I Chr 11:31).

RIBBAND. An archaic form of "ribbon," used in KJV to translate *pāthîl,* "line" or "cord" (Num 15:38). It refers to the blue thread to be worked into the tassels on the hems of Israelite garments (NEB).

RIBLAH (rĭb'lȧ)

1. A Syrian city in the land of Hamath, near Lebo-hamath (*q.v.*) and Kadesh-on-the-Orontes. Now known as Ribleh, it is situated in the Bekaa, the broad plain between the Lebanon and Anti-Lebanon Mountains, *c.* 65 miles N of Damascus. Located in a wide and fertile valley, Riblah was an ideal spot for the headquarters of an army. Here Pharaoh-Necho, after the death of Josiah, deposed Josiah's son Jehoahaz, who had been chosen king of Judah.

He made him a captive and appointed his brother Jehoiakim king (II Kgs 23:31-34). Here also Nebuchadnezzar of Babylon brought Zedekiah and his sons, first killing the sons and then blinding the king (II Kgs 25:6-7). Later, numerous prominent men of Judah were killed there (II Kgs 25:18-21). Riblah is called Shabtuna in the Egyptian records of Thutmose III and Rameses II (ANET, p. 256).

2. A location on the N boundry of Canaan assigned by the Lord to Israel (Num 34:11), unknown unless it is the same as Riblah 1.

S. C.

RICHES. The practical problems and dangers of riches are often mentioned in Scripture. They are a source or root from which every kind of evil can stem (I Tim 6:10). They can prevent a person from accepting Christ (Mt 13:22; Mk 4:19); they can thwart spiritual growth (Ps 62:10).

Notably in the Gospel of Luke, several of Jesus' parables warn against the danger of becoming consumed with a desire for wealth, or of wrongfully using material gain: the rich farmer (Lk 12:13-21), the rich man and Lazarus (Lk 16:19-31), the rich ruler (Lk 18:18-30). See also the story of Zacchaeus (Lk 19:1-10), and the widow's mites (Lk 21:1-4).

The term riches is also used metaphorically to speak of the blessings of God in the Christian life. There are the riches of His goodness (Rom 2:4), of His glory (Rom 9:23), of His grace (Eph 1:7; 2:7), of His wisdom and knowledge (Rom 11:33); the riches of Christ (Eph 3:8), of His presence (Col 1:27), of His reproach (Heb 11:26); the riches of the Gentiles (Rom 11:12).

See Wealth.

R. A. K.

RIDDLE. The ancient Greeks, Romans, Egyptians, Assyrians and Hebrews were fond of the use of the riddle, which sometimes they employed as games (*q.v.*) and sometimes as "enigmas," "dark sayings" or "hard questions." On occasion in the OT the riddle appears as a pointed or pithy saying which hints at some deeper or more profound reality or teaching, as in the case of the riddles put to the wise Solomon by the Queen of Sheba (I Kgs 10:1). The historian Josephus comments that Solomon was particularly fond of the riddle (*Ant.* viii.5.3).

A remarkably interesting riddle is Samson's famous one: "Out of the eater came forth food, and out of the strong came forth sweetness" (Jud 14:14, ASV). Samson is challenging his wedding guests to identify the meaning of the honey he found in the slain lion carcass. His wife gave the solution to the guests: "What is sweeter than honey? and what is stronger than the lion?" Surmising they had been prematurely informed of the riddle's meaning, Samson accused his guests by giving them an additional puzzle: "If ye had not plowed with my heifer, ye had not found out my riddle" (v. 18).

Riddles (Heb. *ḥîdôt*) not only were used as a form of humor and challenge in games but also as a test of wisdom (I Kgs 10:1; II Chr 9:1). The wise deal in "dark" or perplexing sayings (*ḥîdôt,* Prov 1:6; Ps 49:4; 78:2). Daniel was shown in vision a future king who would be "of bold countenance, one who understands riddles" (Dan 8:23, RSV), i.e., one "skilled in intrigues" (Berkeley). The riddle was at times a literary device conveying divine revelation ("showing of dark sentences," Dan 5:12, ASV, referring of course to the prophetic skills of Daniel). God spoke to Moses without employing such "dark speech" (Num 12:8).

The NT reference in I Cor 13:12 ("darkly," Gr. "in a riddle" or "enigma") to the enigmatic nature of our "sight" might well indicate that while God in His revelation may be known by man, yet His ways and nature remain partially a mystery until "that which is perfect is come" (cf. Rom 11:33).

See Proverb.

A. M.

RIDER. Used in the OT almost always of those mounted on horses or in chariots; but mules, camels, and dromedaries are also mentioned. The ass was early used for riding, and the camel for long distances. Horses were generally used in war, or by kings. "Riding on an ass" by a king was an act of humility (cf. Zech 9:9).

Sometimes "rider" is used figuratively, as in Gen 49:16-17: "Dan shall judge his people . . . he shall be a serpent by the way . . . that biteth the horse heels, so that his rider shall fall backward." Perhaps this is a reference to Samson the judge, greatest of the tribe of Dan, who slew many Philistines in his life, but more in his death (cf. Jud 16:30).

RIGHT. In the OT at least six distinct Heb. word roots denote the concept of what is morally good, just, legal, proper, or fitting. The two most important words are *yāshār* and *mishpāṭ*.

With its cognate words the root *yāshār* means to be smooth, level, straight, direct, and thus to be right (e.g., I Sam 6:12; Ps 107:7; Isa 45:2; Jer 31:9). The one who walks on such a path is straightforward, just, upright (I Kgs 9:4; Job 1:1, 8); doing what is "right" in God's sight (Ex 15:26). This path is equivalent to the way of wisdom (Prov 4:11). God takes pleasure in man's uprightness or honesty (I Chr 29:17), and such a heart attitude is a product of true wisdom and fear of the Lord (Prov 14:2). The corresponding Gr. word is *euthus,* a "straight" path or street (Mt 3:3; cf. Isa 40:3; Acts 9:11), the "right" way (II Pet 2:15), a heart "right" before God (Acts 8:21).

The word *mishpāṭ* is a forensic term from the root *shāpaṭ,* "to judge, govern." It signifies what is legally or judicially right: "Shall not the Judge of all the earth do right?" (Gen 18:25); "I know that the Lord will maintain the cause of the afflicted, and the right of the poor" (Ps 140:12). It is the social justice which God requires of man, "to act justly" or "do justice" (Mic 6:8, NEB, NASB).

In the NT the Gr. *dikaios* carries the similar idea of being right or just: a fair wage (Mt 20:4), judging what is right (Lk 12:57), the law-abiding, righteous man (I Tim 1:9), a just, honest, good man such as Joseph (Mt 1:19), doing what is ethically right (Eph 6:1; Rev 22:11).

Usually, however, in the NT the Gr. adjective and its noun *dikaiosynē* bear the meaning of righteousness (*q.v.*) in a moral, religious, or theological sense, based on the Heb. terms *ṣedeq* and *ṣᵉdāqâ*. The Gr. word *orthōs* in Lk 10:28 means to answer "correctly" (NASB), an answer which is straight up or erect (cf. Acts 14:10) and thus right or correct (cf. Lk 7:43; 20:21). In II Tim 2:15 "rightly dividing" (from *orthotomeō*) means to cut a path in a straight direction through a country that is forested or full of other obstacles. The meaning here seems to be to guide and teach the word of truth along a straight course without being turned aside by useless arguments about words or by worldly chatter (Arndt, p. 584).

See Righteousness.

J. R.

RIGHT HAND. The Heb. *yāmîn*, "right hand," and *yᵉmānî*, the "right" as opposed to the left direction, occur *c.* 170 times in the OT. The corresponding Gr. term *dexios* appears over 50 times in the NT. Because the Israelites faced E when considering the primary direction, the term *yāmîn* sometimes indicates the S (I Sam 23:19, 24, NASB marg.; Ps 89:12); and the more usual word *têmān* for "south" is derived from *yāmîn*. *See* Left; Left-handed.

These Heb. and Gr. words are often used in a figurative sense. The right hand is the hand of strength, skill, and authority (Job 40:14; Ps 45:4; 89:42; 137:5; Prov 27:16; Mt 27:29; Rev 1:16); the one of love and tenderness (Song 2:6; 8:3); the one which bestows the greatest blessings (Gen 48:13–18; Rev 1:17); the place of greatest favor or honor or influence (I Kgs 2:19; Mt 25:33; Ps 45:9; 109:6). Being the more important hand or side, it is the one by which a man is led (Ps 73:23); on which a man is endangered (Job 30:12; Ps 91:7) or accused (Ps 109:6; Zech 3:1); and where his protector must stand to help him (Ps 16:8; 109:31; 121:5; Isa 41:13; 63:12).

The "right hand of God" is a favorite OT expression for His almighty power in creation (Isa 48:13) and in war and deliverance (Ex 15:6, 12; Ps 17:7; 18:35; 20:6; 44:3; 78:54; 98:1; 118:16; 139:10), as well as for His sovereign beneficence (Ps 16:11; 48:10; 80:15, 17). To be seated at the right hand of God signifies the position of greatest honor, reserved only for the royal figure of Messiah (Ps 110:1): "Jehovah saith unto my Lord, Sit thou at my right hand, until I make thine enemies thy footstool" (ASV). This verse is quoted and referred to more often in the NT than any other single verse in the OT, showing that the exaltation of Jesus Christ to reign in power and glory at the Father's right hand is the direct fulfillment of this prophetic psalm (Mt 22:44; 26:64; Mk 16:19; Acts 2:34–35; 7:55–56; Rom 8:34; I Cor 15:25; Eph 1:20; Col 3:1; Heb 1:3, 13; 8:1; 10:12–13; 12:2; I Pet 3:22).

See Hand; Prophecy, Fulfillment of.

J. R.

RIGHTEOUSNESS. In the OT several Heb. words set forth the biblical concept of what is right (*q.v.*). Heb. *yāshār* denotes the "straight, smooth" way (Prov 9:15; 15:21; Isa 26:7, all NASB), and what is agreeable or pleasing to God because it is right (Deut 12:25, 28). One who follows such a path and performs such deeds is called "upright" (Job 1:1).

The judge (*shōphēṭ*) in deciding a case and executing judgment (*mishpāṭ*) was expected to have the attribute of *mishpāṭ*, "justice, right, rectitude." Yahweh is a God of justice (Isa 30:18, NASB), and it was inconceivable that He as the Judge of all the earth would not do right or deal justly (Gen 18:25). He requires that man, who was created in His image, should seek and practice justice also (Isa 1:17; 56:1; Mic 6:8).

A third term is *ṣedeq*, designating what is just, right, or normal, such as full and "just" weights and measures (Deut 25:15). God sits on His throne judging what is "right" (Ps 9:4), so that David had confidence to ask the Lord to hear his "right" or just cause (Ps 17:1). God's judgments are "right" or fair, executed in faithfulness for our ultimate good (Ps 119:75).

Cognate with the third word is the noun *ṣᵉdāqâ*, "righteousness." Because of its wide range of meanings in the OT, and its later use in Jewish intertestamental and rabbinic literature as a term for approved ethical conduct, its basic concept has been difficult to discover. Elizabeth and Paul Achtemeier have argued that in both the OT and the NT "righteousness" is a concept of relationship, and that "he who is righteous has fulfilled the demands laid upon him by the relationship in which he stands" (IDB, IV, 80).

The righteous person does what is right, fair, or necessary to uphold harmonious relationships within his family and community (e.g., Tamar, Gen 38:26). He is concerned for the rights of the poor (Prov 29:7, NASB) and speaks up for them to plead their case (Prov 31:8–9). Righteousness is closely linked with giving to the poor (Ps 112:9; II Cor 9:9–10). The prophets repeatedly warned against the lack of righteousness in the gate (where legal trials were usually held), for the very foundations of communal life were being destroyed (Isa 29:21; 59:4, 14; Amos 5:10, 12, 15; Hab 1:4).

With respect to God, the Israelite was considered righteous when he fulfilled the demands of his covenant relationship with Yahweh. God had chosen Israel in His grace and gave the

RIGHTEOUSNESS

nation the law at Mount Sinai in order to guide them as His covenant people. Its purpose was to make Israel holy even as Yahweh their God is holy (Lev 19:2; 20:26; 21:6-8). Therefore a righteous relationship with God included obedience to and love for His law (Deut 6:25; Ps 1). But the essential element in the covenant relationship was trust in the Lord and submission of one's life to His lordship. Thus the relationship of faith was primary (Hab 2:4). "He who does not in faith accept the context of the law, the lordship of Yahweh, cannot be righteous before Yahweh, though he fulfill all other precepts of the law" (IDB, IV, 82).

God's righteousness is not an abstract quality or attribute but His fulfillment of the covenant which He has made with His chosen people (Neh 9:8, 32-33; Ps 103:6-7, 17-18). The Lord upholds the right, and helps those who have had their right taken from them by His judging the wicked (Ps 72:2-4; 94:14-23). His righteous judgments are *saving* judgments (Ps 36:6). As a righteous God He is a Saviour (Isa 45:21). "Yahweh's salvation of Israel is his righteousness, his fulfilment of his covenant with her" (IDB, IV, 83). The Lord's "righteous acts" concerning which Samuel reasoned with all the people were His acts of deliverance and redemption in bringing Israel out of Egypt (I Sam 12:7; cf. Ps 65:5; Isa 46:13; 51:5-6, 8; 62:1). He continues to execute judgment in favor of the oppressed and to show His love to the righteous, whose right has often been taken from them in their unfortunate circumstances (Ps 146:7-9).

Both nationally and individually, however, the people of God fail. There is none who is truly righteous: "there is no one who does good, not even one" (Ps 14:1-3, NASB; cf. Rom 3:10-12; 7:18). "There is not a righteous man on earth who continually does good and who never sins" (Eccl 7:20, NASB). "All our righteous deeds are like a filthy garment," wrote Isaiah (64:6, NASB).

Accordingly, whatever righteousness man may have, is his only by virtue of his relationship with God. It must be given to him from God. This is called imputed righteousness by the theologians. The doctrine is based on Abraham's experience in Gen 15:6: "Then he believed in the Lord; and He reckoned it to him as righteousness' (NASB). Because he exercised faith in the Lord and His promises, Abraham—who was by no means yet sinless (cf. Gen 20)—nevertheless was in covenant relationship with God. This relationship, stemming entirely from God's gracious election and call (Gen 12:1-3; Josh 24:2-3; Neh 9:7-8), is termed "righteousness."

In like manner every repentant sinner enters this state of righteousness when by faith he accepts it as God's gracious gift. "Zion will be redeemed with justice, and her repentant ones with righteousness. But transgressors and sinners will be crushed together, and those who forsake the Lord shall come to an end" (Isa 1:27-28, NASB). "The salvation of the righteous is from the Lord . . . because they take refuge in Him" (Ps 37:39-40, NASB).

It is God who maintains His righteousness by justifying Israel. He keeps His chosen people in covenant relationship with Himself by imputing righteousness to them who have no righteousness. It is equivalent to granting them His salvation (Isa 46:12-13). In the new covenant God will impart Himself to them, for He will be called "the Lord our righteousness" (Jer 23:6; 33:16); and in that righteousness His believing remnant will be established (Isa 54:14).

J. R.

In the NT the most frequent Gr. word for righteousness is *dikaiosynē*, the regular translation in the LXX of Heb. *ṣ^edāqâ*. Just as in the OT, the term "righteousness of God" does not refer specifically to God's inherent perfection of character. Rather it speaks of His righteous provision of salvation for sinners (Rom 1:17; 3:5, 21-22, 25-26; 10:3; II Cor 5:21). In the gospel, which is the power of God for salvation to every one who believes, the righteousness of God is revealed (Rom 1:16-17). It is made operative among men who, because of their sin, are subject to the wrath of God and far off from Him. By the gracious extending of the righteousness of God to them they are brought into a saving relationship with Him.

God's self-righteousness depends on His being true to His own good and holy nature, on the one hand, and His dealing righteously with His creatures, on the other hand. In God's righteous provision of a way of salvation, He cannot forgive sin without both satisfying His justice and maintaining His holiness. The righteousness of God, manifested in His righteous plan of salvation through the substitutionary death of Christ, satisfies both. The sinner's acceptance of this provision enables God to impute to him all that Christ did for him to achieve his salvation. In his acceptance of Christ as his Sin-bearer and Saviour by faith, man receives "the righteousness which is by faith," a term expressing the righteousness of Christ which is imputed to the believer (Rom 4:5 ff.; 9:30; Phil 3:9).

In OT times the sins of the believer were forgiven through the forbearance of God (Rom 3:25), for God applied the atonement in a proleptic, anticipatory manner. In the Gospel Age sins are remitted on the basis of the salvation already completed at Calvary. In both cases God's righteousness and justice were satisfied: in the one as God looked forward to the cross; in the other as He looks back. Therefore Paul writes of Christ, "Whom God hath set forth to be a propitiation through faith in his blood, *to declare his righteousness* for the remission of sins that are past, through the forbearance of God; to declare, I say, at this time *his righteousness:* that he might be just, and the justifier of him which believeth in Jesus" (Rom 3:25-26).

Whereas Yahweh is called "our righteousness" in the OT (Jer 23:6; 33:16), in the NT Christ is specified to be our righteousness (I Cor 1:30). He is the termination of the law, resulting in righteousness for every one who believes (Rom 10:4), so that every one who has faith may be justified (RSV). This saving righteousness is imputed when man believes in his heart that God raised Christ from the dead (Rom 10:9–10).

See Imputation; Justification; Right.

R. A. K.

Bibliography. Elizabeth R. Achtemeier, "Righteousness in the Old Testament," IDB, IV, 80–85. Paul J. Achtemeier, "Righteousness in the New Testament," IDB, IV, 91–99. Abraham Cronbach, "Righteousness in Jewish Literature, 200 B.C.–A.D. 100," IDB, IV, 85–91. David Hill, *Greek Words and Hebrew Meanings,* Cambridge: Univ. Press, 1967, chapter on *dikaiosynē*. John Murray, *The Epistle to the Romans,* NIC, 2 vols., Grand Rapids: Eerdmans, 1963, 1965. J. Barton Payne, *The Theology of the Older Testament,* Grand Rapids: Zondervan, 1962, pp. 155–161, 415–418. Gottlob Schrenk, "*Dikaios,* etc.," TDNT, II, 182–225. Norman H. Snaith, *The Distinctive Ideas of the Old Testament,* London: Epworth Press, 1944, pp. 51–93, 161–173.

RIMMON (rĭm'ŏn)

1. A Benjamite, the father of the two captains of Ishbosheth who murdered their master (II Sam 4:2, 5–9).

2. A city located in Judah's inheritance near the town of Ain (Josh 15:32) but also in Simeon's territory (Josh 19:7; I Chr 4:32). Judah and Simeon were closely connected in regard to their inheritances. Later Ain and Rimmon were joined as one town, En-rimmon (*q.v.;* Neh 11:29). It is identified with the site of Khirbet Umm er-Ramamin, nine miles N of Beer-sheba.

3. A city of the Merarite Levites located in the tribe of Zebulun (I Chr 6:77; Rimmono in RSV, NASB), the present village of Rumaneh, six miles NNE of Nazareth. It is the Rimmon of Josh 19:13 in RSV and NASB, called Remmon-methoar in KJV. The second term is translated in NASB as "which stretches," referring to the border of Zebulun which proceeds to Rimmon and stretches to Neah. The RSV renders the same term "it bends toward."

4. The rock of Rimmon was located 15 miles N of Jerusalem and seven miles NE of Gibeah. It was there that the 600 surviving Benjamites took refuge for four months (Jud 20:45, 47; 21:13). It has been identified with the village of Rammûn, three and a half miles NE of Bethel. It is situated on a limestone outcropping with steep ravines on the N, S, and W. In the hill are many caves where fugitives could hide.

5. Rimmon was the name of a Syrian god connected with fertility. It appears in Mesopotamian inscriptions as Ramânu, "the thunderer," the deity of the storm responsible for rain, and thus for the vegetation he stimulated. The name occurs in combination with Hadadrimmon (*q.v.*), linking Rimmon to Hadad, the proper name of Baal in the Ras Shamra (*q.v.*) texts. A temple of Rimmon stood in Damascus in the time of Naaman (II Kgs 5:18). *See* Gods, False.

R. G.

RIMMON-PEREZ (rĭm'ŏn-pĕr'ĕz). The KJV spelling is Rimmon-parez. The literal meaning is "pomegranate of the breach or pass." It was the 15th camping place of Israel from Egypt, and the fourth after Sinai, between Rithmah and Libnah (Num 33:19–20). While not identified with any certainty, it may have been Naqb el-Biyar, *c.* 20 miles SW of Ezion-geber (Grollenberg, *Atlas of the Bible,* map 9).

RIMMON, ROCK OF. *See* Rimmon 4.

RING. In the OT the word "ring" most often translates Heb. *ṭabba'at,* derived from the root *ṭāba',* "to sink." The name is evidently based on the ring's original function as a seal sinking into impressionable material such as clay or wax, hence a signet ring. Such rings carried the name or symbol of the owner, and so constituted his signature for legal transactions or were a means of designating ownership. Giving such a ring to another granted that one the authority to act in behalf of the owner. Thus Ahasuerus empowered Haman to issue an edict in his behalf (Est 3:10, 12) and likewise Mordecai (Est 8:2, 8, 10). Pharaoh did the same with Joseph (Gen 41:42).

Rings are most frequently mentioned in the OT in connection with articles of furniture in the tabernacle and the priestly vestments, such as the curtains, ark, breastplate, and ephod (Ex 25–28, 30, 36–39 *passim*). Rings were often simply articles of adornment (Isa 3:21). Other ornaments of the ring type are, e.g., "earrings" (Ex 32:2–3; 35:22; Hos 2:13) and "bracelets" (Ex 35:22; II Sam 1:10; Gen 24:22; 38:18, 25). The "rings" of Ezk 1:18, KJV, should be rendered "rims" (RSV), and in Song 5:14 the "rings" are probably rods of metal (RSV marg., NASB). For nose rings (Isa 3:21, RSV; cf. Gen 24:47, ASV; Ezk 16:12, RSV) *see* Nose Jewel.

In the NT the ring *(daktylios)* symbolized the full position and privileges of sonship (Lk 15:22), and in Jas 2:2 the golden ring *(chrysodaktylios)* suggested wealth, position, and privilege.

R. V. R.

RINGSTRAKED. The translation of Heb. *'āqōd* which means "banded," "striped," or "streaky" (Gen 30:35, 39–40; 31:8, 10, 12). The term describes the (normally black) goats in Jacob's flocks which were marked with white stripes and the sheep with brown or black stripes.

RINNAH (rĭn′ȧ). In Heb. this word means "a shouting," either a cry of joy (Ps 30:5) or of grief (Jer 14:12). It is the name of a son of Shimon, who was a descendant of Caleb, son of Jephunneh (I Chr 4:20).

RIOT. There are two basic ideas which are expressed by the English word riot. The major use of the word in the Bible is to express excessiveness in pleasure and moral laxity. It is thus used to translate the Gr. *asōtia,* "debauchery" (Tit 1:6; I Pet 4:4; Eph 5:18); *kōmos,* "revelry" (Rom 13:13); and *tryphē,* "indulgence," "reveling" (II Pet 2:13). The Heb. *zālal* is used in Proverbs of gluttony (BDB, p. 272): "Be not among winebibbers, among gluttonous [riotous, KJV] eaters of flesh" (Prov 23:20, ASV); "But he that is a companion of gluttons [riotous men, KJV] shameth his father" (Prov 28:7, ASV). The prodigal son "wasted his substance with riotous [*asōtōs*] living" (Lk 15:13), i.e., "dissolute, profligate" (Arndt, p. 119).

The other meaning of riot is found in Acts 19:40 (NASB: Gr. *stasis,* KJV "uproar"). This meaning is also conveyed by the Gr. *thorybos* (Mt 26:5 and Mk 14:2, NASB; Acts 17:5 and 20:1, "uproar").

RIPHATH (rī′făth). A son of Gomer and grandson of Japheth (Gen 10:3). By scribal error the name was misspelled Diphath in most MSS of I Chr 1:6 (see RSV, NASB). Riphath is non-Semitic and his descendants were probably Anatolian. Josephus (*Ant.* i.6.1) placed them in Paphlagonia, W of the lower Halys River in Asia Minor. They are thought to have marched across the Riphaen Mountains, which are said to be part of the Ural chain in Russia, into the farthest regions of Europe.

RISSAH (rĭs′ȧ). The 17th station of Israel from Egypt, and sixth after Sinai, between Libnah and Kehelathah (Num 33:21–22). Grollenberg (*Atlas of the Bible,* map 9) suggests as a possible location modern el-Kuntilla, *c.* 35 miles NW of Ezion-geber. It is also called Jarasa, with a number of water holes in the area, and where numerous trails from the Sinai and the Negeb converged (Nelson Glueck, *Rivers in the Desert,* New York: Farrar, Straus & Cudahy, 1959, p. 237).

Falls on the Cydnus River above Tarsus. HFV

RITHMAH (rĭth′mȧ). The name of this place means "broom bush." It was the 14th station of Israel from Egypt, and the third after Sinai. Its location was between Hazeroth and Rimmon-parez (Num 33:18–19). It must have been along one of the wadis 15–25 miles N of 'Ain Khadra (Hazeroth) on the E side of the Sinai peninsula.

RIVER OF EGYPT

1. The KJV term for the brook or stream marking the SW border of Canaan (Num 34:5; I Kgs 8:65; II Kgs 24:7; II Chr 7:8; Isa 27:12) and of the tribe of Judah (Josh 15:4, 47). The Heb. *naḥal Miṣrayim* denotes a wadi or streambed, not a true river. In Assyrian records it is called *naḫal (māt) Muṣri.* The Wadi el-'Arîsh is almost certainly the geographical feature meant by this term. It is a seasonal stream that flows only after heavy rains, running N out of Sinai and ending at the Mediterranean 90 miles E of the Suez Canal and 50 miles SW of Gaza. It forms a logical boundary, for to the W lies only barren desert and scrub, while to the E are meadows and arable fields (see K. A. Kitchen, "Egypt, River of," NBD, pp. 353 f.).

2. The SW boundary of the ultimate territory promised to Abram's descendants (Gen 15:18). Since the Heb. is *nahar Miṣrayim,* an actual river, the probable reference is to the eastern or Pelusiac branch of the Nile. It may be the same as the Shihor (*see* Sihor) of Egypt (Josh 13:3; I Chr 13:5; Isa 23:3; Jer 2:18). The "flood of Egypt" (Amos 8:8; Heb. *yᵉʼôr Miṣrayim*) refers to the Nile River proper (see RSV, NASB).

J. R.

RIVERS. Streams or their channels conveying water to the sea. Rivers have always been of prime importance in the life of mankind, and this was especially true in the semiarid Middle East. At least seven different Heb. words used in Scripture mean "river." In the NT, *potamos* is the only Gr. word (K. H. Rengstorf, "*Potamos,* etc.," TDNT, VI, 595–623).

There were rivers in the antediluvian earth (Gen 2:10–14), but these must have been destroyed in the Deluge, along with all other surface features of the heavens and earth which were of old (II Pet 3:5–6). The continental uplifts terminating the Deluge year resulted in the formation of new drainage channels (Ps 104:6–9), so that the earth's present river system dates from these events (see John C. Whitcomb and Henry M. Morris, *The Genesis Flood,* Nutley, N. J.: Presbyterian and Reformed, 1961, pp. 311–330).

The most modern scientific studies of rivers indicate that their size, form, slope, and other characteristics have definite relationships that can be explained and predicted in terms of the universal first and second laws of thermodynamics (Luna B. Leopold, "Rivers," *American Scientist,* L [Dec., 1962], 511-537). It is significant that out of all the hundreds of biblical references to rivers, there are none which are not in full concord with a scientific understanding of their behavior (note Eccl 1:7).

In addition to the many obviously literal references, "river" is frequently used in a symbolic sense. Since rivers can be sources of both calamities and blessings, they symbolize both judgment (Hab 3:9-10) and prosperity (Isa 66:12). The withholding of God's provisions is likened to the drying up of a river (Isa 19:5-8).

But the most important figurative usage is undoubtedly that which describes the eternal pouring forth of the Holy Spirit as a mighty river of life (Henry M. Morris, "Water and the Word," *Bibliotheca Sacra,* CXVIII [July, 1961], 203-215). This is typified by the first river in Eden (Gen 2:10) and by the river from the millennial temple (Zech 14:8; Ezk 47:1-12). It was specifically promised by Christ (Jn 4:13-14; 7:37-39), and provided through His atoning death on Calvary; when He poured out His soul unto death (Isa 53:12; Ps 22:14), then both blood and water poured forth from His side (Jn 19:34-37; I Jn 5:6-8). As a result, God could then pour out His Spirit upon all flesh (Acts 2:16-21).

This is consummated in the great river of the water of life out of the throne of the Lamb (Rev 22:1-2) which has its source in the Lamb Himself (Rev 7:17; 21:6), and which will last eternally. It is significant that the last invitation of the Bible is from the Lord Jesus, offering this water of life freely to whosoever will come (Rev 22:17).

See Brook; Canal; Channel; Eden; Euphrates; Jordan; Nile; River of Egypt; Tigris; Water.

H. M. M.

RIZIA. *See* Rezia.

RIZPAH (rĭz'pȧ). A concubine of King Saul. She was a descendant of Aiah, a Hivite, and hence a foreigner. Her story is one of tragedy.

First, Ishbosheth accused Abner of taking her after Saul's death, fearing that Abner planned to make a bid for the throne. Being offended, Abner transferred his allegiance to David (II Sam 3:7-12).

Later, a famine during David's reign lasted three years. At last he inquired of the Lord for the cause. God told him it was the result of Saul having slain the Gibeonites after Israel had vowed to protect them. David asked the Gibeonites what could be done, and they replied that seven of Saul's sons should be delivered to them for execution. David granted their request, because according to the law (Num 35:33) blood-guiltiness could only be cleansed

The Appian Way near Rome. Black top covers the Roman road. HFV

by the blood of the criminal. Two sons of Rizpah whom she had borne to Saul and five sons of Michal, daughter of Saul, were delivered to the Gibeonites, and they were hanged in the spring of the year and left unburied. Rizpah watched over the bodies from the time of execution until the autumn rains began and lovingly protected the corpses from birds and beasts (II Sam 21:1-10). Yet the attitude of the Lord did not change. David was told of the devotion of Rizpah, and he had the bones of Saul and Jonathan brought from Jabesh-gilead and with the bones of the seven sons had them honorably buried in the family grave at Zelah. Then "God was intreated for the land" (II Sam 21:11-14).

R. H. B.

ROAD. Roads tied the ancient biblical cities together for purposes of trade. When empires arose, these trade routes became the primary concern of kings for the stability of their governments. Roads served the needs of commerce, the military, and the pilgrim. Jerusalem, Damascus, Haran, Babylon, and other ancient cities were important terminals on these roads.

Palestine, situated between Africa and Asia, inevitably was crossed by main roads on which flowed much traffic between these areas. Advantages for exacting tribute from caravans became obvious early in the history of the land. For protection, either of others or himself, the collector erected fortresses at strategic points to enforce tax collections. Caravansaries, or inns, sprang up to service the pilgrim and caravanees. The fortresses controlled both trade and immigration. The road from Egypt to Babylon went from the Nile delta either along the coast or across the Wilderness of Shur and the Negeb up to the Shephelah, or foothills of Judah; then northward along the Plain of Sharon from Philistia and across the pass near Megiddo, eastward past Beth-shan and across the Jordan, or northeastward past Capernaum N of the Sea of Galilee (Isa 9:1), ascending the plateau and continuing up to Damascus. Branches turned off to various places W of Beth-shan. In Abraham's time the king's high-

Original Roman paving of a road at Ostia, Italy. HFV

way traversed southward through the highlands E of the Dead Sea (Gen 14). Later, Petra was a city center on this route, and a road connected it with Gaza after crossing the Arabah S of the Dead Sea. Eastward a road led into Arabia and Yemen. *See* Highway; cf. CornPBE, pp. 626–630.

Some roads within cities took on a sacred character. In Jerusalem it is the Via Dolorosa, the way of Christ from judgment to crucifixion. In Rome it is the Via Sacra through the Roman Forum to the temples of Castor and Pollux. In Babylon the sacred way passed the Ḫanging Gardens and passed out of the city through the beautiful Ishtar gate. Cumae, Athens, and Delphi also had their sacred ways, used for religious processions particularly.

The Romans built roads paved with stone to serve the interests of empire, as did the Hittites, Babylonians, Assyrians, and Persians before them, though not with stone. Many of the Roman roads are still to be seen, one of which is the Via Appia leading into Rome, and portions of another between Aleppo and Antioch. Milestones were also erected by the Romans (approx. 4850 feet apart) showing on them distances, the year of their erection, and the emperor's name. Ramsay uses them to define the boundaries of Roman provinces in Asia Minor (see William Ramsay, *Cities of St. Paul* and *St. Paul, Traveler and Roman Citizen*).

Figuratively, "road" (way) denotes the manner of life of mankind (Gen 6:12); God's purposes and actions (Ex 33:13; Ps 67:2); His commandments (Gen 18:19; Ex 18:20); the things He is ready to teach men (Ps 25:8; Isa 30:21; Mk 12:14).

There is the "evil" way or way of unrighteousness (Ps 119:101; Isa 53:6); the way of righteousness (Mt 21:32); of peace (Lk 1:79); of understanding (Isa 40:14).

Regarding the way of righteousness, Jesus is the only entrance to it as well as being the way itself (Jn 14:6), it being defined as the way of truth and (eternal) life. Contrary to Thomas' question, it is plainly evident to the seeker (Isa 35:8). In the process of repentance men are to consider their "ways" (Ezk 20:43) and turn from them (II Kgs 17:13; Isa 55:7).

H. G. S

ROAST. *See* Food: Cook, Cooking.

ROBBER, ROBBERY. Robbery is taking another's property by force or threat. The word "robber" does not represent any particular Heb. word in the OT (cf. the RSV changes from the KJV in such passages as Job 5:5; 18:9; Prov 21:7; Nah 3:1).

Job 1:15, 17; Num 31:1–54. and the book of Judges bear witness to the frequency of robbery among the nomads of the ancient Near East. The prophets complained frequently about it (e.g., in Hos 4:2; 6:9; Mic 2:8). Banditry continued through the Roman period, when corrupt administrations fostered bands of robbers by accepting bribes. Plundering bands infested Palestine, some motivated by sheer desire for gain, others by desire for national independence (Lk 10:30; Acts 5:36–37; 21:38).

Ex 22 contains Mosaic legislation on theft. Restitution was mandatory, the amount varying according to the type of animal stolen and whether it had been killed, sold, or recovered. When necessary, a thief's property and person could be sold to make restitution (Ex 22:3). Killing a burglar in the act at night was justifiable homicide (22:2), and man stealing a capital offense (Ex 21:16; Deut 24:7). Stolen property was to be restored with the addition of one-fifth of its value (Lev 6:5). Altering land boundaries was strictly forbidden (Deut 27:17).

In the KJV the Gr. word *lēstēs* is 11 times translated "thief" and four times "robber" (Jn 10:1, 8; 18:40; II Cor 11:26), meaning plunderer, highwayman, brigand, or bandit. There may have been a distinction between the common thief (Gr. *kleptēs*) who took property by stealth and the "robber" who in NT times was often a rebel against Roman power. Like Barabbas (Jn 18:40), the two "thieves" crucified with the Lord were possibly robbers, or rebels. Capital punishment indicates that they were guilty of major crimes, and their admission of the justice of their penalty tends to verify this (Lk 23:41). *See* Crime and Punishment; Law; Thieves.

I. R.

ROBE. *See* Dress; Priest, High: Dress.

ROBOAM. The KJV NT form of Rehoboam (*q.v.*).

ROCK. In the OT two Heb. words are regularly translated "rock," *sela'*, "crag, cliff" (*see* Sela; Petra) and *ṣûr,* "rocky wall, cliff; large piece of rock, boulder." The Gr. word for both is *petra*. Sandstone formations are predominant in the region of Petra in Edom, and in parts of Galilee and Bashan there are volcanic outpourings of basalt. But limestone, which being

ROD

softer, weathers easily, and permits caves to develop in its cliffs, is the principal rock of western Palestine. *See* Minerals and Metals. There were numerous crags and prominent rocks, some of which bore names (e.g., Jud 15:11; 21:13; I Sam 14:4). The abundance of rocks produced striking and beautiful imagery in the minds of God's people.

God is spoken of in the OT as a rock of refuge (II Sam 22:2), a fortress (Ps 18:2; 71:3; cf. Ps 61:2; 62:2; 95:1), and "the rock of my salvation" (Ps 89:26; cf. 62:2, 6–7; 95:1). In the song of Moses in particular, He is called Israel's rock (Deut 32:4, 15, 18, 31). The expression in Isa 26:4, "For in God the Lord, we have an everlasting Rock" (NASB), is the basis for the title of A. M. Toplady's famous hymn, "Rock of Ages." Likewise Christ is spoken of as a rock both in the OT and the NT. He was the rock which would be rejected by Israel (Ps 118:22; Isa 8:14; 28:16), who would become the chief cornerstone at His resurrection (Rom 9:33; I Pet 2:6–8). It was Christ as the Rock who, Paul says, nourished Israel in the wilderness (I Cor 10:1 ff.; cf. Ex 17:6; Num 20:11).

It is important to determine what Christ meant by the term in Mt 16:17–19, particularly since the Roman Catholic church bases its claim to supremacy on the argument that Peter himself was the rock on which the Church was to be built. When Jesus said, "Thou art Peter, and upon this rock I will build my church" (Mt 16:18), He could not mean that Peter was the rock, because *petros,* "Peter," is a diminutive and means only a fragment of a greater rock, a small rock or stone, while the Gr. *petra,* "rock," signifies a great rock, bedrock, or cliff. Light is thrown on this passage by the fact that Peter explains in his epistle that Christ Himself is the cornerstone and believers are living stones built upon Him (I Pet 2:4–8; cf. Eph 2:20). Peter could then be regarded as the first NT stone placed upon the cornerstone Christ.

Another interpretation is that the confession of Jesus as the Christ, the Son of God and Saviour is the rock upon which the Church is built, rather than on Christ Himself. Peter's own explanation in his epistle points more clearly to the latter, however, though the confession of Christ as Saviour is certainly not excluded. *See* Church.

At the first advent, Christ was a stumbling stone to the Jews (Ps 118:22; Rom 9:32; I Cor 1:23). To the unbeliever Christ the Rock is a stone of judgment (Mt 21:44).

Daniel speaks of the messianic kingdom which is to be set up at Christ's second coming as a rock which fills the whole earth (Dan 2:34–35).

See Cornerstone; Headstone; Stone; Stumbling Block; God, Names and Titles of.

R. A. K.

ROD. The translation of five Heb. and Gr. words.

1. Heb. *ḥōṭer,* "rod," properly, "shoot," "sprout," "twig." The two occurrences of this word in the OT are figurative, the first indicating the product of thoughtlessness, the second indicative of the purpose of God in grace. Pride shows itself as a sprout out of the mouth of the fool (Prov 14:3). Though the house of David shall fall, it shall not remain prostrate, for a "rod" (shoot) shall come forth, the Christ (Isa 11:1*a*). The designation of "shoot" reflects the humble nature of the life of Christ. The grandeur of His future reign is suggested in the word "branch" (*nēṣer,* Isa 11:1*b*).

2. *Heb. maqqēl,* "rod," "stick," is a shorter portion of a branch (Jer 1:11, almond; Gen 30:37, poplar), or a longer portion (Jer 48:17, a staff). The shorter portion is that used by Jacob in Padan-aram in conformity with the local custom of belief in prenatal influence. In this case the rod was peeled in a certain manner and arranged in a particular fashion before the herds (Gen 30:37–38, 41) so as to influence the character of the offspring (30:39, 41). It was also Jacob's walking staff (Gen 32:10).

3. Heb. *maṭṭeh,* "staff," "rod," the word most frequently used, designates the walking staff of the pilgrim and herdsman (Ex 4:2); of the soldier (I Sam 14:27, 43; the latter are seen in models of Egyptian soldiering of ancient times); the rod of the oppressor (Isa 9:4; "staff"); the symbol of leader or ruler (Jer 48:17). The two most important usages are in the contest with Pharaoh, and in the contest over Aaron as high priest. In Moses' hand, his rod became the symbol of the authority by which God demanded the release of Israel and also the symbol of God's power against which Egypt could not stand (Ex 4:2; 7:9, 12; 8:16). *See* Staff.

In the case of Aaron, the fact that his rod alone among all the rods budded, though all were cut off from the supply of fruit-producing energy, was proof from Yahweh that Aaron was high priest and the priesthood was limited to his house (Num 17:2–9). The rod was laid up before the people as a warning to rebels (v. 10). A rod symbolized God's authority (Isa 10:26); man's wickedness (Ezk 7:11); when broken, the loss of power (Ezk 19:12); and a scepter (Ezk 19:11, 14).

4. Heb. *shēbeṭ,* "rod," "scepter," is used in connection with beating people (Ex 21:20; Prov 13:24); to beat out cummin (Isa 28:27); as a weapon (II Sam 23:21); as the emblem of national chastisement (Isa 10:24; Ps 89:32; 110:2). It is the shepherd's club (Ps 23:4), and is used to count sheep (Lev 27:32). This term signifies a shorter stick than a staff; it usually had a knobbed end which was studded with nails or flint. It could refer to a mace with a stone head. It is also the scepter (Isa 14:5), the symbol of conquest (Num 24:17), and of the power of Christ (Ps 2:9). *See* Armor.

5. Gr. *rhabdos,* "rod," "staff," "scepter," is the symbol of chastisement (I Cor 4:21). The reed of measurement is similar to a staff (Rev 11:1). Gathering up into itself all the strength of

OT uses as a symbol of power and might, Christ's power to rule the world is symbolized as an unbreakable rod of iron, the fulfillment of Ps 2:9 (Heb 1:8; Rev 2:27; 12:5; 19:15).

H. G. S.

ROE. *See* Animals: Gazelle, II. 15.

ROEBUCK. *See* Animals: Deer, II.10.

ROGELIM (rō'gĕ-lĭm). Literally, "a place of fullers." It was a city in Gilead, the home of Barzillai, who befriended David when he arrived in Mahanaim in flight from Absalom (II Sam 17:27–29; 19:31). It was probably located near the Jabbok, in the hills E of Mahanaim.

A location at or near Tell Bersinya has been suggested, however, because of its proximity to the Wadi er-Rujeili, which appears to preserve the ancient name. Bersinya is E of Beth-shan and 25 miles N of Mahanaim.

ROHGAH (rŏ'gȧ). The firstborn son of Shemer, and a member of the tribe of Asher (I Chr 7:34).

ROLL. The usual form of a book in biblical times consisted of a long piece or sheets of leather or papyrus sewn together and rolled up on a stick. The reader would simply unroll the scroll as he read. The Heb. word *m^e^gillâ* implies the existence of a soft pliable material which may be rolled up. The words were written in horizontal lines and arranged in vertical columns. (See Isa 34:4; Ezr 6:2; Jer 36:2–32; Ezk 2:9–3:3; Zech 5:1–2.) In Isa 8:1 the "roll" (*gillāyôn*) is a tablet or smooth surface, and the "house of the rolls" (Ezr 6:1) refers to the royal archives or library in Babylon. *See also* Scroll; Writing.

ROLLER. The KJV translation of Heb. *ḥittûl,* a bandage to be wrapped around a broken arm (Ezk 30:21).

ROLLING THINGS. *See* Plants.

ROMAMTI-EZER (rō-măm'tĭ-ē'zĕr). A Levite; the name of this son of Heman means "I have exalted help." He was the musician whom David appointed as head of the last of the 24 courses of singers to serve in the sanctuary (I Chr 25:4, 31).

ROMANS, EPISTLE TO THE. By common consent this is the most important of Paul's writings from the theological standpoint. Its exposition of salvation is broad in its sweep and detailed in its application.

Founding of the Church

The beginnings of gospel testimony in the capital of the empire are veiled in mystery. At the time he wrote, Paul could speak of a long-desired visit to the church (15:23). Its faith was known far and wide (1:8).

Just before the middle of the 1st cen. the emperor Claudius expelled the Jews from Rome. Their turbulence may well have resulted from their violent disagreement over the preaching of Jesus as the Christ. Aquila and his wife Priscilla were forced out at this time and went to Corinth. Since Paul lived and labored with them, they must have been believers (Acts 18:2–3).

The evangelization of the capital cannot be attributed to Peter, since he was in Palestine up to the time of the decree of Claudius (Acts 15). In writing to the church at Rome, Paul has nothing to say about Peter, which is a strong hint that he had no knowledge of activity by Peter in that area. The most helpful information comes from Ambrosiaster (4th cen.) to the effect that the Romans believed apart from apostle and miracle. His testimony seems to point to Jewish Christians as the missionaries to the metropolis, perhaps converted on the day of Pentecost (Acts 2:10).

Purpose

Although he had a number of friends and acquaintances in the Roman church, Paul was unknown by face to most of the believers. He wrote, in part, to acquaint the church with his long-standing desire to visit them (1:13), and then proceeded to set down a rather lengthy statement of the gospel. Presumably this was not because he felt the church was poorly informed on this subject. More likely it was because he sought the hearty cooperation of this group of believers in extending the gospel throughout the western Mediterranean area, to which he was about to give his undivided attention as soon as his ministry at Jerusalem had been completed. The apostle seems to envision Rome as a missionary base, such as Antioch had been in the E. From this center he and others could reach out even as far as Spain (15:23 ff.).

It is barely possible that Paul wrote as fully as he did because of an underlying anxiety that he might be prevented from reaching Rome (15:30–32; cf. Acts 23:11). In that case the church would at least have his letter for its instruction and inspiration, and might take up his burden.

The alternative, that Paul wrote as he did in order to deal with conditions in the church at Rome, is not borne out by the epistle itself. There is almost nothing which suggests that the apostle is addressing himself to specific problems of the Christian community there. It would hardly be expected of him anyway, since this church was not of his own planting.

Authorship

There is no debate on this subject today. The epistle claims Paul as its author (1:1), and its great similarity to Galatians, another acknowledged product of his pen, helps to establish its authenticity. Certain agreements with the book of Acts are helpful also, such as the collection

ROMANS, EPISTLE TO THE

for the poor saints at Jerusalem (15:25-26; cf. Acts 24:17); Paul's long-cherished desire to go to Rome (1:13; 15:23-24; cf. Acts 19:21); and his foreboding about trouble facing him at Jerusalem (15:30-31; Acts 20:22-23).

Date and Place of Writing

Paul's major task awaiting completion in the E before he could comfortably leave for the W was the gathering of the fund for the poor of the Jerusalem church. When he wrote II Corinthians, this project was nearing completion (chaps. 8-9). As Paul writes Romans, this fund has been raised and is ready to be delivered (15:25-28). Therefore, Romans was written after II Corinthians. The apostle seems to be in Corinth as he writes, for Phoebe, a worker in the church at nearby Cenchrea, is being entrusted with the letter (16:1-2). Since he spent only three months in Corinth at this period (Acts 20:3), the date can be roughly set as early in A.D. 56, just before the departure for Jerusalem. The idea that Paul was already en route to Jerusalem when he wrote (15:25) is not a necessary conclusion, since intention rather than location seems to be the force of his statement.

Nature of the Epistle

This letter is decidedly doctrinal in character, yet not lacking in teaching about the implications of the message for Christian life. Paul expounds the gospel in terms of the key word *salvation,* and that in the light of righteousness (1:16-17). A righteous God has a plan whereby He is able to redeem an unrighteous world in terms of righteousness, namely, the sacrificial death of His righteous Son. The fundamental response demanded of sinful men is faith, with all that this suggests of obedience to the divine will as well as acceptance of salvation in Christ (1:5, 16-17). This plan is basically that which God used in the case of Abraham (chap. 4), who was justified by faith rather than by works.

As suggested by the reference to Jew and Greek in 1:16, the epistle has much to say about the sinful condition of both groups in the sight of God and their common privilege to partake of the proffered salvation. Notable features are the large use of the OT in quotation and allusion; also the framework of debate in which the doctrinal teaching is set. The truth is advanced often by means of questions which are raised and then answered. This may reflect Paul's actual experience in coping with objections during his missionary preaching.

Outline

Introduction and Theme: God's righteousness has been revealed and may be obtained by faith, 1:1-17

I. The Universal Need of Righteousness: both Jews and Gentiles are condemned as sinners, 1:18–3:20

II. The Divine Provision of Righteousness Through Salvation, 3:21–8:39
   1. Justification: righteousness is imputed on the basis of faith in Christ and is received as a gift, 3:21–5:21
   2. Sanctification: God's Spirit acts as a transforming power in the new life of the believer to produce righteousness and holiness, 6:1–8:30
   3. Preservation: God allows nothing to separate the redeemed from His love, 8:31-39

III. The Vindication of God's Righteousness: His dealings with the nation Israel are explained, 9:1–11:36

IV. The Responsibilities of Righteousness, 12:1–16:27
   1. Complete dedication of oneself to God, 12:1-2
   2. Humility in relation to the church, 12:3-8
   3. Love to other believers, 12:9-16
   4. Goodness in relation to society, 12:17-21
   5. Subjection to governing authorities, 13:1-14
   6. Tolerance toward weaker brothers, 14:1–15:13

Conclusion and Greetings, 15:14–16:27

Integrity

Does the whole of the present text really belong to Romans as Paul wrote it? The problem affects chiefly the closing chapter, which some scholars think was intended for Ephesus. Priscilla and Aquila (16:3-4) were last seen in Ephesus (I Cor 16:19). Epaenetus is called the firstfruits of Asia unto Christ (Rom 16:5). It seems strange that Paul would know as many people at Rome, which he had not visited, as he greets in this chapter, whereas it is natural for Ephesus, where he had labored for three years. He seems to know something of the nature of their labors also, in many cases.

On the other hand, it was not Paul's habit to greet individuals in writing to churches he had founded. In view of the ease of travel in those days, many whom the apostle had known in the E may have returned to Rome or moved there. Several of the names are Roman, and what is more important, a few are names associated with the early history of Christianity in Rome. A possible solution of the problem is that Paul sent a copy of the epistle to Ephesus as well as to Rome, in the former case adding this chapter. But the case for a Roman destination of the entire epistle is fairly strong.

Bibliography. C. K. Barrett, *The Epistle to the Romans,* HNTC, New York: Harper, 1957. F. Godet, *Commentary on St. Paul's Epistle to the Romans,* 2 vols. (1883), Grand Rapids: Zondervan, 1956 (reprint). Charles Hodge, *Commentary on the Epistle to the Romans,* reprint rev. ed. of 1864, Grand Rapids: Eerdmans, 1964. H. C. G. Moule, *The Epistle to the Romans,* London: Pickering & Inglis, n.d. John Murray, *Commentary on the Epistle to the Ro-*

mans, 2 vols., NIC, Grand Rapids: Eerdmans, 1959, 1965. Wm. Sanday and A. C. Headlam, *A Critical and Exegetical Commentary on the Epistle to the Romans* (1895), ICC, New York: Scribner's, 1915. Wm. G. T. Shedd, *A Critical and Doctrinal Commentary upon the Epistle of St. Paul to the Romans,* New York: Scribner's, 1879. W. H. Griffith Thomas, *St. Paul's Epistle to the Romans,* Grand Rapids: Eerdmans, 1953 (reprint).

E. F. Har.

ROME, ROMAN EMPIRE. Rome and her empire have meant many things to many people. To Constantine it meant a restoration of greatness and a creation of a new Rome on the Bosporus. To Charlemagne it meant establishment of a Holy Roman Empire in the image of the first Rome. To Innocent III, other popes and faithful Catholics through the ages the term has become synonymous with the mother church. To many contemporary students of prophecy, the Roman Empire is an object of speculation: when and how will it be restored? To most Romans of the 1st and 2nd cen. A.D. it was "the world," and the Mediterranean *Mare Nostrum,* our sea. To the apostle Paul the empire meant a place to preach and to suffer; its citizenship meant protection from undue harassment and Rome a place to seek legal vindication, and eventually to die. For early Christians the empire was not only home but a persecutor for belief in Christ. Of course it is because of Christian involvement in the empire that this article appears here.

Early Development

Rome was strategically placed to dominate the Italian peninsula and Italy (*q.v.*) strategically located to dominate the Mediterranean world. Moreover, the Mediterranean is surrounded by a rim of deserts and mountains and other natural barriers that made possible in ancient times unification of the land around the sea by a superior political power.

In a very real sense Roman beginnings date from the entrance of Italic tribes into the peninsula from the N between 1000 and 750 B.C. These peoples intermarried with the Mediterranean and Indo-European stock already in the land, and began settlements on the hills of Rome. Earliest settlements in the area of Rome were located on the Palatine Hill, where the Caesars later built their palaces, and date to about 900 B.C. Visitors to Rome may see remnants of these excavated villages on the Palatine today.

About 800 B.C. Etruscan peoples moved into W and NW Italy, apparently from the Near East. These people made numerous contributions to Roman civilization and development, not the least of which was urbanization of the city of Rome. The great Etruscan period at Rome was the 6th cen. B.C.

During the 8th cen. B.C. Gr. migrations began to hit the Italian mainland and continued for a couple of centuries. They located primarily in SW Italy and Sicily. Gauls or Celts moved into the Po Valley in the N at the end of the 6th cen. B.C. and posed a threat to the Romans for some three centuries thereafter.

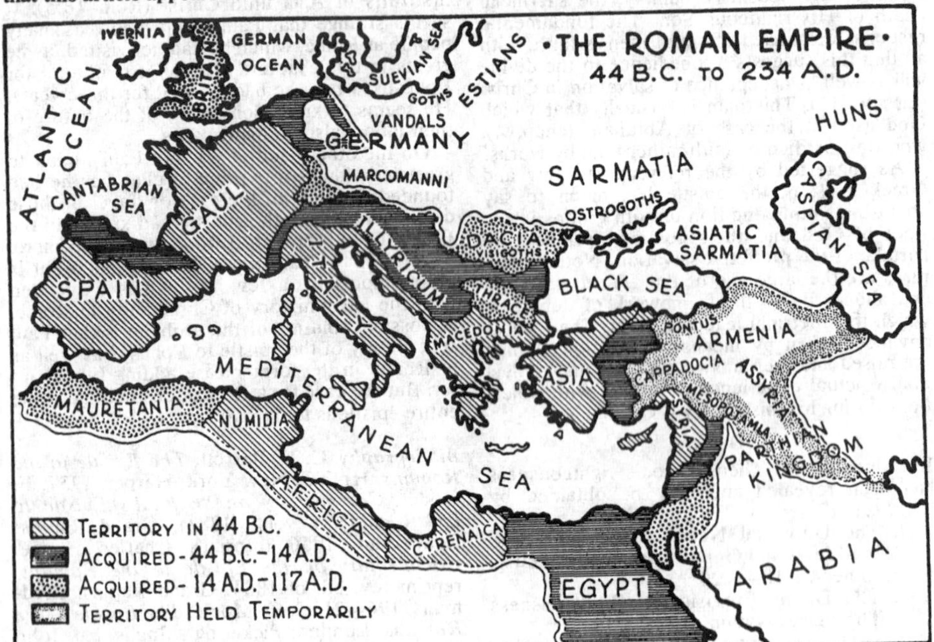

During her early centuries, Rome was occupied by Latins (one of the Italic tribes) and Etruscans, who apparently dominated after *c.* 600 B.C. Kings ruled during these early years, assisted by their councils of nobles. Then, as the traditional view has it, around 500 B.C. the Latins successfully revolted against the Etruscans and set up a republic, ruled by consuls, the senate and assembly. The tendency now is to hold that the change from monarchy to republic was more evolutionary and required a considerable period of time. At any rate, Rome found herself almost incessantly at war with a variety of powers for hundreds of years.

There was nothing very planned about this struggle that first brought her the peninsula and the western basin of the Mediterranean. Every time she conquered a new tribe or city-state she faced new enemies; she never felt safe or secure until she reached natural boundaries of the sea or the Alps and had finally reduced the Carthaginians, her powerful opponents in the western Mediterranean. Even then her fears and insecurity and the insatiable greed of her ruling classes continued to drive her on until the entire Mediterranean world had been secured.

As already noted, Rome's first struggle was with the Etruscans. First wresting control of Rome from these people, the Latins of the city were forced to war upon them intermittently for about 200 years. During the early days of the Etruscan conflict, Romans were aided by a league of Latin towns. But ultimately these people felt that Rome was merely using them for her own advantage and rebelled against Roman leadership. In the ensuing struggle the Romans were successful and absorbed the territory of Latium into the Roman state. Now Rome had new borders and became embroiled in struggles with neighboring Italic tribes. Meanwhile a new threat blew in from the N. Gauls descended from the Po Valley on the largely defenseless city in 390 B.C. The Romans ultimately got rid of them by paying a ransom. But the Gauls made an indelible impression on Roman development, first by destroying all early records of the city and with them a factual knowledge of much of early Roman history, and second by instilling a fear and insecurity that would affect Roman affairs for a long time.

The ancient Senate House, Roman Forum. HFV

During the 4th cen. Rome overcame one after another of the Italic tribes of the peninsula. By the end of the century most of the peninsula was hers except the toe, heel and instep of the boot of Italy. In the process she had virtually brought to an end the Etruscan and Italian threats. Then as she sought to protect Italian allies in the S, Rome became embroiled in war with the Greeks of southern Italy early in the 3rd cen. The struggle was fierce, especially because troops from Epirus came in to help their Gr. compatriots. But by 265 B.C. the Romans had taken control of the entire peninsula and had shut up the Gauls in the Po Valley.

Rome organized this territory in a threefold way. Some towns had full Roman citizenship and rights. Others were known as Latin allies and had lesser privileges. The vast majority, however, were Italian allies and had no special benefits except the Roman peace imposed on the peninsula, with the degree of prosperity and security which Roman control brought. All these peoples were confederated with Rome by a treaty relationship.

Conquest of the Mediterranean World

Hardly had Rome united the peninsula when she became involved in a series of wars (the Punic Wars) with the Carthaginians. As Rome's power grew she came increasingly into conflict or competition with these prosperous Phoenician peoples centered in modern Tunisia. The immediate issue before them was who would control Sicily—at that time a rich agricultural region. This question was of great moment for Rome because Sicily was then within shouting distance of the Italian coast, though today the straits are a little wider. During the first war with Carthage (264–241 B.C.) Rome took Sicily, developed a first-rate navy and became the dominant naval power in the western Mediterranean. Subsequently she took Sardinia and Corsica and pushed her boundaries in the N to the Alps, thereby erasing the Gallic threat.

The second war with Carthage (218–202 B.C.) was essentially a land war. Hannibal marched from Spain, through southern France and over the Alps into Italy. His war elephants helped to terrorize his opponents. Hannibal counted heavily on a revolution of the Gauls and numerous Italian cities to bring Rome to her knees. Many Gauls and Italians did join his armies, and numerous Italian towns did rise in rebellion; but somehow the Romans managed to fight on, subduing the rebellious towns one by one. Ultimately Rome won the war by invading the Carthaginian homeland and decisively defeating her enemy there. She now annexed Spain and a piece of France. Much later (149–146 B.C.) Rome fought a third war with Carthage, destroyed the city and Phoenician power in the W, and annexed Carthaginian territory in N Africa.

ROME, ROMAN EMPIRE

Interior of the Roman Senate. Chairs of the senators stood on the steps on either side of the chamber. HFV

Meanwhile Rome had been forced to turn her attention to the eastern Mediterranean. Macedonia had allied with Hannibal during the second Carthaginian war and Rome had neutralized the threat by making alliances with other Greeks who then engaged the Macedonians. But she was also faced with the possible destruction of balance of power in the E.

Background for the situation was this. After Alexander the Great died in 323 B.C., his empire broke up and ultimately fell into three major divisions: Macedonia, Seleucia (including initially Syria, Mesopotamia, Asia Minor and other territories), and Egypt. As long as a balance of power was maintained between these empires, Rome was safe. Should that balance of power be upset, one eastern nation might become strong enough to defeat Rome. It should be remembered that the E was more wealthy and more populous than the western Mediterranean.

Just before 200 B.C. a boy king ascended the throne of Egypt. Seeking to take advantage of the situation, Seleucia and Macedonia went into action. Egypt appealed to Rome. The latter felt obliged to intervene to restore the balance of power and to settle accounts with Macedonia for declaring war on Rome in one of her darkest hours. A series of wars ensued; these finally ended when in 146 B.C. Rome destroyed the venerable old city of Corinth in an effort to cow the Greeks, who periodically had risen against Roman power. Rome annexed all of Greece, but allowed other eastern Mediterranean powers to remain independent and allied to Rome. A few years later (133 B.C.) the king of Pergamum willed his kingdom to Rome and it came into the empire as the province of Asia. Encompassing the western third of Asia Minor, it constituted the brightest jewel in the imperial crown.

Demise of the Republic

As is clearly evident, Rome had been involved in prolonged warfare, during which time she used her allies without properly sharing the booty of war with them. As a result of imperial acquisitions, numerous problems rose in Rome, on the Italian peninsula and in the empire. The senatorial class and republican institutions proved incapable of handling the increasing emergencies. A series of revolutions broke out which gradually destroyed the republic. One of the most important involved an Italian revolt (90–88 B.C.) during which most of the peninsula rose against Roman domination. Rome was forced to grant full citizenship to all free Italians in order to quell the uprising. The activities of Marius, Sulla, Pompey, Julius Caesar, Crassus, Mark Antony and others cannot be commented on in detail here. But select activities require attention if one is to gain some idea of Roman development.

Pompey was granted emergency powers to exterminate the pirate threat to Roman shipping. As a by-product of that campaign, he took several eastern provinces in 64–63 B.C., including Syria and Palestine. Subsequently (in 60 B.C.), Pompey, Julius Caesar and Crassus organized a triumvirate. By pooling their political support they sought to gain certain personal concessions. The most important was the grant of an army to Caesar to conquer Gaul. The triumvirate was renewed in 55 B.C., but it gradually disintegrated in the heat of personal ambition. The civil war with which it ended left Julius Caesar ruler of the empire in 48 B.C., when he defeated Pompey at Pharsalus in Greece.

Granted dictatorship, Caesar set about with great vigor and ability to restore order and prosperity to the Roman state, governing it as an empire. Not the least of his reforms was the Julian calendar, which remained in effect for several centuries. Unfortunately Caesar was assassinated in 44 B.C. by men distraught over demise of the republic. But they did not realize it was impossible to restore the old political institutions. Octavius, Caesar's adopted heir, Mark Antony and Lepidus in 44 B.C. had themselves appointed by the Senate to rule the state and in 42 B.C. destroyed the republican forces led by Brutus and Cassius. Soon Octavius and Antony pushed Lepidus into the background and began to square off for the ultimate struggle between them. Again the decision as to who would rule the empire was made in Greece, this time at a naval battle at Actium in western Greece, 31 B.C. Octavius pursued the fleeing Antony and Cleopatra to Egypt, where they both subsequently committed suicide; Egypt came into the empire in 30 B.C.

Government Under the Principate

Now Octavius was free to restore the empire, which by this time was in a very disheveled condition. Wracked by civil war for decades, the Mediterranean world suffered severe economic dislocation and some provinces tottered on the brink of bankruptcy. Political and social evils or needs long unattended in the midst of military activity and political uncertainty now received needed attention. Augustus brought in the *Pax Romana* or Roman Peace, which was to grace the Mediterranean area almost without interruption for some two centuries. He wiped out debts of many towns that were virtually bankrupt. When he had restored order, he appeared before the Senate in 28 B.C. to return to that body rule of the state. But they were neither able nor willing to reassume the full burden of administration. So they conferred upon him numerous powers, to which they periodically added. Thus, although Augustus (a title bestowed by the Senate) was the real ruler, his power was legally conferred upon him by the Senate. And he shared rule with the Senate both in Italy and the empire. Of special importance in this arrangement is the fact that Augustus became in effect commander-in-chief of all armed forces.

Augustus. BM

Augustus proceeded to carry out numerous programs initiated by Julius and to launch some of his own. He brought peace and prosperity to the empire, reorganized political institutions everywhere, provided the first real police and fire protection for Rome, and in many other ways benefited the empire. A grateful populace revered him greatly, and some (especially in the East) actually worshiped the cult of the divine Augustus. Thus emperor worship was born. But during his reign, so was the Prince of Peace born in Bethlehem, where Joseph and Mary reported for a census-taking ordered by Augustus as part of his effort to tidy up the empire.

Augustus (27 B.C.–A.D. 14) was succeeded by his adopted heir, Tiberius (a stepson by his third wife). In adopting his heir before his death and associating him with himself, Augustus guaranteed a regular and peaceful succession and set a precedent that was to characterize subsequent imperial administrations. Augustus also inaugurated what is known as the Principate (rule of princeps, first citizen), an arrangement in which the ruler was to be viewed as

Tiberius. BM

first citizen of the empire rather than dictator. In practice, however, the princeps enjoyed increasing power either because he preempted it or because he gained it by senatorial default.

Tiberius (A.D. 14–37) is especially significant for the NT student because Christ was crucified during his reign. He also appointed Pontius Pilate procurator of Judea (A.D. 26–36). Though much maligned as an embittered and suspicious ruler, Tiberius' greatest difficulty was with the Senate; he gave good government to the empire.

Caligula (A.D. 37–41), grandson of Augustus' daughter Julia, next occupied the imperial chair. As a result of a serious illness he seems to have become mentally deranged. Among his wilder projects was the erection of a temple to himself out of public funds and appointment of his favorite horse as high priest of the cult. In order to obtain needed funds, he resorted to new taxes and confiscations, and used treason laws as a means of seizing money and property.

Claudius. LM

Caligula therefore incurred the wrath of many of the most prominent members of government and society. A plot against his life, carried out by a member of the Praetorian Guard, elite corps of the army, was successful on January 24, A.D. 41.

Caligula had alienated not only the Romans but Jews as well. Their monotheistic beliefs prevented them from worshiping images of the princeps, and his statues were forcibly erected in the synagogues in Alexandria. Before the order to set up his statue in the temple in Jerusalem could be carried out, news of the emperor's death arrived.

The Praetorian Guard elevated Caligula's uncle, Claudius (41–54) to the imperial office. The Senate had no choice but to rubber stamp the action. Claudius seems to have provided a high quality of administration for the empire. He adjusted tax burdens and inaugurated an extensive program of public works. This involved building new aqueducts, roads and canals, and especially the development of Ostia (*q.v.*) as a harbor for Rome. For some decades, however, Puteoli (modern Pozzuoli), near Naples, was to remain the chief port of the capital. Paul landed at this far away port, some 150 miles distant from the capital, when he came to Rome (Acts 28:13). Claudius also added Britain and Thrace to the empire and extended Roman citizenship in the provinces.

Claudius' activities crossed paths with the NT narrative on at least two occasions. He permitted Judea a brief experience as a client kingdom under Herod Agrippa I (A.D. 41–44) and then restored it to its position as an imperial province under the rule of procurators. Pursuant to some trouble with Jews in Rome, he expelled them all from the capital (Acts 18:2; the historian Suetonius confirms this action).

Claudius adopted as his son and successor Nero, son of his second wife by a previous marriage. Nero (A.D. 54–68) ruled well during his first five years, when he was under the domination of his mother and capable heads of the executive departments of government, chief of whom was the Stoic philosopher Seneca. When Nero became his own man, he came increasingly into conflict with various individuals and factions in the government. As he did he became fearful of plots against his life, and his rule took on aspects of a reign of terror. Ultimately he disposed of his mother, his wife and his stepbrother.

One hot July night in 64, fire broke out in Rome in the slums E of the Circus Maximus and burned with unabated force for nine days, gutting more than half the city. No effort to check it succeeded. Even Nero's palace lay a charred mass. In spite of the emperor's measures to alleviate the sufferings of the homeless, he could not allay the people's suspicion that he had started the fire in order to have the glory of rebuilding Rome along grander lines. To divert criticism from himself, he laid blame for the fire on Christians of the city and initiated the first official persecution of them. This began in the latter part of 64 and lasted until 66; it was restricted to Rome because those elsewhere could hardly have had a part in the catastrophe. Paul and Peter were apparently martyred in Rome during this persecution.

Nero ultimately managed to alienate important segments of society in Rome and Italy and the empire. Of special importance was his failure to hold allegiance of the military, who launched a successful rebellion in 68. Nero committed suicide, and with him died the Julio-Claudian line. The year 68/69 is often known as the Year of the Four Emperors, as Galba, Otho, Vitellius and Vespasian followed each other in rapid succession. Finally Vespasian, commander of the armies of the E, won undisputed control of the empire and ruled 69–79.

Vespasian could have followed the path of military dictatorship or cooperation with civilian administrators. He chose the latter and became a kind of second Augustus, dividing rule of Rome and the empire with the Senate. Vespasian faced a herculean task in lifting the empire from its disheveled state. But he was equal to the emergency. He put down rebellions, reformed the army, built extensive fortifications, restored the economy, and built numerous public buildings in the capital. His most famous structure, which he was not able to finish, was the great Colosseum, built on the site of one of the lakes on the grounds of Nero's palace.

The most significant of Vespasian's activities for the Bible student was his suppression of the Jewish revolt. This rebellion had broken out in 66, and Vespasian had reduced all of Judea but Jerusalem by the time he made his bid for the imperial chair in 69. His son Titus assumed command of the armies that finally destroyed the city and the temple in A.D. 70. To commemorate this victory, Titus erected a triumphal arch adjacent to the Forum in Rome. One of the reliefs of this arch shows plunder from the temple, including the golden lampstand and the silver trumpets.

Titus ruled the empire briefly during the years 79–81. He completed the Colosseum and delighted the populace with a festival of 100 days' duration on that occasion. Obviously the structure did not exist during the Neronian persecution and had nothing to do with Paul's execution. Moreover, there is no firm evidence that it was ever used for martyrdom of Christians. The short reign of Titus was saddened by the eruption of Vesuvius and the consequent burial

Titus. LM

Personification of the Tiber River, which flows through Rome. LM

of Pompeii and nearby cities, and by another great fire which roared through the capital for three days.

Titus was succeeded by his younger brother Domitian (81–96), who was received without opposition by the Praetorian Guard and the Senate. Very soon he won the undying hostility of the Senate by his autocratic ways, which indicated his intention of absolute dictatorship. After 86 he seems to have required officials of his household to address him as "Lord and God." A persecution of Jews broke out in the empire about A.D. 90 and soon engulfed Christians. The apostle John was exiled to the Isle of Patmos at this time.

But Domitian cannot be dismissed as a mere tyrant. In Rome he was an able administrator and built extensively in an effort to erase the scars left by the great fire of 80. He ruled the empire well, and it prospered under his administration. But ultimately no one felt safe from his suspicion and purges. His own wife, believing she was to be the next victim, launched a conspiracy that resulted in his assassination on September 16, 96. Thus had come virtually to an end the first Christian century. The apostle John was freed to return to his beloved Ephesus where he probably finished writing the book of the Revelation and died a natural death.

Demise of the Empire

During the first decades of the 2nd cen. the empire reached its greatest extent under Trajan (98–117) and for some decades thereafter enjoyed its height of prosperity. But toward the end of the 2nd cen. the Principate was on its way out. The economic base of the municipalities began to show increasing signs of strain; this was coupled with the militarization of the state. The latter situation was largely the fault of Lucius Septimius Severus (193–211), who was put into power by the army of the Danube and felt that he had to favor the army. He increased its size and improved its conditions of service and discharge benefits. From this time on, officers moved directly into important positions in the civil service on retirement from

ROME, ROMAN EMPIRE

army life. The effects of this militarization were soon felt.

The years 235–283 constituted a period of anarchy, of barrack-room emperors, many of whom bought their position from the armies. Some 40 of them were put forward by the armies during those years. At last Diocletian established order out of confusion and reorganized the state. This reorganization was not very effective because civil war started again at the end of his reign. Peace was restored when Constantine established himself as sole ruler and moved the capital of the empire to Constantinople.

During the decades just before Diocletian took office, barbarian tribes moved against the northern frontiers of the empire, especially in the Danubian region. Some of these had been permitted to move into the empire and to settle along the frontiers where they would serve as a buffer against other barbarians. Before these tribes were completely Romanized, a new wave of barbarian infiltration began in the 4th cen. during the days of Constantine. This was too much of a strain for the empire, and it began to disintegrate into semibarbarian states. Although Rome had no Roman ruler after A.D. 476, and the empire is commonly said to have fallen in that year, the empire continued on in the E, with its capital at Constantinople, until 1453.

Rome and the New Testament

Rome provides the political, religious and geographical context for much of the New Testament. Her power and influence pervade almost every book of the NT canon. A Roman emperor gave the order that resulted in Christ being born in Bethlehem instead of Nazareth. A Roman official arranged for His crucifixion. Roman engineers had built the roads on which the apostle Paul traveled to preach the gospel; Roman citizenship protected the apostle as he ministered. Roman governors administered all the provinces where the gospel went in its earliest days; Greco-Roman religious cults were the gospel's chief opponents during the church's first decades.

Temple of Saturn, Roman Forum, where part of the treasury of Rome was kept. HFV

As to specific early references to Rome, Claudius expelled all the Jews from Rome (Acts 18:2); but they must have returned soon, for some were there again a decade or two later when Paul arrived. Primarily Rome figures in the NT in connection with Paul. He traveled the famous Appian Way into Rome (Acts 28:15). He was imprisoned in the city for some two years and probably on two occasions. The first time occurred when he appealed to Caesar for adjudication of a question of Jewish law. Acts 28 gives some of the detail. Indications are that he enjoyed considerable freedom at that time, and that he was released and went on a fourth missionary journey.

During his first imprisonment Paul rejoiced over the spread of the gospel in Rome. Phil 1:13 refers to his having evangelized "the palace"; but the Gr. says "the praetorium," which probably refers to the Praetorian Guard, the crack imperial legion, members of which were assigned to guard him during the imprisonment. No doubt Paul had in mind the results of his witnessing to his guards. Paul's second epistle to Timothy was probably written during a second Roman imprisonment; chap. 4 anticipates the apostle's early martyrdom. On this occasion he is thought to have been incarcerated in the Mamertine Prison, which any visitor to Rome may see today.

Much has been written about the connection of the apostle Peter with Rome. Probably he did visit the city and may very likely have been martyred there during the Neronian persecution. This is not tantamount to saying that he founded the Roman church or was its first bishop, however. St. Peter's and the Vatican are today built over the circus and the gardens of Nero where Christians were martyred, and Peter may indeed have been buried somewhere in that part of Rome. But acceptance of the claim that Peter's grave lies under the high altar of the basilica stretches the credulity of most. Excavations have been conducted there and many in the Catholic church believe his remains have actually been found. But in the face of conflicting scholarly opinion, conclusions are difficult. A reading of the evidence does not seem completely convincing that Peter's tomb has been found. On the other hand, it does not seem to close the door conclusively to the possibility that Peter was buried there (see bibliography for a few of the relevant books on the subject).

Rome in the First Century

When Paul came to Rome about A.D. 60 it had not yet reached its height. That would come during the first decades of the 2nd cen. But Rome was a great city that dominated the Mediterranean world and commanded the fear, admiration and respect of millions of people beyond imperial frontiers. For instance, regular contacts were made along the silk route with China.

The city stood on the banks of the Tiber

ROME, ROMAN EMPIRE

some 16 miles from its mouth and was supplied by ports at Puteoli on the Bay of Naples and Ostia (*q.v.*) on the Tiber. The built up area covered not only the traditional seven hills but stretched far beyond in all directions. The political, legal, commercial and religious life still centered on the Forum area. The Roman Forum (some 300 by 150 feet) had been augmented by other adjacent forums constructed by Julius and Augustus and would be further enhanced by the fora of Nerva and Trajan around the beginning of the 2nd cen. *See* Forum.

Overhanging the Roman Forum on the S were the palaces of the Caesars on the Palatine Hill. Towering over it on the W was the Capitoline Hill with its great temple to Jupiter. Along the S slope of the Palatine sprawled the Circus Maximus, where some 200,000 could be entertained with chariot races, wild beast hunts and the like. After Paul's day but before the end of the century the Colosseum stood proudly near the E end of the Forum; its capacity was about 50,000.

In the Forum itself at the W end stood the Rostra from which crowds could be harangued. The Rostra was flanked by the Senate and law courts. Temples in the Forum honored Saturn (where one of the state treasuries was housed), Vesta (where the perpetual flame was maintained), the divine Julius, and Castor and Pollux. There was also the house of the Vestal Virgins and a great commercial building among other structures. Very likely Paul's trial was held on the S side of the Forum in the Basilica Julia, begun by Julius Caesar. The Mamertine Prison was located at the NW corner of the Forum. *See* Archaeology: Rome.

The population of Rome probably reached something like 1,500,000 early in the 2nd cen., and of course structures of all kinds multiplied with the increasing needs and affluence of the populace.

The Colosseum. HFV

Christianity and the Official Cult

As already noted, official persecution of Christians began with Nero after the fire of Rome. But that persecution could never have succeeded if antipathy had not developed between Christians and the general populace. Christians alienated some people with their exclusivistic claims for Christ and the gospel. The religious eclecticism of the age did not jibe with the assertion that Christ was *the* way, *the* truth and *the* life. Christians alienated others with their antisocial ways. Since almost everything in Greco-Roman life—whether drama, sports events or public festivals—was carried on in the name of some pagan deity and began with sacrifice to a deity, true Christians found it difficult to participate in almost every aspect of social life.

Then, of course, Christians could not worship in shrines of the ruler cult and the goddess Roma (personification of the state). As long as this practice was somewhat informal or at least voluntary, the difficulty was not so great. But there was some suffering during the brief attempt of Caligula to have himself worshiped, and Domitian brought great hardship to many, especially in the province of Asia. After Domitian, persecution became more pronounced, but it was often quite local in character and inspired more by a local situation than imperial edict. A few local persecutions broke out in the E during the administrations of Trajan and Antoninus Pius (138-161). Marcus Aurelius (161-180) took imperial initiative against Christianity and the great apologist Justin Martyr lost his life in 165.

But persecutions were still generally local or regional until Decius (249-251) launched a general attack. His orientation was somewhat the same as Nero's: both were looking for a scapegoat. Nero needed someone on whom to place blame for the fire of Rome, Decius someone on whom to lay blame for Rome's general decline. During Decius' reign began the millennial celebration of the founding of Rome (traditionally 753 B.C.). Rome was obviously on the skids and someone was at fault. Christians were compelled to share a large part of the blame, for they had turned away from worship of the old gods; those gods were angry and therefore were punishing all of society. Decius' fierce, empire-wide persecution was followed by sporadic and somewhat local attacks on Christians during the next half century.

Then Diocletian initiated the last and worst persecution in 303-305. He aimed at complete destruction of the church, martyring leaders and members, leveling church buildings and burning copies of Scripture. But his efforts proved futile, and with Constantine came toleration as exemplified in the Edict of Milan in 313 and his subsequent actions. The sons of Constantine began to persecute heathenism and Theodosius the Great (381 ff.) launched an attack on heathenism designed to destroy it and create a state church. Constantine himself had assumed the position of head of the Christian church and subsequent rulers followed suit. *See* Persecution.

Bibliography. J. Carcopino, *Daily Life in Ancient Rome,* New Haven: Yale Univ. Press, 1941. CornPBE, "Rome and the Jews," pp. 630–635. Oscar Cullmann, *Peter,* trans. by Floyd V. Filson, 2nd rev. ed., Philadelphia: Westminster Press, 1962. Jack Finegan, *Light from the Ancient Past,* 2nd ed., Princeton: Univ. Press, 1959, pp. 363–384, 451–491, 501–526. Margherita Guarducci, *The Tomb of St. Peter,* trans. by Joseph McLellan, London: George G. Harrap & Co., 1960. Fritz M. Heichelheim and Cedric A. Yeo, *History of the Roman People,* Englewood Cliffs, N. J.: Prentice-Hall, 1962. Engelbert Kirschbaum, *The Tombs of St. Peter and St. Paul,* trans. by John Murray, London: Secker and Warburg, 1959. Paul MacKendrick, *The Mute Stones Speak,* New York: St. Martin's Press, 1960. Albert G. Mackinnon, *The Rome of Saint Paul,* Philadelphia: John C. Winston Co., 1930. Carl Roebuck, *The World of Ancient Times,* New York: Scribner's, 1966. A. N. Sherwin-White, *Roman Society and Roman Law in the New Testament,* Oxford: Clarendon Press, 1963; "Roman Public Law," HDB rev., pp. 855–859. Graydon F. Snyder, "Survey and 'New' Thesis on the Bones of Peter," BA, XXXII (1969), 1–24. Chester G. Starr, *A History of the Ancient World,* New York: Oxford Univ. Press, 1965. Jocelyn Toynbee and John Ward Perkins, *The Shrine of St. Peter and the Vatican Excavations,* London: Longmans, Green & Co., 1956. T. G. Tucker, *Life in the Roman World of Nero and St. Paul,* New York: Macmillan, 1911.

H. F. V.

ROOF. *See* House.

ROOM. The rendering of nine Heb. and Gr. words.

1. Heb. *maqôm,* "place," "standing-ground." A place for a traveler and his camels (Gen 24:23, 31), requested by Abraham's servant from Rebekah.

2. Heb. *qēn,* "room" (properly, "nest"). The separate compartments in the ark prepared by Noah in which to quarter the animals (Gen 6:14).

3. Heb. *merḥāb,* "broad place." The term denotes David's freedom from the confining powers of a pursuer (Ps 31:8) as he felt them in the days of Saul (cf. II Sam 22:20).

4. Heb. *taḥath,* "room" ("instead of"). David desired to replace the troublesome Joab with Amasa as head of the army (II Sam 19:13).

5. Gr. *anti,* "room" ("in place of"). Archelaus had become king after Herod the Great (Mt 2:22).

6. Gr. *diádochos,* "room" ("successor"). The term designates the governor succeeding Felix, namely, Porcius Festus (Acts 24:27). As Felix did, so he also left Paul bound, favoring the Jews (cf. Acts 24:27; 25:9).

7. Gr. *prōtoklisia,* "room" ("foremost seat for reclining"). The honored place at a dinner or banquet, sought by the Pharisees (Mt 23:6; Mk 12:39; Lk 14:7).

8. Gr. *topos,* "room" ("place"). Expressive of the ample quarters in God's heaven for the elect (Lk 14:22). Figurative of the status of the ignorant, like to a dwelling place (I Cor 14:16).

9. Gr. *huperōon,* "room" ("upper room"). The place where Matthias was chosen to fill Judas' apostleship (Acts 1:13, 23–26). It was most likely reached by an outside stairway. The place where Dorcas' body was laid and where Peter raised her to life (Acts 9:37). The upper level in a building of at least three stories (Acts 20:8).

H. G. S.

ROOT. The underground part of a plant or tree, which secures it in the earth and through which it draws nourishment. It is often used figuratively both in the OT (Heb. *shōresh*) and in the NT (Gr. *hriza*).

1. The "root" of a family is the ancestor from whom the descendants derive their name or character; e.g., "if the root be holy, so are the branches" (Rom 11:16; cf. vv. 17–18); "a root that beareth gall and wormwood" (Deut 29:18); "from Ephraim those whose root is in Amalek came down" (Jud 5:14, NASB); "from the serpent's root a viper will come out" (Isa 14:29, NASB), meaning that though Tiglath-pileser III had died, another, namely, Sargon II, would arise to pillage Philistia.

The term can also mean a descendant or branch of the family. Messiah is called the "root of Jesse" (Isa 11:10; Rom 15:12) in the sense that He is a branch from the roots and stem of Jesse (Isa 11:1). In like manner He is "the root and the offspring of David" (Rev 22:16; cf. 5:5). *See* Branch.

2. The "root" means the essential cause of anything; e.g., "the love of money is a root of all kinds of evil" (I Tim 6:10, ASV); "lest any root of bitterness spring up" (Heb 12:15). It is equivalent to the very core, heart, or foundation of a matter (Job 19:28), a mountain (Job 28:9), or a nation: "Ephraim is smitten, their root is dried up" (Hos 9:16); "the axe is laid unto the root of the trees" (Mt 3:10), prophesying the coming judgment of the Jewish people with all their leaders.

3. To be "rooted" or "take root" means to be firmly established, "being rooted and grounded in love" (Eph 3:17); "rooted and built up in Him" (Col 2:7). Thus the "root of the righteous" will not be moved, but yields fruit (Prov 12:3, 12). The vine of Israel took deep root and filled the land of Canaan (Ps 80:9; cf. Hos 14:5; Isa 27:6; 37:31). Jeremiah complained to God that He had planted those who had become wicked in Judah, and they had taken root (Jer 12:2).

4. Opposed to this is "to root up," "root out," which has the sense of to destroy or remove (Deut 29:28; I Kgs 14:15; Job 31:8, 12; Ps 52:5; Prov 2:22; Mt 13:29; 15:13). Similar is the expression to be "plucked up by the roots" (II Chr 7:20; Dan 7:8; Lk 17:6; Jude 12).

5. The roots of a tree planted near water is symbolic of prosperity: "my root was spread out by the waters" (Job 29:19). The man who trusts in the Lord is like a tree planted by the water "that extends its roots by a stream" (Jer 17:8, NASB). God described Assyria as a tree with long branches because its roots extended to many waters (Ezk 31:7). The opposite figure is of roots that are "dried up" (Job 18:16; cf. 14:8; Hos 9:16; Isa 5:24).

6. Jesus Christ in His humiliation (*see* Christ, Humiliation of) was prefigured as "a tender plant, and as a root out of dry ground" (Isa 53:2), depicting His lowly birth and unpretentious family background and home of His early years.

Bibliography. Christian Maurer, *"Riza,* etc.," TDNT, VI, 985–991.

J. R.

ROPE. Ropes or cords are represented by five Heb. words (*ḥebel, 'ăbōt, yether, mêtār, ḥûṭ*) and one Gr. word (*schoinion*). Various materials and methods used by ropemakers have caused translators to give indistinct translations at times. The "string" of a bow (Ps 11:2) and "green withs" (Jud 16:7) were probably made alike (both, Heb. *yether*), of animal sinew or gut. Tent "cords" (Isa 33:20), ship "tacklings" (Isa 33:23), and ropes associated with "shipmaster" (lit., "master of the ropeholders" in Jon 1:6) are the same word (Heb. *ḥebel*, in this and the next sentence), probably all made of twisted flax. These were strong enough to lower a man (Josh 2:15; Jer 38:11–13), to drag the building stones of a city into the valley (II Sam 17:13), or to ensnare animals or men (Job 18:10). The "threefold cord" of Eccl 4:12 (Heb. *ḥûṭ*) was strong, possibly made of twisted palm fiber, goat's hair, or leather strands.

Men wound rough cords (KJV "ropes") around their heads, as well as put sackcloth on their bodies, as a sign of mourning, repentance, or surrender (I Kgs 20:31–32, NEB). Josephus calls it "the ancient manner of supplication among the Syrians" (*Ant.* viii.14.4).

See Cord.

J. W. W.

ROSE. *See* Plants.

ROSETTA STONE. *See* Writing.

ROSH (rŏsh)

1. The name of Benjamin's seventh son (Gen 46:21). The LXX, however, lists him as the son of Bela, which would make him the grandson of Benjamin. Rosh seems to have died childless, for no descendants of his are listed in Num 26:38–41.

2. The name of a people or land mentioned in Ezk 38:2–3; 39:1 (ASV, JerusB, NASB). Because Heb. *rō'sh* is the word for head, often with derived meanings such as "first" or "chief," KJV and RSV have translated the text to read, "Gog . . . the chief prince of Meshech and Tubal." However, the name of a third northerly people is more likely. Rosh was probably one of the Sarmatian or Iranian tribes around the Caspian Sea. Sargon II of Assyria defeated the Mannaeans (*see* Minni) and Rusas of Urartu in 719–714 B.C. In his Khorsabad inscription (l. 18) he mentions "the land of Rašu, on the [NW] boundary of Elam, which is beside the Tigris." Other Assyrian and Babylonian records (700–600 B.C.) also mention the Rašu. Apparently they migrated into the Crimean area *c.* 200 B.C. (John Ruthven, "Ezekiel's Rosh and Russia: a Connection?" BS, CXXV [1968], 324–333). The Heb. scholar Gesenius suggested identifying Russia with Rosh, but the Heb. word has no relationship to the modern European country. *See* Gog; Magog.

J. R.

ROT, ROTTENNESS. As a translation of *nāphal,* "to rot" means lit., "to fall," i.e., "to wither" or "waste away" (Num 5:21–22, 27). Heb. *'ābash* means "to shrivel" (Joel 1:17). In Jer 38:11–12 the reference of *melāḥîm* is to worn-out rags or tattered clothing. Heb. *rāqab* refers to the decay that takes place in dead wood (Job 41:27; Isa 40:20), or to caries in living bones (Prov 12:4; 14:30; Hab 3:16), or to the putrefaction of flesh by worms, gangrene, or boils (Job 13:28; cf. 2:8).

ROW, ROWERS. *See* Ship.

RUBY. *See* Jewels.

RUDDER. *See* Ship.

RUDDY. The translation of Heb. *'ādōm,* which means "to be red," and *'admōnî,* "red, ruddy," describing an attribute of man's complexion. Most references are to vigorous health (Lam 4:7; I Sam 16:12; 17:42; Song 5:10), although one reference is possibly to red hair (Gen 25:25). *See* Colors: Red.

RUDE. The KJV translation of *idiōtēs* (II Cor 11:6). A Gr. word meaning "private," "uninstructed," it is the word from which we derive the English word "idiot." With reference to Paul's manner of speaking it is translated "unskilled" (RSV, NASB).

RUDIMENTS. This word occurs only in Col 2:8, 20 as the KJV rendering of the Gr. word *stoicheion.* Translated in Heb 5:12 as "principles" and in Gal 4:3, 9 as "elements," *stoicheion* means "elementary teachings." It denotes what an initiate or observer encounters first. In Galatians and Colossians Paul's thought is inclusivistic, covering any tendency in pre- and non-Christian religions that shows itself to be in opposition to Christ and that binds and enslaves men. In Gal 4:3, 9 he is opposing religious ordinances and ritualism; in Col 2:8, 20, asceticism and incipient Gnosticism. The RSV rendering "elemental spirits" therefore would unnecessarily restrict Paul's meaning. See Arndt, p. 776; G. Delling, *"Stoicheion,"* TDNT, VII, 670–687.

Stoicheion also occurs in II Pet 3:10, 12, where "elements" refer to the basic physical substances of the material world.

See Elements.

RUE. *See* Plants.

RUFUS (rū'fŭs). The Rufus mentioned in Mk 15:21 was one of two sons of Simon of Cyrene who carried the Lord's cross to Golgotha. Perhaps this is the same man as the one mentioned in Rom 16:13 as being "chosen in the Lord." Paul sent salutations to the latter, and to his mother, who seems to have acted in some way as a mother to Paul—perhaps giving him lodging and otherwise ministering to his needs.

RUHAMAH (rōō-hā'mȧ). A symbolic name ("she has obtained mercy") applied to the daughters of the prophet Hosea. It was a prophecy and promise of the restoration of Israel when they should have repented and returned to God (Hos 2:1, 23). It is the counterpart to the judgment pronounced by God upon Israel signified in the name given to Hosea's daughter, Lo-ruhamah (Hos 1:6, "she has not obtained mercy"). *See* Lo-ruhamah. Both Paul (Rom 9:25–26) and Peter (I Pet 2:10) refer to the prophecy as evidence of God's great mercy, applying it, however, to Gentile as well as Jewish believers.

Six columns of the Temple of Jupiter still stand majestically among the ruins of Baalbek. HFV

RUIN. This rendering of several Heb. and Gr. words has both literal and figurative usage in Scripture.

Literal ruin may come to strongholds or fortifications (Ps 89:40), cities (Isa 17:1; 25:2), or nations (Ezk 31:13). While the ruin of cities or nations may be very literal, often prophets hurled predictions of destruction against them because of their sin—especially the sin of idolatry or of severe treatment of Israel (e.g., prophecies against Tyre, Isa 23:13; Ezk 27:27; and Egypt, Ezk 31:13). All over the Middle East one may see evidence of the ruin of ancient cities and nations. As early as the time of Abraham the site of the Early Bronze Age city of Ai (*q.v.*) was so named because of its ruined condition (Heb. *hā'ay,* "the ruin"). Uninhabited mounds (called *Tell* in Arabic, *Tepe* in Persian, and *Hüyük* in Turkish), encasing ancient cities, dot the landscape of the entire area. Only a small percentage of these have been excavated by the archaeologists. *See* Tell.

Often figurative or spiritual aspects of ruin in Scripture are more pronounced than literal aspects, though the ruin is no less real. On the individual level, a "flattering mouth worketh ruin" (Prov 26:28); so does strong drink, as attested by numerous passages in Proverbs. Jesus in a parable also likened the spiritual ruin of an individual to the collapse of a house built on sand; such a collapse would certainly occur if an individual did not receive the teachings of Christ and live according to them (Lk 6:49). A nation could come to ruin as well as an individual; Ezekiel warned that iniquity would bring about the ruin of the house of Israel (Ezk 18:30).

H. F. V.

RULER. The translation of some 19 words in the Bible. As rulers they were protectors (*māgēn,* "shield," Hos 4:18). The king was so designated (*māshal,* Ps 105:20), or was called "leader" (*nāgîd,* I Sam 25:30). The ruler was called *nāṣî* ("one lifted up," Ex 16:22), or "captain" (*qāṣîn,* Isa 1:10), or "head" (*rō'sh,* Deut 1:13, ASV, RSV). In administration of the realm he was denoted *śar,* "officer" (Gen 47:6; Ex 18:21). In Persian times the local rulers were called "prefects" (*segānîm,* "rulers," Ezr 9:2). In the NT they are called *archōn* (Mt 9:18) and *politárchai* (Acts 17:6).

See Authority; Captain; Governor; King; Lead, Leader; Officer.

RUMAH (rōō'mȧ). Rumah, which means "height," was the town of Zebudah, the mother of Jehoiakim, and her father Pedaiah (II Kgs 23:36). If it is the same as Arumah, its location was near Shechem. Otherwise, it may be identified with Khirbet Rumeh, near Rimmon in Galilee, *c.* six miles N of Nazareth. Or it may be a scribal error for Dumah SW of Hebron (*see* Dumah 3).

RUMP. The "fat-tail" (Heb. *'alyâ*) on oriental sheep. Weighing ten or 12 pounds, the entire rump was burnt as a sacrifice (Ex 29:22; Lev 3:9; 7:3; 8:25; 9:19).

RUNNER. The NASB translation in II Sam 15:1 of the 50 men who ran before Absalom's chariot. The Israelite royal guards were called *hārāṣîm,* which literally means "the runners," i.e., the outrunners or royal escorts (I Sam 22:17; I Kgs 1:5; 14:27-28; II Kgs 10:25; 11:4, 6, 11, 19). They kept watch at the palace doors, had charge over the room in which the king kept his treasures, and accompanied the royal chariot. *See* Footman; Forerunner; Guard 2. For the concept of running as a sport (I Cor 9:24-27; Heb 12:1) *see* Games.

Bibliography. Otto Bauernfeind, *"Trechō,* etc.," TDNT, VIII, 226-235.

RUSH. *See* Plants: Reed.

RUST. In the NT *brōsis* ("eating," "a devouring," Mt 6:19-20) and *ios* ("metallic rust," Jas 5:3) are the Gr. words for "rust," with reference to the tarnishing of earthly treasures and of gold and silver, respectively. In Ezk 24:6-13 the rust (ASV, RSV, etc.; KJV "scum," *q.v.*) of a pot was a symbol of Jerusalem's "filthy lewdness" (v. 13, RSV) which even repeated intense heatings would not remove. The Heb. word *ḥel'â* is derived from a verb root meaning "to be sick, diseased," and denotes the greenish oxide of copper as well as the brown rust of iron. Thus, the use of the English word in the Bible refers in a general way to the corrosion of various metals.

RUTH (rōōth). A Moabitess who had the unique distinction of marrying two Jewish farmers, Mahlon (Ruth 4:10), one of the sons of Elimelech and Naomi (1:2), and Boaz, a kinsman of Elimelech (4:3). In wholeheartedly endorsing these marriages, Elimelech's family either ignored the statute preserved in Deut 23:3-4 forbidding Jews to accept Moabites into their assembly, or was unaware of this prohibition.

Ruth was remarkable in her willingness to forsake her own environment for a foreign one, somewhat like Abraham's venturing into a land he had never seen (Gen 12:1 ff.; cf. Ruth 2:11). She resisted the undoubtedly strong temptation of her sister-in-law (Orpah) to return to her own people. Because of her love for Naomi Ruth desired to remain with her mother-in-law, to become a Jew, to exchange her

Fields of Boaz near Bethlehem. HFV

god (probably Chemosh, Num 21:29; I Kgs 11:7, 33) for Naomi's God (Yahweh) (cf. Ruth 2:12-13), and to be buried in the burying place of Naomi (Ruth 1:14-17). Ruth's devotion transcended Naomi's pessimism, which ascribed her utter "emptiness" to the Almighty and urged the women of Bethlehem to call her Mara ("bitter," 1:19-21).

Although she was under no obligation, Ruth immediately took advantage of the season of the year in Bethlehem (barley harvest—from the middle to the end of May, preceding wheat harvest) to glean to support herself and her mother-in-law. The Israelite laborers were impressed by her devotion and told Boaz (2:11), who gave her special privileges (2:14 ff.).

The apex of Ruth's devotion was reflected in her compliance with Naomi's suggestion that she go to the threshing floor at night when Boaz would be merry with wine to try to persuade him to accept the responsibility of a kinsman. He assented, and when the nearest kinsman waived his responsibility, Boaz voluntarily assumed it, bought the property of Elimelech, Chilion, and Mahlon, and married Ruth (4:7-12). He followed the custom of the levirate (*q.v.*) law of Deut 25:5-10, even though he was not Mahlon's brother but only a close relative.

In due time, Obed ("servant") was born to Boaz and Ruth. Naomi's "bitterness" was assuaged in her joy over the child, who became an ancestor of David (4:18-22) and of the Messiah. Ruth was one of four women specifically mentioned in Matthew's genealogy of Jesus (1:5). All these women were Gentiles, and apparently Matthew's intention was to emphasize the universal dimension of Jesus' background. *See* Ruth, Book of.

J. T. W.

RUTH, BOOK OF. The Heb. Bible places the book of Ruth in the last major division (Writings) as one of the five Megilloth. English Bibles place it after the book of Judges, following the LXX, Vulgate, and Josephus. It is doubtful that the book of Ruth was once a part of the book of Judges. It is a short story containing four scenes, with a concluding genealogy.

Outline

I. The Sojourn in Moab and Return Home, 1:1–22
II. Ruth the Gleaner, 2:1–23
III. Ruth's Request of Boaz at the Threshing Floor, 3:1–18
IV. Boaz Performs the Function of a Kinsman, 4:1–17
V. A Genealogy from Pharez to David, 4:18–22

Purpose

Scholars differ widely as to the purpose of the book. We may dismiss the views that (*a*) the author simply wanted to tell an interesting story; (*b*) the book is a midrash on an alleged cult myth of a Bethlehem fertility cult (Staples); (*c*) it is a propaganda pamphlet intended to emphasize the duty of marriage to a near kinsman (Driver); (*d*) the author wishes to extol a widow's faithfulness.

Several scholars (e.g., R. H. Pfeiffer and G. A. F. Knight) contend that the book of Ruth is a polemic against the demands of Ezra (chaps. 9–10) and Nehemiah (13:23–31) that Jews put away their foreign wives. The author often mentions that Ruth is a Moabitess (Ruth 1:4, 22; 2:2, 6, 11–13, 21; 4:5, 10), and there is no indication that the Jews involved in this story disapproved of the marriages of Chilion to Orpah, Mahlon to Ruth, and Boaz to Ruth. However, there is no polemic in the book—even in the passages where it is expected. We would expect the author to indicate that the nearest kinsman rejected Ruth *because she was a Gentile,* or that Boaz married her *in spite of her Gentile origin,* but there is no hint of this (Hertzberg).

Many scholars think that the purpose of the book was connected with the ancestry of David. But there is no general agreement as to the author's intention. Did he wish to bridge the gap which existed in his day (the genealogical table in 4:18–22 is also found in expanded form in I Chr 2:5–15) between Pharez and David? Or did he want to establish a relationship between David's house and that of Moab, perhaps to provide a basis for the two nations uniting against a common enemy, or for Moab to submit to Israel? This type of relationship might explain why David entrusted his parents to the care of the king of Moab (I Sam 22:3-4), although that event has other plausible explanations. Or was he trying to deny that David should be considered a Moabite, since he was a descendant of Boaz (a Jew) who had simply married a Moabite, in order to avoid the stigma which might be attached to David because of the statute preserved in Deut 23:3-4 forbidding a Moabite to enter the assembly of Yahweh to the tenth generation? It seems likely that the author of the book was interested in providing information about David's background, but subordinated this to a more imposing purpose.

The author's primary purpose was to emphasize the providential care of Yahweh for two widows in desperate circumstances (Hertzberg), and thus to show that the appearance and rise of David at a crucial period in Israel's history was not accidental (similarly Ringgren). This theme is beautifully capsulated in Boaz's statements to Ruth in his field (2:11–12), and is explicit throughout the book (cf. 1:8, 16-17; 2:3–4, 20–23; 3:1–4, 7–13; 4:13–15).

Date

The Talmud (Baba Bathra 14*b*) makes Samuel the author of the book, but this is unlikely. The date of the book is dependent on the understanding of its purpose. If it were a polemic against the measures of Ezra and Nehemiah, it would belong to the post-Exilic period, probably in the 4th cen. B.C. If the author intends, however, to emphasize the providence of God, it can certainly be pre-Exilic. Under close scrutiny, the alleged late words and expressions fail to refute an early date (see Driver), and the Aramaisms in the book may be later attempts

Barley harvesting in the fields of Bethlehem. JR

to clarify obscurities in the earlier text. The similarities between Ruth 4:7 ff. and Deut 25:5 ff. do not demand a date after King Josiah's reform in 621 B.C. (triggered by the discovery of the book of the law, which presumably included Deuteronomy), because the custom in Ruth rests on earlier legal codes, and the circumstances underlying these two passages are not really the same. *See* Ruth. The Heb. vocabulary and syntax, the idiomatic expressions, and the purity of style (see Driver) support an early date of the book. Its present form cannot be earlier than the time of David (4:18-22).

Bibliography. Stephen Bertman, "Symmetrical Design in the Book of Ruth," JBL, LXXXIV (1965), pp. 165-168. John J. Davis, *Conquest and Crisis: Studies in Joshua, Judges, and Ruth,* Grand Rapids: Baker, 1969, pp. 155-170. S. R. Driver, *An Introduction to the Literature of the Old Testament,* New York: Scribner's, 1893, pp. 453-456. J. Vernon McGee, *In a Barley Field,* Glendale: G/L Publications, 1968. Leon Morris, *Ruth,* London: IVCF, 1968. Charles F. Pfeiffer, "Ruth," WBC, pp. 267-272. W. E. Staples, "The Book of Ruth," AJSL, LIII (1937), 145-157. *See also* under Judges, Book of.

J. T. W.

RYE, RIE. *See* Plants.

S

SABACHTHANI. *See* Eli, Eli, Lama Sabachthani.

SABAEANS. *See* Sabeans.

SABAOTH. The transliteration of the plural form of the Heb. word meaning "army" or "host." The connotation of organization as applied to creation, angels, heavenly bodies, or the migrating Israelites (Num 1:3) points to a leader or one of superior station. Accordingly the word gains prominence in the name Lord of hosts (Sabaoth), occurring first in the books of Samuel, but used freely (247 times) by the prophets. Isaiah declares directly, "Our redeemer, the Lord of hosts is his name, the Holy One of Israel" (47:4). It is indefinite what hosts are meant in this epithet of sovereign might and majesty. This word occurs as such in the KJV in Rom 9:29 and Jas 5:4. *See* Host.

SABBATH. *Its meaning*. From the Heb. *shabbāt,* which means "to cease" or "to desist." The Gr. word is *sabbaton,* but the plural *sabbata* is sometimes used to designate a single sabbath (Arndt, p. 746). The word is applied to several festivals in the OT, but principally and usually it refers to the seventh day of the week, the Jewish day of rest and worship.

Its origin. The sabbath was instituted at creation (Gen 2:2, where the root occurs from which the word is derived). God ceased from His labor on the seventh day of creation and set a pattern for man to follow. The incorporation of the sabbath into the Decalogue was based on God's resting at the time of creation and on His deliverance of Israel from Egypt (Ex 20:11; Deut 5:15). Some have tried to derive the institution of the sabbath from Babylonia. Although the word appears in Babylonian inscriptions, it was not attached to the seventh day of the week (the Babylonians had a five-day week), nor was it a day of cessation from labor. J. R. Sampey remarks: "Hence the assertions of some Assyriologists with regard to the Bab. origin of the Sabbath must be taken with several grains of salt" (ISBE, IV, 2630). The Bible attributes the origin of the sabbath to God's example at creation.

Its mention and purpose. After the creation account, the sabbath is next mentioned in relation to the giving of the manna (Ex 16:23-30); then at Sinai, when it became part of the Decalogue (Ex 20:8-11). God ordained sabbath-keeping as the sign of His covenant relationship with Israel (Ex 31:12-17; Ezk 20:12, 20). Thus it acted as the seal of the Mosaic covenant (cf. Isa 56:4, 6), corresponding to circumcision as the seal of the Abrahamic covenant (cf. Gen 17:11).

The other books of the Pentateuch contain legislation for sabbath observance. The Day of Atonement was designated a sabbath of complete rest (Lev 16:31; 23:32), and the first, fifteenth, and twenty-third days of the seventh month (Feast of Trumpets, Feast of Tabernacles) were to be observed with a sabbath rest (Heb. *shabbātôn*; Lev 23:24, 39). The seventh year was to be a sabbatical year (Lev 25:2-7). The fields were to enjoy a rest from cultivation (Ex 23:10-11), and the debts of fellow Israelites were to be remitted (Deut 15:1-9). After every series of seven sabbatical years the fiftieth year was to be observed as a year of jubilee when property reverted to its original owner and Israelites in servitude regained freedom (Lev 25:8-54). The sabbath is also mentioned in Kings, Chronicles, Nehemiah, Ps 92 (title), Isaiah, Jeremiah, Ezekiel, Hosea, and Amos. *See* Festivals: Sabbatical Seasons.

With the development of the synagogue during the intertestamental period, the sabbath became a day of worship and study of the law as well as cessation from work. The beginnings of legalism and petty restrictions on sabbath observance began during this period. Jesus declared Himself to be Lord of the sabbath (Mk 2:28), and that the sabbath was made for man, and not man for the sabbath (v. 27), though He did nothing to violate the Mosaic law. Instead He pointed the Jews back to the original intent of the sabbath ordinance, viz., to provide rest for man, and taught that the higher principle of mercy should take precedence (Mt 12:5–7, 10–12; Lk 13:15; 14:1–6).

Early Christians may have used the sabbath for witnessing to Jews (Acts 13:14), but the first day of the week was their day of worship (Acts 20:7). It is significant that the decrees of the council of Jerusalem made no mention of sabbath-keeping in the requirements laid on Gentile Christians (Acts 15:28 ff.). However, the sabbath will apparently be part of worship in the future (Isa 66:22–23).

Its observance. Numerous biblical regulations governed the observance of the sabbath. In addition, many traditions were added in the intertestamental period. Two tractates of the Mishnah, *Shabbath* and *'Erubin*, are devoted to the detailed observances of the sabbath. The details include the 39 classes of prohibited actions with much hairsplitting as to the working out of these matters.

1. The chief biblical prohibition concerning the sabbath was against work on that day (Ex 20:10). The OT does not define work in detail except that it specifically forbids the kindling of a fire for cooking (Ex 35:3) and the gathering of wood (Num 15:32 ff.). However, in keeping with the purpose of the sabbath, burden-bearing (Jer 17:21 ff.), traveling (Ex 16:29), and trading (Amos 8:5; Neh 10:31; 13:15, 19) were also forbidden.

2. The Jewish sabbath was also to be observed with a holy assembly, the doubling of the daily offerings, and the placing of new showbread in the holy place (Num 28:9 ff.; Lev 24:5–8). This made it a day of gladness (Num 10:10), for it provided man an opportunity to put aside the duties of life and concentrate on spiritual activities for the refreshing of his soul. In the time of Christ sumptuous feasts were held on the sabbath although the actual cooking had to be done previous to the day (Lk 14:1; cf. E. Schurer, *The Jewish People in the Time of Jesus Christ*, II, ii, 99). *See* Festivals: Weekly Sabbaths.

Its commemoration. For Israel, the sabbath commemorated God's creation rest (Ex 20:11) and their deliverance from Egypt (Deut 5:15). For the believer in Christ, the sabbath rest of God at the original creation is made an illustration of the rest into which the believer enters in the new creation when "he also hath ceased from his own works" by trusting Christ (Heb 4:1–10).

C. C. R.

Its relevance today. Two views are held today concerning the sabbath: (1) That it has been done away with completely, and that, though man needs one day of rest in seven, it and all of the Mosaic law—and the Decalogue in particular—are no longer binding (II Cor 3:6–11). Many Reformed theologians believe, however, that it is not possible to maintain that the Ten Commandments are no longer valid. They point out that Christ kept them in our stead for our justification—that they are done away with only as far as justification is concerned—and that the NT writers quote them as applicable for our sanctification. Christ uses them in the Sermon on the Mount (Mt 5:21, 27), Paul in Rom 13:8–10, and James in Jas 2:10–12. (2) That since the Son of Man is Lord of the sabbath He had the right to change the day of its keeping for His Church from the last day of the week to the first, and did so in order that it might become a commemoration of His rising from the dead. This appears to many to be the only explanation that fits all the facts. Since the sabbath was made for man, Christ changed its celebration to bless man. *See* Lord's Day.

R. A. K.

Bibliography. Gary G. Cohen, "The Doctrine of the Sabbath in the Old and New Testaments," *Grace Journal*, VI (1965), #2, pp. 7–15. Alfred Edersheim, *The Life and Times of Jesus the Messiah*, 2 vols., Grand Rapids: Eerdmans, reprint, 1956. Paul K. Jewett, *The Lord's Day*, Grand Rapids: Eerdmans, 1971, pp. 13–51. E. Lohse, "*Sabbatismos*, etc.," TDNT, VII, 1–35. Julius Morgenstern, "Sabbath," IDB, IV, 135–141. W. W. Prescott, "Sabbath: Seventh-Day Adventist Position," ISBE, IV, 2632 ff. John R. Sampey, "Sabbath," ISBE, IV, 2629–2632.

SABBATH, COVERT FOR THE. The word "covert" (Heb. *mûsāk*) means a covered place or way, probably screened off from the public. The phrase "covert for the sabbath" is found only in II Kgs 16:18 in the KJV and has been translated "covered way for the sabbath" (ASV, RSV, NASB). The removal of this covert was one of the infamous acts of the wicked king Ahaz. The significance of the act is in doubt, for the original purpose of the covert is unknown. The best explanation seems to be that it was a stand, covered place, or hall used by the king when he visited the temple with his retinue on the sabbath or on feast days.

SABBATH DAY'S JOURNEY. This expression is used only once in Scripture, at Acts 1:12, where it is said that the ascension from the Mount of Olives took place a "sabbath day's journey" from Jerusalem, the distance a Jew might travel on the sabbath without breaking the law. This distance of 2,000 cubits or 3,000 feet was arrived at on the basis of Josh 3:4, where it is said that the ark traveled 2,000 cubits ahead of the Israelite camp. Since Jews were allowed to go to the tabernacle on the sabbath, this distance became fixed as a sabbath day's journey.

Today in the Chapel of the Ascension on the

Mount of Olives one may see a footprint in the top of the mount that some of the pious believe is the footprint of Jesus, made when He ascended. In reality it is probably a mark to indicate the extent of a sabbath day's journey from Jerusalem and may be the spot from which Jesus ascended.

H. F. V.

SABBATICAL YEAR. *See* Festivals.

SABEANS (sȧ-bē'ȧnz). The Sabeans were a group of Arab tribes who formerly roamed far and wide over Arabia and eventually settled in the wooded hill country in the SW corner of Arabia now known as Yemen. They were mentioned for the first time in the annals of one of the priest-kings of Lagash which go back to the 21st cen. B.C. The priest-king claimed that he ruled over the Sabeans and received incense from them as tribute. Some Sabeans attacked the servants of Job (Job 1:15). Nothing further was recorded about them until the age of Solomon, when the Queen of Sheba (or Saba) visited Judah and entered into a trade agreement with Solomon (I Kgs 10:1–13), bringing with her spices, almug trees, precious stones, and gold. *See* Sheba 4–7. Subsequently the Sabeans paid tribute in gold and incense to the Assyrian kings Tiglath-pileser III (745–727 B.C.) and Sargon II (722–705 B.C.). Sabeans are mentioned as dealers in slaves in Joel 3:8.

The Sabeans made their living mainly from the incense trade. The almug tree which grew profusely in their land, when tapped, yielded a gummy substance that had a rich fragrant aroma. Incense produced in S Arabia was exported to Mesopotamia and Egypt in substantial quantities from time immemorial, and the Sabeans thrived on its trade.

The Assyrian invasion of the 8th cen. evidently brought with it knowledge of the Phoenician alphabet, because from the 7th cen. onward we find a new alphabet used in S Arabia based on the Phoenician. Some 2,000 inscriptions have been collected so far in the territory of the Sabeans which have added greatly to our knowledge about this people.

The Sabeans have left behind a great monument in the form of a dam near Marib, their ancient capital. This dam was probably built soon after the Assyrian invasion, and finally became ruined through neglect sometime during the 6th cen. A.D.

The Sabeans worshiped a number of deities including al-Uzza, goddess of fertility; ath-Thurayya, goddess of rain; and Manat, goddess of doom and death. The most important deities were the moon-god Ilumquh symbolized by the bull, his consort the sun-goddess Shams, and their child, the male morning star which we know as the planet Venus. Besides these deities they placated a number of spirits that were supposedly resident in stones, trees, and springs. Judaism and Christianity penetrated into Yemen at an early date, and there were communities belonging to both sects down to the advent of Islam. Archaeological expeditions in 1950–52 cleared away sand from a huge ovoid temple nearly 1,000 feet in circumference at Marib. It was dedicated to the chief god Ilumquh.

The Sabeans at the outset appear to have been ruled by a priest-king called "Mukarrib." However, with the growth of the prosperity and power of the country, *c.* 450 B.C. the rulers assumed the title of "melek" or king. About the beginning of the 1st cen. A.D. Saba appears to have brought some of its neighbors under its suzerainty and the title was changed from "king of Saba" to "king of Saba and Raydan."

Bibliography. Wendell Phillips, *Qataban and Sheba,* New York: Harcourt, Brace, 1955. Gus W. Van Beek, "Sabeans," IDB, IV, 144–146.

D. C. B.

SABTA, SABTAH (săb'tȧ). The descendants of this third son of Cush probably lived on the SW coast of Arabia along the Red Sea (Gen 10:7; I Chr 1:9).

SABTECHA (săb'tĕ-kȧ). The fifth son of Cush, whose descendants presumably were one of the S Arabian tribes (Gen 10:7; I Chr 1:9). The name is otherwise unknown.

SACAR (sā'kär)

1. A Hararite, he was the father of Ahiam, who was one of David's valiant men (I Chr 11:35). In II Sam 23:33 his name appears as Sharar.

2. The name of a Korahite, son of Obed-edom, who was a gatekeeper of the tabernacle in the days of David (I Chr 26:4).

SACCUTH, SICCUTH. *See* Gods, False.

SACKBUT. *See* Music.

SACKCLOTH. The English word "sack" is derived from Heb. *sáq* and Gr. *sakkos,* a "mesh," i.e., coarse loose cloth. Sackcloth was a coarse-textured cloth of a dark color, composed of goat's or camel's hair (cf. Isa 50:3; Rev 6:12). It resembled the Roman "cilicium."

It frequently was worn as a symbol of mourning for the dead (Gen 37:34; II Sam 3:31; Joel 1:8); of lamentation for personal or national disaster (Job 16:15; Lam 2:10; Est 4:1); of penitence for sins (I Kgs 21:27; Neh 9:1; Jon 3:5; Mt 11:21); and of special prayer for deliverance (II Kgs 19:1–2; Dan 9:3). Frequently those wearing the sackcloth of mourning or penitence put ashes or earth on themselves. Sometimes they tore their clothing before donning the symbolic sackcloth (II Kgs 6:30; Isa 32:11).

The use of sackcloth spanned many centuries and the exact shape of the garment is uncertain. It may have been a rectangular piece of cloth in the shape of a grain bag sewn on both sides and on one end, leaving space for the head and arms (cf. Gen 42:25, 27, 35; Josh 9:4; Lev 11:32). It could have been a smaller garment such as loin cloth worn close to the skin (cf. I Kgs 21:27; II Kgs 6:30; Job 16:15; Isa 32:11). The sackcloth may have been a large garment worn over the coat instead of the outer garment (cf. II Kgs 19:1-2; I Chr 21:16; Est 4:2; Ps 69:11; Isa 37:1-2).

See Dress.

Bibliography. G. Stählin, "*Sakkos,*" TDNT, VII, 56-64.

D. W. D.

SACRAMENTS. One of certain religious acts, ceremonies, or practices distinguished from all others in Christian rites as having been observed or recognized by Christ and given a certain character by Him. According to some, sacraments were instituted by Christ as the visible means by which divine grace is sought and conferred; according to others, they are observed in memory of Him and as a sign, seal, or symbol of a Christian experience or profession. Many in the latter group prefer to call them ordinances. In most cases, a sacrament is administered by a clergyman, and to those only who have fulfilled the conditions considered proper to its valid reception.

The Roman Catholic and the Eastern churches recognize seven sacraments (usually called Mysteries in the latter church), viz., baptism, confirmation, the Eucharist, penance, extreme unction, holy orders, and matrimony. In general, Protestants accept only two sacraments, baptism and the Lord's Supper, but among members of certain churches, as the Anglican and Lutheran, others of the seven are recognized as of a salutary but subordinate character, though not usually regarded as having been instituted by Christ Himself.

Calvin (*Institutes,* IV, 14, 1-24) discusses the sacraments in general; baptism (IV, 15, 1-22; IV, 16, 1-32) and the Lord's Supper (IV, 17, 1-50) specifically. The Apology of the Augsburg Confession (Art. XIII) and the Formula of Concord (Art. VII) set forth the Lutheran view. *See* Baptism; Lord's Supper; Ordinances, Christian.

Bibliography. P. W. Evans, *Sacrament in the New Testament,* London: Tyndale Press, 1947.

C. S. M.

SACRIFICE, HUMAN. A perverted expression of religious devotion and means of seeking divine favor. It has been found in several primitive religions, as well as in heathenism of biblical times, such as in the case of the Ammonites to Molech (Lev 18:21; 20:2) and the Phoenicians to Baal (cf. Jer 19:5; 32:35). Greek and Roman authors wrote extensively about the practice of sacrificing children as burnt offerings in Phoenicia and the Punic colonies of N Africa, especially at Carthage (W. F. Albright, *Yahweh and the Gods of Canaan,* Garden City: Doubleday, 1968, pp. 234-244).

Human sacrifice was often done in an endeavor to placate a god who was considered to be showing his anger in a particular trial or danger. Because it was practiced both by the Canaanites (Ps 106:37-38) and their immediate neighbors, it was specifically mentioned and forbidden in the law of Moses (Lev 18:21; 20:2-5; Deut 18:10). A terrible example of this is given in II Kgs 3:27, when during a seige Mesha, king of Moab, sacrificed his eldest son and heir apparent to the throne upon the city wall as a burnt offering. Israel and her allies withdrew in horror.

Some of the Israelites adopted the practice of sacrificing sons and daughters. Many scholars believe that Jephthah carried out his vow to sacrifice whatever came out of his house to meet him, even though it was his daughter, his only child (Jud 11:30-40); others question the interpretation (*see* Jephthah). Both Ahaz (II Kgs 16:3; II Chr 28:1-3) and Manasseh (II Kgs 21:6; II Chr 33:6) fell into this heathen custom and "made their sons to pass through the fire"—a term used to express the horror of human sacrifice. Josiah, a godly king who succeeded them, "defiled Topheth, which is in the valley of the children of Hinnom, that no man might make his son or his daughter to pass through the fire to Molech" (II Kgs 23:10; cf. II Chr 34:3-5). Though no specific example is given of its occurrence in the N after the division of the kingdom, still it is stated as a cause of their captivity (II Kgs 17:17). The people were even practicing it at the time of the Babylonian Exile as witnessed by the prophets of that day (Jer 7:31; 17:1-2; 19:5; 32:35; Ezk 16:21; 20:31; 23:37; cf. Isa 57:5). The Lord clearly pronounced through Micah that the sacrifice of his firstborn would not atone for one's sins (Mic 6:7-8).

An ethical issue has been raised by Sören Kierkegaard in his *Fear and Trembling.* God commanded Abraham, he argued, to depart from what is ethical, to break the commandment and to do the contradictory, the paradoxical, the absurd! As Abraham went to sacrifice he was a murderer! Kierkegaard sees this as an example of the nature of faith. True faith demands a leap into the absurd and the acceptance of what goes contrary to our categories of reason.

In answer to this it should be pointed out that God had a dual purpose in asking Abraham to offer up his son. God wanted to test Abraham's faith and also to teach him that He did not want human sacrifice. While Abraham believed that God could raise his son from the dead, and would do so if he were sacrificed since Isaac was the child of the promise (Heb 11:17-19; cf. Gen 17:19), he also believed that God would supply a substitutionary sacrifice in place of his son. This is proved by his answer to Isaac's query, "Where is the lamb for a burnt offering?" "God," Abraham replied, "will provide himself a lamb for a burnt offering" (Gen 22:7-8). That God did not intervene until

SACRIFICES

Abraham raised the knife to slay his son only proves the extremity of God's test on the one hand, and the perfection of Abraham's obedience on the other. On what did Abraham's faith rest? Upon God's direct revelation (Gen 12:1-3, 7; 15:1-6, 18 ff.; 17:4-8; 18:10-14) and His proved faithfulness. Biblical faith is based upon reasonable evidence (cf. Jn 20:30-31; I Jn 1:1-2) and not upon the ridiculous, the absurd, the contradictory, and the paradoxical.

R. A. K.

SACRIFICES

Terms and Procedures

The basic Heb. terms in the OT for the sacrificial offerings are: (1) *minḥâ,* "gift" (II Chr 32:23), "present" (Jud 6:18), "offering" (Gen 4:3-5; Num 5:15-26), "sacrifice" (I Kgs 18:29, 36), the gift presented to the deity; (2) *qorbān,* "offering" (Lev 1:2; etc.), that which is brought near (cf. Mk 7:11; *see* Corban); (3) *zebaḥ,* "sacrifice" (Gen 31:54; Ex 10:25; 12:27; 23:18; etc.), a slaughtered animal (from *zābaḥ,* "to slaughter for sacrifice"), the remainder of which could be eaten by the worshiper in fellowship with his god (Deut 12:27) and called a sacrifice of peace offering (Lev 3); (4) *'ōlâ,* "burnt offering" (Gen 8:20; 22:2-13), that which goes up as a soothing aroma to the Lord (see Ex 29:25, NASB), burned to ashes (Lev 6:10) in order to make it an irrevocable gift and to give it a spiritual form as it rises in smoke from the altar toward God; (5) *'āshām,* "trespass offering" (Lev 5:6, KJV, ASV), "guilt offering" (RSV, NASB), a blood sacrifice made to atone for sins which were a breach of faith against God *and* man and produced guilt serious enough to demand the death penalty, used with reference to the vicarious sacrifice of Christ (Isa 53:10, NASB); (6) *ḥaṭṭā't,* "sin offering" (Ex 29:14, 36; Lev 4), "for sin," a blood sacrifice made to atone for unintentional sins.

In Heb. the first two terms are combined *(qorban minḥâ)* to form the expression for the meal or grain offering (Lev 2). Such an offering was usually in the form of unleavened perforated cakes (*ḥallôt*) of fine flour mixed with oil and seasoned with salt (*see* Food: Cake) or of flat thin wafers (*r^{e}qîqîm*) spread with oil. It might also consist of roasted heads of newly ripened grain with oil and incense put on it and burned on the altar. A meal offering was always accompanied by a drink offering or libation of wine (Ex 29:40-41; Lev 23:13, 18; Num 15:4-10; 28:1-31).

A more general term is *'isheh,* "fire (offering)," an offering consumed by fire, including both animal sacrifices (Ex 29:18) and baked goods (Lev 2:11; 24:7). The *n^{e}dābâ,* a "freewill offering," was purely voluntary, given as an expression of devotion (Lev 22:18-23); as such, the animal could be overgrown or stunted (v. 23, NASB). A votive offering (*neder*) was a kind of peace offering (Lev 7:15-16) presented either when making a vow or when

An altar of sacrifice in the Canaanite Obelisk Temple at Byblos, with a receptacle to catch the blood in front and a water jar at right. HFV

the vow was performed (Num 15:3; Jon 1:16). The *zebaḥ hattôdâ,* "the sacrifice of thanksgiving" (Lev 7:12-13; Ps 50:14, 23; 107:22; 116:17; Jer 17:26; Amos 4:5), was another form of peace offering and often became part of the fellowship meal eaten by the worshiper. *See also* Firstfruits; Tithes.

In the NT the most common Gr. word for "sacrifice" is *thysia* (Mt 9:13; Rom 12:1; Eph 5:2; Heb 7:27; etc.), from *thyō,* "to sacrifice" (Acts 14:13, 18; I Cor 5:7), "to butcher" (Mt 22:4, NASB; cf. Lk 15:23, 27, 30), "to kill" (Jn 10:10). Referring to Christ's sacrifice as the Lamb of God *sphagē* is the word for "slaughter" (Acts 8:32, quoting Isa 53:7). A more general term for "offering" is *prosphora* (Acts 21:26; Rom 15:16; Eph 5:2; Heb 10:5, 8, 10, 14, 18), signifying that which is brought forward. The term *dōron,* "gift," is used in the epistle to the Hebrews as a parallel term to "sacrifices" (Heb 5:1; 8:3-4; 9:9).

According to Lev 1 and 3 the worshiper first of all "offered" (*hiqrîb,* 1:3) his animal in the sense of bringing it near (1:2, same Heb. verb), bringing it to the N side (1:11) of the forecourt of the tabernacle or temple. He then laid (*sāmak*) his hand on the head of the animal, evidently to identify himself with his offering which would become his substitute. It is not certain whether this act also signified a transferring of sin and guilt. The victim was "killed" or slaughtered (*shāḥaṭ*) by the worshiper himself, except for the national sacrifices (Lev 16:15; II Chr 29:24). The priest collected the blood in a basin and sprinkled (*zāraq*), i.e., dashed or tossed it by handfuls (cf. use of this verb in Ex 9:8) against the altar. The remainder of the blood was poured out (*shāpak*) at the base of the altar.

Next, the worshiper flayed or skinned (*hiphshîṭ*) the animal and cut (*nātaḥ*) it into its pieces, i.e., dividing it by the joints (Lev 1:6, 12). In every case the kidneys along with the fat or suet of the kidneys, liver, and entrails, and the entire fat tail of a sheep (1:8; 3:3-4, 9-10; 4:8-10; cf. Gen 4:4; I Sam 2:16) were presented to the Lord (in the whole burnt offering no distinction was necessary). The priest "burned" (*hiqṭîr*), "offered up in smoke" (NASB), all of it on the altar. In the burnt offering all the parts of the animal, except for the skin, were wholly burnt on the altar in similar fashion. In the sin offering, after the fat and kidneys were removed, the entire carcass including the hide was taken outside the camp and burned (*śārap*, 4:11–12).

In the case of peace offerings the remaining pieces of the slaughtered animal were eaten in a sacrificial meal by the priests and worshipers together; such a meal was considered as a means of fellowshiping with the Lord (Deut 12:6–7; Ex 18:12; 24:5, 11).

In Lev 7:28–34 the portions of the sacrificed peace offerings especially reserved for the priest and his family were called the wave offering (*t^{e}nûpâ*) and the heave offering (*t^{e}-rûmâ*). The former was the breast of the animal, so called because it was "waved," i.e., moved toward the altar and back, as a symbol of presenting the offering to God and His returning it to the priest. Such an offering has been recognized in the Ugaritic term *šnpt*, occurring in a ritual text following a list of *šelem* (peace) sacrifices (BASOR # 198 [1970], p. 42). The heave offering was the right shoulder or thigh (*shôq*), something "heaved" or lifted up (from Heb. *rûm*; see both noun and verb in Num 15:20; 18:30, 32, NASB) to the Lord and set aside as a "contribution" to Him (Lev 7:14, 32, 34, NASB) for the use of the priests (Num 18:8–19).

J. R.

The Origin of Sacrifices

Concerning the origin of sacrifices two views are held: (1) that sacrifices were originated by men and that Israel actually only reorganized and adopted the customs of other religions when they inaugurated their system of sacrifices; (2) that sacrifices were inaugurated by Adam and his descendants in response to a revelation from God.

Possibly the first sacrificial act in Genesis occurred when God clothed Adam and Eve in skins to cover their nakedness (Gen 3:21). The second sacrifice mentioned was that of Cain, who came with an offering of "the fruit of the ground," namely, of what he had produced, expressing self-satisfaction and pride. His brother Abel, however, brought "of the firstlings of his flock and of the fat thereof," expressing contrition of heart, repentance, and need for the expiation of his sins (Gen 4:3–4). [It is also possible that the reason Abel's sacrifice was acceptable to God in contrast to His rejection of Cain's was the fact that Abel brought his best to God ("firstlings" and "fat thereof") while Cain simply went through the motions of worship. – Ed.]

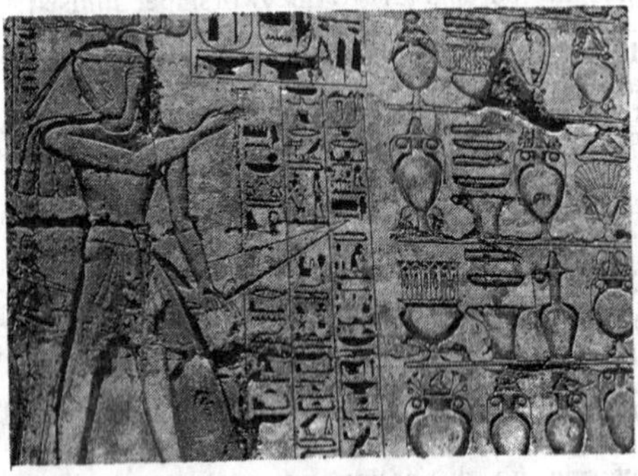

Rameses III makes an offering to Amon, portrayed on the temple of Medinet Habu at Luxor. HFV

In Rom 1:21 Paul refers to the primal revelation and the knowledge of God possessed by the patriarchs, and explains man's sin and apostasy on the basis that "when they knew God, they glorified him not as God, neither were thankful." After the Flood, Noah "builded an altar unto the Lord; and took of every clean beast, and of every clean fowl, and offered burnt-offerings on the altar" (Gen 8:20). The patriarchs also offered true sacrifices long before the time of Moses: Abraham (Gen 12:8; 13:18; 15:9–17; 22:2 ff.), Isaac (Gen 26:25), Jacob (Gen 33:20; 35:3).

A great advance in the organization and differentiation of sacrifices occurred with the giving of the law at Mount Sinai. A study of the different sacrifices prescribed reveals their final development to meet the needs of both the individual and the community.

Sacrifices for All Israel

Regular daily sacrifices were to be performed by the priests at the tabernacle while in the wilderness and at Shiloh, and later in the temple. These were offered both morning and evening, and each consisted of a yearling lamb as a burnt offering, a tenth of an ephah of flour as a meal offering, a fourth of a hin of wine as a drink offering (Num 28:3–8).

On the sabbath the daily offerings were all to be doubled (Num 28:9; Lev 24:8). Remember that all the other sacrifices for the whole of Israel were additional to the daily sacrifices; they did not supplement them.

At the new moon (monthly) the offerings were to be two young bullocks, one ram, seven lambs, three-tenths of an ephah of flour for each bullock, two for the ram, and one for each lamb, plus a drink offering, and a kid of the goats as a sin offering (Num 28:11–15).

Whenever a new supply of ashes was needed for mixing in water as a ceremonial agent for purification, the priest was to slaughter a red heifer and burn all of it (Num 19:2–10).

Five annual religious assemblies or holy convocations were held: Passover and the Feast of Unleavened Bread, Feast of Weeks, Feast of Trumpets, Day of Atonement, Feast of Tabernacles.

1. The Passover or Feast of Unleavened Bread, held the fourteenth day of the first month, had two phases, national and family. Each home was to slay its lamb (Ex 12), strike some of the blood on the sides and top of the doorframe, and eat the flesh roasted with fire with unleavened bread and bitter herbs, with

shoes on their feet and staff in their hand. Following this, there were to be seven days when they ate only unleavened bread (Ex 12:1-20). Because of the two parts, the celebration is often divided into the Feast of the Passover and the Feast of Unleavened Bread, and said to form two feasts.

The national celebration consisted in the addition of certain special sacrifices to those already offered daily at the temple. The first day (a sabbath) there was to be a holy convocation with the special offering of two bullocks, one ram, seven lambs of the first year without blemish, along with a meal offering of flour mixed with oil—three-tenths of an ephah for each bullock, two-tenths for each ram, one-seventh for each lamb—and one goat as a sin offering. The Passover celebration was concluded by a second public convocation on the seventh day (Num 28:16-25).

The offering of the firstfruits of the barley harvest (Lev 23:10) appears to have taken place in conjunction with the Feast of Unleavened Bread, since the Feast of Pentecost with the firstfruits of the wheat harvest (Ex 34:22) was to be seven weeks later (Lev 23:15), and since Pentecost was seven weeks after Christ's resurrection in the NT. The barley firstfruits were offered on the sixteenth of Nisan, or two days after the Passover, and had the identical offerings of unleavened bread prescribed for the rest of the week (Num 28:26-31). The timing fits with Christ's death and resurrection in the NT, 50 days before Pentecost. In this offering a sheaf of newly harvested grain was waved before the Lord as a sign of new life, and as typical of the resurrection of our Lord (Lev 23:9-14).

2. The Feast of Weeks or Pentecost was called this because it came seven weeks or 50 days after that of the Passover and the Firstfruits. It was to be initiated with a holy convocation and no work done on that day. Besides the regular morning and evening sacrifices, there were to be offered two more loaves baked with leaven, a burnt offering of seven lambs, one bullock, two rams, along with their meat and drink offerings, one kid for a sin offering, and two lambs for peace offerings (Lev 23:15-22; Num 28:26 ff.). The leaven in the loaves signified the believer with his sin. Christ is the firstfruits and sinless, the believers are the harvest and sinful (I Cor 15:22-23).

3. The Feast of Trumpets came on the first day of the seventh month. It was a celebration of thanks in anticipation of the final regathering of Israel (cf. Isa 18:3; 27:12-13; Joel 2:15-32). No work was to be done, but a holy convocation held with the blowing of trumpets. The addition to the daily offerings consisted of one young bullock, one ram, seven lambs of the first year with their meal offering, and one goat kid as a sin offering (Lev 23:24-25; Num 29:1-6).

4. The Day of Atonement was held on the tenth day of the seventh month. It was marked by a time of extreme soul-searching, and points to the sorrow and repentance of Israel at Christ's second coming (Lev 23:29; Num 29:7; Zech 12:10 ff.; 13:6; Mt 25:30; Rev 1:7). The addition to the regular daily offerings consisted of one bullock, one ram, seven lambs, with their meal offering mixed with oil, and one goat kid as a sin offering (Num 29:7-11).

5. The Feast of Tabernacles, held on the fifteenth day of the seventh month after all the harvest was in, was the greatest of all. It started with a holy convocation and lasted seven more days, closing the eighth day with another solemn assembly. During this feast the people were to live in tents made from boughs of trees in remembrance of their deliverance from Egypt. The special offering, besides the regular daily ones, started with 13 bullocks, two rams, 14 lambs with their appropriate meal offerings mixed with oil, and one goat kid for a sin offering, and tapered off on the last day to one bullock, one ram, seven lambs, and one goat kid. This feast was a memorial for Israel of her deliverance from Egypt and also a prophecy of the final coming Kingdom Age (Lev 23:33-44; Num 29:12-38; Zech 14:16, 19).

Public Sacrifices on Special Occasions

At the making of a covenant. Such was the case when a covenant was made between God and Abraham (Gen 15:9 ff.), between God and Israel at Sinai under Moses' leadership (Ex 24:1-8), and reenacted at Mount Ebal under Joshua (Josh 8:30; cf. chap. 24). The sacrifice offered included both burnt offerings and peace offerings, and therefore was first expiatory and then an act of thanks and praise. Moses sprinkled the blood of this offering upon both the book and the people (Ex 24:8; Heb 9:18-19) as a sign of cleansing from sin (Heb 9:22).

At a dedication or consecration. Examples of this are seen at the consecration of a priest (Lev 8-9) or a Levite (Num 8); at a coronation (I Sam 11:15; II Sam 6:13; I Kgs 1:9); at the dedication of Solomon's temple (I Kgs 8:5 ff.).

See Altar; Atonement; Blood; Festivals; Priest, Priesthood. For the sacrifices offered by individuals, *see* Worship, particular sacrifices.

R. A. K.

Bibliography. Johannes Behm, "*Thyō,* etc.," TDNT, III, 180-190. CornPBE, pp. 638-648. T. H. Gaster, "Sacrifices and Offerings, OT," IDB, IV, 147-159. F. D. Kidner, *Sacrifice in the Old Testament,* London: Tyndale Press, 1952. Otto Michel, "*Sphazō, Sphagē,*" TDNT, VII, 925-938. Leon Morris, "*'Asham,*" EQ, XXX (1958), 196-210. H. H. Rowley, "The Meaning of Sacrifice in the Old Testament," BJRL, XXXIII (1950), 74-110. Norman H. Snaith, "The Sin-Offering and the Guilt-Offering," VT, XV (1965), 73-80. R. J. Thompson and R. T. Beckwith, "Sacrifice and Offering," NBD, pp. 1113-1123. Roland de Vaux, *Ancient Israel,* trans. by John McHugh, New York: McGraw-Hill, 1961, pp. 415-456.

SACRILEGE. The Gr. verb *hierosyleō* is used once in Rom 2:22, the adjective once in Acts 19:37. It is translated "commit sacrilege" in Rom 2:22, KJV, but more literally it is "rob temples" as in RSV. Since it is used to refer to a sin that is the antithesis of abhorring idols, a better translation yet might be "profane sacred places." *See* Abomination; Abomination of Desolation.

SADDLE. The noun "saddle" (Heb. *merkāb*) appears only in Lev 15:9. It means "riding seat," and refers to a leather or cloth seat strapped to the back of an animal. This riding seat bore virtually no resemblance to the modern saddle. There was, however, a gradual improvement in design, so that the saddle during the early Christian era was quite similar to the present model.

The Heb. verb *ḥābash,* which literally means "to bind up, gird," is always used of saddling asses (Gen 22:3; Num 22:21; Jud 19:10; II Sam 16:1; 17:23; 19:26).

SADDUCEES. This name (Heb. *ṣᵉdûqîm*, Gr. *saddoukaioi*) refers to the priestly aristocratic party in the latter part of the second temple period. They emerged after the Maccabean rebellion and during the Hasmonean attempt for national freedom from the Syrians. They were in many ways opposed to the Pharisees, although many influential Pharisees were members of the Sanhedrin.

The Name

A rabbinic tradition (*Abot Rabbi Natan* 5) names Zadok, a disciple of Antigonus of Soko, the father of the Sadducees. Zadok supposedly misunderstood his teacher, denied the resurrection and afterlife, and so founded the party espousing these views. Epiphanius in *Heresies* I, 14 stated that the name is derived from the Heb. *ṣadîq* (or, "righteous"). There is a problem, however, in explaining the vowel change from *î* to the *û* in Sadducee.

The more plausible view is that the name came from Zadok the priest chosen by Solomon as the high priest (I Kgs 2:35), and descendants of this family assumed the temple leadership for centuries. Ultimately the term Sadducee could then apply to anyone in sympathy with the Zadokites, descendants of Zadok, i.e., the Sadducee political party which emerged during the Hasmonean period.

History

Origin. By *c.* 190 B.C. there is testimony to the supremacy of the Zadokite priesthood that extols and sings the praises of the line of Phinehas and Zadokite priest Simon II as the chief ones for the spiritual office (Sir 45:25; 50). In 175 B.C. Antiochus IV Epiphanes deposed Onias III, a Zadokite, in favor of the Hellenized house of Tobias, and over the next several years, because of Syrian influence, the position of high priest was held by men who did not represent the high traditions of the Zadokites. The last pre-Hasmonean of Aaronic legitimacy was Alkimos (162–159 B.C.), but he brought the priesthood into disrepute by his harsh reforms (I Macc 7:13–18).

With these distressing affairs, Onias IV, son of Onais III, fled into Egypt (*Ant.* xii.9.7; xiii.3.1–2), while other Zadokites might have been responsible for founding the Qumran community, since in a number of passages the leadership is depicted as sons of Zadok (Damascus Document 4:2 f.; 6:1 f.; 1QS 5:2, 9). Presumably, most godly Zadokite priests did not flee from the mainstream, even though they were no longer in full control.

In 152 B.C. the Hasmonean Jonathan was appointed high priest (I Macc 10:18–21), and in 140 B.C. Simon became high priest by popular acclaim (I Macc 14:25–29). The sons of Mattathias were priests, but they were of the priest Hasmon of Jehoiarib (*Ant.* xii.6.1). In tracing the line we find Jehoiarib second to Jedaiah because he failed to return with Ezra to Jerusalem (I Chr 24:7; Ezr 2:36–39; *Ta'anît 27b*), thus raising a serious question in that the pure Zadokite claim to priesthood was set aside when the public acknowledged the Hasmonean Simon as the high priest. The acclamation could not be otherwise when the family fought for the country's freedom.

It is this fight for national freedom that began to alienate the religious elements of the nation as well as the stricter of the Zadokite priesthood. In the thrust for religious freedom, the nation stood together even though there were the corrupting Hellenistic influences. As soon as religious freedom was atained, the more spiritual of the Zadokites and the *hasīdîm* (spiritual successors to the previous movement of *Sôpherim* which ended *c.* 180 B.C.) were content. The Maccabees wanted to continue the struggle, but the more religious element did not favor a secular fight, which became a factor that eventually led to an alienation of interests of various groups and was a reason for party formations.

Out of these dissensions, Hellenized Zadokites in Jerusalem linked themselves with the Hasmoneans to continue their posterity and influence and not be dismembered by the in-fighting within their group. The Hasmoneans, on the other hand, needed a ready ally with Zadokite elements and became known as those of Zadokite persuasion, although the earlier Hasmoneans, Judah, Jonathan, and Simon, followed the more strict religionists except for the fight for political freedom. By creating this union, i.e., Sadducees, this party eventually, beginning with John Hyrcanus I (135–104 B.C.), was very much like the religious oppressors they had set out to conquer, even though their ideal was a Jewish state with the temple at its center and with the minimum of foreign influence.

The Hasmonean and Roman period. The Sadducees were first mentioned during the reign of John Hyrcanus I (*Ant.* xiii.10.5–7), indicating that by this point the religious parties were already well formed, the Sadducees the result of the aforementioned union and the Pharisees as the spiritual successors of the *Hasīdîm*. John Hyrcanus, an admirer and disciple of the Pharisees, went completely over to the Sadducees after a gross insult by a leading Pharisee. The Hasmonean house now functioned as a questionable priesthood in the eyes of godly elements in both parties. The Hasmoneans sought to increase the territory of Judah, to strengthen the temple center of the state, and to involve the people to realize a kingdom as the one David once ruled. The Sadducee party leaders became the aristocratic heads of the country, although the Pharisees did have representation on the Sanhedrin. With successive reigns, the regime became unstable when contestants for power called on foreign nations to arbitrate against each other, with the result that Rome was able to obtain a stranglehold on the country through the Hasmoneans. By 37 B.C. the last Hasmonean king was beheaded and Herod the Great was made ruler over Judah.

With Herod, the Sadducees were no longer able to maintain their original goal of a theocratic state independent of foreign domination. Herod's politic was a state as part of the Roman Empire and not the pursuit of an original Sadduceeism, although he was clever enough to provide a stately temple to hold the people. The function of the Sadducees now became a holding maneuver to protect the temple center from any further inroads by alien authorities. So, while the party remained the titular leaders of the nation, they began to command less respect by the people. Pharisee dogma was increasingly accepted by the people, and when the temple was destroyed in A.D. 70 the Sadducees ended as a party while the Pharisees were the dominant leaders among Jewish people.

Beliefs

The law. Surprisingly, the Sadducees were considered the conservatives in holding to older doctrines and regarding as supreme the temple sacrificial system. They opposed the Pharisees, and the main point of division was the understanding of the law. Both parties acknowledged the supremacy of Torah, but the Sadducees held only to the written law while the Pharisees put the long development of traditions alongside the written law (*Ant.* xiii.10.6). The Sadducees accepted only what could be based directly on the written law. The Pharisee basically was a mild critic while the Sadducee was regarded as stern (*Ant.* xiii.10.6; xx.9.1), because the Pharisee's "hedge about the law" was to help people in everyday living while the Sadducee saw the Pharisee method a weakening of genuine piety (although at times *some* Pharisees could be stern too). If the Sadducee had not been so secularized and so removed as aristocrats from the people, this emphasis on only written law could have been commendable in many ways.

Bias prevents an objective analysis of the Sadducees since information about them comes from their opponents. Therefore one needs to be careful in assessing beliefs attributed to the Sadducees since to date there are no materials in which they present their own side. A few differences will be noted.

In the *lex talionis* (Ex 21:23; Deut 19:21; *Mᵉgīllâh Ta'anît* 4; *Baba Kamma* 84*a*) the Sadducee insisted on the more literal fulfillment while the Pharisees were more lenient with a graduated monetary compensation of the extent of the crime. In the case of false witnesses, the Sadducees would not ask for their death penalty unless their testimony was clearly responsible for the execution of the accused, and furthermore, that it be carried out after the accused was killed; the Pharisees wanted the false witnesses to die as soon as sentence was passed (*Makkôt* 1:5–8; *Tôsefta Sanhedrin* 6:6). Here the Pharisees were more severe. The Sadducees held an owner more responsible to compensate not only where damage was done by an ox or ass (Ex 21:32, 35) but compensate even more for the slave who injured anyone; the Pharisees replied that the slave should be held equally responsible, so as to prevent a disgruntled slave from involving his master in further lawsuits (*Yadaim* 4:7).

In inheritance rights, Jewish law specified that only the son, not the daughter, could inherit the father's property. In a special case, when a father was deceased, and his son was also dead, leaving only a daughter (the granddaughter), the Pharisees felt that the granddaughter was the sole heir to the exclusion of any daughter of the deceased father while the Sadducees held that daughter and granddaughter should share equally *(Baba Batra* 115*b)*.

In further complicated inheritance rights of the Levirate marriages, the Sadducees had a peculiar interpretation concerning the question asked of Jesus about the woman and seven husbands (Mt 22:23–33; Lk 20:27–38). The Sadducee belief was that Levirate marriage was granted only in cases with a *betrothed* wife and not to one who had actually been married (*Yᵉrûshalmî Yᵉvamôt* 1:6). In their question, they believed that the woman was only married to the seventh husband. The Pharisees didn't have this restriction, and thus the Sadducees wanted to ridicule the Pharisees where one woman could have seven husbands, as well as the dogma concerning the resurrection.

In matters of ritual, the differences seem minor. The main objection on the part of the Sadducees was to the minutiae of the oral law and they did not regard this as binding, although in certain instances the Sadducees could also be subject to many restrictions, e.g., Levitical purity. The cost of the daily offerings was a controversy where the Pharisees wanted the offerings paid from the general treasury while their opponents wanted the offerings paid by freewill offerings (*Mᵉgīllâh Ta'anît* 1). The Sadducees ridiculed the Pharisees for their constant washings, yet the Sadducees took greater pains for purity in the red heifer offering (*Parâh* and *Tôsefta Parâh* chap. 3). The Pharisees had many restrictions about touching sacred things that "defiled" their hands while the Sadducees ridiculed the notion where the Scriptures "defiled" the hands from handling them.

Doctrinal. Because of the Sadducees' strong emphasis on humanism, their view of God was thereby affected. While there was a belief in God, yet God was one who never interfered in the course of history or the fortunes of men, and thus there was no foreordination (*Ant.* xiii.5.9). There was no divine cooperation in human action, and good and evil lay within the prerogative of man's free will and self-determination. The Pharisees felt some actions were the result of divine providence but some human actions were in man's free will.

Concerning man, he had no immortal soul since the soul died with the body (*Ant.* xviii.1.4) and therefore the Sadducees did not believe in any future judgment (*Wars* ii.8.14).

The existence of angels and other spirits was denied by the Sadducees (Acts 23:8) since this was in the same class as the spirits of deceased people. The doctrines of angels and spirits were regarded as developments of the oral law and were not to be accepted, while the mention of angels in the OT was seen as the representation of God in some kind of unsubstantial form.

In Sadduceean eschatology, there was no belief in the resurrection of the dead, while the Pharisees did believe this (*Ant.* xviii. 1.3; Mt 22:33; Acts 23:8). The Pharisees felt that the resurrection could be found in the Law, Prophets, and Writings, but the Sadducees would not accept their point since they insisted that the supreme authority was the Torah alone. Jesus did use striking passages from the Law in His discussions with the Sadducees concerning the subject (Ex 3:6; Mk 12:26-27; Lk 20:37), but these passages only *imply* this doctrine; if Moses never really proclaimed the doctrine then there was no compulsion to believe it. The charge once more is that the resurrection came from the Pharisee tradition development.

The Sadducees in the NT

The NT materials do not treat the complicated relationship of the parties and Sadduceeism is not considered in its many-sided character. The resurrection is given as the main point which the Sadducees denied. Both Pharisees and Sadducees are considered jointly many times. John the Baptist condemned both in sharp terms (Mt 3:7 f.). Jesus grouped both parties when He denounced their doctrines. Both groups are described in their questions to test Jesus' ability to handle the teachings of the law (Mt 15:1). In the Acts, Peter and John were detained by them (Acts 4:1-2; 5:17-18). Since the early Jewish believers in Jesus had many doctrines in common with the Pharisees, e.g., resurrection, their greatest difficulties were with Sadducees. It must be stressed, however, that not all Sadducees and Pharisees were hostile to Jewish believers in Jesus. The NT tells a story written by ordinary men who did not present a scholarly study of the parties. They spoke of the parties in a very general way, but this literary style does not condemn outright many fine men in both parties; in fact, many of these became believers in Jesus.

Bibliography. B. Z. Bokser, *Pharisaic Judaism in Transition,* New York: Bloch Publishing Co., 1935. V. Eppstein, "Sadducees," JBL, LXXXV (1966), 213-224. L. Finkelstein, *The Pharisees,* New York: Devin-Adair, 1938. R. Meyer, "*Saddoukaios,*" TDNT, VII, 35-54. R. T. Herford, *The Pharisees,* New York: Macmillan, 1924. J. W. Lightley, *Jewish Sects and Parties in the Time of Christ,* London: Epworth Press, 1925. T. W. Manson, "Sadducees and Pharisees," *Bulletin of the J. Rylands Library,* No. 22 (1938), pp.144-159. Emil Schurer, *Jewish People in the Time of Jesus Christ,* Vol. II. New York: Scribners, 1891.

L. Go.

SADOC (sā'dŏk). The NT form of Zadok. This ancestor of Jesus was the son of Azor, and the father of Achim (Mt 1:14).

SAFFRON. *See* Plants.

SAIL. In the OT only the noun is found (Heb. *nēs*), meaning "sign," "ensign," or "banner" (Isa 33:23; Ezk 27:7). As a Gr. noun in the NT *skeuos* is a "vessel" or "instrument" (Acts 27:17, KJV "sail"). Therefore the RSV has "they lowered the gear," and the NASB translates "they let down the sea anchor." The basic Gr. verb is *pleō*, "to sail," with various prefixes, as in Acts 27:4-7. *See* Ship.

SAILOR. *See* Occupations: Mariner; Ship.

SAINT. English versions of the Bible have rendered three words by the term "saint." They are the Heb. words *ḥāsîd* and *kādôsh* as well as the Gr. word *hagios* (e.g., KJV and ASV in Ps 30:4; 106:16; Rom 1:7). The RSV differentiates between the Heb. words, rendering *ḥāsîd* as "saint" (e.g., Ps 132:9), also "faithful" ones (e.g., Ps 50:5; 149:1, 5, 9), and "godly" (e.g., Ps 52:9), while *kādôsh* is sometimes translated "saint" (e.g., Ps 16:3), and at other times "holy one" (e.g., Ps 106:16).

By definition *ḥāsîd* means "pious," hence, the pious worshipers of Yahweh (I Sam 2:9; II Chr 6:41; Ps 30:4; 31:23; 37:28; 50:5; 52:9; 79:2; 85:8; 97:10; 116:15; 132:9, 16; 145:10; 148:14; 149:1, 5, 9). By definition *kādôsh* means "holy," "pure," or "clean," hence, is especially appropriate to describe those individuals consecrated to Yahweh's service: priests (Ps 106:16; Ex 28:41–29:1; Lev 21:6; I Sam 7:1), angels (Deut 33:2-3), the firstborn (Ex 13:2).

Some feel that *ḥāsîd* in certain of the psalms (79:2; 97:10; 149:5, 9) represents the concept of the "faithful" during the intense struggles of the Maccabean period when the *ḥasidim* were the loyalists, nationalists, strictly separated to the worship of Yahweh. Some have professed to find an eschatological significance in Daniel (7:21-22), where the term *kādôsh* describes the saints who receive the kingdom in the great day of the Lord's righteous judgment. *Kādôsh* is also applied to sacred places (Ex 29:31; Lev 6:16), sacred days (Neh 8:10-11), and to Yahweh Himself as the "most holy" (Hos 11:9; Josh 24:19; Prov 9:10).

In the LXX *ḥāsîd* is rendered chiefly by *hosios*, which by definition means "undefiled by sin," "free from wickedness," or "religiously observing every moral obligation"; hence, it came to represent those who were holy or pious. In the LXX *kādôsh* is rendered chiefly by *hagios*, which refers to reverence or religious awe, hence, to those who venerate Yahweh.

In the NT the Gospels make little use of the term "saint," the one reference being to the bodies of the saints which arose (Mt 27:52), and this may well be a reference to OT usage, those who were faithful before the NT age. Christ Himself is, however, referred to as the "Holy One of God" (Mk 1:24; Lk 1:35).

Christians in general are "saints" in NT usage, and the term is common in reference to the inclusive membership of a local church (Rom 1:7; I Cor 1:2; II Cor 1:1; Eph 1:1; Phil 1:1; Col 1:2). Other references in the NT equate Christians in general with "saints" (II Cor 13:13; Rom 16:15; Acts 9:13; Heb 13:24; Rev 5:8). All these are identified as saints because they are in Christ Jesus.

In keeping with both OT and NT usage it is to be observed that those who are called to be saints are to give themselves to the highest ethical standard of life (Eph 5:3), which is revealed through love of others expressed in practical and helpful service (see Rom 12:13; 15:25-26; 16:2; Eph 1:15; Col 1:4; I Tim 5:10; Heb 6:10; II Cor 8:4; 9:1). *See* Consecration.

In the NT Christ's saints are to be associated with Him in the fullness of His final triumph and victory, giving an eschatological meaning to the term (I Thess 3:13; II Thess 1:10; I Cor 6:2-3; Col 3:4). *See* Holiness.

H. L. D.

SALA, SALAH (sā'lȧ). The son of Arphaxad, who was the third son of Shem and the father of Eber (Gen 10:24; 11:12-15; Lk 3:35-36). The name is spelled Shelah in the ASV and all newer versions.

SALAMIS (săl'ȧ-mĭs). The greatest port and commercial center of Cyprus (*q.v.*) when Paul

The forum at Salamis.

and Barnabas landed there on their first missionary journey (Acts 13:5). The city is commonly assumed to be the home of Barnabas. Numerous destructions and rebuildings plus partial excavation make it difficult to picture how Salamis appeared in Paul's day. Paul would have known the great limestone forum (750 × 180 feet) surrounded with shops, at the S end of which stood a temple to the Olympian Zeus.

SALATHIEL. *See* Shealtiel.

SALCAH, SALCHAH (săl'kȧ). A city on the extremity of Gad in the NE of Bashan (Deut 3:10; Josh 12:5; 13:11; I Chr 5:11). The name is spelled Salecah in the ASV and all newer versions. Salecah is now known as Salkhad, which is seven miles E of the Bostra of Roman times.

The city was built in a circular volanic hill of basalt, rising over 300 feet above the surrounding plain. It is the strongest site in the Jebel el-Druze.

SALEM (sā'lĕm). The city, whose name means "peace," was ruled by Melchizedek to whom Abraham paid tithes (Gen 14:18; Heb 7:1-2). It is usually identified with Jerusalem after Josephus (*Ant.* 1.10.2) and with the Jebusite city on the border between Judah and Benjamin, which was captured by Joab and became the "city of David" (*see* Jerusalem).

SALIM (sā'lĭm). This place was near Aenon (*q.v.*) on the W side of the Jordan. John baptized here "because there was much water" (Jn 3:23). While Jerome placed Aenon and Salim (Umm el-'Amdan) eight Roman miles S of Scythopolis (Beth-shan), W. F. Albright believed the springs near Tirzah and the headwaters of the Wadi Far'ah are a more likely possibility for the area of John the Baptist's ministry (*Archaeology of Palestine,* Harmondsworth: Penguin, 1960, p. 247). In this case Salim may be identified with the Salem *c.* four miles E of Nablus and Shechem which the Samaritans claimed was the Salem of Gen 14:18. Nearby is a present-day village called 'Ainûn, preserving the name Aenon. M. Avi-Yonah, however, favors a location in Perea E of the Jordan, opposite Jericho ("Aenon," IDB, I, 52).

SALLAI (săl'ī)

1. A leading Benjamite, son of Meshullam, who dwelt in Jerusalem (Neh 11:8).

2. The name of a priest who returned with Zerubbabel (Neh 12:20); he is also called Sallu (Neh 12:7). *See* Sallu.

SALLU (săl'o͞o)

1. A priest who returned with Zerubbabel (Neh 12:7).

2. The name of a Benjamite, a grandson of Joed, who dwelt in Jerusalem after the Exile (I Chr 9:7; Neh 11:7).

SALMA (săl'mȧ)

1. A son of Hur and grandson of Caleb. Salma was the "father" or founder of Bethlehem and the ancestor of several other clans and town groups (I Chr 2:51, 54).

2. An alternate form of Salmon (*q.v.*), father of Boaz (I Chr 2:11).

SALMON (săl'mŏn)

1. As the father of Boaz the husband of Ruth, and the great-grandfather of Jesse the father of David, Salmon is included in the genealogy of Jesus (Ruth 4:20-21; I Chr 2:11). According to Mt 1:4-5 he was the husband of Rahab (*q.v.*), doubtless the former harlot of Jericho.

2. The name of a mountain, perhaps in Samaria near Shechem (Ps 68:14, KJV). It is spelled Zalmon (*q.v.*) in the ASV and other newer versions.

SALMONE (săl-mō'nē). A promontory at the E tip of Crete which Paul and his companions passed en route to Rome. They sailed by this point, probably the modern Cape Sidero, in an effort to gain protection from the adverse Aegean winds (Acts 27:7).

SALOME (sȧ-lō'mĭ)

1. One of the women who followed Jesus from Galilee, and who stood afar off witnessing His crucifixion (Mk 15:40-41). She came with other women on the morning of the resurrection to anoint Jesus' body with spices (Mk 16:1). She was probably the wife of Zebedee and the mother of James and John (Mt 27:56).

2. The daughter of Herodias who asked for the head of John the Baptist after dancing before Herod Antipas (Mt 14:3-11; Mk 6:17-28). She is unnamed in the Gospels, but her name is known from Josephus (*Ant.*xviii.5.4).

SALT. A number of different uses of salt are disclosed in the Bible. A common association with food in the life of the ancient Near East is intimated by Job's query, "Can that which is tasteless be eaten without salt?" (Job 6:6, RSV). Its sacred use is seen in connection with the ceremonial offerings in Israel's worship of God. Salt was to be mixed with the cereal offering (Lev 2:13) and in later times was sprinkled on the burnt offering (Ezk 43:24). It was a commodity to be kept on hand in the temple (Ezr 6:9). Sometimes it was mixed with incense as well (Ex 30:35, RSV).

The expression "covenant of salt" (Num 18:19; Lev 2:13; II Chr 13:5) likely refers to an ancient custom of confirming a pact between parties by eating food. This is a practice still continued in our day by the Arab, who says: "There is salt between us," after eating with another. The adversaries of the Jewish returnees claimed loyalty to the Persian king by saying they ate "the salt of the palace" (Ezr 4:14, RSV).

Salt was also rubbed on the newborn infant

(Ezk 16:4), suggesting some medicinal or religious significance. As to the latter, some think heathen parents had originally applied salt as a deterrent to potential attacks of demons.

Perhaps the most significant and familiar use of salt in the Bible occurs in those contexts dealing with salt's preservative and fertilizing (Lk 14:34-35) qualities (see Eugene P. Deatrick, "Salt, Soil, Savior," BA, XXV (1962), 41-48). Elisha healed the waters of Jericho with it (II Kgs 2:20-21). The fact that good salt has curative and seasoning properties is used as an illustration by our Lord to enjoin His followers to responsible living (Mt 5:13; Mk 9:50; Lk 14:34-35; Col 4:6). He was alluding to one of the impure complex salts of Palestine which can lose its saltiness through physical disintegration or through mixture with gypsum. Such salt was usually procured from salt pits near the Dead Sea (Zeph 2:9; Ezk 47:11, RSV).

One final use is embodied in our Lord's statement: "Every one shall be salted with fire" (Mk 9:49), which associates salt with impending divine judgment. A vivid illustration of this figurative use of salt is seen in the unusual reference to the transformation of Lot's wife into a pillar of salt (Gen 19:26). The incident is shockingly descriptive of the spiritual disobedience of her neighbors as well as that of her own life, for the wrath of God fell on the whole area in the form of utter devastation and barrenness (Deut 29:23; Ps 107:34, NASB; Jer 17:6; Zeph 2:9). In this sense Abimelech scattered salt on the ruins of Shechem as a sign of cursing the city or perhaps of "consecrating" it to his god so that it would not be rebuilt (Jud 9:45; see Stanley Gevirtz, "Jericho and Shechem: a Religio-Literary Aspect of City Destruction," VT, XIII [1963], 52-62). *See* Minerals and Metals.

A. M.

SALT, CITY OF. A city of Judah in the wilderness district near the W shore of the Dead Sea (Josh 15:62). By transliterating the Heb. the NEB calls it Ir-melach. It was first identified with modern Khirbet Qumran by Martin Noth in 1938. While the site of the monastery that produced many of the Dead Sea scrolls (*q.v.*) was occupied with a fortress during Iron Age II (930-586 B.C.), no evidence of settlement so early as Joshua's time has as yet been discovered. Frank M. Cross, Jr. and J. T. Milik therefore believe that the list of Josh 15:61-62 goes back only to the time of King Jehoshaphat ("Explorations in the Judaean Buqe'ah," BASOR #142 [1956], 5-17). Perhaps, however, earlier inhabitants in the time of the Israelite conquest lived in an unwalled village whose occupation debris has been entirely eroded. *See* Nibshan.

SALT, COVENANT OF. *See* Covenant of Salt.

SALT SEA. *See* Dead Sea.

SALT, VALLEY OF. A valley in the vicinity of the Dead Sea, the scene of two Israelite victories over the Edomites. Here David's army slew 18,000 Edomites (II Sam 8:13, RSV; I Chr 18:12; Ps 60, title), and two centuries later Amaziah king of Judah defeated another 10,000 Edomites before capturing Sela (II Kgs 14:7; II Chr 25:11). While the valley has been identified because of the correspondence in names (Heb. *gê' hammelaḥ*) with the Wadi el-Milḥ E of Beer-sheba in the Negeb, it was more likely on the route of the Israelite invaders into Edomite territory. Therefore geographers Denis Baly (*The Geography of the Bible*, New York: Harper, 1957) and Yohanan Aharoni (*The Land of the Bible*, Philadelphia: Westminster, 1967, pp. 263, 313) identify it with the Arabah S of the Dead Sea, and with the desolate Sebkha, a barren saline stretch, in particular.

SALTWORT. *See* Plants: Mallow.

SALU (sä'lo͞o). A Simeonite, and the father of Zimri (*q.v.*) who was slain by Phinehas the priest (Num 25:14).

SALUTATION. The elaborate and courteous oral greeting on meeting or parting is recorded in ancient cultures of Bible times. Rebekah was blessed as she left home (Gen 24:60). Laban complained that Jacob had not allowed him to kiss his sons and daughters in farewell (Gen 31:28, 55).

Greetings in epistolary correspondence are also recorded in antiquity, as in the Amarna letters and in Ugaritic epistles. In the latter, the form was "(*a*) Salutation(s) and/or (*b*) divine blessings: a:'at the feet of [N's title] (seven times this way and seven times that way) I/we bow down.' 'To N let there be peace!' b: 'May the gods guard and preserve thee!'" (C. H. Gordon, *Ugaritic Literature*, p. 116).

The epistolary greeting thus appears in the ancient Semitic world, but was only gradually adopted in Gr. and Rom. culture. Such greetings were not common in the pre-Christian period.

The use of the epistolary greeting in the NT, especially by Paul, is typical of his enlargement and enrichment of the form of the epistle to convey the affection and concern felt among Christians. According to Hans Windisch ("*Aspazomai*," TDNT, I, 496), there were no lengthy greetings in Gr. and Rom. correspondence. Paul's use of such a long series in Rom 16 was most unusual. The standard form of Greco-Roman business and personal letters, followed in the NT, came into vogue a few decades before the birth of Christ. The greeting was more brief and simple than Semitic greetings, however.

The salutation at meeting or farewell was charged with emotion and affection, especially in Christian circles, as shown in the departure of Paul's party from Miletus (Acts 20:36-38) and Tyre (21:5-6). This emotional content of the words for greeting is reflected in Heb 11:13: the ancient patriarchs, seeing from afar the city with foundations, hailed with delight (greeted) the promises and died in faith.

Prominent in the ideas conveyed in the salutation was honor or even reverence. The implications of peace, friendship, and good will should be extended even to one's enemies, Christ said (Mt 5:47). So also the suggestion of divine blessing was conveyed in the angel Gabriel's address to Mary, as he spoke of the grace given to her, causing her to wonder at the amazing salutation (Lk 1:26-29).

Paul calls special attention to his salutation in his own handwriting in certain of his epistles (I Cor 16:21; Col 4:18; II Thess 3:17). In this last reference, Paul gives mark and proof of the genuineness of the epistle, to guard against the acceptance of a forgery. The technique was to add to a dictated letter a few concluding words in the author's own handwriting (see also Gal 6:11; Phm 19).

The injunction of Paul and Peter to greet with a kiss (Rom 16:16; I Cor 16:20; II Cor 13:12; I Thess 5:26; I Pet 5:14) raises an interesting problem of cultural change. The application of the principle of greeting fellow believers has caused some to stumble. Is not the essential which the apostle enjoined preserved by the handclasp and the personal touch and word as brethren meet together?

The importance of the salutation throws light on numerous passages of the NT. Jesus had received no kiss (Lk 7:44-46) and so had been slighted by this hurt. He said the Pharisees loved greetings in the market (Mk 12:38). The implication is that they desired to be greeted first, since the greeting was directed to the one to be honored. In Lk 10:4 the command to greet no one by the way means to avoid time-wasting ceremonies, and hasten to execute the mission.

W. B. W.

SALVATION. The biblical doctrine of salvation is technically called soteriology (*q.v.*). Understood actively, salvation is the total work of God in bringing men from the state of sin to the state of glory through Jesus Christ the God-man. In the former state men are spiritually dead and subject to divine wrath; in the latter, they are under God's grace and experiencing eternal life. Understood passively, salvation is the total present and future enjoyment by true believers in Christ, of God's self-giving through His Son (J. I. Packer, BS, CXXIX, 293, 295).

Various terms for salvation occur frequently throughout the Bible. In the OT the most important Heb. word root is *yāsha'*, which signifies freedom from what binds or restricts. Hence the verb means to deliver, liberate, give width and breadth to (BDB, p. 446). The several nouns derived from this root mean both the act of deliverance or rescuing (I Sam 11:9, KJV "help"), the resultant state of safety, welfare, and prosperity (II Sam 23:5; Ps 12:6), and victory over one's foes (II Sam 23:10, 12; Ps 98:1). The Hiphil participle of this verb is the word for "Saviour," *môshîa'* (*see* Saviour), and from it comes the name Joshua (*q.v.*) and its Grecized form Jesus, both meaning "Yah(weh) saves."

In the LXX and NT the Gr. verb *sōzō* and its cognates *sōtēr*, "saviour," and *sōtēria*, "salvation," usually translate *yāsha'* and its respective nouns. A number of times, however, the *sōzō* group are translations of *shālôm*, "peace" or "wholeness," and its cognates. Thus *sōtēria* can mean "cure," "recovery," "remedy," "rescue," "redemption," or "welfare." *Sōzō* signifies the act or result of deliverance or preservation from danger, disease, or death (Acts 27:20, 31, 34, NASB; Mt 9:22; 14:30; Lk 8:50; 18:42; Heb 5:7) and implies safety, health, and even victory (Rev 12:10; 19:1, NEB). In Christian usage the verb came to mean saving from eternal death and endowing with everlasting life (Rom 5:9; Jas 5:20; Heb 7:25). In II Tim 4:18 (see NASB; cf. marg.) it means to bring one safely to Christ's heavenly kingdom. In the NT *sōtēria* is found only in connection with Jesus Christ as Saviour and not in any merely temporal or physical sense.

A personification of salvation (Soteria) in a fifth century floor mosaic from a suburb of Antioch of Syria. HFV

Salvation brings the righteousness of God to man when he meets the condition of faith in Christ (Rom 1:16-17; I Cor 1:21). It is based on the death of Christ for the remission of sins in accord with the just requirements of a holy God (Rom 3:21-26). The basic accomplishments of salvation include redemption, reconciliation, and propitiation. Redemption (*q.v.*) means full release because of the payment of a ransom price (II Pet 2:1; Gal 3:13; Mt 20:28). Reconciliation (*q.v.*) means that because of Christ's death, man's relationship with

God has been changed from a state of enmity to one of fellowship (Rom 5:10). Propitiation (*q.v.*) means that God's wrath has been turned away by the offering of Christ (Rom 3:25; I Jn 4:10).

When a man believes in the Lord Jesus Christ he is saved (Acts 16:31); therefore he is already justified, redeemed, reconciled, and cleansed (Jn 13:10; I Cor 6:11). Yet salvation is also progressive (I Cor 1:18, NASB), and man needs the sanctifying work of the Spirit in the working out of his salvation (Rom 8:13; II Cor 3:18; Phil 2:12). In addition, salvation in its fullness is to be realized in the future when Christ comes (Heb 9:28).

The need for salvation is found in the sinful nature of man (*see* Sin). The single condition for salvation is faith. This is both the gift of God and the responsibility of man (Eph 2:8; Jn 3:16). The responsibility of a saved man is to live a godly life in separation from the world and in anticipation of the future consummation of his hope (Tit 2:12-13). *See* Atonement; Justification; Sanctification; Soteriology.

With regard to the eschatological aspect of redemption Peter speaks of the "salvation ready to be revealed in the last time" (I Pet 1:5). The believer has received the Holy Spirit as the earnest or the down payment of his salvation (Rom 8:23; Eph 1:13-14). Two further blessings remain for the future: the removal of the fallen nature completely and the reception of a resurrection body. Paul calls the latter "the redemption of our body" (Rom 8:23), and explains that it will occur at the return of Christ when He will remove the curse which was placed upon both man and nature after Adam fell. Both OT and NT speak of this removal of the curse from nature (Rom 8:18-23; Isa 11:1-16; 65:25) as well as of the resurrection (Dan 12:2). *See* Resurrection.

Bibliography. Werner Foerster and Georg Fohrer, "*Sōzō, Sōtēria,* etc.," TDNT, VII, 965-1024. Charles M. Horne, *Salvation,* Chicago: Moody, 1971. Wilhelm Kasch, "*Ruomai,*" VI, 998-1003. James I. Packer, "The Way of Salvation," BS, CXXIX (1972), 195-205, 291-306; CXXX (1973), 3-11, and continuing. Alan Richardson, "Salvation, Savior," IDB, IV, 168-181. George B. Stevens, *The Christian Doctrine of Salvation,* Edinburgh: T. & T. Clark, 1905. A. H. Strong, *Systematic Theology,* 11th ed., Philadelphia: Judson, 1947, pp. 665-886. B. B. Warfield, *The Plan of Salvation,* Grand Rapids: Eerdmans, 1942.

C. C. R.

SAMARIA (sȧ-mâr'ĭ-ȧ)

1. *The city*—founded *c.* 880 B.C. by Omri, king of Israel. It remained the capital of the northern kingdom until its fall in 722/21 B.C. After reigning for six years at Tirzah (*c.* six miles NNE of Shechem), Omri purchased a hill (*c.* six miles NW of Shechem) and began building his new residence. According to I Kgs

Ruins of the gate of Samaria with a Hellenistic round tower at left. HFV

16:24, he named the city Samaria (Heb. *shōmerôn*), "after the name of Shemer, the owner of the hill," but the name may also mean "watch-post, lookout." This excellent site, with a lovely view of the Mediterranean Sea to the W, rises *c.* 300 feet above a fertile valley of olive orchards and vineyards.

Archaeological evidence indicates that there was a small settlement on the hill prior to Omri's purchase, but in any case he and his son Ahab leveled the top of the hill and fortified this summit with inner and outer walls (ANEP #718). The palace was built on the western side of the enclosed area. Since there was no natural water supply, cisterns had to be dug for collecting rain water. Later fortifications on the slopes of the hill gave the city superior defenses. Samaria withstood the attack by Ben-hadad, king of Syria (II Kgs 6:24-25), but it finally fell to the Assyrians after a three-year siege (II Kgs 17:5). The earliest extrabiblical mention of the city of Samaria by name appears on a stele, found in 1967, of Adad-nirari III inscribed after 798 B.C. In cuneiform the name is Sa-me-ri-na (*Iraq,* XXX [1968], 139-149).

The Israelite capital was noted for its idolatry. Ahab built a temple and altar for Baal (I Kgs 16:32), and his wife Jezebel supported 450 prophets of Baal and 400 prophets of Asherah (I Kgs 18:19). Elijah and Elisha contested the royal patronage of the Canaanite religion; and later prophets, declaring the doom of Samaria, often referred to its corruption and luxury (e.g., Hos 8:5-6; Amos 3:15; 6:1, 4, 6; Isa 7:8-9; Mic 1:5-7).

Excavations at Samaria have unearthed some ostraca (pieces of broken pottery used for writing) which probably date from the reign of Jeroboam II (793-753 B.C.), the period of greatest Israelite prosperity. These ostraca, with a number of personal and place names found in the Bible, are accounts of wine and oil received as part of the royal revenue. Amos pronounced woe on the inhabitants of Samaria who drank "wine in bowls" and anointed themselves with "the finest oils" (6:6). He also referred to their "beds of ivory" (6:4), and numerous ivories have also been found in the ruins of Samaria. Depicted in relief are the Egyptian gods Isis and Horus, sphinxes, bulls, deer, lions, papyrus, lotus, lilies, and palmettes (ANEP #129, 130, 566, 649). These ivories, probably reproduced by Phoenician artists from Egyptian originals, were most likely inlaid in furniture and wall paneling. It is in this sense that the references to "the ivory house" built by Ahab (I Kgs 22:39) and the later "houses of ivory" (Amos 3:15) are to be understood. *See* Ivory. Remains of the palace begun by Omri and finished by Ahab have also been found. For a drawing of the heavily fortified E gateway of Samaria, where Elisha predicted correctly that food would be sold cheaply on the morrow (II Kgs 7:1), see VBW. II. 262.

After its fall, Samaria was rebuilt as the capital for the Assyrian province of Samaria. It also served as a provincial capital during most of the Persian period. Nehemiah's foe Sanballat probably resided here as governor of the area (Neh 4:1-2). Alexander the Great took the city and imported peoples from Syria and Macedonia after having deported many of the resident Samaritans (*q.v.*) to Shechem. Alexander's followers strengthened Samaria's fortifications with a number of magnificent circular towers (ANEP #720). The city was devastated (from 111 to 107 B.C.) by John Hyrcanus, the Hasmonean ruler of the Jews; but after 63 B.C., when the region of Samaria became a part of the Roman province of Syria, reconstruction of the city was begun by Pompey.

It was Herod the Great, however, who restored (from 30 to 20 B.C.) the splendor of the city. A great temple was constructed over the Israelite and Hellenistic remains on the summit, and an extensive fortification system of walls and towers was erected around the lower slopes of the hill. Within this enclosure appeared landscaped residential areas, colonnaded streets, a forum, a theater, and a stadium. Six thousand of Herod's mercenary troops were settled there and given land. Herod dedicated the city and temple to his patron, Caesar Augustus; therefore the city was renamed Sebaste, "Venerable, August" (the Gr. form of Latin Augusta). The pagan culture of Sebaste and its environs may be part of the reason why Jesus and the Twelve are never reported to have entered the city. It may, however, have been the city where Philip preached and encountered Simon the magician (Acts 8:5-24).

Ruins of the palace of Omri and Ahab at Samaria. HFV

Sebaste received some damage during the Jewish revolt (A.D. 66-70), but between A.D. 180 and 230 the Antonine and Severi emperors refurbished and enlarged it to its greatest splendor. During the Byzantine period the city fell into decay, and in the time of Arab control it dwindled to a hamlet. The village Sebastiyeh, which exists today near the ruins of Samaria, preserves in its name the Herodian designation.

Archaeological knowledge of Samaria derives from two major series of excavations. The first (1908-1910), by Harvard University under the direction of Reisner, Fisher, and Lyon, was published in 1924. The second (1931-1935), sponsored by a number of institutions under the direction of Crowfoot, Sukenik, and Kenyon, was published in 1938, 1942, and 1957.

2. *The region*—which derived its name from the city of Samaria (see section above). It was the geographical center of Palestine. Lying between Galilee to the N and Judah to the S, it extended from the Mediterranean to the river Jordan. Its northern limits were clearly defined by the Mount Carmel and Mount Gilboa ranges. Since Samaria and Judah constituted one geographical unit, there was no natural southern boundary. Over the centuries it varied (either N or S of Bethel) depending on military and political conditions. In this region, predominantly hill country (rising to 3333 feet at Baal-hazor), were located the twin peaks Ebal and Gerizim with ancient Shechem guarding the pass between them. *See* Palestine, II, B, 2, *c*.

At the conquest of Canaan most of Samaria was occupied by Ephraim and the half tribe of Manasseh. Inasmuch as these Joseph tribes were large, Joshua instructed them to make more room by clearing the forests (Josh 17:15, 18). During the divided monarchy Samaria was the political and economic heart of the northern kingdom of Israel (Hos 7:1; 8:4-6), and during the reign of Jeroboam II (793-753 B.C.) the area reached its zenith. By *c.* 732 Tiglath-Pileser III (745-727) had overrun the region, and with the fall of Samaria (the capital, in 722/21) it became a province in the Assyrian Empire (II Kgs 17:24-26). When Assyrian control weakened after Josiah became king of Judah (640-609 B.C.), this godly ruler was able to dismantle the high places in the cities of Samaria (II Kgs 23:19). Political subservience continued on through the Babylonian, Persian, Greek, and Roman Empires.

During the intertestamental and NT times the region as the territory of the Samaritans (*q.v.*) was increasingly bypassed when Jews traveled between Judea and Galilee. Jesus, however, passed through Samaria (Jn 4:4-43; Lk 17:11) and commanded His disciples to witness in that area (Acts 1:8). Here Philip and

The Roman theater of Samaria built by Herod the Great. HFV

other Christians preached Christ and established churches after being scattered by the persecutions of Saul (Acts 8:1-13; 9:31; 15:3).

Bibliography. P. R. Ackroyd, "Samaria," TAOTS, pp. 343-354. André Parrot, *Samaria: The Capital of the Kingdom of Israel*, London: SCM Press, 1958. G. Ernest Wright, "Samaria," BA, XXII (1959), 67-78; "Israelite Samaria and Iron Age Chronology," BASOR #155 (1959), 13-29.

D. M. B.

SAMARITANS (sá-măr'ĭ-tánz). In the OT period a term referring to the residents of the city or province of Samaria (II Kgs 17:29). Some estrangement between the residents of middle and southern Palestine was evident in the period of the judges, but the feelings were intensified with the formation of the northern kingdom of Israel under Jeroboam I.

In general, residents of Israel and the Canaanites practiced racial, social, and religious intermingling. In 732 B.C. the Assyrians under Tiglath-pileser III conquered the NE portion of Israel and followed its established policy of deporting local residents and replacing them with foreign captives (II Kgs 15:29). This syncretistic process was augmented when Sargon II in 721 B.C. deported many inhabitants of the region of Samaria and imported other peoples (II Kgs 17:24). Intermarriage gradually took place. Because lions played havoc among the new residents, one of the deported priests was returned to Bethel in order to "teach them the law of the God of the land" (II Kgs 17:25-28). He was only partially successful, however, for while they "feared the Lord," they also "served their own gods" (II Kgs 17:29-33). Ezr 4:2, 10 indicate that the Assyrian practice of mixing populations was continued under Sargon's grandson (Esar-haddon) and great-grandson (Ashurbanipal, called Asnapper).

Descendants of this mixed population desired to help Zerubbabel build the temple because they claimed to worship the same God, but when their offer was rejected, they opposed and delayed the construction (Ezr 4:2-5). After Nehemiah began to rebuild the walls of Jerusalem (*c*. 444 B.C.), he was opposed by the triumvirate of Sanballat, Geshem, and Tobiah (Neh 2:10, 19; 4:1; 6:1; etc.).

One of the letters found at Elephantine (Syene of Isa 49:12, RSV, near modern Aswan) in Upper Egypt informs us that in 408 B.C. Sanballat was governor of Samaria and that his sons Delaiah and Shelemiah assisted him (*see* Elephantine Papyri). Although Sanballat had a good Babylonian name, Sin-uballit "(the god) Sin has given life," he was probably a worshiper of Yahweh because he gave his sons names ending in *iah* (i.e., Yah, a shortened form of Yahweh). The same may have been true for Tobiah since he named his son Johanan (where *Jo* is another shortened form of Yahweh).

Nevertheless, the Yahwism of these leaders was repugnant to Nehemiah. In his attempt to cleanse the people "from everything foreign" (Neh 13:30) he demanded the dissolution of all mixed marriages. One of the grandsons of Eliashib the high priest was married to the daughter of Sanballat, but apparently he refused to put her away because Nehemiah chased him from Jerusalem (Neh 13:28). Josephus (*Ant*. xi.7.2; 8:2-7) relates how Manasseh, brother of Jaddua the high priest, married Nikaso, the daughter of (a later?) Sanballat, and founded the temple worship on Mount Gerizim. The story is tied in with the activities of Darius III (335-331 B.C.) and of his conqueror, Alexander the Great (336-323 B.C.); but since the account swarms with historical improbabilities, it is preferable to follow the biblical data and date the beginning of the Samaritan schism *c*. 445 B.C.

Subsequently, the term "Samaritans" came to refer specifically to this religious group, not to the inhabitants of the city or province of Samaria in general. Only the Torah or the Pentateuch was accepted as Scripture, and in the growing conflict with the Jews, the Samaritans rejected the rest of the Jewish OT as being authoritative. It is difficult to determine whether this limitation was premeditated by the banished priest or whether it was accidental; i.e., possibly the only MS he could obtain at his expulsion was a copy of the Torah. In any case, the mutual esteem of the law accounts for the features common to the Samaritans and the Jews: belief in one God, veneration of Moses, and concern for the sabbath, the major feasts, and circumcision.

The irreconcilable heresy of the Samaritans was their claim that Mount Gerizim, not Mount Zion in Jerusalem, was the true place to worship God. According to Deuteronomy, Moses made a number of references to "the place which the Lord your God will choose, to make his name dwell there" (e.g., 12:11), but the place was not specifically designated. He instructed the people, however, that on entering the land they should "set the blessing on Mount Gerizim and the curse on Mount Ebal" (Deut 11:29; 27:12-13). The context implied that

Ruins on the site of the Samaritan Temple on Mount Gerizim. HFV

Mount Gerizim, the place of blessing, was the site for the altar and, according to the Samaritan Pentateuch, Moses commanded that an altar be built on Mount Gerizim (Deut 27:4–8). The Jews rejected the claim, however, because their copies of the Torah had Mount Ebal instead. Yet the intent of the passage, in either case, authorized worship near Shechem (*q.v.*), that ancient religious center which lay in the pass between Mount Ebal to the N and Mount Gerizim to the S.

The claim of Shechem's priority over Jerusalem appeared to have historical bases as well. Shechem was the first place in Canaan visited by Abram, and here he built an altar and sacrificed (Gen 12:6–7). Jacob bought a piece of land at Shechem and erected an altar there (Gen 33:18–20). After the conquest of Canaan, Shechem became the central city of refuge W of the Jordan (Josh 20:7). It was at Shechem that the bones of Joseph were buried (Josh 24:32), and there Joshua renewed the covenant with the Israelites (Josh 24:25).

According to their own account, the Samaritans originated with those faithful Israelites and descendants of Joseph who refused to follow Eli when he moved the ark S from Shechem to the apostate sanctuary at Shiloh.

When Alexander the Great invaded Palestine (332 B.C.) he found many Samaritans residing in the city of Samaria. These he deported to Shechem, which thus became more than ever before a Samaritan city. In 1952 a collection of Aramaic papyrus fragments was found in a cave *c.* nine miles N of Jericho. These were legal and administrative documents of the Samaritans dated from *c.* 375–335 B.C. and written in the province and/or the city of Samaria. They were deposited in the cave when some 200 Samaritans fled from Alexander and were finally massacred here.

Jesus, the son of Sirach, writing *c.* 180 B.C., expressed the mounting hatred between the Jews and the Samaritans: "With two nations my soul is vexed, and a third is no people: those who live on Mt. Seir, and the Philistines, and the foolish nation which dwells in Shechem" (Sir 50:25–26). This was probably a reference to God's promise, "I will stir them to jealousy with those who are no people; I will provoke them with a foolish nation" (Deut 32:21, RSV).

Notwithstanding the enmity between the Jews and the Samaritans, both were oriented in the Pentateuch and both mounted opposition to the Hellenizing campaign of Antiochus Epiphanes. Accordingly, the Seleucid ruler desecrated both temples (167 B.C.), dedicating the one in Jerusalem to Zeus Olympios and the other on Gerizim to Zeus Xenios, the Friend of Strangers (II Macc 6:2). But the Samaritan temple did not have the protection of Zeus for long, because strife within the Seleucid kingdom permitted John Hyrcanus, the Hasmonean ruler of the Jews, to destroy the sanctuary in 128 B.C.

The Samaritan temple was built by permission of Alexander the Great (Jos*Ant.* xi.8.2. 6–7; xii.5.5; xiii.9.1). Its ruins, 1,000 feet above Shechem at Tell er-Ras on the northern peak of Mount Gerizim, were investigated in 1966 and 1968. It lies under the foundations of a Roman temple of Zeus built by Hadrian, and consists of a massive altar podium of solid masonry, *c.* 65 feet by 65 feet by 26 feet high, dated by pottery to the Hellenistic period (Robert J. Bull, "The Excavation of Tell er-Ras on Mount Gerizim," BA, XXXI [1968], 58–72). Their temple was never rebuilt; however, its loss did not mean the end of the Samaritans. Public worship was transferred to a synagogue and the Samaritan sect continued as a religious thorn in the side of the Jews. Rather than risk ceremonial contamination from the heretical Samaritans, pious Jews of Judea and Galilee traveled through Transjordan or along the W bank of the Jordan.

The NT makes it quite clear, however, that John the Baptist and Jesus did not share this antipathy. John's early ministry of baptism was at the Jordan River, and there Jesus was baptized. But later, while Jesus and His disciples were in Judea, "John also was baptizing at Aenon near Salim, because there was much water there" (Jn 3:23). Tradition located Aenon up the Jordan toward the Sea of Galilee. Yet if the Jordan area was meant, then why add "because there was much water there"? Just a few miles E of Shechem is the most likely site of Salim (*q.v.*) and nearby lies the modern village of 'Ainûn. The latter name probably derives from Aramaic *'ainon*, "little spring"; it is significant that the area, lying at the headwaters of the *Wadi Far'ah*, has many springs. It is most likely, therefore, that part of the ministry of John the Baptist and his disciples was in Samaritan territory, not far from Shechem.

The Bible does not indicate where John was beheaded or where his body was buried. While Josephus locates his death at Machaerus (*q.v.*), the Herodian palace and fortress E of the Dead Sea, there is a strong tradition that John's body was buried in the city of Sebaste (Samaria) a few miles NW of Shechem. The desire to inter the body outside the jurisdiction of Herod Antipas, the tetrarch of Galilee and Perea, would

SAMARITANS

be expected, but the selection of Samaria instead of Judea may be additional evidence that John had close contacts with that region.

Jesus also had interest in the Samaritans. Early in His ministry He came to a city of Samaria near Jacob's well. While the Gr. MSS designate the city as Sychar, the old Sinaitic Syriac text has "Sychem," i.e., Shechem. The latter is most likely correct because recent excavations and explorations at the modern village of Balatah, just to the NW of Jacob's well, have shown it to be the site of Shechem in the Roman period. It was adjacent to the tell of OT Shechem destroyed by John Hyrcanus in 107 B.C. (G. E. Wright, *Shechem,* New York: McGraw-Hill, 1965, pp. 5-6 and n. 6, pp. 243 f.). "Sychar" probably resulted from some tired scribe who intended to write "Sychem," but after copying *Sych* he accidentally added *ar* (from "Samaria," which occurs twice just above). *See* Sychar.

The Samaritan woman had come out to the ancient well for water, and Jesus asked her for a drink. Knowing that "Jews have no dealings with the Samaritans" (Jn 4:9), she was suspicious; but she continued the conversation in hope of relief from the arduous task of carrying water from the well. When Jesus confronted her with one of her secrets, she turned at once to the old theological argument: "Our fathers worshiped on this mountain; and you say that in Jerusalem is the place where men ought to worship" (Jn 4:20, RSV). Jesus affirmed that true worship would not be confined to either site because He, the Messiah, had come. After the startled disciples returned, the woman left her water jar and went into the village. As a result of her witness Jesus stayed in the vicinity for two days (Jn 4:40). There at the foot of Mount Gerizim, He began the missionary outreach which was to characterize His Church.

Christ's concern for the Samaritans is also indicated by the number of times He cited them as examples for the Jews; for instance, the true neighbor (Lk 10:30-37) and the leper who returned to thank Jesus (Lk 17:11-19). Moreover, He rebuked James and John when they wanted to call down fire on an inhospitable Samaritan village (Lk 9:52-56).

In the early church there were some Jewish Christians called the Hellenists, who indicated their broader outlook by missionary activity among the Samaritans. Philip, one of the seven deacons chosen when "the Hellenists murmured against the Hebrews" (Acts 6:1, RSV), proclaimed Christ in a city of Samaria (Acts 8:5). When Saul began his great persecution of the church, all except the apostles were scattered throughout Judea and Samaria (Acts 8:1). On hearing of Philip's success, Peter and John went to Samaria and laid their hands on the new converts that the latter might receive the Holy Spirit (Acts 8:14-17). Thus, as Jesus had told His disciples at Jacob's well, "Others have labored, and you have entered into their labor" (Jn 4:38). On their return to Jerusalem, Philip,

The Samaritan Synagogue at Nablus. HFV

Peter, and John preached the gospel in "many villages of the Samaritans" (Acts 8:25).

Evidently the Samaritans, like the Jews, desired to throw off the Roman yoke, for they foolishly resisted Vespasian's army. Josephus reports (*Wars* iii.7.32) that 11,600 of them were slain. The Roman emperors Hadrian (A.D. 117-138) and Commodus (A.D. 180-193) opposed the Samaritans and apparently destroyed much of their sacred writings. After the Arab conquest of Palestine (*c.* A.D. 634), the Samaritans, refusing to become converts to Islam, were subjected to many cruelties. By A.D. 1099 the main community of Samaritans came under the jurisdiction of the small Christian kingdom ruled by the crusader Godfrey of Bouillon. About 1259 the Mongol successors of Genghis Khan gained control over the area; but the period of greatest persecution was under the fanatical Muslim rule of the Ottoman Turks.

By the beginning of the 19th cen. all the synagogues and communities of the Samaritan dispersion (e.g., at Damascus, Cairo, and Gaza) had been wiped out and only the synagogue and dwindling group of Samaritans at Nablus (Neapolis) remained. They numbered 152 in 1901 (with only 55 females), and by 1930 the group was less than a hundred. Now a revitalized Samaritan community claims more than 300 adherents, with *c.* 250 living in Nablus and another 50 residing in Tel Aviv.

The sacred document of the Nablus synagogue is the Abisha scroll of the Pentateuch. It is written in a modified form of the Old Heb. or Canaanite script. Because of some catastrophe much of the original scroll was destroyed, and so only the last three chapters of Numbers and all of Deuteronomy are really ancient. The oldest known book-form of the Samaritan Pentateuch (SP) has a sale notice dated A.D. 1150, but the manuscript was probably written some centuries earlier.

The text of the SP represents a distinct recension of the Pentateuch. At times it differs from either the LXX or the standard Heb. text, and in some cases it diverges from both of them. *See* Bible Manuscripts: The OT, III, 12 Samaritan Pentateuch. Since the Samaritans employed Aramaic, Greek, and Arabic at various periods in their history, their Pentateuch was translated into each of these languages. Although the canonical book of Joshua was not accepted as Scripture, Joshua was highly regarded and much of the conquest account is incorporated, along with apocryphal additions, in the Samaritan book of Joshua (a 13th cen. A.D. document in the Arabic language written in the old Samaritan script). Also dating from this period and later are a number of commentaries on the Pentateuch.

While much early Samaritan literature perished, the rather extensive liturgy extant today has preserved a great deal of relatively old material. Some of the poems in the so-called *Defter,* "The Common Prayers," stem from Marqa (4th cen. A.D.), whom the Samaritans acknowledge as their great theologian. The old Samaritan creed affirmed faith in: one only God, Yahweh; one only lawgiver, Moses; one only sacred book, the Torah; and one only holy place, Mount Gerizim (the true Beth-el, "house of God"). Later theological development established belief in angels, immortality (but not resurrection), and a day of vengeance and judgment. The Samaritan Messiah, called *Thaheb,* possibly meaning "restorer," was expected from the tribe of Joseph. As a prophetic leader instructed by God, he would restore unity to Israel and subdue "seven nations," i.e., convert all peoples to Samaritanism.

Although Jewish tradition condemned the Samaritans for pronouncing the sacred name "Yahweh" (instead of substituting "Lord") in oaths, Judaism never considered them idolaters. In fact, the Samaritans were extreme monotheists and they avoided, wherever possible, all anthropomorphisms (descriptions of God in terms of human form or characteristics). They were more strict than the Jews in observance of the law, especially the sabbath. Their religious calendar revolved around the three great feasts commanded in Lev 23: Passover, Day of Atonement, and Feast of Booths. After destruction of the Gerizim temple, Passover was not transferred to the synagogue as was the rest of the ritual. Today, much like their ancestors, the Samaritan community (in the SW quarter of Nablus) makes its annual pilgrimage up the nearby slopes of Mount Gerizim. There, near the ruins of the ancient temple, the great feast is celebrated with an elaborate ritual in which seven lambs are slain, plucked of wool, disemboweled, roasted, and eaten.

Bibliography. CornPBE, "Samaritans," pp. 649–652. Frank M. Cross, "Papyri of the Fourth Century B.C. from Däliyeh," *New Directions in Biblical Archaeology,* D. N. Freedman and J. C. Greenfield, eds., Garden City: Doubleday, 1969, pp. 41–62. Moses Gaster, *The Samaritans,* London: H. Milford, 1925. Joachim Jeremias, "*Samaritēs,* etc.," TDNT, VII, 88–94. L. A. Mayer, *Bibliography of the Samaritans,* D. Broadribb, ed., Leiden: Brill, 1964. James A. Montgomery, *The Samaritans,* Philadelphia: Winston, 1907 (New York: Ktav, 1968 reprint). J. E. H. Thomson, *The Samaritans,* Edinburgh: Oliver and Boyd, 1919. Bruce K. Waltke, "The Samaritan Pentateuch and the Text of the Old Testament," NPOT, pp. 212–239.

D. M. B.

SAMECH (sä'mĕk). The 15th letter of the Heb. alphabet, in KJV placed as the heading of the 15th section of Ps 119 (vv. 113–120). As a numeral it denotes 60. The Heb. word for which this is a transliteration means "a prop" or "support," and the cognate verb *sāmak* appears in v. 116 as "uphold me."

SAMGAR-NEBO (săm'gär-nē 'bō). A prince of the king of Babylon, who sat in the middle of the gate of Jerusalem during the seige of 588–586 B.C. (Jer 39:3, KJV).

According to the NEB, the above name was misunderstood by the Masoretic scholars and should be separated to give the following translation: "Nergalsarezer of Simmagir, Nebusarsekim the chief eunuch, Nergalsarezer the commander of the frontier troops. . . ." Samgar, then, is the place name of a city and province of Babylonia known in a cuneiform text from Nebuchadnezzar's reign as Sin-magir. Nebo is the first element of the following personal name. *See* Nergalsharezer.

SAMLAH (săm'lȧ). The fifth of the ancient kings of Edom, of the city of Masrekah (Gen 36:36–37; I Chr 1:47–48).

SAMOS (sā'mŏs). An island in the Aegean Sea, about a mile off the coast of Lydia in Asia Minor, SW of Ephesus and NW of Miletus. Its city of the same name was noted in ancient times for its fine pottery and wine, and was a noted center for the worship of the goddess Juno. There is a strait about a mile wide between Samos and the promontory of Trogyllium, and it was probably here that Paul's ship anchored as he stopped on his way homeward on the third missionary journey (Acts 20:15). It is not known whether Paul evangelized during his brief stay here, but there had been a settlement of Jews on the island for many years (cf. I Macc 15:23).

SAMOTHRACE (săm'ŏ-thrās). The KJV spelling is Samothracia. It is a small island with high mountains (up to 5,250 feet) off the coast of Thrace in northern Greece; hence, its name, "Samos of Thrace." It lay near a much traveled sea route from Macedonia to the Hellespont (Dardanelles) on the way to the Black Sea and therefore was a well-known landmark. The island was important as the home of a famous mystery cult featuring two pre-Greek deities known as the Cabiri. These were reverenced as the guides and protectors of sailors. Another attraction of the cult was the enactment of a ritual drama representing the sacred marriage of the Great Mother. Numerous prominent per-

The victory of Samothrace. LM

sonages, including Philip of Macedon and the Roman emperor Hadrian, were initiated into the Samothracian mysteries.

The ship in which Paul sailed from Troas to Neapolis on his second missionary journey anchored off the shore for the night (Acts 16:11), since the island has no harbor. Presumably he stopped here on his voyage to Troas during his third journey, as the five day trip of Acts 20:6 implies.

J. R.

SAMSON (săm′sŏn). An Israelite hero from the tribe of Dan, the son of Manoah; one of the last of the judges before Samuel (Jud 13:24 – 16:31). The derivation of his name *Shimshôn* is uncertain. It may be from Heb. *shemesh*, "sun," meaning "sun-like," given by his parents in anticipation of his heroic, sun-like energy, and corresponding to the Ugaritic name *špšyn*, derived from *špš*, "sun." Or it may be from Heb. *shāmam*, "to destroy," hence, "Destroyer."

Samson was born *c.* 1090 B.C. at the beginning of the Philistine oppression (Jud 13:1) in Zorah. It lay across the valley of Sorek from Beth-shemesh, very near the Israelite-Philistine border in those days. Beth-shemesh (*q.v.*) was then in Israelite hands (I Sam 6:12–16), but the archaeological remains of Stratum III (1200–1000 B.C.) reveal it was under strong Philistine influence (*see* Philistines).

Samson's parents dedicated him to be a life-long Nazirite (*see* Nazarite) even before his conception (Jud 13:3–7). When he was grown, the Spirit of the Lord repeatedly came upon him to enable him to perform amazing feats of physical strength (13:25; 14:6, 19; 15:14). Because of this seemingly superhuman prowess many have relegated the "Samson stories" to Hebrew myth or folklore (e.g., C. F. Kraft, "Samson," IDB, IV, 198–200). Others assert that the Greek myth of the 12 labors of Hercules provides the pattern for the Samson narrative. But the parallels between the careers of Samson and Hercules are superficial, and the Greek poets did not embellish the memory of Hercules with a story of 12 mighty works until the 6th cen. B.C., much too late to influence the writing of the book of Judges (Gary G. Cohen, "Samson and Hercules," EQ, XLII [1970], 131–141).

In spite of his godly upbringing and charismatic empowering Samson was careless about honoring God as a Nazirite. As a young man he secretly disobeyed the prohibition against approaching a dead body (I Sam 14:8–9) and publicly provided wine for a feast or drinking bout (Heb. *mishteh*, 14:10). He violated the Nazirite principle of living separated unto Yahweh by his immoral relations with the Gaza harlot and with Delilah (16:1–20). His spiritual indifference was climaxed by the cutting of his long hair, the characteristic sign of Nazirite consecration (Num 6:5, 9, 18–19).

Samson probably became involved with the Philistines soon after the disastrous battle near Aphek *c.* 1070 B.C. when the Israelites lost the ark and thousands of their men (I Sam 4:1–11). The demoralized nation took no steps toward repentance or prayer for deliverance from the Philistines during Samson's 20-year ministry (Jud 15:20; 16:31; cf. 14:4; 15:9–13; I Sam 7:2). His victory in which he sacrificed his own life at the Gaza temple decimated the ranks of Philistine leaders and probably contributed to the Israelite victory in the battle of Ebenezer soon afterward (I Sam 7:7–14). But because of his lack of self-control his ministry was largely ineffective, and accordingly he wrought no permanent deliverance for Israel.

The narrative of Samson centers around his experiences with three Philistine women. In connection with his marriage to a woman of Timnath he killed a lion with his bare hands (Jud 14:5–6) and slew 30 Philistines of Ashkelon for their clothing (14:19). Because his father-in-law gave his wife to his best man ("companion," 14:20; 15:2), Samson took revenge by catching 300 foxes, tying firebrands to their tails, and turning them loose in the grain fields and orchards of the Philistines. When they punished his wife and her father by burning, he avenged this with a great slaughter and went to hide in the cliff of Etam (15:3–8).

Soon the Philistines invaded Judah to capture Samson. The fearful Israelites bound him with two new ropes to surrender him to the enemy. As the Philistines met him, he snapped his fetters and, seeing a jawbone of an ass, killed a thousand of them with it (15:9–16).

The next recorded event tells of his visit to a harlot in the Philistine stronghold of Gaza. Upon learning of his presence in the city the officials had him surrounded. At midnight he arose and carried off the city's two gate doors, doorposts, and bars toward Hebron. In so doing he humiliated the Gazites beyong measure because the gates symbolize the strength of a city (16:1–3).

Once more Samson let his passions go unchecked. He became infatuated with Delilah (*q.v.*), a woman near his home. The Philistines bribed her to learn from him the secret of his strength. Three times her charms and coaxings failed to get a true answer, but he finally gave in to her persistent nagging and revealed to her that as a Nazirite his unshorn hair was the key to his strength. While he was asleep Delilah shaved his head and he was helpless, for the Lord forsook him. The Philistines blinded him and consigned him in the Gaza prison to a woman's task of grinding grain (16:4–21).

On the occasion of a national festival in honor of the god Dagon, a multitude of Philistines gathered in the temple, with about 3,000 more on the roof. They brought Samson to make sport of him before the crowd. Meanwhile his hair (along with inner repentance) had grown, and his strength had returned. Calling upon Yahweh, Samson braced himself against the two middle pillars at the entrance of the temple building, and pushed them off their bases. In 1972 at Tell Qasile, in the ruins of the first Philistine temple ever found in Palestine, two such stone pedestals were discovered, placed only a yard apart. The roof of the portico fell, burying the five Philistine lords and all who were inside, including Samson. Thus at one stroke he was avenged for his two eyes, as he had prayed, by killing more enemies in his death than the total he had killed during his life (16:22–30).

In spite of his failings Samson is listed with the heroes of faith in Heb 11(v. 32). It was by his dependence on God's gifts and calling that he was empowered to perform mighty exploits, and this faith was manifested in his dying act.

See Judge, The; Judges, Book of.

J. R.

SAMUEL (săm'yo͞o-ĕl). One of the greatest leaders of Israel (II Chr 35:18; Ps 99:6; Jer 15:1; Acts 3:24; Heb 11:32). Samuel came to Israel in one of her darkest hours. The Philistines, who for a long time had menaced the Israelites, were threatening to engulf them. But Hannah, the wife of Elkanah of Ramathaim-zophim in Mount Ephraim, was more concerned about her childlessness. While worshiping at the tabernacle in Shiloh, she vowed to make any man child the Lord would give her a Nazarite (Num 6) for life. This son became Samuel the king maker, the last of the judges, and the first of the prophets after Moses.

From early childhood he ministered in the tabernacle wearing a linen ephod (I Sam 2:18; 3:1) and became the protegé of the old priest Eli. It was a time of spiritual decline in the nation: "word from the Lord was rare in those days" (I Sam 3:1, NASB). But the Bible says that "the Lord revealed himself to Samuel in Shiloh by the word of the Lord. And the word of Samuel came to all Israel" (I Sam 3:21*b*–4:1*a*). The theocracy worked exactly so, for Israel had the theocratic ideal; only God was king and His will was communicated to the people through prophets or dreams or by the Urim (I Sam 28:6, 15; Ex 28:30).

When Israel misused the ark of God by taking it into battle for protection, God showed His displeasure by delivering them and the ark over to the Philistines. Samuel's mentor Eli proved too old to endure the shock of this tragic news. The capture of the ark meant that God had forsaken Shiloh (Ps 78:60; Jer 7:12, 14; 26:6,9), and Samuel was left without a place to minister. He returned to Ramah his home, where he built an altar and judged Israel from there, making a regular yearly circuit of towns near Ramah, *c.* eight miles N of Jerusalem (I Sam 7:15–17).

Samuel's task was the reviving of true worship in Israel. He besought the people to put away the images of the Canaanite deities Baal and Ashtoreth (Astarte) and to serve only the Lord (*see* Gods, False). At a general convocation at Mizpeh, one of the circuit towns, Samuel preached and prayed for the people (I Sam 7). This resulted in a spirit of repentance, renewed trust in the Lord, and consequent victory over the Philistines at a place called Ebenezer, "the stone of help," for the people said, "Hitherto hath the Lórd helped us" (I Sam 7:9–12).

After years of faithful administration of the law and giving of the word of the Lord, Samuel failed in the same way Eli had failed. His sons "walked not in his ways," but took bribes and perverted judgment (I Sam 8:3). Although God forced the Philistines to abandon the ark (I Sam 5–6), it nevertheless remained for 20 years in Abinadab's house in apparent disuse.

With no possible successor to Samuel and with no central shrine for worship, the Israelites found themselves increasingly at the mercy of the Philistines. Feeling their need for strong leadership and copying the nations about them, they clamored for a king. Monarchy was inherently distrusted by the Israelites. Moses had warned them of this pitfall (Deut 17:14), for it went against the theocratic ideal that anyone but the Lord should be king (I Sam 8:7). However, under pressure of the times the people forced a reluctant Samuel to find a king. Before privately anointing Saul first in Ramah (I Sam 9:1 – 10:6), Samuel preached a sermon of warning; but it fell on deaf ears (I Sam 8:9–22; cf. I. Mendelsohn, "Samuel's Denunciation of Kingship in the Light of the Akkadian Documents from Ugarit," BASOR #143 [1956], pp. 17-22).

Saul proved that he had charismatic gifts for leadership when he responded to the plight of the people of Jabesh-gilead (I Sam 11). He was an attractive man in appearance (I Sam 9:2), in his humility (I Sam 9:21; 10:16), and in courage. Furthermore, Samuel had the Lord's leading in choosing this man (I Sam 9:17). Samuel therefore called the people to Mizpeh again and publicly announced the anointing (I Sam 10:17-24). After victory over the Ammonites, a coronation service was held (I Sam 11:15).

The long sermon of I Sam 12 seems to be proof that in all this Samuel still had misgivings. Here he testifies of his own integrity, and again reproves the people for wanting a king. His moving conclusion is, "God forbid that I should sin against the Lord in ceasing to pray for you" (I Sam 12:23).

Saul usurped the function of the priesthood (I Sam 13:4-15), and in the holy war against the Amalekites he violated the *ḥerem* (the things devoted to the Lord and consequently consigned to utter destruction, I Sam 15:3, 8, 9, 15, 20, 21; *see* Accursed; Devote, Devoted). Samuel therefore announced that the Lord had rejected Saul from being king (I Sam 15:26-28).

An example of Samuel's great stature among the people at this time is seen in I Sam 16:4 where the elders of Bethlehem trembled at his presence for fear they had displeased him. The occasion was to anoint David, the youngest of Jesse's eight sons, to succeed Saul. This was the last of Samuel's recorded official acts. The last glimpse of him is at Ramah in "Naioth," the huts of a primitive abbey or monastery (I Sam 19:18, JerusB). Here David with great perplexity fled from Saul's presence, and here Samuel is pictured as temporary leader of a school of ecstatic prophets. Saul and his messengers were caught up in the spirit of this ecstatic prophesying, God thus providing David time to escape (I Sam 19:18-24).

A single verse (I Sam 25:1) tells of Samuel's death and burial in Ramah. Samuel's voice is heard again in a posthumous appearance before the witch of Endor (I Sam 28:15). In reply to Saul's request for help against the Philistines, Samuel asks why he who would not listen to him in life should disturb him in death. The last words of Samuel predict Saul's defeat and reassert David's accession to the throne.

See Saul; David; Samuel, Books of.

E. B. S.

SAMUEL, BOOKS OF. The Hebrews originally treated the books of I and II Samuel as one book, as seen from Josephus' canon (*Contra Apion* I.8) and in the Masoretic note on I Sam 28:24 which takes this as the middle verse of the book. The Gr. translation (LXX) and other versions call I and II Samuel the First and Second Books of the Kingdoms. The Bomberg Rabbinic Bible published in Venice in 1516-17

Ramah, Samuel's home town. HFV

divided the book into I and II Samuel as in Heb. Bibles today.

Text

The Masoretic text of Samuel seems to have suffered in transmission, for the LXX has addenda which has been generally recognized as belonging to the original text, according to F. M. Cross, Jr. The Dead Sea Scroll material containing numerous fragments of I and II Samuel has proved to be of great value in showing that the Heb. text behind the LXX of Samuel is an equally important text (*The Ancient Library of Qumran and Modern Biblical Studies,* Garden City: Doubleday, 1958, pp. 133-145).

Authors

The books of Samuel do not form an unbroken narrative in strict chronological order, but almost all scholars recognize I Sam 15 – II Sam 5 as a continuous narrative by one writer and II Sam 9-20 as a continuous narrative possibly by the same writer. Although we do not know for sure who wrote these books, there are indications in the Scripture that the prophets Samuel, Nathan, and Gad were the authors. I Sam 10:25 says that Samuel wrote a book and laid it up before the Lord, while I Chr 29:29 states that the acts of David were "written in the book of Samuel the seer, and in the book of Nathan the prophet, and in the book of Gad the seer" (cf. II Chr 9:29 *re* the acts of Solomon). It is not likely that Samuel could have been responsible for more than the early part of I Samuel since his death is recorded in chap. 25. II Sam 5:5 speaks of the complete reign of David in the past tense, so someone who outlived David wrote this section.

Critics claim there are two principal sources of the books of Samuel, the later one having what is called Deuteronomistic affinities dated from about 550 B.C. Here they place such chapters as I Sam 2, 12, 15, and II Sam 7. They claim the books of Samuel came from many hands and have contradictory and conflicting accounts. They allege two different descriptions of the origins of Heb. kingship, one being in I Sam 7, 8, and 12 which looks on the kingship as a defection from the Lord, and the other in I Sam 9-11 which regards kingship as given by the Lord for the good of the people. It is not difficult to see that there is no real contradiction in these accounts; they merely stress different aspects of God's relationship with His people. Other alleged contradictions, such as David's maturity as a warrior and musician in 16:14-23 and his coming as a youth to Saul in 17:55 may be explained by the unchronological order of some of the material in I and II Samuel.

The books of Samuel represent the earliest true form of the art of historiography. The ancient Egyptian and Assyrian kings wrote annals which are important historical documents but are manifestly one-sided propaganda pieces. Here in the Bible we have the hero David presented as a complete man capable of good and evil. The forceful literary style, amazing psychological insight, and dramatic pathos is unsurpassed in the world literature of such an early date.

Outline

I. The Early Life and Ministry of Samuel, I Sam 1:1–7:14
 A. The birth and youth of Samuel, 1:1–4:1*a*
 B. Wars with the Philistines, 4:1*b*–7:14
II. Samuel's Ministry to Saul, I Sam 7:15–15:35
 A. Israel's request for a king, 7:15–8:22
 B. Saul chosen and installed as king, 9:1–12:25
 C. War of independence from the Philistines, 13:1–14:52
 D. Holy war to destroy Amalek, 15:1–35
III. Saul and David, I Sam 16:1–31:13
 A. David anointed to be future king, 16:1-13
 B. David brought into Saul's court, 16:14–19:17
 C. David as a fugitive, 19:18–26:25
 D. David in Philistine territory, 27:1–30:31
 E. Death of Saul and Jonathan, 31:1-13
IV. The Early Years of David's Reign, II Sam 1:1–8:18
 A. David, king at Hebron, 1:1–5:5
 B. Jerusalem, the new capital of all Israel, 5:6–7:29
 C. Further victories of David, 8:1-18
V. The Court Life of King David, II Sam 9:1–20:26
 A. David's treatment of Mephibosheth, 9:1-13
 B. War against Ammon and David's sin, 10:1–12:31
 C. The rebellion of Absalom, 13:1–18:33
 D. David's return and Sheba's revolt, 19:1–20:26
VI. Appendices: Aspects of David's Reign, II Sam 21:1–24:25
 A. The famine, 21:1-14
 B. Exploits of David's warriors, 21:15-22
 C. Psalm of thanksgiving, 22:1-51
 D. The testament of David, 23:1-7
 E. Catalogue of David's mighty men, 23:8-39
 F. The census and plague, 24:1-25

Content

Three main characters are presented in the account, Samuel, Saul, and David. I Sam 1-7 deals with the role of Samuel as that great leader who made possible the transition from the judges (charismatic leadership) to the kings (dynastic kingship). At the same time, as seen in I Sam 8-15, he forwarded the prophetic office to a point where ever after Heb. kings had to face the strictures of God's holy prophets when they went astray. I Sam 16-31 tells largely of the reign of Saul and his neurotic hatred and hounding of David the fugitive. II Samuel deals with the history of David as king. Chaps. 1-4 outline the transition of the dynasty from the line of Saul to David. The rest of II Samuel gives the events of David's reign; for example, his wars in chaps. 10-12 and the rebellion of Absalom and its aftermath in chaps. 14-20. David's royal thanksgiving hymn is recorded in II Sam 22 (also in Ps 18), but his death does not take place until I Kings 2. II Samuel ends with the purchase of the Jebusite Araunah's threshing floor as the proposed site for the building of the temple of the Lord.

Bibliography. Peter R. Ackroyd, *The First Book of Samuel,* Cambridge Bible Commentary on the NEB, Cambridge: Univ. Press, 1971. W. F. Albright, "Reconstructing Samuel's Role in History," *Archaeology, Historical Analogy, and Early Biblical Tradition,* Baton Rouge: Louisiana State Univ. Press, 1966, pp. 42-65. John J. Davis, *The Birth of a Kingdom,* Grand Rapids: Baker, 1970. S. R. Driver, *Notes on the Hebrew Text and the Topography of the Books of Samuel,* Oxford: Clarendon Press, 1913. S. Goldman, *Samuel,* London: Soncino, 1951. F. B. Meyer, *Samuel the Prophet,* New York: Revell, n.d. D. F. Payne, "I and 2 Samuel," NBC, 3rd ed. rev., pp. 284-319. H. P. Smith, *The Books of Samuel,* ICC, Edinburgh: T. & T. Clark, 1899.

E. B. S.

SANBALLAT (săn-băl'*ă*t). A man of political importance in Samaria at the time of Nehemiah's successful attempt to rebuild the walls of Jerusalem (Neh 2:10, 19). He is referred to as a Horonite, which probably means merely that he resided at Beth-horon in Samaria rather than in the town of that name in Moab. He and Tobiah tried to convince the Persian king that the people of Jerusalem were planning to revolt against him (Neh 2:19); then when that plan did not succeed, they tried jeering at Nehemiah's efforts, saying even a fox could break down those walls (Neh 4:3). The two enemies tried to entice Nehemiah to Ono where they could molest him, but Nehemiah replied that his work was too important (Neh 6:2–4). They were very much dismayed when the wall was completed in 52 days (v. 15).

Sanballat's daughter married the grandson of a high priest (Neh 13:28). In the Elephantine papyri, dating from the seventeenth year of the Persian king Darius II (*c.* 407 B.C.), mention is made of Sanballat as governor of Samaria along with his two sons whose Heb. names suggest that he kept at least some relationship to the Jewish faith.

Evidently one of his grandsons bore the name Sanballat, as recorded in one of the Aramaic papyri of refugees from Samaria who hid from Alexander the Great in caves in Wadi Daliyeh (Frank M. Cross, Jr., "The Discovery of the Samaria Papyri," BA, XXVI [1963], 110–121). In turn his grandson, Sanballat III, would have been the one appointed governor by Darius III and who began the Samaritan temple on Mount Gerizim (Jos *Ant.* xi.7.2; 8.2).

A. W. W.

SANCTIFICATION. Derived from the Lat. *sanctus;* Heb. verb *qādash,* "to be set apart, consecrated"; Gr. noun *hagiasmos,* "consecration," "purification," "sanctification"; verb *hagiazō,* "to hallow," "to separate from profane things or consecrate," "to purify or sanctify." The Shorter Westminster Catechism defines sanctification as "the work of God's free grace, whereby we are renewed in the whole man after the image of God, and are enabled more and more to die unto sin and live unto righteousness." This definition, however, while it is helpful in that it draws attention to both the sovereign grace of God and the responsibility of every Christian, tends to confuse regeneration with sanctification. The main ideas in sanctification are separation from what is sinful, on the one hand, and consecration to what is righteous and according to God's will, on the other.

Sanctification needs to be distinguished from justification. In justification God attributes to the believer, at the moment he receives Christ, the very righteousness of Christ and sees him from that point on as having died, been buried, and raised again in newness of life in Christ (Rom 6:4–10). It is a once-for-all change in forensic, or legal status, before God. Sanctification, in contrast, is a progressive process which proceeds in the life of the regenerated sinner on a moment-by-moment basis. In sanctification there occurs a substantial healing of the separations which have occurred between God and man, man and his fellowman, man and himself, and man and nature.

Varying Views

Three main views need to be mentioned:

1. *Baptismal sanctification.* This is the Roman Catholic view, which holds that at baptism not only the guilt but also the depravity of sin is removed. This claim is of course negated by their teaching that ensuing sins must be constantly confessed at the confessional, forgiven by the priest, and satisfied by penance.

2. *Perfectionism.* Those who hold this view teach that the Christian can become perfectly sanctified, or attain perfection, in this life. In order to sustain this conviction it is necessary to minimize the strenuous demands of the law in some way, such as requiring obedience only to the extent of our human ability (Finney); obedience to the new commandment or law of Christ; the exercise merely of love in all we do (Paul Tillich). Such interpretations of God's demands fail to satisfy Christ's own application of the sixth and seventh commandments in Mt 5:17–48, where He exegetes these two laws as the basis of a perfection in which we are exhorted to become perfect like our heavenly Father (v. 48). Methodists, and other Christian churches in the Arminian or Wesleyan tradition in general, teach perfectionism of some sort.

3. *Progressive sanctification.* This is the view of Calvin and all Christians who hold a Reformed theology. It can only be properly understood when realized that they point out that sanctification, as taught in the Bible, appears in three aspects:

a. Positional. All who are regenerated or saved are positionally seen as totally sanctified in Christ. Therefore, though Paul reprimands the Corinthian Christians as carnal (I Cor 5:1; 6:1–8), still he says they are "sanctified in Jesus Christ, called saints" (I Cor 1:2; 6:11; cf. Acts 20:32; Heb 10:10; I Pet 1:2; Jude 1). The book of Hebrews acts as a bridge between this aspect and the experiential sanctification which follows (Heb 2:17; 9:13 ff.; 12:14). The knowledge of positional sanctification, since it depends on a mental grasp of a biblical truth, has an instantaneous, once-for-all nature, as is true of the perception of all other knowledge, which some confuse with perfection itself.

b. Experiential. In the development of a holy life the Christian reckons upon his position in Christ as given in such passages as Rom 6:2–10 and Col 2:9–13 (cf. II Thess 2:13; I Pet 1:2). Christ Himself gives the basic teaching on sanctification in Mt 5:17–48 and Paul in Rom 6–8. The believer is commanded to be holy (Ex 19:6; Lev 11:44; I Pet 1:15), but his growth in holiness rests on a dependence upon his position and a moment-by-moment surrender to God's will and His ways. Since God has chosen to leave him with a fallen nature (Rom 7; Gal 5:17 ff.), he can never attain perfection until this is finally removed, though hopefully there is progress toward perfection.

c. Ultimate. When the believer goes to be with Christ or He comes for His Church at the rapture, whichever comes first, the fallen nature of believers will be completely removed and they shall receive resurrection bodies, be glorified, and become like the Saviour (Rom 8:29–30; I Jn 3:1–3; Jude 24).

Means of Sanctification

The external means is the Word of God. Christ prayed, "Sanctify them through thy

SANCTUARY

truth: thy word is truth" (Jn 17:17). Since He has given the Scriptures by inspiration, He never works against but through them. The internal means is the presence and guidance of the Holy Spirit in our hearts. It is He who keeps the law of God, as revealed by Himself, in and through us. "For what the law could not do, in that it was weak through the flesh, God sending his own Son in the likeness of sinful flesh, and for sin, condemned sin in the flesh: that [in order that] the righteousness of the law might be fulfilled in us [by the Holy Spirit], who walk not after the flesh, but after the Spirit" (Rom 8:3-4). This is the key to and is the very Spirit-filled life itself. In conclusion, God's sovereign work by His Spirit and man's responsive action are to be combined in a proper view of sanctification (Phil 2:12-13).

See Hallow: Holiness, Holy.

Bibliography. G. C. Berkouwer, *Faith and Sanctification,* Grand Rapids: Eerdmans, 1952. C. G. Finney, *Views of Sanctification,* Toronto, 1877. Charles H. Hodge, *Systematic Theology,* Grand Rapids: Eerdmans, 1952, III, 213-258. K. F. W. Prior, *The Way of Holiness,* Chicago: Inter-Varsity, 1967. W. E. Sangster, *The Path to Perfection,* London: Epworth, 1957. Daniel Steele, *A Defense of Christian Perfection,* New York: Hunt and Eaton, 1896. A. H. Strong, *Systematic Theology,* Philadelphia: Judson Press, 1953, pp. 868-881. B. B. Warfield, *Perfectionism,* New York: Oxford Univ. Press, 1931.

R. A. K.

SANCTUARY. In the Bible a place set apart, usually as the place of the Lord's presence among His people. Examples are the tabernacle of Moses (Ex 25:8; Lev 16:33) and the temple of Solomon with its precincts (I Chr 22:19; Isa 63:18; Ps 74:7). Heb. *qōdesh* and *miqdāsh* (137 times) and Gr. *hagion* (four times) have the idea of apartness, later narrowed to separation from sin. *See* Holiness; Sanctify. These terms are also used of the heathen high places and sanctuaries (Isa 16:12; Ezk 28:18; Amos 7:9).

The Canaanite sanctuary at Ai. HFV

Excavations have uncovered a wide variety of Canaanite sanctuaries at, e.g., Megiddo, Ai, Hazor, Lachish, Shechem, and Beth-shan, and an Israelite sanctuary within the royal citadel at Arad. (For details see articles on these cities.)

Other places on earth which God's presence has sanctified, such as Jerusalem, Zion, and Shiloh, are called the Lord's sanctuaries. But heaven especially is His holy abode (Deut 26:15; Ps 68:4-5), His holy temple (Mic 1:2; Hab 2:20; Jon 2:4, 7). His high sanctuary (Ps 102:19), and His holy heaven (Ps 20:6) with His holy throne (Ps 47:8). Indeed, Ps 150:1 simply calls heaven God's sanctuary.

Sanctuary of the Eleusinian Mysteries near Athens. HFV

God told the Israelites how to make the tabernacle (Ex 25-27), instructing them to reverence it (Lev 19:30) and not to profane it (Lev 21:12, 23). The ceremonies of the Mosaic law were, in part, a grand object lesson; their purpose was to teach the nation something of the holiness of God and His total separation from sin. When Israel fell into apostasy and her priests profaned the temple (Zeph 3:4), God announced through His prophets that Israel's adversaries would desecrate the sanctuary (Isa 63:18; Jer 51:51; Dan 8:11-14), for He had rejected it as the place of His special presence. *See* High Place; Tabernacle; Temple.

To the Jews in captivity God tenderly declared that He Himself was "a sanctuary for them a little while in the countries where they had gone" (Ezk 11:16, NASB; cf. Isa 8:14). He also promised Israel to make "a covenant of peace with them" and to "set my sanctuary in the midst of them for evermore" (Ezk 37:26, 28). Ezekiel describes this revived, ideal temple in chaps. 40-48. He ends with a vision of a healing river that flows from the holy sanctuary (47:12) where the messianic Prince dwells (48:21).

The NT teaches that the believer's body is, in a real sense, a sanctuary of God (e.g., II Cor 6:16). Yet the sanctuary also continues to be heaven, where Jesus our great High Priest is "set on the right hand of the throne of the

A sanctuary of the cult of emperor worship at Ostia, Italy. HFV

Majesty in the heavens; a minister of the sanctuary, and of the true tabernacle, which the Lord pitched, and not man" (Heb 8:1-2).

E. B. S.

SAND. The product of the erosive action of waves upon rock, consisting largely of insoluble quartz which is left when the more soluble constituents of rock are carried away in the water. In the Bible sand is almost always associated with the seashore and is frequently a figure for numbers too large to be counted (Gen 22:17; Josh 11:4; Jer 15:8; Heb 11:12; Rev 20:8). The term is used once for heaviness (Job 6:3).

SAND FLEAS. *See* Animals, IV.13.

SANDAL. In the KJV the word sandal is used only to translate Gr. *sandalion* (diminutive of *sandalon*), "small sandal or slipper" (Mk 6:9; Acts 12:8). However, most of the "shoes" of the Bible are patently of the sandal type. Heb. *na'al* is the OT word for footwear. Heb. *min'āl* (only in Deut 33:25) is obscure and may refer to a metal (locking) bar for a gate or door. The more usual NT word for "shoe" is Gr. *hypodēma,* normally used for *na'al* in the LXX.

Both *na'al* and *hypodēma* ("that which is bound under") are demonstrably used for sandals (identified by the "latchet" or leather thong fastened over the foot in Gen 14:23; Isa 5:27; Mk 1:7; Lk 3:16; Jn 1:27), although they may also have designated some types of boots (*q.v.*). A distinction was apparently made between *sandalion* and *hypodēma* by the evangelists, for they report that when our Lord charged the Twelve being sent out to preach, He instructed them to have small sandals (*sandalia*) on their feet (Mk 6:9), but He also told them in Mt 10:10 not to provide themselves with "shoes" (*hypodēmata*), which may have been sandals of a heavier type or even boots. *See* Dress.

The sandal was usually constructed with a flat sole of leather, wood, dried grass, reeds, or bark, fastened to the foot by means of a leather thong ("latchet") attached to the sole at several points. Even though such sandals were rather crude they were often a luxury item to the poor (Lk 15:22). Amos says the poor were sold for a mere pair of shoes (Amos 2:6; 8:6). The black obelisk of Shalmaneser III pictures in row 2 the 13 tribute-bearing envoys of Jehu as wearing better-made sandals with upturned toes (ANEP, figs. 351-355).

In ancient Israel, sandals were ordinarily for protection of the feet outdoors. They were removed upon entering a house. Special occasions for removing footwear included standing on holy ground (Ex 3:5; Josh 5:15; Acts 7:33), captive status in war as a sign of shame (II Chr 28:15; Isa 20:2-4), and mourning (II Sam 15:30).

Early Israelite custom and law seem to have attached significance to the shoe as a symbol of ownership and of the levirate marriage responsibility (Deut 25:9; Ruth 4:7; Ps 60:8). John the Baptist used the loosening of the sandals (at the door), a slave's task, as a figure of humility to set off his own unworthiness in relation to Christ (Mk 1:7; Lk 3:16; Jn 1:27). *See* Latchet. Another figurative use is that of Paul for readiness to (go out and) proclaim the gospel (Eph 6:15). *See* Armor, Spiritual.

W. R. L. McL.

Two pairs of papyrus sandals from the tomb of Tutankhamen with a single sandal at left made of vegetable fibers. LL

SANDALWOOD. *See* Plants: Almug.

SANHEDRIN (săn-hē'drĭn). Originally a Gr. term used to indicate such separate bodies as assemblies, councils, and courts of justice in Hellenistic and rabbinical literature. Some scholars have held that in every instance the same body of legalists is indicated. But the contradictions between the Hellenistic and rabbinical sources are so great that most writers have followed the lead of Adolf Büchler, who concluded that there were two distinct bodies by that name, one political and the other religious, which existed side by side in the last centuries before the destruction of the temple in A.D. 70.

The Political Sanhedrin

The Gr. term *synedrion* (from *syn,* "with," and *hedra,* "seat") is frequently used in Gr. literature in the sense of an assembly, especially one summoned for a special purpose. Thus Herodotus mentions such an assembly of the Gr. city-states during the war with Persia (*Histories* viii.56).

The term occurs frequently in the writings of Josephus in the sense of a council, such as that which Augustus invoked after seeing a Jewish embassy; it was "composed of the Roman magistrates and his friends" (*Ant.* xvii.11.1). Such a council is reported to have met on various occasions as a representative of the Jewish people in their relations with their Roman overlords. The head of this council was the high priest or the local king, who chose its members. There is no indication in Josephus as to how these members were selected, but it is most likely that they were close friends of the high priest or king, and mainly from the priestly class, though toward the end of its existence this Sanhedrin included some of the Pharisees or popular leaders, as well as its majority of priestly Sadducees (cf. Paul's appeal to the Pharisees in Acts 23:6–10). This council had no permanent status, nor did it meet regularly; it was convoked by the king or high priest whenever a political occasion arose (cf. the council convened after Lazarus' resurrection, Jn 11:47), and met in a place convenient to him. This body was empowered to examine charges of rebellion against individuals. It could render a verdict, but had no power to impose a sentence of capital punishment, a right which was retained by the Roman authorities.

The Religious Sanhedrin

This body, of 70 or 71 members, was the highest Jewish court of law, and was always called a court (Heb. *bêt dîn,* lit., "house of justice") prior to the destruction of the second temple. Since civil cases in Jewish law were settled by arbitration on the part of a panel of three judges chosen by the litigants, Sanhedrins concerned themselves only with the trials of individuals on the charge of violating the Jewish religious and criminal laws. Every important city had such a court with up to 23 elders.

The highest court, which had the power to settle all matters beyond the ability of the local courts (Mt 10:17; Mk 13:9; probably Mt 5:22) and to hand out the correct interpretation of Jewish law, was that which met at Jerusalem in the chamber of hewn stone near the SW corner of the temple area. This was the Great Sanhedrin (*sanhedrîn haggᵉdōlâ*) of later rabbinical literature, which gives a detailed description of its membership and proceedings, especially in the tractate Sanhedrin of the Talmud. It is recorded that the court was seated in three semicircles, so that the members could see one another at all times. The first row of 23 was evidently composed of those judges who began the trials; the others were added to it, pair by pair, in cases where the decision was not definite.

The members of this court were chosen from the most learned teachers of the country, and it co-opted new members in case of the death or retirement of the older ones. Its heads were elected by the members and usually served as long as they lived. Thus the Sanhedrin remained an aristocratic institution up to the time of the destruction of the temple in A.D. 70. This judicial body was in permanent session, but did not meet at night nor on sabbaths and holidays. It also did not start a trial on the days preceding these rest periods since, according to Jewish law, a verdict of guilty could not be given unless the trial lasted at least two days (Sanhedrin 4:1). This court was free of Roman supervision and had the power of imposing capital punishment, the four forms of which (stoning, burning, beheading, and strangulation) are expressly indicated in rabbinic literature (see Sanhedrin 6 and 7).

Thus the two kinds of Sanhedrin had completely different fields of action. The political council was concerned only with secular problems, while the religious court dealt only with the enforcement of the laws of the Pentateuch. In order to understand how this division arose, it is necessary to retrace the development of the Jewish community during the period of the second temple.

History

When the Jews returned from the Babylonian Exile in the 6th cen. B.C., they had no kings of their own, but were ruled by governors appointed by their overlords. The Persians and Greeks for the most part gave them complete freedom to follow their religion. Thus a theocracy developed with the Torah (Pentateuch) as its constitution and the high priest as its head. The latter seems to have received the title *nāśî'* ("prince"; see Ezk 44–46), a distinct title from that of king (*melek*). Rabbinical sources speak of a Great Assembly, a ruling body consisting of the priests, who were solely responsible for religious instruction and court procedure (Aboth 1:1). The latter is clear from the fact that one of their principles was deliberateness in judgment (*ibid.*).

Only the names of the high priests in this

period are known; the other teachers were grouped anonymously under the appellation of *sōpherîm*, the interpreters of the *sēpher* ("book") of the Torah (cf. Ezr 7:6, 11; Neh 8:1–9; Mal 2:6–7). At the same time courts for the administration of the law as applied to individuals became a necessary part of the system of government, and in fact their existence had been expressly ordered in the Torah (Dt 16:18–20; 17:8–13; 19:16–19). At first these courts must have consisted solely of priests, and it was only gradually that laymen were included.

This arrangement seems to have lasted satisfactorily until the rise of the Maccabees in the 2nd cen. B.C. and the recovery of national independence. As the books of Maccabees dramatically relate, the last high priests of the old line, especially Jason, Menelaus, and Alcimus, completely lost by their actions the support of the people. The result was a religious revolution: the old line of Zadokite high priests was terminated, and Simon the Maccabee was chosen in their stead "until there should arise a faithful prophet" (I Macc 14:41).

In the next decades the high priest (later the king as well) became immersed more and more in purely political affairs and left religious matters entirely to the *Bêt Dîn*. The latter organization became more and more composed of lay teachers, the Pharisees, while the influence of the priests and their supporters, the Sadducees, was proportionately diminished. Rabbinical sources from this time on expressly report the names of the leaders of the religious Sanhedrin (Aboth 1:4 *et seq.*). First come five pairs (*zugoth*) of teachers, the first of whom took the former high priestly title of nasi (the new high priests had the title *kōhēn gādôl*) and the second the title of *'Āb Bêt Dîn* ("father of the court"; Hagigah 2:2). By about the end of the 1st cen. A.D., the office of nasi became hereditary in the family descended from the famous teacher Hillel, and that of *'Āb Bêt Dîn* ceased to exist.

During the period when Herod was king of Judea (37–4 B.C.), the prestige of the high priest diminished even more. After the end of the Maccabean line, Herod appointed and deposed high priests at will, and the Sanhedrin over which they presided became his tool to use as he pleased. After his death and during the time when one or another of his sons were permitted to appoint high priests, the position of the priests was somewhat better, but they never again became leaders of the people, either in political or religious affairs.

Thus, in the 1st cen. A.D., the two Sanhedrins, the council and the court, existed side by side. The political Sanhedrin was convoked only on special occasions; the religious Sanhedrin was continually supreme in religious affairs. The Mishnah minutely describes the instructions given by the representatives of the rabbinical court to the high priest in regard to

Remains at Beit Shearim, seat of the Sanhedrin in the second century A.D. IIS

his duties on the Day of Atonement (Yoma 1:5).

Typical Proceedings of the Sanhedrins

The historian Josephus gives all the important instances in which the political Sanhedrin took action. He recounts that in 57 B.C., when the kingship in Judea was suspended, Gabinius, the Roman proconsul, divided the country into five councils, thus diminishing the position of Jerusalem as the capital; but by the time of Herod this division had ceased to exist. Herod himself convoked such councils on such occasions as when he presented a case against his sons (*Wars* i.27.1), when he accused the wife of his brother Pheroras (*ibid.* i.29.2), or when he wanted to condemn his oldest son, Antipater (*ibid.* i.32.1).

There is little information about the acts of the religious Sanhedrin, but there are references to a priest's daughter who was condemned to burning (Sanhedrin 7:2) and to women whose bodies were hung up after death because they had been convicted of witchcraft (*ibid.* 6:4). The proceedings of this Sanhedrin, as described in rabbinical literature, were inclined to make a death sentence less likely and acquittal easier. It was always permissible to advance a new argument for acquittal, even after a sentence had been passed; the majority in favor of conviction had always to be greater than that for acquittal. The impression received from these sources is that the religious Sanhedrin very seldom imposed capital punishment. Indeed, one passage declares that a Sanhedrin that inflicted such punishment once in seven years would be called "a Sanhedrin careless of human life"; one teacher went so far as to extend the term to once in 70 years (Makkoth 1:10).

The Trial of Herod

About the year 50 B.C., Herod, who appears here in history for the first time, was brought to trial on a charge of summarily executing a certain Hezekiah and his followers who were "robbers," i.e., revolutionaries. The trial was held before the "Sanhedrin in Jerusalem" (*Wars* i.10; *Ant.* xiv.9); from the nature of the charge, which amounted to manslaughter, this was probably the religious Sanhedrin. Although the trial was brought about by the high priest and Herod's acquittal was ordered by the Roman authorities, the fact that mention is made of the words of the teacher Sameas, who is probably the same as the Nasi Shemaiah, would point definitely to the religious court rather than the political council.

The Trial of Jesus

On the other hand, the trial of Jesus certainly took place before the political Sanhedrin. The accounts of it that are given in the Gospels (Mt 26:57–27:2; Mk 14:53–15:1; Lk 22:54–23:2; Jn 18:12–28) differ as to details, but the main points are sufficiently clear. The trial took place before an assembly summoned by the high priest, and the charges on which Jesus was arraigned were those of advocating the non-payment of tribute to the Roman government (Lk 23:2) and of proclaiming Himself king (*ibid.* and the *titulus* on the cross).

The trial was conducted in a manner entirely contradictory to the regulations of the religious court. It was held at night, on the eve of a festival, and did not extend over two days. It did not take place in the chamber of hewn stone, but was held in the house of the high priest, whither were summoned only those whom the high priest could depend upon to do his will. The mode of execution was a purely Roman one, carried out by Roman soldiers, and not one of the four to which the religious court was limited. It is obvious, therefore, that the trial of Jesus could not have taken place before the religious court; rather His trial was solely the product of a packed high priest's council that dreaded the popularity that Jesus had attained, resented His criticism of the conduct of the temple authorities, and desired to get rid of Him as expeditiously as possible. [A later meeting at daybreak of the entire religious Sanhedrin seems to have been held hastily in their regular council chamber (Lk 22:66, NASB; Mt 27:1; Mk 15:1). In fact, many have understood the above details as illegal proceedings on the part of the religious Sanhedrin rather than as evidence that the political Sanhedrin was the body involved.—Ed. note]

The Trials of Peter

Somewhat less is known about the trials of the disciples of Jesus. The first arrest of Peter and his followers is described in Acts 4. The mention of the high priests would perhaps indicate that the trial was before the political Sanhedrin. Since this had no jurisdiction over religious matters, the defendants were allowed to go, with a warning. But they continued to preach and were again hailed before the council of the high priests, who then convened the Great Sanhedrin, i.e., the full senate of the Israelite nation (Acts 5:21, NEB). This time they were saved by the intervention of the Pharisee Gamaliel, who warned the Sanhedrin that they might possibly be fighting against a work of God (Acts 5:21–41).

The Trial of Stephen

This trial is described in Acts 6 and 7. In this case the charge was blasphemy and of prophesying that the temple would be destroyed and the laws of Moses would be changed. The punishment inflicted on Stephen was death by stoning. All this indicates that the trial took place in the religious Sanhedrin, despite the assertion that it was conducted by the high priest (Acts 7:1). The writer here apparently included only the long and elaborate speech of Stephen and omitted any detailed description of the trial itself.

The Procedure in the Case of Paul

This appears in Acts 21–26. As in the trial of Stephen, the writer quotes Paul's defense but omits details of the procedure. It is possible that Paul may have previously been summoned before the religious courts of several Jewish communities, as he refers to occasions when he was flogged (II Cor 11:24). When he arrived in Jerusalem he was seized by a mob, was rescued by a Roman tribune and kept in protective custody. Eventually he was brought before a political council, headed by the high priest. This body apparently did not find that he was in the class of political offenders, and turned him over to the Roman officials, who returned him to custody. He then "appealed to Caesar" for a further trial (Acts 25:11–12) and was eventually sent to Rome. As in the case of all the acts of the political Sanhedrin, Paul was referred to the Roman authorities to decide his punishment, if any (Acts 25:16). There is not the slightest suggestion that Paul was ever brought before the religious Sanhedrin in Jerusalem.

The End of the Sanhedrins

The great war against Rome (A.D. 66–73) not only destroyed the second temple and reduced the Jews to the status of provincials, but also brought an end to the political Sanhedrin, since the Jews had no political power at all. The leadership fell into the hands of the religious Sanhedrin which, under the direction of Johanan ben Zakkai, now became the supreme authority. It assumed not only the status but also the name of Sanhedrin. In later rabbinical literature this term appears side by side and with the same meaning as the old *Bêt Dîn*, and the Talmudic tractate which describes the ancient court is actually called Sanhedrin. This changeover seems to have been completed by the end of the 1st cen. A.D., as appears from the rabbinic writings. But the term was only a historical one, since the court became more and more an academy discussing the details of the Jewish religious law. The academy considered itself the successor of the Sanhedrin; it retained its titles and its manners; but by the 2nd cen. A.D. the religious Sanhedrin, as such, had followed the political Sanhedrin into oblivion.

Bibliography. A. Büchler, *Das Synedrion in Jerusalem und das grosse Beth-Din in der Quader-kammer des jerusalemischen Tempels*, Wien: A. Hölder, 1902. Sidney B. Hoenig, *The Great Sanhedrin*, New York: Block Pub. Co., 1953. Jacob Z. Lauterbach, "Sanhedrin," JewEnc (1905), XI, 41–44. Eduard Lohse, "*Synhedrion*," TDNT, VII, 860–871. Solomon Zeitlin, "The Political Synedrion and the Religious Sanhedrin," JQR, XXXVI (1945), 109–140.

S. C.

SANSANNAH (săn-săn'*ȧ*). A city in the S part of Judah, near Madmannah (Josh 15:31). It has been identified with Khirbet esh-Shamshaniyat, *c*. nine miles NE of Beer-sheba.

SAPH (săf). A descendant of the *rāphâ*, the progenitor(s) of the giants. He was slain by Sibbechai the Hushathite in an encounter at Gob (II Sam 21:18). In I Chr 20:4 he is called Sippai.

SAPHIR (sā'f*ȧ*r). Spelled Shaphir in the ASV and all newer versions. The name of this city in Judah means "beautiful" or "pleasantness" (Mic 1:11), figuring in the word-play section of Micah's prophecy (1:10–15). A suggested location is Khirbet el-Kôm, *c*. eight miles WNW of Hebron, which dominates the Wadi es-Saffar (an Arabic adaptation of Saphir?).

SAPPHIRA (s*ȧ*-fī'r*ȧ*). The name appears on Jerusalem ossuaries in both Gr. and Aram. forms. In the NT only one Sapphira, the wife of Ananias (*q.v.*), is mentioned (Acts 5:1–11). Like her husband, she was struck dead by divine judgment for lying. Other persons in the early church at Jerusalem were contributing all their proceeds to the common treasury, whereas Sapphira and Ananias, pretending to give the total price from their sale of property, held back a portion by previous mutual agreement.

Their deceit was so severely judged because it was the first offense in the infant Jerusalem church; it served as a warning to all others. It is to be noted that Peter predicted rather than decreed the deaths of Sapphira and her husband. Sapphira may have been judged in the mercy of God and hence taken to heaven, rather than condemned to eternal perdition as is sometimes assumed. The basis for this opinion is Paul's teaching in I Cor 11:29–32 that those guilty of profaning the holy communion table may be punished by illness or even death in order that they may not be condemned along with unbelievers.

T. B. C.

SAPPHIRE. *See* Jewels.

SARA (sâr'*ȧ*). The KJV NT form of Sarah (Heb 11:11). *See* Sarah.

SARAH (sâr'*ȧ*)

1. The later name of Sarai (Heb. *śāray*, the old Semitic feminine form), the principal wife of Abraham (*q.v.*), and the mother of Isaac (*q.v.*). Both Sarah and Sarai mean "princess."

About ten years younger than Abraham, Sarah was his half sister on his father Terah's side (Gen 20:12). She was still considered a very beautiful woman when Abraham took his household to Egypt to escape famine in Canaan (Gen 12:10–11), even though she was already over 65 years of age. He persuaded her to pose as his sister lest the Egyptians kill him to get her, and, whatever her inner feelings, she submitted to her husband's plan. The pharaoh was attracted to her and took her into his harem. Pharaoh returned her, however, when the truth became known, and he sent Abraham and his party away with a strong rebuke (12:12–20). More than 20 years later Abraham again suffered a lapse of faith regarding Sarah and his own safety. In this case Abimelech, the ruler of Gerar, was warned in a dream by God that Sarah was married to Abraham (Gen 20).

While Abraham's actions on these two occasions appear to us to be deliberate subterfuge, his purpose in introducing Sarah as his sister may have been to invoke the special protection which the "sister-wife" status afforded according to the laws then current in Mesopotamia. The Nuzu (*q.v.*) texts demonstrate that in the Hurrian and culturally related societies the bonds of marriage were most solemn when the wife had the simultaneous legal status of sister. But this status, and its consequent safeguard, was not recognized either by the Egyptians or the Philistines.

While in Egypt Abraham had obtained the Egyptian girl Hagar (*q.v.*) to be Sarah's personal slave. Because of her barrenness Sarah despaired of herself giving birth to the heir which God had promised Abraham. Sarah therefore urged her husband to beget a child by Hagar (Gen 16:1–3), following a normal legal expedient frequently attested in Old Babylonian (e.g., the code of Hammurabi, #146, 170, 171; ANET, pp. 172 f.) and Nuzu texts (ANET, p. 220). By law the sonless wife was to provide her husband with a woman, usually a slave, who would bear offspring in the name of her mistress. Sarah also acted within her rights according to common Mesopotamian law in treating Hagar harshly for despising her barren mistress (Gen 16:4; code of Hammurabi, #146). When the pregnant Hagar fled, it took a divine visitation to bring her back to Abraham's household where Ishmael was born (Gen 16:5–15).

When she was 90 Sarai's name was changed to Sarah. At this time and another, she received divine promises that she would bear a son within a year, to become a "mother of nations" (Gen 17:15–17; 18:9–15). On the second occasion Abraham was granted a theophany and asked Sarah to bake some cakes for the divine visitors. Listening from inside the tent door, in unbelief she laughed to herself at the incongruity of the prophecy about her son. The

Phoenician sarcophagi at Byblos. HFV

Lord knew her innermost scoffing attitude, even though she tried to deny it. The rebuke "Is anything too hard for the Lord?" changed her doubting to faith, and her physical vigor was divinely renewed, thus enabling her to conceive (Heb 11:11). The promise was fulfilled in the birth of Isaac (Gen 21:1-7).

During Isaac's weaning feast Sarah noticed Ishmael mocking (Gen 21:9; cf. Gal 4:29). Incensed, she demanded that Hagar and Ishmael be expelled from the family so that Ishmael would not share in Isaac's inheritance. In this Sarah acted contrary to Mesopotamian law (code of Hammurabi, #170, 171), for Abraham had already acknowledged Ishmael as his (legal) son (Gen 17:23-26). It therefore required a special command from God for Abraham to send Hagar and Ishmael away (Gen 21:10-12). *See* Patriarchal Age.

Sarah lived to be 127 years old, the only woman whose age at death is recorded in the Bible. She was buried near Hebron in the cave of Machpelah (*q.v.*), which Abraham purchased for a family sepulcher after her death (Gen 23).

Sarah is named in Isa 51:2 as the one who gave birth to the Israelite nation. In the NT Paul refers to the deadness of Sarah's womb as an obstacle to Abraham's faith (Rom 4:19). He quotes Gen 18:10 with reference to her being the mother of the child of promise (Rom 9:9). Without naming her in Gal 4:21-31, Paul uses Sarah as an illustration in his allegory of the children of the bondwoman and of the free woman: "Hagar's children" are born of the flesh and slaves to the law, while "Sarah's children" are born of the Spirit (i.e., supernaturally) according to the promise.

Peter mentions Sarah as an example of a wife's proper regard for her husband (I Pet 3:6), and in Heb 11:11 she is praised for her faith. Among the Dead Sea Scrolls (*q.v.*) the Genesis Apocryphon gives a detailed description of Sarah's charming beauty.

2. Daughter of Asher (Num 26:46, KJV), spelled Serah in the ASV and all newer versions.

Bibliography. N. Avigad and Y. Yadin, *A Genesis Apocryphon,* Jerusalem: Magnes Press, 1956, col. xx:2-8. Harold J. Ockenga, *Women Who Made Bible History,* Grand Rapids: Zondervan, 1962, pp. 19-28. E. A. Speiser, "The Wife-Sister Motif in the Patriarchal Narratives," *Oriental and Biblical Studies,* Philadelphia: Univ. of Pennsylvania Press, 1967, pp. 63-82. Donald J. Wiseman, *The Word of God for Abraham and To-day,* London: Westminster Chapel, 1959, pp. 13, 15-18.

J. R.

SARAI (sâr'ī). The original name of Abraham's wife. *See* Sarah.

SARAPH (sâr'if). A descendant of Shelah, son of Judah, who had dominion in Moab (I Chr 4:22), possibly governing that country when it was ruled by David or Solomon.

Gold sarcophagus of King Tutankhamen. LL

SARCOPHAGUS (sär-kŏf'*a*-gŭs). A coffin, originally of stone. The Gr. word has the sense of "eating flesh," for coffins of limestone hastened the decomposition of the corpse. Usually, however, sarcophagi were intended to protect and preserve the body, as in the case of the inscribed stone sarcophagus of King Ahiram of Byblos, dated *c.* 1000 B.C. (ANEP #456-459). The Philistines (*q.v.*) apparently made anthropoid pottery coffins with a human face on the lid for some of their dead (ANEP #641). *See* Beth-shan.

Many sarcophagi are known from ancient Egypt, and there the term is applied to coffins of many kinds. The word does not appear in the English Bible, though "coffin" occurs once (Gen 50:26) in connection with the burial preparations for Joseph. The Heb. *'ārôn* means essentially a chest or box, probably of wood. In view of the Egyptian setting, "sarcophagus" may be a possible translation here. If, however, Joseph was prime minister during the 12th Dynasty (1991–1786 B.C.), his "coffin" was very likely a wooden rectangular chest with flat or vaulted lid and four or more battens on its underside. While the most common form of coffin in the Middle Kingdom period was decorated with elaborate painted panels and hieroglyphic texts, the nobility began to use a less gaudy coffin employing fine dark woods or cedar, relieved and accented by narrow bands of gold. Although the anthropoid coffin came into use in Egypt during the 12th Dynasty, it did not become popular until the New Kingdom and later (William C. Hayes, *The Scepter of Egypt:* Part I, New York: Harper, 1953, pp. 310–320). *See* Coffin.

C. E. D.

SARDINE. *See* Jewels.

Remains of an early Christian church built into a corner of the Temple of Artemis at Sardis, symbolizing the triumph of Christianity over paganism there. HFV

Reconstructed monumental entrance to the Roman gymnasium at Sardis. HFV

SARDIS (sär'dĭs). Sardis was located about 50 miles E of Smyrna. The earliest city stood on a 1,000-foot hill five miles S of the Hermus River, the basin of which was the broadest and most fertile of the river valleys of Asia Minor. Sardis commanded the great trade and military road from the Aegean islands to the interior of the Roman provinces of Asia and Galatia. As the city grew it spread northward into the valley of the Hermus, where ruins of great structures of the Roman period may be seen.

The site first achieved greatness as the capital of Lydia (*see* Lud), which with its king Croesus fell to Cyrus of Persia in 546 B.C. Destroyed by earthquake in A.D. 17 (during Roman rule), it was rebuilt by Tiberius and was a thriving city when John addressed the church there (Rev 3:1–6).

Before World War I, H. C. Butler of Princeton excavated at Sardis (1910–14). G. M. A. Hanfmann of Harvard began to excavate there again in 1958. The city of John's day has not yet been laid bare, but John would have known the great temple of Artemis (160–300 feet) with its 78 Ionic columns, each 58 feet high. Begun in the time of Alexander the Great but never finished, it was erected over the 6th cen. B.C. foundations of the temple built by Croesus. In 1962 the archaeologists discovered a large Jewish synagogue dating to the first half of the 3rd cen. A.D. Its wealth and size indicate a rather large and prosperous Jewish community in the early Christian era.

Bibliography. George M. A. Hanfmann, "Excavations at Sardis, 1958," BASOR #154 (1959), pp. 5–35; for subsequent campaigns see BASOR, #157, 162, 166, 170, 174, 177, 182, 186, 191, 203, 206. W. M. Ramsay, *The Letters to the Seven Churches of Asia,* London: Hodder & Stoughton, 1904. Bastian Van Elderen, "Sardis," BW, pp. 497–499. Howard F. Vos, WHG, pp. 397–400.

H. F. V.

SARDITE (sär'dīt). The name ascribed to members of the family of Sered, a son of Zebulun (Gen 46:14; Num 26:26).

Human-headed winged bull from the palace of Sargon
II. LM

SARDIUS. *See* Jewels.

SARDONYX. *See* Jewels.

SAREPTA (sȧ-rĕp'tȧ). The KJV form of Zarephath (*q.v.*), a city located midway between Tyre and Sidon (Lk 4:26). Its present-day name is Sarafand.

SARGON (sär'gŏn). With the single exception of Isa 20:1 the name Sargon (Heb. *sargôn*) was not attested in ancient literature. Because of cuneiform records unearthed since 1843 it is now known that three different Mesopotamian rulers, two of them illustrious in their own way and in their own eras, bore that throne-name (for such it actually was). Since the careers of these two impinge, however slightly, on biblical history, it will be profitable to discuss them.

1. *Sargon* of Agade or Akkad (see Accad), was the first Semitic ruler to reign over all of Mesopotamia. Late Assyrian and Babylonian cuneiform texts record a legend about his origin that is reminiscent of the story of Moses' birth (Ex 1:22–2:10). The mother of Sargon is said to have conceived and borne him in secret, set him in a basket of rushes, and cast him into a river from which Akki, a drawer of water, lifted him out, subsequently to raise him as his son (ANET, p. 119).

On attaining to manhood, Sargon I is known to have become a cunning politician and brilliant military strategist. At first the cupbearer of Urzababa, the last king of Kish, Sargon deposed the latter and then eliminated his only other rival for power, Lugalzaggisi of Uruk (*see* Erech). Transferring his capital from Kish to Akkad, he founded the First Dynasty of Akkad (*c.* 2360–2180 B.C.) over which he ruled for 56 years. His was the first true world empire in history; he subdued all of Sumer as far as the Persian Gulf, and then embarked on a series of conquests that made him a figure of story and legend. The glories of Sargon were recorded in texts up to the time of Nabonidus, almost 2,000 years after his death. The most famous and widespread of the stories concerning his exploits is the *shar tamḫāri* ("King of Battle") epic, according to which Sargon, at the request of Mesopotamian merchants plying their trade in Anatolia, invaded that country to champion their cause.

Comparing the career of this Sargon with the terse account of Gen 10:8-13, some scholars have been tempted to equate him with Nimrod (*q.v.*), though without compelling reasons.

2. *Sargon II* of Assyria was king from 722/1 to 705 B.C. Prior to the discovery and decipherment of his inscriptions, some scholars identified him with his predecessor, Shalmaneser V (*q.v.*), formerly and erroneously called IV. Others equated him with his son and successor, Sennacherib (*q.v.*). Then in 1843 Paul-Emile Botta, the French consul in Mosul, Iraq, began the excavation of Khorsabad, which turned out to be the ancient city of *Dūr-Sharrukēn* ("The Fortress of Sargon," "Sargonsburg"). It is located 12 miles NNE of Mosul on the W bank of the Tigris River across from the ruins of Nineveh. There Botta uncovered the remains of the palace of Sargon II, thereby paving the way for the rediscovery of Sargon himself and his restoration to his rightful place in secular history. The palace area alone consists of more than 25 acres, while the palace is the best preserved of the Assyrian royal edifices.

From 1852 to 1854 Victor Place completed the excavation of Sargon's palace, removing additional important reliefs and sending them down the Tigris to Basra, from there to be exported to the Louvre Museum. In the present century the Iraq Expedition of the Oriental Institute of the University of Chicago under the direction of the late Henri Frankfort did some important further exploration at Khorsabad. Two years after Botta's work, Austen Henry Layard, the pioneer British archaeologist, undertook the excavation of Calah (modern Nimrud), 20 miles SE of Mosul. There he uncovered the imperial residences of several Assyrian kings, that of Sargon among them. As a result of the labors of these and other excavators, a fairly complete résumé of Sargon's life and times may now be sketched.

Not long after the accession of Shalmaneser to the throne of Assyria (727 B.C.), Hoshea (*q.v.*), the last king of Israel, withheld tribute from Assyria and sought to join forces with Egypt for defensive purposes against the common enemy. Hoshea's miscalculations of the relative strength of Assyria and Egypt proved fatal for Israel, however. Egypt, in a weakened condition at this time, could not be expected to offer any real assistance to Hoshea, and so it was that in 724 B.C. Shalmaneser attacked Israel. Meeting with relatively little resistance, the Assyrians occupied the entire land with the exception of the capital city. Well fortified, Samaria managed to withstand the invader for over two years, finally capitulating in 722/1 B.C.

The identity of the actual conqueror of Samaria is still a matter of some dispute. Most scholars take at face value the claim of Sargon as recorded in annalistic reports late in his reign to the effect that he besieged and conquered Samaria (Assyrian *Samerīna*) at the beginning of his rule, deporting 27,290 of its inhabitants in the process (ANET, pp. 284 f.). Others, however, have noted that II Kgs 17:3-6 gives *prima facie* support to Shalmaneser as Samaria's captor, it being unlikely that the phrase "the king of Assyria" in v. 6 refers to a different antecedent than does the same phrase in the preceding verses. Moreover, the Babylonian Chronicle seems to corroborate the biblical account in this regard, for it notes that Shalmaneser destroyed the city of *Sha-ma-ra-in* (Samaria?).

It may be that the solution to this problem lies imbedded in II Kgs 18:10, where the Masoretic Text informs us that "they" (RSV, vocalizing differently, reads "he") took Samaria;

Sargon II and his commander-in-chief. BM

While it is possible that "they" might be simply an indefinite reference to the Assyrian captors, it is also conceivable that Shalmaneser and an associate, perhaps Sargon, are intended. At any rate, Sargon's claim to sole credit for the conquest of Samaria is doubtless exaggerated. (For a sober discussion of this whole problem cf. especially Edwin R. Thiele, *The Mysterious Numbers of the Hebrew Kings,* pp. 121–128.) After Samaria's destruction, the administration of Israel was reorganized and the land was made an Assyrian province (called Samaria) under the control of an Assyrian governor.

Immediately upon his accession to the throne, Sargon was confronted with insurrection and rebellion throughout his vast empire. In 721 B.C. Marduk-apla-iddina (Merodach-baladan, *q.v.*), in league with the Elamites, revolted against him. The revolt was successful and served to encourage dissenters in other parts of Sargon's realm. Marduk-apla-iddina seized power in Babylon and ruled an independent Babylonian state for over ten years. It was not until 710 that Sargon, free at last from troubles in the W, was able to uproot the usurper and drive him from the land, at least for a time.

Meanwhile, in 720 B.C. revolts had broken out in Hamath, Gaza, Arpad, Simirra, Damascus, and Samaria itself. Sargon roundly defeated the rebels of the northern provinces at Qarqar; then marched southward and at Raphia inflicted a severe defeat upon Sib'e, the *turtanu* (Tartan, *q.v.*) of the Egyptian Pharaoh, whose forces had come to the aid of King Hanno of Gaza (ANET, p. 285). II Kgs 17:24 relates the fact that in succeeding years people were deported from Babylon, Hamath, and elsewhere to colonize Samaria, there to mingle with the remnant of the native population and become the Samaritans of later times.

In 717 B.C. Mitâ (Midas), king of the Phrygian Musku in Asia Minor, in collusion with the vassal Hittite state of Carchemish in Syria, rebelled against the hegemony of Sargon. The latter thereupon destroyed Carchemish and deported its population to Assyria. At about the same time Sargon attacked Urartu (*see* Ararat) as well, breaking the power of that already weakened state.

Sargon's preoccupation with northern affairs may have encouraged the southern provinces to make one last attempt to free themselves from the Assyrian yoke. Azuri of Ashdod, who had been promised assistance from the vigorous new leadership of Egypt's 25th Dynasty, revolted against Sargon in 714/3 (ANET, pp. 286 f.). The Egyptian aid did not materialize, however, and Sargon crushed the revolt in 711 (Isa 20:3). Apparently Judah took the advice of Isaiah and his supporters at this point not to concur in Ashdod's rebellion (Isa 20:1–6), for she escaped harm.

The last few years of Sargon's life were spent in relative tranquillity. During this period his building projects proceeded apace, and he turned his attention toward recording his exploits for posterity. He was to meet a violent end, however; in 705 B.C. he was slain during a border skirmish and was buried far from his homeland. Sennacherib, his son, succeeded him on the throne of Assyria.

Bibliography. A. G. Lie, *The Inscriptions of Sargon II, King of Assyria,* Part I: The Annals, Paris, 1929. D. D. Luckenbill, *Ancient Records of Assyria and Babylonia,* 2 vols., Chicago: Univ. of Chicago Press, 1926, 1927. H. R. Moeller, "Sargon of Akkad, Sargon II," BW, pp. 499–508. A. T. Olmstead, "The Text of Sargon's Annals," AJSL, XLVII (1931), 259 ff. H. Tadmor, "The Campaigns of Sargon II of Assur," JCS, XII (1958), 22–40, 77–100.

R. F. Y.

SARID (sâr'ĭd). A border town in the territory of Zebulun (Josh 19:10, 12). It is identified with Tell Shadud, six miles NNE of Megiddo, on the

N edge of the valley of Jezreel, *c.* four miles SW of Nazareth.

SARON (sâr'ŏn). In the KJV the NT form of Sharon. This is the name of the sea coast between Joppa and Caesarea (Acts 9:35). *See* Sharon.

SARSECHIM (sär'sĕ-kĭm). A prince of Babylon who came with Nebuchadnezzar to Jerusalem and who sat at the gate. His title, the Rab-saris (*q.v.*), meant "chief of the eunuchs" (Jer 39:3). The "nebu" of the preceding name should be included as part of this man's name, so that he was called Nebusarsekim (NEB). *See* Samgar; Nergalsharezer.

SARUCH (sâr'ŭk). The KJV NT form of Serug (*q.v.*), who was the father of Nachor and son of Ragau. Thus he was an ancestor of Jesus (Lk 3:35).

SATAN (sā'tán). The Heb. *śāṭān,* "adversary," "accuser," human or angelic (Ps 109:6, ASV, NASB, 29; Num 22:22), and Gr. *Satan(as)* is the leader of fallen spirits (Mt 12:24). More than other angels, Satan "excels in strength" (Ps 103:20; Jude 9), yet is spacially limited (Job 1:7) and can operate only by divine permission (Job 1:12; cf. I Cor 10:13). He dominates all kingdoms of mankind (Lk 4:6), seeking their alienation from God and their destruction (I Pet 5:8). His biblical career covers four successively degenerating stages.

1. While Genesis nowhere names Satan, it does describe a serpent that tempted man in Eden (Gen 3:1; cf. II Cor 11:3). But behind the reptile (Gen 3:14) lay a spiritual personality (witness its ability to speak, 3:1-5, and its assumed equality with men, impossible for mere beasts, 1:28). The primary tempter was Satan (Rom 16:20), "that old serpent" (Rev 12:9).

Satan's prior status is undefined; but Isaiah describes the proud king of Babylon in superhuman terms: "How you have fallen from heaven, O star of the morning [Heb. *hêlēl,* Venus, the morning star; Lat., *lucifer*], son of the dawn" (Isa 14:12, NASB). He is pictured as saying, "I will exalt my throne above the stars of God . . . I will be like the most High" (vv. 13-14). God concludes, "Yet thou shalt be brought down to hell" (v. 15). But the explanation that this is a reference to the literal planet Venus seems to be inadequate, and Satan's attempt to rival God (I Tim 3:6) may be the ultimate point of the comparison (Rev 9:1). Gen 3:1 seems furthermore to date this fall (all was still "very good" in Gen 1:31). Satan's attempt to win over the allegiance of mankind may thus have precipitated his loss of angelic status, for both the serpent and the humans were cursed simultaneously (3:14-19). But while man received hope of reconciliation to God, the tempter was condemned to be trampled and crushed (3:15). *See* Lucifer.

2. The term *śāṭān* appears in Job 1-2, but always as *haśśāṭān* ("the adversary," *q.v.*), not yet a proper noun (cf. Zech 3:1, ASV marg., and NT Gr. *diabolos,* "slanderous, the slander," *see* Devil). This "accuser" (Zech 3:1-2; cf. Rev 12:10; *see* Accuser) had access to heaven, and evolutionary liberalism pictures him as still simply an angel who prosecutes (Millar Burrows, *Outline of Biblical Theology,* Philadelphia: Westminister Press, 1946, p. 125). But though serving (unwittingly) as a tool of providence (Job 42:11; cf. "the spirit" in I Kgs 22:19-22), he was insolent toward God (Job 1:7, 9; 2:5) and slanderous against Job (1:11; 2:4; cf. Edmond Jacob, *Theology of the Old Testament,* New York: Harper, 1958, pp. 70-72). *Śāṭān* (now a personal name, I Chr 21:1) was Israel's implacable enemy.

3. With Christ's incarnation, Satan's dominion (Acts 26:18, NASB) received further restriction. Thwarted in his temptations of Jesus (Mt 4:1-11; Lk 4:1-13), he and his demons suffered defeat by Christ's miracles of healing and exorcism (Mt 12:26-29; Lk 13:11, 16; 22:31-32). Even of Satan's apparent triumph at Calvary (Lk 22:53) Christ said, "Now is the judgment of this world: now shall the prince of this world be cast out" (Jn 12:31; cf. Rev 12:10-11). Believers therefore no longer suffer accusation in heaven, where Christ ever lives to make intercession for us (Heb 2:14-15; 7:25).

Satan still incites people to evil (Acts 5:3; I Cor 7:5; II Cor 2:11) and is able to disguise himself as an angel of light (II Cor 11:14). He continues to hinder Christians (I Thess 2:18), and is still the prince of the power of this terrestrial air (Eph 2:2); but if we resist the devil he will flee from us (Jas 4:7). Satan knows that his time is short (Rev 12:12). *See* Satan, Depths of; Satan, Synagogue of.

4. With the return of Christ, Satan is to be bound, that he "deceive the nations no more, till the thousand years should be fulfilled" (Rev 20:2-3; cf. Isa 24:21-22). His final release will accomplish only the destruction of those he deceives, after which he is cast into the lake of fire forever (Rev 20:9-10).

See Demonology; Devil.

Bibliography. W. Foerster and K. Schäferdiek, "*Satanas,*" TDNT, VII, 151-165. William G. Heidt, *Angelology of the Old Testament,* Washington: Catholic Univ. of America, 1949. Edward Langton, *Essentials of Demonology,* London: Epworth, 1949. Leon Morris, "Satan," NBD, pp. 1145-1147. J. Barton Payne, *Theology of the Older Testament,* Grand Rapids: Zondervan, 1962, pp. 289-295. John H. Raven, *History of the Religion of Israel,* New Brunswick: New Brunswick Seminary, 1933, pp. 612-618. Merrill F. Unger, *Biblical Demonology,* Wheaton: Van Kampen, 1952. Owen C. Whitehouse, "Satan," HDB, IV, 407-412.

J. B. P.

SATAN, DEPTHS OF. This expression appears just once in the NT (Rev 2:24). Its counterpart is "the depths . . . of God" (Rom 11:33), though "the deep things of God" (I Cor 2:10) is similar. "Depths" seems to refer to sinful experience rather than false doctrine, though both false doctrine and seduction to evil deeds are attributed to Jezebel (Rev 2:20). Moreover, the text of Rev 2:24 would suggest that "have . . . this doctrine" refers to the teaching, while "have . . . known the depths" refers to the practice. The victims claimed "the depths" of experience with God, but Christ labels this "the depths of Satan." The doctrine was the germ principle of Gnosticism arguing for a supposedly new, deep, and hidden philosophy of life. But in practice it was the degeneracy of false religion, which lowered the standard of separation between the church and the world by denying the sinfulness of sin and the sacredness of holy things.

H. A. Hoy.

SATAN, SYNAGOGUE OF. There is identity of meaning in the two appearances of this term in the NT (Rev 2:9; 3:9), pointing to a group outside the church. This is implied in the description of the Smyrna church, but clearly stated in the description of the Philadelphia church. The word "synagogue" is the counterpart in Gr. speaking communities for the Heb. word "congregation" (cf. Ex 12:3 in LXX). In rebellion against God it was referred to as "the evil congregation" in the OT (Num 14:27, 35), but by Christ as the "synagogue of Satan." Claiming to be Jews means they were descendants of Abraham according to the flesh. Lacking the spiritual quality to make them true Jews (Rom 2:28–29), they were charged with lying. Evidence of this lack was their open and determined opposition to the church, opposing its doctrines by blasphemy, its progress by hindrance, and its very existence by persecution.

H. A. Hoy.

Gibeah, home of Saul. HFV

SATISFACTION. *See* Atonement; Propitiation.

SATYR. *See* Animals, II. 35.

SAUL (sôl)

1. Saul or Shaul of Rehoboth, one of the early kings of Edom (Gen 36:37–38; I Chr 1:48–49).

2. The son of Kish of the tribe of Benjamin, the first king of Israel. Since the days of Moses God had governed Israel through the priests and judges specially endowed with power and ability. When Samuel, last of the judges, became old, the people demanded a king that they might be like the nations around them. Their demand was a repudiation both of God and of a walk by faith. They desired to imitate the nations not simply in government but in spirit, depending on their own might and power rather than on Yahweh (I Sam 8). In acceding to their request God provided the Israelites with exactly the kind of king they desired. Saul was a man of courage and strength, a man of great ability as an administrator and a warrior. He was natural man at his best, but he had a fatal flaw. Saul acted not in the power and wisdom of the Lord but in dependence on his own judgment and strength; this led to eventual disaster.

Saul's first appearance is as a young country-man from the city of Gibeah. In searching for his father's straying asses, he encountered Samuel, who anointed him and prophesied that he would be king of Israel (I Sam 9:1–10:16). Later, Samuel called the tribes together at Mizpeh to cast lots in the ancient manner. The lot fell upon Saul, and Samuel presented him as the king God had chosen (I Sam 10:17–25).

Very shortly Saul was put to the test; Nahash, king of Ammon, besieged Jabesh-gilead, and the city sent for help. Saul proved himself a king indeed; he gathered an army and, surprising Nahash, destroyed the Ammonites. After the battle all Israel acknowledged Saul as their king and held a great celebration at Gilgal (I Sam 11). For a description of Saul's rustic palace-citadel which he built in his home town, *see* Gibeah.

Saul spent his entire reign defending Israel against the encroachments of the surrounding nations (I Sam 14:47–48, 52). Yet at the end of his life, Israel was more harassed by her enemies, especially the Philistines, than she had been at the beginning.

Scripture mentions only the critical events of Saul's reign which determined the course of his career. His first great failure occurred at the beginning of war against the Philistines (I Sam 13). His son Jonathan provoked the war by a daring raid against the Philistine garrison at Geba. As the Philistine armies gathered, Saul tried to rally his people too. But fear caused the Israelites to desert, until Saul was left with only a handful at his headquarters in Gilgal. Impatient because Samuel delayed in coming to seek God's favor, Saul performed a perfunctory sacrifice and was ready to start his campaign when Samuel finally appeared. Samuel pronounced God's judgment: "Thou hast not kept the commandment of the Lord thy God . . . now thy kingdom shall not continue" (I Sam 13:13-14). Although the ensuing battle was a success, primarily because of the boldness of Jonathan near Michmash, no lasting peace resulted from it.

Saul was evidently a stern disciplinarian of others, if not of himself. During the rout of the Philistines Jonathan unknowingly disobeyed the king's orders by eating. Saul would have executed his own son had it not been for the intercession of his army (I Sam 14:24-45).

Saul's first great failure was one of usurping the priestly office; his second was outright disobedience (I Sam 15). Commanded by God to destroy all the Amalekites, Saul won a crushing victory, then failed to carry out fully God's instructions by sparing Agag the king and the best of the animals. Samuel again came as God's spokesman of judgment. The prophet brushed aside Saul's excuses that he had saved the spoil because of pressure by the people and that he intended to sacrifice it all to the Lord: "Behold, to obey is better than sacrifice. . . . Because thou hast rejected the word of the Lord, he hath also rejected thee from being king" (I Sam 15:22-23). Samuel's next act was to anoint Saul's successor, David (I Sam 16).

The rest of Saul's reign is tragic. The king drifted farther and farther from God, becoming ever more despondent and fearful. There is little question that he was mentally ill. He became progressively worse, subject to periods of blackest depression (I Sam 16:14; 19:9); yet he refused to humble himself before God. He realized that God must have provided a successor and became jealous of any rival. David, Israel's hero after the defeat of Goliath, was the special object of his enmity and fear. Saul sought to kill David, pursued him as an outlaw, and eventually drove him from the kingdom though he was now his son-in-law (I Sam 18-20). Because the high priest Ahimelech had aided David, Saul had the whole priestly family at Nob slaughtered (I Sam 21-22). Although David twice spared Saul's life, the king failed to recognize in this the warning of God and continued on his way to final destruction (I Sam 24, 26).

Saul's reign ended as it began, in battle; but what a difference! The young king went forth to victory; the old king, discredited and rejected, went out to death and defeat. In desperation before his last battle Saul sought help in witchcraft, though in better days he had driven such practices from the kingdom (I Sam 28). On the eve of the battle he appealed to the witch of Endor for some word of hope. But Samuel, dead for many years, appeared to pronounce Saul's doom: "Tomorrow shalt thou and thy sons be with me" (I Sam 28:19).

The next day Saul met the Philistines on the slopes of Mount Gilboa, and there he and his sons died. Wounded and unwilling to be captured and tortured by the enemy, Saul fell upon his own sword. The Philistines hung his body on the wall of Beth-shan. The men of Jabesh-gilead rescued it, repaying by their brave act the ruler whose first kingly act had been to rescue them (I Sam 31).

David, who had never lost his love for the king, grieved over this man who might have been so great and fell so far short, and chanted a lament: "Your beauty, O Israel, is slain on your high places! How have the mighty fallen! . . . Saul and Jonathan, beloved and pleasant in their life, and in their death they were not parted; they were swifter than eagles, they were stronger than lions. O daughters of Israel, weep over Saul" (II Sam 1:19, 23-24, NASB).

3. The Heb. name of the apostle Paul (*q.v.*).

P. C. J.

SAVE. *See* Salvation; Saviour.

SAVIOUR. The Gr. word *sōtēr,* "saviour," "deliverer," "preserver," was employed widely and used of the gods (Zeus, Asclepius), of the divinities in the mystery religions (Serapis, Isis), of philosophers (Epicurus), of rulers and deserving men (Nero). In the OT it is used of men such as judges (Jud 2:16; 3:9; 12:3; Neh 9:27) in the sense that these men were instruments of God for salvation. Otherwise, the OT is emphatic that God is the only Saviour and man's salvation is vain (Isa 43:11; 45:21; Ps 60:11). Messiah is also spoken of as Saviour in the OT (Zech 9:9; Isa 49:6, 8).

In the NT God the Father is designated Saviour in that He provided salvation by sending His Son (Lk 1:47, 67-69; I Tim 1:1; 2:3; 4:10). But generally it is Christ who is spoken of as the Saviour. Although He never used the word of Himself, others did freely (Jn 4:42; Acts 5:31; Eph 5:23; I Jn 4:14). *See* Salvation.

Theologically, the person of the Saviour required the union in one person of Deity and humanity (Rom 1:3-4) and involved the kenosis (*q.v.*) or emptying of Christ (Phil 2:6-7) and the impeccability, or inability to sin, of the Person (II Cor 5:21; Heb 4:15).

C. C. R

SAVORY MEAT. *See* Food.

SAVOUR. The OT translates *rēaḥ* "smell," "savor," "fragrance," and *niḥôaḥ,* "sweetness" (once, Ezr 6:10). Some 36 times the two words stand together and are translated by the expression "sweet savor."

The associations of this latter expression are sacrificial, as noted in Gen 8:21. The explanatory phrase, "a sweet savor," is attached to descriptions of the burnt offering. S. H. Kellogg (*Expositor's Bible,* Leviticus, pp. 50 ff.) argues that since the burning of the sacrifice followed the killing of the animal, the fire was not appropriate as a symbol of God's punitive wrath against sin, nor was there any thought of expiation in the cereal offering which was burnt. Kellogg concludes, "We must hold, therefore, that the burning can only mean in the burnt offering that which alone it can signify in the meal offering; namely, the ascending of the offering in consecration to God, on the one hand; and, on the other, God's gracious acceptance and appropriation of the offering." So the pleasing fragrance of the meat, wine, and cereal thus consumed had its symbolic significance.

The fuller implications are seen in Paul's passing remark in Eph 5:2: the fragrance of love in the Christian life is like the fragrance of the loving sacrifice of Christ in our stead, "an offering and a sacrifice to God for an odor of a sweet smell" (ASV). So in Rom 12:1 the consecration of the Christian's personality is acceptable to God. The whole burnt offering of the Levitical ritual spoke of the perfect obedience of the great sacrifice to which it pointed. Also, His perfect obedience is our one perfect example of what consecration to God really is.

In II Cor 2:14–16, the imagery is probably not sacrificial. The human vessel in whom Christ dwells is the instrument of releasing the fragrance of the knowledge of Christ among those who are being saved and among those who are perishing (v. 15, NASB).

The word "savor" also refers to taste (Mt 5:13), smell (Joel 2:20), and figuratively, to reputation (Ex 5:21).

W. B. W.

SAW. Saw (Heb. *m^egērâ*) is mentioned in II Sam 12:31; I Kgs 7:9 (along with Heb. *gārar,* "to saw") and I Chr 20:3, and in Isa 10:15 (Heb. *maśśôr*). A Gr. verb *prizō,* "to saw," is used only in Heb 11:37.

Saws usually consisted of flint knives with irregular edges until the Iron Age when iron saw blades were introduced, although bronze blades with wooden handle were used during the 18th Dynasty in Egypt. Saws were used for cutting stones and wood. The stone-cutting technique likely involved the use of water and of sand as an abrasive.

David probably put the captive Ammonites *to* the saw and other tools as laborers (II Sam 12:31; I Chr 20:3, RSV, NEB), not "under saws" as in the KJV. Forced labor is described here rather than torture. The allusion in Heb 11:37 to those "sawn asunder" has not been identified with other historical information. A Jewish tradition relates that the prophet Isaiah was sawn apart as he hid in a hollow tree during the reign of Manasseh. This story is not necessarily related to Heb 11:37, however.

W. R. L. McL.

SCAB. *See* Diseases.

SCABBARD, SHEATH. *See* Armor.

SCAFFOLD. The bronze platform (NASB) on which Solomon stood and kneeled (II Chr 6:13). Because Heb. *kiyyōr* usually means a cooking pot or basin, it was probably round.

SCALES. The Hebrews were allowed to eat only that fish which had both fins and scales (Lev 11:9–12; Deut 14:9–10).

The scales of "Leviathan" (*q.v.*) served as strong shields or armor (Job 41:15), suggesting this was a crocodile. In Isa 40:12, the reference is to the yard or beam from which the scales hang down. This same word, Heb. *peles,* is translated "balance" in Prov 16:11.

SCALL. *See* Diseases.

SCALP. The crown of the head or the pate (Ps 68:21, Heb. *qodqōd;* cf. Gen 49:26; Job 2:7; Ps 7:16; etc.). The American Indian custom of taking scalps as trophies of war was not practiced in the ancient Near East. Instead, the Egyptians cut off the hands of their defeated enemies and counted these (ANEP #319, 340, 348), while the Assyrians mutilated prisoners and decapitated conquered kings and hung the heads in public view (ANET, p. 291; ANEP #361, 375, 451). David gave to King Saul the foreskins of 200 Philistines whom he killed, and brought the head of Goliath to Jerusalem (I Sam 18:27; 17:54).

SCAPEGOAT. *See* Azazel; Festivals; Day of Atonement.

SCARLET. *See* Colours.

SCENT. In Hos 14:7 Heb. *zēker* (KJV, "the scent thereof") should be translated "his renown," as in the NASB, in keeping with the meaning of a remembrance or a memorial (cf. Ps 9:6; Ex 3:15). Heb. *rêaḥ* describes smell, odor, or fragrance (Job 14:9; Jer 48:11; Gen 27:27).

SCEPTER. Often ornate, a king's rod or mace used as a symbol of royal authority. The word *shēbeṭ* more often denotes ordinary rods (e.g., for punishing slaves, Ex 21:20; for numbering sheep, Lev 27:32; shepherd's rod, Ps 23:4; Mic 7:14; for disciplining children, Prov 10:13; 22:15; flail, Isa 28:27) than the symbol of kingship. It is also a frequent term for the unit or tribe governed. *See* Tribe.

Breaking a scepter pictures the downfall of him who wields it (Isa 14:5). This is the picture Ezekiel gives to the princes of Israel (Ezk 19:1, 11–14) and which Amos prophesies concerning her neighbors (Amos 1:5, 8).

Gen 49:10 and Num 24:17 look forward to the establishment of kingship in Israel, and the term "scepter" acquires Messianic significance (*see* Shiloh). Heb 1:8 (the only place "scepter" occurs in the NT) applies Ps 45:6 directly to Christ as the Son who rules with a scepter of righteousness. The Roman soldiers placed a crown of thorns on His head and a reed instead of a scepter in Jesus' hand to mock Him as the King of the Jews (Mt 27:29).

The form *shar^ebîṭ,* influenced by Aramaic, occurs only in Est 4:11; 5:2; 8:4. Heb. *m^eḥō-*

qēq, formerly rendered "lawgiver," is now taken to mean a ruler's staff or scepter in Gen 49:10; Num 21:18; Ps 60:7; 108:8 (RSV, NASB).

D. P. B.

SCEVA (sē'vȧ). A Jewish high priest at Ephesus whose seven sons attempted to cast out a demon in the name of Jesus. Instead, they were wounded by it and had to flee humiliated and naked. God used this experience to turn many people of Ephesus unto Himself (Acts 19:11-20). Since he lived in Ephesus and had a Gr. name, Sceva was probably not related in any way to the official high priestly family in Jerusalem. He seems to have adopted the title of high priest in order to impress the superstitious pagan (A. F. Walls, "Sceva," NBD, p. 1149).

SCHIN (shĭn). The 21st letter of the Heb. alphabet, represented by *sh* in English. Another sibilant a variation of this letter is *sin,* represented in English by *ś.* The schin (or 21st) stanza of Ps 119, the great acrostic or alphabetic psalm, is contained in verses 161-168. The letter *schin* also came to represent the numeral 300. *See* Alphabet.

SCHISM. *See* Heresy.

SCHOOL. The only place this word occurs in the Bible is Acts 19:9, where Paul is said to have left the synagogue in Ephesus and continued his ministry in the "school of one Tyrannus." The word comes from Gr. *scholē,* meaning leisure, and indicates a place where men would take the time to listen to learned discussions. It was not what we usually think of as a school, so perhaps the rendering "lecture hall" of the NEB is better.

See Education; Schools, Hebrew.

SCHOOLMASTER. *See* Education; Schools, Hebrew; Occupations: Schoolmaster.

SCHOOLS, HEBREW. Although there is no trace of schools for public instruction in ancient Israel, religious instruction of children was a responsibility laid upon parents personally (Gen 18:19; Deut 6:7). Reading and writing with some mathematics apparently were also a part of the instruction given in the home (Deut 6:9; 11:20). Some provision was also made for public religious instruction at the time of the great festivals, which were in themselves means of such instruction (Deut 31:10-13; 31:19, 30; 32:1-43; Neh 8:1-8, 18). Much business and most legal actions were pursued in public places, the gate of the city, and the streets of the villages, and thereby provided constant instruction for the people through the process of observation.

At a later time the prophets assisted in religious instruction of the people through public preaching. References to bands of prophets at

Qumran Scriptorium where many of the Dead Sea Scrolls were copied

Ramah under Samuel and possibly at Gibeah, though referred to as schools of the prophets, are not to be thought of in the same sense as the later scribal colleges which characterized Judaism. They were rather occasioned by the decline of the priesthood under Eli and his sons and again during the monarchy (I Sam 10:5,10; 19:20; II Kgs 2:3,5,7,15; 4:1; 9:1) and the resulting need for public religious instruction. These associations of the prophets are not to be thought of as monastic but actually existed for the very purpose of bringing about a greater religious influence upon their times. There must have been some teaching and training in connection with them, but nothing like a formal curriculum. It is to be noted, however, that the cultivation of music may have resulted from these activities of the prophets (I Sam 10:5).

Probably in the time of Ezra religious instruction came to be a scholastic endeavor among the Jews (Ezr 7:10). Associated with the rise of the synagogues and other post-Exilic institutions, elementary education in a scholastic framework was to become compulsory as revealed in the Talmud (Bab. Bath. 21, *a*). Theoretically, the parent was still responsible for the education of the children; but, practically, all the father did in all probability was teach his sons the Shema (Deut 6:4-5), turning the more technical subjects over to the elementary school when the boy was five or six years of age. The education of daughters remained almost entirely the responsibility of the mother since the rabbis did not approve the same amount of instruction for girls as for boys. In addition to domestic duties girls were taught the written but not the oral law.

Tradition testifies to the existence of a school whenever there were as many as 25 children to be taught or 120 families resided. It was also expected that an additional teacher woud be provided for each increase of 25 students. It was forbidden to a family to send its children to schools other than those of its own town, apparently with the intention of assuring support for the local school and thereby lifting the standard of education.

In general the elementary school was attached to the synagogue, and quite commonly the teacher of the school was a minister of the synagogue. The salary of the teacher was provided by the congregation, and only under very rare circumstances was it permitted that he receive fees from the parents of the students which he taught. Other expenses were met by voluntary contributions. The teacher had a socially respectable though humble position and was entitled to be addressed as "Rabbi" by his pupils. No teacher was employed who was not a married man. In matters of discipline, the teacher was authorized to punish the offending student with a strap but never with a rod. If the teacher were ineffective or inadequate, he could be removed from his position, and nothing was valued more than experience in the securing of such a person for a school. The teacher had as much responsibility to provide moral education as to impart information.

The school day was rather uniformly limited to the hours between 10:00 A.M. and 3:00 P.M. except for the summer months, during which the period of daily instruction was shortened to four hours because of the intense heat.

Ordinarily the teacher sat cross legged on a low platform with a rack before him which held the scrolls to be used in the teaching of the day. Students sat on the floor or ground in a half-circle facing the teacher. Much of the instruction was carried on in question and answer form. When the teacher had spoken about the subject, the students were permitted to ask questions; and often the reverse process was employed by which the teacher raised the question and answers were suggested by the pupil.

Attendance in such schools for boys six to 16 years of age (cf. II Tim 3:15) became compulsory *c.* 75 B.C., with the exception of the very rich who employed slaves and others as tutors for their children (*see* Occupations: Schoolmaster). Although it is thought to be an exaggeration, the Jewish legend which says that Jerusalem possessed 480 such schools at the time of its destruction gives some indication of the importance placed on education by Jews in Greco-Roman times.

The beginning student was confronted with an alphabet which was taught by drawing letters on a board until the child remembered them. The child pointed to words as he learned to spell them, and he had also to learn to pronounce the words reverently and correctly. By NT times the Heb. language, with which training in the school began, was strange to the student because at home he spoke Aramaic. Hebrew was primarily for the synagogue, but the teacher taught the student to identify individual words of Scripture passages that had already been memorized at home. The Gr. language of the market place, which many Jews could use to one degree or another, was not taught in the synagogue schools.

The book of Leviticus was the place of beginning in the Scriptures, probably because it was believed necessary for every Jew to know its contents in order to regulate his life acceptably to God. After Leviticus the other books of the Pentateuch were studied. Following this study came the Prophets, and next the Hagiographa (Psalms and other remaining books of the OT). By the age of ten more advanced students had the school day divided into two sections, studying the OT and the Mishna. The Mishna was reduced to writing only about A.D. 200; but in oral form it was subject matter for students long before that time. By the age of 15 the study of the Talmud was added, to make a threefold division of emphasis in the school day for such a student.

After learning to read, the beginning student was introduced to writing, probably in both Heb. and Aramaic. Some work in mathematics was also given. The study of foreign languages had even been declared unlawful and therefore was not a part of the curriculum. In spite of the admonition of fathers to teach their boys to swim, gymnastic exercises were banned, no doubt because of the heathen emphases and practices associated with them.

There were higher schools, scribal colleges which were available to the gifted student. The principal schools of this description were located in Jerusalem (before A.D. 70) and Babylon, although there were similar institutions in some other foreign cities inhabited by Jews. Famous theological teachers attracted their students from great distances. In addition to theology, the colleges of Babylon developed other sciences and were felt by Eastern Jews to be equal, if not superior, to those of Palestine. As a whole, however, the great teachers were at Jerusalem. In their work they treated the written law, the oral traditions, and the interpretations of other scholars. These were the teachers who came to set the standard for Jews everywhere. At the time of the NT the best known of these great teachers were Hillel and Shammai, who were contemporaries of Herod the Great. The name of the famous Gamaliel (*q.v.*), who was a grandson of Hillel, is associated with Paul. Much of the teaching of these great men was carried on in public in the porches and chambers of the temple, having thereby an even wider and more significant effect.

See Education.

Bibliography. Nathan Drazin, *History of Jewish Education from 515 B.C.E. to 220 C. E.*, Baltimore: Johns Hopkins, 1940. K. A. Keith, *The Social Life of a Jew in the Time of Christ*, 3rd ed. rev., London: Church Missions to Jews, 1929, pp. 46–56. John A. Maynard, *A Survey of Hebrew Education*, Milwaukee: Morehouse Pub. Co., 1924.

H. L. D.

SCIENCE. The word is not used in the English Bible in the modern sense of the term, but occurs in two places in the KJV (Dan 1:4; I Tim 6:20). In both cases it has the Old English meaning of knowledge in the broader sense. Dan 1:4 renders the Heb. *maddā'*, which usually (II Chr 1:10–12; Dan 1:17) is translated "knowledge" in conjunction with the terms "wisdom" and "learning." In Eccl 10:20 (KJV) it is translated "thought"; but the NASB, following K-B, renders it "bedchamber" in the sense that it signifies a place of sexual knowledge. I Tim 6:20 renders the Gr. *gnōsis*, which is here translated "knowledge" by all modern translations (ASV, NASB, RSV, Berkeley NEB). It is uniformly translated "knowledge" the other 28 times in the NT.

Paul is warning against "oppositions of knowledge (science) which is falsely so called," i.e., against a false not a true knowledge. He opposes the so-called higher or esoteric knowledge which the false teachers claimed they possessed in distinction from others. This is an incipient form of Gnosticism (*gnōsis*), springing from a native spirit of scientism delving into the areas of religion and philosophy (G. van Groningen, *First Century Gnosticism: Its Origins and Motifs*, Leiden: Brill, 1967). The tragedy of this false knowledge which opposes the true knowledge of Christianity is that "some have professed" it "and thus gone astray from the faith" (I Tim 6:21, NASB).

See Gnosticism; Know, Knowledge.

G. W. K.

SCOFF. The Heb. word *qālas* translated "scoff" in the KJV means to hold in contempt, to deride, as the Babylonians are said to scoff at the kings who dared stand in their path (Hab 1:10). The word is also translated "mock" (II Kgs 2:23; Ezk 22:4–5), and "derision" (Ps 44:13; 79:4; Jer 20:8). It contains more the idea of despising the worth of another than of treating lightly.

SCOFFER. The Gr. word *empaiktēs*, translated "scoffer" in II Pet 3:3 (KJV) and "mocker" in Jude 18, means to treat as a child, to take lightly as though of no account, to refuse to take seriously. The same root word is uniformly translated "mock" in the KJV (e.g., Mt 2:16; 20:19; Lk 18:32; 22:63; 23:11, 36), and occasionally as "ridicule" (Lk 14:29, NASB) or "tricked" (Mt 2:16, RSV).

SCORN, SCORNER. An expression used especially in Psalms and Proverbs to describe the man who is abusive, sarcastic, and the opposite of happy (Ps 1:1), or one who is foolish rather than wise (Prov 1:22). Such a person refuses advice and suggestions from others, and although he may be punished (Prov 19:25; 22:10), he continues his quarrelsome ways. A scorner will be despised for his proud arrogance (Prov 21:24); he is an abomination to men (Prov 24:9) and will bring upon himself the scorn of God (Prov 3:34). Scorners were ridiculed and often friendless (Job 16:20). The enemies of Nehemiah tried to frighten and trick him so he would be scorned by those he led (Neh 6:13). To scorn an enemy meant complete defeat or devastation, either by man or at the hand of God.

A. W. W.

SCORPION. *See* Animals, IV. 29.

SCOURGE. The Heb. verb *nākâ*, "to smite," also conveys the sense of "to beat or scourge" (Hiphil). The nouns *shôṭ* and *shōṭēṭ* signify a whip or scourge. The scourge was usually a whip of thongs used to inflict punishment. It consisted of a handle to which leather cords or thongs were attached. These were sometimes knotted or weighted with pieces of metal. Scourging could also consist of a beating with "rods," the apostle Paul thus distinguishing between being beaten with "forty stripes" (the whip) and "beaten with rods" (II Cor 11:23–25).

The Mosaic law authorized scourging as punishment for certain offenses and prescribed its use, limiting it to 40 stripes (Deut 25:1–3). Its familiarity in Israel is seen from Rehoboam's threat (I Kgs 12:11), and later from its customary use by the Jewish religious authorities and synagogue (Mt 10:17; Acts 5:40; 22:19).

Examples of scourging under Roman law are found in the NT (Gr. *mastigóō; mastízō; phragellóō*). Christ was scourged, as was the custom, before His crucifixion by Pilate (Jn 19:1). The "stripes" inflicted on the suffering Servant of the Lord foretell the whiplashes received by Jesus (Isa 53:5; I Pet 2:24). Scourging was frequently used to obtain confessions from the accused (Acts 22:24), but was illegal to inflict upon a Roman citizen (Acts 22:25–29).

Figuratively, "scourge" may refer to divine national punishment (Josh 23:13; Isa 10:26), the "lash" of the tongue (Job 5:21), or calamity (Job 9:23).

See Beating; Crime and Punishment; Punishment.

H. E. Fr.

SCREECH OWL. *See* Night Monster.

SCRIBE. In the OT the scribe (Heb. *sōphēr*) was originally one who took a count, a muster officer (II Chr 26:11; II Kgs 25:19; cf. Gen 41:49; II Sam 24:10). As a royal official or "secretary" with cabinet status (II Sam 8:17; I Kgs 4:3; II Kgs 18:18), such a scribe might serve as the state treasurer (II Kgs 12:10). In the NT Gr. *grammateus* was one who could write numbers and the letters (*gramma*) of the alphabet, hence, a secretary or clerk. As such he might be a high official, e.g., the "townclerk" of Ephesus (Acts 19:35).

The importance of the law of Moses stimulated its study and transmission in Israel. At first, this was done by the priests. Ezra was a priest but also an early scribe (Ezr 7:6) who studied and taught the law to Israel (Ezr 7:11). In this manner, the religious and civil law was applied to the lives of the people, and at the same time the interpretations and decisions of the scribes became oral law and tradition themselves.

At times the scribe seemed to be a mere secretary to write a letter (Ezr 4:8), whereas at other times he was an inscriber of Scripture like Baruch (Jer 36:26, 32; cf. v. 4). Therefore, a scribe could take dictation, copy, study, interpret, and teach Scripture (Jer 8:8–9).

After the Exile and the end of the prophets, the law assumed more prominence. The influence of the scribes as teachers and interpreters of the law increased accordingly. By the 2nd cen. B.C. they were recognized as constituting an honored profession (I Macc 7:12; Sir 39:1–11). In the modern sense they were the religious scholars or theologians. Such a man is sometimes called in the NT a *nomikos*, "lawyer" (Mt 22:35; Lk 10:25; etc.), or *nomodidaskalos*, "teacher of the law" (Acts 5:34, NASB; I Tim 1:7). Paul's use of the word "scribe" in I Cor 1:20 implies an expert in the law. Thus "lawyer" is an exact synonym for "scribe," and the two terms are never found together.

During the time of Christ the scribes exerted a powerful religious influence as teachers, and because of their ability to make judicial decisions based on scriptural exegesis, occupied important positions in the Sanhedrin (Mt 16:21; 26:3). In the latter capacity they played a major role in bringing on the crucifixion of Jesus (Mk 14:43; 15:1). They and the Pharisees (*q.v.*), to whose party they mainly belonged (Mk 2:16, NASB; Acts 23:9), usually opposed Jesus (Mt 7:29) because He exposed their traditions and the false exegesis they used in order to preserve a legal system. Later they persecuted the apostles (Acts 4:5) and Stephen (Acts 6:12) for the same reason.

However, a few of them followed Jesus (Mt 8:19). Others helped defend Paul's position against that of the Sadducees (Acts 23:9). Converted scribes would be able to use their knowledge of the Word of God to "bring forth out of his treasure things new and old" (Mt 13:52; cf. 23:34).

The most famous scribes of Jewry were the great teachers, such as Hillel, Shammai, and Gamaliel I (Acts 5:34; *see* Gamaliel). These lived in Jerusalem at the time of Christ's birth and shortly thereafter. Many believe that, having studied at the feet of Gamaliel (Acts 22:3), the apostle Paul had been a scribe and a member of the Sanhedrin (*q.v.*) before his conversion. According to Acts 26:10–11 he seems to have served in criminal cases as a judge appointed by the high priests, the ruling members of the Sanhedrin.

E. B. R.

In the time of Christ there were scribes all over the land of Palestine, for Luke speaks of scribes as teachers of the law "who had come

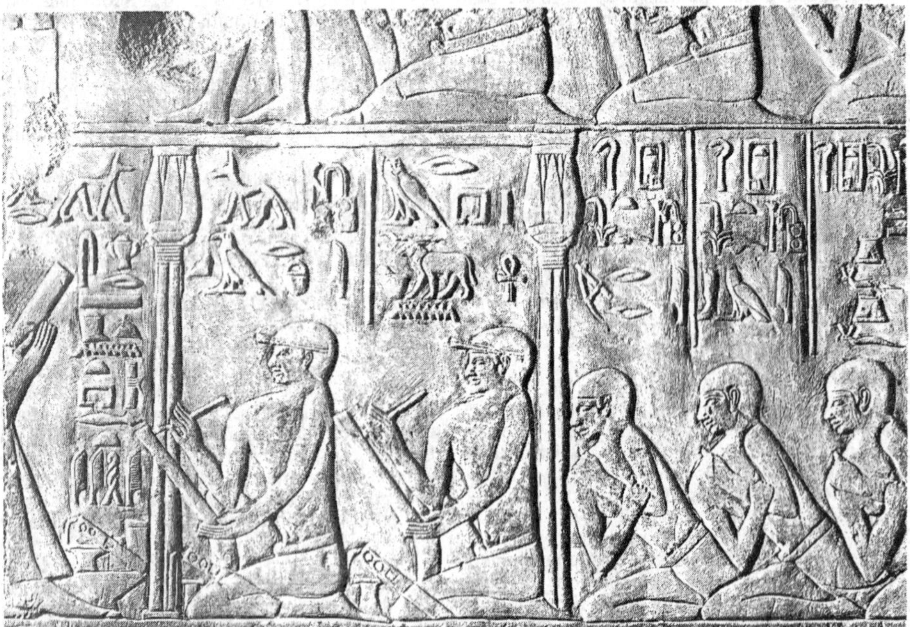

Scribes portrayed in the tomb of Mereruka at Sakkara, Egypt, third millennium B.C. LL

from every village of Galilee and Judea and from Jerusalem" (5:17, RSV). Also there were scribes among the Dispersion. Babylonian scribes in subsequent centuries put into writing the great rabbinic formulations known as the Talmud.

The scribes contributed to the ongoing of Judaism in several ways. First of all, they preserved the law. They were scribes in the literal sense and gave much of their time to copying and transmitting the OT Scriptures. In doing this they invented a number of counting devices to guarantee the preservaton of the authentic Heb. text. Beyond this, however, was their extreme concern to uphold the oral law—the many unwritten legal decisions that touched on every phase of daily life. They adhered strictly to these traditions and lifted them above the written law; for this they were severely reprimanded by Jesus (Mk 7:1-13).

The scribes also taught the law. As doctors of the law they seated themselves as teachers in the temple and in the synagogues (Lk 2:46). They were supposed to teach without pay. Rabbi Zadok said: "Make the knowledge of the law neither a crown in which to glory nor a spade with which to dig." But in actual practice the scribes undoubtedly received, indirectly at least, fees for their services. This perhaps is implied in passages like Mt 10:10 and I Cor 9:3-18; certainly Jesus condemned the scribes for their greed (Mk 12:38-40; Lk 16:14; 20:47).

Finally, the scribes acted as judges of the law. They were reputed to be the true interpreters of the law. Their traditional legal interpretations were known as *Halachah,* as distinguished from their religious devotional instructions known as *Haggadah.*

The scribes were granted extraordinary respect from the people. They were honored with and took pride in the title "rabbi," meaning "my lord" (Mt 23:7). As teachers they were to be accorded more honor than that received by parents. It was said: "The honor of thy teacher must surpass the honor bestowed on thy father; for son and father are both in duty bound to honor the teacher." They dressed in long, flowing robes and always desired the places of eminence (Mt 23:5-6; Mk 12:38-39; Lk 20:46). Jesus did not contest their authority but spoke against their example (Mt 23:2-3).

N. R. L.

See Occupations: Doctor, Lawyer, Secretary; Rabbi; Writing.

Bibliography. Matthew Black, "Scribe," IDB, IV, 246-248. Joachim Jeremias, *Jerusalem in the Time of Jesus,* Philadelphia: Fortress, 1969, pp. 233-245, 379-380.

SCRIP. Gr. *pēra* is translated "scrip" in KJV; "wallet" in ASV: "bag" in RSV; "pack" in NEB. It was used to refer to the provision bag shepherds carried with them (I Sam 17:40). The word commonly referred to a traveler's bag in which clothes or provisions for a journey were taken. In the instructions for their preaching tours to the Twelve and later to the Seventy, Jesus forbade taking such a bag with them (Mt 10:10; Mk 6:8; Lk 9:3; 10:4; cf. 22:35-36). They were to place their full trust in God in carrying out their commissions. Deissmann (LAE, pp. 108-110), citing a Syrian inscription of a pagan priest begging on behalf of his goddess, gave it the specialized meaning of a begging bag in which gifts for pagan temples were collected. According to this view, Jesus was forbidding His disciples to beg their support as did the pagan priests and traveling teachers.

F. P.

SCRIPTURE. *See* Bible. The term "scripture" is derived from Lat. *scriptura,* "a writing," and is used to render the Gr. *graphē,* "a writing, thing written," or (in one case, Dan 10:21) the Heb. *k^etāb.* Almost invariably this word occurs with the definite article "the" (thus: "the scripture"—*hē graphē,* indicating the authoritative written matter of the Bible itself). The term *hakkātūb,* "that which was written," is often (as in Josh 1:8) used to refer to the text of the Torah as constituting a text of final and binding authority.

In the NT *hē graphē* may pertain to a specific passage in the Heb. Scriptures, as in Mk 12:10: "And have ye not read this scripture; The stone which the builders rejected . . . "—a quotation from Ps 118:22. Or else *hē graphē* may include the OT as a whole, as in Gal 3:22: "But the scripture hath concluded all under sin." In Gal 3:8 "the scripture" is spoken of as possessing a unified, organic personality partaking of God's own foreknowledge and authority (precisely because it is the Word of God written): "And the scripture, foreseeing that God would justify the heathen through faith, preached before the gospel unto Abraham, saying, In thee shall all nations be blessed" (see Gen 12:3).

Most frequently, of course, the term is used in the plural: "the scriptures" (Gr. *hai graphai*), suggesting the many different books of which the OT is composed. So employed, it became the NT equivalent to our term "Bible," and was invested with the same connotations of divine authority. In one instance (II Pet 3:15-16), the NT writings themselves (or more specifically, the epistles of Paul) are classed with the Heb. Scriptures as of binding authority.

See Bible Manuscripts; Versions, Ancient and Medieval; Bible, English Versions.

Bibliography. Gottlob Schrenk, "*Graphō,* etc.," TDNT, I, 742-773.

G. L. A.

SCROLL. Before the invention of books as we know them, namely, codexes which are bound at one edge, writing was done on long documents made of either leather or papyrus, which were rolled up on round sticks for ease of handling and storage. The writing was sometimes only on one side, but often on both front and back as in Rev 5:1, where the book handed to the Lamb was "written within and on the backside" (cf. Ezk 2:10). *See* Writing; Book.

SCULL. *See* Golgotha.

A granite bust of King Tutankhamen, from Karnak, Egypt. LL

SCULPTURE. Many of the products of ancient sculpture were carved images or idols (Deut 7:25). Jud 3:19 (RSV) makes specific reference to the "sculptured stones" (KJV, "quarries") of a place near Gilgal. Other usages were in decorative work for temples and palaces (I Kgs 6:35) and engravings on signets (Ex 28:11). *See* Seal.

Sumerian sculpture dates back some 5,000 years. Great numbers of sculptured statues, monuments, idols, and models found in tombs have come from ancient Egypt, Assyria, and Babylonia (ANEP, see table of contents), as well as from the Greeks and Romans. It is to be expected that the Israelites produced very little sculpture. This was true not because of Israelite artistic inability, but because of the commandment prohibiting "graven images."

See Occupations: Carving, Engraver.

SCUM. A soiling or rust described as being on the inside of the caldron (figurative of the city of Jerusalem). As a symbol of lewdness (Ezk 24:13), God promised to burn it out of the city (Ezk 24:6, 11-12). *See* Rust.

SCURVY. *See* Diseases.

SCYTHIANS (sĭth'ĭ-ȧns). Horse-riding nomadic Indo-Aryan tribes, first traced in Central Asia near the border of Siberia and Outer Mongolia *c.* 1700 B.C. Frozen burial chambers, such as in the Pazyryk valley of the Altai Mountains, built *c.* 500-300 B.C., reveal their characteristic art, customs, and possessions. The Scythians are probably first mentioned in the OT as "Ashkenaz," descended through Japheth from Noah (Gen 10:3; I Chr 1:6). When they tried to move SW of the Caspian Sea they were checked by the Assyrians whose records refer to them as *I/Ashguza.* About 715 B.C. they broke with the Mannai tribe (*see* Minni) and under Partatua moved into Urartu (*see* Ararat), capturing Sakiz. This action may lie behind the prophecy of Jer 51:27. In the 7th cen. B.C. the Scythians were strongly influenced by the culture of NW Iran, and it is now generally agreed that the Scythian language was an Iranian dialect.

According to Herodotus (*History* I, 104-105) the Scythians swept down on Mesopotamia and *c.* 611 B.C. were bought off from invading Egypt by Psammetichus I. They subsequently remained in W Asia for 28 years. It has been argued that during this period they sacked the temple of Venus at Ashdod and settled in Beth-shean, called Scythopolis (Jud 1:27, LXX; cf. II Macc 12:29). It is thus assumed by some that it is this Scythian foe which is described by Zephaniah and Jeremiah. The events of the period *c.* 630-617 B.C. in N Assyria are, however, little known. The Scythians may be included in the confederation of tribes (*umman-manda*) who helped As-

This statue of Gudea is a good example of Sumerian sculpture. LM

syria against the Medes and later sided with the Babylonians against them at Harran, but no contemporary texts give details by which they may be identified. The northern foe described by these two prophets can equally well be the Babylonians.

The warlike Scythians are described as barbarians (II Macc 4:47; III Macc 7:3). Since they sacrificed to a sword (Herodotus, *History* IV, 62) some have inferred a reference to them in Hab 1:16, but this is doubtful. By 110 B.C. these nomadic horsemen had settled in the Crimea (Neapolis) and traded with the Russian steppes in grain, horses, and slaves, intermarrying with Greeks. In Col 3:11 Paul either cites the Scythians as typical barbarians or refers to them as a well-known group of nomadic freemen.

Bibliography. M. I. Artamonov, "Frozen Tombs of the Scythians," *Scientific American*, CCXX (May, 1965), 101-109. T. Talbot Rice, *The Scythians*, London: Thames & Hudson, 1957. Maurita Van Loon, review of *Die Skythen in Südrussland* by J. A. H. Potratz, Basle, 1963, in JNES, XXIX (1970), 66-72.

D. J. W.

SEA. This word is applied to many different bodies of water in the OT, even including lakes and large rivers. *The* sea in the Bible is usually the Mediterranean (Num 13:29). It is also called "the great sea" (Ezk 47:10), the "sea of the Philistines" (Ex 23:31), and "the hinder sea," that is, the western sea as contrasted with the "former sea," which is the Dead Sea (Zech 14:8). *See* Great Sea.

The Dead Sea (*q.v.*) goes by the name of the "Salt Sea" (Gen 14:3), the "east sea" (Joel 2:20), and "the sea of the Arabah" (II Kgs 14:25, RSV). The Lake of Galilee (*q.v.*) is also called a sea and goes by various names: "Chinnereth" (Num 34:11), "Gennesaret" (Lk 5:1), and "Tiberias" (Jn 6:1).

The Red Sea (*q.v.*; Ex 10:19) is thought by some scholars to mean the "sea of reeds." In Isa 18:2 the Nile is clearly referred to by the term "the sea," and in 21:1 either the Euphrates River or the Arabian Sea is meant.

The word is also used frequently in a figurative sense. The Heb. word *yam* is used *c.* 70 times as a term for "the west" (e.g., Gen 12:8). The vast size of the laver in Solomon's temple led the priests to call it the "brazen sea" (I Kgs 7:23-26). To the land-loving Hebrews the sea was a dangerous and stormy place, and it furnished an apt simile for the troubled, restless soul of the sinner (Isa 57:20) and for the rebellious, seething nations of the world (Dan 7:2; Mt 13:47; Rev 13:1). The statement in Rev 21:1 that in the world to come there shall be no more sea probably refers to this figure of restless godlessness rather than the physical sea.

P. C. J.

SEA, BRAZEN. *See* Tabernacle: Laver.

The Mediterranean at Caesarea with ruins of the days of Herod the Great still to be seen in the water.

SEA MONSTER. *See* Animals: Jackal, II. 23.

SEA OF CHINNERETH. *See* Galilee, Sea of.

SEA OF GALILEE. *See* Galilee, Sea of.

SEA OF GLASS. The scenes in the Revelation where the expression "sea of glass" occurs (Rev 4:6; 15:2) have parallels with OT visions. Those most strikingly similar are Ezk 1; Ex 24; Dan 7; Isa 6. All these postulate the reality of an invisible, supernatural world which men can experience. The opening of the eyes enables men to see and hear the supernatural realities (II Kgs 6:17; II Cor 12:2-4; Rev 4:1-2). The fact that the visions of the throne in Revelation have similarities to other such visions would argue that it is essentially one reality revealed to the prophets and apostles.

The nearest verbal parallel to the sea of glass is the "paved work of a sapphire stone" of Ex 24:10. In Ezk 1:22-26, there is portrayed an expanse like "terrible crystal" on which was the sapphire throne. These visions can be assimilated to the vision in Revelation: the sapphire throne comparable to the throne encircled by an emerald-colored rainbow (Rev 4:3), the lightning and fire (Ezk 1:4, 13 with Rev 4:5; 15:2), the four living creatures (Ezk 1:5-12; Rev 4:6-8), and the majestic one brought before the throne (Dan 7:13-14; Rev 5:5-8); all make it plain that John is viewing the same supernatural verities revealed to Moses, Isaiah, Ezekiel, and Daniel.

The mention of the sea of glass in Rev 4 enables us to identify the setting of the "sea of glass mingled with fire" of Rev 15:2. Most plausibly those seen standing by the sea are raptured saints in glory. The mention of the sea gains its significance from the parallel evoked by the mention of (1) their victory over the beast and his image, and (2) their singing the song of Moses. Just as the people of Israel sang a song of triumph when safe on the farther side of the sea (Ex 15), so these stand by the crystal sea in glory to sing a song of praise and deliverance.

W. B. W.

SEA OF TIBERIAS. *See* Tiberias, Sea of; Galilee, Sea of.

SEAH. *See* Weights, Measures, and Coins.

SEAL, SEALSKIN. *See* Animal: Badger, II.4; Animal: Dugong, V.3.

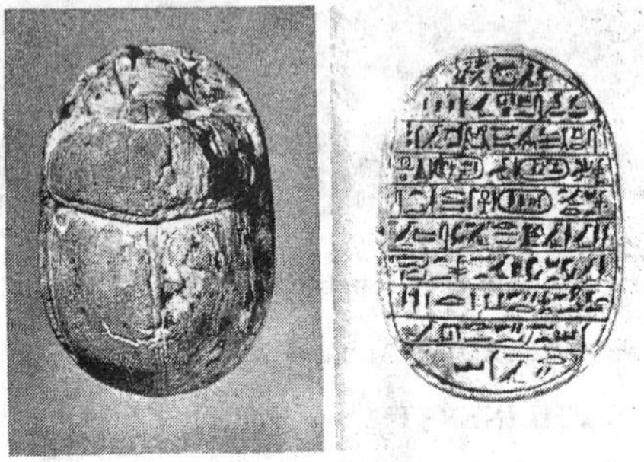

A scarab seal from Egypt.

SEAL, SIGNET. Heb. *ḥôtām* and Gr. *sphragis* describe the seal impression itself or the instrument by which it was made (I Kgs 21:8).

Form. The instrument was a carved or engraved device used to make a distinctive design in clay, wax, etc. Ex 39:6, 14, 30 speak of engraving a seal, which took various shapes. In the Bible it was often a stone ("signet") set in a ring (Est 3:12; Jer 22:24) and worn on the "arm" or hand (Song 8:6). The use of a ring seal is indicated in the case of Pharaoh giving his ring to Joseph (Gen 41:42) as a badge of his delegated authority; of Jezebel sending out letters in Ahab's name when she determined to obtain Naboth's vineyard by false accusation and unlawful seizure (I Kgs 21:8-16); of Ahasuerus giving his ring to the wicked Haman (Est 3:10, 12), then giving it to Mordecai after Haman's perfidy was exposed (Est 8:2); of the sealing of the lions' den after Daniel was placed in it by Darius (Dan 6:17).

In other cases the seal was a stamp type, frequently conical in shape, examples of which have been found (ANEP #237). In Babylonia it was generally a cylinder with a hole through its length to take a cord for wearing around the neck (Gen 38:18), or an axle. The latter arrangement facilitated rolling the instrument across the wet clay to reproduce the image carved on the surface (cf. ANEP #239-240 for cylinder seals, and #276-278 for stamp seal impressions).

Materials. Various materials were used to make seals. Terra cotta, bitumen, and limestone were often found, used by poorer people. The well-to-do had them made out of carnelian, chalcedony, agate, jasper, rock crystal, and hematite. The engraver often had to use a "diamond" or corundum point on his small bow-drill to work the hard gem stones (Jer 17:1; *see* Jewel). Sometimes the engraving was sharp and clear, sometimes less so (cf. ANEP #703 and 704).

Usage. The manner of forming a seal in clay to authenticate a document was early known to the Bible (Job 38:14). Not only documents (Isa 8:16) but containers of all sorts were shut with a closing plug placed in position and then stamped with an identifying seal. In Israel, jug containers were stamped by the potter with a seal impression on their handles to designate the owner. In other cases the door to a granary was sealed by being closed and the sealing placed across the gap and given a seal impression. Sometimes the sealing was a cord, held in place by clay on either side and both patches of clay given the impression. Books were fastened shut with seals (Rev 5:1).

An example of the use of a seal in a business transaction is that of Jeremiah using his seal when he purchased, according to his right of redemption, the field of Hanameel while the city of Jerusalem was still under siege and he was still in prison (Jer 32:10). The use of a seal also acts as the confirmation of a covenant (Neh 9:38; 10:1). The importance of a seal as something of the greatest personal value is expressed in Hag 2:23 and the seriousness of its loss in Jer 22:24.

Designs and inscriptions. Patterns of seals before the monarchy were similar to Mesopotamian seals, having well-filled areas, or rows of men or humans and animals. Later Palestinian seals showed lion heads or lions, sphinxes, griffons, etc. After the 7th cen. B.C. there was a change to an inscriptional type, usually two lines. One such is that reading "Belonging to Shema', servant of Jeroboam," found at Megiddo. Egyptian scarab seals often bore the name of the reigning Egyptian king, and this has been helpful in identifying conquerors and conquest dates of Palestinian towns.

Palestinian excavations have uncovered at least a thousand jar handles bearing several kinds of seal impressions. Of special interest are royal seal impressions stamped on storage jars found at various Judean sites. Above the design—either a four-winged scarab or a double-winged sun disk—appears the phrase *l-m-l-k*, "belonging to the king," and below it is

A stamp seal from Egypt, second millennium B.C. BM

one of four place names, viz., Hebron, Socoh, Ziph, or the enigmatic *m-m-sh-t*. Aharoni believes the four-winged variety dates to Hezekiah's reign prior to Sennacherib's invasion in 701 B.C. and that the other kind is subsequent to that event. The four place names point to store cities which served as tax collecting centers of the four zones in Hezekiah's newly reorganized administrative system. Hebron, Socoh, and Ziph were the respective centers of the hill country, the Shephelah, and the wilderness of Judah zones, while *m-m-sh-t* is a shortened form of Heb. *memshelet*, "government," and signifies Jerusalem (*Land of the Bible*, pp. 340–346).

Yigael Yadin, however, believes the four zones were organized for the defense of the southern kingdom and that *m-m-sh-t* should be located in such a zone in the Negeb. He proposes to identify it with the large fortified Iron Age site Khirbet al-Gharra, nine miles E of Beer-sheba ("The Fourfold Division of Judah," BASOR #163 [1961], pp. 6–12). A. D. Tushingham prefers to date all the royal jar handle stamps found in cities of Judah to the reign of Josiah on the basis of their paleography, archaeological evidence at Ramat Rahel, and the occurrence of such seal impressions at Gezer and Jericho (BASOR #201 [1971], pp. 23–35).

Figurative use in the NT. The Gr. verb *sphragizō* is used literally several times, e.g., of the sealing of the tomb after Jesus' burial (Mt 27:66), the sealing of Satan in the abyss (Rev 20:3), and the command not to seal up the contents of the book of Revelation (Rev 22:10).

Most of the references to seals in the NT, however, are figurative. The one who accepts Christ's testimony certifies ("has set his seal," NASB) that God is true (Jn 3:33). Circumcision was the confirming seal of the righteousness which was imputed and received by faith, before the rite itself was instituted (Rom 4:11). Paul authenticates, or validates, his ministry by calling his converts a seal (I Cor 9:2). The Christian is given the double seal of assurance of belonging to God in that he is known of God, and that he abstains from wickedness (II Tim 2:19).

God set His seal of approval on His Son when He sent the Holy Spirit in the form of a dove upon Jesus at His baptism (Jn 6:27). In somewhat similar fashion, by being baptized in the Spirit Christian believers are sealed by the Holy Spirit unto the day of their full redemption (Eph 1:13; 4:30; II Cor 1:22). This emphasizes both the authenticity and the security of their salvation, for the Holy Spirit remains with them always (Jn 14:16–17) and they belong to God forever. The Holy Spirit may be grieved (Eph 4:30) or quenched (I Thess 5:19), but not removed, because salvation is permanent (Jn 10:28–30; 14:16–17).

In the end time, when the Antichrist shall have tremendous power and control, God will seal 144,000 of the tribes of Israel with His name upon their foreheads (Rev 7:4–8; 14:1).

An Akkadian cylinder seal: the killing of the Hydra, from Asmar, Iraq. ORINST

This seal seems to be a mark of safeguard as well as of ownership. Satan, too, will seal his own with the terrible mark of the beast (Rev 13:16–17; 14:9, 11; 15:2; 16:2; 19:20; 20:4). Revelation also mentions the book with the seven seals, which contains the history of the end times (Rev 5:1–2) and which only Christ can open (5:5).

Bibliography. Yohanan Aharoni, *The Land of the Bible*, Philadelphia: Westminster, 1967. N. Avigad, "Ammonite and Moabite Seals," *Near Eastern Archaeology in the Twentieth Century* (Glueck Festschrift), J. A. Sanders, ed., Garden City: Doubleday, 1970, pp. 284–295. CornPBE, "Seals," pp. 656–659. David Diringer, "Hebrew Seals," DOTT, pp. 218–226. G. Fitzer, "*Sphragis*, etc.," TDNT, VII, 939–953. Siegfried H. Horn, "Scarabs, Seals," BW, pp. 508–515. G. W. H. Lampe, *The Seal of the Spirit: A Study in the Doctrine of Baptism and Confirmation in New Testament and the Fathers*, London: Longmans, Green, 1951. Olga Tufnell, "Seals and Scarabs," IDB, IV, 254–259. D. J. Wiseman and S. S. Smalley, "Seal, Sealing," NBD, pp. 1153–1156.

H. G. S.

SEAM. The coat of Jesus, for which the soldiers cast lots, was "without seam, woven from the top throughout" (Jn 19:23–24).

SEAMEW or SEA GULL. *See* Animals: Cuckoo, III.8.

SEAR. The meaning is "to brand" or "to burn with a hot iron." Paul counseled Timothy that a day would come when some would fall away and speak lies, "having their conscience seared with a hot iron" (I Tim 4:2). The resultant condition was one of callousness and insensitivity to the truth.

SEASON. *See* Time, Division of.

SEAT. *See* House.

SEAT, CHIEF. The *protokathedria*, the "chief seat" in the synagogue (*q.v.*), is noted once in Matthew and in Mark, and twice in Luke, there translated "uppermost seats" (11:43) and "highest seats" (20:46). It is separate and distinct from "chief place" (*protoklisia*). Both words occur in Mt 23:6; Mk 12:39; Lk 20:46, but *protokathedria* only in Lk 11:43. There is nothing in these references to describe the construction of the seat. Its importance, of course, was the prominent feature, along with the attitude of the Pharisees toward themselves and others as expressed in their desire to have the chief seats. Always they appropriated these places to themselves as their right and prerogative. The chief seats in the synagogues were those nearest the pulpit or reader's desk, reserved for the elders of the people. The early Christians were sometimes prone to offer the best seats in their assembly to the wealthy visitor (Jas 2:1-4).

The places of honor at banquets were at the head of the table or to the right of the host when reclining. The Pharisees were also roundly condemned for their seeking these chief places, for Jesus taught that there is no inherent right to them (Lk 14:7-11). Position based on theological concepts of superiority are not proper bases for preference. Such does not guarantee purity of life or real spiritual attitudes (Mk 12:38-40).

Jesus said on another occasion that the scribes and Pharisees seated themselves in "Moses' seat" (Mt 23:2). This chair in a synagogue was a symbol of the legal authority of Moses which the scribes (*q.v.*) and Pharisees felt they inherited as teachers of Jewish law. It was the seat for the most distinguished elder, and was next to the ark of the Torah in the synagogue at Dura Europos (Emil G. Kraeling, *Bible Atlas*, Chicago: Rand McNally, 1956. p. 378). Such chairs of solid stone have been found in synagogue ruins at Chorazin and Hammath, S of Tiberias.

H. G. S.

SEAT OF MOSES. *See* Seat, Chief.

SEBA (sē'bȧ). The Heb. spelling is *s^ebā'* (cf. Sheba 4).

1. The first-named descendants of Cush, son of Ham, who settled in S Arabia before the time of Moses (Gen 10:7; I Chr 1:9).

2. The name of a land, the Sudan or northern part of Ethiopia, including Meroe (Ps 72:10; Isa 43:3). The inhabitants (known also as Sabeans, *q.v.*) were wealthy, and tall in stature, and will someday acknowledge Israel's God (Isa 45:14). The name may be assumed to have been given the area by Sabean colonists coming from SW Arabia.

SEBAT (sē'băt), **SHEBAT** (shē'băt). The eleventh month of the Jewish religious year, beginning with the new moon of February (Zech 1:7). *See* Calendar.

SECACAH (sē-kā'kȧ). A town in the wilderness of Judah near Nibshan and Middin (Josh 15:61). It has been identified by Cross and Milik with Khirbet es-Samrah, five miles SW of Qumran in the Buqê'ah valley (BASOR, #142 [1956], p. 16). On the other hand, it may be one of the three Iron Age sites along the W shore of the Dead Sea investigated in 1965-66 (*see* Nibshan).

SECHU, SECU (sē'kū). A town in Benjamin near Ramah. It was here that Saul, in pursuit of David, sought information relative to his whereabouts (I Sam 19:22). The site remains unidentified.

SECOND COMING OF CHRIST. *See* Christ, Coming of.

SECRET. *See* Mystery.

SECRETARY. *See* Occupations: Secretary.

SECT. The Gr. word *hairesis* translated "sect" in the KJV means literally "division" or "party" with no disparaging connotation. It was used to speak of the various philosophical schools of thought. It is used in this neutral sense concerning the Pharisees and Sadducees in Acts 5:17; 15:5. In the latter chapters of Acts where it is used of the Christians it is beginning to take on a more judgmental tone (24:5; 26:5; 28:22). In I Cor 11:19; Gal 5:20; II Pet 2:1 the KJV translates "heresies." While it is questionable whether the word had come to be synonymous with false doctrine this early, it is used here in the sense of "dissension" or "destructive opinions" (Arndt, p. 23).

Bibliography. H. Schlier, "*Airesis*," TDNT, I, 180-184.

SECUNDUS (sē-ko͝on' dŭs). A believer from Thessalonica, and a companion of Paul on his return from Greece. He, Aristarchus, and others accompanied Paul on his journey to Syria en route to Jerusalem with the offering for the poor (Acts 20:4).

SECURITY. When related to the believer's position which results from the regenerating work of the Holy Spirit, this is the doctrine which means that once a sinner has trusted Christ as Saviour he is eternally saved. Some deny the doctrine completely, while others accept it as entirely biblical; still others, of the latter group, distort and misuse it to find shelter for their loose living.

Those who reject the doctrine of eternal security are often referred to as Arminian, though Arminianism embraces far more than a failure to believe in the eternal security of the believer. It is true, though, that after the death of James Arminius (1560-1609), his followers, led by Episcopius, drew up five articles of faith called the Remonstrance. They were in direct opposition to the Belgic Confession of Faith and the Heidelberg Catechism which stressed what came to be known as the five points of Calvinism set forth at the Synod of Dordt

(1618–1619). In Calvin's system of theology, the fifth point deals with "final perseverance," which is the term generally used for the security of the believer. The term Calvinist is usually applied to those who accept the doctrine. But it should also be kept in mind that Calvinism as a system of theology involves far more than this one doctrine.

This doctrine must not be confused with the doctrine of assurance (*q.v.*). Security is God's work, while assurance results from man's acceptance of and rest in that work. There is no security apart from genuine salvation, i.e., regeneration. The doctrine does not provide a license to sin. God never condones sin and this doctrine in no way implies that He does. Nor does the truth of security mean that the believer will always feel saved and secure. It does unquestionably mean, though, that those who have been truly born again through personal faith in Jesus Christ as Saviour will never be lost. They are eternally saved.

Though the doctrine has suffered much from neglect, misuse and confusion, it remains a clear teaching of the Word of God. The central question is, did Christ do enough on the cross to make it possible for God the Father to keep the believing sinner saved? If it be admitted that the sinner can do nothing to merit or earn salvation, then it must logically and scripturally also be admitted that the saved sinner can do nothing to keep himself saved.

Since the believer is related to the Godhead, his security is certain. The believer is related to God the Father in His purpose (Eph 1:4), His power (Eph 1:19–20), and His love (Rom 5:7–10). The Father also heard the prayer of His Son for His own (Jn 17:9–12). The believer is related to God the Son since He died for the sinner (Rom 8:34); He arose from the grave providing victory over death (Col 3:1); He is the believer's advocate (I Jn 2:1–2) and his intercessor (Heb 7:25). The believer is also related to God the Holy Spirit through regeneration (Tit 3:5), indwelling (Rom 8:9), baptism (I Cor 12:13), and sealing (Eph 4:30).

Those who reject this doctrine usually find support from passages of Scripture taken out of context completely or from passages which emphasize the importance of a Christian virtue as the evidence of a real work of regeneration. Scripture abounds with evidence for the security of the believer, but there are three central passages teaching this doctrine (Jn 10:27–30; Rom 8:35–39; I Pet 1:3–5). *See* Perseverance.

R. P. L.

SEDITION. In Ezr 4:15, 19; Lk 23:19, 25; Acts 24:5 the idea expressed is revolt or rebellion against the government; in Gal 5:20, causing dissension among believers.

SEDUCER. One who leads others astray by his chant or cry as in sorcery and enchantment (II Tim 3:13; I Tim 4:1). To lead astray or seduce (I Jn 2:26; Rev 2:20; Mk 13:22) in the sense of causing to wander from the truth.

SEED. In Scripture the word "seed" is used literally of the essential plant organism which enables the species to reproduce itself (Gen 1:11) and of the human male semen (Lev 15:16, 18). It is also used in many figurative ways: of human offspring, descendants, progeny (Gen 3:15; 13:15); of "the word of the kingdom" (Mt 13:3–23); of "the children of the kingdom of heaven" (Mt 13:38); of "the word of God" (Lk 8:11; I Pet 1:23); and of "the kingdom of heaven" itself (Mt 13:31–32).

In Gal 3:16 Paul, in order to show that the promises made to Abraham were realized in Christ and not in Israel, calls attention to the singular number of the word "seed." Jesus Christ was recognized by the early church as being the seed of David who would reign forever (Ps 89:4; II Tim 2:8). In I Cor 15:35 ff. Paul indicates that the difference between the resurrection body of the believer from that buried in the grave is like the difference between a seed and the full-grown plant. *See* Agriculture.

Bibliography. S. Schultz and G. Quell, "*Sperma*, etc.," TDNT, VII, 536–547.

F. C. K.

SEEDTIME. *See* Agriculture.

SEER. *See* Prophet.

SEETHE. The Heb. verb *bāshal* means to cook by boiling or stewing, whether the food is manna (Ex 16:23) or vegetables (II Kgs 4:38) or meat (Ex 29:31) or bones (Ezk 24:5). The Israelites were forbidden to seethe a young goat in the milk of its mother (Ex 23:19; 34:26; Deut 14:21), which according to the Ras Shamra (*q.v.*) tablets was a Canaanite fertility rite to insure a good crop by sprinkling over one's field broth obtained in such a manner.

Another Heb. word, *zîd,* also can mean to seethe or boil (Gen 25:29, KJV "sod"). It is expressive of the hissing or sizzling of boiling water. Usually it means "to act arrogantly or presumptuously" as if to boil over with passion (Deut 1:43; 18:20; Neh 9:10, NASB). The adjective form referred to the raging of waves (Ps 124:5) and to insolent, arrogant people (Mal 3:15; 4:1, NASB).

SEGUB (sē′ gŭb)

1. The youngest son of Hiel the Bethelite. Segub died for the sin of his father in rebuilding Jericho. According to the word of God through Joshua, "Cursed be the man before Jehovah that . . . buildeth this city Jericho; with the loss of his firstborn shall he lay the foundations thereof, and with the loss of his youngest son [Segub] shall he set up the gates of it" (Josh 6:26, ASV; I Kgs 16:34). Many believe that these sons were offered as human sacrifices and buried in the foundations of the walls and gate of the city to placate the gods.

2. The son of Hezron (grandson of Judah) and the daughter of Machir who was father of

The Khazneh, or treasury, at Petra (capital of Seir or Edom), probably a tomb of a Nabataean king.
MIS

Gilead. Segub became the father of Jair, who possessed, probably by conquest, a great many cities in Gilead (I Chr 2:21-22).

SEIR (sē'ĭr)

1. A mountainous land inhabited by the Edomites. The etymology (Heb. *śē'ir*) suggests something hairy or shaggy and may be descriptive of the former wooded nature of the landscape. However, the name may be eponymous since Seir is mentioned once in Amarna letter #288 written from Jerusalem (ANET, p. 488) and in an ancient Egyptian inscription which recounts a victory in this vicinity by Ramses III (*c.* 1200 B.C.) over a Bedouin tribe named Saira or Seirim (JewEnc, IX, 462). Ashurbanipal perhaps refers to Seir as Sa'arri in the record of his campaign against the Arabs; the name occurs after the Hauran and Moab (ANET, p. 298). Gen 36:8-9, 30 connect the name with Edom ("red") and Esau ("hairy").

The primary biblical reference is geographical, designating the mountainous region SW of the Dead Sea. *See* Halak. One of the highest points of Seir was Mount Hor where Aaron was buried (Num 20:27-28). Apparently the name Seir was later applied to the entire territory of Edom both SE and SW of the Dead Sea.

The earliest inhabitants of the area known to the OT were the Horites (Gen 14:6; Deut 2:12). Seir is listed as grandfather of the Horites (Gen 36:20-21; I Chr 1:38). The children of Esau replaced them (Gen 32:3; 33:14, 16; Deut 2:4-5, 8, 29; Josh 24:4). The Edomites (Num 24:18) were Israel's neighbors in this area until about the middle of the 5th cen. B.C. when they were overcome by Arabian tribesmen, later known as the Nabataeans (*q.v.*).

Seir is significant in the OT as a synonym for Edom and Esau. The people to whom all three names apply stood in a unique relation to Israel. The three terms are related in the genealogy of Esau (Gen 36). The ambivalent attitudes of brotherhood and competitive enmity are reflected in the cycle of the Jacob narratives in Gen 25–36. The same tension is revealed when Moses and the Israelites were forced to detour around Edom (Num 20; Deut 2:4-8).

David brutally subjugated Edom (II Sam 8:14), and successive generations of Judean kings struggled in vain to maintain this subjection (II Kgs 8:20-22; 14:7-10; II Chr 20). The tension continued through the centuries. Lam 4:21 f. and Ps 137:7 accuse Edom of perfidious collaboration with the common enemy during the sack of Jerusalem in 586 B.C.

Seir (= Edom) also stands in the prophetic denunciations of this people (Ezk 25:8; 35:1-15). No other people except Philistia is mentioned so often in the prophecies against the nations (Amos 1:11-12; Isa 21:11-12; 34; 63:1-6; Jer 49:7-22; Ezk 32; Obadiah; Joel 3:19; Mal 1:2-5; Zech 9:5 ff.; Ps 60).

Mount Seir conveys another meaning. It stands with Sinai and Paran as a mountain particularly related to Yahweh. In the song of Deborah He is described as "going forth from Seir" (Jud 5:4) in a context which mentions Sinai as well. The blessing of Moses (Deut 33:2) has a similar passage with all three mountains named. *See* Edom; Petra.

2. A mountain ridge near Jerusalem on the N border of Judah (Josh 15:10). Modern Saris near Chesalon *c.* ten miles W of Jerusalem may preserve the name.

Bibliography. Denis Baly, *The Geography of the Bible,* New York: Harper, 1957, pp. 239-251. L. H. Grollenberg, *Atlas of the Bible,* tr. and ed. by Joyce M. H. Reid and H. H. Rowley, New York: Thomas Nelson & Sons, 1956, p. 161. J. Simons, *The Geographical and Topographical Texts of the Old Testament,* Leiden: E. J. Brill, 1959, pp. 68, 435. G. A. Smith, *The Historical Geography of the Holy Land,* London: Hodder & Stoughton, 25th rev. ed., 1931, pp. 557-576.

J. D. W. W.

SEIRATH (sē-ī'răth). The name is spelled Seirah in the ASV and all newer versions. A place (the name means "wooded") in the hill country of Ephraim to which Ehud the judge escaped after having assassinated Eglon (Jud 3:26); not yet identified. From Seirah Ehud rallied the Israelites to pursue the Moabites (vv. 27-29).

SELA, SELAH (sē'lȧ). An Edomite stronghold whose Heb. name *sela'* (LXX: Fr. *petra*) means "rock" or "crag." Since soundings in 1929, 1933, and 1934 on the top of Umm el-Bayyarah, a flat-topped mountain at Petra where Edomite pottery was discovered, most scholars have accepted the identification of that acropolis with biblical Sela. It is the only site in the Petra area with Edomite remains.

According to II Kgs 14:7 King Amaziah of Judah captured Sela *c.* 790 B.C. and changed its name to Joktheel; II Chr 25:11-12 states that he threw down his Edomite captives from the top of "the rock" (Heb. *hassāla'*). The prophet Obadiah *c.* 840 B.C. condemned the Edomites who dwelt in the clefts of "the rock" (Heb. *sela'*, Ob 3; cf. Jer 49:16). Referring to coming judgment on Moab, Isaiah mentioned the fleeing Moabites taking refuge at Sela (in Edom) and sending tribute from there to Jerusalem (Isa 16:1; WBC, p. 622). Later he called upon the inhabitants of Sela to add their songs of praise to the Lord of the whole earth (Isa 42:11, ASV). A difficult passage to interpret regarding the border of the Amorites mentions Sela (Jud 1:36, RSV), but this may refer to another otherwise unidentified place.

Umm el-Bayyarah (3,700 feet above sea level) towers a sheer 950 feet above the valley floor of the Nabataean (*q.v.*) and Roman city of Petra (*q.v.*) and commands a fine view of the Arabah to the W. Further excavations in 1960, 1963, and 1965 on the summit of this natural stronghold proved that the Edomite settlement was essentially of a domestic nature and belonged to the later 8th and 7th cen. B.C. Among the finds was a seal impression of Qos-gabr, king of Edom, a contemporary of King Manasseh of Judah (Crystal-M. Bennett, "Exploring Umm el-Biyars, the Edomite Fortress-rock Which Dominates Petra," ILN, Apr. 30, 1966, pp. 29-31). Nabataean building remains on the summit concur with the statement of Diodorus Siculus that the Nabataeans had occupied the stronghold and repulsed an attack by Antigonus in 312 B.C.

Since no sherds earlier than the end of the 8th cen. B.C. have been found on Umm el-Bayyarah, another site for biblical Sela has been suggested. A small village in Edom 30 miles N of Petra, near Buseirah (*see* Bozra 1), is called Sela'. Nearby is a rock massif or crag, with only one possible route of ascent. Sherds picked up on its surface appear to be from an earlier date than those found at Umm el-Bayyarah. Geographically this site would be more in line with the OT passages than one in the Petra region (PEQ, XCVIII [1966], 123-126). There is evidence at this northern Sela' of a sanctuary which may be of Edomite origin.

J. R.

SELAH (sē'lȧ). A musical notation (Heb. *selâ*) found primarily in the Psalter, denoting an intended pause either in the singing of the psalm or in the instrumental accompaniment. *See* Music.

SELA-HAMMAHLEKOTH (sē'lȧ-hȧ-mä'lĕ-kŏth). Meaning "rock of the divisions or separations" (I Sam 23:28), this was a cliff in the wilderness of Maon, a section of the wilderness of Judah (v. 25). It was to this place that David fled from Saul and the division between them was intensified. The RSV and NASB translations use "the Rock of Escape." It perhaps may be identified with the Wadi el-Malâqi, a deep gorge *c.* eight miles ENE of Maon toward En-gedi.

SELED (sē'lĕd). The childless descendant of Jerahmeel. His grandfather was Pharez, son of Judah. Nadab was Seled's father (I Chr 2:30).

SELEUCIA (sē-lōō'shȧ). The name given to nine cities of the Seleucid kingdom by Seleucus I Nicator. Of these only Seleucia Pieria figures in the NT. Built by Seleucus in 300 B.C. at a point five miles N of the mouth of the Orontes, it guarded the river mouth and served as the port of Antioch of Syria. Above the harbor Mount Pieria rose from the sea in a series of ledges. The lower city with the harbor and warehouses stood on a level about 20 feet above the quay; on a much higher shelf of the mountain perched the upper city. The elevation displayed to best advantage the magnificence of the public buildings and temples of the city. Paul and Barnabas embarked on their first missionary journey from Seleucia (Acts 13:4) and apparently returned to it from that journey.

SELF-CONTROL. *See* Temperance.

SELF-DENIAL. To deny oneself is to repudiate the gratification of those desires and values which are exclusively self-centered rather than God-centered. This is not to say that the believer can have no personal values, desires, or goals which may exist legitimately; but it does mean that such should exist within the context of God's will. It does not imply that personal needs should not be met; but these will be viewed in the context of God being glorified (I Cor 10:31).

Self-denial is to take self out of the driver's seat so that God might occupy that place. It is to deny self the right or mastery over one's life. Peter's denying Jesus illustrates that denial involves a decision to dissociate oneself from the person or object denied (Mt 26:69-75). Christ taught that the decision to deny self should be radical and decisive (*aparnēsasthō*, aorist middle imperative verb, Mt 16:24; Mk 8:34) and renewed daily (Lk 9:23), so that the disciple could continually follow Christ. The implications of this concept are far-reaching indeed, involving repudiation of the old self-righteousness (Phil 3:7-11) and the old life of sin (Tit 2:12; Rom 6:6; 8:12-13; Gal 5:16-17, 24; Col 3:5-9; I Pet 2:11). However, this repudiation achieves its goal only when the life becomes Christ oriented (which is expressed in various manners in the NT—Mt 16:24 and parallels; Rom 12:1-2; 13:14; Gal 2:20; 4:19; 5:16; Col 3:1-4, 10-17; Phil 2:5; *et al.*). The believer who does this has Christ's promise that this is the only way to have a full life either now or in the future (Mt 16:25-26 and parallels; Lk 18:27-30; Jn 12:25; cf. Phil 3:7-11).

S. N. G.

SELF-WILL. According to II Pet 2:10, those who walk after the flesh are "self-willed" (Gr. *authadēs*), stubborn, arrogant. In contrast, those chosen for bishops or elders are not to be self-willed or easily angered (Tit 1:7), but humble (I Pet 5:5-6) and patient (I Tim 3:3). The term is found once in the OT in Jacob's poetic description of his sons Simeon and Levi (Gen 49:6).

SELVEDGE. In the tabernacle, loops of blue were to adorn the edge of the curtain beginning at the selvedge (end, extremity) in the coupling (Ex 26:4; 36:11). It refers to the edge of the outermost hanging in each set of curtains, comparable to the ornamental fringe at either end of an oriental carpet.

SEM. *See* Shem; Semite.

SEMACHIAH (sĕm'ȧ-kī-ȧ). The son of Shemaiah, a Korahite (NASB), he was a gatekeeper of the tabernacle in the days of David (I Chr 26:1, 7).

SEMEI (sĕm'ī). An ancestor of Jesus (Lk 3:26) who lived during the intertestamental period.

The name is spelled Semein in the ASV and all newer versions.

SEMITE (sĕm'īt). The name Semite was suggested by the fact that most of the nations listed in the Table of Nations (Gen 10:21 ff.) were descendants of Shem. The origin of the term has been credited to A. L. Schlözer (1781). However, the classification of modern scholars does not wholly coincide with the table of Genesis but has been revised in light of linguistic considerations. Thus, Elam is classified with the descendants of Shem in Genesis, but today, because of linguistic reasons, is not considered as Semite. On the other hand, the Canaanites were of Hamitic origin, but spoke a Semitic language.

Semitic peoples were found primarily in W Asia and E Africa. Their territory stretched from the Mediterranean on the W to Persia (modern Iran) on the E, while their N boundary was Armenia, with the Arabian Sea and Persian Gulf on the S.

The principal theories as to their original homeland are: (1) Babylon (von Kremer, Guidi and Hommel); (2) Arabia (Sprenger, Sayce, Schrader and Wright); (3) Africa with Arabia as their first Asiatic home (Jastrow, Ripley, Barton, Palgrave); (4) Arabia was the original home with the Egyptians originating from an intermingling of migrating Semites and the earlier Negroid population (Wiedemann, Breasted); (5) Amurru (the cuneiform Uru) which is between Syria and Mesopotamia. The second view is favored by most today.

Semitic peoples have made a profound impact upon ancient history. The Akkadians (Babylonians and Assyrians) were prominent in the affairs of the Fertile Crescent between 2350 and 538 B.C. For more than a millennium their language was the *lingua franca.* Noted rulers were Sargon I, Hammurabi, Tiglath-pileser I, Shalmaneser III, Sennacherib, and Nebuchadnezzar. Sophisticated cultures were found at Ur, Nineveh and Babylon. The Akkad. civilization is also noted for the codified laws of Hammurabi and the diversified literary works in the library of Ashurbanipal.

Another Semitic people, the Arameans, were traders who were carriers of foreign cultures. Their homeland was Syria, with Damascus becoming their capital in Solomon's time. The zenith of their power was reached in the 9th cen. B.C. Their language, Aramaic, was adopted by the Jews after the Exile, and was the language of portions of the books of Daniel and Ezra and the Talmud.

Returning from Haran in Padan-aram (Gen 28:6), a part of Mesopotamia (*'Aram-nahărayim,* Gen 24:10), Jacob was called "a wandering Aramean" (Deut 26:5, RSV). Thus the Israelites who spoke Heb., a NW Semitic dialect, were Semites in the racial, linguistic, and geographical senses of the term.

Of lesser importance in ancient history were the Canaanites (whose culture we have learned of in Ugarit), the Arabs, and the Ethiopians. The Phoenicians were the seafaring descendants of the Canaanites.

The chief contributions of the Semites were their languages and religions. The best known Semitic languages are Akkadian, Aramaic, Syriac, Hebrew, Arabic and Amharic. Roots in these languages are usually triconsonantal with parts of speech made by affixes.

While polytheism was practiced by many Semitic people, it is noteworthy that the three great monotheistic religions of the world (Judaism, Christianity and Islam) have come through them.

See Hebrew People; Nations.

P. D. F.

SENAAH (sē̆-nā'ă). A town perhaps also called Hassenaah (*q.v.*) in Judah, to which nearly 4,000 Jews returned with Zerubbabel from Exile (Ezr 2:35; Neh 7:38; note that all the proper names in Ezr 2:21–35 seem to be names of towns). Men of Hassenaah helped Nehemiah repair the wall of Jerusalem (Neh 3:3). It has been tentatively identified with the small site of Khirbet ʿAuja el-Foqa, *c.* 17 miles NE of Jerusalem and six miles N of Jericho on the W edge of the Jordan Valley.

On the other hand, the extraordinarily large number of people may indicate that the term "Hassenaah" describes a certain category or group of returning exiles (GTT, ¶1035, pp. 382 f.). On the basis of the name *s^enā'â* perhaps meaning "hated," BDB (p. 702) suggests they were the poorer classes of Jerusalem.

SENATE. The Gr. word *gerousia* in Acts 5:21 means "body or assembly of elders." The text speaks of "the council" (lit., Sanhedrin, Gr. *synedrion*) and "all the senate." The two terms are in apposition, as the NEB indicates: "they summoned the 'Sanhedrin,' that is, the full senate of the Israelite nation." The term Sanhedrin (*q.v.*) was beginning to replace the older term "senate of elders" (Gr. *gerousia*), used in Judith 4:8; I Macc 12:6; II Macc 1:10; 4:44.

SENATORS. The Heb. word *zāqēn* translated thus in Ps 105:22 means simply "elders," the original meaning of the Latin "senator," as in the ASV and most newer versions.

SENEH (sĕ'nă). A jagged rock in Benjamin near Gibeah, at the pass of Michmash, where the Philistines had a garrison in the days of Saul (I Sam 14:4). It was one of the two cliffs (*see also* Bozez) at Michmash (*q.v.*) in the Wadi es-Suweinit, which Jonathan and his armor bearer had to climb on hands and feet in order to attack the Philistines.

SENIR (sĕ-nîr'), **SHENIR** (shĕ-nîr'). A peak or mountain, probably snow-capped, NE of Jordan, between Amana (*q.v.*) and Hermon (I Chr 5:23; Song 4:8). Senir was famous for its fir trees used in shipbuilding (Ezk 27:5). This was also the name by which the Amorites called

Mount Hermon (Deut 3:9); in Akkadian it was called Saniru. The Sidonians called it Sirion, and in Ps 29:6 Sirion is used poetically for Mount Hermon.

SENNACHERIB (sě-năk'ĕr-ĭb). This king reigned over the Assyrian Empire 705–681 B.C. His predecessor, Sargon II (*q.v.*), had laid a good foundation and as a result the Assyrian army stayed at home for the first two years of Sennacherib's reign. In this time the king devoted himself to rebuilding Nineveh (*q.v.*). He had a passion for building and an interest in engineering. At Nineveh he constructed a system of water works, restored temples, and built a magnificent palace. Many friezes of Sennacherib's palace excavated by A. H. Layard were badly damaged, but they show that this was a high period of Assyrian art. His interest in art and literature is only equaled by that of his grandson, Ashurbanipal, whose palace was much better preserved. Sennacherib was probably the administrator who most often sang his own glories in Assyrian annals.

His reign began with marked absence of the diplomatic procedure carefully followed by his father Sargon, i.e., the ceremony of taking the hands of the god Bel in Babylon to indicate continued kingship there. His purpose, however, was to set up a separate Babylonian kingdom in order to restrict Assyrian commitments but still have a strong ally. To do this he had to crush the persistently troublesome Chaldeans who sought and often maintained control of the southern region.

Clay prism from Sennacherib's palace telling of his attack on Judah in 701 B.C. BM

Sargon had allowed the former Chaldean ruler of Babylon, Merodach-baladan (II Kgs 20:12), to remain head of his tribe Bit-Yakin. But the latter revolted against Sennacherib. In wrath the Assyrian marched against the Babylonian cities, taking 88 fortified towns and finally entering Babylon where he got a friendly reception. He therefore limited his booty-taking to Merodach-baladan's palace.

Unfortunately for the Assyrians, the wily Chaldean ruler escaped to the marshlands at the head of the Persian Gulf where he awaited the opportunity to stir up revolt again. This opportunity came when Bel-ibni, the pro-Assyrian governor of Babylon, proved weak and incompetent. Sennacherib responded by sending one of his younger sons, Ashur-nadin-shum, on a campaign in the year 700 B.C. His campaign, however, had limited success because Merodach-baladan escaped again to Elam, and though Ashur-nadin-shum became ruler of Babylon the nobles there were unwilling to support an Assyrian king.

Sennacherib later abandoned his policy of making Babylonia an independent kingdom and set out in 694 B.C. on a long and difficult operation. He brought sailors and shipbuilders from Tyre, Sidon, and Cyprus to build boats on the upper Euphrates, and on the Tigris near Nineveh. The latter sailed down the Tigris to a place called Opir, crossed over to the Euphrates to bypass the enemy, and proceeded to the Persian Gulf. With these boats Sennacherib was now able to overpower the marsh area where the Chaldeans took refuge. While this arduous campaign was taking place, however, the situation in Babylon deteriorated badly when Ashur-nadin-shum was carried off captive by the Elamites. The Assyrian army was too weary from its long campaign on the gulf to set things in order before returning home.

In 693 B.C. a Mushezib-Marduk set himself up as ruler of Babylon with a strong pro-Chaldean policy. Sennacherib's annals speak strongly against Mushezib-Marduk, probably because he himself directed a hate campaign against the Assyrians, even forbidding Assyrian traders entrance to Babylon. Mushezib was very successful in organizing the traditional enemies of the Assyrians, the Elamites, the Arameans E of the Tigris, and all the Chaldean clans into a large army. In the year 691 the opposing armies met at a place called Halule. Though Sennacherib's annals claim a great victory, it is apparent that the losses on both sides were very heavy and that the Assyrians could not immediately consummate the war.

A stroke of fortune helped Sennacherib's cause when the Elamite king became ill in 689, with resultant internal confusion and a great weakening of Mushezib's forces. After nine months of continuous siege, Babylon racked with famine and pestilence finally yielded and was sacked and leveled by Sennacherib's army. The other idols were smashed and the statue of Marduk, the chief city-god of Babylon, was taken captive to Assyria; to this historic event Isaiah very likely refers (Isa 46:1-2), for Cyrus *honored* the gods of Babylon (ANET, p. 316). This was the turning point in Sennacherib's policy: for the first time the mighty Assyrian proclaimed himself "King of Sumer and Akkad." Sennacherib immediately set about to rebuild the city of Babylon. For the next eight years (689-681) peace prevailed in Babylonia. During this time Sennacherib gave complete authority over the southern provinces to his son Esar-haddon and by this indicated that he was to become his father's successor.

The E and N frontiers were never very troublesome to Sennacherib, for he pursued a rather cautious policy in these areas. In the W, notably Syria and Palestine, this was not to be the case. Chaldean emissaries, like those from Merodach-baladan who visited Hezekiah (II Kgs 20:12-13), helped stir up intrigue and rebellion against Sennacherib. In the year 701 Sennacherib was unable to deal with the problems of Babylonia because of the disorders brewing in the westlands.

In his third campaign (ANET, pp. 287-288), the king tells how he marched against Hatti, the Assyrian name for the western country derived from earlier Hittite domination. Luli, the king of Sidon and leading ruler of the Phoenician coastal cities, fled to Cyprus. Sennacherib overwhelmed the area and set up a puppet in Sidon, one Tuba'lu (Ethba'al). Most of the rulers nearby, like Arvad, Byblos, and Ashdod (called kings of Amurru), capitulated immediately. Others from Edom, Moab, etc., brought heavy tribute and kissed Sennacherib's feet.

To the S several of the Philistine cities chose to resist the Assyrian yoke as did Hezekiah of Judah. Before the arrival of Sennacherib in the area Ekron had deposed its pro-Assyrian king, Padi, and turned him over to Hezekiah in chains. Ashkelon with its ruler Sidqia also remained obstinate. Sennacherib marched S taking numerous strategic cities. Ashkelon fell and Sidqia was carried away. A battle developed near Eltekeh (cf. Josh 19:44) as the Assyrian force marched toward Ekron. A large force led by various princes of Egypt and the cavalry of the king of Ethiopia, Shabataka, perhaps led by his younger brother Tirhakah (*q.v.;* II Kgs 19:9), was soundly defeated by Sennacherib. He then besieged Eltekeh and Timnah (cf. Jud 14:1), conquered them, and carried away their spoils. Ekron was assaulted and its officials impaled on poles around the city. In all, Sennacherib claimed to have taken 46 fortified cities and countless villages, and a total of 200,150 captives. Next came Jerusalem.

Hezekiah had instituted many religious reforms and had therefore the wholehearted support of the great prophet Isaiah. He had also strengthened the water supply of Jerusalem by blocking the eastern flow of the Gihon spring and successfully digging a tunnel through rock to bring water inside Jerusalem's walls (II Kgs 20:20; II Chr 32:30). Expansion of power into Philistia (II Kgs 18:8) and alliances with the Chaldeans (Isa 39:1) and the Egyptians (Isa 30:1; 31:1) had made Hezekiah the leading ruler of Palestine. His overthrow was certainly a major objective of Sennacherib. The dealings between these two historic figures is highly documented, sources being the Bible, the annals of Sennacherib, and the Gr. historian Herodotus. Scholars have detected some problems, however, in putting the sources together to obtain a unified account.

It does not seem necessary to posit two sources to the biblical account in II Kgs 18 and 19 as some do (Emil G. Kraeling, *Rand McNally Bible Atlas,* 1956, p. 302). Kraeling supposes there was an annalistic source based on dependable records which tells of a complete surrender by Hezekiah to Sennacherib while the latter was at Lachish (II Kgs 18:13-16). Then follows a patriotic legend which makes Isaiah the hero who predicts the deliverance of Jerusalem (II Kgs 18:17 – 19:37). This second source is divided into two versions; in the one Sennacherib's plan to take Jerusalem is frustrated by his hearing a rumor of the coming of Pharaoh Tirhakah (II Kgs 19:9); and in the other, Jerusalem is saved by the angel of the Lord, presumably using a pestilence. While it is not easy to solve all the detailed obscurities in a very brief account of complicated events, it seems that II Kgs 18:13-16 is simply a summary statement of the full effect of Sennacherib's dealings with Hezekiah while at Lachish. The Judean king did pay tribute, but the rest of the account (18:17 – 19:37) is given to assure the reader that Sennacherib never took Jerusalem. This fact is strongly implied in Sennacherib's earlier statement in his annals: "I shut up Hezekiah like a bird in a cage."

It is not characteristic of Assyrian annals to miss exploiting any event which would have increased the glory of the Assyrian monarch and his god. If Hezekiah had completely capitulated at any time much would have been made of it. A corollary to this is the reluctance of Assyrians to admit any failure, so that though the disaster to Sennacherib's army was so famous that Herodotus heard about it 250 years later in Egypt, yet Sennacherib himself makes no mention of it. Furthermore, Isaiah's bit of predictive prophecy in one terse statement hints at several aspects of Sennacherib's troubles which began in Palestine. II Kgs 19:7 (RSV) speaks first of the Lord's putting "a spirit" in Sennacherib, or better a "blast" (a wind) against him; the latter would refer to the decimation of his army. Secondly, a rumor was to be heard of the coming of Tirhakah (either as a general in 701 B.C. or as Pharaoh during a second campaign of Sennacherib). Thirdly, Isaiah predicts his assassination after he returned home (Isa 37:7). Such a combination of disastrous events and forewarnings would certainly lead to a hasty retreat.

Hence it seems reasonable to posit a second

campaign into Judah for II Kgs 19:8-36 (or 18:17–19:36), possibly in connection with a suspected campaign against Arabia *c.* 688 B.C. Sennacherib does not report it, but it seems most likely for the following reasons:

1. Herodotus knew of a disaster to Sennacherib's army (II.141). The Gr. historian speaks of mice gnawing the leather shields, the bowstrings, and quivers, which may possibly allude to bubonic plague carried by mice as the instrument of the angel of the Lord.

2. Assyrian kings never report disaster in their annals. Parallel sources show how defeat is often reported as a great victory.

3. Sennacherib omits a report of the siege of Lachish and Libnah from his annals which describe the campaign of 701 B.C., and the biblical account omits the battle at Eltekeh which was so important in 701. Yet Lachish was one place where the king himself directed the siege, and he considered it so important he had it vividly carved in bas-relief on the walls of his palace at Nineveh (now in the British Museum).

4. Another basic part of the biblical account omitted in the annals is the role of the Rabshakeh or chief officer and his psychological warfare so effectively used against Hezekiah when the former insisted on speaking in Heb. rather than in the diplomatic tongue, Aramaic. The Jews on the walls of Jerusalem were undoubtedly impressed with Rabshakeh's speech (II Kgs 18:26-35). This omission, however, might be plausible if it was a common procedure, as seems likely.

The assassination of Sennacherib by two of his sons (II Kgs 19:36-37) is confirmed by several Babylonian sources, though the Babylonian sources make it singular, a son, and the biblical names of the sons remain unconfirmed. Also the god Nisroch is unknown in any source. The name is probably the result of a textual corruption. An inscription of Esar-haddon describes the fight for the throne (ANET, p. 289), which tells how his brothers plotted against him after Sennacherib his father named him successor to the throne. In the winter of 680 B.C. Esar-haddon organized an expedition against the rebellious brothers and overthrew them. They "fled to an unknown land" according to the annal, but the Bible says it was Ararat (Urartu). This inscription does not mention the actual assassination, but this is in keeping with the policy of such annals never to record a disaster.

[The principal argument in favor of a two-campaign theory to explain the biblical account of Sennacherib's invasion of Judah concerns the age of Tirhakah in 701 B.C. (John Bright, *A History of Israel,* Philadelphia: Westminster, 1959, pp. 268-271, 282-287). Formerly it was thought that this Ethiopian king of Egypt was only 20 years old at the time of his accession to the throne as co-regent of his brother Shabataka in 690/689, so that he would have been too young to lead an army to aid Hezekiah in 701. Now, however, it is recognized Tirhakah was 20 when he began to lead an army as his brother's representative in 701 (G. L. Archer, "Old Testament and Recent Archaeology–from Solomon to Zedekiah," BS, CXXVII [1970], 209 f.). – Ed.]

See Assyria; Hezekiah; Israel, Kingdom of.

Bibliography. Raymond P. Dougherty, "Sennacherib and the Walled Cities of Judah," JBL, XLIX (1930), 160-171, D. D. Luckenbill, *The Annals of Sennacherib,* Chicago: Univ. of Chicago, 1924.

E. B. S.

SENSE

1. Understanding or meaning of a statement. Heb. *śekel* is used in Neh 8:8 of Ezra and others who "read in the book in the law of God distinctly, and gave the sense."

2. Mental faculty, organ of perception. Gr. *aisthētērion* is used in Heb 5:14 to describe those who are sufficiently awakened and enlightened morally to discern good and evil.

SENSUAL. The KJV translation of *psychikos* in Jas 3:15 and Jude 19. Elsewhere the KJV uses "natural" for this Gr. word (I Cor 2:14; 15:44, 46). The NASB renders *aselgeia* as "sensuality" in Mk 7:22; Rom 13:13; II Cor 12:21; Gal 5:19; Eph 4:19; I Pet 4:3; II Pet.2:2, 7 ("sensual conduct"), 18.

Sensuality issues from the "flesh" (Mk 7:22-23; Gal 5:19), dominates the unregenerate (Eph 4:19; I Pet 4:3), characterizes the

Sensuality issues from the "flesh" (Mk 7:22-23; Gal 5:19), dominates the unregenerate (Eph 4:19; I Pet 4:3), characterizes the

The sexual overtones of sensuality are seen in its close association (in NASB) with "impurity," "immorality," and "sexual promiscuity" (Rom 13:13; II Cor 12:21; Gal 5:19; Eph 4:19).

Sensual men, devoid of the Holy Spirit (Jude 19) and blind to spiritual truth (I Cor 2:14; Jas 3:15), possess no inner power to restrain their sinful inclinations. Such people "have abandoned themselves to sensuality, so as to practice with eagerness all kinds of impurity" (Eph 4:19, Berkeley).

SENTRY. *See* Occupations: Sentry.

SENUAH. *See* Hasenun.

SEPARATION

1. The KJV translation of Heb. *niddâ*, the state of being shunned, is better translated "impurity." Separation from the worship of the Lord, and sometimes from the community of Israel, was caused by a state of ritual uncleanness. Such things as contact with the dead (Num 19), childbirth (Lev 12), menstrual or other discharges from the sexual organs (Lev 15), or leprosy (Lev 13-14) excluded the Israelite from normal communion with God and men. The term "days of separation" might better be translated "days of uncleanness," as in

RSV. This state was not one of sin, but a reminder to the people that they were to be in all things holy and pure before God. The ashes of a red heifer mixed with water made the "water of separation" or "uncleanness" used to cleanse one from the defilement of death (Num 19). *See* Uncleanness.

2. Another Heb. word is used (*nēzer*) to define another type of separation. The Nazarite (*q.v.*), who by a vow separated himself unto the Lord for a longer or shorter period, spoke of these days as the days of his separation (Num 6). *See* Dedication; Holiness, Holy.

P. C. J.

SEPHAR (sē'fär). This was a mount of the E in the SW section of Arabia. It was probably located in the southern interior of Yemen. It could, however, be Isfar, situated near the port of Mirbat (Gen 10:30).

SEPHARAD (sĕf'ȧ-răd). The proper name of a region to which exiles were taken from Jerusalem (Ob 20). Its exact location is uncertain. Possible sites include Sparad on the Bosphorus, Sardis, Sparta, and Spain (as seen in the term Sephardic Jews, who lived in Spain in the Middle Ages). Most likely it is the country near Media mentioned in the Assyrian records of Sargon and Esar-haddon, called Sapparda in Persian.

SEPHARVAIM (sĕf'ȧr-vā'ĭm), **SEPHARVITE** (sĕf'ȧr-vīt). A city mentioned as having been conquered by the Assyrians according to the boasts of Rabshakeh and Sennacherib to Hezekiah (II Kgs 18:34; 19:13; Isa 36:19; 37:13). The place also furnished colonists to repopulate Samaria (II Kgs 17:24). Its people the Sepharvites worshiped the gods Adrammelech and Anammelech (v. 31).

Because of the dual form of the name, Sepharvaim was at first identified with the twin Sipparas, Sippara of Shamash and Sippara of Anunitu, the site of which was discovered in 1881 by Hormuzd Rassam at Abu Habba, about 16 miles SE of Baghdad. The cities were located on opposite sides of a canal, and excavations revealed numerous monuments and inscriptions. In the reign of Nabonidus, the Sipparas were the place where the Babylonians, under the king's son, fought with the army of Cyrus the Persian, and their defeat there paved the way for the quick surrender of Babylon.

On the other hand, the Sippara cities worshiped the sun-god rather than the deities mentioned in the Bible. The fact that Sepharvaim is mentioned in connection with Hamath and Arpad suggests that its location is rather to be sought in Syria. A place named Shabarain was captured by Shalmaneser III, and this is probably the same as the Sibraim of Ezekiel (47:16) on the border between Damascus and Hamath. It has been suggested, therefore, that Sibraim was the original reading, and that later scribes confused the name with that of the larger and more famous Sippara cities.

S. C.

SEPTUAGINT. *See* Versions, Ancient and Medieval.

SEPULCHER. *See* Grave; Tomb.

SERAH (sē̆r'ȧ). A daughter of Asher (Gen 46:17; I Chr 7:30; Num 26:46, Sarah), a sister of Imnah, Ishuah, Ishuai, and Beriah, with whom she went into Egypt with Jacob. In Num 26:46 her name occurs in a census reportedly taken from Moses in the wilderness.

Because of the prominence of her name in the genealogical table, the rabbis suggested that she was an extraordinary historical person. Hence Jewish legend has her, because of her virtue and piety, as the first person to inform Jacob that his son Joseph was still living. Because of this she was translated to paradise where there are four mansions, according to the ancient book Zophar. Each of these mansions is presided over by an illustrious woman: Sarah the daughter of Asher, the daughter of Pharaoh who reared Moses, Jochebed the mother of Moses, and Deborah the prophetess.

SERAIAH (sē-rā'yȧ)

1. The scribe or secretary of David (II Sam 8:17). The name appears as Sheva in II Sam 20:25, Shavsha in I Chr 18:16, and perhaps as Shisha in I Kgs 4:3 where his sons appear as secretaries to Solomon.

2. The son of Azariah and high priest in the days of Zedekiah (I Chr 6:14). When Jerusalem fell to Babylon he was taken captive with others to Riblah where he was put to death (II Kgs 25:18–20; Jer 52:24–26). He was the "father," that is, ancestor of Ezra (Ezr 7:1).

3. The son of Tanhumeth of Judah, the leader of one of the guerilla bands still existing after the fall of Jerusalem. He and the other leaders were advised by Gedaliah to submit to and serve Babylon (II Kgs 25:23–24; Jer 40:8–9).

4. The second son of Kenaz and brother of the first judge Othniel. Seraiah's son Joab is called the father of Ge-harashim, "the valley of craftsmen," perhaps because he brought the Kenezite (*q.v.*) metal working skill into Israel (I Chr 4:13–14, RSV).

5. The son of Asiel and father of Josibiah of the tribe of Simeon (I Chr 4:35).

6. A prominent priest who returned from Babylon with Zerubbabel (Ezr 2:2; Neh 12:1; called Azariah in Neh 7:7). He is probably the same man mentioned as the head of a priestly house whose son or descendant, Meraiah, served in the days of Joiakim (Neh 12:12).

7. The son of Hilkiah who sealed the covenant of Nehemiah. He is called "the ruler of the house of God" (Neh 10:2; 11:11). It is highly improbable that he could be the same as #6 who returned almost a century earlier.

8. The son of Azriel who with others was ordered by Jehoiakim to apprehend the prophet Jeremiah after reading and burning the prophet's words of judgment (Jer 36:26).

9. The son of Neriah, an important official in

the court of Zedekiah (Jer 51:59). He is called a *śar m^enûhâ* which the KJV translates "a quiet prince." The literal translation is "prince of rest." He was probably the quartermaster (RSV) or chamberlain (ASV) who was responsible for determining the nightly encampments or "resting places" when he accompanied Zedekiah on the long journey to Babylon in the fourth year of his reign. Seraiah was commissioned by Jeremiah to take with him the prophecy of judgment written against Babylon. When he reached the city he was to tie a stone to the scroll and cast it into the Euphrates as a symbol that Babylon would fall never to rise again (Jer 51:59-64).

P. C. J.

SERAPHIM (sĕr'*a*-fĭm). The plural form of a Heb. word which is translated "fiery serpents" in Num 21:6, but is simply transliterated "seraphim" in Isa 6:2. The creatures thus designated appear in the vision of Isaiah, the description of which shares in the obscurity of symbolism: they have six wings, a face, hands, and feet; they fly, speak, stand reverently in the presence of Yahweh, and dramatize the word of the Lord; they proclaim antiphonally and ministrate effectively the holiness of God. (*See* Angel.) Whatever else one might say about them must be inferred from etymology or Near Eastern lore.

The Heb. verb composed of the three consonants of the singular form means "to burn." This burning was not for the purpose of making light, never the burning of a sacrifice on the altar, but usually to destroy and to eradicate uncleanness and refuse. So one of the seraphim touched the lips of the prophet to burn away the uncleanness. Likewise the fiery serpents of Num 21:6 were sent to rid the Israelite camp of unwholesome attitudes, and those attacking Philistia would destroy that exultant nation (Isa 14:29; cf. 30:6). In the reference in Numbers the word *s^eraphim* has a somewhat adjectival function modifying the word serpent, thus emphasizing the aspect of its fiery sting or the resulting inflammation and burning fever (*see* Animals, IV.8).

It is possible that the elements of fire and the serpentine figure are derived from the celestial phenomenon of lightning, which may have been personified in Near Eastern mythology. Archaeologists have uncovered a stone slab showing a six-winged figure with human body at Tell Halaf (ANEP #655) and a two-winged griffin named "seref" in Egypt.

J. D. Y.

SERED (sĕr'ĕd). The firstborn son of Zebulun (Gen 46:14; Num 26:26). The name is attested in Ugarit as *S-r-d*.

SERGIUS PAULUS (sûr'jĭ-*ŭ*s pôl'*ŭ*s). The Roman governor of Cyprus who sent for Barnabas and Paul at Paphos, sought "to hear the word of God," and became a believer in Christ (Acts 13:7, 12). Luke's characteristic accuracy is shown in calling him a "proconsul" (*anthypatos*) because Cyprus had been a senatorial province since 22 B.C. He is probably to be identified with L. Sergius Paullus, one of the curators of the Tiber during the reign of Claudius (Pliny, *Natural History*, ii.90, 97, 112). He must have gone to Cyprus after his curatorship. Also a Latin inscription mentions an L. Sergius Paulus, who may be the same man with alternate spelling of his family name. On the basis of this inscription his term of office has been dated in A.D. 46/47 or 49/50. Another inscription mentioning a "Paulus proconsul" has been found at Soloi on the N coast of Cyprus.

SERJEANT. The word translated "serjeant" in Acts 16:35, 38 is literally "rod-bearers," the officers called "lictors" by the Romans. These were attendants on the chief magistrates and bore as their sign of office a bundle of rods bound around an axe. The translation "police" in RSV is a good modern equivalent.

SERMON ON THE MOUNT. The passages in Mt 5:1–7:29 and Lk 6:20–7:1 were accorded that designation as early as the 4th cen. A.D. by Augustine in his commentary (*De Sermone domini in monte*). The discourse was delivered from some eminence, probably in the high plateau country of Galilee. A 13th cen. tradition locates the setting as the "horns of Hattin." The significant preface is "seeing the multitude." Percy C. Ainsworth observes: "The great commentary on the Sermon on the Mount is life–life as we all must live it–daily bread, simple fellowship, neighborhood toils and tears."

The account opens with the Beatitudes (Mt 5:3-12) in which Jesus claims to know just what life means and how it ought to be lived, holding that the answer to the universal quest for happiness can be found as men identify themselves with the kingdom of God. (See F. Hauch, *"Makarios,"* TDNT, IV, 362-370.)

In this sermon, which Lord Acton defined as the real revelation of a morally new society, Jesus contrasts the spiritual ideals underlying moral conduct with the mere external requirements of the law. He teaches that the anger which fructifies in murder is wrong; that reconciliation with a brother is more essential than the performance of outward acts of worship; that the entertainment of lascivious thoughts makes one as guilty as committing adultery; that His followers are to be so devoted to truthfulness that oath taking is rendered unnecessary; that revenge is evil; that enemies quite as much as friends and benefactors are to be recipients of our love; that magnifying the defects in others' lives and officiously attempting to remodel their lives, and that in a censorious attitude, are reprehensible; that pious exercises, such as almsgiving, prayer, and fasting, are to be devoid of ostentation; that only one master is possible for the Christian.

Many noteworthy passages appear in this sermon. There are the parables of the inner light (Mt 6:22–23) and the two houses (Mt 7:24–27). The Lord's Prayer, cited by Matthew, in its first section deals with duties to God, and in its second, duties to fellowmen. Jesus derived this model from a Jewish background, giving an example of how the soul with economy of words can speak to God. (See Frederick W. Farrar, *The Lord's Prayer,* 1894, and J. D. Jones, *The Lord's Prayer,* 1903.)

The Golden Rule (Mt 7:12) was termed the Golden Law in the 18th cen. by Richard Godfrey and Isaac Watts, whereas William Dean Howells in his novel *Silas Lapham* (1885) uses the now familiar phrase. This principle of reciprocity, which Wesley said commends itself to every man's conscience, was made the basis of John Stuart Mill's ethical system and is reflected in Kant's dictum that one ought so to act as though the maxim of his conduct were destined by the force of his will to become a universal law of nature. The difference between Kant's categorical imperative and Christ's Golden Rule is that Kant's maxim is contentless, while Christ's is the summary of the contents of the second table of God's moral law. Jesus exemplified the Golden Rule in the parable of the Good Samaritan (Lk 10:25 ff.).

Mt 5:41 enunciates the principle of the second mile, enjoining an unstinted willingness to do more than anyone can ask, and of kindness to the one who oppressed you; it is the cheated client doing good to the man who harmed him; it is what Shakespeare causes Iago to declare concerning Desdemona that "she holds it a vice in her goodness not to do more than is requested."

Mt 7:11 is one of the most telling revelations of God's nature, with the analogy of earthly parenthood tinctured by sin, yet ever manifesting goodness to the offspring.

Mt 5:48 presents the ideal of the Christian life, that the children of God be like their heavenly Father, perfect in holiness. It represents an obligation resting upon us presently, and a prophecy of what Christians are to be eternally.

Mt 7:20 commands that preachers, healers, and miracle workers be judged by the fruit of their works rather than their words. It is the basis for warning and criticism against modern so-called faith healers.

Advocates of a non-doctrinal Christianity tend to exalt the morals of the Sermon on the Mount as the essence of our religion, disregarding Christ's claims to deity. They fail to note that the entire discourse is pervaded by Jesus' ringing affirmations of His divine nature and power. J. Gresham Machen observes that the Beatitudes contain a strong note of authority, which would be overwrought and pathological in any other person than the Jesus of the Bible. Machen inquires: "Who is there who tells with such extraordinary assurance what

Church atop the Mount of Beatitudes. HFV

sort of persons will be in the kingdom of God? Who is this that announces to men rewards that only God can give?" (J. Gresham Machen, *The Christian Faith in the Modern World,* p. 163). Further, Jesus implies His deity as He declares that His teaching has superseded the OT standard: "Ye have heard that it was said . . . but I say unto you." The Sermon on the Mount is unmistakable testimony of Jesus to His deity, apart from which His ethic, however admirable and unsurpassed, would be without authority.

For all who understand the principle that the covenant of works promulgated in Eden must be kept perfectly by man, Christ proves His deity when He says: "Think not that I am come to destroy the law, or the prophets: I am not come to destroy, but to fulfill," and immediately adds, "Till heaven and earth pass, one jot or one tittle shall in no wise pass from the law, till all be fulfilled" (Mt 5:17–18). He was intimating He would keep them. Since Christ dealt directly with two of the Ten Commandments (vv. 21, 27) and the second table of the law (v. 43), we must conclude He had specific reference to them as well as to the rest of the OT. He exegeted the commandments as rules for the child of God for his progressive growth in grace in sanctification. At the same time when He said, "I am come . . . to fulfill," He was intimating He would keep the law Himself in our stead for our justification—and this is just what we find taught in the rest of the Gospels and the Epistles in particular.

G. H. T.

SERPENT, SNAKE. *See* Animals: Cobra, IV. 8; Viper, IV. 34.

SERPENT, BRAZEN. *See* Brazen Serpent.

SERPENT, FIERY. During Israel's fortieth year in the wilderness, they journeyed toward the Promised Land in the barren Arabah (between the Dead Sea and the Red Sea, Akaba). When they complained about the food and water, God sent a plague of fiery serpents so that many

Israelites died (Num 21:8; Deut 8:15). Some scholars believe the snakes were called "fiery" because of their color, but this does not seem to fit Heb. usage. More probably it refers to the burning pain caused by their venomous bite. Isa 14:29; 30:6 refer to fiery flying serpents. It is not known whether "flying" refers to their speed or to a hood (as of a cobra) that gave the appearance of wings.

See Brazen Serpent.

SERUG (sêr'ŭg). The firstborn son of Reu and great-grandfather of Abraham (Gen 11:20; I Chr 1:26; Lk 3:35, RSV). The Akkadian city and district of Sarugi, situated W of Haran, is thought to have been named after Serug.

SERVANT. *See* Occupations: Servant; Service.

SERVANT OF THE LORD. The Heb. *'ebed YHWH* is a designation of one who stands in special relationship to Yahweh and is charged with a special mission. The full formal employment of the term appears prominently with the name Moses (cf. Josh 1:1 ff., ASV; I Chr 6:49; II Chr 1:3; Neh 1:7; 10:29).

The plural, servants, occurs several times as the humble self-designation of worshipers. Much wider is the circle of persons who stand as servant of Yahweh in those passages where, for the divine name, there is substituted the possessive pronoun. So the Lord addresses David as "My servant"; Solomon in speaking to the Lord refers to himself as "Thy servant"; both Elijah and Jonah are designated by another as "His servant." While the word "servant" may be used by anybody to express an inferior position, the full sense of the word denotes ownership by the one of whom he is the servant. In the term under discussion, this ownership arises from God's gracious call to perform a special service such as leader, prophet, and king.

The term has currency in those elevated passages in Isaiah where the Lord describes prophetically the unique role of "My servant" (42:1-7; 49:1-6; 50:4-9; 52:13–53:12). While scholarship debates the original reference of the writer, the NT writers applied the title (Gr. *pais*) to Jesus as the Messiah, thus making Him the fulfillment and par excellence the Servant of the Lord, the Suffering Servant (Mt 12:18, from Isa 42:1; Acts 3:13, 26; 4:27, 30–ASV and newer versions).

Modern Jewish scholars usually interpret all references to the "servant(s) of the Lord" in Isa 41-66 to mean Israel as God's chosen people in a collective sense. Older Jewish expositors (e.g., the Targum of Isaiah; in the Midrash, *q.v.*), however, commonly applied Isa 52:13–53:12 to a future Messiah.

See Service.

Bibliography. David Baron, *The Servant of Jehovah,* 3rd ed., Grand Rapids: Zondervan, 1954. C. R. North, *The Suffering Servant in Deutero-Isaiah,* 2nd ed., Oxford: Clarendon Press, 1956, with full bibliography; "Servant of the Lord, The," IDB, IV, 292-294. H. H. Rowley, *The Servant of the Lord and Other Essays on the Old Testament,* London: Lutterworth Press, 1952, pp. 1-88. Edward J. Young, *Isaiah 53,* Grand Rapids: Eerdmans, 1952. W. Zimmerli and J. Jeremias, *"Pais Theou,"* TDNT, V, 654-717.

J. D. Y.

SERVICE. The terms "service" and "servant" in the Bible are used in the sense of both servitude and ministry. Slavery, bondage, or enforced service is attested from the earliest times throughout the ancient Near East. Slave labor was utilized mainly by wealthy families and in royal building projects, such as the construction of the pyramids in Egypt and pharaoh's store cities before the Exodus.

In Palestine and Syria the slave was usually a domestic servant rather than an agricultural or industrial worker. In the Alalakh tablets from Syria in the 18th and 15th cen. B.C. the highest number of slaves belonging to one master was three. The big landowners, like those of Babylonia and Assyria, seem to have preferred free tenants to slave labor (I. Mendelsohn, "On Slavery in Alalakh," IEJ, V [1955], 65-72).

The average price of slaves rose gradually like that of other commodities during the 2nd and 1st mils. B.C. For the remarkable correspondence between the prices of slaves mentioned in Scripture and those recorded on inscriptions contemporary with the biblical incidents, see K. A. Kitchen, "Slave," NBD, p. 1196.

The most frequent Heb. verb for "serve" is *'ābad,* "to work," "labor" (Ex 5:18; 20:9; 34:21). Commonly it meant to serve a master as a slave (Ex 21:6; Deut 15:12, 18; Jer 34:14); but the noun *'ebed,* in addition to "slave," has a variety of meanings. For example, in II Sam 9:2*a* Ziba was Saul's "servant" or retainer; in v. 10 Ziba's 20 "servants" were bondmen; and in vv. 2*b,* 11 "thy servant" is a polite expression of humility. Because of the king's powerful control, the word *'ebed* also means the king's subjects, especially his mercenaries, officers, and ministers, those who had joined his service.

Heb. *na'ar,* "young man," "servant," suggests that often one's attendant was youthful and unmarried (Gen 22:3; Num 22:22; Jud 7:10 f.). The verb *shārat* means "to minister," to serve in a personal way, as Joshua waited upon Moses (Ex 24:13; 33:11). The female slave or handmaid was called *shipḥâ* (e.g., Hagar, Gen 16:1; 25:12) or *'āmâ* (Gen 20:17; Ex 23:12), whose status was often that of a childbearing concubine to her master.

Service in the OT

Secular service

1. A work agreement (Heb. *'ăbôdâ*) between two parties for a stipulated period of time (Gen 29:27; 30:26; cf. Hos 12:12).

2. The work (*'ăbôdâ*) of a servant, i.e., heavy, menial work (Lev 23:7-8, 21, 25, 36).

3. Work of the hired servant or hireling (Heb. *śākîr,* Ex 12:45; Job 7:1-2; Isa 16:14; Gr. *misthios,* Lk 15:17, 19), who, though he is used as an example of one who takes no real interest or responsibility (Job 7:2; 14:6; Jn 10:12-13), still is to be treated fairly and handled with kindness (Mal 3:5; cf. Eph 6:5-9), and not as a bondservant (Lev 25:39).

4. Israelitish slave servants. Men became slaves of their brethren for the following reasons: (*a*) Poverty, the inability to sustain oneself and one's family. This was regarded as a kind of sale, in that the person sold the right to his labor to one of his brethren in return for provision of sustenance for himself and his family (Lev 25:39, 47; cf. Deut 15:12-13). Exorbitant interest rates on loans, although forbidden under the statutes regulating usury, often brought a man to insolvency and subsequent slavery. Some of David's followers were defaulting debtors who had fled their creditors (I Sam 22:2). (*b*) Restitution for theft. Restitution by law required the return of at least double the amount stolen. Should the thief be unable to make the required restitution, he was sold for his theft and made the restitution by his work (Ex 22:1-4). (*c*) Birth. Children of a Heb. slave became slaves of his master by birth (Ex 21:4), though this could not have been permanent except in the case of one who had chosen permanent slavery (Ex 21:6; Deut 15:17). (*d*) Children of a defaulting debtor were sold to pay the debt or were claimed along with their father as slaves till the next year of jubilee (Ex 21:7; Lev 25:39-41, 47, 54; II Kgs 4:1; Neh 5:5; Isa 50:1; Job 24:9). (*e*) Abduction. Joseph's brothers essentially stole him and sold him as a slave (Gen 37:27-28; cf. 45:4). To reduce a kidnapped person to slavery was a crime punishable by death in the laws both of Hammurabi (#14, ANET, p. 166) and of Moses (Ex 21:16; Deut 24:7).

There were limits to slave service under the Mosaic law. Besides freedom granted in the year of jubilee, a relative might redeem the slave (Lev 25:48-49). If not redeemed, however, a person would receive freedom after six years' service together with a gift of cattle or fruits from his master (Ex 21:2; Deut 15:12-15). A man's wife, and her children also, went free with him (Ex 21:3). If, however, the slave had received her from her master, then she and her children remained with the owner (Ex 21:4).

In his seventh year, an Israelitish servant could choose to become a permanent slave instead of accepting freedom. If so, he came before the elders and had his ear bored through with an awl against a doorpost, and thereby became a lifelong servant (Ex 21:6; Deut 15:17; cf. Christ in Ps 40:5-8; Heb 10:5 f.).

5. Special provisions covered a maid sold as a household slave or concubine. Should she not please her master, she could not be resold but was to be immediately redeemed (Ex 21:7-11; Deut 21:14). Yet if her master kept his contract, she could not leave either at six years or in the year of jubilee. He must give her the same dowry as a daughter if he betrothed her to his son. He must treat her equally with any other wife he took. Should he fail in any of the above, she was to be set free without any payment to him as owner.

Prisoners of Rameses II at Abu Simbel, Egypt. Prisoners of war commonly sold into slavery.
LL

6. Non-Israelitish slaves, purchased from heathen nations or captured in the conquest of Palestine (Num 31:9, 18, 35; Deut 20:14) or in later wars, remained permanent slaves along with their children (Lev 25:44-46). The Gibeonites and their descendants were permanently assigned to be public slaves to cut wood and carry water for Israel's central shrine (Josh 9:23, 27; Neh 7:57-60; *see* Nethinim). In contrast, Israelites who were slaves of non-Israelites living in the land could obtain their freedom either at the year of jubilee, or by paying the purchase price less the value of years of service already given (Lev 25:47-55).

Besides all the provisions mentioned for slaves, there was also the possibility of manumission, i.e., receiving freedom from the hand of the owner of the slave (Ex 21:26-27). Rabbinists have suggested four ways to gain freedom: (*a*) Redemption by a payment of money (already mentioned). (*b*) Granting of a bill of freedom. (*c*) Disposition through a testament or will. (*d*) Making a slave one's heir (cf. Gen 15:2). To these should be added: (*e*) By command of the Lord, as through the prophet Jeremiah (Jer 34:8-10).

7. Service as royal officials and military officers (Heb. *'ăbôdâ,* I Chr 26:30; *shārat,* I Chr 27:1; 28:1; II Chr 17:12-19).

Protection was provided for the slave in the law of Moses. Loss of an eye or a tooth entitled the slave to freedom (Ex 21:26-27; cf. Ex 21:20; Lev 24:22). Extradition of fugitive slaves seeking shelter in an Israelite home was prohibited (Deut 23:15-16). The slave of an Israelite was to be circumcised. He was thereby entitled to the pascal sacrifice (Ex 12:44), all the Jewish festivals (Deut 12:12, 18; 16:11, 14), and the sabbath rest (Ex 20:10–11; Deut 5:14).

Religious service

1. Family observance (Heb. *'ăbôdâ*) of the Passover (Ex 12:14–27; 13:5).

2. Service or care (*'ăbôdâ*) of the tabernacle by Levites (Num 3:7–8; 18:7, 23).

3. Service in music in the temple (*'ăbôdâ*, I Chr 25:1–7; II Chr 35:15).

4. Priestly service in worship of the Lord (*'ăbôdâ*, I Chr 24:1–31; II Chr 8:14; *shārat*, II Chr 29:11; Isa 56:6; *latreia*, Heb 9:1, 6, 9).

5. Work as a builder on the tabernacle or temple (Ex 36:1, 3, 5; I Chr 28:20).

6. Moses as an exceptional leader was often called the servant of the Lord (e.g., Ex 14:31; Num 12:7; Deut 34:5; Josh 1:1, 15; 8:31). God called all Israelites "My servants" (Lev 25:42), and such an appellation was common for the worshiper of a deity in the ancient Near East (see Yamauchi, "Slaves of God"). Later the term "Servant of Jehovah" (*q.v.*), Heb. *'ebed Yāhweh*, became a prophetic designation of Jesus Christ—a title stressing His absolute obedience to the Father (Isa 42:1–4; quoted in Mt 12:18–21; Isa 49:1–9; 50:10; 52:13–53:12).

Service in the NT

In the Hellenized cities of the NT period slaves constituted a large part of the population. Jesus ministered to Roman slaves (Lk 7:2–10) and often mentioned slaves in His teaching (e.g., Mt 10:24 f.) and parables (e.g., Mt 18:23–34), yet He never criticized the institution of slavery. Many slaves at that time were well-educated men who had been captured or had fallen upon lean days; they were capable of managing large estates and business affairs (Mt 25:14–23). But unlike classical Greece or imperial Rome, the economy of Israel never became dependent on slave labor. The benevolent requirements toward slaves in the Mosaic law prevented profitable large-scale dealing in slaves.

The term "servant" or "bondslave" (Gr. *doulos*) is often used by a man of God such as Paul to describe his total dedication (Rom 1:1; Phil 1:1; Tit 1:1). Such submission to Christ is called in Rom 12:1 our "reasonable service" (*latreia*, the performance of religious rites and duties).

Paul warns against the slavery (NASB, Gr. *douleia*) of legalism (Gal 4:24; 5:1), and likens the one held in the grip of sin to a slave (Rom 6:6, 16–20). All of creation will at Christ's return be delivered from the slavery of corruption (Rom 8:21). Unregenerate men today are enslaved all their lives by the fear of death (Heb 2:15, NASB).

Another Gr. root that often is translated "to serve" or "service" is *diakoneō*, to serve by waiting on someone, as in Martha's preparing food for the table (Jn 12:2; Lk 10:40; cf. 12:37; 17:8; 22:26 f; Acts 6:2). By extension the term came to mean any ministry of physical or financial help to others (Mt 8:15; 25:44; Lk 8:3; Acts 11:29; 12:25; 19:22; Rom 15:25, 31; II Tim 1:18; Heb 6:10). In its highest usage in the NT it is a ministry (*diakonia*) of the gospel (Acts 6:4; 20:24; 21:19), received from the Lord (Col 4:17; II Tim 4:5; II Cor 5:18) and directed by the Spirit (I Cor 12:4–7; II Cor 3:8). *See* Minister.

Other Gr. words for "servant" emphasize service with care and loving treatment (*therapeia*, Lk 12:42; Mt 24:45), his household status (*oiketēs*, Lk 16:13; Rom 14:4; I Pet 2:18), or his assisting role (*hypēretēs*, Acts 13:5; Lk 4:20).

As the gospel message with its social implications reached into the Roman Empire it became increasingly necessary to define what the attitude of the church toward slavery should be. Many slaves were turning to Christ in the households of Christian masters (Rom 16:10–11; I Cor 1:11). Some of the slaves certainly were desiring emancipation, but Paul counseled the Christian slave to be willing to remain in that condition in which he was "called," i.e., when he was converted, with the right to accept manumission when it was offered him (I Cor 7:20–23). The apostle kept repeating only one great principle—in Christ there is neither bond nor free, all are alike (I Cor 12:13; Gal 3:28; Col 3:11). Thus he ordered slaves to be obedient for the Lord's sake, as a testimony (Eph 6:5–9; Col 3:22–4:1; I Tim 6:2), and at the same time he instructed the masters to treat believing slaves fairly and justly.

In the case of Philemon and Onesimus, Paul exemplifies his attitude toward slavery. He did not ask his friend to free the runaway slave, but commended Onesimus to him as a beloved brother (Phm 16). In such a fraternity all its members would eventually be freed of their bonds without hatred and resorting to violence and bloodshed.

See Occupations: Servant.

Bibliography. CornPBE, "Slavery," pp. 663–666. H. L. Ellison, "The Hebrew Slave: a Study in Early Israelite Society," EQ, XLV (1973), 30–35. I. Mendelsohn, *Slavery in the Ancient Near East*, New York: Oxford Univ. Press, 1949; "Slavery in the OT," IDB, IV, 383–391. A. F. Rainey, "Compulsory Labor Gangs in Ancient Israel," IEJ, XX (1970), 191–202. Karl H. Rengstorf, "*Doulos*, etc.," TDNT, II, 261–280. H. Strathmann and R. Meyer, "*Leitouregeō*, etc.," TDNT, IV, 215–231. William L. Westermann, *The Slave System of Greek and Roman Antiquity*, Philadelphia: American Philosophical Soc., 1955 (with full bibliography). Edwin Yamauchi, "Slaves of God," Bul ETS, IX (1966), 31–49.

R. A. K. and J. R.

SERVITOR. An attendant, but not in a menial capacity (II Kgs 4:43).

SERVITUDE. *See* Service.

SETH (sĕth). The son of Adam and father of Enosh (Gen 4:25–26; 5:3–8; I Chr 1:1). After the murder of Abel, another son was born to Adam and Eve. They named him Seth, meaning "set" or "appointed," because they saw in him the God-appointed "seed" through whom the promise of God was to be fulfilled (Gen 3:15). In the fullness of time, it was indeed through the line of Seth that Christ came (Lk 3:38). Seth died at the age of 912 years (Gen 5:8).

SETHUR (sē'thŭr). Son of Michael, the representative of the tribe of Asher among the 12 spies sent by Moses to view the Promised Land (Num 13:13).

SEVENEH (sē-vē'nĕ). The town at the First Cataract of the Nile on the Ethiopian side, the modern Aswan. KJV reads "the tower of Syene" in Ezk 29:10; 30:6; ASV reads "the tower of Seveneh"; RSV, NEB, and NASB read "from Migdol to Syene." It was a stronghold opposite the island of Elephantine where the Elephantine papyri were found in 1903. *See* Syene.

SEVENTY DISCIPLES OF OUR LORD. The specific group sent forth by Jesus Christ as recorded only in Lk 10:1–20. The work of the Seventy, while similar in major detail to the work of the Twelve, was aimed specifically at preparing the way for Messiah in the villages He was to visit prior to His death. The ministry of the Twelve was more generally to preach the gospel and engage in healing (Lk 9:2); the activity of the Seventy was more limited geographically. The Seventy fulfilled a temporary need, while the Twelve were the selected companions of Messiah on a longer basis.

SEVENTY WEEKS. In general there are three schools of interpretation concerning the eschatology of Dan 9:24–27: (1) the traditional, which recognizes Daniel as the writer and locates the seventieth week near the first advent of Christ; (2) the critical, which places the book as late as 150 B.C. and insists that this passage is history; (3) the premillennial, which accepts Daniel as author and introduces a parenthesis between the sixty-ninth and seventieth week. Of these the third possesses the greatest uniformity and the most consistency with Scripture and history.

"Seventy weeks" renders the Heb. expression "seventy sevens." Prevailing among interpreters is the view that this refers to years, so the RSV has translated the phrase by "seventy weeks of years." The 490 years in this prophecy are for the purpose of finishing the course and career of Israel under the OT law (Dan 9:24). These years begin with the decree of Artaxerxes "to restore and to build Jerusalem" (v. 25), and conclude with a seventieth week when conditions for Israel will have changed for the worse (v. 27).

There are at least two segments in this span of 490 years. The first consists of 69 weeks or 483 years, beginning with the decree and concluding on that day when "Messiah the Prince" made triumphal entry into the city of Jerusalem (Sir Robert Anderson, *The Coming Prince,* pp. 95–105). Messiah is then "cut off" (v. 26). But the seventieth week, unlike the first 69, does not follow immediately and consecutively. In the subsequent 1900 years there is not one seven year period that satisfactorily fulfills the prophecy of v. 27. It is a fair conclusion that this period is yet future and is to be identified with the tribulation ushered in by the rapture of the Church, and is described and unfolded in Rev 6–19.

See Christ, Coming of; Daniel, Book of; Eschatology; Rapture; Tribulation, Great.

H. A. Hoy.

SHAALBIM (shā-ăl'bĭm), **SHAALABBIN** (shā'ȧ-lăb'ĭn). When the Amorites forced the tribe of Dan into the mountains, they came and dwelt in Mount Heres, Aijalon, and Shaalbim (Jud 1:35; cf. Josh 19:42, Shaalabin). In the time of Solomon it was included in the administrative district supervised by Ben-deker (I Kgs 4:9). It has been identified with Selbît, eight miles SE of Lydda and two and a half miles NW of Aijalon.

One of David's mighty men is called Eliahba the Shaalbonite (II Sam 23:32), whose town may have been the same as Shaalbim.

SHAALBONITE (shā-ăl'bŏ-nīt). An inhabitant of Shaalabbin (II Sam 23:32; I Chr 11:33). *See* Shaalbim.

SHAAPH (shā'ăf)

1. A son of Jahdai (I Chr 2:47), descendant of Caleb.

2. The son of Maacah, a concubine of Caleb, the brother of Jerahmeel. He is called the "father" or founder of the city of Madmannah (I Chr 2:48–49).

SHAARAIM (shā'ȧ-rā'ĭm), **SHARAIM** (shȧ-rā'ĭm)

1. A city in the Shephelah or "lowland" of Judah (Josh 15:36) mentioned in close association with Socoh and Azekah. After the defeat of Goliath the Philistines fled along the Shaaraim road on their way to Gath and Ekron (I Sam 17:52). It is unidentified.

2. One of the towns of Simeon (I Chr 4:31), evidently identical with Sharuhen (*q.v.*; Josh 19:6), between Gaza and Beer-sheba.

SHAASHGAZ (shā'ăsh'găz). The eunuch of the Persian king Ahasuerus who was overseer of the concubines, the maidens who had visited the king but had failed to win his approval (Est 2:14).

SHABBETHAI (shăb'ĕ-thī). A Levite who opposed Ezra in dealing with those who had married Gentile wives (Ezr 10:15, RSV, NASB).

He is listed also among those appointed to explain the law (Neh 8:7), and as one of the chiefs of the Levites who had the oversight of "the outward business," i.e., the outside work of the house of God (Neh 11:16). This name, meaning "born on the sabbath," is found in cuneiform inscriptions as *Shabbatai* and in Nabataean and Palmyrene inscriptions as *shbty*.

SHACHIA (shȧ-kī'ȧ). A name in a genealogy of Benjamin, the sixth named of seven sons of Shaharaim by his wife Hodesh (I Chr 8:10). The name is spelled Sachia in RSV and NASB.

SHADDAI (shăd'ī). The transliteration of the Heb. word *shadday* regularly translated "almighty." The root idea of the verb form *shādad* from which it probably is derived means to deal violently; thus the derived substantive describes one who possesses such overwhelming power. The word itself does not appear in the KJV but stands as a footnote in the RSV in the compound form El Shaddai (cf. Gen 17:1; Ex 6:3; *et al.*). The majority of the 48 occurrences of the term are found in Job (31 times) independent of El, while the compound expression is confined to Genesis (five times), Ex 6:3 and Ezk 10:5.

Because the compound term is used several times in Genesis and Exodus in identification of Deity, there is a problem to determine the function of the word Shaddai. Is it adjectival, modifying El, or is it to be treated as a proper name? As a Mesopotamian word it means "mountain." Joined, therefore, with El it would mean "the god of the mountain(s)," and by analogy of Mesopotamian practice might be taken to refer to a tribal deity. In keeping with Genesis usage, however, Shaddai describes God's character from the angle of power that cannot be obstructed. It seems to be an epithet intensifying the thought of power or strength inherent in the generic word El for God in NW Semitic languages (Heb. and Ugaritic). This distinctive aspect of unlimited power is placed in the context of a new aspect of God's character about to be revealed in the name Yahweh, the covenant-keeping God (Ex 6:3). *See* God; God, Names and Titles of.

Bibliography. W. F. Albright, *Yahweh and the Gods of Canaan,* Garden City: Doubleday, 1968, pp. 108,155,188f. Lloyd R. Bailey, "Israelite *'Ēl Šadday* and Amorite *Bêl Šadê*," JBL, LXXXVII (1968), 434-438. Jean Ouellette, "More on *'Ēl Šadday* and *Bêl Šadê*," JBL, LXXXVIII (1969), 470f.

J. D. Y.

SHADES. *See* Rephaim 2.

SHADOW. The Heb. *ṣēl,* "shadow, shade," and Gr. *skia* are used literally, figuratively, and theologically in Scripture. The word is used literally of a tree (Dan 4:12; Hos 4:13; Mk 4:32), a plant (Jon 4:5-6), a mountain (Jud 9:36), a sundial (II Kgs 20:9-11; Isa 38:8), a person (Acts 5:15), a booth (Jon 4:5).

It is used figuratively of the brevity of life (I Chr 29:15; Job 8:9; 14:2; 17:7; Ps 102:11; 109:23; 144:4; Eccl 8:13), of God's protection (Ps 17:8; 36:7; 57:1; 91:1; 121:5; Isa 4:6; 25:4; 49:2), of evil (Isa 30:3; Jer 48:45), of the Messiah's blessings (Isa 4:6; 32:2; 51:16), of physical weakness and death (Job 14:2; 17:7), of spiritual death (Mt 4:16; Lk 1:79). The Heb. *ṣalmāwet,* translated "shadow of death" 18 times in the KJV, more exactly means total, deep, or thick darkness. The KJV rendering is retained by RSV only in the familiar Ps 23:4. The term implies intense darkness, whether literal (Job 28:3; Amos 5:8) or figurative. The ideas of distress and misery (Ps 44:19; 107:10, 14), loneliness and privation (Jer 2:6), and spiritual dearth (Isa 9:2) are implicit in the expression.

It is used theologically of the unchangeableness of God (Jas 1:17), and of the OT types as something that was temporary and preparatory to the NT revelation in Christ (Col 2:17; Heb 8:5; 10:1). The rites and ceremonies in the OT pointed to the realities in the NT, concerning which the book of Hebrews offers the fullest explanation. *See* Type.

R.A.K.

SHADRACH (shăd'răk). The Babylonian name given to Hananiah (Dan 1:7), one of the princes of Judah taken captive to Babylon, 603 B.C. He with the others stands out as a testimony to a believer's courage in severe trial when true faith is exercised. His Heb. name means "Jah [Yahweh] has been gracious," but no satisfactory meaning has been found for "Shadrach." *See* Hananiah 7.

With Daniel and the others he refused the diet prescribed by the king (Dan 1:8). The successful outcome demonstrates that God works on behalf of those who trust Him, though they be in completely adverse circumstances; that though not free, yet such a one need not give up his convictions in the face of seemingly insuperable power.

Shadrach joined the other two in prayer to God that Nebuchadnezzar's dream be revealed to Daniel so that it might be shown who was the God of heaven (Dan 2:17-18). The outcome of this uninvited test demonstrated the reality of God and the efficacy of the prayer of the righteous man.

The other uninvited test, that of the fiery furnace (Dan 3:8-18), demonstrated the character of faith that shuns apostasy for the sake of God and frequently finds deliverance. He and the other two stood as witnesses to the fact that God's hand prepares His servants for events most unexpected.

H. G. S.

SHAFT

1. The central stem or "thigh" (Heb. *yārēk*) of the golden "candlestick" or lampstand (Ex 25:31; 37:17; Num 8:4).

2. An arrow or dart, used by the Servant of the Lord as an expression of His readiness to minister (Isa 49:2).

SHAGE (shā'gī). Spelled Shagee in ASV, RSV, and NASB. A Hararite and father of Jonathan, one of David's mighty warriors (I Chr 11:34).

SHAHARAIM (shā'*ȧ*-rā'*ĭ*m). A Benjamite who divorced two Israelite wives and in Moab married a third woman, Hodesh (I Chr 8:8, RSV). By Hushim (v. 11) he had had two sons, and by Hodesh (vv. 9-10) he had seven more sons.

SHAHAZIMAH (shā'*ȧ*-zī'm*ȧ*). A town in the territory of Issachar, between Tabor and the Jordan (Josh 19:22). A possible identification is with Tell el Muqarqash, five miles ESE of Mount Tabor, where surface exploration shows pottery typical of most of the 2nd mil. B.C. The name is spelled Shahazumah in the ASV and all newer versions.

SHALEM (shā'lĕm). Named in the KJV as a place near Shechem, but translated in most of the later versions as "in peace" or "safely" (Gen 33:18).

SHALIM, LAND OF (shā 'lĭm). The region through which Saul passed in the search for the lost asses of his father (I Sam 9:4). It probably was in the land of Benjamin, although some scholars believe it is a shortened form of Shaalbim (*q.v.*) in the territory of Dan. Others identify the district with Shual (*q.v.*) N of Michmash. In the ASV and all newer versions it is spelled Shaalim.

SHALISHA (shăl'*ĭ*-sh*ȧ*). A district NE of Lydda on the W slope of the central ridge of Israel. It is mentioned as one of the regions through which Saul passed in his futile search for the asses of his father (I Sam 9:4).

SHALLECHETH, GATE OF (shăl-lē'kĕth). One of the gates of Solomon's temple on the W side, which fell by lot to the porters Shuppim and Hosah (I Chr 26:16).

SHALLUM (shăl'*ŭ*m). Some 12 to 15 people are identified by this name in the OT. The two best known by this name are the king of Israel and the king of Judah. All the others are little known beyond their identity in genealogies.

1. A son of Jabesh. He assassinated Zachariah, who had reigned only six months as successor to Jeroboam in the Jehu dynasty in 753 B.C.(II Kgs 15:10-15). Shallum was king of the northern kingdom ruling in Samaria only one month when he was killed by Menahem. His father's name, Jabesh, may indicate that he was a Gileadite.

2. A son of Josiah. Shallum, better known as Jehoahaz (*q.v.*), was enthroned by the people in Judah in 609 B.C. but deposed after three months' reign by Necho, king of Egypt (I Chr 3:15; II Chr 36:1-4). He was taken as a prisoner to Riblah in Hamath and finally to Egypt where he died, as indicated by Jeremiah (Jer 22:10-12; II Kgs 23:30-34).

3. A son of Naphtali (I Chr 7:13; Shillem in Gen 46:24 and Num 26:49).

4. A descendant of Simeon (I Chr 4:24-25).

5. A son of Sisamai (I Chr 2:40-41), of the tribe of Judah.

6. A Levite and a gatekeeper during David's reign. He was a son of Korah (I Chr 9:17, 19, 31; Ezr 2:42; Neh 7:45; cf. also Meshelemiah in I Chr 26:1 and Shelemiah in I Chr 26:14).

7. A son of Zadok (I Chr 6:12-15). He served as high priest several generations before the Babylonian Captivity in 586 B.C. He was an ancestor of Ezra (Ezr 7:2; cf. also I Esd 8:1 and II Esd 1:1). He is called Meshullam in I Chr 9:11.

8. An Ephraimite whose son Jehizkiah was an official of Samaria during the reign of Pekah (II Chr 28:12).

9. The husband of Huldah the prophetess (II Kgs 22:14; II Chr 34:22), and keeper of the sacerdotal wardrobe. This may also be Jeremiah's uncle by that name (Jer 32:7; cf. also Jer 35:4; 52:24).

10. A son of Bani, a priest, who had married a heathen woman and was compelled to put her away during Ezra's reform (Ezr 10:42).

11. A son of Halohesh, a ruler who aided by his daughters helped to rebuild the walls of Jerusalem under Nehemiah (Neh 3:12).

12. A Levite who served as a gatekeeper of the temple in the time of Ezra and had married a foreign wife (Ezr 10:24).

13. District officer of Mizpah in the time of Nehemiah (Neh 3:15, RSV, NASB); spelled Shallun (*q.v.*) in KJV, ASV, NEB.

S. J. S.

SHALLUN (shăl'ŭn). The ruler of the district of Mizpah in the days of Nehemiah's governorship (Neh 3:15). His responsibility in the rebuilding of the wall of Jerusalem was the Fountain Gate, together with the wall of the pool of Shelah (Shiloah) by the king's garden. His name is Shallum in the RSV and NASB (*see* Shallum 13).

SHALMAI (shăl'mī). The ancestor of the "children of Shalmai" who were among the Nethinim, a group who returned with Zerubbabel after the Exile (Ezr 2:46; Neh 7:48).

SHALMAN (shăl'm*ȧ*n). The destroyer of Beth-arbel (Hos 10:14). The name is either an abbreviated form of the name Shalmaneser, a king of Assyria (*see* Shalmaneser III); a Moabite king, Salamanu, whose name occurs in an inscription of Tiglath-pileser III (ANET, p. 282); or the Shallum who assassinated Zachariah, son of Jeroboam II of Israel (*see* Shallum 1). The third interpretation is strengthened by the LXX, which for Beth-arbel reads "the house of Jeroboam." If Beth-arbel (*q.v.*) is the modern town of Irbid in Gilead, either of the first two kings could have razed it during a campaign against Israel in Transjordan, but no record survives to corroborate such military action.

SHALMANESER (shăl'mȧ-nē'zẽr). The Heb. name *Shalman'eser* is a transliteration of Akkad. *Shulmânu-asharid,* "(the god) Shulman is supreme." This was the name of five Assyrian kings.

1. *Shalmaneser I* (1273–1242 B.C.), son of Adad-nirari I. He restored Assyrian power after a period of impotence during which time it had been overshadowed by the kingdom of Mitanni and by the Hittites. Some detailed records of Shalmaneser's military campaigns have survived. They reveal that he fought against the Urartians (the people of biblical Ararat) in the Armenian mountains, against the land of Hanigalbat, as Mitanni was then called, and against the Aramaeans of northern Mesopotamia. Although the Hittite king, the most powerful monarch of Asia at that time, refused to recognize Shalmaneser I as king of a great power, he could prevent neither the downfall of his own nation which took place within half a century, nor the rise of Assyria as a world power.

The Monolith Inscription of Shalmaneser, which describes the battle of Qarqar and Assyrian contact with Ahab of Israel. BM

2. *Shalmaneser II* (1031–1019 B.C.), son of Ashur-naṣirpal I, lived in one of the darkest periods of Assyrian history. Of him no more is known than that he carried out building operations at Calah (now Nimrud), and that he seized fortresses in the land of Nairi during a military campaign.

3. *Shalmaneser III* (859–824 B.C.), son of Ashur-naṣirpal II. He was a great warrior, one of the founders of the Neo-Assyrian Empire, and the first king of Assyria to come in active contact with Israel. His military campaigns reached into Urartu in the N, Babylonia in the S, and deep into Syria and Cilicia in the W.

During the first three years of his reign he fought against the Aramaeans of Bit-Adini on the upper Euphrates. After he conquered the capital Til-Barsib, now Tell Aḥmar, in 856 B.C., he deported its population, and called the city after his own name, *Kar-Shulmânu-asharid,* "Port of Shalmaneser."

His successes in northern Mesopotamia had the result that the independent Syrian states became alarmed and formed a league under the leadership of Irhuleni of Hamath and Adad-'idri (the Ben-hadad of the OT) of Damascus to resist any advance of the Assyrians. The expected invasion of Shalmaneser came in 853 B.C. He took Aleppo and Hamath and advanced as far as Qarqar on the Orontes River in central Syria, where a fierce battle of the allied nations and the Assyrians took place. The 12 nations of the league from Cilicia in the N to the Ammonites in the S opposed the Assyrians with an army consisting of more than 60,000 infantry and almost 4,000 chariots. Among the allies, King Ahab of Israel is mentioned as having furnished 10,000 foot soldiers and 2,000 chariots, about half of all the chariots of the allied army. Shalmaneser, as was customary for every Assyrian king after a battle, claimed to have won a splendid victory (ANET, pp. 278 f.); but the truthfulness of his claim is doubted, for he returned home with his army immediately after the battle and did not invade Syria again until five years later, in 848 B.C. When this second showdown came the armies of the Syrian coalition were again able to stop the Assyrian advance, this time at Ashtamuka near Hamath (ANET, pp. 279 f.). Three years later Shalmaneser appeared once more in the W, this time with an enormous army of over 120,000 soldiers, but again he did not have the expected success.

The Black Obelisk of Shalmaneser III, showing Jehu paying tribute to Shalmaneser in the second register. BM

After Ben-hadad's death the Syrian alliance seems to have fallen apart. When Shalmaneser reappeared with his army in Syria in 841 B.C., several Syrian kings offered tribute and submission. Among them was King Jehu (*q.v.*) of Israel (ANET, pp. 280 f.). On the famous Black Obelisk, found in 1845 by Henry Layard at Nimrud, and now in the British Museum, the payment of Jehu's tribute is depicted in sculpture. On the second of five rows of relief King Jehu is seen kissing the ground at the feet of Shalmaneser and offering him, as tribute, bars and vessels of precious metals, which are carried by Israelite courtiers (ANEP #351,355). However, Hazael, the new king of Damascus, did not submit, but met the Assyrian army at Mount Hermon, where he was defeated. Shalmaneser advanced toward Damascus, Hazael's capital, and devastated the gardens surrounding the city, but was unable to conquer the fortified city itself. He then marched to the coast and had his victory monument carved in the rocks of the promontory at Dog River, *Nahr el-Kelb*, N of Beirut.

In Babylonia, Shalmaneser interfered in the fight for the throne between the two sons of Nabu-apla-iddin, in 851 B.C., and helped to establish the legitimate heir as king of Babylon (ANET, pp. 276f.). During his last year Shalmaneser had much internal trouble with several rebellions against his regime.

4. *Shalmaneser IV* (783–772 B.C.), son of Adad-nirari III, was the first of three weak rulers who preceded the reign of the great Tiglath-pileser III. He fought several defensive wars against Argistis, king of Urartu, in which he lost some Assyrian territory.

5. *Shalmaneser V* (727–722 B.C.), son of Tiglath-pileser III. Of this king only one inscription is extant, a fragmentary memorial cylinder found at Ezida, the Nabu temple at Borsippa, which shows that Babylonia was secure in his hand. He reigned over that country under the name of Ululai, as is known from the Babylonian King List. All other information about Shalmaneser V comes from the Bible (II Kgs 17:3; 18:9), from Josephus (*Ant.* ix.14.1–3), and from the Babylonian chronicle. These sources reveal that early in his reign he carried out a campaign against the Phoenicians. At that time King Hoshea of Israel assured Shalmaneser of his loyalty, but later, trusting in the pharaoh of Egypt, rebelled against his Assyrian overlord. Shalmaneser marched into Israel and began the three-year siege of Samaria which ended with the destruction of that city, the deportation of its population, and the cessation of the kingdom of Israel (II Kgs 17:3–6). Sargon II, the successor of Shalmaneser V, claimed later in his inscriptions to have conquered Samaria in his first regnal year; but the chronological data of the OT indicate that Samaria fell shortly before Shalmaneser's death, in 723/22 B.C. Whether the king died a natural death or was murdered by Sargon, his successor, is not certain. *See* Sargon 2; Tiglath-pileser.

See Assyria; Israel, Kingdom of.

S. H. H.

SHAMA (shā'mȧ). One of David's mighty men, a son of Hotham (I Chr 11:44).

SHAMARIAH. *See* Shemariah.

SHAMBLES. A British term for meat market, the KJV translation of Gr. *makellon* in I Cor 10:25. Originally it meant a "bench," or "stall" for marketing merchandise, especially meats. Hence it was any place where butcher's meat was sold, a meat market such as every city of the time could boast. The idea of slaughter house is associated.

The South Stoa or Shambles of Corinth. HFV

Such markets were unknown in Judea prior to the Roman conquest. Jews were forbidden by the Talmud to deal there because the flesh of unclean beasts was offered. The flesh of animals sacrificed to idols was also brought for sale. Therefore Paul counseled that the Christians of Corinth should not stop to ask concerning the meat "for conscience sake" and thus become overscrupulous.

The *makellon* or shambles of Corinth was in a large structure called a stoa located on the S side of the agora or marketplace. Similar shops with deep wells for cooling foods and beverages were in the NW stoa at the foot of the hill on which stood the temple of Apollo. An inscription found in fragments near the Lechaion Road leading to the agora mentions a shop with the Latin word *macellum,* the equivalent of Gr. *makellon.* It dates to the last years of Augustus or to the reign of Tiberius. Another has the word *piscario,* "fish market." *See* Corinth.

I. R.

SHAME. The English word translates many different Heb. and Gr. words in the Bible. The biblical concept of shame is primarily that of an inner consciousness of guilt, failure, or unworthiness, and the frequent humiliation and reproach connected with it.

Subjectively, one feels a sense of shame because of sin (Ezr 9:6; Jer 2:26; 31:19), because of defeat (II Chr 32:21; Jer 9:19), because one's personal modesty is violated (II Sam 10:5; 13:11-13; I Cor 11:6), or because of keen disappointment (Jer 2:36; 14:3-4; 48:13; Ps 119:31, 116). With shame is often a sense of confusion (Jer 3:25; Ps 44:15). Shame may be produced in order to lead someone to repentance (I Cor 6:5; 15:34; II Thess 3:14). While many feel ashamed of Christ and His words (Mk 8:38), the true believer will not be embarrassed to confess Him before men (Rom 1:16; II Tim 1:12) or to stand with persecuted fellow Christians (II Tim 1:8, 16).

Objectively, shame is the disgrace or reproach which sinners bring upon themselves (Prov 14:34). This is especially true in the area of sexual sins (Lev 20:17) and the idolatrous practices of the heathen fertility cults (Ezk 16:52, 54, 63). Nakedness or nudity was particularly disgraceful (Isa 20:4; 47:3; Rev 3:18; Jer 13:26). God sends shame as a judgment upon sinners (Ps 44:9, 13-16) and upon the enemies of His people (Ps 71:13, 24; 132:18).

The shame attached to the cross (Heb 12:2) consisted of the curse of God on one considered to be so criminal that he was hanged on a tree (Gal 3:13 with Deut 21:23; Phil 2:8); the despised condition of one accused of blasphemy (Isa 50:6; Mt 26:65-67); the ignominy of the nakedness of the crucified one as symbolic of his being utterly forsaken by God (Isa 53:3-4; Ps 22:6-8, 16-17; Mt 27:35, 41-46); and the reproach of dying outside the city in fulfillment of the type of the sin offering (Heb 13:12-13; Lev 4:11-12).

See Reproach; Christ, Humiliation of.

J. R.

SHAMED (shä'mĕd). Son of Elpaal and builder of Ono and Lod (I Chr 8:12); spelled Shemed in ASV and later versions.

SHAMEFACEDNESS. The Gr. *aidōs,* "modesty," is an attribute paired with sobriety as a description by Paul of the proper adornment of the women professing godliness (I Tim 2:9).

SHAMER (shä'mĕr)

1. The son of Mahli and father of Bani of the tribe of Levi (I Chr 6:46). *See* Shemer 2.

2. An Asherite with four sons (I Chr 7:34), alternately, Shomer (v. 32). *See* Shemer 3.

SHAMGAR (shăm'gär). The son of Anath. Only one verse is allotted to Shamgar, asserting that he killed 600 Philistines with an ox goad and delivered Israel (Jud 3:31). Another reference in the song of Deborah (Jud 5:6) indicates that highway travel was endangered by marauding bands but again made possible through the heroic exploits of Shamgar. He may have belonged to the tribe of Naphtali since the city of Beth-anath was located in its border and tributary to the Israelites (Josh 19:38; Jud 1:33). Shamgar's aggressive warfare may have prepared the way for the defeat of the Canaanites by the Naphtalites under Barak.

Shamgar is linked by some scholars to the Hurrian Simiqari, a personal name occurring in the Nuzian texts (cf. E. A. Speiser and R. H. Pfeiffer, AASOR, XVI [1936], 161). His father's name may be associated with Anath, a goddess of war at Ugarit. Or, the Heb. term *ben 'anat* may be a military title based on the warlike character of the goddess indicating he was a mercenary soldier (P. C. Craigie, JBL, XCI [1972], 239 f.).

Shamgar is not identified as a judge, although he is listed between Ehud and Barak in the biblical account. Since his tribal connection is not given specifically, some scholars have suggested that he was a Canaanite.

Bibliography. Eva Danelius, "Shamgar Ben 'Anath," JNES, XXII (1963), 191–193. A. van Selms, "Judge Shamgar," VT, XIV (1964), 294–309.

S. J. S.

SHAMHUTH (shăm 'hŭth). The officer serving David as captain of the fifth national guard unit for the fifth month (I Chr 27:8).

SHAMIR (shā'mĭr)

1. One of the cities of Judah in the hill country, possibly identified with Khirbet Somerah (Josh 15:48), *c* 13 miles WSW of Hebron.

2. A place in the hill country of Ephraim, the birthplace of Tola, a judge (Jud 10:1–2), unidentified.

3. A Kohathite Levite in David's time (I Chr 24:24).

SHAMMA (shăm'*à*). Son of Zophar, An Asherite (I Chr 7:37).

SHAMMAH (shăm'*à*)

1. Son of Reuel, who was a son of Esau and Basemath, daughter of Ishmael (Gen 36:3–4, 13; I Chr 1:37). He became an Edomite chief (Gen 36:17).

2. Third son of Jesse, father of David (I Sam 16:9). He was in Saul's army fighting the Philistines when David visited the camp and killed Goliath (I Sam 17:12–19). He was the father of Jonadab, Amnon's friend (II Sam 13:3; variant spellings, "Shimeah," "Shimei"). His son Jonathan slew a Philistine giant (II Sam 21:21; I Chr 20:7). *See* Shimeah 1.

3. Son of Agee, the Hararite, the third of David's three chief "mighty men." Single handedly, after an Israelite rout, he defended a lentil field at Lehi, slaying many Philistines (II Sam 23:11–12). According to the NEB his son Jonathan was one of the thirty "mighty men" (II Sam 23:32–33, emended to read: "Jonathan, the son of Shammah, the Hararite").

4. One of the "thirty," a Harodite (II Sam 23:25). In I Chr 11:27 his name is spelled in plural form, "Shammoth," followed by "the Harorite." The relatively common confusion in Heb. of "r" and "d" has caused the textual error. It may be corrected to "of Harod" as in RSV. If "Shamhuth" (I Chr 27:8) is another variant spelling, he was also commander of a 24,000 man division of David's army on active duty the fifth month of each year.

R. V. R.

SHAMMAI (shăm'ī)

1. The elder son of Onam, a Jerahmeelite of the tribe of Judah (I Chr 2:28).

2. Son of Rekem and father of Maon, a Calebite of the tribe of Judah (I Chr 2:44–45).

3. Son of Ezra, a descendant of Caleb, son of Jephunneh, of the tribe of Judah (I Chr 4:17).

SHAMMOTH (shăm 'ŏth). One of David's band of 30 select warriors, a Harorite (I Chr 11:27). *See* Shammah 4.

SHAMMUA, SHAMMUAH (shă-mū'*à*)

1. Son of Zaccur, of the tribe of Reuben; one of the 12 scouts sent by Moses from the wilderness of Paran to "spy out the land of Canaan" (Num 13:4). He concurred in the majority report of certain failure if entrance should be attempted.

2. First son born to David after he moved to Jerusalem (II Sam 5:14; I Chr 14:4; I Chr 3:5, variant spelling, "Shimea").

3. Son of Galal and father of Abda ("Obadiah," I Chr 9:16); one of the Levites who returned to Jerusalem from captivity (Neh 11:17; I Chr 9:16, variant spelling, "Shemaiah").

4. Son of Bilgah, a priest who returned to Jerusalem from Captivity with Zerubbabel (Neh 12:18).

SHAMSHERAI (shăm'shĕ-rī). The eldest of the six sons of Jeroham, of the tribe of Benjamin (I Chr 8:26).

SHAPHAM (shā'f*à*m). A Gadite, second-in-command of his clan in Bashan (I Chr 5:11–12).

SHAPHAN (shă'f*à*n). A prominent official in the court of King Josiah, whose sons and grandsons were also involved in the events of the last days of Judah.

Shaphan, the "scribe" to Josiah, was in all probability the holder of that office which was at once private secretary to the king and secretary of state, for he seems to have been officially involved in many of the activities (see R. de Vaux, *Ancient Israel,* pp. 129–131). Shaphan read the book of the law found by Hilkiah and made the decision to bring it to King Josiah (II Kgs 22:3–13; II Chr 34:8–21). This discovery brought the reformation under Josiah to its peak. Shaphan and his son Ahikam along with others went to consult the prophetess Huldah in regard to their procedure. This same Ahikam, son of Shaphan, protected the prophet Jeremiah from death (Jer 26:24).

It was in the chambers of another son of Shaphan, Gemariah, that Baruch read the scroll of Jeremiah to the people, and Micaiah, the son of Gemariah, who reported the prophecy to his father and the other princes gathered in the king's house in the days of Jehoiakim. By the hand of Elasah, son of Shaphan, and Gemariah son of the high priest Hilkiah, Jeremiah sent his letter to the captives in Babylon (Jer 36:10–12; 29:3).

The line of this illustrious family ends with Gedaliah son of Ahikam and grandson of Shaphan, who was appointed governor of Judah after the fall of Jerusalem, and unto whom was entrusted the care of the prophet Jeremiah (II Kgs 25:22; Jer 39:14; 40:5, 9, 11; 41:2; 43:6).

The same Shaphan, or another, was the father of Jaazaniah, who was seen in the vision of Ezekiel standing in the midst of the elders and leading them in abominable idolatry (Ezk 8:11). Because of Jaazaniah's opposition to the worship of Yahweh, many believe he must have belonged to a different family than that of Ahikam, Elasah, and Gemariah.

P. C. J.

SHAPHAT (shā'făt)

1. The son of Hori of the tribe of Simeon, one of the 12 spies sent out to explore the Promised Land (Num 13:5).

2. The father of Elisha (*q.v.*) the prophet. He lived in Abel-meholah, a village in the Jordan Valley on the border of Issachar and Ephraim (I Kgs 19:16,19; II Kgs 3:11; 6:31).

3. One of the sons of Shemaiah, a descendant of David, after the return from Exile (I Chr 3:22).

4. One of the chiefs of the tribe of Gad, dwelling in Bashan in the days of Jotham of Judah (I Chr 5:12).

5. The son of Adlai, one of the chief herdsmen of David (I Chr 27:29).

SHAPHER (shā'fẽr). A mountain between Kehelathah and Haradah, stations mentioned in the wilderness wanderings of Israel (Num 33:23–24). It is spelled Shepher in the ASV and most newer versions. It is not identified, but probably was on the route of travel between Mount Sinai and Kadesh-barnea. *See* Wilderness Wandering.

SHAPHIR. *See* Saphir.

SHARAI (shâr'ī). One of the sons of Bani, who put away his Gentile wife during Ezra's reform (Ezr 10:40).

SHARAIM (sha-rā'ĭm). One of the cities in the Shephelah of Judah (Josh 15:36), spelled Shaaraim (*q.v.*) in I Sam 17:52 and I Chr 4:31.

SHARAR (shâr'är). A Hararite, father of Ahiam, one of David's mighty warriors (II Sam 23:33), called Sacar (*q.v.*) in I Chr 11:35.

SHARE. The ancient Israelite plow was not much more than a pointed stick, fitted over the end with a metal "share" or point. During the early monarchy, the Philistines had a monopoly on the skills of working with iron and the Israelites were forced to go to them for their tools (I Sam 13:20).

SHAREZER (sha-rē'zẽr)

1. A son of Sennacherib who, with his brother Adrammelech, murdered their father while he was worshiping in the house of Nisroch, his god. They then escaped to Armenia (II Kgs 19:37; Isa 37:38). The name Sharezer is known only from these references. It is probably an abbreviation of the Akkad. *šar-uṣur,* "he has protected the king," normally prefixed by the name of a deity.

2. A man sent from Bethel during the time of Zechariah to appease the face of the Lord (Zech 7:2, RSV, NASB). The KJV spelling is Sherezer (*q.v.*).

SHARON (shăr'ŭn). The coastal plain running *c.* 50 miles from S of the Carmel range to the vicinity of Jaffa, and extending inland six to 12 miles to the hill country of Ephraim. It was well known for its great suitability for agriculture, both sedentary (Isa 33:9; 35:2; Song 2:l) and pastoral (I Chr 27:29; Isa 65:10). It appears once in the NT in connection with Lydda (Acts 9:35, KJV Saron). It is possible that the LXX is correct in taking Lasharon (Josh 12:18) as a simple indication that the preceding town is "Aphek of the Sharon," at the source of the Yarkon. However, an Egyptian papyrus listing rations issued to Palestinians in the time of Thut-mose III mentions a town called Sharon. *See* Palestine, II. B. 1. *e.*

The reference in I Chr 5:16 seems to be to a locality in Transjordan in the territory of Gad which had good pasture lands. One interpretation emends the name from Heb. *sh r ô n* to *Sh r y ô ṇ,* Sirion, an alternate name of Mount Hermon; but this would lie well beyond the N border of Gad.

A. F. R.

SHARUHEN (sha-rū'ĕn). A town in territory of Simeon (Josh 19:6), modern Tell el-Far'ah, 18 miles SE of Gaza. About 1550 B.C., after expelling them from Avaris in the Delta, the Egyptians defeated the Hyksos here after a three-year siege (ANET, p. 233). Sir Flinders Petrie uncovered a 23 foot thick brick wall around it, presumably built by Shishak as the base of his operations in a campaign against Rehoboam (I Kgs 14:25–26) in which Megiddo, Debir, Ezion-geber, and possibly other sites were destroyed. Sharuhen was destroyed in the 9th cen. B.C. and not reoccupied for four centuries. It may be identical with Shaaraim (I Chr 4:31), and Shilhim (Josh 15:32).

When Petrie excavated the site of Tell el-Far'ah in 1927–29, he was under the impression that it was the ancient Beth-pelet. Therefore his excavation reports are entitled *Beth-Pelet* I (1930) and II (1932). He also found a typical Hyksos defense system with a sloping glacis, and 114 scarabs, one bearing the name of the Hyksos king Khian. Therefore it is quite certain this was the Hyksos bastion of Sharuhen in S Palestine, and the government of Israel has changed the name of the site to Tell Sharuhen.

A. K. H

SHASHAI (shā'shī). One of the sons of Bani, who put away his Gentile wife after the Exile (Ezr 10:40).

SHASHAK (shā'shăk). A son of Elpaal, a Benjamite (I Chr 8:12, 14), who had 11 sons (vv. 22–25).

SHAUL (shôl)

1. A king of Edom (I Chr 1:48–49; spelled Saul in Gen 36:37–38).
2. A son of Simeon by a Canaanitish woman (Gen 46:10; Ex 6:15; I Chr 4:24), and ancestor of a tribal family, the Shaulites (Num 26:13).
3. A son of Uzziah, a Kohathite Levite, and ancestor of Samuel (I Chr 6:24).

SHAULITES. *See* Shaul 2.

SHAVEH, VALLEY OF (shā'vĕ). A place where the king of Sodom and Melchizedek met Abraham (Gen 14:17–18), also called the "king's dale" or "King's Valley" (RSV, NASB). Here Absalom erected a monument to himself (II Sam 18:18). It is one of the valleys surrounding Jerusalem, possibly the Kidron Valley. *See* King's Dale; Kidron.

SHAVEH KIRIATHAIM (shā'vĕ kĭr'ĭ-*a*-thā'*ĭ*m). A plain near the city of Kiriathaim of Moab, where Chedorlaomer defeated the Emim (Gen 14:5). Later Reuben was assigned this site and rebuilt it (Num 32:37; Josh 13:19). The town site has been variously identified with el-Qereiyat, *c.* five miles NW of Dibon, or with Qaryat el-Mekhaiyet, *c.* four miles NW of Medeba. *See* Kirjathaim.

SHAVING. *See* Hair.

SHAVSHA (shăv'sh*a*). State secretary or scribe during the reign of David (I Chr 18:16). The obvious omission of his parentage in a list of officers otherwise well documented has led to the speculation that he was of foreign birth and especially suited to handle David's foreign correspondence. His name is Aramaean. His sons served as Solomon's secretaries (I Kgs 4:3, where Shisha is possibly an alternate spelling of Shavsha). He may also be identical with Sheva (II Sam 20:25), an abbreviated form of Shavsha, and with Seraiah (II Sam 8:17; *see* Seraiah 1). If he is identical with Seraiah, it would indicate that at some time he adopted a Heb. name.

SHEAF. *See* Plants.

SHEAL (shē'*a*l). One of the sons of Bani who put away his foreign wife (Ezr 10:29).

SHEALTIEL (shē-ăl'tĭ-ĕl), **SALATHIEL** (s*a*-lā'thĭ-ĕl). KJV has Shealtiel except in I Chr 3:17. The Gr. of the NT calls him Salathiel (KJV, Mt 1:12; Lk 3:27). The ASV and all newer versions uniformly call him Shealtiel.

According to a number of references, Shealtiel was the son of Jeconiah (Jehoiachin) the king of Judah taken captive to Babylon in 597 B.C., and the father of Zerubbabel, leader of the first Israelites to return from Exile (Ezr 3:2, 8; 5:2; Neh 12:1; Hag 1:1, 12, 14; 2:2, 23). In the genealogy of Christ in Matthew the same relationship is given (Mt 1:12). There would be no problem except that (1) I Chr 3:19 names Pedaiah, another son of Jeconiah, as the father of Zerubbabel, and (2) the genealogy in Luke calls Shealtiel the son of Neri (Lk 3:27). Most modern versions translate I Chr 3:17, "Jeconiah the captive" (ASV, RSV); left untranslated as in the KJV, however, it would make it a question whether Shealtiel was son of Jeconiah or of a son of Jeconiah named Assir.

Luke traces the ancestry of Shealtiel back to Nathan the son of David rather than through the line of Judaic kings that descended from Solomon. One explanation is that Jehoiachin died childless, fulfilling the prophecy of Jeremiah that Coniah (i.e., Jehoiachin) should have no direct descendants on the throne of David (Jer 22:24–30). With the end of Solomon's line, the royal line would continue by adopting Shealtiel descended from Nathan. Clay tablets found in the Ishtar gate of Babylon speak of Jehoiachin king of Judah and the five sons of the king of Judah (ANET, p. 308), but the names of the princes are not given and they need not be assumed to be his actual offspring.

Another explanation is that Jehoiachin did have sons born in Babylon by his wives taken into exile with him (II Kgs 24:15). He was considered "childless," however, in having no son to succeed him on the throne. One of Jeconiah's sons may have died without offspring, and Neri married the widow and Shealtiel was born to this union. Neri would thus be the actual father (according to Luke), but Jeconiah (according to Matthew) a legal ancestor (SDA Dict., p. 991).

Whether Shealtiel or Pedaiah was the actual father of Zerubbabel (*q.v.*) is also in question. Since Luke gives the blood line rather than the royal legal ancestry of Christ, we may presume that Shealtiel, who begat Zerubbabel, died soon afterward and that the boy was reared by Pedaiah and counted as the "son" of his foster father.

P. C. J. and J. R.

SHEAR. *See* Sheepshearing.

SHEARIAH (shē'*a*-rī'*a*). A son of Azel, a descendant of King Saul (I Chr 8:38; 9:44).

SHEARING HOUSE. The site of the murder of the 42 kinsmen of Ahaziah by Jehu (II Kgs 10:12–14). Because the Heb. is *bêt 'ēqed hārō'îm* it is identified by some with Beit Qad, *c.* 16 miles NE of Samaria, and called Beth-eked of the Shepherds in the RSV and NASB.

SHEAR-JASHUB (shē'*a*r-jā'sh*ŭ*b). The little son of Isaiah who accompanied the prophet when he went before King Ahaz (Isa 7:3). His name, meaning "a remnant shall return," was a sign and prophecy to Israel (Isa 8:18). It is possible that Isaiah pointed to Shear-jashub when speaking the words of 7:15–17, thereby indicating that this child, and not the future Immanuel of v. 14, was the one he meant as a sign of how soon the king of Assyria would march on Syria, Israel, and Judah.

SHEATH. The case or covering for the blade of a sword, a scabbard (I Chr 21:27; Ezk 21:3–5; Jn 18:11). The leather or metal sheath was attached to the belt or girdle, usually on the left side.

SHEBA (shē'bȧ). In Heb. there are two distinct spellings of this name, *sheba'* (see 1–3 below) and *sh^{e}bā'* (see 4–7).

1. A descendant of Abihail of the tribe of Gad who lived in Gilead (I Chr 5:13, 16).

2. A son of Bichri of the tribe of Benjamin. After Absalom's rebellion had been quelled, Sheba took advantage of the unrest and confusion that followed to stir up further trouble for David (II Sam 20:1–22). He called the tribes of the northern part of the kingdom to join him in overthrowing the king. Although his battle cry of rebellion had little rallying effect at the time, it was later used by Jeroboam quite successfully (I Kgs 12:16). However, enough of those who had come to welcome David home did turn and follow Sheba so that David became fearful. Since Sheba was from the tribe of Benjamin he received some support from the house of Saul, and he capitalized on the rivalry that had always existed between Judah and the N.

Since David did not want to admit to Joab his mistake of choosing Amasa to be the new army commander, he called Joab's brother Abishai to lead the campaign against Sheba, knowing he would get Joab's help. As David expected, Abishai went to Joab, and Joab lost no time in pursuit of Amasa. When they met, Joab pretended friendship by dropping his sword and reaching out to kiss Amasa. Presumably he had a second sword hidden in his cloak with which he slew his rival. He then proceeded to pursue Sheba to Abel of Beth-maacah in the far N of Israel.

The only men still with Sheba were the Berites, his own clan. Even though the rebellion seemed about to die for want of aid, Joab decided to stamp it out completely. Abel was one of the villages known for keeping the tradition of the Israelites, and disputes of the various tribes were often taken there to be settled. A wise woman of the village asked Joab if he was going to punish the innocent also, and he was wise enough to reply that he only wanted the guilty one. He realized that the kingdom had trouble enough and that the northern tribes needed to be pacified rather than incensed over new quarrels. The people of Abel threw the head of Sheba over the wall to Joab, and the rebellion ended.

3. A town of Simeon, S of Judah (Josh 19:2), generally believed to have been confused with Beer-sheba, or Shema according to the LXX of I Chr 4:28 and the parallel list in Josh 15:26. If it is near or part of Beer-sheba, it may be Tell es-Saba', where occupation began in the Middle Bronze Age (2100–1550 B.C.), *c.* two miles E of the traditional well of Beer-sheba.

4. A people of Cushite genealogy, descended through Raamah, a Semite group of SW Arabia (Gen 10:7; I Chr 1:9). *See* Sabeans. They were probably related by ancestry or trade with the people of Seba (*q.v.*), across the straits of Bab al Mandeb in E Africa, equivalent to modern Sudan to which the biblical term Cush sometimes applied.

5. A Semitic people, descended from Shem through Joktan (Gen 10:28; I Chr 1:22), perhaps to be identified with No. 6. These are likely to have been the nomadic Sabeans who marauded the livestock of Job (Job 1:15), since he lived in N Arabia early in the 2nd mil. B.C.

6. A son of Jokshan, son of Abraham by Keturah, who presumably lived in Edom or N Arabia (Gen 25:3; I Chr 1:32).

7. At present it seems impossible to determine which of the last three above-named persons or peoples was the ancestor of the people of Sheba of the 1st mil. B.C. They are mentioned a number of times in the OT in connection with their caravans and trade in incense, gold, and precious stones (Job 6:19; Ps 72:10, 15; Isa 60:6; Jer 6:20; Ezk 27:22–23; 38:13). *See* Sabeans.

While the Sabeans were originally nomads, it is now fairly certain that they had settled in S Arabia by the 12th cen. B.C. In the 10th cen. Sheba was so well established that one of their monarchs, the Queen of Sheba of I Kgs 10:1–13, journeyed *c.* 1,200 miles by camel to visit King Solomon. *See* Queen 3. Most scholars believe a major purpose of her trip was to negotiate a trade agreement with Israel in order to protect the vital spice traffic of the caravans of Sheba. Her interest in the wisdom of Solomon was contrasted by Christ to the complacency of the Jews of His day who refused to recognize that One greater than Solomon was present (Mt 12:42). Both Assyrian and S Arabic inscriptions testify to the presence of queens in Arabia as early as the 8th cen. B.C. (NBD, p. 1172).

A. W. W.

SHEBAM (shē'băm). A town in the upland pastoral district on the E of Jordan which was requested by and given to the tribes of Reuben and Gad (Num 32:3). It is probably the same place as Shibmah or Sibmah (Num 32:38). The latter name is used for a city famous for its luxuriant vines and summer fruits (Isa 16:8–9; Jer 48:32). It has been tentatively identified with Qurn el-Kibsh, near Mount Nebo and three miles SW of Heshbon.

The Shebna inscription from the British Museum. BM

SHEBANIAH (shĕb'ȧ-nī'ȧ)

1. A priest in the time of David; one of those who blew the trumpet before the ark as it was brought from the house of Obed-edom to Jerusalem (I Chr 15:24).

2. A Levite in the days of Nehemiah. He stood with other Levites on "the stairs" offering prayers of confession and adoration in the great national day of repentance. He also signed the covenant of Nehemiah (Neh 9:4-5; 10:10).

3. A priest who signed the covenant of Nehemiah. His son Joseph is mentioned as a prominent priest in the days of the high priest Joiakim (Neh 10:4; 12:14).

4. Another Levite who signed the covenant of Nehemiah (Neh 10:12).

SHEBARIM (shĕb'ȧ-rĭm). After the repulse of the first attack on Ai, the men of the city chased the Israelites "even unto Shebarim" (Josh 7:5). No trace of such a city has yet been found, and it may be correctly translated as "stone quarries" or "the Quarries" (NEB). Or it may mean "broken places" or defiles in cliffs, as in those along the gorge of Wadi Lereid or Wadi Sneisil leading down from Bethel and Ai toward Gilgal and Jericho (WBC, p. 214; E. G. Kraeling, *Bible Atlas,* Chicago: Rand McNally, 1956, p. 135).

SHEBAT. *See* Sebat.

SHEBER (shē'bẽr). A son of Caleb by his concubine Maacah (I Chr 2:48).

SHEBNA (shĕb'nȧ). A high official in the court of King Hezekiah. At first he held the office called in Scripture "treasurer" (Isa 22:15; Heb. *sōkēn,* "steward," RSV) or "who is over the house," i.e., the master of the palace. The position was in fact second only to the king and would more nearly correspond to the office of prime minister.

A sweeping denunciation of Shebna was proclaimed by Isaiah, condemning him for his pride and arrogance, and he was deposed and replaced by Eliakim (Isa 22:15-20). Shebna doubtless advocated ignoring Isaiah's warnings against alliance with idolatrous Egypt (Isa 30:1-5; 31:1-3; 36:6-9), for he seems to have been a leader in the pro-Egyptian faction in the Judean councils of state (WBC, p. 625). As a leader of the godly remnant who still trusted in Yahweh, Eliakim (*q.v.*) stood in contrast to the worldly minded Shebna.

Shebna was particularly condemned for the ornate sepulchre he was building, perhaps to the neglect of his official duties. The inscribed lintel of such a tomb in Phoenician style, set in a prominent place in a necropolis of about 50 such tombs, was found in 1870 by C. Clermont-Ganneau in the village of Silwan E of the Kidron Valley. The badly weathered and damaged inscription has been deciphered and reads as follows: "This is [the sepulchre of. . .] yahu who is over the house. There is no silver and gold here, but [his bones] and the bones of his slave-wife with him. Cursed be the man who will open this!" Because the name Shebna in Isa 22:15 is apparently an abbreviation of "Shebanyahu," and there is no mention in the OT of another royal official "over the house" with a name ending in -yahu who was buried near Jerusalem, and since the style of the lettering fits the time of Hezekiah, scholars believe an identification of this inscription with the biblical Shebna is quite likely.

Shebna's demotion was in fact only one step lower. The office of "scribe" or "secretary" in which he served was actually more nearly that of secretary of state (see R. deVaux, *Ancient Israel,* New York: McGraw-Hill, 1961, pp. 129-131). Shebna was active in the tense negotiations with Sennacherib (II Kgs 18:18, 26, 37; 19:2; Isa 36:3, 11, 22; 37:2).

The name Shebna or Shebaniah (cf. I Chr 15:24) is found on several Palestinian seals and on an inscribed jar handle.

Bibliography. N. Avigad, "The Epitaph of a Royal Steward from Siloam Village," IEJ, III (1953), 137-152; "The Second Tomb-Inscription of the Royal Steward," IEJ, V (1955), 163-166. David Ussishkin, "On the Shorter Inscription from the 'Tomb of the Royal Steward,'" BASOR #196 (1969), 16-22; "The Necropolis from the Time of the King

The Fortress Temple at Shechem. HFV

dom of Judah at Silwan, Jerusalem," BA, XXXIII (1970), 33-46.

P. C. J.

SHEBUEL (shē-bū'ĕl)

1. A descendant of Gershom and Moses who was ruler of the treasury of the house of God (I Chr 23:16; 26:24). In I Chr 24:20 he is called Shubael.

2. One of the 14 sons of Heman the minstrel (I Chr 25:4); called Shubael in v. 20, where he is mentioned as the ancestor and head of one of the 24 courses of temple singers.

SHECANIAH, SHECHANIAH (shĕk'ȧ-nī'ȧ)

1. The exact meaning of the text is not clear, but apparently Shechaniah in the days of Ezra was the son of Obadiah a descendant of David and Zerubbabel (I Chr 3:21-22; cf. RSV, Berkeley). He may have been one of those listed below, 4-7.

2. The head of the tenth course of priests appointed by lot by David for their service in the temple (I Chr 24:11).

3. A priest in the days of Hezekiah, one of those appointed to distribute the tithes among their brethren (II Chr 31:15).

4. One of the sons of Pharosh and ancestor of the returnee Zechariah who, with 150 males, accompanied Ezra from the Exile (Ezr 8:3; cf. NASB).

5. Either the forefather of the son of Jahaziel who with 300 men returned with Ezra (NASB), or (RSV following I Esd 8:32) Shechaniah the son of Jahaziel who returned (Ezr 8:5).

6. The son of Jehiel of the sons of Elam who as spokesman for the repentant assembly proposed to Ezra that the Jews covenant with God to put away their Gentile wives (Ezr 10:2-4).

7. The "keeper of the east gate" in the days of Nehemiah. His son Shemaiah helped in the restoration of the wall (Neh 3:29).

8. The son of Arah and the father-in-law of Tobiah, the Ammonite official in the days of Nehemiah who opposed the work, and by his family connections caused much trouble for the Jews (Neh 6:18).

9. One of the chiefs of the priests who returned from Babylon with Zerubbabel (Neh 12:3).

P. C. J.

SHECHEM (shĕk'ĕm)

1. The seducer of Dinah, the daughter of Jacob (Gen 34). Son of Hamor, a Hivite prince (Gen 33:19; Jud 9:28), he along with all the men of the town was slain by Simeon and Levi, Dinah's brothers (Gen 34:25-26).

2. A man of the tribe of Manasseh descended from Gilead (Num 26:31; Josh 17:2).

3. A son of Shemidah of the tribe of Manasseh (I Chr 7:19).

4. An important city situated in the central part of Palestine. It was in Ephraim near the border with Manasseh (Josh 17:7; I Chr 7:28), at the junction of important roads, and between Mount Ebal and Mount Gerizim (Jud 9:7). It is twice spelled Sychem in the KJV of Acts 7:16.

a. Biblical importance. Abram first camped in Canaan at Shechem (KJV Sichem), and here he built his first altar to the Lord (Gen 12:6-7). Jacob returned here from Padan-aram and bought a piece of land where Joseph was later buried (Gen 33:18-19; Josh 24:32). Shechem was already a walled city with a gate (Gen 32:20, 24). Simeon and Levi massacred its male population in revenge for the defilement of their sister Dinah (Gen 34:25). Later Joseph looked for his brothers near the town (Gen 37:12-14). The rehearsal of the law, with the blessings acknowledged from Mount Gerizim and the cursings from Mount Ebal, was enacted near Shechem (Deut 27:11-13; Josh 8:33-35). It was appointed a city of refuge (Josh 20:7; 21:21). Joshua's farewell address was delivered in the vicinity (Josh 24:1, 25). Later it was destroyed by Abimelech, the son of Gideon, when the populace turned against him after he had made himself its king (Jud 9:1-7, 23-57). Rehoboam was crowned here just before the division of the kingdom (I Kgs 12:1). Jeroboam I of the northern kingdom rebuilt it and made it his initial residence (I Kgs 12:25). Villagers inhabiting the ruined site are mentioned by Jeremiah (Jer 41:5). After the Captivity it became the chief city of the Samaritans, whose temple was erected on Mount Gerizim (Jos *Ant.* xi.8.6; xii.1.1; xiii.3.4). It was captured by John Hyrcanus (*Ant.* xiii.9.1; *Wars* i.2.6).

b. Location. A mile or two E of modern Nablus, Shechem was situated at the eastern entrance to the valley which lies between Ebal and Gerizim. As its name Shechem ("shoulder") implies, it was built on the lower SE slope or shoulder of Mount Ebal. Its site lies *c.* 31 miles N of Jerusalem and *c.* eight miles by road SE of Samaria. Sychar must have been nearby (Jn 4:5); in fact, many identify Sychar (*q.v.*) with Shechem, or with the site of the present village of Balâṭah at the foot of the city mound.

c. Archaeology. Shechem was first identified with Tell Balâṭah in 1903. The tell was excavated by the German archaeologists Sellin,

Walter, and Steckeweh in 1913–14, 1926–27, 1928, 1932, and 1934. The Drew-McCormick-Harvard Archaeological Expedition worked there in 1956, 1957, 1960; 1962, 1964, 1966, 1968, and 1969 under the direction of G. Ernest Wright, Lawrence E. Toombs, and Edward F. Campbell, Jr.

Evidence points to a sizable Chalcolithic Age village during the 4th mil. B.C. The Amorites or Hyksos were probably the founders of the town when it assumed historical importance in the Middle Bronze II Age (1900–1550 B.C.). Shechem is first mentioned outside the Bible by an officer of Pharaoh Sesostris III (1878–1843 B.C.), who claimed that "Sekmem" fell to the Egyptian forces (ANET, p. 230). The ruler of Shechem, Abesh-hadad, was cursed on one of the execration figurines dating *c.* 1800 B.C. (ANET, p. 329). The Hyksos remains (1750–1550 B.C.) include those of an earlier courtyard temple, a fortress-temple built over it, and the thick city wall with a two-entry gate on the E side and a three-entry gate on the NW.

A century after its destruction *c.* 1550 B.C. Shechem was rebuilt by the Canaanites. The fortress-temple, with walls seven to seven and a half feet thick, was 53 feet wide and 41 feet deep with entrance on the long side. It had three sacred standing stones in the open court with a platform for a stone altar. This temple is undoubtedly that called the house of Baal-berith or of El-berith (Jud 9:4, 46), destroyed by Abimelech. In keeping with the inference of the book of Joshua that Shechem was not captured, there is no archaeological evidence of destruction for 300 years when the city was friendly to the Israelites. An Amarna letter (#289) written by the king of Jerusalem states that the land of Shechem was given to the 'Apiru or Habiru, who in this case may be Heb. Israelites.

The destruction of Shechem by Abimelech *c.* 1150 B.C. is abundantly attested. Its sacred area was never revived. Solomon apparently rebuilt Shechem as a provincial capital and administrative center, but it was violently destroyed presumably by Pharaoh Shishak *c.* 926 B.C. (I Kgs 14:25). Later, Jeroboam I or a successor refortified the city and erected a large government warehouse on the ruins of the temple. But it was destroyed several more times, including its leveling by Shalmanezer V (*c.* 724 B.C.). Shechem did not regain its glory again until the 4th cen. B.C. At that time the Samaritans moved from Samaria and settled Shechem. Evidently John Hyrcanus destroyed the city when he did the same to Samaria in 107 B.C.

Neapolis, now Nablus, began during the Roman period, and is located W of the ruins. The modern village of Balâṭah is immediately S of the tell.

Bibliography. Excavation reports: BA, XX (1957), 82–105; XXIII (1960), 102–126; XXVI (1963). BASOR #144 (1956), pp. 9–20; #148 (1957), pp. 11–28; #161 (1961), pp. 11–54; #169 (1963), pp. 1–60; #180 (1965), pp. 7–41; #190 (1968), pp. 2–41; #204 (1971), pp. 2–17. *Archaeology,* XIV (1961), 171–179. W. Harrelson, *et al.,* "Shechem, Navel of the Land," BA, XX (1957), 1–32. G. Ernest Wright, *Shechem,* London: Duckworth, 1964; "Shechem," TAOTS, pp. 355–370. G. R. H. Wright, "Temples at Shechem," ZAW, LXXX (1968), 1–34.

W. C. and J. R.

SHECHEMITES. *See* Shechem 2.

SHECHINAH. *See* Shekinah.

SHEDEUR (shĕd'ē-ĕr). The father of Elizur, chief of the tribe of Reuben at the time of the Exodus (Num 1:5; 2:10; 7:30, 35; 10:18).

SHEEP. *See* Animals, I. 15; Occupations: Shepherd.

SHEEPCOTE, SHEEPFOLD. Also referred to as fold or cote. Various kinds of enclosures were used to protect the sheep at night from weather, wild animals, and thieves. The general term for "fold" in Heb. is *miklâ'*, a confined place (Ps 50:9; 78:70; Hab 3:17). The permanent type (Heb. *gᵉdērâ*, enclosing wall) often consisted of an area enclosed by stone walls open to the sky (Num 32:16, 24, 36; Zeph 2:6). In some instances the fold may have been a low, shed-like building with stalls (Heb. *'arwâ*, II Chr 32:28; cf. 9:25). The wide usage of caves, enclosed with a short wall and gate at the mouth, is indicated by Scripture (I Sam 24:3), tradition, and archaeology. Temporary sheepfolds were sometimes made of branches woven together. The Heb. *nāweh,* KJV "sheepcote" or "fold," refers to the meadow or pasture for sheep (II Sam 7:8; Isa 65:10; Jer 23:3; Ezk 34:14; see newer versions).

It was customary for the shepherd to sleep with his sheep, either in the open or in a small hut built within the fold. Features of the sheepfold are evident in Christ's allegory of the good Shepherd (Jn 10), where He apparently had in mind an open-court fold (Gr. *aulē,* enclosed courtyard, vv. 1, 16) with one shepherd ("the porter," v. 3) guarding several flocks through the night. In the morning each flock was led out to pasture by its own shepherd (vv. 2–4).

For the prophecy regarding the future remnant of Israel pictured as a flock in its fold (Mic 2:12–13) *see* Breaker, The. For sheep *see* Animals, I.15. For shepherd *see* Occupations: Shepherd. Also see Joachim Jeremias, *"Poimēn,* etc.," TDNT, VI, 485–502.

D. W. B.

SHEEP GATE, SHEEP MARKET. *See* Jerusalem: Gates and Towers 1.

SHEEPMASTER. *See* Occupations: Herdman, Sheepmaster.

SHEEP, MOUNTAIN. *See* Animals, II. 36.

A sheepfold at Dothan. JR

SHEEPSHEARING. Like the harvest season, sheepshearing in the spring was a time of great festivity and joy in Israel. Relatives and friends were invited, and several days would be spent not only in shearing but in feasting and merry-making (Gen 31:19; 38:12 f.; I Sam 25:2-11, 36; II Sam 13:23-28*a*).

When a sheep is being shorn its front legs are usually tied by the shepherd to prevent it from jumping up, but it emits no sound (Isa 53:7; Acts 8:32). The firstborn of the flock were to be consecrated to the Lord and therefore not shorn (Deut 15:19).

SHEEPSKINS. A sheepskin prepared with the wool still on it, used for a crude garment by the very poor (Heb 11:37).

SHEERAH. *See* Sherah.

SHEET. In the OT the word "sheet" (Jud 14:12-13) refers to the *sādîn*, a plain piece of cloth of fine linen used as an upper garment (Prov 31:24). The Gr. word used in these passages in the LXX (*sindōn*) appears in the NT referring to the shroud in which Jesus was wrapped (Mt 27:59) and the garment or perhaps bed sheet wrapped around the youth almost apprehended in the garden with Jesus (Mk 14:51).

Another word (Gr. *othonē*), used in Acts 10:11; 11:5 of the great sheet let down from heaven in Peter's vision, also means a linen cloth and is used in secular literature for the sail of a ship.

SHEHARIAH (shē'*ȧ*-rī'*ȧ*). A son of Jeroham, a Benjamite residing in Jerusalem at the Captivity (I Chr 8:26).

SHEKEL. *See* Weights, Measures, and Coins.

SHEKINAH (shĕ-kī'n*ȧ*). A word used by later Jews and Christians to express the visible divine presence, especially when resting between the cherubim over the mercy seat. *See* Light.

SHELAH (shē'l*ȧ*)

1. The third son of Judah by the daughter of the Canaanite Shuah (Gen 38:5, 11, 14, 26; 46:12; Num 26:20; I Chr 2:3; 4:21-23).

2. The son of Arphaxad and father of Eber (Gen 10:24 and 11:13, spelled Salah; I Chr 1:18).

SHELANITE (shē'l*ȧ*-nīt). A descendant of Shelah (*q.v.*) son of Judah (Num 26:20).

SHELEMIAH (shĕl-ĕ-mī'*ȧ*). A biblical name somewhat common at the time of the Exile.

1. A shorter form of Meshelemiah, a Levite appointed gatekeeper in the tabernacle during the reign of David (I Chr 26:1-2, 14).

2. Son of Cushi and grandfather of Jehudi whom the princes sent to bring Baruch with the writings of Jeremiah (Jer 36:14).

3. Son of Abdeel sent to arrest Jeremiah and his secretary Baruch (Jer 36:26).

4. Father of Jehucal (Jucal) who was sent by King Zedekiah to request Jeremiah to pray for Judah (Jer 37:3) and who later reported Jeremiah's words of warning to the officials (Jer 38:1).

5. Son of Hananiah and father of Irijah, the captain of the guard who accused Jeremiah of traitorous influence (Jer 37:13).

6. and 7. Two sons of Bani (Binnui, RSV) who agreed to put away their foreign wives (Ezr 10:39, 41).

8. Father of Hananiah who assisted in rebuilding Jerusalem's wall (Neh 3:30).

9. A priest appointed by Nehemiah as treasurer in charge of tithes (Neh 13:13).

D. W. B.

SHELEPH (shē'lĕf). The second of the 13 sons of Joktan (Gen 10:26; I Chr 1:20). A Yemenite tribe by this name is mentioned in Sabaean inscriptions found in S Arabia.

SHELESH (shē'lĕsh). An Asherite, son of Helem (I Chr 7:35).

SHELOMI (shē-lō'mī). One of the 12 commissioners appointed to divide the Promised Land; an Asherite (Num 34:27).

SHELOMITH (shē-lō 'mĭth)

1. The daughter of Dibri of the tribe of Dan. She married an Egyptian and their son was stoned to death for blaspheming the name of God (Lev 24:11).

2. The daughter of Zerubbabel (I Chr 3:19).

3. The son of Shimei, chief of the Levitical family of Gershon in the time of David (I Chr 23:9). In v.10 Shimei should probably be Shelomith.

4. Chief of the sons of Izhar, of the Levitical family of Kohath, in the time of David (I Chr 23:18). In I Chr 24:22 he is called Shelomoth.

5. The son of Zichri, a descendant of Eliezer the son of Moses. A prominent Levite in the time of David, he was one of the keepers of the temple treasure (I Chr 26:25–26, 28).

6. The last child of Rehoboam by his wife Maacah, the granddaughter of Absalom (II Chr 11:20).

7. According to KJV, the descendants of Shelomith, led by the son of Josiphiah, returned with Ezra from Babylon. RSV following I Esd 8:36 gives what may be the correct reading, "Shelomith the son of Josiphiah, and with him a hundred and sixty men" (Ezr 8:10).

P. C. J.

SHELOMOTH. *See* Shelomith 4.

SHELUMIEL (shĕ-lū'mĭ-ĕl). The son of Zurishaddai, and prince of the tribe of Simeon at the time of the Exodus (Num 1:6; 2:12; 7:36, 41; 10:19).

SHEM (shĕm). The first son of Noah (Gen 5:32; 6:10; 9:18; 10:1; I Chr 1:4). With Noah his father, and Japheth and Ham his brothers, he went through the Flood in the ark (Gen 7:13; 8:18). After the Flood Noah planted a vineyard and from the vintage became drunk. Upon report of his nakedness, Shem took the lead with Japheth in covering their father (Gen 9:20–23). For his filial respect, Shem is given the blessing of Yahweh, and Japheth shall "dwell in his tents," i.e., find shelter and provision (Gen 9:26–27). That this is primarily a spiritual blessing is seen in that the gospel was taken by Jews to the Gentiles in the Apostolic Age.

Two years after the Flood at age 100 Shem begat Arphaxad, the ancestor of Abraham (Gen 11:10–26), from whom came the Messiah (Lk 3:23, 36). Shem lived to age 600 (Gen 11:10–11).

The genealogy of Shem's descendants in Gen 10 is given after Japheth and Ham in accord with the author's method of dealing with subordinate elements first and then returning to the main line of the people of Yahweh.

Many of the descendants of Shem (Gen 10:21–31) are known to have spoken cognate languages in antiquity, and these languages have been conveniently designated "Semitic." This is a modern term, however, and does not imply that all of Shem's descendants spoke a Semitic language.

H. G. S.

SHEMA (shē'mȧ)

1. A city of Judah in the extreme S near the border of Edom (Josh 15:26). The site is unknown; it may be the same as Sheba, listed in Josh 19:2 as a Simeonite city within the borders of Judah.

2. One of the sons of Hebron, son of Caleb, of the tribe of Judah. He was father of Raham (I Chr 2:43–44).

3. A Reubenite, the son of Joel and father of Azaz (I Chr 5:8). In I Chr 5:4 apparently the same man is called Shemaiah (*q.v.*).

4. A Benjamite, the son of Elpaal. He is listed as a tribal leader who drove the men of Gath from the valley of Aijalon (I Chr 8:13).

5. This man stood with others at the right hand of Ezra as he read the Scriptures to the people in the days of Nehemiah (Neh 8:4).

SHEMAAH (shē̆-mā'ȧ). A Benjamite of Gibeah, father of Ahiezer and Joash who joined David at Ziklag (I Chr 12:3).

SHEMAIAH (shē̆-mā'yȧ). The name of several priests, Levites, and prophets.

1. A prophet who told Rehoboam he was not to take the soldiers of Judah to war against Jeroboam, for God had said, "Ye shall not go up, nor fight against your brethren the children of Israel: return every man to his house; for this thing is from me" (I Kgs 12:21–24; II Chr 11:2). He is mentioned again in Scripture as coming to Rehoboam and his officers who were in Jerusalem because of the invasion of Shishak, king of Egypt, and his siege of Jerusalem. Shemaiah's message from God was that God had permitted the siege because Judah had forsaken Him. Upon Judah's repentance, the wrath of God was turned away (II Chr 12:5–7). Shemaiah wrote a record of the acts of Rehoboam (II Chr 12:15).

2. The son of Shechaniah, a descendant of Zerubbabel (I Chr 3:22). He is thought by some to be one of the men who helped repair the wall and was the keeper of the east gate (Neh 3:29).

3. Father of Shimri and an ancestor of Ziza, a prince of the tribe of Simeon (I Chr 4:37).

4. A member of the tribe of Reuben (I Chr 5:4). Probably the same as Shema (v. 8).

5. A son of Hashub, a Levite descendant of Merari who dwelt in Jerusalem (I Chr 9:14; Neh 11:15). He was among those who had "the oversight of the outward business of the house of God."

6. A Levite of the family of Jeduthun and father of Obadiah (or Abda). He is also called Shammua (I Chr 9:16; Neh 11:17).

7. Son of Elizaphan and head of the house of 200 men. He took part in the removal of the ark from Obed-edom (I Chr 15:8,11).

8. Son of Nethaneel, a scribe, who in the time of David registered the names of the priestly courses (I Chr 24:6).

9. A Korahite Levite, eldest son of

Obed-edom, the Gittite, and a gate keeper of the temple (I Chr 26:4, 6).

10. One of the Levites commissioned by Jehoshaphat in his third year to teach the people the book of the law (II Chr 17:8).

11. A Levite of the family of Jeduthun, the singer, who assisted in the purifying of the temple in the reign of Hezekiah (II Chr 29:14).

12. One of the men in charge of the "free-will offerings of God" (II Chr 31:15). Some think he is the Shemaiah of II Chr 29:14.

13. A chief of the Levites in the reign of Josiah who, with others, made large contributions of sacrifices for the Passover (II Chr 35:9).

14. A son of Adonikam who, with his two brothers, brought 60 men from Babylon with Ezra (Ezr 8:13).

15. A "chief man" under Ezra who was sent with others to Iddo at Casiphia to get ministers for the house of God (Ezr 8:16).

16. A priest of the family of Harim who put away his Gentile wife at the order of Ezra (Ezr 10:21).

17. A layman of the family of Harim who had also married a Gentile wife (Ezr 10:31).

18. A prophet who was bribed by Tobiah and Sanballat to suggest to Nehemiah that all should seek safety in the temple and thus hinder the rebuilding of the wall (Neh 6:10).

19. Head of a priestly house who returned with Zerubbabel from Babylon (Neh 12:6, 18). Some think he is the same as the one mentioned in 10:8 and 12:35.

20. One of the princes of Judah at the time of the dedication of the wall around Jerusalem (Neh 12:34).

21. A priest and a descendant of Asaph (Neh 12:35; see 19).

22. A singer who took part in the dedication of the wall (Neh 12:36).

23. One of the priestly trumpeters who took part in the dedication of the wall (Neh 12:42).

24. Father of the prophet Urijah of Kirjath-jearim (Jer 26:20).

25. A Nehelamite, a false prophet in the time of Jeremiah who upbraided him for trying to hinder God's work. Jeremiah foretold the complete destruction of his family (Jer 29:24–32).

26. The father of Delaiah who was a prince in the reign of Zedekiah (Jer 36:12).

R. H. B.

SHEMARIAH (shĕm'*ȧ*-rī'*ȧ*)

1. A Benjamite warrior who joined David at Ziklag (I Chr 12:5).

2. The second son of Rehoboam by his wife Abigail (II Chr 11:19, spelled Shamariah).

3. One of the sons of Harim who had married foreign wives (Ezr 10:32).

4. One of the sons of Bani who had married foreign wives (Ezr 10:41).

SHEMEBER (shĕm-ē'bẽr). King of Zeboiim and ally of the king of Sodom when he was attacked by the kings of the East under Chedorlaomer (Gen 14:2).

SHEMER (shē'mẽr)

1. The owner of the hill which Omri bought and which became the site of Samaria (I Kgs 16:24).

2. A Merarite (I Chr 6:46, RSV; *see* Shamer 1).

3. An Asherite (I Chr 7:34, RSV; *see* Shamer 2).

SHEMIDA, SHEMIDAH (shē-mī'*dȧ*). One of the six sons of Gilead, of the tribe of Manasseh (Num 26:32; Josh 17:2). In I Chr 7:19 the name is given as "Shemidah."

SHEMIDAITES (shē-mī'd*ȧ*-īts). Descendants of Shemida (*q.v.;* Josh 17:2).

SHEMINITH (shĕm'ĭ-nĭth). A musical term (I Chr 15:21; Ps 6, title; 12, title), perhaps referring to eight strings or octaves.

SHEMIRAMOTH (shē-mĭr'*ȧ*-mŏth)

1. A Levite musician of the second rank in the choir founded by David (I Chr 15:18).

2. One of the Levites sent by Jehoshaphat in the third year of his reign to teach the law to the inhabitants of Judah (II Chr 17:8).

SHEMUEL (shĕm'ū-ēl)

1. A chief of the Simeonites, appointed to divide the land W of the Jordan (Num 34:20).

2. Samuel the prophet, father of Joel (I Chr 6:33, KJV).

3. A son of Tola; head of a clan in Issachar (I Chr 7:2).

SHEN (shĕn). A geographical location meaning "tooth," apparently referring to a projecting rock. Between this spot and Mizpah Samuel set up the stone Ebenezer commemorating Israel's victory over the Philistines (I Sam 7:12). The RSV identifies it with the Jeshanah (*q.v.*) of II Chr 13:19.

SHENAZAR (shē-năz'*ȧ*r). A son of Jeconiah or Jehoiachin (I Chr 3:18).

SHENIR. *See* Senir.

SHEOL (shē'ōl). The Heb. word *shᵉʼôl* is of uncertain derivation and was apparently not used in Semitic languages outside of Jewish circles. It is used in the OT 65 times, translated in the KJV 31 times by "grave," 31 times by "hell," and three times by "pit." The ASV and RSV uniformly transliterate it by "Sheol." There are difficulties with its interpretation. The best tool in its study is a concordance.

The usual view is that Sheol is the place of departed spirits (BDB, ISBE, HDB, etc.). Both the righteous (Gen 37:35) and wicked go there (Prov 9:18). The Scofield Reference Bible, advancing a very old view, equates Sheol with the NT Hades. It holds that this was in two compartments before the cross, but that Christ freed the righteous in Hades and took them to heaven at His ascension (comment on Lk 16:23). Naturalistic views equate Sheol with the Babylonian underworld or the Hades of Gr. myths.

Another view (BulETS, IV [1961], 129–134) holds that Sheol is the place of the bodies of the dead, i.e., the grave. In most biblical passages this agrees very well, and is the translation half the time in the KJV. This view also fits those verses which speak of Sheol as a place of silence (Ps 31:17) where God is not praised (Ps 6:5; Isa 38:18), a place of sorrows (II Sam 22:6; Ps 18:5; 116:3) or inactivity (Eccl 9:10). These passages have sometimes been alleged for soul sleep. But if Sheol means the grave, it refers only to the sleep of the body in death. Other verses refer to the worm (Job 17:14; 21:13, 26; Isa 14:11), the consuming of the body (Ps 49:14), and the presence of kings with their bones and armor (Ezk 32:27).

One problem is that Sheol is used in figurative ways which could fit either the concept "grave" or "place of spirits." Jonah cried "out of the belly of Sheol" (Jon 2:2, RSV). Sheol is a prison with bars and gates (Job 17:16; Isa 38:10). It is personified as an insatiable creature (Prov 30:16; 27:20; Isa 5:14; Hab 2:5). Several references picturing Sheol as beneath, or as the opposite of heaven, may also be considered as arising from the reference to the tomb, remembering that in antiquity burial shafts were often deep in the earth (Deut 32:22; Ps 139:8; etc.). There is no hint of a large subterranean netherworld.

Special passages include Num 16:30, 33, where Korah was buried alive with his possessions; and Ps 16:10, which we should translate "Thou wilt not leave me in the grave" (*see* Soul). This accords with Acts 2:29–31, RSV, where Hades equals "the grave." Hades elsewhere in the KJV of the NT is "hell."

Several passages in Proverbs speak of Sheol as the reward of the wicked (1:12; 5:5; 7:27; 9:18; 23:14). This may only refer to the judgment of premature death. Isa 14:9–20 and Ezk 31:14–18; 32:18–32 probably have a figurative reference to dead kings in the tomb greeting a new arrival. Note in Isa 14:19 that the king of Babylon was denied decent burial.

Sheol is much used in poetry and often parallels "death" or the "grave." A uniform translation "grave" would solve several problems of interpretation. *See* Abaddon; Abyss; Burial; Dead, The; Grave; Hades; Hell; Intermediate State; Pit; Tomb.

Bibliography. R. Laird Harris, "The Meaning of the Word Sheol as Shown by Parallels in Poetic Texts." *Evangelical Theological Society Bulletin,* IV (1961), 129–134; *Man--God's Eternal Creation,* Chicago: Moody, 1971, pp. 162–184.

R. L. H.

SHEPHAM (shē'fȧm). A place, probably a hill town on the ideal eastern boundary of Israel, named in Num 34:10 but omitted in Ezk 47:15–18. It may have been in the vicinity of Hermon.

SHEPHATIAH (shĕf'*ȧ*-tī'*ȧ*), **SHEPHATHIAH** (shĕf'*ȧ*-thī'*ȧ*)

1. The fifth son of David. His mother's name was Abital (II Sam 3:4; I Chr 3:3).

2. The Haruphite, a Benjamite warrior who joined David at Ziklag. He was one of those skilled in using either right or left hand in slinging stones or shooting arrows (I Chr 12:2,5).

3. The son of Maachah. He was prince of the tribe of Simeon in the time of David (I Chr 27:16).

4. One of the seven sons of King Jehoshaphat. Having been richly endowed by their father, he was slain with the others when their brother Jehoram became king (II Chr 21:2,4).

5. The son of Mattan, one of the princes of Judah, who heard the words of Jeremiah counseling surrender to Babylon, and counseled Zedekiah to put the prophet to death for hindering the war effort (Jer 38:1,4).

6. The family of Shephatiah, 372 of whom returned with Zerubbabel in the first return from the Exile (Ezr 2:4; Neh 7:9). Another group of 81 from this family returned with Ezra, with Zebadiah as their chief (Ezr 8:8).

7. Another family of Shephatiah, listed among the "children of Solomon's servants," a menial class, who returned with Zerubbabel (Ezr 2:57; Neh 7:59).

8. The father of Meshullam and son of Reuel, a chieftain of the tribe of Benjamin who returned to live in Jerusalem after the Captivity (I Chr 9:8).

9. A descendant of Perez, son of Judah whose descendants are listed among the inhabitants of Jerusalem in the days of Nehemiah (Neh 11:4).

P. C. J.

SHEPHELAH (shē-fē'l*ȧ*). The name given in the RSV and NASB (e.g., I Chr 27:28) to the lowlands or foothills of southern Palestine, between the central mountainous ridge and the Mediterranean. It contained the strategic defense centers of Lachish, Debir, Libnah, and Beth-shemesh. *See* Palestine II.B.2.*e*.

SHEPHER. *See* Shapher.

SHEPHERD. *See* Occupations: Shepherd; Herdman.

SHEPHI (shē'fī). A son of Shobal, the son of Seir of Edom (I Chr 1:40). He is called Shepho in the parallel passage (Gen 36:23).

SHEPHO. *See* Shephi.

SHEPHUPHAN (shē-fū-'f*ȧ*n). One of the sons of Bela, the firstborn son of Benjamin (I Chr 8:5). He became the ancestral head of the Shuphamites (Num 26:39, where his name is spelled Shephupham [NASB] or Shupham [KJV]). In Gen 46:21 he is called Muppim and in I Chr 7:12, 15, Shuppim. The variant names may be explained as the result of an exchange of the letters *m* and *sh*, which were similar in the Phoenician alphabet used in pre-Exilic Israel.

SHERAH (shē̆r′ȧ). A daughter of Ephraim who built the two Beth-horons, Upper and Lower, and Uzzen-sherah (I Chr 7:24).

SHERD. *See* Potsherd.

SHEREBIAH (shĕr′ĕ-bī′ȧ).

1. A Levite who returned from Babylon with Zerubbabel (Neh 12:1, 8) and became a head of the Levite singers (Neh 12:24).

2. A Levite of the family of Merari who joined Ezra in his return to Jerusalem, with 18 of his sons and brethren. With 11 others, he was entrusted with the great treasure of silver and gold that Ezra was bringing to the temple (Ezr 8:18, 24). He was a leading figure during the reform carried on by Ezra and Nehemiah. With other Levites, he "caused the people to understand the law" as it was read by Ezra (Neh 8:7). He took part in the great hymn of confession and thanksgiving proclaimed at the Feast of Tabernacles (Neh 9:4–5). He is also listed among those who signed the covenant made by Nehemiah (Neh 10:12).

SHERESH (shē̆r′ĕsh). A son of Machir the Manassite by his wife Maacah, or Maachah (I Chr 7:16).

SHEREZER (shĕ-rē′zĕr). A messenger sent from Bethel to inquire at the temple concerning the day of mourning in the fifth month, a time commemorating the fall of Jerusalem to Nebuchadnezzar (Zech 7:2). Because the Heb. text is difficult the NEB translates, "Bethel-sharezer sent Regem-melech with his men to seek the favour of the Lord." This suggests that the man's name may originally have been the common Babylonian name *Bel-šar-uṣur* (*see* Belshazzar; Sharezer).

SHERIFF. One of the offices represented in the distinguished group which Nebuchadnezzar had assembled for the dedication of his golden image (Dan 3:2). The RSV and NASB render the Aramaic term by "magistrates."

SHESHACH (shē′shăk). A cryptic term generally believed to be a reference to Babylon (Jer 25:26; 51:41). Delitzsch believed that the term represents an old Babylonian register of kings which may have ruled over part of the city of Babylon. Most scholars, however, believe that it is an artificial word formed by the device known as Atbash in which the last letter of the alphabet is substituted for the first letter of the name, the letter next to the last for the second, and so forth. If this theory is true, the Heb. consonants represent Babel (see the NASB marg. notes at Jer 25:26; 51:41).

SHESHAI (shē′shī). One of the sons of Anak, perhaps an old Hebronite clan name (Num 13:22). The clan was expelled from Hebron by Caleb at the time of the conquest.

SHESHAN (shē′shăn). A Jerahmeelite who had no sons (I Chr 2:34). He gave his daughter to his Ethiopian servant Jarha, and the lineage is continued through their son Attai.

SHESHBAZZAR (shĕsh-băz′ĕr). Apparently the Chaldean name given to Zerubbabel, the leader of the return to Jerusalem from Babylon after the edict of Cyrus (Ezr 1:8; 5:14). This name is thought to be a corruption of Akkad. *Sin-ab-uṣur*, "May Sin [the moon deity] protect the father." That the two names apply to the same person is suggested by a comparison of the description in Ezr 5:14–16 of Sheshbazzar with that of Zerubbabel in Hag 2:2–4 and Zech 4:9. *See* Zerubbabel.

SHETH (shĕth). Another form of the name of Seth, a son of Adam (I Chr 1:1).

The mention of the word in Balaam's prophecy (Num 24:17) may refer to "tumult, confusion, strife" (ASV, NEB) rather than to a people parallel with the name of Moab. On the other hand, an ancient nomadic tribe known as the Shutu or Sutu is mentioned on at least one occasion in the Mari tablets as ranging in the Syrian steppe and the Bishri mountains and raiding the adjacent oasis of Tadmor (*q.v.*). As many as 2,000 might march at a time. The land of the Shutu is mentioned in connection with the Beni Hasan tomb painting and in the Posener execration texts from Egypt dating to the Patriarchal Age. Their name also appears in the Amarna letters (# 16, 11, 38, 40) and in the inscription on the base of the statue of Idri-mi (l. 15). See W. F. Albright, "The Land of Damascus Between 1850 and 1750 B.C.," BASOR # 83 (1941), p. 34.

J. R.

SHETHAR (shē′thär). One of the seven princes of Persia who had the right of entrance to the king (Est 1:14).

SHETHAR-BOZNAI (shē′thär-bŏz′nī). An official associated with Tatnai, Persia's governor of the province "beyond the river" (i.e., across the Euphrates from Persia; the KJV incorrectly translates "this side the river": Ezr 5:3–6:13). When the rebuilding of the Jerusalem temple, after long delay, was moving forward under the impetus of the post-Exilic prophets Haggai and Zechariah, he joined Tatnai in an inquiry to Darius I, king of Persia, regarding the royal authority the Jews claimed for their project. Darius confirmed their claim and instructed him and the other local officials not only to refrain from interference but to assist the Jews in completing the temple and to provide materials for sacrifice.

SHEVA (shē'vȧ)

1. A son of Caleb by his concubine Maacah (I Chr 2:49).

2. The scribe or royal secretary in David's cabinet (II Sam 20:25).

SHEWBREAD. *See* Tabernacle; Bread of Faces.

SHIBBOLETH (shĭb'ŏ-lĕth). A Heb. word which means "flood" (Ps 69:2), "river" (Isa 27:12), "ear of corn" (Job 24:24), or "branches" (bunch of twigs) of olive trees (Zech 4:12). The untranslated form appears in the story of the Gileadite Jephthah and the protesting Ephraimites (Jud 12:6) as a password used to detect the Ephraimites who were attempting to escape from Gilead by way of the fords of the Jordan. Although the Ephraimite denied his tribal connection, he would betray his true identity by his inability to pronounce the word "shibboleth" correctly, saying instead "sibboleth." Difference in dialect between Semitic peoples forms the basis of the story.

SHIBMAH. *See* Sibmah.

SHICRON (shĭk'rŏn). A town near the W end of the northern boundary of Judah (Josh 15:11), spelled Shikkeron in the ASV, etc.

SHIELD. *See* Armor.

SHIGGAION (shĭ-gā'yŏn). A term which occurs in the title of Ps 7. It may be a musical notation, perhaps a rhapsody.

SHIGIONOTH (shĭg'ĭ-ō'nŏth). The plural of Shiggaion (*q.v.*), used in the introduction to the prayer of Habakkuk in 3:1.

SHIHON (shī'hŏn). A city mentioned in the description of the borders of Issachar (Josh 19:19), whose identification is uncertain; spelled Shion in ASV, etc.

SHIHOR. *See* Sihor.

SHIHOR-LIBNATH (shī'hôr-lĭb'năth). A term generally believed to designate a river S of Carmel, on the S border of Asher (Josh 19:26). It is thought to be modern Nahr ez-Zerka, "Crocodile River."

SHIKKORON. *See* Shicron.

SHILHI (shĭl'hī). The father of Jehoshaphat's mother, Azubah (I Kgs 22:42; II Chr 20:31).

SHILHIM (shĭl'hĭm). A city in southern Judah not far from Ziklag assigned to the tribe of Judah at the time of the conquest of Canaan by the Israelites (Josh 15:32). In Josh 19:6 this city is called Sharuhen (*q.v.*) and is assigned to the tribe of Simeon; in I Chr 4:31 it is called Shaaraim.

SHILLEM (shĭl 'ĕm). The fourth son of Naphtali, among the descendants of Jacob who went into Egypt (Gen 46:24; Num 26:49; called Shallum in I Chr 7:13).

SHILLEMITE (shĭl'ĕ-mīt). A descendant of Shillem. The name appears in the plural form, "the family of the Shillemites," in Num 26:49 where the census was taken of all the families of the Israelites.

SHILOAH. *See* Siloam, Pool of.

SHILOH (shī'lō)

1. The enigmatic term Shiloh probably comes from the Heb. root *sh-l-h* meaning "to be secure, tranquil, at rest." In Gen 49:10 it seems to refer to a person whom many identify as the coming Messiah. As a proper name, it could be translated "rest giver." As Jacob looked to the future, he might well have wondered from which of his sons the Messiah would come. The three eldest sons, Reuben, Simeon, and Levi, had forfeited their rights by their sins, so as Jacob prophesied on his deathbed the honor fell to Judah. The right to rule would not depart from Judah until Shiloh (the Rest Giver) would come, and the people would obey Him.

The Persians had allowed the Jews to have their own governors, such as Zerubbabel, Ezra, and Nehemiah. Under the Hasmonaean (Maccabean) priest-kings Judah was temporarily independent. Even under the Herods the Jews had a measure of local autonomy. In A.D. 6 (after Jesus' birth), however, Herod Archelaus was deposed as ruler of Judea by Caesar Augustus, and Judea became a Roman province governed by procurators appointed by the emperor. At that time the Jewish Sanhedrin (*q.v.*) lost the power of pronouncing the death sentence, so that it no longer could be considered the supreme governing body of domestic affairs. According to Rabbi Rachmann, "When the members of the Sanhedrin found themselves deprived of their right over life and death, a

Plain of Shiloh with mound of the city in background.
HFV

Sanctuary of Shiloh. HFV

general consternation took possession of them; they covered their heads with ashes and their bodies with sackcloth, exclaiming, 'Woe unto us, for the scepter has departed from Judah and the Messiah has not come!' "

A further factor in determining the time of Shiloh's coming is the fact that the tribal traditions and genealogies of Judah remained intact only until A.D. 70 when the temple with its many records was destroyed. The final fulfillment of this prophecy, the time when Shiloh will receive the obedience or homage of the peoples (Gen 49:10*b*, NASB), awaits the second coming of Christ.

Many other interpretations of Gen 49:10 have been given. Only three of them will be considered. (1) The scepter would not depart from Judah until he (Judah) came to Shiloh. This is untenable, for nothing happened at Shiloh (in the territory of Ephraim) with special reference to Judah. (2) The scepter would not depart from Judah until Israel found rest in Canaan. Again this interpretation takes no note of the reference to Judah nor to the prediction of his supremacy. (3) The scepter would not depart from Judah until he come whose right it is to reign. This rendering retains the messianic import of the prediction and is supported by Ezk 21:27. The RSV and JerusB approximate this interpretation by translating "until he comes to whom it belongs." The Heb. expression of Gen 49:10, however, does not favor this translation because it involves a minor emendation.

2. Everywhere else in the OT the word Shiloh refers to a place. It may well have been named after the prophetic figure of Gen 49:10, for Shiloh seems according to OT records to have been a town founded by the Israelites, not one captured directly from the Canaanites. According to Jud 21:19 it was located N of Bethel, S of Lebonah, and on the E side of the highway connecting Bethel with Shechem, in the territory of Ephraim. The present village called Seilûn is adjacent to the ancient ruins.

After the initial conquest of Canaan the tabernacle was moved from Gilgal to Shiloh (Josh 18:1). Here the last seven tribes received their allotments (Josh 18:8-10). From Shiloh the tribes of Reuben, Gad, and half of Manasseh returned to their inheritances (Josh 22:9), and at Shiloh the other tribes gathered to war on those tribes for erecting an altar at the Jordan (Josh 22:12).

The tabernacle was located at Shiloh throughout the period of the judges, which included the days of Eli and Samuel. Virgins were brought to Shiloh from Jabesh-gilead to provide wives for 400 of the Benjamites who had survived the civil war (Jud 21:12); and from the local maidens dancing at the annual vintage festival at Shiloh, wives were secured for the last 200 (21:21). It was at Shiloh that Hannah prayed for a child (I Sam 1:3, 11), and to this place she brought Samuel to minister before Eli (1:24). The ark was taken from Shiloh during a battle with the Philistines, was captured, and was not returned to Shiloh. Ps 78:60 attributes the fall of Shiloh to the judgment of God, and Jeremiah cites its fall as an illustration of God's judgment (Jer 7:12, 14; 26:6, 9).

Shiloh became an inhabited town again in Hellenistic times and continued to be occupied into the Byzantine period.

A Danish expedition directed by H. Kjaer and A. Schmidt excavated parts of the site in 1926, 1929, and 1932. The results seemed to show that Shiloh was destroyed *c.* 1100 B.C. and left desolate for many centuries. A brief supplementary campaign in 1963 revealed evidence of Middle Bronze II occupation and throughout the Late Bronze II period (1400-1200 B.C.), in addition to an abundance of potsherds from the Iron II (900-600) period, while those of Iron I (1200-900) were relatively scarce. The destruction of which Jeremiah speaks may therefore have been a much more recent event, especially since Shiloh was the home of the prophet Ahijah in the reign of Jeroboam I (I Kgs 14:2, 4).

Bibliography. Marie-Louise Buhl and Svend Holm-Nielsen, *Shiloh: The Danish Excavations at Tall Sailūn, Palestine, in 1926, 1929, 1932, and 1963: The Pre-Hellenistic Remains,* Copenhagen: The National Museum of Denmark, 1969. R. A. Pearce, "Shiloh and Jer. VII, 12, 14 & 15," VT, XXII (1973), 105-108.

R. G. and J. R.

SHILONI (shĭ-lō'nī). This word occurs only in the KJV in Neh 11:5 (ASV and RSV read Shilonite, which is preferable). It refers to a descendant of Shelah. In Num 26:20 the descendants of Shelah are called Shelanites (*see* Shilonite 2).

SHILONITE (shī'lō-nīt)

1. A native or resident of Shiloh, applied only to the prophet Ahijah, "the Shilonite" (I Kgs 11:29; 12:15; 15:29; II Chr 9:29; 10:15).

2. The descendants of Judah through Shelah,

dwelling in Jerusalem at a time difficult to determine, are called Shilonites (I Chr 9:5). These people are more properly called Shelanites in Num 26:20.

SHILSHAH (shĭl'shȧ). The ninth son of Zophah, of the tribe of Asher (I Chr 7:37). People named in the genealogical list where this name is found probably lived during the time of David.

SHIMEA (shĭm'ē-ȧ)

1. Son of David and Bathsheba (I Chr 3:5), called Shammua in II Sam 5:14 and I Chr 14:4.
2. A Levite, descendant of Merari, son of Uzza, father of Haggiah (I Chr 6:30).
3. A Levite, descendant of Gershon, son of Michael, father of Berachiah, grandfather of Asaph, famous musician of David's time (I Chr 6:39).
4. Brother of David and father of Jonathan who slew "the son of the giant" (I Chr 20:6–7); called Shimma in I Chr 2:13, Shammah in I Sam 16:9, and Shimeah (*q.v.*) in II Sam 13:3.

SHIMEAH (shĭm'ē-ȧ)

1. Brother of David, father of Jonadab (II Sam 13:3) and of Jonathan who slew one "born to the giant" (II Sam 21:20–21; *see* Shimea 4.) He is called Shammah in I Sam 16:9 and Shimma in I Chr 2:13.
2. A Benjamite, descendant of Jehiel who was either the father or founder of Gibeon (I Chr 8:29–32). He is called Shimeam in I Chr 9:38.

SHIMEAM (shĭm'ē-ȧm). A descendant of Jehiel of the tribe of Benjamin (I Chr 9:38). He is called Shimeah in I Chr 8:32. *See* Shimeah 2.

SHIMEATH (shĭm'ē-ăth). Feminine form of Shimeah, an Ammonitess, the mother of one of the two murderers of King Joash of Judah. This murderer of King Joash is called Jozachar in II Kgs 12:21, but in II Chr 24:26 he is Zabad. In Heb. there is little difference in these two names.

SHIMEATHITES (shĭm'ē-ȧ-thīts). One of three families of scribes that dwelt at Jabez, evidently in Judah (I Chr 2:55). The Shimeathites made up one of the subdivisions of the Calebites (see I Chr 2:18–20, 50–55). The other two Calebite families of scribes in I Chr 2:55 are Tirathites and Suchathites.

SHIMEI (shĭm'ē-ī). A name occurring frequently in the OT before and after the Exile. It has various spellings, such as Shimi in Ex 6:17 KJV, but Shimei in ASV; Shimhi in I Chr 8:21 KJV, but Shimei in ASV; Shimeah in II Sam 21:21 KJV, but Shimei in ASV; Shimei in Zech 12:13 KJV, and Shimeites in ASV; Shimites in Num 3:21 KJV, but Shimeites in ASV. Shimei was a family name among the Levites given to a number of men. Scholars say it is difficult to trace the genealogies and identification of many.

1. The second son of Gershon, son of Levi (Num 3:18; I Chr 6:17; 23:7, 10). The Shimei of I Chr 23:9 seems to be a scribal error for some other name, perhaps Jehiel of v. 8.
2. A descendant of Merari, one of the sons of Levi (I Chr 6:16, 29).
3. A descendant of Asaph the musician (I Chr 6:42), thought by some to be the same person as 1 above, although here he is mentioned as a son of Jahath, the son of Gershom (v. 43).
4. One of the 288 trained singers under Asaph and head of the tenth of the 24 courses of musicians for the temple worship (I Chr 25:17).
5. A Levite who helped cleanse the temple in the reign of Hezekiah (II Chr 29:14), and who later appointed him with Cononiah to have the oversight of the dedicated things brought into the Lord's house (II Chr 31:11–12).
6. A Levite who put away his Gentile wife at the order of Ezra (Ezr 10:23).
7. The man with this name best known is the son of Gera, a Benjamite of the house of Saul, who during David's reign lived on the other side of the Mount of Olives. He hated David who had become the leader of Israel in the place of Saul the kinsman of Shimei. When David was fleeing from Absalom, Shimei cursed David as he passed through a narrow ravine and threw rocks at him from a place of relative safety as he ran along the top. David's faithful men wanted permission to pursue and kill him, but David forbade saying, "Behold, my son, who came forth from my bowels, seeketh my life: how much more may this Benjamite now do it? Let him alone, and let him curse; for Jehovah hath bidden him. It may be that Jehovah. . .will requite me good for his cursing" (II Sam 16:11–12, ASV). After Absalom's overthrow, when David recrossed the Jordan, Shimei was the first to welcome the returning king and fell at his feet earnestly begging for pardon. Against Abishai's advice to execute Shimei for cursing the Lord's anointed, David extended clemency, saying, "Shall there any man be put to death this day in Israel? for do not I know that I am this day king over Israel?" Therefore the king said unto Shimei, "Thou shalt not die" (II Sam 19:16–23).

   David still suspected Shimei, however, and on his deathbed he cautioned Solomon about him. Solomon gave Shimei orders to build a house in Jerusalem, and to remain in it under penalty of death (I Kgs 2:36–38). After three years Shimei left his house to recapture some escaped slaves and was immediately executed (I Kgs 2:39–46).
8. A brother of King David (II Sam 21:21).
9. An officer of David and a follower of Solomon at the time of the rebellion of Adonijah (I Kgs 1:8), identified by some with the son of Elah whom Solomon had appointed as one of the 12 chief commissary officers over Israel (I Kgs 4:18).
10. Son of Pedaiah and brother of Zerubbabel (I Chr 3:19).

11. A Simeonite, son of Zacchur (I Chr 4:26–27). He is remembered as the father of 16 sons and six daughters.

12. A Reubenite, son of Gog and father of Micah (I Chr 5:4).

13. A Benjamite clan chieftain (I Chr 8:21), called Shema in v. 13.

14. The man in charge of David's vineyards, a Ramathite (I Chr 27:27).

15. A member of the family of Hashum who put away his Gentile wife at the order of Ezra (Ezr 10:33).

16. A son of Bani who divorced his foreign wife at the order of Ezra (Ezr 10:38).

17. A son of Kish, a Benjamite, and an ancestor of Mordecai (Est 2:5).

R. H. B.

SHIMEON (shĭm'ē-ŏn). A contemporary of Ezra, a layman in Israel, of the family of Harim, who had married a foreign wife and divorced her (Ezr 10:31).

SHIMHI (shĭm'hī). A Benjamite, father of Adaiah, Beraiah, and Shimrath (I Chr 8:21). This name appears in the KJV; other versions have Shemei. This is apparently the same person who in I Chr 8:13 is called Shema (*q.v.*).

SHIMI. *See* Shimei.

SHIMITE (shĭm 'īt). The Shimites were Levites, descendants of Gershon and Shemei (Num 3:18, 21). Shimites is the form of this name in the KJV; other versions have Shemeites.

SHIMMA. *See* Shimeah.

SHIMON (shī 'mŏn). The father of four sons whose names are enumerated in an obscure genealogy of the tribe of Judah (I Chr 4:20). It is possible that Carmi in I Chr 4:1 stands for Caleb; if so, Shimon was a Calebite.

SHIMRATH (shĭm'răth). The youngest of nine sons of Shimhi, a descendant of Benjamin (I Chr 8:21).

SHIMRI (shĭm'rī)

1. Son of Shemaiah and head of a Simeonite family (I Chr 4:37).

2. Father of Jediael, one of David's valiant men of the armies (I Chr 11:45).

3. A Levite of the family of Elizaphan who aided in the purification of the temple during the reign of King Hezekiah (II Chr 29:13).

SHIMRITH (shĭm'rĭth). A Moabitess, mother of Jehozabad, one of the conspirators who killed King Joash of Judah (II Chr 24:26). Alternately this woman is called Shomer in II Kgs 12:21.

SHIMROM. *See* Shimron 1.

SHIMRON (shĭm'rŏn)

1. The fourth son of Issachar (Gen 46:13; Num 26:24) and ancestor of the Shimronites (Num 26:24). In I Chr 7:1 he is called Shimrom.

2. A Canaanite royal town whose king entered into a confederacy with Jabin, king of Hazor, against Joshua and was defeated (Josh 11:1). The town was later allotted to Zebulun (19:15), more fully called Shimron-meron (12:20). The site has not yet been identified with certainty.

SHIMRONITE (shĭm'rŏ-nīt). A descendant of Shimron. This name appears in the plural form, "of Shimron, the family of the Shimronites" (Num 26:24).

SHIMRON-MERON (shĭm'rŏn-mēr-ŏn). A royal town of the Canaanites whose king was defeated by Joshua (Josh 12:20), probably the same town as Shimron (*q.v.*) in Josh 11:1.

SHIMSHAI (shĭm'shī). A state secretary of the Persian government in the province "Beyond the River" which included Palestine. He, along with Rehum, his superior, wrote a letter to Artaxerxes opposing the rebuilding of post-Exilic Jerusalem by the Jews (Ezr 4:8–16). The royal reply supported their position and they, along with their associates, stopped the rebuilding of Jerusalem by force (Ezr 4:17–24).

SHIN. *See* Schin.

SHINAB (shī'năb). King of Admah, one of the five kings in southern Canaan during the days of Abraham (Gen 14:2) who rebelled against Chedorlaomer, king of Elam. Chedorlaomer took punitive action against Shinab and his allies.

SHINAR (shī'när). The land of Shinar is the OT name for the alluvial plain between the Tigris and the Euphrates rivers commonly known as Babylonia in ancient times. The Table of Nations in Gen 10 locates here the cities of Babel (Babylon), Erech (Sumerian Uruk, modern Warka), Accad (Agade, the capital of the great Semitic conqueror Sargon of the 3rd mil.), and Calneh (a city not yet conclusively identified, possibly the same as Calno of Isa 10:9). *See* Nations. Gen 10:9–10 states that these cities marked the beginning of Nimrod's kingdom. Since these ancient centers did not all come into prominence at the same time, one might assume that Nimrod (*q.v.*) is the name of that people who brought these cities of the plain of Shinar into prominence. Since Sargon of Agade came from Kish (possibly Cush of Gen 10:8) and he himself tells of his victory over the Sumerians at Uruk (ANET, p. 267), perhaps one is justified in seeing Nimrod as symbolic of those who brought an end to Sumerian power in the land of Shinar. The land of Shinar at this early period must have comprised the territory known in ancient texts as Sumer and Akkad (*see* Sumer), the later area of Babylonia.

The OT writers continued to refer to Babylonia as Shinar throughout the OT period. Isa 11:11; Zech 5:11; and Dan 1:2 name Shinar as the place where the Jews were to be carried into captivity.

In Gen 14:1, 9 Amraphel (*q.v.*) is named as king of Shinar. Quite certainly he was a ruler of that Semitic stock called Amurru. It is thought that after 2000 B.C. the term Shinar became localized to an area in NW Mesopotamia or northern Syria.

The Code of Hammurabi (*c.* 1700 B.C.) was one of the most important contributions of the land of Shinar. ORINST

Egyptian kings beginning with Thutmose III compiled lists of countries over which they claimed dominion. In such lists may be found the name Shankhar as the equivalent of biblical Shinar (ANET, pp. 242–243). The eminent Egyptologist Alan H. Gardiner believed that the mention by Amenhotep II (1450–1425 B.C.) in the Memphis stele of the prince of Shanhar (ANET, p. 247) was indeed a reference to Babylonia. Since the Egyptian king includes with this prince the prince of Naharin (northern Mesopotamia) and the prince of Hatti (the Hittites), it is most reasonable to assume that Shanhar is Heb. *Shin'ār*. It is also highly probable that the Shanḫar of Tell el-Amarna letter #35 (line 49) is the same (BDB, p. 1042). The name also appears as "the country of Shanhara" in a Hittite text, along with such countries as Ashur, Babylon, Alashiya (Cyprus), Alziya (upper Tigris), and Egypt (ANET, p. 352). Therefore the term equivalent to Shinar did not have reference to all of Babylonia in the 2nd mil. B.C.

E.B.S.

SHION. *See* Shihon.

SHIPBUILDER. *See* Occupations: Shipbuilder.

SHIPHI (shī'fī). A Simeonite who lived during the time of Hezekiah (I Chr 4:37), a descendant of Shemaiah, father of Ziza.

SHIPHMITE (shĭf'mīt). A native either of Shepham in NE Canaan or of Siphmoth in S Canaan. This adjective form is applied to Zabdi, one of David's officials who was in charge of "the increase of the vineyards for the wine cellars" (I Chr 27:27).

SHIPHRAH (shĭf'rȧ). One of the two Heb. midwives who, fearing God, defied the order of the king of Egypt to put to death the male children of the Hebrews and saved them alive (Ex 1:15).

SHIPHTAN (shĭf'tăn). Father of Kemuel who was a prince of the tribe of Ephraim selected by Moses to help superintend the distribution of W Canaan among the tribes of Israel (Num 34:24).

SHIPS. Ships and shipping have been known from very ancient times. As early as 3500 B.C. ships with a square sail and a forked stern (to hold a steering paddle) were depicted in Egyptian paintings or modeled for use in tombs. By the time of Snefru in the Old Kingdom (*c.* 2650 B.C.) large ships 170 feet long engaged in trading between Egypt and Byblos in Syria (ANET, p. 227). From a cylinder seal comes evidence that boats with high prow and stern were used in Assyria as early as 3200 B.C. (ANEP #104). The Egyptian Wen-Amon tells in detail of his voyage from Tanis to Dor, Tyre, and Byblos to procure lumber *c.* 1100 B.C. (ANET pp. 25–29; cf. ANEP #111).

Although the Israelites were acquainted with ships and sailing, they were not a seafaring people. The lack of good natural harbors on the Mediterranean S of Mount Carmel and the presence of alien maritime peoples (Philistines and Phoenicians) kept the Israelites away from the sea for the most part. Excavations of the small harbor at Tell Abu Hawam at the mouth of the Kishon River near Haifa tend to confirm, however, that Asher "sat at the seashore, and remained by its landings" (Jud 5:17, NASB; cf. Gen 49:13). Only during the reign of Solomon (I Kgs 9:26–28; 10:22) did Israel engage in commerce on the high seas, and then not so much from Mediterranean ports as from

Model of an Egyptian ocean-going vessel of *c.* 2500 B.C. Department of Classics, New York University.

Ezion-geber (*q.v.*) on the Gulf of Aqabah. An attempt was made to revive Israel's navy by Jehoshaphat (I Kgs 22:47–48), but the fleet was wrecked at Ezion-geber.

In spite of not engaging heavily in maritime commerce, the Israelites were familiar with the terminology relating to ships at sea. Several terms are used for ships in the OT. The most common term *'ŏniyyâ* (e.g., Jon 1:3; I Kgs 9:26) may be related to the Indo-European *naus, navis.* Another word meaning "covered ship," *s^epînâ,* occurs only in Jon 1:5, but is common in Aramaic and Arabic. An Egyptian loan-word for ship, *ṣî,* is found in Num 24:24; Isa 33:21; Ezk 30:9; Dan 11:30. One other general term, *k^elî,* "vessel," is used to refer to a papyrus boat in Isa 18:2 (*see* Papyrus; ANEP #109).

"Ships of Tarshish" (I Kgs 10:22; Isa 2:16; Ezk 27:25) were large ocean-going vessels capable of carrying heavy cargo. "Tarshish" (*q.v.*), which is a Phoenician word meaning "mine" or "smelting plant" (W. F. Albright, BASOR #83 [1941], pp. 21f.), probably refers to Tartessus in Sardinia or to the ancient Tartessus, a Phoenician settlement on the Guadalquivir, in SW Spain. For a colored photograph of a model of an 8th cen. B.C. Phoenician ship of this type, with 20 oars, crow's nest on single high mast at midships, steering oar, and high prow and stern, see VBW, II, 222f.

Although the OT relates the story of a great vessel which spared eight people from the Flood, Noah's ark (*tēbâ*), strictly speaking, cannot be classified as a ship. It was nothing more than a floating house. Its function was simply to stay above water, not to sail or travel. *See* Ark, Noah's.

In addition to these words for "ship," other nautical terms such as oar, mast, sail, pilot, and mariner are used in the OT (Ezk 27:5ff.; Isa 33:21, 23; Jon 1:3ff.). The Israelites knew what it was to be in a storm at sea (Ps 48:7; 107:23–30; Prov 23:34). The ability of a ship to sail the ocean was considered a wonder (Prov 30:19). Life itself was compared to the passing of a ship (Job 9:25–26). The city of Tyre was described dramatically and poetically as a ship (Ezk 27:3–9).

The NT also has a number of different terms for "ship." The Gr. word *naus* generally refers to a large ship. It occurs only in Acts 27:41 in the account of Paul's journey to Rome. The usual NT word for "ship" is *ploion* (66 times). It can refer to a large or small vessel. *Ploiarion* is the diminutive of *ploion* so should mean only "little boat," but it is used frequently of Galilean fishing boats (Mk 3:9; Lk 5:2; Jn 6:22–24; 21:8). Gr. *skaphē,* "a small boat or skiff," appears only in Acts 27:16, 30, 32 as the ship's dinghy or lifeboat.

In the NT ships are mentioned most frequently in the Gospels and in the book of Acts. Most of the references in the Gospels deal with boats on the Sea of Galilee. For the most part, these were small boats used for

"The situation of the ship [Paul's] on the fifteenth morning," painted by H. Smartly

fishing (Mt 4:21; Mk 1:19; Jn 21:3). Sometimes the boats were used for communications (Mt 8:23; 9:1; 14:13; Mk 8:10). On occasion Jesus even used a boat for a pulpit (Mk 4:1; Lk 5:2–3). *See* Boats.

Roman ships are mentioned in connection with Paul's first missionary journey and his voyage to Rome, and small island-hopping ships appear in connection with his second and third missionary journeys. Ships carrying official government cargoes during the 1st cen. A.D. were commonly 340 tons. Those of Rome's grain fleet ran to 1,200 tons and were sometimes about 200 feet long. What type of ship the apostle sailed on to Cyprus is not known, but he evidently was on board a fairly large ship when traveling to Rome. In the latter case there were 276 persons aboard (Acts 27:37). "A ship of Alexandria" (Acts 27:6) may imply that this was one of the grain ships bringing supplies to the capital. In spite of their size, such ships probably had very little in the way of accommodations for passengers, so that the majority of the 276 persons were probably crewmen. Josephus, however, claims that he once sailed to Rome on a ship carrying 600 passengers which sank in the Adriatic Sea (*Life* 3). Such merchant vessels had anchors (*q.v.;* Acts 27:29, 40), a sounding bell (v. 28), rudders and sails (v. 40). The mainsail (v. 40, Gr. *artemōn*) is more correctly translated "foresail" (ASV, etc.). Ships were normally dismasted and put in storage from mid-November to mid-February to avoid the winter storms (Acts 20:3, 6; 28:11; I Cor 16:6; II Tim 4:21; Tit 3:12). The periods of about a month before and after this season were also considered dangerous (Acts 27:9–13) because the prevalent storm clouds were apt to obscure the sun and stars and thus hinder navigation.

Nautical metaphors are used only sparingly in the NT. Hope is called the "anchor of the soul" in Heb 6:19, and James compares the tongue with a ship's rudder (3:4).

See Travel and Communication; Occupations: Shipbuilder.

Bibliography. CornPBE, "Ships and Navigation," pp. 659–663. B. Landström, *Ships of the Pharaohs,* Leiden: Brill, 1970. K. L. McKay, "Ships and Boats," NBD, pp. 1178–1181. James Smith, *The Voyage and Shipwreck of St. Paul,* 4th ed., London: Longmans, Green, 1880.

R. L. S.

SHIRT. *See* Dress.

SHISHA (shī'shă). Father of two of King Solomon's high officials, Elihoreph and Ahiah, who were royal secretaries (I Kgs 4:3). This is apparently the same person as Shavsha (*q.v.*), who was royal secretary for King David (I Chr 18:16).

Shishak shown leading Palestinian towns captive, from a wall at Temple of Karnak. HFV

SHISHAK (shī'shăk). Known as Sheshonk I by Egyptologists. He was a Libyan-Egyptian noble who founded the Twenty-second Dynasty of Egyptian Pharaohs with its capital at Bubastis.

At two points his reign (945–924 B.C.) touched recorded OT history: (1) He granted political asylum to the rebellious Jeroboam when the latter fled to Egypt to escape the displeasure of King Solomon (I Kgs 11:40); (2) late in his reign, in the fifth year of Rehoboam (925 B.C.), he invaded Palestine with a great army, seized Rehoboam's fortified cities (cf. II Chr 11:5–12), advanced to Jerusalem, and exacted heavy tribute from that king of Judah (I Kgs 14:25–26; II Chr 12:2–9).

Shishak recorded his military triumphs on the S wall of the temple of Amon at Karnak (ancient Thebes), mentioning more than 150 sites, some of which are Rehoboam's fortified cities, viz., Soco, Adoraim, and Aijalon, thereby supporting the biblical record (ANET, pp. 242f., 263f.). Furthermore, evidence from this triumphal relief scene which cites such biblical place-names as Shechem, Beth-shean, and Megiddo, and from a fragment of a monumental victory stele discovered at Megiddo which bears his name, indicates that his Palestinian invasion penetrated into the northern kingdom of the late-befriended Jeroboam.

Shishak doubtless intended his military conquests to restore Egyptian influence in Palestine as in the "empire era" of the Eighteenth Dynasty, but according to II Chr 12 God providentially instigated and intended Shishak's invasion as a means of punishing Judah for its apostasy from Him. Shishak's campaign had little more effect than a raid, for internal conditions in Egypt prevented him or his successor from establishing rule over Palestine.

A golden bracelet given by Shishak to one of his grandsons was found in the tomb of the latter at Tanis by Pierre Montet. Siegfried H. Horn suggests it may have been made with gold taken from Jerusalem during Rehoboam's reign ("Bracelet," *Seventh-day Adventist Bible Dictionary*, p. 154 and fig. 80).

R. L. R.

Detail of Shishak's relief. HFV

SHITRAI (shĭt'rī). A Sharonite, one of David's royal stewards who had charge of the herds that pastured in Sharon (I Chr 27:29).

SHITTAH TREE, SHITTIM WOOD. *See* Plants.

SHITTIM (shĭt'ĭm). A place name given for the acacia trees growing there (*see* Plants: Shittah, Shittim).

1. Israel's last camp before crossing the Jordan (Josh 3:1), also called Abel-shittim (*q.v.*; Num 33:49). While here, the Israelites joined in the immoral idolatry of the Moabites (Num 25:1; 31:16; Mic 6:5). From here Joshua sent two spies to Jericho (Josh 2:1). Identified by Josephus as Abila, possibly Tell el-Kefrein six miles E of the Jordan, but placed by Nelson Glueck at Tell el-Hammam *c.* two miles further ESE, and *c.* seven miles NW of Mount Nebo.

2. Another location, the valley of Shittim (Joel 3:18), was a barren valley at the NW end of the Dead Sea, possibly the Wadi Nar (the Kidron) flowing from Jerusalem.

S. M. H.

SHIZA (shī'zȧ). A Reubenite, father of Adina, a captain of the Reubenites, one of David's leading warriors (I Chr 11:42).

SHOA (shō'ȧ). A people mentioned in Ezk 23:23, along with the Babylonians, Chaldeans, Assyrians, Pekod, and Koa, who would rise against Judah. They have not been definitely identified, but may be the Sutu mentioned in the Amarna letters, an Aramean people who were never conquered by the Assyrians. *See* Sheth.

SHOBAB (shō'băb)

1. One of the sons of Caleb, the son of Hezron by his first wife Azubah (I Chr 2:18).

2. The second of four sons born to David and Bathsheba in Jerusalem (II Sam 5:14; I Chr 3:5; 14:4).

SHOBACH (shō'băk). Commander of the Syrian forces of Hadarezer, king of Zoba, in his military campaign against David. The Syrians were defeated and Shobach was killed in battle against David and his warriors at Helam. The Syrians who had been tributary to Hadarezer became subject to David (II Sam 10:15-19). This Syrian commander is called Shophach in I Chr 19:16, 18.

SHOBAI (shō'bī). The father (or forebear) of a family of porters (doorkeepers of the temple) who returned from the Babylonian Captivity to Jerusalem with Zerubbabel among the first group of returnees (Ezr 2:42; Neh 7:45).

SHOBAL (shō'bȧl)

1. One of the sons of Seir, the Horite (Hurrian) who ruled in the country later possessed by Edom. Shobal and his brothers are called dukes (KJV) or chiefs (ASV), heads of the various tribes of their people (Gen 36:20,23,29; I Chr 1:38,40).

2. One of the sons of Hur, the son of Caleb. He was the father or founder of the city of Kirjath-jearim (I Chr 2:50,52).

3. One of the descendants of Judah, possibly the same as 2 (I Chr 4:1-2).

SHOBEK (shō'bĕk). One of the chiefs of the people who signed the covenant of Ezra (Neh 10:24). Apparently the document was a pledge in support of certain laws that needed confirmation during or after Nehemiah's second term as governor (Neh 13).

SHOBI (shō'bī). An Ammonite, son of King Nahash of Rabbah, who, along with others, generously supplied David and his men with food and equipment at Mahanaim during the rebellion of Absalom (II Sam 17:27-29).

SHOCHO, SHOCHOH. *See* Socho.

SHOCK OF CORN. A small stack or heap of reaped grain. In Jud 15:5 and Job 5:26 the KJV translates the Heb. *gādîsh* "shock" and in Ex

22:6 "stack." This Heb. word is used for "tomb" in Job 21:32 and "mound" over a grave in Job 5:26.

SHOCO. *See* Socho.

SHOE. *See* Dress; Sandal.

SHOE LATCHET. *See* Latchet, Shoe.

SHOHAM (shō'hăm). A Levite descendant of Merari, son of Jaaziah, who, along with other Levites, cast lots for service in the house of the Lord during David's time (I Chr 24:27).

SHOMER (shō'mĕr)

1. The father of Jehozabad who with Jozachar, the son of Shimeath, murdered King Joash of Judah (II Kgs 12:21). In the parallel passage in II Chr 24:26 the feminine form, Shimrith, is given and is called a Moabitess. Some scholars believe that Chronicles gives the mother of the regicide. Others think it is a case of scribal confusion since the name Shimeath could be either masculine or feminine.

2. One of the sons of Heber of the tribe of Asher (I Chr 7:32). Called Shamer in v. 34.

SHOPHACH. *See* Shobach.

SHOPHAN (shō'făn). In the KJV the name of a fortified town in Gad E of the Jordan (Num 32:35), but is probably a suffix of the preceding word and should be read "Atroth-shophan" as in the RSV. *See* Atroth.

SHORE. Various words are rendered by the word "shore" in KJV. In the OT the Heb. *hôph* (Jud 5:17; Jer 47:7) is translated "coast" in RSV; in Josh 15:2 *qāṣeh* is rendered more accurately "end" in RSV. The main Heb. word translated "shore" or "seashore" in KJV and RSV alike is *śāphâ* (lit., "lip," Gen 22:17; Ex 14:30; Josh 11:4; I Sam 13:5; I Kgs 4:29; 9:26). The reference in I Kgs 9:26 states that Ezion-geber was "on the shore of the Red Sea in the land of Edom." The location of Ezion-geber at Tell Kheleifeh by the researches of Fritz Frank and Nelson Glueck greatly illustrates the meaning of the term "shore" in the OT, since this site was located directly overlooking the Gulf of Aqabah, only 500 meters (*c.* 1,630 ft.) from the actual shore line (Nelson Glueck, *The Other Side of the Jordan,* New Haven: ASOR, 1940, p. 91). The Heb. term therefore seems to refer to the shoreline itself or its near vicinity. The LXX translates the Heb. term by the Gr. term *cheilos* (cf. Heb 11:12).

The regular term for shore in the NT of the KJV is *aigialos* (translated "beach" in the RSV and NASB; Mt 13:2, 48; Jn 21:4; Acts 21:5; 27:39, 40). Thus the term refers to beaches of both fresh water bodies of water (such as the Sea of Galilee) or salt water beaches (of the Mediterranean). The area of the "sandy beach"

The shore at the ancient port of Salamis where Paul and Barnabas landed. HFV

where Paul's ship came aground and suffered shipwreck (Acts 27:39–40) has been carefully investigated (James Smith, *The Voyage and Shipwreck of St. Paul,* 4th ed., London: Longman, Green, 1880). Smith points out that the sand of "St. Paul's Bay," as this area is designated today, is "now worn away by the wasting action of the sea" (p. 172).

E. J. V.

SHOSHANNIM (shō-shăn'ĭm), **SHOSHANNIM-EDUTH** (shō-shăn 'ĭm-ē'dūth). Shoshannim, in the superscriptions of Ps 45 and 69, and Shoshannim-Eduth, in the superscription of Ps 80, probably refer to the melodies according to which the psalms were to be sung, although now the melodies are lost.

SHOULDER. The Gr. word for shoulder (*ōmos*) occurs from Homer down and was frequent in the LXX (47 times in the OT and Apocrypha, HR) and in contemporary writers (Jos *Ant.* iii.7.2; 8.9). In the NT it occurs only in Lk 15:5 (the good shepherd lays the lost sheep on his shoulders) and in Mt 23:4 (figuratively of burdens heaped on people by Pharisees).

It is the usual translation of three Heb. words in the OT: *shôq* (more literally "leg" or "thigh," e.g., Ex 29:22,27; Lev 7:32–34; 10:14–15, shoulder of sacrificial animal); *shekem* (the upper part of the back below the neck, e.g., Gen 21:14; 24:15; 49:15; Josh 4:5; hence always singular); and in the ordinary sense *kātēp* (e.g., Ex 28:12; Num 7:9; Jud 16:3; Isa 46:7). Twice when referring to a part of a sacrificed animal, "shoulder" is used to translate *zᵉrôa'*, regularly rendered "arm" (Num 6:19; Deut 18:3).

The shoulder was used for many things, including bearing burdens, supporting garments, and thrusting. It is applied to inanimate things; e.g., in ASV marg. the side of a building (I Kgs 6:8); the Sea of Galilee (Num 34:11); the "side" or slope of a city built on a hill (Josh 15:8, 10f.; 18:12); the slope of a mountain (Gen 48:22; Isa 11:14); poetically "dwell between his shoulders," i.e., between the mountains He loves--Zion and Moriah (Deut 33:12); the sides of a gate (Ezk 41:2,26); the bearings of an axle (I Kgs 7:30,34); and the shoulder pieces of the priest's dress (Ex 28:7).

Numerous metaphorical uses occur: (1) The member on which a burden is laid (Isa 9:6, "The government shall be upon his shoulder"; Isa 22:22, "The key of the house of David will I lay upon his shoulder"). From this comes "serve God with the shoulder" (Zeph 3:9, ASV marg.), and also "withdrew the shoulder" (Neh 9:29--i.e., refused the responsibility of keeping the law). (2) The member on which blows or punishment falls (Isa 9:4, the rod which threatened his shoulder). (3) "Turn his back [shoulder]" meant "to go away" (I Sam 10:9; Josh 7:12; Jer 48:39); hence Ps 21:12, "make them turn their back [shoulders]" means "put them to flight" (RSV).

J. W. R.

SHOULDER BLADE. The only reference to "shoulder blade" in the Bible is in Job 31:22 and means the socket or the bone to which the arm is attached.

SHOULDER PIECE. The two shoulder pieces or straps of the upper part of the high priest's ephod came over the shoulders from the back and fastened in front. They were made of blue, purple, scarlet, and fine twined linen. An onyx stone (or beryl) bearing the name of six of the tribes of Israel was attached to each shoulder piece. These stones were called "stones of memorial" (Ex 28:7, 12, 25; 39:4, 7, 18).

SHOVEL. The OT mentions two kinds of shovels: (1) Heb. *yāʿ* denotes one of the bronze "vessels of the altar," used in the tabernacle (Ex 27:3; 38:3; Num 4:14) and in the temple (I Kgs 7:40, 45; II Kgs 25:14; etc.) for placing coals on, and removing the fat-soaked ashes from, the altar. At Megiddo was found a bronze shovel 22 inches long, consisting of a rectangular scoop with a long, thin handle. (2) Heb. *raḥath* is a broad shallow wooden scoop used with a winnowing fork in threshing grain (Isa 30:24).

SHOWBREAD. *See* Bread of Faces; Tabernacle.

SHOWER. *See* Rain.

SHRINE. This word does not appear in the KJV of the OT. It is used in the RSV for *bēth 'ĕlōhîm* in Jud 17:5 (KJV lit., "house of gods") referring to Micah's family shrine which contained several images; for *bēth bāmôth* in II Kgs 17:29, 32 (KJV "houses of the high places") referring to Samaritan shrines which housed their idols); and for *bāmôth* in Ezk 16:16 (KJV "high places"), shrines of gaily colored cloth. For pagan shrines in Palestine, *see* Temple and bibliography for article about tribal league shrines in Amman and Shechem.

SHROUD. This word appears only once in the KJV of the OT. In Ezk 31:3 it is used to translate the Heb. word *ḥōresh,* a thicket, or a forest; ASV and RSV translate "shade." It may also mean a cover, a shelter, a wooded place. The KJV translates this word "forest" in II Chr 27:4 and "bough" in Isa 17:9.

SHRUB. *See* Plants: Bush.

SHUA (shōō'*à*)

1. A Canaanite of Adullum, the father of the wife of Judah (Gen 38:2,12; I Chr 2:3). The KJV incorrectly renders this name "Shuah" in Gen 38:2, 12. In I Chr 2:3 where the KJV has "the daughter of Shua the Canaanitess" the RSV treats the word as a proper name, "Bath-shua."

2. The daughter of Heber, an Asherite (I Chr 7:32).

SHUAH (shōō'*à*)

1. A son of Abraham and Keturah (Gen 25;2; I Chr 1:32), evidently progenitor of the Shuhites (*q.v.*), to which tribe Bildad the Shuhite belonged (see Job 2:11).

2. Father of the wife of Judah, but this is an incorrect rendering of "Shua" in Gen 38:2, 12 of the KJV.

3. A brother (or son) of Chelub, one of the descendants of Judah (I Chr 4:11). Both the ASV and the RSV render this name "Shuhah."

SHUAL (shōō'*à*l)

1. The third of eleven sons of Zophah, an Asherite (I Chr 7:36).

2. The "land of Shual" (I Sam 13:17) was a region near Ophrah to which the first of three marauding companies of Philistines from Michmash went. Although this region has not been definitely identified, possibly it was N of Michmash in the vicinity of Bethel in Benjamin.

SHUBAEL (shōō'bă-ĕl)

1. A Levite, a descendant of Amram and of Moses (I Chr 24:20); called "Shebuel" in I Chr 23:16 and 26:24.

2. A Levite, a son of Heman, one of the leaders of song in the temple during the time of David (I Chr 25:20); called "Shebuel" in I Chr 25:4.

SHUHAM (shōō'hăm). A descendant of Dan, head of the family of the Shuhamites (Num 26:42); called "Hushim" in Gen 46:23.

SHUHAMITE (shōō'hăm-īt). The Shuhamites were the descendants of Shuham of the tribe of Dan (Num 26:42–43). This is the only Danite clan named in this Danite genealogy. It numbered 64,400 when the Israelites entered Canaan.

SHUHITE (shōō'hīt). A descendant of Shuah, son of Abraham and Keturah (Gen 25:2; I Chr 1:32), applied only to Bildad, a friend of Job

(Job 2:11; 8:1; 18:1; 25:1), who then would have been a member of this Arab tribe. If the Shuhites are to be equated with the people known to the Assyrians and Babylonians as *Sûḫu* (ANET, pp. 275, 304, 482), they are to be located in northern Syria near the Euphrates, below the mouth of the Khabur River. This may give some clue as to the location of the story of Job, or at least to the extent of the area from which Job's friends came to visit him.

SHULAMITE (shōō'lȧ-mīt). A title used to designate the maiden who figures prominently in the Song of Solomon (Song 6:13). The form "Shulammite," as in the ASV and RSV, is to be preferred. It is widely regarded as the equivalent of "Shunammite," a woman from the town of Shunem. Solomon may have used the term because beautiful women were known to have come from that town (cf. I Kgs 1:3). It is also possible that "Shulammite" is the feminine form of "Solomon" and designates the bride in her honorary role as princess, companion to the bridegroom as king. *See* Shunammite.

SHUMATHITES (shōō'mȧ-thīts). A Calebite family of Kirjath-jearim; descendants of Shobal, a son of Hur (I Chr 2:53).

SHUNAMMITE (shōō'nȧ-mīt). A native of Shunem.

1. A woman of Shunem whose son Elisha raised from the dead (II Kgs 4:8–37). Later, Elisha's intervention secured the restoration of her property (II Kgs 8:1–6).

2. Abishag a Shunammite, a beautiful young woman, was secured as a nurse for David in his old age (I Kgs 1:3,15). Adonijah's love for this Shunammite led to his doom (I Kgs 2:17ff.).

3. The Shulamite (*q.v.*) of Song 6:13 is widely regarded as a Shunammite by means of the common exchange of *l* for *n*.

SHUNEM (shōō'nĕm). A town in the territory assigned to the tribe of Issachar (Josh 19:18). The Canaanite city of this name is mentioned in the Egyptian records of Thutmose III, and in the Amarna letters as *Shunama*. The Philistines encamped at Shunem before Saul's last battle against them at Gilboa (I Sam 28:4). This town was the home of the woman whose son Elisha restored to life (II Kgs 4:8–37); of Abishag, David's nurse in his old age (I Kgs 1:3, 15); and possibly of the Shulamite (or Shunammite) of Song 6:13. Shunem has been identified with the modern Solem which overlooks the valley of Jezreel on the SW slope of the hill of Moreh; it lies seven miles E of Megiddo. *See* Shunammite.

SHUNI (shōō'nī), **SHUNITE** (shōō'nīt). Shuni was the third son of Gad, ancestral head of "the family of the Shunites" (Gen 46:16; Num 26:15).

SHUPHAM (shōō'făm). Son of Benjamin and progenitor of "the family of the Shuphamites" (Num 26:39, KJV; ASV and RSV have "Shephupham"); evidently the same person as Shephuphan in I Chr 8:5. In this later reference Shephuphan is listed as a son of Bela and therefore as a grandson of Benjamin.

SHUPHAMITE (shōō'fȧ-mīt). The Shuphamites were the descendants of Shupham (or Shephupham) who was either the son or grandson of Benjamin (Num 26:39; I Chr 8:5).

SHUPPIM (shŭp'ĭm)

1. A great-grandson of Benjamin, son of Ir, or Iri, grandson of Bela, and brother of Huppim (I Chr 7:7, 12, 15).

2. A Levite, one of the gatekeepers at the temple who, along with Hosah, had charge of the gate Shallecheth, on the W side of Jerusalem (I Chr 26:16).

SHUR (shŏŏr). The name of a desert region between Palestine and Egypt. In poetry the word is used meaning "wall" (Gen 49:22; Ps 18:29), and some scholars believe the name was derived from a line of border fortresses between Egypt and the Sinai desert. This was merely a disconnected line of forts which the Egyptians seem to have known as the "Wall of Tharu" (Egyp. *th* corresponds to *sh* in Heb.). One of these forts was called Tjel or Zilu (Tell Abu Seifeh, probably the biblical Etham, Ex 13:20; Num 33:8). Some also identify Shur with a line of white cliffs 12 to 14 miles E of the Gulf of Suez, which they claim are still called Jebel es-Shur in Arabic today. Other scholars, however, question both explanations.

"The way to Shur," where the angel found Hagar by the spring of water (Gen 16:7), was apparently the road from Beer-sheba, through Khalasa, Ruheibeh, Bir Birein, and Muweilleh, to Egypt. At one time Abraham "dwelt between Kadesh and Shur" (Gen 20:1), and it is said also to have been the home of the Ishmaelites, who "dwelt from Havilah to Shur, which is opposite Egypt in the direction of Assyria" (Gen 25:18, RSV); of the Amalekites, whom Saul defeated "from Havilah as far as Shur, which is east of Egypt" (I Sam 15:7, RSV); and of the Geshurites, the Girzites, and the Amalekites, upon whom David and his men made raids "as far as Shur, to the land of Egypt" (I Sam 27:8, RSV). The Exodus story suggests that Shur was the land directly E of the "Reed Sea," for the Israelites entered the Wilderness of Shur immediately after escaping from the Egyptians (Ex 15:22). This would place it E of Lake Timsah. Apparently the Wilderness of Shur extended eastward to the "River of Egypt" (Wadi el-'Arish). *See* Wilderness Wandering.

D. B.

SHUSHAN (shōō'shăn), **SUSA** (sōō'sȧ). The capital of ancient Elam in SW Persia, which lay near the rivers Ulai (Eulaeus, modern Karun) and Shapur, *c.* 150 miles N of the Persian Gulf. It was one of the royal residences of the Achaemenid kings in whose reigns the city flourished. Here Daniel had a vision (Dan 8:2), Nehemiah was in exile (Neh 1:1), and Ahasuerus (Xerxes) and Esther lived (Est 1:2). *See* Esther. It was the name of both a citadel-palace, the center of government (Est 3:15; 8:14; 9:6, 11-12), and of a large city (Est 3:15; 8:15) situated at the junction of royal roads leading to Sardis and the contemporary capitals of Ecbatana and Persepolis.

The site at modern Shushan (Heb. and Akkad. *shûshan*) has been explored since 1851 by W. K. Loftus, de Morgan, de Macquenem and R. Ghirshman. *See* Archaeology. From the early 4th mil. B.C. occupation of the site was almost continuous. Parts of the royal palace (*apadana*), treasury (Herod. v.49), artisan's quarters and of the royal city have been uncovered. The ruins cover more than five square miles. Here de Morgan found the diorite stele containing the code of Hammurabi, broken in three pieces. It had been taken by the Kassites from Babylon as a trophy of war.

The magnificent palace built by Darius I was embellished by craftsmen with materials brought from many distant countries. Inscriptions help to give a picture of the daily life in Shushan. When this palace was severely damaged by fire in the time of Artaxerxes I (464-423 B.C.) it was rebuilt by Artaxerxes (II) Mnemon, who reigned there in 404-359 B.C. This palace figures prominently in the Esther story.

Earlier palaces on the same site had been occupied by the Kassite kings who sacked Babylon. Babylonian treasures were recovered by Nebuchadrezzar I in his raid on Shushan about 1120 B.C. The Assyrian Ashurbanipal (biblical Osnapper) sacked the city in 640 B.C. removing some of its inhabitants (Shushanites) to exile in Samaria (Ezr 4:9, RSV).

Alexander entered Shushan in 331 B.C. and seized its great treasures. He later used the great columned hall, perhaps the scene of Esther's feast, for a mass wedding of his troops with Persian girls. After the city had been occupied by Antigonus in 317 B.C. it suffered a gradual decline, precipitated by the Parthian establishment of Ctesiphon as the capital. *See* Elam.

A bronze lion from Susa, 5th century B.C. LM

A bull capital for a column at the palace of Susa. LM

Bibliography. Roman Ghirshman, *Iran*, Baltimore: Penguin Books, 1961, pp. 127-205.

D. J. W.

SHUSHAN-EDUTH (shōō'shăn-ē'dŭth). Musical terminology, probably meaning "lily of the testimony." These are cue words in the title of Ps 60, probably referring to the melody according to which the psalm was to be sung, although now the melody is lost.

SHUTHALHITE (shōō'thȧl-hīt). The Shuthalhites were the descendants of Shuthelah of the tribe of Ephraim (Num 26:35).

SHUTHELAH (shōō'thĕ-lȧ). The first son of Ephraim, father of Eran, and head of "the family of the Shuthalhites" (Num 26:35-37; I Chr 7:20-21).

SHUTTLE. A weaver's tool used to shoot the thread of the woof from one side to the other through the threads of the warp. In Job 7:6 the Heb. word *'ereg*, "a weaving," is translated "shuttle" in the KJV. It is used figuratively to show that the days of one's life pass as swiftly as the shuttle moves back and forth in the warp. In Jud 16:14 Heb. *'ereg* is translated a weaver's "pin." *See* Occupations: Weaver.

SIA (sī'*ȧ*), **SIAHA** (sī'*ȧ-hȧ*). A chief among the Nethinim, or temple servants, whose children returned from the Babylonian Exile with Zerubbabel (called Sia in Neh 7:47 and Siaha in Ezr 2:44).

SIBBECAI, SIBBECHAI (sĭb'ē-kī). One of "the valiant men of the armies" of David (I Chr 11:29). He was a Hushathite (of the town of Hushah), a Zarhite (or Zerahite) of the tribe of Judah. He slew the Philistine giant Saph, or Sippai, in a campaign against the Philistines at Gob, or Gezer (II Sam 21:18; I Chr 20:4). He was the captain over David's army of 24,000 men which served during the eighth month (I Chr 27:11). In II Sam 23:27 his name is given as Mebunnai (*q.v.*).

SIBBOLETH (sĭb'ō-lĕth). A variation in the spelling of the password "Shibboleth" (*q.v.*) as mispronounced by the Ephraimites (Jud 12:6).

SIBMAH (sĭb'mȧ). Also called Shebam (Num 32:3) and Shibmah (Num 32:38). A city E of the Jordan which was claimed by the tribe of Reuben and rebuilt. It has not been positively identified but was somewhere on the Moabite hills (Num 32:3, 38; Josh 13:19). The place became famed for its wine, and both Isaiah (16:8–9) and Jeremiah (48:32) speak of it in connection with the destruction of Moab. *See* Shebam.

SIBRAIM (sĭb-rā'ĭm). A Syrian city between Damascus and Hamath (Ezk 47:16). In Ezekiel's ideal delineation of the Holy Land, Sibraim is a northern boundary town of Palestine between Syria and the territory to be allotted to the tribe of Joseph.

SICCUTH. *See* Gods, False: Saccuth.

SICHEM. *See* Shechem.

SICK, SICKNESS. *See* Diseases.

SICKLE. The Heb. words *ḥermēsh* (Deut 16:9; 23:25) and *maggāl* (Jer 50:16; Joel 3:13) mean simply "sickle." The Gr. word *drepanon* is defined by Thayer as "sickle, pruning hook, hooked vine knife" (Mk 4:29; Rev 14:14–19). The sickle consisted of a blade made in different periods of flint, bronze or iron, fastened into a handle of bone or wood. The cutting edge was either plain or toothed. A larger sickle was used for grain, a smaller one for grapes. In a figurative sense, the putting in of the sickle symbolized the infliction of judgment.

SIDDIM, VALE OF. *See* Vale of Siddim.

SIDON (sī'dŏn). An ancient Phoenician city located about 20 miles N of Tyre and a like distance S of Beirut. Backed by the Lebanon Mountains, Sidon faces the Mediterranean and anciently controlled the Plain of Sidon, a strip of coastal plain about 20 miles long and two miles wide.

Apparently the oldest of Phoenician cities, Sidon was founded by the son of Canaan (Gen 10:15). Gradually it assumed domination of the Phoenician coast and maintained it for several centuries, finally losing it to Tyre. So great was this ascendancy that "Sidonian" and "Phoenician" largely became interchangeable terms. This was true for the early period when Sidon was predominant in Phoenicia (Deut 3:9; Josh 13:4, 6), as well as long after Tyre attained the hegemony. Thus Ethbaal, king of Tyre, is called king of the Sidonians in I Kgs 16:31. This equation of Sidonians and Phoenicians also appears in Homer.

Sidon figured in the division of Canaan after the Heb. conquest, when it was described as at the northernmost point of the territory of Asher (Josh 19:28; cf. Jud 1:31). During the Amarna period (*c.* 1400–1360 B.C.), the city threw off the Egyptian yoke and participated in an effective siege of Tyre. Sidon's ruler, Zimreda,

An archer, from the palace of Susa, portrayed in colored enameled brick. LM

Ruins of the Crusader castle at Sidon. HFV

professed devotion to the pharaoh, but in reality was in league with King 'Aziru the Amorite. Thereafter she dominated Tyre until about 1200 B.C., when sea raiders (Philistines and others) sacked Sidon and left it very largely in ruins. At that juncture many Sidonians migrated to Tyre, which then took the leadership among the Phoenician city-states and retained it during the era of Phoenician independence (*c.* 1200–870 B.C.).

When the Assyrians began under Ashurnasirpal II (883–859 B.C.) to exert pressure in W Asia, Sidon was among the principalities to feel their power. Sidon paid tribute to Ashurnasirpal in 868 B.C. and to Shalmaneser III in 842. Sidon felt the weight of other Assyrian conquerors also, but suffered especially for rebellion against Esarhaddon (*c.* 678). In his fury the Assyrian absolutely obliterated the city. Most of the inhabitants were killed or sold into slavery; some escaped to nearby cities.

Sidon rose from the ashes but came under the severe condemnation of Ezekiel (28:21–23), who declared that judgments would be executed in her and that pestilence and slaughter would descend upon her. Sidon became involved in rebellion against Persia in 352 B.C., and when the population saw that all further resistance was useless, they determined to set fire to their homes and perish with them. It is said 40,000 died in the conflagration – certainly a sufficient fulfillment of Ezekiel's prophecy.

Sidon was largely rebuilt by the time Alexander the Great marched through Phoenicia (332 B.C.), and the inhabitants welcomed him as a deliverer. They even helped Alexander besiege Trye, but secretly spirited away to safety about 15,000 Tyrians. From the Hellenistic period comes the great inscribed black basalt sarcophagus of Eshmun'azar, king of Sidon; it was found in 1855 (ANET, p. 505; ANEP #283). The stone coffin of his father Tabnit (*c.* 300 B.C.) was excavated in 1887 (ANET, p. 505).

Under the Romans Sidon was given rights of self-government and seems to have enjoyed a flowering of culture during the period. Strabo (d. A.D. 24) spoke in glowing terms of Sidonian philosophers in the sciences of astronomy and arithmetic. Sidon had a law school which was famed throughout the classical East.

People of Sidon came to Galilee to listen to the preaching of Christ and to be healed (Mk 3:8; Lk 6:17). Jesus went to the borders of Tyre and Sidon (Mt 15:21; Mk 7:24–31), where He healed a Syrophoenician woman's daughter. King Herod Agrippa I of Judea was offended by the people of Tyre and Sidon, but their representatives won over his chamberlain Blastus and begged for peace (Acts 12:20). The apostle Paul stopped briefly at Sidon on his way to Rome and met certain friends there (Acts 27:3). The city became an important center of Christianity, as is demonstrated by the fact that it had a bishop present at the Council of Nicea in A.D. 325. Modern Saida boasts a population of some 40,000. *See* Phoenicia; Lebanon; Tyre.

H. F. V.

SIEGE. *See* Warfare.

SIEVE. A wooden box with a bottom of string netting or coarser material used in threshing to separate the grain from small stones and other foreign objects. The Heb. word *nāpâ*, "sieve," is used figuratively in Isa 30:28, referring to the day of judgment when the Lord will sift the nations with "the sieve of vanity," or of destruction. In Amos 9:9 by usage of the Heb. word *k^e^bārâ* for "sieve," a similar sifting of the house of Israel is foreseen.

SIGHT. The term sight in the English Bible translates many Heb. and Gr. words and is used in various ways. In addition to the normal meaning of what the eye sees, there are numerous references to blind people who receive sight (Lk 4:18; cf. Mk 10:51–52; Jn 9:11–18; Acts 9:18).

Paul's statement in II Cor 5:7 is of special interest: "For we walk by faith, not by sight." Here the word for "sight" is *eidos*, "appearance, form," which refers not to the act of seeing, but rather to the facts which one sees. Our Christian walk on earth is guided by faith in eternal things which cannot now be seen (II Cor 4:18; Heb 11:1, 13), not by the outward appearance of present things. Our unseen hope (Rom 8:24) is that we shall see Christ face to face and know fully even as we are fully known (I Cor 13:9–12; I Pet 1:8; I Jn 3:2–3).

Bibliography. W. Michaelis, "*Horaō,* etc.," TDNT, V, 315–382.

SIGN. The principal words translated "sign" in the KJV are Heb. *'ôth*, "sign, token"; *môphēth*, "wonder, sign, portent"; and Gr. *sēmeion*, "sign, mark, signal." These terms may appear as synonyms with others denoting miracles (*q.v.*), wonders (*see* Wonder, Wonderful), and the mighty works of God (Acts 2:22) and of

His apostles (II Cor 12:12). A sign is a distinguishing mark, a symbol, or a portent or omen of something momentous or calamitous to occur in the future. It may be of a miraculous nature to confirm an inspired message or the divine authority of its bearer, or to warn or to encourage obedience to God's will.

Many different kinds of signs are found in the Bible.

1. Objective signs, e.g., stones taken from the crossing of the Jordan dryshod (Josh 4:6).
2. Ensigns used by the tribes (Num 2:2).
3. Religious signs such as circumcision (Gen 17:11).
4. Physical phenomena, e.g., the sun and the moon (Gen 1:14), the rainbow (Gen 9:12).
5. Omens given by the prophets, e.g., the death of Eli's sons (I Sam 2:34), the gift of the Spirit to Saul (I Sam 10:7), the sign of the virgin bearing a son (Isa 7:11–14; cf. Mt 1:22–23).
6. Visible works of God which were attestations of His active presence, such as the ten plagues in Egypt (Ex 7:3; 10:2; Ps 78:43), and the dividing of the Red Sea and the destruction of the Egyptian army (Deut 7:19).

The prophets foretold specific signs and wonders which were to accompany both the first coming of Christ and also His second coming (Joel 2:28–32). Peter pointed to this prophecy as being partly fulfilled at Pentecost, saying, "This is that which was spoken by the prophet Joel" (Acts 2:16); but he was careful not to say this is all of that, because the "wonders in heaven above, and signs in the earth beneath . . . the sun turned into darkness, and the moon into blood . . . " (vv. 19–20) were not fulfilled at that time. Jesus spoke of the "sign of the Son of man in heaven," namely, the sign of His second coming (Mt 24:30). There is much about the signs of Christ's return in Mt 24 and 25 and throughout the book of Revelation.

See Miracles; Symbol, Symbolism.

Bibliography. Karl H. Rengstorf, "*Sēmeion,* etc.," TDNT, VII, 200–261; "*Teras,*" TDNT, VIII, 113–126.

R. A. K.

SIGNET. *See* Seal.

SIHON (sī'hŏn). An Amorite king whose realm lay E of the Jordan between the Arnon and the Jabbok Rivers. Having attacked the Israelites as they were led by Moses toward the Promised Land, Sihon and his hosts were defeated at Jahaz (Num 21:21–30). Sihon, with his capital at Heshbon (*q.v.*), had been proverbial as a mighty king (Num 21:27 ff.), and his defeat is mentioned often in the OT (Deut 1:4; 2:24–32; Josh 2:10; 9:10; Jud 11:19–21; Neh 9:22; Ps 135:11; Jer 48:45). The territory of Sihon and his confederate to the N, Og king of Bashan, was settled by the tribes of Reuben, Gad, and half of Manasseh (Num 32).

SIHOR (sī'hôr). Sihor, or more correctly Shihor (ASV, etc.), is the name applied in a few places apparently to the Nile River. It is sometimes used as an expression of the southern boundary of Israel (I Chr 13:5), and at times stands for Egypt itself (Isa 23:3; Jer 2:18). The origin of the name may possibly be from the Egyptian name Shi-Ḥor ("lake of Horus") given to a stream on the eastern border of Egypt, a part of the Pelusiac branch of the Nile delta. This seems to be the reference in Josh 13:3.

SILAS (sī'lȧs). Silas first appears (Acts 15:22, 27, 32) in the NT narrative as one of the leading men sent to carry the decree of the Jerusalem council to the Gentile believers of Antioch, Syria, and Cilicia. He was probably a Hellenistic Jew since his name is the Gr. form of the Aram. *She'îla'*, equivalent to Heb. *Sha'ûl*, "Saul." He was a Christian prophet, able to exhort and strengthen by his preaching. Like Paul, he enjoyed Roman citizenship (Acts 16:37–38). Silas appears as Silvanus (the Lat. form of his name) in II Cor 1:19 (cf. Acts 18:5); I Thess 1:1; II Thess 1:1; I Pet 5:12.

After Paul and Barnabas parted (Acts 15:39), Paul chose Silas to accompany him on the second missionary journey (v. 40). Silas was Paul's companion in the dramatic events of the Philippian imprisonment (Acts 16:19, 25, 29).

There is a suggestion that Silas had a significant position of leadership in the missionary task: at Thessalonica some were persuaded and consorted with Paul and Silas (17:4). He and Paul left Thessalonica together (v. 10), and came to Berea. When Paul was forced to leave, Silas and Timothy remained (v. 14). Those who accompanied Paul to Athens conveyed Paul's command back to Silas that they (Silas and Timothy) should join Paul speedily. Silas and Timothy brought news to Paul of what had happened in Thessalonica, and Paul's first epistle to the Thessalonians was the result (cf. I Thess 3:2, 6). The failure to mention Silas here may suggest that he was busy elsewhere in Macedonia, and only Timothy ministered to Thessalonica. Silas may have gone to Philippi, later bringing a gift of money to Paul (cf. II Cor 11:8 f.; Phil 4:15).

There is a problem connected with the movements of Silas and Timothy after Paul left them at Berea. Kirsopp Lake (*The Beginnings of Christianity,* IV, 224) may be correct in insisting that I Thess 3:1 implies that Paul and Silas were left alone at Athens when Timothy was sent back to Thessalonica, and that Timothy's return was to Athens, with the writing of I Thessalonians immediately afterward. Lake sees, however, that "Acts represents Silas and Timothy as coming from Berea to join Paul in Corinth." But when he adds regarding Silas "and never in Athens at all," he is building on the silence of Acts. Acts says that Timothy and Silas joined Paul at Corinth, while I Thess 3:6

says, "Timothy came even now unto us." On Lake's assumption that the plural in I Thess 3:1 includes Silas, the "us" in 3:6 probably includes him also. If we furthermore assume that these (Acts 18:5 and I Thess 3:6) are probably *not* the same events (as is often argued), Lake's criticism will then be against the usual assumption, and not necessarily against the accuracy of Acts. He holds that the writer of Acts "made a mistake in thinking that Silas and Timothy did not join Paul before he had reached Corinth." As remarked above, this rests on the silence of Acts. It is always possible, of course, to argue that Paul was using the editorial "we" in I Thess 3, and adopt the simpler traditional explanation that this epistle was written from Corinth.

Conjecturally adopting, then, Lake's suggestion that I Thessalonians was written from Athens, and rejecting the argument from the silence of Acts concerning Silas' ever coming to Athens, the following sequence would be possible: (1) Timothy and Silas join Paul at Athens. (2) Timothy is sent to Thessalonica (I Thess 3:1–2). (3) Timothy rejoins Paul and Silas at Athens after a brief visit to Thessalonica. (4) I Thessalonians is written. (5) Timothy bears the epistle to Thessalonica; Silas visits other churches. (6) Paul proceeds to Corinth and begins work there. (7) Timothy and Silas rejoin Paul at Corinth (Acts 18:5). (8) II Thessalonians is written.

Silas is not mentioned in the remaining stages of the second journey, and it is conjectured that he and Timothy left Corinth, engaging in missionary work in the province of Achaia.

Silas reappears some ten or 12 years later as the co-author and bearer of I Peter (5:12). He wouldhave been known to the believers in some of the provinces mentioned in I Pet 1:1, having accompanied Paul on the second journey.

Silas is one of the many links between the earliest church in Jerusalem and Paul. Paul's witness to Christ is buttressed by the fact that he had many lines of connection with the Jerusalem church.

W. B. V.

SILENCE. Several terms signify silence (Heb. *hāsâ, ḥārash, dûmîyâ, dûmâ, dûmām;* Gr. *sigē, hēsuchia*). The first term as a command in Hab 2:20 (*has*) sounds like our order to "hush"! *Dûmâ* is used only metaphorically: of Edom in Isa 21:11, "the oracle of Dumah" (lit. silence), having figurative reference to the desolation to fall upon Edom (Dumah); of death (Ps 94:17), "Unless the LORD had been my help, my soul had almost dwelt in silence" (death); and of Sheol (Ps 115:17), "The dead praise not the LORD, neither any that go down into silence" (i.e., the place of silence). The other terms are used for the literal act of refraining from speaking (Ps 39:2; Acts 21:40); women's silent reserve in the church (I Tim 2:11–12); figuratively of Babylon's silence (of extinction, Isa 47:5); dumb idols ("stone of silence," Hab 2:19); and quiet resignation of faith (Ps 62:1). Another term, Heb. *d*^{e}*māmâ*, "whisper," carries practically the force of "silence" (Ps 107:29; I Kgs 19:12), as in Job 4:16.

H. E. Fr.

SILK. The thread produced by caterpillars that feed on the leaves of the mulberry, which thread in turn is woven into a fine fabric identified in English by the word "silk" (Prov 31:22; Ezk 16:10, 13; Rev 18:12). The KJV renders the Heb. *shêsh* in Prov 31:22 as "silk," but the RSV properly translates "fine linen." The references in Ezk 16 are to Heb. *m*^{e}*shî* which concerns basically that which is drawn out, hence a very fine thread. Therefore it is frequently questioned that Ezekiel refers to silk as the term is used today, in spite of indications that this commodity reached Greece and the markets of the W by the time of Aristotle. The rabbinical interpreters understood the word to mean silk. Rev 18:12 has the Gr. *sirikos,* from *sērikos,* meaning "silken" and derived from *Sēres,* an Indian race of people from whom the Greeks first bought silk, though undoubtedly it had come originally from China. In fact, the silk worm is called the Seric worm. In NT times silk was a highly valued article of trade fit for

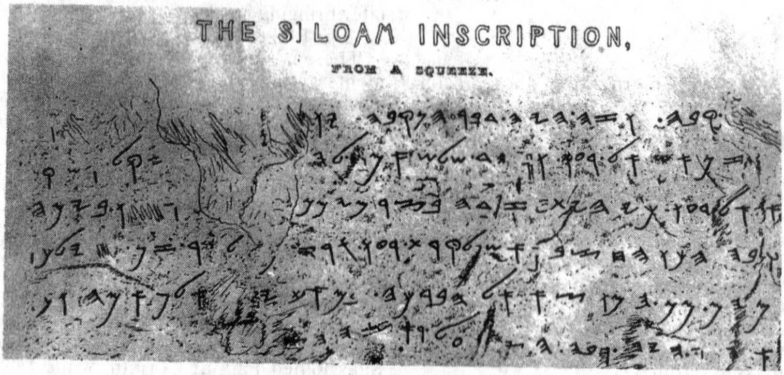

The Siloam Inscription

the clothing of the emperor and literally worth its weight in gold.

H. L. D.

SILLA (sĭl'ȧ). Possibly a portion or a suburb of Jerusalem, mentioned in connection with the house of Millo in which Joash, king of Judah, was murdered (II Kgs 12:20). Nothing is known definitely as to what Silla was or where it was. Some speculate that it was a road, while others surmise that it was a place.

SILOAH, SHILOAH. *See* Siloam, Pool of.

SILOAM, POOL OF (sī-lō'ȧm). The name Siloam or Shiloah means "send" or "conducted," especially applied to the sending of water through an aqueduct. In Jn 9:7 this name is given to the pool of water S of the temple in Jerusalem. Josephus says that this pool was situated at the extremity of the Tyropean Valley (valley of the cheesemongers) near a bend in the old wall beneath Ophel (*Wars,* v.4.1–2). Many identify this with the waters of Shiloah mentioned in Isa 8:6 referring to an open surface aqueduct practicable only in the peaceful reign of Solomon, and with the pool of Shelah in Neh 3:15 (RSV). Others associate this pool with the bringing of water into Jerusalem by Hezekiah (II Kgs 20:20).

The present reservoir that bears this name is rectangular, being 58 feet long, 18 feet wide, and 19 feet deep, built of masonry which is considerably broken down on the W side. This reservoir is fed by a tunnel which was cut for a distance of 1,780 feet through solid rock, beginning at Gihon (*q.v.*), the Virgin's Spring, the only spring of fresh water in the immediate neighborhood of Jerusalem. In 1880 an inscription of six lines was discovered on the walls of this tunnel, written in Heb. that probably dates from the time of Hezekiah. A portion of the first three lines has been worn away, but the remaining letters in the prong-like characters of old Heb. tell about the making of the tunnel. The inscription was cut out by vandals but was recovered in 1890 by Turkish officials and removed to a museum in Istanbul.

Siloam was especially important in time of siege. At the threat of invasion the Virgin's Spring rising outside the walls of the city was covered with masonry, and its waters were fed underground to the pool inside the city. The pool also played an important part in the ritual associated with the Feast of Tabernacles, for it was here that the water was drawn in a golden pitcher which was carried in procession to the temple as part of the week-long ceremony (Jn 7:2, 37–38).

Recent excavations at the southern end of the SE hill suggest that the pool lay outside the city wall in biblical times; that it must therefore either have been covered over for protection, or have been a vast underground cistern completely cut out of the rock.

See Siloam, Tower of; Jerusalem.

H. L. D.

The Siloam Tunnel. Palestine Archaeological Museum

SILOAM, TOWER OF. Reference is made by Jesus (Lk 13:4) to this tower as having recently fallen upon and killed 18 persons. Possibly part of the ancient system of fortifications on the walls of Jerusalem near the pool of Siloam. Or it may have been within the area of the present village of Silwân on the steep E slope of the Kidron Valley. Apparently the incident was well known to Jesus' hearers, but is not mentioned elsewhere. *See* Siloam, Pool of; Kidron.

SILVANUS (sĭl-vā'nŭs). Another name for Silas (*q.v.*).

SILVER. *See* Minerals and Metals.

SILVERLING. A silver coin (Isa 7:23), probably a shekel, as in the NASB translation: "a thousand shekels of silver." *See* Weights, Measures, and Coins.

SILVERSMITH. *See* Minerals and Metals: Silver; Occupations: Metalsmith, Purifier of Silver, Refiner.

SIMEON (sĭm'ē-ŏn)

1. The second son of Jacob by his wife Leah (Gen 29:33), but not one of the major figures in Israel's history. He is better known as a secondary figure in his association with his brother Judah. With his full brothers Reuben, Levi, and Judah, he became the leader in avenging the rape of their sister Dinah by Shechem (Gen 34:24–31). When one of Jacob's sons was to be detained in Egypt as hostage, Joseph held Simeon for security (Gen 42:24).

2. Simeon was the progenitor of the tribe by that name. He had six sons: Jemuel (or Nemuel), Jamin, Ohad, Jachin (or Jarib), Zohar (or Zerah), and Shaul. All of the sons with the exception of Ohad became tribal chiefs (Gen 46:10; Num 26:12–14; I Chr 4:24). When the land was distributed by lot at Shiloh, the second lot in the extreme S within the border of Judah was given to Simeon (Josh 19:1–9). These two tribes made a united effort in subduing the Canaanites (Jud 1:1–3, 17). Among the Simeonite cities were Beer-sheba, Ziklag, and Hormah (Josh 19:1–9) in southern Judah.

At the first census the tribe numbered 59,300 men of military age (Num 1:23; 2:13); at the second numbering the tribe had reduced to 22,200 (Num 26:12–14), making it then the smallest of the tribes. Many of the tribe may have been executed along with Zimri the Simeonite leader because of involvement in the sin of Baal-peor (Num 25:1–15). Nevertheless the tribe of Simeon had the honor of standing at the foot of Mount Gerizim to pronounce blessings (Deut 27:12). When Moses blessed the tribes before his departure, however, he did not mention Simeon specifically (Deut 33). The tribe of Simeon could best be omitted because according to Jacob's dying blessing on his sons it was to be scattered in Israel (Gen 49:5–7). Yet, though Simeon suffered humiliation in not being granted an independent possession or territory, the Simeonites did retain their identity. The tribe was recognized by Ezekiel in his prophetic statement of Canaan's future, and the tribe is also mentioned in the Apocalypse (Ezk 48:24–25, 33; Rev 7:7).

During the reign of Hezekiah the Simeonites conquered the people of Ham (Egyptians) and the Meunites living in the valley of Gedor (LXX: Gerar; I Chr 4:39–41, NASB). A large number of Amalekites were also slaughtered by them in Mount Seir (vv. 42–43). It is apparent that the tribe of Simeon did not gain a great deal of recognition, and it is likely that the tribe partly merged into the tribe of Judah.

When the nation of Israel was divided into two parts after the death of Solomon, the prophet Ahijah revealed to Jeroboam (I) that God had given him ten tribes over which he was to rule (I Kgs 11:28–39). Only nine tribes, however, had had territories assigned to them N (or E) of Judah and Benjamin. Therefore it is probable that, like the Danites, a majority of the Simeonites had migrated northward from the Negeb looking for better pasturelands. This movement evidently took place after David's early reign in Hebron, for Simeon provided more men for David than did Judah (I Chr 12:23–25). That such a migration occurred is corroborated by two passages which mention Simeon in a context of the northern kingdom of Israel or its tribes (II Chr 15:9; 34:6). It seems very likely, therefore, that Simeon was the tenth of the northern ten tribes during the monarchy period (see Leon J. Wood, "Simeon, the Tenth Tribe of Israel," JETS, XIV [1971], 221–225).

3. An ancestor of Jesus Christ and descendant of David, who evidently lived during the Judean monarchy (Lk 3:30).

4. A devout Jew who lived in Jerusalem at the time of the birth of Christ and was looking for the "consolation" or salvation (Lk 2:30) of Israel. Having received a revelation by the Holy Spirit that he would not die until he had seen the Messiah, he was led by the Spirit to the temple at the very time Joseph and Mary brought the infant Jesus to dedicate Him. Simeon recognized Him to be Messiah and prophesied concerning the Child (the hymn of praise now known as the *Nunc Dimittis*) and Mary His mother (Lk 2:25–35).

5. A Christian prophet and/or teacher in the church at Antioch at the time of the call of Barnabas and Paul to missionary service. He was also known by his Latin name Niger, meaning "black," suggesting that he may have been an African (Acts 13:1). Spelled Symeon in ASV and RSV.

6. An alternate spelling for Simon (Symeon in ASV, RSV; Acts 15:14). *See* Peter.

H. A. Han.

SIMILITUDE. Heb. *d^e^mûth* is used with the idea of exact likeness (II Kgs 16:10–11; Gen 5:3). Especially interesting is its use in Gen 1:26: man is made after the "likeness" of God, where it is parallel to *ṣelem,* "image" (lit., something cut out). Dan 10:16 states that a similitude or exact likeness of a human being, an angel in a tangible appearance, touched Daniel as he received a revelation.

Heb. *tabnîth* is related to the idea of construction or structure. In Ps 106:20 it parallels "molten image" of v. 19; in the elaborate simile of Ps 144:12, BDB (p. 125) suggests "carved according to the construction of a palace, palace-fashion."

The meaning of Heb. *t^e^mûnâ* is clarified by a comparison of Num 12:8 and Deut 4:12, 15–16. Moses reiterates that Israel saw no *t^e^mûnâ*, only hearing a voice (Deut); but Moses looked upon the *t^e^mûnâ* of the Lord, thus marking the directness and intimacy of Moses' communion with God (Num). Note also Ps 17:15 where the word is translated "likeness." Important also is its occurrence as a key word in the Decalogue (Ex 20:4) translated "likeness."

Paul's use of the Gr. word *homoioma* bears out the idea of exact likeness (Rom 5:14). The sin of other men is not in all respects exactly like that of Adam. "The doctrine of particular significance to the argument being developed is that death came to all men, not by reason of their own actual transgression or individual sin, but because of their involvement in the sin of Adam; in other words, by reason of solidaric sin" (John Murray, *Romans,* NIC, 1960, p. 187).

James 3:9 refers to Gen 1:26, where the Gr. word *homoiōsis* is used in the LXX to translate the climactic, more precise word of the parallel, Heb. *ṣelem.* James thus graphically emphasizes the enormity of the sin of the tongue which curses man, made in the very image of God.

The use of *homoiotēs* in Heb 7:15 seems to emphasize the close correspondence between Christ and Melchizedek. Heb 7:15 may be a clarifying comment on Ps 110:4, substituting *homoiotēs* for Gr. *taxis* of the LXX rendering.

W. B. W.

SIMON (sīʹmŏn). This name occurs in the Bible only in the NT, designating a number of different persons. Perhaps it is a contraction of the Heb. "Simeon," which occurs mostly in the OT, although occasionally in the NT. *See* Simeon.

1. The best known Simon was the apostle, often called Peter; so named by Jesus (Mt 16:18; Mk 3:16). He was the son of Jonas (Mt 16:17; Jn 21:15) and brother of the apostle Andrew (Jn 1:40). *See* Peter.

2. Simon Zelotes (Lk 6:15), also called "the Cananaean" (Mt 10:4; Mk 3:18, RSV). The latter term is not from "Cana" or "Canaanite" but from an Aramaic word meaning "zealot, enthusiast." Both terms indicate that Simon belonged to a faction called Zealots (*q.v.*) who were fanatical opponents of Roman rule in Palestine.

3. Father of Judas Iscariot (Jn 6:71; 13:2, 26), sometimes called Simon Iscariot (see Jn 6:71; 13:26, RSV).

4. Brother of Jesus (Mt 13:55; Mk 6:3).

5. A Pharisee in whose house Jesus was anointed by a sinful woman (Lk 7:36-50). The location of the house is not mentioned, though it seems to have been in Galilee and possibly in Capernaum. The Pharisee was shocked at Jesus' attitude toward sinners, for Pharisaic tradition forbade association with those disregarding the law. Jesus rebuked Simon by means of a parable and commended the woman for her loving act.

6. A leper in whose home in Bethany Jesus was entertained. It was here Jesus was anointed by Mary (Mk 14:3-9; cf. Jn 12:1-8). Very likely Simon had been miraculously healed by Jesus (Mt 26:6).

7. Simon of Cyrene (Mt 27:32; Mk 15:21; Lk 23:26), who was compelled to carry Jesus' cross. Mark describes him as the father of Alexander and Rufus, known to the Roman Christians (Rom 16:13).

8. A sorcerer in Samaria, who professed faith in Christ when Philip preached in his city (Acts 8:9, 13). Later, when Peter and John came, he wanted to purchase the power of the Holy Spirit (Acts 8:18-19). His object evidently was to apply the power to the working of his magical arts. Peter bitterly denounced him (vv. 20-23). Our word "simony" is derived from Simon's endeavor to obtain spiritual power by a bribe. The Church Fathers (Justin Martyr, Irenaeus, etc.) held him to be the first Christian Gnostic (*see* Gnosticism). Their writings tell much about his teachings in which he identified himself with God Almighty or the chief angelic power who created subordinate angels. He identified his harlot Helena with Divine Wisdom and the Holy Spirit (*Acts*, Anchor Bible, XXXI, 305-308).

9. A tanner in Joppa (Acts 9:43; 10:6, 17, 32) with whom Peter was staying when he received word from Cornelius of Caesarea that he should come and show him the way of salvation.

J. A. S.

SIMPLE, SIMPLICITY. Heb. *tōm* has the idea of integrity and completeness. The meaning of integrity is illustrated in such passages as Gen 20:5-6; I Kgs 9:4; Ps 78:72. This same word very logically carries the idea of simplicity and innocence (II Sam 15:11).

Another Heb. word, *peṯî*, is translated simplicity in Prov 1:22 and means lack of wisdom. As an adjective the word occurs in Ps 19:7; 116:6; 119:130 and frequently in Proverbs.

The Gr. word *haplotēs* occurs only seven times in the NT. In three of these it has the idea of sincerity, simplicity and singleness of mind (II Cor 11:3; Eph 6:5; Col 3:22). In four, the concept of generosity or liberality is conveyed (Rom 12:8; II Cor 8:2; 9:11, 13). The basic idea is absence of duplicity and double motives. It refers to a basic singleness of heart and life.

SIMRI (sĭmʹrī). A Levite, one of the descendants of Merari who, although he was not the firstborn, was made the chief by Hosah his father; he was appointed a doorkeeper of the temple by David (I Chr 26:10). The form of this name in the ASV and the RSV is "Shimri."

SIN

Definition

Most definitions of sin are too restricted. For instance, a usual definition that sin is selfishness would mean that a father's stealing food for a starving child would not be sin. Sin is lawlessness declares I Jn 3:4, but this is usually understood in too narrow a sense. The law against which sin is measured is not simply the Mosaic law, but every revelation of God during all time. This includes specific biblical commandments (both negative and positive), biblical principles of conduct (e.g., I Cor 10:31), and laws not specifically mentioned in the Bible but in the sense of directives given by God's appointed leaders (e.g., Heb 13:17; Eph 6:1). Sin, therefore, is not only anything contrary to what God has *said* man should not do, but it is also anything contrary to what God *would not want* man to do on the basis of revealed principles. Thus, a completely inclusive definition of sin would be: Sin is anything contrary to the character of God. Since God's glory is the revelation of His character, sin is a coming short of the glory or character of God (Rom 3:23).

Reformed theologians stress that the character of God is revealed in the law of God. They teach that this is presented both positively in a general way in the Ten Commandments, which enjoin love to God and love to man (cf. Rom 13:8–10); and negatively (except for the fourth and fifth commandments) in a more specific way in the eight prohibitions contained in the two tables of the law. It is on this basis that the Westminster Shorter Catechism defines sin as "any want of conformity unto or transgression of the law of God." In the Sermon on the Mount, Christ sets up the two promulgations of the law, the negative and the positive, as the basis of the Christian life and the standard of likeness God desires of His children (Mt 5:17, 21–22, 27–28, 43–48).

Origin of Sin

God is nowhere said to be the author or responsible originator of sin. He tempts no one to do evil (Jas 1:13). When God says, "I create evil" (Isa 45:7) He is speaking of woe or calamity (RSV, NASB, JerusB). No view is acceptable which in any way makes God the author of sin, even in the sense that He is unable to prevent its occurrence or appearance.

Barth's view is therefore unacceptable when he speaks of God thinking of all the possible worlds, good, bad and indifferent, and then pushing to the farthest point of existence the indifferent and the evil worlds and holding them off by His infinite power. These form the chaos, *Das Nichtige*, which presses in upon poor little finite man as he comes into the world. Finite man tries to hold off *Das Nichtige* by his own power, and thereby sins and falls. Such a view makes God either the originator of the chaos or a God unable to create without creating evil.

Instead, the Bible indicates that sin originated with Satan in his rebellion against God. All the OT suggests about Satan's responsibility is that "iniquity was found" in the king of Tyre (Ezk 28:15), an evident figure of the devil. In his pride he sought to make himself like the Most High (Isa 14:12–14; cf. I Tim 3:6). In human experience sin originated in the temptation of Adam and Eve in Eden when they rebelled against God by heeding the voice of Satan (Gen 3:1–6). The effect of Adam's sin on the moral life of his descendants is the problem involved in original sin and is the subject of differing viewpoints.

The Extent of Sin

Calvinists hold that Adam's sin was immediately imputed to the whole race, with the result that not only is the entire human family depraved, but it is also guilty of Adam's sin by participation (Rom 5:12). The Arminian view declares that the primary effect of Adam's sin on the race was to give man a proneness to sin without implying guilt. The Pelagian view attributes inherent goodness to man, which opens to man the possibility of living in a state free from sin if he so wills.

However, the Bible teaches the fact and universality of sin (I Kgs 8:46; Prov 20:9; Eccl 7:20; Rom 3:23; 5:12, 19; Eph 2:1–3; Jas 3:2; I Jn 1:8, 10). This is what is meant by total depravity or total inability—the unmeritoriousness of man in the sight of God. The term depravity refers to the corruption or pollution of human nature as the result of Adam's fall. According to the Shorter Catechism original sin consists both in the guilt of Adam's first sin and in the ensuing corruption of his whole nature.

Total depravity speaks of the pervasiveness of evil in man, and in all that he does, with the resultant impossibility on man's part to perform what is truly and spiritually good in the eyes of the all-holy God. It does not mean, however, that man is utterly evil in every way and that he cannot do good things. He can admire and emulate many things that are noble and perform natural good such as acts of civil righteousness and social justice. But all his good is of no avail in meriting favor with God. He is incapable of acting from purely unselfish motives in order to glorify only his Creator, and in his sinful state he is totally unable to reconcile himself to the righteous Ruler of the universe.

This doctrine rests upon clear biblical statements. Gen 6:5 declares, "The Lord saw that the wickedness of man was great on the earth, and that every intent of the thoughts of his heart was only evil continually," supplemented by Gen 8:21, "For the intent of man's heart is evil from his youth" (both NASB). These verses reveal the inwardness of man's sin—"of his heart"; its constancy—"continually"; its completeness—"only evil"; and its totality—"every imagination, intent, or purpose." Isaiah confesses that all our righteous deeds are like filthy rags (64:6), teaching that man cannot perform any good deeds which are really acceptable in God's sight. Man is sinful from his birth, from the very moment of conception (Ps 51:5), and his "heart" (his inner nature) is more deceitful or insidious than anything else, and is desperately corrupt, incurably sick (Jer 17:9, NASB).

In Romans Paul devotes the first main section (1:18–3:20) to the proof of the proposition that "all have sinned and come short of the glory of God" (3:23). He argues that the heathen are without excuse (1:18–32), the moral or self-righteous man stands condemned because of disobedience to his conscience (2:1–16), and the religious Jew breaks the very written law he boasts in (2:17–3:8). He concludes that all are depraved totally, because none are righteous, none do good, all are unprofitable or useless, and their bodily members are instruments of iniquity (3:9–20). John concludes that the whole world, apart from the regenerate children of God, lies (helpless) in the power of the evil one (I Jn 5:19, NASB).

Terminology

Terms denoting sin and evil are numerous in Heb. Indeed, there are more words for evil than for good. There are at least eight basic words: (1) Heb. *ra'*, "bad" (Gen 28:17), "evil" (444 times in KJV), is used to denote anything harmful and is not restricted to things morally bad. (2) Heb. *rāshā'*, "wickedness" (Ex 2:13), is always used in a sense of moral guilt resulting from the confusion of loose living. (3) Heb. *'āshām*, "guilt" (Gen 26:10), is almost always confined to the ritual connected with the tabernacle and temple in Leviticus, Numbers, and Ezekiel. (4) Heb. *ḥāṭā', ḥaṭṭā't* (Ex 20:20) literally means "to lose the path," "miss," or "miss the mark" (Jud 20:16; Job 5:24, RSV; Prov 8:36, NASB), and includes the concept of making a deliberate mistake—not merely an innocent failure. (5) Heb. *'āwôn*, "iniquity" (I Sam 3:13), often means "guilty," the two ideas of iniquity and guilt being very closely connected. It has the connotation of crookedness, of twisting away intentionally from God's straight path of righteousness. (6) Heb. *shâgag, shāgâ*, "err" (Isa 28:7), when used in connection with the law, clearly implies that the sinner in his ignorance was responsible for knowing that law (Lev 5:18; cf. 4:2, 13). (7) Heb. *tā'â*, "wander away" (Ezk 48:11), indicates the error is always deliberate, not accidental. (8) Heb. *pāsha'*, "rebel" (II Kgs 3:5, 7; Isa 1:2), is usually translated "transgress" (I Kgs 8:50; Jer 2:8, 29).

The usage of these words leads to certain conclusions relative to the doctrine of sin as revealed in the OT. (1) Sin was conceived of as being fundamentally disobedience to God. (2) While disobedience involved both positive and negative aspects, the emphasis was definitely on the positive commission of wrong and not merely the negative omission of good. In other words, sin was not simply missing the mark (as it is so frequently defined), but deliberately and knowingly hitting the wrong mark. (3) Sin took many forms, and the Israelite was made keenly aware of the particular form his sin took by the availability of these various words.

The NT uses 13 basic words to describe sin. (1) Gr. *kakos*, "bad" (Rom 13:3), means moral evil, though occasionally it is used to denote physical evil. (2) Gr. *ponēros*, "evil" (Mt 5:45), with two exceptions is used of moral evil. (3) Gr. *asebēs*, "godless" (Rom 1:18), is the opposite of *eusebēs*, "pious," and often occurs with other words for sin as in I Tim 1:9. (4) Gr. *enochos*, "guilty" (Jas 2:10; Mt 26:66), usually denotes a guilt which is worthy of death. (5) Gr. *hamartia*, "sin" (I Cor 6:13), any departure from the way of righteousness, is the most inclusive word for sin. (6) Gr. *adikia*, "unrighteousness" (I Cor 6:9), means any unrighteous conduct in the broadest sense. (7) Gr. *anomos*, "lawlessness" (I Tim 1:9), sometimes is translated "iniquity." (8) Gr. *parabatēs*, "transgressor" (Jas 2:9, 11), usually refers to the transgression of the Mosaic law, and always some specific law. (9) Gr. *agnoeō*, "to be ignorant," sometimes is used to describe innocent ignorance (Rom 1:13) and sometimes culpable ignorance (Rom 10:3; Eph 4:18). (10) Gr. *planaō*, "to go astray" (I Pet 2:25), always means culpable error or being deceived (e.g., Tit 3:3), except possibly in Jas 5:19. (11) Gr. *paraptōma*, "a fault" (Gal 6:1), in most references is a deliberate trespass or transgression. (12) Gr. *hypocritēs*, "hypocrite" (I Tim 4:2). (13) Gr. *parapiptō*, "to fall away" (Heb 6:6), implies a deliberate turning aside in apostasy (*q.v.*).

From the uses of these words certain conclusions may be drawn concerning the doctrine of sin in the NT. (1) There is always a clear standard against which sin is committed. (2) Ultimately all sin is a positive rebellion against God and a transgression of His standards. (3) Evil may assume a variety of forms. (4) Man's responsibility is definite and clearly understood.

Penalty and Remedy

The Bible is consistent that the punishment of sin is death—both physical and spiritual (Ezk 18:4, 20; Rom 5:12; 6:16, 21, 23; Jas 1:15). When Adam and Eve sinned they eventually died physically (Gen 2:17; 3:19), but they immediately experienced spiritual death, alienation from God (Gen 3:8–10; cf. Eph 2:1, 5, 12; 4:18). *See* Death.

The remedy for sin is twofold: (1) forgiveness (*q.v.*) which erases the guilt of sin, and (2) justification (*q.v.*) which is a declaration of the positive righteousness imputed by God to the believer. All of this is based on the work of Christ in His death (Rom 3:24-26) and is secured by believing in Him. *See* Atonement.

Sin is never eradicated in the believer in this life (I Jn 1:8–10). The Holy Spirit is given so that the believer may not let sin reign in his body (Rom 6:1–13; 8:1–4). His enemies, nevertheless, are powerful and constant. The temptations of the world, the devil, and the flesh can only be met by utilizing God's provision (Gal 5:16, 24; Eph 6:10 ff.). Persistent sin in the Christian's life brings chastisement (Heb 12:6) and sometimes physical death (I Cor 11:30), but never total separation from God and spiritual death. The intercession of Christ guarantees the security of his salvation (Heb 7:25; I Jn 2:1), though confession is necessary for restoration of fellowship (I Jn 1:9). Rewards may be lost for failing to maintain fellowship (I Cor 3:15). For the unpardonable sin, *see* Holy Spirit, Sin Against.

See Evil; Fall of Man; Iniquity; Judgment; Trespass; Wicked(ness).

Bibliography. G. C. Berkouwer, *Sin*, Grand Rapids: Eerdmans, 1971. J. Oliver Buswell, *A Systematic Theology of the Christian Religion*, Grand Rapids: Zondervan, 1962, I, 255–320; II, 87–88. W. Grundmann, "*Kakos*, etc.," TDNT, III, 469–487. G. Harder, "*Ponēros, Ponēria*," TDNT, VI, 546–566. Leon Morris, *The Wages of Sin*, London: Tyndale Press, 1954; *The Apostolic Preaching of the Cross*, Grand Rapids: Eerdmans, 1956, pp. 125–185. J. Barton Payne, *The Theology of the Older Testament*, Grand Rapids: Zondervan, 1962, pp. 194–221. G. Quell, G. Bertram, G. Stählin and W. Grundmann, "*Amartanō*," TDNT, I, 267–316. K. H. Rengstorf, "*Amartōlos*," TDNT, I, 317–335. Gottlob Schrenk, "*Adikos*," TDNT, I, 149–163.

C. C. R. and R. A. K.

SIN (CITY). An Egyptian city (Egyp. *si'nw, swn*) slated for judgment according to Ezk 30:15-16. Called by the Greeks Pelusium (so translated in RSV), it is Tell Farama, near the mouth of the E branch of the Nile in the Delta region about a mile from the Mediterranean. Linked as it was with No (Thebes) and Noph (Memphis), it was to be included in a comprehensive judgment on the land of Egypt. Ezekiel called it the "strength" or stronghold (NASB) of Egypt; it was a virtually impregnable frontier fortress against invasion from the E through Palestine. In spite of that fact it had fallen to the Assyrian king Esar-haddon in 671 B.C. Ashurbanipal reinstalled the "king" of Si'nu in his office after a rebellion by Tirhakah (ANET, p. 294). Ezekiel's prophecy was fulfilled either during the campaign against Pharaoh Hophra by Nebuchadnezzar (who does not mention Pelusium) or in the fierce battle in 525 B.C. between the Persian forces of Cambyses and the Egyptians under Psammetichus III (Herodotus iii.10-13). Antiochus IV marched through Pelusium when he invaded Egypt in 170 B.C., and the Romans under Gabinius defeated the Egyptians in the same neighborhood.

H. F. V.

SIN OFFERING. *See* Sacrificial Offerings.

SIN UNTO DEATH. An expression employed in I Jn 5:16-17 in reference to assurance in prayer (cf. 5:14-15). A person may confidently expect that God will answer prayer in behalf of a Christian who commits sin which is not unto death (5:16*a*), since this request is in accord with the will of God. On the other hand, the person whose sin tends toward death cannot be the object of confident intercession (5:16*b*).

Several views concerning the nature of this sin have been advanced. (1) It is sin in which a Christian persists until God finds it necessary to visit him with physical death (cf. I Cor 11:30). (2) It is the sin of a Christian which results in the loss of salvation, that is, in eternal death. Some find the same phenomenon in Mt 12:31 or in Heb 6:4-6. (3) The sin is said to be the persistent, adamant denial of the incarnation of God's Son on the part of a person who professes to be a Christian. Such sin, if persisted in, will result in eternal death. The advantage of the latter view is that it is based on the context of I Jn. The recipients of the epistle were familiar with such sin, having witnessed it in the persons of the early Gnostic teachers, whom John designates as antichrists (I Jn 2:18-19) and false prophets (4:1-3). The apostle does not say that one should not pray for such persons, but only that there is no assurance of an answer.

D. W. B.

Plain of el-Merkah, possible Wilderness of Sin.
JR

SIN, WILDERNESS OF. The desert region between Elim and Sinai through which the Israelites journeyed en route to Mount Sinai (Ex 16:1; 17:1; Num 33:11-12). The exact location is far from certain, though it is often identified with Debbet er-Ramleh, a sandy tract on the fringe of the plateau Et Tih in the SW peninsula. It was near Dophkah (Num 33:12), probably in the vicinity of the Egyptian mines at Serabit el-Khadem. The similarity between the two names suggests that "Sin" and "Sinai" are connected, "Sinai" being a derivative of the word "Sin," which itself, it is suggested, may be related to the worship of the moon-god Sin. The name should not be confused with that of the Wilderness of Zin (*q.v.*), which lay farther N, to the S of Judah. *See* Wilderness Wandering.

SINA (sī'nȧ). Designation of Sinai in the KJV of Acts 7: 30, 38 following the Gr. form of the word. The ASV and RSV have "Sinai" (*q.v.*).

SINAI (sī'nī). The Sinai peninsula is an inverted triangle between the two arms of the Red Sea, with the Gulf of Suez on the W and the Gulf of Aqabah on the E. The base of the triangle is approximately 150 miles long and forms a barrier between Palestine and Egypt. The whole triangle is referred to as the Wilderness of the Wandering, although the NE portion, with its sterile tableland rising to 2,500 feet and its rolling plains with few springs, is generally considered the "great and terrible wilderness" (Deut 1:19), home of the Israelites for 38 years. It is also referred to as the Wilderness of Paran (*see* Paran).

On the N the Sinai plateau slopes away to a plain of white sand reaching to the Mediterranean. Sand also lines the shores of both Suez and Aqabah. At the N end of the Gulf of Aqabah the city of Ezion-geber was located, once the seaport of Solomon. Through this area ran the trade route between Egypt and Arabia. Further N was the Way of Shur from Beer-sheba through the Wilderness of Shur (*see* Shur) to Etham (*q.v.*) and Bubastis, and along the Mediterranean coast was the usual line of march, the Way of the land of the Philistines (*see* Exodus, The: Route). Near the Gulf of Suez the Egyptians mined valuable turquoise and some copper at Serabit el-Khadem. Here inscriptions of Semitic slave laborers from *c.* 1500 B.C. have been discovered, written in a hieroglyphic alphabetic script (*see* Writing). The Pharaoh's army was sent in great numbers to guard both the treasure from the mines and the goods carried along the trade routes by Egyptian caravans.

Near the S end of the peninsula rises a series of granite peaks 5,000–9,000 feet high, standing in stark grandeur and brilliant color in the sandy waste. This group of mountains is triangular in form and consists of ranges radiating from the center. The names Horeb and Sinai seem to have been used interchangeably for them, though some consider the former the name of the group and Sinai one of the peaks. Sinai is the name of the sacred mountain before which the Israelites as a nation made their covenant with God as their king (Ex 19:24). Moses as mediator between God and the people went up the mountain where, according to the narrative, he received the Ten Commandments (19:20; 24:18).

There is some difference of opinion as to the actual site of the Israelite encampment and the summit which Moses ascended, but since the 4th cen. A.D. the sacred mount traditionally has been located in the high mountains at the apex of the Sinai Peninsula. Eusebius stated that Jebel Serbal (6,791 feet high), S of the Wadi Feiran (*see* Rephidim), was the mount of lawgiving. The valley, however, is narrow with no plain in the vicinity large enough for the year-long encampment of the 12 tribes of Israel.

The second tradition, going back to the time of Justinian (6th cen. A.D.), identifies Mount Sinai with Jebel Musa (*c.* 7,500 feet high). It is one of a cluster of three peaks, Jebel Katarin (*c.* 8,600 feet) lying about two miles to the SW, and Ras es-Safsafeh (6,540 feet) equidistant to the NNW. At the foot of the latter peak to the N is the only broad plain in the vicinity; it is called er-Raha, about two miles long and a half mile wide, spacious enough for the tents of all Israel. Bedouin today reach water here for their

The Sinai Peninsula and adjacent areas photographed by satellite. National Aeronautics and Space Administration.

needs by digging shallow wells. Many explorers believe that Ras es-Safsafeh with its steep cliffs rising directly from the plain (cf. Ex 19:12) is the Mount Sinai of Ex 19, for its summit is clearly visible from the plain er-Raha, whereas that of Jebel Musa itself is not. In oases around the plain and in neighboring valleys grow date palms, cypress trees, tamarisks, reeds, and vegetable gardens, and acacia trees, shrubs, and grasses dot the otherwise barren landscape.

On the E slope of Jebel Musa, 5,014 feet above sea level, is St. Catherine's Monastery. Legend says that Catherine of Alexandria, a Christian martyr, was beheaded in A.D. 307 and her body carried by the angels to the top of the peak which bears her name (Jebel Katarin). Her head, however, is said to be buried in the monastery chapel. Tradition says that the oldest part of the structure is the Chapel of the Burning Bush, on the reported site of the event it commemorates.

The monastery library contains many valuable old manuscripts, including a palimpsest discovered by Mrs. A. S. Lewis and her sister in 1892, containing the text of the old Syriac Gospels. The 4th cen. A.D. Codex Sinaiticus of the Gr. NT was found here by Dr. Tischendorf in 1844 and 1859. Valuable icons are preserved in the icon tower, some among the oldest in the world, giving an excellent sample of early Christian art. The monastery is surrounded by high majestic granite walls, naturally well fortified. St Helena, the mother of Constantine, is said to have built the first tower there in the 4th cen. The present foundations are ascribed to the emperor Justinian in A.D. 527, although he may have built only a wall for the protection of the Gr. monks who have lived there since the 4th cen.

Traditional Mount Sinai. MPS

Several other theories of the location of Mount Sinai have been advanced. Some scholars prefer NW Arabia, the biblical land of Midian (*q.v.*). Volcanic eruptions have occurred in this area to give credence to the idea (Ex 19:16, 18). The argument is also presented that Moses made his residence with the Midianites after his first escape from Egypt and is likely to have returned to the same site. There are also several mountains in the land near Kadesh-barnea which some associate with the Seir of two old Israelite poems (Deut 33:2; Jud 5:4-5). Rephidim (Ex 17:1-7) is also associated with Meribah (*see* Massah), a site said to exist near Kadesh-barnea (*q.v.*) where water is more easily obtained from rock than in the S. There is not enough evidence, however, in any of the passages of Scripture to warrant an absolutely certain identification of the peaks involved in the narrative.

See Desert; Horeb; Sin, Wilderness of; Wilderness Wandering.

Bibliography. Emil G. Kraeling, *Bible Atlas,* Chicago: Rand McNally, 1956, pp. 107-113. Beno Rothenburg, *God's Wilderness: Discoveries in Sinai,* London: Thames & Hudson, 1961; "An Archaeological Survey of South Sinai," PEQ, CII (1970), 4-29. H. Clay Trumbull, *Kadesh-Barnea,* London: Hodder & Stoughton, 1884.

A. W. W.

SINCERITY. That quality of life which manifests itself not only in the absence of all hypocrisy, pretense or deception but also in the possession and unostentatious display of such traits as integrity, truthfulness and genuineness. Sincerity is of the very essence of God's dealings with mankind and of the believer's relationship with God and with men.

A person can be sincerely wrong, as Paul was when he had thought he "ought to do many things contrary to the name of Jesus of Nazareth" (Acts 26:9). The religious life of the Pharisees generally, however, was essentially one of inner sham, a spurious imitation of God's truth (Mt 23).

Sincerity of life occupies an important place in the Christian faith. Christians are urged to be sincere (*gnēsios,* "legitimate, genuine") in brotherly love (II Cor 8:8), and to demonstrate sincerity (*eilikrineia,* "purity of motives") in fellowship (I Cor 5:8), manner of life (II Cor 1:12; Phil 1:10), mental attitudes (II Pet 3:1, ASV), and preaching (II Cor 2:17). Some were proclaiming Christ out of selfish ambition, not sincerely (*hagnōs,* from pure motives, Phil 1:17, NASB). God must be worshiped "in sincerity [*beṯāmîm,* completely, in a way free from objection] and in truth" (Josh 24:14).

Bibliography. John Flavel, "The Touchstone of Sincerity," *The Works of John Flavel,* London: The Banner of Truth Trust, 1968, V, 509-683. R. L. Scheef, Jr., "Sincerity," IDB, IV, 379. John Tillotson, "Of Sincerity Toward God and Man," *The Works of Dr. John Tillotson,* London: Richard Priestley, 1820, IV, 1-25.

W. B.

SINEW. The Heb. word *gîd,* "sinew," in Job 10:11 and Ezk 37:6,8 refers to tendons and other connective tissues of the body. The Talmudic identification of "the sinew that shrank" (Gen 32:32) with the sciatic nerve seems to rest upon ancient cultic practice. In poetical description the sinews of the thighs of the hippopotamus are knit together (Job 40:17). Gnawing pains are described in terms of sinews in Job 30:17, and the neck of an obstinate person as an "iron sinew" in Isa 48:4.

SINGER. Individuals in early Israel sometimes sang secular, military, working, and religious songs. The Israelites celebrated God's victories on their behalf in song. Women in Israel celebrated David's victory over Goliath with song (I Sam 18:6-7). There were both singing men and women at Jerusalem during David's time (II Sam 19:35). David appointed Levites as singers for religious worship (I Chr 15:16). These skillful Levitical singers were trained in the songs of the Lord (I Chr 25:7) and were organized for their service (I Chr 25:1). *See* Minstrel; Music; Occupations: Musician.

SINGING. The ancient Israelites expressed their emotions in the singing of songs, both as individuals and as groups. The people of Israel expressed their gratitude and faith in song as they celebrated God's deliverance of them through the Red Sea (Ex 15:1-21), the finding of water at "Beer" in the wilderness (Num 21:17-18), and the triumph of Deborah and Barak (Jud 5:1-31). During and after the reigns of David and Solomon elaborate singing became a part of the worship of Yahweh at Jerusalem (I Chr 25; II Chr 5:12-13; Ezr 2:41; 3:11; Neh 7:44; 10:28). *See* Music.

SINGLE EYE. The Gr. *ophthalmos haplous* in Mt 6:22 and Lk 11:34 of the KJV is translated "single eye." The word *haplous* means "simple," and represents the eye as giving an image of an object that is seen clearly and steadily. The "single eye" as the light or lamp of the body is sound; it is not confused and can focus with healthy, unclouded vision upon its object.

SINIM (sī'nĭm). The Heb. *sînîm* refers to a remote place or nation from which God's people return to their homeland (Isa 49:12). Sinim possibly lay either E or S of Palestine since Isaiah refers to others as coming from the N and W. Some scholars have identified Sinim with "Sina" (or China). However, no Jews had gone to China at this time. Early interpreters understood a place to the S of Israel in Egypt, either Sin (Pelusium) or Syene (modern Aswan). The Heb. manuscript 1QIs[a] among the Dead Sea Scrolls reads *swnyym* (*seweniyîm*), the people of Seweni, which definitely favors an identification with Syene (*q.v.*).

SINITES (sĭn'īts). The Canaanite people located near Arqa and Arvad in Phoenicia (Gen 10:17; I Chr 1:15). Tiglath-pileser III mentions it as the city of Siannu on the Phoenician coast (ANET, pp. 282 f.). The name is found in the place names *Nahr-as-Sinn* and *Sinn-ad-darb*, and possibly in the names *Asnu* (Phoenician), Ugaritic *'sn*.

SINLESSNESS OF CHRIST. *See* Christ, Sinlessness of.

SION, MOUNT (sī'ŭn)

1. One of the names by which Mount Hermon was anciently called (Deut 4:48). The Sidonians called Mount Hermon "Sirion" and the Amorites called it "Shenir" (Deut 3:9).

2. The Gr. form for Mount Zion (Jerusalem) appearing in Ps 65:1; Heb 12:22; and Rev 14:1 of the KJV. Elsewhere it is "Mount Zion." The form "Sion" appears many times in the Apocrypha.

SIPHMOTH (sĭf'mŏth). A town, not identified, in S Judah with which David shared some of the booty that he had taken from the Amalakites. This he did to show his appreciation of their kindness during the time he was fleeing from Saul (I Sam 30:28). This town is not mentioned elsewhere, unless it was the home of Zabdi, the Shiphmite, steward of David's wine cellars (I Chr 27:27).

SIPPAI (sĭp'ī). One of the sons of the Philistine giants slain at Gezer by Sibbechai (I Chr 20:4). In II Sam 21:18 he is called Saph.

SIRAH (sī'rȧ). Joab called Abner by messengers from the well of Sirah to Hebron and treacherously murdered him (II Sam 3:26–27). The well of Sirah has been identified with the modern 'Ain Sarah, a mile or more NW of Hebron.

SIRION (sĭr'ĭ-ŏn). One of the names of Mount Hermon by which it was called anciently by the Sidonians (Deut 3:9). Since in Ps 29:6 Sirion is mentioned together with Lebanon, it has been suggested that Sirion designates the Anti-Lebanon Range.

SISAMAI (sĭs'ȧ-mī). A Judahite, the son of Eleasah and father of Shallum, one of the descendants of Pharez through Jerahmeel (I Chr 2:40); form used in KJV. The ASV and RSV have "Sismai" as the preferred form.

SISERA (sĭs'ĕ-rȧ)

1. A general of the armies of a Canaanite alliance (Jud 5:19) under Jabin (Jud 4:2), a second king by that name (title?) ruling in Hazor (cf. Josh 11:1 ff.), and leading an ill-fated league against Israel. Sisera's 900 iron chariots had oppressed Israel for 20 years. He was baited into battle in the valley of Jezreel by the marshaling of the Israelites under Barak and Deborah. Barak rallied troops from Naphtali and Zebulun of his native N (Jud 4:6), and Deborah from her area (Benjamin and Ephraim) and Issachar (Jud 5:14–15). They descended from Mount Tabor upon Sisera's men in the valley. Routed by a sudden storm and flash flood of the meandering river Kishon (Jud 5:20–21) and fleeing westward to their base at Harosheth-hagoiim, Sisera's armies met destruction. Defeated, Sisera fled afoot for refuge with neutral Heber the Kenite. Sensing the flight, Jael, Heber's wife, expediently abandoned neutrality. Harboring Sisera, she exploited his misplaced trust and slew him as he slept by driving a tent peg through his temples into the ground (Jud 4:17–22; 5:24–27). Sisera's typical Oriental character is revealed in the vain attempt to comfort his waiting mother by her maidens. They suggest that revelry with captive women and spoil-gathering for the women at home detain him (Jud 5:28–30).

2. Name of a post-Exilic clan of temple servants (Ezr 2:53; Neh 7:55).

R. B. D.

SISMAI. *See* Sisamai.

SISTER. The term is used almost entirely in both OT and NT to mean, as it does in English, one's own sister or at least half sister, the daughter of both or at least one of the same parents. The word is also used poetically and endearingly to refer to one's beloved (Song 4:9–12, *et al.*). and in the NT it is used several times to refer to a sister in the Lord (Mt 12:50; Mk 10:29–30; Rom 16:1; I Cor 7:15; I Tim 5:2; Jas 2:15). Because of normal usage, the word in such passages as Mt 13:56 and Mk 6:3 ought to be taken as indicating the actual sisters of Jesus. *See* Family.

SISTRUM (sĭs'trŭm). A musical instrument, a rattling type of noisemaker used for both joyous and sad occasions. The instrument came from Mesopotamia via Palestine to Egypt. The Heb. word *m^ena'an'îm* in II Sam 6:5 is properly translated "sistra" (pl. of sistrum) in the Vulg., but is incorrectly translated "cornets" in the KJV. The "castanets" of modern versions (ASV, etc.) is only an approximate term for the ancient instrument. The ancient Egyptian sistrum consisted of a thin oval-shaped metal frame with a handle, and several metal rods that passed loosely through holes in the frame. When shaken, the rods would rattle. *See* Music.

SIT, SITTING. The act of assuming a position of rest. In ancient times, in houses or tents, these words referred to sitting on the ground or floor with the legs crossed in front. During travel these terms referred to sitting on the ground along the way, or, if the ground was too stony, to sitting in a full squatting position. Abraham sat in the tent door in the heat of the day (Gen 18:1).

This expression was used also of a person in authority. The elders "sat at the gate" (Gen 19:1; Ruth 4:1; II Sam 19:8). Moses sat before the people to hear cases and to pass judgment (Ex 18:13). God sits upon the throne of His holiness (Ps 47:8). Israel's kings sat upon their thrones (e.g., I Kgs 1:46).

Thus the statement that God "made us sit together in heavenly places in Christ Jesus" (Eph 2:6) implies that He has enthroned us together with His resurrected Son in the spiritual realm, delegating to us His authority over evil principalities and powers.

H. E. Fi.

SITNAH (sĭt'nȧ). One of the wells the herdsmen of Isaac dug or unstopped which occasioned the enmity of the herdsmen of Gerar. The well was thus named to remind Isaac's herdsmen of the contention and strife which the opposing herdsmen caused them (Gen 26:21). *See* Well.

SIVAN (sī'vǎn). The third month of the Jewish religious year, ninth month of the civil year (Est 8:9). It corresponds roughly with the latter part of May and the first part of June.

SKIN. The rendering of several Heb. and Gr. words.

1. Generally Heb. *'ôr* (perhaps from *'ûr*, "to be naked, bare"), meaning the skin or hide of man, the hide of animals, and treated hide or leather (Ex 22:27; 29:14; Gen 3:21; etc.). The various colors of the skin of infected persons helped to determine the varieties or stages of leprosy (Lev 13; *see* Diseases).

2. Heb. *bāśār* (generally "flesh"), but rendered "skin" once in Ps 102:5, "My bones cleave to my skin" (flesh).

3. Heb. *geled*, "I have sewed sackcloth over my skin" (Job 16:15, NASB).

4. Gr. *derma* ("skin"), "They wandered about in sheepskins and goatskins" (Heb 11:37, lit., "skins of goats").

5. Gr. *dermatinos* (made of leather, "leathern"); John had a "girdle of a skin about his loins" (Mk 1:6).

Of significance are several metaphorical expressions. "The skin of my teeth" (Job 19:20) may signify that Job had scarcely a sound spot in his body, or it may refer to the membrane which surrounds the roots of teeth in the jaw, i.e., the periosteum. Disease could have destroyed the gums and wasted them away from the teeth, leaving only the periosteum. "Can the Ethiopian change his skin, or the leopard his spots?" (Jer 13:23) denotes the inability of one to change his evil character. "Skin for [in behalf of] skin" (Job 2:4) is a phrase of barter, signifying that everything has its price. One will give up part of his skin to save the whole skin, i.e., one will suffer damage to his hand in order to protect his face.

E. C. J.

SKIRT. *See* Dress.

SKULL. *See* Golgotha.

SKY. Used in the plural sometimes to express the clouds (Deut 33:26; Ps 18:11; Isa 45:8; II Sam 22:12), and at other times the sky or the firmament (Job 37:18; Jer 51:9). NT references to heaven and sky are Mt 16:2-3; Lk 12:56; to firmament, Heb 11:12. *See* Heaven.

SLANDER. A malicious statement designed to injure the person of whom it is said. The Bible frequently warns against slander (Ex 20:16; Lev 19:16; Ezk 22:9; Eph 4:31; Col 3:8; Jas 4:11).

SLAUGHTER. *See* Sacrifice.

SLAUGHTER OF INNOCENTS. *See* Innocents, Slaughter of.

SLAVE. *See* Service; Occupations: Servant.

SLEEP. This word is used in both OT and NT to describe the sleep or repose of the body (I Sam 26:7; Jon 1:5-6; Mk 14:37). God gives peaceful sleep to those who trust Him (Ps 4:8; cf. 127:2); not to sleep is a sign of readiness (Ps 121:4; Isa 5:27). To be tormented in bed where men sleep signifies great anguish of mind and body (Job 33:19; Ps 41:3; Isa 28:20).

Of interest is God's causing a deep sleep to fall upon Adam while He made Eve (Gen 2:21-22). Also, divine revelation was disclosed to men while they slept (Gen 15:12; 28:12; Dan 8:18; 10:9; Mt 1:24).

A metaphorical sense is the sleep of death both of the wicked and saved (Dan 12:2; I Thess 5:10). This is the meaning of the OT phrase, "He slept with his fathers" (Deut 31:16; I Kgs 2:10; 11:43), and the NT description of the body of the believer between death and the resurrection (I Thess 4:14; I Cor 15:51).

This word also denotes spiritual laziness and indifference. For this Jesus chided Peter (Mk 14:37) and Paul admonished Christians (Rom 13:11; I Thess 5:6). The spiritual condition of the unsaved is likewise expressed in the quotation from an early unknown hymn (Eph 5:14).

Bibliography. Christian Maurer, "*Hypnos*, etc.," TDNT, VIII, 545-558. Albrecht Oepke, "*Katheudō*," TDNT, III, 431-437.

E. C. J.

SLIME. *See* Minerals and Metals.

SLIME PITS. *See* Siddim.

SLING. Made either of a strip of leather, or several thongs woven together, with a widened pouch to hold a stone. Both ends were held in the hand and the sling was swung in a circle either horizontally or vertically around the head and one end suddenly released to eject the stone. It was chiefly used by shepherds, such as David against Goliath (I Sam 17:40), but also as a weapon of war by Assyrian, Babylonian, and Egyptian armies. A band of 700 Benjamites could sling stones at a hair and not miss (Jud 20:16). *See* Armor. The sling is also used metaphorically (Jer 10:18; I Sam 25:29).

SLIP. A cutting made from a plant. Used once in the Bible in Isa 17:10 to describe replanting after a judgment of devastation.

SLOTHFUL. The principal Heb. root denoting "slothful, sluggish, lazy, indolent" is *'āsal,* "to be slothful" (Jud 18:9). In the KJV the adjective *'āṣēl* appears eight times in the book of Proverbs as "slothful" (15:19; 19:24; 21:25; 22:13; 24:30; 26:13, 14, 15). The noun form occurs in Prov 19:15 and Eccl 10:18. The term is used in contrast to righteousness and is an attribute of the fool.

Another Heb. word, *r^{e}mîyâ,* denotes laxness, negligence, or slackness, but is translated "slothful" in Prov 12:24, 27. Heb. *rāphâ,* "slothful" in Prov 18:9, means to let (the hands) drop because of feebleness or becoming disheartened.

In the NT Gr. *nōthros* (Heb 6:12) means sluggish or lazy, and Gr. *oknēros* (Mt 25:26; Rom 12:11) is similar, meaning indolent, idle, or delaying, the opposite of being fervent in spirit. *See* Sluggard.

SLOW. The translation of two words in the OT and two in the NT.

1. Heb. *'erek,* a derivative of the word meaning "to be long," "prolong," "continue." "Slow to anger" is used to refer to forbearance or self-restraint. As a divine attribute, it is at times used in series with "gracious," "merciful," and "full of compassion" (see Neh 9:17; Ps 103:8; 145:8; Joel 2:13; Jon 4:2; Nah 1:3). In human relationships a person "slow to anger" is one possessing great understanding (Prov 14:29); he is one who quiets contention (Prov 15:18); and he is one who is better than the mighty (Prov 16:32).
2. Heb. *kābēd,* "heavy," "weighty." Moses was slow in mouth and tongue (Ex 4:10), having difficulty in speaking.
3. Gr. *argos,* "inactive," "unprofitable." Paul referred to the Cretans as "slow bellies" (Tit 1:12; cf. RSV "lazy gluttons").
4. Gr. *bradys,* "heavy," "slow," "sluggish." "Slow of heart" (Lk 24:25) is a description of the unreceptive, unbelieving heart. "Slow to speak" and "slow to wrath" (Jas 1:19) are parts of an exhortation concerning the godly life.

H. E. Fi.

SLUGGARD. The Heb. word *'āṣēl,* "stupid, indolent; to be sluggish," is translated "sluggard" in the KJV in Prov 6:6, 9; 10:26; 13:4; 20:4; 26:16 (elsewhere "slothful"); it is often translated "sluggard" in RSV where the KJV has "slothful." The way of the sluggard, which is to be shunned, is the opposite of the way of the diligent man. The noun form of the Heb. word appears in Prov 19:15, which the NASB renders as follows: "Laziness casts into a deep sleep, and an idle man will suffer hunger."

The slug is any one of a number of slow-moving mollusks with no external shell, which provide the basis for the English word "sluggard." The "snail which melteth" in Ps 58:8 may be a slug.

SMELTING. *See* Minerals and Metals; Mining; Occupations: Refiner, Smelting.

SMITE. The translation of a large number of words in Heb. and Gr. which describe all sorts of blows: to slap, strike, beat, bruise. It is used frequently for a judgment inflicted by the Lord on a person or nation (e.g., Ex 12:23).

SMITH. *See* Occupations: Smith.

SMYRNA (smûr'nȧ). One of the seven cities that John addressed (Rev 2:8–11), Smyrna was located on the same site as the modern city of Izmir, Turkey, at the SE edge of the Gulf of Smyrna. The city curved around the edge of the bay at the base of the 525-foot Mount Pagus, its splendid acropolis. Its streets were excellently paved and drawn at right angles. One of them was known as the "Street of Gold" and ran from W to E, curving around the lower slopes of Pagus. This famous street was lined with fine buildings and at each end was a temple. Probably the temple of Zeus stood at the western end and the temple of the mother goddess Cybele Sipylene (patron of the city) at the eastern end. The city had several squares, a public library, numerous temples, and other public buildings.

While Smyrna contested with Ephesus and Pergamum the rank "First of Asia," some of her coins defined her rank as "First of Asia in beauty and size." Her prestige was also enhanced by her claim to have been the birthplace of Homer. In John's day the population may have approached 200,000.

Modern Izmir covers the site of New Testament Smyrna. Foto Esen

Roman aqueduct at Smyrna. HFV

The apostle John was wholly commendatory of believers at Smyrna, who suffered much for their Christian testimony. Sir William Ramsay suggests that the word "faithful" (Rev 2:10) would have had a special appeal to people of Smyrna because they had been known for their faithfulness to Rome over a period of more than two centuries. Excavations in the central part of the city have uncovered the Roman agora with buildings reconstructed during the 2nd cen. A.D.

H. F. V.

SNAIL. Found in Lev 11:30. It is translated "lizard" in NASB and "sand lizard" in RSV. *See* Animals, IV.21.

SNAKE. *See* Animals, IV.30.

SNARE. Any one of several devices designed to catch birds (Ps 91:3; 124:7) or animals (Job 40:24); sometimes baited. Exact distinctions between the terms so translated are uncertain; some seem to be used synonymously, but parallelism may not be a safe guide.

Some snares were loops of wire or rope which tightened around the neck or feet of the victim; some had two jaws which clamped together like a trap (Job 18:9; 40:24, NEB); nets fell on and enclosed the victim in its meshes (Ezk 17:20), or sprang up from below (Amos 3:5, RSV). The snare might be a camouflaged net over a pit into which the victim fell (Ps 141:9–10), or it might be set to one side of the pit (Jer 18:22; 48:43–44). These devices were triggered automatically (Amos 3:5) or might be operated from a distance (Jer 5:26). See ANEP #189.

The elements of concealment, surprise, and an attractive bait that leads to dire consequences made metaphorical use obvious: the Canaanites (Deut 7:16) and their gods (Jud 2:3) would be snares to Israel; the harlot to the one who follows her (Prov 7:23); riches to the man who seeks wealth (I Tim 6:9). The snare's speed and finality made it an apt metaphor for death (Ps 18:5) and the return of Christ (Lk 21:35). (Cf. also Josh 23:13; Job 22:10; Ps 119:110; Ex 10:7; Isa 8:14.)

See Fowler; Gin; Hunt; Net; Trap.

R. V. R.

SNOUT. The Heb. word *'aph,* "nose, nostril," is translated "snout" in Prov 11:22. The proverb points up that it is as incongruous to find a jewel of gold in a swine's snout as a fair woman who is without discretion. A nose ring of gold in a swine's snout is as out of place as a beautiful woman without intellectual and moral discrimination.

SNOW. The OT indicates that snow (Heb. *shĕlĕg*) fell only occasionally in Palestine, but that sometimes there was a heavy fall (II Sam 23:20; I Chr 11:22; cf. I Macc 13:22). Snow-covered Mount Hermon was visible from many parts of the land and was a source of water supply in Palestine (Jer 18:14). God's power over nature provided the snow (Job 37:6; 38:22). Snow is noted for its whiteness (Ex 4:6; Num 12:10; Ps 51:7; Isa 1:18), its cleanness (Job 9:30), its refreshing coolness (Prov 25:13). It symbolizes brilliance (Dan 7:9), purity (Ps 51:7; Isa 1:18), and cleansing (Job 9:30).

SNUFF. Two Heb. words are translated by the term snuff. The first means to sniff, and is used by Malachi (1:13) to indicate the contempt Jews had toward the sacrifices of God in the time of that prophet. The second word means to snuff up the wind as the wild ass pants after the wind (Jer 2:24; 14:6).

SNUFF-DISH; SNUFFER. The snuff-dish was made of gold and was used in the tabernacle and later in the temple for holding the snuffer or the tongs used to trim the wick of the lamps (Ex 25:38;37:23).

The snuffer (I Kgs 7:50; II Kgs 12:13) was a set of tongs or forceps used in trimming wicks.

SO (sō). The name (Heb. *sō'*, possibly to be vocalized *sĕwĕ'*) occurs in a passage about an Egyptian king whose aid Hoshea, the last king of Israel, sought to enlist against the Assyrians. Hoshea's actions precipitated an Assyrian invasion which eventuated in the fall of Samaria and the northern kingdom (II Kgs 17:4 ff.).

The identification of So has long been uncertain. That So was Shabaka, a king of the 25th or "Ethiopian" Dynasty, has always been improbable. Formerly the name was identified as Sib'e, an Egyptian leader who in 720 B.C. joined forces with the king of Gaza against the Assyrian Sargon, at Raphia. Sargon defeated this combine and Sib'e fled, but tribute was later paid by the Egyptians (ANET, p. 285). R. Borger, however, has demonstrated that Sib'e is a misreading in Sargon's text (JNES, XIX [1960], 49–53).

In 1963 Hans Goedicke demonstrated that So must be the Egyptian political center of Sais in the western Delta and that the passage should be read: "he had sent messengers to So, to the king of Egypt." The king of Egypt at the time of Hoshea was Tefnakhte, who resided in Sais. The Egyptian name of this town is *S3w*, spelled *Sai* in Assyrian and *Sô'* in Heb. and Phoenician ("The End of 'So, King of Egypt,'" BASOR #171, pp. 64–66).

C. E. D.

SOAP. The translation in Jer 2:22 and Mal 3:2 of the Heb. *bōrît* derived from the root *bārar*, meaning to purify. In Jer 2:22 the first line of the couplet uses the term "nitre" (Heb. *neter;* RSV "lye," i.e., natron or soda, a mineral alkali) as the parallel of "soap," suggesting that the biblical soap is hardly the combination of oils and sodium salts basic to our modern product. Rather it is an aqueous solution of alkaline salts, chiefly potassium carbonate which would act as a detergent. In the ancient Near East soap was also obtained by decomposing olive oil with salts from the ashes of local saliferous plants.

There are two occurrences of the Heb. cognate *bôr* (RSV "lye"). In Job 9:30 Job declares that no outward cleansing of his hands even with "lye" would suffice for the inner impurity. In Isa 1:25, just as "lye" is used as a flux in the smelting process, so the wrath of God will purge away all impurity from Israel. *See* Potash.

R. V. R.

SOBER, SOBERLY

1. Gr. *nēphō* with its derivatives means to be free from drunkenness and every form of excess; hence to be calm, mild, collected, self-controlled, and even-tempered in mind and action (I Thess 5:6, 8; I Tim 3:2, 11; II Tim 4:5; Tit 1:8; 2:2; I Pet 1:13; 4:7; 5:8).

2. Gr. *sōphroneō* with its derivatives means to be of a sound mind, be reasonable or sensible, act prudently or carefully (Mk 5:15; I Tim 3:2; Tit 1:8; 2:2, 12; I Pet 4:7). It is the antithesis of *existēmi,* "to be beside oneself" (II Cor 5:13); therefore it signifies to exercise self-control by curbing passions (Tit 2:6) and pride (Rom 12:3). Its noun form, *sōphrosynē,* "sobriety" (I Tim 2:9, 15) has the sense of moderation, and then modesty and chastity (cf. Tit 2:5, KJV "discreet").

Bibliography. Ulrich Luck, "*Sōphrōn,* etc.," TDNT, VII, 1097–1104.

SOCHO (sō'kō). The word means "branches" and has several alternate spellings, i.e., Soco, Socoh, Shochoh. Three towns in Palestine have the name Socho:

1. A city of the Shephelah of Judah close to Adullam and Azekah (Josh 15:35). Here the Philistines camped before David's contest with Goliath (I Sam 17:1). Rehoboam strengthened its fortifications (II Chr 11:7), but the Philistines captured it during the reign of Ahaz ((II Chr 28:18). It has been identified with Khirbet 'Abbad, *c.* 14 miles WSW of Bethlehem.

2. A city in the hill country of Judah close to Shamir and Jattir, identified with Khirbet Shuweikeh, about ten miles SSW of Hebron (Josh 15:48).

3. A place ten miles WNW of Samaria, mentioned in the Egyptian lists of towns captured in Palestine by Thutmose III and Shishak.

4. Mention of Socho in I Chr 4:18 seems to be a person named in the genealogy of Judah, but some of the other names in the context are names of places in S Judah found also in Josh 15:48. It is therefore possible that the Socho of I Chr 4:18 was a town in Judah whose "father" or founder was Heber.

D. M. R.

SOCHOCH. *See* Socho.

SOCKET. *See* Tabernacle.

SOCOH. *See* Socho.

SODI (sō'dī). The father of Gaddiel, one of the spies representing the tribe of Zebulun (Num 13:10).

SODOM (sŏd'ŏm). One of the five cities of the plain or valley of the Jordan, i.e., the Dead Sea basin (Gen 10:19; 13:10; 14:2). Lot chose this area for his residence when he broke company with Abraham, even though Sodom was a very wicked city (Gen 13:1–13). It was sacked by Chedorlaomer (*q.v.*) and his allies early in the 2nd mil. B.C. (Gen 14:11). Later it and several other cities of the plain were destroyed by fire and brimstone as a judgment of God, because of their abject immorality (*see* Sodomite). Lot and his two daughters were spared (Gen 19:1–29; Mt 10:15). The divine judgment by fire completely devastated the area (Gen 19:24; Deut 29:23), and Lot's wife was turned into a pillar of salt (Gen 19:26).

A workers' camp at Sedom with salt hill in background. IIS

Tradition locates Sodom at the S end of the Dead Sea. The barren desolation in this area gives mute testimony of judgment by "fire and brimstone." Geological evidence in this region of salt formations, asphalt, sulfur, and petroleum support the biblical record. The W part of the area is within the bounds of modern Israel. The town of Sedom serves as a health resort and rest camp. A peculiar mountain of almost pure salt identifies Sodom and it is referred to as "Lot's wife" by the local guides.

The exact site of Sodom is not certain but most scholars favor a locality around the S end of the Dead Sea. On the E shore is a large peninsula called el-Lisan ("the Tongue"), an alluvial fan at the mouth of a wadi coming from Kerak. The basin to the S is thought to be the Vale of Siddim (Gen 14:3). Five streams, including Wadi Zered (Num 21:12, NASB), flow toward the SE and S shores of the Dead Sea, suggesting a source of water for irrigating the fields of each of the five cities. Further confirmation is supplied by the pilgrimage and burial site of Bab edh-Dhra (*q.v.*), five to ten miles NE of the area of Sodom and Gomorrah. Its destruction *c.* 2000/1900 B.C. coincides with biblical data for the time of Sodom's catastrophe.

The ruins of the cities of the plain may have been covered over with water from the Dead Sea after the cataclysmic upheaval. The shallow waters S of Masada and el-Lisan (two to 18 feet) suggests such a possibility. According to Josephus (*Wars* iv. 8.4), in his day Zoar, one of the cities of the plain (Gen 13:10; 14:2), was still visible at the S end. Sensational reports of the discovery of Sodom at the shallow S end of the Dead Sea have appeared in the press from time to time but no authentic scholarly evidence has thus far been produced to substantiate these claims.

See Gomorrah; Cities of the Plain.

Bibliography. J. Penrose Harland, "Sodom and Gomorrah: The Location and Destruction of the Cities of the Plain," BA, V (1942), 17–32; VI (1943), 41–54; "Sodom," IDB, IV, 395–397.

H. A. Han.

SODOMA (sŏd'ō-mȧ). An alternate spelling for Sodom used in Rom 9:29, referring to one of the five cities of the plain. *See* Sodom.

SODOMITE. One who practiced that unnatural sexual perversion which characterized ancient Sodom (*q.v.*), namely, carnal copulation between male persons (Gen 19:5 ff.). The English term translated Sodomite in the OT is from the Latin *sodomita,* derived from the Heb. *s^e^dōm,* Sodom. A Heb. word for "sodomite" derived from this root does not occur in Scripture, the Heb. term so translated being *qādēsh,* which means a male temple prostitute who was attached to the heathen sanctuaries and consecrated to the impure rites of pagan worship. The term is from a root meaning "to be set apart or consecrated," in this case for immoral purposes.

Sodomy, universally prevalent (cf. Rom 1:27), was forbidden in Israel (Deut 23:17; cf. Lev 18:22;20:13), but was present as early as Rehoboam's reign (I Kgs 14:24). Both Asa (I Kgs 15:12) and Jehoshaphat (22:46) temporarily removed the Sodomites, but by Josiah's time they were found in the temple itself (II Kgs 23:7). The feminine form, *q^e^dēshâ*, signifies a "prostitute" or "harlot" (Gen 38:21; Hos 4:14).

The English term "homosexual" is used in I Cor 6:9 by RSV and NASB, and in I Tim 1:10 (NASB) to translate Gr. *arsenokoitai,* male bed partners.

H. E. Fr.

SOJOURNER. *See* Alien; Foreigner.

SOLDER. The metal substance used by idol craftsmen to connect metals together (Isa 41:7).

SOLDIER. *See* Army; Mercenary; War; Occupations: Soldier.

SOLOMON (sŏl'ŏ-mŏn). The name of Solomon occurs *c.* 300 times in the OT and 12 times in the NT (cf. I Kgs 1–11; 14:21,26; II Chr 1–11; II Sam 12:24; I Chr 3:10; 22:5–19; 28:5–11, 20; Ps 72; 127 (titles); Prov 1:1; 10:1; Mt 6:29; 12:42; *et al.*).

Solomon, the "man of sunset and shadows," was the second son of David by Bath-sheba. Their first son died soon after birth (II Sam 12:18). Solomon was the fourth son born to King David in Jerusalem (II Sam 5:14; 12:24). The third king of Israel, Solomon reigned for 40 years (*c.* 971–931 or *c.* 960–922 B.C.). He was also known as Jedidiah, meaning "beloved of Jehovah."

Early Life

Little is known of the early life of Solomon. He was the son of King David's favorite wife Bath-sheba, an intelligent, charming woman who wielded tremendous influence over the king and exerted power in the court. Solomon grew up in a polygamous house. King David married often (Scriptures record 18 times). There were constant tensions among the wives and their respective children. The king's harem became the scene of all kinds of plots and counterplots of those jockeying for favor and places of prestige. So Solomon grew up in the type of environment which educated and seasoned him in the art of rough and tumble practical politics.

Struggle for the Throne (I Kgs 1–2)

During David's final illness there was a mad scramble for the throne between Adonijah, the oldest son, and Solomon, the next in line of succession. It was an open secret that after Amnon and Absalom had liquidated themselves David had promised the throne to Solomon.

Adonijah solicited the assistance of Joab, the

general of the army, and Abiathar, the priest. His friends met at En-rogel, below Jerusalem, to sacrifice sheep, oxen, and fatlings. This abortive coronation feast did not include Solomon and those favorable to his cause. Also, Nathan the prophet, Zadok the priest, and Benaiah the chief of David's bodyguard were conspicuously absent. When they heard of Adonijah's plot to seize the throne, they spearheaded a counterplot with the assistance of Bath-sheba. Armed with David's orders, Solomon mounted the royal mule and rode in the midst of his regal supporters down to the spring Gihon in the Kidron Valley on the E side of Zion. There Zadok anointed the royal lad with a horn of sacred oil in the midst of trumpet blasts and people's shouting "Long live King Solomon!" Adonijah's abortive *coup d'etat* collapsed. He in turn begged for mercy and promised allegiance to Solomon.

After King David's death (I Kgs 2:10), Solomon moved swiftly to solidify his hold on the throne. Being a mere boy (I Kgs 3:7), 18 at the most, his dying father gave him some instructions to dispose of those who might wrest the government out of his hands (I Kgs 2:1-9). Solomon saw the wisdom of David's counsel and as a typical oriental despot he quickly liquidated his chief rivals. Adonijah was executed on the mere suspicion that by his asking the king for Abishag (David's chief concubine) for a wife he was plotting intrigue (I Kgs 2:13-25). Because of his part in Adonijah's plot to snatch the throne, venerable Abiathar was deposed from the priesthood and banished to his native town of Anathoth (Anata, cf. I Kgs 2:26-27), making this house extinct (I Sam 2:27-36). Zadok assumed Abiathar's place. Joab, in fear for his life, fled to the horns of the altar for refuge. But Solomon commanded Benaiah to cut him down. Benaiah in turn succeeded Joab as commander-in-chief of Israel's hosts (I Kgs 2:28-35). Shimei, a Benjamite who violently cursed King David during Absalom's rebellion, was kept under surveillance in Jerusalem for three years and was killed when he sought to recover two renegade servants who had fled to Gath (I Kgs 2:36-46).

The Dream at Gibeon (I Kgs 3; II Chr 1

The crowning event of Solomon's formative regal years was his choice of wisdom. Because of Nathan the prophet's influence, Solomon was deeply religious. One of his earliest acts was to visit the high place of Gibeon and sacrifice 1,000 burnt offerings upon the ancient altar that stood before the tent of meeting (I Kgs 3:4; cf. I Chr 21:29). On the following night, Solomon had a dream in which Yahweh asked him what he desired most. Instead of asking for long life, or riches, or honor, the young king asked for "practical" wisdom to govern his people wisely. His request pleased the Eternal and it was granted. Not long after, two mothers stood before him accusing each other of the same crime. There were no witnesses; a modern judge would have dismissed the case for lack of evidence, but Solomon quickly devised a strategem which revealed the real mother. The decision spread like wildfire from village to village. Now the king was revered as a wise and fair ruler.

The Administration (I Kgs 4)

King David's kingdom fell full-orbed into Solomon's lap. It totaled *c.* 50,000 square miles (a little less than the area of Illinois and a little more than New York state). Under David, domestic conditions in Israel remained patriarchal and primitive. David gave birth to the Israelitish nation; Solomon produced the Israelitish state. His government was an absolute monarchy. The members of his enlarged cabinet were called princes. With the exception of two carry-overs from David, they were all new, consisting of: (1) the (chief) priest, Azariah son of Zadok; (2) two secretaries, Elihoreph and Ahiah; (3) a chronicler or recorder, Jehoshaphat; (4) the generalissimo of the army, Benaiah; (5) priests Zadok and Abiathar; (6) an overseer of the 12 commissary officers, Azariah, son of Nathan the prophet; (7) the "king's friend" or counselor, Zabud (son of Nathan the prophet); (8) a court chamberlain, Ahishar; and (9) a superintendent of slave service, Adoniram (I Kgs 4:2-6). *See* Solomon's Servants.

Ignoring the old tribal divisions, Solomon divided the entire country into 12 administrative districts, nine W of the Jordan and three E of it. Over each district was stationed a commissary officer whose responsibility was to provide the king's court with provisions for one month each year. A single day's provisions were 337 bushels of fine flour, 674 bushels of meal, 10 fat stall-fed oxen, 20 pastured oxen, 100 sheep, besides harts, gazelles, roebucks and fatted owls; also barley and straw for the animals in government stables.

Solomon introduced chariots and cavalry in his army: 40,000 stalls of horses, 12,000 cavalry men, and 1,400 chariots. These were kept in Jerusalem or in his fortified cities ready for distribution in time of danger. These necessitated new, unparalled roads. Border fortresses such as at Arad with its small temple in the citadel (*see* Temple) were built to guard the trade routes.

Building Program (I Kgs 5-7; II Chr 2-4)

Early in his reign Solomon resolved to fulfill the promise of his father to build a temple in Jerusalem to house the ark. Solomon re-established the alliance which David had made with Hiram of Tyre (not to be confused with Hiram the skilled craftsman, I Kgs 5:1; 7:13-14), in which Solomon supplied Hiram with food in return for cedars from Mount Lebanon (I Kgs 5:1-12). The king's greatest need was workmen. To secure an adequate construction force, he resorted to corvée or forced labor. He reduced the Canaanites to the grade of state slaves (I Kgs 9:20-21). Since these were insufficient for his grandiose plans, he drafted free-born Israelites also, compelling

The Dome of the Rock now stands on the site of Solomon's Temple. MIS

them to work in sections of 10,000 every third month (I Kgs 5:13-18; II Chr 2:17-18). In all, his task force was composed of 80,000 stonecutters, 70,000 common laborers, and 3,600 overseers or slave drivers.

Like Rameses II of Egypt, Solomon was a great builder. The temple was the most important of his public work projects. It was located on Mount Moriah, the site of Araunah's threshing floor where King David had erected an altar to Yahweh for staying the plague (II Sam 24:16-25; I Chr 21:15-25), and possibly where Abraham had offered Isaac (II Chr 3:1; Gen 22:2). Materials were collected by David (I Chr 22:2-4), but actual work began in Solomon's fourth year (I Kgs 6:1). Although the temple was a large edifice for its day, it was rather small by modern standards: 90 feet long, 30 feet wide, and 45 feet high.

Seven years were spent in its construction. Its floor plan was modeled after the tabernacle of Moses. The architectural prototype of this shrine was the Syrian or Canaanite style of temple (e.g., as found at Ugarit, Qatna, and Hazor). Neither hammer nor axe nor any tool of iron was heard in the house while it was building (cf. I Kgs 6:7). The sanctuary proper was inlaid with gold as though carved out of one solid mass. Two immense pillars stood at the entrance of the court as guardians of the sanctuary (I Kgs 7:21). The temple centralized and fixed Jerusalem as the center of Yahweh worship, as the focal point for all 12 tribes to migrate and worship at the same altar and shrine. (See Ira M. Price, *Old Testament History*, p. 237 for specifications of the temple.) *See* Temple.

Dedication of the Temple
(I Kgs 8-9; II Chr 5-7)

On the completion of the "royal chapel" in the eleventh year of his reign (I Kgs 6:38), Solomon planned a great celebration (I Kgs 8). Before a convocation of convocations composed of the heads of the tribes and the princes of the fathers of the Israelites, the ark of the covenant was transferred from the city of David to the holy of holies beneath the cherubim. All this was executed in the midst of hecatombs of sacrifices by all the congregation. A cloud filled the building to screen the glory of Yahweh. The king blessed the assembled multitudes, recited the history of the temple's construction and his part in the process. Then standing before the altar of Yahweh, Solomon spread his hands toward heaven and offered a dedicatory prayer unsurpassed in all religious literature (I Kgs 8:23-53). He requested Yahweh to hear and answer prayers made (1) by the oath of ordeal, (2) under defeat. (3) during drought, (4) under several distressing calamities, (5) for the army, and (6) in captivity. His conclusion appealed to the attentiveness and continued presence of Yahweh, that He might clothe His priests with salvation and His saints with goodness. Solomon's final acts of the dedicatory service were the offering of numerous sacrifices of peace, burnt, and meal offerings (I Kgs 8:62-66).

Other Buildings (I Kgs 7-11)

Among the numerous buildings and public works in Jerusalem, Solomon constructed the house of the forest of Lebanon (150 feet long, 75 feet wide, and 45 feet high, containing an audience room and an armory); a pillared hall (75 by 45 feet); another porch or hall for his throne where he was to pronounce judgment; a house for Pharaoh's daughter (cf. I Kgs 7:2-8) close by his own house with the splendor befitting an Egyptian king's daughter. He spent 13 years building his own house to accommodate 700 wives and 300 concubines and the necessary servants (I Kgs 11:3), and Millo, a huge fortress to protect the temple (I Kgs 9:24). Also Solomon built military defenses and fortified cities throughout his kingdom (I Kgs 9:15, 17-19; II Chr 8:1-6). *See* Gezer; Hazor; Megiddo.

The final dedicatory building celebration was rounded off by a colossal banquet shared by all Israel from Hamath to the brook of Egypt. The eighth day was a solemn assembly, after which the people returned to their houses. Solomon spent 14 years in these building operations and spent the staggering sum of *c.* \$4,400,000,000.

Commerce and Revenue

Solomon was a shrewd diplomat. Through his marriages he drove international bargains, thereby insuring peace for his nation. During the 40 years of his reign (I Kgs 11:42) Israel rarely had to fight a battle.

Solomon's first commercial contract was with King Hiram of Tyre. He paid annually to Hiram 225,000 bushels of wheat and 1,800 gallons of beaten olive oil for Hiram's timber, stonecutters, and erected buildings. Solomon paid Hiram 20 cities in Galilee in lieu of contracted indebtedness. Later Hiram loaned Solomon 60 talents of gold (*c.* \$2,000,000). Solomon made a contract with Egyptian traders (Muṣri of Asia Minor?) for horses and chariots. The king in turn distributed them to the Hittites and Aramaeans for a handsome profit (I Kgs 10:28 f.).

Solomon's most profitable commercial enterprise was his maritime trade. He built ships of the Tarshish type at Ezion-geber at the head of the Gulf of Aqabah. This city was developed into a great seaport and became the home base for Solomon's fleet. Hiram's experienced sailors manned and sailed these ships on the Red Sea, the Indian Ocean, and even to Ophir in three-year round trips.

The store cities or warehouses (II Chr 8:4-6) built in strategic areas were filled with revenue (tariff) collected from caravans crossing Solomon's dominion. Solomon's annual gold revenue, exclusive of his traders' profits, his merchants' traffic, and the king's tribute from the mixed population and the governors of the country, reached the incredible sum for that day of *c.* \$25,000,000.

Wisdom and Splendor

The wisdom of Solomon is celebrated in the Bible (I Kgs 4:29-34) and in legend. The book of Proverbs begins with the statement: "The proverbs of Solomon the son of David, king of Israel." (A large section of the book is accredited to him, cf. Prov 25:1.) The title verse of Ecclesiastes is meant to refer to Solomon. He is credited with the Song of Solomon and the apocryphal book Wisdom of Solomon. The compiler of I Kgs 4 states that Solomon was responsible for 3,000 proverbs and 1,005 songs. The superscriptions of the psalms give him two psalms (72, 127). The obituary of Solomon (I Kgs 11:41) refers to his wisdom as recorded in the Acts of Solomon—the official record in the royal archives.

During the middle of Solomon's reign he received a notable visit from the Queen of Sheba, who came from "the ends of the earth" to hear of his wisdom (Mt 12:42). Solomon showed her Jerusalem, its temple, palaces, and fortifications. The queen was so overwhelmed by the beauty of his capital, the food on his table, the array of his servants, and the general magnificence of his court, that "there was no more spirit in her" (I Kgs 10:5). But it was Solomon's wisdom that profoundly impressed her. She bombarded him with questions and enigmas. All of her riddles and conundrums were so cleverly answered she finally exclaimed congratulatory words: "Happy are thy men . . . thy servants, which stand continually before thee, and that hear thy wisdom" (I Kgs 10:8). In keeping with the oriental custom, she presented Solomon with rich gifts besides 120 talents of gold (*c.* \$4,800,000, I Kgs 10:8-10). *See* Sheba.

Decline and Fall (I Kgs 11)

Many of Solomon's policies were unsound: (1) his forced labor disrupted the family life of his people; (2) his foreign trade brought in foreign gods and encouraged idolatry; (3) his excessive building program overextended his resources; (4) his court of splendor overtaxed his people and overburdened them; (5) his gross polygamy was unwise (in his old age his foreign wives turned his heart after other gods, I Kgs 11:1-8). Though angry with him, Yahweh graciously did not rend the kingdom from him but from his son.

But Yahweh raised up "adversaries" to goad Solomon. These found support among the populace. The first was Hadad the Edomite who fled to Egypt in David's reign. As soon as news of David's death reached him, he returned home, despised Israel, and became king of Edom. The second was Rezon, who established himself in Damascus and was a thorn in Solomon's side all his days (I Kgs 11:9-25). The third and most dangerous was a strong labor leader named Jeroboam, son of Nebat an Ephrathite, the overseer of Solomon's public works program. Jeroboam inwardly rebelled against the king's policy, and the prophet Ahijah encouraged him in his patriotism and assured him the kingship over the ten northern tribes. When Solomon suspected him, Jeroboam fled to Egypt and waited (I Kgs 11:26-40).

With all his weaknesses, Solomon made great contributions to Israel: (1) He was responsible for establishing the temple as the central religious shrine of the nation. (2) He hastened the transition of Israel from an agricultural people to a commercial people. (3) He placed Israel in international affairs. (4) He championed the ideal of justice in the courts. (5) In his proverbs he championed common sense in religion.

So Solomon closed his career worn out by excessive self-indulgence, leaving behind him an impoverished treasury, a discontented people, and a tottering empire ready to fall apart—it did collapse under Rehoboam. However, he made immortal contributions: Solomon was the father of Hebrew wisdom literature, and builder of the temple. Also, Solomon with all his glory and splendor became the type of Him who is to rule in peace one day "from sea to sea" (Ps 72:8).

Bibliography. John Bright, *A History of Israel,* Philadelphia: Westminster, 1959, pp. 190-208. Nelson Glueck, *The Other Side of the Jordan,* New Haven: ASOR, 1940, pp. 89-113. James Fleming, *Personalities of the Old Testament,* New York: Scribner's, 1939, pp. 149-165. W. S. LaSor, *Great Personalities of the Old Testament,* New York: Revell, 1959, pp. 125 ff. Abraham Malamet, "Organs of Statecraft in the Israelite Monarchy," BA, XXVIII (1965), 34-65. J. M. Meyers, "Solomon," IDB, IV, 399-408. Martin Noth, *The History of Israel,* 2nd ed., New York: Harper, 1960, pp. 204-224. I. M. Price, *The Dramatic Story of Old Testament History,* 5th ed., New York: Revell, 1935, pp. 230-251. G. Ernest Wright, *Biblical Archaeology,* Philadelphia: Westminster Press, 1959, pp. 120-144.

D. W. D.

SOLOMON, SONG OF. This book, also called the Song of Songs or Canticles, is one of the smallest, loveliest, and most controversial books of the OT.

Canonicity

In a discussion about what writings "rendered the hands unclean" because they were holy, the rabbis were divided about the status of the Song and of Ecclesiastes. Rabbi Akiba declared, "All the ages are not worth the day on which the Song of Songs was given to Israel, for all the Writings are holy, but the Song of Songs is the holy of holies" (Mishnah Yadaim 3:5; cf. M. Eduyoth 5:3; Tosefta Sanhedrin 12:10).

Many writers hold that these disputes indicate that the canonicity of the Song was not settled until the Council of Jamnia (*c.* A.D. 90). W. Rudolph, however, maintains that these discussions actually assume the prior canonicity of the book ("Das Hohe Lied im Kanon," ZAW, LIX [1943], 195).

Solomonic Authorship

It is generally held that a factor favoring the acceptance of the Song into the canon was the traditional ascription of its authorship to Solomon. Some conservative writers see no reason for denying this tradition (E. J. Young, *An Introduction to the Old Testament;* M. G. Kline, ChT, April 27, 1959, p. 39). Other conservatives point out that the Heb. phrase in 1:1, *lishᵉlōmōh,* can mean "for Solomon" instead of "by Solomon" (D. A. Hubbard, NBD, p. 1204; S. Schultz, *The Old Testament Speaks,* p. 295).

Many writers hold that the opening verse was a later addition and that Solomon was not the author for the following reasons: (1) Song 1:1 uses the long form of the relative pronoun *'ăsher* whereas the short form *she* is used elsewhere (cf. 3:7). (2) The five other occurrences of the name Solomon (1:5; 3:9, 11; 8:11-12), and the three occurrences of the word "king" (1:4, 12; 7:5) view him as the one addressed or described rather than as the one who is speaking. Further, the name Solomon is missing from the superscription of the Syriac Peshitta (Joshua Bloch, "A Critical Examination of the Text of the Syriac Version of the Song of Songs," *American Journal of Semitic Languages,* XXXVIII [1921], 108).

Solomonic Setting

Whereas most writers would question the Solomonic authorship of the Song, many are willing to agree that the setting of the Song accords well with the Solomonic age. The references to the many locations in northern Palestine (especially to Tirzah in 6:4, which was abandoned by Omri in 876 B.C. when he made Samaria his capital), and the references to the king's harem and furnishings, to the wealth of perfumes and other goods, and the impression of a time of general happiness, confirm this belief (see H. M. Segal, "The Song of Songs," VT, XII [1962], 481 f.; D. A. Bruno, *Das Hohe Lied, Das Buch Hiob,* pp. 20 f.). W. F. Albright detects in 1:2*b*-3*a*; 2:15; 4:8-12; 5:9; 6:8; 7:1 f.; 8:5-7 texts which he believes go back to the 13th-11th cen. B.C. on the basis of their type of parallelism and their references to Canaanite mythology ("Archaic Survivals in the Text of Canticles," *Hebrew and Semitic Studies,* ed. D. Winton Thomas and W. D. McHardy, pp. 1-7). Albright and others hold that the final editing of the text, however, must have taken place in the 5th or 4th cen. B.C. on the basis of certain linguistic features.

Linguistic Features

The Song contains a number of words and constructions which are akin to the forms used in later Mishnaic Hebrew (Segal, p. 478) and in Aramaic (Pouget, pp. 78–81). This has inclined scholars to favor a post-Exilic date for the book. More recently, however, such Aramaisms have been shown to be indications of a northern locale rather than signs of a later date (cf. A. Hurvitz, " 'Aramaisms' in Biblical Hebrew," IEJ, XVIII [1968], 236). The explanation of a northern origin would also fit well with the predominance of northern sites in the book.

In addition to the Aramaisms, scholars believed that they could detect Gr. words in the text. Pouget listed four (p. 82). More recently Albright has stated, "Contrary to assertions in the past, there is not a single Gr. loan-word, and therefore there is no evidence for the frequently assumed Hellenistic date (i.e., 3rd or 2nd cen. B.C.)" ("Archaic Survivals," p. 1).

Interpretations

Allegorical. The view which interpreted the Song as an allegory of the love between God and Israel or between Christ and the Church prevailed for centuries as the orthodox interpretation among Jews, Catholics, and Protestants. The Targum or Aramaic paraphrase (6th cen. A.D.) saw in the "eyes like doves" the wise men in the Sanhedrin, and in the "neck like a tower of David" the chief of the academy. A Jewish scholar in the 12th cen., Saadia Gaon (892–942), saw in the Song the complete history of Israel up to the coming of the Messiah.

The first allegorical commentary in the church was that of Hippolytus of Rome early in the 3rd cen. The classic work on Canticles, however, was that by Origen (d. 254). The Song was the favorite book of Bernard of Clairvaux, who preached 86 sermons on the first two chapters. Luther saw in the bride the personification of Solomon's kingdom.

In modern times, the allegorical view is maintained by some Catholics—Jouon, Feuillet, Buzy, and Robert. The parabolic or typological interpretation espoused by a number of recent writers—Ellis, Ambroggi, Weber, Murphy—differs from the above in accepting the Song basically as a literal love song and in seeking a spiritual sense not from the details but from the more general analogies between man's love and God's.

Narrative. The earliest proponent of a literal view, Theodore of Mopsuestia (d. 429) was condemned a century after his death by the church for proposing such a view. In modern times literal interpretations began with Chatellon in 1544. Ewald (1826) and Delitzsch (1875) popularized a dramatic view of the Song. Delitzsch maintained that the lover was Solomon in the dual role of king and shepherd; Ewald distinguished a voluptuous Solomon and a rustic shepherd who were contending for the hand of the maid. The constancy of the maid to her shepherd is taken as a lesson of fidelity. This three-character view involves more dramatic tension and at the same time requires more sophisticated ingenuity to contrive than the two-character plot.

Leroy Waterman offers the novel interpretation that the Song was designed as a political polemic against Solomon, with the description of the bride actually intended as grotesque caricatures ("The Role of Solomon in the Song of Songs," JBL, XLIV [1925], 171–187).

Lyrical. A number of writers from the 16th to the 18th cen. had described the Song as a collection of madrigals, idyls, or eclogues. Then in 1873 Wetzstein published his observations of Syrian wedding customs, which included the singing of *wasfs* or songs describing the beauty of the bride. Others, including Theodore of Mopsuestia, Herder (1778), and in modern times Haupt, Jastrow, Baumgartner, Gottwald, Gordis and Segal, have held that the Song was a collection of popular love songs. Gordis, for example, perceives 28 separate songs which span five centuries. Rowley, May, and others object that this kind of analysis does not do justice to the uniform style and characterization of the work.

Cultic. The most novel attempt to unravel the meaning of the Song is the liturgical or Tammuz cult interpretation. In the 1920's Theophile Meek suggested that the Song is a Yahwistic modification of the liturgies of a pre-Israelite fertility cult, similar to those of the Tammuz cult of Babylon. This view has captured the allegiance of a number of scholars, among them Snaith, Oesterley, Wittekind, Margoliouth, and Ebeling. The basic objection to such a view is the improbability of the revisions necessary to introduce such a cultic liturgy into the canon. For a criticism of the cultic interpretation see H. H. Rowley, "The Song of Songs': an Examination of Recent Theory," *The Journal of the Royal Asiatic Society,* April, 1938, pp. 251–276; Edwin Yamauchi, "Cultic Clues in Canticles?" BETS, IV (1961), 80–88.

Comparisons with Other Love Songs

The earliest literature—that of the Sumerians—has given some love songs (from *c.* 1750 B.C.) associated with the Tammuz cult which present some striking parallels (S.N. Kramer, "The Biblical 'Song of Songs' and the Sumerian Love Songs," *Expedition,* V, pp. 25–31). One of the objections to the two-character view was that it made Solomon both a king and a shepherd. It is noteworthy that in these songs Dumuzi, the king of Erech who was later deified, is also addressed as a shepherd. W. G. Lambert recently pieced together fragments of Akkad. love songs (from *c.* 1000 B.C.) which were used in the Tammuz cult. In comparing them with the Song he remarks: "Both are love poetry with no apparent sequence or development. In both there is a frequent change of speaker, and at times narrative or monologue occurs. In both the scene changes, and the lovers appear to have left their metropolitan environment" ("Divine Love Lyrics from Babylon," JSS, IV [1959], pp. 1-15). The Egyptian love songs (1200 B.C.) in ANET are not cultic but secular.

Conclusion

The Song seems most likely to be a composition of a north Palestinian writer in Solomon's court (cf. Prov 25:1) about a maid—perhaps his sister—celebrating her espousal to Solomon. The casting of Solomon as a shepherd would be intended as a poetic figure, even as King Dumuzi was likewise addressed in the Sumerian lyrics. The literary form of the Song would be based on contemporary Akkadian and Egyptian models. However, to insist that therefore the Song must conceal the cultic function of the pagan models would be as unreasonable as to insist that the plays of Aeschylus retained the Dionysiac character of the original tragedies.

Outline

As the analysis of the Song depends largely on one's point of view, simply the speakers involved are indicated. It would help the English reader to note that the maid addresses her lover as *dôdî*, which the KJV renders "my beloved"; the man addresses the maid as *ra'yātî*, which the KJV renders "my love."

The Maid	*The Man*	*Other*
1:2-4*a*,5-7	1:8-11	1:4*b*
1:12-14	1:15	
1:16-2:1	2:2	
2:3-10*a*	2:10*b*-14	
2:15-3:5		3:6-11
4:16	4:1-15	5:9
5:2*a*,3-8,10-16	5:1,2*b*	6:1,10
6:2-3	6:4-9,11-12	7:1-6
7:11-14	7:7-10	8:5*a*
8:1-4,5*b*		
8:6-7,10-12	8:13	8:8-9
8:14		

Bibliography. ALLEGORICAL VIEW: Origen, *The Song of Songs,* trans. by R. P. Lawson, London: Longmans, Green & Co., 1957. A. Robert, *et al., Le Cantique des Cantiques,* Paris: Lecoffre, 1963. NARRATIVE VIEW: William Pouget and Jean Guitton, *The Canticle of Canticles,* trans. by Joseph L. Lilly, New York: D. X. McMullen Co., 1948. LYRICAL VIEW: Robert Gordis, *The Song of Songs,* New York: The Jewish Theological Seminary of America, 1954. CULTIC VIEW: Samuel N. Kramer, "The Biblical 'Song of Songs' and the Sumerian Love Songs," *Expedition,* V (1962), 25-31. Theophile Meek, "The Song of Songs," *The Interpreter's Bible,* Vol. V, New York: Abingdon Press, 1956. RECENT SURVEYS: Roland E. Murphy, "Recent Literature on the Canticle of Canticles," CBQ, XVI (1954), 1-11. H. H. Rowley, "The Interpretation of the Song of Solomon," *The Servant of the Lord,* London: Lutterworth, 1952, pp. 189-234.

E. M. Y.

SOLOMON'S PORCH

1. The "porch of judgment" which Solomon built and lined with cedar as part of his palace (I Kgs 7:7). *See* Palace; Solomon.

2. Outer corridor of the temple on the E side (Jn 10:23; Acts 3:11; 5:12). The outer court of the temple was surrounded by two rows of pillars to form corridors or porticos within the temple walls. *See* Temple.

R. A. K.

SOLOMON'S SERVANTS. King Solomon, like all ancient rulers, had many servants who were delegated certain responsibilities. Some were foreign slaves who did the menial tasks in both the palace and the temple, while a number were Israelite princes and officers (I Kgs 4:1-19). Of these, some were priests who officiated in the temple; some were princes who advised the king on foreign or domestic policies. Others were overseers of certain land areas charged with the collection of supplies or military protection.

The overseer of the homeland labor force had charge of 12 districts, but these divisions did not coincide with the old tribal boundaries. This system probably resulted from Solomon's policy of breaking up old loyalties of the tribes to insure greater loyalty to the court, and it perhaps gives some reason for the dissatisfaction of the northern tribes at the close of Solomon's reign. Also, there was no overseer for Judah, which was evidently exempt from tax and labor. The list of officials in I Kgs 4 seems to be included in order to indicate the greatness of Solomon. Also designated as Solomon's servants were some descendants of foreign slaves who came back from the Babylonian Captivity (Ezr 2:55-58; Neh 7:57-60). They worked for the Levites and priests in the temple, and may have been those of Canaanite descent who had been enslaved in the time of Solomon. *See* Nethinim; Solomon.

A. W. W.

SON. There are more than 3,700 occurrences of son in the OT (Heb. *ben*) and more than 350 in the NT (Gr. *huios*).

1. The natural use is, of course, very numerous. The first occurrence is in Gen 4:17, used of Enoch, son of Cain. A son-in-law was regarded as a son, e.g., David to Saul (I Sam 24:16). *See* Family.

2. Direct descendants are called sons, as the grandsons of Laban (Gen 31:28), or Jesus of David and Abraham (Mt 1:1).

3. Sons often denote ethnic or racial descendants, as "the children [sons] of Israel asked the Lord" (Jud 1:1), i.e., the Israelites; so, "sons of Ammon" (Jer 49:1, ASV); "sons of the Anakims" (Deut 1:28). The ethnic use may become geographic, as "the children of Jerusalem" (Joel 3:6).

4. The phrase "son of man" may be used generally to denote any human being, as "God is not a man, that he should lie; neither the son of man, that he should repent" (Num 23:19;

also Ps 146:3; Isa 51:12). It is also used of Ezekiel whom God addresses as son of man more than 80 times, and once of Daniel (Dan 8:17).

5. Sons may refer to a member ot a class or group, as "the sons of the prophets" (*q.v.*; II Kgs 2:3-5), or to members of a wedding party (Mt 9:15).

6. Son at times expresses one who is affectionately regarded by an elder, as Samuel to Eli (I Sam 3:6), or Timothy to Paul (I Tim 1:2).

7. Son used with any noun of quality ascribes a moral trait to that person, as "king over all the sons of pride" (Job 41:34, RSV), i.e., proud men; "if the son of peace be there" (Lk 10:6), i.e., a peaceable man.

8. Infinitely most meaningful are the expressions "Son of Man" and "Son of God," messianic and redemptive epithets of Jesus. *See* Sonship of Christ; Son of Man.

As Son of Man, Jesus was subject to human conditions and experiences: "nowhere to lay his head" (Mt 8:20); He was one with His disciples as He sent them out (Mt 10:1, 18-25, 40); He ate and drank with sinners (Lk 7:33-34); blasphemy "against the Son of man" may be forgiven (Mt 12:31-32); He experienced death and the grave, as do all men (Mt 12:40); He came to serve others, not to be served (Mk 10:45).

"Son of God" is used less than half as often as "Son of Man" in the four Gospels, but occurs 17 times from Acts to Revelation. Another contrast is that in the Gospels the term is used by others of Jesus except in Jn 5:25; 9:35; 10:36; 11:4; and possibly 3:18. As Son of God, Jesus explicitly declared to His disciples that He is the Messiah (Mt 16:16-20). The redeeming function is plain, especially in the Johannine writings, in Paul's epistles, and in Hebrews. The pagan and demonic testimony, however, to Jesus as Son of God is unusual: Satan (Mt 4:3, 6), the Gadarene demoniacs (Mt 8:29), the centurion (Mt 27:54).

As Son of Man He was tested in all respects as we are, yet without sin (Heb 4:15). As Son of God, He is the Lamb of God who takes away the sin of the world (Jn 1:29, 34). Being both, He is the mediator of the new covenant (I Tim 2:5; Heb 8:6; 9:15; 12:24).

Bibliography. Peter Wülfing von Martitz, *et al.*, "*Huios*, etc.," TDNT, VIII, 334-399.

L. R. E.

SON OF GOD. *See* Sonship of Christ.

SON OF MAN. A translation of the Aram. *bar 'enāš* and the Gr. *huios tou anthrōpou*. The expression has various meanings in Scripture depending on the context. In Ps 8:4 it means "man" generally; in Ezk 2:1 it emphasizes the difference between the human prophet and the Lord who speaks to and through him; in Dan 7:13 the phrase refers to a human-like figure, but also a supernatural one, Head of the saints of the Most High (Dan 7:18); while in the NT it is generally used as a title for Jesus (except in Rev 1:13; 14:14). *See* Son.

The title appears over 80 times in the NT, all but one in the Gospels (see Acts 7:56, the only place where it is not used by our Lord Himself; Jn 12:34 is no real exception, for here it is used as a quote from Jesus' words). Some writers (e.g., R. Bultmann, *Theology of the New Testament*, I, 30; B. M. Metzger, *The New Testament*, p. 153) see three meanings of the phrase: (1) as descriptive of the Coming One (eschatological, Mt 24:27); (2) referring to Jesus' suffering and death (Mk 8:31); and (3) as descriptive of His earthly ministry of teaching and healing (Mk 2:10, 28). Others (e.g., O. Cullmann, *Christology of the New Testament*, p. 155) differentiate two categories: (1) the eschatological sayings; and (2) the sayings referring to Jesus' earthly task.

A recent study by J. M. Ford (JBL, LXXXVII [1968], 257-266) contends that Jesus used the title as a euphemism for "the Son of God," for in Palestine the latter would sound blasphemous to a Semitic audience. When Christianity spread into the Gentile world the latter was used, and it is notable that "the Son of man" never occurs in the NT letters. What was original in Jesus' use of the title? W. Barclay (*The Mind of Jesus*, p. 155) argues that it was the fact that He connected it with His sufferings and death (see also A. M. Hunter, *The Work and Words of Jesus*, p. 87; O. Cullmann, p. 161). Yet others see that idea *already* present in Dan 7, namely, that it is through suffering that the "one like unto a Son of man" (there identified with the "saints of the Most High") is vindicated and glorified (R. Longenecker, JETS, XII [1968], 154).

Why did He use a title so enigmatic as this? Probably for at least two reasons: (1) it was general enough to include all the aspects of His person and work, whether present or eschatological; and (2) it caught His hearers by surprise, jolted them into attention and forced them to ask, "Who is this Son of man?" (Jn 12:34).

While some have denied that Jesus ever used this title for Himself, rather the Palestinian church attributed it to Him (e.g., Bornkamm, *Jesus of Nazareth*, p. 230), the majority of writers today accept it as a genuine, in fact, the most outstanding self-designation of our Lord (e.g., Hunter, Barclay, Klausner, Cullmann). E. Stauffer (*New Testament Theology*, p. 108) even writes: "But the contribution of the history of religions has taught us better than that. 'Son of Man' is just about the most pretentious piece of self-description that any man in the ancient East could possibly have used."

Bibliography. W. Barclay, *The Mind of Jesus*, London: SCM, 1960. G. Bornkamm, *Jesus of Nazareth*, trans. by I. and F. McLuskey and J. M. Robinson, New York: Harper, 1960. R. Bultmann, *Theology of the New Testament*, trans. by K. Grobel, Vol. I, New York: Scribner, 1951. R. H. Charles, *The Book of Enoch*,

Oxford: Clarendon Press, 1893. Carsten Colpe, "*Ho Huios tou Anthrōpou,*" TDNT, VIII, 400–477. O. Cullmann, *The Christology of the New Testament,* trans. by S. C. Guthrie and C. A. M. Hall, London: SCM, 1963. J. M. Ford, "'The Son of Man'–A Euphemism?" JBL, LXXXVII (1968), pp. 257–266. E. D. Freed, "The Son of Man in the Fourth Gospel," JBL, LXXXVI (1967), pp. 402–409. A. M. Hunter, *The Work and Words of Jesus,* London: SCM, 1950. F. J. F. Jackson and K. Lake, *The Beginnings of Christianity,* Part I, Vol. I, London: Macmillan, 1920. J. Klausner, *Jesus of Nazareth,* trans. by H. Danby, Boston: Beacon Press, 1964. R. N. Longenecker, "'Son of Man' As a Self-Designation of Jesus," JETS, XII (1969), pp.151–158. I. Howard Marshall, "The Son of Man in Contemporary Debate," EQ, XLII (1970), 67–87. B. M. Metzger, *The New Testament,* New York: Abingdon, 1965. E. Stauffer, *New Testament Theology,* trans. by J. Marsh, London: SCM, 1963. William O. Walker, "The Origin of the Son of Man Concept as Applied to Jesus," JBL, XCI (1972), 482–490. B. F. Westcott, *The Gospel According to St. John,* London: J. Clarke & Co., 1958.

W. M. D.

SON OF PERDITION. *See* Judas 8; Perdition, Son of.

SONG. Singing had as important a place in Heb. culture as it does in our own, and the variety of songs in Scripture testify to the musical aptitude of the people. Song was used to express praise, thanksgiving, adoration, triumph, joy, love, indeed all the emotions of life. Song was used extensively in the worship of Israel and the Psalms are still the hymnal of the church. Much of the message of the prophets is poetic and may have been delivered at times in song (Ezk 33:32). Moses taught the people a song to keep before them the commandments of the Lord (Deut 31:19), and Paul exhorts us to communicate our Christian love and joy in song (Eph 5:19). There is song in heaven where the redeemed give praise to their Saviour-God (Rev 4 and 5). *See also* Music.

SONG OF DEGREES. *See* Degrees, Song of.

SONG OF SONGS. *See* Solomon, Song of.

SONGS OF ASCENT. *See* Degrees, Song of.

SONS OF GOD. *See* Children of God.

SONS OF THE PROPHETS. This phrase first appears in association with Elijah and Elisha. These sons of the prophets were located at Bethel, Jericho, Gilgal and elsewhere (I Kgs 20:35; II Kgs 2:3, 5, 7, 15; 4:1, 38; 6:1). Rather than indicating physical descent, the phrase seems to refer to prophetic guilds or schools which may have had their origin in the time of Samuel. I Sam 10:5, 10 (RSV) speaks of a "band of prophets" (*ḥebel n^e^bîʾîm*) at Gibeah, and I Sam 19:20 of a "company of the prophets" (*q^e^hillath hann^e^bîʾîm*) at Ramah. Samuel and later accredited prophets seem to have attracted young men with the prophetic call who wanted to learn from them. Possibly the writing prophets, many of whom seem to have been well educated, obtained their training in one of these schools. On the other hand, God did raise up men (Amos 7:14) who never attended one of these schools.

For the view that the sons of the prophets had become largely a hereditary guild in which the young men were trained in the external art of prophecy and became attached as professionals to the main sanctuaries in Israel, see H. L. Ellison, *The Prophets of Israel* (Grand Rapids: Eerdmans, 1969), pp. 36–42.

H. W. H.

SONS OF THUNDER. *See* Boanerges.

SONSHIP OF BELIEVERS. *See* Adoption.

SONSHIP OF CHRIST. Three main views have been presented of the sonship of Christ.

1. *Creation in time past.* This was the view of Arius as he argued that Jesus Christ was created in time past in the likeness of God the Father and is *homoiousios* with Him. It was rejected at the Council of Nicea because it made Christ into a created being and denied His deity. While it perhaps claimed that Christ was the first and the greatest, still it did not recognize that He is very God of very God. The council said He was *homoousios,* i.e., of the same substance with the Father, but adopted Origen's view that He proceeded from the Father by "eternal generation." It refuted Arius' arguments on the basis of the scriptural proofs that Christ is eternal and that there never was a time when Christ did not exist.

2. *Eternal generation.* Origen and those who held this view considered the Gr. word *monogenēs* to be a derivative of *gennaō,* "to beget" (the translators of the KJV following in their footsteps) and translated it "only begotten" (Jn 1:14, 18; 3:16, 18; Heb 11:17; I Jn 4:9). However, it is actually a derivative of *genos* and therefore means "unique" or "the only one of its kind." Because of this the French Bible translates it "*Son Fils Unique,*" meaning "His unique Son" (see NASB marg. at Jn 3:16, 18). In Heb 11:17 with reference to Isaac *monogenēs* must mean "unique," because Abraham begat other sons (Ishmael and the sons of Keturah).

3. *The unique Son of God.* This view is supported by the above arguments. Examples of such usage in Scripture are to be found in the OT Heb. expression "sons of . . .," meaning "of the order of . . ." in such phrases as sons "of the prophets" (I Kgs 20:35; II Kgs 2:3, 5, 7, 15; 4:38; 5:22; etc.); "of the apothecary" (Neh 3:8); "of the singers" (Neh 12:28). From this it can be understood how the contemporaries of Christ in the NT could take His declaration

that He was the Son of God to mean He claimed to be equal with God or to be God.

The Gospel of John shows this to be the case. Christ said that God was His own Father, and the Jews therefore sought to kill Him since they concluded that He was "making himself equal with God" (Jn 5:18). He also claimed to be worthy of equal honor and said that "all men should honour the Son, even as they honour the Father," for "He that honoureth not the Son honoureth not the Father which hath sent him" (Jn 5:23). Again, when He said, "I and my Father are one," the Jews accused Him of blasphemy and took up stones to stone Him because, they said, "Thou, being a man, makest thyself God" (Jn 10:30, 33). Of course it must be recognized that in other contexts the term "son of" may have another meaning, as when Scripture speaks of believers as sons of God or children of God by regeneration (Jn 1:12; I Jn 3:1-2; Rom 8:14; cf. 8:29).

What, however, is the meaning of the declaration in Ps 2:7, "Thou art my Son; this day have I begotten thee"? This is quoted in both Heb 1:5 and 5:5. The Gr. *gennaō* is used, and it is applied to Christ, but the timing and meaning are difficult to determine. However, in Acts 13:33 Paul connects it with the resurrection of Christ. In doing so he makes clear that its meaning is to be connected with the declaration of Christ's divine sonship rather than as becoming man in the incarnation.

Never has the church, nor have even heretics, spoken of the Holy Spirit as the father of Jesus Christ, though He was "conceived by the Holy Ghost, born of the virgin Mary" (Apostles' Creed). In Lk 1:35*b* Christ is specifically called the Son of God. Westcott and Hort's punctuation of this verse, which is supported by Nestle's margin, would make this answer to Mary's question as to how she could be mother of the Messiah, read, "The Holy Ghost shall come upon thee, and the power of the highest shall overshadow thee; therefore, also that which is born shall be called holy, the Son of God." Christ's holiness was preserved by the virgin birth. His unique relationship and equality with God were expressed by the term Son of God, and yet the term "only begotten" is applied to Him after His resurrection (cf. Ps 2:7 ff.) and used of His resurrection (cf. Acts 13:33) and exaltation.

The term "first begotten, firstborn," *prototokos*, is easier to define. It clearly refers to His being the first to rise from the dead (Rom 8:29; Col 1:15,18; cf. Heb 1:6; Rev 1:5), and fits in with the revelation in I Cor 15:22-23, "For as in Adam all die, even so in Christ shall all be made alive. But every man in his own order: Christ the firstfruits; afterward they that are Christ's at his coming."

See Christ, Deity of; Christ, Humanity of; Jesus Christ.

R. A. K.

SOOTHSAYER. *See* Magic; Observer of Times.

SOP. A thin morsel of bread used as a spoon to secure food from the common dish (Ruth 2:14; cf. Jn 13:26).

SOPATER (sō'pȧ-tẽr). A man from Berea, the son of Pyrrhus, one of Paul's traveling companions on his last missionary journey (Acts 20:4, RSV). He is probably the same person as the Sosipater of Rom 16:21 who sent greetings to the Romans with Paul.

SOPHERETH (sŏf'ĕ-rĕth). The name probably means "learning" and has the alternate form of Hassophereth (Ezr 2:55, RSV). One of the remnant returning from the Babylonian Captivity with Zerubbabel (Neh 7:57).

SORCERER, SORCERY. A sorcerer is one who is said to have superhuman or occult power by virtue of spells, magic, or secret knowledge obtained from evil spirits. The Heb. term for "sorceries" is *k^eshāpîm* (Isa 47:9, 12), translated in the KJV as "witchcrafts" in II Kgs 9:22; Mic 5:12; Nah 3:4. The same root is rendered either as "sorcerer" (Ex 7:11; Jer 27:9; Dan 2:2; Mal 3:5) or as "witch" (Ex 22:18; Deut 18:10; II Chr 33:6). These terms have their cognate in Akkad. *kišpu* and *kaššāpūtu*, "sorcery, magic." The other root common in ancient Semitic languages for magic or sorcery is *ḥ-r-š*, noted in Ugaritic in the Legend of King Keret (ANET, p. 148*b*) as well as in Aramaic and Syriac. It appears in Heb. in Isa 3:3 in the phrase *ḥăkam ḥărāshîm*, "the skillful magician" (RSV) or, lit., one skilled in magical arts or potions.

The practice of sorcery was widespread in the surrounding ancient cultures, but Israel was prohibited from allowing sorcerers, spiritists, mediums, or such like in their midst (Ex 22:18; Lev 19:26, 31; 20:27; Deut 18:10-14). It was a crime punishable by death (Ex 22:18); true also under the Middle Assyrian law code for makers of magical preparations (ANET, p. 184*b*).

The reason God condemned all such practices is that magic and sorcery are rivals to true religion. The believer's life is to be centered in a personal experience with the one, true, living God. He walks humbly and trustingly with his Lord, and looks only to Him in prayer for the supply of his needs. He accepts his circumstances as part of the sovereign design of God for his life. The magician or sorcerer, on the other hand, seeks to alter circumstances by trying to "compel a god, demon, or spirit to work for him; or he follows a pattern of occult practices to bend psychic forces to his will" (J. S. Wright, "Magic and Sorcery," NBD, p. 766).

It has become apparent in the modern revival of the occult that magic and sorcery, including horoscopes, Ouija boards, and various card games, are not always mere superstition or trickery, but have a demonic reality behind them. These forces must be resisted and renounced if one has had contact with them, overcoming them through the power of God in the name of Jesus Christ and applying the cleansing and protective efficacy of His blood (Rev 12:11).

See Demonology; Familiar Spirit; Magic.

J. R.

SOREK (sôr'ĕk). A fertile agricultural valley W of Jerusalem. Its name could also have been associated with the village known to Jerome as Kephar or Capharsorech near the ancient town of Zorah. Zorah was the home of Samson (Jud 13:2 ff.). It was in this valley that Samson found two of the Philistine girls he loved, one at Timnath (Jud 14:1), and Delilah in the "valley of Sorek" (Jud 16:4).

Traveling SW from Jerusalem, one is conscious of converging watersheds which begin shortly to form a ravine and then a valley. This watershed reaches N as far as Bethel and S as far as Bethlehem. The valley is irregular in its course, but the general direction is NW, making its way across the plain of Sharon and emptying into the Mediterranean about ten miles S of Joppa (modern Tel Aviv). The railroad built in 1889 from Jerusalem to Joppa followed the valley until it reached the plain of Sharon.

J. W. C.

SORES. *See* Diseases.

SORROW. An emotion common to humankind and referred to in the Bible by a number of Heb. and Gr. words, which range in their primary meanings through work, affliction, distress, tribulation, sadness, grief, evil. *See* Grief; Suffering. Though generally disagreeable, sorrow may vary in cause, degree, and effect. II Cor 7:10 speaks of a godly sorrow that results in repentance and salvation, while I Thess 4:13–18 distinguishes the sorrow of the Christian and that of the unbeliever on the death of a loved one. The sorrow of the Christian is assuaged by the sure hope of the Lord's return and of the accompanying resurrection. For the expression or demonstration of sorrow, *see* Mourn, Mourning.

Bibliography. R. Bultmann, "*Lypē*, etc.," TDNT, IV, 313–324.

SOSIPATER (sō-sĭp'ȧ-tẽr). A traveling companion of Paul who sent greetings to the Christians at Rome (Rom 16:21). *See* Sopater.

SOSTHENES (sŏs'thĕ-nēz). The name occurs twice in the NT. The man in Acts 18:17 was chief ruler of the synagogue at Corinth when Gallio was proconsul of Achaia. He may have become a Christian believer through Paul's preaching, as had his predecessor Crispus (Acts 18:8). If so, he quickly suffered for his faith, for when trouble broke out Sosthenes was beaten before the judgment seat of Gallio, who failed to intervene. It is possible that he did not become a Christian at this time, however, and that he was beaten because he was a Jew stirring up trouble in Corinth. It seems strange that Paul was not beaten too. The word "Greeks" is omitted in Acts 18:17, ASV.

If I Cor 1:1 refers to the same man, Sosthenes remained (or became) a firm believer, however; for several years later when Paul wrote his first letter to the Corinthians, Sosthenes was not only with Paul but Paul bracketed his name with his own in saluting the church in Corinth. It is not to be understood that Paul meant that he and Sosthenes enjoyed joint inspiration in writing I Corinthians, but it does indicate Sosthenes' stature as that of a traveling companion of Paul.

J. A. S.

SOTAI (sō'tī). One who returned from Babylon with Zerubbabel and was classed as one of "Solomon's servants" (Ezr 2:55; Neh 7:57).

SOTERIOLOGY. The doctrine of salvation as revealed in the Bible and formulated by an inductive study of the Scriptures. Three theories of salvation are particularly important, the idealistic, the governmental, and the federal headship, particularly since they distinguish the liberal and neoorthodox theologians on the one hand from the orthodox on the other hand.

The Idealistic View of the Atonement

This view was classed as realistic by Hodge and the older theologians who used the terms "realistic" and "idealistic" in the Platonic sense—which is just the opposite of our common philosophic usage. According to this view, which was held in its straightforward form by Schleiermacher but only in part by Barth and Brunner, Adam partook of a transtemporal eternal form of ideal humanity or generic humanity; that is, of a humanity which existed in heaven before man was created. When Adam sinned and fell, he polluted not only himself but the common pool of this ideal humanity. Christ also partook of this polluted pool in becoming man and came to this earth as a sinner among sinners or "one in the series of sinners" (Barth). But He overcame sin and in doing so cleansed both Himself and all those affected by the pool.

This view is clearly unscriptural:

1. It makes Christ a sinner among sinners, whereas the Bible says that He was "holy, harmless, undefiled, separate from sinners" (Heb 7:26). Christ challenged men to point out any sin in Him (Jn 8:46). He was the Lamb of God that takes away the sin of the world (Jn 1:29). As the type, the sacrificial lamb, had to be spotless and without blemish, so was He.

2. If Christ were a sinner among sinners, "one in the series of sinners" (Barth), then this would necessitate that He first atone for His own sin before He could atone for that of others.

3. The theory leads to Universalism, i.e., to the salvation of all men, and this directly contradicts the teaching of the Bible, and of Christ in particular, that the lost will suffer eternal punishment (Mt 25:41, 46; Rev 20:14–15).

Several attempts have been made to rework the theory and thus overcome its weaknesses. William G. Shedd in his *Dogmatic Theology* tried to adjust it to an otherwise orthodox view of his own. Shedd said that Adam was undifferentiated humanity, and that when he sinned all humanity therefore sinned in him. Each individual descendant of Adam, being a differentiation of Adam, as if he were a section of an orange, therefore partook of Adam's sin. Christ as He became man was in His human nature also a differentiation of Adam. Thus Christ came as a sinner among sinners, but He was different in that, according to Shedd, His atoning death was applied by *prolepsis,* i.e., by its application before it happened, to the Adamic sin assumed by Christ. This view is as unsatisfactory as Schleiermacher's in that it partakes of the same dangers of Universalism and of declaring Christ a sinner. It has the one merit that it does recognize the difficulty in Christ assuming sinful fallen nature.

A synthesis may be made between Schleiermacher and Kierkegaard. Karl Barth, along with Emil Brunner, makes a synthesis between a view of the solidarity of the human race in original sin (Kierkegaard) and generic humanity. Adam was simply the first in his class to sin and each man repeats his sin and falls individually. Brunner says, "Each one of us is 'Adam' just as we all together are Adam" (*Man in Revolt,* p. 149). Christ became the rejected one and the elected one, the one to whom the Father said no, and then said yes, and in whom He said the same to every man in the "eternal Now" of God (Barth). In Christ every man has been justified, then, from eternity past and is redeemed whether he believes it or not. Therefore Barth can say that every man who remains an unbeliever exists in the "impossible possibility of sin" and in "the impossible possibility of unbelief." In Christ, as God sees him united with Christ, he cannot be unbelieving or sin, but in himself he is unbelieving and sinful.

Barth's view is to be rejected for the following reasons:

1. It has a defective view of the sin and fall of man. Adam becomes only a type of every man and not the representative of the human race as clearly taught in Rom 5:12 and I Cor 15:22. Every man is really the cause of his own fall. This contradicts the parallel between what Adam did and how it affected the human race, and what Christ did as set forth in Rom 5:12 ff.

2. It substitutes the mere idea of Christ's death on the cross, as it existed in the mind of God for eternity past, for the historical fact as it occurred at Calvary. The cross itself becomes only a shadow, an *epiphenomenon* as Barth calls it, of what God planned in eternity past. At this point Barth has adopted pure idealism, with its attendant problem of being unable to distinguish between fairy tales and fancies and mere ideas, on the one hand, and fact and history, on the other.

3. Christ is called "one in the series of sinners" and becomes a sinner among other sinners in His incarnation. Barth does not even try to overcome this difficulty as Shedd has done. Christ cannot offer Himself as the sinless, spotless Son of God on whom the sins of the world were placed when He became a sacrifice.

4. Barth ends in *apokatastasia,* or the restoration and salvation of all men; but this contradicts the clear teachings of Christ and the Bible. Barth's hyphenated theory of God's salvation of man fails both as solidarity proves unscriptural and as generic humanity fails.

The Governmental Theory

A view elaborated by Hugo Grotius in which God's character as a moral governor acting in the best interests of His subjects is so overstressed that God's absolute holiness and justice are obscured and lost. All that is seen as necessary with regard to sin is that public justice be upheld by God, and the dignity of His laws vindicated in an outward manner. Christ's death is regarded as an acceptable payment for a debt rather than as a true sacrifice to satisfy divine justice (Isa 53:11). It is only a demonstration of the dire consequences of sin. God forgives sin because of His love apart from logical justification or true satisfaction.

The view was accepted by many of the Remonstrants and Jonathan Edwards, Jr. Charles Finney also held substantially the same view, as do many Arminians still. It denies any real ontological reason for Christ's death, since the death of anyone else would have been of equal value if it would have convinced men of the consequences of sin.

Federal Headship View

This is the orthodox and biblical view. Adam and Eve were the first of the human race, and all men are descended from them. Adam acted as the representative and federal head of the race which was to follow. To each of his descendants Adam's sin is directly imputed by God, for all are seen as sinning in him (Rom 5:12).

Christ, as the second Adam, took upon Himself a true human nature; but no sin was imputed to Him since He did not have a human father, being "conceived of the Holy Ghost" (Apostles' Creed). He was "made of a woman, made under the law, to redeem them that were under the law" (Gal 4:4). He came into the world by the virgin birth free of all sin, so that He as the perfect man might first keep the law of God perfectly, and then die under the penalty of the law as broken by man, bearing our sins in His own body on the tree. He acted as the representative of all who choose to accept Him as their own personal Saviour. While Adam's sin is imputed directly to all his posterity, Christ's righteouness is imputed only to those who individually elect to accept Him as their own substitutionary sacrifice and Redeemer. *See* Salvation.

Bibliography. Karl Barth, *Church Dogmatics,* Edinburgh: T. and T. Clark, 1956, IV, 1. Emil Brunner, *Man In Revolt,* London: Lutterworth Press, 1947. J. Oliver Buswell, Jr., *A Systematic Theology of the Christian Religion,* Grand Rapids: Zondervan, 1963, II, 70 ff. Charles Hodge, *Systematic Theology,* Grand Rapids: Eerdmans, 1952, II, 51 ff., 469 ff.

R. A. K.

SOUL. In the OT the word "soul" almost always translates Heb. *nephesh,* which is also many times translated "life"; also by various other words like "person," "self," "creature," etc. *Nephesh* is used 756 times. The word occurs in other Semitic languages and dialects (including Ugaritic) to mean person, life, or perhaps breath.

In its most common usage, *nephesh* means "the man himself" (BDB), the "individual." It often is used as the reflexive pronoun; e.g., "Backsliding Israel hath justified *herself*" (Jer 3:11); "seventy *persons*" (Deut 10:22). Related to this usage are numerous places where the word designates the seat of appetites and desires: "Eat . . . whatsoever thy *soul* lusteth after" (Deut 12:20), and "my *soul* shall weep" (Jer 13:17). In Old English, "soul" was used more often for "individual" than it is today.

Probably a more basic, though less common, meaning for *nephesh* is "life" or "living being"; e.g., "*life* for *life*" (Ex 21:23). Thus, the word characteristically means the person as a living being. It is even used of a dead person, i.e., a corpse (Num 6:6)! It is occasionally applied to the life of animals, particularly in the phrase, "the life of the flesh is in the blood" (Lev 17:11). Possibly it means just "life" in the phrases "her *soul* was in departing" (Gen 35:18), and, "the *soul* of the child came into him again" (I Kgs 17:22). Seldom if ever is the word clearly used for the non-material part of man. It seldom equals "soul" in the theological sense. However, that the OT teaches that believers are in God's presence now and will be resurrected in glory at last, is taught by the examples of Enoch and Elijah and in references such as Isa 25:8; 26:19. This is apart from the usage of *nephesh.*

In the NT, the OT usage of *nephesh* is continued to an extent in the Gr. word *psyche.* Paul's ship had 276 "souls" aboard (Acts 27:37). Jesus asked if it were lawful "to save *life,* or to kill" on the Sabbath (Mk 3:4). The word is seldom if ever used of animal life.

But the NT usage goes further and refers sometimes to the immaterial part of man. Men can "kill the body, but are not able to kill the *soul*" (Mt 10:28). Peter refers to lusts "which war against the *soul*" (I Pet 2:11). John saw in heaven the "souls" of the martyrs (Rev 6:9). Usually man is said to have a body and soul. Another view calls man tripartite, with body, soul, and spirit. *See* Anthropology; Spirit.

R. L. H.

SOUND MIND. *See* Sober.

SOUR. The translation of Heb. *bōser,* used of unripe or ripening grapes (Isa 18:5), which are sour and bitter. The person who ate such grapes found that the tartness of the unripe grapes caused a reaction described as "setting the teeth on edge." This became a figure to express a belief which Jeremiah and Ezekiel exposed as a partial truth. That is, the people believed that the actions of their fathers had determined their reactions. The proverbial saying was: "The fathers have eaten sour grapes, and the children's teeth are set on edge" (Jer 31:29; Ezk 18:2). This vitiating belief absolved persons of individual moral responsibility. Jeremiah denounced it and declared: "Every man that eateth the sour grape, his teeth shall be set on edge" (Jer 31:30). He thus pointed out that everyone shall suffer the consequences of his own iniquity. Ezekiel proclaimed: "As I live, saith the Lord Jehovah, ye shall not have occasion any more to use this proverb in Israel" (Ezk 18:3, ASV).

Sour is also the translation of Heb. *sûr* (Hos 4:18). It describes the turn Ephraim's idolatry had taken, the bitterness to which it had turned.

H. E. Fi.

SOUTH. *See* Negeb.

SOVEREIGNTY OF GOD. This term expresses the biblical teaching concerning the absolute, irresistible, infinite, and unconditional exercise of God's self-will over every area of His creation. God is the Disposer of all events throughout both time and eternity, as well as the Creator and Sustainer of all that exists. God "worketh all things after the counsel of his own will" (Eph 1:11). *See* Will of God.

God's names ("the most high God," Gen 14:18; "the blessed and only Potentate, the King of kings, and Lord of lords," I Tim 6:15), attributes (omnipotence, Rom 11:36; omniscience, Prov 15:3; omnipresence, Ps 139:7-12), works (creation, Gen 1–2; salvation, Eph 2:8; judgment, Rom 2:16), dominion (over men, Dan 4:25, 35; over Satan, Job 1:12; over nature, Ps 89:9), and providence (Gen 50:20; Rom 8:28) all attest to divine sovereignty.

There is nothing which lies outside the realm of God's sovereignty, including even the evil acts of men. Though God does not approve these evil acts, He permits, governs, and uses them for His own purposes and glory. The crucifixion, the most heinous crime of all time, was committed within the boundaries of "the determinate counsel and foreknowledge of God" (Acts 2:23). Jesus told Pilate that it was not within the realm of human power to crucify the Son of God, but that that power could come only from God (Jn 19:11). The crucifixion, despite its evil nature, was the most important aspect of God's plan to establish Christ as Lord and Saviour (Acts 2:36).

Another important aspect of this doctrine is God's exercise of this sovereignty over the eternal destinies of men. The gift of eternal life is the possession of those whom God, before the foundation of the world, "predestinated . . . unto the adoption of children by Jesus Christ to himself, according to the good pleasure of his will" (Eph 1:5). God's choice of those who are to receive the gift of eternal life has not been determined by a blind, arbitrary sovereignty, but by a sovereignty which operates in conformity with divine wisdom, holiness, and justice. *See* Election.

Bibliography. Loraine Boettner, *The Reformed Doctrine of Predestination,* 7th ed., Grand Rapids: Eerdmans, 1951. Arthur W. Pink, *The Sovereignty of God,* Cleveland: Bible Truth Depot, 1930.

W. M.

SOW. *See* Animals, I.14, 16.

SOWER. *See* Agriculture; Occupations: Farmer.

SPAIN (spān). The Gr. term *spania* designates the peninsula now comprising Spain and Portugal, called by the Greeks *Iberia* and the Romans *Hispania*. The early Phoenician colonies on the S coast (*see* Tarshish) were absorbed by Carthage. In the second Punic War (218–202 B.C.) Rome conquered the part ruled by Carthage (cf. I Macc 8:3), but the conquest of the NW was not completed until the time of Augustus, who divided the country into three provinces. The products of Spain were gold, silver, tin, copper, lead, grain, wine, olives, fruit, and wool. The populace of native Iberians, immigrant Celts, and Roman colonists became thoroughly Romanized (especially in the S).

Some of Paul's famous contemporaries were from Spain: Gallio, Seneca, and Lucan. It was natural that Paul should desire to evangelize Spain (Rom 15:24, 28; cf. II Cor 10:16). Such a visit to Spain by Paul is implied in First Clement (5) and stated in the Muratorian Canon. Irenaeus (*Against Heresies,* I.x.2) and Tertullian (*Against Jews,* 7) confirm the presence of Christians there in the 2nd cen. A.D.

E. F.

SPAN. *See* Weights, Measures, and Coins.

SPARKS. The English translation of several Heb. words.

1. Heb. *bᵉnê-reshep,* lit., "sons of the flame" (Job 5:7). means bits of flaming coal which leap from a burning faggot or brush fire. Just as it is natural for them to leap from the fire, so it is the order in which man lives to experience troubles.

2. Heb. *shabîb* (Job 18:5) refers to the remaining glow of the wick of a lamp hanging in a tent (cf. Job 18:6; 29:3). When this goes out, the tent is plunged into darkness (Job 21:17). It is used figuratively of what happens to the wicked man who pursues his ungodly ways.

3. Heb. *kîdôd* (Job 41:19) refers to what leaps out of the mouth of the leviathan, either a fabled sea monster or a crocodile. At times a crocodile will expel streams of steam-like breath from its nostrils with a snort or bellow. This therefore would give the appearance of smoke and perhaps incline toward the poetic suggestion of sparks or flames.

4. Heb. *niṣoṣ* (Isa 1:31) is a figure of the quick passing of the strong or haughty person under the consuming fire of divine judgment.

5. Sparks, also firebrands or fiery darts, *zîqôt* (Isa 50:11), are symbols of the invectives and blasphemies which the ungodly cast at God's servant. This may be compared with the hellish fire of an evil tongue (Jas 3:6).

H. E. Fi.

SPARROW. *See* Animals, III. 46.

SPARROW HAWK. *See* Animals: Hawk, Sparrow, III. 19.

SPEAR. *See* Armor.

SPECKLED

1. Speckled, *nāqōd* (Gen 30:32–33, 35, 39; 31:8, 10), is used only of sheep or goats and means "spotted" or "marked." It seems to refer to sheep or goats which are mostly black with white spots or vice versa.

2. Heb. *ṣābûaʻ* (Jer 12:9) is used in the phrase "speckled bird" of prey and is difficult to interpret. It parallels the thought of verse 8: "My heritage is become unto me as a lion in the forest" (ASV). That is, his people and his associates out of the past had turned against him; thus his heritage was about to hunt him out as the speckled or colored vulture seeks its prey. Another interpretation is that Israel was being likened to a colorful or speckled bird standing out sharply against a different background and therefore an easy bird of prey. Further, due to the difficulty of the Heb. text and the difference in the LXX, *ṣābûaʻ* is rendered hyena by some rather than speckled.

3. Speckled or bay, *sārōq* (Zech 1:8), pertains to the sorrel-colored horses along with the red and white horses of Zechariah's vision.

H. E. Fi.

SPECTACLE. The word is used twice in the NT. In Acts 19:29 it is the place where a show is put on, a theater. In I Cor 4:9 Paul describes the life of an apostle as a spectacle to the world.

SPELT. *See* Plants: Rye.

SPICE, SPICERY. Spices were extensively used in the ancient Near East for a wide variety of purposes. The Bible mentions the use of spices in connection with anointing oils and ointments (Ex 25:6; 35:8; I Chr 9:30), in the materials compounded for incense (Ex 25:6; 35:8), perfumes (Song 4:14, 16), cosmetics (Est 2:12, NASB), mixed with wine (Song 8:2), in cooking (Ezk 24:10), and in preparation of the dead (II Chr 16:14; Mk 16:1; Lk 23:56; Jn 19:40).

The spices were of aromatic vegetable substance or the fragrant gums of various plants. Biblical lists (Ex 30:23–24, 34; Song 4:13–14) include a wide variety: myrrh, cinnamon, aromatic cane, cassia, stachte, onycha, galbanum, frankincense, nard, saffron, calamus, aloes. The identification of some of these is in question. In addition, spices such as mint, dill, and cummin (Mt 23:23, RSV) were used in the preparation of foods. *See* Plants: Spice, and the separate subheadings of the above substances.

The spice trade was a very lucrative one (I Kgs 10:25), most of the spices coming by caravans either from Arabia (I Kgs 10:2, 10; *see* Sheba), or from India via Persia and Mesopotamia. There was great rivalry for that trade, just as there was for the same trade in the 13th to 18th cen. between European nations. King Hezekiah with great pride showed his stores of spices to the Babylonian ambassadors from Merodach-baladan (II Kgs 20:13; Isa 39:2).

P. C. J.

SPIDER. *See* Animals, IV. 31.

SPIKENARD. *See* Plants.

SPIN, SPINNING. *See* Dress; Occupations: Spinning.

SPINDLE. A shaft-like instrument used for winding loose fibers into thread. The size of the spindle varied from eight to 12 inches, and often possessed a stone or other heavy object to maintain the momentum of a turn. Two or three feet of thread could be prepared as the spindle was twirled and the string twisted around it. The spindle is mentioned in Prov 31:19 in connection with the virtuous woman who puts her hand to the spindle.

The ASV, etc., translates the Heb. word *kîshôr* as "distaff" (*q.v.*) and the parallel term *pelek* as "spindle." The latter is thought to refer to the spindle-whorl which enables the spinner to twirl the distaff.

See Occupations: Spinning.

SPIRIT. The essential and activating principle or animating force within living personal beings.

In the OT. The Heb. noun *rûaḥ* occurs 377 times in the OT, and usually is translated "breath," "wind," or "spirit" (e.g., Gen 6:17; 8:1; 41:8). In Ezk 37:1–14 the three different meanings may be observed: in v. 9*b* it means "winds," in vv. 5, 6, 8, 10 "breath," and in v. 14 "spirit." The noun derives from a verb meaning to breathe out through the nose with violence. With respect to human beings *rûaḥ* sometimes stands for the "life center" and is practically synonymous with *nephesh*, "soul." Generally, however, *nephesh* is the person himself as an individual, whereas *rûaḥ* is to be regarded as the animating principle (Job 32:8, 18; Ps 143:4, 7). Man has no power to retain his spirit (Eccl 8:8; Ps 104:29), and when he dies his spirit leaves the body (Ps 146:4).

Heb. *rûaḥ* is also used as a psychological term to denote vitality, animation, or vigor (Jud 15:19; I Kgs 10:5), morale or courage (Josh 2:11; 5:1; Isa 19:3), temper or anger (Jud 8:3), basic disposition or temperament (Num 14:24; Ps 51:10; Isa 54:6), moral character (Ezk 11:19; 36:26), and dominant impulse or attitude (Prov 16:18, 19; Num 5:14; Isa 57:15). Several times an evil spirit or demon is indicated by *rûaḥ* (I Sam 16:14–16, 23; 18:10; 19:9; Hos 4:12; 5:4), and the lying spirit of I Kgs 22:19–25 is obviously a personal being. Over 80 times the word refers to God's Spirit, the Spirit of the Lord, the Holy Spirit.

In the NT. Gr. *pneuma* has a similar range of meanings to that of *rûaḥ*. "Wind" is obviously meant in Jn 3:8*a*: "The wind blows where it wishes and you hear the sound of it. . . ." (NASB). II Thess 2:8 speaks of "the breath of his mouth." More important theologically, the spirit is that which gives life to the body. The spirit of Jairus' daughter returned to her body and she rose up immediately (Lk 8:55). After the righteous person's death, his *pneuma* lives on as an independent being in heaven (Heb 12:23).

Psychologically, the *pneuma* denotes the immaterial part of the human personality in such expressions as "let us cleanse ourselves from all defilement of flesh and spirit" (II Cor 7:1, NASB) and "that she may be holy both in body and spirit" (I Cor 7:34). It can mean simply a person's true self: "For they have refreshed my spirit and yours" (I Cor 16:18; cf. II Tim 4:22). More specifically, however, the *pneuma* is the source or seat of one's insight (Mk 2:8), emotions (Mk 8:12; Jn 11:33; 13:21; Acts 17:16; 18:25), and will (Mt 26:41; Acts 19:21). It is the man's spirit within him that can "know" his thoughts, i.e., comprehend his human state (I Cor 2:11).

Through the new birth man's spirit is made alive to God and sensitive to the inner voice of the Holy Spirit (Rom 8:16). As the spirit is constantly being renewed it is able to govern the attitudes of the mind (Eph 4:23). One's spirit enables him to think along spiritual lines because it is in turn controlled by the Spirit of Christ who imparts the mind and attitude of Christ to the believer (I Cor 2:16). Thus the regenerated human spirit when humbly submitted to Christ is capable of meekness and gentleness toward others (I Cor 4:21; Gal 6:1). Such a disposition is characterized as a "meek and quiet spirit" (I Pet 3:4).

The NT often refers to spirits as independent non-physical beings. Usually these spirit-beings are evil, or demons; but angels are also classed as spirits (Heb 1:4, 14). For a discussion of the Spirit of God *see* Holy Spirit.

See Angel; Anthropology: the nature of man; Inner Man; Ghost; Holy Spirit; Soul; Demonology; Winds.

J. R.

SPIRIT, HOLY. *See* Holy Spirit.

SPIRITS, DISCERNING OF. *See* Discerning of Spirits.

SPIRITS IN PRISON. The interpretation of "the spirits in prison" (I Pet 3:19) has been debated throughout church history. One view is that the spirits refer to unregenerate deceased individuals confined in the prison of Hades awaiting their final destination (cf. Lk 16:19–31). To these Jesus went and announced victory over sin and death during the three days He was in the grave (cf. I Pet 4:6; Eph 4:9–10). The primary objection to this view centers in the purpose for Christ's preaching. Did His preaching grant to these spirits a second chance for salvation? Heb 9:27 rules out this possibility. If not, then what value does the news of His victory hold for them?

A better interpretation springs from the context. I Pet 3:20 explains these spirits. They were people living in the time of Noah who were preached to by the Spirit of God and of Christ working in Noah's life (cf. II Pet 2:5). Noah was a testimony to the fact that there is a God who demands righteous living. Scripture relates, however, that these individuals rejected Noah's testimony and consequently died in the flood God sent. Because of their rejection, they perished and are now spirits confined in prison.

A third view holds that the spirits in prison are fallen angels or demonic beings, Satan's evil spirits, that masterminded the corruption and wickedness of the whole human race before the Flood (II Pet 2:4; Jude 6). Christ as Victor over Satan and sin descended in His spirit to their prison to make proclamation of His cosmic triumph (Jn 12:31; 16:11; Col 2:15; Heb 2:14; I Jn 3:8). E. G. Selwyn argues that in the NT *pneumata,* unless qualified (as in Heb 12:23), refers only to supernatural beings (e.g., Lk 10:20) and never to departed human spirits (*The First Epistle of St. Peter,* London: Macmillan, 1958).

L. B.

SPIRITUAL BODY, TERRESTRIAL BODY. In his classic discussion of the resurrection Paul speaks to the question of the nature of the resurrection body (I Cor 15:35). The body of this life is said to be a natural (*psuchikon,* 15:44) body, a member of that class of bodies known as terrestrial bodies (15:40, KJV). In other words, it is a body that is adapted to life as it presently is lived on this earth. The natural body is subject to corruption, lacking in honor, weak, and subject to death. In short, it is made in the image of the earthy man, Adam.

By way of contrast the resurrection body is a spiritual body, which probably means that it is transformed and governed by the Spirit and thus adapted to the conditions of heaven and eternity. Hence, it is incorruptible, raised in glory and power, and no longer subject to death. In short, it will bear the image of Christ, the Heavenly One (15:42–54). This is not to say that they are two distinct bodies, for there is an unbroken continuity between the natural and the spiritual body in spite of differences that exist (cf. 15:36–38, 42; Phil 3:21). Since the resurrection body is transformed into the likeness of Christ's resurrection body, perhaps something of its specific characteristics can be discerned in Lk 24:29–43. But the picture is incomplete and confusing, being beyond the realm of our present experience and comprehension.

See Resurrection of the Body.

S. N. G.

SPIRITUAL GIFTS. *See* Gifts, Spiritual.

SPIRITUALITY. God, who is spirit, regenerates sinful man and also makes it possible for him to attain true spirituality. "It is the Spirit who gives life; the flesh profits nothing" (Jn 6:63, NASB). God gives to the believer spiritual understanding (Col 1:9), and also a spiritual vocabulary so that he may express divine truths in a spiritual way (I Cor 2:12–13). The spiritual man is the Christian who has come to maturity (I Cor 2:15; 3:1; Gal 6:1), in whom the fruit of the Spirit abounds. The carnal Christian, on the contrary, is one who has remained immature and is still a child spiritually. He can be fed only milk. Jealousy, quarreling, pride, impurity mark his life (I Cor 3:1–3; 5:1–2). However, it is possible to walk by the Spirit, to be filled with the Spirit, to possess His power, to own His gifts—all marks of true spirituality (Gal 5:16; Eph 5:18; Acts 1:8; I Cor 12:7, 11).

R. P.

SPIT, SPITTLE. The act of spitting on or toward a person is an expression of extreme contempt and rejection throughout the Bible (Num 12:14; Job 17:6, ASV, NASB; 30:10). A man refusing to enter into levirate marriage was to be shamed publicly by having the wife of his deceased brother spit in his face (Deut 25:9). Isaiah prophesied that the suffering Servant would submit to this indignity (Isa 50:6), and Jesus Himself foretold He would be thus humiliated (Mk 10:34; Lk 18:32); both the Jews and the Roman soldiers so mocked Him (Mt 26:67; 27:30; Mk 14:65; 15:19). The Essenes punished spitting in their gatherings with a 30-day penance (Jos *Wars* ii.8.9; *Manual of Discipline,* vii.13, *see* Dead Sea Scrolls).

Spittle, or saliva, is mentioned in I Sam 21:13 (Heb. *rîr*); Job 7:19, and was considered slimy like the white (*rîr*) of an egg (Job 6:6). Jesus applied His saliva (Gr. *ptysma*) in several instances when healing an individual (Jn 9:6; Mk 7:33; 8:23). In so doing He followed a widespread practice common to both Jewish and Graeco-Roman healers. For example, according to the Talmud the rabbis condemned the use of spittle only when accompanied with incantations. Therefore our Lord undoubtedly employed saliva not as a medicine but as an aid to faith.

J. R.

SPOIL. More than a dozen Heb. and Gr. words are rendered by the English word "spoil" in the KJV. The spoil, sometimes referred to as the booty of warfare, could consist of various commodities contained in a plundered city. Of special importance were such goods as armor and all types of clothing, money and jewels, metals, animals of various types, and even human beings of both sexes.

Certain restrictions were given for the nation of Israel with regard to the spoil. The normal pattern was that no captives were to be made inside the limits of Canaan (Deut 20:14–16); however, in the case of warlike resistance, all men were to be put to death and the women and children were to be made captives. This normal pattern was not always followed by the nation, however (cf. II Sam 8:2; II Kgs 15:16).

When spoil or booty was secured, there were certain rules laid down for its distribution. First of all, the army and the people of the nation were to share equally in the spoil. But a further distinction was drawn for the army in that the spoil was to be divided between those who had actually taken part in the battle and those who had been left behind to guard and care for the camp (I Sam 30:24–25). A portion of the entire spoil was reserved for the Lord as follows: from the spoil of the army, one share in every 500 was given to the Lord, and from the spoil of the people, one share in every 50 was set aside (Num 31:26–47). These portions for the Lord were given to the Levites. Under the monarchy, a portion of the spoil was given to the king also. The king in turn could dedicate the spoil to the Lord or make use of it as he saw fit (I Chr 18:7, 11). There is some intertestamental evidence that a spoil was reserved for the oppressed, the aged, widows and orphans.

L. B.

SPOKE. The rod running from the hub to the outer rim of a wheel. In Solomon's temple the lavers were set upon elaborate bases with moving wheels. The spokes were the connecting rods of the wheels (I Kgs 7:32–33).

SPONGE. *See* Animals, V. 12.

SPOON. *See* Censer; Tabernacle.

SPORT. The word sport translates three different terms in the Bible: (1) to hold in derision, as in Jud 16:25 concerning Samson; (2) to laugh in jest, as in Gen 26:8 when Isaac "sported" or expressed affection to Rebecca; (3) to delight in self, as in Prov 10:23 where "it is as sport to a fool to do mischief."

SPOT. The Heb. *mûm* means a blemish or defect, either physical (Lev 21:17 f.; Num 19:2; II Sam 14:25; Song 4:7; Dan 1:4) or moral (Prov 9:7; Job 11:15; 31:7; Deut 32:5). Other uses in the OT are loose translations: the term in Jer 13:23 means "of varied color"; "without spot" (Heb. *tāmîm*) in Num 19:2 simply means "perfect." For the spots of leprosy (Lev 13) *see* Diseases.

The NT *spilos* is used for the sign of sin (II Pet 2:13; Eph 5:27). Jude (v. 23) speaks of a "garment spotted by the flesh," but the word in v. 12 may mean "hidden rocks" or "reefs" in the surf (ASV, NASB). The negative form (*aspilos*) occurs in I Tim 6:14; II Pet 3:14; Jas 1:27 in passages exhorting the Christian to keep himself unstained morally, and in I Pet 1:19 of Christ as a spotless sacrifice.

See Blemish.

SPOUSE. *See* Marriage; Sister.

SPREADINGS. This translates three OT terms: (1) it has the idea of letting out a sail of a ship (Ezk 27:7); (2) a spreading place where fishing nets are unrolled in the sun to dry (Ezk 26:5); (3) a branch that grows and continues to cover a larger area (Ezk 17:5–6).

SPRING. Spring translates a number of different words in the OT, such as fountain, source, stream (Deut 4:49; Josh 15:19; Ps 104:10), as well as verbs of activity such as "the pastures do spring" (Joel 2:22). *See* Fountain; Water; Well.

SPRINKLING. In the OT this involves the use of blood, water, or oil. Connected with the sacrificial system, sprinkling of blood took place in sacrifice and in consecration of the priesthood, as well as garments and vessels. Sprinkling could be done with a sprinkler, the finger, or in handfuls (Ex 24:6–8; Num 19:13; Ex 29:21).

Bibliography. Claus-Hunno Hunzinzer, *"Rantizō, Rantismos,"* TDNT, VI, 976–984.

SPY. A word translating several OT words with the meaning of (1) to see, i.e., he spied an Egyptian smiting a Hebrew (Ex 2:11); (2) to search out a country or city for invasion purposes (Num 21:32).

STABLE. An enclosed area in which animals are fed, as a camel stable (Ezk 25:5). Caves were also used as stables and corrals.

STACHYS (stā'kĭs). A Roman Christian, a friend of Paul, to whom he sent greetings (Rom 16:9).

STACTE, STORAX. *See* Plants.

STAFF. Various Heb. and Gr. words in many passages in the Bible refer to the staff in a literal sense. These include association with or use by shepherds, travelers, warriors and soldiers. The predominant biblical uses, however, are figurative. Moses' rod, for instance, symbolized the presence of God and His covenant concern for His people (Ex 14:16; 17:5, 9). Aaron's rod was God's miracle-working instrument (Ex 7:9 f.). Elisha's staff conveyed his healing power (II Kgs 4:29, 31).

The shepherd's staff symbolizes security, protection, and perhaps the nearness of God (Ps 23:4). From such symbolism the believer takes courage as he faces life's demands and disappointments. Since a staff supports its user, the figurative expression "staff of bread" came to mean one's daily supply of food (Lev 26:26; Ps 105:16; Ezk 4:16; 5:16; 14:13). On occasion the rod and staff emblemized God's power in judgment. Assyria was the rod of God's anger, like a staff to execute His indignation (Isa 10:5, 15). *See* Armor; Rod.

A. M.

STAG. *See* Animals, II. 10.

STAIR. A word used to translate three OT terms: (1) winding stairs (I Kgs 6:8); (2) an ascent, going up, step (II Kgs 9:13; Neh 3:15); (3) rocky ascent (Song 2:14). The basic idea is step upon step leading upward.

STAKE. The tent pin or peg used to anchor tents. Isaiah refers to the stakes of the whole city of Jerusalem (Isa 33:20; 54:2).

STALL. A place where livestock could be tied and housed during the winter season. Solomon (I Kgs 4:26) and Hezekiah (II Chr 32:28) had extensive "stalls" for animals. The Heb. word *'urāyôth* may instead mean "pens," as in NASB of II Chr 32:28. Calves were kept in "stalls" (Heb. *marbēq*, from *rābaq*, "to tie fast") to complete the fattening before slaughter (Amos 6:4; Mal 4:2; cf. Prov 15:17).

STAMMERING. The Heb. word *la'ag* implies a sense of scorn and derision in the OT (cf. Ps 2:4). In two passages (Isa 28:11; 33:19) it has the idea of God speaking in judgment through the foreign language(s) of conquering armies. Because Israel refused to listen to God's prophets in the native Heb. language promising rest and refreshing, God would send against His people the Assyrians and their mercenary troops of various nationalities, whose strange words would sound as though pronounced "by stammering lips" (Heb. *bᵉla'ăgê śāphâ*). Thus Israel would be hardened in its unbelief by the tongues of the foreign invaders.

STANDARD. *See* Ensign; Banner.

STAR. The Hebrews grouped all heavenly bodies except the sun and moon under the term "star." While the OT makes numerous references to the stars or planets, the Israelites evidently did not give as much attention to the study of astronomy (*q.v.*) as many other Near Eastern peoples. This was no doubt due in large part to the biblical injunction against worship of the stars (Deut 4:19; 17:2–5; II Kgs 17:16; Isa 47:13; Jer 44:19, 25). In spite of such condemnation, King Manasseh introduced it into Judah (II Kgs 21:5).

Scripture specifically mentions Arcturus or the Bear, Pleiades, and Orion (Job 9:9; 38:31; Amos 5:8), but most of the references to stars or planets are figurative or symbolic. Seven stars represent angels or messengers of the seven churches of Revelation (Rev 1:16, 20). Eleven stars stand for the brothers of Joseph who did obeisance to him in his dream (Gen 37:9). At the battle between Barak and Sisera the stars are viewed as fighting against Sisera (Jud 5:20), indicating that divine power was on the side of the Hebrews. The prophecy of a star to come out of Jacob (Num 24:17) is interpreted as referring to the first coming of Christ. Jesus Christ refers to Himself as the bright and morning star (Rev 22:16).

Stars also denoted rulers of earth (Dan 8:10; Rev 6:13) and fallen angels (Rev 12:4). Lucifer (Isa 14:12, KJV) is called "star of the morning" in the NASB. The innumerable stars are used as an indication of the extent of Abraham's posterity (Gen 15:5).

Considerable attention has been devoted to the "star in the east" (Mt 2:2, 7, 9). While much has been written in an effort to equate its appearance with conjunction of two or three planets, it does not seem that such an explanation meets the requirements of the situation. Although such a conjunction may have been interpreted by the Magi as indicating the birth of the King of the Jews and may have sent them to Palestine looking for Him, it could hardly have stood over the house where He lay and to have pointed to that specific house. It is of course possible that the first time the star appeared it was a conjunction of planets and the second time (when it specified an exact house) it was some supernatural light.

H. F. V.

STAR GAZER. *See* Astronomy; Magic.

STATER. The term is used only once, in Mt 17:27 (NASB). The RSV translates it "shekel" and the KJV as "a piece of money."

See Weights, Measures, and Coins.

STATURE. The basic Heb. and Gr. words for "stature" suggest the idea of a vertical distance whether great or small. A measurement of height is obviously intended in some passages (cf. II Sam 21:20; Ezk 17:6; Lk 2:52; 19:3). A simple measurement of height, however, does not exhaust all the uses of the original words. Some references imply the principle of life itself, the "length of life" (ISBE), as illustrated in passages like Jn 9:21, 23 and Heb 11:11. There the words translated "of age" and "past age" are the same Gr. word (*hēlikia*) translated elsewhere as "stature." The idea of length of life is more in keeping with the words of the Lord in Mt 6:27 and Lk 12:25, that it is not possible for a man to add one cubit (18 inches) to his stature or life span. The Lord is stressing the fact that a man cannot do one small thing to prolong the length of his life, rather than add an impossible number of inches to his height.

L. B.

STATURE

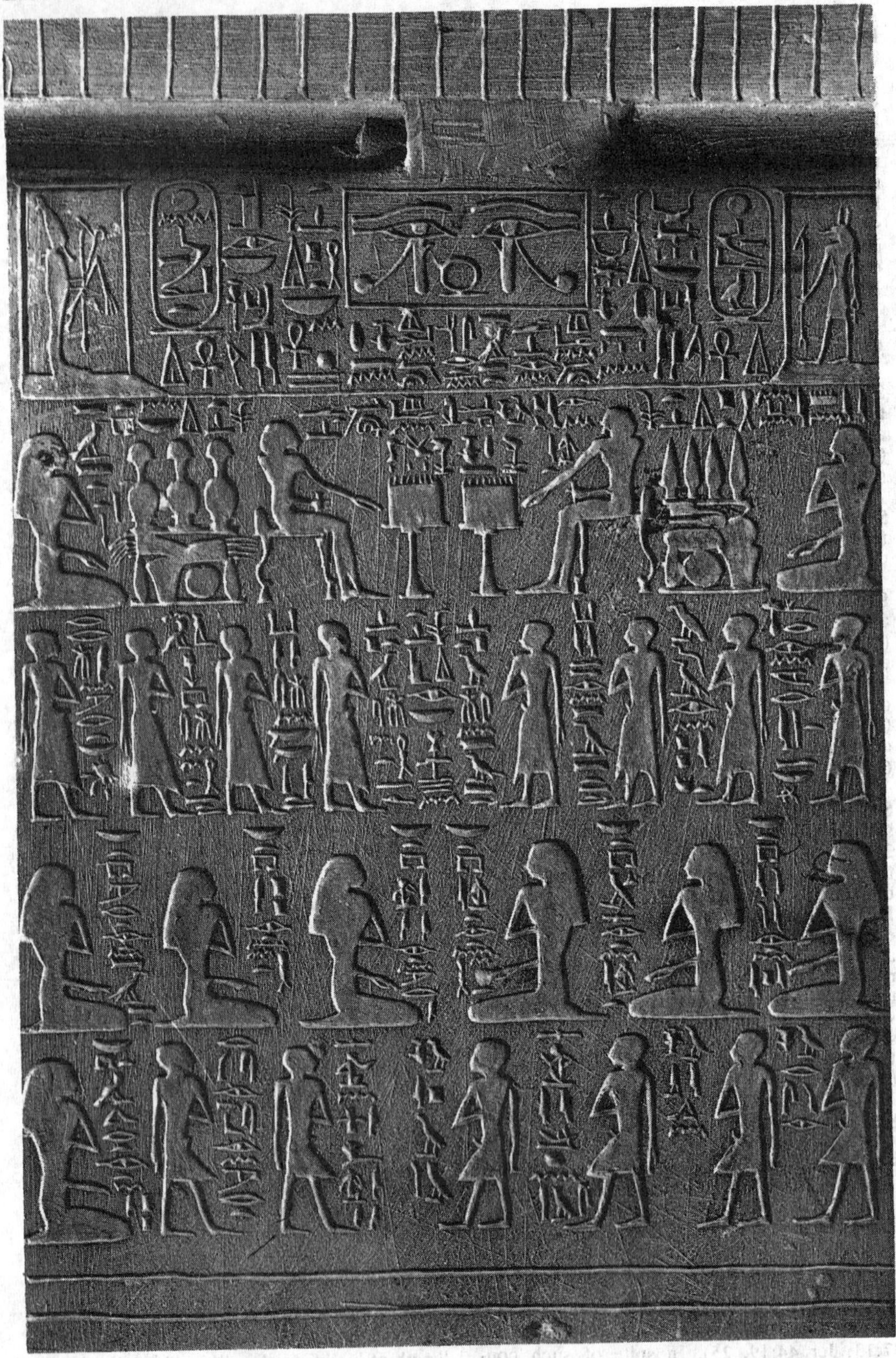

Stele of the Cartouches of Amenemhet III, *c.* 1900 B.C. LM

STATUTE. *See* Law; Law of Moses; Ordinance.

STAVES. *See* Staff; Tabernacle.

STAY. A thing or a person used to strengthen, steady, or support something. It is used of the arms on Solomon's throne (I Kgs 10:19); the bread and water that sustains life (Isa 3:1); the Egyptian princes that "corner" or support the tribes (Isa 19:13); and the Lord Himself, the support of His people (II Sam 22:19; Ps 18:18).

STEADFASTNESS. God provides the basis of steadfastness in the firm foundation of Christian truth. Apart from this foundation, steadfastness is impossible, for it involves being "rooted and built up in him, and stablished in the faith" (Col 2:5-7). The Christian's obligation is to hold fast to the foundation provided by God (II Pet 3:17). Though seldom used in Scripture, this word is expressive of a concept which appears repeatedly throughout the Bible.

See Patience; Perseverance.

STEEL. *See* Minerals and Metals.

STELE. The Gr. word *stēlē* means an upright stone or post. To the archaeologist a stele or stela is a rock or stone set up and inscribed as a monument. An example is the large stone with the law code of Hammurabi (*q.v.*). The famous stela of Merneptah (*c.* 1220 B.C.) contains the first mention of Israel outside the Bible; claiming an Egyptian victory over Israel which by then was located in Palestine (ANET, p. 378). The Moabite Stone (*q.v.*) records the Moabite account of the story found in II Kgs 3:4-27. The stone Ebenezer (*q.v.*) erected by Samuel (I Sam 7:12) would be a biblical stele, in addition to the stones on which the law of Moses was copied and set up by Joshua at Mount Ebal (Josh 8:32; cf. Deut 27:2-4).

STEPHANAS (stef'ă-năs). Paul calls Stephanas and his household "the firstfruits of Achaia" (I Cor 16:15) and lists him as one of the few in Corinth that he had personally baptized (I Cor 1:16). As one of the leading members of the Corinthian church, Stephanas was sent with two others to Paul in Ephesus, bringing news of the church, questions on doctrine and practice, and perhaps gifts (I Cor 16:17). Our I Corinthians was, at least in part, a response to these messengers.

STEPHEN (stē'vĕn). A Hellenist member of the primitive Jerusalem church. He first appears as one of the seven almoners or deacons appointed to supervise the daily distribution of charity to the widows and other poor members of the church and to ensure that there was no unfairness in the allocation between the Hellenists and Hebrews among the recipients. All seven of the almoners seem to have been Hellenists (Acts 6:1-6).

Following the view of Abram Spiro, W. F. Albright and C. S. Mann argue that Stephen was a Samaritan who based his arguments on the Samaritan Pentateuch (J. Munck, *The Acts of the Apostles,* Anchor Bible, 1967, Appendix V, pp. 285-300). W. Harold Mare, however, effectively refutes this view by showing that peculiarities in the Acts 7 quotations favor the LXX text ("Acts 7: Jewish or Samaritan in Character?" WTJ, XXXIV [1971], 1-21).

It was not as an almoner, however, that Stephen made his mark in early church history, but as an uncompromising apologist for the Christian way. He evidently appreciated more clearly than many—including even the apostles—how decisive a breach with Jewish tradition and the temple cult was involved in the new faith introduced by Jesus. He voiced his convictions in a manner that stirred up keen opposition among the Hellenistic Jews in Jerusalem. A debate was held in a synagogue which was attended by many Jews from the western provinces (probably including Saul of Tarsus). Stephen's arguments about the temporary character of the temple worship and the supersession of the ancient customs by Jesus, the second Moses (Deut 18:15 ff.), proved difficult to confute—largely, no doubt, because of his facility in quoting OT prophets in his support.

The synagogue authorities therefore laid information against him before the Sanhedrin. The accusation was twofold: (1) he had committed blasphemy against God by saying that Jesus of Nazareth would destroy the temple (note the close similarity between this charge and that brought against Jesus in Mk 14:58); (2) he had committed blasphemy against Moses by saying that Jesus would change the customs delivered to them by Moses. (That blasphemy against the lawgiver was regarded as a capital offense in some Jewish circles is evident from the account of the Essenes in Jos *Wars* ii.8.9.)

Brought before the Sanhedrin on this serious charge, Stephen was invited to reply. His answer (Acts 7:2-53) was by no means a forensic defense aimed at procuring an acquittal, but a reasoned defense of his teaching. It takes the form of an historical retrospect of God's dealings with His people Israel. Its two dominant themes are: (1) God has never restricted His presence to one place only, and to think of Him as doing so makes His people static in their religious ideas and practices, whereas His call to them is to strike camp and go out at His bidding, like Abraham, not knowing where that bidding may lead; (2) the people of Israel have always rebelled against God and persecuted His messengers, and their recent rejection of Christ is consistent with their fathers' treatment of those who foretold His coming.

The speech concentrates on three phases of Israelite history: the Patriarchal Age, Moses and the wilderness wanderings, the tabernacle and the temple.

1. In the Patriarchal Age God revealed Himself to Abraham in Mesopotamia, and was

with Joseph in Egypt. The patriarchs were pilgrims, possessing not a square foot of land, always on the move at the call of God, yet never deprived of His presence. Even in the Patriarchal Age, however, opposition to God's appointed man was evident in Joseph's persecution by his brothers; but Joseph was ultimately vindicated in their sight (Acts 7:2-16).

2. Moses too was rejected by his people when he attempted to protect them, but he also was vindicated. He received a revelation from God—not in the Holy Land but in the wilderness of Sinai—and returned to Egypt to deliver his people from bondage. Even then he was repudiated by them, although he was God's prophet and lawgiver to them, a predecessor in this respect of Christ Himself. Their rejection of Moses was therefore a rejection of God, as their worship of the golden calf foreshadowed their subsequent idolatrous course (vv. 17-43).

3. The mobile tent shrine of wilderness days was a more suitable sanctuary for a pilgrim people than the more permanent structure built by Solomon. A fixed temple like Solomon's tempted them to imagine that God was always at their disposal in that place. But now He was calling them to leave the supposed security of their traditional cult and go forth where He might lead (vv. 44-50).

The charges of blasphemy came fittingly indeed from the descendants of those who blasphemed God by worshiping idols and blasphemed Moses by repudiating his divinely appointed leadership! These descendants, moreover, had but lately shown themselves to be of the same mind as their ancestors by their rejection of Christ. The whole speech is a magnificent sample of early Hellenistic Christian apologetic.

Stephen suffered the blasphemer's penalty of death by stoning, but in death he was vindicated by his vision of the glorified Son of Man. His death was not in vain: it was followed quickly by the Gentile mission, led by like-minded Hellenistic Christians. His teaching continued to bear fruit; echoes of it were heard in the next generation in the Epistle to the Hebrews.

Bibliography. F. F. Bruce, *The Book of the Acts,* Grand Rapids: Eerdmans, 1954, pp. 127 ff. W. L. Knox, *The Acts of the Apostles,* Cambridge: University Press, 1948, pp. 23 ff., 71 ff. W. Manson, *The Epistle to the Hebrews,* London: Hodder, 1951, pp. 25 ff. M. Simon, *St. Stephen and the Hellenists in the Primitive Church,* London: Longmans, 1958.

F. F. B.

STEWARD. *See* Occupations: Steward.

STIFFNECKED. The term stiffnecked (Heb. *q^e^shēh 'ōreph;* Gr. *sklerotrachēlos* is applied in the OT and NT only to the nation Israel. It is derived apparently from the idea of a rebellious and stubborn ox which refused to receive the yoke. When used metaphorically, the expression conveys the idea of stubbornness or obstinacy along with arrogance, and is associated with unbelief in God and rejection of His revealed will.

God Himself first employed this denunciatory term (Ex 32:9; 33:3, 5). Moses then used it of Israel in prayer (Ex 34:9), afterward directly in addressing the nation (Deut 9:6; cf. 9:13; 10:16; 31:27). Hezekiah employed this figure in II Chr 30:8, and the concept appears also in II Chr 36:13; Prov 29:1; and Jer 17:23. Stephen in Acts 7:51 calls his generation stiffnecked for their stubborn unbelief. For a similar expression *see* Hardness of Heart.

STOA. A long open rectangular structure, with one or two rows of columns in front, and backed by either a solid wall or a row of small rooms used as shops or offices. While they could be built anywhere, these characteristically Gr. porticoes commonly stood along the sides of a marketplace (*agora*) where they provided convenient places for conversation and the conduct of business, protected from rain and the hot Mediterranean sun.

Probably the most magnificent stoa available

Stoa of Attalos in the Athenian Agora. Spyros Meletzis

to a tourist today is the rebuilt stoa of Attalos along the E side of the Athenian agora. Built in the 2nd cen. B.C., it was still in a good state of repair when Paul ministered in Athens. Two stories in height, it is 385 feet long. Paul would also have known the great S stoa at the agora of Corinth; 539 feet long, it was probably the largest secular structure in mainland Greece and presumably was the "shambles" (KJV) or "meat-market" (NEB) of I Cor 10:25. These are only two examples of the scores of stoas to be found all over the Greco-Roman world. The school or lecture hall of Tyrannus may have been in a rented room of such a stoa in Ephesus (Acts 19:9).

H. F. V.

STOCK. This term has several meanings.

1. The base of a tree (Isa 40:24; Job 14:8).
2. A family genealogy (Lev 25:47; Phil 3:5).
3. An instrument for punishment in prison comparable to shackles (Job 13:27; *see* Stocks).

STOCKS. A device used for detention and torture. The usual form was that of a wooden framework in which the legs, and sometimes the wrists and neck, were fastened. In Job 13:27; 33:11 the feet only were placed in the stocks (Heb. *sad*). The word translated "stocks" in Prov 7:22, KJV, is *'ekes,* probably a type of ankle fetters. Jeremiah was placed in the stocks (Jer 20:2-3). Here the word is *mahpeketh,* which refers to a twisting and thus probably to an instrument which twisted the body into a painful position (cf. II Chr 16:10, RSV). Others suggest that the word speaks of a cramped room of a prison (M. Greenberg, "Stocks," IDB, IV, 443). In Jer 29:26 the KJV renders the word as "prison" and translates *ṣînōq* as "stocks." The latter was probably an instrument for fastening the neck. In Philippi the feet of Paul and Silas were placed in stocks (Gr. *xylon,* Acts 16:24).

D. W. B.

STOICS (stō'iks). Philosophers who, with Epicureans, confronted Paul at Athens (Acts 17:18 f.). The poets cited by Paul (Acts 17:28) were the Stoics Aratus (*Phaenomena*) and Cleanthes (*Hymn to Zeus*). Begun as a Gr. school of philosophy by Zeno of Citium *c.* 336-260 B.C., it was embraced by many Romans, including Seneca, tutor to Nero, and the emperor Marcus Aurelius. Other great Stoics were Chrysippus, Epictetus, Cornutus, and Musonius Rufus.

The name was derived from *stoa* (porch) at Athens where Zeno lectured. The most influential philosophy of the Hellenistic period, it embraced elements of the Socratic, Aristotelian, and Cynic schools. Essentially it was a rational pantheism though with rare approximations to monotheism. In Stoicism God was not a personal Being but a spiritual force or soul-power immanent in men and things. He was given many names—Logos or Reason, Nature, Providence, divine Spirit, *et al.* His substance was the whole world and the heavens. An elaborate pantheon was developed to agree with God's total immanence. The highest good was to follow reason or virtue, suppress the emotions, and conduct oneself according to what nature wills. In the end there was reabsorption into the world Soul, but no individual immortality. The greatness of Stoicism was found in its high ethical concepts and doctrine of human brotherhood.

R. L. J.

STOMACHER. The KJV term for the decorative covering worn on the upper front part of the body. The RSV calls it a "rich robe" (Isa 3:24).

An ancient stone cup for watering sheep and goats at the well of Abraham in the Plains of Mamre. HFV

STONE. The chief biblical words are Heb. *'eben* and Gr. *lithos.* For the various kinds of stone, *see* Minerals and Metals.

Stones had a great variety of uses throughout the ancient Near East. In its natural state, or only slightly shaped, a stone could serve as a pillow (Gen 28:18) or a seat (Ex 17:12), for covering the mouth of a well (Gen 29:2), or for closing the entrance of a cave (Josh 10:18) or of tombs (Jn 11:38; Mt 27:60, 66; 28:2), although 1st cen. A.D. tombs in the vicinity of Jerusalem had cut stones that rolled on a track hewn out of the rock. Small stones made convenient missiles to use in slings (I Sam 17:40, 49) or when stoning a criminal (Josh 7:25; *see* Crime and Punishment; Punishment). Larger stones were hurled at cities by means of catapult machines (II Chr 26:15; I Macc 6:51).

Stone vessels found in Egypt (cf. Ex 7:19) are often of superb craftsmanship. Waterpots (Jn 2:6) and troughs hollowed out of stone were used, as well as hand mills to grind grain (Deut 24:6). Cutting blades were fashioned from flint (Josh 5:2; *see* Knife), sickles being made by inserting several flints along the length of a stick.

A farmer preparing new land for cultivation had first to clear it of stones (Isa 5:2). With these he could build walls for a sheepfold or vineyard (Prov 24:30–31; Isa 5:5).

Stones were gathered to make cairns for memorials or markers (Gen 31:46–52; Josh 4:9, 20; 7:26). Usually, however, a single stone, whether carved or natural, was set up as a boundary marker (Deut 19:14; 27:17; Josh 15:6), similar in function to the Babylonian *Kudurru* stone (ANEP #518–521); as a guidepost along a highway (Jer 31:21); or as a plain (I Sam 7:12; *see* Ebenezer) or inscribed monument (Deut 27:2–4; *see* Moabite Stone; Stele; Writing). In many parts of Palestine have been found dolmens (*q.v.*) made of large slabs of stone, dating evidently to pre-Abrahamic times.

Pillars or standing stones (Heb. *maṣṣēbôt*; *see* Pillar) often had specifically religious associations (Gen 28:18–22; 35:14; Ex 24:4; Isa 19:19). Many such Canaanite pillars have been found in excavations, some broken as at Shechem, perhaps by Israelite reformers (cf. Deut 12:3; Ex 23:24, NASB). The heathen worshiped idols of stone (Isa 37:19; Acts 17:29). Meteorites were especially venerated as having come from heaven (*see* Gods, False: Artemis). The Israelites built altars of uncut stone and without steps to obviate heathen practices (Ex 20:25–26; I Kgs 18:31–32).

Stones of various sizes, often inscribed, were used as weights on balance scales (Lev 19:36; Prov 11:1; 16:11, where "weight[s]" = Heb. *'eben*). *See* Weights, Measures, and Coins. Semiprecious stones were commonly used in jewelry (*see* Jewels) and as seals (*q.v.*).

Above all, stone was employed in building. Masonry and stonecutting were regular trades (II Sam 5:11; II Kgs 12:12; I Chr 22:2; *see* Occupations: Mason). Houses (Lev 14:40–45; Hab 2:11), city walls (II Chr 16:6; Neh 4:3), and especially the temple (I Kgs 5:17–18; 6:7; 7:9–12; II Kgs 22:6; Mk 13:1–2) were con-

Assyrian kings frequently erected great human-headed stone bulls (30–40 tons in weight) at the entrances to their palaces. This one is from the palace of Sargon II at Khorsabad. ORINST

Cultic standing stones from a temple at Hazor. IIS

structed of stone (*see* Architecture). Public buildings had foundations laid with cut stones (I Kgs 5:17; 7:10; Rev 21:14, 19), a cornerstone (*q.v.*; Ps 118:22), a headstone (*q.v.*) or finial or coping stone which completes a building (Zech 4:7), and in some cases a stone pavement (II Kgs 16:17; Jn 19:13; *see* Gabbatha).

In the NT Christians are pictured as living stones who are being built up in union with Christ, the precious cornerstone, to form a spiritual "house" or temple, so that they as priests may offer up spiritual sacrifices to God (I Pet 2:4–6; cf. Eph 2:19–22; I Cor 3:9*b*–16).

See Rock.

J. R.

STONECUTTER. *See* Occupations: Mason, Stonecutter.

STONING. *See* Punishment.

STOOL. In older English usage the term stool was used for various types of seats or chairs. The Heb. word translated "stool" or "chair" (RSV) in II Kgs 4:10 is used for a seat (I Sam 1:9) and is most often translated "throne" (*q.v.*).

The Heb. word *'obnayim* in Ex 1:16 means literally "two stones" and refers to the birth stool, two stones or blocks of wood upon which women in ancient times sat or stooped when giving birth.

STORAX. *See* Plants: Stacte, Storax.

STORE CITY. Cities where great deposits were located of goods, arms, treasures, or food for distribution or safekeeping (Ex 1:11, RSV; I Kgs 9:19; II Chr 8:4, 6; 16:4; 17:12; 32:28).

Pithom (*q.v.*) and Rameses (*q.v.*) are two examples of Egyptian store cities or "treasure cities" (KJV). In Palestine government or royal storehouses have been excavated at such sites as Ezion-geber, Hazor, and Beer-sheba. At Megiddo a large silo pit for grain storage was found belonging to the time of the Israelite monarchy, in addition to other administrative buildings. *See* City, Treasure; Storehouse.

STOREHOUSE. Heb. *(bêt)hâ'ôsār,* "house of the treasure," was a government or temple warehouse serving as a treasury or magazine for all kinds of products (I Kgs 7:51; 15:18; I Chr 27:25; Neh 10:38; 13:12–13; Joel 1:17; Mal 3:10).

The *'ăsāmîm* probably were underground silos or storage pits for grain, found so frequently in excavated Palestinian cities (Deut 28:8; Prov 3:10, "barn"). While different Heb. terms, the "storehouses" (RSV, "granaries") of Jer 50:26, and the "garners" of Joel 1:17, and "barns" of Hag 2:19 were also most likely storage pits. The "garner" or "barn" (Gr. *apothēkē*) of Mt 3:12; 6:26; 13:30; Lk 12:18, 24 was either a building or a pit, and the term is used in other Gr. literature of a cellar for oil and wine. In Lk 12:24 the "storehouse" (Gr. *tameion*) is more correctly a storeroom (NASB; cf. its translation as "closet" in v. 3). For photo of a larger storage pit at Megiddo from *c.* 700 B.C., holding up to 12,800 bushels, see ANEP #743.

The Egyptians were well known for their storehouses of jewels, gold, preserved fruits, grain, liquors, etc. The Israelites before the Exodus worked as slave laborers on Pharaoh's store cities of Pithom and Rameses (Ex 1:11; *see* Store City). King David built warehouses extensively in Israel (I Chr 27:25), as did Solomon (I Kgs 9:19; II Chr 8:4–6). Also Baasha of Israel (I Chr 16:4), Jehoshaphat (II Chr 17:12–13), and Hezekiah of Judah (II Chr 32:27–29) are mentioned as builders of storehouses.

Mal 3:10 refers to the storehouse as a repository for the tithe; it was probably located in the temple area (cf. Lk 21:1) and supervised by the Levites (cf. I Chr 9:26, 29).

See Agriculture; City, Treasure; Garner; Treasure.

D. W. D.

STORK. *See* Animals, III. 48.

STRAIGHT STREET. A term (Gr. *eutheia*) used to name one of the main streets traversing Damascus (Acts 9:11). The traditional street called "Straight" is *c.* two miles long crossing the city from NE to SW, beginning at the present East Gate of the old walled city that dates from Roman times (*see* Damascus). Today the street is named *Sultaniyeh,* and the "Long Bazaar" (Sûq et-Tawîleh) occupies a considerable portion of its length. Excavations indicate that it was once a beautiful avenue flanked by colonnades.

STRAIN. The Gr. word *diulízō,* meaning "strain," is used by Jesus in Mt 23:24 in speaking of the Pharisees, who "strained at a gnat and swallowed a camel." It means to filter through or strain thoroughly. The idea is that a small gnat will be strained or filtered out before the wine is used. *See* Animals, III. 16.

STRANGE VINE. *See* Plants.

STRANGER. This OT term is most commonly a translation of Heb. *gēr,* usually rendered "sojourner" in the ASV and RSV, and frequently has the meaning of foreigner (*q.v.*). There was a substantial number of foreigners among the Israelites when they left Egypt (Ex 12:38; Num 11:4), and this number was augmented by such groups as the Gibeonites (Josh 9).

The *gēr* had no inherited rights with respect to his new land. However, strangers or resident aliens in Israel were to receive hospitality, the inviolate right of a guest lodging in one's tent or house (Job 31:32), in part because the Israelites themselves had been strangers in the land of Egypt (Ex 23:9; Lev 19:33 f.). In fact, they were classed with widows and orphans as needing special consideration (e.g., Ex 22:21–24; Deut 10:18; 14:29; Jer 22:3). People migrated to sojourn in another land to escape famine (Gen 12:10; 47:4; Ruth 1:1) and personal enemies (Ex 2:21–22), as well as for religious reasons (II Chr 15:9).

Strangers within Israel had numerous responsibilities. For instance, they had to rest on the sabbath (Ex 20:10; 23:12); to observe the Day of Atonement (Lev 16:29); and to avoid the use of leaven on the Feast of Unleavened Bread (Ex 12:19). In addition, they were permitted to attend the three great Heb. feasts (Deut 16:11 ff.).

The law permitted some marriage unions between Israelites and foreigners, and this seems to have been quite common during the period of the monarchy. During the restoration, however, Ezra and Nehemiah carried on a vigorous campaign against the practice (Ezr 10; Neh 13:23–31).

Some foreigners could obtain full citizenship in Israel if they submitted to circumcision and agreed to keep the law (Ex 12:48; Num 15:14–16). There were restrictions, however, on the achievement of citizenship by Edomites and Egyptians (Deut 23:7–8). By NT times the naturalized alien, who became a member of the covenant nation by circumcision and adopting the Mosaic code, was considered a convert or proselyte (*q.v.*) to Judaism.

Of the three other Heb. words translated "sojourner," "stranger" or "foreigner," *tôshāb* seems to be roughly synonymous with *gēr*; *nokrî* is definitely a foreigner and outside Heb. religious society; *zār* must be understood from the context as referring to complete strangers to Israel (often hostile enemies) or a non-member of some defined family (e.g., Deut 25:5).

The Israelite was considered to be a stranger and sojourner with the Lord in the land of Canaan which belonged to Him (Lev 25:23; I Chr 29:15), a "passing guest" of His (Ps 39:12, RSV). In like manner the Christian believer is a stranger and pilgrim or alien in the earth (I Pet 2:11; cf. 1:17; Heb 11:9, 13; Ps 119:19), for his true citizenship is in heaven (Eph 2:19; Phil 3:20, NASB).

H. F. V.

STRANGLE. The means of killing by choking

or cutting off the breath. Jewish law prohibited strangling of animals for sacrifice or food, because they would thereby eat of the blood of the animal yet in the body (Lev 17:12). The influence of the precept was carried over into the early Christian church and the Jerusalem council listed a prohibition against food that was strangled (Acts 15:20).

STRAW. The mixture of chopped straw and chaff that was left after the grain was threshed out. This was used as fodder for the cattle when mixed with grain (Gen 24:25; Jud 19:19; I Kgs 4:28; Isa 11:7). The ancients harvested their grain by cutting the stalk close to the head, so that "straw" would not have the great bulk of dried stalk that the modern term implies.

In Egypt straw was mixed with clay to give strength to the bricks (*q.v.*). When the Israelites were no longer given straw, they had to go out into the fields and gather "stubble," the stalks still left in the fields after harvesting (Ex 5). *See* Plants: Straw.

STREAM OF EGYPT. *See* River of Egypt.

STRIKER. A contentious person always looking for a fight, a bully. It is one of the characteristics no bishop should possess (I Tim 3:3; Tit 1:7). The word is also translated "violent" (RSV) and "pugnacious" (Goodspeed).

STRINGED INSTRUMENTS. *See* Music.

STRIPES. *See* Punishment.

STRONG DRINK. *See* Drink, Strong.

STUBBLE. *See* Plants.

STUMBLING BLOCK. The Heb. noun *mikshôl* designates that against or over which someone stumbles (Lev 19:14). Several different stumbling blocks are mentioned metaphorically in Scripture.

1. Christ was a stumbling block to unbelieving Israel. This had been foretold in the OT (Isa 8:14; Rom 9:32–33; 11:9), and was fulfilled in Christ's death on the cross (I Cor 1:23; I Pet 2:8). It was a stumbling block to Israel that they could not be saved by their own good works, but must be saved by the righteousness of another (Rom 9:32–33; 10:3–4).

2. The Christian can become a stumbling block (Gr. *proskommatos*, an obstacle or occasion causing stumbling by striking the foot against it) to a weaker brother when he insists upon exercising all his freedom regardless of another person's conscience. The idol a man formerly worshiped may be nothing, and the dance before that idol or the offering given it may really mean nothing to the redeemed person; but his using the food or taking part in the ritual taken from paganism can be a real cause of stumbling to a person recently converted from his paganism (Rom 14:13; I Cor 8:9).

3. Believers can tempt others to sin. Christ called Peter a cause of offense, a *skandalon* ("trap, snare"), when Peter urged Him not to die (Mt 16:23). Balaam, a heathen prophet used at one time by God, later showed Balak how to cause Israel to stumble (Rev 2:14; Num 31:15–16). The sins of professing believers can be a stumbling block to others, as Israel's iniquity was (Ezk 7:19; 14:3–4).

R. A. K.

STUMP. Used only in Dan 4:15, 23, 26 to describe figuratively the king's seven-year mental breakdown.

STYLUS. An instrument used for writing, simply pointed for writing on a wax tablet such as the Assyrians and Romans used (Isa 8:1, NASB marg.), or with a triangular end for making cuneiform impressions on a clay tablet. An iron stylus was an engraving tool used for cutting letters on stone (Job 19:24; Jer 17:1, both NASB). *See* Writing.

SUAH (sū'ȧ). The name means "riches" or "distinction," and refers to one of the descendants of Asher (I Chr 7:36).

SUBSTANCE. This is the KJV translation of several Heb. and Gr. words which generally refer to material goods or possessions. In Job 30:22 it apparently designates the human body. The translation of Gr. *hypostasis* in Heb 11:1 presents a special problem, however. In what sense can faith be called "the substance of things hoped for"? The difficulty of interpretation there seems beautifully solved by the papyri which points to a translation, "Faith is the title deed [a legal term] of things hoped for." Thus faith is the substantiation or assurance of things hoped for, the making real of God's promises in one's own experience.

SUBSTITUTION. *See* Atonement; Reconciliation; Salvation.

SUBURBS. This word in the KJV ordinarily has reference to the open area around the city which was used as a common grazing ground for cattle. ASV and RSV translate it "pasture lands" (Num 35:2–7; Josh 21). *See* City.

In II Kgs 23:11 the word *parwār* is translated "suburb" and seems to mean the porticoes and small chambers that border the temple courts. The RSV and NASB translate the word "precincts" here. In I Chr 26:18 the KJV and NASB simply transliterate it as a proper noun, "Parbar"; the RSV has "the parbar" and says in a footnote that the meaning of the word is unknown. *See* Temple.

SUCCOTH (sŭk'ŏth). As a common noun it is the plural of Heb. *sukkâ*, "thicket, booth," and is frequently used of temporary shelters for man or beast. It appears in the name of the harvest festival, Feast of Booths (Tabernacles), which also commemorated the wilderness wanderings of the Exodus, during which the Israelites lived in such structures (see Lev 23:33 ff., esp. vv. 42–43; Deut 16:13 ff.).

1. Succoth is mentioned as a site in Transjordan. In Gen 33:17 the origin of the name is explained from Jacob's building shelters for his cattle while returning to Canaan from Aram Naharaim.

In the tribal division the city of Succoth was allotted to the tribe of Gad (Josh 13:27). During the period of the judges this city was severely punished by Gideon because the people refused to aid him in his pursuit of the defeated Midianites (Jud 8:5–7, 13–16). At the time of the construction of the Solomonic temple, the bronze decorations and service utensils were cast "in the plain of Jordan . . . in the clay ground between Succoth and Zarthan" (I Kgs 7:46; II Chr 4:17). The term "valley of Succoth" is used in Ps 60:6 and 108:7.

The Transjordanian Succoth usually is identified as Tell Deir 'Allā, one mile N of the Jabbok River (Nahr ez-Zerqa), and certainly must be in this locality. Tell Deir 'Allā is the largest and most prominent mound in the Succoth valley. Excavations at the site by H. J. Franken, 1960–64, revealed no fortified city but mainly a Late Bronze Age sanctuary surrounded by dwellings and storehouses.

Bibliography. H. J. Franken, "The Excavations at Deir 'Allā in Jordan," VT, X (1960), 386–393; VT, XI (1961), 361–372; VT, XII (1962), 378–382; VT, XIV (1964), 377–379, 417–422; *Excavations at Tell Deir 'Allā I: A Stratigraphical and Analytical Study of the Early Iron Age Pottery*, Leiden: Brill, 1969.

2. Succoth is named as the first stop in the itinerary of the Exodus. Its location must be in the NE part of the Egyptian delta (Ex 12:37; 13:20; Num 33:5–6), a short distance from the city of Rameses. Tell el-Maskhutah in the Wadi Tumeilat has been proposed as the site. J. Simons holds that the name Succoth indicates only a temporary camp and that it is therefore not to be identified with a permanent settlement in this area (*Geographical and Topographical Texts of the OT*, pp. 246–247). *See* Exodus, The: Route.

C. E. D.

SUCCOTH-BENOTH. *See* Gods, False.

SUCHATHITE (sū'kă-thīt). One of three families dwelling at Jabez, descendants of Caleb (I Chr 2:55).

SUFFERING

The Fact of Suffering

In the Bible both man and the whole physical creation are spoken of as suffering. Man suffers from physical calamities resulting from the curse, such as storms, droughts, heat, cold, wars, famines, diseases, etc., as well as from the effects of his own individual sin.

Creation suffers, Paul tells us, from the curse which God placed on the world because of man's sin (Gen 3:14–19). He says it "groaneth and travaileth in pain together until now," waiting for "the manifestation of the sons of God," and "the adoption, to wit, the redemption of our body" (Rom 8:19 ff.). This will happen when the saints receive their resurrection bodies at Christ's coming for His own at the rapture (Rom 8:18–23; I Thess 4:14–18; I Cor 15:20–55). Isaiah prophesied what this would mean to nature, particularly to the animals (Isa 11:6–9; 65:25).

Causes of Suffering

Sin. Sin has brought untold suffering to mankind as well as to the whole of creation. When man fell his whole nature became totally corrupt, and this led to those sufferings which beset man as a result of his fallen nature (Rom 7:15 ff.). Besides this, individual sins lead to personal guilt complexes (Pss 32; 51) and the excruciating pangs of remorse revealed in several of the psalms (28; 32; 77), where David writes of his anguish and repentance. Many are overcome with fear because of their unforgiven sins, and this may lead to very serious consequences in the health of the individual in the form of psychosomatic illnesses, that is, physical ailments brought on by mental and emotional difficulties.

The curse. It was placed upon the earth by God because of man's sin. All that God had made was good, as proved by the fact that He reviewed His work six times and each time found it to be good (Gen 1:4, 10, 12, 18, 21, 25), and then placed man on the earth and found it all to be "very good" (Gen 1:31). The fall brought sickness, corruption, and death. It even led to disorders within the animal kingdom, which await removal at the second coming of Christ (Isa 11:6-9; 65:25; Rom 8:18–23). Toil and drudgery in his work are consequences of the curse for man in his labors to feed and clothe himself (Gen 3:18–19).

Diseases. One of the things to be removed when man receives his full redemption is the suffering from disease. This will occur first for those who receive their resurrection bodies at the rapture, as revealed in II Cor 4:16–5:4; Phil 3:20–21; Rom 8:18, 23; it will be the portion of all the redeemed in the new heavens and the new earth (Rev 22:2; cf. Ezk 47:12). *See* Diseases; Resurrection.

God's Purpose in Ordaining Suffering

Suffering borne by creation. According to Rom 8:18–23, God subjected nature to the curse and to the suffering brought on by the curse, "in hope," that is, as a means toward a real goal that would be attained first in the Millennium and then in the new heavens and the new earth.

God's direct purpose for man. Suffering can

be a warning that man is disregarding the laws set up by God. Whatever a man sows, that he also reaps (Gal 6:7-9). At the same time man may set himself up in rebellious defiance of the laws, as Israel did so often (Heb 3:7-15). Suffering can be the result of God's punishment of man's sin. David suffered much as he experienced God's punishment for his sins of adultery and murder, after he took Uriah the Hittite's wife and had him slain (II Sam 12:7-12). Israel suffered along with its king as God punished David for disobeying Him in numbering the people (II Sam 24:1-17; I Chr 21:8-17).

Chastisement. This is part of the training of a child and particularly of a child of God. All believers whom God loves suffer chastening and discipline (Heb 12:5-11; cf. I Cor 11:31-32; I Pet 4:16-17). *See* Chastisement.

To develop character. Paul says "Tribulation worketh patience; and patience, experience; and experience, hope; and hope maketh not ashamed; because the love of God is shed abroad in our hearts by the Holy Ghost which is given unto us" (Rom 5:3-5). Thus suffering is sent to the believer for the development of his character. Too often we think only of what we can do for the Lord as soul winners and servants, and forget what He must do in us to develop our characters. Suffering is used by God, then, to develop faith, meekness, patience, etc. God has great eternal tasks for His redeemed, but the believer can enter into these only insofar as he is sufficiently matured in character through chastisements and sufferings (Job 23:10; Jas 1:2-12).

The eternal value of suffering. Each Christian's sufferings form a part of the sufferings of Christ (Phil 3:10; Col 1:24; I Pet 4:13), for each one is a part of His Body, the Church, and the Church is appointed to much suffering. This suffering is not of a sacrificial, propitiatory character as if the cross were insufficient, but rather of a purifying, refining nature (I Pet 1:7; 4:1; 5:10). The sufferings of Christ and of the Christian not only bring present glory to God (I Pet 1:7) but also eternal glory (I Pet 1:11; Rom 8:17-18). The patient suffering of grief wrongfully inflicted is well pleasing to God (I Pet 2:19-20).

The Mystery of Suffering

Though the causes and purpose of suffering have been seen, yet there is a mystery to suffering. The sufferings to which the individual Christian is subjected are a mystery to him in that he cannot see why he should be chosen to suffer more than, or differently from, others. Sometimes he cannot see the imperfections which God is endeavoring to correct. At other times he cannot see the goal God is trying to accomplish in his life. No one knows the specific task for which God would prepare him to the fulfilling of His own glory.

The experience of Job is the classic example. His friends tried to rationalize his sufferings and to place the blame for them upon Job, but this was not the answer. Finally Job saw the hand of God through it all in an exposure of his own sinfulness and weakness (Job 40:4), and bowed to God's superior authority and wisdom, even as Paul in Rom 11:33, "O the depth of the riches both of the wisdom and knowledge of God! how unsearchable are his judgments, and his ways past finding out!" Faith was the answer in Job's case as it was in Abraham's and Paul's. As God revealed Himself to Job, Job's faith grew till he cried, "Though he slay me, yet will I trust in him" (Job 13:15-16). In like manner, after years of suffering Joseph could say to his brethren, "God meant it unto good" (Gen 50:20). *See* Job.

Christ's Sufferings

In order to be a sacrifice sufficient to satisfy divine justice, Christ had to keep the law of God perfectly in His life; to be "tempted like as we are, yet without sin" (Heb 4:15); to suffer all sorts of testings, opposition, and rejection; and finally to endure cruel scourging, buffeting, and scorn in His trials before Caiaphas, Pontius Pilate, and Herod. Then He had to die the most painful type of death as He hung nailed to a wooden cross, His body racked by pain, His mouth by thirst, His soul by taunts and sneers. Yet there was a purpose in all this, for on that cross He bore the penalty of the law which men had broken, and bore their sins in His own body. As a result, Paul could write, "For he hath made him to be sin for us, who knew no sin; that we might be made the righteousness of God in him" (II Cor 5:21). *See* Christ, Passion of; Cross.

Cross Bearing

This refers to that particular individual suffering which Christ expects each believer to bear, as he dies to himself and his own wishes and desires in order to live as God wants him to live. Jesus said, "If any man will come after me, let him deny himself, and take up his cross daily, and follow me" (Lk 9:23; cf. Mt 16:24). This is to be done daily; i.e., as often as the temptation to succumb to self comes to mind. The believer is to deny his "flesh" or selfish old nature, and is to walk the path which Christ directs him to take with its particular suffering, which forms that particular cross.

See Affliction; Agony; Grief; Sorrow; Tribulation.

Bibliography. William Goulooze, *Victory Over Suffering,* Grand Rapids: Baker, 1949; *Blessings of Suffering,* Baker, 1951. Hugh Evan Hopkins, *The Mystery of Suffering,* Chicago: Inter-Varsity, 1959. C. S. Lewis, *The Problem of Pain,* New York: Macmillan, 1947. W. Michaelis, "*Paschō,* etc.," TDNT, V, 904-939. Roy Yates, "A Note on Colossians 1:24," EQ, XLII (1970), 88-92. L. Paul Trudinger, "A Further Brief Note on Colossians 1:24," EQ, XLV (1973), 36-38. Rolf L. Veenstra, *The Secret of Suffering,* Grand Rapids: Eerdmans, 1948.

R. A. K.

SUICIDE. The act of killing oneself voluntarily and intentionally. While there is no specific law recorded in the Bible against suicide, nevertheless such prohibition is to be regarded as an expansion and extension of the commandment, "Thou shalt not kill" (Ex 20:13). The manner in which Christ develops the application of several commandments in Mt 5 warrants this view.

Though suicide was regarded as a noble act in a time of adversity by many of the pagans, by the Romans, and some of the Greek philosophers (even Socrates administered his own death by willingly taking the potion of hemlock), both the Israelites and the early Christians regarded the taking of one's own life as entirely wrong.

There are two notable instances of suicide in the Bible: Saul (I Sam 31:4) and Judas (Mt 27:5; Acts 1:16–20), and in both cases they were driven to their act of self-destruction by the remorse of the damned. The modern rise in suicides has made this an acute problem for today.

R. A. K.

SUKKIIM (sŭk'ĭ-ĭm). A tribe which with the Libyans and the Cushites joined in an attack in 926 B.C. against Judah led by the Egyptian Pharaoh Shishak (II Chr 12:3). They were probably a people known from Egyptian texts of the 13th and 12th cen. B.C. as Tjuku or Tjukten, who served as scouts or light-armed auxiliaries, perhaps of Libyan origin (K. A. Kitchen, *Ancient Orient and Old Testament,* Chicago: Inter-Varsity, 1966, p. 159). Others believe that the *Sky'* mentioned in a 5th cen. B.C. Aramaic papyrus from Elephantine (*q.v.*) may be identified with the Sukkiim.

That the LXX renders the term Troglodytes is possibly because a place called Suche is named among the possessions of the Troglodytes (Pliny, *Natural History,* vi.172). According to Strabo, the fortress of Suchus is named for a sacred crocodile. Some geographers identify the place with modern Suakin, located in N Africa.

G. A. T.

SULFUR. *See* Minerals and Metals.

SUMER (sōō'mẽr). The earliest known nation of Mesopotamia (*q.v.*). It was situated in the S part of Babylonia (*q.v.*), the S half of modern Iraq. The later kingdom of Akkad lay to the NW. Sumer is mentioned only indirectly in the Bible; Shinar (*q.v.*) in Gen 10:10 apparently includes the area of both Sumer and Akkad. Yet one of the great ancient civilizations is involved in this passing reference. The Sumerians still cannot be classified with certainty, either ethnically or linguistically (Sumerian is an agglutinative rather than an inflected language). But a great deal is known about their history, religion, way of life, etc.

Outline of Sumerian History

The original homeland of the Sumerians is not known, but quite likely it was in mountainous territory somewhere beyond Iran. They seem to have arrived at the head of the Persian Gulf and began to dominate the earlier settlers at the close of the Ubaid period.

1. *Protoliterate Period (3300–2800* B.C.*).* All dates are approximate. In the system adopted here, the period before 3500 B.C. is the Ubaid (or Obeid), that of 3500–3300 B.C. is the Warka, and that of 3300–2800 B.C. is the Protoliterate. The period of 3300 B.C. marks the introduction of writing, hence "Protoliterate." *See* Writing.

This was a period of tremendous advances. Already in this phase most of the pertinent, distinctive elements of later Mesopotamian civilization may be observed. It includes the late Uruk (Erech in Gen 10:10 and modern Warka) and Jemdet Nasr cultures. The greatest achievement was the appearance of writing in the form of pictograms (i.e., picture writing), an early form of Sumerian. Present also are lists of signs (syllabaries). Later, the Semitic Akkadians added to these lists equivalent words in their own speech.

2. *Early Dynastic Period (2800–2360* B.C.*).* Also called the Classical Sumerian Age, this period is subdivided archaeologically according to building levels and cylinder seals into Early Dynastic I, II, and III (ED III = Ur I). Sources for the study of this period include the Sumerian King List (supplemented by Berossus, a Babylonian priest of the 3rd cen. B.C.), cylinder seals, pottery, and the Vulture Stele of Eannatum. The King List (ANET, pp. 265 f.) somewhat parallels the biblical antediluvian genealogies in that the life spans of these kings before their "flood" are phenomenal, each recorded as having ruled many thousands of years. Genesis, though not going to the extremes of the Sumerian King List, likewise indicates a remarkable longevity before the Flood.

In 1965 a large number of Sumerian tablets were found at Tell Abu Salabikh, *c.* 12 miles from Nippur. Dated to a period *c.* 2600 B.C., the tablets are difficult to read, but some are literary texts 800 years older than the classical

Gold vases from Ur, *c.* 2500 B.C. BM

period of Sumerian literature. The "Instructions of Shuruppak" and the "Kesh Temple Hymn," known previously from that later period, are now shown to be traditional texts of high antiquity.

Some of the kings of this period were Urnanshe of Lagash, Eannatum, Entemena, and Eannatum II. Finally, the throne was usurped by Urukagina, then by Lugalzaggesi, the *ensi* ("governor") of Umma. The time of the latter's rule is known as the Proto-Imperial Period because he succeeded in establishing the first Sumerian Empire. He conquered Lagash and the other Sumerian towns and made Uruk his capital. But he was soon defeated by Sargon the Great of Akkad (Akkad is the Akkadian form; the Sumerian name was Agade), who began not only a new dynasty but also a new era with Semites in control.

3. *First Dynasty of Akkad (2360–2180 B.C.)*. Sargon's Akkadian name was Sharru(m)-kin, meaning "the king is legitimate." He took the name because he was, as an usurper, not at all legitimate! His period of rule was considered the "Golden Age" of all Babylonian history. Sources for this dynasty include several inscriptions written in Old Akkadian, by Sargon and his successors. Several legends grew up about Sargon. He was succeeded by his son Rimush, who was in turn followed by another son of Sargon, Manishtusu. Then came Naram-Sin, probably a grandson of Sargon. Like Sargon, he was depicted as a hero (on his victory stele, ANEP #309, and in later literary tradition). He was succeeded by Sharkalisharri, who was followed by four short-lived minor kings. This dynasty was eventually swept away by outside powers, among them the Gutians, a people from the Zagros Mountains to the E. Indeed, the last four kings paralleled the following dynasty.

4. *Guti Period (2180–2060 B.C.)*. The fall of Akkad to outside forces, principally the Gutians, lived on in tradition as a great catastrophe, for here were uncivilized, barbarian hordes replacing the civilized dynasty of Akkad. The inscriptions from this period are few and difficult to correlate with the names in the King List. Apparently, however, Lagash and Uruk had their own rulers. Thus the Gutians did not exercise hegemony over the whole country. They were finally defeated and expelled by Utuhegal of Uruk. Under his rule there was an *ensi* of Ur (Sumerian Urim) named Ur-Nammu, who at first recognized Utuhegal's suzerainty but later defeated him. He then made Ur the capital and inaugurated the Third Dynasty of Ur (or the Ur III Period).

5. *Third Dynasty of Ur (2060–1950 B.C.)*. This dynasty had five kings: Ur-Nammu, Shulgi, Amar-Sin, Shu-Sin, and Ibbi-Sin. Apparently, by the middle of the dynasty it became the custom to give children Akkadian names, for the last three names are Akkadian. Ur-Nammu is now well known for his law code (see below) and because he *may* have been a contemporary of Abraham. Beginning with Ur-Nammu, who conquered most of the country, the kings of Ur titled themselves "king of the land of Sumer and Akkad." This was also the period of statism, a state economy run by the king (see below). The most conspicuous achievement of this period was the great buildings, some still standing, such as the ziggurat (i.e., stage tower or high place with a temple or shrine on top) of Ur, built originally by Ur-Nammu. A tremendous number of economic texts from this period have been discovered.

One of the most famous Sumerian rulers was Gudea, *ensi* of Lagash, whose reign (or vice-royalty) probably should be placed near the beginning of the Third Dynasty of Ur. He has left numerous and extensive inscriptions, as well as several portrait statues, all made of a hard black stone called diorite.

The last few years of the reign of Ibbi-Sin witnessed the emergence of another period, so that in his rule he was confined to Ur. Eventually, he lost his kingdom and was carried captive to Susa in Elam. Ur was completely destroyed by the Elamites (who also seem to have been one of the foreign powers responsible for the fall of Akkad before the Gutians took control). In their overthrow of Ur the Elamites were joined by an unknown people called the Sua.

About this same time W Semitic proper names appear. The people bearing them, ac-

Gudea of Lagash. LM

tually Amorites (Sumerian Martu; Akkadian Amurru), must have spoken a Canaanite dialect somewhat akin to Phoenician, Ugaritic, and Hebrew.

6. *Isin-Larsa Period (1950–1700* B.C.*).* At the end of the above struggle Ishbierra emerged as *ensi* of Isin. He drove out the Elamite garrison that had been stationed at Ur and established the Dynasty of Isin. The fifth king of Isin, Lipit-Ishtar, produced a law code (see below). But co-existing with this dynasty in the S was a Dynasty of Larsa. Finally, the last king of Larsa, Rim-Sin, defeated the last king of the Isin Dynasty and united the country. This union was short-lived, however, as Rim-Sin was in turn defeated by Hammurabi, an Amorite (or E Canaanite). The latter was king of the northernmost Babylonian city, Babylon. The Dynasty of Babylon had actually existed a hundred years before Hammurabi, but it was Hammurabi who succeeded in finally unifying all of Babylonia.

Generally speaking, beginning in the 19th cen. B.C. all three major dynasties of this period, Isin, Larsa, and Babylon, belonged to the Old Babylonian Period. (To the NW, Assyria and Mari had their own rulers, too.) With the conquests of Hammurabi (1792–1750; or, 1728–1686) the First Dynasty of Babylon (which had started about 1850) became supreme, and historians refer to the next period as that of the Old Babylonian Kingdom. But this survey stops here, for in the words of Kramer, "With Hammurabi the history of Sumer comes to an end, and the history of Babylonia, a Semitic state built on a Sumerian foundation, begins" (*The Sumerians,* p. 72). John Bright also aptly observes, "In Mesopotamia, by the age of Israel's origins, a whole tide of civilization had flowed and ebbed; Sumerian culture had come into being, run a magnificent course of over fifteen hundred years, and finally played itself out. Israel was born into a world already ancient" (*A History of Israel,* Philadelphia: Westminster Press, 1959, p. 36).

Sumerian Religion

Sources for the study of Sumerian religion include myths, prayers, and votive inscriptions. The Sumerians had a pantheon of "great gods." The three principal male deities were the sky-god An (later called Anu by the Akkadians), whose chief city or cult center was Uruk; the air-god Enlil, whose cult center was Nippur; and the god of the abyss (*abzu*) and of wisdom Enki (Ea in Akkadian), whose main seat of worship was Eridu. The god An appears as the overlord of the pantheon in the earliest periods. Later, Enlil was the prime god. Then, under Hammurabi during the Old Babylonian Period, Marduk was elevated to the position of chief god of the pantheon.

One of the great female deities was Nintu(d) (*nin,* "lady"; *tud,* "birth"; hence, "lady of birth," i.e., the mother goddess). Her main cult center was Dilmun (according to some, the island of Bahrein in the Persian Gulf), though she also had cult centers at Lagash and Kish. Another female deity was Inanna ([*n*]*in,* "lady"; *an,* "sky" or "heaven"; hence, "lady of the sky," i.e., queen of heaven). She was the goddess of love and war. Her main cult center was that of An, viz., Uruk. The relationship between them was that of father and daughter. Inanna's Akkadian name was Ishtar. A temple to her (called Eanna, "house of heaven") was found at Uruk, dating from the Protoliterate Period.

A triad of lesser importance to the Sumerians is represented by the gods of natural phenomena: (1) Utu, the sun-god (Semitic Shamash), whose cult centers were Sippar and Larsa; (2) Nanna(r), the moon-god (the Akkadian Sin, worshiped at Ur and Haran), whose main cult center was Ur; and (3) Ishkur, the weather-god (Akkadian Adad or Hadad, Canaanite Baal).

Each of these "great gods" was thoroughly anthropomorphic. They are never depicted with animal characteristics, as in Egypt (e.g., with the head of an animal).

In addition to the above gods, there were certain lesser deities, such as the vegetation deity Dumuzi (the Tammuz of Ezk 8:14; this god corresponds to Gr. Adonis). He died and was revived or reborn every year; thus his story is the symbolic representation of the seasons. Other lesser gods were the demons and genii.

Life in Sumer

1. *The King*

a. The words used. The most frequent term in Sumerian for king or ruler is *ensi* (*en,* "lord"; the meaning of *si* is uncertain) or *en* alone (but this was originally used mainly of priests). Another term is *lugal* (*lu,* "man"; *gal,* "great"; hence, "the great man"). The latter was probably originally used of a king who united more than one city under his rule. *Ensi,* on the other hand, seems to have been employed only of the ruler of a single city-state.

b. Divine or not divine? In Egypt the pharaoh, or ruler, was deified. But in Mesopotamia in early dynastic times there is no trace of the deification of the ruler, nor is there a cult of the ruler, though in later periods this does appear (e.g., within the period of the First Dynasty of Akkad and Ur III). Such deification, however, disappears completely from the time of Hammurabi on.

c. His duties. The king was supposed to act as priest to the city-god; administer the city-state in the name of the deity; supervise all state machinery; be concerned with the building of temples, the digging of canals, and the erection of dikes; and control the military forces. He was also the supreme judge and was responsible for the administration of justice.

d. His palace. The king's residence or palace was called *egal* (*e,* "house"; *gal,* "great"; hence, "the great house"; Heb. *hêḵāl,* "palace," "temple," is ultimately to be derived from this word). In earliest times, the king may have resided in the temple.

2. *The Temple*. Before the Ur III period there had been in Sumer a large number of small city-states, within each of which the spiritual, economic, and political center was the temple. That is to say, it was essentially a temple economy, with temple or religious control, including the ownership of much land. Large numbers of people were necessary for the maintenance of all this land, and they became dependent on the temple, which apparently had about 1,000–1,200 working persons (not including families). Almost the entire population of Lagash seems to have been in some way dependent on the temple. There (Lagash) several crafts are enumerated: field hands, plowmen, shepherds, herdsmen, gardeners, and fishermen. Hierarchies of officials also existed: bakers, cooks, brewers, artisans, goldsmiths, and stone and seal cutters. Women were employed to do the milling, spinning, and weaving. There were also messengers ("chariot riders") and boatmen. All these had inspectors and overseers.

The highest official, though, was the priest. The priest and priestess were actually king and queen, for the king was the priest of the chief male deity and the queen was the priestess of the chief female deity. However, the king often delegated his priesthood to another. Those dependent on the temple should not be regarded as slaves, for they enjoyed the status of freemen. Slaves were usually imported and were only a minor element in Sumerian society.

Revenue was derived from the land, not only from the crops harvested but also from rent, which was sometimes paid, interestingly enough, in silver. Another source of revenue was fishing (the temple at Lagash employed 100 fishermen). There were also taxes. Foreign trade for stone, timber, and metal, of which S Mesopotamia had practically none, was conducted as a monopoly of the temple. Trade was extensive, having been carried on with Elam, areas along the Persian Gulf, Syria, N Mesopotamia, and even the Indus Valley.

During the Ur III period the above system became even more elaborate, as well as more secularized, so that it had an even greater number of officials. This period also witnessed the beginning of *state* control.

3. *The Law*. Two incomplete Sumerian law codes are extant: that of Ur-Nammu, the founder of the Third Dynasty of Ur, to be dated *c.* 2050 B.C., and that of Lipit-Ishtar, the fifth king of Isin, to be dated *c.* 1850 B.C. The laws from the available parts of the texts deal with such matters as marriage, sexual offenses, divorce, assault and battery, slaves, perjury, lawsuits, hiring of boats, real estate, defaulting on taxes, inheritance, rented oxen, etc. These codes were the forerunners of later, more famous codes, such as the well-known code of Hammurabi (many parts of which are similar to the civil laws in the Book of the Covenant, i.e., Ex 20:22–23:33).

Bibliography. Henri Frankfort, *Kingship and the Gods,* Chicago: Univ. of Chicago Press, 1948; *The Birth of Civilization in the Near East,* New York: Doubleday Anchor Books, 1956; *The Problem of Similarity in Ancient Near Eastern Religions,* Oxford: Clarendon Press, 1951. C. J. Gadd, *Ideas of Divine Rule in the Ancient Near East,* London: British Academy, 1948. Thorkild Jacobsen, *The Sumerian King List,* Chicago: Univ. of Chicago Press, 1939. Samuel Noah Kramer, *History Begins at Sumer,* New York: Doubleday Anchor Books, 1959; *Sumerian Mythology,* New York: Harper Torchbooks, 1961; *The Sumerians: Their History, Culture and Character,* Chicago: Univ. of Chicago Press, 1963. A. Leo Oppenheim, *Ancient Mesopotamia,* Chicago: Univ. of Chicago Press, 1964. André Parrot, *Sumer,* trans. by Stuart Gilbert and James Emmons, London: Thames & Hudson, 1960. E. A. Speiser, "The Sumerian Problem Reviewed" (1952), in *Oriental and Biblical Studies,* Philadelphia: Univ. of Pennsylvania Press, 1967, pp. 213–231; "Some Factors in the Collapse of Akkad" (1952), ibid., pp. 232–243.

K. L. B.

SUMMER. *See* Agriculture; Palestine.

SUN. The heavenly body of light which is the center of the solar system, around which the earth travels and receives energy in the form of light and heat. The sun was created by God (Gen 1:16) and is preserved and regulated by Him (Jer 31:35; Ps 104:19). The apparent rising and setting of the sun furnish the most obvious natural phenomena for divisions of the day. Between sunrise and sunset the Hebrews recognized at least three periods: the early morning until the sun is hot (I Sam 11:9; Neh 7:3); the heat of the day in late morning and early afternoon (Gen 18:1; I Sam 11:11; II Sam 4:5); and the cool of the day (Gen 3:8). Twilight (lit., "between the two evenings") was the period after sunset before dark (Ex 12:6, NASB; cf. Deut 16:4, 6). The sun was also used as a means of telling time on sun dials (II Kgs 20:8–11; *See* Sun Dial; Time).

In its majesty in the heavens the sun is beautifully pictured as inhabiting a tent (Ps 19:4). Its radiance was a figure used to describe deity (Ps 84:11). "The righteous" will shine as the sun (Mt 13:43), as did the face of Jesus at His transfiguration (Mt 17:2; cf. Rev 1:16). "The Sun of righteousness shall arise with healing in his wings" (Mal 4:2), indicating a desire for a messiah to help the people and a prophecy of His coming. The sun was compared to a strong man running a race, going completely around the earth (Ps 19:5–6). The expression "under the sun," which occurs nearly 30 times in the book of Ecclesiastes, may imply figuratively that the sun is a witness of human conduct limited to this earth and world system.

Because it was so scorching, the midday sun was regarded as evil (Ps 91:6; 121:6; Isa 49:10; Jon 4:8). The sunspot activity may be involved in the intense heat of Rev 16:8–9. But the blotting out of the sun is also to be associated with judgment on sin in the day of the Lord (Isa 13:10). The Gospels say that the sun was darkened at the crucifixion of Jesus when He bore the judgment of man's sin (Mt 27:45–56; Mk 15:33–41; Lk 23:44–49). *See* Eclipse. In the eternal state there will be no need of the sun, for the glory of God and of Christ is declared to be greater and more enduring than sunlight (Rev 21:23–25; 22:5; cf. Isa 24:23; 60:19–20; Acts 26:13).

In a quotation from the lost Book of Jasher (Josh 10:12–15) the sun is said to have "stood still" at the command of Joshua until the Israelites had defeated their enemies fleeing from Gibeon. It is not known how God intervened to cause the sun to "stop in the middle of the sky" (v. 13, NASB). It is usually assumed that the purpose of the miracle was to prolong the daylight to enable Israel to pursue the Amorites, and that either the rotation of the earth was halted or the sunlight was refracted. Another interpretation is to consider the miracle as one which stopped the sun from its normal shining in order to provide relief from its heat during the dry summer season to the weary Israelite troops who had been marching all night from Gilgal. The verb "stand still" (Heb. *dāmam*) means to be silent, dumb, suggesting that Joshua prayed for the "voice" of the sun's shining (cf. Ps 19:2–6) to be silenced. The second occurrence of "stood still" in Josh 10:13 (NASB "stopped," Heb. *'āmad*) can also mean "ceased." Joshua prayed at sunrise, and the Lord answered by sending a destructive hailstorm, extremely rare in the summer months in Palestine (v. 11). This interpretation considers the passage from the Book of Jasher (vv. 12–14) to be an explanation of the main narrative in vv. 10–11 (see NBC, p. 231; WBC, pp. 217 f.). *See* Beth-horon; Joshua, Book of.

Since the sun was so important to Israel it is no wonder that under the influence of their neighbors at times some of the Israelites apostatized to worship the sun. Various towns and villages were named for the sun, such as Beth-shemesh, "house of the sun" (Josh 15:10), and En-shemesh, "spring of the sun" (Josh 15:7; 18:17). The worship of the sun was forbidden by Heb. law (Deut 4:19), but some instances are indicated, as in the case of Manasseh, king of Judah, who adopted sun worship officially (II Kgs 21:3) and encouraged the people and the leaders who followed him to do likewise. The term "sun-images" which the ASV employed to translate Heb. *ḥammānîm* (Lev 26:30; II Chr 14:5; 34:4, 7; etc.) is better rendered "incense altars," as in RSV, NASB (*see* Altar). *See* Sun, Worship of.

A. W. W.

SUN DIAL. An instrument for the measuring of daytime. The term "sun dial" (*ma'ălōt*) occurs once in the KJV in Isa 38:8 and "dial" in the parallel passage in II Kgs 20:11. The ASV and RSV render *ma'ălôt* by "dial" in both instances. In his prayer, Hezekiah requested that God cause the shadow cast by the pointer to return ten degrees, or steps, indicating an earlier time of day again.

Sun umbrella of King Tutankhamon of Egypt.
LL

This dial, associated with Ahaz, may have been the Babylonian type with a pointer and hour gradations (Herodotus II, 109), which the Latin Vulg. favors. Or, more likely, *ma'ălôt* refers to steps (as in II Kgs 20:9–10; 9:13; Ezk 40:6, all RSV) on which the shadow of a wall or of some other object opposite the steps fell. The LXX favors this alternative by its use of *bathmous* in II Kgs 20:9–10 and *anabathmous* (steps) in II Kgs 20:11 and Isa 38:8, as do Josephus' comments (*Ant.* x.2.1) and the Dead Sea Isa scroll. Y. Yadin believes Ahaz had twin flights of stairs leading to the roof of his palace, one facing E, the other W. A low wall bordered each flight. As the morning sun rose higher, the shadow traveled down the E steps; in the afternoon the shadow ascended the W steps (CornPBE, p. 178 and fig. 261). The possibility of a parahelion, or "false sun," casting a shadow while the sun itself was temporarily obscured by a cloud has been suggested (JBL, LXXXVII [1968], 173, n. 31).

W. H. M.

SUN, WORSHIP OF. The sun, known by several names in the OT (*shemesh, ḥeres, ḥammâ*) and recognized by the ancients as one of the most powerful of nature's forces, was widely worshiped as a god. The Babylonians and Assyrians regarded the sun as a male deity named Shamash, who was a god of justice. At Ugarit the sun-god was called Shapshu. Sacrifices to him are prescribed in ritual texts, and mention is made of worshiping him on rooftops (cf. Jer 19:13; Zeph 1:5). In Egypt the sun was worshiped as the god Re at Heliopolis (biblical On). Joseph's father-in-law, Potipherah ("gift of Re"), was priest of Re at On (Gen 41:45). Pharaoh Akhenaton (*c.* 1367–1350 B.C.) attempted to introduce a kind of monotheism into Egypt, when he worshiped the sun disc Aton as the sole deity, but his reforms did not last beyond his lifetime. The Hittites worshiped several sun-deities, both male and female, the most prominent of which was Istanu.

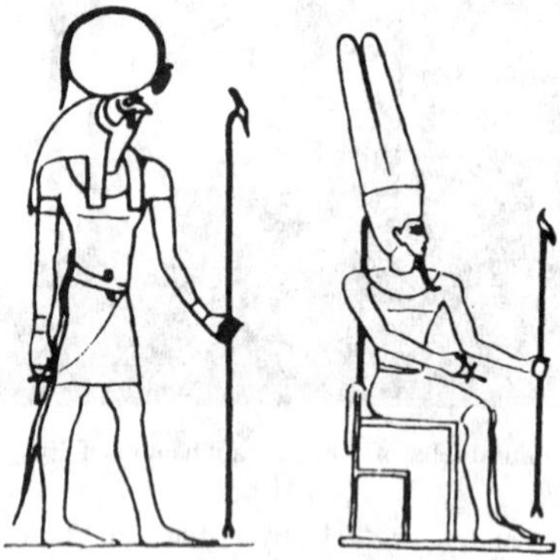

Stylized figures of Egyptian sun gods

The popularity of the sun cult in pre-Israelite Palestine may be adjudged by the names of villages, such as Beth-shemesh ("house of the sun") and En-shemesh ("spring of the sun"). Although such practices were forbidden to Israelites by God's law (Deut 4:19; 17:3; II Kgs 23:5), some engaged in them (Ezk 8:15–16; Job 31:26–27), including Manasseh, king of Judah (II Chr 33:3). The horses and chariots which the kings of Judah had dedicated to the sun and placed at the gate of the sanctuary were probably models (comparable in purpose to the sun barques of Egyptian worship), which represented the conveyance of the sun in which it was thought to traverse the sky each day. Similar pottery models of horses and chariots have been found in pre-Israelite levels on several Palestinian sites. The godly king Josiah removed and destroyed these cult objects, so that no Israelite might be tempted to worship a created object rather than the Creator (II Kgs 23:11; Rom 1:25).

For a bronze model found in a 12th cen. B.C. level at Susa representing the cult of the dawn, see VBW, II, 294. Two naked male figures are seen in a kneeling posture. One is worshiping with outstretched hands while the other is holding a basin of water for lustration. The surface of the model is covered with altars, ritual pillars, asherah trees, a large laver, and libation basins.

See Sun.

H. A. Hof.

SUNDAY. *See* Lord's Day.

SUNSTROKE. A condition arising from exposure of the body and particularly the head to the heat of the sun. Heat exhaustion with fainting can result from a mild case of sunstroke. A severe case of sunstroke can be fatal, as was the case of the Shunammite's son (II Kgs 4:19; cf. Ps 121:6; Jon 4:8; Isa 49:10).

SUPERSCRIPTION. The title or inscription written upon something. It is used of the name found upon a coin (Mt 22:20; Mk 12:16; Lk 20:24), and it describes the writing affixed to a sign over the cross of Christ indicating the crime for which He was executed (Mk 15:26; Lk 23:38). A verb form is used to indicate the inscription on an altar in Athens (Acts 17:23), the law of God that is written on the heart and mind (Heb 8:10; 10:16), and the names of the tribes of Israel inscribed on the gates of the heavenly Jerusalem (Rev 21:12).

SUPERSTITION. The word which is literally, "fear or reverence toward the gods," is used in both a bad sense as "superstition" or in the good sense of "religion." In the two places it is found in the NT it ought probably to be translated "religious" and "religion" (Acts 17:22; 25:19).

SUPH (so͞of). The location "beyond the Jordan" where Moses addressed the Israelites before their entry into the land (Deut 1:1). The exact location is unknown. The KJV uses Red Sea instead of Suph (RSV).

SUPHAH (so͞o'fȧ). The area in which Waheb is located, probably Moab (Num 21:14). The term is not to be equated with the Red Sea (see RSV).

SUPPER. *See* Food: Banquet; Food: Meals; Lord's Supper.

SUPPLICATION. A humble, earnest request or petition, as by one begging on bended knee. The Heb. nouns *t*[e]*ḥinnâ* and *taḥănûnim* both mean supplications for grace, and are derived from a stem of the verb *ḥānan* (to be gracious, show favor) that means to seek favor. Gr. *deēsis,* "supplication," "humble entreaty," is in distinction to *proseuchē* which is a prayer given in real reverence to God. The first Gr. word then simply signifies a humble request to meet a personal need (Eph 6:18; Phil 4:6; I Tim 2:1); the second a reverent prayer to God with a strong element of devotion (Jas 5:16; I Pet

3:12). The OT words are both used almost identically (I Kgs 8:28, 33, 47, 59; 9:3; II Chr 6:24; Job 8:5; 9:15; Ps 6:9; 28:2, 6; 30:8; 142:1; Dan 9:3, 17, 18, 20). In supplication man seeks some special grace or blessing from God. In the NT supplication is coupled with the idea of importunity in prayer (Eph 6:18; I Tim 5:5). *See* Prayer.

R. A. K.

SUR, GATE OF. A gate in Jerusalem (II Kgs 11:6), called the Gate of the Foundation in II Chr 23:5. It probably led from the king's palace to the temple of Solomon.

SURETY. In the OT Heb. *'ārab* means to become surety (Gen 43:9; 44:32; Job 17:3; Ps 119:122; Prov 6:1; 11:15; 20:16); *'ărrubâ*, a pledge, surety (Prov 17:18); *tāqa'*, to strike hands, be surety in a deal (Prov 11:15). To these should be added the Heb. words translated "pledge," since surety and pledge are almost synonymous terms: *ḥăbōl*, that which binds, a pledge (Ezk 18:12, 14, 16); *'ăbôṭ* (Deut 24:10–13); *'ērābôn*, surety (Gen 38:17–18, 20). In the NT Gr. *'egguos* occurs once for "surety" (Heb 7:22). A surety is a person who takes responsibility either for a person or for his responsibilities or debts.

The Scripture warns against hastily becoming a surety by striking hands for another's responsibilities or debts (Prov 11:15; 17:18; 22:26–27). Judah became surety for Benjamin's safety (Gen 43:9; 44:32). Hostages were given as a surety (II Kgs 18:23; Isa 36:8). Christ became surety for the new covenant which replaces the Mosaic covenant of the law (Heb 7:22).

A pledge was something given as an assurance that a loan would be repaid. No man could seize anything in another's house for a pledge (Deut 24:10). The owner must himself deliver the pledge. The poor man's pledge of his clothing or his blanket must be returned by sundown (Deut 24:12–13), and the failure to do so was one of the sins most severely judged by God (Ezk 18:12, 18). *See* Debt; Loan; Mortgage.

R. A. K.

SURFEITING. Overindulgence in either food or drinking which causes dissipation, intoxication, or a severe headache or hangover (Lk 21:34).

SURNAME. An additional name as in the case of Simon who was surnamed Peter (Mk 3:16). In Isa 44:5 the heathen surname themselves by the name of Israel because of the blessing of God upon the Israelites. In the NT there are a number of surnames: James and John were given the name of Boanerges (Mk 3:17), Barsabas is called Justus (Acts 1:23), and Joseph is surnamed Barnabas (Acts 4:36).

SUSA. *See* Shushan.

SUSANCHITES (sōō'sǎn-kīts). The term for the inhabitants of Susa of Elam. They were colonists removed to Samaria from Susa when the Israelites were deported (Ezr 4:9–10).

SUSANNA (sōō-zǎn'ȧ)

1. An early follower of Christ, who helped support Jesus and His disciples from her personal resources (Lk 8:3). Nothing further is known of her.

2. A much better known Susanna is the heroine of the apocryphal story concerning Daniel called "Susanna and the Elders" or "The Story of Susanna."

SUSI (sū'sī). Father of Gaddi, one of the 12 spies sent into the land to ferret information prior to the Israelites' entry into Canaan. He was from the tribe of Manasseh (Num 13:11).

SWADDLE, SWADDLING BANDS. To swaddle is to wrap up tightly and fully, and is used in the Bible to refer to the custom of wrapping an infant in long "bands" or "cloths" that completely enveloped him (Ezk 16:4; Lk 2:7, 12). The term is used figuratively in Job 38:9 of the clouds wrapping up and obscuring the waters in darkness.

A different Heb. word translated "swaddle" in Lam 2:22 is more properly given as "fondle" (Berkeley) or "dandle" (ASV, RSV), as it means to carry in the arms or hands.

SWALLOW. *See* Animals, III. 49.

SWAN. *See* Animals, III. 50.

SWEAR. *See* Oath.

SWEAT. Perspiration caused by exertion is used as the symbol of God's judgment upon man for his disobedience in Eden that brought toil and labor into man's life. Perhaps it is because of this that the regulation is given in Ezk 44:18 that the clothes of the priests as they minister before the Lord shall not be made of any material that causes one to sweat.

The bloody sweat of our Lord in Gethsemane was a token of the intense agony of spirit with which He faced bearing the burden of our sins (Lk 22:44). *See* Bloody Sweat.

SWEAT, BLOODY. *See* Bloody Sweat.

SWEET CANE, SWEET CALAMUS. *See* Plants.

SWEET STORAX. *See* Plants: Stacte.

SWELLING. This word in the KJV translates two Heb. and two Gr. words, all with the basic concept of pride. In Ps 46:3 Heb. *ga'ăwâ* evidently refers to the "swelling pride" (NASB) or "tumult" (RSV) of the sea, whose roaring waters cause the mountains to quake. The Gr. *physiōsis* (II Cor 12:20) occurs in a list of sins of the tongue and refers specifically to being puffed up with "conceit" (RSV) or "arrogance" (NEB. NASB). False teachers are said to speak out "great swelling words of vanity" (II Pet 3:18; Jude 16). where Gr. *hyperogkos* (lit., over-swollen) means bombastic or "arrogant" (NASB).

The expression "the swelling of the Jordan" occurs three times in Jeremiah (12:5; 49:19; 50:44) and once as "pride of Jordan" (Zech 11:3). The Heb. *gā'ôn* literally means exaltation, and usually refers to pride. But in this context it refers to the majesty of the Jordan, which consisted of the trees, shrubs, and reeds which grew along its banks in the river bottom area (cf. II Kgs 6:4). Therefore the RSV translates the "jungle of the Jordan," and NASB has "thicket of the Jordan." In OT times wild beasts including lions still made their covert here and went up to prey on the sheepfolds.

For swelling as a physical malady (Num 5:21-22, 27) *see* Diseases.

J. R.

SWIFT. *See* Animals, III. 51.

SWINE. *See* Animals: Pig, I. 14.

SWORD. *See* Armor.

SYCAMINE. *See* Plants.

SYCAMORE. *See* Plants.

'Askar (Sychar?) at the foot of Mount Ebal.
HFV

SYCHAR (sī'kär). A city of Samaria "near the parcel of ground that Jacob gave to his son Joseph" (Gen 48:21-22), near Jacob's well (Jn 4:5). The name does not occur elsewhere in either the OT or the NT. Some have identified Sychar with 'Askar, which lies at the foot of Mount Ebal, on the caravan route between Jerusalem and Damascus, a little N of Jacob's well. Arguing against this identification is the fact that 'Askar has an abundant water supply of its own and it would have been unnecessary for the woman of Jn 4 to go such a distance for water.

Jerome, translator of the Vulgate, said that Sychar is to be identified with Sychem (Shechem) and that the former was a scribal error. A great many tend to follow this view, especially since the excavations at Tell Balâṭah have identified it as Shechem, just one-half mile W of Jacob's well.

Excavations of the Drew-McCormick-Harvard Expedition at Shechem since 1956 proved that no city existed on Tell Balâṭah by the 1st cen. A.D. As G. E. Wright says, however, it is highly probable that a village existed then where the modern village of Balâṭah is. Roman-Byzantine remains in this village are still to be found (*Shechem,* New York: McGraw-Hill, 1965, p. 244). *See* Shechem.

A. W. W. and H. F. V.

SYCHEM. *See* Shechem.

SYENE (sī-ē'nē). The Gr. form of the Egyptian town of *Swn* located on the E bank of the Nile just below the first cataract, now called Aswan (ASV, Seveneh, *q.v.*). Because it was on the ancient border between Egypt and Cush, it was an important military and commercial town. The site was further protected by the fortress Yeb or Elephantine, on an island in the midst of the river. Ezekiel uses the expression "from Migdol to Syene" (29:10; 30:6, RSV) to indicate that all of Egypt shall fall under God's judgment. During the Persian Empire there was a considerable Jewish colony at Elephantine and Syene, and even today it retains its importance and name as the site of the great Aswan dam. *See* Elephantine Papyri.

The Dead Sea IQ Is[a] scroll uses a Heb. spelling which suggests Syene instead of Sinim in Isa 49:12, but the reference is still in question. *See* Sinim.

See Egypt; Pathros.

P. C. J.

SYMBOL(ISM). This word does not occur in the Bible, but the use of symbols and emblems is very frequent.

Definition

A symbol is that which stands for or represents another thing. It is a visible object or representation of a process, idea, quality or of another object. Symbols are unlike types (*see* Type) in that they are not usually prefigurative, but represent things already existing. Etymologically the English word "symbol" is traced to the Gr. *sumballein,* which means to throw or place together as, for example, for purposes of comparison. In one of its noun forms the term referred to the two halves of a coin or other like object which any two contracting parties broke between them; hence the idea of "token" or symbol.

Nature

Symbols in Scripture generally appear as literal objects and always denote something different from themselves. Candlesticks or lampstands, olive trees, beasts, horses, trees, birds, stones are a few examples of objects used for symbols. These are the objects the prophets saw, but, of course, they represented something else. Symbols *suggest* ideas and concepts rather than *state* them. There is generally some conceptual parallel between the symbol and the thing symbolized.

Interpretation

The great differences of opinion which exist between scholars should alert one to the fact that this is a difficult and complex subject. Biblical symbolism, like typology, has at times been carried to extremes by imaginative writers, and rather than clarifying the revelation of truth as found in the Bible they have obscured it. The interpretation of symbols is immediately made difficult by virtue of a cultural gap which exists between East and West. The more remote the culture, the more difficult it is to interpret its symbols. Several rules or principles for the proper interpretation of biblical symbols can be established, however. They are as follows: (1) The interpreter must carefully examine the historical-cultural background of the writer using the symbol for clues as to its significance. (2) The nature and scope of the context in which the symbol is found must also be considered. (3) Symbols which are interpreted by Scripture should be the foundation for all other studies in symbolism. (4) A symbol is often interpreted by its own nature. Such symbolism is made obvious by some outstanding feature of the object employed. (5) Be sure to allow for double imagery in a symbol inasmuch as it may have more than one interpretation. For example, the lion is used to symbolize Christ ("the lion of the tribe of Judah," Rev 5:5) and Satan ("a roaring lion . . . seeking whom he may devour," I Pet 5:8). (6) Items used as symbols are not always symbolic. Be sure that symbolism is clearly intended before a normal or literal interpretation is abandoned.

Examples

Proper names. Sodom and Gomorrah are many times used to symbolize moral and spiritual corruption (cf. Isa 1:9–10; Jer 23:14; Ezk 16:44–59; Rev 11:8). The name Egypt appears to be symbolic of captivity and exile (cf. Hos 8:13; 9:3). Other names which have been suggested as having symbolic value are Babylon, Ariel and Leviathan.

Objects. Various objects are used for symbols both in visions and in actual life. In many cases these symbols are explained in the immediate context. Examples of this type are found in Jer 1:11 ("rod of an almond tree"), Jer 1:13 ("a seething pot"), Jer 24:1-3 (good and bad figs), Amos 8:1 ("a basket of summer fruit"), Ezk 37:1–14 (the dry bones), and Rev 1:12–20 (stars and lampstands). In other instances symbols used in the OT find their full explanation in NT revelation. For example, the rich typology of the tabernacle (*q.v.*), its furniture and the priesthood is unveiled in the book of Hebrews. *See* Type.

Special acts and rituals. Various acts provide the basis for dramatic symbolism in both the OT and NT. A clear example of this type is found in the rending of Jeroboam's garment signifying the separation between Israel and Judah (I Kgs 11:29–31). Emblematic actions are also common to Ezekiel's prophecy. In 4:1-3 he built a miniature of a city under siege. According to 4:4–8 the prophet lay on his left side 390 days and on his right side for 40 days (4:9–17; cf. also 5:1-4). The command to take a scroll and eat it was given to both Ezekiel (2:8 – 3:3) and John (Rev 10:2, 8–11). All these symbolic acts are properly understood by virtue of the explanations given in the immediate context.

The sacrificial rituals and ordinances also have obvious symbolical and genuine typological value as explained in the NT in general and the book of Hebrews in particular. The Lord's Supper (I Cor 10:16–18; 11:23-34) and Christian baptism (Mt 28:19; cf. Rom 6:1–10) are important symbols reflecting on the salvation of the individual. They are especially significant because both the material and the act have symbolic value.

Numbers. Much of what has been regarded as symbolism in numbers is actually only a schematic, idiomatic or rhetorical use of numbers. However, some numbers do seem to exhibit some symbolism in Scripture. The number seven is quite clearly used to convey the idea of "completeness" or "fullness." The number three at times is symbolic of the concept of "a few" or "completeness." Nowhere in Scripture is any number given theological values, such as holiness, sin, perfection, etc. No NT writer ever interprets OT numbers in this manner, even though many other objects and acts are given symbolic value. This is an indication that the interpreter should exercise great reserve in this matter. *See* Number, Numerology.

Colors. It is quite difficult to be sure of the symbolism intended by the reference to certain colors. Since scholars are not agreed as to the precise translation of certain words relating to colors, one must approach this subject with great care. Some colors, however, do have obvious symbolic value in Scripture. Purple and scarlet, as the colors of the dress of kings, suggested royalty and majesty (Jud 8:26; Est 8:15; Dan 5:7; Nah 2:3). Black usually signified death, evil or mourning (Rev 6:5–6; Jer 14:2), and red, war and bloodshed (Rev 6:4; 12:3). *See* Color.

Bibliography. Alexander Altmann, *Biblical Motifs: Origins and Transformations*, Cambridge: Harvard Univ. Press, 1966. Frederick W. Dillistone, *Christianity and Symbolism*, Philadelphia: Westminster Press, 1955. Patrick Fairbairn, *The Typology of Scripture*, 2 vols., 6th ed., Edinburgh: T. & T. Clark, 1882. Maurice H. Farbridge, *Studies in Biblical and Semitic*

Symbolism, London: Kegan Paul, Trench, Trubner & Co., 1923. Francis Foulkes, *The Acts of God,* Tyndale Old Testament Lectures for 1955, London: Tyndale House, n.d. Norman L. Geisler, *Christ: The Theme of the Bible,* Chicago: Moody Press, 1968. Anthony T. Hanson, *Jesus Christ in the Old Testament,* London: S.P.C.K., 1965. Abraham Kuyper, *The Antithesis Between Symbolism and Revelation,* Edinburgh: T. & T. Clark, n.d. Geoffrey W. H. Lampe, *Essays on Typology,* Naperville: Allenson, 1957. A. Berkeley Mickelsen, *Interpreting the Bible,* Grand Rapids: Eerdmans, 1963, pp. 236–279. Walter L. Wilson, *Wilson's Dictionary of Bible Types,* Grand Rapids: Eerdmans, 1957.

J. J. D.

SYNAGOGUE. In Gr. "synagogue" means simply "a place of assembly," though it came to be the technical name for an immeasurably important institution in Judaism. *See* Congregation; Worship.

Origin. This is a matter of considerable dispute. Jewish tradition is strong that the synagogue is at least as old as the time of Ezra. In fact, there was a tradition among the Jews in NT times that Moses had established it; this is historically unreliable. References to the synagogue in the Talmud in temple times are almost nonexistent. The NT itself with over 50 mentions of synagogues presents the first coherent accounts of its services.

The synagogue was such an extensive and developed institution by NT times that it must have had a history of some length prior to the 1st cen. The two most ancient synagogues in Babylonia were those of Nahardea and Huzal, and tradition says the former of these was founded by King Jehoiachin. As early as the time of Augustus Caesar, there were many synagogues in Rome. Those scholars who deny that there were any synagogues in Palestine prior to the time of the Maccabees are probably incorrect, although it does appear that there were synagogues outside Palestine before there were synagogues inside that land. It seems, rather, that this institution grew to maturity and underwent its most important development during the period of Jewish history that falls between the close of the OT and the Maccabeean revolt (444–168 B.C.).

Four pillars supported the roof of a synagogue built into the palace of Herod the Great (the Herodium) near Bethlehem. HFV

Ps 74:8 is considered by some to be the only specific mention of a synagogue occurring in pre-Christian literature, though this reference cannot be proved to apply to it. The Heb. words translated "the synagogues of God," following the Gr. translations of Symmachus and Aquila, are *mô'ădê -'ēl,* "the meeting places of God" (RSV) or "every shrine of God" (JerusB). The Heb. for synagogue, *bêt-hakk*^{e}*nēset,* "house of the assembly," is nowhere used in the OT.

The synagogue probably grew out of two situations: first, the Exile in Babylon, when it may be presumed that the Jews gathered together for prayer and to strengthen themselves and each other in their devotion to the religion of their fathers; second, the emphasis of Ezra on the law at the time of the restoration. A possible clue for the origin of the institution in Babylonia is to be found in Ezk 14:1: "Then came certain of the elders of Israel unto me, and sat before me" (cf. also 20:1). Although there is no mention of the synagogue in records of the restoration, the entire history of the return presupposes the habit of periodic assemblies of the people (Ezr 8:15; Neh 8:2; Zech 7:5) which could well have been akin to the synagogue; and, indeed, has been identified by some with it.

Function. Strictly speaking, the temple was the place of worship in Judaism, while the synagogue became the educational institution, providing a place to study the law. As the institution for the study and inculcation of the law the synagogue was especially suited to the Pharisaic interest; and from the 2nd cen. B.C. onward, this institution was dominated by the Pharisees. In practice, however, the distinction between worship and instruction disappeared; the Jews who lived at great distances from Jerusalem found it difficult, if not impossible, to worship there. It was only natural that the synagogue, as the place of religious association and fellowship, should early be adapted to the common need which the people felt for the worship experience; thus, this element became increasingly a part of synagogue life as expressed in its services.

It must also be noted that synagogues were more than religious institutions. Among the Jews dispersed around the Roman world, the synagogue generally served as the civic center of the Jewish community, especially providing the schools necessary for the teaching of the young. In fact, the atmosphere of this institution among the dispersed Jews tended toward the secular rather than the religious.

Requirements. It was required that any community of Jews that contained ten males above 12 years of age support a synagogue (some say ten families, assuming the leadership of a family for each man). It was expected that ten or more men be present for each service. In some communities wealthy men of leisure habitually represented the congregation at the services, supplying regularly the required number. Evidently Philippi did not have ten such male Jews to form a synagogue, because the few followers of Judaism met for prayer outside the city by a river (Acts 16:13). The larger towns, of course, would be able to support more than one synagogue, although the 480 synagogues reported for Jerusalem by the Talmud (Megillah 73) is probably an exaggeration.

There was no fixed size or shape for a synagogue, such as that associated with the temple and the tabernacle. According to the Talmud (*Shabbat* 11*a*), however, it was required that the building should be erected on the highest possible point in the community, the thought being that no building was worthy to look down upon this holy house. It was also desired that the chest which contained the Scriptures referred to as the "ark," should face toward Jerusalem. The building was usually made of stone. In Galilee the synagogue would be oriented on a N and S axis, with the entrance to the building at the S end.

Services. Earliest indications reveal services in the synagogues on three days of the week: the sabbath, Monday and Thursday. Later, the synagogues located in populous centers held three services each day at the times of the three daily temple sacrifices, the extra services being greatly abbreviated and consisting principally of prayers (cf. Acts 3:1 with 10:2-4). The main service of the synagogue was held on the sabbath morning, but the services on the sabbath afternoon and Monday and Thursday mornings were more extended than the daily times of prayer, containing in addition to prayers a short reading from the Pentateuch.

Prior to NT times it became the custom to conduct services on the great feast days for the benefit of the people who could not go up to Jerusalem. The services on these festive occasions were substantially the same as the sabbath morning service; the main difference was the selection of the appropriate section of the Hallel (Ps 113-118) to be read after the prayer of benediction which began the service.

It seems probable that the order of service of the synagogue gradually developed with the passing of the years. The earliest element in this development was, no doubt, the reading of the law in the Heb. tongue, followed by an explanation in the vernacular Aram.

Note how Ezra read the book of the law to the assembled people, "distinctly" (KJV) or "with interpretation," translating into Aram. and "giving the sense" so that the people understood the reading (Neh 8:8). By NT times, in the Gr. synagogues, it was the custom to read the Scriptures in the Gr. translation (LXX). Paul, e.g., quotes directly from the LXX version of Hab 1:5 in his sermon in the synagogue in Antioch of Pisidia (Acts 13:41).

The reading of the law at the public gathering in the earliest instance was probably on the occasion of certain festivals. In the course of time, these readings were extended to four special sabbaths in the last month of the civil year, Adar, and finally to every sabbath. Eventually, in Palestine the entire law was arranged in portions to be read sabbath by sabbath, completing the whole in a period of three years. Finally, there came a time when the reading of the law was concluded with a verse or two from the Prophets. It is not known at what period the reading of the Prophets came to be part of the service, but it was certainly well before the end of the 1st cen. A.D. Some scholars have conjectured that the Psalter was also read through, sabbath by sabbath, over a three year period; but in spite of the prominence of the Psalter in the synagogue service, there is no conclusive evidence that it was systematized and used in its entirety.

During NT times, a typical service on a sabbath morning in a large synagogue would have followed this order more or less exactly. Since the synagogue was essentially a lay institution, any Jew could read the Torah or the Prophets, lead the congregation or, if gifted, speak to the assembly. Jesus took advantage of this freedom in His home synagogue at Nazareth when He read from Isa 61 and preached (Lk 4:16-27).

The service began with an invitation to prayer given as a proclamation in the words: "Bless ye the Lord who is to be blessed." To this the people replied: "Blessed be the Lord who is to be blessed forever." This was followed by the confession of faith that has from the first word become known as the "Shema" (Deut 6:4-9, to which later was added Deut 11:13-21 and Num 15:37-41). Following the Shema was the prayer proper, which consisted of benedictions ascribed in authorship to the men of the Great Synagogue in the time of Ezra. The prescribed reading from the law followed. The prophetical reading (of much later origin than the reading of the law) came next. In both readings an interpreter more or less paraphrased the passage in the vernacular of the people. A homily, or sermon, immediately followed the prophetic passage which in essence was usually an exposition of the Scriptures read or a hortatory comment based on the same material. This on occasion might be given by a visiting Jew, as often in the case of Paul (Acts 13:14-16; 14:1; 17:1-4, 10; 18:4, 19). The close of the service consisted of a benediction given by a priest if one were present, to which the congregation responded with "Amen" after each verse. Where there was no priest in attendance, the benediction was probably not given, though some evidence points at a later time to its transformation into a prayer given by any member of the congregation in the absence of a priest.

Officers. The synagogue was controlled by a

Colonnaded courtyard and entrance to the second century A.D. synagogue at Sardis. HFV

body of elders presided over by a "ruler of the synagogue" (*archisynagōgos,* Mk 5:22; Lk 8:49; 13:14; Acts 13:15; 18:8, 17), probably chosen from among them. These elders had the general supervision of the services and the building. It was the ruler who invited different members of the congregation to lead in prayer and to read the Scriptures. If a stranger were invited to give the sermon, it was at the invitation of the ruler.

The only paid officer of the synagogue was the minister or attendant (Lk 4:20, Heb. *ḥazzan*). In the modern synagogue this term is used for the "reader" or "cantor," but in NT times the minister would have been a reader in the service only on exceptional occasions. It was his work to supervise the building and its furniture, special attention being given to the sacred scrolls. He blew the trumpet from the roof of the synagogue to indicate the beginning and ending of the sabbath. Sometimes this person served as schoolmaster to the young in the synagogue school. It was also the minister's responsibility to carry out any punishment of a member of the congregation which had been decided upon by the elders.

A fully organized synagogue also had officers called "receivers" who were responsible for the receiving and distributing of alms. The recitation of prayers tended to settle upon one individual who became known, because of this function, as "the reciter of prayers." This individual functioned also as a secretary of the congregation, taking supervision of its necessary transactions with the outside world.

Furnishings. The early synagogues were quite simple. Since there was no sacramental focus, a basilica style of architecture was usually adopted, sometimes with two rows of columns and with one or more rows of benches along the walls. Later synagogues boasted of elaborate mosaic floors and a sculptured frieze decorating the façade.

The portable chest or Torah shrine which contained the sacred scrolls wrapped in a linen covering was separated from the rest of the room by a curtain or kept in a side room. In the 2nd cen. A.D. some Jews began to call this chest the "ark" and placed it in a "sanctuary" or permanent repository, reminiscent of the ark in the tabernacle.

In the center of the room was a raised platform upon which was a reading desk used by the one reading from the scrolls. Also the preacher who delivered the homily sat upon this platform while he spoke. The men who served as elders occupied the "chief seats" (Mt 23:6; Lk 11:43; 20:46; cf. Jas 2:2–3), which were benches arranged just below the chest near the reader's desk or on either side of the ark, facing the congregation. The seat of Moses (Mt 23:2) was a stone chair, as found in synagogue ruins at Chorazin and Hammath near Tiberias. It stood next to the ark of the Torah in the 3rd cen. A.D. synagogue at Dura-Europos on the Euphrates River. It was the seat for the most distinguished elder, a symbol of the legal authority of Moses inherited by the scribes and Pharisees as teachers of Jewish law.

The congregation was divided, with the men and women sitting on different sides of the assembly room. By the 3rd cen. A.D. a gallery was often built running around three sides of the room, which was reserved for the women. It was fitted with a grill of wood so that its occupants could look down through it but could be seen only dimly themselves. The lamps, trumpets and other items needed for the services completed the few furnishings of the synagogue.

Importance. The synagogue even more than the temple determined the religious life of the Jewish people. After the destruction of the temple in A.D. 70, it was the synagogue that kept Judaism alive. An important development associated with the synagogue was the growth of the Targums. These were Aram. paraphrases of the original Heb. texts used in the synagogue services, which by the 2nd cen. A.D. were written.

The importance of the synagogue in the propagation of Christianity cannot be overemphasized. Jesus taught in the synagogues; Paul found a ready-made audience for his preaching in the synagogues that were scattered throughout the Roman world. Not only so, but the order of worship and the type of service conducted in the synagogue greatly influenced the communal worship as expressed in Christianity (cf. Jas 2:2–6), and Islam also. Its general outline in the service of worship is to be seen in the Christian and Moslem worlds today.

Ruins. Remains of synagogues have been found at more than 50 places in modern Israel and Jordan. Since Jews were allowed to settle in Galilee during the Byzantine period (A.D. 300–650), the majority are in this region. Evidence of a synagogue was uncovered on the Masada bastion, destroyed in A.D. 73, thus being the earliest extant ruins of a synagogue in Palestine. In Ostia, the seaport of Rome, a 1st cen. A.D. synagogue was discovered, decorated with a marble bas-relief representing the golden candelabrum. The size and workmanship of the ruins indicate a prosperous Jewish community. The largest and most elaborate synagogue of the Mediterranean world has recently been unearthed at Sardis in western Turkey. Dating from the late 2nd cen. A.D., the main room is a great hall nearly 200 feet long with a broad apse at its western end (BASOR #174, pp. 30–44; #187, pp. 9–50).

Bibliography. S. W. Baron, *A Social and Religious History of the Jews,* 2 vols., New York: Columbia Press, 1952. CornPBE, pp. 667–672. W. D. Davies, *Christian Origins and Judaism,* Philadelphia: Westminster Press, 1962. Frederick C. Grant, *Ancient Judaism and the New Testament,* New York: Macmillan, 1959. G. F. Moore, *Judaism in the First Centuries of the Christian Era,* Vol. I, Cambridge: Harvard Univ. Press, 1927. W. O. E. Oesterly, *The Jewish Background of the Christian Liturgy,* Oxford: Clarendon Press, 1925. W. Schrage, "*Synagōgē,* etc.," TDNT, VII, 798–852. Emil Schürer, *A History of the Jewish People in the Time of Jesus Christ,* Edinburgh: T. & T. Clark, 1885. I. Sonne, "Synagogue," IDB, IV, 476–491. Roy A. Stewart, "The Synagogue," EQ, XLIII (1971), 36–46.

H. L. D.

SYNAGOGUE OF SATAN. *See* Satan, Synagogue of.

SYNOPTIC GOSPELS. *See* Gospels, Synoptic.

SYNTYCHE (sĭn'tĭ-kē). The name of a Christian woman in Philippi. She was at variance with another believer, Euodias, and Paul urges them to be reconciled. He describes the women as those "who labored with me in the gospel," and the disagreement of such leaders in the church would have deeply hurt the struggling Philippian community (Phil 4:2–3).

SYRACUSE (sĭr'*ȧ*-kūs). Syracuse was a city of eastern Sicily where Paul stopped en route to Rome. For three days his ship lay in the harbor there waiting for favorable winds (Acts 28:12). Nothing is said about his preaching there; presumably Christianity spread to Sicily from the mainland at a later time. A Corinthian colony founded in the 8th cen. B.C., Syracuse became one of the most magnificent Gr. states. It successfully fought off the Athenian expedition of 415–13 but fell to Rome in 241 B.C. at the end of the First Punic War. The city suffered terribly during the Roman civil wars of the 1st cen. B.C., but Augustus made efforts to restore it.

SYRIA (sĭr'ĭ-*ȧ*)

Geography

Boundaries. The boundaries of Syria have fluctuated over the centuries according to political arrangements. Originally Syria was a term which applied only to a powerful state whose center was in the Lebanon district and whose capital was Damascus. The Assyrians called this country W of the Euphrates the land of Amŭrrû. But geographers commonly, following such ancient authorities as Strabo and the Arab geographers, consider the limits of Syria to be the Taurus Mountains and the Euphrates on the N, the Sinai Desert on the S, and the Mediterranean and the Syrian Desert on the W and E.

Biblical students generally, and many others as well, make a distinction between Syria and Palestine. Syria is restricted to the territory at the arch of the Fertile Crescent, bounded on the W by the Mediterranean, on the S by what became known as Galilee and Bashan, on the E by the Syrian Desert, and on the N by the Euphrates and the Amanus Mountains. Sometimes it is considered to include Phoenicia. In this volume Syria is not generally used to include either Palestine or Phoenicia; separate articles are devoted to those areas. The SW boundary is set at the Lebanon Mountains which effectively shut off Syria from the coast.

Geographical divisions. Syria consists of a series of strongly marked zones—coastal plain, mountain ranges, valleys with luxuriant vegetation, and stony or sandy tracts in the E which are either desert or largely unproductive.

The coast of the eastern Mediterranean, some 400 miles from Alexandretta to the Egyptian border, is one of the straightest in the world, with no deep estuary or gulf and no protecting island of any size. In Syria proper there were small harbors at such places as Latakia (ancient Laodicea) and Ras Shamra (ancient Ugarit); Seleucia (the port for Antioch) was hardly more than a roadstead. The coastal plain, never more than a few miles wide, was largely inconsequential to Syrian (as opposed to Phoenician) history. Much of it is merely a broad strip of sand dunes covered by short grass and low bushes.

Overlooking the coastal plain is a line of mountains that begins with the Amanus in the N and extends all the way to the towering massif of Sinai in the S. The Amanus Mountains (rising to a height of some 5,000 feet) are a southward offshoot of the Tauric system. Separating Syria from Asia Minor, the Amanus are cut on their southern fringe by the Orontes gorge and are crossed by roads to Antioch and Aleppo. The chief pass over the mountains is at Beilan, the Syrian Gates, at an altitude of 2,400 feet. South of the Orontes the range is continued by Jebel Akra, which rises to a height of 5,750 feet and extends to Latakia, S of which it bears the name of Nuṣayrīyah. The Nuṣayrīyah chain is broken on the S by the river Nahr el Kebeer, which today forms the border between Syria and Lebanon and to the S of which extend the Lebanon Mountains.

Behind the western mountain range is a deep valley, a great "fault," extending from Armenia to the Gulf of Aqaba on the Red Sea. Starting in the neighborhood of Antioch, where the

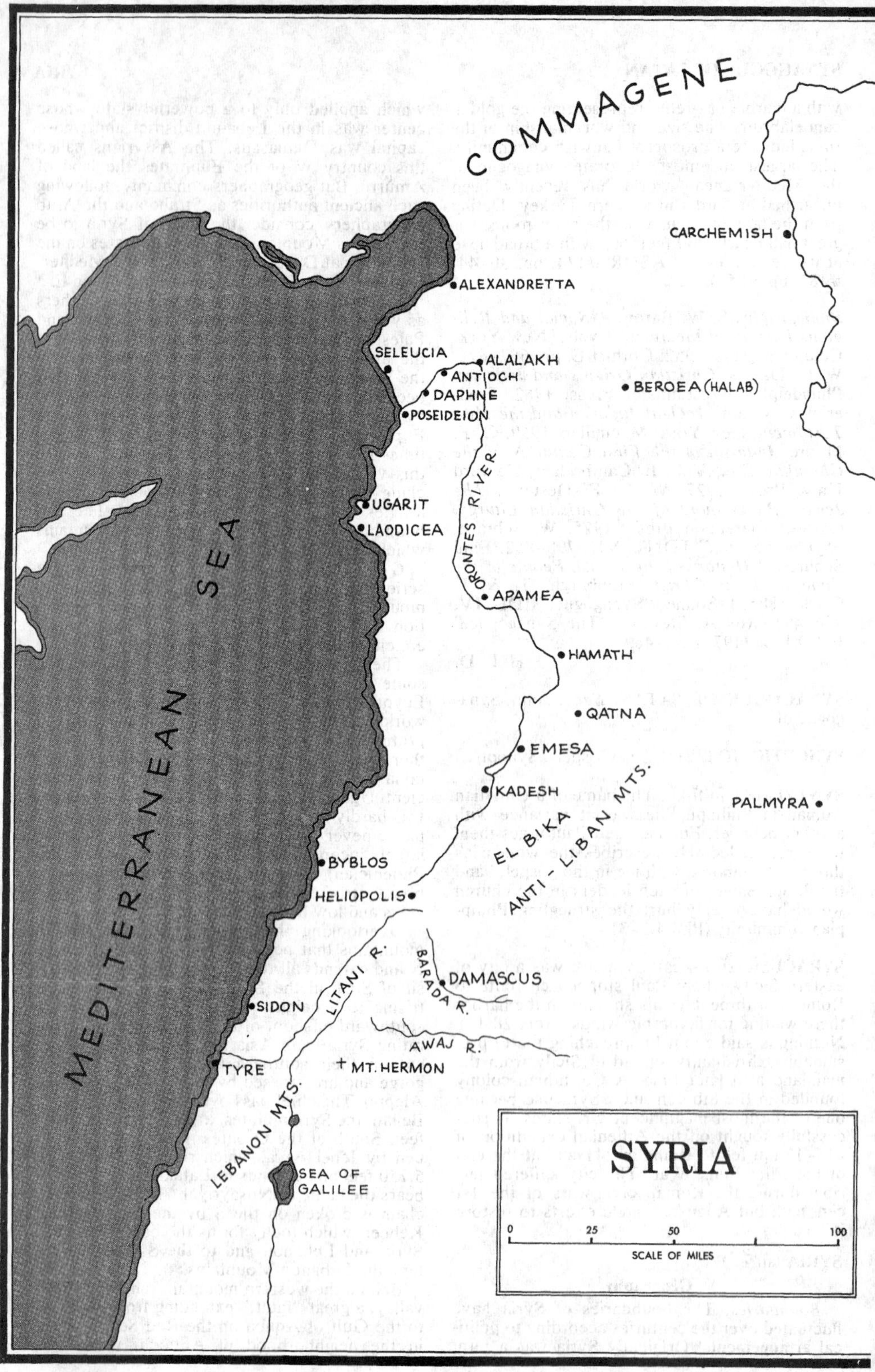
COMMAGENE
CARCHEMISH
ALEXANDRETTA
SELEUCIA
ALALAKH
ANTIOCH
DAPHNE
BEROEA (HALAB)
POSEIDEION
ORONTES RIVER
UGARIT
LAODICEA
MEDITERRANEAN SEA
APAMEA
HAMATH
QATNA
EMESA
KADESH
PALMYRA
EL BIKA
ANTI - LIBAN MTS.
BYBLOS
HELIOPOLIS
BARADA R.
LITANI R.
DAMASCUS
SIDON
AWAJ R.
TYRE
MT. HERMON
LEBANON MTS.
SEA OF GALILEE
SYRIA
0
25
50
100
SCALE OF MILES

SYRIA

Orontes turns westward to cut through the mountains to the sea, the inland plain is broad and extremely rich. From Antioch the valley of the Orontes ascends slowly between the western range and the high plateau of N Syria. At Hamah (Hamath) the altitude is 1,015 feet and at Homs (Emesa) it has risen to 1,660 feet.

After Homs the valley becomes the Beqa'a or "cleft" between the Lebanon and Anti-Lebanon Mountains. Varying in breadth from six to ten miles, the Beqa'a is some 75 miles long and has always been a rich agricultural and pastoral region.

The eastern mountain range (Anti-Lebanon) has no counterpart to the northernmost sections of the western mountain range. Rising from the Syrian plateau S of Homs, it opposes the Lebanons in almost equal length and height. This mountain complex is divided into two parts by the broad plateau and gorge of the Barada or Abana River flowing eastward to Damascus. The southern part of the eastern range, Mount Hermon, rises to a height of 9,232 feet and is the highest and most majestic peak in Syria.

On the S and E the slopes of Hermon fall swiftly to the vast plateau of Hauran, the treeless surface of which is volcanic and its soil is rich, red loam. The lava field covers an area almost 60 miles long by as many wide. The Hauran has some of the best wheat land in the Near East.

The Anti-Lebanons collect their waters and send them far out into the desert (Damascus is about 30 miles E of Mount Hermon) in the channel of the Barada or Abana. On a lofty and drainable plateau some 2,200 feet in altitude it has created 150 square miles of fertility, from which rises the city of Damascus, civilization's outpost in the desert. The Abana (*c.* 45 miles long) divides into five branches in the Damascus oasis and finally loses itself in the desert. Another river which rises in the Anti-Lebanons is the Pharpar, identified with the Awaj. This flows some distance S of Damascus and disappears in swamps E of the city. Naaman was immensely proud of both these life-giving rivers of his homeland (II Kgs 5:12).

East of the Hauran lies the Syrian Desert, which is a continuation of the great Arabian Desert. In this region lay Palmyra, the ancient caravan center of Tadmor (*q.v.*), 135 miles NE of Damascus. A new dam on the Euphrates 25 miles upstream from the mouth of the Balikh River will help to irrigate parts of N Syria, but the waters of the proposed lake will cover ancient ruins as far as Carchemish.

History

In the earliest periods of its known history Syria was dominated by Canaanites, Amorites, Hyksos, Mitanni, Hittites, and especially Egyptians. But limitations of space do not permit discussion of these early times; attention is first focused here on the Arameans (*see* Aram, Arameans). The Canaanite city of Ugarit at the site of Ras Shamra (*q.v.*) is discussed in a separate article. For the discoveries at Alalakh, an ancient city (3100–1200 B.C.) near the bend of the Orontes E of Antioch, important for OT studies, see D. J. Wiseman, "Alalakh," TAOTS, pp. 119–135. Aleppo, Carchemish (*q.v.*), and Mari (*q.v.*) were other important ancient cities in Syria.

The Beqa a (El Bika) and the Lebanon Mountains. HFV

The Arameans (whose ancestry is traced to Shem, Gen 10:22–23) were Bedouins who spread from the fringe areas N of the Syro-Arabian desert into the more settled region of the Fertile Crescent. They were established in upper Mesopotamia from early patriarchal times, as the accounts of Isaac and Jacob and a Naram-Sin inscription indicate. There Aram-naharaim (Gen 24:10, ASV marg.) or Padan-aram (Gen 25:20; 28:2) had as its center the biblical Haran. Perhaps the Arameans moved into N and central Syria earlier, but events of the 12th cen. offered them an unparalleled opportunity to settle in the area. Hittite power had collapsed; the Egyptian Empire in western Asia was gone; the Hebrews were a politically ineffective collection of tribes living under the leadership of the judges.

Most powerful of the Aramean kingdoms of Syria in the latter 11th cen. was that of Zobah, which now is known to have been considerably N of Damascus, probably in the region of Emesa (Homs). Damascus must at that time have been part of the kingdom of Zobah. The states of Maacah (Deut 3:14; Josh 12:5; 13:11, 13), Geshur, and Tob (Jud 11:3 ff.) are located by Unger to the E of the Jordan and S of Damascus (Merrill F. Unger, *Israel and the Aramaeans of Damascus,* p. 43).

Relations with David and Solomon. As Heb. power advanced under David, Hanun of Ammon made an alliance with the Aramean kingdoms of Zobah, Rehob, Tob, and Maacah (II Sam 10:8), which were no doubt also fearful of increasing Israelite power. David utterly defeated the Arameans, with heavy casualties suffered both by Zobah and Damascus, and stationed occupation troops in the latter city (II Sam 10:18–19; 8:3–6). After David worsted Zobah (which lay to the N of Damascus, as noted above), King Toi of the Hittite kingdom of Hamath apparently acknowledged Heb. suzerainty (II Sam 8:9–11). It would seem that the districts under Israelite rule in the days of David can be divided into two categories: those in which occupation troops were stationed (e.g., Damascus), and those which were satellites (e.g., Zobah).

Apparently Solomon (970–931 B.C.) expanded the kingdom bequeathed to him and ruled the entire area from the border of Egypt to the Euphrates, including Transjordan (II Chr 9:26). He even brought the Phoenicians within his sphere of influence. And his geographical position gave him a good opportunity to make his state chief middleman for overland trade between Arabia, Egypt, Phoenicia, and the Aramean and Hittite states of Syria and Asia Minor.

Relations with the divided kingdom. All peoples of Palestine and Syria were not docile followers of the great king in the Holy City. Apparently Zobah rebelled against Solomon and had to be subdued (II Chr 8:3). As the state disintegrated late in Solomon's reign, Rezon of Zobah headed a rebel movement that captured Damascus (I Kgs 11:23–24). There Rezon set up a new dynasty. With the death of Solomon the subject states all seem to have reestablished their independence.

After Rezon's revolt against Solomon, his son Tabrimon and grandson Ben-hadad I ruled after him (I Kgs 15:18). Apparently Rezon set a pattern of Syrian animosity to the Hebrews from the beginning (I Kgs 11:25). Although the kingdom of Damascus gradually increased in power, its big chance came as a result of an animosity between Israel and Judah. When Asa of Judah found himself in dire straits because of the invasion of Baasha of Israel, Asa sent a large gift to Ben-hadad of Syria and asked for help. The Syrian king advanced into Israel and took cities in the N, perhaps *c.* 885 B.C.

Near the end of Ahab's reign (*c.* 855 B.C.) Ben-hadad advanced on Israel and met defeat. Seeking revenge in the following year, the Syrians attacked again and suffered even worse defeat. Ahab was now in a position to humiliate his northern rival, but chose not to do so because it was clear that all possible aid would be needed to meet the imminent Assyrian invasion of the westlands (I Kgs 20). So in 853 B.C. the inveterate enemies marched side by side in the coalition that met Shalmaneser III at Qarqar N of Hamath. The Assyrian apparently won a victory on that occasion, but it was not sufficiently overwhelming to assure him control of Syria. Five years later Shalmaneser met another Syrian confederacy of 12 kings, again headed by Ben-hadad. In 845 B.C. Shalmaneser found it necessary to engage in another major campaign against Syria. Again he met and defeated a coalition of a dozen kings headed by Ben-hadad of Damascus and Irhulenu of Hamath. About two years later the usurper Hazael (*q.v.*) killed Ben-hadad and brought a new dynasty to power in Syria.

Within the next few years Shalmaneser won two great victories over Hazael, but soon other problems occupied the Assyrians, so there were no more campaigns into Syria for the moment. Hazael now determined to settle a score with Jehu and took all of Israel's holdings E of the Jordan in Gilead and Bashan (II Kgs 10:32–33). Subsequently Hazael brought Israel very low indeed, apparently reducing her to a puppet. Then he moved southward and defeated King Jehoash of Judah (II Kgs 12:17–18). But the fortunes of Syria were destined to take a downturn once more. Hazael died about 800 B.C. and the Assyrians renewed campaigns against Syria. Joash or Jehoash of Israel defeated Ben-hadad II, son of Hazael, and retrieved territory lost previously to the Damascenes (II Kgs 13:24–25). Jeroboam II (793–753 B.C.) continued Israelite victories over Syria. Details are wanting, but Damascus and Hamath apparently became tributary to Jeroboam for a time (II Kgs 14:28).

Probably about 750 B.C. Damascus became independent of Israel, with Rezin as king. Soon thereafter, Tiglath-pileser III (744–727 B.C.) determined to bring the moribund Assyrian Empire back to vigorous life. Rezin of Damascus and Menahem of Israel were among those forced to pay tribute to him. Then, while Assyria turned to other enemies along the NW frontier, Rezin and Pekah of Israel moved to punish Ahaz of Judah for refusing to support them in the struggle against Assyria. The allies besieged Jerusalem and pushed past the capital to take Judah's Red Sea port, Ezion-geber. The slaughter and pillage in Judah were great (II Chr 28:5–8). Desperate, Ahaz of Judah sent an embassy to Tiglath-pileser, professing to be a vassal of Assyria and bearing tribute (II Kgs 16:7–8). The Assyrian was only too glad to intervene. He descended on the foes of Judah,

Antiochus IV. G. L. Archer and W. S. LaSor

destroying the rich gardens of Damascus and bringing the kingdom of Damascus to an end in 732 B.C. (II Kgs 16:9).

Foreign domination. Syria remained part of the Assyrian Empire until its fall to Babylon in 612 B.C. Subsequently it remained part of the Neo-Babylonian Empire until it fell to the Persians in 539 B.C. Damascus was the capital of the Fifth Satrapy (province) of the Persian Empire, but unfortunately we know little of the city during either the Babylonian or Persian periods.

The Seleucid Empire. When Alexander the Great moved against the Persian Empire, he brought Syria under his control along with the rest of the vast Persian domains. On his death in 323 B.C. he left behind a group of ambitious generals, each of whom sought mastery of the empire Alexander had carved out. From the anarchy that followed, a workable arrangement finally emerged with Ptolemy controlling Egypt, Cyrene, Cyprus, and Palestine; Antigonus ruling Macedonia; and Seleucus founding a dynasty at Babylon in 312 B.C. At their height the Seleucids ruled over most of the old Persian Empire except Egypt. Under Seleucus II (264–226 B.C.) the empire was greatly diminished; a Parthian revolt pulled Iran out of the Seleucid orbit. But Antiochus III (223–187 B.C.) gave promise of complete recovery. He managed to reconquer Iranian territory and extend Seleucid borders to the Indus once more. In 198 B.C. he defeated Ptolemy and won Palestine and, for all his successes, won the epithet of "Great." Soon, however, Antiochus overreached himself. Tangling with the Romans, he lost all Seleucid lands W of the Taurus Mountains and was forced to pay a huge indemnity.

By the time of Antiochus IV Epiphanes (175–164 B.C.), Syria was strong enough once more to take the offensive. Learning that Egypt was preparing for war, Antiochus beat Ptolemy Philometer to the draw and took nearly all the delta region except Alexandria. When Rome made Antiochus go back home, he turned his attention to more effective Hellenization of his subjects and touched off the Maccabean or Jewish revolt in 168 B.C. This eventuated in Jewish independence and further truncation of Seleucid domains. In subsequent decades the Seleucid Empire continued to disintegrate and Pompey brought what was left into the Roman Empire in 64 B.C.

Roman domination. One of the most important features of Seleucid administration was the establishment of cities, which could act as centers for the spread of Hellenistic culture and garrison points to hold the surrounding countryside. Two of the most important of these cities were Antioch on the Orontes and its seaport of Seleucia. Antioch was destined to become the third city of the Roman Empire, after Rome and Alexandria. And it was destined to become a great center of Christianity. Antioch was the birthplace of foreign missions; all three of Paul's missionary journeys were launched from there (Acts 13:1–4; 15:35–36; 18:22–23).

Antioch and Mount Stauris, where stood the acropolis of ancient Antioch. HFV

Disciples of Jesus were first called "Christians" there (Acts 11:26). It was among the Antiochians that the question of Gentile relation to the Mosaic law first arose, with the resultant decision at the Jerusalem council that Gentiles were not under the law (Acts 15).

Never was Syria so effectively ruled or so populous as under the Romans. After initial disorders, peace was established and the capital of the province moved from Damascus to Antioch. The general curve of prosperity continued to rise and reached its height in the 2nd cen. A.D. Areas of the country which now present a barren appearance were then covered with thriving towns. Fruits, vegetables, and cereals grew in abundance. Advanced methods of fertilization and irrigation were employed. Among chief industries were leather, linen, and wine production. A chief source of Syrian wealth was the trade that flowed along her busy caravan routes and through her ports. In addition to the thousands of villages which studded the Syrian countryside (in which little Hellenizing or Romanizing influence was felt), there were large and populous cities which were centers of Hellenistic culture. Of course the greatest of all Syrian cities was Antioch, the capital. But Seleucia, Berea (modern Aleppo), Laodicea, Apamea, Epiphania (modern Hama), Emesa (modern Homs), Heliopolis (Baalbek) with its magnificent temples, Damascus, and Palmyra should not be ignored.

Bibliography. E. S. Bouchier, *A Short History of Syria,* Oxford: Basil Blackwell, 1921; *Syria as a Roman Province,* Oxford: Basil Blackwell. 1916. Glanville Downey, *A History of Antioch in Syria,* Princeton: Princeton Univ. Press, 1961. Jack Finegan, *Light from the Ancient Past,* 2nd ed., Princeton: Princeton Univ. Press, 1959. F. M. Heichelheim, *Roman Syria,* Vol. IV of *An Economic Survey of Ancient Rome,* ed. by Tenney Frank, Baltimore: Johns Hopkins Press, 1938. Philip K. Hitti, *History of Syria,* New York: Macmillan, 1951. Theodor Mommsen, *The Provinces of the Roman Em-*

pire from Caesar to Diocletian, trans. by William P. Dickson, Vol. 2, New York: Scribner's, 1906. A. T. Olmstead, *History of Palestine and Syria,* New York: Scribner's, 1931. Richard Stillwell, ed., *Antioch-on-the-Orontes,* Princeton: Princeton Univ. Press, 1938. Merrill F. Unger, *Israel and the Aramaeans of Damascus,* Grand Rapids: Zondervan, 1957.

H. F. V.

SYRIA MAACHAH. *See* Maacah.

SYRIAC; SYRIAN LANGUAGE. The Syrian language referred to in the KJV (II Kgs 18:26; Ezr 4:7; Isa 36:11; Dan 2:4) is Aramaic, not the modern Syriac. It is a Semitic language widely used in numerous dialects through the ancient Middle East. During the Exile it displaced Hebrew as the spoken language of the Jews. *See* Aram; Aramaic.

SYRIAN (sĭr′ĭ-ȧn). The word refers to (1) terms translating the names Aram and Arameans; (2) the language of Syria, Aramaic (II Kgs 18:26; Ezr 4:7); (3) the inhabitants of Syria (Gen 25:20; II Sam 8:5).

SYROPHOENICIAN (sī′rō-fĭ-nĭsh′ȧn). A name applied to a Gentile woman from the region of Tyre and Sidon who came to Jesus for the healing of her daughter (Mk 7:26; cf. Mt 15:21–22). A study of the Matthew and Mark passages together leads one to the conclusion that the woman was a Greek (i.e., non-Jewish or pagan) who had been born in this region. She could be classified as Syrophoenician because she was from the old area of Phoenicia which by NT times had been conquered by Rome and included in the province of Syria. Jesus tested the woman's faith, but she met the test and healing occurred. Her faith is all the more remarkable because the woman accepted Jesus' pronouncement of healing without opportunity to know if a cure had actually been effected until she arrived home. This is one of the few examples of Jesus performing a miracle by "remote control."

SYRTIS (sûr′tĭs). The shoals or sandbanks lying off the northern coast of Africa. They undoubtedly lay in one of the two shallow gulfs along the coast of Libya. The larger, Syrtis Major, W of Cyrenaica, is probably the one intended in Acts 27:17; it is now called the Gulf of Sidra. In it is a moveable bar of sand that stretches for *c.* 125 miles. When Paul and his companions were driven by the storm S from Crete, not knowing the direction they were traveling, the sailors feared lest they strike these "quicksands" (KJV), "the shallows of Syrtis" (NEB, NASB, Acts 27:17) and be destroyed.

T

TAANACH (tā′ȧ-năk). A Canaanite city in the hills just S of the Jezreel Valley, located at Tell Ta'annak. Its commanding position on one of the entrances to the valley occasioned its first appearance in historical records. Thutmose III's commanders suggested its pass as an alternative approach to attack Megiddo five miles to the NW (ANET, p. 235). Later it appears as one of Thutmose's conquered towns (No. 42, ANET, p. 243) and on a list of chariot warriors receiving rations in Egypt. Twelve cuneiform tablets in the Akkadian language were found by Sellin in 1903-04 at Tell Ta'annak. Two of these are letters from a certain Amenhotep instructing the ruler of Taanach to send men and supplies, first to Gaza and then to Megiddo. Their script and language strongly suggest a date early in the reign of Amenhotep II. One Amarna letter testifies that the men of a town which some scholars read as Taanach had robbed and plundered a neighboring king (EA 248:14).

The king of Taanach was defeated by Joshua (Josh 12:21). Though it was in the inheritance of Issachar, its territory was transferred to Manasseh (Josh 17:11; I Chr 7:29), who failed to conquer the town until later (Jud 1:27; cf. 5:19). The Kohathite Levites were assigned residence in the town itself (Josh 21:25), which may explain why it became an important center in Solomon's fifth administrative district (I Kgs 4:12). Shishak of Egypt listed Taanach (No. 14) as one of the towns conquered by him in his swing through the Jezreel Valley, *c.* 926 B.C.

A. F. R.

Prof. Ernst Sellin of Vienna conducted three archaeological campaigns there (1902–04), finding numerous Canaanite and Israelite remains. But this work was done before the days of scientific archaeology. Beginning in 1963 a series of three campaigns (also 1966, 1968) was held by a joint Concordia-ASOR team directed by Paul W. Lapp.

The excavations show that occupation began at Taanach with a well-planned, heavily fortified Early Bronze Age city. It was an active, thriving town from 2700 to perhaps 2400 B.C. Taanach again became prosperous during the Hyksos period of the 17th–16th cen. B.C. It had typical sloping Hyksos fortifications and a large nobleman's house (the West Building) measuring 70 by 60 feet with walls four feet thick. Occupation continued probably to the time of Thutmose III when the city seems to have been destroyed (*c.* 1479 B.C.). The Canaanites, however, rebuilt at once, and it is to this period that the cuneiform tablets belong. One additional such tablet was discovered in 1968.

The site seems to have had little importance during the Amarna age (mid-14th cen.) and down to the 12th cen. B.C. Some very interesting discoveries were made in connection with a 10th cen. building which Lapp calls the "Cultic Structure." Here Sellin had unearthed a terra cotta stand *c.* 36 inches high bearing animal figures, a snake, and a tree of life in ornamental relief. He called it an incense altar. But a similar cultic stand found in 1968 (BASOR #195, fig. 29) shows no evidence of burning or incense; therefore Lapp believes these stands were used for libations. His expedition also discovered 108 anthropomorphic clay figurines, many of the Astarte type, from both the 15th and 12th cen. B.C.

The city was evidently destroyed once again by Shishak's army on his campaign in 926 B.C. Thereafter it was sparsely settled during the Israelite monarchy and Persian periods. Its occupational history throughout the OT closely parallels that of Megiddo.

Bibliography. Albert E. Glock, "A New Ta'annek Tablet," BASOR #204 (1971), pp. 17–30. Carl Graesser, Jr., "Taanach," BW, pp. 556–563. Paul W. Lapp, "The 1963 Excavation at Ta'annek," BASOR #173 (1964), pp. 4–44; "The 1966 Excavations . . . ," BASOR #185 (1967), pp. 2–39; "The 1968 Excavations . . . ," BASOR #195 (1969), pp. 2–49; "Taanach by the Waters of Megiddo," BA, XXX (1967), 1–27.

J. R.

TAANATH-SHILOH (tā'*a*-năth-shī'lō). A city or region located on the NE boundary of Ephraim, between Michmethath and Janoah (Josh 16:6). Its earliest identification is found in the Talmud (Zebahim 118*b*), which interprets the phrase as "mourning of Shiloh," and thinks of it as a strip of Ephraimite territory which ran into that of Benjamin and included the site of Shiloh. On the other hand, both Eusebius and Jerome regard it as a city called Thena ten miles E of Neapolis (Nablus) on the road to the Jordan. Pliny also mentions a town named Thena in Samaria. Accordingly, the site has been identified as the modern Khirbet Ta'nah el-Foqa, seven miles SE of Shechem. This is located on a mountain which could have served as a fortress guarding the latter town. The name may mean "approach to Shiloh."

Massive walls of the Early Bronze Age period at Taanach. JR

TABBAOTH (tăb'ā-ŏth). The head of a family of temple servants who returned from the Exile with Zerubbabel (Ezr 2:43; Neh 7:46).

TABBATH (tăb'*a*th). A place on the route of Gideon's pursuit of the Midianites after his victorious strategy at Jezreel (Jud 7:22). It has been identified with Ras Abu Tabat in Gilead, five miles E of the Jordan and ten miles N of Succoth.

TABEEL (tăb'ē-ĕl). The Aramaic name Tabeel may be translated "God is good." The KJV spelling Tabeal (Isa 7:6) reflects the Masoretic pointing, changing the meaning to "no good," a rendering limited to the first of the two to bear the name.

1. The "son of Tabeel" was a pawn in the Syro-Ephraimitic war against Judah. The allies, Pekah of Israel and Rezin of Syria, had united with others to form a common front against the great threat of the day, Assyria. To strengthen their position they desired to add Judah to the alliance, but Ahaz, king of Judah, refused. He had already determined to save himself and his country by coming to terms with the Assyrian. In order to force Judah into the alliance, Israel and Syria went to war against Ahaz, planning when they had conquered the country to put "the son of Tabeel" upon the throne as a willing puppet. The plan failed and the son of Tabeel disappears from history (Isa 7:1–6).

There is no certain identification of this man. Some have supposed him to be Zichri, an Ephraimite who slew Ahaz' son in the battle (II Chr 28:7), though there seems to be no reason for the conjecture. Because an Assyrian letter (*c.* 730 B.C.) from Calah mentions a little district of Tabel (*Ṭâbilâya*) in N Transjordan or S Syria, it has been suggested that possibly he was the son of Uzziah and a princess of Tabel, and thus would have a certain legitimacy to be king (W. F. Albright, BASOR #140 [1955], pp. 34 f.). Tabel would have been the name of a province in the Assyrian administration of conquered Transjordan, however, and not that of an independent political state. Probably it took its name from the family of Tabeel which formerly had governed the region on behalf of King Uzziah of Judah (B. Oded, "Assyrian Rule in Transjordan," JNES, XXIX [1970], 180).

2. A Persian official in Palestine who attempted to halt the rebuilding of the temple. With others, he wrote a letter to King Artaxerxes accusing the Jews of rebellion, which brought a royal command to stop the work (Ezr 4:7). P. C. J.

TABERAH (tăb'ĕ-rȧ). An unknown site in the itinerary of the Israelites soon after they left Mount Sinai on their trek to Kadesh. As a judgment of the people because they had complained concerning their misfortunes, the fire of the Lord is said to have burned among them and consumed some outlying parts of the camp. The place was consequently called Taberah ("burning") because the fire of the Lord burned among them (Num 11:1 ff.). Taberah is mentioned in conjunction with Massah and Kibroth-Hattaavah in the second discourse of Moses as places where the Israelites provoked the Lord to wrath (Deut 9:22). However, it is omitted from the itinerary in Num 33.

TABERING. An obsolete rendering in the KJV of a participial form of Heb. *tāpap,* meaning "beating (incessantly) on a drum (top)" (Nah 2:7). Nahum decries the fall of the city of Nineveh when in utter bewilderment the Assyrian queen(?) is led forth with her maidens, who lament and moan like doves, tabering (KJV) or beating (ASV,RSV) upon their breasts in anguish.

TABERNACLE. The tabernacle (Heb. *'ōhel* and *mishkān*) was the place where Yahweh dwelt and met with His people after the exodus from Egypt. It later became the prototype of subsequent Jewish temples.

The most comprehensive source of information about the tabernacle is Ex 25-28, where there is prescribed in minute detail instructions for the construction of the sanctuary and its furniture. Ex 35-40 describes the execution of the task of building the structure. Since the tabernacle was the model for subsequent temples, the specifications given in I Kgs 6; II Chr 3-4 are an aid to understanding its function and certain details, as well as Ezk 41-43. Apart from the Scriptures, the principal source of information is Josephus, who in his description of the sacred buildings of the Jews (*Ant.* iii.6.2-7:7) essentially repeats the statements of the OT.

Structure

The ground plan of the Mosaic tabernacle can be made out with reasonable certainty. The primary features were:

The court. The court was an enclosed space 100 × 50 cubits around the tabernacle, which was placed in the W half of the courtyard. The long sides faced N and S, i.e., ran E and W (Ex 27:9-19; 38:9-20). This space was enclosed by a fence whose framework consisted of pillars of acacia wood five cubits high (Ex 27:18). The bottom was secured by sockets or bronze plates, evidently laid flat on the ground. These sockets had a hole to receive the tenon which was in the bottom end of each pillar. The pillars were stabilized by ropes and pegs, and had hooks overlaid with silver, and silver bands, called fillets, around the neck.

On this fence were hung sheets of "fine twined linen," sewn end to end so that they formed a continuous screen from the doorway all around the corners to the doorway again. The hanging for the doorway was in the middle of the E end. Its size was five cubits high and 20 cubits long. One entered the court by lifting this curtain at the bottom.

In the E half of the court stood an altar, called either the "brazen" (copper) altar after the plating material, or the altar of burnt offering after the chief type of sacrifice offered on it (Ex 27:1-8; 38:1-6). *See* Altar. Between the altar and the door of the tabernacle stood the laver (Ex 30:17-21; 38:8; 40:30-32).

When in camp, the tabernacle was surrounded by two ranks of tents. The Levites were the first and the 12 tribes were the second, three tribes camping on each side (Num 2:1-3:39).

The tabernacle. The tabernacle was composed of two parts, the tabernacle proper (Heb. *mishkān*, referring to the wooden frame and linen curtains) and the tent (RSV; Heb. *'ōhel*, which the KJV calls a "covering upon the tabernacle," Ex 26:7).

The tabernacle proper was made of planks or boards of acacia wood, ten cubits long and one and a half cubits wide, which were plated with sheets of gold (Ex 26:16). Each side wall consisted of 20 planks, and each plank had two tenons at its foot to enter the socket. Eight planks formed the rear; six were identical in size to those on the sides, and two were one-half cubit wide.

In order to keep these boards in place, three series of bars, made from acacia overlaid with gold, were provided to pass through rings on the outside of the planks (Ex 26:26-29; 36:31-34).

Another view of the construction of the tabernacle building, advocated by A. R. S. Kennedy, sees the wooden framework as consisting of skeleton panels or open frames, not solid boards. Since the acacia trees used for wood do not grow large in the Sinai peninsula, no boards 27 inches (one and a half cubits) wide would have been obtainable. But open panels could have been easily made. These would allow the linen curtains with their embroidered cherubim to have been seen when they were draped over the framework.

An example of such panel construction may be found in the innermost of four concentric burial shrines of gilded wood over the sarcophagus of Pharaoh Tutankhamen (*c.* 1390 B.C.). It was made from a set of demountable wooden panels, with sliding bolts to hold them together. A linen veil or canopy decorated with tiny golden rosettes covered the second shrine. The RSV and JerusB ("frames," Ex 26:15–25) have adopted this explanation, and it is accepted by D. W. Gooding and R. Laird Harris ("Archaeology and the Wilderness Tabernacle," *Bulletin of the Near East Archaeological Society,* VII [1964], 3–4).

Most likely the structure was stayed with cords, one end fastened to the copper knobs used in connection with the tent cloth and the other to pins which were driven into the ground.

The roof consisted of an inner covering of goats' hair canvas. The material was woven in 11 pieces, each 30 cubits long and four cubits wide (Ex 26:7–13; 36:14–18). The tent extended one cubit over the sides allowing an extra fold at the front and overlapping at the back (Ex 26:9, 12). According to Ex 26:14 and 36:19 additional coverings for the tent were made of rams' skins dyed red and of porpoise or dugong skins (*see* Animals, V.3). The roof was held up by posts, one of them being the extension of the central doorpost.

The entrance to the tabernacle was much like that of the court. It was closed by a screen, which was supported by five pillars that were covered with gold (Ex 26:36–37; 36:37–38).

The inside of the tabernacle was decorated with wall draperies. A particular dignity was bestowed on these ten curtains of fine twisted linen over that of the door curtains, by their embroidery of "cherubim of cunning work" (Ex 26:1; 36:8) rather than the simple tracery on the latter.

The tabernacle proper was divided into two compartments, the holy place and the holy of holies. If the proportions of these areas were analogous in the tabernacle and temple, then the holy of holies was square, and the holy place was twice as long as it was broad.

These two compartments were separated by the veil (Heb. *pārōket*). The veil was made from the same materials as the entrance screen, except it was embroidered with cherubim. It is generally believed that there were two with their wings extended touching one another (Ex 26:31–33; 36:35–36).

The furniture. Furniture was placed both within the court and the tabernacle. The pieces were as follows:

1. The altar of burnt offering was found in the E half of the court (Ex 27:1–8; 38:1–7). It was a hollow framework of acacia wood, five cubits square and three cubits high, and was plated with copper or bronze. Each of the top corners had a triangular extension in the shape of a horn. Halfway up the altar was a ledge (KJV, "compass"). Below this, a grating of bronze network around the four sides allowed the sacrificial blood to be poured out and sprinkled or dashed against the base of the altar

Shick's model of the Tabernacle. MPS

through the network (Ex 29:12, 16). By means of a ring at each of the corners of the grating provision was made so that poles could be used in transporting it.

Apparently the altar had no top, because none is mentioned, whereas the top of the golden altar is specifically mentioned. Consequently, some have suggested that the hollow framework was filled with earth. The other alternative is to assume that the sacrifice was burned on the ground inside the altar, which acted as a kind of incinerator.

The utensils used in the service of the altar were made of bronze or copper and included pots and shovels to remove the ashes, basins for the blood of the sacrifice, fleshhooks, and firepans in which the fire was carried when the camp was on the move. The fire on this altar was never allowed to go out.

2. Between the altar and the tabernacle door was placed a copper or bronze laver (Ex 30:17-21; 38:8; 40:30-32). It was a large basin and stood on a copper "foot." The laver was made from the bronze mirrors of the serving women (Ex 38:8; *see* Mirror). It held water for the priests' ablutions. The Scripture tells us nothing of its size or shape. As a matter of fact, it is also missing from the marching instructions set out in the Heb. text of Num 4, but is mentioned in the LXX Version. The omission is probably without significance, as all other parts of the tabernacle have detailed instructions for transport.

3. The table of showbread (Num 4:7; II Chr 29:18) was located in the holy place (Ex 25:23-30; 37:10-16). It was set on the N or right side as one entered, and faced the lampstand (Ex 40:22). The table was made of acacia wood overlaid with pure gold, two cubits long, one cubit wide, and one and a half cubits high. The top of the table rested upon a frame, and around it ran a "crown" or molding of gold, projecting above the top to keep articles from falling off. Rings were placed at each corner to make transportation possible.

On the table was placed bread made of fine wheat flour (unleavened), baked in 12 loaves or cakes, each containing one-fifth ephah of flour. These cakes were renewed every sabbath to be eaten only by priests (only in the sanctuary). The task of preparing the loaves fell to the Levites (I Chr 9:32). To each pile of cakes incense was added, most likely in bowls which were placed beside the bread, "for a memorial, even an offering made by fire unto the Lord" (Lev 24:5-9). *See* Bread of Faces.

In the service of the table of showbread three kinds of pure gold vessels were used: dishes or flat plates which were probably employed in carrying the bread to and from the table, and possibly to contain the bread while on the table; spoons, or perhaps cups, probably for incense (Lev 24:7); and flagons and bowls, perhaps for wine.

4. The candlestick (KJV; or lampstand) (Heb. *m^e^nôrâ*) stood on the S or left side of the holy place, directly across from the table of showbread (Ex 40:24). The details of construction with the exception of its size are given in Ex 25:31-40; 37:17-24. An entire talent of pure gold was used in the construction of the lampstand and its vessels. The different parts were of "beaten work," that is, hammered out of sheets. It consisted of a pedestal, a shaft, and three branches projecting from either side of the shaft. The shaft and branches terminated in sockets, into which seven lamps were set. The ornamentation of the lampstand was quite intricate. The seven-branched candelabrum of Herod's temple was apparently made to resemble that in the tabernacle, as shown by the relief in the Arch of Titus at Rome where it was taken as a trophy of war after A.D. 70. The form of the gold lampstand seen by Zechariah in vision was quite different (Zech 4:2, NASB). A bowl on top supplied oil to its seven lamps, each of which had seven wick-spouts after the pattern of seven-lipped pottery lamps found in 2nd mil. B.C. tombs at Dothan and elsewhere. *See* Lamp, Lampstand.

The lamps were supplied with pure beaten olive oil (Ex 27:20). They were lit at the time of the evening sacrifice (Ex 30:8), and extinguished, trimmed and filled at the time of the morning sacrifice (Ex 30:7; I Sam 3:3).

Tongs and snuffdishes were the utensils belonging to the service of the lampstand (Ex 25:38). They too were made of the same gold that was used in the construction of the lampstand (Ex 25:38). The tongs or tweezers were used to adjust the wick and to hold it while blowing to light the lamp. The snuffdishes were trays for holding the tongs and pieces of wick trimmed off, such as the fire pans used to carry coals from the altar (Ex 27:3; Lev 16:12).

5. The altar of incense occupied the middle space in the holy place, close to and in front of the veil leading to the holy of holies (Ex 30:1-6; 37:25-28; 40:5; Lev 16:18). However, it was counted as belonging to the holy of holies (I Kgs 6:22; Heb 9:4), perhaps on account of its great sanctity. It was a simple box of acacia wood, two cubits high, one cubit wide, and one cubit deep, with a top similar to that of the altar of burnt offering (the top corners had horns projecting). The entire altar was covered with gold. It had a molding around the top, and provisions for transporting it. No special utensil was used in its service. No sacrifice was offered on it, as it was reserved exclusively for burning incense each morning and evening. *See* Incense.

6. The ark, sometimes called the ark of the covenant (Num 10:33) or the ark of the testimony (Ex 25:22), was the only piece of furniture which was located in the holy of holies proper. The ark was made of acacia wood, two and one-half cubits long, one and one-half cubits deep, and one and one-half cubits high, and overlaid with pure gold within and without.

There was also a gold border which extended above the top of the ark to keep the lid from moving. The ark had gold rings on each side so that it could be transported. *See* Ark of the Covenant.

The ark had a lid called the mercy seat or covering (Ex 25:20, 22). It was identical in length and width to the ark, and was acacia wood covered with gold. *See* Mercy Seat.

On the ends of the lid were placed two cherubim, probably beaten out of gold as was the lampstand. These cherubim (*q.v.*) most likely had a human shape with the exception of their wings, although some authorities understand Ezk 1:5-14 as a general description of their appearance. They are always pictured as maintaining a standing position (II Chr 3:13), and facing one another, looking down upon the mercy seat with their wings forward in a brooding position (Ex 25:20; cf. Deut 32:11).

It was betweeen these cherubim that the shekinah glory rested (Ex 25:22; cf. Ex 40:34-35; Lev 16:2). This was a visible manifestation of Yahweh's presence among His people. Because the ark was the divine dwelling place, not only could no ordinary man come before the mercy seat, but even the high priest was not to come before the ark at his own pleasure or without the blood of sacrifice. The penalty for so doing was death.

Within the ark were kept the two tablets of stone upon which Moses copied the Ten Commandments (Ex 31:18; 34:29; Deut 9:10-11; 10:1-5), a copy of the law written by Moses, perhaps containing the entire Pentateuch thought to have been rediscovered in the time of Josiah (II Kgs 22:8), a golden pot of miraculously preserved manna (Ex 16:33-34), and "Aaron's rod that budded" (Heb 9:4; cf. Num 17:10).

Care of the Tabernacle

Directions for the care of the tabernacle are given in Num 3:25–4:33; 7:3-9; 10:17, 21.

When the tabernacle was to be taken down for moving, the Kohathite Levites were charged with the job of disassembling the structure. They were to cover the furniture with dugong or porpoise skin. The only piece of furniture not mentioned is the laver, perhaps because it was carried without covering.

Having completed the preparations, the Kohathites carried the furniture, while the Gershonites were assigned the tapestry of the tabernacle. The Merarites were charged with care of the tabernacle bars, pillars and sockets, and pins and cords.

History

The date for the introduction of the tabernacle will vary with the date one accepts for the Exodus (*See* Exodus, The). The tabernacle was set up at Sinai on the first day of the first month of the second year (Ex 40:2, 17), i.e., 14 days before the celebration of the Passover on the first anniversary of the Exodus. When the Israelites resumed their journey, six wagons carried everything except the ark and the two altars (Num 7). Before leaving Sinai, the altar of burnt offering and utensils of gold and silver were dedicated. The tabernacle had been standing at Sinai for 50 days (Num 10:11).

From Sinai to Canaan took 39 more years. Of this, nearly 38 years were spent at Kadesh. The ordinary sacrifices were not offered during this period (Amos 5:25). Little is recorded concerning these years, and little mention is made of the tabernacle except that the ark of the covenant preceded the host of Israel when marching (Num 10:33-36).

When Israel finally came into the land of Canaan, one of the first considerations was to find a resting place for the tabernacle. It had to be a place which had not been inhabited and which was free from the defilement of human graves. Such a place was found at Gilgal (Josh 4:19; 5:10; 9:6; 10:6, 43). Gilgal, however, was never considered as a permanent site. The question of a permanent location was a matter of intertribal jealousy, and was at last settled by the removal of the tabernacle to Shiloh (Josh 18:1). Shiloh was in the territory of Ephraim, and was conveniently located for the attendance of male adults at the three yearly festivals. While at Shiloh, the tabernacle seems to have gained some more permanent accessories such as doorposts (I Sam 1:9), which led to its being called a "temple" (I Sam 1:9; 3:3).

During the early years of Samuel, war broke out anew with the Philistines. At a council of war it was proposed that the ark of the covenant should be brought to the war zone, in an attempt to insure victory. The two sons of Eli, Hophni and Phinehas, carried the ark, and it arrived in the camp to shouts that were heard in the hostile camp. It was no longer Yahweh in whom the Israelites were trusting for victory, but a material ark that was the hope of Israel. The episode ended in disaster. The ark was captured, Eli's sons were killed, and Israel was routed (I Sam 4:1-11). The tabernacle, however, does not seem to have been taken, and the date of Shiloh's destruction is uncertain (*see* Shiloh).

The ark was soon restored to Israel by the Philistines, and remained at Kirjath-jearim for a number of years. The tabernacle was moved to Nob (I Sam 21:1 ff.). There it remained until the massacre by Saul of the high priests of Nob (I Sam 22:1 ff.). Subsequently, it was moved to Gibeon (I Chr 16:39; 21:29). Gibeon was six miles from Jerusalem and seven miles from Bethel.

After David captured Jerusalem, he prepared a place for the ark of God and pitched a tent on Zion to imitate the tabernacle in Gibeon (II Sam 6:17 ff.; I Chr 16:1). There must have been an altar, as burnt offerings and peace offerings are recorded. Meanwhile, the ark was brought down from Kirjath-jearim. It remained for three months in the house of Obed-edom. It was then carried into the Davidic tabernacle, so that there were now two tabernacles, one with the original tabernacle and altar, and another with the original ark. Both, however, were superseded with the building of Solomon's temple. Of all the materials in the original tabernacle, only the ark was incorporated into the temple. The tabernacle was finally brought to Jerusalem, and kept as a relic in the temple (I Kgs 8:4). In all, the tabernacle had a history of nearly 500 years (I Kgs 6:1).

Significance

Quite frankly, the exact nature of the significance of the tabernacle is a matter of dispute. Formerly, some have argued that every detail, even to the pegs used to hold the tent of meeting, were of the utmost importance. In response to this excessive typology, the pendulum has swung in the other direction. Either extreme seems to be in error, as the NT clearly teaches that the tabernacle speaks typologically of Christ (Heb 9:23–24). The tabernacle, then, is significant in these ways:

1. It was a portrayal of heavenly reality (Heb. 9:23–24).
2. The tabernacle was typical of the Church, which is "a habitation of God through the Spirit" (Ex 25:9; Eph 2:19–22).
3. The tabernacle was typical of the individual believer who is "a temple of the Holy Spirit" (I Cor 6:19; II Cor 6:16).
4. The holiness of God was vividly portrayed in the tabernacle. The entire service should have shown the godly Israelite that Yahweh exists apart from the sinfulness of man, and could only be approached after the most elaborate preparations. Further, the high priest was not allowed into the holy of holies, which was the place where God dwelt among His people, except once a year and then only with sacrificial blood.
5. The tabernacle at the same time was a demonstration of the grace of God. When one contemplates the greatness of God and the sinfulness of man, he is indeed amazed that God should deign to dwell with men.
6. The chief significance of the tabernacle belongs to the theology of the incarnation (*q.v.*). In the NT the idea of the divine presence culminates in the person of Jesus Christ, in whom "the Word was made flesh, and dwelt [lit., tabernacled] among us" (Jn 1:14), and in whom "all the fullness of God was pleased to dwell" (Col 1:19, RSV; cf. 2:9).

The tabernacle was, then, a principal bridge between the OT and the incarnation. The furniture of the court symbolized man's approach to God. Man must have his sin problem dealt with. At the altar there was forgiveness of sin through sacrifice (Heb 9:22), and cleansing from daily defilement at the laver (Jn 13:2–10).

On the other hand, the furniture of the holy of holies spoke of God's approach to man. Here the holiness, grace, and sovereignty of God were demonstrated in God's provision. Christ as our High Priest took the blood of His sacrifice and sprinkled it over the broken law that we might be regarded as perfect in God's eyes (Heb 9:11–15; 10:19).

The furniture of the holy place pictured Christ's work as Mediator between God and man. The table of showbread symbolized Christ as the bread of life (Jn 6:29–38; 12:24–33). By the golden lampstand He is shown to be the light of the world (Jn 8:12) as well as the light "who lights every man who comes into the world" (Jn 1:9), in the sense that He is God's final and ultimate revelation (Heb 1:1–2). Finally, the altar of incense portrayed Christ as our Intercessor (Jn 17:1–26; Heb 7:25). It is through Him that our prayers ascend to God (Heb 13:15).

Problems

There are some literary and historical problems surrounding the tabernacle. However, they are a part of the much larger problem of the OT, and as such, would be incapable of complete discussion here, let alone solution. Nevertheless, a few observations are in order on the more prominent features.

1. Some have alleged that the instructions given for the tabernacle are impractical and the work of an idealist. Whether one accepts or rejects this view will depend greatly on what he sees as God's purpose in including such a record in Scripture. Indeed, the primary purpose must have been "for our learning." Furthermore, during the same period in Egypt, it is known that portable shrines quite similar in constructional techniques to the tabernacle were in use. A portable pavilion of Queen Hetep-heres (*c.* 2600 B.C.), large enough for an ornate chair and bed, consisted of a gilded wooden framework with hooks on all sides for hanging the curtains. The beams and rods were fitted into sockets for easy erecting and dismantling. A bas relief of Rameses II (*c.* 1285 B.C.) depicts the tent of the divine king placed in the center of the Egyptian military camp (Harrison, IOT, pp. 404 f.). Therefore it is certain that structures like the tabernacle not only could be built but were built (K. A. Kitchen, "Some Egyptian Background to the Old Testament," *Tyndale House Bulletin*).
2. In the Heb. text the altar of incense and laver come in Ex 30 rather than as expected in Ex 25 and 27. This is thought by some to show that Ex 30 is a later addition to the writings of P, which are already late as to date. However, such is not warranted by the context. As a matter of fact, there are good reasons for accepting the order as deliberate and orignal (see A. H. Finn, "The Tabernacle Chapters," JTS, XVI (1915), pp. 449–482, and *Westminster Dictionary of the Bible* on "tabernacle").
3. There is a wide divergence between the LXX and the Heb. in the last chapters of Exodus. Therefore, it has been argued that the last chapters had not yet reached their final Heb. form, and that the LXX was translated from another Heb. tradition which knew nothing about an altar of incense. These conclusions are unfounded (see D. W. Gooding, *The Account*

of the Tabernacle, 1959).

4. Finally, it is claimed that in the Pentateuch as we have it there is a conflict and discrepancy between the primitive "tent of meeting" found in the E source and the ornate and unhistorical tabernacle of the later P sources. Here again, the conclusion is unjustified (see J. Orr, *The Problem of the Old Testament,* 1906, pp. 165–73, and A. H. Finn, *The Unity of the Pentateuch,* 1917, pp. 255–85).

Bibliograpny. "Tabernacle, Ark and Cherubim," CornPBE, pp. 673–677. G. Henton Davies, "Tabernacle," IDB, IV, 498–506. D. W. Gooding, "Tabernacle," NBD, pp. 1231–1234. R. K. Harrison, *Introduction to the Old Testament,* Grand Rapids: Eerdmans, 1969, pp. 403–408. A. R. S. Kennedy, "Tabernacle," HDB, IV, 653–668. K. A. Kitchen, "Some Egyptian Background to the Old Testament," *Tyndale House Bulletin,* Nos. 5, 6 (1960), pp. 7–13. W. Michaelis, "*Skēnē,* etc.," TDNT, VII, 368–394. Marten H. Woudstra, "The Tabernacle in Biblical-Theological Perspective," NPOT, pp. 88–103.

P. D. F.

TABERNACLES, FEAST OF. *See* Festivals.

TABITHA (tăb'ĭ-thȧ). An Aramaic word which Luke, the writer of Acts, rendered "Dorcas" in the Gr. (Acts 9:36). He did this apparently for the benefit of his readers. The name means "gazelle," a feminine name of endearment among both Jews and Greeks, and thus an appropriate name for the woman whom Peter raised from the dead. This was a noteworthy miracle since it was the first raising from death performed by an apostle (cf. Mt 10:8; Acts 20:9–10). The news of it spread all over Joppa and many believed on the Lord Jesus as a result of it (Acts 9:42).

Nothing is known about Tabitha except that which is given in Acts 9:36–42. She is called a "disciple" (*mathētria,* the feminine form used only here in the NT), i.e., a Christian, an actual believer in Jesus Christ. Her kindness and helpfulness had touched the lives of many persons around her. There was widespread sorrow when she died and a sense of great loss. Peter, who had healed Aeneas at Lydda ten miles to the SE, was called by the bereaving friends of the deceased Tabitha. It is not known exactly why they brought him to Joppa, whether to be a consolation to them or to attempt a miracle for them. But Peter responded to their plea. They took him to the upper room where the corpse lay; after dismissing her friends and kneeling to pray, he turned to the body and said, "Tabitha, arise." She opened her eyes and sat up. The widows whom Dorcas had helped by giving them garments and coats rejoiced, as well as the other believers.

H. E. Fi.

TABLE. The translation of seven Heb. and Gr. words.

1. Heb. *lûaḥ,* "tablet" (Ex 24:12; 31:18), the tablets of stone on which Yahweh inscribed the Ten Commandments. They were put in the ark (Deut 10:5). The heart is to be like a table, but impressionable, not adamantine like stone, that God may impress on it His law so that it governs one's life (Jer 17:1). *See* Tablet.

2. Heb. *mēsab,* "round table" (Song 1:12).

3. Heb. *shulḥān,* "table," the usual OT word, designating the table of showbread, i.e., the bread of the "Presence" (Ex 25:23 ff.), a ritual table in the tabernacle, in the holy place (Ex 26:35). Solomon made ten for the temple (II Chr 4:8); Ezekiel's temple has 12 (40:39–43).

An idolatrous table to Gad, the god of fortune, is condemned in Isa 65:11. The table of Mal 1:7 is the temple altar, a figurative use. The tables of kings are noted: Adoni-bezek (Jud 1:7), whose enemies were under it, the earliest noted table in the Bible; King Saul's at which many ate and was therefore large (I Sam 20:29, 34); the food of Solomon's table amazed the queen of Sheba (I Kgs 10:4–5); David was host to various persons at his table (II Sam 9:7), as also were Jezebel (I Kgs 18:19) and Nehemiah (Neh 5:17). Commoners had tables (I Kgs 13:20) and one provided a table for Elisha (II Kgs 4:10).

4. Gr. *anakeimai,* "recline," "table" (Jn 13:28), a couch at table height, indicative of the usual reclining posture of diners. The table often was u-shaped, allowing access to it by servants (cf. also Lk 7:38; Jn 13:23). Usually it was high enough to permit dogs under it (Mt 15:27).

5. Gr. *klinē,* "reclining couch," "table" (Mk 7:4).

6. Gr. *plax,* "table," "slab," "tablet" (II Cor 3:3; Heb 9:4). Gr. for 1 above.

7. Gr. *trapeza,* "table," with four legs, used for eating (Mt 15:27; Mk 7:28); those used by money changers in the temple (Mt 21:12; Mk 11:15); the table of the last supper (Lk 22:21); the communion table (I Cor 10:21), figurative of God's provision for the soul. See L. Goppelt, "*Trapeza,*" TDNT, VIII, 209–215.

H. G. S.

TABLE OF SHOWBREAD. *See* Tabernacle.

TABLECLOTH. According to Num 4:7 f., when the camp of Israel was to set forth on its journeys, Aaron and his sons were to place over the table of showbread a cloth of blue upon which they were to place the plates, the incense dishes, the bowls, the drink-offering flagons, and the continual bread. This cloth of blue and the utensils were then covered by a cloth of scarlet, over which was imposed a covering of goatskin. *See* Tabernacle.

TABLET

1. In the lower Tigris-Euphrates valley where clay is very plentiful, tablets of clay became the most common (and perhaps earliest) writing (*q.v.*) material. Thousands of inscribed

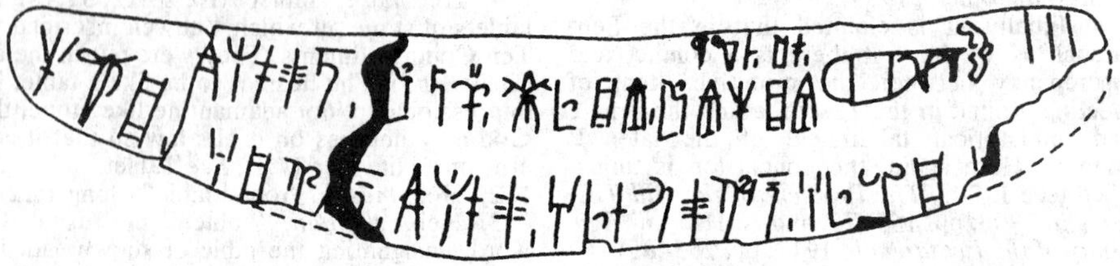

A Linear B tablet from the Mycenaean period.

tablets have survived from antiquity, giving an insight into ancient everyday life, containing receipts, literary masterpieces, business documents, wills, lawsuits, letters, word lists, etc. Some of these cuneiform tablets, such as those from Nuzu (*q.v.*) and Mari (*q.v.*), have direct bearing on the patriarchal narrative. *See* Cuneiform.

2. The correct rendering of Heb. and Gr. words improperly rendered "table" in Isa 30:8; Prov 3:3; Hab 2:2; Lk 1:63. Wooden writing tablets with a coating of wax which could easily be inscribed are known to have been in use in Assyria before Isaiah's time. Also limestone tablets have been found in Israel (e.g., the Gezer calendar, *c.* 950 B.C.), and the two "tables" (tablets, NASB, Ex 24:12; *et al.*) on which the Ten Commandments were inscribed were of stone.

3. The inaccurate rendering of Heb. *kûmāz* (Ex 35:22; Num 31:50). Those pieces of gold shaped like beads and worn as pendants around the neck or on bracelets are intended.

4. Inaccurate rendering of Heb. *bêt nephesh* (Isa 3:20), which may refer to a small perfume bottle worn around the neck.

H. F. V.

TABOR, MOUNT (tā'bŏr). A dome-shaped mountain in Galilee known in Arabic as Jebel et-Tor. Isolated from other mountains, it stands like a sentinel in the NE part of the plain of Jezreel, *c.* 12 miles N of Mount Gilboa. It is situated *c.* six miles SE of Nazareth and *c.* 12 miles SW of the Sea of Galilee.

Its highest elevation is 1,843 feet above sea level and it is some 1,350 feet above the plain of Jezreel. Its sides are steep and ascent is usually made on the W. The top is more or less flat and elliptical, stretching a half mile E-W and a quarter mile N-S.

Some suppose it to be the mountain of Deut 33:19 where an early sanctuary was to be located. It is first mentioned by name at the time of the division of the land to the tribes of Israel (Josh 19:12, 22) as the meeting place of the territories of Issachar, Naphtali, and Zebulun. Barak gathered 10,000 men here from Issachar and Zebulun in order to engage Sisera and the Canaanites near Megiddo (Jud 4:6, 12, 14). At Mount Tabor the brothers of Gideon were slain by Zebah and Zalmunna (Jud 8:18–19). In the time of the prophets it was a sanctuary for idolatry (Hos 5:1).

Dominating two important roads, the N-S route from Jezreel to the Sea of Galilee and the E-W route coming N of Megiddo from Mount Carmel and the Bay of Accho (modern Haifa), Tabor was frequently fortified. In 218 B.C. Antiochus the Great captured a town which had been built on its summit and fortified the top. During the Jewish rebellion, Josephus also encircled the top with a wall. The Mohammedan leader Saladin fortified the area in the 12th cen.

Tabor is chiefly remembered as the traditional site of the transfiguration of Christ. Helena, mother of Emperor Constantine, built a church there in A.D. 326, and subsequently shrines were dedicated to Moses and Elijah. Since the site of the transfiguration is not named in the Gospels (Mt 17:1–8; Mk 9:2–8; Lk 9:28–36), this traditional location is open to question. The two chief difficulties are the distance from Caesarea-Philippi and the probability that a town occupied the top of Tabor in NT times.

The summit is presently occupied by a Greek Orthodox church and a Franciscan monastery, in addition to the ruins of the structures previously mentioned.

H. L. D.

The Franciscan Convent on Mt. Tabor. IIS

TABRET. *See* Music.

TABRIMON (tăb-rĭm'ŏn). An Aramean ruler in Damascus during the last quarter of the 10th cen. B.C. In I Kgs 15:18 he appears as the son of Hezion and the father of Ben-hadad (I), the king of Syria. A league between Tabrimon and Rehoboam and/or Abijah is mentioned in the overtures of Asa to Ben-hadad (v. 19).

It was formerly thought that the Aramaic Melkart Stele (ANEP #499) from *c.* 850 B.C., found near Aleppo, was erected by the above Ben-hadad "the son of Tabrimmon, the son of Hezion" (ANET, p. 501; W. F. Albright, BASOR #87 [1942], pp. 23–29). Further study by Frank M. Cross indicates that the stele was misread and that instead it was erected by a certain Ben-hadad (III) who was crown prince and co-regent with his father Ben-hadad (II), a contemporary of King Ahab and enemy of Shalmaneser III (BASOR #205 [1972], 36–42).

J. R.

TACHE. An archaic rendering of the KJV to indicate that by which a thing is attached (Ex 26:6; etc.). The Heb. term appears to be a hook or "clasp" (ASV, RSV) which joined together two sets of curtains in the tabernacle *(q.v.)*. The two sets of five linen curtains each were coupled together by 50 golden taches (Ex 26:6). Under these taches the veil was hung to divide between the holy place and the holy of holies (26:33). Fifty bronze taches joined the outer goat-hair curtains (26:11), which formed a tent over the tabernacle structure. *See* Clasp.

TACHMONITE (tăk'mō-nīt). ASV, RSV and NASB spell the name Tahchemonite. A gentilic epithet attached to the first named hero in the list of David's 30 mighty men (II Sam 23:8). To judge from the parallel passage in I Chr 11:11, Tachmonite appears to be a corrupt reading of "the Hachmonite" or "(the son of) Hachmoni" (I Chr 27:32).

TACKLING. RSV and NASB use the word "tackle." Tackling is an obsolete word used in the plural in the KJV of Isa 33:23 to describe the rigging or gear of a ship consisting in ropes or cables (Heb. *ḥebel*) used as shrouds and stays to hold the mast firmly in its place and to control the sails. The same general meaning obtains for the singular tackling (Gr. *skeuē*) in Acts 27:19, but may include as well all dispensable equipment (cf. ASV marg. and Jon 1:5, LXX).

TADMOR (tăd'môr). An oasis city in the Syrian desert *c.* 135 miles NE of Damascus, halfway between the valleys of the Orontes and the Euphrates. In patriarchal times it lay on the old caravan route that led from Haran to Damascus and SW. It was also a major trading center for commerce that moved both N-S and E-W. Tadmor is first mentioned in the Assyrian texts

Airview, Temple of Bel, Palmyra. J. H. Breasted, Jr.

from Cappadocia (19th cen. B.C.), again in the Mari tablets (18th cen. B.C.), and then by Tiglath-pileser I (*c.* 1100 B.C.). Following David's victorious wars against Hamath and Zobah in Syria (II Sam 8), Solomon included Tadmor in his empire (II Chr 8:4).

The greatest era of Tadmor (renamed Palmyra by the Greeks) began with the downfall of Nabataean Petra in A.D. 105 and reached its peak under Odenatus (d. A.D. 267) and his widow, Queen Zenobia. She assumed the role of leadership on the assassination of her husband. Her court retinue included the Greek philosopher Longinus, and she was reputed to have been fluent in at least five languages. She attempted to free Tadmor from Roman influence, but was defeated in A.D. 273 by Aurelian. He completely destroyed the site in revenge for the massacre of a Roman garrison stationed there following the surrender to the Romans. Among its many ruins today stand the Temple to the Sun, a row of Corinthian columns, an aqueduct, and remnants of a wall built by Justinian. Numerous Roman tombs dot the surrounding area, while an oil pipeline from Iraq to Tripoli passes near the ancient city.

The Tamar of I Kgs 9:18 (ASV, etc.) was vocalized by the Jewish Masoretes to read Tadmor (KJV). Some scholars feel that this site was situated on the road from Hebron to Elath, and was fortified by Solomon to protect the trade route from S Arabia via Elath to Jerusalem. *See* Tamar 5.

F. E. Y.

TAHAN (tā'hăn)

1. One of the sons of Ephraim and eponymous ancestor of the Tahanites, one of the clans of the tribe of Ephraim (Num 26:35).

2. One of the ancestors of Joshua the son of Nun (I Chr 7:25).

TAHAPANES. *See* Tahpanhes.

TAHASH (tā'hăsh). The third son of Reumah, the concubine of Nahor, the brother of Abraham (Gen 22:24).

TAHATH (tā'hăth)

1. A Levite, the son of Assir, who is mentioned among the descendants of Kohath (I Chr 6:24, 37).

2–3. Two of the descendants of Ephraim. If I Chr 7:20 ff. is conceived of as a genealogy of Joshua, then Tahath is the son of Bered and the grandfather of a namesake. If this passage is treated as a list of the sons of Ephraim, then the second mention of Tahath is apparently a dittography. On the whole, the former seems preferable.

4. One of the encampments during the wandering of Israel in the wilderness (Num 33:26 f.), whose location is presently unknown.

TAHPANHES (tä'pȧ-nēz). Tahpanhes is found in Jer 43:7, 8, 9; 44:1; 46:14; Tahapanes, in Jer 2:16; Tehaphnehes, in Ezk 30:18. An Egyptian city located in the Delta, ESE of Tanis. It was the Gr. Daphnai (Herodotus II. 30) and today is known as Tell Defenneh, "mound of the grave-diggers." The Judean remnant fled to this city after the murder of Gedaliah (Jer 43:7). Jeremiah was taken along with these refugees, and at Tahpanhes he was told by the Lord to prophesy an invasion of Egypt by Nebuchadnezzar. He was also to hide large stones under the brickwork of the pavement of the palace entrance and here Nebuchadnezzar would set up his royal pavilion (43:8–10).

Sir W. M. Flinders Petrie excavated at Tell Defenneh in 1883–84 and found a fortress which probably is the building mentioned in Jer 43:9. The name of the fortress mound, Kasr el Yehudi ("the palace of the Jew's daughter"), was regarded by Petrie as a reminiscence of Jewish habitation (*Egypt and Israel,* London: SPCK, 1923, pp. 84–90). In Jer 44:1–2 Tahpanhes and several other Egyptian cities are named as residences of the displaced Jews, against whom a prophecy is directed. Ezk 30:18 refers to the city in a passage which declares judgments on the leading cities of Egypt.

C. E. D.

TAHPENES (tä'pĕ-nēz). A queen of Egypt who lived during the time of David and Solomon (I Kgs 11:19–20). The name does not appear in the historical records of Egypt. Her husband is referred to only by title ("Pharaoh king of Egypt"), but according to the chronology he must have been a king of the 21st Dynasty of Egypt (BASOR #140 [1955], p. 32). When Hadad, of Edomite royal descent, fled to Egypt for political asylum from the Israelites, Pharaoh gave him the sister of Tahpenes as his wife. This sister bore a son, Genubath, who was weaned by Tahpenes and reared in the royal household among the sons of the king.

TAHREA (tär'ē-ȧ). A Benjamite, one of the sons of Micah, whose great-grandfather was Jonathan the son of Saul (I Chr 9:41). In the parallel genealogy his name appears as Tarea (I Chr 8:35).

TAHTIM-HODSHI (tă'tĭm-hŏd'shī). The phrase "the land of Tahtim-hodshi" in the KJV and NASB of II Sam 24:6 is a transliteration of the Heb. and presumes a northern locale somewhere between Gilead and Dan to be included in the Davidic census. Following Lucian's recension of the Gr. OT, the RSV proposes the translation: "to Kadesh in the land of the Hittites." This conjecture is not without difficulties, however, since Kadesh is admittedly too far N. Others emend the difficult text to read "to the land beneath Hermon."

TAIL

1. The Heb. noun *zānāb* is used literally of the tail of a serpent (Ex 4:4), of foxes (Jud 15:4), and of the hippopotamus (Job 40:17). The word is used figuratively of a depressed people (Deut 28:13, where tail is opposed to head; cf. Deut 28:44), of degraded folk (Isa 9:14, where tail is apposite to reed, and head to palm branch, and identified in this context as "the prophet who teaches lies"), and of derogatory impotence (Isa 7:4, RSV "stumps"; Isa 19:15). The nominal verb form is translated "smite the hindmost" (KJV, Josh 10:19; Deut 25:18), but means literally "to cut off the tail."

2. The Heb. word *'alyâ* is rendered by "fat tail" in the RSV, but is translated "rump" (*q.v.*) in the KJV (Ex 29:22; *et al.*).

3. The Gr. noun *oura* is used to describe the tails of the locusts from the bottomless pit (Rev 9:10, 19) and the tail of the great red dragon (Rev 12:4).

E. R. D.

TALENT. The talent was the largest weight used by the Hebrews and was used to measure gold (I Kgs 9:14), silver (II Kgs 5:22), lead (Zech 5:7), iron (I Chr 29:7), and bronze (Ex 38:29). It is not certain whether the talent was the same in each of these cases, although Ex 38:24–29 would seem to imply this. In the OT the weight of a talent was 3,000 shekels (Ex 38:25–26) and therefore equal to *c.* 75 pounds. The discovery of a number of labeled weights in Babylonia has revealed that there was a heavy talent of *c.* 132 pounds and a light talent of *c.* 66 pounds. By knowing which of these weights was being used, the value in modern currency can be computed from the contemporary value of gold or silver. *See* Weights, Measures, and Coins.

In the NT the talent as a weight was equal to 125 *librae,* or Roman pounds of 12 ounces each, thus *c.* 94 pounds. This would be a huge weight for a hailstone (Rev 16:21; cf. the RSV paraphrase, "heavy as a hundred-weight"). As a unit of coinage its value differed considerably from place to place, but it was always comparatively high. The silver talent of Aegina was worth *c.* $1,625, while a Syrian talent was only *c.* $250 (Arndt, p. 811). The "ten thousand talents" of Mt 18:24 is obviously meant to represent an impossibly huge debt that no man could ever repay, illustrative of everyone's sin-debt to God.

The parable of the talents (Mt 25:14–30) speaks of varying numbers of talents being given by a master to his servants, to each one according to his own personal ability or potential (Gr. *dynamis*). In exegesis the talent may be considered to be worth a thousand dollars. With these large sums of money the servants were to do business by trading and investing during the master's absence. The talents are representative of the spiritual gifts and opportunities which are given to the believer, taking into account his natural abilities, intellect, and background. The "talents" are a sacred trust to be employed in the service of Christ our Master, with great reward for faithfulness as a servant. *See* Parables of Jesus.

J. R.

TALITHA CUMI (tăl'ĭ-thȧ ko͞o'mī). An Aramaic expression found in Mk 5:41 meaning "maiden, or little girl, arise." The more reliable MSS make it clear that *kum* (masculine imperative) instead of *kumi* (feminine imperative) was the original reading; therefore the NASB has "Talitha kum!" These tender words spoken to the daughter of Jairus furnish good evidence that the normal language of Jesus was Aramaic.

TALMAI (tăl'mī)

1. One of the three sons of Anak who dwelt in Hebron. Their gigantic size terrified the Israelites, but in faith Caleb went up against them and drove the three brothers out (Num 13:22; Josh 15:14; Jud 1:10). A tall, fair-skinned race called Tammahu, pictured on the Egyptian monuments, has been thought by some to refer to this family.

2. The king of Geshur, a small Aramaean kingdom NE of the Sea of Galilee. He was the father of Maacah, the wife of David and mother of Absalom. Absalom fled to Geshur's court after the murder of Amnon (II Sam 3:3; 13:37; I Chr 3:2).

TALMON (tăl'mŏn). The eponymous ancestor of a Levitical family which was associated with the office of gatekeepers of the temple and which returned with Zerubbabel to Jerusalem (I Chr 9:17; Ezr 2:42; Neh 7:45; 12:25), where they continued that ministry in post-Exilic times (Neh 11:19).

TALMUD (tăl'mŭd). The Heb. term *talmûd* is derived from *lāmad,* "to study," "to learn." It is applied to the second greatest literary achievement in Heb. and Aramaic after the Bible, and is an interpretation of the Law, as well as the repository of a vast fund of wise counsel, covering the period from Ezra (*c.* 450 B.C.) to about A.D. 500.

Development of the Traditional Materials

Before the post-Exilic prophetic period came to an end, there was the institution and development of a new force among the Jewish people. Ezra came from Babylon in 458 B.C. with the ideal of directing the reorganized Jewish settlement in Israel based on the principles and institutions of *Tôrâ* (the Law). Ezra marks the beginning of the movement of the *Sôph^{e}rîm* (the scribes, *q.v.,* the religious leadership), who popularized the knowledge and appreciation of the Scriptures. Public readings were instituted, of which Neh 8 was a beginning example. This was the start of the oral transmission of *Targûmîm* ("interpretations," the transliterations and paraphrases of Scripture), especially that of the Pentateuch.

The development of *Targûmîm* and Oral Law was possible because of the Midrash (*q.v.*), a running commentary on the biblical text probably started by Ezra and his companions. The Midrash covers a wide scope, not only including legal matters but also ethics and theology. When the Midrash treated legal matters, it was known as *Midrash Halakah* (from Heb. *hālak,* "to walk," hence to walk within the law); in the other areas it was *Midrash Haggadah* (the latter word *'agadâ* meaning "narration").

In developing the traditions, generations of teachers did not reach their decisions on individual impulse. Just as Ezra had a group about him, so in every succeeding generation there were corporate bodies that deliberated and acted in unison. Such successive corporate bodies functioned during the time of the *Sôph^{e}rîm*. There is no extant material of these sessions and there is no significant information about any of its members except fragments of assertions in the writing of a later age, especially the material of *Pirkē 'Abôt* ("Sayings of the Fathers"). The *Sôph^{e}rîm* laid the basis for the future literary collections of Judaism.

The *Sôph^{e}rîm* continued until about 180 B.C. and were succeeded by the *Hasidîm* ("Pious Ones") of the Maccabean Age, and then in turn by the Pharisee party. From the time of the *Hasidîm* until Hillel (d. A.D. 10) and Shammai there were five pairs of leaders; thus the period is known as the *Zûgôt* ("pairs"). These pairs of leaders carried on the work of tradition, adding new concepts of interpretation.

The *Zûgôt* teachers developed a new method of instruction rivaling the Midrash. The Oral Law was now taught without referring to the Scriptures, although it was asserted that Scriptures support the teaching of the traditions. With the growing mass of tradition it was easier to handle the various topics as needed, rather than follow the tedious order of the Scriptures. By this topical study, the teaching and memory work was done through continuous repetition, and the name Mishnah (from Heb. *shānâ,* "to repeat") was applied to the new method of teaching. Beginning at the end of the 1st cen.

B.C., especially with the schools of Hillel and Shammai, and proceeding to *c.* A.D. 200, the teachers who taught by this new method were called *Tannaîm* (from Aramaic *teₙn'a,* Heb. *shānâ,* "to teach orally").

Midrash study, however, was not set aside by the Mishnah approach. It continued to be used in the *haggadâh* area as well as in the *halakah* area of teaching, side by side with the Mishnah method.

From Hillel onward, and perhaps even before, there was a process of organization and codification of the growing mass of *halakah* according to the method of Mishnah. An important collection was made by Akiba (martyred in A.D. 135), and continued by his disciple Meir. In turn, Judah HaNasi's labors and final development of the Mishnah collection was committed to written form in post-biblical Hebrew *c.* A.D. 200. This Mishnah makes use of many of the *halakah* decisions so that it is a digest of the work of scholars from the *Sôpherîm, Hasidîm, Zûgôt,* and *Tannaîm* periods. The work became the basis of authority on the Jewish traditions over the next several centuries, and was one of the chief pieces of literature for study and research in the academies in the lands of Israel and Babylon.

Judah HaNasi, however, did not include all the Mishnah collection and *halakôt* (pl. of *halakah*) collection current in his day. As the scholars in the rabbinic academies continued to add explanations and interpretations of the Mishnah in the succeeding period (*c.* A.D. 200–500), they used the additional material, *Tosefta* (Aramaic *tûseft'a,* "additions") and *Baraita* (Aramaic *barêt'a,* or individual *halakôt*), together with their own opinions. Many *haggadah* as well as Midrash sources were also used. The scholars who carried on these studies in the academies were called *Amōraîm* ("interpreters"). Their work was necessary in order that the Mishnah could be adequately explained, that many old *halakôt* be reinforced, and that many new *halakôt* be formulated for new problems which Judaism encountered in its ever changing historical and cultural situations. The work of these scholars in Aramaic is called Gemara (Aramaic *gemara',* "completion"). The combination of HaNasi's Mishnah text with the Gemara is designated Talmud.

Two Versions of the Talmud

There were two active schools in the *Amōraîm* period, in the land of Israel as well as in the cities of Babylon. These two sets of scholars worked with the Mishnah of Judah HaNasi to produce two versions of Gemara; therefore there are two versions of the Talmud. One is the *Yerûshâlmi,* or "Jerusalemite," of Israel and the other is known as the Babylonian Talmud. The latter is three times as long, for the Babylonian Jews had greater freedom and less persecution than their counterparts in Israel to produce a work that reflected the entire secular and religious knowledge of the period in successive *halakah* and *haggadah.* The *Yerûshâlmi* in Western Aramaic was finished shortly after A.D. 425, and the final redaction of the more authoritative Babylonian Talmud in Eastern Aramaic was finally redacted about A.D. 500.

Orders of Division

The Mishnah is divided into six orders. Since the Gemara is the commentary on the Mishnah, the commentary also follows this division. Each order is further subdivided into tractates for a total of 63 tractates, ten to 11 tractates for each order. Each tractate is still further divided into chapters. When references are made to material in the Talmud they are designated by tractate followed by either chapter and verse or by page number. The orders are (1) *Zeraîm,* or "seeds," the laws of agriculture; (2) *Mô'ēd,* or "festivals," the regulations of the sabbaths; (3) *Nashîm,* or "women," laws concerning women, marriage and divorce; (4) *Nezikîm,* or "damages," the civil and criminal law; (5) *Qōdashîm,* or "things sanctified," laws that treat the sanctuary and sacrificial rites; and (6) *Tōhōrôt,* or "purity," laws of Levitical purity.

Value and Influence

Both versions of the Talmud were completed *c.* A.D. 450–500. These became the guide of main stream Judaism in the centuries of the Middle Ages, especially in Europe when secular scholarship became virtually nonexistent. In this period when Jewish missionary activity ceased and the soul of the Jew went inward, he had a repository of literature to engage his religious and intellectual yearning. In this way he had an escape from the world around him with its brutal hate and persecution. The Talmud also had its influence on the Renaissance, and through the new thrust in intellectual pursuits the Talmud helped in shaping these new values ultimately to have an impact on the modern era. Finally, the Talmud provides Christian scholars with the means to understand the practice of Judaism as well as to have access to ancient Jewish insights into scriptural exegesis and practice. The Mishnah in particular gives a great deal of knowledge on Jewish belief and practice in the lst cen. A.D., e.g., temple life and practice.

Bibliography. Translation of the Talmud in English: I. Epstein, ed., *The Babylonian Talmud with Indices,* 18 vol., London: Soncino Press, 1961. Translation of the Mishnah in English: H. Danby, trans., *The Mishnah,* Oxford: Univ. Press, 1950. J. Bowker, *The Targums and Rabbinic Literature and Introduction to Jewish Interpretation of Scripture,* New York: Cambridge Univ. Press, 1961. I. Epstein, *Judaism,* Baltimore: Penguin, 1959; "The Rabbinic Tradition," *The Jewish Heritage,* Washington, D.C.: *Bnai Brit* Adult Jewish Education, 1955, pp. 51–69. J. Kaplan, *The Redaction of the Babylonian Talmud,* New York: Bloch, 1933. S. M. Lehrman, *The World of the*

Midrash, Cranbury, N.J.: A. S. Barnes, 1961. G. F. Moore, *Judaism in the First Centuries of the Christian Era,* Vol. I, Cambridge: Harvard Univ. Press, 1927. H. L. Strack, *Introduction to Talmud and Midrash,* Philadelphia: Jewish Publication Society, 1931. M. Waxman, *A History of Jewish Literature,* Vol. I, New York: Thomas Yoseloff, 1960.

L. Go.

TAMAH (tā'mȧ). The eponymous ancestor of a family of temple servants who returned from Babylon with Zerubbabel (Ezr 2:53; Neh 7:55). The name Tamah (Neh 7:55, KJV) or Thamah (Ezr 2:53, KJV) is an inconsistent and erroneous rendering of Temah (ASV, RSV).

TAMAR (tā'mȧr)

1. The daughter-in-law of Jacob's son Judah and widowed wife of Judah's son Er. When Er's brother Onan refused to be a husband to Tamar and died, Tamar returned to her Canaanite home with Judah's promise that she should have his third son Shelah when he was old enough. When this promise was not fulfilled and Judah's wife died, Tamar seduced Judah by veiling her identity and pretending to be a harlot of the heathen worship cult. She became pregnant and when Judah was going to have her put to death, Tamar revealed that she had conceived by Judah himself. She showed the pledges Judah had given her. Judah was convicted by the wrong he had done her and she was spared. One of the twins born to Tamar was Perez (Phares, KJV) who through Judah was in the direct line of the ancestry of David, and hence of Christ (Gen 38; Mt 1:3–6; Lk 3:31–33).

2. A beautiful daughter of David, sexually assaulted by her half brother Amnon through a deceiving plot. Infatuated before that, he then bitterly rejected her. Tamar's brother Absalom then protected her and vengefully effected Amnon's murder after two years (II Sam 13).

3. A beautiful daughter of Absalom, possibly named for his beloved sister (II Sam 14:27).

4. A town of unknown site near the border of Judah and Edom at the S end of the Dead Sea. Mentioned by Ezekiel as a border place of the future restored Israel (Ezk 47:19; 48:28).

5. A place in the wilderness of Judah, fortified by Solomon (I Kgs 9:18, ASV, RSV), perhaps the same as Tamar 4 or Hazezon-tamar (*q.v.*). The KJV, however, reads Tadmor (*q.v.;* cf. II Chr 8:4), following the suggestion of the Jewish masoretes.

N. B. B.

TAMARISK. *See* Plants.

TAMBOURINE. *See* Music.

TAMMUZ. *See* Gods, False.

TANACH. *See* Taanach.

TANHUMETH (tăn-hū'mēth). The father of Seraiah, who was one of the military commanders in support of Gedaliah, the gubernatorial nominee of Nebuchadnezzar over Judah. In II Kgs 25:23 Tanhumeth is a Nethophathite (i.e., from Nethophah, a village halfway between Bethlehem and Tekoa). However, the insertion of the words "the sons of Ephai" after Tanhumeth in Jer 40:8 makes Nethophathite refer not to Tanhumeth, but to Ephai.

TANNER. *See* Occupations: Tanner.

TAPHATH (tā'făth). The daughter of Solomon who was married to Ben-abinadab, the prefect in charge of the royal revenues from the district of Naphath-dor (I Kgs 4:11).

TAPPUAH (tăp'ū-ȧ)

1. One of the sons of Hebron (I Chr 2:43), a descendant of Caleb.

2. A town mentioned in Josh 15:34 as lying in the Shephelah W of Jerusalem. Its site has not been identified with certainty, but it lies in the group of towns including Jarmuth, Adullam, Socoh, and Azekah, all located in the foothills separating the Maritime plain from the hill country of Judea.

3. A town on the N border of Ephraim which belonged to Ephraim but whose land was in the territory of Manasseh (Josh 16:8; 17:8). Its king was among the many Canaanite rulers slain by Joshua (Josh 12:17). Its location is near the brook Kanah which empties into the Mediterranean. It has been identified with the large Tell Sheikh Abu Zarad, *c.* ten miles SSW of Shechem and five miles NW of Shiloh. It is perhaps the Tiphsah that was pillaged by Menahem (II Kgs 15:16; cf. RSV). *See* En-tappuah.

G. A. T.

TARAH (târ'ȧ). More correctly Terah as used in RSV and ASV. An unidentified encampment of the Israelites in area of Kadesh-barnea during the 38 years of wandering (Num 33:27 f.).

TARALAH (tăr'ȧ-lȧ). One of the 14 cities in the land of Canaan allotted to the tribe of Benjamin (Josh 18:27). From other cities in the list it appears to be in the hill country, NW of Jerusalem. Père Abel locates the village in the vicinity of *Khirbet Erha* below the hill *er-Ram* to the SW, where reservoirs and a large cistern as well as evidence of occupation from Israelitic times through the Roman period are discoverable (*Géographie de la Palestine,* Paris: Gabalda, 1933–1938, II, 480).

TAREA (târ'ē-ȧ). A member of the royal Benjamite lineage whose father Micah was the grandson of Jonathan, the son of Saul (I Chr 8:35). In the parallel genealogy his name appears as Tahrea (I Chr 9:41).

TARES. *See* Plants.

TARGET. In the KJV of I Sam 17:6 "target" is

a mistranslation of the Heb. *kîdôn,* which means javelin or spear (ASV, RSV). Target is a misrendering also in the KJV of the Heb. *ṣinnâ* in I Kgs 10:16; *bis* in II Chr 9:15 and 14:8; and is correctly translated as "shield" in ASV and RSV. In Job 16:12 the RSV and NASB render the Heb. noun *maṭṭārâ* as "target" for arrows, while the KJV and ASV have "mark."

TARGUM. *See* Talmud; Versions, Ancient and Medieval.

TARPELITES (tär'pĕ-līts). One of the official (RSV "officials") or ethnic (KJV "tarpelites") groups associated with Rehum the Persian commander and Shimshai the scribe in writing a defamatory letter to Artaxerxes I (465–425 B.C.) against the rebuilding activities of the returned exiles (Ezr 4:9).

TARSHISH (tär'shĭsh). The term has a fourfold usage in Scripture.

1. A "son" or descendant(s) of Javan, grandson of Japheth, and great-grandson of Noah (Gen 10:4; I Chr 1:7), probably also referring to the land (see 4).
2. A son of Bilhan, and grandson of Benjamin (I Chr 7:10).
3. One of the seven notable princes of Ahasuerus, ruler of Persia (Est 1:14).
4. A place in the western Mediterranean region, and thought by many (Herodotus IV.152) to have been identified with Tartessus, an ancient city or region located along the Guadalquivir River near the SW coast of Spain (*q.v.*), W of Gibraltar. Because several of the OT references are concerned with merchants, trade, and ships (I Kgs 10:22; Jon 1:3), it has been suggested that Tarshish was a land bordering on the sea (also Isa 60:9; 66:19). The land was rich in metals such as silver, iron, tin, and lead (Jer 10:9; Ezk 27:12). It was the place to which Jonah planned to flee from Joppa, on the Mediterranean coast of Palestine, when he was trying to run away from God (Jon 1:3; 4:12).

The word Tarshish is a Phoenician term traced from the Akkadian word meaning "to melt or to be smelted," thus the noun form would be "a smelting plant or refinery." On the basis of this meaning of the word William F. Albright has suggested that the term Tarshish could refer to any land which contained natural minerals, or any place where mining and smelting operations were carried on (BASOR #83 [1941], pp. 21–22). However, a land in the western Mediterranean area having good deposits of minerals would be a very good identification. It seems evident that the mineral wealth of Spain attracted the Phoenicians who founded colonies there as early as the 10th or 9th cen. B.C. Rio Tinto, 85 miles N of Cadiz in Spain, is the richest mining district around the Mediterranean. Today one million tons of silver, gold, and copper ores are mined there each year. An 8th cen. B.C. cemetery with Phoenician objects was excavated at this site (AJA, LXXI [1967], 183). A Phoenician inscription known as the Nora Stele, dating from the 9th cen. B.C., seems to tell of their capture of Tarshish, a smelting site on the island of Sardinia, which is also located in the western Mediterranean. Evidently, then, Tarshish was the name of at least two Phoenician mining cities.

The term "navy" or "ships of Tarshish" seems to refer to the large ships used in the Tarshish trade which carried smelted metal from Solomon's seaport at Ezion-geber, on the Gulf of Aqabah, to distant lands (I Kgs 10:22; 22:48; II Chr 9:21). Nelson Glueck's work at Ezion-geber (*q.v.*) has uncovered the extensive warehouse at this seaport where Solomon based his navy of Tarshish. The ships of Tarshish were thus identified with the transportation of minerals, and came to be symbols of wealth and power (Ezk 27:25). They were also used as illustrations of proud human inventions receiving divine judgment and destruction in the past and in the future day of the Lord (Ps 48:7; Isa 2:16; 23:1). *See* Ships.

Bibliography. Frank M. Cross, "An Interpretation of the Nora Stone," BASOR #208 (1972), pp. 13–19. David Neiman, "Phoenician Place Names," JNES, XXIV (1965), 113–115. J. M. Sola-Sole, "Semitic Elements in Ancient Hispania," CBQ, XXIX (1967), 487–494.

P. S. H.

TARSUS (tär'sŭs). Tarsus lay astride the Cydnus River in Cilicia about ten miles from the Mediterranean at 80 feet above sea level. Normally the oppressive atmosphere of such a place would be most destructive of vigorous municipal or commercial life. But about two miles N of the city the hills begin to rise gently and extend in undulating ridges until they meet the Taurus Mountains. And about ten miles N of the lowland city a second Tarsus rose. Partly a summer residence, it served a considerable population as a year-round home. The more bracing climate of the upland town offset the enervating climate of the lower region. Some 20 miles N of the upland town were the Cilician Gates, a narrow gorge through which cut the only good trade route between Syria and Asia Minor. Its location on this route brought great wealth to Tarsus.

While the Cydnus was navigable by light vessels right up into the middle of Tarsus in Roman times, most ships docked at the harbor, which was five or six miles S of the city. At that point was the spring-fed lake Rhegma, surrounded on all but the S side by the harbor town and the wharf installations. Great skill and diligence must have been expended on maintaining the channel of the Cydnus and the harbor. In later centuries slackness required an auxiliary channel to reduce flooding. The cut to the E of town (made by Justinian, A.D. 527–563) in time became the main bed of the river and remains so today.

With a continuous history of six millenniums Tarsus is one of the oldest cities in the world. It was probably the capital of Kizzuwatna, ancient Cilicia, in Hittite times. Shalmaneser III captured the city in 832 B.C., and in 696 B.C. it was plundered by Sennacherib. Greek merchants established a colony there early in the 7th cen. B.C. to be near the silver and high quality iron resources of the Taurus Mountains (JNES, XXX [1971], 99–109). Alexander saved the city from destruction at the hand of the retreating Persians. Tarsus became self-governing in the Seleucid period, but Pompey annexed it for Rome in 64 B.C. Antony granted Tarsus the status of a free city in 41 B.C. and exempted it from taxes.

During the 1st cen. A.D., Tarsus was the capital and only great city of Cilicia. Along with its commercial and agricultural wealth, it boasted a great university and ranked with Athens and Alexandria as an intellectual center. The city's fine scholars were numerous. Athenodorus the Stoic was the companion of Cato the Younger; Athenodorus Kananites was tutor and adviser of Augustus; Nestor taught Augustus' nephew Marcellus and reportedly Tiberius; and Antipater was head of a school in Athens.

The apostle Paul was born in Tarsus, and was a Roman citizen. It seems evident that many citizens of Tarsus received Roman citizenship at the hands of Pompey, Julius Caesar, Antony, and Augustus. Paul's ancestors may have been among them. Excavation has so far been unable to recreate the city of Paul's day, which lies under the modern town and adjacent farmland.

H. F. V.

TARTAK. *See* Gods, False.

TARTAN (tär'tăn). The title (Heb. *tartān* from Assyrian *turtānu* or *tartanu*) of an Assyrian army general (cf. RSV "commander-in-chief," Isa 20:1), a rank borne by two individuals mentioned in the Bible. One, serving under Sargon II, effected the capture of Ashdod (*c.* 711 B.C., Isa 20:1); the other was dispatched by Sennacherib (*c.* 701 B.C.) with two other high ranking Assyrian officers to demand of Hezekiah the capitulation of Jerusalem (II Kgs 18:17).

TASKMASTERS. Petty Egyptian officials (Heb. *nōgēś*, "taskmaster," "oppressor") who had general superintendence of the labor gangs of enslaved Israelites (Ex 3:7; 5:6, 10, 13 f.). Immediately subordinate to them in charge of the actual work were Israelite gang-masters (Heb. *shōṭēr;* Ex 5:14). The cruelty of Egyptian overseers is reflected in the OT and is confirmed by Egyptian reliefs and by the very name they bore (lit., "drivers to work"; cf. LXX *ergodiōktēs*). The same Heb. word is used of "oppressors" in Job 3:18 ("taskmaster," RSV,

A Roman arch in Tarsus. HFV

NASB), and of "exactors" in Isa 60:17 ("taskmasters," RSV, ASV marg.; "overseers," NASB). An equivalent term to the foregoing is the Heb. *śārê missîm,* captains of the corvée or levy (Ex 1:11).

David and Solomon organized enforced Israelite labor gangs over which they placed officers such as Adoram and Adoniram (II Sam 20:24; I Kgs 4:6; 5:14, 16). When King Rehoboam determined to make this service even more severe, the people stoned his overseer Adoram and rebelled (I Kgs 12:4–18). *See* Levy.

TATNAI (tăt'nī). The Persian governor of the district of Samaria, who stopped the rebuilding of the temple under Zerubbabel (Ezr 5:3, 6) until he had the matter of Cyrus' permission to the Jews investigated in the archives of Darius (Ezr 6:6–13). He was identified with the satrap over Babylon and Trans-Euphratia, Ushtannu (Hystanes), e.g., in the ICC volume on Ezra (1913), until Olmstead in 1944 pointed out the correct identification. In a document dated June 5, 502 B.C., he is specifically cited as "Ta-at-tan-ni," the *paḫatu* or governor subordinate to the satrap over Ebir-nari. Thus he acted as the deputy of Ushtannu in the W, since the two satrapies were too large for one man to administer successfully. The full phrase corresponds exactly with the Heb. phrase which is rendered by the KJV, "governor on this side the river." Ebir-nari should be rendered "across the river," i.e., Samaria as viewed from the E.

Bibliography. A. T. Olmstead, "Tattenai, Governor of 'Across the River,'" JNES, III (1944), 46.

E. M. Y.

TATTLER. One who utters silly talk or nonsense, hence a prater or babbler (I Tim 5:13, KJV, ASV; gossip, RSV). The cognate verb is used to describe the malicious conduct of Diotrephes who "prated" or brought unjustified charges against the elder John with evil words (III Jn 10).

TATTOOING. An indelible mark upon the surface of the body caused by the insertion of pigment beneath the skin. The word "tattoo" (Heb. *qa'ăqa'*, "incision") occurs only in the RSV (cf. NEB, NASB) of Lev 19:28: "You shall not . . . tattoo any marks upon you" (KJV, ASV: "print any marks"), where it is closely related to "cuttings in the flesh." While "cuttings in the flesh" have reference here to mourning customs, the tattooing does not appear to pertain to such practice. Indeed, "gashing" (RSV, Jer 41:5; 47:5; 48:37), "cuttings in the flesh" (Lev 19:28*a*; Lev 21:5; Deut 14:1), and mutilation (Ex 21:6) must be differentiated from tattooing. The above word for "incision" occurs elsewhere only in late Heb.

The practice of tattooing may be comprehended by a passage in the Mishnah: "If a man wrote [on his skin] pricked-in writing [he is culpable]. If he wrote but did not prick it in, or pricked it in but did not write it, he is not culpable, but only if he writes it and pricks it in with ink or eye-paint or aught that leaves a lasting mark. R. Simeon b. Judah says in the name of R. Simeon: he is not culpable unless he writes there the name [of a god], for it is written, Nor print any marks upon you: I am the Lord" (Makkoth 3, 6).

In the ancient Near East tattooing and branding were widely practiced. Slaves had marks placed upon them to indicate their status and their owners (Code of Hammurabi, 226-227, ANET, p. 176; Breasted, *Ancient Records of Egypt*, iii. 414; iv. 405). From secular usage the custom migrated to the sacral personnel who are mentioned occasionally as receiving stigmata upon the head or face or arms to indicate their status in respect to their god. They may be viewed, accordingly, as the slaves and property of the god whose name or mark they bear (cf. Herodotus II. 113; Lucian, *The Syrian Goddess*, 59; III Macc 2:29). Although branding and the imposition of indelible marks perhaps served also as a penalty for crime (cf. Code of Hammurabi #146, ANET, p. 172), its usage in the Bible is sacral throughout.

In its literal sense this practice is referred to in Lev 19:28*b*, where the prohibition forbids the printing or tattooing of any marks upon the person; in Gen 4:15, where the Lord put a mark on Cain; and in I Kgs 20:41, where the prophet appears to have disclosed to the king a marking peculiar to his office.

In a figurative sense, which presupposes the actual custom, the custom is mentioned in Ex 13:9, 16, where the feast of Mazzoth and the redemption of the firstborn are to be as a mark on the hand and as a memorial or frontlets between the eyes (cf. Deut 6:8; 11:18; 14:1). Ezekiel sees in vision a mark of inviolability placed upon the foreheads of those who groaned over the abominations of Judah (Ezk 9:4; cf. Rev 7:3-8). In Rev 13:16 the mark of the beast is defined as its name or the number of its name. In Isa 44:5 the prophet envisions the willing response to Yahweh of those who will write on their hands, "Belonging to the Lord" (RSV). Even Yahweh Himself assures the discouraged that He has graven them on the palms of His hands (Isa 49:16). Paul states that he bears on his body the marks (Gr. *stigmata*) of Jesus (Gal 6:17). *See* Mark (sign).

Bibliography. Otto Betz, "*Stigma*," TDNT, VII, 657-664.

E. R. D.

TAU (tô). The 19th letter of the Gr. alphabet. The Greeks borrowed their alphabet from the Phoenicians presumably sometime in the 8th cen. B.C.; consequently, the 22nd or last letter of the Heb. alphabet, *taw*, is generally related to the Gr. letter *tau*. Originally, the Semitic *taw* was represented by an upright or oblique cross (cf. Ezk 9:4, 6). The Greeks transmuted the letter somewhat, preferring the upright form but deleting the projection of the vertical line above the transversal – hence the form T.

TAVERN. *See* Appii Forum; Inn.

TAX, TAXES. In patriarchal times, for the semi-nomadic Hebrews taxation was spasmodic. Instead, voluntary gifts were made in return for protection or other advantage (Gen 32:13-21; 33:10; 43:11; cf. I Sam 10:27). Because of the severe famine in Egypt during Joseph's term of office as vizier, he bought all except the land of the priests for the crown. The people gave 20 percent of their crop to the pharaoh (Gen 47:20-26).

Compulsory taxation is first seen imposed on others by Israel when the Canaanites were compelled to serve under tribute (Heb. *mas*, "task-work," Josh 16:10; 17:13; Jud 1:28-35). This system of corvée or forced labor is known to have been imposed on the common people of Palestine and Syria in the 2nd mil. B.C., as mentioned in the Amarna and Ugaritic tablets. Jacob foretold that the tribe of Issachar would be subjected to slave labor (Gen 49:15, RSV).

Under the Mosaic law. According to theocratic law, each male above 20 years of age was assessed a fixed sum of one-half shekel (Ex 30:11-16). This was for the service of the tabernacle. After a lapse it was reinstated for the repair of the temple during Joash's reign (II Chr 24:6, 9). There were also tithes, first fruits, redemption money of the firstborn, and special offerings.

Under the monarchy. The chief fixed means of taxation were: (1) tithe of produce of soil and livestock (I Sam 8:15, 17), similar to the one-tenth tax levied by the king of Ugarit; (2) forced military service of one month each year (I Chr 27:1; cf. I Sam 8:12; I Kgs 9:21-22); (3) annual gifts or tribute to the king from subject peoples (I Kgs 4:21; 10:25) or in time of war (I Sam 16:20; 17:18); (4) import duties (I Kgs 10:14-15); (5) monopoly of certain branches of commerce, as gold (I Kgs 9:28; 22:48), and

The Black Obelisk of Shalmaneser III of Assyria, showing tribute bearers. BM

horses and chariots from Egypt and Kue (I Kgs 10:28–29, NASB); (6) Amos 7:1 suggests that the early crop of hay was appropriated for the king's use.

Special taxation was demanded in emergencies (II Kgs 15:20). It seems to have been annual (II Kgs 17:4). Exemption from taxes was given as a reward for military service (I Sam 17:25).

Solomon's "glory" demanded excessive taxation, causing later rebellion (I Kgs 12:4). He had 12 officers, each having to provide the court provisions for one month of the year (I Kgs 4:7 ff.). For the first time Israelites gave forced labor (I Kgs 5:13 ff.). Amos warned Israel that the men of rank were exacting illegal taxes from the poor people (Amos 5:11).

The Black Obelisk of Shalmaneser III portrays in bas-relief the kneeling figure of King Jehu of Israel presenting tribute to that Assyrian king. Thirteen Israelite porters are shown bringing vessels of silver and gold, a royal staff or scepter, and various animals such as camels, antelope, and monkeys (ANEP #351–355).

Menahem of Israel exacted 50 talents of silver each from men of wealth to pay 1,000 talents to Assyria (II Kgs 15:20). Ahaz of Judah robbed the temple treasury to do likewise (II Kgs 16:8). When the tribute was not paid, the suzerain king would invade the country of his vassal to collect it and inflict punishment (II Kgs 17:4–5; Hos 8:10, NASB).

Under the Persians. Jews paid tribute in kind for maintenance of the king's household. Added was a monetary payment of 40 shekels a day (Neh 5:14–15). Ezr 4:13 indicates three branches of revenue: (1) toll—probably collected at bridges and on main roads; (2) tribute—fixed payments to the suzerain ruler; (3) custom—excise tax on articles consumed. Ministers of the house of God were immune (Ezr 7:24).

Under Egypt and Syria. The Ptolemies introduced the farming out of taxes to the highest bidder, who gained the right to squeeze his own margin of profit.

Under the Romans. In Judea direct taxes were collected by imperial officers. A poll tax, or head money, was levied on all persons up to 65 years, women from 12 years, men from 14. Ground tax was one-tenth of all grain, one-fifth of wine and fruit. Customs or tolls on imports and exports and on goods passing through the country were sold to the highest bidders. These men were the hated publicans or tax collectors (Gr. *telōnēs*), noted for their extortion (cf. Mt 10:3; Lk 19:8). *See* Publican.

In the time of Nehemiah, the people agreed to an annual contribution of one-third shekel for the house of God (Neh 10:32; Ezr 6:8). Since Ex 30:13 required payment according to the standard of the sanctuary, money changers were found in the temple to convert the hated Roman coins used in daily commerce to the less offensive coins minted in Tyre (cf. Jn 2:14). Jews of the Dispersion sent this temple tax to

Jerusalem after they became 20 years of age (Jos *Ant.* xiv.7.2). It was concerning the temple tax of two drachmas or a half-shekel that the Lord was asked in Mt 17:24.

See Weights, Measures, and Coins.

I. R.

TAX COLLECTOR. *See* Publican.

TAXING. Used twice in the KJV (Lk 2:2; Acts 5:37), the word means the formal registration and enrollment of population and property. Census is probably a current equivalent. It was the first step toward complete statistical returns in the empire.

Lk 2:1 refers the taxing to the decree of Caesar Augustus, presumably at the approximate time of the birth of Jesus Christ. As quoted in Acts 5:37, Gamaliel, the "doctor of the law," associates it with the revolt of Judas of Galilee, which took place in A.D. 6. The accuracy of Luke the historian, however, is unquestionable. Secular history relates that Herod had fallen into disrepute with Augustus. As a result, Judea was treated as a Roman province and all Jews had to take an oath of fidelity to the emperor. Six thousand Pharisees refused to comply and caused trouble. Josephus, the Jewish historian, coincides this incident with the birth of Christ. Cyrenius (Quirinius), a senator or procurator, was involved in the registration. It took place in the thirty-third year of Herod's reign. The enrollment of the people, "each in his own city" (Lk 2:3), was carried out as the first step of this census. Herod, however, succeeded in mollifying Caesar, and the decree was suspended. It was later completed when Judea was settled as a Roman province. At that time Cyrenius was sent, as president of Syria, to complete the census and impose the tax. This caused the revolt headed by Judas, A.D. 6, and mentioned in Acts 5:37. *See* Census; Cyrenius.

I. R.

TEACH, TEACHER, TEACHING

In the Old Testament

Terminology. In various English versions 12 Heb. terms in the OT are rendered by some form of the word "teach." The more important are as follows:

1. Heb. *'ālap*, "get familiar with" (Job 33:33; 35:11). The verb is used four times in the OT and is rendered in Prov 22:25 as "learn" and in Job 15:5 by the verb "uttereth" (RSV, NASB "teach").

2. Heb. *bîn* occurs *c.* 125 times in the OT in the general sense of "understand." In two instances the causative tense has been translated as "taught" (II Chr 35:3; Neh 8:9).

3. Heb. *dābar.* Appearing nearly 1,500 times in its various forms in the OT, it is rendered as "speak" 814 times and as "say" 119 times. The KJV translated the verb idiomatically as "taught" in Jer 28:16 (ASV "hast spoken"; RSV "uttered") and in Jer 29:32 (ASV "hath spoken"; RSV "has talked"). The RSV also uses "taught" (KJV, ASV "spoken") to render the verb in Deut 13:5.

4. Heb. *yāda'* occurs over 940 times and is translated 662 times by the verb "know." The causative form of the verb is rendered as "teach" in nine instances in the KJV (Deut 4:9; Jud 8:16; II Chr 23:13; Job 32:7; 37:19; Ps 90:12; Prov 9:9; Isa 40:13 [RSV "instruct"], and Ezr 7:25 where it represents the cognate Aramaic *yeda'*). In addition, the RSV uses the word "teach" as the translation of the causative tense in Ps 51:6; 78:5; 143:8.

5. Heb. *yāsar,* "chasten, correct, instruct," in one instance is translated by the verb "teach" (Prov 31:1).

6. Heb. *śākal,* "to have insight," is rendered in the KJV as "taught" in II Chr 30:22 (NASB "show good insight") and "teacheth" in Prov 16:23 (RSV "makes judicious").

7. Heb. *ḥākam,* "to be wise," is causative in Prov 5:13 ("teachers"), and is idiomatically rendered in Ps 105:22 as "to teach wisdom."

8. Heb. *yārâ,* "direct, teach, instruct." The causative form of the verb is correctly rendered over 40 times in the KJV by some form of the verb "teach."

9. Heb. *lāmad* is translated 57 times in the KJV by some form of the word "teach." In addition the RSV uses the word "taught" to render the verb in Isa 50:4, where it occurs twice (ASV, KJV "learned").

It is apparent that some of the foregoing Heb. words are rendered periphrastically by some form of the word "teach" in order to render into English the nuance of the particular passage. However, *yārâ* and *lāmad* are basically the Heb. terms which may be generally equated with the English word "teach" and its cognates.

God as teacher. God is the incomparable teacher (Job 36:22). None can teach Him knowledge (Job 21:22; Isa 40:14). On the contrary, it is He who teaches man knowledge (Ps 94:10), and the farmer the art of agriculture (Isa 28:24–26). God taught Moses what to say and do (Ex 4:12, 15), and Israel concerning the law and the commandments (Ex 24:12). He promised to teach the royal Davidic heirs His covenant and His testimonies (Ps 132:12) and Israel how she might profit (Isa 48:17). Even the apostate Judah, said Jeremiah, had been persistently taught by the Lord, but to no avail (Jer 32:33). In the last days Yahweh will be sought by the nations in order to be taught by Him (Isa 2:3; Mic 4:2; cf. Isa 30:20; 54:13).

But God teaches the individual as well as the nation. The humble and the sinner He teaches in His way (Ps 25:8–9), the psalmist from his youth up out of the law (Ps 71:17; 94:12), and the one who fears God in the way he should choose (Ps 25:12). The psalmist praises the Lord that He has taught him His statutes (Ps 119:171), and because of this teaching he has not departed from the ordinances (Ps 119:102).

We may petition God to teach us His statutes (Ps 119:12, 64, 68, 124, 135), to teach good judgment and knowledge (Ps 119:66), and how to perform His will (Ps 143:10).

Man as teacher. Moses taught Israel the statutes, the commandments, and the ordinances (Deut 4:1,5,14; 5:31; 6:1; 11:19). The parents, in turn, were instructed to teach these to their children (Deut 4:10; 11:19). The Levitical order was to teach Israel all the statutes, ordinances, and the law of Yahweh (Lev 10:11; Deut 33:10). Mention is made of the ministry of a teaching priest (II Chr 15:3; cf. Mal 2:6-7).

The song of Moses was to be taught to the people (Deut 31:19,22). David taught the people of Judah the lament over Saul and Jonathan (II Sam 1:18, NASB; cf. Jer 9:20 and Ps 60 title). The judges were to teach the instructions concerning decisions (Deut 17:11). In his valedictorian address before turning over the reins of governing the people to young King Saul, Samuel promised to continue to teach Israel in the good and right way (I Sam 12:23). Jehoshaphat commanded the Levites to teach the law in the cities of Judah (II Chr 17:7,9), while Ezra taught the people the statutes and ordinances of the Lord (Ezr 7:10). The Assyrian king requested of the Judean monarch that one of the Israelitic priests might teach the Assyrian immigrants in Samaria the law of the God of the land (II Kgs 17:27 f.).

David invited his children to listen to him as he taught them the fear of the Lord (Ps 34:11); later he vowed that if Yahweh would bestow upon him moral renewal, he would teach transgressors the ways of God (Ps 51:13). He also proposed to teach the penitent the way he should go (Ps 32:8).

In the Wisdom Literature the preacher taught the people knowledge, weighing and studying and arranging proverbs with great care (Eccl 12:9). Solomon disclosed that his father had taught him adherence to paternal instruction (Prov 4:4), while in another place the writer asserts that he has taught his son or disciple the way of wisdom (Prov 4:11). Job petitioned his friends to teach him his error (Job 6:24). Bildad commended to Job the experience of former ages as a source of authoritative teaching (Job 8:10). Job indicated that even the fauna and flora join to instruct man (Job 12:7-8), and proposed to teach his friends the hand of God (Job 27:11). Jeremiah prophesied that the knowledge of Yahweh would not be taught in the days of the new covenant because all would know Him personally (Jer 31:34; cf. Heb 6:11 and Isa 54:13).

Unfortunately, however, it is possible to teach evil things as well as good things. The captured cities were put under the ban lest they should teach Israel their pagan abominations (Deut 20:18). Judgment is predicted upon the prophet who teaches lies (Isa 9:15) as well as on the priests who teach solely for hire (Mic 3:11). A worthless person is represented as teaching (or pointing) contemptuously or mischievously with his finger (Prov 6:13). Idolators are held up to ridicule for their credulity that idols of wood and stone can teach aught to their devotees (Hab 2:19).

Education. Primary education took place in the home (Deut 4:10; 11:19). The parents combined in this early training of the child (Prov 4:4,11; 31:1; Song 8:2). Leaders of the nation, priests, prophets, psalmists, and the wise contributed to the general education of Israel. In addition, some had undoubtedly the advantage of the specialized training in the palace school or in other seats of learning, particularly in the later history of Israel (e.g., Prov 1:1-4; I Chr 25:7f.). Daniel attended the royal academy of Babylon and was taught the language and literature of the Chaldeans (Dan 1:4). The characteristics of one who was taught are receptiveness toward instruction and the ability to embody it in expression (Isa 50:4).

In the New Testament

Terminology. Some form of the word "teach" is used in the KJV to render five Gr. terms, four of which are otherwise more precisely translated by the RSV.

1. Gr. *mathēteuō,* "to be" or "to make a disciple" (Mt 28:19; Acts 14:21).
2. Gr. *paideuō,* "to educate" or "train" (Acts 22:3; Tit 2:12).
3. Gr. *katēcheō,* "to instruct" (I Cor 14:19; Gal 6:6 twice; RSV "taught").
4. Gr. *kataggellō,* "to proclaim" (Acts 16:21; RSV "advocate").
5. Gr. *sōphronizō,* "to encourage," "advise" (Tit 2:4).

The RSV renders the normal term for "word" (*logos*) idiomatically in Lk 10:39 as "teaching."

Apart from these inexact renderings in the KJV, the idea conveyed by the word "teach" and its cognates and compounds rests entirely upon some form of the verb *didaskō.*

God as teacher. Paul maintained that his preaching was not in words taught by human wisdom but by the Spirit (I Cor 2:13). The apostle refrained from discoursing on brotherly love to the Thessalonians because he affirmed that they were taught of God to love one another (I Thess 4:9). Jesus encouraged His disciples not to worry about what they would say in the perils of persecution, for in that very hour the Holy Spirit would teach them what to say (Lk 12:12). The Holy Spirit, said our Lord, would come as the Paraclete and would teach His disciples all things (Jn 14:26). The anointing of the Spirit is the perennial tutor of the believer (I Jn 2:27).

Jesus as teacher. The ministry of Jesus throughout Palestine is described as essentially one of teaching, whether to the casual crowds or to His own disciples; whether in the synagogues, public places, or in the audience of the religious leaders (Lk 5:17). The effect upon His gatherings was impressive, and forced the conviction that He taught not as the scribes but as one who possessed authority (Mt 7:28 f.; 13:54; Mk 1:22; 6:2; cf. Lk 4:32). *See* Authority. Jesus asserted that God had taught Him the words that He spoke (Jn 8:28) and that His teaching was from the Father (Jn 7:16 f.). His teaching was characterized by the frequent use of parables (Mk 4:2).

Nicodemus acknowledged Jesus to be a teacher come from God and attested by mighty works (Jn 3:2). The chief priests and scribes interrogated Him as to the source of His teaching authority (Mt 21:23; cf. Jn 18:19). Even His opponents frankly admitted that the Lord taught the way of God impartially, regardless of the fear or the favor of man (Mk 12:14; Lk 20:21; Mt 22:16; cf. Jn 18:19). Indeed, all were astonished at His teaching (Mt 7:28; 13:54; 22:33; Mk 1:22; 11:18) and asked whether it was a new teaching (Mk 1:27). In His early circuit of Galilee Christ was glorified by all for His teaching (Lk 4:15). In the last days of His ministry He was daily in the temple teaching (Lk 19:47; 20:1; cf. Mk 14:49; Jn 18:20). His ministry was characterized by such activity that the Jews, misunderstanding one of His statements, queried whether He would go to teach the Diaspora and the Gentiles (Jn 7:35).

Christ's reputation as a teacher quickly won for Him the respectful title of rabbi (*q.v.*) or rabboni ("my lord," an outstanding title for a distinguished teacher) from His disciples (Mk 9:5; 11:21; Jn 1:49), His audiences (Mk 12:14; Jn 3:2), and even His enemies (Lk 10:25; 11:45; 19:39; 20:28). This Aramaic title is at times left untranslated, at times it is interpreted, but more often it is rendered by the Gr. word *didaskalos* (KJV, "master"; RSV "teacher"), which though not a literal rendering is true to the sense of the original. Jesus accepted this title as indicative of the true relationship existing between Himself as teacher and His followers as disciples (Jn 13:13; Lk 6:40; Mt 10:24 f.).

The central theme in the teaching of Jesus was the kingdom of God (Mt 5:2; 9:35). Luke described his Gospel account as pertaining to all that Jesus began both to do and to teach (Acts 1:1). Among the many lessons Jesus taught His disciples, the evangelists have singled out several for particular mention; e.g., the Sermon on the Mount (*q.v.*); the request of His disciples to be taught how to pray (Lk 11:1); His rejection, death, and resurrection at Jerusalem (Mk 8:31; 9:31); and His second coming (Mt 24–25; Mk 13: Lk 17:20–27; 21).

The apostles as teachers. During His ministry Jesus sent His disciples out to teach (Mk 6:30). They were later commanded by Jesus to make disciples of all nations and to teach them to observe all He had commanded (Mt 28:20). After Pentecost, following the ascension, the apostles taught the people the resurrection of Jesus from the dead (Acts 4:2). Peter and John were commanded by the Jewish council to desist from teaching in the name of Jesus (Acts 4:18), a command they did not heed, and were apprehended in the temple as they taught further (Acts 5:21, 24 f.). Despite another stern warning from the authorities, the apostles continued to teach and preach Jesus Christ (Acts 5:42) until all Jerusalem was filled with their teaching (Acts 5:28).

Barnabas and Paul taught an entire year in the church at Antioch (Acts 11:26; cf. 15:35). The proconsul Sergius Paulus was astonished at Paul's teaching of the Lord (Acts 13:12). When the Athenians heard Paul, they brought him to the Areopagus so that he might expound to them his new teaching (Acts 17:19). Paul spent eighteen months at Corinth teaching the Word of God (Acts 18:11), and later reminded the Ephesian elders that he had taught them publicly and from house to house during his stay at Ephesus (Acts 20:20). Apollos, though he knew only the baptism of John, taught diligently at Ephesus the things of the Lord (Acts 18:25). The Jewish disciples accused Paul before James and the elders at Jerusalem of having taught the Gentiles to abandon the law of Moses, to cease the practice of circumcision, and to forsake Jewish customs (Acts 21:21). This same charge was leveled by the Jews themselves when they discovered Paul in the temple and cried out against him as one who had taught men everywhere against the Jews, the law, and the temple (Acts 21:28). By the spoken and written word the apostles taught the message of Christianity to their contemporaries.

Teachers in the church. Paul refers repeatedly to his commission as a teacher, "a teacher of the Gentiles in faith and truth" (I Tim 2:7; II Tim 1:11) and to his doctrine (II Tim 3:10; I Cor 4:17). He denied that the gospel he preached was taught him by man; on the contrary, he stated that he received it by revelation of Jesus Christ (Gal 1:12). Paul's teaching was to all men in all wisdom that every man might become mature in Christ (Col 1:28; cf. Heb 6:1–2).

Among the gifts of the ascended Christ in order to equip and train the members of His Body were pastors and teachers (Eph 4:11). Since the apostles, prophets, and evangelists were primarily mobile, very likely many of the teachers in the early church had a traveling ministry, visiting the believers in a certain city for a shorter or longer period of time. In the church at Antioch it is probable that most or all of the five men named in Acts 13:1 were not permanently residing there.

The role of the teacher in the church was through divine appointment and endowment of the Spirit (I Cor 12:28). Integrity and fidelity to the task of teaching are strongly enjoined (Rom 12:7; I Tim 4:11, 13, 16), both in preparation and in content (Tit 2:1, 7; II Tim 4:2). Those who teach are to be considered worthy of double honor (I Tim 5:17) and merit the support of those who are taught (Gal 6:6). The aspirant teacher is solemnly warned that it will ultimately involve him in a more stringent judgment (Jas 3:1).

But while there are those specially selected to teach in the church, every believer is to engage in this ministry (Col 3:16; I Cor 14:6, 26; Heb 5:12). This is to be of benefit to all, and must not be compromised by disorder in the worship of the church (I Cor 14:6, 19, 26). The servant of the Lord must be an apt teacher and avoid contentions (II Tim 2:24). While women are forbidden to teach men in the church (I Tim 2:12), Paul bids older women to teach what is good as they educate the younger women (Tit 2:3).

The teaching in the church. There is reference in the NT to an apostolic Christian tradition termed variously the sound doctrine (Tit 2:7) or the faithful word (Tit 1:9), which had been delivered to the church (Rom 6:17; 16:17; Eph 4:21; Col 2:7; II Thess 2:15; II Tim 2:2; Tit 1:9). The early disciples at Jerusalem devoted themselves to the teaching of the apostles (Acts 2:42). Part of this tradition was the OT, which is profitable, says Paul, for teaching (Rom 15:4; II Tim 3:16; cf. I Tim 1:8-10). The Christian teaching and that alone (I Tim 1:3) is to be entrusted to believing men who shall in turn be able to teach others also (II Tim 2:2; cf. I Tim 4:11). The elder, therefore, must be an apt teacher (I Tim 3:2), who is to hold fast to the faithful word which he has been taught so that he may give instruction in sound doctrine and offer an effective apology for the faith (Tit 1:9). Obedience to the standard of doctrine is credited with the moral power to liberate the believer from the thraldom of sin (Rom 6:17). The doctrine is according to godliness (I Tim 6:3) and supplies the necessary spiritual nourishment to the believer (I Tim 4:6).

Other usage. The boy Jesus was found by His family sitting among the teachers in the temple (Lk 2:46). Nicodemus is called the teacher of Israel by our Lord (Jn 3:10, ASV, etc.). John the Baptist taught his disciples how to pray (Lk 11:1). Jesus warns that he who breaks the least commandment and teaches men so will be least in the kingdom, and, conversely, he who observes and teaches men so concerning the least commandment will be great in the kingdom (Mt 5:19). Jesus censured the scribes and the Pharisees for worshiping God vainly, teaching as doctrines the precepts of men (Mt 15:9; Mk 7:7; cf. Isa 29:13).

False teaching. There were those among the Christians in Judea who taught the necessity of circumcision for salvation, a doctrine later repudiated by the Jerusalem council (Acts 15:1). Paul makes mention of human precepts and teachings which prescribe cultic regulations to which the Christian must not submit (Col 2:20-22). He warns Timothy that in the latter times some will depart from the faith giving heed to doctrines of demons (I Tim 4:1), while others will accumulate for themselves teachers to suit their own likings (II Tim 4:3). False teachers who will bring in destructive heresies are elsewhere forecast to arise in the church (II Pet 2:1).

Paul urged Timothy to teach the sound words of Jesus and to reject those who teach otherwise (I Tim 6:2 f.). He instructed that there were those who must be silenced since they were upsetting whole families by teaching for base gain what they had no right to teach (Tit 1:11), and he warns Timothy against the Judaizers who desire vainly to become teachers of the law (I Tim 1:7). The same apostle urged upon the Ephesians the spiritual integration and vital participation of all within the church so that they would not be tossed to and fro and carried about with every wind of doctrine (Eph 4:14).

The author of the Epistle to the Hebrews warns his audience not to be led away by diverse and strange doctrines (Heb 13:9), while John bids his readers not to associate with anyone who does not abide in the doctrine of Christ (II Jn 9-10). The church at Pergamum is criticized for having some who adhered to the teaching of Balaam and the doctrine of the Nicolaitans (Rev. 2:14), while the church at Thyatira is censured for tolerating the teaching of the woman Jezebel (Rev 2:20,24).

See Chastisement; Disciple; Education; Lead, Leader; Parable; Parables of Jesus; Rabbi.

Bibliography. Karl H. Rengstorf, "*Didaskō*, etc.," TDNT, II, 135-165.

E. R. D.

TEARS. *See* Mourn.

TEBAH (tē'bȧ). One of the sons of Nahor, the brother of Abraham, whom Reumah his concubine bore to him (Gen 22:24). It is suggested by modern scholars that Betah (II Sam 8:8), which appears as Tibhath in the parallel passage in I Chr 18:8, should be read as Tebah. Accordingly, the patrimony of Tebah would be identified with a city of Hadadezer, king of Aram-zobah, located in the Anti-Lebanon region, and mentioned in the Amarna letters and in Egyptian sources. *See* Tibhath.

TEBALIAH (tĕb'ȧ-lī'ȧ). One of the sons of Hosah, a Merarite, who was chosen to serve as a gatekeeper of the temple in the Davidic organization of the Levites (I Chr 26:11).

TEBETH (tē'bĕth). The tenth month of the Heb. sacred calendar, corresponding generally to Dec.-Jan. of our calendar, and equivalent to the Babylonian month *Ṭebītu* (Est 2:16; spelled Tebet in the ASV, etc.). In the pre-Exilic period the months were named according to the Canaanite calendar (cf. Ex 13:4; 23:15; 34:18; Deut 16:1; I Kgs 6:1,37 f.; 8:2), but increasingly the Jews adopted the names of the months of the Babylonian calendar. *See* Calendar.

TEHAPHNEHES. *See* Tahpanhes.

TEHINNAH (tē-hĭn'*ȧ*). One of the descendants of Judah and the father of Irnahash (KJV, RSV) or the father (founder) of the city of Nahash (ASV marg.; I Chr 4:12).

TEIL. *See* Plants.

TEKEL. *See* Mene, Mene, Tekel, Upharsin.

Octagonal baptismal font belonging to a Byzantine church at Tekoa. HFV

TEKOA, TEKOAH (tĕ-kō'*ȧ*). The KJV has Tekoah in II Sam 14:2,4,9.

Tekoa was a town in Judah (I Chr 2:24; 4:5), six miles S of Bethlehem and ten miles S of Jerusalem, on a hill in the area of the wilderness of Tekoa (II Chr 20:20). It was the birthplace of the prophet Amos (Amos 1:1) and the home of a wise woman for whom Joab sent to turn David's heart back to Absalom (II Sam 14:1-24). It is identified with Khirbet Taqu'a, the ruins of which cover four or five acres. Excavations begun in 1968 by Wheaton College discovered tombs used in Iron Ages I and II as well as the Roman period, indicating that occupation of the site began *c.* 1200 B.C.

The site was eventually occupied by a Christian community. A complex of Byzantine church and monastery ruins undoubtedly represent the Propheteum of Amos, a memorial church to the prophet. The most interesting object in the ruins is an octagonal baptismal font cut out of a single block of rose-red limestone. The last occupation of the site was apparently in the 12th cen.

Tekoa's elevation of 2,790 feet above sea level led to its development as a station for trumpet-blown signals (Jer 6:1), and it was fortified by King Rehoboam to protect Jerusalem (II Chr 11:6). Tekoites helped to rebuild the walls of Jerusalem under Nehemiah (Neh 3:5,27).

Bibliography. Martin H. Heicksen, "Tekoa: Historical and Cultural Profile," JETS, XIII (1970), 81-90.

A. C. S.

TEKOITE (tē-kō'īt). One who was a resident in or whose antecedents were from the village of Tekoa (*q.v.*). Tekoite is the gentilic form of Tekoa and is used as such of the wise woman (II Sam 14:4,9), of Ira the son of Ikkesh (II Sam 23:26; I Chr 11:28; 27:9), and as a substantive describing those who assisted in the repair of the wall of Jerusalem (Neh 3:5,27).

TEL-ABIB (tĕl'*ȧ*-vĭv'). A town on the banks of the Chebar canal, which flowed into the river S of Babylon. Here Ezekiel lived with his fellow exiles from Judah (Ezk 3:15). The name of the largest city in modern Israel, Tel Aviv, is taken from this.

TELAH (tē'l*ȧ*). The son of Resheph and father of Tahan, a descendant of Ephraim and ancestor of Joshua (I Chr 7:25).

TELAIM (tē-lā'ĭm). A city in the Negeb of Judah near Ziph where Saul summoned and numbered the people in preparation for his campaign against the Amalekites (I Sam 15:4). Some cursive Gr. MSS of the LXX support the idea that the phrase "from of old" in I Sam 27:8 (MT) should read "from Telem." Telaim has been identified by some scholars with Telem mentioned in Josh 15:24.

TELASSAR (tēl-ăs'*ȧ*r). One of the cities in N Mesopotamia inhabited by the people of Eden (Heb. *b^enê Eden*, abbreviation of *b^enê-Beth-Eden;* cf. Amos 1:5; Ezk 27:23) mentioned in the letter of Sennacherib to Hezekiah as conquered by the previous Assyrian kings (Isa 37:12; II Kgs 19:12, KJV "Thelasar"). In the area of Akkadian Bît-Adini (Beth-eden) along the middle Euphrates was situated Til Ashûri, "mound of Ashur," mentioned in inscriptions of Tiglath-pileser III.

TELEM (tē'lĕm)

1. A city of the tribe of Judah in the Negeb toward the border of Edom (Josh 15:24). Some scholars have identified it with Telaim (*q.v.*; I Sam 15:4).

2. One of the gatekeepers who dismissed his foreign wife in accordance with the policy instituted by Ezra (Ezr 10:24).

TEL-HARESHA. *See* Tel-harsa.

TEL-HARSA (tĕl-här's*ȧ*). A Babylonian city from which certain Jews returned to Jerusalem after the Exile, but were unable to establish their Israelitic identity (Ezr 2:59; Neh 7:61, KJV "Tel-haresha"). The site of the city is presently unknown.

TELL. An Arabic word meaning "mound of a ruined city," related to Babylonian *til* and Syriac *telālâ*, and corresponding to Persian *tepe* and Turkish *hüyük*.

In the Bible the related Heb. *tēl* is used of

the "heap" of a destroyed city (Deut 13:16; Josh 8:28, the ruin of Ai; Josh 11:13, RSV, where KJV mistranslates "strength"; Jer 30:18, RSV "mound"; Jer 49:2, RSV "mound"). This word is part of the name of several biblical cities: Tel-assar in northern Mesopotamia, and Tel-abib, Tel-harsha, and Tel-melah (all three in Babylonia).

The typical tell in the Near East is a flat-topped mound with sloping sides, like a truncated cone. It may be composed of the ruins of one or more layers of occupation. Tell el-Huṣn (biblical Beth-shan) has 18 successive layers, totaling 70 feet in thickness. The oldest level is naturally on the bottom and the newest on top. The size of tells varies not only in height but also in area: Tell el-Hesy (biblical Eglon) covers two and a half acres and Tell el-Qedaḥ (biblical Hazor) 40 acres. The known characteristics of a tell have helped archaeologists to locate many biblical cities.

In 1890 W. M. F. Petrie, while excavating Tell el-Hesy in southern Palestine, worked out a pottery chronology. He noted several characteristic pottery types in the various occupational levels at the site. Some of these could be assigned dates because they were found in association with specifically dated objects. It stood to reason that these same pottery types would have similar dates if found in other tells. Soon Petrie had worked out a pottery chronology useful in dating many finds in Palestine. And principles have been applied in working out pottery chronologies for other Near Eastern lands.

Bibliography. W. F. Albright, *The Archaeology of Palestine,* rev. ed., London: Penguin, 1960, pp. 16–18. K. M. Kenyon, *Beginning in Archaeology,* London: Phoenix, 1953, pp. 98–107. G. E. Wright, "Cities Standing on Their Tells," BA, II (1939), 11–12; *Biblical Archaeology,* Philadelphia: Westminster, 1957, pp. 23–24.

J. A. T.

TELL EL-AMARNA. *See* Amarna, Tell el-.

TEL-MELAH (tĕl-mē'*lȧ*). A Babylonian city whose location is presently unknown from which certain Jews returned to Jerusalem after the Exile, but were unable to establish their Israelitic identity (Ezr 2:59; Neh 7:61).

TEMA, TEMAH (tē'*mȧ*). The ninth son of Ishmael who was subsequently regarded as one of the 12 princes of Ishmael and whose name identified the village and encampment of his descendants (Gen 25:15; I Chr 1:30). The residence of the clan is to be identified with the modern Teima, an oasis caravansary in NW Arabia *c.* 260 miles SE of Ezion-geber (Job 6:19). It lay on the caravan route between the land of spices and incense in S Arabia and the countries to the N such as Egypt, Israel, and Syria.

Excavations at the tell of New Testament Jericho. J. L. Kelso

In an oracle concerning Arabia the inhabitants of the land of Tema were urged to succor the Dedanites and Kedarites who were soon to flee from a crushing rout (Isa 21:14), perhaps a reference to the campaign of Tiglath-pileser III who claimed to have received tribute from the inhabitants of Tema (ANET, pp. 283 f.). In Jer 25:23 Tema is numbered among those peoples who were to drink of the cup of the wine of the wrath at the hand of the Lord, which apparently has reference to the conquests of Nebuchadnezzar.

Nabonidus, the last king of Babylon, lived at Tema for a decade (ANET, p. 306), building his palace there and beautifying and fortifying the city to rival Babylon itself (ANET, pp. 313 f.).

E. R. D.

TEMAN (tē'*mȧn*). An Edomite name meaning "on the right, southern."

1. A son of Eliphaz and grandson of Esau (Gen 36:11) called in v.15 an Edomite "chief" (RSV) or "duke" (KJV).

2. An important city in Edom. Husham, a king of Edom, was a Temanite (Gen 36:34). Temanites were famed for their wisdom (Jer 49:7; Baruch 3:23), and Eliphaz, the wisest of Job's comforters, was a Temanite (Job 2:11). Habakkuk (3:3) sees the Lord coming from Teman, recalling God's acts in that area during the journey to the Promised Land. The prophetic warnings of judgment on Teman (Jer 49:20; Ezk 25:13; Amos 1:12; Ob 9) have been fulfilled, for its site is uncertain. Glueck identifies it with Tawilan, about five miles E of Petra. Abel favors Shôbek, about 25 miles N of Petra.

Bibliography. Nelson Glueck, "Explorations in Eastern Palestine, II," AASOR, XV (1935), 82–83. F. M. Abel, *Géographie de la Palestine,* 2 vols., Paris: Gabalda, 1933, 1938, I, 284; II, 479–480.

TEMENI (tĕm'*ĕ*-nī). A descendant of Judah whose father was Ashhur and whose mother was Naarah (I Chr 4:6).

TEMPERANCE. The Gr. word *egkrateia* signifies moderation, continence, or self-restraint, especially curbing one's impulses for the sake of worthier ends (I Cor 7:9, RSV; cf. 7:5). The term "temperance" occurs only in the NT, although readers of Solomon's proverbs had long been familiar with the idea. Paul, in reasoning with Felix, stressed self-control along with justice and future judgment (Acts 24:25, RSV). In Titus he lists it among the marks required of a church leader (l:7-8) and enjoins it for the aged men (2:2). It is an outgrowth of the Spirit's work in the believer (Gal 5:22-23), to be actively sought by Christians (II Pet 1:5ff.), and essential in the Christian ministry (I Cor 9:25-27). The biblical usage of the term suggests self-crucifixion and submitting to control by the indwelling Spirit rather than spartan self-denial.

TEMPLE. The principal Heb. word for "temple" is *hêkāl,* "palace, large building" (cf. I Kgs 21:1; Ps 45:8, 15; Isa 39:7). It is a loan-word from Akkadian *ekallu,* in turn borrowed from Sumerian *E-GAL,* "great house." In addition to its references to the temple in Jerusalem the word is used of the sanctuary at Shiloh (I Sam 1:9; 3:3), of God's heavenly abode (II Sam 22:7; Ps 11:4; 18:6; Isa 6:1), and of heathen temples (Joel 3:5). Heb. *bayith,* "house," is also frequently used of a temple, either that of a pagan deity (Jud 9:46; II Kgs 10:21; etc.) or of God's temple in Jerusalem (I Kgs 6:2-10; II Chr 35:20; etc.).

As contrasted to the open-air "high place" (*q.v.*), a temple was considered primarily a "house" or dwelling place of the deity, and only secondarily a place of worship. Therefore the inner sanctuary where the image of the god (or the ark of the covenant of the Lord) was placed, was usually a rather small room set apart from the people.

In Gr. there are two terms that mean "temple." The more general is *hieron,* the place of the priest, which applies to the entire temple complex with all its courts and auxiliary buildings. The more specific is *naos,* "sanctuary, shrine," the chief temple building itself. The biblical use of these terms is primarily in reference to the national sanctuary of the Jews in Jerusalem, located on Mount Moriah.

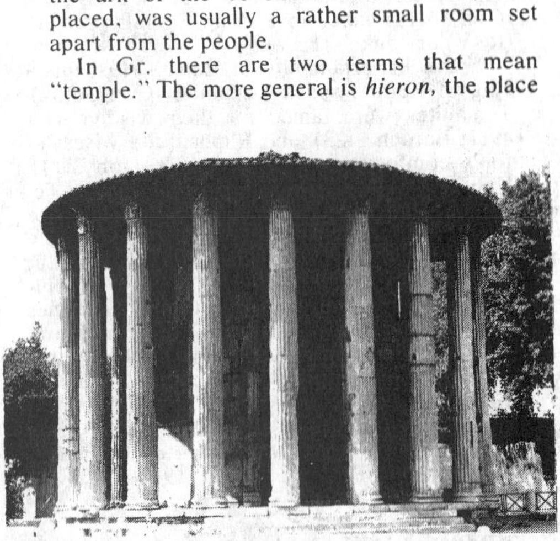

The so-called Temple of Vesta by the Tiber River in Rome. HFV

Pagan Temples

The OT occasionally mentions temples of the non-Israelite population of Canaan, as well as the temples of Babylon (II Chr 36:7; Ezr 5:14) and of Egypt (Jer 43:12-13). In Palestine a number of Canaanite shrines or temples have been excavated, revealing the typical floor plan of a heathen sanctuary. In general they consisted of three main rooms: an antechamber or porch giving admittance to the main sanctuary, whose entrance was sometimes flanked with columns; the sanctuary, usually with posts to support the roof beams and stone benches against one or more of the walls, and often with an altar for offerings; and the innermost holy of holies or shrine, usually on a raised platform approached by steps, containing a pedestal or niche for the image of the deity.

The temple of El-berith (Jud 9:46, NASB) at Shechem (*q.v.*) has been excavated and appears to have been a large fortress-temple (Heb. *migdal*) with a sacred pillar (Heb. *maṣṣēbâ*) in the courtyard. The temple of Dagon at Ashdod (I Sam 5:2-4) was probably similar to the temples of Dagon (I Chr 10:10) and of Ashtaroth (I Sam 31:10) at Beth-shan; the latter structures probably were the twin temples found in Level V dating to the 11th cen. B.C.

Israelite Border Sanctuaries

At several Israelite sites from the period of the divided monarchy evidence of enclosed sanctuaries have been found. Amos denounced the worship at Beer-sheba and Gilgal and compared it with the temples which Jeroboam I built at Dan and Bethel on the N and S borders of his kingdom (Amos 5:5; 8:14). The walls forming an Israelite high place enclosure (*c.* 20 by 61 feet) at Dan have been discovered (IEJ, XXII [1972], 165), but no temple building has yet been located.

Excavations begun in 1969 at Tell Beer-sheba have uncovered a large four or five room building in which many cult objects of Egyptian and of Assyro-Babylonian style were found. In a nearby house was an Iron Age jar with the incised Heb. inscription *q-d-sh,* "holiness." The archaeologist in charge, Yohanan Aharoni, believes that there was no Israelite sanctuary at Beer-sheba which had been corrupted by pagan influence ("Excavations at Tel Beer-sheba," BA, XXXV [1972], 123-127).

Aharoni's re-examination of the so-called "solar shrine" at Lachish indicates that there was probably a series of Jewish temples at this chief fortress on the Philistine border. Sennacherib's bas-reliefs of the capture of Lachish depict two large incense burners carried as part

Reconstruction of the Temple of Venus at Baalbek. National Museum, Beirut

of the spoil from the city (VBW, II, 286 bottom). Such a cult at Lachish may be alluded to by Micah: "She was the beginning of sin to the daughter of Zion; for the transgressions of Israel were found in thee" (1:13, ASV). Pottery figurines of the mother goddess from the time of King Josiah and more than 150 incense altars of the Persian period, one inscribed with a dedication to Yah(weh), were found in tombs and caves at Lachish. The "solar shrine" itself, while dating to the Hellenistic period and thus contemporary with Onias' temple at Leontopolis in Lower Egypt (Jos *Ant.* xiii.3.1-3; *Wars* vii.10.3-4), bears a striking resemblance to the earlier Israelite sanctuary at Arad (Y. Aharoni, "Trial Excavation in the 'Solar Shrine' at Lachish," IEJ, XVIII [1968], 157-164).

In the 1960's at Tell Arad, *c.* 20 miles E of Beer-sheba, Aharoni directed excavations of the citadel first built in the Solomonic period. A square fortress *c.* 165 by 165 feet guarded the main trade route descending to the Arabah and Edom. In the NW corner of this 10th cen. B.C. royal fortress was found a temple as an integral and prominent part of it. It was constructed over an earlier high place, perhaps that of the Kenites who moved to the Negeb of Arad in the time of the judges (Jud 1:16), and was rebuilt several times along with the citadel preceding the reform movement of King Josiah.

Like the tabernacle and Solomon's temple, the Arad sanctuary had an entrance on the E, with the holy of holies toward the W. In the courtyard stood an altar of earth and small uncut stones (cf. Ex 20:25) for burnt offerings. Flanking the doorway into the main room (Heb. *hêkāl*) were stone bases for pillars, calling to mind the biblical Jachin (*q.v.*) and Boaz. The *hêkāl* was a broad room (*c.* nine by 30 feet) instead of a long room, and the inner sanctuary (Heb. *d^ebîr*) was a small projecting cella in the center of the western side, preceded by three steps. Inside the *d^ebîr* was a well-finished and rounded cult pillar (Heb. *maṣṣēbâ*).

Both its architectural history and the ostraca found at Arad indicate that this sanctuary was a genuinely Israelite temple. Several Heb. ostraca mention names of priestly families. Therefore Arad must have been one of a number of royal border fortresses with an altar and/or sanctuary to give both divine and royal authority to the national boundary (cf. Josh 22:11, 25; Isa 19:19-21). These were apparently constructed by apostate kings of Judah such as Solomon in his latter reign and Rehoboam after Shishak's devastating campaign. Hezekiah removed high places and altars (II Kgs 18:22), and Josiah destroyed "the high places where the priests had burned incense, from Geba to Beer-sheba" (II Kgs 23:8) as well as the "houses" of the high places in the cities of Samaria (v. 19; cf. I Kgs 12:31; 13:32). See Y. Aharoni, "Arad: Its Inscriptions and Temple," BA, XXXI (1968), 1-32; "The Israelite Sanctuary at Arad," *New Directions in Biblical Archaeology*, ed. by D. N. Freedman and J. C. Greenfield, Garden City: Doubleday, 1969, pp. 25-39.

Solomon's Temple

On the site sacred in Jewish memory as the place of intended sacrifice of Isaac by Abraham there was begun in April/May of 967 B.C. the building of the temple that was destined to bear the name of the king, Solomon. The building was completed in Oct./Nov., 960 B.C., requiring a total of seven and a half years (I Kgs 6:1, 37 f.).

The origin of this house of worship is credited to David; it is observed in I Chr 28 that the Spirit suggested to him the necessity for replacing the tabernacle with a permanent building. Although David was forbidden to build this house because he was a warrior and had shed blood (v. 3), he purchased the site (II Sam 24:18-24), collected much of the material to be used in its construction (I Chr 22:2-16), and committed the task to his son Solomon (I Chr 28:1-29:19).

The plan of this edifice was similar to that of the tabernacle; but the dimensions were doubled, with the height triple that of the former sanctuary. It is quite probable that Josephus (*Ant.* viii.3.2) gives the external dimensions, 60 cubits in height as well as length and 20 cubits in width, with a second story of equal floor plan, while the book of Kings gives the internal height (30 cubits) of each story (I Kgs 6:2). Probably the royal cubit of 20.9 inches was used, "according to the old standard" (II Chr 3:3, NASB).

The stone walls were lined with carved cedar which was overlaid with gold (I Kgs 6:22); the ceilings and even the floor were covered with gold also. The partition separating the holy of holies from the holy place apparently was also of gold-covered cedar wood (I Kgs 6:16, 20,

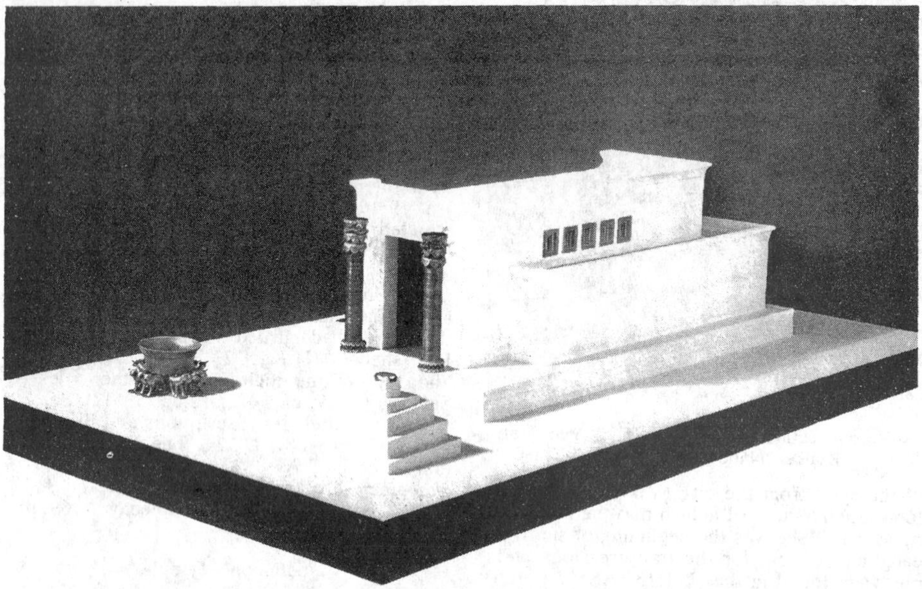

Howland-Garber model of Solomon's Temple. E. G. Howland

Howland-Garber model interior. E. G. Howland

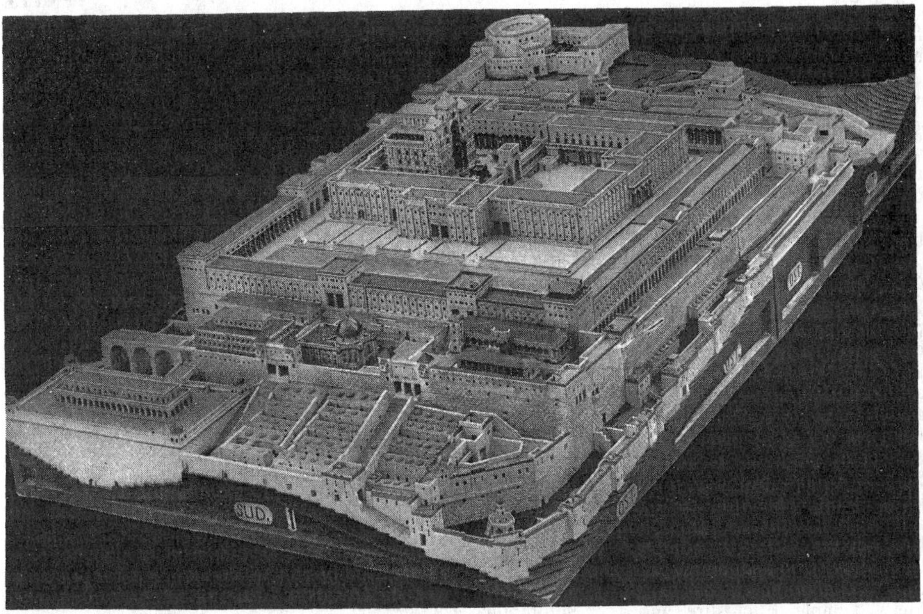

Shick's reconstruction of Solomon's Temple. MPS

NASB). The entrance to the holy of holies consisted of a double door of olive wood with carvings and overlaid with gold (I Kgs 6:31–32). This doorway stood open, but was veiled with material similar to that in the tabernacle, evidently held in place by gold chains in front of the partition (6:21). *See* Veil.

In the holy of holies or inner sanctuary (RSV; "oracle," KJV; Heb. *d^ebîr*) was placed the ark of the covenant, its top or lid being called the mercy seat. It stood between two cherubim which were ten cubits high, being made of olive wood covered with gold. It is believed that these appeared as winged sphinxes, with a lion's body and human face. The wings of the cherubim were outstretched and touched each other over the ark (I Kgs 6:23–28; II Chr 3:10–13). Here God especially manifested His presence in the Shekinah glory.

In the holy place or nave (RSV; Heb. *hêkāl*) were the altar of incense, ten golden lampstands (with seven lamps to each stand) and ten tables for the showbread. Five of the lampstands and tables were on each side of the holy of holies. The holy place, being higher than the side chambers, had upper windows like a clerestory (I Kgs 6:4–5).

If the temple stood on a raised platform (cf. Ezk 41:8), then a flight of steps would have led up from the inner court to the porch or vestibule (Heb. *'ûlām*). The porch was equal in length to the width of the temple and ten cubits in depth along the front of the building (I Kgs 6:3). Its height is a subject of controversy because the figure of 120 cubits in II Chr 3:4 seems overly large. No tower(s) or pylon commonly at the entrance to Egyptian temples is mentioned anywhere in the OT. Flanking the entrance to the porch were a pair of huge, free-standing bronze pillars with great capitals. These were named Jachin (*q.v.*) and Boaz (I Kgs 7:15–22; II Chr 3:15, 17; Jer 52:21–23), perhaps the initial words of Heb. inscriptions carved on the pillars. Such free-standing columns were a common feature of ancient Near Eastern temples.

There were two courts (II Kgs 23:12), an inner court which surrounded the holy area which was reserved for the exclusive use of the priests (I Kgs 6:36; II Chr 4:9), and an outer court or "great court" (II Chr 4:9) which was for the use of the people. The inner court was called the "upper" or "higher" court (Jer 36:10), and here were found the huge basin called the molten (cast-metal) sea and the bronze altar of sacrifice, as well as lesser items of equipment, including ten lavers. It is thought that the inner court was at least 100 cubits wide and 200 cubits in length, while the outer or "lower" court for the people was at least 400 cubits long and 200 cubits wide.

This magnificent edifice was dedicated in a week-long ceremony of solemn thanksgiving and prayer. As Solomon prayed in consecration of the building in front of the altar, fire fell from heaven and consumed the burnt offering (II Chr 6:13–7:1). When Jerusalem was destroyed by Babylon in 586 B.C., Solomon's temple was plundered of its wealth, and the building was burned to the ground (II Kgs 25:9 ff.; Jer 52:13

ff.). Periodic plundering had occurred earlier, however, e.g., in the days of Shishak's invasion, *c.* 925 (I Kgs 14:25–28).

Ezekiel's Temple

The temple which the prophet Ezekiel saw in vision (Ezk 40:2–47:2) apparently belongs to the eschatological age following the destruction of Gog and his hordes (Ezk 38–39). Therefore premillennial interpreters of Scripture usually believe this will be a literal temple built for worship during the millennial reign of Christ (*see* Ezekiel, Book of).

In its essential features Ezekiel's temple was patterned after Solomon's temple. The gates, described in great detail (Ezk 40:6–44), match almost exactly the city gates built by Solomon's architects, which archaeologists have excavated at Megiddo, Hazor, and Gezer. Carl G. Howie reconstructed a plan of the East Gate (vv. 6–16) and noted the amazing resemblance between it and the Solomonic gate of Megiddo level IVB. Both have the same number of piers and recessed chambers (KJV "little chambers"; NASB "guardrooms"), both have a double vestibule or porch, and the over-all measurements are similar ("The East Gate of Ezekiel's Temple Enclosure and the Solomonic Gateway of Megiddo," BASOR #117 [1950], pp. 13–19). It is surmised then that as a young man Ezekiel had known the actual temple of Solomon before he was taken captive from Jerusalem.

The main feature of Ezekiel's temple is its perfect symmetry throughout. The whole precinct, 500 cubits square (42:15–20), faces E. Perhaps the chief point of difference from Solomon's temple is the absence of the great "sea" or laver (cf. I Kgs 7:23–26). Its place seems to be taken by the river of living water flowing eastward from the threshold of the temple toward the Dead Sea, making its waters fresh and bringing life to the barren wilderness (47:1–12).

The Second Temple

For information about this building Josephus is the principal source. Indeed, except for occasional references in the Talmud and the shadowy image of this structure in the background of the NT, there is no other information about it. The foundation was laid in 535 B.C., the second year after the initial return of exiles from Babylon (Ezr 3:8–12), but Zerubbabel and Jeshua the priest encountered so much opposition from local adversaries that the work was halted. The rebuilding of the temple was resumed in 520 B.C. upon the exhortation of the prophets Haggai and Zechariah and by decree of the Persian king himself (Ezr 5–6). The rebuilding was completed (Ezr 6:15) on the third day of the month Adar in the sixth year of Darius I (Mar., 516 B.C.), this in spite of Josephus' note that the rebuilding required seven years.

This second building could not be compared in splendor with that of Solomon, but occupied the same location and was developed on the same plan generally. It would seem from Zech 6:9 ff. that this work was generously supported by the people who remained in Babylon.

This temple, sometimes called the temple of Zerubbabel according to the Talmud, lacked five items that had been in Solomon's temple. They were the ark of the covenant, the sacred fire to consume the initial burnt offering and sacrifices, the Shekinah glory, the Holy Spirit, and the Urim and Thummim. There was nothing, according to Josephus, in the holy of holies where the ark of the covenant had stood. A stone was placed there for the use of the high priest, but no article of furniture appeared. On this stone the atoning blood was sprinkled on the Day of Atonement instead of on the mercy seat of the ark as in the former temple.

It is evident that the temple suffered damage more than once in the years that followed its rebuilding. Probably the buildings of the temple suffered during the suppression by Artaxerxes III of the rebellion of 351 B.C. Also when Ptolemy I severely damaged Jerusalem in 312 B.C., the temple no doubt received its share. During the time of Antiochus IV (175–163 B.C.) these buildings received their most serious blows. Pompey also breached its walls in 63 B.C. after a three month siege. Crassus plundered the temple in 54 B.C., and its buildings also suffered much when Herod stormed the city of Jerusalem in 37 B.C., assisted by the Roman general Sosius from Syria.

Considerable additions were made to the temple compound during these centuries, and it was renovated in the time of Simeon ben-Jochanan, who also fortified it and dug out a huge reservoir for water needed in the religious services (*c.* 223–187 B.C.). After this temple was desecrated by Antiochus IV, it was restored by Judas Maccabeus (I Macc 4:36), which event provided the occasion for the annual Jewish Feast of Dedication (cf. Jn 10:22).

In later years other fortifications were added to the temple buildings by Jonathan Maccabeus, and also by John Hyrcanus (134–103 B.C.), who was the first of the Hasmonean priest-kings. It is generally agreed that Hyrcanus built the great bridge which crossed the Tyropoean Valley at the SW corner of Mount Moriah and connected with the court of the Gentiles. Alexander Jannaeus (101–75 B.C.) caused the balustrade to be built which separated the court of the priests from the court of Israel.

Herod's Temple

In Jan., 19 B.C., Herod initiated the rebuilding of the temple, which subsequently became known by his name. His interest in this structure has been explained in many ways, but none that would hint at the religious. He was by temperament a builder; this also was the national shrine which must have suffered much since the Captivity and so brought little glory to the

Reconstruction of Herod's Temple, Holyland Hotel, West Jerusalem. Holyland Corporation.

land. Sometimes it is suggested that this was Herod's way of placating the Jewish people, but the truth is that he began the work in the face of strong opposition. In fact, his proposal to rebuild the temple met with such strong opposition that in order to conciliate the Jews, he caused 1,000 priests to be trained as stonecutters, carpenters, and decorators, insuring that no profane hand would touch the holy place. The work on the sanctuary was completed in 18 months, but the rest of the building was still being rebuilt in the time of Jesus (cf. Jn 2:20, RSV) and was not finished until A.D. 64, being destined to continue for only six years in its finished state.

The area on which the temple was constructed was not large enough to accommodate the plan which Herod determined to carry out. Rock was pushed back to fill a deep valley that brought an area of approximately 35 acres within the temple compound. Although the exact dimensions of the new structure are disputed, it seems probable that it was 351 yards on the N, 309 yards on the S, 518 yards on the E, and 536 yards on the W. This increased area was built upon with hard white stones of enormous size; these giant limestone blocks are attested by the wailing or western wall today which was a part of Herod's western retaining wall.

On the highest level of the area stood the sanctuary itself, divided as it was in the days of Solomon and built to the same dimensions. It was now, however, covered with plates of gold, and generally more richly adorned than was possible at the time of reconstruction following the Captivity. The sanctuary, containing the holy of holies and the holy place, stood in the northern half of the court of the Gentiles, and to the W rather than to the E of that part. Twelve steps down, on the second level, was the court of the priests. This court contained the great laver and the altar of burnt offering. Three flights of steps below lay the court of the Israelites, which seems to have been divided so that the eastern part was designated the court of the women while the western part was for the men. Around this court were the residences of the priests, various temple offices, and the hall of the Sanhedrin. Against the wall of the court of the women were located 13 chests. Nine of these were to receive that which was legally due from the worshipers; the other four were for strictly voluntary gifts (Lk 21:1–4). The specific object of each was carefully marked on it. Fourteen steps below was the court of the Gentiles, which was open to anyone, Jew or Gentile, except to those who happened to be ceremonially unclean.

Around the temple proper was a breast-high, carved marble balustrade with four gates on the N and S, one on the E, and none on the W. At each gate stood a notice, engraved on stone in Latin and Greek: "Let no stranger come within the barrier and the court which surrounds the temple. Every trespasser who is caught will be himself responsible for his ensuing death." The gate on the E was known as the Beautiful Gate (Acts 3:2) or Nicanor's Gate. Three of the four remaining gates on both the N and S opened directly into the court of Israel, while the fourth in each instance entered the court of the women.

The court of the Gentiles was especially of interest to Herod; and upon it he exhausted his taste, lavishing upon it his personal attention. He so enlarged this court that it was twice the size that it had been. All around this court was a magnificent colonnade of white marble pillars, Corinthian columns, each made of a single piece, being three pillars deep on three sides and four deep on the S side. The timbered ceiling of this cloister was connected by a runway with the fortress of Antonia at the NW corner of the temple compound, which was also connected with the floor level of the court of the Gentiles by two staircases. All of the court of the Gentiles was paved with marble of many elegant colors.

The porticoes on three sides were about 45 feet wide. Within the wider southern section, which was commonly called the "royal porch," was found the temple market. Between some of these pillars were permanent booths, while other spaces in the area were occupied only temporarily. It was here that the money changers and the dealers in sacrificial animals were to be found (Mk 11:15-18; Jn 2:14-16). The E portico was called "Solomon's porch" (Jn 10:23; Acts 3:11; 5:12). Here the teachers held forth; any rabbi might seat himself with his back to one of the pillars and instruct the people seated in front of him in a circle. The eastern portico ended in a tower that was known as the Tower of the Pinnacle, on the SE extremity (cf. Mt 4:5).

The massive walls which surrounded the entire temple area were pierced by four gates on the W; two of these led to the suburbs of the city, the third to the Tyropoean bridge, and the fourth led to steps that descended into the valley itself. There were two additional gates in the S wall, known by the name of Huldah. The Shushan or Golden Gate was in the E wall (Ezk 10:19; 11:1; 43:1), and Josephus mentions one other in the N wall (*Wars* vi.4.1).

It seems that the "bridge" (perhaps a monumental staircase, incorporating "Robinson's Arch") over the Tyropoean Valley was the most used entrance to the temple area. Ordinarily a worshiper, entering from the W and leaving by the E, crossed the bridge which led straight into the royal porch along the S edge of the outer temple courtyard. Next the court of the Gentiles was crossed diagonally; and, after almost a full left turn, the worshiper stood before the Beautiful Gate which led into the court of the women.

Fourteen officials constituted the standing council of the temple which regulated everything connected with its affairs and services. Its members were also called the "elders of the priests," or "the counselors." The high priest, a suffragan or subordinate high priest, two overseers or treasurers, seven who were keepers of the gates, and three under-treasurers made up the council.

Next in rank to the members of the council were the heads of each course of the priests. Many other officers and subordinates served as instructors, examiners of sacrifices, artificers, and assistants to the priests.

Destruction came to these buildings at the hands of the Romans under Titus in A.D. 70. The Jews were using the temple as a fortress and were responsible themselves for setting the outer cloisters on fire. The sanctuary area was burned by the Romans, who later pulled down its walls also. The triumphal arch of Titus in Rome reveals carvings which show the Roman soldiers carrying away the furnishings of the temple.

The emperor Hadrian caused a temple dedicated to Jupiter Capitolinus to be built on the former site of the Jewish temple in A.D. 136. In A.D. 691 the Muslims built the Dome of the Rock, sometimes erroneously called the Mosque of Omar, over this same area; it is this structure, built by Caliph Omar, that presently occupies the ancient site of the Jewish shrine and sanctuary.

See Architecture; Church; Jerusalem; Sanctuary; Tabernacle; Worship.

Bibliography. Georges A. Barrois, "Temples," IDB, IV, 560-568. E. F. Campbell, Jr., and G. E. Wright, "Tribal League Shrines in Amman and Shechem," BA, XXXII (1969), 104-116. CornPBE, "Temple," pp. 680-687. Alfred Edersheim, *The Temple*, New York: Revell, 1874 (Eerdman's reprint, 1950). Paul L. Garber, "Reconstructing Solomon's Temple," BA, XIV (1951), 1-24. Siegfried H. Horn, "Temple," SDABD, pp. 1069-1080. R. J. McKelvey, " 'Temple' in the New Testament," NBD, pp. 1247-1250; *The New Temple, the Church in the New Testament*, London: Oxford, 1969. Otto Michel, *"Naos,"* TDNT, IV, 880-890. André Parrot, *The Temple of Jerusalem*, London: SCM Press, 1957. Gottlob Schrenk, "*Hieron*, etc.," TDNT, III, 221-283. Emil Schürer, *A History of the Jewish People in the Time of Jesus Christ*, Edinburgh: T. & T. Clark, 1885. W. F. Stinespring, "Temple, Jerusalem," IDB, IV, 534-560. Roland de Vaux, *Ancient Israel: Its Life and Institutions*, trans. by John McHugh, New York: McGraw-Hill, 1961, pp. 271-344. G. E. Wright, *Biblical Archaeology*, rev. ed., Philadelphia: Westminster, 1962, pp. 137-146. G. R. H. Wright, "Temples at Shechem," ZAW, LXXX (1968), 1-34.

H. L. D. and J. R.

TEMPLE SERVANTS. *See* Nethinim.

TEMPT, TEMPTATION. The Heb. and Gr. terms for "tempt" (Heb. *massâ*, Gr. *peirazō*, *ekpeirazō*) and "temptation" (Heb. *nāsâ*, Gr. *peirasmos*) may at times have the meaning "enticement to sin," which so strongly colors our English words "tempt" and "temptation." But their main and overriding meaning is that of "testing the worth and character" of men and, sometimes, of God. In this sense Christians are to examine themselves to see that their words and actions evidence that they are genuine believers (II Cor 13:5; cf. II Pet 1:10).

Likewise, God in the OT tests the reality of His people's trust in Him, as in the case of Abraham (Gen 22:1), Israel (Ex 15:25; 16:4), the tribe of Levi (Deut 33:8), Hezekiah (II Chr 32:31), and the psalmist (Ps 26:2). The NT speaks of God's (or Christ's) proving the faith of Philip (Jn 6:6) and of Abraham (Heb 11:17; cf. Gen 22:1).

In His providence God uses the events of everyday life to test professed Christian faith and character. Testing can result in severe physical and spiritual torment (Heb 11:37; I Pet 4:12). God used severe natural disturbances (Ex 20:18-20), the hardships of the wilderness wanderings (Deut 8:2), and oppression by the Canaanite tribes to test Israel (Jud 2:21-22). Christians are promised not exemption from testing but strength to endure it (I Cor 10:13; II Pet 2:9; cf. I Pet 4:1, 12-16). Christ Himself, in becoming man, underwent all sorts of physical and mental testings (Heb 2:18; 4:15).

Even *things* are sometimes thought of as being tested or proved, such as a sword (I Sam 17:38), a reputation (I Kgs 10:1; II Chr 9:1), and convictions (Dan 1:12, 14).

Both the Heb. and the Gr. words at times carry the meaning of attempting to do something. In a rhetorical question God asks, "Or has a god tried to go to take for himself a nation . . ." (Deut 4:34, NASB). Men try to communicate with (Job 4:2) or to join others (Acts 9:26).

The Heb. and Gr. words translated "tempt" and "temptation" also occur with the bad sense of "enticement to sin." The devil is named as an instigator of such trials (Mt 4:3; I Thess 3:5-6). Even on the Christian, he exerts great pressure to sin (I Cor 7:5; I Thess 3:5; Rev 2:10). Succumbing to such temptations may show one's Christian profession to be insincere (Lk 8:13).

Temptation to sin often originates from evil thoughts and lust (Jas 1:14), provocations that a strong desire for riches may well compound (I Tim 6:9). However, temptation to sin never comes from God (Jas 1:13). From all such temptations the Christian should pray for deliverance (Mt 6:13; Lk 11:4).

Temptation in the bad sense may also take the form of testing another with the hope of exposing his weak points and using them against him. The enemies of Christ frequently tried to employ this tactic against Him (cf. Mt 16:1; 19:3; 22:35; Lk 20:23).

On occasion the Bible speaks of men's testing or tempting God. For instance, Israel tested God in the wilderness (Ex 17:2, 7; Num 14:22; Ps 95:8-9; I Cor 10:9), and the Pharisees and Sadducees tempted Jesus (Mt 16:1; Mk 8:11; 10:2). Furthermore, professing Christians can tempt God. Ananias and Sapphira did so by lying (Acts 5:9). Jewish Christians did so by hindering Gentile believers (Acts 15:10). Paul warned the Corinthians against unbelief, idolatry, ungodly living, tempting Christ, and murmuring (I Cor 10:7-10; cf. Num 21:4-9).

In the face of temptations the Christian draws encouragement from the knowledge that he does not face them alone. God has already removed the believer from Satan's realm and put him in His own kingdom and family (Col 1:12-13). The temptations that Satan brings are always within the limits God allows him (Job 1:8-12; 2:3-6). Further, the Christian has the example of Christ's victory over sin (Heb 4:15) and the promise of His aid (Heb 2:18).

When the Christian does succumb to temptation and sin, there is the promise of forgiveness available through Christ's continual, efficacious, redeeming grace (Heb 4:14-16; I Jn 2:1).

The Christian's reward for faithfully enduring all kinds of temptation is a crown of life (Rev 2:10).

The best-known examples of temptation in Scripture are Satan's enticement of Adam and Eve in the garden of Eden to sin (Gen 3:1-7; I Tim 2:13-14) and the temptation of Christ in the wilderness (Mt 4:1-11; Mk 1:12-13; Lk 4:1-13).

In comparing these temptations, note that Eve (with Adam's agreement) succumbed to temptation by paying excessive attention to physical desires (e.g., for food) and to the material possessions of this life (the beautiful fruit which she wanted), and by indulging in rash pride (the fruit was to make one wise). While feeling the full weight of the test, Christ, the second Adam (Rom 5:12-21; I Cor 15:22), completely overcame temptation in each of these areas (i.e., turning stones into bread; obtaining the kingdoms of the world; and in presumptuous pride, throwing Himself down from the temple).

Because He experienced and triumphed over these and other temptations, Christ is able to sympathize with and help His people in their temptations.

Bibliography. H. Seeseman, "*Peira*, etc.," TDNT, VI, 23-36.

W. H. M.

TEMPTATION OF CHRIST. This expression is often spoken of as if confined to that temptation which our Lord experienced immediately after His baptism (Mt 4:1-11; Mk 1:12-13; Lk 4:1-13), but it actually extended through His life. The devil only "departed from him for a season" (Lk 4:13), and therefore at the last supper Christ said, "Ye are they which have continued with me in my temptations" (Lk 22:28).

The temptation Christ endured following His baptism is, however, of such importance that it deserves special attention. From His experience it is clear that temptation in itself is not sin, since Christ was led to His temptation by the Holy Spirit. "Then Jesus was led up by the Spirit into the wilderness to be tempted by the devil" (Mt 4:1, RSV). Sin is not the fact of being tempted (cf. Adam and Eve, Gen 3:1 ff.), but of yielding to the temptation. Though God may lead us into a place of testing (Mt 6:13; cf. Jas 1:2-12), He does not Himself tempt us. Rather it is the devil, our own fallen nature, and our lusts (I Pet 5:8; Jas 1:14-15) which tempt us.

The question has been raised as to whether the devil actually bore Christ up to the pinnacle of the temple. And did he take Christ to a high mountain and show Him the kingdoms of this world? Are these experiences to be interpreted figuratively as Oriental imagery, or literally? There appears to be a combination here of the figurative and the literal. The devil challenged Christ to go up on the pinnacle of the temple

Traditional Mount of Temptation near Jericho with its Greek Orthodox monastery. HFV

and also to climb a mountain and look at a portion of the world, and Christ did so. He repelled both the temptation to make a spectacular leap and to worship the devil, by means of quotations from the Word of God (Mt 4:4, 7, 10). Even if the temptation is regarded as vision or allegory, as by Calvin, still the devil was the adversary and it was a real temptation. But there is no reason to take it other than literally as it is written.

The nature of Christ's threefold temptation. The order of the specific temptations varies in Matthew and Luke, but this is not of real importance. The length of Christ's fast, namely, 40 days, though formerly stressed by infidels, is no longer considered a problem. The nature of the three temptations is the most important thing.

Had Christ turned the stones to bread He would have used His miraculous power to escape suffering and to supply His own need, and no longer have acted as the perfect man meeting testing and temptation as the last Adam. He would not have been "tempted like as we are" (Heb 4:15). His miraculous power was to be used to help others and not for Himself (*see* Humiliation of Christ: Kenosis).

The temptation to exhibit His deity by jumping from the temple was an enticement to presume upon God with unwarranted confidence, in contrast to the first temptation which was to distrust His ability to withstand hunger. It would also have led Him to step aside from the path of duty. In it the devil quoted Scripture but only in a fragmentary form: "He shall give his angels charge concerning thee" (Mt 4:6; cf. Lk 4:10). The tempter omitted the words "to keep thee in all thy ways" (Ps 91:11). In this lay the devil's lie, for he is a liar from the beginning (Jn 8:44; cf. Gen 3:4-5).

The temptation to secure immediate rulership and power by bowing to the devil is the argument of expediency: do evil that good may come – in this case, sooner. Christ was divinely decreed to be the King of the very ends of the earth (Ps 2), and this was a temptation to take a shortcut to His rightful kingship.

The purpose of testing and temptation. God has always tested each order of rational beings that He has created. This test has consisted of proof of perfect trust and obedience. A test in itself is not a cause of sin. Only the action of the one tested can turn it into an occasion to sin. The angels were the first order. Those who believed God and obeyed Him were confirmed in righteousness and became the holy angels; those who disobeyed and rebelled along with Satan fell. Adam and Eve faced a test of obedience, and disobeyed and fell. Christ, in order to redeem men, faced testing, and came out victorious (Heb 5:7-9). As by the disobedience of the first Adam all fell, so by the obedience of the last Adam salvation is offered to all who will believe in Him as personal Saviour (Rom 5:19).

The nature of Christ's sinlessness. There has

been much theological debate over Christ's ability to sin, *posse peccare,* and over three possibilities: (1) Christ *could have sinned* but did not; (2) Christ was able *not* to sin; (3) Christ was *not able* to sin. The crux or heart of the debate centers in what constitutes real temptation. If Christ could not have sinned, did He then ever really face a genuine temptation? If, on the other hand, in order to make the temptation real, He could have sinned, is this not blasphemy? How could Christ sin since He is God? Even if we choose the second alternative and say Christ was able *not* to sin, do we not then imply He was able also to sin and thus still impugn His inherent holiness?

The dilemma can be solved if we first recognize that, though according to the human nature no man would be able not to sin, Christ's human nature along with His divine belongs to the one divine person and is ruled by that person. It is the divine person of the Christ who hated sin and could not countenance it in His divine nature, who out of love suffered temptation in all points like as we without succumbing to sin (Heb 4:15). In the human nature Christ could have sinned, but because of His divine person He could not. Therefore we do not say either that Christ was able to sin, or that Christ was able *not* to sin, but that Christ could not sin. Abraham Kuyper wrote, "But since Jesus did not assume a human person, a 'homo,' but human nature, and since there was in him no human ego (to realize this *possibilitas*) but, on the contrary, the human nature remained eternally united to the second person of the Trinity, therefore the control of this divine person makes it absolutely impossible for the *possibilitas* to become reality" (*Loci* III, Cap., III, par. 6. p. 11, cited by G. C. Berkouwer, *The Person of Christ,* Grand Rapids: Eerdmans, 1955, p. 259). Berkouwer puts it in more existential terms as he writes, "The inability to sin is that of His person, of His full and inviolable willingness to do the will of the Father. It is the inability to desist from His love, which He brings to its final, its consummating realization" (*op. cit.*, p. 262).

It may be concluded that Christ did experience a real testing and temptation commensurate with that required of rational creatures, but that He was victorious in every area of temptation. It was the fact that He was a divine person which made Him not able to sin in spite of the fact that He assumed a human nature which could otherwise have sinned. *See* Christ, Sinlessness of.

R. A. K.

TEN. *See* Number.

TEN COMMANDMENTS

History of Interpretation

The OT holds the law to be the standard of acceptable behavior. Occasionally the ceremonial aspect is prominent, but the prophets emphasized the ethical aspects. Their messages are best understood against the backdrop of the Decalogue (e.g., Jer 7:9).

Jesus applied the Decalogue to the realm of motivation. Paul in his epistles to the Romans and Galatians emphasized that the law is written on the heart and was proclaimed to give knowledge of sin. The NT, as well as the OT, links the Decalogue with Moses.

Excepting the gnostics (*see* Gnosticism), the Church Fathers generally acknowledged the law's Mosaic origin. Justin maintained a distinction between moral and ceremonial laws. Medieval Jewish and Christian scholars taught the Mosaic origin of the law. Aquinas introduced a threefold division of the law: moral, ceremonial, and judicial.

The reformers expounded the Decalogue, declared its Mosaic authorship, and echoed the Pauline emphases. Wesley promulgated the views of Paul, Justin, and the reformers, holding that the law leads to the gospel, while the gospel leads to a greater keeping of the law.

Higher criticism brought the first denial of the Mosaic tradition. Portions of the Decalogue were considered the result of the evolutionary development of ancestor worship, nomadic environment, or a settled agricultural life. Some felt that Moses originally gave the law and that it evolved upward. Others maintained that the law is so highly developed that Moses had no connection with it, but that Moses gave only a ritual Decalogue.

Present trends in biblical studies indicate growing support of a Mosaic origin. The noble qualities of the Decalogue are being dated earlier and earlier.

Traditional View of Origin

The traditional view claims that God gave the law through Moses. The two versions of the Decalogue have come from Moses—the Exodus version (Ex 20:1–17) as quoted from the stone tables, and the Deuteronomy account (Deut 5:6–21) as Moses recited it. The traditional view is supported by three millennia of tradition, and by stylistic arguments. The Deuteronomy version has a hortatory style. The Mosaic tradition coincides with this fact. Every variation in Deut 5:6–21 can be interpreted as hortatory. Furthermore, most scholars recognize an underlying style common to both versions.

The witness of history substantiates the traditional position. In Israel's own history the ministry of the prophets becomes an enigma without the law's existence. The prophets declare the ideal that Israel has not reached, indicting her for breach of covenant. Mendenhall avers that Hittite suzerainty treaties of the 2nd mil. B.C. contain parallels with the Decalogue. This means that the Decalogue was historically appropriate to the Mosaic era. *See* Covenant.

Some claim that the Decalogue in Ex 20 interrupts the narrative, but a reading of Ex 20:19, 22 indicates that the Decalogue is no interruption. Wellhausen stressed contradictions about authorship in Ex 34:1 (indicating that God wrote on the tablets) and 34:28 (that Moses wrote on them), claiming that such a glaring inconsistency in so short a span is unlikely. But the Lord, not Moses, is the logical subject of "And he wrote . . ." in the second half of v. 28.

Critical Views of Origin

There are two basic critical views of the Decalogue's origin. Some consider it a primitive legislative code traceable to Moses, which has expanded through the years. Others hold that the Decalogue was not preceded by ten terse Mosaic commands, but a ritual decalogue.

The former view stresses the brevity of several commandments, and the fact that in the longer ones a short command is evident. However, when the supposed accretions are removed, there are 13 commands. Thus, three commands must be arbitrarily eliminated. The so-called interpretive material is essential to having ten commands.

Those who feel that the precursor to the Decalogue was ritualistic, appeal to Ex 20:23–26; 22; 23:10–19; 34 to prove it, but do not agree as to which are the original ten commands. These men fail to account adequately for the narrative sections. Furthermore, the two supposedly "late" commands, the second and fourth, are in evidence in these ritual decalogues.

The critical positions on the origin of the Decalogue all have an underlying commitment to the evolutionary development of law and religion, and to a disbelief in supernatural revelation.

Division of the Decalogue

The Jews, Catholics, and Lutherans combine the prohibitions against polytheism and idolatry into one. The Jews establish the introductory statement (Ex 20:2) as the first commandment, while Catholics and Lutherans divide the commandment against coveting. The Orthodox and Reformed churches consider Ex 20:2 as introductory, the prohibition of polytheism as the first commandment, and the prohibition against idolatry as the second commandment.

The latter view is superior because it distinguishes between polytheism and idolatry. This view avoids artificially dividing the tenth commandment, and making a commandment out of Ex 20:2, which is neither a command nor a prohibition.

Contents of the Commandments

1. *First commandment* (Ex 20:3; Deut 5:7). This commandment declares the obligation of loyalty to Yahweh. The Israelite was to have no other god. God expected undivided fidelity to Himself. The term "before" signifies being before one's face. Thus it means "in front of" or "in the presence of." There was to be no rival to Yahweh for the heart's affection.

2. *Second commandment* (Ex 20:4–6; Deut 5:8–10). This is a dual command that prohibits the making and worshiping of images. Since Yahweh is the Creator, to represent Him as created is blasphemy. The commandment reminds one that his life is inescapably involved with others. His conduct has implications for himself and for others, not in terms of guilt but of consequences.

3. *Third commandment* (Ex 20:7; Deut 5:11). This commandment calls for reverence of Yahweh by refraining from the abuse of His name, which reveals His nature. The words "in vain" have several possible meanings. Some suggest that His name was not to be used with witchcraft. Others maintain that God's name was not to be used with inconsequential matters. Still others believe that profane swearing is meant, that "in vain" means to appear empty-handed before the Deity, or to use God's name in an oath one fails to perform. The commandment probably has no particular kind of misuse of God's name in view, but forbids any misuse of His name.

4. *Fourth commandment* (Ex 20:8–11; Deut 5:12–15). This is a positive commandment concerning the proper use of time. A man's work is to occupy six days, but the seventh is to be hallowed unto God, following the pattern of creation.

The accounts in Ex 20:11 and Deut 5:14–15 are not contradictory. Both call for one day in seven and declare the sabbath an occasion for rest. Deuteronomy gives no reason for the pattern of one day in seven. Deut 5:14–15 repeats the command without the pattern, citing the impetus of the Exodus. In Deuteronomy the Exodus is consistently cited as a motivation for many religious observances, so it is not of peculiar significance here. Ex 20:2 and Deut 5:6 also claim the Exodus as an impetus to obedience. This commandment in Exodus is couched in universal language. When Moses exhorts to "remember," however, he adapts it to Israel (Deut 5:15).

There are many opinions concerning the manner of observing the sabbath. However, the Decalogue simply commands that it be kept holy, i.e., set apart unto God. This involves physical rest from daily labors for man and beast. The references to the creation and the Exodus imply a religious content is to be given to the sabbath. The head of the household is responsible for the observance of the sabbath throughout his household.

5. *Fifth commandment* (Ex 20:12; Deut 5:16). The Israelite is to honor both parents. The fourth commandment cites the responsibility of the parents to provide a proper climate including rest for their young, while this commandment deals with the offspring's responsibility. Honoring one's parents involves respect and obedience. One's offspring have a duty so to live that they will bring honor to their parents.

6. *Sixth commandment* (Ex 20:13; Deut

5:17). The most accurate translation is "Do not murder" (from *rāṣaḥ*). It does not prohibit taking animal life, nor even human life under certain circumstances. It was directed against murder which grows from hatred.

7. *Seventh commandment* (Ex 20:14; Deut 5:18). This commandment forbids adultery. Some believe that adultery is committed with another man's wife, while intercourse with a single woman is permissible (fornication). Others hold that the commandment bans intercourse with anyone other than one's spouse.

The words for adultery and fornication are occasionally used interchangeably, so there is no complete distinction. Hosea and Jeremiah condemn fornication, yet in their lists of sins, the only sexual sin is adultery, suggesting that it is inclusive (cf. Hos 4:2, 12; Jer 2:20; 7:9; 23:14). Since adultery is the only sexual perversion mentioned in the Decalogue, it should be understood to include fornication.

8. *Eighth commandment* (Ex 20:15; Deut 5:19). This commandment prohibits theft, i.e., the taking of property that belongs to another. Therefore it approves the right of owning property. A man may possess that which is the just result of his labor, or a gift. Man is forbidden to steal that which is another's possession.

9. *Ninth commandment* (Ex 20:16; Deut 5:20). This commandment is an exhortation to honest speech. While dealing specifically with court testimony, it prohibits all false witnessing as unbecoming to God's people. A man's words are of concern to God.

10. *Tenth commandment* (Ex 20:17; Deut 5:21). This commandment carries the divine standard into the inner life. The commandment does not oppose all desire, but only forbids the craving for things that are not ours with such intensity that it becomes the dynamic of our life. The heart's desires are to accord with God's desires for one's life (Ps 37:4; 10:17).

R. B. D.

NT Attitude Toward the Decalogue

It must be remembered that the Decalogue is not a self-contained unit standing in isolation; it is an integral part of the Mosaic Law. The contexts of Exodus and Deuteronomy are sufficient to indicate this, but the fourth commandment (sabbath observance) makes this especially obvious, for it is elsewhere in the Mosaic law that we find the detailed prescriptions regarding its observance. In a sense, this commandment, though included in what is commonly called the ethical or moral law, is more ceremonial than moral, and its violation was punishable by civil sanctions. The point is that dividing the Mosaic law into moral law, ceremonial law, and civil law can become quite artificial. The law as a governing economy over God's people stands or falls as a whole system (cf. Jas 2:11-12), the Jews themselves regarding it as an indivisible unit. That system as such has come to an end inasmuch as it was fulfilled by Christ, its goal and end (Rom 10:4; Gal 2:19-21; 3:13; 5:11).

This does not mean, however, that the commandments relating to morality in the law are abrogated in the sense that immorality is now legitimate. Quite the contrary, for the timeless principles of right and wrong embodied in the Decalogue are in essence repeated in the NT as part of the rule of life for Christians (there is no commandment corresponding to the fourth commandment). But even this is not simple repetition, for there is an advance beyond the OT statements. Though Christ quotes the fifth through ninth commandments as summarizing man's duties to man, it is following Jesus that leads to salvation (Mt 19:16-30; Mk 10:17-29; Lk 18:18-30).

In the Sermon on the Mount Christ placed Himself as a higher authority than the law, correcting the Jewish misinterpretations of the law and clarifying the true intent and meaning of the law (Mt 5:17-46; cf. Mt 15:3-6; Mk 2:23-28). Specifically, He quotes the sixth and seventh commandments and then asserts that anger is incipient murder and that lust is adultery in the heart. Thus He radicalizes the Decalogue statements on these points by extending the commands into the realm of thought-life (Mt 5:21-32). He also summarized man's obligation to God and fellowman in the one word "love," for the man who has love in his heart for God and neighbor will not trespass against either of them (Mt 22:36-40; cf. Jn 13:34-35). Paul develops the same concept (Rom 13:8-10; Gal 5:14).

While there are principles of right and wrong in the Ten Commandments that are eternally valid, the NT does not merely repeat those precepts which are still the believer's duty, but it also internalizes them and points to love as the essence that fulfills all requirements towards our fellowman and God. The Decalogue should not be regarded as the highest summation of a Christian's duty. This will be found in the NT, which spells out the implications of love being lived out as one is led by the Holy Spirit.

See Covenant; Grace; Law of Moses.

Bibliography. Alva J. McClain, *Law and Grace*, Chicago: Moody Press, 1967. G. Schrenk, *"Entole,"* TDNT, II, 544-556.

S. N. G.

TENDERHEARTED. The Gr. *eusphlanchnos* for "tenderhearted" in Eph 4:32 literally means "kindly bowels," hence "compassionate." A similar expression, *splanchna eleous,* in Lk 1:78 (KJV "tender mercy"), means "bowels of mercy or kindness." The bowels are regarded as the source of kindness and longing in Scripture (Gen 43:30; I Kgs 3:26; Lam 1:20; 2:11; Phm 7, 12, 20; Phil 1:8). In Jas 5:11 Gr. *oiktirmōn* from *oiktos,* "pity," is translated "of tender mercy" (cf. Rom 12:1, "mercies"). The two

Gr. words are combined in the expression "bowels of mercies" (Col 3:12) and "bowels and mercies" (Phil 2:1). *See* Bowels.

TENONS. The term is used of the two projections at the end of each of the 28 upright acacia boards of the tabernacle (*q.v.*). Each tenon was fitted into a mortise in a base of silver. The mortise-tenon arrangement held firmly in place the lower part of the frame structure of the tabernacle (Ex 26:17, 19; 36:22, 24).

TENT. The tent (Heb. *'ōhel,* Gr. *skēnē*) was the characteristic dwelling of the keepers of cattle, the nomad races, of whom Jabal was the father (Gen 4:20). The pastoral tribes of Reuben, Gad, and the half tribe of Manasseh, for the most part retained the tent life E of Jordan (Josh 22:4-8). Jacob was characterized as a "quiet man," "dwelling in tents" (Gen 25:27). The settled Israelites preserved a reminder of their nomad ancestry in such phrases as "going to one's tent" for to "go home" (Jud 20:8), and in the call "to thy tents [i.e., to your homes], O Israel" (I Kgs 12:16). Agriculture was sometimes associated with tent life, as in Isaac's case (Gen 26:12, 25). After settlement in Canaan, the Israelites would return at harvesttime to their tents, camping near the crops.

The typical tent of Semitic nomads was made by sewing together strips or curtains (Jer 49:29) of the native black goat's hair cloth (Song 1:5), such as the Bedouin still use in Palestine. Poles were placed under this covering at intervals to hold it from the ground, and it was suspended between these poles by ropes of goat's hair or hemp (Isa 54:2; Jer 10:20). The loose ends of the ropes were fastened to hardwood pins driven into the ground with a large wooden mallet (Jud 4:21; 5:26). Some tents were circular, resting on one central pole. The usual tent was oblong and held up by nine poles, six to seven feet high, arranged in three rows of three. The tent was divided by a curtain partition—the front division open and free to all, the back closed and reserved for the women and privacy of domestic life (Gen 18:9).

A typical Bedouin tent in Palestine

The women's quarters were called *ḥarem* ("banned" to other men). The patriarchs were wealthy enough to afford separate tents for their wives (Gen 24:67; 31:33). In early times it was also customary to pitch a special tent for a newly wedded pair (Ps 19:5; Joel 2:16; cf. II Sam 16:22), as is still the practice among the Arabs. The canopy under which Jewish couples are married today is a survival of the ancient *ḥuppâ* (bridal tent). The tent (Heb. *qubbâ*) of Num 25:8 was probably a portable tent-shrine of the nomadic Midianites (JBL, XC [1971], 200-206).

The equipment for nomadic living was meager. The stove or oven consisted of a few stones placed at the tent entrance or simply a hole in the ground. Objects were easily hidden in the dirt floor of the tent, albeit with the knowledge of the family members, as in the case of Achan (Josh 7:20-25). Coarse straw mats served as beds which could be rolled up during the day. A piece of leather spread on the floor was the table (Ps 23:5; Isa 21:5). Bags of goatskins, earthen pots, bowls, water jars, two grinding stones for a grain mill, simple pottery lamps or torches, and a few other crude instruments completed the belongings of the tent dwellers.

The finest picture of tent life in patriarchal times is found in Gen 18. The tent dweller usually looked for a clump of oaks for a site to provide shade as at Mamre near Hebron, and it was especially choice if a water supply was nearby (Isa 13:20). Aquila and Priscilla, as well as the apostle Paul, were tentmakers (*see* Occupations: Tentmaker). The quickness and ease with which tents can be struck, leaving their tenants without covering in the lonely deserts, is Paul's image for the speedy dissolution of our mortal body, preparatory to our abiding resurrection body (II Cor 5:1).

See Tabernacle.

Bibliography. Wilhelm Michaelis, "*Skēnē,* etc.," TDNT, VII, 368-394.

R. L. D.

TENTH DEAL. The Heb. word *'iśśārôn,* "tenth," occurs 28 times in the priestly instructions of the Pentateuch regarding the amount of flour for grain offerings. The English word "deal" (KJV), "part" (ASV), or "measure" (RSV, in Ex 29:40 only) does not occur in the Heb., but is supplied to give the sense. The RSV, however, with the exception noted, renders the Heb. by the fraction and supplies "of an ephah," which the ASV and NASB add in italics. The English word "deal" means part or portion, but is obsolete as a translational expletive of the Heb. term. *See* Weights, Measures, and Coins.

TENTMAKER. *See* Tent; Occupations: Tentmaker.

TERAH (tĕr'ȧ)

1. Father of Abraham, Nahor, and Haran (Gen 11:26). Terah's family settled in Haran in Mesopotamia after migrating from Ur. Abraham, with his nephew Lot, later migrated further to Canaan. From Gen 11:31; 24; 31:53; Josh 24:2; Acts 7:2-3 it appears that Abraham's religious experience was the reason the family moved out of polytheistic and idolatrous Ur to Haran. Terah evidently became a worshiper of Yahweh.

The ancient city Til Turaḫi, located in the vicinity of Haran according to Mesopotamian cuneiform tablets, may have been named after him.

2. A desert station (Num 33:27-28; "Tarah" of KJV is "Terah" in ASV).

TERAPHIM (tĕr'ȧ-fĭm). The Heb. pl. noun *t^erāpîm* (a word of unknown derivation) is rendered in the KJV seven times as "images" and once each as "idols" and "idolatry," while six times it is simply transliterated as "teraphim." The teraphim images of ancient Israel were household idols (cf. Gen 31:19 with 31:30, 32; Jud 18:17 with 18:24) whose primary function in the apostate element of Israel's population seems to have been that of divination (*q.v.;* I Sam 15:23; II Kgs 23:24; Ezk 21:21; Zech 10:2); note their connection with the ephod in Jud 17:5; 18:14, 17-18, 20; Hos 3:4. They were probably of Mesopotamian origin (Gen 31:19-21; Ezk 21:21) and came under frequent prophetic condemnation (I Sam 15:23; II Kgs 23:24; Zech 10:2). *See* Amulet.

Recent scholarship asserts, on the basis of certain Nuzu texts (ANET, pp. 219 f.), that Rachel stole Laban's teraphim (Gen 31:17-50) to guarantee Jacob's title to Laban's estate upon the latter's death. Nuzu law, however, implies that bequeathal, rather than mere possession, of household gods determined family inheritance rights. It is therefore perhaps better to assume that Rachel, not yet fully separated from her polytheistic heritage, took the gods for religious or divinatory purposes. Josephus (*Ant.* xviii.9.5) states that it was customary even in much later times for inhabitants of Mesopotamia to carry their household gods along with them wherever they traveled (cf. M. Greenberg in JBL, LXXXI [1962], 239-248). Harry A. Hoffner, Jr., modifies the opinion that teraphim were objects of worship by showing from a parallel Hittite term that they were mantic devices employed for cultic inquiry ("Hittite *Tarpiš* and Hebrew *Terāphîm*," JNES, XXVII [1968], 61-68).

It is scarcely possible that the teraphim of I Sam 19:11-17 were household deities since archaeologists have found no such images of the size of a full-grown man (cf. W. F. Albright, *Archaeology and the Religion of Israel,* 4th ed., p. 114; cf. also Gen 31:34). It has therefore been suggested (Albright, *op. cit.,* p. 207, n. 63) that Michal's teraphim were "old rags."

R. Y.

Terracing along the edge of the Shepherds Fields, Bethlehem. HFV

TEREBINTH. *See* Plants.

TERESH (tĕr'ĕsh). One of the two disaffected royal eunuchs of Ahasuerus charged with the responsibility of guarding the threshold of the palace, who plotted the assassination of the king. Mordecai exposed the plot and the conspirators were hanged. This meritorious service of Mordecai was overlooked for a time, but later it became the cause of his singular advancement (Est 2:21-23; 6:2).

TERRACE. The Heb. term *m^esillâ* appears in the plural in II Chr 9:11 and is translated in the KJV as "terraces" (marg., "highways" or "stairs") and in the RSV as "steps," which follows the versional readings. The word is normally rendered "highway" 20 out of 28 occurrences, but the precise nuance of the usage in II Chr 9:11 is illusive. The corresponding Heb. term of the parallel passage in I Kgs 10:12 is *mis'ād,* "prop" or "support," which is rendered by "pillars" in the KJV (marg., "rails"). But here it appears in the singular. Two things are evident: the object was made of expensive almug wood, and it embodied the ideas of support and of elevation. It appears best, therefore, to translate the term as "balustrade" (Moffatt) or "a railing" (Rudolph), since such includes both of these ideas (Anchor Bible, XIII, 53).

TERRESTRIAL BODY. *See* Spiritual Body.

TERROR. Several Heb. terms and their Gr. synonym, *phobos,* are used to express the concept of terror, fear, dread, consternation, or fright. The more important OT terms are *ḥittît,* "terror," which occurs only in Ezekiel and usually refers to the terror caused by the great heathen nations and kings (Ezk 26:17; 32:27). Heb. *'êmâ* frequently signifies the terror or dread inspired by human enemies (Josh 2:9; Isa 33:18), or by God: "Let not thy terror make me afraid" (Job 13:21, ASV; cf. Ex 15:16; 23:27, ASV; Ps 88:15), or figuratively of idols (lit., "terrors," i.e., dreadful things, Jer 50:38). The term *ballāhâ* expresses figuratively the idea of death: "the terrors of the shadow of death" (Job 24:17; cf. 18:14); or destruction, as when the ruin of Tyre is foretold, "I will make thee a terror" (i.e., a desolation, Ezk 26:21). Fear in the sense of reverence or holy respect toward God is expressed by *yir'â* (e.g., Gen 20:11; Ps 2:11; 5:7; Prov 1:7).

In the NT Gr. *phobos* is three times translated "terror" in the KJV: in Rom 13:3, "for rulers are not a cause of fear for good behavior, but for evil" (NASB); in II Cor 5:11, speaking of the Christian's fear of the Lord because of the judgment to come; and in I Pet 3:14, exhorting believers not to be afraid of the terror or intimidation of their persecutors. *See* Fear.

H. E. Fr.

TERTIUS (tûr'shĭ-ŭs). The manuensis of Paul who wrote the letter to the Romans and added his own personal greetings to the church at Rome (Rom 16:22).

TERTULLUS (tĕr-tŭl'ŭs). An orator (legal advocate) engaged by members of the Sanhedrin to accuse Paul before Felix (procurator of Judea). *See* Orator. The name, occurring in the NT only in Acts 24:1-2, was common, a Gr. diminutive form of the Latin *Tertius*. Whether he was Jewish, Greek or Roman is unknown. Verses 2 ("this nation") and 5 ("the Jews") may indicate he was not a Jew; vv. 3-4 and 6 ("we") have been taken to indicate he was (although it may simply indicate a professional identification with his clients). The end of v. 6, "we . . . would have judged according to our law" (KJV), possibly the strongest argument for his Jewishness, is placed in the margin in the ASV, RSV and NASB, along with v. 7 and part of v. 8, which are found only in some later MSS.

TESTAMENT. The Gr. noun *diathēkē* is translated "testament" 13 times in the NT (KJV), though elsewhere it is rendered "covenant." The noun is itself the LXX rendering of Heb. *b^e^rît* when signifying God's self-imposed obligation for the reconciliation of sinners to Himself (Gen 17:7; Deut 7:6-8; Ps 89:3-4). The LXX here avoided the usual Gr. term for covenant, *synthēkē* (mutually "put together"), as inappropriate for God's sovereign activity and substituted *diathēkē* (an arrangement, lit., "put through"), the primary meaning of which is "a disposition of property by a will." The term seems providentially chosen, because salvation springs historically from a specific form of covenant, namely, a bequest. "For where a testament is, there must also of necessity be the death of the testator" (Heb 9:16); and it is Christ's death alone that accomplished redemption, both for ourselves and for "the transgressions that were under the first testament" (Heb 9:15; cf. Heb 11:40; Jn 14:6; J. B. Payne, *Theology of the Older Testament*, pp. 78-87).

The testament thus constitutes the heart of all God's redemptive revelation, and Scripture consists of "the Old Testament" and "the New Testament." For while there can be but one testament (one death: "My blood of *the* testament," Mt 26:28, best MSS), revelation yet organizes itself under the older testament, with its anticipatory symbols of Christ's sacrifice (II Cor 3:14, Jer 31:32), and the newer testament, commemorative of His accomplished atonement (II Cor 3:6; Jer 31:31).

God's testamentary arrangement contains the following elements: a testator, God the Son, "the mediator" (Heb 9:15); heirs, "the called" ones (9:15); an objective method of effectuation, namely, a gracious bequest (9:16); subjective conditions by which heirs qualify for the gift, by commitment to Christ (9:28); and an inheritance of reconciliation, "eternal salvation" (9:15,28).

Its objective effectuation is always marked by: monergism, "one worker," God exercising pure grace (Gen 15:17; Ex 19:4; Jer 31:2-3), unassisted by man's works (Eph 2:8-9); the death of the testator (Ex 24:8; Heb 9:18-22); promise, "I will be their God, and they shall be my people" (Gen 17:7 through Rev 21:3); eternity (Ps 105:8-10; cf. Lev 2:13, "the salt [eternal preservation] of the testament"); and a confirmatory sign, such as the rainbow to Noah (Gen 9:12-13), the exodus to Moses (Ex 20:2), or Christ's resurrection to us (Rom 1:4). Subjective appropriation of the testament is likewise marked by unchangeable features of human response: faith (Gen 15:6; Deut 6:5; Heb 11:6) and obedience, both moral (Gen 17:1; Mt 7:24; Eph 2:10) and ceremonial (Gen 17:10-14; Acts 22:16; I Cor 11:24); for genuine faith must be demonstrated by works (Jas 2:14-26).

Yet God's revelations of His testament also exhibit historical progression (testaments, plural, Rom 9:4). Under the older testament appear the Edenic (Gen 3:15), Noachic (9:9), Abrahamic (15:18), Sinaitic (Ex 19:5-6), Levitical (Num 25:12-13), and Davidic (II Sam 23:5). Each anticipated the same redemptive death; yet differences appear, particularly in their ceremonial response. Even our own, newer testament thus exhibits two stages: the present new testament in Christ (Jer 31:33-34; Heb 8:6-13), with its ceremony, the Lord's Supper, exhibiting "the Lord's death *till he come*" (I Cor 11:26). For Scripture also speaks of a future testament of peace among all nations (Ezk 34:25-31), when spiritual communion with Christ will become "face to face" (Ezk 37:27; 39:29).

Bibliography. Meredith G. Kline, "Dynastic Covenant," WTJ, XXIII (1960), 1-15. John Murray, *The Covenant of Grace*, London: Tyndale Press, 1954.

J. B. P.

TETH (tĕth). The ninth letter of the Heb. alphabet which may be considered an explosive palatal with the general sound of *t*, but with firmer articulation and produced by pressing the tongue against the roof of the mouth. It appears in the KJV as a heading for Ps 119:65-72.

TETRARCH. Originally the ruler of a fourth part of a region. It may be used in this sense for Herod Antipas, tetrarch of Galilee (Mt 14:1; Lk 3:1, 19; 9:7; Acts 13:1), and Herod Philip, tetrarch of Ituraea and Trachonitis (Lk 3:1), sons of Herod the Great, each of whom inherited a fourth of his father's kingdom (Jos *Ant.* xvii.11.4; *Wars* ii.6.3). The title became loosely employed for a petty ruler of a small district, e.g., of Lysanias as tetrarch of Abilene (Lk 3:1). "Tetrarch" may, however, also have been applied to Antipas (also styled "king" in Mt 14:9; Mk 6:14) in a general sense, for their father had received the same title (Jos *Wars* i.12.5). A third brother, Archelaus, to whom was assigned Judea, Samaria, and Idumaea, was given the superior title "ethnarch." *See* Herod.

TEXT OF THE BIBLE. *See* Bible Manuscripts; Versions, Ancient and Medieval.

THADDAEUS (thă-dē'*ŭs*). One of the Twelve mentioned only in Mt 10:3 and Mk 3:18. In the corresponding lists in Lk 6:16 and Acts 1:13 the name "Judas (the son) of James" occurs. Possibly Matthew and Mark used the other name because of the possible confusion with Judas the traitor.

In Jn 14:22 he is described as "Judas (not Iscariot)," thus also showing the distinction. The question which he posed in the last passage showed his misunderstanding of the nature of Jesus' promised manifestation of Himself. He was virtually urging Jesus to make a public, dramatic appearance.

For a history of attempted solutions see E. Nestle, "Thaddaeus," HDB, IV. 741-42.

THAHASH (thā'hăsh). KJV form of Tahash (*q.v.*) in Gen 22:24.

THAMAH. *See* Tamah.

THAMAR. *See* Tamar.

THANK OFFERING. *See* Sacrificial Offerings.

THANKSGIVING. The expression of gratitude or appreciation to God. It is acknowledged by man universally, but only known in its fullest degree by the Christian believer who sees God as the Creator of a world that was "good" (Gen 1:4, 31), the Provider of salvation to man immediately after he sinned and fell, and the Giver of every good and perfect gift.

The Bible is full of thanksgiving, the most pronounced examples of which are found in a special OT offering of thanksgiving (Lev 7:12-15; 22:29; II Chr 29:31; Amos 4:5), in the many feasts instituted for Israel (Ex 23:14 ff.; 34:22-23; Lev 23; Num 29; Deut 16), and in psalms of thanksgiving (Ps 34:3; 50:14; 92:1-5; 100; 107; 136). In the NT the believer is never to pray without giving thanks (Phil 4:6; Col 4:2) for the things God has done for him (I Cor 15:57; II Cor 2:14; 8:16; 9:15; I Tim 4:3-4). Our gifts to others are to be the cause of their rendering thanksgiving (Gr. *eucharistia)* to God for His abundant grace (*charis*) and favor (II Cor 4:15; 9:11-12). Heaven will be filled with the voices of angelic creatures and of the redeemed giving thanks to God (Rev 4:9; 7:12; 11:17).

Our national celebration of thanksgiving is an echo of two OT feasts: of Harvest (Ex 23:16), called also the Feast of Pentecost and the Feast of Weeks (Ex 34:22), since it was seven weeks or 50 days after the Passover; and of the Feast of Tabernacles (Lev 23:34-43), also called the Feast of Ingathering (Ex 23:16; 34:22) at the end of the agricultural year. Pentecost marked the end of the wheat harvest in Israel and came in June, while our thanksgiving marks the end of the entire harvest season and comes in the fall, as did the Feast of Tabernacles after the olives, grapes, and other fruits were picked (*see* Festivals).

See Praise; Prayer; Worship.

R. A. K.

THANKWORTHY. The Gr. *charis,* "grace," "worthy of thanks, or gratitude," "thankworthy" (I Pet 2:19) is translated "approved" by RSV. Berkeley chooses the literal translation "grace," considering that to endure grief wrongfully takes grace.

THARA. *See* Terah.

THARSHISH. *See* Tarshish.

THEATER

1. A place where dramatic productions were held. Dramatic exhibitions were originally held in honor of the god Dionysus on the days of his festivals. The ruins are of two types--structures built primarily for drama, and those built for other purposes and used for plays. As a general rule the theater was the largest building in a city. Hence, among the Greeks, it was a common practice to use the theater for public assemblies and the transaction of public business (as in Acts 19:29, 31).

Gr. assemblies were known for their demonstrativeness. An inscription at Ephesus mentions a civic assembly at the theater. Josephus (*Ant.* xix.8.2) relates that it was in the recently excavated Herodian theater at Caesarea (*q.v.*) that the events of Acts 12:20-23 took place. He also states that Herod the Great built a theater and an amphitheater in Jerusalem (*Ant.* xv.8.1).

The Gr. theater had three parts. The *orchēstra* was a circular dancing place for the chorus and actors, with an altar in the center. The

Theater of Dionysus, Athens. HFV

origin of drama is commonly found in the hymns celebrating the deeds of Dionysus sung to the accompaniment of flute and a dance around the altar. The *theatron* proper or auditorium was the place for the spectators, extending around two-thirds or more of the orchestra. The seats were stone slabs except where natural rock was cut to shape and wooden seats were added. The seats arose one above another in concentric tiers, frequently constructed against a concave hillside so as to take advantage of the natural slope. The *skēnē* (lit., "tent," "booth") or stage building was later added at the edge of the circle opposite the seats as a retiring room for the actors and as a background to the action. The *skēnē* developed a raised stage on the audience side which shared the acting with the orchestra.

The late Hellenistic theater gave impetus to the Roman theater, but the latter was an original construction of the Roman spirit. The Roman theater instead of being placed against a hillside was erected as a free-standing building supported by arched construction. The auditorium and scene or stage buildings were linked to make one structure and were roofed in contrast to the open-air Gr. theaters. The auditorium formed only a semicircle, as did the orchestra which was included in the seating space, so that all the acting took place on the platform stage. Whereas the Greeks reserved only a few chief seats for magistrates and dignitaries, the Romans (at least from the time of Augustus) made an elaborate classification of seats by sex, age, profession, and rank. The Romans also built amphitheaters with arenas for gladiatorial and athletic contests. Professional combats are first mentioned *c.* 30 B.C. Admission was free.

The theater at Ephesus (*q.v.*) mentioned in Acts 19 was located on the western slope of Mount Pion overlooking the harbor with which it was connected by a main street. It was built by Lysimachus in the early 3rd cen. B.C., and has been estimated to have held more than 24,000 people. The construction was of stone.

2. The Gr. word also referred to the show itself, a "spectacle," and is so figuratively used by Paul of the apostles who were exhibited to be gazed at and made sport of (I Cor 4:9).

E. F.

THEBES. *See* No, No-Amon.

THEBEZ (thē'bĕz). A fortified city in the territory of Manasseh on the road from Shechem to Beth-shan, mentioned in connection with Abimelech, son of Gideon, who was seeking to set himself up as king in Israel (Jud 9:50–57). Thebez refused submission to Abimelech. The city was conquered with the exception of a strong tower where many of the inhabitants had fled for safety, and had climbed onto the roof. Abimelech, in the process of the siege, carelessly ventured near the tower and a woman cast an upper millstone striking him upon his head, breaking his skull. To avoid the shame of perishing by the hand of a woman, Abimelech persuaded his armor bearer to thrust him through with his sword. The story seems to have been well known as it was recalled by David some 200 years later (II Sam 11:21). The place is now represented by Tubas *c.* ten miles NE of Shechem, where roads from Shechem and Dothan converge on the way to the Jordan Valley.

R. L. D.

THEFT. *See* Law.

THEISM. Defined by Charles Hodge as "the doctrine of an extramundane, personal God, the creator, preserver and governor of the world"(*Systematic Theology,* I, 205). It includes the study of the rational arguments and reasons for belief in the reality of God, and the proofs for His existence as a triune God.

The theistic arguments. In the history of Christian thought certain of the theistic proofs used to support belief in the existence of God appeared quite early. Anselm was the originator of the ontological argument: that which exists in actuality is greater than that which exists merely in the mind. For example, we have an idea of an infinitely perfect being. But since real existence is included in perfect being, if God does not actually exist, then we must conceive of a being greater than God.

Thomas Aquinas is noted for five arguments: (1) Motion requires a first mover, and this is God. (2) The world as an effect requires a sufficient cause, and this is God. (3) The world as contingent demands a self-existent cause, and this is God. (4) In the world are grades of perfection which require something that is altogether perfect, and this is God. (5) Purposeful results demand an intelligent purposeful cause, and this cause is God.

Modern apologetics use the ontological, cosmological, teleological, and moral arguments. Of these the ontological is the weakest, because the idea of a perfect being is no more a proof of the same than the idea of a perfect kingdom, such as Atlantis, is proof of its existence. This argument, it is pointed out, appears convincing only to those who consider the existence of God to be the most evident of all facts. Calvin spoke of the "seed of religion," namely, that man naturally conceives of and believes in a God and can only take refuge in atheism temporarily. This is probably a sounder basis of proof since it rests upon the phenomenon of belief in deity which we observe in the entire history of mankind.

The cosmological argument is that every effect requires a sufficient cause. The world is an effect, therefore the world must be the result of an outside cause sufficient and adequate to account for its existence; this must be God. This argument is essentially sound in itself, though insufficient as usually expressed in that it is confined to the explanation of the physical world. It is much better when framed thus: Everything that exists requires a sufficient cause. The world and rational beings called men exist. Therefore there must exist an adequate cause for these, namely, a rational, personal God.

The teleological argument is that anything that reveals purpose and order demands a planner. The world, including man, reveals purpose and order. Therefore there must exist an intelligent, purposeful cause, and this cause is God.

The moral argument claims that the possession of a moral nature, namely, the ability to distinguish between good and evil, requires a first moral cause. Man has a moral nature; therefore man must be the product of a personal, moral cause—God.

The value of the theistic arguments. Opinions vary widely as to the value of the theistic arguments. Immanuel Kant, for example, attacked the ontological and the cosmological arguments violently. He insisted that the cosmological argument is essentially only an extension of the ontological. However, he did accept the teleological argument and also favored the moral argument.

The orthodox Christian does not simply plead for these arguments individually, but for a cause sufficient to account for and explain a universe in which teleology is manifest, and also to account for man who reveals in his makeup both purpose and a moral nature. This involves the combined use of the cosmological, teleological, and moral arguments to form a greater argument for God's existence. This might be called the "cosmo-teleo-moral argument." Some orthodox theologians have bowed to a greater or lesser degree to Kant's attacks, and as a result consider the arguments either worthless or of value only to a man who is already a Christian.

Another reason for discounting the value of the arguments is the overemphasis placed on them by the Roman Catholic church which claims they are sufficient to prove the existence of God and thereby to know Him. The natural theology which results is sufficient to save man, it maintains. However, it immediately qualifies this statement by saying that those mentally able to come to a knowledge of God in this way are too lazy in their thinking to do so, and the rest too dull; therefore God reveals Himself in the special revelation found in the Scriptures.

The evangelical points out that man may prove to his rational satisfaction that God exists, but that this conviction cannot save him. Even if man can form a natural theology with the arguments, nevertheless since man is a sinner and fallen he must have a Saviour. He can know this Saviour and the plan of salvation only through revelation.

Not only is it reasonable on the basis of the arguments to believe in a personal God, but God holds man responsible to come to this conclusion. Rom 1:19 f. states: "That which may be known of God is manifest in them [the heaven]; for God hath showed it unto them. For the invisible things of him from the creation of the world are clearly seen, being understood by the things that are made, even his eternal power and Godhead; so that they are without excuse." The mind of man is so constituted that as he looks at the universe he is able to come to the conclusion that it is the result of the omnipotent power of a personal, moral being, namely, God. If he does not, man is inexcusable so far as God is concerned.

Theistic proof of God's triune nature. Theism next presents arguments for the triune nature of God, and proofs that this is the view given of God in the Bible. If God were unitarian in nature and existed from eternity as one individual unitary person, He would have experienced the three great personal relationships—the I-It, the I-Thou, and the We-You relationships—only after He had created the world and man. As only one person God would have added to Himself the I-It relationship by creating the world, the I-Thou relationship by creating man, and the We-You social relationship by cooperating with Adam and Eve in the procreation of their first child.

Even Aristotle, the heathen philosopher, saw the problems in such a view. Therefore he placed his Unmoved Mover as it were in a space capsule and closed the windows, lest He learn of the existence and development of the world. Such increase in knowledge would destroy his God by adding new things to Him. He saw that a unitary person would need the world and man, but would cease to be infinite when these three relationships would be added as a result of the existence and development of the universe and man.

Christianity's doctrine of a triune God alone satisfies the requirements for an infinite, self-sufficient God. The Son is an object to the Father, and therefore the I-It relationship existed for God from eternity past. The Son and the Father as well as the Holy Spirit communicate in an I-Thou relationship, and the Father and the Son unite to minister to the Spirit, so that all three personal relationships have always existed in the God of the Bible. The world therefore adds nothing to God. Muhammadanism, Judaism, and all unitarian views of God make shipwreck upon this problem and end up with a finite God.

The I-It or subject-object relationship within the Godhead is revealed in such scripture as Heb 1:13, "But to which of the angels said he at any time, Sit on my right hand, until I make thine enemies thy footstool?" (cf. Ps 110:1; Heb 1:6-8). The I-Thou or the personal encounter is revealed when the Son in eternity past discusses His sacrificial death on the cross in Ps 40:5-8 (cf. Heb 10:5-13). The We-You or the social relationship is proved as God says in Gen 1:26, "Let us make man in our image, after our likeness," and again in Gen 11:7. "Let us go down, and there confound their language." Further, all the Scripture proofs for the deity of Christ and of the Holy Spirit support the doctrine of the Trinity. *See* Trinity; Christ, Deity of; God; the Holy Spirit.

Bibliography. J. Oliver Buswell, Jr., *Systematic Theology,* Grand Rapids: Eerdmans, 1962, I, 72-126. John E. Carnell, *An Introduction to Christian Apologetics,* Grand Rapids: Eerdmans, 1950. Stuart C. Hackett, *The Resurrection of Theism,* Chicago: Moody Press, 1956. Charles Hodge, *Systematic Theology,* Grand Rapids: Eerdmans, 1952, I, 191-240.

R. A. K.

THELASAR. *See* Telassar.

THEOCRACY. This term, meaning "the rule of God," generally refers to the government of a state by God or to the state so governed. The word is not biblical in origin, but the idea of God being the ruler of His people is basic to the thought of the OT. Josephus seems to have been the first to have used the term. He contrasted the theocracy with other forms of government, such as oligarchy, monarchy, and republic (*Contra Apion* II.16).

Theoretically, a theocracy would be a state over which God rules directly without human mediators or representatives. Israel was never a true theocracy in this sense. Although Israel always thought of herself as under the rule of God, that rule was always mediated through a judge, a king, or a priest.

In a political sense, a theocracy could be possible only during times of Israel's independence. When Israel was a vassal state or a province of some foreign power such as Egypt, Assyria, Babylon, Persia, Greece, or Rome, the rule of God could only be spiritual.

Israel's longest period of independence was from the conquest of Canaan in Joshua's time to the fall of Jerusalem (*c.* 586 B.C.). During these years Israel had two forms of government: the amphictyony or tribal league; and the monarchy. During the period of the amphictyony, God raised up special charismatic (spiritual) rulers called "judges" to deliver His people from oppression. However, much of the actual ruling was left to the elders of each tribe in this period.

In the period of the monarchy, the rule of God was carried on through the role of the king. The office of king in Israel was a sacral office (cf. A. R. Johnson, *Sacral Kingship in Ancient Israel,* Cardiff, 1955). The king was the anointed one of God. He was God's representative. Even though Israel's form of government was a monarchy for several centuries, theoretically it was also a theocracy.

The whole concept of Israel's basic relationship to God which is seen in the covenant is really related to the idea of the theocracy. One of the cardinal elements in the covenant between God and Israel is God's sovereignty. This fact has been clarified and emphasized in recent years by the discovery of the similarities in form between the Hittite vassal or suzerainty treaties and Israel's covenant with God (see Meredith Kline, *Treaty of the Great King,* Eerdmans, 1963).

In the NT the idea of the rule of God is taken out of the realm of the political and is made synonymous with the kingdom of God, which is the rule of God within and among individual believers now, but which will only come to final fruition when Jesus Christ returns to inaugurate the millennial kingdom. *See* Covenant; King; Kingdom of God.

Bibliography. CornPBE, "Government, Authority, and Kingship," pp. 354-369.

R. L. S.

THEOLOGY

Definition

The term theology comes from two Gr. words: *theos,* "God," and *logos,* "word," and means when compounded, the study of or science of God. However, this is a very restricted meaning of the term since it is generally used to cover not only the study of God, His nature, existence, and revealed plans and actions, but also His relation to and dealings with the world and man. In line with this, J. O. Buswell defines it very simply and clearly as "the study which treats directly of God and His relationship to the world and to man" (*A Systematic Theology of the Christian Religion,* I, 13).

The term theology can be used either to cover a dogmatic study of a part of Scripture or of the whole. Thus it is correct to speak of OT theology, e.g., J. Barton Payne, *The Theology of the Older Testament* (Zondervan, 1962); or of NT theology, e.g., C. C. Ryrie, *Biblical Theology of the New Testament* (Chicago: Moody Press, 1959); or of Johannine theology. In this article the term is considered in its broader sense, to cover the total content of what the Scriptures teach and man can know concerning God and His relation to all that He has made.

A good comprehensive definition of theology is hard to find since nearly every one offered is either too meager, or tends to stress one of the sources of a fully developed theology to the exclusion of others. A glance over the seven possible sources of theology discussed below, before some specific definitions are considered, will elucidate this point.

In *Encyclopedia of Religion and Ethics* (1924 ed.) it is defined thus: "Theology may be briefly defined as the science which deals, according to scientific method, with the facts and phenomena of religion and culminates in a comprehensive synthesis or philosophy of religion, which seeks to set forth in a systematic way all that can be known regarding the objective grounds of religious belief" (XII, 293). If the words "science" and "scientific method" are to be understood in their strictest sense, this definition stresses a phenomenological approach, i.e., an approach which admits as the content of theology only what appears in some material way or form. Since this emphasizes the position taken by the philosophical positivists and their successors, the logical positivists, it must essentially rule out the supernatural, particularly in revelation.

A very different definition is given by the Presbyterian theologian Charles Hodge as he answers the question, "What is theology?" "If natural science be concerned with the facts and laws of nature, theology is concerned with the facts and principles of the Bible. If the object of the one be to arrange and systematize the facts of the external world and to ascertain the laws by which they are determined, the object of the other is to systematize the facts of the Bible and ascertain the principles or general truths which those facts involve" (*Systematic Theology,* I, 18). In this definition all the stress is laid on the Bible as the source and content of theology.

Lewis Sperry Chafer offers the following definition: "Systematic theology may be defined as the collecting, scientifically arranging, comparing, exhibiting, and defending of all facts from any and every source concerning God and His works. It is *thetic* in that it follows a humanly devised thesis form and presents and verifies truth as truth" (*Systematic Theology,* I, 6). This definition broadens the source to include "all facts from every source concerning God and his works." If consistently applied it would include the pertinent material which can be gathered from each source stressed in the historical development of theology given below. In practice, however, Hodge came closer to fulfilling the definition of Chafer, and Chafer that of Hodge, since Chafer confined his theology to a biblical theology presented in systematic form, while Hodge, though devoting large sections to biblical theology, did not hesitate to venture into history and philosophy, and to use psychology in his concept of the common consciousness of man.

Before going further it is important to clear up a misunderstanding which may arise over the terms biblical theology and theology. A strictly biblical theology would be one which is based entirely on an inductive study of Scripture, i.e., a study which collects and organizes the doctrinal facts found in the Bible. Possibly Chafer's eight volume *Systematic Theology* comes closest to being the perfect extant example. The term biblical theology has reference to the source of materials. However, since doctrines deduced from the Scriptures lend themselves to an orderly development and reveal a logical relation with each other, a systematic presentation is called for. This leads to the setting up of what is called systematic theology. Every science presents its facts in an orderly manner, and theology, as a particular kind of science, ought to do so also. A good theology cannot be convincing if it is not based on a well-thought-out and carefully presented biblical theology, on the one hand, and is not organized into a progressive and logically developed system, on the other. The one should not exclude but rather complement the other.

In the light of the above, and in anticipation of what follows, systematic theology may be defined as: A methodical study of God, who He is, the proofs of His existence, and His relationship to the world and man, which gathers its material inductively from the Bible, the facts of science, psychology, history, the other sciences and philosophy, and examines, evaluates, and organizes all in the light of the Bible as God's revealed norm of truth. This definition is broad enough to allow for the inclusion of all that the sciences and philosophy can contribute to theology, and yet it gives divine revelation, as found in the Bible, its correct normative place, and biblical theology its proper function.

The Content of Theology

In order to understand what is demanded of a good theology, the sources of the facts on which it is constructed, together with its correct content, must be determined. A history of the growth of theology, and the movements to which it has been subjected, is therefore in order. At the same time a careful consideration of the motives which have governed its history is important. The two can be combined through a chronological study of the great emphases evident in theology at different times, and a description of the motives or stresses lying behind each. These can be organized and classified under the following seven headings: (1) The Bible and biblical theology. (2) Tradition. (3) The creeds and confessional theology. (4) Philosophy and philosophical theologies. (5) Science and liberal theology. (6) History of religions and comparative religion. (7) Psychology and the psychological approach.

It is to be noticed each stresses a different source and adds an additional content to theology. At the same time, it should be recognized that they do not necessarily exclude one another, except as certain extremists choose to make one or more sources exclude others. Several are generally found combined in any one theologian or theological system.

In the construction of a sound orthodox system it must be realized that even if some starting point, such as a particular philosophy, be destructive of the key to all (viz., the Bible as the God-given norm), still it may be important in that it contributes in a negative manner to a more fully developed theology. As its errors are exposed by a thorough analysis, and the Bible's revealed answer alone shown to be adequate, increased value and respect accrue to God's revelation in Scripture.

1. *The Bible and biblical theology.* The early Christian church had as the content of its theology the OT, the preaching of the apostles, and the gradually increasing number of books which were to be finally set apart as the NT canon. They accepted the OT as the divine, infallible revelation of God, and the guide and norm of both what was preached and what was written. This could well be called the age of biblical theology. To the extent that all attempts to return to the teaching and theology of the NT church stress the need to base theology on the Bible, they are commendable. At the same time, however, it must be seen that even the apostles were not without their philosophical problems. For example, the teachings of Colossians, I John, and II John deal with the errors of Gnosticism, a philosophical system which was based on a theory of emanations and cannot be understood fully apart from a knowledge of the same. This leads us to recognize that any theology we may develop, in order to follow the biblical example, ought to consider the philosophical views of its day and their relationship to theology and doctrine.

2. *Tradition.* This could be considered under the Bible and biblical theology except that, like philosophy, it offers only a negative contribution to theology. The Roman Catholic church places the church above Scripture instead of subject to it, as in Protestantism. The church, Catholics maintain, gave us the Bible. The Scriptures, however, they contend, do not contain all that the apostles taught, nor do they develop many doctrines which are given only in germinal form. Some doctrines have been transmitted by tradition, some have been developed from their germinal form by the early Church Fathers, and others are still being worked out. Examples of those based on tradition are purgatory, prayers for the dead, the worship of Mary, indulgences, and the Papacy itself. Examples of development of Roman Catholic doctrines from germinal ideas and tradition are the immaculate conception of Mary, her translation directly to heaven, and the declaration of her mediatorship between God and man. The Council of Trent declared in 1546 that the Word of God contained in the Bible *and* in tradition are of equal authority.

3. *The creeds and confessional theology.* Though all the facts of divine revelation are to be found in the Scriptures of the OT and NT, still it was not long till the Christian church found that much study and careful consideration were called for if the fundamentals of the faith were not to be destroyed by erroneous deductions. First of all, problems arose as to the person of Christ. Was He really God in the same sense as God the Father, or was He only the highest created being? At the Council of Nicea (325) where Athanasius stood at first almost alone against the world, and against Arius in particular, the church decided Jesus Christ was "very God of very God" and of the same substance with the Father. At the Council of Chalcedon (451) it determined the relationship which exists between the two natures in Christ. Each nature is real, but the two exist in such a manner together as to be indivisible and inseparable, yet unmixed and unchanged.

The Apostles' Creed developed slowly from what may have been just a confession of faith in the Father, the Son, and the Holy Spirit in the 2nd cen. A.D. Today it is repeated by Christian congregations in many orthodox churches every Lord's day. The confessional movement, though it started with the great creeds of the first six centuries—Nicean Creed at 325, Chalcedonian 451, and Athanasian Creed about 500—actually received its greatest impetus from the confessions which were written as a result of the Protestant Reformation. The more important of these, which are still in active use, are the Augsburg (1530), the Genevese (1549), the Belgian Confession (1561), the Heidelberg Catechism (1563), the 39 Articles, the Westminster Confession of Faith, and the Larger and Shorter Catechism (1648).

The tendency to establish theology very largely upon the creeds and confessions has been much stronger in Continental Europe than in English-speaking countries. As a result, Lutheran and Christian Reformed theologians stress catechism and catechetical teaching much more than Presbyterians. Baptists and Methodists practically ignore the confessions except as a check upon the accepted doctrines of Christendom. Yet liberals, and in particular neoorthodox, in Europe show the creeds and confessions great respect, especially in their preaching. As a result there often appears to be a great discrepancy between what some Europeans preach and teach, and what they write about the creeds and confessions and express in their lectures.

The value of the creeds and confessions in the writing and teaching of theology is certainly very great. They express briefly and clearly the faith and doctrine agreed upon, either by church councils or by large numbers of Christian scholars and theologians, and accepted by the leading Protestant denominations. The theologies written by English-speaking non-confessional theologians tend to show a real lack as a result of their failure to use the creeds fully.

4. *Philosophy and philosophical theologies.* Since very early in the history of the Christian church philosophy has had a great influence on the formulation of theology. Even the NT epistles, as already seen, are in part a result of some of the philosophical teachings of their day. Philosophy can influence theology either negatively, as did Gnosticism by evoking the answers given in Ephesians, Colossians, and I and II John, or it can influence it positively. The latter occurs when a synthesis is made between theology and philosophy.

The first important attempt at synthesis, but one which did not prove too dangerous, was made by Augustine in an attempt to fit Platonism into Christianity. A much more serious synthesis was consummated when, with the use of the pseudo-Dionysian letters (which though questioned much earlier were only finally proved to be forgeries at the time of the Reformation), Christianity and neo-Platonism were wedded together. To this day the Roman Catholic church reflects the result in her teaching of degrees of being, and the corollary theory that it is a lack of being which makes the material (i.e., man's body and the universe) inherently evil. Rome's views on sin, salvation, celibacy, and cleansing are affected by this philosophical error.

Thomas Aquinas attempted the next great synthesis. In it he retained the Plotinian influence in his theory of degrees of being, but added Aristotelian methods and philosophy to form what is now known as Thomism. This has become the philosophical basis of the theology of the Roman Catholic church. As a philosophy it has until recently reigned almost supreme in Roman Catholic institutions, and has gained a strong foothold even in some secular universities.

Hegel went very much further than any before him in the actual imposition of philosophy upon theology. In his system, a rationalistic philosophy became the very source of theology. He set up a triadic or three point dialectic: (1) thesis, God is Being; (2) antithesis or contradictory thesis, *Non-Being;* (3) synthesis, or the contradiction of the contradiction, *Becoming*. Hegel then proceeded to explain the creation and the development of man on a similar basis. God, the creation, the Fall, Christ, and salvation are all to be explained with dialectic triads according to Hegel and the Hegelian theologians.

Harnack applied triads to early church history and the formulation of dogma. Paul Tillich followed Hegel even more closely. He saw God as developing from Being, the Unmoved Mover of Aristotle, to Creative Being through a triad of Being, Non-Being, Power of Being. Not content to stop at this point he continued on to make Power of Being the Father, and then set it up as a new thesis standing in antithesis to the Logos, from which comes a synthesis, the Spirit. The Spirit represents God as unambiguously creative.

Three philosophical systems, the last two having a very dangerous influence on theology, have been mentioned. A fourth has proved of perhaps even greater significance. It is Immanuel Kant's. He taught that man can have no real knowledge of the *Ding-an-zich,* the thing-in-itself, and that therefore there can be no real knowledge of God. This view led to two main philosophical reactions which entered systematic theology and can be observed in (1) those who saw no way to know God or about Him by revelation and turned completely from revelation to psychology and feeling; (2) those who were impressed by the causes of the actual epistemological problem stated by Kant and endeavored to overcome it by a theory of revelation. Since the theologians who turned to psychology will be treated under Psychology, point 7, only the others will be dealt with here.

Sören Kierkegaard reasoned that the problems facing man in receiving revelation from God arise because he has no categories in which to receive timeless, spaceless truth. Like Kant, but using other terminology, he argued that truth, as it comes from God, is timeless and spaceless and thus cannot be grasped by finite man. Man therefore forces divine revelation into his own categories of time and space, with the result that it appears dressed in the garments of space—as having location and place—and extended in the continuum of time—appearing as if it takes time to occur.

In order to explain the Bible's presentation in time-space categories of its content and teachings concerning original sin, miracles, heaven, and hell, Kierkegaard invented such concepts as indirect communication (because God cannot reveal Himself directly in speech and words) and myth, symbol and saga. He believed that revelation can only come in these peculiar literary forms because man has no containers in which to receive timeless, spaceless truth. The interpretation of myth, symbol, and saga has been called demythologization by Rudolf Bultmann and Paul Tillich. The "myths" in Scripture are to be recognized and then deciphered. *See* Myth, Mythology.

Kierkegaard's view was refined and adopted by Karl Barth and the neoorthodox theologians. To Barth, revelation is something that occurs as one reads the Bible, or hears the Word of God in proclamation or preaching. It is an event in which the fallible Word of God, the Bible, becomes the real Word of God, or Christ, in a moment of time. Emil Brunner agrees with Barth very closely at this point, and Tillich, though much further to the left, differs only in that he fits the same views into his own ontological Hegelian system.

The place of philosophy in systematic theology is largely negative, in the sense that a good theology considers the philosophy and philosophic ideas behind erroneous views of doctrine mainly in order to refute them. It discusses the philosophy showing how well or how poorly it stands up as a philosophy, and then shows how it agrees or disagrees with the teachings of the Bible. Usually a theory based upon philosophy can be shown to be untenable in its own field before being shown to be in conflict with the teachings of the Scripture. If a systematic theology refuses to enter the lists of combat with philosophy, as well as in its own field, it proves inadequate to meet both the worldly philosophies of its own day and those of other times. The systematic theologies written by such men as Charles Hodge, Herman Bavinck, Louis Berkhof, and J. O. Buswell, Jr., together with the biblical theology of B. B. Warfield, are notable for their able work in this field. It is the proper handling of the philosophy popular in the day when it is written, that makes a systematic theology timely and of value for its own age.

5. *Science and liberal theology.* Since the times of Copernicus and Galileo, the church has constantly struggled with the question as to whether theology and science negate each other or can be reconciled. Do the laws of physics exclude miracles? Does matter deny metaphysics? Materialism has constantly raised its head to challenge theism. The theory of evolution in particular has been used to challenge the Genesis account of revelation, the discovery of anthropological remains to contest the Genesis record of the creation of man and the Fall.

The methods of science appear to deny the possibility of basing theology upon provable facts. Philosophical positivism insists on limiting knowledge to the phenomena or known facts of existence, and logical positivism goes even further and questions the very meaningfulness of statements about God because they are based on ideas which cannot be proved like physical phenomena by laboratory tests. Therefore both of these philosophies deny the reality of God and the possibility of theology.

This means that proper regard must be taken of scientific discovery, and a view of the spiritual and transcendent must be presented which does not confuse the physical realm with the higher one of the immaterial and spiritual. When the Bible says God is Spirit, and that He is omnipresent, this ought to warn the theologian not to confuse his concept of God and of the spiritual with material dimensions. Arguments against the Christian God "up there" or "out there" by Tillich and his school, and repeated by Bishop Robinson's *Honest to God,* lead the Christian to see that his God transcends space and dwells, according to Scripture, in an entirely different realm from man. Some have suggested that the spiritual realm is so different that it might even interpenetrate the physical.

Under the scientific approach, though it is a question whether they are truly scientific at all, must be taken up the attacks of higher criticism against the Bible. The Graf-Wellhausen theory of the OT, the JEDP theory of the sources of the Pentateuch, and the Deutero-Isaiah theory, together with Form Criticism of the Gospels, have led to an intensive study of the OT and NT and their origin. The methods used by the critics, though once applied even to Shakespeare's plays, are now generally discarded in the study of other literature. They have also been losing support as applied to the Bible. Able defenses against each of the above-mentioned higher critical theories have been produced and published by evangelicals.

Lower criticism, or the study of the Bible texts and contents, has received a great stimulus from the discovery of the Dead Sea Scrolls, and the papyri, and the authenticity of the texts of the Bible has been wonderfully confirmed.

Systematic theology does not ignore science or the scientific method. It accepts the facts proved by science, though it questions all theories which do not agree with Scripture. It maintains that the methods it uses in gathering the contents of its doctrines are those suited to and appropriate in its field, and that they are in this sense truly scientific.

6. *History of religions and comparative religion.* Those who use these sources teach that Christianity is the result of a long evolution of religion, from a primitive state up through polytheism and monotheism to its present form. A study of comparative religion shows, they maintain, that Christianity lacks any absolute distinctiveness and exclusive values. This view developed in the following manner. The stress was laid on the historical development of Christianity by such a man as Otto Pfeiderer in Germany and the men of the Leiden School of Theology in Holland. Compendiums in comparative religion by Cornelius Petrus Tiele, P. D. Chantepie de la Saussage, and G. van der Leeuw's *Godsdiensten Der Wereld* added a wealth of material concerning all the major religious movements in the world. This led many to the conclusion that Christianity is the result of a long process of development from pure paganism to its present form.

Some, such as Ernst Troeltsch, came to the conclusion that Christianity possesses no really distinctive unique quality which can set it above other religions. In the theology of Paul Tillich many passages are found which illustrate the religious-historical theory of the origin and nature of Christianity.

In a good systematic theology, references to the teachings of pagan religions have their place when used to illustrate the OT struggles with idolatry and the differences between revealed truth and the heathen practices man has developed to replace the true worship of God (Rom 1:23).

7. *Psychology and the psychological approach.* Kant said that all that man could know was the appearances of things, or phenomena. Everything that enters the human mind is stamped upon, like a letter at the post office, by the outer form of the mind (space) and the inner form (time). Since the latter is within the mind, even what is conceived of within the mind is suspect since it is branded with time. Thus man cannot know the noumenon, the thing-in-itself, either by theoretical reason (i.e., reason which

is knowledge of external reality) or by pure reason (i.e., knowledge conceived within the mind). It follows, for Kant, that God who is timeless and spaceless certainly cannot be known. He falls in the category of the noumenon. How then can man have religious faith? Kant replied by saying that each man finds within himself a categorical imperative, a *Du solst,* a Thou-shalt which leads him to the formulation of the rule or the Categorical Imperative, "Act as if the maxim of thy action were to become by thy will a universal law of nature."

There were two reactions by those who accepted Kant's reasoning. Some, as mentioned above, worked out solutions to the philosophical-epistemological problem, the problem of knowing God if He is in the category of the noumenon. Kierkegaard and the neoorthodox took this approach. Others turned, as Kant had done, to man himself and tried to solve the problem through a psychology of religious experience. Kant's categorical imperative is actually a rewording of the Golden Rule (Mt 7:12), but falls far short of the latter since it offers only a contentless concept, while Christ's rule is given as the consummation and summary of the content of the second table of God's law (cf. Mt 5:21, 27, 43).

To fill the void in the knowledge of God caused by Kant's view, Schleiermacher put forth the theory that Christianity and religion are based not just on a *Du solst* but on an inherent feeling of dependence in man which calls for the gospel. This is the basis of the religious consciousness from which we must start. Ritschl took up Kant's challenge to establish religion upon subjective experience but chose another origin. Man's goal is the kingdom of God on earth, but it should be based on value judgments, i.e., the value man obtains by making his own decisions about God. Schleiermacher's view made shipwreck on the fact that man can just as well set up a pagan religion as Christianity in his desire to express his feeling of dependence on a superior power; Ritschl's on the fact that, if value judgments be true, a child can as well be saved by believing in Santa Claus as in Jesus Christ.

The attempts to base theology upon what can be found in the psychology of religious experience have all failed. Nevertheless psychology has much of value to offer in the formulation of a good theology. Man's feelings of estrangement from his fellow man and God, the persistent anxiety which haunts him till the grave, and his guilt feelings are all witnesses to the sin and depravity of the human heart. They reveal the existential predicament to which a sound, biblically grounded theology must give the answers.

Modern Theology

Modern theology is to be distinguished from evangelical and orthodox theology which hold to the infallibility of the Bible in the original writings.

Modern theology is a multidimensional affair. Perhaps it can best be understood by first singling out some of its common denominators, and then considering its more significant variants. In every case it is marked by its acceptance in a greater or lesser degree of the radical theories of the higher criticism of the last two centuries. The neoorthodox do not concern themselves with its development or consequences in the same way as the liberals, because they teach that man receives the true Word of God whenever the fallible Bible becomes the Word of God in the subjective but ineffable so-called "event of revelation." It is only by tacit acceptance of the critical theories that they generally show their attitude. Both are strongly opposed to supernaturalism and belief in miracles, and teach the Scriptures are full of contradictions, errors, and paradoxes.

Three main streams exist: the old-fashioned liberals of whom Nels Ferré is the best present exponent, the neoorthodox, and a hybrid American synthesis of liberalism and neoorthodoxy. The liberal school is a continuation of the old German liberalism. The neoorthodox are the followers of Karl Barth, though most of them are separated from him on particular details. All the neoorthodox base their theology more or less on Kierkegaardian existentialism (e.g., Barth and Brunner in particular) and its development by such a later existentialist as Heidegger (e.g., Bultmann and Tillich). The American school of synthesis is centered in Union Theological Seminary, and had for many years as its most important leaders Reinhold Niebuhr and Paul Tillich. The latter went so far beyond either liberalism or neoorthodoxy that he became the founder of an entirely new school of theology, namely, ontological theology. He presented a system based on a synthesis of Hegel's views of God, the world and man, and Aristotle's evolving pyramid of potentiality-actuality, starting with potential being and rising through the different dimensions—inorganic, organic, psychological, spirit—up to that of New Being, and the actualization of all essential potentialities, and then returning to God or the Power of Being to enjoy "eternal life."

It becomes the challenge and task of present-day systematic theology to expose the philosophical foundations of modern theologies, show the errors in their philosophies, and then present the biblical doctrines on the same subjects, pointing out the way in which the revealed doctrines of the Scriptures answer the philosophical errors of modern theology and yet escape their devastating consequences.

Conclusion

A presentation of theology is called for which is based on a thorough biblical theology, and which takes advantage of the great creeds and confessions of the orthodox churches and the developments in doctrine which have been accomplished thereby. In order to be effective for our times, theology needs to consider the philosophy behind all variant and erroneous views. Philosophy thus becomes a negative source of theology. Tradition, as used in the Roman Catholic formulation of its dogmas, falls in a negative category, but demands proper attention in order to expose the errors of Rome. The proved facts of science demand their place, but what are only theories must be most carefully examined (e.g., evolution). The history and data of primitive and pagan religions must be considered and biblically explained.

Finally, psychology presents the theologian with man's existential dilemma with his feelings of "estrangement," his "guilt complex," his *angst zum tode* ("fear of death"), his inherent "need of religion" and his inborn "categorical imperative." Man's psychological problems pose the existential questions to which a thorough systematic theology alone can give the full theological answer.

See Existentialism; God is Dead; Liberalism; Neoorthodoxy.

R. A. K.

Bibliography. L. Berkhof, *Systematic Theology*, Grand Rapids: Eerdmans, 1941. J. O. Buswell, Jr., *A Systematic Theology of the Christian Religion*, Grand Rapids: Zondervan, 1962. Lewis Sperry Chafer, *Systematic Theology*, 8 vols., Dallas: Dallas Seminary Press, 1947–57. D. S. Clark, *A Syllabus of Systematic Theology*, Philadelphia: Presbyterian and Reformed, n.d. A. A. Hodge, *Outlines of Theology*, London: Hodder and Stoughton, 1878. Charles Hodge, *Systematic Theology*, New York: Scribner's Sons, 1872–1909. F. L. Patton, *A Summary of Christian Doctrine*, Philadelphia: Westminster Press, 1916. William G. T. Shedd, *Dogmatic Theology*, New York: Scribner's Sons, 1889. A. H. Strong, *Systematic Theology*, rev., Westwood, N.J.: Revell, 1963.

THEOPHANY. The word theophany combines two Gr. words, *theos*, "God," and *phainein*, "to show, to manifest," thus meaning "God manifest." From this general definition, however, limitations must be applied. (1) There must be an indication that the biblical passage deals with a true manifestation of God and not simply an anthropomorphism. (2) The manifestation need not appear in human form but may appear in symbolic form. (3) It also may appear in a dream or vision as well as in physical sight. (4) The manifestation must be identified with God either in self-affirmation or by a statement of identification from the recipient of the theophany or from a biblical writer's interpretation of the event. (5) The manifestation exists to make known the divine will to the recipient. A theophany, then, is a manifestation of God to man either in human or symbolic form in order to impart God's will to that person.

On the basis of this definition a theophany may be manifested in human form or in symbolic form. The human form is characterized by one of two descriptions. (1) It is characterized by the use of the verb "appear" with Yahweh as the subject. The verb is the Niphal (passive) form of *rā'â*, "to see," and means literally, "He let Himself be seen." Such an appearance is limited in general to the patriarchs in Gen 12.17,18.26,28.35, although the expression is also used in regard to Solomon (I Kgs 9:2; II Chr 7:12). (2) A theophany in human form may also be characterized by the terms *mal'ak Yahweh*, "the Angel of Yahweh," or *mal'ak 'ĕlōhîm*, "the Angel of God." In many cases the angel in Scripture is a created being, but at times the angel is theophanic.

Four tests may be applied in determining the theophanic Angel: (1) "He explicitly identifies Himself with Yahweh on various occasions. (2) Those to whom He makes His presence known recognize Him as divine. (3) The biblical writers call Him Yahweh" (H. C. Leupold, *Exposition of Genesis*, p. 500). (4) He also makes Himself distinct from Yahweh. Thus the theophanic Angel appears in such passages as Gen 16,21.32 (cf. Hos 12:4); Ex 3:1–6; 23:20–23 (cf. Isa 63: 8–9); Josh 5:13–15; Jud 6:12–23; 13:2–23; Mal 3:1; etc. *See* Angel of the Lord.

The symbolic form of theophany must be understood in terms of real presence through a symbol used to express that real presence. In Gen 15 the symbolic form—"a smoking oven and a flaming torch" (v. 17, NASB)—is nonetheless permeated by the real presence. The more permanent symbolic form is the "glory" cloud, called in post-OT times the Shekinah. This is equated with the pillar of cloud and fire (Ex 13:21–22), the glory which appeared on Mount Sinai (Ex 24:16), the cloud which entered the tabernacle (Ex 40:34–38; Lev 16:2) and which also entered Solomon's temple (I Kgs 8:11).

The abiding value of the theophanic appearance is threefold. (1) It is eschatological. The theophanic revelations contain a hope which finds fulfillment in the universal blessing stemming from the first coming of the Messiah. (2) It is redemptive. The theophanic appearances were not only concerned with the redemption of the recipients (Gen 48:16), but the redemption manifested in the eschatological period. (3) It is Christological. The more permanent theophanies of the OT—the theophanic Angel and the Shekinah—find their fulfillment in Jesus Christ. Thus these theophanies are pre-incarnate appearances of Christ.

H. E. H.

THEOPHILUS (thē-ŏf'ĭ-lŭs). The person to whom the books of Luke and Acts are addressed (Lk 1:3; Acts 1:1). There have been many conjectures concerning the identity of Theophilus. It has been suggested that the word Theophilus, which means "friend of God," refers to Christians in general and not to any one individual. Thus Luke-Acts would be written to all Christians. On the other hand, there is good evidence to show that Theophilus was a real person. The name was common among both Greeks and Jews in NT times. Besides, Theophilus is addressed as "most excellent" (Gr. *kratiste*), a term of unique importance that would scarcely apply to an imaginary figure. The manner in which Luke uses "most excellent" to designate governors (Acts 23:26; 24:2, RSV; 26:25, RSV), and the fact that the term is nearly always applied to persons of equestrian rank, makes it likely that Theophilus was a man of distinction, perhaps a Roman official.

If a real person, then, what else is known of Theophilus? Aside from the many fanciful theories and suppositions, it can be said that Theophilus was an acquaintance of Luke who had received instructions about the Christian way (Lk 1:4). Whether or not he was a Christian when Luke wrote to him cannot be determined.

N. R. L.

THESSALONIANS, FIRST EPISTLE TO THE
(thĕs'ȧ-lō'nĭ-ȧns)

Date

This epistle was written in A.D. 50 or thereabouts. With the possible exception of Galatians, I Thessalonians was the earliest of Paul's letters.

Authenticity

Its authenticity is not seriously disputed. It claims to have been written by Paul (in conjunction with Silvanus and Timothy, but all agree these could have had little part in the composition of the letter). The book is included in the canon accepted by Marcion (*c.* A.D. 140) and in the Muratorian Fragment. Irenaeus in the late 2nd cen. quoted it by name, after which it was universally accepted. There seems no reason for its composition unless it is a genuine letter of the apostle.

Occasion of Writing

The report brought by Timothy and Silvanus (Acts 18:5; I Thess 3:6) occasioned the writing of this epistle. Acts 16 and 17 reveal that Paul had been forced to leave Philippi, Thessalonica (*q.v.*), and Berea by opposition from fanatical Jews after promising beginnings in each city. Then in Athens he had little success. Small wonder that when he came to Corinth it was "in weakness, and in fear, and in much trembling" (I Cor 2:3). Here he was clearly in doubt as to his whole mission. But he then received reports from Silas and Timothy that his converts in Thessalonica were standing firm. This epistle was written out of his great sense of relief.

The letter was aimed at meeting the needs of Paul's converts as revealed by the messengers. It is clear that Paul was being slandered by opponents who sought to undermine his work by discrediting his motives. So he took space to remind his readers of the way the preachers had behaved when establishing the church in Thessalonica. They had worked hard and refused to accept maintenance. It was important that nothing be allowed to impair the usefulness of the first preaching.

The Egmatian Way, main road across ancient Greece, runs through modern Thessalonica on the same roadbed as in ancient times. HFV

Paul also encouraged the Thessalonians in the face of the opposition they were meeting. He went on to deal with the importance of Christian living, for it was important that they accept no low pagan standards. Then he came to questions about the second coming. Some seem to have given up working for their living in view of the expected nearness of Christ's return. Paul urged them to work. Others apparently thought that all Christians would live until the second coming. When some died, they thought that these would miss their share in the happenings of the great day. Paul reassured them that the dead in Christ would rise first. He urged watchfulness and went on to general exhortations on several aspects of Christian living.

Outline

I. The Exemplary Missionary Church, 1:1-10
II. The Good Missionary, 2:1-20
III. The Love and Concern of the Good Missionary, 3:1-13
IV. Admonitions and Exhortations to Believers, 4:1-12
V. Christ's Coming for Believers, 4:13-18
VI. Further Admonitions for Christian Living, 5:1-22
VII. Closing Words, 5:23-28

Bibliography. F. F. Bruce, "The Epistles to the Thessalonians," NBC, pp. 1052-1062. D. Edmond Hiebert, *The Thessalonian Epistles,* Chicago: Moody, 1971 (with full bibliography). C. F. Hogg and W. E. Vine, *The Epistles of Paul the Apostle to the Thessalonians,* reprint, Grand Rapids: Kregel, 1959. George Milligan, *St. Paul's Epistles to the Thessalonians,* reprint, Grand Rapids: Eerdmans, 1952. Leon Morris, *The Epistles of Paul to the Thessalonians,* TNTC, Grand Rapids: Eerdmans, 1957; *The First and Second Epistles to the Thessalonians,* NIC, Grand Rapids: Eerdmans, 1959.

Alfred Plummer, *A Commentary on St. Paul's First Epistle to the Thessalonians,. . . Second Epistle to the Thessalonians,* London: Robert Scott, 1918. Charles C. Ryrie, *First and Second Thessalonians,* EBC, Chicago: Moody, 1959.

L. M.

THESSALONIANS, SECOND EPISTLE TO THE. This letter carries on from I Thessalonians. It seems that some aspects of the teaching of that first letter were not fully understood, so Paul wrote again. The interval could not have been a long one, a few months at most, and probably only a few weeks.

Occasion

For the most part, Paul discusses again questions that were raised in the first epistle. After his opening prayer the most important part of the epistle deals with the second coming. Some of the Thessalonians had evidently come to the conclusion that the day of the Lord had already come (or perhaps was imminent). Paul points out that it could not arrive until "the man of sin" (better, "of lawlessness") is revealed. He gives information about the kind of rebellion this man will lead, and reminds his converts that this could not be yet.

He goes on to give thanks for his converts and to exhort them to stand fast. He reminds them of the faithfulness of God, and the letter is brought to an end with some exhortations about godly discipline. The most important part of this section deals with the disorderly, those who had begun to abstain from work in view of the nearness of the Lord's coming (as they thought), and with the disobedient.

Authenticity

The letter is generally accepted as genuine. Its early attestation is very good. Polycarp, Ignatius, and Justin all appear to have known it. It is in the Marcionite canon and the Muratorian Fragment. It is quoted by name by Irenaeus and later writers. It claims to have been written by Paul (II Thess 3:17 purports to be his signature), and the style and language are Pauline.

However, some scholars raise questions. (1) There is the problem of the resemblances to and differences from I Thessalonians. It is suggested that a man like Paul would not repeat himself, and that there are differences, e.g., in eschatology. The inference is that someone was deliberately imitating the apostle. But the resemblances can be exaggerated, and in any case most scholars feel that they are best explained as natural when the same man writes on the same subjects after an interval of a few weeks. For the differences, see next section. (2) Some think the eschatology is different from that in I Thessalonians, since in the second epistle the *parousia* is to take place only after signs, and in the first epistle it is to be sudden. But this combination of ideas is often found and is no proof of divergence of authorship. (3) The tone of the two epistles is said to be different, but this proves little, even if it be accepted. There is no real reason for doubting the authenticity of this epistle.

Outline

I. Comfort in Tribulations, 1:1–12
II. The Day of the Lord and the Man of Sin, 2:1–12
III. Exhortations and Instructions, 2:13–3:15
IV. Benediction and Closing Words, 3:16–18

Bibliography. *See* Thessalonians, First Epistle to.

L. M.

Ancient walls of Thessalonica

THESSALONICA (thĕs'ȧ-lō̆-nī'kȧ). Cassander named the city after his wife, half sister of Alexander the Great, when in 315 B.C. he grouped together villages of the area. But a much older settlement called Therma (after the adjacent hot springs) existed nearby. The two appear to have continued side by side (Pliny refers to them as existing together, *Natural History,* iv. 17). But Thessalonica eventually absorbed the older center.

The city has a strategic situation at the head of the Thermaic Gulf, about midway between the Hellespont and the Adriatic Sea, and astride land trade routes. Its harbor is excellent, and it has thus through the centuries been the natural port for the trade of Macedonia. In Roman times it was always important. The Romans first made it the capital of one of the four parts of Macedonia, and when they reorganized the four into a single province Thessalonica was its capital. Pompey made it his base during the first civil war, but in the second it supported Octavian, and his victory led to its being made a free city.

Luke tells in Acts 17:6 that its rulers (known to have numbered five or six) were called *politarchoi* (KJV "rulers of the city," RSV "city

A pulpit in stone from a fifth century church in Thessalonica. Istanbul Museum

authorities"), a term found also in inscriptions. The city was basically Greek, though there was a Roman element in the 1st cen. and enough Jews to have a synagogue. A church established in such a center could influence the whole province. Paul ministered there on his second missionary journey and had considerable success. A "great multitude" of proselytes to Judaism became Christians during the apostle's stay (Acts 17:4). Subsequently Paul wrote two epistles to the church there.

Almost no visible ruins at Thessalonica date to the 1st cen. Excavation is not feasible because the modern city covers the ancient one. The current population of *c.* 400,000 is approximately double that of NT times.

L. M.

THEUDAS (thōō'dȧs). The leader of an unsuccessful insurrection against the Romans. He is cited along with Judas of Galilee, another revolutionary, in Gamaliel's speech in Acts 5:36 urging the Sanhedrin to let the Christian movement alone.

Josephus (*Ant.* xx.5.1) also mentions a Theudas, a charlatan who led a revolt by pretending that he was able to cause the Jordan to part, but was beheaded by Fadus. If the Theudas of Acts and the Theudas of Josephus are the same, Luke is guilty of a glaring anachronism. Since the revolt under Judas—whom Luke places after Theudas—took place in A.D. 6, Gamaliel's speech between A.D. 30 and 37, and Fadus' procuratorship between A.D. 44 and 46, Luke makes Gamaliel say something which did not happen till later; and he reverses the order of the two revolts and misplaces that of Theudas about 40 years too early.

This difficulty was perceived as early as Origen (185–254). Blass suggested that a later reviser made the blunder. Holtzmann in 1873 suggested that Luke misread Josephus. The simplest solution, offered as early as Origen, is that there were two persons named Theudas, one early (Acts) and one later (Josephus). In a period of 40 years there were four Simons and within ten years three Judases who were leaders of insurrections.

It is difficult to see how Luke could have committed so gross an error regarding Gamaliel's speech when he had a student of Gamaliel with him—Paul. It is also difficult to believe that Acts was written after the *Antiquities* (A.D. 93), or that Luke was dependent on Josephus, superficial similarities notwithstanding (cf. Theodore Zahn, *Introduction to the NT*, III, 132 f.). Finally, the Theudas of Josephus was beheaded, a fact which would nullify the reason for Gamaliel's citation, which was to show that the Sanhedrin should *not* punish the Christian leaders.

Bibliography. W. M. Ramsay, *Was Christ Born at Bethlehem?* New York: Putnam's, 1898, pp. 252 f. Joseph W. Swain, "Gamaliel's Speech and Caligula's Statue," HTR, XXXVII (1944), 341–349.

E. Y.

THICKET. Dense growth of shubbery. Thicket is used to translate five Heb. terms: (1) *s^{e}bāk* and (2) *s^{e}bōk.* These two related terms have for their meaning the interwoven undergrowth such as might catch a ram by its horns (Gen 22:13), or provide a lair for a lion (Jer 4:7), or simply refer to the dense growth of a forest (Isa 9:18; 10:34; Ps 74:5, ASV). (3) Heb. *ḥōaḥ*, lit., "thistle, brier," is translated "thicket" in I Sam 13:6; RSV and NEB render it "hole" (Heb *ḥôrîm*) on the basis of I Sam 14:11. (4) Heb *ʿāb* (Jer 4:29) from a root meaning thickness (of a forest). (5) Heb. *ya'ar* (Isa 21:13, ASV marg., RSV, NASB), which normally means "forest." *See* Plants.

THIEF. One Heb. and two Gr. words are so translated in KJV, but one of the latter is "robbers" in ASV, which accords better with the precise meaning of that word. "Thief" suggests stealth; "robber" suggests violence. Jesus, in Jn 10:8, speaks of both "thieves and robbers," referring to those who had come before Him claiming to be the Shepherd of Israel, the Messiah. In Mt 6:19–20 "thieves" is still "thieves" in ASV. But in Mt 21:13; Mk 11:17; Lk 19:46, "den of thieves" is "den of robbers" in ASV; in Mt 27:38, 44 and Mk 15:27, the "thieves" crucified with Christ are "robbers"; in Lk 10:30, 36, the man who fell among "thieves" fell among "robbers."

The thieves (or robbers) crucified with Jesus are called "malefactors" in Luke. Although both of these wicked men began by deriding Jesus (Mt 27:44), one later repented, rebuked his fellow criminal, appealed to Jesus for mercy, and was forgiven (Lk 23:39–43).

See Crime and Punishment; Law; Rob, Robber.

J. A. S.

THIGH. This word is used for part of the sacrificial animal (Ex 29:22, RSV), and for the part of the body of man from the legs to the trunk. It was the portion that a weapon covered when suspended from the waist (Jud 3:16, 21: Ps 45:3). The thigh of a rider on horseback could be covered by a sword and a loose girdle on which his name would be embroidered (Rev 19:16).

When the angel touched the hollow of Jacob's thigh, it was put out of joint (Gen 32:24–32). This experience showed Jacob that he had lived his previous life in his own strength instead of relying upon God. By wrestling with the angel, Jacob entered a new stage in his life as signified by his name change from Jacob to Israel. The custom grew up among Jacob's descendants of not eating the *nervus ischiadicus* (cf. Gen 32:32), the principal nerve in the area of the hip which is easily injured by violent strain in wrestling. *See* Sinew.

The phrase "hip and thigh" is an expression for a cruel and devastating slaughter (Jud 15:8). "Smiting on the thigh" denotes penitence (Jer 31:19), grief, and mourning (Ezk 21:12).

The word is also used euphemistically for the loins (*q.v.*) or sexual organs as the seat of procreative power (cf. Gen 35:11; 46:26). Thus, it was the custom to put the hand under the "thigh" in taking an oath, perhaps to signify that if the oath was violated, the man's children, yet unborn, would avenge the act of disloyalty (WBC, p. 28). Abraham required this of his servant when he sent him forth to secure a wife for Isaac (Gen 24:2, 9), and Jacob required it of his son Joseph when he asked him not to bury him in Egypt (Gen 47:29).

To "uncover the thigh" (Isa 47:2), which exposed the female captive's genital area, was a sign of greatest shame (v. 3). Part of the curse pronounced by the priest to a woman accused of infidelity was that her "thigh" should "rot" (Num 5:21–22). If she were guilty, a falling or wasting away (Heb. *nāphᵉlâ*) of her reproductive organ would occur (Num 5:27, NASB). On the other hand, the falling thigh may mean a premature birth or miscarriage (NEB). The word *nēphel* from the same root as "rot" or "waste away" means "untimely birth" or miscarriage in Job 3:16; Ps 58:8; Eccl 6:3. In Isa 26:18 (NASB) the verb *nāphal* is also used of birth, in the context of v. 17 (see WBC, p. 120).

E. C. J.

THIMNATHAH. *See* Timnah.

THIRST. A painful sensation caused by lack of water or liquids in the stomach (Ex 17:3; Deut 28:48; Jud 15:18). Since it can be accompanied by vehement passions, it is used in Scripture figuratively of desire for spiritual food or nourishment (Ps 42:2; 63:1; Amos 8:11, 13; Mt 5:6; Jn 7:37), of the complete satisfaction of man's spiritual needs (Isa 49:10; Jn 4:13–14; 6:35), and of insatiable desire for evil (Jer 2:25). Solomon urges young husbands to drink water out of their own cisterns (Prov 5:15), that is, control their passions and be satisfied with and faithful to their wives.

THIRTY. *See* Mighty Men.

THISTLE. *See* Plants: Thorns.

THOMAS (tŏm'as̀). One of the 12 apostles (Mt 10:3; Mk 3:18; Lk 6:15; Acts 1:13); also called Didymus, meaning "twin," in Jn 11:16; 20:24; 21:2. He was pessimistic but was loyally prepared to die with Jesus when the Lord intended to go to Judea in the face of a threat of stoning (Jn 11:8, 16). Later he was uncertain about the Lord's meaning and inquired further when Jesus said He was going away and that the disciples knew His destination (Jn 14:5).

Thomas was skeptical about the Lord's resurrection when the other disciples reported that Jesus met with them in his absence. He demanded tangible evidence if he was to believe. But when Jesus appeared again to them all and invited Thomas to touch His wounds, he exclaimed with the highest declaration of faith, "My Lord and my God!" (Jn 20:24–28). Thomas was with six other disciples fishing in a boat on the Sea of Galilee when Jesus again revealed Himself (Jn 21:1 ff).

Tradition holds that Thomas evangelized in Parthia and India. A present-day Christian community in India claims derivation from him. The apocryphal Gospel of Thomas is unreliably attributed to him.

N. B. B.

THORN IN THE FLESH. This expression is found in II Cor 12:7 where Paul writes that he was given "a thorn in the flesh, a messenger of Satan to buffet" him in order to keep him from spiritual pride.

Four main types of interpretation have been suggested: (1) persistent carnal desires or fleshly temptation; (2) feelings of guilt stemming from his having formerly persecuted the church; (3) some form of physical or nervous ailment; or (4) a personal enemy who sought to slander and discredit him. Numerous diseases have been suggested, such as epilepsy, acute ophthalmia or eye trouble, malarial fever, hysteria or melancholy, sick headache, or nervous exhaustion. Regarding the first, he found victory through the indwelling Spirit of God (Rom 8:5–13). Regarding the second, he knew that the grace of Jesus Christ had fully absolved him of his past crime (I Tim 1:13–16). Whatever was the nature of his thorn, it did not prevent his continuing in an extremely active ministry which included long journeys on foot.

A study of the phrase "thorn in the flesh" (Gr. *skolops tē sarki*) and of its context in Paul's defense of his apostleship (II Cor 10–13) indicates that it probably refers to a person, not an illness. In the OT a "thorn" was a rather common idiom for a human enemy. The Canaanites would become "pricks [LXX, *skolops*] in your eyes, and thorns in your sides" (Num 33:55; cf. Josh 23:13). Ezekiel refers to the enemies of Israel as "a pricking brier" (LXX, *skolops pikrias*) and "any grieving thorn" (28:24; cf. 2:6; Mic 7:4).

In II Cor 12:7 Paul characterized his thorn as a messenger of Satan (*angelos satana*). The Gr. *angelos* occurs 188 times in the NT, translated 181 times in the KJV as "angel" and seven times as "messenger." In no other verse does *angelos* refer to anything but an earthly or a heavenly personal being. Therefore the "messenger" in II Cor 12:7 most likely refers to an actual human being or to an oppressing spirit operating through such a person. Paul describes the false teachers at Corinth as deceitful workers who masqueraded as apostles of Christ. "And no wonder, for even Satan disguises himself as an angel of light" (II Cor 11:13-14, NASB). Satan was represented by his "ministers" who also disguised themselves as ministers of righteousness (v. 15). These were probably Judaizers who attempted to require Christian converts to keep the Mosaic law and thus were perverting Paul's ministry of the grace of God. Paul's "thorn" was perhaps the ringleader of this opposition at Corinth or Ephesus.

In his response to his thorn in the flesh Paul demonstrated the proper Christian response to frustration, whatever form it may take. After earnest prayer for its removal, he accepted it and made the best of the situation by the grace of Christ (II Cor 12:8-10).

See Paul.

Bibliography. Norman V. Hope, "Paul's Thorn and Ours," CT, XIV (Dec. 5, 1969), 222-223 [14-15]. Terence Y. Mullins, "Paul's Thorn in the Flesh," JBL, LXXVI (1957), 299-303.

J. R.

THORNS. *See* Plants.

THREE. *See* Number.

THREE TAVERNS. *See* Appii Forum.

THRESHING. The process of separating the edible grain from the husk and stock in which it grew. Some crops might be plucked up by the roots and threshed where they were, but usually the grain was cut with a sickle and bound into sheaves which would be taken to a threshing floor (*q.v.*). There a small crop might be beaten with sticks or flails (Isa 28:27*b*). The sheaves of a larger harvest would be spread out and cattle driven back and forth over them (Deut 25:4). Or a pair of animals would draw over them a board with the underside made rough with pieces of stone or iron (II Sam 24:22). More elaborate threshing instruments had stone or iron-toothed rollers supporting a platform on which the driver would ride (Isa 28:27-28; 41:15). *See* Threshing Sledge.

During the threshing the sheaves would be turned over frequently with some sort of fork. A brisk breeze would help by blowing away the light husk or chaff, especially when the material was tossed in the air (cf. Ps 1:4; Isa 41:16). In

A winnowing scene near Shechem. JR

the latter case, the heavier grain would drop down, nicely separated. Tossing grain into the air for this purpose is called winnowing (Ruth 3:2). *See* Agriculture.

N. B. B.

THRESHING FLOOR. A good hard floor (Heb. *gōren*) was essential to efficient threshing. Circular in form and *c.* 50 feet in diameter, it was best to have a slightly raised center to allow moisture to drain off. The surface could either be hard beaten earth (Jer 51:33) or be paved with hard stones. David raised an altar on a threshing floor which he bought from Araunah the Jebusite (II Sam 24:18-25). More often it belonged to the whole community. As in the case of the threshing floor of Samaria, where Ahab and the visiting Jehoshaphat sat on their portable throne chairs (I Kgs 22:10, RSV), it was frequently just outside the city gate, placed to receive the prevailing west wind to aid in winnowing (Hos 13:3). During the threshing season the owners of the crop would sleep at the floor to prevent stealing (Ruth 3:2; cf. I Sam 23:1). Because it was bare ground and open to the sky, Gideon placed his fleece on a threshing floor to receive the dew (Jud 6:37).

N. B. B.

THRESHING SLEDGE. A threshing device (Heb. *morag*) composed of two heavy, oblong planks, secured by two cross-pieces and raised slightly at the front end (II Sam 24:22). It was drawn by draught animals over the grain on the threshing floor (Deut 25:4) and set with sharp stones (Isa 41:15) or pieces of iron (Amos 1:3) on its underside. It is to be distinguished from the threshing cart with several rollers (Heb. *ăgālâ*, Isa 28:17*b*; Prov 20:26, NASB). The threshing sledge appears to have been used figuratively to describe the extermination of inimical populations (Amos 1:3; Jud 8:7, NASB; II Kgs 13:7) and as such it became a metaphor for complete annihiliation of one's foes (Isa 41:15). The crocodile (Leviathan) is likened to a threshing sledge as it spreads itself upon the mire (Job 41:30, RSV). *See* Threshing; Threshing Floor.

Draught animals pulling a threshing sledge near Amman. A woman stands on it to weight it down. HFV

THRESHOLD. The sill of a doorway (Jud 19:27), consisting of a heavy piece of timber or stone which lies under the door. Adjacent to the end(s) would be the stone door socket(s) of the door(s) swung by pivot instead of hinges (Isa 6:4, NASB marg.). Two Heb. words, *saph* and *miphtān*, are used for threshold in the KJV, RSV, and NASB; it is possible that *miphtān* refers to the platform or podium of an idol (I Sam 5:4-5) or the platform or terrace on which the temple was elevated (Zeph 1:9; Ezk 9:3; 10:4, 18; 46:2; 47:1, all NEB).

As the first part of the house on which one would step when entering, the threshold symbolized the entrance itself. Therefore the gatekeepers of the temple and of the royal palace are referred to as "keepers of the threshold" (II Kgs 22:4; 25:18; I Chr 9:19, 22; II Chr 34:9, all RSV; cf. II Kgs 12:9; Est 2:21; 6:2). The threshold of the temple would be considered sacred, as the place where shoes must be removed before advancing to stand on holy ground (cf. Ex 3:5; Josh 5:15). Ezk 43:8 compared to II Kgs 16:14; 21:5, 7 indicates that the setting up of idols and pagan altars in the temple area is like setting a threshold (Heb. *saph*), i.e., building a shrine in opposition to God's house.

When the image of Dagon in the Philistine temple at Ashdod fell and was smashed upon the threshold, the superstitious priests and worshipers of Dagon avoided stepping on the threshold when entering (I Sam 5:4–5), or on the "platform" (NEB). It is not certain whether "leaping on the threshold" (Zeph 1:9) signifies an idolatrous practice, as indicated in the NEB by its translation, "I will punish all who dance on the temple terrace", an act of irreverence—"all who leap on the temple threshold" (NASB); or an act of violence committed in housebreaking and robbery of homes or in demanding repayment of loans (cf. Deut 24:10-11).

J. R.

THRONE

1. Heb. *kissē'*, an ordinary chair; when applied to the king's public seat, it means "throne." It is the symbol of authority (Gen 41:40; Deut 17:18) and of the perpetual supremacy of David's line above others (II Sam 3:10; 7:13; I Kgs 2:45; Isa 9:7). Its continuity in David's house was predicated on obedience to God's laws (I Kgs 8:25; 9:4-5), and therefore was called the throne of the Lord (I Chr 29:23). The governor's seat is designated a throne (Neh 3:7). Yahweh's throne in His heavenly temple (Isa 6:1) is the source of judgment for the people (Ps 9:4; 97:2; etc.), for He is holy (Ps 47:8). Jerusalem is to be His throne (Jer 3:17), i.e., the place where the Lord will rule the earth.

2. Aramaic *korsē'* means "throne" (Dan 5:20; 7:9).

3. Gr. *bēma*, the portable throne chair on which Herod Agrippa I sat in the theater at Caesarea (Acts 12:21), is elsewhere translated "judgment seat" (*q.v.*).

4. Gr. *thronos* is the place where Christ will rule the earth (Mt 19:28; 25:31). It is the ultimate place of appeal for the certainty of an oath (Mt 23:22). Christ inherits David's throne (Lk 1:32; Acts 2:30). To be seated at the right of God's throne signifies complete approval (Heb 8:1; 12:2). It is symbolical of God's right to judge men and to rule the world (Rev 4:2 ff.), and of the future authority of Christ's disciples (Mt 19:28; Rev 20:4).

Throne of Tutankhamon. LL

Solomon's royal throne was placed in a special room in his palace called the porch or hall of judgment (I Kgs 7:7; *see* Palace). Made with ivory work and overlaid with gold, it was on a dais six steps high and had flanking lions (I Kgs 10:18–20), with wide armrests, and a back with a carved bull's head, the ancient symbol of strength. Representations of thrones seen on ancient monuments show similar features. A 13th cen. B.C. ivory plaque from Megiddo shows a king or prince on a throne, the side of which is a winged lion with human head (ANEP, #332). Decoration consisted of varieties of gold, ivory, lapis lazuli, frequently worked into intricate patterns or showing human and animal figures, in an attempt to glorify the owner.

The wooden throne of Tutankhamon discovered intact in his tomb is overlaid with sheet gold and has feline legs, surmounted by lions' heads. On the inside of the back a family scene in bas-relief depicts the seated king wearing a composite crown and the queen standing before him (ANEP, #415–417). For a representation of King Ahiram of Byblos seated on his sphinx throne, with his feet resting on a footstool, see ANEP, #458. Just as Ahab and Jehoshaphat sat on thrones outside Samaria planning a military campaign (I Kgs 22:10), so a bas-relief from the palace of Sennacherib at Nineveh depicts him sitting on a high, portable, ornate throne overlooking Lachish, as he received prisoners and spoils from the Judean city (ANEP, #371). A bas-relief at Persepolis shows King Darius I of Persia seated on an elaborately carved throne with his feet on a footstool (ANEP, #463). *See* Footstool.

Bibliography. Otto Schmitz, *"Thronos,"* TDNT, III, 160–167.

H. G. S.

THUMMIM. *See* Urim and Thummim.

THUNDER. The English translation of two Heb. words, *qôl* and *ra'am,* and of the Gr. *brontē.* It was most often heard in Palestine and the surrounding area during spring and autumn, while its summer occurrence was so rare that Samuel invoked it as a means of conveying God's disapproval of Israel (I Sam 12:17–18).

Thunder occurred several times in the OT as a literal accompaniment of electrical storms. It added a violent effect to the seventh plague of Egypt when hail smote the land, killing men and beasts (Ex 9:22–34). Thunder and lightning accompanied the giving of the law at Sinai a short time later (Ex 19:16–18; 20:18). These occurrences apparently were natural phenomena controlled by the Lord (Job 28:26; 38:25). *See* Lightning; Thunderbolt.

Figuratively, thunder was explained as the "voice" (*qôl*) of Yahweh," especially in the poetical books (Job 37:2–5; 40:9; Ps 18:13; 29:3–9). As such, it symbolized divine power and vengeance (I Sam 2:10; II Sam 22:14; Isa 30:30–31). In the NT Jesus depicted James and John as "sons of thunder" (Mk 3:17), conceivably because of their brash and spontaneous temperaments (Lk 9:54–55).

J. Ma.

Baal of Thunder from Ugarit. LM

THUNDERBOLT. Literally a "flame" or "burning arrow," it is a picturesque description of what might better be called a bolt of lightning (Ps 78:48), as in NASB. *See* Lightning.

THYATIRA (thī-*à*-tī'r*à*). Thyatira was located 52 miles NE of Smyrna on a main road joining the Caicus and Hermus river valleys. A great trading city, its height came about A.D. 100. There is evidence of more trade guilds there than in any other Asian city. Lydia, a seller of purple from Thyatira, probably represented her guild at Philippi (Acts 16:14). The purple she sold was probably made in the region of Thyatira, which produced the well-known Turkey red, obtained from the

Ancient ruins at Thyatira. Robert Cooley

madder root. Perhaps the city was evangelized from Ephesus. John addressed himself to the church there (Rev 2:18–29), scoring it for too much conformity to the pagan customs and practices of the day.

THYINE. *See* Plants.

TIBERIAS (tī-bĭr'ĭ-*ă*s). Tiberias stands on the W shore of the Sea of Galilee about 12 miles S of where the Jordan flows into the sea. Its location at 682 feet below sea level gives it a delightful winter climate but an oppressive one in summer.

In OT times Rakkath stood on this site and was one of the walled cities given to the tribe of Naphtali (Josh 19:35). In A.D. 20 (perhaps A.D. 18), Herod Antipas (*q.v.*) began to build a new town there and named it after the ruling emperor, Tiberius (A.D. 14-37). Herod made Tiberias his capital for the administration of Galilee and Perea, and the town gave its name to the sea (of Galilee, Jn 6:1; 21:1). Despite its importance it is mentioned only once in the NT (Jn 6:23) and apparently was not visited by Christ during His ministry. Perhaps avoidance of the site resulted from the fact that Herod had to remove many tombs in order to make room for his city. Strict Jews did not go there.

After the destruction of Jerusalem in A.D. 70, Tiberias became a seat of rabbinic learning. Here the Mishna was completed about A.D. 200 and the Jerusalem Talmud about 400. Here too the system of vowel markings and the punctuated Heb. script of the Masoretes later originated. Destroyed during the Crusades of the 12th cen., the town was rebuilt in the 16th cen. Destroyed by an earthquake in 1837 it was again rebuilt and is today a thriving center. Tombs of several famous rabbis are shown in the town, including Maimonides, Yohanan Ben Zakkai, Eliezer the Great, and Akiva.

H. F. V.

TIBERIAS, SEA OF. Another name for the Sea of Galilee (*see* Galilee, Sea of) as explained by John in his Gospel (6:1; 21:1). The name is that of the Roman emperor Tiberius and came from the city of Tiberias, built by Herod Antipas and named for the emperor. The modern name is still *Bahr Tabariyeh.*

TIBERIUS (tī-bĭr'ĭ-ŭs). Tiberius Claudius Nero (42 B.C.–A.D.37) was second emperor of Rome (A.D. 14-37). Son of Tiberius Claudius Nero and Livia Drusilla, he was adopted by Augustus Caesar when the latter married Tiberius' mother. Thus the younger Tiberius was a stepson of Augustus. Made Augustus' heir in A.D. 4, Tiberius came to the imperial chair in A.D. 14. He is mentioned specifically in Scripture only in Lk 3:1, where it is said that John the Baptist began his ministry in the fifteenth year of Tiberius' reign. This chronological note is very useful in establishing the chronology of Jesus' life and ministry. Tiberius was the "Caesar" referred to in the narrative of Jesus' ministry, and it was during his reign that Jesus was crucified. Tiberius appointed Pilate procurator of Judea in A.D. 26 and removed him from office in 36.

As a result of the evaluation of Tiberius' reign by the historian Tacitus, "a masterpiece of malice and innuendo," the emperor has been roundly condemned. In recent years, however, it has become clear that as a senatorial partisan (and a member of a group that did not get along well with Tiberius), Tacitus greatly exaggerated Tiberius' faults. The emperor is now viewed as a conscientious ruler showing prudence in expenditure and excellence in civil and imperial administration.

H. F. V.

TIBHATH (tĭb'hăth). A city of Hadadezer, the powerful Aramaean king of Zobah, which was conquered by David and from which he removed much bronze (I Chr 18:8). The parallel passage in II Sam 8:8 gives the name of the city as Betah, which is no doubt a corruption of the name Tibhath (cf. LXX *Metebac*). Tibhath has been identified with Tubiḫi mentioned in the Tell el-Amarna letters and with the Egyptian city *d-b-ḫ* (ANET, p. 477), and is to be located

Tiberias and the Sea of Galilee. ISS

somewhere in the valley between the Lebanon and the Anti-Lebanon ranges. Some scholars propose that the name should be read Tebah (*q.v.*) in accordance with Gen 22:24.

TIBNI (tĭb'nī). The son of Ginath who was one of the three contenders for the throne of Israel following the regicide of Elah (*c.* 886 B.C.). In the ensuing civil war Omri, the commander of the army, promptly liquidated Zimri, and then during the next three years gradually prevailed over the unquestionably powerful forces under the command of Tibni (I Kgs 16:21f.). Tibni and his brother Joram (so LXX) apparently perished after their defeat.

TIDAL (tī'dăl). The last of the four kings who under the leadership of Chedorlaomer (*q.v.*) invaded Palestine *c.* 2000 B.C. (Gen 14:1, 9). *See* Abraham. Scholars are quite well agreed that Tidal (Heb. *tid'āl*) represents the cuneiform Tudḫaliya, the name of four or five Hittite kings in the 18th to 13th cen. B.C. Tudḫaliya I reigned *c.* 1740 B.C., not early enough for the time of Abraham. The name itself goes back to pre-Hittite Anatolia, and is perhaps Hattian or proto-Hittite rather than strictly Hittite.

His title "king of nations" (Heb. *gōyîm*) does not specify over what country he ruled. There is a parallel to this title, however, in the Mari (*q.v.*) tablets, in which the word *gâ'um* means "group" or "gang." This suggests that Tidal was ruler over a nomadic people which had not yet established a settled kingdom. Such were the Umman-Manda (Akkad. "Manda-people"), barbarians who very early destroyed the empire of Akkad and who are later cited by name in the Hittite code. Thus Tidal may well have been an early Tudḫaliya ruling a group of Indo-Europeans, perhaps in the process of migrating from N of the Caucasus, on the borders of N Syria and SE Asia Minor, heading eventually for the future Hittite homeland in Anatolia.

Bibliography. K. A. Kitchen, "Tidal," NBD, p. 1276; *Ancient Orient and Old Testament,* Chicago: Inter-Varsity, 1966, p. 44. E. A. Speiser, *Genesis,* Anchor Bible, Garden City: Doubleday, 1964, pp. 107f.

J. R.

TIGLATH-PILESER (tĭg'lăth-pĭ-lē'zĕr). Three kings of Assyria bore the throne name *Tukultī-apil-Esharra,* "My Confidence Is (in) the Firstborn Son of Esharra" (the name of a famous Mesopotamian temple). The career of Tiglath-pileser I (*c.* 1114-1076 B.C.) was the highwater mark of Assyrian power in the 12th cen. B.C. He conquered Babylon, campaigned northward into Armenia and Anatolia, and westward to the N Phoenician coast. At the end of his reign Assyrian might declined slowly, partly because of the rising power of the Aramaeans.

Tiglath-pileser III in a war chariot. BM

The fortunes of Assyria reached their lowest ebb under the inept Tiglath-pileser II (*c.* 966-935), who was helpless to prevent the other nations of the Fertile Crescent from attempting to realize their destinies. Israel's era of expansion during the reigns of David and Solomon thus providentially coincided with a period of impotence in the history of Assyria, which was unable to regain the Upper Euphrates Valley until after 875 B.C.

Perhaps the ablest of all Assyrian rulers was Tiglath-pileser III (745-727B.C.), the only one of the three rulers bearing that name to whom the OT refers. In II Kings he is called Tiglath-pileser (Heb. *Tiglat-pil'eser,* 15:29; 16:10; *Tiglat-pᵉleser,* 16:7), while the Chronicler uses the later dialectal variant Tilgath-pilneser (*q.v.*; Heb. *Tillegat-pilnē'eser,* I Chr 5:6; II Chr 28:20;*Tillᵉgat-pilneser,* I Chr 5:26). He was referred to as Pul (Heb. *Pûl,* II Kgs 15:19; I Chr 5:26; Akkad. *Pūlu;* Ptolemaic Canon *Pōros*) by the Babylonians, to whose throne he acceded late in his reign (cf. below). I Chr 5:26 apparently distinguishes between Pul and Tilgath-pilneser, but since the verb following the names is singular ("*he* carried them away") we are obliged to translate "the spirit of Pul king of Assyria, *even* the spirit of Tilgath-pilneser king of Assyria" (cf. similarly RSV), thus demonstrating the supposed distinction to be more superficial than real.

The history of the reign of Tiglath-pileser III is imperfectly known because of the fragmentary nature of his inscriptional remains, most of which were found at Calah (*q.v.*), modern Nimrud, excavated by Austen Henry Layard over a century ago and by M. E. L. Mallowan in 1949-61. This was the site of his palace, from which have been recovered reliefs portraying the king and his military campaigns. Despite the poor state of preservation of his inscriptions, however, the main outline of his career is given in the Assyrian eponym list.

By the time of the accession of Tiglath-pileser III to the Assyrian throne in 745 B.C., a significant series of events had taken place in the northern kingdom of Israel. Jeroboam II, her most powerful ruler, had died, and Israel was in dire need of another strong king. None was forthcoming, however, and thus she entered upon a period of anarchy and civil strife. Jeroboam's son Zachariah was murdered by the usurper Shallum following a six-month reign. After ruling for only one month, Shallum was in turn assassinated by Menahem, who then seized the throne. Such was the situation in Israel when Tiglath-pileser rose to power in Assyria.

The Assyrian monarch coveted the territories of Syro-Palestine not only for the wealth (mineral and timber, primarily) that they contained but also because they constituted the corridors through which his armies would be able to march into Anatolia and Egypt. After seizing the throne of Assyria, he soon subdued Babylon (though not actually acceding to the Babylonian throne until 729 B.C.), and in so doing protected his realm on the SE. He then turned his attention to the W, pushing into Syria in 743 B.C. and defeating a Syrian ally, Sarduri II of Urarṭu (Ararat, *q.v.*), en route.

Upon the capitulation of Sarduri, Tiglath-pileser campaigned against Arpad (in northern Syria) and in Armenia, turning toward southern Syria to crush a revolt instigated by *Azriyā'u* (probably Azariah [Uzziah], *q.v.*) of *Ya'ūdu* (probably Judah; ANET, p. 282*b*; for a recent discussion of this problem of identification cf. H. Tadmor, "Azriyau of Yaudi," *Scripta Hierosolymitana,* VIII, 232-271; cf. II Chr 26:6-15 for the biblical account of Uzziah's military prowess). Tiglath-pileser destroyed the Syrian confederacy by 738 B.C., if not before (cf. Edwin R. Thiele, *The Mysterious Numbers of the Hebrew Kings,* pp. 75-98). Menahem (Assyrian *Meniḫimmu*), who had usurped Israel's throne, averted the capture of the northern kingdom by surrendering a huge tribute (ANET, p. 283*a*). It has been estimated that Menahem exacted 50 shekels of silver from as many as 60,000 "mighty men of wealth" to raise the necessary funds to appease Tiglath-pileser (II Kgs 15:19-20). A recently discovered stele of Tiglath-pileser III points to this tribute as having been paid in 737 B.C. (BASOR,#206 [1972], pp. 40-42; *see* Menahem).

Menahem was succeeded by his son Pekahiah. The latter was murdered by Pekah who usurped his throne (II Kgs 15:23-25) and, perhaps, his name as well, since Isaiah, while introducing him to us as "Pekah the son of Remaliah" (Isa 7:1), consistently and contemptuously alludes to him in all subsequent references simply as "the son of Remaliah" (e.g., 7:4).

Pekahiah, like his father, had been tributary to Assyria; Pekah, on the contrary, together with Rezin of Damascus, became the principal instigators of a coalition to oppose Tiglath-pileser. It would seem (II Kgs 15:37) that they sought the aid first of Jotham (ruling Judah as co-regent with his ailing father Uzziah, who had been smitten with leprosy by the Lord for having arrogated to himself priestly prerogatives; cf. II Kgs 15:1-5; II Chr 26:16-21), and then that of his co-regent Ahaz to insure the success of their enterprise. Supported in his decision by the prophet Isaiah, Ahaz in 734 B.C. refused to join the Syro-Ephraimite alliance. Pekah and Rezin invaded Judah and besieged Jerusalem (II Kgs 16:5; II Chr 28:5-15) in an attempt to force the issue, intending to place a Syrian, the son of Tabeal (Isa 7:6), on the throne in the place of Ahaz should the latter refuse to capitulate.

Understandably, Ahaz became alarmed (Isa 7:2) at the attack by his northern neighbors. Isaiah attempted to allay his fears by urging him to avoid all entangling alliances and to trust in the Lord, assuring him that the careers of Israel and Damascus were soon to be extinguished (7:4). This time, however, Ahaz refused to heed the prophet (7:12) and decided on another course of action. He requested the assistance of Tiglath-pileser against Rezin and Pekah by offering a sizable tribute (II Kgs 16:7-8; II Chr 28:16, 20-21). Vainly Isaiah tried to dissuade Ahaz from allying Judah with Assyria, but to no avail. Tiglath-pileser now had an excuse for executing his already-formulated plan, while in addition Ahaz would in effect be financing the venture.

The immediate result of Ahaz' submission was that *c.* 733 B.C. Tiglath-pileser moved down the Mediterranean seacoast and invaded Philistia, thereby cutting off Israel and Syria from any possible Egyptian aid that they might have hoped to obtain. Ashkelon and Gaza were quickly reduced (ANET, p. 283*b*), after which Tiglath-pileser attacked Queen Samsi of Arabia, driving her peoples inland (ANET, p. 284*a*).

His next stratagem was to turn northward into Israel itself, where he captured "Ijon, and Abel-beth-maachah, and Janoah, and Kedesh, and Hazor, and Gilead, and Galilee, all the land of Naphtali, and carried them captive to Assyria" (II Kgs 15:29). This passage illustrates one of the distinctive administrative policies inaugurated by Tiglath-pileser in Assyria to establish his undisputed control over dependent states: deporting to other lands the prominent and influential segments of the native population. Native rulers of conquered states were then normally succeeded by Assyrian administrators, who in turn were kept in rein by an elaborate system of checks and balances; and foreign elements, as part of a policy designed to avert rebellion and insure non-resistance, were imported to repopulate the land (B. Oded, "Observations on Methods of Assyrian Rule in Transjordania After the Campaign of Tiglath-pileser III," JNES, XXIX [1970], 177-186; for his capture of Astartu, biblical Ashtaroth in Bashan, see ANEP #366).

After Tiglath-pileser's foray into Israel, Hoshea, a usurper, conspired against Pekah, "slew him, and reigned in his stead" (II Kgs 15:30). In his annals, Tiglath-pileser credits himself with placing *Ausī'u* (Hoshea) on the throne after the overthrow of *Paqaḫu* (Pekah), perhaps indicating only that such an accession could not have taken place without his attendant blessing (ANET, p. 284*a*). In Tiglath-pileser's view, then, Hoshea was in effect his puppet on Israel's throne. Only the death of the violently anti-Assyrian Pekah kept Israel from total destruction at this time. In 733 B.C. Tiglath-pileser annexed portions of the northern kingdom, creating from them the provinces of Megiddo, Dor, and Gilead (which corresponded closely in extent to the fourth, fifth, and seventh administrative districts of Solomon's reign two centuries earlier).

Damascus, left without allies, became the next object of Tiglath-pileser's attention. In 732 B.C. he attacked and destroyed the city and slew Rezin (II Kgs 16:9), and the ancient Syrian kingdom ceased to exist. As a vassal of Assyria, Ahaz was then summoned to Damascus to pledge his political loyalty to Tiglath-pileser. He soon came to understand, however, that religious loyalty was required of him as well, for on returning to Jerusalem he found himself obliged to offer sacrifices on a replica of an Assyrian altar that he had seen in Damascus. He then apparently instructed it to be installed on the site of the altar of the Lord in the Jerusalem temple, removing the Lord's altar to a subsidiary position (II Kgs 16:10-18). Ahaz was by this time completely apostate, having substituted foreign gods for the one true God of his fathers (cf. also 16:3-4; II Chr 28:1-4, 22-25). Since Tiglath-pileser referred to him in his inscriptions as *Ya'uḫāzu* (ANET, p. 282*a*), it would seem that his full name was Jehoahaz and that the Hebrew scribes dropped the divine prefix from it to express their abhorrence of his evil memory. He was buried in a common grave, away from the royal tombs (II Chr 28:27).

Israel and Judah were now both tributary to the Assyrian Empire, which had reached the zenith of its power and prestige. Like his great namesake of four centuries earlier, Tiglath-pileser III remained master of all he surveyed until the day of his death.

See Assyria.

R. F. Y.

TIGRIS (tī'grĭs). The Tigris River derives its name from the Gr. *Tigris* and Old Persian

Tigris River at Baghdad. JR

Tigrā. The modern Arabic name is Dijlah, which comes from the original Sumerian name for the river (*Idigna*), rendered in Assyrian and Babylonian as *Idiqlat* and by the Heb. *ḥiddeqel*.

The Tigris has two sources: the western, rising on the S slopes of the Armenian Anti-Taurus Mountains near Diarbekr; the eastern (Bitlis Chai and Bohtan Chai), S of Lake Van. After these unite in the northern Kurdistan hills, the river flows swiftly ESE to join the Euphrates in the marshes 40 miles N of the Persian Gulf. In antiquity it ended in this area. At the time of the March-May floods, caused by the melting snows at its sources or at the sources of its principal tributaries (the Greater and Lesser Zab, Adhem, and Diyala rivers), the 1,146 mile long river is navigable up to modern Mosul. The ancient Assyrian capitals lay on its upper course, Nineveh on the left bank opposite Mosul, Calah 25 miles downstream near the junction of the Greater Zab, and Asshur on the right bank opposite the Lesser Zab. Thus the Tigris is well described as one of the four rivers branching out of Eden and flowing to the E of Assyria (or, of Asshur, Gen 2:14). Its twin river (hence Mesopotamia, "the land of the two rivers") was the Euphrates to the W.

In its lower reaches in the level terrain the Tigris is a "wide river" (Dan 10:4). On these banks were built various capital cities, among the more famous being Seleucia (Hellenistic), Ctesiphon (Parthian) across the river on the E side, and Baghdad (Islamic or Arabic, and capital of modern Iraq) 20 miles upstream at the junction of the Diyala.

D. J. W.

TIKVAH (tĭk'vȧ)

1. The son of Harhȧs (Hasrah, II Chr 34:22) and father of Shallum, keeper of the wardrobe (II Kgs 22:14). Shallum was the husband of Huldah the prophetess who flourished in the time of Josiah. Tikvah is called Tokhath in II Chr 34:22 (RSV, NASB; KJV, Tikvath).

2. The father of Jahzeiah who opposed the edict of Ezra concerning the banishment of foreign wives (Ezr 10:15).

TIKVATH (tĭk'văth). The rendering of the name Tokhath (RSV, NASB) in the KJV of II Chr 34:22. As the marginal reading of the MT suggests and as the parallel passage in II Kgs 22:14 indicates, the name should be read Tikvah.

TILE, TILING

1. Heb. *l*ᵉ*bēnâ*, "a tile" (Ezk 4:1; RSV, NASB, "brick"), elsewhere translated "brick" (*q.v.*) in the KJV. Ezekiel was instructed to inscribe Jerusalem on a clay brick and lay siege to it, so as to emphasize his preaching that Jerusalem would be captured because of Israel's sins (4:4ff.). Plans on clay bricks or tablets have been found in Mesopotamia (see ANEP #260) and give supporting evidence of the Babylonian milieu of this activity of the prophet.

Tiles in the sense of glazed bricks were also known in the OT world. Glazed bricks were used to face the Ishtar gate of Babylon (ANEP, #760–762). At Qantis in the Egyptian Delta Rameses II had his dais covered with blue glazed tiles (W. C. Hayes, *Glazed Tiles from a Palace of Rameses II at Kantir,* New York: Metropolitan Museum of Art, 1937); this may be compared with the "pavement of sapphire" which Moses and the 70 elders of Israel saw under God's feet (Ex 24:10, NASB).

2. Gr. *keramos,* "tiling" (ceramic; a baked thing), in Lk 5:19 the tiles (NASB) used for roofing. Graeco-Roman temples were roofed with tiles. Luke is specific as to material, while Mark (2:4) is specific as to method (digging, NASB) by which the opening was made in the roof by the four friends of the paralytic, to let him down into the presence of Jesus. Ordinarily tiles were not used on the flat roofs of Palestine. A Jew influenced by Hellenistic culture may, however, have had tiles covering the normal roof made of thick clay laid on branches over wooden beams. On the other hand, there may have been a slightly sloping tile roof overhanging the courtyard of the house. This arrangement would suffice to allow the men access to the place above where Jesus sat out of the sun.

H. G. S.

TILGATH-PILNESER (tĭl'găth-pĭl-nē'zẽr). An alternate form of Tiglath-pileser (*q.v.*) which appears in I Chr 5:6 and II Chr 28:20. The interchange of *g* and *l* was no doubt made in the interests of Heb. euphony, a course the LXX and Vulgate follow, while the *n* in *pilne'eser* represents the Akkadian *ina,* meaning "in," found in one reading of the name: *Tukulti-apil-ina-Ešarra.* The form Tilgath-pilneser found in I Chr 5:26 omits the letter *aleph* altogether (cf. Zenjirli Stele, line 16).

TILLAGE. The practice of tilling the land or the cultivated land itself. As a translation of Heb. *'ăbôdâ,* meaning "labor, service, work," it is used in I Chr 27:26 of the "work of the field for tillage of the ground" (KJV, ASV; RSV) "tilling the soil") and in Neh 10:37 in the phrase "cities of our tillage" (KJV, ASV; RSV "our rural towns"). The Heb. *nîr* is incorrectly rendered tillage (so KJV, ASV; cf. ASV marg. "tilled land") in Prov 13:23 and should be translated as "fallow ground" (cf. Jer 4:3; Hos 10:12). Tillage is the marginal reading of Prov 21:4 (ASV), but should be rendered "lamp" (so ASV, RSV).

TILON (tī'lŏn). A Judahite who is named among the sons of Shimon (I Chr 4:20).

TIMAEUS, TIMEUS (tĭ-mē'ŭs). The father of an unnamed blind beggar of Jericho (Mk 10:46). In the parallel passages (Mt 20:29-34; Lk 18:35–43) no name is given at all. Mark identifies the beggar simply as Bartimaeus (*q.v.*) which he translates for his readers as "the son of Timaeus."

TIMBREL. *See* Music.

TIME. In the Bible a number of Heb. and Gr. words denote various aspects of time. The most important terms are Heb. *yôm,* day, time; *'ēth,* time; Gr. *kairos,* time, a fixed time or point of time; *chronos,* time, extended time. The Gr. words definitely show a certain distinction between punctiliar time or points in time (*kairoi*), and time as duration (*chronos*). Christ used both words when He said to His disciples, "It is not for you to know the times [*chronous*] or seasons [kairous]" (Acts 1:7), and appears to have been distinguishing between periods of time, such as the Church Age and the Millennium, and points in time such as His return and the day of judgment.

God and time. In the Bible God is revealed as creating and acting in time. He created the world in six days and rested the seventh. Even before creation, time appeared as He and the Son planned our redemption and recorded it in His book (Ps 40:7). After Christ's second coming, time will continue as the redeemed live and reign with God forever, lit., "to the ages of the ages" (Rev 11:15; 22:5). The use of the term "day" for each of the six steps of creation does not militate against the application of time to God and His actions, even if "one day is with the Lord as a thousand years, and a thousand years as one day" (II Pet 3:8; Ps 90:4). God can stretch out time and examine each moment meticulously (as we can write a book on the experience of a moment), or compress it so that a thousand years appear as a day (as we can summarize a millennium in a sentence). But this does not deny the existence of time; it only reveals its importance.

Philosophy and time. Aristotle struggled with the problem of time. In order to express the passage of time, he reasoned, we must use numbers. Do numbers and counting come before or after countables? Can we have arithmetic without things to count, without creation? If not, we cannot have time, since it is a "countable," before creation. Aristotle decided, therefore, that counting and mathematics and time as something countable did not exist before creation. He failed to see that counting and mathematics are possible also as the theoretical possibility to count; and that time, therefore, can be the mere possibility of before and after, and of succession, entirely apart from the countables of creation.

Immanuel Kant complicated the philosophical picture when he argued, from another angle, against the eternal existence of time. God is infinite. If time and space are also infinite—as they must be if eternal—then we have three infinites. But this is impossible because two or more things cannot all be infinite. Therefore, God must be infinite, and time and space are finite. It follows, there is then no time or space to God. Time and space are categories of finitude, and anything known in time-space terms is finite knowledge. Since God is timeless and spaceless, and man knows things only in time-space categories, according to Kant it follows that God cannot ever be known because there is a complete disjunction between His realm of knowledge and ours.

Theology and time. Three theological views are held concerning time. (1) There is no time to God, and yet He works and reveals Himself in time. Augustine and many Reformed theologians take this view. It can only mean that there is no time to God only with respect to His essence, since we know God in time and He has dealt with man in time. Since we do not know our closest friend in his essence, certainly we will never know God in His essence, but only as He reveals Himself, and this has occurred only in time. This being so, one may say there is no time for God, while another says that there is time for Him; and yet we must agree that it really makes no difference to our view of revelation since all He has done and revealed comes to us in time-space terms.

(2) There is no time to God in any sense. He is timeless and spaceless (S. Kierkegaard, Karl Barth and other neoorthodox theologians, and Paul Tillich). Because God is timeless and spaceless, and man only knows things in time and space, He cannot communicate directly with man. Revelation must be in the form of myth, symbol, or saga, and requires "demythologization" and interpretation (Rudolph Bultmann and Paul Tillich). *See* Myth, Mythology.

(3) There is time for God. This view is held by J. O. Buswell, Jr., a Reformed theologian. He reasons that the definition given of time by Aristotle is erroneous because based upon a mistaken view of counting and mathematics. Time (cf. counting) is the mere possibility of a before and an after, "the mere abstract possibility of relationships in sequence" (J. O. Buswell, Jr., *Thomas and the Bible,* p. 68). Space likewise is the mere possibility of a relationship between objects. With such a definition neither time nor space limit God. They only exist as relationships.

What of the charge of Kant that they still are infinites and therefore limit God? Not all infinites exclude each other. We can have an infinite number of infinite lines. Moreover God's omniscience overcomes any limiting aspect of time and His omnipresence of space. Are not infinite time and infinite space encompassed in the definition of an omnipotent, omniscient, omnipresent God in the sense they exist as relationships within Him even before they are manifest in His creation? Furthermore, we speak of God as eternal in His being (Ps 102:24-27; Jer 10:10) and as inhabiting eternity (Isa 57:15). Eternity and time are not opposites, because eternity ("from everlasting to everlasting," Ps 90:2) must include time.

Conclusion. Time has become a very acute problem for theologians in our day. Aristotle and Kant raised the philosophical difficulties; Augustine, Kierkegaard and the neoorthodox, the theological ones. A definition of counting and mathematics and of time is demanded which is broad enough to extend to eternity past (before the creation) as well as to creation and eternity to come. If time and mathematics are relationships which have been existent always in God, then the problem is solved and neoorthodoxy refuted.

On the other hand, if time and space only exist as a result of God's creation—since God certainly has known these relationships from creation—the world and man added these to God. God only knew time and space, then, because of creation. It added to Him something He did not have before. He needs creation to be fully God! This is dangerous thinking because it means we experience relationships God did not have till He had us. We are superior to, or at least equal with, God at this point. The only safe answer is a re-examination of the biblical relationship between God and time, and the formulation of a definition which fits revelation. When time and space are removed from the realm of creation, and seen as relationships existing in God before creation, the problems are solved.

See Aeon; Calendar; Eternity; Existentialism; Neoorthodoxy; Theology; Time, Division of.

Bibliography. James Barr, *Biblical Words for Time,* rev., London: SCM Press, 1969. J. Oliver Buswell, Jr., *Being and Knowing,* Grand Rapids: Zondervan, 1960, pp. 41–45; *Systematic Theology,* Grand Rapids: Zondervan, 1963, I, 45–48, 127; *Thomas and the Bible* (mimeographed), St. Louis: Covenant Theological Seminary, n.d. Oscar Cullmann, *Christ and Time,* London: SCM Press, 1951. Gerhard Delling, *"Hēmera,"* TDNT, II, 943–953. Carl F. H. Henry, "Time," BDT, pp. 523–525. E. Jenni, "Time," IDB, IV, 642–649. John R.

Wilch, *Time and Event,* Leiden: Brill, 1969 (an exegetical study of the use of *'ēth* in the OT).

R. A. K.

TIME, DIVISIONS OF. The attitude of various cultures toward time differs. For this reason scholars have been unable to fully explain the exact usage of the tense system of classical Heb. The Hebrews were not avid seekers after impersonal causes, and time as an abstract concept was outside their interest. They did, however, have a rustic interest in the measurement of time.

1. *Day.* The basic unit of time, because the most obvious, was the day. Like all ancients, the Israelites watched the movement of the sun (and shadow) as a mark of the passing of the day. They counted days, months, and years, and divided the nights into three watches (Jud 7:19; Ps 90:4; 119:148; Jer 51:12; Hab 2:1). So far as we know, the divisions of the day were not into exact hours; but evening and morning, midday and dawn were the usual designations. In II Kgs 20:9 (cf. Isa 38:8) mention is made of the so-called sundial of Ahaz. Careful reading of the Heb. text reveals that the sundial was steps (*ma'ălōt*) on which the shadow moved down. Though not a dial as such, yet the passing of the day could be roughly measured by how many steps the shadow had moved.

2. *Hour.* The Babylonians divided their days into 12 *beru* (the Gr. *hōra;* English "hour"). These were two of our hours in duration, for a certain Babylonian astrologer reports that at the equinox the six *bere* of the day and the six of the night were exactly equal (CAH, III, 239). There is no evidence in the OT that the Hebrews had any such hour or double hour, though by NT times the hour was well established and they had become single hours, 12 for the day and 12 for the night (Jn 11:9).

The original division of the day into 12 parts comes from the Sumero-Babylonian sexagesimal system of numbering, which some believe may have originally derived from the obvious 12 lunations of the moon through each seasonal cycle. Curiously this system survives to the present day not only in our measurement of the day in hours but hours into minutes and minutes into seconds.

3. *Week.* The next division of time, the week (*shābûa',* meaning a heptad of days), was used throughout the biblical world from time immemorial. Yet it has no connection with astronomical phenomena.

The biblical record clearly teaches that the origin of the week rests squarely on God's sovereign choice to create all things in six days and to cease from His creative work the seventh, and His subsequent command to man to emulate Him in His labors. So the week as a divider of time was strictly a religious matter having no other basis. The period from sabbath to sabbath in the NT is called a *sabbaton* (Mt 28:1), which word derives from the Heb. *shabbāt,* meaning "rest," rather than *sheba'* meaning "seven." The Israelites had other periods of time in their religious calendar which were based on the seven cycle, such as the seven sabbaths from the Day of Atonement to the Feast of Pentecost (Lev 23:15-16), and the seven heptads of years which measured the time to the year of jubilee when debts were cancelled and bond servants were freed (Lev 25:8ff.).

4. *Month.* The common Heb. word for "month" was *ḥōdesh,* which referred to the renewal of the moon. Watching carefully for the first sign of the moon's renewal, the Israelites celebrated the beginning of each month with the blowing of trumpets (Num 10:10; 29:1). Hence, the Heb. month was wholly lunar. This meant that there was a fraction over 29 days in each month, making 12 months plus some extra days in each solar year. Being agriculturalists, the Israelites recognized this discrepancy and made up for it by intercalating, that is, putting in an extra month when needed. The Jews today still intercalate in their religious calendar, having a second Adar at regular intervals. The Egyptians were pioneers in nonlunar months which we have inherited through the Romans.

The names of the months in the Heb. calendar were borrowed from the Babylonians after the Exile. Before this the months were usually numbered, although during the building of Solomon's temple Phoenician month names were used (Zif, Ethanim, and Bul, I Kgs 6:1, 38; 8:2) because Phoenician artisans were doing the work. In the earliest times the Hebrews undoubtedly had various agricultural menologies (lists of month names). Abib, the first month of the year, was in the spring and marked the time of the Passover. After the Jews adopted the Babylonian system, the first month of the year came in the fall. The little inscription discovered at Gezer in 1908 represents a local agricultural menology of 12 months used by simple folk to mark the passing of the various crop seasons. *See* Calendar.

5. *Year.* As the Heb. name for month derived from the renewal of the moon, the word for year seems to be derived from the change of the seasons (BDB, p. 1039). Unlike the Egyptians who had a solar year based on observation of the star Sirius, the Hebrews with agricultural simplicity watched for the seasonal change to keep their lunar year correct, intercalating when necessary.

For longer periods of time, the Bible does not divide into decades and centuries but uses terms in common with Near Eastern culture. For example, a period used to measure a lengthy span of service or servitude is 40 years (Jud 3:11; I Sam 4:18; Mesha Inscription, line 8, ANET, p. 320). Daniel in prophetic context uses the heptad of years and 70 heptads to divide time into periods before the consummation of the ages (Dan 9:24-27). John in the Apocalypse tells of the final thousand year reign of Christ following Daniel's last heptad of years (Rev 20:4). Such a thousand year span has ancient literary tradition (Ps 90:4), although there is no evidence that the Hebrews ever reckoned with such large eras of time in daily practice.

The passing of long periods of time was often measured in generations (Deut 32:7; *see* Generation). Adding generation to generation is the Heb. way (*dōr wādōr*) of expressing an aeon of time. Such aeons expressed the concept of eternity both in the NT (Gr. *aiōnios*) and in the OT (Heb. *'ōlām*). The psalmist parallels a thousand generations to an *'ōlām* (Ps 105:8). That undoubtedly means "forever," for it is referring to God's faithfulness.

E. B. S.

Other terms and expressions. "Dawn" or "dawning" signifies the beginning of the day when activity can begin (Josh 6:15), literally "when the dawn arose" (Gen 19:15; etc.). Heb. *shaḥar,* KJV "morning," is better translated "dawn" as in Neh 4:21; Ps 139:9; Isa 58:8; Joel 2:2; etc. (all NASB).

"Even, evening, eventide" are KJV renderings of Heb. *'ereb* and Gr. *opse* or *opsia* and *hespera.* The terms have several meanings: (1) late afternoon, when shadows lengthen (Jer 6:4) and women go to the well (Gen 24:11); (2) sunset (Lev 22:6–7, NASB), at which time the Jewish day began; (3) twilight, the period between sunset and dark (Prov 7:9; Gen 29:23). The third of these was evidently the original meaning of the Heb. expression "between the two evenings," the time when the lamps were lit in the tabernacle (Ex 30:8, NASB and marg.) and the time of the slaying of the Passover lamb (Ex 12:6, NASB and marg.). According to Deut 16:6, this took place "at even, at the going down of the sun." On the other hand, the fact that the Passover was sacrificed on the 14th of the month, not after sunset that began the 15th, caused the rabbis in later times to interpret the expression as meaning between the declining of the sun and sunset. By this exegesis the time was extended to allow for the various ceremonies, and the lamb was offered from the 9th to the 11th hour, *c.* 3:00–5:00 P.M. (Jos *Ant.* xiv.4.3; *Wars* vi.9.3).

"Midday" is an alternate term for noon (Neh 8:3). One Heb. term, *ṣohŏrayim,* a dual form, means "double brightness" (I Kgs 18:29); it is usually translated "noon" (see below). Saul of Tarsus was converted at midday, the brightest part of the day, when a far greater light shone on him (Acts 26:13; cf. 22:6, 11).

"Midnight" (Heb. *ḥăṣî hallayᵉlâ*) means literally "half of the night" (Ex 12:29; Jud 16:3; Ruth 3:8). The ancients thought of midnight more as the middle of the night (I Kgs 3:20) rather than as an exact hour (12:00 P.M.). The Lord struck all the firstborn in Egypt "about midnight" (Ex 11:4), and the psalmist rose at midnight to praise God (Ps 119:62). The Gr. *mesonuktion* was perhaps more precise, referring to the midnight watch (Mk 13:35). At Troas Paul continued preaching until midnight (Acts 20:7).

"Moment" is the translation of several Heb. and Gr. words used to designate a very small interval of time. Like the English word moment, they do not indicate a measurable period but only imply its swift passing. The Heb. *rega'* means "wink of an eye," and is used to describe the sudden coming of God in judgment (Ex 33:5) or the swiftly passing triumph of the wicked (Job 21:13). It is also used of the sorrows of the righteous (Ps 30:5; Isa 26:20) and of God's ceaseless, moment-by-moment care (Isa 27:3). In the NT the Gr. is similar. The word *stigmē* is a point of time, the flashing vision which Satan gave to Christ of the world's kingdoms (Lk 4:5). In II Cor 4:17 Paul calls our present "light afflictions" only momentary (*parautika*). The Lord will return and we shall be changed in a moment (*atomos,* "indivisible"), so short a period it cannot be measured (I Cor 15:51–52). *See* Twinkling.

"Morning" is the translation of Heb. *bōqer* (over 200 times in the OT), and of Gr. *prōios,* "early," and *orthros,* "dawn, early morning." Jesus was known to arise in the early morning, a great while before day, to go out by Himself to pray (Mk 1:35). In the early morning the sky appeared red on a stormy day (Mt 16:3). Both Jesus and the apostles taught in the temple early in the morning (Lk 21:38; Acts 5:21). The Sanhedrin could not hold a formal session until daybreak (Mk 15:1). Jesus had already risen before the women came to the tomb very early in the morning just after the sun had risen (Mk 16:2). The risen Christ appeared on the shore of Galilee so early in the morning that the night-time fishermen could not discern His features (Jn 21:4). Our idea of mid-morning is indicated by the expression "when the sun is hot" (I Sam 11:9; Neh 7:3).

"Night" (Heb. *layᵉlâ,* Gr. *nyx*) is the period between sunset and sunrise, especially the hours of darkness. The alternation of day and night was divinely ordained (Gen 1:5, 14, 16; Jer 33:20, 25). Time was normally counted by so many days and nights (Gen 7:4, 12; Ex 24:18; I Sam 30:12; I Kgs 19:8; Job 2:13; Jon 1:17). The beginning of the night was called "evening" and its end "dawn" (see above); "twilight" (Heb. *neshep*) was the period of semidarkness after sunset (I Sam 30:17; II Kgs 7:5, 7; Job 3:9; 24:15) and before dawn (Job 7:4 "till morning twilight" NEB; Ps 119:147, lit., "I rise to meet [Thee] in the pre-dawn twilight"). The night was divided into watches (Ps 63:6; 90:4; 119:148; Lam 2:19; Lk 12:38; cf. Isa 21:11–12, NASB and marg.). Apparently the Israelites had three (the night watch; "the middle watch," Jud 7:19; "the morning watch," Ex 14:24; I Sam 11:11), and the Graeco-Roman system four watches (Jos *Ant.* xviii.9.6; Mt 14:25; cf. the four groups of soldiers guarding Peter, Acts 12:4), called evening, midnight, cockcrowing, and morning (Mk 13:35). Roman army officers also designated the time of night by hours (Acts 23:23). *See* Night.

"Noonday" or "noon" (Heb. *ṣōhar*) was not just a point of time but a period, as is indicated by the phrase in Isa 16:3, "in the midst of the noonday." The noon period was known as "the heat of the day," the time for a midday rest (II Sam 4:5; I Kgs 20:16; cf. Gen 18:1; I Sam 11:11), probably lasting from *c.* 10:00 A.M. to *c.* 2:00 P.M. It came between the "morning" and the time of the evening sacrifice (I Kgs 18:26–29). It was a resting time for flocks (Song 1:7) and one of the three times of daily prayer (Ps 55:17; Acts 10:9; Dan 6:10; cf. morning prayer, Ps 5:3; 88:13; evening prayer, Acts 3:1; 10:30). *See* Midday above.

The word "season" is used in the Bible both of climatic divisions of the year and periods of harvest, and of definite shorter periods of time as opposed to the longer "ages" (*see* Time). In the former sense God governs the seasons by the sun and moon (Gen 1:14–16; Ps 104:19), and spoke to Job of the "season" or zodiacal period of a constellation (Job 38:32).

The climatic seasons in Palestine are principally the rainy season (Nov.–Apr.) and the dry season (May–Oct.). The early or former rain (Joel 2:23; Jas 5:7; Jer 5:24) softens the sun-baked soil to permit plowing and sowing, and the latter rain (Feb.–Mar.) matures the grain before barley harvest in the spring (Deut 11:14). God promised to give these rains "in their season" (Lev 26:4, ASV; Ezk 34:26). Therefore crops were harvested in regular seasons (Job 5:26; Ps 1:3;Hos2:9; Mt 21:41; Acts 14:17; Gal 6:9), and each Jewish festival was kept at its "appointed season" (Heb. *mô'ēd;* e.g., Num 9:2–3). *See* Calendar; Festivals.

In the NT the phrase "the times and the seasons" (Gr. *hoi chronoi kai hoi kairoi*) has an eschatological sense referring to the events which must be completed before the second coming of Christ and the restoration of the kingdom to Israel (I Thess 5:1; Acts 1:7). The expression may originate in Dan 2:21. D. Edmond Hiebert believes that "times" (*chronoi*) designates the chronological periods which may intervene before Christ returns, while "seasons" (*kairoi*) indicates the critical nature of the occurrences which distinguish these "times"; hence his rendering "the eras and the crises" (*The Thessalonian Epistles,* Chicago: Moody, 1971, pp. 208f.). *See* Times of the Gentiles.

In prophetic passages of the Bible "time" seems to be equivalent to "year." In apocalyptic passages is found the expression "a time, and times, and half a time" (Rev 12:14; Dan 7:25; 12:7). It means the eschatological period of $1 + 2 + \frac{1}{2} = 3\frac{1}{2}$ years, during which the Antichrist is to reign on the earth. That three and a half years is the length of time to be understood is proved by this period being equated with the 42 months of Rev 11:2; 13:5 and the 1260 days (42 months of 30 days each) of Rev 11:3; 12:6). In other passages a "day" may be designated to represent a literal year (Num 14:34; Ezk 4:6), and in Dan 9:24–27 a week represents a period of seven years.

For "twilight" and "watches" see above under "Night."

See Time; Calendar. For historical periods of time *see* Chronology, OT; Chronology, NT.

Bibliography. Roger T. Beckwith, "The Day, Its Divisions and Its Limits, in Biblical Thought," EQ, XLIII (1971), 218–227. Jack Finegan, *Light from the Ancient Past,* 2nd ed., Princeton: Princeton Univ. Press, 1959, pp. 552–598.

J. R.

TIMES, OBSERVER OF. *See* Magic.

TIMES OF THE GENTILES. The period of history referred to by Christ in Lk 21:24 in which the Gentiles will be in the supremacy. During this time God will deal with Jew and Gentile alike so far as salvation is concerned, because the middle wall of partition has been broken down and there is one Church of those saved by grace through faith (Eph 2:13–15). But during this period the Gentiles will be the great world rulers. It is variously said to extend from the fall of Jerusalem in 586 B.C., or from its later fall in A.D. 70, till the full restoration of the city of Jerusalem under the Messiah.

Paul speaks of the "fulness of the Gentiles" coming in and says when the time of Gentile supremacy is completed "all Israel shall be saved" (Rom 11:25–26). Zechariah describes the repentance of Israel when Christ appears at the second coming (Zech 12:10–11), and Isaiah asks, "Shall a land be born in one day? Shall a nation be brought forth in one moment?" (66:8, RSV). After Christ's return, the regenerated nation and the resurrected saints whom Christ will bring with Him will rule together with Him as their Saviour and King (Dan 7:22, 27; Zech 14:5; Mt 19:28; I Thess 3:13; Jude 14; Rev 20:4, 6).

R. A. K.

TIMNA (tĭm'nȧ)

1. A daughter of Seir the Horite and sister of Lotan (Gen 36:22; I Chr 1:39). She became a concubine of Esau's son Eliphaz and bore Amalek to him (Gen 36:12).

2. A son of Eliphaz (I Chr 1:36) and a chieftain (KJV "duke") of Edom (Gen 36:40; I Chr 1:51; spelled Timnah in KJV). The capital of Qataban in S Arabia was named *Timna'*, perhaps going back to a tribal name received from this biblical person. Also the location of some 2nd mil. B.C. copper mines is called Timna, 15 miles N of Ezion-geber, likely named after the Edomite leader.

TIMNAH (tĭm'nȧ)

1. A town near Beth-shemesh on the northern border of Judah (Josh 15:10), now identified with Tell el-Batashi in the Sorek Valley (Y. Aharoni, "The Northern Boundary of Judah," PEQ, XC [1958], 27–31). Note the variant forms of the name: construct, Timnath; locative, Timnatha.

The town had been assigned to the tribe of

Dan as a residence (Josh 19:43); but it is evident that they failed to conquer it (cf. Jud 1:34), and in Samson's day it was occupied by Philistines (Jud 14:2). It was there that Samson made his first marriage and propounded his famous riddle about the lion and the honey (Jud 14:1ff.). Doubtless Timnah was incorporated into Judah after David's victories. When Ahaz was under pressure from Samaria and Damascus, the Philistines used the opportunity to recapture Timnah and several neighboring towns (II Chr 28:18). Hezekiah may have regained it later, but it was lost to Sennacherib in 701 B.C. (ANET, p. 288).

2. A town in the hill country of Judah (Josh 15:57), probably Khirbet at-Tabbana, ten miles W of Bethlehem, if it can be associated with the Timnah (KJV, Timnath) of Gen 38:12–14 which is mentioned in connection with Adullam and Enaim. This was probably one of the cities fortified by Bacchides to pacify Judea (I Macc 9:50; *see* Timnath-serah).

3. An improper spelling for Timna, a chief of Edom (Gen 36:40; I Chr 1:51, KJV; *see* Timna 2).

A. F. R.

TIMNATH. *See* Timnah.

TIMNATH-HERES. *See* Timnath-serah.

TIMNATH-SERAH (tĭm'năth-sēr'*ȧ*). A town in the hill country of Ephraim, probably Khirbet Tibna, which was given to Joshua as his inheritance (Josh 19:50) and where he was buried (Josh 24:30). Tibna is on the old Roman road from Caesarea to Jerusalem, *c.* 12 miles NE of Lydda (Lod) and 12 miles SW of Shiloh. It is referred to as Timnath-heres (hēr'ēs), the second element probably being written backward by mistake (Jud 2:9). In the last days of Jewish independence before Judea became completely subjugated to Rome, it had become the administrative center of a Judean toparchy (Pliny, *Natural History,* v. 70; Jos *Wars* iii.3.5; *Ant.* xiv.11.2), replacing the former center of Aramatha (I Macc 11:34). It formerly was identified with the *Thamna* fortified by Bacchides along with several other Judean towns for the purpose of pacifying Judea (I Macc 9:50). However, Michael Avi-Yonah has shown that this was more likely Timna 2 (*q.v.; Historical Geography of Palestine,* Jerusalem: Bialik Inst., 1962, pp. 36–37 [Hebrew]).

A. F. R.

TIMNITE (tĭm'nīt). A Gentilic epithet used by the Philistines to describe the father-in-law of Samson (Jud 15:6) and which is derived from Timnah, the place of his residence (Jud 14:1–2, 5; KJV, Timnath). Timnah was formerly a Danite village on the northern border of Judah near Beth-shemesh (Josh 15:10; 19:43) and has been identified with Tell el-Batashi in the Wadi eṣ-Ṣarar.

TIMON (tī'mŏn). One of the seven men chosen by the church in Jerusalem and consecrated by the apostles to have oversight of a more equitable distribution of the daily rations. Timon was no doubt a Hellenist, i.e., a Greek-speaking Jew, to judge by the Gr. character of his name. He shared with his associates in office a favorable reputation and is described as Spirit-filled and wise (Acts 6:5).

TIMOTHEUS. *See* Timothy.

TIMOTHY (tĭm'ō-thĭ). From the affectionate way in which Paul wrote of him, it would seem that Timothy was his favorite disciple. Timothy's father was a Greek, but his mother Eunice and his grandmother Lois were Jewesses (II Tim 1:5). They were probably converted during Paul's first visit to Derbe and Lystra (Acts 14:6–22). It is generally accepted that Timothy was born in Lystra (Acts 16:1–2). When Paul returned to that region on his second missionary journey after a couple of years, he was so impressed with young Timothy that he resolved to take him with him, probably to replace John Mark.

Timothy had excellent spiritual training under his mother and grandmother, and was "well reported of by the brethren" (Acts 16:1–2; II Tim 1:5; 3:14–15). Strangely enough, he had never been circumcised, perhaps because his father was a Greek. But the father had little to do with his son's religious education and may have died early. There were certain prophetic indications that the young man was destined to important service in the cause of Christ (I Tim 1:18; 4:14). When Paul joined the local elders in laying hands on Timothy he received a charismatic gift, probably to equip him for his ministry as an evangelist (II Tim 1:6; 4:5). Before ordaining him, however, the apostle circumcised him, since he was going to labor in regions where many Jews dwelt. Normally, Paul held strongly that circumcision was unnecessary for the Christian, and strenuously opposed the demands of Judaizers that Gentiles should be circumcised before admission to church membership. In the present instance, however, he had Timothy submit to the rite so as not to arouse unnecessary prejudice among the many Jews to whom he would proclaim the gospel.

Paul, Silvanus, and Timothy traveled northwestward across the high tableland of Asia Minor and descended to Troas. There Paul had his significant vision of "the man of Macedonia" beckoning him to "come over and help" them (Acts 16:9). It was a call to evangelize Europe. They were joined by Luke, and hastened across the Aegean Sea to Neapolis.

There is no mention of Timothy in connection with the subsequent events in Philippi and Thessalonica, but it is virtually certain that he was in the company. He is next found at Berea where he was left by Paul to continue the work (Acts 17:10–14). Timothy later followed Paul to Athens and from there he was sent back to Thessalonica to help the brethren. Having fulfilled the mission, Timothy joined Paul at Corinth bringing a good report (I Thess 3:6–7).

Timothy was ministering to the church at Ephesus when Paul wrote I Timothy to him. Here the main street of ancient Ephesus passes the Greek agora on the left and the theater on the right. Foto Esat Balim

As the name of Timothy appears in the salutations of both the epistles to the Thessalonians written from Corinth, and as he preached much in that city (II Cor 1:19), it is clear that he labored in Corinth with Paul for some time.

The next mention in Acts of Timothy is in connection with his ministry to Paul during his long stay at Ephesus on Paul's third missionary tour (Acts 19:22). As there is no record of his ministering elsewhere in the intervening period, he probably accompanied Paul from Corinth to Ephesus, and then by ship to Caesarea on the journey to Jerusalem as recorded in Acts 18:18-23. After returning with Paul to Ephesus, Timothy was sent on a special mission across the Aegean Sea with Paul's first epistle to the Corinthian church (I Cor 4:17; 16:10-11). He evidently did come back to Ephesus as planned (I Cor 16:11), and then was sent with Erastus into Macedonia to prepare the way for a new stage of Paul's third journey (Acts 19:22; I Cor 16:5).

Timothy was with Paul in Macedonia when II Corinthians was written (1:1). He was again in Corinth with Paul when Romans was written (16:21). Then Timothy, with others, preceded Paul on his way back through Macedonia to Jerusalem, waiting for him at Troas (Acts 20:4-5). Timothy is not heard of between Paul's arrest at Jerusalem and his arrival at Rome, but he was with the apostle in Rome when Colossians, Philippians, and Philemon were written (Col 1:1; Phil 1:1; Phm 1). Paul expressed his intention of sending Timothy to Philippi in order to express his concern for the believers in that city (Phil 2:19-23).

During Paul's period of freedom after his first imprisonment, he left Timothy at Ephesus to attend to necessary church affairs (I Tim 1:3). The tradition that he was the first bishop of Ephesus is unsound, for his stay there was only temporary. As the apostle John soon afterward resided there permanently, Timothy would not have been the ruling elder or bishop.

In his last imprisonment in Rome, Paul had a tender yearning to see Timothy and he urged him to come "before winter." Where Timothy was then we do not know. Neither do we know whether he arrived before Paul's martyrdom (II Tim 4:6-9).

The numerous exhortations and injunctions to Timothy have caused many to believe that he was timid (cf. also I Cor 16:10-11) and needed Paul's support. The perilous times of Nero's reign called for exhortations to constancy, especially as Timothy was young and not robust in health (I Tim 4:12; 5:23). On the other hand, none of Paul's co-workers was more active than he, and none more trusted and beloved by the apostle (Phil 2:19-22).

Tradition alleges that he, like Paul, died as a martyr.

A. M. R.

TIMOTHY, FIRST EPISTLE TO. The epistles to Timothy and Titus are classed as Pastoral Epistles. The introductory matters pertaining to the three letters are considered together. *See also* Pastoral Epistles.

Genuineness

The authenticity of the epistles to Timothy and Titus is very strongly supported by external evidence. Testimony is given by the Peshito (Syriac) Version (2nd cen.), the Old Latin Version (2nd cen.), the Muratorian Fragment (A.D. 170), Theophilus of Antioch (A.D. 181), Irenaeus (A.D. 178). Clement of Rome (A.D. 93-95), Clement of Alexandria (A.D. 194), Tertullian (A.D. 200), and many more. That Gnostic heretics rejected these books proves nothing, for their settled policy was to cut out all Scripture that contradicted their own views.

Only at the beginning of the 19th cen. was the universal view of the church challenged as to the Pauline authorship and genuineness of these books. Schmidt and Schleiermacher began the attack, followed by Eichhorn, De Wette, and F. C. Baur. Then came H. J. Holtzmann, P. N. Harrison, and M. Dibelius.

Objections alleged have been:

1. That vocabulary and style are different from the other Pauline epistles; that, for example, they contain 165 classical Gr. words not found elsewhere in Paul. But no writer exhausts his vocabulary all at once, and vocabularies are enlarged in course of time. In Rome Paul would be visited by cultured Greeks and he may have increased his knowledge of classical authors. In the Pastorals, too, Paul was writing to close friends with an intimate knowledge of Gr. Changes in vocabulary and style are not surprising. After the rise of Karl Barth in Europe the style and terminology of many theologians changed drastically. Why deny the apostle the right to vary his style a little? The general tone and sentiment of the Pastorals, as well as their words and style, remained, however, markedly similar to that in earlier epistles.

2. That the references to heresies in the Pastorals prove the letters must have been as late as mid-2nd cen. Passages such as I Tim 1:4 and 6:20 are alleged to refer to Gnosticism. But it is known that the first manifestations of Gnosticism (*q.v.*) came early. Some nominally Jewish Christians were becoming very degenerate in morals. At the same time Gnostic tendencies were growing, and Paul's warnings against false teachings were perfectly in keeping with such a situation.

3. That the ecclesiastical organization in the Pastorals is much later than the Apostolic Age. In reality the church organization was primitive. The terms bishop and presbyter (or elder) are still interchangeable. There were no diocesan bishops before the late 2nd cen. W. F. Albright (*New Horizons in Biblical Research,* London: Oxford, 1966, p. 49) has shown that the NT office of ruling elder closely follows that of the *m*[e]*baqqer* who presided over the Qumran community, according to the Dead Sea Scrolls (*q.v.*).

4. That the data in the Pastorals cannot be fitted into the narrative in Acts. But Philemon (v. 22) and Philippians (2:24) show that Paul was fully expecting his release from the first imprisonment in Rome. Clement of Rome (A.D. 95), the Muratorian Fragment (A.D. 171), and Eusebius all declare that this actually took place. Ancient tradition said he then went to Spain, and the Pastorals strongly point to later journeys in the East as Paul had intended (I Tim 1:3; Tit 1:5). He hoped to winter in Nicopolis (Tit 3:12) but instead went to Rome, probably as a prisoner.

The Pastorals express the urgent exhortations which Paul wished to give to his beloved helpers in time of danger, toward the end of his life. No forger could have invented the intimate personal touches of these epistles.

Date

The Pastorals show strong evidence of having been written in the reign of Nero and at short intervals, probably between A.D. 62 and 65.

Outline

I. Salutation, 1:1–2
II. Paul's Commandment to Timothy, 1:3–20
  A. To teach only sound doctrine, 1:3–11
  B. To observe Paul as God's pattern, 1:12–17
  C. To wage successful warfare, 1:18–20
III. Exhortation for Proper Order in Public Worship, 2:1–15
  A. Prayers for all people and for rulers, 2:1–8
  B. Conduct of the women, 2:9–15
IV. Requirements for Church Officers, 3:1–13
  A. For elders, 3:1–7
  B. For deacons and deaconesses, 3:8–13
V. Proper Ministerial Conduct in the Church, 3:14–6:19
  A. Because the church is the pillar and bulwark of the truth, 3:14–16
  B. Because of demon-inspired doctrines, 4:1–5
  C. Disciplining oneself unto godliness, 4:6–12
  D. Giving attention to public ministry and teaching, 4:13–16
  E. Instructions for men and women, especially widows, in the church, 5:1–16
  F. Rewarding, disciplining, and ordaining elders, 5:17–25
  G. Instructing Christian slaves, 6:1–2
  H. Warning about the love of money, 6:3–19
VI. Closing Exhortation to Avoid False "Science" (*Gnōsis*), 6:20–21

Bibliography. J. H. Bernard, "The Pastoral Epistles" (1899), *Cambridge Greek Testament,* Cambridge: Univ. Press, 1922 reprint. B. S. Easton, *The Pastoral Epistles,* New York: Scribner's, 1948. Donald Guthrie, *The Pastoral Epistles,* TNTC, Grand Rapids: Eerdmans, 1957. P. N. Harrison, *The Problem of the Pastoral Epistles,* Oxford: Univ. Press, 1921. William Hendriksen, *Exposition of the Pastoral Epistles,* NTC, Grand Rapids: Baker, 1957. D. Edmond Hiebert, *First Timothy,* EBC, Chicago: Moody, 1957; *Second Timothy,* 1958; *Titus and Philemon,* 1957. H. A. Kent, Jr., *The Pastoral Epistles,* Chicago: Moody, 1958. H. P. Liddon, *Explanatory Analysis of St. Paul's First Epistle to Timothy,* London: Longmans, Green, 1897. Walter Lock, *A Critical and Exegetical Commentary on the Pastoral Epistles,* ICC, New York: Scribner's, 1924; 1936 reprint. E. K. Simpson, *The Pastoral Epistles,* Grand Rapids: Eerdmans, 1954. Theodor Zahn, *Introduction to the New Testament,* Vol. II, translated 1909, Grand Rapids: Kregel, 1953 reprint.

A. M. R.

TIMOTHY, SECOND EPISTLE TO. This epistle was written from Rome where Paul was a prisoner. He knew that his end was at hand (II Tim 4:6–7) and urged his beloved Timothy to hasten to his side. In the Neronian persecution many Christians were being hurried to the most brutal deaths which could be invented for them. Even when he wrote I Timothy and the letter to Titus, Paul must have known the character of Nero and the dangers which might come to leading Christians from such a ruler.

Written under these circumstances, it was natural that the Pastorals should be urgent and appealing, and go directly to the point. Hence, the pressing calls to Timothy to be a good soldier of Christ. In that awful time, he must strain every nerve to fight the good fight. It is not necessary to assume, as some do, that all these exhortations imply definite weakness or timidity in Timothy, although he seems to have had a tendency in this direction (*see* Timothy).

From the Pastorals it is clear that Paul had recently visited Crete, Miletus, Troas, Macedonia, and Corinth. From Corinth a short journey would take him to Nicopolis in Epirus whither he had summoned Titus (Tit 3:12). There Paul may have been arrested at the outbreak of the Neronian persecution in A.D. 64.

In Rome he was forsaken by false friends. Only Luke was with him (II Tim 4:11). He longed for the company of the faithful Timothy in the hour of danger and possible death (II Tim 4:9).

It is known that Paul suffered martyrdom at Rome, probably in A.D. 65. Timothy too was arrested but was liberated (Heb 13:23). There is no later knowledge of him.

Outline

I. Greeting and Thanksgiving for Timothy, 1:1–5
II Paul's Charge to be Unashamed, 1:6–18
  A. The endowment of the Holy Spirit, 1:6–7
  B. Paul's example of suffering and commitment, 1:8–14
  C. Onesiphorus' steadfastness amid defections, 1:15–18
III. The Charge to be Strong, 2:1–13
  A. As a teacher, 2:2
  B. As a soldier, 2:3–4
  C. As an athlete, 2:5
  D. As a farmer, 2:6–7
  E. Because of Jesus Christ, 2:8–13
IV. The Charge to Withstand False Teaching, 2:14–3:17
  A. By right handling of the Word of truth, 2:14–18
  B. By abstaining from the pollutions of error, 2:19–22
  C. By refusing foolish speculations, 2:23
  D. By correcting others with kindness and meekness, 2:24–26
  E. By avoiding the apostates of the last days, 3:1–9
  F. By following Paul's course during persecution, 3:10–13
  G. By continuing in the inspired Scripture, 3:14–17
V. The Charge to Preach the Word, 4:1–8
  A. Because many will no longer tolerate sound doctrine, 4:1–4
  B. Because Paul's departure is at hand, 4:5–8
VI. Personal Instructions to Timothy and Conclusion, 4:9–22

Bibliography. *See* Timothy, First Epistle to.

A. M. R.

TIN. *See* Minerals and Metals.

TINKLING

1. The nominal Heb. verb *'ākas* is derived from the noun *'ekes,* "ankle ring," "bangle" (Isa 3:18) and means the tinkling or jingling sound produced by the contact of the metal anklets with one another as the women walked. Isaiah censures this type of suggestive behavior practiced by the wanton women of Jerusalem (Isa 3:16).

2. The Gr. participle *alalazon,* "clashing, clanging," modifies cymbal in I Cor 13:1 (cf. Ps 150:5), where the gift of tongues without love is compared to a noisy gong or a clanging cymbal.

TIPHSAH (tĭf'sȧ)

1. A town situated on the right bank of the Euphrates *c.* 40 miles W of its confluence with the Balikh River and which constituted the extreme NE boundary of the kingdom of Solomon (I Kgs 4:24). Later called Thapsacus, it guarded an important river crossing where Cyrus the Younger and Alexander forded the Euphrates with their armies.

2. A town sacked by the Israelitic king Menahem (II Kgs 15:16). Since it is clearly associated with Tirzah in the territory of Manasseh, it is not to be identified with the city on the Euphrates. However, the variant readings of the name in the Gr. versions and the otherwise singularity of its reference have led the RSV to adopt the Lucianic reading *Taphōe* and to identify the name with Tappuah, a town in the N of Ephraim not far from Shiloh (cf. Josh 16:8; 17:7f.).

TIRAS (tī'rȧs). One of the descendants of Japheth, the son of Noah (Gen 10:2; I Chr 1:5). The eponym appears to refer to an Aegean sea-people on the W coast of Asia Minor, and is plausibly identified with the Tursha (Tw-rw-š3), who are mentioned in Egyptian inscriptions of the 13th cen. B.C. Rameses III lists them as one of the Peoples of the Sea who invaded Syria and Palestine on their way to attack Egypt. They are the Tyrsenians (later, Tyrrhenians) of Gr. sources (Homer; Herodotus I.57, 94) in which they are described as sea pirates of the Aegean. This agrees with the notice in the Book of Jubilees (9:13) that Tiras comprehended four great islands in the midst of the sea. *See* Nations.

TIRATHITES (tī'rȧ-thīts). A scribal family of Kenite origin dwelling at Jabez (I Chr 2:55).

TIRE. An archaic English word used for dress or adornment. Three words are so translated.

1. Heb. *yāṭab,* to attire, dress, or adorn the head or hair (II Kgs 9:30).

2. Heb. *pe'ēr,* some sort of headdress or covering; RSV translates "turban" (Ezk 24:17, 23; 44:18; KJV "bonnets").

3. Heb. *śahărōn,* crescent-shaped ornaments or amulets, "round tires like the moon" (Isa 3:18); RSV has "crescents."

TIRHAKAH (tûr-hā'kȧ). The Egyptian Taharka, third king of (Ethiopian) Dynasty XXV of Egypt. He is first mentioned as "Tirhakah king of Ethiopia" leading Egyptian forces against Sennacherib (II Kgs 19:9). The latter claimed to have defeated the Egyptian chariotry and cavalry at Eltekeh in 701 B.C. (ANET, pp. 287 f.) while Jerusalem was being besieged. Dates on Apis stelae indicate that Tirhakah began to reign in 689 B.C., continuing until 664 B.C. Five large stelae excavated at Kawa in the Sudan clarify other broken stelae of his. It is now certain that he was 20 years old when his brother Pharaoh Shebitku (701–690 B.C.) summoned him from Nubia to Thebes to assist. not that he was 20 when he became king (Alan Gardiner, *Egypt of the Pharaohs,* Oxford: Clarendon Press, 1961, pp. 342 ff.). Thus Tirhakah was old enough to lead an army from Egypt as the representative to his brother, King Shebitku, in 701. Ancient Oriental writers, as well as modern, frequently referred to persons by titles acquired later than the period being described (K. A. Kitchen, *Ancient Orient and Old Testament,* Chicago: Inter-Varsity, 1966, pp. 82-84).

In 670 B.C. Esarhaddon, son of Sennacherib, led an army to Egypt. He boasts that he conquered Egypt, wounded its king, Tirhakah, five times with arrowshots, and ruled over all his land (ANET, p. 290). When Esarhaddon died, Tirhakah again returned to Egypt. Ashurbanipal met his army at Kar-Baniti in the Delta and defeated it. Then Tirhakah, who had remained in Memphis, fled to Thebes. After his plot with some of the Egyptian governors to revolt against Assyria was thwarted, Tirhakah retired to Ethiopia.

R. E. H.

TIRHANAH (tẽr-hā'n*ȧ*). A son of Caleb by his concubine Maacah (I Chr 2:48).

TIRIA (tĭr'ĭ-*ȧ*). One of the sons of Jehaleleel of the Judahite family of Caleb (I Chr 4:16).

TIRSHATHA (tûr-shā'th*ȧ*). The KJV transliteration of Heb. *tirshāthā',* honorific title of the Persian governor of a province, given to Zerubbabel (Ezr 2:63) and Nehemiah (Neh 7:65, 70; 8:9; 10:1) as governors of Judah. It is from the Persian *tarshta* meaning "the feared one," equivalent to "his excellency."

TIRZAH (tûr'z*ȧ*)

1. The youngest of the five daughters of Zelophehad of the tribe of Manasseh (Num 26:33; 27:1; 36:11; Josh 17:3).

2. A royal city of the Canaanites, one of the 31 subdued by Joshua (Josh 12:24). Situated in the western tribal territory of Manasseh, it superseded Shechem as capital of the northern kingdom (I Kgs 14:17) and was the royal residence of the kings of Israel from Jeroboam to Omri. After Omri moved the capital to Samaria, Tirzah faded into insignificance in spite of its beauty and the charm of its location. Its last mention is in the time of Menahem *c.* 752 B.C. (II Kgs 15:14, 16). The word Tirzah may mean "delight"; the place must have been noted for its beauty, since Solomon compared his beautiful Shulamite woman to the beauty of Tirzah (Song 6:4).

In Tirzah reigned Jeroboam I, Nadab his son, Baasha, Elah, and Zimri (I Kgs 14:17, 20; 15:21, 33; 16:6-9, 15). Baasha was buried here. Here Elah was assassinated while "drinking himself drunk" in the house of his steward, and likely was buried here. Zimri was besieged here by Omri and perished in the flames of his palace rather than fall into Omri's hands. Tirzah thus maintained its leadership in Israel for almost 40 years, only to be superseded by Samaria.

House remains of the days of Omri at Tell el-Far'ah, probable Tirzah. HFV

Today the site is uncertain, although archaeological evidence seems to favor the northern Tell el-Far'ah *c.* seven miles NE of Nablus and Shechem. It lies at the head of the well-watered and fertile Wadi Far'ah, the only wide pass leading from the Jordan valley (near Succoth) into the heart of Canaan. This was almost certainly the route which Abraham and Jacob took in traveling to Shechem from Mesopotamia.

Excavations at Tell el-Far'ah during nine seasons between 1946 and 1960 unearthed well-preserved remains from the Chalcolithic, Early Bronze, and Iron Ages. In the Israelite level dating to the time of Solomon, Jeroboam I, and Baasha (*c.* 950-885 B.C.), the houses were quite uniform in size, showing there was no great social inequality among the inhabitants. This level (Stratum III) was violently destroyed by fire, corresponding to Zimri's death in the burning of his own palace (I Kgs 16:18). An intermediate stratum revealed walls of new buildings. One large structure had been started, but it never rose above the foundations and the thresholds. De Vaux suggests this was a palace for Omri left unfinished when he transferred his capital to Samaria and abandoned Tirzah. The 8th cen. B.C. level had a large two-story building near the city gate, perhaps the residence of Menahem, if he was the governor of Tirzah. This city was destroyed at the time of the Assyrian invasion, and the last period was a poor, unfortified city, finally abandoned *c.* 600 B.C. (R. de Vaux, "Tirzah," TAOTS, pp. 371-383).

R. L. D. and J. R.

TISHBITE (tĭsh'bīt). Elijah the prophet is said to be a Tishbite from Gilead (I Kgs 17:1; 21:17, 28; II Kgs 1:3, 8; 9:36). In I Kgs 17:1 the RSV, NEB, and JerusB, following the LXX, have "of Tishbe in Gilead" in place of the KJV "of the inhabitants of Gilead." The location of Tishbe(h) in Gilead is unknown. On evidence from ancient Jewish and Christian writers, some scholars place it at the modern site of Lisdib (also called el-Istib), a little E and S of Jabesh-gilead. The ruins of a Christian church and convent at this location are called Mar Ilyas. Nelson Glueck suspects a scribal error and concludes it is actually "Elijah the Jabeshite of Jabesh-gilead." *See* Elijah.

TISHRI (tĭsh'rĭ). Name of the seventh month of the Heb. calendar after the Exile. It was the first month of the civil year and during it the great festivals of Atonement and Feast of Tabernacles fell, the Day of Atonement occurring on the tenth. This month coincides with parts of September and October of the current international calendar. *See* Calendar.

TITHE. The Heb. word *'āśar,* "to tithe," is derived from the word signifying "ten," which also means "to be rich." The basic principle in tithing is the acknowledgment that everything rightly belongs to God, including a man's own property, and that men are only stewards. The tithe is a token brought to honor the Lord and to recognize Him as owner of all.

The custom of tithing was common among Semitic peoples, and antedated the Mosaic law. Abraham gave to Melchizedek one-tenth of all the spoils taken from Chedorlaomer (Gen 14:20; cf. Heb 7:4-10). The way in which this is mentioned seems to indicate that it was an established custom. Jacob's vow (Gen 28:22) adds weight to this view.

Tithes in Israel consisted of one-tenth of all yearly produce and of the increase of flocks and cattle. This was declared to be sacred to Yahweh as rent or feudal fee to Him who was really the owner of the land. Certain scriptures suggest that these tithes consisted of one-tenth of all that remained after "the first of the firstfruits" and the priestly heave offering had been separated (Ex 23:19; Deut 26:1ff.). Since the law did not set the amount to be given as the firstfruits, some regard the tithing regulations as a defining of the amounts to be given. Others see the tithes as additional to the firstfruits. Jewish sources indicate that the second thought is true, and that the "first of the firstfruits" generally amounted to one-fiftieth of the produce.

In the Pentateuch, legislation as to tithes was as follows:

1. Lev 27:30-33. One-tenth of all produce (crops, fruit, oil, wine) and of all animals was to be devoted to the Lord. The tithe of the produce of the land could be redeemed if one-fifth of its value was added. The animal tithe was not redeemable. The increase of the herd was counted, and every tenth animal was reckoned holy to the Lord. This was in keeping with the pre-Sinaitic instruction to Israel that the firstlings of the flock belong to the Lord (Ex 13:12-13). Any attempt to replace a good with a bad was punishable by the forfeit of both (Lev 27:32-33). "Whatsoever passeth under the rod" was assigned to the Levites, to do with as they pleased, since they had received no land (cf. Num 18:21-32). Out of this tithe, the Levites paid a tithe or heave offering to the priests. This had to be brought to the temple in Jerusalem. Neh 10:38 suggests that there was supervision of this division of tithes.

2. Deut 12:5-6, 11, 18 (cf. Amos 4:4). The festival tithe was one-tenth of the nine-tenths that remained. It had to be set apart and taken to Jerusalem. There it was eaten as a sacred meal by the offerer and his household, together with "the Levite within his gates." If the distance was prohibitive, the tithes could be sold and the money used for purchase of food or animals for offerings in Jerusalem (cf. Deut 14:22-27).

3. Deut 26:12-15; 14:28-29. The triennial or charity tithe given during the third year was for the Levite, the stranger, the fatherless, and the widow.

Opinions differ regarding this third tithe. According to Josephus it was actually a third tithe offered every third year, in which priests and Levites were obliged to participate. Others state that every third year the second, or festival tithe, was given to the poor at home instead of being taken to Jerusalem.

Payment of tithes was not forced; it was a matter of conscience before the Lord. The people were to perform these ordinances with all their heart and soul (Deut 26:16). Every third year a solemn declaration was to be made on the last day of the Passover: "I have done according to all that thou hast commanded me" (Deut 26:14).

I. R.

Because of Israel's negligence during the period of the judges, Levites often did not receive enough tithes to live on. As a result some began wandering in order to find some means of livelihood, and even entered idolatrous relationships (Jud 17:7-10; 18:18-20). The laws of the tithes were not meant to impose a hardship, but the additional expenses of the kingdom changed the picture. A tax of one-tenth usually had to be paid to the kings, plus terms of enforced labor (I Sam 8:11-18). Only in times of revival did the people bring their tithes faithfully and in abundance (II Chr 31:5-12; Neh 10:37-38; 12:43-47). Under foreign occupation, such as by the Romans, there was an especially heavy burden of taxes; yet in spite of this the Pharisees were scrupulously careful in the payment of their tithes (Lk 18:12). Jesus rebuked them, however, because in so doing they were taking pride in their righteous acts while neglecting the more important principles of the Mosaic law–justice and mercy and faithfulness (Mt 23:23; Lk 11:42).

Other teaching in the OT regarding the principle of tithing as stewardship may be found in

David's prayer of thanksgiving for the materials for the future temple: "All things come from Thee, and from Thy hand we have given Thee" (I Chr 29:14, NASB). The principle of honoring God from one's wealth and with a token of all one's income, followed in turn by the promise of His blessing, is taught in Prov 3:9–10. In post-Exilic times the people were robbing God by not paying their tithes and offerings. The prophetic admonition was to bring all the tithes into the temple storehouse (cf. Neh 13:12–13), and God would bless them until there was no more need (Mal 3:8–11).

Though the NT does not prescribe the tithe in a legal sense for the follower of Christ, yet he is taught to give systematically, bountifully, and cheerfully (I Cor 16:2; II Cor 9:6–7). He is commanded to preach the gospel and perform acts of deliverance without demanding payment, because he himself has freely received from the Lord (Mt 10:7–8). On the other hand, the principle that the laborer is worthy of his support is drawn from the OT and applied to the servants of the Lord (Mt 10:10; Lk 10:7; I Cor 9:7–14; I Tim 5:17–18).

Since tithing was practiced before the giving of the law of Moses, many have argued that it affords a timeless pattern for the Christian, rather than being merely a part of OT ceremonial law which has already been fulfilled. The NT believer, like the Israelite, must recognize that he is a steward (e.g., I Cor 4:1–2; *see* Occupations: Steward) and that God is owner of all.

Bibliography. B. E. Cowell, "Should a Christian Tithe?" *Footnote,* Wheaton College Graduate School, V (1965), 17–25.

J. R.

TITTLE. In the nuance of Mt 5:18 and Lk 16:17 the Gr. term *keraia,* "little horn," means a small stroke, crown, or hook which serves as an ornament to some letters of the Heb. alphabet, a serif. In rabbinical sources it is designated as "thorn" (*qôṣ, qôṣâ*), "crown" (*keter*), *and "point"* (*n^eqûdâ*). The distinctive peculiarities which differentiated, say, *dāleth* from *rēsh, bêth* from *kaph,* are not considered tittles (cf. SBK *in loco cit.*). Jot (the Heb. letter *yôdh*) and tittle form a hendiadys in Mt 5:18 which is used metaphorically to assert that the most minute detail of the Torah has an imperishable character awaiting its fulfillment. *See* Jot.

TITUS (tī'tŭs). A very highly valued friend and helper of Paul. He was probably one of Paul's converts (Tit 1:4). Although active in Christ's service, he is not mentioned in Acts but appears in II Corinthians, Galatians, II Timothy, and Titus. He accompanied Paul and Barnabas on their visit to Jerusalem to discuss with the apostles and elders the obligations of the Christian to the Mosaic law (Acts 15; Gal 2:1–4). Paul strenuously resisted the Judaizers who wanted Gentile converts to be circumcised and to observe other Jewish rites. The case of Titus (a Gentile) was a test case, and Paul won a complete victory in the council. The church was not to be in subjection to Jewish ordinances, and the gospel was to be preached freely to Jews and Gentiles (Acts 15:13–29).

An important work was done by Titus in Corinth. He is mentioned eight times in II Corinthians and the apostle refers to him as "my partner and fellow worker" (II Cor 8:23, ASV). The situation in Corinth was very unsatisfactory. Not only was there division, there was also gross immorality. Sent to that center bearing a severe letter from Paul, Titus had magnificent success. He and the Corinthians became mutually attached to one another, and his good report brought great comfort to Paul in his anxiety. Titus seems to have visited Corinth three times, superintending on two occasions the collection for the poor saints at Jerusalem (II Cor 8:6, 10–11, 22–24). He and another Christian brother carried the second epistle to Corinth (II Cor 8:18).

Titus disappears until the epistle which bears his name was written. After his first imprisonment Paul took him to Crete and, on his own departure from the island, left Titus behind to complete the work and organize the church by having elders appointed in every city (Tit 1:5). His ecclesiastical position in Crete was much the same as that of Timothy in Ephesus. *See* Titus, Epistle to. The strong, steadfast Titus was the right man to work among the ungodly Cretans. He was asked by Paul to meet him at Nicopolis, and it was probably from there that he went to nearby Dalmatia (II Tim 4:10).

Bibliography. *See* Timothy, First Epistle to.

A. M. R.

TITUS, EPISTLE TO. One of the three Pastoral Epistles (*q.v.*) of Paul in the NT. The letter to Titus (*see* Titus) was written before II Timothy. Paul wrote him concerning the work allotted to him in Crete (Tit 1:5). He was to "appoint," or make, elders in every city. It is clear that for Paul the terms elder (*presbyteros*) and bishop (*episkopos*) were interchangeable, because in explaining the qualifications required in an elder, he says, "For a bishop must be blameless, as the steward of God," etc. (Tit 1:5–9). He had said previously to the elders of Ephesus, "Take heed unto yourselves, and to all the flock, in the which the Holy Ghost hath made you bishops" (Acts 20:28, ESV). This seems to confirm Bishop Lightfoot's contention that in the early church the terms were synonymous. Titus was no more a diocesan bishop in Crete than Timothy was in Ephesus. In each case their stay was temporary (cf. Tit 3:12). They were the apostle's representatives doing the work he assigned them.

The work called for wisdom, grace, and fortitude, for the Cretans were then a rude and licentious race as even their own poet Epimenides declared (Tit 1:12). There were strange Judaistic aberrations among them, and idiotic discussions on false science and "genealogies" (Tit 3:9), pointing to the beginnings of Gnosticism.

Contents

Much of the epistle consists of personal instruction for Titus. However, it contains a great deal that is relevant to all Christians. The gospel is truth and brings eternal life. Paul prescribes qualifications for church elders: blameless reputation, well-disciplined homes, temperate, self-controlled, hospitable. The doings of false teachers called for sharp rebuke (chap. 1).

Paul next instructed Titus that he must show an example of sound doctrine and good works, for teaching is useless without good example (chap. 2). The fruits of God's mercy must be seen in good conduct, otherwise Christian profession will become a reproach. Titus was to avoid senseless disputations with heretics about nonsensical matters. Incorrigible heretics were to be rejected as church members (3:1–11).

We can well believe that Titus repeated in Crete his success in Corinth (*see* Titus). He was urged by Paul to meet him in Nicopolis (Tit 3:12).

Outline

I. Salutation, 1:1–4
II. Godliness in the Leaders of the Church, 1:5–16
  A. Qualifications for elders, 1:5–9
  B. Need for godly elders to combat disorderly teachers, 1:10–16
III. Godliness in the Christian Family, 2:1–15
  A. Adorning sound doctrine in the home, 2:1–10
  B. Grace as the basis of all Christian conduct, 2:11–15
IV. Godliness in the World, 3:1–11
  A. Be subject to rulers and considerate of all men, 3:1–7
  B. Engage in good deeds and shun foolish arguments, 3:8–11
V. Conclusion, 3:12–15

Bibliography. See Timothy, First Epistle to.

A. M. R.

TIZITE (tī'zīt). A Gentilic name attached to Joha, one of David's mighty men (I Chr 11:45).

TOAH (tō'*ȧ*). The great-great grandfather of the prophet Samuel (I Chr 6:34). The name appears elsewhere as Nahath (I Chr 6:26) and as Tohu (I Sam 1:1).

TOB (tŏb). A region E of the Jordan River to which Jephthah exiled himself after his father's death when his brethren disowned him (Jud 11:3–5). Later the elders found him there, and in desperation they constrained him to take command of their army. Hanun, the king of Ammon, drafted soldiers from this area with which to fight David (II Sam 10:6, ASV; KJV "Ishtob"). This would suggest that it was beyond the borders of Israel, probably NE of the district of Gilead.

The name appears in Egyptian records as Tu-by (#22 in the list of Thutmose III), and in the Amarna letters (#205) as Dubu. It is best identified with et-Taiyibeh over ten miles E of Edrei and Ramoth-gilead, near the headwaters of the Yarmuk River. The OT Tob seems to be the Toubion of I Macc 5:13 and II Macc 12:17, mentioned in connection with the campaign of Judas Maccabaeus in Gilead.

H. A. Han.

TOB-ADONIJAH (tŏb'ăd-ō-nī'*jȧ*). One of the Levites whom Jehoshaphat sent in an itinerant teaching mission throughout all the cities of Judah (II Chr 17:8). However, the unusual name appears to be a scribal dittography occasioned by the preceding names, Tobijah and Adonijah.

TOBIAH (tō-bī'*ȧ*)

1. The head of a family who returned from the Babylonian Captivity but could not prove its descent (Ezr 2:60, 62; Neh 7:62, 64). He may be related to the Tobiad family mentioned below, but no definite relationship can be proved.

2. A Jewish-Ammonite governor who joined forces with Sanballat (*q.v.*) in trying to prevent Nehemiah and the Israelites from rebuilding the temple (Neh 2:10; 6:1–19). During Nehemiah's absence from Jerusalem, Tobiah had been given a room in the temple area, formerly used as a storeroom, since he had a relative in the priesthood (6:17–18; 13:6). Evidently he was on friendly terms with the priesthood and nobility in Jerusalem. When Nehemiah returned he tossed out the goods of Tobiah, had the room cleansed and purified, and then once more used it as a storeroom for vessels, frankincense, and meat offerings (13:6–9). Most biblical scholars believe him to be an ancestor of the house of Tobiah which in the 3rd cen. became a rival of the house of Onias for the Jewish high priesthood in Palestine (II Macc 3:11).

According to W. F. Albright (*The Archaeology of Palestine*, Baltimore: Penguin, 1960, pp. 149f.), the family mausoleum of the Tobiads is the most interesting ruin of the Seleucid period since it carries an inscription of the name Tobiah in deeply cut Aramaic characters of the 3rd cen. B.C. (for photo see VBW, IV, 237). This was evidently a descendant of the enemy of Nehemiah. Near the tomb at 'Araq el-Emir, 15 miles WSW of Amman in Transjordan, is a structure that archaeologists believe belongs to the era when Hyrcanus, the last of the Tobiads, was taking part in the Maccabean revolt. It is believed that the Tobiads were tax collectors. After the plunder of Palestine by Antiochus Epiphanes of Syria, the family disappears from the pages of history.

A. W. W.

TOBIJAH (tō-bī'*jȧ*)

1. One of the Levites whom Jehoshaphat

sent on an itinerant teaching ministry throughout the cities of Judah (II Chr 17:8).

2. One of the Jewish exiles from whom the prophet Zechariah received an offering of silver and gold to make an ornate crown (KJV "crowns") for Joshua the high priest (Zech 6:10, 14).

TOCHEN (tō'kĕn). One of the Simeonite villages in S Judah (I Chr 4:32); unidentified. In the parallel list in Josh 19:7 the name is omitted in the MT, but occurs in the LXX^B. It is possible that Tochen (I Chr 4:32) should be equated with Ether (Josh 19:7) since in the lists both are preceded and followed by the same cities.

TOGARMAH (tō-gär'mȧ). The third son of Gomer, brother of Ashkenaz, the Scythian progenitor (Gen 10:3; I Chr 1:6; Ezk 38:6). (Beth)-Togarmah (RSV) was one of the many far-flung nations which traded with Tyre (Ezk 27:14), providing horses and mules and soldiers to Gog (*q.v.*; Ezk 38:6). Murshilis II the Hittite king knew it as Tegarama situated between Carchemish and Haran. The Assyrians knew it as Tilgarimanu, according to the records of Sargon and Sennacherib; the latter conquered the land in 695 B.C. It was known in classical times as Gauraena (modern Gurun), approximately 70 miles W of Malatya. The Armenians trace their ancestry back to Haik, the son of Torgom; thus they may be descended from the ancient inhabitants of Togarmah.

TOHU (tō'hū). One of the ancestors of Samuel (I Sam 1:1). The name appears elsewhere as Toah (I Chr 6:34) and Nahath (I Chr 6:26).

TOI (tō'ī). The king of Hamath (II Sam 8:9-10; Tou, I Chr 18:9-10), probably a Hittite (*q.v.*), who sent his son Hadoram (Hadadram[?]; Joram, II Sam 8:10) with gifts of gold, silver, and bronze to congratulate or tacitly to recognize the suzerainty of David after the latter had overwhelmingly defeated Hadadezer, the Aramaean king of Zobah and perpetual foe of Toi.

TOKEN

1. The KJV rendering of the Heb. word *'ôt*, which occurs 79 times in the OT and is translated 11 times by "token," 60 times by "sign," twice by "ensign," twice by "miracle," and once by "mark." The various nuances of the word are as follows:

(a) A memorial symbol or identifying sign. The rainbow is the token of the Noahic covenant (Gen 9:12-13, 17). Circumcision is the identifying mark of the Abrahamic covenant (Gen 17:11). The account of the redemption of the firstborn Jewish sons in Egypt was to be a reminiscent mark upon the Israelite hand (Ex 13:16). The blood upon the Israelite houses served as the distinguishing mark on the night of the Passover (Ex 12:13).

(b) Tangible evidence. The divine authentication of the mission of Moses is guaranteed by the promised return of Moses with his people to the scene of the inaugural vision (Ex 3:12). The psalmist prayed for an authenticating, sensible sign from God (Ps 86:17). Aaron's rod was to be an evidential witness against the rebels (Num 17:10). The oath sworn to Rahab by the spies formed the assurance or pledge of her security (Josh 2:12). Token is used in the sense of testimony or evidence in Job 21:29.

(c) Omen, portent, or *miracle.* Token refers to occult heathen prognostication in Isa 44:25, to divine miracles or acts in Ps 135:9, and to divine portents in Ps 65:8.

2. Token is used in the RSV of I Sam 17:18 as the rendering of *'ărubbâ*, KJV "pledge," as a sign or assurance of welfare.

3. In the phrase "tokens of virginity" (Deut 22:14ff.), the word "tokens" is supplied by the translators in the idiomatic rendering of the Heb. word *b^{e}tûlîm*, "virginity," which refers to the cloth upon which the nuptial pair consummated their marriage and, hence, by virtue of the hymeneal issue bore evidence of the bride's virginity (Deut 22:17).

4. In the KJV of the NT "token" is used to translate *sussēmon*, "a sign" (previously agreed upon) in Mk 14:44; *endeixis*, "omen" or "sign" (Phil 1:28); *endeigma*, "evidence" or "plain indication" (II Thess 1:5); and *sēmeion*, "sign" or "distinguishing mark" by which Paul authenticated his epistle (II Thess 3:17).

E. R. D.

TOKHATH. *See* Tikvath.

TOLA (tō'lȧ)

1. A son of Issachar (Gen 46:13; I Chr 7:1-2), and ancestral head of the family of Tolaites (Num 26:23).

2. A judge who was of the lineage of Issachar. His father's name was Puah the son of Dodo (Jud 10:1). Tola lived and was buried in Shamir in the hill country of Ephraim. Following the era of Gideon and Abimelech, Tola rose to leadership and served as judge for 23 years. There is no mention of any enemy oppression and deliverance. Some scholars suggest that the unknown site of Shamir may have been in the vicinity of Samaria.

TOLAD (tō'lăd). A city of the tribe of Simeon in the extreme S toward the boundary of Edom, mentioned with Ezem, Ziklag, Hormah, and other cities which the Simeonites inherited within the territory of Judah (I Chr 4:29; elsewhere Eltolad, *q.v.*, Josh 15:30; 19:4). It has been tentatively identified as Khirbet Erqa Saqra by F.-M. Abel (*Geographie de la Palestine*, Paris: 1938, II, 314).

TOLAITES (tō'lȧ-īts). A family descended from Tola (*q.v.*), one of the sons of Issachar (Num 26:23).

TOLL. *See* Tax; Tribute; Publican.

TOMB. A burial place, larger and more complex in plan or structure than a simple grave dug in the earth. Tombs usually are associated with the burial of persons of position or wealth, and are designed to serve as a monument or memorial to the deceased. In the Bible a number of Heb. and Gr. words refer to burial places; these may have overlapping, synonymous, or complementary meanings, as in English. In the English versions the words tomb, grave, sepulcher, burial, burying place, monument appear often in reference to the same place.

In Palestine both natural caves and rock-cut tombs were used for burial. Abraham purchased the cave of Machpelah in which to bury Sarah (Gen 23:9). Because of the lack of space within a walled city and because of the possibility of ceremonial defilement, tombs usually were grouped in a cemetery outside the city walls. Often they are found farther down the slope of the city hill from the fortifications of the era of their first use. Sometimes they were associated with a garden (II Kgs 21:18, 26; Jn 19:41). The tombs of the kings of Judah at Jerusalem (II Chr 21:20; 24:25; 28:27; 32:33; 35:24) have not been identified with any certainty, although some tombs plundered long ago and partially quarried away in Roman times are located on the SE hill of Jerusalem where David's city stood.

The Israelites knew and respected tombs of earlier times. Rachel's tomb near Bethlehem was known by the writer of Genesis (Gen 35:20) and also in the days of Saul (I Sam 10:2). David's tomb was well-known in NT times (Acts 2:29; Jos *Ant.* vii.15.3; xiii.8.4; xvi.7.1).

In the NT we read of demoniacs who lived in tombs (Mt 8:28; Mk 5:2-5; Lk 8:27). Tombs are referred to in the preaching of Jesus (Mt 23:27, 29), who upbraided the scribes and the Pharisees for being "whitewashed tombs" (RSV), beautiful outwardly but inwardly de-

During the Egyptian Empire period, kings, queens and nobles were buried in tombs cut in the cliffs around Thebes. In foreground is tomb of Tutankhamon, behind which is tomb of Rameses VI. HFV

Ancient Phoenician sarcophagi at Gebal. HFV

filed. He accused them of hypocritically building the tombs of the prophets and adorning the monuments of the righteous.

More information is given concerning the tomb of Jesus than any other mentioned in the Bible. It was located in a garden near Golgotha (Jn 19:42) and was rock-cut (Mt 27:60; Mk 15:46; Lk 23:53). No one had been buried there previously (Lk 23:53; Jn 19:41), for Joseph of Arimathea had made this for his own burial (Mt 27:60). A large rolling stone closed the doorway (Mt 27:60; Mk 15:46; cf. Mk 16:3). Upon His resurrection the tomb was empty (Mt 28:6; Mk 16:6; Lk 24:3, 6, 12; Jn 20:1-8).

An enormous amount of research has sought to establish the exact location of this tomb, but the problem remains inconclusive. The so-called Garden Tomb N of the present walled city, advocated by General Charles Gordon, has no historical or archaeological evidence in favor of its site. The traditional site within the ancient Church of the Holy Sepulchre remains a plausible general location for Jesus' tomb.

See Burial; Coffin; Funeral; Grave; Mourning.

Bibliography. L. E. Cox Evans, "The Holy Sepulchre," PEQ, C (1968), 112-136. Kathleen Kenyon, *Digging Up Jericho,* London: Benn, 1957. Robert H. Smith, "The Tomb of Jesus," BA, XXX (1967), 74-90.

C. E. D.

TONGS

1. The English rendering of the Heb. word *malqāḥayim,* a dual noun from the verb *lāqaḥ,* "take" or "seize," and denoting a device used at the temple altar for taking hold of objects such as a live coal (Isa 6:6).

2. The same Heb. term appears in Ex 25:38; Num 4:9; I Kgs 7:49; II Chr 4:21, where it refers to an instrument for holding the wick of a lamp while it was being trimmed. The rendering as "snuffers" in the RSV of Ex 25:38 and Num 4:9 is not warranted either by the root derivative of the term or by the contrary fact that in I Kgs 7:50 (cf. II Chr 4:22) a device for cropping the snuff or charred part of the

lampwick is mentioned in addition to "tongs" in the previous verse.

3. The Heb. term *ma'ăṣād,* translated "tongs" in KJV of Isa 44:12, is a mistranslation and should be rendered by "axe" (ASV) or "cutting tool" (NASB).

E. R. D.

TONGUE. This word is used to denote the physical organ of man in such actions as thirst (Lam 4:4), dumbness (Job 29:10), holding a choice morsel (Job 20:12), and lapping, "Every one that lappeth of the water with his tongue, as a dog lappeth, him shalt thou set by himself" (Jud 7:5).

It is also used by synecdoche for the person as in "my tongue was glad" (Acts 2:26; cf. Ps 52:2; Prov 26:28; Isa 45:23; Jas 1:26). Sometimes "every tongue" means "every person" regardless of the language he speaks (Isa 45:23; Phil 2:11).

Another use is as the organ of speech, both good and bad. Love and kindness may be in the tongue, i.e., speech (I Jn 3:18; Prov 31:26) as well as insolence, falsehood, and slander (Josh 10:21; Ps 78:36; 15:3). It may be slow (Ex 4:10) or as swift as the pen of a ready writer (Ps 45:1). Moral qualities are ascribed to it, such as arrogance (Ps 12:3), deceit (Ps 52:4), and lying (Prov 6:17). It is also the organ of singing (Ps 51:14; 126:2; Isa 35:6).

The word is also used as a synonym for language or dialect (Deut 28:49; Acts 1:19).

Another use is for the tongue of animals, including the dog (Ex 11:7; Ps 68:23), viper (Job 20:16), and crocodile (Job 41:1).

The word is also used to denote that which resembles a tongue in shape. Thus, "a wedge [tongue] of gold" (Josh 7:21, 24) and "the bay [tongue] of sea" (Josh 15:2, 5; 18:19; cf. Isa 11:15).

Of significance are some of the metaphorical uses of the word. The "rage of the tongue" signifies verbal abuse (Hos 7:16), while the "strife of tongues" and "scourge of the tongue" mean cursing and wrath (Ps 31:20; Job 5:21). To "bend the tongue" signifies the telling of malicious falsehoods (Jer 9:3) and to "sharpen the tongue" denotes cutting speech (Ps 140:3). To "use the tongue" means flattery (Jer 23:31) and to "smite with the tongue" signifies slander (Jer 18:18). To "hide under the tongue" means to hide within wickedness (Job 20:12) and "the word of God in the tongue" is a sign of inspiration (II Sam 23:2). To "stick out the tongue" means to mock (Isa 57:4) and to "divide the tongues of the wicked" is to raise up dissension among them (Ps 55:9). To "gnaw one's tongue" is a sign of fury, despair, and torment (Rev 16:10).

The most important biblical passage concerning the right and wrong use of the mouth and tongue is Jas 3:1-12. James likens the power or influence of the tongue to that of the rudder of a ship, to a spark which sets a forest ablaze, and to an untamable serpent full of deadly poison.

See Tongues, Confusion of; Tongues, Gift of; Tongues of Fire; Languages; Mouth.

E. C. J.

TONGUES, CONFUSION OF. The divine judgment of Gen 11 took place in the land of Shinar (i.e., Mesopotamia). The rationale for building a city and a tower was twofold: to preserve the unity and social solidarity of the human race, and to glorify human achievement in a structure that would reach into the heavens. *See* Babel, Tower of. The tower would serve the surrounding area as a center and rallying point. It characterized the urban rather than the nomadic spirit.

The human prerogative shows man's rebellion against the divine command in Gen. 1:28 to fill the earth. The city builders in the early Genesis stories were evil men, while the later Genesis narratives reflect the Heb. thinking about departing from cities for a more devout life under God in nomadic surroundings. This religious concept is recurrent in OT literature.

The original unity of human speech is suggested on the basis of the unity of creation as seen in Adam and Eve, and in Noah and his family, the only survivors of the Flood. No system of philology can by empirical research prove the unity of language through historically preserved languages. The only logical argument, then, is that of faith.

This event thus emphasizes the breaking up of the human family by God. The anthropomorphic element is seen in the Lord's coming down to inspect their building program. Man has ever tried to build permanent physical structures. The Pharaohs built colossal pyramids; the Greeks, their pyramids of human wisdom; the Assyrians and the Romans, their military empires with divine emperors; 20th cen. man, his atomic "pyramids" that extend to the moon and beyond. The record of Gen 11 is the same: confusion, frustration, dispersion, and displacement. The gateway to heaven (*Bab-el*) is not built with human hands, nor on material foundations, but is reached in the pilgrimage by faith. Any other way leads only to confusion (*bālāl*) and alienation of man from man, and man from God.

F. E. Y. and E. L. C.

TONGUES, GIFT OF. This is twice noted as one of the spiritual (charismatic) gifts given to and operative within the church (I Cor 12:10, 28). It is usually referred to as speaking in tongues, though it is also designated glossolalia (Gr. *glōssa,* "tongue"; *lalein,* "to speak"). The chief biblical references are Acts 2:1-13 and I Cor 12-14.

Occurrence

The Gr. word *glōssa* ("tongue") appears some 50 times in the NT with various usages.

It is used 17 times of the speech organ of the body (e.g., Mk 7:33; Lk 1:64), once figuratively of cloven tongues of fire (Acts 2:3), and seven times in the book of the Revelation in an ethnic sense (e.g., 5:9; 7:9). The remaining 25 times it describes the phenomenon of speaking in tongues (Mk 16:17; Acts 2:4, 11; 10:46; 19:6; I Cor 12:10 [twice], 28, 30; 13:1, 8; 14:2, 4, 5 [twice], 6, 13, 14, 18, 19, 22, 23, 26, 27, 39).

The constructions vary. It is described as "new tongues" (*glōssais . . . kainais,* Mk 16:17), "other tongues" (*heterais glōssais,* Acts 2:4), "kinds (diversities) of tongues" (*genē glōssōn,* I Cor 12:10, 28), and simply "tongue" or "tongues" (e.g., I Cor 14:19, 22). The adjective "unknown" which appears in the KJV at I Cor 14:2, 4, 13, 14, 19, 27 is not found in the original but is an interpretative addition of the translators. Most often the word is found in the singular or plural with the verb "to speak" (*laleō*) (e.g., I Cor 14:2, 4, 5, 6). Once it is used with the verb "to pray" (I Cor 14:14) and once with the verb "to have" (I Cor 14:26).

Lexicographers are in general agreement that *glōssa* can be classified in three ways: (1) literally as the organ of speech (or figuratively of forked tongues of flame); (2) of languages (and as a synonym for an ethnic distinction); and (3) of unintelligible or ecstatic utterance (Arndt, p. 161).

Identification

The phenomenon of speaking in tongues did not occur in the OT or during the period of the Gospels. Some interpreters identify certain OT instances of prophesyings with the phenomenon of glossolalia (Num 11:26-30; 23:7-10, 18-24; 24:3-9, 15-24; I Sam 10:1-13; 19:18-24; I Kgs 18:26-29), but there is no explicit statement that the men mentioned spoke in tongues, nor can such be demonstrated. (For historical instances of glossolalia in non-Christian religions see Robert Gromacki, *The Modern Tongues Movement,* pp. 5-10.) The only reference to glossolalia in the Gospels (Mk 16:17) is prophetic and is found in the disputed portion of Mark's Gospel (16:9-20).

The first biblical occurrence of glossolalia was on the day of Pentecost in Jerusalem (Acts 2:4-13). In addition, only two other historic occasions and one didactic section are found in the biblical record. Those who believed at the house of Cornelius in Caesarea spoke with tongues (Acts 10:46) as did those of John's disciples when they believed at Ephesus (Acts 19:6). The practice of speaking in tongues at Corinth was cause for the lengthiest treatment of the subject (I Cor 12-14). No other specific instances are noted, though some commentators believe that it occurred in Samaria (Acts 8:17-18; NBD, p. 1286) and on the occasion of Paul's conversion (Acts 9:1-17).

Paul's instructions concerning glossolalia in I Cor 14 are evidently made for all the churches (vv. 33-34), which would imply that the gift was not limited to Corinth. Some interpreters see the phenomenon in certain distinctive phrases of Scripture (e.g., "spake the word of God with boldness," Acts 4:31; "the Spirit itself maketh intercession for us with groanings which cannot be uttered," Rom 8:26; "spiritual songs," Eph 5:19; cf. I Cor 14:15; "Quench not the Spirit. Despise not prophesyings," I Thess 5:19-20; "let him speak as the oracles of God," I Pet 4:11). Such identification, if not dubious, is at best uncertain, since no specific reference to tongues is made.

How are these occasions of glossolalia to be identified? Are these occasions of a miraculous gift of speaking previously unknown foreign languages? Are they occasions of humanly unknown but miraculous ecstatic speech? Or both? Aside from those who would deny any miraculous element and explain the events on some purely naturalistic basis, there are three basic positions as to identification.

Ecstatic speech. A few interpreters see all the instances of and references to glossolalia as ecstatic utterances, that is, some humanly unintelligible speech, perhaps heavenly (cf. I Cor 13:1, "tongues. . .of angels"). In the case of the foreigners in Acts 2 when "every man heard them speak in his own language" (v. 6; cf. vv. 8, 11), there would have to have occurred a miracle of the hearing as well as the speaking. This miracle of the hearing, however, would appear untenable in that the speaking with tongues began before there was any audience (cf. v. 4 with v. 6).

Some modern scholars contend for an "original" account of Pentecost (Acts 2:1-6*a*, 12ff. and without the *heterais* ["other"] of v. 4) which would mean then only ecstatic utterances, and that Luke later added the references to foreign languages (Acts 2:6*b*-11 and the *heterais* of v. 4). This supposed later addition would serve as a more favorable explanation when glossolalia had fallen into disrepute, or as a symbolic interpretation of Pentecost as a reversal of Babel, or as a parallel to the Midrash record of the giving of the law at Sinai in the 70 languages of man. This theory lacks any further evidence. (For further discussion of this theory and notations of those who subscribe to it see NBD, p. 1286.)

Foreign languages. A second and more commonly held view is that all the biblical accounts of glossolalia were foreign languages miraculously bestowed. That there are some easily detectable differences between the pheonomena in Acts and those in I Corinthians is not denied. For example: (1) In Acts whole companies on whom the Spirit came immediately broke into tongues, whereas in Corinth not all possessed this gift (I Cor 12:10, 30). (2) In Acts tongues appear to have been an irresistible and temporary initial experience, whereas in Corinth it was a continuing gift under the control of the speaker (I Cor 14:27-28). (3) In Acts the tongues were readily understood by the hearers, whereas at Corinth the additional gift of interpretation was required to make the speaking intelligible (I Cor 14:5, 13, 27). But it is argued that these differences are of such a nature as not to require that the tongues in Corinth are different in kind from those in Acts (which are clearly designated as foreign languages). For argumentation of this position see Charles Hodge, *An Exposition of the First Epistle to the Corinthians*, pp. 248–252, and R. C. H. Lenski, *The Interpretation of St. Paul's First and Second Epistles to the Corinthians*, pp. 504–509.

Foreign languages and ecstatic speech. By far the most commonly held interpretation is that the Acts phenomena are to be identified as foreign languages and the Corinthian phenomena as ecstatic speech. For argumentation of this position see H. A. W. Meyer, *Critical and Exegetical Hand-Book to the Epistles to the Corinthians*, pp. 284–287.

Purpose

The gifts of the Spirit were given in order that the members of the one body of Christ might function properly and harmoniously (I Cor 12:12, 27; cf. Rom 12:3–8), and that God might be glorified (I Pet 4:10–11). In addition to these general purposes, it is possible to note at least two distinct purposes for the gift of tongues in particular.

An evidential purpose. Several passages indicate clearly that tongues were given primarily to serve in an evidential or verifying capacity. In Acts 2 tongues were a sign of confirmation to the Jewish people of the truth of the Christian message (vv. 5–12). Peter clearly used this miracle in an evidential manner with regard to Christ's resurrection and ascension (vv. 32–36; v. 33*b* – "this, which ye now see and hear"), and it certainly played an important part in the result of 3,000 responding in belief (v. 41). Tongues, since they fall in the general category of miracles, seem also to have served as a means of verifying the messenger as well as his message (cf. Heb 2:3–4; Acts 2:22; II Cor 12:12).

Whereas in Acts 2 the tongues were a sign to the unsaved, in Acts 10 they served as a sign to believing Jews that Gentile believers had received identical privileges with them (Acts 10:46–47; cf. 11:15–18). In Acts 19 tongues served to verify to those believers the reality of the presence and ministry of the Holy Spirit in their lives (vv. 2, 5–6). Some commentators have suggested that tongues served also as a sign of judgment upon unbelievers for their failure to respond in belief to the gospel (I Cor 14:21–22 [cf. historical background to v. 21 which is from Isa 28:11–12]; cf. Acts 2:13).

A devotional purpose. Though certainly not primary, there is indication that tongues could serve in a totally personal capacity. The one who speaks in a tongue "edifies himself" (I Cor 14:4). One could pray and praise in a tongue (vv. 14–17). Thus one could speak "to himself and to God" (v. 28). Although Paul himself had the gift (I Cor 14:18), his preference was that in public one should speak so that all may understand and join in (v. 16). If the one speaking in a tongue could not interpret (I Cor 14:13), or if no interpreter was present, he was to exercise this gift in private (v. 28). A very limited, and certainly not preferred, instructional value may be seen if the tongue is interpreted (I Cor 14:2–6, 12–13, 19, 28).

Regulation

Paul recognized this gift as a genuine gift of the Holy Spirit (I Cor 14:5) with definite value (see section above on purpose), and he cautioned against the prohibition of its exercise (v. 39). But Paul also saw dangers in the practice, perhaps even more than its values. He did not give it precedence or even encouragement in the public worship (I Cor 14:19, 28), because by nature this gift is individualistic (v. 4) and its main characteristic is its unintelligibility (vv. 15–16). In both lists of gifts where tongues are mentioned (I Cor 12:8–10, 28–30) this gift (and its accompanying gift of interpretation) is placed last (lowest?) in the scale. This gift is not to be desired and is relatively unimportant in value (I Cor 14:1, 5, 19, 39). The exercise of spiritual gifts was to be measured against their capacity to build up the church in love (I Cor 13; 14:4–5, 12–19, 26).

In view of their limited value in public worship and that "all things be done decently and in order" (I Cor 14:40), Paul set down certain regulations for the exercise of this gift in public. (1) The exercise of this gift must, as must all the other shared elements, contribute to the edifying (building up) of those present (I Cor 14:26). (2) In public worship no more than two or three should speak in a tongue (v. 27). (3) Those who so speak are to do so in turn, not simultaneously (v. 27). (4) If no interpreter is present the tongue speaker should keep silent (v. 28).

In addition to these very clear and explicit regulations some commentators have suggested two other regulations. From the last clause of v. 27, "and let one interpret," some have concluded that there should be no more than one interpreter in a meeting. Others have concluded from the command that "women keep silence in the churches" (vv. 34–35) that women are never to exercise the gift of tongues in public worship. Though such interpretations are possible, other equally good (if not better) interpretations are also possible for these expressions.

It is to be noted in concluding this section that the four explicit regulations indicate that tongues are not exercised in a state of uncontrolled (or uncontrollable) unconscious excitement, but in a state of self-determined control.

Continuance

Is glossolalia a continuing gift for the church or is it to be viewed in some sense as one of the temporary (or foundational) gifts? Clearly, tongues shall cease (I Cor 13:8), but the question is *when*? Three answers are commonly proposed.

Already ceased. It is contended that tongues are among the temporary gifts, limited to the apostolic era (i.e., to A.D. 100). More specifically it is argued that since the NT was not yet completed and since there were a limited number of apostles and prophets around, God revealed Himself and His truth through certain gifts which were temporary, while other gifts were to be a permanent part of church life. The question is one of purpose. If the purpose is no longer needed, then the gift was temporary and will not be seen throughout the history of the church.

Other arguments commonly proffered are as follows: (1) The statement that tongues shall cease (I Cor 13:8) when that which is perfect is come (v. 10) looks to the completed canon of Scripture which brought the climax to the maturing process of the church. (2) In books written after I Corinthians which also deal with church problems and the Christian life, there is no mention of tongues. (3) In later listings of spiritual gifts tongues are not included (cf. Rom 12:3–8; Eph 4:7–11). (4) In the three centuries following the apostolic era there are no genuine cases of glossolalia. Speaking in tongues apparently had ceased by the end of the 1st cen.

Continuing. A second position contends that all spiritual gifts, including tongues, will cease only at the second coming of Christ and are necessary today. Arguments advanced are: (1) "That which is perfect" (I Cor 13:10) can refer only to the perfect age ushered in by Christ's second advent (cf. v. 12). (2) Paul was concerned that the church "come behind in no gift; waiting for the coming of our Lord Jesus Christ" (I Cor 1:7). (3) Tongues were given to the church, and so long as the church continues so must tongues. (4) The gift of tongues is an integral part of the great commission (Mk 16:15–20 [a disputed passage]). (5) The purpose of the gifts was for the confirmation, not the substitution, of the Word to a pagan world, which confirmation is continually needed.

Continuing but limited. A third position, somewhat moderating, posits that tongues are permanent and possible today, though neither necessary (in the sense that they were in the 1st cen.) nor normal. Some writers suggest a continual decreasing based on the illustration in I Cor 13:10–11 (F. Godet, *Commentary on the First Epistle to the Corinthians*, II, 321). In addition to at least some of the arguments the following are offered. (1) There is *no* scripture which explicitly states that tongues would cease with the end of the apostolic era. (2) In view of the sovereignty of God it is presumptuous to impose a limitation upon God's power or purposes. If He has accomplished His divine intent by this gift at one time, He may well continue to do so.

Bibliography. Johannes Behm, "Glōssa," TDNT, I, 719–726. Frederick Dale Bruner, *A Theology of the Holy Spirit*, Grand Rapids: Eerdmans, 1970. Robert G. Gromacki, *The Modern Tongues Movement*, Philadelphia: Presbyterian and Reformed Pub. Co., 1967. Charles Hodge, *An Exposition of the First Epistle to the Corinthians*, Grand Rapids: Eerdmans, 1953. H. A. W. Meyer, *Critical and Exegetical Hand-Book to the Epistles to the Corinthians*, New York: Funk and Wagnalls, 1884.

H. D. F.

TONGUES OF FIRE. Tongues as of fire (cf. Isa 5:24, ASV and newer versions) appeared divided or distributed and resting upon each of the 120 disciples at Pentecost (Acts 2:3). This particular manifestation which accompanied the initial baptism in the Holy Spirit was never repeated in visible form, and therefore its explanation must be sought in similar phenomena in the Scriptures. This was a manifestation of the Holy Spirit, the third member of the Trinity.

There was a similar appearance of God (the Father) at Mount Sinai who "descended upon it in fire: and the smoke thereof ascended as the smoke of a furnace" (Ex 19:18; cf. 24:17; Dan 7:9; Ezk 1:4; Mal 3:2), in the burning bush at Mount Horeb (Ex 3:2; *see* Burning Bush), at the dedication of Solomon's temple (II Chr 7:1), and on Mount Carmel (I Kgs 18:38).

Later, in the book of Revelation, John saw the glorified Christ whose "eyes were as a flame of fire" (1:14; 2:18; cf. Mal 3:2). Thus, in the appearing of each of the three Persons of the Trinity, their deity and holiness were manifested as fire (cf. Isa 10:17). Only because Christ had emptied Himself and laid aside His glory in order to become man (Phil 2:6–8) and die for our sins, did He appear without such blazing, blinding glory, and even then it returned momentarily at the transfiguration (Mt 17:2; Lk 9:29).

The tongues of fire on the day of Pentecost (*q.v.*) were a fulfillment of John the Baptist's pronouncement that Jesus Christ would baptize in the Holy Spirit and fire (Mt 3:11; Lk 3:16). Many believe that the tongues of fire are symbolic of the purifying, sanctifying work of the Holy Spirit (*q.v.*; cf. Isa 6:6–7). *See* Fire; Sanctification.

R. A. K.

TOOL. The two words rendered "tool" in the Bible are very general. The first (Heb. *ḥereb*) in Ex 20:25 refers to any cutting instrument and is the ordinary word for "sword." The second (Heb. *k^{e}lî*) is even more general and might be translated "thing." In I Kgs 6:7 it means any kind of tool for building. *See* Occupations: Craft, Craftsman.

TOOTH. This word is used for the hard bony appendages set in the jaw of man and used for biting, tearing, and chewing (Num 11:33; Song 4:2; Rev 9:8). The teeth are white (Gen 49:12) and may be irritated by acid (Prov 10:26). The word is also used of beasts (Deut 32:24), including the crocodile and lion (Job 41:14; cf. 4:10; Joel 1:6). Another use is to describe the wicked (Job 29:17; Ps 3:7; 58:6; 124:6), false prophets (Mic 3:5), and foes (Zech 9:7). The sharpness of the wicked's teeth is likened to their weapons (Ps 57:4; Prov 30:14). The word is also used to denote that which resembles a tooth in shape, such as the tine or prong of a fleshhook (I Sam 2:13) and the crag (tooth) of the rock (Job 39:28).

Of significance are several expressions, including the *lex taliones* (law of retaliation), "tooth for tooth," in the law of Moses (Ex 21:24; Lev 24:20; Deut 19:21; Mt 5:38). This means that the injured party was only to be compensated equally, not to take undue revenge. A "broken [bad] tooth" denotes decay (Prov 25:19) and "to break the teeth" means to disgrace and disable (Ps 3:7). "Wherefore do I take my flesh in my teeth?" signifies risk of life (Job 13:14), and "the skin of my teeth" may mean that Job had scarcely a sound spot in his body or that the flesh which surrounds the teeth in the jaw (gums) was destroyed by disease (Job 19:20).

Beautiful teeth are compared to newly washed sheep (Song 6:6) and "iron teeth" are a symbol of destructive power (Dan 7:7, 19). "Cleanness of teeth" is a sign of hunger and famine (Amos 4:6). The "gnashing [grinding] of teeth" denotes the suffering and anguish of hell (Mt 13:42, 50; 22:13; 24:51; 25:30; Lk 13:28).

E. C. J.

TOPAZ *See* Jewels.

TOPHEL (tō'fĕl). Mentioned once (Deut 1:1), it apparently is a locale in the Arabah marking the N end—and Paran the S end—of the general border (Heb. *sûph* can mean "end," "border") of the region opposite which Moses addressed all Israel "beyond the Jordan" (RSV).

It has been identified with eṭ-Ṭafileh, a modern Arab village about 15 miles SE of the Dead Sea on the road from Kerak to Petra. The initial dental of the Arabic (*ṭ*) is an emphatic sound and does not correspond with the simple dental of the Heb. (*t*). The identification is therefore questioned on linguistic grounds as well as on the basis of context.

It appears that it is to be identified more appropriately as a site somewhere in the plain of Moab opposite Jericho. It may be an alternate spelling of the Heb. area term *diblathaim* (cf. Num 33:46f.; Jer 48:22), and it may be referred to as a territory in a cuneiform letter sent to the Assyrian king at Calah, speaking of a messenger from Moab as a "Dabilite" (Henri Cazelles, "Tophel," *Essays in Honour of Miller Burrows*, Leiden: Brill, 1959, pp. 76–79).

H. E. Fi.

TOPHET (tō'fĕt), **TOPHETH** (tō'fĕth). An area in the valley of Hinnom, just S of Jerusalem, where child sacrifices were made to the deity Molech (II Kgs 23:10; Jer 7:31). The meaning and etymology of the name are uncertain. Some identify it with the root meaning "spittle," while others explain it as based on the Aramaic root *t-ph-t*, "to burn," and therefore signifying "a place of burning and burying dead bodies" (cf. Isa 30:33). The name occurs only in the OT.

Tophet was not identical with Hinnom but was a sacrificial area located in the valley of Hinnom. The high places of Baal are mentioned in connection with Tophet (Jer 19:5), and there the pagan deity Molech (Jer 32:35) was worshiped by the ancient Canaanites, and later by the idolatrous Israelites. Ahaz and Manasseh were especially noted for this in that they made their sons pass through the fire (II Kgs 16:3; 21:6). This wicked practice was an abomination in Israel, and provoked the Lord to anger.

In the precinct of Tanit at Carthage, going back to the 8th cen. B.C., has been found evidence of child sacrifice. An early Punic shrine was surrounded by thousands of urns containing the cremated bones of small children, some up to 12 years old but mostly under the age of two. Other Phoenician sanctuaries or sacrificial precincts have been discovered on Sicily and Sardinia and at several sites in N Africa, one with a cremation pit full of burnt matter (Donald Harden, *The Phoenicians*, London: Thames & Hudson, 1962, pp. 94–104; W. F. Albright, *Yahweh and the Gods of Canaan*, Garden City: Doubleday, 1968, pp. 237f.). *See* Sacrifice, Human.

Jeremiah predicted that the name Tophet would be changed to "the valley of slaughter" because many people would be killed there (Jer 7:32–33; 19:6). The good kings of Judah, such as Josiah (II Kgs 23:10), defiled the place by throwing down the altars and high places so that it could no longer be used for idolatrous practices. So thorough was the destruction, there is no definite indication of the exact location of the site.

P. S. H.

TORAH (tôr'ȧ). The Heb word for "law" perhaps comes from the causative form of the verb *yārâ*, "to throw," "to shoot (arrows)"; at any rate, the Hiph'îl verb form *hôrâ* means "to point, guide, instruct, teach." Hence, authoritative guidance is law. The noun *tôrâ* appears 215 times in the OT. Torah is used in the singular 172 times to refer to the whole law of God or Moses, and in the plural 11 times with the same meaning. It is used in Leviticus 15 times, Numbers seven times, and elsewhere 26 times to refer to a specific law in the code. In Proverbs it is used six times to refer to the laws or rules of parents (1:8; 3:1), or traits of character such as kindness (31:26).

Thus, because of its overwhelming usage to refer to the law of the Lord that was given to Israel through Moses, the Torah became the name for the Pentateuch. The term Torah sometimes stood for the whole OT (in Jn 10:34 Jesus referred to Ps 82:6 as "your law"; cf. also Jn 12:34), and at times it was even applied to the whole body of ancient Jewish literature written and oral. However, it is still chiefly used to refer to the Pentateuch alone.

The expression "the book of the law" clearly

indicates its written form. According to the Talmud the Heb. Pentateuch was divided into 154 sections for the systematic reading of the Torah in weekly worship services. By this system, it would be read through once every three years. *See* Canon of Scripture, the OT; Law.

R. B. D.

TORCH. A flaming light produced by some highly flammable substance such as resinous wood or tow affixed to the end of a rod and soaked in tallow or oil, carried usually in the hand. The Heb. word *lappîd* occurs in Gen. 15:17, where "a flaming torch" (ASV, etc.) passed between the severed parts of the covenantal sacrifice (KJV "lamp"); in Ex 20:18, where it is uniformly rendered "lightnings"; in Jud 7:16, 20, where "torches" (ASV, etc.) were part of the military strategy of Gideon; and in Jud 15:4-5, where firebrands or "torches" (RSV, NASB) formed part of the ruse of Samson. "Torch" (ASV, etc.) is used as a simile of the flame between the cherubim (Ezk 1:13), of the eyes of the angel (Dan 10:6), of flashes reflected from the darting chariots (Nah 2:3f.), of the flashing water vapor expelled by the snortings of the crocodile (Job 41:19), of Zion's deliverance (Isa 62:1, RSV), and of the victorious power of the clans of Judah (Zech 12:6).

In Jn 18:3 torches are mentioned with lanterns as providing light for Judas and his companions during their seizure of Jesus. The marginal reading of the ASV of Mt 25:1, 3, 4, 7, 8 suggests "torches," but it is more correctly translated "lamps." In Rev 4:5 (RSV) seven torches of fire burn before the divine throne, while in Rev 8:10 the great star that falls from heaven is described as "blazing like a torch" (RSV). *See* Lamp.

E. R. D.

TORMAH (tôr'mȧ). The marginal reading of the KJV ("to Tormah") and of the ASV ("in Tormah") for the KJV text "privily" and the ASV "craftily" of Jud 9:31. Three solutions have been proposed for this difficult text.

1. Tormah is the name of a place to which Zebul sent messengers to Abimelech. But Tormah is not mentioned elsewhere and Abimelech dwelt in Arumah (Jud 9:41).

2. Tormah, prefixed by the Heb. preposition *b*^{e} meaning "with," is considered a noun derived from the Heb. verb *rāmâ* meaning "deceive"; therefore Zebul sent messengers with deception, i.e., secretly or craftily (so LXX^{B}). But the unparalleled form of the supposed noun militates against such a view.

3. The RSV corrects the text to read "at Arumah," a change that involves but one letter and agrees with the text of Jud 9:41. Arumah has been identified with Khirbet el-'Ormeh, *c.* five miles SSE of Shechem.

E. R. D.

TORMENTOR, One who extracts the truth by means of torture on the rack, or by scourging, or by some other means. It is used only once in the NT by Christ in the parable of the debtor delivered to the rough jailers (Mt 18:34). Claudius Lysias, the chief captain, was planning to have Paul "examined by scourging" (Acts 22:24) before he learned he was a Roman citizen. Christ our Saviour was scourged for our sins, even as Isaiah had prophesied in the words "with his stripes we are healed" (Isa 53:5; I Pet 2:24).

TORTOISE. *See* Animals: Lizard, Dabb, IV.22.

TOU. *See* Toi.

TOUCH. The principal OT verb translated "touch" is Heb. *nāga',* "to touch, reach, strike." The woman told the serpent that she was not even to handle the forbidden fruit in the garden of Eden (Gen 3:3). The word is used of sexual fondling or intercourse (Gen 20:6; 26:11; Ruth 2:9; Prov 6:29); of coming in contact with anything ceremonially unclean, whether it be the carcass of an unclean animal (Lev 5:2; 11:8), a human corpse (Num 19:11, 13; 31:19), bodily discharges (Lev 15), bloody garments (Lam 4:14-15), or a leper (Lev 22:4); and of divine chastisement (Job 19:21) or Satanic attack (Job 1:11; 2:5). It can also signify harming someone (Ps 105:15; Zech 2:8) or spiritual revival (I Sam 10:26).

The commonly used word in the NT is Gr. *haptomai,* "to touch, take hold of, hold." The LXX generally translates *nāga'* by this verb; hence it has the above wide range of meaning. It is used of sexual intercourse (I Cor 7:1), of contact with unclean things (II Cor 6:17; Col 2:21), and of the harm produced by the devil (I Jn 5:18). The risen Lord Jesus commanded Mary Magdalene not to touch Him (Jn 20:17), evidently telling her to stop clinging to Him (NASB). The intimate fellowship she craved with Him had to wait His ascension and the sending of the Holy Spirit.

Elsewhere in the NT "touch" is used in the Synoptic Gospels of the healing work of Christ and of the people's reaching out to receive help from Him. Here also the verb implies holding the person, not a light touch. In stretching out His hand to the leper Jesus must have held the man without being quick to withdraw from contact with him (Mt 8:3), and gripped the hand of Peter's feverish mother-in-law (Mt 8:15). He grasped the bier of the widow's son (Lk 7:14) and hugged the little children to Himself when He blessed them (Lk 18:15), so that there was nothing distant in His manner. All of this suggests that the transfigured Jesus came to embrace His three fear-stricken disciples, not just to prod them (Mt 17:7). Likewise, the woman with the hemorrhage and other sick folk gripped His garment (Mk 5:27-31; Mt 14:36) or took hold of Jesus Himself (Mk 3:10; Lk 6:19), perhaps in similar fashion to the woman who came in to anoint His feet (Lk 7:39).

J. R.

TOW. The Heb. word *n*^{e}*'ōret* means the refuse of the flax produced in the manufacture of linen and occasioned by the processes of pounding and carding the fibers. Its highly inflammable nature was proverbial (Jud 16:9), and it was used as an effective emblem of the speedy disintegration of the unrighteous (Isa 1:31). The KJV of Isa 43:17 uses "tow" to render the Heb. *pishtâ* ("flax"), but it is more correctly translated as "a wick" (ASV, etc.). *See* Plants.

TOWEL. The linen cloth (Gr. *lention,* a loan-word from the Latin *linteum*) with which Jesus girded Himself, when He had removed His outer garments, and wiped the feet of the disciples after He had washed them at the last supper (Jn 13:4–5).

TOWER. The biblical tower, whether free-standing or surmounting a wall or other edifice, served for purposes of surveillance (cf. Isa 5:2; Mt 21:33) and/or defense (cf. II Chr 26:9, *et al.*). Heb. *migdāl,* the most common OT word for "tower," is derived ultimately not from the Heb. root *gdl,* "to be great" (as per the lexicons), but rather by metathesis from the root *dgl,* "to see, look (out)" (so always in Amarna Canaanite; cf. also Akkadian *madgalu/madgaltu,* "watchtower," and note Heb. *miṣpeh,* "watchtower," from *ṣāpâ,* "to look about"). The word *bāḥôn,* rendered "tower" in Jer 6:27, is better translated "assayer" (cf. RSV).

Defensive towers played an important role in ancient Near Eastern fortifications from the earliest times through the NT period. Jericho, as early as 7000 B.C., boasted a large stone tower as part of its defenses, while city walls of later periods had towers at regular intervals to strengthen them. Even Saul's small highland castle at Gibeah apparently had a tower at each of its four corners. In the early Hellenistic period, towers became increasingly popular and well-constructed, while the three towers bordering Herod's Jerusalem palace on the N were described in glowing terms by Josephus (*Wars* v.4.3–4).

Tower flanking lower entrance to acropolis of Pergamum.

The remains of a massively contructed build ing found just inside the city wall of Balâṭah may be the Tower of Shechem mentioned in Jud 9:46–49 (*see* Shechem). The "tower [Gr. *pýrgos*] in Siloam" (Lk 13:4) is perhaps to be equated with the remains of a large round tower standing over against the village of Silwan (*see* Siloam, Tower of).

"Tower" is used figuratively in Ps 61:3; Prov 18:10; Song 4:4; 7:4; 8:10.

See Babel, Tower of; Fort, Fortification, Fortress; Gate; Wall.

R. Y.

TOWER OF BABEL. *See* Babel, Tower of.

TOWER OF SILOAM. *See* Siloam, Tower of.

TOWN. The various Heb. words employed for "city," "town," and "village" in the OT do not appear to have been used unambiguously. Basically, the "city" (Heb. *'îr*) was walled, the "village" (*ḥāṣēr*) unwalled (Lev 25:30–31), and this distinction served as a broad, practical means of differentiating these two terms. Several factors, however, complicate the matter. Deut 3:5 and Est 9:19 speak of the "unwalled town" or, more literally, "rural city" (*'îr happ*^{e}*-rāzî*), which might become the basis for a further (though less precise) distinction, the "town" (cf. "rural towns," Est 9:19, NASB). The English term "town," then, might well serve to refer to those communities which are neither cities nor villages, but rather intermediate entities.

The *ḥāṣēr* was located in the area surrounding the *'îr* (Josh 19:8; I Chr 4:33; Neh 12:29) and was frequently denoted in Heb. by the *bat* ("daughter"; cf. Num 21:25, marg.) of the city, which in turn was called its "mother" (*'ēm;* cf. II Sam 20:19, RSV). Heb. *bat* and *ḥāṣēr* may therefore in some cases be used as equivalent terms (Neh 11:25, 30). On the other hand they may be distinguished from each other (cf. Josh 15:45, 47, in which *bat* is best translated "town" and *ḥāṣēr* "village"). Nor is *'îr* itself free from ambiguity. It is found as a generic term including *bat* (I Chr 2:23) and *ḥāṣēr* (I Chr 4:32; Isa 42:11); it means both "city" *and* "town/village" in Jer 19:15; and in I Sam 6:18 it is a generic term for all the cities of the Philistines including both the fortified city (*'îr mibṣār*) and the unwalled village (*kōper happ*^{e}*-rāzî*).

The NT makes a threefold distinction between city, village, and countryside (cf. Mk 6:56) with "city" rendering Gr. *polis* and "village" rendering *kōmē*. Unfortunately, the English versions have introduced unnecessary ambiguity by sometimes adding a fourth category, "town," as their translation of *polis* and/or *kōmē*. The resulting confusion is perhaps best illustrated by referring to Mt 10:11 in which *polin ē kōmēn* is rendered "city or town" by KJV, "city or village" by ASV and NASB, and "town or village" by RSV. It would seem that "town" should be reserved for the translation of *kōmopolis* (Mk 1:38), a hybrid between "village" and "city."

See City; Village.

R. Y.

TOWNCLERK. The townclerk (*grammateus*) of Acts 19:35 was the most important official in Ephesus. As secretary to the city's council, he was responsible for accurately recording its minutes and filing the council's decisions and the decrees, treaties, and edicts of the Roman emperors. He acted as a liaison officer between the civic administration and the Roman provincial administration, whose headquarters were also in Ephesus. In the case mentioned in Acts, the townclerk appeased and dispersed the mob, for the provincial administration would have held him responsible for a riot. He encouraged Demetrius and the craftsmen to avail themselves of the Roman courts and proconsuls for their grievances.

TOYS. *See* Games.

TRACHONITIS (trăk-ŏ-nī'tĭs). Meaning "rough" or "hilly," the word is a Gr. adjective applied to the territory 25 miles SE of Damascus that is mentioned in Lk 3:1 along with Iturea as making up the tetrarchy of Philip, son of Herod the Great and brother of Herod Antipas. It is sometimes referred to as Trachon, which simply makes a noun of the adjective. In fact, Strabo, the geographer of antiquity, uses the noun in the plural, speaking of two such districts (Strabo, xvi.2.20). The extensive mass of volcanic rock, black basalt, which covers approximately 350 square miles, is the distinguishing feature of the district.

It is understood to be a portion of the ancient territory known as Bashan in the OT (Deut 3:4), which now is called the Hauran. Josephus notes that it was a hideout for robbers and desperados. The ruins of the area indicate that in antiquity it supported a population considerably larger than now. There seems to have been some agriculture, small grain, and vineyards, but the husbandry of sheep and goats was especially suited to the terrain.

Emperor Augustus gave Trachonitis to Herod the Great who in turn willed it to his son Philip in 4 B.C. Philip ruled this territory for nearly 40 years. After his death in A.D. 34 it was absorbed into the Roman province of Syria (Jos *Ant.* xviii.4.6). In A.D. 37 Emperor Caligula transferred it to Herod Agrippa I who ruled until A.D. 44. Roman officials once again governed following Herod Agrippa, until it was made a part of the kingdom of Herod Agrippa II in A.D. 53 and remained so until A.D. 100 when it was returned to the province of Syria. In A.D. 106 Emperor Trajan made Trachonitis a part of the new province of Arabia.

H. L. D.

TRADE. *See* Commerce; Loan; Occupations: Merchant.

TRADE ROUTES. *See* Travel and Communication.

TRADITION. The Gr. word *paradosis* occurs 13 times in the NT and is used in the sense of a teaching that is handed down from one person or group to another. In the NT the term has two general meanings. It is used to refer to the oral interpretation of the OT, particularly of the law of Moses, and the teachings of the Jewish elders and rabbis. It was called Halakah in Jewish literature, and was later written down and preserved in the Mishnah and the Talmud (*q.v.*). These traditions were often accorded authoritative status equal to that of the OT Scriptures. Jesus sternly rebuked the Pharisees for such an attitude toward tradition: they had forsaken the commandments of God in order to keep their own traditions, the "tradition of men" (Mk 7:3ff.; Mt 15:1ff.). The "tradition of the elders" blinded men to their basic spiritual need by making the observance of many external forms the essential qualification in order to be accepted with God. The word is also found in Col 2:8 in a slightly broader sense that includes all merely human teaching.

On three occasions Paul uses the word to denote his teachings (I Cor 11:2; II Thess 2:15; 3:6). They were the teachings of an inspired apostle and were to be received and held on to because the authority of heaven was behind them. In the early church the oral tradition of eyewitnesses to the acts and teachings of Jesus was considered authentic and of great importance (Heb 2:3–4). Luke made use of such tradition, which was "handed down" (from Gr. *paradidomi,* the verb corresponding to *paradosis*) in the writing of his Gospel (Lk 1:2, NASB).

N. R. L.

TRAIN

1. From a Heb. word *ḥānak* formerly thought to have a meaning "to fill the mouth," it came to be used for filling the mind, to instruct or educate (Gen 14:14; Prov 22:6). S. C. Reif has recently argued for the basic meaning "to initiate" for all the passages where the Heb. word occurs (also Deut 20:5; I Kgs 8:63; II Chr 7:5); in Prov 22:6 he suggests, "Start a boy on the right road" (VT, XXII [1972],

495-501). The word in Gen 14:14 may have an Egyptian origin, with the sense of "retainers," according to W. F. Albright (BASOR, #94 [1944], p. 24, n. 87).

2. The "train" or "retinue" (RSV) of the queen of Sheba as she came to visit Solomon refers to the might or wealth and resources displayed in the caravan of men and animals she brought with her (I Kgs 10:2). It is the word *ḥayil* used in Zech 4:6, "not by might . . .," and appearing in Deut 8:17-18 as "wealth."

3. Another word, Heb. *shûl*, is used in Isa 6:1 to describe the "train" of the Lord of glory that "filled the temple." The word is used for the skirt of a robe (Lam 1:9) or the hem of a garment (Ex 28:33-34). It has been suggested (Delitzsch, G. A. Smith, *et al.*) that these robes of glory filling the temple veiled the full, unbearable sight of God from the prophet's eyes.

P. C. J.

TRANCE. The Gr. word *ekstasis* denotes a supernaturally induced state of being, in which consciousness is wholly or partially suspended (Arndt). It is caused by sudden emotion and the person is transported, as it were, out of himself so that although he is awake, his mind is drawn off from all surrounding objects and wholly fixed on things divine, thinking he perceives with his bodily eyes and ears realities shown him by God (Thayer).

The KJV uses the word twice in the OT (Num 24:4, 16). In both instances it was supplied by the translators since it was not in the original. It occurs three times in the NT in the KJV and ASV (Acts 10:10; 11:5; 22:17). Elsewhere it is translated "astonishment" or "amazement" (Mk 5:42; Lk 5:26). *See* Vision.

TRANSFIGURATION OF CHRIST. The word transfiguration is derived from the Latin term used to translate the Gr. *metamorphoō*, "to change into another form." The transfiguration of Christ is mentioned in all the Synoptic Gospels and also by Peter in his second letter (Mt 17:1ff.; Mk 9:2ff.; Lk 9:28ff.; II Pet 1:16-18).

Four possible locations have been suggested: the Mount of Olives, Mount Tabor, Mount Hermon, and Jebel Jarmuk. Mount Hermon seems to some to be the most likely because of its great height (9,232 feet) and its proximity to Caesarea Philippi, which place is mentioned immediately before (Mt 16:13; Mk 8:27). Both the Mount of Olives and Mount Tabor appear to have been too inhabited for an event that called for such privacy and quiet as the transfiguration. Jebel Jermaq (3,962 feet), the highest mountain in Upper Galilee, is suggested by W. Ewing (ISBE, V, 3006). He reasons that Hermon lay outside Palestine, and therefore was unlikely. Further, since Christ went up the mountain to pray (Lk 9:28) and came down next day to meet a multitude (Lk 9:37), Hermon appears to be too inaccessible. On the other hand, our Lord may have ascended Mount Hermon part way, without climbing to the summit ("brought them up to a high mountain by themselves," Mt 17:1, NASB).

Christ took His three closest disciples, Peter, James, and John, with Him on this occasion. The transfiguration occurred as He was praying (Lk 9:29). The disciples, who were asleep (Lk 9:32), awakened to see Christ transformed. His face shone with a brightness like the sun, even as it was to shine after His ascension and glorification as revealed in the book of Revelation, and His raiment was white as snow (cf. Rev 1:14-16). The glory which the Son of God possessed in His own right returned for a moment to enshroud Him (cf. Jn 17:5). The heavenly voice which spoke, "This is My beloved Son, with whom I am well pleased; hear Him!" (Mt 17:5, NASB), was the same as at Jesus' baptism (Mt 3:16-17). It identified Jesus not only as the Messiah but also as the Prophet of Deut 18:15-19, the One who was truly proclaiming that the Messiah must suffer death, that the cross was the will of God.

The transfiguration marks an important stage in the ministry and revelation of Jesus Christ. At it the two greatest OT representatives, one of the law, namely, Moses, and one of the prophets, namely, Elijah, joined with Christ in consummating the plan for Christ's atoning death, burial, and resurrection—His exodus (Lk 9:31, Gr. *exodos*). Thus His passion was foretold to be the means of redemption of His people as typified by the OT Exodus from Egypt. Moses and Elijah were alike in that each had had a vision of God on a mountain, Moses on Sinai (Ex 24:15ff.), Elijah on Horeb (I Kgs 19:8ff.); each had no known grave (Deut 34:6; II Kgs 2:11); each was mentioned in the closing verses of the OT (Mal 4:4-6). Some think they are to appear again on earth in the end time (Rev 11).

The transfiguration is regarded by Christ as a revelation of the coming of His kingdom (Mt 16:28; Mk 9:1; Lk 9:27).

Bibliography. E. F. Harrison, "Transfiguration," BDT, pp. 528f. A. M. Ramsey, *The Glory of God and the Transfiguration of Christ*, London: Longmans, Green, 1949.

R. A. K.

TRANSFORM. The Gr. word used in Phil 3:21; II Cor 11:13-15; I Cor 4:6 is *metaschēmatizō*. It means "to change the outward appearance of that which itself remains the same," "to assume the appearance of another." The Gr. *metamorphoō* is used in Mt 17:2; Mk 9:2; Rom 12:2; II Cor 3:18. It is used in the latter two passages of the change of the moral character for the better through the renewal of the innermost nature, but always of a transformation that is visible.

In Phil 2:6-8 Gr. *morphē*, "form," is contrasted with *schēma*, "fashion," as that which is "intrinsic and essential with that which is accidental and outward" (Lightfoot, *Philippians*, p.

131). The use of *morphē* is of the visible expression of the character or essence of the thing (vv. 6–7); *schēma* is of the transitory appearance of the thing, its "fashion" (v. 8; I Cor 7:31). *See* Kenosis.

Bibliography. J. Behm, "*Morphē*, etc., " TDNT, IV, 742–759.

TRANSGRESSION. *See* Sin.

TRANSJORDAN. *See* Ammon; Bashan; Edom; Gilead; Hauran; Jordan; Moab; Palestine: II.B.4.

TRANSLATE. The Heb. and Gr. words which appear as "translate" in the English connote the idea of change of something or someone from one condition to another. Usually the change is very definite, determined, and drastic. Though the term does relate to the transference of words from one language to another (i.e., translations of the Bible), that meaning is not discussed in the Scriptures. Enoch and Elijah are both said to have been translated. Both of these OT saints escaped death through translation. Enoch (Gen 5:24; Heb 11:5) and Elijah (II Kgs 2:11) were suddenly changed from an unglorified state to a glorified state by God.

Believing sinners who do nothing more than place their faith in Christ as Sin-bearer are said to be "translated" from Satan's kingdom to the Saviour's (Col 1:13). This change results in the forgiveness of sins and the change of citizenship from earth to heaven. Such a translation is spiritual in nature.

There is also a physical and final translation of believers. Often this great event is spoken of as the rapture of the Church. When the Lord returns for the Church which is His body (Jn 14:1–3; I Thess 4:13–18), the members of that body will experience a complete change (I Cor 15:51–57). Paul calls this translation of those who are "in Christ" and alive when the Lord returns, "a mystery." In this way he indicates that the truth of the translation of living saints at the Lord's return was not revealed in the OT.

R. P. L

TRANSLATIONS, ENGLISH BIBLE. *See* English Versions.

TRAP. A hunting device for capturing game, made of a wooden frame strung with mesh and sprung so as to be triggered by the quarry in its attempt to obtain the bait, or set off manually by the hunter. "Trap" is used five times in the KJV and ASV, and 12 times in the RSV. It is the rendering in these three versions of the Heb. *môqēsh* (Josh 23:13; Ps 69:22), *mashḥit* (Jer 5:26), *malkōdet* (Job 18:10), and the Gr. *thēra* (Rom 11:9, a free quotation of Ps 69:22, LXX, in which *thēra* is an expletive which does not occur in the original text). In the RSV "trap" is used to translate the Heb. *paḥ* (Job 18:9; Ps 140:5; 141:9; 142:3: Isa 8:14; Amos 3:5) and *māzôr* (Ob 7; cf. KJV "wound"; ASV "snare"). "Trap" often occurs with the synonymous word "snare" and is used metaphorically of sudden and unforeseen disaster or of the plots of the wicked against the godly. *See* Gin; Hunting; Snare.

E. R. D.

TRAVEL AND COMMUNICATION. In ancient Bible times travel and communication were not always easy. Means of transportation were quite primitive, according to modern standards, but at an early time countries developed both land and sea transportation and communication for political, military and commercial purposes.

Palestine was ready for the early development of roads for travel since the country was the land bridge between the area of Mesopotamia and Syria to the NE, Arabia to the SE, and the land of Egypt and N Africa to the SW. This land, promised to Abraham (Gen 12:1–3; 17:8), could be called in the 2nd and 1st mil. B.C. "the international race track" and "the apple of discord," as nations fought with one another on its soil and vied with one another for its possession. It is to be noted that in the first three quarters of the 2nd mil. B.C. there were serviceable, well-guarded travel routes throughout much of the Near East.

In addition to the more traveled roads, there were caravan routes upon which merchants carried their goods, and desert paths upon which Bedouin and nomadic tribes went in search of pasture and water.

In contrast to the people of Tyre (cf. Ezk 27) and Phoenicia, the Israelites cannot be said to have made significant advance in sea travel in this early period. Although knowing of ships and sailing from contact with the Phoenicians, Israel failed to develop sea power because of the lack of good natural harbors S of Mount Carmel and because of Philistine domination along the Mediterranean Coast. Thus, even when Solomon developed some sea power in the 10th cen. B.C., he did so not from the Mediterranean Sea but from the Gulf of Aqaba at Ezion-geber near Elath (cf. I Kgs 9:26–28).

Land Travel in OT and NT Times

There was considerable travel in Palestinian and other lands in very early times, as exampled by Cain (Gen 4:14-16) and those who scattered from the tower of Babel (Gen 11:9). During the 3rd mil. B.C. traveling merchants of Sumer conducted a thriving business both domestic and foreign. Assyrian traders shortly after 2000 B.C. regularly traveled 500 miles from Ashur the capital to their merchant colony at Kanish in central Anatolia. Midianite caravans traversed Palestine bearing spices, balm and slaves for trade with Egypt (Gen 37:25–28). *See* Commerce.

Individuals with their families and possessions made extensive trips, as Abraham into Canaan and Egypt (Gen 12–13), Jacob from Padan-aram to Canaan (Gen 31–33), Ruth and Naomi from Moab to Bethlehem (Ruth 1), Joseph and Mary from Nazareth to Bethlehem and then later into Egypt (Lk 2; Mt 2).

Sometimes large groups of people traveled from one country to another, either voluntarily or as captives, as the Israelites in the Exodus journeys (Ex 12ff.) and the captives taken at the fall of the northern kingdom of Israel (II Kgs 17) and of the southern kingdom of Judah (II Kgs 24–25).

Disasters such as famine often resulted in travel and exchange of food and goods as, for example, Jacob and his sons trading spices, honey, nuts, etc., for Egyptian grain (Gen 43:11ff.) and then immigrating into Egypt (Gen 46:1-6). Frequently military operations would bring about the movement of large bodies of troops and equipment (cf. the Assyrian attack against Jerusalem (II Kgs 18:17; 19:35).

Following Jewish dispersions to various regions of the Near East in the Hellenistic and NT periods, additional travel in Palestine was stimulated, as Jews returned to their home land to participate in the annual feasts. For example, Jews from various lands were present at Jerusalem for Pentecost (Acts 2:5, 9–11); and commercial transactions at the temple, including money changing, evidence the presence of many foreign visitors (Jn 2:13–16; Mt 21:12–13).

Sea Travel in OT and NT Times

Egypt and Sumer yield evidence of sailing boats before 3000 B.C. Pharaohs of the Old Kingdom imported timber from the Lebanon Mountains for shipbuilding and their palaces. The annals of Snefru (*c.* 2650 B.C.) tell of bringing 40 ships filled with cedar logs, each ship over 170 feet long (ANET, p. 227).

Familiarity with sea travel among the Israelites may be noted when Jacob prophesied of Zebulun, whose territory bordered on the area of Tyre and Sidon, as becoming a "haven of ships" (Gen 49:13), and when Asher (to the N) and Dan (on the coast) likewise were associated with sea travel (Jud 5:17). Traces of small Canaanite ports have recently been discovered on the coastline S of Mount Carmel at the mouth of nearly every estuary and small river.

Considerable sea trade developed in Solomon's time, evidenced by his fleet built at Ezion-geber and used for trade with Ophir in S Arabia or W India (I Kgs 9:26–28) and by his navy united with that of Hiram, king of Tyre, trading with Tarshish (I Kgs 10:22; II Chr 9:21). Jehoshaphat in his time also desired trade with Ophir, but his "ships of Tarshish" were broken at Ezion-geber (I Kgs 22:47–48; II Chr 20:35–37).

The extent of Phoenician sea power and the maritime activity of Tyre is seen by a study of Ezk 27. See "Ships and Navigation," CornPBE, pp. 659-663.

Roads, Highways and Sea Lanes

Palestine being the international link that it was between countries in the Middle East, it was natural that important roads and highways should develop early in various parts of its territory. The Heb words *m^e^sillâ*, meaning "a raised, built-up way, highway," used in Num 20:19; Jud 20:31, etc. (cf. the metaphorical use in Isa 40:3), suggests developed road systems. Frequently there were caravansaries (or inns for caravans) and fortresses built along these roads.

Dominant road systems in Palestine included:

1. The great trunk road, or "the way of the sea" (Isa 9:1), used by the armies of Egypt, Assyria and Babylon, which led through Damascus and ran SW to Hazor (where it was joined by a route from the N past Mount Hermon), past the Sea of Galilee and via the pass of Megiddo to the coastal plain through Lydda, Ashkelon, Gaza and along "the way of the land of the Philistines" (Ex 13:17) into Egypt.

2. The hill country road, connecting near Kadesh-barnea with the way of Shur (Gen 16:7) to Egypt, through the Negeb desert to Beer-sheba in the S, up the ridge going N through Hebron, Bethlehem, Jerusalem, Gibeah of Saul, Ramah, Mizpah, Bethel (Jud 21:19), Shiloh, Shechem, Samaria, Dothan, Ibleam, and on.

3. The king's highway (*q.v.*; Num 21:22, 27–30; Deut 2:26 f.), which ran S from Damascus through Karnaim in Bashan, following the W edge of the Transjordan plateau through Medeba, Heshbon, Kir-Harosheth, and Petra to Elath by the Red Sea (the Gulf of Aqaba) and on to Arabia. At Bozrah near Punon in Edom a branch of this route crossed the Arabah to Tamar, climbing again into the central Negeb to join the way of Shur at Kadesh-barnea. It was this route that the Edomites denied to Israel on her circuitous march toward the land of Canaan (Num 20:17).

4. The way of the Red Sea (Ex 13:18; Num 14:25; 21:4; Deut 1:40; 2:1), which crossed the Sinai desert from the present Port Suez to Elath at the head of the Gulf of Aqaba on the way to Arabia.

5. West-east roads from Joppa through Lod (Lydda), then either up the Valley of Ajalon ("the way of the ascent of Beth-horon" of Josh 10:6–14) through Bethel to Jericho, or S to Beth-shemesh and up the Valley of Sorek (I Sam 6:12) through Jerusalem to Jericho (Lk 10:30). (For further details on roads see Denis Baly, *The Geography of the Bible,* 1957, chap. ix; Y. Aharoni and M. Avi-Yonah, *Macmillan Bible Atlas,* maps 9, 10.)

Although Jesus often used bypaths, He undoubtedly traveled on some of these important roads, such as the one from Jericho up the Wadi Qelt (the Jericho road) to Jerusalem. Paul traveled on many of the great paved Roman roads of Palestine, Asia Minor and SE Europe, and also on a portion of the famous Appian Way near Rome (Acts 28:15). See "Roads, Transportation, Trade Routes," CornPBE, pp. 626–630.

Well-known sea lanes included:

1. The route from Egypt to Rome for grain imports, which because of unfavorable head

TRAVEL AND COMMUNICATION

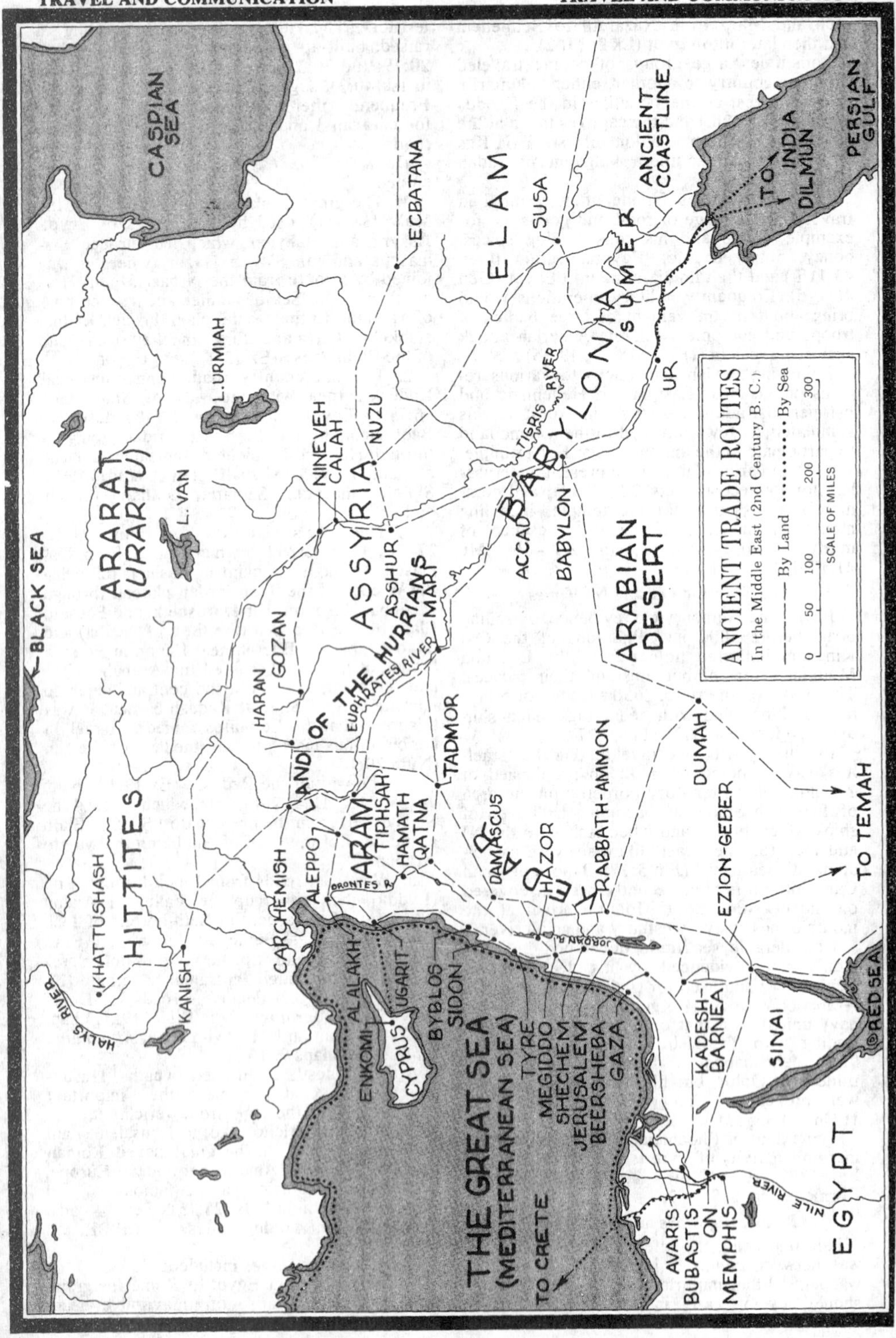

 TRAVEL AND COMMUNICATION

A section of the Egnation Way near Philippi. This was the main Roman road across Greece and Paul certainly traveled on it. HFV

winds frequently caused ships to travel from Alexandria to Rome via Syria and Asia Minor. It was one of these ships on which Paul embarked on his way from Melita to Rome (Acts 28:11). It was well-known that traveling by ship in the winter was dangerous (cf. Acts 27).

2. The lane from the Crimean Lake Maeotis or Sea of Azov above the Euxine or Black Sea down through the Aegean and Mediterranean Seas to Alexandria.

Well-known ports and maritime cities in ancient times included Tyre of the OT (cf. Ezk 27) and NT times (Acts 21:1–8), and in the Hellenistic and NT periods such ports as Seleucia near Antioch, Ephesus, Corinth (cf. Acts 18:18, Cenchrea, a port close to Corinth), Alexandria, Puteoli, Ostia near Rome, and Caesarea (a harbor which Herod the Great had built, cf. Jos *Ant.* xv.9.6). Into this last port Paul came at the end of his second missionary journey (Acts 18:22) and from it he sailed on his journey to Rome (Acts 23:33; 27:2).

Modes of Transportation

Walking. The easiest and most common mode of transportation in ancient times was walking, as exhibited by the frequent use of the word "walk" in the OT and the NT. Abraham was encouraged to walk through Canaan to see what land God had given to him (Gen 13:17). The palsied man was commanded by Jesus to rise, take up his pallet, and walk home (Mk 2:9–11). With metaphorical reference to this frequent mode of transportation, often God's people are encouraged to walk in God's way (cf. Gen 17:1; I Kgs 2:4; Lk 1:6). The hill country, rugged wilderness of Judea, and the rising Transjordan area no doubt made walking arduous, although it was the most frequent and least expensive way of traveling. Jesus walked everywhere with His disciples (cf. Mt 4:18; Mk 10: 32; Jn 1:36).

Animals for riding and as beasts of burden. The two Testaments indicate that people rode on a variety of animals, such as the ass (Num 22:22; Mt 21:7), the mule (II Sam 18:9), the horse (Zech 1:8; Rev 6:4), and the camel (Gen 24:61). These and other animals were used also as beasts of burden.

Reference to the *horse* (Heb. *sûs,* Gr. *hippos*) is found early in the OT, such as horses of the Egyptians (Ex 9:3; 15:21) including their chariot horses (Ex 14:9, 23), the chariot horses of the Canaanites (Jud 5:22) and also of Absalom (II Sam 15:1), and the many horses of Solomon (I Kgs 10:25–26). The Palestinian horse was a light breed like the Arabian. Horses seem to have been used extremely early in Palestine, evidenced by the discovery of bones of horses (domesticated) in a Negeb settlement dating from the Chalcolithic period before 3000 B.C. (cf. "Fauna," IDB, II, 248). But horses did not become well known in the Near East until after 2000 B.C. when they came to be employed chiefly for drawing war chariots. Mounted cavalry first appeared in northern Mesopotamia after 1000 B.C. Horses used in postal service are mentioned in Est 8:10.

The importance of horses in the NT period is seen in various references to them in Revelation (6:4; 9:9; 14:20; 18:13; 19:18). The white horse (Rev 19:11) was for the conquering commander. This common animal guided by a bit in its mouth makes a fitting illustration for James (3:2–3).

The Palestinian *ass,* found in all periods, very possibly a descendant of the Nubian variety of Africa recognized for its black shoulder and black stripes (F. S. Bodenheimer, "Fauna," IDB, II, 248), is spoken of in Scripture as : (1) the ass or he-ass (Heb. *ḥămôr*) used as a beast of burden (Gen 22:3, 5; 44:13) and for riding (Ex 4:20; Josh 15:18; II Sam 16:2); (2) the she-ass (Heb. *'ātôn*), also a beast of burden (Gen 45:23) and an animal for riding (Jud 5:10); (3) the young male ass (Heb. *'ayir*) used for the same two purposes (Jud 10:4; Isa 30:6), (4) and the onager or wild ass (Heb. *pere'*), tamed by some in Mesopotamia (W. S.

Neapolis was the port of Philippi. HFV

McCullough, "Ass," IDB, I, 260), but evidently used very little if at all in Palestine as a domesticated animal for travel or burden bearing (cf. Job 6:5; 39:5; Isa 32:14; Jer 2:24; 16:6; Ps 104:11).

The NT Gr. word for male and female ass is *onos*, an animal used in Christ's triumphal entry into Jerusalem (Mt 21:2; Jn 12:15), the "colt" of the ass being the young donkey. (The Gr. word is *pōlos* which means "young animal," but when another animal is in the context it can mean a "horse colt.")

The *mule* (Heb. *pered*) was also used for riding (II Sam 13:29), for battle (II Sam 18:9) and as a beast of burden (II Kgs 5:17). Sometimes a she-mule (Heb. *pir^{e}ddâ*) was used for riding (as by the king, I Kgs 1:33). This animal is not mentioned in the NT.

The *camel* (Heb. *gāmāl*), the one humped or dromedary variety, is referred to in Gen 12:16; 31:17; 37:25; etc., and is not to be taken as an anachronism since there is archaeological evidence for the camel from the early 2nd mil. and before (cf. J. P. Free, "Abraham's Camels," JNES, III [1944], 187–193; K. A. Kitchen, *Ancient Orient and OT*, 1966, pp. 79f.). This animal was used as a beast of burden (Gen 24:10ff.; I Kgs 10:2; Isa 30:6) and for riding when speed, not comfort, was primary (Gen 24:64; 31:17–21; I Sam 30:17). The young camel or dromedary (Heb. *bik^{e}râ*) is referred to in Jer 2:23 and Isa 60:6; also possibly Isa 66:20, "swift beasts" (KJV), has reference to the dromedary (Heb. *kirkārâ*; see RSV).

The importance of the camel in the NT period (Gr. *kamēlos*) is seen in its use in illustrations (Mt 19:24; 23:24) and the use of its hair in clothing (Mt 3:4; Mk 1:6). *See* Animals, I.5.

Vehicles. Various kinds of vehicles were developed in ancient times both for carrying passengers and goods. Archaeological remains show a very early four solid-wheeled covered *wagon* at Tepe Gawra (3rd mil. B.C., ANEP, fig. 169), and two-wheeled Assyrian *carts* with four, six and eight spokes, drawn by oxen (cf. ANEP, figs. 167, 367) and also by mules, and even by two men (J. Davis, *A Dictionary of the Bible*, 4th rev. ed. p. 123). Carts in the OT might be of wood (I Sam 6:14), covered (Num 7:3) or uncovered, and drawn by cattle (Num 7:7) or horses (Isa 28:28). They were used to haul various objects (I Sam 6:7; II Sam 6:3) including grain (Amos 2:13), and to convey persons (Gen 45:19).

Carts of Bible times included:

1. The *'ăgālâ* (Heb. word coming from the concept of "rolling of wheels"), used of vehicles drawn by cattle (I Sam 6:7; Num 7:3) for the transporting of persons and things (Gen 46:5; I Sam 6:8; II Sam 6:3), and even used as a war chariot or military transport wagon (Ps 46:9), as well as a threshing wagon (Isa 28:27–28).

2. A Gr. equivalent for cart or wagon, *hamaxa*, occurs in the LXX but not in the NT. Another Gr. word, *rhedē* (from Celtic and then Latin *reda* or *raeda*), a four-wheeled carriage, is used in Rev 18:13. Although not mentioned in the NT, there were a number of Roman vehicles with two or four wheels, such as: the *carpentum*, a two-wheeled covered carriage used as a state-carriage and also for general traveling; the *carruca*, a large four-wheeled carriage (something like the *reda*); the light, uncovered two-wheeled open front *cisium* used for swift travel; the familiar two-wheeled chariot, the *currus* (the Gr. *harma*) used for racing and war; the *tensa*, a two-wheeled stately carriage pulled by four horses and used in state affairs and for religious purposes, etc.

The *chariot* was a specialized vehicle for general riding, though mainly for military purposes. Ancient chariots included the 3rd mil. Sumerian disk-wheeled chariot drawn by four asses, found at Ur (ANEP, fig. 163); the spoked-wheeled chariots of Hammurabi's time (*c.* 1750 B.C.); the four, six, and eight spoked-wheeled Egyptian chariots of the middle and late 2nd mil. B.C. (ANEP, figs 314–316, 327, 345). By the time of the Assyrian military ascendancy in the early 9th cen. B.C. the six- and eight-spoked chariots were in vogue (ANEP, figs. 204, 356–367). The Elamite 12-spoked wagon (or chariot) was an oddity (ANEP, fig. 168). The chariot was manned by one (ANEP, fig. 300), two (ANEP, figs. 172, 184), and three men (J. W. Wevers, "Chariot," IDB, I, 553).

The OT war chariot, the *rekeb*, the vehicle used by the Egyptians (Ex 14:7; Josh 24:6) and by the Canaanites (Josh 11:4; Jud 4:7), was made mainly of wood (Josh 11:6; II Kgs 23:11), and was ironbound or studded (Josh 17:16; Jud 1:19; 4:3, 13). The use of this vehicle was slow in developing in Israel (1) because the constant movement in the Exodus wanderings did not warrant the building of such vehicles (Joshua with his foot soldiers had to defeat Jabin of Hazor with his chariots by surprise in a mountain valley, Josh 11:4–9), and (2) because of the uneven terrain of the hill country basically inhabited by Israel (Josh 17:16–18; Jud 1:19). Israel was so unprepared for chariot warfare that it achieved victory under Deborah and Barak against Sisera and his 900 chariots only with the help of flash flooding (Jud 4-5). It was not until David's and Solomon's time that Israel used chariots effectively (II Sam 8:4; I Kgs 9:19). In a figurative sense the Lord is said to show His power and sovereignty by using the chariot (II Kgs 2:11-12; 6:17; Ps 68:17).

Chariots could be used also as a symbol of pomp and royal dignity, as in the case of Joseph's riding in an Egyptian chariot (Gen 41:43; cf. also Jer 17:25), as well as a vehicle for travel (as in the case of the Ethiopian eunuch, Acts 8:28; the Gr. word is *harma*, used also as a war chariot in Rev 9:9).

The *litter* could be a portable bed (as the Heb. *mittâ* in I Sam 19:15) or a canopied couch or sedan chair, borne on men's shoulders. The palanquin (Heb. *'appiryôn*) of Song 3:9-10 (RSV) seems to be an equivalent expression to the "litter" (*mittâ*) of Song 3:7 (RSV) or "traveling couch" (NASB). Another expression for the same thing is the Heb. *ṣāb* (litter) of Isa 66:20.

Vessels for sea travel. Seafaring vessels, of course, included ships for commercial and military purposes. Archaeology and literary sources reveal that there was considerable naval activity among the Egyptians and the Assyrians. The 3rd mil. shows evidence of Canaanite shipping to Egypt, and in the 18th Dynasty a tomb painting of Egyptian sea-going vessels shows single-mast ships, with crow's nest, large rectangular sail, high prows and stern, guided by oars as rudders (ANEP, fig. 111). In the time of the Philistines ships appear with a row of oars as well. Assyrian ships could be either a small variety with a helmsman at the stern and oarsman near the prow; larger transport ships with high horse-headed prows and high sterns propelled by both oars and sail attached to a center mast with crow's nest; or three-decked warships with pointed ram, consisting of two rows of oarsmen and armed warriors on the top deck (ANEP, fig. 106).

Pictures of ships from archaeological remains in Phoenicia and Palestine are few. From later times, a 4th cen. B.C. Byblos coin depicts a Phoenician war galley with lion-head prow and ruddered by an oar (ANEP, fig 225), and a 1st cen. A.D. Sidon sarcophagus shows a high curved prowed (with attached flag) ship with an unfurled sail connected with a single mast and a spanker sail attached to a small mast aft. From Tell Sandahannah (200 B.C.–A.D. 200) in Palestine comes a graffito scratched on a stone depicting a ship with a sail and oars and two anchors at the stern (J. B. Pritchard, "Ships, OT," IDB, IV, 335). (Cf. Acts 27:29 where four anchors were at the stern of the ship.)

Although no warships are mentioned in the NT, the Roman navy had various sized vessels, such as biremes (two tiers of oars), triremes, and even quinqueremes (five-tiered). Merchant ships plied the Mediterranean, like the grain ship Paul traveled on which carried a crew and passengers totaling 276 (Acts 27:2,37). Merchant ships also carried cargos of wine and similar items in amphorae and pithoi (Gr. jars) from the island of Rhodes (which produced many stamped, dated amphorae) and other places. Remains of these jars which stood in racks have been found in archaeological excavations and on underwater wrecks.

The merchant ship carried the figurehead of the deity from whom it got its name, as Castor and Pollux was the name for the ship on which Paul sailed from Sicily to Puteoli (Acts 28:11). Pictures of grain ships show a great square mainsail with a raked foremast and a small square sail (the foresail, *artemōn*, Acts 27:40).

Smaller vessels carried goods between the Decapolis and Galilee and fishing boats plied the waters of the Sea of Galilee (cf. Mt 4:18-22; Lk 5:1-11).

In the OT, sea vessels (Heb *'aniyyâ*) were military ships for captives (Deut 28:68) or merchant ships (II Chr 9:21), and they could be propelled by oars (Isa 33:21). The Heb. *ṣî*, a loan-word from Egyptian, is also used for ship (cf. Num 24:24; Isa 33:21).

Greek ship of the fifth century B.C.

In the NT, emphasis is placed on smaller vessels or boats (Gr. *ploion*, Mt 4:21f.; Mk 1:19; Lk 5:3; etc.; and *ploiarion*, Mk 3:9; Jn 6:22-23) such as would sail the Sea of Galilee; as well as on the larger sea-going vessel (Gr. *naus*, Acts 27:41, and also *ploion*, Acts 20:13, 38; 21:2f.; 27:2-44; Rev 8:9; etc.) which would ply the Mediterranean. None of these ships were military, and the ones on which Paul traveled to Rome were definitely grain ships (Acts 27-28). The "boat" of Acts 27:16, 30, 32 (Gr. *skaphē*) was the ship's lifeboat. *See* Ship.

Types of Communication

Verbal and written communication between persons, groups and states in ancient times could be maintained in several ways. First, the communication could be made by *personal visit*, as illustrated by the visit of the Queen of Sheba to Solomon (I Kgs 10:1-10), and Paul's projected visits to the Philippians (Phil 1:24-25) and to the Romans (Rom 1:15).

Another means of communication was the use of the *personal messenger,* as the one sent by Joab to David regarding the battle at Rabbah (II Sam 11:18–25).

A third basic method of communication was that accomplished through the *dispatching of letters.* This was done by governments and governmental officials, as is evidenced in Est 3:13; 8:10 where in the Persian system letters were dispatched by foot runners or mounted couriers (cf. also runners, "posts" in KJV, used by Hezekiah to deliver letters to the nation, II Chr 30:6, 10); and in Acts 23:15, 25ff, where the military tribune (Gr. *chiliarchos*) sent an official letter regarding Paul to the governor Felix. The official postal system of the Roman Empire did not handle other than official mail. Thus to accomplish the task of delivering letters wealthy families used slaves, and companies employed letter carriers called *tabellarii* (from the wooden tablet called *tabella* upon which were written brief communications).

In Christian circles a selected group could be charged with delivering a communication (as the decree of the Jerusalem council, Acts 15:22–23). Paul had his letters to churches delivered by private friends and associates, such as the Corinthian epistle probably by Titus (II Cor 8:16–18), the one to Philippi by Epaphroditus (Phil 2:25–30), and the ones to Ephesus and Colossae by Tychicus (Eph 6:21; Col 4:7–8).

Bibliography. Yohanan Aharoni, *The Land of the Bible,* trans. from Heb. by A. F. Rainey, Philadelphia: Westminster Press, 1967. F. S. Bodenheimer, *Animal and Man in Bible Lands,* Leiden: E. J. Brill, 1960. R. J. Forbes, "Land Transport and Road Building," *Studies in Ancient Technology,* Leiden: E. J. Brill, 1955, II, 126–186. J. P. Free, "Abraham's Camels," *Journal of Near Eastern Studies,* 1944, pp. 187–193. E. G. Kraeling, *Bible Atlas,* New York: Rand McNally and Co., 1956. James B. Pritchard, *The Ancient Near East in Pictures,* Princeton: Princeton Univ. Press, 1954. G. E. Wright and F. V. Filson, *The Westminster Historical Atlas to the Bible,* rev. ed., Philadelphia: Westminster Press, 1956. Yigael Yadin, *The Art of Warfare in Biblical Lands,* Vols. 1 and 2, New York: McGraw-Hill, 1963.

W. H. M.

TREAD, TREADER. *See* Winepress.

TREASURE, TREASURY. "Treasure" is the translation of several Heb. and Gr. words, *'ôṣār* and *thēsauros* being the chief ones. It refers to a valuable accumulation of money or other forms of wealth such as gems, rich clothing, or precious metals. It could be the treasure of kings (Isa 39:2), or temple (I Kgs 14:25–26), or of a rich man (Lk 12:21). The word may be used figuratively, as of Israel as God's treasure (Ex 19:5; Ps 135:4), or of one's heavenly treasure of salvation or virtue (Mt 6:19–21; Lk 12:33), or of the gospel (II Cor 4:7), or of the quality of one's heart (Lk 6:45).

The above-mentioned Heb. and Gr. terms can also mean the place where treasure is stored. The "treasures" which the magi opened in the presence of the infant Jesus and Mary were probably jewel caskets (Mt 2:11). Both Solomon's temple and the royal palace had treasuries for the sacred vessels and valuables held in store (I Chr 28:11–13; II Chr 32:27–28). The treasury of Herod's temple where the people brought their monetary gifts was in the Court of the Women (Mk 12:41–44; Jn 8:20). Pithom and Rameses were treasure or store cities for Pharaoh (Ex 1:11).

See Storehouse; Occupations: Treasurer.

N. B. B.

The Temple of Saturn in the Roman Forum was one of the ancient Roman treasuries.
HFV

TREASURE CITY. *See* City, Treasure; Store City.

TREASURER. *See* Occupations: Treasurer.

TREATY. *See* Alliance; Covenant.

TREE. *See* Plants.

TREE OF KNOWLEDGE, TREE OF LIFE. Two trees planted by God in the midst of the garden in Eden (Gen 2:9; 3:22, 24). The tree of life was so called because its fruit conferred immortality upon the person who ate it. In Proverbs (3:18; 11:30; 13:12; 15:4) it is a symbol of health and long life, success and happiness. In apocalyptic visions (I Enoch 24:4–25:6; II Enoch 8:3; II Esdras 8:52; Testament of Twelve Patriarchs: Levi 18:1; Rev 2:7; 22:2, 14, 19 [ASV, etc.]), the tree of life is reserved for the righteous after the last judgment.

Plants whose fruit conferred life upon the one who ate it were a popular theme in ancient Mesopotamian literature. Gilgamesh acquired a plant from the bottom of the sea which could give him immortality, but while he was taking it home a snake stole it from him (ANET, p. 96). In the myth of Adapa, there is mention of magical bread and water which can bestow immortality (ANET, pp. 101f.). In ancient art, representations of the tree of life or a sacred tree flanked by two rearing goats are known from Assyria and Crete. The tree is usually stylized, sometimes representing a date palm, economically the most important tree grown in Mesopotamia (VBW, I, 21–22). At Calah in the palace of Ashurnasirpal II two-winged goddesses stand on either side of a sacred tree (ANEP, #656; see also#654, 667, 706). *See* Trees, Sacred.

The tree of knowledge plays a lesser role in the Bible than the tree of life. In Gen 2 and 3 it constituted a test of obedience for Adam and Eve. When the couple disobeyed God and ate of the tree of knowledge, they were deceived by Satan into obtaining an experiential knowledge of evil and thus fell into sin (Gen 3:22). The possibility of eating of the tree of life was then withdrawn, lest man become immortalized in his sinful condition and sin propagate itself forever. Eternal life then had to be gained through redemption (James J. Reeve, "Tree of Life," ISBE, V, 3009f.).

Of the various theories about the nature of this knowledge the following are the most important:

1. Sexual knowledge. Adam and Eve became conscious of sex and were ashamed of their nakedness. The Heb. word "know" often implies sexual intercourse. But this could not make man like God since it is not appropriate for God (Gen 3:22).

2. Universal knowledge. "Good and evil" constitutes an antonymic pair (or merism) implying totality (cf. II Sam 14:17, 20). But Adam and Eve clearly did not become omniscient (Gen 3:8ff.). The characteristic feature of this knowledge was a consciousness of sin and guilt (Gen 3:7ff.).

3. Moral judgment and conscience. God knows good experientially but evil only intellectually and never experientially. Man is like God (Gen 3:22) in his ability to discern between right and wrong. He differs from God in that his knowledge of evil involves guilt and shame since it was obtained not by revelation and observation, but by participation in sin.

H. M. Hof.

TREES, SACRED. Sacred trees and groves are known among many ancient peoples. They were found among the Canaanites and became a snare for Israel. It is not altogether clear why the trees were considered as having sacred significance. Some think that it was simply the refreshing shade of a grove of trees that attracted worshipers to the site, the trees being only incidental (Hos 4:13). It is more likely that certain trees and places were believed to be the abode of powerful gods or spirits, and the people came to worship the spirit there. Certain noted trees in Scripture may have gained their fame for this reason, or they may also have marked the home of some well-known man (Gen 12:6; 13:18; Jud 4:5; 9:37, all RSV).

The word "asherah," often mistakenly translated "grove" in the KJV, was the Heb. name for the female consort of the Canaanite god El. (*See* Gods, False: Asherah; Plants: Grove.) The translators' confusion is understandable for the goddess was worshiped in the thick groves and she was symbolized by a pole or even a living tree planted by a sanctuary (Ex 34:13; Deut 12:3; 16:21). The sacred prostitution carried on in the name of this fertility goddess made the groves of green trees notorious, and this is the reason why, on the lips of the prophets, the phrase "under every green tree" became the symbol of Israel's spiritual adultery from Yahweh (Isa 57:5; Jer 2:20; Ezk 6:13; 20:28). *See* Plants: Tree.

P. C. J.

TRENCH. A narrow ditch or excavation. It is used to translate the following terms.

1. Heb. *ma'gāl*. In I Sam 17:20 and 26:5, 7 the KJV renders the term by "trench" with a marginal reading of "place of carriages" ("midst of his carriages," I Sam 26:5). The ASV translates it as the "place of the wagons" with a marginal reading of "barricade," while the RSV uses the word "encampment." The root of the term ' *-g-l* may conceivably be related to *'ăgālâ*, "wagon or cart," and mean the formation of wagons surrounding the Israelite army as a protective barricade. But the same root may more appropriately be taken to mean "round" (cf. the Hexaplaric recension of the LXX: Gr. *stroggylōsin*, "a rounding") and refer generally to the encampment in its circular form. Moreover, the word "trench" creates a wrong impression in the mind of the English reader; consequently, the word "encampment" or "circle of the camp" (NASB) is to be preferred.

2. Heb. *ḥêl*. In the KJV of II Sam 20:15 Joab and his men in the investment of the city of Abel of Bethmaacah cast up a bank against the city and "it stood in the trench." While the ASV, RSV, and NASB translate the term by "rampart," it is more precisely to be conceived of as a small outer wall (JerusB) or outwork.

3. Heb. *te'ālâ*. In I Kgs 18:32, 35, 38 Elijah commanded a large trench (so KJV, ASV, RSV) to be made about the altar, which subsequently became filled with the water of the 12 jars poured upon the sacrifice.

4. Heb. *gēbîm*. In II Kgs 3:16 the ASV renders the repeated term as "full of trenches" (KJV "full of ditches"; RSV "full of pools"). A literal translation of the divine oracle is: "A making of this wadi trenches upon trenches." The trenches served for the collection of the anticipated water for the desiccated armies.

In the NT Jerusalem is represented as about to have a trench (so KJV; RV, RSV "bank"; ASV marg. "palisade") cast up against her by her enemies (Lk 19:43). The Gr. term *charax* is here used in a military sense of a palisade or a fence of stakes preventing entrance to or exit from the beleaguered city.

E. R. D.

TRESPASS. A trespass (Heb. *ma'al*, a treacherous, unfaithful act; or *pesha'*, a transgression) is a sin committed against either God (Num 31:16) or man (Gen 31:36; Ex 22:9; Num 5:12, 27).

In addition to the atonement necessary for the guilt involved, the Levitical system required a repayment or restitution when men trespassed against others (Lev 5:15–6:7; 7:1–10). This trespass offering (Heb. *'āshām*) typified the payment made by Christ for our sins (Isa 53:10f.). *See* Sacrifices and Offerings. The spiritual counterpart of the OT rite is exemplified in the restitution and reconciliation required of Christians before their trespasses are forgiven (Mt 6:14f.; 18:15–17, 21–35; Eph 4:32).

Joab warned King David not to be a cause of trespass or guilt to Israel (I Chr 21:3). On other occasions whole tribes or nations were warned not to act unfaithfully and increase their guilt (Josh 22:16, 20; II Chr 28:12f.) of their trespasses. Leaders are especially responsible for their trespass or unfaithfulness (II Chr 33:19; Ezr 9:2, 6f.). All trespasses bring wrath from the Lord (II Chr 24:18; Ezk 14:13f.).

Men by nature are dead in their trespasses (Eph 2:1). Only God can forgive them (Col 2:13) and make them righteous in Christ by no longer accounting their trespasses against them (II Cor 5:19–21).

See Sin.

W. B.

TRESPASS OFFERING. *See* Sacrificial Offerings.

TRIAL. *See* Law, Administration of; Temptation.

TRIAL OF JESUS. *See* Christ, Passion of; Jesus Christ.

TRIANGLES. One of the two marginal readings suggested by the ASV and RSV for the rendering of the Heb. term *shālish* in I Sam 18:6. The KJV, ASV, and RSV have as their text "instruments of music" and agree in appending the alternate translation of "three-stringed instruments." The Heb. term is definitely connected with *shālôsh*, "three," but its precise meaning is unknown. What can be inferred with certainty is that the instrument was played by women at a joyful occasion to accompany songs of joy and dancing. It has been tentatively identified with a three-stringed lute (Kolari) or a sistrum (Amer. trans.).

See Music.

TRIBE. The normal unit of social organization among the Semitic nomads and seminomads. The staff was symbolic of the leader's authority. Thus the two Heb. words for rod regularly denote a tribe (*maṭṭeh*, "staff, rod"; *shēbeṭ*, "rod, scepter"). The Gr. word in the NT is *phylē* (e.g., Lk 2:36; Heb 7:13).

Josh 7:14 displays the skeleton of the Israelite tribe. In descending order it was composed of the clan (Heb. *mishpāḥāh;* cf. Ex 6:14; Jud 9:1, NASB), the household or family (Heb. *bayit*), and the individual man (Heb. *geber*). A few times the Heb. term *'elep* (thousand) also carries the meaning "clan" (cf. Jud 6:15, RSV; I Sam 10:19, NASB; Mic 5:2, NASB). The clan or group of families (cf. Reuben in Ex 6:14) mediated between the larger tribal unit and the smaller familial units. The term *bêt-'ābôt* ("fathers' houses," Ex 6:14) in the sense of father-households was ambiguous, referring to groups from a tribe (Num 1:4) to a clan (Num 3:24, NASB) to a home unit (Ex 12:3). Married brothers with few sons might be reckoned together as forming one such "father's household" (I Chr 23:11, NASB). Although large, and even including the servants or retainers "born in the house" as in Gen 14:14, the household centered around a patriarch or sheik such as Abraham or Jacob, and traveled with him (Gen 12:1; 31:17–18).

Possession of similar religious convictions and an ancestry and economic and military purposes in common contributed to tribal unity. Groups of tribes might be united under an amphictyonic covenant, such as states in ancient Greece as at Delphi and the 12 tribes of Israel at Shiloh (Josh 18:1; 21:2; I Sam 1:3). In Israel's case their covenant with Yahweh was first instituted in the Promised Land at Shechem (Josh 8:30–35) and later renewed there as their leader Joshua approached death (Josh 24:1–28). *See* Covenant.

At the time of the Exodus, the Israelite tribal structure included a council of elders (Ex 3:16; 34:31). *See* Elder. The leader of each tribe was termed a prince (Num 34:18). The "princes of the tribes," the "heads of thousands," aided Moses and Aaron in numbering the people (Num 1:4–16). By the period covered in Judges, decentralization, and with it lawlessness, had set in. Individual judges periodically exercised centralized authority (cf. Jud 3:15; 4:6; 13:2, 24–25). Samuel, the prophet-judge (I Sam 3:20; 7:15), solidified the tribes preceding the inception of the kingdom under Saul (I Sam 9:27–10:1; 11:15). David and Solomon, however, like other monarchs of the ancient Near East, deliberately undermined tribal foundations in order to foster nationalism.

The memory of the tribal divisions remained alive in later OT history (cf. II Chr 5:2; Zech 9:1). Even later, the NT both identifies individuals with their tribes (cf. Lk 2:36; Acts 4:36; Phil 3:5; Heb 7:14) and refers to the 12 tribes (Mt 19:28; Jas 1:1; Acts 26:7; Rev 7:1–4). Jewish genealogical records were largely destroyed with the burning of the temple in A.D. 70, however, so that the modern Jew cannot be sure of his tribal ancestry.

Conceptually, the tribe is linked to an ancient progenitor so that in NT times the Jews still considered themselves children of Abraham, Isaac, and Jacob (Jn 8:33; Acts 3:13). Paul associates the NT believers with the patriarch Abraham, "the father of all them that believe" (Rom 4:11–16; Gal 3:6–7, 16–29). Thus all

TRIBES, TERRITORIES OF THE

Christians belong to the same spiritual "household of the faith" (Gal 6:10, NASB; cf. Heb 3:6; I Pet 2:5).

The OT generally mentions 12 tribes of Israel (e.g., Gen 35:22-26; Deut 27:12-13; I Chr 2:1-2; Ezk 48:1ff.). Sometimes Levi (the special priestly tribe) drops out and the two sons of Joseph appear separately (Num 1:20-47). When all three are mentioned, the count is 13 (Gen 46:8-24).

The OT contains evidence of the ancient tribal patterns of some non-Israelite peoples, e.g., the Edomites in Gen 36:1-19; the semi-nomadic Midianites in Num 25:15; 31:7-10; the Ishmaelites in Gen 25:12-18; and the Arabians in Gen 25:1-3. The latter people illustrate the change from tribal chieftains to kings and governors as they settle and turn to agriculture and trade (II Chr 9:14; Ezk 27:20-22). This breakdown of tribal organization was also true of Amorite tribes as they came in contact with civilization at Mari (*q.v.*) early in the 2nd mil. B.C.

See Family; House; Household; Israel; Tribes, Territories of the.

W. H. M.

TRIBES, TERRITORIES OF THE. The territories of the tribes of Israel do not represent fixed areas with permanent borders. Instead, they were subject to frequent change from the time of the conquest of Canaan under Joshua to the reign of King David.

The Ideal Borders of Israel

The northern border of the land of Canaan into which the Israel tribes migrated is delimited by Mount Hor (probably a prominent summit of the Lebanon range near the coast of the Mediterranean N of Byblos), Aphek on the Amorite border, Lebo-hamath, Zedad, Ziphron, and Hazar-enan. From Hazar-enan, located approximately 100 miles E of the Mediterranean coast, the ideal border turns southward to Sepham and Riblah, sites as yet unidentified. It is generally agreed that the border along the Syrian desert turns westward at about the latitude of Beth-shean and proceeds WNW to the Sea of Galilee at Ain. The eastern border continues S through the Jordan Valley and the Salt (Dead) Sea. At the S end of the Dead Sea the border is contiguous with the border of Edom, and then it turns W to Hazar-addar and Kadesh-barnea and finally to the brook of Egypt. The Mediterranean serves as the western border. These mark the general external borders of the land of Israel (Num 34:1-12; Gen 15:18-21; Josh 15:1-5; Ezk 47:13-21; 48:28). It must be noted, however, that these were never the actual borders.

Stages of Settlement

In the early years of Israelite settlement the actual borders as such were rather nondescript and quite flexible. The term "land of Israel," which came into use during the Israelite settlement of Canaan, at first referred only to the Israelite sectors of occupation in contrast to the Canaanite sectors, etc. (cf. I Sam 13:19).

During the first stages of settlement the typical tribal territory was not made up of broad territorial provinces, but rather of cities or groups of cities with their adjacent lands. Some of these holdings were isolated from other holdings of the same tribe.

The first tribes to possess territory were Gad, Reuben, and Manasseh in Transjordan. Gad occupied the land of Jaazer, the land of Gilead, and the land of Dibon (Num 21:32; 32:1, 34-36; 33:45-46; Josh 13:24-28). Reuben occupied the land of Heshbon and several surrounding cities (Num 32:37-38; Josh 13:15-23; I Chr 5:8-10). Thus the territories of the two tribes overlapped. The Machir clan of the tribe of Manasseh occupied portions of Gilead and Bashan in northern Transjordan (Num 32:33, 39-42).

In Cisjordan only those regions which were without strong Canaanite settlements were at first occupied and held by the Israelites. These regions were located in the mountains and hill country (Josh 17:18; Jud 1:19). Israelite settlement chiefly in the mountains kept them removed from Egyptian administrative centers in Canaan. This isolation in mountain enclaves explains, in part, the absence in the Bible of the mention of a number of external affairs known to us from extrabiblical records such as the Amarna letters (*q.v.*).

The Judah-Simeon coalition settled in the mountains and wilderness W of the Dead Sea. Their northern border ran N of Bethlehem and Beth-shemesh. The western border in actuality then ran S through the Shephelah into the Negeb to approximately the latitude of the S shore of the Dead Sea.

Benjamin was allotted land in the hill country N of Jebus (Jerusalem). The Josephite tribes occupied most of the mountains N of Benjamin to Mount Gilboa. Manasseh, as mentioned above, also occupied areas in Transjordan. In the Cisjordan it settled the northern section of the "hills of Ephraim" and along the coast of Sharon from Asher at Dor S of Mount Carmel to Michmethah, opposite Shechem, *c.* eight miles N of Tel Aviv (Josh 17:2-10). The tribe of Ephraim occupied primarily the southern hills of the region later called Samaria, though settlement was intermingled with Manasseh (Josh 17:9-10). Asher, Naphtali, Zebulun, and Issachar settled the Galilee region (see map).

As some of the tribes and clans outgrew their original settlements they were to expand by clearing the forests and driving out the Canaanites (Josh 17:14-18). Other tribes, such as Dan, moved to new regions for failure to actually possess their proper allotment (Jud 17, 18). Clans or parts of clans shifted locations so that some had representatives in more than one tribe (cf. Tola, a man of Issachar living in Ephraim, Jud 10:1; Gen 46:13; Num 26:23; cf. also the clans of Achan, Hezron, and Bela). Thus even after the tribal league met at Shiloh, its new religious center (Josh 18:1; 21:1-2), to

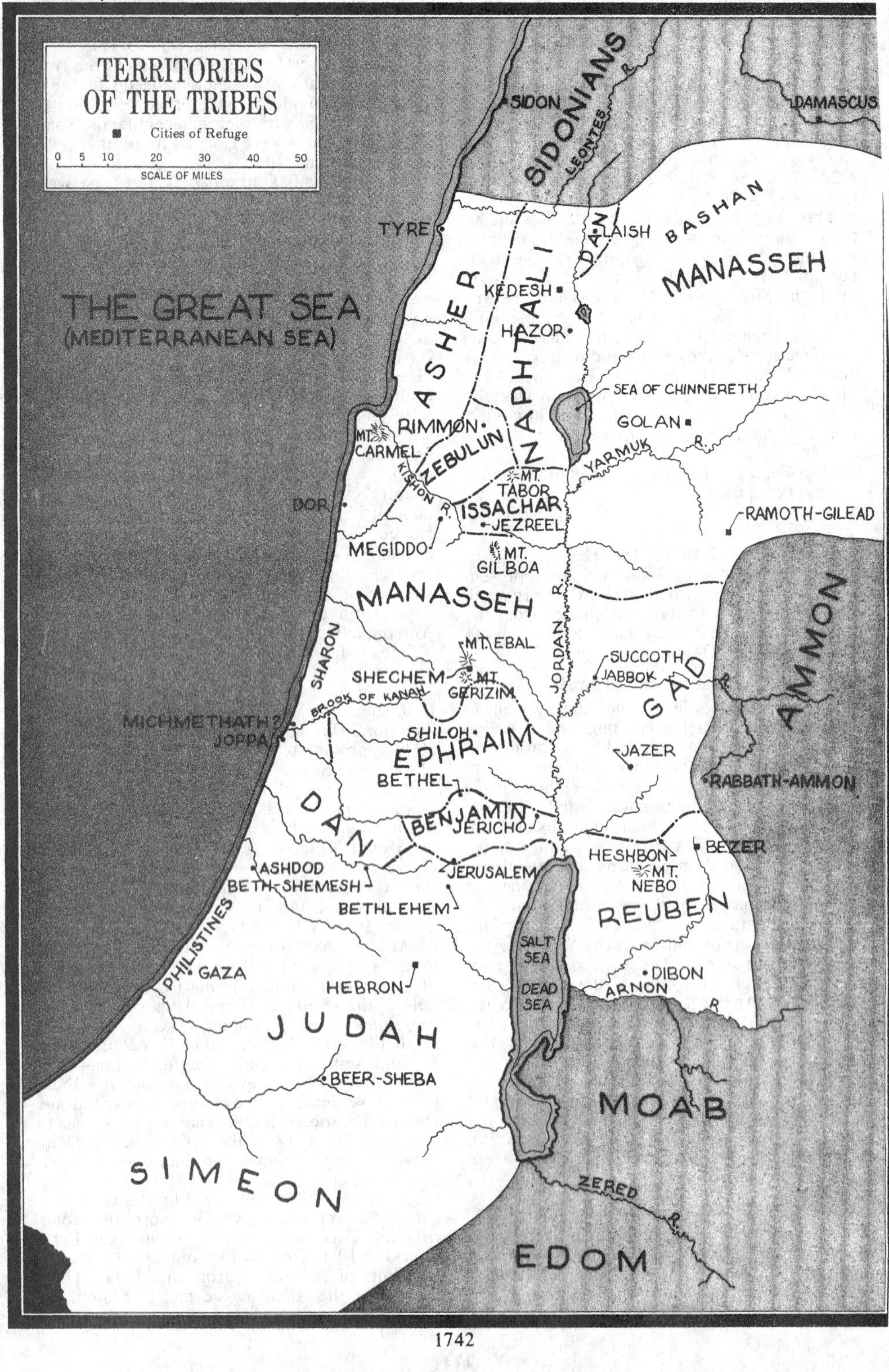
TERRITORIES OF THE TRIBES
Cities of Refuge
0 5 10 20 30 40 50
SCALE OF MILES
THE GREAT SEA
(MEDITERRANEAN SEA)
SIDON
SIDONIANS
LEONTES R.
DAMASCUS
TYRE
DAN
LAISH
BASHAN
MANASSEH
ASHER
NAPHTALI
KEDESH
HAZOR
SEA OF CHINNERETH
GOLAN
YARMUK R.
RIMMON
MT. CARMEL
ZEBULUN
KISHON R.
MT. TABOR
DOR
ISSACHAR
JEZREEL
RAMOTH-GILEAD
MEGIDDO
MT. GILBOA
MANASSEH
JORDAN R.
AMMON
SHARON
MT. EBAL
SUCCOTH
JABBOK
SHECHEM
MT. GERIZIM
BROOK OF KANAH
GAD
MICHMETHATH?
JOPPA
SHILOH
EPHRAIM
JAZER
RABBATH-AMMON
BETHEL
DAN
BENJAMIN
JERICHO
HESHBON
BEZER
ASHDOD
JERUSALEM
MT. NEBO
BETH-SHEMESH
BETHLEHEM
REUBEN
PHILISTINES
SALT SEA
GAZA
HEBRON
DEAD SEA
DIBON
ARNON R.
JUDAH
BEER-SHEBA
MOAB
SIMEON
ZERED R.
EDOM

apportion land to the seven remaining tribes (Josh 18:1-10) by casting lots, the political geography changed quite extensively. During the later stages of settlement in the period of the judges the assigned borders remained the same. However, the local wars described in the book of Judges seem to indicate that those borders were not secure.

Assigned Tribal Boundaries

The records of the boundary delineations preserved for us in Josh 13-22 vary considerably in detail. The record contains two types of lists. One type notes the reference points of the boundary delineations (e.g., Josh 15:1-12; 16:1-3, 5-8; 17:7-9). This method of describing borders—proceeding from town to mountain to town to river, etc.—is almost exactly paralleled in Ugaritic records of the boundary agreement accorded by the Hittite king to Niqmadu, ruler of the vassal city-state of Ugarit (WBC, pp. 223 f.).

The second type is merely a town list which serves as a description of the tribal inheritance (e.g., Josh 19:1-9, *et al.*). The latter makes it obviously more difficult to reconstruct the precise borders. Further, only seven tribes' inheritances are given with boundary descriptions. As mentioned above, the holdings of the tribes or clans were often interspersed. Occasionally a town would belong to one tribe while the lands that had previously belonged to that town in the Canaanite period were held by another tribe.

The border arrangement conformed to the requirements of the pastoral-agrarian economy of Palestine in such a way that a tribe was not dependent on only one or two kinds of farming. Almost without exception a tribe held some rich valleys or plains where grain could be cultivated, some hill country conducive to groves and vineyards, and some fringe areas for grazing their flocks and herds. Thus their welfare was not jeopardized by the failure of one type of farm produce.

Borders of David's Kingdom

Jud 1 and Josh 13:1-6 describe the land that remained in Canaanite, Amorite, and Philistine hands. This area, apart from the pockets of "foreign" settlement that existed within the Israelite occupied territory, consisted of the Philistine plain along the Mediterranean coast stretching S of the Yarkon River, and the area N of Ahlab (Jud 1:31) near Misrephoth-maim (Josh 11:8; 13:6) on the Sidonian coast and stretching eastward toward Damascus.

Skirmishes continued more or less constantly until the wars of David, when he subdued the Philistines and greatly expanded the territory of his kingdom. By the reign of Solomon the borders of Israel extended in the N to include Hamath and Tadmor all the way to the Euphrates River. In the S they reached the Red Sea. In the E Israel encompassed the Arameans, Ammonites, Moabites, and Edomites, thus extending to the Arabian Desert (II Sam 8:1-14; I Kgs 4:24; 9:26).

Both David and Solomon used the basic tribal establishment as the basis for their provincial administration of the home territories (I Chr 27; I Kgs 4:7-19).

Bibliography. Y. Aharoni, *The Land of the Bible*, London: Burns and Oates, 1966. Karl Elliger, "Tribes, Territories of," IDB, IV, 701-710. John Rea, "Joshua," WBC, pp. 205-231. G. A. Smith, *The Historical Geography of the Holy Land*, London: Hodder & Stoughton, 1931.

P. W. F.

TRIBULATION. This word occurs three times in the KJV of the OT and is the translation of *ṣar* in Deut 4:30, and of the cognate *ṣārâ* in Jud 10:14 and I Sam 26:24. The plural form of the latter is rendered "tribulations" in the KJV of I Sam 10:19 (RV, RSV "distresses"). The basic notion in these terms is the unpleasant sensation of claustrophobia, which occurs when one is confined in a narrow place; cf. the Engish word "anguish," from the Latin *angustia*, "narrowness." The two Heb. terms derived from the root *ṣ-r-r*, "to be cramped, narrow," mean "straits" or "distress." In addition, the RSV uses the word "tribulation" (KJV, "travail") in Lam 3:5 to render the Heb. *t^elā'â*, "weariness, hardship," though the text is not without its difficulties.

The English versions of the NT use "tribulation" as a translation of the Gr. *thlipsis* from *thlibō*, which has the same general connotation as the Heb *ṣar, ṣārâ*; and frequently renders these terms in the LXX. Gr. *thlipsis* occurs *c.* 45 times in the NT and is rendered in the KJV as "tribulation" (21 times), "affliction" (17 times), "trouble" (3 times), "persecution" (once), "anguish" (once), "to be afflicted" (once), and "burdened" (once). The word is found in association with "persecution" (Mt 13:21; II Thess 1:4), with "anguish" or "distress" (Rom 2:9), with "distress, persecution, famine, nakedness, peril, and sword" (Rom 8:35); and as "afflictions" along with "necessities, stripes, imprisonments, and tumults" (II Cor 6:4f.).

Although "tribulation" or "affliction" in the NT may be occasioned by natural causes, such as widowhood (Jas 1:27), childbirth (Jn 16:21), famine (Acts 7:10), and carnal drives (I Cor 7:28, KJV "trouble"), its usage is predominately related to the tribulation which the Christian encounters in the world because of the Word (Mt 13:21; cf. Mk 4:17; I Thess 1:6; Jn 17:14) and for the sake of Christ's name (Mt 24:9; Jn 15:21; II Cor 12:10; Rev 1:9). The tribulation is identifiable with "bearing one's cross" (cf. Mt 10:34-38; 16:24; Gal 6:12) or the antagonism which devolves upon the Christian as a result of the tension between the gospel and the world. It is not tribulation in a general sense, but the specific tribulation occasioned by the believer's identification with Christ (II Tim 3:12). It follows as the logical consequence of the nature of the gospel that, as our Lord said, "In the world ye shall have tribulation" (Jn 16:33; cf. I Thess 3:4). Paul warned the faithful that "through many tribulations" one must enter the kingdom of God (Acts 14:22; cf. Lk 14:27–33; Heb 10:32f.). The apostle felt that he had received the sentence of death (II Cor 1:8) and reminded the Thessalonians that tribulation is "to be our lot" (I Thess 3:3).

The inevitable tribulation of the Christian is viewed, however, as his identification with the sufferings of Christ. Paul considered that tribulation is a sharing in the sufferings of Christ (II Cor 1:4f.), a perennial carrying in the body the death of our Lord (II Cor 4:8ff.; cf. Rom 8:35), and a completion of the tribulations of Christ as regards the church (Col 1:24).

This tribulation is to be patiently endured (Rom 12:12; Rev 1:9; Eph 3:13; cf. Heb 12:7; II Thess 1:4) since escapism would rob the Christian of his true development. Tribulation segregates the false and true followers (Mt 13:21; I Thess 1:6); it commends to the world the true nature of the faith through the testing (II Cor 6:4; 8:2; Rev 2:10). Moreover, if the Christian carries in the body the death of the Lord Jesus, paradoxically he discovers that the life of Jesus is made manifest in his mortal flesh (II Cor 4:10f.). As he shares abundantly in Christ's sufferings, so through Christ he shares abundantly in comfort (II Cor 1:5). While Paul describes his tribulation as a "sentence of death," he indicates its didactic purpose: that he should not rely in himself but in God, who raises the dead (II Cor 1:8–9).

The inevitable tribulation which the believer must patiently endure identifies him with the eternal order of God. He is assured that the light and momentary tribulation of this presently unresolved age is actually working in his favor in terms of a far more and exceeding weight of glory (II Cor 4:17). If he is treated by the world as an imposter, as unknown, dying, punished, sorrowful, and possessing nothing, he discovers himself paradoxically to be true, well-known, alive, indestructible, joyful, rich, and possessed of all things in the eternal order. He knows that nothing shall separate him from the love of God—not even tribulation—and that no tribulation can do other than augment his joyful hope (Rom 5:3; cf. Rev 2:9). In the world he may have tribulation, but in Christ he has peace, and is encouraged that he will participate in the triumph of his Lord over the world (Jn 16:33; cf. 16:21ff.).

The present ambiguity involved in Christian tribulation will be ultimately resolved (Rom 2:9; II Thess 1:6; cf. Rev 2:22). In apocalyptic language the Olivet discourse pictures the final tension between the world and the kingdom of God as producing great tribulation (Mt 24:21), but the coming of the Son of Man will ultimately and forever deliver the elect (Mt 24:29ff.; Mk 13:24ff.; cf. Rev 7:14). *See* Tribulation, Great; Affliction; Persecution; Suffering.

Bibliography. Heinrich Schlier, "*Thlibō*, etc.," TDNT, III, 139–148.

E. R. D.

TRIBULATION, GREAT. The Tribulation is the seven-year period falling between the rapture of the Church and the second advent of Jesus Christ to the earth. It is the concluding period of Daniel's prophecy of 70 weeks (Dan 9:24–27). The seven years are divided into two equal periods, the latter being called the Great Tribulation (Mt 24:21).

The character of the period is clearly revealed in Scripture. It is a time of "wrath" (Zeph 1:15–18; I Thess 1:10; 5:9; Rev 6:16–17; 11:18; 14:10, 19; 15:1, 7; 19:2); "indignation" (Isa 26:20–21; 34:1–3); "trial" (Rev 3:10); "trouble" (Jer 30:7; Zeph 1:14–15; Dan 12:1); "destruction" (Joel 1:15; I Thess 5:3); "darkness" (Joel 2:2; Amos 5:18; Zeph 1:14–18); "desolation" (Dan 9:27; Zeph 1:14–15); "overturning" (Isa 24:1–4, 19–21); "punishment" (Isa 24:20–21). *See* Tribulation.

Two main purposes are stated for the Tribulation. First, God will prepare a believing remnant in the nation Israel to whom Messiah will come and in whom all Israel's covenants will be fulfilled. The gospel of the kingdom, the good news that the King is coming, will be preached universally (Mt 24:14), and multitudes will accept by faith the offered salvation. God will again do for Israel what He did through John the Baptist at the first advent (Mt 3:1–10; Lk 3:3–14; cf. Mal 4:5–6). Second, God will pour out judgment upon unbelieving men and nations (Rev 3:10; Jer 25:32–33; Isa 24:1; II Thess 2:12). These judgments will fall both directly from God and indirectly through men and armies.

The seventieth week of Daniel's prophecy officially begins when the last head of the fourth world empire (Rome) makes a covenant with Israel, guaranteeing them their right in Palestine and the resumption of sacrifices (Dan 9:27). This covenant is broken after three and one-half years, and the Great Tribulation falls upon the earth.

Events within the Tribulation period are set forth in Scripture in great detail. The nations proceeding out of the Roman Empire will be federated into a world power again (Dan 2 and 7; cf. Rev 17:12, 16–17). The head of the empire is known as the little horn (Dan 7:8), the abomination of desolation (Mt 24:15), the man of sin (II Thess 2:3), the Antichrist (I Jn 2:18), and the beast (Rev 13:1–10). This political ruler will make a covenant with Israel (Dan 9:27). The king of the N, also known as Gog (Ezk 38), will oppose him (Dan 11:40) but will be destroyed by the Lord upon invading Palestine (Ezk 39). With that strong power removed, the Antichrist will be able to control world government. A great religious system, centering in the worship of this political figure, will be promoted by the false prophet (Rev 13:11–18) which will become worldwide. At the return of Christ this

Black Obelisk of Shalmaneser of Assyria, detail showing Jehu of Israel prostrate before Shalmaneser as he brings his tribute. BM

politico-religious system will be destroyed (Rev 19:20).

During the Tribulation God will pour out judgment on the earth through the breaking of the seals (Rev 6), the blowing of the trumpets (Rev 8-11), and the emptying of the vials (Rev 16). Through the preaching of the 144,000 sealed witnesses (Rev 7:1-8), the gospel will be proclaimed to the ends of the earth and multitudes will be turned to the Lord (Rev 7:9-10).

The Tribulation will be terminated by the second advent of the Lord Jesus Christ to the earth (Mt 24:22, 29-30; Rev 19:11-16; cf. Zech 14:1-7).

See Antichrist; Christ, Coming of; Eschatology; Rapture.

J. D. P.

TRIBUNE. This word appears in the RSV at Acts 21:31, etc. (KJV, "chief captain"), as the officer in charge of a Roman cohort, which usually consisted of *c.* 600 men. The Gr. *chiliarchos* literally means "commander of a thousand"; it is also found in Jn 18:12 with reference to the captain who arrested and bound Jesus. It is used of high-ranking military officers in a general sense in Mk 6:21; Rev 6:15; 19:18. The Latin term *tribunus,* "head of a tribe," originated with the appointment of commanders (NASB) over certain of the troops provided by aboriginal tribes for the Roman army. Twenty-four tribunes—enough to command four legions—were appointed by popular vote, the rest by the consuls. There were also tribunes whose task it was to administer law and government. For example, there were ten tribunes of Rome appointed for this purpose who even held a veto power which, when the Caesars were weak, they exercised quite fully.

See Captain.

R. A. K.

TRIBUTARY, TRIBUTE. A tributary (Heb. *mas*) was a people or nation in subjection to another to whom they paid tribute, a compulsory levy or tax, as a sign of their relationship (Deut 20:11; Jud 1:30, 33, 35; Lam 1:1). Tribute had a twofold goal: to keep a nation in subjection, and to enrich the conqueror's own revenues and supply needed resources (Est 10:1; Rom 13:6-7).

The cities of the plain which were delivered by Abraham had been tributaries for 13 years and then rebelled (Gen 14:1-5). King Jehu of Israel was a tributary of Shalmaneser III; Menahem, of Tiglath-pileser (II Kgs 15:19); Israel, of Sargon; Manasseh king of Judah, of Esar-haddon. The Assyrian kings boasted of the tribute which they exacted from Israel and other conquered peoples (ANET, pp. 275-301; ANEP #350-356). Because of her position astride the line of march between the great powers of Egypt and Babylonia, and her smallness, Israel was prone to be made a tributary.

On the other hand, when Israel was strong, her kings received tribute from foreign princes and peoples. After David stationed garrisons in Damascus, etc., the Syrians became vassals and brought "gifts" (ASV, etc., "tribute") to him (II Sam 8:6). All the kingdoms from the Euphrates to Egypt brought "presents" or tribute to Solomon (I Kgs 4:21; cf. II Chr 8:7-8). Jeshoshaphat received tribute from the Philistines and Arabs (II Chr 17:11), and Uzziah from the Ammonites (II Chr 26:8). In addition to silver, gold, and cattle, tribute could be paid in the form of forced labor or a levy (*q.v.*) on manpower. *See also* Taxes.

For the tribute money due Caesar (Mt 22:17, 19), *see* Weights, Measures, and Coins.

R. A. K.

TRINITY. The early church, opposing polytheism with the OT teaching that there is only one God, was soon forced to ask, Who is Jesus Christ? Was He a mere man? Is He an angel? Or is He God? And if He is God, are there two Gods?

Near the beginning of the 4th cen. a strong party in the church, under the leadership of Arius, maintained that Christ was a created angel. Athanasius championed orthodoxy and secured the condemnation of Arianism at the Council of Niceae in A.D. 325. The decision was repeated and the Nicene Creed received its final form at the Council of Constantinople in A.D. 381.

The debate in the council centered on the meaning of the title Son of God. The Arians held that the Son had not always existed; the Son or Word is a creature and a work, not the same in substance with the Father, and therefore not true God.

Athanasius, on the contrary, drew a disjunction between moral sonship, in which sense every believer is a son of God, and a natural sonship, as Isaac was the son of Abraham. Now, if Christ was son only in a moral sense, He would not differ from us and would not be the only begotten Son.

To this the Arians replied that Christ is only begotten because He came into being from the Father alone, while all others are begotten by the Father through the Son. But this construction, Athanasius claimed, would make us sons of Christ instead of sons of God. Christ then would separate us from God rather than unite us to God.

The debate went into great detail. Arius used Prov 8:22, "The Lord created me at the beginning of his work" (RSV), to prove that Christ was a creature. Athanasius referred the verse to Christ's human nature.

The council finally rejected Arius' assertion that the Son is like the Father, as tin is like silver, and adopted the Nicene Creed in which the Son is said to be one in substance with the Father.

Some critics ridicule theology and the council for having quarreled so violently over nothing more important than the letter "i." The point of debate was whether Jesus Christ was of the "same substance" (*homoousios*) as the Father (and hence fully God) or of "like substance" (*homoiousios*) to the Father (and hence something less than God). The difference the "i" makes is greater than the difference between silver and tin; it is the difference between God and a creature.

The doctrine of the Trinity is also attacked on the ground that it introduced into Christianity pagan themes from Gr. philosophy. Nothing could be further from the truth. In the first place, Athanasius' arguments use neither the language nor the concepts of Gr. philosophy, but are completely biblical. Second, it was Arius, rather than Athanasius, who held pagan principles, in that he allowed divine honors to be paid to a being whom he regarded as less than God. And third, the Nicene Creed removed pagan elements that had appeared in Origen and other early theologians.

For example, the doctrine of the eternal generation of the Son, indicated in the Nicene words, "Begotten of His Father before all worlds," avoids the error that the Logos, instead of being an eternal Son, is a voluntary production by which God insulates Himself from contamination in creating the world. As the emphasis on *eternal* generation avoids this error, so emphasis on eternal *generation* shows that the Son is not a step in a descending series of emanations, and that while generation filiation is a necessary relationship, creation is a voluntary act.

For active Christians today the question of the Trinity most often takes the form of defending the deity of Christ and the personality of the Spirit. This defense is called for in two cases. Liberal theology tends toward a purely human Christ, and Jehovah's Witnesses resurrect Arianism in making Christ a created angel. The scriptural material is the same, regardless of which group is envisaged, though Jehovah's Witnesses are more likely to pay attention to the Scripture than the liberals are.

The first verse of John's Gospel is frequently quoted by a Jehovah's Witness. He inevitably argues that it should be translated, "In the beginning was the Word, and the Word was with God, and *the Word was a god.*" The Christian's answer starts right with the verse. Here we find a particular Gr. idiom, the *anarthous* use of the noun, i.e., the use of the noun without the definite article. In Gr. when the speaker wanted to point out or designate a person or object, he used the article; but when he wanted to bring out the inherent quality or nature of the same he left it out. A literal translation of Jn 1:1 would therefore be, "and the Word was of the very nature or quality of God" (cf. the same idiom in Heb 1:2, where the KJV has correctly translated "his Son," though the Gr. says merely "son").

Further evidence to prove that John could not teach that Christ was a created being upon whom the title "God" was honorifically bestowed, is clearly found in the verses immediately following Jn 1:1. Other passages directly state His deity, such as Heb 1:5-8, "Unto which of the angels said he at any time, Thou art my Son?. . .But unto the Son he saith, Thy throne, O God, is forever and ever" (cf. Tit 2:13). Another supportive verse, whose two parts liberals have tried to separate by inserting a period between them, is, "Christ, who is over all, God blessed forever" (Rom 9:5). Other well-known assertions of the deity of Christ are contained in the apostolic benediction (II Cor 13:14) and the baptismal formula (Mt 28:19). Additional references, selected from a great number, are: Mt 11:27; Jn 5:23; Acts 10:36; 20:28; Rom 10:9; Col 2:9; I Thess 3:11; I Pet 1:2.

The fact that the term Lord is the Gr. translation for the OT Yahweh is in itself an evidence of the deity of Christ and also invites us to compare OT and NT passages; e.g., Isa 40:3 with Mt 3:3; Ps 24:7, 10 with I Cor 2:8; Jer 23:5-6 with I Cor 1:30; and Prov 16:4 with Col 1:16.

One may also suppose that the OT anticipates the doctrine of the Trinity in the plural *Elohim* of Gen 1:26, and more clearly in the angel of the Lord in Gen 16, 18, 19.

In the case of the Holy Spirit, it is not so much His deity that is called in question as His distinct personality. That the Spirit is a person is seen first of all in the fact that although the

Triumphal arch of Titus, Roman emperor who destroyed Jerusalem and the Temple. HFV

noun Spirit is neuter in Gr., the pronouns referring to the Spirit are masculine (contrary to the mistranslation of Rom 8:16 in the KJV). That He is a person distinct from both the Father and the Son is clear in Mt 3:16; Lk 4:18; Jn 15:26; 16:7; Acts 5:32; Heb 9:14; etc.

Sometimes the doctrine of the Trinity is rejected on the grounds that it is not explicitly spelled out in Scripture (I Jn 5:7 is not in the best Gr. texts). But the doctrine is clearly implicit in that Scripture testifies to the full and real deity of the Father, the Son, and the Spirit while maintaining a distinction of persons; in other words, three persons, one God.

See Christ, Deity of; God; Godhead; Holy Spirit; I Am; Jesus Christ.

Bibliography. Edward H. Bickersteth, *The Rock of Ages*, rev. ed., New York: The Bible Scholar, n.d. Loraine Boettner, *Studies in Theology*, Grand Rapids: Eerdmans, 1947, pp. 79–139. Richard N. Davies, *Doctrine of the Trinity*, Cincinnati: Cranston & Stowe, 1891. Leonard Hogsden, *The Doctrine of the Trinity*, London: Nisbet. George A. F. Knight, *A Biblical Approach to the Doctrine of the Trinity*, Edinburgh: Oliver & Boyd, 1953. A. H. Strong, *Systematic Theology*, Philadelphia: Judson Press, 1956. Arthur W. Wainwright, *The Trinity in the New Testament*, London: S.P.C.K., 1962.

G. H. C., S. G., R. A. K.

TRIUMPH. The translation of seven Heb. and Gr. words. In the OT the thought of shouting or exulting predominates over the thought of actual triumph or victory, representing the attitude of the victor.

The kings of ancient Egypt and Assyria, and later Rome, celebrated their military victories by gorgeous processions in which were displayed their captives and booty, culminating in a solemn religious service of thanksgiving and sacrifice to their gods.

The earliest victory song in the Bible is that of Moses and Miriam who led the people of Israel in singing after the destruction of Pharaoh's host (Ex 15:1–18), accompanied by music from the timbrel, celebrating the judgment of God upon the wicked king. The hymn of Deborah and Barak (Jud 5) and of Miriam (Ex 15:20–21) are splendid examples of triumphal hymns. In Ex 15:1, 21 *gā'â*, "triumphed," expresses the exaltation of Yahweh above Egypt, her king, and her gods. In Jud 5:3 the exultation at victory is expressed by singing praise to the Lord, the following verses detailing the various parts played by the tribes, etc.

In keeping with the thought of shouting out the victory, David prays that the wicked may not shout over him in victory (*'ālaz,* Ps 25:2); that the enemy does not triumph (rûa', "shout," Ps 41:11) over him is a sign of Yahweh's favor.

The common expression in early times was to place the foot on the neck of the captive (Josh 10:24) and in many cases to utter one's war cry, in evidence of the complete subjection of the enemy (cf. Ps 110:1, "footstool"; Isa 60:14, "soles of thy feet"; I Cor 15:25, "under his feet"). In the days of the successors of Alexander, triumphs were symbolized by the wearing of robes having symbols of the palm tree woven into them. John uses an adaptation of this symbol where he speaks of the martyrs having "palms in their hands" (Rev 7:9).

The Romans, more recently than the Egyptians, were foremost in expressing the importance of the triumph. They took great care through the triumphal parade to bestow honor upon the victor, so that he could be said to have triumphed openly, that is, be recognized in fact as the victor. In similar fashion Christ is pictured as leading captive in His victory procession the hostile "principalities and powers" of the spiritual realm. He had disarmed and made a public display of them, having triumphed (from Gr. *thriambeuō*) over them by the cross (Col 2:15).

In addition to conquered foes to be executed, the possessions being retained by the victor, particularly captives, were also a part of the procession. This aspect is seen in Eph 4:8, which tells of Christ leading captive a host of captives, not to slavery or death but to liberty and life in Him. Respecting the gospel, the spread of it by Christ's followers is a "triumph" (II Cor 2:14–16), for His victory sets the sinner free in Christ.

Finally, in attestation of His kingship and the ultimate victory of Him who was born King of the Jews, Christ made His "triumphal" entry into Jerusalem. Palms were used to greet Him,

Panel from Arch of Titus showing the seven-branched lampstand and silver trumpets from the Temple being paraded in Titus' triumphal procession. HFV

emphasizing His royal dignity and victory (Mt 21:1–9). *See* Triumphal Entry. In a final victorious conquest He shall cast Satan into hell (Rev 20:10), and shall wipe away all tears, thus swallowing up in victory the death that till then attaches to men.

Bibliography. H. S. Versnel, *Triumphus, An Inquiry into the Origin, Development, and Meaning of the Roman Triumph,* Leiden: Brill, 1970.

H. G. S.

TRIUMPHAL ENTRY. The entrance of Jesus into Jerusalem which commenced His passion week. Each Gospel writer records the event (Mt 21:1–11; Mk 11:1–11; Lk 19:28–44; Jn 12:12–19). Two perspectives of the event are given. The Synoptic writers follow Christ from Bethany, while John records the entry as the multitude which went out from Jerusalem to meet the procession saw it.

As Jesus neared Jerusalem on His last trip into the city, He sent two disciples to get a colt, the foal of an ass, for Him to ride. Matthew adds the detail that the colt's mother was also to be brought. Some scholars have contended that Matthew misunderstood the synonymous parallelism of Zech 9:9 ("humble and riding on an ass, even on a colt the foal [lit., son] of a she-ass") as referring to two different animals with Christ riding both as a contrived fulfillment of the misunderstood prophecy. But Matthew's information about the mother animal is intended to emphasize that the colt (Heb. *'ayir,* Gr. *pōlos,* a vigorous young animal able to be used, as in Jud 10:4; 12:14) was previously unridden. The presence of the mother ass would have calmed the young colt in the tumultuous crowd so that Jesus could ride it. Far from adding an invention to make a contrived fulfillment of a misunderstood OT prophecy, Matthew understood Zech 9:9 correctly and included the additional details about the mother ass to clarify how it was that an unbroken colt would allow Jesus to ride it in the midst of the crowd.

After the animals were brought, garments were placed on them, and Christ sat on them (Mt 21:7, NASB marg., following the best attested Gr. reading), i.e., on the garments. The disciples had placed their garments on both animals, not knowing which animal Jesus would ride; but He chose the colt (Zech 9:9, ASV, RSV, NEB, Mk 11:7; Lk 19:35; Jn 12:14). As the procession neared Jerusalem, a great multitude met them, casting in the way clothes and branches of palm trees. As the crowd followed Christ into the city, they shouted, "Hosanna to the son of David! Blessed is he that cometh in the name of the Lord! Hosanna in the highest!" These words were taken from Ps 118, considered by the Jews as messianic.

This event was important, because it was Jesus' final and official offer of Himself to Israel as their King and Messiah (cf. Zech 9:9). The manner of His arrival (e.g., on a donkey rather than on a horse) was not what the Jews had expected, but rather was in keeping with His purpose of bringing salvation and peace. That it was His official offer of Himself to Israel as their Messiah-King is clear from the details contained in the Gospels: (1) The reference to "this day" in Lk 19:42 (cf. v. 44) at least suggests the possibility that the first 69 weeks of Daniel's prophecy are coming to a close (Dan 9:24–27). (2) Jesus intentionally fulfilled Zech 9:9, and Matthew believed He had fulfilled it (Mt 21:4–5). (3) Though their understanding was limited and deficient, the words and actions of the people indicate that they were celebrating the coming of their King (Jn 12:13). The Pharisees recognized the messianic and kingly implications of these actions and words, and asked Jesus to repudiate them. But He rejected the suggestion, saying that "if these become silent, the stones will cry out!" (Lk 19:39–40, NASB). (4) Mt 21:41–45 shows that the Jewish leaders had rejected Christ's offer of Himself to the nation to be their King.

Some have questioned how Jesus could have received such an enthusiastic welcome by the inhabitants of Jerusalem just a week before His crucifixion. The answer seems to be in the composition of the crowd that went to meet Him on Palm Sunday. John (12:12–13) indicates that the majority was drawn from those who had come to Jerusalem for the Feast of Passover. Josephus claims that nearly three million people came to the city for such feasts. Even Joachim Jeremias' more likely figure of 125,000 pilgrims indicates a great crowd (*Jerusalem in the Time of Jesus,* Philadelphia: Fortress Press, 1969, pp. 77–84). These, then, were not citizens of Jerusalem whose enmity was set, but pilgrim strangers whose curiosity had been aroused (note the Pharisees' different attitude, Lk 19:39; Jn 12:19). A week later, however, these country people and foreign Jews did not dare resist the combined power of the Sanhedrin and Rome.

P. D. F.

TROAS (trō'ăs). The name occurs in four passages in the NT (Acts 16:8, 11; 20:5–6; II Cor

2:12; II Tim 4:13), all in connection with Paul's life and travels. A port city in Mysia (*q.v.*), founded in the 4th cen. B.C. by Antigonus, it was located about ten miles S of the ancient Hellespont (Dardanelles). Constituted a Roman colony by Augustus, it was a prominent center, even having been the object of a rumor that Julius Caesar "intended to move the seat of government to Troy or Alexandria" (Suetonius, *The Twelve Caesars,* "Julius Caesar," p. 79). Ruins of a wall six miles in circumference, a theater, and an aqueduct are still visible. In the NT, Troas was a pivotal point in Paul's travels. Here he turned to the W (Europe) after having tried to enter the Roman provinces of Asia and Bithynia (Acts 16:6–8), and it was at this time that Luke first joined the missionary party (Acts 16:10, notice the "we").

After his long stay in Ephesus (Acts 19), Paul headed N looking for Titus' return from Corinth. He came to Troas and had opportunity to evangelize, but stayed only a brief time (II Cor 2:12–13). Later he returned after a visit in Greece (Acts 20:2–3) and visited the church for seven days (20:6). It was at this time the incident concerning Eutychus (*q.v.*) occurred (20:9–12).

Troas was situated about ten miles SW of Hissarlik, the ruins of ancient Troy made famous in Homer's *Iliad.* Excavations begun in 1870 by Heinrich Schliemann have traced at least nine cities there, the Homeric level being fourth from the top.

W. M. D.

TROGYLLIUM (trō-jĭl'ĭ-ŭm). A stopping point on Paul's journey from Troas to Miletus (Acts 20:15, KJV; the ASV, RSV, and NASB place the phrase in the margin). It was about a mile opposite Samos. William M. Ramsay (*St. Paul the Traveller and the Roman Citizen,* pp. 293–94) suggests that the ship stopped here for the night when becalmed.

TROOP. A collection of people, a company; then, soldiers collectively, an armed force, usually in the plural. The following are some of the Heb. terms rendered "troop" in the various English versions.

1. The noun *gad.* In Gen 30:11 the KJV erroneously translates the word as "troop" and adds in the margin that the name Gad means "a troop" or "company," thus indicating the word-play involved in the two words. However, the ASV renders the term as "Fortunate!" with the marginal readings "with fortune!" and "fortune is come," while the RSV translates it as "good fortune." It would appear that the Semitic root *g-d* meant "fortune" and that it became associated with the Phoenician god of fortune. Accordingly, in Isa 65:11 the term *gad* is translated in the ASV and RSV as "Fortune," thus indicating the pagan deity whom the apostate Jews worshiped, which is in juxtaposition with another such deity named "Destiny" (Heb *m*^{e}*ni*). While the KJV renders the term *gad* as "troop" in this reference, it provides the marginal reading of "Gad." *See* Gad 1; Gods, False.

2. The noun *g*^{e}*dûd,* "band," "troop." In II Sam 22:30 (cf. Ps 18:29) and Job 19:12 the term is uniformly rendered as "troop," as the troops of an army. In I Chr 12:18 "band" is used in the KJV and ASV, and "troops" in the RSV (cf. I Chr 7:4; II Chr 25:9–10, 13; 26:11). The term may also refer to a marauding band, e.g., of the Amalekites (I Sam 30:8, 15, 23) or the one led by Rezon (I Kgs 11:24); or to a troop or band of robbers (Hos 6:9; 7:1). In II Sam 3:22 the KJV renders the term by "troop"; the ASV, while noting the Heb. meaning of the term as "troop" in the margin, uses the expletive "foray" (RSV "raid"). The Heb. term is translated as "army" in the KJV and ASV of Job 29:25, but as "troops" in the RSV. In the word-play on the name Gad in Gen 49:19 the KJV and ASV render the Heb. term as "troop," whereas the RSV and NASB translate it as "raiders," noting in the margin "a raiding troop." In Mic 5:1 the KJV, ASV, and NASB use the phrase "O daughter of troops"; however, the RSV translates otherwise on the basis of a conjectural text.

3. The verb *gādad* has the sense of "gather in troops" in Mic 5:1. In Jer 5:7 the verb is translated "to assemble by troops" in the KJV and ASV, while the RSV and NASB have simply "trooped."

4. The noun *'ăguddâ,* "band," is translated in the KJV in II Sam 2:25 as "troop," while the ASV and RSV render it "band." The same term is translated as "troop" (marg., "bundle") in the KJV of Amos 9:6, while the ASV and RSV agree in their translation as "vault," i.e., as banded together.

5. The noun *'ōraḥ,* "path," then by metonymy "traveler," is rendered "troops" in the KJV, but as "caravans" in the ASV and RSV (Job 6:19).

The RSV differs from the KJV and ASV in the additional use of "troop" in *c.* 15 other instances to translate various Heb. terms. This procedure is generally justified in order to bring out the military nuance involved in the passages.

In the NT the KJV and ASV translate the Gr. term *strateúmata* in Mt 22:7 and Rev 9:16 as "army" or "armies"; the RSV uses "troops" in both instances.

See Army.

E. R. D.

TROPHIMUS (trŏf'ĭ-mŭs). An Ephesian Christian, and a companion of Paul on his voyage from Greece to Troas (Acts 20:1–6). Later he was seen with Paul in Jerusalem (21:29), and the Jews accused Paul of defiling the temple by bringing a Gentile into the court of Israel, an act forbidden by the temple authorities. A notice (written in Greek and Latin), now preserved in a museum in Istanbul, reads: "Let no foreigner enter within the screen and enclosure surrounding the sanctuary. Whosoever is taken so doing will be the cause that death overtaketh him" (translation in A. Deissmann, *Light From the Ancient East,* 2nd ed., 1927, p. 80) The resulting uproar led to Paul's being taken into custody by the Roman soldiers and ultimately being sent to Rome for trial. After Paul was released from his first Roman imprisonment, Trophimus was left by Paul in Miletus ill (II Tim 4:20), presumably shortly before Paul's final trip to Rome and his execution there.

TROUGH. A large hollowed stone or box-like water receptacle used for watering animals. "Trough" is used to render Heb. *shōqet* in Gen 24:20 and 30:38 as well as Heb. *rahaṭ* (used only in the plural) in Ex 2:16. The latter word occurs also in Gen 30:38, 41, where it is translated "gutters" (KJV, ASV) or "runnels" (RSV). Scholars are generally agreed that the words are synonymous, as may be illustrated by the new Jewish Publication Society's translation of Gen 30:38: ". . .in troughs [rahaṭ]--the water receptacles [shōqet] that the flocks came to drink from."

TROW. An archaic word used in Lk 17:9 (KJV) meaning "think," "believe," or "suppose"; cf. German *trauen.* However, the Gr. words *ou doko* ("I trow not") are clearly an interpolation of a copyist since they do not occur in the most ancient Gr. MSS, and are correctly omitted consequently by the ASV, etc.

TRUCE BREAKER. The KJV translates the Gr. *aspondos* "implacable" in Rom 1:31 following the Textus Receptus, but the RSV follows Nestle's reading, *astorgos,* and therefore translates it "heartless." In II Tim 3:3 the KJV translates *aspondos* "truce breakers," but the RSV gives the more literal translation, "implacable."

TRUMP, TRUMPET. *See* Music.

TRUMPETS, FEAST OF. *See* Festivals.

TRUST. *See* Believe; Faith.

TRUTH. Heb. *'ĕmûnâ,* "steadfastness, stability, truth"; *'ĕmet,* "steadfastness, truth"; Gr. *alētheia,* "truth." In 1912 Webster's Dictionary defined truth as: "Conformity to fact or reality; exact accordance with that which is, or has been, or shall be." While possibly satisfactory when formulated, such a definition proves too vague for today when logical positivists deny all evidence not empirically verifiable.

Carnell holds that "truth is a property of that judgment which coincides with the mind of God" (*An Introduction to Christian Apologetics,* p. 47). While Webster errs in an overstress of the factual, this definition errs in overstress of the metaphysical. However, when Carnell expands his definition to: "correspondence with the mind of God; test: systematic consistency" (p. 369) and explains systematic consistency, he offers possibly the best definition of truth at present obtainable. By systematic consistency he means that a statement must: first, meet and clear with the laws of logic, that is, be horizontally consistent—which is the test of formal truth; second, fit the facts, that is, agree vertically with all the facts, which is the test of material truth.

Aspects of Truth

In a satisfactory definition of truth, such as the above, three aspects and elements of truth are included.

1. *Ontological or metaphysical truth.* This expresses the ultimate relationship of truth, and the nature as well as the relationship of religious and moral truth in particular, to the very character, will, and mind of God. Religious and moral truth is what God is, and agrees with His character. Scientific and social truth is what God wills, and is also in consistency with His character. God is truth in His own person (Deut 32:4; Ps 31:5; Isa 65:16), and this is particularly revealed in Jesus Christ (Jn 1:14, 17; 14:6); His revealed Word is truth (I Kgs 17:24; Jn 17:17); His moral law is truth (Ps 119:142, 151).

2. *Logical truth.* Two extremes occur. (*a*) Some apply logic and deny revelation. For example, the (logical) positivists stress meaningful logical expression that is empirically verifiable and deny metaphysical and moral truth, saying it is illogical and meaningless since it cannot be scientifically examined like material phenomena. The Christian replies that metaphysical and moral truth comes to man by revelation and cannot be known other than as *a priori* since it forms the very basis of knowledge and existence itself. Their proof rests upon the reasonable evidence supporting revelation. He points out that the logical positivist assumes the basic propositions of morality and ethics, and uses them without requiring proof. (*b*) Others attempt to accept revelation while denying logic its proper function. The neoorthodox speak of God's truth as timeless and spaceless. Man has no categories in which to receive such truth and therefore it appears in the forms of contradiction, paradox, and the absurd, and therefore cannot be judged by logic. The evangelical says the problem of the neoorthodox stems from the acceptance of a faulty philosophy of time and space introduced to theology by Sören Kierkegaard and from a modernistic approach to the Bible. God is rational and logical, and the Bible proves not to be full of paradoxes and contradictions when accepted by faith as written. He has given credible evidences of the truth and infallibility of His Word. This conclusion is the witness of believers of both Testaments (Ps 108:4; Jn 20:30–31; I Jn 1:1–3).

3. *Factual truth.* Truth must fit the facts of life and existence. This means propositional correspondence to reality. Truth cannot satisfy

itself with universals and generalities, useful as they may be, nor with mere individuals and particulars, but must vertically fit the facts while organizing them correctly through the use of universals.

Attitudes to Truth

Hearing and being the truth. One can hear the truth, believe that it is true, even teach it, and still refuse or fail to act upon it. This is to hear the truth and yet not be the truth. Truth that is known, in the sense it is both believed and acted upon, then satisfies three tests: logical consistency, factual consistency, and practical consistency. The first two have been discussed above under logical and factual truth. The third is what Christ speaks of as the basis of salvation, namely, experiencing the truth by acting upon it (Jn 8:32). It entails a content of knowledge upon which the action is taken.

The Scriptures give all three their proper place. They expect faith to be based upon reasonable evidence and action to follow the reception of clear self-consistent revelation.

Many modern theologians of the neo-orthodox and liberal schools deny that truth is absolute. Paul Tillich, for example, sees it as necessarily relative, arguing that were it absolute and unchangeable it would make God, who is The Ultimate and The Absolute, relative. Such a view really denies the possibility of real truth, substituting for it *kairotic* or temporary truth – things may be true for today but wrong for tomorrow. The Christian answer points out several things:

1. If truth is dependent upon God and God is truth in His person, then absolute truth does not limit but rather reveals God. God is love, but love does not steal, lie, etc., and the commandments only state these truths which already exist in the character of God. They are not limiting but revealing statements which have their basis in His nature.

2. Because God is truth, Christ is truth, both in His person and His revelation (Jn 1:14, 17; 14:6). His character and His words thus complement each other, and His teaching reveals His holy character and that of the Father (Mt 5:43–48). Existential theologians have tried to stress the importance of *being* the truth while denying that truth has a propositional content, i.e., a content which is contained in revealed statements in Scripture. Their attempt fails when one realizes that Christ, using the language of the schoolroom, maintains in Jn 8 that His record is true. He teaches only what He has heard (vv. 26, 40), seen (v. 38), and been taught by the Father (v. 28). He can confirm what He says because the Father has not left Him alone (v. 29).

In Jn 14, where Christ declares He is the truth (v. 6), He again refers to the content of His teaching, showing that He is not merely the truth personally, but also teaches propositional truth. It is in the context of Jn 8, when as seen above He is defending the truth of His teachings, that He says, "And ye shall know the truth, and the truth shall make you free" (v. 32). This makes it clear that He is not speaking of some mystical personal knowledge of Himself which will save a man, but a knowledge whose content is composed of what He teaches.

Bibliography. E. J. Carnell, *An Introduction to Christian Apologetics,* Grand Rapids: Eerdmans, 1950; *A Philosophy of the Christian Religion,* Grand Rapids: Eerdmans, 1952, pp. 449ff. Charles Hodge, *Systematic Theology,* Grand Rapids: Eerdmans, 1952. G. Quell, G. Kittel, and R. Bultmann, "*Aletheia,* etc.," TDNT, I, 232–251.

R. A. K.

TRYPHENA (trī-fē'nȧ). A woman who worked along with Tryphosa in Rome to whom Paul sent greetings (Rom 16:12). Tryphena was also the name of a queen of Thrace who befriended the heroine Thecla in the apocryphal Acts of Paul and Thecla. Both names have been found on burial plates in a cemetery used chiefly for servants of the royal household (cf. Phil 4:22). Since the name Tryphosa comes from the same Gr. word root (meaning "luxuriant"), it has been supposed that the two women were sisters, perhaps twins, "for it was usual to designate members of the same family by derivations of the same root" (Lightfoot, *Philippians,* p. 175).

TRYPHOSA. *See* Tryphena.

TSADHE. *See* Tzaddi.

TUBAL (tū'bȧl). The fifth son of Japheth (Gen 10:2; I Chr 1:5). *See* Nations. The country traded with Tyre in slaves and brass (Ezk 27:13). At one time Gog ruled Tubal (Ezk 38:2–3) and Meshech (39:1). Isa 66:19 declared it shall hear of the grace of Yahweh. It is the Tabali of the Assyrian inscriptions. The country was located in the Cappadocian region of Asia Minor.

Shalmaneser III (859–824 B.C.) received presents from 24 kings of Tubal. In the following century Uassurme united the country but was dethroned in 732 B.C. by the Assyrians. Sargon refers to precious metal vessels from Tubal. A rebellion against Sargon led by Ambaris, involving the Mushki (Meshech) and Ararat, was put down.

TUBAL-CAIN (tū'bȧl-kān'). The son of Lamech, a descendant of Cain, by his wife Zillah (Gen 4:22). The name means "Tubal the smith" and he is called the "forger of all instruments of bronze and iron" (RSV), the first man to learn how to smelt and use metals.

TUNIC. *See* Dress.

TURBAN. *See* Dress; Mitre.

TURPENTINE. A resinous juice extracted by making incisions in the trunk of a turpentine or terebinth tree. *See* Plants: Terebinth.

TURQUOISE. *See* Jewels.

TURTLE, TURTLEDOVE. *See* Animals: Dove, III.9.

TWELVE. *See* Number.

TWELVE, THE. *See* Apostle.

TWILIGHT. *See* Time, Divisions of.

TWINKLING. The Gr. *hripē,* "a sudden motion," is used along with the Gr. *en atomō,* "in an indivisible instant of time." In I Cor 15:52 it is used to explain the sudden, instantaneous change which will occur at the resurrection of the dead and the transformation of the living believers at Christ's second coming. *See* Rapture.

TYCHICUS (tĭk′ĭ-kŭs). One of the most frequently mentioned of Paul's companions and delegates (Acts 20:4; Eph 6:21; Col 4:7; II Tim 4:12; Tit 3:12). He was an Asian (Ephesian?) who probably accompanied Paul as he carried the collection to the church in Jerusalem (I Cor 16:1-4).

High praise is given Tychicus by the apostle: "the beloved brother and faithful minister and fellowservant in the Lord" (Col 4:7; cf. Eph 6:21). He was sent, together with Onesimus, from Paul (in prison) to the church at Colossae (and possibly to the one at Ephesus), to deliver the apostle's letters and to inform the believers of his state.

According to Tit 3:12, Tychicus was a possible replacement for Titus in Crete, for Paul wanted Titus to join him during his stay in Nicopolis.

TYPE. The English word "type" has its derivation in the Gr. *typos,* which is used 16 times in the NT. In the KJV this Gr. word is variously translated "print" (Jn 20:25); "figure" (Acts 7:43; Rom 5:14): "pattern" (Tit 2:7; Heb 8:5); "fashion" (Acts 7:44); "manner" (Acts 23:25); "form" (Rom 6:17); "example" (I Cor 10:6, 11; Phil 3:17; I Thess 1:7; II Thess 3:9; I Tim 4:12; I Pet 5:3). Thus the meanings of the Gr. word differ significantly from its corresponding English word in that they lack a predictive sense.

There are three other Gr. words used in the NT which more closely express the idea involved in typology. They are *skia* ("shadow," Heb 8:4-5; 10:1; Col 2:16-17), *parabolē* ("figure" or "symbol," Heb 9:9), and *hypodeigma* ("copy" or "pattern," Heb 9:23).

A type is best defined as a historical person, event or object which, as designed by God, has an essential feature which corresponds to another person, event or object yet future. The term "antitype" is used to describe that future fulfillment. Evangelical scholars have usually limited the application of types to various aspects of the person and work of Christ, since such types are the only ones clearly recognized in the NT. Others see in the OT additional types that are of the Holy Spirit and of the Church.

A true biblical type is generally characterized by at least three elements: (1) There is some notable point of resemblance between the type and its antitype. It should be noted, however, that there will also be points of dissimilarity. For example, Adam is made a type of Christ (Rom 5:14), but only in his headship of the race, as the first representative of humanity. (2) There should be evidence that the type is of divine appointment. (3) It must prefigure something in the future.

There are four basic categories of types found in Scripture: (1) Persons. According to Rom 5:14 Adam, as the head of the race, is a type of Christ. Moses (Heb 3:1-6), Melchizedek (Heb 5:6-10; 7:1-28), and Aaron (Heb 5:4-5) are types pointing to Christ. (2) Institutions and rituals. The Passover, special offerings, sacrifices and the priesthood all appear to point to various aspects of Christ's person and ministry. (3) Special acts or events. The lifting up of the brazen serpent in the wilderness by Moses (Num 21:8-9) is considered a type of Christ's crucifixion (Jn 3:14-16). Israel's entrance into the Promised Land is a type of the believer's "rest" in salvation and the victory won for us by our "Joshua," Jesus Christ (Heb 4). (4) Structures and objects. The book of Hebrews views the tabernacle and its furniture as typical of the person and work of Christ.

In the history of typological exegesis a number of schools of interpretation have appeared. One group, best represented by Origen of the 3rd cen. A.D., has tended to see too much as typical in Scripture, resulting in an extreme allegorization of OT history (*see* Allegory). Another group, more inclined to a skeptical rationalism, considers the whole idea of typology as completely artificial and denies any such phenomenon to Scripture.

In order to achieve balance in this matter, Bishop Marsh proposed in his *Lectures on the Criticism and Interpretation of the Bible* that a type is a type only if the NT specifically so indicates. Many have felt that this definition is too narrow and have sought to propose a more moderate view following Patrick Fairbairn. This latter group sees two kinds of types in the Bible: (1) Innate, i.e., a type specifically declared to be so in the NT; and (2) inferred, or a type which is recognized because of the nature of NT discussions of this subject. Recent scholars who accept the conclusions of modern literary criticism (W. H. Lampe, G. von Rad, W. Eichrodt, H. W. Wolfe) recognize typology in the OT in the sense of "analogy" and "corresponding reality" but not as truly predictive (as discussed in article by Gundry in bibliography).

See Bible Interpretation.

Bibliography. Lewis S. Chafer, *Systematic Theology,* Dallas: Dallas Seminary Press, 1948, III, 116–125; IV, 136–141; VI, 47–66. Patrick Fairbairn, *The Typology of Scripture,* 2 vols., New York: Funk & Wagnalls, 1900. Francis Foulkes, *The Acts of God,* London: Tyndale, 1955 (a study of the basis of typology in the OT). Leonhard Goppelt, "*Typos,* etc.," TDNT, VIII, 246–259. Stanley N. Gundry, "Typology as a Means of Interpretation," JETS, XII (1969), 233–240. For additional bibliography *see* Symbol (ism).

J. J. D.

TYRANNUS (tī-răn'ŭs). Aside from Acts 19:9 no mention is made of this man. The phrase "the school [Gr. *scholē*] of Tyrannus" is ambiguous. Did he lecture in the hall? Or was he the owner of it? Either is possible.

The Western Gr. text (Codex Bezae) of Acts adds several words at the end of v. 9: ". . . of one (or, a certain) Tyrannus, from the fifth to the tenth hour" (*Tyrannou tinos apo hōras e heōs dekatēs*). If this addition were accepted, we would know that Paul used this hall between the hours of 11:00 A.M. and 4:00 P.M., a time of day when people were not working. Thus it served the same purpose as the house of Titus Justus in Corinth (cf. Acts 18:6–7 with 19:8–9). This went on for two years with great success (19:10).

TYRE (tīr). An ancient Phoenician city-state on the Mediterranean between Acre and Sidon. In control of only the plain of Tyre (*c.* 15 miles long and two miles wide) in the early days, the city eventually established leadership over all the cities of the Phoenician coast, but did not unify them into a national state.

Origins of Tyre date to very early times, probably the 3rd mil. B.C. During the Amarna age (*c.* 1400–1360 B.C.) Sidon successfully besieged the town and maintained an ascendancy over it thereafter. The temple of Asherah in Tyre was well known to the people of ancient Ugarit (ANET, p. 145). When sea raiders left Sidon largely in ruins about 1200 B.C., many of her people migrated to Tyre, contributing to its ascendancy. Thus it could be said that Tyre was the "daughter of Sidon" (Isa 23:12).

The story of the period of Phoenician independence (*c.* 1200–870 B.C.) is largely the story of the expansion of Tyre. The great period of advance seems to have come with Hiram I (*q.v.*) soon after 1000 B.C. The dates of his reign have recently been set at 980–947 B.C. by Frank M. Cross (BASOR, #208 [1972], p. 17). He seems to have begun the colony of Tarshish (*q.v.*) in distant Spain. In those days Tyre consisted of two small islands off the Phoenician coast. (Whether or not there was a Tyre on the mainland at that time is uncertain.) Hiram united the islands and presumably gave attention to the fortifications and harbors as well. A Sidonian harbor lay on the N and an Egyptian harbor on the S.

Friendly relations existed between the Hebrews and Tyrians. Hiram provided carpenters, masons, and wood for the construction of David's palace (II Sam 5:11–12; I Chr 14:1–2), and he provided men and materials for the construction of Solomon's palace and the temple (II Chr 2; I Kgs 5:1–12). Hiram and Solomon also engaged in joint commercial endeavors (I Kgs 9:26–28). Hiram's line was brought to an end early in the 9th cen. B.C. by the revolt of a priest named Ethbaal, who assumed the throne and married his daughter Jezebel to Ahab of Israel (I Kgs 16:31). By this means Baal worship was introduced to Israel.

Phoenician independence ended with the reign of Ashurnasirpal II (883–859 B.C.) of Assyria. In 876 he received tribute from Tyre, as well as other Phoenician towns. Later in that century, as tradition has it, Pygmalion (831–785 B.C.) founded Carthage in his seventh year of reign. Tyre attained the height of her prosperity during the 8th cen. under Assyrian suzerainty, probably because Assyrian power brought a high degree of peace and safety for the commerce of western Asia. But Tyrian history during the Assyrian period was punctuated with several rebellions against the foreign overlords. With the decline of Assyria after the middle of the 7th cen., Tyre obtained her independence and retained it for *c.* 40 years. Ezekiel, who lived during those decades of independence, penned a remarkable description of Tyre's attainments (Ezk 27).

Ezekiel also prophesied the destruction of Tyre (26:3–21). The first stage of fulfillment came with Nebuchadnezzar of Babylon who besieged the mainland city for 13 years (585–572 B.C.) and ultimately destroyed it. Without a fleet he could not take the island city, which surrendered on favorable conditions. Tyre's greatest days were gone. Her commerce was ruined by the siege, as well as by the fact that Gr. merchants had captured Phoenician trade in the NE Mediterranean and to some extent elsewhere. Her role in international

A Roman street from the island city of Tyre.
HFV

The great Roman circus or hippodrome from the mainland city of Typre. HFV

trade was further usurped on land by Aramean merchants and on sea by the Carthaginians.

The second stage of fulfillment of Ezekiel's prophecy came in 332 B.C., when Alexander the Great for seven months besieged the island city and ultimately took it by building to the island a causeway composed of remains of the mainland city and scraping the area as "bare as the top of a rock" in the process. Most of the population was killed or sold into slavery.

Although the city was rebuilt and was fairly prosperous by 315 B.C., the colonists were largely Carian rather than Phoenician. Thus there was little ethnic connection with ancient Tyre. During the Roman period Tyre attained a degree of prosperity, Tyrian purple being much in demand (*see* Purple). A Roman colony was established at the city, which subsequently became largely Hellenized. At the close of Paul's third missionary journey he stopped for a week at Tyre (Acts 21:3-4). Tyre suffered numerous attacks and partial destruction in subsequent centuries and was almost completely destroyed by the Muslims in 1291, after which it lay in ruins for centuries. The modern town has a population of *c.* 12,000. The Lebanese government has been excavating remains of the city. *See* Phoenicia; Sidon; Lebanon.

H. F. V.

TZADDI (tsä'dĭ). The 18th letter of the Heb. alphabet. *See* Alphabet. This letter is used in the KJV as the heading of the 18th section of Ps 119 (vv. 137-144), where each verse begins with this letter. It has a numerical value of 90.

U

UCAL (ū'kăl). According to the usual translation, Ucal is one of the two men to whom the words of Prov 30 are addressed, "The man spake to Ithiel, even unto Ithiel and Ucal" (Prov 30:1). If this is correct, then Ucal may have been a sage known to Agur, who is the author of this chapter. Nothing more is known concerning any of these named in connection with the chapter.

Very early, however, scholars felt that the passage was obscure, and since the days of the LXX various attempts have been made to translate these words rather than take them as proper names. There is no unanimity among translators because the phrase requires some emendation to make a meaningful statement. Since the time of Cocceius, his translation, "I have labored on account of God and I have obtained," has been widely accepted. Other suggestions are: "I wore myself out and, O God, I languish" (Berkeley); "I have wearied myself, O God, and am consumed" (ASV marg.); "I am wearied, O God, and spent" (American). The word is still taken as a proper name, however, by most standard versions.

P. C. J.

UEL (ū'ĕl). One of the sons of Bani who had taken a foreign wife (Ezr 10:34).

UGARIT. *See* Ras Shamra.

UKNAZ (ŭk'năz). KJV marginal note at I Chr 4:15 refers to Kenaz (*see* Kenaz 2).

ULAI (ū'lī). A river near which Daniel saw himself in a vision (Dan 8:2, 16). This is described only as a river of Elam that flowed near Susa (bibical Shushan), a winter capital of the Persians located *c.* 150 miles N of the Persian Gulf. Some would identify the Ulai with the Eulaeus of Pliny (vi. 135), the modern Karûn which is a 450-mile-long river of Persia that empties into the Shatt-al-Arab, the single stream that bears the waters of the Tigris and Euphrates into the Persian Gulf. But there is nothing in Scripture to require that Daniel was referring to the largest river of that area. Called *Ulai* in Assyrian inscriptions, it is illustrated in reliefs depicting Ashurbanipal's victory in 640 B.C. when he drove the Elamites into that river (R. D. Barnett, *Assyrian Palace Reliefs,* London: Batchworth, 1960, plates 118-129; Y. Yadin, *The Art of Warfare in Biblical Lands,* New York: McGraw-Hill, 1963, II, 442–444).

H. F. V.

ULAM (ū'lăm)

1. Eponym of a family of Manasseh (I Chr 7:16–17).

2. The firstborn son of Eshek, a descendant of Benjamin. Ulam's sons became famous as great archers and men of valor (I Chr 8:39–40).

ULLA (ŭl'*ă*). A family of the tribe of Asher (I Chr 7:39).

UMMAH (ŭm'*ă*). One of the cities belonging to the tribe of Asher (Josh 19:30). Its location is unknown unless one follows the indication of a few LXX MSS which identify it with Accho (*q.v.*).

UNCIAL LETTERS. *See* Writing.

UNCIRCUMCISED. The word occurs frequently and signifies a condition in which there is a lack of circumcision (*q.v.*), either literal or figurative. Literal circumcision was required of all Abraham's male descendants plus any "bought with money" from outside (Gen 17:12–14). Anyone not circumcised was to be "cut off from his people," because he had broken God's covenant. The Israelites despised Gentiles as being outside the pale of God's concern and blessing, referring to them as "uncircumcised" (Gen 34:14; Ex 12:48; Jud 14:3; I Sam 17:26). Stephen speaks of his fellow Jews as being figuratively "uncircumcised in heart and ears" (Acts 7:51). The former applies in general to a God-offending condition, and the latter to ears closed to the message of God, as if closed with a foreskin (cf. Lev 26:41; Ezk 44:9; Jer 4:4).

UNCLEAN, UNCLEANNESS. Heb. *tāmē'* has the sense of profane, unclean, defiled. Gr. *akathartos* has the sense of impure, idolatrous, or demonic; while *koinos* denotes something profane or desecrated (Acts 21:28) because it is common or has been made ordinary. To be unclean means to be contaminated by physical, ritual, or moral impurity. Uncleanness is displeasing to deity; it may belong in the sphere of demons (Zech 13:2; Mt 10:1; 12:43; etc.) Ritual impurity is contagious and transferable from one object or person to another (Hag 2:10 f.).

The idea of uncleanness is consistently defined in relation to God and His will. Ritual uncleanness is the opposite of purity or sanctity. It may be understood as being over against the sacred in the sense of that which is contaminated or profaned by contact with the common. Those things, such as meats, which are not consistent with the requirements of holiness, are declared ceremonially unclean. Moral uncleanness is understood as opposed to goodness, justice, uprightness. Clinical uncleanness describes that which is diseased as opposed to that which is healthy and whole (*see* Diseases).

Uncleanness calls for measures for purification. The principal means of purification include abstaining from that which profanes, such as unclean foods, and from certain activities, such as copulation for an appropriate time after childbirth and menstruation; washing with water after touching unclean objects; and bringing a sacrifice to purge from iniquity and restore the holiness lost through defilement or profanation. These measures may be applied to an object, to the body, or to the spirit, mind, and soul of the unclean person (Ps 79:9; Ezk 43:20, 26; Heb 9:14, 22; II Pet 1:9).

A major function of priesthood was the definition of the difference between clean and unclean (Lev 10:10; 11:47; 20:25; Ezk 22:26). Priestly injunction and sacrifice provided the means of purification (cf. Lev 16 especially). It is natural then that priestly legislation should contain the major treatments of the subject in the OT.

The major collection of the rules concerning the unclean is found in Lev 11–15. Chap. 11 contains the divine instruction regarding clean and unclean beasts. The general rule decreed that animals without cloven hoofs or which did not chew the cud were unclean (vv. 3–8) as were sea creatures without scales or fins (vv. 9–12). Birds of prey and some others were forbidden (vv. 13–19), along with all winged creatures having four legs, except locusts and crickets (vv. 20–23). The creeping animals were tabu (vv. 29–31, 41–44). It is to be noted that unclean animals were neither to be eaten nor touched (vv. 24–28, 32–38, 41–42). Any dead animal was judged to be unclean whether it normally belonged to this class or not (vv. 28, 39–40). Deut 14:3–21 contains a much shorter parallel to this chapter.

Lev 12 describes the condition of uncleanness incurred by a mother in childbirth. The difference in length of time for a son or a daughter is remarkable. The fact that birth contaminates is an illustration of the many-faceted picture of uncleanness. It is probably to be explained as belonging with other issues from the body as described in chap. 15.

Lev 13–14 gives the minute prescriptions concerning leprosy. This too leads to eruptions and issues from the body resulting, however, from a horrible disease rather than natural functions. Leprosy not only contaminates the person afflicted (Lev 13:1–46) but also clothes (vv. 47–59) or a house (14:33–53). The careful provisions for priestly examination and for isolation show a recognition of the nature of the disease. In the very nature of the case uncleanness from leprosy is usually permanent. However, provision is made for those suspected of leprosy to prove their health (14:1–3) and to be restored through rites of purification (14:4–32). *See* Leper, Leprosy.

Lev 15 adds prescriptions for uncleanness caused by a bodily discharge (15:1–15) or by the emission of semen in copulation or otherwise (vv. 16–18) or by menstrual discharges (vv. 19–30).

Num 19:11–19 treats uncleanness resulting from death. Any person who comes in contact with a dead body is deemed unclean with a long period required for purification. The Mosaic religion did not yet deal positively with death and the issues raised by it. It reacted against every evidence of the cult of the dead (as practiced in Egypt), and simply decreed that Israelites should have as little to do with dead bodies as possible. God's people had to await further revelation in order to learn the hope of the resurrection.

These passages outline the major areas to which uncleanness pertained: eating of meat, sex and birth, leprosy, and death. They define limits of behavior and life for the Israelite.

The interpretation of uncleanness is peculiarly ambivalent. On the one side it is treated as a breach of the realm of holiness, as a physical quality which must be washed away or burned away (Num 19:20–22; Lev 15:31). On the other hand it is interpreted as a breach of covenant, as a personal break in one's relationship to the holy God (Lev 11:44–45). This difference arose because of the parallel ambivalence in the understanding of holiness as related to a place or object and as a personal characteristic of God.

The idea of uncleanness as a breach in personal relations because of sin allows it to transcend the purely ritual ideas and to make a positive contribution to the thought of the whole Bible. Yet one should beware of viewing this as an evolutionary development. Ritual requirements against uncleanness were even stricter in later Judaism than in old Israel, as the Zadokite Document and the Manual of Discipline of the Dead Sea Scrolls (*q.v.*) now show.

In the NT uncleanness is viewed in internal spiritual terms rather than outer ritual prescriptions (II Cor 7:1). Cleansing is understood to be the work of Christ through His atoning death (Heb 10:22; Jas 4:8; I Jn 1:7, 9).

See Ablution; Clean, Cleanness; Defile; Holiness; Purity; Separation.

Bibliography. CornPBE, "Impurity and Purification (Ritual)," pp. 403–405. Edward Neufeld, "Hygiene Conditions in Ancient Israel (Iron Age)," BA, XXXIV (1971), 42–66.

J. D. W. W.

UNCTION. Anointing was a part of the inaugural ceremony of priests (Ex 29:7; 40:13; Lev 6:22; Num 35:25), of kings (I Sam 9:16; 10:1; 15:1), and sometimes of prophets (I Kgs 19:16; cf. Isa 45:1). John speaks of an unction or anointing (Gr. *chrisma*) of the Holy Spirit (I Jn 2:20, 27) which gives knowledge and discernment of the true Church in contrast to schisms (2:19), and a sound doctrine of the incarnation vs. heresy (2:22). John is referring to the gift of the Holy Spirit who leads us into all truth (Jn 14:26; 16:13).

Is baptism a sign of anointing, or is it the laying on of hands, or some special initiation ceremony? It is none of these. Baptism typifies the cleansing power of the blood of Christ when sprinkling is the mode; identification with Christ's death, burial, and resurrection when immersion is the mode; the infilling of the Holy Spirit when pouring is the mode. No mode can signify all that the Holy Spirit accomplishes in applying Christ's death to our sins, though the user of each mode acknowledges that the Holy Spirit does the three things signified above to all who believe. *See* Anoint; Baptism of the Spirit; Holy Spirit, Filling of the.

R. A. K.

UNDEFILED. In the OT Heb. *tām* or *tāmîm* usually means "perfect" and is translated "undefiled" in Ps 119:1 in KJV, but "blameless" in the RSV. Song 5:2 and 6:9 are rendered "perfect" in the RSV. The NT Gr. *hamiantos* designates the undefiled or unstained Christ in Heb 7:26, the marriage act as guiltless in Heb 13:4, perfect religion in Jas 1:27, and the heavenly inheritance in I Pet 1:4.

UNDERGIRDING. *See* Ship.

UNDERSETTERS. Supports at the four corners of each of the ten bronze lavers in the temple (I Kgs 7:30, 34). RSV uses the word "supports."

UNDERSTANDING. The English word denotes comprehension of knowledge resulting from intelligence and reason. It implies a mental grasp of the nature and significance of something, along with discernment and good judgment. In short, it is common sense, closely akin to wisdom (*q.v.*), not the mere accumulation and possession of knowledge. "Understand" and "understanding" translate a number of Heb. and Gr. words that mean either to grasp the full meaning or to have the knowledge or skill needed to accomplish a task (*re* God with respect to creation and providence, Ps 147:5; Prov 3:19; Isa 40:28; *re* Bezaleel as a craftsman, Ex 31:3; 35:31; 36:1). In the OT the principal words are Heb. *bîn* and *śākal* and their derivatives; in the NT, Gr. *nous* and *synesis*.

Heb. *bîn* and the nouns *bînâ* and *tᵉbûnâ* suggest discernment or perception with the senses (II Sam 12:19; Job 6:30; Prov 7:7), and then close attention or careful consideration (Deut 32:7; Ps 50:22; Prov 23:1; 24:12; Isa 14:16). Finally the terms mean the gaining or giving of comprehension both in the intellectual (Job 38:18, NEB; Dan 1:17, 20) and moral and spiritual spheres of life (Prov 2:11; 29:7, NASB; Isa 6:9–10). Such understanding is gained from the Lord (I Chr 22:12) through knowledge of the Holy One (Prov 9:10; 2:6) and by paying attention to parental instruction (Prov 4:1, 5, 7). The evidence of having understanding is to depart from evil (Job 28:28), to be slow to anger (Prov 14:29; 17:27), to accept chastening

(Prov 17:10), and to acquire wise counsel (Prov 1:5). Men of Issachar who sided with David "had understanding of the times, to know what Israel ought to do" (I Chr 12:32).

The noun *śekel* means intelligence or prudence (I Sam 25:3). This leads to the wisdom and understanding of experience, gained through doing God's commandments (Ps 111:10; II Chr 30:22).

A third OT term for "understanding," Heb. *lēb,* means "heart," used often in a figurative sense of the "deepest recesses of the human personality where man's being centers and where the issues of his life are determined" (IDB, IV, 733; cf. Prov 4:23). This term most clearly depicts the moral and spiritual nature of biblical understanding. The one who commits or even considers adultery lacks understanding (Prov 6:32; 7:7; 9:16). The one who lacks "heart" is not only physically lazy but morally as well (Prov 24:30; Jer 5:21). One acquires heart understanding by heeding reproof (Prov 15:32).

Gr. *nous,* "mind," denotes the faculty of thinking and intellectual perception (I Cor 14:14, 15,19), and then the ability to make moral judgments. Jesus "opened" the disciples' "understanding" or minds so that they could understand the scriptures about Him (Lk 24:45). The peace of God surpasses all power of human reasoning and understanding (Phil 4:7). Gr. *synesis* denotes insight leading to comprehension (Eph 3:4, RSV), such as the boy Jesus evidenced in the temple (Lk 2:47). Paul prayed that we might receive spiritual understanding for full insight into God's will (Col 1:9, NEB); such understanding is the basis for full assurance (Col 2:2). It is the Lord who gives us understanding in everything (II Tim 2:7).

See Heart; Knowledge; Mind; Wisdom.

J. R.

UNICORN. *See* Animals: Ox, Wild, II. 30.

UNITY. The Gr. word *henotēs,* "oneness, unity," is used in Eph 4:3, 13 to describe that unity which is to exist within the Christian church. It is based upon the clear doctrines of one Saviour, one heavenly Father, one Holy Spirit, one baptism, and only one Church in God's sight (Eph 4:4-6). It is made possible by the Holy Spirit enabling Christians to exercise forbearance and love to each other (vv. 2-3), and by the humble, intelligent use of the gifts given to the church (vv. 7-11). Its grand goal is accomplished as, in the unity of the faith, the individual Christian comes to "the measure of the stature of the fulness of Christ" (v. 13).

This goal is the fulfillment of David's psalm extolling the excellencies of brotherly unity (Ps 133:1 ff.), and of our Lord's high priestly prayer "that they all may be one" (Jn 17:21-22). Paul urges the believers at Philippi to realize Christian unity "by being of the same mind, maintaining the same love, united in spirit, intent on one purpose" (Phil 2:2, NASB). It becomes possible when each has the attitude of humility which was characteristic of Christ (Phil 2:3-5; *see* Mind and Attitudes).

R. A. K.

UNIVERSALISM. *See* Restoration, Restitution.

UNKNOWN GOD. An inscription from an Athenian altar, employed by Paul as the basis for his Areopagus address, read "to an unknown god" (Gr. *agnōstō theō;* Acts 17:23 ff.). Apparently the altar had been erected in honor of a supposed divine benefactor whose identity was unknown. In this confession of ignorance the apostle saw an opportune occasion to make known the true God.

References to altars to unknown gods are found in several early writings. Pausanius speaks of altars "to gods called unknown" (*Description of Greece,* i.1.4). Philostratus states that such altars were to be seen in Athens (*Life of Apollonius of Tyana,* vi.3.5). Diogenes Laertius recounts the slaughter of sheep at various spots in Athens to avert a plague. At each of these places an "anonymous altar" was dedicated (*Lives of Philosophers,* i.110). The fact of altars to unknown gods is confirmed by a mutilated Gr. inscription from Pergamum which appears to have read, "To unknown gods" (Deissmann, *Paul,* pp. 287 ff.).

Such modern writers as Eduard Norden and Albert Schweitzer have disputed the historicity of the Areopagus sermon on the ground that no evidence of an altar to an unknown god (singular) has ever been found outside Acts. This, however, is an argument from silence which does not prove the point.

D. W. B.

UNKNOWN TONGUE. *See* Tongues, Gift of.

UNLEARNED. The members of the Sanhedrin who questioned the disciples in Acts 4:13 were amazed that such "illiterate" (Gr. *agrammatos*) men, and Peter in particular, could present their case so well. The NT speaks of the unsaved as unlearned, using the Gr. *idiōtes,* which means unskilled and unlearned in divine truth (I Cor 14:16, 23-24).

There are foolish and "unlearned" (Gr. *apaideutos*) questions, the thoughts of an untaught child, which we are warned to avoid (II Tim 2:23). Unlearned people, *amathēs,* "untaught," "uneducated," cause dissensions (II Pet 3:16).

UNLEAVENED BREAD. This was bread made from dough which had not been caused to rise with yeast or "leaven." *See* Food: Bread; Leaven. Although the cracker-like bread was known earlier (Gen 19:3), at the time of the Exodus it became a symbol not only of the Israelites' haste in leaving (Ex 12:39) but their separation from all the sin for which Egypt stood. The bread became the symbol of the Feast of Unleavened Bread, the memorial of the Passover (*q.v.*). The bread as a symbol of purity, unmixed with the leaven of sin, was used to accompany certain of the offerings (Lev 2:4-5; 6:16; 7:12). Since the last supper of Jesus with the apostles was the Passover (Mt 26:17 ff.), they used unleavened bread, and this has governed the usage of unleavened bread for the Lord's Supper in many Christian churches.

UNNI (ŭn'ī)

1. One of the musicians who accompanied the ark of the covenant brought by David to Jerusalem (I Chr 15:18, 20).

2. A Levite of the post-Exilic period (Neh 12:9), spelled Unno in ASV and RSV.

UNPARDONABLE SIN. *See* Holy Spirit, Sin Against the.

UNTEMPERED MORTAR. Translated "whitewash" in RSV. It was probably mortar made of clay rather than slaked lime. This mortar was smeared over mud brick walls for enhancement and prolongation of the life of the wall. The coating was not permanent and required yearly attention. *See* Mortar. Ezekiel used untempered mortar to allegorize the preaching of false prophets. Their prophecies seemed plausible but were in fact flimsy and unreliable. They affirmed peace when there was no peace (Ezk 13:10-15; 22:28).

UPHARSIN. *See* Mene, Mene, Tekel, Upharsin.

UPHAZ (ū'făz). A place (Heb. *'ûphāz*) mentioned as a source for gold (Jer 10:9; Dan 10:5). Its location is not known, although it is thought by some that "Uphaz" is an error for the well-known gold area of "Ophir" (*q.v.*), or for Heb. *ûpaz*, meaning "and pure gold." The NEB and JerusB adopt the former alternative on the basis of the Targum and Syriac version.

UPPER CHAMBER, ROOM. The translation of several Heb. and Gr. words.

1. Heb. *'ăliyyâ*, "upper chamber," indicating at least a second story. King Eglon was sitting in his cool roof chamber with doors open when Ehud came to kill him (Jud 3:20-25). The Shunammite woman had a walled upper chamber built on her house for Elisha (II Kgs 4:10-11), and Elijah stayed in a similar room at Zarephath (I Kgs 17:19, 23). An upper chamber could be over the gateway (II Sam 18:33) or on the corner of the city wall (Neh 3:31-32). Ahaziah, king of Israel, had an upper chamber with a latticed window (II Kgs 1:2). He fell through it by accident and was so injured by the fall that eventually he died. Ahaz had erected a multi-storied structure and placed an altar on it (II Kgs 23:12). It was these altars which Josiah destroyed among others. Jeremiah rebuked King Jehoiakim for building himself a spacious palace with airy roof chambers without paying the laborers (Jer 22: 13-14, NEB).

The temple of Solomon was flanked by rooms opening to the outside, possibly as much as three stories high, reached by one or more stairs inside the thick walls; they served as treasuries (I Chr 28:11) and were gold leafed (II Chr 3:9).

2. Gr. *anōgeon*, "upper room," that provided by some friends of Jesus to celebrate the Passover with His disciples alone (Mk 14:15; Lk 22:12).

3. Gr. *huperōon*, the place of assembly of the disciples where Matthias was chosen to fill Judas' place (Acts 1:13); the place where Peter raised Dorcas from the dead (Acts 9:37-38); the room where Paul preached (Acts 20:8), this one in the third story (v. 9). *See* Room 9.

H. G. S.

Royal lyres from Ur give some indication of the high level of civilization there c. 2500 B.C.
BM

UR (ûr)

1. The city of Ur plays only a minor role in OT history, but a significant one. When it pleased God to choose one man and one family as ancestors to the later nation of Israel, that man was Abram and that family the family of Terah. They were all western Semites (Amorites), although living at that time in S Mesopotamia, in or near the Sumerian city of Ur (Gen 11:27-31). *See* Abraham.

Ur at the time of Abram (*c.* 2000 B.C.) was in a serious decline politically. [Other systems of chronology would put Abraham at Ur during or before the city's golden age. – Ed.] The once proud Third Dynasty of Ur, which marked a major military and cultural peak in the history of Mesopotamia, was disintegrating rapidly under the impact of Guti and Elamite invaders. Ibbi-Sin, king of Ur at this time, saw one after another of the city-states, long controlled by Ur, break away and become independent political units. Nevertheless, the economic and cultural level of the people of Ur remained at a comparatively high level.

It seems certain that Abram's ancestors migrated S down the Euphrates Valley along with thousands of other Amorites toward the close of the 3rd mil. B.C. Evidence for this migration is found in the increasing number of Amorite personal names occurring in the business documents of S Mesopotamia.

The ruins of ancient Ur are known today as Tell el-Muqayyar (mound of pitch) by the Arabs because many of the bricks in these mounds are bound together by bitumen. These ruins lie some 220 miles SE of Baghdad and cover an area roughly 1,000 by 800 yards. *See* Archaeology. Today, little can be seen apart from the remains of the great ziggurat, low foundation walls of a palace, and a temple. But 4,000 years ago, the city covered nearly four square miles with an estimated population of 300,000. The Euphrates River which once flowed along the W side of the city now follows a course 12 miles to the E. So today there is no sign of habitation as far as the eye can see.

Yet in its heyday, Ur was one of the most important cities in the world. At the dawn of recorded history in Iraq, there were three main centers: Kish, Ur, and Uruk (biblical Erech). Around 2600 B.C. Mesannepadda king of Ur defeated Agga king of Kish to found the First Dynasty of Ur. There were at least five kings of this dynasty, which is the first historical dynasty in Mesopotamian history known both from later chronicles and contemporaneous archaeological materials.

In fact, the treasures found in the so-called Royal Tombs (together with rich private graves), which come largely from the First Dynasty, are among the richest finds in archaeological history. Although nearly all these tombs were plundered in antiquity, an amazing collection of gold and silver, vessels, jewelry, musical instruments, and richly inlaid furniture was recovered, testifying to the skill of the ancient craftsmen and the extent and volume of trade. Mass burials pose intriguing problems regarding religious customs. One tomb contained the bodies of seven men and 68 women in addition to the main burial. Others contained oxen hitched to chariots. *See* Burial.

The best known period in the history of Ur was the Third Dynasty (*c.* 2100-2000 B.C.) founded by Ur-Nammu. This was the most prosperous and literate period in Sumerian history. Nearly 100,000 cuneiform tablets have been recovered chiefly from Ur, Umma, Lagash, Nippur, and Puzrish-Dagan, which permit a detailed reconstruction of religious, business, and family life. Ur was never again a leading city in its own right. But palaces and temples were built there in later periods of Old Babylonian, Kassite, Assyrian, Chaldean, and even Persian kings. The latest dated tablet comes from the 12th year of Alexander the Great.

The ziggurat at Ur is the best preserved example in Mesopotamia. The present structure dates to the rebuilding of Nabonidus *c.* 560 B.C. It was roughly 60 by 40 meters at the base, of an undetermined height, with probably seven stages surmounted by a small temple of blue glazed brick. It was dedicated to the worship of the moon-god whose Sumerian name was Nanna, the Semitic god Sin. Nanna was the tutelary deity of Ur. The first major construction of the ziggurat dates to King Ur-Nammu. Earlier buildings from the Uruk and early dynastic periods remain buried beneath the core of the later structures.

Excavations at Ur began in 1854 under J. E. Taylor, British consul at Basra. He discovered the so-called Nabonidus cylinders which disclosed the ancient name of the city and indicated its relationship to biblical Ur. Following the short season by Dr. H. R. Hall in 1919, the major expedition uniting the British Museum with the University Museum of the University of Pennsylvania began in 1922 under the direction of Mr. (later Sir) C. Leonard Woolley and carried out 12 seasons up to 1934. Ten magnificent volumes recording the excavations and recovered objects have been published, in addition to six volumes of cuneiform texts discovered in the ruins.

Some scholars have discounted a southern location for the Ur of Gen 11. One of their arguments was that an Arab tradition arising in the 8th or 9th cen. A.D. believed that Abram's Ur was Urfa, a city 20 miles NW of Haran, called Edessa by the Greeks. More recently Cyrus H. Gordon has sought to identify the Ur of Abram with one or the other of two towns called Ura in Hittite and Ugaritic texts dated *c.* 1400 B.C. One was a fortress in NE Anatolia or Armenia, the other a seaport near Tarsus (BASOR #163, p 44, n. 42). His arguments are rather effectively answered by H. F. W. Saggs. Abraham would have had to travel eastward to Haran before setting out W to go to Canaan.

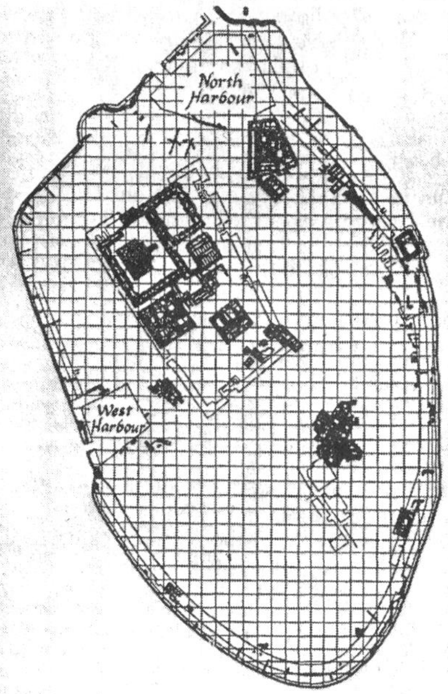

Plan of Ur in Abraham's day. The enclosed area in the center is the great worship center with its ziggurat.

Street of Ur in Abraham's day. Note windowless house fronts. Houses faced inward on courtyards. University of Pennsylvania Museum

Furthermore, the tablets mentioning Ur date 500 years or more after the probable time of Abraham. *See* Chaldeans; Patriarchal Age; Sumer.

2. The father of Eliphal (I Chr 11:35), one of David's mighty men. He is called Ahasbai (*q.v.*) in II Sam 23:34.

Bibliography. C. J. Gadd, "Ur," TAOTS, pp. 87–101. Cyrus H. Gordon, "Abraham and the Merchants of Ura," JNES, XVII (1958), 28–31. M. E. L. Mallowan, D. J. Wiseman, *et al.*, "Ur in Retrospect," *Iraq*, XXII (1960), 1–236 (28 important articles). H. F. W. Saggs, "Ur of the Chaldees, A Problem of Identification," *Iraq*, XXII (1960), 200–209. C. Leonard Woolley, *Excavations at Ur, A Record of Twelve Years' Work*, London: Benn, 1954 (a good popular summary). K. M. Yates, Jr., "Ur," BW, pp. 596–603.

F. R.S.

URBANE (ûr'bān). A believer in Rome to whom Paul sends greetings in Rom 16:9. Deissmann sees this as a Latin servant's name, Urbanus, since it is found on inscriptions in the imperial household (e.g., CIL. VI. 4237). If this is correct, it would show that the gospel had already reached Caesar's household on this lower level by A.D. 55 (cf. also Phil 4:22).

URI (ūr'ī)

1. The father of Bezalel, one of the builders of the tabernacle (Ex 31:2; 35:30; 38:22; I Chr 2:20; II Chr 1:5).

2. The father of Geber, the district officer in Gilead under Solomon (I Kgs 4:19).

3. A gatekeeper in the restored temple. Ezra induced him to put away his foreign wife (Ezr 10:24).

URIAH (yo͞o-ri'ȧ), **URIJAH** (yo͞o-ri'jȧ). In the OT the name refers to at least four and perhaps five men.

1. A Hittite and one of David's mighty men (II Sam 23:39; I Chr 11:41). From his name and conduct it appears that he was a proselyte to the Heb. religion, for he seems to have been concerned about observing the Feast of Tabernacles (cf. II Sam 11:11, RSV). His primary importance in the Bible is in connection with David's sin of adultery. His wife was Bath-sheba. David's sin occurred while Uriah was at war. To cover the sin, David called him from the battlefield at the seige of Rabbah, the Ammonite capital, so that it would appear that he was the father of the child that would be born. However, Uriah refused, even when David made him drunk, to go to his house, choosing rather to sleep at the door of the king's house to maintain his consecration as a soldier (II Sam 11:6–13). Whereupon David told Joab to place him in the "forefront of the hottest battle," and then retreat so that he would be killed. These instructions were duly followed (II Sam 11:14–25). When Bath-sheba heard of the death of her husband, she lamented. But afterward she became the wife of David (II Sam 11:26–27). God sent Nathan the prophet to declare to David that he had sinned against the Lord, and to announce the punishment of God upon his house. The child of that union was born sick and died (II Sam 12:1–23).

2. A priest in the time of Isaiah and Ahaz (Isa 8:2; II Kgs 16:10–16). He was one of the two faithful witnesses taken by Isaiah to confirm the prophetic oracle in the matter of Maher-shalal-hash-baz (Isa 8:2). In II Kgs 16 he appears in an unfavorable light, as he complies without complaint with certain undesirable changes in the temple worship at the request of Ahaz. Some have suggested that this explains the omission of his name from the list in II Chr 6:10–14. However, this omission is probably without significance, as Chronicles records only nine names from Solomon to the Exile.

3. A prophet, a son of Shemaiah of Kirjath-jearim (Jer 26:20–23). He, along with Jeremiah, faithfully proclaimed the word of God. He was opposed by Jehoiakim and his court, arrested, even at the trouble of a pursuit into Egypt, and finally put to death. The story is related by Jeremiah to show the gravity of his danger and the goodness of Ahikam, Jeremiah's protector.

4. A priest, the father of Meremoth, a descendant of Hakkoz (Ezr 8:33; Neh 3:4, 21).

5. A man named without title who stood at Ezra's side at the reading of the law (Neh 8:4). It is quite possible that he is identical with 4 above.

P. D. F.

URIEL (ūr'ĭ-ĕl)

1. A Levite of the family of Kohath. Although the lines of descent are somewhat obscure, he would appear to be a lineal ancestor of Samuel and the musician Heman (I Chr 6:24).

2. The chief of the Levitical family of Kohath in the days of David. He was one of those called upon to sanctify themselves to carry the ark of God to Jerusalem (I Chr 15:5, 11).

3. A man of Gibeah, father of Michaiah, the wife of Rehoboam (II Chr 13:2).

URIJAH. *See* Uriah.

URIM AND THUMMIM (ŭr'ĭm, thŭm'ĭm). Transliterated forms of the Heb. *'ûrîm* and *tummîm,* which designate some now unknown objects contained in the breastplate of the high priest for ascertaining the will of God by inquiry.

There is dispute over the meaning of the original words. The majority take "urim" from the root for "light" (so the LXX, Ezr 2:63; Neh 7:65; and Aquila and Theodotion). But the LXX usually translates by *dēlōsis,* "explanation" (Ex 28:30). Thummim is usually derived from the word for "perfection" or "completeness," also meaning "integrity" (*q.v.*). The LXX once uses *teleios,* "perfect," but prefers *alētheia,* "truth." The Vulgate rendered *doctrina et veritas.* "Light and perfection" are probably the best English representations. Some take the two words as hendiadys yielding the meaning "perfect illumination," but this is rejected by Plumptre in *Smith's Bible Dictionary.* The order is reversed in Deut 33:8. Urim occurs alone in Num 27:21; I Sam 28:6. Thummim alone is possible the meaning in I Sam 14:41; the RSV (with NEB and JerusB), following the longer text of the LXX, translates: "If this guilt is in me or in Jonathan my son, O Lord, God of Israel, give Urim; but if this guilt is in thy people Israel, give Thummim."

The biblical data is as follows: Upon the high priest's ephod a "breastplate of judgment" was to be worn (Ex 28:15 ff.). It was said, "Thou shalt put in the breastplate of judgment the Urim and the Thummim; and they shall be upon Aaron's heart, when he goeth in before the Lord"(Ex 28:30; Lev 8:8). Later scriptures imply that all the priestly tribe participated (Deut 33:8; Ezra 2:63; Neh 7:65), though on important matters inquiry was directed to the high priest (cf. Num 20:28; 27:21).

The Urim and Thummim were the glory of Levi (Deut 33:8). At first mention the articles are not described, implying their earlier use and familiarity. A single instance of their use by name is described after Joshua, when Saul in his sin could receive no answer (I Sam 28:6), though instances of "inquiring" occur often (e.g., Jud 1:1; 18:5-6; 20:18; I Sam 14:3, 18; 23:2 ff.; 30:7 f.), and references to the practice are frequent. Usually the question asked was one of strategy, often requiring merely a "yes" or "no" answer (I Sam 14:36 f.). But sometimes different answers were obtained; e.g., the inquiry might detect the guilty (I Sam 14:41-42).

There is no mention of consultation of the medium after David's time. The teraphim were seemingly used as an unlawful substitute (Jud 17:5; 18:14, 20; cf. Hos 4:12, RSV). It became proverbial that answers could not be given "until a priest with Urim and Thummim should arise" (Ezr 2:63; Neh 7:65, RSV; cf. Ezr 2:63; Hos 3:4). Giekie conjectures that the instruments may have been overlooked in the restoration of the sacred objects by Cyrus but that more likely they had been destroyed with the temple (*Hours with the Bible,* V.5, 413). Josephus (*Ant.* iii.8.9) says that they had been out of use for 200 years, having been replaced by prophecy.

There have been several theories as to the exact nature and workings of these objects. (1) Some have considered them supernaturally created and given to Moses. (2) They have been thought to be stones or images which produced some sort of physical effect to the eye or ear to indicate the answer. (3) Others have thought that they were symbols which by being observed produced an effect on the priest, leading to prophetic utterance or ecstatic speech. (4) Others would identify them with the object for casting lots (Josh 7:16-18; Prov 16:33), consisting in some sort of cube or dice with the answer obtained by the "roll" or the particular one of the objects drawn or cast out. The evidence is not definite enough to help reach a choice among these positions.

See Ephod; Priest, High.

J. W.R.

USURY. The translation of Heb. *neshek,* a "biting," from its painfulness to the debtor; and *nāshā',* "to lend on interest," "be a creditor. The Heb. words *marbît* (KJV "increase," Lev 25:37) and *tarbît* (KJV "increase," Lev 25:36; Ezk 18:8, 13, 17; 22:12) are synonyms which denote gain on the creditor's side.

In Jewish law, "interest" and "usury" may be used indiscriminately. "Usury" suggests the taking advantage of another's need to gain a disproportionate remuneration in return for some service, usually a loan. Among the Israelites, borrowing might become necessary as a result of crop failure (Neh 5:3), or becoming security for a friend (Prov 6:1), or for payment of tax (Neh 5:4). Commercial borrowing is not mentioned in the OT. Ex 22:25-27 and Lev 25:35-37 forbid the taking of any kind of interest from a fellow Israelite. Deut 23:20 (cf. 15:6) adds, "Unto a stranger thou mayest lend upon usury [or interest]."

There is no mention of rate for loans, nor concerning punishment for taking usury. The translation (KJV) of Neh 5:11 is questioned, but even 12 percent per annum would have been low for that period. Rates of interest for money loans ranged from 20 to 30 percent; for grains, 25 to 33 1/3 percent. The practice of mortgaging land at exorbitant interest grew up among Jews during the Captivity. Nehemiah denounced it, as did Ezekiel (Neh 5:3-13; Ezk 18:8, 13, 17).

In the NT gratuitous giving is encouraged (Lk 6:30-31). The taking of reasonable rates, however, is not forbidden (Mt 25:27; Lk 19:23). The question is not concerning "interest," but exorbitant interest, which is a moral rather than an economic problem. Against this the early Church Fathers were vehement in denunciation.

See Debt; Loan; Surety.

I. R.

UTHAI (ū'thī)
1. The son of Ammihud of the tribe of Judah, a resident who returned to Jerusalem after the Exile (I Chr 9:4).
2. A son of Bigvai. With his brother Zabbud and 70 men he returned to Jerusalem with Ezra (Ezr 8:14).

UZ (ŭz). Three men in the Bible are named Uz.
1. The oldest son of Nahor (Gen 22:21, RSV; Huz in KJV).
2. Grandson of Seir (Gen 36:28; I Chr 1:42).
3. Son of Aram in the Table of Nations (Gen 10:23). Thus the name is of an ancient Aramaic tribe, probably the same as the Ausitai who lived in the desert W of the Euphrates.
4. Job's homeland (Job 1:1), usually identified with the homeland of the Aramaic tribe of Uz. Although Uz cannot be located precisely, it probably lay in the Arabian or Syrian Desert E of Palestine. Such a site meets the requirements of the biblical narrative which indicate Uz was within striking distance of the Sabeans and Chaldeans (Job 1:15, 17). It was probably adjacent to the Transjordan trade route of the Middle Bronze I Age (2100–1900 B.C.), the route taken by the four kings of Gen 14. Job seems to have been in contact with traders and travelers to and from Mesopotamia, Egypt, and Arabia (Job 6:18–19; 31:32; 28:19).

More specific suggestions are: (*a*) Based on Lam 4:21 and Gen 36:28, Uz has been located in the vicinity of Edom, confirmed by Eliphaz coming from Teman (Job 2:11; cf. Gen 36:11; Amos 1:12). (*b*) Alternatively, early Christian tradition pointed out the dunghill on which Job sat in the desert E of Lake Semechonitis (Huleh). (*c*) The most recent suggestion is that Uz (Heb. *'ûṣ*) should be related to the Arabic god *'Awḍ*. This, together with acknowledged Arabic linguistic influence in the language of Job, suggests a southern location closer to or in Arabia.

A. B.

UZAI (ū'zī). The father of Palal, a helper of Nehemiah in the repairing of the Jerusalem wall (Neh 3:25).

UZAL (ū'zăl). The name of a son of Joktan (Gen 10:27; I Chr 1:21), and probably the ancestor of an Arabian tribe. According to Arabian tradition Uzal or Auzal was the ancient name of Sana'a, the capital of Yemen in Arabia.

UZZA, UZZAH (ŭz'ȧ)
1. A Levite of the family of Merari (I Chr 6:29–30).
2. A descendant of Ehud and the head of a Benjamite clan (I Chr 8:7).
3. One of two brothers who accompanied the ark (*q.v.*) on its journey from Kirjath-jearim toward Jerusalem (II Sam 6:3-8; I Chr 13:7–11). The ark of the covenant had remained for two decades at the house of Abinadab. In arranging to bring the ark to Jerusalem, David assigned Uzza and Ahio to drive the oxcart carrying the ark amid the accompanying festal march. Upon arriving at the threshing floor at Chidon (Nacon in II Sam 6:6) the oxen stumbled. Uzza rashly put forth his hand to steady the ark and was smitten by the Lord for touching the sacred object, which only a priest was permitted to handle (Num 4:15). Displeased with the incident, David canceled the journey and left the ark at the house of Obed-edom. He called the place of the incident Perez-uzzah, meaning "the breaking forth upon Uzzah." David's failure to obey God's word regarding the proper method of transporting the ark on the shoulders of Levites was therefore severely judged. The death of Uzza directed David to the Scripture (I Chr 13:12; 15:2), and the ark was then properly and safely moved to Jerusalem.
4. The owner of a garden which served as the burial place for kings Manasseh and Amon (II Kgs 21:18, 26).
5. The ancestral head of a Nethinim family who returned from the Babylonian Exile with Zerubbabel (Ezr 2:49; Neh 7:51).

G. E. W.

UZZEN-SHERAH (ŭz'ĕn-shē'rȧ). Sherah, a female descendant of Ephraim, built this unidentified town along with the upper and lower cities of Beth-horon, according to I Chr 7:24. Some believe this town was located at modern Beit Sira, W of Beth-horon.

UZZI (ŭz'ī)
1. A high priest, the great-grandson of Phinehas the son of Eleazar. He was an ancestor of Ezra (I Chr 6:5–6, 51; Ezr 7:4). Josephus records (*Ant.* v.11.5) that after Uzzi, the high priesthood was transferred to the family of Ithamar.
2. The grandson of Issachar and founder of one of the families of that tribe (I Chr 7:2–3).
3. A Benjamite founder of one of the families of that tribe (I Chr 7:7).
4. A Benjamite, the father of Elah who returned to Jerusalem after the Exile (I Chr 9:8).
5. The son of Bani, a Levite of the musician family of Asaph. He was overseer of the Levites in Jerusalem under Nehemiah (Neh 11:22).
6. A priest of the course of Jedaiah in the days of the high priest Joiakim. He took part in the dedication of the wall of Jerusalem (Neh 12:19, 42).

UZZIA (ŭ-zī'ȧ). A man from the town of Ashtaroth who served as one of David's mighty men (I Chr 11:44).

UZZIAH (ŭ-zi'ȧ)
1. Son and successor of Amaziah as king of Judah *c.* 792–740 B.C. He is called Azariah in II Kgs 14:21; 15:1, 6–8, 17, 23, 27, and Ozias in Mt 1:8–9. Uzziah, "Yah(weh) is my strength." was probably his throne name.

Uzziah reigned during a period of temporary resurgence for both Israel and Judah in the 8th cen. B.C. Under Jeroboam II of Israel (*c.* 793–753) and Uzziah of Judah, these kingdoms reached the greatest heights of power and prosperity since the death of Solomon. Archaeological excavations at Samaria and other sites have confirmed the biblical picture of this period as one of unusual prosperity and luxury (at least for those in power, viz., the leaders and the wealthy). The world political situation at the time was partly responsible for making this possible. Adad-nirari III of Assyria (*c.* 811–783) had broken the power of Damascus, laid Ben-hadad III under tribute, and thus removed the Arameans (Syria) as a serious threat to Israel and Judah. Assyria itself did not continue to be a dangerous foe, for Adad-nirari's next three successors (down to *c.* 745) were not able to maintain much control W of the Euphrates.

Uzziah ascended the throne at the age of 16. He repaired the defenses of Jerusalem, reorganized and refitted the army, and used "engines" (II Chr 26:15) in battle. The latter seem to have been wooden structures built on the towers and battlements to hold protective shields, thus giving protection to the archers and "stone-throwers" as they shot the arrows and threw the stones down on the heads of the assault troops (see Yigael Yadin, *The Art of Warfare in Biblical Lands,* New York: McGraw-Hill, 1963, II, 326 f.).

Uzziah was also able to maintain control of Edom and further consolidate his position along the trade routes by operations against NW Arabian tribes and the Ammonites (II Chr 26:7–8). He again opened up the port and industries of Ezion-geber (Elath) (II Kgs 14:22). Strong fortresses from this period have been excavated at Arad and a nearby site and at Kadesh-barnea, and indicate that the Negeb and the southern desert were firmly in his control, as were the northern and eastern parts of the Philistine plain (he seized Gath, Jabneh, and Ashdod, II Chr 26:6).

Late in his reign Uzziah was stricken by the Lord with leprosy because he entered the temple in pride to burn incense on the altar of incense. Because of this affliction, he was forced to yield the public administration of the affairs of the kingdom to his son Jotham (II Chr 26:16–21). He lived in a separate house (II Kgs 15:5, ASV, RSV), perhaps in a palace built for him outside Jerusalem (cf. the later 7th cen. B.C. royal palace at Ramat Raḥel, Y. Aharoni, "Beth-haccherem," TAOTS, pp. 178–184). But he appears to have remained the real ruler until his death.

In spite of the picture of outward peace, power and prosperity just presented, the protests of Amos and Hosea make it clear that all was not well. Internally, there was social, moral and spiritual decay. Politically, in the third quarter of the 8th cen. Assyria began to take the matter of empire seriously. Tiglath-pileser III (*c.* 745–727 B.C.) was the true founder of the Assyrian Empire which annexed conquered territories as provinces. Beginning in 743 he conducted a number of campaigns in Syria. At first he was met by a coalition led by one Azriau of Yauda (ANET, pp. 282 f.). This almost certainly is a reference to Azariah (Uzziah) of Judah. As John Bright explains, "The probability is that Uzziah, though old and incapacitated by leprosy, as ruler (after Jeroboam's death) of one of the few stable states left in the west, understood the danger and took the lead in attempting to meet it . . . The attempt, however, failed to stem the Assyrian advance. By 738, if not before, Tiglath-pileser had taken tribute from most of the states of Syria and northern Palestine, including Hamath, Tyre, Byblos, Damascus—and Israel. Uzziah presumably died (*c.* 742) [740 according to Thiele] before Assyrian reprisals could reach him" (*A History of Israel,* p. 253).

In 1931 E. L. Sukenik recognized a stone tablet from the time of Christ in the Russian Archaeological Museum on the Mount of Olives with this inscription in Aramaic: "Hither were brought the bones of Uzziah king of Judah—do not open!" This inscription suggests that Uzziah's original tomb had recently been disturbed and his bones moved to a new resting place marked by the tablet.

2. Father of one of David's overseers or stewards (I Chr 27:25).

3. A Kohathite Levite and ancestor of Samuel (I Chr 6:24–28).

4. A priest of the sons of Harim who had married a foreign woman in the days of Ezra (Ezr 10:21).

5. A Judahite, father of Athaiah, who lived in Jerusalem after the return from Exile in the time of Nehemiah (Neh 11:4).

Bibliography. Y. Aharoni and M. Avi-Yonah, *The Macmillan Bible Atlas,* New York: Macmillan, 1968, pp. 90–92. John Bright, *A History of Israel,* Philadelphia: Westminster, 1959, pp. 238–240, 252 f. Samuel J. Schultz, *The Old Testament Speaks,* New York: Harper, 1960, pp. 205–207. E. R. Thiele, *The Mysterious Numbers of the Hebrew Kings,* 2nd ed., Chicago: Univ. of Chicago Press, 1965. G. E. Wright, *Biblical Archaeology,* rev. ed., Philadelphia: Westminster, 1962, pp. 161 ff.

K. L.B.

UZZIEL (ŭz'ĭ-ĕl)

1. One of the four sons of Kohath and founder of the family of Uzzielites (*q.v.*), one of the four into which the Kohathite Levitical family was divided for service (Num 3:27). He was the uncle of Aaron and the father of Elizaphan, prince of all the families of Kohath (Ex 6:18, 22; Lev 10:4; Num 3:19, 30).

2. A Simeonite in the days of Hezekiah. With his brothers, the sons of Ishi, he smote the Amalekites (I Chr 4:42).

3. One of the five sons of Bela, the Ben-

jamite, head of one of the tribal families (I Chr 7:7).

4. A son of Heman, one of the temple musicians in the days of David (I Chr 25:4) called Azareel in v. 18.

5. A Levite of the family of Jeduthun in the days of Hezekiah. With the other Levites he carried out a thorough cleansing and reconsecration of the temple (II Chr 29:14–19).

6. The son of Harhaiah, the goldsmith; he helped in the rebuilding of the wall under Nehemiah (Neh 3:8).

P. C. J.

UZZIELITE (ŭz'ĭ-ĕ-līt). A member of the family of Uzziel (*see* Uzziel), who was the founder of a subdivision of the families of Levites. The Uzzielites as descendants of Kohath (Ex 6:22; Lev 10:4; *et al.*) were assigned to encamp on the S side of the tabernacle (Num 3:27, 29). Num 3:31 describes their role in the service of the ark and tabernacle. Members of this Levite subdivision were among those who transported the ark when King David brought it to Jerusalem (I Chr 15:10). They were among the Levites whose duties were set out by David as he made preparatory arrangements for the temple (I Chr 23:12, 20, 24:24).

V

VAGABOND. IN KJV Heb. *nûd* is rendered "vagabond," referring to God's punishment of Cain (Gen 4:12, 14); RSV has "wanderer." Cain is said to have dwelt in the land of Nod, that is, "wandering" (Gen 4:16). The word "vagabond" does not have the connotation of a dishonest or idle rascal that the English "vagabond" does.

In Ps 109:10 the word is used as an imprecation to render Heb. *nûa'*. In Acts 19:13 it refers to the itinerancy of Jewish exorcists.

VAIL. *See* Veil; Dress.

VAINGLORY. Paul tells the Christian not to do anything for the mere glory (Gr. *kenodoxia,* "empty glory, conceit, boasting") that he will receive, nor out of envy or jealousy (Gal 5:26), but to do all in humility while regarding others as better or more important than himself (Phil 2:3).

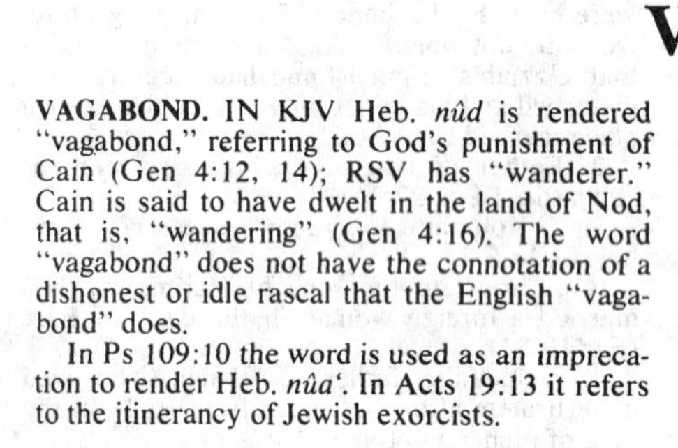

So-called Valley of Dancers near Shiloh (for background see Jud 21). HFV

VAJEZATHA (vȧ-jĕz'ȧ-thȧ). One of the sons of Haman slain by the Jews in the general reprisal resulting from Haman's frustrated attempt to liquidate the Jewish people in the Persian kingdom (Est 9:9), spelled Vaizatha in ASV, etc.

VALE, VALLEY. Words normally used of a riverbed and its adjoining land; but as the translation of various Heb. and Gr. words, the opposite of hill or mountain. It is a term referring to isolated, mountain-enclosed areas, to broad plains, narrow ravines, and lowland or foothill terrain. The Holy Land is described as a "land of hills and valleys" (Deut 11:11); it is therefore not surprising that "valley" translated a number of words of the original languages which sometimes overlap in meaning.

1. Heb. *biq'â*, from the Heb. root *bq'*, "to cleave, break open." Used as the opposite of *har,* "mountain" (Deut 8:7; Isa 41:18; Ps 104:8), it applies in most instances to rather extended, lower-elevation areas that break open or divide parallel or surrounding ranges; hence, "valley-plain" or "broad valley" (Gen 11:2—"plain," RSV; Ezk 3:22–23; 8:4; 37:1–2). It is used frequently with proper names; e.g., Valley of Jericho (Deut 34:3), the broad Jordan Valley in the Jericho region; Lebanon (Josh 11:17), the six to ten mile wide valley called the Biqa' between the Lebanon and Anti-Lebanon ranges; Megiddo (II Chr 35:22; Zech 12:11), the broad valley or plain of Armageddon.

The Kidron Valley, foreground separates Jerusalem from the Mount of Olives. In center is Garden of Gethsemane and Church of All Nations. MPS

2. Heb. *gay'*, "valley," sometimes called a wadi in Arabic. It is a restricted fertile area between mountains, often extending out from or around a city; e.g., one of the tributary valleys opposite Beth-peor (Deut 3:29; 4:46; 34:6; cf. II Kgs 2:16), leading into the Jordan Valley; in the vicinity of Ai (Josh 8:11); the Valley (*'emeq*) of Elah (I Sam 17:2) which separated Philistines and Israelites as the prelude to the David and Goliath incident (I Sam 17:3); the productive plain surrounding Samaria (Isa 28:1, 4; Mic 1:6). It is included with mountains, hills, and rivers ("ravines," NASB) as a description of the land (Ezk 6:3; 35:8; 36:4). As the term used in the name of the Valley of Hinnom on the S and W sides of Jerusalem (Josh 15:8; 18:16; Neh 11:30; Jer 7:31; 19:2; etc.), it is a point of reference for a gate of the city wall of Jerusalem—"gate of the valley" (II Chr 26:9; Neh 2:13, 15; 3:13). It is the term for the future great split in the Mount of Olives (Zech 14:4). It occurs in Ps 23:4 as the "valley of the shadow of death."

3. Heb. *naḥal,* "brook, river, stream, valley." It may be a torrent-valley or wadi which remains dry except during the rainy season or after a cloudburst (I Kgs 17:7, "brook"; II Kgs 3:16–17). Also it is specifically the torrent of rushing water of the Qishon in its channel (Jud 4:7, 13; 5:21; Ps 83:9–10) or of a gushing mountain stream (Deut 9:21; etc.), rendered "river" or "brook" in the KJV. With the connotation of the streambed of a wadi, it is the place where David picked up stones for his sling (I Sam 17:40), where Isaac's servants dug for water (Gen 26:19), and a ravine where idolatrous worship was conducted along with child sacrifice (Isa 57:5–6). It can be a valley with running water, as where elders of a city should slay a heifer to affirm their innocence concerning a slain man (Deut 21:4, NASB), and a place of springs (Ps 104:10), ravens (Prov 30:17; I Kgs 17:4–6), and fruits (Song 6:11). With proper names it is rendered "valley": Valley of Eschol (Num 32:9; Deut 1:24), Gerar (Gen 26:17), Shittim (Joel 3:18), Sorek (Jud 16:4), Zared (Num 21:12); "river": Arnon (Deut 2:24), Jabbok (Deut 2:37), the River of Egypt (*q.v.*; Josh 15:4); "brook": Besor (I Sam 30:21), Cherith (I Kgs 17:3), Kidron (II Sam 15:23).

4. Heb. *'ēmeq,* "dale, vale, valley." From the verb root *'āmōq,* "to be deep," the term generally means a vale or lowland, the opposite of mountain. It can refer to the Jordan Valley (Josh 13:27). "Valleys" specified the lower areas of Palestine occupied principally by the Amalekites and Canaanites (Num 14:25; cf. 13:29); where the Midianites encamped at the base of Moreh, threatening the Israelites (Jud 7:1, 8, 12); where there was plowing, sowing, and harvesting of grains (I Sam 6:13; Job 39:10; Ps 65:13); where herds were pastured (I Chr 27:29); where lilies grew (Song 2:1); the region not inhabited by Israel's God, according to the Syrians (I Kgs 20:28). It is also used with proper names; e.g., Valley of Achor (Josh 7:24, 26; 15:7; Isa 65:10; Hos 2:15); Ajalon or Aijalon (Josh 10:12); Berachah (II Chr 20:26); Elah (I Sam 17:2, 19); Jezreel (Josh 17:16; Jud 6:33; Hos 1:5); King's Dale (Gen 14:17; II Sam 18:18); Rephaim (II Sam 5:18; 23:13; I Chr 11:15; 14:9; Isa 17:5); Siddim (Gen 14:3, 8, 10).

5. Heb. *sh^{e}pēlâ,* "low country, plain, vale, valley." It was used frequently as a technical term applying to the western slopes or foothills of the Judean hill country. Its exact limits have been defined well by different geographers (e.g., George Adam Smith, *Geography,* pp. 201 f.). It

is distinguished from the hill country, the South, and the Arabah (Deut 1:7; Josh 9:1; 10:40; 11:2, 16; 12:8; Jud 1:9). It is perhaps a proper name (as in the NEB), the region of Eshtaol, Zoreah, Ashnah, and other cities (Josh 15:33).

6. Gr. *pharagx*, "a valley shut in by cliffs; a ravine." It is the translation of *gay'* in the quotation of Isa 40:3-5 (Lk 3:5).

7. Heb. *'āphîq* "brook, channel, river, stream," while never translated "valley," is used of a ravine (Ezk 6:3; 35:8; 36:4, 6, NASB) or of dry streambeds or wadis in the Negeb (Ps 126:4, NASB marg.).

See the various valleys listed under their proper names; Palestine.

Bibliography. Denis Baly, *The Geography of the Bible*, New York: Harper, 1957. George Adam Smith, *Historical Geography of the Holy Land*, New York: Doran, 1918.

H. E. Fi.

VALE OF SIDDIM. An area around the S end of the Dead Sea. Jutting out from the E bank of the Dead Sea is a tongue-shaped peninsula, called the Lisan. The W end of this peninsula comes within about four miles of the W shore, just opposite the rock citadel of Masada. It is believed that this "tongue" once made contact with the western shore and that the area southward was dry land on which Sodom (*q.v.*) and the cities of the plain–Gomorrah, Admah, Zeboiim, and Zoar–stood. Geological evidence shows a great cataclysmic upheaval, probably in the time of Abraham. It is thought that during this upheaval the area S of the Lisan became flooded, thereby covering the cities of the plain. It is mentioned in Genesis as the battleground of the four kings against the five kings (Gen 14:3, 8, 10) where the slime pits (bitumen or asphalt?) proved disastrous. *See* Dead Sea.

H. A. Han.

VALLEY GATE. *See* Jerusalem: Gates and Towers 9

VALLEY OF DECISION. *See* Decision, Valley of.

VANIAH (vȧ-nī'ȧ). One of the sons of Bani, who married a foreign wife (Ezr 10:36).

VANITY. The most significant Heb. word for "vanity" is *hĕbel*, a term which characterizes man's life as a vapor or "breath" (Job 7:16; Ps 39:5, 11; 62:9; 78:33; 94:11; 144:4, all in RSV). The "vanity" of man's life "under the sun" is repeatedly described by this term in Ecclesiastes (1:2, 14; 2:1, 11, 15, 17; etc.). The RSV translates *hĕbel* as "idols" (Deut 32:21; II Kgs 17:15; Jer 8:19; 10:8; Jon 2:8), "worthlessness" (Jer 2:5; 10:8), "worthless" (Jer 10:15; 51:18), and "nonsense" (Zech 10:2) to show the unreality of pagan gods and their supposed utterances.

Another Heb. term for "vanity" is *shāw'*, which actually designates what is unfounded, i.e., a "baseless" rumor (Ex 23:1, NEB), or "empty" (Ps 41:6, RSV). This word tragically describes man's life as "emptiness" (Job 7:3; 15:31, both in RSV). In most places, as in ASV and RSV, "false" or "falsehood" is a preferred translation for *shāw'*. This term thus describes what false prophets see or speak (Ezk 13:6, 8, 9, 23; 21:29; 22:28, all in ASV). It also sets forth man's speech as "falsehood" (Ps 12:2, ASV) and man's world as "vanity" (Ps 119:37).

Heb. *tōhû*, meaning "a waste" (Gen 1:2), graphically describes the "confusion and emptiness" of nations (Isa 40:17), judges (40:23), idolaters (44:9), and man's sinful ways (59:4).

Heb. *rîq* designates "vanity" in Ps 4:2 ("vain words" in RSV) and in Hab 2:13 ("nought" in RSV).

The NT categorizes idols as "vanities" (Acts 14:15). The Gr. noun *mataiotēs* describes the "futility" of the world under the curse (Rom 8:20, NASB), the "purposeless lives" of non-Christians (Eph 4:17, 20th Century NT), and the "nonsense" of false teachers (II Pet 2:18, Phillips).

W. B.

VASHNI (văsh'nī). Firstborn son of Samuel the prophet (I Chr 6:28). But I Sam 8:2 lists his firstborn as Joel and the second Abiah. The usual explanation is that a copyist's error appears in the I Chronicles reference, where the name Joel (cf. I Chr 6:33) has been accidentally omitted and a word meaning "and the second" (Vashni) was converted into a proper name. See ASV, RSV, NASB and margins.

VASHTI (văsh'tī). The queen of the Persian king Ahasuerus (Xerxes). When the king commanded her to appear with her royal crown at his banquet in order to display her beauty to his nobles, she refused (Est 1:9-12*a*). The angered monarch was advised to depose her (vv. 12*b*-19). She was replaced by the beautiful young Jewish woman Esther (2:1-4, 15-17). The name of only one wife of Xerxes is known from other sources, that of Queen Amestris (Herodotus vii.61; ix.108-112), whom he had married before becoming king. Vashti must have been one of Xerxes' other wives, unknown from extrabiblical records. *See* Esther.

VAT. The term wine vat is often synonymous with winepress. It was a round or square cavity cut into the rock where the juice of grapes or the oil of olives was received (Num 18:27; Mk 12:1, NASB). Where there were no rocks close to the surface, vats were dug in the earth, lined with stone, and made watertight with pitch or plaster. *See* Winepress.

VAU, VAV (vô). The sixth letter of the Heb. alphabet. This letter begins each verse of the sixth section (vv. 41-48) of the acrostic poem in Ps 119. It is transliterated *w* or *v*, and has the numerical value of six.

VEIL, VAIL. A covering or wrapping; a curtain.

1. Article of clothing. The Middle Assyrian laws (12th cen. B.C.) state that wives and daughters of Assyrian citizens must veil themselves when they go out on the street alone, but that harlots and female slaves must not veil themselves. When a citizen veiled his concubine in the presence of neighbors and pronounced, "She is my wife," the woman became his legal wife (ANET, p. 183).

Among nomadic peoples veiling was less common, so that Rebekah put on a veil or shawl (Heb. *ṣa'îp*) only as she was approaching Isaac before their marriage (Gen 24:65). The veil here appears to have been the sign of her marriageability, which was then taken off at the consummation of the marriage; Jacob's unexpected receiving of Leah as his bride would suggest this custom (Gen 29:21-25). In the Beni-Hasan tomb painting (19th cen. B.C.) depicting Amorite men and women walking into Egypt, the women have no covering on their heads even though they are out in public. Contrary to the above-mentioned Assyrian law, Tamar disguised herself with a large veil not only to hide her identity from Judah but also to cause him to think that she was a harlot (Gen 38:14-15). After she left him she removed her veil and resumed her widow's garb (v. 19).

Moses put on a veil (Heb. *masweh)*, like a head scarf to protect one from the sun's glare, in order to hide the radiance of his face after speaking to the Israelites (Ex 34:33-35, RSV). Since he removed it when he entered God's presence, it had no religious significance. Paul likened Moses' veil to the figurative veil (Gr. *kalumma*) or covering over Jewish hearts when the Scriptures are read (II Cor 3:13-18).

Ruth's "vail" (Ruth 3:15) was actually her cloak or large shawl (Heb. *miṭpaḥat*), large and strong enough to hold six measures of barley. It would appear from chap. 2 that she was not veiled while she was gleaning in Boaz' field in the presence of male reapers. The women's "vails" (Heb. *rādîd*) in the KJV of Isa 3:23 and Song 5:7 were more accurately long shawls or scarves to wrap around the upper body, similar to the modern stole. A sheer face veil (Heb. *ṣammâ*) seems to be the article mentioned in Song 4:1, 3; 6:7 (ASV, etc.; KJV "locks"), for the bridegroom could see the eyes and temples of his bride through her veil (see also Isa 47:2). There is no evidence in the OT, however, for the total veiling demanded of Muslim women in public.

According to sculpted Roman portrait busts (VBW, V, 259) and scenes painted on Grecian pottery, by NT times cultured women often set their hair in elegant styles and wore no head coverings. Other women, however, did wear a veil, as seen in a fresco showing a young woman dressed in a long violet garment and modestly veiled. The painting was discovered in the ruins of a patrician home of the late Augustan period in Rome (VBW, V, 99). A painting in the catacomb of St. Callixtus at Rome (4th cen. A.D.) represents a modestly dressed Christian woman with a sheer veil over her entire head (VBW, V, 246). *See* Dress.

It is believed that during worship and prayer both Jewish and Roman men covered their heads. The Jews spread the long rectangular outer garment or mantle (Gr. *himation*), with tassels or fringes (Mt 23:5), over their head as a sign of reverence. This garment is the *tallith* of the Talmud and modern Judaism. Roman men would draw a fold of their voluminous toga over the head when praying or sacrificing to the official gods of Rome; a statuette from the early empire shows a Roman so garbed performing a libation (VBW, V, 228). Therefore, when Paul writes that "every man praying or prophesying, having his head covered, dishonoureth his head" (I Cor 11:4), he cannot be telling men not to put any cloth on their heads while worshiping. He himself must have done so as he continued to go to the temple in Jerusalem and to synagogues in order to reach Jews for Christ. Instead he must have meant by Gr. *kata kephalēs echōn* that every man who "has (hair) hanging down from his head" (in a womanly fashion) while praying or prophesying disgraces Christ his Head (see Arndt, p. 406*a*).

On the other hand, women in the Graeco-Roman world sacrificed with their heads uncovered (VBW, V, 175, 228). Therefore James B. Hurley (WTJ, XXXV, 193-204) has recently argued that the Gr. term *akatakalyptos* translated "uncovered" or "unveiled" (RSV) regarding the condition of the head of the woman who is praying or prophesying in public worship (I Cor 11:5), really refers to hair that is "disheveled" or "hanging loose." The Gr. word is so used in the LXX of Lev 13:45 (see NASB marg.) concerning the hair of the unclean leper. The same original Heb. term (*pārûa'*) occurs in Num 5:18 of the accused adulteress who must let her hair go loose (NASB). Paul's teaching, then, that a woman should cover her head pertains to a proper feminine style of hair, rather than to a veil or head covering. A modest feminine coiffure is the sign that the Christian wife is in submission to the authority of her husband. This conclusion tends to agree with Paul's figurative statement that all Christians behold the glory of the Lord "with unveiled face" (II Cor 3:18, ASV, etc.). *See* Covering the Head.

2. Veil of the temple. A thick curtain separated the holy of holies from the holy place in both the tabernacle (Ex 26:33) and later the temple (II Chr 3:14). This veil (Heb. *pārōket*) was made of blue, purple, and scarlet material, embroidered with figures of cherubim, representative of the angelic beings around God's throne (Ex 26:31). It veiled the immediate presence of God from the officiating priest who daily burned incense and ministered in other ways in the holy place (Ex 40:26; Lev 4:6). Only on the annual Day of Atonement could

the high priest enter within the veil to bring incense and to sprinkle blood on the mercy seat (Lev 16:12, 15). When the tabernacle was transported from one place to another the veil was taken down and used to drape the ark of the covenant (Num 4:5). At the time of Christ's death the veil of Herod's temple was rent from top to bottom, thus exposing the most holy place to view (Mt 27:51; Mk 15:38; Lk 23:45).

In the LXX the two curtains of the tabernacle were called in Gr. *katapetasma*, the outer one screening the entrance to the holy place from the outer court (Ex 38:18), and the other separating the two sections of the sanctuary (Ex 26:31). Therefore in Heb 9:3 the designation "second veil" occurs for the inner curtain.

As our High Priest the ascended Christ has entered "within the veil" (Heb 6:19-20), into the very presence of God in our behalf. We also may now enter that holy place by virtue of the blood of Jesus, "by a new and living way which He inaugurated for us through the veil, that is, His flesh" (Heb 10:20, NASB). "As [Christ's] body was torn on the cross, so the veil between God and men was torn, giving immediate access to God" (WBC, p. 1420).

See Curtains; Tabernacle; Temple.

Bibliography. James B. Hurley, "Did Paul Require Veils or the Silence of Women? A Consideration of I Cor 11:2-16 and I Cor 14:33*b*-36," WTJ, XXXV (1973), 190-220.

J. R.

VEIN. A streak or shaft of silver in a mine (Job 28:1). The Heb. *môṣā'*, "source, place of outgoing," is translated "mine" in ASV, etc.

VENGEANCE. The Heb. verb *nāqam*, with its derived nouns, means "to avenge, vindicate." In the ancient Mari and Amarna tablets *n-q-m* can mean to champion, vindicate, or save.

Vengeance belongs to God (Deut 32:35) as part of His righteous nature (Isa 59:17; Jer 11:20; Nah 1:2 f.) and as part of His care over His children (Jer 11:18-23; Lam 3:58-66; Lk 18:7 f.). Vengeance on God's part was considered to be the evidence of His zeal in His just dealings with Israel and the nations according to His covenant (Lev 26:25; Isa 59:15*b*-18). The concept stemmed from the action deemed necessary to heal the breach made in the solidarity of the family as a result of manslaughter (Deut 32:41-43). Thus it may be defined as righteous retribution.

God sometimes uses men as agents of His vengeance (Num 31:1 f.; Josh 10:12-14; Jud 11:36; Jer 51:11) and even commissions them to act thus (Num 35:9-34; II Kgs 9:1-10; Jer 50:14-15). *See* Blood, Avenger of. The state, under God, has the right to take vengeance (Rom 13:4; cf. Gen 9:5 f.). This right is exercised by kings (I Sam 14:24), by a national entity (Est 8:13), and even by individuals (Jud 16:28). However, vengeance maliciously executed brings retribution (Ezk 25:12-17).

Sin brings God's vengeance (Jer 5:7-9, 25-29; 9:8 f.). This vengeance is threatened (Lev 26:23-25; Deut 32:41, 43) and fulfilled historically (Ps 99:8; Nah 1:2-8; Lk 21:22) and eternally (Jer 20:10-12; II Thess 1:8; Jude 7). God's vengeance is distributed equally (Ps 137:8; Jer 50:15, 28 f.) or in larger measure (Gen 4:15, 24; Rev 18:6). God's righteous nature (Nah 1:2 f.) and the deserts of men (Isa 59:17 f.) determine its distribution upon the nations (Isa 34:8-10; 47:1, 3, 10-11; Mic 5:15), upon Israel (Isa 61:2; Lk 21:20-22; I Thess 2:14-16), and upon individuals (Lk 18:1-8).

Men are forbidden to take vengeance with a vindictive or revengeful motive (Lev 19:18; Rom 12:19; Heb 10:30). Sometimes this prohibition is disobeyed (Jud 15:7 f.), but disobedience usually brings judgment (II Sam 4:8-12; Ezk 25:12-17).

The righteous cry out to God for Him to execute His vengeance (I Sam 24:12; Ps 94:1-10; Jer 15:15; 20:10-12; Rev 6:9 f.). Such vengeance causes them to rejoice (Deut 32:43; Ps 58:10 f.; 149:5-9; Jer 20:12 f.) and to take courage (Isa 35:3 f.; 61:2).

W. B.

VENISON. *See* Food.

VERMILION. *See* Colours.

VERSIONS, ANCIENT AND MEDIEVAL

Introduction

The present-day text of the Bible manifests the various alterations and corruptions resulting from the vicissitudes of many centuries of transmission. Consequently, early translations of the Bible assist in reconstructing an older text of the OT and NT, or in correcting later Heb. and Gr. MSS. Therefore, they are of considerable importance to the student of the Bible.

Two important facts about ancient and medieval versions or translations should be stressed when considering their role in the transmission of the biblical text. First, their purpose. They were works used to disseminate the message of the autographs to the followers of Judaism and Christianity and to assist them in keeping their religion pure. As such, the Targums came into use before the time of Christ. After the introduction of Christianity, versions and commentaries were employed by the church for proselyting, organizing, and establishing the new religion. Second, the ancient renderings are important because of their proximity to the autographs. In general, the older a MS is the more valuable it is in terms of textual criticism and reconstruction. The ancient translations often take the biblical scholar back to the very threshold of the autographs and render invaluable collaborating testimony to the authenticity of the biblical text.

It must be admitted, however, that there are a whole series of difficulties involved in the use of any particular translation, since each one is

VERSIONS, ANCIENT AND MEDIEVAL

the product of an individual or a group of individuals living at various periods of time and in particular cultural contexts. Within each translation there is both the underlying Heb. or Gr. text, with the peculiar problems of its own textual tradition, and the translator's own comprehension and communication of that text to his readers. Care should be taken therefore not to treat the versions naively by using them directly in textual criticism, as has been customary in the past. There are too many unsolved and possibly insoluble problems in discerning what belongs to the original textual tradition and what is to be attributed to the ancient translators, since most of those men are anonymous and leave little if any trace of their cultural outlook, intellectual presuppositions, religious opinions, prejudices, aspirations, or their education and ability to express themselves (see Ernst Würthwein, *The Text of the Old Testament*, pp. 33–34). Nevertheless, such works as the Targums, the LXX, and some early NT versions warrant consideration by the careful student of Scripture.

Definitions

In addition to the above considerations, certain distinctions should be borne in mind in order to avoid unnecessary confusion in this complex issue. The *autographs* are the original manuscripts of the writers of inspired Scripture. A *translation* is simply the rendering from one language into another any given composition or text. If any item were rendered from the second language into a third, or even back into the original language, it too would be a translation. A specific kind of translation is the *literal translation*. Its object is to provide, as far as possible, the exact meaning of the words of the original language. Such a word-for-word translation is much more rigid than a simple translation and results in the transmission of exact word order rather than ideas from one language into another. As a result of this process many Hebraisms and Gr. idioms have been translated into the English language.

In *transliteration* a word is transposed from one language into another by writing it with those letters or characters which have the closest phonetic value. In other words, translations attempt ideological equivalency, and transliterations strive for phonetic equivalency. The net result of transliteration is the crossing over of many foreign words into other languages. Such words as *aggelos* (messenger, angel), *biblos* (book, Bible), *diakonos* (minister, deacon) and *martys* (witness, martyr) are examples of certain Gr. words which have been transliterated into English.

A *version* is a translation. Strictly speaking, it is a translation only from the original language of a literary text into any other language. In this technical sense, the KJV and the Rheims-Douay Version would not actually be versions; the former being the fifth revision of Tyndale's Version, and the latter being a translation of the Latin Vulgate Version. In general usage, however, a version simply means any translation of the Bible or a part of it. Terms used to describe a translation from another language (usually from the original) which is systematically and critically reviewed and examined with a view to correcting errors or making other necessary emendations, are *revision, revised version*, and *recension*. A recension is a critical revision of any text whether in the original language or in translation.

A *paraphrase* is a free, loose translation. It is a restatement of sentences, passages, or words so that while attempting to retain the original sense, the meaning is expressed more clearly or intelligibly to the reader. Since paraphrases allow more leeway to the translator, they can be lacking in accuracy. Such works appeared quite early in the transmission of the Bible in English. An *expanded* or *amplified translation* of the text borders on explaining or commenting on it, and thus comes close to being a *commentary*. These too appear quite early in the history of Bible transmission.

Some scholars have mistakenly classed the Samaritan Pentateuch among the versions of the OT. Strictly, however, it is a revised Heb. MS of the five books of the law (*see* Bible Manuscripts: III.12. Samaritan Pentateuch).

The Aramaic Targums

During their Babylonian Exile the Jewish people began to forsake their ancestral tongue for Aram., the international diplomatic and commercial language of their suzerains. After the Exile the practice arose among Palestinian Jews of accompanying the public reading of the Heb. Scriptures in the synagogue with an oral paraphrase or interpretation in the Aram. vernacular for the benefit of the growing number of Jews who were becoming less and less familiar with Heb. There is evidence that the scribes were making oral paraphrases into Aram. as early as the time of Ezra (Neh 8:1–8). The paraphrases were not strictly translations, but were actually aids in understanding the archaic forms of the Torah. The translator or interpreter involved in this work was called a *methurgeman*. By the close of the last centuries B.C., a gradual process culminated in the existence of oral translations or paraphrases of almost every book of the OT. During the early centuries A.D., these Targums were committed to writing, and an official text came forth, since the Heb. canon, text and interpretation had become well identified by the time the rabbinical scholars met at Jamnia (*c.* A.D. 90) and the Jews were expelled from Palestine in A.D. 135.

The earliest Targums were apparently written in Palestinian Aram. during the 2nd cen. A.D., although there is evidence of Aram. Targums from the pre-Christian era. These early official Targums contained only the Law and the Prophets, but the Writings were included in later unofficial Targums. One pre-Christian Targum of Job written in Palestinian Aram. was found in Cave XI at Qumran, and Cave IV contained a Targum of the Pentateuch. These DSS specimens were among the unofficial Aram. Targums which were superseded by the official texts in the 2nd cen. A.D. The official Palestinian Targums of the Torah and the Prophets were practically swallowed up by the Babylonian Aram. Targums of the Torah and the Haphtaroth (Prophets) during the 3rd cen. Targums of the Writings (Hagiographa) were apparently done on an unofficial basis and none of the extant Targums of the Hagiographa, except for the above mentioned DSS, is older than about the 5th cen.

During the 3rd cen. A.D., there appeared in Babylonia an Aram. Targum on the Torah which may have been a recension of an earlier Palestinian tradition. It has been ascribed to Onkelos (Ongelos) by tradition, a name probably confused with Aquila who made a slavishly literal Gr. translation of the Heb. OT as a substitute for the LXX (see discussion below). Another Babylonian Aram. Targum accompanies the Prophets (Former and Latter), and is known as the Targum of Jonathan ben Uzziel. This Targum dates from the 4th cen. and is a freer and more paraphrastic rendering of the text. Both of the above named Targums were read in the synagogues as the Torah and the Haphtaroth respectively.

During the mid-7th cen. another Pentateuchal Targum appeared called the Pseudo-Jonathan Targum. This work is a mixture of the Onkelos Targum and materials from the Midrash (*q.v.*). Still another Targum appeared *c.* A.D. 700. It is known as the Jerusalem Targum, but survives in fragments only.

The Targums are useful for the light they cast on traditional Jewish interpretations of their Scriptures. They are of more value, however, for their contributions to the study of hermeneutics than to textual criticism.

The Talmud and Midrash

There were three periods of OT scribal tradition: the Sopherim (*c.* 400 B.C.-*c.* A.D. 100), the Talmudic (*c.* A.D. 200-*c.* 500), and the Masoretic (*c.* 500-*c.* 1000). During the first of these periods the Sopherim ("scribes") were regarded as the custodians of the Heb. Scriptures. Ezra was apparently one of the Sopherim, and their contribution included the Targums. During the Talmudic period the Talmud became crystallized as a body of Heb. civil and canonical law based upon the Torah.

The Talmud (instruction, teaching) represents the opinions and decisions of Jewish teachers from *c.* 300 B.C. to *c.* A.D. 500, and consists of two basic divisions: the *Mishnah* and the *Gemara*. The *Mishnah* (repetition, explanation, teaching) was the oral law which was in existence by the end of the 2nd cen. A.D. and collected by Rabbi Judah the Prince. It was regarded as the Second Law of the Jews, the Torah being the First, and was written in Heb. It included traditions as well as explanations of the oral law. The *Gemara* (to complete, accomplish, learn) consisted of the comments of the rabbis on the *Mishnah* during the period after A.D. 200. These expanded commentaries on the *Mishnah* were written in Aram. rather than Heb. Like the Targums, the *Gemara* was transmitted in two traditions: the Palestinian *Gemara* (*c.* A.D. 200) and the larger and more authoritative Babylonian *Gemara* (*c.* A.D. 500).

The Midrash (textual study, interpretation, commentary, from the Heb. root meaning "to search out," "investigate") was actually a formal doctrinal and homiletical exposition of the Heb. Scriptures written in both Heb. and Aram. These textual studies and interpretations were collected between 100 B.C. and A.D. 300. Within the Midrash are two major sections: the *Halakah* (procedure) and the *Haggada* (declaration, explanation). These are commentaries on the Torah and on the entire OT, respectively. The Midrashim differ from the Targums in that they are actually commentaries, while the Targums are paraphrases. The Midrash contains some of the earliest extant synagogue homilies on the OT, including such items as proverbs and parables. Midrashic activity came to an end after the completion of the Babylonian Talmud, and was replaced by the disciplines of history, grammar, and theology. *See* Talmud.

The Septuagint (LXX)

Just as the post-Exilic Jews had abandoned their native Heb. tongue for Aram. in the Near East, so they abandoned Aram. in favor of Gr. in such Hellenistic centers as Alexandria, Egypt. The Jews had received considerable favor from Alexander the Great as a result of their policies toward him during the siege of Tyre (332 B.C.). In the new centers established by him during his extensive conquests, he frequently included areas for Jewish inhabitants.

After Alexander's sudden death (323 B.C.) his empire was divided into several dynastic units: the Ptolemies in Egypt, the Seleucids in Asia Minor, the Antigonids in Macedonia, and several minor kingdoms. It was to Ptolemaic Egypt, named after Ptolemy I Soter, son of Lagus, that many Jews migrated; they settled especially in the new city of Alexandria. Ptolemy I was governor of Egypt (323–305 B.C.) before becoming king. In 285 B.C. his son, Ptolemy II Philadelphus, succeeded to the throne. He reigned until 246 B.C. and followed the Pharonic practice of marrying his sister, Arsinoë II. During this reign Egypt experienced a cultural and educational revival, and the Jews were granted religious and political privileges. One of the achievements of this reign was the translation of the Heb. Scriptures for the benefit of the Gr.-speaking Jews who were unable to use the Heb. text. The standard Gr. version produced in Alexandria is known as the Septuagint (LXX), the Gr. word for "seventy." The translation was undoubtedly ac-

VERSIONS, ANCIENT AND MEDIEVAL

complished during the 3rd and 2nd cen. B.C., and is purported to have been done as early as the time of Ptolemy II Philadelphus, according to the so-called *Letter of Aristeas to Philocartes* (*c.* 130–100 B.C.).

According to the *Letter of Aristeas*, the librarian at Alexandria persuaded Ptolemy II Philadelphus to translate the Torah into Gr. for use by the Alexandrian Jews. The letter relates that six translators from each of the 12 tribes were selected and that they completed the translation in just 72 days. While the details of this story are undoubtedly fictitious, the nucleus of fact contained in it appears to be that the Pentateuch was translated into Gr. sometime during the first half of the 3rd cen. B.C. During the next two centuries the remainder of the OT was translated, as well as some apocryphal and noncanonical books (Sirach, Tobit, etc.). Subsequently the name LXX was extended to cover all these translations, with the apocryphal books interspersed among the canonical books according to their general character or subject matter.

As to quality of translation, the LXX is not consistently executed, leaving room for several observations at this juncture. The LXX varies from slavishly literal renderings of the Torah to free translations in the Writings. The LXX was not designed to have the same functional purpose as the Heb. OT, since it was probably designed for public readings in the synagogues in contrast to the more scholarly purposes of those having need of the Heb. text.

The LXX is the product of a pioneer venture in the transmission of the OT Scriptures, and an excellent one at that. In terms of textual criticism, the LXX is generally loyal to the original Heb. text (*see* Bible Manuscripts). The LXX bridged the religious gap between the Heb. and the Gr.-speaking peoples as it met the needs of the Alexandrian Jews. The LXX bridged the historical gap between the Heb. OT of the Jews and the Gr.-speaking Christians who would use it in conjunction with their own NT text. The LXX also provided the precedent for missionaries who would later make translations into various languages and dialects. Finally, the LXX bridges the textual criticism gap by its substantial agreement with the OT Heb. MSS. Together with the SP and a few of the DSS fragments, the LXX provides the earliest link available to the autographs of the OT (see Norman L. Geisler and William E. Nix, *A General Introduction to the Bible*, pp. 308–309).

It was as a result of Jewish criticism and reaction during the early centuries of the Christian era that a reaction against the LXX occurred among the Jews. This reaction produced a new wave of translations and versions of the OT.

Greek OT Versions in the Christian Era

Two reasons for Jewish rejection of the LXX during the first centuries of Christianity were its adoption by Christians for apologetic and polemic purposes, and the appearance *c.* A.D. 100 of an acceptable translation by a Jew from a Heb. text which would eventuate in the MT. Justin Martyr's *Dialogue with Trypho the Jew* and his *First Apology* (*c.* A.D. 150) followed the pattern of NT writers in citing the LXX rather than the Heb. text and provided the basis for Trypho's charge that the Christian text was not authoritative.

The result of these circumstances, along with the rapid emergence of Christianity from its Judaistic antecedents, was the appearance of several translations which would help to preserve the OT for future generations. Of the several rival renderings of the OT produced, three are known today by the name of their translators. Three other Gr. translations are anonymously known. Unfortunately, all of these works are preserved only in relatively small fragments and in a limited number of citations by the Church Fathers.

Aquila's version was produced by Aquila, a native of Pontus, *c.* A.D. 130–150. He is said to have been a relative of the emperor Hadrian, and a civil servant who moved to Jerusalem from Sinope. While in Jerusalem he was converted to Christianity, but was unable to extricate himself completely from his pre-Christian ideas and habits. As a result, he was publicly rebuked by the elders of the church. He took offense, forsook Christianity, and turned to Judaism. As a proselyte he studied under the famed Rabbi Aqiba and produced a new translation of the Heb. OT into Gr.

Although much of this story lacks credence, Aquila appears to have been a Jewish proselyte from the region of the Black Sea. During the first half of the 2nd cen. he did make a Gr. translation of the OT. It was the translator of this extremely literal rendition of the OT who has been wrongly associated with the Targum Onkelos, as mentioned above. Although Aquila produced a Gr. translation, it is so slavishly literal and rigid that the thought patterns and sentence structures follow Heb. rules of composition rather than Gr. Aquila displayed his antagonism toward Christianity by rendering some of the LXX messianic passages differently. As a result, his version became the official Gr. translation of the Scriptures used among non-Christian Jews. Only fragments and isolated citations of this version have survived.

Theodotion's revision was produced during the second half of the 2nd cen. by a native of Ephesus who was either a Jewish proselyte or an Ebionite Christian. Although authorities are divided over the particular text which he used, Theodotion appears to have revised either the LXX, Aquila's version, or some other early Gr. translation (see Geisler and Nix, p. 310, n. 22, for an exposition of the views of various authorities on this issue). Theodotion's revision is much freer than Aquila's, and in some instances he replaced the reading of the LXX. The book of Daniel as revised by Theodotion soon replaced the older LXX in usage and even super-

VERSIONS, ANCIENT AND MEDIEVAL

seded it in Christian catalogs of OT books. It is possible that his revision of Ezra-Nehemiah also superseded the LXX. One of the characteristics of this revision is the frequency with which Heb. words are transliterated rather than translated.

Symmachus' revision appeared toward the end of the 2nd cen. and follows Theodotion in time as well as theological commitment. Symmachus was an Ebionite or perhaps a Jewish proselyte who attempted to produce an idiomatic Gr. rendition of the OT which reflects the pole opposite to Aquila's version. Being concerned with the sense of his rendering of Heb. terms rather than with the actual letter of the Heb. word did not keep Symmachus from exhibiting a high standard of accuracy, which was to have influence on subsequent Bible translators, including Jerome.

Origen's Hexapla grew out of the need to render to the Christian world a satisfactory Gr. text of the OT in an age when the many divergencies between the existing MSS of the LXX, the discrepancies between the Heb. text and the LXX, and the attempts at revising the OT in Gr. translations had resulted in general confusion. In addition to the above mentioned translations, Origen uncovered three anonymous Gr. translations while preparing to produce the first really outstanding attempt at textual criticism, the *Hexapla*, during the second quarter of the 3rd cen. Hence, he decided upon an attempt to unify the Gr. and Heb. texts by correcting textual corruptions, and his *Hexapla* is essentially a recension rather than a version. It is arranged in six parallel columns: Heb., a Gr. transliteration, Aquila's version, Symmachus' revision. Origen's personal revision of the LXX, and the revision of Theodotion, respectively. In the Psalms Origen added three additional columns, but only two are different translations. Still another work by Origen is the *Tetrapla*, a shorter version of the *Hexapla* having the first two columns omitted.

Neither of these works has survived the ravages of time, but Eusebius of Caesarea and Pamphilus did publish Origen's own translation (the fifth column of the *Hexapla*). The entire work was too voluminous to be marketable in Origen's day, but part of the fifth column has survived in the 4th or 5th cen. Codex Sarravianus (G). A 7th cen. Syriac translation of a large portion has also survived in several MSS (cf. Gleason L. Archer, Jr., *A Survey of Old Testament Introduction*, p. 39). Enough of Origen's *Hexapla* has survived so that his diacritical markings have been preserved.

Other recensions of the LXX appeared after the turn of the 4th cen. A.D. Early in that century Eusebius and Pamphilus each published his own edition of Origen's fifth *Hexapla* column. In so doing they advanced the LXX Version which was to become the standard in many places. The Egyptian bishop Hesychius (d. 311) attempted his own recension of the LXX, but it survives only in citations made by such Egyptian writers as Cyril of Alexandria (d. 444). Lucian of Samosata and Antioch (d. 311) made another recension of the LXX which has been preserved in portions cited in the works of John Chrysostom (d. 407) and Theodoret (d. *c.* 457). Thus by the time of Jerome there were three basic recensions of the LXX available to the church: Lucian's in N Syria, Asia Minor, and Greece; Hesychius' in Egypt along the Nile Valley and in the Delta; and Origen's Hexaplaric edition for the area of Jerusalem and Caesarea (cf. Henry Barclay Swete, *An Introduction to the Old Testament in Greek*, p. 85).

Old and New Testament Translations

1. *Syriac versions* provide the oldest and most important translations of the Heb. Scriptures after the LXX. Syriac, a Semitic language, was an Aram. dialect similar to but not identical with the Aram. dialect used in Palestine during the time of Jesus and His disciples. Since Palestinian Jews spoke Aram., it is reasonable to assume that the Jews in nearby Syria also spoke it. In fact, Josephus indicates that the Jews were engaged in proselyting activity in the area to the E of ancient Nineveh near Arbela, during the mid 1st cen. A.D.

This movement of Judaism in the mid 1st cen. paved the way for the spread of Christianity into Syria, from where it spread into central Asia, India, and as far as China. Contemporary to the formation of the Jewish Targum into Aram., Christian missionaries were translating the Bible into a more usable dialect of the same language, although they used a distinctive variation of the Aram. alphabet. The dialect these Christians used was Syriac, and it corresponded in Aram. to Koine in Greek and Vulgar in Latin, i.e., it was the common language of the marketplace. The translation used by the Syriac church has been designated *Peshitta*, meaning "simple." While this name dates from the 9th cen., and is of uncertain origin, the Syriac text of the OT undoubtedly stems from the mid 2nd to early 3rd cen., and appears to have been the work of many hands in the area at or near Edessa.

The translation of the OT was probably from the Heb. language, but was later revised in conformity with the LXX. The Syriac Pentateuch resembles the Targum of Onkelos, following the MT, but subsequent books demonstrate a rather unsystematic and not too thorough an influence from the LXX. Thus it is not too reliable as an independent witness to the text of the OT. It does, however, provide valuable assistance in the study of canonicity, as it omits the apocryphal books of the Alexandrian Canon. When the Christian faith was declared to be an official religion of the Roman Empire at the beginning of the 4th cen., codices of the Scripture (LXX) were produced in great numbers (cf. Eusebius, *Ecclesiastical History*

VERSIONS, ANCIENT AND MEDIEVAL

[Loeb], VIII, 2). It is reasonable to suppose that a similar development occurred with the Peshitta version.

The standard Syriac edition of the NT is generally believed to stem from a 5th cen. revision by Rabbula, bishop of Edessa (411-435). It is actually a recension of earlier Syrian versions which were brought into approximation with the Gr. MSS then in use in Constantinople (Byzantium). This recension, plus the Christian recension of the Syriac OT, has come to be known as the Peshitta. Rabbula ordered a copy of his recension placed in every church in his diocese, resulting in widespread circulation during the mid to the late 5th cen.

At the end of the first quarter of the 5th cen. a schism took place in the Syrian church, resulting in the Nestorian withdrawal into the E. When Nestorius was expelled from his bishopric of Constantinople in 431, he took with him the Peshitta Bible. In 489 the Nestorian school at Edessa was destroyed, and they fled into Persia where they established another school at Nisibis. The two branches of the church kept their own Bible texts, which became distinctly Eastern (Nestorian) and Western (Jacobite). The Nestorian texts have undergone fewer revisions, based on Heb. and Gr. MSS and versions, because of the more isolated circumstances of the church in the E. The Jacobite text is in the stream of the Byzantine text type.

The Syro-Hexaplaric version of the OT was a translation into Syriac of the fifth column of Origen's *Hexapla*. This work was done under the sponsorship of Paul, bishop of Tella in Mesopotamia, *c.* 616. It is an excessively literal rendering of the Gr. text which violates the Syriac idiom, and as a result this translation never actually took root in the Syrian churches. Extant copies of most of the OT books may be found in the Syro-Hexaplaric version, while the oldest MS (only a century younger than the original translation) is currently in the Ambrosian library in Milan. The Milan MS contains the poetical and prophetical books, and provides an early and extensive witness to the Hexaplaric text of the LXX as well as the diacritical signs and the original LXX text of the book of Daniel which had by this time become almost completely superseded in the church by Theodotion's version. The text type is basically Byzantine, with a marked Western influence.

Related to the Old Syriac version is Tatian's *Diatessaron* (Gr. "through the four"), or harmony of the Gospels. This work was drawn up *c.* A.D. 170, following Tatian's return to Assyria after having followed Justin Martyr to Rome. Although this work enjoyed wide circulation in the Near East, it is known mainly through indirect references. Tatian's "scissors and paste" harmony may have been originally written in Syriac, although it is more likely to have been wirtten in Gr. and later translated into Syriac.

Tatian belonged to an heretical sect called the Encratites, and this appears to have been the underlying factor for Rabbula and Theodoret, bishop of Cyrrhia in 423, abolishing its use in the early 5th cen. The *Diatessaron* was so popular that Ephraem, a Syrian Father, wrote a commentary on it. Nevertheless, Theodoret had all of the known copies (about 200) destroyed because of the potential danger of their corrupting influence. In its stead Theodoret presented another translation of the *Gospels of the Four Evangelists.*

Although both the *Diatessaron* and Ephraem's commentary have been lost, an Armenian translation of the commentary and two Arabic translations of the *Diatessaron* itself have survived (see Bruce M. Metzger, *The Text of the New Testament,* pp. 91-92; also see Metzger's *Chapters in the History of New Testament Textual Criticism,* pp. 97-120, for up-to-date treatments of this subject). No MS of the *Diatessaron* is extant, but a small fragment of a Gr. MS dating *c.* 220 has survived.

Three other Syriac versions require brief comment, although they date from later times. In 508 Zenaia (Philoxenus), Jacobite bishop of Mabbug (Hierapolis), directed his coadjutor to prepare another translation of the Gr. Bible, the Philoxenian Syriac Bible. It was a revision of the entire Bible designed to supplant the popular Peshitta version. It included several books of the NT omitted by the Peshitta (II Peter, II John, III John, Jude, and Revelation). This revision indicates that it was as late as the 6th cen. before the Syrian church accepted all the books of the NT canon.

About a century after the Philoxenian revision, the work of revision was again resumed. In 616, Thomas Harkel (Heraclea), also bishop of Mabbug, reissued the Philoxenian revision with marginal notes of the variant readings from several Gr. MSS. This Harklean Version, as it is called, is especially important for its witness to the Western text in the book of Acts. The OT portion of the Harklean revision was done under Paul of Tella, as indicated above.

Still another Syriac version is known as the Palestinian Syriac. It was actually an Aram. rendition of lectionaries (oral readings) of the Gospels written in a Syriac-type script. No complete book of the NT exists in this version. It appears to have been accomplished by Melchite Christians of Palestine toward the close of the 4th cen. The present witness to this text is in three 11th and 12th cen. lectionaries, which follow the pattern of the earlier Gr. lectionaries.

2. *Coptic versions* reflect the latest form of Egyptian writing. Prior to Christian times, Egyptian writing was done in hieroglyphic, hieratic, and demotic scripts. At the beginning of the Christian era the Gr. alphabet, with seven characters added, became the standard written mode. This system of writing became known as Coptic, and the Bible was translated into its several dialects, with portions of the Bible being extant in six of these dialects.

Of the dialects to emerge along the Nile River, Sahidic (Thebic) and Bohairic (Memphic) are the most important, while "Middle Egypt-

VERSIONS, ANCIENT AND MEDIEVAL

ian" includes several other minor dialects: Fayumic, Achmimic, and sub-Achmimic. Only fragments of the "Middle Egyptian" dialects have been discovered. No complete book of the NT survives in "Middle Egyptian" dialect, but the Gospel of John is nearly complete. One 4th cen. papyrus codex in Fayumic contains Jn 6:11–15:11, and the text lies closer to the Sahidic than to the Bohairic text.

In Upper (southern) Egypt near Thebes, virtually all the NT was translated into Sahidic by the beginning of the 4th cen. Portions of the NT were translated into this dialect as early as the 3rd cen., earlier than into any other Egyptian dialect. In Lower (northern) Egypt near Memphis and the Delta region, the Bohairic dialect became the basic vernacular tongue of the Egyptian church. Although the centrality of this region would tend to make Bohairic the most basic Egyptian dialect, the persistence of Gr. as the language of the Alexandrian church tended to account for the somewhat later appearance of Bohairic versions of the Bible. The only early MS in Bohairic is a Bodmer papyrus codex of the Gospel of John. In all, more Bohairic MSS survive than any other, but they are almost all relatively late (dating from the 12th to 14th cen.). In the NT, both the Sahidic and the Bohairic reflect the Alexandrian type Gr. text (*see* Bible Manuscripts).

3. *The Ethiopic version* of the Bible began to appear during the 4th cen., as a result of the spread of Christianity through Egypt into Ethiopia. The OT was translated soon after the consecration of Frumentius as bishop of Aksum by the patriarch of Alexandria, Athanasius. The OT appears to have been based on the LXX primarily, with revisions based upon the Heb. text. During the Monophysite controversy, 5th and 6th cen., Syrian monks moved into Ethiopia and probably worked on the translation. During the emergence of Islam, 7th and 8th cen., translation of the NT was completed. The text of the NT was later influenced by Coptic and Arabic versions, and may have been based on Syriac rather than Gr. MSS. These MSS were undoubtedly 4th or 5th cen. texts, resulting in the almost complete negation of the Ethiopic text for critical value. Of the more than 100 extant MSS, none are earlier than the 13th cen., and these were copied from late sources. The OT includes the noncanonical books of I Enoch and Jubilees, and the NT text is basically Byzantine with admixtures from other families.

4. *The Gothic version* was translated from the Gr. by the second Ostrogothic bishop, Ulfilas (311–81), known as the "Apostle of the Goths." It is not clear exactly when Christianity penetrated into the Germanic tribes in the regions of the Rhine and Danube Rivers, but Ulfilas was engaged in translating the Bible for his people when they moved from the lower Danube into the region known as Bulgaria. If Ulfilas accomplished what is generally attributed to him, namely, creating a Gothic alphabet and reducing the spoken language to writing, this enterprise was of great moment. At any rate, his OT translation was a remarkably faithful rendering of the Lucian recension. Although this translation was done in the mid 4th cen., very little remains of the OT (only six fragmentary MSS survive). The most complete MS is the Codex Argenteus, "the silver codex," written on purple vellum in silver and some gold letters.

Like Coptic, Gothic is a language whose script was expressly devised for the writing of the Scriptures. In addition, the NT is the earliest known literary monument in the Germanic dialect. It is significant because it is the earliest literary work in the Germanic group, to which English belongs, as well as the earliest version of which there is information regarding the identity of its translator. It is also the only version of any considerable extent of which all the known MS evidence has been utilized.

5. *The Armenian version* of the Bible is actually a secondary translation. As the Syrian churches carried out their work of evangelization they laid the foundations for several secondary translations. These secondary translations are so named because they were not really translated from the original languages. Not all scholars agree that the Armenian version is a translation of a translation, and there are two basic traditions concerning the origin of this version. One attributes it to Mesrob (d. 439), a soldier turned missionary who created a new alphabet to assist Sahak the Patriarch (Isaac the Great, 390–439) in translating the Bible from the Gr. text. The other tradition asserts that Sahak himself translated the Bible from the Syriac text. While both views have merit, the latter has the better position, since it stems from the nephew and disciple of Mesrob himself.

The OT rests upon the Hexaplaric recension, while portions disclose evidence of a revision from the Syriac, and stems from an early 5th cen. translation. The earliest NT translations appear to have undergone subsequent revision between the 5th and 8th cen., and provide the basic Armenian text today. Included in the Armenian translation is the apocryphal Third Letter of Paul to the Corinthians, which follows the tradition of both the Syrian and the Armenian churches. The oldest MS of the revised Armenian translation dates from the 9th cen. Its NT text type is either Caesarean or Byzantine and does not weigh heavily in textual criticism.

6. *The Georgian version* is definitely a translation of a translation, and thus a secondary translation. During the 4th cen. the mountainous region between the Black and Caspian Seas, Georgia, to the N of Armenia, received the Christian message. By mid 5th cen. it had its own translation of the Bible. Just as the message of Christianity passed into Georgia

from Armenia, so did its Bible translation. Thus, regardless of the underlying source of the Armenian Bible, the Georgian translation was actually from the Armenian. Therefore, if the Armenian translation were based on the LXX or the Syriac Peshitta, it would be a secondary translation, and the Georgian would be at best tertiary. Like the Coptic, Gothic, and Armenian, the Georgian alphabet was expressly developed for purposes of translating the Bible into the vernacular.

7. *The Sogdian versions* arose as a result of the Nestorian controversy in the 4th cen. When Nestorius (d. *c.* 451) was condemned by the Council of Ephesus (431) and placed in a monastery, many of his supporters were drawn into the camp of his opponents by compromise. The Persian Nestorians, however, broke away and became a separate schismatic church. They spread into central and even eastern Asia during the following period, and translated the Scriptures into several languages as they went. These translations are known as the Sogdian versions, but they are based on the Syriac Scriptures rather than either the Heb. or the Gr. Testaments. Scant remains of their work date from the 9th to 10th cen. and later, and represent late and tertiary evidence to the text. The devastating work of Tamerlane, "the Scourge of Asia," almost exterminated the Nestorians toward the close of the 14th cen.

8. *The Arabic version* of the Bible came about subsequent to the rise of Islam (after the *hejirah,* flight of Muhammad, 622). It was translated into Arabic from Gr., Syriac, Coptic, and Latin translations as well as various combinations of these works. The earliest of the numerous Arabic translations appears to have been from Syriac, which was probably the ecclesiastical language of the church in Arabia before the rise of Islam and the success of its Koran had made Arabic into a literary language. Muhammad (570–632), the founder of Islam, knew the gospel story from oral tradition only, and this was based on the Syriac sources left by missionaries.

The earliest extant biblical references in Arabic are in citations made by 9th cen. writers. The first and most important rendering of the OT was the translation from Heb. by the Jewish scholar Saadia Gaon (d. 942). Other than this, the OT was not standardized in its Arabic translations. In 946 Isaak the son of Velásquez, a Spanish Christian from Córdoba, made Arabic translations of the Gospels based on a Latin MS containing Old Latin and Diatessaronic readings (cf. B. M. Metzger, "Versions, Ancient," IDB, IV, 758). Arabic MSS range from the 9th to the 13th cen. and offer little if any assistance to the textual critic, since the NT is a translation of a translation, and the OT is quite late.

9. *The Slavonic version* was begun shortly after the mid 9th cen. In the middle of that century a Moravian empire was formed in east-central Europe which espoused Christianity. The leaders of this church used Latin in their liturgy, but the native people were not familiar with it. Rostislav, the founder of the kingdom, requested that Slavonic priests be sent to conduct the liturgy in the language of the people. At this time only one tongue was native to the region of eastern Europe, namely, Slavonic. Thus, in response to Rostislav's request, the Byzantine emperor, Michael III, sent two monks from Byzantium to Moravia. These monks were the brothers Methodius and Cyril, natives of Thessalonica. They devised a new alphabet for their translation. It became known as the Cyrillic alphabet, containing 36 letters, and is still used in the Russian, Ukranian, Serbo-Croatian, and Bulgarian languages. The Glagolithic alphabet, which was superseded by the Cyrillic in the 10th cen., is also attributed to these two brothers, the "Apostles to the Slavs." Their OT used to be regarded as a translation of the LXX, although more recent evidence indicates that it was translated from Latin. The NT follows the Byzantine type of Gr. text, with many readings from Western and Caesarean types. Most of the Slavonic MSS still extant are lectionaries, and the first translation itself may have been in the form of a lectionary.

10. *Miscellaneous versions* need mention only in passing since they perform little useful function in terms of textual criticism. The Nubian version has been found in fragmentary form only, and has not yet been analyzed. An Anglo-Saxon translation from the Latin Vulgate opens the area of English versions (*see* Bible, English versions). Two Old Persian versions of the Gospels are known, but they are actually translations of a 14th cen. version based on the Syriac and from a later version based on the Gr. One fragmentary 8th cen. MS preserves portions of Matthew in Frankish, a west-central European language. This is actually a bilingual edition, with the Frankish text on the page facing the Latin text.

11. *Latin versions* of the OT and NT resulted in the one great translation of the Scriptures by the Western church during the Middle Ages (A.D. 400–1400). The Latin Vulgate of Jerome was destined to reign unchallenged for a thousand years before the invention of movable type by Johann Gutenberg in the middle of the 15th cen. Before Jerome was able to perform his monumental task, however, there were several Old Latin versions translated. It appears that the OT Scriptures were translated into Latin first in N Africa during the last quarter of the 2nd cen. A.D. The OT section was translated from the LXX. This Old Latin translation was widely cited in N Africa in the period previous to Origen's *Hexapla*. It may have been the translation used by such Church Fathers as Tertullian (*c.* 160–*c.* 220) and Cyprian (*c.* 200–258). It was probably the unrevised apocryphal books of this translation that Jerome reluctantly added to his Vulgate OT. By Jerome's time, however, the remainder of the OT translated in the 2nd cen. fell into disuse.

During the 3rd cen. several Old Latin ver-

VERSIONS, ANCIENT AND MEDIEVAL

sions circulated in Europe, including versions of diverse quality current in Spain, Italy, and Gaul. It is apparently this wide discrepancy among the Latin translations which led Jerome to complain that there were almost as many versions as there were MSS. Nothing except citations of the Old Latin OT remain. Since they represent a translation of a translation, however, there is no great value in them for the textual critic.

The case of the NT is an entirely different matter. Some 27 MSS of the Gospels have survived, with seven of Acts, six of the Pauline epistles, and fragments of the Catholic Epistles and of Revelation. While no codex of the entire NT is extant, MS witnesses from the 4th to the 13th cen. indicate that the Old Latin version continued to be copied long after it had been displaced by Jerome's Vulgate. Textual evidence indicates that the African and European texts of the Old Latin NT appeared before the beginning of the 3rd cen. The Italian version, used most notably by Augustine (354–430), seems to have appeared about two centuries later. In the 3rd and 4th cen. a multiplicity of Old Latin texts appeared which created an intolerable situation by the late 4th cen. As a result, Damasus, bishop of Rome (366–84), commissioned Jerome to make a revision of the Old Latin in 382.

The Latin Vulgate Bible prepared by Sophronius Eusebius Hieronymus (*c.* 340–420), better known as St. Jerome, has exerted a profound and pervasive influence on western Europe. It grew out of the unbearable situation in the late 4th cen. when the language of the Old Latin had suffered spoilage from the multiplicity of hands stirring the kettle of translation. Instead of being the polished, literary language of the time, the Old Latin had become the vernacular and often the uncouth dialect of the common people. In addition, the OT was merely a translation of the LXX rather than the Heb. and both Testaments suffered from scribal corruptions which cried out for revision.

In 383 Jerome sent Damasus the first installment of his new assignment, a slight revision of the Gospels. In this enterprise he undoubtedly used the European Latin text and revised it in accordance with a Gr. MS following the Alexandrian text. Shortly after Jerome completed his revision of the Gospels, Damasus died (384). Jerome, who had aspired to the Holy See and had hastily revised the Roman Psalter, now returned to the East where he settled down at Bethlehem. Before setting out, however, he completed a cursory revision of the rest of the NT. In 387 he completed a more thorough revision of his Roman Psalter, subsequently known as the Gallican Psalter and the translation of the Psalms which is currently employed in the Vulgate OT. It was translated from the fifth column of Origen's *Hexapla,* Origen's own revision of the LXX.

As soon as his Psalter was completed, Jerome turned to a revision of the LXX. This was not his original objective, so he devoted his energies to perfecting his knowledge of Heb. while staying at Bethlehem. While his friends praised his endeavor, those less sympathetic began to suspect him of Judaizing, and became enraged that he should cast doubt on the "divine inspiration of the LXX" (cf. Philip Schaff, *History of the Christian Church,* 5th ed., rev., III, 974, n.3). After completing his translation of the Heb. Psalter, Jerome pursued his objective of translating the Heb. OT in spite of opposition and illness. Finally, in 405, his Latin translation of the Heb. OT was completed. It was not readily received, but he continued his revision work after the completion of the OT translation.

The sweeping nature of some of the changes introduced by Jerome, as well as the marked difference of the text he used for his translation, alienated those who loved the Old Latin versions and who were not able to understand the critical reasons for his alterations. Even Augustine, and the large majority of influential leaders in the church, opposed the translation because it was not based on the LXX. Shortly after Jerome's death, however, his OT gained a complete victory in the field of Bible translations. During subsequent centuries the intrinsic worth of his translation came to be more widely appreciated, and eventually it was accepted throughout Western Christendom as the standard text of the Bible. At the mid 16th cen. Council of Trent (1545–1563), it was officially placed in that position by the Roman Catholic church.

It was perhaps inevitable that in the course of its transmission scribes would corrupt Jerome's original translation. Sometimes this would occur by oversight, sometimes by intention. As a result, there were several medieval attempts at recension of the Vulgate. After the 6th cen., the overall character of the Vulgate text became rather faulty. Editorial work by such scholars as Alcuin of York, Theodulf, Lanfranc, and others was done. Then in the 13th cen. numerous "Correctoria" were collected at Paris and other centers of learning. These attempts resulted in further contamination rather than purification. With the introduction of movable type, several editions of the printed text appeared.

Bibliography. Gleason L. Archer, Jr., *A Survey of Old Testament Introduction,* Chicago: Moody Press, 1964. F. F. Bruce, *The Books and the Parchments,* rev. ed., Westwood, N. J.: Revell, 1963. Eusebius, *Ecclesiastical History,* Loeb ed. Vol. I, trans. by Kirsopp Lake, 1926; Vol. II, trans. by J. E. L. Oulton, 1932, London: Heinemann. Elmer Flack, *et al., The Text, Canon, and Principal Versions of the Bible,* Grand Rapids: Baker, 1956. A. von Gall, *Der hebräische Pentateuch der Samaritaner,* Geissen, 1914–18. Norman L. Geisler and William E. Nix, *A General Introduction to the Bible,* Chicago: Moody Press, 1968. J. Harold Greenlee, *Introduction to New Testament Textual Criticism,* Grand Rapids: Eerdmans, 1964. Sidney Jellicoe, *The Septuagint and Modern Study,* Oxford: Clarendon, 1968; "Septuagint Studies in the Current Century," JBL, LXXXVIII (1969), 191–199. Paul E. Kahle, *The Cairo Geniza,* 2nd ed., Oxford: Blackwell, 1959. Frederic Kenyon, *Our Bible and the Ancient Manuscripts,* rev. by A. W. Adams, New York: Harper, 1958. Geddes MacGregor, *A Literary History of the Bible, from the Middle Ages to the Present Day,* Nashville: Abingdon, 1968. Bruce M. Metzger, *Chapters in the History of New Testament Textual Criticism,* Grand Rapids: Eerdmans, 1963: *The Text of the New Testament,* New York: Oxford Univ. Press, 1964; "Versions, Ancient," IDB, IV, 749–760. Philip Schaff, *History of the Christian Church,* 7 vols., 5th ed. rev., New York: Scribner's, 1910. Henry B. Swete, *An Introduction to the Old Testament in Greek,* 2nd ed., Cambridge: Univ. Press, 1902. Bruce K. Waltke, "Prolegomena to the Samaritan Pentateuch," unpublished doctoral thesis, Harvard Univ., 1965. Ernst Würthwein, *The Text of the Old Testament,* trans. by Peter R. Ackroyd, Oxford: Blackwood, 1957.

W. E. N.

VERSIONS, ENGLISH. *See* Bible, English Versions.

VESSEL. A hollow utensil made of leather, cloth, wood, stone, straw, or metal, including copper (Ex 27:3), silver (Num 7:13), and gold (II Chr 4:8). Pottery served as the best and most popular vessel. The vessel was so well known among the people that it was used as illustrative of nations (Jer 18:4; Hos 8:8) and individuals (Isa 22:24; Acts 9:15), as well as of the human body (II Cor 4:7; I Thess 4:4). The common Heb. word for "vessel" is *kelî*, "article, utensil, vessel, instrument, weapon, etc." In the NT Gr. *skeuos,* "thing, object, equipment, instrument, jar, etc.," seems to have the same wide range of meaning.

Pottery vessels used for grain storage often were very large. This one, (dating c. 1500 B.C.) from the palace at Knossos, Crete, is almost five feet high. BM

VESTRY, VESTMENT, VESTURE. "Vestry" is an old English word for clothes or attire, like "vestment" and "vesture," all of which occur in the KJV.

"Vestry" (II Kgs 10:22, KJV) is an old English word for "wardrobe" (RSV, etc.; cf. II Kgs 22:14). Here the "vestments" or sacred robes for the worshipers of Baal were kept. The Heb. *l^ebûsh,* however, is simply a common word for clothing, as in Ps 22:18; 102:26 (KJV "vesture"). The Gr. *himatismos,* quoting Ps 22:18, has the same general meaning (Mt 27:35; Jn 19:24). The Gr. *himation* refers simply to a garment of any sort (Rev 19:13, 16) while *peribolaion* refers to a robe or mantle (Heb 1:12). *See* Dress; Garments.

VIAL

1. A small container or flask (Heb. *pak*) used for perfume or oil (I Sam 10:1; II Kgs 9:1–3, ASV).

2. A broad shallow vessel (Gr. *phialē*) used for drinking as well as for libations (Rev 5:8; 15:7; 16:1–3; 17:1; 21:9). RSV "bowl."

3. An alabaster flask (Gr. *alabastron)* for ointment (Mt 26:7; Mk 14:3; Lk 7:37, all NASB). *See* Minerals: Alabaster; Pottery.

VICTUALS. *See* Food.

VILLAGE. Some of the earliest known villages were located at Jericho and Beidha (near Petra) in Palestine, at Catal Huyuk (SE of Iconium) in Anatolia, and at Jarmo in NE Mesopotamia, all *c.* 7000 B.C. Jericho and Catal Huyuk became cities, while Jarmo and Beidha were abandoned and passed out of existence (CAH, 3rd ed., I [Part I], 248–317, 499–520). The first villages in Egypt are not yet closely dated. In ancient Israel the unwalled village was to the walled city (cf. Lev 25:30–31) as a daughter (e.g., Num 21:25 Heb.) is to her mother (cf. II Sam 20:19, RSV). A group of villages tended to cluster around a mother city (Josh 19:8; I Chr 4:33; Neh 12:29) to which their inhabitants might resort for protection and sustenance in times of danger.

"Village" in the OT translates several Heb. words, among them *bat* (lit.,"daughter"), *ḥāṣēr* (cf. Hazar-gaddah [Josh 15:27], "the village of Gaddah"), and various vocalizations of the root *kpr* (cf. Capernaum, "the village of Nahum"). Although *p^erāzāw* is rendered "his villages" in the KJV of Hab 3:14, the meaning of the Heb. word is uncertain (cf. ASV and RSV). In the

NT "village" translates Gr. *kōmē*.
See City; Town.

R. Y.

VILLANY. Jeremiah (29:23) warns that the false prophets Zedekiah and Ahab the son of Kolaiah "have committed villany," have done what was senseless ("folly," RSV) in breaking the seventh commandment and in lying. The vile person or fool speaks "villany" (Isa 32:6, KJV; "folly," RSV; "nonsense," NASB).

VINE. Any plant with a long, slender stem that trails or creeps on the ground or climbs by winding itself about a support holding fast with tendrils or claspers. The most common vine of the Bible was the grapevine, although other vines such as gourd (II Kgs 4:39), cucumber, and melon (Num 11:5) are mentioned. Palestinian soil and climate were favorable to grapes, and these were early grown in Canaan (Gen 14:18). The vines of Eschol in the hill country of Judah produced superior fruit (Num 13:23). *See* Agriculture; Plants.

VINE OF SODOM. *See* Plants.

VINEDRESSER. *See* Occupations: Farmer, Husbandman; Plants: Vine.

VINEGAR. *See* Wine.

VINEYARD. A plantation of grapevines for producing grapes for wine or other uses. The vineyard (Heb. *kerem;* Gr. *ampelōn*) was usually planted on a hill (Isa 5:1; Joel 3:18), often terraced, and was surrounded by a protective wall made of stone or bushes (Num 22:24; Isa 5:5; Ps 80:8-13; Song 2:15). A stone watchtower (*see* Tower) was erected for the watchman whose duty it was to guard the ripening grapes during the vintage season (Mt 21:33). At harvest time the grapes were processed in the winepress (*q.v.*) on the premise of the vineyard (Isa 5:2). Vineyards were cultivated by their owners or by hired hands (Mt 20:1-16). At times a large land owner rented out his vineyard on a sharecropper basis (Song 8:11; Mt 21:33-43).

That the vineyard played a large part in the life of the Israelites may be seen from the law making a person who had recently planted a vineyard exempt from the military service (Deut 20:6). An owner was required to leave the gleanings for resident aliens, widows, and orphans (Lev 19:10; Deut 24:21).

Naboth owned a vineyard in Jezreel next to the winter palace of King Ahab (I Kgs 21:1-2). He refused to sell it to the king because Israelites were forbidden by the Mosaic law to sell their paternal inheritance (v. 3; Lev 25:23-28; Num 36:7 ff.; *see* Land and Property).

Biblical writers used vines and vineyards to illustrate spiritual truths. In the OT Israel was compared to a vine (Isa 5:1-7; Ps 80:8-16). In the NT Christ based some of His parables around the vineyard (Mt 20:1 ff.; 21:28-32) and spoke of Himself as the vine and His followers as the branches (Jn 15:1 ff.).
See Plants.

Bibliography. J. P. Brown, "The Mediterranean Vocabulary of the Vine," VT, XIX (1969), 146-170.

G. E. W.

VINEYARDS, PLAIN OF THE. The plain mentioned in connection with Jephthah delivering Israel from the Ammonites (Jud 11:33). It is called Abel-keramim in ASV, etc. Its location may be sought in the general vicinity of Amman in Transjordan.

VINTAGE. *See* Vine.

VIOL. *See* Music.

VIOLENCE. Violence began in Satan's fall (Ezk 28:15 f.). It caused man's first civilization to be destroyed (Gen 6:11, 13). It still prevails wherever sinful men are found (Ps 58:1-3), for men love violence (Ps 11:5; 73:6; Prov 13:2, RSV) and are not satisfied unless they are doing it (Prov 4:14-17).

Violence mars personal relations in society (Gen 21:25). It comes upon a nation (Deut 28:31, 45) as a retribution for violating God's law (Zeph 3:4). It enters the very citadel of a nation's religion and government in times of moral and spiritual decay (Ezk 8:16 f.; Amos 3:10; 6:1, 3-6). Such a nation soon becomes a cesspool of violence (Isa 59:6-8). Jerusalem, in her degenerate years, became such a place (Jer 6:6 f.; Ezk 7:10 f., 23). Some nations have become notorious for their violence (Hab 1:9). Divine judgment comes upon nations for their violence (Jer 51:34-36; Joel 3:19; Ob 10; Hab 2:8, 17). God Himself uses violence (Lam 2:6) in destroying violent nations (Ezk 12:19 f.). Violent men are likewise destroyed (Jer 22:17-19). In fact, violence is self-retributive (Ps 7:16; 140:11; Amos 6:3).

God's servants must ever cry out concerning violence (Jer 20:8; Hab 1:2). They pray for deliverance from violent men (Ps 140:1, 4), knowing that only God can deliver them (II Sam 22:3, 49; Ps 72:14; 86:14). Rulers must suppress violence (Jer 22:2 f.; Ezk 45:9). Cities must repent of it (Jon 3:8). However, its presence in human society still creates a problem regarding God's theodicy (Eccl 5:8; Hab 1:2-4). Only Christ was free of it (Isa 53:9); and in the new earth it will cease to exist (Isa 60:18 f.).

It should be noted that the violence of Noah's time (Gen 6:11, 13) will be repeated in the last days before the second advent of Christ (Mt 24:12, 37, NASB,).

The difficult statements found in Mt 11:12 f. and Lk 16:16 probably mean that men of violence (i.e., publicans, harlots and the like) are violently (i.e., aggressively; with great zeal and determination) seeking to enter God's kingdom, bringing persecution upon themselves in the process (cf. Mt 7:7; Lk 13:24; I Cor 9:24; I Tim 6:12).

W. B.

VIOLET. *See* Colours.

VIPER. *See* Animals, IV. 34.

VIRGIN. A virgin is one who has never had sexual intercourse, in usage usually a woman. The word itself is a translation of two Heb. words in the OT and one Gr. word in the NT: (1) Heb. *b^{e}tûlâ*, "virgin." It is also used figuratively of nations and place-names. (2) Heb. *'almâ*, "young woman, virgin." This word is the feminine form of *'elem*, "young man." As to the much debated question of whether or not the word means always and only "virgin," etymology offers no help and even usage is not all-determinative in this instance. However, it may be said correctly that it is used only of unmarried women. (3) Gr. *parthenos*, "virgin." This is the word employed in the LXX translation of Isa 7:14 and in its quotation in Mt 1:23; and is used to describe Mary in Lk 1:27 (cf. v. 34), Philip's daughters (Acts 21:9), and members of the Bride of Christ (II Cor 11:2).

The second word above, *'almâ*, is the one used in Isa 7:14, where it has the article (probably generic). Mt 1:23 definitely indicates that Isa 7:14 is messianic. But among those who accept the NT authority that the prophecy applies to the Messiah, there are three principal views:

1. The strictly messianic view. The passage is predictive of the Messiah alone. This position was championed by E. J. Young in *The Book of Isaiah*, I. The two articles by Hindson (cf. the bibliography) also provide a useful survey. Those who oppose this view insist on rather convincing hermeneutical grounds that the context and argument of Isa 7-8 do not yield readily to the idea that the Messiah alone is in view, for Isaiah certainly seems to be predicting the birth and growth of an observable, contemporary child who can serve as a sign of Judah's deliverance from the Syrian and Israelite threat, a sign that "God is with us" (Immanuel). For this reason, the following two other possible major positions have been taken.

2. The "compenetration" view. Some elements apply to the Messiah, while other aspects are fulfilled in a child born in the prophet's day. A slight variation of this view is the double reference or double fulfillment view (the present writer prefers the expression, the progressive fulfillment view). J. Taylor, in his article in *Christianity Today*, summarizes this approach: "The prophetess bears a son. . .and this son is the promised sign to King Ahaz. If, therefore, we insist that Isaiah 7:14 be translated with 'virgin' and never with 'young woman,' we find ourselves with two virgin births recorded in Scripture, while we hold that the birth of Christ was unique. By acknowledging that *almah* can mean either 'young woman' or 'virgin,' we avoid this inconsistency. But Matthew, faced with the twin meaning of the word ['young woman of marriageable age' and 'virgin'], by the inspiration of the Spirit chose 'virgin.'

3. The typically messianic view. The entire prophecy refers initially to an 8th cen. B.C. child, who then serves as a perfect type of the messianic deliverer to come. The most recent comprehensive treatment of this explanation is by McIntosh (cf. bibliography). Archer also accepts this view: "Judging from Isaiah 8:1-4, the typical mother was the prophetess who became Isaiah's wife within a short time after this prophecy was spoken. Therefore, she was a virgin at the time this promise was given. She serves as a type of the Virgin Mary, who remained a virgin even after her miraculous conception by the Holy Spirit. The son of this prophetess, correspondingly, is a type of the Messianic Immanuel. . ." ("Isaiah," WBC, p. 618).

Of course, totally aside from Matthew's use of Isa 7:14 in Mt 1:23, the doctrine of the virgin birth of Christ is still plainly taught in Mt 1:18, 20, 25; Lk 1:34-35.

See Incarnation.

Bibliography. Gleason L. Archer, Jr., "Isaiah," WBC, pp. 605-654. Gerhard Delling, *"Parthenos,"* TDNT, V, 826-837. Charles L. Feinberg, "The Virgin Birth in the Old Testament and Isaiah 7:14," BS, CXIX (1962), 251-258. Edward E. Hindson, "Development of the Interpretation of Isaiah 7:14," *Grace Journal*, X (Spring, 1969), 19-25; "Isaiah's Immanuel," *Grace Journal*, X (Fall, 1969), 3-15. P. D. McIntosh, "The Immanuel Prophecy of Isaiah," unpublished master's thesis, Dallas Theolog. Sem., Mosher Library, 1971. J. Taylor, "Born of a Virgin," *Christianity Today*, IX (Dec. 18, 1964), 9-10. Gordon J. Wenham, "*B^{e}tûlah*, 'A Girl of Marriageable Age,'" VT, XXII (1972), 326-348. Herbert M. Wolf, "A Solution to the Immanuel Prophecy in Isaiah 7:14—8:22," JBL, XCI (1972), 449-456. Edward J. Young, *Studies in Isaiah*, Grand Rapids: Eerdmans, 1954, pp. 143-198; *The Book of Isaiah*, Grand Rapids: Eerdmans, 1965, pp. 283-291.

K. L. B.

VIRGIN BIRTH OF CHRIST. *See* Incarnation.

VIRGINITY. A virgin (*q.v.*) is one who has had no sexual intercourse. The reference is usually to the female sex. His fiancée's virginity was especially important to the Israelite before marriage (Lev 21:13; Deut 22:13-21). Therefore proof of virginity could be demanded by the groom before the consummation of the marriage. The bride's parents would then have to exhibit evidence of her "virginity" (Heb. *b^{e}tûlîm*), probably one of her garments stained with her menstrual blood to prove she was not pregnant. Her crime would have been sexual relations with a third party when she was already betrothed but still living with her parents (G. J. Wenham, "*Beṯûlāh*," VT, XXII [1972], 330-337). On the other hand, childlessness was considered such a misfortune that death before marriage, as in the case of Jephthah's daughter, was tragic (Jud 11:37-38).

The "breasts of one's virginity" would be the small, firm breasts of the young girl not yet fully developed, a mark that she was still childless and a virgin (Ezk 23:3, 8).

J. R.

VIRTUE. Formerly virtue sometimes meant "manly power," "valor," and "efficiency." The adjective "virtuous" (Heb. *ḥayil,* "strength, ability") is used to describe Ruth as a worthy woman (Ruth 3:11). The word is used of women three other times in the OT (Prov 12:4; 31:10, 29). Occasionally "virtue" is used in the KJV in the sense of miraculous power (Gr. *dynamis,* Mk 5:30; Lk 6:19; 8:46). In its ordinary meaning it translates Gr. *aretē* and projects the idea of moral excellence or goodness (Phil 4:8; II Pet 1:3, 5). This Gr. word, connoting moral energy, manliness, and integrity, appears in Wisd 8:7: "And if a man loves righteousness, the fruits of wisdom's labors are virtues: for she teaches soberness and understanding, righteousness and courage; and there is nothing in life for men more profitable than these."

VISION. According to the biblical records visions were often used by God to reveal His word or will to His servants. Whatever the form of the vision, whether it was the action type as was Jacob's dream of the angels ascending and descending on the heavenly ladder (Gen 28:12; *see* Dream), or the still life type like Amos' basket of summer fruit (Amos 8:1), or simply a vision of a man speaking such as the Macedonian who called to Paul in Acts 16:9, it was always a message from God.

The various words translated vision in the English Bible all come from roots having to do with seeing. Visions were often dreams or dream-like and always involved direction, instruction, or prediction. They are not to be confused with visitations, such as Peter's deliverance from prison at the hand of the angel (Acts 12:7) or Moses' encounter with the burning bush (Ex 3:2).

Visionaries of the Bible were not the sort who wasted their days in idle contemplation. They were men of action. With one exception (Balaam) visions were given only to men dedicated to the service of God. In OT days prophets received visions, and Jeremiah and Ezekiel denounced false prophets for feigning visions (Jer 14:14; 23:16; Ezk 13:7). In the NT the books of Acts and Revelation are replete with visions primarily given to the apostles.

Biblical visions concerned the present as in Gen 15:1 and Acts 9:10-11, and also the future as evidenced by the writings of Isaiah, Ezekiel, Daniel, and John.

Bibliography. Carmen Benson, *Supernatural Dreams and Visions,* Plainfield: Logos, 1970. Wilhelm Michaelis, "*Horaō,* etc.," TDNT, V, 315-382.

G. E. W.

VISITATION. God's divine visit for inspection (Heb. *pᵉquddâ* ò Gr. *episkopē*) and judgment in order to punish or reward people for their deeds (Jer 8:12; 10:15; 11:23; 50:27; Hos 9:7; Mic 7:4; Lk 19:44; I Pet 2:12). Thus the "day of visitation" (Isa 10:3) is the time of one's punishment.

VOCATION. The word occurs only once in KJV (Eph 4:1; rendered "calling" in NASB). The same Gr. word *klēsis,* is frequently rendered "calling" elsewhere (e.g., Eph 4:4) in both KJV and NASB. In Scripture, vocation or calling has to do with God's invitation, and has nothing to do with a man's vocation in the sense of his business or profession or employment. God calls or invites lost men to be saved (Mt 11:28), and saved men to serve Him (Gal 1:15-16) and to "walk worthy" (I Thess 2:12). "Chosen" in Eph 1:4 means "called out" or "selected."

Vocation in Eph 4:1 has to do with God's calling of believers to a suitable walk. Paul urges believers to live in a manner worthy of the calling with which they have been called. They have been called to an exalted standing: perfection in Christ. Thus it should be the aim or goal of every believer that his walk should correspond with his vocation. *See* Calling; Perfection.

J. A. S.

VOID. *See* Chaos.

VOLE. *See* Animals, IV. 35.

VOPHSI (vŏf'sī). The father of Nahbi, the Naphtalite spy, sent out to survey the Promised Land (Num 13:14).

VOW. This word has three different grammatical usages: verb transitive, verb intransitive, and noun. The words used express the idea of a verbal promise made generally to God, but not exclusively so.

In the OT three Heb. words were used. One is the verb *nādar.* Another is the noun *neder* derived from this verb. The third is *'issār,* a negative meaning—a vow of abstinence. The NT noun, used only twice, is Gr. *euchē,* translated "a vow."

OT vows seem to take three basic forms: bargain type, acts of selfless devotion, and those for the purpose of abstaining.

1. Bargains were made with God in the form of vows to insure His presence, protection, pro-

vision, etc. The promises made under these circumstances were always conditional.

Person	*Promise*	*Condition*
Jacob	House of worship to God and personal worship of God	Safe return (Gen 28:20-22)
Jephthah	Sacrifice of first thing seen at home	Victory over the Ammonites (Jud 11:30-31)
Hannah	To give her son to God	Make possible for her to have a son (I Sam 1:11)
Absalom	Worship to God	That he be reinstated with David (II Sam 15:7-12)

2. Vows as acts of selfless devotion can best be illustrated by David's vow not to rest until the ark was returned to Jerusalem (Ps 132:2-5). Num 6 records the laws concerning the Nazarite vow (*see* Nazarite).

3. Vows of abstinence were a sort of bargain, but rather than "do this for that," it was "refrain from this for that" (Num 21:1-3; I Sam 14:24).

Certain laws in the OT governed vows. The scope of these laws indicates how vital vows were to Jewish life.

Lev 7:16-17—the flesh from sacrifices was to be retained only two days.

Lev 22:17-25—all sacrifices were to be without blemish.

Lev 27—an appendix of laws relating to vows and tithes.

Num 30—fulfillment of vows was imperative, not optional.

Num 15:1-10—sacrifice was to accompany a vow.

Deut 12—vows were to be controlled by the laws of the central sanctuary.

In summary, several observations can be made concerning OT vows. Making a vow was not a religious duty, but fulfilling it was both a sacred and a binding duty. A vow was as binding as an oath (*q.v.*), but only when actually spoken. It could be redeemed with money, the amount to be set by the priest. Vows arose from mixed motives, and therefore should not be considered determinative in matters of Christian piety.

In the NT the term "vow" appears only twice as such (Acts 18:18; 21:23). Both references refer to Paul's taking a vow. It is said to have been a gesture on the part of Paul to show his Jewish friends that he was willing to keep the forms of Jewish piety so long as they did not conflict with Christian convictions.

There seems to have been serious misuse of vows in the days of Jesus. The current practice regarding "corban," or money dedicated to temple use rather than given to aid aged parents, was denounced by Jesus in Mt 15:3-6 and Mk 7:9-11. *See* Corban.

R. O. C.

VULGATE. *See* Versions, Ancient and Medieval.

VULTURE. *See* Animals, III. 10, 11, 52, 53, 54.

W

WADI. *See* Brook; Valley 2, 3.

WAFER. A thin, flat piece of bread. Heb. *rāqîq* is used of the unleavened wafers offered ceremonially in connection with the consecration of priests (Ex 29:2, 23; Lev 8:26), the fulfillment of Nazarite vows (Num 6:15, 19), or as part of a grain or meal offering (Lev 2:4; 7:12). Heb. *ṣappîḥit* is used once to describe the taste of manna (Ex 16:31). *See* Bread; Sacrificial Offerings.

WAGES. Compensation paid to a hired worker, either in money or goods. Coined money was not the common kind of payment in Palestine before the Gr. period. Men were hired for a variety of services in Bible times, and while commonly paid by the day, there is reference to yearly pay (Isa 16:14; 21:16). Paid workers were free men, sometimes foreigners, but ordinarily poor people who had lost their land. *See* Hireling.

Jacob served 14 years for his wives Rachel and Leah, and then agreed with Laban on wages in the form of selected livestock for caring for the flocks (Gen 29:15; 30:28, 32 f.). Paid laborers included, among others, agricultural workers (Mt 20:1-16); masons, carpenters, and metal workers, as those who repaired the temple under King Joash (II Chr 24:12); nurses (Ex 2:9); soldiers (Lk 3:14); shepherds (Jn 10:12); and fishermen (Mk 1:20). Even a harlot's hire is referred to (Ezk 16:31).

The OT gives no information on the amounts regularly paid. In any case, money equivalency to our time is not known, and rates would doubtless vary over the centuries. One writer estimates that in NT times an ordinary day laborer would be paid nine cents a day. Skilled workers would be paid more. Individual agreements would govern. The parable in Mt 20:1-16 has a man paying vineyard workers a denarius a day, thought to be worth from 16 to 20 cents (living costs would be proportionately low). By paying all his men the same amount at the end of the day, though some were hired much later than others, the employer represents God's gracious generosity, and perhaps also His provision for the minimum needs of His people.

The law of Moses protected workers against unfair treatment. The daily wage was to be paid in the evening, not kept till the next morning (Lev 19:13; Deut 24:14 f.). But the hired servant was thought to have a difficult life (Job 7:1 f.). Employers did not always keep their agreements, as in the case of Laban with Jacob (Gen 31:7). The prophets denounced those who withheld wages or otherwise oppressed the wage earner (Jer 22:13; Mal 3:5; cf. Jas 5:4).

The term "wages" is also used figuratively, as of the compensation received by those who gather a harvest of lives for Jesus Christ (Jn 4:36), and of death as the wages of sin (Rom 6:23).

See Recompense; Reward.

Bibliography. Leon Morris, *The Wages of Sin*, London: Tyndale Press, 1954.

N. B. B.

WAGON. The translation of several words in Heb. and Gr. The one most frequently used is *'ăgālâ* (from *gll*, "roll"), "cart" or "wagon"—the distinction between a two-wheeled vehicle for lighter loads and a four-wheeled vehicle for heavier loads being made not by the different words but by analysis of context. For the most part, the words in the original refer to a two-wheeled, animal-drawn vehicle.

The walls of the Old City of Jerusalem with the blocked up Golden Gate date to the sixteenth century. MIS

Carts or wagons were used for transporting both persons and things (Gen 45:19), principally, however, for carrying bulky sheaves to the threshing floor (Amos 2:13). A "covered wagon" was used for moving the tabernacle and its objects (Num 7:3-9). The two-wheeled cart, replacing the sledge and becoming common in Babylonia, Egypt, and Palestine *c.* 3000 B.C., first had wheels of solid wood and later wheels with spokes, hub, and rim (Isa 28:27-28).

WAIL. *See* Mourning.

WALK. The word is first used of God in the garden of Eden: "And they heard the voice of the Lord God walking in the garden" (Gen 3:8). It is often used symbolically or figuratively of a believer's conduct or spiritual state. It was said of Enoch, the first prophet of whom we have record (cf. Jude 14), "And Enoch walked with God: and he was not; for God took him" (Gen 5:24). "Can two walk together, except they be agreed?" (Amos 3:3). "Noah walked with God" (Gen 6:9). Abraham was told by God, "Walk before me, and be thou perfect" (Gen 17:1).

We are admonished to "walk in love, as Christ also hath loved us" (Eph 5:2). "And this is love, that we walk after his commandments" (II Jn 6). Walking in truth is held up as an example in Ps 26:3. Again in II Cor 5:7, "We walk by faith, not by sight." Other admonitions are: "Walk in the Spirit, and ye shall not fulfil the lust of the flesh" (Gal 5:16); "Walk worthy of the vocation wherewith ye are called" (Eph 4:1); "Walk circumspectly, not as fools, but as wise" (Eph 5:15). "As ye have therefore received Christ Jesus the Lord, so walk ye in him" (Col 2:6). "He that saith he abideth in him ought himself also so to walk, even as he walked" (I Jn 2:6).

See Conversation; Way.

L. A. L.

WALL. The city wall (Heb. *ḥômâ*; Gr. *teichos*) was used very early (*c.* 7000 B.C. at Jericho) to supplement the fortification of an inhabited site selected originally for its natural strength. Many ancient city walls seem to have been constructed of mud bricks on foundations of uncut stones. The earliest stone walls tended to be faced on both sides with huge blocks and filled in with packed earth and stones. Early Bronze Age (3100-2100 B.C.) Palestine exhibited most frequently the single vertical construction without exterior protective revetment. The S wall of Ai was widened several times until in at least one area its total width exceeded 60 feet. Megiddo and Tell el-Far'ah (Tirzah, *q.v.*) also had massive walls 25 to 30 feet thick during this period.

The latter Middle Bronze Age (1900-1550 B.C.) witnessed the introduction of battered (sloping) walls, fine examples of which may be seen at Shechem (Tell Balaṭah) and Jericho. Cyclopean masonry, consisting of great boulders fitted together to form the main structure while smaller stones filled in the chinks, was characteristic of this type of wall. The Hyksos also erected massive sloping ramparts around huge enclosures in these centuries, as at Hazor and Ashkelon. During the Late Bronze Age (1550-1200) the double brick wall on a stone foundation with space between the walls, providing width suitable for the support of houses (cf. Josh 2:15), came into prominence.

Saul's castle at Gibeah exemplifies the Iron Age innovation (perhaps originally a Hittite invention) of casemate wall construction, consisting of two thin parallel walls joined at intervals by transverse partitions. The Solomonic city wall at Megiddo (cf. I Kgs 9:15) was built of drafted stones, each one set a little ahead or back of its neighbors in staggered fashion and providing strength of construction as well as forming a series of small salients or bastions (Heb. *pinnôt*; cf. II Chr 26:15, NEB; KJV "bulwarks") for more effective defense. Rehoboam's wall at Lachish was built (*c.* 920 B.C.) of sun-dried mud brick (cf. II Chr 11:5-11). Carefully hewn stones became more commonly used in wall construction after Solomon's time as a result of Phoenician influence (cf. the 9th-cen. wall of Samaria). This stone masonry is of such superb workmanship that nothing has been found in Palestine to surpass it.

Jerusalem's Wailing Wall was built during the NT period by Herod the Great, while Herod Agrippa I was probably responsible for the so-called Third Wall (cf. Jos *Wars* v.4.1-2 for a contemporary description of the walls of Jerusalem).

Early house wall (Heb. *qîr*) construction was of mud brick, sometimes on a foundation of uncut stones. Later walls were made of stones which, in the homes of the wealthy, tended to be hewn and dressed (cf. I Kgs 5:17; 7:9). Mortar employed was of clay or bitumen. Wooden walls on hewn stone foundations were not unknown (cf. 7:12). Walls were often painted, plastered, or paneled (cf. Hag 1:4, RSV), or in extreme cases inlaid with ivory (cf. I Kgs 22:39; Amos 3:15).

Heb. *ḥômâ* is used figuratively in such striking passages as Ex 14:22, 29; Isa 26:1; 60:18; Jer 1:18; 15:20; Zech 2:5. Gr. *toichos,* "wall," is used as a term of invective in Acts 23:3.

See Architecture; City, Fenced; Fort, Fortification, Fortress; Gate; House; Tower; Jerusalem: Walls and Gates.

R. Y.

WANDERING IN THE WILDERNESS. *See* Wilderness Wandering.

WAR, WARFARE. War is a part of the history of man as recorded in the Bible. The ideal described by the psalmist, "Behold, how good and how pleasant it is for brethren to dwell together in unity" (Ps 133:1) remained as elusive for him as for modern man. War was a very significant part of the experience of the Israelites, particularly during the time of the Conquest, of the judges, and of the kings. It has also provided figurative language for NT writers' comments about spiritual warfare.

The Western Wall (Wailing Wall) of the Temple area dates to New Testament times. HFV

The main Heb. root for words of war in the OT, *l-ḥ-m,* "to fight, do battle," is used mostly in the *niphal* stem as a verb, *nilḥam,* "to wage war." Heb. *milḥāmâ,* "war," is the regular noun. Two verbs used frequently in the NT are (1) Gr. *polemeō,* "to wage war, fight," and its cognate noun *polemos,* "war, battle, strife, contention"; and (2) *strateuomai,* "to war, wage war."

History of Wars in the OT

The early biblical period (to c. 1700 B.C.*).* During the early biblical period civilization developed and radiated out from two main centers, one along the Nile in Africa and the other in Mesopotamia along the Tigris and Euphrates. City-states arose and expanded in some instances into empires through the use of force. Weapons, soldiers, strategy, battles, campaigns—all elements of war became vital to the establishment and continued existence of such peoples as the Sumerians, Elamites, Akkadians, Amorites, early Babylonians, and Assyrians of Mesopotamia, and of the Egyptians along the Nile in Africa. The history of these peoples makes up the background of the early biblical record.

Man killing man is traceable from the biblical viewpoint to the Fall (Gen 3). The first incident of bloodshed recounted in the Bible is, of course, the Cain and Abel incident (Gen 4:1-15). Killing on a mass scale became a part of man's tragic experience long before Abraham. While the Bible does not make specific reference to wars or battles before the time of Abraham, there is probably an allusion to military tyranny in the ancient saying "Like Nimrod a mighty hunter before the Lord" (Gen 10:9).

During the time of Abraham and his descendants. The expression "made war" occurs first in the Bible in the account of the foray of an alliance of four Mesopotamian kings into Palestine who despoiled the cities of the fertile region at the S end of the Dead Sea, and who carried off Lot among their captives (Gen 14). Abram led forth his 318 "trained men" (*ḥanîkim,* Gen 14:14, i.e., retainers or mercenaries as this word means in contemporary texts found in Egypt and at Taanach), men of his household, in order to pursue these kings and to bring Lot back (Gen 14:13–16). It is indicative of unsettled times that Abram should have his own contingent of armed men who were in readiness to protect his rights and possessions and to fight for him when necessary. Other men also had their trained followers; e.g., Esau and 400 men at the time Jacob was anticipating a battle with his brother (Gen 32:6). Simeon and Levi killed every male in Shechem with the sword and looted the town in retaliation for the rape of their sister Dinah, so that Jacob feared an all-out attack by the Canaanites and Perizzites (Gen 34:25–30).

From the sojourn to the death of Moses. The sojourn of Jacob and his descendants in Egypt was for the most part a time of co-existence with the Egyptians without actual warfare. During the peaceful time of the sojourn and the time of oppression, the Israelites apparently were in no position to wage war if they so desired. However, the Egyptians were prepared to go to war or to fight, for this is illustrated in the readiness of chariotry which was used to pursue the Israelites during the Exodus (Ex 14:6–9). Light military chariots were introduced into Egypt by the Hyksos in patriarchal times.

Led by Moses, the Israelites in making their way to the Promised Land fought a number of battles along the way. They were forced to fight with Amalek at Rephidim on the way to Mount Sinai (Ex 17:8 f.). They obtained or possessed weapons of some sort (probably short swords for the most part) from an unexplained source; they were victorious because God gave them victory through Moses.

Amenhotep II of Egypt (possible Pharaoh of the Exodus) engaged in target practice from his chariot. The chariot was used effectively in making war by Egyptians, Hittites, Assyrians and Babylonians. ORINST. For other illustrations see: Armor, Ashurbanipal, Bow and Arrow, Captivity, Harness, Tiglath-pileser

They also fought against King Arad of the Negeb who had come against them and had taken some Israelites as captives (Num 21:1). They vowed they would "utterly destroy" (from the root *ḥ-r-m,* "to devote, utterly destroy") Arad's cities (Num 21:2). God gave them victory, enabling them to destroy his cities. The region was therefore called Hormah (Num 21:3), from the root *ḥ-r-m,* "devoted to destruction." This incident marked the beginning of Israel's practice employed in the Conquest, that of utterly destroying Canaanite cities and anything that might corrupt life under the Mosaic covenant. The requirement of *ḥerem,* "devoting to the sword" or "putting under the ban," meant that anything which had been dedicated to any heathen deity was hostile to true theocracy and must either be destroyed or rededicated to Yahweh, but not allowed to be used in civilian life (Josh 6:17–19, 21, 24). *See* Devote. In Transjordan N of Moab, the Israelites fought and defeated Sihon of the Amorites (Num 21:21–32) and Og of Bashan (Num 21:33–35).

In these instances, battles of conquest were presumably undertaken with an underlying religious motivation and sanction, for the understanding was that God was leading and that He would deliver the enemy into Israel's hands (e.g., Num 21:34).

The conquest of west bank Jordan territory. In the conquest of the territory W of the Jordan River, Joshua led the Israelites forth with the conviction that God would keep His word in giving them the land and therefore He would direct them in their moves against the Canaanites (Josh 1:2–9). Further, they went forth with the divine directive to "utterly destroy" the Canaanite cities with their kings and inhabitants. They did this to Jericho (6:17), Ai (8:24–29), the five kings under Adoni-zedek at Makkedah (10:22–27), and numerous other cities and kings in the S section of Canaan and the Negeb (10:28–43), as well as Hazor and the cities in the N (11:1–20). These were victories which God had given His people: God had delivered Israel from the hands of enemies (Josh 3:10; 10:8, 25; 11:6) "because Jehovah, the God of Israel, fought for Israel" (10:42, ASV). Further, the Lord fought for Israel at times in terms of creating terror in the hearts of the Canaanites and making them an easy prey to Israel by rumors or by storms (Josh 2:9; 10:10; cf. also "the hornet" sent before them, Deut 7:20; Josh 24:12).

The time of the judges. The period of the judges as presented in the book of the Judges was a time of new incidents of warfare and new understanding of the purpose of war. This was apparently the period which rounded out the biblical viewpoint of war. First, it was a means of establishing a tribe's claim to its territory which Canaanites sometimes recovered and tenaciously tried to hold; e.g., Judah against Canaanites (Jud 1:1–10). Second, the forceful oppression by an enemy was a means of divine judgment upon rebellious, idolatrous Israel (Jud

2:11-15). Third, the use of arms was the means by which God gave deliverance to a repentant Israel through the Spirit-anointed judge or "saviour" (Jud 2:16-18; Othniel, 3:7-11; Ehud, 3:15-30; etc.). Fourth, war or internal strife was the means whereby an undesirable leader was removed and wrongs which he had perpetrated were righted, as in the case of Abimelech (Jud 9). Fifth, the fighting between the combined forces of the other tribes and of the tribe of Benjamin was an instance of war being used as a means of dealing drastically and radically with an intolerable social condition (Jud 19-20). Sixth, Israel's battles with the Philistines during the time of Eli and Samuel resulted in defeat when Israel had been self-reliant and unfaithful (I Sam 4), or in victory when Israel was trustful and obedient (I Sam 7:5-14).

The time of the kings. The ideas expressed for understanding and explaining war during the time of the kings are basically the same as those used with respect to Israel's earlier fighting with other peoples. There is perhaps more pointed explanation in terms of Israel's covenant responsibilities and her destiny as a nation among nations than in the explanation for earlier periods of her history. This is understandable, for this period was crucial for Israel as a special people, and wars were the determining factor in the realization of her destiny or in the failure of achieving it.

First, victories on the battlefields were understood as an aspect of God's favor and blessing upon His covenant people; e.g., David's victory over Goliath (I Sam 17); David's great conquests and expansion of the kingdom (II Sam 8); victories over the Syrians during the time of Elijah (I Kgs 20) and of Elisha (II Kgs 6:8–7:20).

Second, defeats suffered in various battles and the downfall of the northern kingdom and of the southern kingdom were understood as aspects of divine wrath, retributive divine judgment upon a faithless and apostate person or people. Examples of this are: for a person, the moves of Hadad the Edomite and Rezon the Syrian against Solomon (I Kgs 11:14-25); the downfall of Samaria under Assyrian blows (II Kgs 17:1-23); and the downfall of Jerusalem (II Kgs 24:1–25:21; see also II Kgs 23:26-27).

Holy War

[Every aspect of life under the theocratic government of ancient Israel was definitely linked with God. Therefore even her wars were waged under His direction (II Chr 6:34-35). Yahweh Himself was considered to be a warrior (Ex 15:3; Isa 42:13; Zeph 3:17, RSV), mighty in battle (Ps 24:8), who shatters and scatters His enemies (Ex 15:6; Num 10:35; Ps 68:1). He appeared to Joshua as the "Captain of the Lord's host" (Josh 5:13-15). God marched forth at the head of the army of His people (II Chr 13:12; cf. I Sam 17:45-47), and will come with His heavenly army to execute judgment (Joel 3:11*b*; Isa 13:3, 5). Such war follows as the result of God's wrath against His enemies (Num 31:3; Ps 110:5; Isa 13:9), against those whose immorality and idolatry might corrupt the life of His chosen people.

[When Israel was loyal to her covenant relationship with Yahweh her enemies were God's enemies. Thus her wars were holy wars. Israel understood warfare as "a divine-human, cosmic-earthly endeavor" (P. D. Miller, VT, XVIII [1968], 103) in which the cosmic forces (Jud 5:20), the chariots of heaven (II Kgs 6:17), and the Lord Himself fought in her behalf (II Chr 20:17). Therefore the call to "prepare war" (Jer 6:4; Joel 3:9) literally meant "sanctify" (Heb. *qaddᵉshû*) war, declare holy war (Mic 3:5, NASB). The military camp was kept ceremonially pure (Deut 23:9-14). The soldiers consecrated themselves to the Lord (Isa 13:3) in this service, abstained from sexual intercourse, and were looked upon as holy "vessels" during the campaign (I Sam 21:4-5). For this reason Uriah the Hittite refused to visit his wife while on leave from the siege of Rabbah (II Sam 11:11). Holy war was conducted with the full encouragement of the priest (Deut 20:2), who at times used the Urim and Thummim in the ephod to ascertain the guidance of the Lord for the ensuing battle (I Sam 28:6; 30:7; cf. II Sam 5:19, 23). Even the battle cries had religious significance; e.g., "A sword for the Lord and for Gideon" (Jud 7:20, RSV).

Methods of Warfare

[After the close of the rainy season in springtime was the best season for beginning a war (II Sam 11:1). War was not declared. A military commander would march into enemy territory, encamp with his army near a city, and demand its surrender, often laying down harsh conditions (I Sam 11:1-2). Because of the strength of city fortifications many ancient wars centered around siege tactics. Israel was given specific instructions for this type of warfare (Deut 20:10-20), but during Joshua's campaigns other tactics proved more successful.

[To guard against chariots and arrows from the invaders' bows during the Middle Bronze Age II (1900-1550 B.C.), cities increased their defenses with sloping embankments (the glacis), stronger gateways, and thicker walls. The attackers would blockade the city and seek to enter it by scaling its walls with ladders, employing battering rams (Ezk 21:22), tunneling to undermine the walls (II Sam 20:15), or making a surprise entry through an existing water shaft (e.g., Joab's means of entering Jebus, II Sam 5:8; I Chr 11:5-6). Often a mound or ramp was piled up outside the wall (Ezk 4:2) to enable the enemy to jump across to engage the defenders in hand-to-hand combat (see ANEP # 159-181; many pertinent illustrations in VBW, 5 vols.).

[Spies were sent out to learn the nature of a nation's military preparedness (Num 13) and of the fortifications of specific cities such as Jericho (Josh 2) and Ai (Josh 7:2). In battle slingers (Jud 20:16; II Kgs 3:25) and archers were used, but Joshua's troops relied principally on the curved sword for slashing or the short two-edged sword for thrusting to pierce the enemy soldier at close quarters. Daring forays (I Sam 14:1-4) and raids by desert bands were frequent tactics (I Sam 30:1-2). Troops were mustered and led in battle by means of trumpet signals (Num 10:9; Josh 6:4-20; Jud 6:34; 7:18; II Sam 2:28). Smoke or fire signals were employed to send messages beyond earshot (Jud 20:38; Jer 6:1).

[Joshua's great victories were gained by a combination of the demoralization of the Canaanites (Josh 2:9-11) and surprise attacks or ambushes. Coming from the desert the Israelites had neither horses and chariots nor heavy siege equipment. It was God who intervened to topple the walls of Jericho. Ruse and ambush worked at Ai (Josh 8). An all-night forced march enabled Joshua to attack the besiegers of Gibeon at dawn and start the rout (Josh 10:9). The Israelites surprised the chariots of Jabin in the mountainous region of Galilee before they could deploy on the broad plain of Jezreel. Such lightning-like tactics permitted Joshua to engage the armies of Canaan in the field before they could reach their fortified cities. When the army of Israel did surround these cities the defenders surrendered through fear, making long sieges unnecessary (*see* Joshua). – J. R.]

Warfare in Eschatology and in Figure

Actual historic wars are not treated by the biblical writers in post-Exilic and subsequent biblical times as they were in the earlier books. There are two main ways in which the later writers considered warfare.

First, apocalyptically and eschatologically. The Gog and Magog prophecy of Ezekiel (chaps. 38-39), and the visions of Daniel, as well as portions of earlier prophetic writings, provide the basis for developing apocalyptic literature of canonical and non-canonical sorts for speaking about conflict between the forces of Satan and evil and those of God and righteousness. In the book of Revelation (especially chaps. 12, 16, 19), victory in war is seen as the means by which God will put an end to the rule of evil and achieve peace in the world, thus establishing His kingdom on earth.

Second, figuratively. War is applied figuratively to the spiritual life, particularly by the apostle Paul. The follower of Christ like a good soldier endures hardship and disentangles himself from the affairs of this life (II Tim 2:3-4). The godly person dons the "whole armor of God" that he may be strong and withstand the spiritual forces that oppose and would otherwise defeat him (Eph 6:10-20). The Christian does not wage a flesh-and-blood war; therefore the weapons of his warfare are not material or human, but are divinely powerful to demolish strongholds of speculation and sophistry and every proud thing raised up against the knowledge of God (II Cor 10:4-5). The church of Jesus Christ is to storm the very gates of hell which will not be able to stand against it (Mt 16:18). *See* Demonology; Devil; Satan.

Summary. War was a part of Israel's history and was given a religious interpretation. There is no basis, however, for understanding and explaining the wars of any particular modern nation in the same way as the wars of ancient Israel. Further, there is no specific statement in the Bible concerning modern pacifism. Many Christians have inferred non-resistance from such commandments as "Thou shalt not kill" (Rom 13:9) and "Put up thy sword. . ." (Mt 26:52), and James' condemnation of fighting in Jas 4:1-4. On the other hand, our duty as citizens to obey the call to arms by our government seems to be taught in Rom 13:1-7 and I Pet 2:13-17.

See Armor, Arms; Enemy; Fortifications; Mighty Men.

Bibliography. Otto Bauernfeind, "*Polemos,* etc.," TDNT, VI, 502-515; "*Strateuomai,* etc.," VII, 701-713. Richard Gale, *Great Battles of Biblical History,* London: Hutchinson, 1968. Norman K. Gottwald, " 'Holy War' in Deuteronomy: Analysis and Critique," *Review and Expositor,* LXI (1964), 296-310. Abraham Malamat, "The *Ḥerem* in Mari and in the Bible," *Yehezkel Kaufmann Jubilee Volume,* ed. by M. Haran, Jerusalem: Magnes Press, 1960. Patrick D. Miller, Jr., "God the Warrior," *Interpretation,* XIX (1965), 39-46; "The Divine Council and the Prophetic Call to War," VT, XVIII (1968), 100-107. Gerhard von Rad, *Studies in Deuteronomy,* trans. by David Stalker, London: SCM, 1953, pp. 45–59; *Der Heilige Krieg im Alten Israel,* 3rd ed., Zurich: Zwingli-Verlag, 1958. Rudolf Smend, *Yahweh, War, and Tribal Confederation,* trans. by Max G. Rogers, Nashville: Abingdon, 1970. Ethelbert Stauffer, "*Agōn,* etc.," TDNT, I, 134-140. L. E. Toombs, "War, Ideas of," and J. W. Wevers, "War, Methods of," IDB, IV, 796-805. Roland de Vaux, *Ancient Israel: Its Life and Institutions,* trans. by John McHugh, New York: McGraw-Hill, 1961, pp. 213-267. Yigael Yadin, *The Art of Warfare in Biblical Lands,* 2 vols., New York: McGraw-Hill, 1963.

H. E. Fi.

WARDROBE. *See* Vestry.

WARS OF THE LORD, BOOK OF. A lost book, evidently a collection of songs on the order of the Book of Jashar (*q.v.*). The only OT reference to it is Num 21:14. The quotation in vv. 14-15 comes from it, as quite possibly do the songs in vv. 17-18 and vv. 27-30. Many scholars regard the book as a later (*c.* 800 B.C.) composition and the excerpts as editorial glosses. E. J. Young (*An Introduction to the*

OT, 1960 ed., p. 98) defends the possibility of its composition in the Mosaic era.

WASHING. *See* Ablution.

WASHPOT. This term occurs only in the KJV and ASV of Ps 60:8 and its parallel Ps 108:9. The Heb. *sîr raḥaṣ* denotes a vessel for washing, usually made of pottery, a "washbasin" (RSV) or "washbowl" (NASB). During the monarchy period the Israelites had oval ceramic footbaths, about two feet long with a raised footrest in the middle and drain-hole at the bottom of one side, according to specimens found at Samaria and Tell en-Nasbeh. God metaphorically declares Moab to be His washbasin, perhaps with an allusion to the "basin" of the Dead Sea, and certainly indicating that after being conquered by David, Moab would perform menial service for His people the Israelites.

WASP or HORNET. *See* Animals, III. 55.

WASTE AND VOID. *See* Chaos.

WATCH. Several words in Heb. and Gr. are rendered watch in English versions as nouns and verbs.

1. *Watch or guard,* "watches of the night" (Heb. *ashmûrâ* or *ashmūrâ*, Ex 14:24; Jud 7:19; I Sam 11:11; Ps 63:6; 90:4; 119:148; Lam 2:19; Gr. *phylakē*, Mk 14:25; 24:43; Mk 6:48; Lk 2:8; 12:38). From very early times the day was counted from sunrise to sunset and various devices were used to designate the time of day; for example, the sundial of Hezekiah's time (II Kgs 20:11; Isa 38:8). For telling time at night the Jews, like the Greeks, divided it into three watches. The first was the "beginning of the watches" (Lam 2:19) from sunset to 10:00 P.M.; the second, the middle watch (Jud 7:19) from 10:00 P.M. to 2:00 A.M.; the third was the morning watch (Ex 14:24; I Sam 11:11) from 2:00 A.M. to sunrise—times approximate, of course. The Romans increased the number of watches to four, referring to them by their numerical order as "fourth watch" (Mt 14:25), or by the terms "even, midnight, cockcrowing, and morning" (Mk 13:35). Presumably each of these ended respectively at 9:00 P.M., midnight, 3:00 A.M., and 6:00 A.M. *See* Time, Divisions of.

2. *Setting or posting a watch.* (*a*) Heb. *mishmār*: Nehemiah set a watch against Sanballat and others (Neh 4:9; 7:3; see also Job 7:12; Jer 51:12). (*b*) Heb. *mishmeret:* Particular persons were assigned the watch or guarding of the young king Joash (II Kgs 11:5 ff.; see also II Chr 23:4–6; Neh 7:3; 12:24 f.). Habakkuk stationed himself on watch (Hab 2:1) to wait and hear from the Lord. (*c*) Heb. *shōmrāh*: The psalmist prayed for a watch to be set before his mouth (Ps 141:3). (*d*) Heb. *coustōdia*, a guard of soldiers: A guard or watch assigned by Pilate accompanied those who sealed Jesus' tomb (Mt 27:65–66; see also 28:11).

3. *A watch tower,* a place of lookout. Heb. *miṣpeh*, "a watch tower." The stone structure, frequently erected in vineyards or along borders, provided the basis for Isaiah to speak of standing continually upon the watch tower (Isa 21:8; see also II Chr 20:24). *See* Tower.

4. *To watch, observe, take heed.* Five words are so translated in the OT of which *shāmar* perhaps is the most common. Five are thus translated in the NT, with *grēgoreō* the most frequently used of these five. This verb means to keep awake, be alert, give strict attention lest through negligence and indolence some destructive calamity overtakes one (Mt 24:42; 25:13; Rev 16:15), or lest one deny or forsake Christ (Mt 26:41), or fall into sin (I Thess 5:6; I Cor 16:13; I Pet 5:8; Rev 3:2 f.).

Bibliography. Harald Reisenfeld, "*Tēreō,* etc.," TDNT, VIII, 140–151.

H. E. Fi.

WATCHER. A watcher is mentioned in Dan 4:13, 17, 23 as a holy angel sent from heaven. The watchers (v. 17) have authority to decree the fate and chastisement of a ruler such as Nebuchadnezzar in order that men may know that God rules. The concept of watchers was developed and elaborated upon in the apocryphal books. In the Book of Jubilees they are regarded as angels sent to instruct the righteous; in Enoch, both as archangels and fallen angels. Mount Hermon is designated as the place of their descent in Enoch 6:6. They can be compared with the guardian angels Jesus speaks of as representing little children before God (Mt 18:10). *See* Angels.

WATCHMAN. *See* Watcher; Occupations: Porter, Sentry; Watch.

WATCHTOWER. *See* Tower.

WATER. To the ancient Israelite, coming from rainless Egypt and traveling through the desert, water assumed great importance because it was so scarce. Water was essential for the daily needs as well as the agricultural pursuits of the people (Ex 15:22; Deut 8:7, 15; 11:10–11). Location of early settlements was determined on the basis of a water supply.

In Palestine the inhabitants and their animals were dependent upon the rain and dew and the flowing springs in the hill country, rather than on irrigation from great rivers as in Egypt and Mesopotamia (Deut 8:9; 11:10–11). Brooks and small streams usually dried up completely in the dry season after the rains had ceased and the melting snow from the mountains had disappeared (Ps 126:4; Jer 15:18; Joel 1:20). In the Negeb deep wells and underground springs were fought over by nearby tribes because they could not exist without them (Gen 21:25; 26:18–22). Frequent droughts wrought further tragedy to the crops and cattle (I Kgs 18:1, 2, 5). As the years passed trees on the hillsides were cut down for houses, firewood, and arti-

Steps leading into the pool at Gibeon. HFV

cles for home and field. Soil erosion and loss of moisture resulted, so that the desert crept slowly over the outskirts of land once arable. Migrations in search of better water supply followed, making the best areas of the Fertile Crescent overpopulated.

Archaeologists have discovered that a good spring was the determining factor where a settlement was to be founded. City reservoirs or pools as well as private cisterns (II Kgs 18:31) were dug to conserve water both for normal use and in case of siege. The OT mentions the pool of Hebron beside which the bodies of the assassins of Ish-bosheth were hung for public display (II Sam 4:12); the large pool in Samaria where Ahab's blood was washed off his chariot (I Kgs 22:38); and a number of pools in Jerusalem (II Kgs 18:17; Isa 7:3; 22:11; Neh 2:14; 3:16; etc.).

The most interesting of all the reservoirs discovered thus far is the one at Gibeon (II Sam 2:13; Jer 41:12). This great pool measures 37 feet in diameter and 33 feet in depth, quarried from the bedrock of the hill. A spiral staircase had been left in the rock to descend along the vertical sides of the pool. The original construction of the pool may be dated somewhere within the 12th–11th cen. B.C. (BA, XXIII [1960], 24). Later builders dug a curving stepped tunnel following the course of the circular stairway, in order to reach a water chamber 45 feet below the floor of the cylindrical pool.

Ways and means of protecting the city water supply from enemy assault were devised both by the Canaanites and by the Israelites. Foot tunnels leading to underground springs or pools have been explored at a number of Palestinian cities. A combination of stepped tunnel and vertical shaft (called Warren's shaft after its discoverer) enabled the Jebusites to reach the water of the Gihon spring from inside the walls of Jerusalem. Later, Hezekiah dug a long tunnel to bring this water to the pool of Siloam (II Kgs 20:20), replacing an earlier conduit or surface canal along the slope of the SE hill of Jerusalem (Isa 7:3). Macalister cleared a tunnel 132 feet long at Gezer which had been cut in the Late Bronze Age to reach water some 130 feet below the present surface of the tell. Gibeon also had a stepped water tunnel with 93 steps and niches to hold oil lamps, entirely separate from the above mentioned pool system. Ibleam, Megiddo, and Zarethan, too, could boast of hidden means of access to their water supplies.

The largest water system discovered (1968–69) to date is that of the citadel mound of Hazor, constructed in the 9th cen. B.C. and in use until the city was destroyed in 732 B.C. It descends *c.* 140 feet to the level of the local water table in three stages: an entrance structure of masonry walls and a doorway, a vertical shaft with five flights of stairs, and a tunnel continuing with a staircase to a large underground room in which the water collected.

Another means of obtaining water from a well or underground water supply has been noted on a 9th cen. B.C. Assyrian bas-relief showing the siege of a Syro-Palestinian city. It is a rope and pulley system to hoist a large bucket to the top of the city wall (BASOR # 206 [1972], 42–48).

Water is mentioned in the Bible more often than any other material resource. It was recognized as essential to man (Gen 21:14–15). The value of water was emphasized by David when his friends brought him some from Bethlehem in spite of their great danger when he hid in the cave of Adullam (I Chr 11:17). Jeremiah in his Jerusalem dungeon (Jer 38:6) and Jesus on the cross (Jn 19:28) indicate man's need for water. Water is sometimes used to express the friendliness of the universe and God's blessing to man (Ps 33:7). The psalmist hints that even the waters praise God (148:4).

Water was part of the original created earth in its formless void (Gen 1:2). Hence it was a symbol of instability (Gen 49:4; Isa 57:20; Jas 1:6).

Water provided many other metaphors for expressing ideas. God exhorted His people to "let justice roll down like waters and righteousness like an ever-flowing stream" (Amos 5:24, NASB), rather than like the small brooks and wadis that dry up rapidly after a rain. Water was a symbol of God's salvation, as in the prophecy that His worshipers would "draw water out of the wells of salvation" (Isa 12:3; cf. Jer 2:13; 17:13). The Jews used it for ceremonial washings, and Christians considered it essential for baptism to indicate the washing away of sin. It was metaphorically used by Jesus when talking to Nicodemus about the new birth (Jn 3:5). To the woman at Sychar Christ spoke of "living water" (Jn 4:10) as His teaching, which springs up within the redeemed unto eternal life (4:14; cf. Prov 13:14; 18:4). Water is also a biblical symbol of the Holy Spirit (Jn 7:37–39), whose coming in the Messianic Age is likened to the pouring out of the liquid (Isa 32:15; 44:3; Joel 2:28).

See Agriculture; Cistern; Conduit; Flood; Pool; Rain; Rivers; Spring; Well.

Bibliography. CornPBE, "Water Supply," pp. 700–704. R. J. Forbes, "Irrigation and Drainage," *Studies in Ancient Technology,* II, Leiden: Brill, 1955, pp. 1–77. L. Goppelt, "*Hy-*

dōr," TDNT, VIII, 314–333. William G. Dever, "The Water Systems at Hazor and Gezer," BA, XXXII (1969), 71–78. James B. Pritchard, *The Water System of Gibeon,* Philadelphia: University Museum, 1961. R. S. Lamon, *The Megiddo Water System,* Chicago: Oriental Institute Publications, 1935. Yigael Yadin, "The Fifth Season of Excavations at Hazor, 1968–1969," BA, XXXII (1969), 63–70.

A. W. W. and J. R.

WATER GATE. *See* Jerusalem: Gates and Towers 12.

WATER OF JEALOUSY OR BITTERNESS. *See* Jealousy Offering.

WATER OF SEPARATION. "Water of separation" (KJV) or "water of impurity" (RSV), i.e., water designed to remove ceremonial impurity, was a Levitical purification agent. Instructions concerning it are found in Num 19 in connection with the red heifer sacrifice (cf. Heb 9:13).

When an Israelite became ceremonially unclean through contact with death (cf. Num 19:11–16 for details), God required that he be purified from his "sin" (vv. 9, 17) by the sprinkling of this specially prepared water upon him.

An unblemished, unbroken red heifer, together with cedar wood, hyssop, and scarlet wool, was *wholly* burned outside the camp of Israel. Its ashes were then gathered and stored in a clean place. As the need arose, a pinch of these ashes was mixed in a vessel with running water, then sprinkled with hyssop upon the unclean person on the third and seventh days of his uncleanness.

As sin in Num 19 is symbolized by death, so this divine remedy for sin's contagion employs details which speak of life and vitality—death's opposites: (1) a heifer, the sex that brings forth life; (2) her red hue and the scarlet wool, colors reflecting life energies having their seat in the blood; (3) her unblemished, unbroken condition speaking of unsapped vital energies; (4) her being burned *with* her blood; (5) the cedar wood, noted for its durability; (6) the hyssop, associated with purification (cf. Ps 51:7); and (7) the water itself being *running* water, literally "water (which is) life."

The symbolism here is rich. The believer's defilement before God arises from contact with sin, here imaged in the corruption of death. Purification from sin's contagion has been divinely provided for the believer in the continuing merits of Christ's blood (I Jn 1:7), symbolized by the "water (designed for) impurity."

R. L. R.

WATERPOT. A jar or earthen vessel used for storing or carrying water. The jars usually had one or two handles and were carried by women on the head or shoulders (Jn 4:28). Large waterpots with a capacity of 10 to 30 gallons were used for the purpose of ceremonial purification (Jn 2:6).

WATERSPOUT. Heb. *ṣinnōr* in Ps 42:7 refers to descent of water over a steep surface, a "waterfall" (NASB) or "cataract" (RSV, NEB). The Heb. word also occurs in II Sam 5:8 as the "gutter" (KJV), "water shaft" (RSV), or "water tunnel" (NASB) leading to the spring Gihon in Jerusalem. In Ps 148:7 the NEB strangely translates Heb. *tannîn*, "dragon, sea monster," as "water-spouts."

WAVE OFFERING. *See* Sacrificial Offerings.

WAY, THE. The words "way" and "path" translate a large number of Heb. and Gr. words. Not the variety of terms but the consistency of their usage throughout the Bible is significant.

The primary or literal meaning is frequent: road, customary path, or course of travel (Gen 3:24; Ex 23:20; I Sam 6:9; II Kgs 3:8; Jer 2:17; Mt 2:12; Acts 25:3; etc.).

The figurative use refers to man's course of conduct or character (Job 17:9; 22:15), divided into the good way (Ex 18:20; 32:8; Deut 31:29; Isa 30:21; Mt 21:32; I Cor 4:17) and the evil way (Num 22:32; Ps 139:24; Isa 65:2; Jer 18:11; Acts 14:16).

Contrasted in both Testaments, the two ways are prominent in Ps 1:1–6 (cf. Prov 4:18–19; 12:28). Jesus also contrasted the two ways (Mt 7:13–14). The way of the good man is the way of life (Prov 15:24; Acts 2:28), faithfulness (Ps 119:30, RSV), peace (Isa 59:8; Rom 3:17), justice (Prov 17:23; Dan 4:37), righteousness (Mt 21:32; II Pet 2:21), and salvation (Acts 16:17). The "way of truth" denotes Christian conduct in II Pet 2:2, but "walk" is the more usual term for it (cf. Eph 4:1, 17; 5:2, 8, 15). *See* Conversation; Walk.

"Way" does, however, refer to the Christian faith six times, each time in a context of non-Christian hostility to the gospel. These six are Acts 9:2; 22:4 (Paul's persecution of Christians); Acts 19:9, 23 (Ephesian opposition to Paul's ministry); Acts 24:14, 22 (Paul's defense before Felix).

God's ways may mean either His own method of procedure and action (Rev 15:3) or the ways which He would have men take. In the former case, the emphasis may be on His actual procedures, whether present (Deut 32:4; Acts 13:10) or future (Isa 40:3; Mt 3:3), or on the manner of His activities (Isa 55:8), or on the purpose of His designs (Isa 58:2; Rom 11:33). In the case of how God commands man to walk (cf. Job 21:14; Jer 7:23; Ps 18:30; 25:4; Prov 8:32), God's ways are good (I Kgs 8:36), right (I Sam 12:23), and perfect (Ps 101:6). Jesus (Mt 22:16) and the law (Deut 8:6) both teach the way of the Lord.

Not only did Jesus teach "the way of God in truth" (Mt 22:16), but He is "the way, the truth, and the life" (Jn 14:6). He is the only way to the Father (cf. Acts 4:12). More precisely, His substitutionary death and present intercession are viewed as the "new and living way" into the very presence of the Father (Heb 10:20; cf. 9:8).

Bibliography. Wilhelm Michaelis, "*Hodos*, etc.," TDNT, V, 42–96.

F. D. L.

WAYFARER, WAYFARING MAN. The KJV renders three Heb. phrases by the term "wayfaring man": (1) *'ōrē(a)ḥ* (lit., "wanderer"), Jud 19:17; II Sam 12:4; Jer 9:2; 14:8; (2) *'ōbēr 'ōraḥ* (lit., "one passing along a path"), Isa 33:8; (3) *hôlēk derek* (lit., "one going on a way"), Isa 35:8. In every case the intended meaning is simply "traveler."

WAYMARKS. A guiding mark or sign set along a path or road. Heaps of stones were often used as guide posts. Jeremiah encouraged the exiles to mark their route into exile so that they could return to Israel by the same road (Jer 31:21). In Ezk 39:15 a "sign" ("marker," NASB) was used to mark unburied bones.

WEAKER BROTHER. In terms of Paul's descriptions a weaker brother is one who is "weak in the faith" (Rom 14:1). He is a believer who is immature in Christian understanding so that his conscience condemns him with regard to matters that are really morally neutral (cf. Rom 14:1–15:1; I Cor 8:7–13). Morally neutral matters that might be important to a weaker brother included abstinence from food other than vegetables (Rom 14:2), special observance of certain days (Rom 14:5), and abstinence from meat that had been sacrificed to idols (I Cor 8:4, 10). But the list is not confined to these matters alone (cf. Rom 14:21) and doubtless would include additional items today.

To both the strong and the weak Paul gives important guidelines. The weak simply are told not to judge the strong (Rom 14:3). The strong, though, have a greater responsibility. They are to accept the weak without passing censorious judgment on their opinions; nor are they to be contemptuous of the weak (Rom 14:1, 3). The strong are to bear others' weaknesses rather than just pleasing themselves (Rom 15:1). In practice this means that the strong will walk in love, being careful not to put stumbling blocks in the way of the weak. The strong should even relinquish the privileges of their liberty if necessary for the well-being of those who are genuinely weak (Rom 14:13–21; I Cor 8:9, 13), remembering that they must "do all to the glory of God" (I Cor 10:31). However, this does not mean that the strong must submit to the arbitrary standards that merely any self-appointed judge would impose. *See* Example.

S. N. G.

WEALTH. Possession of something in quantity represents wealth or riches. To have an abundance of something means one is wealthy or rich. In Scripture the idea of wealth or riches is used in various ways—of things material and things spiritual.

Though custody of portions of material wealth is given to man, it is God who, by virtue of His sovereign creatorship, owns "the cattle upon a thousand hills" (Ps 50:10). God the Father also possesses all spiritual wealth and thus bestows it upon His own. He is "rich in mercy" (Eph 2:4). The confession of David's heart was that "riches and honor" come from God (I Chr 29:12*a*). According to His "riches in glory by Christ Jesus" He has promised to supply all the needs of His own (Phil 4:19).

Scripture has a great deal to say about the possession and use of economic or material wealth and also about spiritual wealth. Possession of great material wealth is not condemned in the Bible. Some of the great stalwarts of the faith were men of means. Abraham, Isaac, Barnabas, Joseph of Arimathea, and Philemon, for example, were all well-to-do people. According to Scripture, God's prime concern is not how much a man has, but how he uses the wealth he possesses. Earthly possessions relate generally to four classes of people. First, those who are rich in the things of this earth and poor in spiritual assets. Second, those poor in this world's goods but rich toward God (Jas 2:5). Third, the host of people who are poor in both heavenly and earthly things. Fourth, those who have a great deal of this world's goods but who are also rich in heavenly blessings.

Times of affluency and great material prosperity create difficulties for Christians to appreciate and enjoy their spiritual wealth in Christ. Biblical warnings abound to guard against trusting in one's wealth (Ps 49:6–7; 52:7; Prov 18:11) and setting the heart on riches (Ps 62:10). The wealthy man is not to glory in his riches (Jer 9:23). Jesus castigated avarice as illustrated by one who selfishly wished to build bigger barns to hoard his crops (Lk 12:13–21). Wealth is often a barrier to entering the kingdom of God (Mt 19:16–24). Many who covet wealth "have erred from the faith" (I Tim 6:10), and the rich tend to become highminded (6:17). The "deceitfulness of riches" stifles the Word and makes it unfruitful in the heart (Mt 13:22). Scripture carefully outlines the dangers associated with earthly riches, and it also presents the proper use of wealth.

James issued strong words of warning to the unsaved wealthy of his day (Jas 5:1). They were probably no more wealthy than the majority of believers in the United States today. These whom James addresses were not judged for being rich but because they had misused their wealth. Christians can also misuse the wealth they have, be it small or large. They can also, like many no doubt in James' day, envy the wealthy. This is just as much a sin as misusing wealth. It is also very important that the means used to acquire wealth be proper. Evidently, those to whom James speaks in 5:1 had exploited the worker to gain their wealth.

Many Christians live below their means when it comes to spiritual wealth. They fail to appropriate and appreciate "the unsearchable riches of Christ" (Eph 3:8). Not only does the believing sinner enjoy redemption according to the riches of God's grace (Eph 1:7), but also the exceeding riches of His grace are showered upon him continually (Eph 2:7-8). Not "out of" the riches of God's grace but "according to," "commensurate with," His riches He gives freely to His own people spiritual blessings to enjoy. Economic wealth is temporary. Spiritual wealth not only pays dividends now but will endure forever. The Saviour was rich. For our sakes He became poor so that we might be spiritually rich (II Cor 8:9).

See Riches.

Bibliography. F. Hauck and W. Kasch, *"Ploutos,"* TDNT, VI, 318-332.

R. P. L.

WEAN, WEANING. *See* Children.

WEAPON. *See* Armor; War.

WEASEL. *See* Animals, IV.36.

WEAVER, WEAVING. *See* Occupations: Weaver.

WEB. *See* Animals: Spider, IV.31; Weaver.

WEDDING. *See* Marriage.

WEDGE. A bar (Heb. *lashôn*, "tongue") of gold probably used as one form of money. A wedge 50 shekels in weight was taken from Jericho by Achan (Josh 7:21, 24). A similar ingot of gold *c*. ten inches long, one inch wide, and one-half inch thick, was found at Gezer by R. A. S. Macalister. A similar wedge is indicated in Amarna letters No. 27, line 61 and No 29, line 39 from the Mitannian king Tushratta to Pharaoh Amenhotep IV. A thin strip of gold with embossed ornamentation, used as a headband, was discovered at Tell el-Ajjul in a Middle Bronze Age tomb (VBW, II, 32).

WEEDS. *See* Plants.

WEEK. A time unit of seven successive days. In the Bible the days of the week were designated by number, "first day," "second day." The seventh day became known as the sabbath (Ex 20:10; 31:15). In Daniel the Heb. word *shābûa'* for "week" refers to a period of seven years (Dan 9:24-27) as well as to one of seven days (Dan 10:2-3, lit., "three weeks, days"). *See* Time, Divisions of; Seventy Weeks.

WEEKS, FEAST OF. *See* Festivals.

WEEPING. *See* Mourning.

WEIGHTS, MEASURES, AND COINS. In biblical times statements of weight or measure were necessarily approximate. Handfuls, the flight of an arrow, a day's journey, and parts of the body such as the finger, the palm, and the span constituted units of measurement. Weights were judged by hand or with portable or standing balances. The potential for fraud was great, and false balances were an object of frequent prophetic denunciation (e.g., Prov 11:1; 20:23; Hos 12:7; Amos 8:5; Mic 6:11). The Mosaic command, "Just balances, just weights, a just ephah, and a just hin, shall ye have" (Lev 19:36), echoed down through the OT (e.g., Deut 25:15; Prov 16:11; Ezk 45:10).

Some units of measurement were common to the whole of the ancient Near East. The cubit, e.g., was used in Egypt, Canaan, and Mesopotamia, although its length varied in each region. In Egypt the common or short cubit equaled 17.7 inches (six palm widths), and the royal or long cubit ran 20.65 inches (seven palms); in Mesopotamia the royal cubit varied from 19.5 to 19.8 inches. In general, Israelite weights and measures were related more closely to the Babylonian-Assyrian system than to the Egyptian.

However, though their units of weight and measurement were basically the same as those in Mesopotamia, the Israelite system of computation differed. The Israelites seem to have used a mixed system, partly following the decimal (by 10's) system, and partly the Babylonian-Assyrian system which was sexagesimal, with 60 shekels to the mina and 60 minas to the talent (cf. our 60-second minutes and 60-minute hours).

That both Sennacherib and the Israelites computed the tribute in gold exacted from Hezekiah at 30 talents is an evidence they were using the same system of measurement (cf. II Kgs 18:14 with ANET, p. 288).

Weights

In the KJV of the OT "weight" usually translates Heb. *'eben* ("stone") or *mishqāl* ("weight"). The latter is from the verb root *shākal*, "to weigh," while the former arises from the common use of stones as balance-weights on the scales. Bronze weights were also sometimes used as royal standards. A bronze lion-weight from Assyria is inscribed, "Palace of Shalmaneser, king of Ashur, two-thirds mina of the king" (ANEP # 119). A reclining bull in bronze from Ugarit weighs 468.5 grams and is inscribed with the Canaanite symbol for "20," evidently 20-shekel weight. Its unit is double the Palestinian shekel (BA, XXII [1959], 21, fig. 1). Israelite and Canaanite weights were usually in simpler forms (e.g., barrel or dome shaped) as compared with the Mesopotamian and Egyptian examples in the shape of ducks, lions, and other creatures.

Scholars have had great difficulty in classifying ancient Heb. weights. Palestine in OT times had many systems of weights during its long history of domination by various peoples. While the Heb. system was modeled on the Babylonian, it may be assumed that there were independent systems which probably varied

Ancient Hebrew weights found in Palestine. Courtesy St. Peter's in Gallicantu, Jerusalem.

slightly from region to region and according to the goods for sale. Even today the druggist, the grocer, and the jeweler use different standards. Furthermore, no two early Heb. stone weights bearing the same inscription have exactly the same weight (DOTT, pp. 227 f.).

In the OT

1. The "talent" (Heb. *kikkār,* meaning "round") was usually a round weight of gold or silver (cf. II Sam 12:30; I Kgs 9:14), but also of iron (I Chr 29:7) and bronze (Ex 38:29). The heavy Babylonian talent weighed 132 pounds; the light talent, 66 pounds. In Israel the talent weighed *c.* 75 pounds.

2. The "mina" (KJV "maneh" and "pound"; Heb. *māneh*) equaled either 50 or 60 shekels (Ezk 45:12, cf. KJV with RSV which follows the LXX). Thus the lighter mina of the common or Phoenician system weighed *c.* one and one-fourth pounds. It was used to weigh gold (I Kgs 10:17) and silver (Ezr 2:69; Neh 7:71). Sixty minas equaled a talent. Inscribed mina weights from Assyria and Babylonia indicate a mina of 60 shekels of *c.* 2.2 pounds (ANEP # 118–119). A round limestone weight found in the Jerusalem region bears a Gr. inscription stating that it is three minas and dated to year 32 of King Herod (9 B.C.). Since it weighs 1233 grams (2.72 pounds), it relates roughly to the Attic mina of 437 grams (*c.* 0.95 pounds or 15.4 ounces).

3. The "shekel" (Heb. *sheqel*) was in early times the standard measure of weight. After the invention of coinage, the name was given to a coin. Many inscribed weights from cities in S Palestine seem to indicate a shekel or its multiples. Some of these stone scale weights are inscribed in ancient Heb. *n-ṣ-p,* a term which apparently means "half." Professor R. B. Y. Scott believes that the *n-ṣ-p* was the old "half" or "light" shekel of the Syro-Palestinian kingdoms witnessed to at Ugarit, and that it was the shekel in common use in Israel and Judah prior to the new standardization of the weight system in Josiah's reign. The new standard shekel weights were heavier and bore a "looped-line" symbol (ɤ), which may represent the tied pouch in which bits of silver were kept.

The ratio between the two systems seems to have been 5:6, one-fifth being added to the mass of the depreciated "light" shekel. An eight-shekel weight of the new standard was then equivalent to the Egyptian *deben* unit of *c.* 91 grams, a matter of great convenience for commercial transactions (BASOR # 200 [1970], pp. 62–64). The *n-ṣ-p* weights have an average mass of *c.* 9.8 grams (ranging from *c.* 9.2 to 10.5 grams). The "looped-line" weights show a variation from *c.* 10.8 to 11.7 grams. Accounting for wear, the official shekel in Judah after Josiah's standardization may be set at 11.35 to 11.4 grams (*c.* 0.4 ounces). There seems also to have been a "heavy" shekel of *c.* 13 grams, perhaps used for weighing a specific commodity (BA, XXII [1959], 32–39).

The shekel was used to weigh bronze armor (I Sam 17:5), an iron spearhead (I Sam 17:7), and, implying value, gold and silver (Josh 7:21; Ex 21:32). Its exact weight, and the worth of the metals varied. In general the shekel in gold was worth *c.* $10; in silver, *c.* 67 cents. The "shekel of the sanctuary" (Ex 30:13; Lev 5:15), i.e., "by the sacred standard" (NEB), was equivalent to 20 gerahs. This was smaller by one-sixth than the common Babylonian shekel of 24 girus in use at that time. One-fourth of a shekel of silver is mentioned in I Sam 9:8; one-third of a shekel appears in Neh 10:32, and seemingly in I Sam 13:21 as the amount to be paid for having axes sharpened (cf. RSV and LXX).

4. The "pim" (Heb. *pîm*) appears in I Sam 13:21 (RSV) as the exorbitant Philistine charge in silver for sharpening plowshares and mattocks. It possibly equals two-thirds of a shekel, or 0.268 ounces. A number of small weights inscribed with *p-y-m* have been found in excavations throughout Palestine. The average weight of these is 7.76 grams, *c.* two and two-third ounces.

5. The term "bekah" (Heb. *beqa'*, meaning "half") is used for a half shekel weight in Ex 38:26; cf. Gen 24:22. It weighed 0.2 ounces.

6. The "gerah" (Heb. *gērâ*) was several times stipulated to be one-twentieth of a shekel, or 0.02 ounces (e.g., Ex 30:13; Ezk 45:12).

7. The "piece of money" of Gen 33:19 and Job 42:11 and the "piece of silver" of Josh 24:32 (Heb. *q^eśîṭâ*) may have been a unit of weight of unknown value. The LXX translates *q^eśîṭâ* by *amnos* (male lamb) in Gen 33:19 and by *amnas* (female lamb) in Josh 24:32 and Job 42:11; thus, possibly the weight was in the form of a metal lamb, or possibly the translators expanded the word *mna*, the Gr. form of mina.

In the NT

8. The "talent" (Gr. *talanton*) varied greatly, ranging from 58 to 80 pounds. The name was later applied to a unit of coinage with differing but comparatively high values. The term occurs only in Mt 18:24; 25:15–28 (of money) and in Rev 16:21 (of weight). *See* Talent.

9. The "pound" (Gr. *litra* from Lat. *libra*, hence our abbreviation for pound) was a Roman pound of 12 ounces. It is mentioned twice, in Jn 12:3 and 19:39, of the ointment poured on Jesus' feet and the spices used for His burial. The "pound" (Gr. *mna*) appears only as a monetary unit in Lk 19:13–25 (cf. Coins below).

Dry Measures

The earliest measures of capacity were natural ones. The "handful" was an obvious container to mete out small amounts of grain. Larger measures depended on the size of familiar household containers such as a "skin" of wine (I Sam 25:18; II Sam 16:1; both RSV).

In the OT

1. The "homer" (Heb. *ḥōmer*, from Akkad. *imeru*, "ass") was a fairly large measure and presumably was the normal load of grain for a donkey. In Middle Assyrian and Nuzian texts the *imeru* seems to equal *c.* 3.8 bushels. A homer of barley was worth 50 shekels of silver in Moses' day (Lev 27:16). In Israel the homer was equivalent to a cor and equaled ten baths or ten ephahs (Ezk 45:11–14), estimated variously from four to six and one-half bushels.

2. The "cor" (Heb. *kōr*) of Ezk 45:14 is translated "measure" in I Kgs 4:22; 5:11; II Chr 2:10; 27:5; Ezr 7:22. Also a liquid measure, the cor was equivalent to the homer (Ezk 45:14).

3. "Half homer" is the assumed meaning given by the KJV and other ancient translations to the Heb. word *letek* (Ugaritic *lṯḥ*). The term occurs only in Hos 3:2 as a measure of barley, when the RSV transliterates it as "lethech." If equal to one-half homer, the *letek* would have been two or three bushels.

4. The "ephah" (Heb. *'êpâ*), a measure of grain, equaled one-tenth of a homer. It was equal in volume to the bath, a liquid measure (Ezk 45:11). Its size was approximately half a bushel, anywhere from 13 to 21 quarts. In Zech 5:6–10 the word "ephah" also appears as the name of a receptacle for holding grain.

5. The "seah" (Gen 18:6, RSV marg.; in KJV and elsewhere in RSV translated "measure"; Heb. *s^e'â*) was a measure of flour and grain. It was one-third of an ephah, or from five to seven quarts.

6. The "omer" (Heb. *'ōmer*; LXX *gomor;* not the same as the homer) was used in the gathering of the manna (Ex 16:13–36). It held one-tenth of an ephah and therefore one-hundredth of a homer, or *c.* two dry quarts.

7. The KJV's "tenth deal" (Heb. *'iśśārôn*) translates a term meaning "a tenth part." The term probably referred to a tenth part of an ephah. If so, the measure would be equal to the omer. It was used in preparing the meal offering (cf. Ex 29:40).

8. The "cab" (Heb. *qab*), a measure of uncertain quantity, appears only in II Kgs 6:25. Josephus (*Ant.* iv.4.4) understands one-fourth of a cab to equal the Lat. *sextarius*, or *c.* one pint. Rabbinical sources suggest the cab equaled one-eighteenth of an ephah, or *c.* 2.3 pints.

9. The "handful" was always an inexact approximation. The KJV's word "handful" renders several different expressions meaning, e.g., what will fit into the two hands cupped together (Ex 9:8), one closed hand (Heb. *qōmeṣ*, Lev 2:2; 5:12; 6:15), and the palm (Eccl 4:6).

In the NT

10. The Gr. word rendered "measure" in Lk 16:7 is *koros*. The name is derived from the Heb. *kōr* (see above). It was a large measure running *c.* 11 to 17 bushels.

11. "Measure" in Mt 13:33 and Lk 13:21 renders the Gr. word *saton* (from the Heb. *se'â*, see above). Equal to one and one-half modii (Jos *Ant.* ix. 4.5), the *saton* held about 12 quarts.

12. The "bushel" (Gr. *modios*, from Lat. *modius*), mentioned in Jesus' illustration (Mt 5:15; Mk 4:21; Lk 11:33), was a small grain measure containing 16 sextarii or eight choinikes, roughly eight dry quarts or a peck.

13. The "measure" of Rev 6:6 is the Gr. *choinix*. Often used for grain, it held *c.* a quart (so RSV, NASB). A *choinix* of grain was considered the daily ration per man in Xerxes' army that invaded Greece (Herodotus vii.187).

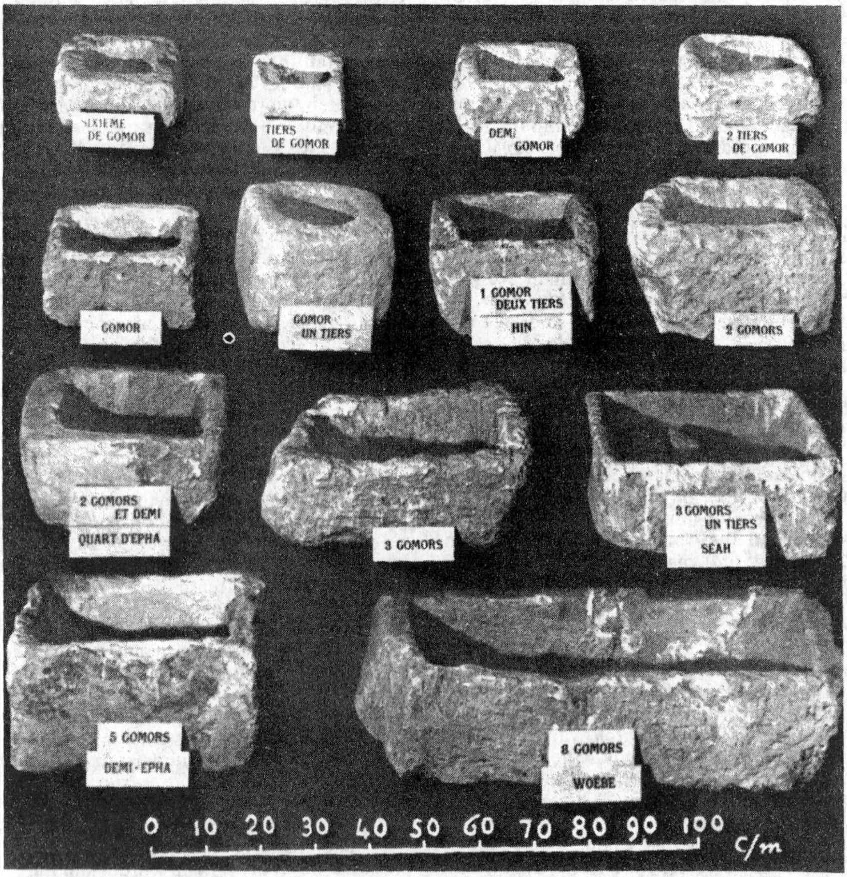

Ancient Hebrew dry measures found in Palestine. Courtesy St. Peter's in Gallicantu, Jerusalem. To interpret the illustration, it is necessary to know that *Gomer* is the Greek for *Omer*. Size is measured in centimeters at the bottom. The French is to be translated as follows: *Sixieme* = sixth; *tiers* =third; *demi* = half; *deux* = two

Liquid Measures

In the OT

1. The "bath" (Heb. *bat*) was equal in volume to the ephah, a dry measure. Since Heb. *bat* also means "daughter," it is conjectured that the term may specify the capacity of the water jars carried from the well by the daughters of the household (BA, XXII [1959], 29; cf. Gen 24:15). Each bath was one-tenth of a homer (Ezk 45:11, 14). Bronze jars marked "bath" found at Tell Beit Mirsim and Lachish are estimated to have held about five and one-half gallons. According to Josephus' information, the term "bath" was apparently applied to a larger standard measure in NT times (see below).

2. An Egyptian example of a "hin" (Egyptian *hn* or *hyn*; Heb. *hîn*) jar held about one pint. According to Josephus (*Ant.* iii.8.3), the Heb. hin was much larger, being one-sixth of a bath, or *c.* a gallon. A sixth of a hin of water was Ezekiel's drinking allotment (4:11), but the measure was usually associated with offerings—in Ex 29:40 and Num 15:6 with the meal offering, in Ex 30:24 with the anointing oil, in Lev 23:13 with the wine drink offering. In Lev 19:36 the word appears as the name of a container with the capacity of a hin.

3. The "log" (Heb. *lōg*; Ugaritic *lg*), the smallest biblical measure of capacity, is mentioned only in specifications of the oil to be used in the rites of purification for lepers (Lev 14:10-24). It held one-twelfth of a hin or *c.* two-thirds of a pint.

In the NT

4. The "firkin" (Gr. *metrētēs*) is mentioned in Jn 2:6. Originally an Attic measure, the *met-*

rētēs held *c.* nine gallons. Thus the six jars of water which Jesus turned into wine would have totaled between 100 and 150 gallons.

5. The "measure" (Gr. *batos,* from Heb. *bat*) of Lk 16:6 had a volume of 72 sextarii, *c.* ten gallons (cf. Jos *Ant.* viii.2.9).

6. The small "pot" (Gr. *xestēs*, possibly a corruption of Lat. *sextarius*) held *c.* one pint. The sextarius was the sixteenth part of a modius. Gr. *xestēs* appears only in Mk 7:4 as the name of a pitcher or jar.

Linear Measures

The cubit was the principal unit of linear measurement in the world of the OT. The length of a man's forearm, it was a natural and always available means of measuring short distances such as the dimensions of a building, the

Ancient Hebrew liquid measures found in Palestine. Courtesy St. Peter's in Gallicantu, Jerusalem

height of a man, the thickness of a wall, or the breadth of cloth.

Longer distances were expressed by such expressions as "a bowshot" (Gen 21:16), "half a furrow's length" (I Sam 14:14, RSV), "a day's journey" (Num 11:31; I Kgs 19:4; Jon 3:4; Lk 2:44), "three days' journey" (Gen 30:36; Ex 3:18; 8:27; Num 10:33; Jon 3:3), "seven days' journey" (Gen 31:23; II Kgs 3:9). A "day's journey" on foot was ordinarily 20 to 25 miles, but it varied according to the terrain, the weather, and the stamina of the persons traveling. A "sabbath day's journey" in NT times was five or six stadia (see 8 below), or between 3,000 and 3,600 feet. The Mount of Olives was a sabbath day's journey from Jerusalem (Acts 1:12). *See* Sabbath Day's Journey. The word rendered "pace" (Heb. *ṣa'ad*, either *c.* 30 or *c.* 60 inches) in II Sam 6:13 more often merely indicates a "step" (cf. II Sam 22:37).

In the OT

1. The "reed" (Heb. *qānĕh*) was primarily an instrument for measuring distances, like our yardstick (Rev 11:1). Such a reed would be found along most river banks in Palestine, where it grows four to ten feet high (Job 40:21; Ps 68:30, ASV, etc.; Isa 35:7). As a unit of measurement it was cut to equal six cubits. Based on the common cubit of 17.5 inches, it would equal eight feet nine inches. The measuring reed or rod (NASB) used in measuring Ezekiel's temple was six long cubits of seven handbreadths each, or 10 feet 2.5 inches (Ezk 40:5). A golden reed or rod is used to measure the holy city of Jerusalem which will descend out of heaven (Rev 21:15).

2. The "cubit" (Heb. *'ammâ*) appears frequently but with differing lengths. The ordinary cubit (e.g., Deut 3:11; Ex 25–27; 36–38) of six handbreadths was probably *c.* 17.5 inches, the length of a man's forearm from elbow to the tip of his middle finger. The longer cubit of Ezk 40:5 and 43:13 (where the expression is a cubit and a handbreadth) was like the Egyptian cubit, *c.* 20.5 inches long. The Siloam Inscription says that the tunnel which Hezekiah built (II Chr 32:30) was 1,200 cubits long. From measurement of the tunnel itself, this works out to *c.* 17.5 inches to a cubit. The length of the identical Solomonic city gates at Megiddo and Hazor was found by archaeologists to be 20.3 meters, or 45 cubits (7.5 reeds) of 17.7 inches. Since this is the length of the Egyptian common cubit, it suggests that Solomon's architect may have been an Egyptian (BA, XXII [1959], 26).

3. The short or two-thirds cubit (Heb. *gōmed*) was the distance from the elbow to the wrist, equal to four handbreadths. The length of Ehud's sword (Jud 3:16; the LXX, however, has "span" [Gr. *spithamēs*]), was about 12 inches.

4. The "span" (Heb. *zeret*), i.e., the distance between the extended thumb and the little finger, was one-half a cubit, or about eight and three-quarter inches. The ephod and breastplate were to be a span square (Ex 28:16; 39:9); Goliath was six cubits and a span in height (I Sam 17:4).

5. The "handbreadth" or "palm" (Heb. *ṭepaḥ* or *ṭōpaḥ*) was the width of a hand at the base of the four fingers. About one-sixth of a cubit, or almost three inches, it was used in measuring the frame around the table in the tabernacle (Ex 25:25), the thickness of Solomon's molten sea (I Kgs 7:26), and the hooks on which to hang instruments of slaughter in Ezekiel's temple (Ezk 40:43).

6. The "finger" (Heb. *'eṣba'*) was the smallest Israelite linear measure. About three-quarters of an inch, it appears only in Jer 52:21, where two hollow pillars are said to be four fingers thick.

In the NT

7. The "mile" (Mt 5:41; Gr. *milion* from Lat. *mille*) equaled the Roman mile. Literally 1,000 paces, the distance was fixed at 4,854 feet.

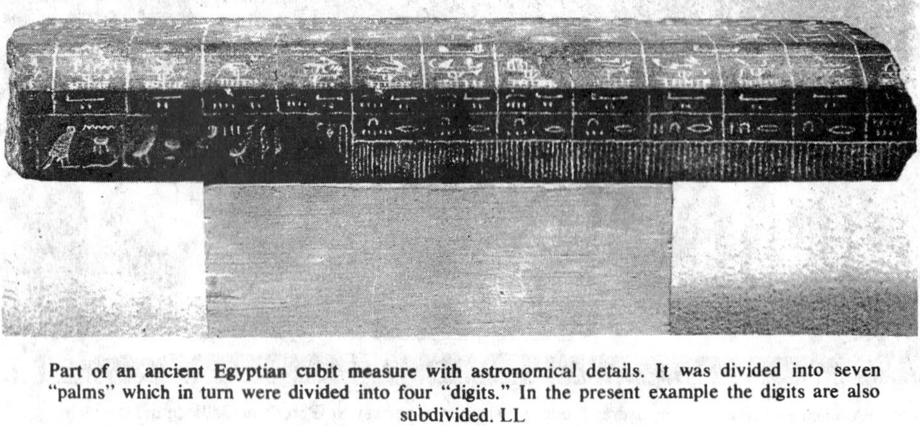

Part of an ancient Egyptian cubit measure with astronomical details. It was divided into seven "palms" which in turn were divided into four "digits." In the present example the digits are also subdivided. LL

TABLES OF WEIGHTS, MEASURES, AND COINS

Weights

Terms: Heb. or Gr.	Terms: KJV	Ratio	Approximate Metric	Equivalent U.S.
In the OT				
Kikkar	talent	3,000 *shekels*	34.2 kg.	75 lb.
Maneh, mina	pound	50 *shekels*	.57 kg.	1.25 lb.
Shekel (official, 625 B.C.)			11.4 gm.	0.4 oz.
Pim		2/3 *shekel*	7.6 gm.	0.27 oz.
Bekah		1/2 *shekel*	5.7 gm.	0.20 oz.
Gerah		1/20 *shekel*	0.57 gm.	0.02 oz.
In the NT				
Litra	pound		0.34 kg.	12 oz.
Talanton	talent			58–80 lb.

Dry and Liquid Measures

Terms: Heb. or Gr.	Terms: KJV	Ratio	Approximate Metric	Equivalent U.S.
In the OT				
Homer— cor		10 *ephahs* 10 *baths*	220 liters	6.25 bu. 58 gal.
Letek		1/2 *homer*	110 lit.	3.12 bu.
Ephah—bath			22 lit.	0.625 bu. 5.8 gal.
Seah		1/3 *ephah*	7.33 lit.	6.67 dry qt.
Hin		1/6 *bath*	3.67 lit.	1 gal.
Omer—'issarôn		1/10 *ephah*	2.2 lit.	2 dry qt.
Qab (cab)		1/18 *ephah*	1.3 lit.	2.3 pt.
Log		1/72 *bath*	0.31 lit.	0.64 pt.
In the NT				
Koros	measure			11–17 bu.
Batos	measure	72 *sextarii*	39.6 lit.	10.4 gal.
Metretes	firkin		35 lit.	9 gal.
Saton	measure	24 *sextarii*	13.2 lit.	12 dry qt.
Modios	bushel	16 *sextarii*	8.8 lit.	1 peck
Choinix	measure	2 *sextarii*	1.1 lit.	1 qt.
Xestes	pot	1 *sextarius*	0.55 lit.	1 pt.

Linear Measures

Terms: Heb. or Gr.	Terms: KJV	Ratio	Approximate Metric	Equivalent U.S.
In the OT				
qaneh	Reed	6 cubits	2.67 m.	8 ft. 9 in.
	Reed (Ezk)	6 cubits	3.12 m.	10 ft. 3 in.
ammâ	Cubit	(6 handbreadths)	44.45 cm.	17.5 in.
	Cubit (Ezk)	(7 handbreadths)	52 cm.	20.5 in.
zeret	Span	1/2 cubit	22.2 cm.	9 in.
tepah	Handbreadth	1/6 cubit	7.4 cm.	3 in.
'esba'	Finger	1/24 cubit	1.85 cm.	3/4 in.
In the NT				
milion	Mile	Roman mile (1000 paces)	1.48 km.	4,854 ft.
stadion	Furlong	1/8 Roman mile	185 m.	607 ft.
orguia	Fathom	4 cubits	1.85 m.	6 ft.
pechys	Cubit		46.25 cm.	18 in.

Coins

Jewish	Greek	Roman	Approximate U.S. Equivalent
Lepton ("mite")		1/2 *quadrans*	*1/8 cent*
		quadrans ("farthing")	1/4 cent
		assarius ("farthing")	1 cent
	drachma	*denarius* ("penny")	16 cents
	didrachma	2 *denarii*	32 cents
	stater	4 *denarii*	64 cents
	25 *drachma*	*aureus*	4 dollars
	mina ("pound")	100 *denarii*	16 dollars
	talent	240 *aurei*	960 dollars

WEIGHTS, MEASURES, AND COINS

8. The "furlong" (Gr. *stadion*) was *c.* 607 feet, or one-eighth of a Roman mile.

9. The "fathom" (Gr. *orguia*) is mentioned only in Acts 27:28. The distance of a man's arms stretched out horizontally, i.e., *c.* six feet, the fathom was used by sailors to measure water depth.

10. The "cubit" (Gr. *pēchys*, lit., "forearm") as a measure of length was *c.* 18 inches (Jn 21:8; Rev 21:17). Jesus' question, "Which of you by taking thought [i.e., worrying] can add one cubit unto his stature?" (Mt 6:27; cf. Lk 12:25), may be a figurative expression regarding adding a single hour to one's life (Arndt, p. 662).

Measurements of Area

The "acre" is the only unit of area mentioned in the Bible (Heb. *ma'ănâ*, I Sam 14:14; Heb. *ṣemed*, lit., "pair," Isa 5:10). Its size is uncertain, but the second Heb. word suggests the amount of land which a yoke of oxen could plow in one day. Land was also measured by the area which could be sown with a specified amount of barley (Lev 27:16).

Coins

Prior to the development of currency, men exchanged goods and services by bartering. Their words for cattle and for money show the central place cattle held in the Roman and Israelite systems of bartering. The Lat. word *pecunia* (money) comes from *pecus* (cattle), while the common Heb. word for cattle, *miqneh*, can mean "purchase price" or "possession (gained by purchase)," as it does in Gen 17:12–13; 23:18; Lev 25:16. Of course, other goods and animals, such as sheep and goats, were used in barter also. Hiram was paid in olive oil and wheat for his assistance in erecting the temple (I Kgs 5:11).

As time passed, men turned to the use of metals, mainly gold, silver, and copper, as media of exchange. At first, before the introduction of coinage, the metal used in exchange was of various sizes, shapes, and weights. Thus Abraham paid for the field of Machpelah by weighing out 400 shekels of silver (Gen 23:16), and Achan pilfered a wedge of gold weighing 50 shekels and a quantity of silver weighing 200 shekels from Jericho (Josh 7:21). The word "shekel" was the name of a unit of weight long before it became the name of a coin. What Abraham gave in payment and what Achan stole were not coins. They were nondescript quantities of gold and silver. Jewelry and other intentionally fashioned objects were also valued in relation to their weight (cf. Gen 24:22).

In business deals the gold or silver was weighed out in the presence of the participants, as Abraham and Ephron did (Gen 23:13). Jeremiah weighed out 17 shekels of silver for the field of Anathoth (Jer 32:9), and Ezra weighed the silver and gold to be taken for the temple at Jerusalem (Ezr 8:24–30). It is difficult to make exact comparisons between the value of a shekel of silver or gold and our modern money, since the purchasing power of each varies and the measures of weight used then would fluctuate with the time and place.

Origin of coins. The first coins were lumps of electrum (a natural alloy of gold and silver) stamped by merchants with their own marks guaranteeing their value. Because they were of a standard size, quality, and weight, coins offered a simpler, more exact medium of exchange.

The first series of coins coming close to being uniform came from Lydia in Asia Minor *c.* 700 B.C. (Herodotus i.94). Greek cities on the coast of Asia Minor and in Greece rapidly adopted this idea. With the Persian conquest of Sardis in 547 B.C. the use of coins spread far and wide (cf. "Coinage: Greek," *Oxford Classical Dictionary*, p. 208). Forgery in coins—e.g., plating inferior metal with silver, shaving edges to lessen the weight—did occur in antiquity, but the gains to commerce of a standard means of exchange were immense.

Coin of Alexander the Great from Persepolis, Persia. ORINST

Coins were not known among the Israelites before the fall of the northern kingdom in 721 B.C. or of the southern kingdom in 586 B.C. Mention of money in our English translations of the OT before those dates is to be understood as references to bars, ingots, and jewelry made of precious metal used in trading.

The first reference to coins in the OT seems to be Ezr 2:69; 8:27; Neh 7:70–72. The Jews offered 61,000 gold darics for the rebuilding of the Jerusalem temple. (The Heb. is *darkemônîm* a rare word, which may come from the word "daric," a name derived from Darius I, or may be related to the Gr. word "drachma." The KJV has "dram"). Examples of the Persian daric have been found. It was an oval shaped coin of pure gold. The obverse shows the king kneeling with a bow in his left hand and a spear in his right (cf. "Money," IDB, III, 431). The reference to darics in David's time (I Chr 29:7) is anachronistic, giving the value in its equivalent at the time the Chronicler was writing. *See* Daric.

Ancient coins were made of gold, silver, electrum, copper, and bronze. They were characteristically round and flat, and of various sizes. The obverse (or inscription) side usually carried a picture of the ruler plus the date and an inscription. On the reverse (or under) side would be further information and a design (for illustrations, cf. "Money," IDB, III, 431–435).

The Persian and intertestamental periods. The reference in Ezr 2:69 to the gold daric has been discussed above. The Persian daric may have been minted at Sardis, in the general area where the craft was developed.

The Persian province of *Yehûd* had a local mint by the 4th cen. B.C. *Yehûd* was the official name for Judea while it was a part of the Persian Empire (cf. Ezr 7:14–16; Dan 2:25; 5:13). A silver coin inscribed with YHD but of Gr. style, apparently found in Gaza, dates to the 4th cen. B.C. (IDB, III, 425, fig. 68), as does another of the Athenian owl style, also bearing the Heb. letters YHD. The oldest Gr. coin yet found in Palestine, at Shechem, dates from the 6th cen. B.C. It came from the island of Thasos and consists of electrum (G. E. Wright, *Shechem,* p. 168). After Alexander's conquest (*c.* 330 B.C.), the gold stater and silver tetradrachma were the dominant coins in Palestine, with the nearest mints at Acre and Sidon.

Late in the 2nd cen. B.C., following the Maccabean revolt from Syrian (Seleucid) rule, John Hyrcanus of the Hasmonean family minted coins with the inscription, "Johanan the high priest and the community of the Jews" (*c.* 111/110 B.C.). These were the first truly Jewish coins, for earlier coins minted by the Jews had been made subject to the permission of foreign overlords. To be consistent with the command of Ex 20:4, the coins omitted the ruler's image on the obverse. They carried a wreath with the inscription inside it instead. The reverse showed a cornucopia and a poppy head (indicating plenty and fertility), the latter frequently used on Syrian coins.

John's successor, Judas Aristobulus, followed the same pattern of coinage. Alexander Jannaeus (105–78 B.C.) was the first to use the term "king" on his coins. Antigonus Mattathias (40–37 B.C.), the last of the Maccabees and ruler just before Herod the Great became king, issued a coin picturing a seven-branched lampstand. This is the oldest known representation of the sacred lampstand belonging to the temple in Jerusalem. Many of Mattathias' coins were an alloy containing lead.

The NT period. In the NT there are various general references to money. The Gr. word *nomisma* comprises one-half of the KJV's expression "tribute money" (Mt 22:19). It is a general term for money. Jesus used the word in asking for the coin suitable for paying the poll tax (NASB). The Gr. word *argyrion* is translated both "silver" (Acts 3:6; 20:33; I Pet 1:18) and "money" (Mt 25:18, 27; Lk 9:3; 19:15, 23; Acts 8:20). Several times it refers to a silver coin without the particular coin being specified, e.g., the 30 coins paid to Judas (Mt 26:15; 27:3–9) and the burning of 50,000 silver coins' worth of books at Ephesus (Acts 19:19).

In telling His disciples not to take gold, silver, or brass along on their preaching missions, Jesus may have been referring either to coins or to supplies of metal which could be used as money (Mt 10:9). When Jesus overturned the money changers' tables (Jn 2:15), John says He poured out their *kerma* (KJV "money"). Referring to pieces of money, usually copper coins, the term carries the idea of small change. Another Gr. word carrying at times the idea of copper coins or small change is *chalkos* (Mt 10:9, KJV "brass"; Mk 6:8; 12:41, KJV "money").

Coins of Brutus (left) and Mark Antony. BM

For a final example, Gr. *chrēma* (KJV "money") is used both of a definite sum of money, what Joses presented to the apostles in Acts 4:37, and of indefinite amounts, e.g., Simon's attempt to buy the gift of the Spirit with money (Acts 8:18, 20) and Felix' hope to receive bribe money from Paul (Acts 24:26).

During the NT era coins could be issued by the Roman government itself, Roman governors, local kings, and free cities. Some important Roman coins, which General Pompey introduced to Israel in 63 B.C., represented the Roman government and emperor directly (cf. Mt 22:19–21). However, from A.D. 6 on, Roman governors could issue coins locally in the name of the emperor. The governor's name did not appear on these issues, and so as not to offend the Jews they generally carried neutral symbols such as the barley ear, palm tree, olive branch, grape leaves, and cornucopia. However, Pilate did antagonize the Jews by using pagan symbols on some of his coins. An example is a *lepton* with the obverse containing the words, "Tiberius Caesar," and an augur's wand (auguring was forbidden to the Jews in Deut 18:10). The reverse had a wreath with the date letter L I Z around it, indicating the 17th year of Tiberius, i.e., A.D. 30–31. L was the Egyptian symbol for year, I and Z for 10 and 7. Coins issued by the Roman governors Coponius (A.D. 6–9), Valerius (15–26), Pilate (26–36), and Felix (52–59) have been found (cf. J. A. Thompson, *The Bible and Archaeology,* pp. 308–309).

WEIGHTS, MEASURES, AND COINS

Local kings also minted coins. Herod the Great was the first Jewish ruler to drop Heb. and use Gr., and his were the first Jewish coins to show a date (cf. "Money," IDB, III, 427, 432). For the most part he did not use Roman symbols, but substituted, e.g., pomegranates and leaves, although on one of his small coins he did use the offensive Roman eagle. Herod the Great's sons Archelaus (ruler over Judea, 4 B.C.–A.D.6) and Herod Antipas (ruler over Galilee and Perea, 4 B.C.–A.D. 39) used neutral symbols. Another son, Herod Philip (4 B.C.–A.D. 34), ruling over the more Gentile area of Ituraea and Trachonitis (Lk 3:1), used the image of the emperor on one side and the temple on the other.

Herod Agrippa I (A.D. 37–44) used pagan symbols. He placed the emperor on the obverse, goddesses and pagan temples on the reverse. Herod Agrippa II (A.D. 50–100) completed the progression. Early in his reign he showed his own image and sometimes the bust of a goddess. One of his coins following Jerusalem's destruction (A.D. 70) shows Agrippa II as a vassal of Rome.

Independent cities such as Ascalon, Antioch, Tyre, Damascus, Sidon, Byblos, Gadara, Seleucia, Beirut, Gaza, and Caesarea also minted coins.

Among the Gr. coins mentioned in the NT, the *drachmē* appears as the "pieces of silver" (KJV) in Jesus' parable of the lost coin (Lk 15:8–9). The commonplace rating of the drachma at less than 20 cents is not illuminating; it would buy a sheep, and five would buy an ox (Arndt, p. 205).

The *didrachma,* a double or two-drachma coin, was equivalent to the Jewish half-shekel and was acceptable as the annual temple tax for individuals (Mt 17:24, KJV "tribute").

The *statēr* (KJV "piece of money") which Peter found in the fish's mouth (Mt 17:27) was worth four *drachmas,* or equal to the temple tax for two persons.

The *mina* (Lk 19:13–25, Gr. *mna,* KJV "pound") was a monetary unit equal to 100 drachmas. The Attic mina was worth *c.* 18 to 20 dollars in normal times (Arndt, p. 526).

A bronze coin of Vespasian, inscribed "Judaea Capta," commemorating the capture of Jerusalem and Judaea. A palm tree, symbol of Judaea, is flanked by mourning Jew and Jewess. BM

The *talent* (Mt 18:24; 25:15–28, Gr. *talanton*) was another large measure of money. It was originally a measure of weight, and the value of a talent varied considerably with the time, area, and type of metal. *See* Talent.

Also, several Roman coins are mentioned in the NT. The *dēnarion* (Lat. *denarius,* KJV "penny" and "pennyweight") was a silver coin. It was normally worth *c.* 18 cents, but Nero debased it, reducing its worth to about 8 cents (Arndt, p. 178). The *dēnarion* was the common daily wage for a working man (Mt 20:2; cf. Mt 18:28; Jn 6:7; Rev 6:6). In the 1st cen. A.D. it was minted mainly at Rome under imperial direction.

When Jesus was asked by the malicious Pharisees and Herodians about the legality of Jews having to pay a census tax (Gr. *kēnsos*) to the Roman emperor, He demanded them to show Him the "tribute money" (Mt 22:17–19). So they brought Him a denarius, the legal coin used to pay the poll tax. He asked whose image and inscription it bore, in order to provide a basis for His answer to their attempt to trap Him. The current denarius would have been inscribed in abbreviated Latin on the obverse around the head of the emperor: "Tiberius Caesar, August Son of the Divine Augustus"; and on the reverse: "Pontifex Maximus" (i.e., high priest), with his mother Livia shown seated in the role of Pax, holding a branch and scepter. The coin therefore represented to the Jews both the hated power of the Roman government and the blasphemous imperial cult which deified the earthly ruler and demanded worship of him. Yet Jesus skillfully avoided condemning the tribute taxation by telling the Jewish leaders, "Render therefore unto Caesar the things which are Caesar's; and unto God the things that are God's" (v. 21).

The sparrows of Mt 10:29 and Lk 12:6 were appraised in terms of the *assarion* (Lat. *assarius,* KJV "farthing"). A copper coin, it was worth about one-sixteenth of a *dēnarion.*

The value of the *kodrantēs* (Lat. *quadrans,* KJV "farthing," Mt 5:26; Lk 12:59) was one-fourth that of the *assarion,* and the value of the copper *lepton* (KJV "mite") one-half that of the *kodrantēs.* The *lepton,* which the widow threw into the temple offering (Mk 12:42; Lk 21:2), was the smallest coin in circulation.

Coins of the Jewish revolts. During both of their uprisings against Rome the Jews stamped coins in their own name. In A.D. 66–70 they minted silver shekel and half-shekel coins using neutral symbols that told of the Jewish hopes for deliverance and other coins in bronze (Y. Yadin, *Masada,* pp. 98, 108–109, 168–171). One silver shekel read on the obverse in ancient Heb. script, "Shekel of Israel I"; on the reverse, "Jerusalem Holy." A bronze coin read on the obverse, "Year 4"; the reverse carried a chalice and the words, "For the Redemption of Zion" (J. A. Thompson, *The Bible and Archaeology,* pp. 310 f.).

After crushing the Jewish revolt in A.D. 70

the Romans minted coins with the letters "s.c.," i.e., "with the consent of the senate." These showed the head of Emperor Vespasian on the obverse with his titles; the reverse pictured a woman (Judea) beneath a palm tree under Roman guard and had the words, "Judaea Capta" (cf. Y. Yadin, *Masada*, p. 215 for picture and caption).

During their revolt of A.D. 132-135 under Ben Kosebah (Bar Kochba), the Jews over-stamped Roman coins and issued some of their own, including a silver tetradrachma and a silver denarius. The tetradrachma bore a star above the temple and the name "Simon" on the obverse. The reverse had the inscription, "For the Liberty of Jerusalem," with the citron and twigs. The denarius had "Simon" on the obverse and "Year of the Liberty of Israel" on the reverse (cf. Thompson, *op. cit.*, p. 311).

After suppressing this rebellion, the Romans issued a special coin showing the emperor with a pair of oxen plowing the borders of a new town bearing the inscription Colonia Aelia, the new name which they gave to Jerusalem.

Archaeological use of coins. The historian studies coins found in archaeological excavations in order to augment our knowledge of biblical times. Some depict historical personages, e.g., coins showing Tiberius, Vespasian, and the Herodian kings. Others reflect the fortunes of regional political and military affairs, e.g., the hope of Israel for independence and the Roman conquest.

Coins can also aid in determining the date of archaeological remains. For example, the occupation of a large building in Roman Jericho can be dated from the last of the 1st cen. B.C. up to *c.* A.D. 65 on the basis of coins found there minted by Herod the Great, Archelaus, Herod Agrippa, and several Roman procurators (cf. James B. Pritchard, "The 1951 Campaign at Herodian Jericho," BASOR # 123 [1951], pp. 14 f.).

Coins found at Qumran, where the Dead Sea Scrolls were copied or used, show that the monastery was intermittently occupied. The occupations were from the early 1st cen. B.C. to *c.* 37 B.C., then from 4 B.C. to A.D. 68, and finally from A.D. 132 to 135. Coins dated A.D. 66-70 indicate the fortress Masada was inhabited at the time of the first Jewish revolt and was in contact with Jerusalem up to A.D. 69-70 (Yadin, *Masada*, pp. 108, 168, 172).

Bibliography. Florence A. Banks, *Coins of Bible Days*, New York: Macmillan, 1955. G. A. Barrois, "Chronology, Metrology, Etc.," IB, I, 153-164. A. Ben-David, "The Standard of the Sheqel," PEQ, XCVIII (1966), 168 f.; "The Talmud Was Right! The Weight of the Biblical Sheqel," PEQ, C (1968), 145-147. CornPBE, "Coins," pp. 228-230; "Weights and Measures," pp. 705-708. David Diringer, "Weights," DOTT, pp. 227-230. H. Hamburger, "Money, Coins," IDB, III, 423-435. A. Kindler, "Coins as Documents for Israel's Ancient History," *Antiquity and Survival*, II (1957), 225-236. Y. Meshorer, "A Stone Weight from the Reign of King Herod," IEJ, XX (1970), 97 f. A. Reifenberg, *Ancient Jewish Coins*, 2nd ed., Jerusalem, 1940; *Israel's History in Coins from the Maccabees to the Roman Conquest*, London: Horovitz, 1953. R. B. Y. Scott, "Weights and Measures of the Bible," BA, XXII (1959), 22-40; "The Scale-Weights from Ophel, 1963-64." PEQ. XCVII (1965), 128-139; "The N-S-P Weights from Judah," BASOR, #200 (1970), pp. 62-66. O. R. Sellers, "Weights and Measures," IDB, IV, 828-839. D. H. Wheaton, "Money," NBD, pp. 836-841. D. J. Wiseman and D. H. Wheaton, "Weights and Measures," NBD, pp. 1319-1325.

W. H. M.

WELL. Wells have always held a prominent place in Bible lands because of the aridity of the land and the scarcity of rainfall. For this reason there are a variety of words used.

The most common Heb. word for "well" is *be'ēr* (Gen 21:30; Num 21:18; etc.), a source of water made by digging. This root is often found in compounds denoting places, such as Beer-sheba (Gen 21:14). Beer-lahai-roi (Gen 16:14), Beeroth (Deut 10:6), and Beer-elim (Isa 15:8). At each of these locations famous wells existed.

Other Heb. terms for "well" are: *bôr* (I Sam 19:22; II Sam 23:15-16; the RSV often replaces the KJV's "well" with "cistern"—e.g., Deut 6:11; II Chr 26:10; Neh 9:25); *ma'yān* (Josh 18:15; II Kgs 3:19; Ps 84:6; Isa 12:3; RSV substitutes "spring"); *māqôr* (Prov 10:11; RSV "fountain"); *'ayin* (Gen 24:13; 49:22; Ex 15:27; Neh 2:13; RSV "spring").

The Gr. also has two words. They are *pēgē* (a well fed by a spring, Jn 4:6) and *phrear* (the shaft or pit of the well, Jn 4:11-12; cf. Lk 14:5).

"Abraham's Well" at Beersheba. HFV

Well in northern Iraq west of Nineveh. JR

Biblical wells were found in diverse places, their depth and shape varying with the soil type and water level. Some were shallow pits, while others reached deep into the earth, even serving as a place of concealment for men (II Sam 17:18-19). Many wells had covers over their mouths, undoubtedly to keep the water pure and to prevent animals and people from falling in (Gen 29:3; Ex 21:33). The Bible speaks of wells being located in the wilderness (Gen 16:14), near cities (Gen 24:11), in valleys (Gen 26:17-18), in fields (Gen 29:2), and in courtyards (II Sam 17:18). They were of particular importance in the patriarchal period as the society was nomadic (Gen 26:18). Wells supplied water for both family and flocks (Gen 29:2). Later they became an important supplement to cisterns and springs in the water supplies of cities and villages (I Sam 19:22; II Sam 23:15; Jn 4:6). *See* Spring.

Bibliography. Wilhelm Michaelis, *"Pēgē,"* TDNT, VI, 112-117.

P. D. F.

WEN. *See* Diseases.

WEST. The ordinary word for west in the OT is Heb. *yām*, "sea" (e.g., Gen 12:8; Deut 3:27). This is a result of the geography of the Holy Land, with the expanse of the Mediterranean Sea on the W. Other Heb. terms translated "west" in the KJV speak of the "going in of the sun" (Josh 23:4; Zech 8:7) or the "setting" of the sun (e.g., Ps 75:6; Isa 45:6). In the NT Gr. *dysmē*, "sinking" of the sun, is the regular word for west (e.g., Mt 8:11; 24:27).

WHALE. *See* Animals, V.13.

WHEAT. *See* Plants.

WHEEL. Wheels were invented by the Sumerians in Mesopotamia before 3000 B.C. Cart wheels were first made of solid, semi-circular halves of wood fastened together with planks and sometimes rimmed with metal (ANEP # 163), later consisting of spokes, hub, and rim. Most references are probably to the spoked wheel.

Heb. *'ôphān* refers to a chariot wheel (Ex 14:25), probably the light six-spoked wheel as on the Egyptian chariot (*q.v.*) found in King Tutankhamen's tomb, or to the heavier eight-spoked wheel of Babylonia and Persia (Nah 3:2); to the wheels for the lavers of Solomon's temple, made of bronze with bronze axles yet like chariot wheels (I Kgs 7:30-33); to the wheels of a threshing cart (Prov 20:26, NASB; Isa 28:27); and to the wheels of Ezekiel's visions (Ezk 1:15-21; 3:13; 10:6-19).

Heb. *galgal* may be the wheel of a war chariot (Isa 5:28) or of wagons to haul away spoils of war (Jer 47:3; Ezk 23:24; 26:10, NASB); it also is used of a waterwheel or pulley wheel for a rope at a cistern (Eccl 12:6). The same Heb. word refers to the whirling motion of dust or chaff (Isa 17:13; Ps 83:13, KJV "wheel").

Heb. *'obnayim* denotes the two discs of a potter's wheel (Jer 18:3), one for the clay and the lower one to rotate the entire device by kicking.

H. E. Fi.

WHELP. The young of the lion (Nah 2:11; Job 4:11); also young of the jackal (Lam 4:3, RSV). Lions figured prominently in Bible lands. Their whelps were used to describe Judah (Gen 49:9), the princes of Israel (Ezk 19:2-9), and Babylonian residents (Jer 51:38).

WHIP. An instrument with which to strike, as in driving animals (Prov 26:3; Nah 3:2), or in punishing or coercing men (I Kgs 12:11, 14; II Chr 10:11, 14). In Jn 2:15 Jesus made a whip of cords (Gr. *phragellion,* from Latin *flagellum,* KJV "scourge," RSV "whip") to drive the money changers and animals from the temple. *See* Scourge.

WHIRLWIND. A mass of air rotating rapidly round and round toward a more or less vertical axis (Isa 17:13, ASV), and having at the same time progressive motion over the surface of land or sea (II Kgs 2:11). The violent tornado with its funnel-shaped cloud is not common in Palestine, however. Most biblical references to whirlwind do not necessarily imply a circular motion but designate several different types of wind and storm. The whirlwind depicted the power and might of God (Nah 1:3) and was used by God for communication with Job (Job 38:1).

Most biblical uses are figurative with the whirlwind portraying destruction (Ps 58:9; Prov 1:27; 10:25; Hos 13:3); quickness (Isa 5:28; 66:15; Jer 4:13); the anger of God (Jer 23:19); and punishment to the wicked (Jer 30:23).

WHITE. *See* Colours.

WHITEWASH. The RSV and NASB translation of Heb. *tāphēl,* KJV "untempered mortar" (Ezk 13:10; 22:28). *See* Untempered Mortar.

WHOLE. *See* Perfect.

WHORE. *See* Fornication; Harlot.

WICK. A wick (Heb. *pishtâ*) of flax or hemp was used in early Palestinian clay lamps to conduct the olive or animal oil to the flame (Isa 42:3, KJV "flax"; Isa 43:17, KJV "tow"). *See* Lamp.

WICKED, WICKEDNESS. These English words and "wickedly" occur over 500 times in the KJV. In the Heb. OT the derivatives of *rā'a'* and *rāsha'* are the words most commonly translated by "wicked" and "wickedness," whereas in the NT *ponēros* and *ponēria* have this distinction. But this is not a hard and fast rule, for both languages, especially Heb., have other words which are more or less synonymous. This situation is complicated by the fact that English has other words that are very close in meaning to wicked and wickedness, so close as to be almost indistinguishable; and these English synonyms are often used to translate the above Gr. and Heb. words. As a result, it often is very difficult to find a clear distinction of meaning among words like wicked, evil, lawless, and sinful in the English text, or their counterparts in the original languages.

But whatever distinction can legitimately be made indicates that wickedness is an active, virulent form of evil. It is that which is evil or false before God (Gen 38:7; Isa 5:20; Amos 5:14–15); that which is contrary to God is wicked. Perversity of mind is wicked (Prov 15:26). In the words of Jesus, "wicked" (Gr.) describes the heart of the Pharisees (Mt 12:34–35; 22:18). The wicked are contrasted with the righteous (Mt 13:49). Wicked works alienate the unbeliever from God (Col 1:21). Apostates and false teachers are wicked (II Tim 3:13; II Thess 3:2).

In Rom 1:29 wickedness is one of a list of terms used to describe the utter depravity of man (see also Jer 17:9). Certainty of punishment faces the wicked (Ps 9:17; Mt 13:49). In this connection it is significant to note that the Gr. *ponēros* is never applied to believers (with the possible exception of I Cor 5:13, though the individual there may be only a nominal Christian). On the opposite side is the fact that *ponēros* (normally adjectival) can be used as a substantive to refer to Satan (Mt 13:19; I Jn 2:13–14; 5:18). The total impression derived from these usages is that wickedness is that which is especially and actively evil in the moral and spiritual realm.

See Evil; Iniquity; Sin.

S. N. G.

WIDOW. The Bible presents a widow as one in need of protection and provision, to be honored and respected. Thus Jerusalem destroyed is shown as a widow: "How doth the city sit solitary . . . how is she become as a widow!" (Lam 1:1).

Under the Mosaic law, care of the widow was left to relatives, and was one of the duties assigned to the eldest son, who received the birthright. Regarding remarriage of a widow, if childless, she was expected to marry the brother or near relative of her deceased husband (Deut 25:5). If anyone harmed a widow or an orphan, and the one afflicted should cry unto the Lord, He promised swift vengeance (Ex 22:22–24; Ps 146:9).

In the early Christian church the care of widows received prompt attention when "there arose a murmuring of the Grecians against the Hebrews, because their widows were neglected in the daily ministration" (Acts 6:1). Seven deacons were appointed to care for such matters. Thereafter special importance was shown in the care of widows. "If any provide not for his own, and specially those of his own house, he hath denied the faith, and is worse than an infidel" (I Tim 5:8). Four classes of widows are mentioned by Paul in this chapter: (1) the widow indeed, who is desolate, trusts in God, and continues in prayer night and day; (2) the widow who has children; (3) the pleasure-seeking widow; (4) the widow entered or enrolled. She must be at least 60 years of age, diligent in good works, have brought up children, lodged strangers, relieved the afflicted, washed the saints' feet, and "been the wife of one man" (cf. I Tim 5:3–10).

"Pure religion and undefiled before God and the Father is this, To visit the fatherless and widows in their affliction, and to keep himself unspotted from the world" (Jas 1:27).

L. A. L.

WIFE. *See* Family; Marriage; Veil; Woman.

WILD ASS. *See* Animals: Onager, II.29.

WILD BEASTS. *See* Animals, II.

WILD GOAT. *See* Animals, I.9.

WILD GOURD. *See* Plants: Gourd.

WILD OX. *See* Animals, II.30.

WILD VINE, WILD GRAPES. *See* Plants.

WILDERNESS. A barren wasteland. The word is used often in a general geographical sense, but there are a number of areas specifically called wildernesses, e.g., Shur, Zin, Paran, Kadesh (*q.v.*).

Several Heb. words vary the description of these areas. The most common word, *midbār,* means a pastureland, an uninhabited land, unsuited for farming but sufficient for grazing (I Chr 5:9; Job 38:26 f.). The word *'ărābâ* means literally "dry" (Job 39:6), and it is used as a proper noun to refer to that arid steppe that stretches from the Jordan Valley and the Dead

Sea S to the Gulf of Aqabah (*see* Arabah). Heb. *ṣiyyâ* also means "dry" and is translated "wilderness" in Job 30:3 and Ps 78:17. The word *tōhû* is used in Gen 1:2 to describe the chaos of God's beginning creation, and also the pathless "waste" of the wilderness of wandering (Deut 32:10; Job 6:18, RSV; 12:24; Ps 107:40). The word *yeshîmôn*, a desolate place (Deut 32:10; Ps 68:7), is also used as a proper noun (*see* Jeshimon). The Gr. words *erēmos* and *erēmia* mean "uninhabited, deserted" (Lk 4:1; 5:16; 8:29; 15:4).

See Desert; Wilderness Wandering.

P. C. J.

WILDERNESS WANDERING. When the Israelites under Moses' leadership fled from Egypt at the time of the Exodus, they passed through the Red Sea into wilderness or desert territory. The crossing probably took place at the N end of the Gulf of Suez (*see* Exodus, The: The Route). They camped for a whole year at the foot of Mount Sinai where they received the Law and built the tabernacle. Under God's direction they marched northward to Kadesh-barnea in order to invade Canaan from the S. But here they rebelled. Then 38 years elapsed until the adults who sided with the ten terror-stricken spies all died. By that time a new generation was willing to make the long circuitous journey around Edom and Moab in order to cross the Jordan River into Canaan from the E. The intervening time was spent in the deserts of the Sinai peninsula, the Negeb, and the Arabah rift valley S of the Dead Sea, wandering from oasis to oasis.

The precise route taken by Israel from the Red Sea crossing to the Jordan Valley opposite Jericho is still a matter of conjecture. The majority of the place names have not yet been identified; nor can we expect much further enlightenment from archaeological research because no remains of settlement would have been left by the trekking Israelites at their brief stopping places. Furthermore, the various biblical accounts do not harmonize easily (see accompanying table). Yet this is no reason to suppose that the several accounts relate the movements of smaller tribal groups at differegt times, as some critics have proposed. It must be remembered that all 12 tribes left Egypt together (Ex 12:41), all were at Mount Sinai when God gave them the Law (Ex 24:4), all were represented on the ephod and breastplate of Aaron (Ex 28:9–21; 39:6–14), all were included in the two national censuses (Num 2:26), all marched from Sinai together (Num 10:11–28), at Kadesh-barnea each tribe furnished a spy to explore Canaan (Num 13:4–16; Deut 1:23), and all 12 tribes crossed the Jordan together (Josh 3:12; 4:2–8, 20–24).

Physical Features

The Sinai peninsula and the Negeb form a large inverted triangle *c.* 22,000 square miles in area. Its base is the SE shore of the Mediterranean Sea with a line extending eastward to the S end of the Dead Sea. Its W side is formed by the Gulf of Suez and Bitter Lakes region, while its E side consists of the Gulf of Aqabah and the Arabah depression. The region is largely barren, with few settlements in ancient times and these of rather short duration.

The road from the Nile delta to Gaza by "the way of the land of the Philistines" (Ex 13:17) parallels the Mediterranean coast. From the Suez Canal to the Wadi el-'Arish (*see* River of Egypt 1) the traveler is wearied by sand dunes unrelieved by vegetation; but beyond that point to Gaza the land is cultivable. Farther S 20-40 miles another ancient caravan route traversed the Wilderness of Shur, from Serapeum (Etham?) between Lake Timsah and the Bitter Lakes to the Kadesh-barnea region and on to Beer-sheba (Gen 16:7; 20:1). The ground is hard and strewn with flints. Since there are presently few if any wells along the W half of this road, W. F. Albright supposed that in Abraham's time there must have been more water sources or else caravan stations spaced a day's journey apart in order to provide the necessary drink and provender for donkeys (BASOR # 163, Oct. 1961, pp. 37–38). But these stations would not have been available to the Israelites in Moses' day.

South of the Way of Shur hills and wadis gradually ascend to the 2,000–2,500 foot high limestone tableland known as Et-Tih, its NE part being the biblical Wilderness of Paran (Num 10:12; 12:16). The S half of the plateau is ringed by a chain of mountains 4,000 feet and more high, called Jebel et-Tih. Across the plateau ran an ancient trade route from Suez to Arabia *via* Ezion-geber, the approximate line of the later road for pilgrims to Mecca. This seems to have been called "the way of the Red Sea" in Deut 2:1. Between the Mitla Pass and the Moslem fortress of Qal'at en-Nakhl, and near the Parker monument, Beno Rothenberg discovered extensive Middle Bronze Age I (2100–1900 B.C.) ruins on the slope of Ruweiset el-Akheider (*God's Wilderness*, pp. 60–62, Pl. 22, 23). Ancient sites and rock-drawings prove that the E end of the road descended to the Gulf of Aqabah 15 miles or so SW of Elath (PEQ, CII, 5, 9).

A sandstone formation crosses the Sinai peninsula just S of Jebel et-Tih, separating the limestone plateau from the granite mountains of the S. In these high sandstone hills (up to 1,500 feet in altitude) the Egyptians mined much turquoise in the vicinity of Wadi Maghareh and Serabit el-Khadem. Actually only one mine for copper, at Bir Nasb, can be attributed to them in this region (PEQ, CII, 15–18). Egyptian mining expeditions were sent out normally during January to March, and did not live permanently at the mines; therefore presumably no detachments of troops would have been present to harass the migrating Israelites.

A region of granite mountains juts up in the S end of the peninsula, 5,000–8,000 feet high. To

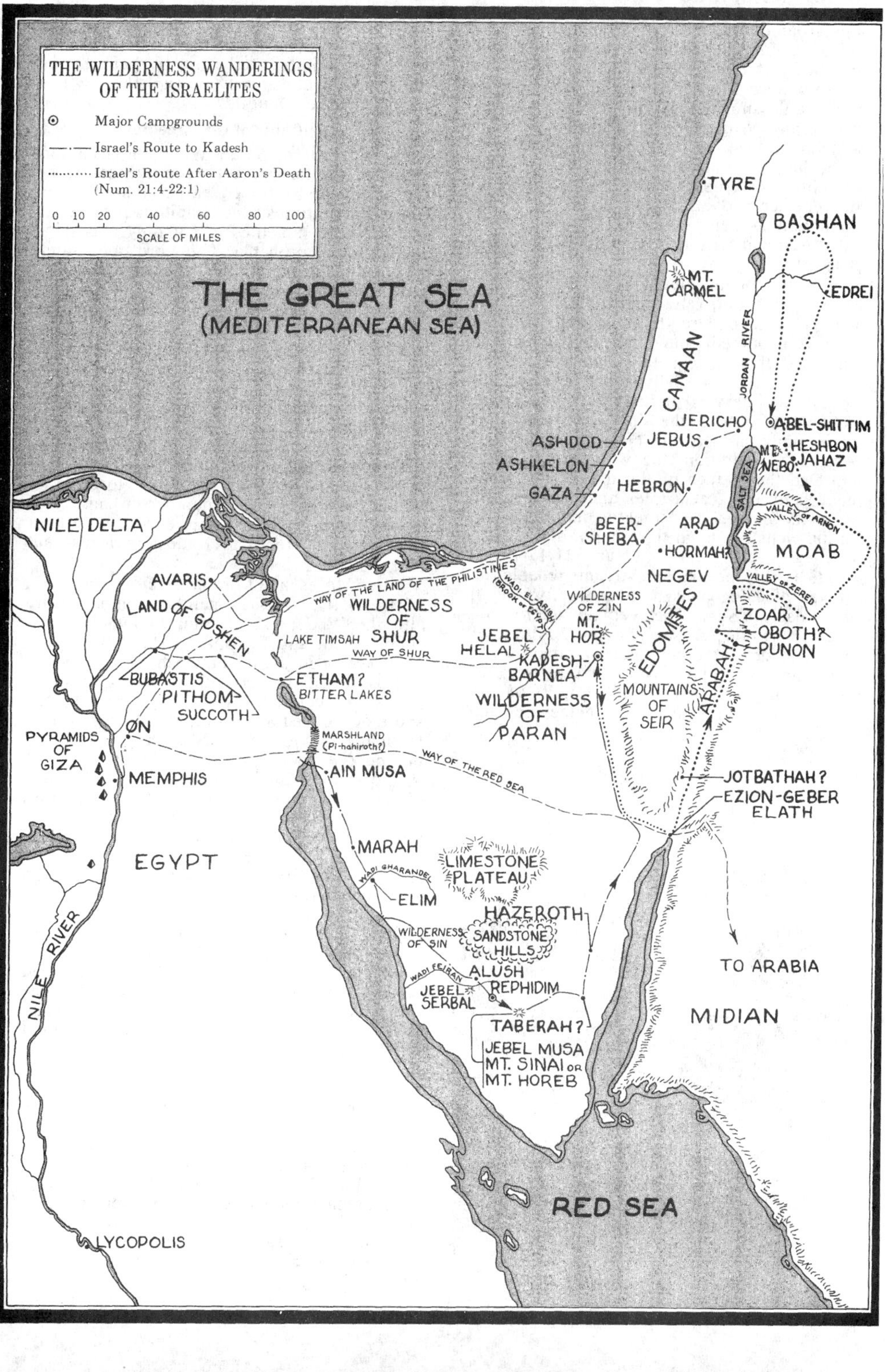
THE WILDERNESS WANDERINGS OF THE ISRAELITES
Major Campgrounds
Israel's Route to Kadesh
Israel's Route After Aaron's Death (Num. 21:4-22:1)
0 10 20 40 60 80 100
SCALE OF MILES
THE GREAT SEA (MEDITERRANEAN SEA)
TYRE
BASHAN
MT. CARMEL
EDREI
JORDAN RIVER
CANAAN
JERICHO
ABEL-SHITTIM
JEBUS
ASHDOD
HESHBON
MT. NEBO
JAHAZ
ASHKELON
SALT SEA
HEBRON
GAZA
VALLEY OF ARNON
BEER-SHEBA
ARAD
HORMAH?
MOAB
NILE DELTA
NEGEV
VALLEY OF ZERED
AVARIS
WAY OF THE LAND OF THE PHILISTINES
WADI EL-ARISH (BROOK OF EGYPT)
WILDERNESS OF ZIN
LAND OF GOSHEN
WILDERNESS OF SHUR
ZOAR
MT. HOR
OBOTH?
JEBEL HELAL
EDOMITES
PUNON
LAKE TIMSAH
WAY OF SHUR
KADESH-BARNEA
BUBASTIS
ETHAM?
PITHOM
BITTER LAKES
MOUNTAINS OF SEIR
ARABAH
SUCCOTH
WILDERNESS OF PARAN
ON
PYRAMIDS OF GIZA
MARSHLAND (Pi-hahiroth?)
MEMPHIS
WAY OF THE RED SEA
AIN MUSA
JOTBATHAH?
EZION-GEBER ELATH
MARAH
EGYPT
LIMESTONE PLATEAU
WADI GHARANDEL
ELIM
HAZEROTH
WILDERNESS OF SIN
SANDSTONE HILLS
NILE RIVER
ALUSH
TO ARABIA
WADI FEIRAN
REPHIDIM
JEBEL SERBAL
TABERAH?
MIDIAN
JEBEL MUSA MT. SINAI OR MT. HOREB
RED SEA
LYCOPOLIS

this group of majestic peaks belongs the traditional Mount Sinai, Jebel Musa, with an altitude of 7,467 feet. *See* Sinai.

How were the needs of the Israelites and their cattle supplied during the long years of wandering? While God daily provided manna and on occasion miraculously supplied water from the rock and meat in the form of quails, life in the wilderness for the most part was one of repeated privation and hardship. Moses could remind them at the end of the 40 years of "that vast and terrible wilderness" (Deut 1:19; 8:15, NEB).

Nomadic peoples learn to get along on very scant amounts of water, and the ability of man and beast to endure thirst is great in desert lands. Undoubtedly they carried goatskin water bags with them, adequate for up to three days (cf. Ex 15:22). Usually there are wells or springs at intervals of about a day's journey down both coasts of the Sinai peninsula, as well as in many parts of the Negeb and along the Arabah. In addition, the water-table is often close to the surface of the dry wadis, as evidenced by the acacia trees and sparse bushes along its course. The Israelites understood how to dig wells to obtain this source of water, according to the song of Num 21:17–18. In Wadi Feiran permanent streams enable lush groves of date palms to flourish, forming the finest oasis in Sinai. The average winter in Sinai has a short rainy season of about 20 days, with mist and dew at other times. And on certain occasions God may have sent rain unexpectedly to help His people (Jud 5:4; Ps 68:7–9). Yet when all allowances are made, one must recognize that the preservation of multiplied thousands of people and their animals for so long a period in that terrain, with their clothing still serviceable, can only be explained by special providence (Deut 8:2–4).

The Oasis of Elim. MPS

The Route of the Israelites

From Egypt to Sinai. While the traditions attaching to the present Mount Sinai (Jebel Musa) cannot be traced earlier than the first Christian centuries, the traditional route ascribed to the Israelites is not only a possible one but quite probable. The Lord deliberately removed the former slaves far from civilization and all caravan routes while He taught them and molded them into a functioning nation. Hence the isolation of the S Sinai peninsula was ideal for His purposes. On the other hand, some explorers such as Major C. S. Jarvis, one-time governor of Sinai, have suggested a northern candidate for Mount Sinai, such as Jebel Helal (2,920 feet). But it is less than 30 miles W of Kadesh-barnea and adjacent to the well-traveled trade route known as the Way of Shur (see above). The traditional location of Mount Sinai best fits the number of camp sites listed in Num 33:8–15 and a journey of at least 11 days from Horeb to Kadesh-barnea (Deut 1:2).

After Moses' and Miriam's victory songs (Ex 15:1–21), the Israelites marched southeastward into the Wilderness of Shur to avoid further contact with any Egyptians. Marah and Elim may be placed at the brackish 'Ain Hawarah and Wadi Gharandel with its oasis of many palms, respectively. A day's journey to the shore of the Red Sea (Num 33:10) would have brought Israel to a point N of the modern port of Abu Zenima, out of sight of Egyptians on the W shore of the Gulf of Suez. Such a huge group of people could only cover from five to 15 miles a day, which compares favorably with the distances between many of these stopping places.

The exact identities of the Wilderness of Sin (*see* Sin, Wilderness of), Dophkah, and Alush are still uncertain. Quail migrating northward in spring from the Sudan in Africa still fly low at night after crossing the Gulf of Suez (Ex 16:13). Thus the Wilderness of Sin where Israel was camping at the time was probably the broad plain known as el-Merkhah along the coast rather than the plain Debbet er-Ramleh farther inland near the Egyptian mines at Serabit el-Khadem.

Almost certainly Rephidim (*q.v.*) is the large oasis in the Wadi Feiran, where Moses would have anticipated finding adequate supplies of water and provender. But perhaps a drought had dried up the usually flowing streams, with the result that the people grumbled at his poor leadership (Ex 17:1–7). The steep, almost precipitous mountains arise directly from the narrow valleys in this region, affording Moses, Aaron, and Hur a safe observation post to watch Joshua's battle with the nomadic Amalekites (vv. 8–13).

At Mount Sinai the multitude no doubt encamped on the extensive plain of er-Râḫah before the jutting peaks of Ras eṣ-Ṣafṣafeh leading up to Jebel Musa. Here the Bedouin still dig shallow wells and obtain provisions from small oases in nearby valleys surrounding the Mount of the Law.

From Sinai to Kadesh-barnea. The itinerary left by Moses in Num 33 covers the journey from Rameses and Succoth in Egypt to the plains of Moab opposite Jericho. The campaign lists of the pharaohs beginning with Thutmose III, found at Thebes in Upper Egypt, also contain series of place names, which are quite certainly the stations along a particular line of march arranged in correct sequence (M. Noth, "Thebes," TAOTS, pp. 29–32). The encampments recorded in Moses' list after Sinai are thought perhaps to indicate the movements of the tabernacle at the command of the Lord: "Moses recorded their starting points in writing whenever they broke camp on Yahweh's orders" (Num 33:2, JerusB). The people, however, often must have scattered widely from the central camp, tending their flocks wherever water and vegetation could be found. The itinerary lists only formal encampments and does not mention every halting place for only a night (cf. Ex 15:22; Num 16:33).

In the accompanying table ten intervening encampments are assigned to the journey to Kadesh-barnea, on the basis of the statement in Deut 1:2 that it normally takes 11 days from Horeb (Mount Sinai), figuring about 20 miles a day for a single traveler or a merchant caravan. The Israelites, however, took much more time, spending perhaps a whole month at Taberah, where they again gathered quail by the shore of the Gulf of Aqabah (Num 11:18–21, 31–33) and at least seven days at Hazeroth (Num 12:15). It is puzzling that Kadesh is not mentioned in Num 33 at the end of this phase of Israel's journey; but Makheloth, which in Heb. means "places of assembly," may be another name for Kadesh-barnea (*q.v.*), considering the fact that several fine springs and oases—around which the people would congregate—are to be found in this vicinity.

Thirty-eight years of wandering in the Negeb. The few encampments which can be tentatively identified in the list of Num 33:26–35 suggest that for 38 years the Israelites meandered aimlessly in the the central and southern Negeb and the Arabah. It has been suggested that the thick, hard crust on certain mudflats in the Arabah could split open and let people sink into a deep mass of liquid mud and ooze, thus explaining the means of the punishment of Korah, Dathan, and Abiram in Num 16:27–33 (NBD, p. 1329). Aharoni identifies Jotbathah (33:33) with Ṭabeh, *c.* seven miles SW of Elath on the W shore of the Gulf of Aqabah (*Land of the Bible,* p. 183). Ebronah may be 'Ain ed-Dafiyeh, six miles N of modern Elath in the Arabah, or UMM Rashrash near the city (*God's Wilderness,* pp. 163 f.). It may be conjectured that at Ezion-geber the Israelites received a command to return to Kadesh, and marched directly to that region without setting up formal camp again.

From the Kadesh area to Gilgal. During the time of Moses the Edomites were still dwelling in the Negeb and the Wilderness of Zin between Kadesh-barnea and the Arabah (*see* Edom; Seir). Not until the 13th cen. B.C., according to Nelson Glueck's explorations, did they expand eastward and fortify the heights of Transjordan against nomadic marauders from the E. As semi-nomads themselves, most of them must still have been living in tent cities (cf. the tent cities of Midian, Num 31:10), which left few if any archaeological remains. Some, however, may have been conscripted to work in the copper mines near the 19th-20th Dynasty Egyptian mining temple at Timna in the Arabah.

The king of Edom refused to grant permission to Moses for the Israelites to march eastward along the "king's highway" to the Arabah (Num 20:14–21). Probably this ancient travel route led past Bir Hafir to Abdah and down the Wadi Fiqreh and the Scorpion Pass to 'Ain Hosb in the Arabah (Glueck, *Rivers in the Desert,* pp. 23, 205 f.). So God's people, after burying Aaron on Mount Hor NE of Kadesh-barnea (*see* Hor, Mount), turned around to head southward to the way of the Red Sea (see above) in order to march round the flank of Edom (Num 21:4, NEB). It took them many days to circle Mount Seir (Deut 2:1, NASB) by going to Ezion-geber and then proceeding northward along the Arabah. The NEB best brings out the geographical significance of Deut 2:8: "So we went on past our kinsmen, the descendants of Esau who live in Seir, and along the road of the Arabah which comes from Elath and Ezion-geber, and we turned and followed the road to the wilderness of Moab."

Before turning right into the Wadi el-Ḥesa and crossing the Zered, Israel camped at Punon (modern Feinan), on the E side of the Arabah. Here copper was mined in the Bronze Age, and it was probably here that Moses made a bronze or copper serpent to erect on a standard. A look at it was the antidote for Israelites bitten by the fiery serpents (Num 21:6-9).

After bypassing the Moabites, Moses led Israel across the gorge of the Arnon, far upstream to the E, into the territory which the Amorites under Sihon had captured from Moab. The order of towns in the table from 49 to 59 is based on the most direct line proceeding northward in accord with the newest evidence for the location of these sites. The last camp of the Israelites before entering Canaan was pitched in the plains or lowlands (*'arbôth*) of Moab at the E edge of the Jordan Valley. Apparently their tents spread over a wide area, from Beth-jeshimoth by the Dead Sea to Abel-shittim, a distance of nearly eight miles. Here Moses reviewed God's dealings with His covenant nation and led Israel to renew their vows to Yah-

40 YEARS OF JOURNEYINGS FROM EGYPT TO CANAAN

Narrative in Ex, Num, and Josh		Formal Encampments—Num 33		Allusions in Deut		Dated Events Mo Day Yr
		From Egypt to Sinai				
Passover	Ex 12:2, 6			Passover	Deut 16:1	1st 14th 1st
1. Rameses	12:37	Rameses	Num 33:3			1st 15th 1st
2. Succoth	12:37;13:20	Succoth	v. 5			
3. Etham	13:20	Etham	v. 6			
4. Pi-hahiroth	14:2	Pi-hahiroth	v. 7			
5. The sea	14:9	The sea	v. 8	Red Sea	11:4	
6. Wilderness of Shur	15:22	Wilderness of Etham	v. 8			
7. Marah	15:23	Marah	v. 8			
8. Elim	15:27;16:1	Elim	v. 9			
9.		Red Sea	v. 10			
10. Wilderness of Sin (manna given)	16:1	Wilderness of Sin	v. 11			2nd 15th 1st
11.		Dophkah	v. 12			
12.		Alush	v. 13			
*13. Rephidim (Massah, Meribah)	17:1–8;19:2	Rephidim	v. 14	Massah	6:16;9:17	
Battle with Amalek	17:8–13			Amalekites	25:17–18	
14. Wilderness of Sinai (Mount Horeb)	19:1–2	Wilderness of Sinai	v. 15	Horeb	4:10–14;5:2–5	3rd 1st 1st
Tabernacle erected	40:1–17					1st 1st 2nd
Passover observed	Num 9:1–5					1st 14th 2nd
Numbering ordered	1:1					2nd 1st 2nd
Departure from Sinai	10:11–12					2nd 20th 2nd
		From Sinai to Kadesh-barnea				
15. Taberah (Kibroth-hattaavah)	Num 11:1–34	Kibroth-hattaavah	v. 16	Taberah, Kibroth-hattaavah	9:22	
16. Hazeroth (at least 7 days)	11:35–12:15	Hazeroth	v. 17	Hazeroth (?)	1:1	
17.		Rithmah	v. 18	Miriam	24:9	
18.		Rimmon-parez	v. 19			
19.		Libnah	v. 20			
20.		Rissah	v. 21	(11 days'		
21.		Kehelathah	v. 22	journey from		
22.		Mount Shapher	v. 23	Horeb to Kadesh-		
23.		Haradah	v. 24	barnea. 1:2)		
24.		Makheloth	v. 25			
25. Wilderness of Paran, Kadesh	12:16;13:26			Kadesh-barnea	1:2,19	
Spies sent out in late summer						
at grape harvest time,	13:17–20					5th-6th 2nd
Israel sentenced to a total of				Rebellion at Kadesh	9:23	
40 years in the wilderness,	14:33–34					
Israel defeated in hill country,	14:45			Routed from Seir to Hormah	1:44	
		38 Years of Wandering in the Negeb				
26. —In the wilderness (Num 15:32)—		Tahath	v. 26	"By the way to the Red Sea"	1:40	
27.		Tarah	v. 27			
28.		Mithcah	v. 28	Dathan and Abiram (with Korah)	11:6	

WILDERNESS, WANDERING

29. – Korah's rebellion in the wilderness, perhaps in the Arabah (16:12)		Hashmonah	v. 29			
30.		Moseroth	v. 30			
31.		Bene-jaakan	v. 31	Beeroth-bene-jaakan	10:6	
32.		Hor-hagidgad	v. 32			
33.		Jotbathah	v. 33			
34.		Ebronah	v. 34			
35.		Ezion-geber	v. 35			
36. Wilderness of Zin, Kadesh	20:1–21	Wilderness of Zin, Kadesh	v. 36	Kadesh	1:46;32:51	1st 40th
Miriam's death; Moses' anger; messengers sent to Edom						
37. Mount Hor (Aaron's death)	20:22–29	Mount Hor	vv. 37–40	Moserah (Aaron's death)	10:6	5th 1st 40th
*38. Hormah (victory over king of Arad)	21:1–3					
		From Kadesh Area to Gilgal				
39. By the way of the Red Sea	Num 21:4			The way of the Red Sea	2:1	
40.				Gudgodah	10:7	
41.				Jotbathah	10:7	
42.				Elath, Ezion-geber along the Arabah road (NEB)	2:8	
43.		Zalmonah	v. 41			
44. Fiery serpents	21:5–9	Punon	v. 42	Fiery serpents	8:15	
45. Oboth	21:10	Oboth	v. 43			
46. Ije-abarim	21:11	Iye-abarim (Iyim)	vv. 44,45			
47. Valley of Zered	21:12			Brook Zered	2:13–15	
				38 years after the condemnation at Kadesh		
48. Valley of the Arnon	21:13–14			Ar. Arnon valley	2:18,24	
Ar of Moab (on S rim?)	21:15,28			Aroer (on N rim)	2:36	
49.		Dibon-gad	v. 45			
50. Beer	21:16					
51. Mattanah	21:18					
52.				Wilderness of Kedemoth	2:36–31	
53.		Almon-diblathaim	v. 46			
*54. Jahaz	21:23			Jahaz	2:32	
55. Nahaliel (a stream flowing SW from Heshbon)	21:19					
56. Bamoth	21:19					
57. Heshbon (Sihon's capital)	21:25					
58. Valley in Moab, below the summit of Mount Pisgah	21:20	Mountains of Abarim before (or E) of Nebo	v. 47			
*59. Jazer	21:32					
*60. Edrei (Og's capital in Bashan)	21:33			War with Og	3:1–10	
61. Plains (lowlands) of Moab beyond the Jordan opposite Jericho	22:1;36:13	Plains of Moab from Beth-jeshimoth to Abel-shittim	vv. 48–50	Land of Moab	1:5;29:1	
Idolatry at Shittim (25:1)						
62. – Moses' death				Mount Nebo the top of Pisgah	32:49;34:1–8	12th? 1st? 40th
30 days of mourning						
63. Shittim, E bank of the Jordan	Josh 2:1					
Crossing the Jordan	3:1–4:18					
64. Gilgal, camp set up	4:19					1st 10th 41st
Passover in Promised Land	5:10					1st 14th 41st
Manna ceases (40th anniv. of the Exodus)	5:11–12					1st 15th 41st

*A battle

weh. From here Moses went up to Mount Nebo's summit at Pisgah to see the Promised Land and then die (Deut 1:1, 5; 34:1–5). After 30 days of mourning Israel prepared to enter Canaan under their new leader Joshua.

See Exodus, Book of; Joshua; Moses.

Bibliography. Y. Aharoni, *Land of the Bible,* Philadelphia: Westminster, 1967. C. R. Conder, "Wanderings of Israel," ISBE, V, 3064–3069. John D. Davis, "Wilderness of the Wandering," *Davis Dictionary of the Bible,* 4th rev. ed., Grand Rapids: Baker, 1972, pp. 860–865. John J. Davis, *Moses and the Gods of Egypt,* Grand Rapids: Baker, 1971, pp. 173–193. Nelson Glueck, *Rivers in the Desert,* New York: Farrar, Straus & Cudahy, 1959. Siegfried H. Horn, "Wilderness Wandering," SDABD, pp. 1145–1148. K. A. Kitchen, "Wilderness of Wandering," NBD, pp. 1327–1330. Emil G. Kraeling, *Bible Atlas,* Chicago: Rand McNally, 1956, pp. 106–128. Beno Rothenberg, *God's Wilderness,* London: Thames and Hudson, 1961; "An Archaeological Survey of South Sinai," PEQ, CII (1970), 4–29.

J. R.

WILL OF GOD. One of the distinctive features of the Christian religion is its teaching that God is both spiritual and personal. This latter characteristic demands a will.

Biblical Terms

The Bible uses a variety of terms to denote the will. Common Heb. and Aram. words are *ḥāpēs* ("to delight, to desire, have pleasure"), *rāṣôn*, and *ṣᵉbā'* ("to will"), while the usual Gr. terms are *boulē, thelēma,* and *eudokia* ("good pleasure"). These words are applied to man as well as to God. Neither Heb. nor Gr. has a word for "will" in the technical psychological sense. In general the biblical languages are functional and practical. Heb. in particular has no words for abstractions, so that the actions ascribed to God and the various roles attributed to Him are of primary importance in the study of God's will.

The Will of God

The concept of "will" as applied to God in theology and the Bible does not always have the same connotation. It may denote His whole moral nature including His attributes, the faculty of self-determination (Ps 115:3; Dan 4:35), a predetermined plan as in the decree (Eph 1:9–10; Rev 4:11, ASV; etc.), the power to realize His plan and purpose (Prov 21:1; Rom 9:19; II Chr 20:6), or the rule of life imposed upon rational creatures, i.e., God's objective will, which one can keep (Mt 7:21; Jn 4:34; 7:17; Rom 12:2).

The divine will is the final cause of all things. It is absolute and unchangeable (Ps 33:11), unconditioned by anything outside Himself. Everything is the outworking of it: creation and preservation (Ps 135:6; Jer 18:6; Rev 4:11); government (Prov 21:1; Dan 4:35); election and reprobation (Rom 9:15–16; Eph 1:5); the death of Christ (Lk 22:42; Acts 2:23); salvation (Jas 1:18); sanctification (Phil 2:13); the sufferings of saints (I Pet 3:17); man's existence, course of life, and end (Acts 18:21; Rom 15:32; Jas 4:15); and even the smallest detail of life (Mt 10:29). *See* Works of God.

Since all things find their ultimate cause in the will of God, it is usual to distinguish between the efficacious and permissive aspects of God's will. The efficacious aspect of His will is accomplished causatively or actively. It is not only that which God wills, but also that which He desires. On the other hand, the permissive aspect of the divine will is permitted to occur by the unrestrained agency of rational creatures.

The will of God is revealed to men in a variety of ways: in the spoken word (Ex 3:14–18; Acts 1:8); in dreams and visions (Gen 41:1–32; Acts 16:6–10); in the natural world and historical events (Ps 89:9–10; Isa 46:10–11; 53:10, RSV); in the future kingdom of God (Eph 1:9–10); and in the sacred Scriptures (cf. Acts 20:27; I Pet 4:17, 19).

The Humanity of Jesus and the Will of God

During the early history of the church, two closely related questions about the person of Christ arose. Did Christ possess one nature or two? And how many wills did the theanthropic person have? The latter question gave rise to a group called the Monothelites. They argued that the unity of the person of Christ demanded a single will. This unity took two forms. Some taught that the human will was so merged with the divine that the latter alone acted, while others regarded the will as a composite, resulting from the fusion of the two wills. Those who opposed the Monothelites were called Duothelites. They argued that since there were two natures in the person of Christ, there must be two wills.

The sixth ecumenical Council of Constantinople (A.D. 680), which was held with the co-operation of the bishop of Rome, adopted the doctrine of two wills as the orthodox position, but also added that the human will of Christ must always be conceived as subservient to the divine. The human will rather than becoming less than human was heightened and perfected through the union, so that the two always acted in perfect harmony.

The Will of God in Relation to Sin

The doctrine of the will of God gives rise to a serious question concerning its relation to sin. If God is the final cause of all things that exist, is He not the author of sin? Such a problem cannot be completely resolved, and man must admit his ignorance in attempting to wholly comprehend God's ways. However, some of the more important proposed solutions are:

1. Augustine, coming from a background which included Manichaeism [a dualistic religious-philosophic school which viewed the uni-

verse as governed by two ultimate and radically opposed principles, good and evil—Editor's note], found this a pressing problem and sought a solution. He taught that good logically precedes evil, and that evil is the privation of some good. Therefore, evil is not something positive but a *nothing* or *lack*.

God created a material universe that was good. However, the creation is mutable, and therein exists the possibility of change. This change may be in the form of privation or evil.

Such an explanation gave Augustine a twofold answer to the aforementioned problem. First, it is meaningless to accuse someone of responsibility for nothing. Second, God created a *good* universe; it only contained the possibility for evil in that it was mutable. Therefore, the entrance of evil was subsequent and the "responsibility" of the creature (e.g., Lk 7:30).

2. Arminians have attempted to escape the difficulty by making the will of God to permit sin dependent upon foreknowledge of human choices. Then, the actions can be certain, but responsibility can be placed upon man.

3. Reformed theology has the greatest difficulty with this problem. These theologians candidly admit that they have no completely satisfactory solution. They hold that the divine decree includes the sinful acts of man (e.g., Acts 2:23), but at the same time they point out that this must be conceived in such a way as to absolve God of responsibility. This is customarily done by suggesting the distinction between that which God effectuates and that which He permits. *See* Sin.

The Will of God and the Will of Man

One of the mysteries concerning the doctrine of the will of God centers about the biblical teaching concerning the sovereignty of God and the responsibility of man. Does man's freedom condition and set limits upon the will of God? Or are all the actions of men determined in the sense that they become mere robots? Again, a solution is beyond the finite mind, as man is unable to understand the nature of divine knowledge and His comprehension of the laws which govern human conduct. Man is unable to comprehend how an act which appears to be free can nevertheless be willed by God and thus certain. No man can fully understand the will and the ways of God (Job 9:10; Isa 55:8-11; Rom 11:33; I Cor 2:9-11). However, the problem of relating the freedom which man thinks he experiences to the sovereignty of God becomes less acute if that freedom is understood as the ability to choose what one desires rather than the power of contrary or arbitrary choice.

How to Know the Will of God

Of great practical consequence to the believer is the question of how one may know the will of God. God does have a plan for the lives of His children which He desires to make known to them (Col 1:9; Heb 13:21). Before the completion of the written revelation of Scripture, God frequently made known His will by direct means (dreams, audible voice, theophanies, angels, etc.), but at best, such seem to be the exception now.

While God's ways of dealing with each person will be unique, there are six principles that are important for all. Briefly stated they are: (1) There must be an honest desire to know and a willingness to do God's will (Rom 12:1-2; Prov 3:5-6; Ps 40:8; 143:10; Jn 7:17). (2) God's will for a person now will always be in harmony with what is revealed in the written Word; God will not contradict Himself. Even Christ acted in complete harmony with the OT. This being the case, it behooves every believer to be saturated with the Bible (Ps 40:8; Josh 1:8). (3) God's will is made known in answer to prayer (I Jn 5:14; Col 1:9). (4) Circumstances *may be* an indication of God's leading, but in themselves they are not a reliable guide; for Satan can create propitious circumstances for his designs, while God may direct one into most difficult situations. (5) The believer should rely on the indwelling Holy Spirit to lead in and through the preceding factors (Rom 8:14; Gal 5:16, 25; I Jn 2:27). (6) Knowledge of God's will will bring with it peace of heart and mind (Phil 4:6-7; Col 3:15). If such assurance is absent, one should seriously question whether or not he has yet discerned the will of God for himself.

See Election; God; Sovereignty of God.

Bibliography. H. Bavinck, *The Doctrine of God,* Grand Rapids: Eerdmans, 1951, pp. 223-241. J. Oliver Buswell, *A Systematic Theology of the Christian Religion,* Grand Rapids: Zondervan, 1962, I, 263-269. J. Barton Payne, "Saul and the Changing Will of God," BS, CXXIX (1972), 321-325. G. Schrenk, *"Boulomai, Boulē,"* TDNT, I, 629-637; *"Eudokeō,* etc.," TDNT, II, 738-751; *"Thelō,* etc.," TDNT, III, 44-62.

P. D. F.

WILLOW. *See* Plants.

WILLOWS, BROOK OF THE. A willow fringed brook which long formed the boundary between Moab and Edom (Isa 15:7). The brook is usually identified with the Wadi el-Hesa or brook Zered.

WIMPLE. *See* Dress.

WINDOW. *See* House; Lattice.

WINDS. The Hebrews recognized four horizontal movements of air which they called wind. The S and SE winds crossing the Arabian Desert were hot and dry (Job 37:17; Lk 12:55). The N wind was cooler being favorable to vegetation (Song 4:16). The W, SW, and NW winds brought rain and accompanied a storm

(I Kgs 18:43–45; Ps 147:18; Ezk 13:13). The E wind was hot, gusty, and laden with sand. It was harmful to vegetation (Gen 41:6; Isa 11:15; Ezk 19:12; Jon 4:8).

The wind was recognized as God's creation (Ps 135:7; Amos 4:13) and was used as an instrument to perform His pleasure (Ex 14:21; Ps 78:26; 148:8; II Kgs 2:11) and His judgment (Ps 48:7; Jon 1:4). Men also used the wind to their advantage. It was important to the farmer in winnowing grain (Ps 1:4; 35:5; Isa 17:13) and to the sailor in sailing the ancient seas (Acts 27:40; 28:13; Jas 3:4).

Because the words for "wind" in the original languages (Heb. *rûaḥ*, Gr. *pneuma*) also mean "spirit" and "breath," the English terms are sometimes interchangeable, as in Ezk 37:5–9, 14. Christ illustrated the working of the Holy Spirit in regeneration by the invisible nature of the wind (Jn 3:8). One manifestation of the coming of the Holy Spirit on the day of Pentecost was described as a noise like a "violent, rushing wind" (Acts 2:2).

See Lightning; Rain; Holy Spirit; Whirlwind.

G. E. W.

Heads representing the four winds in a floor Mosaic at ancient Ostia, Italy. HFV

The NE wind about to unload hailstones, from the Tower of the Winds, Athens, first cen. B.C. HFV

WINE. Eleven different Heb. words are thus translated in the OT. The exact distinction between all these is difficult, indeed perhaps impossible to determine now. However, most of these are used only a few times. The main interest attaches to two OT words which are used a great many times: *yayin* (134 times) and *tîrôsh* (38 times). The NT counterpart is *oinos* (used 33 times).

Heb. *yayin* "seems to be used to describe 'all sorts of wine' (Neh 5:18), from the simple grape juice, or a thickened syrup, to the strongest liquors with which the Israelites were acquainted, the use of which often led to deplorable scenes of drunkenness" (Fairbairn, *Imperial Standard Bible Encyclopedia,* VI, 341). This is the word used in the first biblical reference to wine (Gen 9:21). It was intoxicating then, and caused Noah to fall into a disgraceful condition which proved the occasion for a serious sin on the part of his son Ham. Melchizedek brought forth bread and *yayin* for the refreshment of Abraham (Gen 14:18). Lot's incestuous daughters used it to bring their father to an inebriated condition (Gen 19:30–38). This word is used of the wine presented as a drink offering to the Lord (Ex 29:40, *et al.*).

The priests were forbidden to drink *yayin* when ministering in the tabernacle (Lev 10:9). It may be inferred that this is what caused the error of Nadab and Abihu which resulted in their destruction (Lev 10:1–2). It was likewise forbidden to the Nazarite during the time of his separation (Num 6:3, 20). The Rechabites refused to drink wine because a notable ancestor had commanded them not to do so (Jer 35:6–7). But his purpose was apparently to have them retain their simple, nomadic life rather than settling down to the dangerous luxuries of civilization.

Heb. *tîrôsh* is used for juice just pressed from the grapes, and frequently translated "new wine." Indeed, it is apparently used even to denote juice not yet squeezed from the grapes (Isa 65:8; Mic 6:15). As the juice was allowed to ferment, the lees, dregs or sediment, in settling to the bottom of the container, gave strength and flavor to the wine. Before being served the wine would be filtered to eliminate the dregs (*see* Dregs; Lees). Only once is intoxication presumably suggested in connection with the word *tîrôsh* (Hos 4:11), but the Talmud makes clear it, too, could be fermented.

Gr. *oinos* is the rendering in the LXX of both Heb. terms. All the NT references to wine except one (Acts 2:13) use this word. The Gr. term refers to "wine, normally the fermented juice of the grape" (Arndt, p. 564). The process of fermentation is evidently referred to in Mk 2:22, and the juice when first placed in the wineskins is called "new *oinos*." At the Cana marriage feast, the Lord Jesus turned the water into *oinos*, and it was praised as far better than that which had been used previously (Jn 2:1-10).

Vinegar (Heb. *ḥōmeṣ*, Gr. *oxos*) in the Bible refers to sour wine, wine vinegar which was cheaper than regular wine and thus a favorite beverage of the lower ranks of society (Ruth 2:14). The prophecy in Ps 69:21, "In my thirst they gave me vinegar to drink," had a fulfillment at the time of Jesus' suffering on the cross (Mt 27:48; Mk 15:36; Lk 23:36; Jn 19:28-30). Roman soldiers drank a thin, sour wine called in Latin *acetum*, "vinegar, sour wine."

Total abstinence or moderation? Much argument has raged among Bible students as to whether the Scriptures teach total abstinence or sanction moderate use of wine. Authorities can be found who insist that when fermented wine is referred to, it is always by way of condemnation, and that the verses which seem to commend the use of wine always have in view the unfermented juice (John W. Haley, *Alleged Discrepancies of the Bible*, p. 252).

It is doubtful that this thesis can be maintained, however. All agree that the Bible uniformly condemns the winebibber or drunkard (Prov 23:20-21) and drunkenness and overindulgence in wine (Prov 20:1; 21:17; 23:30-31; Isa 5:22; 28:7; Joel 1:5; Amos 6:6; Hab 2:5; Eph 5:18; I Tim 3:8; Tit 2:3). But wine is suggested for medicinal purposes by Paul to Timothy (I Tim 5:23). Jesus Himself must have partaken of some wine in order to be wrongfully classed among the "winebibbers" (Mt 11:19; Lk 7:34). Believers, however, are recommended to abstain from wine if it should put a stumbling block before a weaker brother (Rom 14:21). Many who acknowledge that the Bible does not absolutely forbid the use of wine, nevertheless feel that "a sound case can be made for total abstinence on the basis of biblical principles" (Roland H. Bainton, "Total Abstinence and Biblical Principles," CT, July 7, 1958, pp. 3-6).

Figurative use. Wine is pictured as "making glad the heart of man" (Ps 104:15). It is thus used as a metaphor for the joy and gladness which the salvation of the Lord brings (Isa 55:1; Zech 10:7). Jesus likened His teaching of the kingdom and a new creation to new wine which would burst the old wineskins of Jewish tradition (Mt 9:17). When nations are inexorably forced to endure awful judgments at the hands of God, this is sometimes pictured as their being made to drink a cup full "of the wine of the fierceness of his wrath" (Jer 25:15; 51:7; Rev 14:10; 16:19). To become intoxicated with false teachings and evil principles is symbolized under the figure of becoming drunk with wine (Rev 14:8; 17:2; 18:3).

See Banquet; Drink; Drink, Strong; Drunkenness; Plants: Grape, Vine; Vineyard.

G. C. L.

WINEPRESS. The vat or trough used for pressing the juice from grapes. Heb. *yeqeb*, used about 16 times in the OT, is from a root meaning "to excavate." "All winepresses [were] sunk in the ground, in a hole that had been dug out or hewn in the rock" (Keil and Delitzsch, *Joshua, Judges, Ruth*, p. 331). In Christ's parable of the vineyard, the owner "digged a winepress [Gr. *lēnos*] in it" (Mt 21:33). *See* Vineyard. *Yeqeb* may refer either to the upper winepress in which the grapes were crushed, or the lower one into which the juice drained. This grape juice in its still unfermented state is sometimes called "must" or, in the English Bible, "new wine."

The method of squeezing out (or expressing) the juice from the grapes was either by the application of a heavy weight or, more frequently, by treading on them with the bare feet. "It was a simple but sufficient arrangement, and modern ingenuity has not much improved on it. Nor has any effectual substitute been found for the human foot as an apparatus for expressing the juice of the grape without crushing the seeds or 'stones'" (Fairbairn, *Imperial Standard Bible Encyclopaedia*, VI, 316). This process of expressing the juice by treading on the grapes with the feet is referred to many times in the OT (e.g., Job 24:11; Neh 13:15).

The "treading of the grapes," so familiar to people of Bible days, is used as a figure for the awful slaughter which took place at the Babylonian destruction of Jerusalem (Lam 1:15). Since this was a judgment from God, He is pictured as the Treader with the blood of the young men gushing forth like the must in the winepress. The same figure is applied to the Messiah when He comes the second time "in flaming fire taking vengeance on them that know not God" (II Thess 1:8; cf. Isa 63:2-3; Joel 3:13; Rev 14:19-20; 19:15). All these prophecies have in view the awful bloodshed which will take place at the battle of Armageddon. Isa 63:2-3 has often been misapplied to Christ's shedding His own blood for us at His first coming when, it is said, He "trod the winepress alone." "The impossibility of such a sense in the original passage cannot be too strongly stated" (J. A. Alexander, *Commentary on the Prophecies of Isaiah*, II, 415). Biederwolf is right when he writes: "He treads the winepress not as a sufferer but as an inflicter" (*The Millennium Bible*, p. 125).

G. C. L.

WING. Heb. *kānāp* and Gr. *pteryx* signify: (1) "wing," as of a bird or insect; or (2) "extremity," as the corner of a garment or temple protuberance (Gr. *pterygion,* "pinnacle," Mt 4:5). Wings, symbolic of swiftness and strength, frequently adorned animal figures in the ancient Near East, e.g., the Assyrian winged lions and bulls, winged sphinxes, etc. In Scripture, the cherubim on the ark possessed wings (Ex 37:9), as did the seraphim of Isaiah's vision (Isa 6:2), and Ezekiel's "living creatures" (Ezk 1:5–6; cf. Rev 4:8). The two women of Zechariah's vision had wings of a stork (Zech 5:9).

Figurative usage conveys various ideas. An invader "shall fly as an eagle, and shall spread out his wings against Moab" (Jer 48:40, ASV). "Hide me under the shadow of thy wings" is David's prayer for divine protection (Ps 17:8; cf. Ruth 2:12; Mt 23:37). The term depicts the swift departure of riches (Prov 23:5); the wind's movements (Ps 18:10); and the sun's beams (Ps 139:9; Mal 4:2). God's deliverance of Israel is described under the figure of bearing them on "eagles' wings" (Ex 19:4; cf. Isa 40:31). In Isa 11:12 *kānāp* signifies the extremity or ends of the earth, and in Ruth 3:9 the corner of Boaz's garment spread over Ruth.

H. E. Fr.

WINNOW. *See* Agriculture.

WINTER. The heaviest rainy season in Palestine is in the winter. This is reflected in both the Heb. and Gr. words which are used. Heb. *ḥōreph* refers to the harvest and to the cold and rain which begin then (Prov 20:4, "cold").

The king enjoyed a winter house (*q.v.*) with its open fire (Jer 36:22). Heb. *s^ethāw,* from Akkad. *šatū,* "be watered," is found only in Song 2:11, and here the basic idea shows forth: "For, lo, the winter is past, the rain is over."

In the NT the distinctive Gr. word for winter is *cheimōn.* Its basic meaning is "winter storm" or "stormy weather." This is evidenced by the fact that while it is four times translated "winter," it is once rendered "tempest" (Acts 27:20) and once "foul weather" (Mt 16:3). And in two of the places where it is translated "winter" (Mt 24:20; Mk 13:18) it means bad traveling weather (cf. Acts 27:12, where the verb "to winter" is used).

R. E.

WINTERHOUSE. A residence for the cold season used by wealthy people (Amos 3:15). In Jer 36:22 the winterhouse probably referred to a part of Jehoiakim's palace exposed to the winter sun and used because of its warmth.

WISDOM (NT). While wisdom is personified in the OT in the book of Proverbs and shown to have existed eternally in God (Prov 8:22–30), it is centered in one person, the Lord Jesus Christ (I Cor 1:30; Col 2:2–3; cf. Lk 11:49).

Christ in His human nature increased in wisdom and stature and in favor with God and man (Lk 2:52), but in His divine nature there rested upon Him the sevenfold Spirit whose primary attribute is wisdom (Isa 11:2). As a result, men asked, "Whence hath this man this wisdom?" (Mt 13:54; Mk 6:2), not realizing that a greater than Solomon was here (Mt 12:42). Of him Paul writes that He is the power and the wisdom of God, stressing that Christ's life and death were God's wise plan of salvation (I Cor 1:24).

The Greeks with their philosophy sought wisdom (I Cor 1:22) and produced such great men as Plato and Aristotle, but did not come to know God. God in His infinite wisdom, by contrast, used the word of the cross to reveal the way man can be saved. The gospel proved to be a stumbling block to the Jews, who were trying to obtain salvation by good works (Rom 9:30–33); and "foolishness" (Gr. *mōria,* the thoughts of a simpleton, too simple altogether to be accepted as the true knowledge of salvation) to the learned Greeks (I Cor 1:23). The Jews were offended at the thought of the crucifixion and that they were so impotent someone must die for their sins. The Greeks considered simple faith in a substitutionary atonement too easy a way to salvation. Yet the atoning death of the Lord Jesus Christ is the epitome of all wisdom (Eph 3:10) since it solves the greatest problem of the world and man, namely, sin.

The deeper man studies into his condition and his need for salvation, and the problem entailed in making this possible, the greater proves to be the wisdom of the cross. Salvation must be equally possible for all, wise and simple, and justification by faith alone meets this need. It must meet the needs of a holy God who required that the covenant of works be kept perfectly, and the perfect sinless Son of God who became man met this need. It must be sufficient not merely for the man who kept the law and fulfilled the covenant of works perfectly, but for all men. Only the infinite satisfaction of one who was both God and man could meet this need.

While Paul did not preach according to the wisdom of the world, still he preached the hidden wisdom of God which can be discerned only as God gives man the guidance and help of the Holy Spirit (I Cor 2:7–14).

God is desirous that man have and know His wisdom (Jas 1:5). It is spiritual and consists in the knowledge of His will (Col 1:9; Eph 1:8–9). It is "from above" and is contrasted with the earthly, human wisdom of this world which can even be demon-inspired (Jas 3:13–17; cf. Col 2:23; I Cor 3:19–20; II Cor 1:12). God's wisdom must be revealed or "given" to men (Rom 11:33–34; II Pet 3:15; Lk 21:15). This may be imparted through the Word of God and by the human teaching of it (Col 3:16; 1:28; Rev 13:18; 17:9). As in the case of the wisdom (Heb. *ḥokmâ*) of the book of Proverbs, it enables the believer to know how to conduct him-

WISDOM LITERATURE, OLD TESTAMENT

self toward other people and make the most of his spiritual opportunities (Col 4:5). *See* Wisdom Literature, OT. For the word of wisdom as one of the charismatic gifts (I Cor 12:8), *see* Gifts, Spiritual.

Bibliography. U. Wilckens and G. Fohrer, "*Sophia,* etc.," TDNT, VII, 465-528.

R. A. K.

WISDOM LITERATURE, OLD TESTAMENT. The main words used for wisdom in the OT are *ḥokmâ* (used 146 times), *bînâ,* and *t^ebûnâ.* The latter two are often translated "understanding" (*q.v.*). The word *tûshiyyâ* is used a few times to mean "sound wisdom," or "enterprise." The adjective *ḥākām,* "wise," is used 102 times and as "wise men" 15 times. Well over half of the instances of the use of these words is found in Job, Proverbs and Ecclesiastes, which are often called the wisdom books. Material of a somewhat similar cast is known both from Egypt and Babylon. Thus, Wisdom Literature is a wide category of writing in the ancient Near East.

The wisdom books of the OT, however, are quite varied in structure and content. The handling of the word "wisdom" is also different in these different books and in the other parts of the OT. In Exodus the skill of the builders of the tabernacle is called wisdom and it is said to be a gift of God. The statecraft and judgment of Solomon, Daniel, and others is likewise regarded as a skill and is called wisdom. It is ascribed to God. This is the usual usage of the OT aside from the wisdom books.

In Ecclesiastes, "wisdom" is considered in contrast to other things as a possible highest goal of life and as such it is rejected. Wisdom excels folly, it is true, but the wise man dies just as does the fool (Eccl 2:16). An example is given of wisdom that does not profit (Eccl 9:17-18). A city was besieged and a wise man delivered it. But the wise man was forgotten. Wisdom here is used to mean intelligence or skill. But it is not highly regarded. "In much wisdom is much grief: and he that increaseth knowledge increaseth sorrow" (Eccl 1:18).

The word is used less often in Job and is not a major feature of the book, which has as a major theme, "Why do the righteous suffer?" Usually the word refers to intelligence and is used by Job and his comforters alike. But there is a very distinctive use in Job 28, a chapter devoted to the praise of wisdom. Wisdom and understanding as used in this chapter, however, are not mere intelligence, but rectitude. Job 28:28 amounts to a new definition, "The fear of the Lord, that is wisdom; and to depart from evil is understanding."

The usage of "wisdom" in Proverbs is quite distinctive and is exactly like that in Job 28. In the first of the book (Prov 1:7), at the end of the first section (9:10), and at the end of the book (31:26-30), "wisdom" is defined in religious terms. "Wisdom" here is not mere skill or intelligence. It is rectitude; it is a moral and religious quality. Proverbs is the wisdom book *par excellence* (cf. "Proverbs," WBC, pp. 553-583). In Proverbs 1-9 "wisdom" is personified as a righteous woman. This is natural, for "wisdom" in Heb. is a feminine noun. The contrast is drawn with the foolish woman, the harlot. Notice that the opposite of "wisdom" is not ignorance, but sin. In Prov 9:4, 16 the contrast is most pointed. Wisdom and the foolish woman give the same call to passersby. The one calls to the fear of the Lord; the other calls to sin. In Prov 8 "wisdom" is presented as the companion of God in creation and providence. The personification is so striking that many have taken Prov 8:22 ff. to be an adumbration of Christ (*see* Wisdom). In the remainder of Proverbs also there are many encomiums of the wise man. He is contrasted with the foolish son in 10:1 and 15:20 (where the foolish son sins in dishonoring a parent). The wise winner of souls in 11:30 is apparently the righteous man of v. 31. The law of the wise in 13:14 is equated with the fear of the Lord in 14:27. A wise king is one who scatters away evil (20:8, 26). Indeed, the words of the wise are an invitation to trust in the Lord (22:17-19).

Parallels of the biblical Wisdom Literature to other wisdom literature of the Orient are not impressive. The *Story of Ahikar* (ANET, pp. 426-430) is a story of a wise man under King Sennacherib who fell out of favor with the king, but was reinstated in due time. A copy was found among the Elephantine papyri dating to about 400 B.C. There is some suggestion that this copy, used by Jews in Egypt, shows a dependence on Prov 23:14 (see the author's commentary, *in loc.*). The *Wisdom of Amen-em-Opet* of Egypt (ANET, pp. 421-424) has some parallels with Proverbs, but more, perhaps, in its arrangement into 30 chapters (like the 30 sections alleged in Prov 22:17–24:22). The Babylonian work *I Will Praise the Lord of Wisdom* (ANET, pp. 434-437) is sometimes called the Babylonian Job. The *Dialogue about Human Misery* (ANET, pp. 438 f.) is likened by some to Ecclesiastes. Various Sumerian proverbs are known, written in the short maxim style. They have been described by S. N. Kramer in *History Begins at Sumer* (Garden City, N. Y.: Doubleday Anchor, 1959), pp. 117-126. All these works have no real relation to the teaching of the biblical books. In general, the biblical Wisdom Literature includes types of literature found in the ancient world, but expresses the unique biblical teaching of the fear of God, the chief end of man, and the triumph of the godly man over suffering and evil.

Bibliography. G. L. Archer, *A Survey of Old Testament Introduction,* Chicago: Moody Press, 1964, pp. 438-472. M. Noth and D. W. Thomas, eds., *Wisdom in Israel and the Ancient Near East,* Leiden: Brill, 1955. R. B. Y. Scott, "The Wisdom Movement and Its Literature," *Proverbs, Ecclesiastes,* The Anchor Bible, Garden City, N. Y.: Doubleday, 1965, pp. xv-liii; *The Way of Wisdom in the Old*

Testament, New York: Macmillan, 1971.

R. L. H.

WISE MEN. *See* Magi.

WITCH. *See* Familiar Spirit; Magic; Saul; Sorcery.

WITHERED. *See* Diseases.

WITNESS. One who gives his witness to the actions and words of others and to events, even to becoming a martyr.

The biblical view. According to the biblical view, the writers of Scripture made their records under the guidance of the Holy Spirit, so that their original writings were infallible both as to word and deed. As true witnesses they recorded the very words of God.

The neoorthodox view. The modernists, and neoorthodox scholars in particular, see the writings of the Bible as a mere witness to the experience of revelation in the lives of the biblical persons and writers. Insisting that God is timeless and spaceless and that truth with Him is contemporaneous—that is, past, present and future are one homogeneous eternal now—they cannot admit direct communication between God and man in any verbalized form. They therefore reject all propositional revelation, that is, revelation of truth in the form of verbalized statements or propositions. When this view is adopted, man's witness can only be to an ineffable, inexpressible, subjective experience. This makes it impossible to accept the words, "Thus spake the Lord," in any real or literal sense.

Different kinds of witness

1. Things can be witnesses, such as the presence of a heap of stones (Gen 31:44-52), a particular stone which "heard" God speak (Josh 24:27), an altar set up on the border of Egypt (Isa 19:19-20), a literary witness such as a song (Deut 31:19-21; Ps 78), or the law of God (Deut 31:26).

2. A witness in the tabernacle to the presence of God (Num 17:7-8; II Chr 24:6). The word for witness (*'ēdût*) is usually translated "testimony," and refers (e.g., Ex 25:16; 31:18) to the two stone tablets of the decalogue, the written witness of the pact between Yahweh and Israel.

3. People are witnesses. The witness of two or more was required in legal proceedings (Deut 19:15; Mt 18:16; II Cor 13:1; I Tim 5:19; Heb 10:28) and in the transfer of property (Jer 32:6-25, 44; cf. Ruth 4:9-11).

4. People as witnesses for God (Isa 43:10, 12; 44:8; Lk 24:48; Jn 1:7; 5:31-35; Acts 1:8). The most important witnesses in the NT were the apostles (Jn 15:27; Acts 1:21-22; 3:15; 5:32; I Thess 2:10; I Pet 5:1; I Jn 1:2), and particularly Paul (Acts 22:15; 26:16). All believers are to be His witnesses also (Acts 1:8; 13:31; Mt 28:19-20). *See* Commission, Great; Evangelist; Martyr.

5. The Holy Spirit gives an inner witness to the believing Christian that he is a child of God (Rom 8:16; I Jn 3:24; 4:13; 5:10). *See* Witness of the Spirit. The Spirit continually bears witness of Christ in this present age (Jn 15:26; I Jn 5:6, 8). Often this is by the Word (Heb 10:15-17). Furthermore, He may witness by means of the charismatic gifts (cf. Acts 4:31, 33; 20:23; Heb 2:4). See Bernard Ramm, *The Witness of the Spirit,* Grand Rapids: Eerdmans, 1960.

True and false witness. Bearing false witness was condemned in the OT (Ex 20:16; 23:1; Deut 5:20) and was to be punished with the same penalty as the crime to which the false witness was given (Deut 19:16-19; cf. Prov 14:5).

Bibliography. R. Kenneth Strachan, *The Inescapable Calling,* Grand Rapids: Eerdmans, 1968. H. Strathmann, "*Martys,* etc.," TDNT, IV, 474-514.

R. A. K.

WITNESS OF THE SPIRIT. The key text for this subject is Rom 8:15-16. The following translation is suggested: "In the fact that we cry 'Father' in familiar language [lit., 'Abba, Father'], the Spirit Himself bears witness with our spirit that we are children of God" (suggested in Nestle's marg.).

It is an observable fact that a born-again person in prayer speaks to God not as to the Judge whose penalties are the sanctions of the law, but as to his Father in whose gracious love he trusts. If a child of God finds himself in sin, his thought is not, "I stand liable to penalty," but, "I have wounded my Father!" The fact that we spontaneously cry to God as to our Father is evidence from the Holy Spirit that we are children of God.

The same teaching is brought out in Gal 4:6, "Because you are sons, God has sent forth the Spirit of His Son into our hearts, crying 'Father' in familiar language" (orig. trans.).

John gives the same thought in different words: "The one who believes in the Son of God has the witness in himself" (I Jn 5:10*a*, NASB). The nature of this witness is revealed in the preceding verses. "It is the Spirit who bears witness, because the Spirit is the truth" (v.7, NASB).

The symbolism of the water and the blood does not involve separate witnesses, because the three are one (v.8). The Spirit does not bear witness in a vacuum, nor merely in our subjective experience, but in historical facts and outward scriptural symbols (water and blood). Nevertheless, it is the inner witness of the Spirit in our hearts which makes these outward historical matters significant.

This witness of the Spirit is the "anointing" referred to in I Jn 2:20-21, 27 (cf. Jn 16:13). A word of caution is necessary in the reading of these promises. We are not given omniscience, but we are given *the* truth. For example, I Jn

2:20–21 does not say "ye know all things" (*panta*), but it says, "ye all (*pantes*) know. . .the truth."

The "understanding" given to us (I Jn 5:20) is from this same witness of the Spirit. "We know that the Son of God has come and has given us understanding [discernment] in order that we might know Him who is true" (NASB).

The witness of the Spirit is given in the Scripture. The words, "The Holy Spirit witnesses to us . . ." (Heb 10:15), introduce an OT quotation, and "the Holy Spirit says . . ." is used similarly (Heb 3:7). The witness of the Spirit in the Word was emphasized by the Westminster churchmen in 1646: "Our . . . assurance of the infallible truth [of the Bible] . . . is from the inward work of the Holy Spirit bearing witness by and with the Word in our hearts." Further, "The Supreme Judge . . . can be no other but the Holy Spirit speaking in Scripture" (*Confession* I:V, X).

The Holy Spirit not only bears witness in the hearts of God's children, but the manifest presence of the Spirit is a witness to their genuine faith. The saying that by faith the elders "received a good report," literally means, "they were attested by witness" (Heb. 11:2, 39). The Holy Spirit in the life of God's children bears "fruit" (Gal 5:22–23), and constitutes a "seal" or evidence or attestation of our regeneration (Eph 1:13; 4:30; II Cor 1:22).

See Holy Spirit.

Bibliography. Bernard Ramm, *The Witness of the Spirit*, Grand Rapids: Eerdmans, 1959.

J. O. B.

WIZARD. The word "wizard" means literally "a knowing one" in Heb., just as it does in its original English meaning. The knowledge is of an esoteric and supernatural nature, and those who possess it are either demons (II Kgs 21:6; II Chr 33:6) or those who through special powers have contact with demons (Lev 20:27; Deut 18:11). The Israelites were forbidden contact with all such beings and warned against such wisdom from below (Lev 19:31; Isa 8:19; 19:3). *See* Demonology; Divination; Familiar Spirit.

WOLF. *See* Animals, II.41.

WOMAN. The Heb. word *'ishshâ*, "woman, wife," is thought to be derived from a root *'-n-sh*, "to be soft, delicate." While it is similar to Heb. *'îsh*, "man," there is an intentional contrast in meaning, for *'îsh* seems to come from a root *'-y-sh*, "to be strong" (BDB, pp. 35, 61). Heb. *n^eqēbâ*, "female," is a term based on a physiological description of the sexual characteristic (from *nāqab*, "to perforate").

It is important to recognize that when God created mankind (Heb. *'ādām*), when He made human beings in His image, He created them both male and female (Gen 1:27; 5:1–2; Mt 19:4), not one or the other. Therefore the image of God appears equally in man the male and woman the female, and the peculiar personality characteristics of each sex are needed fully to mirror the nature of God. The very word *'ishshâ* for "woman" suggests her special God-given sensitivities and gifts in the emotional realm. These serve to enhance mankind. Woman has a special sensitivity to human needs which enables her to understand intuitively the situations and feelings of other people.

Because the woman was formed out of the man (Gen 2:21–23) and for the man's sake, the Bible assigns headship to the man (I Cor 11:7–9). In the divine order man's authority over his wife is based on priority of creation, not on superiority (I Tim 2:12–13). As in the case of the Son to the Father within the triune Godhead, the woman's position of dependence indicates a difference of function, not inferiority. Woman was created to be man's partner, a "help meet" for him (Gen 2:18, 20), i.e., "a helper suitable for him" (NASB), literally, "corresponding to him." Thus "she is man's complement, essential to the perfection of his being. . . Man and woman are endowed for equality, and are mutually interdependent" (Dwight M. Pratt, "Woman," ISBE, V, 3100). The husband's delegated rulership over his wife was made necessary by the fall, not creation (Gen 3:16; I Tim 2:14).

In Hebrew society the ordinary woman had a secondary position legally and was considered part of a man's property (Gen 31:14–15; Ruth 4:5, 10). Normally daughters received no inheritance when their father died (cf. Num 27:1–8). Practically, however, the woman's status was one of dignity, especially as a wife and mother in the home (Ex 20:12; Lev 19:3; Deut 21:18). Disrespect toward her was severely punished (Lev 20:9; Deut 27:16). She also shared in the religious life of the community (Deut 12:12, 18; I Sam 1:7–19, 24; 2:19).

Women participated in the arts such as in singing and dancing (Ex 15:20; Jud 21:19–21; II Chr 35:25) and in skilled weaving for the tabernacle (Ex 35:25–26). They could take part in business such as in real estate ventures (Prov 31:16; Acts 5:1) and in the manufacture and sale of linen garments and tents (Prov 31:24; Acts 16:14; 18:2–3). Some even played a significant role in political and military life, e.g., Deborah, Bathsheba (I Kgs 1:11 ff.), and two wise women in Israel (II Sam 14:2–20; 20:16–22). Huldah the prophetess was consulted regarding the newly found book of the law and prophesied a message for the king (II Kgs 22:14–20).

Only the men in Israel were required to attend the three annual festivals (Ex 23:17), but this ordinance seems to have been a humane concession because of the inconveniences of childbirth and the woman's responsibility for the children in the home (cf. I Sam 1:22). She possessed full rights of participation when she could attend (Num 6:2; Deut 16:11, 14). She could even go without her husband to monthly (new moon) and weekly (sabbath) services (II Kgs 4:23). Women could "publish the word" (Ps 68:11, KJV) or "proclaim the good tidings" (NASB). Their restriction to a separate "court of the women" in Herod's temple (Jos *Ant.* xv. 11.5; *Wars* v.5.2) was an intertestamental and unbiblical innovation that developed out of Judaism corrupted by contact with the Hellenistic world (J. B. Payne, *The Theology of the Older Testament,* Grand Rapids: Zondervan, 1962, p. 229). In ancient Gr. society women were considered inferior to men, intermediate between freemen and slaves. Wives led lives of seclusion and practical slavery. "Chastity and modesty, the choice inheritance of Heb. womanhood, were foreign to the Gr. conception of morality, and disappeared from Rome when Gr. culture and frivolity entered" (ISBE, V, 3101).

The gospel of Christ brought a revolution in the status of women, God's favor to the Virgin Mary being the starting point (Lk 1:28, 30, 42, 48). Jesus taught women (Jn 4:10–26; 11:20–27) and received their acts of kindness and financial support (Lk 8:3; 10:38–42: 23:56). They are to be considered as spiritual equals in Christ (Gal 3:28).

After Jesus' resurrection the women united with the other disciples in prayer and full fellowship (Acts 1:14). Therefore they evidently helped to elect Matthias (1:15–26). They received the power and gifts of the Holy Spirit along with the men on the day of Pentecost (Acts 2:1–11, 17–18). In the life of the early churches women were always among the first believers (Acts 5:14; 12:12; 16:14–15; 17:4, 34). Some like Lydia, Priscilla, and Phoebe were outstanding as fellow-workers with Paul and as women in whose homes churches met (Rom 16:1–5). While Christian women were permitted to pray and prophesy in the church meetings (I Cor 11:2–16; Acts 21:9), the NT does not allow them to usurp leadership in public worship (I Tim 2:12) or to exercise authority over men in the matter of judging the prophets (I Cor 14:29–35).

See Eve; Family; Marriage; Mother; Veil.

Bibliography. Argye M. Briggs, *Christ and Modern Woman,* Grand Rapids: Eerdmans, 1958. C. E. Cerling, Jr., "An Annotated Bibliography of the New Testament Teaching About Women," JETS, XVI (1973), 47–53. Jean Danielou, *The Ministry of Women in the Early Church,* London: Faith Press, 1961. James B. Hurley, "Did Paul Require Veils or the Silence of Women? A Consideration of I Cor 11:2–16 and I Cor 14:33b–36," WTJ, XXXV (1973), 190–220. J. Jeremias, *Jerusalem in the Time of Jesus,* Philadelphia: Fortress, 1969, Appendix I (pp. 359–376). L. M. Muntingh, "The Social and Legal Status of a Free Ugaritic Female," JNES, XXVI (1967), 102–112. Eugenia Price, *God Speaks to Women Today,* Grand Rapids: Zondervan, 1964. Harold J. Ockenga, *Women Who Made Bible History,* Grand Rapids: Zondervan, 1962. A. Oepke, *"Gynē,"* TDNT, I, 776–789. Russell Prohl, *Women in the Church,* Grand Rapids: Eerdmans, 1957. Charles C. Ryrie, *The Place of Women in the Church,* New York: Macmillan, 1958. Krister Stendahl, *The Bible and the Role of Women,* trans. by E. T. Sander, Philadelphia: Fortress, 1966. Clarence J. Vos, *Woman in Old Testament Worship*, Delft: Judels & Brinkman, 1968.

J. R.

WONDER, WONDERFUL. Among the many terms in the Bible expressing the greatness of God is the word "wonderful." This is one of the names of Messiah. "His name shall be called Wonderful, Counsellor. . ." (Isa 9:6), or, as RSV and NASB translate, "Wonderful Counselor" (cf. Isa 28:29). It is also the way in which the angel of the Lord revealed himself to Manoah, "Why do you ask my name, seeing it is wonderful?" (Jud 13:18, RSV, NASB). The Lord is "the God that doest wonders" (Ps 77:14), who alone "doeth wondrous things" (Ps 72:18; cf. 136:4). He refers to the miraculous judgment which He will execute against Egypt and His mighty deeds of deliverance for Israel as His wonders (Ex 3:20; cf. Ps 106:7). *See* Miracles.

The most frequently used Heb. root meaning "wonder" is *pālā'*. It indicates something unusual (a "singular" vow, Lev 27:2), extraordinary (Jonathan's love for David, II Sam 1:26), beyond one's power and hence difficult (II Sam 13:2; Zech 8:6, NASB), or something hard to be understood (Job 42:3; Ps 139:6; Prov 30:18). When used of God it speaks of His supernatural acts and of His omnipotence. Jeremiah knew God well enough to say, "Behold, Thou hast made the heavens and the earth by Thy great power and by Thine outstretched arm! Nothing is too difficult for thee" (Jer 32:17, NASB; KJV "too hard for thee"; cf. 32:27; Gen 18:14). *See* Marvel.

The Heb. word *mōpēt* means a wonder, a sign or symbol (Isa 20:3; Zech 3:8, NASB) or a portent of a future event (I Kgs 13:3, 5). As "wonder" it points to a special display of supernatural power performed directly by God (Ex 7:3; 11:9; Joel 2:30), by one of His servants (Ex 4:21; 11:10), or by a false prophet (Deut 13:1–2). It is usually translated in the LXX by Gr. *teras,* a strange phenomenon to be watched or observed. In the NT this word always appears in the plural in conjunction with "sign" (*sēmeia*). *See* Sign.

J. R.

WOOD. *See* Plants.

WOOD OF EPHRAIM. *See* Ephraim, Wood of.

WOODCUTTER. *See* Hew; Occupations: Woodcutter.

WOOL. *See* Dress; Animals: Sheep, I. 15.

WORD. The "word" is the characteristic means whereby God makes known His will to man. The form may vary. It may be spoken through the prophets, written in the law and other Scriptures, or living in the person of Jesus Christ. It is also the means by which God accomplishes His providential purposes in the world.

Biblical Terms

In the OT the most important terms are from the Heb. root *dbr,* although *'ōmer, 'imrâ,* and *mālâ* are also found. The etymology of *dbr* is a matter of dispute. Probably, it is wisest to associate the root meaning with "to speak." A "word" is essentially an utterance. This root is also sufficient to explain the derivative words "matter," "affair," or "thing," as a "thing about which one speaks."

In the LXX *hrēma* and *logos* are the Gr. equivalents. The Pentateuch more commonly uses *hrēma,* while in the prophets *logos* is preferred. The former lays stress on the dynamic effect of God's revelation, while the latter stresses its character and means.

The most common term in the NT is *logos. Logion,* a derivative of *logos* or the related adjective *logios,* appears four times (Acts 7:38; Rom 3:2; Heb 5:12; I Pet 4:11). In each instance it is plural and means "oracles." Gr. *hrēma* is also found in the NT translated "word" over 50 times as well as in connection with Hebraisms (e.g., Lk 1:37, ASV; 2:15, 19, "thing" or "saying," ASV marg.).

Old Testament Usage

"Word" has three significant uses in the OT:

1. Usually it occurs in connection with divine revelation. God speaks and His prophets hear. Jeremiah, Hosea, Joel, Jonah, Zephaniah, Haggai and Zechariah all begin their prophecy with "The word of the Lord came to . . ." or some slight variation. This expression appears about 130 times in the OT.

Not only was the "word of God" given in visions to His prophets but it also accompanied His acts so that these acts were not incomprehensible and so that those who witnessed them had an authoritative explanation. God's word is thus connected with His activities in history.

The purpose of this revelation is to make known His will concerning man's conduct in this world. It is noteworthy that the content of revelation does not usually concern the ethereal but the practical. It is therefore not unexpected that Deut 18:18–19 demands obedience to the prophetic word, and that the content of the "word" is characteristically in the imperative mood.

2. God's word was the means of creation. The creation of God is vividly contrasted with that of men. Men must labor and strive to create, and their creations are only the refashioning of existing materials, while the God of the Bible merely speaks and it is done (e.g., Gen 1:3; Ps 33:6).

3. It is used of the words of false prophets (Num 22–24). The false prophet spoke favorable words to those who sought his services, while the true prophet could only say what God commanded (Num 22:38; I Kgs 22:14). For this reason, God gave Israel tests so that they might discern what was of God and what was not (Deut 13:1–5; 18:2–22).

Non-Biblical Greek Usage

It is necessary to survey non-biblical Gr. usage of *logos,* because some have argued that it throws light on Johannine usage. These are the important instances:

1. The earliest appearance of *logos* is in the writings of Heraclitus of Ephesus about 500 B.C. The Stoics thought he anticipated their view that the universe was operated by "reason" or "law." Plato, on the other hand, who knew the teaching of Heraclitus did not agree, so that it is quite likely that the Stoics read their view back into admittedly obscure words.

2. The Stoicism of Zeno and his immediate successors held a form of pantheistic hylozoism. The universe was composed of matter, and permeated and controlled by a fiery vapor which was also material, called the *logos.*

Later, the *logos* lost its material associations and became the divine reason which governs the world. It was this latter idea that influenced Philo.

3. Philo taught that the *logos* was an intermediary between a wholly transcendent God and the material universe. It was unthinkable that God should be involved in the created order. Therefore, God conceived the ideal universe which was the pattern followed in creation of the actual world by His intermediary the *logos.* The *logos* is both the pattern and agent of God in creation. Some of the titles which Philo employs to describe the *logos* are God's "firstborn son," "image," "shadow," "God" without the article to distinguish him from *the* God, "ambassador," "suppliant," "advocate," and "high priest."

Nevertheless, it is very questionable whether Philo is indeed a bridge between OT Wisdom Literature and the writings of John. John had access to the identical materials which Philo had, but in addition he held the firm belief that God had spoken, acted and revealed Himself in a new way in Jesus Christ. So John goes beyond Philo, who does no more than personify the *logos.* If Philo could have formed John's conception of the *Logos,* Philo would have rejected it.

New Testament Usage

In the NT "word" has both general uses and a specific function as a title for Jesus Christ. Its meanings are colored by the OT associations with *dbr* rather than *logos* of classical Gr. The important uses are:

1. As in the OT, the most frequent NT function is to describe the medium of divine revelation. This revelation contains God's will for

mankind in general (Lk 11:28), Israel (Rom 9:6), and the Church (Col 1:25–27). It may refer to a written revelation such as the OT law (Mt 15:6; Mk 7:13) or a particular OT passage (Jn 10:35, referring to Ps 82:6). Divine revelation comes also in the spoken word of Jesus (Lk 5:1; Jn 5:38; 8:55; 17:6; etc.; Acts 20:35) and of the apostles (I Thess 1:8; II Thess 3:1).

2. Closely related to the above, the Christian message is called the "word of God" (Lk 8:11; Acts 4:31; I Cor 14:36), "word of Christ" (Col 3:16; Heb 6:1) and "word of the Lord" (Acts 8:25). The "word" contained in the Christian message is characterized as "the gospel" (Gal 2:2; Col 1:23; I Thess 2:9), "life" (Phil 2:16), "living and active" (Heb 4:12, NASB), "the power of God" (I Cor 1:18) and "truth" (Eph 1:13; Col 1:5; II Tim 2:15).

3. Three passages in the NT use *logos* as a title for Jesus Christ (Jn 1:1–14; I Jn 1:1; Rev 19:13). The KJV uses the term in I Jn 5:7; however, the MS evidence is against the authenticity of this verse. The significance of this title cannot be overestimated, for John puts into language acceptable to pagan, Jew, and Christian the truth that in the incarnation, life, death and resurrection of Jesus Christ a new revelation of God had been given (cf. Heb 1:1–2). *See* Logos.

Bibliography. A. Debrunner, *et al.*, *"Legō, Logis,* etc.," TDNT, IV, 69–143. C. H. Dodd, *The Interpretation of the Fourth Gospel,* Cambridge: Univ. Press, 1953, pp. 263–285. Merrill C. Tenney, *The Bible–The Living Word of Revelation,* Grand Rapids: Zondervan, 1968, pp. 11–27.

P. D. F.

WORK. *See* Labor.

WORKMAN. The various words used for a worker or workman all denote the arduous working with one's hands, an active engagement in performing a task or producing a product (I Chr 22:15; Jer 10:3; II Chr 24:13). This active, energetic usage is applied also to "workers of iniquity" (Ps 6:8; 14:4; Lk 13:27), and to the hardworking man of God, laboring in the Word to show himself approved to his Master (II Tim 2:15). *See* Occupations.

WORKS OF GOD. The doctrine of God is often divided into the nature of God and the works of God. The former deals with ontology, while the latter is interested in God's relation with the universe. The primary works of God are as follows:

1. The decree. The decree in its primary sense is singular as God has only one all-inclusive plan whereby He "worketh all things after the counsel of his own will" (Eph 1:11). For convenience, however, the individual features of this plan may be called decrees.

Reformed theology places great emphasis on the doctrine of the decree, while in Arminian theology it is of less importance. It is because of this difference in emphasis that much of the tension between these two schools of theology arises.

The Scriptures teach that the decree of God was made in eternity past (Acts 15:8; Eph 1:4; II Tim 1:9), was grounded in the wisdom of God (Ps 104:24; Prov 3:19; Eph 3:10–11), and is all-comprehensive (Eph 1:11).

Important features within the decree of God are His choice to create, to permit man to fall, to justify the elect, and to pass over the non-elect and to subject them to eternal punishment which their sin rightfully deserves.

While it is difficult for the finite mind to grasp God's infinite plan, and while nothing happens apart from God's will or decree, it helps to remember that *God did not will everything He desired* (II Pet 3:9) and *He does not desire everything He has willed* (II Pet 3:7). For this reason, it is convenient to distinguish between those things which are willed directively or efficaciously (actively), and those willed permissively (passively). *See* Will of God.

2. Creation. Creation is an act of the triune God: of the Father (Gen 1:1), of the Son (Jn 1:3), and of the Holy Spirit (Gen 1:2). It was a free act of the will of God, as there was nothing in the divine nature which necessitated it. The Bible teaches that creation was *ex nihilo* and by divine fiat or command (Gen 1:1,3, *et al.*).

Among those things which were created by God are angels (Ps 148:2, 5; Col 1:16), Satan and the demonic hosts (Isa 14:12–15; Ezk 28:12–19; II Pet 2:4; Jude 6), the heavens and earth (Gen 1:1), plant and animal life (Gen 1:11–12, 20–22, 24–25), and man and woman (Gen 1:26–27; 2:21–24).

Since the universe was created by God, the Bible teaches that it is a means of revealing God to man (Ps 19:1–3). The content of this revelation is "His eternal power and Godhead," and on this ground all "are without excuse" (Rom 1:20).

Finally, because of man's sin the creation has been cursed (Gen 3:14, 17–19) and at present "groaneth and travaileth" for its redemption (Rom 8:19–22). Further, during this present age, Satan rules it (Jn 14:30; 16:11; II Cor 4:4), but at some future time it shall be restored to God and ruled by Jesus Christ (Rev 11:15; 19:6–21; 20:4). After the millennial reign of Christ, the heavens and earth will be cleansed or destroyed by fire (II Pet 3:7). *See* Creation.

3. Preservation. This is the activity of God whereby He maintains all that He has created (Neh 9:6; Col 1:17; Heb 1:3). While all theists agree that God preserves His creation, there is disagreement over the method whereby He does this. The deist claims that it is by natural law. Others have suggested that maintenance is through continuous creation. The best answer is that God concurs in all the operations of matter and mind. Without this concurrence no force or person could continue to exist or to act (Acts 17:28; I Cor 12:6).

4. Providence. Not only does God preserve His creation, but He exercises sovereign control over it (Ps 103:19). This control is called providence. God's providence is His operation within time to execute His decree.

The means employed in the exercise of providence may be the laws of nature (Gen 8:22; Ps 107:24), miracle (Ex 14:21-31; Josh 24:31; Jud 2:7, 10), His word (Deut 17:18-20), His judgments (Isa 10:12; 28:21-22; Jer 50:25), man's reason (Isa 1:18; Acts 6:2), outward circumstances (I Cor 16:9; Gal 4:13, NASB), dreams and visions (Mt 2:13, 19-20; Acts 16:9-10; 22:17-18), and special agents, particularly angels (Dan 6:22; 10:5-21; 12:1). *See* Providence.

5. Salvation. While the work of creation is spoken of as the work of God's hands (Ps 8), salvation is accomplished by the arm of God (Ex 15:16; Jn 12:38) and by (Jn 5:36; 10:25, 38; 17:4) and at the cost of His Son.

While salvation was finished with Christ's death (Jn 19:30), the complete realization of its benefits is future. At the Lord's return the Christian will be saved from bodily infirmities and God's curse upon the world (Rom 8:18-23; I Cor 15:42-44), and brought into the perfect likeness of Christ (Rom 8:29; 13:11; Heb 10:36; I Pet 1:5; I Jn 3:2).

Scripture teaches that salvation is on the basis of grace through the means of faith, wholly apart from works (Rom 3:27-28; 4:1-8; 6:23; Eph 2:8). It is only after salvation that the believer is commanded to produce good works (Eph 2:9-10; Tit 3:5-8; Jas 2:20); in fact, such works are the natural product and evidence of new life in Christ (Gal 5:16, 22-24; I Jn).

See God; Miracles; Salvation; Works.

P. D. F.

WORKS OF MAN. Heb. *ma'aśeh, melā'kâ,* and Gr. *ergon* are generally the words that stand behind the words "work" and "deed" in the English text of Scripture. Though Scripture refers to the works of God and the works of our Lord on earth, in this article consideration is restricted to the works of men; and not so much with works in the sense of toil and occupation as in the sense of actions which exhibit the moral character of men. Such works are referred to collectively, usually in the plural, though the singular may be used (Gal 6:4).

There is a whole class of usages referring to the sinful deeds of men which exhibit their moral and spiritual wickedness. Included here are wicked or evil works (Col 1:21 and II Jn 11; cf. Lk 13:27; Jn 3:19; 7:7; I Jn 3:12), works of the flesh (Gal 5:19), ungodly or impious deeds (Jude 15), works of darkness (Rom 13:12), and unfruitful works of darkness (Eph 5:11).

By way of contrast, good works are those actions of which God approves in His children. Good works are the evidence of a walk worthy of the Lord (Col 1:10); they are to be the adornment of women and that by which widows are known (I Tim 2:10; 5:10), even as Dorcas is called one who was "full of good works" (Acts 9:36). But the men are not left out, for Titus is exhorted to be an example of good works (Tit 2:7).

Good works are to be regarded as the consequence of salvation ("works worthy of repentance," Acts 26:20); indeed, the performance of good works is one of the purposes for which believers are saved (Eph 2:10; Tit 2:14). Such deeds are produced in the life not by any innate goodness in man but by the right use of Scripture (II Tim 3:17) and the grace of God working within (II Cor 9:8; cf. II Thess 2:17; Phil 1:6). They may be considered as being, or resulting from, the fruit of the Spirit (Gal 5:22 f.). The example of Jesus Christ who cast out demons by the Spirit of God (Mt 12:28; cf. Lk 4:14; Acts 10:38) and the instruction of the apostle Paul in I Cor 12:1-11 reveal that all genuine, lasting work for God must be done in the power of the Holy Spirit (cf. I Thess 1:5; Rom 15:18 f.; I Cor 2:4; II Cor 6:6; II Tim 1:7; Acts 4:29-31, 33; Heb 2:4).

It is to such works that Paul refers when he speaks of the "work of faith" and "faith working through love" (I Thess 1:3; II Thess 1:11; Gal 5:6), the reference being to good works that spring from faith. This is precisely what James refers to when he speaks of those works which show that faith is vital and real; indeed, a faith that does not give such evidence is no faith at all—it is dead (Jas 1:21-25; 2:14-26). Since good works are the evidence of faith and the product of the grace of God, they bring glory to God rather than man (Mt 5:16). *See* Conversation; Faith.

But there are those who suppose that their own works are good and sufficient to gain merit and acceptance with God. Such individuals are said to be "of the works of law" (Gal 3:10). Works of law are those legal performances by which men seek to be accepted of God (ISBE, V, 3105). They are the course of action demanded by the law (Rom 3:27; Gal 2:16; 3:2, 5, 10; sometimes simply called "works," cf. Rom 4:2, 6; Eph 2:8-9). That which God did lay down as a requirement is misused by man in his arrogant striving after self-righteousness. But such a course is useless and can only result in God's curse and condemnation (Gal 2:16, 21; 3:10-14).

The works of law along with the works of flesh are also called "dead works" in that they are works devoid of faith in the saving grace of God (Heb 6:1; 9:14).

Bibliography. Herbert Braun, *"Poieō,* etc.," TDNT, VI, 458-484. Georg Bertram, *"Ergon,"* TDNT, II, 635-655. John Gerstner, "Good Works," BDT, pp. 253 f. W. L. Walker, "Work, Works," ISBE, V, 3105.

S. N. G.

WORLD. The English word is used in the Bible with various meanings and is the translation of the following words: Heb. *'ereṣ,* "land" or "earth" (*c.* 400 times), "world" (four times); Heb. *tēbēl,* "fruit-bearing" or "habitable earth" (35 times); Gr. *aiōn,* "age," "dispensation," "world" (32 times, KJV); Gr. *gē,* "earth" (over 150 times), "world" (once in Rev 13:3); Gr. *kosmos,* "ordered world," "world system" (over 170 times); Gr. *oikoumenē,* "inhabited earth" or "world" (14 times). The Gr. words prove of the greater importance, the words *aiōn* and *kosmos* in particular.

Though the Gr. *aiōn* is translated "world" 28 times in the KJV, a study of its basic meaning, "aeon" or "age," plus its use in each context, leads to the conclusion that in over half the instances it refers specifically to a period or age of time rather than to the earth. For example, the disciples asked Christ, "When shall these things be? and what shall be the sign of thy coming, and of the end of the *aeon*?" (Mt 24:3). Since the OT and NT speak of a millennial reign of Christ (Isa 11; 65–66; Zech 14:9–21; Rev 20:4–6; cf. Rom 8:18–25; 11:26–29), since the disciples believed this was to occur (Acts 1:6–8), and since Christ Himself went to heaven without in any way denying this truth when questioned about it at His ascension 40 days after His resurrection, it is only reasonable to translate the word *aiōn* by "age" in Mt 24:3. In many other passages the use of the word clearly indicates a concept which stresses the idea of a period of time (cf. Mt 13:40, 49; 28:20; Mk 10:30; Lk 18:30; 20:35; II Cor 4:4; Gal 1:4; Eph 1:21). At the same time, however, the word is also used without any apparent time content (cf. Heb 1:2; 11:3).

The Gr. word *kosmos* was used from Homer on to express "an apt and harmonious arrangement or constitution, order" (Thayer's Lexicon, p. 356), and also meant the universe, the world. It is theologically important because its study in the NT reveals much concerning the world, mankind, and man's fallen condition, the temptations and problems of the Christian, as well as Christ's work in relation to the fallen cosmos and to its prince Satan. This can be considered under the following headings:

1. The physical world. The world had a beginning (Mt 24:21; 25:34). God (Acts 17:24) through Christ created the *kosmos,* the world (Jn 1:3, 10; cf. Heb. 1:2, "through whom he made the aeons"). This *kosmos,* or earth, Peter says, was destroyed by the Flood in Noah's day (II Pet 2:5; 3:6). However, even before God founded the *kosmos* He had planned the atonement for the sins of fallen mankind (Eph 1:4; I Pet 1:20; Rev 13:8).

When first created, the earth was good: at each stage of the creation God re-examined it and found it good (Gen 1:4, 10, 12, 18, 21, 25, 31). The principle of evil first entered it as Adam, rebelling against God, opened the doors to the floodgates of sin which originated in heaven by Satan and his fallen angels (Rom 5:12; cf. Ezk 28:12–18). The day will come when the created world (*ktisis*) will be freed again from the curse brought by sin. Today it groans and travails in agony, but then, after the resurrection, it will again be freed (Rom 8:21–23; cf. Isa 11:6–9; 65:25).

2. The world of mankind. Men and women are born into the human race or world of mankind (Jn 16:21). This world is organized into kingdoms or states (Mt 4:8–9), and it was these that Satan offered to Christ if He would only accept Satan's overlordship and worship him (Mt 4:8–10). Through his followers, namely, unsaved worldly rulers, Satan reigns over this world system. And yet it was the world of fallen mankind God loved so much that He sent His Son to die that they might have redemption (Jn 3:16).

3. The fallen world. Sin entered the *kosmos* when Adam, following the leadership of Satan, disbelieved God and rebelled. Since that time the unregenerate are the children of Satan (Jn 8:44) and can become the children of God only by the new birth (Jn 3:3–7). Thus the term "world" very frequently designates humanity as a whole in rebellion against God and destined for judgment.

The *kosmos* has become the domain of Satan: "the whole world lies in the power of the evil one" (I Jn 5:19, NASB). He is its prince (Jn 12:31; 14:30). He has become the god of this world (II Cor 4:4), and has raised up many antichrists (I Jn 4:1 f.) to deceive the lost. The world system has its own wisdom (I Cor 1:21) in contrast to the knowledge of Christ as God's wisdom and power for salvation (I Cor 1:24). This deficient wisdom leads to pride and lust (I Jn 2:16) and covetousness which becomes a form of idolatry (Col 3:5), because man tends to worship what he covets. This fallen world has a spirit of its own in contrast to the Holy Spirit (I Cor 2:12), offers an ungodly friendship to the sinner (Jas 4:4), and holds the unregenerate in its bondage (Gal 4:3; Col 2:20). Only by regeneration can man be delivered from the system of the world (I Jn 5:4–5).

4. Christ and the world. God loved the fallen world enough to send His Son to redeem out of it His elect (Jn 3:16; I Jn 4:14). Jesus came to bring judgment on this fallen world (Jn 9:39) and on its prince Satan (Jn 12:31; 14:30). This was accomplished at the cross (Jn 16:11). Christ's death is sufficient for all (I Jn 2:2), but efficient only for the believer. It was for His own that He prayed His high priestly prayer (Jn 17:9) and intercedes constantly at God's throne (Heb 7:25). At His second advent the kingdom of the world will become His kingdom (Rev 11:15). The believers, along with their father Abraham, are to be heirs of this world and to reign over it with Christ (Mt 5:5; Rom 4:13; 8:17; cf. Rev 5:10).

5. The Christian's present relationship to the world. The believer has been delivered from the meshes of the fallen world system and can overcome it by faith in Christ (I Jn 5:4–5). The teachings of the fallen world are characterized by two extremes, rigid legalism (Gal 4:9–10; cf. Jn 8:41–44) on the one hand, and licentious lust

on the other (Jn 8:44; Jas 4:1-4). While in this world the Christian, like his Lord, will suffer tribulation since it hates Him (Jn 15:18-19; 16:33) and does not know Him (I Jn 3:1). Through the presence and power of the Holy Spirit, who is greater than the devil, the believer conquers (I Jn 4:4). But Christ warns against seeking prosperity in worldly things (Mt 16:26). Paul recognizes that a married person is in danger of being distracted from devotion to the Lord by concern for the things of the world (I Cor 7:31-35). John strictly forbids the believer to love the world, but intimates that the love of God, being that of a higher affection, is able to drive out the love of the world (I Jn 2:15-17).

6. The Christian's responsibility for the world. He is to remain in it and let his light shine (Mt 5:14) but not become a part of it (Jn 17:15). It is his field of service (Mt 13:38). The gospel is to be preached to the whole world (Mk 14:9; 16:15), for it is still God's world and only lies temporarily in Satan's power (I Jn 5:19). It is the task of the Christian not only to be a light to the world (Mt 5:14-16; Phil 2:15) but also to plead with fallen mankind to be reconciled to God through the cross (II Cor 5:19-20). God will deliver the whole creation from both Satan and the curse of sin, first by putting Satan into the bottomless pit (Rev 20:3), later in the lake of fire and brimstone (Rev 20:10), and then by removing the curse from both nature and man (Rom 8:21-24; cf. Jer 31:33-34).

Gr. *oikoumenē,* the third Gr. word, refers to the inhabited or civilized earth. In Caesar's decree in Lk 2:1 it refers to the Roman Empire. The term is used in this sense in Acts to describe the extent of a drought (Acts 11:28), the effects of Paul's missionary messages (17:6), the extent of the pagan worship of Diana (19:27), and the dispersion of the Jews (24:5).

Bibliography. Hudson T. Armerding, ed., *Christianity and the World of Thought,* Chicago: Moody Press, 1968. Karl Heim, *Jesus the World's Perfecter,* trans. by D. H. van Daalen, Philadelphia: Muhlenberg Press, 1961. G. Nagel, J. Hering, Christian Senft, "World," *A Companion to the Bible,* ed. by J. J. Von Allmen, New York: Oxford Univ. Press, 1958, pp. 466-471. Hermann Sasse, "*Kosmos,* etc." TDNT, III, 867-898.

R. A. K.

WORM. *See* Animals, IV. 37.

WORMS. *See* Diseases.

WORMWOOD. *See* Plants.

WORSHIP. The purpose of worship is to establish or to give expression to a relationship between creature and deity. Worship is practiced by paying religious reverence and homage to God (or a god) in thought, feeling, or act, with or without the aid of symbols and rites. *See* Religion. Pure worship expresses adoration (*q.v.*) and veneration without making petition, and predicates self-renunciation and sacrificial giving to God. Strictly speaking, worship is the occupation of the soul with God Himself and does not include prayer for needs and thanksgiving for blessings.

Worship is represented in the Bible principally by two words: in the OT the Heb. word *shāḥâ* (more than 100 times), meaning "to bow down," "prostrate oneself" (Gen 22:5; 42:6; 48:12; Ex 24:1; Jud 7:15; I Sam 25:41; Job 1:20; Ps 22:27; 86:9; etc.), and in the NT the Gr. word *proskyneō* (59 times), meaning "to prostrate oneself," "do obeisance to another" (Mt 2:2, 8, 11; 4:9; Mk 5:6; 15:19; Lk 4:7-8; Jn 4:20-22; etc.). These two words are consistently rendered in the English versions by the word "worship," which in Old English was spelled "worthship," denoting the worthiness of the one receiving the special honor or devotion. The two terms "worship" and "worthy" may be seen together in the grand description of the 24 elders falling down before the One who sits on the throne (Rev 4:10-11; cf. 5:8-14). *See* Bowing; Knee; Kiss.

In addition to the two principal words there is an extensive vocabulary in both Heb. and Gr. further defining the activity of worship. Words commonly used are the Heb. *'ābad,* meaning "to work," "to serve," "to worship" (II Kgs 10:19-23) with its Gr. counterpart *latreuō,* meaning "to render religious service or honor to God" (Acts 24:14; Phil 3:3). A Heb. and Aram. word *sāgad,* meaning "to fall down in adoration," is found in Isa 44:15, 17, 19; 46:6; Dan 2:46 and frequently in the following chapter. To fear the Lord is a close synonym, as one learns by comparing Deut 6:13 with Jesus' quotation of this verse in Mt 4:10. Here fear has the sense of awe and reverence (cf. Ps 5:7). *See* Fear. Other Gr. words of importance are *sebomai* and its various cognates, meaning "to hold in awe," "to revere," and *threskeia,* meaning "religion," "ceremonial worship" (Col 2:18; Acts 26:5; Jas 1:26 f.).

Worship in the OT

OT worship may be divided into two main periods, patriarchal and theocratic. Prior to the Mosaic institutions there are few indications of formal and public worship among the patriarchs. The times of the patriarchs reveal rather the individual, personal, and occasional acts of worship that would characterize a seminomadic people living apart from organized society (e.g., Abraham at Moriah, Gen 22:1-5; Jacob at Bethel, Gen 28:18-22). Genesis does, however, picture the beginnings of ritualistic religion in the institution of sacrifices and the building of altars (Gen 4:3-4, 26; 8:20-22).

During the theocratic period the corporate and ritualistic concept of worship became prominent. A very highly organized and comprehensive system of worship was revealed to Moses by God at Sinai, which included:

1. Special kinds of offerings and sacrifices

for the whole nation: (*a*) daily (Num 28:3-8); (*b*) each sabbath (Num 28:9-10; Lev 24:8); (*c*) at the new moon (Num 28:11-15); (*d*) the Passover or the Feast of Unleavened Bread (Num 28:16-25; Ex 12:1 ff.) on the fourteenth day of the first month, which is the prototype of Christ and was succeeded by the Lord's Supper (Mt 26:17-29); (*e*) Feast of Weeks or of the Firstfruits of the wheat harvest (Lev 23:15-20; Num 28:26-31), which is the prototype of the coming of the Holy Spirit at Pentecost: in that Christ was to be sinless, only unleavened bread was to be used in the Passover; in that we are sinful, leavened bread was to be used for Pentecost; (*f*) Feast of Trumpets on the first day of the seventh month, which is prophetic of the final future regathering of Israel (Lev 23:23-25; Num 29:1-6; cf. Isa 18:3; 27:12-13; Joel 2:15-32); (*g*) Day of Atonement (Lev 23:26-32; Num 29:7-11) on the tenth day of the seventh month, which was to be a time of repentance and was prophetic of Israel's final repentance at Christ's second coming (Zech 12:10 ff.; 13:6; Mt 24:30; Rev 1:7); (*h*) the Feast of Tabernacles, when on the fifteenth day of the seventh month just after the harvest was in, while the people dwelt in booths made with boughs of trees in remembrance of their deliverance from Egypt, the priests offered seven days of special sacrifices (Lev 23:33-44; Num 29:13 ff.). *See* Festivals; Sacrifices.

2. Particular sacrifices to be offered by an individual for himself and his family, such as the Passover meal and the Passover itself (Ex 12; cf. Lev 23:5); a burnt offering of a male of the flock without blemish, for himself and his family (Lev 1:1 ff.) with which he identified himself and upon which both his and their sins were typically placed as he put his hand on the head of the offering as it was slain; a meal offering as an offering of praise pointing to the perfections of God and of Christ (Lev 2); a peace offering pointing to Christ as our peace (Lev 3). For sins of ignorance there were appropriate offerings (Lev 4-5) and for trespasses (Lev 6:1-7).

3. Special sacrifices for the priests themselves at the consecration of Aaron and his sons (Lev 8:2, 14, 15); at the anointing of a priest (Ex 29:15 ff.; Lev 6:19-23); when a priest had sinned (Lev 4:3 ff.); at the purification of women (Lev 12:6, 8); for the cleansing of lepers (Lev 14:19); to remove ceremonial uncleanness (Lev 15:15, 30); at the conclusion or the breach of a Nazarite vow (Num 6:11-14). *See* Sacrifices; Sacrificial Offerings.

There was undoubtedly much confusion during the period of the judges, and the dispersion of the tribes throughout the land further unsettled the religious picture. The corporate concept of worship, in spite of everything,, was destined to increase. Sanctuaries were established and sought out by the people year after year; Dan, Gilgal, Shechem, Shiloh, and Beersheba, to name the more important. Syncretistic tendencies in religion constantly corrupted the worship at these places, infusing pagan practices into the religion of Israel.

Because of constant and increasing corruption, Israel's religion was at a low ebb when Saul and the monarchy arrived. Indeed, David's reign could be viewed as a time of religious revival which culminated in the erection of the temple under Solomon's authority. Undoubtedly David's own experience of worship in private and fellowship with the Lord in the most trying circumstances gave him the desire to lead others to praise and worship God (Ps 42:1-4; 122:1; II Sam 6:12-18; I Chr 16:1-36).

The effect of the temple on Israel's worship is unequaled by any other factor. Gradually all other places of worship were eliminated, and the temple in Jerusalem remained as the only place for sacrifice, the basis of worship.

Besides all the offerings and sacrifices specified by God in the Mosaic law, there developed a system of public worship in such things as: (1) Special sacrificial acts for extraordinary occasions such as the consecration of the tabernacle (Num 7) or of Solomon's temple (II Chr 7:5 ff.). (2) Particular ceremonial acts at which the people expressed unusual reverence, such as when the high priest offered incense in the holy place, when Solomon blessed the people (I Kgs 8:14), and when the priests sounded the silver trumpets (II Chr 7:6). (3) Services of praise at the temple when vocal song and musical instruments of every sort were employed (II Chr 5:13). Moses had composed a song of deliverance after God had led the people dryshod through the Red Sea, and Miriam, his sister, and the women accompanied their antiphony with timbrels (Ex 15:1, 20). David had appointed a choir of Levites to minister before the ark of the Lord after its recovery from the Philistines (I Chr 16:4), and had set up an orchestra (I Chr 16:6, 42-43; cf. II Sam 6:5). The last psalm commands that musical instruments of every sort be used to praise the Lord (Ps 150). There are possibly some antiphonal psalms (Ps 20, 21, 24, 107, 118). (4) Public prayer as when the people were led by Moses (Deut 26:15), by Solomon (I Kgs 8:23-54), and as found in Ps 51, 60, 79, 80 and many others. (5) Public addresses, such as Moses' summation of his work with five discourses in the book of Deuteronomy; Solomon speaking to the congregation (II Chr 6:4-11); Nehemiah having the law read and then having the Levites pray (Neh 9:3-38; cf. 13:1-5). *See* Temple.

After the captives returned from Babylon, the rebuilding of the temple was in a sense the rebirth of national religion. In the centuries following the return, Israel's worship became even more highly developed and ritualistic. The religious calendar was expanded to include the post-Exilic feasts and holy observances. The temple was not just a building, but the center that brought the worship of the entire nation into focus. It is true evidence reveals that some sects of Judaism (such as the Essenes) were anti-temple in their expression of worship, but the main stream of Jewish life, fed by many and differing tributaries (such as the Sadducees and the Pharisees), flowed through the temple.

After the return from the Babylonian Exile, the synagogue (*q.v.*) appeared as a rival to the temple. Strictly speaking the synagogue was designed for instruction and not worship; but practically, there appears to have been some element of worship in the synagogue service from its beginning. In fact, it was an increasing element; and after the destruction of the temple in A.D. 70 the synagogue appropriated to itself all that remained of Jewish worship.

Worship in the NT

With the death, burial, and resurrection of Christ, all the OT sacrifices and offerings became a thing of the past. There is now "no more sacrifice for sins," for the Lamb of God has taken away the sin of the world (Heb 10:26; Jn 1:29). Now the believer has an advocate before God in Christ to plead for him when he repents of his sin (I Jn 1:9; 2:1), and he needs no earthly priest. Therefore the form of worship soon began to change.

Public worship, however, in the first days of Christianity was still associated with the temple. The book of Acts pictures Jewish Christians continuing their worship in the temple (Acts 2:46; 3:1; 5:20, 42), even to the time of Paul's arrest (Acts 21:26–33). Only the hostility of those who controlled the temple seemingly kept the first Christians from that holy place.

At the same time Christianity began to turn toward private residences for places of assembly (Acts 2:46; 5:42; 12:12). The element of sacrifice which was basic in the temple was perpetuated only in the supper which memorialized the sacrificial death of Christ. This observance seems to have been at first a part of a communal meal which Christians shared (I Cor 11:20–34). Later it became associated especially with the Lord's day, the day that soon was set aside for Christian worship. The Jewish sabbath was gradually displaced by the first day of the week, resting as that day did upon the earliest Christian experience with the resurrected Christ (Jn 20:19, 26; Acts 20:7; I Cor 16:2; Rev 1:10).

Preaching and teaching were elements of supreme importance in public meetings for the young churches (Acts 11:26; 15:35; 18:25; 20:7). Those elements that were part of worship in Judaism also appear in early Christian services: reading of the OT (I Tim 4:13, NASB), prayer (Acts 2:42; I Cor 14:14–16), singing (Eph 5:19; Col 3:16), and giving of alms (I Cor 16:1–2).

Actual congregational worship is regulated in I Cor 11–14. Any member was free to take part as the Spirit might prompt (I Cor 14:26), especially as he sought to minister to the others by his spiritual or charismatic gift (I Pet 4:10 f.). A woman who prayed or prophesied ought to have her head covered (I Cor 11:5). A message in an unrecognized tongue must be interpreted, and all prophesying should be subject to the prophets in the assembly (I Cor 14:27–33). *See* Music; Praise; Prayer; Spiritual Gifts; Thanksgiving.

Christ did not Himself prescribe for His disciples specific forms of public worship, no doubt assuming that His own example and the Holy Spirit would bring it about spontaneously. He did stress that worshipers must worship God "in spirit and in truth" (Jn 4:23 f.) and sought to guard their worship from merely outward forms, emphasizing privacy and reality before God (Mt 6:1–18). The apostle Paul permits us to glimpse something of his private devotional life when he tells of speaking mysteries to God by his spirit and of praying, singing, and blessing God both with the spirit and with the mind (I Cor 14:2, 14–19).

Some scholars have professed to find in the mystery religions several practices that have, they think, influenced Christian worship. The ceremonial bath or baptism (such as the blood bath of Mithraism); the sacred meal, sometimes with memorial significance (such as elevation of the ear of wheat as a symbol of death and rebirth in the Eleusinian rite). It is clearly certain that these religions were utterly inferior to Christianity in that the basis of Christian worship lay in historical fact rather than in myth and theory. By its own inherent merits Christianity won its victory over the rival religions of the ancient world, and such expressions of worship as are similar to Christianity only point to the broad religious basis which is inherent in human nature.

One of Christianity's greatest trials came early and in connection with its worship. Rome decreed a universal religion for the world: the cult of the emperors. It was Roman policy to draw the attention of all people to the center of power, and the Imperial cult was one means of giving cohesion to the vast empire.

This cult was never intended to persecute or displace national religions, nor was it intended to impose religious dogma. Actually, Imperial apotheosis was political in nature and purpose, coming into existence as a result of flattery, gratitude, and historic precedent. The emperors reacted to apotheosis in different degrees. Of all the emperors, though probably encouraging worship of himself as little as any, Augustus received the most genuine adoration. Tiberius refused divine honors in Rome, but encouraged the cult in the provinces. Caligula was insistent upon his divinity. Nero was the first living emperor to wear the *corona radiata* which was symbolic of descent from the sun-god. Domitian claimed the title *dominus et deus* in his lifetime. Although never possessed of any religious value, the cult became in the provinces a convenient means of detecting disloyalty to Rome. The chief nonconformists were Republicans, Jews and Christians. Christianity was never willing to ascribe lordship to Caesar, which brought untold suffering and wide-spread persecution at the close of the 1st cen. The worship of Christians in a polytheistic age was reserved exclusively for Christ. *See* Persecution.

Bibliography. Oscar Cullmann, *Early Christian Worship,* trans. by A. S. Todd and J. B. Torrance, Chicago: H. Regnery Co., 1953. G. Henton Davies, C. C. Richardson and Abraham Cronbach, "Worship, etc.," IDB, IV, 879–903. Gerhard Delling, *Worship in the NT,* trans. by Percy Scott, Philadelphia: Westminster Press, 1962. Roland de Vaux, *Ancient Israel,* trans. by John McHugh, New York: McGraw-Hill, 1961, pp. 271–517, 537–552. George Evans, *The True Spirit of Worship,* Chicago: Bible Inst. Colportage Assn., 1941. Alfred P. Gibbs, *Worship: The Christian's Highest Occupation,* 2nd ed., Kansas City, Kan.: Walterick Publ., n.d. Oscar Hardman, *A History of Christian Worship,* Nashville: Cokesbury Press, 1937. Arthur S. Herbert, *Worship in Ancient Israel,* Richmond: John Knox Press, 1959. Yehezkel Kaufmann, *The Religion of Israel,* trans. and abridged by Moshe Greenberg, Chicago: Univ. of Chicago Press, 1960. Franklin M. Segler, *Christian Worship: Its Theology and Practice,* Nashville: Broadman Press, 1967. H. Strathmann, *"Latreuō, etc.,"* TDNT, IV, 58–65. Jean J. von Allmen, *Worship, Its Theology and Practice,* New York: Oxford Univ. Press, 1965.

H. L. D. and R. A. K.

WORTH. *See* Honor.

WOUNDS. *See* Diseases.

WRATH. While the positive attributes of God are His wisdom, power, holiness, justice, goodness, and truth, His negative attribute is wrath against sin. It is as much a part of His character as His love and mercy. However, unlike anger in man, God's anger is not capricious, spasmodic, or changing; but constant and unchanging against sin, though wholly tempered by His justice. Anger or wrath is an essential element of divine love, and realization of it produces a wholesome fear of God.

God's wrath is against those who refuse to believe He exists and who do not recognize His power and deity through nature. It is revealed both in the Bible and through the fact that God has abandoned men to ever deeper degrees of degradation in sin (Rom 1:18, 21–32). At different times and in different ways He has displayed His wrath; e.g., in the Flood (Gen 6:5–7); the destruction of Sodom and Gomorrah (Gen 19:1 ff.); the downfall of Nineveh (Nah 1:2–6). Still His wrath remains tempered by His mercy right down through the ages until He will finally pour out the seven bowls of wrath in the time of the Tribulation (Rev 15–16). This is particularly the case for Israel (Hos 11:8 ff.). When the sinner presumes upon the mercy of God and refuses to repent, he only treasures up wrath unto the day of wrath (Rom 2:5).

Nevertheless, the good news of the gospel is to be preached to men. God has been reconciled to the sinner through the death of His Son. He is propitious or kindly disposed toward man. The sinner is therefore urged to be reconciled to God (II Cor 5:20). It is only the continued willful rejection of Christ which prevents a man from knowing peace and redemption, for the price has been paid at Calvary.

In his unredeemed state man is an object of God's wrath, a child of disobedience and wrath (Eph 2:2–3), a vessel destined to wrath (Rom 9:22). Nor does the law rescue man from this condition by his own works, because "the law worketh wrath" rather than redemption (Rom 4:15), and is a ministration of condemnation (II Cor 3:9; cf. Rom 3:19–20) and death (II Cor 3:7). It requires perfect obedience, which could only be offered by Christ, and an infinite atonement for sin which could only be accomplished on His cross.

The love of God for sinners, as He sent His Son to bear their sins in His own body on the tree, is the main theme of the NT. Christ endured misery, suffering, and death in their stead; and God promises immediate salvation to all who will acknowledge their sins, believe Christ died for them, and accept Him as their personal Saviour. For such there is no condemnation (Rom 8:1). Thus, Jesus can be described as the deliverer "from the wrath to come" (I Thess 1:10), and Paul can say of the believer: "Being now justified by his blood, we shall be saved from wrath through him" (Rom 5:9). And yet the wrath of God remains for those who refuse to accept His revealed plan of salvation.

See God; Judgments; Love; Salvation; Sin.

Bibliography. H. Kleinknecht, *et al., "Orgē,* etc.," TDNT, V, 382–447. R. V. G. Tasker, *The Biblical Doctrine of the Wrath of God,* London: Tyndale Press, 1951.

R. A. K.

WRESTLING. The OT speaks metaphorically of Rachel's wrestlings (*naphtûlîm*) with her sister Leah (Gen 30:8) and refers to Jacob's wrestling (from Heb. root *'ābaq*) in Gen 32:24–25. The name of the stream Jabbok (Heb. *yabbōq*) seems to have been given it as a result of Jacob's experience (*see* Jabbok). It has been suggested that the tournament between the 12 men of David and the 12 of Ishbosheth at Gibeon began as a wrestling match (II Sam 2:14). The expression "hip and thigh" (Jud 15:8) may be a technical wrestling term, for Babylonian cylinder seals depict the hero Gilgamesh overthrowing a lion or a buffalo with which he is wrestling by grasping its hind leg to rend it limb from limb with his bare hands (A. Parrot, *Sumer,* London: Thames & Hudson, 1960, pp. 186 f.).

In OT times the form of wrestling was usually belt-wrestling, in which the otherwise nude male contestant wore a special belt which his opponent would grasp. From the early 3rd mil. B.C. at Khafajah in Sumer come a limestone plaque and a bronze statuette, both depicting belt-wrestlers (ANEP # 218, 219). Such wrestling was very popular in Egypt, according to 12th Dynasty tomb murals at Beni Hasan (*Everyday Life in Ancient Times,* Natl. Geog. Soc., 1951, pp. 76–77, 116).

Paul's metaphor in Eph 6:12 for the believer's conflict with demonic powers is the only NT reference to wrestling (*palē*). He draws his figure of speech from the Gr. games. Wrestling was by far the most popular sport among the Gr. athletes themselves. Palaestras or wrestling schools abounded in Gr. cities from the 6th cen. B.C. to the end of the Roman imperial epoch. In Gr. wrestling the purpose was to throw one's opponent and pin his shoulders to the ground. A match was for the best of three falls. The pankration, a favorite event for the spectators, was a combination of boxing and wrestling, with kicking and hitting allowed but biting and gouging illegal. This event afforded the supreme test of strength and skill in combination (H. A. Harris, *Greek Athletes and Athletics,* London: Hutchinson, 1964, pp. 102–109). The believer's struggle requires the strength of the Lord (Eph 6:10), the perseverance of prayer (v. 18), and the dexterity of faith to meet all the fiery darts of the wicked one (v. 16). Paul also uses the complementary metaphor of boxing (I Cor 9:26).

Gr. tragedy used the term *palē* in the more general sense of conflict. Philo wrote of the wrestling of the ascetic, again probably with the general moral "conflict" in view. In their writings the Stoics felt they were wrestlers or warriors as they endured in the world, and likewise the devotees of the mystery religions.

See Armor, Spiritual; Games; War.

F. D. L.

WRINKLE. Used once in Eph 5:27 to describe the Church as if it were a garment to be made spotlessly clean and ironed free of every defect and wrinkle.

WRITING. The ability to record thoughts by means of marks on some more or less durable material, so that the marks will later recall these thoughts to the mind of the author or convey them to someone else, is easily the greatest single achievement of man's intelligence. It is probably to the ancient Sumerians that we owe this great discovery. Their earliest known tablets have been found at Erech and date to a period *c.* 3500 B.C.

Development and History of Writing in Bible Times

In earliest Sumerian writing a picture of an object may represent that object, or it may represent merely the sound of the name of that object, or it may represent some concept that is somehow logically related to the object. Thus a picture of a star might represent the sky and call to mind the word *an* or it might represent the word for god (associated with the sky) and be read *dingir.* This method of extending the value of a given sign opened the way for the writing of many words that could not in themselves be pictured, but it also added to the difficulty of reading by making the value of the signs ambiguous. To eliminate this ambiguity the Sumerians and their neighbors in Mesopotamia, the Akkadians, developed a group of so-called determinatives which indicated the class to which the following word belonged.

Since the inhabitants of Mesopotamia did most of their writing on clay with a reed stylus, curved lines were harder to make than straight ones, and soon the original pictures were stylized into a group of wedge-shaped impressions formed by the point of the reed. Later the pictorial character of the script was completely lost and only a set arrangement of wedges remained. This kind of writing, called cuneiform (Latin *cuneus,* "wedge"), became very widespread in the Near East. The Semites who spoke Akkadian (the Assyrians and Babylonians) passed it on to the Hurrians (*see* Horites) and Hittites (*q.v.*). *See* Cuneiform Writing.

Meanwhile toward the end of the 4th mil. B.C. the Egyptians learned of the Sumerian accomplishment. They developed their own hieroglyphic method of writing along similar lines, using pictures, determinatives, and signs to be read phonetically, but with a very important

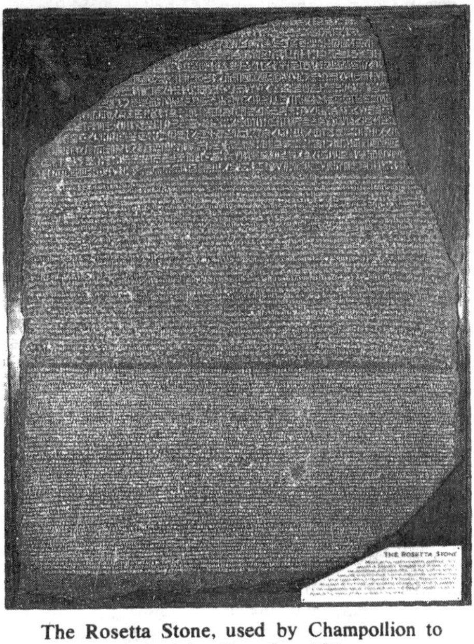

The Rosetta Stone, used by Champollion to decipher Egyptian. BM

difference from cuneiform. Whereas in cuneiform a sign, taken phonetically, might represent a certain consonant plus a certain vowel (and perhaps a second consonant), the Egyptian sign represented one or more consonants regardless of the accompanying vowels. Since Egyptian contained a number of words that had only one consonant (plus one or more vowels), the signs for these words virtually represented single consonants.

The key to deciphering the Egyptian hieroglyphic language was the Rosetta Stone. It was discovered in 1799 by an officer in Napoleon's army near the mouth of the Rosetta branch of the Nile. It had been written in 196 B.C. in three languages: hieroglyphic, Demotic Egyptian, and Koiné Greek. The young French scholar J. F. Champollion is credited with the successful decipherment of the hieroglyphic script.

Exactly when, where, or how the alphabet (*q.v.*) originated is not yet known. Perhaps it originated in Egypt or Canaan. The earliest known alphabet is Canaanite and consonantal. It certainly came into existence between 2000 and 1500 B.C. and was transmitted subsequently by the Phoenicians to the Greeks, probably in the 8th cen. B.C. The Greeks added vowels and changed the direction of writing to what the West now follows—left to right. The order of the Canaanite alphabet, essentially that of the Heb. alphabet, is known from a 14th cen. B.C. clay tablet from Ugarit (*q.v.*) written in cuneiform signs.

The syllabic cuneiform of Mesopotamia and the Egyptian hieroglyphic systems of writing were so complicated that a scribe working in either medium took years to learn to read and write. Therefore only very few could afford the luxury of such an education. The alphabet, however, put literacy within the reach of the masses, and there is some indication that this was true even in antiquity. The casual report in Jud 8:14 (RSV) that Gideon's young captive wrote a list of the 77 leading citizens of Succoth seems to imply that it was not especially unusual for a young man to be able to write.

That Moses could write (Ex 24:4; Num 33:2; Deut 31:22, 24) is hardly surprising. Indeed, since he was trained in Pharaoh's court it would be very surprising if he could not write. Long before Moses' time there were scribes in Egypt who could write Akkadian, speak Canaanite, and at least read Hurrian, not to mention Egyptian. Multi-language dictionaries were in use at Ugarit. *See* Languages.

Moses' successor could also write (Josh 8:32), and according to Deut 17:18 f. anyone who was to be king over Israel should be able to read and write so that he might make and use his own copy of the law.

Writing retained its importance in Israel throughout the biblical period. An interesting account of the relationship between the prophet Jeremiah and his secretary Baruch is given in Jer 36. Jeremiah also mentions the legal use of sealed documents (32:9 ff.), an institution now known to have been very widespread in the ancient biblical world, especially in Mesopotamia. The use of official documents by the Persian government is alluded to several times in the OT (e.g., Ezr 1:1; 5:6 f.; Est 3:12–15; Dan 6:8–10) as is the keeping of an official journal, both at the Persian court (Est 6:1) and at the courts of Israel (e.g., I Kgs 22:39) and Judah (e.g., I Kgs 22:45).

In the 1st cen. A.D. writing was very common, and it is alluded to often in the NT. Letters or epistles at that time would normally be written in a non-literary script of cursive style. When the NT books were copied in later centuries the scribes would naturally use a literary bookhand with capital or uncial letters. Although Paul used an amanuensis (Rom 16:22) he could also write himself (Gal 6:11), and he carried books with him on his travels (II Tim 4:13). Thousands of Gr. papyri from the Roman period have been discovered in the dry sands of Egypt, written by peoples from all walks of life. *See* Papyrus.

G. G. S.

An Amarna letter written in Cuneiform c. 1400 B.C. BM

Writing Materials

In biblical times in the Near East many varieties of writing materials and implements were employed by the scribes. Numerous inscriptions chiseled on the stone surfaces of temple and tomb walls and smoothed cliff faces, as well as on stelae, belonged to rulers of both Egypt and Mesopotamia. Others might use a small stone, as did the school boy who wrote his Heb. exercise on a limestone tablet known today as the Gezer Calendar. It is illustrative of the two stone covenant tablets containing the Decalogue (Ex 24:12; 34:1; Deut 4:13).

Cuneiform inscriptions in Sumerian, Akkadian, Hittite, and Old Persian have been found on metal objects and plaques (cf. Ex 28:36). An extensive copper scroll discovered in a cave near Qumran claims to describe the hiding places of buried Jewish treasures.

A sharpened reed was used as a stylus to impress cuneiform characters on clay tablets while they were still moist. Clay from the alluvial soil of the Tigris-Euphrates valley was the cheapest material for writing in Mesopotamia. Its use spread along with the adoption of Akkadian as the language of international diplomacy in the 2nd mil. B.C. Where more than one tablet was needed to complete a literary work, each text in the series was marked by a catch line, or colophon, from its adjacent tablet to indicate its proper order.

The poorer classes often utilized potsherds, always available around any town. On these they wrote messages or receipts with pen and ink. Important collections of these ostraca (*q.v.*) have been unearthed at Samaria, Lachish, and Arad in Palestine.

People even wrote on pieces of wood and sticks (Num 17:2–3; Ezk 37:16–17). Wooden tablets coated with a layer of wax were used as writing boards; often two such tablets were hinged together. The wax could be rubbed smooth to give a fresh surface. Such a waxed writing board and stylus were known to Isaiah (8:1; 30:8, both RSV), Habakkuk (2:2), and Zacharias (Lk 1:63).

Papyrus was made in Egypt by splitting reeds which grew in profusion along the Nile and laying the strips side by side with a second layer at right angles. When pounded and smoothed a material not unlike heavy wrapping paper was produced. The Egyptians used a reed cut obliquely and frayed to form a brush pen (Ps 45:1; Jer 8:8) to apply a black ink made from soot mixed with a thin solution of gum. The scribe carried his equipment on his hip in a writing case (Ezk 9:2–3, NASB; KJV "inkhorn"). From Egyptian tombs have come sets of such instruments, including a slate palette for holding red and black pigments, a water jar, and a long tubular case for pens and brushes. The Roman historian Pliny mentions the use of metallic lead to rule a papyrus sheet with guide lines in preparation for writing a text in ink.

While papyrus rolls are not mentioned in the OT, papyri were found among the Dead Sea Scrolls. Many believe that the scroll burned by King Jehoiakim was of papyrus rather than leather (Jer 36:23), for the stench of burning leather would have been intolerable. Papyrus is almost certainly the paper of II Jn 12. Evidently there were some papyrus books or scrolls in addition to the parchment ones that Paul asked Timothy to bring (II Tim 4:13).

The use of tanned skins goes back to the 3rd mil. B.C. in Egypt. Skins of goats and sheep were more durable than papyrus, and perhaps more available to the Israelite. That most of the Dead Sea Scrolls (*q.v.*) were of leather suggests that the Scriptures were commonly written on this material in the OT period. Parchment, a better prepared and smoother animal skin, began to replace leather *c.* 200 B.C. *See* Scroll.

An inscription in Greek from the theater of biblical Hierapolis. James L. Boyer

Bibliography. Y. Aharoni, "Three Hebrew Ostraca from Arad," BASOR # 197 (1970), pp. 16–42. CornPBE, "Alphabet and Writing," pp. 30–40; "Inscriptions," pp. 407–415. Frank M. Cross, Jr., "The Development of the Jewish Scripts," *"The Bible and the Ancient Near East,* ed. by G. E. Wright, Garden City: Doubleday, 1961, pp. 133–202. David Diringer, "The Biblical Scripts," *Cambridge History of the Bible,* I, ed. by P. R. Ackroyd and C. F. Evans, Cambridge: Univ. Press, 1970. G. R. Driver, *Semitic Writing from Pictograph to Alphabet,* London: Oxford Univ. Press, 1948. I. J. Gelb, *A Study of Writing,* London: Routledge & Kegan Paul, 1952. A. R. Millard, "The Practice of Writing in Ancient Israel," BA, XXXV (1972), 98–111. Joseph Naveh, "The Scripts in Palestine and Transjordan in the Iron Age," *Near Eastern Archaeology in the Twentieth Century,* Essays in Honor of Nelson Glueck, ed. by J. A. Sanders, Garden City: Doubleday, 1970, pp. 277–283. R. J. Williams, "Writing and Writing Materials," IDB, IV, 909–921. D. J. Wiseman, "Writing," NBD, pp. 1341–1351. *See also* under Alphabet.

J. R.

WRITING TABLE. *See* Tablet; Writing.

X

XERXES. *See* Ahasuerus.

Y

YAHWEH. *See* God; God, Names and Titles of; Lord.

YARN. The only use of the word "yarn" in the KJV occurs in the expression "linen yarn" of I Kgs 10:28 and II Chr 1:16. The Heb. word *miqwēh* thus translated appears to have been misinterpreted. It may instead be read "from Kue" (cf. LXX *ek thekoue* and Vulg. *de Coa*). Kue is a name for Cilicia (*q.v.*).

Yarn and/or thread in biblical times was spun on a simple hand spindle from wool and linen fiber, and also from the hair of goats and camels. The "fine linen" of Est 1:6 may have been cotton. Another fiber appears in Ezk 16:10, 13. The meaning of Heb. *meshî* there (KJV, etc., "silk") is uncertain. *See* Occupations: Weaver, Weaving.

YEAR. *See* Time, Divisions of.

YELLOW. *See* Colours.

YODH (yōd). The tenth letter of the Heb. alphabet. This letter begins each verse of the tenth section of the acrostic poem in Ps 119. It has the numerical value of 10. Since it is the smallest letter in the Aramaic or square script of the Heb. alphabet, and is equivalent to the Gr. *iōta*, many believe that Jesus referred to the *yôd* in His statement that not one jot (Gr. *iōta*) or tittle of the law would pass away until all would be accomplished (Mt 5:18). *See* Jot; Alphabet.

YOKE. A wooden frame placed over the neck of an animal, or necks of two or more animals (Num 19:2; Deut 21:3). The yoke (Heb. *'ōl*) was attached by ropes to the draft animals, and with a bar or shaft (Lev 26:13; Ezk 34:27, RSV) attached to the frame of a plow or cart (I Sam 6:7). In this manner the latter were pulled by the shoulders of the animal or animals. There was different construction of yokes for different purposes depending on how many animals were used, e.g., one, two, or four.

Heb. *ṣemed*, a couple or pair bound together, signifies a "yoke" or team of oxen (I Sam 11:7; I Kgs 19:19, 21; Job 1:3). Twice the KJV translates *ṣemed* as "acre" (I Sam 14:14, RSV; Isa 5:10), signifying the amount of land a pair of oxen could plow in one day. Yokes (Heb. *mōṭâ*, "bar") were also used on people when taken captive (Isa 58:6, 9; Jer 28:10, 12) and slaves many times had a yoke (Gr. *zygos*) put on them to restrain them (I Tim 6:1).

Figuratively, a people burdened with taxes are under a yoke (I Kgs 12:11, 14). When a nation was subjugated by another, it was considered being under the yoke of bondage (Jer 17:8); and when a nation was able to free itself from servitude to another, it was regarded as breaking the yoke (Isa 9:4). In the religious sense one can be yoked (KJV "joined") to Baal, considered a sin (Num 25:3, 5), while to apostatize from God in rebellion is considered breaking His yoke (Jer 5:5). God's sovereignty could be directed to breaking the yoke of Egypt, i.e., her power (Ezk 30:18). A mark of true spiritual worth is one's power to break the yoke of wickedness and to let the oppressed go free (Isa 58:6).

Being yoked to Christ in obedience is an easy and light burden (Mt 11:29–30), but it is a bondage to be yoked to legalism (Gal 5:1; Acts 15:10). The Christian is warned not to be "unequally yoked" with unbelievers (II Cor 6:14; cf. Deut 22:10). Finally, another believer in Christ serving together with one as a unit is considered his yoke fellow or comrade (Phil 4:3). Some believe that Paul is here referring to Luke, who had first served the Lord with the apostle at Philippi.

Bibliography. G. Bertram and K. H. Rengstorf, *"Zygos,"* TDNT, II, 896–901.

L. Go.

Z

ZAANAIM. *See* Zaanannim.

ZAANAN (zā'*ȧ*-năn). An unidentified town in western Judah (Mic 1:11). It is perhaps the same as Zenan (Josh 15:37).

ZAANANNIM (zā'*ȧ*-năn'ĭm). A point on the SE border of the territory of Naphtali (Josh 19:33). This is the site of the tent in which Sisera was slain by Jael (Jud 4:11, 18 ff.).

ZAAVAN (zā'*ȧ*-văn). A son of Ezer, the Horite (Gen 36:27; I Chr 1:42).

ZABAD (zā'băd)

1. The son of Nathan and father of Ephlal of the tribe of Judah. Zabad's grandfather was Attai the son of a daughter of Sheshan and an Egyptian slave Jarha (I Chr 2:31. 34–37).
2. The son of Tahath and father of Shuthelah of Ephraim (I Chr 7:21).
3. One of David's mighty men, the son of Ahlai (I Chr 11:41).
4. The son of Shimeath the Ammonitess. He conspired with Jehozabad to assassinate King Joash of Judah, and was put to death for the murder (II Chr 24:25–26; 25:3–4). In II Kgs 12:21 his name is given as Jozachar, perhaps his Israelite name.

5, 6, 7. Sons of Zattu, Hashum, and Nebo who put away their Gentile wives in the days of Ezra (Ezr 10:27, 33, 43).

ZABBAI (zăb'ī). A son of Bebai induced by Ezra to put away his foreign wife (Ezr 10:28). He is perhaps the same individual listed as the father of a certain Baruch who worked on the Jerusalem wall during the days of Nehemiah (Neh 3:20).

ZABBUD (zăb'ŭd). One of the sons of Bigvai who accompanied Ezra from Babylonia to Jerusalem (Ezr 8:14); RSV Zakkur. *See* Zaccur 5.

ZABDI (zăb'dī)

1. The son of Zerah of the tribe of Judah. He was the father of Achan whose trespass brought trouble to Israel (Josh 7:1, 17–18).
2. One of the sons of Shimhi of Benjamin (I Chr 8:19).
3. An inhabitant of Shepham, appointed by David as custodian of the royal wine cellars (I Chr 27:27).
4. A Levite, the son of Asaph, one of whose descendants, Mattaniah, was prominent in the time of Nehemiah (Neh 11:17).

ZABDIEL (zăb'dĭ-ĕl)

1. Father of Jashobeam (I Chr 27:2).
2. An overseer of a group of priests (Neh 11:14).

ZABUD (zā'bŭd). A son of Nathan who served as friend and chief minister to King Solomon (I Kgs 4:5).

ZABULON. The Gr. spelling of Zebulun (*q.v.*).

ZACCAI (zăk'ī). Head of a family, 960 members of which returned from Babylonian Captivity (Ezr 2:9; Neh 7:14).

ZACCHAEUS (ză-kē'*ŭ*s). A tax collector at Jericho who became a disciple of Jesus (Lk 19:1–10). He is identified as the chief tax collector (*architelōnēs*), which implies he was head over the other tax collectors of that district. Two to four trade routes converged at Jericho and a Herodian palace was located there (Jos *Ant.* xvii.10.6; 13.1). Also, Jericho was the center of famous productive palm and balsam groves (Jos *Ant.* xiv.4.1; xv.4.2). Thus Jericho provided abundant sources for tax revenue.

Comparison of Lk 18:35–19:2 with Mk 10:46 indicates that Bartimaeus (*q.v.*) was sitting by the road between the older town of Jericho and the new city built by Herod the Great where Zacchaeus lived (*see* Jericho). Zacchaeus, of short stature, climbed a sycamore tree in order to see Jesus, who in turn asked to stay at his house. Besides Zacchaeus' genuine repentance, the story shows Jesus' willingness to mingle with the despised tax collectors.

H. W. H.

Great sycamores, like the one Zacchaeus climbed, still grow in the Jericho oasis. HFV

ZACCHUR. *See* Zaccur.

ZACCUR (zăk'ûr)

1. The father of Shammua, the Reubenite spy of Num 13:4.
2. A Simeonite (KJV "Zacchur") descended through Mishma (I Chr 4:26).
3. A son of Jaaziah, a Merarite Levite (I Chr 24:27).
4. A son of the musician Asaph (I Chr 25:2, 10; Neh 12:35), perhaps to be identified with the Zichri of I Chr 9:15 and the Zabdi of Neh 11:17.
5. According to Ezr 8:14, RSV (which follows the *qerê;* cf. ASV marg.), a descendant of Bigvai. KJV reads "Zabbud" with *ketîb.*
6. A son of Imri who helped to rebuild the walls of Jerusalem (Neh 3:2).
7. A Levite who set his seal to the post-Exilic covenant (Neh 10:12).
8. An ancestor of Hanan, who was appointed an assistant treasurer by Nehemiah (Neh 13:13).

ZACHARIAH. *See* Zechariah 15, 16.

ZACHARIAS (zăk'á-rī'ás). In the KJV NT Zacharias, equivalent to Zechariah (*q.v.*) in the OT, is the name of two men.

1. Father of John the Baptist (Lk 1:5–25). Zacharias received a visit by the angel Gabriel while engaged in his ministry in the temple as a priest of the course of Abijah. Zacharias was given the angelic assurance that he should become the father of John the Baptist, and his initial unbelieving response was met by his being rendered speechless until after Elizabeth gave birth to a son. Then, filled with the Spirit, he prophesied the beautiful words known in the Latin church as the Benedictus (Lk 1:68–79).
2. Mt 23:35, apparently a reference to II Chr 24:20–22, refers to the Zacharias who was slain in the temple precincts. In Matthew's account he is called the son of Barachias, while in Chronicles Jehoiada the priest is named as his father. The Chronicler may have selected his prominent grandfather (cf. II Chr 24:15) to cite in the genealogy, whereas Matthew gives Barachias' name as his actual father (cf. Broadus, *Commentary on Matthew* for a full discussion). In the statement "from the blood of righteous Abel unto the blood of Zacharias" Jesus no doubt had reference to the first murder found in the beginning of the Bible (Gen 4:8) and the stoning of the prophet recorded in the last book of the Heb. OT (II Chr 24:21). *See* Zechariah 1, 13.

F. R. H. and A. F. J.

ZACHER (zā'kẽr). A Benjamite of the family of Jehiel of Gibeon (I Chr 8:31); an alternate form of his name Zechariah in I Chr 9:37. RSV Zecher.

ZADOK (zā'dŏk)

1. A priest during the Davidic and Solomonic reigns. Zadok is first identified as a valiant leader among the Levites who came to Hebron to make David king over all Israel (I Chr 12:26–28). His lineage is traced directly to Eleazar and Aaron (I Chr 6:1 ff., 50 ff.).

During David's reign Zadok and Abiathar, who traced his lineage as son of Ahimelech (I Sam 21–22) back through Eli to Ithamar the son of Aaron, served as priests in charge of the ark (I Chr 15:11–13). Both Zadok and Abiathar, together with their sons Ahimaaz and Jonathan, led the Levites in support of David when fleeing from Jerusalem during Absalom's revolt. At David's command they returned to Jerusalem with the ark and subsequently supplied vital information to David (II Sam 15:24–36; 17:15–21). David also appealed to Zadok and Abiathar in regaining recognition from Judah (II Sam 19:11).

In the crucial transition of royal leadership, Zadok, supported by Nathan the prophet, anointed Solomon as king, whereas Abiathar was associated with Adonijah in his attempt to succeed Solomon to the throne (I Kgs 1:1–53). As a result, Abiathar was deposed (I Kgs 2:26–27) while Zadok became the sole occupant of the high priestly office (I Kgs 2:35). In this manner the office of high priest was restored to the lineage of Eleazar, the son of Aaron. The demotion of Abiathar, a descendant of Eli, was effected in accordance with the warnings to Eli by an unnamed man of God (I Sam 2:27–36).

Zadok and his descendants continued as high priests in the Solomonic temple until its destruction in 586 B.C. Ezekiel in his message of restoration designates the Zadokites as faithful priests during the apostasy of Israel (Ezk 44:15; 48:11).

When the second temple was built 520–515 B.C. the Zadokite Jeshua, a son of Jehozadak, who had been taken into Babylonian Captivity in 586 B.C., served as high priest. The Zadokites continued in this office until 171 B.C. when it was transferred to Menelaus by Antiochus IV. After that the Zadokite line continued at the Jewish temple at Leontopolis in Egypt until this temple was closed by Vespasian shortly after A.D. 70. The Qumran community apparently supported the Zadokite priesthood and hopefully anticipated its restoration. *See* Priest, Priesthood.

2. A son of Ahitub in the lineage of Zadok (I Chr 6:12; 9:11; Ezr 7:2; Neh 11:11).
3. The father of Jerusha, the mother of Jotham king of Judah (II Kgs 15:33; II Chr 27:1).
4. Descendant of Baana who helped repair the wall of Jerusalem (Neh 3:4; cf. Ezr 2:2).
5. A descendant of Immer who helped repair the walls of Jerusalem (Neh 3:29; cf. Ezr 2:37).
6. A signer of the covenant of Ezra (Neh 10:21), who may have been either 4 or 5.
7. A sc ibe appointed treasurer by Nehemiah (Neh 13:13; cf. Neh 3:29), who may nave been either 4, 5, or 6.
8. An ancestor of Jesus (Mt 1:14, RSV).

S. J. S.

ZAHAM (zā'hăm). A son of King Rehoboam of Judah (II Chr 11:19).

ZAIN. *See* Zayin.

ZAIR (zā'ĭr). An unknown place near Edom where King Joram met the Edomites in an unsuccessful attempt to crush their revolt against Judah (II Kgs 8:20 ff.).

ZALAPH (zā'lăf). The father of a certain Hanun who helped repair the wall of Jerusalem following the Babylonian Captivity (Neh 3:30).

ZALMON (zăl'mŏn)

1. A hill covered with snow where God scattered enemy kings of Israel (Ps 68:14, KJV "Salmon"). This may be a reference to a hill in Bashan (v. 15).

2. A hill near Shechem where Abimelech gathered brushwood to burn the city (Jud 9:48–49).

3. A warrior of David, "Zalmon the Ahohite" (II Sam 23:28), who may have been named Zalmon to indicate his strength, called Ilai in I Chr 11:29.

ZALMONAH (zăl-mō'nȧ). The first stopping place of the Israelites following their departure from Mount Hor (Num 33:41–42). The place cannot be identified with certainty although it is probably one of the desert wells or oases in the Arabah S of Punon (*q.v.*).

ZALMUNNA (zăl-mŭn'ȧ). One of the two kings of Midian who was pursued, captured, and slain by Gideon in his great victory (Jud 8). This striking victory was long remembered in Israel (cf. Ps 83:11; Isa 9:4; 10:26). *See* Zebah.

ZAMZUMMIM (zăm-zŭm'ĭm). The Ammonite name given to the Rephaim, the earlier inhabitants of the land of the Ammonites (Deut 2:20), who drove them out. They were a people of giant stature (2:21), of which Og, king of Bashan, was left of the remnant (3:11). They were remembered down into David's time (II Sam 21:16, 20, 22). The Rephaim had been smitten by Chedorlaomer which weakened them, enabling the Ammonites to dispossess them. The bed of Og appears to have been an object of veneration because of his prowess or his size as the last living example of the Rephaim known to the Ammonites. *See* Giant; Zuzim.

ZANOAH (zȧ-nō'ȧ)

1. A city in the Shephelah of Judah near En-gannim (Josh 15:34). It was resettled after the Babylonian Exile (Neh 3:13). It may probably be identified with the foothill city of Khirbet Zanu', where there is pottery from the time of the kings. It is two miles S of Beth-shemesh.

2. A city in the hill country of Judah near Juttah (Josh 15:55–56). It has been identified with Zanuta, SW of Hebron, but this is probably too far S. A more probable site is that of Khirbet Beit Amra, one and a quarter miles NW of Yatta (Juttah).

ZAPHNATH-PAANEAH (zăf'năth-pȧ-nē'ȧ). The Egyptian name given to Joseph by the king of Egypt at the time of Joseph's elevation to the viziership (Gen 41:45; spelled Zaphenath-paneah in RSV, etc.). Various meanings have been proposed for the name; most commonly it is interpreted as "the god speaks (and) he lives" (Steindorff, Griffith, Crum, *et al.*). Other more correct renderings include "Nourisher of the land of the living one" (Archer, SOTI, p. 102), "the giver of the nourishment of the land," etc. In later times the Jews surmised that it meant "the revealer of secrets" (Jos *Ant.* ii.6.1; Targum of Onkelos).

ZAPHON (zā'fŏn). A town of the Gadites N of Succoth in the Jordan Valley (Josh 13:27). It is mentioned in the Amarna letters as Ṣapuna. Jud 12:1–6 lists this town as the site of a battle between the jealous Ephraimites and the army of Jephthah. A clan of Gad known as the Zephonites (Num 26:15) or Ziphionites (Gen 46:16) may have taken its name from the city.

The site of Zaphon has been identified with Tell el-Qos on the N side of the Wadi Rajeb, *c.* four miles N of Succoth near the Jabbok (cf. N. Glueck, "Explorations in Eastern Palestine IV," AASOR, XXV-XXVII [1951], pt I. 297–300, 334–355); BASOR # 90 [1943], pp. 20 f.). Y. Aharoni, however, chooses to identify Zaphon with nearby Tell Sa'idiyeh (*Land of the Bible*, pp. 115, 190), which site is usually identified with Zarethan (*q.v.*).

G. E. W.

Heb. *ṣāphôn* means "north," literally the hidden or remote area (cf. Ezk 38:6, 15, NASB). In this sense it appears in Isa 14:13 in connection with "the mount of assembly" (RSV; *see* Congregation, Mount of the). Here and in Ps 48:2 is found the Heb. phrase *yarkᵉthêṣāphôn*, "the sides of the north," "the recesses of the north" (NASB). Because the concept of north does not figure elsewhere in Scripture in relation to God's dwelling, the expression should perhaps be translated "the cloisters of Zaphon" in parallel with "Mount Zion" and with "the city of the great King" (Ps 48:2). This would suggest the sanctity and the seclusion of the divine abode, both in heaven and in the holy of holies of the temple in Jerusalem.

Zaphon was an ancient term among the Semites for the dwelling place or "aerie" of their god(s). Mount Zaphon (present day Mount Casius, 30 miles N of Ras Shamra in Syria) was to the Canaanite religion what Mount Zion was to the worship of Yahweh, namely, the most hallowed spot of the land because God dwelt there (M. Dahood, *Psalms I*, Anchor Bible, XVI, 289 f.; John Gray, *The Legacy of Canaan*, Leiden: Brill, 1957, p. 209). In the Ugaritic texts Baal is said to dwell upon Zaphon's summit, and Baal asked that a palace be built for him "in the midst of the fastness of Zaphon" (ANET, pp. 133*b*, 134*a*). He describes his abode as "in the midst of my mount Godly Zaphon: in the sanctuary, mount of my portion, in the pleasant place, the hill I possess" (ANET, p. 136*b*). *See* North.

J. R.

ZARA, ZARAH (zâr'*ȧ*). Alternate forms of Zerah (*see* Zerah 3). One of the twin sons born to Judah and Tamar (Gen 38:30; 46:12; I Chr 2:4). He was the ancestor of Achan (Josh 7:1, 18, 24; 22:20) and Pethahiah (Neh 11:24), and the founder of the tribal family called Zarhites (Num 26:20) also referred to as the "sons of Zerah" (I Chr 9:6; Neh 11:24).

ZAREAH (zâr'ĭ-*ȧ*). Found only in Neh 11:29. *See* Zorah.

ZAREATHITE (zā-rē'*ȧ*-thīt). Descendant of Shobal and the inhabitants of Zorah (I Chr 2:52-53). *See* Zorathites.

ZARED. *See* Zered.

ZAREPHATH (zăr'ĕ-făth). During the three-year drought suffered by Israel in the days of Ahab, God sent Elijah, by whom the judgment had been pronounced on Israel, to the Phoenician city of Zarephath for sustenance. There the widow with whom the prophet lived enjoyed a perennial supply of oil and meal and experienced the joy of having her son raised from the dead (I Kgs 17:8-24). The town was located about eight miles S of Sidon, along the Mediterranean coast, on the road to Tyre. Known as Zarephath in the OT (Ob 20), it is called Sarepta in the NT (Lk 4:26) and is the modern Sarafand.

Zarephath is mentioned in Ugaritic texts of the 14th cen. B.C. and in an Egyptian papyrus of the 13th cen. B.C. along with Byblos, Beirut, Sidon and Tyre as one of the principal cities of the coast (ANET, p. 477). Both Sennacherib and Esar-haddon claim to have captured Zarephath, according to Assyrian inscriptions (called Zaribtu, ANET, p. 287).

In 1969 James Pritchard began a series of excavations for the University Museum of the University of Pennsylvania at the ancient site adjacent to the village of Sarafand. It is the best stratified mound so far explored in the original homeland of the Phoenicians. There are numerous links with Phoenician and Punic cities in the western Mediterranean area. At Zarephath certain unusual pottery styles and building methods and the sign of the goddess Tanit—all found earlier at Carthage and sites in Sicily and Sardinia—attest that Phoenician culture spread westward from the Lebanese coast. *See* Phoenicia.

Bibliography. James B. Pritchard, "The Phoenicians in Their Homeland," *Expedition*, XIV (1971), 14-23.

H. F. V.

ZARETAN. *See* Zarethan.

ZARETHAN (zăr'ĕ-thăn). A town name, also spelled Zaretan, Zarthan, Zererath, Zartanah, or Zeredathah in different places or versions.

When Joshua led Israel across the Jordan, the waters were stopped at Adam, which is said to be "beside Zaretan" (Josh 3:16, KJV). Adam is at the confluence of the river Jabbok and the Jordan. There is some difference of opinion whether Zarethan was just E or W of the Jordan. Nelson Glueck identified it with a site (Tell es-Sa'idiyeh) about 14 miles N and a little E of Adam (Tell ed-Damiyeh), which was on the E side of the Jordan. Yohanan Aharoni, however, believes Zarethan may be the large mound of Tell Umm Ḥamad, only two miles NE of Adam.

Bronze pots, basins, and other equipment for Solomon's temple were cast on the clay ground between Succoth and Zarethan on the Jordan plain (I Kgs 7:46; KJV "Zarthan"; II Chr 4:17, KJV "Zeredathah"). The nature of the ground made the region an active center of industry in those days. Solomon's Beth-shean administrative district border ran near Zarethan (I Kgs 4:12, KJV "Zartanah"). The Midianite invaders fled before Gideon and his 300 men in the direction of Zererath (Jud 7:22), usually considered to be Zarethan.

The site of Tell es-Sa'idiyeh is an imposing one, covering 25 acres and rising over 130 feet above the floor of the Jordan Valley. It strategically overlooks the Jordan River a mile to the W and the Wadi Kufrinjeh 100 yards to the N. James B. Pritchard directed three seasons of excavations of this mound in 1964-66. A walled stairway, originally covered over to hide and protect it, led down the N side to a copious spring. A partition divided the six-foot-wide steps for easier two-way traffic. Most important was the discovery of a 13th-12th cen. B.C. cemetery. In one tomb a queen or noblewoman was buried with beautiful jewelry and ivory cosmetic objects, and four bronze vessels plus a bronze tripod of Cypriot design supporting a bronze dish. One cauldron with two handles is the largest bronze vessel ever discovered in Palestine. Other tombs contained a bronze wine-drinking set, a bronze cup with a gazelle's head handle, bronze bowl and mirror, and bronze swords, all confirming the accuracy of the biblical statement that the area of Succoth and Zarethan was a center of bronze-working in Solomon's day (ILN, Mar. 28, 1964, pp. 487-490; July 2, 1966, pp. 25-27; BA, XXVIII [1965], 10-17).

N. B. B. and J. R.

ZARETH-SHAHAR (zâr'ĕth-shā'här). A town in the territory of Reuben (Josh 13:19). The location of the town is probably on a hill overlooking the basin of the Dead Sea (v. 27). It has been identified by some as the modern Zarat on the E shore of the Dead Sea, due E of Tekoa in Judah. *See* Mount of the Valley.

ZARHITES (zär'hīts). Descendants of the family of Zerah. There were two families of this name, one of the tribe of Simeon (Num 26:13) and the other of the tribe of Judah (Num 26:20; Josh 7:17). Two of the "mighty men" of David belonged to this family (I Chr 27:11, 13).

ZARTANAH. *See* Zarethan.

ZARTHAN (zär'thăn). A city located on the E side of the Jordan Valley (I Kgs 7:46, KJV). *See* Zarethan.

ZATTHU (zăth'o͞o), **ZATTU** (zăt'o͞o). The head of an Israelite family, members of which returned to Jerusalem from the Captivity (Ezr 2:8; Neh 7:13). Some of the family put away their foreign wives in accordance with Ezra's reform banning foreign marriage (Ezr 10:27). Zattu is named as one of the chiefs who signed Nehemiah's covenant (Neh 10:14).

ZAVAN. *See* Zaavan.

ZAYIN (zä'yĭn). The seventh letter of the Heb. alphabet. Zayin begins each verse of the seventh section of the acrostic poem in Ps 119. It has a numerical value of seven.

ZAZA (zā'zȧ). A man of Judah and the house of Jerahmeel (I Chr 2:33).

ZEAL. In classical Gr. usage, *zēlos* denoted "the capacity or state of passionate committal to a person or cause" (Albrecht Stumpff, "*Zēlos*, etc.," TDNT, II, 877–888), either as a noble impulse toward the development of character or as the opposite and poisonous passion of jealousy (*q.v.*). The context determines the significance of this human emotion. In koinē Gr. the term has both a good sense—"ardor, zeal," and a bad sense—"jealousy, envy."

In the OT God declares that He Himself manifests ardor, zeal or jealousy (Heb. *qin'â*) in behalf of His people (Isa 9:7; 37:32; 42:13; 59:17; 63:15; Ezk 5:13; Zech 1:14; 8:2). In like manner Paul writes he was jealous for the Corinthian believers with "godly jealousy" (*theou zēlo,* II Cor 11:2). Some other NT uses of *zēlos* call to mind the passionate concern or zeal of certain OT individuals for maintaining God's honor and doing His will (Num 25:6–13; II Sam 21:2; I Kgs 19:10, 14; II Kgs 10:16; Ps 119:139). The disciples, thinking of Ps 69:9, saw such a parallel in Jesus' cleansing of the temple (Jn 2:17). Similar zeal of the Jews toward Christians was a mistaken zeal or jealousy (RSV, Acts 5:17; 13:45). Paul himself had been guilty of such a misplaced zeal (Gal 1:14; Phil 3:6). He nevertheless commended the Jews for their zeal for God (Rom 10:2; Acts 22:3; cf. 21:20).

Christians are to be zealous to repent (Rev 3:19), to correct wrongs (II Cor 7:11) and to give (II Cor 9:2). They are to be zealous of spiritual gifts, earnestly to desire (from *zēloō*) these and especially that they may prophesy (I Cor 14:12; 12:31; 14:1, 39).

F. D. L.

ZEALOT. A name generally applied to devoted Jewish patriots of the 1st cen. A.D. To many of them, violence was justified as long as it accomplished a good end—deliverance from foreign oppressors. *Sanhedrin* 9:6 and *Sanhedrin* 82*a* give an indication of the original meaning of Zealots (Heb. *qannā'îm*) in a deed of valor that recalls the zeal of Phinehas (Num 25:7–13). Phinehas is praised for his zeal (Heb. *beqanô*) in the defense of God's cause. He became the prototype of the zealot who defends the honor of God, Torah, and Israel. This concept of zeal characterized many great leaders, prophets, priests, wise men and military men.

Specifically, the term applied to the members of an extremist party active since A.D. 6 when Judah the Galilean, a rabbi, urged resistance to the Romans taking a census when Judah became a Roman province directly under the emperor. Judah the Galilean laid down the principles for a zealot cause: that the Jews not pay taxes to Rome, nor give allegiance to the emperor as their master since he was a mere man. Judah's point was that the land of Israel is the Holy Land and its produce and resources were not to go to a foreign ruler; furthermore, Israel was a theocracy and anything deviating from this norm was apostasy. Many men took up the cause, and these became an active group known as Zealots. They gave the Romans much difficulty and resorted many times to violence, sometimes even to assassination.

It has been suggested that Jesus favored the Zealots and picked Simon the Zealot to indicate approval of their tactics. Nothing could be further from the truth since Jesus' whole ministry was based on peaceful means and Simon probably had a change of heart about the whole Zealot activity, although his designation continued to show his former involvement. *See* Simon 2; Zelotes.

The Zealots took control in Jerusalem in A.D. 66, which eventually led to the downfall of Judah and Jerusalem in A.D. 70. Therefore they have been remembered for being the direct cause of Jerusalem's destruction by bringing on the war. Josephus would not regard them as really zealous for God, and referred to them as *sicarii* (Lat., "daggermen"), actually assassins (*Wars* iv.3.9; vii.10.1). Their last stronghold, Masada (*q.v.*), fell in May, A.D. 73.

L. Go.

The error of the zealots was not in their enthusiasm but in the motive which prompted it. Properly motivated zeal is an honor to the Lord. God expects His children to have a zeal for Him. They are commissioned to be "not slothful in business" but "fervent in spirit serving the Lord" (Rom 12:11). Christ gave Himself for us to redeem us from iniquity and purify unto Himself a people "zealous of good works" (Tit 2:14). Like the Corinthian Christians, all believers should be "zealous of spiritual gifts" so that the church can be edified (I Cor 14:12).

R. P. L.

Bibliography. W. R. Farmer, *Maccabeans, Zealots and Josephus,* New York: Columbia Press, 1967. K. Kohler, "Zealots," JewEnc.

ZEBADIAH (zĕb-*ȧ*-dī'*ȧ*)

1. A Benjamite, one of the sons of Beriah (I Chr 8:15).

2. A Benjamite, one of the sons of Elpaal (I Chr 8:17).

3. One of the two sons of the Benjamite Jeroham of Gedor. With his brother, Zebadiah joined David at Ziklag (I Chr 12:7).

4. One of the sons of Meshelemiah the Korhite, whose Levitical responsibility was to be doorkeepers of the temple (I Chr 26:2).

5. A captain of the fourth division of David's army. He took the place of his father Asahel, David's cousin, who was killed by Abner (I Chr 27:7).

6. One of the Levites sent out by Jehoshaphat throughout Judah to teach the people the law of the Lord (II Chr 17:8).

7. The son of Ishmael and chief of the tribe of Judah in the reign of Jehoshaphat. He was appointed as a judge "in all the king's matters" (II Chr 19:11).

8. The son of Michael, of the sons of Shephatiah, who returned with Ezra in a group of 80 (Ezr 8:8).

9. A priest in the time of Ezra who vowed to give up his foreign wife (Ezr 10:20).

P. C. J.

ZEBAH (zē'b*ȧ*). Zebah is always mentioned with Zalmunna as one of the two kings of Midian who led the hosts put to rout by Gideon (Jud 8; Ps 83:11). These Midianites had joined with the Amalekites to keep the Israelites in the great central valley of Esdraelon in bondage and terror for seven years. Each year at harvest time they came sweeping in like locusts, pillaging and devouring the Israelite crops. After Gideon and his 300 had put to rout the Midianite army, they fled back across the Jordan. Great numbers of them were slain by the Ephraimites at the fords of the Jordan, including the minor chiefs Oreb and Zeeb. Zebah and Zalmunna escaped with a remnant to Karkor, a stronghold not yet identified with certainty (Qarqar in the Wadi Sirhan, 200 miles to the SE in the Arabian desert, as suggested in the *Westminster Atlas,* seems too far distant). They were taken by surprise by Gideon, who had pursued them, and the two kings were captured. When Zebah and Zalmunna described the men they had captured and slain at Tabor. Gideon recognized they were his own brethren. Had they spared his brethren, he would have spared them. The two desert chieftains died, proudly defying their captor.

P. C. J.

ZEBAIM (zē-bā'ĭm). The name of a group of descendants of Solomon's temple servants who returned from Captivity (Ezr 2:57; Neh 7:59). Little is known of their history or function. They may have been Canaanite prisoners of war who became state slaves (Isaac Mendelsohn, "State Slavery in Ancient Palestine," BASOR #85 [1942], pp. 16–17). The RSV has Pochereth-hazzebaim.

ZEBEDEE (zĕb'*ĕ*-dē). This is probably the Gr. form of the Heb. name Zebediah which means "Yahweh has endowed." The name is assigned to the husband of Salome (Mt 27:56; Mk 15:40) and the father of James and John, disciples of Christ (Mt 4:21). Apparently, he was quite well-to-do since he had "hired servants" (Mk 1:19–20) and was a Galilean fisherman (Mt 4:21–22). It has been conjectured that since his son John knew Annas the high priest (Jn 18:15), Zebedee may have conducted a business of selling fish in Jerusalem. He is seen in Scripture with his two sons in the fishing boat mending the nets. There is no record of his raising any objection to his sons' immediately leaving him and following the Saviour when He summoned them to do so.

ZEBINA (zē-bī'n*ȧ*). One of the Jews contemporary with Ezra who had married a foreign wife (Ezr 10:43).

ZEBOIM (zē-bō'ĭm)

1. A town near Hadid and Naballat in the Sharon plain which was occupied by some of the returnees from the Babylonian Exile (Neh 11:34). The location of its ancient site is unknown. There is some uncertainty as to whether it and the town in its immediate vicinity were part of the Persian province of Judah or not, but at least their Jewish occupants were permitted to participate in the religious life of the community at Jerusalem (contrast the Samaritans, Ezr 4:1–3, 10).

2. The valley of Zeboim (Heb. *s^e^bō'îm,* "hyenas") between Michmash and the wilderness to the E (I Sam 13:16–18), identified with the Wadi Abu Daba .

ZEBUDAH (zē-bū'd*ȧ*). The mother of King Jehoiakim (II Kgs 23:36); RSV "Zebidah."

ZEBUL (zē'bŭl). The governor of Shechem who warned Abimelech of a rebellious plot planned by Gaal and his adherents, and then drove Gaal out of the city (Jud 9:28–41).

ZEBULONITE. *See* Zebulunite.

ZEBULUN (zĕb'yŭ-lŭn). The tenth son of Jacob, the sixth borne to him by Leah in Padan-aram. His full brothers were Reuben, Simeon, Levi, Judah, and Issachar. In Canaan he had three sons (Sered, Elon, and Jahleel) who accompanied him into Egypt. These became the ancestors of the three main divisions of the tribe (Gen 46:14). Scripture gives no record of Zebulun's personal activities. These can only be deduced from accounts involving the other sons of Jacob (e.g., the sale of Joseph into slavery).

During the wilderness march the tribe of Zebulun camped on the E side of the tabernacle and thus moved among the first group under the standard of Judah. When the first census was taken, Zebulun had 57,400 males above 20 years of age (Num 1:31) and at the second census had 60,500 (Num 26:27). Zebulun's representative among the 12 spies who entered Canaan was Gaddiel (Num 13:10). When the tribe entered Palestine, they received an allotment of land in the Galilee hills, but it did not at that time extend to either the Sea of Galilee or the Mediterranean as Jacob had prophesied (Gen 49:13; Josh 19:10–16). They were not able to dislodge the Canaanites from all this territory.

Zebulun sent a distinguished corps to Barak in his struggle with Sisera (Jud 4:10–16; 5:18), and later provided Gideon with aid against the Midianites (Jud 6:35). Elon, one of the minor judges, came from this tribe (Jud 12:11). Later, Zebulun sent 50,000 warriors to join David at Hebron (I Chr 12:33). In the later days of the northern kingdom the territory of Zebulun apparently suffered depopulation and annexation to Assyria at the hands of Tiglath-pileser III in 732 B.C. (II Kgs 15:29). Some people from Zebulun accepted King Hezekiah's invitation to come to Jerusalem for the renewal of the Passover celebration (II Chr 30:10–11, 18).

Nazareth and Cana both lay in Zebulun, and Christ's ministry there fulfilled such prophecies as Isa 9:1–2 (cf. Mt 4:12–16). Ezekiel (48:26–33) and John (Rev 7:8) included Zebulun in their predictions concerning the end times.

H. F. V.

ZEBULUNITE (zĕb'ū-lū-nīt). A member of the tribe of Zebulun (Num 26:27; Jud 12:11–12). *See* Zebulun.

ZECHARIAH (zĕk'*á*-rī'*á*). The name means "Yahweh remembers" or "whom Yahweh remembers." Many persons in the OT bore this name.

1. The greatest of the prophets who ministered in the days of the restoration from Babylonian Exile. He was a contemporary of Zerubbabel, the political leader of the returned exiles; Joshua the son of Josedech was the priestly head of the nation; and Haggai was also a prophet (Zech 3:1; 4:6; 6:11; Ezr 5:1–2).

Zechariah was born in Babylon, and was a member of a priestly family which returned from exile to Jerusalem when about 50,000 exiles made their way home by the permission of King Cyrus. Zechariah's father Berechiah is supposed to have died young, so that the prophet is designated as the son of Iddo, who was his grandfather (see Ezr 5:1; 6:14; Neh 12:4, 16; cf. Zech 1:1). He was, like Jeremiah and Ezekiel before him, both a prophet and priest, a fact which reveals that these divinely ordained offices were not antagonistic to each other, as liberal scholars have repeatedly claimed.

Some interpreters consider Zechariah to have been a very young man at the commencement of his ministry (Zech 2:4), but no definite age can be deduced from this reference. Jewish tradition makes him a member of the Great Synagogue, a group that is supposed to have collected and preserved the sacred writings and traditions of the Jews after the Exile. He began his prophetic ministry two months after Haggai had begun his service (cf. Hag 1:1 and Zech 1:1). It was in the second year of the reign of the Persian Darius (Hystaspes) I (521–485 B.C.). The first recorded prophecy of Zechariah was in the second year of the reign of Darius, in 520 B.C. His work and that of Haggai was to encourage the building of the restoration temple, and to reveal the hope of the nation for the future. The length of his ministry is unknown.

Some have tried to identify this prophet with the Zechariah referred to in Isa 8:2, but the chronological considerations are against it. This tradition of the Jews refutes another which held that Zechariah prophesied in the second temple.

Although the latest notation of time in the book is the fourth year of Darius (7:1), it is probable that Zechariah saw the completion of the temple of Zerubbabel two years later (Ezr 6:14–15). His later prophecies must have come from his pen a number of years after the first visions granted him. Tradition has it that he lived to an extreme old age, died in Judea, and was buried near Haggai in the vicinity of Eleutheropolis.

This prophet is probably not to be identified with the Zacharias son of Barachias mentioned by the Lord in Mt 23:35, who was slain between the sanctuary and the altar (cf. II Chr 24:20–22), an event of pre-Exilic days. Although the Targum to Lam 2:20, Chrysostom, and Jerome made such an identification, it can hardly be correct. Furthermore, if the prophet had been martyred in post-Exilic times, we should have expected some word concerning it in the books of Ezra and Nehemiah or Malachi. The Lord was evidently speaking of Zechariah the son of Jehoiada (II Chr 24:20). [But see J. Barton Payne, "Zachariah Who Perished," *Grace Journal*, VIII (1967), 33–35. – Ed.]

Zechariah's ministry was carried on in an especially significant period of Israel's history. When Cyrus sent forth his edict (between 538 and 536 B.C.), some 50,000 exiles returned to Palestine from Babylon (Ezr 1:1–4; 2:64–65). With high enthusiasm they determined to rebuild the temple of the Lord in Jerusalem, and to repossess the land. They began the work and in the second month of 535 B.C. they laid the temple foundation (Ezr 3:8–13).

The Samaritans, who offered to help in the work and were denied, opposed the work relentlessly. They succeeded in stopping the work even in Cyrus' reign (Ezr 4:5). For about 14 years nothing was done on the building. When Darius Hystaspes came to the throne in 521 B.C., Zechariah and his contemporary Haggai assumed that the prohibitory decrees of the former monarch were no longer valid. Therefore they exhorted their fellow countrymen to begin the work anew. The work was started under the leadership of Zerubbabel and Joshua, but was again interrupted when an inquiry concerning the purpose of the work was made by Tatnai, the Persian governor W of the Euphrates. The matter was referred to Babylon, and the original decree of Cyrus was brought to light. Darius confirmed the permission in the second year of his rule (Ezr 6:1–14).

But outward obstacles were only part of the difficulty, for now there had come a change in the attitude of the people, who saw in the hindrances to the work the restraint of the Lord, forbidding them to go on with the enterprise. Haggai and Zechariah tried to turn the nation from their indifference. The Lord blessed their ministry, and in 515 B.C. the work was completed. Zechariah later gave himself under God to revealing to the people what glorious things the Lord had in store for the godly under Messiah and His benevolent reign (*see* Zechariah, Book of).

C. L. F.

2. The chief of the tribe of Reuben who lived around the time of the invasion of Tiglath-pileser III *c.* 740 B.C. (I Chr 5:6–7).

3. A son of Meshelemiah, a Kohathite Levite; keeper of the N gate of the tabernacle in David's reign, who also served as a wise counselor (I Chr 9:21; 26:2, 14).

4. A son of Jehiel the first Israelite settler of Gibeon (I Chr 9:35, 37). His shorter name Zacher (ASV, Zecher) appears in I Chr 8:31.

5. A Levite musician of the second rank whom David appointed to play at the bringing of the ark to Jerusalem (I Chr 15:14, 18, 20), and later to minister "before the ark of the Lord" (I Chr 16:5).

6. One of the trumpet-playing priests who accompanied the ark from the house of Obed-edom (I Chr 15:24).

7. A son of Isshiah, a Kohathite Levite in David's reign (I Chr 24:25), perhaps the same as 5

8. Fourth son of Hosah, a Merarite Levite; one of the chief gatekeepers during David's administration (I Chr 26:11).

9. The father of Iddo the chief officer of the half tribe of Manasseh in Gilead under David (I Chr 27:21).

10. A prince of Judah sent by King Jehoshaphat to teach the law to the people (II Chr 17:7).

11. A Levite of the family of Asaph; his son Jahaziel was Spirit-anointed to encourage the army of Jehoshaphat against the invading Moabites (II Chr 20:14).

12. A son of King Jehoshaphat (II Chr 21:2).

13. A son of the high priest Jehoiada in the reign of Joash, king of Judah (II Chr 24:20), and therefore the king's cousin. After the death of Jehoiada (24:15–16), Zechariah probably succeeded to his office. At that time the officials of Judah returned to idolatry (24:17–18), and Zechariah was moved by the Spirit of God to rebuke the nation for its transgressions. This aroused such resentment that the nobles conspired with the king to have him stoned to death in the court of the temple. As he died he cried out, "May the Lord see and avenge!" (24:22, RSV). For the problem regarding the identification of this Zechariah with the Zacharias of Mt 23:35; Lk 11:51, *see* Zechariah 1 above.

14. A prophet in the reign of Uzziah whose counsel brought prosperity as long as the king heeded it (II Chr 26:5).

15. One of the last kings of the northern kingdom of Israel, who succeeded his father Jeroboam II in 753 B.C. (II Kgs 14:29); called Zachariah in the KJV. With him ended the dynasty of Jehu (cf. II Kgs 10:30), when Shallum assassinated him after a brief reign of only six months (II Kgs 15:8–12).

16. The father of Abi (or Abijah), Hezekiah's mother (II Kgs 18:2, KJV "Zachariah"; II Chr 29:1).

17. A Levite of the house of Asaph who aided King Hezekiah in cleansing the temple (II Chr 29:13).

18. The son of Jeberechiah; one of the witnesses to a tablet written by Isaiah concerning the name Maher-shalal-hash-baz for the prophet's yet unconceived son (Isa 8:2); perhaps the same as 14 or 17.

19. A Kohathite Levite, an overseer of the workmen who repaired the temple in the reign of Josiah (II Chr 34:12).

20. A chief officer of the temple, probably a priest, in the reign of Josiah (II Chr 35:8).

21. A descendant of Pharosh; he returned to Jerusalem with 150 male members of his clan under Ezra's leadership (Ezr 8:3).

22. The son of Bebai; accompanied by 28 male members of his family he also returned with Ezra from Babylon (Ezr 8:11).

23. One of the prominent men sent by Ezra to persuade Levites and temple servants to return to Jerusalem (Ezr 8:16); possibly either 21 or 22 above.

24. One of the sons of Elam; he had married a foreign wife in Ezra's time (Ezr 10:26).

25. A leading priest or Levite who stood at Ezra's left hand at the reading of the law (Neh 8:4); perhaps 23 above.

26. The grandfather of Athaiah who lived in Jerusalem in post-Exilic times, of the tribe of Judah (Neh 11:4).

27. An ancestor of Maaseiah who lived in

ZECHARIAH, BOOK OF

Jerusalem at the same time (Neh 11:5).

28. A priest, ancestor of Adaiah, in Nehemiah's time (Neh 11:12).

29. The representative of the priestly family of Iddo in the time of Joiakim (Neh 12:16), perhaps a descendant of Zechariah 1.

30. A Levite, son of Jonathan, of the clan of Asaph; he led a group of musicians at the dedication of the wall of Jerusalem (Neh 12:35-36).

31. A priest who played the trumpet at the same dedication ceremony (Neh 12:41).

32. The father of John the Baptist (Lk 1:5; 3:2, RSV). *See* Zacharias.

J. R.

ZECHARIAH, BOOK OF. Zechariah's book is the eleventh of the so-called Minor Prophets, or "the Twelve," as they were called by the Jews.

Style and Value

Because the prophet (*see* Zechariah 1) used the apocalyptic form to convey prophetic truth, his book has been called the Apocalypse of the OT. His revelations are succinct and terse, hence he has been called the epitomist of the prophets. His style varies from direct prophetic address to the presentation of visions and the recording of symbolic acts.

Many have complained in ancient and modern times over the obscurity of the book. Especially have Jewish commentators expressed their inability to fathom the visions and prophecies of the book. The outlook and framework of the prophecy are so definitely messianic, that there should be no surprise that an unbelieving approach to the message should yield little results.

However, if the book is difficult of exposition, it has not forfeited its importance. Luther referred to this book as *Der Ausbund der Propheten*, the quintessence of the prophets. Its contribution to messianic prophecy is all out of proportion to its size. Only Isaiah has a fuller portrayal of the person and work of the Messiah. Zechariah treats both the first and second comings of Israel's Redeemer: Messiah's coming in lowliness, His shepherd ministry to His people, their rejection of Him, the Father's smiting of His equal with the consequent scattering of the sheep, His return in glory to repentant Israel, His establishment of peace among the nations, and the inauguration of His blessed millennial rule over all the earth. Other eschatological themes receive attention also.

Authorship and Date

The critical questions concerning the book are second in importance only to those related to Mosaic authorship of the Pentateuch, and the single or multiple authorship of Isaiah, together with the late dating of the book of Daniel. In brief, chaps. 1-8 have been assigned to Zechariah, whereas chaps. 9-14 are said to be either pre-Exilic or post-Zecharian.

The critical position is based on several arguments, the most important of which deal with the matters of style and historical references. As has been demonstrated many times, the style of a writer is directly related to the subject or theme under treatment. It cannot be proved that Zechariah used language inappropriate or out of keeping with the truths he sought to present. As to subject matter or historical references, the critical animus against the supernatural in predictive prophecy is immediately discernible. To argue that the reference to Greece in 9:13 makes it impossible for the chapter to be written before Alexander the Great, is valid only if predictive prophecy be ruled out as a possibility in a record admittedly supernatural. Incidentally, others have argued on the basis of 9:13 and 10:7, where mention is made of Ephraim and Judah, for a pre Exilic date. Both parts of the prophecy have thought and style resemblances, indicating unity. The prophecy is undoubtedly post-Exilic and by Zechariah.

Contents

Zechariah is recognized as the prophet of comfort, hope, and glory. The introduction to the prophecy (1:1-6) opens on the ethical note of the need for repentance and a full return to the Lord. Then follows a series of eight night visions, all granted the prophet in one night. The purpose of the visions was to comfort and encourage the returned exiles in their task of rebuilding the restoration temple, and to set their hope in the larger framework of OT expectation in the Messiah and His coming reign over all the earth.

The first night vision underscores the concern of the Lord for His distressed people so recently returned to the land. They need not be disturbed over the disparity between their distraught condition and the ease of the nations about them (1:7-12), for the Lord has purposes of blessing in store for them (1:13-17) and wrath upon their enemies.

The second night vision discloses that every foreign power that has oppressed Israel will in turn suffer the visitation of the Lord (1:18-21).

The third night vision continues the theme of blessing by showing how the city of Jerusalem will be enlarged because of the multiplication of man and beast in her midst. The dwelling presence of the Lord will assure both safety and glory for them in the day of fulfillment (2:1-13).

However, before these promised blessings can become actual, sin must be radically dealt with in Israel. The high priest's cleansing in the fourth vision is symbolic of the cleansing of the nation and their reinstatement to their intended priestly position among the nations (3:1-10). All is a picture of Messiah's cleansing of His land and people.

The fifth vision was intended to encourage Zerubbabel in his work of building the temple by disclosing to him the infinite resources in the Spirit of God and His power committed to the work (4:1-14).

Again, sin is a reality to be dealt with, so the sixth and seventh visions show how the Lord will summarily extirpate sin and sinner from the land of promise (5:1-11).

The final vision returns in general form to the first, showing a completion of the work promised, namely, the subjugation of Israel's enemies (6:1–8).

The series is concluded by a symbolic crowning of Joshua the high priest, foreshadowing the priestly and kingly ministry of the Messiah in the coming kingdom of righteousness (6:9–15).

In chaps. 7 and 8 the prophet answers questions concerning fasting, pointing to the shallowness of these observances, the sins of their ancestors which brought the judgment of God upon them, the way of blessing for them in the then present hour, and the time when all the fasts will be turned by God into feasts.

No prophetic portion in the Bible condenses so much eschatological revelation as the last six chapters of this prophecy. Against the backdrop of Alexander's conquests in the 4th cen. B.C. (9:1–8), Zechariah foretells the coming of Israel's King of peace (9:9–10), and His benefits to be bestowed on His people (9:11–17).

Zech 10 occupies itself with a delineation of the manifold blessings of Messiah upon Israel. Chap. 11 is one of the most somber in the book. It depicts, first of all, a thorough devastation of the land (vv. 1–3), which befell them in the Judeo-Roman war of A.D. 67–70. Then the cause of the visitation is revealed as their rejection of the Good Shepherd (vv. 4–14); for this wickedness there will be sent in a coming day a foolish shepherd who will oppress them (vv. 15–17).

The last chapters bring us to the threshold of the kingdom. Zechariah vividly pictures the world confederacy against Jerusalem, which is completely routed by the Lord (12:1–9), at which time He deals with Israel concerning their rejection of their Messiah (12:10–14). Israel's Day of Atonement issues in their national conversion. The people are cleansed of their sins (13:1–6), and the method is stressed again, namely, the death of Messiah (13:7–9).

Finally, in bold and dramatic strokes the prophet unveils the return of the Messiah to the Mount of Olives to His beleaguered people, the complete devastation of the forces of the enemy, and the cleansing of the land to conform to God's infinite holiness (14:1–21). The book began with a call to repentance and holiness, and closes with the realization of this holiness in God's people dwelling in Messiah's kingdom of righteousness.

Outline

I. Introduction: Exhortation to Repentance, 1:6

II. The Prophet's Eight Night Visions, 1:7–6:8
   - A. The Angel of the Lord among the myrtles (true Israel), 1:7–17
   - B. The four horns (powers) and the four smiths, 1:18–21
   - C. The surveyor (promise of Jerusalem's future prosperity), 2:1–13
   - D. Joshua the high priest and the Angel of the Lord, 3:1–10
   - E. The lampstand (Israel) and the two olive trees (the two anointed ones, Joshua and Zerubbabel), 4:1–14
   - F. The flying scroll (curse of God on those who break the two parts of the Decalogue in the land), 5:1–4
   - G. The woman in the ephah (religious wickedness of the Jews), 5:5–11
   - H. The four colored horses and chariots (symbols of God's wrath going forth to destroy Gentile nations), 6:1–8

III. The Symbolic Coronation, 6:9–15

IV. The Deputation from Bethel Concerning Fasting, 7:1–8:23
   - A. Their question: Should they continue the national fast in the fifth month? 7:1–3
   - B. The answer: God has already expressed through the earlier prophets His mind on mere form worship, 7:4–14
   - C. A promise of restoration: God will save His people and dwell with them, 8:1–8
   - D. A reaffirmation of God's purpose to rebuild a house of the Lord, 8:9–17
   - E. The promise that their fasts will become feasts, 8:18–23

V. The Future of the World Powers and of Israel Predicted, 9:1–14:21
   - A. The burden concerning the Gentiles, 9:1–11:17
     1. Judgment on the lands of Syria, Phoenicia, and Philistia by Alexander the Great, 9:1–8
     2. Israel's far greater King, who will bring peace to the nations after smiting the enemies of His people, 9:9–17
     3. God's work of delivering Israel from her own leaders and from the nations when Messiah returns, 10:1–12
     4. Parenthetical: Rejection of the Good Shepherd and rule of the wicked one, 11:1–17
   - B. The burden concerning Israel, 12:1–14:21
     1. Israel's end-time conflict and her physical and spiritual deliverance, 12:1–14
     2. Israel's future cleansing from sin and from idolatrous prophets, 13:1–6
     3. Israel's Shepherd smitten and her remnant refined, 13:7–9
     4. The great climax of the day of the Lord: the Lord's coming to deliver Israel and to set up His earthly millennial kingdom, 14:1–21

Bibliography. David Baron, *The Visions and Prophecies of Zechariah*, London: Hebrew Christian Testimony to Israel, 1919, reprinted 1951. Charles L. Feinberg, *God Remembers: A Study of the Book of Zechariah*, Wheaton: Van

Kampen Press, 1950, reprinted 1965. R. E. Higginson, "Zechariah," NBC, 2nd ed. H. C. Leupold, *Exposition of Zechariah,* Grand Rapids: Baker, 1965. F. B. Meyer, *The Prophet of Hope: Studies in Zechariah,* New York: Revell, 1900. George L. Robinson, *The Prophecies of Zechariah,* Chicago: Univ. of Chicago Press, 1896. Merrill F. Unger, *Commentary on Zechariah,* Grand Rapids: Zondervan, 1962.

C. L. F.

ZEDAD (zē'dăd). A place or tower located on the N borderline of the Promised Land (Num 34:8; Ezk 47:15). It is identified by many with Sadad in the desert E of the road from Damascus to Homs and Qatna, *c.* 65 miles NE of Damascus.

ZEDEKIAH (zĕd'ĕ-kī'*á*)

1. Son of Chenaanah (I Kgs 22:1–28; II Chr 18:1–27); one of Ahab's 400 court prophets who were consulted prior to the planned expedition against Ramoth-gilead. At first all the prophets prophesied, and then Zedekiah became spokesman for the group, placing upon his head "horns of iron," symbolic of power. He then predicted victory over the Syrians. When Micaiah, on the other hand, delivered a prophecy of defeat for Ahab, Zedekiah stepped forward and struck him, asking, "Which way went the Spirit of the Lord from me to speak unto thee?" (II Chr 18:23).

2. A contemporary of Jeremiah the prophet and son of Maaseiah (Jer 29:21). In association with another false prophet named Ahab, Zedekiah uttered lying prophecies among the captives in Babylon and also committed adultery. Apparently Zedekiah attempted to raise the hopes of the captives with delusive predictions of an early restoration. Jeremiah denounced the false prophets sternly, and declared that their names and their terrible fate would become proverbial in Israel (Jer 29:21–23).

3. Son of Hananiah (Jer 36:12), a prince of Judah in the days of Jehoiakim who gathered with other princes in the scribe's chamber to hear Baruch read the scroll of Jeremiah's prophecies.

4. The last king of Judah (597–586 B.C.). The account of his 11-year reign is found in II Kgs 24; II Chr 36; Jer 39 and 52. Twenty-one years of age when he became king, Zedekiah was the third son of Josiah to come to the throne. He was the younger brother of Jehoahaz and Jehoiakim and the uncle of Jehoiachin, kings of Judah who had in turn been deposed by Pharaoh-necho and deported to Egypt, died in office, or had been taken captive to Babylon. The removal of Jehoiachin to exile included the deportation of the chief men of Judah. Zedekiah was made king over the remnant left behind in 597 B.C., and his previous name, Mattaniah, was changed to Zedekiah (II Kgs 24:17). The situation he inherited was a tenuous one and in fact too difficult for Zedekiah to control.

At the outset of his reign Zedekiah gave some signs of intention to obey the Mosaic law and to heed the advice of Jeremiah with respect to foreign policies. He urged those who held slaves to set them free (Jer 34), and sent an embassy to Babylon to advise the Jews there to settle down to normal living and seek the peace of the city and to pray for it (Jer 29).

It soon became apparent, however, that the court of Zedekiah was a center of intrigue and plotting against Babylon. In the fourth year of Zedekiah, ambassadors gathered at Jerusalem from the surrounding nations of Edom, Moab, Ammon, Tyre, and Sidon urging the king of Judah to join them in a conspiracy against Babylon. Jeremiah opposed this foolish scheme, and appeared before the envoys bearing upon his shoulders a yoke of wood to dramatize his declaration that God had given the nations into the hands of Nebuchadnezzar. Those who submitted would be allowed to live, but those who rebelled and refused submission to the yoke would perish (Jer 27). News of the impending revolt may have reached Nebuchadnezzar, who apparently then summoned Zedekiah to Babylon (Jer 51:59). This would seem to explain, at least in part, why the proposed insurrection did not materialize at this time.

The next step toward overt rebellion was taken when Zedekiah leagued with Egypt—a treacherous and defiant move in the eyes of Nebuchadnezzar, the result of which was an invasion of Palestine which reduced all Judea apart from Jerusalem, Lachish, and Azekah. The scriptural record of this event is found in Jer 34 and 37, and in Ezk 17. Josephus declares that the date was the eighth year of the reign of Zedekiah.

The final siege of Jerusalem began in the ninth year of Zedekiah's reign on the tenth day of the tenth month. The account of the siege and fall of the city is found in II Kgs 25 and also in Jer 39 and 52. Because of a report that Hophra of Egypt was on his way to aid the beleaguered city, the siege was lifted for a short time as the Babylonian army deployed to meet this threat. Although details are not available, it may be assumed that Egypt was summarily defeated, for Babylon resumed its siege of Jerusalem as Jeremiah had solemnly predicted would be the case (Jer 37:8–10).

Conditions now became desperate. The strongly fortified city held out for nearly a year and a half, during which time the population suffered all the horrors of famine and pestilence. A breach was finally made in the walls, and Zedekiah, seeing that all was lost, attempted to escape to the Jordan Valley. Pursued and captured by the Chaldeans, he was brought before Nebuchadnezzar at Riblah, and there sentence was passed upon him. The sons of Zedekiah were slain before him, after which his eyes were put out and he himself was taken in chains to Babylon, where he later died. Thus were fulfilled the prophecies of Jer 34 and Ezk 12 concerning the fate of Judah's last king.

5. A prominent Jewish official who was among the sealers of the renewed covenant after the Exile (Neh 10:1, RSV; KJV "Zidkijah").

D. K. C.

ZEEB (zē′ĕb). One of two Midianite princes (*see* Oreb) captured and beheaded by men of Ephraim "at the winepress of Zeeb" near the Jordan (Jud 7:25). Their heads were taken across the river to Gideon. Josephus (*Ant.* v. 6.5) defines this as "in a certain valley encompassed in torrents, in a place which these could not get over." Also he words Israel's battlecry as "Victory to Gideon, by God's assistance." Under the hand of the Lord, Gideon with 300 men put to rout and slew the Midianite army of 135,000. In Ps 83:11 we read of Israel's enemies: "Make their nobles like Oreb, and like Zeeb."

ZELAH (zē′lȧ). A town in the territory of Benjamin (Josh 18:28), the site of the tomb of Kish in which the bones of Saul and Jonathan were buried (II Sam 21:14). The location of the city is uncertain except that it is listed among 14 cities generally located in the hill country N and W of Jerusalem. Khirbet Salah, a few miles NW of Jerusalem, is a possible identification of the site.

ZELEK (zē′lĕk). An Ammonite who was one of David's mighty men known as the "Thirty" (II Sam 23:37; I Chr 11:39).

ZELOPHEHAD (zē-lō′fē-hăd). A Gileadite of the tribe of Manasseh. Zelophehad, who came out of Egypt with Moses, had no sons but five daughters who set two legal precedents in Israel. When the people were numbered in Moab in order to determine the inheritance each family was to possess in the Promised Land, the girls, whose father had died in the wilderness, appealed to Moses. If the inheritance was to be determined solely through the male line, the family of Zelophehad would disappear. The decision was made that in such cases the inheritance would go to the daughters (Num 27:1-11).

Later the question of the marriage of such daughters arose. In order to keep the inheritance within the tribe, it was determined that they must marry only members of their own tribe (Num 36).

ZELOTES (zē-lō′tēz). The Gr. word *zēlōtēs*, twice associated with one of the 12 disciples of Jesus (Lk 6:15, "Simon called Zelotes"; Acts 1:13, "Simon Zelotes"), marks this man as being jealous for the honor of God. The term translates the Heb. *qannā'*, "jealous," "zealous," which Matthew and Mark preserve by transliteration, speaking of "Simon the Canaanean " (Mt 10:4; Mk 3:18, ASV, etc.), i.e., Simon, the one zealous for God's honor.

The name suggests that Simon patterned his life after the patriarch Phinehas, whose indignation and decisive action in the face of Israelite idolatry God said had "turned away My wrath from the sons of Israel, in that he was jealous with My jealousy among them . . . and made atonement for the sons of Israel" (Num 25:10-13, NASB). Phinehas' zeal for God was remembered in Scripture, being "reckoned to him for righteousness" (Ps 106:30-31, NASB), inviting emulation. When Jesus drove the money changers from the temple, the disciples remembered the word, "Zeal for Thy house has consumed me" (Ps 69:9, NASB; Jn 2:17), an association which may have first attracted Simon to Jesus. *See* Simon 4; Zealot.

W. L. L.

ZELZAH (zĕl′zȧ). An unidentified place located in the territory of Benjamin near Rachel's tomb. It was the site of one of the promised signs to Saul that he was to be the king of Israel (I Sam 10:1-2).

ZEMARAIM (zĕm-ȧ-rā′ĭm)

1. A city of the tribe of Benjamin (Josh 18:22). Some writers identify it with Ras ez-Zeimara, a ruin *c.* three miles NE of Bethel.

2. A mountain in the hill country of Ephraim (II Chr 13:4) on which King Abijah stood to harangue Jeroboam and his men, urging them to repent of their rebellion.

ZEMARITES (zĕm′ȧ-rīts). A Canaanite people of the city of Ṣimura (Assy. Ṣimirra; Amarna, Ṣumur) (Gen 10:18; I Chr 1:16). It is a town six miles S of Arvad. The town today is known as Sumra. Tiglath-pileser I (1114-1076 B.C.) invaded Sumur by sea (Luckenbill, *Anc. Rec. of Assyr. & Baby.*, I, 98). Genesis indicates the early and close relationship between this people and Hamath, which long figured in Canaanite history. It was important enough to be sought by both Pharaoh and his adversaries as shown by the Amarna letters, suggesting the reason why the Zemarites are listed in the Table of Nations (*see* Nations).

ZEMIRA (zē-mī′rȧ). A Benjamite of the family of Becher (I Chr 7:8).

ZENAN zē′nȧn). A town of Judah in the Shephelah district of Lachish (Josh 15:37), not identified. It is probably identified with Zaanan (Mic 1:11).

ZENAS (zē′nȧs). In Tit 3:13 Zenas is described as a lawyer or jurist by way of identification. Paul admonishes Titus to send forward Zenas and Apollos on their journey, doing everything possible to make adequate provisions for them. If Zenas was a converted Jew, he may have retained his former designation as a scribe or lawyer. If a Gentile, the law he practiced would have been Gr. or Rom.

ZEPHANIAH (zĕf'*ȧ*-nī'*ȧ*)

1. A Levite descended from Kohath (I Chr 6:36–38).

2. Son of Maaseiah and second priest under the high priest Seraiah during the reign of King Zedekiah. On two occasions he helped bear requests for prayer from the king to Jeremiah; and brought back oracles of the prophet denouncing further defense against Nebuchadnezzar's army and hoping for Egyptian aid (Jer 21:1; 37:3). Once Zephaniah received a letter from Shemaiah already in Babylon, rebuking him for not imprisoning Jeremiah who was accused of sending discouraging letters to the exiles (Jer 29:25–29). After the Babylonians captured Jerusalem Zephaniah was among the Jewish leaders taken to Riblah in Syria and executed by Nebuchadnezzar (II Kgs 25:18–21; Jer 52:24–27).

3. The prophet, son of Cushi, who prophesied in the 7th cen. B.C. in the days of Josiah. His descent is traced back four generations to Hezekiah (Zeph 1:1; KJV "Hizkiah"), probably the king, in view of the fact that the genealogy is followed to so distant a time, and because the chronology tallies. He lived in Judah, and showed familiarity with the physical features of the city of Jerusalem (Zeph 1:10–11). There are no means of determining the length of his prophetic ministry. The reign of Josiah would set it between 640 and 609 B.C. (1:1). His ministry may have been carried on in the early years of Josiah's rule before the reform, beginning in 622 B.C. or earlier (cf. II Kgs 22:3 ff.; II Chr 34:3–7, 8 ff.). The enemy threatening Judah at that time has been taken by some to be the Scythians who dominated western Asia in the last quarter of that century. However, they were probably the Babylonians. If the date of the commencement of his preaching is placed *c.* 625 B.C., then he began his ministry at the time Jeremiah did. *See* Zephaniah, Book of.

4. Father of Josiah, an exile who returned from Babylon (Zech 6:10, 14).

C. L. F.

ZEPHANIAH, BOOK OF. Ninth book among the Minor Prophets. The author was the son of Cushi and descendant of Hezekiah (Zeph 1:1, ASV), probably the king of Judah. Being of royal lineage, he was able with impressive force to rebuke the sins of the princes (1:8).

There is verification of the date in 1:1 by the mention of Nineveh (2:13), which was not destroyed until 612 B.C., and the absence of direct reference to the Babylonians. *See* Zephaniah 3.

Authenticity

The authenticity of parts of the book has been questioned by an over-active criticism, but the trustworthiness of the prophecy has been vindicated. The book portrays a society plagued by social inequities, complacent luxury, and religious declension in the aftermath of the long idolatrous reign of Manasseh.

Contents

After announcing the soon coming of the day of the Lord with the abolition of idolatry (1:2–6), the prophet declares judgment on Judah's leaders (1:7–13), and a time of distress for all. The visitation may be averted by turning to the Lord (2:1–3); Philistia will feel the brunt of the stroke (2:4–7); it will touch Moab and Ammon (2:8–11), and go N to Assyria with the resultant destruction of Nineveh, its capital (2:12–14).

Again, the prophet rebukes the sins of Jerusalem and its leaders (3:1–8), announcing wrath upon the ungodly, but immunity for the righteous remnant (3:9–13). The prophecy closes with the promise of the latter days when Israel will be restored to their own land, and enjoy the blessing of God (3:14–20).

Theme

The central theme of the prophecy is the day of the Lord. The phrase occurs more often in this book than in any other in the OT. His teaching on the day of the Lord is explicit: (1) it is a day of wrath and terror (1:15); (2) it is imminent (1:14); (3) it is a visitation for sin (1:8, 17); (4) it touches all creation (1:2–3); and (5) it spares a remnant in Israel and among the nations (2:3; 3:9–13). Zephaniah's messages have a comprehensive and universal outreach. The book has points of contact with the messages of the earlier prophets. Although 3:14–20 describes the blessings of the messianic reign, the messianic King Himself is mentioned nowhere in the prophecy.

Outline

I. Preface, 1:1
II. The Pronouncement of Universal Judgment, 1:2–3:8
  A. Judgment of the whole earth, 1:2–3
  B. Judgment upon Judah, 1:4–2:3
    1. The cause—idolatry and apostasy, 1:4–7
    2. The extent—including all the wicked of Jerusalem, 1:8–13
    3. The nature—the great day of the Lord, 1:14–18
    4. The way of escape—seek the Lord, 2:1–3
  C. Judgments upon Gentile nations, 2:4–15
    1. Philistia (to the west), 2:4–7
    2. Moab and Ammon (to the east), 2:8–11
    3. Egypt (ruled by the Ethiopian dynasty, to the south)), 2:12
    4. Assyria (to the north), 2:13–15
  D. Judgment upon Jerusalem restated, 3:1–7
  E. God's final plea, 3:8
III. The Promise of Millennial Joy, 3:9–20
  A. The future conversion of the Gentiles, 3:9–10
  B. The future conversion of Israel, 3:11–13

C. Zephaniah's hymn concerning the Lord's Salvation of Israel, 3:14–20

Bibliography. J. T. Carson,, "Zephaniah," NBC. pp. 736-742. H. A. Hanke, "Zephaniah," WBC, pp. 883-888. Theodore Laetsch, "Zephaniah," *The Minor Prophets,* St. Louis: Concordia, 1956. E. A. Leslie, "Zephaniah, Book of," IDB, IV, 951-953. J. M. P. Smith, W. H. Ward, and J. A. Bewer, *et al., A Critical and Exegetical Commentary on Micah, Zephaniah, Nahum, Habakkuk, Obadiah, and Joel,* ICC, Edinburgh: T. & T. Clark, 1951. Donald L. Williams, "The Date of Zephaniah," JBL, LXXXII (1963), 77–88.

C. L. F.

ZEPHATH (zē'făth). A Canaanite city in the extreme S of Judah which was utterly destroyed by the tribes of Judah and Simeon (Jud 1:17). It was later named Hormah, i.e., "denoted to destruction." *See* Hormah. It has been identified with Khirbet el-Meshash, *c.* eight miles E of Beer-sheba.

ZEPHATHAH (zĕf'*a*-th*a*). A valley near Mareshah where Asa met and defeated an Ethiopian army under the leadership of Zerah (II Chr 14:10).

ZEPHI (zē'fī), **ZEPHO** (zē'fō). A son of Eliphaz and grandson of Esau (Gen 36:11, 15; I Chr 1:36).

ZEPHON (zē'fŏn). A son of Gad and founder of the tribe of Zephonites (Num 26:15). In Gen 46:16 he is called Ziphion.

ZER (zûr). A fortified city in the territory of Naphtali (Josh 19:35). Its location was probably on the slopes W of the Sea of Galilee. It has been suggested that Zer may be another name for Madon (*q.v.*; Josh 11:1; 12:19), which is not listed in Josh 19.

ZERAH (zĕr'*a*)

1. A chief of Edom (perhaps the same as 2 below), son of Reuel, and descendant of Esau and Bashemath (Gen 36:13, 17; I Chr 1:35, 37).

2. The father of Jobab, second of the early kings of Edom (Gen 36:33; I Chr 1:44).

3. Son of Judah and Tamar and twin of Pharez (Gen 38:30; I Chr 2:4). A scarlet thread was tied on his hand before his brother was born. Zerah therefore may mean "scarlet" (Gen 38:27–30). He was the father of the Judean clan of Zarhites (Num 26:20), among whom was Achan who sinned at Jericho (Josh 7:1, 17–18). His name along with that of his brother Pharez appears in the genealogy of Jesus (Mt 1:3). *See* Zara, Zarah.

4. A son of Simeon and father of the Simeonite clan called Zerahites (Num 26:13, ASV, etc.). Zohar (Gen 46:10; Ex 6:15) is an alternate spelling of this man's name.

5. A Levite, descendant of Gershom (I Chr 6:21, 41).

6. An "Ethiopian" or Cushite (Heb.) who invaded Judah with a large army and chariots and was defeated by Asa in a battle at Mareshah (II Chr 14:9–12; 16:8).

There is some debate as to the exact identity of this Zerah. Some (IDB, IV, 953 f.) believe he was merely the leader of raiding Arabian Bedouin or "Cushite" tribes, pointing to tents and camels as evidence (cf. II Chr 14:15). Others, noting the presence of Libyan troops in his army (II Chr 16:8), argue that he was a commander of mercenary troops for Egypt in the reign of Osorkon I (914–874 B.C.). Since Zerah is not called king, it would probably be better to regard him as an Ethiopian general leading the Egyptian forces of Osorkon I, who was likely trying to follow up the success of his father Shishak, first ruler of the 22nd or Libyan Dynasty (K. A. Kitchen, "Zerah," NBD, p. 1359). His forces evidently included Bedouin as well as Egyptian mercenaries who had been settled in Gerar with their families to form a buffer state after Shishak's campaign against Rehoboam (Jacob M. Myers, *II Chronicles,* Anchor Bible, XIII, 85).

R. L. S.

ZERAHIAH (zĕr'*a*-hī'*a*)

1. A priest of the line of Eleazar and son of Uzzi, and one of the ancestors of Ezra (I Chr 6:6, 51; Ezr 7:4).

2. The father of the head of the clan of Pahath-moab that returned with Ezra from the Captivity (Ezr 8:4).

ZERED (zē̆r'ĭd). The valley where Israel encamped before they reached the Arnon gorge (Num 21:12; KJV "Zared"). In Deut 2:13 ff., the crossing of the brook Zered marks the end of the Israelites' 38 years of wandering in the wilderness (*see* Wilderness Wandering). The Zered has been identified with the Wadi el-Ḥesa, the southernmost of the four main streams of Transjordan (Yarmuk, Jabbok, Arnon, Zered). It formed the natural ancient boundary between Edom and Moab. Since it flows into the SE end of the Dead Sea, water for one or more of the cities in league with Sodom (*q.v.*) and Gomorrah was undoubtedly obtained from the Zered. During its 35 mile long course it descends nearly 4,000 feet from the plateau of Moab. The deep canyon is *c.* four miles wide where the modern road to Petra crosses it.

The "brook of the willows" (Isa 15:7; NASB "brook of Arabim") is thought to be the lower course of the Zered, here called the Seil el Qerahi, where there is a small plain with some swamps suitable for willows.

J. R.

ZEREDA (zĕr'ĕ-d*a*). The home town of Jeroboam I, the first ruler of the northern kingdom (I Kgs 11:26). Since Jeroboam was an Ephraimite, the city was evidently located in the territory of that tribe. The name of the town has been preserved in the spring of 'Ain Şeridah at Deir Ghassaneh. It is in western Samaria in the Wadi Deir Ballut, 17 miles SW of Shechem and 12 miles W of Shiloh.

ZEREDATHAH (zĕr'ĕ-dā'thȧ). A city in the plain of the Jordan. In the vicinity, Huram made the instruments of brass for the temple (II Chr 4:16-17). It is thought that Zeredathah is either another name or a scribal error for Zarethan (*q.v.*), as the city is called in the parallel passage in I Kgs 7:46.

ZERERATH (zĕr'ĕ-răth). A place through which the Midianite host fled on its first defeat by Gideon and his band of 300 (Jud 7:22), usually considered to be another name for Zarethan (*q.v.*); spelled Zererah in the ASV, etc.

ZERESH (zē'rĕsh). The wife of Haman. She counseled him to build a gallows to hang Mordecai, and warned him of his defeat when Mordecai became the object of the king's honor (Est 5:10, 14; 6:13).

ZERETH (zē'rĕth). A descendant of Judah; the first son of Ashur by Helah (I Chr 4:7).

ZERI (zē'rī). A member of a family of temple musicians; a son of Jeduthun (I Chr 25:3). The name appears as Izri in v. 11, the difference in spelling perhaps resulting from the dropping of the initial *yodh* from *Yiṣrî*, "Izri."

ZEROR (zē'rôr). An ancestor of King Saul; the son of Bechorath and the father of Abiel (I Sam 9:1).

ZERUAH (zē-roo'ȧ). The mother of Jeroboam, the first king of divided Israel (I Kgs 11:26).

ZERUBBABEL (zē-rŭb'ȧ-bĕl). A prince of Judah, a grandson of the captive king Jehoiachin. Under Zerubbabel and Jeshua, the high priest, the Jews returned from Babylon (Ezr 2:2; Neh 7:6-7; 12:1). Zerubbabel was appointed governor of Jerusalem.

Cyrus' decree in 538 B.C. permitted the Jews to return to Jerusalem. With great enthusiasm they started on the task of rebuilding the temple. First they restored the altar of sacrifice on its original site and began again to observe the regular sacrifices and holy days which had been impossible since the fall of Jerusalem in 586 B.C. (Ezr 3:1-6). The returnees gathered materials and in the second year Zerubbabel laid the foundation of the temple with solemn ceremony. The great task was begun (Ezr 3:8 ff.; Zech 4:9).

The rebuilding aroused the concern of the settlers then living in Samaria. They approached Zerubbabel with an offer to help in the work. Their offer was refused because the Jews did not consider them to be true worshipers of Jehovah (Ezr 4:1-3). The Samaritans then began openly to oppose the rebuilding by threats and particularly through legal obstacles (Ezr 4:4-5). Because of this opposition, Zerubbabel and his people abandoned their sacred task. From the latter years of Cyrus (d. 530 B.C.) until the second year of Darius the Great (520 B.C.) no work was done on the Lord's house (Ezr 4:24). Zerubbabel's own lack of faith and courage must have contributed to this failure (cf. Hag 2:4-5; Zech 4:6-7).

In the second year of Darius the prophets Haggai and Zechariah began their ministry. The Jews, no longer occupied with the temple, had set to work providing fine houses for themselves, and their interest in the things of the Lord had grown cold (Hag 1:1-6). The exhortations and encouragement of the prophets, however, stirred the spirits of the people, and the work began anew.

As soon as the work commenced the opposition also revived, but even interference on the part of the highest officials failed to halt the Jews now (Ezr 5:3-5). An official letter sent by Tatnai, Shethar-boznai, and other Persian officials to King Darius was of no avail (Ezr 5:6-17). Darius found the original decree of Cyrus in the archives and gave orders that the work was to be permitted and that all Persian officials were required to give all aid required for the task (Ezr 6:1-12).

The temple was finally completed in 516 B.C., fulfilling God's promise that Zerubbabel who had begun the work would bring it to completion (Zech 4:9). With the great feast of dedication for the completed temple, Zerubbabel disappears from history, though it may be assumed that he remained for some years in Jerusalem as the governor (Ezr 6:16 ff.; Neh 12:47).

There are two problems related to Zerubbabel that need to be considered. The first is his relationship to Sheshbazzar (*q.v.*). In Ezr 1:8, 11 the leadership of the returning exiles is given by Cyrus to Sheshbazzar, the prince of Judah. In the letter of Tatnai also he is designated as the man who laid the foundation of the temple (Ezr 5:14, 16).

Two solutions have been offered to the problem. One is that Zerubbabel and Sheshbazzar are two names for the same man. This is reasonable since many Jews had both a Jewish and a Persian or Babylonian name; e.g., Daniel—Belteshazzar. It has been objected, however, that in this case both names are Persian, a very strange possibility. The other solution is that Sheshbazzar, as the head of the tribe of Judah, was the titular leader recognized by the king. Some have identified him with Shenazar, Zerubbabel's uncle (I Chr 3:18). The actual leader was Zerubbabel, who is the only one mentioned in the actual building of the temple. The older man may have died, or simply have been unable to take part in the work. Both men are called governor, so eventually Zerubbabel must have taken over whatever official position Sheshbazzar held.

Another question has to do with the paternity of Zerubbabel. He is consistently called the "son of Shealtiel" (Hag 1:1, 12, 14; *et al.;* Mt 1:12, RSV; Lk 3:27, RSV; Jos *Ant.* xi.3.10), but in I Chr 3:19 his father is said to be Pedaiah. The probable explanation is that Shealtiel died, and his brother Pedaiah, in accordance with the Levirate law, married the widow and was the actual father of Zerubbabel. Shealtiel would always be considered the father, how-ever, according to Jewish law and custom. In either case, of course, Zerubbabel was a direct descendant of David and in the lineage of Christ.

P. C. J.

ZERUIAH (zĕ-rōō'ĭ-*ȧ*). A sister of David the son of Jesse (I Chr 2:16–17). According to II Sam 17:25 she was the sister of Abigail who is said to be the daughter of Nahash. Thus she was only a half sister either of David or of Abigail. She was the mother of Joab, Abishai, and Asahel (II Sam 2:18). These loyal nephews of David are consistently identified as sons of Zeruiah rather than sons of their father, perhaps because of her relationship to David (I Sam 26:6; II Sam 2:13; 3:39; 8:16; etc.).

ZETHAM (zē'th*ȧ*m). A Levite of the Gershonites (I Chr 23:8; 26:22).

ZETHAN (zē'th*ȧ*n). Head of a Benjamite family (I Chr 7:10).

ZETHAR (zē'th*ȧ*r). One of the seven chamberlains who served King Ahasuerus (Est 1:10).

ZEUS. *See* Gods, False.

ZIA (zī'*ȧ*). A head of a family in the tribe of Gad (I Chr 5:13).

ZIBA (zī'b*ȧ*). A servant of Saul (II Sam 9:2). After Saul's death Ziba apparently retained contact with the courtiers of the new king, David. When David, after securing his kingdom, wished to fulfill his pledge of friendship with Jonathan (I Sam 20:42), he called for Ziba. Ziba reported that Mephibosheth, a son of Jonathan, was still living in Lo-debar. David made Mephibosheth a member of his personal court and restored to him the estates of Jonathan and Saul. He appointed Ziba, who evidently was a superior manager and not just a common servant, steward of Mephibosheth's affairs (II Sam 9).

When Absalom rebelled against his father, David fled from Jerusalem. Ziba met David with much-needed supplies and told him that Mephibosheth considered the rebellion his chance to regain the throne. David repaid Ziba by promising him all his master's property (II Sam 16:1–4). After David returned to Jerusalem, Mephibosheth appeared before him in mourning. He said that Ziba had abandoned him, a cripple, and had brought David a false report. Mephibosheth had remained faithful to his benefactor.

Faced with the problem of deciding which of the two stories was true, David solved the difficulty by awarding half the estates to each man, a decision which Mephibosheth gladly accepted (II Sam 19:24–30).

P. C. J.

ZIBEON (zĭb'ĭ-ŏn). A son of Seir; a chieftain of the Horites, native inhabitants of Edom (Gen 36:20, 24, 29; I Chr 1:38, 40). He is probably the same as Zibeon the Hivite, grandfather of Aholibamah, one of Esau's wives (Gen 36:2, 14). In Heb. the spelling of Hivite and Horite is similar, and some scholars think the two terms are interchangeable (*see* Hivite; Horite).

ZIBIA (zĭb'ĭ-*ȧ*). Head of a family in the tribe of Benjamin; a son of Shaharaim, born in the land of Moab (I Chr 8:9).

ZIBIAH (zĭb'ĭ-*ȧ*). The mother of Joash, king of Judah; she came from Beer-sheba (II Kgs 12:1; II Chr 24:1).

ZICHRI (zĭk'rī)

1. One of the three sons of Izhar, the grandson of Levi (Ex 6:21).
2. One of the sons of Shimhi, a Benjamite (I Chr 8:19–21).
3. One of the sons of Shashak, a Benjamite (I Chr 8:23–25).
4. One of the sons of Jeroham, a Benjamite (I Chr 8:27).
5. A Levite, son of Asaph, whose descendants lived in Jerusalem after the Exile (I Chr 9:15). His name also appears as Zabdi (Neh 11:17) and Zaccur (Neh 12:35).
6. A descendant of Eliezer, the son of Moses, and father of David's treasurer, Shelomoth (I Chr 26:25–26).
7. Father of Eliezer, a chief officer of Reuben in the days of David (I Chr 27:16).
8. The father of Amasiah of Judah, "a volunteer for the service of the Lord" (RSV), who led 200,000 men in the army of Jehoshaphat (II Chr 17:16).
9. The father of Elishaphat, who in the time of Jehoiada aided in restoring Joash to the throne of Judah (II Chr 23:1).
10. A mighty man of Ephraim. In the war between Pekah of Israel and Ahaz of Judah he killed Ahaz's son Maaseiah, as well as Azrikam, "commander of the palace," and Elkanah, "next in authority to the king" (II Chr 28:7, RSV).
11. The father of Joel who was leader of the Benjamites living in Jerusalem after the Captivity (Neh 11:9).
12. A priest of the family of Abijah when Joiakim was high priest in the time of Nehemiah (Neh 12:17).

P. C. J.

ZIDDIM (zĭd'ĭm). A fortified city allotted to the tribe of Naphtali (Josh 19:35). According to the Talmud it is to be identified with Caphar Hittaia, modern Hattin el-Qadim, *c.* six miles NW of Tiberias. The *Oxford Bible Atlas* identifies it with Kadish, a site W of the S end of the Sea of Galilee.

ZIDKIJAH. *See* Zedekiah.

ZIDON (zī'dŏn). An alternate designation for the Phoenician city of Sidon. Although the KJV uses both Sidon and Zidon, the newer versions tend to standardize by using Sidon, which is the common name employed in secular references. Therefore discussion of the city appears in this work under Sidon (*q.v.*).

ZIDONIANS. *See* Sidon.

ZIF (zĭf). The name (spelled Ziv in ASV, etc.) for the second month in the Heb. calendar; later called Iyyar (I Kgs 6:1, 37). *See* Calendar.

ZIHA (zī'*ȧ*)

1. The ancestral head of a family of temple servants who returned from Babylon (Ezr 2:43; Neh 7:46).

2. An overseer of the temple servants (Neh 11:21).

ZIKLAG (zĭk'lăg). A city in S Judah (Josh 15:31), allotted to the Simeonites (Josh 19:5; I Chr 4:30) but controlled by the Philistines during the reign of Saul. It was given to David by Achish, king of Gath (I Sam 27:6; I Chr 12:1–22). Amalekites captured and plundered it, but David pursued the attackers, captured them, and regained most of the spoil. Under David the city was separated permanently from the Philistines and placed under the kings of Judah. It was inhabited after the Captivity (Neh 11:28).

ZILLAH (zĭl'*ȧ*). The second wife of Lamech; the mother of Tubal-cain and Naamah (Gen 4:19, 22–23).

ZILPAH (zĭl'p*ȧ*). The mother of Gad and Asher (Gen 30:9–13; 35:26). She was one of Leah's maidservants given her by her father Laban (Gen 29:24; 46:18), and given by her to Jacob as a secondary wife to bear sons for her (Gen 30:9; 37:2).

ZILTHAI (zĭl'thī). The name is spelled Zillethai in the ASV, etc.

1. The family of the tribe of Benjamin (I Chr 8:20).

2. A Manassite, a captain of a thousand who joined David at Ziklag and assisted in the recovery of the families and property taken by the Amalekites (I Chr 12:20).

ZIMMAH (zĭm'*ȧ*)

1. The son of Jahath and father of Joah of the Levitical family of Gershom (I Chr 6:20). In I Chr 6:42 he is called the grandson of Jahath and son of Shimei.

2. A Gershonite in the days of Hezekiah. Both his son Joah and grandson Eden were active in carrying out the reform of Hezekiah (II Chr 29:12, 15).

ZIMRAN (zĭm'răn). The first son of Abraham and Keturah (Gen 25:2; I Chr 1:32), and probably the ancestor of an Arabian tribe, possibly the Zimri of Jer 25:25. The name may be recognized in Zambran, a town W of Mecca on the Red Sea (Ptolemy vi.7.5) and/or in Zamareni, an Arabian tribe (Pliny, *Natural History,* vi.32).

ZIMRI (zĭm'rī)

1. One of the five sons of Zerah; grandson of Judah and Tamar (I Chr 2:3–4, 6). In Josh 7:1, 17–18 he is called Zabdi.

2. Son of Salu, a Simeonite leader. Zimri was executed while engaged in idolatrous sexual intercourse, by the priest Phinehas (Num 25:6–18). The occasion for the slaying of Zimri was his bringing to his family a Midianite woman named Cozbi, apparently to be his harlot, while Israel was still lamenting its earlier apostasy to the Moabite Baal. This unholy union, perhaps in a Midianite tent-shrine, incurred the wrath of the Israelite leaders (Num 25:14). See S. C. Reif, "What Enraged Phinehas? A Study of Numbers 25:8," JBL, XC (1971), 200–206.

3. The fifth king of Israel, who reigned in 885 B.C. for only seven days (I Kgs 16:9–20). Elah, the son of Baasha, had reigned scarcely two years when Zimri, captain of half his chariots, conspired against him. Omri, commander of the army, was besieging the Philistines at Gibbethon, and Elah was at Tirzah in the house of Arza, his steward, debauching himself. Zimri took advantage of the situation, murdered Elah and all the male descendants, and established himself on the throne. News reached Omri and the army, and they exalted Omri to kingship. Omri with the army returned to the capital and captured it. When it became evident to Zimri that his cause was lost, he retreated into the king's castle, set fire to it, and perished in the flames. Thus in the death of Elah and the destruction of the house of Baasha Jehu's prophecy (I Kgs 16:7, 12) was fulfilled, and in his own death Zimri's sins were visited upon him (I Kgs 16:19).

4. A descendant of Jonathan, Saul's son. His father's name was Jehoadah (I Chr 8:36; 9:42).

5. A people of Arabia (Jer 25:25); *see* Zimran.

H. A. Hoy.

ZIN, WILDERNESS OF (zĭn). A desert region S of Judah, usually regarded as being the northern half of the Negeb. It marked the southern edge of the Israelite territory, according to both Num 34:3–4 and Josh 15:1–3, which suggest that Zin may have been a place near the ascent of the Akrabbim, giving its name to the surrounding desert. It was probably a frontier region rather than an exact line. In Num 13:21 Zin forms the southern edge of the land which the Israelite spies explored. Elsewhere it is mentioned in connection with Kadesh (Num 20:1; 27:14; 33:36; Deut 32:51), indicating that the word referred loosely to the region between Kadesh-barnea on the border of Sinai and the passes through the cliffs rising from the Arabah. The terrain W of the Kurnub and Khurashe upwarps of jagged rock is marked by broad cultivatable wadis divided by wide level spurs.

D. B.

ZINA (zĭn'ȧ). A Levite, son of Shimei (I Chr 23:10), called Zizah (*q.v.*) in v. 11.

ZION (zī'ŏn). A name applied to Jerusalem or portions thereof since the time of David. Because usage of the word has changed during the succeeding centuries, considerable uncertainty persists as to its precise location. Originally it designated a Jebusite fortress located on the SE spur of the hill at the junction of the Kidron and Tyropoean valleys which David captured and renamed "the city of David" (II Sam 5:6-9). It was an elongated enclosure, about a mile in circumference, shaped like a human foot with the heel to the S. The precipitous valleys on three sides and a dependable source of water at the spring Gihon made the position almost impregnable.

In prophecy the name was the poetic designation of the hill on which the temple stood, and was metaphorically extended to mean the headquarters of Israel's God (Isa 2:2-4; 8:18; Mic 4:1-5; Jer 31:6). In Heb. psalmody the term stood for the entire city (Ps 48; 125:1-2), as it does in Christian hymnody. From the 4th cen. A.D. until recently, "Mount Zion" was erroneously associated with the SW corner of the "Upper City" to the W. *See* Jerusalem; Jerusalem, New.

Bibliography. G. Fohrer and E. Lohse, "*Sion*, etc.," TDNT, VII, 292-338.

G. A. T.

ZION, DAUGHTER OF. This phrase occurs in the singular form (*bat ṣiyôn*) 24 times in the OT. It is a poetic synonym for Jerusalem, being a personification of the city rather than referring to the inhabitants of that city. Hence, it could be translated "daughter Zion" or "daughter who is Zion." Cities to be designated as women is common in OT poetry (cf. II Sam 20:19; Ps 87:5; Isa 47:1).

The phrase occurs twice in the Gospels: Mt 21:5 and Jn 12:15, which quote Zech 9:9 in connection with Jesus' triumphal entry.

The plural form "daughters of Zion" (*b^enôt ṣiyôn*) occurs only four times in the Bible (Song 3:11; Isa 3:16-17; 4:4). It refers to the inhabitants of Jerusalem, and more specifically to the women of that city. *See* Jerusalem; Zion.

H. W. H.

ZIOR (zī'ôr). A town in the hill country of Judah (Josh 15:54), perhaps the same as Zair (*q.v.*), the modern village of Si'ir, *c.* five miles NE of Hebron.

ZIPH (zĭf)

1. A family or clan of the tribe of Judah (I Chr 4:16).

2. A town in the Negeb of Judah, 25 to 30 miles SW of the Dead Sea and near the "ascent of Akkrabim," identified as es-Zeifeh (cf. Josh 15:24).

3. A town in the hill country of Judah (Josh 15:55), five miles SSE of Hebron, sometimes thought to be the same as Tell Zif, which had a strategic location commanding the desert. It was founded by Mesha, a son of Caleb (I Chr 2:42, NEB). It was near here that David twice hid from Saul (I Sam 23:14-15; 26:2). *See* Ziphites. Later it was fortified by Rehoboam to guard the approach to Jerusalem from the S (II Chr 11:8). Ziph is one of four cities named in seals on the handles of royal storage jars from the time of Hezekiah: Hebron, Socoh, Ziph, and Memshe(le)th (meaning "government," probably referring to Jerusalem); these were the four new administrative centers of the kingdom of Judah (*Macmillan Bible Atlas*, p. 98).

J. R.

ZIPHAH (zī'fȧ). A descendant of Judah; son of Jehaleleel (I Chr 4:16).

ZIPHIMS. *See* Ziphites.

ZIPHION. *See* Zephon.

ZIPHITES (zĭf'īts). Citizens of the town of Ziph 3, SE of Hebron. They were a family or clan from the tribe of Judah, descendants of the house of Jehaleleel (I Chr 4:16). They also appear in the KJV as Ziphims in the superscription to Ps 54. They informed Saul of David's hiding place on two different occasions (I Sam 23:19-24; 26:1).

ZIPHRON (zĭf'rŏn). A place on the N border of the Promised Land (Num 34:9), a desert post *c.* 75 miles NE of Damascus, perhaps modern Ḥawwarin (*Macmillan Bible Atlas*, map # 50).

ZIPPOR (zĭp'ôr). The father of Balak, king of the Moabites who called upon Balaam to curse the Israelites (Num 22:2, 4, 10, 16; 23:18; Josh 24:9; Jud 11:25).

ZIPPORAH (zĭp'ŏ-rȧ). One of the seven daughters of Jethro, priest of Midian; the wife of Moses and mother of his sons, Gershom and Eliezer (Ex 2:16, 21-22; 18:2-4). When God's displeasure was upon Moses because of his neglect to circumcise his younger son as the divinely ordained sign of the covenant, Zipporah attended to the matter, but apparently without respect for the ordinance (Ex 4:25).

During the time of the ten plagues in Egypt Moses evidently sent his wife and children away to Jethro for their safety. After Israel had escaped from Egypt and come into the Sinai desert, Jethro brought them back to Moses where he was camped "at the mount of God" (Ex 18:1-6).

Num 12:1 states that Moses had married an Ethiopian (KJV) or Cushite (ASV, etc.) woman. It is possible that Zipporah, a Midianite, was also designated a Cushite, for Midian (*q.v.*) included part of NW Arabia where some Cushite tribes lived. Furthermore, she may have been called a Cushite because her complexion may have been darker than that of most Israelites. *See* Ethiopian Woman.

J. R.

ZITHRI (zĭth'rī). A descendant of Levi; son of Uzziel (Ex 6:22). Spelled Sithri in ASV, etc.

ZIV. *See* Zif.

ZIZ (zĭz). "The cliff [better "ascent"; cf. ASV, RSV] of Ziz" translates Heb. *ma'ălēh haṣṣîṣ* in II Chr 20:16. The term refers to an acclivity used by Moabites, Ammonites, and Meunites (*see* Meunim) as they advanced against the army of Jehoshaphat. Wadi Ḥaṣâṣah, located W of the Dead Sea about halfway between En-gedi (v. 2) and Tekoa (v. 20), is the most likely identification of the site. It is perhaps better to read *ḥaṣṣîṣ* (with *ḥ* rather than *h*) in II Chr 20, or to consider the name as Hazziz (cf. Anchor Bible, XIII, 111) in keeping with the Assis of various LXX MSS.

ZIZA (zī'zȧ)

1. A prince of the tribe of Simeon who participated in an expansion of the tribe's land toward Gedor (I Chr 4:37).

2. A son of Rehoboam, king of Judah, by Maachah (II Chr 11:20).

ZIZAH (zī'zȧ). A Gershonite Levite, among those whom David divided into courses for the temple service (I Chr 23:11). In v. 10 the name is Zina.

ZOAN (zō'ȧn). An Egyptian city of apparently many names, but perhaps best known under its Gr. name Tanis. Situated in the NE section of the Delta, the site of this ancient city is often identified as the modern San el Hagar. Building remains here date as early as Dynasty IV (*c.* 2600 B.C.), and the site has had a rich and varied history.

Others identify Zoan as Qantir, *c.* 11 miles S. It served as the capital of the Hyksos under the name Avaris (*c.* 1720-1570 B.C.). The native king Ahmose successfully besieged the city and expelled the Hyksos from Egypt.

In Dynasty XIX the city saw much building activity; Zoan became the Egyptian capital, perhaps because of its somewhat central location in the empire. P. Montet, Sir Alan Gardiner, and others identify the city as the "House of Rameses" of Rameses II. Many therefore regard it also as the Raamses of Ex 1:11; but there are differences of opinion concerning both of these identifications. *See* Rameses. Montet excavated at San el Hagar and found tombs of the kings of Dynasties XXI and XXII, and remains of a great temple.

In the Bible the name Zoan first appears in Num 13:22, where it is stated that Hebron was founded seven years before Zoan. It is also mentioned in Ps 78:12, 43. Here it is twice said that the Lord did marvels in "the field of Zoan" at the time of the Exodus. Isaiah, in his "burden of Egypt," calls the princes of Zoan fools (Isa 19:11, 13) and in 30:3-5 says that Israelites who return to Egypt will come to shame, even though Pharaoh's officials are at Zoan. Ezekiel also prophesied against Egypt and declared that the Lord "will set fire to Zoan" (30:14).

See Exodus, The: Route; Goshen.

C. E. D.

ZOAR (zō'ȧr). A town also known as Bela, apparently located at the S end of the Dead Sea (Jos *Wars* iv.8.4), perhaps near Khirbet esh-Sheik 'Isa. In patriarchal times the environs of Zoar were very attractive (Gen 13:10). It was on the route followed by the five invading kings (Gen 14:5-9). Lot's intercession saved Zoar from the destruction that fell on Sodom and Gomorrah (Gen 19:20-23).

As Moses viewed the Promised Land from Mount Nebo, Dan was the northernmost city and Zoar the southernmost which he could see (Deut 34:1-3). Prophetic oracles during the Judean monarchy refer to Zoar as part of Moab (Isa 15:5; Jer 48:34). In the Hellenistic period it was part of the Nabataean kingdom (Jos *Ant.* xiii.15.4; xiv.1.4). During the Middle Ages it was an important station on the highway connecting the seaport of Elath with Jerusalem.

J. P. Harland outlines the evidence for the occupation of the site of es-Safi around the time of Abraham. It is near the present mouth of the stream Seil el-Qurahi, the lower end of the Wadi el-Hesa (*see* Zered), which flows into the Dead Sea through a once fertile region ("Zoar," IBD, IV, 961 f.).

A. F. R.

ZOBAH (zō'bȧ). One of the smaller Aramean kingdoms of the 11th-10th cen. B.C. Its name in Heb. is an abbreviated form of *ṣᵉhôbâ*, "bronze"; thus it is an appellative meaning "the copper country" (M. F. Unger, *Israel and the Aramaeans of Damascus*, London: James Clarke, 1957, p. 44). Saul is said to have been victorious over Zobah (I Sam 14:47). David later came into collision with its king Hadadezer, who was pursuing a career of conquest. David defeated him and made heavy captures of men and horses (II Sam 8:3–8; I Chr 18:3). Later in his reign, the Ammonites, who had provoked David to attack them, hired some 20,000 foot soldiers of Zobah to come to their aid. Joab defeated the combined forces of the enemy in two battles, after which the Arameans hastened to make peace with Israel and acknowledge its sovereignty (II Sam 10:6–19; I Chr 19:6; title of Ps 60).

In II Sam 23:36 a certain Igal, the son of Nathan of Zobah, is mentioned as one of David's "mighty men." Reson, who founded the Aramean kingdom of Damascus, is reported to have been a servant of Hadadezer of Zobah (I Kgs 11:23). Soon after Solomon's time Zobah was evidently swallowed up by the growing kingdom of Damascus to the S.

Since Zobah is spoken of as bordering Hamath (II Sam 8:9–10; I Chr 18:3, 9), it must have been located S of that city, probably in the Biq'ah between the Lebanon and Anti-Lebanon Mountain ranges E of Byblos. Formerly it was assumed that David's conquests were all S of Damascus in the Hauran region (biblical Bashan). Egyptian lists and the Amarna letters, however, prove that Tibhath and Chun, cities of Hadadezer (I Chr 18:8), were in the territory S of Hamath and Homs. Analysis of the Assyrian provincial organization, which was constructed on older foundations, confirms that Zobah (Assyrian *Subatu*) lay N not S of Damascus ("Zoba," UBD, p. 1191).

S. C.

ZOBEBAH (zō-bē'b*ȧ*). A man of the tribe of Judah (I Chr 4:8).

ZODIAC. *See* Astronomy.

ZOHAR (zō'här)

1. The father of Ephron, the Hittite prince from whom Abraham bought the cave of Machpelah (Gen 23:8; 25:9).

2. A son of Simeon (Gen 46:10; Ex 6:15). The spelling Zerah (Num 26:13; I Chr 4:24) apparently resulted from a transposition of the Heb. letters *ḥ* and *r*. *See* Zerah 4.

ZOHELETH (zō'*ĕ*-lĕth). Evidently a sacred stone ("Serpent's Stone," RSV) near En-rogel in the Kidron valley of Jerusalem. Here Adonijah prepared his inaugural celebration when he attempted to succeed David as king (I Kgs 1:9).

ZOHETH (zō'hĕth). Head of a family in the tribe of Judah (I Chr 4:20).

ZOPHAH (zō'f *ȧ*). Head of a family of the tribe of Asher (I Chr 7:35–36).

ZOPHAI (zō'fī). Alternate form of Zuph (I Sam 1:1; I Chr 6:35). A descendant of Levi; son of one Elkanah who was an ancestor of Samuel (I Chr 6:26). *See* Zuph 1.

ZOPHAR (zō'făr). A Naamathite, friend and counselor of Job (Job 2:11; 11:1; 20:1; 42:9). Conjectured to be in Edom or N Arabia, the site of Naamah, his home, is unknown. The LXX (Job 2:11) calls Zophar "king of the Minaeans," a people from S Arabia.

Zophar agrees with Job's other friends in attributing Job's sufferings to his sins. Zophar is the least tactful, speaking bluntly and harshly. His two speeches arouse Job's indignation as those of the other friends do not, and they receive withering answers. Zophar does not appear in the third cycle of speeches. This may be a textual confusion, or it may indicate that the least able and spiritual of Job's friends had nothing more to say.

ZOPHIM (zō'fĭm). Balak took Balaam "into the field of Zophim, to the top of Pisgah" for a second view of the Israelites and hopefully for a cursing of Israel. From here Balaam blessed Israel as before (Num 23:14). Its exact location has not been identified.

ZORAH (zôr'*ȧ*). A city allotted to the tribe of Dan (Josh 19:41); the home of Manoah, the father of Samson (Jud 13:2, 25), and the place of Samson's burial (Jud 16:31). Some Danites of Zorah sought additional land in the N and migrated there, capturing Micah's Levitical priest of his private temple en route (Jud 18:2, 8, 11). Zorah, which lay in the Shephelah, apparently came to belong to Judah (Josh 15:33, spelled Zoreah). After the division of Israel, Rehoboam fortified the city (II Chr 11:10). It was reoccupied after the Exile (Neh 11:29, spelled Zareah). *See* Zorathites.

It was a city mentioned in the Amarna letters as *Ṣarḫa*. It has been identified with Ṣar'ah, 15 miles W of Jerusalem, on the N side of the valley of Sorek (Wadi es-Sarar) opposite Beth-shemesh.

ZORATHITES (zôr'*ȧ*-thīts). A clan of the tribe of Judah, reported as being descendants of Shobal (I Chr 2:53; 4:2). Their name is probably derived from the city of Zorah (Josh 15:33) in the lowland of Judah. It has been suggested that the Zorites in I Chr 2:54 are the same group, but this is unlikely as the line of their descent is a different one.

ZOREAH. *See* Zorah.

ZORITES (zôr'īts). Descendants of Salma of the tribe of Judah (I Chr 2:54).

ZOROBABEL. *See* Zerubbabel.

ZUAR (zo͞o'*ȧ*r). The father of Nethaneel, chief of the tribe of Issachar in the wilderness (Num 1:8; 2:5; 7:18, 23; 10:15).

ZUPH (zŭf)

1. An ancestor of Samuel who lived in Ephraim (I Sam 1:1). He was a Levite of the family of Kohath (I Chr 6:35). I Chr 6:26 refers to him as Zophai (*q.v.*).

2. A district of Palestine apparently N of Benjamin in the territory of Ephraim. It was probably named for the family of Zuph I, who presumably settled there. The town of Ramathaim-zophim (I Sam 1:1) received its designation from lying in the land of Zuph; hence Zuph must have been located *c.* 15 miles W of Shiloh. In the village of this district Saul and his servant found Samuel, who anointed young Saul king of Israel (I Sam 9:5; cf. 10:1-2).

ZUR (zûr)

1. A Midianite chieftan, father of Cozbi who was slain with her Israelitish husband Zimri in connection with the purging of the idolatry into which Israel had fallen. Zur, an ally of the Amorite king Sihon, fell in the ensuing battle (Num 25:14-15; 31:8 Josh 13:21).

2. A Benjamite; brother of Kish, the father of Saul (I Chr 8:30; 9:36).

ZURIEL (zŏŏr'ĭ-ĕl). A Levite; chief of the house of Merari during the wilderness wanderings. In the marches the Merarites were in charge of the framework of the tabernacle and of the sacred vessels (Num 3:35-37).

ZURISHADDAI (zŏŏr'ĭ-shăd'ī). The father of Shelumiel, the leader of the tribe of Simeon in the wilderness (Num 1:6; 2:12; 7:36, 41; 10:19).

ZUZIM (zū'zĭm). A people who dwelt in the city of Ham (*q.v.*) *c.* five miles SSW of Irbid in Transjordan. The ancient city mound (Tell Ham) goes back to the Bronze and Iron Ages. The Zuzim were conquered by Chedorlaomer (Gen 14:5). Distinct from the Rephaim, they may have been their allies. The *Genesis Apocryphon (see* Dead Sea Scrolls) indicates that the Jews later identified them with the Zamzummim of Deut 2:20.